W9-BBM-332

Baker's Biographical Dictionary of Musicians

Sixth Edition

Baker's Biographical Dictionary of Musicians

Sixth Edition

Completely Revised by
Nicolas Slonimsky

SCHIRMER BOOKS
A Division of Macmillan Publishing Co., Inc.
NEW YORK

Collier Macmillan Publishers
LONDON

Schirmer Books
A Division of Macmillan Publishing Co., Inc.
866 Third Avenue, New York, N.Y. 10022

Collier Macmillan Canada, Ltd.

Library of Congress Catalog Card Number 78-3205

Printed in the United States of America

printing number
1 2 3 4 5 6 7 8 9 10

Library of Congress Cataloging in Publication Data

Baker, Theodore, 1851-1934.
    Baker's Biographical dictionary of musicians.

    1. Music--Bio-bibliography. I. Slonimsky, Nicolas

ML105.B16 1978   780'.92'2 [B]   78-3205
ISBN 0-02-870240-9

Preface
to the Sixth Edition

If I were to write an autobiography (which God forbid!) I would call it *I am a footnote,* or *I am a parenthesis.* I am a footnote in the entry on Carl Maria von Weber in the Fifth Edition of *Grove's Dictionary* and a parenthesis in the article on Lully in *Die Musik in Geschichte und Gegenwart.* And I am a paragraph in the Fifteenth Edition of the *Encyclopædia Britannica* under Pandiatonicism, which is my polysyllabic brainchild.

Dr. Samuel Johnson defines a lexicographer in his famous dictionary as "a harmless drudge." Harmless? Not necessarily. In fact, lexicography, when practiced in excess, may well be harmful to the lexicographer's psyche. Consider the melancholy case of John Wall Callcott (1766-1821) as related in *Baker's Biographical Dictionary of Musicians:* "His mind gave way from overwork on a projected biographical dictionary of musicians, ... He recovered, but not sufficiently to continue his work." Callcott reached the letter Q, associated with such disturbing images as queer, quaquaversal, and quagmire, and then quit.

One of my predecessors in editing *Baker's* jotted down these words in the margin of the galley proofs: "I will go mad if I have to continue this for a long time." Another music editor, working on another dictionary, deliberately rented a room on the ground floor lest he should be tempted to jump out the window in despair over the contents of the book.

Although most of my friends regard me as an eccentric, I am not given to suicidal impulses while working on a dictionary. But I am rather paranoiac in my suspicions about melodrama, except in opera librettos. I never believed that Salieri poisoned Mozart, even though I memorized, as part of my school assignment in St. Petersburg, Salieri's monologue in Pushkin's play *Mozart and Salieri,* in which Salieri explains his reason for poisoning Mozart lest his blazing genius should eclipse the work of such humble votaries in the divine art of harmony as himself. In another tale of Mozart, I became suspicious of the reports in practically every reference work and every biography that a fierce snowstorm was raging in Vienna on the day of his funeral in December 1791, which made it impossible for his friends to follow his body to the cemetery (the snowballs were as large as tennis balls, the top Vienna Mozartologist Erich Schenk asserts). Why wasn't this meteorological phenomenon as much as mentioned in early Mozart biographies? It would have at least explained why Mozart's widow did not attend the funeral, if not her failure to pay dues for keeping Mozart's grave in perpetuity, which was the reason why he was eventually moved to the place of common burial. The snowstorm episode appears for the first time in Otto Jahn's monumental biography of Mozart, and the only source to substantiate it was an anonymous article published in a Vienna newspaper on the occasion of Mozart's centennial in 1856. Some Mozartologists identified the writer (who signed his report as "a man of the people") as the bartender of Mozart's favorite Vienna tavern, although by the time of Mozart's centennial he himself, if still living, would have been about a hundred years old. To resolve my puzzlement, I wrote to the Vienna Weather Bureau for a report on the climatic conditions on that December day in

1791. Great was my malicious sense of gratification when I received a report that the temperature on that day was well above freezing and that a gentle Zephyr wind blew from the West. No snowballs. No frigid weather which frightened away Mozart's friends. No melodrama, except the tragedy of Mozart's death so young. Encouraged by the prompt response of the Vienna Weather Bureau (which had kept records for more than two centuries), I inquired about another melodramatic episode: an electric storm on the afternoon of Beethoven's death. Yes, there was an electric storm, even though it was hardly likely that Beethoven in his debilitated physical condition could have lifted his clenched fist toward heaven in a gesture of defiance of *Jupiter tonans*.

Not every melodramatic report is necessarily a pabulum for the gullible. I became incredulous of the tale told in *Baker's* about the French singer Alexandre Taskin who reportedly displayed an untenorlike bravery during a conflagration at the Opéra-Comique in Paris on the night of May 25, 1887, when he sang in *Mignon*. The lives of hundreds of panic-stricken opera-goers were supposedly saved thanks to his *sang-froid*. Well, it turns out that there was a rather horrendous fire at the Opéra-Comique on that night, and that "le beau Taskin," as he was known to his admirers, did display courage in calming down the audience, and was commended for it by the French government.

I was smugly confident of the accuracy of the report that the Italian conductor Gino Marinuzzi was assassinated by the anti-Fascist partisans in Milan on August 17, 1945, as duly noted in *Baker's*, and also in *Grove*, in *Riemann's Musik-Lexikon* ("ermordet") and in the Italian encyclopedia *La Musica* ("morì assassinato"). But why did the anti-Fascist partisans wait so long after the end of the Mussolini regime to shoot him? True, he was the author of a triumphal ode on the occasion of the historic meeting between Hitler and Mussolini in an Alpine tunnel, but many other Italian composers expressed a similar lack of precognition in glorifying the Fascist regime. I received many letters from Italian composers during the Fascist years, dated E.F. XV, E.F. XVIII, etc., i.e., Era Fascista followed by the year, in Roman numerals, since Mussolini's march on Rome ("tough on Jesus Christ," a witty Bostonian remarked when I showed him these letters), and they remained unscathed. However that might be, the publishers of *Baker's* received an irate letter from a Milan lawyer, acting on behalf of the Marinuzzi family, protesting that the account of the assassination was false and demanding an immediate rectification. Gino Marinuzzi, the letter said, died peacefully in a Milan hospital on the date correctly given in *Baker's*, succumbing not to a bullet wound but to hepatic anemia. Fortunately, *Baker's* VI was still in a fluid state, and the publishers were able to pacify the Marinuzzi family lawyer, promising to make a correction. But why did the Marinuzzis wait all these years for firing their salvo, and why zero in on *Baker's* rather than on their own Italian dictionaries? And where did the original report of assassination come from? The *Corriere della Sera*, Milan's major newspaper, carried an *R.I.P.* notice of Marinuzzi's death, with no mention of the cause. The case was clinched eventually by the Servizio Mortuario of the city of Milan, stating that Marinuzzi had indeed died of acute atrophy of the liver. No bullets, no assassination, no melodrama.

Beware of false suspicions! Could Raselius have written a book on Roselius? He could, and he did. Could Gabriel Faure (no accent) have written a monograph on Gabriel Fauré (accent)? He could and he did. Was Schubart really the author of the words of *Die Forelle* by Schubert? Yes, he was. Could two composers, each named Victor Young, have been active in the movies in Hollywood during the same period? They were. Could I myself have had a classmate, in a St. Petersburg high school, called Nicolas Slonimsky? I had, and since I joined the class after him, my name was registered as Nicolas II, which was the official name of the then reigning Czar of all the Russians.

Among the many persistent errors plaguing musical biography is the belief that Wagner originated the term *Leitmotiv*. He did not; it was first proposed by Friedrich Wilhelm Jähns in the preface to his book on Weber published in 1871. Bizet did not write the famous *Habanera* in *Carmen*. He took it from a collection of Spanish songs by Sebastián Yradier, without any alteration of key, harmonization, tempo, rhythm, and dynamics.

The Russians have a marvelously expressive word for a story unsupported by evidence— "nyebylitsa," an "un-was-ity." Famous last words by historic personages are almost all such un-was-ities. Madame Roland's exclamation on her way to the guillotine, "Liberty, how many crimes are committed in thy name!" first appeared in print in Lamartine's *Histoire de la Révolution française,* or so it is cited in *Bartlett's Familiar Quotations.* But browsing through the 1793 volume of *The Annual Register* of London I came upon a Paris dispatch quoting the famous phrase. Is one to suppose then that the British Paris correspondent actually followed the tumbril taking Madame Roland to the place of execution and actually heard her utter the famous apostrophe? Not bloody likely.

"Lexicographis secundus post Herculem labor" was the judgment pronounced by Joseph Justus Scaliger (1540–1609), himself a lexicographer of stature. The mythological reference is, of course, to the labor performed by Hercules in cleaning up the manure-filled stables of King Augeus, son of the sun god Helius. Hercules did the job in twenty-four hours; to clean up a clogged music dictionary takes a little longer. But sanitation must be done with circumspection; one never knows what shining gems, what bits of fascinating tektite, are embedded in rejected debris. Take the story of the Italian singer Giulio Rossi as related by *Baker's.* He started out as a tenor, but unintentionally plunged into the Tiber on a cold day and as a consequence became a *basso profondo.* Incredible? Yes, incredible, but what lexicographer would have the heart to throw it into the pile of refuse? I couldn't. So—*stet!*

There should be no such spirit of acceptance for the purple prose that some editors indulged in while describing the life and works of admired persons. I had to deflate somewhat the verbal effusions in the original *Baker's* entry on A. W. Thayer, biographer of Beethoven. Here is a sample: "Unhappily, his wonderful capacity for work was overtaxed, and volume IV of his nobly conceived Beethoven biography, executed with a painstaking thoroughness and scrupulous fidelity beyond praise, was left unfinished. Though he lived for years in straitened circumstances, he resolutely refused offers from firms like Novello & Co. and G. Schirmer, Inc., hoping to recast entirely the English version of his *Beethoven.''* Suffocating! Give us air to breathe!

A biographical dictionary ought to be a democratic assembly of factual information. Great masters are by right to be given preferential treatment, but opaque luminaries, e.g., Bibl, Kittl, Lickl, or Titl, ought to be tendered hospitality, if not lavish accommodations. Ay, there's the rub! Proportionate representation is the ideal desideratum, but availability of information and productivity of work determine the space allowance. One would fain wish that there were more biographical information on Shakespeare than on Pepys, on Josquin Desprez than on a whole gallery of later madrigalists, on Bach than on Reger. As it is an unhappy editor must gather every bit of information on the great masters of the past and make a judicious selection of biographical data and a list of works of *dii minores* in the arts.

One must also beware of lexicographical zombies, typographical clones and monsters. The great Eitner, who spent a lifetime in tabulating manuscripts in European libraries, was also progenitor of such teratological creatures. Working on a pile of anonymous French songs, he apparently mistook the nouns in their titles for names of composers. Thus we learn from Eitner that "La Chanson d'un gai Berger" was a song by Ungay Berger, and that "La Chanson de l'Auberge Isolée" was composed by Mlle. Isolée L'Auberge. There must be a number of desperate music researchers trying to find out who Mr. Gay Shepherd and Miss Isolated Tavern were in life. *Cobbett's Cyclopedia of Chamber Music* is responsible for spawning D. Michaud (a misprint for D. Milhaud), Marcel Babey (for Marcel Labey), and, most intriguing, a famous violinist, Heinrich Wehtan, generated through the transliteration of the Russian spelling in Cyrillic letters of the name of Henri Vieuxtemps via a German translation of an article originally written in Russian by a contributor to *Cobbett*.

To exorcise such vampires and to drive a stake through their hideous hearts I myself decided to create a monster as the last entry of the 1958 edition of *Baker's*. Never fear: I killed it in page proofs. But here it is *à titre documentaire:*

Zyžik, Krsto, Czech composer; b. Pressburg, Feb. 29, 1900. [1900 was not a leap-year in the West.] He traveled widely to Pozsony and Bratislava [Pozsony and Bratislava are respectively the Hungarian and Slovak names of Pressburg], and back to Pressburg. He attracted attention with his oratorio *Dieta Wormsová* written for the quadricentennial of the Diet of Worms in a vermicular counterpoint. [Diet of Worms was an actual historic assembly, held in the city of Worms in 1521; it condemned Luther as a heretic]; then brought out a bel canto work *Strč prst skrz krk* (a Czech tongue-twister, meaning *put your finger on your throat*), using only consonants in consonant harmony. His works include *Pinč mj šuga* (*Pinch me, Sugar,* or *Pinch Meshuga* in phonetical transcription) for chorus and pinched strings; *Smyccový Kvartet* (string quartet) for woodwind quintet; *Sappho LXIX* for 2 female participants (Lesbos Festival, 1955); *Macho* for large secular organ (male player), etc. In 1979, after many years of aggravated floccillation and severe dyscrasia, he was committed to a dissident asylum. See Sol Mysnik [rather obvious anagram of Slonimsky], *A Czech Checkmate: The Story of Krsto Zyžík* (Los Angeles, 1979).

The most authentic sources of information ought to be diaries and autobiographies, correspondence and reminiscences of friends and relatives. But much too frequently, at least in musical biography, accounts by musicians themselves are tainted by a desire for self-glorification hidden behind a mask of assumed modesty. "Look at me," they seem to tell the reader, "and marvel at my accomplishments; starting out in poverty, privations and need, and by dint of faith in my destiny and hard work, rising to the top of the pyramid of fame, recognition and even wealth." Wagner's autobiography abounds in trivia, including some tedious pages about his pet dogs, but he never mentions the episode of his incarceration at the Clichy prison in Paris from October 28 to November 17, 1840, for non-payment of debt. True, it was one of those permissive jailings, with easy family furloughs, but still the episode is a legitimate part of Wagner's biography. Naturally, Wagner never gave an account in his autobiography of his cavalier treatment of the women in his life, nor did he make clear the circumstances of the birth of his natural daughter Isolde born to Cosima on April 10, 1865, while she was still married to Hans von Bülow. In 1914 Isolde petitioned the Bavarian Civil Court to grant her a share in Wagner's royalties; her claim was rejected on the grounds that there was no evidence that Cosima had ceased all communication with her legitimate husband Hans von Bülow within the period of ten months before Isolde's birth, a legal maximum for the length of gestation. The court also overruled the evidence submitted by Isolde's lawyer husband, based on the phrenological and hemological similarities between Wagner and Isolde.

It was fashionable among artists of the nineteenth century to claim paternity from celebrated or titled persons. Was the French cellist François Servais actually a bastard child of Liszt, as was claimed for him in various sources, including *Baker's*? He was born in St. Petersburg, or so the dictionaries said, in 1846, a date that fits the chronology of Liszt's liaison with Princess Sayn-Wittgenstein. But nothing in the voluminous correspondence between her and Liszt during that period indicated that she was a prospective mother. My earnest inquiries in Russia brought no results. The verdict in this case, therefore, must remain unproven.

A more involved claim of desirable paternity concerns the once famous pianist Sigismond Thalberg who apparently authorized the report that he was the son of a Prince Dietrichstein and a baroness. Further inquiries were discouraged by a footnote in the 1954 edition of *Grove's Dictionary* stating that Thalberg's birth certificate (he was born in Geneva) was unobtainable. Distrustful of this notice, I wrote to Geneva and obtained a copy of the certificate by airmail within a matter of days. I discovered later that the document had been previously published in a Belgian magazine on the occasion of Thalberg's centenary in 1912. The certificate stated that Thalberg was a legitimate son of Joseph Thalberg and Fortunee Stein, both of Frankfurt-am-Main, and that he was born in Geneva on January 8, 1812. The case was further complicated by the publication in various sources of a letter allegedly written by Thalberg's natural mother to Prince Dietrichstein at the time of Thalberg's birth, suggesting that he should be given the name Thalberg, so that he would grow as peacefully as a Thal (valley) and would tower over humanity as high as a Berg (mountain). Just who fabricated this letter and for what purpose remains unclear. The Supplement to *Riemann's Musik-Lexikon*, published in 1975, adds an intriguing bit of information that Thalberg was indeed adopted by Prince Dietrichstein later in life.

The strange lure of aristocratic birth seems to be undiminished even in our own century. An English singer who was active in recital and on the light opera stage in the early 1900's under the name Louis Graveure declared in an interview published in *The New York Times* in 1947 that he was of royal or possibly imperial birth, and that it would be worth a fortune to him to find out who he really was. Well, for the modest sum of two shillings and sixpence I obtained from London a copy of his birth certificate which dispelled the mystery. His real name was Wilfrid Douthitt, and he used it in his early appearances in England as a baritone; later he changed to tenor and gave concerts as Louis Graveure, which was his mother's maiden name.

Much more honest was the search for true paternity undertaken by the American folk songster and poet Rod McKuen. He knew he was illegitimate, and his mother never told him who his father was. He undertook a long quest, almost epic in its simple grandeur, and in the end established the identity of his father, a backwoods lumberjack.

The desire to recreate one's life according to one's fancy is universal, and artists are particularly apt to imagine, and at times consciously to contrive, the tales of might-have-been. Was Liszt actually kissed on the brow by Beethoven at the concert he played in Vienna as a child? There is a charming lithograph of the supposed event, which is reproduced in several Liszt biographies. But the evidence of Beethoven's archives suggests that Beethoven was annoyed by Liszt's father's bringing the child Liszt to Beethoven's quarters, and that he never went to the concert despite Schindler's efforts to persuade him to attend. Liszt did play for Beethoven in private, but whether he was kissed on the brow or not remains uncertain.

Preface

Working on a biographical dictionary of musicians, I have found myself in the uncomfortable position of private detective. Some years back I received a letter from a Russian woman living in Rome, Italy. She asked my help to find out whether her father, the Russian violinist Bezekirsky who emigrated to America when she was a child, was still alive. Since Bezekirsky was in *Baker's*, I had to search for him anyway to bring him up to date, dead or alive. Tracking him down through several music schools where he taught violin, I finally reached him in a small locality in upstate New York. Delighted that I could restore a missing father to an anxious daughter, I wrote to both giving their mutual addresses. Frankly, I expected letters full of emotional gratitude for my humanitarian endeavor, but I got none from either father or daughter. I do not relish unfinished human symphonies, so I wrote to Bezekirsky again asking him to let me know whether he established contact with his long-lost offspring. Great was my shock when I received from him a postcard scribbled in English in a senile hand, saying as follows: "Your mission was successful, if you call several unpleasant and demanding letters from my daughter a success. I am in no position to help her in any way." I never heard from the daughter.

One of the sharpest rebukes I ever received for trying to obtain information was administered by the remarkable English composer Kaikhosru Sorabji. I made the terrible *faux pas* of describing him as an Indian composer. "Do not dare to call me an Indian," he thundered in reply. "We are Parsi, followers of Zarathustra." He flatly refused to supply biographical data about himself, but he sent me a signed copy of his formidable *Opus Clavicembalisticum,* and pointed out for my information that it is the greatest polyphonic work since Bach's *Kunst der Fuge.* For all I know, it may be exactly that, at least in the grandeur of conception and extraordinary skill of its structure. But his rebuke to me was mild in comparison with the eruption of invective he poured on Percy Scholes for what he deemed to be an undignified and inadequate entry on him in the *Oxford Companion to Music.* Scholes sent the letter to me with the inscription "For your delectation." It is worth reproducing *in toto:*

Corfe Castle, Dorset, XXII.II.MCMLII A.D.

My Good Sir:

A valued friend draws my attention to a lucubration of yours under the entry of my name in a recently published book of reference. One is hard put to it at which to marvel the more, the exiguity of your sense of proportion or the poverty of your taste in devoting double the amount of space to cheap impertinences regarding the place and date of my birth (which is as little business of yours as of any other prying nosey busybody) to that which is devoted to my work, which is all that concerns anyone and which carefully conveys inaccurate and false information by leaving out material facts. Formerly I used to consider it enough when dealing with these stupid and impudent enquiries from lexicographical persons, deliberately to mislead them as to dates and places. This is a mistake: their enquiries should either be ignored or refused. And the sooner folk of their kidney grasp the fact that one is under no moral obligation to provide them with accurate, or indeed any information at all just because they choose to ask for it, the very much better for all concerned.

I have the honour to be, Sir, Yours very faithfully,
Kaikhosru Shapurji Sorabji

Sorabji is a unique figure in music, and his full biography would be fascinating. Erik Chisholm, who knew him personally, told me that the gate of Sorabji's castle in Dorset bears this legend: "Visitors Unwelcome. Roman Catholic Nuns in Full Habit May Enter Without An Appointment." In reckless disregard of Sorabji's demurrer at biographical information about him, I wrote to the London registry of birth to find out at least when and where he was born. To my surprise the document stated that his real name was Leon Dudley Sorabji; Kaikhosru was apparently his Parsi name assumed later in life. I informed Eric Blom, who was then working on the Fifth Edition of *Grove*, of my findings. His response was prompt. "I knew right along," he wrote, "that Sorabji's name was Leon Dudley, but if you value your life I would not advise you to put it in print, for I fear that if you do he would take the next plane to America and assassinate you personally." And Samuel Johnson said that a lexicographer is a "harmless drudge!"

Once in a while in a beleaguered lexicographer's life the subject of an entry in a biographical dictionary voices his gratitude for the honor. A letter I received from Walter Stockhoff, an American composer whose music was praised by Busoni as "a fresh voice from the New World that could revitalize the tired art of Europe," certainly warmed the cockles of my heart. "As pure, cool, crystal-clear water," he wrote me, "revives one thirsting in the desert, so intelligence, understanding, sympathy and sense of values come to brighten one's pathway. There is a noble generosity in your giving thought to my work. Through the greatness of your nature you strengthen others."

Chronological memory is treacherous. Casals owned the manuscript of the B-flat major string quartet, op. 67, of Brahms, given to him by a Vienna collector. It was, he told me, mysteriously connected with his life, for he was conceived when Brahms began the composition of the quartet, and was born when Brahms completed it. Leaving aside the problem of knowing the date of one's conception, the chronology does not support this fancy. Brahms wrote the work during the summer and fall of 1875, and it was first performed in Berlin on October 30, 1876. Casals was born two months after its performance and could not have been conceived fourteen or fifteen months previously.

Lexicographical cross-pollination of inaccurate information in similar wording is a hazard. Philip Hale used to say that when several mutually independent reference works vouchsafe identical data, he deems the information reliable. Not necessarily so. If we consider the case of Mascagni, one comes upon a curious iteration of idiom that arouses suspicion. The 1906 edition of *Grove's* states that Mascagni was compelled to study music "by stealth" because his father, a baker, wanted him to be a lawyer. The *Oxford Companion to Music* paraphrases *Grove's:* "Mascagni was the son of a baker who took music lessons by stealth." The 1940 edition of *Baker's* echoes: "Mascagni's father (a baker) wished him to study jurisprudence, but he learned piano-playing by stealth." What is this obsession with the quaint locution "by stealth" in all these reference works? In point of fact, Mascagni's father was quite proud of his achievement as a musician and eagerly supported his studies at the Conservatory of Milan, as attested by their published correspondence.

If autobiographies are inevitably images of one's life as refracted through a prism resulting in an attractive and colorful spectrum, it is nevertheless strange that a composer would alter the history of the creation of a particular work. Berlioz did so paraleptically in his most famous score *Symphonie fantastique* by leaving out of its program the fact that one of the movements was taken from his early school work and that he implanted the unifying *idée fixe* surgically in a vacant measure containing a fermata, in order to justify its inclusion. And yet this manipulation creates the false impression of coherence. Of course, composers need not apologize to their biographers and analysts for revising their works in the light of later wisdom. Mahler denied the programmatic intent of several of his symphonies even though the descriptive titles appeared in the manuscripts. Beethoven carefully disavowed the pictorial nature of his *Pastoral Symphony* by stating that the music represented an impression rather than a description of a day in the country, and this despite the birdcalls and the electric storm in the score. Schoenberg, who was opposed to representational music, nevertheless yielded to the importunities of his publishers in authorising romantic titles for the individual movements of his *Five Orchestral Pieces.*

On the other hand, Stravinsky's latter-day denial that his early *Scherzo fantastique* was inspired by his reading of Maeterlinck's *La Vie des Abeilles* is puzzling. In Robert Craft's *Conversations with Igor Stravinsky,* in reply to the question about the subject matter of the work, Stravinsky replies unequivocally: "I wrote the *Scherzo* as a piece of pure symphonic music. The bees were a choreographer's idea . . . Some bad literature about bees was published on the fly-leaf of the score to satisfy my publisher who thought a 'story' would help to sell the music." This declaration was most unfair to the publisher and to the choreographer. In his own letters to Rimsky-Korsakov at the time of composition of the score (1907), published in Moscow in 1973, Stravinsky writes: "I intended to write a scherzo already in St. Petersburg, but I lacked subject matter. It so happens that I have been reading *La Vie des Abeilles* by Maeterlinck, a half-philosophical, half-poetic work, which captivated me completely. At first, I intended to use direct quotations so as to make the program of my piece quite clear, but then I realized that it would not do because in the book the scientific and poetic elements are closely interwoven. I decided therefore to guide myself by a definite programmatic design without actual quotations, and to entitle the work simply *The Bees,* after Maeterlinck, a fantastic scherzo."

In the nineteenth century America was, to all practical purposes, a German colony in instrumental music and an Italian colony in opera. Lillian Norton would have never made a singing career had she not changed her name to Nordica. Conductors had to be German or Austrian (Damrosch, Muck, Henschel, Nikisch, Mahler). Pianists prospered when their last names ended with "sky" or "ski." Paderewski was a shining example of grandeur and glory. (I myself profited peripherally when I entered the United States in 1923 exempt from the rigid quota imposed by the Immigration Office on Slavs and such, exception being made for "artists," particularly those whose names looked and sounded artistic.) Ethel Liggins, an Englishwoman, intent on making an American career was advised to change her name to Leginska ("ska" being the feminine counterpart of "ski"). She told me interesting stories about herself; among her many memories, she said that as a child she was bounced by Winston Churchill on his knee after his return as a hero from the Boer War. She volunteered her own date of birth, April 13, 1886, and I checked on it by securing her birth certificate; it was correct. Now, Churchill came home in glory in 1899, and since it is unlikely that he proceeded right away to bounce Liggins (not yet Leginska) on his knee, she must have reached a nubile adolescence at the time, and the whole episode assumed a totally different complexion. "Botheration!" she exclaimed when I pointed out the embarrassing chronology to her. "How do you know when Churchill returned to England from South Africa? You are not British!"

No greater splendor among contemporary orchestral conductors surrounded the career of Leopold Stokowski, who lived to be 95, working in music to the last days of his life. And his name ended in "ski"! Invidious rumors had it that his real name was Stokes, and that he polonized it as many other artists did. False! He was born in London, the son of a Polish cabinet maker named Kopernik Joseph Boleslaw Stokowski and an Irish woman Annie Marion Moore-Stokowski, on April 18, 1882. Not satisfied with his true half-Polish origin, he for some reason chose to maintain that he was totally Polish, born in Cracow in 1887 (rather than 1882), and that his name was Leopold Boleslawowicz Stokowski. This bit of fantasy appears in the main volume of *Riemann's Musik-Lexikon.* When I sounded the alarm, pointing out that the patronymic ending on "which" or "wicz" or "witch" is possible in Russian, but not in Polish, the *Riemann's* editors sent me a photostat copy of the original questionnaire in Stokowski's own hand embodying all this fanciful information. By way of rebuttal, I forwarded to the *Riemann's* people a copy of Stokowski's birth certificate which I had obtained from London. The 1975 supplement to *Riemann's* carries a corresponding correction.

Among many fantastic tales that accompany musical biographies there is one concerning Werner Egk. The name sounded like a manufactured logograph, or an acronym for "ein guter Künstler," and even more self-anointed "ein genialer Künstler." I wrote to the director of the archives of the City of Augsburg where Egk was born, and elicited information that his real name was Mayer. If so, whence Egk? The composer himself came forward with an explanation that was more puzzling than the original riddle: he changed his name from Mayer to Egk after his marriage to Elisabeth Karl; the initials of her first and last name formed the outer letters of Egk, and the middle "g" was added "for euphony." Guttural euphony?

No experience in my "harmless drudgery" equaled the Case of Walter Dahms, an obscure German author of musical biographies. According to musical lexika that listed his name, including *Baker's,* he went to Rome in 1922, and promptly vanished. I did not care to leave him dangling like an unshriven ghost, an elusive zombie. I used to mention Dahms to every musicologist I met as a disappearing act, and one of them told me that there was nothing mysterious about Dahms, that he went to Lisbon, Portugal, adopted a Portuguese-sounding pseudonym and continued publishing books on music. I inserted this seemingly innocuous bit of information in my 1965 Supplement to *Baker's,* but unbeknownst to myself it unleashed a fantastic chain of events. The editors of the Supplement to *Riemann's Musik-Lexikon* who were also interested to bring Dahms up to date seized upon my addendum and inquired through Santiago Kastner, London-born German-educated music scholar resident in Lisbon, to find out facts about Dahms. But no one in the rather flourishing German colony in Lisbon, not even anyone at the German Embassy, knew anything about Dahms. The *Riemann* editors would not be pacified. "Baker (really Slonimsky)," they wrote Kastner again, "is greatly valued here because of its reliability. Behind the bland statement that Dahms was still in Lisbon in 1960 must lie a lot of painstaking research." Kastner volunteered a guess that Dahms may be a German-speaking Portuguese citizen named Gualterio Armando, Gualterio being a Portuguese form of Walter, and Armando containing three letters of the name Dahms. He addressed the question directly to Dahms, whether he was or was not Dahms. All hell broke loose thereafter. "I am not identical with anyone but myself," replied Gualterio Armando. "I have absolutely nothing to say about Herr W. D. mentioned in your letter because I know nothing about him. I hope that this will put an end to this whole business once and for all." Kastner reported his failure to the *Riemann's* editors, and announced that he was through with his investigation, but voiced his conviction that Dahms "must be identical with that ass Gualterio Armando after all." Why was he so vehement in denying his real identity? He died on October 5, 1973, carrying the secret to his grave.

Among the unburied musical ghosts that haunted me through the years was Alois Minkus, an Austrian composer of operas and ballets who spent most of his career in Russia. For a hundred years, first under the Czars, then under the Soviets, his ballets never ceased to be the favorite numbers in the Russian ballet repertory. Not a year passed without my receiving an insistent inquiry from Russia and abroad as to the fate of Minkus after he left Russia in 1891. Some reference works have him dead in that year; others prolong his life until 1907, with the date accompanied by a parenthetical question mark. I must have written a dozen letters to various registries of vital statistics in Vienna on the supposition that Minkus returned to Vienna where he was born and died there. I did obtain his birth certificate ascertaining that he was born on March 23, 1826, rather than 1827 as most Russian and other music reference sources have it, but the Vienna archivists could tell me nothing as to his date of death. Then in the summer of 1976 I made one more half-hearted inquiry in Vienna. To my astonishment I got a clue that all death notices before 1939 were moved from the Stadtarchive, the Landesarchiv, and from the Vienna Rathaus and its numerous subdivisions to the corresponding parochial registries. Hot on the scent, I wrote to the proper Lutheran parish, and to my absolute joy of discovery I received a document certifying that Alois Minkus died at Gentzgasse 92 in Vienna, on December 7, 1917, in the 92nd year of his life, from pneumonia, and that his mortal remains were deposed at the cemetery of Döbling. I immediately rushed this information and the pertinent documentation to the editors of the big Russian musical encyclopedia which had just reached the letter M, and the date got in at the last moment before going to press, with an appropriate proud parenthetical clause testifying to its authenticity.

One of the most fantastic episodes in my hunt for missing musical persons was the search for Heinrich Hammer, German conductor and composer who emigrated to the United States about the turn of the century, and then vanished from the musical scene. I appealed for help to William Lichtenwanger, who combines profound erudition with a detective flair that would have made him a rich man had he dedicated himself to the search for missing heirs and holders of unused bank accounts. Quick as a panther, he produced a clipping from *The Los Angeles Times* of October 25, 1953, which carried on its society page a photograph of Heinrich Hammer, 91, and his young bride Arlene, 22. Their address was given in the story, but when I wrote to him my letter came back with the notation "Deceased." But when and where? Lichtenwanger got on the telephone, and after a few inquiries got hold of Hammer's son, a repair worker of the California telephone company. Unbelievably, contact was established with him atop a telephone pole, and he gave Lichtenwanger the needed information. Hammer had moved to Phoenix, Arizona, where he died on October 28, 1954, just a year after his marriage.

How much of personal life ought to be reported in a dignified biographical dictionary? Volumes have been written speculating about the identity of Beethoven's "Immortal Beloved," even though the famous letter addressed to her was never sent off. Should a biographer be so bold as to doubt a great man's own confession of love? A conscientious biographer took exception to Goethe's declaration that he had never loved anyone as much as Lili Schönemann. "Here the great Goethe errs," he commented: "His greatest love was Frederike Drion." From the sublime to contemporary love lore. The formidable Hungarian pianist Nyiregyhazi was married nine times, and admitted to 65 extra-marital liaisons. Is this proper information in a biographical dictionary? The marriages, perhaps; the liaisons, only famous ones, like Liszt's and Chopin's.

It was only recently that the known homosexuality of Tchaikovsky became a matter of open discussion in his biographies; first inkling of it appeared in the preface to the 1934 edition of Tchaikovsky's correspondence with his benefactress Madame von Meck. In 1940 a collection of his letters to the family, including those to his brother and biographer Modest who was also a homosexual, was published in Russia, but it was soon withdrawn from publication and became a sort of bibliographical phantom; an expurgated edition was published later. In subsequent books on Tchaikovsky published in Russia the matter is unmentioned. But a strange mass of unfounded rumors began circulating both in Russia and abroad shortly after Tchaikovsky's death that he committed a "suicide by cholera," that he deliberately drank unboiled water during a raging cholera epidemic in St. Petersburg, and this despite his fear of cholera which had been the cause of his mother's death. The stories that I heard during my visit to Russia in 1962 were right out of Gothic horror tales. It seems that Tchaikovsky became involved in a homosexual affair with a young member of the Russian Imperial family, and that when Czar Alexander III got wind of it, he served the Tchaikovsky family an ultimatum: either have Tchaikovsky take poison, or have him tried for sodomy and sent to Siberia. Tchaikovsky accepted the verdict, and with the connivance of his personal physician Dr. Bertenson, was given a poison that produced symptoms similar to those of cholera. As additional evidence that Tchaikovsky did not die of cholera, the proponents of this theory argue, was the fact that his body was allowed to lie in state and that several of his intimates kissed him on the mouth, as the Russian death ritual allows, whereas cholera victims were buried in zinc-lined sealed coffins to prevent contagion.

Dramatic deaths should rightly be noted in biographies, but grisly details had better be left out. It is not advisable to follow the type of reporting exemplified in an obituary of Sir Armine Woodhouse in *The Annual Register of London* for the year 1777, noting that his death "was occasioned by a fishbone in his throat."

Percy A. Scholes took credit for sending the British writer on music, Arthur Eaglefield Hull, to his death under the wheels of a train. He wrote me: "Hull's suicide was the result of my exposure of his thefts in his book *Music, Classical, Romantic and Modern*. He threw himself under a train."

A suicide directly connected with a musical composition was that of Rezső Seress, Hungarian author of the sad, sad song "Gloomy Sunday." At one time the playing of the tune was forbidden in Central Europe because it drove several impressionable people to suicide. Seress himself jumped out the window, on a Monday, not gloomy Sunday.

Musical murders are surprisingly few; singers are occasionally murdered out of jealousy, but not famous singers. The most spectacular murder, never conclusively solved, was that of the French eighteenth-century musician Jean Marie Leclair, stabbed to death in his own house. Since nothing was taken, it could not have been a burglary. I proposed a theory that he was done to death by his estranged wife who was a professional engraver and publisher of some of Leclair's music, and had sharp tools at her disposal, but my painstaking argumentation in favor of this theory was pooh-poohed by the foremost French music historian Marc Pincherle and others.

Dementia, insanity and bodily disintegration are scourges that hit many composers, and in most cases they were caused by syphilis. Undoubtedly, the tragic illnesses of Schumann, Smetana, Hugo Wolf and MacDowell were all caused by the lues, the *morbus gallicus* as it was usually described in the past centuries. In his book on Delius, Sir Thomas Beecham remarks ruefully that the goddess Aphrodite Pandemos repaid Delius cruelly for his lifelong worship at her altar. Delius died blind and paralyzed.

In light of recent disclosures, free from displaced piety for a great man, it appears that Beethoven, too, was the victim of syphilis. His deafness was only a symptom (as in the case of Smetana) which does not necessarily indicate a venereal infection. But there are too many other circumstances that lead to this sad conclusion, recounted in the recent study by Dieter Kerner, *Krankheiten grosser Musiker.*

Even the worshipful speculation as to psychological causes of physical decline and death, so cherished in old-fashioned biography, has no place in a book of reference. I brushed aside such probings into a person's psyche as found in an old entry on the eighteenth-century French composer Isouard, to the effect that he was so deeply "mortified" by his failure to be elected to the French Academy that "although a married man," he abandoned work, "plunged into dissipation, and died."

Triskaidecaphobia, an irrational fear of number 13, demonstrably affected the state of mind of two great composers, Rossini and Schoenberg. In addition to his superstition about the malevolent character of 13, Rossini was also fearful of Friday. He died on November 13, 1868, which was a Friday. Numerologists could cite his case to prove predestination. Schoenberg's case is remarkable because there is so much recent evidence that his triskaidecaphobia was not a whimsical pose. He was born on the 13th of the month of September in 1874, and he regarded it ominous in his personal destiny. He sometimes avoided using 13 in numbering the bars of his works. When he realized that the title of his work *Moses und Aaron* contained 13 letters, he crossed out the second "a" in Aaron, even though the spelling Aron can not be substantiated either in German or in English. When someone thoughtlessly remarked to him on his 76th birthday that $7 + 6 = 13$, he seemed genuinely upset; he died at that age. On his last day of life, July 13, 1951, he remarked to his wife that he would be all right if he would survive the ominous day, but he did not, and died.

Going over my list of *morituri,* centenarians or near-centenarians, I came upon the name of Victor Küzdö, a Hungarian-American violinist born, or so the old edition of *Baker's* said, in 1869. I wrote to Küzdö at his last known address which I found in an old musical directory, in effect asking him whether he was living or dead. A few days later I received from him a dictated postcard saying that, although practically blind, he was still alive and well in Glendale, California. Furthermore, he took the opportunity to correct his date of birth: he was born in 1863, not in 1869, and had shortly before celebrated his 100th anniversary! But this was not the end of the story; soon afterwards I got a letter from a real-estate man in Glendale notifying me that Küzdö was in the habit of diminishing his age, and that he was actually 103, not 100! How could he be sure? Simple: he was a numerologist. When the inevitable end came to Küzdö on February 24, 1966, his death certificate gave his age as 106. He was born in 1859, not in 1860, not in 1869.

The most remarkable woman centenarian on my list was Margaret Ruthven Lang, of the Boston musical dynasty of Lang, who died at the age of 104 in 1972. She was a regular symphony goer since the early days of the Boston Symphony. On her 100th birthday the orchestra played the hymn *Old Hundred* in her honor. The Russian-French singer Marie Olénine d'Alheim lived to be 100. Among other recent centenarians was the French conductor and composer Henri-Paul Busser who died in 1973 at the age of 101.

It would be most interesting to compile actuarial tables of life expectancy of musicians according to their specialties. One thing appears certain: great musicians die young; consider Mozart, Schubert, Chopin, Mendelssohn, Scriabin. It is a fascinating speculation to project

Mozart's life from 1756 into 1840, and Schubert's life to an even later date! One may indulge in a revery that very great musicians are summoned to Heaven because they would be more at home there.

Statistically speaking, organists live the longest lives, perhaps because their sedentary occupation keeps them from wasting their energy on idle pastimes. Scholars and pedagogues come next in longevity; conductors are fairly durable, too; among instrumentalists, those handling big instruments, like the double bass or trombone, live longer than violinists who in turn live longer than flutists and oboe players who are apt to be frail in physique. Among singers, tenors dissipate their vitality faster than bass singers. In all musical categories mediocrities outlive great artists by a large margin.

In addition to all the troubles involved in the compilation of a biographical dictionary, there are people who concoct sinister plots to further bamboozle the proverbial "harmless drudge." Mikhail Goldstein, a respectable Russian violinist, annoyed by his unfair treatment by the Soviet Music Publishing House in systematically rejecting his compositions, decided to take revenge on them. He invented a Russian composer named Ovsianiko-Kulikovsky, furnished him with a plausible biography, obtained a quantity of old manuscript paper and composed a symphony in his name, pretending that he found the score in the archives of the Odessa Conservatory where he was librarian at the time. The Soviets swallowed the bait and published the score, proclaiming it to be a major discovery; it was also recorded, and greeted with enthusiastic reviews, not only in Russia but elsewhere. (Shall I confess, blushingly? I reviewed the recording for *The Musical Quarterly,* and announced with some reservations that if the work were genuine it would be the first Russian symphony ever written.) A doctoral dissertation was published on the work. When Goldstein admitted the hoax, he was accused of trying to appropriate an important piece of national legacy. The situation degenerated into a farce, and Goldstein got out of Russia as soon as he could get an exit visa. But, as in Prokofiev's *Lieutenant Kije,* it was too late to kill off Ovsianiko-Kulikovsky, and his symphony is still listed in some record catalogues and is kept on the shelves of music libraries.

An even more dangerous mystification was perpetrated by the eminent Italian music scholar Alberto Cametti who claimed discovery of an important biographical notebook of Palestrina, which established the elusive exact date of Palestrina's birth. He said he purchased the document from one Telemaco Bratti, and even went to the trouble of reproducing, or rather forging, part of the manuscript in an article he wrote on the subject. Another Italian music scholar Raffaele Casimiri embraced the "discovery" as a gift of God to all true Palestrinologists. Then Alberto Cametti let it pass through various channels that the name of the alleged discoverer of the document, Telemaco Bratti, was an anagram of Alberto Cametti. A great inner storm ensued in the confined company of Italian music scholars, but in the meantime the hoax found its way into reputable bibliographies. (It was thanks to a knowledgeable friend that I myself did not fall into the trap in giving the exact date of Palestrina's birth in my edition of *Baker's;* this date remains unknown to this day.)

It is amazing that grown men and women would deliberately falsify their vital statistics, particularly their dates of birth, in order to appear younger in a reference work. The gambit is understandable among actressses and prima donnas; and it has been said that a woman has the privilege of improvising her age. It would also be understandable for men in their dotage who marry girls in their nonage, but both men and women of music rejuvenate themselves lexicographically even when they are not stage performers.

The Spanish composer Oscar Esplá produced his passport to prove to me that he was born in 1888 and not in 1886 as I had it in *Baker's*. But I had obtained a copy of his birth certificate which confirmed the accuracy of the earlier date.

Mabel Daniels, the Boston composer, once included in a piece a C-sharp against C, explaining that she "had to use a dissonance," since she was living in the same town with me. She petulantly accused me of being "no gentleman" in putting her down as born in 1878 rather than 1879, her own chosen year. She was born in November 1878, just a few weeks away from 1879, so why should I not accept the later year, she pleaded. Poor Mabel! She lived a full life until well into her tenth decade, dying in 1971.

A desire to appear young, if only on paper, is not a modern phenomenon. Since time immemorial, musicians, poets, painters, actors, even politicians, exercised their unquestionable prerogative to fib about their age. Johann Jakob Froberger gave the date of May 18, 1620 as that of his birth to his physician, but his certificate of baptism reveals that he was baptized on May 19, 1616. It is a reasonable assumption that the day and the month of his birth, as given by himself, were correct, and that he was baptized on the next day, in 1616, not 1620.

In his handwritten autobiographical note for Mattheson's *Grundlage einer Ehrenpforte,* Telemann stated that he was born in 1682, whereas he was born a year earlier; as in many such cases, the day and the month of his birth, March 14, were given correctly.

The Italian composer and conductor Angelo Mariani, who was born on October 11, 1821, insisted in his communications to Francesco Regli, editor of an Italian biographical dictionary, that he was born on October 11, 1824. Mariani's birth certificate proves that he was born in 1821.

It was common practice in Catholic families to give identical Christian names to infants born after the death of a previous son, or a daughter, so as to perpetuate the memory of the lost child. This has led to a number of mistaken identities. The bicentennial of Giovanni Battista Viotti was widely celebrated in 1953, commemorating the birth in Fontanetto, Italy, of an infant of that name born on May 23, 1753, who died in the following year, on July 10, 1754. On May 12, 1755, another child was born to the Viottis and was given the names Giovanni Battista Guglielmo Domenico, retaining the first two names from those of their deceased son. This second similarly-named child was the composer whose bicentennial was celebrated two years early.

Biographical notices for Giacomo Insanguine found in old music dictionaries list his year of birth variously between 1712 and 1742. I applied for a copy of his birth certificate from the registries of his native town of Monopoli, and received a document purporting to show that he was born in 1712, a date that did not seem to agree with the known facts of his education and career. I pressed for further search, which revealed that a Giacomo Insanguine who was born in 1712 died in 1726 at the age of 14. On March 22, 1728, a boy was born to the bereaved parents, and was given the names Giacomo Antonio Francesco Paolo Michele. This was the composer Insanguine.

Beethoven was eager to prove that he was born in 1772, not in 1770, and that he had an older brother who was born in 1770. It was discovered that a Ludwig Maria van Beethoven was born on April 1, 1769, but he died a few days later. The great Beethoven was born in the following year.

Next to birth certificates, the best sources of information are family bibles, marriage certificates and school registries. The date of birth of Kaspar Othmayr, March 12, 1515, is verified by his astrological chart, and one can be sure that in those remote times no one would hoodwink one's own astrologer. Even in modern times there are practicing astrologers among composers; of these, Dane Rudhyar is professionally the most successful.

In one famous event the correct age of the protagonist became a matter of life or death. On June 28, 1914, Gavrilo Princip, a young Serbian patriot, assassinated Crown Prince Franz Ferdinand of Austria. His act precipitated World War I, which precipitated the Russian Revolution, which precipitated the rise of Hitler, which precipitated World War II, etc., etc., etc. According to the Austrian law of the time no person less than twenty years of age could be executed for a capital crime. Gavrilo Princip was born on July 25, 1894, according to the Gregorian calendar, and was not quite twenty when he turned the world upside down. This saved him from execution, and he died in prison of tuberculosis of the bone marrow on April 28, 1918.

Oscar Wilde was not so lucky in his own chronology. He had whittled two years off his true age, claiming that he was born in 1856, whereas his real year of birth was 1854. Owing to a peculiar twist of English law, persons under forty indicted for immorality were granted leniency. Oscar Wilde was arrested for sodomy in 1895, and would have benefited by the law had it not been for the prying investigation of the court clerk who secured Wilde's birth certificate proving that he was over forty at the time of his offense. This precluded leniency, and Wilde got a severe sentence. Despite the availability of the correct date, the *Encyclopædia Britannica* carried the 1856 date in its article on Oscar Wilde right through its thirteenth edition. The *Century Cyclopedia* still gives the wrong date.

Much confusion is created in musical biography by the discrepancy in dating past events according to the Russian and Western calendars. The Greek Orthodox Church refused to accept the Gregorian calendar, and continued to use the Julian calendar until 1918. The Julian calendar was also in force in Bulgaria and Rumania during the same period. As a result, the dating of Russian births and deaths lagged behind the Western calendar, by 11 days in the 18th century, 12 days in the 19th century and 13 days in the 20th century. (The increase in discrepancy was caused by the fact that the years 1800 and 1900 were leap-years in Russia but not in the West.) Stravinsky was born on June 5, 1882, according to the Julian calendar, which corresponded to June 17 of the Western calendar. But after 1900, when the difference between the two calendars increased by a day, he began celebrating his birthday on June 18. As his 80th anniversary approached in June 1962, he let it be known that he was going to celebrate it on June 18, which gave occasion to *The New York Times* to say that the faces of some lexicographers would be red on June 18, Stravinsky's preferred date for his birth, seeing that most dictionaries, including two edited by me, gave this date as June 17. I sent a rebuttal explaining my reasons for sticking to the June 17 date, and *The New York Times* published it under the caption, "It Is All Clear Now." This aroused Stravinsky's anger, and he shot off a wire to the paper reasserting his prerogative to celebrate his birthday on any date he wished. He declared his intention to mark the date in the twenty-first century on June 19, assuming that the difference between the two calendars would continue to increase a day each century, but he overlooked the fact that the year 2000 will be a leap year according to both Gregorian and Julian calendars, because Pope Gregory ruled on the advice of learned astronomers that the year divisible by 400 must be reckoned as a leap year.

Are trivia worth mentioning in a biographical dictionary? It all depends. If such trivia have significant bearing on the subject's life and career, they should be given consideration. The unique case of the male castrato Tenducci who eloped with a young girl and subsequently married her, deserves comment to dispel incredulity. He was a triorchis, and was therefore capable of marriage even after he was two-thirds castrated. His wife wrote a book of memoirs on the affair.

There remain a few categories that ought to be dealt with in separate rubrics.

INCLUSION AND EXCLUSION. *Baker's Biographical Dictionary of Musicians* must necessarily include men and women active in music who were not professional musicians, such as aristocratic patrons and patronesses, wealthy promoters of musical events, impresarios, music publishers, ballet masters who played important roles in commissioning and performing works from composers, and of course music critics. A practical criterion for including names of little-known composers, performers and pedagogues should be the degree of likelihood that a music student, or a concert goer, or a person who wants to know who is who in music would look it up in a dictionary. Thousands of names hover in the perifery of the music world and many more populate the index pages of biographies of famous composers. Still more are modest members of world orchestras who have distinguished themselves in various ways. Hugo Leichtentritt told me that Riemann, with whom he studied, used to play chamber music with amateurs and professionals at his home in Leipzig, and after each session, would ask them to fill out questionnaires for inclusion in his *Musik-Lexikon*. Theodore Baker, the compiler of the original edition of the present dictionary, collected biographical data from his friends who played in the Boston Symphony Orchestra. As a result, the early editions of both lexica became over-populated with individuals who were perfectly honorable practitioners of their art, but who failed to leave an indelible, or even delible, mark on the sands of music. Most of these long-dead servants of music, whether borrowed by Baker from Riemann and other collectors of musical flesh, or installed anew by Baker and his successors out of personal friendship, have been allowed in the present edition to remain under their individual lexicographical tombstones for humanitarian reasons, rather than relegated to the common graves of crumbling newspaper clippings in public libraries; still, the paragraphs devoted to them originally have been mercifully cut down to commensurate size. No more will the impatient user of the dictionary be offered long lines of printed matter dealing with this or that obscure orchestral player, church organist or provincial music teacher, relating in stultifying detail the advancement of their dull careers. But musical, or even unmusical, figures that multidentally smile on us from huge posters or gold-rimmed record albums, the glamorized purveyors of popular subculture of whatever degree of vulgarity, the Beatles and other singing coleoptera, are welcomed to this edition of *Baker's* even more liberally than they were to the 1958 edition and to the 1965 and 1971 supplements. When, overcoming a natural revulsion, I dictated to my California secretary a paragraph on Humperdinck, the pop singer whose manager had the supreme *chutzpah* to appropriate the honored name of the composer of *Hänsel und Gretel* because it sounded "funny" and would attract attention, she was genuinely surprised at my liberality, but revealed her complete ignorance as to the existence of an earlier musician of the same name as the glorified rock singer.

DATES OF PERFORMANCE. A determined effort has been made in the present edition to list as many exact dates as possible of first performances of major works, especially operas and symphonies, not only by celebrated masters but also by modern composers. Care had to be taken to avoid duplication, for many composers are, and have been, in the habit of changing the titles of their works and then presenting them as new compositions. For instance, Don Emilio Arrieta y Corera wrote an opera, *La Conquista de Granada*, which was produced in Madrid in 1850 and revived under the title *Isabel la Católica* in 1855. The opera got a double billing in the valuable compilation *Cronica de la Opera italiana en Madrid* published in 1878, the index of which correctly lists the two titles interchangeably, but this precaution has failed to deter other publications from duplicating the work. Quite often, composers append an optional descriptive title to an earlier work, which is apt to be duplicated in the catalogue.

SPELLING OF NAMES. Variants of spelling of celebrated musical names cause uncertainty, and choice had to be made in the present edition of *Baker's* guided by common usage; alternative spellings are then cross-referenced. Spanish, Portuguese and Latin American names commonly include both the paternal and maternal surname; a selection has to be made according to preferred usage. Thus, Alejandro García Caturla is listed under Caturla, the name he used in his published works; Oscar Lorenzo Fernandez is listed under Fernandez. In some instances, a musician changes the form of his name in the middle of his career. In the earlier editions of this dictionary the main entry on Edmund Rubbra appeared under Duncan-Rubbra; Duncan was the name of his first wife, which he adopted in some of his works; later he reverted to the legal name Rubbra, which is therefore used in the present edition of *Baker's*. Philip Heseltine published most of his music under the witching surname Peter Warlock, but Heseltine would seem preferable for a biographical dictionary. Americanization has produced several changes in the spelling of names; Arnold Schoenberg changed the spelling of his last name from Schönberg to Schoenberg when he emigrated to the United States. Carlos Salzedo dropped the acute accent that marked the antepenultimate letter of his original name. Eugen Zádor dropped the accent and changed his first name to Eugene when he came to America. Aladár Szendrei made his career in Europe under his original Hungarian name and surname, but changed it phonetically to Sendrey when he emigrated to the United States; a cross-reference has been made in the present edition under Sendrey to his original name. Edgar Varèse was baptized as Edgard Varèse, but most of his works were published with the first name spelled Edgar; in 1940 or thereabouts he changed it back to his legal name Edgard. However, the present edition of *Baker's* keeps the familiar form Edgar. The existence of alternate spellings Carl and Karl in many German names creates considerable confusion. The 1958 edition of *Baker's* modernized virtually all Carls to Karls, with some curious results, such as the spelling Karl Philipp Emanuel Bach instead of the standard Carl; the traditional spelling has been restored in the present edition. A curious case is that of Carl Ruggles, the American composer, whose real first name was Charles. He changed it to Carl as a youth when he decided to devote himself to music; he hoped that the Germanic form of the name would give him a better chance to succeed in the highly German-minded musical world of early twentieth-century America.

NOBILIARY PARTICLES. Early in this century it was common in American and British usage to put the nobiliary particle "von" in front of German names, such as "Von Bülow" and the like. In the wake of World War I the "von" became unpopular among the Allied nations. The original full name of the English composer Gustav Holst, who was of Swedish ancestry, was Von Holst. During the war, at the suggestion of Percy A. Scholes, he dropped the objectionable "von" from his name. Anton von Webern eliminated the "von" after the fall of the Austro-Hungarian Empire in 1918; the present edition lists his name under Webern, Anton von, in appreciation of the fact that he used the full name in titles of many of his early works. A more difficult problem is encountered in the Dutch and Flemish nobiliary particle Van. Beethoven was very proprietary about his own "van" and regarded it as a proof of his noble origin, an important claim at the time when he tried to assure the guardianship of his nephew. The French and Spanish "de" and the Italian "di" often become coalesced with the last name. Debussy was Bussy to friends in his youth; Madame von Meck, the patroness of Tchaikovsky, who employed Debussy as a house musician and teacher in Moscow, referred to him as Bussy. No book of reference would list Bussy as an alternative for Debussy, but in some other names, not necessarily French, this nobiliary particle retains its independent existence. De Koven is an example. But De Falla is improper; his name should be listed under Falla, Manuel de.

RUSSIAN NAMES. The Russian alphabet has two untractable letters: one is represented by the Cyrillic symbol "ы," the other by a fence of three sticks with a line underneath it, and a wriggle, or a cedilla, on the right of the protracted horizontal line. Only Turkish has the phonetic equivalent of "ы," represented by an undotted "i" in the new Turkish alphabet. As for the second Cyrillic symbol aforementioned, it can be very adequately represented by the coalescence of the sounds "sh" and "ch" in a compound word such as fish-chips. The Russian sound for "e" is palatalized into "yeh" as in the now accepted English spelling of Dostoyevsky. English and American music dictionaries have inherited the spelling of Russian names of composers and performers from German, which has no "ch" sound, and in which the Russian (and English) "v" sound is represented by "w." As a result, we had Tschaikowsky for at least half a century. British and American librarians, realizing that Tsch = Ch, began spelling Tchaikovsky as Chaikovsky. But if we follow phonetics, then why do we need the diphthong "ai"? Why not plain "i" as in China? Here we come to the antinomy of sound, sight and audio-visual association: Chikovsky has an impossible look. A compromise is necessary: hence, Tchaikovsky in *Baker's*. "Ch" in Rachmaninoff has a guttural German sound that English does not possess. The spelling Rachmaninoff is part-German ("ch") and part-French ("ff"), but this is the way he signed his name, familiar from printed music and concert programs. Most British sources prefer Rakhmaninov.

Once we start on the road to phonetics we will be bound for disaster. The name of the poet Evtushenko is pronounced Yevtushenko, but the eye rebels against its aspect. Besides, an unpalatalized "e" in such an initial sound is not necessarily un-Russian; some people from the northern provinces or from Siberia would say Evtushenko, just as if it were written in English. Another thing: the final diphthong "iy," as it is often represented phonetically in names like Tchaikovsky (or for that matter in Slonimsky), is nearest to the French "ille" in "volaille," but it is not as emphatically articulated. There is no reason to add ugliness to a name like Tchaikovsky by spelling it Tchaikovskiy. Then there is the vexing problem of transliterating Russian names of French or German origin back into their original languages. Some music dictionaries transliterate Cui as Kyue, a visual monstrosity. Cui was the son of a Napoleonic soldier who remained in Russia after the campaign of 1812 and married a Russian woman. His French name Cui ought to stay. The Soviet composer Shnitke (spelled phonetically in English) was of German origin, and his father signed his name in German as Schnittke; this spelling ought to remain even in an English reference work. The same consideration holds for names like Schneerson (Jewish-German) or Steinpress (pronounced Shteinpress in Russian) and Steinberg (for Shteinberg). If we try to transliterate foreign names in Russian back and forth, we will arrive at mutations such as Betkhoven and (yes, unbelieveable but true) Poochcheenee, used for a time in the bibliography of *Notes.* I am proud to say that I opened such a vigorous letter-writing campaign against this practice that it was stopped. To conclude, the transliteration of Russian names and Russian titles of works should be guided by ear and by sight. There are seasonal changes and fashions for some Russian names. It used to be Sergey, Bolshoy Theater, etc. Now it is Sergei, Bolshoi, etc. Both visually and phonetically, these altered spellings are fine. In this edition of *Baker's* the paternal names have been omitted in listings of Russian composers, except in that of Piotr Ilyich Tchaikovsky which has become traditional. The pronunciation of Russian names has been indicated only when mispronunciation is common, as for instance in Balakirev (stress on the second syllable, not the third), Borodin (stress on the last syllable). The pronunciation of Khachaturian's name, with the accent on the third syllable, has become so common that it would be idle to try to change it to the proper pronunciation with the accent on the last syllable; equally futile would it be to persuade people to compress the last two vowels into one: "yan." The doubling of "s" between vowels in Russian names such as Mussorgsky is admittedly Germanic in origin; but in seeking to avoid the vocalization of the middle "s" in Mussorgsky the doubling of "s" becomes essential. Thus it is Mussorgsky rather than Musorgsky, Vassily rather than Vasily; but in less familiar names like Stasov, a single "s" is postulated. Illogical? So is the language itself.

GEOGRAPHIC NAMES. Place names have been playing musical chairs during the wars and revolutions of the first half of the present century. I was born in St. Petersburg, left Petrograd in 1918, and revisited Leningrad in 1962. One can travel from Pressburg to Bratislava to Pozsony without budging an inch. A person born in Klausenburg finds himself nominally transferred to Kolozsvár and then to Cluj without moving from one's house. Sometimes a town renamed to honor a current revolutionary figure resumes its original name when the eponymous hero falls into disfavor. Perm was renamed Molotov after the Soviet Revolution, but became Perm once more when Molotov faded out in 1956. In Poland, Katowice was named Stalinogorod in 1953 but became Katowice once more in 1956 when Stalin was posthumously disfranchised. In all such cases, common sense is the only guide in tracing the movements of a biographical subject. Then there is Liège. For over a century it bore an unnatural acute accent over its middle letter. In 1946 its Municipal Council resolved that the accent should be changed to the grave one. A Belgian musician born in a town with an acute accent may die there with a grave.

ABBREVIATIONS. All abbreviations except the obvious ones, like vol., prof., symph. orch., etc., and the names of the months (except March and April, which remain unabbreviated) have been eliminated from this edition. No more the impenetrable jungle of Ztsch. Vsch., vcs., mvt. or Kgl.

BIBLIOGRAPHY. In listing sources of information pertaining to the subject of an entry, a conscientious bibliographer ought to use common sense. It would serve no rational purpose to cite general histories of music for references to Bach, Mozart or Beethoven in the bibliographical section; obviously each of such books will have extended chapters on great masters of music. But in bibliographies on modern composers, it is worthwhile to mention collections of articles containing informative material relating to such composers. The same consideration would apply to books on great conductors, great instrumentalists, or great singers; they ought to be listed if they contain useful biographical information. Magazine articles of extensive length are also proper bibliographical material. Title pages are sometimes deceptive. A brochure on Louis-Gilbert Duprez by A. A. Elwart bears the claim on its title page "avec une biographie authentique de son maître A. Choron." Upon examination, it turns out that it contains only a couple of pages on Choron. On the other hand, there are books modestly titled that provide a wealth of biographical information not available in special monographs on the subject. Since it is patently impractical to append an evaluation of each bibliographical item in a book of general reference, a reader's attention can be called to a particularly valuable publication by a word or two, such as "important," "of fundamental value," etc. Conversely, a warning should be given against worthless publications of a biographical nature that for some reason have become widely read. A famous, or infamous, example is a purported book of memoirs attributed to the nineteenth-century German prima donna Wilhelmina Schröder-Devrient and duly listed under her name in the bibliography of a number of respectable music dictionaries. It is a mildly pornographic (as pornography went at the time of its publication a hundred years ago) volume recounting her amours with famous people. It was made available in German and French; there is even a French edition in existence illustrated with erotic drawings. Less obvious in intent, but much more harmful in its effect, is the notorious correspondence between Chopin and Potocka manufactured by a Polish woman in 1945 and broadcast over the Warsaw Radio during the first months after the liberation of Poland from Nazi occupation. Respectable music scholars and Chopinologists eagerly accepted these letters, which portrayed Chopin as a sex maniac given to verbal obscenities, as genuine. In one of Chopin's alleged letters he is made to use a sexual pun on a vulgar Polish word that was not in use until 1900; and there were other indecencies. The poor woman who concocted these letters committed suicide, but even then some people refused to give up their faith in the authenticity of this clumsy forgery.

Archaic spelling of the titles of old books is preserved in the present edition of *Baker's*. Martin Agricola's work, *Ein deudsche Musica,* retains its ancient title. Varieties of spelling in different editions of old English books are indicated, as in Christopher Simpson's *Practicall Musick.* Inordinately long book titles are abbreviated unless they contain some specific limiting clauses. For instance, Karl Grunsky's volume, *Die Technik des Klavierauszuges entwickelt am dritten Akt von Wagners Tristan und Isolde,* treats the problem of piano reduction only of the third act of *Tristan,* and it would be misleading to list it as *Die Technik des Klavierauszuges* plain and simple. In all such cases, practical sense rather than pedantic considerations should guide the compiler.

POLTERGEIST. Typographical errors are not just human failures of perception. They are acts of a malevolent mischievous spirit that lays its eggs in the linotype ribbon. Or else how are we to account for alterations that are obviously intended as mockery? Such fanciful conceits as "scared music," "pubic rectal," or "anals of music" cannot be accidents endemic to the typesetter. Avaunt! Avaunt! (Memo to proofreader: typos intentional to illustrate the dreadful dangers in writing books; do not change to "sacred music," "public recital" and "annals of music.")

I have a recurrent dream: I am in the dock facing a trio of stern judges vaguely resembling my school teachers of long ago, about to hear a sentence pronounced upon me for incompetence, negligence, dereliction of duty, fraudulent pretense at lexicographical expertise. The judges exhibit grotesquely enlarged entries from my edition of Baker's, engraved on huge slabs of granite, as evidence against me. In my anguish I plead extenuating circumstances.

Yes, I was guilty of procrastination, sloth, accidie, pigritude (a lovely old word for laziness), stupidity perhaps, but did I not try? Did I not get from Naples the birth certificates of 13 Enrico Carusos before giving up? Did I not locate Edward Maryon in England after his publisher told me he had been dead for years? Maryon bequeathed to me his manuscripts and other memorabilia, going back to the seventeenth century (he was of nobility; his full name was Maryon d'Aulby), which were sent to me in a huge trunk by his executors after his death. I donated the materials to the Boston Public Library.

At least one living composer showed kindness to me in appreciation of my efforts to get his biography right (and failing), Ezra Sims of Massachusetts. I got his string quartets all mixed up in my 1971 Supplement to *Baker's,* and created a non-existent String Quartet No. 2, composed according to my mistaken impression in 1962. In an unparalleled act of forgiveness, Sims composed a piece scored for a quintet for winds and strings, called it String Quartet No. 2, dated it 1962, although he wrote it in 1974, and dedicated it to me so that I "may be now less in error."

De minimis non curat lex, says an old legal maxim. But still there are minutiae that ought to be attended to in a reference work. The title of Leoncavallo's most famous opera is *Pagliacci,* without the definite article, not *I Pagliacci.* The original manuscript score is in the Library of Congress in Washington, D.C., and the title page can be examined by any doubting person. But the bronze plaque underneath the precious relic bears the wrong title *I Pagliacci!* Aaron Copland's best known work *Lincoln Portrait* was listed in *Baker's* 1958 as *A Lincoln Portrait,* and Copland specifically pointed out to me that the score has no such indefinite article in its title. And yet the program of its very first performance carried an intrusive "A," and many symphony programs repeated the error.

My medulla oblongata, or whatever part of the brain controls lexicographical reflexes, overflows with gratitude to many unselfish people who have helped me in putting together the 1958 edition of *Baker's,* its two supplements, of 1965 and 1971, and, most importantly, the present swollen edition. First to be thanked are the multitudinous registrars, clerks and keepers of city or state archives all over the habitable world who have provided me with copies of birth and death certificates that have made it possible to establish correct chronology in the lives of thousands of musicians represented in *Baker's.* The editors of the *Riemann Musik-Lexikon* have most generously let me have hundreds of documents pertaining to musical biography and copies of a number of birth and death certificates which I had not had in my possession—a most extraordinary example of scholarly cooperation. Boris Steinpress, editor of the Soviet musical encyclopedia, patiently collected for me dates of first performances of Russian operas and symphonies and corrected numerous errors encountered in the articles on Russian composers in the previous editions of *Baker's.* Grigori Schneerson of Moscow was a great lexicographical and personal friend during many years of our correspondence. And there were many others in Russia and in other countries in Europe.

How can I thank William Lichtenwanger, that magus of musical, and not only musical, encyclopedias, the polynomial scholar who possesses in his head a cross-reference to all subjects biographical, historical and lexicographical? A polymath, a polyglot at home in all European languages, an enlightened opsimath in Russian and a philological connoisseur of Turkish and Japanese, he was willing to read and to critically annotate the galley proofs of the entire bulk of the present edition of *Baker's;* he got for me precious biographical data on *Baker* inmates who dwelt in the lexicographical nirvana for decades. To quote from James

Preface

Joyce's "work in progress," written in bird language, "Have you *aviar* seen any*wing* to *eagle* it?" Lichtenwanger is unique.

Much as I welcome people volunteering corrections in *Baker's* and other lexicographical publications of which I have been in charge, I admit that I was somewhat startled when in August 1972 I received a letter from Stephen W. Ellis of Glenview, Illinois, in which he tore to pieces my 1971 Supplement to *Baker's*, sideswiping also at the basic 1958 volume. "Grossly incomplete," "flagrantly inaccurate," "absurd," "shockingly out of date," "sadly inadequate," "ridiculous," "disgraceful," and even "criminal," were some of his expletives. The 1971 Supplement must have been a "one-man job," he correctly surmised. But who *was* Stephen W. Ellis? I had never heard of him, and I could not find his name in any index of articles on music. Yet the man exhibited such precise knowledge of so many obscure items of music history and musical biography that he could not have been just an amateur. My first impulse was to respond with lofty indignation: "Sirrah! Do you realize that you are addressing one whom the *Penguin Dictionary of Music* called 'a modern prince of musical lexicography,' and for whom Percy A. Scholes invoked, in a personal letter *(rubesco referens),* the famous lines of Goldsmith, 'and still the wonder grew that one small head could carry all he knew?' One, who . . ." But I quickly cooled down, realizing how valuable Ellis could be for the completely new edition of *Baker's*. I wrote him with genuine curiosity, asking how on earth he could have collected such a mountain of information on music and musicians, which he dispensed with such certainty of his sources. I was sure he was not an academic person, I wrote him, but I guessed that he was a record collector, that he was about 42 years old, married, and had two children. I was right, as it turned out, that he was not a professional musicologist (no professional musicologist would possess such a variety of knowledge), that he was an ardent collector of records, and subscribed to bulletins issued by unions of composers all over the world. He was not 42, but only 30 years old at the time; yes, he was married, but had only one child (a second child came along soon). By profession, he was a copy reader for a small publishing house. A fortunate publishing house it was indeed! It did not take me long to persuade Ellis to help me in putting together the present edition of *Baker's;* in fact he was eager to help. His proofreading ability, I soon found out, was prodigious, but what was most remarkable, and what still astounds me, is his uncanny knack for digging up information about contemporary composers, in precise detail, and his perseverance in getting these data for *Baker's* from reluctant, recalcitrant and unwilling musicians. The wealth of information about modern Finns, Swedes, Norwegians and Danes which he was able to gather for me was truly comprehensive; he was comparably "teeming with the news," to borrow a phrase from Gilbert and Sullivan, about composers of Iceland, Japan, Belgium, Holland, Spain and Portugal; he seemed to be able to get more information about the musicians of Rumania than I could after my trip to Rumania in 1963; he was equally successful with Poles, Yugoslavs, Czechs and Bulgarians, not to mention Americans. His special contribution was information on hard-to-get Australians. All told, he sent me about 1250 biographies, each having a very complete list of works. I could not use all this material, and I had to cut down drastically on some catalogues of works. Inevitably, I had to use my own verbiage for the introductory paragraphs of each entry, but the hard core of information on hundreds of these contemporary composers from all lands under the lexicographical sun was furnished by Ellis.

My effusive thanks are owed to Samuel Sprince of Boston, Massachusetts. Like the Canadian Royal Mounties, he never failed to get his man; in this context, the man (or the woman) was some obscure musician whose opaque name made an insignificant blur on a page in an old edition of *Baker's* and who somehow remained unnoticed by subsequent editors. Still, such unfortunates had to be taken care of, dead or alive, to preserve the continuity of *Baker's* heritage. Sprince tracked down for me quite a number of such personages, most of them in a nursing home hovering between uncertain life and certain death. Several of them met their Maker without the benefit of an obituary, and were lost until some relative could be found to supply the missing obit. It is unfortunate that so many musicians die out of alphabetical order, so that when a dictionary is already half-printed, a *revenant* from the early part of the alphabet is apt to make a belated appearance. The entries under the early letters of the alphabet in the present edition of *Baker's* already constitute a sizable mortuary.

The following individuals and institutions have lent their most valuable assistance in preparing the present edition of *Baker's:*

Patsy Felch, Head Reference Librarian, and Don Roberts, Head Music Librarian, Northwestern University Music Library, Evanston, Illinois
Centre Belge de Documentation Musicale, Brussels
Per Olof Lundahl, Executive Secretary, Swedish Music Information Center, Stockholm
Bálint András Varga, Head of Promotion, Editio Musica Budapest, Budapest
Jarmo Sermilä, former Executive Secretary, Finnish Music Information Centre, Helsinki
Kimiko Shimbo, Secretary General, The Japan Federation of Composers, Tokyo
Rina Smits-Westhof, Librarian, Foundation Donemus, Amsterdam
Canadian Music Centre, Toronto
Timothy Rice, faculty of music, University of Toronto
Czechoslovak Music Information Centre, Prague
Magnhild Stoveland, Society of Norwegian Composers, Oslo
Secretaria de Estado da Comunicação Social, Lisbon
Union of Rumanian Composers, Bucharest
Iceland Music Information Centre, Reykjavik
Dimiter Christoff, Secretary General of the UNESCO International Music Council in Sofia, Bulgaria
Teresa Mochtak, Head of the Music Department, Polskie Wydawnictwo Muzyczne Edition, Warsaw
James Murdoch, National Director, Australia Music Centre, Ltd., Sydney
Wilhelm Hansen Edition, Copenhagen
Esperanza Pulido, editor, *Heterofonía,* Mexico City
Hellenic Association for Contemporary Music, Athens
Instituto de Cultura Puertorriqueña, San Juan
Benjamin Bar-Am, Secretary, League of Composers in Israel, Tel Aviv

I conclude this rather inflated preface, as I did my 1971 Supplement to *Baker's,* with a cherished quotation from a letter I received from Alfred Einstein shortly before his death. In his characteristic mood of gentle humor, he wondered "ob wir, und natürlich vor allem Sie, im Himmel einmal dafür belohnt werden, dass wir einige Ungenauigkeiten aus der Welt geschafft haben. . . ." Onward to a heavenly reward!

Los Angeles, California
September 1978

Biographical Dictionary of Musicians

A

Aaltonen, Erkki, Finnish composer; b. Hämeenlinna (Tavastehus), Aug. 17, 1910. He studied violin at the Helsinki Cons. and composition privately with Väinö Raitio and Selim Palmgren. In 1966 he became music director of the city of Kemi. His music often reflects topical subjects.

WORKS: 5 symphonies: No. 1 (1947); No. 2, *Hiroshima* (1949); No. 3, *Popular* (1952); No. 4 (1959); and No. 5 (1964); *Hämeenlinna,* rhapsody for orch. (1945); 2 piano concertos (1948, 1954); *Folk Music* for orch. (1953–60); 2 ballet suites from *Lapponia* (1956, 1959); Violin Concerto (1966); Piano Sonata (1932, revised 1972); Oboe Sonata (1945); 5 string quartets; piano pieces; songs.

Aaron, abbot of the monasteries of St. Martin and St. Pantaleon at Cologne, where he died on Dec. 14, 1052. He was the author of two historically important treatises: *De utilitate cantus vocalis et de modo cantandi atque psallendi* and *De regulis tonorum et symphoniarum.* He is believed to be the first cleric to introduce the Gregorian evening service *(nocturns)* into Germany.

Aaron, Pietro, Italian theorist; b. Florence, 1489; d. Venice, 1545. He was cantor at the cathedral of Imola in 1521; at the Rimini cathedral in 1523. In 1525 he was 'maestro di casa' in a Venetian house; in 1536 entered the Order of Jerusalem. He published *Libri tres de institutione harmonica* (Bologna, 1516); *Thoscanello de la musica* (Venice, 1523; 4 reprints, 1525–62); *Trattato della natura et cognitione di tutti gli tuoni di canto figurato* (Venice, 1525; reproduced in part, in an English translation, in O. Strunk's *Source Readings in Music History,* N.Y., 1950); *Lucidario in musica di alcune opinione antiche e moderne* (Venice, 1545); *Compendiolo di molti dubbi, segreti, et sentenze intorno al canto fermo et figurato* (Milan, posthumous; title page bears the inscription: 'In memoria eterna erit Aron').

BIBLIOGRAPHY: J. W. Link, Jr., *Theory and Tuning: Aaron's Mean Tone Temperament* (Boston, 1963); Peter Berquist, "Mode and Polyphony Around 1500; Theory and Practice," *Music Forum* I (1967).

Aav, Evald, Estonian composer; b. Reval, Feb. 22, 1900; d. there, March 21, 1939. He studied composition in Reval with Arthur Kapp; wrote mostly vocal music to words in the Estonian language. In 1928 he composed the first national Estonian opera, *The Vikings* (Tallinn, Sept. 8, 1928). In his style of composition he followed the model of Tchaikovsky.

Aavik, Juhan, Estonian composer; b. Reval, Jan. 29, 1884. He studied at the St. Petersburg Cons.; was a conductor in Dorpat (1911–25); settled again in Reval (1928–44) as prof. and director of the Conservatory there; in 1944 he went to Sweden; was conductor of the Estonian song festivals there from 1948–61 before retirement. He celebrated his 92nd birthday in 1976. A highly prolific composer, he wrote about 200 opus numbers, among them 2 symphonies; Cello Concerto (1949); Doublebass Concerto (1950); Piano Trio (1957); *Requiem* (1959); and numerous choral works, songs and pieces of chamber music. He published a history of Estonian music in 4 vols. (Stockholm, 1965–69).

Abaco, Evaristo Felice dall', Italian composer, b. Verona, July 12, 1675; d. Munich, July 12, 1742. He was in Modena from 1696–1701. In 1704, he was at the Bavarian Court in Munich; then he followed the Duke of Bavaria to Belgium and France, where he became acquainted with French music, which left some influence on his later works. In 1715 he returned to Munich, and was active as leader of the Court orchestra. He wrote 12 violin sonatas, with cello or cembalo, op. 1 (1706); *Concerti da chiesa* for 4 string instruments, op. 2 (1714); *6 Sonate da chiesa* and *6 Sonate da camera* for 3 string instruments, op. 3 (1715); *12 Sonate da camera* for violin and cello, op. 4 (1716; arranged by Chédeville for musette, flute, oboe and continuo); *6 Concerti* for 7 instruments (4 violins, viola, bassoon or cello and bass), op. 5 (1717); Concerto for Violin Solo with Instruments, op. 6 (1730), his most important work. Sandberger published a biographical sketch and a selection from op. 1–4 in vol. 1 of *Denkmäler der Tonkunst in Bayern,* and a second selection in vol. 16 (9.i); Riemann edited 3 trio sonatas.

BIBLIOGRAPHY: R. Brenzon, "Un grande musicista veronese, Ev. Fel. dall'Abaco," *Note d'Archivio* XII

(1935); K. G. Fellerer's article in *Die Musik in Geschichte und Gegenwart.*

Abaco, Joseph Marie Clément dall', Belgian violoncellist; son of **Evaristo Felice dall'Abaco;** b. Brussels, March, 1710 (baptized March 27); d. at Arbizzano di Valpolicella, near Verona, Aug. 31, 1805. He studied with his father; as a small boy played in the orchestra of the Prince Elector at Bonn; in 1738 he was appointed music director there. He was in England in 1740; in 1753 he went to Verona; was given the title of baron by Prince Maximilian of Bavaria (1766). His works comprise more than 30 cello sonatas and other compositions.

Abbadia, Natale, Italian composer; b. Genoa, March 11, 1792; d. Milan, Dec. 25, 1861. He composed the opera *Giannina di Pontieu* (1812), the musical farce *L'imbroglione ed il castigamatti*; Masses, motets and other religious music.

Abbado, Claudio, Italian conductor, brother of **Marcello Abbado;** b. Milan, June 26, 1933. He received his early training from his father; then enrolled in the Milan Cons., graduating in 1955 as pianist; in 1957 he studied conducting with Swarowsky in Vienna. In 1958 he won the Koussevitzky conducting prize in Tanglewood and in 1963 the Mitropoulos prize in New York. He rapidly established himself as a fine symphonic conductor; his guest appearances with the N.Y. Philharmonic and the Boston Symphony were acclaimed. He also conducted opera at La Scala in Milan. In 1971 he was engaged as permanent conductor of the Vienna Philharmonic. As a symphonic conductor, he particularly distinguished himself in his fine and subtle interpertations of Mahler's symphonies. In 1973 and again in 1977 he made a series of extremely successful U.S. appearances conducting the Cleveland and Philadelphia orchestras.

Abbado, Marcello, Italian pianist and composer; brother of **Claudio Abbado;** b. Milan, Oct. 7, 1926. He studied at the Cons. in Milan with Gavazzeni (piano) and Ghedini (composition), graduating in 1947. In 1951 he was appointed instructor at the Cons. of Venice; from 1958–66 he was director of the Liceo Musicale in Piacenza, and in 1966 appointed director of the Rossini Cons. in Pesaro. He has written a cantata *Ciapo* (1945); *Lento e Rondo* for violin and piano (1949); *Costruzioni* for 5 small orchestras (1964); Double Concerto for Violin, Piano and 2 Chamber Orchestras (1967); Quadruple Concerto for Piano, Violin, Viola, Cello and Orch. (1969); 3 string quartets (1947, 1953, 1969); and piano pieces.

Abbatini, Antonio Maria, Italian composer; b. Tiferno (Città di Castello), c.1597; d. there, c.1679. He was maestro di cappella at the Lateran (1626–28), and other Roman churches; was at the church of Loreto from March, 1667. He wrote 3 operas, *Dal male al bene* (Rome, 1654; one of the earliest comic operas, and historically important as introducing the final ensemble); *Ione* (Vienna, 1666); *La comica del cielo* or *La Baltasara* (Rome, 1668); and a dramatic cantata *Il Pianto di Rodomonte* (Orvieto, 1633). He published 3 books of Masses, 4 books of psalms, various antiphons (1630, 1638, 1677) and 5 books of motets (1635).

BIBLIOGRAPHY: H. Goldschmidt, *Studien zur Geschichte der italianischen Oper im 17. Jahrhundert* (Leipzig, 1901–04); F. Coradini, *A. M. Abbatini* (Arezzo, 1922).

Abbey, John, noted English organ-builder; b. Whilton, Northamptonshire, Dec. 22, 1785; d. Versailles, Feb. 19, 1859. He went to Paris in 1826 at the invitation of Sébastien Erard to construct an organ for the Paris Exposition. He remained in France and built organs for the cathedrals of many French cities. In 1831 he installed an organ at the Paris Opéra. His innovations in the English type of bellows were adopted by many French organ builders. His sons, **E.** and **J. Abbey,** inherited the business, situated at Versailles.

Abbott, Emma, American soprano; b. Chicago, Dec. 9, 1850; d. Salt Lake City, Jan. 5, 1891. She was taken to Peoria as a child; studied music with her father who was a singer, and played the guitar with him and her brother, a violinist, at hotels and clubs. Her first regular employment was with Chapin's choir in New York (1870–72) at a salary of 1,500 dollars a year. In March, 1872 she went to Europe where she studied with Sangiovanni in Milan and with Delle Sedie in Paris. From then on, she rapidly advanced as an opera singer. Her London debut was on May 2, 1876. Returning to America, she made her first appearance in N.Y. on Feb. 8, 1877, and sang thereafter with great acclaim in the U.S. and in Europe. In 1875 she married E. Wetherell of New York (d. 1889). She was in some ways an American primitive in opera, traveling with her own small opera company across the United States. She was prone to interpolate her "specialties" into opera scores, such as her singing the hymn "Nearer My God to Thee" in *Faust.*

BIBLIOGRAPHY: Sadie E. Martin, *The Life and Professional Career of Emma Abbott* (Minneapolis, 1891).

Abe, Komei, Japanese composer; b. Hiroshima, Sept. 1, 1911. He studied cello at the Tokyo Academy of Music, graduating in 1933; took post-graduate composition courses there with Klaus Pringsheim (1933–36); conducting with Joseph Rosenstock (1935–39); then became prof. at the Elizabeth Music College at Kyoto; was from 1969 to 1974 prof. at Kyoto Municipal Univ. of Arts.

WORKS: *Theme and Variations* for orch. (Tokyo, Feb. 8, 1936); *Kleine Suite* for orch. (Tokyo, Feb. 27, 1937); Cello Concerto (Tokyo, March 31, 1942); Piano Concerto (1945; Tokyo, March 27, 1947); 2 symphonies: No. 1 (Tokyo, May 9, 1957) and No. 2 (Tokyo, Oct. 10, 1960); *Serenade* for orch. (Tokyo, Oct. 7, 1963); *Sinfonietta* (Tokyo, Jan. 14, 1965); 9 string quartets (1935, 1937, 1939, 1943, 1946, 1948, 1950, 1952, 1955); 2 flute sonatas (1942, 1949); Clarinet Quintet (1942); *Divertimento for saxophone and piano* (1951; orchestrated, 1953); *Divertimento for 9 instruments* (1954); Sextet for Flute, Clarinet, Violin, Viola, Cello and Piano (1964); *A Picture Book for Chil-*

dren for piano (1967); Piano Sonatina (1970); 3 piano sonatinas for children (1971); *Variation on a Subject by Grieg* for 4 trumpets, 4 horns, 3 trombones and tuba (1972); choral music; songs; film music.

Abeille, Johann Christian Ludwig, German organist and composer; b. Bayreuth, Feb. 20, 1761; d. Stuttgart, March 2, 1838. He was educated in Stuttgart, and was leader of the private orchestra of the Duke of Württemberg; in 1802 became court music director, retiring in 1832. He published several albums of songs which found their way into vocal anthologies and wrote 2 light operas *Amor und Psyche* (1801) and *Peter und Ännchen* (1809); also composed concerted music for small groups, and harpsichord pieces.

Abel, Carl Friedrich, German viola da gamba player and composer; b. Köthen, Dec. 22, 1723; d. London, June 20, 1787. He studied with his father, a renowned player on the gamba, and later went to Leipzig where he enrolled in the Thomasschule. From 1746–58 he was a member of the Dresden Court Orchestra. In 1759 he settled in London as court musician of the Queen Charlotte. He also became associated with Bach's son John Christian, and with him organized a series of concerts, which became known as Bach-Abel Concerts (1765–82). Subsequently he traveled as a concert player; he was guest in Goethe's house in Frankfurt. He wrote a number of instrumental works, among them several symphonies; a *Sinfonia concertante;* piano concertos; string quartets; trio sonatas; piano sonatas; violin sonatas; as well as pieces for the gamba. In his style of composition he followed the Mannheim School, emphasizing the symmetric instrumental forms and varied dynamics. Several of his works were erroneously ascribed to Mozart, which is a strong albeit oblique testimony to the intrinsic worth of his music. Apart from his instrumental works, he also contributed sections for the light operas *Love in a Village* and *Berenice*. Abel is generally regarded as the last great virtuoso on the viola da gamba.
BIBLIOGRAPHY: G. Beechey, "Carl Friedrich Abel's Six Symphonies, op. 14," *Music & Letters* (July 1970); P. M. Young, "Johann Christian, der englische Bach," in H. Wegener, ed. *Musa—Mens—Musici. Im Gedenken an Walther Vetter* (Leipzig, 1969).

Abel, Ludwig, German violinist; b. Eckartsberg, Thuringia, Jan. 14, 1834; d. Neu-Pasing, Bavaria, Aug. 13, 1895. He studied with Ferdinand David; played in the Gewandhaus orch. in Leipzig, and was later violinist in Weimar and Munich. He published a method of violin playing.

Abell, Arthur M., American music critic; b. Norwich, Conn., April 6, 1868; d. Hastings-on-Hudson, N.Y., Feb. 8, 1958. He studied in Weimar with Carl Halir (violin), Wilhelm Saal (piano), and Fritz Hartmann (theory); remained in Europe for 28 years (1890–1918) as a correspondent for the *Musical Courier* and other publications. He knew Brahms, and was a friend of Richard Strauss, Max Bruch, Joseph Joachim and other celebrated musicians. Upon his return to the U.S. he lived in retirement in Hastings-on-Hudson. In 1955 he published a book of memoirs, *Talks With Great Composers.*

Abell, John, celebrated Scottish lute player; b. Aberdeenshire, 1652; d. Cambridge, 1724. He was a chorister in the Chapel Royal in London; in 1679 received a stipend from Charles II which enabled him to study in Italy. He returned to London in 1681; suspected of Roman Catholic adherence, he was compelled to seek employment on the continent; served as intendant of music at Kassel (1698–99); was back in London shortly afterwards, able to resume his career (he was described in a contemporary report as "a harmonious vagabond"). He gave his last London concert in 1716. Abell published *A Collection of Songs in Several Languages, A Collection of Songs in English, A Choice Collection of Italian Ayres.*
BIBLIOGRAPHY: H. G. Farmer, "John Abell," in *Hinrichsen's Music Book VII* (1952).

Abendroth, Hermann, conductor and pedagogue; b. Frankfurt, Jan. 19, 1883; d. Jena, May 29, 1956. He studied in Munich (1900–1905); was active in Lübeck (1905–11); Essen (1911–15); Cologne (1915–34); also conducted at the Berlin State Opera (1923–34). From 1934–42 he was director of the Leipzig Cons. and conductor of the Gewandhaus Concerts. In 1947 he was appointed director of the Musikhochschule in Weimar; in 1949, music director of the Leipzig Radio.

Abendroth, Walter, German composer and writer on music; b. Hannover, May 29, 1896. He studied music in Berlin and Munich; was active in Hamburg and Berlin; in 1945 established himself in Hamburg. He wrote 5 symphonies, a concerto for orch., a viola concerto, 5 string quartets; several violin sonatas and numerous songs; but he is known chiefly as a musical biographer. He published monographs on *Pfitzner* (Munich, 1935); *Brahms* (Berlin, 1939); *Bruckner* (Berlin, 1940); and several collections of essays, among them *Deutsche Musik der Zeitwende* (Hamburg, 1937); *Vom Werden und Vergehan der Musik* (1948); *Selbstmord der Musik?* (Berlin, 1963); also published an autobiography entitled *Ich warne Neugierige* (Munich, 1966).

Aber, Adolf, musicologist; b. Apolda, Germany, Jan. 28, 1893; d. London, May 21, 1960. He studied with Kretzschmar, Stumpf and Wolf in Berlin; was music critic in Leipzig (1918–33). In 1936 he settled in London and became connected with the Novello publishing firm.
WRITINGS: *Handbuch der Musikliteratur* (1922); *Die Musikinstrumente und ihre Sprache* (1924); *Die Musik im Schauspiel, Geschichtliches und Ästhetisches* (1926); *Verzeichnis der Werke von Brahms* (1928); also articles in various journals.

Abert, Anna Amalie, musicologist; b. Halle, Sept. 19, 1906. She studied at Berlin Univ. (Ph. D., 1934). In 1943 was appointed instructor at the Univ. of Kiel; 1950, prof. there; became assistant editor of the musical encyclopedia *Die Musik in Geschichte und Gegenwart.* She has edited several collections of German choral music, written many articles, and has published several important books, among which are

Claudio Monteverdi und das musikalische Drama (Lippstadt, 1954); *Gluck* (Munich, 1959), and *Die Opern Mozarts* (Wolfenbüttel, 1970).

Abert, Hermann, German music scholar; b. Stuttgart, March 25, 1871; d. there, Aug. 13, 1927. He studied with his father, **Johann Joseph Abert;** then at Tübingen Univ. (*Dr. phil.*, 1897). He was Dozent of musical science at Halle Univ. (1902); prof. there (1909). In 1919 he was appointed prof. at Heidelberg Univ.; 1920, at Leipzig Univ. (succeeding Hugo Riemann); 1923, at Berlin Univ. (succeeding Kretzschmar).
WRITINGS: *Die Lehre vom Ethos in der griechischen Musik* (1899); *Die Musikanschauung des Mittelalters und ihre Grundlagen* (Halle, 1905); *Nic. Jommelli als Opern-Komponist* (Halle, 1908); *Nic. Piccinni als Buffo-Komponist* (1913); biography of his father, Johann Jos. Abert (1916); revision of Otto Jahn's biography of Mozart (1919-21 and several later editions); *Goethe und die Musik* (1922); *Luther und die Musik* (1924); *Illustriertes Musiklexikon* (1927). His collected writings were posthumously edited by F. Blume *(Gesammelte Schriften,* 1929).

Abert, Johann Joseph, German composer; b. Kochowitz, Sept. 20, 1832; d. Stuttgart, April 1, 1915. He was a choirboy until 15 at Gastdorf and Leipa monasteries; then studied double bass and composition at the Prague Cons. (1846-53). In 1853 he was engaged as double-bass player in the court orchestra at Stuttgart; in 1867 he became its conductor and also led the Stuttgart Opera. He produced several of his operas in Stuttgart: *Anna von Landskron* (1859); *König Enzio* (1862) and the 'romantic opera' *Astorga,* on the life of the composer Astorga (May 27, 1866; very successful at the time). His 5-act opera *Ekkehard* (Berlin, Oct. 11, 1878) also attracted considerable attention, as did his 'musical sea picture' *Columbus,* in the form of a symphony (1864). He also wrote 6 symphonies, several overtures and chamber music, and pieces for double bass. Abert's style, influenced by Mendelssohn, Schumann, and to some extent Liszt, follows the romantic tradition. His son, Hermann Abert, wrote a detailed biography: *Johann Joseph Abert, sein Leben und seine Werke* (Leipzig, 1916).

Abos, Girolamo (baptismal name **Geronimo**), Maltese composer; b. Valetta, Nov. 16, 1715; d. Naples, Oct., 1760. He studied with Leonardo Leo and Francesco Durante in Naples. In 1756 he went to London as 'maestro al cembalo' at the Italian Theater. Returning to Naples in 1758 he taught at the Cons. della Pietà de' Turchini. Among his pupils was Paisiello. Abos wrote 15 operas which were produced in Naples, Rome and London; of these, *Tito Manlio* (Naples, May 30, 1751) was successful; also composed 7 Masses and other church music.

Abraham, Gerald, eminent English musicologist; b. Newport, Isle of Wight, March 9, 1904. He studied piano; became interested in philology; mastered the Russian language and made a profound study of Russian music which has become his specialty. From 1935-47 he was connected with the BBC in London; then was appointed prof. of music at Liverpool Univ.

(1947-62); then returned to work with the BBC (1962-67). He has publ. the following books: *Borodin* (1927); *This Modern Stuff* (1933; revised edition under the title *This Modern Music,* 1952); *Masters of Russian Music* (in collaboration with M. D. Calvocoressi, 1936; revised, 1958); *A Hundred Years of Music* (1938); *On Russian Music* (1939); *Chopin's Musical Style* (1939); *Beethoven's Second-Period Quartets* (1942); *8 Soviet Composers* (1943); *Rimsky-Korsakov: A Short Biography* (1945); also edited collections of articles on Tchaikovsky (1945), Schubert (1946), Sibelius (1947), Schumann (1952), Handel (1954), and *The Age of Humanism,* vol. IV of the *New Oxford History of Music* (Oxford, 1968).

Abraham, Max, German publisher; b. Danzig, June 3, 1831; d. Leipzig, Dec. 8, 1900. He became a partner in C. F. Peters's 'Bureau de Musique' in 1863, and sole proprietor in 1880. On Jan. 1, 1894, his nephew, Heinrich Hinrichsen, of Hamburg, entered the firm and, upon Abraham's death, became its head. The famous 'Edition Peters' was inaugurated by Abraham.

Abraham, Otto, German specialist in tone psychology; b. Berlin, May 30, 1872; d. there, Jan. 24, 1926. He studied medicine; became an associate of Stumpf at the Berlin Psychological Institute from 1894; then collaborated with Hornbostel in building up the Archive of Phonographic Recordings in Berlin. He published several valuable treatises on acoustics and primitive music, among them *Wahrnehmung kürzester Töne und Geräusche* (1898); *Studien über das Tonsystem und die Musik der Japaner* (1904); *Phonographierte Indianermelodien aus Britisch-Columbia* (1905; with Hornbostel). He also wrote studies on recorded Turkish, Siamese and Hindu melodies; a paper on Chinese musical notation, etc.

Abraham, Paul, Hungarian composer of light operas; b. Apatin, Nov. 2, 1892; d. Hamburg, May 6, 1960. He studied in Budapest and wrote chamber music before turning to light opera. His first successful operetta was *Victoria und ihr Husar* (Vienna, Dec. 23, 1930); his other popular productions were *Die Blume von Hawaii* (Leipzig, July 24, 1931) and *Ball im Savoy* (Vienna, Dec. 25, 1933). In 1938 Abraham went to the U.S., but suffered a mental breakdown, and was in 1955 committed to a sanitarium in Hamburg, where he died.

Abramsky, Alexander, Russian composer; b. Lutsk, Jan. 22, 1898. He studied with Miaskovsky at the Moscow Cons., graduating in 1926. Commissioned to do research work in Asian folklore, he traveled to Uzbekistan; wrote a music drama on native themes, *Laylikhon and Anarkhon* (Andizhan, Dec. 28, 1943). He also composed a piano concerto (1941); *Laconic Sonata* for piano solo; a cantata, *Land of the Silent Lake* (1971); and many choruses.

Ábrányi, Cornelius, Hungarian pianist, composer and writer on music; grandfather of **Emil Ábrányi;** b. Szentgyörgy-Ábrányi, Oct. 15, 1822; d. Budapest, Dec. 20, 1903. He came of an ancient Magyar family whose name was originally **Eördögh.** He was first destined to a legal profession, but in 1834 a meeting with the Hungarian national composer, Erkel, made him decide to study music. In 1843 Ábrányi went abroad; in Munich he met Liszt, and became his lifelong friend. He went to Paris and took lessons with Chopin and Kalkbrenner for a short time, returning to Hungary in 1845. He took a leading part in the formation and encouragement of the Hungarian national school of composition. His own compositions (130 opus numbers) emphasize the Hungarian national elements; the most ambitious of these works being his *Hungarian Millennial Sonata*, op. 103. His books (all in Hungarian) include: *Art and Revolution* (1867); *Biography of Franz Liszt and Survey of His Oratorio Christus* (1873); *General History of Music* (1886); *History of Hungarian Music in the Nineteenth Century* (1900). He also wrote an autobiography, *From My Life and Memories* (1897).

Ábrányi, Emil, composer and conductor; b. Budapest, Sept. 22, 1882. His father was Emil Ábrányi, the poet, and his grandfather, **Cornelius Ábrányi.** In 1902 he went to Germany and studied under Nikisch in Leipzig. He was engaged as conductor to the Municipal Theater at Cologne (1904) and at Hannover (1907). Returning to Budapest (1911) he became conductor at the Royal Opera House; he was also active as music critic. He was director of the Budapest Municipal Theater (1921–26); conducted various orchestras in the provinces. As a composer, Ábrányi follows the tradition of Wagner. The following stage works were performed at the Royal Hungarian Opera House, Budapest: *The King of the Mist,* ballet (Oct. 17, 1903); the operas *Monna Vanna* (March 2, 1907); *Paolo e Francesca* (Jan. 13, 1912); *Don Quixote* (Nov. 30, 1917); *Ave Maria* (1922). Other operas are *Singing Dervishes* (1935); *The Prince with the Lilies* (1938); *Byzantium* (1942); *Sorceress Eve* (1944); *The Tale of Balaton* (1945) and *The Cantor of St. Thomas Church* (1947; the first opera written on the life of J. S. Bach).

Abravanel, Maurice, distinguished American conductor; b. Saloniki, Greece, Jan. 6, 1903, of Sephardic Jewish parents (an ancestor is reputed to have been chancellor to Ferdinand and Isabella of Spain). He was taken to Switzerland at the age of 6, and studied general subjects at the Univ. of Lausanne; in 1922 he went to Berlin where he took composition lessons with Kurt Weill; with the advent of the Nazi regime in 1933, Abravanel moved to Paris, where he conducted ballet; in 1934–35 he toured Australia as conductor of the British National Opera Co.; in 1936 he received an offer to join the staff of the Metropolitan Opera in N.Y.; made his debut there on Dec. 26, 1936, conducting *Samson et Dalila;* generally adverse reviews compelled him to leave the Metropolitan Opera in 1938. He turned to leading Broadway musicals; conducted a season with the Chicago Opera Co. (1940–41). In 1947 he became conductor of the Utah State Symph. Orch. at Salt Lake City, and revealed a great talent for building up the orchestra; in 30 years of his conductorship it has become one of the finest symphony orchestras in the U.S.; he also introduced many modern works in its repertory. In 1976 he underwent open-

heart surgery, but recovered completely and returned to his post in Utah.

Abreu, José Antonio, Venezuelan composer; b. Valera, Venezuela, May 17, 1939. He studied with local teachers before going to Caracas, where he took courses with Vicente Emilio Sojo. His works follow the traditional line of tonal composition. They include *Sinfonieta Neoclásica,* 2 symphonies, a symphonic poem *Sancta et Immaculata Virginitas; Tríptico* for 11 instruments; Quintet for Wind Instruments; String Quartet; choruses.

Absil, Jean, eminent Belgian composer; b. Bonsecours, Oct. 23, 1893; d. Brussels, Feb. 2, 1974. He studied organ and composition at the Brussels Cons.; later took lessons in advanced composition with Gilson. He won the Prix Agniez for his First Symphony (1921); in 1922 won a 2nd Prix de Rome for the cantata *La Guerre;* also received Prix Rubens. His 1st Piano Concerto was commissioned by the 1938 Concours Ysaÿe in Brussels as the compulsory work for the 12 finalists in the contest eventually won by Emil Gilels. He was music dir. of the Academy of Etterbeek in Brussels (1922–64); taught at the Brussels Cons. (1931–59); was also one of the founders of the *Revue Internationale de Musique.* Absil evolved an individual style, characterized by rhythmic variety, free tonality and compact counterpoint.

WORKS: FOR THE STAGE: *Peau d'âne,* lyrical poem in 3 acts (1937); *Ulysse et les sirènes,* radio play (1939); *Fansou ou le chapeau chinois,* musical comedy (1944); *Le Miracle de Pan,* ballet (1949); *Pierre Breughel l'Ancien,* radio play (1950); *Épouvantail,* ballet (1950); *Les Voix de la mer,* opera (1951; Brussels, March 26, 1954); *Les Météores,* ballet (1951). FOR ORCH.: 5 symphonies (1920, 1936, 1943, 1969, 1970); *La Mort de Tintagiles,* symph. poem (1923–26); *Rapsodie Flamande* (1928; also for wind ensemble); *Berceuse* for cello (or saxophone) and small orch. (1932); 2 violin concertos (1933, 1964); *Petite Suite* for small orch. (1935; also for wind ensemble); 3 piano concertos (1937, 1967, 1973); *Rapsodie No. 2* (1938); *Hommage à Lekeu* (1939); Cello Concertino (1940); *Sérénade* (1940); *Variations Symphoniques* (1942); Viola Concerto (1942); *Rapsodie roumaine* for violin and orch. (1943); *Concerto Grosso* for wind quintet and orch. (1944); *Jeanne d'Arc,* symph. poem (1945); *Rites,* triptych for wind ensemble (1952); *Rapsodie brésilienne* (1953); *Mythologie,* suite (1954); *Croquis sportifs* for wind ensemble (1954); *Divertimento* for saxophone quartet and chamber orch. (1955); *Introduction et valses* (1955); *Legend* for wind ensemble (1956); *Suite,* after Romanian folklore (1956); *Suite bucolique* for strings (1957); *Fantaisie concertante* for violin and orch. (or piano, 1959); *Danses bulgares* (1959; also for wind quintet or piano); *Rapsodie bulgare* (1960); 2 *Danses Rituelles* for small orch. (1960); *Triptyque* for small orch. (1960); *Fantaisie-humoresque* for clarinet and strings (or piano, 1962); *Rapsodie No. 6* for horn and orch. (or piano, 1963); Viola Concertino (1964); *Nymphes et Faunes* for wind orch. (1966); *Allegro brillante* for piano and orch. (1967); *Fantaisie-caprice* for saxophone and strings (1971); Guitar Concerto (1971); *Ballade* for saxophone, piano

and small orch. (1971); *Déités,* suite (1973). VOCAL MU-SIC: *La Guerre,* cantata (1922); *Philatélie,* chamber cantata (1940); *Les Bénédictions,* cantata (1941); *Le Zodiaque,* symph. variations with chorus and piano concertante (1949); *Phantasmes* for contralto, saxophone, piano and percussion (1950); *Le Cirque volant,* cantata (1953); *Petites polyphonies* for 2 voices and orch. (1966); *À cloche-pied* for children's chorus and orch. (1968). CHAMBER MUSIC: 4 string quartets (1929, 1934, 1935, 1941); 2 piano trios (1931, 1972); 2 string trios (1935, 1939); *Rapsodique* for 4 cellos (1936); Cello Quartet (1937); Quartet for Saxophones (1937); Piano Quartet (1938); *Fantaisie* for piano quartet (1939); *Concert à cinq* for flute, violin, viola, cello and harp (1939); 2 suites for cello and piano (1942, 1968); *Chacone* for solo violin (1949); 3 *Contes* for trumpet and piano (1951); Suite for Trombone and Piano (1952); *Sonatine en duo* for violin and viola (1962); Saxophone Sonata (1963); 3 *Pieces for Organ* (1965); Quartet for Clarinets (1967); Solo Violin Sonata (1967); *Croquis pour un carnaval* for 4 clarinets and harp (1968); *Suite mystique* for 4 flutes (1969); Violin Sonata (1970); *Esquisses* for wind quartet (1971); *Images stellaires* for violin and cello (1973). PIANO MUSIC: 3 *Impromptus* (1932); 3 sonatinas (1937, 1939, 1965); 3 *Marines* (1939); Bagatelles (1944); 2 *Grand Suites* (1944, 1962); *Sketches on the 7 Capital Sins* (1954); Variations (1956); *Chess Game,* suite (1957); *Passacaglia* (1959); Rhapsodie No. 5 for 2 pianos (1959); *Humoresques* (1965); Ballade (1966); *Asymetries* for 2 pianos (1968); *Alternances* (1968); *Féeries* (1971); *Poésie et vélocité,* 20 pieces (1972); also numerous pieces for guitar, a cappella choral works, songs.
    BIBLIOGRAPHY: J. Dopp, "Jean Absil," *La Revue Musicale* (Oct./Dec. 1937); R. deGuide, *Jean Absil* (Tournai, 1965).

Abt, Franz, German song writer and conductor; b. Eilenburg, Dec. 22, 1819; d. Wiesbaden, March 31, 1885. His father, a clergyman, sent him to Leipzig Thomasschule to study theology; later obtained an excellent musical education both there and at the Univ. He became a choral conductor in Zürich (1841). In 1852 he was appointed second conductor at the Brunswick Court; in 1855 became first conductor. In 1869 he traveled, as a choral conductor, to Paris, London and Russia; in 1872 he made a highly successful tour in America. He retired on a pension from Brunswick in 1882. Abt wrote over 600 works, comprising more than 3,000 numbers; the largest are the 7 secular cantatas. His popularity as a song writer is due chiefly to the flowing, easy and elegant style of his vocal melodies, some of which *(Wenn die Schwalben heimwärts zieh'n, Gute Nacht, du mein herziges Kind, So viele Tausend Blumen,* etc.) have become so well known as to be mistaken for genuine folksongs.
    BIBLIOGRAPHY: B. Rost, *Vom Meister des volkstümlichen deutschen Liedes, Franz Abt* (Chemnitz, 1924).

Achron, Isidor, Russian-American pianist; brother of **Joseph Achron;** b. Warsaw, Nov. 24, 1892; d. New York, May 12, 1948. He studied at the St. Petersburg Cons. with Anna Essipoff (piano) and with Liadov (composition). In 1922 he settled in the United States;

naturalized in 1928. From 1922–33 he was accompanist to Jascha Heifetz; was also active as piano teacher in New York. He was also a composer; played his piano concerto with the New York Philharmonic Orchestra on Dec. 9, 1937; his *Suite Grotesque* for orch. was first performed in St. Louis, Jan. 30, 1942. He also wrote a number of piano pieces, all in a moderate romantic manner in the prevalent tradition of the time.

Achron, Joseph, Russian-American violinist and composer; brother of **Isidor Achron;** b. Losdseje, near Suwalki, Poland, May 13, 1886; d. Hollywood, April 29, 1943. In 1890 the family moved to Warsaw. He studied violin there, and gave his first public concert at the age of 7. In 1898 he entered the St. Petersburg Cons. as a student of Leopold Auer in violin and with Liadov in music theory. Graduating in 1904 he went to Berlin where he appeared as a soloist with orchestras. In 1907 he returned to St. Petersburg to continue his studies in theory and orchestration at the conservatory there. In 1911 he organized, along with several Jewish musicians, a Society for Jewish folklore. One of the products of his research was the popular *Hebrew Melody* for violin and piano (1911), based on a Hasidic theme. During World War I he was a member of the music corps of the Russian Army. In 1919–21 he was active as composer for the Hebrew Chamber Theater in Petrograd; in 1922 he went again to Berlin; in 1924 he was in Palestine, and in 1925 emigrated to the United States; became a naturalized American citizen in 1930. He lived in New York until 1934, when he went to Hollywood where he earned his living as a violinist in film studios, and continued to compose energetically. His early compositions are marked by characteristic Russian harmonies with a distinctly romantic aura, but under the impact of modern techniques he developed a strong idiom based on purely structural principles employing atonal and polytonal devices. Schoenberg wrote about him in the program book of a memorial concert of Achron's compositions given in Los Angeles in 1945: "Joseph Achron is one of the most underestimated of modern composers, but the originality and profound elaboration of his ideas guarantee that his works will last." Achron's major compositions include a suite for chamber orchestra, *Golem* (1932), the last section of which is the exact retrograde movement of the first section, to symbolize the undoing of the monster Golem; 3 violin concertos in which he appeared as soloist; No. 1 (Boston, Jan. 24, 1927); No. 2 (Los Angeles, Dec. 19, 1936); No. 3 (Los Angeles, March 31, 1939); *4 Tableaux fantastiques* for violin and piano (1907); *Chromatic String Quartet* (1907); 2 violin sonatas (1910, 1918); *Hazan* for cello and orch. (1912); *2 Hebrew Pieces* for violin and piano (1912); *Suite bizarre* for violin and piano (1916); *Scher* for violin and piano (1916); *Elegy* for string quartet (1927); *Statuettes* for piano (1929); *Sextet* for flute, oboe, clarinet, bassoon, horn and trumpet (1938); Piano Concerto (1941); *Evening Service for the Sabbath* (1930); songs and choruses.
    BIBLIOGRAPHY: Ph. Moddel, *Joseph Achron* (Tel Aviv, 1966).

Ackté (real name **Achté**), **Aïno,** Finnish dramatic soprano; b. Helsinki, April 23, 1876; d. Nummela, Aug. 8, 1944. She studied at the Paris Cons. and made her debut at the Paris Opéra as Marguerite (Oct. 8, 1897). She sang the same role at her first appearance in America at the Metropolitan Opera (Feb. 22, 1904). Her performance of Salomé in Strauss's opera at Covent Garden (1913) led to an invitation from Richard Strauss to sing the part in Dresden and Paris. Her other roles were Juliette, Ophélie, Gilda, Nedda, Elsa, Elisabeth and Sieglinde. Her memoirs are published in Finnish, Swedish and German.

Adachi, Motohiko, Japanese composer; b. Osaka, Jan. 3, 1940. He studied composition with Yori-Aki Matsudaira, Y. Shimaoka and S. Yamagata.
  WORKS: Concerto for 5 Violins, 4 Violas and 5 Cellos (1962); Concerto Grosso for String Orch. (1966); *Air* for solo violin (1968); Toccata for 4 Japanese Instruments (1968); *Monodia* for piano (1968–69); *Concertanto* for string quintet (1969); *Carmina Burana,* trio for male voice, piano and double bass (1971); *Talking the Future Out* for soprano, baritone, children's chorus and instrumental ensemble (1971); Chaconne for Japanese Instruments (1971); *Capriccio* for cello and dai-byoshi (1971); *Per Pianoforte* (1972); *Chase the Pigeon* for 2 folk singers, 4 actors, chorus and instrumental ensemble (1972).

Adam de St. Victor, French Augustine monk who developed the rhymed liturgical sequence; b. c.1110; d. possibly, July 8, 1192. He was cantor at the St. Victor Cloister in Paris. His significance lies in his decisive introduction of rhymed "proses," or sequences, each consisting of 12 or more stanzas, in which the first half was given a new melody, while the second half was set to the same melody. Adam de St. Victor wrote a great many of such sequences, and influenced their further development.
  BIBLIOGRAPHY: L. Gautier, *Œuvres poétiques d'Adam de St. Victor* (Paris, 1858); E. Misset and P. Aubry, *Les Proses d'Adam de St. Victor* (Paris, 1900); F. Wüllner, *Adam de St. Victor, Sämtliche Sequenzen* (Vienna, 1937).

Adam, Adolphe-Charles, celebrated French opera composer; b. Paris, July 24, 1803; d. there, May 3, 1856. He entered the Paris Cons. in 1817 and studied with Boieldieu, whose influence was a determining factor in his career. His first opera was *Pierre et Catherine* (Opéra-Comique, Feb. 9, 1829). The one-act comic opera, *Le Chalet* (Opéra-Comique, Sept. 25, 1834), marked his first success (1400 performances of this opera were given before 1899). With the production of *Le Postillon de Longjumeau* (Opéra-Comique, Oct. 13, 1836) Adam achieved international fame. Of his other operas (he wrote 53 in all), the following, all produced at the Opéra-Comique, are the most important: *Le Fidèle Berger* (Jan. 6, 1838); *Le Brasseur de Preston* (Oct. 31, 1838); *Régine, ou Les Deux Nuits* (Jan. 17, 1839); *La Reine d'un jour* (Sept. 19, 1839); *Le Roi d'Yvetot* (Oct. 13, 1842); *Cagliostro* (Feb. 10, 1844); *Le Toréador, ou L'Accord parfait* (May 18, 1849); *Giralda, ou La Nouvelle Psyché* (July 20, 1850); *Le Farfadet* (March 19, 1852); *Le Sourd, ou L'Auberge pleine* (Feb. 2, 1853). His comic opera *Si j'étais roi* (Théâtre-Lyrique, Sept. 4, 1852) was also very popular; his tragic opera *Richard en Palestine* was produced at the Paris Opéra (Oct. 7, 1854) with considerable success, but was not retained in the repertoire. Adam was also a very successful ballet composer; his *Giselle,* produced at the Paris Opéra (June 28, 1841) became one of the most celebrated and enduring choreographic scores. His song *Cantique de Noël,* in numerous arrangements, still enjoys great popularity. In 1847 Adam ventured into the field of management with an operatic enterprise, the Théâtre National; the revolutionary outbreak of 1848, however, brought financial ruin to his undertaking. In 1849 he was appointed prof. of composition at the Paris Cons. He traveled widely in Europe, visiting London, Berlin and St. Petersburg. As one of the creators of French comic opera, Adam ranks with Boieldieu and Auber in the expressiveness of his melodic material if not in originality or inventive power. Adam's memoirs were published posthumously in 2 volumes under the titles *Souvenirs d'un musicien* (1857), and *Derniers souvenirs d'un musicien* (1859).
  BIBLIOGRAPHY: A. Pougin, biography (Paris, 1877); P. Hering, "Louis Joseph Ferdinand Herold (1791–1833), Adolphe Adam (1803–1856), Emile Waldteufel (1837–1915)," in *La Musique en Alsace hier et aujourd'hui* (Paris, 1970).

Adam, Claus, American cellist and composer; b. on a kapok plantation in Central Sumatra, of Austrian parents, Nov. 5, 1917; his father was an ethnologist and photographer in Indochina. When Claus Adam was six years old, he was taken to Europe; he received his early musical training at the Salzburg Mozarteum, where he sang in a school choir. In 1931 the family moved to the U.S.; he studied cello with E. Stoffnegen; progressing rapidly, he joined the National Orchestral Association in New York, eventually becoming its first cellist. He continued to study cello with Emanuel Feuermann; in 1940 he was engaged by Dmitri Mitropoulos as first-desk cellist in the Minneapolis Symph. Orch. During World War II he served in the U.S. Air Force. Returning to New York he studied composition with Stefan Wolpe. He was the cellist in the New Music Quartet (1948–55) and in the Juilliard String Quartet (1955–74). He received a Guggenheim Foundation grant in 1975; was also appointed to the faculty of the Juilliard School of Music; was elected President of the Violoncello Society of New York. His music is marked by pragmatic modernism free from doctrinaire adherence to any particular technique of composition; his mastery of the instrumental and vocal idiom is evident in all his works. He wrote a String Trio (1967); 2 string quartets; Cello Concerto (1973); Piano Sonata (1952); Concerto-Variations for Orch. (N.Y., April 5, 1977).

Adam (or Adan) de la Halle (or Hale), called "Le Bossu d'Arras" (Hunchback of Arras); b. Arras, c.1237; d. Naples, c.1287. A famous trouvère, many of whose works have been preserved; the most interesting is a dramatic pastoral *Le Jeu de Robin et de Marion* (1285), written for the Anjou court at Naples and resembling an opéra comique in its plan. He was gifted in the dual capacity of poet and composer. Both monodic and polyphonic works of his survive. A facsimile reprint of one of the important MS sources of Adam's works is issued as *Le Chansonnier d'Arras,* intro. A. Jeanroy (Paris, 1925). For transcriptions of most of the extant music, see E. de Coussemaker, *Oeuvres complètes du trouvère Adam de la Halle* (1872); F. Gennrich, *Rondeaux, Virelais und Balladen* (Dresden, I, 1921; II, 1927); J. Chailley, *Adam de la Halle: Rondeaux* (Paris, 1942); F. Gennrich, *Le Jeu de Robin et de Marion,* in *Musikwissenschaftliche Studienbibliothek* (Langen, 1962); N. Wilkins, *The Lyric Works of Adam de la Halle: Chansons, Jeux-Partis, Rondeaux, Motets* (Dallas, 1967). Transcriptions of the texts only: R. Berger, *Canchons und Partures des altfranzösischen Trouvère Adan de la Halle le Bochu d'Arras* (1900); L. Nicod, *Les Partures Adan: les jeux-partis d'Adam de la Halle* (Paris, 1917); E. Langlois, *Le Jeu de la Feuillée* (Paris, 1923); id., *Le Jeu de Robin et de Marion* (Paris, 1924); A. Langfors, *Recueil général des jeux-partis français* (2 vols., Paris, 1926). A new edition of the complete works, using all known music and text sources, including those never before transcribed, is being prepared by a consortium of music and language specialists at City University of New York.

BIBLIOGRAPHY: H. Guy, *Essai sur la vie et les œuvres littéraires d'Adam de la Hale* (Paris, 1898); J. Tiersot, *Sur le Jeu de Robin et Marion* (1897).

Adam, Jenö, Hungarian conductor, composer and writer on music; b. Szigetszentmiklós, Dec. 13, 1896. He studied composition in Budapest with Kodály (1921–25) and conducting in Basel with Felix Weingartner (1933); was associated with Kodály in a program reorganizing the system of musical education. He was a professor at the Academy of Music in Budapest (1929–59); was awarded the Kossuth Prize in 1957. He wrote 2 operas: *Magyar Karácsony (Hungarian Christmas;* Budapest, Dec. 22, 1931) and *Mária Veronika* (1936–37; Budapest, 1938); 2 string quartets (1924, 1930); *Dominica Suite* for orch. (1925; transcribed as *My Village,* 1963); Cello Sonata (1926); *Lacrima Sonata* for baritone, and orch. or piano (1927); choral works; also wrote musical textbooks for schools.

Adam, Louis, Alsatian pianist, teacher and composer; father of **Adolphe-Charles Adam;** b. Müttersholz, Dec. 3, 1758; d. Paris, April 8, 1848. He went to Paris in 1775; was later prof. of piano at the Paris Cons. (1797–1842). He was the teacher of Kalkbrenner and Hérold; was also known as composer of virtuoso piano pieces, some of which (especially variations on *Le Roi Dagobert*) were very popular. He was the author of two standard manuals for piano: *Méthode générale du doigté* (Paris, 1798) and *Méthode nouvelle pour le Piano* (5 editions, 1802–32), which he wrote for his pupils at the Paris Conservatory.

Adam, Theo, German bass-baritone; b. Dresden, Aug. 1, 1926. He was a chorister in Dresden; made his operatic debut at the Dresden Opera in 1949; in 1954 he appeared in Bayreuth and in the course of a few years established himself as a leading Wagnerian heroic bass-baritone. He also distinguished himself in the modern opera repertory, and sang the title role in *Wozzeck* in Salzburg in 1972.

Adam von Fulda, German theorist and composer; b. Fulda, c.1440; d. (of the plague) Wittenberg, 1505. His tract on music theory is published in Gerbert's *Scriptores ecclesiastici;* his works were highly prized in their day.

BIBLIOGRAPHY: H. Riemann in *Kirchenmusikalisches Jahrbuch* (1879); W. Niemann (ibid., 1902); W. Gurlitt in *Luther Jahrbuch* (1932); W. Ehmann, *Adam von Fulda* (1936).

Adamis, Michael, Greek composer of ultramodern music; b. Piraeus, May 19, 1929. While studying theology at the Athens Univ. (1948–54), he took music courses at the Athens Cons. (1947–51) and Byzantine music and harmony at Piraeus Cons. (1951–56); studied composition with Papaioannou at the Hellikon Cons. in Athens (1956–59), followed by advanced studies in electronic music and Byzantine musical palaeography at Brandeis Univ. in Waltham, Mass. (1962–65). His works are derived from a universal spectrum of musical techniques and sonorous resources: dodecaphonic, electronic, liturgical, neo-baroque, choreographic.

WORKS: *Liturgikon Concerto* for oboe, clarinet, bassoon and string orch. (1955); *2 Pieces for Violin and Piano* (1958); Variations for String Orch. (1958); *Suite in ritmo antico* for piano (1959); *Sinfonia da camera* for flute, clarinet, horn, trumpet, percussion, piano and string orch. (1960–61); Duo for Violin and Piano (1961); *3 Pieces for Double Bass and Piano* (1962); *Anakyklesis* for flute, oboe, celesta, violin and cello (1964); *Perspective* for flute, piccolo and percussion (1965); *Apocalypse (Sixth Seal)* for chorus, narrator, piano and tape (1967); *Byzantine Passion* for 6 soloists, chorus and percussion (1967); *Genesis* for 3 choirs, narrator, tape, painting, projection and dance (1968); *Lamentation* for 2 chanters, 2 drone chanters, percussion and tape (1970); *Tetelestai* for narrator, 3 choirs, tape and bells (1971); *Iketirion* for women's choir, percussion and tape (1971); *Kratima* for narrator, oboe, tuba and tape (1971); *The Fiery Furnace* for chanters' choir and 3 children (1972; based on a 15th-century manuscript that is the only extant specimen of Byzantine liturgical drama); *Orestes* for baritone, percussion and tape (1972); *Photonymon* for narrator, chorus and percussion (1973). He also has numerous pieces for tape alone, and tape and voice, and has produced electronic stage music for plays by Aeschylus, Euripides, Shakespeare and others.

Adamowski, Joseph, American cellist, brother of **Timothée Adamowski;** b. Warsaw, July 4, 1862; d. Cambridge, Mass., May 8, 1930. He studied at the Warsaw Cons. (1873–77) with Goebelt; and at the Moscow Cons. with Fitzenhagen; also attended Tchaikovsky's classes there. He gave concerts from 1883–89 in Warsaw. From 1889 to 1907 he played in the Boston Symph. Orch. In 1896 he married the pianist, **Antoinette Szumowska.** With his wife and brother, Timothée, he formed the Adamowski Trio.

Adamowski, Timothée, American violinist, brother of **Joseph Adamowski;** b. Warsaw, March 24, 1857; d. Boston, April 18, 1943. He studied in Warsaw and at the Paris Cons.; in 1879 gave concerts in the U.S. with Maurice Strakosch and Clara Louise Kellogg, and settled in Boston, where he taught at the New England Cons. (until 1933). In 1888 he organized the Adamowski String Quartet which gave about 30 concerts annually; he also conducted several summer seasons of popular concerts given by the Boston Symph. Orch. (1890–94 and 1900–07). He published songs and violin pieces (*Barcarolle, Polish Dance,* etc.)

Adams, Charles, American dramatic tenor; b. Charlestown, Mass., Feb. 9, 1834; d. West Harwich, Mass., July 4, 1900. He studied in Vienna with Barbieri; was engaged for three years by the Royal Opera, Berlin, and for nine years by the Imperial Opera, Vienna; sang at La Scala, at Covent Garden, and in the U.S. He settled in Boston as a teacher in 1879.

Adams, Horst, German musicologist; b. Merzig, Saar, Jan. 29, 1937. He studied musicology with Müller-Blattau. In 1962 he joined the Schott publishing house and participated in the editorship of the supplement to *Riemann's Musik Lexikon* (2 vols., 1972, 1975).

Adams, Suzanne, American soprano; b. Cambridge, Mass., Nov. 28, 1872; d. London, Feb. 5, 1953. She studied with J. Bouhy in N.Y.; went to Paris in 1889; made her debut at the Paris Opéra as Juliette (Jan. 9, 1895), and subsequently was engaged to sing there for 3 more seasons; appeared at the Metropolitan Opera House as Juliette on Jan. 4, 1899.

Adams, Thomas, eminent English organist; b. London, Sept. 5, 1785; d. there, Sept. 15, 1858. He studied with Dr. Busby; was organist at various London churches. His publ. organ works include fugues, voluntaries, 90 interludes, and variations on popular airs; he also wrote anthems, hymns, and sacred songs.

Adaskin, Murray, Canadian violinist and composer; b. Toronto, March 28, 1906. He studied violin with his older brother Harry; then went to Paris where he took lessons with Marcel Chailley. Returning to Toronto he continued his lessons with Luigi von Kunits and Kathleen Parlow. He subsequently played the violin in the Toronto Symph. Orch. (1926–36). He studied composition with John Weinzweig (1944–48); also took a course with Darius Milhaud (1949–50, 1953). In 1952 he was appointed head of the music dept. at the Univ. of Saskatchewan; in 1966–73 was composer-in-residence there. He writes music in a facile laissez-faire manner, enlivened by a rhythmic pulse.
WORKS: chamber opera, *Grant, Warden of the Plains* (Winnipeg, July 18, 1967); *Ballet Symphony* (1950–51); Violin Concerto (1956); *Algonquin Symphony* (1957–58); *Saskatchewan Legend* for orch. (1959); Bassoon Concerto (1960); *Qalala and Nilaula of the North,* symphonic poem based on Eskimo tunes (1969); *Fanfare* for orch. (1970); *There Is My People Sleeping,* symphonic poem (1970); *Nootka Ritual* for small orch. (1974); *Adagio* for cello and orch. (1973–75); Violin Sonata (1946); Piano Sonata (1950);

Sonatine Baroque for solo violin (1952); 4 Divertimentos: No. 1 for 2 violins and piano (1956); No. 2 for violin and harp (1964); No. 3 for violin, horn and bassoon (1965); No. 4 for trumpet and orch. (1970); *Introduction and Rondo* for piano quartet (1957); String Quartet (1963); *Calisthenics* for violin and piano (1968); Trio for Flute, Cello and Piano (1970); *2 Pieces for Viola da Gamba* (1972); *2 Portraits* for violin and piano (1973); Wind Quintet (1974); and songs.

Adderley, Julian Edwin (Cannonball), American jazz alto saxophonist player; b. Tampa, Florida, Sept. 15, 1928; d. Gary, Indiana, Aug. 8, 1975. He began his career as a member of a jazz group at a Greenwich Village Club in New York City; in 1956 he formed his own combo with his brother **Nat Adderley** (b. Tampa, Florida, Nov. 25, 1931) who plays the cornet. He achieved fame mainly through his recordings, beginning with *African Waltz* in 1961. He received an academic education, graduating from Florida A. & M. with a B.A. in music. For 8 years (1948–56) he was a band director at Dillard High School in Ft. Lauderdale, Florida. After leaving his school position he lectured frequently in colleges on the subject of his "black experience in music." He owes his nickname Cannonball to the mispronunciation of cannibal, a slurring reference to his voracious eating habits. He suffered a stroke during a concert engagement in Gary, Indiana. Among his most successful recordings were *Dis Here, Sermonette, Work Song, Jive Samba, Mercy, Mercy, Mercy,* and *Walk Tall.* He also wrote *Suite Cannon,* with its title alluding to both his academic background and to his popular nickname.

Addinsell, Richard, English composer of theater and film music; b. London, Jan. 13, 1904; d. there, Nov. 15, 1977. He studied law at Oxford Univ. and music at the Royal College of Music in London. His first theater score was incidental music for Clemens Dane's play *Come of Age,* produced in London in 1928; in 1929 he went to Berlin and Vienna for further musical study. In 1933 Eva Le Gallienne commissioned him to write the score for her production of *Alice in Wonderland.* Addinsell then went to Hollywood where he wrote the scores for the films *A Tale of Two Cities, Blithe Spirit* and others. During World War II he wrote film music for several patriotic documentaries, among them *Siege of Tobruk* and *We Sail at Midnight.* He achieved sudden fame with his score for the film *Dangerous Moonlight* (released in the U.S. as *Suicide Squadron*), containing a movement for piano and orch., which became immensely popular as *Warsaw Concerto.* Stylistically, its melody, harmony and pianistic technique follow with remarkable fidelity the familiar outlines of Rachmaninoff's Second Piano Concerto.

Addison, John, English composer; b. Cobham, Surrey, March 16, 1920. He was educated at Wellington College, and in 1938 entered the Royal College of Music. His studies were interrupted by World War II, during which he served in a cavalry regiment. After the war he continued his musical education with Gordon Jacob in composition, Leon Goossens in oboe and Frederick Thurston in clarinet. In 1951 he joined the staff of the Royal College of Music, until 1958, when he decided to devote himself mainly to composition for the films. He wrote music for more than 60 motion pictures, both in England and the U.S., including such popular productions as *Tom Jones* (1963), which won for him an Academy Award Oscar, *The Loved One* (1965), *Torn Curtain* (1966), *The Charge of the Light Brigade* (1968), *Sleuth* (1972) and *Seven Per Cent Solution*, a comedy involving Sherlock Holmes and Freud (1976). His film music is particularly effective in epical subjects with understated humor. Apart from film music, he wrote *Variations for Piano and Orch.* (1948), a concerto for trumpet, strings and percussion (1949), a woodwind sextet (1949), a trio for oboe, clarinet and bassoon (1950), a trio for flute, oboe and piano; *Serenade and Conversation Piece* for 2 soprano voices, harpsichord, organ and harp. He also wrote music for television documentaries. Since 1975 Addison has divided his time between Los Angeles and a small village in the French Alps where he does some skiing and mountaineering.

Adelburg, August Ritter von, violinist and composer; b. Constantinople, Nov. 1, 1830; d. Vienna, Oct. 20, 1873. He studied the violin with Mayseder in Vienna (1850–54), and composition with Hoffmann; then toured Europe as violinist. He wrote 3 operas: *Zrinyi* (Budapest, June 23, 1868; his most successful work), *Martinuzzi* (1870), and *Wallenstein* (on Schiller's drama); an oratorio *War and Peace;* 5 string quartets and *School of Velocity* for violin.

Adgate, Andrew, American church organist and choral conductor; b. Philadelphia c.1750; d. there of yellow fever, Sept. 30, 1793. In 1784 he organized, in Philadelphia, the Institution for the Encouragement of Church Music; in 1785 he founded there the Free School for Spreading the Knowledge of Vocal Music, reorganized in 1787 as The Uranian Academy, the purpose of which was to urge the incorporation of musical study with general education. On May 4, 1786, he presented in Philadelphia "A Grand Concert of Sacred Music," with a chorus of 230 voices and an orchestra of 50, featuring works by Handel, Billings and others. Adgate compiled several publications: *Lessons for the Uranian Society* (1785); *Select Psalms and Hymns* (1787); *Rudiments of Music* (1788); *Selection of Sacred Harmony* (1788).

Adler, Clarence, American pianist; b. Cincinnati, March 10, 1886; d. New York, Dec. 24, 1969. He studied at the Cincinnati College of Music (1898–1904); then in Berlin with Godowsky (1905–09). He toured in Europe as pianist in the Hekking Trio. Returning to America in 1913, he settled in New York; made his American debut with the N.Y. Symph. Orch. (Feb. 8, 1914). In 1941 he broadcast all of Mozart's 28 piano concertos. He published an album of piano pieces; also arrangements of works by Dvořak and Franck.

Adler, F. Charles, conductor; b. London, July 2, 1889; d. Vienna, Feb. 16, 1959. He studied piano with August Halm in Munich, theory with Beer-Walbrunn, and conducting with Mahler. He was assistant to Felix Mottl at the Royal Opera in Munich (1908–11); in 1913 he became first conductor of the Municipal Opera, Düsseldorf. Conducted symphonic concerts in Europe (1919–33). He was owner of Edition Adler in Berlin until 1933 when he came to America. In 1937 he founded the Saratoga Springs Music Festivals, N.Y.

Adler, Guido, musicologist; b. Eibenschütz, Moravia, Nov. 1, 1855; d. Vienna, Feb. 15, 1941. He studied at the Vienna Cons. under Bruckner and Dessoff; entered Vienna Univ. in 1874 and founded, in coöperation with Felix Mottl and K. Wolf, the academical Wagner Society; took the degree of *Dr. jur.* in 1878, and in 1880 that of *Dr. phil.* (dissertation on *Die historischen Grundklassen der christlich-abendländischen Musik bis 1600*), and in 1881 qualified as instructor, lecturing on musical science (thesis, *Studie zur Geschichte der Harmonie*). With Chrysander and Spitta he founded, in 1884, the *Vierteljahrsschrift für Musikwissenschaft.* In 1885 he was appointed prof. of musicology at the German Univ. at Prague. In 1892 he was elected President of the Central Committee of the Internationale Ausstellung für Musik und Theater. In 1895 he succeeded Hanslick as prof. of music history at the Univ. of Vienna, retiring in 1927. Important books by Adler are *Methode der Musikgeschichte* (1919); *Der Stil in der Musik* (1911; 2nd ed., 1929); *Gustav Mahler* (1914); *Handbuch der Musikgeschichte* (1 vol., 1924; 2nd ed. in 2 vols., 1930); *Wollen und Wirken* (memoirs; Vienna, 1935). He was also editor of the monumental collection *Denkmäler der Tonkunst in Österreich* from its inception (the first volume appeared in 1894) to 1938 (83 vols. in all). He contributed many articles to periodic music publications.
  BIBLIOGRAPHY: C. Engel, "Guido Adler in Retrospect," *Musical Quarterly* (July 1941); R. Heinz, "Guido Adlers Musikhistorik als historistisches Dokument," in W. Wiora, ed. *Die Ausbreitung des Historismus über die Musik* (Regensburg, 1969).

Adler, Kurt, American pianist and conductor; b. Neuhaus, Bohemia, March 1, 1907; d. Butler, New Jersey, Sept. 21, 1977. He was educated in Vienna, where he studied musicology with Guido Adler and Robert Lach at the Vienna Univ. He served as assistant conductor of the Berlin State Opera (1927–29) and at the German Opera in Prague (1929–32). In 1933, with the advent of the Nazi regime, he went to Russia where he was principal conductor of the Kiev State Opera (1933–35); then organized and conducted the Philharmonic Orch. of Stalingrad (1935–37). In 1938 he came to the U.S., and first appeared as a pianist; then conducted in Canada and Mexico. In 1943 he joined the staff at the Metropolitan Opera as choirmaster and assistant conductor; made his conducting debut at the Metropolitan Opera, N.Y., on Jan. 12, 1951 in Mozart's *Die Zauberflöte*, and led about 20 different operas there until he resigned in 1973. He edited several collections of vocal works: *Operatic Anthology, The Prima Donna Album, Arias from Light Operas, Famous Operatic Choruses;* also brought out *The Art of Accompanying and Coaching* (Minneapolis, 1965); *Phonetics and Diction in Singing* (Minneapolis, 1967).

Adler, Kurt Herbert, opera conductor; b. Vienna, April 2, 1905. He studied at the Vienna Cons.; was a theater conductor in Vienna (1925–28), in Prague and in Germany. He served as assistant to Toscanini at the Salzburg Festival in 1936; then settled in the U.S.; was with the Chicago Opera Company (1938–43); in 1943 joined the staff of the San Francisco Opera; in 1953 he became its artistic director. He is no relation to Kurt Adler.

Adler, Larry (Lawrence), harmonica player; b. Baltimore, Feb. 10, 1914. He won a harmonica contest at 13 for the best rendition of Beethoven's Minuet in G. He has appeared in numerous revues; also gave concerts as soloist with piano and with orchestra, as well as command performances for King George VI, King Gustav of Sweden and Presidents Roosevelt and Truman. In 1940, determined to learn to read music, he took lessons with Ernst Toch. Darius Milhaud wrote a Suite for Harmonica and Orch. for Adler, which he played on Nov. 16, 1945 with the Philadelphia Orch. In 1949 he was viciously attacked by a wolf pack of right-wing agitators who accused him of communistic leanings and un-American thoughts. Unable to get any engagements from frightened American managers, he went to England. When the winds of national hysteria subsided, he returned to the United States and resumed his concert career.

Adler, Peter Herman, conductor; b. Jablonec, Czechoslovakia, Dec. 2, 1899. He studied in Prague with Fidelio Finke, Vítězlav Novák, and Alexander von Zemlinsky; conducted opera in Brno (1923); later was first conductor of the Bremen State Theater (1928–31). In 1932 he went to Russia; was chief conductor of the Ukrainian State Orch. in Kiev (1932–37) and taught conducting at the Kiev Cons.; also conducted symph. concerts in Moscow and Leningrad. He was in Prague in 1938; then settled in the U.S.; made his American debut as conductor at a concert for Czech relief in N.Y., Jan. 24, 1940; appeared as guest conductor with the Cleveland Orch., Detroit Symph., and other organizations. He then became active in the opera; in 1949 he became musical director of the NBC Opera Theater; from 1959–67 he was music director of the Baltimore Symphony Orch.; since 1967 he has been active in educational broadcasting.

Adler, Samuel, German-born American composer; b. Mannheim, March 4, 1928. After the advent of the Nazi regime, he was taken to America. He studied at Boston Univ. with Karl Geiringer, and at Harvard Univ. with Walter Piston, Randall Thompson and Paul Hindemith; also worked with Aaron Copland at Tanglewood. In 1950 he joined the U.S. Army; was stationed in Germany where he organized the Seventh Army Symph. Orch. and conducted in Germany and Austria; received the Medal of Honor. In 1953 he was appointed music director at the Temple Emanu-El in Dallas, Texas; in 1966 he became Professor of Composition at the Eastman School of Music, Rochester, N.Y. A prolific composer in all genres, he evolved a sui generis idiom of composition with a realistic regard for effective instrumental writing.
WORKS: 1-act opera *The Outcasts of Poker Flat,*

after Bret Harte (1959; Denton, Tex., June 8, 1962); *The Wrestler,* a sacred opera (1971); *The Lodge of Shadows,* a music drama for baritone solo, dancers, and orch. (1973); *The Disappointment,* a reconstruction of an early American ballad opera of 1767 (1974); five symphonies: *No. 1* (1953); *No. 2* (1957); *No. 3, Diptych* for wind orch. (1960); *No. 4, Geometrics* (1967); *No. 5, We Are The Echoes,* for mezzo-soprano and orch. (Fort Worth, Tex., Nov. 10, 1975); *Toccata* for orch. (1954); *Rhapsody* for violin and orch. (1961); *Song and Dance* for viola and orch. (1965); *City by the Lake,* "a portrait of Rochester, N.Y." (1968); Organ Concerto (1970); *Sinfonietta* (1970); Concerto for Orchestra (1971); much music for brass instruments including *Five Vignettes* for 12 trombones (1968); *Brass Fragments* for 20 brass instruments (1970); *Histrionics* for brass and perc. (1971); *Déjà Vu* for 6 recorders (1975); a great deal of chamber music, including 6 string quartets (1945, 1950, 1953, 1963, 1969, 1975), the last one with mezzo-soprano; Piano Trio (1964); three violin sonatas; Sonata for Horn and Piano (1948); Sonata for Cello Unaccompanied (1966); 8 pieces, each titled *Canto,* most of them for a single unaccompanied instrument (trumpet, bass trombone, violin, saxophone, double bass, tuba, piano), composed between 1970 and 1975, also one for soprano, flute, cello and percussion; *Four Dialogues* for euphonium and marimba (1974); an untold amount of organ music; sacred vocal works, among them *From Out of Bondage,* biblical cantata (Temple Sinai, Brookline, Mass., April 4, 1969). He published *Anthology for the Teaching of Choral Conducting* (1971).

Adlgasser, Anton Cajetan, German organist and composer; b. Inzell, Bavaria, Oct. 1, 1729; d. Salzburg, Dec. 22, 1777. He studied with Johann Eberlin in Salzburg; on Dec. 11, 1750 was appointed organist at Salzburg Cathedral and held this post until his death (he died of a stroke while playing the organ). Adlgasser enjoyed a great reputation as a musical scholar and was admired by the young Mozart. He wrote an opera *Nitteti* (Salzburg, 1767); several oratorios and sacred dramas; 7 symphonies; piano sonatas and church works.
BIBLIOGRAPHY: C. Schneider, *Die Oratorien und Schuldramen A. C. Adlgassers* (Vienna, 1923); id., *Musikgeschichte von Salzburg* (1936).

Adlung, Jakob, German music scholar; b. Bindersleben, near Erfurt, Jan. 14, 1699; d. Erfurt, July 5, 1762. He studied with Christian Reichardt; in 1727 became organist at the Erfurt Lutheran Church; in 1741 was named prof. at the town school. A man of wide erudition, Adlung gave language lessons as well as musical instruction. He built 16 clavichords with his own hands. Among his writings, three have historical value: *Anleitung zu der musikalischen Gelahrtheit* (Erfurt, 1758; 2nd ed., revised by J.A. Hiller, 1783; facsimile ed. by H. J. Moser, Kassel, 1953); *Musica mechanica organoedi* (1768; facsimile ed. by Chr. Mahrenholz, Kassel, 1931); *Musikalisches Siebengestirn* (1768). His autobiographical sketch was publ. by Marpurg (*Kritische Briefe,* II).
BIBLIOGRAPHY: E. Valentin, s.v., *Die Musik in Geschichte und Gegenwart.*

Admon-Gorochov, Jedidiah, Israeli composer; b. Ekaterinoslav, Russia, Dec. 5, 1894. He settled in Palestine as a child and studied music in Jerusalem; lived in the U.S. in 1923-27. His works, mostly for voices, are thematically derived from traditional Jewish cantillation. His chamber music is more cosmopolitan in nature.

Adolphus, Milton, American composer; b. New York, Jan. 27, 1913. In 1935 he moved to Philadelphia, where he studied composition with Rosario Scalero; was subsequently director of the Philadelphia Music Center; in 1938 he went to Harrisburg where he was engaged in an administrative capacity by the Department of Labor and Industry of the Commonwealth of Pennsylvania. Although he never practiced music vocationally, he is extremely prolific in composition. He wrote 13 symphonies (1930-54) and 28 string quartets (1935-64) as well as other pieces of symphonic and chamber music. Some of his works show a measure of sophisticated humor, exemplified by *Bitter Suite* for oboe, 4 clarinets and strings (1955) and *Petits fours* for cello and piano (1960); *United Nations Suite* for orch. (1962); and *Sinfonietta* for chamber orch. (1970).

Adomián, Lan, American composer; b. in the county of Mogiliov-Podolsk, in the Ukraine, April 29, 1905. After completing his high school education he went to Czernowitz, Moldavia, where he studied violin. He emigrated to the U.S. in 1923, and studied at the Peabody Cons. of Music in Baltimore (1924-26), and at the Curtis Institute of Music in Philadelphia (1926-28), where his teachers were Bailly (viola), and R. O. Morris (composition). He moved to New York in 1928; conducted working class choruses and bands; in 1936 he joined the Abraham Lincoln Brigade and went to Spain to fight on the Republican side during the Spanish Civil War. Upon return to America, he wrote music for documentary films. In 1952, his radical politics made it prudent for him to leave the U.S. Accordingly, he moved to Mexico, and became a Mexican citizen. Adomián is uncommonly prolific as a composer. He wrote 8 symphonies between 1950 and 1966. His other major works include *Lincoln's Gettysburg Address* for baritone solo and strings (1946); *Cantata de la Revolución Mexicana* for mixed chorus and orch. (1960); *Cantata de las Ausencias* for tenor, chorus and strings (1964); an opera, *La Macherata,* to an Italian libretto after Alberto Moravia (1969-72); *Auschwitz,* for solo voice and chamber orch. (1970); *Clavurenito,* for soprano and orch. (1973); *Una Vida* for 7 instruments (1975); numerous songs to texts in Spanish, English, Italian and French.

Adorno (real name **Wiesengrund**), **Theodor,** significant German musician and philosopher; b. Frankfurt, Sept. 11, 1903; d. Visp, Switzerland, Aug. 6, 1969. He studied music with Sekles in Frankfurt and with Alban Berg in Vienna; was for several years prof. at the Univ. of Frankfurt. Devoting himself mainly to music criticism he was editor of the progressive music journal *Anbruch* in Vienna (1928-31). In 1933 he went to the U.S. and later became connected with radio research at Princeton Univ. (1938-41); subsequently

lived in California. He returned to Germany in 1949 where he became active as a lecturer on modern music. He published numerous essays dealing with the sociology of music, among them *Philosophie der neuen Musik* (Tübingen, 1949); *Dissonanzen: Musik in der verwalteten Welt* (Göttingen, 1956); *Arnold Schönberg* (Berlin, 1957); *Klangfiguren* (Berlin, 1959); *Einleitung in die Musiksoziologie* (Frankfurt, 1962); *Moments musicaux* (Frankfurt, 1964); *Form in der Neuen Musik* (Mainz, 1966); *Impromptus* (Frankfurt, 1968); *Alban Berg, der Meister des kleinsten Übergangs* (Vienna, 1968). Adorno advised Thomas Mann in the musical parts of his novel *Doktor Faustus.* He exercised a deep influence on the trends in musical philosophy and general esthetics, applying the sociological tenets of Karl Marx and the psychoanalytic techniques of Freud. In his speculative writings he introduced the concept of "cultural industry" embracing all types of musical techniques, from dodecaphony to jazz. A Festschrift was published in honor of his 60th birthday under the title *Zeugnisse* (Frankfurt, 1963). Numerous articles in several languages have been published on Adorno's theories in various music journals. In his early writings he used the hyphenated name **Wiesengrund-Adorno.**

BIBLIOGRAPHY: R. Stephan, "Theodor W. Adorno (1903-1969)," *Die Musikforschung* (July/Sept. 1969); E. Werner, "Zu Theodor W. Adornos *Impromptus,*" *Die Musikforschung* (April/June 1970); R. Weitzman, "An Introduction to Adorno's Music and Social Criticism," *Music & Letters* (July 1971); C. Rittelmeyer, "Dogmatismus, Intoleranz und die Beurteilung moderner Kunstwerk," *Kölner Zeitschrift für Soziologie und Sozialpsychologie* XXX/1 (1969); H. Sabbe, "Philosophie der neuesten Musik—ein Versuch zur Extrapolation von Adornos *Philosophie der neuen Musik,*" *Philosophica Gandensia* 9 (1972); F. C. Reininghaus and J. H. Traber, "Musik als Ware—Musik als Wahre. Zur politischen Hintergrund des musiksoziologischen Ansatzes von Theodor W. Adorno," *Zeitschrift für Musiktheorie* IV/1 (1973).

Adriaensen (Adriaenssen, Hadrianus), Emanuel (Emmanuel), Flemish lutenist; b. in Antwerp in the 16th century; d. Antwerp, in 1604; date of burial Feb. 27, 1604. In 1584 he published *Pratum musicum,* a collection of songs and dances for 2, 3, and 4 lutes; in 1592 he brought out another collection entitled *Novum pratum musicum,* containing canzonets, dances, fantasias, madrigals, motets and preludes by Cipriano de Rore, Orlando di Lasso, J. de Berchem, H. Waelrant and others, freely arranged by him for lute in tablature.

Adrio, Adam, German musicologist; b. Essen, April 4, 1901; d. Ritten, Bozen, Sept. 18, 1973. He studied at Berlin Univ. (1927-34) and took his Ph.D. there. In 1951, appointed prof. at the Univ. of Berlin-West. Contributor to *Die Musik in Geschichte und Gegenwart.* Author of *Die Anfänge des geistlichen Konzerts* (Berlin, 1935), many articles, and editor of collections of old German music.

Aerts, Egide, Belgian flutist; b. Boom, near Antwerp, March 1, 1822; d. Brussels, June 9, 1853. A precocious musician, he studied as a child at the Brussels Cons.; gave a concert in Paris at the age of 15. In 1847 he was appointed teacher of flute at the Brussels Cons. He wrote numerous works for flute, most of which remain in manuscript.

Aeschbacher, Adrian, Swiss pianist; b. Langenthal, May 10, 1912. He studied at the Zürich Cons. with Emil Frey and Andreae; later took lessons with Schnabel in Berlin. He toured in Europe from 1934 to 1939; then taught and gave concerts in Switzerland. In 1965 he was appointed prof. of piano at the Musikhochschule in Saarbrücken.

Aeschbacher, Niklaus, Swiss conductor; b. Trogen, April 30, 1917. He studied in Zürich and Berlin. Was active as theater conductor in Germany; appointed conductor of the Municipal Theater in Bern in 1949; in 1959 became music director and conductor of symph. concerts in Kiel; in 1964 became music director at the Detmold Opera. He wrote a radio opera *Die roten Schuhe* (1943) and chamber music.

Aeschbacher, Walther, Swiss conductor and composer; b. Bern, Oct. 2, 1901; d. Bern, Dec. 6, 1969. He studied music theory with Ernst Kurth, and conducting in Munich and then settled in Basel. He wrote much choral music and several orchestral pieces in old forms.

Afanassiev, Nikolai, Russian composer; b. Tobolsk, Jan. 12, 1821; d. St. Petersburg, June 3, 1898. He studied violin with his father, an amateur musician, and joined the orchestra of the Moscow Opera at the age of 17. Later he conducted Italian opera in Moscow and St. Petersburg. He traveled in Europe in 1857. Afanassiev was regarded as the first Russian composer to write a string quartet (1860), but this is refuted by the discovery of 3 string quartets by Aliabiev. He further wrote a cantata, *The Feast of Peter the Great,* and an opera *Ammalat-Bek,* which was produced at the Imperial Opera in St. Petersburg on Dec. 5, 1870, and three more operas, *Stenka Razin, Vakula the Smith,* and *Taras Bulba,* which were never performed; also wrote some children's songs.

Afranio de Pavia (family name **Albonese**), Italian theologian, reputed inventor of the bassoon; b. Pavia, 1480; d. Ferrara, c.1560 as canon of Ferrara. His claim to the invention of the bassoon is based on the attribution to him of the instrument Phagotus, in the book by his nephew Teseo Albonese, *Introductio in chaldaicam linguam* (Pavia, 1539).

Agay, Dénes, Hungarian-American pianist, composer and arranger; b. Budapest, June 10, 1911. He studied at the Budapest Academy of Music, graduating in 1933. In 1939 he went to the U.S. and settled in New York as piano teacher. Since 1950, he is active mainly as editor of educational material for piano students; compiled several collections of piano music adapted for beginners (*Easy Classics to Moderns, The Young Pianist's Library,* etc.).

Agazzari, Agostino, Italian composer; b. Siena, Dec. 2, 1578; d. there, April 10, 1640. He entered the service of Emperor Matthias as a professional musician; proceeding to Rome, he was in turn maestro di cappella at the German Collage there (1602–06), the church of St. Apollinaris, and the 'seminario romano'; intimacy with Viadana led to his adoption of the latter's innovations in sacred vocal music (writing church concerti for one or two voices with instrumental harmonic support). From 1630 he was maestro di cappella at Siena Cathedral. His works, variously reprinted in Germany and Holland, were in great favor and very numerous (madrigals, psalms, motets and other church music). His treatise *La musica ecclesiastica* (Siena, 1638) is a theoretical endeavor to bring the practice of church music into accord with the Resolution of the Council of Trent; he was also among the first to give written instructions for performing the basso continuo, presented in the tract *Del sonare sopra il basso con tutti gli strumenti e del loro uso nel concerto* (Siena, 1607); in English, O. Strunk, *Source Readings in Music History,* N.Y., 1950). His pastoral drama, *Eumelio* (1606) is one of the earliest operas.

BIBLIOGRAPHY: A. Adrio, s.v., *Die Musik Geschichte und Gegenwart;* M. F. Johnson, "Agazzari's *Eumelio,* a 'Dramma pastorale,'" *Musical Quarterly* (July 1971).

Ager, Milton, American composer of popular music; b. Chicago, Oct. 6, 1893. He began his career as pianist in silent film theaters and accompanist to singers in vaudeville. He served in the U.S. Army Morale Division during World War I. His song *Happy Days Are Here Again* was selected by Franklin Roosevelt as his campaign song in 1932, and became an anthem of the Democratic Party in subsequent election campaigns. Ager also wrote the greatly popular ballads *Ain't She Sweet, Crazy Words, Crazy Tune,* and *Hard-Hearted Hannah.*

Agnew, Roy, Australian composer and pianist; b. Sydney, Aug. 23, 1893; d. there, Nov. 12, 1944. He went to London and studied with Gerrard Williams (1923–28); gave concerts in England (1931–34). He then returned to Australia; was appointed dir. of the Australian radio (1938–43) and taught at the Sydney Cons.

WORKS: *Breaking of the Drought* for mezzo-soprano and orch. (1928); many piano works, including *Dance of the Wild Men* (1920); *Fantasia Sonata* (1927); *Sonata Poem* (1935); *Sonata Ballade* (1936); *Sonata Legend "Capricornia"* (1940).

Agostini, Lodovico, Italian composer and poet; b. Ferrara, 1534; d. there Sept. 20, 1590. He served as maestro di cappella to Alphonso II of Este, Duke of Ferrara. A number of his sacred and secular vocal works (madrigals motets, Masses, Vespers, etc.) were published in Milan, Ferrara and Venice (1567–86).

Agostini, Mezio, Italian composer; b. Fano, Aug. 12, 1875; d. there, April 22, 1944. He studied with his father and with Carlo Pedrotti at the Liceo Rossini in Pesaro (1885–92). He was prof. of harmony there from 1900–09 when he was appointed as successor of Wolf-

Ferrari in the position of director of the Liceo Benedetto Marcello in Venice (1909-1940). He was active as an opera conductor in Venice and other Italian cities; also gave chamber music concerts as pianist. His *Trio* won first prize at the international competition in Paris in 1904. His works include the operas *Iovo e Maria* (1896), *Il Cavaliere del Sogno* (Fano, Feb. 24, 1897), *La penna d'Airone* (1896), *Alcibiade* (1902), *America* (also entitled *Hail Columbia*, after Longfellow, 1904), *L'Ombra* (1907), *L'Agnello del sogno* (1928), *La figlio del navarca* (Fano, Sept. 3, 1938); a symphony, 4 orchestral suites, a piano concerto, 2 string quartets, 2 piano trios, cello sonata, violin sonata, a cantata *A Rossini*, numerous piano pieces and songs.

Agostini, Paolo, Italian organist and composer; b. Vallerano, 1583; d. Rome, Oct. 3, 1629. He studied with Giovanni Bernardino Nanino in Rome; was organist at S. Maria in Trastevere, in Rome, and at S. Lorenzo in Damaso. He succeeded Vincenzo Ugolini as maestro di cappella at the Vatican in 1626. Agostini's published works, 7 books of psalms (1619), 2 books of Magnificats and antiphons (1620), and 5 books of Masses (1624-28), are only a small portion of his total output. Most of his manuscripts are preserved in various Roman libraries. His music displays great ingenuity of contrapuntal structure; some of his choral works are written in 48 independent parts.

Agostini, Pietro Simone, Italian composer; b. near Pesaro, in the first half of the 17th century; d. Parma, Oct. 1, 1680. He was in the service of the Duke of Parma as maestro di cappella during the last year of his life. He wrote 6 operas, some of which were written in collaboration with Busca, Ziani and others: *Argia principessa di Negroponte* (probably Milan, 1669); *La Regina Floridea* (Milan, 1669); *Eliogabalo*, to his own libretto (Genoa, Jan. 28, 1670); *Ippolita regina delle Amazzoni* (Milan, 1670); *La Costanza di Rosmonda* (Genoa, 1670); *Gli inganni innocenti* or *L'Adalinda* (Rome, 1673); and *Il Ratto delle Sabine* (Venice, 1680); he also wrote oratorios, motets and secular cantatas.

Agrell, Johan Joachim, Swedish composer; b. Löth, Feb. 1, 1701; d. Nuremberg, Jan. 19, 1765. He studied at Uppsala Univ.; later he was active in Kassel (1723-46) and in Nuremberg (from 1746). Among his published works are 5 concertos for cembalo and strings, 2 sonatas for violin and cembalo, 6 sonatas for cembalo solo, and pieces for cembalo in dance forms. His symphonies and cantatas are preserved in various European libraries (Stockholm, Uppsala, Brussels, Berlin, Königsberg, Munich and Darmstadt).

Agricola, Alexander, composer of the Netherland school; sometimes said to have been of German extraction, but referred to as a Belgian in his epitaph; b. Flanders, c.1446; d. 1506 at Valladolid, Spain. He was in the service of the Duke of Milan from 1472-74; then went to Cambrai; in 1476 he is mentioned as "petit vicaire" at Cambrai Cathedral. He later traveled in Italy; entered the service of Philip I of Burgundy in 1500 and followed him to Spain in 1502, returning to

Belgium in 1505. He went to Spain again in January 1506 and died shortly afterward. Thirty-one of Agricola's songs and motets were printed by Petrucci (Venice, 1501-03), who also published a volume of 5 Masses based on chanson material: *Le Serviteur, Je ne demande, Malheur me bat, Primi toni, Secundi toni* (Venice 1503).

Agricola, Johann Friedrich, German organist and composer; b. Dobitzschen, near Altenburg, Jan 4, 1720; d. Berlin, Dec. 2, 1774. He entered the Univ. of Leipzig as a law student in 1738, studying music meanwhile with J. S. Bach, and later (1741) with Johann Quantz in Berlin. In 1751 Agricola was appointed court composer to Frederick the Great; in 1759 he succeeded Karl Graun as director of the Royal Chapel. Agricola wrote 8 operas (produced between 1750-1772 at Berlin and Potsdam) and church music; he also made arrangements of the King's compositions. He taught singing and translated (1757) Pier Tosi's *Opinioni de' cantori.* Under the pseudonym **Flavio Amicio Olibrio** Agricola printed some polemical pamphlets directed against the theorist Friedrich Marpurg; he was also a collaborator with Jakob Adlung in the latter's *Musica mechanica organoedi* (1768).

Agricola, Martin, important German music theorist and writer; b. Schwiebus (Brandenburg), Jan. 6, 1486; d. Magdeburg, June 10, 1556. His real name was **Sore,** but he adopted the Latin name Agricola to indicate his peasant origin. Mattheson says that he was the first to abandon the old tablature for modern notation, but this is not quite accurate; Agricola merely proposed an improved system for lute tablature. From 1510 he was a private music teacher in Magdeburg. In 1527 was cantor at the first Lutheran church there. His friend and patron, Rhaw of Wittenberg, published most of Agricola's works, the magnum opus being *Musica instrumentalis deudsch* (i.e., 'set in German'; 1st ed., Wittenberg, 1529; 4th ed., considerably revised, 1545; modern reprint, Leipzig, 1896). This work, although derived from Virdung's *Musica getutsch,* contains much new material and is set in couplet verse in the German vernacular. Further works are: *Ein kurtz deudsche Musica* (1529; 3d ed. as *Musica choralis deudsch,* (1533); *Musica figuralis,* with a supplement *Von den proportionibus* (1532); *Scholia in musicam planam Venceslai Philomatis* (1538); *Rudimenta musices* (1539); *Quaestiones vulgatiores in musicam* (1543); *Duo libri musices* (posthumous; Wittenberg, 1561; includes reprints of *Musica choralis* and *Musica figuralis;* and 54 *Instrumentische Gesänge* as a supplement). Compositions: *Ein Sangbüchlein aller Sonntags-Evangelien* (1541); *Neue deutsche geistliche Gesänge* (1544); *Hymni aliquot sacri* (1552); *Melodiae scholasticae* (1557).

BIBLIOGRAPHY: Heinz Funck, *Martin Agricola* (Wolfenbüttel, 1933).

Aguado, Dionisio, Spanish guitar virtuoso and composer; b. Madrid, April 8, 1784; d. there Dec. 29, 1849. He studied with Manuel Garcia; went to Paris in 1825; gave numerous concerts there, attracting the attention of Rossini and Paganini. Returning to Madrid in 1838, he became a teacher of guitar. He wrote *Estudio* *para la guitarra* (Madrid, 1820); *Escuela o método de guitarra* (Madrid, 1825); also 45 waltzes; 6 minuets, etc.

Aguilar, Emanuel Abraham, English pianist and composer of Spanish descent; b. London, Aug. 23, 1824; d. there Feb. 18, 1904. He wrote a collection of canons and fugues as preparatory exercises for the playing of Bach; also composed 3 symphonies, 2 overtures, much chamber music and the operas, *Wave King* (1855) and *The Bridal Wreath* (1863).

Aguilar-Ahumada, Miguel, Chilean composer; b. Huara, April 12, 1931. He studied composition with Domingo Santa Cruz and Orrego-Salas in Santiago and later took a course in conducting in Cologne. Returning to Chile, he occupied various posts as a teacher, also giving piano recitals. Under the influence of the German avant-garde, he adopted an advanced atonal idiom.
WORKS: *Obertura al Teatro Integral* for orch. (1954); Septet for Wind Instruments and Double Bass (1954); *Sonatina concertante* for clarinet and piano (1956); *Simetrias* for piano (1958) and an orchestral work entitled *Música aleatoria* (1969); in one of his electronic pieces he introduced tape recordings of a mooing cow, exploding balloons and the recording of an orchestra while tuning up before a rehearsal. He wrote several vocal works to texts by the Chilean poet Vicente Huidobro, among them *Torre Eifel* (1967).

Aguilera de Heredia, Sebastian, b. in Aragon, c.1565; d. in Saragossa, Dec. 16, 1627. He was organist at Huesca (1585–1603) and then 'maestro de musica' at Saragossa cathedral. He published there his collection *Canticum Beatissimae Virginis Deiparae Mariae octo modis seu tonis compositum, quaternisque vocibus, quinis, senis et octonis concionandum* (1618). It contains sacred choruses in 4, 5, 6 and 8 parts, derived from 8 church modes. His music is notable for skillful use of dissonances ('falsas').
BIBLIOGRAPHY: H. Anglès, "Orgelmusik der Schola Hispanica von XV–XVII. Jahrhunderte," in *Peter Wagner-Festschrift* (Leipzig, 1926).

Aguirre, Julián, Argentine composer; b. Buenos Aires, Jan. 28, 1868; d. there, Aug. 13, 1924. He was taken to Spain as a child; studied at the Madrid Cons., returning to Buenos Aires in 1887. His works are mostly miniatures for piano in the form of stylized Argentine dances and songs. He wrote 61 opus numbers; *Gato* and *Huella* (op. 49), his most popular pieces, were orchestrated by Ansermet, who performed them in Buenos Aires (April 6, 1930); the *Huella* was also arranged for violin and piano by Jascha Heifetz. Other notable works are *Aires nacionales argentinos* (op. 17) and *Zamba* (op. 40).
BIBLIOGRAPHY: J. F. Giacobbe, *Julián Aguirre* (Buenos Aires, 1945); C. García Muñoz, *Julián Aguirre* (Buenos Aires, 1970).

Agujari, Lucrezia (known as **La Bastardina,** or **Bastardella,** being the natural daughter of a nobleman), a brilliant Italian singer; b. Ferrara, 1743; d. Parma, May 18, 1783. Her father entrusted her instruction to

P. Lambertini; in 1764 she made a triumphant debut at Florence, followed by a succession of brilliant appearances in Milan and other Italian cities; also in London. Mozart wrote of her, that she had "a lovely voice, a flexible throat, and an incredibly high range." In 1780 she married the Italian composer, **Giuseppe Colla,** whose songs she constantly performed at her concerts. Her compass was phenomenal, embracing 3 octaves (C¹–C⁴).

Ahle, Johann Georg, German organist and composer (son of **Johann Rudolf Ahle**); b. Mühlhausen, June, 1651 (baptized June 12); d. there, Dec. 1, 1706. He succeeded his father as organist in Mühlhausen, and was made poet laureate by Emperor Leopold I. Among Ahle's works published during his lifetime are *Musikalische Frühlings-, Sommer-, Herbst-, und Wintergespräche* (1695–1701; written to illustrate his method of composition); *Instrumentalische Frühlingsmusik* (1676); *Anmuthige zehn vierstimmige Viol-di-gamba Spiele* (1681) and many volumes of dances, sacred and secular songs.

Ahle, Johann Rudolf, German composer; b. Mühlhausen, Dec. 24, 1625; d. there, July 9, 1673. From 1646 he was cantor in Erfurt. He was organist of St. Blasius, Mühlhausen, in 1654, and in 1661 was elected burgomaster of the town. Ahle was a diligent composer of church music and writer of theoretical works. His *Compendium pro tonellis* (1648) ran through 4 editions; 2nd (1673) as *Brevis et perspicua introductio in artem musicum;* 3rd and 4th (1690 and 1704) as *Kurze und deutliche Anleitung.* His principal compositions include: *Geistlich Dialoge,* songs in several parts (1648); *Thüringischer Lustgarten* (1657); *Geistliche Fest- und Communionandachten* (posthumous). Many of his songs are still popular in Thuringia. A selection from his works was published by J. Wolf in *Denkmäler deutscher Tonkunst* (vol. V).
BIBLIOGRAPHY: J. Wolf, "Johann Rudolf Ahle," *Sammelbände der Internationalen Musik-Gesellschaft* II/3 (1920); A. Adrio, s.v., *Die Musik in Geschichte und Gegenwart.*

Ahna, Heinrich Karl Herman de. See **De Ahna, Heinrich Karl Herman.**

Aho, Kalevi, Finnish composer; b. Forssa, March 9, 1949. He studied at the Sibelius Academy in Helsinki with E. Rautavaara; then went to Berlin and took a course in composition with Boris Blacher. He has written 4 symphonies (1969, 1970, 1971, 1972); 3 string quartets, a quintet for oboe and string quartet (1974), and sonata for solo violin (1974).

Ahrens, Joseph Johannes Clemens, eminent German organist and composer; b. Sommersell, Westphalia, April 17, 1904. He received his early instruction in music from his father; in 1925 went to Berlin where he studied choral music with Sittard and Wilhelm Middelschulte. He displayed an early talent for improvisation on the organ; in 1934 he became organist at St. Hedwiga Cathedral in Berlin; later was prof. of Catholic church music in the Berlin Hochschule für Musik. In 1968 he received the silver pontifical medal in

Rome. In his works, almost exclusively for organ and chorus, he maintains the strict form of the Gregorian chorale within the framework of complex polyphony, applying advanced melodic, rhythmic and harmonic formulas, including the 12-tone technique. His works include a number of toccatas, partitas and fugues for organ, couched in a modern Baroque style, which are highly esteemed by professional organists; several Masses: *Missa choralis* (1945); *Missa dorica* (1946); *Missa gotica* (1948); *Missa hymnica* (1948); *Missa Salvatoris* (1949); *Missa pro unitate* (1963); *Missa dodekaphonica* (1966, in which Gregorian chant is combined with 12-tone melodic patterns); *Passion of St. Matthew* (1950); *Passion of St. John* (1961); and numerous motets and solo cantatas. He published a handbook on improvisation as a basic science in music pedagogy.

Aibl, Joseph, founder of a music publishing firm, established in Munich in 1824; his successors were **Eduard Spitzweg** (from 1836), and his sons, **Eugen** and **Otto.** In 1904 Universal Edition bought the Aibl firm.

Aiblinger, Johann Kaspar, German conductor and composer; b. Wasserburg, Bavaria, Feb. 23, 1779; d. Munich, May 6, 1867. He studied music in Munich, then at Bergamo under Simon Mayr (1802); lived at Vicenza (1803–11), then became second maestro di cappella to the viceroy at Milan; founded the 'Odeon' (a society for the cultivation of classical vocal music) at Venice, in collaboration with Abbé Trentino; was engaged (1819) for the Italian opera in Munich as maestro al cembalo; returned in 1833 to Bergamo, and amassed a fine collection of ancient classical music, now in the Staatsbibliothek at Munich. He wrote many sacred compositions (Masses, Requiems, liturgies, psalms, etc.), which were very popular. He also wrote an opera, *Rodrigo e Ximene* (Munich, 1821), and 3 ballets.

Aichinger, Gregor, important German church composer; b. Regensburg, 1564; d. Augsburg, Jan. 21, 1628. At the age of 13 he went to Munich where he was under the tutelage of Orlando Lasso; then entered the Univ. of Ingolstadt. He made two journeys to Rome; visited Venice where he mastered the art of Venetian polyphony. He eventually settled in Augsburg as choir master and vicar of the Cathedral. He wrote almost exclusively for voices, to Latin texts; his sacred works are remarkable for their practical value and for the excellence of their musical content. Among his many published works are 3 books of *Sacrae cantiones* (Venice, 1590; Augsburg, 1595; Nuremberg, 1597); *Tricinia Mariana* (Innsbruck, 1598); *Divinae laudes* (Augsburg, 1602); etc. His publication *Cantiones ecclesiaticae cum basso generali et continuo* (Dillingen, 1607) is noteworthy as one of the earliest works in which the term 'basso continuo' appears in the title. A selection of Aichinger's works is included in Vol. 18 (formerly 10.i) of *Denkmäler der Tonkunst in Bayern,* prefaced with a biographical article by the editor, Th. Kroyer.
BIBLIOGRAPHY: E. Fr. Schmid, s.v., *Die Musik in Geschichte und Gegenwart.*

Aigner, Engelbert, Austrian composer and conductor; b. Vienna, Feb. 3, 1798; d. there, Aug. 27, 1866. He studied with Stadler, from whom he received a thorough training in church music; also wrote for the stage. Among his works are the operettas *Die Wunderlilie* (Vienna, 1827); *Das Hochzeitskonzert* (Vienna, 1829); *Der Angriffsplan* (Vienna, 1829); *Das geheime Fenster* (Vienna, 1829); several ballets; a canonic Mass (1823); cantata, *Lob der Musik; Kontrapunktischer Scherz* for piano; Quintet for Piano, Flute, Violin, Viola and Cello; some orchestral pieces. He also participated in a society for the propagation of church music.

Aitken, Hugh, American composer; b. New York, Sept. 7, 1924. He studied music with his father, a professional violinist, and his mother, a pianist. He served in the U.S. Army Air Force in World War II as a navigator; after the war he enrolled in the Juilliard School of Music, N.Y., where he attended classes in composition with Bernard Wagenaar and Vincent Persichetti; upon graduation in 1950, he became a member of its faculty. In 1971 he was appointed chairman of the music dept. of William Paterson College, Wayne, New Jersey.
WORKS: 5 cantatas; 5 partitas for various ensembles; a choreographic work, *The Moirai* (New London, Conn., Aug. 18, 1961); Piano Concerto; Oboe Quintet; 8 pieces for wind quintet; Quartet for Clarinet and Strings; *Montages,* for solo bassoon; Suite for Solo Clarinet; *Trumpet!* for unaccompanied trumpet (1974); *Fables,* a diversion for 4 singers and 9 instruments to words by La Fontaine (1975); Quintet for Oboe and Strings (1975); Quintet for Trumpet and String Quartet (1976).

Aitken, Robert, Canadian composer; b. Kentville, Nova Scotia, Aug. 28, 1939. He studied flute and, at the age of 19, became principal flutist of the Vancouver Symphony Orchestra; then played in the Canadian Broadcasting Corporation Symphony Orch. (1959–64), and the Toronto Symph. (1965–70). He was a student of composition with Barbara Pentland at the Univ. of British Columbia in Vancouver, and later took courses with John Weinzweig; also studied electronic music with Myron Schaeffer at the Univ. of Toronto (1961–64). In 1972 he was appointed to the faculty of the Univ. of Toronto. His early works are in a traditional romantic vein, but about 1970 he evolved a decidedly advanced method of composition, exploring unusual instrumental combinations and spatial concepts of antiphonal groupings.
WORKS: *Rhapsody* for Orch. (1961); Quartet for Flute, Oboe, Viola and Double Bass (1961); *Music for Flute and Tape* (1963); Concerto for 12 Soloists and Orch. (1968); *Spectra* for 4 mixed chamber groups (1969); *Nekuia* for orch. (1971); *Kebyar* for flute, clarinet, trombone, 2 double basses, percussion and tape (1971); *Shadows* for flute, 3 cellos, 2 harps and percussion (1973).

Aitken, Webster, American pianist; b. Los Angeles, June 17, 1908. He studied in Europe with Sauer and Schnabel; made his professional debut in Vienna (1929). Returning to America, he played a concert in

N.Y. (Nov. 17, 1935); in 1938 gave a series of recitals in N.Y. in programs comprising all of Schubert's piano works. He has also appeared with chamber music ensembles.

Akeroyde, Samuel, English composer of songs; b. Yorkshire, about 1650; d. London after 1706. He was in the service of James II in 1687 as 'Musician in Ordinary,' and wrote songs for at least eight plays produced in London between 1685 and 1706. His songs were printed in several contemporary collections: Durfey's *Third Collection of Songs* (1685); *The Theatre of Musick* (1685–87); *Vinculum Societatis* (1687); *Comes Amoris* (1687–94); *The Banquet of Musick* (1688); *Thesaurus Musicus* (1693–96).

Akimenko (real name **Yakimenko**), **Fyodor,** Russian composer; b. Kharkov, Feb. 20, 1876; d. Paris, Jan. 3, 1945. He studied with Balakirev at the Court Chapel in St. Petersburg (1886–90), then with Liadov and Rimsky-Korsakov at the St. Petersburg Cons. (1895–1900). He was the first composition teacher of Stravinsky, whom he taught privately. After the Russian Revolution he emigrated to Paris, where he remained until his death. He wrote mostly for piano in the manner of the Russian lyric school, and had the good fortune of having had his pieces and songs published by Belaiev; some of them were included in anthologies of Russian music. He wrote an opera, *The Fairy of the Snows* (1914); a concert overture, which was conducted by Rimsky-Korsakov in St. Petersburg on Nov. 20, 1899; an orchestral fantasy conducted by Glazunov in St. Petersburg on Oct. 28, 1900; *Petite ballade* for clarinet and piano; *Pastorale* for oboe and piano; Piano Trio; Violin Sonata; Cello Sonata; 2 *Sonata-Fantasias* for piano, numerous character pieces for piano and songs.

Akiyama, Kuniharu, Japanese composer; b. Tokyo, May 22, 1929. After taking lessons in academic musical subjects, he dedicated himself to a thorough study of advanced trends in music, surrealist literature and abstract expressionist painting. In 1967 he was one of the chief organizers of a modern series of performing arts in Tokyo, called Cross-Talk, with the participation of Japanese and American avant-garde artists and musicians. His own compositions make use of both electronic and primitive Japanese instruments; in this respect a characteristic item is *Music for Meals* (1964) for tape and stone instruments, which he prepared for a cafeteria at the Olympic Games in Tokyo in 1964 even more physiologically specific is his *Onara no uta* (*Music for Farting and Belching,* 1971).

Akses, Necil Kâzim, Turkish composer; b. Istanbul, May 6, 1908. He studied cello and theory at the Istanbul Cons. In 1926 he studied in Vienna with Joseph Marx; in Prague, with Alois Hába and Josef Suk (1931). Returning to Turkey in 1935, he became instructor at the Teachers' College in Ankara; he also took lessons with Hindemith, who was teaching there at the time. In 1936 Akses was appointed prof. of composition at the Ankara State Cons., and was its director in 1948–49. His music, derived from Turkish folk rhythms, is in the modern idiom.

WORKS: *Mete,* one-act opera (1933); *Bayönder,* opera (Ankara, Dec. 27, 1934); incidental music to *Antigone* and *King Oedipus* (Sophocles); *Çiftetelli,* dance for orch. (1933); *Ankara Castle,* tone poem (Ankara, Oct. 22, 1942); *Poem* for cello and orch. (Ankara, June 29, 1946); *Ballade* for orch. (*Ankara,* April 14, 1948); String Quartet (1946); *Allegro feroce* for saxophone and piano (1931); Flute Sonata (1939); *Poem* for cello and orch. (1942–46); *Ballads* for orch. (1947); *Symphony* (1966) and piano pieces.

Akutagawa, Yasushi, Japanese composer; b. Tokyo, July 12, 1925. He is the third son of the famous writer Ryunosuke Akutagawa, author of *Rashomon*. Yasushi studied composition (with Hashimoto and Ifukube), conducting, and piano at the Tokyo Academy of Music (1943–49); was active in Tokyo as a conductor and organizer of groups promoting the cause of Japanese music.

WORKS: 2 operas: *Kurai Kagami* (*Dark Mirror;* Tokyo, 1960), and *L'Orphée in Hiroshima* (1967; Tokyo Television, Aug. 27, 1967); 4 ballets, all produced in Tokyo: *The Dream of the Lake* (Nov. 6, 1950), *Paradise Lost* (March 17, 1951), *Kappa* (July 21, 1957), and *Spider's Web* (March 17, 1969); *Prelude* for orch. (1947); *3 Symphonic Movements* (Tokyo, Sept. 26, 1948); *Music for Orchestra* (1950); *Triptyque* for string orch. (1953); *Sinfonia* (1953); Divertimento for Orch. (1955); *Symphony for Children* (*"Twin Stars"*) for narrator and orch. (1957); *Ellora Symphony* (1958); *Music for Strings* No. 1 for double string quartet and double bass (1962); *Gengaku no tame, no inga (Negative Picture)* for string orch. (1966); *Ostinato Sinfonica* (Tokyo, May 25, 1967); *Concerto Ostinato* for cello and orch. (Tokyo, Dec. 16, 1969); *Ballata Ostinata* for orch. (1970); *Rhapsody* for orch. (Tokyo, Oct. 4, 1971); *Ballata* for violin and piano (1951); film music, including the prize-winning *Gate of Hell.*

Alain, Jehan, French composer, b. Paris, Feb. 3, 1911; killed in action at Petits-Puis, near Saumur, June 20, 1940. He composed his first piece *Étude sur un thème de quatre notes* at the age of 8; studied with his father, an organist; later with Marcel Dupré, Paul Dukas and Roger-Ducasse. Alain wrote 127 opus numbers, mostly for organ or piano.

BIBLIOGRAPHY: B. Gavoty, *Jehan Alain, Musicien Français* (Paris, 1945); F. Sabatier, "A propos de l'oeuvre d'orgue de Jehan Alain," *Jeunesse et Orgue* (1973).

Alaleona, Domenico, Italian theorist and composer; b. Montegiorgio, Nov. 16, 1881; d. there, Dec. 28, 1928. He studied organ and clarinet in his native town; in 1901 went to Rome where he studied piano with Sgambati, organ with Renzi and theory with De Sanctis at Santa Cecilia; was then active as choral conductor in Leghorn and Rome; in 1911 obtained the post of prof. of musical esthetics at Santa Cecilia. He wrote an opera *Mirra* (1912; produced in Rome, March 31, 1920, with critical acclaim, but not revived); a *Requiem; Sinfonia italiana;* 12 *Canzoni italiane* and 4 *Laudi italiane* for various instrumental groups; a cycle of 18 songs *Melodie Pascoliane* and other works. However, his importance lies in his theoretical writings. His valuable book *Studii sulla storia dell'oratorio musicale in Italia* (Turin, 1908) was reprinted in Milan (1945) as *Storia dell'oratorio musicale in Italia*, and is now a standard work. A believer in musical progress, he contributed several original ideas to the theory of modern music, notably in his article "L'armonia modernissima," *Rivista Musicale* (1911), and originated the term "dodecafonia." He also contributed articles on Italian composers to Eaglefield-Hull's *Dictionary of Modern Music and Musicians* (London, 1924). The entry on Alaleona in that dictionary contains a detailed list of his works and bibliography.

Alard, Jean-Delphin, a distinguished violinist of the French school; b. Bayonne, March 8, 1815; d. Paris, Feb. 22, 1888. He was a student of Habeneck at the Paris Cons. He succeeded Baillot as violin teacher there in 1843, and as leader of the royal orchestra, teaching in the Cons. till 1875. A fine instructor (Sarasate was his pupil), he publ. *Violin School*, a manual of high merit; *Les Maîtres classiques du violon*, a selection from 18th-century classics; and numerous brilliant and popular pieces for violin (concertos, études, fantasias, etc.).

Alary, Jules (Giulio) Eugène Abraham, Italian-French composer; b. Mantua, March 16, 1814; d. Paris, April 17, 1891. He studied at the Cons. of Milan; then played the flute at La Scala. In 1838 he settled in Paris as a successful voice teacher and composer. He wrote numerous operas, among them *Rosamunda* (Florence, June 10, 1840); *Le tre nozze* (Paris, March 29, 1851; a polka-duet from it, sung by Henrietta Sontag and Lablache, was highly popular), and *Sardanapalo* (St. Petersburg, Feb. 16, 1852). His opera *La Voix humaine* had the curious distinction of being staged at the Paris Opéra (Dec. 30, 1861) with the sole purpose of making use of the scenery left over after the fiasco of *Tannhäuser* (the action of Alary's opera takes place in Wartburg, as does that of *Tannhäuser*). It held the stage for 13 performances (*Tannhäuser* had three). Alary also wrote a mystery play *Redemption* (Paris, April 14, 1850), much sacred music and some chamber works.

Albanese, Licia, Italian-American soprano; b. Bari, July 22, 1913. She studied with Giuseppina Baldassare-Tedeschi; made her opera debut at Parma in *Madama Butterfly* (Dec. 10, 1935); sang the same role in her first appearance with the Metropolitan Opera (Feb. 9, 1940). In 1945 she sang with Toscanini and the NBC Symphony; also continued to appear with the Metropolitan Opera.

Albani, Emma (stage name of **Marie Louise Cecilia Emma Lajeunesse**), Canadian dramatic soprano; b. Chambly, near Montreal, Nov. 1, 1847; d. London, April 3, 1930. She sang in a Catholic church in Albany, N.Y. in 1864; was then sent to Europe for study, first with Duprez in Paris, and then with Lamperti in Milan (Lamperti dedicated to her his treatise on the trill). She made her debut as Amina in *La Sonnambula* in Messina in 1870, under the name of Albani, in honor of the American city in which she had her first job as a singer. After further appearances in Italy, she made her London debut, again as Amina (Covent Garden, April 2, 1872). In 1873 she sang in Moscow and St. Petersburg. Her American operatic debut was in the same role at the New York Academy of Music, in Max Strakosch's company (Oct. 21, 1874). It paved the way for later successes with the Metropolitan Opera, where she made her first appearance as Gilda (Dec. 23, 1891). Her last important operatic engagement was as Isolde at Covent Garden (June 26, 1896). She sang in concerts, however, for several years longer. Her repertoire included Marguerite, Mignon, Ophelia, Elsa, Elisabeth, Lucia and Desdemona. Albani married Ernest Gye, the lessee of Covent Garden, in 1878. In her singing, she combined high technical skill with profound feeling. She was equally successful on the operatic stage and in oratorio. In appreciation of her services to British art, she was made a Dame of the British Empire (1925). She published her memoirs, *Emma Albani: Forty Years of Song* (London, 1911).

Albani, Mattia (real name **Mathias Alban**), violin maker; b. S. Niccolo di Kaltern (Alto Adige) March, 1621 (baptized March 28); d. Bolzano, Feb. 7, 1712. Pupil of Jakob Stainer. Violins of his are extant dating from as early as the end of 1644. His best examples date from 1680 onward. Owing to the great vogue his violins enjoyed, many Albani forgeries are in existence. A son, **Giuseppe,** his pupil, worked from 1680 to 1722 at Bolzano, and another son, **Michele** (1677–1730) at Graz. Other violin makers named Albani, or at least using the name on their instruments (perhaps for its commercial value) are the following, none appearing to have been connected with the family of the original Mattia: Mattia (Rome, c.1650–1715); Nicola (worked at Mantua, c.1763); Filippo (active c.1773); Francesco (active at Graz, c.1724); Michele (at Palermo, 18th cent.); and Paolo (at Palermo and Cremona, 1630–70).

Albéniz, Isaac, eminent Spanish composer; b. Camprodón, May 29, 1860; d. Cambo-les-Bains (Pyrénées), May 18, 1909. He exhibited precocious musical ability. When he was six, his mother took him to Paris, where he had a few private lessons with Marmontel. Upon his return to Spain, he gave concerts with his sister **Clementine,** also a child prodigy. In 1868 the family moved to Madrid, and Albéniz entered the Conservatory there. Possessed by a spirit of adventure, he ran away from home at the age of 13, and traveled in Spain, giving concerts. He then stowed away on a ship for Puerto Rico; from there he went to Cuba and to the U.S., supporting himself by playing concerts in private and in public. He returned to Spain in June, 1875, and was befriended in Madrid by Count Guillermo Morphy, who enabled him to undertake serious study, first at the Brussels Cons. with Brassin (piano) and Dupont and Gevaert (composition); and then at the Leipzig Cons. with Jadassohn and Reinecke. He went to Budapest in 1878 to meet Liszt, but it is doubtful that he actually became Liszt's pupil. Albéniz married Rosita Jordana in 1883; their daughter, Laura Albéniz, became a well known painter. In 1893 he settled in Paris; he also gave frequent piano recitals in Spain, and visited London. His early works were for the theater; he wrote several operas: *The Magic Opal* (London, Jan. 19, 1893); *Enrico Clifford* (Barcelona, May 8, 1895); *San Antonio de la Florida* (Madrid, Oct. 26, 1894; also staged in Brussels, Jan. 3, 1905 under the title *Ermitage fleuri*): *Pepita Jiménez* (Barcelona, Jan. 5, 1896). He undertook the composition of an operatic trilogy *King Arthur*, of which only the first part, *Merlin*, was completed. In the meantime he met Felipe Pedrell, and was greatly influenced by Pedrell's passionate championship of national Spanish music. Albéniz's first nationalistically inspired composition was the rhapsody *Catalonia* for piano and orch. (1899). In 1906–09 he wrote his most remarkable national work *Iberia*, a set of 12 piano pieces: *Evocación, El Puerto, Fête-Dieu à Séville, Rondeña, Almeria, Triana, El Albaicín, El Polo, Lavapiés, Málaga, Jérez, Eritaña*. In this suite, which is a brilliant example of virtuoso writing for the instrument, Albéniz applied the impressionistic technique as developed by Debussy. He left unfinished two other piano works, *Azulejos* (completed by Granados) and *Navarra* (completed by D. de Sévérac; orchestrated by Fernández Arbós). Arbós also made effective orchestral transcriptions of *Evocación, Triana*, and *Fête-Dieu à Séville* (also orchestrated by Stokowski). Among Albéniz's smaller piano pieces, the *Seguidillas, Córdova*, and the Tango in D have attained wide popularity.

BIBLIOGRAPHY: J. de Marliave, *Etudes musicales* (Paris, 1917); G. Jean-Aubry, "Isaac Albéniz," *Musical Times* (Dec. 1917); H. Klein, "Albéniz's Opera, *Pepita Jiménez*," *Musical Times* (March 1918); G. Jean Aubry, *La Musique et les Nations* (Paris, 1922; English translation, 1923); Henri Collet, *Albéniz et Granados* (1925); E. Istel, "Albéniz," *Musical Quarterly* (Jan. 1929); A. de las Heras, *Vida de Albéniz* (Barcelona, 1940); M. Raux Deledicque, *Albéniz, su vida inquieta y ardorosa* (Buenos Aires, 1950); A. Sagardia, *Isaac Albéniz* (Buenos Aires, 1951); G. Laplane, *Albéniz* (Paris, 1956).

Albéniz, Mateo (Antonio Perez de), Spanish composer; date of birth unknown; d. St. Sebastian, June 23, 1831; was a church organist; published *Instrucción melódica especulativa y practica para enseñar a cantar y a tañer la música antigua* (St. Sebastian, 1802). His Sonata for Piano was published by Joaquín Nín in *16 Sonates anciennes d'auteurs espagnols* (Paris, 1925).

Albéniz, Pedro, Spanish organist and composer; son of **Mateo Albéniz**; b. Logroño, April 14, 1795; d. Madrid, April 12, 1855. He studied with his father; from his early youth played the organ in various Spanish towns; later studied piano in Paris with Kalkbrenner and Henri Herz. In 1830 he was appointed prof. of piano at the Madrid Cons.; in 1834 became court organist. He was an energetic promoter of modern methods of piano playing in Spain. He published a manual (1840) which was adopted at the Madrid Cons.; also wrote some 70 piano pieces in a highly developed technical style (rondos, variations, medleys, etc.).

Albergati, Pirro Capacelli, Conte d', Italian composer; b. Bologna, Sept. 20, 1663; d. there, June 22, 1735. He wrote 2 operas, *Gli amici* (Bologna, Aug. 16, 1699) and *Il Principe selvaggio* (Bologna, 1712), and numerous oratorios which were regularly performed at various churches in Bologna (1686–1732): *Nabuccodonosor; Giobbe; S. Orsola; Il convito di Baldassare; L'innocenza di S. Eufemia; S. Catarina; S. Eustachio; Maria annunciata dall'angelo; La morte di Cristo;* etc. Besides these works, Albergati published during his lifetime 15 opus numbers, consisting of vocal and instrumental music, among them *Balletti, Correnti, Cantate morali, Cantate spirituali, Messa e salmi, Cantate da camera, Motetti et antifone, Capricci,* 12 sonatas for 2 violins and bass, etc.

Alberghetti, Anna Maria, Italian soprano; b. Rodi, May 5, 1936. She first sang in public at the age of 6; gave recitals in Milan at 9. She came to America in 1950; made her debut in Carnegie Hall; then became a film vedette.

Albersheim, Gerhard, German-American pianist and musicologist; b. Cologne, Nov. 17, 1902. He studied at Vienna Univ.; emigrated to the U.S. in 1940. From 1953–56 he was on the staff of Univ. of Calif., Los Angeles; in 1956 appointed prof. at Calif. State College at Los Angeles. He began his career as an accompanist, playing for Lotte Lehmann, Elisabeth Schumann, Ezio Pinza and other eminent artists. He publ. *Zur Psychologie der Ton- und Klangeigenschaften* (Strasbourg, 1939); contributed numerous essays on musicial esthetics to American and German publications.

Albert, Prince Consort of Queen Victoria, b. Rosenau, Coburg, Aug. 26, 1819; d. Windsor, Dec. 14, 1861. He married Queen Victoria on Feb. 10, 1840; lent energetic support to musical activities in England, sponsoring orchestras and choral societies. He studied organ and theory, and acquired an estimable technique of composition; wrote *Invocazione alla armonia* for chorus and orch. His songs were published in 1881 under the title *The Collected Compositions of His Royal Highness the Prince Consort*. They reveal a romantic musical temper, influenced by Mendelssohn.

d'Albert, Eugène (Francis Charles), British-born German pianist and composer; b. Glasgow, April 10, 1864; d. Riga, March 3, 1932. His father, **Charles Louis Napoleon d'Albert** (b. Nienstetten, near Hamburg, Feb. 25, 1809; d. London, May 26, 1886), was a dancing master who wrote popular music; it was from him that d'Albert received his early instruction in music. At the age of 12 he entered the National Training School in London, where he studied piano with Pauer and theory with Stainer, Prout and Sir Arthur Sullivan. He made extraordinary progress both as pianist and composer, and after several appearances at the Popular Concerts, was the soloist in Schumann's concerto at the Crystal Palace, London (Feb. 5, 1881). On Oct. 24, 1881, when only 17, he played his own piano concerto at one of Hans Richter's concerts, arousing great enthusiasm; the press compared him to Mozart and Mendelssohn. He received a Mendelssohn fellowship and went to Vienna; later he studied with Liszt, who was greatly impressed by his technique and often referred to him as "the young Tausig." In 1895, d'Albert was appointed conductor at Weimar; in 1907, became director of the High School for Music in Berlin. In the wake of his success, he repudiated his English birth, adopting German citzenship, and made repeated statements derogatory to English culture and even to his former English teachers. He was vocal in his enmity to England during the first World War, which led in turn to an understandable repugnance among British musicians to accept his music.

WORKS: D'Albert composed industriously. He published two piano concertos (in B minor and E); Cello Concerto in C; 2 overtures (*Hyperion* and *Esther*); Symphony in F; an orchestral suite in 5 movements (1924); Piano Sonata; a piano suite in 5 movements; 2 string quartets; *Der Mensch und das Leben* for 6-part chorus and orch. (op. 14); 4 piano pieces, op. 16 (Waltz, Scherzo, Intermezzo, Ballade), minor piano pieces and songs. However, his main interest was in the field of opera. Of his 20 operas, the most successful were: *Tiefland,* first staged at the German opera in Prague (Nov. 15, 1903), and *Die toten Augen* (Dresden, March 5, 1916). The list of his other operas includes: *Der Rubin* (Karlsruhe, Oct. 12, 1893); *Ghismonda* (Dresden, Nov. 28, 1895); *Gernot* (Mannheim, April 11, 1897); *Die Abreise* (Frankfurt, Oct. 20, 1898); *Kain* (Berlin, Feb. 17, 1900); *Der Improvisator* (Berlin, Feb. 20, 1902); *Flauto solo* (Prague, Nov. 12, 1905); *Tragaldabas* (or *Der geborgte Ehemann;* Hamburg, Dec. 3, 1907); *Izeyl* (Hamburg, Nov. 6, 1909); *Die verschenkte Frau* (Vienna, Feb. 6, 1912); *Liebesketten* (Vienna, Nov. 12, 1912); *Der Stier von Olivera* (Leipzig, March 10, 1918); *Revolutionshochzeit* (Leipzig, Oct. 26, 1919); *Sirocco* (Darmstadt, May 18, 1921); *Mareike von Nymwegen* (Hamburg, Oct. 31, 1923); *Der Golem* (Frankfurt, Nov. 14, 1926); *Die schwarze Orchidee* (Leipzig, Dec. 1, 1928); *Mister Wu* (unfinished; completed by Leo Blech; Dresden, Sept. 29, 1932). Despite a brilliant beginning, Eugène d'Albert did not justify his early promise, and his operas and other works are rarely revived. His musical idiom oscillates between the Italian melodic style and German contrapuntal writing, and fails to achieve originality. A considerable corpus of his autograph music manuscripts, including 11 of his operas (though not *Tiefland*), was acquired in 1963 by the Library of Congress. Eugène d'Albert's personal life was a stormy one. He was married six times; his first wife (1892–1895) was Teresa Carreño; his second was the singer, Hermine Finck.

BIBLIOGRAPHY: W. Raupp, *Eugen d'Albert: ein Künstler- und Menschenschicksal* (Leipzig, 1930).

Albert, Heinrich, German composer; b. Lobenstein, Saxony, July 8, 1604; d. Königsberg, Oct. 6, 1651. In 1622 he went to Dresden to study music with his cousin Heinrich Schütz; then studied law at the Univ. of Leipzig; traveled to Warsaw with a peace delegation in 1627, but was seized as a prisoner of war by the Swedes; upon his release in 1628 he settled in Königsberg; was appointed cathedral organist in 1631; took courses with Johann Stobäus. He publ. in Königsberg 8 books of arias (1638–50); a cantata *Musi-*

kalische Kürbs-Hütte (1645) consisting of a cycle of 12 terzets to Albert's own texts (a modern reprint was issued by J. M. Müller-Blattau in 1932). A selection of his songs is found in the *Neudrucke deutscher Litteraturwerke* (Halle, 1883); the arias in volumes XII and XIII of *Denkmäler deutscher Tonkunst.*

BIBLIOGRAPHY: L. H. Fischer, *Gedichte des Königsberger Dichterkreises* (Halle, 1883); H. J. Moser, *Corydon* (1933).

Albert, Karel, Belgian composer; b. Antwerp, April 16, 1901. He studied with Marinus de Jong at the Royal Flemish Cons. in Antwerp; in 1933 became associated with the music service of the NIR, predecessor to the Belgian Radio and Television, until his retirement in 1961.

WORKS: an opera buffa *Europa ontvoerd* (1950); 2 ballets: *De toverlantaarn* (The Magic Lantern, 1942), and *Tornooi* (1953); ORCH. WORKS: 4 symphonies (1941, 1943, 1945, 1966); Sinfonietta (1968); *Pietà* (1933); *Wilde jacht* (1933); the overture *Ananke* (1934); *Lentewandeling* (1935); *Humoresque* (1936); *Het Land* (1937); *Impulsions* (1939); *Suite flamande* (1947); *De Nacht* (1956); Suite (1958); *Dansende beeldekens* (1959); *3 Constructions* for strings (1959); *In the Beginning Was the Word* for baritone and orch. (1962); Chamber Symphony (1932); 2 string quartets (1929, 1941); Trio for Oboe, Clarinet and Bassoon (1930); Quintet for Flute, Oboe, Violin, Viola and Cello (1954); *Étude* for alto and wind quintet (1958); Quartet for 4 Saxophones (1960); Brass Quintet (1962); Wind Quintet (1963); Brass Quartet (1964). He publ. *De evolutie van de muziek van de Oudheid tot aan Beethoven aan de hand van fonoplaten* (Brussels, 1947).

Albert, Stephen, American composer; b. New York, Feb. 6, 1941. He studied composition privately with Elie Siegmeister (1956–58); then took courses with Bernard Rogers at the Eastman School of Music in Rochester (1958–60), with Joseph Castaldo at the Philadelphia Musical Academy (1960–62), and with George Rochberg at the Univ. of Pennsylvania (1963); was a Fellow of the American Academy in Rome (1965–67); held a Guggenheim Fellowship (1968–69); taught at Smith College (1974–76). His style of composition is omnimodern without overflowing into the crepuscular regions of atonal glossolalia; in his idiom he accepts all utilitarian means of production, even neo-classical and neo-romantic types of melody and harmony.

WORKS: *Illuminations* for 2 pianos, brass and percussion (1962); *Supernatural Songs* for soprano and chamber orch. (1964); *Imitations* for string quartet (1964); *Winter Songs* for tenor and orch. (1965); *Leaves from the Golden Notebook* for orch. (1970); *Cathedral Music* for amplified flutes, amplified cellos, brass, percussion, amplified guitar, amplified harpsichord, electronic piano, electronic organ, and 2 grand pianos (1972); *Voices Within* for a concertino ensemble encased in a large orch. (1975); and *To Wake the Dead* for soprano and orch. to a text from James Joyce's *Finnegans Wake* (1977).

Alberti, Domenico, Venetian composer; b. Venice, 1710; d. Formio, or Rome, c.1740. He studied with Lotti, and won considerable renown as singer and harpsichord player; wrote 3 operas, *Endimione, Galatea,* and *Olimpiade.* In 1737 he was a member of the Venetian Embassy in Rome, and made several appearances there as singer and player. His fame in music history rests on his reputed invention of the arpeggio style of keyboard accompaniment, which became known as the 'Alberti Bass.' His set of 8 sonatas, published by Walsh in London, gives many illustrations of this device.

Albicastro, Henricus (real name **Heinrich Weissenburg**), Swiss violinist and composer; b. Switzerland at an uncertain date; d. c.1738 in Holland where he was a court musician. His works for string instruments were publ. in Amsterdam between 1700 and 1706; of these, 12 concertos *a 4,* a trio sonata and several violin sonatas with basso continuo are available in modern editions.
BIBLIOGRAPHY: W. S. Newman, *The Sonata in the Baroque Era* (Chapel Hill, 1959; pp. 343–44); M. Talbot, "The Concerto Allegro in the Early Eighteenth Century," *Music & Letters* (Jan., April 1971).

Albini, Srecko, Croatian composer and conductor; b. Zupanja, Dec. 10, 1869; d. Zagreb, April 18, 1933. He studied music in Vienna; then was theater conductor in Graz and Zagreb. He composed an opera *Maricon;* a ballet *The Lake of Plotvice;* the operettas *Nabob, Madame Troubadour, Baron Trenk* (1908; achieved considerable popularity); piano pieces and songs.

Albinoni, Tomaso, Italian violinist and composer; b. Venice, June 8, 1671; d. there, Jan. 17, 1750. Between 1694 and 1740 he produced 45 operas, most of them in Venice. He rarely absented himself from Venice, but it is known that he attended the premiere of his opera *Griselda* in Florence (1703); in 1722 he was in Munich where he presented his festive opera *I veri amici.* It is, however, as a composer of instrumental music that he is significant; Bach, his close contemporary, admired Albinoni's music; made arrangements of two fugues from Albinoni's trio sonatas.
BIBLIOGRAPHY: A detailed catalogue of Albinoni's works and a thematic analysis are given by R. Giazotto in his exhaustive monograph, *Tomaso Albinoni* (Milan, 1945); M. Talbot, "Albinoni: The Professional Dilettante," *Musical Times* (June 1971); id., "Vivaldi and Albinoni," *Informations de la Société Int. Antonio Vivaldi* (1972); id., "Albinoni's Oboe Concertos," *Consort* (July 1973).

Alboni, Marietta (real name **Maria Anna Marzia Alboni**), famous Italian contralto; b. Cesena, March 6, 1823; d. Ville d'Avray, France, June 23, 1894. She studied in Bologna with Monbelli; in 1841 was introduced to Rossini who agreed to give her lessons. She made her debut in Bologna, in Pacini's opera *Saffo* (Oct. 3, 1842); shortly afterwards sang at La Scala in Rossini's *Assedio di Corinto* (Dec. 30, 1842). She then sang in Russia and obtained great success during the season of 1844–45 in St. Petersburg, appearing at the Italian opera with Tamburini, Rubini and Mme. Viar-

dot. After appearances in Prague, Berlin and Hamburg, she appeared in the spring of 1847 in Rome and at Covent Garden where she became a rival of Jenny Lind with the public. So successful were her London appearances that her fees were increased to 2,000 pounds a season. She gave four 'concerts-spectacles' in Paris in Oct. 1847; made her Paris opera debut in Rossini's *Semiramide* (Dec. 2, 1847). Auber wrote the opera *Zerlinda* for her and she sang at its premiere (May 16, 1851). She made an American tour from June, 1852, till May, 1853, in concert and opera, appearing in N.Y., Boston and other cities. On July 21, 1853, Alboni married Count Pepoli (d. Oct. 10, 1867); on Jan. 22, 1877 she married Charles Ziéger, a French officer, and settled in France. Suffering from excessive obesity, she gradually retired from the stage, but continued to appear occasionally in concert, singing while sitting in a large chair. Her vocal range was exceptional, from the contralto G to high soprano C, enabling her to sing soprano parts. She bequeathed a large sum of money to the City of Paris. In appreciation, the City Council, on Oct. 15, 1895, named a street in Passy after her. Arthur Pougin's monograph *Marietta Alboni* (Paris, 1912) quotes many of her autobiographical notes and presents a documented outline of her career.

Albrecht, Evgeny, Russian violinist; son of **Karl Albrecht** and brother of **Konstantin Albrecht;** b. St. Petersburg, July 16, 1842; d. there, Feb. 9, 1894. He studied violin with Ferdinand David at the Leipzig Cons. (1857–60). Upon his return to Russia he conducted the Italian opera in St. Petersburg (1860–77); was also musical director of military schools there (1872–77). In 1877 he became inspector of the Imperial Orchestras; in 1892 was music librarian of the Imperial Theaters. He published 3 albums of Russian folksongs and a book of 128 children's songs.

Albrecht, Hans, German musicologist; b. Magdeburg, March 31, 1902; d. Kiel, Jan. 20, 1961. He studied at the Univ. of Berlin (1921–25); then taught music in Essen (1925–37). During World War II was prof. at the State Institute in Berlin (1939–45); from 1947 prof. at the Univ. of Kiel. He publ. a valuable monograph *Kaspar Othmayr, Leben und Werke* (Kassel, 1943).
BIBLIOGRAPHY: W. Brennecke and H. Haase, eds., *Hans Albrecht in Memoriam* (Kassel, 1962).

Albrecht, Johann Lorenz, German music scholar; b. Görmar (Thuringia), Jan. 8, 1732; d. Mühlhausen, Nov. 29, 1768. He studied at Leipzig; edited Adlung's *Musica mechanica* and *Siebengestirn* (Berlin, 1768); wrote an essay *Abhandlung über die Frage: ob die Musik beim Gottesdienst zu dulden sei oder nicht* (1764), a manual *Gründliche Einleitung in die Anfangslehren der Tonkunst* (1761), and a treatise *Vom Hasse der Musik* (1765); contributed articles to Marpurg's *Kritische Beiträge,* etc. He also composed several cantatas.

Albrecht, Karl, German-Russian conductor; father of **Konstantin** and **Evgeny Albrecht;** b. Posen, Aug. 27, 1807; d. Gatchina, Feb. 24, 1863. He came to Russia in 1838; for 12 years (1838–50) was conductor at the Imperial Theaters, and gave the first performance of Glinka's opera *Russlan and Ludmilla* (1842).

Albrecht, Konstantin, Russian cellist; son of **Karl Albrecht** and brother of **Evgeny Albrecht;** b. Elberfeld, Oct. 4, 1835; d. Moscow, June 26, 1893. He was brought to Moscow by his father at the age of 2 and received his musical education from him. In 1854 he became a member of the orch. of the Moscow Opera. In 1860 he collaborated with Nicholas Rubinstein in organizing the Moscow Cons.; in 1866 he was appointed inspector there; also taught elementary theory. He was an intimate friend of Tchaikovsky and was a notable figure in the Moscow musical world. He published a manual on solfeggio and compiled several collections of choral works.

Albrecht, Max, German composer and conductor; b. Chemnitz, March 14, 1890; d. Dresden, Feb. 13, 1945. He studied in Leipzig with Reger; conducted opera in Chemnitz (1911–13), and in Neisse (1914–15); then lived in Dresden. He wrote the operas *Neros Ende* (1927); *Rama und Sita* (1929); *Amosa* (1930); *Die Brücke* (1932); a cantata *Marathon;* 2 symph. poems, and a number of songs.

Albrecht, Otto Edwin, American musicologist; b. Philadelphia, July 8, 1899. He studied at the Univ. of Pennsylvania (A.B., 1921; M.A., 1925; Ph.D., 1931); then became lecturer in music and curator of the Music Library there and in 1941 vice-pres. of the Music Library Association.
WRITINGS: *Four Latin Plays of St. Nicholas* (Philadelphia and London, 1935); *Brahms and von Bülow; 18th-century Music in the Univ. Library;* "Francis Hopkinson," Univ. of Pennsylvania Library *Chronicle* (1934, 1936, 1938); "Microfilm Archives and Musicology," American Musicological Soc. *Papers, 1938; A Census of Autograph Music Manuscripts of European Composers in American Libraries* (Philadelphia, 1953); *The Mary Flagler Cary Music Collection* (N.Y., 1970).

Albrechtsberger, Johann Georg, famous Austrian theoretical writer, composer and teacher; b. Klosterneuburg, near Vienna, Feb. 3, 1736; d. Vienna, March 7, 1809. After holding positions as organist and musicmaster in smaller towns (especially 12 years in Melk, where his fine playing attracted the Emperor Joseph's notice), in 1772, he was engaged in Vienna as 'Regens chori' to the Carmelites; was appointed court organist in the same year, and, in 1792, music director at St. Stephen's cathedral. His important theoretical writings (complete ed. publ. by Seyfried) are: *Gründliche Anweisung zur Composition* (1790 and 1818; French ed., 1814); *Kurzgefasste Methode, den Generalbass zu erlernen* (1792; also in French); *Clavierschule für Anfänger* (1808); and some lesser essays. A selection from his instrumental works is publ. in *Denkmäler der Tonkunst in Österreich,* vol. 33 (formerly 16.ii); the MS scores (in the possession of Prince Esterhazy-Galantha) comprise 26 Masses, 43 graduals, 34 offertories, 6 oratorios; 28 trios, 42 quartets, and 38 quintets for strings; besides a great variety of church music. He had many celebrated pupils, among whom was Beethoven (from Jan. 1794 to March 1795). Scholars regard the quality of instruction he gave to Beethoven as of a very high order.
BIBLIOGRAPHY: G. Nottebohm, *Beethovens Unterricht bei J. Haydn, Albrechtsberger und Salieri* (Leipzig, 1873); R. Oppell, "Albrechtsberger als Bindeglied zwischen Bach und Beethoven," *Neue Zeitschrift für Musik* (May 18, 1911); A. Weissenbäck, "J. G. Albrechtsberger als Kirchenkomponist," *Studien zur Musikwissenschaft* (1927).

Albright, William, American composer; b. Gary, Indiana, Oct. 20, 1944. He studied at the Juilliard School of Music (1959–62); then at the Univ. of Michigan (1963–70) where his teachers in composition were Ross Lee Finney and Leslie Bassett. He spent a year in Paris in 1968 where he took lessons in composition with Olivier Messiaen at the Paris Cons. In 1970 he was appointed associate director of the Electronic Studio at the Univ. of Michigan. In his compositions he pursues the most extreme experimental notions of the cosmopolitan avant-garde using varied techniques according to need.
WORKS: *Foils* for wind instruments (1964); *Salvos* for flute, clarinet, bassoon, violin, viola, cello, percussion (1964); *Juba* for organ (1965); *2 Pieces for Nine Instruments* (1966); *Caroms* for 7 instruments (1966); *Tic* for soloists, 2 jazz-rock improvisation ensembles, films and tape (1967); *Beulahland Rag* for narrator, jazz quartet, improvisation ensemble, tape, film and slide projections (1969); *Alliance* for orch. (1970); *Grand Sonata in Rag* for piano (1968); *Marginal Worlds* for winds, strings, piano and percussion (1970); *Gothic Suite* for organ, percussion and strings (1973); also 2 organ collections (1967, 1972).

Alcock, John, Sr., English organist; b. London, April 11, 1715; d. Lichfield, Feb. 23, 1806. He was a chorister at St. Paul's Cathedral; then studied with the blind organist, Stanley. Subsequently he held positions as organist at St. Andrew's Church, Plymouth (1737), St. Lawrence's Church, Reading (1742), Lichfield Cathedral (1750), etc. In 1761 he took the degree of D. Mus. at Oxford. He published several suites for harpsichord, and collections of anthems and other sacred choral works. He wrote numerous glees, for which he obtained prizes from the Catch Club. His son, also named **John** (b. Plymouth, 1740; d. Walsall, Staffs., March 30, 1791) was organist at various churches and author of anthems.

Alda, Frances (real name **Frances Davies**), lyric soprano; b. Christchurch, New Zealand, May 31, 1883; d. Venice, Sept. 18, 1952. She studied with Marchesi in Paris, and made her debut as Manon at the Opéra-Comique (April 15, 1904). She later sang in Brussels, London, Milan, Warsaw and Buenos Aires. Her debut at the Metropolitan Opera was on Dec. 7, 1908 (opposite Caruso in *Rigoletto*); her farewell appearance there, on Dec. 28, 1929 in *Manon Lescaut.* She also made numerous recital tours in the U.S. Her principal roles included Louise, Mimi, Manon, Marguerite, Juliette, Gilda, Violetta and Aida. She married Giulio Gatti-Casazza, manager of the Metropolitan Opera, on April 3, 1910; divorced, 1928; married Ray Vir Den in

1941. In 1939 she became an American citizen. She wrote an autobiography *Men, Women and Tenors* (Boston, 1937).

Alden, John Carver, American pianist and teacher; b. Boston, Sept. 11, 1852; d. Cambridge, Mass., Oct. 20, 1935. He studied with Carl Faelten and was later associated with him at the New England Cons.; also took lessons with Plaidy at the Leipzig Cons. He wrote a piano concerto and several songs to German texts.

Alderighi, Dante, Italian composer and pianist; b. Taranto, July 7, 1898; d. Rome, Dec. 12, 1968. He went to Rome as a child and studied with Giovanni Sgambati; from 1911–14 he was in Leipzig, studying piano with Teichmüller and theory with Krehl. Returning to Italy, he took lessons in composition with Malipiero; gave many recitals and began to write music criticism. In 1936 he was appointed prof. of piano at Santa Cecilia in Rome.
WORKS: two piano concertos; *Fantasia* for piano and chamber orch. (1932); *Rococo Suite* for band (1932; revised 1952); oratorio, *Maria a Nazareth* (1949); *Divertimento* for piano and strings (1952); many choral works.

Aldrich, Henry, English music scholar; b. Westminster, 1647 (baptized Jan. 22, 1648); d. Oxford, Dec. 14, 1710. A man of versatile talents, excelling in music, he was also distinguished as an architect, theologian, linguist and logician. He was educated at Christ Church, Oxford, receiving the degree of M.A. in 1669; in 1681 he became a canon, and in 1689, Dean of Christ Church, and exercised decisive influence on the teaching of music and other arts. He wrote the learned works: *On the Commencement of Greek Music*; *Theory of Organ-building*; *Theory of Modern Instruments*; composed several services (one of which, in G, is still sung); in a lighter vein, glees and catches (among them the popular *Catches on Tobacco*). The collections of Boyce, Arnold and Page contain numerous pieces by Aldrich.
BIBLIOGRAPHY: W. G. Hiscock, *Henry Aldrich of Christ Church* (Oxford, 1960).

Aldrich, Perley Dunn, American vocal teacher; b. Blackstone, Mass., Nov. 6, 1863; d. Philadelphia, Nov. 20, 1933. He studied at the New England Cons. (1883–86); then took singing lessons with William Shakespeare in London (1892–95) and with Sbriglia in Paris (1903); acted as Sbriglia's assistant in the summer classes in 1904 and 1908. He settled as vocal teacher in Philadelphia; was the first head of the vocal dept. at the Curtis Inst. He published a volume *Vocal Economy* (1895); composed several choruses, among them *The Sleeping Wood Nymph* for mixed voices (1896).

Aldrich, Putnam (Calder), American harpsichord player and musicologist; b. South Swansea, Mass., July 14, 1904; d. Cannes, France, April 18, 1975. He studied at Yale Univ. (B.A., 1926); then went to Europe and took piano lessons with Tobias Matthay in London (1926–27) and harpsichord with Wanda Landowska in Paris (1929–33); later took his Ph.D. at Har-

vard Univ. (1942). He has given harpsichord recitals and played harpsichord solos with the Boston Symph. Orch.; in 1950 he was appointed associate prof. at Stanford Univ., California. He published a brief treatise, *Ornamentation in J. S. Bach's Organ Works* (N.Y., 1950) which is part of an important and much larger work (his Harvard dissertation) on 17th- and 18th-century ornamentation, which has not yet been published; also, *Rhythm in 17th-century Italian Monody* (London, 1965).

Aldrich, Richard, American music critic; b. Providence, July 31, 1863; d. Rome, June 2, 1937. He studied with Paine at Harvard Univ., graduating in 1885. He then was music critic of the *Providence Journal* (1885–89) and *Evening Star* (1889–91). From 1891–1901 he was assistant to H. E. Krehbiel on the *N.Y. Tribune*, then became music editor of the *N.Y. Times* (1902–23). A selection of his articles from the *N.Y. Times* was published in *Musical Discourse* (1928) and, posthumously, in *Concert Life in New York, 1902–1923* (1941). He also wrote *Guide to Parsifal* (1904) and *Guide to the Ring of the Nibelung* (1905). His critical writings were urbane and witty; while liberal minded in regard to milder types of modern music, he vehemently opposed its extreme trends.

Aldrovandini, Giuseppe (Antonio Vincenzo), Italian composer; b. Bologna, 1665; d. there, Feb. 9, 1707, when, under the influence of alcohol, he fell into a canal and was drowned. He studied with Giacomo Perti at the Bologna Philharmonic Academy, taught there from 1695, and in 1702 became its head ('principe'). Among his 15 operas, the following were produced in Bologna: *Gli inganni amorosi* (Jan. 28, 1696); *Dafni* (Aug. 10, 1696); *Le due Auguste* (Aug. 16, 1700); *I tre rivali in soglio* (posthumously, Jan. 2, 1711). He also wrote a 'sinfonia' and much church music (6 oratorios, motets, etc.), some published in his lifetime.

d'Alembert, Jean-le-Rond, French philosopher and encyclopedist; b. Paris, Nov. 16, 1717; d. there, Oct. 29, 1783. He was the illegitimate child of one Mme. de Tencin and an artillery officer named Destouches; his mother abandoned him on the steps of the church of St. Jean-le-Rond, which name was subsequently attached to him. Later, his father acknowledged him, and enabled him to study. He was sent to the Mazarin College, and progressed rapidly in mathematics. He also was interested in theoretical musical subjects, and published several treatises on acoustics and on the theory of music: *Recherches sur la courbe, que forme une corde tendue mise en vibration* (1749); *Recherches sur les vibrations des cordes sonores*, and *Recherches sur la vitesse du son* (both in *Opuscules mathématiques* [Paris, 1761–80]); *Reflexions sur la musique en général et sur la musique française en particulier* (1754); *Reflexions sur la théorie de la musique* (1777). His best known work on music was *Éléments de musique, théorique et pratique, suivant les principes de M. Rameau* (1752), which went into 6 editions. He contributed several articles on music to the famous *Encyclopédie*, which he edited with Diderot.

BIBLIOGRAPHY: J. Bertrand, *d'Alembert* (Paris, 1889).

Alemshah, Kourkene M., Armenian composer; b. Erevan, May 22, 1907; d. Detroit, Dec. 14, 1947. He studied in Milan with Pizzetti (1924–30); in 1931 he settled in Paris. He died during an American tour which he undertook as a choral conductor. His music is strongly permeated with Armenian melos, and the settings are impressionistic.

WORKS: symph. poem *Légende* (Paris, June 19, 1932); symph. poem *La Bataille d'Avarayr* (Paris, June 2, 1934); *Danses populaires arméniennes* for orch. (Paris, June 2, 1934). A memorial festival of his music was presented in Paris on Feb. 19, 1950.

Alessandrescu, Alfred, eminent Rumanian composer and conductor; b. Bucharest, Aug. 14, 1893; d. there, Feb. 18, 1959. He studied piano and theory at the Bucharest Cons. with Kiriac and Castaldi (1903–11); then went to Paris where he took composition courses with Vincent d'Indy at the Schola Cantorum and with Paul Vidal at the Paris Cons. (1913–14). Returning to Bucharest he was active as pianist. In 1921 he was appointed conductor of the Rumanian Opera in Bucharest, retaining this post until his death; also conducted the Budapest Philharmonic Orch. (1926–40) and was artistic director of the Bucharest Radio (1933–59); appeared as conductor in Germany and France; was piano accompanist to George Enesco, Jacques Thibaud and others.

WORKS: *Amurg de toamnă* (*The Twilight of Autumn*), for string orch. (1910); *Didona*, symph. poem (1911); *Fantezie română* for orch. (1913); Violin Sonata (1914); *Acteon*, symph. poem (Bucharest, Dec. 20, 1915); *Pièce pour quatuor à cordes* (1921); a number of songs; also orchestrated many works by Rumanian composers, as well as classical compositions; translated into Rumanian the libretti of *Parsifal, La Traviata, Aida,* etc.

BIBLIOGRAPHY: V. Tomescu, *Alfred Alessandrescu* (Budapest, 1962).

Alessandri, Felice, Italian opera composer; b. Rome, Nov. 24, 1747; d. Casinalbo, Aug. 15, 1798. He studied music in Naples; then lived in Paris (1765–68) and in London (1768). From 1784–89 he was in Russia; then in Berlin as a second conductor at the Royal Opera (1789–92), finally returning to Italy. Alessandri wrote about 30 operas in all. Two were produced in London: *La Moglie fedele* (1768) and *Il re alla caccia* (1769); and two at La Scala in Milan: *Calliroe* (Dec. 26, 1778) and *Ezio* (Feb. 1, 1782). In Potsdam he produced *Il ritorno di Ulisse* (Jan. 25, 1790); *Dario* (1791), and the comic opera *La compagnia d'opera a Nanchino* (1790), which exhibited the colorful effects of pseudo-Chinese music. His opera *Virginia* was given in Venice (Dec. 26, 1793). He also wrote an oratorio *Betulia liberata* (1781); *6 sinfonie* in 8 parts; 6 trio sonatas for 2 violins and basso continuo, etc., all in the then prevalent Italian manner.

BIBLIOGRAPHY: L. Valdrighi, *Felice Alessandri* (1896).

Alessandro, Victor, American conductor; b. Waco, Texas, Nov. 27, 1915; d. San Antonio, Nov. 27, 1976 (on his 61st birthday). He studied French-horn playing with his father; then took composition courses with Howard Hanson and Bernard Rogers at the Eastman School of Music, Rochester, N.Y.; subsequently attended classes at the Santa Cecilia Academy in Rome; returning to the U.S. he was conductor of the Oklahoma Symph. Orch. (1938–51); in 1952 was appointed conductor of the San Antonio Orch., a position which he held until his death.

Alexander, Josef, American composer; b. Boston, May 15, 1907. He studied piano at the New England Cons., graduating in 1925; then entered Harvard Univ., where he took composition with Walter Piston and orchestration with Edward B. Hill; received his B.A. in 1938 and his M.A. in 1941. In 1939 he went to Paris where he studied with Nadia Boulanger; also took a course with Aaron Copland at Tanglewood in 1940. In Boston he taught piano and composition; in 1943 became a member of the music faculty at Brooklyn College. As a composer he adopts a facile laissez-faire idiom in a tolerably modern manner, marked by a pleasing admixture of fashionable dissonances.

WORKS: 4 symphonies (1951, 1954, 1961, 1968); Piano Concerto (1938); *Epitaphs* for orch. (1947); *Celebrations* for orch. (1960); *Quiet Music* for strings (1966); String Quartet (1940); Piano Quintet (1942); Piano Trio (1944); Wind Quintet (1949); Piano Quartet (1952); Clarinet Sonata (1957); *4 Movements for Brass* (1958); *Concertino* for trumpet and strings (1950); Trombone Sonata (1959); *Nocturne and Scherzo* for violin and piano (1963); *3 Pieces* for 8 instruments (1965); *Gitanjali* for soprano, harpsichord and percussion, based on texts from Rabindranath Tagore (N.Y., Nov. 14, 1975).

Alexandre, Jacob, French organ builder; b. Paris, 1804; d. there, June 11, 1876. In 1829 he established a firm of harmonium manufacturers, which introduced the 'Alexandre' organ, a development of the so-called 'American organ' (1874).

Alexandrov, Alexander, Russian composer; b. Plakhino (Riazan Govt.), April 1, 1883; d. Berlin, during a concert tour, July 8, 1946. He studied with Rimsky-Korsakov and Glazunov at the St. Petersburg Cons. (1899–1901) and later at the Moscow Cons. with Vassilenko (1909–1913). In 1928 he organized the Red Army Ensemble and conducted it on numerous tours in Russia and abroad. His song *Hymn of the Bolshevik Party*, with a new set of words, was proclaimed as the Soviet national anthem on March 15, 1944.

Alexandrov, Anatoly, eminent Russian pianist and composer; b. Moscow, May 25, 1888. He studied with Taneyev (1907–10); in 1916 graduated from the Moscow Cons. as pianist in the class of Igumnov and in composition with Vassilenko. In 1923 he became prof. at the Moscow Cons. Alexandrov is particularly distinguished as a composer of piano music; he wrote 14 piano sonatas (1914–1971) and many smaller works for the instrument; in his style, he follows the main line of Rachmaninoff and Scriabin. His other works include the operas, *Two Worlds* (1916), *Bela* (Moscow, Dec. 10, 1946); *Wild Bara* (Moscow, March 2, 1957); 4 string quartets (1914–53); *Romantic Suite* for orch. and chorus (1920); *Classical Suite* for orch. (1926); *Dithyramb* for double bass and piano (1959); also film scores, several song cycles and incidental music for theatrical plays.

Alfano, Franco, eminent Italian composer; b. Posilippo (Naples), March 8, 1876; d. San Remo, Oct. 27, 1954. He studied composition with Paolo Serrao in Naples, and with Jadassohn and Hans Sitt in Leipzig. From the beginning of his musical career, Alfano was interested in opera. His first stage work *Miranda* was produced in Leipzig when he was barely 20; another opera, *La Fonte di Enscir*, followed (Breslau, Nov. 8, 1898). In 1900 he went to Paris and became fascinated by light theater music. While in Paris he wrote *Napoli*, a ballet in the folk manner, which was staged at Folies-Bergères (Jan. 28, 1901), proving so successful that it ran for 160 successive performances. Returning to Italy, he began work on an opera based on Tolstoy's novel *Resurrection*. It was produced as *Risurrezione*, in Turin (Nov. 4, 1904) with sensational acclaim; the American premiere (Chicago, Dec. 31, 1925) was equally successful; there were also numerous performances in Germany and France. The opera was widely praised for its dramatic power and melodic richness in the best tradition of realistic Italian opera. Alfano continued to compose industriously for another half-century, but his later operas failed to equal the success of *Risurrezione*. They are: *Il Principe Zilah* (Genoa, Feb. 3, 1909); *L'ombra di Don Giovanni* (La Scala, Milan, April 3, 1914); *La Leggenda di Sakuntala* (Bologna, Dec. 10, 1921); *Madonna Imperia*, lyric comedy (Turin, May 5, 1927; Met. Opera, N.Y., Feb. 8, 1928); *L'Ultimo Lord* (Naples, April 19, 1930); *Cyrano de Bergerac* (Rome, Jan. 22, 1936); *Il Dottor Antonio* (Rome, April 30, 1949). Alfano also wrote 3 symphonies (1909; 1932; 1934); 3 string quartets, a violin sonata, a cello sonata, and a ballet *Vesuvius* (1938; a symphonic poem was drawn from it in 1946). One of Alfano's signal achievements was that he completed Puccini's last opera, *Turandot*, adding the last scene. His *Hymn to Bolivar*, for chorus and orch., written for the centennial of Bolivar's death, was performed in Caracas, Venezuela, on Dec. 22, 1930. He was also active in the field of musical education; was successively director of the Liceo Musicale in Bologna (1919–23); of the Turin Cons. (1923–39); superintendent of the Teatro Massimo in Palermo (1940–42), and from 1947, director of the Rossini Cons. in Pesaro.
BIBLIOGRAPHY: G. M. Gatti, "Franco Alfano," *Musicisti moderni d'Italia e di fuori* (Bologna, 1920; also in the *Musical Times*, March 1921); G. Cesàri, "La leggenda di Sakuntala di Franco Alfano," *Rivista Musicale Italiana* (1921); Andrea della Corte, *Ritratto di Franco Alfano* (Turin, 1935). Ettore Desderi published a list of Alfano's works in *Bolletino bibliografico musicale* (Milan, 1931).

Alfarabi (or **Alpharabius**, properly **Al Farabi**), **Abu Nasr,** so named from his birthplace Farab (now transoxine Othrâx), Arabian music theorist; b. c.870;

d. Damascus, c.950. Of Turkish descent, he became renowned through his writings on philosophy, political science and the arts. He was a Greek scholar and attempted unsuccessfully to introduce the Greek musical system into his country. His principal work is *Kitab al-Musiqi al-Kabir* ('Greater Book about Music,' repr. with commentary, Cairo, 1967) dealing with acoustics, intervals, scales, instruments and rhythm. The 2nd volume of this work was lost. Excerpts from this book are contained in Kosegarten's *Alii Ispahanis Liber Cantilenarum Magnus* (1840) and in J. Land's *Recherches sur l'histoire de la gamme arabe* (Leyden, 1884). Another treatise, *Kitab al-Iqua'at* has been translated into German by E. Neubauer, in *Oriens* (1968/69).
BIBLIOGRAPHY: M. Steinschneider, *Al-Farabi* (St. Petersburg, 1869); Baron d'Erlanger, *La Musique arabe*, vol. I (Paris, 1930); E. A. Beichert, *Die Wissenschaft der Musik bei Al-Farabi* (Regensburg, 1931); H. G. Farmer, *Al-Farabi's Arabic-Latin Writings on Music* (Glasgow, 1934).

Alferaki, Achilles, Russian composer of Greek origin; b. Kharkov, July 3, 1846; d. Petrograd, Dec. 27, 1919. He studied philology at the Univ. of Moscow; simultaneously he took lessons in piano and music theory. He joined the group of composers whose works were published by Belaiev, and wrote numerous songs and piano pieces in the manner of the Russian national school, many of them also published by Belaiev. He furthermore wrote an opera *St. John's Eve*, which remains in manuscript.

Alfieri, Pietro, Italian music scholar; b. Rome, June 29, 1801; d. there, June 12, 1863. He was a member of the Camaldolese Order; taught Gregorian music at the English College in Rome. His major work is *Raccolta di musica sacra* (1841–46), a collection of 16th-century church music in 7 vols., which includes virtually all representative works of Palestrina; other collections are *Excerpta ex celebrioribus de musica viris* (Rome, 1840), containing works by Palestrina, Victoria and Allegri; *Raccolta di motetti* (1841), etc. His essays on Gregorian chant are very valuable: *Ristabilimento del canto e della musica ecclesiastica* (1843); *Saggio storico del canto gregoriano* (1855); *Prodromo sulla restaurazione de' libri di canto ecclesiastico detto gregoriano* (1857), etc.; he also publ. a biography of N. Jommelli (1845) and contributed articles on musical subjects to Italian periodicals.

Alfvén, Hugo, outstanding Swedish composer; b. Stockholm, May 1, 1872; d. Falun, May 8, 1960. He studied violin at the Stockholm Cons. (1887–91); continued these studies with Lars Zetterquist until 1896, while taking composition lessons from Johan Lindegren. He was then sent by the government to Brussels to complete his violin studies with César Thomson (1896–99). Government scholarships in 1896, 1897 and 1899, as well as the Jenny Lind stipend (1900–03), enabled him to study composition in many European countries. In 1910 he became musical director at the Univ. of Uppsala and conductor of the student chorus until his retirement in 1939; continued to conduct various mixed choruses.

WORKS: His best known work is *Midsommarvaka* (*Midsummer Vigil*; Stockholm, May 10, 1904), the first of his three Swedish rhapsodies for orch. It was produced as a ballet, *La Nuit de Saint-Jean*, by the Ballets Suédois in Paris, Oct. 25, 1920, and had over 250 performances in four years. His other works include the second and third Swedish rhapsodies: *Uppsala* (1907) and *Dalecarlian* (1937); 5 symphonies: No. 1 (1896–97; Stockholm, Feb. 9, 1897); No. 2 (1898–99; Stockholm, May 2, 1899); No. 3 (1905–06; Göteborg, Dec. 5, 1906); No. 4, with soprano and tenor (1918–19; Stockholm, Nov. 16, 1918); and No. 5 (1942–52; first complete performance, Stockholm, April 30, 1952); 2 ballet pantomimes, *Bergakungen* (*The Mountain King*, 1923) and *Den förlorade sonen* (*The Prodigal Son*, 1957); *En skärgårdssägen* (*A Tale of the Skerries*), symph. poem (1905); *Festspel* (*Festival Music*) for orch. (1907); suite of incidental music to the play *Gustaf II Adolf* (1932); *Synnöve Solbakken*, Suite for Small Orch. (1934); 10 cantatas, many contributed for various occasions, patriotic anniversaries and the like—among them one celebrating the 450th year since the founding of Uppsala Univ. (1927) and another on the 500th jubilee of the Swedish Parliament (1935); Violin Sonata (1896); *Elegie* for horn and organ (1897); *Skärgårdsbilder* (*Pictures from the Skerries*) for piano (1902); a ballad on Gustaf Vasa for soloists, mixed chorus and organ (1920); and numerous male choruses and folk song arrangements. The music of Alfvén represents the best traits of Scandinavian national art, along the lines of Grieg and Sibelius. He published 4 volumes of memoirs: *Första satsen* (Stockholm, 1946); *Tempo furioso* (1948); *I dur och moll* (1949) and *Finale* (1952).

BIBLIOGRAPHY: S. E. Svensson, *Hugo Alfvén, som människa och konstnär* (Uppsala, 1946); J. O. Rudén, *Hugo Alfvéns kompositioner. Käll- och verkförteckning* (thematic index; Stockholm, 1972).

Algarotti, Francesco, Italian musician and scholar; b. Venice, Dec. 11, 1712; d. Pisa, May 3, 1764. The fame of his great knowledge reached Frederick the Great who invited him to Berlin in 1740 and gave him the title of Count, and, in 1747, that of 'Chevalier de l'ordre pour le mérite.' In 1753 Algarotti returned to Italy. His musical monument is the *Saggio sopra l'opera in musica*, published in 1755; also in many later editions, including German and French translations. The English text of the *Saggio . . .* is reproduced in part in O. Strunk's *Source Readings in Music History* (N.Y., 1950).

BIBLIOGRAPHY: D. Michelessi, *Memorie intorno alla vita ed agli scritti del Francesco Algarotti* (Venice, 1770); R. Northcott, *Francesco Algarotti, A Reprint of His 'Saggio . . .' and a Sketch of His Life* (London, 1917).

Ali Akbar Khan, Hindu instrumentalist; b. Shibpore, Bengal, April 14, 1922. He studied dhrupad, dhamar, khayal and sarod with his father; pakhawaj and tabla with his uncle. He founded the Ali Akbar College of Music in Calcutta in 1956; toured widely in Europe, America and Japan as a virtuoso; held the post of court musician in Jodhpur. He has written a number of new ragas. Several of his students achieved prominence as Indian instrumentalists in their own right.

Aliabiev, Alexander, Russian song composer; b. Tobolsk, Siberia, Aug. 15, 1787; d. Moscow, March 6, 1851. His father was the governor of Tobolsk, and Aliabiev spent his childhood there. In 1796 the family went to St. Petersburg, and in 1804 settled in Moscow. He studied music in Moscow and had his first songs published in 1810. During the War of 1812, he served in the Russian Army, and participated in the entry of the Russian Army into Dresden and Paris. Returning to Russia he lived in St. Petersburg, in Voronezh, and in Moscow. In 1825 he was arrested on suspicion of murder after a card game, was sentenced to prison, and in 1828 was deported to his birthplace in Siberia. There he organized concerts of popular music and also composed. In 1831 he was allowed to return to European Russia and lived in the Caucasus and in Orenburg. In 1843 he returned to Moscow, but was still under police surveillance. He wrote more than 100 songs, of which *The Nightingale* became extremely popular; it is often used in the music lesson scene in Russian productions of Rossini's opera *The Barber of Seville*. Glinka and Liszt made piano arrangements of it. He also wrote a symphony, 3 string quartets, 2 piano trios, piano quintet, violin sonata, quartet for 4 flutes, quintet for wind instruments, piano sonata, choruses. Among his works for the theater are scores of incidental music to *The Prisoner of the Caucasus* and to Shakespeare's plays; the stage ballads, *The Village Philosopher*, *The Moon Night*, and *Theatrical Combat* (with Verstovsky and Mauer), etc.

BIBLIOGRAPHY: Igor Ilyin, "Aliabiev in Siberia" (with a facsimile reproduction of the registry of Aliabiev's birth), *Sovietskaya Musica* (Aug. 1952); Boris Steinpress, *Aliabiev in Exile* (Moscow, 1959); B. Dobrohotov, *Alexander Aliabiev* (Moscow, 1966).

Alió, Francisco, Spanish composer; b. Barcelona, March 21, 1862; d. there, March 31, 1908. He studied piano with Vidiella and composition with Anselmo Barba. He subsequently was active as a music critic in Catalan newspapers. A determined believer in the importance of folk songs, he traversed Catalonia, notating folk songs and dance tunes, which he later incorporated in his collections, among them *Cansons populars catalanas* (Barcelona, 1891). He also published his own piano pieces and songs based on Catalan melodies.

Aliprandi, Bernardo, Italian cellist and composer; b. Milan, c.1710; d. Frankfurt, c.1792. In 1732 he became a member of the Court Orchestra in Munich, retiring in 1780. He wrote 3 theatrical works with music: *Apollo tra le Muse in Parnasso* (Munich, Aug. 6, 1737); *Mitridate* (Munich, 1738); *Semiramide riconosciuta* (Munich, 1740); and a *Stabat Mater* (1749).

Alkan (real name **Morhange**), **Charles-Henri Valentin,** French pianist and composer of Jewish extraction; b. Paris, Nov. 30, 1813; d. there, March 29, 1888. His three brothers were also musicians; his father was the founder of a school for Jewish children. Alkan's talent was precocious; he was accepted at the Paris Cons. at the age of six and studied piano with Zimmermann. In 1833 he visited London, then returned to Paris, where his main activities were playing concerts in the fashionable salons and teaching piano. He entered the brilliant circle of musicians and littérateurs, among whom were Chopin, George Sand, Hugo and Liszt.

WORKS: Like Chopin, Alkan wrote almost exclusively for piano; the list of his works includes 76 opus numbers, in addition to many pieces not numbered by opus. His pieces are programmatic, bearing such titles as *Désir,* a set of variations, *Les Omnibus*; *Le vent* (op. 15); *Le Tambour bat aux Champs* (op. 50); he was the first composer to write a piece descriptive of the railroad (*Le Chemin de fer,* op. 27). His 2 sets of études, in all major and minor keys (op. 35 and 39), of transcendent difficulty, present great interest as examples of modern piano technique. Other works are *3 Études de bravoure* (op. 16); *Le preux, étude de concert* (op. 17); *3 pièces poétiques* (op. 18); *Bourrée d'Auvergne* (op. 29); a sonata (op. 33, subtitled *Les quatre âges*); *Les mois* (op. 8, 74), comprising 12 pieces, etc. He also wrote 2 piano concertos, a piano trio, a cello sonata and vocal music. César Franck arranged several of his pieces for organ. For a long time Alkan's music was completely forgotten, but its significance as an inventive composer became more evident in the 20th century.

BIBLIOGRAPHY: Sorabji, *Around Music* (London, 1932); Bernard van Dieren, *Down Among the Dead Men* (London, 1935); Ronald Smith, *Alkan,* vol. 1, *The Enigma* (London, 1976).

Alldahl, Per-Gunnar, Swedish composer; b. Solna, Oct. 11, 1943. He studied organ and composition at the Royal College of Music in Stockholm (1968–71); later joined its staff as instructor. In his music, he pursues the twin goals of total freedom of realization and strict observance of minuscule tonal data.

WORKS: *Nulla ars . . .* for string orch. (1966; Helsinki, Feb. 24, 1967); *Biceps* for chamber orch. and tape (1968–69; Swedish Radio, Dec. 7, 1969); *Music for Solo Cello* (1968); *Light Music* for 5 flutes, Hammond organ and vibraphone (1968); *Play* for orch. (Bollnas, April 4, 1970); *Ad lib,* for any instruments, though originally for bass clarinet, trombone and cello (1971); *Bruspolska* for nyckelharps (1972); *Stämma blod* for chorus and percussion (1972); *Unisona* for alto voice, flute, trombone, double bass and vibraphone (1972); *Från när och fjärran* for jazz quartet (1973); *Mot värk* for chorus and percussion (1973; a sequel to *Stämma blod.*)

Allegri, Domenico, Italian composer; b. Rome, 1585; d. there, Sept. 5, 1629. He was maestro di cappella at S. Maria Maggiore from 1610–29, and was one of the first to provide vocal music with an independent instrumental accompaniment. A few of his *Mottetti* are extant (a soprano solo with violins, a tenor duet and a bass solo, each accompanied by 2 violins).

Allegri, Gregorio, Italian composer; b. Rome, c.1582; d. there, Feb. 17, 1652. He was a choir boy in Rome from 1591–96; then studied with Giovanni Maria Nanino (1600–07). He entered the Papal Chapel in 1629 after serving for some years as chorister and composer for the cathedral at Fermo. He is chiefly known as the composer of the celebrated *Miserere* in 9 parts (i.e., for two choirs singing 4 and 5 parts respectively), regularly sung during Holy Week at the Sistine Chapel, and surreptitiously written out by Mozart after hearing it twice, though its publication was forbidden on pain of excommunication; since then it has been frequently published. Many other works by Allegri are preserved in MS; 2 books of *Concertini* and 2 of *Mottetti* have been printed, also a 4-part sonata for strings which might be regarded as the prototype of the string quartet.

BIBLIOGRAPHY: A. Cametti, "La scuola dei pueri cantus di S. Luigi dei Francesi in Roma," *Rivista Musicale Italiana* (1915); J. Amann, *Allegris Miserere und die Aufführungspraxis in der Sixtina* (Regensburg, 1935); A. Eaglefield-Hull, "The Earliest Known String Quartet," *Musical Quarterly* (Jan. 1929).

Allen, Creighton, American pianist and composer; b. Macon, Miss., March 26, 1900. He made his first public appearance at the age of nine; studied with Hutcheson in New York; then settled there as teacher and composer. He has written a piano concerto, a violin concerto, 17 settings of the poems of Edgar Allan Poe, piano pieces and many songs, some of which have acquired considerable popularity.

Allen, George Benjamin, English singer and composer; b. London, April 21, 1822; d. Brisbane, Queensland, Nov. 30, 1897. He was active successively as chorister, conductor, and organist in England, Ireland, and Australia; managed a light opera company, producing several of Sullivan's operas. He composed the operas *Castle Grim* (London, 1865), *The Viking* (not performed), *The Wicklow Rose* (Manchester, 1882); 3 cantatas and songs.

Allen, Sir Hugh Percy, eminent English organist and educator; b. Reading, Dec. 23, 1869; d. Oxford, Feb. 20, 1946. He studied with Dr. F. Read in Reading, and at Oxford Univ. (Mus. Doc., 1898). At the age of 11 he acted as church organist in Reading. Thereafter he was organist at various churches and cathedrals until the turn of the century. He was appointed organist at New College, Oxford (1901–18), and later (1908–18) director of music at University College, Reading. In 1918 he succeeded Sir Walter Parratt as prof. of music at Oxford, and in the same year became director of the Royal College of Music, London, from which he resigned in 1937 (succeeded by George Dyson). He was knighted in 1920. For many years he conducted the London and the Oxford Bach Choirs; he was an ardent promoter of British music.

BIBLIOGRAPHY: C. Bailey, *Hugh Percy Allen* (London, 1948).

Allen, Nathan H., American organist and choral conductor; b. Marion, Mass., April 14, 1848; d. Hartford, Conn., May 9, 1925. He studied organ in Berlin; was active as church organist and teacher in Hartford, Conn. From 1906–11 he was organist at Worcester, Mass., then returned to Hartford. He wrote church music (including a cantata, *The Apotheosis of St.*

Dorothy), and concert pieces for organ, violin and piano.

Allen, Paul Hastings, American composer; b. Hyde Park, Mass., Nov. 28, 1883; d. Boston, Sept. 28, 1952. He studied at Harvard Univ. (A.B., 1903), then in Italy. During World War I was in the American diplomatic service there; returning to the U.S. in 1920 and settling in Boston.
WORKS: A prolific composer, he wrote 12 operas, mostly in Italian, several of which were performed in Italy. They include *Il Filtro* (Genoa, Oct. 26, 1912); *Milda* (Venice, June 14, 1913); *L'Ultimo dei Mohicani* (Florence, Feb. 24, 1916); *Cleopatra* (1921); *La piccola Figaro* (1931). His *Pilgrim Symphony* received the Paderewski prize (1910); other orchestral works are largely unperformed. Allen wrote much chamber music, some for unusual combinations, such as a quartet for 2 clarinets, basset horn and bass clarinet; several piano sonatas and a great number of other piano pieces; choral works and songs. His writing is marked by technical mastery in a romantic style.

Allen, Warren D., American musicologist; b. San Jose, Cal., Aug. 3, 1885; d. Olympia, Wash., June 21, 1964. He studied at the Univ. of California, Berkeley; later took theory lessons with Fielitz in Berlin and with Widor in Paris. Returning to America he was Dean of Music at the College of the Pacific in San Jose (1913–18). In 1918 he was appointed choral director at Stanford Univ.; from 1940 to 1949 was on the faculty there, and from 1949 to 1955 was Prof. at Florida State Univ.; after retirement in 1955 he lived in Seattle. He published the books *Philosophies of Music History* (1939) and *Our Marching Civilization* (1943).

Allende, Sarón, (Pedro) Humberto, eminent Chilean composer; b. Santiago, June 29, 1885; d. there, Aug. 16, 1959. He studied violin and theory at the National Cons. in Santiago (1899–1908); then taught in public schools there. Elected member of the Chilean Folklore Soc. in 1911. He was in France and Spain (1922–23); appointed Chilean delegate to the Congress of Popular Arts in Prague, under the auspices of the League of Nations (1928); in 1929 he took part in the Festival of Ibero-American Music in Barcelona. He was prof. of composition at the National Cons. in Santiago from 1928–45. In 1945 he received the Chilean Government Prize. In his music, Allende combines authentic national sentiment with a modern treatment, often in an impressionistic manner.
WORKS: Symphony in B-flat (1910; awarded Chilean Centennial Prize); *Campesinas Chilenas* for orch. (1913); Cello Concerto (1915); *La Voz de las Calles*, symphonic poem utilizing street cries of Chilean cities (Santiago, May 20, 1921); *La Despedida* for 2 sopranos, contralto and orch. (Santiago, May 7, 1934); Violin Concerto (Santiago, Dec. 4, 1942); String Quartet (1947); 3 piano sonatas (1909–15); *12 Tonadas de carácter popular chileno* for piano (1918–22; his most distinctive work in a national style; also arranged for orch.) and songs. He also published a teaching manual *Método Original de Iniciación Musical* (Santiago, 1937).
BIBLIOGRAPHY: Special issue of *Revista Musical Chilena* (Sept. 1945); N. Slonimsky, "Humberto Allende, First Modernist of Chile," *Musical America* (Aug. 1942); V. S. Viu, *La Creación Musical en Chile*, pp. 115–129 (Santiago, 1952).

Allers, Franz, conductor; b. Prague, Aug. 6, 1905. He studied violin at the Prague Cons. and later in Berlin; was a member of the Berlin Philharmonic for a season; then conducted theater orchestras in Germany (1926–38). He left Germany in 1938 and conducted ballet in London, South America and Canada, eventually settling in the U.S. as conductor of musical shows on Broadway; also appeared as symphonic conductor in Europe and America.

d'Allesandro, Raffaele, Swiss composer; b. Gallen, March 17, 1911; d. Lausanne, March 17, 1959 (on his 48th birthday). He studied music with Victor Schlatter and Willi Schuh in Zürich, then went to Paris where he studied composition with Nadia Boulanger and organ with Marcel Dupré. In 1940 he returned to Switzerland and settled in Lausanne, where he became active as a pianist, organist and composer.
WORKS: BALLET, *Isla persa* (1952); FOR ORCH.: *Rumba sinfonica* (1940); *Conga contrapuntique* (1941); *Thème et variations* (1944); Symph. No. 1 (1948); Symph. No. 2 (1953); *Tema variato* for orch. (1957); Piano Concerto No. 1 (1939); Violin Concerto (1941); Flute Concerto (1943); Piano Concerto No. 2 (1945); Piano Concerto No. 3 (1951); Bassoon Concerto (1955); Oboe Concerto with string orch. (1958); CHAMBER MUSIC: 2 violin sonatas (1936, 1953); Cello Sonata (1937); Piano Trio (1940); Flute Sonata (1943); 2 string quartets (1947, 1952); Oboe Sonata (1949); Sonatina for Oboe solo (1953); Sonatina for Clarinet and Piano (1953); Bassoon Sonata (1957); Sonata for Flute, Viola and Piano (1958); FOR PIANO: Sonatina for left hand alone (1939); 24 Preludes (1940); Sonatina for 2 pianos (1943); 12 Etudes (1952); *Contes drolatiques* (1952); *6 Klavierstücke* for left hand alone (1958); many pieces for organ, choruses; several songs with orch., organ or piano. A catalogue of his works is obtainable from the Association des Amis de Raffaele d'Alessandro in Lausanne.

Allihn, Heinrich (Max), German music scholar; b. Halle-on-Saale, Aug. 31, 1841; d. there, Nov. 15, 1910; from 1885 pastor and school inspector at Allenstedt; edited the 2nd edition (1888) of Töpfer's *Lehrbuch der Orgelbaukunst* (*Theorie und Praxis des Orgelbaues*); publ. *Die Hausinstrumente Klavier und Harmonium* (1892), and *Die Pflege des musicalisches Teils des Gottesdienstes* (1906); contributed many essays to De Wit's *Zeitschrift für Instrumentenbau*.

d'Almeida, Fernando, Portuguese composer; b. Lisbon, c.1618; d. Thomar, March 21, 1660. Distinguished pupil of Duarte Lobo; in 1638, entered the Order of Christ at Thomar. Of his many church compositions, only one folio vol. in MS is known: *Lamentacões, Responsorias e Misereres das tres officias da Quarta, Quinta e Sexta-feria da Semana Santa.*

Almeida, Renato, Brazilian music historian; b. S. Antonio de Jesus, Bahia, Dec. 6, 1895. He studied law;

worked as a journalist in Rio de Janeiro. He is the author of the standard work on Brazilian music: *Historia da musica brasileira* (1926; new enlarged ed., 1942); *Danses Africaines en Amerique Latine* (Rio de Janeiro, 1969); *Vivência e projeção do folclore* (Rio de Janeiro, 1971).

Almenräder, Karl, German bassoon virtuoso; b. Ronsdorf, near Düsseldorf, Oct. 3, 1786; d. Biebrich, Sept. 14, 1843. Was prof. of bassoon at Cologne, theater conductor in Frankfurt and regimental bandmaster; started a factory for wind instruments (1820) at Cologne, but gave it up in two years, entering the Nassau Court Orch. at Biebrich. He materially improved the bassoon, wrote a treatise on it (Mainz, 1824), and a method for it; publ. a bassoon concerto; variations for bassoon and quartet; Duettinos for 2 bassoons, etc.; and the popular ballad, *Des Hauses letzte Stunde.*

Almquist, Carl Jonas Love, Swedish composer and writer on music; b. Stockholm, Nov. 28, 1793; d. Bremen, Sept. 26, 1866. He studied at Uppsala Univ.; wrote songs to his own words, but refused to study music for fear that his instinct for simple melody might be destroyed by learning. He published these songs in a collection *Törnrosens bok* (1838); he also published 11 albums of piano pieces under the title *Fria Fantasier* (1848). Almquist's life was an adventurous one; he was forced to leave Sweden, where he was accused of forgery; lived in America (1851-65); then went to Germany, where he died.

Alnaes, Eyvind, Norwegian composer; b. Fredriksstad, April 29, 1872; d. Oslo, Dec. 24, 1932. He studied in Oslo with Ivar Holter (1889-92) and in Leipzig with Carl Reinecke (1892-95). From 1895 he occupied various positions as church organist in Norway.
WORKS: 2 symphonies (1898 and 1923); *Variations Symphoniques* (1898); Piano Concerto (Oslo, Feb. 7, 1914); *Marche symphonique* for 2 pianos, and several choruses and songs. He also published a collection of Norwegian folk songs (1922).

Alnar, Hasan Ferid, Turkish composer; b. Istanbul, March 11, 1906. As a child he played authentic Turkish instruments; at 16 composed an operetta in oriental style. In 1927 he went to Vienna, where he studied with Joseph Marx (composition) and Oswald Kabasta (conducting). Returning to Istanbul in 1932, he taught at the Municipal Cons. He was associate conductor of the Presidential Philh. Orch. in Ankara from 1936-49, and its director from 1949-52. He also taught composition at the Ankara Cons. (1937-46). Alnar's music reflects Turkish melodic and rhythmic patterns.
WORKS: *Prelude and Two Dances* for orch. (1935); *Istanbul Suite* for orch. (1938); Cello Concerto (Ankara, Feb. 15, 1943); Concerto for Kanun (Turkish psaltery) and Orch. (1951); Piano Trio (1967), etc.

Alpaerts, Flor, Belgian composer; b. Antwerp, Sept. 12, 1876; d. there, Oct. 5, 1954. He studied composition with Benoit and Blockx and violin at the Flemish Cons. in Antwerp; in 1903 he joined its staff; was its director from 1934 until 1941. He conducted the local orch. at the Zoological Gardens (1919-51); was in

charge of the edition of works by Peter Benoit. His own music is marked by an intense feeling for the modalities of Flemish folksongs.
WORKS: an opera *Shylock,* after Shakespeare (Antwerp, Nov. 22, 1913); a *Symphonie du printemps* (1906); symph. poems *Psyche* (1900), *Herleving* (1903), *Cyrus* (1905), *Pallieter* (1921), *Thijl Uilenspiegel* (1927), *Avondindruk* (1928), and *Zomeridyll* (1928). Other symph. works include *Poème symphonique* for flute and orch. (1903); *Karakterstuk* for trumpet and strings (1904); *Bosspeling* (1904); *Salome's danse,* theme and variations (1907; based on incidental music to the Wilde play); *Vlaamse Idylle* (1920); *Romanza* for violin and small orch. (1928); *James Ensor Suite* for orch. (1929); 2 *Suites* for small orch. (1932); *Humor* (1936); *Serenade* for cello and orch. (1936); *Small Suite* for strings (1947); Violin Concerto (1948); *Capriccio* (1953). He also wrote *Kolonos* for soloists, chorus and orch. (1901); a cantata, *Het schoner vaderland* (1912); 2 *Pieces* for piano trio (1906); *Avondmuziek* for 8 woodwinds (1915); 4 string quartets (1943, 1944, 1945, 1950); 3 *Petite Pieces* for violin and piano (1944); 4 *Bagatelles* for string quartet (1953); incidental music to 6 plays; *Kinderleideren,* in 4 sets (1915-16). His 5-volume treatise *Muzieklezen en Zingen* was adopted as the official textbook in all Flemish music institutions.

Alpaerts, Jef, Belgian conductor and pianist; son of Flor Alpaerts; b. Antwerp, July 17, 1904; d. there, Jan. 15, 1973. He studied in Paris with Isidor Philipp and Cortot (piano) and with Vincent d'Indy (comp.). In 1936 he was appointed prof. at the Antwerp Cons.; in 1938 he inaugurated the Collegium Musicum Antverpiense for performances of old music.

Alsen, Elsa, opera singer; b. in Obra, Poland, April 7, 1880; d. in New York, Jan. 31, 1975. She was trained as a contralto and made her debut in Germany in 1902. In 1912 she changed to soprano parts and established herself as an opera singer, excelling in Wagnerian roles. She made her American debut in 1923, and sang with the Manhattan Opera House and the Chicago Civic Opera Company until 1928. She also appeared in the movies as a singer in musical comedies and gave song recitals until her retirement at an advanced age.

Alsina, Carlos Roqué, Argentine composer; b. Buenos Aires, Feb. 19, 1941. He studied piano and music theory with various local teachers; was an assistant conductor at the Teatro Colón in Buenos Aires (1960-64). He traveled to Berlin (1964-66); subsequently was a member of the Center of the Creative and Performing Arts at the State Univ. of N.Y. at Buffalo (1966-68); then was again in Berlin; both in Europe and America he gave piano recitals in programs of modern music. His works are of a functional nature, in the manner peculiar to the cosmopolitan avant-garde; among them to be noted are *Funktionen* for winds, strings, piano and percussion (1965); *Texts, a* theater piece (1967); *Symptom* for orch. (1969); *Rendez-vous* for wind instruments, piano and percussion (1970); *Schichten* for chamber orch. (1971); *Approach* for piano, percussion and orch. (West Berlin, March 14, 1973); *Sinfonia* (Royan, France, April 4, 1977).

Alsleben, Julius, German pianist and pedagogue; b. Berlin, March 24, 1832; d. there, Dec. 8, 1894. He studied piano with Zech, and theory with S. Dehn. In 1865 he became president of the Berlin Tonkünstlerverein; in 1879 he was president of the Musiklehrerverein of which he was also a founder. From 1874 he edited the periodical *Harmonie.* Alsleben published 12 *Vorlesungen über Musikgeschichte* (1862); *Über die Entwickelung des Klavierspiels* (1870), *Licht- und Wendepunkte in der Entwickelung der Musik* (1880). He wrote a Requiem, a liturgy, choral pieces and some orchestral overtures.

Alsted, Johann Heinrich, German music scholar; b. Ballersbach, Nassau, in March, 1588; d. Weissenburg, Transylvania, Nov. 8, 1638. He taught philosophy and theology in Weissenburg. His articles on music are found in his *Encyclopädie der gesammten Wissenschaften* (1610) and in his *Elementale mathematicum* (1611), translated into English by Birchensha (1644).

Alt, Hansi, American pianist and composer; b. Vienna, Feb. 25, 1911. She studied music at the Univ. of Vienna. In 1941 she went to the United States. She taught at several private schools in New York before moving to Washington. She publ. a number of piano pieces pleasingly adapted to popular tastes, among them *Parade, Sleepyhead, Splashing,* etc.

Altar, Cevat Memduh, Turkish writer on music; b. Constantinople, Sept. 14, 1902. He studied in Leipzig (1922–27); taught music theory in Ankara (1927–35), and was a founder of the Ankara State Cons. (1936). In 1951 he was appointed director of Turkish theaters; in 1954 he visited the U.S. under the Educational Exchange Program. He has translated several German books into Turkish; wrote several essays on Beethoven's use of so-called Turkish music, and initiated a 6-volume edition of musical biography.

Altenburg, Johann Ernst, German trumpet player and composer; b. Weissenfels, June 15, 1734; d. Bitterfeld, May 14, 1801. He was a field-trumpeter during the 7 Years' War; then became organist at Bitterfeld. He wrote the first special manual on playing the trumpet and kettledrums, *Versuch einer Anleitung zur heroisch-musikalischen Trompeter- und Paukerkunst* (Halle, 1795; reprinted, Dresden, 1911); also pieces for 2, 4, 6, and 8 trumpets, and a concerto for 7 trumpets and kettle-drums.
BIBLIOGRAPHY: A. Werner, "Johann Ernst Alternburg," *Zeitschrift für Musikwissenschaft* (1933).

Altenburg, Michael, German church musician; b. Alach, near Erfurt, May 27, 1584; d. Erfurt, Feb. 12, 1640. He studied theology at Halle (1601); became pastor at Tröchtelborn (1611), then at Gröss-Sommerda (1621), and finally in Erfurt (1637). He published a Wedding Motet in 7 parts; a collection of songs 'for Church and Home' in 6, 7, 8, and 9 voices (3 vols.; Erfurt, 1620–21); 16 instrumental *Intraden* in 6 parts (Erfurt, 1620) and numerous church anthems some of which have been permanently incorporated in the Lutheran service. For a detailed list of works, see Adrio's article in *Die Musik in Geschichte und Gegenwart.*

Altès, Ernest-Eugène, French violinist and conductor; brother of **Joseph-Henri Altès;** b. Paris, March 28, 1830; d. St.-Dyé, near Blois, July 8, 1899. He studied with Habeneck at the Paris Cons., where he won first prize for violin playing in 1848. In 1871 he joined the staff of the Paris Opéra as conductor, retiring in 1887. He composed a symphony, chamber music, and an orchestral *Divertissement* on ballet airs by Auber on the occasion of Auber's centennial (1882).

Altès, Joseph-Henri, French flutist; brother of **Ernest-Eugène Altès;** b. Rouen, Jan. 18, 1926; d. Paris, July 24, 1895. He studied at the Paris Cons.; then became flutist at the Paris Opéra. He was appointed prof. of flute at the Paris Cons. in 1868, holding this post to the end of his life. He published a number of flute pieces.

Altglass, Max, lyric tenor; b. Warsaw, Feb. 16, 1886; d. New York, Feb. 15, 1952. He studied at the Berlin Cons.; sang in Berlin and Prague, and made his American debut with the Metropolitan Opera in 1924. Later he was active as vocal teacher in New York.

Althouse, Paul, American tenor; b. Reading, Pa., Dec. 2, 1889; d. New York, Feb. 6, 1954. He studied with O. Saenger, and made his debut as Dimitri in the American premiere of *Boris Godunov* at the Metropolitan Opera on March 19, 1913; later undertook Wagnerian tenor roles there; was also for a time a member of the Chicago Civic Opera and of the San Francisco Opera. He sang with Toscanini and the N.Y. Philh. as soloist in Beethoven's Ninth Symphony; also appeared with other U.S. orchestras. He gave two recital tours in Australia and New Zealand. In the last years of his life Althouse was mostly active as vocal teacher in New York.

Altmann, Wilhelm, German music bibliographer, b. Adelnau, near Posen, April 4, 1862; d. Hildesheim, March 25, 1951. He studied philology and government in Marburg and Berlin, and in 1885 received his *Dr. phil.* He served as librarian in Greifswald (1889–1900). In 1900 he was appointed a librarian of the Prussian State Library in Berlin; in 1915 he became director of the music dept., retiring in 1927. In 1906 he founded, in cooperation with Breitkopf & Härtel, the 'Deutsche Musiksammlung,' at the Berlin library. From 1945 he lived in Hildesheim. Altmann compiled a number of valuable bibliographical works; among them *Chronik des Berliner Philh. Orchesters* (1902); *Richard Wagners Briefe* (1905; a list of 3143 letters with brief synopses); *Brahms Briefwechsel* (1908); *Wagners Briefwechsel mit seinen Verlegern* (2 vols., 1911); *Kammermusik-Literatur-Verzeichnis* (1910; a list of chamber music published since 1841; 6 revisions up to 1945); *Max-Reger-Katalog* (1917 and 1923); catalogue of music for viola and viola d'amore (1937) and a catalogue of piano music for 4 and 6 hands and 2 pianos (1943). Altmann also edited Paul Frank's *Tonkünstler-*

Lexikon (1926, 1927, 1936, 1949). Furthermore, he published bibliographies of books on instruments; also made arrangements of classical works.

Altnikol, Johann Christoph, German organist and composer; b. Berna (Silesia) in December 1719 (baptized Jan. 1, 1720); d. Naumburg, July 25, 1759. In 1744–48 he studied with J. S. Bach; was then organist at St. Wenzel's Church in Naumburg. On Jan. 20, 1749 Altnikol married Bach's daughter, Elisabeth. In a letter of recommendation Bach describes him as "quite skillful in composition." As Bach's copyist, Altnikol established authentic texts of many of Bach's works. See *(passim)* H. David and A. Mendal, *The Bach Reader* (N.Y., 1945); also F. Blume's article in *Die Musik in Geschichte und Gegenwart.*

Altschuler, Modest, Russian cellist and conductor; b. Moghilev, Feb. 15, 1873; d. Los Angeles, Sept. 12, 1963. He studied cello at the Warsaw Cons. as a child; then went to Moscow where he took courses in composition with Arensky and Taneyev and in piano and conducting with Safonov at the Moscow Cons., graduating in 1890. After touring Russia as a cellist, he emigrated to America, and in 1903 organized in New York the Russian Symphony Society. He conducted its first concert on Jan. 7, 1904; for some 12 years the concerts of this organization became an important cultural medium for performances of Russian music in America. One of Altschuler's most signal accomplishments was the world premiere of Scriabin's *Le Poème de l'Extase* which he gave in New York on Dec. 10, 1908, in advance of its Russian performance. At the same concert Mischa Elman made his American debut as a concert violinist. Altschuler also conducted the first American performance of Scriabin's *Prométhée* in N.Y. on March 20, 1915, at which he made an unsuccessful attempt to include the part of *Luce* (a color organ) prescribed by Scriabin in the score. Among other Russian composers whose works Altschuler presented for the first time in America were Rachmaninoff, Liadov, Vasilenko and Ippolitov-Ivanov. Altschuler eventually retired to Los Angeles; he wrote an autobiography which remains unpublished.

Alva, Luigi, Peruvian tenor; b. Lima, April 10, 1927. He made his operatic debut in Milan in 1954; appeared in London in 1960, and sang at the Metropolitan Opera in New York in 1964. He excels in the Italian repertory; his interpretations of Mozart have won praise.

Alvarado, Alberto, Mexican composer; b. Durango, Dec. 10, 1864; d. there, June 18, 1939. He wrote nearly 1000 pieces of various types ranging from waltzes to symphonic works, mostly of a descriptive nature: (*El principe de Asturias; Angel Mujer; Almas Destrozadas; La Fiesta encantadora; Suite Tropical, Corazón latino*).

Alvarez (real name **Gourron**), **Albert Raymond,** French tenor; b. Cenon, near Bordeaux, May 16, 1861; d. Nice, Feb. 1, 1933. He started his musical career as the leader of a military band in France; then began his vocal studies in Paris; made his debut at the Paris Opéra in 1892. He made successful appearances at Covent Garden in London; made his American debut at the Metropolitan Opera in N.Y. on Dec. 18, 1899, remaining with the Met until 1903, when he returned to Paris to become a singing teacher. His repertory included about 60 roles.

Alvary (real name **Achenbach**), **Max,** German tenor; b. Düsseldorf, May 3, 1856; d. near Gross-Tabarz, Thuringia, Nov. 7, 1898. His father was a well known painter. Alvary studied with Stockhausen; made his debut at Weimar. On Nov. 25, 1885 he made his American debut at the Metropolitan Opera as Don José singing in German; later he specialized in Wagnerian roles, in which he was eminently successful in America and in Germany.

Alwin, Karl (original name **Alwin Oskar Pinkus),** German conductor; b. Königsberg, April 15, 1891; d. Mexico City, Oct. 15, 1945. He studied composition in Berlin with Humperdinck and Hugo Kaun; later he dedicated himself mainly to conducting. He was Kapellmeister in Halle (1913), Posen (1914), Düsseldorf (1915–17) and Hamburg (1917–20). From 1920 to 1938 he served as conductor of the Vienna Staatsoper. He left Austria in 1938, after the *Anschluss,* and went to Mexico where he conducted opera from 1941 until his death. He was married to the singer Elisabeth Schumann (1920–36).

Alwyn, William, English composer; b. Northampton, Nov. 7, 1905. He studied at the Royal Academy in London with McEwen; in 1928 he was appointed to its faculty. A prolific composer, he wrote an opera, *The Libertine* (1969); 4 symphonies (1951, 1953, 1956, 1959); the oratorio *The Marriage of Heaven and Hell* (1936); a piano concerto (1930); a violin concerto (1938); an oboe concerto (1944); *Lyra Angelica* for harp and string orch. (1954); *Autumn Legend* for English horn and string orch. (1956); chamber music, piano pieces and songs. Alwyn achieved his greatest successes as a composer of film music; his most popular film scores include *Desert Victory* and *Odd Man Out.* In these scores he demonstrated his ability to write effective music in an ingratiating modern manner.

Alypios, Greek musical theorist, who flourished in the middle of the 4th century. His *Introduction to Music* is the chief source of specific information regarding ancient Greek notation; it contains a summary of Greek scales in all their transpositions, both for voices and instruments. This treatise was published by Meursius (Leyden, 1616); by Meibom in his *Antiquae musicae auctores septem* (Amsterdam, 1652); and reprinted by F. Bellermann in *Die Tonleitern und Musiknoten der Griechen* (Berlin, 1847). A new critical edition is found in Jan's *Musici scriptores graeci* (1895). A graphic explanation of the notation of Alypios is presented by A. Samoiloff in his article "Die Alypiusschen Reihen der altgriechischen Tonbezeichnung," *Archiv für Musikwissenschaft* (1924; pp. 383–400).

Amadei, Filippo, Italian opera composer; b. Reggio, c.1670; he probably died in Rome about 1729. His claim to attention is that under the name of **Signor Pippo** (diminutive of Filippo) he wrote the first act of the opera *Muzio Scevola,* for which Bononcini wrote the second act, and Handel the third, which was produced at the Royal Academy of Music in London, April 15, 1721. His other works are the opera *Teodosio il Giovane* (Rome, 1711), the oratorio *Il trionfo di Tito* (Rome, 1709), and the cantata *Il pensiero* (Rome, 1709). Amadei's name was erroneously converted into **Filippo Mattei** by Mattheson in his *Critica musica,* and the mistake was carried into reference works and Handel's biographies.

Amalia Catharina, Countess of Erbach; b. Arolsen, Aug. 8, 1640; d. Cuylenburg, Netherlands, Jan. 4, 1697. She was the daughter of Count von Waldeck; in 1664 she married Count Georg Ludwig von Erbach; of her 16 children only a few survived perilous infancy. She merits attention of musical biographers as one of the few women of the German nobility who actually composed all by herself a number of singable religious anthems.

Amalia Friederike, Princess of Saxony who wrote comedies under the name of **Amalie Heiter;** b. Dresden, Aug. 10, 1794; d. there, Sept. 18, 1870. She composed several light operas (*Una donna, Le tre cinture, Die Siegesfahne, Der Kanonenschuss,* etc.) and church music.

Amani, Nikolai, Russian composer; b. St. Petersburg, April 4, 1872; d. Yalta, Oct. 17, 1904. He studied piano with Anne Essipova and composition with Rimsky-Korsakov and Liadov at the St. Petersburg Cons. (1890–1900); then went to Italy and played a concert of his piano works at Naples (July 29, 1900); in 1901–02 he traveled in Germany. Tuberculosis forced him to stop working; he lived his last two years in the Crimea. Amani's music is close in style to Tchaikovsky; but he wrote only in small forms. He composed a string trio (1900) and a number of harmonious piano pieces and songs, many of them published. A memoir of his short life was published in Italian by S. Gentile, *Breve ricordo della vita e opere di Nicolas Amani, musicista russo* (Palermo, 1911).

Amar, Licco, Hungarian violinist; b. Budapest, Dec. 4, 1891; d. Freiburg-im-Breisgau, July 19, 1959. He studied with Henri Marteau in Berlin and in 1912 joined the Marteau Quartet as second violinist. He subsequently was appointed concertmaster of the Berlin Philharmonic (1915–20) and at the National Theater in Mannheim (1920–23). In 1921 he organized the Amar Quartet, with Paul Hindemith as the violist, Walter Caspar as second violinist and Maurits Frank as cellist. In 1933 he was compelled to leave Germany; in 1935 he was engaged as prof. of the Cons. of Ankara, Turkey. In 1957 he returned to Germany and taught at the Hochschule für Musik in Freiburg-im-Breisgau.

Amara (real name **Armaganian**), **Lucine,** American soprano; b. Hartford, Connecticut, March 1, 1927, of Armenian parentage. She studied in San Francisco and at the Univ. of Southern California in Los Angeles; made her operatic debut at the Metropolitan Opera House, in N.Y., in 1950; then traveled to Europe; sang at Edinburgh (1954) and at the Vienna State Opera (1960).

Amat, Juan Carlos, Spanish physician and writer on guitar playing; b. Monistrol, 1572; d. there, Feb. 10, 1642. His book *Guitarra Española en cinco ordenes* (Barcelona, 1596) has been reprinted many times.

BIBLIOGRAPHY: E. Pujol, "Significación de Juan Carlos Amat (1572–1642) en la historia de la guitarra," *Anuario Musical,* vol. V (Barcelona, 1950).

Amati, a renowned Italian family of violin makers working at Cremona. (1) **Andrea,** b. between 1500 and 1505; d. before 1580. He was the first violin maker of the family who established the prototype of Italian instruments with characteristics found in modern violins. His two sons were (2) **Antonio,** b. c.1538; d. c.1595, who built violins of varying sizes, and (3) **Girolamo,** b. c.1561; d. Nov. 2, 1630. The latter continued the tradition established by his father, and worked together with his brother Antonio. (4) **Nicola** (or **Niccolò**), was the most illustrious of the Amati family; b. Dec. 3, 1596; d. April 12, 1684. He was the son of Girolamo Amati, and signed his labels "Nicolaus Amati Cremonens, Hieronimi filius Antonii nepos." He built some of the "grand Amatis," large violins of powerful tone surpassing in clarity and purity those made by his father Girolamo and his grandfather Andrea. In his workshop both Andrea Guarneri and Antonio Stradivari received their training. (5) **Girolamo,** son of Nicola; b. Feb. 26, 1649; d. Feb. 21, 1740. The last of the family, his violins were inferior to those of his father, his grandfather and his great-grandfather; in his work he departed from the family tradition in many respects and seemed to be influenced by Stradivari's method without equaling Stradivari's superb workmanship.

BIBLIOGRAPHY: G. de Picolellis, *Genealogia degli Amati e dei Guarneri* (Florence, 1886); L. von Lütgendorff, *Die Geigen- und Lautenmacher vom Mittelalter bis zum Gegenwart* (2 vols., in dictionary form; Frankfurt, 1904; 4th edition, 1922); D. D. Boyden, *The History of Violin Playing from Its Origins to 1761* (London, 1965).

Amato, Pasquale, Italian baritone; b. Naples, March 21, 1878; d. New York, Aug. 12, 1942. He studied at the Cons. of Naples (1896–99); made his debut in *La Traviata* in Naples in 1900. He later sang at leading European opera houses, and in Russia, England, Egypt and Argentina. He made his American debut at the Metropolitan Opera in *La Traviata* (Nov. 20, 1908) with Sembrich and Caruso. Amato remained a member of the Metropolitan Opera until 1921 and then settled in New York as voice teacher.

Ambros, August Wilhelm, eminent musical historiographer; b. Mauth, near Prague, Nov. 17, 1816; d. Vienna, June 28, 1876. He studied law and music; rapidly rose in the legal profession; was appointed Public Prosecutor in Prague (1850), but continued to devote

much time to music; published his *Die Grenzen der Musik und Poesie* (Leipzig, 1856; English translation, N.Y., 1893) as a reply to Hanslick's views on esthetics; followed by a brilliant collection of essays under the title, *Culturhistorische Bilder aus dem Musikleben der Gegenwart* (Leipzig, 1860); also published two collections of articles, *Bunte Blätter* (1872–74; 2nd ed. by E. Vogel, 1896). In 1869 Ambros was appointed prof. of music at Prague Univ. and Prague Cons.; in 1872 received a post in the Ministry of Justice in Vienna; he also taught at Vienna Cons. His major work was the monumental *Geschichte der Musik* commissioned by the publisher Leuckart in 1860. Ambros spent many years of research in the libraries of Munich, Vienna, and several Italian cities for this work, but died before completing the 4th volume, which was edited from his notes by C. F. Becker and G. Nottebohm; a 5th volume was published in 1882 by O. Kade from newly collected materials. W. Langhans wrote a sequel in a more popular style under the title *Die Geschichte der Musik des 17., 18. und 19. Jahrhunderts,* bringing the work up to date (2 volumes, 1882–86). A list of names and general index were issued by W. Bäumker (1882). A 2nd edition of the original 4 volumes (Leipzig, 1880) contain the following: Vol. I, The Beginnings of Music; Vol. II, From the Christian Era to the First Flemish School; Vol. III, From the Netherlands Masters to Palestrina; Vol. IV, Palestrina, his contemporaries and immediate successors. Volume I has been rewritten, not always for the better, by B. Sokolovsky; 2nd volume was reprinted in a new revision by Reimann (1892); volume IV by Leichtentritt (1909); volume V was revised and enlarged by O. Kade (1911). Ambros was also an excellent practical musician, a proficient pianist, and composer. He wrote an opera in Czech, *Bretislaw a Jitka;* overtures to *Othello* and the *Magico prodigioso,* numerous songs, and religious music.
BIBLIOGRAPHY: Guido Adler, "August Wilhelm Ambros," *Musical Quarterly* (July 1931).

Ambrose (Ambrosius), Christian saint and creator of 'Ambrosian Chant'; b. Trier (Trèves), c.333; d. Milan, April 4, 397. He was elected Bishop of Milan in 374; canonized after his death. In 384 he became responsible for the regulation and development of singing in the Western Church by the introduction and cultivation of ritual song (antiphonal and congregational) as practiced at the time in the Eastern Church. His indisputable authorship of several sacred songs has earned him the title of 'Father of Christian Hymnology,' but his reputed composition of the 'Ambrosian Chant,' *Te Deum laudamus* (said to have been sung by St. Ambrose and St. Augustine at the baptism of the latter) is mythical.
BIBLIOGRAPHY: Biraghi, *Inni sinceri e carmi di S. Ambrogio* (Milan, 1862); G. M. Dreves, *Aurelius Ambrosius, der Vater des Kirchengesanges* (Freiburg, 1893); A. Mocquereau, *Notes sur l'influence de l'accent et du cursus tonique latins dans le chant ambrosien* (Paris, 1897); A. Steier, *Untersuchungen über die Echtheit der Hymnen des Ambrosius* (Leipzig, 1903); P. Wagner, *Introduction to the Gregorian melodies,* part 1, *Origin and Development of the Forms of Liturgical Chant.* (London, 1907); E. Garbagnati, *Riviste*

sull'antica salmodia ambrosiana (Rome, 1912); A. S. Parodi, *S. Ambrogio e la sua età* (Milan, 1941).

d'Ambrosio, Alfredo, Italian violinist and composer; b. Naples, June 13, 1871; d. Nice, Dec. 29, 1914. He studied with E. Bossi at the Cons. of Naples (comp.); violin with Sarasate in Madrid and with Willhelmj in London. Settled in Nice as teacher, and leader of a string quartet. He wrote an opera *Pia de Tolomei;* a ballet *Ersilia;* a string quintet; a string quartet; 2 violin concertos, and many smaller compositions for violin (*Romanza, Canzonetta,* etc.).

Ambrosius, Hermann, German composer; b. Hamburg, July 25, 1897. He studied at the Univ. of Leipzig; later took master courses with Pfitzner (1921–24). In 1925 he joined the faculty of the Leipzig Cons.; after the end of World War II he settled in Engen, devoting himself mainly to composition. He has written 12 symphonies, 5 piano concertos, numerous concertos for a variety of other instruments, including the electronic Trautonium, and an untold number of solo piano pieces, songs and choruses; not content with traditional formats, he has experimented with monothematic symphonic composition. His fecundity astounds many of his colleagues. An admiring Festschrift, edited by F. Hirtler, was published on his 70th birthday.

Ameller, André (Charles Gabriel), French composer; b. Arnaville, Jan. 2, 1912. He studied composition with Roger-Ducasse and Gaubert at the Paris Cons.; also violin and double bass. He was taken prisoner of war in Germany in 1940; after the end of the war he returned to France, and in 1953 was appointed director of the Cons. in Dijon. He wrote the operas *La Lance de Fingal* (1947), *Sampiero Corso, Monsieur Personne* (1957), and *Cyrnos* (Nancy, April 6, 1962); ballets: *La Coupe de sang* (1950); *Oiseaux du vieux Paris* (1967); *Jeux de table* for saxophone and piano (1955); *Terre secrète,* 6 poems for voice and orch. (1956); *Airs hétérogènes* for wind ensemble (1966); *Hétérodoxes* for 2 flutes, 2 trumpets, string quartet and string orch. (1969).

Amengual, René, Chilean composer; b. Santiago, Sept. 2, 1911; d. there, Aug. 2, 1954. He studied with Humberto Allende at the National Cons. in Santiago. His compositions are few, and mostly in small forms; their style shows influences of the modern French school. He wrote a Piano Sonatina (1938); *Introduction and Allegro* for 2 pianos (1939); Piano Concerto (Santiago, June 30, 1942); *El Vaso* for voice and chamber orch. (Santiago, Aug. 25, 1944), etc. His *Burlesca* for piano is included in the album *Latin American Art Music for the Piano* (N.Y., 1942).

Amfiteatrov, Daniele, composer and conductor; b. St. Petersburg, Russia, Oct. 29, 1901; studied composition in St. Petersburg with Wihtol, in Prague with Křička, and in Rome with Respighi. He stayed in Italy until 1937 when he came to America as assistant conductor of the Minneapolis Symph. Orch. (1938–41). In 1941 he settled in Hollywood as composer of film music; became an American citizen in 1944. He has written for orch. *Poema del Mare* (1925), *Miracolo delle Rose* (1927), *American Panorama* (1934), and some chamber music, as well as numerous film scores.

Amiot, Père Joseph Marie, French ecclesiastic; b. Toulon, Feb. 8, 1718; d. Peking, Oct. 9, 1793. He was Jesuit missionary to China; while there, he translated Li Koang Ti's work on Chinese music: *Commentaire sur le livre classique touchant la musique des anciens;* also wrote *Mémoires sur la musique des Chinois, tant anciens que modernes* (vol. VI of *Mémoires concernant l'histoire, les sciences, les arts, . . . des Chinois;* Paris, 1780, edited by Abbé Roussier).

Amirkhanian, Charles, American avant-garde composer of Armenian extraction; b. Fresno, Calif. Jan. 19, 1945. He began experimenting in composition without outside help, probing the potentialities of sound phenomena independently from traditional musical content. His *Composition No. 1* was a solo for an acoustically amplified ratchet (1965). His *Symphony I* (1965) is scored for 12 players and 200-odd non-musical objects, ranging from pitchpipes to pitchforks. In collaboration with the painter Ted Greer, Amirkhanian developed a radical system of notation in which visual images are transduced by performers into sound events. Representative of this intermedia genre are *Micah, the Prophet,* a cantata for 4 intoning males, 2 accordions, 2 drummers and 2 painters (1965), and particularly *Mooga Pook,* a tetraphallic action for dancers, realistically notated on graph paper, which was produced in San Francisco, Dec. 12, 1967. He also evolved the art of "text-sound composition" for magnetic tape; to this category belong such pieces as *Words* (1969); *Oratora Konkurso Rezulto: Autoro de la Jaro,* an Esperanto recitation (1970); *If In Is* (1971); *Spoffy Nene* (1971); *Just* (1972); *Heavy Aspirations* (1973); *Seatbelt Seatbelt* (1973); *MUGIC* (1973); *Muchrooms* (1974); *Beemsterboer* (1975); *Mahogany Ballpark* (1976); *Dutiful Ducks* (1977). In 1969 Amirkhanian became Sound Sensitivity Information Director of radio station KPFA in Berkeley, California; produced Ode to Gravity, a weekly program of avant-garde music. In 1975 he organized, with the visual artists Carol Law and Jim Petrillo and poet Betsy Davids, a group called, with a deliberate letter substitution, "Mugicians Union." In 1977 he was appointed to the faculty of the Interdisciplinary Creative Arts Dept. of San Francisco State University.

Amirov, Fikret Dzhamil, Azerbaijan composer; b. Kirovabad, Nov. 22, 1922. He received his early musical instruction from his father who was a singer and guitarist; he then studied composition at the Cons. of Azerbaidzhan, graduating in 1948. His compositions reflect the melorhythmic patterns of popular Azerbaidzhan music, marked by characteristic Oriental inflections, while retaining a classical format and development, particularly in variation form. Among his works are a symphonic poem *To the Memory of the Heroes of the Great National War* (1944); Double Concerto for Violin, Piano and Orch. (1948); *The Pledge of the Korean Guerrilla Fighter* for voice and orch. (1951); several symphonic suites based on the national modes "mugamas," of which *Shur* is the best

known; and the opera *Sevil* (Baku, Dec. 25, 1953). He also wrote a piano concerto on Arab themes (1957; in collaboration with Nazirova). In 1959 he visited the U.S. as a member of the Soviet delegation of composers under the auspices of the State Dept.
BIBLIOGRAPHY: D. Danilov, *Fikret Amirov* (Moscow, 1958).

Ammann, Benno, Swiss composer and conductor; b. Gersau, June 14, 1904. He studied composition with Karg-Elert at the Leipzig Cons., and later in Paris with Honegger, Milhaud and Albert Roussel. He was chorus leader in Basel (1936–39) and at the Teatro Real in Rome (1939–42); then was active as conductor and instructor at the International Festival Courses for New Music in Darmstadt. He composed a Mass *Defensor Pacis* (Rome, 1947); *Vision pastorale* for orch. (1954); Wind Quintet (1956); a ballet, *Zweimal Besuch* (1961); *Successions* for flute solo (1966); and numerous pieces for miscellaneous instruments, such as *Dialogues et Décisions* for 2 guitars; *Composition en Mouvement* for double-bass solo; *Remove* for oboe solo; etc.

Ammerbach, Elias Nikolaus, German organist and contrapuntist; b. Naumburg, c.1530; d. Leipzig, Jan. 1957 (buried Jan. 29). From 1560 he was organist of the Thomaskirche, Leipzig. He published *Orgel oder Instrument Tabulatur* (Leipzig, 1571; repr. 1583), a work of importance regarding progress and development in the practice of tuning, the fingering of keyboard instruments, execution of graces, etc. (described by Becker in *Die Hausmusik in Deutschland,* Leipzig, 1840); and *Ein neu künstlich Tabulaturbuch* (1575; 2nd ed., 1583; a copy of the original 1575 edition is preserved in the Royal Library in Copenhagen.) He also published numerous compositions for organ and clavichord.

Ammon, Blasius, contrapuntist; b. 1558 at Hall, Tirol; d. Vienna, June, 1590. He was a choir boy in the service of Archduke Ferdinand of Austria, who sent him to Venice for his musical education. In 1578 he returned to Innsbruck and joined the Franciscan Order. In 1587 he went to the Franciscan monastery in Vienna, where he entered the priesthood. He printed a book of 5-part Introits (Vienna, 1582); a book of 4-part Masses (Vienna, 1588); 2 books of 4, 5 and 6-part motets (Munich, 1590). A number of works in MS are in the libraries of Munich and Vienna. A volume containing his church music was published by Caecilianus Huigens in *Denkmäler der Tonkunst in Österreich* 73 (38.i).

Amon, Johann (Andreas), German musician; b. Bamberg, 1763; d. Wallerstein, Bavaria, March 29, 1825. He studied horn with Giovanni Punto and traveled with him on tours in France and Germany. From 1789 till 1817 he was music director at Heilbronn; then became court conductor to the Prince of Öttingen-Wallerstein. He wrote 2 operas, 3 Requiems (one of which he intended for performance at his funeral), and many pieces of chamber music.

Amram, David Werner, American composer; b. Philadelphia, Nov. 17, 1930. He learned to play piano, trumpet and French horn; took courses at the Oberlin Cons.; after serving in the U.S. Army in Europe (1952-55) he studied composition with Vittorio Giannini in New York. He then began to compose prolifically and flexibly for theater, television, motion pictures and jazz bands; also played in various jazz combos. Among his works are a Trio for Saxophone, French Horn and Bassoon (1958); Violin Sonata (1960); Overture and Allegro for Unaccompanied Flute (1960); many jazz pieces. His 'Passover opera,' *The Final Ingredient,* was produced on television in N.Y., April 11, 1965. Other works include: *King Lear Variations,* for winds and percussion (1967); String Quartet (1968); opera, *Twelfth Night* (1968); *Triple Concerto* for woodwinds, brass, jazz quintet and orch. (N.Y., Jan. 10, 1971). He publ. an autobiography *Vibrations: The Adventures and Musical Times of David Amram* (N.Y., 1968).

Amy, Gilbert, French composer; b. Paris, Aug. 29, 1936. He studied composition with Darius Milhaud and Olivier Messiaen. His principal works are *Œil de fumée* for soprano and piano (1955); *Variations* for 4 instruments (1956); *Cantate brève* to words by García Lorca (1957); *Mouvements* for 17 instruments (1958); *Alpha-Beth* for 6 wind instruments (1963); *Antiphonies* for 2 orch. (1963); *Triade* for orch. (1964); *Trajectoires* for violin and orch. (1966); *Cycle* for 6 percussion players (1967); *Chant* for orch. (Donaueschingen, Oct. 20, 1968); *Relais* for 5 brass instruments (1969). In his music he follows the baroque precepts of antiphony and concertante, but applies then in combination with modern serialism.

Ančerl, Karel, Czech conductor; b. Tučapy, April 11, 1908; d. Toronto, Canada, July 3, 1973. He studied at the Prague Cons., taking courses in composition with Alois Hába and Křička and percussion playing with Šourek; at the same time he practiced conducting. He devoted himself mainly to the modern repertory, and conducted several concerts at the festivals of the International Society for Contemporary Music. He held the post of music director on the Prague Radio, but as a Jew was removed from this position when Czechoslovakia was occupied by the Nazis in 1939. In 1942 he was deported to the Jewish ghetto camp in Theresienstadt, and was later transported to Auschwitz; his entire family was put to death there but, providentially, he was spared. After the war he resumed his activities as conductor; was at the Prague Opera from 1945 to 1947; then with the Radio Orch. (1947-50), and from 1950 until 1968 was appointed conductor of the Czech Philharmonic, with which he traveled through Europe, Canada, the U.S., Australia and Japan. In 1970 he was appointed conductor of the Toronto Symphony Orch., and lived there until his death. He was distinguished mainly for his congenial interpretation of the music by Czech composers; in appreciation of his service he was named in 1966 People's Artist.
BIBLIOGRAPHY: K. Šrom, *Karel Ančerl* (Prague, 1968).

Ancina, Giovanni Giovenale, Italian choral composer; b. Fossano, Oct. 19, 1545; d. Saluzzo, Aug. 31, 1604. He studied medicine and theology; became interested in music when he met Filippo Neri; in 1578 he joined the Congregazione dell'Oratorio, founded by Neri. Ancina wrote church music; published *Tempio armonico della beata Vergine* (Rome, 1599).
BIBLIOGRAPHY: J. Bacci, *Vita di G. G. Ancina* (Rome, 1671); Pietro Damilano, *G. G. Ancina e la lauda cinquecentesca* (Milan, 1953).

Ancona, Mario, Italian baritone, b. Leghorn, Feb. 28, 1860; d. Florence, Feb. 22, 1931. He studied social sciences and law, and started his career as a diplomat. He soon turned to the study of singing, however, and made his debut at Trieste; then sang at the principal opera houses of Italy. He appeared as Tonio at both the London (1892) and New York (1894) premieres of *Pagliacci;* for nine seasons he was a member of Covent Garden; he spent five seasons at the Metropolitan Opera, and two at the Manhattan Opera House. He also appeared in Spain, Portugal, Russia and Argentina. His repertoire included such various roles as Amonasro, Sachs, Wolfram, etc. After retiring from opera he was active as vocal teacher in Italy.

Ancot, a family of musicians at Bruges. **Jean** (*père*), b. Bruges, Oct. 22, 1779; d. there July 12, 1848; violin virtuoso, pianist and composer; studied (1799-1804) in Paris under Baillot, Kreutzer, and Catel; then settled in Bruges as teacher. Publ. 4 violin concertos; overtures, marches, sacred music, etc.; most of his works are still in MS. Taught his sons: (1) **Jean** (*fils*); b. Bruges, July 6, 1799; d. Boulogne, June 5, 1829; finished his education at the Paris Cons. under Pradher and Berton; an accomplished pianist, he was successful in London (1823-25); eventually settled in Boulogne. Considering that he died short of his 30th birthday, he was an astonishingly prolific composer (225 works; a piano concerto, sonatas, etudes, 4-hand fantasias, also violin concertos); and (2) **Louis;** b. Bruges, June 3, 1803; d. there, 1836; for a time pianist to the Duke of Sussex, London; made extended continental tours, taught at Boulogne and Tours, and finally returned to Bruges. He wrote piano music in salon style.

Anda, Géza, Hungarian pianist; b. Budapest, Nov. 19, 1921; d. Zürich, June 13, 1976. He studied with Dohnányi at the Royal Music Academy in Budapest; won the Liszt Prize. During World War II he escaped from Hungary and settled in Switzerland; became a Swiss citizen in 1955. He toured widely in recitals and as soloist with major orchestras in Europe and America; made his American debut with the Philadelphia Orch., Oct. 21, 1955. He was an ardent champion of the music of Béla Bartók, and performed all of Bartók's three piano concertos numerous times. He also was a congenial interpreter of the music of Brahms. In Switzerland he conducted annual summer classes in piano music.

Anderberg, Carl-Olof, Swedish composer; b. Stockholm, March 13, 1914; d. Malmö, Jan. 4, 1972. He studied composition with Broman in Stockholm, piano in Copenhagen and conducting with Weingartner, in Salzburg. His early compositions are permeated with a romantic "Scandinavian" idiom; among them was an opera *Hilde.* In the 1950's he joined various avant-garde groups active in Sweden. These associations led to a radical change in his style of composition towards advanced forms of musical expression.

WORKS: *Music I* and *II* for strings (1949, 1957); *Episode,* chamber opera (1952); 3 piano sonatas (1950, 1952, 1956); *Tre Estampies* for piano, percussion and violins (1953); 2 string quartets (1955, 1957); Cello Sonata (1956); *4 Serious Caprices* for clarinet and piano (1956); *Fyra legeringar (4 Alloys)* for soprano and 5 instruments (1958); Duo I for Flute and Piano (1958); *Teater,* suite for orch. (1958); *Höstens Hökar,* metamorphoses for narrator and 5 instruments (1959); *Triad* for solo violin (1959); *Variationer över Variationer* for clarinet, bassoon, violin, cello and harp (1959); *Transfers* for symphonic groups (1960); *Di Mi Se Mai* for soprano, narrator and orch. (1963); *Hexafoni* for 6 instruments (1963); *Execution I* for clarinet, piano and percussion (1963); *Strändernas svall (The Surge of the Seaside),* cantata for soprano, baritone, narrator and instrumental ensemble (1963-64); *Acroama I* and *II* and orch. (1965-66); Duo II and III for Violin and Piano (1968); *Klangskap I (Soundscape)* for piano (1968); Piano Concerto (Malmö, March 18, 1969); *Concerto for a Ballet* for piano, winds, percussion and double basses, Swedish Radio performance, March 4, 1972); *Orkesterspel I* and *II (Orchestral Game,* 1969-70); *Music* for piano, winds and tape (1970); *Dubbelspel (Double Play)* for soprano, baritone, clarinet, cello, piano and tape (1971); piano pieces, songs.

Andersen, (Carl) Joachim, Danish flute player and composer; b. Copenhagen, April 29, 1847; d. there, May 7, 1909; son and pupil of the flutist **Christian Joachim Andersen.** From 1869-77, member of the Royal Orch.; 1881 in Berlin, where he was co-founder, and for 10 years first flutist and assistant conductor of the Philh. Orch.; from 1893, cond. of the Palace Orch. at Copenhagen. He wrote solo works for the flute; also pieces with orch.: *Hungarian Fantasia; Ballade; Dance of the Sylphs;* 24 easy and 24 difficult etudes, etc. His brother, **Vigo,** was an eminent flute player; b. Copenhagen, April 21, 1852; d. by suicide in Chicago, Jan. 28, 1895. He was first flutist in the Thomas Orch. in Chicago.

Andersen, Karl August, Norwegian composer and cellist; b. Oslo, Sept. 29, 1903; d. there, Aug. 15, 1970. He studied cello and composition in Oslo and later cello with Hugo Becker in Berlin (1921-22); then became a cellist in the Oslo Philh. Orch. (1924). From 1946 to 1962 he was a member of the governing board of the Society of Norwegian Composers.

WORKS: 3 string quartets (No. 1, 1934; No. 3, 1961-67); Symphony for Chamber Orch. (1936); Suite for Orch. (1937); Trio for Flute, Clarinet and Cello (1939); *Vårdagen* for male chorus (1942); *Allegro festivo e solenne Norwegese (Festforspill)* for orch. (1950); *Variations Over Theme and Rhythm* for wind quintet (1966).

Anderson, Arthur, American bass; b. Harvey, Ill., Aug. 16, 1898. He studied at Cincinnati Cons. and later in Italy. He made his debut in Malta; then toured Italy. Upon his return to America he made his debut at the Metropolitan Opera as Donner in *Das Rheingold* (Feb. 26, 1932). Eventually he settled in New York as a vocal teacher.

Anderson, Emily, English musicologist; b. Galway, Ireland, March 17, 1891; d. London, Oct. 26, 1962. She studied music in Berlin; upon return to England, she was employed in the British Foreign Office, without abandoning her musical research. The result of this work was the publication of two monumental collections, translated and annotated by her: *Letters of Mozart and His Family* (3 vols., London, 1938); and *The Letters of Beethoven* (3 vols., London, 1962).

Anderson, Laurie, American composer of avant-garde persuasion; b. Chicago, June 5, 1947. Renouncing the tradition of conventional musical modernism, she set for herself a goal of union of all arts as they were in ancient music, but co-opted the various techniques of new arts, from topical pop to electronics, playbacking with herself on magnetic tape. In her performing techniques she combines speech, song and facial mesmerization of the audience; gave successful exhibitions of her psychomusicurgy at the Berlin Akademie der Kunst in 1976. Some of her works demand violent action, as in her "reggae" piece, *It's Not the Bullet that Kills You, It's the Hole,* in which the singer is required to shoot himself in the arm. Her satirical piece *New York Social Life* is for voices and tamboura; another piece, *Time to Go* for guitar, violin and organ, is a repeated exhortation of a museum guard to visitors to leave at the closing time.

Anderson, Leroy, American composer of light instrumental music; b. Cambridge, Mass., June 29, 1908; d. Woodbury, Conn., May 18, 1975. He received his first musical training from his mother, an organist, and studied double bass with Gaston Dufresne in Boston. He then took courses in theory of composition with Walter Spalding, Edward Ballantine and Walter Piston at Harvard Univ., obtaining his B.A. *magna cum laude* in 1929, and M.A. in 1930. From 1932 to 1935 he was conductor of the Harvard Univ. Orchestra. In 1935 he became an arranger for the Boston Pops. In 1942 he entered the U.S. Army and was stationed in Iceland. A linguist, he acted as translator, particularly in Scandinavian languages (Anderson was of Swedish extraction). In 1939 he wrote a piece for string orch. called *Jazz Pizzicato,* which was played at the Boston Pops and became an immediate hit. This was followed by a number of similar inventive instrumental novelties, among them *Jazz Legato, The Syncopated Clock* (1950), *Fiddle Faddle, Sleigh Ride* (1950), *Serenata, A Trumpeter's Lullaby, China Doll, A Bugler's Holiday, Blue Tango* (his greatest success, 1952); *The Typewriter;* he also wrote a musical, *Goldilocks* (New York, Oct. 11, 1958).

Anderson, Marian, American contralto; b. Philadelphia, Pa., Feb. 17, 1902. She studied voice with Giuseppe Boghetti; won a vocal competition against 300 entrants and was soloist at the Lewisohn Stadium with the N.Y. Philh. on Aug. 27, 1925. She later appeared in programs with Roland Hayes. In 1930 she made her European debut in Berlin. 1930–32, she gave 52 concerts in Scandinavia and again in 1933–34 (142 concerts); in 1934 she sang in Paris, London, Holland and Belgium; in 1934–35, made a tour of Poland, Russia, Latvia, Switzerland, Belgium, Austria, Hungary, Italy and Spain. From 1935–36 she toured America, giving a concert in Carnegie Hall on Jan. 30, 1936; another European tour followed including Vienna, Budapest and The Hague. From Jan. to May, 1938, she gave 70 concerts in the U.S. and South America, and again in Europe (1938–39). In Feb. 1939 Marian Anderson became a center of national attention when she was forbidden to sing at Constitution Hall in Washington. In protest against this case of racial discrimination, a distinguished group of citizens, headed by Mrs. Franklin D. Roosevelt, sponsored her concert at the Lincoln Memorial (April 9, 1939), which was attended by 75,000 persons. She was the first black American singer to be engaged as a permanent member of the Metropolitan Opera Co., making her debut as Ulrica in *The Masked Ball* (Jan. 7, 1955). She received the honorary degree of Mus. Doc. from Howard Univ., Washington, D.C. in June, 1938. On the occasion of her 75th birthday, in 1977, the resolution was passed by Congress to strike a gold medal in her honor.

BIBLIOGRAPHY: Kosti Vehanen, *Marian Anderson* (N.Y., 1941).

Anderson, Ruth, American composer of the avantgarde; b. Kalispell, Montana, March 21, 1928. She studied flute with Jean-Pierre Rampal; received her M.A. from the Univ. of Washington in Seattle; did post-graduate work at Columbia Univ. and Princeton; also took private lessons with Darius Milhaud; was associate prof. at Hunter College, N.Y., where she designed and installed the Hunter College Electronic Music Studio in 1970; also organized meditation workshops, and taught listening techniques; made use of human and artificial electronic sound for healing ailments. Her most successful composition in these fields is *Points* (1974) for multi-channel electronic sound built entirely on sine waves. She utilizes the collage technique in her work *SUM* (State of the Union Message), incorporating television commercials in a presidential address.

Anderson, T. J. (Thomas Jefferson), black American composer; b. Coatesville, Penn., Aug. 17, 1928. He graduated from West Virginia State College in 1950; received his M.Ed. from Penn. State Univ. in 1951, and his Ph.D. from the Univ. of Iowa in 1958; in the summer of 1964 he took lessons in composition with Milhaud at the Aspen School of Music. He taught at West Virginia State College (1955–56), Langston, Oklahoma, Univ. (1958–63), Tennessee State Univ. (1963–69), Morehouse College in Atlanta (1971–72); in 1972 he was appointed chairman of the music dept. of Tufts Univ. in Medford, Mass. He was chairman of the Advisory Board of the Black Music Center at the Univ. of Indiana (1969–71) and lecturer for the U.S. State Department in Brazilian universities (1976). He

played a major role in the revival of interest in the music of Scott Joplin, and orchestrated Joplin's opera *Tremonisha* for its production in Atlanta (Jan. 28, 1972). His own style of composition is audaciously modernistic, while preserving the basic tonal framework.

WORKS: *New Dances* for orch. (1960); *Trio Concertante* for orch. (1960); *Classical Symphony* (1961); *6 Pieces* for clarinet and chamber orch. (1962); Symph. in 3 Movements (1964; in memory of J. F. Kennedy); *Squares,* essay for orch. (1965); *Rotations* for symph. band (1967); *Chamber Symphony* (1968); *Intervals* for orch., in 7 sets (1970–71); *In Memoriam Malcolm X* for voice and orch. (1974); *Horizons '76* for soprano and orch. (1975; a U.S. Bicentennial Commission); *Fanfare* for solo trumpet and 4 mini wind bands (1976); *5 Bagatelles* for oboe, violin and harpsichord (1963); *5 Etudes and a Fancy* for wind quintet (1964); *Personals* for chorus and brass septet (1966); *Connections,* fantasy for string quintet (1966); *Variations on a Theme by M. B. Tolson* for soprano, violin, cello, saxophone, trumpet, trombone and piano (1969); *Transitions* for chamber ensemble (1971); *Block Songs* for voice and children's toys (1972); *Swing Set* for clarinet and piano (1972); *Beyond Silence* for chamber ensemble (1973); *5 Easy Pieces for Violin, Piano and Jew's Harp* (1974); *5 Portraitures of Two People* for piano, 4 hands (1965); *Watermelon* for piano (1971); an operetta, *The Shell Fairy* (1976).

Anderson, Thomas, English organist; b. Birmingham, April 15, 1836; d. there, Sept. 18, 1903. He served as organist in Birmingham churches; was also music critic there. He composed several cantatas: *The Song of Deborah and Barak; The Wise and Foolish Virgins; The Wreck of the Hesperus; John Gilpin; The Three Jovial Huntsmen; The Norman Baron; Yuletide; English Requiem;* and instrumental music.

Anderssén, Alfred, Finnish composer; b. Pietarsaari rural communal, Aug. 4, 1887; d. Turku (Åbo), Sept. 10, 1940. He studied in Helsinki and in Munich; settled in Turku as a music critic and was a conductor of the Swedish Theatre there (1927–40). In 1926 he married the singer Karin Limnell. He wrote an opera *Kohtalo (Destiny on Board)* (1928–32), 2 symphonies (1927, 1938), 15 cantatas, and many choral works.

d'Andrade, Francesco, Portuguese baritone; b. Lisbon, Jan. 11, 1859; d. Berlin, Feb. 8, 1921. He studied in Italy; made his debut in San Remo (1882); then lived in Berlin. He was well known as a successful singer in Europe; his most famous role was that of Don Giovanni.

Andrade, Mario de, Brazilian poet and writer on music; b. S. Paulo, Oct. 9, 1893; d. there, Feb. 25, 1945. He studied at S. Paulo Cons.; in 1935 he was appointed director of the S. Paulo Dept. of Culture. Andrade spent much time on special research and reconstruction of Brazilian folk songs and dances; he was also active as music critic. Among his publications are *Carlos Gomes* (Rio de Janeiro, 1939); *Musica do Brasil* (1941); *Pequeña Historia de Música* (1942).

BIBLIOGRAPHY: B. Kiefer, "Mário de Andrade e o

modernismo na música brasileira," *R. Bimestra Cubana* (Jan./March 1971).

André, Anton (Johann Anton), third son of **Johann André**; b. Offenbach, Oct. 6, 1775; d. there April 6, 1842. A precocious talent, he studied with Vollweiler in Mannheim (1793–96); was a fine pianist, violinist and composer before entering the Univ. of Jena; after completing his studies he made extensive travels, and on his father's death took charge of the business, adding particular lustre to its good name by the purchase (1800) of Mozart's entire musical remains. He publ. Mozart's autograph thematic catalogue, and supplemented it by a list of the works so acquired. By accepting the application of the lithographic process to music-engraving (1799), he took another long stride towards placing his firm in the front rank. He was also a composer (2 operas, symphonies, songs, etc.), a successful teacher, and a noteworthy theorist. He wrote 2 vols. on harmony, counterpoint, canon and fugue, (1832-43; new revised ed. 1875); and *Anleitung zum Violinspiele.* His sons were: (1) **Carl August,** b. Offenbach, June 15, 1806; d. Frankfurt, Feb. 15, 1887; head (from 1835) of the Franfurt branch opened in 1828, and founder of a piano factory ('Mozartflügel'); author of *Der Klavierbau und seine Geschichte* (1855). (2) **Julius,** b. Frankfurt, June 4, 1808; d. there, April 17, 1880; a fine organist and pianist, pupil of Aloys Schmitt (his grandfather's pupil), author of a *Praktische Orgelschule,* composer of several interesting organ compositions, and arranger of Mozart's works for piano, 4 hands. (3) **Johann August,** b. Offenbach, March 2, 1817; d. there, Oct. 29, 1887; his father's successor (1839) in the publishing establishment. His two sons, **Karl** (b. Aug. 24, 1853; d. June 29, 1914) and **Adolf** (b. April 10, 1885; d. Sept 10, 1910), succeeded to the business. (4) **Jean Baptiste** (*de St.-Gilles*), b. Offenbach, March 7, 1823; d. Frankfurt, Dec. 9, 1882; pianist, and composer of various pieces for piano and voice, was a pupil of A. Schmitt, Taubert (piano), and Kessler and Dehn (harmony); lived for years in Berlin; had the honorary title of 'Herzoglich Bernbergischer Hofkapellmeister.'

André, Franz, Belgian conductor; b. Brussels, June 10, 1893; d. there, Jan. 20, 1975. He studied violin with Eugène Isaÿe; in 1912 was violinist in the Blüthner Orch. in Berlin. Returning to Brussels in 1913, he became assistant to César Thomson at the Brussels Cons.; was mobilized and spent the years 1914–18 on the crucial front in the trenches at Ypres. After the war, he resumed his teaching of violin classes. In 1923 he joined the Radio Belgique, first as a violinist in the Radio Orch., and from 1930 as conductor. He trained the orchestra in difficult modern works which he insisted on reading *à livre ouvert* at rehearsals. He cultivated particularly the works of modern French and Belgian composers, but also conducted many Schoenberg works.

André, Johann, German composer, publisher, and father of a musical family; b. Offenbach, March 28, 1741; d. there, June 18, 1799. He founded (Sept. 1, 1774) at Offenbach a music publishing house under his name and had publ. 1,200 compositions by the time of his death. For seven years (1777–84) he was Kapellmeister of Döbblelin's Theater in Berlin. He was a prolific composer, author of 19 Singspiele and 14 miscellaneous scores for the stage, among them *Der Töpfer* (Hanau, Jan. 22, 1773) and *Der Liebhaber als Automat* (Berlin, Sept. 11, 1782). Bretzner wrote the libretto of *Die Entführung aus dem Serail,* or *Belmont und Constanze* for him; the opera was produced in Berlin, May 25, 1781. The same text was used the following year by Mozart for his celebrated work, which elicited Bretzner's haughty protest against "a certain man named Mozart" for the unauthorized use of his libretto. Among André's songs, the *Rheinweinlied* ('Bekränzt mit Laub') was widely performed. André is credited with being the composer of the first 'durchkomponierte Ballade,' *Die Weiber von Weinsberg* (1783).

Andreae, Volkmar, Swiss conductor and composer; b. Bern, July 5, 1879; d. Zürich, June 18, 1962. He studied music with Karl Munzinger in Bern and later with Wüllner at the Cologne Cons. In 1901 he decided to devote himself mainly to conducting; was assistant conductor at the Munich Opera; in 1902 he went to Zürich where he conducted the Municipal Chorus until 1949; at the same time he also led the orchestra of the Tonhalle-Gesellschaft. In 1914 he was appointed director of the Zürich Cons., a post he held until 1939. In 1949 he retired but continued to teach private lessons. He distinguished himself particularly by his performances of oratorios and became known as one of the best conductors of Bruckner's choral works. In his compositions Andreae reflects the post-romantic tendencies of German music.

WORKS: 2 operas: *Ratcliff* (Duisburg, May 25, 1914), and *Abenteuer des Casanova* (Dresden, June 17, 1924); several choral works: *Der Göttliche, Charons Nachen, Magentalied,* etc.; 2 symphonies; a violin concerto; a concertino for oboe and orch.; 8 Chinese songs, *Li-Tai-Po;* 2 string quartets; 2 piano trios; a string trio; a violin sonata; piano pieces.

BIBLIOGRAPHY: F. Seiler, *Dr. Volkmar Andreae ... zum Juviläum seiner 25 jährigen Tätigkeit* (Zürich, 1931); R. Schoch, *Hundert Jahre Tonhalle Zürich* (Zürich, 1968).

Andrée, Elfrida, Swedish organist and composer; b. Visby, Feb. 19, 1841; d. Stockholm, Jan. 11, 1929. She studied at the Stockholm Cons. and with Gade in Copenhagen; at the same time studied telegraphy, and was the first woman telegrapher in Sweden. In 1867 she obtained the post of organist at the Göteborg Cathedral. She established a series of popular concerts, and presented about 800 programs. She was a member of the Swedish Academy of Music. A pioneer among women musicians, she was the first Swedish woman to write an organ symphony, and wrote a Swedish Mass, which had frequent performances, and chamber music.

Andreis, Josip, Croatian music historian; b. Split, March 19, 1909. He studied philology in Zagreb and Rome, and later composition in Zagreb and Split. In 1941 he was appointed Professor of Music History at the Music Academy in Zagreb. His most important lexicographical work is an encyclopedia of music in the Croatian language, issued in 2 volumes in Zagreb (1958–63); he further published a 3-volume edition of music history, also in the Croatian language (Zagreb, 1951–54; second edition 1966). He is the author of a valuable pamphlet in English, *Yugoslav Music* (Belgrade, 1959), a monograph on the Yugoslav composer Gotovac (Split, 1957), and numerous musicological articles in various journals.

Andrevi, Francisco, prominent Spanish church composer; b. Sanahuja, near Lérida, Nov. 16, 1786; d. Barcelona, Nov. 23, 1853. He started as choir boy, and from his earliest years devoted himself to the study of church music. At the age of 22 he became director of music at the Cathedral of Segorbe; then held similar posts at the churches at Barcelona, Valencia and Seville. During the civil war in Spain he was in Bordeaux (1832–42); later in Paris (1845–49), where he published his *Traité d'Harmonie et de Composition* (1848); in the same year it was also published in Spanish. Andrevi returned to Barcelona in 1849. He wrote a sacred drama *Juicio universal*; also much choral music, most of which is in MS; two of his sacred choruses *(Nunc dimittis* and *Salve regina)* are included in Eslava's *Lira Sacra-Hispana.*

Andricu, Mihail, Rumanian composer; b. Bucharest, Jan. 4, 1895; d. there, Feb. 4, 1974. He studied at the Bucharest Cons. (1903–09); later became a teacher there (1926–59). For many years he was an accompanist for Georges Enesco.
    WORKS: the ballets, *Cenuşăreasa (Cinderella,* 1929), *Taina (The Secret,* 1933; Bucharest, Feb. 8, 1936) and *Luceafărul (The Planet Venus;* Bucharest, Sept. 24, 1951). His orch. works include 11 symphonies: No. 1 (1944); No. 2 (1947); No. 3 (1950); No. 4 (1954); No. 5 (1955); No. 6 (1957); No. 7 (1958); No. 8 (1960); No. 9 (1962); No. 10 (1968); No. 11, *In Memoriam* (1970); 3 chamber symphonies (1927, 1961, 1965); 11 sinfoniettas (1945–71); 9 suites (1924–58); *Poem* for piano and orch. (1923); *3 Symphonic Pictures* (1925); *Serenade* (1928); 2 sets of *3 Symphonic Sketches* (1936, 1951); *Fantezie* for piano and orch. (1940); *3 Symphonic Pieces* (1950); *Rapsodie* (1952); Violin Concerto (1960); Cello Concerto (1961); *6 Portraits* (1969); *Evocation* (1971); *Miniatures and Images* (1971). He also wrote *4 Novelettes* for piano quartet (1925); Octet (1928); String Quartet (1931); Piano Sextet (1932); 2 piano quintets (1938, 1956); Violin Sonata (1941); Sonata for Piano, 4 hands (1946); Piano Sonata (1949); *3 Pieces* for piano and winds (1964); choral pieces and songs. A detailed list of his works, with exact dates of their first performances is given in Viorel Cosma's *Muzicieni Romani Lexicon* (Bucharest, 1970).

Andries, Jean, Belgian musician; b. Ghent, April 25, 1798; d. there, Jan. 21, 1872. He played violin in a local theater from 1813 till 1848, at the same time taught at the Ghent Cons.; in 1851 became director, retiring in 1859. He published the following treatises: *Aperçu historique de tous les instruments de musique actuellement en usage* (1856); *Précis de l'histoire de la musique depuis les temps les plus reculés* (1862); *Instru-*

ments à vent: La Flûte (1866); *Remarques sur les cloches et les carillons* (1868).

Andriessen, Hendrik, Significant Dutch organist and composer, brother of **Willem Andriessen;** b. Haarlem, Sept. 17, 1892. He studied with his brother; then with Louis Robert and J. B. de Pauw (piano and organ) and Bernard Zweers (composition) at the Amsterdam Cons. (1914–16); later taught harmony there (1928–34). He succeeded his father as organist at St. Joseph's Church in Haarlem (1916–34); was then organist at Utrecht Cathedral (1934–49) while serving as director of the Utrecht Cons. (1937–49). He was director of the Royal Cons. in The Hague (1949–57) and special professor at the Catholic Univ. in Nijmegen (1952–63). His own music is romantically inspired; some of his instrumental works make use of modern devices, including melodic atonality and triadic polytonality.
    WORKS: 2 OPERAS: *Philomela* (Holland Festival, June 23, 1950), and *De Spiegel uit Venetië (The Mirror from Venice,* 1964; Dutch Television, Oct. 5, 1967). FOR ORCH.: 4 symphonies (1930, 1937, 1946, 1954); *Variations and Fugue on a Theme of Kuhnau* for string orch. (1935); *Capriccio* (1941); *Variations on a Theme of Couperin* for flute, harp and strings (1944); *Ballet Suite* (1947); *Ricercare* (1949); *Wilhemus van Nassouwe,* rhapsody (1950); Organ Concerto (1950); *Symphonic Etude* (1952; The Hague, Oct. 15, 1952); *Libertas venit,* rhapsody (1954); *Mascherata,* fantasy (1962); *Symphonie Concertante* (1962); Violin Concerto (1968–69); Concertino for Oboe and String Orch. (1969–70); Concertino for Cello and Orch. (1970); *Chromatic Variations* for flute, oboe, violin, cello and strings (1970); *Canzone* (1971); *Chantecler,* overture (1972). CHAMBER MUSIC: Cello Sonata (1926); Violin Sonata (1932); *3 Inventions* for violin and cello (1937); Piano Trio (1939); Suite for Violin and Piano (1950); Solo Cello Sonata (1951); Suite for Brass Quintet (1951); Wind Quintet (1951); Ballade for Oboe and Piano (1952); Theme and Variations for Flute, Oboe and Piano (1953); *Quartetto in stile antico,* String Quartet (1957); *Il peniero,* string quartet (1961); *Pezzo festoso* for organ, 2 trumpets and 2 trombones (1962); *Canzonetta* for harpsichord (1963); *Canzone, Trio No. 2* for flute, oboe and piano (1965); Viola Sonata (1967); *Concert spirituelle* for flute, oboe, violin and cello (1967); *Haydn Variations* for English horn and piano (1968); *L'Indifférent,* string quartet (1969); Clarinet Sonata (1971); *Choral Varié* for 3 trumpets and 3 trombones (1973). SOLO SONG CYCLES, MOST WITH ORGAN OR ORCH.: *L'Aube spirituelle* (1916); *L'Invitation au voyage* (1918); *Magna res est amor* (1919); *L'Attente mystique* (1920); *Miroir de peine* (1923); *Cantique spirituel* (1924); *La Vièrge à Midi* (1966). CHORAL WORKS: *Missa Simplex,* a cappella (1927); *Missa Sponsa Christi* for male chorus with organ (1933); *Missa Christus Rex* for double chorus with organ (1938); 2 Madrigals with Strings (1940); *Te Deum Laudamus I,* with organ or orch. (1943–46) and *II,* with orch. (1968); *De Zee en het land (Declamatorium),* with speaker and orch. (1953); *Veni Creator,* with orch. (1960); *Psalm IX,* with tenor and orch. (1968); *Lux Jocunda,* with tenor or orch. (1968); *Carmen Saeculare (Horatius),* with soprano, tenor, winds, harpsi-

chord and double bass (1968). FOR ORGAN: 4 Chorales (1913, c.1918, 1920, 1952), Toccata (1917), *Fête-Dieu* (1918), *Sonata de Chiesa* (1927), Passacaglia (1929), *Sinfonia* (1940), *Intermezzi* (1943), Theme and Variations (1949), 4 Studies (1953). FOR PIANO: 2 sonatas (1934, 1966), Pavane (1937), Serenade (1950).

BIBLIOGRAPHY: J. Wouters, *Negen portretten van Nederlandse componisten* (Amsterdam, 1971).

Andriessen, Jurriaan, Dutch composer, son of **Hendrik Andriessen;** b. Haarlem, Nov. 15, 1925. He studied theory with his father; took lessons in conducting with Willem van Otterloo at the Utrecht Cons. After graduating in 1947, he went to Paris to study film music; a Rockefeller Foundation Fellowship enabled him to come to the U.S., where he studied composition with Copland at the Berkshire Center, Tanglewood, during the summers of 1949 and 1950. Returning to Holland, he was active mainly as music consultant on the national radio and television.

WORKS: He wrote the first television opera, *Kalchas,* to be produced in Holland (June 28, 1959); an opera buffa, *Het Zwarte Blondje (The Black Blonde)* (1964); Piano Concertino (1943); Concerto for 2 Pianos Alone (1944); *Hommage à Milhaud* for 11 instruments (1945; also for flute and string quartet, 1948); Violin Sonata (1946); *Symphonietta Concertante* for 4 trumpets and orch. (1947); Piano Concerto (1948); *Het wonderlijk uur (The Strange Hour),* Suite No. 1 for orch. (1948); *Octet Divertissement* for winds (1948); 5 symphonies: No. 1, *Berkshire Symphonies* (1949; produced as a ballet under the title *Jones Beach,* in New York, March 12, 1950); No. 2 for wind orch. (1962); No. 3, *Symphonyen fan Fryslàn* (1963); No. 4, *Aves (The Birds),* after Aristophanes, with chorus (1963); No. 5, *Time Spirit,* after M. C. Escher's prints, for clarinet, wind orch., pop group and 6 dancers (Rotterdam, Nov. 19, 1970); *Magnificat* for soprano, chorus and orch. (1950); Flute Concerto (1951); *Les Otaries (The Seals),* classic ballet fantasy (1951); *Cymbeline,* overture (1954); *Rouw past Electra (Mourning Becomes Electra),* suite for 11 winds and percussion (1954); 2 piano sonatas; 5 trios: No. 1 for flute, oboe and piano (1955); No. 2 for flute, viola and piano (1955); No. 3 for 3 recorders (1957); No. 4 for flute, oboe and bassoon (1957) and No. 5, *Sonata da Camera,* for flute, viola and guitar (1959); *L'incontro di Cesare e Cleopatra,* sextet for winds and piano (1956); *Astrazione* for piano (1957); *Inno della Tecnica,* introduction and scherzo for orch. (1957); *Ritratto di una città (Ouverture Den Haag)* (1957); *Duo* for 2 violins (1958); *Balocco* for solo oboe (1960); *Thai,* symph. rhapsody based on jazz tunes by King Phumiphon Aduldet of Thailand, written for a special performance during the King's visit in the Netherlands (The Hague, Oct. 25, 1960); Concertino for Bassoon and Winds (1962); *Fantasy* for piano, 4 hands (1962); *Respiration,* suite for double wind quintet (1962); *Sciarada Spagnuola* for wind quintet (1962); *Movimenti I,* for trumpet, horn, trombone, strings and timpani (1965), *II,* for oboe, clarinet, bassoon, strings and percussion (1972) and *III,* for violin, viola, cello, winds and percussion (1974); Trio for Clarinet, Cello and Piano (1965); *Concerto Rotterdam* for jazz combo and orch. (Rotterdam, June 20, 1966); *Entrata festiva* for brass and timpani (1966); *Antifono e Fusione* for wind quintet, brass quartet and timpani (1966); *In Pompa Magna* for brass and percussion (1966); *Summer-Dances* for 7 percussionists, harp and guitar (1966); *Les bransles erotiques,* pantomime of the 16th century, for 8 performers (1967); *Contra-Bande,* a "rapsodia interrotta" for Sousaphone and orch. (1967); *Il divorcio di Figaro,* variations for amateur orch. (1967); *Omaggio à Sweelinck* for harpsichord and 24 strings (1968); *Trelleborg Concerto* for harpsichord and 3 orch. groups (Amsterdam, Sept. 27, 1969); *Antifona dell'Aja* for orch. (1969); *Beestenkwartet (Animal Quartet)* for amateur orch. (1972); *Een Prince van Oraengien (Wilhelmus-Phantasy)* for chorus and orch. (1973); *Pasticcio-Finale* for orch., dixieland band and tape (1974); *Quartetto Buffo* for clarinet and string trio (1974); incidental music for over 60 plays.

BIBLIOGRAPHY: W. Paap, "Jurriaan Andriessen and Incidental Music," *Sonorum Speculum* (Autumn 1969).

Andriessen, Louis, Dutch composer, son of **Hendrik Andriessen;** b. Utrecht, June 6, 1939. He first studied with his father and with Kees van Baaren at the Royal Cons. in The Hague (1957–62); also took lessons with Luciano Berio in Milan (1962–63). He was a co-founder of a Charles Ives Society in Amsterdam. His works are conceived in an advanced idiom.

WORKS: Flute Sonata (1956); *Séries* for 2 pianos (1958); *Percosse* for flute, trumpet, bassoon and percussion (1958); *Nocturnes* for Soprano and Chamber Orch. (1959); *Aanloop en sprongen* for flute, oboe and clarinet (1961); *Ittrospezione I,* for 2 pianos (1961); *II,* for orch. (1963) and *III,* for 2 pianos, and chamber ensemble or saxophone (1964); *A Flower Song I,* for solo violin (1963), *II,* for solo oboe (1963) and *III,* for solo cello (1964); *Sweet* for recorder or flute (1964); *Double* for clarinet and piano (1965); *Paintings* for recorder or flute, and piano (1965); *Souvenirs d'enfance* for piano and tape (1966); *Anachronie I,* to the memory of Charles Ives, for orch. (1965–55; Rotterdam, Jan. 18, 1968) and *II,* for solo oboe, 4 horns, piano, harp and string orch. (1969); *Contra-tempus* for 23 musicians (1968); the anti-imperialist collective opera, *Reconstructie* (1968–69; Holland Festival, June 29, 1969; in collaboration with Reinbert de Leeuw, Misha Mengelberg, Peter Schat and Jan van Vlijmen); *Hoe het is (What It's Like)* for live-electronic improvisers and 52 strings (Rotterdam, Sept. 14, 1970); *Spektakel (Uproar)* for 16 winds, 6 percussionists and electronic instruments (1970); *The Nine Symphonies of Beethoven* for promenade orch. and ice cream bell (1970); *De Volharding (The Persistence)* for piano and winds (1972); *On Jimmy Yancey* for chamber ensemble (1973); *Il Principe,* after Machiavelli, for 2 choirs, winds, piano and bass guitar (1974); *Symphonieën der Nederlanden* for brass band (1974).

Andriessen, Willem, Dutch pianist and composer, brother of **Hendrik Andriessen;** b. Haarlem, Oct. 25, 1887; d. Amsterdam, March 29, 1964. He studied piano and composition at the Amsterdam Cons. (1903–08); taught piano at The Hague Cons. (1910–17) and at the Rotterdam Cons.; from 1937 to 1953 was director of the Amsterdam Cons. He was a professional pianist of a high caliber. He wrote a Piano Concerto (1908); *3 Songs* for voice and orch. (1911); *Hei, 't was de Mei*, scherzo for orch. (1912); Piano Sonata (1938); Piano Sonatina (1945).

Anerio, Felice, Italian composer; brother of **Giovanni Francesco Anerio;** b. Rome, c.1560; d. there, Sept. 27, 1614. He studied with G. M. Manni; was a chorister at Santa Maria Maggiore in Rome (1568–75); then sang at St. Peter's under Palestrina (from May, 1575 to March, 1579). In 1584 he became maestro di cappella of the English College in Rome. After Palestrina's death, Anerio was appointed by Clement VIII to succeed him as composer to the Papal Chapel (April 3, 1594). His eminence as composer is best attested by the fact that several of his compositions were for a long time supposed to be Palestrina's own. Besides MSS in Roman libraries, many of Anerio's works are extant in printed collections. They include: *Madrigali spirituali a 5* (1585, reprinted 1598); *Canzonette a 4* (1586, reprinted 1603, 1607); *Madrigali a 5* (1587); *Madrigali a 6,* book I (1590, reprinted 1599); *Concerti spirituali a 4* (1593); *Sacri hymni e cantica a 8,* book I (1596); *Madrigali a 3* (1598); *Madrigali a 6,* book II (1602); *Responsorii per la Settimana Santa a 4* (1602); *Sacri hymni e cantica a 8,* book II (1602) and *Responsoria a 4* (1606).

BIBLIOGRAPHY: L. Torri, "Nei parentali di Felice Anerio," *Rivista Musicale Italiana* (1914): A. Cametti, "Nuovi contributi alle biografie de Felice Anerio," *Rivista Musicale Italiana* (1915).

Anerio, Giovanni Francesco, Italian composer; younger brother of **Felice Anerio;** b. Rome, c.1567; d. June, 1630, on his way from Poland to Italy (buried in Graz, June 12, 1630). He was a chorister at St. Peter's (1575–79) and sang with his brother under Palestrina; later he became maestro di cappella at the Lateran Church (1600–1603). He was at the court of King Sigismund III of Poland in Cracow (1607); in 1608 he returned to Rome; then became choirmaster at Verona cathedral (1609); at the Seminario Romano (1611–12) and at the Jesuit church of S. Maria dei Monti in Rome (1613–20). He became a priest in 1616; visited Treviso (near Venice) in 1624. He was a prolific composer in all forms of sacred music; many of his works were printed by leading Italian publishers. He also arranged Palestrina's 6-part *Missa Papae Marcelli* for 4 voices (Rome, 1600).

BIBLIOGRAPHY: G. Liberali, "Giovanni Francesco Aneria," *Note d'Archivio* (Dec. 1940).

Anet, Baptiste (actually **Jean-Baptiste**), French violinist, son of **Jean-Baptiste Anet,** *père;* b. Paris, and was baptized on Jan. 2, 1676; d. Lunéville, Aug. 14, 1755. He was a pupil of Corelli in Rome; upon return to France he was a member of the Royal Chapel in Paris; in 1736 he went to Lunéville as court musician to the former Polish King Stanislas Leszczynski. He published 3 sets of sonatas for violin with basso continuo (1729) and 3 collections of duets for musettes (1726, 1730, 1734).

BIBLIOGRAPHY: L. de La Laurencie, *L'École française de violon* (vol. 1, Paris, 1922).

Anet, Jean-Baptiste, *père,* French violinist; b. about 1651; d. Paris, April 28, 1710. He was known as a teacher beginning 1673; in 1699 he became a member of the 24 Violons du Roi. He was the father of another **Jean-Baptiste Anet,** who was known simply as Baptiste.

Anfossi, Pasquale, prolific Italian opera composer; b. Taggia, near Naples, April 25, 1727; d. Rome, Feb., 1797. Originally a violinist, he studied composition under Piccinni, and brought out two unsuccessful operas, but with his third opera, *L'incognita perseguitata* (Rome, 1773) won popular approval. This opera was written on the same subject as Piccinni's previously staged opera and Anfossi had a greater success, backed by a powerful clique hostile to Piccinni. Anfossi then proceeded to bring out opera after opera. He wrote 76, which were successful in Rome for a time; later he sought new fields: in Paris (1779), London (1781–83, as director of the Italian Opera), then in Prague, Dresden and Berlin. Returning to Italy in 1784 he was appointed maestro di cappella at the Lateran in 1791, and turned his attention to sacred composition (12 oratorios, Masses, psalms, etc.). Mozart wrote two arias for use in Anfossi's opera *Il curioso indiscreto* (Vienna, 1783) and for *Le Gelosie fortunate* (Vienna, 1788).

Angeles, Victoria de Los (real name **Victoria Gómez Cima**), famous Spanish soprano singer; b. Barcelona, Nov. 1, 1923. She studied at the Barcelona Cons.; made her debut in 1945. After appearances in concerts she sang the role of Marguerite in Gounod's *Faust* at the Paris Opéra in 1949; made her American debut at the Metropolitan Opera in New York again as Marguerite on March 17, 1951, and sang soprano roles (among them, Mimi, Cio-Cio-San and Mélisande) during her three seasons with the Metropolitan (1951–54); was engaged there again in 1957–58 and 1961. From 1949 to 1957 she made guest appearances at La Scala, Milan, at Covent Garden in London and at the Vienna Opera; in 1961–62 she sang Elisabeth in *Tannhäuser* at the Bayreuth Festival. She made concert tours all over the world. On Nov. 28, 1948 she married Enrique Magrina Mir.

d'Angeli, Andrea, Italian composer and writer on music; b. Padua, Nov. 9, 1868; d. S. Michele, near Verona, Oct. 28, 1940. He studied at the Univ. of Padua; then was instructor at the Liceo Rossini in Pesaro. He wrote several operas: *L'Innocente; Il Negromante; Al Ridotto di Venezia; Fiori e Colombi; Maurizio e Lazzaro;* also a number of libretti. He published monographs on Verdi (Milan, 1924) and Benedetto Marcello (Milan, 1930), and numerous essays on music in *La Cronaca Musicale* of which he was editor (1907–14).

Angelini, Bontempi Giovanni Andrea. See **Bontempi, Giovanni Andrea.**

d'Angelo, Louis, Italian baritone singer; b. Naples, May 6, 1888; d. Jersey City, N.J., Aug. 9, 1958. He was brought to the U.S. as a child, and was first apprenticed as a glove cutter in Gloversville, New York; then sang in a local church choir. He went to New York at the age of 18 and appeared in vaudeville; in 1917 he joined the staff of the Metropolitan Opera, retiring in 1946. He had more than 300 operatic roles in his repertoire and was particularly successful in his interpretation of Bartolo in *The Barber of Seville*.

Angeloni, Carlo, Italian composer; b. Lucca, July 16, 1834; d. there, Jan. 13, 1901. He wrote a number of operas, several of which were performed in Lucca: *Carlo di Viana* (1855); *Asraele degli Abenceragi* (1871); *Dramma in montagna* (posthumous, 1902).
BIBLIOGRAPHY: L. Landucci, *Carlo Angeloni* (Lucca, 1905).

Angeloni, Luigi, Italian writer on music; b. Frosione, Papal States, 1759; d. London, Feb. 5, 1842. He wrote a valuable monograph, *Sopra la vita, le opera ed il sapere di Guido d'Arezzo, restauratore della scienza e dell'arte musica* (Paris, 1811).

Angerer, Paul, Austrian conductor and composer; b. Vienna, May 16, 1927. He studied violin, piano and composition in Vienna; played viola in the Vienna Symphony Orch. (1953–57). He then devoted himself to conducting; was theater conductor in Bonn (1964–66) and Ulm (1966–68); in 1968 was appointed opera conductor at the Landestheater in Salzburg. He has written a number of instrumental works in the Baroque manner, and theater pieces, often of a humorous type.
WORKS: His television opera *Passkontrolle* received first prize at an opera competition in Salzburg (1959); he also wrote a musical, *Hotel Comédie* (Salzburg, 1970). Other works include: Quartet for Oboe, Horn, Viola and Cello (1951); *Serenata* for violin, viola, horn and bassoon (1951); Trio for Recorder, Viola d'amore and Lute (1953); *Musica examinata* for cello and piano (1953); *Agamemnon muss sterben*, dramatic cantata (1954); *Musica ad impulsum et pulsum* for strings and percussion (1955); *Musica fera* (*Feral Music,* for orch. 1956); *Concerto pour la jeunesse* for orch. (1956); *Gloriatio* for double bass and chamber orch. (1957); Concerto for Piano and String Orch. (1962); Viola Concerto (1962); *Chanson gaillarde* for oboe, cello and harpsichord (1963); *Cogitatio* for wind quintet and strings (1964).

d'Anglebert, Jean-Henri, French clavecin player; b. Paris, probably in 1628; d. there, April 23, 1691. He studied with Champion de Chambonnières; in 1664 he succeeded his teacher as clavecinist to Louis XIV. In 1689 he published a collection, *Pièces de clavecin avec la manière de les jouer,* containing original suites, arrangements of airs from Lully's operas and also 22 variations on *Folies d'Espagne* (the theme later used by Corelli); the same volume contains instruction on figured bass. D'Anglebert contributed greatly to the establishment of the French method of performance on the clavecin. His extant compositions were published in 1934 by Marguerite Roesgen-Champion in *Publications de la Société Française de Musicologie,* also containing biographical information. His son **Jean-Baptiste Henri** (b. Paris, Sept. 5, 1661; d. there, March 9, 1747) succeeded his father as court musician.

BIBLIOGRAPHY: Ch. Bouvet, "Les Deux d'Anglebert," *La Revue de Musicologie* (May 1928).

Anglès, Higini (Catalan form; in Spanish, **Higinio Anglés**), distinguished musicologist; b. Maspujols, Catalonia, Jan. 1, 1888; d. Rome, Dec. 8, 1969. He studied philosophy at Tarragona (1900–13); musicology with Felipe Pedrell and composition with V. M. Gibert in Barcelona (1913–19). In 1917 he became head of the Music Dept. of the Barcelona library. In 1923 he went to Germany and studied with W. Gurlitt at Freiburg and F. Ludwig at Göttingen. In 1924 he returned to Barcelona and in 1927, became prof. of music history at the Cons. With the outbreak of the Spanish Civil War in 1936, he went to Munich; returned to Barcelona in 1939. In 1943 he was appointed director of the Instituto Español de Musicologia; in 1947 he became director of the Pontifical Institute of Sacred Music in Rome. His most important publication is *El Códex Musical de Las Huelgas* (3 vols., 1928–31), containing facsimiles and transcriptions of Spanish music of the 13th and 14th centuries. Part of the text of this edition was published in the *Musical Quarterly* (Oct. 1940). He has published the following books: *Cantigas del Rei N'Anfos el Savi* (Barcelona, 1927); *Historia de la musica española* (Barcelona, 1935); *La música a Catalunya fins al segle XIII* (Barcelona, 1935); *La música española desde la edad media hasta nuestros dias* (Barcelona, 1941), and many smaller works. He edited the collected works of J. Pujol (1925); the organ works of Cabanilles (1926); *La Música en la Corte de los Reyes Católicos* (2 vols.; Madrid, 1941, Barcelona, 1947); *Recopilación de Sonetos,* etc. by Juan Vásquez (Barcelona, 1946); *El cancionero musical de Palacio* (Barcelona, 1947). Anglès has contributed to many music journals and has written articles on Spanish music for *Die Musik in Geschichte und Gegenwart.* He is regarded as an outstanding expert on Spanish music of the Middle Ages.

Anglès, Rafael, Spanish organist and composer; b. Rafales (Teruel), 1731; d. Valencia, Feb. 19, 1816; was organist at Valencia Cathedral from 1762–72. He devoted his life to liturgical music; also wrote keyboard pieces, four of which are printed by J. Nín in his collection, *17 Sonates et pièces anciennes d'auteurs espagnols* (Paris, 1929).

Anhalt, István, Hungarian-born Canadian composer; b. Budapest, April 12, 1919. He studied with Kodály at the Budapest Academy (1937–41); took lessons in Paris with Nadia Boulanger (1946–48). He came to Canada in 1949, settling in Montreal; was appointed to the faculty of music at McGill Univ., where he founded the electronic music studio in 1963. In 1971 he became head of the music department of Queen's Univ. at Kingston, Ontario. His music reflects serial procedures; in his works of a later period he applies electronic techniques and speech-sounds.
WORKS: *Concerto in stilo di Handel* for 2 oboes, 2 horns and strings (1946); *Interludium* for strings, piano and timpani (1950); *Arc en Ciel,* ballet for 2 pianos (1951); Piano Sonata (1951); *Funeral Music* for chamber ensemble (1951); Piano Trio (1953); *Fantasia* for piano (1954); Violin Sonata (1954); *Comments* for

alto and piano trio (1954); *3 Songs of Death* for a cappella chorus (1954); *Chansons d'Aurore* for soprano, flute and piano (1955); Symphony (1954–58); 4 *Electronic Compositions* (1959, 1959, 1960, 1962); *Symphony of Modules* for chorus, orch. and tape (1967); *Cento (Cantata Urbana)* for 12-part chorus and tape (1967); *Foci* for soprano, 10 instrumentalists, off-stage percussionist and tape (1969); *La Tourangelle* for 3 sopranos, tenor, bass, chamber ensemble and tape (1972–74; Toronto, July 17, 1975).

Animuccia, Giovanni, Italian composer of sacred music; b. Florence, c.1514; d. Rome, March 25, 1571. In 1555 he was appointed maestro di cappella at St. Peter's as successor to Palestrina (who returned to that post after Animuccia's death in 1571). He worked with Filippo Neri for whom he composed his *Laudi spirituali* (2 vols.; publ. 1563 and 1570), which were performed by Neri in his "oratorium." These are contrapuntal hymn-like songs of praise, rather than forerunners of true oratorio. Other published works are 4 books of madrigals (1547, 1551, 1554, 1565); a book of Masses (1567) and a book of Magnificats (1568). Animuccia's compositions mark a gradual emancipation from the involved formalism of the Flemish School in the direction of a more practical style, which approached that of Palestrina. Animuccia possessed a great skill in polyphony, demonstrated especially in his ingenious canonic writing.
BIBLIOGRAPHY: L. Cervelli, "Le Laudi spirituali di Giovanni Animuccia," *Rassegna Musicale* (1950); Gustave Reese, *Music in the Renaissance* (N.Y., 1954; pp. 453–55).

Anka, Paul, popular Canadian singer and composer; b. Ottawa, July 30, 1941, of Syrian parentage. He began improvising songs as a child; at the age of 15 he recorded his song *Diana*, to his own lyrics, and it became a substantial hit. He then embarked on a highly successful career as a ballad singer; acquired considerable musical ability, and wrote some 300 songs. In 1962 he incorporated himself to manage his growing fortune. He had his nose remodeled in 1958 for television appearances. He married Anne de Zogheb on Feb. 16, 1963.

Anna Amalia, Princess of Prussia, sister of Frederick the Great; b. Berlin, Nov. 9, 1723; d. there, Sept. 30, 1787. She received her general musical training from her brother; then studied with the cathedral organist, Gottlieb Hayne, and with Joh. Ph. Kirnberger. She wrote music to Ramler's *Tod Jesu* which was later set also by Graun; she also composed some instrumental works and many chorales. Her sonata for flute, a trio sonata and 4 military marches have been published. She assembled a great library of manuscripts, including some of Bach; a catalogue was published by Eitner (Berlin, 1884).

Anna Amalia, Duchess of Saxe-Weimar; b. Wolfenbüttel, Oct. 24, 1739; d. Weimar, April 10, 1807. She was the mother of the Grand Duke Charles Augustus, who was Goethe's protector. Goethe supplied her with a libretto for *Erwin und Elmire,* a Singspiel; first performed at the Weimar Court (May 24, 1776), it had

numerous revivals. Max Friedländer publ. its vocal score in 1921. She also wrote some instrumental music (*Divertimento* for piano, clarinet, viola and cello, etc.).
BIBLIOGRAPHY: W. Bode, *Amalie, Herzogin von Weimar* (3 vols. Berlin, 1908); O. Heuschele, *Herzogin Anna Amalia* (Munich, 1947).

Annibale (Il Padovano, from his birthplace, Padua), Italian organist and composer; b. Padua, c.1527; d. Graz, March 15, 1575. He was organist at San Marco, (1552–66); from 1566 Kapellmeister ('Obrister Musicus') to the Archduke Carl at Graz.
WORKS: a book of Ricercari *a* 4 (1556; modern ed. by N. Pierront and J. P. Hennebains, 1934); a book of madrigals *a* 5 (1564); a book of motets *a* 5–6 (1567); a book of Masses *a* 5 (1573); a book of *Toccate e Ricercari* for organ (1604). Two *Ricercari* for organ are reprinted in vol. III of Torchi's *L'Arte musicale in Italia.*
BIBLIOGRAPHY: G. del Valle de Paz, *Annibale Il Padovano, nella storia della musica del cinquecento* (Turin, 1933; contains complete bibliography and musical examples).

Anrooy (properly Anrooij), Peter van, Dutch conductor and composer; b. Zalt-Boomel, Oct. 13, 1879; d. in The Hague, Dec. 31, 1954. He studied with Johan Wagenaar in Utrecht; in 1899 he went to Moscow where he studied violin and conducting with Willem Kes and Taneyev. He played the violin in the orchestras of Glasgow and Zürich (1902), then was active as conductor in Groningen (1905), Arnhem (1910), and in 1917 became conductor of the Residentie Orch. at The Hague, retiring in 1935. He wrote an orchestral rhapsody on Dutch themes, *Piet Hein* (1901); Ballade for Violin and Orch. (1902); several pieces of chamber music.

Anschütz, Johann Andreas, German musician; father of **Karl Anschütz;** b. Koblenz, March 19, 1772; d. there, Dec. 26, 1856. In 1808 he founded a school for vocal music at Koblenz. He was a lawyer by profession, but was also a pianist and conductor, and composed numerous vocal works.

Anschütz, Karl, German conductor; son of **Johann Andreas Anschütz;** b. Koblenz, Feb., 1815; d. New York, Dec. 30, 1870. He studied with Friedrich Schneider. In 1844 he assumed the directorship of the music school founded by his father, in 1848 went to London (where he conducted the Wednesday Concerts for a time). In 1857 he went to America and settled in New York as opera conductor. He was a cultivated musician; apart from his activity as conductor he published several piano pieces.

Ansermet, Ernest, celebrated Swiss conductor; b. Vevey, Nov. 11, 1883; d. Geneva, Feb. 20, 1969. He studied mathematics with his father who was a school teacher, and received his musical training from his mother. He became himself a mathematics teacher, and taught school in Lausanne (1906–10). At the same time he took courses in music with Denéréaz, Barblan and Ernest Bloch. He also studied conducting with Mottl in Munich and with Nikisch in Berlin. From then on he devoted himself mainly to conducting. He led the summer concerts in Montreux (1912–14), and from 1915 to 1918 was conductor of the regular symphony concerts in Geneva. In 1918 he organized the prestigious Orchestre de la Suisse Romande in Geneva, at which he performed a great deal of modern French and Russian music. He met Stravinsky who introduced him to Diaghilev, and subsequently conducted Diaghilev's Ballet Russe. On Sept. 28, 1918 he presented in Lausanne the first performance of Stravinsky's *L'Histoire du soldat*. He made numerous guest appearances as conductor with the Ballet Russe in Paris, London, Italy, Spain, South America and the U.S., and also conducted performances with major American symphony orchestras, attaining the reputation of a scholarly and progressive musician capable of fine interpretations of both classical and modern works. He himself composed a symphonic poem, *Feuilles de printemps*, orchestrated Debussy's *6 epigraphes antiques*, and 2 Argentinian dances by Julian Aguirre. He published *Le Geste du chef d'orchestre* (Lausanne, 1943) and *Les Fondements de la musique dans la conscience humaine* (2 vols.; Neuchâtel, 1961), making use of mathematical formulations to demonstrate the lack of validity in 12-tone technique and other advanced methods of composition.

Ansorge, Conrad (Eduard Reinhold), German pianist; b. Buchwald, near Löbau, Silesia, Oct. 15, 1862; d. Berlin, Feb. 13, 1930. He studied at the Leipzig Cons. (1880–82) and was one of the last pupils of Liszt in Weimar (1885). He toured in Russia and America; then lived in Weimar (1893–95) and in Berlin (from 1895). From 1898 he taught at the Klindworth-Scharwenka Cons. In 1920 he gave courses at the German Cons. in Prague. Ansorge excelled as an interpreter of romantic compositions; he was called "a metaphysician among pianists" for his insight into the inner meaning of the music of Beethoven, Schubert and Schumann. He wrote a piano concerto, a string sextet, 2 string quartets and a cello sonata; *Ballade, Traumbilder, Polish Dances*, and 3 sonatas for piano, and a Requiem.

Antegnati, Costanzo, Italian organist and composer; b. Brescia, baptized on Dec. 9, 1549; d. there, Nov. 14, 1624. He was descended from a family of organ builders, and served as apprentice to his father. In 1584 he became organist at Brescia cathedral. His madrigals and sacred compositions (Masses, motets, psalms and canzoni) were published in Venice (1571–1608) with pieces in organ tablature; he also published an important treatise, *L'Arte organica* (Brescia, 1608; new ed. by Renato Lunelli, Mainz, 1938). His *3 Ricercari* for organ are reprinted in vol. III of Luigi Torchi's *L'Arte musicale in Italia.*
BIBLIOGRAPHY: D. Muoni, *Gli Antegnati* (Milan, 1883).

Antes, John, American Moravian (*Unitas Fratrum*) minister; b. Frederickstownship, Pa., March 24, 1740; d. Bristol, England, Dec. 17, 1811. He left America in 1764, and was a missionary in Egypt where he was beaten and crippled by order of a bey who tried to extort money from him. He spent the rest of his life in England. Watchmaker by trade, he was an inventive artisan. He constructed several string instruments; one violin, made by him in Bethlehem in 1759, is preserved in the Museum of the Moravian Historical Society at Nazareth, Pa. A contribution by Antes to the *Allgemeine musikalische Zeitung* in 1806 describes a device for better violin tuning, as well as improvements of the violin bow and of the keyboard hammer. Antes also invented a machine with which one could turn pages while playing. He wrote about 25 melodious short anthems to German or English words for chorus, winds, strings, and organ. All of his MS compositions are in the Archives of the Moravian Church at Bethlehem, Pa. and Winston-Salem, N.C. His three string trios were discovered in 1949. They are the earliest chamber works by a native American. His interesting autobiography was publ. in *Nachrichten aus der Brüder-Gemeine* (1845).
BIBLIOGRAPHY: D. M. McCorkle, "John Antes, 'American Dilettante,'" *Musical Quarterly* (Oct. 1956; repr. as No. 2 in the series Moravian Music Foundation Publications, Winston-Salem, N.C.).

Antheil, George, remarkable American composer who cut a powerful swath in the world of modern music; b. Trenton, N.J., July 8, 1900; d. New York, Feb. 12, 1959. He studied theory with Constantine von Sternberg in Philadelphia and later took lessons in composition with Ernest Bloch, and also with Clark Smith. From his earliest years he was attracted to modernistic experimentation. In 1922 he made a tour of Europe as a pianist and composer playing his own pieces, works in an ultra-modern idiom with such pointed titles as *Mechanisms, Airplane Sonata, Sonate sauvage*. Settling in Paris he joined a group of famous literary figures, among them James Joyce, Ezra Pound, and Jean Cocteau, becoming a self-styled *enfant terrible* of modern music, who enjoyed the art and science of "épater les bourgeois." The culmination of his Paris period was marked by the performance of his orchestral suite *Ballet mécanique* on June 19, 1926, with musical materials taken from his score for a film by Fernand Léger. He subsequently returned to New York, where he staged a spectacular production of the *Ballet mécanique* at Carnegie Hall on April 10, 1927, with noisy airplane propellers, 8 pianos and a lot of drums in the score, creating an uproar in the audience and much publicity. A revival of this work in a prudently scaled-down version, using only 4 pianos and replacing the obsolescent propellers by a recording of the noise of a jet plane, staged at the Composers' Forum in New York on Feb. 20, 1954, aroused no hoped-for hostile reactions, but was accepted as a curiosity, a period piece. Other works composed by Antheil in Europe included a "symphony" for 5 instruments, usually referred to as "Quintet" (1923); an orchestral work *Zingareska* (Berlin, Nov. 21, 1922); a jazz symphony for chamber orch. (1925, later revised for large orch., and first performed in the new version in New York, Dec. 14, 1960); Symphony in F Major, No. 1 (1926); a piano concerto (1926); and a group of pieces for piano solo under the title *La Femme 100 Têtes*, inspired by Max Ernst's book of collages of that title (1933). In 1924 Antheil began the composition of the opera *Mr.*

Bloom and the Cyclops, based on James Joyce's novel *Ulysses,* but it never progressed beyond fragmentary sketches. His first complete opera *Transatlantic,* to his own libretto, portraying the turmoil attendant on the presidential election, and employing jazz rhythms, was performed for the first time in Frankfurt, Germany, on May 25, 1930, and aroused considerable interest. A second opera, *Helen Retires,* with a libretto by John Erskine, was produced in N.Y. on Feb. 28, 1934. In 1936 Antheil moved to Hollywood, where he wrote for films. For a time he ran a syndicated column of advice to perplexed lovers; another of his whimsical diversions was working on a torpedo device, in collaboration with the motion picture actress Hedi Lamarr. In the meantime he abandoned the extreme modernism of his Paris days, and adopted an effective style of composition with elements of classicism, romanticism and impressionism freely intermingled and arranged in moderately advanced harmonies. His works of this period include Symphony No. 2 (1937); Symphony No. 3 (1942); Symphony No. 4 (NBC Symph. Orch., N.Y., Stokowski conducting, Feb. 13, 1944); Violin Concerto (Dallas, Feb. 9, 1947); Symph. No. 5 (Philadelphia, Dec. 31, 1948); Symph. No. 6 (San Francisco, Feb. 10, 1949); a ballet *The Capital of the World* (N.Y., Dec. 27, 1953); the operas *Volpone,* after Ben Jonson (Los Angeles, Jan. 9, 1954); *The Brothers* (Denver, July 28, 1954) and *The Wish* (Louisville, Ky., April 2, 1955); *Cabeza de Vaca,* opera cantata (produced posthumously on CBS Television, June 10, 1962). Antheil also wrote three string quartets, 4 violin sonatas, in one of which the pianist is required to double on a set of drums; 4 piano sonatas; a concerto for flute, bassoon and piano; and various other pieces and songs. He is the author of an autobiographical volume, *Bad Boy of Music* (N.Y., 1945). On Nov. 4, 1925 Antheil married Böski Markus. The poet Ezra Pound published a pamphlet entitled *Antheil and the Treatise on Harmony, with Supplementary Notes* (Chicago, 1927), which, however, has little bearing on Antheil's compositions or, indeed, on Antheil himself.

Antill, John Henry, Australian composer; b. Sydney, April 8, 1904. He received his early musical training at the St. Andrew's Cathedral Choir School; for a time was apprenticed to the New South Wales Government Railways as a mechanical draftsman, and designed a steam whistle capable of producing a major ninth-chord. He then entered the Sydney Cons. (1925) and studied with Alfred Hill; sang tenor in the J. C. Williamson Imperial Opera Co. (1932-34); from 1949 to 1969 was Federal Music Editor for the Australian Broadcasting Corporation. He became greatly interested in indigenous Australian music and attended the rural festivals of the Aborigines, the Corroborees. The outcome of these explorations was the composition of a ballet *Corroboree;* Eugene Goossens, conductor of the Sydney Symph. Orch., played a suite from this work on Aug. 18, 1946; a complete ballet was produced in Sydney, July 3, 1950; Antill revised the score in 1960. Other works: 3 operas: *Endymion* (1920; Sydney, July 22, 1953), *The Music Critic* (1953) and *The First Christmas* (commissioned by the New South Wales Government; produced by the Australian Broadcasting Corporation, Dec. 25, 1969). 5 other ballets: *G'Day Digger* (1953), *Sentimental Bloke* (1955), *Wakooka* (1957), *Black Opal,* for chorus and timpani (1961) and *Snowy,* with soprano voices (1961); an oratorio, *The Song of Hagar* (1958); Variations for Orch. (1953); *Momentous Occasion Overture* (1957); *Symphony for a City* (1959); *Music for a Royal Pageant* for orch. (1962); Harmonica Concerto (1964); *Paean to the Spirit of Man* for orch. (1968); *The Unknown Land,* suite for string orch. (1968); songs, including *5 Australian Lyrics* for baritone, and piano or string ensemble (1953); *Cantate Domino,* anthem for chorus, brass, timpani and organ (1970). He also wrote numerous film scores.

BIBLIOGRAPHY: James Murdoch, *Australia's Contemporary Composers* (Melbourne, 1972; pp. 9-15).

Antiquus, Andreas (also **A. de Antiquiis Venetus,** or **Andrea Antico**), Italian music printer and composer; b. Montona (Istria) in the latter half of the 15th century. He printed music in Rome and Venice (1520), and was probably one of the earliest in his trade after Petrucci, who himself published many of Antiquus's *Frottole* (Venice, 1504-08). His collection of *Canzoni, Sonetti, Strambotti e Frottole, libro tertio,* was edited by A. Einstein (Northampton, Mass, 1941).

Antoine, Georges, Belgian composer; b. Liège, April 28, 1892; d. Bruges, Nov. 15, 1918 (of an ailment acquired during World War I). He studied at the Cons. of Liège (1902-13) with Sylvain Dupuis; joined the Belgian Army in 1914. He wrote a Piano Concerto (1914); *Vendanges* for voice and orch. (1914); *Veillée d'Armes,* symph. poem (1918); a Piano Quartet (1916); a Violin Sonata (1912-15), and songs.

BIBLIOGRAPHY: M. Paquot, *Georges Antoine* (Brussels, 1935).

Anton, Karl, German musicologist; b. Worms, June 2, 1887; d. Weinheim/Bergstrasse, Feb. 21, 1956. He studied voice in Heidelberg and Halle, as well as music history and theology. In 1912 he received his degree of *Dr. Phil.* with the thesis *Beiträge zur Biographie Carl Loewes.* In 1919 he was appointed to the faculty of the Hochschule für Musik in Mannheim; at the same time he served as a cleric in the Lutheran Church. Most of his publications deal with church music; among them are *Luther und die Musik* (1917); *Angewandte Liturgik* (1918) and *Erneuerung der Kirchenmusik* (1932).

Anton, Max, German conductor and pedagogue; b. Bornstedt, Aug. 2, 1877; d. Bonn, Aug. 18, 1939. He studied with Stavenhagen in Munich and James Kwast in Frankfurt; then taught at Gladbach and Detmold. From 1922 was active in Bonn as choral conductor until his retirement in 1934. A prolific composer, he wrote an opera *Die Getreuen;* an oratorio *Ekkehard;* several instrumental concertos, piano pieces and songs. He published *Versuch einer Kunstanschauung* (1922).

Antoniou, Theodore, Greek composer of advanced tendencies; b. Athens, Feb. 10, 1935. He studied violin, voice and theory at the Cons. in Athens (1947-58); then took courses in composition with Papaioannou

(1958–61). In 1961 he went to Germany where he studied conducting and composition with Günter Bialas at the Hochschule für Musik in Munich (1961–65) and attended summer courses in Darmstadt (1963–65). Returning to Greece, he taught in Athens. In 1969 emigrated to the U.S., where he was a member of the faculty at Stanford Univ (1969–70) and at the Philadelphia Musical Academy (1970–74). In 1974 he was appointed conductor and assistant director of contemporary activities at the Berkshire Music Center, Tanglewood. In his compositions he follows a mathematically oriented method, intermingling dodecaphony, modality and folk-like motivic configurations, often involving mixed media.

WORKS: 2 "sound-actions" (ballets): *Clytemnestra* for actress, dancers and orch., with tape (1967; Kassel, Germany, June 4, 1968), and *Cassandra* for dancers, actors, choir and orch., with tapes, lights and projections (1969; Barcelona, Nov. 14, 1970); 3 cantatas: *Melos* (1962); *Nenikikamen (We Are Victorious)* (commissioned for the Munich Olympics, and performed there, July 25, 1972); and *Die weisse Rose* (Philadelphia, April 25, 1976); Triple Concerto for Violin, Trumpet, Clarinet and Orch. (1959); *Overture* (1961); Concertino for Piano, String Orch. and Percussion (1962); *Antithesis* for small orch. (1962); Concertino for Piano, 9 Winds and Percussion (1963); *Jeux* for cello and string orch. (1963); *Micrographs* for orch. (1964); *Kontakion* for soloists, chorus and string orch. (1965); Violin Concerto (1965); *Kinesis ABCD* for 2 groups of strings (1966); *OP Overture* for orch. and tape (1966); *Events I* for violin, piano and orch. (1967–68), *II* for orch. (1969) and *III* for chamber orch., with tapes and slides (1969); *Climate of Absence* for medium voice, and orch. or piano (1968); *Katharsis* for flute and orch., with tapes and projections (1968); *Threnos* for wind orch. (1972); *Fluxus I* for orch. (1974–75) and *II* for piano and chamber orch. (1975); *Scherzo* for violin and piano (1958); Violin Sonatina (1958); *Suite* for 8 Instruments (1960); String Quartet (1960); Trio for Flute, Violin and Cello (1961); Sonata for Solo Violin (1961); *Dialogues* for flute and guitar (1962); *Epilogue* for mezzo-soprano, narrator and 6 instruments (1963); *Music* for harp (1965); *Quartetto giocoso* for oboe, violin, cello and piano (1965); *6 Likes* for solo tuba (1967); *Lyrics* for violin and piano (1967); *5 Likes* for solo oboe (1969); *Lamentations for Jani Christou* for medium voice and piano (1970); *Parodies* for actor and piano (1970); *Protest I* for actors and tape (1970) and *II* for 16 instruments, medium voice, actors, tape and lights (1971); *Synthesis* for 4 instruments and 4 synthesizers (1971); *4 Likes* for solo violin (1972); *Chorochronos I* for baritone, narrator, 4 percussion, 4 trombones, tape, films, slides and lighting effects (1973), *II* for narrator and instrumental ensemble (1973) and *III* for voice, pianist for percussion and tape (1975); *3 Likes* for solo clarinet (1973); *Aquarelles* for piano (1958); Piano Sonata (1959); *Syl-la-bles* for piano (1965); tape pieces; theater and film music.

Antony, Franz Joseph, German organist and writer on music; b. Münster, Westphalia, Feb. 1, 1790; d. there, Jan. 7, 1837. He was appointed music director at Münster cathedral in 1819; in 1832, succeeded his father Joseph Antony (1758–1836) as organist. He published *Archäologisch-liturgisches Gesangbuch des Gregorianischen Kirchengesangs* (1829) and *Geschichtliche Darstellung der Entstehung und Vervollkommnung der Orgel* (1832).

Apel, Johann August, German scholar; b. Leipzig, Sept. 17, 1771; d. there, Aug. 9, 1816. He is important in music history for his collection *Gespensterbuch* (1810–14), dealing with supernatural tales, which was the inspiration for Weber's *Der Freischütz*. Apel also published several treatises on music, among them a series of articles on rhythm, in *Allgemeine musikalische Zeitung* (1807–08) and a large work in 2 volumes, *Metrik* (1814–16).

Apel, Willi, eminent music scholar; b. Konitz, Germany, Oct. 10, 1893. He studied mathematics at Bonn Univ. (1912), Munich (1913), and Berlin (1918–21), and took piano lessons. He taught mathematics and music in Germany; in 1935 he came to the U.S. He gave lectures at Harvard Univ. (1938–42); in 1950 he was engaged as prof. of musicology at Indiana Univ., Bloomington. While in Germany he edited 2 volumes of early music, *Musik aus früher Zeit* (Mainz, 1934), and published 2 treatises: *Die Fuge* (1932) and *Accidentien und Tonalität in den Musikdenkmälern des 15. und 16. Jahrhunderts* (Strasbourg, 1936); he also contributed to German music magazines. In America he published the extremely valuable treatises and compilations, *The Notation of Polyphonic Music, 900–1600* (Cambridge, Mass., 1942); *The Harvard Dictionary of Music* (Cambridge, Mass. 1944; 2nd ed., rev. and enl., Cambridge, 1969; a prime reference work of musical terminology); *Historical Anthology of Music*, 2 vols. (with A. T. Davison; Cambridge, Mass., 1946 and 1949); *Masters of the Keyboard* (Cambridge, Mass., 1947); *Gregorian Chant* (Bloomington, Ind., 1957). A Festschrift in Apel's honor, *Essays in Musicology*, ed. H. Tischler (Bloomington, Ind., 1968), contains a bibliography of his writings.

Aperghis, Georges, avant-garde Greek composer; b. Athens, Dec. 23, 1945. He studied music privately with Yannis Papaioannou in Athens; in 1963 went to Paris and became a student of Xenakis, who initiated him into the mysteries of ultra-modern techniques involving such arcana as musical indeterminacy and audio-visual coordinates in spatial projection.

WORKS: *Bis, spectacle musical* for 10 actors and 10 instruments (1968); *The Tragic Story of the Necromancer Hieronimo and His Mirror* for puppets, voice, guitar and piano (1971); *Funeral Oration* (1971); *Concerto Grosso* (Paris, May 29, 1972); *Ouverture* (1973); *Pandaemonium* (1973) and *Jacques le Fataliste* (1973). He has also written *2 Movements* for string quartet (1964); *Dialogues* for flute, harpsichord and xylophone (1965); *Antistixis A* for 3 string quartets (1964–65), *B* for 4 flutes, 4 percussionists, celesta, harp, Ondes Martenot and double bass (1965) and *O* for orch. (1966); *Contrepoint for Orch.* (1967); *Libretto* for orch. in 4 groups (1968); *Anacrusis* for chamber ensemble (1967); *Eluding Game* for instrumental ensemble (1968); *Freak Map* for 6 instruments and 3 percussionists (1968); *Contrepoint for 3 String*

Quartets, Piano, Trombone and Percussion (1968); *Plastic Piece* for 2 orch. (1968); *Music for an Orange Girl* for chamber ensemble and tape (1968); *Color Music* for 19 instruments (1966–69); *Musique Automatique,* suite of 6 pieces for female voice and chamber ensemble (1969); *Boogie-Woogie* for chamber ensemble (1969); *Variations* for 10 Musicians (1969); *B.A.C.H.* for chorus and orch. (1969); *4 Pièces Superposables* for conductor, percussion, voice and strings (1969); *La Création* for speaker and instrumental ensemble (1969); *Variations sur un portrait de Bach* for any instrument (1970); *Le Fil d'Ariane* for Ondes Martenot (1970); *Variations 1 and 2* for 5 Percussionists and 5 Xylophones (1970); *Variations 3 and 4 (Awake)* for 6 Oboes (1970); *Music Box* for harpsichord (1970); *Vesper,* oratorio (1970); *Quartet for 4 Double Basses* (1970); *Quartet for 4 Percussionists* (1970); *Symplexis* for 22 jazz soloists and orch. (Paris, Nov. 3, 1970); *Puzzles* for 5 woodwinds, 5 brass and percussion (1971); *Die Wände haben Ohren (The Walls Have Ears)* for orch. (Metz, France, Nov. 26, 1972); *BWV* for 6 singers and instrumental ensemble (1973).

ApIvor, Denis, Irish-born English composer; b. Collinstown, West Meath, April 14, 1916. He studied music theory privately in London with Patrick Hadley and Alan Rawsthorne (1937–39); adopted a fairly advanced technique of composition while adhering to tradition in formal design; his pieces are quite playable, and the associations he brings out with extramusical elements, painting, etc. are most ingenious.

WORKS: 4 operas: opera-buffa *She Stoops to Conquer* (after Goldsmith's play; 1943–47, revised 1976–77); *Yerma* (after García Lorca's play; 1955–58); *Ubu Roi* (1965–66) and *Bouvard and Pecuchet* (after Flaubert, 1970); 5 ballets: *The Goodman of Paris* (1951); *A Mirror for Witches* (1951), *Blood Wedding* (1953; after Lorca), *Saudades* (1954), and *Corporal Jan* (1967); cantata, *The Hollow Men,* after T. S. Eliot's poem (1939; BBC Radio, London, Feb. 21, 1950); *Cantata,* to poems by Dylan Thomas (1960); Piano Concerto (1948); Concerto for Violin and 15 instruments (1950); 2 symphonies (1952, 1963); Guitar Concertino (1953); *Overtones,* 9 short pieces for orch., based on Paul Klee's paintings (1961–62); *String Abstract,* concerto for string trio and orch. (1967); *Tarot,* variations for chamber orch. (1968); *Neumes,* variations for orch. (1969); *The Tremulous Silence* for guitar and chamber orch. (1972); *Exotics Theater,* 10 pieces for chamber ensemble (1972; Klee pieces: iii); *Resonance of the Southern Flora* for wordless chorus and orch. (1972; Klee pieces: iv); *Fern Hill,* after Thomas, for tenor and 11 instruments (1973); Violin Concerto (1975); Violin Sonata (1944–45); *Concertante* for clarinet, piano and percussion (1944–45); *Variations* for solo guitar (1958); wind quintet (1960); *Mutations* for cello and piano (1962); 2 string quartets (1964, 1976); *Crystals* for percussion, Hammond organ, guitar and double bass (1964–65); *Harp, Piano, Piano-Harp* (1966); *Ten String Design* for violin and guitar (1967); *Discanti,* 5 pieces for solo guitar (1970); *Saeta* for solo guitar (1972); *Psycho-pieces,* 8 pieces for clarinet and piano (1973; Klee pieces: v); *Studies for Wind,* 7 pieces, one each for flute, oboe, clarinet, bassoon, horn, trumpet and trombone (1974); Clarinet

Quintet (1975); *Liaison,* duo for guitar and keyboard (1976); *Animalcules,* 12 piano pieces (1962); *5 Piano Pieces* (1968); *Orgelberg* for organ (1971; Klee pieces: ii); songs.

Aponte-Ledée, Rafael, Puerto Rican composer; b. Guayama, Oct. 15, 1938. He studied composition with Cristóbal Halffter at the Madrid Cons. (1957–64); then took courses with Ginastera at the Latin American Center of Advanced Musical Studies at the Di Tella Institute in Buenos Aires (1965–66). Returning to Puerto Rico, he founded in San Juan, with the collaboration of Francis Schwartz, the "Fluxus" group for the promotion of new music (1967); taught composition and theory at the Univ. of Puerto Rico (1968–74). His music is highly advanced, employing nearly every conceivable technique of the cosmopolitan avant-garde.

WORKS: *Tema y Seis Diferencias* for piano (1963); *Dialogantes 1* for flute and violin (1965); *Elejía* for 13 strings (1965; version for 50 strings, 1967); *Presagio de Pájaros muertos* for narrator and tape (1966); *Epíthasis* for 3 oboes, 2 trombones, double bass and 3 percussionists (1967); *Dialogantes 2* for 3 flutes, 3 trombones and 3 clarinets (1968); *La Ventana abierta* for 3 mezzo-sopranos, 3 flutes, clarinet, trumpet, 2 percussionists, celesta, piano, violin, cello and double bass (1968; alternate version for 3 mezzo-sopranos, flutes, clarinet, 2 trumpets, horn, 2 percussionists, guitar, piano and 2 string quartets, 1969); *Streptomicyne* for soprano, flute, clarinet, trumpet and piano (1970); *SSSSSS²* for double bass solo, 3 flutes, trumpet and percussion (1971); *Volúmenes* for piano (1971); *Elvira en sombras* for piano and orch. (1973); *Estravagario, in memoriam Salvador Allende* for orch. and tape (1973); *Cuídese de los angeles que caen,* musique concrète (1974); *Los huevos de pandora* for clarinet and tape (1974); *El palacio en sombras* for orch. without violins and cellos (1977).

Apostel, Hans Erich, Austrian composer; b. Karlsruhe, Jan. 22, 1901; d. Vienna, Nov. 30, 1972. After early studies in Karlsruhe he went to Vienna in 1921, and became a pupil in composition of Schoenberg and Alban Berg. He served as a reader in Universal Edition and in that capacity prepared for publication the posthumous works of Berg. He was also active as a teacher. He received numerous prizes for his own works, among them, the Grand Prize of the City of Vienna (1948) and the Grand Prize of the Republic of Austria (1957). In 1951 he adopted the method of composition with 12 tones according to Schoenberg's precepts, without however avoiding tonal combinations. He experimented in Klangfarbe effects, and applied audible overtones in his piano pieces by holding down the keys without striking them. His music was often performed at international festivals, but never penetrated beyond the confines of Central Europe.

WORKS: *Requiem,* to Rilke's words (1933); *Sonatina ritmica* for piano (1934); 2 string quartets (1935, 1957); *Adagio* for strings (1937); *Kubiniana* for piano (1945–47); Quartet for Flute, Clarinet, Horn and Bassoon (1949); Sonatina for Flute Solo (1951); Sonatina for Clarinet Solo (1951); Sonatina for Bassoon Solo (1951); *Intrada* for brass and percussion (1954); *Bal-*

lade for orch. (1955); *Suite concise* for piano (1955); *Rondo ritmico* for orch. (1957); Piano Concerto (1958), *6 Epigrammes* for string quartet (1962); Cello Sonata (1962); *Kleines Kammerkonzert* for flute, viola and guitar (1964); Sonatina for Oboe Solo (1964); *Kammersymphonie* (1968); *Epitaph* for strings (1969); *Haydn Variations* for orch. in 2 parts, the 2nd of which is named "Paralipomena dodekaphonica" (1969).

BIBLIOGRAPHY: H. Kaufmann, *Hans Erich Apostel* (Vienna, 1965).

Appel, Richard Gilmore, American music librarian and organist; b. Lancaster, Pa., April 25, 1889; d. Cambridge, Mass., Nov. 18, 1975. He studied organ with Wallace Goodrich in Boston and Karl Straube in Germany; received his M.A. from Harvard Univ. in 1912; was church organist in Boston and vicinity; composed various pieces for the organ. From 1922 to 1954 he was head of the Music Dept. of the Boston Public Library. In 1975 he published *The Music of the Bay Psalm Book: 9th Edition (1698)* (No. 5, I.S.A.M. Monograph Series).

Appeldoorn, Dina, Dutch composer; b. Rotterdam, Feb. 26, 1884; d. The Hague, Dec. 4, 1938. She was the composer of several works in romantic style, including 2 symphonic poems, *Noordzee* and *Volkfeest;* she also wrote chamber music and songs, and taught piano at The Hague.

Appenzeller (Appencellers, Appenzelder, Appenzelders), Benedictus, Franco-Flemish composer of the first half of the 16th century. Possibly a pupil of Josquin, he served Mary of Hungary as court musician and master of the choir boys at her chapel in Brussels (1539–c.1554) and probably accompanied her on her visit to Spain (1551). Appenzeller's works were formerly attributed to Benedictus Ducis, a German composer whose identity was confused with his. Among Appenzeller's extant compositions are a book of chansons (1542; two of the chansons from this collection had been published by Attaingnant in 1529 without being ascribed to Appenzeller); a lament on the death of Josquin (1521) which uses half of the *Musae Jovis* text; and a double canon on *Sancta Maria* embroidered on a tablecloth for Mary of Hungary (1548). Pieces by him are included in the second *Musyckboexken* of Susato; the *Hortus Musarum,* part I (1552), published by Phalese, contains a transcription for two lutes of a piece by him.

BIBLIOGRAPHY: E. van der Straeten, *La Musique aux Pays-Bas* (Brussels, 1867–8; volumes 3, 7, and 8); D. Bartha, *Benedictus Ducis und Appenzeller* (Wolfenbüttel, 1930); G. Reese, *Music in the Renaissance* (N.Y., 1954).

Appia, Edmond, Italian Swiss violinist and conductor; b. Turin, May 7, 1894; d. Geneva, Feb. 12, 1961. He studied violin wth Henri Marteau at the Cons. of Geneva, in Paris with Lucien Capet, and at the Brussels Cons. obtaining Premier Prix in 1920; toured Europe (1920–35); taught violin in Geneva and Lausanne. In 1935 he became a conductor of Radiodiffusion Suisse in Lausanne; in 1938 was appointed conductor of the Geneva Radio Orch. He also wrote articles on Swiss music for *Musical Quarterly* and many European publications.

Applebaum, Edward, American composer; b. Los Angeles, Sept. 28, 1937. He studied at the Univ. of California at Los Angeles, acquiring his Ph.D. in composition in 1966; was composer-in-residence of the Oakland Symphony (1969). Among his works are Piano Sonata (1965); String Trio (1966); Variations for Orch. (1966); Concerto for Viola and Chamber Orch. (1967); *Montages* for clarinet, cello and piano (1968); *Shantih* for cello and piano (1969); Symph. No. 1 (1970); *Foci* for viola and piano (1971); . . . *When Dreams Do Show Thee Me. . .*, concerto for clarinet, cello, piano, chamber orch. and 9 vocal soloists (1972); Piano Trio (1972).

Applebaum, Louis, Canadian composer; b. Toronto, April 3, 1918. He studied with Healy Willan, Leo Smith and Sir Ernest MacMillan at the Toronto Cons., graduating in 1940; then with Bernard Wagenaar and Roy Harris in New York (1940–41). He returned to Canada in 1949 and was a member of the board of directors of the Composers, Authors and Publishers Association of Canada (1956–68) and then its musical executive (1968–71).

WORKS: A musical comedy, *Ride a Pink Horse* (1960); 3 ballets: *Dark of the Moon* (1953; revised in 1960 as *Barbara Allen;* concert suite, 1965), *Legend of the North* (1957) and *Homage* (1969); *East by North* for orch. (1947); *Variations on a Theme from a Film Score* for oboe, piano and string trio (1948, revised 1953); *Christmas Overture* (1951); *Suite of Miniature Dances* for orch. (1958; arr. for band, 1964); *3 Greek Dances* for orch. (1958); *Moments from "Romeo and Juliet"* for wind quintet cello, harp and percussion (1961); *Action Stations* for orch. (1962); *Concertante* for Small Orch. (1967); *Fanfare and Anthem* for orch. (1969); incidental music for plays and over a hundred films; piano pieces; songs.

Appledorn, Mary Jeanne van, American pianist and teacher; b. Holland, Michigan, Oct. 2, 1927. She studied piano at the Eastman School of Music in Rochester; also received her M.M. in theory there (1950) and Ph.D. in composition (1966). Among her works are *Burlesca* for piano, brass and percussion (1951); Piano Concerto (1954); Trumpet Concerto (1960); Passacaglia for Chamber Orch. (1958); and a number of piano pieces in a facile Western manner, such as *Apache Echoes, Indian Trail, Boots 'n' Saddles* and *Wagon Train.* She published *Keyboard, Singing and Dictation Manual* (Dubuque, Iowa, 1968). In 1975 she held the position of Chairman of the Music Literature and Theory Division at Texas Tech. University in Lubbock, Texas.

Aprile, Giuseppe, Italian male contralto; b. Martinafranca, Apulia, Oct. 28, 1731; d. there, Jan. 11, 1813. From c.1763 he sang at the principal theaters of Italy and Germany; then settled in Naples as teacher; among his pupils was Cimarosa. Aprile's vocal treatise, *The Modern Italian Method of Singing, with 36 Solfeggi,* first published by Broderip in London (1791), has been reprinted in many editions and several languages.

Apthorp, William Foster, American music critic; b. Boston, Mass., Oct. 24, 1848; d. Vevey, Switzerland, Feb. 19, 1913. A graduate of Harvard Univ. (1869), he studied music with Paine. He taught music at the New England Cons. and lectured on music history at Boston Univ. He wrote music criticism for the *Atlantic Monthly* (1872–77); was music and drama critic on the *Boston Evening Transcript* (1881–1903). In his criticisms Apthorp violently opposed new Russian, French and German music (his intemperate attacks on Tchaikovsky elicited protests from his readers). Apthorp was also the annotator of the Boston Symph. programs (1892–1901). He published several books: *Musicians and Music Lovers* (N.Y., 1894); *By the Way,* a collection of short essays in 2 vols.: I. *About Music,* II. *About Musicians* (Boston, 1898); *The Opera, Past and Present* (N.Y., 1901). He was co-editor of *Scribner's Cyclopedia of Music and Musicians* (N.Y., 1888–90).

Ara, Ugo, Italian violinist; member of the Flonzaley Quartet; b. Venice, July 19, 1876; d. Lausanne, Switzerland, Dec. 10, 1936. He studied violin with Tirindelli in Venice; at the age of 13 played in theater orchs. In 1894 he went to Liège where he studied with César Thomson; he then took lessons in composition with R. Fuchs at the Vienna Cons. When the Flonzaley Quartet was established, he joined it as a viola player, (1903–17). He later returned to Italy.

Araja, Francesco, Italian composer; b. Naples, June 25, 1709; d. in Bologna in 1770. He produced his first opera *Lo matremmonejo pe' mennetta* in the Neapolitan dialect (Naples, 1729); his subsequent operas were *Berenice* (Florence, 1730); *La forza dell'amore e dell'odio* (Milan, 1734); *Lucio Vero* (Venice, Jan. 4, 1735). In 1735 he was engaged as musical director and court composer in St. Petersburg. There he wrote annual pieces for court occasions, beginning with the cantata *La gara dell'amore e del zelo* (April 28, 1736). Among his operas given at the Russian court were *La Semiramide riconosciuta* (Feb. 9, 1737); *Artaserse* (1738); *Seleuco* (1744); *Scipione* (1745); *Mitridate* (1747); *L'asilo della pace* (1748); *Bellerofonte* (1750); *Eudossa incoronata* (1751). He wrote 22 operas; *La Clemenza di Tito,* attributed to him by some, was the work of Hasse. On Feb. 27, 1755, Araja presented in St. Petersburg the first opera ever composed to a Russian text to a libretto in the Russian language on the story of Cephale and Procris, written by the famous Russian dramatist Sumarokov. He was in Italy in 1741–42 and 1759–61; in 1762 he revisited Russia briefly at the summons of Peter III, his great admirer, returning to Italy after the Czar's death. Nothing is known of Araja's last years.
BIBLIOGRAPHY: A. Mooser, *Annales de la musique des musiciens en Russie au XVIII siècle,* vol. I, pp. 121–131 (Geneva, 1951).

Arakishvili, Dmitri, Georgian composer; b. Vladikavkaz, Feb. 23, 1873; d. Tbilisi, Aug. 13, 1953. He studied composition at the Moscow Philharmonic Institute with Ilyinsky and also took private lessons with Gretchaninov. At the same time he studied archeology and ethnic sciences; in 1901 he became a member of the Musical Ethnographic Commission at the Univ. of Moscow. In 1906 he took part in the organization of the Moscow People's Cons., which offered free music lessons to impecunious students. He was editor of the Moscow publication *Music and Life* (1908–12). In 1918 he moved to Tbilisi, where he was active as a teacher and conductor. He composed one of the earliest national Georgian operas, *The Legend of Shota Rustaveli* (Tbilisi, Feb. 5, 1919), a comic opera *Dinara* (1926), 3 symphonies (1934, 1942, 1951), *Hymn of the New East* for orch. (1933), and film music. But his best compositions are some 80 art songs in a lyrico-dramatic manner reflecting the Georgian modalities.

Aranyi, Francis, Hungarian violinist; b. Budapest, March 21, 1893; d. Seattle, May 5, 1966. He studied at the Royal Academy of Music in Budapest, and later took violin lessons in Berlin with Willy Hess and Henri Marteau. His career as violinist took him to Vienna, Stockholm and Zagreb. In 1935 he emigrated to America; taught at Duquesne Univ., in Pittsburgh, Pa. (1935–40) and at Michigan State College (1940–41); was concertmaster at the Seattle Symph. Orch. during the season 1941–42. In 1942 he organized the Youth Symph. Orch., of the Pacific Northwest, in Seattle, where he remained until his death.

d'Aranyi, Jelly, Hungarian violinist; grandniece of **Joachim,** and sister of the violinist **Adila Fachiri;** b. Budapest, May 30, 1895; d. Florence, March 30, 1966. She studied violin with Hubay in Budapest; after some concerts in Europe, she went to America and made her debut in a solo recital in New York on Nov. 26, 1927; made her second American tour in 1932. She frequently appeared in joint recitals with Myra Hess. A pioneer in modern music, she gave first performances of many new works. Béla Bartók's First Violin Sonata, Ravel's *Tzigane* and the Violin Concerto by Vaughan Williams are dedicated to her. She attracted considerable attention in 1937 when she proclaimed that Schumann's spirit appeared to her during a séance and revealed the secret of his unpublished Violin Concerto; but Schumann's ghost spoke ungrammatical German, which aroused suspicion concerning the authenticity of the phenomenon; besides, the manuscript of the concerto had long been known to be preserved at the Berlin State Library; its first performance was eventually given in Germany by another violinist. Jelly d'Aranyi was given a chance, however, to perform it with the BBC Orch. in London on Feb. 16, 1938.
BIBLIOGRAPHY: J. Macleod, *The Sisters d'Aranyi* (London, 1969).

Arapov, Boris, Russian composer; b. St. Petersburg, Sept. 12, 1905. He studied at the Leningrad Cons. with Vladimir Stcherbatchev, graduating in 1930; then joined its teaching staff. He spent several years in Central Asia, collecting and codifying indigenous folk melodies; several of his works are based on Central Asian themes. He wrote an opera *Hodzha-Nasreddin* (1943); 3 symphonies (1947, 1959, 1962); *Free China,* symph. poem (Leningrad, Oct. 2, 1960); Trio for Clarinet, Violin and Piano, on Mongol themes (1942); Violin Concerto (1965); chamber music; piano pieces and film scores.

Arauxo (or **Araujo**), **(Francisco).** See **Correa de Araujo, (Francisco).**

Arbatsky, Yury, Russian music scholar; b. Moscow, April 15, 1911; d. New Hartford, N.Y., Sept. 3, 1963. His family left Russia in 1919, and proceeded to Dresden, where Arbatsky began to study music; later he enrolled at the Cons. of Leipzig, studying composition with Grabner. In 1932 he went to Yugoslavia, where he was active as choral conductor and cathedral organist in Belgrade, receiving his doctorate in 1944. In 1942 he went to Prague, and studied at the German Univ. there. After the end of the war he emigrated to the U.S.; was active as church musician in Chicago (1950–53), and later was consultant with the Newberry Library. He published several valuable tracts on folk music, among them *Beating the Tupan in the Central Balkans* (Chicago, 1953), and also essays on *The History of Russian Music* (publ. in Russian, N.Y., 1956). He was also a composer; he wrote at least 8 symphonies and much choral music. See "The Arbatsky Collection," *Bulletin of the Newberry Library* (July 1954).

Arbeau, Thoinot (anagram of real name **Jehan Tabourot**), French writer; b. Dijon, c.1519; d. Langres, c.1595. He owes his fame to his unique treatise in dialoque form, *Orchésographie, et traité en forme de dialoque par lequel toutes personnes peuvent facilement apprendre et pratiquer l'honnête exercise des danses* (Langres, 1589; 2nd ed., 1596), which contains not only instruction for dancing (indicating dance steps by a simple system of initial letters) but also valuable observations on the dance music of his time. It was publ. in English translations by C. W. Beaumont (London, 1925) and M. Evans (N.Y., 1948).

Arbo, Jens, Norwegian music critic; b. Kristiansand, Aug. 20, 1885; d. Oslo, Jan. 8, 1944. He studied in Oslo; then in Germany (1911–14). He was music critic of *Musikbladet* (1917–24) and of *Morgenbladet* (1924–43).

Arbós, Enrique Fernández, Spanish violinist and conductor; b. Madrid, Dec. 24, 1863; d. San Sebastian, June 2, 1939. He studied violin with Monasterio in Madrid, with Vieuxtemps in Brussels, and with Joachim in Berlin. After successful tours in Europe he returned to Spain in 1888; taught violin at the Madrid Cons. In 1889 he was concertmaster of the Glasgow Symph. Orch.; from 1894–1916 he held the post of honorary prof. at the Royal College of Music in London. He was appointed conductor of the new Madrid Symph. Orch. in 1904; conducted in the U.S. (1928–31); then in Europe. At the outbreak of the Spanish Civil War in 1936 he retired to San Sebastian. Arbós was the author of a comic opera *El Centro de la Tierra* (Madrid, Dec. 22, 1895). He was a brilliant orchestrator; his arrangement of the music from *Iberia* by Albéniz is very popular.

BIBLIOGRAPHY: V. Espinós Moltó, *El Maestro Arbós* (Madrid, 1942).

Arbuckle, Matthew, American cornet player and bandmaster; b. 1828; d. New York, May 23, 1883. He published a manual under the title *Complete Cornet Method.*

Arbuthnot, John, British physician and musical amateur; b. Arbuthnot, Scotland, in 1667; d. London, Feb. 27, 1735. He was one of the founders of the Scriblerus Club in London (1714), and was friendly with Handel during the composer's difficulties with his opera company. Arbuthnot's publication entitled *Miscellaneous Works* throws sharp sidelights on various persons of interest at the time. He wrote several anthems, glees, etc.

Arcadelt, Jacob (or **Jachet Arkadelt, Archadet, Arcadet, Harcadelt),** great Flemish composer; b. probably in Liège, c.1505; d. Paris, Oct. 14, 1568. He was "magister puerorum" to the Papal Chapel (1539), and choirmaster (1540). In 1544 he held the office of 'Camerlingo.' He went to France in 1546; returned to Rome in May, 1547. In 1555 he again went to France, this time with the Duc de Guise. Arcadelt is mentioned in Paris as *Regis musicus* in 1557. In the domain of secular music, his Roman period was, in the main, devoted to the madrigal; his Paris period to the French chanson.

WORKS: He wrote 20 motets, about 120 French chansons and 200 madrigals. Of his extant works, the most important are 6 books of 5-part madrigals (Venice, 1538–56; his finest and most characteristic compositions) and 3 books of Masses in 3–7 parts (Paris, 1557).

BIBLIOGRAPHY: W. Klefisch, *Arcadelt als Madrigalist* (Cologne, 1938); A. Einstein, *The Italian Madrigal* (Princeton, 1949); F. Lesure, "Notes et Documents," *Revue de Musicologie* (Dec. 1961).

d'Archambeau, Iwan, Belgian cellist; member of the Flonzaley Quartet; b. Hervé, Sept. 28, 1879; d. Villefranche-sur-Mer, France, Dec. 29, 1955. He studied music at home; played in a family quartet with his father and two brothers. He then studied cello with A. Massau in Verviers and with Hugo Becker in Frankfurt. In 1903 he became a member of the Flonzaley Quartet, until it disbanded in 1929; in 1935 he joined the Stradivarius Quartet in New York. From 1939 until 1950 he lived in Cambridge, Mass.; then returned to Belgium.

Archangelsky, Alexander, Russian choral conductor; b. near Penza, Oct. 23, 1846; d. Prague, Nov. 16, 1924. He studied singing and theory of music at the Court Chapel in St. Petersburg; in 1880 organized a chorus there, toured Russia with it in 1899–1900, presenting 110 concerts; also gave concerts with his chorus in Western Europe (1907 and 1912). Archangelsky was the first choir leader in Russia to include women's voices in performances of sacred works. He supported (with Gretchaninov) the reform movement in Russian church music; wrote a number of choral pieces for his organization and made transcriptions of

Russian church hymns. In 1923 he went to Prague as conductor of a students' choir, and died there the following year.

Archer, Frederick, English-American organist, conductor and composer; b. Oxford, June 16, 1838; d. Pittsburgh, Oct. 22, 1901. He studied organ in Leipzig, and in 1873 was appointed organist of Alexandra Palace in London; then became conductor of a Glasgow choir (1878–80). In 1881 he came to America; was active as church organist in Brooklyn and, from 1895, at Carnegie Institute in Pittsburgh. He was the first conductor of the newly organized Pittsburgh Symphony Orchestra, from Feb. 27, 1896, to 1898, when he was succeeded by Victor Herbert. A prolific composer, he published a cantata, *King Witlaf's Drinking-horn;* organ and piano pieces and songs. The bulk of his music remains in MS. He was the author of the manuals *The Organ* (1875) and *A Complete Method for the American Reed Organ* (1899), and founder and editor of the music magazine *The Keynote* (1883).

Archer, Violet, Canadian pianist and composer; b. Montreal, April 24, 1913. She studied composition with Champagne, and piano at the McGill Cons. in Montreal (1930–36); took private lessons with Bartók in New York (1942) and attended courses in composition with Hindemith at Yale Univ. (1948–49). She taught at McGill (1944–47), at North Texas State College (1950–53); Univ. of Oklahoma (1953–61) and, since 1962, at the Univ. of Alberta, Edmonton, as chairman of theory and composition. Her music is tonally organized, although she occasionally applies modified methods of composing with 12 tones.
WORKS: a comic opera, *Sganarelle* (Edmonton, Feb. 5, 1974); Timpani Concerto (1939); *Scherzo Sinfonico* (1940); *Poem* (1940); *Fantasia concertante* for flute, oboe, clarinet and strings (1941); *Britannia, a Joyful Overture* (1941); Fantasy for Clarinet and Strings (1942); Clarinet Concertino (1946); Symphony (1946); *Fantasy on a Ground* (1946); *Fanfare and Passacaglia* (1949); Piano Concerto (1956); Divertimento (1957); Violin Concerto (1959); *3 Sketches* (1961); *Prelude-Incantation* (1964); *Sinfonietta* (1968); *Sinfonia* (1969; Edmonton, Oct. 24, 1970); Clarinet Concerto (1971); *Choruses from "The Bacchae"* for chorus and orch. (1938); *Leaves of Grass,* after Whitman, for chorus and orch. (1940); *Lamentations of Jeremy* for chorus and orch. (1947); *The Bell,* cantata (1949); *Apocalypse* for soprano, chorus, brass and timpani (1958); *Cantata Sacra* for 5 soloists and small orch. (1966); songs, choruses and anthems, and much chamber music: *6 Pieces* for piano and timpani (1939); 2 string quartets (1940, 1948–49); Theme and Variations for String Quartet (1942); Sonata for Flute, Clarinet and Piano (1944); Quartet for Wind instruments (1945); Divertimento No. 1 for oboe, clarinet and bassoon (1949); *Fugue Fantasy* for string quartet (1949); 2 string trios (1953, 1961); 2 piano trios (1954, 1957); *Prelude and Allegro* for violin and piano (1954); Cello Sonata (1956); Violin Sonata (1956); Divertimento No. 2 for oboe, violin and cello (1957); Divertimento for Brass Quintet (1963); Horn Sonata (1965); Clarinet Sonata (1970); Suite for 4 Violins (1971); Fantasy for Violin and Piano (1971); Saxophone Sonata (1972); Oboe Sonata (1973); for piano: 3 sonatinas (1945, 1946, 1973); sonata (1945); *3 Sketches* for 2 pianos (1947); 6 Preludes (1947); Fantasy (1947); Suite (1947); *11 Short Pieces* (1960); Theme and Variations (1963); *Improvisations* (1968); *Lydian Mood* (1971).

Ardévol, José, Cuban composer; b. Barcelona, March 13, 1911. In 1930 he went to Cuba; in 1942 he organized in Havana the Grupo de Renovación Musical, dedicated to the modernization of composition. He adopted a neo-classical idiom in his own compositions. After the Cuban Revolution of 1959 he was appointed National Director for Music, a post which he held until 1965. He wrote several works of political content, such as *Cantos de la revolución* (1962); *Por Viet-Nam,* to words by Fidel Castro (1966); cantata *Ché comandante* (glorifying the revolutionary role of Ché Guevara, 1968) and *Cantata Lenin* (1970). Other works are: Concerto for 3 Pianos and Orch. (1938); *Ballet forma* with chorus (Havana, May 18, 1943); 3 symphonies (1943, 1945, 1946); 3 concerti grossi (1937–46); 6 trio sonatas (1937–46); *Movimiento sinfónico No. 1* (1967); *No. 2* (1969); 3 string quartets; Cello Sonata; Sonata for Guitar Solo.

Arditi, Luigi, Italian composer and conductor; b. Crescentino, Piedmont, July 22, 1822; d. Hove, near Brighton, England, May 1, 1903. He studied violin, piano and composition at the Milan Cons., where he also produced his first opera, *I Briganti* (1841). He then embarked on a career as operatic conductor. From 1846 he traveled in Cuba (where he produced his opera *Il Corsaro,* Havana, 1846), and visited New York and Philadelphia. In New York he produced his opera *La Spia* (March 24, 1856). He finally settled in London (1858) as conductor and vocal teacher, while making annual tours with the Italian Opera in Germany and Austria. He conducted in St. Petersburg in 1871 and 1873. His operas and other works were never revived, but he created a perennial success with his vocal waltz *Il Bacio.* He wrote his autobiography *My Reminiscences* (N.Y., 1896).

Arel, Bülent, Turkish composer and musicologist; b. Constantinople, April 23, 1919. He studied composition with Necil Kazim Akses at the Ankara State Cons., and also took courses in piano, conducting and acoustics. From 1951 to 1959 he was employed as sound engineer at the Ankara Radio. At the same time he occupied various teaching posts in Ankara and Istanbul. In 1961 he went to America as instructor in electronic music at Yale Univ. and Columbia Univ. In 1971 he was appointed to the faculty of the State Univ. of N.Y. at Stony Brook. In his early works he explored Turkish folksongs; then wrote pieces alternatively in a neo-classical and impressionistic manner; also experimented with serial techniques; eventually turned to electronic composition; a typical score of this period is *Impressions of Wall Street* on tape (1961). His other works include Piano Concerto (1946); *Suite intime* for orch. (1949); 2 symphonies (1951, 1952); *Stereo Electronic Music I* (1961); *For Violin and Piano* (1966); *Mimiana I* for tape, dance and film (1968); *Mimiana II* on tape (1969); *Stereo Electronic Music II* (1970).

BIBLIOGRAPHY: R. Teitelbaum, *Perspectives of New Music* III (1964–65).

Arens, Franz Xavier, German-American composer; b. Neef (Rhenish Prussia), Oct. 28, 1856; d. Los Angeles, Jan. 28, 1932. His family came to the U.S. and settled in Milwaukee when he was very young; he studied with his father and later in Germany with Rheinberger. Upon his return to America he was active as conductor of various choral and instrumental groups. He led the Gesangverein in Cleveland (1885–88); from 1890–92 he was again in Europe; he was the first to present complete programs of orchestral music by American composers in Germany. He was president of the Indianapolis College of Music (1892–96), and later settled in N.Y. as vocal teacher. In 1900 he established a series of People's Symph. Concerts, with low admission prices (from 5¢ to 50¢). He wrote orchestral music, a string quartet and numerous songs.

Arensky, Anton, Russian composer; b. Novgorod, July 12, 1861; d. Terijoki, Finland, Feb. 25, 1906. He studied at the St, Petersburg Cons. with Johanssen and Rimsky-Korsakov (1879–82); then taught harmony at the Moscow Cons. (1882–94). Returning to St. Petersburg, he conducted the choir of the Imperial Chapel (1895–1901); a victim of tuberculosis, he spent his last years in a sanatorium in Finland. In his music he followed Tchaikovsky's lyric style.
WORKS: 3 operas: *A Dream on the Volga* (Moscow, Jan. 2, 1891); *Raphael* (Moscow, May 6, 1894); *Nal and Damayanti* (Moscow, Jan. 22, 1904); 2 symphonies (he conducted the first performances of both in Moscow, Nov. 24, 1883 and Dec. 21, 1889). He was more successful in his works for smaller forms; his *Variations* for string orch. on Tchaikovsky's song, *The Christ Child had a Garden* (originally the *Variations* formed the slow movement of Arensky's Quartet, op. 35, in A minor for violin, viola and 2 cellos) became a standard work. His Piano Trio also retains its popularity. His 4 suites for 2 pianos, expertly written, are often heard; he also arranged these suites for orch. Some of his songs are included in vocal anthologies. Other works are: music to Pushkin's poem *The Fountain of Bakhtchissaray*; ballet *Egyptian Nights* (St. Petersburg, 1900); *The Diver*, ballad for voices and orch.; *Coronation Cantata*; *Marche solennelle* for orch.; *Intermezzo* for string orch.; Piano Concerto; Violin Concerto in A minor; a fantasy on epic Russian songs, for piano and orch.; Piano Quintet in D; String Quartet in G, op. 11; pieces for cello, for violin, and many pieces for piano solo. He also published a *Manual of Harmony* (translated into German) and *Handbook of Musical Forms*.
BIBLIOGRAPHY: G. Tzypin, *Arensky* (Moscow, 1966).

d'Arezzo, Guido. See **Guido d'Arezzo.**

Argenta, Ataulfo, Spanish conductor; b. Castro Urdiales, Santander, Nov. 19, 1913; d. Madrid, Jan. 21, 1958. He first sang in a church choir; in 1926 he entered the Madrid Cons., studying piano, violin and composition. He continued his musical education in Germany and studied conducting. Returning to Spain in 1939, he conducted various small groups; in 1945 became director of the National Orch. in Madrid.
BIBLIOGRAPHY: A. Fernandez-Cid, *Ataulfo Argenta* (Madrid, 1958).

Argento, Dominick, outstanding American composer; b. York, Pennsylvania, Oct. 27, 1927. He studied at the Peabody Cons. in Baltimore between 1947 and 1954 where his composition teachers were Hugo Weisgall, Nicolas Nabokov and Henry Cowell. In the interim he also studied in Florence with Luigi Dallapiccola; returning to America he took courses with Howard Hanson and Bernard Rogers at the Eastman School of Music in Rochester (Ph.D. 1957). He was a co-founder of the Hilltop Opera Company in Baltimore (1950) and the Center Opera Company (now the Minnesota Opera) in Minneapolis. In 1958 he was appointed to the faculty at the Univ. of Minnesota in Minneapolis. In 1975 he received the Pulitzer Prize for his song cycle *From the Diary of Virginia Woolf*. In his compositions, Argento has developed a style that is constructively eclectic, ranging from expansive Italianate cantabile to tense and acerb polyphony; by the nature of his talent he is most successful in vocal composition, particularly opera.
WORKS: 8 operas: *The Boor* (Rochester, May 6, 1957), *Colonel Jonathan the Saint* (1958–61; Denver Lyric Opera, Dec. 31, 1971), *Christopher Sly* (Univ. of Minn., May 31, 1963), *The Masque of Angels* (Minneapolis, Jan. 9, 1964), *Shoemakers' Holiday* (Minneapolis, June 1, 1967), *Postcard from Morocco* (Minneapolis, Oct. 14, 1971), a monodrama *A Water Bird Talk* (1974), and *The Voyage of Edgar Allan Poe* (Minnesota Opera, April 24, 1976; achieved an extraordinary critical acclaim). He also composed *Songs About Spring*, cycle for soprano and chamber orch. (1950, revised 1954 and 1960); *Divertimento* for piano and strings (1954); *The Resurrection of Don Juan,* ballet (1955) *Ode to the West Wind,* concerto for soprano and orch., (Rochester, N.Y., April 20, 1957); String Quartet (1956); *6 Elizabethan Songs* for high voice and piano (1958); *Royal Invitation (or Homage to the Queen of Tonga)* for chamber orch. (1964); *Variations (The Mask of Night)* for orch., with soprano solo in the final variation (Minneapolis, Jan. 26, 1966); *Revelation of St. John the Divine,* rhapsody for tenor, male chorus, brass ensemble and percussion (1966); *Letters from Composers* for high voice and guitar (1968); *A Nation of Cowslips,* 7 bagatelles for chorus a cappella (1968); *Bravo Mozart!,* an imaginary biography for oboe, violin, horn and orch. (1969; Minneapolis, July 3, 1969); *Tria Carmina Paschalia,* cantata for female chorus (1970); *A Ring of Time,* preludes and pageants for orch. (1972); *To Be Sung Upon the Water* for high voice, clarinet and piano (1972); *Jonah and the Whale* for narrator, soli, chorus and chamber ensemble (Minneapolis, March 11, 1974); *From the Diary of Virginia Woolf* for medium voice and piano (1974; Minneapolis, Jan. 5, 1975).

Argento, Pietro, Italian conductor; b. Gioia del Colle, March 7, 1909. He received his early musical training from his father; then entered the San Pietro a Majella Cons. of Naples, where he studied piano, oboe, organ, composition and conducting. He subsequently became a student in conducting of Bernardino Molinari at Santa Cecilia in Rome. He conducted orchestras in Germany, Austria, France and Czechoslovakia; made 7 tours in Russia. Since 1953 he has been a conductor of the Orchestra of Italian Radio-Television.

Aria, Cesare, Italian singing teacher; b. Bologna, Sept. 21, 1820; d. there, Jan. 30, 1894. He studied at the Bologna Cons. with Mattei. Rossini helped him in his career. For a number of years he was a voice teacher in France and England. He composed some church music; his *Dies irae* is particularly noteworthy.

Aribon (Aribo Scholasticus, Aribon de Liège, Aribon de Freising, and **Aribon d'Orléans),** medieval scholar; b. probably in Liège, about the year 1000; d. in Orléans, about 1078. In 1024 he was chancellor to the Bishop of Liège; after a short period of service he went to Italy, where he acquired a knowledge of the methods of Guido d'Arezzo. From 1060-70 he was again in Liège as preceptor at the Cathedral school; then went to Orléans. Aribon was the author of the important treatise *De Musica,* written in Liège about 1065. It is reproduced in Gerbert's *Scriptores* (vol. II, pp. 197-230) and in J. Smits van Waesberghe's *Corpus Scriptorum de Musica* (vol. II, Rome, 1951).
BIBLIOGRAPHY: Waesberghe, *Muziekgeschiedenis der Middeleeuwen* (1936).

d'Arienzo, Nicola, Italian composer; b. Naples, Dec. 22, 1842; d. there, April 25, 1915. He composed an opera in the Neapolitan dialect at the age of 18; a series of Italian operas followed: *I due mariti* (Naples, Feb. 1, 1866); *Il cacciatore delle Alpi* (Naples, June 23, 1870); *Il cuoco* (Naples, June 11, 1873); *I Viaggi* (Milan, June 28, 1875); *La figlia del diavolo* (Naples, Nov. 16, 1879; his most successful opera, which aroused considerable controversy for its realistic tendencies); *I tre coscritti* (Naples, Feb. 10, 1880), etc. He also wrote 2 symphonies and much choral music. He published a treatise *Introduzione del sistema tetracordale nella moderna musica,* favoring pure intonation; a historical essay, *Dell' opera comica dalle origini a Pergolesi* (1887; German translation, 1902), several monographs on Italian composers and numerous articles in periodicals.

Ariosti, Attilio, Italian opera composer; b. Bologna, Nov. 5, 1666; d. c.1740. He joined the Servite Order in 1688, but later abandoned it. He served as organist in Bologna in 1693; in 1697 he was in Berlin as court musician. From 1703 till 1711 he was in Vienna, then returned to Bologna. He was in London in 1716 and again from 1723-27. A volume of his cantatas and 'lessons' for the viola d'amore, on which he was an accomplished performer, was publ. in London in 1728. Ariosti then disappeared, the most probable conjecture being that he returned to Italy and died there in obscurity. Burney's attribution to Ariosti of one act of the opera *Muzio Scevola* (produced in London on April 15, 1721) is an anachronism, for Ariosti was not in London at the time.
WORKS: A list of his known operas includes the following: *Tirsi* (erroneously named *Dafne* by many

music historians; Venice, 1696, in collaboration with Lotti and Caldara; *Mars und Irene* (Berlin, July 12, 1703); *Marte placato* (Vienna, March 19, 1707); *Artaserse* (London, Dec. 1, 1724); *Dario* (London, April 5, 1725); *Lucio Vero, imperator di Roma* (London, Jan. 7, 1727). He also wrote 5 oratorios, some instrumental works and numerous cantatas (many of which are preserved in various European libraries).
BIBLIOGRAPHY: G. Weiss, "57 unbekannte Instrumentalstücke (15 Sonaten) von Attilio Ariosti . . .," *Die Musikforschung* (April-June 1970).

Aristides Quintilianus, Greek writer on music; lived about 200 A.D. in Smyrna. His treatise *De Musica libri VII* was printed in Meibom's *Antiquae Musicae Auctores Septem* (1652) and by A. Jahn (1882); R. Schäfke published it in German (1937) with a commentary. Despite the dubious authenticity of some of his descriptions of Greek scales, the work is one of the basic sources of our knowledge of ancient Greek music.

Aristotle, famous Greek philosopher, pupil of Plato; b. Stagira, 384 B.C.; d. Chalcis, 322 B.C. The 19th section of the *Problems,* once ascribed to him, is the product of a much later follower of his theories; the English translation, by E. S. Forster, is found in *The Works of Aristotle,* vol. 7 (Oxford, 1927); the Greek text with French translation and commentary by F. A. Gevaert and C. Vollgraff is published in *Les problèmes musicaux d'Aristote* (3 vols., 1899-1902). Aristotle's actual writings on music are reproduced by K. von Jan in his *Musici Scriptores Graeci* (1895). The name Aristotle was also used by a writer on mensurable music of the 12th-13th centuries, whose treatise is published by E. de Coussemaker in his *Scriptores,* vol. I.

Aristoxenos, one of the earliest Greek writers on music; b. Tarentum, 354 B.C. His *Harmonic Elements* (complete) and *Rhythmical Elements* (fragmentary) are among the most important treatises on Greek musical theory that have come down to us. They have been published by R. Westphal and F. Saran (2 vols., 1883, 1893); also by H. S. Macran, with English and Greek text and a commentary (1902). The *Harmonic Elements* are included, in an English translation, in O. Strunk's *Source Readings in Music History* (N.Y., 1950). See also L. Laloy, *Aristoxène de Tarente* (1904); C. F. A. Williams, *The Aristoxenian Theory of Musical Rhythm* (Cambridge, 1911).

Arizaga, Rodolfo, Argentinian composer; b. Buenos Aires, July 11, 1926. He studied philosophy at the Univ. of Buenos Aires and composition with Luis Gianneo; then went to Paris where he took lessons with Nadia Boulanger and Messiaen. Beginning with folkloric composition of the traditional Latin American type, he traversed the entire gamut of modern techniques, including 12-tone structures and aleatory composition, and applied these diverse methods liberally according to need and intention.
WORKS: cantatas *Martirio de Santa Olalla* (1952) and *Delires* (1957); *Prometeo 45,* opera (1958); Piano Concerto (1963); 2 string quartets (1968, 1969); var-

ious vocal works and piano pieces. Arizaga also published the monographs *Manuel de Falla* (Buenos Aires, 1961) and *Juan José Castro* (Buenos Aires, 1963) and edited *Enciclopedia de la música argentina* (Buenos Aires, 1971).

Arkhipova, Irina, Russian mezzo-soprano; b. Moscow, Dec. 2, 1925. She attended the vocal classes at the Institute of Architecture in Moscow, graduating in 1948; in 1953 entered the Moscow Cons.; in 1956 made her operatic debut as Carmen at the Bolshoi Theatre. Since then, she has appeared in opera and song recitals at La Scala, Milan, in Vienna, Paris, and in the U.S. She excels in the Russian repertoire, but has also distinguished herself in French and Italian operas.

Arkwright, Godfrey Edward Pellew, English music editor; b. Norwich, April 10, 1864; d. Highclere, near Newbury, Aug. 16, 1944. He studied at Eton and at Oxford. His most important publication is *The Old English Edition,* in 25 volumes (1889–1902), containing masques, ballets, motets and madrigals by English composers of the 17th and 18th centuries. He also edited Purcell's church music published by the Purcell Society. He was the editor of *Musical Antiquary* from 1909–13.

Arlen, Harold (real name **Hyman Arluck**), American composer of popular music; b. Buffalo, Feb. 15, 1905. He studied music privately with Simon Bucharoff. As a small child he joined the choir of a synagogue where his father was cantor. At 15 he began to earn a living as a pianist on lake steamboats and in nightclubs. Then he went to New York where he became engaged in a variety of professions, as singer with jazz bands, pianist, arranger, and finally composer. Possessing a natural gift of melody, he created numerous song hits, of which *Stormy Weather* (1932), became a classic of American popular music. He wrote several successful musicals for Broadway, among them *Bloomer Girl* (1944); *St. Louis Woman* (1946); *House of Flowers* (1954); *Jamaica* (1957). He also wrote music for films, among them the score for *The Wizard of Oz* (1939).
BIBLIOGRAPHY: Edward Jablonski, *Happy with the Blues* (Garden City, 1961); A. Wilder, *American Popular Song* (N.Y., 1972).

Arma, Paul (real name **Imre Weisshaus**), composer; b. Budapest, Oct. 22, 1904. He studied with Béla Bartók at the Budapest Academy of Music (1921–24). He then went to New York (1925–30); later settled in Paris, where he assumed the pseudonym Paul Arma, under which he published a *Nouveau Dictionnaire de Musique* (Paris, 1947). A composer of empiric music exploring the ultimate in complexity, he has developed a compromise method evocative of folk songs in an advanced rhythmic style.
WORKS: Concerto for String Quartet (1947); Concerto for String Quartet and orch. (1947); Sonatina for Flute solo (1947); Violin Sonata (1949); Symphony (1950); *31 instantanés* for woodwind, percussion, celesta, xylophone and piano (1951); *Polydiaphonie* for orch. (1962); *Structures variées* for orch. (1964); *Convergences de mondes arrachés* for speaker and orch.

(1968); *7 Variations spatiophoniques* for tape; *Transparencies* for various ensembles; numerous piano pieces; choruses.

Armbruster, Karl, conductor; b. Andernach-am-Rhine, Germany, July 13, 1846; d. London, June 10, 1917. He studied piano in Cologne; at the age of 17 settled in London, where he made propaganda for Wagner by means of numerous lectures. He was Hans Richter's assistant at the Wagner concerts in London in 1884; later conducted operas at London theaters. He was also one of the conductors of the Wagner cycles at Bayreuth (1884–94).

Armes, Philip, English organist and composer; b. Norwich, Aug. 15, 1836; d. Durham, Feb. 10, 1908. He received his early musical education from his father, a singer; was chorister at the Cathedrals of Norwich (1846) and Rochester (1848); for his work as a boy soloist he received the gift of a grand piano. He subsequently was organist in London, Chichester and Durham, retiring shortly before his death. He wrote the oratorios *Hezekiah* (1877), *St. John the Evangelist* (1881), *Barnabas* (1891). His madrigal *Victoria* won the first prize of the Madrigal Society in 1897.

Armin, Georg (real name **Hermann**), German singer and pedagogue; b. Brunswick, Nov. 10, 1871; d. Karlslunde Strand, Denmark, Feb. 16, 1963. He studied architecture; then turned to singing. He settled in Berlin as voice teacher; from 1925 he edited the periodical *Der Stimmwart.* His home was destroyed in Berlin during an air raid in World War II; in 1949 he settled in Denmark. He published several papers on voice production, among them *Das Stauprinzip* (1905) and *Von der Urkraft der Stimme* (1921).
BIBLIOGRAPHY: J. Berntsen, *Ein Meister der Stimmbildungskunst* (Leipzig, 1936).

Armingaud, Jules, French violinist; b. Bayonne, May 3, 1820; d. Paris, Feb. 27, 1900. He began his career as a member of the orch. at the Paris Opéra. In 1855 he organized a string quartet, which he later enlarged by adding wind instruments, and named the 'Société classique.' He published some violin pieces, and 2 musico-philosophical books of essays: *Consonances et dissonances* and *Modulations.*

Armstrong, Louis, black American jazz trumpeter, familiarly known as "Satchmo" (for "Satchel Mouth," with reference to his spacious and resonant oral cavity); b. New Orleans, July 4, 1900; d. in New York, July 6, 1971. At age 13 he was arrested for firing his stepfather's gun during a New Year's Eve celebration, and was placed in the colored Waifs Home for Boys; there he learned to read music and play several instruments, excelling on the cornet. After his release he worked as a musician, mostly in Storyville, the brothel district of New Orleans; in 1922 went to Chicago, where he played cornet in King Oliver's Creole Jazz Band; in 1925 he organized his own band—the Hot 5, and then the Hot 7—and rapidly earned fame; set an endurance record when he sounded high C on the trumpet 280 times in succession. His style of improvisation revolutionized jazz performance—on all instruments—in the 1920s, and he won admirers all over the world (including Russia), some critics hailing him as "The Einstein of Jazz." From the mid-1930s on he was no longer an innovative jazz influence, but he retained his popularity; he continued participating in jazz festivals into the 1960s, and his recording of the song *Hello Dolly* was a best-seller in 1964. His wife during the years 1924–32 was **Lil Hardin** (b. Memphis, Tenn., 1903), who was the pianist for King Oliver's group from 1920–23, and then with the Hot 5 and Hot 7 combos. He wrote an autobiography, *Satchmo, My Life in New Orleans* (N.Y., 1954).

BIBLIOGRAPHY: R. Goffin, *Horn of Plenty, The Story of Louis Armstrong* (N.Y., 1947); H. Panassié, *Louis Armstrong* (Paris, 1947; N.Y., 1971); A. McCarthy, *Louis Armstrong* (London, 1960); G. Schuller, *Early Jazz* (N.Y., 1968); M. Jones *et al. Salute to Satchmo* (London, 1970); R. Merryman, *Louis Armstrong—A Self-Portrait* (N.Y., 1971); J. G. Jepsen, *Louis Armstrong Discography, 1923–1971* (Rugsted Vyst, Denmark, 1973).

Armstrong, William Dawson, American organist and composer; b. Alton, Ill., Feb. 11, 1868; d. there, July 9, 1936. He studied with Clarence Eddy; occupied posts at various churches in Alton and St. Louis from 1890–1908; established a music school at Alton. He was active in local pedagogical groups. He wrote an opera *The Specter Bridegroom* (St. Louis, 1899); published some church music and many pieces for organ, and songs. He was the author of *The Romantic World of Music* (N.Y., 1922) and *Rudiments of Musical Notation, an Elementary Handbook*.

BIBLIOGRAPHY: W. T. Norton, *W. D. Armstrong* (N.Y., 1916).

Arne, Michael, English opera composer (natural son of **T. A. Arne**); b. London, 1741; d. there, Jan. 14, 1786. He was trained in his youth as an actor and a singer, and made his debut in London on April 2, 1750. He also acquired considerable skill as a harpsichord player. He wrote much stage music; among his operas (all produced at Drury Lane or at Covent Garden) are: *Hymen* (Jan. 20, 1764); *Cymon* (Jan. 2, 1767); *The Artifice* (April 14, 1780); *The Choice of Harlequin* (Dec. 26, 1781) and *Vertumnus and Pomona* (Feb. 21, 1782). He collaborated with other composers in the music of 14 other productions. In 1771–72 he traveled in Germany as conductor; from 1776 he was in Dublin; from 1784 again in London. He was an eccentric person, and among his vagaries was a preoccupation with alchemy, and a search for the philosopher's stone to convert base metals into gold.

BIBLIOGRAPHY: J. F. Parkinson, *An Index to the Vocal Works of Thomas Augustine Arne and Michael Arne* (Detroit, 1971).

Arne, Thomas Augustine, famous English dramatic composer; b. London, March 12, 1710; d. there, March 5, 1788. His father, an upholsterer, sent him to Eton College; he then spent three years in a solicitor's office. He studied music on the side, much against his father's wishes, and acquired considerable skill on the violin. He soon began to write musical settings "after the Italian manner," to various plays. His first produc-

tion was Addison's *Rosamond* (March 7, 1733). He renamed Fielding's *Tragedy of Tragedies* as *Opera of Operas*, and produced it at the Haymarket Theatre (May 31, 1733); a masque *Dido and Aeneas* followed (Jan. 12, 1734). His most important work was the score of *Comus* (Drury Lane, March 4, 1738). On Aug. 1, 1740, he produced at Clivedon, Bucks., the masque *Alfred*, the finale of which contains the celebrated song *Rule Britannia*, which became a national patriotic song of Great Britain. In the meantime Arne married Cecilia Young (March 15, 1737), daughter of the organist Charles Young, and herself a fine singer. In 1742 he went with her to Dublin, where he also stayed in 1755 and 1758. Of his many dramatic productions the following were performed at Drury Lane, London: *The Temple of Dullness* (Jan. 17, 1745); *Harlequin Incendiary* (March 3, 1746); *The Triumph of Peace* (Feb. 21, 1749); *Britannia* (May 9, 1755); *Beauty and Virtue* (Feb. 26, 1762); *The Rose* (Dec. 2, 1772). The following were staged at Covent Garden: *Harlequin Sorcerer* (Feb. 11, 1752); *The Prophetess* (Feb. 1, 1758); *Thomas and Sally* (Nov. 28, 1760); *Love in a Village* (Dec. 8, 1762); *The Fairy Prince* (Nov. 12, 1771). He further contributed separate numbers to 28 theatrical productions, among them songs to Shakespeare's *As You Like It;* 'Where the Bee Sucks' in *The Tempest,* etc. He wrote 2 oratorios: *Abel* (Dublin, Feb. 18, 1744); and *Judith* (Drury Lane, Feb. 27, 1761), the latter remarkable for the introduction of female voices into the choral parts. He also wrote numerous glees and catches, and miscellaneous instrumental music. He received the honorary degree of Doc. of Mus. from Oxford Univ. (July 6, 1759), which accounts for his familiar appellation of 'Dr. Arne.'

BIBLIOGRAPHY: J. F. Parkinson, *An Index to the Vocal Works of Thomas Augustine Arne and Michael Arne* (Detroit, 1971).

d'Arneiro, (José Augusto) Ferreira Veiga, Viscount, distinguished Portuguese composer; b. Macao, China, Nov. 22, 1838; d. San Remo, July 7, 1903. He studied with Botelho, Schira and Soares in Lisbon. The production of his ballet *Gina* (Lisbon, 1866) attracted attention; he then produced an opera *L'Elisire di Giovinezza* (Lisbon, March 31, 1876), followed by *La Derelitta* (Lisbon, 1885). *Te Deum,* performed in Lisbon and in London in 1871 was very successful; it was later given in Paris under the somewhat affected title of 'Symphonie-Cantate.'

Arnell, Richard, English composer; b. London, Sept. 15, 1917. He studied with John Ireland at the Royal College of Music (1935–38). In 1939 he went to America; when Winston Churchill had a reception at Columbia Univ. in 1946, Arnell wrote *Prelude and Flourish* for brass instruments, performed at the occasion. In 1948 Arnell returned to London. A prolific composer, he wrote 5 symphonies, 2 piano concertos, Harpsichord Concerto, Violin Concerto, overtures and miscellaneous pieces of chamber music and also music employing electronic instruments. He particularly excelled in his stage works. He composed a 1-act opera *Moon Flowers* (1958); the ballets *Punch and the Child* (1948); *Harlequin in April* (1951); *The Great Detective* (about Sherlock Holmes, 1953); a multi-media score, *Combat Zone,* for 2 speakers, vocal soloists, chorus, wind instruments, a jazz group, tape and film (1969); an overture *Food of Love* (1968); a television opera, *Love in Transit* (1955); and *The Petrified Princess* (1959).

Arnestad, Finn, Norwegian composer; b. Oslo, Sept. 23, 1915. He studied violin and piano in Oslo and, briefly, composition from Bjarne Brustad; pursued his studies in Paris, Germany, Holland and Belgium. His works carry an aura of impressionism.
WORKS: *3 Intermezzi for Orch.* (1947); *I.N.R.I.,* 2 concert suites from a symph. mystery play (1952–55); Violin Concerto (1957); *Aria Appassionata* for orch. (1962); *Cavatina Cambiata* for orch. (1965; originally titled *Dopplersonance*); *Smeden og Bageren (The Blacksmith and the Baker)* for baritone, flute, oboe, harpsichord and strings (1966); *Overture* (1970); *Vaeletjennet* for orch. (1970); *Toccata for Orch.* (1972); String Quartet (c.1947); *Missa Brevis* for chorus and 6 instruments (1951); Sextet for flute, clarinet, bassoon, violin, cello and piano (1959); 2 piano sonatas (1967); Trombone Sonata (1971).

Arnič, Blaž, Slovenian composer; b. Luče, Jan. 31, 1901; d. in Ljubljana, Feb. 1, 1970. He studied composition and organ at the Cons. of Ljubljana (1925–29) and at the New Vienna Cons. (1929–32). Later he took courses in Warsaw and Paris. In 1945 he was appointed prof. at the Music Academy of Ljubljana. He wrote 9 symphonies, all with meaningful subtitles: *Te Deum,* with chorus (1932), *Symphonic Rhapsody* (1933), *Resurrection* (1935), *Reverie* (1940), *The Whirlwind of War* (1941), *Pioneer* (1948), *Symphony of Labor* (1950), *In the Fatherland's Soul* (1951), *War and Peace* (1960); 2 symph. poems, *Memento mori* (1934), *Witch Dance* (1951); Organ Concerto (1931); Cello Concerto (1960); Clarinet Concerto (1963); 3 violin concertos (1953, 1953, 1966); Viola Concerto (1967); chamber music; piano pieces; songs. All of his music is permeated with folk motives; his last works reflect the revolutionary era after the end of the war.

Arnold, Byron, American composer; b. Vancouver, Wash., Aug. 15, 1901. He studied at Willamette Univ. (B.A., 1924) and later at the Eastman School of Music, with Bernard Rogers and Howard Hanson. From 1938 to 1948 he was on the faculty of the Univ. of Alabama. One of his most original pieces is a symphonic suite entitled *Five Incapacitated Preludes,* each portraying a serious incapacitation (deafness, blindness, paralysis, etc.; the deaf prelude instructs the players to pretend they are playing music, but without producing any sounds); it was performed in Rochester, N.Y. on April 19, 1937. He also wrote *Three Fantasticisms* for orch., piano pieces and songs. He published *Folk Songs of Alabama* (1950).

Arnold, Frank Thomas, English music scholar; b. Rugby, Sept. 6, 1861; d. Bath, Sept. 24, 1940. He studied at Trinity College, Cambridge, and was lecturer in German literature at the University College of South Wales at Cardiff (1886–1926). He wrote a valuable book, *The Art of Accompaniment from a Thorough-Bass, as Practiced in the 17th and 18th Centuries* (London, 1931), and contributed numerous papers on Bach, Viadana, Corelli, etc. to various music journals. He was also a collector of rare editions.
BIBLIOGRAPHY: D. R. Wakeling, "An Interesting Music Collection," *Music & Letters* (July 1945).

Arnold, Georg, Hungarian composer; b. Paks, June 5, 1781; d. Subotica, Oct. 25, 1848. Adopting an operatic method in religious music, he created some unusual effects. His 3 operas were never performed, and the MSS seem to be lost, but his church music is extant. Arnold completed a music dictionary (1826) which, however, was never published. His songs, in the Hungarian style, were once very popular.
BIBLIOGRAPHY: K. Isoz, *Georg Arnold* (Budapest, 1908).

Arnold, Gustav, Swiss organist and composer; b. Altdorf, Uri, Sept. 1, 1831; d. Lucerne, Sept. 28, 1900. He studied at Innsbruck; in 1850 he went to England, where he was choirmaster and organist at various churches. He returned to Switzerland in 1865 and settled in Lucerne as organizer of choral festivals and conductor. He wrote some sacred music and piano pieces.

Arnold, Johann Gottfried, German violoncellist and composer; b. Niederhall, near Öhringen, Feb. 1, 1773; d. Frankfurt, July 26, 1806. He studied with Willmann and Bernhard Romberg; after a brief concert career he became a theater cellist in Frankfurt. He wrote a *Symphonie concertante* for 2 flutes and orch.; several cello concertos; 6 sets of variations for cello, and various pieces for the guitar and other instruments.

Arnold, Karl, German organist and conductor; son of **Johann Gottfried Arnold;** b. Neukirchen, near Mergentheim, Württemberg, May 6, 1794; d. Christiania (Oslo), Norway, Nov. 11, 1877. He studied with J. A. André and Vollweiler; then occupied various positions in St. Petersburg, Russia (1818), Berlin (1824) and Münster (1835). In 1847 he went to Norway where he became conductor of the Philharmonic Society in Christiania, and also was a church organist there. He wrote an opera *Irene* (Berlin, 1832), a piano sextet, and numerous works for piano solo.

Arnold, Malcolm, prolific and versatile English composer; b. Northampton, Oct. 21, 1921. He studied composition (with Gordon Jacob), conducting (with Lambert) and trumpet at the Royal College of Music in London (1938–40); was principal trumpeter with the London Philharmonic (1942–44, 1946–48); received additional conducting tutelage from Eduard van Beinum.
WORKS: 2 operas: *The Dancing Master* (1951), and *The Open Window* (1956); ballets, *Homage to the Queen* (1953; London, June 2, 1953: evening of the Coronation of Queen Elizabeth II), *Rinaldo and Armida* (1954), *Sweeney Todd* (1958) and *Electra* (1963); the nativity play *Song of Simeon* for chorus, mime and orch. (1958); a children's play *The Turtle Drum* for mime, children's voices and percussion band (1967). His orchestral works include a Symphony for Strings (1946); 7 numbered symphonies: No. 1 (Chel-

tenham Festival, July 6, 1951), No. 2 (Bournemouth, May 25, 1953), No. 3 (London, Dec. 2, 1957), No. 4 (London, Nov. 2, 1960), No. 5 (Cheltenham Festival, 1961), No. 6 (Manchester, 1968), No. 7 (1973; London, 1974); 14 solo concertos: 2 for horn (1945; 1956); 2 for clarinet (1948, 1974); one for piano duet (1951); one for oboe (1952), 2 for flute (1954); one for harmonica (1954; London, Aug. 14, 1954, Larry Adler soloist); one for organ (1954); one for guitar (1958); one for 2 violins (1962); one for 2 pianos, 3-hands (1969); one for viola (1970). He furthermore wrote 10 overtures: *Beckus the Dandipratt* (1943); *Festival Overture* (1946); *The Smoke* (1948); *A Sussex Overture* (1951); *Tam O'Shanter* (1955); *A Grand, Grand Overture* for 3 vacuum cleaners, 1 floor polisher, 4 rifles and orch. (1956); *Commonwealth Christmas Overture* (1957); *Peterloo* (1968); *Anniversary Overture* (1968); *The Fair Field* (1972). Other orchestral works are: the tone poem *Larch Trees* (1943); Serenade for Small Orch. (1950); 8 *English Dances* in 2 sets (1950-51); *The Sound Barrier*, rhapsody (1952); 3 sinfoniettas (1954, 1958, 1964); 2 *Little Suites* (1955, 1962); Serenade for Guitar and Strings (1955); *4 Scottish Dances* (1957); *4 Cornish Dances* (1966); Concerto for 28 Players (1970); *Fantasy for Audience and Orch.* (1970); *A Flourish for Orchestra* (1973); Fantasy for Brass Band (1974). CHAMBER MUSIC: Trio for Flute, Viola and Bassoon (1943); *3 Shanties* for wind quintet (1944); Wind Quintet (1944); Duo for Flute and Viola (1945); 2 violin sonatas (1947, 1953); Viola Sonata (1947); Flute Sonatina (1948); String Quartet No. 1 (1949); Oboe Sonatina (1951); Clarinet Sonatina (1951); Recorder Sonatina (1953); Piano Trio (1955); Oboe Quartet (1957); *Toy Symphony* for 12 toy instruments, piano and string quartet (1957); Brass Quintet (1961); *5 Pieces for Violin and Piano* (1965); 9 solo Fantasies: for bassoon, clarinet, horn, flute, oboe, trumpet, trombone, tuba, and guitar; *Trevelyan Suite* for wind instruments (1968); piano pieces; songs; music for films, notably *The Bridge on the River Kwai*, in which he popularized the rollicking march tune, *Colonel Bogey*, originally written by Kenneth Alford in 1914. In his music, Arnold retains a happy common touch without attendant vulgarity. His experience as an orchestral trumpet player and conductor has enabled him to acquire a facility for instrumental writing and versatility of styles, ranging from English folksong modalities to quasi-modernistic and occasionally humorous expositions. As a result, his works enjoy frequent performances, particularly in England.

Arnold, Maurice (real name **Maurice Arnold Strothotte**), American violinist and composer; b. St. Louis, Jan. 19, 1865; d. New York, Oct. 23, 1937. He studied in Cincinnati; then in Germany with several teachers, including Max Bruch. The performance of his orchestral work *American Plantation Dances* (New York, 1894) aroused the interest of Dvořák, because of the Negro melodies used in it, and he engaged Arnold to teach at the National Cons. of which Dvořák was then head. Arnold subsequently was active as conductor of light opera, and as violin teacher. He wrote a comic opera *The Merry Benedicts* (Brooklyn, 1896); a grand opera *Cleopatra*; a symphony; a cantata *The Wild Chase*; *Minstrel Serenade* for violin and piano; and a fugue for piano 8 hands.

Arnold, Richard, German-American violinist; b. Eilenberg, Prussia, Jan. 10, 1845; d. New York, June 21, 1918. He emigrated to the U.S. in 1853, but returned to Germany in 1864 to study with Ferdinand David in Leipzig. He was a violinist in the Theodore Thomas Orch. (1869-76), and concertmaster of the New York Philharmonic Orch. (1880-1909). Then lived in New York as violin teacher.

Arnold, Samuel, celebrated English composer, organist and music scholar; b. London, Aug. 10, 1740; d. there, Oct. 22, 1802. He received his musical training from Gates and Nares as a chorister of the Chapel Royal. He early showed a gift for composition, and was commissioned to arrange the music for a play *The Maid of the Mill*; for this he selected songs by some 20 composers, including Bach, and added several numbers of his own; the resulting pasticcio was produced with success at Covent Garden (Jan. 31, 1765). This was the first of his annual productions for Covent Garden and other theaters in London, of which the following were composed mainly by Arnold: *Harlequin Dr. Faustus* (Nov. 18, 1766); *The Royal Garland* (Oct. 10, 1768); *The Magnet* (June 27, 1771); *A Beggar on Horseback* (June 16, 1785); *The Gnome* (Aug. 5, 1788); *New Spain, or Love in Mexico* (July 16, 1790); *The Surrender of Calais* (July 30, 1791); *The Enchanted Wood* (July 25, 1792); *The Sixty-Third Letter* (July 18, 1802). He also wrote several oratorios, among them *The Cure of Saul* (1767); *Abimelech*; *The Resurrection*; *The Prodigal Son*; and *Elisha* (1795; his last oratorio). On the occasion of a performance of *The Prodigal Son* at Oxford Univ. in 1773, Arnold was given the degree of D. Mus. In 1783, he became the successor of Nares as composer to the Chapel Royal, for which he wrote several odes and anthems. In 1789 Arnold was engaged as conductor of the Academy of Ancient Music; in 1793 he became organist of Westminster Abbey. He was buried in Westminster Abbey, near to Purcell and Blow. Arnold's edition of Handel's works, begun in 1786, was carried out by him in 36 volumes, embracing about 180 numbers; it is, however, incomplete and inaccurate in many respects. His principal work is *Cathedral Music* (1790, 4 vols.); its subtitle describes its contents: "A collection in score of the most valuable and useful compositions for that Service by the several English Masters of the last 200 years." It forms a sequel to Boyce's work of the same name. A new edition of Arnold's *Cathedral Music* was issued by Rimbault (1847).

Arnold, Youri, Russian opera composer and theorist; b. St. Petersburg, Nov. 13, 1811; d. Karakash, Crimea, July 20, 1898. He was of German extraction; studied at the German Univ. of Dorpat, Estonia; from 1863 to 1871 he lived in Leipzig; then returned to Russia; he lived in Moscow until 1894, when he moved to St. Petersburg. He wrote a comic opera *Treasure Trove* (St. Petersburg, Feb. 1, 1853), the manuscript of which was lost in the fire of the St. Petersburg Opera Theater in 1859, together with the manuscript of his other opera *St. John's Eve.* He further composed an overture, *Boris Godunov.* Arnold was the author of the first book in the Russian language dealing with the theory of composition (1841); also published *Theory of Old Russian Religious Dance* (Moscow, 1880) and many articles on Russian music for German periodicals. Among his publications in German was *Der Einfluss des Zeitgeistes auf die Entwickelung der Tonkunst* (Leipzig, 1867). He translated into German the librettos of operas by Tchaikovsky and Glinka, and published the historically valuable memoirs (3 vols.; Moscow, 1893).

Arnoldson, Sigrid, Swedish dramatic soprano; b. Stockholm, March 20, 1861; d. there, Feb. 7, 1943. She was the daughter of the celebrated tenor **Oscar Arnoldson** (b. 1830; d. Carlsbad, July 8, 1881). She studied with Maurice Strakosch and Désirée Artôt; made her debut in Moscow in 1886 as Rosina in *Il Barbiere di Siviglia*; then sang as prima donna in London (June 20, 1887), at the Opéra-Comique in Paris, in Nice and in Rome with brilliant success. In 1888 she was engaged at Covent Garden as successor to Patti. On Nov. 29, 1894, she made her debut at the Metropolitan Opera. In 1910 she was elected member of the Stockholm Academy; in 1922 settled in Vienna as a singing teacher; later taught in Berlin. On June 16, 1888, she married the Austrian impresario, Alfred Fischhof, a nephew of Maurice Strakosch.

Arnould, (Madeleine) Sophie, French operatic soprano; b. Paris, Feb. 14, 1740; d. there, Oct. 18, 1802. She studied singing with Mme. Fel and acting with Mlle. Clairon; made her debut at the Paris Opéra on Dec. 15, 1757. She created the title role in Gluck's *Iphigénie en Aulide* (April 19, 1774), and after a highly successful career retired in 1778 with a pension of 2,000 livres. Gabriel Pierné wrote a one-act 'lyric comedy,' *Sophie Arnould* (1926), based on incidents of her life.
BIBLIOGRAPHY: *Arnouldiana,* a large collection of anecdotes, published anonymously (Paris, 1813; real author, A. Deville); E. and J. de Goncourt, *Sophie Arnould d'après sa correspondance et ses mémoires* (Paris, 1877); R. B. Douglas, *Sophie Arnould, Actress and Wit* (Paris, 1898).

Arquier, Joseph, French opera composer; b. Toulon, 1763; d. Bordeaux, Oct., 1816. He played the cello in a theater at Lyon; then lived in Marseilles and Paris. After 1800 he went to New Orleans as director of an opera troupe, but failed and returned to France in 1804, holding various positions in Paris, Toulouse, Marseilles and Perpignan; he died in poverty. Arquier wrote about 16 comic operas.

Arrau, Claudio, eminent Chilean pianist; b. Chillán, Feb. 6, 1903. He received his early training from his mother, an amateur pianist, and as a child played a program of pieces by Mozart, Beethoven and Chopin at a public performance in Santiago. In 1910 he was sent by the Chilean government to Berlin where he took lessons with Martin Krause. In 1914-15 he gave piano recitals in Germany and Scandinavia, attracting attention by his precocious talent. In 1921 he returned

to Chile, making his first professional appearances there and elsewhere in South America. In 1923 he made his first American tour as soloist with the Boston Symph. Orch. and the Chicago Symph. In 1925 he was appointed to the faculty of the Stern Cons. in Berlin. He won the Grand Prix International des Pianistes at Geneva in 1927; in 1929 he made a tour of Russia, returning for a second tour the following year. During the season 1935-36 he presented in Berlin the complete keyboard works of Bach in 12 recitals; in 1936 he performed all keyboard works of Mozart in 5 recitals in Berlin. In 1938 he played all 32 piano sonatas, and all 5 piano concertos of Beethoven in Mexico City, and in 1939 repeated this series in Buenos Aires and Santiago. In 1941 he settled permanently in New York, devoting himself to concert appearances and teaching. In 1947 he made a tour of Australia, and in 1949 gave a series of concerts in South Africa. In 1951 he toured in Israel. In 1956 he played in India; in 1958 he gave concerts in Prague and Bucharest. In 1965 he made his first tour in Japan. In 1973 he made a complete recording of Beethoven sonatas. He also supervised the edition of the Urtext of Beethoven's piano sonatas. In his playing Arrau combines a classical purity and precision of style with a rhapsodic éclat.

Arregui Garay, Vicente, Spanish composer; b. Madrid, July 3, 1871; d. there, Dec. 1, 1925. He studied in Paris and Rome; was active in Madrid as music critic; wrote a symph. poem *Historia de una madre* (after H. C. Andersen, 1910); *Sinfonia vasca* for orch.; the operas *Yolanda, La Maya* and *El Cuento de Barba Azul*; a cantata *El Lobo ciego*; chamber music and choral works. His music follows the romantic school of programmatic writing.

Arriaga, Juan Crisóstomo, precocious Spanish composer; b. Rigoitia, near Bilbao, Jan. 27, 1806; d. Paris, Jan. 17, 1826 (10 days before his 20th birthday). At the age of 11, he wrote an Octet for French horn, strings, guitar and piano subtitled *Nada y Mucho*, and a 2-act opera, *Los esclavos felices*, at 13. On the strength of these works he was accepted at the Cons. of Paris where he studied with Baillot and Fétis. In Paris he wrote a Symphony, a biblical scene *Agar*, 3 string quartets, several fugues, piano pieces and songs. On Aug. 13, 1933, a memorial was unveiled to him in Bilbao and a Comisión Permanente Arriaga was formed to publish his works. Under its auspices, the vocal score of the opera and the full scores of his Symphony and Octet were printed. A bibliographical pamphlet *Resurgimiento de las obras de Arriaga* by Juan de Eresalde was also published (Bilbao, 1953).

Arrieta y Corera, Pascual Juan Emilio, Spanish composer; b. Puente la Reina, Oct. 21, 1823; d. Madrid, Feb. 11, 1894. He studied at the Milan Cons. (1842-45) with Vaccai; returned to Spain in 1848; was prof. at the Madrid Cons. in 1857; became its director in 1868. He wrote more than 50 zarzuelas and several grand operas in Italian. Of these productions the most important is *La conquista de Granada*, produced in Madrid (Oct. 10, 1850) with Arrieta himself conducting, and revived five years later under the title *Isabel la Católica* (Madrid, Dec. 18, 1855). Other successful zarzuelas and operas are *Ildegonda* (Milan, Feb. 28, 1845); *El Domino Azul* (Madrid, Feb. 19, 1853); *El Grumete* (Madrid, June 17, 1853; its sequel, *La Vuelta del Corsario*, was performed in Madrid, Feb. 18, 1863); *Marina* (Madrid, Sept. 21, 1855; revised and produced as a grand opera, Madrid, Oct. 4, 1871); *S. Francesco da Siena* (Madrid, Oct. 27, 1883).

Arrieu, Claude, French composer and pianist; b. Paris, Nov. 30, 1903. She studied piano with Marguerite Long, and composition at the Paris Cons. with Roger-Ducasse and Noël Gallon, graduating with Premier Prix in 1932. Among her many works are a music drama, *Noë* (Strasbourg, Jan. 29, 1950); comic operas *Cadet Roussel* (Marseille, Oct. 2, 1953), *La Cabine téléphonique* (Paris Radio, March 15, 1959), and *La Princesse de Babylone* (Reims, March 4, 1960); numerous scores of incidental music for radio; 2 violin concertos; a piano concerto; a flute concerto; chamber music; songs.

Arrigo, Girolamo, Italian composer; b. Palermo, April 2, 1930. He studied at the Palermo Cons., and later in Rome and Paris. His works are mostly in small form, and virtually all with programmatic connotations. The most important among them are *Tre occasione* for soprano and 32 instruments (1958); *Quarta occasione* for 7 voices, horn, viola, mandolin, guitar and celesta (1959); *Fluxus* for 9 instruments (1959); *Episodi* for soprano and flute to texts by ancient Greek poets (1963); *Shadows* for orch. (1965) and *Infrarosso* (*Infrared*) for 16 instruments (1967). He also wrote a "collage opera" entitled *Orden* (1969), consisting of several not necessarily related numbers, to texts in French, Italian and Spanish.

Arrigoni, Carlo, Italian composer; b. Florence, Dec. 5, 1697; d. there, Aug. 19, 1744. He left Italy as a young man; in 1728 he was in Brussels. In 1732 he was invited to London by a group favorable to Italian composers in opposition to Handel; there he produced an opera *Fernando* (Feb. 8, 1734). Arrigoni then went back to Italy through Vienna, where he produced an oratorio *Esther* (1737); returning to Florence, he staged his new operas *Sirbace* and *Scipione nelle Spagne* (1739). His 10 *Cantate da camera* were published in London (1732). Several airs from his opera *Fernando* are preserved in the British Museum; Burney mistakenly attributed the music of this opera to Porpora.

l'Arronge, Adolf, German conductor and composer; b. Hamburg, March 8, 1838; d. Berlin, Dec. 25, 1908. He studied at the Leipzig Cons.; then conducted opera in Cologne, Danzig, Berlin, Breslau and Budapest. He wrote a number of light operas which, however, failed to obtain any degree of success.

Arroyo, João Marcellino, eminent Portuguese composer, writer and statesman; b. Oporto, Oct. 4, 1861; d. there, May 18, 1930. A member of a musical family, he first took lessons with his father; at the same time he studied law. From 1884-1904 he was a member of the Portuguese parliament; in 1900-01 he held the posts of minister of foreign affairs and public educa-

tion. A royalist, he abandoned politics after the revolution of 1910, and received a professorship of law at the Univ. of Coimbra.
WORKS: 2 operas: *Amor de Perdição* (Lisbon, March 2, 1907; Hamburg, Jan. 25, 1910), regarded as the first modern Portuguese opera, and *Leonor Teles*; two symphonic poems; several choral works and songs; also compiled a manual of solfeggio for primary schools.
BIBLIOGRAPHY: article on him, E. Amorim, *Dicionário biográfico de músicos do Norte de Portugal* (Oporto, 1941); C. A. Dos Santos, *João Arroyo* (Lisbon, 1941).

Arroyo, Martina, American soprano; b. in New York, Feb. 2, 1940. She made her debut at the age of 18; sang with the N.Y. Philharmonic and other orchestras as soloist. In 1965 she was called upon to substitute for Birgit Nilsson at the Metropolitan Opera as Aida, scoring spontaneous acclaim. This marked the beginning of a spectacular operatic career, and she has since made successful appearances in America and in Europe.

Artaria, music publishing house in Vienna, founded by the cousins **Carlo A.** (1747-1808) and **Francesco A.** (1744-1808). They opened a music shop on Kohlmarkt in 1769, and in 1778 began printing music; they introduced the method of zinc plating for the first time in Vienna. In 1779 the firm acquired some of Haydn's works, which brought them fame; music of Clementi, Salieri and Boccherini was published later. Artaria publ. Mozart's 6 violin sonatas (K. 296, 376-80), the *Haffner-Sinfonie* and 6 string quartets dedicated to Haydn, among other works, thus becoming Mozart's most important publisher in his lifetime. Other first editions in Artaria's catalogue were several songs by Schubert, Beethoven's C major Quintet, op. 29, and string quartets, op. 130 and 133. The last owners were **Carl August Artaria** (d. 1919); **Dominik Artaria** (d. 1936) and **Franz Artaria** (d. 1942). After 1932, the old house became an art gallery and an auction bureau, preserving the name Artaria.
BIBLIOGRAPHY: F. Artaria and Hugo Botstiber, *Joseph Haydn und das Verlagshaus Artaria* (Vienna, 1909); D. MacArdle, "Beethoven, Artaria, and the C major Quintet," *Musical Quarterly* (Oct. 1948); A. Weinmann, *Vollständiges Verlagsverzeichnis, Artaria & Comp.* (Vienna, 1952).

Arteaga, Esteban de, Spanish writer on music; b. Moraleja de Coca, Segovia, Dec. 26, 1747; d. Paris, Oct. 30, 1799. He joined the Jesuit Order at 16, and was banished to Corsica when they were proscribed in Spain. He left the Order in 1769; from 1773-78 he studied philosophy at the Univ. of Bologna; there he formed a friendship with Padre Martini, and at his behest undertook a history of the musical theater in Italy. The resulting work, *Le rivoluzioni del teatro musicale italiano dalla sua origine fino al presente,* was published in 3 volumes in Bologna and Venice (1783-86; the materials in the Bologna edition partly overlap, partly supplement those in the Venice edition); it was brought out in German by J. Forkel (2 vols., Leipzig, 1789); a summary was published in

French (1802). Arteaga's strong and often critical opinions expressed in this work antagonized many Italian writers who resented the intrusion of a foreigner into their own field. A polemical exchange of considerable acrimony followed; Arteaga's views were attacked by Matteo Borsa in a tract *Del gusto presente in letteratura italiana . . .* and by Vincenzo Manfredini in *Difesa della musica moderna . . .* (Bologna, 1786). After a sojourn in Venice (1785), Arteaga lived in Rome (1786–87); in 1796 he went to Florence and later to Paris. In addition to his magnum opus, he published a book on esthetics, *Investigaciones filosóficas sobre la belleza ideal . . .* (Madrid, 1789; new ed., Madrid, 1943). A book of essays *Lettere musico-filologiche* and the treatise *Del ritmo sonoro e del ritmo muto nella musica degli antichi* (long regarded as lost) were published in Madrid in 1944, with an extensive biographical account by the editor Miguel Battlori, who also gives the bibliographical synopsis of the Bologna and Venice editions of *Rivoluzioni*.

Arthur, Alfred, American composer and choral conductor; b. Pittsburgh, Pa., Oct. 8, 1844; d. Lakewood, Ohio, Nov. 20, 1918. He studied with Eichberg at the Boston Cons.; sang at Boston churches; then moved to Cleveland where he was conductor of the Vocal Society (from 1873) and director of the Cleveland School of Music. He wrote 3 operas which remain unperformed and unpublished: *The Water-carrier* (1876); *The Roundheads and Cavaliers* (1878) and *Adaline* (1879); brought out *Progressive Vocal Studies* (1887) and other manuals on singing.

Artôt, Alexandre-Joseph Montagney, Belgian violinist; b. Brussels, Jan. 25, 1815; d. Ville-d'Avray, July 20, 1845. He studied with his father, **Maurice Artôt,** and with Snel; then took lessons from Rodolphe and Auguste Kreutzer at the Paris Cons., obtaining first prize (1828). He then played concerts on the continent; made his debut in London (June 3, 1839) in his own *Fantaisie* for violin and orch. In 1843 he embarked on an American concert tour. He wrote a violin concerto, several sets of variations for violin, and some chamber music.

Artôt, Désirée (baptismal name **Marguerite-Joséphine Désiré Montagney**), Belgian mezzo-soprano (daughter of **Jean-Désiré Artôt**); b. Paris, July 21, 1835; d. Berlin, April 3, 1907. She studied with Mme. Viardot-Garcia; sang in Belgium, Holland and England (1857). Meyerbeer engaged her to sing in *Le Prophète* at the Paris Opera (Feb. 5, 1858); she was greatly praised by Berlioz and other Paris musicians and critics. In 1858 she went to Italy; then made appearances in London. In 1868 she was in Russia, where she was briefly engaged to Tchaikovsky; however, this engagement was quickly disrupted by her marriage (on Sept. 15, 1869) to the Spanish singer **Padilla y Ramos** (1842–1906). Their daughter is **Lola Artôt de Padilla.**

Artôt, Jean-Désiré, Belgian horn player and composer; b. Paris, Sept. 23, 1803; d. Brussels, March 25, 1887. He was a pupil and successor of his father, **Maurice Artôt.** From 1843 he taught at the Brussels Cons.; also played in the Court Orch. He published fantasias and études for horn and quartets for cornets à pistons.

Artôt, Maurice Montagney, ancestor of a celebrated line of musicians (the true family name being Montagney); b. Gray (Haute-Saône), Feb. 3, 1772; d. Brussels, Jan. 8, 1829. He was a bandmaster in the French Army; then went to Brussels where he became first horn player at the Théâtre de la Monnaie. A versatile musician, he also played the guitar and taught singing.

Artusi, Giovanni Maria, Italian contrapuntist and writer on music; b. Bologna, c.1540; d. there, Aug. 18, 1613. He became canon-in-ordinary at S. Salvatore in Bologna in Feb., 1562. A capable musician and writer, a pupil of Zarlino, Artusi was reactionary in his musical philosophy. His first publication, *L'Arte del contrappunto* (in 2 parts, Venice, 1586 and 1598) has considerable theoretical value. He then published several polemical essays directed mainly against the innovations of Monteverdi and others: the characteristically named volume *L'Artusi, ovvero delle imperfettioni della moderna musica* (Venice, 1600; reproduced in part in English by O. Strunk in *Source Readings in Music History,* N.Y., 1950); a posthumous attack on his teacher Zarlino in *Impresa del R. P. Gioseffo Zarlino* (Bologna, 1604); *Considerazioni musicali* (1603; as part II of *L'Artusi,* etc.); *Discorso musicale . . .* (1606); *Discorso secondo musicale* (both attacking Monteverdi); and further polemical essays against Bottrigari and Vincenzo Galileo. Monteverdi replied to Artusi in a leaflet entitled *Ottuso accademico* and in the preface to his 5th book of madrigals; this reply is reproduced in Strunk's *Source Readings in Music History.* Bottrigari replied in a pamphlet entitled *Ant' Artusi.* As a composer, Artusi followed the old school; he published a set of 4-part *Canzonette* (1598), and an 8-part motet *Cantate Domino* (1599).
BIBLIOGRAPHY: H. Redlich, *Claudio Monteverdi, Life and Works* (London, 1952).

Artzibushev, Nikolai, Russian composer, music editor and pedagogue; b. Tsarkoe-Selo, March 7, 1858; d. Paris, April 15, 1937. He studied with Rimsky-Korsakov and Soloviev; in 1908 was elected president of the St. Petersburg Royal Music Society. After the revolution he went to Paris where he was in charge of the Belaiev publishing house. As a composer he is chiefly known for his melodious piano pieces and songs in a distinct style of the Russian national school; he also wrote a *Valse Fantasia* for orch. and was one of the group of composers who contributed to a collection, *Variations on a Russian Theme* for string quartet; other variations were by Rimsky-Korsakov, Glazunov, Liadov and Scriabin.

Arutiunian, Alexander, Armenian composer; b. Yerevan, Sept. 23, 1920. He studied piano and composition at the local cons.; later went to Moscow where he took a course in composition with Litinsky. Returning to Armenia, he was appointed musical director of the Armenian Philharmonic Society. In his works he utilizes authentic folksong inflections of Armenian popular music; his *Cantata of the Fatherland* on native themes (1948) achieved considerable success. His other important works are a Piano Concerto (1941); Trumpet Concerto (1950); *Chronicle of the Armenian People*, a symph. poem (1961); Horn Concerto (1962); an opera, *Sayat-Nova* (1967); *Ode to Lenin* (1967); *Hymn to Brotherhood* (1970); a cycle for chorus a cappella, *My Armenia* (1971); chamber music. A monograph on him was published in the Armenian language in Yerevan (1962).

Asafiev, Boris, Russian composer and writer on music; b. St. Petersburg, July 29, 1884; d. Moscow, Jan. 27, 1949. He studied with Kalafati and Liadov at the St. Petersburg Cons., graduating in 1910; at the same time he studied philology and history at St. Petersburg Univ. He then became a ballet coach at the Opera. In 1914 he began writing music criticism under the pseudonym **Igor Glebov.** Subsequently he published his literary writings under that name, sometimes indicating his real name as well. He always signed his musical works, however, with the name Asafiev. In 1920 he was appointed Dean of the dept. of music of the Institute of History of Arts in Petrograd. He was also an editor of the journal *Novaya Musica* (1924–28); within a few years he published brief monographs on Mussorgsky, Scriabin, Rimsky-Korsakov, Liszt, Chopin, etc.; translated articles from German, French and Italian. At the same time he continued to compose, mostly for the stage. The following ballets by him were performed in Leningrad: *Flames of Paris* (Nov. 7, 1932); *The Fountain of Bakhtchisaray*, after Pushkin (Sept. 28, 1934; very popular); *The Partisan Days* (May 16, 1937); *The Prisoner of the Caucasus* (April 14, 1938). Altogether he wrote 9 operas, 27 ballets, works for orch. and chamber music. But it is as a historian of Russian music that Asafiev-Glevob is especially important. He continued the tradition of Vladimir Stasov in his ardent advocacy of the national Russian style. He published *The Russian Poets in Russian Music* (with a valuable catalogue of Russian vocal works; 1921); *Symphonic Études* (an account of the evolution of the Russian operatic style; 1922); *Stravinsky* (a comprehensive analysis of Stravinsky's works; Leningrad, 1929; later he repudiated the favorable view of Stravinsky expressed in this book); *Russian Music from the Beginning of the Nineteenth Century* (1930; English transl. by A. Swan; American Council of Learned Societies, 1953); *Musical Form as a Process* (2 vols., 1930 and 1947) and *Glinka* (Moscow, 1947; the only book on music to receive the Stalin Prize). A 7-volume edition of Asafiev's collected writings was begun in Moscow in 1952.

Aschaffenburg, Walter, German-born American composer; b. Essen, May 20, 1927. He came to America when he was 11; served in the U.S. Army in Germany in 1947; upon returning to America, he studied music at Oberlin College (B.A., 1951) and at the Eastman School of Music in Rochester, N.Y. (M.A., 1952). In 1952 he was appointed to the faculty of the Oberlin Cons.; in 1968 became chairman of the dept. of composition there. WORKS: opera, *Bartelby* (Oberlin, Nov. 12, 1964); *Ozymandias*, "symphonic reflections after Shelley" (Rochester, N.Y., April 22, 1952); *Oedipus Rex*, overture (1952); Piano Trio (1951); *Divertimento* for trumpet, horn and trombone (1951); Cello Sonata (1954); Sonata for solo violin (1954); String Quartet (1955); Woodwind Quintet (1967).

Aschenbrenner, Christian Heinrich, German violinist and composer; b. Altstettin, Dec. 29, 1654; d. Jena, Dec. 13, 1732. He studied with Schütz; was active as violinist at Zeitz (1677–81) and Merseburg (1683–90); then served as music director to the Duke of Zeitz (1695–1713) and later to the Duke of Merseburg (1713–19); finally retired on a pension to Jena. His only known work is *Gast- und Hochzeitsfreude, bestehend in Sonaten, Präludien, Allemanden, Couranten, Balletten, Arien, Sarabanden mit 3, 4 und 5 Stimmen, nebst dem Basso continuo* (1673).

Ascher, Joseph, Dutch pianist and composer; b. Groningen, June 4, 1829; d. London, June 20, 1869. He studied with Moscheles; went to Paris in 1849 and was Court pianist to the Empress Eugénie. He wrote numerous pieces of salon music (études, nocturnes, galops, etc.).

Ascher, Leo, Austrian composer of light operas; b. Vienna, Aug. 17, 1880; d. New York, Feb. 25, 1942. His first successful operetta was *Vergeltsgott* (Vienna, Oct. 14, 1905); *Soldat der Marie* and *Hoheit tanzt Walzer* followed. Altogether he composed some 50 stage works, and film music. In 1938 he left Austria to live in New York.

Ascone, Vicente, Uruguayan composer of Italian parentage; b. Siderno, Italy, Aug. 16, 1897. He was brought to Uruguay as a child; studied trumpet and music theory in Montevideo; was conductor of the Municipal Band of Montevideo (1940–54). Most of his works are based on Uruguayan motives; stylistically, they follow the traditional Italian formulas. He composed five operas, of which *Paraná Gauzú*, based on an Indian subject, was produced in Montevideo on July 25, 1931. He further wrote three symphonies, a Trumpet Concerto, a Violin Concerto, *Suite uruguaya* for orch. (1926); *Acentos de America* for orch. (1940); *Sobre el Rio Uruguay* for orch. (1946); and numerous songs.

Ashdown, Edwin, London music publisher; successor (1884) of Ashdown & Parry, who were the successors (1860) of Wessel & Co. (founded 1825). Two grandsons of Edwin Ashdown inherited the company, and incorporated into it the catalogue of Enoch & Co., and also of J. H. Larway & Co. (1936), the official name of the enlarged business remaining Edwin Ashdown, Ltd. Their list of publications contains mostly pedagogical works.

Ashkenazy, Vladimir, Russian pianist; b. Gorki, July 6, 1937. He studied with Oborin at the Moscow Cons.; at the age of 19 won the first prize at the Brussels International Competition under the auspices of Queen Elisabeth of Belgium (1956); he also won the Chopin International Prize in Warsaw (1955). His pianistic style combines the traditional school with the digital precision demanded for performance of modern music. From 1963 he has lived mostly in England.

Ashley, Robert, American composer; b. Ann Arbor, Michigan, March 28, 1930. He studied music at the Univ. of Michigan (Mus. B., 1952) and The Manhattan School of Music (Mus. M., 1954); took post-graduate courses in psychoacoustics at the Univ. of Michigan (1957-60). In his independent composition, he pursues the ideal of 'total musical events' which absorbs gesticulation, natural human noises and the entire planetary environment. In 1961 he became co-founder of the ONCE group in Ann Arbor, dedicated to such actions; from 1958 to 1966 he operated an electronic music studio in association with the composer Gordon Mumma; in 1970 was appointed co-director of the Center of Contemporary Music at Mills College, Oakland, Calf.
WORKS: Most of his works utilize electronic sounds; of these the following are notable for the totality of their envergure: *The Fourth of July* (1960); *Something* for clarinet, piano and tape (1961); *Detroit Divided* (1962); *Complete with Heat* (1962); *Kitty Hawk,* an 'anti-gravity piece' (1964); *Untitled Mixes* (1965); *Night Train* (1966); *The Trial of Anne Opie Wehrer and Unknown Accomplices for Crimes Against Humanity* (1968); *Purposeful Lady Slow Afternoon* (1968); *Illusion Models* for hypothetical computer (1970); several film scores: *The Image in Time* (1957); *The Bottleman* (1960); *Jenny and the Poet* (1964); *My May* (1965); *Overdrive* (1968); *Portraits, Self-Portraits and Still Lifes* (1969); *Battery Davis* (1970). He also composes music performable on traditional instruments, among them *Maneuvers for Small Hands* for piano (1961), Quartet for Any Number of Instruments (1965), and organ pieces.

Ashton, Algernon (Bennet Langton), English composer; b. Durham, Dec. 9, 1859; d. London, April 10, 1937. His family moved to Leipzig and he studied at the Leipzig Cons. with Reinecke and Jadassohn (1875-79); later took lessons with Raff in Frankfurt (1880). Returning to England, he obtained the post of piano teacher at the Royal College of Music (1885-1910). He was a prolific composer, having written more than 160 opus numbers, mostly in a conventional German style: 5 symphonies, 3 overtures, a piano concerto, a violin concerto, 3 piano quintets, 3 piano quartets, 3 piano trios, trio for clarinet, viola and bassoon, trio for piano, horn and viola, 5 violin sonatas, 5 cello sonatas, a viola sonata, and more than 200 piano works (among them a sonata, 3 fantasias, and various picturesque pieces such as *Idyls; Roses and Thorns,* etc.); also more than 200 songs, choral pieces and organ works. Many of his chamber music compositions were published, but he was never given recognition as a composer; however, he acquired notoriety by his curious letters in the English press dealing with a variety of subjects. Many of these letters he collected in his volumes *Truth, Wit and Wisdom* (London, 1904) and *More Truth, Wit and Wisdom* (London, 1905).

Asioli, Bonifazio, Italian composer; b. Correggio, Aug. 30, 1769; d. there, May 18, 1832. A precocious talent, he began writing music at a very early age. He studied with Angelo Merighi in Parma (1780-82); then lived in Bologna and Venice as a harpsichord player. His first opera *La Volubile* was produced in Correggio (1785) with marked success; it was followed by *Le nozze in villa* (Correggio, 1786); *Cinna* (Milan, 1793); and *Gustavo al Malabar* (Turin, 1802). From 1796-99 he was private maestro to the Marquis Gherardini in Turin; then went to Milan and taught at the Cons. (1808-14). Asioli wrote 7 operas in all, an oratorio *Giacobbe in Galaad,* many cantatas, instrumental music and sacred choral works, etc. He was the author of several textbooks: *Principi elementari di musica* (Milan, 1809; also in English, German and French); *Trattato d'armonia e d'accompagnamento* (1813); also manuals for harpsichord, voice and double bass. His theoretical book *Il maestro di composizione* was published posthumously (1836).
BIBLIOGRAPHY: A. Coli, *Vita di Bonifazio Asioli* (Milan, 1834); O. S. Ancarani, *Sopra alcune parole di Carlo Botta intorno al metodo musicale di Bonifazio Asioli* (1836); A. Amadei, *Intorno allo stile della moderna musica di chiesa* (1841).

Asola (Asula), Giovanni Matteo, Italian composer; b. Verona, c.1530; d. Venice, Oct. 1, 1609. An ordained priest; in 1566 he acceded to the position of chaplain at the Church of S. Stefano in Verona; was at Treviso in 1578; then at Vicenza (1581). Later he lived in Venice. Asola's importance in music history lies in his early use of a basso continuo for the organ accompaniment of sacred vocal music. He composed a great deal of church music; his two books of madrigals were published in Venice (1587; 1596; also later editions).
BIBLIOGRAPHY: F. Caffi, *Della vita e delle opere di Giammateo Asola* (Padua, 1862).

Asow, Erich H. Müller von. See **Mueller von Asow, Erich H.**

Aspa, Mario, Italian opera composer; b. Messina, 1799; d. there, Dec. 14, 1868. He studied with Zingarelli in Naples. He produced 42 operas, of which the most successful were *Paolo e Virginia* (Rome, April 29, 1843) and *Il muratore di Napoli* (Naples, Oct. 16, 1850). His last opera *Piero di Calais* was produced posthumously in his native town (Messina, March 6, 1872).

Aspestrand, Sigwart, Norwegian opera composer; b. Fredrikshald, Nov. 13, 1856; d. Oslo, Dec. 31, 1941. He studied at Leipzig and Berlin and spent 30 years of his life (1885-1915) in Germany. Of his 7 operas *Die Seemansbraut,* produced in Gotha (March 29, 1894) and later in Oslo (March 18, 1907) was the most successful. His other operas, all in German, are: *Der Recke von Lyrskovsheid, Freyas Alter, Die Wette, Der Kuss auf Sicht, Robin Hood,* and *Pervonte.*

Asplmayr, Franz, Austrian composer; b. 1728; d. Linz, July 29, 1786. He was composer of ballets at the Austrian Court; the scores of his ballets *Agamemnon, Iphigenia, Flora, Acis and Galatea* and others have been preserved. He also wrote the Singspiel, *Die Kinder der Natur,* and the music for two of Shakespeare's plays: *Macbeth* (1777) and *The Tempest* (1781). Historically, Asplmayr was important as one of the earliest Austrian composers to adopt the instrumental style established by the Mannheim school. He composed *6 Serenate*, op. 1; *6 Quatuors concertants*, op. 2; *6 Trios*, op. 5; *6 Quatuors*, op. 6. A trio (op. 5, no. 1) and a quartet (op. 6, no. 2) were published by Riemann in *Collegium Musicum.*

Asriel, André, Austrian composer; b. Vienna, Feb. 22, 1922. He studied piano and music theory at the State Academy in Vienna; in 1939 he went to England where he took courses at the Royal College in London. After the war he moved to East Berlin; was appointed to the Faculty of the Hanns Eisler Hochschule in 1950. He wrote a number of songs on socialist themes; also film music for documentaries, produced in East Germany. Among his purely instrumental works are *Four Inventions* for trumpet, trombone and orch. (1963) and *Serenade* for 9 instruments (1969). In many of his works he applies jazz rhythms. He published a book *Jazz, Analysen und Aspekte* (Berlin, 1966).

Assmayer, Ignaz, Austrian composer; b. Salzburg, Feb. 11, 1790; d. Vienna, Aug. 31, 1862. He studied with Michael Haydn; in 1808 became organist at Salzburg. In 1815 he moved to Vienna, where he studied additionally with Eybler. In 1825 was appointed Imperial organist; in 1838 was made one of the court conductors. He wrote the oratorios *Saul und David, Sauls Tod* and *Das Gelübde*, and performed them with the Vienna Tonkünstler Society. He further wrote 15 Masses, 2 Requiems, other church works, and some 60 instrumental compositions, many of which were published.

Aston, Hugh, English composer; b. c.1480; d. York, Dec. 9, 1522. These dates apply to the son of a certain Richard Aston of Mawdesley in Lancashire. After obtaining his B.A. (1505–06) and M.A. (Oct. 30, 1507) from Oxford, he moved to Cambridge to study canon law; he was throughout his life associated with St. John's College, Cambridge. On May 27, 1509, he became Prebend of St. Stephen's, Westminster, and in 1515, Archdeacon of York. Among Aston's authentic works are 2 Masses (*Te Deum* for 5 voices and *Videte manus meas* for 6 voices); two other vocal works for 5 voices (*Gaude Virgo Mater Christi* and *Te Deum laudamus*) and 3 fragments published in *Tudor Church Music* (vol. X). More unusual for the time is Aston's *Hornpipe* for virginal, which is preserved in a manuscript at the British Museum; it is the earliest known piece for the instrument. Of the ten other dances in this manuscript, some, notably *My Lady Carey's Dompe* may also be Aston's work.

BIBLIOGRAPHY: W. H. Grattan Flood, *Early Tudor Composers* (London, 1925, pp. 30–33).

d'Astorga, Emanuele (Gioacchino Cesare Rincón), Italian composer of operas; b. Augusta, Sicily, March 20, 1680; d. probably in Madrid, after 1757. Of a noble Spanish family which had settled in Augusta, Sicily, early in the 17th century; he was a baron in his own right, from his estate Ogliastro, nearby. Later in life he moved to Palermo; during the revolution of 1708 he was an officer in the municipal guard. In 1712 he went to Vienna; and was in Znaim in 1713. He was in London in 1714–15; and returned to Palermo where he became senator. It is known that he sold his Sicilian estate in 1744 and went to Spain, where he was in the service of the king. D'Astorga was widely known as a versatile and highly educated person; he was also adept as a singer and a cembalo player, but never regarded music as his primary profession. He composed at least 3 operas: the first, *La moglie nemica*, was produced at Palermo in 1698; the 2nd and most notable, *Dafni*, was staged at Genoa on April 21, 1709; it was probably also heard in Barcelona (1709) and in Breslau (1726); the third, *Amor tirannico*, was given in Venice in 1710. He also wrote numerous chamber cantatas and published himself 12 of them in one volume (Lisbon, 1726). His best known work is *Stabat Mater* for 4 voices; it was first heard in Oxford in 1752; a new edition of it was published by R. Franz in 1878. In his 2-volume biography of d'Astorga (Leipzig, 1911 and 1919), Hans Volkmann refutes the unsupported statement of R. Pohl in the 1st edition of Grove's Dictionary, that d'Astorga died at Raudnitz on Aug. 21, 1736; Volkmann also exposes the romantic account of d'Astorga's life published by Rochlitz in volume II of *Für Freunde der Tonkunst* (1825) as a fanciful invention. An opera *Astorga*, based on his life, was written by J. J. Abert (1866). See also O. Tiby, "E. D'Astorga," *Acta Musicologica* (1953).

Asuar, José Vicente, Chilean composer; b. Santiago, July 20, 1933. He studied engineering and music, first in Santiago, then in Berlin. He also took special courses in electronic music, taking advantage of his training as an engineer. In 1969 he was placed in charge of the Dept. of Acoustics at the Univ. of Chile. His works are prepared mostly on tape; his *Estudio aleatorio* (1962) makes use of random devices. Among his purely instrumental works are *Heterofonías* for orch. (1965), *Octet* for four flutes and four percussion players (1966) and *Guararia repano* for indigenous Indian instruments (1968).

Atanasov, Georgi, Bulgarian composer; b. Plovdiv, May 18, 1881; d. Fasano, Nov. 17, 1931. He studied in Italy; was one of the first Bulgarian composers to be fully equipped with the technique of composition. He wrote the early national Bulgarian operas *Borislav* (Sofia, March 4, 1911) and *Gergana* (Stara Zagora, July 1, 1925); other operas are *Zapustialata Vodenitza* (The Abandoned Mill); *Altzek; Tzveta*; also 2 children's operas: *The Sick Teacher* and *About Birds.*

Atherton, Percy Lee, American composer; b. Boston, Mass., Sept. 25, 1871; d. Atlantic City, N.J., March 8, 1944. He studied music at Harvard Univ.; then with Rheinberger in Munich, with Sgambati in Rome and with Widor in Paris. Returning to America he served on various advisory boards in Boston. He wrote 2 operas *The Heir Apparent* (1890) and *Maharajah* (1900), a symph. poem, *Noon in the Forest*, and numerous songs.

Atlantov, Vladimir, Soviet tenor; b. Leningrad, Feb. 19, 1939. He was brought up in a musical atmosphere; his father was a professional singer. He studied voice at the Leningrad Cons., graduating in 1963. He made his operatic debut at the Kirov Opera House in Leningrad; then appeared at La Scala, Milan (1963-65); in 1967 became a member of the Bolshoi Theater in Moscow. He also gave concert recitals in Italy, Austria, Hungary, France and Japan. He is especially praised as a lyrico-dramatic tenor; his best parts are Don José in *Carmen*, Alfred in *La Traviata*, Cavaradossi in *Tosca* and Lensky in *Eugene Onegin*.

Attaignant (also Attaingnant, Atteignant), Pierre, French printer of music who lived during the first half of the 16th century; d. 1552. He was probably the earliest printer in France to employ movable type in music printing. His first publication was a *Breviarium Noviomense* (1525). He continued to publish a great many works, including 18 dances in tablature for the lute (1529); 25 pavans (1530); a folio edition of 7 books of Masses (1532); 13 books of motets (1535) and a series of 35 books of chansons (1539-49) containing 927 part songs by French and Flemish composers. Reprints: E. Bernoulli, facsimile edition of 4 books under the title *Chansons und Tänze* (Munich, 1914); 31 chansons in Henry Expert's *Les Maîtres Musiciens de la Renaissance française* (1894-1908); D. Heartz, *Preludes, Chansons, Dances for Lute (1529-30)* (1964); *Danseries à 4 parties,* in *Le Pupitre* 9 (Paris, 1969).

BIBLIOGRAPHY: Yvonne Rihouet (Rokseth), "Note bibliographique sur Attaignant," *Revue de Musicologie* (1924); F. Lesure, "Pierre Attaignant, notes et documents," *Musica Disciplina* (1949); D. Heartz, *Pierre Attaingnant, Royal Printer of Music* (Berkeley, Calif., 1969).

Attenhofer, Karl, Swiss conductor and composer; b. Wettingen, May 5, 1837; d. Zürich, May 22, 1914. He studied in his native city and later at the Leipzig Cons. (1857-58) with Richter and Dreyschock. Returning to Switzerland he developed vigorous activity as choral conductor and teacher. He settled in Zürich in 1867; was appointed director of the Cons. in 1896. Attenhofer wrote mainly for chorus; his cantatas *Hegelingenfahrt* (1890), *Frühlingsfeier*, and *Der deutsche Michel* for men's voices have achieved great popularity. For women's voices he wrote *Beim Rattenfänger im Zauberberg, Das Kind der Wüste, Prinzessin Wunderhold*, and *Rütlifahrt*; he also compiled a manual, *Liederbuch für Männergesang* (1882).

BIBLIOGRAPHY: Ernst Isler, *Karl Attenhofer* (Zürich, 1915).

Atterberg, Kurt, eminent Swedish composer; b. Göteborg, Dec. 12, 1887; d. Stockholm, Feb. 15, 1974. He studied engineering and was employed in the wireless service; then took courses in composition at the Stockholm Cons. with Hallén, and in Berlin with Schillings (1910-12). From 1913-22 he conducted at the Dramatic Theater in Stockholm; from 1919-57 he wrote music criticism for a Stockholm newspaper and from 1912-68 also served in the Swedish patent office. From 1940 to 1953 he was secretary of the Royal Academy of Music; was one of the founders of the Society of Swedish composers (chairman, 1924-47).

WORKS: His 6th Symphony was the winner of the first prize given by the Columbia Phonograph Co. (1928) for the Schubert centennial contest. Atterberg subsequently declared that he had consciously imitated the style of the members of the jury (Glazunov, Alfano and Nielsen) in order to ingratiate himself in their judgment. His other symphonies are, however, marked with the same expansive, romantic qualities as the winning work. They are: No. 1 (1909-11; Stockholm, Jan. 10, 1912); No. 2 (1911-13; Sondershausen, Germany, July 27, 1913); No. 3 (1914-16; Stockholm, Nov. 28, 1916); No. 4, *Sinfonia piccola* (1918; Stockholm, March 27, 1919); No. 5, *Sinfonia funèbre* (1919-22; Stockholm, Jan. 6, 1923); No. 6 (1927-28; Stockholm, Oct. 15, 1928); No. 7, *Sinfonia romantica* (1942; Frankfurt, Feb. 14, 1943); No. 8 (1944; Helsinki, Feb. 9, 1945); No. 9, *Sinfonia visionaria*, with mezzo-soprano, baritone and chorus (1955-56; Helsinki, Feb. 26, 1957); also a *Sinfonia* for strings (1952-53). His orchestral rhapsody on Northern Swedish folk tunes, *Varmlandsrhapsodi*, written in honor of Selma Lagerlöf's 75th birthday (broadcast over the Swedish radio, Nov. 20, 1933) became one of his most popular works. Atterberg wrote 5 operas, all produced in Stockholm: *Härvard Harpolekare (Harvard the Potter*, 1915-17; Sept. 29, 1919; revised as *Härvard der Harfner* and produced in German at Chemnitz, 1936; a later version with new third act produced in Linz, Austria, June 14, 1952); *Bäckahästen* (1923-24; Jan. 23, 1925); *Fanal* (1929-32; Jan. 24, 1934); *Aladdin* (1936-41; March 18, 1941); *Stormen*, after Shakespeare's *Tempest* (1948; Sept. 19, 1949). OTHER WORKS: the ballet, *Per Svinaherde (Peter the Swineherd*, 1914-15); ballet-pantomime, *De fåvitska jungfruna (The Wise and Foolish Virgins,* 1920; Paris, Nov. 18, 1920); 9 suites for orch., among them No. 3, for violin, viola and strings (1917); No. 5, *Suite Barocco* (1922); and No. 8, *Suite Pastorale* (1931); Rhapsody for Piano and Orch. (1909); Violin Concerto (1913); Cello Concerto (1917-22); 2 incidental-music suites to the play *Stormen*, after Shakespeare's *Tempest*: No. 1 (1921, revised 1962-63), No. 2 (1964-65); *Rondeau rétrospectif* for orch. (1926); Horn Concerto (1926); *Älven (The River)*, symph. poem (1929-30); Piano Concerto (1927-35); *Ballad and Passacaglia* for orch. (1936); *Rondeau caractéristique* (1939-40); *Indian Tunes* for orch. (1950); *Ballad utan ord (Ballad Without Words)* for orch. (1957-58); Concerto for Violin, Cello or Viola, and Orch. (1959-60; version with string orch., 1963); *Vittorioso* for orch. (1962); *Adagio Amoroso* for flute and strings (1967); a *Requiem* (1913); a cantata, *Järnbäraland* (1919); 2 string quartets (1915, 1937); Cello Sonata (1925); Piano Quintet (1927); *Variations and Fugue* for string quartet (1943); *Trio Concertante* for violin, cello and harp (1959-60; revised 1965). A list of his works is contained in G. Percy, "Kurt Atterberg 85 år," *Musikrevy* XXVIII/1 (1973).

Attwood, Thomas, English organist and composer; b. London, Nov. 23, 1765; d. London, March 28, 1838. He was a chorister at the Chapel Royal under Nares and Ayrton from the age of nine. Following a performance before the Prince of Wales (afterwards George IV), he was sent to Italy for further study; there he received instruction in Naples from Filippo Cinque and Gaetano Latilla. He then went to Vienna, where Mozart accepted him as a pupil; his notes from these theory and composition lessons are printed in the *Neue Mozart Ausgabe* X/30/1. In 1787 he returned to London and held various posts as organist. He was also music tutor to the Duchess of York (1791) and to the Princess of Wales (1795). A founder of the London Philharmonic Society (1813), he conducted some of its concerts. He occupied an important position in the English musical world; when Mendelssohn came to London as a young man, Attwood lent him enthusiastic support. Attwood was a prolific composer of operas, of which many were produced in London, including *The Prisoner* (Oct. 18, 1792); *The Mariners* (May 10, 1793); *The Packet Boat* (May 13, 1794); *The Smugglers* (April 13, 1796); *The Fairy Festival* (May 13, 1797); *The Irish Tar* (Aug. 24, 1797); *The Devil of a Lover* (March 17, 1798); *The Magic Oak* (Jan 29, 1799); *True Friends* (Feb. 19, 1800); *The Sea-Side Story* (May 12, 1801); *The Curfew* (Feb. 19, 1807). In all, Attwood wrote 32 operas, in some of which he used material from other composers (he included music by Mozart in *The Prisoner* and *The Mariners*). He also wrote church music, piano sonatas, songs and glees.

Auber, Daniel-François-Esprit, prolific French composer of comic operas; b. Caen (Normandy), Jan. 29, 1782; d. Paris, May 12, 1871. His father, an art dealer in Paris, sent him to London to acquire knowledge of business. Auber learned music as well as trade and wrote several songs for social entertainment in London. Political tension between France and England, however, forced him to return to Paris in 1804; there he devoted himself exclusively to music. His pasticcio *L'Erreur d'un moment,* a resetting of an old libretto, was produced by an amateur group in Paris in 1806; his next theatrical work was *Julie,* performed privately, with an accompaniment of 6 string instruments, in 1811. Cherubini, who was in the audience, was attracted by Auber's talent and subsequently gave him some professional advice. Auber's first opera to be given publicly in Paris was *Le Séjour militaire* (1813). Six years later the Opéra-Comique produced his new work *Le Testament et les billets-doux* (1819). These operas passed without favorable notice, but his next production, *La Bergère châtelaine* (1820) was a definite success. From that time until nearly the end of his life, hardly a year elapsed without the production of a new opera. Not counting amateur performances, 45 operas from Auber's pen were staged in Paris between 1813 and 1869. He was fortunate in having the collaboration of the best librettist of the time, Scribe, who wrote (alone, or with other writers) no fewer than 37 libretti for Auber's operas. Auber's fame reached its height with *Masaniello, ou la Muette de Portici,* produced at the Opéra, Feb. 29, 1828. Its success was enormous. Historically, it laid the foundation of French grand opera with Meyerbeer's *Robert le Diable* and Rossini's *Guillaume Tell.* Its vivid portrayal of popular fury stirred French and Belgian audiences; revolutionary riots followed its performance in Brussels (Aug. 25, 1830). Another popular success was achieved by him with his romantic opera *Fra Diavolo* (Opéra-Comique, Jan. 28, 1830), which became a standard work. Despite these successes with grand opera, Auber may be rightfully regarded as a founder of the French comic opera, a worthy successor of Boieldieu and at least an equal of Adam and Hérold. The influence of Rossini was noted by contemporary critics, but on the whole, Auber's music preserves a distinctive quality of its own. Rossini himself remarked that although Auber's music is light, his art is profound. Auber was greatly appreciated by the successive regimes in France; in 1829 he succeeded Gossec at the Academy; in 1842 he was appointed director of the Paris Cons. by Louis Philippe, and retained this post until his death. In 1857 Napoleon III made him imperial maître de chapelle. At the age of 87 he produced his last opera *Rêves d'amour.* Auber lived virtually all his life in Paris, remaining there even during the siege by the Germans. He died, during the days of the Paris Commune, in his 90th year. His memory was honored by the Academy. Among his operas (most of which were produced at the Opéra-Comique) are also the following: *Le Cheval de bronze* (March 23, 1835); *Le Domino noir* (Dec. 2, 1837); *Les Diamants de la couronne* (March 6, 1841); *Manon Lescaut* (Feb. 23, 1856); *Le Premier Jour de bonheur* (Feb. 15, 1868), etc.

BIBLIOGRAPHY: A. Pougin, *Auber* (Paris, 1873); A. Kohut, *Auber* (Leipzig, 1895); Ch. Malherbe, *Auber* (Paris, 1911); J. Klein, "Daniel-François Auber (1782-1821)," *Opera* (Aug. 1971).

Aubert, Jacques (called 'le vieux'), celebrated French violinist; b. Paris, Sept. 30, 1689; d. Belleville, near Paris, May (buried May 19), 1753. He was a pupil of Senaillé; in 1719 he bacame band leader to the Duke of Bourbon; in 1727 was one of the King's 24 violinists; he played in the orch. of the Grand Opéra as first violinist from 1728-52, and took part in the Concerts Spirituels (1729-40). He published 33 separate instrumental works; was also the first in France to write instrumental concertos (scored for 4 violins and a bass). His music, distinguished by elegance, contributed to the formation of the French 'style galant.'

BIBLIOGRAPHY: L. La Laurencie, *L'École française de violon de Lully à Viotti* (Paris, 1922-23).

Aubert, Louis-François-Marie, French composer; b. Paramé, Ille-et-Vilaine, Feb. 19, 1877; d. Paris, Jan. 9, 1968. Of precocious talent, he entered the Paris Cons. as a child, and studied piano with Diémer, theory with Lavignac and advanced composition with Gabriel Fauré; he also sang in church choirs. His song, *Rimes tendres* was published when he was 19. His *Fantaisie* for piano and orch. was performed in Paris by the Colonne Orch. with his teacher Diémer as soloist (Nov. 17, 1901). His *Suite brève* for 2 pianos was presented at the Paris Exposition, 1900; an orchestral version of it was performed for the first time in Paris on April 27, 1916. Aubert's major work is an operatic fairy tale *La Forêt bleue* (Geneva, Jan. 7, 1913); an American production was staged in Boston, March 8, 1913, attracting considerable attention. The Paris production of *La Forêt bleue,* delayed by the war, took place on June 10, 1924, at the Opéra-Comique. Aubert's style is largely determined by the impressionistic currents of the early 20th century; like Debussy and Ravel, he was attracted by the music of Spain and wrote several pieces in the Spanish idiom, of which the symph. poem *Habanera* (Paris, March 22, 1919) was particularly successful.

WORKS: The list of Aubert's works further includes: *La Légende du sang* for narrator, chorus and orch. (1902); 3 ballets, *La Momie* (1903), *Chrysothémis* (1904), and *La Nuit ensorcélée* (1922); *6 poèmes arabes* for voice and orch. (1907); a song cycle *Crépuscules d'automne* (Paris, Feb. 20, 1909); *Nuit mauresque* for voice and orch. (1911); *Dryade* for orch. (1921); *Caprice* for violin and orch. (1925); *Feuilles d'images*, symph. suite (Paris, March 7, 1931); *Saisons* for chorus and orch. (1937); *Offrande aux victimes de la guerre* for orch. (1947); *Le Tombeau de Châteaubriand* for orch. (1948); *Cinéma*, ballet (1953); a set of 3 piano pieces *Sillages* (1913); a piano quintet, songs, etc.

BIBLIOGRAPHY: L. Vuillemin, *Louis Aubert et son œuvre* (Paris, 1921); Marcel Landowski and Guy Morançon, *Louis Aubert* (Paris, 1967).

Aubéry du Boulley, Prudent-Louis, French composer; b. Verneuil, Eure, Dec. 9, 1796; d. there, Jan. 28, 1870. He studied at the Paris Cons. with Momigny, Méhul and Cherubini. He wrote much chamber music, in which he used the guitar; published a guitar method and a text book *Grammaire musicale* (Paris, 1830). He was an active teacher in his native province, and contributed much to the cultivation of music there.

BIBLIOGRAPHY: J. de L'Avre, *Aubéry du Boulley* (Paris, 1896).

Aubin, Tony, French composer; b. Paris, Dec. 8, 1907. He studied at the Paris Cons. with Samuel Rousseau, Noel Gallon and Paul Dukas; in 1930 he won the first Grand Prix de Rome. Upon return from Rome he studied conducting with Philippe Gaubert, and later was in charge of the music division at the Paris Radio, until 1940. After the liberation of Paris in 1944 he joined the faculty of the Paris Cons. In 1968 he was elected member of the Académie des Beaux-Arts. A utilitarian composer par excellence, Aubin cultivates a pragmatic idiom of composition calculated to achieve a desired effect.

WORKS: *Symphonie Romantique* (1937); another symphony (1951); *Suite éolienne* for clarinet, flute and strings (1958); *Concertinetto dell'amicizia* for flute and piano (1964); *Concertinetto* for violin and piano (1964); *Brughiera* for bassoon and piano (1966); and an opera *Goya* (1970). He also composed several ballet scores after musical materials taken from Schubert, Rossini, Brahms and others.

Aubry, Pierre, French music scholar; b. Paris, Feb. 14, 1874; d. (following a fencing accident) Dieppe, Aug. 31, 1910. He began his education as a philologist; studied oriental languages, and traveled to Turkestan on a research project. He then became interested in medieval music; was, for a time, lecturer on music history at the École des hautes études sociales. His theories of notation are based on a plausible interpretation of medieval writers.

WRITINGS: His many publications, distinguished by profound scholarship, include: *Huits Chants héroiques de l'ancienne France* (1896); *Mélanges de musicologie critique*, in 4 vols.: I. *La Musicologie médiévale* (1899); II. *Les Proses d'Adam de Saint-Victor* (1900, with Abbé Misset); III. *Lais et descorts français du XIIIᵉ siècle* (1901, with Jeanroy and Brandin); IV. *Les Plus Anciens Monuments de la musique française* (1903, with 24 facsimiles); *Essais de musicologie comparée*, 2 vols.: I. *Le Rhythme tonique dans la poésie liturgique et dans le chant des églises chrétiennes au moyen-âge* (1903); II. *Esquisse d'une bibliographie de la chanson populaire en Europe* (1905); *Les Caractères de la danse. Histoire d'un divertissement pendant la première moitié du XVIIIᵉ siècle* (1905); *Au Turkestan. Notes sur quelques habitudes musicales chez les Tadjikes et chez les Sartes* (1905); *La Musique et les musiciens d'église en Normandie au XIIIᵉ siècle* (1906); *Estampies et danses royales. Les Plus Anciens Textes de musique instrumentale au moyen-âge* (1907); *Recherches sur les ténors français dans les motets du XIIIᵉ siècle* (1907); *Recherches sur les ténors latins dans les motets du XIIIᵉ siècle* (1907; facsimile ed. of the Parisian MS, with index and editorial explanations); *Cent motets du XIIIᵉ siècle* (1908; 3 vols.; photographic facsimile of Bamberg Codex E. d. IV. 6, with annotations; a most important work); *Refrains et rondeaux du XIIIᵉ siècle* (1909, in the Riemann Festschrift); *Trouvères et troubadours* (1909; English ed. N.Y., 1914); and a number of essays on kindred topics, publ. in the *Mercure Musical* (1903–08).

Auda, Antoine, French-Belgian organist and music scholar; b. at St. Julien-in-Jarez (Loire), Oct. 28, 1879; d. Brussels, Aug. 19, 1964. He studied music at Marseilles; then established himself at Liège as organist; published important studies on the musical history of the city: *Etienne de Liège* (1923); *La Musique et les musiciens de l'ancien pays de Liège* (1930); and the valuable theoretical works: *Les Modes et les tons* (1931); and *Les Gammes musicales* (1947). A complete bibliography of his writings appears in *Archiefen Bibliotheckwezen in Belgie* (1967).

Audran, Edmond, French composer of light opera; son of **Marius Audran**; b. Lyons, April 12, 1840; d. Tierceville, Aug. 17, 1901. He studied at the École Niedermayer in Paris (grad. in 1859). In 1861 he was appointed organist at St. Joseph's Church in Marseilles where he produced his first operetta *L'Ours et le Pacha* (1862). He wrote a funeral march on Meyerbeer's death (1864). After the production of *Le Grand Mogol* (Marseilles, Feb. 24, 1877), he returned to Paris, and staged *Les Noces d'Olivette* (Nov. 13, 1879). With the production of *La Mascotte* (Bouffes-Parisiens, Dec. 28, 1880), Audran achieved fame; this operetta became immensely popular; thousands of performances were given in Paris and all over the world. He continued to produce new operettas almost annually; of these, the following were successful: *Gillette de Narbonne* (1882); *La Cigale et la fourmi* (1886); *Miss Hélyett* (1891); *Sainte Freya* (1892); *Madame Suzette* (1893); *Mon Prince* (1893); *La Duchesse de Ferrare* (1895); *Photis* (1896); *La Poupée* (1896); *Monsieur Lohengrin* (1896); *Les Petites Femmes* (1897).

Audran, Marius-Pierre, French operatic tenor and composer of songs; father of **Edmond Audran;** b. Aix, Provence, Sept. 26, 1816; d. Marseilles, Jan. 9, 1887. He began his career in the provinces (Marseilles, Bordeaux, Lyons); then became first tenor at the Opéra-Comique, Paris. After a period of travel (1852-61), he settled in Marseilles and in 1863 became prof. of voice and dir. of the Marseilles Cons.

Auer, Leopold, celebrated Hungarian violinist and pedagogue; b. Veszprém, June 7, 1845; d. Loschwitz, near Dresden, July 15, 1930. He studied with Ridley Kohnel in Budapest and with Dont in Vienna; later lessons with Joachim. From 1863-65 he was in Düsseldorf as concertmaster of the orchestra; in 1866 in Hamburg. In 1868 he was called to St. Petersburg as soloist in the Imperial Orch., and prof. of violin at the newly founded Cons. He became one of the most famous violin teachers in Russia; among his pupils were Elman, Zimbalist, Heifetz and many other virtuosos. Tchaikovsky originally dedicated his Violin Concerto to Auer, but was offended when he suggested some revisions and changed the dedication to Brodsky. Nevertheless, the Concerto became Auer's favorite work, and he made it a *pièce de résistance* for all his pupils. After the revolution he left Russia. On March 23, 1918, he played a concert in New York City; settling permanently in America, he devoted himself exclusively to teaching. He published the manuals *Violin Playing as I Teach It* (N.Y., 1921), *Violin Master Works and Their Interpretation* (1925), and an autobiography *My Long Life in Music* (1923).

Auer, Max, Austrian writer on music; b. Vöcklabruck, May 6, 1880; d. Vienna, Sept. 24, 1964. He studied in Vienna; later taught in provincial public schools; settled in Bad Ischl. He is the foremost authority on Bruckner; published *Anton Bruckner; Sein Leben und Werk* (Vienna, 1923); *Anton Bruckner als Kirchenmusiker* (Regensburg, 1927); completed vols. 2-4 (1928, 1932, 1937) of Göllerich's monumental biography, *Anton Bruckner; Ein Lebens- und Schaffensbild.*

Augener, George, English publisher, founder of Augener & Co.; b. Germany, 1830; d. London, Aug. 25, 1915. He organized the firm in 1853 (incorporated Oct. 11, 1904), and was its head until he retired in 1910. In 1870, Augener started publishing the music periodical *Monthly Musical Record.* In 1896 the firm purchased the catalogue of Robert Cocks & Co.

Augustine (Augustinus), Aurelius (known as **St. Augustine**), b. Tagaste, Numidia, Nov. 13, 354; d. as bishop, at Hippo (now Bona), Algeria, Aug. 28, 430. St. Augustine was one of the four great fathers of the Latin Church. He was educated at Madaura and Carthage. He became a Christian in 387, receiving his baptism from St. Ambrose. His writings contain valuable information concerning Ambrosian song; the book entitled *De Musica* treats largely of meter. It is printed in Migne, *Patrologiae cursus* (vol. 32); German translation by C. J. Perl (Strasbourg, 1937); English translation by R. Catesby Taliaferro in *The Classics of the St. John's Program* (1939). A synopsis of *De Musica* in English (with commentaries and translation by W. F. Jackson Knight) was published by the Orthological Institute (London, 1949).
BIBLIOGRAPHY: J. Huré, *Saint Augustin Musicien* (1924); H. Edelstein, *Die Musikanschauung Augustins* (Freiburg, 1928); W. Hoffmann, *Philosophische Interpretation der Augustin-Schrift De Musica* (Freiburg, 1930); H. Davenson, *Traité de la musique selon l'esprit de Saint Augustin* (Neuchâtel, 1944).

Aulin, Tor, Swedish violinist and composer; b. Stockholm, Sept. 10, 1866; d. there, March 1, 1914. He studied with C. J. Lindberg in Stockholm (1877-83) and with Sauret and Scharwenka in Berlin (1884-86). In 1887 he established the Aulin String Quartet, and traveled with it in Germany and Russia. He was concertmaster at the Stockholm Opera from 1889 till 1902, but continued his concert career, and was considered the greatest Scandinavian violinist since Ole Bull. Aulin was appointed conductor of the Stockholm Philharmonic Soc. in 1902; became leader of the Göteborg Orch. in 1909. As conductor and violinist, he made determined propaganda for Swedish composers. He wrote incidental music to Strindberg's *Mäster Olof,* 3 violin concertos, several suites of Swedish dances for orch., a violin sonata, a violin method and songs. His sister **Laura Aulin** (b. Gävle, Jan. 9, 1860; d. Örebro, Jan. 11, 1928), was a well known pianist; she also composed chamber and piano music.

Aurelianus Reomensis (Aurelian of Réomé), French scholar; monk at Réomé in the 9th century. His treatise *Musica disciplina* (published by Gerbert in *Scriptores* I) contains the earliest information on the melodic character of the church modes.
BIBLIOGRAPHY: H. Riemann, *Handbuch der Musikgeschichte* I (Leipzig, 1919).

Auric, Georges, brilliant French composer; b. Lodève, Feb. 15, 1899. He began to compose spontaneously as a child, and later studied in Paris with Vincent d'Indy and Albert Roussel at the Schola Cantorum. Between the ages of 12 and 16 he wrote nearly 300 songs and a number of piano pieces; at 18 he composed a ballet *Les noces de Gamache,* and at 20 completed a comic opera *La Reine de Cœur*; dissatisfied with this early effort he destroyed the manuscript. One of his major influences was that of Erik Satie; he pursued a manner of composition that would, in his own words, produce "auditory pleasure without demanding a disproportionate measure of attention from the listener." Auric became associated with Milhaud, Poulenc, Honegger and others in the celebrated group known as "Les Six." He established the connection with Diaghilev, the Russian impresario of the Ballet Russe, and wrote several ballets for Diaghilev's productions in Paris and elsewhere, among them *Les Fâcheux* (Monte Carlo, Jan. 19, 1924); *Les Matelots* (Paris, June 17, 1925); *La Pastorale* (Paris, May 26, 1926) and *Les Enchantements d'Alcine* (Paris, May 21, 1929); subsequent ballet scores were: *Les Imaginaires* (Paris, May 31, 1934); *Le Peintre et son modèle* (Paris, Nov. 16, 1949); *La Pierre enchantée* (Paris, June 23, 1950); *Chemin de lumière* (Munich, March 27, 1952); *Coup de feu* (Paris, May 7,

1952); *La Chambre* (Paris, 1955); *Le Bal des voleurs* (1960). He also wrote a number of brillant film scores, of which *A nous, la liberté* (1932) was greatly acclaimed; other film scores were *Les Mystères de Paris* (1936); *Symphonie pastorale* (1946); *Moulin Rouge* (1952); *Gervaise* (1956); and several films to Jean Cocteau's scenarios: *Le Sang d'un poète* (1930), *La Belle et la bête* (1946), *Les Parents terribles* (1949) and *Orphée* (1950). He also wrote some chamber pieces, among them Flute Sonata (1964); Partita for 2 Pianos (1958); and some songs. In 1962 he was appointed general administrator of the Grand Opéra and Opéra-Comique, holding the posts until 1968. In 1962 he was elected member of the Académie des Beaux-Arts.

BIBLIOGRAPHY: Anton Goléa, *Georges Auric* (Paris, 1959).

Aus der Ohe, Adele, German pianist; b. Hannover, Dec. 11, 1864; d. Berlin, Dec. 7, 1937. She studied as a child with Kullak in Berlin; at the age of 12 became a pupil of Liszt for seven years. She then played concerts in Europe; made her American debut with Liszt's 1st Piano Concerto in New York (Dec. 23, 1886) and continued her American tours for 17 consecutive years. She played 51 times with the Boston Symph. Orch. between 1887 and 1906. One of the highlights of her career was her appearance as soloist in Tchaikovsky's 1st Piano Concerto under Tchaikovsky's own direction at his last concert (St. Petersburg, Oct. 28, 1893). Because of a crippling illness, she was forced to abandon her concert career; she lost her accumulated earnings in the German currency inflation in the 1920s, and from 1928 till her death, subsisted on a pension from the Bagby Music Lovers Foundation of New York.

Austin, Ernest, English composer, brother of **Frederick Austin**; b. London, Dec. 31, 1874; d. Wallington, Surrey, July 24, 1947. He had no formal musical education; began to compose at the age of 33 after a business career. His compositions, therefore, acquired an experimental air; he was particularly interested in a modern treatment of old English tunes.

WORKS: *The Vicar of Bray* for string orch. (1910); *Hymn of Apollo* for chorus and orch. (Leeds, 1918); *Stella Mary Dances* (London, 1918); *Ode on a Grecian Urn*, after Keats (1922); 14 Sonatinas on English folk songs for children; a cycle of organ works in 12 parts (inspired by Bunyan's *Pilgrim's Progress*); chamber music and songs. He published a book, *The Fairyland of Music* (1922).

Austin, Florence, American violinist; b. Galesburg, Mich., March 11, 1884; d. (in a railroad accident) Fairchild, Wis., Aug., 1926. She studied with Schradieck in New York, and with Musin at Liège Cons., winning first prize (for the first time by an American). Upon her return to New York (1901) she appeared in recitals, then settled in Newark, N.J., as violin teacher.

Austin, Frederick, English baritone and composer; brother of **Ernest Austin**; b. London, March 30, 1872; d. there, April 10, 1952. He studied with his uncle, Dr. W. H. Hunt; became an organist and also taught music at Liverpool. In 1902 he appeared as a singer in

London, and participated in many choral festivals in later years. He sang in opera at Covent Garden, and with the Beecham Opera Co. At the same time he became known in England as a composer. He wrote a symphony, a symph. poem *Isabella*, a choral work *Pervigilium Veneris*, and an overture *The Sea Venturers* and composed incidental music for the stage.

Austin, Henry Richter, English-American organist, music publisher and editor; b. London, May 17, 1882; d. Marblehead, Mass., May 13, 1961. He was organist at the English Royal Church in Berlin (1904–06); then settled in the U.S., occupying positions as church organist in and around Boston until 1948. He conducted experiments with the acoustical characteristics of non-tempered scales and devised a keyboard *Novaton*, of 16 keys (8 white, 8 black) providing the true seventh partial tone. Became president of the Arthur P. Schmidt Co. in 1954, after many years with the firm; after his death the firm was bought out by Summy-Birchard, Inc., of Evanston, Illinois.

Austin, John Turnell, English-American organist; b. Poddington, Bedfordshire, May 16, 1869; d. Hartford, Conn., Sept. 17, 1948. He came to the U.S. in 1889 and worked for various organ building firms. On March 3, 1899 he founded an organ company under his own name at Hartford, Conn., retiring in 1935. He patented the Austin Universal Air Chest. The Austin Organ Co. supplied organs for many concert halls in the U.S.

Austin, Larry, American avant-garde composer; b. Duncan, Oklahoma, Sept. 12, 1930. He studied at the North Texas State Univ., Denton (B.M. 1951; M.M. 1952); at Mills College with Darius Milhaud, and at the Univ. of California, Berkeley (1955–58) with Seymour Shifrin; in 1969 he took a course in computer-generated music systems at Stanford Univ. He was on the faculty of the Univ. of California at Berkeley (1956–58); in 1958, joined the staff of the Univ. of California at Davis; in 1972 he moved to the Univ. of Florida at Tampa. From 1967 to 1970 he was an editor of the *ne plus ultra* modern unperiodical publication *Source*. He held several creative fellowships, among them one in Rome (1965). Most of his works are cast for mixed media in which theatrical, acoustical and dynamic elements are integrated into manifestations of universal vitality. He makes use of traditional instrumental, as well as electronic, computerized and aleatory resources. In order to attain a maximum impact with a minimum of anarchy, he introduced the concept of coordinated improvisation which he termed "Open Styles."

WORKS: Among his works, both in the playable and moderately unplayable categories, are: Woodwind Quartet (1948); Woodwind Quintet (1949); Brass Quintet (1949); String Trio (1952); Concertino for flute, trumpet and strings (1952); *Prosody* for orch. (1953); *Improvisations for Orchestra and Jazz Soloists* (1961); *Collage* for assorted instruments (1963); *Continuum* for 2, 3, 4, 5, 6 or 7 instruments (1964); *In Memoriam J. F. Kennedy* for band (1964); Piano Variations (1964); *A Broken Consort* for 7 instruments (1964); *Open Style for Orchestra and Piano Soloists* (1965); *The Maze: A Theater Piece in Open Style*

(1967); *Catharsis: Open Style for Two Improvisation Ensembles, Tapes and Conductor* (1967; Oakland, Nov. 11, 1969); *Accidents* for electronically prepared piano, magnetic tape, mirrors, actions and counteractions and black light (1967; *Piano Set in Open Style* (1968); *Current* for clarinet and piano (1968); *Transmission One*, a video-audio electronic composition for color television (1969); *Agape*, a celebration for priests, musicians, dancers, a rock band, actors and poets (Buffalo, Feb. 25, 1970); *Plastic Surgery* for electric piano, percussion, magnetic tape and film (N.Y., March 1, 1970); *Heaven Music* for a condominium of flutes (Tampa, Fla. June 3, 1975). In 1974–77 Austin integrated fragments of the *Universe Symphony* of Charles Ives in the form of 3 fantasies for various ensembles, under the title *Phantasmagoria*.

Austin, William W., American musicologist; b. Lawton, Oklahoma, Jan. 18, 1920. He studied at Harvard Univ., obtaining his Ph.D. in 1951. In 1947, he was appointed to the faculty of Cornell Univ. In 1961–62 he was the recipient of a Guggenheim Fellowship. He wrote *Music of the 20th Century from Debussy through Stravinsky* (N.Y., 1966); *Susanna, Jeanie and The Old Folks at Home: The Songs of Stephen Foster from His Time to Ours* (N.Y., 1975); edited *New Looks at Italian Opera* (Ithaca, N.Y., 1968) and the Norton Critical Score edition of Debussy's *Prelude to "The Afternoon of a Faun"* (N.Y., 1970); contributed numerous articles to the *Musical Quarterly* and other journals.

Austral (real name **Wilson), Florence,** Australian soprano; b. Melbourne April 26, 1894; d. Sydney, May 15, 1968. She studied at the Melbourne Cons. (1914–18) and in New York (1918). She made her operatic debut as Brünnhilde at Covent Garden (May 16, 1922); later she sang the roles of Isolde and Aida. She toured in the U.S. between 1925 and 1931 with her husband, the flutist John Amadeo. She returned to Australia after World War II.

Auteri Manzocchi, Salvatore, Italian opera composer; b. Palermo, Dec. 26, 1845; d. Parma, Feb. 21, 1924. He studied in Palermo with Platania, and with Mabellini in Florence. His first opera *Marcellina* was never performed; his second, *Dolores* (Florence, Feb. 23, 1875) enjoyed considerable success, as did *Stella* (Piacenza, May 22, 1880). His other operas are *Il Negriero* (Milan, 1878); *Il Conte de Gleichen* (Milan, 1887); *Graziella* (Milan, Oct. 23, 1894) and *Severo Torelli* (Bologna, April 25, 1903).

Autori, Franco, Italian-American conductor; b. Naples, Nov. 29, 1903. After study in Italy, he emigrated to America in 1928. He conducted the Chicago Civic Opera Co. (1928–32), the summer series of the Dallas Symph. Orch. (1932–34); was staff conductor of the Federal Music Project in New York (1934–36); then held the post as conductor and music director of the Buffalo Philharmonic (1936–45); subsequently was active as guest conductor in Poland and Argentina; from 1949 to 1959 served as associate conductor of the N.Y. Philharmonic. From 1961 to 1971 he was conductor of the Tulsa, Oklahoma, Philharmonic.

Aventinus (real name **Turmair), Johannes,** German theorist; b. Abensberg (whence Aventinus), July 4, 1477; d. Regensburg, Jan. 9, 1534. His treatise *Annales Boiorum* (1554) contains considerable information (not always trustworthy) about musical matters. He also edited Nicolaus Faber's *Musica rudimenta admodum brevia* (1516).

Averkamp, Anton, Dutch choral conductor and composer; b. Willige Langerak, Feb. 18, 1861; d. Bussum, June 1, 1934. He studied with Daniel de Lange in Amsterdam, with Friedrich Kiel in Berlin, and with Rheinberger in Munich. In 1890 he founded the famous chorus 'Amsterdam A Cappella Coor,' with which he traveled in Europe, presenting programs of early polyphonic music. He wrote an opera *De Heidebloem* (not produced); a symph. poem *Elaine and Lancelot*; 2 choral works with orch., *Decora Lux* and *Die versunkene Burg*; a symphony; a *Te Deum*; a violin sonata and songs. He contributed numerous historical articles to music periodicals, and published a manual for singers, *Uit mijn practijk* (Groningen, 1916).

Avidom (original name **Mahler-Kalkstein), Menahem,** Polish-born Israeli composer; b. Stanislawow, Jan. 6, 1908. He studied in Beirut (1926–28) and at the Paris Cons. (1928–31). In 1935 he settled in Tel-Aviv, teaching music theory at the Cons. there until 1946. From 1955 to 1970 he was the chairman of the Israeli Composers' League. His early works reflect the influences of expressionism; in several of them he made explicit use of dodecaphonic techniques. After his settlement in Israel, he turned to the exploration of authentic Israeli folkways.
WORKS: *Alexandra*, opera (Tel-Aviv, Aug. 15, 1959); *In Every Generation*, opera (Ein-Gev Passover Festival, 1955); *The Crook*, comic opera (Tel-Aviv, April 22, 1967); *The Farewell*, a radiophonic opera (1969; broadcast performance, Nov., 1971); *The Pearl and the Coral*, ballet for 12 instruments (1972). FOR ORCH.: 9 symphonies: No. 1, *A Folk Symphony* (Prague Spring Festival, 1946); No. 2, *David Symphony* (Tel-Aviv, Dec. 1, 1949); No. 3, *Mediterranean Sinfonietta* (1951); No. 4 (1955); No. 5, *The Song of Eilat*, for voice and orch. (1956–57); No. 6 (1960); No. 7, *Philharmonic* (1961); No. 8, *Festival Sinfonietta* (Jerusalem, July 27, 1966); No. 9, *Symphonie Variée*, for chamber orch. (1968); Concerto for Flute and Strings (1946); *Music for Strings* (1949); *Jubilee Suite* (1959); *Triptyque Symphonique* (1966); *Spring*, overture (Jerusalem, Dec. 13, 1973). CHAMBER MUSIC: Concertino for Violin and Piano (1950; also with chamber orch., 1972); *Concertino for Piatigorsky* for cello and piano (1952); 2 string quartets (1953; *Metamorphoses*, 1960); *Adagio* for harp (1962); *Enigma* for 5 winds, percussion and piano (1962); *Reflexions* for 2 flutes (1963); Brass Quartet (1963); *B-A-C-H*, suite for woodwinds, strings, piano and percussion (1964); *Triptyque* for solo violin (1967). FOR PIANO: 2 sonatinas (1939, 1945); *12 Changing Preludes* (1965); *6 Inventions on the Name of Artur Rubinstein* (1973); *Yemenite Wedding Suite* (1973).

Avison, Charles, English organist and composer; b. Newcastle-upon-Tyne, 1709 (old style; baptized, Feb. 16); d. there, May 9, 1770. He acquired the rudiments of music at home; in 1736 he was appointed organist at St. John's Church, Newcastle. An enterprising musician, he organized in Newcastle a series of subscription concerts, one of the earliest musical presentations of its kind in Great Britain. He wrote a large number of concertos employing various combinations of strings with harpsichord continuo, and sonatas in which the keyboard instrument is given a predominant function. These works were published between 1740 and 1769; in 1758 Avison collected 26 concertos in 4 books, arranged in score, for strings *a* 7 (4 violins, viola, cello, bass), with harpsichord; other works were 12 keyboard concertos with string quartet, 18 quartets for keyboard with 2 violins and cello, and 3 volumes of trio sonatas for keyboard with 2 violins. His *Essay on Musical Expression* (London, 1752) is historically important as an early exposition of relative musical values by an English musician. His views were opposed by an anonymous pamphlet, *Remarks on Mr. Avison's Essay . . . in a Letter from a Gentleman in London,* which was probably written by Professor William Hayes of Oxford (London, 1753). Not to be thus thwarted, Avison published a rebuttal that same year, reinforced by a statement of worth contributed by a Dr. Jortin. He renewed his demurrer by publishing in 1775 another edition of the polemical exchange. Among his scholarly publications is Marcello's *Psalm-Paraphrases* with an English text, containing a biography of Marcello (jointly with John Garth, 1757).
BIBLIOGRAPHY: A. Milner, "Charles Avison," *Musical Times* (Jan. 1954); Ch. Cudworth, "Avison of Newcastle," *Musical Times* (May 1970); L. Lipking, "Charles Avison and the Founding of English Criticism of Music," chapter 8 of *The Ordering of the Arts in Eighteenth-Century England* (Princeton, 1970); O. Edwards, "Charles Avison: English Concerto-Writer Extraordinary," *Musical Quarterly* (July 1973).

Avni, Tzvi, German-born Israeli composer; b. Saarbrücken, Sept. 2, 1927. He emigrated to Palestine in 1935; studied composition with Seter, Ehrlich and Ben-Haim in Tel-Aviv (1954–56); then attended the courses of Aaron Copland and Lukas Foss at the Berkshire Music Center in Tanglewood, Mass. (1963) and the classes in electronics with Ussachevsky at Columbia Univ. (1963-64) and with Myron Schaeffer at the Univ. of Toronto. Returning to Tel-Aviv, he became director of the Central Music Library; in 1971 was appointed instructor in electronic music at the Rubin Music Academy in Jerusalem; also acted as music adviser to the Bat-Dor Ballet Company, for which he wrote special scores. In his music he makes use of Middle-Eastern folk motives, in ultra-modern coloristic arrangements.
WORKS: *Songs* for soprano and orch. (1957); Wind Quintet (1959); *Prayer* for strings (1961); 2 string quartets (1962, 1969); *2 Pieces for 4 Clarinets* (1965); *Meditations on a Drama,* metamorphoses for chamber orch. (1965–66); *Elegy* for solo cello (1967); *Collage* for voice, flute, percussion and tape (1967); *5 Pantomimes* for 8 players (1968); *Churban Habayit*

(Destruction of the Temple) for chorus and orch. (1968); *Akeda (Sacrifice)* for 4 chamber groups and narrator (1969); *Requiem for Sounds,* ballet music (1969); *Holiday Metaphors* for orch. (1970); *All the King's Women,* ballet music (1971); *By the Waters of Babylon,* prelude for chamber orch. (1971); *From the Valley of Shadows I Shall Sing Thee a Song of Love,* ballet music for 10 players (1971); *De Profundis* for strings (1972); *Lyric Episodes,* ballet music for oboe and tape (1972); *Gilgulim (Reincarnations),* radiophonic poem for narrator and tape (1973); *On That Cape of Death* for chamber orch. (1974); *Frames,* ballet music (1974); *Retrospections* for cello, percussion and tape (1975); *Michtam for David* for harp and string quartet (1975); 2 Psalms for Oboe and Strings (1975); *Synchromotrask,* musical theater for a woman, tape and a door (1976); *He and She,* ballet music for 7 instruments (1976); *Leda and the Swan* for voice without text, and clarinet (1976); numerous a cappella choruses; songs.

d'Avossa, Giuseppe, Italian opera composer; b. Paola, Calabria, in 1708; d. Naples, Jan. 9, 1796. He wrote 4 comic operas and much religious music. For many years he was a teacher at the Cons. in Naples.

Avramov, Eugenii, Bulgarian composer; b. Svishtov, Sept. 13, 1929. He graduated in political science from the Sofia Univ. in 1952; then studied composition with Vladigerov and Raichev at the Bulgarian State Cons., graduating in 1958; then taught harmony there.
WORKS: Piano Sonata (1960); Piano Trio (1963); Clarinet Concerto (1964); Symph. (1969); *Inventions* for oboe, clarinet and bassoon (1972); *A Mummer's Dance* for piano (1974).

Avshalomov, Aaron, Russian-American composer; b. Nikolayevsk, Siberia, Nov. 11, 1894; d. New York, April 26, 1965. He studied at the Zürich Cons.; in 1914 he went to China where he wrote a number of works on Chinese subjects, making use of authentic Chinese themes. On April 24, 1925 he conducted the first performance in Peking of his first opera on a Chinese subject *Kuan Yin;* his second opera, also on a Chinese subject, *The Great Wall,* was staged in Shanghai on Nov. 26, 1945, and also was presented in Nanking under the sponsorship of Madame Chiang Kai-Shek, the wife of the then powerful generalissimo. His other works composed in China, were also performed for the first time in Shanghai, among them: *Peiping Hutungs,* symph. sketch (Feb. 7, 1933; also given by Stokowski with the Philadelphia Orch., Nov. 8, 1935); *The Soul of the Ch'in,* ballet (May 21, 1933); *Incense Shadows,* pantomime (March 13, 1935); Piano Concerto (Jan. 19, 1936); Violin Concerto (Jan. 16, 1938); First Symphony (March 17, 1940, composer conducting); *Buddha and the Five Planetary Deities,* choreographic tableau (April 18, 1942). In 1947 Avshalomov came to America, where he continued to compose works in large forms; among them were: Second Symphony (Cincinnati, Dec. 30, 1949); Third Symphony (1950); Fourth Symphony (1951).

Avshalomov, Jacob, American composer, son of **Aaron Avshalomov;** b. Tsingtao, China, March 28, 1919;

his mother was American; his father, Russian. He studied music in Peking; in 1936 he was in Shanghai, where material circumstances forced him to work for a time in a slaughterhouse. In 1937 he came to U.S.; studied with Ernst Toch in Los Angeles; then with Bernard Rogers in Rochester, N.Y. From 1943–45 he was in the U.S. Army as interpreter. From 1947–54 he was instructor at Columbia Univ.; received a Guggenheim Fellowship in 1952; in 1954 he was appointed permanent conductor of the Portland Junior Symphony. His music reflects the many cultures with which he was in contact; while the form is cohesive, the materials are multifarious, with tense chromatic harmonies and quasi-oriental inflections.

WORKS: *Sinfonietta* (1946); *Evocations* for clarinet and chamber orch. (1947); Sonatina for Viola and Piano (1947); *Prophecy* for chorus, tenor and organ (1948); *Taking of T'ung Kuan* for orch. (1948); *Tom o' Bedlam* for chorus (N.Y., Dec. 15, 1953; received the N.Y. Music Critics Award); *The Plywood Age* for orch., commissioned for the 50th anniversary of the Fir Plywood Corp. (Portland, June 20, 1955); *Psalm 100* for chorus and wind instruments (1956); *Inscriptions at the City of Brass* for chorus, narrator, and large orch., to a text from the *Arabian Nights* (1956); *Quodlibet Montagna* for brass sextet (1975).

Ax, Emanuel, American pianist; b. Lvov, June 8, 1949. He studied with his father who was a coach at the Lvov Opera House. The family moved to Warsaw when Ax was 8 years old, and later to Winnepeg in Canada. In 1961 the family settled in New York, where Emanuel Ax enrolled at the Juilliard School of Music as a pupil of Mieczyslaw Munz. In 1969 he went on a tour of Latin America. In 1970 he competed at the Chopin contest in Warsaw, but gained only seventh place; in 1971 he participated in the Vienna da Motta competition in Lisbon, and was placed third; in 1972 he entered the Queen Elisabeth Contest in Brussels, where he again received a remote place. A long awaited victory came in 1973 when he won first prize at the Artur Rubinstein International Competition in Tel-Aviv. Among his awards was a contract for an American concert tour. Ax received a tremendous accolade from the critics at his first New York recital in 1975, which proved the starting point for him of a brilliant career.

Axman, Emil, Czech composer; b. Rataje, June 3, 1887; d. Prague, Jan. 25, 1949. Of a musical family, he began to compose at an early age. He studied musicology with Nejedlý at the Prague Univ., obtaining his Ph.D. in 1912; took private composition lessons with Novák (1908–10) and Ostrčil (1920). In 1913 he was appointed keeper of the musical archives at the National Museum in Prague. He participated in the modern musical movement typified by Janáček but was not attracted to any spirit of experimentation, his music remaining highly lyrical.

WORKS: 6 symphonies: No. 1, *Tragic* (1925–26); No. 2, *Giocosa* (1926–27; International Society for Contemporary Music fest., Frankfurt, July 3, 1927); No. 3, *Spring* (1928); No. 4, *Eroica* (1932); No. 5, *Dithyrambic* (1936); No. 6, *Patriotic* (1942); the symph. poems *Sorrows and Hopes* (1919–20) and *A Bright Sky* (1921–22); 5 cantatas: *My Mother* (1926), *A Ballad on the Eyes of a Stoker* (1927), *Ilonka Beniačová* (1930), *The Cemetery of Sobotka* (1933) and *Stabat Mater* (1938); *From the Beskids* for chamber orch. (1934); Violin Concerto (1936); Piano Concerto (1939); Cello Concerto (1940); Double Concerto for Violin, Cello and Orch. (1944); Suite in the Form of Variations for Orch. (1948); Violin Sonata (1923); Cello Sonata (1924); 4 string quartets (1924, 1925, 1929, 1946); Piano Trio (1924–25); Wind Quintet (1938); Suite for String Quartet (1940); *Divertimento* for nonet (1944); *3 Moravian Dances* for nonet (1944); Variations for String Quartet (1944); 3 piano sonatas: No. 1, *Appassionata* (1922); No. 2, *To the Memory of a Great Man* (1922); No. 3 (1924); *Sonatina charakeristicka* for piano (1922); *Moravia Sings* for piano (1925; orchestrated, 1935); several choruses and song cycles. His musicological writings include *Moravian Operas of the 18th Century* (1912) and *Moravia in Czech Music of the 19th Century* (1920).

BIBLIOGRAPHY: F. Pala, *Emil Axman. Židot a dílo* (Prague, 1966).

Ayala, Daniel, Mexican (Indian) composer; b. Abalá, Yucatán, July 21, 1906; d. Veracruz, June 20, 1975. He went to Mérida, Yucatán, to study music; entered the National Cons. in Mexico City in 1927; studied violin with Ezequiel Sierra and Revueltas; composition with Ponce, Huízar and Carrillo. He played in night clubs in Mexico City; in 1931 became a violinist with the *Orquesta Sinfónica de México*; in 1934, together with Moncayo, Contreras and Galindo, formed the *Grupo de los Cuatro* (Group of the Four). He became conductor of the *Banda de Policía* in Mérida in 1940 and in 1942 founded the Yucatán Orch. His music, inspired by ancestral melos of the Mayan civilization and legends, is cast in pentatonic modes and possesses a vigorous rhythmic pulse.

WORKS: 2 ballets: *El Hombre Maya* (as a symph. suite, Mexico City, Nov. 21, 1940), and *La gruta Diabólica* for chamber orch. (1940); the symph. poems *Tribú* (Mexico City, Oct. 18, 1935), *Paisaje (Landscape,* 1935; Mexico City, June 2, 1936), *Panoramas de México* (1936; Dallas, Dec. 1, 1940) and *Mi viaje a Norte America* (1947). For voice: *4 Canciones* with piano (1932); *Uchben X'Coholte (Ancient Cemetery)* for soprano and chamber orch. (Mexico City, Oct. 13, 1933; ballet version, 1936; Mexico City, March 6, 1936); *El grillo (Cricket)* for soprano, clarinet, violin, timbrel and piano (1933); *U Kayil Chaac,* an incantation for rain, for soprano, Mexican percussion instruments and chamber orch. (1934); *Brigadier de Choque* for chorus and percussion (1935); *Suite infantil* for soprano and chamber orch. (1937); *Los Yaquis y los Seris,* 2 suites for voice, chamber ensemble and Mexican percussion instruments (1938; Mérida, July 31, 1942); *Radiograma* for piano, imitating radio code signals (1931).

Ayesterán, Lauro, Uruguayan musicologist; b. Montevideo, July 9, 1913; d. there, July 22, 1966. He studied voice and music history; became instructor of choral music in municipal schools in Montevideo. He is the author of the important monograph *Domenico Zipoli, el gran compositor y organista romano en el Rio* *de la Plata* (Montevideo, 1941); *El Folklore Musical Uruguayo* (Montevideo, 1967).

Ayres, Frederic (real name **Frederick Ayres Johnson**), American composer; b. Binghamton, N.Y., March 17, 1876; d. Colorado Springs, Nov. 23, 1926. He studied with Edgar S. Kelley (1897–1901) and Arthur Foote (1899). His works include an overture *From the Plains;* 2 string quartets, 2 piano trios, 2 violin sonatas, a cello sonata and numerous songs. In his later music he showed a tendency towards impressionism, and used moderately complex harmonic combinations.
BIBLIOGRAPHY: Wm. T. Upton, "Frederick Ayres," *Musical Quarterly* (1932).

Ayrton, Edmund, English organist and composer; father of William Ayrton; b. Ripon, Yorkshire, baptized on Nov. 19, 1734; was probably born the day before; d. London, May 22, 1808. He studied organ with Nares; from 1755 was organist in various churches; in 1764 was appointed Gentleman of the Chapel Royal, and in 1780 was appointed lay Vicar at Westminster Abbey. He was in charge of the Chapel Royal from 1780 until 1805. In 1784 he was given the degree of Mus.D. at Trinity College in Cambridge, and in 1788, Mus.D. at Oxford. He wrote a number of anthems, of which *Begin unto my God with Timbrels,* scored for 4 vocal soloists, mixed choir, 2 oboes, 2 bassoons, 2 trumpets, timpani and strings, obtained great success at its performance on June 29, 1784 in St. Paul's Cathedral, London. His glee *An Ode to Harmony* (1799) was also popular. He was admittedly a faithful imitator of Handel, but the judgment of Wesley, who described Ayrton as "one of the most egregious blockheads under the sun," seems unduly severe.

Ayrton, William, English organist; son of **Edmund Ayrton;** b. London, Feb. 24, 1777; d. there, March 8, 1858. He received a fine education; was one of the original founders of the London Philharmonic Soc. in 1813; wrote music criticism for *Morning Chronicle* (1813–26) and for *Examiner* (1837–51). In 1823 he started the publication of the historically important London music periodical *Harmonicon,* and was its editor; from 1834–37 edited *The Musical Library,* which published vocal and instrumental music. He also compiled a practical collection, *Sacred Minstrelsy* (2 vols., 1835).

Azantchevsky, Mikhail, Russian music educator and composer; b. Moscow, April 5, 1839; d. there, Jan. 24, 1881. He studied composition with Richter and Hauptmann at the Leipzig Cons. (1861–64), and piano with Liszt in Rome. After a sojourn in Paris (1866–70) he returned to Russia, where he became an executive director of the St. Petersburg Cons. (1871–76). A disciplinarian by nature, he raised the minimal requirements for acceptance of new pupils and engaged important teachers, among them Rimsky-Korsakov. In

Paris he purchased the important music library of Anders which he later presented, together with other acquisitions, to the St. Petersburg Cons. He composed a concert overture, 2 string quartets, 2 piano trios, a cello sonata, a *Festival polonais* for 2 pianos and numerous piano solo pieces and songs.

Azevedo, Alexis-Jacob, French writer on music; b. Bordeaux, March 18, 1813; d. Paris, Dec. 21, 1875. He was a prolific contributor to *Le Ménestrel* and other French music magazines; published monographs on Félicien David (1863) and Rossini (1864); a pamphlet, *La verité sur Rouget de Lisle et la Marseillaise* (Dieppe, 1864); *La transposition par les nombres* (Paris, 1874); a collection of articles *Les doublescroches malades* (1874), etc.

Azkué, Resurrección María, Spanish composer and musicologist; b. Lequeitio, Aug. 5, 1864; d. Bilbao, Nov. 9, 1951. He studied theology in Spain, then went to Paris and studied music at the Schola Cantorum. He wrote 2 operas to Basque texts: *Ortzuri* (Bilbao, 1911) and *Urlo* (Bilbao, 1913); an oratorio *Daniel* and a *Te Deum;* also several zarzuelas. He published a valuable collection *Cancionero Vasco* (11 vols.) and *Literatura popular del país Vasco* (4 vols., the last containing musical examples).

Azmayparashvili, Shalva, Georgian conductor and composer; b. Tiflis, Jan. 7, 1903. He studied trumpet and kettledrums at the Tiflis Cons.; from 1938 to 1954 was conductor of the Tiflis Opera Theater.
WORKS: opera, *The Village Elder* (Tbilisi, Jan. 21, 1951); musical comedy, *Times are Different* (Tbilisi, Feb. 12, 1952); symph. suite, *Pictures of Old Tiflis* (1941); a group of mass songs.

Aznavour (real name **Aznavurian**), **Charles,** French chansonnier; b. Paris, May 22, 1924. A son of an Armenian baritone from Tiflis, he received his early musical training at home; acted in Paris variety shows at the age of 5; learned to play the guitar. He made several American tours as a night club entertainer with a valuable French accent; also acted in films. He composed a great number of songs, of the genre of "tristesse chansons" and frustration ballads, among them the popular tunes *On ne sait jamais, Comme des étrangers* and *Ce jour tant attendu.* His operetta *Monsieur Carnaval* was produced in Paris on Dec. 17, 1965. He wrote an autobiography, entitled *Aznavour par Aznavour* (Paris, 1970).

Azzopardi, Francesco, Italian (Maltese) music theorist and composer; b. Rabat, Malta, May 5, 1748; d. there, Feb. 6, 1809. His fame rests on the school manual *Il musico prattico* (1760), published by Framéry in French translation (Paris, 1786) and quoted by Cherubini in his course on counterpoint and fugue, and by Grétry. He also composed sacred music, including an oratorio *La Passione di Cristo.*
BIBLIOGRAPHY: P. Pullicino, *Notizia biografica di Francesco Azzopardi* (1876).

B

Baaren, Kees van, Dutch composer; b. Enschede, Oct. 22, 1906; d. Oegstgeest, Sept. 2, 1970. He studied at the Hochschule für Musik in Berlin and later for 4 years with Willem Pijper in Rotterdam. His early works are in the lyric tradition of Grieg. However, he destroyed his early works in 1933 and started afresh in the direction of structural techniques, following the precepts of Schoenberg and Anton von Webern. His Trio (1936) shows traces of serialism, and his Septet (1952) is the first work by a Dutch composer written in an integral serial style, in which not only the 12 tones of the chromatic scale, but durations, dynamics and meters are organized according to a unifying thematic set. Baaren was director of the Amsterdam Music Academy (1948–53), the Cons. of Utrecht (1953–57) and the Royal Cons. of The Hague (1957–70).

WORKS: Piano Concertino (1934); a cantata, *The Hollow Men,* after T. S. Eliot (1948); *Sinfonia* (1956–57); 5 *Variazioni* for orch. (1959); Piano Concerto (1964); *Musica for Orch.* (Rotterdam, May 18, 1966); 2 string quartets (1932–33; *Sovraposizioni I,* 1962); Trio for Flute, Clarinet and Bassoon (1936); Piano Sonatina (1948); Septet for Concertante Violin, Wind Quintet and Double Bass (1952); *Sovraposizioni II,* wind quintet (1963); *Musica for Solo Flute* (1965); *Musica for 72 Carillons* (1964–68; alternate version for 47 carillons, 1964–69); *Musica* for organ (1968–69).

Babadzhanian, Arno, Armenian composer; b. Erevan, Jan. 22, 1921. He studied at the Erevan Cons. and, after graduation in 1947, went to Moscow where he took courses in piano with Igumnov and composition with Litinsky at the Moscow Cons. In 1950 he returned to Armenia and joined the faculty of his alma mater. His music continues the line of modernism cultivated by Khachaturian, with emphasis on rhythm and color in a characteristic quasi-oriental manner. Babadzhanian also wrote numerous popular songs and ballads, under such titles as *The Song of First Love, Make a Wish,* etc. His more ambitious works include a Violin Concerto (1949); *Heroic Ballad* for piano and orch. (1950); Cello Concerto (1962); 2 string quartets (1942, 1947); Piano Trio (1952); Violin Sonata, etc. A monograph on Babadzhanian was published in Erevan in 1961 in the Armenian language.

Babbitt, Milton Byron, American composer and theorist; b. Philadelphia, May 10, 1916. He received his early musical training in Jackson, Mississippi; at the same time he revealed an innate flair for mathematics; this double faculty determined the formulation of his musical theories, in which he promulgated the principle of melodic and rhythmic sets and such concepts as time points relating pitch to duration, ultimately leading to the technique of integral serialism. His academic studies included courses with Philip James and Marion Bauer at N.Y. Univ. (B.A. 1935), and Princeton Univ. (M.A. 1942); at Princeton he also took private lessons with Roger Sessions. He taught music theory and mathematics at Princeton (1943–45); in 1960 was named prof. of music. He received the New York Music Critics' citation in 1949 and 1964; held a Guggenheim grant in 1961; was elected member of the National Institute of the Arts and Letters in 1965. He organized the council for the electronic music center at Columbia and Princeton, and inaugurated an experimental program of electronic music, with the aid of a newfangled electronic synthesizer. Taking as the point of departure the Schoenbergian method of composition with 12 tones, he extended the serial principle inherent in it to embrace 12 different note values, 12 different time intervals between instrumental entries, 12 different dynamic levels and 12 different instrumental timbres. In order to describe the fractional combinations of the basic 4 aspects of the tone-row, he introduced the term "combinatoriality" with symmetric parts of a tone-row being termed "derivations." As in classical dodecaphony, Babbitt subdivides the 12-tone series into groups, used horizontally as melody and vertically as counterpoint. His paper, "Twelve-Tone Invariants as Compositional Determinants," *Musical Quarterly* (April 1960), outlines the fundamental tenets of his total serialism. The serial application to rhythm is expounded in Babbitt's paper "Twelve-Tone Rhythmic Structure and the Electronic Medium," *Perspectives of New Music* (Fall 1962). Most of his compositions are slim but pregnant with potential embryonic development. They include *Three Compositions for Piano (1947); Composition* for 4 Instruments (1948); *Composition* for 12 instruments (1948); *Composition* for viola and piano (1950); *The Widow's Lament in Springtime* for voice and piano (1950); *Du,* a song cycle (1951); Quartet for Flute, Oboe, Clarinet and Bassoon (1953); String Quartet No. 1 (1954); String Quartet No. 2 (1954); *Two Sonnets* for voice and 3 instruments (1955); *Semi-simple Variations* for piano (1956); *All Set* for jazz ensemble (1957); *Sounds and Words,* to text of disparate syllables for voice and piano (1958); *Composition* for voice and 6 instruments (1960); *Composition* for synthesizer (1961); *Vision and Prayer,* song for soprano and synthesized magnetic tape (1961); *Philomel* for voice and magnetic tape (1964); *Ensemble* for synthesizer (1964); *Relata I* for orch. (1965); *Post-Partitions* for piano (1966); *Sextets* for violin and piano (the title refers to the sextuple parameters of the work, 1966); *Correspondences* for string orch. and synthesized magnetic tape (1967); *Relata II* for orch. (1968); *Occasional Variations,* a compost collated by synthesizer (1969); String Quartet No. 3 (1970); *Phonemena* for soprano and piano (1970); *Reflections* for piano and synthesized tape (1975); Concerti for Violin, Small Orch. and Synthesized Tape (N.Y., March 13, 1976). Babbitt's scientific sounding theories have profoundly impressed the musical thinking of young American composers; a considerable literature, both intelligible and unintelligible, is devoted to Babbitt's theories. For a detailed list of Babbitt's writings, see article by B. Boretz in J. Vinton, ed., *Dictionary of Contemporary Music* (N.Y., 1974).

Babić, Konstantin, Serbian composer; b. Belgrade, Feb. 10, 1927. He studied in Belgrade; wrote a number of symphonic pieces in a neo-Classical vein; of these, *Konzertna Intrada* (Belgrade, Sept. 30, 1955) is the most effective. His *Levačka Svita (Suite from Levač)* for mixed choir (1966), in 3 classical sections, *Passacaglia, Fuga* and *Toccata,* uses folkloric texts.

Babin, Victor, Russian pianist and composer; b. Moscow, Dec. 13, 1908; d. Cleveland, March 1, 1972. He studied at the Riga Cons.; in 1928 went to Berlin where he took lessons with Artur Schnabel. On Aug. 31, 1933 he married the pianist Vitya Vronsky; they emigrated to the U.S. in 1937, and toured widely as a duo piano team. Babin wrote several pieces for 2 pianos for their concerts.

Babini, Matteo, famous Italian tenor; b. Bologna, Feb. 19, 1754; d. there, Sept. 22, 1816. He studied with Cortoni; made his debut in 1780; then toured England, Russia, Germany and Austria with great acclaim. He settled in Paris as a court favorite until the Revolution forced him to leave France; he was in Berlin in 1792 and in Trieste in 1796. Brighenti published an "Elogio" in his memory (Bologna, 1821).

Babitz, Sol, American violinist; b. Brooklyn, Oct. 11, 1911. In 1932 he went to Berlin where he studied violin with Carl Flesch and composition with Paul Juon; also musicology with Curt Sachs. In 1933 he proceeded to Paris where he took violin lessons with Marcel Chailley. Shortly afterwards he returned to America, where he became violinist in the Los Angeles Philharmonic Orch. (1933–37). From 1942 to 1961 he played violin in studio orchestras in Hollywood. He has written numerous articles dealing with violin technique and edited many violin works by contemporary composers; also published a manual of modern violin playing, *Principles of Extensions in Violin Fingering* (New York, 1947). See his autobiographical entry in the supplement to *Die Musik in Geschichte und Gegenwart.*

Bacarisse, Salvador, Spanish composer; b. Madrid, Sept. 12, 1898; d. Paris, Aug. 7, 1963. He studied at the Cons. of Madrid with Conrado del Campo; received the Premio Nacional de Música three times, in 1923, 1930 and 1934. During the Spanish Civil War he was active in the music section of the loyalist army, and after its defeat in 1939 went to Paris where he remained until his death. He wrote music in all genres; among his works are an opera *Charlot* (1933); the symphonic poem *La tragedia de Doña Ajada* (1929); *Corrida de feria,* a ballet (1930); Piano Concerto (1933); *Tres Movimientos Concertantes* for string trio and orch. (1934); a cantata, *Por la Paz y Felicidad de las Naciones* (1950); Concerto for Guitar and Orch. (Paris, Oct. 22, 1953); 2 string quartets, piano pieces and songs.

Baccaloni, Salvatore, Italian bass singer; b. Rome, April 14, 1900; d. New York, Dec. 31, 1969. He sang as a child in the Cappella Sistina; then studied to be an architect, but returned to singing. He made his debut in Rome as Bartolo in *The Barber of Seville;* in 1927 he appeared at La Scala in Milan. In 1931 he went to America; sang for a season at the Chicago Opera, and in 1940 made his debut with The Metropolitan Opera in Philadelphia; he remained on its staff until 1954. He specialized in comic roles; his repertory was very large, comprising some 150 roles in several languages.

Bacchius, Greek theorist who flourished c. 350 A.D. His treatise, *Isagoge musicae artis,* was publ. by Mersenne (1623); with Latin translation and commentary by Morellus (1623); also by Meibom (1652) and Carl von Jan (with German translation and analysis in the Program of the Strasbourg Lyceum, 1890; Greek text alone in Jan's 'Scriptores,' 1895). French translations have been publ. by Mersenne (in Book I of his *Harmonie universelle,* 1627) and Ruelle (1896). The work is a musical catechism in dialogue form. Another treatise attributed to Bacchius, having no dialogue, and edited by Bellermann (in German, 1841) and Vincent (in French, 1847) is not by Bacchius, but by his contemporary, Dionysios.

Baccusi, Ippolito, Italian composer; b. Mantua, 1530; d. Verona, Sept. 2, 1608. He served as maestro di cappella at San Marco in Venice. In 1570 he was in Ravenna as an organist and in 1572 in Verona; from 1584 to 1587 he was maestro di cappella in Mantua; in 1591 went to Verona. He published 5 books of Masses (1570–96); 7 books of madrigals (1570–1605); also numerous other choral works. His music shows the influence of the Venetian school; his motets have considerable expressive power.

Bacewicz, Grażyna, significant Polish composer; b. Lódź, May 5, 1913; d. Warsaw, Jan. 17, 1969. She studied composition and violin at the Warsaw Cons., graduating in 1932; continued her study of composition with Nadia Boulanger in Paris (1933–34); upon her return to Poland she taught at the Lódź Cons.; in 1966 she was appointed professor at the State Academy of Music in Warsaw. A prolific composer, she adopted a neo-Classical style, characterized by a firm rhythmic pulse and crisp dissonant harmonies. WORKS: a comic radio opera *Przygody króla Artura (The Adventures of King Arthur,* 1959); 3 ballets: *Z chlopa Król (A Peasant Become King,* 1953); *Esik in Ostende* (1964) and *Pozqdanie (Desire)* (1968); Sinfonietta (1937); 7 violin concertos (1938, 1946, 1948, 1952, 1954, 1957, 1965); Overture (1943); 4 numbered symphonies (1942–45, 1950, 1952, 1953); an unnumbered Symphony for string orch. (1943–46); *Olympic Cantata* (1948); Concerto for String Orch. (1948); Piano Concerto (1949); 2 cello concertos (1951, 1963); *Polish Overture* (1954); Partita for Orch. (1955); Variations for Orch. (1957); *Muzyka* for strings, 5 trumpets and percussion (Warsaw, Sept. 14, 1959); *Pensieri notturni* for chamber orch. (1961); Concerto for Orchestra (1962); *Cantata,* after Wyspiański's "Acropolis" (1964); *Musica Sinfonica* (1965); Divertimento for String Orch. (1965); *Incrustations* for horn and chamber ensemble (1965); *Contradizione* for chamber orch. (1966; Dartmouth College, Hanover, N.H., Aug. 2, 1967); 2-piano concerto (1966); *In una parte* for orch. (1967); Viola Concerto (1967–68); Wind Quintet (1932); Trio for Oboe, Violin and Cello

(1935); 7 string quartets (1938, 1942, 1947, 1950, 1955, 1960, 1965); 5 violin sonatas (1945, 1946, 1947, 1951, 1955); Quartet for 4 Violins (1949); 2 piano quartets (1952, 1965); solo Violin Sonata (1958); Quartet for 4 Cellos (1964); Trio for Oboe, Harp and Percussion (1965); *4 Caprices* for solo violin (1968); 3 piano sonatas (1935, 1949, 1952); *10 Concert Studies* for piano (1957); *Esquisse* for organ (1966).

Bach is the name of the illustrious family which, during two centuries, supplied the world with a number of musicians and composers of distinction. History possesses few records of such remarkable examples of hereditary art, which culminated in Johann Sebastian.

The genealogy of the family is traced to **Johannes** or **Hans Bach,** mentioned in 1561 as one of the guardians of the municipality of Wechmar, a little town near Gotha. **Veit Bach** (d. March 8, 1619), the presumed son of this Hans, and Caspar, a town-musician ("Stadtpfeifer") at Gotha, are the first of the family concerning whose musical tendencies we have any information. Veit was a baker by trade, and emigrated to Hungary; returning to Wechmar, he settled there as a miller and baker. His chief recreation consisted in playing the zither. His son, **Hans** (b. c.1580, d. Dec. 26, 1626), was known as 'the minstrel' ('der Spielmann'), although he followed the supplementary occupation of carpetweaver. He received instruction from the above-mentioned Caspar, possibly his uncle. On numerous occasions he was called to various places in Thuringia to assist the town-musicians. His three sons **Hans, Christoph** and **Heinrich,** inherited his ability. (See W. Wolffheim, "Hans Bach, der Spielmann," *Bach-Jahrbuch* [1910].) The Bach genealogy mentions a second son of Veit, presumably **Lips Bach** (d. Oct. 10, 1620), who had three sons, who were sent to Italy, by the Count of Schwarzburg-Arnstadt, to study music. From Hans and Lips, the two sons of Veit, sprang the main branches of the Bach family, whose male members filled so many positions as 'Stadtpfeifer' throughout Thuringia, that, in some instances, even after there had ceased to be any member of the family among them, the town-musicians were known as "the Bachs." When the family became numerous and widely dispersed, they agreed to assemble on a fixed date each year. Erfurt, Eisenach and Arnstadt were the places chosen for these meetings, which are said to have continued until the middle of the 18th century, as many as 120 persons of the name of Bach then assembling. At these meetings, a cherished pastime was the singing of 'quodlibets,' comic polyphonic potpourris of popular songs. An amusing example attributed to J. S. Bach, is publ. in *Veröffentlichungen der Neuen Bach-Gesellschaft* (vol. XXXII, 2).

Johann Sebastian was very interested in the history of his family. A collection of notes on members of the family, entitled *Ursprung der musikalisch-Bachischen Familie,* and known as 'the genealogy,' was, according to Carl Philipp Emanuel, who made additions to the copy preserved (written in 1735), started by Johann Sebastian. This 'genealogy' is reproduced in *Veröffentlichungen der Neuen Bach-Gesellschaft* (vol. XVII, 3). It has also been edited and translated by C. S. Terry as *The Origin of the Family of Bach Musicians* (Oxford, 1929).

A valuable collection of compositions by Hans Bach (1), his sons and grandsons, possibly also begun by J. S. Bach, is partly preserved. The remainders of this collection were edited by M. Schneider as 'Altbachisches Archiv' in *Das Erbe deutscher Musik, Reichsdenkmale* (vols. I and II, Breitkopf & Härtel, 1935). See also *Die Familie Bach,* a collection of excerpts from works by 12 Bachs, edited by Karl Geiringer (Vienna, 1936); also his books *The Bach Family* (N.Y., 1954) and *Music of the Bach Family* (Cambridge, Mass., 1955).

The principal members of the Bach family are enumerated below, in alphabetical order, with their list numbers according to the family tree.

17. Carl Philipp Emanuel
2. Christoph
5. Georg Christoph
1. Hans
3. Heinrich
6. Johann Ambrosius
10. Johann Bernhard
19. Johann Christian
8. Johann Christoph
7. Johann Christoph
11. Johann Christoph
18. Johann Christoph Friedrich
4. Johann Egidius
15. Johann Ernst
14. Johann Ludwig
9. Johann Michael
13. Johann Nikolaus
12. Johann Sebastian
16. Wilhelm Friedemann
20. Wilhelm Friedrich Ernst

1. Bach, Hans (eldest son of Hans, the "Spielmann"), b. Wechmar, Nov. 26, 1604; d. Erfurt, May 13, 1673. Apprentice to an organist at Suhl; then organist at Schweinfurt. In 1635, director of the 'Raths-Musikanten' of Erfurt; 1647, also organist of an Erfurt church.

2. Bach, Christoph (2nd son of Hans, the "Spielmann," and grandfather of Johann Sebastian), b. Wechmar, April 19, 1613; d. Arnstadt, Sept. 12, 1661; instrumentalist, serving as town-musician at Weimar, Erfurt and Arnstadt. No compositions by him seem to be preserved.

3. Bach, Heinrich (3rd son of Hans), b. Wechmar, Sept. 16, 1615; d. Arnstadt, July 10, 1692. From 1641, organist at Arnstadt for 51 years. M. Schneider publ. a thematic index of his works in *Bach-Jahrbuch* (1907, pp. 105–9). A cantata of his is found in the Bach Archives.

4. Bach, Johann Egidius (2nd son of Hans, 1), b. Erfurt, Feb. 9, 1645; d. there, 1716. Succeeded his father as municipal music director; was organist of an Erfurt church.

5. Bach, Georg Christoph (eldest son of Christoph, 2), b. Eisenach, Sept. 6, 1642; d. April 24, 1697, at Schweinfurt, where he was cantor. A cantata is in the Bach Archives.

6. Bach, Johann Ambrosius (2nd son of Christoph, 2), father of Johann Sebastian, b. Erfurt, Feb. 22, 1645; d. Eisenach, Feb. 20, 1695. (Exact date of death is found in his widow's petition for support, *Bach-Jahr-*

buch, [1927].) At the age of nine, he was taken to Arnstadt where he was trained as a town piper ('Stadtpfeifer'). In 1667 he was engaged at Erfurt to play the viola ('Altgeige') in the town band; in 1671, he moved to Eisenach, where he was active as town-musician. He was married twice: on April 8, 1668, to Elisabeth Lämmerhirt (b. Feb. 24, 1644; d. May 3, 1694), who was the mother of Johann Sebastian; and on Nov. 27, 1694 to the widow of his cousin, Johann Günther Bach.

BIBLIOGRAPHY: F. Rollberg, "J. A. Bach," *Bach-Jahrbuch* (1927).

7. Bach, Johann Christoph, twin brother of Johann Ambrosius; b. Erfurt, Feb. 22, 1645; d. Arnstadt, Aug. 25, 1693. He entered the town service at Arnstadt as 'Stadtpfeifer' in 1671. The physical resemblance between him and his twin brother (father of Johann Sebastian) was such that, according to the testimony of C. P. E. Bach, even their wives had difficulty distinguishing between them.

8. Bach, Johann Christoph (eldest son of Heinrich, 3), organist and instrumental and vocal composer of the highest rank among the earlier Bachs; b. Arnstadt, Dec. 3, 1642; d. Eisenach, March 31, 1703. From 1665, town organist of Eisenach; from 1700, court musician. A thematic catalogue of his compositions was publ. by M. Schneider in *Bach-Jahrbuch* (1907, pp. 132–77). C. P. E. Bach described him as a 'great and expressive composer'; his works are printed in the Bach Archives and separate editions; several of his motets were publ. by V. Junk (Breitkopf & Härtel, 1922); his *Choräle zum Praeambulieren* by M. Fischer (Bärenreiter-Verlag, 1929).

BIBLIOGRAPHY: F. Rollberg, "Johann Christoph Bach" in *Zeitschrift für Musikwissenschaft* (vol. XI, pp. 549–61); M. Fischer, "Die organistische Improvisation . . .," *Königsberger Studien zur Musikwissenschaft* (1919).

9. Bach, Johann Michael, brother of the preceding Bach, and father of Maria Barbara, first wife of Johann Sebastian; b. Arnstadt, Aug. 9, 1648; d. Gehren, May 17, 1694. Organist and town clerk of Gehren from 1673; also maker of clavichords, violins, etc. His works are listed in *Bach-Jahrbuch* (1907, pp. 109–32); many of them are included in the Bach Archives; also represented by motets publ. in *Denkmäler deutscher Tonkunst* (vols. 49–50). Organ compositions are found in *Das Erbe deutscher Musik, Reichsdenkmale* (vol. IX). A published work consisting of sonatas for 2 groups of instruments is not preserved.

10. Bach, Johann Bernhard (son of Johann Egidius, 4), organist and organ composer, one of the best of his generation; b. Erfurt, Nov. 23, 1676; d. Eisenach, June 11, 1749. Organist at Erfurt, Magdeburg, and the successor of Johann Christoph (8), at Eisenach (1703); also served the Duke of Saxe-Eisenach. He wrote harpsichord pieces; several organ-chorales, a few of which are published; and 4 orchestral suites, one of which was published by A. Fareanu (1920).

11. Bach, Johann Christoph (brother of Johann Sebastian, and eldest son of Johann Ambrosius, 6), b. Erfurt, June 16, 1671; d. Ohrdruf, Feb. 22, 1721. He was a pupil of Pachelbel; then organist at Erfurt, for a short time at Arnstadt, and finally at Ohrdruf, where

Johann Sebastian stayed with him for almost five years.

12. Bach, Johann Sebastian, the most famous of the family, and one of the great masters of music; b. Eisenach, March 21 (bapt. March 23), 1685; d. Leipzig, July 28, 1750. He first learned the violin from his father (Joh. Ambrosius, 6). His mother, Elisabeth, *née* Lämmerhirt, was a native of Erfurt. Both parents dying in his tenth year, he went to Ohrdruf to live with his brother, Johann Christoph (11), who taught him to play on keyboard instruments; but the boy's genius soon outstripped his brother's skill, and, if we may trust the somewhat fanciful tale first appearing in the 'Nekrolog,' led to somewhat harsh treatment by the latter. Unable to obtain the loan of a MS volume of works by composers of the day, Sebastian secretly obtained possession of the work, and, by the light of the moon, painfully and laboriously copied the music within six months, only to have it taken from him, when his brother accidentally found him practicing from it. He recovered it only after his brother's death. In 1700 Bach went to Lüneburg with a fellow-student named Erdmann, and both were admitted as choristers at St. Michael's Church, also receiving gratuitous scholastic education. The fame of the family had preceded Sebastian, for in the choice collections of printed and MS music of the church were to be found the compositions of Heinrich (3) and J. Christoph Bach (8). A fellow-Thuringian, Georg Böhm, was the organist of St. John's Church, and Bach attentively studied his compositions. He also went, occasionally, on foot to Hamburg to hear the famous old organist, J. A. Reinken, and to Celle, where the court music adhered completely to the French style. In 1703 Bach became violinist in the orch. of a brother of the Duke of Saxe-Weimar, but the following year left the post for the more congenial one of organist of the new church at Arnstadt. In 1705 he obtained leave of absence, and walked to Lübeck, to make the acquaintance of the famous organist Dietrich Buxtehude. He was so impressed with this master's work that he trebled his leave of absence, and returned only after a peremptory summons from the church consistory of Arnstadt. In 1707, Bach accepted the appointment as organist of St. Blasius' Church at Mühlhausen. On Oct. 17 he married his cousin Maria Barbara Bach, daughter of Johann Michael (9). The following year he went to Weimar, played before the reigning duke, and was offered the post of court organist and "Kammermusicus." In 1714 he was made "Concertmeister." A considerable series of compositions and arrangements, especially for organ, date from his Weimar period. Almost annually he made tours as an organ inspector and virtuoso. In 1714 he visited Kassel, Halle and Leipzig (where he furnished the music for a service in the Thomaskirche, including a cantata), Halle again in 1716, and Dresden in 1717. In this town his challenge to J. L. Marchand, a French clavecinist and organist of high reputation, was evaded by the latter's failure to appear. In 1717 Bach was appointed Kapellmeister and director of the 'Kammermusik' to Prince Leopold of Anhalt, at Cöthen, and this period is especially rich in the production of orchestral and chamber music. In 1718 he revisited Halle, hoping to meet Handel; but the latter had just left for England. In

1720, during his absence at Carlsbad, his wife died suddenly. In November of the same year he applied, though (owing to bribery) without success, for the organistship of the Jacobikirche, Hamburg. Here he again met the aged Reinken, whose admiration he excited by his brilliant playing. In 1721 he married his second wife, Anna Magdalena Wülken, a daughter of a court trumpeter at Weissenfels. Thirteen children were born to them. Of highly-cultured musical taste, she participated in his labors, and wrote out the parts of many of his cantatas. She also left 2 books of music in which her own hand appears as well as her husband's. In May, 1723 Bach succeeded Johann Kuhnau as cantor at the Thomasschule, Leipzig, becoming also organist and director of music at the two principal churches, the Thomaskirche and the Nicolaikirche, and continuing in the service of Prince Leopold of Anhalt as 'Kapellmeister von Haus aus.' He further received the appointment of honorary Kapellmeister to the Duke of Weissenfels, and in 1736, that of court composer to the King of Poland, Elector of Saxony. He remained in his post at Leipzig for 27 years, and there composed most of his religious music. Several times, he visited Dresden, where his eldest son, Wilhelm Friedemann, was appointed in 1733 organist of the Sophienkirche. On these occasions he attended the Italian opera, then conducted by Hasse. His second son, Carl Philipp Emanuel, was appointed in 1740 chamber musician to Frederick II of Prussia. He communicated to his father the king's oft-expressed wish to see and hear him; and on May 7, 1747, with his son Wilhelm Friedemann, Bach arrived at Potsdam. Here at the king's request, he improvised upon the various Silbermann pianos in the different rooms of the palace, to the admiration of his royal host and of the musicians who followed them from room to room. Among Bach's improvisations was a fugue, presumably in 3 parts, on a theme proposed by the king, and a fugue in 6 parts on a theme by Bach himself. The next day Bach tried also the principal organs in Potsdam. On his return to Leipzig he used the king's theme for a Ricercare in 3 parts, a Ricercare in 6 parts, a series of ten canons and a Trio for flute, violin and basso continuo, dedicating the whole to Frederick as a *Musikalisches Opfer.* Bach was nearsighted from childhood, and later his eyes showed symptoms of weakness; in 1749 an unsuccessful operation resulted in total blindness, and his hitherto robust health also declined. His sight was suddenly restored on July 18, 1750; but immediately afterwards he was stricken by apoplexy, and ten days later he died. He worked to the end, dictating the chorale prelude *Vor deinen Thron tret' ich hiermit,* his last composition, a few days before his death.

Clearness and acuteness of intellect, strength of will, a love of order, and a high sense of duty, were Bach's leading characteristics. His home life was always of the happiest. Among the long list of his distinguished pupils were Johann Friedrich Agricola, Johann Christoph Altnikol, Heinrich Nikolaus Gerber, Johann Theophilus Goldberg, Gottfried August Homilius, Philipp Kirnberger, Johann Christian Kittel, Johann Tobias Krebs and his son Johann Ludwig; also his own sons Wilhelm Friedemann, Carl Philipp Emanuel and Johann Christoph Friedrich, and his

nephew Bernhard, son of Johann Christoph (11). Many of Bach's works were written with educational intent, among them the 2- and 3-part inventions which first appear in the *Clavierbüchlein für Wilhelm Friedemann Bach* (now at Yale Univ.). Only a small number of works were publ. during Bach's life; among them are 4 parts of the *Clavierübung,* including 6 Partitas, Overture in the French manner and the Italian Concerto; music for organ; the Goldberg Variations; Musical Offering; Canonic Variations upon *Vom Himmel hoch;* and six chorale preludes. A few pages of these publications were evidently engraved by Bach himself. (See G. Kinsky, *Die Originalausgaben der Werke J. S. Bachs,* 1937.) Bach promoted the adoption of the tempered system of tuning keyboard instruments, and introduced the style of fingering which, with comparatively few modifications, is still in use.

Bach's compositions mark an epoch. His originality and fecundity of thematic invention are astounding; the mastery of his polyphonic art remains a marvel of the ages. Indeed, the rhetorical phrase "Nicht Bach aber Meer haben wir hier" (Not a stream, but an ocean have we here) offers an eloquent metaphor for Bach's greatness. His style is elevated and of sustained harmony; the momentum of his grand fugues is as inexorable as the march of Fate. Bach's importance was but meagerly appreciated by his contemporaries, and for half a century after his death he was practically ignored. Some works were then occasionally performed, or even published; but Mendelssohn, by a performance of the *St. Matthew Passion* at Berlin, in 1829, first drew general attention to the great value of Bach's music. The centenary of Bach's death (1850) was marked by the formation, at Leipzig, of the Bach-Gesellschaft, a society founded by C. F. Becker, M. Hauptmann, O. Jahn, R. Schumann and the publishers Härtel, in order to publish a complete edition of Bach's works. When the purpose of this society had been fulfilled, a Neue Bach-Gesellschaft was founded in 1900. It seeks to popularize Bach's works through Bach festivals, the *Bach-Jahrbuch* (begun 1904) and practical editions. A Bach-Society was active in London from 1849 to 1870; numerous Bach Vereine and similar institutions aiming at the cultivation and production of Bach's music existed, or exist, in many European and American cities. The most famous of such societies in the U.S. is the Bach Choir at Bethlehem, Pa. (See R. Walters, "Bach at Bethlehem, Pa.," *Musical Quarterly* [April 1935].)

WORKS: VOCAL: Bach wrote 5 sets of sacred compositions for every Sunday and feast-day of the year, and not less than 5 Passions. Many of these works are lost. We have approximately 190 sacred 'concertos' or 'cantatas' (now all called cantatas); the *St. Matthew* and *St. John Passions* (the *St. Luke* is probably spurious); 'oratorios' for Christmas, Easter and Ascension (the latter known as Cantata No. 11); 2 Magnificats; a Grand Mass in B minor; several short Masses; 5 Sanctus; motets; vocal works written for special occasions, e.g., the 'motetto' *Gott ist mein König* (written for the inauguration of the new council members of Mühlhausen in 1708; the only one among the works now called cantatas which was printed during Bach's life) and the *Tombeau de S. M., la Reine de Pologne;* many secular cantatas, including the *Dramma per musica, Der Streit zwischen Phoebus und Pan,* the 'Coffee' Cantata and the *Cantate en burlesque,* known as the 'Peasant' Cantata.

INSTRUMENTAL: Numerous pieces for organ, including a collection of chorale settings entitled *Orgelbüchlein;* many other chorale fantasias, preludes and fugues, toccatas; a set of 6 trios; Passacaglia, Canzona and Pastorale; numerous pieces for keyboard instruments (mostly for harpsichord or clavichord; a few definitely require a harpsichord with 2 keyboards), including the 2 collections of 24 Preludes and Fugues in all keys entitled *Das Wohltemperierte Clavier* (i.e., the well-tempered keyboard; the common translation, 'clavichord', is wrong), the series of 15 Inventions and 15 Sinfonias (now known as 3-part inventions), the 6 English suites, the secular works contained in the *Clavierübung,* a number of suites, 6 of which became known as French suites, toccatas and various other works.—Among Bach's chamber-music works are a number for obbligato harpsichord and another instrument (violin, flute, or viola da gamba); a set of 6 suites for cello alone; a set of 3 sonatas and 3 partitas for violin alone. He dedicated a set of 6 *Concertos pour plusieurs instruments* to a Margrave of Brandenburg, whence they became known as *Brandenburg Concertos.* He wrote 4 overtures or orchestral suites, concertos for 1 and 2 violins, violin and oboe, violin, flute and harpsichord, and for from 1 to 3 harpsichords; also a concerto for 4 harpsichords which is an arrangement of a work by Vivaldi.

The monumental edition of Bach's works, published by the Bach-Gesellschaft, is in 47 volumes, including a volume of facsimile reproductions of original manuscript pages. A completely revised edition, the *Neue Bach-Ausgabe,* began publishing in 1954. Bach's instrumental works were also completely publ. by C. F. Peters. There are innumerable reprints of many of his works. Deserving of special mention are the following: the edition of organ works, by C. M. Widor and A. Schweitzer with voluminous notes and directions for playing (G. Schirmer); that of the *Well-tempered Clavier,* in score, annotated by F. Stade (Steingräber); the *Kunst der Fuge* by H. T. David (Peters, 1928); the same work by Roy Harris and M. D. Herter Norton (G. Schirmer, N.Y., 1936); and Bach's 4-part chorales by C. S. Terry (5 vols., London, 1929). The *Goldberg Variations* have been published in an edition by Ralph Kirkpatrick (G. Schirmer, N.Y., 1938).

Several works, including the *St. Matthew Passion,* the cantatas *Ach Herr, mich armen Sünder, Ich will den Kreuzstab gerne tragen,* the 'Coffee' Cantata, and Prelude and Fugue in B minor for organ, are publ. in facsimile reproduction of the original manuscripts.

A thematic catalogue of Bach's instrumental works was publ. by A. Dörffel in 1882, one of his vocal works by C. Tamme in 1890. A thematic index to 120 cantatas is included in vol. 27 of the Bach-Gesellschaft ed., such an index to Bach's other works in vol. 46 of the same edition. A valuable systematic *Melodic Index to the Works of J. S. Bach* was publ. by May de Forest Payne (N.Y., 1938). A complete thematic catalogue of Bach's works was drawn up by W. Schmieder: *Thematisch-systematisch Verzeichnis der musikalischen Werke von Johann Sebastian Bach* (Leipzig, 1950).

BIBLIOGRAPHY: BIOGRAPHICAL: Bach's earliest biographers were his son, C. P. E. Bach, and J. F. Agricola in Mizler's *Musikalische Bibliothek* (Leipzig, 1754; reprint in *Bach-Jahrbuch,* 1920, pp. 13–29); J. N. Forkel, *Über J. S. Bachs Leben, Kunst und Kunstwerke* (a very lively account of Bach's career, and an invaluable source; Leipzig, 1802; Engl. transl., London, 1820; transl. with notes by C. S. Terry, 1920); C. L. Hilgenfeldt, *Bachs Leben, Wirken und Werke* (Leipzig, 1850); C. H. Bitter, *J. S. Bach* (2 vols., Berlin, 1865; 2nd ed., 4 vols., 1880); Ph. Spitta, *J. S. Bach* (the standard work on Bach's life and work, and one of the masterpieces of musical biography; 2 vols., Leipzig, 1873–80; rigidly shortened ed. in 1 vol., ib., 1935; Engl. transl. by C. Bell and J. A. Fuller-Maitland, 3 vols., with many additions, London, 1884–5; 2nd ed., 1899; reissued, N.Y., 1951). There are numerous other biographies of Bach, all based on Spitta. Most widely known is A. Schweitzer's book, originally publ. as *J. S. Bach, le musicien-poète* (Paris, 1905; augmented German editions, 1908, 1915; English translation by E. Newman, 2 vols., London, 1911; new English edition, 1923). Other biographies in English: R. L. Poole, *J. S. Bach* (London, 1882; 2nd ed., 1890); C. F. Abdy Williams, *Bach* (London, 1900; rev. ed., 1934); C. H. H. Parry, *J. S. Bach: The Story of the Development of a Great Personality* (N.Y. and London, 1909; new ed., 1934); Rutland Boughton, *Bach, the Master. A New Interpretation of His Genius* (N.Y. and London, 1930); T. Scott Buhrmann, *Bach's Life Chronologically as he lived it* (illustrated chronological tables; N.Y., 1935); H. T. David and A. Mendel, *The Bach Reader,* a life of Bach in letters and documents (N.Y., 1945); K. Geiringer, *The Bach Family* (N.Y., 1954). A work based on original research is C. S. Terry's *Bach, a Biography* (the finest and most thorough description of Bach's life; London, 1928; new edition, 1933; German edition, prefaced by Straube, Leipzig, 1929); W. Neumann, *Bach: A Pictorial Biography* (N.Y., 1961); Imogen Holst, *Bach* (London, 1965). Biographies in French are: André Pirro, *Bach* (Paris, 1906); T. Gérold, *Bach* (Paris, 1925); J. Tiersot, *Bach* (Paris, 1934); P. Collaer, *Bach* (Brussels, 1936); W. Cart, *J. S. Bach* (Lausanne, 1946); E. E. Buchet, *Jean-Sébastien Bach, l'œuvre et la vie* (Paris, 1963). Of German biographies the following are valuable: Ph. Wolfrum, *J. S. Bach* (2 vols., Leipzig, 1910); H. Kretzschmar, *Bach-Kolleg* (Leipzig, 1922); W. Dahms, *J. S. Bach, Ein Bild seines Lebens* (Munich, 1924); R. Steglich, *J. S. Bach* (Potsdam, 1935; richly illustrated); H. J. Moser, *Bach* (Berlin, 1935); W. Gurlitt, *Bach* (Berlin, 1935); H. and E. H. Müller von Asow, *J. S. Bachs Briefe* (Regensburg, 1950); H. Franck, *J. S. Bach: die Geschichte seines Lebens* (Berlin, 1960); A. Mendel, "Recent Developments in Bach Chronology," *Musical Quarterly* (July 1960); F. Blume, *Der junge Bach* (Wolfenbüttel, 1967); F. Smend, *Bach-Studien: Gesammelte Reden und Aufsätze* (Kassel, 1969). A unique and fascinating volume is W. His, *J. S. Bach, Forschungen über dessen Grabstätte, Gebeine und Antlitz* (Leipzig, 1895; dealing with the state of Bach's mortal remains, including many striking photographs of Bach's skull and bones at the time of his exhumation and reinterment).

CRITICAL, ANALYTICAL: F. Rochlitz, *Wege zu Bach* (extracted from 'Für Freunde der Tonkunst', Leipzig, 1824–37, by J. M. Müller-Blattau; Augsburg, 1926); A.

Pirro, *L'esthétique de J. S. Bach* (Paris, 1907); E. Kurth, *Grundlagen des linearen Kontrapunkts. Einführung in Stil und Technik von Bachs melodischer Polyphonie* (Berlin, 1917); C. S. Terry, *Bach: The Historical Approach* (London, 1930); id., *The Music of Bach* (London, 1933); A. E. F. Dickinson, *The Art of J. S. Bach* (London, 1936); M. Hauptmann, *Erläuterungen in J. S. Bachs Kunst der Fuge* (Leipzig, 1841); H. Riemann, *Handbuch der Fugenkomposition* (vols. I and II, analysis of *Das wohltemperierte Klavier* [Berlin, 1890–91; 3rd ed., 1914; Engl. transl. by J. S. Shedlock, 2 vols., London, 1893, several eds.]; vol. III, analysis of the *Kunst der Fuge* [Berlin, 1894; 3rd ed., 1921]); F. Iliffe, *The 48 Preludes and Fugues of J. S. Bach* (London, 1897); W. Werker, *Bachstudien* (2 vols., Leipzig, 1922); D. F. Tovey, *A Companion to the Art of Fugue* (London, 1931); also various vols. of the Musical Pilgrim Series; R. Wustmann, *J. S. Bachs Kantatentexte* (Leipzig, 1913); C. S. Terry, *Bach's Chorals* (3 vols., Cambridge, 1915, 1917, 1921); id., *J. S. Bach's Original Hymn-Tunes for Congregational Use* (1922); id., *Bach's Mass in B minor*; id., *A Bach Hymnbook of 16th-Century Melodies* (1923); W. G. Whittaker, *Fugitive Notes on Certain Cantatas and the Motets of J. S. Bach* (London, 1924); C. S. Terry, *J. S. Bach's Cantata Texts, Sacred and Secular* (London, 1926); id., *Bach's Four-Part Chorals* (complete ed., with German and English words, 1928); A. Eaglefield Hull, *Bach's Organ Works* (London, 1929); C. S. Terry, *Bach's Orchestra* (London, 1932); Cecil Gray, *Bach's 'Forty-Eight'* (London, 1937); H. T. David, "Zu Bachs Kunst der Fuge," *Peters Jahrbuch* (1928); H. T. David, "Zur Gesamtgestalt von Bachs H-moll Messe," *Festschrift für Johannes Wolf* (1929); J. Schreyer, *Beiträge zur Bach-Kritik* (2 vols., Leipzig, 1911–13); H. E. Huggler, *J. S. Bachs Orgelbüchlein* (Bern, 1930); L. Landshoff, *Urtextausgabe der Inventionen und Sinfonien J. S. Bachs* (Leipzig, 1933; with Revisionsbericht); G. Herz, *J. S. Bach im Zeitalter des Rationalismus und der Frühromantik* (Würzburg, 1935); L. Landshoff, *Musikalisches Opfer* (Leipzig, 1936); A. Schering, *J. S. Bachs Leipziger Kirchenmusik* (Leipzig, 1936); E. Thiele, *Die Chorfugen J. S. Bachs* (Bern, 1936); A. Schering, *Das Zeitalter J. S. Bachs und Johann Adam Hillers* (Leipzig, 1940); H. Rutters, *J. S. Bach en onze tijd* (Amsterdam, 1941); H. T. David, *J. S. Bach's Musical Offering* (N.Y., 1945); Marie M. Meyer, *J. P. Rameau; J. S. Bach* (Chambéry, 1946); N. Dufourcq, *J. S. Bach, le maître de l'orgue* (Paris, 1948); H. Besseler and G. Kraft, *J. S. Bach in Thüringen* (Weimar, 1950); A. Dürr, *Studien über die frühen Kantaten J. S. Bachs* (Leipzig, 1951); F. Hamel, *J. S. Bach: Geistige Welt* (Göttingen, 1951); Paul Hindemith, *J. S. Bach* (N.Y., 1952); F. Rothschild, *The Lost Tradition in Music: Rhythm and Tempo in J. S. Bach's Time* (N.Y., 1953); G. von Dadelsen, *Beiträge zur Chronologie der Werke J. S. Bachs* (Trossingen, 1958); W. G. Whittaker, *The Cantatas of J. S. Bach, Sacred and Secular* (2 vols., London, 1959); E. Bodky, *The Interpretation of Bach's Keyboard Works* (Cambridge, Mass., 1960); R. Steglich, *Tanzrhythmen in der Musik J. S. Bachs* (Wolfenbüttel, 1962); J. Day, *The Literary Background to Bach's Cantatas* (London, 1962); P. Aldrich, "On the Interpretation of Bach's Trills," *Musical Quarterly* (July 1963); N. Car-

rell, *Bach the Borrower* (London, 1967). Two titles in the Norton Critical Score series, both ed. by G. Herz, contain valuable background, analysis, and commentary: *J. S. Bach. Cantata No. 4. Christ lag in Todesbanden* (N.Y., 1967), and *J. S. Bach. Cantata No. 140. Wachet auf, ruft uns die Stimme* (N.Y., 1972).

13. Bach, Johann Nikolaus (eldest son of Johann Christoph, 8), b. Eisenach, Oct. 10, 1669; d. there, Nov. 4, 1753. In 1695, appointed organist of the city and university in Jena. He was an expert on organ-building and also made keyboard instruments for secular use, especially lute-clavicymbals. J. Adlung highly praises him.

WORKS: A fine *Missa* (Kyrie and Gloria), edited by A. Fareanu and V. Junk (Breitkopf & Härtel, 1920); a comic cantata, *Der Jenaische Wein- und Bier-Rufer*, a scene from Jena college life (ed. by F. Stein, 1920); suites for a keyboard instrument, which are not preserved, and organ chorales, of which only one is known.

14. Bach, Johann Ludwig (son of Jakob, a grandson of Lips, and cantor at Steinbach and Ruhle), b. Thal, Feb. 4, 1677; d. Meiningen (buried, March 1), 1731; was Court Kapellmeister at Saxe-Meiningen.

15. Bach, Johann Ernst (only son of Johann Bernhard, 10), b. Eisenach, Jan. 28, 1722; d. there, Sept. 1, 1777. Attended the Thomasschule and then the Leipzig Univ. He studied law and, after his return to Eisenach, practiced as advocate. In 1748 he was appointed assistant, and then successor, to his father, organist of St. George's Church; 1756, appointed Kapellmeister at Weimar. Publ. a *Sammlung auserlesener Fabeln mit Melodeyen* (ed. by H. Kretzschmar in *Denkmäler deutscher Tonkunst*, vol. 42) and other works; prefaced one of J. Adlung's books, and left a number of compositions in manuscript.

16. Bach, Wilhelm Friedemann ('Bach of Halle'), eldest son of J. Sebastian; b. Weimar, Nov. 22, 1710; d. Berlin, July 1, 1784. Pupil of his father and, at 15 years of age, J. G. Graun at Merseburg. Also studied at the Thomasschule, and at the Univ. of Leipzig, taking courses, among others, in mathematics. Organist of the Sophienkirche, Dresden (1733–47), and at the Marienkirche, Halle (1747–64). A composer of superior gifts, he unfortunately gave way to dissipation, lost his positions, and died in misery. An edition of selected works was started by the Abteilung für Musik der Preussischen Akademie der Künste; vol. I contains 4 trios (Leipzig, 1934). Among other compositions available in modern editions are an impressive Sinfonia (Wunderhorn Verlag, 1910) and a collection of fugues and polonaises edited by W. Niemann (1914); also, piano compositions in *Die Söhne Bachs*, ed. by W. Rehberg (1933); three excerpts in Karl Geiringer, *Music of the Bach Family* (Cambridge, Mass., 1955).

BIBLIOGRAPHY: K. H. Bitter, *K. P. E. Bach und W. Friedemann Bach und deren Brüder* (2 vols., Berlin, 1868); M. Falck, *W. F. Bach; sein Leben und seine Werke* (Leipzig, 1913); K. Stabenow, *J. S. Bachs Söhne* (Leipzig, 1935); K. Geiringer, *The Bach Family* (N.Y., 1954); Hans Franck, *Friedemann, der Sohn J. S. Bachs* (Berlin, 1963).

17. Bach, Carl Philipp Emanuel ("the Berlin or Hamburg Bach"), 3rd (and 2nd surviving) son of J. Sebastian; b. Weimar, March 8, 1714; d. Hamburg, Dec. 14, 1788. He studied philosophy and law at Leipzig and Frankfurt-on-the-Oder, but the inherited passion for music, and completeness of musical study under his father, decided his profession. He conducted a singing society at Frankfurt, for which he also composed. In 1738 he went to Berlin and, in 1740, was appointed chamber musician and clavecinist to Frederick the Great. In 1767 he went to Hamburg, succeeding Telemann as 'Musikdirector' of the principal church there, a position he held until death. He was one of the most brilliant performers of his day, creator of the modern expressive school of piano writing, and the outstanding master of 'Empfindsamkeit' (intimate expressiveness), the North German counterpart of the rococo; his work was of great significance in the establishment of the style as well as the forms of the classical school; Haydn and Mozart were indebted to him. His *Versuch über die wahre Art, das Clavier zu spielen* (2 parts, 1753-62, clumsily reedited by Schelling in 1857; new, but not complete, ed. by W. Niemann, 1906) is an important theoretical work and yields much information about musical practice of the time. An English translation of the *Versuch . . .,* entitled *Essay on the True Art of Playing Keyboard Instruments,* was made by W. J. Mitchell (N.Y., 1948). His compositions are voluminous (thematic list by A. Wotquenne, Leipzig, 1905); for clavier they comprise 210 solo pieces; 52 concertos with orch.; quartets; trios, duets; also 18 orchestral symphonies; 34 miscellaneous pieces for wind instruments; trios for flute, violin and bass; flute, oboe, cello concertos; soli for flute, viola da gamba, oboe, cello, harp; duets for flute and violin; for 2 violins; also for clarinets. Vocal works: 2 oratorios, *Die Israeliten in der Wüste,* and *Die Auferstehung und Himmelfahrt Jesu;* 22 Passions; cantatas; etc. Reprints of sonatas for clavier have been edited by Bülow, C. F. Baumgart ('für Kenner und Liebhaber', 6 vols.), H. Schenker (9 sonatas), R. Steglich and others. There are also reprints of concertos and chamber music works.

BIBLIOGRAPHY: C. H. Bitter, *C. P. E. Bach und W. Friedemann Bach und deren Brüder* (2 vols., Berlin, 1868); M. Fleuler, *Die norddeutsche Symphonie zur Zeit Friedrichs des Grossen, und besonders die Werke Ph. E. Bachs* (Berlin, 1908); O. Vrieslander, *C. P. E. Bach* (Munich, 1923); H. Wien-Claudi, *Zum Liedschaffen C. P. E. Bachs* (Reichenberg, 1928); H. Miesner, *P. E. Bach in Hamburg* (Leipzig, 1929); E. F. Schmid, *C. P. E. Bach und seine Kammermusik* (Kassel, 1931); H. Schenker, *Ein Beitrag zur Ornamentik; Als Einführung zu P. E. Bachs Klavierwerke* (Vienna, 1904); Karl Geiringer, *The Bach Family* (N.Y., 1954). C. P. E. Bach's Autobiography was reprinted by Willi Kahl in *Selbst-Biographien Deutscher Musiker* (Cologne, 1948).

18. Bach, Johann Christoph Friedrich ("the Bückeburg Bach"), 9th son of J. Sebastian; b. Leipzig, June 21, 1732; d. Bückeburg, Jan. 26, 1795. He studied law at Leipzig, but adopted the profession of music and, presumably in 1750, was appointed 'Kammermusicus' at Bückeburg. Although less brilliant in composition than his brothers, he was an excellent musician and thorough composer. An exhaustive biographical study was publ. by G. Schünemann in the *Bach-Jahr-*

buch (1914, pp. 45-165). The same author also prepared an edition of selected works by Johann Christoph Friedrich Bach, sponsored by the Fürstliches Institut für musikwissenschaftliche Forschung, in 1920, but abandoned after the publication of 2 motets, 4 piano sonatas and 4 chamber-music works. Schünemann also edited 3 oratorios by J. C. F. Bach in the *Denkmäler deutscher Tonkunst* (vol. 56; contains a thematic index of his compositions). G. A. Walter edited the cantata *Die Amerikanerin* (1920) and L. Duttenhofer a set of 6 quartets (Paris, 1922).

19. Bach, Johann (John) Christian (the "London Bach"), 11th and youngest surviving son of Sebastian; b. Leipzig, Sept. 5, 1735 (bapt. Sept. 7); d. London, Jan. 1, 1782. He went to Berlin to study with his brother, Carl Philipp Emanuel Bach, after the death of his father in 1750. He became music director to Count Antonio Litta in Milan in 1754; was organist at the cathedral there (1760-62); studied with Padre Martini in Bologna. He traveled through Italy; his opera *Alessandro nell'Indie* was produced at Naples (Jan. 20, 1762). In 1762 he went to England, and in London produced his most successful opera, *Orione* (Feb. 19, 1763); shortly afterwards he was appointed music master to the Queen. Beginning in 1764 he gave, together with K. F. Abel, a famous series of London concerts. Christian Bach was a prolific composer, and immensely popular in his day; he was master of the light and charming 'rococo' style; his music was an important source of the classical idiom, and influenced Mozart's development. His surviving works, many of them reprinted, include symphonies, concertos, operas, piano compositions and chamber music. Among his 13 operas are *Lucio Silla* (Mannheim, Nov. 20, 1776); *La Clemenza di Scipione* (London, April 4, 1778); *Amadis des Gaules* (Paris, Dec. 14, 1779), etc. His quintets for flute, oboe, violin, viola, and thoroughbass are reprinted in *Das Erbe deutscher Musik, Reichsdenkmale* (vol. I).

BIBLIOGRAPHY: C. S. Terry, *Johann Christian Bach* (London, 1929); H. P. Schökel, *Johann Christian Bach und die Instrumentalmusik seiner Zeit* (Wolfenbüttel, 1926); F. Tutenberg, *Die Sinfonik Johann Christian Bachs* (Kiel, 1926); G. de Saint-Foix, "A propos de J. Ch. Bach," *Revue de Musicologie* (1926); A. Wenk, *Beiträge zur Kenntnis des Opernschaffens von Johann Christian Bach* (Frankfurt, 1932); Karl Geiringer, *The Bach Family* (N.Y., 1954).

20. Bach, Wilhelm Friedrich Ernst (son of Johann Christoph Friedrich, 18, and grandson and last male descendant of J. Sebastian), b. Bückeburg, May 23, 1759; d. Berlin, Dec. 25, 1845. Studied with his father, and his uncle Johann Christian (19), in London. After his uncle's death, he traveled giving concerts. In 1787 he is mentioned as music director at Minden; later, became Kapellmeister to the Queen of Prussia, consort of Friedrich Wilhelm III, and also music master to the royal princes. He was pensioned after the Queen's death. Few of his compositions have been published.

Bach (real name **Bak**), **Albert,** Hungarian singer; b. Gyula, March 24, 1844; d. Edinburgh, Nov. 19, 1912. He studied at the Vienna Cons.; gave his first concert there in 1871; continued his studies in Italy. He sang opera in Italy, Russia, Germany and England. In his recitals he always performed Loewe's songs. He was a member of the Loewe-Verein in Berlin and edited three volumes of Loewe's ballades with English translations; also published several papers on music.

Bach, August Wilhelm, German organist; b. Berlin, Oct. 4, 1796; d. there, April 15, 1869. After a period of organ playing in churches and in concert, he became teacher and later director (1832) of the Royal Institute for Church Music in Berlin. Mendelssohn was his pupil in organ playing.

Bach, Leonhard Emil, German pianist and composer; b. Posen, March 11, 1849; d. London, Feb. 15, 1902. He studied with Th. Kullak (piano) and with Kiel (theory); in 1869 became teacher at Kullak's Academy in Berlin. He settled in London; from 1882 taught at the Guildhall School of Music. He wrote several short operas: *Irmengard* (London, 1892); *The Lady of Longford* (London, 1894); *Des Königs Garde* (Cologne, 1895) which were fairly successful at their first productions.

Bacharach, Burt, American composer of popular songs; b. Kansas City, May 12, 1928. He was raised in a cultural atmosphere (his father was a newspaper columnist). He played jazz piano in night clubs; then studied music seriously at McGill Univ. in Montreal; also attended courses of Darius Milhaud and Henry Cowell at the New School for Social Research in N.Y. From 1958 to 1961 he traveled with Marlene Dietrich as her accompanist. In 1962 he joined forces with the lyricist Hal David with felicitous results; together they produced such fine songs as *Reach Out for Me, Trains and Boats and Planes, Make It Easy on Yourself, Blue on Blue, Walk on By, Always Something There to Remind Me, What the World Needs Now Is Love, Do You Know the Way to San Jose?, Raindrops Keep Fallin' on My Head, The Look of Love, I'll Never Fall in Love Again, Our Little Secret, She Likes Baseball.* He wrote the title songs for the films *What's New Pussycat?, Wives and Lovers, Alfie, Send Me No Flowers, Promise Her Anything* and *Butch Cassidy and the Sundance Kid.* With Hal David again as his lyricist, he produced the highly successful Broadway musical *Promises, Promises* (1968). He is married to the actress Angie Dickinson.

Bachauer, Gina, eminent Greek pianist; b. Athens, May 21, 1913; d. there, Aug. 22, 1976. Her father was of Austrian descent; her mother, an Italian. She showed her aptitude as a pianist at the age of 5; entered the Athens Cons. where her teacher was Waldemar Freeman. She then went to Paris where she took lessons with Alfred Cortot at the École Normale de Musique. In 1933 she won the Medal of Honor at the International Contest for Pianists in Vienna; between 1933 and 1935 she received occasional instructions from Rachmaninoff in France and Switzerland; in 1935 she made her professional début with the Athens Symph. Orch. under the direction of Mitropoulos; she was also piano soloist in Paris in 1937 with Monteux. During World War II she lived in Alexandria, Egypt, and played several hundred concerts for the Allied

Forces in the Middle East. On Jan. 21, 1946 she made her London debut with the New London Orch. under the direction of Alec Sherman who became her second husband. Her first American appearance took place in New York on Oct. 15, 1950. Only 35 people attended this concert, but she received unanimous acclaim from the critics, and her career was assured. The uncommon vigor of her technique suggested comparisons with Teresa Carreño; her repertoire ranged from Mozart to Stravinsky; in both classical and modern works she displayed impeccable taste. She died suddenly of a heart attack in Athens on the day she was to appear as soloist with the National Symph. Orch. of Washington at the Athens Festival.

Bache, Constance, English writer and musician; b. Birmingham, March 11, 1846; d. Montreux, Switzerland, June 28, 1903. She was the sister of the English pianists **Francis Edward Bache** (1833–1858) and **Walter Bache** (1842–1888). She studied at the Munich Cons. and later with Klindworth; planned a piano career, but was forced to abandon it owing to an accident to her hand. In 1883 she settled in London. She published a vivid book of memoirs *Brother Musicians* (London, 1901), describing the lives of her brothers; translated the letters of Hans von Bülow and Franz Liszt, and Heintz's analyses of Wagner's operas; also translated the libretto of Humperdinck's *Hänsel und Gretel.*

Bachelet, Alfred, French composer; b. Paris, Feb. 26, 1864; d. Nancy, Feb. 10, 1944. He studied at the Paris Cons.; received the Grand Prix de Rome for his cantata, *Cléopatre* (1890). From his earliest works, Bachelet devoted himself mainly to opera. In his youth, he was influenced by Wagnerian ideas, but later adopted a more national French style. During World War I he conducted at the Paris Opéra; in 1919 became director of the Nancy Cons.; in 1939, elected a member of the Académie des Beaux Arts.
WORKS: lyric drama *Scémo* (Paris Opéra, May 6, 1914); *Quand la cloche sonnera,* one-act music drama, his most successful work (Opéra-Comique, Nov. 6, 1922); lyric drama *Un jardin sur l'Oronte* (Paris Opéra, Nov. 3, 1932); ballets: *La fête chez la Pouplinière; Castor et Pollux* by Rameau (adapted and rewritten); orchestral works with voices: *L'amour des Ondines, Joie, Le Songe de la Sulamith, Noël; Surya* for tenor, chorus and orch. (1940); *Ballade* for violin and orch.; songs.

Bachmann, Alberto Abraham, violinist and composer; b. Geneva, March 20, 1875; d. Neuilly-sur-Seine, Nov. 24, 1963. He studied violin at the Cons. of Lille, then took courses in succession with Ysaÿe, César, Thomson, Hubay and Adolf Brodsky. He was in the U.S. from 1916–26; since then living near Paris. He composed 3 violin concertos (the last of which is called *American Concerto*); 12 improvisations for solo violin; about 250 various pieces and as many transcriptions for violin. He published *Le violon* (1906); *Les grands violonistes du passé* (1913); *Gymnastique à l'usage des violonistes* (1914); *L'École du violoniste* (in 4 parts); and *Encyclopedia of the Violin* (N.Y., 1925).

Bachrich, Sigismund, violist and composer; b. Zsambokreth, Hungary, Jan. 23, 1841; d. Vienna, July 16, 1913. He studied violin with Böhm in Vienna; after several years in Paris, played with the Hellmesberger and Rosé quartets; was first violist of the Vienna Philh.; taught at the Vienna Cons. until 1899. His memoirs were posthumously published under the title *Aus verklungenen Zeiten* (Vienna, 1914). He wrote the comic operas *Muzzedin* (1883); *Heini von Steier* (1884); *Der Fuchs-Major* (1889); the ballet *Sakuntala* and other theatrical works.

Bäck, Knut, Swedish pianist and composer; b. Stockholm, April 22, 1868; d. Göteborg, Oct. 27, 1953. He studied music in Stockholm; later took lessons with Max Bruch in Berlin. He eventually settled in Göteborg as a music critic and teacher. Among his works are songs and piano pieces.

Bäck, Sven-Erik, significant Swedish composer; b. Stockholm, Sept. 16, 1919. He studied violin at the Royal Academy of Music in Stockholm (1938–43); composition with Hilding Rosenberg (1940–45); then went to Switzerland and took courses in medieval music at the Schola Cantorum in Basel (1948–50); later studied advanced composition with Petrassi in Rome (1951). Returning to Sweden, he played violin and also viola in two local string quartets and conducted the "Chamber Orchestra 1953" until 1957. In 1959 he was appointed director of the Swedish Radio music school at Edsberg Castle outside Stockholm. As a composer, he at first embraced the Scandinavian romantic manner, but soon began experimentation in serial procedures, later annexing electronic sound. WORKS: His first important work which attracted merited praise was the radio opera *Tranfjädrarna (The Crane Feathers)*, a symbolist subject from Japanese Noh drama (1956; Swedish Radio, Feb. 28, 1957; first stage performance, Stockholm, Feb. 19, 1958). His other works are: a scenic oratorio, *Ett spel om Maria, Jesu Moder (A Play About Mary, Mother of Jesus;* Swedish Radio, April 4, 1958); a chamber opera, *Gästabudet (The Feast;* Stockholm, Nov. 12, 1958); a radio opera, *Fågeln (The Birds;* Swedish Radio, Feb. 14, 1961; later versions for stage and commercial recording, 1969); a ballet, *Ikaros* (Stockholm, May, 1963); a television ballet, *Movements* (Swedish television, Feb. 27, 1966); a ballet, *Kattresan (Cat's Journey,* 1969; original version was a "concerto per bambini" for children's chorus, 2 recorders, violin and percussion, 1952); 2 electronic ballets, *Mur och port (Wall and Gate;* Stockholm, Jan. 17, 1971) and *Genom Jorden genom havet (Through the Earth, Through the Sea,* 1971; Stockholm, June, 1972); also, 3 string quartets (1945, 1947, 1962); string quintet, *Exercises* (1948); solo Flute Sonata (1949); *Expansive Preludes* for piano (1949); *Sonata alla ricercare* for piano (1950); *Sinfonia per archi* (1951); *Sinfonia Sacra* for chorus and orch. (1953); Trio for Viola, Cello and Double Bass (1953); *Sinfonia da camera* (1954); Sonata for 2 Cellos (1957); Violin Concerto (1957); *Impromptu* for piano (1957); *A Game Around a Game* for strings and percussion (Donaueschingen, Oct. 17, 1959); *Arkitektur* for 2 wind orchs. and percussion (1960); *Favola* for clarinet and percussion (1962); *In-*trada for orch. (Stockholm, April 26, 1964); Cello Concerto (1965); *O Altitudo I* for organ (1966; orch. version, *O Altitudo II,* 1966); *5 Preludes* for clarinet and percussion (1966); *Humlan* for chorus, cello, piano and percussion (1968); *... in principio ...* for tape (1969); String Trio (1970); *for Eliza* for organ or tape ad lib. (1971); *Aperio* for 3 orch. groups, each including electronic sound (1973); *Decet* for wind quintet, string quartet and double bass (1973); *Där fanns en brunn* for chorus, flute, clarinet, cello, percussion and piano or organ (1973); many motets and religious cantatas; short electronic pieces. A list of works is printed in "Verkerförteckning 1945–1966," *Nutida Musik* (1966/67).

Backer-Grøndahl, Agathe, Norwegian composer and pianist; b. Holmestrand, Dec. 1, 1847; d. Ormöen, near Oslo, June 4, 1907. She studied in Norway with Kjerulf and Lindemann, in Florence with Hans von Bülow, and in Weimar with Liszt; married the singing teacher Grøndahl (1875). Among her piano works, *Études de Concert, Romantische Stücke,* and *Trois Morceaux* became well known and have been frequently reprinted. She also wrote a song cycle, *Des Kindes Frühlingstag.*
  BIBLIOGRAPHY: Ole M. Sandvik, *Agathe Backer-Grøndahl* (Oslo, 1948), a centennial biography.

Backers, Cor, Dutch music historian and composer; b. Rotterdam, June 5, 1910. He studied piano with Dirk Schäfer and composition at the Rotterdam Cons. He gave piano recitals in Holland; also traveled through Europe and East Africa; conducted the chamber choir "Haags kamerkoor" (1950–60), specializing in the forgotten masterpieces of the past. He published a valuable compendium *Nederlandse Componisten van 1400 tot op onze Tijd* (The Hague, 1941; 2nd enlarged ed., 1948), which details the evolution of music in the Netherlands, with particular emphasis on modern Dutch music; he also published monographs on Handel, Puccini, Gershwin and others. He composes mostly for voices and organ; among his works are a "declamatorio," *Joost de Decker,* for narrator and piano; piano sonata (1935); *6 Goethe-Lieder* for chorus a cappella (1969); *Missa Sancta* for soloists, chorus and organ (1973–74); *Te Deum Laudamus* for chorus and organ or orch. (1973–75).

Backhaus, Wilhelm, German pianist and pedagogue; b. Leipzig, March 26, 1884; d. in Villach, Austria, July 5, 1969. He studied with Reckendorf (1891–98), and in 1899 took lessons with Eugene d'Albert in Frankfurt. He began his concert career at the age of 16, and traveled widely around the world. He made his last American tour at the age of 72, displaying undiminished vigor as a virtuoso. He was particularly distinguished in his interpretations of Beethoven and Brahms, combining impeccable technical efficiency with romantic ardor. He eventually settled in Lugano, where he continued to teach.
  BIBLIOGRAPHY: F. W. Herzog, *Wilhelm Backhaus* (Berlin, 1935).

Bacon, Ernst, remarkable American composer; b. Chicago, May 26, 1898. He studied music theory at

Northwestern Univ. with P. C. Lutkin (1915–18), and later at Univ. of Chicago with Arne Oldberg and T. Otterstroem; also took private piano lessons in Chicago with Alexander Raab (1916–21). In 1924 he went to Vienna where he took private composition lessons with Karl Weigl and Franz Schmidt. Returning to America he studied with Ernest Bloch in San Francisco, and conducting with Eugene Goossens in Rochester, N.Y. From 1934 to 1937 he was supervisor of the Federal Music Project in San Francisco; simultaneously deployed numerous related activities, as conductor and music critic. He was on the faculty of Converse College in South Carolina (1938–45) and Syracuse Univ. (1945–63). He also engaged in literary pursuits—wrote poetry and published a book of aphorisms—and espoused radical politics. A musician of exceptional inventive powers, he published a brochure *Our Musical Idiom* (Chicago, 1917) when he was 19; in it he outlines the new resources of musical composition. In some of his piano works he evolved a beguiling technique of mirror reflection between the right and the left hand, exact as to the intervals, with white and black keys in one hand reflected respectively by white and black keys in the other hand. However, Ernst Bacon is generally regarded as primarily a composer of lyric songs. In 1963 he went to California and lived in Orinda, near San Francisco.

WORKS: Symphony No. 1 for piano and orch. (1932); Symph. No. 2 (1937; Chicago, Feb. 5, 1940); Symph. No. 3, *Great River,* for narrator and orch. (1956); Symph. No. 4 (1963); a musical play, *A Tree on the Plains* (Spartanburg, South Carolina, May 2, 1942); a folk opera, *A Drumlin Legend* (N.Y., May 4, 1949); *By Blue Ontario,* oratorio to words by Walt Whitman (1958); *The Last Invocation,* a requiem, to poems by Walt Whitman, Emily Dickinson and others (1968–71); *Nature,* a cantata cycle (1968); the ballets, *Jehovah and the Ark,* (1968–70) and *The Parliament of Fowls* (1975); songs to words by Emily Dickinson and Walt Whitman: *From Emily's Diary* for soprano, alto, women's chorus and orch. (1945); *The Lord Star,* cantata (1950); *Songs of Eternity* (1932); *Black and White Songs* for baritone and orch. (1932); *Twilight,* 3 songs for voice and orch. (1932); *Midnight Special,* 4 songs for voice and orch. (1932); Piano Quintet (1946); Cello Sonata (1946); String Quintet (1951); *Riolama,* for piano and orch., in 10 short movements (1964); *Spirits and Places,* a cycle with geographical connotations for organ (1966); *Saws,* a suite of canons for chorus and piano (1971); *Dr. Franklin,* music play for the bicentennial (1976), to text by Cornel Lengyel. Among Bacon's published books are *Words on Music* (1960) and *Notes on the Piano* (1963). A collection of his songs, *Grass Roots* for soprano, alto and piano, was published in 2 volumes in 1976.

Bacon, Richard Mackenzie, English writer on music; b. Norwich, May 1, 1776; d. Cossey, Nov. 27, 1844. He publ. *Elements of Vocal Science* (London, 1824); *Art of Improving the Voice and Ear* (London, 1825); was the founder and editor (1812–28) of the *Quarterly Music Magazine and Review,* the first music periodical in England; the organizer of the triennial Music Festivals at Norwich.

Badarzewska, Thekla, Polish composer of salon music; b. Warsaw, 1834; d. there, Sept. 29, 1861. At the age of 17 she published in Warsaw a piano piece *Molitwa dziewicy (A Maiden's Prayer),* which was republished as a supplement to the Paris *Revue et Gazette Musicale* in 1859, and unaccountably seized the imagination not only of inhibited virgins, but of sentimental amateur pianists all over the world. More than 100 editions of this unique piece of salon pianism, dripping maudlin arpeggios, were published in the 19th century, and the thing was still widely sold even in the 20th century. Badarzewska wrote 34 more piano pieces in the salon style, but none of them matched *A Maiden's Prayer.* An ungentlemanly German critic opined in an obituary that "Badarzewska's early death saved the musical world from a veritable inundation of intolerable lachrymosity."

Baden, Conrad, Norwegian composer, organist and music critic; b. Drammen, Aug. 31, 1908. After studies in his home town, he took advanced training in Leipzig (1931–32) and later in Paris with Honegger and Rivier (1951–52). He was organist in Drammen from 1943 and in Oslo since 1961; also taught at the Oslo Cons. since 1946. He writes in a neo-Classical idiom.

WORKS: Mass for soloists, chorus and orch. (1949); Divertimento for Orch. (1950); *Overtura Gioia* (1951); 3 symphonies (1952, 1957, 1970); Concertino for Clarinet and Strings (1953); *Pastorale and Fugue* for chamber orch. (1957); 3 anniversary cantatas: for the city of Skien's 600th (1958), for Strömsö Church's 300th (1966–67) and for Dröbak Church's 200th (1973); *Eventyr-Suite (Fairytale Suite)* for orch. (1960); *Fantasia Brevis* for orch. (1965); *Concerto for Orchestra* (1968); *Intrada Sinfonica* for orch. (1969); *Mennesket (The Human Being),* cantata for chorus and orch. (1971); Violin Sonata (c. 1942); 3 string quartets (1944, 1946, 1961); 2 trios for flute, oboe and clarinet (1957, 1964); Sonata for Solo Flute (1958); Divertimento for Flute, Oboe and Clarinet (1964); *Hymnus* for alto voice, flute, oboe and viola (1966); Wind Quintet; Piano Trio; piano pieces; *Sonata Sacra* for organ (1974); choral works.

BIBLIOGRAPHY: B. Kortsen, *Contemporary Norwegian Orchestral Music* (Bergen, Norway, 1969); id., *Contemporary Norwegian Chamber Music* (Bergen, Norway, 1971); H. Herresthal, "Kirckemusikeren og komponisten Conrad Baden," *Norsk musiktidsskrift* (1971/72).

Badings, Henk, eminent Dutch composer; b. Bandung, Indonesia, Jan. 17, 1907, of Dutch parents. He was orphaned at an early age and came to the Netherlands. He first studied mining engineering at the Delft Polytechnic Univ.; then began to compose without any formal study and produced a symphony which was performed in Amsterdam by Mengelberg with the Concertgebouw on July 6, 1930; however, he discarded the work, and wrote another symphony 2 years later to replace it. At the same time he began taking lessons in composition with Willem Pijper (1930–31); afterwards taught music at the Rotterdam Cons. (1934–37), at the Lyceum in Amsterdam (1937–41) and at the Cons. of The Hague (1941–44). He was temporarily barred from professional activities after the end of World War II on charges of cultural collaboration with the Germans during Holland's occupation, but regained his status in 1947. In 1961 he was appointed prof. of acoustics at the Univ. of Utrecht. In 1962 he was guest lecturer at the Univ. of Adelaide, Australia. His style of composition may be described as romantic modernism marked by intense dynamism. In melodic progressions he often employs the scale of alternating major and minor seconds known in Holland as the "Pijper scale." After 1950 he began experimenting with electronic sound and microtonal divisions, especially the 31-tone scale devised by the Dutch physicist Adriaan Fokker.

WORKS: 6 operas: *De Nachtwacht (The Night Watch,* 1942; Antwerp, May 13, 1950); *Liebesränke (Love's Ruses,* 1944-45; Hilversum, Jan. 6, 1948); *Orestes,* radio opera (Florence, Sept. 24, 1954); *Asterion,* radio opera (Johannesburg, April 11, 1958); *Salto mortale,* chamber opera, for television (Netherlands Television, Eindhoven, June 19, 1959; first opera to be accompanied solely by electronic sound); and *Martin Korda, D.P.* (Amsterdam, June 15, 1960; includes electronic sound). Ballets for instruments: *Balletto Grottesco* for 2 pianos (1939); *Orpheus und Eurydike* for soloists, chorus and orch. (1941; Amsterdam, April 17, 1941); *Balletto Serioso* for orch. or 2 pianos (1955); *Balletto Notturno* for 2 pianos (1975). Ballets for electronic sound: *Cain and Abel* (The Hague, June 21, 1956; first all-electronic sound ballet); *Variations électroniques* (1957; originally film music, performed as a ballet *Marionetten,* Salzburg, 1961); *Evolutions* (Hannover, Sept. 28, 1958); *Genèse* for 5 audio-frequency oscillators in quadrophonic sound placement (Brussels, Oct. 7, 1958; produced as a ballet under the title *Der sechste Tag* at Innsbruck, Nov. 7, 1959; new choreography produced under the title *Mikrobiologisches,* Linz, Feb. 22, 1960); *Jungle* (Amsterdam, 1959); *The Woman of Andras,* with voices (Hannover, April 14, 1960). Oratorios: *Apocalypse* (1948; Rotterdam, Nov. 25, 1959) and *Jonah* (Adelaide, Australia, Sept. 30, 1963; includes electronic sound); *St. Mark Passion* for soloists, male chorus, orch. and tape (1971; Rotterdam, May 18, 1972); 8 cantatas (1936-73); 14 symphonies: No. 1 for 16 solo instruments (1932; Hilversum, March 19, 1959); No. 2 (1932; Amsterdam, Oct. 5, 1932); No. 3 (1934; Amsterdam, May 2, 1935); No. 4 (1943; Rotterdam, Oct. 13, 1947); No. 5 (1949; Amsterdam, Dec. 7, 1949); No. 6, *Psalm,* with chorus (1953; Holland Festival, Haarlem, June 25, 1953); No. 7, *Louisville* (1954; Louisville, Ken., Feb. 26, 1955); No. 8, *Hannover* (1956; Hannover, Jan. 11, 1957); No. 9, for string orch. (1959; Amsterdam, Dec. 17, 1960); No. 10 (1961; Rotterdam, Jan. 29, 1962); No. 11, *Sinfonia Giocosa* (Eindhoven, Oct. 26, 1964); No. 12, *Symphonische klangfiguren* (The Hague, Nov. 20, 1964); No. 13 for wind orch. (Pittsburgh, June 29, 1967); No. 14, *Symphonische Triptiek* (Ghent, Sept. 4, 1968); Sinfonietta for Small Orch. (1971); 4 violin concertos (1928, 1933-35, 1944, 1947); 2 cello concertos: No. 1 (1930) and No. 2 (1939); *Symphonic Variations* (1936-37); 6 overtures, including *Tragic* (1937), *Heroic* (1937), *Symphonic Prologue* (1942), and *Irish* (1961); 2 piano concertos (1939, 1955); Concertino for Violin, Cello, Piano and Chamber Orch. (1942); Divertimento (1949); Ballad, symph. variations (1950); Saxophone

Concerto (1951-52); 2 organ concertos (1952, 1966); Serenade (1953); *Symphonic Scherzo* (1953); 2 concertos for 2 violins (1954; 1969, in the 31-tone temperament); *Dance Variations* (1956); 2 flute concertos (1956; 1963); *Mars* for small orch. (1957); *Nederlandse dansen* for orch. (1957); Partita for Wind Orch. (1960); *Symph. Variations on a South African Theme* (1960); Concerto for Bassoon, Double-Bassoon and Wind Orch. (1964); 2-Piano Concerto (1964); Concerto for Viola and String Orch. (1965); *Pittsburgh Concerto* for solo clarinet, brass, percussion and tape (1965); Concerto for Violin, Viola and Orch. (1965); Concerto for Harp, and small orch. (1967); *Tower Music* for wind orch. and tape (1969); Concerto for 3 Horns, Wind Orch. and Tape (1970); *Variations on Green Sleeves* for wind orch. (1970); *Transitions* for wind orch. (1972); Concerto *(American Folk Song Suite)* for English Horn and Wind Orch. (1975); *Nederlandse dansen* for small orch. (1975); *Lieshout and Its Windmills,* suite for wind orch. (1976). For voice and orch.: *The West Wind,* for narrator and orch. (1936); *Songs of Life and Death* for tenor and orch. (1940); *Psalm 147* for chorus, children's chorus and orch. (1959); *Te Deum* for male chorus and orch. (1961); *Hymnus, Ave Maris Stella* for female chorus and orch. (1965); *Genesis* for baritone, tenor, male chorus, tape and 4 percussionists (1967); *Armageddon* for soprano, wind orch. and tape (1968); Chamber and solo works in the 31-tone temperament: *Contrasts* for a cappella chorus (1952); *Series of Small Pieces* for organ (1954); 2-violin sonatas Nos. 2 and 3 (1963, 1967); String Quartet No. 4 (1966); *Variations on Seikilos Skolion* for 2 violins (1975); *Archifonica* for organ (1976). Other chamber and solo works: 3 sonatas for solo violin (1940, 1951, 1951); 2 sonatas for solo cello (1941, 1951); Sonata for Solo Harp (1944); Toccata for Solo Marimbaphone (1973); *Capriccio* for violin and tape (1959); Chaconne for Trumpet and Tape (1965); Sonata for Violin and Cello (1927); Sonata for Violin and Viola (1928); Sonata No. 1 for 2 violins (1928); 2 cello sonatas (1929, 1934); 4 violin sonatas (1933; 1939; 1952; originally 1931, rescored, 1966); *Capriccio* for flute and piano (1936); Ballade for Harp and Flute (1950); Viola Sonata (1951); Passacaglia for Timpani and Organ (1958); Canzona for Horn and Organ (1967); *It Is Dawning in the East,* balladic variations for guitar and organ (1967); 9 trios for varying instrumental combinations (1934-62); Nocturne for 3 Horns and Tape (1970); 4 string quartets (1931, 1936, 1944; No. 4, in the 31-tone temperament, 1966); Piano Quartet (1973); Brass Quartet (1947). 5 quintets: No. 1 for flute, piano and string trio (1928); No. 2 for wind quintet (1929); No. 3 for harp, flute and string trio (1936); No. 4 for wind quintet (1948); No. 5 for piano quintet (1952); Sextet for Wind Quintet and Piano (1952); Octet (1952); *Twentse Suite* for 4 soloists and 4 groups of accordions (1976); 6 piano sonatas (1934, 1941, 1944, 1945, 1945, 1947); 3 piano sonatinas (1936, 1945, 1950); Suite for Piano (1930); Theme with Variations for piano (1938); *Arcadia,* little piano pieces for beginners, in 7 volumes (1945-67); *5 Small Pieces* for Piano (1967); Concertino for Piano and tape (1967); *Kontrapunkte* for piano and tape (1970); Preludes for Piano (1976); *Preludium and Fuga I-IV* for organ (1952, 1952, 1953, 1956); Toccata for Organ (1929); *Ricercare* for organ (1973). Many songs and choruses; pieces for tape alone; piano pieces. Badings is the author of a book on contemporary Dutch music, *De Hedendaagsche Nederlandsche Musiek* (Amsterdam, 1936), and *Elektronische Muziek* (Amsterdam, 1958).

BIBLIOGRAPHY: Cor Backers, *Nederlandse Componisten* (Amsterdam, 1949); Jos Wouters, "Henk Badings," *Sonorum Speculum* 32 (1967), pp. 1–23. A complete catalogue of his works, in German and English, was issued in 1965, listing all publishers and recordings (supplement, 1965–70).

Badura-Skoda, Paul, eminent Austrian pianist, music editor and pedagogue; b. Vienna, Oct. 6, 1927. He was brought up by his stepfather Skoda, whose name he adopted professionally. He studied mathematics and engineering as well as music; his piano teacher in Vienna was Viola Therns; he graduated from the Vienna College of Music in 1948. He won numerous prizes: The Austrian Music Competition (1947); International Music Contest in Budapest (1948), and one in Paris (1949). On Sept. 19, 1951 he married **Eva Halfar,** who collaborated with him in his various editions of Mozart's piano concertos. He made his New York debut on Jan. 10, 1953. In 1966 he became artist-in-residence at the Univ. of Wisconsin.

WRITINGS: *Mozart-Interpretation, Anregungen zur Interpretation der Klavierwerke* (Vienna, 1957; in collaboration with Eva Badura-Skoda; revised and published in English as *Interpreting Mozart on the Keyboard,* N.Y., 1962; also in Japanese, Tokyo, 1963); *Die Klaviersonaten von Ludwig van Beethoven* (with J. Demus, Wiesbaden, 1970).

Baervoets, Raymond, Belgian composer; b. Brussels, Nov. 6, 1930. He studied composition with Absil, Bourguignon and Barbier, and conducting with Defossez at the Brussels Cons.; later took a course with Petrassi at the Santa Cecilia Academy in Rome (1961–62). In his music he follows the classical forms, while its content evolves in an ultra-chromatic coloristic idiom, including the use of quarter-tones.

WORKS: 2 ballets, *Metamorphose* (1963) and *La Chasse Fantastique* (Antwerp, Sept. 28, 1968); *Concerto da Camera* for violin and chamber orch. (1955); *Mouvement Symphonique* (1955); *Petite Suite* for chamber orch. (1955); *Elégie et Passacaille* for orch. (1956); *Rhapsodie* for viola and chamber orch. (1957); Concerto for Guitar and Chamber Orch. (1958); Fantasia for String Orch. (1958); Sinfonietta for String Orch. (1959); Violin Concerto (1961); *Improvvisazioni concertanti* for cello and 19 instruments (1962); *Musica for 14 Instruments* (1962); *Composizione* for orch. (1962); *Espressioni* for orch. (1966); *Constellations* for orch. (1966); *Notturno* for chamber orch. (1971; performed as a ballet, Antwerp, Nov. 10, 1973); *Musica 1972* for chamber orch.; *Magnificat* for soprano and orch. (1964); *Erosions I* for alto and 6 performers, and *II* for female chorus and orch. (both 1965); *Les Dents de la terre* for narrator, soloists, chorus and 2 orch. (1968); *Impromptu* for trombone and piano (1958); Etude for String Quartet (1961); *Musica Notturna* for harpsichord, violin, cello and flute (1969); *Figures* for 4 trombones, 4 horns and 4 trumpets (1973); Quartet for Flute, Clarinet, Violin and Piano (1974); *Scherzo*

for 2 pianos (1957); *Hommage à Serge Prokofieff* for piano (1958); *Inventions* for piano (1964); **Immagini** for chamber orch. (1976).

Baeyens, August, Belgian composer; b. Antwerp, June 5, 1895; d. there, July 17, 1966. He studied at the Royal Flemish Cons. in Antwerp; beginning in 1911 he was a viola player in Belgian orchestras. In 1932 he became secretary of the Royal Flemish Opera, later serving as director (1944–48 and 1953–58). Despite his intimate association with the Flemish currents in the music of Belgium, he turned away from the dominant national direction and wrote music of distinctly expressionistic type, rooted in a quasi-atonal chromaticism.

WORKS: 2 operas, *De Ring van Gyges* (1943) and *De Triomferende Min* (1948); a radio opera, *Coriolanus,* after Shakespeare (1941); a ballet, *De Dode Dichter* (*The Dead Poet,* 1920); *De Liefde en de Kakatoes* (*Love and the Cockatoos*), a "grotesque" in one act (1928); 8 symphonies (1923, 1939, 1949, 1952, 1954, 1955, 1958, 1961); a *Sinfonia Breve* (1928); *Arkadia,* chamber symphony for 19 soloists (1951); 6 orch. scores: *Entrata* (1917); *Niobé* (1918); *4 Small Pieces* (1923); *Arlequin* (1924); *Cyclops* (1925); *Notturno* (1953); *Viola Concerto* (1956); Trumpet Concerto (1959); Horn Concerto (1960); *Rhapsodie* for clarinet and orch. (1966); *Lofzang aan de haven* (*Hymn of Praise for the Port*), cantata (1929); *Barabbas,* for narrator and orch. (1949); 6 string quartets (1922, 1925, 1927, 1949, 1951, 1962); Wind Quintet (1950); Concertino for Oboe, Clarinet and Bassoon (1951); *Piranesi Suite* for flute and cello (1951); Violin Sonata (1952); Piano Sonata (1930); songs.

Baez, Joan, politically active American folk singer of English, Irish and Mexican descent; b. Staten Island, N.Y., Jan. 9, 1941. She played the guitar by ear; then studied folk singing at Boston Univ. She made her first impact on American mass consciousness in 1959 when she appeared at the Newport Folk Festival. In 1965 she founded the Institute for the Study of Non-Violence; joined the struggle against the Vietnam War and supported the organizing fight of the United Farm Workers' Union. Accompanying herself on the guitar she appeared at numerous concerts promoting topical humanitarian causes.

Bagby, Albert Morris, American pianist and concert manager; b. Rushville, Illinois, April 29, 1859; d. New York, Feb. 26, 1941. He studied in Berlin, and with Liszt in Weimar. Returning to America in 1891, he organized in New York the Bagby Morning Musicales, presenting 428 concerts; directed them until a few weeks before his death.

Bagge, Selmar, composer and music pedagogue; b. Coburg, June 30, 1823; d. Basel, July 16, 1896. He studied at the Prague Cons. and in Vienna with Sechter; later taught at the Vienna Cons. (1851–55); was editor of the *Allgemeine Musikzeitung* in Leipzig (1863–66). Became director in 1868 of the Basel Music School, and retained this post until his death. He publ. several books: *Lehrbuch der Tonkunst* (1873); *Die geschichtliche Entwickelung der Sonate* (1880); *Die*

Symphonie in ihrer historischen Entwickelung (1884); wrote a symphony, piano pieces, and other works. His biographical sketch (by Eglinger) was publ. in Basel (1897).

Baggiani, Guido, Italian composer; b. Naples, March 4, 1932. He studied composition at Santa Cecilia in Rome; then attended courses given by Stockhausen in Cologne, which were crucial for his further development. In Rome he organized a group for the propaganda of contemporary music with the meaningful Nuova Consonanza. In 1970 he was appointed prof. of composition at the Cons. of Pesaro. In 1972 he formed a group with the curious Italian-American name Gruppo Team for performances of electronic music. His principal works are *Mimesi* for strings and woodwinds (1967); *Metafora* for solo strings (1968); *UBU-ng* for soprano, piano, vibraphone, electric guitar and 6 Chinese gongs (of indeterminate duration; 1970); *Twins* for piano and magnetic tape (1971); *Memoria* for chamber orch. and 2 magnetic tapes (1972); *Accordo Presunto* for 2 instrumental groups and electronic media (1973).

Bagier, Guido, German musicologist; b. Berlin, June 20, 1888; d. Düsseldorf, April 3, 1968. He studied at the Univ. of Leipzig with Max Reger and Riemann; taught at the State Academy of Arts in Düsseldorf; settled in Berlin, where he was connected with a motion picture company. He published a biography of Max Reger (Stuttgart, 1923).

Bai, Tommaso, Italian musician; b. Crevalcore, near Bologna, c. 1660; d. Rome, Dec. 22, 1714. He was a tenor at the Vatican where he became maestro di cappella Nov. 19, 1713. A follower of Palestrina, Bai's best known composition is a five-part *Miserere* sung during Holy Week in the Papal Chapel alternately with those by Allegri and Baini. It is reprinted in various collections (Choron, Burney, Peters); other works of Bai are included in C. Proske's *Musica Divina* (1853–63).

Baïf, Jean-Antoine de, French composer and poet; b. Venice, Feb. 19, 1532; d. Paris, Sept. 19, 1589. He was brought to Paris as a child, and formed a friendship with Ronsard and other eminent poets. In 1570 he founded the Académie de Poésie et de Musique, with the aim of reviving the music and poetry of ancient Greece. He developed a system of 'musique mesurée' which he believed would possess a moral force similar to the Greek ideas of 'ethos.' Settings of his poems were composed by Jacques Maudit in *26 Chansonnettes mesurées* (1586) for 4 voices; and by Claude Le Jeune, in *Le Printemps* (1603). Both of these collections have been reprinted in Henri Expert's *Maîtres Musiciens* (1899–1901; vols. X, XII, XIII and XIV). Baïf's musical works comprise 12 sacred songs and several works in lute tablature.
BIBLIOGRAPHY: M. Auge-Chiquet, *La Vie, les idées et l'œuvre de Jean-Antoine de Baïf* (Paris, 1909); W. Müller-Blattau, "Chanson, Vaudeville, und Air de cour," *Volks- und Hochkunst in Dichtung und Musik* (Saarbrücken, 1968).

Bailey, Parker, American lawyer and musician; nephew of Horatio Parker; b. Kansas City, March 1, 1902. He studied at Yale Univ. with D.S. Smith (1919–23) and with Ernest Bloch in Cleveland; also studied piano with Beryl Rubinstein there. At the same time he took courses in law at Cornell Univ. (LL.B., 1934). In 1942 he settled in New York as a practicing lawyer. He was on the Board of Directors of the Edward MacDowell Association from 1954 to 1962. Among his compositions are a flute sonata (1929); *Variations symphoniques* on a theme of Chambonnières (1930); several choruses and songs.

Baillot, Pierre-Marie-François de Sales, celebrated French violinist; b. Passy, near Paris, Oct. 1, 1771; d. Paris, Sept. 15, 1842. The son of a schoolmaster, he received an excellent education; at the age of nine he became a pupil of the French violinist, Saint-Marie; he later was sent to Rome where he studied under Pollani; returned to Paris in 1791. He met Viotti who obtained for him a position in the orchestra of the Théâtre Feydeau; later he served as a clerk in the Ministry of Finance. In 1795 he received the important appointment as violin teacher at the newly opened Paris Cons.; but continued to study comp. with Cherubini, Reicha and Catel. In 1802 he joined Napoleon's private instrumental ensemble; toured Russia with the cellist Lamarre (1805–1808). Upon his return to Paris, he organized chamber music concerts which enjoyed excellent success; also gave concerts in Belgium, Holland and England. In 1821 he became first violinist at the Paris Opéra; from 1825 he was also solo violinist in the Royal Orch. Baillot's musical compositions, rarely performed, comprise 10 violin concertos, 3 string quartets, 15 trios, a symphonie concertante for 2 violins with orch.; 6 violin duos, etc. Baillot's name is chiefly remembered through his manual *L'Art du Violon* (1834); with Rode and Kreutzer he wrote a *Méthode du Violon*, adopted by the Paris Cons., and republished in numerous editions and languages; he also edited the *Méthode de Violoncelle* by Levasseur, Catel and Baudiot.

Bailly, Louis, French viola player; b. Valenciennes, June 13, 1882; d. Cowansville, Quebec, Nov. 21, 1974. He studied violin and viola at the Paris Cons., graduating with first prize in 1899; was subsequently the violist in the Capet, Flonzaley (1917–24), Elman and Curtis quartets; served as head of the viola and chamber music dept. at the Curtis Institute of Music in Philadelphia; in 1954 went to Canada and taught in Montreal.

Baines, Anthony, English music scholar, conductor and bassoon player; b. London, Oct. 6, 1912. He studied at the Royal College of Music in London, and played the bassoon in the London Philharmonic Orch. (1935–39 and 1946–48). In 1949 he became associate conductor of the International Ballet Company, and in 1970 was appointed curator of the Bate Collection of Historical Wind Instruments of the Faculty of Music of Oxford Univ. He published several valuable monographs on musical instruments: *Bagpipes* (Oxford, 1960); *Woodwind Instruments and Their History* (London, 1957); *European and American Musical In-*

struments (London, 1966); *Musical Instruments Through the Ages* (Baltimore, 1961).

Baini, Giuseppe (also known as **Abbate Baini**), Italian writer on music and composer; b. Rome, Oct. 21, 1775; d. there, May 21, 1844. He received rudimentary training from his uncle, Lorenzo Baini; then entered the Seminario Romano, where his instructor, Stefano Silveyra, indoctrinated him with the spirit of Palestrina's music. In 1795 he became a member of the papal choir at St. Peter's; he continued his studies there with Bianchini; in 1802 he took courses with Jannaconi, whom he succeeded as maestro di cappella at St. Peter's (1818). In 1821 he wrote his masterpiece, a 10-part *Miserere*, which was accepted for singing at the Sistine Chapel during Holy Week, in alternation with the *Misereres* of Allegri and Bai. He also wrote many psalms, hymns, masses and motets. His great ambition was to publish a complete edition of Palestrina's works, but he was able to prepare only two volumes for publication. The monument of his devotion to Palestrina was his exhaustive biography *Memorie storico-critiche della vita e delle opere di Giovanni Pierluigi da Palestrina* (Rome, 1828; German translation by Kandler, with notes by Kiesewetter, 1834), which remains extremely valuable despite its occasional inaccuracies. He also wrote a *Saggio sopra l'identità de' ritmi musicali e poetici* (1820). Haberl published an essay on Baini in the *Kirchenmusikalisches Jahrbuch* (1894).

Bainton, Edgar Leslie, English composer; b. London, Feb. 14, 1880; d. Sydney, Australia, Dec. 8, 1956. He studied piano and composition at the Royal College of Music with Walford Davies and Charles Stanford. He taught piano and composition at the Cons. of Newcastle-on-Tyne from 1901 until 1914. The outbreak of World War I found him in Berlin, and he was interned as an enemy alien. After the end of the war he resumed his pedagogical activities as director of the Newcastle Cons. In 1934 he went to Australia and was director of the State Cons. at Sydney until 1947.
WORKS: 3 symphonies (1903–56); *Before Sunrise,* for voice, chorus and orch. (1917); symph. poem, *Paracelsus* (1921); and a *Concerto-Fantasia* for piano and orch. (Carnegie Award, 1917; London, Jan. 26, 1922); 2 operas: *Oithona* after Ossian (Glastonbury, Aug. 11, 1915); and *The Pearl Tree* (Sydney, May 20, 1944); chamber music and songs. In his style he followed the tenets of the British national school, writing in broad diatonic expanses with a Romantic élan.
BIBLIOGRAPHY: H. Bainton, *Remembered on Waking: E. L. Bainton* (Sydney, 1960).

Baird, Martha, American pianist and music patroness; b. Madera, Calif., March 15, 1895; d. New York, Jan. 24, 1971. She studied at the New England Cons. and with Artur Schnabel in Berlin; appeared as soloist with Sir Thomas Beecham in London and Koussevitzky in Boston. In 1957 she married John D. Rockefeller, Jr. and became a benefactress of opera and concert music.

Baird, Tadeusz, eminent Polish composer; b. Grodzisk Mazowiecki, July 26, 1928. He studied composi-

tion privately with K. Sikorski and Woytowicz in Lodz (1943–44) and later with Rytel and Perkowski at the State College of Music in Warsaw (1947–51); took a course in musicology with Zofia Lissa at the Warsaw Univ. (1948–52). His early music followed the spirit of Socialist Realism, with an emphasis on folksong patterns within a Romantic mode; in his later works he adopted a lyrico-dramatic style marked by a dynamic expressionism, with a moderate application of dodecaphony.
WORKS: a one-act opera, *Jutro (Tomorrow),* after a short story by Conrad (1964–66); Sinfonietta (1949); Piano Concerto (1949); 3 numbered symphonies (1950; *Sinfonia quasi una fantasia,* 1952; 1969); *Overture in Old Style* for small orch. (1950); *Colas Breugnon,* suite in the old style for flute and string orch. (1951); *Overture Giocosa* (1952); Concerto for Orch. (1953); *Lyrical Suite,* 4 songs for soprano and orch. (1953); *Cassazione* for orch. (1956); *4 Love Sonnets,* after Shakespeare, for baritone and chamber orch. (1956; second version with strings and harpsichord, 1969); *4 Essays* for orch. (1958); *Espressioni Varianti* for violin and orch. (1958–59); *Egzorta (Exhortations),* on old Hebrew texts, for narrator, chorus and orch. (1959–60); *Erotyki (Love Songs),* cycle of 6 songs for soprano and orch. (1961); *Study* for vocal orchestra of 28 mixed voices, 6 percussionists and piano (1961); *Variations without a Theme* for orch. (1961–62); *Epiphany Music* for orch. (1963); *4 Dialogues* for oboe and chamber orch. (1964); *4 Songs* for mezzo-soprano and chamber orch. (1966); *4 Novelettes* for chamber orch. (1967; Dartmouth College, Hanover, N.H., July 16, 1967); *5 Songs* for mezzo-soprano and chamber orch. (1968); *Sinfonia breve* (1968); *Goethe-Briefe (Goethe's Letters),* cantata (1970; Dresden, June 6, 1971); *Psychodrama* for orch. (1971–72); Oboe Concerto (1973; Warsaw, Sept. 23, 1973); *Elegeia* for orch. (1973); *Concerto lugubre* for viola and orch. (1974–75; Nuremberg, May 21, 1976); Double Concerto for Cello, Harp and Orch. (1976); *4 Preludes* for bassoon and piano (1954); *Divertimento* for flute, oboe, clarinet and bassoon (1956); String Quartet (1957); *Play* for string quartet (1971); Piano Sonatina No. 2 (1952).

Bairstow, Sir Edward Cuthbert, English organist and composer; b. Huddersfield, Aug. 22, 1874; d. York, May 1, 1946. He received his Mus. B. at Durham Univ. in 1894; his Mus. D. in 1900; was organist at Wigan (1899–1906), Leeds (1906–13) and at the York Minster. He composed church music, anthems, part songs, and an organ sonata (1937); author of *Counterpoint and Harmony* (1937) and *The Evolution of Musical Form* (1943).
BIBLIOGRAPHY: E. Bradbury, "A Birthday Tribute," *Musical Times* (Aug. 1944).

Bakala, Břetislav, Czech conductor; b. Fryšták, Feb. 12, 1897; d. Brno, April 1, 1958. He studied organ at the Cons. of Brno, and composition with Janáček in Prague. He was for a season organist in Philadelphia (1925–26); upon return to Brno he was active as a pianist, accompanist and choral conductor. In 1956 he was appointed music director at the State Philharmonic Orch. in Brno. He composed a few orchestral pieces and some chamber music, but his chief merit is editing works by old Czech composers and arranging vocal scores of several operas by Janáček.

Bakaleinikov, Vladimir, Russian-American viola player and conductor; b. Moscow, Oct. 12, 1885; d. Pittsburgh, Nov. 5, 1953. He studied violin with Michael Press; graduated from the Moscow Cons. in 1907; subsequently played the viola in the Grand Duke of Mecklenburg Quartet (1910-20); taught at the Cons. of St. Petersburg (1913-20); conducted opera at the Musicalnaya Drama in St. Petersburg (1914-16). Returning to Moscow, he taught at the Moscow Cons. (1920-24); was in charge of the opera branch of the Moscow Art Theater (1920-27). He came to America in 1927; was associate conductor of the Cincinnati Symph. Orch.; eventually settled in Pittsburgh as conductor and teacher; among his pupils was Lorin Maazel. He wrote a viola concerto (1937) and a suite of oriental dances for orch.; published several arrangements of works by Bach and Beethoven; also *Elementary Rules of Conducting* (1937); *The Instruments of the Band and Orchestra* (with M. Rosen, N.Y., 1940), and an autobiography, *A Musician's Notes* (N.Y., 1943; in Russian).

Baker, Benjamin Franklin, American music pedagogue; b. Wenham, Mass., July 10, 1811; d. Boston, March 11, 1889. He was a singer in various churches in Salem, Boston and Portland; in 1841 he succeeded Lowell Mason as teacher of music in the public schools; sang with the Handel and Haydn Society. He founded the Boston Music School (1851-68) and edited the *Boston Musical Journal;* composed 3 cantatas: *The Storm King, The Burning Ship* and *Camillus;* also published a text book *Thorough-Bass and Harmony* (1870).

Baker, George, English organist; b. Exeter, 1768; d. Rugeley, Feb. 19, 1847. He studied in Exeter with William Jackson; was organist at Stafford (1795), Derby (1810) and Rugeley, Staffordshire (1824). The opera *The Caffres, or Buried Alive* (produced at Covent Garden in London, June 2, 1802) is often listed as a work by Baker but was really written by John Davy. Among Baker's own works are numerous anthems and glees.

Baker, Janet, British mezzo-soprano; b. York, England, Aug. 21, 1933. She studied in England; then at the Mozarteum in Salzburg; attended a master class of Lotte Lehmann; received the Queen's Prize from the Royal College of Music in 1959. She made her American debut in 1966, singing to tumultuous applause; her interpretations of classical opera parts received great acclaim from the public and praise from sophisticated critics. She also distinguished herself in modern operatic repertory, particularly in Britten's works. In 1970 she received the Order of Commander of the British Empire.
BIBLIOGRAPHY: A. Blyth, *Janet Baker* (1973).

Baker, Michael, American-born Canadian composer; b. West Palm Beach, Florida, March 13, 1942. He moved to Canada in 1958; studied composition with J. Coulthard and E. Weisgarber at the Univ. of British Columbia in Vancouver (1962-66); later on took private lessons with Lennox Berkeley during a year in London (1974-75); then settled in Vancouver as a teacher.
WORKS: *Dialogues* for orch., choir and solo baritone (1970-71); *Counterplay* for viola and string orch. (1971); *Okanagan Landscapes* for piano and orch. (1972); *Contours,* for double-bass, harpsichord and string orch. (1973); Concerto for Flute and String Orch. (1974); *Point No Point* for viola and string orch. (1975); Concerto for Piano and Chamber Orch. (1976); *Duo Concertante* for violin, viola and string orch. (London, Aug. 19, 1976); *A Struggle for Dominion* for piano and orch. (Vancouver, Sept. 26, 1976); *Ballade* for cello and piano (1961); Flute Sonata (1963); *5 Epigrams* for woodwind trio (1965); Wind Quintet (1965); Piano Quartet (1966); *Scherzo* for trumpet and organ (1967); String Quartet (1969); *Concert Piece* for organ, piano and timpani (1969-70); Piano Trio (1972); *Elegy* for flute and organ (1972); *Counterplay* for viola and piano (1973); *Music for Six Players* for flute, oboe, harpsichord and string trio (1973); *Combinations* for double bass and harpsichord (1974); *En Rapport* for 2 guitars (1974); *4 Views from a Nursery Tune* for violin, horn and piano (1975); *Dance Sequences* for solo cello (1975); *Capriccio* for 2 pianos (1964); Piano Sonata (1975).

Baker, Theodore, American writer on music, and the compiler of the 1st edition of the present dictionary; b. New York, June 3, 1851; d. Dresden, Germany, Oct. 13, 1934. As a young man, he was trained for business; in 1874, decided to study music; went to Leipzig, became a pupil of Oskar Paul and received his Dr. phil. there in 1882 (thesis: *Über die Musik der nordamerikanischen Wilden,* the first serious study of American Indian music); lived in Germany until 1890; returned to the U.S. in 1891, and became literary editor and translator for the publishing house of G. Schirmer, Inc. (1892); retired in 1926 and returned to Germany.
WRITINGS: *A Dictionary of Musical Terms* (1895; highly popular: 25 editions before 1939); *A Pronouncing Pocket Manual of Musical Terms* (1905); *The Musician's Calendar and Birthday Book* (1915-17). *Baker's Biographical Dictionary of Musicians* was first published in 1900 by G. Schirmer, Inc. It included the names of many American musicians, theretofore not represented in musical reference works; 2nd edition was published in 1905; the 3d edition, revised and enlarged by Alfred Remy, in 1919; the 4th edition in 1940, under the general editorship of Carl Engel; a supplement 1949 was compiled by Nicolas Slonimsky; he undertook in 1958 a completely revised Fifth Edition of the Dictionary, and compiled the supplements 1965 and 1971. The present edition (1978) has also been in his care.

Bakfark, Valentin, celebrated Hungarian lutenist; b. Kronstadt, 1507; d. Padua, Aug. 15, 1576. He was brought up by the family of his brother's wife Greff (or Graew), and used that name in conjunction with his own; the spelling Bacfarc or Bekwark is also encountered. As a youth he was in the service of the King of Hungary in Buda (1526-40), where he studied lute. He was later attached to the court of Sigismund

Augustus of Poland in Wilna (1549–66). He subsequently traveled in Germany, France and Italy, eventually settling in Padua where he died of the plague. He published works for the lute in tablature: *Intabulatura* (Lyons, 1552; reprinted as *Premier Livre de Tablature de Luth,* Paris, 1564). A second book *Harmonicarum Musicarum . . . tomus primus* appeared in Cracow in 1564, and was reprinted in Antwerp in 1569. Some of his works are included in *Denkmäler der Tonkunst in Österreich* (vol. XVIII, 2).

BIBLIOGRAPHY: H. Opienski, *Bekwark lutinista* (Warsaw, 1906; also in German as *Valentin Greff-Bekwark,* Leipzig, 1914); Otto Gombosi, *Der Lautenist Valentin Bekfark, Leben und Werke* (Budapest, 1935; in Hungarian and German).

Baklanov, George, Russian baritone; b. Riga, Jan. 17, 1881; d. Basel, Dec. 6, 1938. He made his debut in St. Petersburg (1905); then sang at various European opera houses; was a member of the Boston Opera Co. (1909) and the Chicago Opera Co. (1917). He was particularly successful in dramatic roles (Scarpia, Boris Godunov, Rigoletto).

Bal y Gay, Jesús, Spanish composer and musicologist; b. Lugo, June 23, 1905. He studied in Madrid. After the outbreak of the Spanish Civil War he went to England, and eventually to Mexico where he was appointed to the staff of the Instituto Nacional de Bellas Artes. He published a number of valuable essays on Spanish music, among them *Tientos* (Mexico City, 1960), which traces the development of the ricercar in Spain. He composed some symphonic and chamber music.

Balada, Leonardo, Spanish composer; b. Barcelona, Sept. 22, 1933. He studied at the Barcelona Cons.; in 1960 he emigrated to America; studied at the Juilliard School of Music and at the Mannes College of Music in New York; his principal instructors in composition were Aaron Copland and Vincent Persichetti; he also studied conducting with Igor Markevitch in Paris.

WORKS: *Música tranquila* for string orch. (1960); Violin Sonata (1960); Concerto for Cello and 9 Instruments (1962); Piano Concerto (1964); Guitar Concerto (1965); *Geometrías I* for 7 instruments (1966); *Geometrías II* for string quartet (1967); *Guernica* for orch. (1966); *Sinfonía en Negro,* homage to Martin Luther King for orch. (1968); *María Sabina* for narrator, chorus and orch. (1969); *Bandoneon Concerto* (1970); *Mosáico* for brass quintet (1970); *Las moradas* for chorus and 7 instruments (1970); *Sinfonía del acero (Symphony of Steel,* 1972); *Apuntes* for guitar quartet (1974); *Música en 4 tiempos* for piano (1959), and other piano pieces; also *End and Beginning* for rock music ensemble (1970); miscellaneous pieces for guitar; songs.

Balakirev, Mily (His name is pronounced Balákirev, not Balakírev.), greatly significant Russian composer, protagonist of the Russian National School of Composition; b. Nizhny-Novgorod, Jan. 2, 1837 (new Gregorian calendar; Dec. 21, 1836, old style); d. St. Petersburg, May 29, 1910. His mother gave him his first piano lessons; he received theory instruction from a local German musician named Karl Eisrich, who put him in touch with Oulibishev, author of a book on Mozart, who owned an estate in Nizhny-Novgorod; Balakirev often took part at private musical evenings at Oulibishev's estate as a pianist. From 1853 to 1855 he attended classes in mathematics at the Univ. of Kazan; in 1855 went to St. Petersburg, where he was introduced to Glinka who encouraged him in his music studies. On Feb. 24, 1856, Balakirev made his first public appearance as a composer, playing the solo part in a movement from his piano concerto; his *Overture on the Theme of Three Russian Songs* was performed in Moscow on Jan. 2, 1859, and his overture *King Lear,* at a concert of the Univ. of St. Petersburg on Nov. 27, 1859. In 1860 he took a boat down the Volga River from his birthplace of Nizhny-Novgorod to the Caspian Sea; during this trip he collected, notated and harmonized a number of Russian songs; among these was the universally popular *Song of the Volga Boatmen,* also known as *Song of Burlaks* (peasants who pulled large boats with grain upstream on the Volga River). In 1862 Balakirev organized in St. Petersburg a musical group, known as the "Balakirev Circle," which became the center of an ardent propaganda of Russian national music, as against the passive imitation of classical German masterpieces which had the commanding influence in Russia. Simultaneously he founded the Free Musical School in St. Petersburg, presenting programs of works of contemporary western composers and also works by young Russian musicians. These activities coincided with the growth of Slavophile sentiments in Russia; Balakirev formed friendships with several young Russian composers who were animated by the same spirit of emancipation from European music. In 1866 he visited Prague and conducted there Glinka's operas *Ruslan and Ludmila* and *A Life for the Czar;* he took this opportunity to invite several Czech musicians to take part in a concert of Slavic music at Balakirev's Free Music School; it took place on May 4, 1867; the program included, besides the works by the Czech guests, compositions by Borodin, Cui, Mussorgsky, Rimsky-Korsakov and Balakirev himself; the occasion proved to be of historical importance, for it moved the critic Vladimir Stasov to write an article in which he proudly declared that Russia, too, had its "mighty little company" (*Moguchaya Kuchka*) of fine musicians; the phrase became a catchword of Russian musical nationalism; in general music histories, it came to be known as "The Mighty Five." In search of new materials Balakirev made several trips to the Caucasus, where he became fascinated by quasi-Oriental melodies and rhythms of the regional music. In 1869 he wrote a brilliant Oriental fantasy for piano entitled *Islamey;* its technical difficulties rival the transcendental studies by Liszt. Among the "Mighty Five" Balakirev was a leader; when Rimsky-Korsakov went on a prolonged cruise as a midshipman in the Russian Imperial navy, he maintained a remarkable correspondence with Balakirev who gave him specific advice in composition. Unaccountably, Balakirev slackened the tempo of his work as a composer, and seemed to have trouble in completing his scores. In 1872 he discontinued his concerts at the Free Music School, and took a clerical job in the railroad transport administration; in 1873 he became music inspector in a women's educational institute in St. Petersburg; in 1875 was inspector of another women's school. In 1881 he returned to musical activities, and on March 29, 1882 conducted at the Free Music School the première of the 1st Symph. by the 16-year-old Glazunov; he also began to work on the revision of his early works. His *Second Overture on Russian Themes,* originally performed in St. Petersburg on April 18, 1865, and retitled *One Thousand Years,* to commemorate the millennium of Russia observed in 1862, was revised by Balakirev in 1882, and renamed *Russia.* It took Balakirev many years to complete his symphonic poem, *Tamara,* which he conducted in St. Petersburg on March 19, 1883; the score, inspired by Lermontov's poem, and permeated by Caucasian melodic inflections, was dedicated to Liszt. Balakirev spent 32 years (1866–98) working on his Symph. in C; he wrote his Second Symph. in D minor at the age of 70 (1907–08); it was performed in St. Petersburg on April 23, 1909. He completed his 1st piano concerto in 1855, and began the composition of his 2nd piano concerto in 1861, but laid it aside until 1909; it was completed after his death by Liapunov. During the last decades of his life, he became increasingly unsocial and morose; his lamentable quarrel with Rimsky-Korsakov was a sad testimony of his decline. While Balakirev's name retains its historical significance in Russian music, his works are but rarely performed. Among his minor compositions to be noted are *Spanish Overture* (1886); *Czech Overture* (1867); octet for flute, oboe, French horn, violin, viola, cello, and double bass (1950–56); 2 piano sonatas (1857, 1905); piano sonatina (1909), transcriptions for piano: *The Lark,* song by Glinka; about 35 original songs; *Collection of Russian Songs* (1865); several choruses a cappella. A complete edition of Balakirev's piano works was published in Moscow in 1952; a collection of all of his songs was published in Moscow in 1937.

BIBLIOGRAPHY: Balakirev, *Autobiography, in Russkaya Musicalnaya Gazeta* (1910); *Correspondence With Tchaikovsky,* edited by Liapunov (St. Petersburg, 1912); *Correspondence with Rimsky-Korsakov,* edited by Liapunov (St. Petersburg, 1915); J. Leyda and S. Bertensson, *The Musorgsky Reader,* (N.Y., 1947); N. Rimsky-Korsakov, *Chronicle of My Musical Life* (St. Petersburg, 1909); M. D. Calvocoressi and G. Abraham, *Masters of Russian Music* (London, 1936); G. Abraham, *On Russian Music,* (London, 1939); G. Kiselev, *Balakirev* (Moscow, 1938); V. Muzalevsky, *Balakirev* (Leningrad, 1938); A. Kandinsky, *Symphonic Works of Balakirev* (Moscow, 1950); G. Fedorova, *Balakirev* (Moscow, 1951); *Correspondence With N. Rubinstein and M. Belaeff* (Moscow, 1956); *Correspondence with Jurgenson* (Moscow, 1958); M. Balakirev, *Reminiscences and Letters* (Leningrad, 1962); *Correspondence with V. Stasov* (2 vols., Moscow, 1970–71); *Balakirev, Essays and Articles* (Leningrad, 1961); I. Kunin, *Balakirev, Life and Works in Letters and Documents* (Moscow, 1967); M. Gordeyeva, *The Mighty Company* (Moscow, 1960); E. Garden, *Balakirev: A Critical Study of His Life and Music* (London, 1967).

Balanchine, George, celebrated Russian-American choreographer, b. St. Petersburg, Jan. 22, 1904. He is a son of the Georgia composer Meliton Balantchivadze, and brother of the Soviet composer Andrei Balantchivadze. He studied at the Imperial Ballet School in St. Petersburg, and later took piano lessons at the St. Petersburg Cons. In 1924 he undertook a tour through Germany and England; then joined the Diaghilev troupe, and staged a number of productions for his Ballet Russe. In 1934 he went to New York where he became the leader of the School of American Ballet; he also directed the Ballet Caravan; eventually became the choreographer of the New York City Ballet; in 1962 he made a tour of Russia with this company. He is greatly distinguished for his modern productions, with music by Stravinsky, Anton Webern, Xenakis, Ives, and other modern composers.

BIBLIOGRAPHY: Lincoln Kirstein, *Blast at Ballet, in: Three Pamphlets Collected* (N.Y., 1967).

Balanchivadze, Andrei, Georgian composer (brother of the choreographer George Balanchine); b. St. Petersburg, June 1, 1906. He studied with his father, the composer **Meliton Balanchivadze;** then entered the Tiflis Cons. where he took courses in piano, and in composition with Ippolitov-Ivanov. In 1935 he joined the staff of the Tiflis Cons., and in 1962 became chairman of the composition department; numerous Georgian composers are his students. In his music he makes use of Georgian folk motives in a tasteful harmonic framework characteristic of the national Russian school of composition. Among his works is the first Georgian ballet, *The Heart of the Mountains* (1936); another ballet, *Mtsyri,* after Lermontov, was produced in Tiflis in 1964. His other works include 2 symphonies (1944, 1959); symph. poem, *The Ocean* (1952); 4 piano concertos (1944, 1946, 1952, 1968); choruses and songs.

BIBLIOGRAPHY: G. Ordzhonikidze, *Andrei Balanchivadze* (Tbilisi, 1967).

Balanchivadze, Meliton, Georgian composer; b. in the village of Banodzha, Dec. 24, 1862; d. in Kutais, Dec. 21, 1937. He was educated at the Seminary in Tiflis, where he sang in a choir. In 1880 he was engaged at the local opera theater as a baritone. At the same time he studied Georgian folk music. In 1891 he went to St. Petersburg where he took lessons in composition with Rimsky-Korsakov. From 1895 to 1917 he organized a series of so-called "Georgian Concerts." After the revolution he returned to Georgia, where he resumed his work on folk music. He composed a national Georgian opera *Tamara the Treacherous* (1897) and a number of songs in the manner of Georgian folk music.

BIBLIOGRAPHY: P. Khuchua, *Meliton Balanchivadze* (Tbilisi, 1964).

Balart, Gabriel, Spanish composer; b. Barcelona, June 8, 1824; d. there, July 5, 1893. He studied at the Paris Cons.; composed various pieces of salon music, which enjoyed some success. In 1849 he went to Milan as theater conductor; in 1853 appointed musical director of the Teatro del Liceo in Barcelona. He wrote 5 symphonies in a romantic vein, which he conducted in Spain; for a time his light opera *Amore y Arte* enjoyed considerable success.

Balassa, Sándor, Hungarian composer; b. Budapest, Jan. 20, 1935. He studied composition with Endre Szervánszky at the Budapest Academy of Music, graduating in 1962. In 1964 he joined the staff of the Hungarian Radio. He writes pragmatic music with a modernistic veneer. Among his works are *Bagatelles and Sequences* for piano (1957); *Locks,* monologue for soprano and chamber ensemble (1963); Violin Concerto (1964); Septet for Brass (1965); *Golden Age,* cantata (1965); *3 Songs* for soprano and string trio (1965); *Dimensioni* for flute and viola (1966); Wind Quintet (1966); *Zenith* for soprano and orch. (1967); *Antinomia* for soprano, clarinet and cello (1968); Quartet for Percussion (1969); Trio for Violin, Viola and Harp (1970); *Xénia,* nonet (1970); *Iris* for orch. (1971); *Lupercalia,* concerto in memory of Stravinsky, for woodwinds and brass (1972); *Tabulae* for chamber ensemble (1972); opera, *Az ajtón Kivül (Beyond the Threshold,* 1973–76); songs and motets.

Balatka, Hans, Czech conductor and composer; b. Hoffnungsthal, Moravia, Feb. 26, 1825; d. Chicago, April 17, 1899. After studying music in Vienna he emigrated to America in 1849; settled in Milwaukee, where he organized the German Musikverein, and in 1860 became conductor of the Chicago Philharmonic Society, which was the nucleus of the Theodore Thomas Symph. Orch. (later Chicago Symph. Orch.). He was an important figure in carrying German musical culture to the American Midwest. He also composed some insignificant choral works.

Balbastre (Balbâtre), Claude, French organist and composer; b. Dijon, Jan. 22, 1727; d. Paris, May 9, 1799. He was a pupil of Rameau (1760); organist at the Church of Saint-Roche in Paris; later alternated with Couperin, Daquin, and Séjan as organist of Notre-Dame. He wrote four piano suites of variations on French *noëls;* also many pieces for organ and harpsichord.

Balbi (Balbus), Lodovico, Italian composer; b. Venice, 1545; d. there, Dec. 15, 1604. He was a pupil of Costanzo Porta; sang in the choir of San Marco in Venice (1570); then was maestro di cappella at the Franciscan monastery there (1578), and at San Antonio in Padua (1585–91); later returned to Venice. He published Masses, motets, canzoni, madrigals, sacred songs, etc.; compiled a collection of graduals and antiphons by celebrated Italian masters, publ. by Gardano (Venice, 1591).

Balbi, Melchiore, Italian theorist and composer; b. Venice, June 4, 1796; d. Padua, June 21, 1879. He was a pupil of Nini, Valeri, and Calegari in Padua; was theater conductor there (1818–53); from 1854 was maestro di cappella at the basilica San Antonio. He wrote 3 operas, all produced in Padua: *La Notte periglosia* (1820); *L'Abitator del bosco* (1821); *L'Alloggio militare* (1825); a requiem (for Rossini, 1868); Masses; psalms; edited Calegari's *Trattato del sistema armonico* (Padua, 1829); and wrote a *Grammatica ragio-*nata della musica considerata sotto l'aspetto di lingua (Milan, 1845), and *Nuova scuola basata sul sistema semitonato equabile* (1872).

Baldwin, Samuel Atkinson, American organist and composer; b. Lake City, Minnesota, Jan. 25, 1862; d. New York, Sept. 15, 1949. He studied organ playing in Dresden; upon return to America, was church organist in Chicago, New York and Brooklyn. He was one of the founders of the American Guild of Organists, and gave something like 1500 organ recitals. He also wrote symphonies and overtures, but is chiefly remembered, if at all, by an innocuous anthem, *Tarry With Me.*

Bales, Richard, American conductor and composer; b. Alexandria, Virginia, Feb. 3, 1915. He studied at the Eastman School of Music in Rochester and took a course in conducting under Koussevitzky at the Berkshire Music Center in Tanglewood. In 1943 he was appointed conductor of the National Gallery Orch. in Washington; at this post he introduced numerous works by American composers, both old and new. His ingenious potpourri of Southern songs, *The Confederacy* (1954), became very popular. Other works include 2 orchestral suites inspired by watercolors in the National Gallery of Art in Washington; *American Design* (Washington, May 26, 1957) and *American Chronicle* (Washington, May 23, 1965).

Balfe, Michael William, Irish composer; b. Dublin, May 15, 1808; d. Rowney Abbey, Hertfordshire, Oct. 20, 1870. He was the son of a dancing-master; at the age of six he played the violin for his father's dancing classes; subsequently studied violin with O'Rourke. After his father's death (Jan. 6, 1823), Balfe went to London where he studied with Charles Edward Horn (violin) and Carl Friedrich Horn (composition); in 1824 was violinist at the Drury Lane Theatre; also sang in London and the provinces. His patron, Count Mazzara, took him to Italy (1825); he studied in Milan with Federici (counterpoint) and Filippo Galli (singing); his ballet, *La Pérouse,* was produced there in 1826. Acting on the advice of Rossini, Balfe further studied singing with Bordogni; then was engaged as principal baritone at the Italian Opera, Paris (1828); also sang in various Italian theaters until 1833. In Italy, he married the Hungarian vocalist **Lina Rosa** (b. 1808; d. London, June 8, 1888). Returning to England in 1835, he began his brilliant career as a composer of English operas with *The Siege of Rochelle* (Drury Lane Theatre, London, Oct. 29, 1835); he was then manager of the Lyceum Theatre in London (1841); went to Paris, where he composed the operas *Le Puits d'amour* (Opéra-Comique, Paris, April 20, 1843; in English as *Geraldine,* Princess's Theatre, London, Aug. 8, 1843), and *Les Quatres Fils Aymon* (Opéra-Comique, Paris, July 15, 1844; in English as *The Castle of Aymon,* Princess's Theatre, London, Nov. 20, 1844); returned to England in 1843 and produced his most famous opera, *The Bohemian Girl* (Drury Lane Theatre, London, Nov. 27, 1843), which was subsequently translated into French, German and Italian, and performed on the chief continental stages with great success. Excepting visits to Vienna (1846), Berlin (1848), to St. Petersburg and to Trieste (1852–6), he stayed in England; retired to his country seat at Rowney Abbey in 1864. His daughter, **Victoire**, made her debut as a singer in 1857 at the Lyceum Theatre, London. The further list of his operas includes three in Italian: *I rivali di se stesso* (Palermo, 1829); *Un avvertimento ai gelosi* (Pavia, 1830); *Enrico IV al Passo della Marna* (Milan, Feb. 19, 1833); and one in French: *L'Étoile de Séville* (Opéra, Paris, Dec. 17, 1845). The following operas were produced in London at Drury Lane, Covent Garden, and other theaters: *The Maid of Artois* (May 27, 1836); *Catherine Grey* (May 27, 1837); *Joan of Arc* (Nov. 30, 1837); *Diadeste, or The Veiled Lady* (May 17, 1838); *Falstaff* (in Italian, July 19, 1838); *Kéolanthe, or The Unearthly Bride* (March 9, 1841); *The Daughter of St. Mark* (Nov. 27, 1844); *The Enchantress* (May 14, 1845); *The Bondman* (Dec. 11, 1846); *The Maid of Honour* (Dec. 20, 1847); *The Sicilian Bride* (March 6, 1852); *The Devil's In It* (July 26, 1852); *Moro, the Painter of Antwerp* (Jan. 28, 1882; originally produced as *Pittore e duca*, Trieste, Nov. 21, 1854); *The Rose of Castille* (Oct. 29, 1857); *Satanella, or The Power of Love* (Dec. 20, 1858); *Bianca, or The Bravo's Bride* (Dec. 6, 1860); *The Puritan's Daughter* (Nov. 30, 1861); *The Armourer of Nantes* (Feb. 12, 1863); *Blanche de Nevers* (Nov. 21, 1863); *The Sleeping Queen*, operetta (Sept. 8, 1864); *The Knight of the Leopard* (Liverpool, Jan. 15, 1891; originally produced in London as *Il Talismano*, June 11, 1874); also *Mazeppa*, a cantata, and 2 other cantatas; ballads, glees, songs, etc.

BIBLIOGRAPHY: Charles Lamb Kenney, *A Memoir of Michael William Balfe* (London, 1875); W. A. Barrett, *Balfe: His Life and Work* (London, 1882).

Balfoort, Dirk Jacobus, Dutch musicologist; b. Utrecht, July 19, 1886; d. The Hague, Nov. 11, 1964. He studied with Evert Cornelis; played violin in various German orchestras; then held teaching posts in Holland; also organized concerts of old music by Dutch composers. He published valuable books (in Dutch) on music making in Holland: *De Hollandsche vioolmakers* (Amsterdam, 1931); *Het Muziekleven in Nederland in de 17e en 18e eeuw* (Amsterdam, 1938); a monograph on Stradivarius (Amsterdam, 1945; also in German and English); etc.

Balfour, Henry Lucas, English organist; b. London, Oct. 28, 1859; d. Croydon, Surrey, Dec. 27, 1946. He studied music in London with Arthur Sullivan; later in Leipzig; was organist at Croydon (1872–1902). In 1902 he became organist at the Church of the Holy Trinity.

Ball, Ernest R., American composer of popular songs; b. Cleveland, July 21, 1878; d. Santa Ana, California, May 3, 1927. He studied at Cleveland Cons.; moved to N.Y., where he earned his living as a vaudeville pianist. His first success came with the song *Will You Love Me in December as You Do in May?* to the words of James J. Walker (later, Mayor of N.Y.). No less successful were his sentimental songs *Mother Machree, When Irish Eyes are Smiling, Little Bit of Heaven, Dear Little Boy of Mine, Till the Sands of the Desert Grow Cold, Love Me and the World is Mine,* etc., sung by John McCormack and other famous artists. Ball was a charter member of ASCAP (1914).

BIBLIOGRAPHY: I. Witmark and I. Goldberg, *The Story of the House of Witmark: From Ragtime to Swingtime* (N.Y., 1939; 1976).

Ballantine, Edward, American composer; b. Oberlin, Ohio, August 6, 1886; d. in Martha's Vineyard, Massachusetts, July 2, 1971. He studied with Walter Spalding at Harvard Univ.; graduated with highest honors in 1907; took piano courses with Artur Schnabel and Rudolph Ganz in Berlin (1907–09). In 1912 he was appointed instructor at Harvard; became assistant prof. in 1926; associate prof. in 1932; retired in 1947. His first published work was a musical play, *The Lotos Eaters* (1907); three of his orchestral pieces were performed by the Boston Symph. Orch.: *From the Garden of Hellas* (Feb. 9, 1923); *Prelude to The Delectable Forest* (Dec. 10, 1914); *The Eve of St. Agnes* (Jan. 19, 1917); and one, *By a Lake in Russia,* at the Boston Pops (June 27, 1922). He also wrote a violin sonata and songs. His most striking work is a set of piano variations on *Mary Had a Little Lamb* (1924) in the styles of 10 composers; a second series of variations on the same tune (1943) includes stylizations of Stravinsky, Gershwin and others.

Ballard, a family of French music printers. The establishment was founded by Robert Ballard in 1552, whose patent from Henri II made him "Seul imprimeur de la musique de la chambre, chapelle, et menus plaisirs du roy"; the patent was renewed to various members of the family until 1776, when it expired. The firm enjoyed a virtual monopoly on French music printing, and continued under the management of the Ballard family until 1788. Until c. 1750, the movable types invented in 1540 by Guillaume le Bé were used; the Ballards printed Lully's operas in this style (from 1700); later printings were from engraved copperplates.

Ballard, Louis W., American Indian composer of Quapaw-Cherokee extraction (his Indian name is Hunka-No-Zhe, which means Grand Eagle); b. Miami, Oklahoma, July 8, 1931. He studied piano and composition at Oklahoma Univ. and Tulsa Univ.; obtained his B.A. in music in 1954, and M.M. in composition in 1962. He subsequently took private lessons with Darius Milhaud, Castelnuovo-Tedesco and Carlos Surinach. In 1964 he traveled in Europe under the auspices of the State Department; was awarded a Ford Foundation grant in 1971. He ws subsequently appointed program director in the Bureau of Indian Affairs at Albuquerque, New Mexico. Virtually all his compositions are musical realizations of authentic Indian melodies and rhythms.

WORKS: *Koshare,* ballet, on Hopi themes (Barcelona, May 16, 1966); *The God Will Hear,* cantata (1966); *The Four Moons,* ballet, commemorating the 60th anniversary of the statehood of Oklahoma (Tulsa, Oklahoma, Oct. 28, 1967); *Devil's Promenade,* for orch. (Tulsa, May 20, 1973); *Incident at Wounded Knee* for orch. in 4 sections dramatizing the rebellion of the Sioux Indians at the locality known as Wounded Knee in South Dakota (partial performance,

St. Paul, Minnesota, April 16, 1974); *Ritmo Indio* for woodwind quintet and a Sioux flute (1968); *Katcina Dances* for cello and piano (1970); *Desert Trilogy* for winds, strings and percussion (1971); *Cacega Ayuwipi (The Decorative Drums)* for percussion ensemble of 35 instruments and standard drums (Washington, July 27, 1973). He published a collection of percussion pieces, *Pan-Indian Rhythms.*

Ballif, Claude, French composer; b. Paris, May 22, 1924. He studied composition at the Paris Cons. with Tony Aubin and Messiaen and later in Berlin with Blacher and Rufer. For several years he was connected with various pedagogical institutes in Paris; in 1964 he was appointed to the staff of the Cons. of Reims. He has also written articles on subjects dealing with modern musical techniques.
WORKS: Several of his works bear surrealist titles, e.g. *Airs comprimés* for piano (1953); *Voyage de mon oreille* for orch. (1957); *Ceci et cela* for orch. (1959); *À cor et à cri* for orch. (1962), and several pieces under the generic title *Imaginaire* for various ensembles; also Quintet for Flute, Oboe and String Trio (1958); and Double Trio for Flute, Oboe, Cello, Violin, Clarinet and Horn (1961). Ballif has also written several books and many articles: *Introduction à la méta-tonalité* (Paris, 1956); *Berlioz* (Paris, 1968); "Claude Ballif: essais études, documents," *Revue Musicale, numéro spécial 263* (1968).

Balling, Michael, German conductor; b. Heidingsfeld, near Würzburg, Aug. 27, 1866; d. Darmstadt, Sept. 1, 1925. He began his career as an orchestral viola player; also enjoyed a fine reputation as a chamber music player. In 1892 he went to Nelson, New Zealand, where he organized a choral society and a music school. Returning to Europe, he conducted Wagner's operas at Bayreuth, Hamburg and Lübeck. In 1911 he succeeded Hans Richter as conductor of the renowned Hallé Orch. in Manchester. In 1919 he went to Darmstadt, where he remained until his death. He was the editor of Wagner's early operas, undertaken by Breitkopf & Härtel in 1912.

Balmer, Luc, Swiss conductor and composer; b. Munich, July 13, 1898. He studied piano and composition with Hans Huber, Egon Petri and Ernst Levy at the Cons. of Basel, and took a course with Busoni in Berlin in 1922. Returning to Switzerland, he devoted himself to conducting; from 1941 to 1964 he conducted the Musical Society of Bern. He composed symphonic and chamber music in a healthy romantic manner; a piano concerto; a violin concerto and a comic opera, after Tirso de Molina, *Die drei gefoppten Ehemänner* (1969).

Balogh, Ernö, Hungarian pianist and composer; b. Budapest, April 4, 1897. A precocious musician, he played in public literally as an infant, and at 7 entered the Royal Academy of Music in Budapest, where he studied piano with Bartók, and composition with Kodály. He further studied piano with Leonid Kreutzer in Berlin. In 1924 he emigrated to America. His violin pieces *Caprice antique* and *Arabesque* were played

by Kreisler; his piano pieces were performed by himself. He also wrote some symphonic miniatures.

Baloković, Zlatko, eminent Yugoslav violinist; b. Zagreb, March 21, 1895; d. Venice, March 29, 1965. He studied at the Zagreb Cons. as a child; then in Vienna with Sevčik. He appeared as soloist all over the world, including Australia where he received a state prize. He gave the first performance of John Alden Carpenter's violin concerto with the Chicago Symph. Orch. on Nov. 18, 1937. From that time on he divided his activities between America and Europe.

Balsam, Artur, Polish pianist; b. Warsaw, Feb. 8, 1906. He studied at the Berlin Hochschule für Musik; in 1930 received first prize at the International Competition in Berlin and in 1931 obtained the prestigious Mendelssohn Prize. With the advent of the Nazi regime he emigrated to America, and distinguished himself mainly as a superlative accompanist; in this capacity he toured with Yehudi Menuhin and Zino Francescatti. He also played much chamber music and appeared in solo piano recitals. In 1970 he joined the staff of the Manhattan School of Music in New York.

Baltzell, Winton James, American music editor; b. Shiremanstown, Pennsylvania, Dec. 18, 1864; d. New York, Jan. 10, 1928. He studied at the New England Cons. and in 1890 went to London where he took lessons in singing with William Shakespeare and composition with Frederick Bridge. Returning to America he devoted himself chiefly to editing school manuals; published *A Complete History of Music for Schools* (1905) and a *Dictionary of Musicians* (1912). He also composed some choral works and songs.

Bamberger, Carl, Austrian conductor; b. Vienna, Feb. 21, 1902. He studied at the Univ. of Vienna; conducted opera in Germany and in Russia. In 1937 he emigrated to the U.S., and conducted sporadically various symphonic and choral groups in New York; later dedicated himself mainly to teaching. From 1938 to 1975 he was on the staff of Mannes College of Music in New York; was also lecturer on music at Louisiana State College in Baton Rouge (1975–76). From 1957 to 1974 he was guest conductor of the Stuttgart Radio Orchestra. He published a useful manual, *The Conductor's Art* (N.Y., 1965).

Bamboschek, Giuseppe, Italian conductor; b. Trieste, June 12, 1890; d. New York, June 24, 1969. He studied at the Trieste Cons., graduating in 1907. In 1913 he went to the U.S. as accompanist for Pasquale Amato; in 1916 he joined the staff at the Metropolitan Opera in New York, specializing in Italian repertory. After 1929 he was active mainly as conductor for radio and motion pictures.

Bampton, Rose, American operatic soprano; b. Cleveland, Nov. 28, 1908. She studied at the Curtis Institute of Music in Philadelphia with Queena Mario, and at Drake Univ. in Des Moines, Iowa, where she obtained a doctorate of fine arts. She sang as contralto with the Philadelphia Opera (1929–32); then changed to mezzo-soprano and soprano; sang the parts of both Amneris (mezzo-soprano) and Aida (soprano). She was on the staff of the Metropolitan Opera, N.Y. from 1932 to 1943 (debut as Laura in *La Gioconda*, Nov. 22, 1932); made annual appearances at the Teatro Colón in Buenos Aires (1942–47); then returned to New York. She is married to the conductor **Wilfrid Pelletier.**

Banchieri, Adriano, Italian organist and composer; b. Bologna, Sept. 3, 1568; d. there, 1634. He studied with Lucio Barbieri and Giuseppe Guami. On Sept. 8, 1589 he took holy orders and entered the monastery of Monte Oliveto. In 1592 he was at the Monastery of S. Bartolomeo in Lucca; 1593, in Siena; was organist at Santa Maria in Regola di Imola in 1600. In 1608 he returned to Bologna, remaining there until his death. Despite his clerical rank (he became abbot in 1620) Banchieri never abandoned music, and was active at the Accademia Filarmonica in Bologna (where he was known as 'Il dissonante'). He wrote numerous stage works, historically important in the evolution of early opera. Among these dramatic works were *La Pazzia senile* (1598); *Il zabaione musicale* (1604); *La barca da Venezia per Padova* (1605); *La prudenza giovanile* (1607); *Tirsi, Filli e Clori* (1614). He wrote a number of Masses for 3 to 8 voices, and other sacred vocal works; also several groups of instrumental works: *I canzoni alla francese a 4 voci per sonar* (1595); *Dialoghi, concentus e sinfonie* (1625); *Il virtuoso ritrovato accademico* (1626), etc. As a theorist, he advocated the extension of the hexachord and proposed to name the 7th degree of the scale by the syllables *ba* and *bi* (corresponding to B-flat and B). Banchieri's theoretical work *L'organo suonarino* (Venice, 1605) gives instructions for accompaniment with figured bass; his *Moderna prattica musicale* (Venice, 1613) contains further elaborations of the subject. Banchieri was the first to use the signs *f* and *p* for loudness and softness (in his *Libro III di nuovi pensieri ecclesiastici*, 1613). He also wrote dramatic plays under the name of **Camillo Scaliggeri della Fratta.** A reprint of his *Sinfonia d'istromenti* (1607) is found in A. Schering's *Geschichte der Musik in Beispielen* (No. 151); the organ pieces from *L'organo suonarino* are reprinted in Torchi's *Arte musicale in Italia* (vol. III). Banchieri further publ.: the treatises *Cartella musicale del canto figurato, fermo e contrappunto* (Venice, 1614); *Direttorio monastico di canto fermo* (Bologna, 1615); and *Lettere armoniche* (Bologna, 1628).

BIBLIOGRAPHY: Max Schneider, *Die Anfänge des Basso continuo* (1918); F. Vatielli, "Il Madrigale drammatico e Adriano Banchieri," in *Arte e vita musicale a Bologna* (1927); F. T. Arnold, *The Art of Accompaniment from a Thorough Bass* (London, 1931); Gustave Reese, *Music in the Renaissance* (N.Y., 1954); E. Capaccioli, "Precisazioni biografiche su Adriano Banchieri," *Rivista Musicale* (Oct.-Dec. 1954); H. J. Wilbert, *Die Messen des Adriano Banchieri* (Mainz, 1969); O. Mischiati, *Adriano Banchieri* (Bologna, 1972).

Band, Erich, German conductor; b. Berlin, May 10, 1876; d. Waidhofen, May 13, 1945. He studied at the Hochschule für Musik in Berlin; was conductor at the Stuttgart Hoftheater (1905); chief of the opera at Halle (1924–32), and later at Berlin. He adapted Auber's *Le Domino noir* for the German stage; also wrote a manual, *Zur Entwickelungsgeschichte des modernen Orchesters* (1910); composed chamber music and songs.

Bang, Maia (Mrs. Charles Hohn), Norwegian-American violinist and teacher; b. Tromsö, April 24, 1879; d. New York, Jan. 3, 1940. She was graduated from the Leipzig Cons. (1897); then studied with Leopold Auer in St. Petersburg. She came to the U. S. in 1919 and became Auer's assistant in New York. She was the author of several violin methods; at the time of her death, she was engaged in writing a biography of Paganini. Her collection of Paganini materials was given to the Library of Congress.

Banister, Henry Charles, English music theorist and teacher: b. London, June 13, 1831; d. Streatham, near London, Nov. 20, 1897. He studied music with his father, a cellist; then with Cipriani Potter at the Royal Academy of Music, where he twice gained the King's scholarship (1846–48); was appointed assistant prof. (1853) of harmony and composition at the Royal Academy; taught harmony at Guildhall School (from 1880) and at the Royal Normal College for the Blind (from 1881). He published a *Textbook of Music* (London, 1872, and 15 editions since); *Some Musical Ethics and Analogies* (1884); *Lectures on Musical Analysis* (1887); *Musical Art and Study* (1888); *George Alexander Macfarren* (1892); *Helpful Papers for Harmony Students,* (1895); *The Harmonising of Melodies* (1897); and *The Art of Modulating* (1901). A collection of his lectures, *Interludes,* edited by Macpherson, appeared in 1898. Banister composed 4 symphonies and 5 overtures, chamber music, cantatas, piano pieces, and songs.

Banister, Henry Joshua, English cellist; b. London, 1803; d. there, 1847. He was a skilled performer, and the author of several books on cello technique. His father, **Charles William Banister** (1768–1831), was a composer who published a *Collection of Vocal Music* (London, 1803).

Banister, John, English violinist and composer; b. London, 1630; d. there, Oct. 3, 1679. After he had received some musical instruction from his father, his skill earned him the patronage of King Charles II, who sent him to France for further study; was later a member of Charles' band, until an outspoken preference for the English over the French musicians playing in it caused his expulsion. Banister was director of a music school, and established the first public concerts not associated with taverns or other gathering places in which music was only of incidental importance, in London (1672–78); was a prominent figure in the English musical life of his day. He wrote music for Davenant's *Circe* and Shakespeare's *The Tempest* (both 1676); composed *New Ayres and Dialogues for voices and viols* (London, 1678); contributed to Playford's *Courtly Masquing Ayres* (1662), and to Lock's *Melothesia* (1673); also wrote music for plays by Dryden, Shadwell and Wycherley.

Banister, John, Jr., English violinist, son of preceding; b. London, c. 1663; d. there, 1735. He studied violin with his father; was a member of the private band under Charles II, James II and Queen Anne; was concert master at the Italian Opera in London. He composed some music for the theater; contributed to Playford's *Division Violin* (1685), the first violin manual published in England.

Bank, Jacques, Dutch composer; b. Borne, April 18, 1943. He studied with Jos Kunst and Ton de Leeuw at the Amsterdam Cons., graduating in 1974. Apart from his musical activities, he taught English in Amsterdam schools.

WORKS: *Blind Boy Fuller I* for recorder, piano and optional voice, being a recording of "Thousand Women Blues" sung by Blind Boy Fuller in Chicago in 1940 (1966); *The Memoirs of a Cyclist* for 2 recorders (1967–70); *Emcée* for voices (1969); *Put Me on My Bike I* for solo baritone, recorder and chorus (1971); *Fan It* for orch. (1973); *Song of Sitting Bull* for recorder player possessing a baritone voice, and organ (1974); *Monk's Blues* for piano, 14 voices and 12 winds (1974); *Blue Mosque* for bass recorder (1974); *Die Ouwe (The Old One)* for bass recorder, bass clarinet and piano (1975); *Hitch* for piano (1975); *Last Post* for bass clarinet and piano (1975); *Thomas* for the recorded voice of poet Dylan Thomas reading his "Lament" and 19 instruments (1975).

Banks, Don, Australian composer, b. Melbourne, Oct. 25, 1923. He began piano lessons at the age of 5; played in dance bands; served in the Australian Army (1941–46). After World War II, he studied composition with Le Gallienne at the Melbourne Cons. (1947–49); went to Europe in 1950; studied composition privately in London with Mátyás Seiber and in Florence with Luigi Dallapiccola. He returned to Australia in 1972. In his works he applies serial methods, modified so as not to destroy the sense of tonality; in some of his music he makes use of electronic sonorities.

WORKS: *4 Pieces for Orch.* (1953; London, June 1, 1954); *Episode* for chamber orch. (1958); *Equation I* and *II* for 12 players (1963, 1969); *Divisions* for orch. (Cheltenham Fest., July 12, 1965); Horn Concerto (London, Feb. 27, 1966); *Assemblies* for orch. (Melbourne, Dec. 3, 1966); Violin Concerto (London, Aug. 12, 1968); *Fanfare* for orch. (1969); *Dramatic Music* for young orch. (1969); *Intersections* for tape and orch. (1969); *Music for Wind Band* (1970); *Nexus* for jazz quintet and orch. (1970–71); *Duo* for violin and cello (1951–52); *Divertimento* for flute and string trio (1951–52); Violin Sonata (1953); *3 Studies* for cello and piano (1955); *Pezzo Dramatico* for piano (1956); *Sonata da Camera* for 8 instruments (1961); Horn Trio (1962); *Elizabethan Miniatures* for flute, lute, viola da gamba and strings (1962); *3 Episodes* for flute and piano (1964); *Sequence* for solo cello (1967); *Tirade,* Triptych for mezzo-soprano, piano, harp and 3 percussionists (1968); *Prologue, Night Piece, 2nd Blues* for 2 clarinets and piano (1969); *Meeting Place* for chamber group, jazz group and synthesizer (1970); *Commentary* for piano and tape (1971); *3 Short Songs* for voice and jazz quartet (1971); *4 Pieces* for String Quartet (1971); *Limbo* for 3 singers, 8 instruments and tape (1971); *Mobil* for tape (1972).

BIBLIOGRAPHY: James Murdoch, *Australia's Contemporary Composers* (Sydney, 1972).

Bannister, Rev. Henry Marriott, English music editor and bibliographer; b. Oxford, March 18, 1854; d. there Feb. 16, 1919. He studied theology; was ordained priest in 1878; publ. the valuable editions, *Monumenti Vaticani di Paleografia Musicale Latina* (Leipzig, 1913; also in Italian transl. by R. Baralli), a catalogue of the music MSS in the Vatican Library, including 141 plates; *Anglo-French Sequelae* (ed. by Dom Anselm Hughes and publ. by The Plainsong and Medieval Music Society in 1934); co-editor of vols. 47, 49, 53 and 54 of *Analecta Hymnica Medii Aevi* (1886–1922); also publ. some MSS of the Abbey of Coupar-Angus in Scotland, with a brief description (Rome, 1910); ed. a Gallican sacramentary, *Missale Gothicum,* with introduction and liturgical notes (London, 1917–19). He was for many years librarian of the Bodleian Library in Oxford.

Banshchikov, Gennady, Soviet composer; b. Kazan, Nov. 9, 1943. He studied at the Moscow Cons. (1961–64) and at the Leningrad Cons. (1965–69). In his works he adopts a fairly progressive, even aggressive, modern idiom, making use of serial techniques. He wrote 5 cello concertos (1962–70); Piano Concerto (1963); Piano Trio (1972); 3 piano sonatas (1972–74); *To the Memory of García Lorca,* cantata (1965); Symphony (1967); and a comic opera, after Gogol, *How Ivan Ivanovich quarrelled with Ivan Nikiforovich* (1971).

Banti-Giogi, Brigida, famous Italian soprano; b. Monticelli d'Ongina (Piacenza), 1759; d. Bologna, Feb. 18, 1806. She sang in Parisian cafés where she was heard by de Vismes, the director of the Opera. Her engagement by him was the beginning of a brilliant career which took her to England, Italy and Germany. She studied with Sacchini, Piozzi and Abel; her abilities were greatly appreciated by composers; Paisiello wrote for her his opera *Giuochi di Agrigento,* and she sang at its premiere (Venice, May 16, 1792). She married the dancer, Zaccaria Banti; her son wrote her biography.

BIBLIOGRAPHY: Giuseppe Banti, *Vita di B. Banti-Giorgi* (Bologna, 1869); Carlo Lozzi, "Brigida Banti," *Rivista Musicale Italiana* (1904): 64–76.

Bantock, Sir Granville, eminent English composer; b. London, Aug. 7, 1868; d. there, Oct. 16, 1946. He studied at the Royal Academy of Music, graduating in 1892; was the first holder of the Macfarren Scholarship. His earliest works were presented at the Academy concerts: an Egyptian ballet suite *Rameses II;* overture *The Fire Worshippers;* and a short opera *Caedmar,* which was later presented at the Crystal Palace (Oct. 18, 1893). He then developed varied activities; he was founder and editor of *New Quarterly Musical Review* (1893–96); toured as a musical comedy conductor (1894–95); organized and conducted concerts devoted to works by young British composers; conducted a military band and later a full orchestra at New Brighton (1897–1901). At the same time he was engaged in teaching activities; in 1907 he succeeded Sir Edward Elgar as prof. of music at Birmingham Univ., a post which he retained until 1934, when he became Chairman of the Board of Trinity College of Music. In 1938, at the age of 70, he undertook a journey to India and Australia, returning to England on the eve of World War II. He was married in 1898 to Helen von Schweitzer, daughter of the poet, Hermann von Schweitzer. Bantock was knighted in 1930. As a composer, Bantock was attracted to exotic subjects with mystical overtones; his interests were cosmopolitan and embraced all civilizations, with particular predilection for the Celtic and oriental cultures; however, his music was set in western terms. He was a strong believer in the programmatic significance of musical images, and most of his works bear titles relating to literature, mythology or legend. Yet he was a typically British composer in the treatment of his materials. His works are brilliantly scored and effective in performance, but few of them have been retained in the repertory of musical organizations.

WORKS: 3 Celtic operas: *Caedmar* (1892); *The Pearl of Iran* (1894); and *The Seal-Woman* (Birmingham, Sept. 27, 1924); ballets: *Egypt* (1892); *Lalla Rookh* (1902); *The Great God Pan* (1902); 5 tone poems: *Thalaba the Destroyer* (1900); *Dante* (1901; revised, 1910); *Fifine at the Fair* (1901); *Hudibras* (1902); *The Witch of Atlas* (1902); overture, *The Pierrot of the Minute* (1908); *Hebridean Symphony* (Glasgow, Jan. 17, 1916); *Pagan Symphony* (1923–28); *Celtic Symphony* for strings and 6 harps (1940); *2 Heroic Ballads* (1944); *The Funeral* (1946); choral works with orch.: *The Time Spirit* (1902); *Sea Wanderers* (1906); *Omar Khayyám* (in 3 parts; 1906–09; Bantock's most ambitious work); *The Pilgrim's Progress* (1928); *Prometheus Unbound* (1936); numerous works for unaccompanied chorus, among them 3 'choral symphonies': *Atalanta in Calydon* (1911); *Vanity of Vanities* (1913); *A Pageant of Human Life* (1913); also *The Golden Journey to Samarkand* (1922); choral suites to words from the Chinese; children's songs to the poems of Helen Bantock; works for brass band, cello and orch., voice and orch.; 2 string quartets; 3 violin sonatas; viola sonatas; cello sonatas; several sets of piano pieces; *Songs of the East* (6 cycles of 6 songs each); several sets of *Songs from the Chinese Poets;* sets of Celtic songs, etc. Bantock also edited albums of keyboard pieces by Byrd, Bull, etc.

BIBLIOGRAPHY: H. O. Anderton, *Granville Bantock* (London, 1915); H. Antcliffe, "A Brief Survey of the Works of Granville Bantock," *Musical Quarterly* (July 1918); P. J. Pirie, "Bantock and His Generation," *Musical Times* (Aug. 1968).

Baranović, Krešimir, eminent Croatian composer; b. Šibenik, July 25, 1894; d. Belgrade, Sept. 1975. He studied piano and theory in Zagreb and Vienna. He was a theater conductor in Zagreb from 1915 to 1927; then traveled with Anna Pavlova's ballet group (1927–28); upon return to Yugoslavia he conducted opera in Zagreb. In 1945 he was appointed prof. at the Musical Academy in Belgrade, and in 1951 became conductor of the newly organized state symphony orchestra. He retired in 1963. A prolific composer, with

a natural flair for opera, he wrote two comic operas *Striženo-Košeno (Clipped and Mowed),* which he conducted for the first time in Zagreb on May 4, 1932 and *Nevjesta od Cetingrada (The Bride from Cetingrad),* written in 1942, which was produced at the Belgrade Opera on May 12, 1951 under his direction. He further wrote several ballets, among them *Kineska priča (Chinese Tale),* in which he made use of the pentatonic scale for local color (Belgrade, April 30, 1955) and *The Gingerbread Heart,* which was produced at the Edinburgh Festival in 1951. Other works include *Pjesma guslara (Song of the Minstrel)* for orch. (Zagreb, Jan. 25, 1947); *Pan,* for narrator, voices and orch. (Belgrade, March 10, 1958); *Oblaci (The Clouds),* for mezzo-soprano and orch. (Belgrade, Oct. 31, 1964), etc.

BIBLIOGRAPHY: V. Peričić, *Muzički Stvaraoci u Srbiji* (Belgrade, 1970).

Barati, George, eminent Hungarian-American cellist and conductor; b. Györ, April 3, 1913. He studied cello and theory at the Budapest Cons., and was first cellist at the Budapest Opera (1936–38). In 1939 he emigrated to America. He then attended courses of Roger Sessions at Princeton Univ. (1939–43); served as bandleader with the U.S. Army (1943–46); from 1946 to 1950 he played the cello with the San Francisco Symph. Orch. In 1950 he was appointed conductor of the Honolulu Symph. Orch. in Hawaii, until 1968, when he became conductor of the Santa Cruz County Symph., California.

WORKS: 2 operas, *The Feather Cloak* (1970) and *Noclani* (1971); Cello Concerto (1957); *The Dragon and the Phoenix* for orch. (1960); Symphony (1964); Polarization for orch. (1965); *The Waters of Kane,* festival ode for chorus and orch. (Honolulu, Sept. 23, 1966); Octet for Harpsichord, Flute, Oboe and String Quintet (1966); Festival Hula, symph. dance (1969); South Sea Suite for guitar and orch. (1971); 2 string quartets (1944, 1962); piano pieces.

Barbaja, Domenico, celebrated Italian impresario; b. Milan, c. 1775; d. Posillipo, near Naples, Oct. 19, 1841. He was a waiter; then became a financial speculator; he accumulated his early fortune as the inventor of whipped cream with coffee or chocolate, which became known as *barbajata,* or granita di caffè. He had a concession for gambling in Naples (1808–21); became so powerful that he was nicknamed 'Viceroy of Naples.' Under the influence of his mistress, the singer Isabella Colbran, he entered the theatrical business, and obtained enormous success with his undertakings in opera. He was impresario of San Carlo and other theaters in Naples (1809–24), two theaters in Vienna (1821–28); also managed La Scala (1829–32). He was a friend of Rossini, Bellini and Donizetti, from whom he commissioned operas. Emil Lucka wrote a novel *Der Impresario* (Vienna, 1937) on his life.

BIBLIOGRAPHY: G. Monaldi, *Impresari celebri del Secolo XIX* (Milan, 1918).

Barbe, Helmut, German composer; b. Halle, Dec. 28, 1927. He studied theory in Berlin with Pepping and conducting with Grote; was active as a church organist and conductor of student orchestras in Berlin.

About 1957 he adopted the 12-tone method of composition, while adhering to structural classicism. He composes mostly sacred choral works; also wrote a violin concerto (1968) and *Hova Hallar* for organ, 12 solo strings and percussion (1970).

Barbeau, Marius, eminent French-Canadian musician and folklorist; b. Ste. Marie de Beauce, Quebec, March 5, 1883; d. in Ottawa, Feb. 27, 1969. He studied at Oxford Univ., obtaining his diploma in Anthropology as a Rhodes Scholar in 1910 and later took courses at the Sorbonne in Paris. In 1911 he was appointed anthropologist at the Victoria Memorial Museum in Ottawa; was pensioned in 1948. His main study was devoted to the codification of folkloric materials of Canadian Indians and the French population of Quebec. He collected more than 6000 melodies and 13,000 texts of French-Canadian folksongs and many thousands of Indian melodies, making use of phonograph recordings. From 1927 to 1930 he was in charge of folk music festivals in Quebec. In 1956 he organized the Canadian Folk Music Society. He published 30 books and 10 anthologies of songs in collaboration with other Canadian folklorists. Among his most important publications are "Chants populaires du Canada," *Journal of American Folklore* (1919); *Folksongs of French Canada* (with E. Sapir; New Haven, 1925); *Jongleur Songs of Old Quebec* (Toronto, 1962). For a bibliography of Barbeau's writings, almost 100 books and 600 articles, see Israel Katz, "Marius Barbeau, 1883–1969," *Ethnomusicology* (Jan. 1970).

Barber, Samuel, eminent American composer; b. West Chester, Pa., March 9, 1910. He came of a musical family; his mother's sister was the well-known singer, Louise Homer. Barber began studying piano at the age of six; at ten he attempted to write an opera, *The Rose Tree.* He played the organ in a local church for a time, until, in 1924, he entered the newly founded Curtis Institute of Music in Philadelphia where he studied piano with Isabelle Vengerova and composition with Rosario Scalero; also took singing lessons with Emilio de Gorgoza. In 1928 he won a prize for his violin sonata. His first work to attract general attention was the *Overture to The School for Scandal,* after Sheridan (Philadelphia, Aug. 30, 1933), which earned him another prize. His *Music for a Scene from Shelley* was performed by the N.Y. Philharmonic (March 23, 1935). He traveled extensively in Europe from 1928 on; received a Pulitzer Traveling Scholarship for 1935–6 and went to Rome; also won the American Prix de Rome (1935) for his Cello Sonata and *Music for a Scene from Shelley.* In Rome he wrote a *Symphony in One Movement,* which was performed there by Molinari (Dec. 13, 1936); Rodzinski conducted its American premiere in Cleveland (Jan. 21, 1937), and also at the Salzburg Festival (July 25, 1937) where it was the first American work to be given a performance. On Nov. 5, 1938, Toscanini, with the NBC Symphony Orch., gave two new works by Barber in New York: *Essay for Orchestra No. 1* and *Adagio for Strings.* The *Adagio* (arranged from Barber's String Quartet) has become one of the most popular American works for a string ensemble. From 1939–42 Barber was on the faculty of the Curtis Insti-

tute, teaching orchestration and conducting a chorus. In the autumn of 1942 he joined the Army Air Forces, by whom he was commissioned to write a symphony, his second. It was performed in Boston by Koussevitzky (March 3, 1944); the original score included a special electronic instrument to imitate radio signals. Another wartime work was *Commando March* for band (1943). In 1945, Barber was discharged from the Air Forces, and settled at Mt. Kisco, N.Y., in a house which he had purchased with Gian Carlo Menotti in 1943. In 1947 he received a Guggenheim fellowship. Barber has written a ballet *The Serpent Heart* for Martha Graham, performed by her group in New York (May 10, 1946); it was later revised and produced under the title *Cave of the Heart* (N.Y., Feb. 27, 1947); an orchestral suite *Medea,* drawn from this ballet, was first played by the Philadelphia Orch. (Dec. 5, 1947). In his *Prayers of Kierkegaard* for soprano, chorus and orch. (Boston Symph., Dec. 3, 1954) Barber essayed the style of modern oratorio with impressive results. His first full-fledged opera, to a romantic libretto by Gian Carlo Menotti, *Vanessa,* was produced at the Metropolitan Opera in New York on Jan. 15, 1958. A much more ambitious opera, commissioned by the Metropolitan Opera House for the opening of the Lincoln Center in New York, was *Anthony and Cleopatra,* in three acts, after Shakespeare's play; it was produced there on Sept. 16, 1966, but it was haunted by all kinds of misfortunes. The revolving stage did not work properly, the acoustics were faulty, and the critics damned the music itself with a curious lack of compassion. Nothing daunted, Barber undertook a radical revision of the opera, with a libretto restructured by Menotti; this new version was produced at the Juilliard School of Music in New York on Feb. 6, 1975. Other works include an effective piano suite *Excursions* (1945) and a highly elaborate piano sonata, which makes full use of the resources of modern music, including an incidental application of dodecaphony; the work became a minor classic of American piano music; it was performed for the first time anywhere by Vladimir Horowitz at his concert in Havana, Cuba, on Dec. 9, 1949. Barber's Violin Concerto was performed for the first time by Albert Spalding with the Philadelphia Orch., conducted by Eugene Ormandy, on Feb. 7, 1941. There followed *Essay No. 2* for orch. (N.Y., April 16, 1942); *Capricorn Concerto* for flute, oboe, trumpet and strings (N.Y., Oct. 8, 1944); Cello Concerto (Raya Garbousova, soloist, with the Boston Symph., conducted by Koussevitzky, April 5, 1946); a radically revised version of his wartime Second Symph. (Philadelphia, Jan. 21, 1948) and *Knoxville: Summer of 1915* for soprano and orch. to the text of James Agee from his novel *A Death in the Family* (Boston, April 9, 1948); *Souvenirs,* ballet suite (Chicago, Nov. 13, 1953); *Summer Music* for woodwind quintet (Detroit, March 20, 1956); *A Hand of Bridge,* one-act opera to a libretto by Menotti, for 4 solo voices and chamber orch. (Festival of Two Worlds, Spoleto, Italy, June 17, 1959); *Toccata Festiva* for orch. (Philadelphia, Sept. 30, 1960); *Die Natali* for orch. (Boston Symph. Orch., Dec. 22, 1960); *Andromache's Farewell* for voice and orch. (1962; N.Y., April 4, 1963); Piano Concerto (Boston Symph. Orch., Lincoln Center, N.Y., Sept. 24, 1962, Erich Leinsdorf conducting, John Browning soloist; a striking modern work, spontaneously successful and acclaimed at many subsequent performances in Europe and America). He further wrote Serenade for String Quartet (1929); *Dover Beach* for voice and string quartet (1931); Cello Sonata (1932); String Quartet (from which the famous *Adagio for Strings* was extracted, 1936); 3 songs to poems by James Joyce (1936); *A Stopwatch and an Ordnance Map* for male chorus, brass and timpani (1940); *Mélodies passagères*, 5 songs to Rilke's words (1951); *Hermit Songs*, a cycle of 10 songs for voice and piano (1953); *Despite and Still*, a song cycle (1969); *Fadograph from a Yestern Scene* for orch., after James Joyce's *Finnegans Wake* (Pittsburgh, Sept.10, 1971); *The Lovers*, for baritone, chorus and orch., to words by Pablo Neruda (Philadelphia, Sept. 22, 1971).

Barber is generally regarded as America's foremost lyricist, possessing a natural gift for melody; perhaps the fact that he studied singing and even performed as a baritone soloist in public as a youth had determined his vocally shaped melos. His harmonies are basically tonal, but he makes free use of chromatic techniques verging on atonality and polytonality, while his contrapuntal technique contains strong canonic and fugal elements; his orchestration is rich and sonorous; his treatment of solo instruments is idiomatic but requires a virtuoso performance. He received the Pulitzer Prize in music twice, for the opera *Vanessa* in 1958, and for the piano concerto in 1963. In 1959 Harvard Univ. conferred upon him an honorary doctor's degree.

BIBLIOGRAPHY: Nathan Broder, *Samuel Barber* (N.Y., 1954); David Ewen, *The World of Twentieth-Century Music* (N.Y., 1968).

Barberá, José, Catalan music theorist; b. Barcelona, Jan. 27, 1874; d. there, Feb. 19, 1947. He studied in Barcelona with Pedrell; in 1924 he was appointed instructor in composition at the Conservatorio del Liceo, and from 1931 until 1938 was its director. He published an important manual *Curso deo Melódica*, in which he derives all rules of music theory from the melodic structure. His *Cuatro lecciones del alta teoría musical* was issued posthumously (1948). He composed a symphony (1928) and some piano pieces and songs.

Barbi, Alice, Italian mezzo-soprano; b. Modena, June 1, 1862; d. Rome, Sept. 4, 1948. She made her debut in Milan on April 2, 1882; sang recitals in England, Germany and Russia. At her concert in Vienna on Dec. 21, 1893, Brahms played the accompaniments to his songs. She was married to Pietro della Torretta in 1920, and spent her last years in Rome.

Barbier, Jules Paul, French librettist and dramatist; b. Paris, March 8, 1822; d. there, Jan. 16, 1901. He was joint author (with Carré) of several librettos for famous operas, among them Gounod's *Faust* and *Roméo et Juliette* and *Hamlet* by Ambroise Thomas.

Barbier, René (Auguste-Ernest), Belgian composer; b. Namur, July 12, 1890. He studied with Paul Gilson at the Brussels Cons. and with Sylvain Dupuis at the Liège Cons.; taught at the Liège Cons. (from 1920) and of the Brussels Cons. (from 1949); concurrently served as director of the Cons. of Namur (1923–63). He received the Belgian Royal Academy Prize for his symph. poem *Les Genies du Sommeil* (1923).

WORKS: 2 operas: *Yvette* (1910) and *La Fête du vieux Tilleul* (1912), an operetta *La Sultane de Paris;* 3 oratorios: *La Tour de Babel* (1932); *Le Chemin de la Croix (The Way of the Cross)*, 14 commentaries for narrator, orch. and organ (1952); and *Lamentation de la 9e heure* (1961); a "pièce radiophonique," *La Mort de Prométhée* (1933); a ballet *Las Pierres magiques* (1957); *Pièce Symphonique* for trumpet and orch. (1918); 2 piano concertos (1922, 1934); *Les Eléments (Suite Platonicienne*, 1935); *Poème* for cello and orch. (1936); *Fantaisie concertante* for violin and orch. (1937); Cello Concerto (1938); *La Voix humaine* for small orch. (1940); *Poco Adagio et Allegro Brillante* for clarinet and orch. (1940); *Diptyque* for orch., with organ (1941); *La Musique de perdition*, symph. poem (1947); *Petite Suite* for orch. (1955); *Introduction (Fanfare) et 3 Esquisses Symphoniques* for orch. (1956); *Pièce Concertante* for violin or saxophone, and orch. (1958); Guitar Concerto (1960); *Te Deum laudamus* for chorus, brass and organ (1962); *3 mouvements symphoniques* for string orch. (1962); *Tableau symphonique* (1963); Horn Concerto (1964); Concertino for Woodwind Quartet or 4 Clarinets, and String Orch. (1964); Sinfonietta for Small Orch. (1966); *Introduction et Allegro symphonique* (1967); Concerto for Organ, Strings and Percussion (1967); *Ouverture concertante* (1969); Concertino for 2 Guitars and String Orch. (1971); Violin Sonata (1914); Piano Quintet (1915); Viola Sonata (1916); Piano Trio (1919); String Quartet (1939); Quartet for 4 Horns (1956); Quartet for 4 Saxophones (1961); *Divertissement* for 4 clarinets (1962); *Petite Suite* for woodwind quartet (1964); 2 *Petites Suites* for 2 guitars (1965, 1969); Trio for Flute, Cello and Piano (1971).

Barbieri, Carlo Emmanuele, Italian conductor and composer; b. Genoa, Oct. 22, 1822; d. Budapest, Sept. 28, 1867. He studied with Mercadante; in 1845 embarked on a career as an opera conductor, eventually settling in Budapest. He wrote 5 operas: *Cristoforo Colombo* (Berlin, 1848); *Nisida, la Perla di Procida* (1851); *Carlo und Carlin* (1859); *Arabella* (Budapest, 1862); and *Perdita, ein Wintermärchen* (Leipzig, 1865); church music, German and Italian songs.

Barbieri, Fedora, Italian contralto; b. Trieste, June 4, 1920. She studied with local teachers; then moved to Milan, where her teacher was Giulia Tess. She made successful appearances as an opera singer, first in Italy, then, already during the raging war, in Germany, Belgium and Holland. After the war she sang at La Scala in Milan, in Vienna, Paris and London. She made her American debut in San Francisco and Chicago; sang with the Metropolitan Opera in New York in 1950-53 and in 1967. Her best roles were Azucena in *Il Trovatore* and Amneris in *Aida;* she also sang the lead in *Carmen*, a rare achievement for a contralto singer.

Barbieri, Francisco Asenjo, Spanish composer; b. Madrid, Aug. 3, 1823; d. there, Feb. 19, 1894. He studied clarinet, voice and composition at the Madrid Cons., then engaged in multifarious activities as a café pianist, music copyist and choral conductor. He found his true vocation in writing zarzuelas, and composed 78 of them. The following, all produced in Madrid, were particularly successful: *Gloria y peluca* (March 9, 1850); *Jugar con fuego* (Oct. 6, 1851); *Los diamantes de la corona* (Sept. 15, 1854); *Pan y Toros* (Dec. 22, 1864) and *El Barberillo de Lavapiés* (Dec. 18, 1874). Barbieri edited a valuable collection *Cancionero musical de los siglos XV y XVI* and published a number of essays on Spanish music.

BIBLIOGRAPHY: A. Martínez Olmedilla, *El maestro Barbieri y su tiempo* (Madrid, 1950); J. Subirá, *Manuscritos de Barbieri, existentes en la Biblioteca Nacional* (Madrid, 1936); Gilbert Chase, "Barbieri and the Spanish Zarzuela," *Music & Letters* (Jan., 1939).

Barbireau (or **Barbirau, Barbarieu, Barbyrianus, Barberau, Barbacola**), **Jacques (Jacobus),** Flemish composer; b. Mons, c.1408; d. Antwerp, Aug. 8, 1491. He was choirmaster at the Antwerp Cathedral from 1447 until his death; Okeghem was one of his pupils. Barbireau enjoyed a great reputation in his time; his opinions are copiously cited by Tinctoris.

WORKS: Mass for 5 voices, *Virgo parens Christi*; for 4 voices: *Missa Pascale; Faulx perverse;* antiphons, psalms, etc.

BIBLIOGRAPHY: H. du Saar, *Het Leven en de composities van Jacobus Barbireau* (Utrecht, 1946); G. Reese, *Music in the Renaissance* (N.Y., 1954).

Barbirolli, Sir John, eminent English conductor; b. London, Dec. 2, 1899, of Italian-French parentage; d. London, July 29, 1970. He studied at Trinity College (1911–12) and at the Royal Academy of Music (1912–17); made his concert debut in Queen's Hall as a cellist at the age of eleven; became cellist in the Queen's Hall Orch. (1915). He then held various positions as a conductor; with the Chenil Orch., Chelsea (1925); British National Opera Co. (1926); achieved recognition when he substituted for Beecham with the London Symph. (1926); in 1933 was appointed conductor of the Scottish Orch., Glasgow, and Leeds Symph. Orch. He made his American debut with the New York Philh. (Nov. 5, 1936) and produced such an excellent impression that he was selected to succeed Toscanini in 1937. He was chief conductor of the N.Y. Philh. until 1943, when he went back to England and was appointed conductor of the Hallé Orch., Manchester. He was knighted in 1949. As a conductor, Barbirolli had a fine pragmatic sense of shaping the music according to its inward style, without projecting his own personality upon it; however, this very lack of subjective interpretation was responsible for the somewhat lukewarm reception he obtained with the New York audiences accustomed to virtuoso conductors. While not by temperament a propagandist of modern music, he introduced several contemporary works during his conductorship with the N.Y. Philh., among them Benjamin Britten's *Sinfonia da Requiem*. He made transcriptions for string orch. and French horns of 5 pieces from the Fitzwilliam Virginal Book (performed by him under the title *Elizabethan Suite*, Los Angeles, Dec. 4, 1941); wrote an oboe concerto on themes by Pergolesi (dedicated to his wife, Evelyn Rothwell, the oboist).

BIBLIOGRAPHY: Charles Rigby, *John Barbirolli* (Altrincham, 1948); Charles Reid, *John Barbirolli* (London, 1971); Michael Kennedy; *Barbirolli: Conductor Laureate* (London, 1971).

Barblan, Otto, Swiss organist and composer; b. Scanfs, Switzerland, March 22, 1860; d. Geneva, Dec. 19, 1943. He studied at the Stuttgart Cons. (1878–84); made his debut as organist at Augsburg (1885); taught at Chur (1885–87); then became organist at the Cathedral of Geneva; prof. at the Cons. and conductor of the 'Sociétéde Chant Sacré' (1887). He wrote an *Ode Patriotique* (1896); a *Festspiel* (Chur, May 28, 1899) commemorating the 400th anniversary of the battle of Calven, and containing the chorus *Terre des Monts* which has attained great popularity, placing it next to the national anthem as a patriotic song; *Post Tenebras Lux,* cantata for the Calvin jubilee (1909); string quartet; variations and triple fugue on B-A-C-H; Passion according to St. Luke (Geneva, April 9, 1919).

BIBLIOGRAPHY: A.-E. Cherbuliez in the *Schweizerische Musikzeitung* (1925, and on Barblan's 70th birthday, 1930); E. Perini, *Otto Barblan* (Zürich, 1960).

Barbot, Joseph-Théodore-Désiré, French tenor; b. Toulouse, April 12, 1824; d. Paris, Jan. 1, 1897. He studied with Garcia at the Paris Cons.; was engaged to sing at the Paris Opéra in 1848; sang Faust at the premiere of Gounod's opera (March 19, 1859). In 1875 he became prof. at the Paris Cons. succeeding Mme. Viardot.

Barbour, Florence Newell, American composer and pianist; b. Providence, Aug. 4, 1866; d. there, July 24, 1946. She received her education in the U.S., then traveled through Europe and the Far East. Her works include the piano suites *Holland, Venice, Forest Sketches, A Day in Arcady, At Chamonix;* children's piano pieces and songs. She wrote *Childland in Song and Rhythm* (1921).

Barbour, J. Murray, American musicologist; b. Chambersburg, Pa., March 31, 1897; d. Homestead, a corporate entity surrounded by, but separate from, Pittsburgh, Jan. 4, 1970. He studied with Otto Kinkeldey at Cornell Univ., and in 1932 received there the first doctorate in musicology awarded by an American university. He taught English at Ithaca College (1932–39) before his appointment as prof. of Musicology at Michigan State College. He published *Tuning and Temperament* (1951), and contributed various learned essays to music journals. He was also a composer; wrote a *Requiem* and some chamber music.

Barce, Ramón, Spanish composer; b. Madrid, March 16, 1928. He studied languages at the Univ. of Madrid; in music he was largely autodidact. In 1958 he organized the group Nueva Música in Madrid; as music critic he supported modern tendencies in Spanish music. The titles of many of his works indicate his trend towards absolute music in abstract modern forms: *Estudio de sonoridades* for piano (1962); *Parábola* for wind quintet (1963); *Objetos sonoros* for chamber orch. and percussion (1964); *Coral hablado (Spoken Chorus*, 1965), *Las cuatro estaciones* for orch. (1966); *Estudio de densidades* for piano (1965); *Obertura fonética* for wind sextet (1968); also a theater piece, *Abgrund Hintergrund* (1964).

Barclay, Arthur (original name **Arthur Barclay Jones**), English choral conductor; b. London, Dec. 16, 1869; d. Purley, Surrey, Oct. 12, 1943. He studied at the Guildhall School of Music, where he later taught piano; served as musical director of the Brompton Oratory Choir (1893-1935). He changed his name from Arthur Barclay Jones to Arthur Barclay about 1900. He wrote a symphony (1896); violin sonata; hymns for children and miscellaneous pieces for organ.

Bardi, Giovanni de', Count of Vernio, Italian nobleman, patron of music and art and composer; b. Florence, Feb. 5, 1534; d. Rome, 1612. He was the founder of the Florentine Camerata, a group of musicians who met at his home (1576–c.1582) to discuss the music of Greek antiquity; this led to the beginnings of opera. Count Bardi was descended from an old Guelph banking family; he was a philologist, mathematician, neo-Platonic philosopher and lover of Dante. He was a member of the Crusca Academy, a literary group founded in 1583 whose ideas had great influence on the Camerata. Bardi is known to have been in Rome in 1567; he lent support to Vincenzo Galilei, a member of the Camerata. In 1580 Bardi married Lucrezia Salvati. The masques of 1589, commemorating the marriage of Grand Duke Ferdinand, were conceived largely by Bardi. In 1592 he left for Rome to become chamberlain at the court of Pope Clement VIII. Caccini was his secretary in 1592. Bardi's writings are: *Discorso sopra il giuoco del calzio fiorentino* (Florence, 1580); *Ristretto delle grandezze di Roma* (Rome, 1600); *Discorso mandato a Caccini sopra la musica antica* in Doni's *Lyra Barberina* (Florence, 1763). Among his compositions are a madrigal in 4 voices *Misere habitator* in Malvezzi's *Intermedi e concerti* (Venice, 1591); the madrigal *Lauro ohime Lauro* in *Il Lauro secco, lib.* I (Ferrara, 1582). Among contemporary documents which refer to him are Vincenzo Galilei's *Dialogo della musica antica e della moderna* (translated in part in O. Strunk's *Source Readings in Music History*, N.Y., 1951; also included is a letter from Bardi's son to G. B. Doni commenting on Bardi's ideas).
BIBLIOGRAPHY: G. Gasperini, *Intorno alle origini del melodramma* (Rome, 1902); Henriette Martin, "La Camerata du comte Bardi et la musique florentine du XVIe siècle," *Revue de musicologie* (Nov. 1932); Nino Pirrotta, "Temperaments and Tendencies in the Florentine Camerata," *Musical Quarterly* (April 1954).

Barenboim, Daniel, Israeli pianist and conductor; b. Buenos Aires, Argentina, Nov. 15, 1942. He studied with his mother and his father; made his debut in Buenos Aires at the age of 7; was taken to Salzburg when he was 9; studied piano there with Edwin Fischer and received first lessons in conducting with Igor Markevitch. In 1952 the family settled in Israel; his subsequent studies were with Nadia Boulanger in Paris and at Santa Cecilia in Rome, where he was one of the youngest students to receive a diploma in 1956. He made his American debut as pianist at Carnegie Hall on Jan. 20, 1957, playing Prokofiev's First Piano Concerto with Leopold Stokowski; gave his first U.S. solo recital in New York on Jan. 17, 1958; made several world tours. He began to conduct orchestras in 1962 and soon established himself as a professional conductor of high caliber. In his piano playing he subordinates romantic passion to classical balance of form and thematic content; his performances of the entire cycle of Beethoven sonatas are notable for technical proficiency and interpretative taste. On June 15, 1967 he married the English cellist **Jacqueline DuPré**.

Barge, Wilhelm, German flute player and composer; b. Wulfsahl, Nov. 23, 1836; d. there, July 16, 1925. He played in a military band before his appointment as first flutist at the Gewandhaus Orch. in Leipzig; retired on pension in 1895. He publ. a method for flute, 4 sets of orch. flute studies based on passages in classical symph. works; also publ. flute arrangements of various famous works (*Sammlung beliebter Stücke*); edited the flute concertos of Frederick the Great.

Bargiel, Woldemar, German composer; b. Berlin, Oct. 3, 1828; d. there, Feb. 23, 1897. He was a half-brother of **Clara Schumann**. As a boy, he sang at the Berlin Cathedral and studied counterpoint with Dehn; and at the Leipzig Cons. (1846-50) with Hauptmann, Moscheles and Gade. He was teacher and conductor in Rotterdam from 1865-74; then returned to Berlin. He was greatly admired by Schumann and Brahms, and his works, in a romantic vein, were frequently performed; almost all of his music was publ. during his lifetime. He wrote a symphony; 3 overtures; string octet; 4 string quartets; 3 piano trios; violin sonatas; numerous piano pieces and songs.
BIBLIOGRAPHY: E. Rudorff, *Aus den Tagen der Romantik; Bildnis einer deutschen Familie* (Leipzig, 1938).

Bargielski, Zbigniew, Polish composer; b. Lomza, Jan. 21, 1937. He studied composition with Szeligowski at the State College of Music in Warsaw; musicology with Szabelsi at the State College in Katowice; completed his studies with Nadia Boulanger in Paris.
WORKS: *Danton, or Some Pictures from the History of the Great French Revolution*, surrealistic historical opera (1968-69); *Le Petit Prince*, after Saint-Exupéry (1970); a children's opera, *Alice in Wonderland* (1971-72); opera, *Phantoms Do Not Lie* (1971-72); *Parades* for orch. (1965); *Espace attrapé* for orch. (1973); Percussion Concerto (1975); Violin Concerto (1975); *Ballad* for winds and percussion (1976); *3 Sonnet-Capriccios* for solo clarinet (1976); *Impromptu* for solo percussion (1976); String Quartet (1976).

Barilli, Bruno, Italian writer on music; b. Fano, Dec. 14, 1880; d. Rome, April 15, 1952. He studied in Parma and later in Munich; his collections of essays are published under the titles *Il sorcio nel violino* and *Il paese del melodramma*. He also wrote 2 operas: *Medusa* (1914; first performed, Bergamo, Sept. 11, 1938) and *Emiral* (Rome, March 11, 1924).

Barini, Giorgio, Italian musicologist; b. Turin, Aug. 23, 1864; d. Rome, Sept. 22, 1944. He is noted for his editions of operas by Paisiello and Cimarosa; was also music critic of various newspapers in Rome. He published *La Donna e L'Artista: Musicisti innamorati* (Rome, 1927) and several essays on Wagner's operas.

Bark, Jan, Swedish composer; b. Härnösand, April 19, 1934. He was first a jazz trombonist; then studied at the Royal Academy of Music in Stockholm, taking courses in composition with Lars-Erik Larsson and Karl-Birger Blomdahl; was initiated into ultra-modern music by György Ligeti in Stockholm; made an American trip in 1962 and worked with avant-garde groups at the Tape Music Center in San Francisco; in 1964 he traveled to the Far East to study oriental music. Returning to Sweden, he joined the radio and television center of the Swedish Broadcasting Service. He was co-founder with Folke Rabe of the Culture Quartet of 4 trombones, which explores the potentialities of modern trombone playing. Many of his pieces are of a theatrical, almost exhibitionistic, nature, often with a healthy radical tinge. WORKS: Piano Sonata (1957); 2 string quartets (1959, 1962); *Metakronismer* for orch. (1960; Oslo, March 4, 1961); 2 works for the Culture Quartet, composed in collaboration with Folke Rabe: *Bolos,* in an anarcho-Dadaistic manner (1962) and *Polonaise* (1965); *Lamento* for percussion, piano and double basses (1962); *Boca Chica* for chamber ensemble (1962); *Pyknos* for orch. (1962); *Eko* for news broadcaster and 5 tape recorders (1962); *Missa Bassa* for small orch. with 7 conductors, six of whom also sing (1964; Swedish Radio, April 1, 1967); *Nota* for "choreographic" mixed chorus (1964); *Ost-Funk* for 8 jazz musicians (1964); *Mansbot* for male chorus and 12 guitars (1964); *Tredjedels Signeri* for 3 Hammond organs (1967); *Bar,* electronic music (1967); *Light Music* for chorus a cappella (1968); *Lyndon Bunk Johnson,* a "poster" work, composed collectively (1968); *Irk-Ork 1970* for chamber ensemble (1970); *Het Jacht von het vliegende Joachim* for trombone, cello and piano (1971).

Barkauskas, Vytautas, Lithuanian composer; b. Kaunas, March 25, 1931. He studied music at the Tallat-Kelpša Music College in Vilnius (1949–53) and mathematics and physics at the State Pedagogical Institute there; then took composition with Raciunas and orchestration with Balsis at the Lithuanian State Cons. (1953–59); then taught classes there. His music employs advanced West-European techniques. WORKS: an opera, *Legend of Love* (1975); *Poem* for piano and orch. (1960); 2 symphonies (1963, 1971); *Poezija (Poetry),* cycle for piano (1964); *Choreographic Miniatures* for orch. (1965); *Partita* for solo violin (1967); Variations for 2 pianos (1967); *Žodis revoliucijai,* cantata for narrator, chorus and orch. (1967); *Intimate Composition* for oboe and 12 strings (1968); *3 Aspects* for orch. (1969); *Pathetique Sonata*

for piano (1969); *Contrast Music* for flute, cello and percussion (1969); *Pro memoria,* 3 movements for flute, bass clarinet, harp and 5 percussionists (1970); String Quintet (1971); *Monologue* for solo oboe (1970); *La vastra nominanza e color d'erba,* musical mirage, after Dante, for chamber chorus and string quintet (1971); string quartet (1972); *Gloria urbi,* Organ Concerto (1972); *Sonata subita* for violin and piano (1974).

Barlow, Fred, French composer; b. Mulhouse, Oct. 26, 1881; d. Boulogne (Seine), Jan. 3, 1951. He was of British parentage; studied engineering; then turned to music; took lessons in Paris with Jean Huré and Charles Koechlin. WORKS: *Sylvie,* comic opera (Paris, March 7, 1924); *La Grande Jatte,* ballet (Paris, July 12, 1950); *Gladys,* ballet (posthumous; Mulhouse, Jan. 7, 1956); several symph. suites; String Quartet (1947); Violin Sonata; Cello Sonata; piano pieces; vocal compositions.

BIBLIOGRAPHY: R. Delage, "Trois figures de musiciens contemporains," *La musique en Alsace hier et aujourd'hui* (Paris, 1970).

Barlow, Harold, American composer of popular songs, bandleader and musical lexicographer; b. Boston, May 15, 1915. He studied violin at Boston Univ., and later played in various orchestras; also led a U.S. Army band. He has compiled two valuable reference works for which he designed an original method of indexing melodic themes by letters plus accidentals: *A Dictionary of Musical Themes* (with Sam Morgenstern; N.Y., 1948); and *A Dictionary of Vocal Themes* (N.Y., 1950).

Barlow, Howard, American conductor; b. Plain City, Ohio, May 1, 1892; d. Bethel, Conn., Jan. 31, 1972. He studied at the Univ. of Colorado and at Columbia Univ. He conducted the American National Orch., N.Y. (1923–25), at the Neighborhood Playhouse (1925–27); was conductor of the CBS Symph. Orch. (1927–43), with which he presented numerous new works.

Barlow, Samuel, American composer; b. N.Y., June 1, 1892; studied music at Harvard Univ. (B.A., 1914); then took lessons with Respighi in Rome. His one-act opera, *Mon ami Pierrot,* was the first by an American composer to be given at the Opéra-Comique in Paris (Jan. 11, 1935); he wrote also 2 more operas, *Eugénie* and *Amanda.* His symphonic concerto *Babar* (1935) employs magic lantern slides. Other works: piano concerto (Rochester, Jan. 23, 1931, composer-soloist); a suite of *Biedermeier Waltzes* for orch. (Rome, 1935); *Circus Overture* (1960); choruses.

Barlow, Wayne, American composer; b. Elyria, Ohio, Sept. 6, 1912. He studied with Bernard Rogers and Howard Hanson at the Eastman School of Music; in 1935 took courses in composition with Schoenberg at the Univ. of Southern California. In 1937 he was appointed to the staff of the Eastman School of Music. He composed *The Winter's Passed* for oboe and strings (Rochester, Oct. 18, 1938); *Three Moods* for orch. (1940); *Lyrical Piece* for clarinet and strings (1945); *Nocturne* for 18 instruments (1946); *Sinfonia in C* (1950); Mass in G (1951); a piano quintet (1951); *Night Song* for orch. (1957); *Sinfonia da camara* for orch. (1962); Trio for Oboe, Viola and Piano (1964); *Elegy* for viola and piano (1967); *Wait for the Promise of the Father,* a ballet (1968); Saxophone Concerto (1970).

Bärmann, Heinrich Joseph, German clarinetist; b. Potsdam, Feb. 14, 1784; d. Munich, June 11, 1847. He was a renowned performer; made extensive tours, and finally settled in Munich as first clarinetist of the court orchestra; his friends, Weber and Mendelssohn, wrote clarinet works for him. He composed concertos, fantasias, quintets, quartets, sonatas, etc. for his instrument, about 90 works in all; 38 have been published; many of his clarinet exercises are still being used for teaching the instrument.

Bärmann, Karl, German clarinetist, son of **Heinrich Joseph Bärmann;** b. Munich, Oct. 24, 1811; d. there, May 23, 1885. He was a pupil of his father, whom he accompanied on his tours; later succeeded him at the Munich court orchestra. He wrote a method for clarinet, with a supplement entitled *Materalien zur weiteren technischen Ausbildung.*

Bärmann (Baermann), Karl, Jr., pianist and music pedagogue, son of the preceding; b. Munich, July 9, 1839; d. Boston, Jan. 17, 1913. He studied piano with Wanner, Wahlmuth and Liszt, and composition with Franz Lachner; was appointed teacher at the Munich Cons., but emigrated to the U.S. in 1881. He settled in Boston.

Barmas, Issaye, Russian violinist and pedagogue; b. Odessa, May 1, 1872; d. London, July 3, 1946. He studied in Moscow and with Joachim in Berlin; toured in Europe; settled in London. Among his publications are *Die Lösung des Geigentechnischen Problems* (1913); *Tonleiter-Spezialstudien; Doppelgriff Spezialstudien;* and many editions of classical works.

Barnard, Charlotte (Mrs. Charles Barnard), English songwriter; b. London, Dec. 23, 1830; d. Dover, Jan. 30, 1869. In 1866 she published under the pen name of **Claribel** the ballad *Come Back to Erin* which attained great popularity. She also wrote poetry.

Barnby, Sir Joseph, English organist, conductor and composer; b. York, Aug. 12, 1838; d. London, Jan. 28, 1896. He was trained as a choirboy; studied with Cipriani Potter at the Royal Academy of Music in London; then held the post of organist at various churches. In 1864 he organized Barnby's Choir, which presented annual concerts in London; in 1874 he inaugurated a series of daily concerts at Albert Hall; was director of music at Eton and at the Guildhall School of Music. He was knighted in 1892. Barnby composed numerous pieces of sacred music, among them *246 Hymn Tunes,* published in 1897.

Barnekow, Christian, Danish composer; b. St. Sauveur, France, July 28, 1837; d. Copenhagen, March 20, 1913. He studied in Copenhagen; from 1871 to 1887 he directed the Society for Publication of Danish Music. He wrote numerous sacred choral works and also Lieder in a folklike manner, as well as some estimable chamber music.

Barnes, Edward Shippen, American organist and composer; b. Seabright, N.J., Sept. 14, 1887; d. Idyllwild, Calif., Feb. 14, 1958. He was a student of Horatio Parker and David Stanley Smith at Yale Univ., and studied organ with Harry B. Jepson there. He was organist at St. Stephen's Episcopal Church in Philadelphia and later at the First Presbyterian Church in Santa Monica, California, retiring in 1954. He wrote 2 organ symphonies, much sacred music and several books of organ arrangements for schools, among them *Bach for Beginners in Organ Playing.*

Barnes, Milton, Canadian conductor and composer; b. Toronto, Dec. 16, 1931. He studied music theory with Weinzweig at the Cons. of Toronto and conducting at the Berkshire Music Center, Tanglewood, Mass. (1958–61); also took a course in conducting with Swarowsky at the Vienna Academy (1959–61). Returning to Canada, he held positions as conductor of the Univ. of Toronto Orch. (1962–63), Toronto Repertory Esemble (1964–70) and St. Catharines, Ontario, Symph. and Chorus (1964–73); concurrently conducted the Niagara Falls, (N.Y.) Philharmonic. In 1968 he was appointed director of the Toronto Dance Theater.

WORKS: the ballet scores: *Masque of the Red Death* (1971); *Three-Sided Room* (1972); and *Amber Garden* (1972); *Invocations* for orch. (1962); Symph. No. 1 (1964); *Children's Suite* for orch. (1966); *Pinocchio,* symp. poem (1966); Variations for Clarinet and Orch. (1968); *Classical Concerto* for piano and orch. (1973); *Psalms of David,* cantata (1972–73); *Shebetim,* tableau for string orch. (1974); Concerto for Saxophone and Strings (1975); Concerto for Violin and Strings (1975); *3 Folk Dances* for violin and piano (1953); *Thespis,* scenic cantata (1956, revised 1973); *Burletta* for string quartet (1957–58); *Lamentations of Jeremiah* for solo viola (1959); Flute Sonata (1965); *Rhapsody on a Late Afternoon* for string quartet (1971); Variations for Solo Violin (1972); Concerto Grosso for Flute, Clarinet, Violin, Cello and 2 Pianos (1973); Serenade for Accordion and Guitar (1973); *Spiral Stairs,* dance septet (1973); *Madrigals* for female chorus, 2 trumpets and 2 trombones (1975); Fantasy for Solo Guitar (1975); Symph. for strings (1976); Chamber Concerto for wind quintet and strings (1976).

Barnett, John, English composer; b. Bedford, July 1, 1802; d. Cheltenham, April 17, 1890. He was a son of the German jeweler named Bernhard Beer, and received his early musical training in Frankfurt. He wrote operettas and various other pieces of light music, before producing his first full-fledged opera *The Mountain Sylph* (London, Aug. 25, 1834); this was followed by 2 more operas *Fair Rosamond* (London, Feb. 28, 1837) and *Farinelli* (London, Feb. 8, 1839). In 1841 he settled in Cheltenham as a voice teacher. Among his works are a symphony, 2 string quartets and something like 4,000 songs. He also published 2 singing methods, *Systems and Singing Masters* (1842) and *School for the Voice* (1844).

Barnett, John Francis, English composer; nephew of John Barnett; b. London, Oct. 16, 1837; d. there, Nov. 24, 1916. He studied piano in London and in Leipzig. In 1883 he was appointed to the staff of the Royal College of Music in London. He wrote a symphony (1864), several playable symphonic overtures and singable cantatas, several of them inspired by literary works. Among his oratorios, *The Raising of Lazarus*, first performed in London on June 18, 1873, was much performed in churches. He published an engaging volume, *Musical Reminiscences and Impressions* (London, 1906).

Barnett, John Manley, American conductor; b. New York, Sept. 3, 1917. He studied piano, violin and trumpet, and took courses in conducting with Leon Barzin in New York, and with Bruno Walter, Weingartner, Enesco and Malko in Europe. He was conductor of the Stamford Symph. Orch. (1939–42) and of the N.Y. City Symph. (1940–42); later conducted occasional concerts at the Hollywood Bowl. In 1976 he was Musical Artistic Consultant for the National Endowment for the Arts.

Barns, Ethel, English violinist and composer; b. London, 1880; d. Maidenhead, Dec. 31, 1948. She studied at the Royal Academy in London; made her debut at the Crystal Palace (1896); toured England (1897) and America (1913). Her compositions include a *Concertstück* for violin and orch.; 2 trios; *Phantasy* for 2 violins and piano; 5 violin sonatas.

Barolsky, Michael, Lithuanian-born Israeli composer; b. Vilna, July 19, 1947. He studied music as a child; then took courses in composition in Warsaw with Lutoslawski; later went to Moscow where he had private lessons with Schnittke and Denisov. He went to Israel in 1971; became instructor in piano, music theory and electronic music at the Music Teachers Training College in Tel Aviv.
WORKS: Violin Sonata (1964); String Trio (1964); Woodwind Quartet (1965); Concertino for solo violin, trumpet, trombone, piano and percussion (1967); *Telefonoballade,* cantata for baritone, 6 narrators and chamber ensemble (1969); *Exodus* for orch. (1970); *Scriptus,* after Kafka's letters, for baritone, mime and chamber ensemble (1972); *Chamber Music* for 4 players and audience (1973); *Photogenesis I, II, III* and *IV* for harpsichord, brass quintet, bass flute, and solo percussion (1973); *Cries and Whispers* for chamber ensemble and tape (1975; Univ. of Chicago, Jan. 24, 1976); *Sublimatio* for flute, cello, 2 pianos, percussion and tape (1975); an opera *Blue Eye, Brown Eye,* to a libretto by the composer (1975–76); *Iris* for flute, oboe, clarinet, violin, cello and piano (1976); *Bible Research* for contralto, clarinet and strings (1977); *Pranah* for violin and tape (1977); *Caramah* for cello solo (1977).

Baron, Ernst Gottlieb, German lutenist; b. Breslau, Feb. 17, 1696; d. Berlin, April 12, 1760. He was a court musician in Gotha (1727); theorbist to the Prussian Crown Prince (later Frederick II) in 1734; wrote *Historisch-theoretische und praktische Untersuchung des Instruments der Laute* (1727); an Appendix (on the lute) to Marpurg's *Historisch-kritische Beiträge,* vol. II; an *Abhandlung von dem Notensystem der Laute und der Theorbe;* other theoretical pamphlets; composed many works for the lute, which remain in MS.

Baron, Maurice, American composer and conductor; b. Lille, France, Jan. 1, 1889; d. Oyster Bay, Long Island, N.Y., Sept. 5, 1964. He studied music in France; emigrated to America where he became a theater conductor. He published several hundred pieces of light music under his own name and the whimsical *noms de plume:* **Francis Delille** (i.e., "de Lille," a native of Lille); **Morris Aborn** (anagram of Baron); also used the name of his wife **Alice Tremblay.** Of his more ambitious works was *Ode to Democracy* for narrator, chorus and orch. (N.Y., Jan. 23, 1949).

Barraine, Elsa, French composer; b. Paris, Feb. 13, 1910. Her father was a cellist, her mother a singer. She studied at the Paris Cons. with Paul Ducat; in 1928 she received the second Prix de Rome; she wrote 3 symphonies (1931, 1938, 1947), a curiously realistic symph. poem *Pogromes (Pogroms;* impressed by the Nazi persecutions of Jews; Paris, March 11, 1939); *Suite astrologique* for orch. (1947); *Atmosphère* for oboe and 10 instruments, on hindu rhythms (1967); *Musique rituelle* for organ, gongs and xylorimba (1968).

Barraqué, Jean, French composer of advanced modern tendencies; b. Paris, Jan. 17, 1928; d. there, Aug. 17, 1973. He studied with Jean Langlais at the Paris Cons., and privately with Olivier Messiaen. From his early works, he devoted himself to experimentation, absorbing all resources of modern music, including dodecaphony and electronics. His major work *Séquence* (1950–55) is scored for soprano, piano, harp, violin, cello and assorted percussion; other works are *Le temps restitué* for voices and orch. (1957) and *Au-délà du hasard* for voices and 4 instrumental groups (Paris, Jan. 26, 1960); *Chant après chant* for voice, percussion and piano (1966); and Concerto for 6 Instrumental Groups, Vibraphone and Clarinet (1968). Barraqué planned the composition of an immense work in 13 parts which was to be the expression of his world philosophy, but the work remained in fragments at his death. A listing of his works is contained in "Propos impromptu. Jean Barraqué," *Courier Musical de France* 26 (1969). Despite the scarcity of his completed works, Barraqué impressed musicians as a potential genius. André Hodeir devotes an enthusiastic chapter to Barraqué in his book *La Musique depuis Debussy* (Paris, 1961).
WRITINGS: *Debussy* (Paris, 1962).

Barraud, Henry, French composer; b. Bordeaux, April 23, 1900. He studied music without a teacher, while engaged in the family wine business in Bordeaux. In 1926 entered the Paris Cons. and studied with Louis Aubert. In 1937 Barraud was appointed Director of Music for the International Exposition in

Paris. He served in the French army during World War II; after the demobilization he lived in Marseilles. After the liberation of Paris in 1944 he was appointed music director of Radiodiffusion Française. In 1967 he received the Grand Prix National de la Musique.

WORKS: *Finale dans le mode rustique* (Paris, 1932); *Poème* for orch. (1934); *Concerto de Camera* for 30 instruments (1936); *Le Diable à la Kermesse*, ballet (1943; a symph. suite from it was broadcast by Paris Radio, April 26, 1945); piano concerto (N.Y. Philh., Dec. 5, 1946); *Offrande à une ombre* (in memory of a brother killed by the Germans as a member of the Resistance; first U.S. performance, St. Louis, Jan. 10, 1947); *La Farce du Maître Pathelin* (Paris, June 24, 1948); *Symphonie de Numance* (Baden-Baden, Dec. 3, 1950); Concertino for piano and 4 winds (1953); *Numance*, opera (Paris, April 15, 1955); Te Deum for chorus and 6 instruments (1955); Symphony for String Orch. (1955); Symph. No. 3 (Boston, March 7, 1958); *Rapsodie cartésienne* for orch. (1959); *Rapsodie dionysienne* for orch. (1961); *Lavinia*, opera-buffa (Aix-en-Provence, July 20, 1961); Divertimento for orch. (1962); Concerto for Flute and Strings (1963); *Symphonie concertante* for trumpet and orch. (1965); *3 Études* for orch.; *Une Saison en enfer*, a symph. suite after Rimbaud (1969). Barraud also published books on Berlioz (Paris, 1955), on the problems of modern music, *Pour comprendre les musiques d'aujourd'hui* (Paris, 1968), and on the analysis of selected operas, *Les Cinq Grands Opéras* (Paris, 1972).

Barrère, Georges, French flute virtuoso; b. Bordeaux, Oct. 31, 1876; d. Kingston, N.Y., June 14, 1944. He studied at the Paris Cons. (1889-95), graduating with first prize; was solo flutist at Colonne Concerts and at the Paris Opéra (1897-1905). He came to America in 1905; played flute with the N.Y. Symph. Orch. (1905-28); taught at the Institute of Musical Art, N.Y., and at the Juilliard School of Music. He was the founder of the Barrère Little Symphony (1914); composed a *Nocturne* for flute; *Chanson d'automne* for voice; also edited classical works for flute.

Barret, Apollon (Marie-Rose), French oboist; b. Paris, 1803; d. London, March 8, 1879. He studied at the Paris Cons.; played in the orchestras at opera houses; in 1874 went to London with the Italian Opera. Barret is the author of a standard manual *Complete Method for the Oboe Comprising All The New Fingerings, New Tables of Shakes, Scales, Exercises.*

Barrett, Reginald, English organist; b. London, Jan. 12, 1861; d. St. Petersburg, Florida, Feb. 7, 1940. He studied at the Guildhall School of Music and at Darmstadt Cons.; came to the U.S. in 1888; was organist in Kansas City until 1898, when he settled in New York City as organist at St. James Church, Fordham. From 1917 until 1925 he played the organ in motion picture theaters. He composed some 100 preludes and interludes for organ, sacred songs, choruses, etc.

Barrett, William Alexander, English writer on music; b. London, Oct. 15, 1834; d. there, Oct. 17, 1891. He was a choirboy in St. Paul's Cathedral; then studied at Oxford. From 1867 he was active mainly as music

critic and editor. He published *English Glee and Madrigal Writers* (1877), *English Church Composers* (1882) and other books of reference. His son, **Francis Barrett,** was also a writer on music; he was born in London, Nov. 14, 1869, and died there Jan. 19, 1925.

Barrientos, Maria, celebrated Spanish coloratura soprano; b. Barcelona, March 10, 1884; d. Ciboure, France, Aug. 8, 1946. She made her operatic debut at the age of 15 in Barcelona on March 4, 1899, and still very young made a successful tour of Europe. She made her first appearance with the Metropolitian Opera House in New York as Lucia on Jan. 31, 1916, and remained with it until 1919; then went to France.

Barrington, Daines, English lawyer and music amateur; b. London, 1727; d. there, March 14, 1800. He was the author of the famous account of Mozart as a child prodigy, published in *Philosophical Transactions* in 1770. He also published an interesting volume, *Experiments and Observations on the Singing of Birds* (London, 1773) and a description of the ancient Welsh crwth and pibcorn.

Barrios, Angel, Spanish composer; b. Granada, Jan. 4, 1882; d. Madrid, Nov. 27, 1964. Of a musical family (his father was a famous guitarist), he studied violin and played in bands as a child. He later studied theory with Conrado del Campo in Madrid and with Gédalge in Paris. At the same time, he perfected his guitar playing; formed a trio, Iberia, and traveled in Europe playing Spanish popular music. He spent his declining years in Madrid. In collaboration with his teacher Conrado del Campo, he wrote a successful operetta *El Avapiés* (Madrid, 1919) and several zarzuelas: *La Suerte, La Romería, Seguidilla gitana, Castigo de Dios, En Nombre del Rey,* and *Lola se va a los puertos;* also numerous overtures and other orchestral pieces based on popular Spanish motives.

Barrows, John, American horn player; b. Glendale, Calif., Feb. 12, 1913; d. Madison, Wisconsin, Jan. 11, 1974. His first instrument was the euphonium; he studied horn playing at the Eastman School in Rochester (1930-32), theory and orchestration at San Diego State Teachers College (1933-34) and composition (with Donovan and Smith) and cello at Yale Univ. (1934-38). He played horn with the Minneapolis Symph. (1938-42); in New York with the City Opera (1946-49) and City Ballet Orch. (1952-55), and in San Juan with the Casals Festival Orch. (1958-61). Barrows was a member of the New York Woodwind Quintet (1952-61); toured Europe with the Marlboro Festival Orch. He taught horn at Yale Univ. (1957-61), at New york Univ. (1958-61) and at the Univ. of Wisconsin (1961-74). He composed 2 string quartets, a string trio, a wind quintet, and made arrangements for band.

Barrozo Netto, Joaquim Antonio, Brazilian composer; b. Rio de Janeiro, Jan. 30, 1881; d. there, Sept. 1, 1941. He studied with Braga, Nepomuceno and others; appeared as pianist in public at an early age; his compositions, in a mildly romantic manner, are mostly for piano. He enjoyed a fine reputation in Brazil as a teacher.

Barry, Charles Ainslie, English organist, and music editor; b. London, June 10, 1830; d. there, March 21, 1915. He studied with Walmisley; later at the Cologne Cons.; also with Moscheles, Plaidy and Richter at the Leipzig Cons. Returning to England, he wrote for various music magazines; was editor of the *Monthly Musical Record* (1875-79); also served as an annotator for orchestral programs conducted by Hans Richter in England.

Barsanti, Francesco, Italian flutist and composer; b. Lucca, c. 1690; d. 1772. He was flutist and, later, oboist at the Italian opera in London; lived in Scotland for a time, and was engaged (1750) as a viola player in London.
WORKS: 6 overtures; 12 violin concertos; 6 flute solos with bass; 6 sonatas for 2 violins with bass; 6 antiphons in Palestrina style; numerous pieces for various instruments. He published *A Collection of old Scots Tunes* (Edinburgh, 1742).
BIBLIOGRAPHY: Henry Farmer, *A History of Music in Scotland* (London, 1947).

Barshai, Rudolf, Soviet conductor; b. Labinskaya, near Krasnodar, Sept. 28, 1924. He studied viola at the Moscow Cons., graduating in 1948. In 1956 he organized the Moscow Chamber Orch., which became extremely successful, not only in Russia, but also abroad; he made tours with it in Western Europe, the U.S. and Australia. In 1977 he emigrated to Israel.

Barsotti, Tommaso Gasparo Fortunato, Italian music teacher; b. Florence, Sept. 4, 1786; d. Marseilles, April, 1868. He founded the Free School of Music in Marseilles (1821), and was its director until 1852; wrote a number of pieces for piano and voice; published a *Méthode de Musique* (1828).

Bárta, Lubor, Czech composer; b. Lubná, Aug. 8, 1928; d. Prague, Nov. 5, 1972. He studied with Řídký at the Prague Academy of Musical Arts (1948-52). His music presents an effective amalgam of modernistic procedures, influenced by Bartók in its rhythm, by Stravinsky in its meters, and by Hindemith in its neoclassical harmony.
WORKS: 2 violin concertos (1952, 1970); 3 symphonies (1955; *The Bitter Summer,* 1969; 1972); Concerto for Chamber Orchestra (1956); Viola Concerto (1957); *Dramatic Suite* for orch. (1958); Piano Concerto (1958-59); *From East Bohemia,* symph. suite (1961); *Concertante Overture* (1964); *Ludi* for 8 winds and string orch. (1964); *Musica Romantica* for strings (1971); 2 cantatas: *Komsomol* (1951) and *Song of the New Age,* inspired by space flight (1962); 2 violin sonatas (1949, 1959); 2 wind quintets (Divertimento, 1949; 1969); 3 string quartets (1950, 1957, 1967); Piano Trio (1955) Trombone Sonatina (1956); Clarinet Sonata (1958); *Ballad and Burlesque* for cello and piano (1963); Concertino for Trombone and Piano (1964); Solo Guitar Sonata (1965); *4 Pieces* for Violin and Guitar (1966); Flute Sonata (1966); *Fragments* for clarinet and piano (1967); *Amoroso* for horn and piano (1970);

Cello Sonata (1971); Variations for Piano (1948); 3 piano sonatas (1956, 1961, 1971); Harpsichord Sonata (1967); songs.

Bartay, Andreas, Hungarian composer; b. in Széplak, April 7, 1799; d. in Mainz, Oct. 4, 1854. He began his career as a civic servant. At the same time he was engaged in collecting Hungarian folk songs and became interested in music in general. In 1829 he became a director of the first Pest singing academy; in 1834 he published one of the earliest collections of Hungarian folksongs and also a Hungarian book on music theory, *Magyar Apollo* (1834). A militant patriot, he participated in the Hungarian struggle for independence of 1848; after its defeat he emigrated to France and eventually to Germany. He wrote three operas: *Aurelia oder das Weib am Konradstein* (Pest, Dec. 16, 1837); *Csel* (*The Ruse*: Pest, April 29, 1839); *A magyarok Nápolyban* (*The Hungarians in Naples;* unperformed).

Bartay, Ede, Hungarian folksong collector; son of **Andreas Bartay;** b. Budapest, Oct. 6, 1825; d. there, Aug. 31, 1901. He studied law and music and was for many years a practicing piano teacher. In 1876 he was appointed director of the National Conservatory in Budapest, a post which he held until his death. In 1863 he founded the Hungarian Pension Fund for Musicians. Like his father, he was a Hungarian patriot. After the defeat of the Hungarian Revolution of 1848 he remained in Budapest dedicating himself to collecting authentic Hungarian folksongs and dances. He also wrote a symphony, an overture *Pericles* and many piano pieces.

Bartels, Wolfgang von, German composer; b. Hamburg, July 21, 1883; d. Munich, April 19, 1938. He studied with Beer-Walbrunn in Munich and with Gédalge in Paris; then became a music critic in Munich. His early works show impressionist influences; later he adopted an eclectic style.
WORKS: melodramas, *The Little Dream,* after Galsworthy (Manchester, 1911); *Li-I-Lan* (Kassel, 1918); song cycles (*Li-Tai-Pe, Baltic Songs, Minnesänge);* Violin Concerto; Viola Concerto, etc.

Barth, Christian Samuel, German oboist and composer; b. Glauchau, Jan. 13, 1735; d. Copenhagen, July 8, 1809. He was a student at the Thomasschule in Leipzig at the time of Bach; played the oboe in various court orchestras: in Rudolfstadt (1753); Weimar (1762); Hanover (1768) and Kassel (1772). In 1786 he joined the court chapel at Copenhagen where he remained until his death. Although he wrote a great number of instrumental works, particularly for the oboe, most of them remain in manuscript.

Barth, Hans, pianist and composer; b. Leipzig, June 25, 1897; d. Jacksonville, Florida, Dec. 9, 1956. When a small child, he won a scholarship at the Leipzig Cons. and studied under Carl Reinecke; came to the U.S. in 1907, but made frequent trips to Germany. His meeting with Busoni inspired him to experiment with new scales; with the aid of George L. Weitz, he perfected a portable quarter-tone piano (1928), on which he played in Carnegie Hall (Feb. 3, 1930); composed a piano concerto for this instrument, with a string orchestra also tuned in quarter-tones (played by him with Stokowski and the Philadelphia Orch., March 28, 1930). Other works using quarter-tones: Suite for Strings, Brass and Kettledrums; Piano Quintet; also a piano concerto for normal tuning (1928) and two piano sonatas; an operetta *Miragia* (1938); a piano manual *Technic* (1935); various essays, etc.

Barth, Karl Heinrich, German pianist and teacher; b. Pillau, near Königsberg, July 12, 1847; d. Berlin, Dec. 23, 1922. He was a pupil of Hans von Bülow in Berlin; also studied with Bronsart and Tausig. He became teacher at Stern Cons., Berlin, in 1868; then at the Hochschule für Musik (1871); established, with De Ahna and Hausmann, the Barth Trio, which enjoyed considerable success.

Barth, Richard, German left-handed violin virtuoso; b. Grosswanzleben, June 5, 1850; d. Marburg, Dec. 25, 1923. He studied with Joachim in Hannover; attracted considerable attention when he gave concerts using the left hand for the bow; was also conductor in Münster, Krefeld and Hamburg. He wrote chamber music in the style of Brahms; edited the correspondence between Brahms and J. O. Grimm (1908); was author of *Johannes Brahms und seine Musik* (1904).
BIBLIOGRAPHY: E. Deggeller-Engelke, *Richard Barth* (Marburg, 1949).

Bartha, Dénes, Hungarian musicologist; b. Budapest, Oct. 2, 1908. He studied musicology at the University of Berlin (1926–30) with Blume, Sachs, Hornbostel and Schering; received his doctorate with the thesis *Benedictus Ducis und Appenzeller* (Wolfenbüttel, 1930). Returning to Budapest he was active as lecturer at the Univ. there and as a music critic. He was visiting professor at Smith College (1964), Harvard Univ. summer school (1964–65), Cornell Univ. (1965–66).
WRITINGS: *Lehrbuch der Musikgeschichte* (Budapest, 1935; in Hungarian); *Franz Liszt* (Leipzig, 1936; in German); *Beethoven* (Budapest, 1939; in Hungarian); *Die ungarische Musik* (with Kodály, Budapest, 1943); *Anthologie der Musikgeschichte* (Budapest, 1948); *J. S. Bach* (Budapest, 1956); *Haydn als Opernkapellmeister* (with L. Somfai; Budapest-Mainz, 1960); edited *Zenei Lexikon* (3 vols., Budapest, 1965).

Barthe, Grat-Norbert, French composer; b. Bayonne, June 7, 1828; d. Asnières (Seine), Aug. 13, 1898. He was a pupil of Leborne at the Paris Cons.; won the Grand Prix de Rome (1854) with the cantata *Francesca da Rimini;* wrote the operas *Don Carlos* and *La Fiancée d'Abydos;* an oratorio, *Judith;* etc.

Barthélémon, François-Hippolyte, French violinist and composer; b. Bordeaux, July 27, 1741; d. London, July 20, 1808. His father was French and his mother Irish. He held posts as violinist in various theater orchestras in London; became intimately acquainted with Haydn during Haydn's London visit in 1792. He was greatly praised as a violinist; Burney speaks of his tone as being "truly vocal." Barthélémon wrote mostly for the stage; among his operas, the most notable are *Pelopida* (London, May 24, 1766); *The Judgement of Paris* (London, Aug. 24, 1768); *Le Fleuve Scamandre* (Paris, Dec. 22, 1768); *The Maid of the Oaks* (London, Nov. 5, 1774); *Belphegor* (London, March 16, 1778). In addition he wrote a violin concerto; 2 sets of duos for violins; 6 string quartets; catches and glees to English words (many of them published). He was married to Mary Young, a descendant of Anthony Young; his daughter contributed a biographical edition (London, 1827) of selections from Barthélémon's oratorio, *Jefte in Masfa.*

Bartholomée, Pierre, Belgian composer; b. Brussels, Aug. 5, 1937. He studied with Louel, Souffrian and Stekke at the Royal Cons. in Brussels (1952–57) and privately with Pousseur and Boulez. In 1960 he founded in Brussels an instrumental ensemble *Musiques Nouvelles.*
WORKS: *Chanson* for solo cello (1964); *Cantate aux Alentours* for voices, instruments and live electronics (1966); *La Ténèbre souveraine* for soloists, double chorus and orch. (1967); *Tombeau de Marin* for violin, 2 violas da gamba and harpsichord (1967); *Premier alentour* for flute, and 2 violas da gamba (1967); *Catalogue* for 4 harps (1968); *Deuxième alentour: "Cueillir"* for mezzo-soprano, piano and percussion (1969); *Harmonique* for orch. (1970); *Fancy I* for solo harp and *Fancy II* for instrumental group (1974–75; can be played together under the title *Sonata quasi una fantasia*).

Bartholomew, Marshall, American choral conductor; b. Belleville, Illinois, March 3, 1885; d. Guilford, Connecticut, April 16, 1978. He studied at Yale University (B. A. 1907) with Horatio Parker and David Stanley Smith, and later in Berlin. Returning to America, he devoted himself mainly to choral conducting and arranging. In 1921 he founded the Yale Glee Club, which he conducted until 1928, and again from 1939–48. He publ. choral arrangements of American folk music; the *Yale Glee Club Series* for male voices (32 numbers); *The Yale Song Book 250th Anniversary Edition* (N.Y., 1953); *Mountain Songs of North Carolina;* various songs for solo voice and piano; *100 Original Songs for Young Voices* (educational).

Bartholomew, William, English violinist, writer and painter; b. London, 1793; d. there, Aug. 18, 1867. A versatile artisan, he was proficient in chemistry, painting and languages. He was a friend of Mendelssohn and translated the texts of his oratorios (including *Elijah*) into English; also wrote the English text for Spohr's *Jessonda,* etc. During the last years of his life he was incapacitated by paralysis.

Bartlett, Ethel, English pianist; b. Epping Forest, June 6, 1896; d. Los Angeles, April 17, 1978. She studied with Matthay; specialized as piano duet player with her husband, **Rae Robertson**; made annual tours in Europe and the U.S.

Bartlett, Homer Newton, American pianist, organist and composer; b. Olive, N.Y., Dec. 28, 1845; d. Hoboken, N.J., April 3, 1920. He studied with Max Braun and Jacobsen; was organist at the Madison Avenue Baptist Church, N.Y., for 31 years. He was one of the founders of the American Guild of Organists. His published works include a cantata, *The Last Chieftain* (Boston, Jan. 29, 1891); a sextet for flute and strings; quartets, anthems, carols, etc.; about 80 songs and piano pieces. The following are in manuscript: opera, *La Vallière;* unfinished Japanese opera *Hinotito;* oratorio, *Samuel;* symph. poem, *Apollo;* a violin concerto; a cello concerto; etc. His first opus number, a *Grand Polka de Concert,* was very popular.

Bartmuss, Richard, German organist and composer; b. Schleesen, Dec. 23, 1859; d. Dessau, Dec. 25, 1910. He studied with Grell and Löschhorn; in 1885 became court organist in Dessau. He wrote numerous organ works that enjoyed considerable popularity, among them 2 organ concertos, 4 sonatas, 2 chorale-fantasias, etc.; also an oratorio *Der Tag der Pfingsten,* a cantata *Die Apostel in Philippi,* motets and songs. His sacred work *Liturgische Vespern* represents a partial formulation of his attempt to modernize the Lutheran musical service.

Bartók, Béla, great Hungarian composer; b. Nagyszentmiklós, Transylvania, March 25, 1881; d. New York, Sept. 26, 1945. His father was a school teacher; his mother was a proficient pianist, and he received his first piano lessons from her. He began playing piano in public at a very early age. In 1894 the family moved to Pressburg, where he took lessons with László Erkel, son of the famous Hungarian opera composer. In 1899 he enrolled at the Royal Academy of Music in Budapest, where he studied piano with István Thomán and composition with Hans Koessler. He began to compose in the style of Brahms, but soon became interested in exploring the resources of national folk music, which included not only Hungarian melorhythms, but also elements of other ethnic strains in his native Transylvania, Rumanian and Slavonic. He formed a cultural friendship with Zoltán Kodály, and together they traveled through the land collecting folk songs, which they published in 1906. In 1907 Bartók was appointed piano instructor at the Royal Academy of Music, and after the end of World War I he was a member of the musical directorate with Dohnányi and Kodály. Although a brilliant pianist, he limited his concert programs mainly to his own compositions; he also gave concerts playing works for 2 pianos with his second wife **Ditta Pásztory.** In his own compositions he soon began to feel the fascination of tonal colors and Impressionistic harmonies as cultivated by Debussy and other French Impressionists. The basic texture of his music remained true to tonality, which he expanded to polytonal structures and unremittingly chordal combinations; he also exploited the extreme registers of the piano keyboard, often in the form of tone clusters, or pitchless drum-beats. He cultivated strong asymmetrical rhythmic figures, often suggesting the modalities of Slavic folk music; these usages imparted an acrid coloring to his music. The melodic line of his works often veers towards atonality in its chromatic involutions; in some instances he employed melodic figures comprising the 12 different notes of the chromatic scale; however, he never adopted the integral techniques of the 12-tone method. Bartók made his first American tour, as a pianist playing his own works in 1927, then returned to Hungary, where he continued to teach and compose music. In the fall of 1940 he went to America where he remained until his death from leukemia. His last completed score, *Concerto for Orch.,* commissioned by Koussevitzky, proved to be his most popular work. His Third Piano Concerto was virtually completed at the time of his death except for the last 17 bars, which were arranged and orchestrated by his pupil Tibor Serly. Throughout his life, even during his last years in America, Bartók constantly experienced financial difficulties, and complained bitterly of his inability to support himself and his family. Ironically, performances and recordings of his works increased enormously after his death, and the value of his estate reached a considerable sum of money. Posthumous honors were also many; Hungary issued a series of stamps with Bartók's image, and a street in Budapest was named Bartók Street.

WORKS: *Kossuth,* symph. poem (Budapest, Jan. 13, 1904); *Scherzo* for orch. (Budapest, Feb. 29, 1904); *Rhapsody for Piano* (1904; also with orch.); Suite No. 1 for Orch. (1905); *20 Hungarian Folksongs* (1906); Suite No. 2 for Orch. (1907; revised 1943); *14 Bagatelles for Piano* (1908); *2 Elegies for Piano* (1908); *2 Rumanian Dances for Piano* (1909); String Quartet No. 1 (1910); *7 Sketches for Piano* (1910; revised 1945); *Deux images* for orch. (1910; Budapest, Feb. 26, 1913); *3 Burlesques for Piano* (1910); *The Castle of Duke Bluebeard,* opera in 1 act (1911; Budapest, May 24, 1918); *Allegro barbaro* for piano (1911; very popular); *4 Pieces* for orch. (1912); *The Wooden Prince,* ballet in 1 act (Budapest, May 12, 1917); String Quartet No. 2 (1917); *3 Etudes for Piano* (1918); *The Miraculous Mandarin,* ballet (1919; Cologne, Nov. 27, 1926); Violin Sonata No. 1 (1921); Violin Sonata No. 2 (1922); *Dance Suite* for orch. (1923); Piano Sonata (1926); Piano Concerto No. 1 (Frankfurt, July 1, 1927, composer as soloist); String Quartet No. 3 (1927); *2 Rhapsodies* for Violin and Piano (1928); String Quartet No. 4 (1928); *Cantata Profana* (BBC, London, May 25, 1934); Piano Concerto No. 2 (1931; Frankfurt, Jan. 23, 1933); String Quartet No. 5 (1934); *Music for String Instruments, Percussion and Celesta* (Basel, Jan. 21, 1937; one of Bartók's most successful works); Sonata for 2 Pianos and Percussion (Basel, Jan. 16, 1938; transcribed as Concerto for 2 Pianos and Orch., first performed in this version in London, Nov. 14, 1942); *Mikrokosmos,* 153 progressive pieces for piano (1926–37; published in 6 vols.; a unique attempt to write simply in a modern idiom with varying meters and dissonant counterpoint); *Contrasts* for violin, clarinet and piano (1938); Violin Concerto (Amsterdam, April 23, 1939; has become a standard piece in the modern repertory); Divertimento for String Orch. (Basel, June 11, 1940); String Quartet No. 6 (1939); Concerto for Orch. (commissioned by Koussevitzky; performed by him, Boston, Dec. 1, 1944; highly successful); Sonata for Solo Violin (1944); Piano Concerto No. 3 (1945; posthumous, Philadelphia, Feb. 8, 1946); Viola Concerto (1945; unfinished; orchestrated by Tibor Serly; first performed Minneapolis, Dec. 2, 1949). The manuscript of an early Violin Concerto, composed in 1908, came to light in 1958, and was first performed in Basel on May 30, 1958. In addition to these Bartók made numerous arrangements of folksongs and dances, of which a set of Rumanian dances, available in various instrumental transcriptions, is particularly popular; further to be noted are: *40 Hungarian Folksongs; 15 Hungarian Peasant Songs; 9 Slovak Folksongs; 8 Improvisations on Hungarian Peasant Songs for Piano*; also arrangements for orch. of many of these songs. Scholarly editions and research publications; *Rumanian Folksongs from the Bihor District* (Bucharest, 1913); *Transylvanian Folksongs* (Budapest, 1923; in Hungarian, French and English; with Kodály); *A magyar népdal* (Budapest, 1924; in German as *Das ungarische Volkslied*, Berlin, 1925; in English as *Hungarian Folk Music*, London, 1931); *Our Folk Music* (Budapest, 1934; in Hungarian, German and French); *Die Melodien der rumänischen Colinde* (Vienna, 1935); *Serbo-Croatian Folk Songs* (with Albert B. Lord; N.Y., 1951); articles in various musical magazines, among them "Hungarian Peasant Music," *Musical Quarterly* (July 1933).

BIBLIOGRAPHY: An entire literature in several languages exists dealing with Bartók's life and music; the most comprehensive biography is by Halsey Stevens, *The Life and Music of Béla Bartók* (N.Y., 1953). Other monographs include E. Haraszti, *Béla Bartók* (Budapest, 1930; in English, 1938); M. Seiber, *The String Quartets of Béla Bartók* (London, 1945); A. Molnár, *The Art of Bartók* (Budapest, 1948, in Hungarian); S. Moreux, *Béla Bartók, sa vie, ses oeuvres, son language* (Paris, 1949; in German, Zürich, 1950; in English, London, 1953); B. Rondi, *Bartók* (Rome 1950); Roswitha Traimer, *Béla Bartóks Kompositionstechnik dargestellt an seinen sechs Streichquartetten* (Regensburg, 1956); R. Pelzoldt, *Béla Bartók's American Years* (Boston, 1958); Willi Reich, ed., *Béla Bartók: Eigene Schriften und Erinnerungen der Freunde* (Basel, 1958); J. Uhde, *Béla Bartók* (Berlin, 1959); *Studia Memoriae Béla Bartók Sacra;* edited by Z. Kodály and L. Lajtha (N.Y., 1959); J. Demény, ed. *Ausgewählte Briefe* (Budapest, 1960; Engl. trans. London, 1971); B. Szabolcsi, *Béla Bartók: Leben und Werk* (Leipzig, 1961); L. Lesznai, *Béla Bartók: sein Leben, seine Werke* (Leipzig, 1961); P. Citron, *Bartók* (Paris, 1963); V. Bator, *The Béla Bartók Archives: History and Catalogue* (N.Y., 1964); F. Bonis, ed. *Béla Bartók. His Life in Pictures* (London, 1964); E. Helm, *Béla Bartók in Selbstzeugnissen und Bilddokumenten* (1965); E. Lendvai, "Duality and Synthesis in the Music of Béla Bartók," in G. Kepes, *Module, Proportion, Symmetry, Rhythm* (N.Y., 1966); *Sesja Bartókowska* (Warsaw, 1967); J. Kárpáti, *Bartók vonósnégyesei* (Budapest, 1967); A. Szöllösy, comp. *Bartók összegyüjtött irásai I* (collected papers; Budapest, 1967); B. Szabolcsi, *Béla Bartók* (Leipzig, 1968); I. Martynov, *Béla Bartók* (Moscow, 1968); J. Demeny, *Bartók, a zongoramüvész* (Budapest, 1968); H. W. Heinsheimer, *Best Regards to Aida* (material on B.'s American travels; N.Y., 1968); T. A. Zielinski, *Bartók* (Krakow, 1969; Zurich, 1973); I. Nestyev, *Béla Bartók* (Moscow, 1969); J. Szego, *Bartók Béla élete* (Budapest, 1969); F. Wesolowski, ed. *Sesja Bartókowska* (Lodz, 1969); J. Ujfalussy, *Bartók Béla* (2d ed., Budapest, 1970; Engl. trans. Boston, 1972); *Béla Bartók: a Complete Catalogue of His Published Works* (London, 1970); P. Petersen, *Die Tonalität im Instrumentalschaffen von Béla Bartók* (Hamburg, 1971); V. Čižik, *Bartóks Briefe in die Slowakei* (Bratislava, 1971); E. Kraus, "Bibliographie und Diskographie: Béla Bartók," *Musik und Bildung* (Oct. 1971); E. Lendvai, *Béla Bartók. An Analysis of His Music* (London, 1971); L. Lesznai, *Bartók* (London, 1972); B. Suchoff, ed. *Béla Bartók's Essays* (B.'s writings on folk music; N.Y., 1977). *Documenta Bartókiana*, a journal devoted to Bartók studies, began publication in Budapest in 1964.

Bartoletti, Bruno, Italian conductor; b. Sesto Fiorentino, June 10, 1926. He studied flute; was flutist in the orchestra of the Maggio Fiorentino; acted as a substitute conductor at these festivals with an instant acclaim, which was an auspicious beginning of his career. He was appointed conductor at the Lyric Opera in Chicago in 1964; in 1965 he became musical director at the Rome Opera; also made frequent appearances at the Teatro Colón in Buenos Aires. He excels equally in the classical Italian opera and the modern repertory; conducted many first performances.

Bartolozzi, Bruno, Italian composer; b. Florence, June 8, 1911. A concert violinist, he turned to composition late in life; studied with Dallapiccola, and followed him along the path of lyric dodecaphony.

WORKS: Concerto for Orch. (1952); *Sentimento del sogno* for soprano and orch. (1954); Concerto for Violin, String Orch. and Harpsichord (San Francisco, Dec. 2, 1957); *Immagine* for women's voices and 17 instruments, to 2 poems by Rilke (1959); String Quartet (1960); *Concertazioni* for oboe and instruments (1966); *Tres recuerdos del cielo* for voice and instruments (1968). He wrote a book, *New Sounds for Woodwind* (in English; London, 1967), demonstrating the possibility of producing simultaneously several pitches on a single woodwind instrument.

Bartoš, František, Czech music critic, editor and composer; b. Brněnec, June 13, 1905; d. Prague, May 21, 1973. He studied composition with Jirák at the Prague Cons. (1921–25), and later with J. B. Foerster (1925–28); wrote music criticism (1931–45); took part in the founding of the annual Prague Spring Festival; was chairman of the editorial committee that arranged for the publication of Dvořák's complete works. He brought out *Mozart in Letters* (Prague, 1937, 1956); *Smetana in Memories and Letters* (Prague, 1939; in English, 1955); *Gustav Mahler's Correspondences* (Prague, 1962).

WORKS: a melodrama *Jaro (Spring,* 1925); String Sextet (1926); 2 string quartets (1928, 1935); *Scherzo* for wind quintet (1932); *Rozhlasová hudba (Radio Music)* for chamber orch. (1936); *Škola žen (The School of Women)*, after Molière, for wind quartet or orch. (1936); Duo for Violin and Viola (1937); *Polka rusticana* for wind trio (1952); several song cycles.

Bartoš, František, Moravian music editor; b. Mlatcová, March 16, 1837; d. there, June 11, 1906. He was a school teacher; published important collections of Moravian folk songs between 1873 and 1901.

Bartoš, Jan Zdeněk, Czech composer; b. Dvůr Králové nad-Labem, June 4, 1908. He played the violin as a youth; then took composition lessons with Otakar Šín and with Jaroslav Křička at the Prague Cons. He earned his living playing in dance orchestras; from 1945 to 1956 he was a member of the Music Section of the Ministry of Education and Culture; in 1958 was appointed teacher of composition at the Prague Cons. In his music he follows the national traditions of the Czech School.

WORKS: the operas *Rýparka (Ripar's Wife,* 1949); *Prokletý zámek (The Accursed Castle,* 1949); *Útok na nebe (The Attack of Heaven,* 1953–54); the operetta, *Je libo ananas? (Do you like pineapples?* 1956); 3 ballets: *Hanuman* (1941); *Mirella* (1956); and *Král manéže (King of the Manege,* 1963); 5 cantatas: *Běžec míru (Peace Runner,* 1948); *Krásná země (Beautiful Land,* 1949); *Poselství (The Message,* 1960); *Country of Comenius* (1961); and *Tractatus pacis* (1973); 2 *Feuilletons* for orch. (1935); *Dvůr Králové* for string orch. (1941); Concertino for Bassoon, and Orch. or Piano (1943); *Song of St. Matthias,* symph. poem (1945); 5 symphonies: No. 1 (1949–52), No. 2, *da camera* (1956); No. 3, *Giocosa,* for strings (1964–65); No. 4, *Concertante,* for oboe d'amore and string orch. (1968); No. 5 for wind orch. (1973–74); *Fronta (The Front),* suite for orch. (1950); *Capriccio* for cello and orch. (1956); *Events of a Single Day* for orch. (1957); *Intermezzo* for orch. (1961); *Concerto da camera* for oboe and strings (1963); 2 viola concertos (1963, 1970); Fantasy for Flute and Orch. (1964); Inventions for Bass Clarinet and String Orch. (1966); *Sonnets of Prague* for narrator, tenor, harp and string orch. (1966); Concerto for Accordion and String Orch. (1966); Horn Concerto (1967); Concerto for Violin and String Orch. (1970); Cello Sonata (1938); 2 nonets (1939, 1974); 9 string quartets (1940; 1946; 1948; 1951; 1952; 1956; 1960; 1963; 1970); *Partita* for solo viola (1944); 3 wind quintets (1946–63); Quintet for Flute, Harp, Viola, Cello and Guitar (1947); Viola Sonatina (1947); *Elegy and Rondino* for horn and piano (1947–48); 12 divertimentos for various combinations of instruments (1956–73); Trio for Violin, Viola and Harp (1961); Double-Bass Sonata (1962); Preludes for Flute and Piano (1963); *Suite Concertante* for viola, double bass and 9 wind instruments (1964); String Trio (1967); Fantasy for Violin and Piano (1967); 3 piano trios (1968, 1969, 1971); 2 piano sonatas (1953, 1959); choruses; songs.

Bartoš, Josef, Czech writer on music; b. Vysoké Myto, March 4, 1887; d. Prague, Oct. 27, 1952. He studied with Hostinsky at the Univ. of Prague (1905–09); was active as a teacher and music critic. He published valuable monographs on Dvořák (1913), Fibich (1914; new edition, 1941), and Otakar Ostrčil (1936); also an important work on the National Opera of Prague (1938).

Barvík, Miroslav, Czech composer; b. Luzice, Sept. 14, 1919. He studied with Kaprál at the Brno Cons. and with Novák in Prague. In 1948 he was appointed instructor in composition at the Prague Cons.; in 1966 was named director of the state theater in Brno. In his works he hews to the prescriptions of Socialist Real-ism, which advocates musical immediate accessability and national reference. In this style he wrote politico-patriotic cantatas *Song of the Fatherland* (1944) and *Thanks to the Soviet Union* (1946). His choral work *Hands Off Korea,* directed against the participation of non-Korean combatants in the Korean Civil War, also belongs to the category of political music. He published a book, *Music of the Revolutionaries* (Prague, 1964).

Bary, Alfred Erwin von, opera singer; b. La Valetta, Malta, Jan. 18, 1873; d. Munich, Sept. 13, 1926. He studied medicine at Munich Univ. (Dr. med., 1898); later developed a dramatic tenor voice, and was engaged at the Dresden Court Opera (1902–12); then at the Court Opera in Munich; sang the roles of Parsifal, Siegmund and Tristan at Bayreuth.

Barzin, Leon, Belgian-American conductor; b. Brussels, Nov. 27, 1900. He was brought to the U.S. in 1902; his father played viola in the orchestra of the Metropolitan Opera; his mother was a ballerina. He studied violin with his father and later in Belgium with Eugène Ysaÿe. In 1925 he was appointed first viola player of the New York Philharmonic, retaining his post until 1929, when he was engaged as assistant conductor of the American Orchestral Society, which was reorganized in 1930 as the National Orchestral Association, with Barzin as principal conductor and musical director; he continued in this capacity until 1959, and again from 1970 till 1976. He was also music director of the Ballet Society and New York City Ballet (1948–58); from 1958 till 1960 he conducted concerts of the Association des Concerts Pasdeloup in Paris, France; and was at the same time instructor at the Scola Cantorum there. He received the order of the légion d'Honneur in 1960. Barzin was particularly successful in training semi-professional and student orchestras; especially with the National Orchestral Association, he attained remarkable results.

Barzun, Jacques, eminent French-American educator and author of books on music; b. Créteil, Nov. 30, 1907. He came to America in 1919; studied at Columbia Univ. (A.B., 1927; Ph.D., 1932); became lecturer in History there in 1927, and professor in 1945. He exercised considerable influence on American college education advocating broad reading in various fields rather than narrow specialization. His books concerned with music include *Darwin, Marx, Wagner* (Boston, 1941) and *Berlioz and the Romantic Century* (Boston, 1950; 2 vols. containing exhaustive documentation); published a new translation of *Evenings with the Orchestra* (N.Y., 1956); also wrote a survey, *Music in American Life* (N.Y., 1956).

Bas, Giulio, Italian organist and music editor; b. Venice, April 21, 1874; d. Vobbia, near Genoa, July 27, 1929. He studied in Munich with Rheinberger and in Venice with Bossi; was organist in the churches of Venice and Rome; in 1908 became a teacher at the Milan Cons. He wrote several textbooks on music theory; was a department editor of *Musica d'oggi.* Among his textbooks are *Metodo per l'accompagna-*

mento del canto gregoriano (Turin, 1920); and *Manuale di canto gregoriano* (Dusseldorf, 1910).

Baselt, Fritz (Friedrich Gustav Otto), composer; b. Öls, Silesia, May 26, 1863; d. Frankfurt, Nov. 12, 1931. He studied with Emil Kohler in Breslau and with Ludwig Bussler in Berlin; was musician, music-dealer, composer, teacher and conductor in Breslau, Essen and Nuremberg; after 1894 he settled in Frankfurt-on-Main, where he conducted the Philharmonischer Verein and the Frankfurt Sängervereinigung. He wrote many light operas: *Der Fürst von Sevilla* (Nuremberg, 1888); *Don Alvaro* (Ansbach, 1892); *Der Sohn des Peliden* (Kassel, 1893); *Die Annaliese* (Kassel, 1896); *Die Musketiere im Damenstift* (Kassel, 1896); *Die Circusfee* (Berlin, 1897); also 2 ballets: *Die Altweibermühle* (Frankfurt, 1906), and *Rokoko* (Frankfurt, 1907); some 100 male choruses; many instrumental pieces; songs.

Basevi, Abramo, Italian composer and writer on music; b. Leghorn, Dec. 29, 1818; d. Florence, Nov. 25, 1885. His 2 operas, *Romilda ed Ezzelino* (Florence, Aug. 11, 1840) and *Enrico Odoardo* (Florence, 1847), were unsuccessful, and he turned to musical journalism; founded the periodical *Harmonia;* publ. a *Studio sulle opere di G. Verdi* (1859); *Studi sul armonia* (1865); *Compendio della storia della musica* (1866); etc.

Bashmakov, Leonid, Finnish composer of Russian extraction; b. Terijoki, April 4, 1927. He studied composition and conducting at the Sibelius Academy (1947–54). In 1960 he became a theater conductor in Tampere.
WORKS: Suite for Marimba and String Quartet (1951); *Fantastic Pictures* for orch. (1953); 2 symphonies (1963, 1965); Violin Concerto (1966); 2 violin sonatinas (1968–69); *Canzona I* for chorus and orch. (1969; Helsinki, Nov. 23, 1971); Octet for Piano, Winds and Brass (1970); Sonata for Percussion (1970); *4 Bagatelles for Flute and Percussion* (1971); *Dialogues* for organ and percussion (1971); *Sinfonietta* (1971); *Canzona II* for soprano and orch. (1971); Overture for wind orch. (1971); Divertimento for Oboe and Strings (1971); Sonata for Viola, Cello and Piano (1971); String Quartet (1972); Fantasia for 3 Different Flutes, One Player (1972); Cello Concerto (1972); Flute Concerto (1973); music for plays and films.

Basie, (Count) (real name **William**), black American bandleader, pianist and composer; b. Red Bank, N.J., Aug. 21, 1904. He played piano as a child; studied organ with Fats Waller; accompanied singers in vaudeville. He organized his own band in Kansas City; in 1936 moved to N.Y.; enlarged his original band, emphasizing the rhythmic element in his arrangements; introduced female ballad singers as soloists. He made a tour of Europe in 1956; played a command performance for the Queen of England during his British tour in 1957. Roulette Records released a two-record set, *The Count Basie Story* (1961), which includes a biographical booklet by Leonard Feather.

Basil (Saint) the Great, b. 329 at Caesarea, Cappadocia; d. there in 379. He was a bishop in Caesarea; is reputed to have introduced congregational (antiphonal) singing into the Eastern Church, thus being the forerunner of St. Ambrose in the Western Church.

Basili, Francesco, Italian composer; b. Loreto, Feb. 3, 1767; d. Rome, March 25, 1850. He studied with his father Andrea Basili and later with Jannaconi. He was active as conductor in various provincial Italian theaters, and himself composed 14 operas and a number of "dramatic oratorios". In 1837 he became conductor at St. Peter's Cathedral in Rome. He wrote a great deal of sacred music, and also some symphonic pieces.

Basiola, Mario, Italian baritone; b. Annico, July 12, 1892; d. there, Jan. 3, 1965. He studied in Rome; was engaged at the Metropolitan Opera in N.Y. (1925–32); at La Scala in Milan and at Rome (1933–38); also sang at Covent Garden, London (1939) and in Australia (1949); then returned to Italy and was active there as a teacher.

Basner, Veniamin, Soviet composer; b. Yaroslavl, Jan. 1, 1925. He studied violin at the Leningrad Cons., graduating in 1949. As a composer, he is best known for lyric songs and film music. His works include 5 string quartets (1948, 1949, 1960, 1969, 1975), a symphony (1958); Violin Concerto (1966); Sinfonietta for flute and strings (1974); *Poem about the Siege of Leningrad* for orch. (1957); *Three Musketeers,* ballet (1964); *Goya,* monologue for bass voice, English horn, bassoon and piano (1965); a choral symphony, *The Eternal Fire* (1971) and 3 musical comedies: *The Polar Star* (1966), *A Heroine is Sought* (1968) and *The Southern Cross* (1970).

Bassani, Geronimo, Italian singer and composer; b. Padua, late in the 17th century. He studied with Lotti; was a fine contrapuntist, singer and singing teacher; produced 2 operas at Venice: *Bertoldo* (1718) and *Amor per forza* (1721); also wrote Masses, motets and vespers.

Bassani (Bassano), Giovanni, Italian composer, singer and violinist. He was a singer at San Marco, Venice, in 1585; singing teacher at the Seminary of San Marco (1595); first violin soloist at the Chapel of the Basilica (1615). The following instrumental works by him are extant: *Fantasie a tre voci per cantar e sonar* (1585); *Il fiore dei capricci musicali a 4 voci* (1588); *Motetti, madrigali e canzoni francesi di diversi auttori . . . diminuiti per sonar con ogni sorti di stromenti* (1591; reprinted in 1602 in an arrangement for one voice with organ ad lib.; containing works of Clemens non Papa, Créquillon, Palestrina and others; the term *diminuiti* refers to ornamentation of the original vocal compositions); 2 volumes of *Motetti per concerti ecclesiastici* for 5–12 voices (1598–99); a volume of *Canzonette* for 4 voices (1587); etc.

Bassani (Bassano, Bassiani), Giovanni Battista, Italian composer, organist and violinist; b. Padua c. 1647; d. Bergamo, Oct. 1, 1716. He studied in Venice with

Castrovillari; was maestro di cappella to the Duke of Mirandola (1678); at the chapel of the Accademia della Morte in Ferrara (1667); at the cathedral of Ferrara (1688) and at the Basilica Maria in Bergamo (1712), where he remained until his death. He was also a member of the Accademia dei Filarmonici in Bologna from 1677. His extant works include the following operas: *Amorosa Preda di Paride* (Bologna, 1683); *Falaride tiranno d'Agrigento* (1684); *Alarico re de Goti* (Ferrara, 1685); *Ginevra, infante di Scozia* (Ferrara, 1690); oratorios: *La morte delusa* (1686); *Giona* (1689); *Nella luna celestiale* (1687); *Il Conte di Bacheville* (1696); *Mosè risorto dalle acque* (1698); *Gl'Impegni del divino amore* (1703); *Il trionfo della fede* (1707). He also wrote numerous Masses, and other sacred music. Of his instrumental works, several suites and trio sonatas are reprinted in Torchi's *L'Arte musicale in Italia* (vol. VII) and in J. W. Wasielewski's *Instrumentalsätze vom Ende des XVI. bis Ende des XVII. Jahrhunderts* (1874). A cantata is included in Riemann's *Kantaten-Frühling* (vol. II); some vocal works are published by G. F. Malipiero in *Classici della musica italiana*.

BIBLIOGRAPHY: J. W. Wasielewski, *Die Violine und ihre Meister* (1883); A. Moser, *Geschichte des Violinspiels* (1923); A Schering, *Geschichte des Oratoriums* (1911); F. Pasini, "Notes sur la vie de G. B. Bassani," *Sammelbände der Internationalen Musik-Gesellschaft* 7 (1906); R. Haselbach, *G. B. Bassani* (Kassel, 1955).

Bassett, Leslie, American composer; b. Hanford, Calif., Jan. 22, 1923. He studied piano; played the trombone in jazz combos; was trombonist during his military service, playing in the 13th Armored Division Band. He then enrolled in Fresno, Calif., State College (B.A., 1947); later studied composition with Ross Lee Finney at the Univ. of Michigan (M.M., 1949; Dr.M., 1956); also took private lessons with Arthur Honegger and Nadia Boulanger in Paris in 1950. In 1952 he was appointed to the faculty of the Univ. of Michigan. He held the American Prix de Rome in 1961–63, and National Institute of Arts and Letters Award in 1964. In 1966 he received the Pulitzer Prize in Music for his *Variations for Orchestra.* He held a Guggenheim fellowship in 1973. In his music, he pursues the ideal of structural logic within the judicial limits of the modern school of composition, with some serial elements discernible in his use of thematic rhythms and motivic periodicity. His works include Suite in G for orch. (Fresno, Dec. 3, 1946); *Five Movements* for orch. (Rome, July 5, 1962); Variations for Orchestra (Rome, July 6, 1963; Philadelphia, Oct. 22, 1965; received the Pulitzer Prize in 1966); *Designs, Images and Textures* for band (1964); *Elaborations* for piano (1966); *Colloquy* for orch. (Fresno, May 23, 1969); *Collect* for chorus and electronic tape (1969); *Music for Saxophone and Piano* (1969); *The Jade Garden* for voice and piano (1973); *Echoes from an Invisible World* for orch. (Philadelphia, Feb. 27, 1975); *Wind Music* for wind sextet (1976).

Bassevi, Giacomo. See **Cervetto, Giacomo.**

Bassford, William Kipp, American pianist, b. New York, April 23, 1839; d. there, Dec. 22, 1902. He was a church organist in New York; also gave piano concerts; composed an opera *Cassilda.* He completed Vincent Wallace's unfinished opera, *Estrella.*

Bassi, Amadeo (Vittorio), Italian operatic tenor; b. Florence, July 20, 1874; d. there, January 14, 1949. His sole teacher was the Marchese Pavese Negri in Florence, where he made his debut in *Ruy Blas* (1899). He toured South America (1902–07); sang at the Manhattan Opera House, N.Y. (1906–08) and at the Chicago Opera Co. (1910–12). His repertoire included more than 50 operas, mostly Italian; he created the following roles: Angel Clare in d'Erlanger's *Tess;* Federico in Franchetti's *Germania;* Giorgio in Mascagni's *L'Amica;* and Lionello in Cilea's *Gloria.*

Bassi, Luigi, Italian opera baritone; b. Pesaro, Sept. 4, 1766; d. Dresden, Sept. 13, 1825. He studied with Pietro Morandi of Bologna; made his debut in Pesaro at the age of thirteen; he then sang in Florence; went to Prague in 1784, where he soon became greatly appreciated. Mozart wrote the part of Don Giovanni for him and heeded his advice in matters of detail. Bassi was in Vienna from 1806–14; then briefly in Prague; in 1815 he joined an Italian opera company in Dresden.

Bastiaans, Johannes Gijsbertus, Dutch organist; b. Wilp, Oct. 31, 1812; d. Haarlem, Feb. 16, 1875. He was a pupil of Schneider at Dessau, and Mendelssohn at Leipzig; was organist at the Zuiderkerk, Amsterdam, and at St. Bavo's, Haarlem (1868); succeeded at St. Bavo's by his son, **Johann** (1854–1885). Bastiaans published a book of chorales and numerous songs.

Baston, Josquin, Flemish composer of the mid-16th century. It is known that from May 1552 to Oct. 1553 he was at the Polish Court of Sigismond Augustus at Cracow. Motets and chansons by Baston appeared between 1542 and 1559 in various collections: Susato's *Het ierste musyck boexken* (Antwerp, 1551); Salbinger's *Concertus* (Augsburg, 1545); also in Louvain (published by Phalèse). His *Lament* has 2 middle voices singing the *Requiem aeternam* in canon 6 times while the other voices have fresh parts. See R. van Maldeghem (ed.), *Trésor musical* (1865–93; vol. XII).

Bate, Stanley Richard, English composer; b. Plymouth, Dec. 12, 1911; d. London, Oct. 19, 1959. He studied composition with Vaughan Williams and piano with Arthur Benjamin at the Royal College of Music in London (1931–35); then took courses with Nadia Boulanger in Paris and with Hindemith in Berlin. During World War II he was in Australia; in 1942 he went to the U.S.; in 1945 he was in Brazil and in 1950 he returned to London. On Nov. 7, 1938 he married the Australian-born composer **Peggy Glanville-Hicks** (divorced 1948). He wrote music in a finely structured cosmopolitan manner, making use of modern devices but observing the classical forms and shunning doctrinaire systems. He wrote several ballets, among them *Goyescas* (1937), *Perseus* (1938), and *Cap Over Mill* (1938). He composed 4 symphonies; of these the 3rd

(1940) was performed 14 years after its composition at the Cheltenham Festival, July 14, 1954, with remarkable success. His 4th Symphony was given in London on Nov. 20, 1955. Other works are 3 piano concertos; he was the soloist in his 2nd Piano Concerto which he performed with the N.Y. Philharmonic, conducted by Thomas Beecham on Feb. 8, 1942. He wrote also 2 sinfoniettas, 3 violin concertos, Viola Concerto, Cello Concerto, Harpsichord Concerto, 2 string quartets, Sonata for Recorder and Piano, Violin Sonata, Flute Sonata, Oboe Sonata, 9 piano sonatinas and other piano pieces.

Bates, Joah, British organist; b. Halifax (England), in March (baptized March 8), 1741; d. London, June 8, 1799. He studied organ with Hartley in Rochdale and Wainwright in Manchester; then went to Eton and Cambridge for further education. In 1760 became a tutor of King's College in Cambridge; received his B.A. in 1764 and M.A. in 1767. He then went to London where he organized the series known as Concerts of Antient Music (1776); also acted as conductor of the famous Handel Commemoration Festivals (1784–87; 1791).

Bates, William, English composer who flourished in the second half of the 18th century. He wrote popular English operas in the ballad opera style. His most popular work was *Flora or Hob in the Well,* which he wrote and arranged in 1760, using 7 of John Hippisley's songs from the 1729 *Flora or Hob's Opera,* together with 8 new songs of his own and a new overture. Neither of his works is to be confused with Thomas Doggett's 1711 farce with songs, a forerunner of the true ballad opera, variously titled *The Country Wake or Hob; or, The Country Wake.* His other stage works are *The Jovial Crew* (1760, altered to *The Ladies Frolick* in 1770); *The Theatrical Candidates* (1775); *The Device, or The Marriage Officer* (1777); *Second Thought is Best* (1778); also a grand opera, *Pharnaces* (London, Nov. 15, 1765).

Bateson, Thomas, English composer; b. in Cheshire County; d. probably in Dublin, in March 1630. He was organist at Chester Cathedral in 1599. In 1609 he became vicar choral and organist of the Cathedral of the Holy Trinity in Dublin. He is said to have been the first music graduate of Trinity College, earning his Mus. B. in 1612 and his M.A. in 1622. As a composer, Bateson is especially noted for his madrigals, although they are regarded as inferior to those by Morley or Weelkes. In 1604 he published a collection of 29 madrigals for 3 to 6 voices; it included the madrigal *When Oriana walked to take the ayre,* originally intended for publication in Morley's *Triumphs of Oriana.* A second set of 30 madrigals was published in 1618. Both sets are reprinted in *The English Madrigal School* (vols. 21–22), edited by E. H. Fellowes.

Bath, Hubert, English composer; b. Barnstaple, Nov. 6, 1883; d. Harefield, April 24, 1945. He studied at the Royal Academy of Music in London; conducted Thomas Quinlan's opera troupe on its world tour in 1913–14. Returning to England he conducted classes in opera at the Guildhall School of Music in London.

As a composer, he showed natural flare for light operas, of which *Bubbles* (Belfast, Nov. 26, 1923) was quite successful. He also wrote a grand opera *Trilby.* He furthermore composed a number of symphonic sketches, several of them on exotic subjects, such as *African Suite;* also 6 cantatas, more than 150 songs, and various pieces of chamber music.

Bathe, William, Irish writer on musical subjects; b. Ireland, April 2, 1564; d. Madrid, June 17, 1614. He was the son of a judge; went to study at Oxford, and remained in England until 1590. He taught mnemonics to Queen Elizabeth and presented her with an Irish harp of his own design. In 1591 he went to Spain; then was in Flanders where he entered the Jesuit order in 1596; was ordained in Padua in 1599; returned to Spain in 1601; was appointed spiritual director of the Irish College in Lisbon in 1604, and lived in Salamanca in 1606 and 1612; eventually went to Madrid. His chief merit as a music theorist lay in fixing definite rules for the placing of accidentals and in changing the system of hexachordal modes to scales based on the octave. He was the author of one of the earliest theoretical works on music, *Introduction to the True Art of Musicke* (London, 1584); also published *A Brief Introduction to the Skill of Song* (London, 1600).
BIBLIOGRAPHY: J. Pulver, "William Bathe," *Musical Times* (Oct. 1934).

Bathori, Jane, French mezzo-soprano; b. Paris, June 14, 1877; d. there, Jan. 21, 1970. After an active operatic career, she devoted herself to the cultivation of modern French music; sang first performances of works by Debussy, Ravel, Satie and Milhaud; gave numerous recitals in England. Returning to Paris, she limited herself to teaching. She published *Conseils sur le chant* (Paris, 1929) and *Sur l'interprétation des mélodies de Claude Debussy* (Paris, 1953).

Batiste, Antoine-Edouard, French organist; b. Paris, March 28, 1820; d. there, Nov. 9, 1876. He studied at the Paris Cons. with Halévy; won 2d Grand Prix de Rome with the cantata *Héloïse de Montfort* (1840); subsequently was organist of St.-Nicolas-des-Champs (1842–54), then of St. Eustache. He composed organ music, piano pieces and songs; also edited the official *Solfèges du Conservatoire* (12 vols.), and published a *Petit solfège harmonique.*

Batistin. See **Stuck, Johann Baptist.**

Batka, Richard, music editor; b. Prague, Dec. 14, 1868; d. Vienna, April 24, 1922. He was trained in the German Univ. in Prague; he went to Vienna, where he became active as music editor and librettist. He published a number of worthwhile monographs on German composers and historical essays, of which *Die Musik in Böhmen* (Berlin, 1906) is of documentary value. He also wrote *Allgemeine Geschichte der Musik* (2 vols., Stuttgart, 1909–11).

Batta, Alexandre, cellist; b. Maastricht, July 9, 1816; d. Versailles, Oct. 8, 1902. He was a pupil of Platel at the Brussels Cons.; settled in Paris (1835); made successful concert tours on the continent; wrote many melodious pieces and transcriptions for cello with piano accompaniment.

Battaille, Charles-Aimable, French bass; b. Nantes, Sept. 30, 1822; d. Paris, May 2, 1872. He was originally a medical student; then studied music; sang at the Opéra-Comique in Paris (1848–57), until a throat disorder ended his public career; taught singing at the Paris Cons. (1851). He published an extensive method of singing in 2 vols.: I. *Nouvelles recherches sur la phonation* (1861); II. *De la physiologie appliquée au mécanisme du chant* (1863).

Battanchon, Félix, French cellist and composer; b. Paris, April 9, 1814; d. there, July, 1893. He studied with Vaslin and Norblin at the Paris Cons.; member of the Grand Opera Orch. (1840). In 1846 he invented, and vainly tried to popularize, a small type of cello called a Baryton.

Batten, Adrian, English organist and composer, b. Salisbury (baptized March 1, 1591); d. London, 1637. He studied at Winchester with the Cathedral organist John Holmes; in 1614 went to London as vicar choral of Westminster Abbey. In 1624 he became vicar choral and organist at St. Paul's Cathedral. A prolific composer, he left 15 services and 47 anthems in manuscript. Some of his pieces are included in Boyce's *Cathedral Music*. A modern reprint of one of his services is included in *The Choir;* several anthems have been published by Novello. Batten also transcribed into organ score numerous sacred choral works, some of which have come down to us only through his transcriptions. His organ book is described in *Tudor Church Music* (1922, vol. II).
BIBLIOGRAPHY: J. B. Clark, "Adrian Batten and John Barnard: Colleagues and Collaborators," *Musica Disciplina* (1968); J. B. Clark and M. Bevan, "New Biographical Facts about Adrian Batten," *Journal of American Musicological Society* (Summer 1970).

Battishill, Jonathan, English organist and composer; b. London, May, 1738; d. Islington, Dec. 10, 1801. He was a chorister in St. Paul's (1747); later apprenticed to William Savage; was deputy organist under Boyce at the Chapel Royal; then harpsichordist at Covent Garden and organist in several London parishes. He wrote an opera with Michael Arne: *Almena* (Drury Lane Theatre, Nov. 2, 1764); a pantomime, *The Rites of Hecate* (1764); many popular anthems, glees and songs.
BIBLIOGRAPHY: J. B. Trend, "Jonathan Battishill," *Music & Letters* (July 1932).

Battista, Vincenzo, Italian composer; b. Naples, Oct. 5, 1823; d. there, Nov. 14, 1873. He studied at the Naples Cons.; wrote 13 operas, eleven of which were produced at Naples (1844–69).

Battistini, Gaudenzio, Italian composer, grandson of Giacomo Battistini; b. Novara, June 30, 1722; d. there, Feb. 25, 1800. He succeeded his father, Giuseppe Battistini, in 1747 as organist of the chapel of San Gaudenzio in Novara, and served for more than 50 years until his death. He wrote numerous church works in a highly developed polyphonic style. A biographical sketch and examples of his music are found in Vito Fedeli, *Le cappelle musicali di Novara* in vol. III of *Istituzioni e monumenti dell' arte musicale italiana* (Milan, 1933).

Battistini, Giacomo, Italian composer; b. 1665; d. Novara, Feb. 5, 1719. He was organist at the Novara Cathedral (1694–1706); then at the church of San Gaudenzio. He is reputed to have been the first to introduce the violoncello into instrumental accompaniment. He composed several masses, motets, organ works; also contributed music to the third act of the drama *Antemio in Roma* (1695; with A. Besozzi and D. Erba). See Vito Fedeli, *Le cappelle musicali di Novara* in vol. III of *Istituzioni e monumenti dell' arte musicale italiana* (Milan, 1933), containing musical illustrations from Battistini's works.

Battistini, Mattia, celebrated Italian baritone; b. Rome, Feb. 27, 1856; d. Collebaccaro, near Rome, Nov. 7, 1928. He first studied medicine at the Univ. of Rome; then began taking singing lessons. He made his debut in Rome in 1878; subsequently appeared at the San Carlo Opera in Naples (1886) and at La Scala in Milan (1888). He then embarked on a worldwide tour, and acquired great popularity in South America, Spain and Russia, and continued his active career until the last months of his life. He was a master of bel canto, with a remarkably expressive high register; was particularly successful in the parts of Rigoletto, Figaro in Rossini's *Barber of Seville,* and Valentin in Gounod's *Faust.*
BIBLIOGRAPHY: G. Fracassini, *Mattia Battistini, profilo artistico* (Milan, 1915); G. Monaldi, *Cantanti celebri* (Rome, 1929); F. Palmegiani, *Mattia Battistini* (Milan, 1948).

Battke, Max, German teacher and writer; b. Schiffuss, near Wandlacken, Sept. 15, 1863; d. Berlin, Oct. 4, 1916. He studied at Königsberg and Berlin, where he later taught at various conservatories. He founded a music seminary in Berlin (1900), which became (1910) the famous "Seminar für Schulgesang." He wrote numerous textbooks on music and methods for voice production; edited (with Humperdinck) collections of folksongs and piano pieces.

Battmann, Jacques-Louis, organist and composer; b. Maasmünster, Alsace, Aug. 25, 1818; d. Dijon, July 7, 1886. He wrote a great quantity of music for the organ and several school manuals on music theory.

Batton, Désiré-Alexandre, French composer; b. Paris, Jan. 2, 1798; d. Versailles, Oct. 15, 1855. He was a pupil of Cherubini at the Paris Cons.; won the Prix de Rome (1816) for his cantata, *La mort d'Adonis;* was inspector of the branch schools of the Cons. from 1842, and teacher of a vocal class at the Cons. from 1849. His most successful opera, *La Marquise de Brinvilliers* (1832), was written jointly with Auber, Hérold and others; his own operas were *La Fenêtre secrète* (Paris, Nov. 17, 1818); *Ethelvina* (1827); and *Le Prisonnier d'état* (1828).

Battu, Pantaléon, French violinist; b. Paris, 1799; d. there, Jan. 17, 1870. He studied with R. Kreutzer at the Paris Cons.; member of the orchestra of the Opéra and the court until his retirement in 1859. He wrote 3 violin concertos; 3 violin duos; etc.

Bätz, Karl, German music editor; b. Sömmerda, March 17, 1851; d. Berlin, 1902. He lived in America (1871–86); then settled in Berlin, where he founded the *Musikinstrumenten-Zeitung* in 1890; published *Die Musikinstrumente der Indianer* (1876); also various pamphlets on instrument-making.

Baudiot, Charles-Nicolas, French cellist; b. Nancy, March 29, 1773; d. Paris, Sept. 26, 1849. He was a pupil of the elder Janson, whom he succeeded as cello professor at the Paris Cons. (1802); from 1816 was first cellist in the royal orchestra; retired in 1832. With Levasseur and Baillot he wrote a cello method which, for a time, was used at the Paris Cons.; also *Instruction pour les compositeurs* (a guide to composers for cello); composed 2 cello concertos; 2 cello concertinos; a great variety of chamber music for cello.

Baudo, Serge, French conductor; b. Marseille, July 16, 1927. He studied at the Paris Cons., conducting with Louis Fourestier, and theory with Jean Gallon and Noël Gallon; received Premier Prix as drummer (1948) and as conductor (1949). He was engaged as pianist and percussion player in the orchestra of the Concerts Lamoureux; then toured as opera conductor. In 1967 he was appointed musical director and conductor of the Orchestre de Paris.

Baudrier, Yves, French composer; b. Paris, Feb. 11, 1906. He was primarily a law student; was mainly autodidact in music. In 1936 he, jointly with Messiaen, Jolivet and Daniel-Lesur, formed a group "La Jeune France," dedicated to the promotion of purely national French music, whether modern or traditional. In 1946 he made a lecture tour in the U.S. He wrote a symph. poem *Eleonora*, after Edgar Allan Poe, a symph. poem *Le Grand Voiler* (1939); a symphony (1945), and a suite for trumpet (1966).

Bauer, Harold, distinguished pianist; b. Kingston-on-Thames, near London, of an English mother and German father, April 28, 1873; d. Miami, March 12, 1951. He studied violin with his father and Adolf Politzer; made his debut as a violinist in London; in 1892 he went to Paris and studied piano for a year with Paderewski; in 1893 made his first tour as a pianist in Russia; gave piano recitals throughout Europe; in 1900 made his U.S. debut with the Boston Symph. Orch.; appeared as soloist with other U.S. orchestras, with eminent chamber music groups, and as a recitalist. He founded the Beethoven Association in New York (1918); was president of the Friends of Music in the Library of Congress, Washington, D.C. Among his writings are: "Self-Portrait of the Artist as a Young Man," *Musical Quarterly* (Oct. 1947); *Harold Bauer, His Book* (N.Y., 1948). He edited works by Schubert and Brahms, and Mussorgsky's *Pictures at an Exhibition*. A considerable corpus of his papers was acquired by the Music Division of the Library of Congress.

Bauer, Marion Eugenie, American composer and writer; b. Walla Walla, Washington, Aug. 15, 1887; d. South Hadley, Massachusetts, Aug. 9, 1955. Her parents were of French extraction; she received her early education from her father who was an amateur musician. She then went to Paris where she took piano lessons with Pugno, and theory with André Gédalge and Nadia Boulanger; also took some lessons with Jean Paul Ertel in Berlin. Returning to America she continued her studies with Henry Holden Huss and others. She was annual lecturer at the summer Chautauqua Institute in 1928 and 1929; from 1933 through 1952 gave lecture recitals each summer; in 1940 joined the faculty at the Institute of Musical Arts in New York. She was a member of the Executive Board of the League of Composers in New York, and had an active teaching career in music history and composition. Her own music oscillates pleasurably between Germanic romanticism and Gallic impressionism. Prudently, she wrote mostly in small forms, and was at her best in her piano pieces; among them were *From New Hampshire Woods* (1921); *Indian Pipes* (1928); *Sun Splendor* (1926; later orchestrated and performed by Stokowski with the New York Philharmonic, Oct. 25, 1947); *Dance Sonata* (1932). Her choral works include *Three Noëls* (1929); *A Garden is a Lovesome Thing* (1938); *The Thinker* (1938) and *China* for chorus with orch. (Worcester Festival, Oct. 12, 1945). She also wrote quite a few pieces of chamber music: String Quartet (1928); *Fantasia quasi una sonata* for violin and piano (1928); Suite for Oboe and Clarinet (1932); Viola Sonata (1936); *Pan*, choreographic sketch for 7 instruments and piano (1937); Concertino for Oboe, Clarinet and String Quartet (1940); Sonatina for Oboe and Piano (1940); Trio Sonata for Flute, Cello and Piano; and an *American Youth Concerto* for piano and orch. (1943). She was a successful popularizer of music history. Her publications include *How Music Grew* (1925; with Ethel Peyser), which had several printings; *Music Through the Ages* (1932; also with Ethel Peyser; revised edition, 1967); *Twentieth Century Music* (1933, and still of use) and *How Opera Grew* (1955; once more with Ethel Peyser) which had, despite the clumsy title, several reprints.

Bauer, Moritz, German teacher and writer on music; b. Hamburg, April 8, 1875; d. Frankfurt, Dec. 31, 1932. He first studied medicine; then turned to music (Mus. Doc., Zürich, 1904). He published *Die Lieder Franz Schuberts* (1915); *Iwan Knorr* (1916); *Formprobleme des späten Beethoven* (1927); also edited songs by Zelter.
  BIBLIOGRAPHY: F. Szymickowski, "Moritz Bauer," *Zeitschrift für Musikwissenschaft* (1933).

Bäuerle, Hermann, German music editor; b. Ebersberg, Oct. 24, 1869; d. Ulm, May 21, 1936. He studied theology and music in Tübingen; in 1895 took holy orders; in 1906 he became Papal Privy Chamberlain. In 1921 he founded the Ulm Cons., of which he remained music director. He published several valuable papers on sacred music, among them *Der Vatikanische Choral in Reformnotation* (1907), *Liturgie,* a manual of the Roman Catholic liturgy (1908), and several school manuals on elementary music theory. His most important work, however, was the series *Bibliothek altklassischer Kirchenmusik in moderner Notation,* which he edited beginning in 1903.

Bauldewijn (Baudoin, Bauldewyn, Bauldeweyn, Balduin, Bauldoin), Noël (Natalis Balduinus), Flemish composer, d. Antwerp c. 1529. From Aug. 31, 1509, to July 29, 1513, he was choir director at the church of Saint-Rombaut at Mechlin. On Nov. 16, 1513 he was appointed choir director at the Cathedral of Antwerp where he probably remained until his death. Two motets by Bauldewijn were included by Petrucci in his collection *Motetti della Corona* (1519); 3 motets were published by Proske; and a chanson was included in Tylman Susato's *Le sixième livre contenant trente et une chansons . . .*(Antwerp, 1545). In addition 10 motets and 6 Masses by Bauldewijn are also known.

Baumbach, Friedrich August, German composer and conductor; b. 1753; d. Leipzig, Nov. 30, 1813. He was conductor at the Hamburg opera (1778–89); then settled in Leipzig; wrote many pieces for various instruments; also contributed musical articles to the *Kurzgefasstes Handwörterbuch über die schönen Künste* (Leipzig, 1794).

Baumfelder, Friedrich, German pianist and composer; b. Dresden, May 28, 1836; d. there, Aug. 8, 1916. He studied at the Leipzig Cons. with Moscheles, Wenzel and Hauptmann; was conductor of the Schumann Singakademie at Dresden. He wrote a cantata *Der Geiger zu Gmünd,* a collection of piano studies, *Tirocinium musicae,* and a great number of piano pieces in the salon style (totaling more than 300 opus numbers).

Baumgarten, Gotthilf von, German composer; b. Berlin, Jan. 12, 1741; d. Gross-Strehlitz, Silesia, Oct. 1, 1813. He wrote 3 operas, produced in Breslau: *Zemire und Azor* (1775), *Andromeda* (1776), and *Das Grab des Mufti* (1778).

Baumgarten, Karl Friedrich, composer; b. Lübeck, 1740; d. London, 1824. He was conductor of the Covent Garden opera orchestra (1780–94); wrote many operas and pantomimes, the best known being *Robin Hood* (London, 1786) and *Blue Beard* (1792).

Baumgartner, August, German composer and writer on music; b. Munich, Nov. 9, 1814; d. there, Sept. 29, 1862. He was choirmaster at the Church of St. Anna in Munich; wrote articles on 'musical short-hand' for the *Stenographische Zeitschrift* (1852); published a *Kurzgefasste Anleitung zur musikalischen Stenographie oder Tonzeichenkunst* (1853), and a *Kurzgefasste Geschichte der musikalischen Notation* (1856); composed an instrumental Mass; a requiem; psalms; many choruses and piano pieces.

Baumgartner, Wilhelm, Swiss composer; b. Rorschach, Nov. 15, 1820; d. Zürich, March 17, 1867. He studied with Alexander Müller; in 1842 was a piano teacher in St. Gall and in Zürich; conducted choruses; wrote pieces on Swiss folk themes. His patriotic song, *O mein Heimatland* (1846) has acquired tremendous popularity in Switzerland, and is regarded as a second national anthem.

BIBLIOGRAPHY: C. Widmer, *Wilhelm Baumgartner, ein Liebensbild* (Zürich, 1868); L. Gross, *Wilhelm Baumgartner, sein Leben und sein Schaffen* (Munich, 1930).

Bäumker, Wilhelm, German writer on music; b. Elberfeld, Oct. 25, 1842; d. Rurich, March 3, 1905. He studied theology and philology at Münster and Bonn; from 1892 was a priest at Rurich. His most important work is *Das katholische deutsche Kirchenlied in seinen Singweisen von den frühesten Zeiten bis gegen Ende des 17. Jahrhunderts* (4 vols., Freiburg, 1883–1911). Vol. II (1883) and vol. III (1891) appeared originally as continuation of the work begun by K. S. Meister, who published vol. I in 1862; Bäumker revised this volume in 1886; vol. IV (1911) was edited by J. Gotzen from Bäumker's notes, and also contains supplements to the preceding volumes. Other works by Bäumker are: *Palestrina, ein Beitrag* (1877); *Orlandus de Lassus, ein historisches Bildniss* (1878); *Zur Geschichte der Tonkunst in Deutschland* (1881); *Der Todtentanz* (1881); *Niederländische geistliche Lieder nebst ihren Singweisen aus Handschriften des 15. Jahrhunderts* (1888); and *Ein deutsches geistliches Liederbuch,* melodies from the 15th century (Leipzig, 1896).

Baur, Jürg, German composer, pianist and choral conductor; b. Düsseldorf, Nov. 11, 1918. He studied theory at the Cons. of Cologne with Philipp Jarnach, and musicology at the Univ. of Cologne with Fellerer. In 1956 he joined the faculty of the Düsseldorf Cons. In 1971 he succeeded Zimmermann as chairman of the composition department at the Musikhochschule in Cologne. The idiom of his works evolved from Lutheran neo-classicism in the manner of Reger and Hindemith, later adopting Schoenberg's method of composition with 12 tones and eventually total serialism.

WORKS: Viola Concerto (1952); *Sinfonia montana* (1953); Concerto for Trautonium and String Quartet (1955); Concerto for Strings (1957); *Quintetto sereno* for 5 wind instruments (1958); *Concerto romano* for oboe and orch. (1960); Divertimento for Harpsichord and Percussion (1962); *Romeo and Juliet* for orch. (1963); *Piccolo mondo* for orch. (1963); *Dialogue* for cello and piano (1963); *Lo specchio* for orch. (1966); *Pentagram* for wind quintet and orch. (1966); *Abbreviations* for 13 string instruments (1969); Piano Concerto (1970); also 3 string quartets; a song cycle to words by García Lorca; *Metamorphosen* for piano trio, and many choruses.

Bausch, Ludwig Christian August, celebrated violin maker; b. Naumburg, Jan. 15, 1805; d. Leipzig, May 26, 1871. He established shops for making and repairing violins in Dresden (1826), Dessau (1828), Wiesbaden (1862) and Leipzig (1863). His son, **Ludwig** (b. Dessau, Nov. 10, 1829; d. Leipzig, April 7, 1871) first lived in New York, later establishing his own violin shop in Leipzig. **Otto,** a younger son (b. Leipzig, Aug. 6, 1841; d. there, Dec. 30, 1875), inherited the business, which then passed to A. Paulus at Markneukirchen.

Baussnern, Waldemar von, German composer; b. Berlin, Nov. 29, 1866; d. Potsdam, Aug. 20, 1931. He studied music in Berlin with Kiel and Bargiel. After graduation he was active mainly as a choral conductor, first in Mannheim (1891), then in Dresden (1895); subsequently taught music at the Conservatories of Cologne, Weimar, Frankfurt, and Berlin (1903–1923). He was a prolific composer; wrote 6 operas: *Dichter und Welt* (Weimar, 1897); *Dürer in Venedig* (Weimar, 1901); *Herbort und Hilde* (Mannheim, 1902); *Der Bundschuh* (Frankfurt, 1904); *Satyros* (after Goethe; Basel, 1922); *Hafis* (1926); 8 symphonies, of which the 3rd and the 5th have choral finales; numerous sacred choral works; 4 string quartets; 4 piano quintets; 2 piano trios. He edited the score of the opera *Der Barbier von Bagdad* by Peter Cornelius and completed his unfinished opera *Gunlöd,* which was produced in this version in Cologne in 1906. Baussnern's symphonies are still regarded as not quite obsolete in Germany.

BIBLIOGRAPHY: G. Wehle, *Baussnerns Sinfonisches Schaffen* (Regensburg, 1931).

Bautista, Julián, Spanish composer; b. Madrid, April 21, 1901; d. Buenos Aires, July 8, 1961. He studied piano, violin and composition at the Madrid Cons., and taught music there during the Spanish Civil War, until the fall of Madrid. He fled to France, and eventually settled in Buenos Aires. His music, delicately colored and rhythmically robust, retained its attraction. He wrote a piano suite, *Colores* (1923), a ballet *Juerga* (produced at the Opéra Comique in Paris in 1929), *Obertura para una ópera grotesca* (1932), *Tres ciudades* for voice and orch. (1937), *Cuatros poemas gallegos* for voice, flute, oboe, clarinet, viola, cello, harp (1946), *Sinfonia breve* (1956); 3 string quartets; songs.

Bavicchi, John, American conductor and composer; b. Boston, April 25, 1922. He studied at the New England Cons. of Music (B.M., 1952); then attended Harvard Univ. Graduate School, taking courses in music theory with Archibald T. Davison, composition with Walter Piston and musicology with Otto Gombosi; concurrently he studied civil engineering; served in the U.S. Navy; was in action in Guadalcanal, Okinawa and Japan (1943–45). Returning to Boston after the war, he devoted himself to teaching and composing; in 1968 became conductor of the Arlington, Mass., Philharmonic Orch.; lectured on music history at the Cambridge Center for Adult Education (1960–73) and in other educational institutions in Boston and vicinity.

WORKS: 2 symphonies for band: No. 1, *Festival Symph.* (Cambridge, Mass., Nov. 6, 1965); No. 2 for brass and percussion (1975); Concerto for Clarinet and String Orch. (Boston, May 14, 1958); Symph. Suite No. 1 (1955); Suite No. 2 for a clarinet ensemble (1961); Suite No. 3 for band (1969); Concert Overture (1957); *Fantasy* for harp and chamber orch. (1959); *Concertante No. 1* for oboe, bassoon and string orch. (1961); *Fantasia on Korean Folk Tunes* (1966); *Caroline's Dance* for orch. (1975); *Concertante No. 2* for band (1975); *Summer Incident* for wind instruments, piano and percussion (1959); *Music for Mallets and Percussion* (1967); chamber music: Divertimento for Violin, Clarinet and Trombone (1950); 3 string quartets (1950, 1952, 1960); Quartet for 2 Trumpets and 2 Trombones (1956); 2 saxophone quartets (1965, 1969); 3 woodwind quintets (1961, 1968, 1973); 6 trios for various instruments (1951–70); *4 Miniatures* for wind quintet (1976); 12 sonatas for various instruments with piano accompaniment (1953–71); duets for wind instruments; numerous choral works and songs; pieces for piano solo, 2 pianos, piano 4-hands, etc.

Bax, Sir Arnold (Edward Trevor), outstanding English composer; b. London, Nov. 8, 1883; d. Cork, Ireland, Oct. 3, 1953. He studied at the Royal Academy of Music with Matthay and Corder. Although not ethnically Irish, Bax became interested in ancient Irish folklore; many of his works are inspired by Celtic legends. In 1910 he visited Russia, and wrote a series of piano pieces in a pseudo-Russian style: *May Night in the Ukraine; Gopak; In a Vodka Shop,* etc.; also wrote music to James M. Barrie's skit, *The Truth about the Russian Dancers.* He was an excellent pianist, but was reluctant to play in public; he also never appeared as conductor of his own works. His position was high in English music and he was knighted at the Coronation of George VI (1937); in 1941 he succeeded Sir Walford Davies as Master of the King's Musick. He was an extremely prolific composer; his style is rooted in neo-romanticism, but impressionistic elements are much in evidence in his instrumental works; his harmony is elaborate and rich in chromatic progressions; his contrapuntal fabric is free and emphasizes complete independence of component melodies.

WORKS: ballets: *Between Dusk and Dawn* (1917); *The Truth About the Russian Dancers* (1920); 7 symphonies: I (London, Dec. 2, 1922); II (Boston, Dec. 13, 1929); III (London, March 3, 1930); IV (San Francisco, March 16, 1932); V (dedicated to Sibelius; London, Jan. 15, 1934); VI (London, Nov. 21, 1935); VII (dedicated to the American people; New York, June 9, 1939); symph. poems: *In the Faery Hills* (1909); *Christmas Eve in the Mountains* (1912); *Nympholept* (1912); *The Garden of Fand* (1916); *November Woods* (1917); *Tintagel* (1917); *Summer Music* (1920); *Mediterranean* (1921); *The Happy Forest* (1922); other orchestral works: 4 orchestral pieces: *Dance in the Sun; Pensive Twilight; From the Mountains of Home;* and *Dance of Wild Irravel* (1912–13); *Scherzo sinfonico* (1913); *Romantic Overture* (1923); *Overture to a Picaresque Comedy* (1930); *The Tale the Pine Trees Knew* (1931); *2 Northern Ballads* (1933; 1937); *Overture to Adventure* (1935); *Rogues' Comedy Overture* (1936); *London Pageant* (1937); *Legend* (1944); *Coronation March* (1953). Instrumental works with orchestra: *Symphonic Variations* for piano and orch. (1917); *Phantasy* for viola and orch. (1920); Cello Concerto (1932); Violin Concerto (1937); Piano Concerto for Left Hand (1948). Vocal music: *Fatherland,* for tenor, chorus and orch. (1907); *Enchanted Summer* (from Shelley's *Prometheus Unbound*), for 2 sopranos, chorus and orch. (1909); *The Bard of the Dimbovitza,* 6 poems for voice and orch. (1915); *Mater Ora Filium,* motet (1920); *Of a Rose I Sing,* for small chorus, harp, cello and double bass (1921); *Now is the Time of Christymas,* for male voices, flute and piano (1921); *This Worlde's Joie,* motet (1922); *The Morning Watch* for chorus and orch. (1923); *To the Name above Every Name,* for soprano, chorus and orch. (1923); *The Boar's Head,* carol for male voices (1923); *St. Patrick's Breastplate,* for chorus and orch. (1923-24); *I sing of a Maiden* for 5 voices unaccompanied (1926); *Walsinghame* for tenor, chorus and orch. (1928); also many solo songs. Chamber music: 3 string quartets (1918; 1924; 1936); Piano Quintet (1915); Quintet for Strings and Harp (1919); Quintet for Oboe and Strings (1923); String Quintet (1931); Trio for Flute, Viola and Harp (1916); *An Irish Elegy* for English horn, harp and strings (1917); Nonet for Winds, Strings and Harp (1931); Octet for Horn, Piano and Strings (1934); Concerto for Flute, Oboe, Harp and Strings (1934); Concerto for Bassoon, Harp and Strings (1936); 3 violin sonatas (1910-27); 2 viola sonatas (2nd with harp; 1921; 1928); Cello Sonata (1923); *Legend Sonata* for cello and piano (1943); Clarinet Sonata (1934); 4 piano sonatas; works for 2 pianos, etc. In his many settings of folksongs, Bax succeeded in adapting simple melodies to effective accompaniments in modern harmonies; in his adaptations of old English songs, he successfully recreated the archaic style of the epoch. In his candid autobiography *Farewell My Youth* (London, 1943), Bax gives a vivid account of his life and travels.

BIBLIOGRAPHY: Edwin Evans, "Arnold Bax," *Mus. Quarterly* (April, 1923); R. H. Hull, *A Handbook on Arnold Bax's Symphonies* (London, 1932); A. Fleischmann, "Arnold Bax," *Recorded Sound* (Jan./April 1968); R.L.E. Foreman, "Bibliography of Writings on Arnold Bax," *Current Musicology* 10 (1970); idem, "The Musical Development of Arnold Bax," *Music & Letters* (Jan. 1971); C. Scott-Sutherland, *Arnold Bax* (London, 1973).

Bay, Emmanuel, Russian-American pianist; b. Simferopol, Crimea, Jan. 20, 1891; d. Jerusalem, Dec. 2, 1967. He was raised in Lodz, Poland, where his father was cantor in the main synagogue. In 1908 he enrolled at the St. Petersburg Cons., and studied piano with Drosdov, graduating in 1913 with the first prize, receiving a grand piano and obtaining the diploma of "free artist." He then embarked on a concert tour in Russia, Germany, and Scandinavia; also took a master class in piano with Leopold Godowsky in Vienna. He continued to give occasional piano recitals throughout his career, but he acquired a fine reputation principally as a superlative accompanist. He toured in Europe, Asia and the U.S. with Efrem Zimbalist (1922-29); then was for 20 years a regular accompanist to Jascha Heifetz (1931-51) on his world tours; other artists with whom he toured were Mischa Elman, Nathan Milstein, Zino Francescatti, Joseph Szigeti, Gregor Piatigorsky, Jan Peerce and Helen Traubel. He died of a heart attack on a trip to Israel.

Bayer, Josef, Austrian composer and conductor; b. Vienna, March 6, 1852; d. there, March 12, 1913. He studied at the Vienna Cons. (1859-70) with Georg and Josef Hellmesberger (violin), Dachs (piano) and Bruckner (theory). He wrote a great number of operettas and ballets which were quite popular owing to his facility for melodic writing and piquant rhythms. He traveled a great deal through Europe as conductor; visited New York in 1881, and conducted there the first performance of his operetta *Chevalier von San Marco* on Feb. 4, 1881. Other operettas successfully produced in Vienna were *Menelaus* (1892), *Fräulein Hexe* (1898); *Der Polizeichef* (1904); he also wrote 2 exotic comic operas *Alien Fata,* on a Bosnian subject, and *Der Goldasoka,* on a Hindu theme. The list of his ballets includes the following, produced in Vienna: *Wiener Waltzer* (1886); *Die Puppenfee* (1888); *Sonne und Erde* (1889); *Ein Tanzmärchen* (1890); *Rouge et Noir* (1892); *Die Donaunixe* (1892); *Eine Hochzeit in Bosnien* (1893, with Bosnian folk melodies); *Burschenliebe* (1894); *Rund um Wien* (1894); *Die Braut von Korea* (1896); *Die kleine Welt* (1904); ballets produced at Berlin: *Deutsche Märsche* (1887); *Die Welt in Bild und Tanz* (1892); *Die Engelsjäger* (1896); *Columbia* (1893).

Bayle, François, French composer; b. Tamatabe, Madagascar, April 27, 1932. He studied academic sciences and music in France; was a student in composition of Olivier Messiaen, and with Pierre Schaeffer whose Groupe de Recherches Musicales he joined in 1966. His works are mostly montages, collages and acoustical barrages. He constructed the following musical compositions: *Points critiques* for horn, piano, cello and percussion (1960); *Pluriel* for 19 instruments and loud-speakers (1963); *L'Oiseau chanteur,* musique concrète (1963); *Espaces inevitables,* musique concrète (1967); *L'Experience acoustique,* musique concrète (1970-77).

Bazelaire, Paul, French cellist and composer; b. Sedan, March 4, 1886; d. Paris, Dec. 11, 1958. He graduated from the Paris Cons. as a cellist at the age of 11, with the Premier Prix; after a concert career became prof. of cello at the Paris Cons. (1918-56); founded a unique ensemble of 50 cellos.

WORKS: *Suite Française sur des chants populaires* for orch.; symph. poem *Cléopâtre* (Paris, Jan. 23, 1908); *Suite Grecque* for small orch. (1910); *Rapsodie dans le style russe* for cello and orch. (Paris, Feb. 2, 1941). He orchestrated Bach's six cello suites; publ. a teaching manual, *Pédagogie du violoncelle.*

Bazelon, Irwin, American composer; b. Evanston, Illinois, June 4, 1922. After graduation from DePaul Univ. of Chicago in 1945 he studied composition with Darius Milhaud at Mills College, Oakland, Calif. (1946-48) and with Ernest Bloch at Univ. of Calif., Berkeley (1947). He went to N.Y. in 1948 where he remained. His style of composition is marked by imaginative eclecticism; he regards music as a practical art.

WORKS: Suite for Clarinet, Cello and Piano (1947); Ballet Suite for small ensemble (1949); *Concert Overture* (1952; revised 1960); *Movimento da Camera* for flute, bassoon, horn and harpsichord (1954); *Adagio and Fugue* for string orch. (1956); suite for small orch.

(1956); Chamber Symphony for 7 instruments (1957); Symph. No. 1 (1960; Kansas City, Nov. 29, 1963); Symph. No. 2 (*Short Symphony;* Washington, Dec. 4, 1962); Symph. No. 3 for brass, percussion, piano and string sextet (1963); Symph. No. 4 (1965); Symph. No. 5 (1966); Symph. No. 6 (Kansas City, Nov. 17, 1970); *Fusions* for orch. (1965); *Ballet Centauri 17* for orch. (1960); *Suite for Merry Wives of Windsor* (1958); *Overture to The Taming of the Shrew* (1960); Brass Quintet (1963); *Excursion* for orch. (Kansas City, March 5, 1966); *Concerto for 14 Players* (N.Y., May 16, 1971); 2 string quartets; 3 piano sonatas; 5 pieces for cello and piano, etc.

Bazin, François-Emanuel-Joseph, French composer; b. Marseille, Sept. 4, 1816; d. Paris, July 2, 1878. He studied with Berton and Halévy at the Paris Cons.; was awarded the Prix de Rome in 1840; in 1844 he was appointed to the faculty of the Paris Cons. He wrote 9 comic operas, none of which was retained in the repertory, although *Le Voyage en Chine,* produced in 1865, was temporarily acclaimed. He also published a manual, *Cours d'harmonie théorique et pratique,* which was adopted at the Paris Conservatory.

Bázlik, Miroslav, Slovak composer and pianist; b. Partizánská Lupča, April 12, 1931. He studied piano at the Bratislava Cons., and became an accomplished concert pianist; then took a course in composition with Cikker at the Bratislava Academy of Musical Arts (graduating in 1961). His musical idiom evolved along modern Romantic lines; in his later compositions he resorts to serial techiques.

WORKS: an opera, after Rolland, *Petr a Lucie* (1962–66; Bratislava, 1967); *Dvanást'* (The Twelve), oratorio after the poem of Alexander Blok (1967; Bratislava, Nov. 4, 1976); *Baroque Suite* for small orch. (1958); *5 Songs on Chinese Poetry* for alto, flute, piano and cello (1960); *Music* for violin and orch. (1961); *3 Pieces* for 14 instruments (1964); *Music for Poetry* for nonet, harp and vibraphone (1966); *Bagatelles* for string orch. or string quartet (1972); *Pastorale* for woodwinds and harpsichord (1972); *Cantata without Words* for mezzo-soprano, madrigal ensemble and chamber orch. (1972); String Quartet (1974); Piano Sonata (1954); *Palette,* 5 bagatelles for piano (1956).

Bazzini, Antonio, Italian violinist and composer; b. Brescia, March 11, 1818; d. Milan, Feb. 10, 1897. Encouraged by Paganini, before whom he played in 1836, Bazzini embarked upon a series of successful tours through Italy, France, Spain, Belgium, Poland, England and Germany (1837–63); taught at the Milan Cons. from 1873, and in 1882 became its director.

WORKS: *Turanda,* opera after Gozzi's *Turandot* (La Scala, Milan, Jan. 13, 1867); *Francesca da Rimini,* symph. poem (1890); symph. overtures to Alfieri's *Saul* (1877) and to Shakespeare's *King Lear* (1880); numerous violin pieces, of which *Ronde des Lutins* became extremely popular.

Beach, Mrs. H. H. A. (maiden name **Amy Marcy Cheney**), American composer; b. Henniker, N. H., Sept 5, 1867; d. New York, Dec. 27, 1944. She studied piano with E. Perabo and K. Baermann; theory with Junius

W. Hill. In composition she was largely self-taught, guiding herself by a study of the masters. She made her debut as a pianist when she was 16. She married Dr. H. H. A. Beach of Boston on Dec. 2, 1885. Her first important work was a Mass in E flat, performed by the Handel and Haydn Society (Boston, Feb. 18, 1892). Her *Gaelic Symphony* (Boston Symph., Oct. 30, 1896), was the first symph. work by an American woman. She also appeared as soloist in her piano concerto (Boston Symph. Orch., April 6, 1900). Other works: cantatas, *The Minstrel and the King, The Rose of Avontown, Sylvania, The Sea Fairies, The Chambered Nautilus;* 2nd Piano Concerto; Piano Quintet; Suite for 2 Pianos; *Variations on Balkan Themes* for 2 pianos; Violin Sonata; numerous choral works, songs and piano pieces, most of them published by Arthur P. Schmidt. Her music, conservative in its idiom and academic in structure, retains its importance as the work of a pioneer woman composer in America.

BIBLIOGRAPHY: Percy Goetschius, *Mrs. H. A. Beach, Analytical Sketch* (Boston, 1906; contains contemporary reviews and a catalog).

Beach, John Parsons, American composer; b. Gloversville, N.Y., Oct. 11, 1877; d. Pasadena, Cal., Nov. 6, 1953. He studied piano at the New England Cons. in Boston; then went to Europe where he took lessons with Gédalge in Paris and Malipiero in Venice. Returning to Boston he took additional lessons with Loeffler. He held various teaching jobs; finally settled in Pasadena. His opera *Pippa's Holiday* was performed in Paris in 1915, and his ballet *Phantom Satyr* was given in Asolo, Italy, July 6, 1925; another ballet, *Mardi Gras,* was staged in New Orleans (Feb. 15, 1926). His orchestral works include *New Orleans Street Cries* (Philadelphia, April 22, 1927; Stokowski conducting); *Asolani* (Minneapolis, Nov. 12, 1926); *Angelo's Letter* for tenor and chamber orch. (N.Y., Feb. 27, 1929). He also composed *Naïve Landscapes* for piano, flute, oboe and clarinet (1917); *Poem* for string quartet (1920); *Concert* for violin, viola, cello, flute, oboe and clarinet (1929); and many songs.

Beale, Frederic Fleming, American organist and composer; b. Troy, Kansas, July 13, 1876; d. Caldwell, Idaho, Feb. 16, 1948. He studied in Chicago with Adolf Weidig and Wilhelm Middelschulte; was church organist in Chicago; taught piano at the Univ. of Washington, Seattle; in 1939 was appointed director of music at the College of Idaho at Caldwell. He wrote 3 operettas: *The Magic Wheel, Fatima* and *Poor Richard; Dance-Caprice* for orch.; numerous songs.

Beale, William, English organist and composer; b. Landrake, Cornwall, Jan. 1, 1784; d. London, May 3, 1854. His early training was as chorister in Westminster Abbey; he then studied with Dr. Arnold and Robert Cooke. In 1813 his madrigal *Awake, sweet Muse* was awarded first prize by the London Madrigal Society; collections of his glees and madrigals were published in 1815 and 1820. From 1816–20 Beale was one of the Gentlemen of the Chapel Royal; served as organist of Trinity College, Cambridge (1820), Wandsworth Parish Church (1821), and St. John's, Clapham Rise.

Beardslee, Bethany, American soprano; b. Lansing, Michigan, Dec. 25, 1927. She studied at Michigan State Univ. and at the Juilliard School of Music in New York; specialized in modern music; evolved an extraordinary technique with a flute-like ability to sound impeccably precise intonation; mastered the art of Sprechstimme, which enabled her to give fine renditions of such works as Schoenberg's *Pierrot Lunaire;* has distinguished herself also in vocal scores by Alban Berg, Anton von Webern, Stravinsky and Krenek.

Beaton, Isabella, American pianist; b. Grinnell, Iowa, May 20, 1870; d. Mt. Pleasant, Henry Co., Iowa, Jan. 19, 1929. She studied in Berlin with Moszkowski (1894–99); received her M.A. and Ph.B. from Western Reserve Univ. (1902); taught many private pupils in Cleveland (1910–19); also gave recitals. She wrote an opera *Anacoana,* a symphony, a scherzo, and piano pieces.

Beaulieu (real name **Martin-Beaulieu**), **Marie-Désiré,** French composer and author; b. Paris, April 11, 1791; d. Niort, Dec. 21, 1863. He studied with Méhul at the Paris Cons.; won the Prix de Rome in 1810; wrote operas *Anacréon* and *Philadelphie;* oratorios *L'Hymne du matin, L'Hymne de la nuit,* etc.; also other sacred music as well as secular songs. He published the essays: *Du rythme, des effets qu'il produit et de leurs causes* (1852); *Mémoire sur ce qui reste de la musique de l'ancienne Grèce dans les premiers chants de l'Église* (1852); *Mémoire sur le caractère que doit avoir la musique de l'Église* (1858); *Mémoire sur l'origine de la musique* (1859). His main contribution to French musical culture was his organizing of annual music festivals in provincial towns; founded the Association Musicale de l'Ouest, to which he bequeathed 100,000 francs.

Bécaud, Gilbert, French composer of popular songs; b. Toulon, Oct. 24, 1927. He studied at the Cons. of Nice; made his debut as a chansonnier in Versailles on Dec. 20, 1952, where he was featured as "Monsieur 100,000 volts." With this sobriquet, he launched a highly lucrative career as a performer of his own songs in music halls, and was accompanist to Edith Piaf on her American tours. He later tried his hand at serious music with a cantata *L'Enfant à l'Étoile* (Paris, Jan. 7, 1962) and *Opéra d'Aran* (Paris, Oct. 22, 1962).

Becerra Schmidt, Gustavo, Chilean composer; b. Temuco, Aug. 26, 1925. He studied at the Santiago Cons., first with Pedro Allende, and then with Domingo Santa Cruz; from 1953 to 1956 he traveled in Europe; from 1968 to 1970 he served as cultural attaché to the Chilean embassy in Bonn. In 1971 he received the Premio Nacional de Arte in music. His early works are set in the traditional manner of neoclassical composition, but soon he adopted an extremely radical modern idiom, incorporating dodecaphonic and aleatory procedures and outlining a graphic system of notation, following the pictorial representation of musical sounds of the European avant-garde, but introducing some new elements, such as indication of relative loudness by increasing the size of the notes on a music staff with lines far apart. His works include the opera *La muerte de Don Rodrigo* (1958); 3 symphonies (1955, 1958, 1960); oratorios *La Araucana* (1965) and *Lord Cochrane de Chile* (1967); Violin Concerto (1950); Flute Concerto (1957); Piano Concerto (1958); 4 guitar concertos (1964–70); Concerto for Oboe, Clarinet and Bassoon with String Orch. (1970); 7 string quartets; Saxophone Quartet; 3 violin sonatas; Viola Sonata; 3 cello sonatas; Sonata for Double-Bass and Piano; pieces for solo oboe and solo trombone; numerous choral works. A special issue of *Revista Musical Chilena* (1972), dedicated to Becerra Schmidt, contains a complete catalogue of his works.

Becher, Alfred Julius, English composer and music critic, who became a martyr of the revolutionary movement in 1848; b. Manchester, April 27, 1803; d. Vienna (executed), Nov. 23, 1848. He studied in Germany; in 1841 went to Vienna; in 1848 he began issuing the revolutionary paper "Der Radikale," and that same year was arrested for treason and shot. He published a monograph on Jenny Lind, in German (Vienna, 1846); he also wrote a symphony, some chamber music and songs.
BIBLIOGRAPHY: H. Ullrich, "Alfred Julius Becher (1803–1848) als Komponist," *Beiträge zur Musikwissenschaft* XIII/3 (1971).

Becher, Joseph, German composer; b. Neukirchen, Bavaria, Aug. 1, 1821; d. Mintraching, Sept. 23, 1888. He was a pastor in Mintraching; wrote 60 Masses and other sacred music.

Bechet, Sidney, black American jazz clarinetist and saxophonist; b. New Orleans, May 14, 1897; d. Garches, France, May 14, 1959. He traveled to Chicago where he played in various bands; in 1947 settled in Paris. In jazz he represented the romantic New Orleans school, playing in an expressively sentimental ballad style.
BIBLIOGRAPHY: E. Ansermet, "Sur un orchestre nègre," *Revue romande* (15 Oct. 1959), trans. by W. J. Schaap as, "Bechet and Jazz Visit Europe," in R. de Toledano, *Frontiers of Jazz* (N.Y., 1962); R. Munly, *Sidney Bechet* (Paris, 1959).

Bechgaard, Julius, Danish composer; b. Copenhagen, Dec. 19, 1843; d. there, March 4, 1917. He studied at the Leipzig Cons. and with Gade in Copenhagen; lived in Germany, Italy and Paris; then settled in Copenhagen. He wrote 2 operas: *Frode* (Copenhagen, May 11, 1893) and *Frau Inge* (Prague, 1894); many piano pieces and songs.

Bechler, Johann Christian, composer; b. Island of Oesel, in the Baltic Sea, Jan. 7, 1784; d. Herrnhut, Saxony, April 15, 1857. He came to the U. S. in 1806 and became a professor of theology at the seminary in Nazareth, Pa.; served as deacon, principal and pastor in Philadelphia; returned to Europe in 1836 as a bishop, and was for some years active in Sarepta and Astrakhan, Russia. Bechler was one of the Moravians active in Pennsylvania. His works, which include anthems, hymns and ariettas, are more interesting from a historic than a musical standpoint.

BIBLIOGRAPHY: A. G. Rau and H. T. David, *A Catalogue of Music by American Moravians, 1742-1842* (Bethlehem, Pa., 1938).

Bechstein, Karl (Friedrich Wilhelm Karl), German piano manufacturer; b. Gotha, June 1, 1826; d. Berlin, March 6, 1900. He worked in German factories; also in London; in 1853 set up a modest shop in Berlin; constructed his first grand piano in 1856; established branches in France, Russia and England. After World War I, the London branch continued under the direction of C. Bechstein, grandson of the founder; following his death (1931), it became an independent British firm, Bechstein Piano Co., Ltd. The firm, one of the largest and best-known in Europe, built, in 1901, the London concert auditorium, Wigmore Hall. The Bechstein piano possesses a particularly harmonious tone, capable of producing a mellifluous cantilena; for many years it was a favorite instrument of pianists of the Romantic school.

BIBLIOGRAPHY: *Bechstein-Chronik* (Berlin, 1926); Count du Moulin-Eckart, *Neue Briefe Hans von Bülow* (containing correspondence with Bechstein; Munich, 1927); W. Huschke, "Zur Herkunft des Klavierbauers Carl Bechstein," *Genealogie* (1969): 709-14.

Beck, Conrad, distinguished Swiss composer; b. Schaffhausen, June 16, 1901; studied at the Zürich Cons. with Andreae, and in Paris with Honegger and Ernst Lévy; lived in Paris and Berlin; in 1939 returned and was appointed radio conductor in Basel, until 1966. A prolific composer, Beck excels in instrumental writing, in a neo-classical style, rich in contrapuntal texture. Several of his works have been featured at the Festivals of the International Society for Contemporary Music: overture *Innominata* (Vienna, June 16, 1932); Chamber Cantata (Warsaw, April 15, 1939), etc. He has written 6 symphonies (1925-53); *Lyric Cantata* (Munich, May 22, 1931); Piano Concerto (1933); *Konzertmusik* for oboe and string orch. (Basel, April 30, 1933); Chamber Concerto for Cembalo and String Orch. (Basel, Nov. 27, 1942); Viola Concerto (1949); oratorio *Der Tod zu Basel* (Basel, May 22, 1953); Concertino for Clarinet, Bassoon and Orch. (1954); Christmas motet, *Es kommt ein Schiff geladen*; Symph. No. 7, *Aeneas-Silvius* (Zürich, Feb. 25, 1958); *Die Sonnenfinsternis*, cantata (Lucerne, Aug. 25, 1967); Clarinet Concerto (1968); *Fantasie* for orch. (1969); *Sonata a quattro* for violin, flute, oboe and bassoon (1970); 4 string quartets; 2 violin sonatas; 2 cello sonatas; 2 string trios; piano music; choral works, etc.

BIBLIOGRAPHY: Willi Schuh, *Schweizer Musiker der Gegenwart* (Zürich, 1948).

Beck, Franz, German violinist and composer; b. Mannheim, Feb. 15, 1734; d. Bordeaux, Dec. 31, 1809. He was a violinist and favorite of the Prince Palatine; after killing his opponent in a duel he fled to France and settled in Bordeaux (1761). In 1783 he went to Paris, where he became a successful teacher. His works include 24 symphonies; several stage works; violin quartets; piano sonatas; church music; the op-

eras *La Belle Jardinière* (Bordeaux, Aug. 24, 1767); *Pandora* (Paris, July 2, 1789); *L'Ile déserte* (unperformed).

BIBLIOGRAPHY: R. Sondheimer, *Die Sinfonien F. Becks* (Basel, 1921).

Beck, Jean-Baptiste, Alsatian-American musicologist; b. Gebweiler, Aug. 14, 1881; d. Philadelphia, June 23, 1943. He studied organ; received his *Dr. phil.* at Strasbourg Univ. with the thesis *Die Melodien der Troubadours* (1908); later publ. a somewhat popularized edition of it in French, *La musique des Troubadours* (Paris, 1910). Beck came to the U. S. after World War I; settled in Philadelphia; taught at the Curtis Institute and at Univ. of Pennsylvania. In 1927 he initiated a project of publishing a *Corpus Cantilenarum Medii Aevi*, in 52 vols., but was able to bring out only 4 vols., under the subtitle *Les Chansonniers des Troubadours et des Trouvères* (all in French), containing phototype reproductions of medieval manuscripts, transcriptions in modern notation and commentary: *Le Chansonnier Cangé* (2 vols.; Philadelphia, 1927); *Le manuscrit du Roi* (2 vols.; Philadelphia, 1938). Among his other important writings is an essay "Der Takt in den Musikaufzeichnungen des XII. und XIII. Jahrhunderts," *Riemann Festschrift* (1909). Beck was an outstanding scholar of medieval vocal music; his application of the modal rhythm of the polyphony of that time to the troubadour melodies was an important contribution to the problem of proper transcription into modern notation.

Beck, Johann Heinrich, American conductor and composer; b. Cleveland, Sept. 12, 1856; d. there, May 26, 1924. He was a pupil of Reinecke and Jadassohn at the Leipzig Cons. (1879-82), subsequently returning to America. In 1895 he was appointed conductor of the Detroit Symph. Orch., and from 1901-12 conductor of the Cleveland Pops Orch.

WORKS: *Moorish Serenade*, for orch. (1889); a cantata, *Deukalion*; String Quartet; String Sextet; Overture to Bryon's *Lara; Aus meinem Leben*, symph. poem; miscellaneous pieces for various instruments.

Beck, Johann Nepomuk, Hungarian singer; b. Budapest, May 5, 1827; d. Pressburg, April 9, 1904. His dramatic baritone voice was "discovered" in Budapest, where he made his professional debut; he then sang in Vienna, Frankfurt, and many other German cities; was a member of the Court Opera in Vienna from 1853; retired in 1885; died insane.

Beck, John Ness, American composer; b. Warren, Ohio, Nov. 11, 1930. He studied composition at the Ohio State Univ. and subsequently taught harmony and theory there, resigning later to assume the management of a retail sheet music business in Columbus, Ohio. He has written mainly sacred choral works, among them *Upon this Rock, Hymn for Our Time, Canticle of Praise, Hymn for Easter Day, Litany of Thanksgiving* and *Exhortation*. Other compositions include *5 Carol Fantasies* for piano (1970); Sonata for Flute and Piano, and pieces for concert band.

Beck, Karl, Austrian tenor; b. 1814; d. Vienna, March 3, 1879. He was the first to sing the role of Lohengrin (Weimar, Aug. 28, 1850).

Beck, Karl, German-American conductor; b. Ilmenau, Thuringia, April 26, 1850; d. San Antonio, Texas, Oct. 2, 1920. He came to the U.S. in 1875; toured with an opera company; in 1884 he moved to San Antonio, Texas, where he was appointed as conductor of the Beethoven Society, a male chorus; he also organized an excellent military band. He was a confirmed Wagnerite, and conducted first Texas performances of several Wagner works.

Beck, Martha, American composer; b. Sodaville, Oregon, Jan. 19, 1900. She studied at the American Cons. in Chicago; eventually she settled in Troy, New York, as a piano teacher. She published a number of piano pieces with exotic titles such as *Chinese Holiday* and *In Old Japan.*

Beck, Thomas Ludvigsen, Norwegian composer; b. Horten, Dec. 5, 1899; d. Olso, Sept. 9, 1963. He studied piano, organ and composition at the Oslo Cons.; also took a course of music theory in Leipzig. From 1930 until his death he was active as organist, choral conductor and music teacher in Oslo; was a member of the board of the Society of Norwegian Composers (1938–46). He wrote many cantatas, among which are *Arnljot Gjelline* (1937); *Höifjell* (*In the Mountains,* 1945; Oslo, 1946) and *Heilag framtid* (*Holy Future*; Oslo, 1954); *Ballad on a Norwegian Folk Tune* for orch. (Oslo, 1940); *3 Dances from Gudbrandsdal* for orch. (Oslo, April 28, 1946); *Andante* for string orch.; *Intrada* for orch. or piano; choruses; songs; film music.

Becker, Albert (Ernst Anton), German composer; b. Quedlinburg, June 13, 1834; d. Berlin, Jan. 10, 1899. He was a pupil of Dehn in Berlin (1853–6); was appointed teacher of composition at Scharwenka's conservatory (1881), and became the conductor of the Berlin Cathedral Choir (1891). His Symphony in G Minor was awarded the prize of the Gesellschaft der Musikfreunde in Vienna (1861); also wrote an opera, *Loreley* (1898), cantatas, and a number of sacred works.

Becker, Constantin Julius, German composer and author; b. Freiberg, Saxony, Feb. 3, 1811; d. Oberlössnitz, Feb. 26, 1859. He studied singing with Anacker and composition with Karl Becker; from 1837–46 edited the *Neue Zeitschrift für Musik,* in association with Schumann; in 1843 settled in Dresden; taught singing, composed and wrote novels on musical subjects. In 1846 he went to Oberlössnitz, where he spent the remainder of his life. He wrote an opera, *Die Erstürmung von Belgrad* (Leipzig, May 21, 1848); a symphony; various vocal works. However, he is best known for his manuals: *Männergesangschule* (1845), *Harmonielehre für Dilettanten* (1842), and *Kleine Harmonielehre* (1844). He also published the novel, *Die Neuromantiker* (1840); translated *Voyage musical* by Berlioz into German (1843).

Becker, Georges, Swiss music editor; b. Frankenthal, Palatinate, July 24, 1834; d. Lancy, near Geneva, July 18, 1928. He was a pupil of Prudent; lived in Geneva most of his life; published *La Musique en Suisse* (Geneva, 1874; reprinted, 1923); *Aperçu sur la chanson française* (from the 11th to 17th centuries); *Pygmalion de Jean-Jacques Rousseau; Les projets de notation musicale du XIXe siècle; La Musique à Genève depuis 50 ans; Eustorg de Beaulieu; Guillaume de Guéroult; Notice sur Claude Goudimel; Jean Caulery et ses chansons spirituelles; H. Waelrant et ses psaumes* (1881); *De l'instrumentation du XVe au XVIIe siècle* (1844); edited the 'Questionnaire de l'Association Internationale des Musiciens-Écrivains'; contributed to the *Monatshefte für Musikgeschichte.*

Becker, Gustave Louis, American pianist and teacher; b. Richmond, Texas, May 22, 1861; d. Epsom, Surrey, England, Feb. 25, 1959. He made his public debut at the age of eleven; studied in New York with Constantin von Sternberg and at the Hochschule für Musik, Berlin (1888–91). Returning to New York, he became Rafael Joseffy's assistant at the National Cons. He continued his teaching activities privately. On May 23, 1952, the 80th anniversary of his public appearance as a child prodigy, he gave a piano recital in Steinway Hall; on his 94th birthday, May 22, 1955, played at a concert in N.Y., arranged by his friends. He wrote 2 suites for string quartet; *Herald of Freedom* for chorus (1925); many vocal and piano pieces, about 200 numbers in all. He published several pedagogic works: *Exercise for Accuracy; Superior Graded Course for the Piano; Musical Syllable System for Vocal Sight Reading;* and many magazine articles.

Becker, Hugo, famous German cellist, son of **Jean Becker**; b. Strasbourg, Feb. 13, 1863; d. Geiselgasteig, July 30, 1941. He first studied with his father; later with Grützmacher; was cellist in the Frankfurt opera orch. (1884–86); was a member of the Heermann quartet (1890–1906); taught at the Königliche Hochschule in Berlin (1909–29). He was not only one of the finest soloists, but also a remarkable ensemble player; was for many years a member of the Marteau-Dohnányi-Becker trio; also played with Ysaÿe and Busoni. Among his compositions are a cello concerto and smaller cello pieces. He publ. *Mechanik und Ästhetik des Violoncellspiels* (Vienna, 1929).

Becker, Jean, German violinist; b. Mannheim, May 11, 1833; d. there, Oct. 10, 1884. He studied with Vincenz Lachner; was concertmaster of the Mannheim Orch. until 1858; later settled in Florence, and established the renowned Florentine Quartet (dissolved in 1880). The remaining years of his life were spent touring with his children: **Jeanne,** pianist, pupil of Reinecke and Bargiel (b. Mannheim, June 9, 1859; d. there, April 6, 1893); **Hans,** violist (b. Strasbourg, May 12, 1860; d. Leipzig, May 1, 1917); and the cellist, **Hugo Becker.**

Becker, John J., remarkable American composer; b. Henderson, Kentucky, Jan. 22, 1886; d. Wilmette, Illinois, Jan. 21, 1961. He studied first in Cincinnati, then at the Wisconsin Cons. in Milwaukee, where he was a pupil of Alexander von Fielitz, Carl Busch and Wilhelm Middleschulte. Upon graduation, he was director of music at Notre Dame Univ. (1918–28) and chairman of the Fine Arts Dept. at the College of St. Thomas in St. Paul (1928–33). He was subsequently Minnesota State Director for the Federal Music Project (1935–41) and prof. of music at Barat College of the Sacred Heart at Lake Forest, Illinois (1943–57), and taught sporadically at the Chicago Musical College. His early works are characterized by romantic moods in a somewhat Germanic manner. About 1930 he was drawn into the circle of modern American music; was on the editorial board of *New Music Quarterly* founded by Cowell and became associated with Charles Ives. He conducted modern American works with various groups in St. Paul. Striving to form a style that would be both modern and recognizably American, he wrote a number of pieces for various instrumental groups under the title *Soundpiece.* He also developed a type of dramatic work connecting theatrical action with music. Becker's music is marked by sparse sonorities of an incisive rhythmic character contrasted with dissonant conglomerates of massive harmonies.

WORKS: FOR THE STAGE: *Dance Figure,* for singer, dance group and orch., on a poem by Ezra Pound (1932); *The Life of Man,* incidental music to the play by Leonid Andreyev (1932–43; unfinished); *Abongo: Dance Primitive,* for 2 solo dancers, dance group and percussion (1933; New York, May 16, 1963); *A Marriage with Space,* "a drama in color, light and sound" for solo and mass recitation, solo and dance group and large orch., to a poem by Mark Turbyfill (1933–35); *Nostalgic Songs of Earth,* 3 dances for solo dancer and piano (Northfield, Minn., Dec. 12, 1938); *Vigilante 1938,* for solo dancer, piano and percussion (Northfield, Minn., Dec. 12, 1938); *Rain Down Death,* incidental music for the play by Alfred Kreymborg (1939); *When the Willow Nods,* incidental music for the play by Kreymborg (1939); *Privilege and Privation,* "a playful affair with music," with libretto by Kreymborg (1940); *Antigone,* incidental music (1940); *Diedre of the Sorrows,* lyric drama in one act, based on the play by John Synge (1945); *Faust,* monodrama (1951); *Madeleine et Judas,* incidental music for the play by Raymond Bruckberger (1958; Paris, radio performance, March 25, 1959). FOR ORCH.: *The Cossacks,* 3 sketches (1912); 7 symphonies: No. 1, *Etude Primitive* (1912–15); No. 2, *Fantasia Tragica* (1920); No. 3, *Symphonia Brevis* (1929; first complete performance, Minneapolis, May 20, 1937, composer conducting); No. 4, *Dramatic Episodes* (1938; uses material from *A Marriage with Space*); No. 5, *Homage to Mozart* (1942); No. 6, *Symphony of Democracy,* with narrator and chorus (1942); No. 7, based on the *Sermon on the Mount,* with narrator and singing and speaking chorus (1953–54; unfinished); *Concerto Arabesque,* for piano and orch. (1930; St. Paul, Minn., Dec. 7, 1931, the composer conducting); *Concertino Pastorale,* "A Forest Rhapsodie" for 2 flutes and orch. (1933; Cincinnati, Jan. 13, 1976); Concerto for Horn and Small Orch. (1933; New York, Feb. 8, 1953); *Mockery,* a scherzo for piano and dance or chamber orch. (1933; first concert performance, New York, March 17, 1974); viola concerto (1937); 2nd Piano Concerto, *Sa-*

tirico (1938; St. Paul, Minn., March 28, 1939); *Rain Down Death,* first orch. suite (1939); *When the Willow Nods,* 2nd orch. suite (1940; Albert Lea, Minn., Jan. 9, 1941); *Antigone,* sym. dances (1940); *Victory March* (1942; last movement of sixth sym.); *The Snow Goose: A Legend of World War II* (1944); Violin Concerto (1948). VOCAL WORKS: *Rouge Bouquet,* for male chorus, with trumpet and piano (1917); *Out of the Cradle Endlessly Rocking,* cantata for speaker, soprano, tenor, chorus and orch. (1929; St. Cloud, Minn., July 19, 1931, composer conducting); *Missa Symphonica,* for male chorus (1933); *Lincoln's Gettysburg Address,* for speaker, chorus and orch. (1941); *Mass in Honor of the Sacred Heart,* for female chorus (1944); *Moments from the Passion,* for solo voice, male and female voices and piano (1945); *Moments from the Liturgy,* for speaker, women's voices, vocal soloist, and singing and speaking choruses (1948). CHAMBER MUSIC: *An American Sonata,* for violin and piano (South Bend, Ind., July 28, 1926, the composer at the piano); 8 *Soundpieces:* No. 1, for piano quintet (1932; New York, Nov. 13, 1933) or for piano and string orch. (1935); No. 2, *Homage to Haydn* (string quartet No. 1, 1936), also for string orch. (1937); No. 3 (Sonata for Violin and Piano, 1936; St. Paul, Minnesota, April 1, 1940); No. 4 (String Quartet No. 2, 1937; Lake Forest, Illinois, Oct. 19, 1947); No. 5 (Sonata for Piano, 1938; St. Paul, Minnesota, April 13, 1943, Ernst Krenek performing); No. 6, for flute and clarinet (1940; Chapel Hill, North Carolina, April 26, 1970); No. 7, for 2 pianos (1949); No. 8 (string quartet No. 3, 1959; unfinished). FOR ORGAN: *Fantasia Tragica* (1920); *Improvisation* (1960). FOR FILM: Incidental music for *Julius Caesar,* a film by David Bradley (1949). In 1934 he scored Ives' song, *General William Booth's Entrance Into Heaven,* for chamber orchestra.

BIBLIOGRAPHY: Don Gillespie, "John Becker, Musical Crusader from Saint Paul," *Musical Quarterly* (April 1976).

Becker, Karl Ferdinand, German organist and writer; b. Leipzig, July 17, 1804; d. there, Oct. 26, 1877. He was church organist at Leipzig and organ teacher at the Cons. (1843). Among his published writings are: *Systematisch-chronologische Darstellung der Musikliteratur* (1836; Supplement, 1839); *Die Hausmusik in Deutschland im 16., 17., und 18. Jahrhundert* (1840); *Die Tonwerke des 16. und 17. Jahrhundert,* etc. He composed piano and organ pieces, and wrote a chorale book. He gave his library, containing valuable theoretical works, to the city of Leipzig.

Becker, Reinhold, German composer; b. Adorf, Aug. 11, 1842; d. Dresden, Dec. 7, 1924. He was originally a violinist, but because of a muscular disorder, was obliged in 1870 to give up his playing; then lived in Dresden as a composer; from 1884–94 was conductor of the Dresdener Liedertafel, for which he wrote numerous choruses.

WORKS: *Frauenlob,* opera (Dresden, 1892); *Ratbold,* opera (Mainz, 1896); *Der Prinz von Homburg,* symph. poem; 2 violin concertos; a string quartet; violin sonata; many works for male chorus.

Becker, René Louis, organist and composer; b. Bischheim, Alsace, Nov. 7, 1882; d. Detroit, Mich., Jan. 28, 1956. He studied in Strasbourg at the Municipal Cons.; settled in the U. S.; taught piano at St. Louis Univ. (1905–11); was organist at the Blessed Sacrament Cathedral, Detroit (1930–42); then at St. Alphonsus Church in Dearborn; retired in 1952.
WORKS: 6 Masses; 4 sonatas for organ; motets; numerous compositions for piano and organ.

Becker, Valentin Eduard, Austrian composer; b. Würzburg, Nov. 20, 1814; d. Vienna, Jan. 25, 1890. He wrote 2 operas: *Die Bergknappen* and *Der Deserteur*; Masses; male choruses.

Beckett, Wheeler, American conductor; b. San Francisco, March 7, 1898; studied at Columbia Univ. and Univ. of California; took a course in conducting with Felix Weingartner in Basel (1928–30); served as organist and choirmaster at Grace Cathedral, San Francisco (1921–25); conducted Young People's Concerts with the San Francisco Symph. Orch. (1927–30); was conductor of the Richmond Symph. Orch. (1932–36); Boston Symph. Youth Concerts (1938–48); in 1957 organized the New York Youth Concerts; under the auspices of the State Dept., conducted in the Far East (1959–62). He composed an opera *Snow White;* an organ concerto; a symphony; church music; songs.

Beckhelm, Paul, American composer; b. Kankakee, Illinois, July 3, 1906; d. Mt. Vernon, Iowa, Nov. 6, 1966. He studied at the Eastman School of Music in Rochester obtaining his Ph.D. there in 1949. He published a number of teaching pieces for piano with romantically fanciful titles and contents such as *Melancholy, Sunday Bells* and *Sidewalk Games.*

Becking, Gustav, German musicologist; b. Bremen, March 4, 1894; lost his life in Prague May 8, 1945, during street fighting. He studied with Riemann, J. Wolf; received his doctorate for a paper on Beethoven (Leipzig, 1921). In 1930 he became professor at the German University in Prague. He edited the collected works of E.T.A. Hoffmann (2 vols.; Leipzig, 1922–23).

Beckmann, Gustav, German musicologist; b. Berlin, Feb. 28, 1883; d. there, Nov. 14, 1948. He studied philology; served as a librarian at the Berlin State Library (1906–11); from 1934 to his death was councillor of the Univ. Library. He wrote some instrumental and vocal music; publ. the valuable paper *Das Violinspiel in Deutschland vor 1700* (Leipzig, 1918) and an essay on Leopold Mozart (1937); edited various bibliographical publications.

Beckmann, Johann Friedrich Gottlieb, German composer and organist; b. Celle, Sept. 6, 1737; d. there, April 25, 1792. He was one of the finest players and improvisers on the organ of his time; was for many years active in Celle. He wrote an opera, *Lukas und Hannchen* (Hamburg, 1782); 6 concertos; 12 piano sonatas; miscellaneous piano pieces.

Beckwith, John, Canadian composer; b. Victoria, British Columbia, March 9, 1927. He studied with Alberto Guerrero at the Cons. in Toronto (1945–50); then with Nadia Boulanger in Paris (1950–52). From 1952 to 1965 he was the music critic of the Toronto *Star,* and from 1952 was on the faculty of the Univ. of Toronto. His music is marked by pragmatic modernism, with ingenious application of urban folklore and structural collage.
WORKS: chamber opera, *Night Blooming Cereus* (1953–58; Toronto radio, March 4, 1959; first stage production, Toronto, April 5, 1960); *Montage* for orch. (1953); *Fall Scene and Fair Dance* for violin, clarinet and string orch. (1956); *Music for Dancing* for small orch. (1959); *Concerto Fantasy* for piano and orch. (1958–59); *Flower Variations and Wheels* for orch. (1962); Horn Concertino (1963); *Jonah,* chamber cantata (1963); *The Trumpets of Summer* for narrator, soloists, chorus and instruments (1964); *Place of Meeting* for narrator, tenor, blues singer with guitar, chorus and orch. (Toronto, Nov. 15, 1967); *Circle, with Tangents* for harpsichord and 13 solo strings (1967); *The Sun Dance* for narrator, 6 soloists, chorus, organ and percussion (1968); *All the Bees and All the Keys* for narrator and orch. (1973); *4 Conceits* for piano (1945–48); *The Great Lakes Suite* for soprano, baritone, clarinet, cello and piano (1949); *5 Pieces* for brass trio (1951); *5 Pieces* for 2 flutes (1951); Woodwind Quartet (1951); *3 Studies* for string trio (1956); 4 "collages" for radio: *A Message to Winnipeg* for 4 narrators, violin, cello, piano and percussion (1960); *12 Letters to a Small Town* for 4 narrators, flute, oboe, guitar and piano-harmonium (1961); *Wednesday's Child* for 3 narrators, soprano, tenor, flute, viola, piano and percussion (1962); and *Canada Dash, Canada Dot* for 8 narrators and singers, and chamber group (1965–67); *Gas!* for 20 speakers (1969; text derives from Ontario street signs); *New Mobiles* for piano (1971); *Taking a Stand* for 5 players, 8 brass instruments, 14 music stands and 1 platform (1972); *Musical Chairs,* string quintet (1973); songs.

Beckwith, John Christmas, English organist; b. Norwich, Dec. 25, 1750; d. there, June 3, 1809. He studied at Oxford; became organist of St. Peter Mancroft (1794); was awarded the degrees Mus. Bac. and Mus. Doc., Oxon. (1803); became organist of Norwich Cathedral (1808). Beckwith's proficiency as an organist was coupled with fine musical scholarship. His collection of chants, *The First Verse of Every Psalm of David, with an Ancient or Modern Chant in Score, adapted as much as possible to the Sentiment of each Psalm* (London, 1808), includes a valuable preface, 'A short history of chanting.' He also published numerous pieces for chorus and organ.

Becquié, A., French flutist; b. Toulouse, 1800; d. Paris, Nov. 10, 1825. He was a pupil of Tulou and Guillou at the Paris Cons.; became first flutist at the Opéra-Comique; wrote many compositions for flute, including *Grande fantaisie et variations* (concerto); *Les Regrets* (sonata); rondos, airs, etc. His brilliant career was cut short by his untimely death at the age of 25.

Becquié ('de Peyreville'), Jean-Marie, brother of **A. Becquié;** French violinist; b. Toulouse, April 28, 1795; d. Paris, Jan., 1876. He studied with R. and A. Kreutzer at the Paris Cons.; wrote chamber music and many pieces for violin.

Bečvařovský, Anton Felix, Bohemian organist; b. Jungbunzlau, April 9, 1754; d. Berlin, May 15, 1823. He was organist at Prague; then at Brunswick (1779–96); after 1800, lived in Berlin; wrote 3 piano concertos, 3 piano sonatas; many songs for voice and piano.

Bédard, Jean-Baptiste, French violinist and harpist; b. Rennes, c.1765; d. Paris, c.1815. He lived in Paris after 1796; wrote 2 *Symphonies périodiques*, and numerous works for the harp.

Bedford, David, English composer; b. London, Aug. 4, 1937. He studied at the Royal Academy of Music, London, with Lennox Berkeley (1958–61); then went to Italy where he took lessons with Luigi Nono in Venice; also worked in the electronic music studios in Milan. Returning to England, he taught at Queen's College in London and played the organ in pop groups.
WORKS: *Concerto for 24 Instruments* (1960); *Piece II* for electronic instruments (1962); *+2, −2,* for orch. (1963); *Piece for Mo* for percussion, vibraphon, accordion and strings (1963); *Music for Albion Moonlight* for soprano and chamber ensemble (1964); *The Great Birds* for 30-part chorus (1964); *Octet for 9* (1964); *A Dream of the Seven Lost Stars* for chorus and instruments (1965); *The Tentacles of the Dark Nebula* for tenor and solo strings (London, Sept. 22, 1969); *The Sword for Orion* for flute, clarinet, violin, cello, 4 metronomes and 32 percussion instruments (1970); *Star's End* for guitar and orch. (London, Nov. 5, 1974); *The Rime of the Ancient Mariner,* opera for children (1975–76).

Bedford, Herbert, English composer; b. London, Jan. 23, 1867; d. there, March 13, 1945. He studied at the Guildhall School of Music; at the same time was active as a painter. He wrote an opera, *Kit Marlowe; The Optimist* for orch.; *Nocturne,* for alto voice and orch.; *Sowing the Wind,* symph. poem; *Over the Hills and Far Away,* symph. interlude; *Queen Mab,* suite for orch.; *Ode to Music* and other songs; also an essay *On Modern Unaccompanied Song* (1923). He married Liza Lehmann in 1894.

Bedos de Celles, Dom François, French organ theorist; b. Caux, near Béziers, Jan. 24, 1709; d. Saint-Denis, Nov. 25, 1779. He was a Benedictine monk at Toulouse; wrote an important treatise, *L'Art du facteur d'orgues* (3 vols.; Paris, 1766–78); a 4th volume, containing historical notes on the organ, appeared in German (1793); a modern edition was publ. in Kassel (1936). He also wrote an account of a new organ at St. Martin de Tours in the *Mercure de France* (Jan. 1762; a German translation is included in Adlung's *Musica mechanica organoedi*).
BIBLIOGRAPHY: Félix Raugel, "Dom Bedos de Celles," *Bulletin de la Société française de Musicologie* (1917); E. Leipp, "La Regale," *Bul. du Groupe d'acoustique musicale* (Dec. 1968); P. Hardouin, "L'Orgue de référence de Dom Bédos aux Jesuits de Paris," *Renaissance de l'orgue* (Nov. 1969); D. Chai-

lley, "Autour de l'edition originale de *L'Art du facteur d'orgues*," *Renaissance de l'orgue* (Nov. 1969).

Beecham, Sir Thomas, eminent English conductor; b. St. Helens, near Liverpool, April 29, 1879; d. London, March 8, 1961. He was educated at Rossall School and at Wadham College, Oxford Univ.; took lessons with Dr. Sweeting and Dr. V. Roberts. Of independent means, he was able to pursue his musical career without regard to economic necessities. In 1899 he founded, chiefly for his own pleasure, an amateur orch. at Huyton. In 1902 he became conductor of K. Truman's traveling opera company, gaining valuable practical experience; after the conclusion of the tour, he resumed further serious study of music. In 1905 he gave his first symph. concert in London with the Queen's Hall Orch.; in 1906 he established the New Symph. Orch., which he conducted until 1908, when he resigned and formed the Beecham Symph. Orch. By that time his reputation as a forceful and magnetic conductor was securely established. His precise yet dramatic interpretive style suits equally well the music of the classics and the moderns, thus closing the esthetic gap between the 18th and 20th centuries. In 1910 Beecham appeared in a new role, that of operatic impresario. With a company of excellent artists and his own well-trained orchestra, he gave a season of opera in London, conducting most of the performances himself; the variety of the repertory and the high level of production made this season a memorable one; he presented the first English performance of *Elektra* at Covent Garden (Feb. 19, 1910); also other Strauss operas (*Salome, Der Rosenkavalier* and *Ariadne auf Naxos*); *A Village Romeo and Juliet* by Delius, *The Wreckers* by Ethel Smyth, *Shamus O'Brien* by Stanford, *Tiefland* by Eugene d'Albert, and *Le Chemineau* by Leroux; in subsequent years he continued to champion English operas, producing *Dylan* by Holbrooke, *The Critic* by Stanford, and *Everyman* by Liza Lehmann. In 1929 he organized and conducted the Delius Festival in London, to which Delius himself, though paralyzed, was brought from his residence in France. Beecham's activities continued unabated for several decades. In 1928 he toured the U. S. for the first time, subsequently continued to appear in America through 1956. He made a tour of Australia and Canada at the outbreak of World War II; was conductor of the Seattle Symph. from 1941–43; also conducted at the Metropolitan Opera House (1942–44). In 1943 he married the British pianist, Betty Humby, after divorcing Utica Welles, whom he had married in 1903. Beecham returned to London in 1945; organized the Royal Philh. Orch. in 1947, and toured in the U.S. and Canada (1949–51); conducted at the Edinburgh Festivals since 1947. On May 4, 1953, he gave in Oxford the first complete performance of the opera *Irmelin* by Delius. Beecham was knighted on Jan. 1, 1916. He published his autobiography, *A Mingled Chime,* in 1943. He also published an extensive biography of Delius (London, 1959). He arranged several orchestral suites from Handel's works, using material from Handel's operas and chamber music, and performed them as ballet scores; of these, *The Great Elopement* (1945) is particularly effective.
BIBLIOGRAPHY: Ethel Smyth, *Beecham and Pha-*

raoh (London, 1935); Ch. Reid, *Thomas Beecham: an Independent Biography* (London, 1961); H. Procter-Gregg, ed., *Sir Thomas Beecham, Conductor and Impresario; As Remembered by his Friends and Colleagues* (London, 1975).

Beecher, Carl Milton, American composer; b. Lafayette, Indiana, Oct. 22, 1883; d. Portland, Oregon, Nov. 21, 1968. He graduated from Northwestern Univ. in 1908; then went to Berlin where he took lessons in piano with Joseph Lhévinne. Returning to America he was on the faculty of his alma mater (1913–36); then spent 11 years in Tahiti. Returning finally to America in 1947, he became prof. at the Portland, Oregon, School of Music. He wrote mainly for piano in miniature forms; among his piano pieces is a suite *Remembrances of Times Past; 9 Musical Profiles* and 5 *Aquatints.*

Beecke, Ignaz von, German clavierist and composer; b. Wimpfen, Oct. 28, 1733; d. Wallerstein, Jan. 2, 1803. He was a captain of dragoons; later became 'Musikintendant' to the prince of Öttingen-Wallerstein. A highly accomplished pianist, he was a friend of Jommelli, Gluck and Mozart. Among his compositions are 7 operas; an oratorio, *Die Auferstehung Jesu;* a cantata; symphonies; quartets; 4 harpsichord trios; 6 harpsichord sonatas; songs; etc.
BIBLIOGRAPHY: L. Schiedermair, "Die Blütezeit der Öttingen-Wallerstein'schen Hofkapelle," *Sammelbände der Internationalen Musik-Gesellschaft* (Oct., 1907).

Beecroft, Norma, Canadian composer; b. Oshawa, Ontario, April 11, 1934. She studied composition with John Weinzweig at the Toronto Cons. (1950–58); took summer composition courses at Tanglewood (1958; with Copland and Foss), Darmstadt (1960; with Maderna); and in Rome (1960–61, with Petrassi). She then attended seminars in electronic music with Myron Schaeffer at the Univ. of Toronto (1962–63) and with Mario Davidowsky at Columbia Univ. (1964). She was subsequently engaged in various organizing activities in Toronto (1965–73) and since 1971 was a member of the board of the New Music Concerts. Her own music takes a modernistic direction without doctrinaire affiliations.
WORKS: Fantasy for Orch. (1958); *3 Pezzi Brevi* for flute, and harp or guitar or piano (1960–61); 3 *Improvvisazioni Concertanti: I* for flute and small orch. (1961), *II* for orch. (1971) and *III* for flute, 2 timpanists and orch. (1973); *Contrasts for 6 Performers* for oboe, viola, xylophone, vibraphone, percussion and harp (1962); *From Dreams of Brass* for narrator, soprano, chorus, orch. and tape (1963–64); *Piece Concertante No. 1* for orch. (1966); *Elegy* and *Two Went to Sleep* for soprano, flute, percussion or piano, and tape (1967); 3 *Rasas: I* for flute, harp, violin, viola, cello, percussion and piano (1968); *II* for contralto, flute, guitar, piano or organ, horn, 2 percussionists and tape (1972–73); and *III* for soprano, flute, trombone, piano, percussion and tape (1974); *3 Impressions* for chorus, piano and/or percussion (1973); *11 and 7 for 5 Plus* for brass quintet and tape (1975).

Beellaerts, Jean. See **Bellère, Jean.**

Beer, Jacob Liebmann. Original name of **Giacomo Meyerbeer** (q.v.)

Beer, Joseph, Bohemian clarinetist, b. Grünwald, May 18, 1744; d. Berlin, Oct. 28, 1812. He was first a trumpet player; served in the Austro-Hungarian army, and later was in the service of France. He learned to play the clarinet in Paris; from 1784 to 1792 he was a chamber musician in St. Petersburg; upon his return he was attached to the court chapel in Potsdam. Beer's principal improvement of the clarinet was the attachment of a fifth key. He wrote many compositions for his instrument.

Beer, Max Josef, Austrian pianist and composer; b. Vienna, Aug. 25, 1851; d. there, Nov. 25, 1908. He was a pupil of Dessoff; wrote the comic operas *Friedel mit der leeren Tasche* (Prague, 1892); *Der Streik der Schmiede* (Augsburg, 1897); *Das Stelldichein auf der Pfahlbrücke;* a cantata, *Der wilde Jäger;* many songs and piano pieces.

Beer-Walbrunn, Anton, German composer; b. Kohlberg, Bavaria, June 29, 1864; d. Munich, March 22, 1929. He was a pupil of Rheinberger, Bussmeyer and Abel at the Akademie der Tonkunst in Munich; from 1901 instructor there; made professor in 1908. He wrote the operas: *Shüne* (Lübeck, 1894); *Don Quixote* (Munich, 1908); *Das Ungeheuer* (Karlsruhe, 1914); *Der Sturm* (after Shakespeare); incidental music to *Hamlet;* a symphony; *Mahomet's Gesang* (for chorus and orch.); *Lustspielouvertüre;* Violin Concerto; Piano Quintet; church music; many compositions for various instruments. He also supervised new editions of works of Wilhelm Friedemann Bach.
BIBLIOGRAPHY: O. G. Sonneck, *Suum cuique: Essays in Music* (New York, 1916).

Beeson, Jack Hamilton, American composer; b. Muncie, Indiana, July 15, 1921. He studied at the Eastman School of Music, Rochester, N.Y. with Burril Phillips, Bernard Rogers and Howard Hanson; received his M.M. in 1943; later studied at Columbia Univ., and took private lessons with Béla Bartók during Bartók's last year of life; in 1945 he joined the staff of Columbia Univ. His music is marked by enlightened utilitarianism; particularly forceful are his operatic compositions. He wrote the operas *Jonah* (1950); *Hello Out There* (N.Y., April 27, 1954); *The Sweet Bye and Bye* (N.Y., Nov. 22, 1957); *Lizzie Borden,* based on a story of the famous murder trial in Fall River, Mass. in 1892 (his most successful opera; first produced, N.Y., March 25, 1965); a musical comedy, *Captain Jinks of the Horse Marines* (Kansas City, Sept. 20, 1975); Symphony in A (1959); *Transformations* for orch. (1959); *Commemoration* for band (1960); 5 piano sonatas; Viola Sonata; many vocal works; also a television opera, *My Heart's in the Highlands,* after a play by William Saroyan (National Educational Television Theater, March 17, 1970).

Beeth, Lola, dramatic soprano; b. Cracow, Nov. 23, 1862; d. Berlin, March 18, 1940. She studied with

Mme. Viardot-Garcia and Désirée Artôt; made her debut as Elsa in *Lohengrin* at the Berlin Court Opera (1882); sang there from 1882 till 1888; and at the Vienna Court Theater (1888–95). After appearances in Paris and New York she settled in Berlin as a teacher.

Beethoven, Ludwig van, the great German composer who represents the fullest maturity (in emotional scope, in formal construction and in instrumental treatment) of the allied classic forms of the sonata, concerto, string quartet and the symphony; b. Bonn, probably Dec. 16 (baptized Dec. 17), 1770; d. Vienna, March 26, 1827. His grandfather, **Ludwig van Beethoven,** was born in Malines, Belgium, Jan. 5, 1712.; moved to Louvain in 1731; went to Liège in 1732. In 1733 he became court musician in Bonn, where he married Marie Poll. The youngest of his three children was **Johann,** father of the composer; he was a tenor singer in the Electoral choir, and married a young widow, Marie Magdalena Laym (born Keverich), daughter of the court cook at Ehrenbreitstein. Ludwig's musical education was taken in hand by his father, a stern master, who was interested in exhibiting the boy in public for profit. Beethoven learned the violin as well as the piano. His instructors, besides his father, were Pfeiffer, a music director and oboist; Van den Eeden, the court organist; and the latter's successor, Christian Gottlob Neefe. He was already a notable improviser on the piano; he could play Bach's *Wohltemperierte Clavier* with fluency; in 1781 he composed his first published pieces (3 piano sonatas); in 1782, during Neefe's absence, Beethoven, then not quite twelve, was formally installed as his deputy at the organ; in 1783 he was appointed cembalist for the rehearsals of the court theater orchestra, as yet without emolument. In 1784 the new Elector Max Franz appointed Beethoven assistant organist at a salary of 150 florins; he held this place till 1792; from 1788 he also played second viola in the theater orchestra under the direction of Reicha. In 1787 he made a visit to Vienna for a few months, and played for Mozart, eliciting from him the oft-quoted exclamation: "This young man will leave his mark on the world." Beethoven's mother died in July 1787 and his father gave way to intemperance, gradually losing his voice. Beethoven's home life became wretched. He found consolation in the family of Frau von Breuning, the widow of a court councillor, to whose daughter and youngest son Beethoven gave music lessons. In their refined society his taste for literature was quickened. About this time he made the acquaintance of the young Count Waldstein, his life-long friend, admirer and benefactor. In his leisure hours he gave other lessons, and occupied himself with composition. Despite his remarkable faculty for improvisation, the number of known works for the period up to the age of 21 is relatively small: half a dozen songs; a rondo; a minuet, and 3 preludes for piano; 3 piano quartets; a piano trio; a string trio; 4 sets of piano variations; a rondino for wind instruments; the *Ritter-Ballet* with orch.; most of the Bagatelles, op. 33; 2 piano rondos, op. 51; the *Serenade Trio,* op. 8. To these should be added the lost cantata praised by Haydn; a lost trio for piano, flute and bassoon, and an Allegro and Minuet for 2 flutes. When Beethoven arrived in Vienna in 1792, he brought with him a considerable number of compositions in MS; some of these early works, e.g., the piano rondos, op. 51, he revised and published later (which accounts for the high opus-number); others were lost. In 1910 Fritz Stein found, in Jena, a set of parts of a Symphony in C, ascribed by the unknown copyist to Beethoven; this so-called "Jena Symphony" was proved to be a work by Friedrich Witt. Beethoven never possessed the fatal facility of invention which rejoices in rapidity rather than solidity of production. His way of working is exhibited in the 'sketch books' of this early period, which contain motives, themes, ideas; fragments jotted down in moods of inspiration, frequently reappearing in modified forms, and in many cases recognizable as the germs of later compositions. This method of tentative notation and careful working-over was typical of Beethoven through his whole life.

The year 1792 marks a turning point. Haydn, passing through Bonn, warmly praised a cantata by Beethoven; the Elector, probably influenced by the master's opinion and the representations of the friendly Waldstein, decided to send Beethoven to Vienna, then the musical center of Europe. Here, a member of the highest circles of artists and art lovers, to which his native genius and letters from the Elector procured speedy admission, Beethoven found himself in a most congenial atmosphere. Besides his salary from the Elector (discontinued in 1794), and an annual stipend of 600 florins from Prince Lichnowsky, one of his truest friends and warmest admirers, his income was derived from the increasing sale of his works. He applied to Haydn for further instruction; but, dissatisfied with his methods of teaching, and angered at his lack of appreciation of compositions submitted to him for approval, he surreptitiously took lessons with Schenk, carrying his exercises, after correction by Schenk, to Haydn. This peculiar arrangement continued for a little more than a year, terminating at Haydn's departure (Jan. 1794) for England. During 1794 he had quite regular lessons in counterpoint with Albrechtsberger, whose verdict, 'He has learned nothing, and will never do anything properly,' can hardly be called prophetic; Salieri gave him many valuable hints on vocal style; and Aloys Förster contributed good counsel on the art of quartet-writing. Beethoven's contrapuntal exercises under Albrechtsberger (publ. Paris, 1832; revised ed. by Nottebohm, in vol. I of his *Beethoven-Studien,* in 1873) illustrate the irrepressible conflict between Beethoven's imagination and the dry course of prescribed study.

A frequent guest at the private musical soirées of the Vienna aristocracy, Beethoven did not play in public until March 29, 1795, when he performed one of his piano concertos (probably op. 19, in B-flat) at a concert in the Burgtheater. In 1796 he visited Nuremberg, Prague and Berlin, and played before King Friedrich Wilhelm II. The publication of the E-flat piano sonata (op. 7) in 1797, a work of strongly individual type, is noteworthy. Two public concerts given by Beethoven in Prague in 1798 are chronicled as making a profound impression. In the same year he met two famed piano virtuosi: Steibelt, whose challenge to Beethoven as an extemporizer and composer resulted in his own overwhelming discomfiture; and Wölffl, a worthier opponent, with whom Beethoven associated and made music on a friendly footing (Wölffl inscribed 3 sonatas to him). To 1798 and 1799 belong the 3 sonatas for piano and violin (op. 12), the *Grande sonate pathétique* (op. 13), the First Piano Concerto (in C) and several lesser publications. About 1800, Beethoven's so-called "first period" of composition (after the generally accepted classification by W. von Lenz in his *Beethoven et ses trois styles*, St. Petersburg, 1852) ends; the "second period" extends to 1815; the "third," to the end of his life in 1827. The works of his first period include opp. 1–13 (4 piano trios, 4 string trios, the first 6 string quartets, 10 piano sonatas), several sets of variations, Septet for Winds and Strings (op. 20), the solo cantata *Adelaide* (op. 46), etc. At that time (1800–1801) a dread malady, which later resulted in total deafness, began to make alarming progress, and caused Beethoven acute mental suffering. From his entrance into Viennese society he demonstrated his spirit of independence, his love of freedom, his refusal to be obsequious, in a world in which even such great musicians as Haydn had to practice subservience. No doubt, he deliberately cultivated his eccentricity. (He remarked that "it is good to mingle with aristocrats, but one must know how to impress them.") His genius as an artist, and his noble generosity, won the hearts of music lovers, and caused them to overlook his occasional outbursts of temper. With increasing deafness, however, his character altered; he gradually grew taciturn, morose and suspicious (traits aggravated by the sordid meanness of his brothers, Karl and Johann, who had also settled in Vienna), and treated his best friends outrageously. When his brother Karl died in 1815, leaving a son to Beethoven's guardianship, Beethoven undertook the boy's education as a sacred trust; his mental anguish at the failure of this task forms one of the saddest chapters in the great man's life, and still further darkened his declining years.

Beethoven's freest and most joyous creative period was his second. It was the period of the fullest flow of ideas, not as yet overcast by the gloom of his anguish. Major works included in it are the six symphonies from the third to the eighth; his opera, *Fidelio;* the music to *Egmont;* the ballet *Prometheus;* the Mass in C, op. 86; the oratorio *Christus am Oelberg* (1803); the *Coriolanus* overture; the piano concertos in G and E-flat; Violin Concerto; the quartets in F minor, E-flat, and those inscribed to Rasumovsky; 3 piano trios (op. 70, nos. 1 and 2; op. 97); and 14 piano sonatas (among them the Sonata *quasi una fantasia,* op. 27, no. 2, commonly known as the *Moonlight Sonata;* the *Pastorale,* op. 28; op. 31, no. 2, in D minor; the one dedicated to Waldstein, op. 53; the *Appassionata,* op. 57; and *Les Adieux, l'absence, et le retour,* op. 81); also the *Liederkreis,* etc.

The third period includes the five piano sonatas opp. 101, 106, 109, 110, 111; also op. 102, nos. 1 and 2; the *Missa solemnis* in D, op. 123; the Ninth Symphony, op. 125; the Orchestral Overture op. 124; the Grand Fugue for string quartet, op. 133; and the great string quartets op. 127 (E-flat), op. 130 (B-flat), op. 131 (C-sharp minor), op. 132 (A minor), and op. 135 (F).

The work on his only opera, *Fidelio,* cost Beethoven more pains and exasperation than any other of his compositions. As early as 1803 he arranged with Schikaneder, manager of the Theater-an-der-Wien, to write an opera; it was produced on Nov. 20, 1805 amid the commotion and gloom incident to the entrance, just a week before, of the French army into Vienna. Originally in three acts, it was withdrawn after three consecutive performances; then, after considerable revisions and cuts, was brought out again (March 29, 1806) with more success, but withdrawn by the composer after only two performances. Once more sweepingly revised, it was staged in 1814, very successfully. The opera was first named *Leonore,* after the heroine; its overture was rewritten twice; the present *Fidelio* overture is quite different. Beethoven's sketch-book for his opera contains 300 large pages of 16 staves each, crammed with heterogeneous notes.

The *Eroica* Symphony (No. 3) has an interesting history. Schindler's report (based on a story told by Lichnowsky and Ries) that Beethoven tore off the title page of the manuscript of the *Eroica* with a dedication to Napoleon after learning of Napoleon's proclamation as emperor, seems apocryphal; while the original MS is lost, a copyist's score (in the library of the Gesellschaft der Musikfreunde in Vienna) shows that Beethoven inked out the title and renamed the symphony as "Sinfonia eroica composta per festeggiare il sovvenire d'un grand' uomo" (heroic symphony, composed to celebrate the memory of a great man). However, in a letter to Breitkopf & Härtel dated Aug. 26, 1804 (long after Napoleon's proclamation) Beethoven still refers to the *Eroica* as "entitled Bonaparte."

With the Ninth Symphony Beethoven achieved a sublime greatness of expression in symphonic form; the choral finale where orchestral and vocal music blend in an outburst of ecstasy (the words are from Schiller's 'Hymn to Joy') is a true apotheosis of musical art.

Up to 1814, Beethoven's material welfare had increased, though hardly in proportion to his artistic triumphs. An honored and frequent guest at the houses of the princes Carl Lichnowsky, Lobkowitz and Kinsky, the counts Moritz Lichnowsky, Rasumovsky and Franz von Brunswick, and Baron von Gleichenstein, Beethoven was treated as a social equal (the nobiliary particle "van" in his full name, Ludwig van Beethoven, made him technically a member of the aristocracy, and Beethoven regarded this sign of nobility with utmost seriousness); at the time of the Vienna Congress, as a guest of Archduke Rudolf, he met the various reigning monarchs as their peers, and even (as he said himself) let them pay court to him. A curious incident was the invitation extended to Beethoven in 1809, by the de facto "King of Westphalia," Jerome Bonaparte, to assume the post of maître de chapelle at Kassel at a salary of 600 ducats; Beethoven never considered accepting this offer; he really wanted to become Imperial Kapellmeister at Vienna; but the bare possibility of losing the great composer so dismayed his Viennese admirers, that Archduke Rudolf and Princes Lobkowitz and Kinsky bestowed on Beethoven an annuity of 4,000 florins (in depreciated currency of fluctuating value). In December, 1826, he caught a violent cold, which developed into pneumonia; dropsy then supervened, and after several unsuccessful operations to let out the accumulating fluid, he succumbed on March 26, 1827.

The primary cause of Beethoven's lingering maladies appears to be syphilis, which he must have contracted in 1796. The converging symptoms were the gradual disintegration of the auditory nerve that resulted in deafness, the painful intestinal disturbances accompanied by diarrhea, enormous enlargement of the pancreas, cirrhosis of the liver, and, most decisively, the porous degeneration of the right temple bone and consequent deterioration of the roof of the cranium, observable in the life mask of 1812 and clearly shown in the photograph of Beethoven's skull taken when his body was exhumed in 1863. That Beethoven himself was fully aware of the nature of his illness appears in his "Heiligenstädter Testament" of October 1802 in which he says that his illness began 6 years before. Numerous other references to the ominous "lues" from which Beethoven suffered are extant in medical recipes prescribing treatment by mercury compounds, regarded as a specific remedy against syphilis in Beethoven's time. A concerted effort was made by Beethoven's intimates to destroy other evidence, including correspondence with his doctors and some of the conversation books referring to the subject; yet Beethoven's biographer A. W. Thayer states plainly in a letter dated Oct. 29, 1880, that it was "well known to many persons" that "his ill health and his deafness perhaps come from some common cause" and names it as "a venereal disease." A full account proving with a finality that Beethoven was indeed a victim of syphilis is found in Dr. Dieter Kerner's publication *Krankheiten grosser Musiker* (Stuttgart, 1973; vol. 1, pp. 89–140).

While Beethoven, in choosing the conventional sonata form as a vehicle for the expression of his thought (in 81 works, i.e., about one-third of all), still belongs to the Classic school, his methods of moulding this form were eminently unconventional; indeed, so much so, that even at the beginning of his 'second period' the progressive *Allgemeine musikalische Zeitung* of Leipzig berated him for his 'daring harmonies and venturesome rhythms'. Even among musicians no genuine appreciation of his last string quartets and piano sonatas was found until half a century after his death. His innovations on the formal key scheme of his predecessors, his original elaboration of connecting links both in thematic development and between separate movements, his fertility in incidental modulation, and the inexhaustible freshness of his rhythms, render the structure of his compositions thoroughly individual. But his loftiest originality, and that whence the differences in formal construction naturally flowed, is the intensity and fervor of subjective emotion which prevades his music. It is this mood of profound subjectivity, of powerful soul-expression, that separates Beethoven's music from the Classical works of Bach, Haydn and Mozart, opening the era of Romantic composition. Technically, Beethoven's art of orchestration reaches a perfection in detail and a grandeur of effect theretofore unknown; his diversified development of the motives (melodic, harmonic, rhythmic) surpasses anything before Wagner. As specimens of what can be done in thematic treatment, his variations on given or original themes are a *ne*

plus ultra of musical ingenuity. It is noteworthy that, according to contemporary accounts, his "free improvisations" at the piano, which held his auditors spellbound, were developments of kindred nature; not mere rhapsodies, but the spontaneous elaborations of a teeming invention; in vocal music, his *Fidelio* and the *Missa solemnis* are creations of unique power.

Monuments were erected to Beethoven in 1845 at Bonn (by Hähnel), and in 1880 at Vienna (by Zumbusch).

Beethoven's works comprise 138 opus numbers, and many unnumbered compositions. A list of his publ. works is given below. Certain works are in both instrumental and vocal categories (the 9th Symphony, *Egmont, Ruins of Athens,* etc.). They have been listed in that group with which they are customarily associated.

WORKS: INSTRUMENTAL: Nine symphonies: No 1, op. 21, in C; 2, op. 36, in D; 3, op. 55, in E-flat (*Eroica*); 4, op. 60, in B-flat; 5, op. 67, in C minor; 6, op. 68, in F (*Pastoral);* 7, op. 92, in A; 8, op. 93, in F; 9, op. 125, in D minor. (*Choral*).—Other orchestral music: *The Battle of Vittoria* (op. 91); music to the ballet *Prometheus* (op. 43), and to Goethe's *Egmont* (op. 84), both with overtures.—Nine further overtures: *Coriolanus* (op. 62); *Leonore* (No. 1, op. 138; Nos. 2 and 3, op. 72a); *Fidelio* (from op. 72b); *King Stephen* (from op. 117); *Ruins of Athens* (from op. 113); *Namensfeir* (op. 115); *Weihe des Hauses* (op. 124).—Other compositions for orch. or band: Allegretto in E-flat; March from *Tarpeia,* in C; Military Marches in D and F; *Ritter-Ballet;* 12 Minuets; 12 *deutsche Tänze;* 12 *Contretänze;* 2 Marches in F; March in C; Polonaise in D; Ecossaise in D.—Concertos: Violin Concerto, op. 61, in D. Two romances for violin and orch. (op. 40, in G; op. 50, in F). Two cadenzas to the Violin Concerto. Five piano concertos: No. 1, op. 15, in C; 2, op. 19, in B-flat; 3, op. 37, in C minor; 4, op. 58, in G; 5, op. 73, in E-flat (*Emperor*); also a piano concerto arranged from the Violin Concerto; a Rondo in B-flat, for piano and orch. (left incomplete and finished by Czerny). 8 cadenzas to the first 4 piano concertos, and 2 cadenzas to Mozart's piano concerto in D minor (K. 466). A Triple Concerto, op. 56, for piano, violin, cello and orch.; a *Choral Fantasia,* op. 80, for piano, chorus and orch.—Chamber music: Two octets for wind, both in E-flat (the first op. 103): Septet for strings and wind, in E-flat, op. 20; Sextet for Strings and 2 Horns, in E-flat, op. 81b; Sextet for Winds, in E-flat, op. 71; March, in B-flat, for 6 woodwinds; three quintets for strings: op. 4, in E-flat; op. 29, in C; op. 104, in C minor; Fugue for string quintet, op. 137. For four trombones: Three *Equale.* Sixteen string quartets: op. 18, nos. 1–6, in F, G, D, C minor, A, and B-flat (first period); op. 59, nos. 1–3, in F, E minor, and C; op. 74 in E-flat (*Harfenquartett*); op. 95, in F minor (second period); op. 127, in E-flat; op. 130, in B-flat; op. 131, in C-sharp minor; op. 132, in A minor; op. 135, in F; Grand Fugue for string quartet, op. 133, in B-flat (third period). Five string trios: op. 3, in E-flat; op. 9, nos. 1–3, in G, D, C minor; op. 8, in D (*Serenade*); 6 *Ländlerische Tänze.* Trio for 2 oboes and Engl. horn, op. 87, in C; Serenade for flute, violin and viola op. 25, in D. Quintet for piano and wind, op. 16, in E-flat; four quartets for piano and strings: in E-flat, D, C (juvenile); in E-flat (arrangement of the piano quintet). Nine trios for piano, violin and cello: op. 1, nos. 1–3, in E-flat, G, C minor; op. 70, Nos. 1–2, in D, E-flat; op. 97, in B-flat; in E-flat, B-flat (both posthumous, the latter in one movement); in D (incomplete). Also for piano, violin and cello: 14 Variations, op. 44, in E-flat; Variations, op. 121a, on 'Ich bin der Schneider Kakadu'; an arrangement of the 2nd Symph., op. 36. Two trios for piano, clar. (or violin) and cello: op. 11, B-flat, op. 38, in E-flat (after the septet, op. 20). Also a Trio for piano, flute and bassoon. Sonatina in C minor, for piano and mandolin; Adagio in E-flat, for piano and mandolin. Ten sonatas for piano and violin: op. 12, nos. 1–3, in D, A, E-flat; op. 23, in A minor; op. 24, in F; op. 30, Nos. 1–3, in A, C minor, G; op. 47 in A (*Kreutzer*); op. 96, in G. Also for piano and violin: Rondo in G; 12 Variations, in F, on 'Se vuol ballare' from Mozart's *Marriage of Figaro;* 6 *Deutsche Tänze.* Five sonatas for piano and cello: op. 5, 1–2, in F, G; op. 69, in A; op. 102, nos. 1-2, in C, D. Also for piano and cello: 12 Variations on 'Ein Mädchen oder Weibchen,' op. 66, in F; 12 Variations in G, on 'See, the Conquering Hero Comes'; 7 Variations, in E-flat, on 'Bei Männern, welche Liebe fühlen.' Sonata for piano and horn, op. 17, in F. Two sets of 'varied themes' for piano with obbligato flute (or violin); op. 105 with 6 themes; op. 107 with 10 themes.—For piano 4 hands: Sonata, op. 6, in D; 3 Marches, op. 45, in C, E-flat, D; Variations, in C, on a theme by Count Waldstein; Song with variations, in D ('Ich denke dein'); Grand Fugue, op. 134 (an arr. of op. 133); an Allegro in B-flat; Gavotte in F; *Marzia lugubre* (incomplete).—Thirty-eight sonatas for piano solo: op. 2, nos. 1–3, in F minor, A, C (ded. to Haydn); op. 7, in E-flat; op. 10, nos. 1–3, in C minor, F, D; op. 13, in C minor (*Pathétique;* ded. to Prince Lichnowsky); op. 14, nos. 1–2, in E, G; op. 22, in B-flat; op. 26, in A-flat (ded. to Prince Lichnowsky); op. 27, nos. 1–2, in E-flat, C-sharp minor; (the latter known as *Moonlight Sonata*); op. 28, in D (*Pastoral*); op. 31, nos. 1–3, in G, D minor, E-flat; op. 49, 2 easy sonatas in G minor, G; op. 53, in C (ded. to Count Waldstein); op. 54, in F; op. 57, in F minor, (*Appassionata*); op. 78, in F-sharp; op. 79, little sonata in G; op. 81a, in E-flat (*Les Adieux, l'absence, le retour;* ded. to Archduke Rudolph); op. 90, in E minor (ded. to Count Lichnowsky); op. 101, in A; op. 106, in B-flat (*Hammerklavier;* ded. to Archduke Rudolph); op. 109, in E; op. 110, in A-flat; op. 111, in C minor. Also three sonatas in E-flat, F minor, D; an easy sonata in C (incomplete); two sonatinas in G, F.—Also for piano solo: 21 sets of variations, including op. 34, in F; op. 35, in E-flat (*Eroica*); op. 76, in D; op. 120, in C (*Diabelli*); Bagatelles, op. 33, 119, 126; 5 rondos, including op. 51, 1–2, and op. 129; Fantasia, op. 77, in G minor; 3 preludes, including op. 39, nos. 1–2 (for piano or organ); Polonaise, op. 89, in C; Andante in F; 7 minuets; 13 Ländler; a *Kleines Stück* in B-flat; a German dance in C; *Letzter Gedanke* in C; 6 easy variations, in F, for piano or harp; *Für Elise* (Bagatelle in A minor); Allegretto in C minor; Allemande in A; 2 Bagatelles in C minor, C; 8 Ecossaisen; 2 *Kleine Clavierstücke* (*Lustig, Traurig*); 2 Waltzes in E-flat, D. For organ: A 2-part fugue.

VOCAL MUSIC: Opera, *Fidelio,* in 2 acts, op. 72b; two Masses, op. 86, in C, and op. 123, in D (*Missa Solemnis*); oratorio, *Christus am Oelberg,* op. 85; cantata, *Der glorreiche Augenblick,* op. 136 (also arr. as *Preis der Tonkunst*); *Meeresstille und glückliche Fahrt,* op. 112 (poem by Goethe); *Ah, perfido!,* scena and aria for soprano with orch., op. 65; *Tremate, empi, tremate,* trio for soprano, tenor and bass, op. 116; *Opferlied,* for soprano, chor. and orch., op. 121b. *Bundeslied,* for 2 soli, 3-part chorus and wind, op. 122; *Elegischer Gesang,* for 4 voices and strings, op. 118; *Cantate auf den Tod Kaiser Joseph des Zweiten; Cantate auf die Erhebung Leopold des Zweiten zur Kaiserwürde; Chor zum Festspiel: Die Weihe des Hauses; Chor auf die verbündeten Fürsten;* for bass and orch: *Prüfung des Küssens;* also *Mit Mädeln sich vertragen;* Two arias for Ignaz Umlauf's Singspiel *Die schöne Schusterin* (O welch ein Leben!; Soll ein Schuh nicht drücken); For soprano and orch.: *Primo amore piacer del ciel;* Music to Friedrich Duncker's drama *Leonore Prohaska. Trauergesang* for 4-part male chor. and 4 trombones; *Lobkowitz-Cantate* for 3 voices and piano; *Gesang der Mönche* for 3 voices; *Abschiedsgesang* for 3 male voices; *O care selve* (song from Metastasio's *Olimpiade*), for unison chorus and piano. Seventy-five songs with piano accomp.; one duet; twenty-three vocal canons; seven books of English, Scotch, Irish, Welsh and Italian songs for voice, piano, violin and cello.

Breitkopf & Härtel were the first to publ. a 'complete edition' in 24 series comprising 40 volumes (1864–67, ed. by Rietz, Nottebohm, David, Hauptmann, Reinecke and others). An additional volume, containing 48 works subsequently found, appeared in 1887.

BIBLIOGRAPHY: BIOGRAPHICAL: F. G. Wegeler and F. Ries, *Biographische Notizen über L. van B.* (Koblenz, 1838; new ed. by A. Kalischer, Leipzig, 1906); A. Schindler, *Biographie von L. van B.* (Münster, 1840; new ed. by A. Kalischer, Berlin, 1909; Eng. transl. by Moscheles, London, 1841); W. v. Lenz, *B.: eine Kunststudie* (2 vols., Kassel, 1855; I. *Das Leben des Meisters,* new ed. by A. Kalischer, Berlin, 1908; II. *Der Stil in B.; Die Mit- und Nachwelt B.s; Der B. Status Quo in Russland*); A. B. Marx, *L. van B.s Leben und Schaffen* (2 vols., Berlin, 1859; 6th ed. Leipzig, 1906); L. Nohl, *B.s Leben* (3 vols., Vienna, 1864–77); id., *B. nach den Schilderungen seiner Zeitgenossen* (Stuttgart, 1877; G. v. Breuning, *Aus dem Schwarzspanierhause* (Vienna, 1874); J. W. v. Wasielewski, *L. van B.* (2 vols., Berlin, 1888); T. von Frimmel, *Neue Beethoveniana* (Berlin, 1887; revised and augmented as *Beethovenstudien,* 2 vols., Munich, 1905–6); id., *B.* (in Riemann's *Berühmte Meister,* Berlin, 1901); R. Rolland, *B.* (Paris, 1903; in English, N.Y., 1917); F. Kerst, *B. im eigenen Wort* (Berlin, 1904; Engl. transl. by H. E. Krehbiel, N.Y. 1905); G. A. Fischer, *B., a Character Study* (N.Y., 1905); E. Walker, *B.* (2nd ed. London, 1907); A. Kalischer, *B. und seine Zeitgenossen* (4 vols., Leipzig, 1910); P. Bekker, *B.* (Berlin, 1911; Engl. transl. and adaptation by M. M. Bozman, London, 1925); M. E. Belpaire, *B., een kunsten levensbeeld* (Antwerp, 1911); V. d'Indy, *B.: Biographie critique* (Paris, 1911; Engl. transl. by T. Baker, Boston, 1913); W. A. Thomas-San Galli, *L. van B.* (Berlin, 1913); A. Hensel, *B. Der Versuch einer musik-philosophischen Darstellung* (Berlin, 1918); J. G. Prod'homme, *La jeunesse de B.* (Paris, 1920; new ed., 1927); G. Bilancioni, *La sordità di B.* (Rome, 1921); T. von Frimmel, *B. im zeitgenössischen Bildnis* (Vienna, 1923); W. Krug, *B.s Vollendung* (Munich, 1924); S. Ley, *B.s Leben in authentischen Bildern und Texten* (Berlin, 1925); L. Schiedermair, *Der junge B.* (Leipzig, 1925; 2nd ed., 1951); B. issue of the *Musical Quarterly* (April 1927); B. Bartels, *B.* (Hildesheim, 1927); L. Bertrán, *Anecdotario completo de B.* (Buenos Aires, 1927); E. Newman, *The Unconscious B.* (N.Y., 1927); A. Orel, *B.* (Vienna, 1927); J.-G. Prod'homme, *B. raconté par ceux qui l'ont vu* (Paris, 1927); A. Schmitz, *Das romantische Beethovenbild* (Berlin, 1927); O. G. Sonneck, *The Riddle of the Immortal Beloved*, a supplement to Thayer's *Life of B.* (N.Y., 1927); W. J. Turner, *B., the Search for Reality* (London, 1927); R. J. J. van Aerde, *Les ancêtres flamands de B.* (Malines, 1928); E. Closson, *L'élément flamand dans B.* (Brussels, 1928; Engl. transl. London, 1934); W. Fischer, *B. als Mensch* (Regensburg, 1928); R. Rolland, *B.: les grandes époques créatrices* (Paris, 1928 ff.); R. Rolland, *B. the Creator* (Engl. transl. by E. Newman, N.Y., 1929); R. H. Schauffler, *B., the Man who Freed Music* (N.Y., 1929); E. Herriot, *La Vie de B.* (Paris, 1929; in English, N.Y., 1935); R. Rolland, *Goethe et B.* (Paris, 1930; Engl. transl. N.Y., 1931); A. Boschot, *B., la musique et la vie* (Paris, 1931); R. Specht, *Bildnis B.s* (Hellerau, 1931; in English, London, 1933); E. Brümmer, *B. im Spiegel der zeitgenössischen rheinischen Presse* (Würzburg, 1932); F. S. Howes, *B.* (London, 1933); M. Scott, *B.* (London, 1934); E. Bücken, *L. van B.* (Potsdam, 1935); C. Carpenter, *French Factors in B.'s Life* (N.Y., 1935); E. Buenzod, *Pouvoirs de B.* (Paris, 1936); K. Kobald, *B.* (Leipzig, 1936); W. Riezler, *B.* (Berlin, 1936; Engl. transl. London, 1938); H. Schultz, *L. van B., sein Leben in Bildern* (Leipzig, 1936); *B. und die Gegenwart* (Berlin and Bonn, 1937); H. Kesser, *B. der Europäer* (Zürich,1937); H. v. Hofmannsthal, *B.* (Vienna, 1938); R. Petzoldt, *L. van B., Leben und Werk* (Leipzig, 1938); R. van Aerde, "A la recherche des ascendants de B.," *Revue belge archéologique* 2 (1939); C. Brandt, *B., su vida, su obra, y el sentido de su música* (Caracas, 1940); A. Orel, *Grillparzer und B.* (Vienna, 1941); L. Schrade, *B. in France* (New Haven, 1942); H. Volkmann, *B. in seinen Beziehungen zu Dresden* (Dresden, 1942); J. N. Burk, *The Life and Works of B.* (N.Y., 1943); E. C. C. Corti, *B.-Anekdoten* (Berlin, 1943); E. Ludwig, *B., Life of a Conqueror* (1943); A. Albertini, *B., l'uomo*, 4th ed. (Milan, 1944); *Les Cahiers de conversation de B. (1819-1827)*, trans. and ed. by J. G. Prod'homme (Paris, 1946); A. Pryce-Jones, *B.* (London, 1948); S. Axnelson, *B.s ferne und unsterbliche Geliebte* (Zürich, 1953; purporting to prove that the "immortal beloved" was Josephine Deym-Stackelberg, sister of Therese Brunswick; that Beethoven was with her in Prague, July 3, 1812, and that Josephine's child Minona, born in Vienna on April 9, 1813, was in fact Beethoven's); Editha and Richard Sterba, *B. and his Nephew, a Psychoanalytical Study of their Relationship* (N.Y., 1954). The standard and most extensive biography is the monumental work of A. W. Thayer, *L. v. B.s Leben* (5 vols., 1866-1908). The English original was never published. The first 3 volumes appeared in a German transl. by H. Deiters (Berlin, 1866, 1872, 1877). After the author's death Deiters completed vols. IV and V from Thayer's material, but died also before their publication. He had also revised

and enlarged vol. I (Leipzig, 1901). Deiters' manuscript was revised and edited by H. Riemann (vol. IV, Leipzig, 1907; vol. V, Leipzig, 1908). Vols. II and III were then revised and enlarged by Riemann along the lines followed by Dieters in the revision of vol. I (Leipzig, 1910-11). The 4th ed. of Thayer's work was revised by Riemann and published in 1919 (abridged English ed. by Krehbiel, in 3 vols., N.Y., 1921).

CORRESPONDENCE: The several partial collections of letters edited by Nohl, Köchel, etc., have been superseded by the following complete editions: A. C. Kalischer, *B.s sämmtliche Briefe* (5 vols., Berlin, 1906-08; partial Engl. transl. by J. S. Shedlock, London, 1909); F. Prelinger, *L. van B.s sämmtliche Briefe und Aufzeichnungen* (5 vols., Vienna, 1907-10); E. Kastner, *L. van B.s sämmtliche Briefe* (Leipzig, 1910). Also A. Leitzmann, *B.s Aufzeichnungen* (Leipzig, 1918); M. Unger, *B. und seiner Verleger Steiner-Haslinger-Schlesinger* (Berlin, 1921); id., *B.s Handschrift* (Bonn, 1926); O. G. Sonneck, *B. Letters in America* (N.Y., 1927); G. Kinsky, *Die Handschriften zu B.s Egmont Musik* (Vienna, 1933). Other letters have been edited by U. Steindorff (in Engl.; Los Angeles, 1933); *Briefe und das heiligenstädter Testament*, ed. by A. Klarer (Zürich, 1944); *L. v. B., ein Bekenntnis mit Briefen und Zeitdokumenten*, edited by H. Freiberger (Berlin, 1951).

CRITICISM, ANALYSIS: —General: L. v. Seyfried, *L. van B.s Studien im Generalbass, Kontrapunkt, und in der Kompositionslehre* (Vienna, 1832; new ed. by Nottebohm, Leipzig, 1873; also by L. Köhler, Leipzig, 1880; W. v. Lenz, *B. et ses trois styles* (St. Petersburg, 1852; new ed. by M. D. Calvocoressi, Paris, 1909); A. v. Oulibicheff, *B., ses critiques et ses glossateurs* (Paris, 1857; Ger. transl. by L. Bischoff, Leipzig, 1859); G. Nottebohm, *Ein Skizzenbuch von Beethoven* (Leipzig, 1865; 2d ed. ib., 1880; new rev. ed. by P. Mies, 1924); R. Wagner, *B.* (Leipzig, 1870; reprinted in vol. IX of *Ges. Schriften und Dichtungen*; Engl. transl., 3rd ed., N.Y., 1883); G. Nottebohm, *Beethoveniana* (Leipzig, 1872; id., *Neue Beethoveniana* (orig. publ. in *Musikal. Wochenblatt*, 1878; revised and enlarged E. Mandyczewski as *Zweite Beethoveniana* (Leipzig, 1887); T. de Wyzewa, *B. et Wagner* (Paris, 1898; 4th ed., 1914); D. G. Mason, *B. and His Forerunners* (N.Y., 1904); H. Berlioz, *A Critical Study of B.'s Nine Symphonies* (transl. by E. Evans; N.Y., 1913); R. Rolland, *B.* (transl. by B. Constance Hull, with a brief analysis of the sonatas, the symphonies and the quartets by A. Eaglefield Hull; N.Y., 1917); H. Mersmann, *B., die Synthese der Stile* (Berlin, 1922); id., *B.s Skizzen* (Basel, 1924); F. Cassirer, *B. und die Gestalt* (Stuttgart, 1925); P. Mies, *Die Bedeutung der Skizzen B.s zur Erkenntnis seines Stiles* (Leipzig, 1925; Engl. transl. London, 1929); T. v. Frimmel, *B.-Handbuch* (2 vols., Leipzig, 1926); J. W. N. Sullivan, *B., His Spiritual Development* (London, 1927); T. Veidl, *Der musikalische Humor bei B.* (Leipzig, 1929); H. Naumann, *Strukturkadenzen bei B.* (Meissen, 1931); W. Haas, *Systematische Ordnung Beethovenscher Melodien* (Leipzig, 1932); D. F. Tovey, *Essays in Musical Analysis* (5 vols., London, 1935-37); A Schering, *B. und die Dichtung* (Berlin, 1936); W. Broel, *Die Durchführungsgestaltung in B.s Sonatensätzen* (Brunswick, 1937); A. Schering, *Zur Erkenntnis B.s; neue Beiträge zur Deu-*

tung seiner Werke (Würzburg, 1938); J. Boyer, Le 'romantisme' de B. (Paris, 1939); Storck-Wieman, Wege zu B. (Regensburg, 1942); D. F. Tovey, B. (London, 1945); L. Misch, B.-Studien (Berlin, 1950; Engl. transl., Norman, Okla., 1954).—Symphonic: G. Erlanger et al., B.s Symphonien erläutert (Frankfurt, 1896); G. Grove, B. and His Nine Symphonies (London, 1896); A. Colombani, Le nove sinfonie di B. (Turin, 1897); J. Hartog, L. van B. en zijne negen symphonieën (Amsterdam, 1904); J.-G. Prod'homme, Les symphonies de B. (Paris, 1906); F. Weingartner, Ratschläge für Aufführungen der Symphonien B.s (Leipzig, 1906; 2d ed. 1916; Engl. transl. N.Y., n.d.); M. H. Barroso, La IX sinfonía de B. (Madrid, 1912); H. Schenker, B.s neunte Symphonie (Vienna, 1912); Eigenhändiges Skizzenbuch zur 9. Symphonie (Leipzig, 1913; facsim. ed.); E. Evans, B.s Nine Symphonies . . . (2 vols., London, 1923–24); E. de la Guardia, Las sinfonías de B. (Buenos Aires, 1927); D. E. Berg, B. and the Romantic Symphony (N.Y., 1927); J. Braunstein, B.s Leonore-Ouvertüren (Leipzig, 1927); W. Hutschenruijter, De symphonieën van B. geänalyseerd (The Hague, 1928); K. Nef, Die neun Sinfonien B.s (Leipzig, 1928); O. Baensch, Aufbau und Sinn des Chorfinales in B.s Neunter Symphonie (Berlin, 1930); J. Chantavoine, Les Symphonies de B. (Paris, 1932); E. Magni Dufflocq, Le sinfonie di B. (Milan, 1935).—Chamber music: J. Matthews, The Violin Music of B. (London, 1902); H. Riemann, "B.s Streichquartette," Musikführer (Leipzig, 1901–7); T. Helm, B.s Streichquartette (2nd ed. Leipzig, 1910); H. Riemann, B.s Streichquartette erläutert (Berlin, 1910); S. Midgley, Handbook to B.'s Sonatas for Violin and Pianoforte (London, 1911); O. Rupertus, Erläuterungen zu B.s Violinsonaten (Cologne, 1915); E. Albini, B. e le sue cinque sonate per violoncello (Turin, 1923); J. H. Wetzel, B.s Violinsonaten, nebst den Romanzen und dem Konzert (Berlin, 1924); J. de Marliave, Les quatuors de B. (Paris, 1925; Engl. transl. by H. Andrews, London, 1928); M. Herwegh, Technique d'interprétation sous forme d'essai d'analyse psychologique expérimentale appliqué aux sonates pour piano et violon (Paris, 1926); W. H. Hadow, B.'s Op. 18 Quartets (London, 1926); W. Engelsmann, B.s Kompositionspläne dargestellt in den Sonaten für Klavier und Violine (Augsburg, 1931); S. Grew, "B.'s 'Grosse Fuge,'" Musical Quarterly (1931); R. Giraldi, Analisi formale ed estetica dei primi tempi dei Quartetti Op. 18 (Rome, 1933); S. Kjellström, B.'s strakkvartetter, en orientering (Stockholm, 1936); G. Abraham, B.'s Second-Period Quartets (1942); D. G. Mason, The Quartets of B. (N.Y., 1947).—Piano Music: E. v. Elterlein, B.s Klaviersonaten (Leipzig, 1856; 5th ed. 1895; Engl. transl. London, 1898); C. Reinecke, Die Beethovenschen Klaviersonaten (Leipzig, 1897; Engl. transl. London, 1898); A.B. Marx, Anleitung zum Vortrag Beethovensche Klavierwerke (Berlin, 1898); W. Nagel, B. und seine Klaviersonaten (2 vols., Langensalza, 1905); R. Nesieht, Das goldene Zeitalter der Klaviersonate (Cologne, 1910); H. Riemann, L. van B.s sämtliche Klavier-Solosonaten (3 vols., Berlin, 1919–20); S. Leoni, Le sonate per pf. di B. (Turin, 1922); F. Volbach, Erläuterungen zu den Klaviersonaten B.s (3d ed. Cologne, 1924); A. F. Milne, B., the Pianoforte Sonatas (London, 1925–28); I. Peters, B.s Klaviermusik (Berlin,

1925); W. Behrend, L. van B.'s Pianoforte Sonatas (transl. from the Danish; London, 1927); J. A. Johnstone, Notes on the Interpretation of 24 Famous Pianoforte Sonatas by B. (London, 1927); H. Westerby, B. and His Piano Works (London, 1931); A. Coviello, Difficulties of B.'s Pianoforte Sonatas (London, 1935); D.F. Tovey, A Companion to B.'s Pianoforte Sonatas (London, 1935); R. Kastner, B.'s Pianoforte Sonatas; a Descriptive Commentary on the Sonatas in the Light of Schnabel's Interpretations (London, 1935); H. Leichtentritt, The Complete Pianoforte Sonatas of B. (N.Y., 1936); J.-G. Prod'homme, Les sonates pour piano de B. (Paris, 1937); E. Blom, B.'s Pianoforte Sonatas Discussed (London, 1938).—Vocal and choral music: M. Bouchor, La messe en ré de B. (Paris, 1886); M. Remy, Missa solemnis (Brussels, 1897); R. Sternfeld, Zur Einführung in L. van B.s Missa solemnis (Berlin, 1900); H. de Curzon, Les Lieder et airs détachés de B. (Paris, 1905); W. Weber, B.s Missa solemnis (Leipzig, 1908); M. Kufferath, Fidelio de L. van B. (Paris, 1913); M. Chop, L. van B.: Missa solemnis geschichtlich und musikalisch analysiert (Leipzig, 1921); H. Böttcher, B.s Lieder (Berlin, 1927); id., B. als Liederkomponist (Augsburg, 1928); J. Schmidt, Unbekannte Manuskripte zu B.s weltlichen und geistlichen Gesangsmusik (Leipzig, 1928); F. Lederer, B.s Bearbeitungen schottischer und anderer Volkslieder (Bonn, 1934).

CATALOGUES, YEAR-BOOKS, ETC.: The first catalogue, revised by Beethoven personally, and completed by A. Gräffer (Vienna, 1828), as well as several published subsequently, leave much to be desired. The first valuable thematic catalogue was issued by Breitkopf & Härtel (Leipzig, 1851). It was thoroughly revised and enlarged by G. Nottebohm and published as Thematisches Verzeichnis der im Druck erschienenen Werke von L. van B. (Leipzig, 1868); new edition, together with Bibliotheca Beethoveniana, by E. Kastner, giving a complete list of all books (and important articles written in periodicals) about Beethoven from 1829–1913 (Leipzig, 1913; 2d ed. by T. von Frimmel, 1925). As a precursor to his great biography, Thayer published a Chronologisches Verzeichniss der Werke L. van B.s (Berlin, 1865), which includes unpublished works. In 1908 T. von Frimmel began the publication of a B.-Jahrbuch, the name of which, in 1911, was changed to B.-Forschung (Vienna). See also the yearly publications of the Beethovenhaus in Bonn (since 1920); especially J. Schmidt-Görg, Katalog der Handschriften des B.-Hauses und B.-Archivs Bonn (Bonn, 1935) and T. Lohmer, Das B.-Haus in Bonn und seine Sammlungen (Bonn, 1936; English transl., 1937); Neues B.-Jahrbuch ed. by A. Sandberger (Augsburg, 1924–); W. Korte, L. van B., Darstellung seines Werkes (Berlin, 1936); A. Bruers, B., Catalogo ragionato delle opere principali (Rome, 1937). Of value and interest also are G. Adler, Verzeichnis der musikalischen Autographe von L. van B. (Vienna, 1890), and A. C. Kalischer, "Die B.-Autographe der Kgl. Bibliothek zu Berlin," Monatshefte für Musikgeschichte (Oct., 1895); report of the Beethoven Centenary (Vienna, 1927); G. Biamonti, Catalogo cronologico di tutte le musiche di B. (Rome, 1952). A thematic and bibliographic index of all Beethoven's works, prepared by Georg Kinsky and completed, after Kinsky's death, by Hans Halm, was published in Munich in 1955.

FURTHER BIBLIOGRAPHY: Paul Nettl, *Beethoven and seine Zeit* (Hamburg, 1958); J. V. Cockshoot, *The Fugue in Beethoven's Piano Music* (London, 1959); R. Bory, *La Vie et l'œuvre de Ludwig van Beethoven par image* (Paris, 1960); Emily Anderson, *The Letters of Beethoven* (3 vols.; highly meritorious; London, 1962); L. G. Bachmann, *Beethoven contra Beethoven; Geschichte eines berühmten Rechtsfalles* (Munich, 1963); Ivan Mahaim, *Beethoven, Naissance et Renaissance des derniers quatuors* (2 vols., Paris, 1964; an original and informative investigation, including valuable biographical documentation on performance of Beethoven's chamber music); G. F. Marek, *Beethoven: Biography of a Genius* (N.Y., 1969); Martin Cooper, *Beethoven: The Last Decade* (with a medical appendix by E. Larkin; London, 1970); Joseph Schmidt-Görg and Hans Schmidt eds., *Ludwig van Beethoven* (N.Y., 1970; pictorial edition with commentaries); Maynard Solomon, *Beethoven* (N.Y., 1977). Other publications of some value are: W. Hess, *Beethoven* (Zürich, 1956); P. Mies, *Text Kritische Untersuchungen bei Beethoven* (Bonn, 1957); H. Unverricht, *Die Eigenschriften und die Originalausgaben von Werken Beethovens in ihrer Bedeutung für die moderne Textkritik* (Kassel, 1960); A. Tyson, *The Authentic English Editions of Beethoven* (London, 1963); J. Schmidt-Görg, *Beethoven: die Geschichte seiner Familie* (Bonn, 1964); L. Misch, *Neue Beethoven-Studien* (Bonn, 1967); J. Kerman, *The Beethoven Quartets* (N.Y., 1967); Pamela Willets, *Beethoven and England; an Account of Sources in the British Museum* (London, 1970). The claim advanced by J. A. Rogers in his book, *100 Amazing Facts About the Negro* (N.Y., c.1930), that Beethoven was of African descent, made largely on iconographic grounds, was moderated by the author in his subsequent publication, *Most Famous People of African Descent*, in which he concedes legitimate dubiety on the subject.

Beffara, Louis-François, French writer on music; b. Nonancourt, Eure, Aug. 23, 1751; d. Paris, Feb. 2, 1838. He was 'Commissaire de Police' in Paris from 1792–1816; left his rare collection of books and MSS to the city of Paris. Practically all of these were burned during the Commune in 1871, but a few are preserved in the Opéra library and at the Bibliothèque Nationale. He wrote a *Dictionnaire de l'Académie royale de Musique* (7 vols.) and 7 vols. of rules and regulations of the 'Académie' (Grand Opéra) also a *Dictionnaire alphabétique des acteurs*, etc. (3 vols.); *Tableau chronologique des représentations journalières*, etc. (from 1671); *Dictionnaire alphabétique des tragédies lyriques . . . non représentées à l'Académie, etc.* (5 vols.); and *Dramaturgie lyrique étrangère* (17 vols.).

Beglarian, Grant, American composer and pedagogue; b. Tiflis, Georgia (Russian Caucasus), Dec. 1, 1927. His family moved to Teheran, Persia; he emigrated to the U.S. in 1947; studied viola with Paul Doktor; then enrolled at the Univ. of Michigan where he was a student of composition with Ross Lee Finney and musicology with Hans T. David, obtaining his doctorate in music in 1957. He was subsequently on the faculty of the Army School of Music in Munich. In 1969 he was appointed Dean of the School of Performing Arts at the Univ. of Southern California in Los Angeles. His compositions include: String Quartet (1948); Violin Sonata (1949); *Symphony in Two Movements* (1950); Cello Sonata (1951); Divertimento for Orch. (1957); *Sinfonia* for winds (1960); Woodwind Quintet (1966); *Diversions* for viola, cello and orch. (1972).

Beheim, Michel, German minnesinger; b. Sulzbach, near Weinsberg, Sept. 27, 1416; d. there (murdered), 1474. He was active as a soldier and singer in the service of various German, Danish and Hungarian princes; was one of the earliest of the Meistersinger who still retained some of the characteristics of the Minnesinger; finally settled in Sulzbach as village major or magistrate. He composed many songs; eleven are preserved at Heidelberg and Munich.

BIBLIOGRAPHY: Alfred Kühn, *Rhythmik und Melodik Michel Beheims* (1907); C. Petzsch, "Text-Form-Korrespondenzen im mittelalterlichen Strophenlied. Zur Hofweise Michel Beheims," *Deutsches Vierteljahrsschrift für Literatur- und Geistesgeschichte* (1967); idem, "Frühlingsteien als Vertragsform und seine Bedeutung im Bîspel," *Deutsches Vierteljahrsschrift für Literaturwissenschaft und Geistesgeschichte* (March 1971).

Behm, Eduard, German composer; b. Stettin, April 8, 1862; d. Bad Harzburg, Feb. 6, 1946. He studied at the Leipzig Cons.; taught at the Erfurt Academy of Music; became director of the Scharwenka Cons. in Berlin (until 1901), and prof. in 1917. He was awarded the Mendelssohn prize for a symphony and the Bösendorfer prize for a piano concerto. He wrote the operas, *Der Schelm von Bergen* (Dresden, 1890), *Marienkind* (1902), *Das Gelöbnis* (1914); a string sextet, using the Stelzner violotta; a piano trio; a clarinet quintet; 3 violin sonatas; a violin concerto; *Frühlingsidylle* for violin and orch.; male choruses, songs, etc. Behm wrote a short autobiography in *Musik in Pommern* (1932).

Behr, Franz, German composer; b. Lübtheen, Mecklenburg, July 22, 1837; d. Dresden, Feb. 15, 1898. He published many salon pieces for the piano, some under the pseudonyms of **Georges Bachmann, William Cooper, Charles Morley** and **Francesco d'Orso**. His waltz *Les Sylphes* became very popular.

Behrend, William, Danish musicologist; b. Copenhagen, May 16, 1861; d. there, April 23, 1940. He studied law; held various government positions. At the same time he took courses in music theory; from 1917 taught music history at the Royal Danish Cons. He was one of the founders of the Wagner Society of Denmark. Under the influence of Niels Gade he turned to music criticism, and became critic of *Politiken*. Among his writings are biographies of J. P. E. Hartmann (1895) and of Gade (1917). He contributed to the Danish *Illustreret Musikhistorie* (1905; Vol. II, from Gluck to modern times); and to Salmonsen's *Konversationslexikon*.

Behrens, Jack, American composer; b. Lancaster, Pennsylvania, March 25, 1935. He studied composition at the Juilliard School of Music, N.Y., with Bergsma, Persichetti and Mennin, graduating in 1959; then took courses at Harvard Univ. with Leon Kirchner and Roger Sessions, obtaining his Ph.D. in composition in 1973. He was subsequently on the faculty of the Univ. of Saskatchewan, Canada (1962–66) and of California State College, Bakersfield (1970–76); in 1976 he was appointed Chairman of the Dept. of Theory and Composition at the Univ. of Western Ontario, London, Canada. In his music he adopts a sophisticated modern idiom without transgressing into the musically unfeasible.

WORKS: *Introspection* for strings (1956); *Quarter-Tone Quartet* (1960); Concertino for Trombone and 8 Instruments (1961); Passacaglia for Piano (1963); *Declaration 1964* for orch. (1964); *Pentad* for vibraphone and piano (1965); *The Lay of Thrym,* opera (Regina, Saskatchewan, April 13, 1968); *The Sound of Milo* for orch. (1970); *Triple Concerto* for clarinet, violin, piano (1971); *The Feast of Life* for piano (1975); and Fantasia on Francis Hopkinson's tune 'My Days Have Been So Wondrous Free' for orch. (Fresno, Calif., March 20, 1976).

Beiderbecke, Bix (Leon Bix), American jazz cornet player; b. Davenport, Iowa, March 10, 1903; d. New York, Aug. 6, 1931. His parents, German immigrants, were amateur musicians, and he began to play as a small child. As he grew he developed a flair for ragtime and jazz. He played cornet in various jazz groups in Chicago and St. Louis, and developed his distinctive style of rhythmic lyricism. In 1928 he joined the Paul Whiteman band. Although lacking a formal musical education, he wrote a number of beguilingly attractive piano pieces of which one, *In a Mist,* shows a curious Impressionistic coloring. Addicted to alcohol, he succumbed at the age of 28. His musical legacy was preserved in recordings, and soon a cult was formed around his name, which was greatly enhanced by the publication of Dorothy Baker's semi-fictional biography, *Young Man With a Horn* (N.Y., 1938). Two factual biographies were published in 1974; R. Berton, *Remembering Bix: A Memoir of the Jazz Age,* and R. Sudhalter and P. Evans, *Bix: Man and Legend.*

Beilschmidt, Curt, German composer; b. Magdeburg, March 20, 1886; d. Leipzig, March 7, 1962. He studied in Magdeburg with Fritz Kauffmann; then in Leipzig (1905–09) with Stephan Krehl (theory), Adolf Ruthardt (piano) and Hans Sitt (violin). He served in the German army in World War I; returned to Leipzig in 1923 and founded a choral-symphonic group which he continued to lead until 1954. His catalogue comprises 141 opus numbers, among them a dance opera *Das Abenteuer im Walde* (Leipzig, 1918); opera buffa *Meister Innocenz;* pastoral play *Der schlaue Amor* (Leipzig, 1921); musical divertimento *Der Tugendwächter* (Halle, 1927) and numerous works for orch. and chamber groups.

Beinum, Eduard van, eminent Dutch conductor; b. Arnhem, Sept. 3, 1900; d. Amsterdam, April 13, 1959. He studied violin with his brother, and piano with J. B. de Pauw; also took lessons in composition from Sem Dresden. He made his first appearance as a pianist with the Concertgebouw Orchestra in Amsterdam in 1920; then devoted himself to choral conducting. In 1931 he was appointed associate conductor of the Concertgebouw; in 1945 he succeeded Mengelberg (who had been disfranchised for his collaboration with the Germans during their occupation of Holland) as principal conductor of the orchestra. He was also a guest conductor of various European orchestras: the Leningrad Philharmonic (1937), the London Philharmonic (1946, 1949, 1950); he made his American debut with the Philadelphia Orch. on Jan. 8, 1954; in the autumn of 1954 toured the U.S. with the Concertgebouw. From 1957 until shortly before his death he was the principal guest conductor with the Los Angeles Philharmonic. Beinum was regarded by most critics as an intellectual conductor whose chief concern was the projection of the music itself rather than the expression of his own musical personality. He was equally capable in the classical, romantic and modern works.

BIBLIOGRAPHY: W. Paap, *Eduard van Beinum. 25 Years Conductor of the Concertgebouw Orchestra* (Amsterdam, 1956).

Beissel, Johann Conrad, German-American composer of religious music; founder of the sect of Solitary Brethren of the Community of Sabbatarians; b. Eberbach on the Neckar, Palatinate, April, 1690; d. Ephrata, Pennsylvania, July 6, 1768. He migrated to America in 1720 for religious reasons. His first attempt to build up a "solitary" residence failed, but in 1735 he started the community at Ephrata which became a flourishing religious and artistic center. Beissel, who styled himself Bruder Friedsam (Brother Peaceful), was a prolific writer of hymns in fanciful German, published in various collections, some printed by Benjamin Franklin, some by the community at Ephrata. He composed tunes for his hymns and harmonized them according to his own rules. His compositions were collected in beautifully illuminated MSS, many of which are preserved at the Library of Congress and the Library of the Historical Society of Pennsylvania. Beissel was not a trained musician, but had original ideas; his religious fanaticism inspired him to write some startling music; in several of his hymns he made use of an antiphonal type of vocal composition with excellent effect. He left a tract explaining his harmonic theory and his method of singing. Beissel's hymns are collected chiefly in *Zionistischer Weyrauchs Hügel* (1739), *Das Gesang der einsamen und verlassenen Turtel Taube, das ist der christlichen Kirche* (1747) and *Paradisisches Wunder Spiel* (two independent publications, 1754 and 1766). Only texts were printed in these volumes, but the 1754 issue was arranged so that the music could be inserted by hand. Beissel's life was first described in the *Chronicon Ephratense,* compiled by the brethren Lamech and Agrippa, published at Ephrata in a German edition in 1786, and in an English translation by J. M. Hark at Lancaster in 1889.

BIBLIOGRAPHY: J. F. Sachse, *The German Sectarians of Pa.* (Philadelphia, 1899–1900); id., *The Music of the Ephrata Cloister* (Lancaster, 1903); *Church Music and Musical Life in Pa. in the 18th Century* (publ. by the Pennsylvania Society of the Colonial Dames of America, vol. II, pp. 26–84 and 242–253; Philadelphia, 1927); W. C. Klein, *J. C. Beissel: Mystic and Martinet* (1942); H. T. David, "Ephrata and Bethlehem in Pennsylvania: A Comparison," *Papers Read by Members of the American Musicological Society, 1941* (1946); T. Mann, *Doktor Faustus* (Stockholm, 1947, pp. 104–9; English trans. by H. T. Lowe-Porter, New York, 1948, pp. 63–68); A. Briner, "Warheit und Dichtung um J. C. Beissel: Studie um eine Gestalt in Thomas Manns 'Dr. Faustus,' " *Schweizerische Musikzeitung* (Oct. 1958); L. G. Blakely, "Johann Conrad Beissel and Music of the Ephrata Cloister," *Journal of Research in Music Education* (Summer 1967).

Bekker, Paul, eminent writer on music; b. Berlin, Sept. 11, 1882; d. New York, March 7, 1937. He studied violin with Rehfeld, piano with Sormann, and theory with Horwitz; began his career as a violinist with the Berlin Philharmonic. In 1909 he devoted himself mainly to writing. In 1934 he left Germany, being unable to cope with the inequities of the Nazi regime. He published biographies of Oskar Fried (1907) and Jacques Offenbach (1909); also *Das Musikdrama der Gegenwart* (1909); *Beethoven* (1911; in English, 1926); *Das deutsche Musikleben, Versuch einer soziologischen Musikbetrachtung* (1916); *Die Sinfonie von Beethoven bis Mahler* (1918; in Russian, 1926); *Franz Schreker* (1919); *Kunst und Revolution* (1919); *Die Weltgeltung der deutschen Musik* (1920); *Die Sinfonien G. Mahlers* (1921); *Richard Wagner* (1924; in English, (1931); *Von den Naturreichen des Klanges* (1924); *Musikgeschichte als Geschichte der musikalischen Formwandlungen* (1926; in French, 1929); *Das Operntheater* (1930); *Briefe an zeitgenössische Musiker* (1932); *Wandlungen der Oper* (Zürich, 1934; English translation by Arthur Mendel as *The Changing Opera*, N.Y., 1935); *The Story of the Orchestra* (his last book; written in English; N.Y., 1936).

Bekku, Sadao, Japanese composer; b. Tokyo, May 24, 1922. He studied theoretical physics at the Tokyo Univ. (1943–50); then studied composition with Milhaud, Rivier and Messiaen at the Paris Cons. (1951–54). Returning to Japan, he became engaged in pedagogy; was also a member of the Japanese section of the International Society for Contemporary Music since 1955 (president, 1968–73). His works are set in neoclassical forms; some of them make use of authentic Japanese modalities.
WORKS: 2 operas: *Le Dit les Trois Femmes (The Story of 3 Women,* opera buffa, 1964; Rome, 1964) and *Prince Arima* (1963–67; Tokyo, March 13, 1967); *Deux Prières (2 Prayers)* for orch. (Tokyo, May 10, 1956); *Symphonietta* for string orch. (Tokyo, Nov. 27, 1959); Symph. No. 1 (Tokyo, Jan. 18, 1962); Violin Concerto (1969; Tokyo radio, Nov. 13, 1969); Viola Concerto (Tokyo, March 3, 1972); Trio for Oboe, Clarinet and Bassoon (1953); Flute Sonata (1954); 2 *Japanese Suites,* No. 1 for wind quintet (1955) and No. 2 for 12 instruments and percussion (1958); String Quartet No. 1 (1955); Piano Sonatina (1965); *Kaleidoscope,* suite for piano (1966); Violin Sonata (1963–67); *3 Paraphrases* for piano (1968); Viola Sonata (1969;

rearrangement of the Violin Sonata); *Sonatina in Classical Style* for piano (1969); choruses. He publ. a book *The Occult in Music* (Tokyo, 1971).

Belafonte, Harry (Harold George, Jr.), American folk singer; b. New York, March 1, 1927, of a Jamaican mother and Martinique father. As a youth he lived partly in New York, partly in Jamaica; worked as a janitor and a cart pusher in Manhattan. When his voice was discovered, he got singing jobs in Greenwich Village restaurants; acted the role of Joe in the film *Carmen Jones* (1954). From 1948 to 1957 he was married to the Negro child psychologist Frances Marguerite Byrd; his second marriage was to Julie Robinson. Belafonte's greatest success came as an interpreter of Calypso songs, which he performed with great dramatic power. He made numerous tours abroad.

Belaiev (Belaieff), Mitrofan, renowned Russian music publisher; b. St. Petersburg, Feb. 22, 1836; d. there, Jan. 10, 1904. His father, a rich lumber dealer, gave Belaiev an excellent education. After his father's death in 1888, Belaiev decided to use part of the income from the business for a music publishing enterprise devoted exclusively to the publication of works by Russian composers (the printing was done in Leipzig); he also established concerts of Russian music in St. Petersburg (ten symphony concerts and four concerts of chamber music each season) and provided funds for prizes awarded for the best compositions. Rimsky-Korsakov, Glazunov and Liadov were placed by Belaiev on the jury for these multifarious activities. The "Belaiev Editions" became a vital factor in the development of Russian national music. Although a conservative, Belaiev was generous towards representatives of the modern school, such as Scriabin, for whom he provided financial means to travel in Europe early in Scriabin's career. The catalogue of Belaiev's publications includes the greatest names in Russian music: Mussorgsky, Rimsky-Korsakov, Borodin, Balakirev, Cui, Scriabin, Glière, Glazunov, Gretchaninov, Liadov, Liapunov, Taneyev, Nicolas Tcherepnin, as well as many lesser and more obscure composers, such as Akimenko, Alferaky, Amani, Antipov, Artzibushev, Blumenfeld, Kalafati, Kopylov, Sokolov, Steinberg, Wihtol, Zolotarev and others. The complete list of Belaiev's editions is available in the *Verzeichnis der in Deutschland seit 1868 erschienenen Werke russischer Komponisten* (Leipzig, 1950).
BIBLIOGRAPHY: M. Montague Nathan, "Belaiev, Maecenas of Russian Music," *Musical Quarterly* (July 1918).

Belaiev, Victor, Russian writer on music; b. Uralsk, Feb. 6, 1888; d. Moscow, Feb. 16, 1968. He studied at the St. Petersburg Cons. (1908–14) with Liadov, Wihtol and Glazunov. In 1923 he was a founder of the Society of Contemporary Music in Leningrad, which presented numerous works by Western modern composers. He wrote about 20 biographical brochures on contemporary composers; also edited the correspondence between Scriabin and M. P. Belaiev (1922); contributed many valuable articles on folk music of Georgia, Caucasus and Central Asia. An annotated bibliography of his ethnomusicological writings is included in B. Krader, "Viktor Mikhailovich Beliaev," *Ethnomusicology* (Jan. 1968).

Belcher, Supply, American hymn writer, dubbed "the Handel of Maine"; b. Stoughton, Mass., March 29 (April 9, new style), 1751; d. at Farmington, Maine, in 1836. He was a tavern keeper and original member (with Billings) of the Stoughton Musical Society. After service in the Revolutionary War under Washington, he went to Farmington, Maine. He published *The Harmony of Maine*, a collection of hymns, in 1794.

Belcke, Friedrich August, German trombone player; b. Lucka, Altenburg, May 27, 1795; d. there, Dec. 10, 1874. He was a member of the Gewandhaus Orch. in Leipzig (1815); a chamber musician in Berlin (1816–58); was the first concert virtuoso on the trombone, for which he wrote concertos and études.

Beliczay, Julius von, Hungarian composer and pedagogue, b. Komorn, Aug. 10, 1835; d. Budapest, April 30, 1893. He was a pupil of Joachim, Hoffmann and Franz Krenn; in 1888 was appointed professor of theory at the National Academy in Budapest. He wrote a Symphony; *Ave Maria* for soprano, chorus and orch.; String Quartet; *Andante* for orch.; Serenade for Strings; many vocal and piano pieces. In 1891 he published the first part of a *Method of Composition* in Hungarian.
BIBLIOGRAPHY: A. Janitschek, *Julius von Beliczay* (Carlsbad, 1889).

Bell, Donald, Canadian bass-baritone; b. South Burnaby, B.C., June 19, 1934. He studied at the Royal College of Music in London; made a brillant debut in a concert at 20. In 1958 he went to Berlin where he made successful appearances at the Berlin State Opera; sang at the Bayreuth Festivals in 1958–61. He made his American debut as a soloist with the Philadelphia Orch. in Carnegie Hall, N.Y., in 1959; toured Russia in 1963. In 1964 he joined the staff of the Düsseldorf Opera Company.

Bell, William Henry, English composer; b. St. Albans, Aug. 20, 1873; d. Capetown, South Africa, April 13, 1946. He studied at St. Albans, and sang in the Cathedral choir; won the Goss scholarship at the Royal Academy of Music, London (1889); studied with Steggall (organ), Burnett (violin), Izard (piano), F. Corder (composition) and Stanford (counterpoint); was prof. of harmony there (1903–12); became director of the South African College of Music, Capetown in 1912; retired in 1936. As a composer, he was extremely self-critical and destroyed almost all of his early works. Most of his compositions were written in South Africa and performed by the Municipal Orch. of Capetown. Among his surviving works are the operas *Hippolytus* (after Euripides) and *Isabeau;* 3 symphonies, including a *Walt Whitman Symphony;* symph. prelude, *Song in the Morning* (1901); music for Ben Jonson's masque, *A Vision of Delight* (1908); *Arcadian Suite* for orch. (1909), symph. poems, *Love Among the Ruins* (1908), *The Shepherd* (1908), *La Fée des sources*

(1912), and *Veldt Loneliness* (1921); Viola Concerto; Violin Sonata.
BIBLIOGRAPHY: M. van Someren Godfrey, "The Symphonic Works of W. H. Bell," *Musical Times* (May and June 1920).

Bella, Johann Leopold, Slovakian composer; b. Lipto-Szentmiklós, Upper Hungary, Sept. 4, 1843; d. Bratislava, May 25, 1936. He was a priest and canon at Neusohl; later cantor and music director at Hermannstadt; retired in 1922 and lived in Vienna. He wrote much church music in the strict style; an opera, *Wieland der Schmied* (Bratislava, April 28, 1926); a symph. poem, *Schicksal und Ideal* (Prague, March 19, 1876); chamber music; numerous songs and piano pieces.
BIBLIOGRAPHY: Dobroslav Orel, *J. L. Bella* (Bratislava, 1924); J. Jindrá, *J. L. Bella* (1933); K. Hudek, *J. L. Bella* (Prague, 1937); E. Zavárský, *J. L. Bella* (Bratislava, 1955).

Bellaigue, Camille, French music critic; b. Paris, May 24, 1858; d. there, Oct. 4, 1930. Originally a law student, he took music courses at the Paris Cons. with Paladilhe and Marmontel; from 1885 was music critic for *La Revue des Deux Mondes*; also wrote for *Le Temps*. He bitterly opposed modern music and was particularly violent in his denunciation of Debussy, his classmate at the Paris Cons. His selected essays are published under the following titles: *L'Année musicale* (5 vols., 1886–91); *L'Année musicale et dramatique* (1893); *Psychologie musicale* (1894); *Portraits et silhouettes de musiciens* (1896; English, 1897; German, 1903); *Études musicales et nouvelles silhouettes de musiciens* (1898; English, 1899); *Impressions musicales et littéraires* (1900); *Études musicales* (2 vols., 1903, 1907); *Mozart: biographie critique* (1906); *Mendelssohn* (1907); *Les Époques de la musique* (2 vols., 1909); *Gounod* (1910); *Paroles et musique* (1925), etc.
BIBLIOGRAPHY: L. Gillel, *Camille Bellaigue* (Paris, 1931).

Bellamann, Henry, American author and pianist; b. Fulton, Missouri, April 28, 1882; d. New York, June 16, 1945. He studied at the Univ. of Denver (1898–1900), also in London and Paris. He was dean of the School of Fine Arts, Chicora College for Women, Columbia, S. C. (1907–24); served as chairman of the Examining Board of the Juilliard School (1924–26) and of the Rockefeller Foundation (1927–28); was dean of the Curtis Institute (1931–32). Among his writings on music are: *A Music Teacher's Notebook* (1920); "Charles Ives, The Man and his Music," *Musical Quarterly* (Jan. 1933); etc. He was the author of a successful novel, *King's Row*.

Bellasio, Paolo, Italian composer; b. Verona, May 20, 1554; d. Rome, July 10, 1594. He was church organist in Rome from 1587; published 5 books of madrigals, beginning with 1578; also *Villanelle alla Romana* (1595).

Bellazzi, Francesco, Venetian composer who flourished in the early 17th century. He was a pupil of Giovanni Gabrieli; later a follower of Monteverdi; published (1618–28) a Mass, psalms, motets and other sacred music.

Bellère (or **Bellerus,** properly **Beellaerts**), **Jean,** music publisher; d. Antwerp, 1595. He was a partner of Pierre Phalèse, *fils*. His son **Balthasar** transferred the business to Douai, and printed much music up to 1625. His catalogue of compositions, published from 1603-5, was found by Coussemaker in the Douai library.

Bellermann, (Johann Gottfried) Heinrich, German music teacher and theorist, son of **Johann Friedrich Bellermann;** b. Berlin, March 10, 1832; d. Potsdam, April 10, 1903. He studied with Eduard Grell; from 1853 taught singing at Graues Kloster and in 1861 was appointed Royal Musikdirektor; in 1866 succeeded Marx as professor of music at Berlin Univ. His book, *Die Mensuralnoten und Taktzeichen des 15. und 16. Jahrhunderts* (Berlin, 1858; 4th enlarged ed., Berlin, 1963) gives an excellent exposition of the theory of mensural music; his treatise *Der Kontrapunkt* (1862; 4th ed., 1901) revives the theories of J. J. Fux's *Gradus ad Parnassum.* Bellermann attempted to justify his adherence to Fux in a pamphlet *Die Grösse der musikalischen Intervalle als Grundlage der Harmonie* (1873). He also contributed valuable articles to the *Allgemeine musikalische Zeitung* (1868-74) and published a biography of Eduard Grell (1899).

Bellermann, Johann Friedrich, German music scholar; b. Erfurt, March 8, 1795; d. Berlin, Feb. 5, 1874. He dedicated himself mainly to the study of ancient Greek music; his chief work was *Die Tonleitern und Musiknoten der Griechen,* explanatory of the Greek system of notation (Berlin, 1847). He further wrote *Die Hymnen des Dionysios und Mesomedes* (Berlin, 1840) and edited essays by authors of classical antiquity: *Anonymi scriptio de musica, Bacchii senioris introductio* (1841).
BIBLIOGRAPHY: "Friedrich Bellermann; seine Wirksamkeit auf dem Gebiet der Musik," reprint from the *Allgemeine Musikzeitung* (Leipzig, 1874, no. 9).

Belleville-Oury, Caroline de. See **Oury, Anna Caroline.**

Bellezza, Vincenzo, Italian conductor; b. Bitonto, Bari, Feb. 17, 1888; d. Rome, Feb. 8, 1964. He studied in Naples; became an opera conductor at various European theaters; was on the staff of the Metropolitan Opera in New York (1926-35).

Bell'Haver, Vincenzo, Italian organist; b. Venice, about 1530; d. there, in Oct., 1587. He was a pupil of Andrea Gabrieli, and upon the latter's death, succeeded him as first organist of San Marco on Oct. 30, 1586; Bell'Haver died a year later, and his position was taken over by Gioseffo Guami. Bell'Haver published several books of madrigals (1567-75), of which only Book II, containing works for 5 voices, is extant; single works survive in various collections.
BIBLIOGRAPHY: G. Benvenuti, *Andrea e Giovanni Gabrieli e la musica strumentale in San Marco,* vol. II

of *Istituzioni e Monumenti dell'arte musicale italiano* (Milan, 1932).

Belli, Domenico, Italian composer of the early 17th century. He lived most of his life in Florence. On Sept. 19, 1619 he and his wife entered the service of the Medici court. As a composer he was one of the earliest representatives of the new monodic style; Caccini praised his music. However, the claim that his short opera, *Il pianto d'Orfeo,* or *Orfeo Dolente* (Florence, 1616; reprinted Brussels, 1927, in Tirabassi's edition) was the earliest ever written is questionable. Among his instrumental works is *Arie per sonarsi con il chitarrone* (Venice, 1616).
BIBLIOGRAPHY: E. Schmitz, *Geschichte der weltlichen Solokantate* (Leipzig, 1914); A. Tirabassi, "The Oldest Opera: Belli's 'Orfeo Dolente,' *Musical Quarterly* (Jan. 1929); M. Bukofzer, *Music in the Baroque Era* (N. Y., 1947).

Belli, Girolamo, composer of the Venetian school; b. Argenta (Ferrara), 1552; d. Ferrara, c. 1618. He was a pupil of L. Luzzaschi; chapel-singer to the Duke of Mantua. Publ. 3 books of madrigals *a* 6 (1583; 1584; 1593), 9 books of madrigals *a* 5 (1584; 1586; 9th ed., 1617); 2 books of canzonets *a* 4 (1584; 1593); *Sacrae cantiones a* 6 (1585), *a* 8 (1589), and *a* 10 (1594); 2 magnificats (1610); and *Salmi a* 5; some 5-part madrigals in the collection *De' floridi virtuosi d'Italia* (1586).

Belli, Giulio, Italian composer, b. Longiano, c.1560; d. c.1621. He was a student of Cimelli and held numerous posts as maestro di cappella: at Imola (1582); at Capri (1590), where he joined the Franciscan order; at Ferrara (1592-3); at the church of Frari in Venice (1594 and 1606); at Montagnana (1596); at Forlì (1599); at the S. Antonio in Padua (1606-8); again at Imola (1613); and at San Marco, Venice (1615). He was a prolific composer; publications of his works appeared between 1584 and 1615; some being reissued several times, among them madrigals and canzonets (1584; 1593); psalms and vespers (1596; 1604); Masses (1586; 1595; 1608); *sacrae contiones* (1600); motets (1605); *falsi bordoni* (1605, 1607); *concerti ecclesiastici* (1613); etc. Many of these works are provided with *basso continuo.*
BIBLIOGRAPHY: A. Brigidi, *Cenni sulla vita e sulle opere di Giulio Belli* (Modena, 1865).

Bellincioni, Gemma, Italian dramatic soprano; b. Monza, Italy, Aug. 18, 1864; d. Naples, April 23, 1950. She studied with her father and with Roberto Stagno whom she later married (1881). She sang Santuzza at the première of *Cavalleria Rusticana* (Rome, May 17, 1890). Her repertoire included virtually all soprano roles; particularly successful in *La Traviata.* She publ. an autobiography, *Io e il palcoscenico* (1920).
BIBLIOGRAPHY: Bianca Stagno Bellincioni, *Roberto Stagno e Gemma Bellincioni* (Florence, 1943).

Bellini, Renato, Italian conductor and composer; b. Naples, March 7, 1895. He studied piano and theory at the Naples Cons.; then was active as opera coach. He was asst. conductor of the Chicago Opera Co.

(1919-21). From 1921-34 he was in Europe; in 1934 he returned to the U.S. for a concert tour with Tito Schipa; settled in New York in 1936 as voice teacher. He has written numerous songs, including the popular *Ninna Nanna a Liana.*

Bellini, Vincenzo, famous Italian opera composer; b. Catania, Sicily, Nov. 3, 1801; d. Puteaux, near Paris, Sept. 23, 1835. He was of a musical family; both his grandfather and his father were organists at the Catania Cathedral; he received his first musical education from them, and when still a child began to compose sacred and secular music. His talent was called to the attention of the Duchess of Sammartino, and she enabled him to enter the Cons. of San Sebastiano at Naples. He studied harmony with Giovanni Furno, counterpoint with Giacomo Tritto and piano with Carlo Conti; he continued his advanced studies with Nicola Zingarelli. At the same time he made a thorough study of the works of Jommelli, Paisiello and Pergolesi. Among his student compositions were a symphony, 2 Masses, several psalms and a cantata *Ismene.* His first opera *Adelson e Salvini* was given at the Cons. (Jan. 12, 1825), and its success encouraged Bellini to continue to write for the stage. The well-known impresario Barbaja commissioned him to write an opera for the San Carlo Theater in Naples; this was *Bianca e Fernando,* staged (May 30, 1826) with considerable approval; this success was followed by a new opera *Il Pirata* presented at La Scala on Oct. 27, 1827, and *La Straniera* (La Scala, Feb. 14, 1829). The series of Bellini's successes was interrupted when he met with his first fiasco, the production of his opera *Zaira* in Parma (May 16, 1829). Undaunted by this reverse, he accepted an offer from La Fenice Theater at Venice for which he rapidly wrote *I Capuleti e i Montecchi* (March 11, 1830), which was acclaimed as a masterpiece. His inspiration seemed to receive a new impetus; he produced in succession two operas destined to become famous: *La Sonnambula* (Teatro Carcano, Milan, March 6, 1831) and *Norma* (La Scala, Milan, Dec. 26, 1831). The celebrated prima donna Giuditta Pasta created the title role in *Norma.* Bellini regarded *Norma* as his greatest achievement; the verdict of the musical public confirmed his judgment, for the popularity of the opera spread quickly throughout Europe. Strangely enough, this supreme achievement was followed by a distinct failure in his next production, *Beatrice di Tenda,* given at La Fenice (March 16, 1833). In 1833 Bellini visited London; then he went to Paris on Rossini's advice. There he wrote his last opera *I Puritani,* which was brilliantly produced at the Théâtre-Italien (Jan. 25, 1835) with such celebrated artists as Grisi, Rubini, Tamburini and Lablache in the cast. Bellini died in his 34th year, at full maturity of his lyric genius. His remains were removed to Catania 40 years after his death. Bellini's music represented the Italian operatic school at its best; together with Donizetti he gave the lyric stage its finest and most singable melodies; harmonic elaboration was not Bellini's aim; hence, the impression of monotony produced on some critics. However, the unassuming grace of Bellini's melodies continues to serve as an unfailing attraction to the musical public at large, and his best operas remain in the repertory of the opera houses in both hemispheres.

BIBLIOGRAPHY: F. Cicconetti, *Vita di V. B.* (Prato, 1859); A. Pougin, *B., sa vie, ses œuvres* (Paris, 1868); F. Clementi, *Il linguaggio dei suoni: Belliniani e Wagneristi* (Rome, 1881); M. Scherillo, *Belliniana* (Milan, 1885); L. Salvioli, *B., Lettere inedite* (Milan, 1885); A. Amore, *V. B.; arti, studi e ricerche* (Cantania, 1894); A. Cametti, *B. a Roma* (Rome, 1900); P. Voss, *V. B.* (Florence, 1901); W. A. Lloyd, *V. B.* (London, 1908); L. Parodi, *V. B.* (Sanpierdarena, 1913); Ild. Pizzetti, *La musica di V. B.* (Florence, 1918; reprinted in his *Intermezzi critici,* 1921); A. Cametti, *La musica teatrale a Roma 100 anni fa* (Rome, 1920); A. Damerini, *Norma di V. B.* (Milan, 1923); A. Rapisarda, *Vita di B.* (Turin, 1925); Cecil Gray, "*V. B.,*" *Music and Letters* (1926); O. Andolfi, *Norma di V. B.* (Rome, 1928); O. Andolfi, *La Sonnambula di V. B.* (Rome, 1930); B. Miraglia, "*V. B.,*" *Rivista Musicale Italiana* (1931); V. Ricca, *V. B.* (Catania, 1932); Luisa Cambi, *B.* (Verona, 1934); G. Ammirata, *La vita amorosa di V. B.* (Milan, 1935); A. della Corte, *V. B., il carattere morale, i caratteri artistici* (Turin, 1935); A. Einstein, "*V. B.,*" *Music and Letters* (1935); G. G. Mezzatesta, *V. B. nella vita a nelle opere* (Palermo, 1935); G. Monaldi, *V. B.* (Milan, 1935); G. Policastro, *V. B.* (Catania, 1935); C. Reina, *Il cigno catanese: B., la vita e le opere* (Catania, 1935); Ild. Pizzetti (ed.), *V. B.: l'uomo, le sue opere, la sua fama* (Milan, 1936); O. Tilby, *V. B.* (Turin, 1938); A. Fraccaroli, *B.* (Verona, 1941); P. Cavazzuti, *B. a Londra* (Florence, 1945); F. Lippmann, "Quellenkundliche Anmerkungen zu einigen Opern Vincenzo Bellinis," *Analecta Musicologica* (1967); L. Orrey, *Bellini* (London, 1969); Herbert Weinstock, *Vincenzo Bellini; His Life and Operas* (N.Y., 1971); P. Petrobelli, "Note sulla poetica di Bellini—a proposito de *I puritani,*" *Muzikološki zbornik* (1972). A collection of Bellini's letters was issued in Catania on the occasion of the centenary of his death (1935); a facsimile reproduction of his opera *Norma* was published in Rome (1936).

Bellison, Simeon, Russian-American clarinetist b. Moscow, Dec. 4, 1883; d. New York, May 4, 1953. He studied at the Moscow Cons.; was first clarinetist at the Moscow Opera (1904-14); toured the Far East and the U.S. with a chamber music group (1917-20); in 1920 became first clarinetist of the N.Y. Philharmonic, retiring in 1948. He made transcriptions for clarinet of Hebrew melodies, and songs by Russian composers.

Bellman, Carl Michael, Swedish poet and composer; b. Stockholm, Feb. 4, 1740; d. there, Feb. 11, 1795. He publ. an important collection of songs to his own words, *Bacchanaliska ordenskapitlets handlingar* (1783); wrote lyric ballads expressive of folk life, *Fredmans epistlar* (1790) and *Fredmans sanger* (1791).

BIBLIOGRAPHY: Hendrik Van Loon, *The Last of the Troubadours, C. M. Bellman, His Life and His Music* (N.Y., 1939). P. B. Austin, *The Life and Songs of Carl Michael Bellman* (London, 1968); C.-G. Stellan, "Några Bellmansmelodiers ursprung 'gripna ur luftan,'" *Bellmansstudier* (1970); K. Johannesson, "Bellman som musikalisk diktare," *Lyrik i tid och otid* (Lund, 1971).

Bellmann, Karl Gottlieb, German organist; b. Muskau, Sept. 6, 1772; d. Schleswig, Dec. 26, 1861. He was organist in Schleswig from 1813; composed the German national song *Schleswig-Holstein meerumschlungen;* a Christmas cantata, motets, etc.

Belloc, Teresa Giorgi, dramatic mezzo-soprano; b. San Benigno, near Turin, July 2, 1784; d. San Giorgio Cavanese, May 13, 1855. She sang with La Scala Milan (1804–24); toured through Italy and to Paris and London; retired in 1827. Her repertory comprised roles in 80 operas, Rossini's being her favorites.
BIBLIOGRAPHY: C. Boggio, *La cantante Teresa Belloc* (Milan, 1895).

Bely, Victor, Soviet composer; b. Berdichev, Ukraine, Jan. 14, 1904. He studied violin at the Kharkov Cons. (1919–22) and the Moscow Cons., where he took courses in composition with Miaskovsky. In 1925, together with other Soviet composers, he organized the so-called Proocoll (Production Collective) in order to promote collective composition by students. From 1929 until 1932 he was a member of the RAPM (Russian Association of Proletarian Musicians). After the dissolution of RAPM, he took part in various other organizations of Soviet composers; in 1957 he became editor-in-chief of the magazine *Musical Life* in Moscow. He also gave courses in composition at the Moscow Cons. (1935-48). In his works, mainly for chorus, he concentrates on the social themes of the revolution and class struggle. Many of his songs became popular. He also published collections of folksongs of the Ural nations.
BIBLIOGRAPHY: Yuri Korev, *Victor Bely* (Moscow, 1962).

Belza, Igor. See **Boelza, Igor.**

Bemberg, Herman, French dramatic composer; b. Paris, March 29, 1859; d. Bern, Switzerland, July 21, 1931. He studied at the Paris Cons. with Dubois, Franck and Massenet; won the Rossini prize in 1885. Among his works are: cantata for soprano and orchestra, *La Mort de Jeanne d'Arc* (1886); short opera, *Le Baiser de Suzon* (Paris, 1888); grand opera *Elaine* (Covent Garden, London, July 5, 1892; N.Y., Dec. 17, 1894). He also published numerous songs, of which *Chant hindou* became extremely popular.

Bembo, Antonia, composer; b. presumably in Venice, c. 1670; death date unknown. Between 1690–95 she went to Paris; sang for Louis XIV, and received a pension from him enabling her to devote herself to composition. Extant works (in the Paris Bibliothèque Nationale): *Produzioni armoniche,* collection of 40 pieces (motets, duets, soli for soprano, etc., with figured bass or instrumental accompaniment, set to sacred Latin, French and Italian texts); *Te Deum* for 3 voices and string orch.; *Divertimento* for 5-voiced chorus with string orch.; *Te Deum,* with large orch.; *Exaudiat* for 3 voices, 2 'symphonie' parts and *basso continuo;* an opera, *L'Ercole Amante* (1707); and *Les sept Pseaumes de David,* for various vocal combinations with instrumental accompaniment.
BIBLIOGRAPHY: Yvonne Rokseth, "A. Bembo,

Composer to Louis XIV," *Musical Quarterly* (April 1937).

Bemetzrieder, Anton, music theorist; b. Alsace, 1743; d. London, 1817. Was at first a Benedictine monk; on leaving the order he became Diderot's pupil and protégé at Paris, and lived from 1782 till 1817 in London. He wrote *Leçons de clavecin et principes d'harmonie* (Paris, 1771; London, 1778), and other textbooks (of doubtful value); also polemical pamphlets.

Benatzky, Ralph, Czech composer of light opera; b. Moravské-Budejovice, June 5, 1884; d. Zürich, Oct. 16, 1957. He studied in Prague with Veit and Klinger and in Munich with Mottl; then lived mostly in Vienna and Berlin. After the annexation of Austria by the Nazis in 1938, he went to America; after the war he settled in Switzerland. An exceptionally prolific composer he wrote 92 stage works, about 250 motion picture scores and perhaps 5,000 songs. His most successful operetta was *Im weissen Rössl,* first produced in Berlin, Nov. 8, 1930. His other operettas are: *Der lachende Dreibund* (Berlin, Oct. 31, 1913); *Yuschi tanzt* (Vienna, April 3, 1920); *Adieu Mimi* (Vienna, June 9, 1926); *Casanova* (Berlin, Sept. 1, 1928); *Bezauberndes Fräulein* (1935); *Kleinstadtzauber* (1947); *Ein Liebestraum* (on Liszt's themes; 1951) and *Don Juans Wiederkehr* (1953).

Benda, Franz (František), famous violinist; b. Alt-Benatek, Bohemia, Nov. (baptized Nov. 22), 1709; d. Neuendorf, near Potsdam, March 7, 1786. He was a pupil of Löbel, Koniček, and of J. S. Graun at Ruppin (1733); was first violinist in the orch. of the Crown Prince (afterwards Frederick II) whom he accompanied in some 10,000 flute concerts during 40 years' service.
WORKS: 2 violin concertos; 6 trio sonatas for 2 violins with basso continuo; 6 sonatas for violin with basso continuo; violin studies; several symphonies and concertos by him are in MS. His autobiography was printed in the *Neue Berliner Musikzeitung* X/32–35; in English, in Paul Nettl's *Forgotten Musicians* (N.Y. 1950).
BIBLIOGRAPHY: F. Berten, *Franz Benda* (Cologne, 1928; F. Lorenz, *Die Musikerfamilie Benda. I. Franz Benda und seine Nachkommen* (Berlin, 1967); J. Müller-Blattau, "Benda — Veichtner — Reichardt — Amenda; Zur Geschichte des nordostdeutschen Violinspiels in der Frühklassik, *Musik des Ostens* (1967).

Benda, Friedrich (Wilhelm, Heinrich), German violinist; son of **Franz Benda;** b. Potsdam, July 15, 1745; d. there, June 19, 1814. He studied music with his father; was a royal chamber musician at Potsdam (1765–1810); wrote the operas *Orpheus* (1785) and *Alceste* (1786); a comic opera, *Blumenmädchen* (Berlin, July 16, 1806); a cantata, *Pygmalion;* much chamber music.

Benda, Friedrich Ludwig, German composer, son of **Georg Benda;** b. Gotha, Sept. 4, 1752; d. Königsberg, March 20, 1792. He was director of the Hamburg opera (1780); court musician at Schwerin (1782); concert director in Königsberg (1789). He wrote incidental music for *The Barber of Seville* (Dresden, 1776); also operas, cantatas, and many works for various instruments.

BIBLIOGRAPHY: H. Güttler, *Königsberger Musikkultur im 18. Jahrhundert* (Kassel, 1925).

Benda, Georg Anton (Jiří Antonîn), brother of **Franz Benda**; b. Alt-Benatek, Bohemia, June 30, 1722; d. Köstritz, Nov. 6, 1795. He was the third son, and pupil, of **Hans Georg Benda**; served as chamber musician at Berlin (1742–49); then at Gotha, where he became court Kapellmeister (1750); in 1764 went to Italy, returning in 1766. He remained in Gotha until 1788, producing 14 *Singspiele* and melodramas (his best works: *Ariadne auf Naxos, Medea, Almansor und Nadine*); then resigned, lived in Hamburg, Vienna and other towns; finally settled in Köstritz. Most of his other works (church music, symphonies, concertos, sonatas, etc.) are in MS in the Berlin Library. He developed the novel idea of the music-drama with spoken words, the music being carried out by the orchestra, only.

BIBLIOGRAPHY: biographies by Hodermann (Coburg, 1895); F. Brückner (Rostock, 1904); see also E. Istel, in *Die Entstehung des deutschen Melodramas* (Berlin, 1906); Vl. Helfert, *G. Benda und J. J. Rousseau* (Munich, 1908); also in his *Zum Problem der böhmischen Musiker-Emigration* (Brno, 1929); H. Martens, *Das Melodram* (Berlin, 1933); Jan van der Veen, *Le Mélodrame musical de Rousseau* (The Hague, 1955); F. Lorenz, *Die Musikerfamilie Benda. II. Georg Anton Benda* (Berlin, 1971); R. Pečman, "Ludwig van Beethoven und Jiří Antonîn Benda," *Beethoven-Kongress 1970* (Berlin, 1971).

Benda, Karl Hermann Heinrich (son of **Georg Benda**), German violinist; b. Potsdam, May 2, 1748; d. there, March 15, 1836. He was the concertmaster at the Royal Chapel and teacher of King Friedrich Wilhelm III, wrote much chamber music.

Bendel, Franz, German pianist; b. Schönlinde, Bohemia, March 23, 1833; d. Berlin, July 3, 1874. He was a pupil of Proksch (Prague) and Liszt (Weimar); from 1862 taught at Kullak's Academy in Berlin.

WORKS: symphonies; 4 Masses; Piano Concerto; Piano Trio; salon pieces for piano; Violin Sonata; nocturnes, romances, several books of songs, etc.

Bendeler, Johann Philipp, German organ theorist; b. Riethnordhausen (near Erfurt), Nov., 1654; d. Quedlinburg, Dec. 26, 1709. He went to Quedlinburg in 1681 as an instructor at the Gymnasium there; in 1687 added the duties of cantor, which post he held for the rest of his life. As an organ theorist he belongs, with Werckmeister, to the middle German group whose ideas were realized in the organs of Arp Schnitger. His most important work is *Organopoeia* (c. 1690; reprinted in 1739 as *Orgelbaukunst*) a treatise on organ building. Other works are *Collegium Musicum de Compositione* (mentioned in Mattheson's *Ehrenpforte*); *Melopeia practica* (1686); and *Aerarium melopoeticum* (1688). In addition, he wrote two books on mathematics.

BIBLIOGRAPHY: Chr. Mahrenholz, *Die Berechnung der Orgelpfeifenmensuren* (Kassel, 1938).

Bender, Paul, German bass singer; b. Driedorf, July 28, 1875; d. Munich, Nov. 25, 1947. He sang at the Bayreuth Festival (1902), and at Munich (from 1903). He made his American debut at the Metropolitian Opera House (Nov. 17, 1922).

Bendix, Max, American conductor and composer; b. Detroit, March 28, 1866; d. Chicago, Dec. 6, 1945. He studied in Germany; was concertmaster of the Metropolitan Opera House (1885), and the Thomas Orch. in New York and Chicago (1886–96); later was opera conductor in New York. He wrote a violin concerto; *Pavlova*, valse-caprice for orch.; also ballet scores for special productions.

Bendix, Otto, pianist; b. Copenhagen, July 26, 1845; d. San Francisco, March 1, 1904. He was a pupil of Niels Gade; then studied with Kullak in Berlin and Liszt at Weimar; taught piano at the Copenhagen Cons., and was oboist in a theater orchestra; came to the U.S. in 1880; settled in Boston as a piano teacher at the New England Cons.; in 1895 moved to San Francisco, where he established his own music school; gave successful concerts in Europe and America; published some piano pieces.

Bendix, Victor Emanuel, Danish composer, brother of **Otto Bendix**; b. Copenhagen, May 17, 1851; d. there, Jan. 5, 1926. He studied with Niels Gade; was active as a choral conductor; wrote 4 symphonies in a romantic vein; piano concerto; church music.

Bendl, Karl, Czech composer; b. Prague, April 16, 1838; d. there, Sept. 20, 1897. He studied with Blažek and Pietsch at Prague; was choirmaster of the German Opera in Amsterdam (1864); returned to Prague in 1865; after 1866 was conductor of the male choral society 'Hlahol.' Jointly with Smetana and Dvořák, he contributed to the general recognition of Czech music.

WORKS: Czech national operas *Lejla* (Prague, Jan. 4, 1868), *Břetislav and Jitka* (1869), *Cernohorci* (1881), *Karel Skréta* (1883), *Dité Tábora* (*Child of the Camp,* 1892), *Mother Mila* (1895), *The Bagpiper* (1907); all produced at the National Theater, Prague, and in its standing repertory; also a ballet, *Bohemian Wedding;* 3 Masses; several cantatas for soli, chorus and orch.; an overture, a *Dithyramb*, a *Concert Polonaise,* a *Slavonic Rhapsody,* etc., for orch.; a string quartet; 200 Czech songs and choruses; piano music.

Benedict, Sir Julius, composer; b. Stuttgart, Nov. 27, 1804; d. London, June 5, 1885. He was the son of a Jewish banker; from his early years he showed a decisive musical talent in various fields. He first studied with J. C. L. Abeille in his native city; then with Hummel at Weimar. Hummel introduced him to Weber, and he became Weber's pupil at the age of 17. In 1823, Benedict was appointed conductor of the Kärnthnerthor Theater in Vienna; in 1825 he received a similar post at the Teatro San Carlo in Naples, where he made his debut as composer with the opera *Giacinta* ed *Ernesto* (1829) without signal success. His second opera in Italian was *I Portoghesi in Goa,* produced in Stuttgart (1830). He went to Paris in 1834; the following year he settled in London, where he remained for the rest of his life. In 1836 he became music director of the Opera Buffa at the Lyceum Theater. His first opera in English, *The Gypsy's Warning,* was produced, April 19, 1838, at Drury Lane, where Benedict was engaged as conductor. He also conducted at Covent Garden; led the Monday Popular Concerts; was musical director of the Norwich Festivals from 1845-78, and the Liverpool Philharmonic Society from 1876-80. In recognition of his services, he was knighted in 1871. Benedict enjoyed a very great reputation as a musician in Europe and in America; he accompanied Jenny Lind on her American tour in 1850-52. Among his operas *The Lily of Killarney* (Covent Garden, Feb. 8, 1862) enjoyed considerable success, and was produced in the U.S. and Australia. Other operas are: *The Brides of Venice* (Drury Lane, April 22, 1844); *The Crusaders* (Drury Lane, Feb. 26, 1846); *The Lake of Glenaston* (1862); *The Bride of Song* (Covent Garden, Dec. 3, 1864); he also wrote the cantatas *Undine* (1860); *Richard Cœur-de-Lion* (1863); *St. Cecilia* (1866); *St. Peter* (1870); *Graziella* (1882); 2 symphonies; 2 piano concertos, etc.; wrote biographies of Mendelssohn (1850) and Weber (1881; 2nd ed., 1913).

Benedictus Appenzeller. See **Appenzeller, Benedictus**

Benedito y Vives, Rafael, Spanish conductor, pedagogue, and editor; b. Valencia, Sept. 3, 1885. He studied at Madrid Cons.; in 1917 he organized an orchestra under his own name and a university chorus. In subsequent years he devoted himself to the organization of music festivals with folk singing. He has published several collections of songs of a popular nature; also pedagogical works: *El piano amigo del niño; Cómo se enseña el canto y la música;* etc.

Benelli, Antonio Peregrino, Italian singer and composer; b. Forlì, Romagna, Sept. 5, 1771; d. Börnichau, Saxony, Aug. 16, 1830. In 1790 he was first tenor at the Teatro San Carlo in Naples; held the same position in London (1798), and in Dresden from 1801-22, when his voice failed; then taught singing at the Royal Theater School in Berlin; was dismissed in 1829 on account of an unjust attack on his benefactor, Spontini. His most valuable work is a vocal method *Gesangslehre* (Dresden, 1819; originally published in Italian as *Regole per il canto figurato,* 1814); also wrote *Bemerkungen über die Stimme* in the *Allgemeine musikalische Zeitung* (Leipzig, 1824); composed many vocal pieces and some piano pieces.

Benet, John, English composer who flourished in the 15th century. He wrote church music, of which the following works are extant: a Mass, 2 motets *(Lux fulget ex Anglia* and *Tellus purpureum),* an isorhythmic motet *Gaude pia Magdalena,* and several numbers from incomplete masses. Stylistically he belongs to the school of John Dunstable and Lionel Power. His *Sanctus* and *Agnus* are found in Wooldridge's *Early*

English Harmony (1897); a *Gloria* is included in *Denkmäler der Tonkunst in Österreich* 61 (31).

Benevoli, Orazio, Italian composer; b. Rome, April 19, 1605; d. there, June 17, 1672; son of a French baker who italianized his name. He studied with Vincenzo Ugolini and sang in the boys' choir at the school 'dei francesi' in Rome (1617-23). He held numerous posts as maestro di capella: at Santa Maria in Trastevere (1624-30); at San Luigi dei francesi in Rome (1638-44); at the Vienna Court (1646); at Santa Maria Maggiore in Rome (1646); and thereafter in the Vatican. His work shows influences of the conservative Palestrina style combined with the polychoral technique of the Venetians; some of his sacred works call for twelve separate choirs. Benevoli's Mass, commissioned for the consecration of the Salzburg Cathedral (1628), was in 52 parts with cembalo; this Mass and a hymn in 56 voices are reprinted in the *Denkmäler der Tonkunst in Österreich* (vol. 20; formerly 10.i). Another Mass (performed at the Church of Santa Maria sopra Minerva, Rome, 1650) is for 12 choirs of 4 voices each.

BIBLIOGRAPHY: A. Cametti, "La Scuola dei pueri cantus di San Luigi dei francesi in Roma e suoi principali allievi" *Rivista musicale italiana* (Oct. 1915); M. Bukofzer, *Music in the Baroque Era* (N.Y., 1947).

Bengtsson, Gustaf Adolf Tiburt, Swedish conductor and composer; b. Vadstena, March 29, 1886; d. Linköping, Oct. 5, 1965. He studied in Stockholm; then in Berlin with Juon and in Leipzig with Riemann; returned to Sweden and settled in Karlstad as composer and teacher; from 1942-46 was conductor of an orchestra in Linköping. He composed 3 symphonies (1908, 1910, 1921); Violin Concerto; Cello Concerto; *Sinfonia Concertante* for violin, viola and orch.; *Canone Concertante* for violin, viola and chamber orch. (1950); *Vettern,* symph. poem (1950); String Quartet (1907); Piano Trio (1916); Violin Sonata; songs.

Benguerel, Xavier, Catalonian composer; b. Barcelona, Feb. 9, 1931. He was a pupil of Cristòfor Taltabull. His early works were influenced by French Impressionism; in 1958 he adopted the dodecaphonic techniques; then tilted towards extreme modernism, often in the manner of the New Polish School.

WORKS: Concerto for Piano and Strings (1955); *Contrasts* for chamber orch. (1959); *Cantata d'Amic i Amat* for chamber group, contralto and chorus (1959); Concerto for 2 Flutes and Strings (1961); *Sinfonia Continua* (Bilbao, Oct. 21, 1962); *Nocturno de los avisos* for soprano, chorus and orch. (1963); Violin Concerto (Barcelona, Oct. 9, 1965); *Sinfonia per a un Festival* (Barcelona, Oct. 30, 1966); *Sinfonia per a Petita Orquestra* (Hagen, Germany, April 24, 1967); *Paraules de Cada Dia* for voice and chamber orch. (1967); *Sinfonia per a Gran Orquestra* (Barcelona, Oct. 2, 1968); *Test Sonata* for 17 instruments and percussion (1968); *Musica per a Oboe* for oboe and chamber group (1968); *Dialogue Orchestrale* (1969); *Musica Riservata* for strings (1969); *Joc* for 7 instruments and percussion (1969); *Consort Music* for strings (1970); Organ Concerto (Baden-Baden, Germany, Sept. 17, 1971); Guitar Concerto (Kassel, Germany,

Feb. 17, 1972); *Quasi una fantasia* for cello and chamber orch. (Barcelona, Oct. 22, 1972); *Arbor,* cantata to words of Goethe, Dante, Shakespeare, Hitler, Mussolini, Martin Luther King and Ché Guevara, for soli, 4 speakers, chorus and orch. (Barcelona, Oct. 22, 1972); *Destructio* for orch. (Madrid, March 23, 1973); *Capriccio Stravagante* for chamber group (1974); *Thesis* for chamber group (1974); Concerto for Percussion and Orch. (1975); 2 violin sonatas (1953, 1959); String Quartet No. 1 (1954); *4 Estructuras: I* for violin (1957), *II* for flute (1959), *III* for cello (1964), *IV* for piano (1966); *Successions* for wind quintet (1960); *Duo* for clarinet and piano (1963); *Musica* for 3 percussionists (1967); *Crescendo* for organ (1970); *Intento a Dos* for guitar and percussion (1970); *Verses* for guitar (1973); *El gran océano* for soprano, guitar and percussion (1975); and *Vermelia* for 4 guitars (1976).

Ben-Haim (original name **Frankenburger**), **Paul**, eminent Israeli composer b. Munich, July 5, 1897. He studied piano and composition at the State Academy of Munich (1915–20); was an assistant conductor at the Munich Opera (1920–24), and at the Opera of Augsburg (1924–31). His career was cut short by the Nazi take-over in 1933, and he went to Palestine, where he devoted himself chiefly to composition. In 1957 he was awarded the state prize of Israel. Apart from his composition, he made a profound study of the folk music of the Middle East. His works, written in a formally sustained neo-classical vein, are nevertheless representative of the modern trends; several of his compositions are written on Hebrew themes. WORKS: 2 symphonies (1941, 1948); Piano Concerto (Tel Aviv, Feb. 1, 1950); *To the Chief Musician* for orch. (1958); *Vision of a Prophet* for tenor, chorus and orch. (1959); Violin Concerto (1960); *Capriccio* for piano and orch. (1960); Cello Concerto (1962); *A Hymn from the Desert* for voices and orch. (1962); *3 Psalms for San Francisco* for voices and orch. (1963); *The Eternal Theme* for orch. (1965); *Myrtleblossoms from Eden* for soprano, alto and piano (1965); *Symphonic Metamorphosis of a Bach Chorale* for orch. (1968); Sonata for String Instruments (1969).

Benincori, Angelo Maria, Italian composer; b. Brescia, March 28, 1779; d. Paris, Dec. 30, 1821. He studied violin with Rolla; spent several years in Spain; in 1803 he settled in Paris, where he was mostly active as a violin teacher. He brought out 3 unsuccessful operas, but performed a meritorious service in completing Isouard's opera *Aladin.*

Benjamin, Arthur, Australian composer and pianist; b. Sydney, Sept. 18, 1893; d. London, April 9, 1960. He received his musical training in Brisbane; then went to London where he studied piano with Frederick Cliffe and composition with Charles Stanford at the Royal College of Music. After serving in the British Army during World War I, he was piano instructor at the Sydney, Australia, Cons. (1919–21). Later he taught at the Royal College of Music in London; was engaged as conductor of the Vancouver, Canada, Symph. Orch. (1941–46); eventually returned to London. WORKS: 5 operas: *The Devil Take Her* (London,

Dec. 1, 1931), *Prima Donna* (1933; London, Feb. 23, 1949), *A Tale of Two Cities,* after Dickens (1949–50; BBC, London, April 17, 1953; prize winner of Festival of Britain opera competition); *Mañana,* a television opera (1956), *Tartuffe,* after Molière (1960; completed by A. Boustead; performed posthumously, London, Nov. 30, 1964) and the ballet *Orlando's Silver Wedding* (London, Festival of Britain, May, 1951); for orch.: Piano Concertino (1927); *Light Music,* suite (1928–33); Violin Concerto (1932); *Heritage,* ceremonial march (1935); *Romantic Fantasy* for violin, viola and orch. (London, March 24, 1938); *Overture to an Italian Comedy* (London, March 2, 1937); *Cotillon,* suite of 9 English dance tunes (1938); *2 Jamaican Pieces* (1938; includes the highly popular *Jamaican Rumba;* arranged also for one or two pianos); *Prelude to Holiday* (Indianapolis, Jan. 17, 1941); Sonatina for Chamber Orch. (1940); Concerto for Oboe and Strings, transcribed from Cimarosa (1942); Symphony No. 1 (1944–45; Cheltanham Fest., June 30, 1948); Suite for Flute and Strings, transcribed from Scarlatti (1945); *Elegy, Waltz and Toccata,* concerto for viola, and orch. or piano (1945); *From San Domingo* (1945); *Caribbean Dance* (1946); Ballade for Strings (1947); *Concerto quasi una Fantasia* for piano and orch. (Sydney, Sept. 5, 1950, composer soloist); Harmonica Concerto (London, Aug. 15, 1953); *North American Square Dances* for 2 pianos and orch. (Pittsburgh, April 1, 1955); *3 Pieces for Violin and Piano* (1919); *3 Impressions* for voice and string quartet (1920); 2 string quartets: No. 1, *Pastorale Fantasia* (1924); No. 2 (1959); Violin Sonatina (1924); Suite for Piano (1927); Cello Sonatina (1938); *2 Jamaican Songs* for 2 pianos (1949); *Le Tombeau de Ravel: Valse Caprice* for clarinet or viola, and piano (1949); Divertimento for Wind Quintet (1960); songs and choral music.

Benjamin, William E., American composer; b. Montreal, Canada, Dec. 7, 1944. He attended McGill Univ. (1961–65) receiving his Mus. Bac. degree; studied composition with István Anhalt; also took piano lessons at the Conservatoire de Musique de la Province de Quebec. In 1966 he enrolled at Princeton Univ., where his teachers were Milton Babbitt, Edward T. Cone, Peter Westergaard and James K. Randall; received the M.F.A. in 1968. In 1970 he was appointed instructor in music at Wellesley College. In his music he strives to fashion a rational multi-dimensional musical space, in which dynamics, rhythm and tonality are functional components in free serial arrangements. His works include *Mah Tovu* for mixed chorus a cappella (1965); *Variations for Four Players* (1967); *At Sixes and Sevens,* a sextet (1968); Piano Concerto (1970).

Bennard, George, American hymn composer; b. Youngstown, Ohio, Feb. 4, 1873; d. Reed City, Mich., Oct. 10, 1958. He served as a Salvation Army officer from 1892–1907; subsequently traveled as evangelist in the U.S. and Canada. He wrote a number of sacred songs, among them *God Bless our Boys, The Old Rugged Cross, Sweet Songs of Salvation.*

Bennet, John, English composer; b. c. 1570, probably in Lancashire. In 1599 he published *Madrigalls to*

Foure Voyces, containing 17 compositions. He contribued a well-known madrigal 'All creatures now are merry minded' to *The Triumph of Oriana* (1601), and composed 6 songs for Ravenscroft's *Briefe Discourse* (1614). Bennet's works have been reprinted by Fellowes in *The English Madrigal School.*

BIBLIOGRAPHY: E. H. Fellowes, *English Madrigal Composers* (Oxford, 1921).

Bennett, George John, English composer and organist; b. Andover, May 5, 1863; d. Lincoln, Aug. 20, 1930. He studied with G. A. Macfarren at the Royal Academy of Music (1878-84); took courses in Berlin (1885) and Munich (1886-87). After returning to London, he was appointed prof. of harmony and composition at the Royal Academy (1888). From 1895 till his death, he was organist of the Lincoln Cathedral.

WORKS: *Festival Evening Service* (for dedication of St. Paul's Cathedral, 1890); 2 overtures: *Jugendträume* (1887) and *Cymbeline* (1895); a piano trio (1893); piano pieces, songs, etc. He was the author of the manuals *Florid Counterpoint* and *Elements of Music for Choir-boys.*

Bennett, Joseph, English critic and writer on music; b. Berkeley, Gloucestershire, Nov. 29, 1831; d. Purton, June 12, 1911. After serving in various musical positions in London, he wrote music criticism for *The Sunday Times, Pall Mall Gazette,* and *The Graphic;* was a contributor to the *Daily Telegraph* and *The Musical Times;* was editor of *Concordia* (1875-6) and *The Lute* (1883-6); annotator of the programs of the Philh. Soc. (1885-1903) and of the Saturday Popular Concerts; also wrote libretti for several English composers.

WRITINGS: *Letters from Bayreuth* (1877); *The Musical Year* (1883); *History of the Leeds Musical Festivals, 1858-1889* (1892; with F. R. Spark); *Story of Ten Hundred Concerts* (1887; an account of the origin and rise of the Saturday Popular Concerts, 1857-87); *Forty Years of Music* (1908).

Bennett, Richard Rodney, English composer; b. Broadstairs, Kent, March 29, 1936. He studied with Lennox Berkeley and Howard Ferguson at the Royal Academy of Music in London (1953-56) and with Boulez in Paris (1957-58); returned to London in 1958; taught briefly at the Royal Academy (1963-65) was a visiting prof. at the Peabody Institute in Baltimore (1970-71). His music may be called "optimistic" in its broad diatonic *envergure* and songful expansion, contrasted with somber chromaticism of dramatic passages; it is intrinsically theatrical.

WORKS: He is particularly successful in film scores; among these are *The Nanny* (1965), *Billion Dollar Brain* (1967), *Nicholas and Alexandra* (1971), *Murder on the Orient Express* (1974) and *Equus* (1977; atonal invocation of erotic hippophilia); for the stage: a chamber opera, *The Ledge* (Sadler's Wells, London, Sept. 12, 1961); a 3-act opera, *The Mines of Sulphur* (1963; London, Feb. 24, 1965); comic opera, *Penny for a Song* (London, Oct. 31, 1967; a children's opera in 1 scene, *All the King's Men* (1968); 3-act opera, *Victory,* after the novel by Conrad (Covent Garden, London, April 18, 1970); Horn Concerto (1956);

The Approaches of Sleep for 4 voices and 10 instruments (1959); *Journal* for orch. (1960); *Calendar* for chamber ensemble (London, Nov. 24, 1960); *Suite Française* for small orch. (1961); *London Pastoral* for tenor and chamber orch. (London, July 13, 1962); Nocturnes for Chamber Orch. (1962); *A Jazz Calendar* for 12 instruments (1963-64; performed as a ballet, Covent Garden, Jan., 1968); *Aubade* for orch. (London, Sept. 1, 1964); 2 symphonies: No. 1 (London, Feb. 10, 1966), No. 2 (N.Y., Jan. 18, 1968); *Soliloquy* for voice and jazz ensemble (1966); *Epithalamion* for chorus and orch. (1966); Piano Concerto (Birmingham, Sept. 19, 1968); *Jazz Pastoral* for voice and jazz ensemble (1969); Concerto for Oboe and String Orch. (Aldeburgh Festival, June 6, 1971); *Party Piece* for young pianist and school orch. (1970); Concerto for Guitar and Chamber Ensemble (London, Nov. 18, 1970); Viola Concerto (York Univ., July 3, 1973); Concerto for Orch. (1973; Denver, Feb. 25, 1974); *Spells* for soprano, chorus and orch. (1974-75); Violin Concerto (1975; Birmingham, March 25, 1976); *Zodiac* for orch. (1975; Washington, D.C., March 30, 1976); *Actaeon* for horn and orch. (London, Aug. 12, 1977); 4 string quartets (1952, 1953, 1960, 1964); *Cantata* for voice and percussion (1954); Sonatina for Solo Flute (1954); *4 Improvisations for Solo Violin* (1955); *Winter Music* for flute and piano (1960); Oboe Sonata (1961); Sonata for Solo Violin (1964); *Conversations* for 2 flutes (1964); Trio for Flute, Oboe and Clarinet (1965); Wind Quintet (1967-68); *5 Impromptus for Solo Guitar* (1968); *Crazy Jane* for soprano, piano, clarinet and cello (1968-69); *Sonnet Sequence* for tenor and instrumental ensemble (1971); *Commedia I* for 6 players; *II* for flute, cello and piano; *III* for 10 instruments; and *IV* for brass quintet (all 1972-73); *Scena II* for solo cello (1973); Piano Sonata (1954); *5 Studies for Piano* (1962-64); *Capriccio* for piano, 4 hands (1968); *Scena I* for piano (1973); *3 Verses,* after Donne, for chorus a cappella (1965); *The Music that Her Echo Is,* cycle for tenor and piano (1967); sets of *5 Carols* and of *2 Carols* for chorus a cappella (1967, 1968); *A Garland for Marjory Fleming,* 5 songs for soprano and piano (1969); *The House of Sleep* for 6 male voices (1971); *Tenebrae* for baritone and piano (1971); *Devotions* for chorus a cappella (1971); *Nightpiece* for soprano and tape (1972); *Times Whiter Series* for counter-tenor and lute (1974).

Bennett, Robert Russell, American composer and arranger; b. Kansas City, June 15, 1894. He studied in New York and in Paris with Nadia Boulanger; held Guggenheim Fellowships (1927-28); worked in film studios in Hollywood; then settled in New York. His main activity was that of expert orchestrator of musical comedies, a field in which he has attained a very high position, financially and artistically. His own music is distinguished by a facile flow of musical ideas.

WORKS: operas, *Maria Malibran* (N.Y., April 8, 1935) and *The Enchanted Kiss* (N.Y., Dec. 30, 1945); operetta *Endymion* (1927); for orch.: *Charlestown Rhapsody* (1926); *Paysage* (1928); *Sights and Sounds* (Victor Contest Award, 1929); March for two pianos and orch. (Los Angeles, July 18, 1930); *Abraham Lincoln Symphony* (Philadelphia, Oct. 24, 1931); *Adagio Eroico* (Philadelphia, April 25, 1935); Concerto Grosso for band (Rochester, Dec. 9, 1932); *Hollywood Scherzo* (NBC, Nov. 15, 1936); Eight Etudes for orch. (CBS, July 17, 1938); Symphony in D "for the Dodgers" (N.Y., Aug. 3, 1941); Violin Concerto (NBC, Dec. 26, 1941); *The Four Freedoms,* symph. sketch after 4 paintings by Norman Rockwell (Los Angeles, Dec. 16, 1943); Symphony (1946); *A Dry Weather Legend* (Knoxville, 1947); Piano Concerto (1948); Violin Sonata (1927); *Toy Symphony* for 5 woodwinds (1928); Organ Sonata (1929); *Water Music* for string quartet (1937); *Hexapoda* for violin and piano (1940); *Five Improvisations* for trio (1946); *Sonatine* for soprano and harp (1947); *Six Souvenirs* for 2 flutes and piano (1948); Concerto for Violin, Piano and Orch. (Portland, Oregon, March 18, 1963); Concerto for Guitar and Orch. (1970); *Suite on Old American Dances* for band (1949); *Symphonic Songs* for band (1958). Concerto for wind quintet and wind orch. (1958); Symphony (1963). He published a book on orchestration, *Instrumentally Speaking* (N.Y., 1975).

Bennett, Sir William Sterndale, English pianist, conductor and composer; b. Sheffield, April 13, 1816; d. London, Feb. 1, 1875. His father, an organist, died when Bennett was three years old, and he was educated by his grandfather, John Bennett. At eight he entered the choir of King's College Chapel, and at ten, the Royal Academy of Music, where he was a pupil of Charles Lucas, Dr. Crotch, Cipriani Potter and William Henry Holmes; performed (1833) his own piano concerto there, which was later published by the Academy. In 1837 the Broadwoods sent him to Leipzig for a year, a visit repeated in 1841–42; he was intimate with Schumann and Mendelssohn, and the influence of both, particularly the latter, is reflected in some of his compositions. From 1843–56 he gave a series of chamber concerts in England; married Mary Anne Wood in 1844; founded the Bach Society in 1849; conducted the concerts of the Philharmonic Society from 1856–66; also led the Leeds Music Festival in 1858; received the degree of Mus. Doc. from Cambridge (1856), after his election to the chair of Musical Professor. In 1866 he was chosen Principal of the Royal Academy of Music, and resigned the conductorship of the Philharmonic. The additional degree of M.A. was conferred on him by Cambridge in 1867; that of D.C.L. by Oxford in 1870; and in 1871 he was knighted. The subscription fund of the Bennett testimonial presented to him at St. James' Hall in 1872 was converted by the recipient into a scholarship at the Royal Academy of Music. He is buried in Westminster Abbey. Sterndale Bennett ranks high among English composers of genuine ability. His compositions are polished and carefully elaborated; a great many of his piano works display the versatility of the piano as a solo instrument.

WORKS: 4 piano concertos; a symphony; 5 overtures: *Parisina* (1834); *The Naiads* (1836; his best work, long in the active orchestral repertory); *The Wood Nymphs* (1841); *Paradise and the Peri* (1862); *Marie du Bois; Caprice* for piano and orch. (1844); *Ode for the Opening of the International Exhibition* (1862); *Cambridge Installation Ode* (1862); a pastoral, *The May Queen* for soli, chorus and orch. (Leeds, 1858); an oratorio, *The Woman of Samaria* (Birming-

ham, 1867; and performed for many years afterwards); music to Sophocles' *Ajax;* Piano Sextet; Piano Quintet; Piano Trio; Sonata-Duo for Piano and Cello; numerous piano pieces, among them a sonata surnamed *The Maid of Orleans;* pedagogical works for piano; anthems, songs.

BIBLIOGRAPHY: J. R. S. Bennett, *The Life of W. S. Bennett* (Cambridge, 1907); C. V. Stanford, "W. S. Bennett," *Musical Quarterly* (Oct. 1916). The *Musical Times* publ. a series of articles on Bennett in its issues of May-August, 1903; and an article by F. Corder (May 1916).

Benoist, André, French pianist; b. Paris, April 4, 1879; d. Monmouth Beach, N.J., June 19, 1953. He studied at the Paris Cons. with Pugno and Saint-Saëns; toured in Europe and America as accompanist to Casals, Heifetz, Albert Spalding, Tetrazzini and other celebrated artists.

Benoist, François, French composer and organist; b. Nantes, Sept. 10, 1794; d. Paris, May 6, 1878. He studied at the Paris Cons. (1811–15) with Adam and Catel, and won the Prix de Rome in 1815 with the cantata *Enone;* returning from Italy in 1819, he was appointed prof. of organ at the Paris Cons.; in 1840, 'chef du chant' at the Opéra; pensioned in 1872.

WORKS: 2 operas, *Léonore et Félix* (1821) and *L'Apparition* (1848); 4 ballets, *La Gipsy* (1839), *Le Diable amoureux* (1840), *Nisida, ou les Amazons des Açores* (1848), and *Pâquerette* (1851); *Bibliothèque de l'organiste* (12 books of organ pieces), etc.

Benoit, Peter, foremost Flemish composer; b. Harlebeke, Belgium, Aug. 17, 1834; d. Antwerp, March 8, 1901. He studied at the Brussels Cons. with Fétis (1851–55); while there he earned his living by conducting theater orchestras. He also wrote music for Flemish plays; at the age of 22 he produced his first opera in Flemish, *Het dorp in't gebergte (A Mountain Village),* staged in Brussels on Dec. 14, 1856. With his cantata *Le Meurtre d'Abel* Benoit obtained the Belgian Prix de Rome (1857); however, he did not go to Italy, but traveled instead in Germany. As part of his duties he submitted a short *Cantate de Noël* to Fétis, who praised Benoit's music; he also wrote an essay *L'École de musique flamande et son avenir* proclaiming his fervent faith in the future of a national Flemish school of composition, of which he was the most ardent supporter. His one-act opera *Roi des Aulnes* was presented in Brussels (Dec. 2, 1859); the Théâtre-Lyrique of Paris tentatively accepted it; Benoit spent many months in Paris awaiting its production, which never took place; in the meantime he acted as second conductor at the Bouffes-Parisiens. In 1863 he returned to Belgium where he produced his second Flemish opera *Isa* (Brussels, Feb. 24, 1867). In 1867 he founded the Flemish Music School in Antwerp; he militated for many years to obtain an official status for it. In 1898 it was finally granted and the school became the Royal Flemish Cons.; Benoit remained its director to the end of his life. In Belgium Benoit is regarded as the originator of the Flemish musical traditions both in composition and in education; but although he cultivated the Flemish idiom in most of his works, his musical style owes much to French and German influences. Apart from his successful early operas, he wrote the opera *Pompeja* (1895) which was not produced; the Flemish oratorios *Lucifer* (Brussels, Sept. 30, 1866; highly successful; considered his masterpiece); *De Schelde* (1869); *De Oorlog (War;* 1873); a dramatic musical score *Charlotte Corday* (1876); historic music drama *De Pacificatie van Ghent* (1876); *Rubens Cantata* (1877; greatly acclaimed); children's oratorio *De Waereld in (In the World;* 1878); cantata *Hucbald* (1880); cantata *De Genius des Vaderlands* (1880); oratorio *De Rhijn* (1889), etc. Of his church music, the most important is his *Quadrilogie religieuse* (Antwerp, April 24, 1864), of which the component parts had been separately performed in 1860, 1862 and 1863; also *Drama Christi* (1871). Benoit wrote relatively little instrumental music; his symph. poems for piano with orch. and flute with orch. have been performed. He also composed many songs in French and in Flemish. In his propaganda for national Flemish music, Benoit contributed numerous papers and articles, among them *Considérations à propos d'un projet pour l'institution de festivals en Belgique* (1874); *Verhandeling over de nationale Toonkunde* (2 vols.; Antwerp, 1877–79); *De Vlaamsche Muziekschool van Antwerpen* (1889; a history of the Antwerp School of Music); *De Oorsprong van het Cosmopolitisme in de Muziek* (1876). In 1880 he was elected a corresponding member of the Belgian Royal Academy; in 1882, full member.

BIBLIOGRAPHY: M. E. Belpaire, *Een vlaamsche meester; Peter Benoit* (Belfort, 1901); C. Stoffels, *P. Benoit et le mouvement musical flamand* (Antwerp, 1901); Th. Radoux, "Paroles prononcées à l'annonce de la mort de P. Benoit," *Bulletins Lettres et Beaux-Arts* (Brussels, 1901); J. Sabbe, *P. Benoit; zijn leven, zijne werken, zijne beteekenis* (Ghent, 1902); L. Mortelmans, *P. Benoit* (Antwerp, 1911); H. Baggaert, *P. Benoit, een kampion der nacionale gedachte* (Antwerp, 1919); H. P. Morgan-Browne, "Peter Benoit, né Pierre Benoit," *Music and Letters* (1929); J. Horemans, *P. Benoit* (Antwerp, 1934); A. M. Pols, *Het leven van P. Benoit* (Antwerp, 1934); Ch. van den Borren, *Peter Benoit* (Brussels, 1942); R. R. Boschvogel, *P. Benoit* (Tiel, 1944); A. Corbet, *P. Benoit, leven, werk en beteekenis* (Antwerp, 1944); G.-M. Matthijs, *P. Benoit* (Brussels, 1944); Floris van der Mueren, *Peter Benoit in het huidig perspectief* (Antwerp, 1968).

Bentoiu, Pascal, Rumanian composer; b. Bucharest, April 22, 1927. He studied composition with Mihail Jora in Bucharest (1943–48); was head of the Folklore Institute there (1953–56). He composed a comic opera, *Amorul doctor (The Love Doctor,* 1964; Bucharest, Dec. 23, 1966); a radio opera, *Jertfirea Ifigeniei (The Immolation of Iphigenia,* 1968); an opera, *Hamlet* (1969; Bucharest, Nov. 19, 1971); Piano Sonata (1947); *Concert Overture* (1948, revised 1959); String Quartet (1953); 2 piano concertos (1954, 1960); *Suite Transylvania* for orch. (1955); *Luceafărul (The Morning Star),* symph. poem (1957); Violin Concerto (1958); *Bucharest Images,* 3 symph. movements (1959); Violin Sonata (1962); Symphony (1965; Bucharest, Sept. 24, 1966). A detailed list of his works is found in Viorel Cosma's *Muzicieni romăni* (Bucharest, 1970).

Benton, Joseph. See **Bentonelli, Joseph.**

Benton, Rita, American musicologist and librarian; b. New York, June 28, 1920. She studied piano with James Friskin and music theory with Bernard Wagenaar at the Juilliard School of Music, N.Y.; then enrolled at the Univ. of Iowa, specializing in musicology (M.A., 1951; Ph.D., 1961). In 1957 she was appointed Music Librarian of the Univ. of Iowa Libraries, and in 1975 prof. of music. In 1976 she became editor of *Fontes Artis Musicae,* quarterly journal of the International Association of Music Libraries; in the same year she was elected General Editor of RISM Series C, Directory of Music Research Libraries. She made several scholarly trips to Europe; worked in France on various problems of French music history of the 18th century; contributed numerous valuable articles to American and French music journals.

WRITINGS: "Nicolas-Joseph Hüllmandel, quelques aspects de sa vie et de son œuvre," *Revue de Musicologie* (1961); "Jean-Frédéric Edelman, A Musical Victim of the French Revolution," *Musical Quarterly* (1964); *Directory of Music Research Libraries* (3 vols.; Iowa City, Univ. of Iowa, 1967–72). "Catalogue of the Early Editions of Ignaz Pleyel," in *Répertoire International des sources musicales* (Kassel, 1976); *Ignace Pleyel: A Thematic Catalogue of His Compositions* (N.Y., 1977); articles for the 6th ed. of *Grove's Dictionary* on music libraries, etc.; published numerous book reviews in the *Journal of the American Musicological Society* and in *Fontes Artis Musicae.*

Bentonelli, Joseph, American tenor; b. Sayre, Oklahoma, Sept. 10, 1900; d. Oklahoma City, April 4, 1975. His real name was **Benton,** but following the frequent practice among American singers, he adopted an Italian sounding name when he entered a singing career. He studied voice with Jean de Reszke in Paris; and made his public debut with the de Reszke Ensemble in Nice in 1925. He returned to the U.S. in 1934; sang with the Chicago Opera; then for 3 seasons sang with the Metropolitan Opera, where he made his debut as Des Brieux in *Manon* (Jan. 10, 1936). He had an extensive opera repertory, and sang all leading Italian tenor parts.

Bentzon, Jørgen, Danish composer; cousin of **Niels Viggo Bentzon**; b. Copenhagen, Feb. 14, 1897; d. Hørsholm, July 9, 1951. He studied music with Carl Nielsen (1915–19), then took a course at the Leipzig Cons. (1920–21). Returning to Denmark, he was active in the field of musical education. As a composer, he followed the romantic school, closely related to Nielsen's ideals; wrote 2 symphonies (the 1st, subtitled *Dickens Symphony,* was performed on the Copenhagen Radio in 1941); the opera *Saturnalia* (Copenhagen, Dec. 15, 1944); Clarinet Concerto (1941); *Symphonic Trio* for 3 instrumental groups (1928–29); 5 string quartets and other chamber music.

Bentzon, Niels Viggo, eminent Danish composer; b. Copenhagen, Aug. 24, 1919. He is a descendant of **Jo-**

hann **Ernst Hartmann** (1726–93), an early German-born Danish composer. The musical tradition of the family continued through many generations (his cousin was **Jørgen Bentzon**). He studied piano with his mother; took classes in music theory with Knud Jeppesen. In 1950 he was appointed to the faculty of the Royal Danish Cons. in Copenhagen. In his early compositions he assimilated a neo-Classical idiom, distinguished by compact contrapuntal writing and harmonic clarity without avoidance of justifiable dissonance; later he adopted a metamorphic technique, characterized by an evolution of varied shapes emanating from the basic musical subject, exemplified in his Symph. No. 4, subtitled *Metamorphoses*; this metamorphism naturally led to the personal formulation of serial techniques.

WORKS: FOR THE STAGE: 4 operas: *Faust III*, after Goethe, Joyce and Kafka (1961–62; Kiel, Germany, June 21, 1964); *Jardin des Plantes* (1969); chamber opera, *Die Automaten* (based on motifs from *The Tales of Hoffmann*, 1973; Kiel, May, 1974) and *The Bank Manager* (1974); 6 ballets: *Metaphor* (Copenhagen, March 31, 1950), *Kurtisanen* (*The Courtesan*, 1952; Copenhagen, 1953), *Døren* (*The Door*; Copenhagen, 1962), *Première* (1964), *Jenny von Westphalen* (1965; Aarhus, Sept. 9, 1965; new version, 1971) and *Jubilaeumsballet 800* (1967; Copenhagen, 1967).

FOR ORCH.: 13 numbered symphonies: No. 1 (1942–43), No. 2 with solo piano (1944–45), No. 3 (1947), No. 4, *Metamorfosen* (1948–49; Copenhagen, June 18, 1949), No. 5, *Ellipser* (1950), No. 6, *Sinfonia piccola* (1950), No. 7, *De tre versioner* (1953, Copenhagen, April 21, 1953), No. 8 *Sinfonia discreta* (1957; Funen, Jan. 21, 1958), No. 9, *Aerosymfonien* (1960–61; Odense, May 29, 1961), No. 10, *Den hymniske* (1963; Aarhus, Oct. 26, 1964), No. 11, *Salzburg* (1965; Hamburg, Dec. 6, 1965), No. 12, *Tunis* (1965; Aarhus, Jan. 31, 1966) and No. 13, *Militaer* (1965; Aalborg, Feb. 2, 1966); *Mini-Symfoni* (1968); *Chamber Symphony* for 17 instruments (1962); 20 concertos: 7 for piano (1947–48; *Piccolo-concerto*, with strings, 1950; 1952; 1954; 1963; 1966; 1967–69), 4 for violin (1951, 1961, 1975, 1976) and one for oboe (with strings, 1952) accordion (1962), flute (1963), clarinet (1970–71), viola (1973), tuba (1975) and a Triple Concerto for Oboe, Clarinet, Bassoon and Strings (1954); *Overture* for chamber orch. (1942); Divertimento for string orch. (1942); *Orchestral Sonata* for flute and stings (1943); *Prelude and Rondo* (1949); Suite for String Orch. (1950); *Intrada* (1950); *Variazione breve* (1950); *Symphonic Variations* (1953); *Symphonic Suite* (1955); *Sinfonia concertante* for violin, viola, cello, clarinet, brass and timpani (1955–56); *Pastorale* (1956); *Pezzi Sinfonici* (1956; Louisville, Kentucky, March 13, 1957); Concerto for Strings (1957); *Mutationer* (1959); *Fem Mobiler* (*5 Mobiles*, 1959; Aarhus, Sept. 9, 1960); *2 Monkton Blues* (1960); *Ostinato* (1961); *Overture for small orch.* (1961); *Rhapsody* for piano and orch. (1961); *Gladsaxe,* concerto for orch. (1963); *Symphonic Fantasy* for 2 pianos and orch. (1958–63; Malmö, Sweden, March 10, 1964); *Meet the Danes* (1964); *Suite for Foreigners* (1964); *Sinfonia concertante* for 6 accordions and orch. (1965; Flensburg, Germany, Jan. 4, 1967); 6 *Copenhagen Concertos* for various solo instruments, strings and harpsichord (all 1965);

Manfred Overture (1967); *Eastern Gasworks No. 2* (1969); *Chorus daniensis No. 2* (1969); *Formula* (in memory of Varèse, 1969; Graz, Austria, Oct. 20, 1970); *Hucbald* for cello and chamber ensemble (1970); *Extracts* (1970); *Ephitaph over Igor Stravinsky* (1971); *Busonism,* audio-visual work for piano and orch. (1971); *Saltholm,* lyric intermezzo (1972); *Reflection Suite* for strings (1972); *Suite as Far as Jazz Music is Concerned* (1973); *Trombones as trotyl* (1973); *Documenta 5, No. 1* (1973); *Feature Article on René Descartes* (1975); *Leipziger Tage* for piano and strings (1976).

FOR VOICE: *Elementi aperti* for mezzo-soprano and orch. (1958); an oratorio, *Torquilla,* after Nevil Shute (1961; Aarhus, Oct. 23, 1961); a surrealistic cantata, *Bonjour Max Ernst* (1961; Aarhus, Oct. 22, 1962); *Sagn* (*Myth*) for male chorus, brass and timpani (1964); *An Arab in Cologne,* 3 psalms of the common man for narrator, flute, violin, viola, xylophone and piano (1964); *Mali* for soprano and chamber ensemble (1967); *Det rustne menageri* (*The Rusty Menagerie*), cantata for narrator and instruments (1972).

CHAMBER MUSIC: *Music* for 7 instruments (1943); *Chamber Concerto* for 3 pianos, 2 trumpets, bassoon, double brass and percussion (1948); *Elegi* for 7 instruments (1954); concerto for 6 percussionists (1957); Double Concerto for solo Violin, Solo Piano and Percussion (1965; Malmö, April 19, 1966); sonata for 12 instruments (1969); Sextet for flute, oboe, clarinet, horn, bassoon and piano (1971); 5 wind quintets (with piano, 1941; Variations 1942; 1943; 1950; 1957); Quintet for piano, flute, violin, viola and cello (1960); Piano Quintet (1966); 10 string quartets (1940; 1944; 1951; 1954; 1956; 1959; 1964; 1967; 1968; 1974); *Bagatelles* for string quartet (1944); Quartet for flute, oboe clarinet and bassoon (1943); *Mosaïque musicale* for flute, violin, cello and piano (1950); *Bop Serenade* for flute, oboe, clarinet and bassoon (1952); Quartet for piano, flute, oboe and bassoon (1952–53); Quartet for 4 flutes (1974); String Trio (1940); Trio for flute, oboe and clarinet (1942); 2 piano trios (1943; 1959); Trio for horn, trumpet and trombone (1952); Trio for violin, cello and English horn (1954); 2 trios for clarinet, cello and piano (1961, 1969); Trio for cello, flute and piano (1971); *Observations, Psycho-biological Suite* for flute, oboe and piano (1974); 7 violin sonatas (1940, 1943, 1943, 1959, 1965, 1971–72, 1973); *Little Suite* for violin and piano (1950); 4 cello sonatas (1946, 1967, 1971, 1972); sonatas for horn (1947), clarinet (1950), English horn (1951), trumpet (1951), trombone (1971), flute (1973), bassoon (1973) and saxophone (1973); 6 *Variations* for flute and piano (1942); *Kvadratrod 3* (*Square Root of 3*) for violin and piano (1944); *2 Pieces* for oboe and piano (1946); Duo for violin and cello (1954); *6 Pezzi* for violin and viola (1956); Duet for viola and organ (1968); Suite for violin and piano (1973); *Duo concertante* for violin and piano (1973); *Dialektism* for violin and harmonica (1975); *Suite in the Form of Variations* for solo violin (1942); Sonatina for violin solo (1950); Variations for solo flute (1953); Solo Cello Sonata (1956); *In the Zoo* for solo accordion (1964); *Portrait of J. P. Sartre* for solo accordion (1967); *In the Forest,* suite for solo horn (1968); *Statics* for solo cello (1972); *3 Sonatas and 3 Partitas* for solo violin (1973).

FOR PIANO: 13 numbered sonatas (1940; 1946; 1946; 1949; 1951; 1952; 1959; 1966; 1966; 1967; 1973; 1974; 1974); *Bonner Sonata* (1967); *Hoffmann Sonata* (1969); *Napolean Sonata* (1970); *Rossini Sonata* (1970); *Devrient Sonata* (1970); *Tekst Sonata* (1972); *Pièce héroïque* for 3 pianos (1967); 2 sonatas for 2 pianos (1949, 1962); *Prolog, Rondo, Epilog* for 2 pianos (1951); Sonata for Piano, 4 hands (1959); *Propostae Novae* for 2 pianos (1960); *Explosions* for 2 pianos (1968); *Mozart Variations* for 2 pianos (1969); *Bones and Flesh* for 2 pianos (1973); *Klaverfantasi* (1939), 7 *Small Pieces* (1940); *Toccata* (1940); *Rhapsody* (1942); *Bagatelles* (1942); *Passacaglia, Prelude and Fugue* (1945); *Partita* (1945); *3 Dance Compositions* (1947); *3 Concert Etudes* (1947); *5 Inventions* (1947); *Traesnit* (*Woodcuts*, 1950); *2 Nocturnes* (1950); *Capriccio* (1952); *Kaleidoscope* (1952); *Pentachord* (1954); *Suite* (1955); *Variazione semplice* (1955); *12 Preludes* (1956-57); *Epitaph* (1962); *Det temperered Klaver* (*The Tempered Clavier*), 24 preludes and fugues (1964); *15 Two-part* and *15 Three-part Inventions* (1964); *2 Suites* (1965); *10 Preludes* (1965); *Information and Scenery* (cycle of 6 pieces in optical notation, 1967; *6 Valses nobles et sentimentales* (1967); *5 Mazurkas délicieuses* (1967); *8 Nocturnes en couleurs* (1967); 7 *Études* (1967); *Scherzo* (1967); *Rondo amoroso* (1967); *Paganini Variations* (1968); *Vibrations* for prepared piano (1969, in two versions); *Hommage à Picasso* (1971); *Variazioni* (1972); *Utilized Termination of a Concert* (1973); *Documenta 5 No. 2* (1973); *Micro-macro* (1973); *Piece for 12 Pianos* (1954).

FOR ORGAN: *Prelude and Fugue* (1942); *Variations* (1955); *Mycelium* (1965); *Trivielle synonymer* (1965); *Toccata, Aria e Fuga* (1968); *Organsazione popolare I-IV* (1974).

Benvenuti, Arrigo, Italian composer; b. Buggiano, Pistoia, May 2, 1925. He settled in Florence in 1945, where he studied advanced composition with Dallapiccola. He has adopted an ultra-modern style of composition, with serial techniques diversified by aleatory permissiveness. His works include *3 Studi* for 11 instruments (1961); *Polymérie* for orch. (1961); *Folia* for piano and string quartet (1963); *Débris* for 24 instruments (1964); *Pop Pourri* for 18 instruments (1967); electronic pieces.

Benvenuti, Giacomo, Italian musicologist, b. Tremosina, Lake Garda, March 16, 1885; d. Salò, Jan. 20, 1943. He studied at the Liceo Mus., Bologna, with M. E. Bossi; edited 2 volumes of selected works by Andrea and Giovanni Gabrieli for the *Istituzioni e Monumenti dell'Arte Musicale Italiana* (with valuable documentary prefaces); 12 harpsichord sonatas by B. Galuppi; works by Cavazzoni (1919) and Paradies (with D. Cipollini; 1920); *35 Arie di vari autori del secolo XVII* (1922), etc. He also wrote an opera *Juan José* and a string quartet.

Benvenuti, Tommaso, Italian opera composer; b. Cavarzere (Venice), Feb. 4, 1838; d. Rome, Feb. 26, 1906. When he was 18 years old, his opera *Valenzia Candiano* was announced for performance in Mantua, but was taken off after a rehearsal. The following year, he succeeded in having his second opera *Adriana Lecou-*

vreur produced in Milan (Nov. 26, 1857). Other productions followed: *Guglielmo Shakespeare* (Parma, Feb. 14, 1861); *La Stella di Toledo* (Milan, April 23, 1864); *Il Falconiere* (Venice, Feb. 16, 1878); *Beatrice di Suevia* (Venice, Feb. 20, 1890); opera buffa *Le baruffe Chiozzotte* (Florence, Jan. 30, 1895). Although Benvenuti's operas are workmanlike and effective, they failed to hold the stage after initial successes.

Benzell, Mimi, American soprano; b. Bridgeport, Conn., April 6, 1922; d. Manhasset, Long Island, N.Y., Dec. 23, 1970. Her grandfather was a Jewish folksong singer in Russia before his emigration to America. She studied at the David Mannes Music School in New York; appeared at the Metropolitan Opera on Jan. 5, 1945 in the role of the Queen of the Night in *The Magic Flute;* in the next five years she sang about 20 different roles with the Metropolitan, including Gilda in *Rigoletto* and Mussetta in *La Bohème.* In 1949 she abandoned grand opera and became a popular singer in Broadway shows and in nightclubs.

Berardi, Angelo, Italian theorist; b. S. Agata, Feltria, about 1630; d. Rome, April 9, 1694. He was maestro di cappella at Spoleto in 1681, and at Viterbo in 1687. In 1693 he was at the Basilica of Santa Maria in Trastevere. He published several treatises on harmony and related subjects: *Ragionamenti musicali* (Bologna, 1681); *Documenti armonici* (Bologna, 1687); *Arcani musicale* (Bologna, 1690); *Il Perché musicale ovvero Staffetta armonica* (Bologna, 1693); composed a *Missa pro defunctis* (1663); *Salmi concertati* (Bologna, 1668); *Concentus cum Missa* (Bologna, 1669); *Musiche diverse variemente concertate per camera* (Bologna, 1689); many canons.

Berat, Frédéric, French song composer; b. Rouen, 1800; d. Paris, Dec. 2, 1855. He was a friend of the poet Béranger, many of whose lyrics he set to music; wrote many popular romances and chansonettes: *À la frontière, Bibi, La Lisette de Béranger, Le Départ, Ma Normandie,* etc.

Berber, Felix, notable German violinist; b. Vienna, March 11, 1871; d. Munich, Nov. 2, 1930. He studied at the Dresden Cons.; was concertmaster at the Gewandhaus Orch. there (1897–1903); taught at the Royal Academy of Music in London (1904–07); at the Hoch Cons. in Frankfurt and at the Geneva Cons. (1908). In 1910 he made a highly successful tour of the U.S.; in 1912 he settled in Munich, teaching privately.

Berberian, Cathy, American mezzo-soprano of Armenian descent; b. Attleboro, Mass. July 4, 1925. She studied singing and dance in the U.S. and in Italy; in 1950 she married the Italian composer Luciano Berio; separated in 1965. An ardent student of ultra-modern music, she has become a foremost exponent of the most complex works by the cosmopolitan avant-garde excelling in rhythmic precision and intonation.

Berbiguier, Benoit-Tranquille, French flutist; b. Caderousse, Vaucluse, Dec. 21, 1782; d. Pont-Levoy, near Blois, Jan. 28, 1838. He was a pupil of Wunderlich at the Paris Cons.; wrote many important works for flute, among them 15 books of flute duos; 2 books of duos for flute and violin; 10 concertos; 7 books of sonatas, with cello or viola; 8 sets of variations with piano or orch.; 6 books of flute trios.

Berchem (or **Berghem**), **Jachet (de)** (also **Jaquet, Jacquet**), Flemish composer; b. Berchem, near Antwerp, early in the 16th century; d. Ferrara, 1580; was in the service of the Duke of Ferrara from 1555. He has been confused with his contemporary Jachet de Mantua; also with Jachet Buus and Giaches de Wert. Berchem's 27 madrigals for 5 voices appeared in 1546, and 24 madrigals for 4 voices in 1555; three books containing settings of stanzas from *Orlando furioso* and dedicated to Duke Alfonso II of Ferrara were publ. in 1561. Modern reprints of Berchem's works are included in the following editions: R. van Maldeghem, *Trésor musical* (1865–93), vols. XI and XX (chansons); vols. XXVII and XXVIII (madrigals); R. Eitner, *Publikationen älterer praktischer und theoretischer Musikwerke* (1873–1905), vols. IX and XI (chansons).
BIBLIOGRAPHY: R. Eitner, "Jachet da Mantua und Jachet Berchem," *Monatshefte für Musikgeschichte* (1889); A. Einstein, *The Italian Madrigal* (Princeton, 1949); G. Reese, *Music in the Renaissance* (N.Y., 1954).

Berens, Hermann, German pianist and pedagogue; b. Hamburg, April 7, 1826; d. Stockholm, May 9, 1880. He studied with his father, Karl Berens, in Hamburg; then studied with Reissiger in Dresden, and with Czerny. In 1847 he settled in Sweden; organized the Quartet Soirées in Stockholm; in 1849 became Royal Music Director in Örebro; taught at the Royal Academy in Stockholm. He wrote the opera *Violetta* (1855) and 3 light operas: *Ein Sommernachtstraum, Lully and Quinault,* and *Riccardo;* some chamber music. His book of piano studies, *Neueste Schule der Geläufigkeit,* has become a standard work for piano students, and has gone through numerous editions.

Beretta, Giovanni Battista, Italian music theorist; b. Verona, Feb. 24, 1819; d. Milan, April 28, 1876. He was director of the Bologna Cons.; then devoted himself to continuing the *Dizionario artistico-scientifico-storico-technologico-musicale* begun by A. Barbieri (publ. Milan, 1869–72), but did not complete it; also wrote a treatise on harmony, and another on instrumentation and orchestration; composed instrumental and sacred music.

Berezovsky, Maximus, Russian singer and composer; b. Glukhov, Russia, Oct. 27, 1745; d. St. Petersburg, April 2, 1777; he studied at the Kiev Ecclesiastic Academy; then was chorister at the Court Chapel in St. Petersburg. He attracted attention by his lyric voice, and in 1765 was sent by the Russian government to Bologna for further study. He became a pupil of Padre Martini, and wrote an opera *Demofoonte* (1773) which was produced in Bologna. Upon his return to Russia, he was unable to compete with Italian musicians who had acquired all the lucrative positions in the field of vocal teaching and opera; he became despondent and cut his throat. In addition to his opera, he left a *Credo* and 17 other sacred works; in these he made an attempt to follow the natural accents of the Russian text, which was an innovation at the time.
BIBLIOGRAPHY: N. Lebedev, *Berezovsky and Bortniansky as Church Music Composers* (St. Petersburg, 1882).

Berezowsky, Nicolai, talented composer; b. St. Petersburg, Russia, May 17, 1900; d. New York, Aug. 27, 1953. He studied singing, violin and piano; graduated from the Court Chapel of St. Petersburg in 1916; played the violin in the orch. of the Opera House in Saratov (1917–19); then in the orch. of the Bolshoi Theater in Moscow. He crossed the border to Poland in 1920 and reached New York in 1922. He found employment as a theater violinist; took a course in the Juilliard Graduate School of Music, where he was a pupil of Rubin Goldmark and Paul Kochanski; was a member of the violin section of the N.Y. Philh. (1923–29); a member of the Elizabeth Sprague Coolidge String Quartet (1935–40); was also active as a radio conductor; held a Guggenheim Fellowship (1948). While he was still living, his music, appealingly Russian in its inspiration and coloristically harmonious, was quite frequently performed, but after his death a change of musical tastes left him in limbo; only some pieces of his chamber music survived oblivion.
WORKS: Sinfonietta (NBC Orch., May 8, 1932; won a prize); Symph. I (Boston Symph., March 16, 1931, composer cond.); Symph. II (Boston, Koussevitzky cond., Feb. 16, 1934); Symph. III (Rochester, Jan. 21, 1937); Symph. IV (Boston Symph., Oct. 22, 1943, composer cond.); *Christmas Festival Overture* (N.Y. Philh., Dec. 23, 1943); *Soldiers on the Town* (N.Y. Philh., Nov. 25, 1943); Violin Concerto (Dresden, April 29, 1930, composer cond., Carl Flesch, soloist); Viola Concerto (Chicago Symph. Orch., Jan. 29, 1942, Stock cond., Primrose soloist); *Concerto Lirico* for cello and orch. (Boston, Feb. 22, 1935, Koussevitzky cond., Piatigorsky soloist); Harp Concerto (Philadelphia Orch., Jan. 26, 1945); *Passacaglia* for the theremin and orch. (N.Y. Philh., Feb. 29, 1948); 2 string quartets, 2 woodwind quintets, string sextet, brass suite, etc. Cantata *Gilgamesh* (New York, May 16, 1947); *Babar the Elephant,* children's opera (N.Y., Feb. 21, 1953; quite successful).
BIBLIOGRAPHY: *Duet with Nicky* (N.Y., 1943) by his first wife, Alice Berezowsky.

Berg, Adam, German music printer who was active at Munich between the years 1567 and 1599; d. Munich, 1610. He published the important collection *Patrocinium musices,* in 12 vols., printed between 1573 and 1598. Of these 7 volumes are devoted to Orlandus Lassus.

Berg, Alban, outstanding Austrian composer; b. Vienna, Feb. 9, 1885; d. there, Dec. 24, 1935. As a young man he met Arnold Schoenberg, who became his teacher and intimate friend. Berg embraced the atonal method of his master, and later adopted the full-fledged 12-tone technique. With Schoenberg, he led the radical movement in Viennese music; was one of the founders of the Society for Private Performances in Vienna, which made propaganda for new music; was also a member of the Austrian section of the International Society for Contemporary Music (from 1925). He taught privately in Vienna; contributed to modern music magazines, gave occasional lectures on modern music. The interest shown in his work by Hertzka, the president of Universal Edition, and the devotion of his friends and admirers enabled him to continue his work. He evolved a markedly individual style of composition, remarkable for its outspoken lyricism and dramatic tension, while using the 12-tone technique as thematic foundation. His early works stem from Wagner and Mahler; in later works tonality is abandoned in favor of a free melodic and harmonic discourse. His major work is the opera *Wozzeck*, after the romantic play by Büchner; the score contains several symphonic sections (a passacaglia with 29 variations; a dance suite; a rhapsody, etc.), while the idiom is starkly dissonant. *Wozzeck* was first produced at the State Opera in Berlin (Dec. 14, 1925) and aroused a storm of protests; the criticisms in the Berlin press, some of extreme violence, were collected and published in a special booklet by Berg's friends as a means of combating the injustice to the work. The production of the opera in Prague was accompanied by similar outbursts. However, the first American performance of *Wozzeck* (Philadelphia, March 19, 1931, Stokowski conducting) aroused tremendous interest; after World War II numerous performances were given in Europe and the U.S. with great acclaim, and *Wozzeck* became recognized as a modern operatic masterpiece. The original score of *Wozzeck* was acquired from the composer by the Library of Congress in Washington. Berg's second opera *Lulu* (derived from two plays by Wedekind) was left unfinished; 2 acts and two fragments of the 3d act were first performed in Zürich (June 2, 1937). Berg's last completed work was a Violin Concerto commissioned by the American violinist Louis Krasner, who gave its first performance at the Festival of the International Society for Contemporary Music in Barcelona (April 19, 1936); the score bears the inscription 'Dem Andenken eines Engels' as a memorial to Alma Mahler's young daughter. The concerto is written in the 12-tone technique, applied with great freedom without avoidance of passing tonality; it has since become part of the modern violinist's repertory. Other works are: *7 frühe Lieder* (1905–8); Piano Sonata (1908); 4 Songs (1909); String Quartet (1910); 5 *Altenberg Lieder* (1912); 4 Pieces for Clarinet and Piano (1913); 3 Pieces for Orch. (1914); *Chamber Concerto* for piano, violin and 13 wind instruments (1925); *Lyrische Suite* for string quartet (1926; Kolisch Quartet, Vienna, Jan. 8, 1927; 3 movements arranged by Berg for string orch.; 1st perf., Berlin, Jan. 21, 1929); *Der Wein* for soprano and orch., after Baudelaire (Königsberg, June 4, 1930). Berg made piano arrangements of Schoenberg's *Gurre Lieder* and compiled analyses of Schoenberg's *Kammersymphonie, Pelleas und Melisande,* as well as the *Gurre Lieder.*

BIBLIOGRAPHY: The basic biography of Alban Berg is by Willi Reich (Vienna, 1937; with contributions by Theodore Wiesengrund-Adorno and Ernst Krenek), which includes musical analyses; Reich also compiled a guide to *Wozzeck* (publ. in English, N.Y., 1931). See also the Alban Berg issue of *Eine Wiener Musikzeitschrift* (Vienna, 1936); Hans Hollaender, "Alban Berg," *Musical Quarterly* (Oct. 1936); René Leibowitz, "Alban Berg's Five Orchestral Songs," *Musical Quarterly* (1948); René Leibowitz, *Schoenberg and His School* (N.Y., 1949); P. J. Jouvé and M. Fano, *Wozzeck, ou le nouvel opéra* (Paris, 1953); H. F. Redlich, *Alban Berg* (Vienna, 1957; condensed English version, New York, 1957); K. Vogelsang, *Alban Berg: Leben und Werk* (Berlin, 1959); Willi Reich, ed., *Alban Berg, Bildnis im Wort* (Zürich, 1959); G. Ploebsch, *Alban Bergs Wozzeck* (Vienna, 1968); G. Perle, *Serial Composition and Atonality*, 4th ed. (Berkeley, 1977); Mosco Carner, *Alban Berg, the Man and His Work* (London, 1975); E. A. Berg, editor, *Alban Berg. Leben und Werk in Daten und Bildern* (Frankfurt, 1976). The International Alban Berg Society (the Graduate Center of The City Univ. of N.Y.) issues a newsletter.

Berg, Conrad Mathias, Alsatian pianist; b. Colmar, April 27, 1785; d. Strasbourg, Dec. 13, 1852. He studied at the Paris Cons. (1806–07); then settled in Strasbourg as a piano teacher (1808). He wrote 4 string quartets; 10 piano trios; 3 piano concertos; sonatas; many other pieces for his instrument. His essay "Ideen zu einer rationellen Lehrmethode der Musik mit Anwendung auf das Klavierspiel" appeared in *Cäcilia* (vol. XVII, 1835); he also wrote an *Aperçu historique sur l'état de la musique à Strasbourg pendant les 50 dernières années* (1840)

Berg, Gunnar, Danish composer; b. St. Gall, Switzerland, to Danish parents, Jan. 11, 1909. He studied composition with Jeppesen and piano with Hermann Koppel in Copenhagen (1935–48); went to Paris in 1948 to study with Honegger and stayed there until 1957; returning to Copenhagen he joined the avant-garde groups with the aim of liberating music from unnecessary academism. In his works he employs a sui generis serial technique in which each theme is a "cell" consisting of 5 to 10 notes, a model suggested to him by the experiments in cellular biology conducted by the bacteriologist Gaffky.
WORKS: *Hymnos* for string orch. (1946); *Prosthesis* for saxophone and piano (1952); *Cosmogonie* for 2 pianos (1952); a ballet, *Mouture* (1953); *5 Etudes* for double string orch. (1955); *El Triptico gallego* for orch. (1957); *Pour Piano et Orchestre* (Danish Radio, Sept. 29, 1966); *Gaffky's,* piano cycle in 10 "assortments" (1959); *Pour violon et piano* (1960); 2 chamber cantatas: *Spring Thaw* (1961) and *Vision,* after Dylan Thomas (1962); *Frise* for chamber orch. and piano (Copenhagen, May 17, 1961); *Pour clarinette et violon* (1962); *Pour quintette à vent* (1962); *Pour quatuor à cordes* (1966); *Uculang* for piano and orch. (1967; Danish Radio, April 15, 1969); *Random* for cello and percussion (1968); *Tronqué* for xylophone, cello and piano (1969).

Berg, Johann von, Flemish music printer; b. Ghent; d. Nuremberg, Aug. 7, 1563. He lived in Ghent; settled in Nuremberg in 1531 where he became Ulrich Neuber's partner.

Berg, Josef, Czech composer; b. Brno, March 8, 1927; d. there, Feb. 26, 1971. He studied with Petrželka at the Brno Cons. (1946–50); was music editor of Brno Radio (1950–53); wrote simple music for the Folk Art ensemble. Later he began using 12-tone techniques. His most original works are the satirical chamber operas, to his own texts: *The Return of Odysseus* (1962); *European Tourism* (1963); *Euphrides in Front of the Gates of Tymenas* (1964); and *Breakfast at Slankenwald Castle* (1966). He also wrote 3 symphonies (1950, 1952, 1955); Viola Sonata (1958); Fantasia for 2 Pianos (1958); Sextet for Piano, Harp and String Quartet (1959); *Songs of the New Werther* for bass-baritone and piano (1962); Nonet for 2 Harps, Piano, Harpsichord and Percussion (1962); *Sonata in Modo Classico* for harpsichord and piano (1963); *Organ Music on a Theme of Gilles Binchois* (1964); String Quartet (1966); 2 *Canti* for baritone, instrumental ensemble, organ and metronome (1966); *Ó Corino* for 4 solo voices and classical orchestra (1967); *Oresteia* for vocal quartet, narrator and instrumental ensemble (1967).

Berg, Natanaël, Swedish composer; b. Stockholm, Feb. 9, 1879; d. there, Oct. 14, 1957. He first studied surgery; then entered the Stockholm Cons., where he studied singing; later he went abroad and took courses in composition in Germany. His works are couched in a characteristically Scandinavian romantic manner.
WORKS: 5 operas, all produced in Stockholm: *Leila* (Feb. 29, 1912); *Engelbrekt* (Sept. 21, 1929); *Judith* (Feb. 22, 1936); *Brigitta* (Jan. 10, 1942); *Genoveva* (Oct. 25, 1947); the ballets *Älvorna* (1914), *Sensitiva* (1919) and *Hertiginnans friare (The Dutchess' Suitors,* 1920): 5 symphonies with subtitles: No. 1, *Alles endet was entstehet* (1913); No. 2, *Årstiderna (The Tides,* 1916); No. 3, *Makter (Power,* 1917); No. 4, *Pezzo sinfonico* (1918); No. 5, *Trilogia delle passioni* (1922); the symph. poems *Traumgewalten* (1911), *Varde ljus* (1914), *Reverenza;* a *Suite* for orch. (1930); oratorios: *Mannen och kvinnan* (Man and Woman, 1911), *Israels lovsång* (Israel's Hymns, 1915), and *Das Hohelied* (1925); Violin Concerto (1918); Serenade for Violin and Orch. (1923); Piano Concerto (1931); Piano Quintet (1917); 2 string quartets (1917, 1919); songs.

Bergamo, Petar, Serbian composer; b. Split, Feb. 27, 1930. He studied at the Music Academy in Belgrade; adopted a neo-classical method of composition. His overture entitled *Navigare necesse est* (Belgrade, Feb. 27, 1962) is one of his most characteristic pieces; his *Musica concertante* for orch. (Belgrade, Feb. 18, 1963) tends toward atonality. He further wrote two symphonies (1961, 1963); *Concerto abbreviato* for clarinet solo (1966); *I colori argentei* for chamber ensemble (1968); *Ritrovari per 3* for violin, cello, piano (1969); *Steps,* ballet (1970).

Berge, Sigurd, Norwegian composer; b. Vinstra, July 1, 1929. He studied composition with Finn Mortensen (1956–59); later took courses in electronic music in Holland and Poland.
WORKS: *Dances from Gudbrandsdal* for orch. (1955–56); Divertimento for Violin, Viola and Cello

(1956); *Episode* for violin and piano (1958); *Pezzo Orchestrale* (1958); *Raga,* a concerto-study in Indian music for oboe and orch. (1959); *Sinus* for strings and percussion (1961); *Tamburo piccolo* for strings and percussion (1961); *Chroma* for orch. (1963); *A* for orch. (1964–65); *B* for orch. (1965–66); *Flute Solo* (1966); *Oboe Solo* (1966); *Yang Guan* for wind quintet (1967); *Ballet* for 2 dancers and percussion (1967–68); *Gamma* for 7 instruments (1970); *Epsilon* for chamber orch. (1970); *Delta* for jazz trio and tape (1970); *Horn Call* for solo horn (1972); over 25 electronic pieces.

Berger, Arthur, American composer and writer on music; b. New York, May 15, 1912. After a preliminary study with Vincent Jones at New York Univ., he moved to Boston and took courses at Harvard Univ. (1934–37) where his teacher was Walter Piston (M.A., 1936); then went to Paris where he took a course with Nadia Boulanger. Returning to America in 1939, he taught at Mills College, San Francisco, at Brooklyn College and at the Juilliard School of Music in New York. In 1953 he was appointed to the staff of Brandeis Univ. in Waltham, Massachusetts. In his style, Berger experienced the divergent influences of the Second Viennese School and the neo-classical pragmatism of Stravinsky. His works, in whatever idiom, are characterized by a strong formal structure; the title of one of his most important compositions, *The Orchestral Ideas of Order,* is pregnant with meaningful suggestions. Arthur Berger is also an able music critic. He published a monograph on Aaron Copland (N.Y., 1953); wrote music criticism for the *New York Sun* (1943–46) and the *New York Herald Tribune* (1946–53); contributed articles to music magazines.
WORKS: *Entertainment Piece* for 3 dancers and "modern-style piano" (1940); *Serenade concertante* for violin, woodwind quartet and small orch. (Rochester, N.Y., Oct. 24, 1945, revised, 1951); *3 Pieces for String Orchestra* (N.Y., Jan. 26, 1946); *Ideas of Order* for orch (N.Y. Philharmonic, April 11, 1953); *Polyphony* for orch. (1956); Woodwind Quartet (1941); 2 duos for violin and piano (1948, 1950); Duo for Cello and Piano (1951); Duo for Oboe and Clarinet (1952); *Chamber Music* for 13 players (1956); Duo for Clarinet and Piano (1957); String Quartet (1958); *Chamber Concerto* (1960); *3 Pieces for 2 Pianos* (1961); Septet for Flute, Clarinet, Bassoon, Violin, Viola, Cello, Piano (1966); a number of piano pieces.
BIBLIOGRAPHY: J. Perkins, "Arthur Berger: The Composer as Mannerist," *Perspectives of New Music* (Fall-Winter 1966).

Berger, Erna, German coloratura soprano; b. in Dresden, Oct. 19, 1900. She joined the staff of the Dresden Opera House in 1926; then sang at the Berlin City Opera (1930–34) and later at the Berlin State Opera. She made her American debut at the Metropolitan Opera in 1949, and remained on its staff until 1951. She returned to Germany in 1959 and became a voice teacher at the Hamburg Musikhochschule. She gave her last solo recital in Munich on Feb. 15, 1968, at the age of 67. Her best operatic parts were Gilda, in *Rigoletto* and Rosina in *The Barber of Seville.*

Berger, Francesco, English pianist and composer; b. London, June 10, 1834; d. there (at the age of 98), April 25, 1933. He studied harmony with Luigi Ricci in Trieste, piano with Karl Lickl in Vienna; later studied with Hauptmann and Plaidy at Leipzig; returned to London, where he was professor of piano at the Royal Academy of Music and at the Guildhall School of Music; made requent concert tours through Great Britain and Ireland; was for some years director, and from 1884–1911 honorary secretary of the Philharmonic. He composed an opera, *Il Lazzarone,* and a Mass; overtures and incidental music to Wilkie Collins' *The Frozen Deep* and *The Lighthouse;* many songs and piano pieces. He published *First Steps at the Pianoforte; Reminiscences, Impressions and Anecdotes; Musical Expressions, Phrases and Sentences;* and a *Musical Vocabulary in 4 Languages* (1922); in 1931 he published his memoirs entitled (with reference to his age), *97.*

Berger, Jean, German-American choral conductor and composer; b. Hamm, Sept. 27, 1909. He studied music theory with Heinrich Besseler at the Univ. of Heidelberg (Ph.D., 1931), and also with Egon Wellesz at the Univ. of Vienna (1928–32). In 1931 he went to Paris where he took lessons in composition with Louis Aubert; was also conductor of Les Compagnons de la Marjolaine, a mixed choral group specializing in his modern harmonizations of French folk-tunes; in 1935 Berger acquired his French citizenship. From 1939 till 1941 he was in Rio de Janeiro where he was employed as French opera coach at the Municipal Theater. In 1941 he went to New York. He taught at Middlebury College in Vermont (1948–59), at the Univ. of Illinois, Urbana (1959–61), at the Univ. of Colorado (1961–68), and other colleges. As a composer he writes mostly for voices, in a melodious pragmatic idiom. In 1937 his work *Le Sang des autres* won first prize at the International Competition in Zurich. His compositions of the American period include: *Brazilian Psalm* for chorus (1941); *Caribbean Concerto* for mouth harmonica and orch., possibly the first of its kind, commissioned by Larry Adler and performed by him with the St. Louis Symph. Orch. on March 10, 1942; *Vision of Peace* for chorus (1948); *Creole Overture* (1949); *Magnificat* for soprano, flute, percussion and chorus (1960); *The Fiery Furnace,* dramatic cantata (1962); *A Song of Seasons* (1967); *The Pied Piper* for vocal groups and orch. (1968); a liturgical drama, *The Cherry Tree Carol* (1975).

Berger, Roman, Slovak composer; b. Těšín, Aug. 9, 1930. He studied piano at the municipal music school in Katowice, Poland (1949–52); then established himself in Bratislava, where he took lessons in composition with Kafenda (1952–56); taught piano at the Bratislava Cons. (1956–65) and theory and composition at the Bratislava Academy of Musical Arts (1969–73). His style of composition follows the tenets of the modern Vienna School, formally well disciplined, melodically atonal and harmonically complex. WORKS: 3 piano sonatas (1960, 1965, 1975), Trio for flute, clarinet and bassoon (1962); *Ukolébavka* (*Lullaby*) for mezzo-soprano and chamber orch. (1962); Suite for strings, piano and percussion (1963);

Transformácie for orch. (1965); *Konvergenzioni I* for violin and *Konvergenzioni II* for viola; electronic pieces.

Berger, Rudolf, Bohemian opera singer; b. Brno, April 17, 1874; d. New York, Feb. 27, 1915. He began his career as a baritone, and was a member of the Berlin Opera from 1904 to 1907. He later went to New York where he studied with Oscar Saenger, and changed his voice to tenor; returning to Germany he sang tenor parts in Wagner's operas. In 1913 he married the soprano singer Marie Rappold; was a member of the Metropolitan Opera during the season 1914–15. He possessed a very large repertory consisting of 96 baritone and 18 tenor roles; sang Jokanaan in *Salome* 79 times.

Berger, Theodor, Austrian composer; b. Traismauer, May 18, 1905. He studied in Vienna with Franz Schmidt; evolved under Schmidt's influence a strong romantic idiom within the framework of classical forms. His music acquired many important supporters in Austria and Germany, but rarely penetrates beyond Central Europe. WORKS: *Malinconia* for string orch. in 25 parts (1938); Ballade for Orch. (1941); *Rondo ostinato* for wind instruments and percussion (1947); *Homerische Symphonie* (1948); *La Parola* for orch. based on the sequitone scale of alternating whole tones and semitones (1955); *Sinfonia Parabolica* (1956); *Sinfonia Macchinale* (1956); *Symphonischer Triglyph,* on themes from Schubert's chamber music (1957); *Jahreszeiten* for orch. (1958); *Frauenstimmen im Orchester* for women's chorus, harps and strings (1959); Violin Concerto (1963), Divertimento for Men's Chorus, 7 Wind Instruments and Percussion (1968).

Berger, Wilhelm, German composer; b. Boston, Mass. (of German parents), Aug. 9, 1861; d. Jena, Jan. 15, 1911. As an infant he was taken to Germany; studied at the Hochschule für Musik in Berlin (1878–81). He was a very prolific composer; wrote 105 opus numbers; his music, though lacking in originality, commanded respect for its technical skill. WORKS: 2 symphonies (No. 1 was performed in Boston on Nov. 4, 1899); oratorio *Euphorion;* 3 Ballades for baritone with orch.; *Gesang der Geister über den Wassern* for chorus and orch.; Piano Quartet; many piano works; choral pieces; about 80 songs. A full catalogue of his works was publ. by W. Altmann (Leipzig, 1920); biography by A. Kohut in the *Neue Musikzeitung* (Stuttgart, 1902, nos. 21–23); see also E. Krause, *W. Berger* in *Monographien moderner Musiker* (Leipzig, 1907); G. Ernest, *W. Berger* (Berlin, 1931).

Berger, Wilhelm Georg, Rumanian composer and musicologist; b. Rupea, Dec. 4, 1929. He studied at the Bucharest Cons. (1948–52); was a viola player in the Bucharest Philh. (1948–57). In 1968 he was elected Secretary of the Rumanian Composers' Union. WORKS: an oratorio, *Stefan Furtună* (1958); *Symphonic Variations* (1958); Concerto for string orch. (1958); 12 symphonies, all bearing descriptive subtitles: No. 1, *Lyric* (1960); No. 2, *Epic* (1962); No. 3,

Dramatic (1964); No. 4, *Tragic* (1965); No. 5, *Solemn Music* (1968); No. 6, *Harmony* (1969); No. 7, *Energetic* (1970); No. 8, *The Morning Star,* with chorus (1971); No. 9, *Melodie* (1974); No. 10, with solo organ (1975-76); No. 11, *Sarmizegetusa* (1975-77); No. 12, for string orch. (1977); 2 viola concertos (1960, 1962); *Rhapsodic Images* for orch. (1964); Violin Concerto (1965; Brussels, Jan. 11, 1966; winner of 1966 Queen Elisabeth of Belgium Composition Contest in the concerto category); Cello Concerto (1967); *Meditations,* cycle of variations for chamber orch. (1968); Variations for Wind Orch. (1968); Concerto for 2 Violas and Orch. (1968); *Concert Music* for flute, strings and percussion (1972); Viola Sonata (1953); 12 string quartets: Nos. 1-8 (1954, 1956, 1957, 1959, 1961, 1965, 1966, 1966), Nos. 9-12 (1967); Violin Sonata (1960); Sonata for Viola and Cello (1962); Piano Sonata (1962); Solo Violin Sonata (1964); Sonata For Flute, Viola and Cello (1965); Solo Cello Sonata (1967); Sonata for Viola and Violin (1967); Solo Viola Sonata (1968). A detailed list of his works and writings on music is found in Viorel Cosma's *Muzicieni români* (Bucharest, 1970).

Berggreen, Andreas Peter, Danish composer; b. Copenhagen, March 2, 1801; d. there, Nov. 8, 1880. He studied law, but turned to music later. He occupied various posts as church organist and teacher of singing in Denmark; in 1859 he became inspector of singing in Danish public schools. His first important work was a comic opera *Billedet og Busten (The Portrait and The Bust),* produced in Copenhagen on April 9, 1832. He also wrote incidental music to various theatrical plays. His most important contribution is the compilation of 11 volumes of folksongs of various nations, published under the title *Folkesange og Melodier* (1842), and 14 volumes of songs for use in schools (1834-76); also edited church anthems. Among his students was Gade. His biographical sketch, by Skou, was published in 1895.

Bergh, Arthur, American composer and conductor; b. St. Paul, Minn., March 24, 1882; d. aboard the S.S. President Cleveland en route to Honolulu, Feb. 11, 1962. He studied violin; played in the orchestra of the Metropolitan Opera (1903-08); then conducted a series of municipal concerts in New York (1911-14); later became associated with various recording companies. Among his works are 2 melodramas with orch., *The Raven* and *The Pied Piper of Hamelin;* a romantic opera *Niorada;* a symphonic chorale *The Unnamed City;* 2 operettas, *In Arcady* and *The Goblin Fair;* about 100 songs; a number of violin pieces, etc. From 1941 Bergh lived in Hollywood as librarian for moving picture companies.

Bergh, Rudolph, composer and writer; b. Copenhagen, Sept. 22, 1859; d. Davos, Dec. 7, 1924. He studied biology and music in Copenhagen and Berlin; in 1922 was a member of the Board of the Copenhagen Cons. He composed the choral works *Requiem für Werther;* *Geister der Windstille;* and an oratorio, *The Mount of Holy Fire;* also about 150 songs; 50 piano pieces; chamber music, etc.

Berghem, Jachet de. See **Berchem, Jachet de.**

Bergman, Erik, Finnish composer, b. Uusikaarlepyy (Nykarleby), Nov. 24, 1911. He studied composition with Erik Furuhjelm at the Helsinki Conservatory (1931-38); then with Heinz Tiessen at the Hochschlue für Musik in Berlin, Joseph Marx in Vienna, and Wladimir Vogel in Switzerland. In 1963 he joined the staff of his alma mater, now assigned the name of Sibelius Academy. Stylistically, Bergman cultivates varied techniques, ranging from medieval modality to dodecaphony. His predilection is for polyphonic vocal music.

WORKS: FOR ORCH.: *Suite* for strings (1938); *Burla* (1948); *Tre aspetti d'una serie dodecafonica* (1957); *Aubade* (1958); *Simbolo* (1960); *Circulus* (1965); *Colori ed improvvisazioni* (1973). CHORAL: *Rubaiyat,* to the text by Omar Khayyam, for baritone, male chorus and orch. (1953); *Adagio* for baritone, male chorus, flute and vibraphone (1957); *Svanbild (Swan Picture)* for baritone, vocal quartet and male chorus (1958); *Aton,* on the text "Hymn to the Sun" by the Pharaoh Echnaton, for baritone, reciter, chorus and orch. (1959); *4 Galgenlieder* for 3 reciters and speaking chorus (1960); *Sela* for baritone, chorus and chamber orch. (1962); *Fåglarna (Birds)* for baritone, male chorus, 5 solo voices, percussion and celesta (1962); *Springtime* for baritone and chorus (1966); *Snö (Snow)* for baritone, male chorus and flute (1966); *Jesurun* for baritone, male chorus, 2 trumpets, 2 trombones and percussion (1967); *Canticum fennicum* for baritone, solo voices, 2 solo quartets, male chorus and orch. (1968); *Annonssidan* for baritone, 3 tenors, reciters and male chorus (1969); *Nox* for baritone, chorus, flute, English horn and percussion (1970); *Requiem for a Dead Poet* for baritone, chorus, brass, percussion and organ (1970); *Missa in honorem Sancti Henrici* for soloists, chorus and organ (1971); *Samothrake,* dramatic scene for reciter, chorus, instrumental ensemble and choreography (1971); *Hathor Suite* for soprano, baritone, chorus and small ensemble (1971). VOCAL WORKS: *Majnätter (May Nights)* for soprano and orch. (1946); *Ensamhetens sånger (Songs of Solitude)* for voice and orch. (1947); *Livets träd (Tree of Life),* chamber cantata for soprano, alto, baritone, horn, clarinet, percussion, harp and string quartet (1947); *Bardo Thödol,* after the Tibetan Book of the Dead, for narrator, mezzo-soprano, baritone, mixed chorus and orch. (1974); *Loleila* for girls' and boys' choruses, girl soprano, tenor and orch. (1974); *Noa* for baritone, chorus and orch. (1976). CHAMBER MUSIC: Piano Trio (1937); Violin Sonata (1943); 3 Fantasies for Clarinet and Piano (1954); *Concerto da camera* for 8 soloists (1961). Solo: Passacaglia and Fugue for Organ (1939); *Intervalles* for piano (1949); Suite for Guitar (1949); *Espressivo* for piano (1952); *Aspects* for piano (1969); *Energien* for harpsichord (1970).

Bergmann, Carl, German conductor; b. Ebersbach, Saxony, April 12, 1821; d. New York, Aug. 16, 1876. He was a pupil of Zimmermann in Zittau, and Hesse in Breslau; emigrated to the U.S. in 1850 and joined the traveling Germania Orch.; later became its conductor until the group disbanded in 1854. Bergmann also conducted the Handel and Haydn Society

(1852-54). In 1854 he was in Chicago; in 1855 became associate conductor (with Theodore Eisfeld) of the New York Philh. Orch.; in 1862 became its sole conductor, retaining this post until his death. He also conducted Arion, a German male chorus. Bergmann played an important role in American music; an ardent admirer of Wagner and Liszt, he introduced their works to American audiences.

Bergmans, Paul Jean Étienne Charles, Belgian musicologist; b. Ghent, Feb. 23, 1868; d. there, Nov. 14, 1935. Studied at the Univ. of Ghent; *Dr. phil.,* 1887; 1892, assistant librarian; 1919, chief librarian and prof. there; member of the Royal Academy of Belgium. He published a number of very valuable studies and books, the most important of which are: *P. J. Leblan, carilloneur de la ville de Gand au XVIIIe siècle* (1884); *H. Waelput* (1886); *Variétés musicologiques* (3 vols., 1891, 1901, 1920); *La Vie musicale gantoise au XVIIIe siècle* (1897); *Peter Philips* (1903); *Les Musiciens de Courtrai et du Courtraisis* (1912); *Notice sur Fl. van Duyse* (1919); *Corn. Verdonck* (1919); *Henri Vieuxtemps* (1920); *Le Baron Limnander de Nieuwenhove* (1920); *Quatorze lettres inédites du comp. Philippe de Monte* (1921); *Tielman Susato* (1923); *Notice sur le chevalier X. van Elewyck* (1925); *De l'histoire de la musique* (1927); *Les Origines belges de Beethoven* (1927); *Une Famille de musiciens belges du XVIIIe siècle: Les Loeillet* (Brussels, 1927; establishes for the first time accurate biographical data on members of the Loeillet family); *La Typographie musicale en Belgique au XVIe siècle* (1930). He also wrote an introduction to vol. I (1932; piano music, ed. by J. Watelet) of *Monumenta musicae Belgicae.*

Bergner, Wilhelm, organist; b. Riga, Nov. 4, 1837; d. there, June 9, 1907. He was organist of the English church at Riga (1861) and at the Riga Cathedral (1868-1906); exercised great influence on the development of musical culture in Latvia.

Bergonzi, Carlo, Italian violin maker; b. Cremona, c.1683; d. there, 1747. He began manufacturing violins in 1716, modeling them after Stradivarius, with whose son he was associated. It is doubtful whether Bergonzi was trained by the master himself. His son, **Michel Angelo Bergonzi** (1722-1770), continued the trade, as did his grandsons, **Carlo, Nicola** and **Zosimo** (sons of Michel Angelo Bergonzi).

Bergonzi, Carlo, Italian opera tenor; b. Parma, July 13, 1924. He studied voice at the Parma Cons., and appeared first as a baritone in the part of Figaro in Rossini's *Barber of Seville;* then sang Andrea Chenier as a tenor in 1951; he then progressed rapidly on his road to success; sang at La Scala in Milan, in England and in South America. On Nov. 13, 1956 he made his American debut singing Rhadames in *Aida* at the Metropolitan Opera in New York, and remained on its staff for more than 20 years. His repertory includes 68 roles.

Bergsma, William, eminent American composer; b. Oakland, California, April 1, 1921. He studied at Stanford Univ., and later with Howard Hanson and Bernard Rogers at the Eastman School of Music in Rochester. He was appointed to the faculty of the Juilliard School of Music, N.Y., in 1946; in 1963 joined the faculty of the school of music at the Univ. of Washington in Seattle. His music is distinguished by its structural pragmatism and a gift for lyrical melodiousness.

WORKS: 2 ballets: *Paul Bunyan* (San Francisco, June 22, 1939); and *Señor Commandante* (Rochester, May 1, 1942); Symphony for Chamber Orch. (Rochester, April 14, 1943); *Music on a Quiet Theme* for orch. (Rochester, April 22, 1943); *Suite from a Children's Film* (1945); Symphony No. 1 (1946-49; CBS, May 20, 1950); symphonic poem, *A Carol on Twelfth Night* (1953); 3-act opera, *The Wife of Martin Guerre* (N.Y., Feb. 15, 1956); Concerto for Wind Quintet (1958); *Fantastic Variations on a Theme from Tristan und Isolde* for viola and piano (Boston, March 2, 1961); *In Celebration: Toccata for the Sixth Day,* commissioned for the inaugural week concert of the Juilliard Orch. during the week of dedication of Philharmonic Hall in Lincoln Center for the Performing Arts, N.Y., and performed there on Sept. 28, 1962; *Confrontation* from the *Book of Job,* for chorus and 22 instruments (Des Moines, Iowa, Nov. 29, 1963); *Serenade, To Await the Moon* for chamber orch. (La Jolla, Calif., Aug. 22, 1965); Violin Concerto (Tacoma, Washington, May 18, 1966); Suite for Brass Quartet (1940); 4 string quartets (1942, 1944, 1953, 1970); 3 Fantasies for Piano (1943); *Showpiece* for violin and piano (1934); *Pieces for Renard* for recorder and 2 violas (1943); 2 choral pieces, *In a Glass of Water* (1945) and *On the Beach at Night* (1946); *Illegible Canons* for clarinet and piano (1969); *Clandestine Dialogues* for cello and percussion (1972); *The Murder of Comrade Sharik,* opera (1973); *Wishes, Wonders, Portents, Charms* for chorus and instruments (N.Y., Feb. 12, 1975); *In Space* for soprano and instruments (Seattle, May 21, 1975).

BIBLIOGRAPHY: A. Skulsky, "The Music of William Bergsma," *The Juilliard Review* (Spring 1956; with a list of works).

Bergson, Michael, composer; b. Warsaw, May 20, 1820; d. London, March 9, 1898. He studied with Schneider in Dessau and with Rungenhagen and Taubert in Berlin. He was in Paris in 1840 and in Italy in 1846; his opera *Luisa di Monfort* was produced in Florence in 1847. He then lived in Vienna, Berlin and Leipzig. On his second visit to Paris he brought out an operetta *Qui va à la chasse, perd sa place* (1859). In 1863 he was appointed professor of piano at the Geneva Cons.; later became its director. He eventually settled in London as piano teacher. He wrote numerous pieces of piano music, clearly in imitation of Chopin (*Polonaise héroïque, 12 Grandes Études caractéristiques,* etc.); also brought out a manual *École du mécanisme.*

Bergt, Christian Gottlob August, noted German composer; b. Öderan, Saxony, June 17, 1771; d. Bautzen, Feb. 10, 1837. He was organist at Bautzen from 1802; also taught music at the Seminary and was conductor of the singing society. He wrote 6 operas; several symphonies; chamber music; songs, of which a set of Lieder, *Congé,* became very popular. His sacred works were for a time constantly performed throughout Germany; he wrote a Passion; the hymns *So weit der Sonne Strahlen* and *Christus ist erstanden* for 4 voices and orch.; the canticle *Herr Gott, dich loben wir*, etc. His book *Briefwechsel eines alten und jungen Schulmeisters* (1838) contains a biographical sketch.

Beringer, Oscar, pianist and pedagogue; b. Furtwangen, Baden, July 14, 1844; d. London, Feb. 21, 1922. His father was a political refugee in 1849, and settled in London; Oscar Beringer received his rudimentary education at home; then enrolled in the Leipzig Cons., where he studied with Plaidy, Moscheles, and Reinecke (1864–66); he further studied in Berlin with Tausig; in 1869 became prof. in Tausig's Schule des höheren Klavierspiels; returned to London in 1871, and in 1873 established an Academy for the Higher Development of Pianoforte Playing, organized on the model of Tausig's Berlin school. From 1885 he was also prof. at the Royal Academy of Music. He was a pianist of great perfection of method; his book of technical exercises is valuable for students. Among his published compositions are a piano concerto; 2 piano sonatinas; various minor piano pieces; songs. He also published *Fifty Years' Experience of Pianoforte Teaching and Playing* (1907).

Berio, Luciano, Italian composer of avant-garde music; b. Oneglia, Oct. 24, 1925. He studied music with his father, an organist, and at the Milan Cons. with Ghedini (comp.) and Giulini (conducting); received a Koussevitzky Foundation Fellowship in 1952; took a summer course with Dallapiccola at the Berkshire Center in Tanglewood. Returning to Italy, he joined the staff of the Italian Radio; founded the Studio di Fonologia Musicale for experimental work on acoustics; edited the progressive magazine *Incontri Musicali*. From 1965 to 1972 he was on the faculty of the Juilliard School of Music in New York; then returned to Italy. The apparatus of sound production in his works consists of every imaginable combination and every feasible application of vocal and instrumental techniques; formal structures extend from deceptively simple Baroque arrangements to theatrical conglomerates of speech, song, spoken melody, rhythmically inflected recitation, mimodrama, choreodrama, abstract opera, concrete noises, electronic effects, aleatory passages.
WORKS: Concertino for Clarinet, Violin, Harp, Celesta and String Orch. (1949); *Opus No. Zoo* for woodwind quintet (1951); *2 pezzi* for violin and piano (1951); *5 Variazioni* for piano (1952); *Chamber Music* to poems by James Joyce for voice, clarinet, cello and harp (1952); *Variazioni* for chamber orch. (1953); *Mimomusique*, ballet (1953); *Nones* for orch. (1954); String Quartet (1955); *Allelujah I* for orch. (1956); *Allelujah II* for 5 instrumental groups (1956–58); *Serenata* for flute and 14 instruments (1957); *Sequenza I* for flute solo (1958); *Tempi concertati* for chamber orch. (1959); *Differences* for 5 instruments and stereophonic tape (1959); *Circles*, to poems by E. E. Cummings, for voice, harp and percussion (1960); *Quaderni* for orch. (1960); *Sequenza II* for harp (1963); *Traces*, for voices and orch. (1964); *Sincronie* for string quartet (1964); *Chemins I, II, III,* for various groups (1965,

1967, 1967); *Sequenza III* for female voice (1966); *Sequenza IV* for piano (1966); *Sequenza V* for trombone solo (1966); *Sequenza VI* for viola (1967); *Sequenza VII* for oboe (1969); *Sequenza VIII* for percussion (1975); *Sequenza IX* for violin (1975); multifarious agglutinations and sonoristic amalgamations for electronic instruments (*Mutazioni, Perspectives, Omaggio a Joyce, Momento,* etc.); *Sinfonia*, containing a movement based on remembered fragments of works by Mahler, Ravel, Richard Strauss, etc. (N.Y., Oct. 10, 1968); *Opera*, spectacle for mixed media (Santa Fe, Aug. 12, 1970; completely revised, 1976); *Memory for Electronic Piano and Electronic Harpsichord* (N.Y., March 12, 1971, with Berio and Peter Serkin at the respective electronic keyboards); *Prayer,* a speech sound event with magnetic tape accompaniment (N.Y., April 5, 1971); Concerto for 2 Pianos and Orch. (1973); *Linea* for 2 pianos, marimba and vibraphone (1974); *Points on the Curve to find. . .* for piano and 22 instruments (1974); *Coro* for 40 voices and 40 instruments (1976); Cello Concerto (1976).

Bériot, Charles-Auguste de, celebrated Belgian violinist; b. Louvain, Feb. 20, 1802; d. Brussels, April 8, 1870. He owed his technical foundation to the careful instruction of his guardian, Tiby, a provincial teacher; as a boy, he had lessons with Viotti, whose concerto he played in public at the age of nine. He made a triumphant debut in Paris (1821); became chamber violinist to the King of France; played successfully in many concerts in England; was solo violinist to the King of the Netherlands; made concert tours through Europe, many with Mme. Garcia-Malibran, whom he married in 1836. From 1843–52 he was prof. of violin at Brussels Cons.; failure of eyesight and paralysis of the left arm necessitated his retirement. Among his compositions are: 7 violin concertos; *duos brillants* for violin and piano; 11 sets of variations for violin. His pedagogical works are still useful; he wrote *Premier guide des violonistes; Méthode de Violon* (3 parts; Paris, 1858; his best work); many studies for violin, etc.
BIBLIOGRAPHY: E. Heron-Allen, "A Contribution towards an Accurate Biography of de Bériot and Malibran," *De fidiculis opuscula,* no. VI (1894); A. Bachmann, *Les grands violonistes du passé* (Paris, 1913); A. van der Linden, "L'Exotisme dans la musique de Charles de Bériot (1802–1870) et d'Henri Vieuxtemps (1820–1881)," *Bulletin de la Classe des Beaux-Arts de l'Académie Royale de Belgique* LII/10–11 (1970).

Bériot, Charles-Wilfride de (son of **Charles-Auguste de Bériot**), French pianist; b. Paris, Feb. 21, 1833; d. Sceaux du Gâtinais, Oct. 22, 1914. He was a pupil of Thalberg (1855); later taught piano at the Paris Cons.; wrote a symph. poem, *Fernand Cortez;* overtures; 3 piano concertos; a collection for violin and piano entitled *Opéras sans paroles,* etc.; was co-author, with his father, of a *Méthode d'accompagnement.*

Berkeley, Sir Lennox, significant English composer; b. Boar's Hill, near Oxford, May 12, 1903. He studied French and philosophy at Merton College, Oxford (1922–26); then took lessons in composition with Nadia Boulanger in Paris (1927–32). Returning to Lon-

153

don in 1935, he was on the staff of the Music Dept. of the BBC (1942–45); then was a prof. of composition at the Royal Academy of Music in London (1946–68). He was attracted from the beginning by the spirit of neo-Classical music, and his early works bear the imprint of the Paris manner as exemplified by the neo-Baroque formulas of Ravel and Stravinsky; but soon he formed an individual idiom which may be termed "modern English," broadly melodious, richly harmonious and translucidly polyphonic. He was knighted in 1974.

WORKS: 4 operas: *Nelson,* in 3 acts (1951; preview with piano accompaniment, London, Feb. 14, 1953; 1st complete performance, London Sept. 22, 1954; an orch. *Suite: Nelson* was drawn from it in 1955); *A Dinner Engagement,* in 1 act (1954; Aldeburgh Festival, June 17, 1954); *Ruth,* in 1 act (1956; London, Oct. 2, 1956); and *Castaway* (Aldeburgh Festival, June 3, 1967); a ballet, *The Judgement of Paris* (1938); an oratorio, *Jonah* (1935); Overture (Barcelona, April 23, 1936); *Domini est Terra* for chorus and orch. (1937; International Society for Contemporary Music Festival, London, June 17, 1938); *Introduction and Allegro* for 2 pianos and orch. (1938); *Serenade* for string orch. (1939); 4 symphonies: No. 1 (1940; London, July 8, 1943), No. 2 (1956–58; Birmingham, Feb. 24, 1959; revised 1976), No. 3 in one movement (1968–69; Cheltenham, July 9, 1969) and No. 4 (1976–77); *Divertimento* for orch. (1943); *Nocturne* for orch. (1946); *4 Poems of St. Teresa* for contralto and strings (1947); *Stabat Mater* for 6 solo voices and 12 instruments (1947); Concerto for Piano and Orch. (1947); 2-Piano Concerto (1948); *Colonus' Praise* for chorus and orch. (1949); Sinfonietta (1950); *Gibbons Variations* for tenor, chorus, strings and organ (1951); Flute Concerto (1952; London, July 29, 1953); Suite for Orch. (1953); Concerto for Piano and Double String Orch. (1958; London, Feb. 11, 1959); *An Overture* for light orch. (1959); *Suite: A Winter's Tale* for orch. (1960); *5 Pieces* for violin and orch. (1961; London, July 3, 1962); Concerto for Violin and Chamber Orch. (1961); *Batter My Heart* for soprano, chorus, organ and chamber orch. (1962); *4 Ronsard Sonnets* (Set 2) for tenor and orch., (1963; London, Aug. 9, 1963; version with chamber orch., Set 1, for 2 tenors and piano, 1952); *Partita* for chamber orch. (1965); *Signs in the Dark* for chorus and strings (1967); *Magnificat* for chorus and orch. (1968; London, July 8, 1968); *Windsor Variations* for chamber orch. (1969); *Dialogue* for cello and chamber orch. (1970); *Sinfonia Concertante* for oboe and chamber orch. (1973; London, Aug. 3, 1973); *Antiphon* for string orch. (1973); *Voices of the Night* for orch. (1973; Birmingham, Aug. 22, 1973); Suite for strings (1974); Guitar Concerto (1974; London, July 4, 1974); 3 string quartets (1935, 1942, 1970); Violin Sonatina (1942); String Trio (1943); Viola Sonata (1945); *Introduction and Allegro* for solo violin (1946); *Theme and Variations* and *Elegy* and *Toccata,* all for violin and piano (all 1950); Trio for violin, horn and piano (1954); Sextet for clarinet, horn and string quartet (1955); Concerto for Flute, Violin, Cello, and Harpsichord or Piano (1955); Sonatina for Solo Guitar (1957); Oboe Sonatina (1962); *Diversions* for 8 instruments (1964); *Nocturne* for harp (1967); Quartet for oboe and string trio (1967); *Theme and Variations* for solo guitar (1970); *Introduction and Allegro* for double bass and piano (1971); Duo for cello and piano (1971); *In memoriam Igor Stravinsky* for string quartet (1971); Quintet for piano and winds (1975); numerous piano pieces, including *Concert Studies,* sets 1 and 2 (1940, 1972), a sonata (1945), sonatina for 2 pianos (1959), Theme and Variations for 2 pianos (1968); *3 Pieces* for organ (1966–68); *Fantasia* for organ (1976); several songs, with piano, organ, harp, or guitar accompaniment; choruses.

Berkenhead, John L., blind organist, who was active in the U.S. towards the end of the 18th century. He arrived in America in 1795; was organist at Trinity Church in Newport from 1796 to 1804. His piece for harpsichord, *Abolition of the Bastille,* was invariably featured at his concerts in Boston and other New England cities.

Berkowitz, Ralph, American pianist and educator; b. New York City, Sept. 5, 1910. He studied at the Curtis Institute of Music, Philadelphia (1933–42); then was instructor at the Berkshire Music Center in Tanglewood; in 1947 was appointed Dean. He made tours as pianist and accompanist in America, Europe and in the Orient; publ. numerous piano arrangements; edited works by Bach, Haydn, Chopin, Debussy, etc. He also wrote a short opera *A Telephone Call* which was performed in Rio de Janeiro on Dec. 15, 1955.

Berlijn, Anton (real name **Aron Wolf**), Dutch composer; b. Amsterdam, May 2, 1817; d. there, Jan. 16, 1870. He studied with L. Erk in Berlin and with G. W. Fink at Leipzig; returning to Amsterdam in 1846, he became conductor of the Royal Theater; wrote 9 operas, two of which (*Die Bergknappen* and *Proserpina*) became popular; 7 ballets; an oratorio, *Moses auf Nebo;* symphonies; chamber music.

Berlin, Irving (real name **Isidore Balin**), famous American composer of popular music; b. Temun, Russia, May 11, 1888; brought to the U.S. in 1893. He received no formal musical training, and never learned to read or write music; nonetheless, he succeeded in producing lyrical songs (to his own words) that are remarkable for their innate feeling, for the melodic phrase and the perfect blend of words and melodies.

WORKS: His first published song was *Marie from Sunny Italy* (1907), for which he wrote only the lyrics; he made his mark with the celebrated song *Alexander's Ragtime Band* (1911); in the same style were *Everybody's Doing It* (1911); *International Rag* (1913); *Ragtime Violin* (1911); *When that midnight choo-choo leaves for Alabam* (1912); *I want to go back to Michigan* (1914); ballads, *When I lost you* (1912), *When I leave the world behind* (1915). His first musical show, for which he composed the entire score, words and music, was *Watch Your Step* (1916); 1917 brought out his war show, *Yip, Yip, Yaphank,* which included the famous song *O how I hate to get up in the morning.* He then wrote the first three of his *Ziegfeld Follies* (1918, 1919, 1920; including the songs, *A pretty girl is like a melody* and *Mandy*); the *Music Box Revues* (1921, 1922; 1923, 1925); built the Music Box Theater with Sam Harris in 1921. His other shows are:

Face the Music (1932); *As Thousands Cheer* (1933, including the songs *Easter Parade* and *Heat Wave*); *Louisiana Purchase* (1939); *This is the Army* (1942); *Annie Get Your Gun* (1946); *Miss Liberty* (1949); *Call me Madam* (1950). Among his songs and ballads that have spread far and wide all over the world are: *What'll I Do* (1924); *All Alone* (1924); *Remember* (1925); *Always* (1925); *The Song is Ended but the Melody Lingers On* (1927); *Russian Lullaby* (1927); *Blue Skies* (1927); and *White Christmas* (enormously popular during World War II). He also composed musical scores for the moving pictures: *Top Hat* (1935); *Follow the Fleet* (1936); *On the Avenue* (1937); *Carefree* (1938); *Second Fiddle* (1939); *Holiday Inn* (1942); *Blue Skies* (1946); *Easter Parade* (1948); etc. To promote the publication and distribution of his music, he founded in 1919 the firm of Irving Berlin, Inc. He was a charter member of ASCAP (1914). In July 1954 he received the Congressional Medal for his patriotic songs, particularly *God Bless America* (composed in 1918; revived in 1938 and made famous during and after World War II). Berlin presented his upright piano, on which he composed most of his memorable tunes, to the Smithsonian Institution in 1973.
BIBLIOGRAPHY: A. Woollcott, *The Story of Irving Berlin* (N.Y., 1925); D. Jay, *The Irving Berlin Songography* (New Rochelle, N.Y., 1969).

Berlinski, Herman, German-American composer; b. Leipzig, Aug. 18, 1910; studied at the Leipzig Cons.; left Germany in 1933, and took lessons with Alfred Cortot (piano) and Nadia Boulanger (composition) in Paris. During World War II he joined the French Foreign Legion; eventually emigrated to the U.S. In his music he emphasizes the rhapsodic element of traditional Jewish cantillation, combining it with dodecaphonic techniques.
WORKS: Flute Sonata (1941); Violin Sonata (1949); *Symphonic Visions* (1949); liturgical compositions: *Kaddish* (1953); *Avodat Shabbat* (1957); *Kiddush Ha-Shem* (1958); songs.
BIBLIOGRAPHY: M. Kayden, "The Music of Herman Berlinski," *Bulletin of the American Composers Alliance* 3 (1959).

Berlinski, Jacques, Polish-American composer; b. Radon, Dec. 13, 1913. He went to France in 1931, and studied theory with Nadia Boulanger and Roger-Ducasse. He fought in the ranks of the French Army, in the artillery unit, during World War II. In 1948 he received first prize in a New York contest for composition, for his first symphony, dedicated to the memory of Churchill and subtitled *Symphony of Glory* (1965). In 1968 he settled in the United States, becoming a naturalized citizen in 1973. For the American Bicentennial he wrote a choral symphony entitled *America, 1976*, which was performed for the first time in San Diego, California, on May 6, 1976.

Berlioz, Gabriel Pierre, French composer (not related to Hector Berlioz); b. Paris, June 25, 1916. He studied in Paris with Roussel and d'Indy. He has written a viola concerto (1935); *Francezaïc*, comic opera (1939); *Symphonie parisienne* (1942); *Jardin hanté* ballet (1943); Piano Trio (1944); *Divertissement* for violin,

cello, piano and string orch. (1945); Concerto for Kettledrums and Orch. (1951; Paris, Jan. 25, 1953); Bassoon Concerto (1952); Symphony No. 2 (1953); pieces for tuba and piano, saxophone and piano, flute and piano, etc.

Berlioz, Hector Louis, great French composer; b. Côte-Saint-André, Isère, Dec. 11, 1803; d. Paris, March 8, 1869. His father, a physician, sent him to Paris to study medicine. But Berlioz took little interest in medicine and became deeply engrossed in music, even though he was not proficient on any instrument except the guitar. Despite his lack of musical training, he entered the Paris Conservatory where he studied with Lesueur and Reicha. He soon became dissatisfied with the formal training given by his teachers and began to compose music in a romantic manner free from all restrictions of the rigorous classical school. From the very first Berlioz endeavored to transcend the limits of practical composition and performance; he dreamed of huge orchestras which could adequately embody his romantic ideas. His first work was an orchestral *Messe solennelle*, which he had produced at the church of St. Roch (July 10, 1825), employing 150 players. Still he was ambitious enough to covet academic honors. He submitted a cantata *La Mort d'Orphée* for the Prix de Rome in 1827; a performance was tentatively scheduled for July 22, 1828, but was cancelled when the music committee declared the score unplayable. The cantata was not performed until a century later, Oct. 16, 1932, when Cortot conducted it in Paris (the MS was regarded as lost, but was discovered by Boschot). Undaunted, Berlioz again applied for the Prix de Rome, and obtained second prize in 1828; he finally carried first prize in 1830 with a more conventional work, *Sardanapale*. In the meantime his overtures *Waverley* and *Les Francs-Juges* were performed at a Conservatory concert on May 26, 1828. He then embarked on his most individual work, the *Symphonie fantastique*, subtitled 'épisode de la vie d'un artiste.' The completion of this score at the age of 26 signalized the opening of a new era in program music; in it Berlioz abandons the classical method of thematic development, and instead establishes what he himself called an *idée fixe*, a basic theme recurring throughout the music. Berlioz gives this description of the *Symphonie fantastique*: "A young musician of morbid sensibility and ardent imagination poisons himself with opium in a fit of amorous despair. The narcotic dose, too weak to result in death, plunges him into a heavy sleep accompanied by the strangest visions, during which his sensations, sentiments and recollections are translated in his sick brain into musical thoughts and images. The beloved woman herself has become for him a melody, like a fixed idea which he finds and hears everywhere." The titles of the 5 movements are: I. *Dreams, Passions*; II. *A Ball*; III. *Scene in the Fields*; IV. *March to the Scaffold*; V. *Walpurgisnight's Dream*. The genesis of the symphony is no less remarkable than its form; it was intended to be an offering of both adoration and condemnation to the Irish actress Harriet Smithson, whose performances of Shakespeare Berlioz had attended in Paris (even though he knew no English). The first performance of the *Symphonie fantastique* was given in Paris on Dec.

5, 1830; Berlioz hoped that Harriet Smithson would attend but she was professionally occupied on that day. Berlioz wrote a sequel to the *Symphonie fantastique* entitled *Lélio;* both parts were performed in Paris on Dec. 9, 1832, creating a sensation, particularly since by that time all Paris knew the story of Berlioz's infatuation. Harriet Smithson was present herself; they met, and over the opposition of both families, they were married Oct. 3, 1833. The marriage proved unhappy; they separated; Harriet Smithson died in 1854. Berlioz remarried that same year; his second wife, Maria Recio, died in 1862.

Berlioz's next significant work was equally unconventional, *Harold en Italie* for solo viola and orch. (Paris, Nov. 23, 1834), inspired by Byron's *Childe Harold;* there followed the dramatic symphony *Roméo et Juliette* for solo voices, chorus and orch. (Paris, Nov. 24, 1839) and *Le Carnaval romain* (Paris, Feb. 3, 1844), the latter destined to become one of the most popular works in the orchestral repertory. Less successful was Berlioz's opera *Benvenuto Cellini,* to which *Le Carnaval romain* originally served as an orchestral introduction (in the 2nd act); it was performed at the Paris Opéra (Sept. 10, 1838) arousing little interest; however, its production by Liszt in Weimar (March 20, 1852) was received with great acclaim; Berlioz conducted it in London, on June 25, 1853. In the meantime Berlioz became a brilliant musical journalist; his articles in the *Journal des Débats* and in the *Gazette Musicale* exercised considerable influence and helped to arouse interest in new musical ideas. To eke out his earnings, Berlioz accepted the appointment as librarian of the Paris Conservatory (1852), and held it until his death. His Paris obligations did not interfere with his travels; he toured Germany and Italy; he also visited Austria, Hungary and Russia. German musicians, led by Liszt, were particularly sympathetic to his music; concerts of his music were organized by Liszt in Weimar (1855). On Aug. 9, 1862, Berlioz conducted in Baden-Baden the première of his opera *Béatrice et Bénédict.*

The creative life of Berlioz is not easily separable into distinct periods. Sometimes he dwelt on a favorite idea for many years before its ultimate embodiment. Still at the conservatory, he presented a cantata *8 scènes de Faust* (Nov. 29, 1829); much later he expanded the materials from this work in *La Damnation de Faust,* which Berlioz termed an "opéra de concert." He conducted it in concert form at the Opéra-Comique on Dec. 6, 1846; the complete work is seldom performed, but its symphonic interlude *Rákóczi March* has become famous; two other excerpts from the score, *Minuet of the Will-o'-the-Wisps* and *Dance of the Sylphs,* are also widely known. A curious destiny was reserved for the opera *Les Troyens,* written in 1856–59, in 2 parts, *La Prise de Troie* and *Les Troyens à Carthage.* Only the 2nd part was performed in Berlioz's lifetime (Paris, Théâtre-Lyrique, Nov. 4, 1863; the 1st part was presented for the first time in Karlsruhe on Dec. 6, 1890; the whole work was produced in Cologne (in German) on two successive nights, March 30–31, 1898; in France, it was not performed in its entirety until 1920 when it was given in Rouen. Other works are: *Messe des Morts* (Paris, Dec. 5, 1837); a sacred trilogy *L'Enfance du Christ* (Paris,

Dec. 10, 1854); symphonic overtures *King Lear* (1831), *Rob Roy* (1832) and *Le Corsaire* (1844); song cycles *Irlande* (1830) and *Nuits d'été* (1834–41; also with orch.); *Te Deum* for tenor, 3 choirs, orch., brass band and organ (1849). His *Traité d'instrumentation et d'orchestration modernes* (1844), a work of fundamental importance, has been translated into all European languages; supplemented editions were issued in German by Weingartner (1904) and Richard Strauss (1905). This treatise, no less than his orchestral music itself, led Weingartner to proclaim Berlioz the "creator of the modern orchestra." The extraordinary versatility of Berlioz's gifts is revealed in his literary writings. He publ. *Voyage musical en Allemagne et Italie* (1844; 2 vols.); *Les Soirées de l'orchestre* (1853; English translation by Ch. E. Roche, with introduction by Ernest Newman; London, 1929; a new translation by J. Barzun, N.Y., 1956); *Grotesques de la musique* (1859); *A travers chants* (1862); *Les Musiciens et la musique* (a series of articles collected from the *Journal des Débats;* 1903, with introduction by André Hallays). His book of *Mémoires* (1870; 2nd ed., 2 vols., 1876; English translation, London, 1884; annotated and edited by Ernest Newman, N.Y., 1932) presents a vivid panorama of the musical life in Europe as reflected in his mind; factually it is not always trustworthy. A complete edition of Berlioz's works (with the exception of the operas *Benvenuto Cellini* and *Les Troyens*) has been publ. by Breikopf & Härtel in 20 vols. under the editorship of Ch. Malherbe and F. Weingartner (but see Supplement 5 in Jacques Barzun's book *Berlioz and the Romantic Century* for the enumeration of musical and other errors). Breitkopf & Härtel also publ. (in German) the literary works of Berlioz in 10 vols., including his correspondence. See C. Hopkinson, *A Bibliography of the Musical and Literary Works of Hector Berlioz* (Edinburgh, 1951).

BIBLIOGRAPHY: BIOGRAPHY: E. Hippeau, *Berlioz, l'homme et l'artiste* (3 vols., Paris, 1883–85); A. Jullien, *H. B.* (Paris, 1888); L. Pohl, *Hector Berliozs Leben und Werke* (Leipzig, 1900); K. F. Boult, *Berlioz's Life as Written by Himself in His Letters and Memoirs* (London, 1903); R. Louis, *H. B.* (Leipzig, 1904); J.-G. Prod'homme, *H. B.* (Paris, 1905); A. Coquard, *Berlioz* (Paris, 1908); B. Schrader, *Berlioz* (Leipzig, 1908); A. Boschot's monumental biography in 3 vols: *La Jeunesse d'un romantique; H. B., 1803–31* (Paris, 1906), *Un Romantique sous Louis-Philippe; H. B., 1831–42* (Paris, 1908), and *Le Crépuscule d'un romantique: H. B., 1842–69* (Paris, 1913), E. Bernoulli, *Berlioz als Ästhetiker der Klangfarben* (Zürich, 1909); A. Boschot, *Une Vie romantique, H. B.* (Paris, 1919; 27th edition, 1951; complete biography in 1 vol.); P.-M. Masson, *B.* (Paris, 1923); J. Kapp, *H. B.* (Berlin, 1922); E. Rey, *La Vie amoureuse de B.* (Paris, 1929); L. Constantin, *B.* (Paris, 1933); W. J. Turner, *B.; the Man and his Work* (London, 1934); Tom Wotton, *H. B.* (Oxford, 1935); J. H. Elliot, *B.* (London, 1938); G. de Pourtalès, *B. et l'Europe romantique* (Paris, 1939); J. Barzun, *Berlioz and the Romantic Century* (2 vols.; Boston, 1950); a most valuable investigation, correcting many accepted but erroneous data); A. W. Ganz, *B. in London* (London, 1950); H. Kuehner, *H. B., Charakter und Schöpfertum* (Berlin, 1952); Henry Barraud, *H. B.* (Paris, 1955).

CORRESPONDENCE: D. Bernard, *Correspondance iné-dite de B.* (Paris, 1878); Ch. Gounod, *Lettres intimes* (Paris, 1882); La Mara, *Briefe von H. B. an die Fürstin Carolyne Wittgenstein* (Leipzig, 1903); J. Tiersot, *Les Années romantiques: Correspondance d'H. B.* (Paris, 1907). All the above-mentioned letters are found in vols. III-V of the Breitkopf & Härtel edition; J. Tiersot, *Le Musicien errant* (Paris, 1919); J. Tiersot, *Corre-spondance inédite de B.* (Paris, 1930); J.-G. Pro-d'homme, *Souvenirs de voyage* (Paris, 1932); G. Clar-ence, "Lettres inédites à Berlioz," *La Revue Musicale* XI/1, S. Ginsburg, "Correspondance russe inédite de Berlioz," *La Revue Musicale* XI/1; J. Barzun, ed., *New Letters of Berlioz, 1830-68* (N.Y., 1954).

ANALYSIS AND CRITICISM: F. Liszt, *Berlioz und seine Harold-symphonie* (1855; reprinted in vol. IV of Liszt's *Gesammelte Schriften*); A. Ernst, *L'Œuvre dramatique de H. B.* (Paris, 1884); R. Pohl, *H. B.: Stu-dien und Erinnerungen* (Leipzig, 1884); E. Hippeau, *Berlioz et son temps* (Paris, 1892); J. Tiersot, *Berlioz et la société de son temps* (Paris, 1904); T. Mantovani, *La dannazione di Faust d'Ettore Berlioz* (Milan, 1923); J. Tiersot, "B. of the Fantastic Symphony," *Musical Quarterly* (1933); P. Schlitzer, *La messa da requiem di Ettore Berlioz* (Florence, 1940).

Berman, Lazar, remarkable Soviet pianist; b. in Len-ingrad, Feb. 26, 1930. He studied at the Moscow Cons. with Goldenweiser, graduating in 1953. He competed at the Queen Elisabeth of Belgium contest in Brussels in 1956, obtaining the fifth prize; at another contest in Budapest in the same year he received third prize. These were the modest beginnings of a brilliant career as a virtuoso pianist. In 1970 he made a highly suc-cessful tour of Italy. His first American tour in 1976 was acclaimed by music critics in undiluted superla-tives. Yet his repertory is not all-embracing; he shows a decided predilection for the music of Tchaikovsky, Rachmaninoff and Scriabin, apart from the German classics; among the modernists his favorite is Prokof-iev. His titanic technique, astounding in the facility of his bravura passages in octaves, does not preclude the excellence of his interpretations of lyric moods.

Bermudo, Juan, Spanish music theorist; b. Ecija, Se-ville, c.1510; d. after 1555. He first studied theology and devoted himself to preaching; later turned to mu-sic and studied at the Univ. of Alcalá de Henares. He spent 15 years as a Franciscan monk in Andalusia; in 1550 he entered the service of the Archbishop of An-dalusia, where Cristóbal de Morales was choir direc-tor. The writings of Bermudo constitute an important source of information on Spanish instrumental music of the 16th century. His most comprehensive work is the *Declaración de Instrumentos Musicales* (Osuna, 1549 and 1555). It deals with theory, in which his au-thorities were Gafurius, Glareanus and Ornithopar-chus; instruments, including problems of tuning, tech-nique of performance, and repertoire; and critical evaluation of contemporary composers, showing fa-miliarity with the works of Josquin, Willaert and Gombert. Bermudo also wrote *El Arte tripharia* (Osu-na, 1550). 13 organ pieces by him are included in F. Pedrell, *Salterio Sacro-Hispano.*

BIBLIOGRAPHY: O. Kinkeldey, *Orgel und Clavier*

in der Musik des 16ten Jahrhundert (1910); H. Collet, *Le Mysticisme musical espagnol au XVIᵉ siècle* (Paris, 1913); R. Mitjana, "La Musique en Espagne," in Lavi-gnac's *Encyclopédie musicale*; H. Anglès and J. Subi-rá, *Catálogo Musical de la Biblioteca Nacional de Madrid* (vol. II); G. Reese, *Music in the Renaissance* (N.Y., 1954); R. Stevenson, *Juan Bermudo* (The Hague, 1960).

Bernabei, Ercole (Giuseppe), Italian composer of vo-cal music; b. Caprarola, Papal States, 1622; d. Munich, Dec. (buried Dec. 6), 1687. He was a pupil of Orazio Benevoli, whom he succeeded in 1672 as chapel mas-ter at the Vatican; 1674, became court conductor at Munich. He wrote 5 operas (produced in Munich); published a book of madrigals, *Concerto madriga-lesco* (1669), etc.; other works (Masses, offertories, psalms) are MS in various libraries.

BIBLIOGRAPHY: R. Casimiri, *Ercole Bernabei, maestro di cappella musicale lateranense* (Rome, 1920); R. de Rensis, *E. Bernabei* (Rome, 1920).

Bernabei, Giuseppe Antonio, Italian composer, son of the preceding; b. Rome, 1649; d. Munich, March 9, 1732. He studied with his father and helped him as second chapel master in Munich from 1677; after his father's death, he assumed his post (1688). He com-posed 14 operas and much sacred music.

BIBLIOGRAPHY: Karl Forster, *G. A. Bernabei als Kirchenkomponist* (Munich, 1933).

Bernac (real name **Bertin**), **Pierre,** French baritone; b. Paris, Jan. 12, 1899. He studied voice with Reinhold von Wahrlich in Salzburg. He started on his career as a singer rather late in life, and assumed the pseudo-nym Bernac in order to avoid confusion with another Pierre Bertin, an actor. He specialized in French and German songs. Between 1936 and 1961 he gave nu-merous song recitals in Europe and America, most of them with Francis Poulenc at the piano; a number of Poulenc's songs were written specially for Bernac. For a number of years Bernac conducted master classes at the American Cons. in Fontainebleau, France. He published a valuable manual *The Interpre-tation of French Song* (N.Y., 1970). See also R. Gelatt, *Music Makers* (N.Y., 1953).

Bernacchi, Antonio, celebrated sopranist *(musico);* b. Bologna, June (baptized June 23d), 1685; d. there, March 16, 1756. He was a pupil of Pistocchi; sang in Venice and Bologna (1709-12); then appeared in Lon-don (1716); was again in Italy (1717-29), also sang in opera in Munich. In 1729 he was specially engaged by Handel as a substitute for Senesino for the Italian Op-era in London; after initial successes, Bernacchi lost his following in London and returned to Italy, where he continued to sing until 1736. He settled in Bologna and opened a singing school. He revived the style of vocal embellishments which the French term 'rou-lades,' and was severely criticized for this practice. He left some compositions, among them *Grave et Fuga a 4; Kyrie a 5;* and *Justus ut palma a 5.*

BIBLIOGRAPHY: L. Frati, "Antonio Bernacchi e la sua scuola di canto," *Rivista Musicale Italiana* (Sept. 1922).

Bernard, Jean Emile Auguste, French composer and organist; b. Marseilles, Nov. 28, 1843; d. Paris, Sept. 11, 1902. He studied at the Paris Cons. with Benoist (organ) and with Marmontel (piano); was organist at Notre Dame des Champs until 1895. He wrote 2 cantatas: *Guillaume le conquérant* and *La Captivité de Babylone*; an overture, *Béatrice*; Piano Quartet; Piano Trio; Cello Sonata; Violin Sonata; a *Divertissement* for wind instruments; etc.

Bernard, Moritz (Matvey), Russian music publisher and pianist; b. Mitau, 1794; d. St. Petersburg, May 9, 1871. He studied piano with John Field in Moscow, and later was active as a piano teacher; in 1822 he moved to St. Petersburg, where he purchased a music store of Dalmas, and began publishing music. Bernard's printing press published songs by Glinka and Dargomyzhsky, piano pieces by Anton Rubinstein and other important Russian composers. In 1840 he began publishing a musical monthly *Nouvelliste*, which continued publication until 1914, many years after his death. Bernard's son took charge of the music store until 1885 when the stock was purchased by Jurgenson. Bernard composed an opera *Olga* which was performed in St. Petersburg in 1845; also published a valuable collection, *Songs of the Russian People* (St. Petersburg, 1847), a collection of children's pieces, *L'Enfant-Pianiste*, and some original piano pieces and songs, some of which were printed in the Soviet Union.

Bernard, Paul, French pianist and teacher; b. Poitiers, Oct. 4, 1827; d. Paris, Feb. 24, 1879. He studied at the Paris Cons. with Halévy and Thalberg; wrote criticisms for the *Ménestrel* and the *Revue et Gazette Musicale*; composed many piano pieces.

Bernard, Robert, Swiss-born composer, editor and writer on music; b. Geneva, Oct. 10, 1900; d. Paris, May 2, 1971. He studied in Geneva with Templeton Strong, Barblan and Lauber. In 1926 he settled in Paris; in 1937 he became a lecturer at the Schola Cantorum and a music critic; for several years he was editor of *La Revue Musicale*. He published monographs on Franck, Aubert, Roussel and other French composers.
WORKS: Piano Concerto; Harp Concerto; Saxophone Quartet; Piano Trio; Trio for Oboe, Clarinet and Trombone; a number of piano pieces.

Bernardi, Bartolomeo, composer; b. Bologna, c.1660; d. Copenhagen, May, 1732. He left Bologna about 1700 and settled in Denmark; two of his operas were performed in Copenhagen in 1703: *Il Gige fortunato* and *Diana e la Fortuna*. He also wrote an opera, *Libussa*, which was produced in Prague; his trio sonatas were published in Bologna (1692; 1696).

Bernardi, Enrico, Italian conductor and composer; b. Milan, March 11, 1838; d. there, July 17, 1900. He toured in Italy with various opera companies as conductor; wrote several operas which he produced himself and nearly 60 ballets, of which the first, *Illusioni d'un pittore* (Milan, 1854), was perhaps the most successful.

Bernardi, Francesco. See **Senesino, Francesco.**

Bernardi, Steffano, Italian composer; b. Verona, c.1575; d. 1636. He served as maestro di cappella at the church of the Santissima Madonna dei Monti in Rome; from 1611–22 was music director at the Cathedral of Verona; became Kapellmeister at the Salzburg Cathedral (1628); left Salzburg in 1634.
WORKS: 2 books of Masses for 8 voices, and one for 4 and 5 voices; a book of madrigals for 3 voices (Rome, 1611) and 2 books for 5 voices (Venice, 1611; Rome, 1612); 2 books of *madrigaletti*; psalms and motets; also instrumental works (trio sonatas, etc.) Reprints of some of his sacred works are to be found in the *Denkmäler der Tonkunst in Österreich* (vol. 69; formerly 36.i). Bernardi was also the author of the manual *Porta musicale per la quale il principiante con facile brevità all'acquisto delle perfette regole del contrapunto vien introdotto* (Verona, 1615; 7 subsequent editions).
BIBLIOGRAPHY: F. Posch, *Steffano Bernardis weltliche Vokal- und Instrumental-Werke* (Munich, 1928).

Bernasconi, Andrea, composer and conductor; b. Milan, 1706; d. Munich, Jan. 29, 1784. He was conductor at the court of Munich from 1755; wrote 18 operas, 14 of which were produced at Munich; also much sacred music.
BIBLIOGRAPHY: E. J. Weiss, *Andrea Bernasconi als Opernkomponist* (Munich, 1923).

Berneker, Constanz, German composer; b. Darkehmen, East Prussia, Oct. 30, 1844; d. Königsberg, June 9, 1906. He studied at the Royal Academy in Berlin; then was organist at the Königsberg Cathedral; also taught at the conservatory.
WORKS: cantatas; *Judith*; *Christi Himmelfahrt*; *Reformations-Kantate*; *Gott unsere Zuflucht*; *Christus ist mein Leben*; *Das Siegefest*; *Hero und Leander*; *Das hohe Lied*; *Mila, das Haidekind*; and many other cantatas.
BIBLIOGRAPHY: O. Laudien, *Constanz Berneker* (Berlin, 1909).

Berner, Friedrich Wilhelm, German organist and composer; b. Breslau, May 16, 1780; d. there, May 9, 1827. He taught at the Breslau Seminary; later became director of the Royal Academic Institute for Church Music; wrote church music and published theoretical essays on music. A biography of him was written by Hientsch (1829).

Berners, Lord (originally **Gerald Tyrwhitt**), eccentric British composer; b. Apley Park, Bridgnorth (Shropshire), Sept. 18, 1883; d. London, April 19, 1950. A scion of nobility and wealth, he was educated at Eton; lived for many years in France, Italy and Germany; studied music and art in Dresden and Vienna; then served as honorary attaché to the British diplomatic service in Constantinople (1909–11) and in Rome (1911–20). Returning to England, he joined the artistic smart set in London; was on intimate terms with George Bernard Shaw and H. G. Wells; took lessons in composition with Vaughan Williams; also had some sporadic advice in orchestration from Casella and Stravinsky. As a composer, he was influenced by Satie's musical nihilism and affected bizarre social behavior; he was fond of practical jokes and grandiloquent spoofs; characteristic of his musical humor is a set of *3 Funeral Marches* for piano (*For a Statesman, For a Canary, For a Rich Aunt*, the latter in raucous dissonances). Gifted in literary expression, he published half a dozen novels and two autobiographical volumes written in an ironic and self-deprecatory vein, *First Childhood* (London, 1934) and *A Distant Prospect* (London, 1945). He was a talented painter who had successful exhibitions of his oil paintings in London, in 1931 and 1936, and an amateur chef de cuisine. He succeeded to the barony of Berners in 1918.

WORKS: opera, *Le Carosse du Saint-Sacrement* (Paris, April 24, 1924); the ballets, *The Triumph of Neptune* (Diaghilev's Ballet Russe production, London Dec. 3, 1926); *Luna Park* (London, 1930); *A Wedding Bouquet* (London, April 27, 1937); *Cupid and Psyche* (London, April 27, 1927, on the same bill as *A Wedding Bouquet*); *Les Sirènes* (London, Nov. 12, 1946); for piano *3 Funeral Marches* (1914); *Le Poisson d'or* (1914); *3 Fragments psychologiques* (1915); *3 Valses bourgeois* for piano 4 hands. (1917).

BIBLIOGRAPHY: J. Holbrooke, *Berners*, in Contemporary British Composers series (London, 1925); Harriett Bridgeman and Elizabeth Drury, *The British Eccentric* (N.Y., 1975).

Bernet Kempers, Karel Philippus, Dutch writer on music; b. Nijkerk, Holland, Sept. 20, 1897; d. Amsterdam, Sept. 30, 1974. He studied in Munich with Sandberger; received his Dr. Phil. in 1926; in 1929 was appointed teacher of music history at the Royal Cons. in The Hague and was secretary of the Federation of Dutch Composers. In 1946 he was appointed prof. at the Amsterdam Univ. Among his writings are: *Jacobus Clemens non Papa und seine Motetten* (1928); *Italian Opera, Peri to Puccini* (1929; English translation, 1947); *Muziekgeschiedenis* (Rotterdam, 1932; 4th ed., 1946); *Meesters der Muziek* (Rotterdam, 1939; 4th ed., 1948).

Bernhard der Deutsche (known also as **Bernardo di Steffanino Murer**), celebrated organist and the reputed inventor of organ pedals; b. Germany, early in the 15th century; d. 1459; was organist of San Marco in Venice.

BIBLIOGRAPHY: Michael Praetorius, *Syntagma musicum* (vol. I, part I, chapter 14, p. 145; vol. II, chapter 5, p. 96).

Bernhard, Christoph, German composer; b. Kolberg, Jan. 1, 1628; d. Dresden, Nov. 14, 1692. He studied with Paul Siefert in Danzig and with Schütz in Dresden. The Elector sent him to study singing in Italy (1649); in 1655 he became second Kapellmeister in Dresden, but was forced to resign through the disaffection of his Italian associates. He then went to Hamburg, where he served as a cantor (1664–74); was recalled by a new Elector to Dresden and was appointed first Kapellmeister, as successor to Schütz. He enjoyed a great respect as composer, particularly for his mastery of counterpoint. He published *Geistliche Harmonien* (Dresden, 1665; new edition, Kassel, 1972) and *Prudentia prudentiana* (Hamburg, 1669); a treatise on composition and another on counterpoint are in MS. Three major treatises in translation with annotation by W. Hilse are published in "The Treatises of Christoph Bernhard," *Music Forum* III (1973). Some of his cantatas were published by M. Seiffert in vol. VI of *Denkmäler deutscher Tonkunst*.

BIBLIOGRAPHY: J. M. Müller-Blattau, *Die Kompositionslehre Heinrich Schützens in der Fassung seines Schülers Christoph Bernhard* (Leipzig, 1926); H. Rauschning, *Musikgeschichte der Stadt Danzig* (1926).

Bernheimer, Martin, American music critic; b. Munich, Germany, Sept. 28, 1936. He was taken to the U.S. as a child in 1940; studied music at Brown Univ. (B.A., 1958) and N.Y. Univ. (M.A., 1962); in the interim took courses in music at the Munich Cons. (1958–59). Returning to the U.S., he was a member of the music faculty of N.Y. Univ. (1960–62); served as contributing critic for the *N.Y. Herald Tribune* (1959–62) and assistant music editor of *Saturday Review* (1962–65). In 1965 he was appointed music editor of *Los Angeles Times*; in 1966 became instructor in the Rockefeller programs for training music critics at the Univ. of Southern California, Los Angeles; also was a member of the faculty of the Univ. of Calif., Los Angeles (since 1969). As a critic, he possesses a natural facility and not infrequently a beguiling felicity of literary style; he espouses noble musical causes with crusading fervor, but he can be aggressively opinionated and ruthlessly devastating to composers, performers or administrators whom he dislikes; as a polemicist he is a *rara avis* among contemporary critics who seldom rise to the pitch of moral or musical indignation nowadays; Bernheimer also possesses a surprising knowledge of music in all its ramifications, which usually protects him from perilous pratfalls.

Bernier, Nicolas, French composer; b. Mantes (Seine-et-Oise), June 28, 1664; d. Paris, Sept. 5, 1734. He studied with Caldara in Rome; in 1692 returned to France; was organist at Chartres Cathedral (1694–98). Bernier was one of the first French composers to cultivate the secular cantata; he published 8 books of such 'cantates profanes,' of which *Les Nuits de Sceaux* is the most remarkable. His *Te Deum* was also much admired.

BIBLIOGRAPHY: P. Nelson, "Nicalos Bernier: A Biblographic Study," in J. W. Pruett, ed. *Studies in Musicology . . . in Memory of Glen Haydon* (Chapel Hill, N.C., 1969).

Bernier, René, Belgian composer; b. Saint-Gilles, March 10, 1905. He studied at the Brussels Cons. and had private lessons from Paul Gilson. In 1925 he and 7 other pupils of Gilson formed the "Groupe des Synthetistes" whose aim was to combine modern technique with classical forms.

WORKS: 3 ballets: *Le Bal des ombres* (1954), *Symphonie en blanc* (1961, derived from the *Sinfonietta*) and *Tanagras* (1969); *Mélopées et Rythmes* for orch. (1932); *Ode à une Madone* for orch. (1938, revised

1955); *Présages* for voice and orch. (1942–46); *Liturgies* for voice and string orch. (1946); *Sortileges ingénus (Ingenuous Charms)*, 14 songs for female or children's chorus, and orch. or piano (1947); *Eclaircies* for voice and orch. (1948); *Le Tombeau devant l'Escaut*, symph. poem (1952); *Notturno* for orch. (1955); *Bassonniere* for bassoon and orch. (1956); *Sinfonietta* for string orch. (1957); *Hommage à Sax*, concertino for saxophone and orch. (1958); *Reverdies*, variations for clarinet and orch. (1960); *Epitaphe II* for wind orch. (1961); *Interludes* for orch. (1966); *Ménestraudie* for violin and orch. (1970); *Sonata à deux* for flute and harp (1939); Trio for Flute, Cello and Harp (1942); Sonatina for Flute and Harp (1943); *Liturgies* for a cappella chorus (1940–41); *Chants Incantations* for a cappella chorus (1968); songs.

Berno von Reichenau, German theorist of the 11th century; b. about 970; d. in Cloister of Reichenau, June 7, 1048. In 1008 he was installed Abbot of the Cloister of Reichenau; accompanied Emperor Henry II to Rome for coronation in 1014, and in 1027 attended the coronation in Rome of Emperor Conrad II. He wrote learned treatises on music, to be found in J. P. Migne's *Patrologiae cursus completus* (vol. 142) and in Gerbert's *Scriptores* (vol. 2). A monograph on his system of music was published by W. Brambach (Leipzig, 1881).

Bernoulli, Eduard, Swiss music scholar; b. Basel, Nov. 6, 1867; d. Zürich, April 17, 1927. He studied at the Univ. of Leipzig, obtaining his doctorate in 1897 with the thesis *Die Choralnotenschrift bei Hymnen und Sequenzen im späteren Mittelalter;* subsequently edited several volumes of *Denkmäler deutscher Tonkunst.* He published the valuable monographs *Berlioz als Ästhetiker der Klangfarben* (Zürich, 1909), *Aus Liederbüchern der Humanistenzeit* (1910), etc. From 1921 till his death, Bernoulli was prof. at the Univ. of Zürich.

Bernstein, Elmer, American composer of film, radio and television music; b. New York, April 4, 1922. Among his film scores are *The Ten Commandments, The Man with the Golden Arm* and *From the Terrace.* He writes music charged with emotional energy, marked by modernistic turns and piquant rhythms.

Bernstein, Leonard, greatly gifted American conductor and composer, equally successful in writing symphonic music of profound content and melodious Broadway shows; b. Lawrence, Mass., Aug. 25, 1918, of a family of Russian-Jewish immigrants. His first piano teachers were Helen Coates and Heinrich Gebhard in Boston. He entered Harvard Univ. in 1935, and studied theory with Tillman Merritt, counterpoint and fugue with Walter Piston and orchestration with Edward B. Hill, graduating in 1939. He then went to Philadelphia where he studied piano with Isabelle Vengerova, conducting with Fritz Reiner, and orchestration with Randall Thompson at the Curtis Institute of Music. During the summers of 1940 and 1941 he attended the Berkshire Music Center at Tanglewood, where he studied conducting with Koussevitzky, who took great interest in his talent and made every effort to promote his career as a professional conductor. He also did some work for publishers, arranging music for band, under the interlingual pseudonym **Lenny Amber** (Bernstein is the German word for amber). In 1943 Bernstein obtained the position of assistant conductor to Artur Rodzinski, then conductor of the New York Philharmonic; on Nov. 14, 1943 he was called upon on short notice to conduct a difficult program in substitution for Bruno Walter who was to lead that particular concert, but who was indisposed. His debut created a sensation, and he was roundly praised for his courage in facing a trying situation and for his professional competence. This was the beginning of one of the most brilliant conducting careers in American music history; Bernstein became the first native born musician to be engaged as conductor of the New York Philharmonic, the post to which he acceded in 1958. In the interim he conducted the N.Y. City Center Orch. (1945–47) and was guest conductor of the International Music Festival in Prague (1946). In 1958 he made a tour with the New York Philharmonic in Latin America; in 1959 he took the orchestra on a grand tour of Russia and 17 other countries in Europe and the Near East; in 1960 he toured Japan, Alaska and Canada; on July 9, 1967, he led a memorable concert with the Israel Philharmonic in Jerusalem, at the conclusion of Israel's "six-day war," in a program of works by Mendelssohn and Mahler. He was the first American conductor to lead a regular performance at La Scala in Milan (1953, in Cherubini's opera *Medea*). In 1969 he resigned as permanent conductor of the New York Philharmonic in order to have more time for composition and other projects. The New York Philharmonic Society bestowed upon him the unprecedented honorable title as "laureate conductor," enabling him to give special performances with the orchestra. In the summer of 1976 he took the orchestra on a Bicentennial tour of 13 concerts in 11 European cities, all in 17 days, in programs of American music. Ebullient with multifarious talents, Bernstein initiated in 1958 a televised series of Young People's Concerts with the New York Philharmonic, in which he served as commentator; these concerts obtained wide popularity, not confined solely to the eponymous youth. His desire, and natural ability to teach others found their expression in the classes he conducted at Brandeis Univ. (1951–55), and at the Berkshire Music Center, in Tanglewood. An excellent pianist in his own right, Bernstein often appears as piano soloist in classical and modern concertos, playing and conducting the orchestra from the keyboard. He prides himself also as a poet, particularly in sonnet form, and has published several of his poems. An artist so fantastically successful in so many fields, Bernstein could not escape some cavilous criticism for his "choreography" in conducting, but even the skeptics express gratification at Bernstein's ardent devotion to modern music, and particularly American music; his interpretations of Mahler's symphonies is also generally admired. Bernstein appears to be a singular, if not a unique, phenomenon in music history, in his easy syndrome of versatile achievements. In New York society he became one of the topmost "beautiful people" (in the sense of attractiveness to popular masses). On Sept. 9, 1951, he married the Costa Rican actress Felicia Montealegre. In 1961 he was elected a member of the National Institute of Arts and Letters. Incidentally, Bernstein prefers the pronunciation of his name in democratic *echt* Yiddish, *Bern-steen,* rather that the patrician *Bern-stine.*

WORKS: Bernstein's list of compositions is not large; it includes the following: Clarinet Sonata (1942); Symphony No. 1, subtitled *Jeremiah* (conducted by Bernstein for the first time by the Pittsburgh Symph. Orch., Jan. 28, 1944; received the N.Y. Music Critics Circle Award in 1944); *The Age of Anxiety,* after a poem by W. H. Auden, traversing many styles and moods, from the religious to the ultra-modern, including a spectacular episode in the jazz idiom; scored for piano and orch. (first performed by Koussevitzky and the Boston Symph. Orch., with Bernstein as pianist on April 8, 1949). He conducted his Serenade for Violin Solo, Strings and Percussion (after Plato's *Symposium*) at the Venice Festival, on Sept. 12, 1954, with Isaac Stern as soloist. Other works: *Kaddish,* oratorio for narrator, chorus and orch. (Tel Aviv, Dec. 9, 1963); *Chichester Psalms* for chorus and orch. (commissioned by the Dean of Chichester, England, but first performed by the N.Y. Philharmonic, Leonard Bernstein conducting, July 14, 1965). For the opening, on Sept. 7, 1971, of the John F. Kennedy Center for the Performing Arts in Washington, he wrote *Mass,* "a theater piece" arranged for chorus, chorus, a group of boy singers, dancers and dancer-singers, to a text partly consisting of the Roman Liturgy in Latin, partly in vernacular. For the stage he wrote *Fancy Free,* a ballet (N.Y., April 18, 1944); *Candide,* musical after Voltaire (N.Y., Dec. 1, 1956); *West Side Story,* social music drama, his most successful production (Washington, Aug. 19, 1957; N.Y., Sept. 26, 1957; also produced as a motion picture). *Facsimile,* "choreographic obervations in one scene" (N.Y., Oct. 24, 1946); a one-act opera to his own libretto, *Trouble in Tahiti* (Brandeis Univ., June 12, 1952); *Dybbuk,* a ballet (N.Y., May 16, 1974); *1600 Pennsylvania Avenue,* a musical (N.Y., May 4, 1976; it closed after a few performances). His score *On the Town* (1944) produced several song hits; even more successful was *Wonderful Town* (1952), which enjoyed a long run on Broadway. Other minor works are a song cycle, *I Hate Music,* subtitled *5 Kid Songs* (1943); *La Bonne Cuisine,* 4 recipes for voice and piano (1945); *4 Anniversaries* for piano (1948); *Prelude, Fugue and Riffs* for large dance band (1949); *2 Love Songs* for voice and piano to texts by Rilke (1949); *5 Anniversaries* for piano (1949–51). He also wrote the film score *On the Waterfront* (1954). Bernstein himself published several books, among them *The Joy of Music,* a collection of his television talks (N.Y., 1959; revised and amplified as *Young People's Concerts,* N.Y., 1970); *The Infinite Variety of Music* (N.Y., 1966); *Six Talks at Harvard* (Cambridge, Mass., 1976).

BIBLIOGRAPHY: D. Ewen, *Leonard Bernstein: A Biography for Young People* (N.Y., 1960); A. Holde, *Leonard Bernstein* (Berlin, 1961); J. Briggs, *Leonard Bernstein, The Man, His Work and His World* (Cleveland, 1961).

Bernstein, Martin, American musicologist; b. New York, Dec. 14, 1904. He was educated at N.Y. Univ.

(grad., 1925; Mus. Bac., 1927); played the double bass in the New York Symph. Orch. (1925); the New York Philh. Orch. (1926–28) and the Chautauqua Symph. Orch. (1929–36). He was for 48 years a member of the faculty of N.Y. Univ. (1924–72); then prof. of music, Lehman College, City Univ. of N.Y. (1972–73). He published *Score Reading* (1932; 2nd ed., 1949); *An Introduction to Music* (successful textbook; N.Y., 1937; 4th ed., 1972); contributed chapters on music to *An Intellectual and Cultural History of the Western World,* edited by Harry Elmer Barnes (N.Y., 1937). A. Festschrift, *A Musical Offering: Essays in Honor of Martin Bernstein,* ed. by E. H. Clinkscale and C. Brook, was publ. in 1977. A brother, **Artie Bernstein** (b. Brooklyn, Feb. 3, 1909; d. Los Angeles, Jan. 4, 1964), a classically trained cellist, became a leading jazz bassist in the 1930s and '40s, playing with many big bands, including Jimmy Dorsey's; from 1939–41 he was part of the Benny Goodman Sextet. After World War II he became a studio musician.

Bernuth, Julius von, German conductor; b. Rees, Rhine Province, Aug. 8, 1830; d. Hamburg, Dec. 24, 1902. He was a practicing lawyer; studied music with Taubert and Dehn in Berlin, and at the Cons. of Leipzig, where he founded a chamber music society, "Aufschwung" (1857) and the "Dilettanten-Orchester-Verein" (1859); later became conductor of the Hamburg Philh. Orch.; in 1873 founded a conservatory in Hamburg.

Berr, Friedrich, clarinetist and bassoonist; b. Mannheim, April 17, 1794; d. Paris, Sept. 24, 1838. He was bandmaster in various French regiments; settled in Paris (1823) as first clarinetist at the Théâtre des Italiens; from 1831 was prof. at the Paris Cons.; in 1836 was appointed Director of the new School of Military Music. He was the author of a *Traité complet de la clarinette à 14 clefs* (1836); also composed many works for clarinet and bassoon, and 500 pieces of military music.

Berré, Ferdinand, Belgian composer, b. Ganshoren, near Brussels, Feb. 5, 1843; d. Brussels, July 29, 1880. He wrote the operas, *L'Orage au moulin; Le Couteau de Castille;* published some 50 songs.

Berry, Chuck, black singer and guitarist; b. San Jose, California, Jan. 15, 1926. He was a carpenter's son; the family moved to Missouri when he was a child; he received his musical training as a chorister at the Antioch Baptist Church in St. Louis; learned to play a six-stringed Spanish guitar, and improvised tunes in a then-current jazz manner. In 1955 he went to Chicago and sold his song *Maybelline* to a record company; it took off like a rocket, and reached No. 1 on the list in the three categories of rhythm-and-blues, country-and-western and pop. This was followed by a brash bragging song, "Roll over, Beethoven, tell Tchaikovsky the news, Roll over, Beethoven, dig these rhythm-and-blues." Moving into the big time, Berry opened in St. Louis the Chuck Berry Club Bandstand; it prospered but he soon ran into trouble when a 14-year-old hatcheck girl employed in the club brought charges that he imported her across the state lines for immoral purposes. He was found guilty and served two years in the federal penitentiary in Terre Haute, Indiana. Jail failed to kill his spirit of happy-go-lucky insouciance, and he rebounded with a sexually oriented song *My Ding-a-Ling,* which made the coveted golden disk record. He became one of the most successful rock singers; when Voyager II was launched into space on Aug. 20, 1977, it carried a sampler of terrestrial music on records, and next to Bach and Beethoven, the package included *Johnny B. Good* by Chuck Berry.

BIBLIOGRAPHY: *Current Biography* (April, 1977).

Bersa, Blagoje, Croatian composer; b. Ragusa, Dec. 21, 1873; d. Zagreb, Jan. 1, 1934. He studied music in Vienna, where he remained until 1919. He wrote 2 operas, *Fire,* and *The Cobbler of Delft;* the symph. poems *Sunny Fields, Ghosts* and *Hamlet;* a string quartet, a piano trio, and songs. Bersa was for many years professor of composition at the Zagreb Cons., and has influenced the development of the new generation of Croatian composers, several of whom were his pupils.

Bertali, Antonio, b. Verona, March 11, 1605; d. Vienna, April 1, 1669. He was a Viennese court violinist from 1637; in 1649 succeeded Giovanni Valentini as court conductor. He produced in Vienna several cantatas (1641–46), 8 operas and 2 oratorios (1653–67).

Berté, Heinrich, Hungarian composer; b. Galgócz, May 8, 1857; d. Vienna, Aug. 23, 1924. He produced the ballets *Das Märchenbuch* (Prague, 1890); *Amor auf Reisen* (Vienna, 1895); *Der Kerneval in Venedig* (Vienna, 1900); and *Automatenzauber* (Vienna, 1901); the operettas *Die Schneeflocke* (Prague, 1896); *Der neue Bürgermeister* (Vienna, 1904); *Die Millionenbraut* (Munich, 1905); *Der schöne Gardist* (Breslau, 1907); *Der Glücksnarr* (Vienna, 1909); *Kreolenblut* (Hamburg, 1911); *Der Märchenprinz* (Hannover, 1914); and *Das Dreimäderlhaus* (Vienna, Jan. 15, 1916), based on Schubert melodies; it was produced in English under the title *Blossom Time,* arranged by Romberg (N.Y., Sept. 21, 1921; very popular); also as *Lilac Time* (London, Dec. 22, 1922), arranged by Clutsam.

Bertheaume, Isidore, violinist; b. Paris, 1752; d. St. Petersburg, March 20, 1802. He was first violinist at the Grand Opéra in Paris (1774); conductor of the "Concert Spirituel" (from 1783); and first violinist at the Opéra-Comique (from 1788). The Revolution forced him to leave Paris in 1791; he settled in St. Petersburg as solo violinist in the Imperial Orch. He composed 2 symphonies concertantes for 2 violins; 3 sonatas for clavecin with violin; violin concerto; many other works for violin.

Berthold, (Karl Friedrich) Theodor, German organist; b. Dresden, Dec. 18, 1815; d. there, April 28, 1882. He was a pupil of Julius Otto and Johann Schneider; in 1864 succeeded Schneider as court organist at Dresden. He wrote an oratorio, *Petrius;* a symphony; much sacred music; was co-author with Fürstenau of the pamphlet *Die Fabrikation musikalischer Instrumente im Vogtlande* (1876).

Bertin, Louise-Angélique, French composer, singer and pianist; b. at Aux Roches, near Paris, Feb. 15, 1805; d. Paris, April 26, 1877. She was a pupil of Fétis; composed the operas *Guy Mannering; Le Loup-garou* (Paris, 1827); *Faust* (after Goethe, 1831); *La Esmeralda* (Libretto adapted by Victor Hugo from his *Notre-Dame de Paris,* 1836); also many minor works, of which *Six Ballades* were published.

Bertini, Benoit-Auguste, French pianist; b. Lyons, June 5, 1780; d. London, after 1830. He was a pupil of Clementi in London (1793); later taught piano there; wrote the pamphlets *Stigmatographie, ou l'art d'écrire avec des points, suivie de la mélographie, nouvel art de noter la musique* (Paris, 1812), and *Phonological System for acquiring extraordinary facility on all musical instruments as well as in singing* (London, 1830).

Bertini, Domenico, Italian composer and music pedagogue; b. Lucca, June 26, 1829; d. Florence, Sept. 7, 1890. He studied at the Lucca Music School; later with Michele Puccini; in 1857 was director of the music institute and maestro di cappella at Massa Carrara; settled in Florence (1862) as singing teacher and music critic; and became director of the Cherubini Society. He contributed to the *Boccherini* of Florence, *La Scena* of Venice, and other musical periodicals; also wrote a *Compendio de' principi di musica, secondo un nuovo sistema* (1866); composed 2 operas; Masses; other sacred music; chamber music.

Bertini, Gary, Russian-born Israeli conductor and composer; b. Bessarabia, May 1, 1927. He went to Palestine (Israel) as a child; studied music in Tel-Aviv and at the Verdi Cons. in Milan; completed his musical education in Paris; graduated from the Paris Cons. in conducting in 1953; studied musicology at the Sorbonne, and took private lessons in composition with Honegger. Returning to Israel, he became conductor of the Israel Chamber Opera (since 1965) and was a frequent guest conductor with the Israel Philharmonic. He also conducted the BBC Symph., the Scottish National Orch., the Scottish Opera and the Hamburg State Opera. He composed a Concerto for Horn, Strings and Timpani (1952), a Solo Violin Sonata (1953), a ballet, *The Unfound Door* (1963); madrigals, songs; incidental music to some 40 plays.

Bertini, Henri (-Jérôme), known as 'Bertini le jeune,' pianist and composer; b. London, Oct. 28, 1798; d. Meylau, near Grenoble, Oct. 1, 1876. When six months old, he was taken to Paris, where he was taught music by his father and his elder brother, **Benoît-Auguste;** at the age of 12 made a concert tour through the Netherlands and Germany; then studied further in Paris and Great Britain; lived in Paris as concert pianist from 1821 till 1859, when he retired to his estate at Meylau. He wrote valuable technical studies, some of which have been published in editions by G. Buonamici and by Riemann; also arranged Bach's *48 Preludes and Fugues* for 4 hands; composed much chamber music; many piano pieces.

Bertoldo, Sperindio (Sper'in Dio), Italian organist and composer; b. Modena, c.1530; d. Padua, Aug. 13, 1570. He served as chief organist at the cathedral of Padua. His surviving compositions include two books of madrigals in 5 voices, published in Venice (book 1, 1561 and book 2, 1562). The first book includes an *Echo a 6 voci* and a *Dialogo a 8 voci;* several other madrigals are included in a collection by Cipriano and Annibale (Venice, 1561). Bertoldo's *Toccate, ricercari e canzoni francese . . . per sonar d'organo* (Venice, 1591) was published posthumously. Two ricercari for organ are included in L. Torchi, *L'Arte Musicale in Italia* (vol. III).

Berton, Henri-Montan, French composer, son of Pierre-Montan Berton; b. Paris, Sept. 17, 1767; d. there, April 22, 1844. He was a pupil of Rey and Sacchini; in 1782 was violinist at the Paris Opéra; in 1795 was appointed prof. of harmony at the Paris Cons.; and in 1818 succeeded Méhul as professor of composition; also conducted the Opera buffa (1807); was choirmaster at the Opéra (1809); in 1815 was made a member of the Academy.
WORKS: 47 operas, of which the best are *Montano et Stéphanie* (1799), *Le Délire* (1799), and *Aline, reine de Golconde* (1803); 5 oratorios; 5 cantatas; ballets; many *romances.* His theoretical works are curious rather than valuable.
BIBLIOGRAPHY: Raoul-Rochette, *Notice historique sur la vie et les ouvrages de M. Berton* (Paris, 1846); H. Blanchard, *Henri-Montan Berton* (Paris, 1839); M. S. Selden, "Henri Berton as Critic," *Journal of American Musicological Society* (Summer 1971).

Berton, Pierre-Montan, French composer; b. Maubert-Fontaines (Ardennes), Jan. 7, 1727; d. Paris, May 14, 1780. He was conductor of the Royal Orch. and of the Grand Opéra at Paris; wrote additions to operas by Lully, Rameau, and Gluck; had a significant influence upon the development of the French opera.
WORKS: the operas *Érosine* (1765) and *Tyrtée* (1772); also *Silvie* (1765) and *Théonis* (1767) in collaboration with Trial; and *Adèle de Ponthieu* (with Laborde).

Bertoni, Ferdinando (Gioseffo), Italian organist and composer; b. Island of Salò, near Venice, Aug. 15, 1725; d. Desenzano, Dec. 1, 1813. He was a pupil of Padre Martini; in 1752 was appointed first organist of San Marco in Venice; made two trips to London, where many of his operas were produced; finally settled in Venice, where he succeeded Galuppi (1784) as maestro di cappella of San Marco; was choirmaster at the Cons. de' Mendicanti from 1757–97.
WORKS: 34 operas, including *La vedova accorta* (Florence, 1745); *Quinto Fabio* (Milan, 1778); *Demofoonte* (London, Nov. 28, 1778); and *Nitteti* (Venice, 1786); also wrote 5 oratorios; much other sacred music; 6 harpsichord sonatas; chamber music; etc.
BIBLIOGRAPHY: *Musica d'oggi* (July 1927); I. Haas, *Ferdinando Bertoni: Leben und Instrumentalwerk* (Vienna, 1958).

Bertouille, Gérard, Belgian composer; b. Tournai, May 26, 1898. While studying philosophy and law, he took lessons in music with Absil, de Bourguignon, Marsick and Souris. He began to compose rather late in life; in his music he pursues a median path in a restrained modern idiom.
WORKS: *Les Tentation de St. Antoine,* choreographic poem for mezzo-soprano, baritone and orch. (1958–59); *Requiem des hommes d'aujourd'hui (Requiem for Men of Today,* 1950); 2 symphonies (1947; 1955); *Sinfonia da Requiem* (1957); *Ouverture* (1937); *Prelude et Fugue* for orch. (1939); *Passacaille* for orch. (1940); *Sinfonietta* (1942); Concerto for Chamber Orchestra (1942); 2 violin concertos (1942, 1970); *Fantaisie* for orch. (1943); 2 piano concertos (1946, 1953); 2 trumpet concertos (with strings, 1946; 1973); *Andante* for strings (1955); *Ouverture* for woodwind trio, strings, timpani and piano (1956); *Aria et Divertimento* for flute and chamber orch. (1956); *Prélude et Scherzo* for flute and string orch. (1958); *Viola Concertino* (1961); *Fantaisie-Passacaille* for orch. (1963); *Fantaisie Lyrique* for orch. (1969); *Concertino* for Clarinet and Strings (1970); *Musique for Orch.* (1972); Concerto for String Orchestra (1974); 7 quartets: Nos. 1–3 and 5–7 are string quartets (1939; 1941; 1942; 1953; *Prélude,* 1953; 1957), No. 4 is for flute and string trio (1948); 5 violin sonatas (1936, 1942, 1946, 1953, 1971); Duo for Violin and Piano (1963–67); 2 string trios (1943, 1945); Trio for 2 Violins and Piano (1955); *Prélude* for 4 Harps (1956); Wind Quintet (1969); *6 Préludes et Fugues* for piano (1940–42); Piano Sonata (1945); *Passacaille et Fugue* for 2 pianos (1959); Concertino for 4 clarinets (1977); songs.

Bertrand, Aline, notable French harpist; b. Paris, 1798; d. there, March 13, 1835. She studied at the Paris Cons. with Naderman; then with Bochsa (1815); made her debut in 1820; then toured all of Europe, winning special acclaim upon her appearance in Vienna (1828). She published a *Fantaisie sur la Romance de Joseph* (on themes of Méhul's opera) for harp, and various other arrangements.

Bertrand, Antoine de, French composer; b. Fontanges (Cantal), c.1540; d. c.1581. He composed 7 books of 4-part chansons: *Les Amours de P. de Ronsard* (2 vols., 1576), *Sonets chrestiens* (2 vols., 1580) and *Chansons* (3 vols., 1578); his music shows harmonic daring in the use of chromatic progressions. Volumes 4–7 of H. Expert's *Monuments de la musique française au temps de la Renaissance* are devoted to Bertrand's works.

Bertrand, Jean-Gustave, French writer on music; b. Vaugirard, near Paris, Dec. 24, 1834; d. Paris, Feb. 9, 1880. He published the following books: *Histoire ecclésiastique de l'orgue* (1859); *Les Origines de l'harmonie* (1866); *De la réforme des études du chant au Conservatoire* (1871); *Les Nationalités musicales étudiées dans le drame lyrique* (1872).

Berutti, Arturo, Argentine opera composer; b. San Juan, March 27, 1862; d. Buenos Aires, Jan. 3, 1938. He was of Italian extraction, and naturalized the spelling of his last name as Beruti. He received his early training in music with his father; then went to Leipzig where he became a student of Jadassohn. He subse-

quently lived in Italy where he produced 3 of his operas: *La Vendetta* (Vercelli, May 21, 1892); *Evangelina* (Milan, Sept. 19, 1893); *Taras Bulba* (Turin, March 9, 1895). Returning to Argentina in 1896, he produced the following operas in various theaters in Buenos Aires: *Pampa* (July 27, 1897); *Yupanki* (July 25, 1899); *Khrise* (June 21, 1902); *Horrida Nox*, the first opera by a native Argentine composer written to a Spanish libretto which was produced in Argentina (Buenos Aires, July 7, 1908); and *Los Heroes* (Aug. 23, 1919; his only opera produced at the Teatro Colón).
BIBLIOGRAPHY: E. M. Navarro, *San Juan en la Historia de la Música* (San Juan, Argentina, 1964).

Berwald, Franz, Swedish composer; cousin of **Johann Friedrich Berwald;** b. Stockholm, July 23, 1796; d. there, April 3, 1868. He was a member of a musical family of German extraction that settled in Sweden in the 18th century. He studied with his father, **Christian Friedrich Berwald;** was a violinist at the Royal Chapel in Stockholm; in 1819 he played in Finland with his brother **Christian August Berwald.** In 1829 he was in Berlin; after a brief return to Sweden, he lived in Vienna and Paris. In 1849 he received the post of musical director at the Univ. of Uppsala, succeeding his cousin Johann Friedrich Berwald. He taught at the Stockholm Academy from 1864–67, and at the Stockholm Cons. (from 1867 until his death).
WORKS: the operas *Estrella di Soria* (1841; Stockholm, April 9, 1862; modern version by Moses Pergament, Göteborg, March 2, 1931) and *Drottningen av Golconda* (1864). His early operas *Gustaf Wasa* (1827), *Leonida* (1829) and *Der Verräter* remain unperformed. He wrote 6 symphonies, of which the most interesting are *Sinfonie sérieuse, Sinfonie capricieuse* and *Sinfonie singulière* (all written between 1842 and 1845). He also composed 5 cantatas; Violin Concerto (1820); *Concertstück* for bassoon and orch. (1827); Piano Concerto (1855); 5 piano trios and other chamber music. Berwald's music is romantic in derivation; his style was determined by the influences of Spohr and Weber, and later by Beethoven and Mendelssohn. A revival of interest in his music in Sweden led to the publication of several of his orchestral and chamber works.
BIBLIOGRAPHY: A. Hillman, *Franz Berwald* (Stockholm, 1920); R. Layton, *Berwald* (Stockholm, 1956; in English, London, 1959); I. Bengtsson, "Franz Berwald från vaggan till graven. En kronologisk tabell," *Musikrevy* XXIII/6 (1968); S. Broman, "Franz Berwalds stanträd," *Svensk tidskrift för musikforskning* (1968); I. Andersson, *Franz Berwald. II: Källhänvisningar och personregister. Diskografi* (Stockholm, 1971).

Berwald, Johann Friedrich, Swedish violinist and composer; cousin of Franz Berwald; b. Stockholm, Dec. 4, 1787; d. there, Aug. 26, 1861. Of precocious talent, he appeared in public at the age of five; studied theory with Abbé Vogler; gave concerts in Finland, Germany and Austria; from 1808–12 was concertmaster at the Imperial Chapel in St. Petersburg; appointed chamber musician to the King of Sweden (1816), and conductor of the Royal Orch. in Stockholm (from 1819). Berwald wrote his first symphony when he was

nine, but in his maturity he devoted himself chiefly to theater music. One of his operettas, *L'Héroïne de l'amour,* was produced in St. Petersburg in 1811.

Berwald, William, German-American composer; b. Schwerin, Dec. 26, 1864; d. Loma Linda, Calif., May 8, 1948. He studied with Rheinberger at the Munich Cons. (1882–87), and with Faiszt in Stuttgart (1887–88). After a series of engagements as orchestral conductor in Germany and Russia, he settled in the U.S. (1892); from 1921–24 he conducted the Syracuse Orchestra. Among his works are 3 cantatas, *Seven Last Words of Christ; Crucifixion and Resurrection; From Old Japan;* a music drama *Utopia* (1936); symph. poem *Eros and Psyche* (1943); numerous choruses and instrumental pieces, and about 250 anthems. He received many prizes for his works, and continued to compose to the end of his life.

Besanzoni, Gabriella, Italian contralto; b. Rome, Nov. 20, 1890; d. there, June 6, 1962. She made her debut as a soprano in *Norma* in 1913; from 1915 appeared as mezzo-soprano and contralto in major opera houses all over the world, making her home principally in Rio de Janeiro, until her return to Italy and retirement in 1938. She was particularly famous in Italy as Carmen.

Besard, Jean-Baptiste, French lutenist and composer; b. Besançon, 1567; d. probably in Augsburg in 1625. He studied philosophy at the Univ. of Dôle; after his marriage in 1602, he went to Rome and studied with the lutenist Lorenzini. Later lived in Germany, publishing at Cologne his *Thesaurus harmonicus* (1603), and at Augsburg his *Novus partus, sive Concertationes musicae duodena trium . . .* (1617) and *Isagoge in artem testudinariam* (1617). Some of the compositions in these works have been translated by O. Chilesotti in *Biblioteca di rarità musicali.*
BIBLIOGRAPHY: O. Chilesotti, *Di G. B. Besardo e del suo Thesaurus harmonicus* (Milan, 1886).

Besekirsky, Vassili. See **Bezekirsky, Vassili.**

Besler, Samuel, composer; b. Brieg, Silesia, Dec. 15, 1574; d. Breslau, July 19, 1625. He was rector (from 1605) of the Gymnasium zum Heiligen Geist in Breslau; wrote a large number of sacred pieces, most of which are preserved at the library of St. Bernardinus in Breslau.

Besly, Maurice, English composer and conductor; b. Normanby, Yorkshire, Jan. 28, 1888; d. Horsham, March 20, 1945. He studied at the Leipzig Cons.; took lessons in conducting with Ernest Ansermet in Switzerland; returning to England he filled in engagements as church organist, and in 1924 was appointed conductor of the Scottish Orch. in Glasgow. He wrote a few orchestral works with picturesque titles such as *Mist in the Valley* and *Chelsea China;* also many anthems, songs and motets. He edited *Queen's College Hymn Book.*

Besozzi, Alessandro, celebrated Italian oboist; b. Parma, July 22, 1702; d. Turin, July 26, 1793. He was a musician at the ducal chapel, Parma (1728–31); made concert tours with his brother, Girolamo (see 3 below); appeared with him in Paris in 1735; then lived in Turin. He published numerous trio sonatas for flute, violin and cello; 6 violin sonatas (with basso continuo), etc. Other members of the family who specialized in woodwinds were: (1) **Antonio**, oboist, nephew of Alessandro (b. Parma, 1714; d. Turin, 1781); (2) **Carlo**, oboist, son of Antonio (b. Naples, c. 1738; d. Dresden, March 22, 1791); played in the Dresden orch. (1754); wrote several oboe concertos; (3) **Girolamo**, bassoonist, brother of Alessandro (b. Parma, April 17, 1704; d. Turin, 1778); (4) **Gaetano**, oboist, nephew of Alessandro (b. Parma, 1727; d. London, 1794); (5) **Girolamo**, oboist, son of Gaetano (b. Naples, c.1750; d. Paris, 1785); (6) **Henri**, flutist, son of Girolamo; played at the Opéra-Comique; (7) **Louis-Désiré**, son of Henri (b. Versailles, April 3, 1814; d. Paris, Nov. 11, 1879), a student of Lesueur and Barbereau; he won the Prix de Rome in 1837, defeating Gounod.

Bessaraboff, Nicholas, Russian authority on musical instruments; b. Voronezh, Feb. 12, 1894; d. New York, Nov. 10, 1973. He was trained as a mechanical engineer and a draftsman, but he also played the French horn and became interested in the mechanics and acoustics of musical instruments. After the completion of his studies at the polytechnical institute in St. Petersburg, he was sent in 1915 with a group of other Russian engineers to the United States in order to expedite the shipping of American military equipment for the Russian armed forces during World War I. He arrived in San Francisco in Dec. 1915, and remained in the United States after the Russian revolution of 1917. He worked as a draftsman in Rochester, N.Y., at the same time doing extensive reading on the subject of musical instruments. In 1931 he moved to Boston, where he began working on cataloguing of the collection of instruments in the Boston Museum of Fine Arts. In 1941 he published his magnum opus, *Ancient European Musical Instruments, an Organological Study of the Musical Instruments in the Leslie Lindsey Mason Collection at the Museum of Fine Arts, Boston.* In 1945 he officially changed his name to Nicholas Bessaraboff Bodley, adopting the maiden name of his American wife, Virginia Bodley.
BIBLIOGRAPHY: David Boyden, "Nicholas Bessaraboff's Ancient European Musical Instruments," *Notes* (Sept. 1971).

Bessel, Vassili, Russian music publisher; b. St. Petersburg, April 25, 1842; d. Zürich, March 1, 1907. He was the founder (1869) of the music publishing firm of Bessel & Co. at St. Petersburg, which has published works by many distinguished Russian composers (Anton Rubinstein, Rimsky-Korsakov, Tchaikovsky, Mussorgsky); also two short-lived periodicals: *Musical Leaflet* (1872–77) and the *Russian Musical Review* (1885–89). Bessel wrote *Reminiscences of Tchaikovsky,* who was his fellow student at the St. Petersburg Cons. In 1920 the firm was transferred to Paris, where it continued under the direction of Bessel's sons, Vassili and Alexander.

Besseler, Heinrich, eminent German musicologist; b. Hörde, Dortmund, April 2, 1900; d. Leipzig, July 25, 1969. He studied mathematics and natural sciences; then turned to musicology; attended the courses of Gurlitt in Freiburg, of Adler in Vienna, and of Ludwig in Göttingen. He received his doctorate in Freiburg in 1923; then taught classes at the Univ. of Heidelberg (1928–48), Jena (1948–56) and Leipzig (1956–65). In 1967 he received the honorary degree of Doctor of Humane Letters of the Univ. of Chicago. A Festschrift in his honor was published on his 60th birthday. He contributed valuable articles to various music journals, mostly on the musical problems of the Middle Ages and the Renaissance, but also on general subjects of musical esthetics; wrote several basic articles for *Die Musik in Geschichte und Gegenwart.* He was also an editor of collected works of Dufay, Okeghem and other musicians of their period.
WRITINGS: *Fünf echte Bildnisse J. S. Bachs* (Kassel, 1956); *Das musikalische Hören der Neuzeit* (Berlin, 1959; in the report of the transactions of the Saxon Academy of Sciences, vol. 104); *Die Besetzung der Chansons im 15.Jahrhundert* (Utrecht 1952); *Singstil und Instrumentenstil in der europäischen Musik* (Bamberg, 1953); "Zur Chronologie der Konzerte J. S. Bachs," in the Festschrift for Max Schneider (Leipzig, 1955); "Das Renaissanceproblem in der Musik," in the Festschrift for Br. Stäblein (Kassel, 1967). He brought out (with Max Schneider) the excellent edition *Musikgeschichte in Bildern* (begun serially in Leipzig, 1961; from 1968, his co-editor was W. Bachmann). A complete list of his writings (up to 1961) and editions is found in the Festschrift issued in his honor (Leipzig, 1961).

Bessems, Antoine, Belgian violinist; b. Antwerp, April 6, 1809; d. there, Oct. 19, 1868. He was a pupil of Baillot at the Paris Cons. (1826); in 1829 was first violinist at the Théâtre-Italien, Paris; then made long concert tours; taught for a time in Paris; returned to Antwerp, and, from 1847–52, conducted the orchestra of the Société Royale d'Harmonie. He composed a Violin Concerto; *12 Grandes Études for Violin with Piano; 12 Grands Duos de concert for Violin with Piano;* many other violin pieces, Masses, motets, psalms, etc.

Best, William Thomas, eminent English organist; b. Carlisle, England, Aug. 13, 1826; d. Liverpool, May 10, 1897. He studied organ in Liverpool; held various posts as church organist in Liverpool and London. At his numerous concerts he introduced arrangements of symphonic works, thus enabling his audiences to hear classical works in musicianly manner at a time when orchestral concerts were scarce. His own works, popular in type, though classical in form, included sonatas, preludes, fugues, concert studies, etc. for organ. He published a *Handel Album* (20 vols.); *Arrangements from the Scores of the Great Masters* (5 vols.); *Modern School for the Organ* (1853); *The Art of Organ Playing* (1870), etc.
BIBLIOGRAPHY: O. A. Mansfield, "W. T. Best," *Musical Quarterly* (April 1918); J. Mewburn Levien, *Impressions of W. T. Best* (London, 1942).

Bethune, Thomas Greene (called **"Blind Tom"**), black American pianist and composer; b. Columbus, Geor-

gia, May 25, 1849; d. 1908. Born blind in slavery, he and his parents (Charity and Mingo Wiggins) were purchased by a Colonel Bethune in 1850. His master's wife was a music teacher who fostered his musical talent. At the age of 9 he was "leased" for 3 years to one Perry Oliver who arranged concert appearances for him throughout the U.S., including a performance at the White House before President Buchanan. Col. Bethune then took full charge of Tom's career, obtaining legal custody and a major part of his earnings. Bethune played in Europe and in America; his programs usually included Bach, Liszt, Chopin, Gottschalk, and his own compositions, mostly improvised character pieces in salon manner, arranged and supplied with appropriate titles by his managers, e.g. *Rainstorm* (1865); *Wellenlänge* (1882; publ. under the pseudonym **François Sexalise**); *Imitation of the Sewing Machine* (1889); *Battle of Manassas* (1894); etc; he also improvised on themes given by members of the audience.
BIBLIOGRAPHY: J. M. Trotter, *Music and Some Highly Musical People* (Boston, 1885); G. Southall, "Blind Tom: A Misrepresented and Neglected Composer-Pianist," *Black Perspective in Music* (May 1975); the July 1976 issue of this journal reprints early letters, testimonials (by Charles Hallé, Ignaz Moscheles, and others), and articles about Blind Tom.

Betti, Adolfo, Italian violinist; b. Bagni di Lucca, March 21, 1873; d. Lucca, Dec. 2, 1950. Of a musical family, he studied violin in Lucca; then with César Thomson in Liège (1892–96). In 1903 he became the first violinist of the famous Flonzaley Quartet and remained with it until it was disbanded in 1929; this group presented some 2500 concerts in America and about 500 concerts in Europe. In 1933 Betti was awarded the Coolidge Medal for eminent services to chamber music in America. He taught in New York before returning to Italy. He published *La vita e l'arte di Francesco Geminiani* (Lucca, 1933); also edited Schubert's string quartets.

Bettinelli, Bruno, Italian composer; b. Milan, June 4, 1913. He studied with Paribeni at the Cons. of Milan; from 1941 until 1961 he was instructor at his alma mater; in 1961 he became a member of the Accademia Nazionale di Santa Cecilia in Rome. In his works he follows the structural forms of classical Italian music while adorning the harmonies with permissible discords; he also explored the resources of Gregorian chant.
WORKS: *Sinfonia da camera* (1939); *Concerto per orchestra* (1940); *Fantasia e Fuga su temi gregoriani* for string orch. (1942); *Sinfonia drammatica* (1943); *Messa da requiem* for chorus a cappella (1945); *Fantasia concertante* for string quartet and orch. (1950); *Concerto da camera* (1952); *Sinfonia breve* (1954); 2 piano concertos (1953, 1968); opera, *La Smorfia* (Como, Sept. 30, 1959); Concerto for 2 Pianos and Orch. (1962); opera, *Il Pozzo e il Pendolo*, after Poe (1958; Bergamo, Oct. 24, 1967); *Improvvisazione* for violin and piano (1968); opera, *Count Down* (Milan, March 26, 1970); *Variante per orchestra* (1970); 2 string quartets (1937, 1960); church music.

Betts, Lorne, Canadian composer; b. Winnipeg, Aug. 2, 1918. He studied music theory, piano and organ in Winnipeg; then took courses in Toronto with John Weinzweig (1947–53). He subsequently settled in Hamilton, Ontario, where he became a teacher and music critic.
WORKS: 2 operas: *Riders to the Sea* (1955) and *The Woodcarver's Wife* (1960); *Suite da Chiesa* for wind ensemble and percussion (1952); *Sinfonietta* (1952); 2 symphonies (1954, 1961); 2 piano concertos (1955, 1957); *2 Abstracts* for orch. (1961); *A Cycle of the Earth*, 4 songs for soprano and orch. (1962–67); *Kanadario: Music for a Festival Occasion* for orch. (1966); *Variants* for orch. (1969); Concertino for Saxophone and Chamber Orch. (1972); *3 Saudades* for 11 strings (1974); *Margarita Sorori* for chorus and orch. (1975); Suite in 3 Movements for Orch. (1975); Concerto for Cello, Piano and orch. (1976); Violin Sonata (1948); Clarinet Sonata (1949); 3 string quartets (1950, 1951, 1970); String Trio (1959); Quartet for Flute, Clarinet, Bass Clarinet and Celesta (1960); Violin Sonatina (1970); Piano Sonata (1950); choruses and songs.

Betz, Franz, distinguished German baritone; b. Mainz, March 19, 1835; d. Berlin, Aug. 11, 1900. He sang from 1856–59 at Hanover, Altenburg, Gera, Cöthen and Rostock; after his debut as Don Carlos in *Ernani* at Berlin (1859), he was permanently engaged at the Royal Opera House until his retirement in 1897; was best known for his performances in Wagner's operas; created the roles of Hans Sachs at Munich (1868) and Wotan at Bayreuth (1876).

Beurle, Jürgen, German composer; b. Ludwigsburg, Feb. 27, 1943. He studied philology and music in Stuttgart, Tübingen and Utrecht; in 1967 he attended Stockhausen's lectures at the Darmstadt Summer School for New Music. He is a confirmed constructionist in his musical design.
WORKS: *Sinus* for soprano, baritone, violin, viola and percussion (1966); *Variable Realizations* for indeterminate performers (1967); *Statischdynamisch* for orch. (1968); *Objets* for chorus, instruments and tape recorder (1968); *Conditional* for voice, piano and tape recorder (1969); *Madrigal* for soprano, 2 choruses, percussion and 5 tape recordings, with audience participation (1969); *Differenz* for indeterminate performers grouped in 5 sections (1970).

Beversdorf, (Samuel) Thomas, American composer and trombone player; b. Yoakum, Texas, Aug. 8, 1924. He began studying music with his father as a child; played several instruments in local bands; studied composition with Kent Kennan, Eric DeLamarter and Anthony Donato at the Univ. of Texas (B.M., 1945), and with Bernard Rogers at the Eastman School of Music in Rochester, N.Y. (M.M., 1946); took a summer course in composition with Honegger and Copland at Tanglewood (1947); also had some lessons with Anis Fuleihan. He was trombone player in the Rochester Philharmonic (1945–46), in the Houston Symph. (1946–48), and in the Pittsburgh Symph. (1948–49); had special engagements as first trombonist with the Metropolitan Opera, Ballet Russe de Monte Carlo and Sadler's Wells Ballet. He was an instructor at the Univ. of Houston (1946–48); in 1949 joined the faculty of Indiana Univ. in Bloomington as prof. of composition; in 1977 lectured at the Univ. of Guadalajara, Mexico.

WORKS: 2 operas: *The Hooligan* (1964–69) and *Metamorphosis,* after Kafka (1968); a mystery play, *Vision of Christ* (Bucknell Univ., Lewisburg, Pa., May 1, 1971); *Essay on Mass Production* for orch. (1946); 4 symphonies: No. 1 (1946); No. 2 (1950); No. 3 for winds and percussion (1954; Bloomington, Ind., May 9, 1954; version for full orch., 1958; Bloomington, Oct. 10, 1958); No. 4 (1958); *Reflections* for small orch. (1947); *Mexican Portrait* for orch. (1948, revised 1952); Concerto Grosso for Oboe and Chamber Orch. (Pittsburgh, April 28, 1950); 2-Piano Concerto (1951; Bloomington, March 17, 1967); *Ode* for orch. (1952); *New Frontiers* for orch. (Houston, March 31, 1953); Serenade for Small Orch. (1956); Serenade for Winds and Percussion (1957); an oratorio, *The Rock,* after T. S. Eliot (Bloomington, March 16, 1958); *Danforth,* a violin concerto (1959); a ballet, *Threnody: The Funeral of Youth,* after Rupert Brooks (Bloomington, March 6, 1963; also known as Variations for Orch.); *Generation with the Torch* for youth orch. (Bayreuth, Germany, Aug. 5, 1965, by the touring Houston All-City Symph. Orch.); *Murals, Tapestries and Icons* for symphonic band, with electric bass and electric piano (1975); Concerto for Tuba and Wind Orch. (Bloomington, Feb. 11, 1976); a horn sonata, *Christmas* (1945); *Suite on Baroque Themes* for clarinet, cello and piano (1947); Prelude and Fugue for Wind Quintet (1950); 2 string quartets (1951, 1955); Sonata for Tuba and Piano (1956); Trumpet Sonata (1962); Violin Sonata (1964–65); Flute Sonata (1965–66); Cello Sonata (1967–69); *Walruses, Cheesecake and Morse Code* for tuba and piano (1973); *La Petite Exposition* for solo violin or clarinet, and 11 strings (Dallas, Feb. 28, 1976); Sonata for Violin and Harp (1976–77). For piano: Sonata (1944), *6 Short Pieces* (1950).

Bevignani, Enrico, Italian conductor and composer; b. Naples, Sept. 29, 1841; d. there, Aug. 29, 1903. He produced an opera *Caterina Bloom* in Naples in 1863; then received an appointment as theater conductor in London; also conducted at the Metropolitan Opera in New York (1894); eventually returned to Naples.

Bevin, Elway, Welsh composer and organist; b. between 1560–70; d. c.1640. He was a pupil of Tallis; was organist of Bristol Cathedral (1589) and Gentleman Extraordinary of the Chapel Royal (1605). His most valuable work is the theoretical pamphlet *A Briefe and Short Introduction to the Art of Musicke* (1631); also wrote a Short Service which is preserved in the collections of Barnard and Boyce; a song *Hark, Jolly Shepherds;* and an anthem, arranged in a canon of 20 voices.

Bewerunge, Henry, German cleric and music editor; b. Letmathe, Westland, Dec. 7, 1862; d. Maynooth, Ireland, Dec. 2, 1923. He was ordained priest in 1885; studied church music in Regensburg; eventually settled in Ireland, where he taught church music at St. Patrick's College in Maynooth (1888–1914). He published *Die Vatikanische Choralausgabe* (Düsseldorf,

1906–07; also in English and French); contributed valuable articles to various ecclesiastical journals; also translated Riemann's *Katechismus der Musikästhetik* into English. From 1891 to 1893 he edited *Lyra Ecclesiastica.*

Bexfield, William Richard, English organist; b. Norwich, April 27, 1824; d. London, Oct. 29, 1853. He was organist in Lincolnshire and in London; took the degrees of Mus. Bac. at Oxford (1846) and Mus. Doc. at Cambridge (1849); wrote an oratorio, *Israel Restored* (1852); a cantata, *Hector's Death;* anthems; organ fugues; songs.

Beydts, Louis, French composer; b. Bordeaux, June 29, 1895; d. Caudéran, near Bordeaux, Sept. 15, 1953. After musical study in Bordeaux he became associated with the popular theater; wrote several operettas, 2 of them on a pseudo-Chinese subject, *Canards Mandarins* (Monte Carlo, 1931) and *Le Voyage de Tchong-Li,* Chinese legend (1932); also wrote pieces for piano, violin, saxophone and other instruments; choruses and songs.

Beyer, Frank Michael, German organist and composer; b. Berlin, March 8, 1928. He received his earliest musical training from his father, a writer and amateur pianist; spent his childhood in Greece, returning to Berlin in 1938. He studied sacred music and organ; took composition lessons with Ernst Pepping (1952–55). In 1960 he was appointed to the faculty of the Berlin Hochschule für Musik. He founded a concert series, *Musica nova sacra.* As a composer, he applies the techniques of Bach's counterpoint to modern structures in the manner of Anton von Webern, with thematic materials based on secundal formations and the tritone; the rhythmic patterns of his music are greatly diversified; in dynamic coloration, he explores the finest gradations of sound, particularly in pianissimo.

WORKS: Concerto for Orch. (1957); 2 string quartets (1957; 1969); *Ode* for orch. (1963); Organ Concerto (1967); *Versi* for string orch. (1968); *Maior Angelis,* cantata (1970); Wind Quintet (1972); *Rondo imaginaire* for chamber orch. (1973).

BIBLIOGRAPHY: W. Burde, "Der Komponist F. M. Beyer," *Musica* (May/June 1975).

Beyer, Johann Samuel, German choir director and composer; b. Gotha, 1669; d. Karlsbad, May 9, 1744. He served as a cantor in various churches in Saxony. Among his publications are *Primae lineae musicae vocalis* (1703) and *Geistlich-musikalische Seelenfreude* (1724).

Beyschlag, Adolf, German conductor; b. Frankfurt, March 22, 1845; d. Mainz, Aug. 19, 1914. He studied in Mannheim; subsequently was active as conductor; then went to England where he conducted the Leeds Philharmonic Society; in 1902 returned to Germany. He published a valuable work, *Die Ornamentik der Musik* (Leipzig, 1908); also wrote dances for piano four-hands, in canon form, songs, etc.

Bezdek, Jan, American pianist and composer; b. St. Louis, Aug. 29, 1896. She studied piano with Rudolf Ganz and composition with Felix Borowski in Chicago; subsequently she obtained her Ph.D. degree at the Eastman School of Music in 1946. She published a number of successful teaching pieces for piano, among them *Bells, The Little Bird* and *Marching.* Under the pseudonym of **Julia Derleth,** she published easy pieces for piano.

Bezekirsky, Vassili, Russian violinist; b. Moscow, Jan. 26, 1835; d. there, Nov. 8, 1919. He studied violin in Brussels; returned to Russia in 1871 and acquired the reputation of a fine concert player. Tchaikovsky wrote about him: "Although not a Czar of the first magnitude, Bezekirsky is brilliant enough on the dim horizon of present violin playing." Bezekirsky was also esteemed as a teacher. He wrote a violin concerto (Moscow, Feb. 26, 1873); published cadenzas to the violin concertos of Beethoven and Brahms. He also published a volume of interesting reminiscences, *From the Notebook of an Artist* (St. Petersburg, 1910).

Bezekirsky, Vassili, Russian violinist, son of the preceding; b. Moscow, Jan. 15, 1880; d. in East Windham, N.Y., Nov. 8, 1960. He studied with his father; made several tours in Europe as a concert violinist; in 1914 he emigrated to the U.S., played in various orchestras and taught in several music schools; from 1930 to 1947 he was violin teacher at the School of Music of the Univ. of Michigan at Ann Arbor.

Biaggi, Girolamo Alessandro, Italian writer on music; b. Calcio, Bergamo, Feb. 2, 1819; d. Florence, March 21, 1897. Wrote an opera, *Martino della Scala.* He then went to Florence to teach at the newly established Reale Istituto Musicale; was active also as contributor to the *Gazetta d'Italia,* under the pen-name **Ippolito d'Albano.** He published a valuable essay *La riforma melodrammatica fiorentina.*

Bial, Rudolf, violinist, composer, and conductor; b. Habelschwerdt, Silesia, Aug. 26, 1834; d. New York, Nov. 13, 1881. He was a member of the Breslau orch.; then toured Africa and Australia with his brother Karl; settled in Berlin as conductor of the Kroll Orch. and conductor of the Wallner Theater, where his numerous farces, operettas, etc. were performed; later conducted at the Italian opera in Berlin. In 1878 he settled in New York.

Bianchi, Bianca (real name **Bertha Schwarz**), German soprano; b. Heidelberg, June 27, 1855; d. Salzburg, Feb., 1947. She studied in Heidelberg and Paris; made her debut as Barberina in *The Marriage of Figaro* at Karlsruhe (1873); sang in Vienna and London; in 1905 settled in Salzburg as a vocal teacher. She married her manager, Pollini, in 1897.

Bianchi, Francesco, Italian composer; b. Cremona, 1752; d. (by suicide) in London, Nov. 27, 1810. He wrote nearly 60 operas, some quite pleasing, if ephemeral. His first opera, *Il Grand Cidde,* was produced in Florence in 1773. He was maestro al cembalo at the Comédie Italienne in Paris from 1775 to 1778, and produced his opera *La réduction de Paris* there on Sept. 30, 1775. In 1778 he went to Florence, and in 1783 became second maestro at the Cathedral of Milan; in 1785 till 1791 he was second organist at San Marco in Venice. There he produced his most significant opera *La Vendetta di Nino* (Naples, 1790). He went to London in 1795, where he officiated as conductor of the King's Theatre; from 1798 till 1800 he was employed as theater conductor in Dublin, returning to London in 1801. Besides his operas, he wrote several pieces of competent chamber music and also a theoretical treatise *Dell' attrazione armonica,* which was partly published in an English version in *The Quarterly Musical Magazine and Review* (1820–21). Bianchi was a successful teacher; among his English pupils was Henry Bishop.

Bianchi, Valentina, Russian soprano; b. Vilna, 1839; d. in Kurland, Feb. 28, 1884. She studied at the Paris Cons.; made her debut as a soprano in Frankfurt (1855); sang at Schwerin (1855–61); St. Petersburg (1862–5); and Moscow (until 1867); retired in 1870. She married chief forester von Fabian in 1865. Her range was extraordinary, extending from low alto through high soprano notes.

Bibalo, Antonio, Italian-born Norwegian composer; b. Trieste, Jan. 18, 1922, of Slovak descent (his family name was **Bibalitsch**). He studied piano and composition at the Trieste Cons.; during the disruption caused by the war, he earned his living as a nightclub pianist and a sanitation worker. He was in Australia briefly before coming to England in 1953; studied advanced composition with Elizabeth Lutyens in London. In 1956 he went to Norway and became a naturalized citizen.

WORKS: He attracted the attention of the musical world with the production of his opera *The Smile at the Foot of the Ladder* (1958–62), after a short story of Henry Miller; the original libretto was in Italian as *Sorrisi ai piedi d'una scala,* but the production was in German under the name *Das Lächeln am Fusse der Leiter* at the Hamburg State Opera on April 6, 1965. His other works include a chamber opera, *Frøken Julie,* after Strindberg (*Miss Julie*; Århus, Denmark, Sept. 8, 1975); a ballet, *Pinocchio* (Hamburg, Jan. 17, 1969); a television ballet, *Nocturne for Apollo* (Norwegian TV, 1971); 2 piano concertos: No. 1 (1953; Oslo, Aug. 1, 1972) and No. 2 (1971; Bergen, Norway, April 27, 1972); Piano Sonatina (1953); 2 chamber concertos: No. 1 for piano and strings (1954) and No. 2 for harpsichord, violin and strings (1954); Fantasy for Violin and Orch. (1954; received 3rd prize at the Wieniawski Composer Competition, Warsaw, 1956); *4 Balkan Dances* for piano or orch. (1956); *12 Miniatures* for piano (1956); *Concerto Allegorico* for violin and orch. (1957); *3 Hommages* for piano (1957); Toccata for Piano (1957); *Pitture Astratte* for orch. (1958); *Elegia per un'era spaziale (Elegy for a Space Age)* for soprano, baritone, chorus and instrumental ensemble (1963); *Sinfonia Notturna* (1968); *Overture,* after Goldoni's "Servant with Two Masters" (1968); *Autumnale,* Suite de Concert for piano, flute, vibraphone and double bass (1968); 2 sonatinas for wind quintet

(1971, 1972); String Quartet No. 1 (1973); 2 piano sonatas (1974, 1975); Suite for Orch. (1974); *Games for trombone and flute* (1975).

BIBLIOGRAPHY: B. Kortsen, *Contemporary Norwegian Orchestral Music* (Bergen, 1969); B. Kortsen, *Contemporary Norwegian Chamber Music* (Bergen, 1971).

Biber, Heinrich Ignaz Franz von, violinist and composer; b. Wartenberg, Bohemia, Aug. 12, 1644; d. Salzburg, May 3, 1704. He was successively in the service of the Emperor Leopold I (who ennobled him), the Bavarian court, and the Archbishop of Salzburg; was one of the founders of the German school of violin playing, and among the first to employ the 'scordatura,' a system of artificial mistuning for purposes of virtuoso performance. He published a number of violin sonatas (reprints in David's *Hohe Schule*; some others in *Denkmäler der Tonkunst in Österreich*, vols. 11, 25 [formerly 5.ii, 12.ii], 92, 96, 97, 106, and 107). There are also preserved in MS the scores of 2 operas, *Chi la dura la vince* (Salzburg, 1681), and *L'ossequio de Salisburgo* (Salzburg, 1699); 2 requiems; offertories *a 4*; etc.

BIBLIOGRAPHY: A. Moser, *Geschichte der Violinspiels* (p. 127 ff.) and an article by Moser in *Archiv für Musikwissenschaft* 1; C. Schneider, "Biber als Opernkomponist," *Archiv für Musikwissenschaft* 8; articles by P. Nettl in *Zeitschrift für Musikwissenschaft* 4 and in *Studien zur Musikwissenschaft* 8; Thomas Russell, "The Violin 'Scordatura,'" *Musical Quarterly* (Jan. 1938); E. Schenk, "Ein Singfundament von Heinrich Ignaz Biber," in H. Becker and R. Gerlach, *Speculum musicae artis. Festgabe für Heinrich Husman* (Munich, 1970).

Bibl, Andreas, Austrian organist; b. Vienna, April 8, 1807; d. there, April 30, 1878. He served for many years as organist at St. Stephen Cathedral in Vienna; was active as a teacher; among his pupils was his son, Rudolf Bibl.

Bibl, Rudolf, Austrian organist and composer; b. Vienna, Jan. 6, 1832; d. there, Aug. 2, 1902. He studied with his father, **Andreas Bibl**; occupied various posts as church organist in Vienna; he wrote 4 Masses with orchestral accompaniment, a Mass a cappella, 2 requiems; much organ music; also a violin sonata and piano pieces. He published a valuable didactic volume, *Orgelschule.*

Bie, Oskar, German music critic; b. Breslau, Feb. 9, 1864; d. Berlin, April 21, 1938. He studied music with Philipp Scharwenka in Berlin; devoted himself principally to musical journalism, and published a number of informative monographs. In the spring of 1940 he accompanied Koussevitzky on his concert tour of the Volga and reported his impressions in a privately published illustrated edition in 1920. Among his publications are: *Das Klavier und seine Meister* (Munich, 1898; published in English as *A History of the Pianoforte and Pianoforte Players*, London, 1899); *Intime Musik* (Berlin, 1904); *Tanzmusik* (Berlin, 1905); *Der Tanz* (Berlin, 1906; later editions, 1919 and 1925); *Die moderne Musik und Richard Strauss* (Berlin, 1906; later editions, Leipzig, 1916, 1925); *Die Oper* (Berlin, 1913; many reprints); *Das Rätsel der Musik* (Leipzig, 1922); *Franz Schubert* (Berlin, 1925; publ. in English under the title *Schubert the Man*, N.Y., 1929); *Das Deutsche Lied* (Berlin, 1926); *Richard Wagner und Bayreuth* (Zürich, 1931).

Biedermann, Edward Julius, American organist and composer; b. Milwaukee, Wis., Nov. 8, 1849; d. Freeport, N.Y., Nov. 26, 1933. He studied with his father, Julius Biedermann, and additionally in Germany (1858–64). Upon return to New York he occupied various posts as church organist and was also active as a teacher. He wrote much sacred music; also choruses for male voices and several Masses.

Biehle, Herbert, German voice teacher and theorist, son and pupil of **Johannes Biehle;** b. Dresden, Feb. 16, 1901. He studied composition with Georg Schumann, and musicology with Johannes Wolf. He became active mainly as a vocal pedagogue. He publ. several monographs dealing with vocal techniques, among them *Die Stimmkunst* (2 vols., Leipzig, 1931); also several informative essays on the role of the "sprechstimme" in vocal literature, and a monograph dealing with the contribution to the science of organ bells invented by his father.

Biehle, Johannes, German organist; b. Bautzen, June 18, 1870; d. there, Jan. 4, 1941. He studied at the Dresden Cons.; served as music director and organist in Bautzen (1898–1914). He publ. two valuable volumes dealing with the acoustics of church and organ building: *Theorie der pneumatischen Orgeltraktur* (Leipzig, 1911) and *Theorie des Kirchenbaues* (Wittenberg, 1913). He was generally regarded as a founder of the modern organ carillon.

BIBLIOGRAPHY: Herbert Biehle, *Johannes Biehle als Begründer der Glockenwissenschaft* (1961).

Bierey, Gottlob Benedikt, German conductor and composer; b. Dresden, July 25, 1772; d. Breslau, May 5, 1840. He was a pupil of Christian E. Weinlig at Dresden; then was director of a traveling opera troupe. He was appointed Kapellmeister at Breslau (1808), succeeding Weber; retired in 1828. He composed 26 operas and operettas; 10 cantatas; Masses; orchestral and chamber music; etc.

Biggs, E. Power (Edward George Power), eminent concert organist; b. Westcliff, England, March 29, 1906; d. Boston, March 10, 1977. He studied at Hurstpierpoint College (1917–24); then entered the Royal Academy of Music in London, graduating in 1929. In 1930 he came to the U.S. and became naturalized in 1937. He made his N.Y. debut as organist at the Wanamaker Auditorium in 1932. He was organist in Newport, R.I. (1929–31); then moved to Cambridge, Mass. where he served as organist at Christ Church, and later became director of the Harvard Church in Brookline. In the interim he toured Europe, and made a wide survey of old church organs in England, Iceland, Sweden, Norway, Denmark, Germany, Holland, Austria, Italy and Spain, in search of the type of organ that Bach and Handel played. His repertory consisted mostly of Baroque masters, but he also commissioned works from American composers, among them Walter Piston, Roy Harris, Howard Hanson and Quincy Porter; Benjamin Britten also wrote a work for him. Biggs became well known to American music lovers through his weekly broadcasts of organ recitals over the CBS network, which he gave from 1942 to 1958; he continued to give concerts until arthritis forced him to reduce his concert activities, but he was able to continue recording organ music, and he also edited organ works for publication. Biggs refused to perform on electronic organs, which in his opinion vulgarized and distorted the classical organ sound. His own style of performance had a classical austerity inspired by the Baroque School of organ playing.

Bignami, Carlo, renowned Italian violinist; b. Cremona, Dec. 6, 1808; d. Voghera, Aug. 2, 1848. He was in turn opera conductor at Cremona (1827), Milan, and Verona (1833); returned to Cremona (1837) as director and first violinist of the orchestra, and made it one of the best in Lombardy. Paganini called him 'il primo violinista d'Italia.' He composed many works for his instrument, including a concerto; a *Capriccio; Studi per violino; Grande Adagio; Polacca;* fantasias; variations, etc.

Bigot, Marie (*née* **Kiéné**), pianist; b. Colmar, Alsace, March 3, 1786; d. Paris, Sept. 16, 1820. After her marriage in 1804, she lived in Vienna, where she was known and esteemed by Haydn and Beethoven; went to Paris in 1808, where she gave piano lessons from 1812 on; Mendelssohn was briefly her pupil in Paris at the age of 7.

Bilhon (or **Billon**), **Jean de,** French composer who flourished c.1530. He was the author of several Masses, Magnificats and motets, which are included in collections of church music published between 1534 and 1554.

Billings, William, pioneer American composer of hymns and anthems; popularizer of "fuging tunes"; b. Boston, Oct. 7, 1746; d. there, Sept. 26, 1800. A tanner apprentice, he acquired the rudiments of music from treatises by Tans'ur; he compensated for his lack of education by a wealth of original ideas and a determination to put them into practice. His first musical collection *The New England Psalm Singer* (Boston, 1770) contained what he described at a later date as "fuging pieces . . . more than twenty times as powerful as the old slow tunes." The technique of these pieces was canonic with "each part striving for mastery and victory." His further published books were: *The Singing Master's Assistant* (1778); *Music in Miniature* (1779); *The Psalm Singer's Amusement* (1781); *The Suffolk Harmony* (1786) and *The Continental Harmony* (1794). In one instance, he harmonized a tune, *Jargon,* entirely in dissonances; this was prefaced by a 'Manifesto' to the Goddess of Discord. There was further a choral work, *Modern Music,* in which the proclaimed aim was expressed in the opening lines: "We are met for a concert of modern invention—To tickle the ear is our present intention." Several of his hymns became popular, particularly *Chester* and *The Rose of*

Sharon; an interesting historical work was his *Lamentation over Boston* written in Watertown while Boston was occupied by the British. However, he could not earn a living by his music; appeals made to provide him and his large family with funds bore little fruit, and Billings died in abject poverty. The combination of reverence and solemnity with humor makes the songs of Billings unique in the annals of American music, and aroused the curiosity of many modern American musicians; Henry Cowell has written a series of "fuging tunes" for orch.

BIBLIOGRAPHY: O. G. Sonneck, *Early Concert Life in America* (Leipzig, 1907; reprinted, 1949); E. H. Pierce, "The Rise and Fall of the Fugue Tune in America," *Musical Quarterly* (April 1930); I. Goldberg, "The First American Musician," *American Mercury* 14; P. Scholes, *The Puritans and Music in England and New England* (Oxford, 1934); C. E. Lindstrom, "William Billings and His Times," *Musical Quarterly* (Oct. 1939); D. McKay and R. Crawford, *William Billings of Boston* (Princeton, 1975); Hans Nathan, *William Billings, Data and Documents* (Detroit, 1976).

Billington, Elizabeth (*née* **Weichsel**), English operatic soprano; b. London, c.1765; d. near Venice, Aug. 25, 1818. Her mother, a singer, was a pupil of Johann Christian Bach. She received her early musical training from her father, a German oboist. She also studied with James Billington, a double bass player by profession, whom she married on Oct. 13, 1783. Her operatic debut took place in Dublin (1784) as Eurydice in Gluck's opera; went to London, where she appeared as Rosetta in *Love in a Village* at Covent Garden on Feb. 13, 1786. Her success was immediate; she was reengaged at Covent Garden and also sang at the Concerts of Ancient Music in London. Her career was briefly disrupted by the publication, in 1792, of anonymous *Memoirs* attacking her private life. This was immediately followed by an equally anonymous rebuttal 'written by a gentleman' defending her reputation. In 1794 she went to Italy where she sang for the King of Naples. He made arrangements for her appearances at the San Carlo, where she appeared in operas by Bianchi, Paisiello, Paer and Himmel, all written specially for her. Her husband died in 1794; she remained in Italy for two more years; then lived in France, where she married M. Felissent. Returning to London in 1801, she sang alternately at Drury Lane and Covent Garden, with great acclaim, at 4,000 guineas a season. This period was the peak of her success. She retired in 1809, except for occasional performances. After a temporary separation from Felissent, she returned to him in 1817, and they settled at their estate at St. Artien, near Venice.

Billroth, Theodor, eminent surgeon and amateur musician; b. Bergen, on the island of Rügen, April 26, 1829; d. Abazzia, Feb. 6, 1894. He received a thorough musical education; was an intimate friend of Hanslick and Brahms; the musical soirées at his home in Vienna were famous. Almost all the chamber music of Brahms was played there (with Billroth as violist), before a public performance. He wrote a treatise *Wer ist musikalisch?* (1896, edited by Hanslick). Two crucial intestinal surgical operations were originated by Billroth, known in medical literature as Billroth I and Billroth II.

BIBLIOGRAPHY: J. Fischer, *Theodor Billroth und seine Zeitgenossen* (1929); A. Fränkel, *Th. Billroth* (1931); Otto Gottlieb, *Billroth und Brahms* (1934); *Briefe Billroths* (1895).

Bilse, Benjamin, German conductor; b. Liegnitz, Aug. 17, 1816; d. there, July 13, 1902. He was "Stadtmusikus" at Liegnitz (1843), and brought his orchestra to a remarkable degree of perfection; then lived in Berlin (1868–84) and conducted at the Concerthaus; retired in 1894 with the title of "Hofmusikus." He composed salon music.

Bilstin (real name **Bildstein**), **Youry,** Russian cellist; b. Odessa, Feb. 10, 1887; d. New York, Dec. 15, 1947. He studied at the Tiflis Cons.; then at St. Petersburg. After the Russian Revolution he lived in Paris; in 1932 settled in the U.S. as a teacher. He wrote several works for cello; also *Invocation to the light* for viola da gamba, flute, and piano (1932); *Variations diaboliques* for cello and piano; and a *Méthode Psycho-Physiologique d'Enseignement Musical.*

Bimboni, Alberto, Italian-American pianist and composer; b. Florence, Aug. 24, 1882; d. New York, June 18, 1960. He studied in Florence; came to the U.S. in 1912 as opera conductor. In 1930 appointed to the faculty of the Curtis Institute in Philadelphia; taught opera classes at the Juilliard School of Music, N.Y., from 1933; appeared as a pianist in concerts with Ysaÿe, John McCormack and other celebrated artists. He wrote the operas *Winona* (Portland, Oregon, Nov. 11, 1926); *Karina* (Minneapolis, 1928); *Il Cancelleto d'oro* (N.Y., March 11, 1936); *In the Name of Culture* (Rochester, May 9, 1949); numerous songs (many of them published).

BIBLIOGRAPHY: E. E. Hipsher, *American Opera and Its Composers* (Philadelphia, 1927; pp. 72–76).

Binchois (de Binche), Gilles, Burgundian composer; b. Mons in Hainaut, c.1400; d. Soignies, near Mons, Sept. 20, 1460. His father was Jean de Binche, counsellor to two rulers of Hainaut. Binchois was in the service of William de la Pole, Earl of Suffolk in Paris (1424). From 1430 he was at the Burgundian court; advanced from fifth to second chaplain; probably visited Italy at some time. Tinctoris considered him the equal of Dunstable and Dufay. He is best known for his secular works; his chansons rank with the finest. Modern reprints of his works are contained in: J. Marix, *Les Musiciens de la cour de Bourgogne au XVᵉ siècle* (1937); L. Feininger (ed.), *Documenta polyphoniae liturgicae Sanctae Ecclesiae Romanae*, Ser. I (1947); W. Gurlitt (ed.), *Gilles Binchois, 16 weltliche Lieder zu 3 Stimmen* in *Das Chorwerk* 22; J. Stainer (ed.), *Dufay and his Contemporaries* (1898); *Denkmäler der Tonkunst in Österreich* (vols. 14/15, 22, 61; formerly 7, 11.i, 31); A. W. Ambros, *Geschichte der Musik*, vol. II (1862–78, 1882); E. Droz and G. Thibault (eds.), *Poètes et musiciens du XVᵉ siècle* (1924); A. Schering (ed.) *Geschichte der Musik in Beispielen* (Leipzig, 1931; reprinted, N.Y., 1950); E. Droz, G. Thibault and Y. Rokseth (eds.), *Trois chansonniers français du XVᵉ siècle* (1927); H. Besseler, *Die Musik des Mittelalters und der Renaissance* in Bücken's *Handbuch* series (1931); C. van den Borren (ed.), *Polyphonia Sacra: A Continental Miscellany of the Fifteenth Century* (1932); O. Dischner (ed.), *Kammermusik des Mittelalters. Chansons der 1. und 2. niederländischen Schule für drei bis vier Streichinstrumenten herausgegeben* (1927); A. Davison and W. Apel (eds.), *Historical Anthology of Music*, vol. I (Cambridge, Mass., 1950); H. E. Wooldridge, *Oxford History of Music*, vol. II (1932); C. Parrish and J. F. Ohl, *Masterpieces of Music before 1750* (N.Y., 1951); G. de Van, "A recently discovered Source of Early Fifteenth Century Polyphonic Music, the Aosta Manuscript," *Musica Disciplina* II (1948); J. Wolf, *Geschichte der Mensural-Notation von 1250–1460* III (1904); J. Wolf (ed.), *Music of Earlier Times* (1946); *Die Chansons von Gilles Binchois*, in *Musikalische Denkmäler* 2.

BIBLIOGRAPHY: E. Closson, "L'Origine de Gilles Binchois," *Revue de Musicologie* V (1924); A. Pirro, *Histoire de la musique de la fin du XIVᵉ siècle à la fin du XVIᵉ* (1940); Aurelio Gotti, *L'Ars Nova e il Madrigale* in *Atti della Reale Accademia di Scienze, Lettere, e Arti di Palermo* (ser. IV, Vol. IV, Part II); W. Gurlitt in *Basler Kongressbericht* (1924); H. Funk, in *Acta musicologica* IV; H. Riemann, *Handbuch der Musikgeschichte* III; G. Reese, *Music in the Renaissance* (N.Y., 1954).

Binder, Abraham Wolfe, American composer and conductor; b. New York, Jan. 13, 1895; d. there, Oct. 10, 1966. He studied at Columbia Univ. (Mus. Bac., 1926); taught liturgical music at the Jewish Institute of Religion, N.Y. He composed the symphonic works *Ha Chalutsim* (The Pioneers, 1931); *Holy Land Impressions* (1932); *The Valley of Dry Bones* (1935); *Dybbuk Suite* for chamber ensemble (1956); opera, *A Goat in Chelm* (N.Y., March 20, 1960).

Binder, Christlieb Siegmund, German organist and composer; b. Dresden, July (baptized July 29), 1723; d. there, Jan. 1, 1789. He was organist at the court church in Dresden from 1753; wrote prolifically, in an "elegant style" akin to that of Carl Ph. E. Bach.

WORKS: sonatas for harpsichord solo, and for harpsichord in various combinations with violin and cello; 76 organ preludes, harpsichord concertos, quartets with harpsichord, and trio sonatas for 2 violins with basso continuo. Some of his compositions have been reprinted by O. Schmid in *Musik am sächsischen Hofe.*

BIBLIOGRAPHY: H. Fleischer, *C. S. Binder* (Regensburg, 1941).

Binder, Karl, Austrian composer; b. Vienna, Nov. 29, 1816; d. there, Nov. 5, 1860. He was a theater conductor by profession; composed mostly for the stage: a melodrama *Der Wiener Schusterhut* (1840); an opera, *Die Drei Wittfrauen* (1841); a vaudeville comedy *Purzel* (1843); overture and choruses for the drama *Elmar.* He wrote a parody on *Tannhäuser* (1857).

Binenbaum, Janco, Bulgarian-French composer; b. Adrianopol, Dec. 28, 1880; d. Chevreuse (Seine-et-Oise), France, Feb. 4, 1956. He studied in Munich with

Rheinberger and others; was active as piano teacher in Germany and France, eventually settling in Chevreuse, where he remained until his death. He wrote a considerable amount of symphonic and chamber music in an impressionistic vein, colored with Balkan rhythms, none of which was published, and little ever performed. Nonetheless, Binenbaum found a number of sincere admirers of his works, among whom M. D. Calvocoressi was the most vocal.

Binet, Jean, Swiss composer; b. Geneva, Oct. 17, 1893; d. Trélex, Switzerland, Feb. 24, 1960. He studied academic subjects at the Univ. of Geneva, and simultaneously obtained a diploma from the Institut Jaques-Dalcroze; then took lessons in musicology and composition with Otto Barblan, William Montillet and Templeton Strong. In 1919 he went to America, where he organized the first school of Dalcroze eurhythmics, and also took lessons with Ernest Bloch. In 1921 he was instrumental in founding, with Ernest Bloch, the Cleveland Cons. In 1923 he returned to Europe, and lived in Brussels where he taught the Dalcroze method. In 1929 he went back to Switzerland, and settled in Trélex. Many of his works are based on a Swiss national folksong. Binet's musical idiom is determined by pragmatic considerations of performance and does not transcend the natural borders of traditional harmonies.

WORKS: Primarily interested in the musical theater, he wrote 6 operettas and radiophonic cantatas, the ballets *L'Île enchantée* (Zürich, 1947); *Le Printemps* (1950) and *La Colline*, for 5 narrators and orch. (1957); also several scores of incidental music for plays of Sophocles, Shakespeare and contemporary writers. Other works include a number of sacred and secular choruses, songs with orchestral accompaniment, String Quartet (1927); *Divertissement* for violin and orch. (1934); Sonatina for Flute and Piano (1942); *6 pieces for Flute Solo* (1947); *Petit concert* for clarinet and string orch. (1950); *Variations sur un chant de Noël* for bassoon and piano (1957); *3 Dialogues* for 2 flutes (1957); educational pieces for piano; also harmonizations of popular melodies for chorus.

Bing, Sir Rudolf, international operatic impresario; b. Vienna, Jan. 9, 1902. He studied at the Univ. of Vienna; took singing lessons, but soon entered the managerial field in opera. He was successively connected with a Vienna concert agency (1923–27); Darmstadt State Theater (1928–30) and the Municipal Opera at Charlottenburg-Berlin (1930–33). In 1934 he went to England, was manager of the Glyndebourne Opera Co. from 1935–39 and 1946–49. He came a British subject in 1946. He was one of the most active organizers of the Edinburgh Festivals in 1947 and was their musical director for 3 seasons. In 1950 he was appointed general manager of the Metropolitan Opera, in New York, inaugurating one of the most eventful and sometimes turbulent periods in the history of the Metropolitan Opera; he resigned in 1972; published an entertaining summary of his experiences in a volume entitled *5000 Nights at the Opera* (N.Y., 1972). In 1971 he was given by Queen Elizabeth II of England the title of Knight Commander of the Order of the British Empire.

Bingham, Seth, American organist and composer; b. Bloomfield, N.J., April 16, 1882; d. New York, June 21, 1972. He studied with Horatio Parker; later in Paris with d'Indy, Widor (composition) and Guilmant (organ). Returning to America, he graduated from Yale University (B.A., 1904); took his M.B. at Yale in 1908, and taught there until 1919; instructor and associate prof. at Columbia University (until 1954).

WORKS: *Wall Street Fantasy* (1912; performed as *Symphonic Fantasy* by the N.Y. Philharmonic, Feb. 6, 1916); *La Charelzenn*, opera (1917); *Tame Animal Tunes* for 18 instruments (1918); *Memories of France*, orchestral suite (1920); *Wilderness Stone* for narrator, soli, chorus and orchestra (1933); Concerto for Organ and Orchestra (Rochester, Oct. 24, 1946); *Connecticut Suite* for organ and strings (Hartford, March 26, 1954); Concerto for Brass, Snare Drum and Organ (Minneapolis, July 12, 1954). Among his compositions for organ the following have been frequently performed: *Suite* (1926); *Pioneer America* (1928); *Harmonies of Florence* (1929); *Carillon de Château-Thierry* (1936); *Pastoral Psalms* (1938); *12 Hymn-Preludes* (1942); *Variation Studies* (1950); *36 Hymn and Carol Canons* (1952).

Binkerd, Gordon, American composer and teacher; b. Lynch, Nebraska, May 22, 1916. He studied piano in South Dakota; composition with Bernard Rogers at the Eastman School of Music, Rochester, and with Walter Piston at Harvard Univ.; from 1949 to 1971, member of the faculty of the Univ. of Illinois; received a Guggenheim Fellowship in 1959.

WORKS: Symph. No. 1 (Univ. of Illinois, Urbana, March 20, 1955); Symph. No. 2 (Univ. of Illinois, Urbana, April 13, 1957); Symph. No. 3 (N.Y., Jan. 6, 1961); Symph. No. 4 (St. Louis, Oct. 12, 1963; dismembered and reduced to a *Movement for Orchestra*); *A Part of Heaven*, 2 romances for violin and orch. (1972); 2 string quartets (1956, 1961); Trio for Clarinet, Viola and Cello (1955); Cello Sonata (1952); 3 Songs for mezzo-soprano and string quartet; *Portrait Intérieur* for mezzo-soprano, violin and cello; Piano Sonata; *Entertainments* for piano; numerous sacred choruses; songs.

Birchall, Robert, English music publisher; d. London, 1819. He founded a music publishing firm in London; published several of Beethoven's works for the first time in England; letters from Beethoven to Birchall are contained in Nohl's collection. The firm, which later became Birchall, Lonsdale & Mills, had one of the first circulating music libraries ever established.

Birchard, Clarence C., American music publisher; b. Cambridge Springs, Pa., July 13, 1866; d. Carlisle, Mass., Feb. 27, 1946. He established his firm in Boston in 1901 and specialized in educational books for public schools; of these, a ten-book series, *A Singing School*, introduced lavish profusion of color in design and illustration; the firm has also issued community song books, of which the most popular is *Twice 55 Community Songs* (several million copies sold). The catalogue includes orchestral scores by many American composers (Berezowsky, Bloch, Converse, Hadley, Ives, Janssen, Josten, Kelley, Loeffler, Mason,

Morris, Shepherd and Sowerby); also cantatas by Cadman, Converse, Hanson, Rogers and Whithorne; and Copland's school opera *Second Hurricane*. After Birchard's death Thomas M. Moran succeeded to the presidency; after his death in 1949, Donald F. Malin became president. The firm publishes a house organ, *The Birchard Broadsheet*.

Bird, Arthur, American composer; b. Belmont, Mass., July 23, 1856; d. Berlin, Dec. 22, 1923. He studied in Berlin with Loeschhorn; spent several months with Liszt at Weimar in 1885; returned to America briefly in 1886, and then lived in Berlin, identifying himself with conservative circles there. He was Berlin correspondent of American music magazines; in his articles he violently attacked Richard Strauss and other modern composers. Among his own works is a symphony, *2 Decimettes* for wind instruments (won Paderewski prize in 1901); a comic opera *Daphne* (N.Y., Dec. 13, 1897), and many piano pieces.
BIBLIOGRAPHY: W. L. Loring, "Arthur Bird, American Composer," *Musical Quarterly* (Jan. 1943).

Bird, Henry Richard, eminent English organist; b. Walthamstow, Nov. 14, 1842; d. London, Nov. 21, 1915. He was a pupil of his father; then studied with James Turle; came to London in 1859, where he held various positions as organist, and conducted the Chelsea Choral and Orchestral Society; was appointed organist at St. Mary Abbott's in Kensington, and occupied this post until his death; was also prof. of piano at the Royal College of Music and at Trinity College from 1896. He was famous throughout England as an unexcelled accompanist, and was in constant demand by the foremost artists.

Biriotti, León, Uruguayan conductor and composer; b. Montevideo, Dec. 1, 1929. He studied oboe, theory and musicology; began to conduct experimentally without preliminary training; founded a string orchestra in Montevideo; conducted the instrumental group Juventudes Musicales of Uruguay.
WORKS: 3 symphonies (1964, 1965, 1968); a *Suite* for violin and cello (1952); String Sextet (1957); Trio for Oboe, Clarinet and Bassoon (1963); String Quartet (1965); Violin Sonata (1967); songs and piano pieces.

Biriukov, Yuri, Russian composer; b. Moscow, April 1, 1908. He studied piano with Feinberg and composition with Miaskovsky at the Moscow Cons., graduating in 1936; then devoted himself to teaching. He wrote two operas, *Peasant Gentlewoman* (after Pushkin's story, 1947) and *Knight of the Golden Star* (1956); a ballet, *The Cosmonauts* (1962); a musical, *The Blue Express* (1971); a symphony on the Ingush themes (1968); 3 piano concertos (1941, 1945, 1970); 24 preludes and 4 toccatas for piano, and much music for the theater and the cinema.

Birkenstock, Johann Adam, German violinist and composer; b. Alsfeld, Feb. 19, 1687; d. Eisenach, Feb. 26, 1733. He studied with Fiorelli; was employed in the Kassel Court orch. (1709-30), and in 1730 went to Eisenach as kapellmeister. His sonatas for violin with basso continuo (Amsterdam, 1722) are included in various anthologies.

Birnbach, Heinrich, German pianist and music pedagogue, son of **Karl Joseph Birnbach;** b. Breslau, Jan. 8, 1793; d. Berlin, Aug. 24, 1879. He studied piano with his father; taught in Breslau from 1814-21; settled in Berlin as music teacher and founded a music institute. Among his pupils were Nicolai, Kücken and Dehn. He composed 2 symphonies; 2 overtures; concertos for oboe, clarinet and guitar; piano concertos; a piano quintet; piano sonatas; piano duos; etc.; also published a treatise, *Der vollkommene Kapellmeister* (1845).

Birnbach, Karl Joseph, German composer; b. Köpernick, Silesia, 1751; d. Warsaw, May 29, 1805. During the last years of his life he was conductor at the German Theater in Warsaw. A prolific composer, he wrote 2 operas; 10 symphonies; 16 piano concertos; 10 violin concertos; cantatas; Masses; chamber music; piano pieces.

Birtwistle, Harrison, English composer; b. Accrington, Lancashire, July 15, 1934. He studied at the Royal Manchester College of Music, and later at the Royal Academy of Music in London. He taught at Salisbury (1962-65); was a visiting prof. at Swarthmore College, Penn. (1973-74); in 1975 joined the faculty of State Univ. of N.Y. of Buffalo.
WORKS: *Refrains and Choruses* for wind quintet (1957); *Monody for Corpus Christi* for soprano solo, flute, violin and horn (1959); *The World is Discovered,* instrumental motet (1960; Festival of the International Society for Contemporary Music, Copenhagen, June 2, 1964); *Chorales* for orch. (1963); *Narration: The Description of the Passing of a Year* for a cappella choir (1964); *Précis* for piano solo; *Punch and Judy,* chamber opera (Edinburgh Festival, Aug. 22, 1968); *Nomos* for orch. (London, Aug. 23, 1968); *Down by the Greenwood Side,* dramatic pastorale (1969); *Medusa* for chamber orch. and percussion (London, Oct. 22, 1969; revised and produced in London on March 3, 1970); *Verses for Ensembles,* for 12 players forming interlocking groups of woodwinds, brass and percussion (London, Aug. 31, 1970); *The Triumph of Time* for orch., after a painting of Bruegel (1970); *Meridian* for mezzo-soprano, chorus and an instrumental ensemble (1971); *Prologue* for tenor, bassoon, 2 trumpets, horn, trombone, violin and double bass (1971); *Grimethorpe Aria* for brass ensemble (1973); *An Imaginary Landscape* for orch. (1971); *Silbury Air* for woodwind quartet, trumpet, horn, trombone, string quintet, piano, harp and percussion (1977).

Bisaccia, Giovanni, Italian singer and composer; b. 1815; d. Naples, Dec. 20, 1897. He studied singing with Crescentini and composition with Raimondi and Donizetti; sang in the Nuovo and San Carlo theaters; later taught singing, and was maestro di cappella at the church of San Fernando, for which he wrote some music. In 1838 he brought out 2 musical farces, *I tre scioperati* and *Il figlio adottivo;* and in 1858 an opera buffa *Don Taddeo.*

Bischoff, Georg Friedrich, German music director; b. Ellrich, Harz Mountains, Sept. 21, 1780; d. Hildesheim, Sept. 7, 1841. He was music director at Hildesheim from 1816; arranged the first Thuringian Festival at Frankenhausen (July 20 and 21, 1810), at which Spohr acted both as conductor and violin soloist.

Bischoff, Hans, German pianist and teacher; b. Berlin, Feb. 17, 1852; d. Niederschönhausen, near Berlin, June 12, 1889. He was a pupil of Theodor Kullak and Richard Wüerst; also studied at Berlin Univ. (*Dr. phil.,* 1873); taught piano at Kullak's Academy from 1873; conducted Monday Concerts of the Berlin Singakademie. He edited the 2nd and 3rd editions of Adolf Kullak's *Ästhetik des Klavierspiels* (Berlin, 1876 and 1889; English translation, N.Y., 1895); also published an *Auswahl Händel'scher Klavierwerke; Kritische Ausgabe von J. S. Bachs Klavierwerken;* etc.

Bischoff, Hermann, German composer; b. Duisburg, Jan. 7, 1868; d. Berlin, Jan. 25, 1936. He was a pupil of Jadassohn at the Leipzig Cons.; lived for a time in Munich, where he was associated with Richard Strauss; then went to Berlin. He composed 2 symphonies; the first symph. had its world première in Essen, May 24, 1906; was given by the Boston Symph. under Karl Muck twice in one season (Jan. 4, 1908 and Feb. 29, 1908); attracted a great deal of attention at the time, but sank into oblivion later on. He also composed the symph. poems *Pan* and *Gewittersegen;* published an essay, *Das deutsche Lied* (1905).

Bischoff, Kaspar Jakob, German composer and teacher; b. Ansbach, April 7, 1823; d. Munich, Oct. 26, 1893. He was a pupil of Franz Lachner in Munich (1842); studied in Leipzig (1848); settled in Frankfurt, where he taught singing, and founded an Evangelical Sacred Choral Society in 1850. He wrote an opera, *Maske und Mantilla* (Frankfurt, 1852); 3 symphonies; overture to *Hamlet;* chamber music; church music; also published a manual of harmony (1890).

Bischoff, Ludwig Friedrich Christian, German editor of music periodicals; b. Dessau, Nov. 27, 1794; d. Cologne, Feb. 24, 1867. He was teacher at Wesel (1823–49); then settled in Cologne, where he founded and edited the *Rheinische Musikzeitung* (1850) and the *Niederrheinische Musikzeitung* (1853).

Bischoff, Marie. See **Brandt, Marianne.**

Bishop, Anna, English soprano; b. London, Jan. 9, 1810; d. New York, March 18, 1884. She was of French descent (her maiden name was Rivière). She studied at the Royal Academy of Music in London; in 1831 married Henry Bishop. She made her London debut in 1834; in 1839 made an extensive concert tour with the harpist, Bochsa; soon afterwards abandoned her husband and went with Bochsa to France; however, she continued to use her married name, and appeared in concerts as Madame Bishop. In 1847 she went to America; in 1858 she married Martin Schultz of New York. In 1866 she toured China and Australia; the ship she was on became grounded on a coral reef in the Marianas for 21 days; but despite this experience she completed her tour, eventually returning to New York.

Bishop, Sir Henry Rowley, noted English composer; b. London, Nov. 18, 1786; d. there, April 30, 1855. He was a pupil of Francesco Bianchi; attracted attention with his first opera, *The Circassian Bride* (Drury Lane, Feb. 23, 1809); was engaged as conductor at Covent Garden in 1810; in 1813 was alternate conductor of the Philharmonic; in 1819 oratorio conductor at Covent Garden; in 1825 conductor at the Drury Lane Theatre; in 1830 Musical Director at Vauxhall; took the degree of Mus. Bac. at Oxford (1839); from 1840 was music director at Covent Garden; then Prof. of Music at Edinburgh (1841–3); was knighted in 1842; engaged as conductor of the Ancient Concerts from 1840–8; then appointed Prof. of Music at Oxford (succeeding Dr. Crotch), where he received the degree of Mus. Doc. in 1853. He was a remarkably prolific dramatic composer, having produced about 130 operas, farces, ballets, adaptations, etc. His operas are generally in the style of English ballad opera; some of the best are: *Cortez or The Conquest of Mexico* (1823); *The Fall of Algiers* (1825); *The Knight of Snowdoun* (after Walter Scott, 1811); *Native Land* (1824). His *Clari, or the Maid of Milan* (Covent Garden, May 8, 1823) contains the famous song *Home Sweet Home,* with text by the American, John Howard Payne; it appears repeatedly throughout the opera. The tune, previously published by Bishop to other words, was thought to have been of Sicilian origin, but after much litigation was accepted as Bishop's original composition (the MS is owned by the Univ. of Rochester, N.Y.). A version of the melody was used by Donizetti in his opera *Anne Boleyn,* thereby causing the erroneous belief that Donizetti was its composer. Bishop also wrote *The Fallen Angel,* an oratorio; *The Seventh Day,* cantata (1834); many additions to revivals of older operas, etc.; his glees and other lyric vocal compositions are deservedly esteemed. Bishop also published vol. I of *Melodies of Various Nations;* and 3 vols. of *National Melodies,* to which Moore wrote the poems.

BIBLIOGRAPHY: F. Corder, "The Works of Sir Henry Bishop," *Musical Quarterly* (Jan. 1918); R. Northcott, *The Life of Sir Henry R. Bishop* (London, 1920).

Bismillah Khan, Indian virtuoso on the shehnai; b. Dumraon, March 21, 1916. He studied instrumental and vocal music; earned a great renown in India; appeared as soloist at the Commonwealth Arts Festival in London in 1965.

Bispham, David (Scull), American baritone; b. Philadelphia, Jan. 5, 1857; d. New York, Oct. 2, 1921. He first sang as an amateur in church choruses in Philadelphia; then went to Milan (1886) where he studied with Vannuccini, and Francesco Lamperti; later studied in London with Shakespeare and Randegger; made his operatic debut as Longueville in Messager's *Basoche* (Royal Opera, London, Nov. 3, 1891), in which his comic acting ability, as well as his singing, won praise; made his first appearance in serious opera as Kurwenal in *Tristan und Isolde* (Drury Lane, June 25, 1892). He was particularly effective in the Wagnerian baritone roles; made his American debut with the Metropolitan Opera as Beckmesser (Nov. 18, 1896). He was a strong advocate of opera in English; a Society of American Singers was organized under his guidance, presenting light operas in the English language. Bispham published an autobiography *A Quaker Singer's Recollections* (N.Y., 1920). A Bispham Memorial Medal Award was established by the Opera Society of America in 1921 for an opera in English by an American composer; among its winners were Walter Damrosch, Victor Herbert, Henry Hadley, Deems Taylor, Charles Cadman, Louis Gruenberg, Howard Hanson, Otto Luening, Ernst Bacon, George Antheil and George Gershwin. Bispham left all the biographical and bibliographical material connected with his career to the Music Division of the N.Y. Public Library.

Bissell, Keith, Canadian composer; b. Meaford, Ontario, Feb. 12, 1912. He studied composition with Leo Smith at the Univ. of Toronto, graduating in 1942; took some instruction in Munich with Carl Orff (1960) and was instrumental in introducing the Orff method of elementary music education to Scarborough (borough of Toronto), where he was chief co-ordinator of music for public schools (1955–76). A great believer in the propagation of music among semi-professionals, he composed works specifically designed for amateur performance.
WORKS: 2 operettas: *Rumpelstiltzkin* (1947) and *His Majesty's Pie* (1966); *3 Pieces* for string orch. (1960); *Little Suite* for trumpet and strings (1962); concertino for piano and strings (1963); *5 Dances* for small orch. (1963); Divertimento for String Orch. (1964); *Canada 1967* for orch. (1967); *A Bluebird in March* for chorus, and orch. or piano (1967); *Christmas in Canada* for narrator, soli, chorus and orch. (1967); *Passion According to St. Luke* for soli, chorus, children's chorus and orch. (Toronto, April 9, 1971); *Andante e Scherzo* for small orch. (1971); *Variations on a Canadian Folksong* for string orch. (1972); *Theme, Variation and Epilogue* for chorus, solo viola and string orch. (1975); *God's Grandeur* for chorus and orch. (1975); *Andante and Allegro* for oboe and strings (1976); *In Praise of Famous Men* for soprano, chorus, organ, brass quintet and string orch. (Toronto, June 1, 1976); Piano Sonata (1947); Violin Sonata (1948); Organ Sonata (1963); Serenade for Wind Quintet (1972); *Trio Suite* for trumpet, horn and trombone (1973); choruses; songs.

Bitsch, Marcel, French composer; b. Paris, Dec. 29, 1921. He entered the Paris Cons. in 1939, studied composition with Busser, and won the second Prix de Rome, 1943; first Prix de Rome, 1945. He has written *Six Esquisses Symphoniques* (1949); *Sinfonietta* (1950); cantata *La Farce du Contrebandier* (1946); *Divertissement* for flute, clarinet, oboe and bassoon (1947); *3 Sonatinas* for flute and piano (1952); Concertino for piano and orch. (Paris, Nov. 28, 1954), etc.

Bitter, Carl Hermann, German writer on music; b. Schwedt-on-Oder, Feb. 27, 1813; d. Berlin, Sept. 12, 1885. He studied at the Berlin Univ.; then in Bonn; pursued a career in government; served in the finance dept.; in 1879 was appointed by Bismarck Prussian Minister of Finance. He retired in 1882.
WRITINGS: *J. S. Bach* (2 vols., Berlin, 1865; abridged English ed., 1873); *Mozarts Don Juan und Glucks Iphigenie* (Berlin, 1866); *C. Ph. E. Bach und W. Fr. Bach und deren Brüder* (2 vols., Berlin, 1868); *Beiträge zur Geschichte der Oper* (1872); *Die Reform der Oper durch Gluck und Wagner* (1884).

Bittner, Julius, Austrian composer; b. Vienna, April 9, 1874; d. there, Jan. 9, 1939. He first studied law; then music with Bruno Walter and Josef Labor; was a magistrate in Vienna until 1920. At the same time he composed industriously. He devoted most of his energy to opera and also wrote his own librettos; composed 2 symphonies; sacred choruses; and numerous songs for his wife, Emilie Bittner, a contralto. During his last years, he suffered from a crippling illness, necessitating the amputation of both legs.
WORKS: operas: *Die rote Gret* (Frankfurt, Oct. 26, 1907); *Der Musikant* (Vienna, April 12, 1910); *Der Bergsee* (Vienna, Nov. 9, 1911; revised, 1938); *Der Abenteurer* (Cologne, Oct. 30, 1913); *Das höllisch Gold* (Darmstadt, Oct. 15, 1916); *Das Rosengärtlein* (Mannheim, March 18, 1923); *Mondnacht* (Berlin, Nov. 13, 1928); *Das Veilchen* (Vienna, Dec. 8, 1934); also operettas, ballets and mimodramas.
BIBLIOGRAPHY: R. Specht, *Julius Bittner* (Munich, 1921); Ullrich Bittner, *Julius Bittner* (Vienna, 1969).

Bizet, Georges (baptismal names **Alexandre-César-Léopold**), great French opera composer; b. Paris, Oct. 25, 1838; d. Bougival, June 3, 1875. His parents were both professional musicians, his father a singing teacher and composer; his mother an excellent pianist. Bizet's talent developed early in childhood; at the age of nine he entered the Paris Cons., his teachers being Marmontel (piano), Benoist (organ), Zimmermann (harmony) and Halévy (composition), whose daughter, Geneviève, he married in 1869. In 1852 he won a first prize for piano, in 1855 for organ and for fugue, and in 1857 the Grand Prix de Rome. In the same year he shared (with Lecocq) a prize offered by Offenbach for a setting of a 1-act opera *Le Docteur Miracle;* Bizet's setting was produced at the Bouffes-Parisiens on April 9, 1857. Instead of the prescribed Mass, he sent from Rome during his first year a 2-act Italian opera buffa, *Don Procopio* (not produced until March 10, 1906 when it was given in Monte Carlo in an incongruously edited version); later he sent 2 movements of a symphony, an overture (*La Chasse d'Ossian*); and a 1-act opera (*La Guzla de l'Emir;* accepted by Paris Opéra-Comique, but withdrawn by Bizet prior to production). Returning to Paris, he produced a grand opera, *Les Pêcheurs de perles* (Th.-Lyrique, Sept. 30, 1863); but this work, like *La jolie fille de Perth* (Dec. 26, 1867) failed to win popular approval. A 1-act opera, *Djamileh* (Opéra-Comique, May 22, 1872) fared no better. Bizet's incidental music for Daudet's play *L'Arlésienne* (Oct. 1, 1872) was ignored by the audiences and literary critics; it was not fully appreciated until its revival in 1885. But an orchestral suite from *L'Arlésienne* brought out by Pasdeloup (Nov. 10, 1872) was acclaimed; a 2nd suite was made by Guiraud after Bizet's death. Bizet's next major work was his masterpiece *Carmen* (based on a tale by Mérimée, text by Halévy and Meilhac), produced after many difficulties with the management and the cast, at the Opéra-Comique (March 3, 1875). The reception of the public was not enthusiastic, and several critics attacked the opera for its lurid subject and the music for its supposed adoption of Wagner's methods. Bizet received a generous sum (25,000 francs) for the score from the publisher Choudens and won other honors (he was named chevalier of the Légion d'honneur on the eve of the premiere of *Carmen*); although the attendance was not high, the opera was maintained in the repertory. There were 37 performances before the end of the season; the original cast included Galli-Marie as Carmen, Lhérie as Don José and Bouhy as Escamillo. Bizet was chagrined by the controversial reception of the opera, but it is a melodramatic invention to state (as has been asserted by some biographers) that the alleged failure of *Carmen* precipitated the composer's death (he died on the night of the 31st perf. of *Carmen*). Soon the opera became a triumphant success all over the world; it was staged in London (in Italian at Her Majesty's Theatre, June 22, 1878); St. Petersburg, Vienna, Brussels, Naples, Florence, Mainz, New York (Academy of Music, Oct. 23, 1878), etc. The Metropolitan Opera produced *Carmen* first in Italian (Jan. 9, 1884), then in French, with Calvé as Carmen (Dec. 20, 1893). It should be pointed out that the famous *Habanera* is not Bizet's own, but a melody by the Spanish composer Yradier; Bizet inserted it in *Carmen* (with slight alterations) mistaking it for a folk song. Bizet also wrote an operetta, *La Prêtresse* (1854); the operas *Numa* (1871) and *Ivan le Terrible*, in 4 acts (Bordeaux, Oct. 12, 1951; the score was believed to have been destroyed by Bizet, but was discovered among the manuscripts bequeathed to the Paris Cons. by the second husband of Bizet's widow); the cantatas *David* (1856) and *Clovis et Clothilde* (1857); *Vasco da Gama*, symph. ode with chorus (1859); *Souvenirs de Rome*, symph. suite in 3 movements (Paris, Feb. 28, 1869; publ. in 1880 as a 4-movement suite, *Roma*); orchestral overture *Patrie* (Paris, Feb. 15, 1874); *Jeux d'enfants* (suite for piano 4 hands); about 150 piano pieces of all kinds (Bizet was a brilliant pianist); etc. Bizet's first symphony, written at the age of 17, was discovered in the Bizet collection at the Paris Cons. in 1933, and was given its first performance anywhere by Felix Weingartner in Basel on Feb. 26, 1935; it rapidly became popular in concert repertory. Bizet also completed Halévy's biblical opera *Noë* (1869).

BIBLIOGRAPHY: E. Galabert, *Georges Bizet* (Paris, 1877); Ch. Pigot, *Bizet et son Oeuvre* (1886; new ed. 1911); C. Bellaigue, *Bizet* (1891); P. Voss, *Bizet* (Leipzig, 1899); A. Weissmann, *Bizet* (Berlin, 1907); O. Séré, "Georges Bizet," in *Musiciens français d'aujourd'hui* (Paris, 1911); H. Gauthier-Villars, *Bizet; biographie critique* (Paris, 1911); R. Brancour, *La Vie et l'œuvre de Bizet* (Paris, 1913); P. Landormy, "Bizet," in *Les Maîtres de la Musique* (1924); Julius Rabe, *Bizet* (Stockholm, 1925); D. C. Parker, *Bizet, His Life and Works* (London, 1926); E. Istel, *Bizet und Carmen* (Stuttgart, 1927); J. Tiersot, "Bizet and Spanish Music," *Musical Quarterly* (Oct. 1925); J. W. Klein, "Nietzsche and Bizet," *Musical Quarterly* (Oct. 1925);

M. Delmas, *Bizet* (1930); R. Laparra, *Bizet et l'Espagne* (Paris, 1934); Bizet issue of the *Revue de Musicologie* (Nov. 1938); M. Cooper, *Bizet* (London, 1938); W. Dean, *Bizet* (London, 1948); Mina Curtiss, "Unpublished Letters by Georges Bizet," *Musical Quarterly* (July 1950); Mina Curtiss, *Bizet and His World* (N.Y., 1958); W. Dean, *Georges Bizet: His Life and Work* (London, 1965).

Bjelinski, Bruno, Croatian composer; b. Trieste, Nov. 1, 1909. He studied law at the Univ. of Zagreb and music at the Cons. there; in 1945 he joined its faculty. His music is marked by romantic coloring, often related to literary subjects. He wrote a children's opera *Die Biene Maja* (1946); *Simfonija Ljeta (Summer Symphony;* Zagreb, Oct. 15, 1956); *In Memoriam Poetae,* with children's chorus (1961); Symph. No. 3 (1964); Symph. No. 4 (1965); Symph. No. 5 (1969); Serenade for Trumpet, Piano, Strings and Percussion (1957); *Mediterranean Sinfonietta* (Zagreb, Dec. 9, 1959); *Sinfonietta brasileira* (1961); operatic fairytale, *Pčelica Maja (Maya the Bee;* 1952); *Sinfonietta concertante* (1967); Concertino for Horn and Orch. (1967); Clarinet Sonata (1966); several song cycles; piano pieces.

BIBLIOGRAPHY: K. Kovačević, *Hrvatski Kompozitori i Njihova Djela* (Zagreb, 1960).

Björkander, Nils (Frank Frederik), Swedish composer; b. Stockholm, June 28, 1893; d. Soedertälje, March 5, 1972. He studied at the Stockholm Cons.; in 1917 he established a music school of his own. Some of his piano pieces achieved considerable popularity, especially *Fyra Skärgårdsskisser (4 Sketches from the Skerries,* 1923); he also wrote a *Concert-Fantasy* for piano and orch.; *Cavatina* for violin and orch.; Piano Quintet; Flute Sonata; Violin Sonata, etc.

Björlin, Ulf, Swedish conductor and composer; b. Stockholm, May 21, 1933. He studied conducting in Salzburg with Igor Markevitch and in Paris with Nadia Boulanger; from 1963 to 1968 he was director of the Royal Dramatic Theater in Stockholm. He has written music mainly for the theater.

WORKS: *Pinocchio,* a children's musical for chamber orch. (1966); *Ekon* for orch. (1967); *Om fem år (In Five Years),* after García Lorca, an opera for actors and chamber ensemble (Stockholm, Oct. 27, 1967); *Aft vaemod (Of Melancholy),* a choreographic oratorio (1970); an opera, *Den stora teatern (The Big Theater;* Göteborg, Feb. 25, 1972); a short opera, *Balladen om Kasper Rosenröd,* for soli and chamber ensemble (Vålberg-Karlstad, Nov. 15, 1972); *Mandala* for orch. (1974).

Björling, Jussi, eminent Swedish tenor; b. Stora Tuna, Feb. 2, 1911; d. Siarö, near Stockholm, Sept. 9, 1960. He studied music with his father, and began his concert career as a member of the vocal Björling Quartet, with his father and two brothers, which became widely known during its European and American tours. He made his operatic debut at the Royal Theater in Stockholm in 1930; also toured in solo recitals. He made his first appearance with the Metropolitan Opera as Rodolfo in *La Bohème* on Nov. 24,

1938; after the interruption caused by the war, he sang with the Metropolitan Opera again in 1947, 1949 and 1950, in the Italian repertory. He publ. an autobiography, *Med bagaget i strupen* (Stockholm, 1945).

Blacher, Boris, outstanding German composer; b. Newchwang, China (of half-German, quarter-Russian and quarter-Jewish ancestry), Jan. 19 (Jan. 6 according to the Russian old-style calendar), 1903; d. Berlin, Jan. 30, 1975. His family moved to Irkutsk, Siberia, remaining there from 1914 until 1920; in 1922 he went to Berlin; studied architecture, and then took a course in composition with F. E. Koch. From 1948 until 1970 he was prof. at the Hochschule für Musik in West Berlin, and from 1953 to 1970 was its director. An exceptionally prolific composer, Blacher was equally successful in writing in classical forms and in original modernistic experimentation. He developed a system of "variable meters" with time signatures following the arithmetical progression, alternatively increasing and decreasing, with permutations contributing to metrical variety. For the theater he developed a sui generis "abstract opera" incorporating an element of organized improvisation. In 1960 he was appointed Director of the Seminar of Electronic Composition at the Technological Univ. in Berlin, and made ample use of electronic resources in his own compositions. WORKS: OPERAS: *Fürstin Tarakanowa* (Wuppertal, Feb. 5, 1941); *Die Flut* (first performed on radio, Berlin, Dec. 20, 1946; first performance on the stage, Dresden, March 4, 1947); *Die Nachtschwalbe* (*The Night Swallow,* "a dramatic nocturne"; Leipzig, Feb. 29, 1948; aroused considerable commotion because of its subject dealing with prostitutes and pimps); *Das preussisches Märchen* (Berlin, Sept. 22, 1952); *Abstract Opera No. 1* (Frankfurt, June 28, 1953); *Rosamunde Floris* (Berlin, Sept. 21, 1960); *Zwischenfälle bei einer Notlandung* (*Incidents at a Forced Landing*), a "reportage" for singers, instruments and electronic devices (Hamburg, Feb. 4, 1966); *200.000 Taler,* after Scholom Aleichem (Berlin, Sept. 25, 1969); *Yvonne, Prinzessin von Burgund* (1972; Wuppertal, Sept. 1, 1973); BALLETS: *Harlekinade* (1939); *Chiarina* (Berlin, Jan. 22, 1950); *Hamlet* (Munich, Nov. 19, 1950); *Lysistrata* (Berlin, Sept. 30, 1951); *Demeter* (1964); *Tristan* (1965). FOR ORCH.: Concerto for 2 Trumpets and 2 String Orchs. (1931); *Kleine Marschmusik* (1932); *Capriccio* (1934); *Concertante Musik* (Berlin, Dec. 6, 1937); Symph. (1939); Concerto for String Orch. (1942); *Partita* for string orch. and percussion (1945); *16 Orchestra Variations on a Theme by Paganini* (Leipzig, Nov. 27, 1947); 1st Piano Concerto (1948); Violin Concerto (1950); Concerto for Clarinet, Bassoon, Horn, Trumpet, Harp and Strings (1950); 2nd Piano Concerto (Berlin, Sept. 15, 1952); *Ornaments,* based on "variable meters" (Venice Festival, Sept. 15, 1953); Viola Concerto (Cologne, March 14, 1955); *Hommage à Mozart* (1956); *Music for Cleveland* (1957); *Musica giocosa* (1959); Cello Concerto (1964); *Collage* (1968); Trumpet Concerto (1970); Clarinet Concerto (1971); *Stars and Strings* for jazz ensemble and strings (1972); CHAMBER MUSIC: *Jazz-Koloraturen,* for soprano, saxophone and bassoon (1929); 3 string quartets (1941–1949); Violin Sonata (1947); Concerto for Bassoon, Horn, Trumpet, Harp and

Strings (1950); Divertimento for 4 Woodwind Instruments (1951); *13 Ways of Looking at a Blackbird* for voice and string orch. (1957); *2 Poems* for vibraphone, double bass, percussion and piano (1957); *Konzertstück* for wind quintet and strings (1963); Octet for Piano, Bassoon, Horn and String Quintet (1965); *Virtuose Musik* for violin solo, 10 wind instruments, percussion and harp (1966); String Quartet No. 4, subtiled *Variationen über einem divergierenden c-moll-Dreiklang* (1967); *Ornamente* for violin and piano (1969); Piano Trio (1970); Sonata for 2 cellos (1971); *Blues and Rumba Philharmonica* for 12 solo cellists (1972); *Duo* for flute and piano (1972). ELECTRONIC MUSIC: *Multiple Raumperspektiven* (*Multiple Space Perspectives*) for piano and magnetic tape (1962); *Electronic Study on a Trombone Glissando* (1962); *Electronic Impulse* (1965); *Electronic Scherzo* (1965); 2 sonatinas for piano (1940); Sonata for piano (1951); songs.

BIBLIOGRAPHY: Karl H. Wörner, *Neue Musik in der Entscheidung* (Mainz, 1954; p. 237 *et seq.*); H. H. Stuckenschmidt, *Boris Blacher* (Berlin, 1964).

Black, Andrew, British baritone singer; b. Glasgow, Jan. 15, 1859; d. Sydney, Australia, Sept. 15, 1920. He studied singing in Milan; made his London debut at the Crystal Palace concert on July 30, 1887. In 1913 he settled in Australia.

Black, Frank, American conductor; b. Philadelphia, Nov. 28, 1894; d. Atlanta, Georgia, Jan. 29, 1968. He studied piano with Raphael Joseffy in New York; then devoted himself chiefly to conducting radio orchestras; in 1928 he organized the music department of the National Broadcasting Company.

Blackwood, Easley, American composer; b. Indianapolis, April 21, 1933. He studied piano in his home town and appeared as a soloist with the Indianapolis Symphony at the age of 14; studied composition during summers at the Berkshire Music Center (1948–50), notably with Messiaen in 1949; then with Bernard Heiden at Indiana Univ. and Hindemith at Yale (1949–51); received his Ph.D from Yale in 1954; then went to Paris to study with Nadia Boulanger (1954–56). In 1958 he was appointed to the faculty of the Univ. of Chicago. His music is marked by impassioned Romantic éclat and is set in a highly evolved chromatic idiom. Blackwood is an accomplished pianist, particularly notable for his performances of modern works of transcendental difficulty, such as the Concord Sonata of Ives and the 2nd piano sonata of Boulez. WORKS: 4 symphonies: No. 1 (1954–55; Boston, April 18, 1958; won the Koussevitzky Music Foundation prize); No. 2 (1960; Cleveland, Jan. 5, 1961; commissioned for the centenary of the music firm G. Schirmer); No. 3, for small orch. (1964; Chicago, March 7, 1965); No. 4 (1972–76); Chamber Symphony for 14 Wind Instruments (1955); Clarinet Concerto (1964); *Symphonic Fantasy* (1965); Concerto for Oboe and String Orch. (1966); Violin Concerto (Bath, England, June 18, 1967); Concerto for Flute and String Orch. (Dartmouth College, Hanover, N.H., July 28, 1968); Piano Concerto (1969–70; Ravinia Festival,

Highland Park, Illinois, July 26, 1970); Viola Sonata (1953); 2 string quartets (1957, 1959); Concertino for 5 Instruments (1959); 2 violin sonatas (1960, 1975); Fantasy for Cello and Piano (1960); *Pastorale and Variations* for wind quintet (1961); Fantasy for Flute, Clarinet, Violin and Piano (1965); *3 Short Fantasies* for piano (1965); *Symphonic Movement* for organ (1966); *Un Voyage à Cythère* for soprano and 10 players (1966); Piano Trio (1968).

Blagrove, Henry Gamble, English violinist; b. Nottingham, Oct. 20, 1811; d. London, Dec. 15, 1872. He studied music with his father and gave public performances as a child. At the age of 12 he was one among the first pupils admitted to the Royal Academy of Music which opened in 1823; later he studied violin with Spohr in Kassel (1833); then returned to London.

Bláha, Ivo, Czech composer; b. Litomyšl, March 14, 1936. He studied with Řídký and Sommer at the Academy of Musical Arts in Prague, graduating in 1958; then joined in the film-music department there.
WORKS: 2 string quartets (1957, 1966); Concerto for Orchestra (1957); *3 Movements* for violin and piano (1961); Wind Quintet (1962); Concerto for Percussion and Orch. (1964); *Solitude*, sonata for solo violin (1965); *Music* for wind quintet (1965); *3 Toccata-Studies* for piano (1967); Violin Concerto (1968); *Music to Pictures of a Friend* for flute, oboe and clarinet (1971); Cello Sonata (1972); *Oh, Love*, music to a poem of J. Prévert, for narrator, flute, oboe, clarinet and tape (1973); *2 Inventions* for solo flute (1974); *Variations on a Czech National Song* for 3 flutes (1975); Duo for Bass Clarinet and Piano (1975).

Bláha-Mikeš, Záboj, Czech composer; b. Prague, Nov. 22, 1887; d. there, April 3, 1957. He was a pupil of Vítězslav Novák. As a composer, he wrote mostly vocal music; also composed a melodrama with orchestra, *Tagore*, and sundry piano pieces.

Blahetka, Marie Léopoldine, Austrian pianist and composer; b. Guntramsdorf, near Vienna, Nov. 15, 1811; d. Boulogne, Jan. 12, 1887. She was a piano pupil of Kalkbrenner and Moscheles; also studied composition with Sechter. In 1840 she settled in Boulogne, France. She wrote a romantic opera, *Die Räuber und die Sänger*, which was produced in Vienna in 1830, and a considerable amount of salon pieces for piano.

Blainville, Charles-Henri, French cellist and music theorist; b. probably in or near Rouen, 1710; d. Paris, about 1770. His claim to musicological attention resides in his "discovery" of a third "mode hellénique" (actually the Phrygian mode); in 1751 he wrote a symphony in which he made use of this mode. Rousseau, always eager to welcome a "historical" discovery, expressed his admiration for Blainville. Among Blainville's theoretical writings are *L'Harmonie théorico-pratique* (1746); *Essai sur un troisième mode* (1751), expounding the supposed "mode hellénique"); *L'Esprit de l'art musical* (1754); and *Histoire générale, critique et philologique de la musique* (1767). He composed 5 symphonies, publ. a book of sonatas "pour le dessus de viole avec la basse continue," and arranged Tartini's sonatas in the form of concerti grossi.

Blamont, François Colin de, French composer; b. Versailles, Nov. 22, 1690; d. there, Feb. 14, 1760. He was a pupil of Lalande; became superintendent of the King's music; wrote many court ballets, cantatas and motets; published an *Essai sur les goûts anciens et modernes de la musique française* (1754).

Blanc, Adolphe, French composer; b. Manosque, Basses-Alpes, June 24, 1828; d. Paris, May 1885. He studied at the Paris Cons. and privately with Halévy; for a short time he was conductor at the Théâtre-Lyrique. In 1862 he was awarded the Prix Chartier for chamber music. He wrote a 1-act comic opera, *Une Aventure sous la Ligue* (1857); 2 operettas, *Les deux billets* (1868) and *Les Rêves de Marguerite;* a burlesque symphony; an overture; trios, quartets, quintets and septets for strings, with and without piano; piano pieces.

Blanc, Giuseppe, Italian song composer; b. Bardonecchia, April 11, 1886; d. Santa Margherita Ligure, Dec. 7, 1969. He studied composition with Bolzoni; produced a number of comic operas, among them *La festa dei fiori* (Rome, Jan. 29, 1913). His only claim to fame is that he was the author of the song *Giovinezza*, which was adopted ex post facto by Mussolini as the national Fascist anthem.

Blancafort, Manuel, Spanish composer; b. Barcelona, Aug. 12, 1897. He studied in Barcelona with Lamote de Grignon. In his music he cultivates national Catalan subjects while adhering to the impressionistic idiom set in neo-classical forms. He wrote *Sardana sinfónica* for orch. (1951); *Rapsòdia Catalana* for cello and orch. (1953); symph. suite, *Evocaciones* (1969); and a number of piano pieces of a descriptive character (*Le Parc d'attractions, Chants intimes, Pastorale, Chemins,* etc.).

Blanchard, Henri-Louis, French musician; b. Bordeaux, Feb. 7, 1778; d. Paris, Dec. 18, 1858. He studied the violin; was conductor at the Théâtre des Variétés in Paris (1818–29); wrote music criticism; produced several operettas.

Blanchet, Emile R., Swiss pianist and composer; b. Lausanne, July 17, 1877; d. Pully, March 27, 1943. He studied with his father Charles Blanchet (1833-1900); with Seiss, Franke and Strässer at the Cologne Cons.; and with Busoni in Weimar and Berlin. From 1904–17 he was teacher of piano at the Lausanne Cons. Among his works are *64 Preludes for Pianoforte in Contrapuntal Style*, a valuable pedagogic work; *Konzertstück* for piano and orch.; Violin Sonata; Ballade for 2 pianos; many etudes and other piano works; songs; etc.

Blanck, Hubert de, conductor and educator; b. Utrecht, June 11, 1856; d. Havana, Nov. 28, 1932. He studied at the Liège Cons. with Ledent (piano) and Dupuy (comp.); subsequently served as theater conductor in Warsaw (1875); toured Europe as a pianist;

visited South America with the violinist E. Dengremont (1880). After teaching at the N.Y. College of Music, he settled in Havana (1883) and founded the first conservatory in Cuba, based upon European models (1885), He was exiled in 1896 for participation in the revolution; after the re-establishment of peace, he reopened his school in Havana and established branches in other towns. He composed piano pieces and songs, but it is as an enlightened educator that he is honored in the annals of Cuban music.

Blanco, Juan, Cuban composer; b. Havana, June 29, 1920. He studied composition with José Ardévol; after a period of writing in traditional forms he devoted himself to experimentation, making use of electronic devices with purposive spatial arrangement. In this manner he constructed *Texturas* for orch. and tape (1964); 4 sets of *Contrapunto espacial,* for different groups distributed through the area of performance (1965–70); *Vietnam,* soundlike composition (1968).

Bland, James A., black American song composer; b. Flushing, N.Y., Oct. 22, 1854; d. Philadelphia, May 5, 1911. He learned to play the banjo and joined a minstrel troupe, improvising songs in the manner of Negro spirituals. His most famous ballad, *Carry Me Back to Old Virginny,* was publ. in 1878; in 1940 it was designated the official song of the state of Virginia. From 1881 to 1901 Bland lived in England, enjoying excellent success as an entertainer, including a command performance for Queen Victoria, but he dissipated his savings and died in abject poverty.
BIBLIOGRAPHY: E. Southern, *The Music of Black Americans* (New York, 1971).

Blangini, Giuseppe Marco Maria Felice, Italian composer; b. Turin, Nov. 18, 1781; d. Paris, Dec. 18, 1841. He was choirboy at the Turin cathedral; in 1799, his family moved to Paris, where he gave concerts, wrote fashionable *romances,* and came into vogue as an opera composer when he completed Della-Maria's opera *La fausse duègne* (1802); he was also popular as a singing teacher. After producing an opera in Munich, he was appointed court Kapellmeister (1806); later was General Music Director at Kassel (1809); and upon his return to Paris in 1814, was made superintendent of the King's music, Court composer, and prof. of singing at the Cons., positions which he held until 1830.
WORKS: 30 operas; 4 Masses with orch.; 170 nocturnes for 2 voices; 174 *romances* for one voice; etc. See his autobiography, *Souvenirs de F. Blangini,* ed. by M. de Villemarest (Paris, 1834).

Blankenburg, Quirin van, Dutch organist; b. Gouda, 1654; d. The Hague, May 12, 1739. He was organist of the Reformed Church in The Hague; wrote *Elementa musica* (1729), and *Clavicembel en Orgelboek der gereformeerde Psalmen en Kerkgezangen* (1732; 3rd edition, 1772); also a method for flute.

Blanter, Matvey, Russian composer of popular songs; b. Potchep, Tchernigov district, Feb. 10, 1903. He studied in Moscow with G. Conius; then devoted himself exclusively to the composition of light music. He wrote an operetta *On the Banks of the Amur* (1939) and some incidental music. Among his songs the most popular is *Katyusha* (famous during World War II), which combines the melodic inflection of the typical urban ballad with the basic traits of a Russian folk song. Blanter is regarded in Russia as a creator of the new Soviet song style.
BIBLIOGRAPHY: V. Zak, *Matvej Blanter* (Moscow, 1971).

Blaramberg, Pavel, Russian composer; b. Orenburg, Sept. 26, 1841; d. Nice, March 28, 1907. His father was a geographer, of French origin; his mother was Greek. At the age of 14 he went to St. Petersburg; later became a functionary of the Central Statistical Committee there. He was largely self-taught in music, apart from occasional advice from Balakirev and Rimsky-Korsakov. In 1878 he settled in Moscow as instructor at the newly founded Philharmonic Institute. In 1898 he went to the Crimea, then to France.
WORKS: the operas *The Mummers* (1881); *Russalka* (Moscow, April 15, 1888); *Maria Tudor,* after Hugo (produced as *Mary of Burgundy* on account of the censor's objection to the original libretto; Moscow, Oct. 29, 1888); *Tushintsy* (Moscow, Feb. 5, 1895; his most successful opera; had several revivals); and *The Waves* (1902). He also wrote a symphonic poem *The Dying Gladiator* (1882), a symphony (1886), and songs.

Blaserna, Pietro, Italian music theorist; b. Fiumicello, near Aquileja, Feb. 29, 1836; d. Rome, Feb. 26, 1918. He studied natural sciences in Vienna and Paris; later taught physics at the Univs. of Palermo (1863) and Rome (1872). An exponent of the acoustic purity of intervals, he made important scientific contributions in the field of acoustics. His principal work is *La teoria del suono nei suoi rapporti colla musica* (1875).

Blasius, Mathieu-Frédéric, French composer; b. Lauterburg, Alsace, April 23, 1758; d. Versailles, 1829. He was a violinist, clarinetist, flutist and bassoonist; taught wind instruments at the Paris Cons. (1795–1802); conducted at the Opéra-Comique (1802–16). He wrote 3 operas; 3 violin concertos; many popular pieces for wind instruments in various combinations.

Blatný, Josef, Czech organist and composer, father of **Pavel Blatný;** b. Brno, March 19, 1891. He studied composition with Janáček at the Brno Organ School (1909–12); then served as his assistant; subsequently became prof. of organ at the Brno Cons., where he taught for 28 years (1928–56).
WORKS: *Sinfonia brevis* for string orch. (1957); 2 Symphonic Dances (1959); chamber symphony (1961); an oratorio, *Lotr na pravici* (*The Thief on the Right,* 1953); 3 violin sonatas (1926, 1957, 1968); 3 string quartets (1929, 1954, 1962); Suite for 2 Flutes, Clarinet and Bassoon (1947); Piano Trio (1950); Piano Quartet (1968); Piano Sonata (1960); many organ pieces; songs.

Blatný, Pavel, Czech composer and conductor, son of **Josef Blatný;** b. Brno, Sept. 14, 1931. He began his musical studies with his father; then studied piano and music theory at the Brno Cons. (1950–55) and musicology at the Univ. of Brno (1954–58); also took composition lessons with Bořkovec at the Prague Academy of Music (1955–59); attended summer courses of new music at Darmstadt (1965–69); in 1968 traveled to the U.S. and took lessons in jazz piano and composition at the Berkeley School in Boston. He became an exceedingly active musician in Czechoslovakia; wrote about 600 works, some of them paralleling the development of "third-stream music" initiated in the U.S. by Gunther Schuller, which constitutes a fusion of jazz and classical forms; played something like 2,000 piano recitals in programs of modern music; conducted a great many concerts and participated in programs of the Czech Radio; in 1971 he was appointed chief of the music division of the television station in Brno.

Works: *Per orchestra sintetica I* for jazz band and wind ensemble (1960); *Per orchestra sintetica II* for jazz band and orch. (1971); *Study* for ¼-tone trumpet and jazz orch. (1964); *Tre per S + H* for jazz septet (1964); *Dialogue* for soprano saxophone and jazz band (1959–64); *Geschichte I* for jazz nonet (1968); *Geschichte II* for jazz septet (1969); *In Modo classico* for string quartet and jazz orch. (1973); *In Modo archaico* for piano and jazz orch. (1976); a children's opera *Domeček* (*Little House*, 1959); opera *Fairy-tales of the Woods* (1976); several musicals; *Kaleidoscope* for orch. (1970); *Continuum pro continuum* for chamber orch. (1973); cantata, *Allende*, dedicated to the memory of the democratic president of Chile (1974); a dozen suites for various instruments with piano; *2:3* for wind quintet (1973); *Discussion* for violin, accordion and guitar (1973); pieces for solo piano, 2 pianos and 4 pianos.

Blauvelt, Lillian Evans, American soprano; b. Brooklyn, N.Y., March 16, 1874; d. Chicago, Aug. 29, 1947. After studying violin for several years she took vocal lessons in N.Y. and Paris; gave concerts in France, Belgium and Russia; made her operatic debut at Brussels (1893); sang before Queen Victoria (1899); sang the coronation ode and received the coronation medal from King Edward (1902); appeared for several seasons at Covent Garden. She married the composer Alexander Savine, in 1914; created the title role in his opera *Xenia* (Zürich, 1919).

Blaze (called **Castil-Blaze**), **François-Henri-Joseph,** French writer on music; b. Cavaillon, Vaucluse, Dec. 1, 1784; d. Paris, Dec. 11, 1857. He studied with his father, a lawyer and amateur musician; went to Paris in 1799 as a law student; held various administrative posts in provincial towns in France. At the same time he studied music and compiled information on the opera in France. The fruit of this work was the publication in 2 volumes of his book *De l'opéra en France* (Paris, 1820; 1826). He became music critic of the influential Paris *Journal des Débats* in 1822, signing his articles 'XXX.' He resigned from this post in 1832 but continued to publish books on music, including valuable compilations of musical lexicography: *Dictionnaire de musique moderne* (1821, 2 vols.; 2nd ed., 1825; 3rd ed., edited by J. H. Mees, with historical

preface and a supplement on Netherlands musicians, 1828, in 1 vol.); *Chapelle-musique des Rois de France* (1832); *La Danse et les Ballets depuis Bacchus jusqu' à Mlle. Taglioni* (1832); *Mémorial du Grand Opéra* (from Cambert, 1669, down to the Restoration); "Le Piano; histoire de son invention," *Revue de Paris* (1839–40); *Molière musicien* (1852); *Théâtres lyriques de Paris,* 2 vols., on the Grand Opéra (1855), and on the Italian opera (1856); *Sur l'opéra français; vérités dures mais utiles* (1856); *L'Art des jeux lyriques* (1858); translated into French many libretti of German and Italian operas. He himself wrote 3 operas; compiled a collection of *Chants de Provence;* some of his popular ballads attained considerable popularity.

Blaze, Henri, Baron de Bury, French music critic; son of **François Blaze;** b. Avignon, May 17, 1813; d. Paris, March 15, 1888. He wrote many essays for the *Revue des Deux Mondes* and other periodicals; these essays were subsequently collected as *Musiciens contemporains* (1856); *Meyerbeer et son temps* (1865); *Musiciens du passé, du présent, etc.* (1880); *Goethe et Beethoven* (1882); his most valuable book is *La Vie de Rossini* (1854).

Blažek, Zdeněk, Czech composer; b. Žarošice, May 24, 1905. He studied composition with Petrželka at the Brno Cons. (1924–29) and with Suk at the Prague Cons. (1933–35); became a prof. at the Brno Cons. in 1941 and was its director from 1947 to 1957; in 1961 was appointed to the staff of the Univ. of Brno.

Works: an opera, *Verchovina,* (*The Highlands,* 1950–51; Brno, 1956); Suite for string orch. (1934); *Funereal Music* for strings, 2 harps, gong and timpani (1968); Divertimento for string orch. (1971); the cantatas, *Song of My Native Land* (1938), *Ode to Poverty* (1958) and *Home* (1962); Piano Trio (1929); 5 string quartets (1943, 1946–47, 1956, 1967, 1969); *Divertimento* for woodwind quartet (1946); String Quintet (1949); *Sonatina giocosa* for clarinet and piano (1949); *4 Romantic Compositions* for horn and piano (1952); *Music at Home* for string trio (1953); *4 Romantic Compositions* for violin and piano (1953–54); Bassoon Sonatina (1958); *Sonatina balladica* for cello and piano (1962); Horn Sonata (1964); Wind Quintet (1971); choruses; songs.

Blazhkov, Igor, Ukrainian conductor and music scholar; b. Kiev, Sept. 23, 1936. He studied at the Kiev Cons., graduating in 1959; appeared as guest conductor in Moscow and Leningrad, specializing in modern music, including American works. From 1958 to 1962 he was assistant conductor of the Ukrainian State Orchestra in Kiev.

Blech, Leo, eminent German opera conductor and composer; b. Aachen, April 21, 1871; d. Berlin, Aug. 24, 1958. After leaving school he tried a mercantile career; then studied briefly at the Hochschule für Musik in Berlin; returned to Aachen to conduct at the Municipal Theater (1893–99); also took summer courses in composition with Humperdinck (1893–96). He was engaged as opera conductor in Prague (1899–1906); at the Berlin Opera from 1906 to 1923, and again from 1926 until 1936. He conducted in Riga

(1938–41) and in Stockholm (1941–49). In 1949 he returned to Berlin, and soon retired.

WORKS: the operas *Aglaja* (1893) and *Cherubina* (1894); "opera-idyl" *Das war ich* (Dresden, Oct. 6, 1902; his most successful stage work); *Alpenkönig und Menschenfeind* (Dresden, Oct. 1, 1903, rewritten and produced as *Rappelkopf* at the Royal Opera, Berlin, in 1917); opera *Aschenbrödel* (Prague, 1905); short opera *Versiegelt* (Hamburg, 1908; N.Y., 1912); an operetta *Die Strohwitwe* (Hamburg, 1920); 3 symphonic poems, *Die Nonne, Waldwanderung, Trost in der Natur;* choruses, songs, piano pieces; *10 Kleinigkeiten* for piano 4 hands; music for children, etc. His music is in the Wagnerian tradition; his knowledge and understanding of instrumental and vocal resources enabled him to produce highly effective works.

BIBLIOGRAPHY: E. Rychnowsky, *Leo Blech* (Prague, 1905); id., *Leo Blech,* in vol. III of *Monographien moderner Musiker* (Leipzig, 1909); W. Jacob, *Leo Blech* (1931).

Bledsoe, Jules, black American baritone and composer; b. Waco, Texas, Dec. 29, 1898; d. Hollywood, July 14, 1943. He studied at the Chicago Mus. College (B.A., 1919); then went to Europe where he took singing lessons in Paris and Rome. Returning to America he distinguished himself as a fine performer in musical comedies and opera. He sang the central role in the premiere of Jerome Kern's *Show Boat* (1927), appeared in grand opera as Rigoletto and Boris and sang the title role in Gruenberg's opera *Emperor Jones.* As a composer, he wrote an *African Suite* for orch. and several songs in the manner of Negro spirituals.

Blegen, Judith, American soprano; b. Missoula, Montana, April 23, 1941. She received her musical training, in violin as well as singing, at the Curtis Institute in Philadelphia (1959–64). In 1962 she won the Philadelphia Award entitling her to appear with the Philadelphia Orch.; she made her concert debut with it in 1963. In 1964 she won a Fulbright Fellowship, and also sang at the Spoleto Festival; subsequently studied voice with Luigi Ricci in Italy. From 1963 to 1966 she was a member of the Nuremberg Opera; in 1968 she made her debut at the Vienna State Opera, singing Rosina in *The Barber of Seville.* On Aug. 1, 1969, she sang at the Santa Fe Opera in the role of Emily in the American premiere of Menotti's satirical opera *Help! Help! the Globolinks!* (a role specially written for her). She made her Metropolitan Opera debut on Jan. 19, 1970 in New York as Papagena in *The Magic Flute,* and has since been one of the principal sopranos of the Metropolitan Opera in such a variety of roles as Marzelline *(Fidelio),* Zerlina *(Don Giovanni),* Sophie *(Der Rosenkavalier),* and Mélisande. She sang Susanna in *The Marriage of Figaro* with the San Francisco Opera in 1972; made her appearance at the Salzburg Festival in 1974; sang at the Edinburgh Festival in 1976 and also at the Paris Opera in 1977.

Bleichmann, Yuly, Russian composer; b. St. Petersburg, Dec. 6, 1868; d. there, Jan. 8, 1910. He studied with Rimsky-Korsakov at the St. Petersburg Cons.; later with Jadassohn and Reinecke in Leipzig. Returning to St. Petersburg, he founded the Popular Symphony Concerts in 1893; also conducted the Philharmonic Symphony Concerts. He composed 2 operas, greatly influenced by Wagner: *St. Sebastian* and *The Dream-Princess* (Moscow, Oct. 23, 1900); also songs.

Blessinger, Karl, German musicologist; b. Ulm, Sept. 21, 1888; d. Pullach, near Munich, March 13, 1962. He studied in Heidelberg and Munich; was theater conductor in Bremen and Bonn; was on the staff of the Akademie der Tonkunst in Munich (1920–45).

WRITINGS: *Ulmer Musikgeschichte im 17. Jahrhundert* (dissertation; Ulm, 1913); *Die musikalischen Probleme der Gegenwart* (1920); *Die Überwindung der musikalischen Impotenz* (1920); *Grundzüge der musikalischen Formenlehre* (1926); *Melodielehre als Einführung in die Musiktheorie* (1930); *Mendelssohn, Meyerbeer, Mahler* (1938); *Judentum und Musik; Ein Beitrag zur Kultur- und Rassenpolitik* (Berlin, 1944; a "scientific" apologia for the anti-Semitic policy of the Nazi regime).

Blewitt, Jonathan, English composer; b. London, July 19, 1782; d. there, Sept. 4, 1853. He studied with his father, and with Battishill; was organist in several churches; served as conductor at the Theatre Royal in Dublin. Returning to London (1825), he was appointed music director at Sadler's Wells Theatre. He composed many popular ballads; was the author of a treatise on singing, *The Vocal Assistant.*

Bleyle, Karl, German composer; b. Feldkirch, Vorarlberg, May 7, 1880; d. Stuttgart, June 5, 1969. He studied with Wehrle (violin) and S. de Lange (comp.) in Stuttgart and with Thuille (comp.) in Munich. He was active as teacher and theater conductor in Graz, Weimar and Munich; in 1923 returned to Stuttgart.

WORKS: 2 operas, *Hannele und Sannele* (Stuttgart, 1923) and *Der Teufelssteg* (Rostock, 1924); many works for soli, chorus and orch. (*An den Mistral, Lernt Lachen, Mignons Beisetzung, Heilige Sendung, Die Höllenfahrt Christi, Ein Harfenklang, Prometheus, Trilogie der Leidenschaft, Requiem,* etc.); orchestral pieces *Flagellantenzug, Gnomentanz, Siegesouverture, Reinecke Fuchs, Legende;* a symphony; violin concerto; string quartet; violin sonata; songs; piano pieces; etc.

Blind Tom. See **Bethune, Thomas Greene.**

Bliss, Sir Arthur (Edward Drummond), eminent English composer; b. London, Aug. 2, 1891; d. there, March 27, 1975. He studied at Pembroke College, Cambridge; then at the Royal College of Music in London with Stanford, Vaughan Williams and Holst. He was an officer of the British Army during World War I; was wounded in 1916, and gassed in 1918. Returning to England after the war, he resumed his musical studies; his earliest works, *Madam Noy,* for soprano and 6 instruments (1918) and *Rout,* for soprano and chamber orch. (1919; Salzburg Festival, Aug. 7, 1922) were highly successful, and established Bliss as one of the most brilliant composers in the modern style. From 1923–25, Bliss was in the U.S.; on a later visit, lived in Hollywood, where he wrote the musical score for the motion picture *Things to Come,* after H. G.

Wells (1935). He returned to London; during World War II he was Musical Director of the BBC (1942–44); knighted in 1950; named Master of the Queen's Musick in 1953 as successor to Sir Arnold Bax.

WORKS: OPERAS: *The Olympians* (London, Sept. 29, 1949); *Tobias and the Angel* (London, BBC, May 19, 1960). Ballets, *Checkmate* (Paris, June 15, 1937); *Miracle in the Gorbals* (London, Oct. 26, 1944); *Adam Zero* (London, April 8, 1946); *The Lady of Shalott* (Berkeley, Cal., May 2, 1958).

FOR ORCH.: *Mélée fantasque* (1920); *Colour Symphony* (the title refers to 4 heraldic colors: purple, red, blue and green; 1st perf., Gloucester, Sept. 7, 1922 under the composer's direction); Concerto for 2 Pianos and Orch. (1924); *Hymn to Apollo* (1926); *Music for Strings* (1935); Piano Concerto (commissioned by the British Council for the British Week at the N.Y. World's Fair, dedicated "to the people of the United States of America"; N.Y., June 10, 1939); Violin Concerto (London, May 11, 1955). Vocal Music: *Madam Noy* (1918); *Rout* (1919); *Rhapsody* for soprano, tenor, flute, English horn, string quartet and double bass (1919; Salzburg Festival, Aug. 5, 1923); *2 Nursery Rhymes* for soprano, clarinet and piano (1921); *The Women of Yueh,* song cycle for soprano and small orch. (1923); *Pastoral* for mezzo-soprano, chorus, strings, flute and drums (1928); *Serenade* for baritone and orch. (1929); *Morning Heroes* (symphony in 6 movements for chorus, orator and orch., dedicated to his brother killed in action; 1st perf., Norwich, Oct. 22, 1930); *The Enchantress* for contralto and orch. (1951); *A Song of Welcome* for soprano, baritone, chorus and orch., composed for the return of Queen Elizabeth II from her Australian voyage (1st perf., London, July 29, 1954); *Discourse* for orch. (Louisville, Oct. 23, 1957); Cello Concerto (Aldeburgh Festival; June 24, 1970, Rostropovich soloist); *Variations* for orch. (London, April 21, 1973, Stokowski conducting); several song cycles (*3 Romantic Songs; The Ballads of the Four Seasons; 7 American Poems*). CHAMBER MUSIC: *Conversations* for violin, viola, cello, flute and oboe, in 5 movements (1919; a humorous work); 3 string quartets (1924; 1941; 1950); Quintet for Oboe and Strings (1927; Vienna Festival, June 21, 1932); Quintet for Clarinet and Strings (1931); Viola Sonata (1932); piano pieces.

BIBLIOGRAPHY: autobiography, *As I Remember* (London, 1970); Percy A. Scholes, *Notes on a Colour Symphony* (London, 1922); Alan Frank, *Arthur Bliss* (London, 1953).

Bliss, P. Paul, American organist and music editor; b. Chicago, Nov. 25, 1872; d. Oswego, N.Y., Feb. 2, 1933. He studied in Philadelphia; then went to Paris where he was a pupil of Guilmant (organ) and Massenet (comp.). Returning to America he was active as organist in Oswego, N.Y.; served as music director with the John Church Co. (1904–10) and the Willis Music Co. (from 1911). He composed 3 operettas, *Feast of Little Lanterns, Feast of Red Corn, In India;* cantatas, *Pan on a Summer Day, Three Springs, The Mound-Builders;* piano suite, *In October;* many songs and choruses; also compiled a *Graded Course for Piano* (4 vols.)

Bliss, Philip Paul, American hymn writer; b. in a log cabin in the woods of Clearfield County, Pennsylvania, July 9, 1838; d. in a train wreck near Ashtabula, Ohio, Dec. 29, 1876. He was an itinerant minstrel, traveling with a mechanical melodeon and an old horse. In 1864 he settled in Chicago, taught singing, and did some preaching. He publ. *Gospel Songs* (1874) and *Gospel Hymns* (1875), both highly successful.

BIBLIOGRAPHY: R. G. McCutchan, *Our Hymnody* (N.Y., 1937).

Blitzstein, Marc, significant American composer; b. Philadelphia, March 2, 1905; d. Fort-de-France, Martinique, Jan. 22, 1964, from a brain injury sustained after a political altercation with a group of men in a bar. He studied piano and organ in Pennsylvania; composition with Scalero at the Curtis Institute, in Philadelphia; also took piano lessons with Siloti in New York. In 1926 he went to Europe where he took courses with Nadia Boulanger in Paris and Schoenberg in Berlin. Returning to America, he devoted himself chiefly to the cultivation of theatrical works of "social consciousness" of the type created in Germany by Bertolt Brecht and Kurt Weill; accordingly he wrote his stage works for performances in small theaters of the cabaret type. In 1940 he received a Guggenheim Fellowship; during World War II he was stationed in England with the U.S. Armed Forces. His theater works include *Triple Sec*, opera-farce (Philadelphia, May 6, 1929); *Parabola and Circula*, 1-act opera-ballet (1929); *Cain*, ballet (1930); *The Harpies*, musical satire commissioned by the League of Composers (1931; 1st production, Manhattan School of Music, N.Y., May 25, 1953); *The Cradle Will Rock*, 1-act opera of "social significance" (N.Y., June 16, 1937, with the composer at the piano); *No For An Answer*, short opera (N.Y., Jan. 5, 1941); the musical play, *I've Got the Tune* (CBS radio, Oct. 24, 1937); also musical revues, one of which, *Regina*, to Lillian Hellman's play *The Little Foxes*, was expanded into a full-fledged opera (Boston, Oct. 11, 1949). Shortly before his death the Ford Foundation commissioned Blitzstein to write an opera on the subject of Sacco and Vanzetti, for production by the Metropolitan Opera House, but the work remained unfinished. Blitzstein further composed *Gods* for mezzo-soprano and string orch. (1926); oratorio, *The Condemned* (1930); *Airborne Symphony* (N.Y., March 23, 1946); *Cantatina* for women's voices and percussion; *Jig-Saw*, ballet-suite (1927); *Romantic Piece* for orch. (1930); Piano Concerto (1931); *Freedom Morning*, symph. poem (London, Sept. 28, 1943); String Quartet; *Percussion Music for Piano* (1929); many other piano pieces. Blitzstein translated Kurt Weill's *Three-Penny Opera* into American (1954), and his version scored great success.

BIBLIOGRAPHY: Henry Brant, "Marc Blitzstein," *Modern Music* (July 1946); *Composers of America*, vol. 5, Washington, 1959; W. Mellers, *Music in a New Found Land* (N.Y., 1967), pp. 414–28.

Bloch, André, French composer; b. Wissembourg, Alsace, Jan. 18, 1873; d. Paris, Aug. 7, 1960. He studied at the Paris Cons. with Guiraud and Massenet; received Premier Grand Prix de Rome in 1893. He was conductor of the orchestra of the American Cons. at

Fontainebleau. His works include the operas *Maida* (1909); *Une Nuit de Noël* (1922); *Broceliande* (1925); *Guignol* (1949); the ballet *Feminaland* (1904); the symphonic poems *Kaa* (1933) and *L'Isba nostaligique* (1945); *Les Maisons de l'éternité* for cello and orch. (1930); *Concerto-Ballet* for piano and orch. (1946); *Suite palestinienne* for cello and orch. (his most successful instrumental work; Paris, Nov. 14, 1948).

Bloch, Augustyn, Polish composer and organist; b. Grudziadz, Aug. 13, 1929. He studied composition with Szeligowski, and organ at the Warsaw State College of Music (1950–58); then was employed at the Polish State Radio as music editor. In his compositions he follows the neo-Romantic trend of modern Polish music.

WORKS: a one-act opera-mystery, *Ayelet, Jephta's Daughter* (Katowice, 1967); children's opera-pantomime, *The Sleeping Princess* (Warsaw, Sept. 29, 1974); 5 ballets: *Voci* (Warsaw television, 1967), *Oczekiwanie* (*The Awaiting,* Warsaw, 1964), *Byk* (*The Bull,* 1965; Holland Festival, Amsterdam, June 24, 1965), *Gilgamesh* (1968); *The Looking Glass,* for tape (1975); Concertino for violin, string orch., piano and percussion (1958); *Meditations* for soprano, organ and percussion (1961); *Télégramme* for children's chorus, 2 pianos and percussion (1963); *Dialogues* for violin and orch. (1963); *Enfiando* for orch. (1970); *Salmo gioioso* for soprano and 5 wind instruments (1970); *Warsaw* for narrator, chorus and orch. (1974); *Wordsworth Songs* for baritone and chamber ensemble (Warsaw, Sept. 23, 1976); *Clarinetto divertente* for solo clarinet (1976); piano pieces; songs.

Bloch, Ernest, remarkable Swiss-born American composer of Jewish ancestry; b. Geneva, July 24, 1880; d. Portland, Oregon, July 15, 1959. He studied solfeggio with Jaques-Dalcroze and violin with Louis Rey in Geneva (1894–97); then went to Brussels, where he took violin lessons with Ysaÿe and composition with Rasse (1897–99); while a student he had already written a string quartet and a "symphonie orientale" indicative of his natural attraction to non-European cultures and coloristic melos. In 1900 he went to Germany, where he studied music theory with Iwan Knorr at the Hoch Cons. in Frankfurt and took private lessons with Ludwig Thuille in Munich; there he began the composition of his first full-fledged symphony, in C-sharp minor, with its 4 movements originally bearing titles expressive of changing moods. He then spent a year in Paris where he met Debussy; Bloch's first published work, *Historiettes au crépuscule* (1903), shows Debussy's influence. In 1904 he returned to Geneva, where he began the composition of his only opera, *Macbeth,* after Shakespeare; the project of another opera, *Jézabel,* on a biblical subject, never materialized beyond a few initial sketches. As a tribute to his homeland, he outlined the orchestral work *Helvetia,* based on Swiss motives, as early as 1900, but the full score was not completed until 1928. During the season 1909–10 Bloch conducted symphonic concerts in Lausanne and Neuchâtel. In 1916 he was offered an engagement as conductor on an American tour accompanying the dancer Maud Allan; he gladly accepted the opportunity to leave war-torn Europe, and expressed an almost childlike delight upon docking in the port of New York at the sight of the Statue of Liberty. Maud Allan's tour was not successful, however, and Bloch returned to Geneva; in 1917 he received an offer to teach at the David Mannes School of Music in New York, and once more he sailed for America; he became an American citizen in 1924. This was also the period when Bloch began to express himself in music as an inheritor of Jewish culture; he explicitly articulated his racial consciousness in several verbal statements. His *Israel Symphony, Trois poèmes juifs* and the "Hebrew rhapsody" for cello and orch., *Schelomo,* mark the height of Bloch's greatness as a Jewish composer; long after his death *Schelomo* still retains its popularity at symphony concerts. In America, he found sincere admirers and formed a group of greatly talented students, among them Roger Sessions, Ernst Bacon, George Antheil, Douglas Moore, Bernard Rogers, Randall Thompson, Quincy Porter, Halsey Stevens, Herbert Elwell, Isadore Freed, Frederick Jacobi and Leon Kirchner. From 1920 to 1925 he was director of the Institute of Music in Cleveland, and from 1925 to 1930, director of the San Francisco Cons. When the magazine *Musical America* announced in 1927 a contest for a symphonic work, Bloch won the first prize for his "epic rhapsody" entitled simply *America;* Bloch fondly hoped that the choral ending extolling America as the ideal of humanity would become a national hymn; the work was performed with a great outpouring of publicity in 5 cities, but as it happens often with prize-winning works, it failed to strike the critics and the audiences as truly great, and in the end remained a mere by-product of Bloch's genius. From 1930 to 1939 Bloch lived mostly in Switzerland; then returned to the U.S. and taught classes at the Univ. of California, Berkeley (1940–52); finally retired and lived at his newly purchased house at Agate Beach, Oregon. In his harmonic idiom Bloch favored sonorities formed by the bitonal relationship of two major triads with the tonics standing at the distance of a tritone, but even the dissonances he employed were euphonious. In his last works of chamber music he experimented for the first time with thematic statements of 12 different notes, but he never adopted the strict Schoenbergian technique of deriving the entire contents of a composition from the basic tone row. In his early Piano Quintet, Bloch made expressive use of quarter-tones in the string parts. In his racially Jewish works, he emphasized the interval of the augmented second, without a literal imitation of Hebrew chants.

WORKS: opera, *Macbeth* (1904-09; Opéra-Comique, Paris, Nov. 30, 1910).

FOR ORCH.: *Poèmes d'automne,* songs for mezzo-soprano and orch. (1906); Prelude and 2 Psalms (Nos. 114 and 137) for soprano and orch. (1912-14); *Vivre-aimer,* symph. poem (1900; Geneva, June 23, 1901); Symphony in C-sharp minor (1901; 1st complete performance, Geneva, 1910; 1st American performance, N.Y. Philharmonic, May 8, 1918, composer conducting); *Hiver-printemps,* symph. poem (1904-05; Geneva, Jan. 27, 1906); *Trois poèmes juifs* (1913; Boston, composer conducting, March 23, 1917); *Israel,* symphony (1912-16; N.Y., May 3, 1917, composer conducting); *Schelomo,* Hebrew rhapsody for cello and orch. (1916; N.Y., May 3, 1917, composer conducting); Concerto Grosso No. 1 for strings and piano (1924–25; Cleveland, June 1, 1925, composer conducting); *America,* symph. poem (1926; N.Y., Dec. 20, 1928; next day simultaneously in Chicago, Philadelphia, Boston and San Francisco); *Helvetia,* symph. poem (1928; Rome, Jan. 22, 1933); *Voice in the Wilderness,* with cello obbligato (1936; Los Angeles, Jan. 21, 1937); *Evocations,* symph. suite (1937; San Francisco, Feb. 11, 1938); Violin Concerto (1938; 1st perf. by Szigeti, Cleveland, Dec. 15, 1938); *Suite symphonique* (Philadelphia, Oct. 26, 1945); *Concerto symphonique* for piano and orch. (Edinburgh, Sept. 3, 1949); *Scherzo fantasque* for piano and orch. (Chicago, Dec. 2, 1950); *In Memoriam* (1952); *Suite hebraïque* for viola and orch. (Chicago, Jan. 1, 1953); *Sinfonia breve* (BBC, London, April 11, 1953); Concerto Grosso No. 2 for string orch. (BBC, London, April 11, 1953); Symphony for Trombone Solo and Orch. (1953–54; Houston, Texas, April 4, 1956); Symphony in E-flat (1954–55; London, Feb. 15, 1956); *Proclamation* for trumpet and orch. (1955). CHAMBER MUSIC: *4 Episodes* for chamber orch. (1926); Quintet for Piano and Strings, with use of quarter-tones (1923, N.Y., Nov. 11, 1923); 1st String Quartet (N.Y., Dec. 29, 1916); 2 Suites for String Quartet (1925); 3 Nocturnes for Piano Trio (1924); Suite for Viola and Piano (won the Coolidge prize, 1919); 1st Violin Sonata (1920); 2nd Violin Sonata, *Poème mystique* (1924); *Baal Shem,* for violin and piano (1923); *Méditation hébraïque* and *From Jewish LIfe,* for cello and piano (1925); Piano Sonata (1935); 2nd String Quartet (1946; received the N.Y. Music Critics Circle Award for chamber music, 1947); 3rd String Quartet (1951); 4th String Quartet (1953); 5th String Quartet (1956); 3 Suites for Cello Unaccompanied (1956); Piano Quintet No. 2 (1956); *Suite Modale* for flute solo and strings (1957; Kentfield, Calif., April 11, 1965); 2 Suites for Unaccompanied Violin, (1958); Suite for Unaccompanied Viola (1958; the last movement incomplete); *2 Last Poems* for flute and chamber orch.: 1. *Funeral Music;* 2. *Life Again?* (1958; anticipatory of death from terminal cancer). PIANO MUSIC: *Poems of the Sea, In the Night, Nirvana, Five Sketches in Sepia.* FOR VOICES: a modern Hebrew ritual *Sacred Service* (1930–33; world première, Turin, Italy, Jan. 12, 1934); *Historiettes au crépuscule,* 4 songs for mezzo-soprano and piano (1903). Bloch contributed a number of informative annotations for the program books of the Boston Symphony, N.Y. Philharmonic and other orchestras; also contributed articles to music journals, among them "Man and Music" in the *Musical Quarterly* (Oct. 1933). An Ernest Bloch Society was formed in London in 1937 with the objective of promoting performances of Bloch's music, with Albert Einstein as honorary president and with vice-presidents including Sir Thomas Beecham, Havelock Ellis and Romain Rolland.

BIBLIOGRAPHY: Paul Rosenfeld, in *Musical Portraits* (N.Y., 1920); G. M. Gatti, "Ernest Bloch," *Musical Quarterly* (1921); Roger Sessions, "Ernest Bloch," *Modern Music* (1927); R. Stackpole, "Ernest Bloch," *Modern Music* (1927); Mary Tibaldi Chiesa, *Bibliografia delle opere musicali di Ernest Bloch* (Turin, 1931); M. T. Chiesa, *Ernest Bloch* (Turin, 1933); Dika Newlin, "The Later Works of Ernest Bloch," *Musical*

Quarterly (Oct. 1947); Henry Cowell, "Current Chronicle," *Musical Quarterly* (1954); D. Z. Kushner, "A Commentary on Ernest Bloch's Symphonic Works," *Radford Review* (Summer 1967); W. M. Jones, "Ernest Bloch's Five String Quartets," *Music Review* (May 1967); M. Griffel, "Bibliography of Writings on Ernest Bloch," *Current Musicology 6* (1968); D. Z. Kushner, "Catalogue of the Works of Ernest Bloch," *American Music Teacher* (Feb./March 1969); A. V. Knapp, "The Jewishness of Bloch: Subconscious or Conscious," *Proceedings of the Royal Music Assoc.* (1970/71); D. Z. Kushner, *Ernest Bloch and His Music* (Glasgow, 1973); R. Strassburg, *Ernest Bloch, Voice in the Wilderness* (Los Angeles, 1977; contains a list of unpublished works and of manuscripts in the Library of Congress, Washington, D.C., and in the Bloch Archive at the Univ. of California, Berkeley); Suzanne Bloch, *Ernest Bloch: Creative Spirit,* a program source book (in collaboration with Irene Heskes; N.Y. 1976).

Bloch, Suzanne, lutenist and harpsichordist; daughter of **Ernest Bloch**; b. Geneva, Aug. 7, 1907. She came to the U.S. with her father; studied with him and with Roger Sessions; then in Paris with Nadia Boulanger. She became interested in early polyphonic music and began to practice on old instruments to be able to perform music on the instruments for which it was written.

Blockx, Jan, significant Flemish composer; b. Antwerp, Jan. 25, 1851; d. there, May 26, 1912. He studied piano at the Flemish Music School with Callaerts and composition with Benoit. In 1886, became teacher of harmony at the Antwerp Cons.; also was musical director of the 'Cercle artistique' and other societies. With Benoit, he is regarded as the strongest representative of the Flemish school in Belgium; however, in his music, he followed traditional European methods; his operas betray a Wagnerian influence. He wrote the operas *Jets vergeten* (Antwerp, 1877); *Maître Martin* (Brussels, Nov. 30, 1892); *Herbergprinses* (Antwerp, Oct. 10, 1896; perf. in French as *Princesse d'Auberge,* N.Y., March 10, 1909); *Thyl Uylenspiegel* (Brussels, Jan. 18, 1900); *De Bruid der Zee* (Antwerp, Nov. 30, 1901; his best work); *De Kapel* (Antwerp, Nov. 7, 1903); *Baldie* (Antwerp, Jan. 25, 1908; revised and perf. in Antwerp, Jan. 14, 1912, under the title *Chanson d'amour*); a ballet *Milenka* (1887); *Rubens,* overture for orch.; *Romance* for violin and orch.; many choral works with orch.: *Vredezang; Het droom vant paradies; De klokke Roelandt; Op den stroom; Scheldezang.*

BIBLIOGRAPHY: L. Solvay, *Notice sur Jan Blockx* (1920); F. Blockx, *Jan Blockx* (1943).

Blodek, Wilhelm, Czech composer; b. Prague, Oct. 3, 1834; d. there, May 1, 1874. He studied with J. B. Kittl and A. Dreyschock; taught for three years in Poland; then returned to Prague, and became prof. of flute-playing of the Prague Cons. (1860–70). In 1870 he became insane and spent the rest of his life in an asylum. His opera in the Czech language *V Studni (In the Well)* was produced with excellent success in Prague (Nov. 17, 1867); it was also given in German under the title *Im Brunnen* (Leipzig, 1893). His second opera,

Zitek, remained unfinished; it was completed by F. X. Vana, and prod. in Prague at Blodek's centennial (Oct. 3, 1934). Blodek also wrote a flute concerto (1862) and a symphony (1866).

Blodgett, Benjamin Colman, American organist; b. Boston, March 12, 1838; d. Seattle, Sept. 22, 1925. He studied organ in Boston and was organist in several churches there; then taught music at Smith College; from 1906 to 1914 he was organist at Stanford Univ., California. He finally settled in Seattle.

Blom, Eric, pre-eminent English writer on music; b. Bern, Switzerland, Aug. 20, 1888; d. London, April 11, 1959. He was of Danish and British extraction on his father's side; his mother was Swiss. He was educated in England. He was the London music correspondent for the *Manchester Guardian* (1923–31); then was the music critic of the *Birmingham Post* (1931–46) and of *The Observer* in 1949; edited *Music & Letters* from 1937 till 1950 and from 1954 to the time of his death; he was also the editor of the Master Musicians series. In 1946 he was elected member of the music committee of the British Council; in 1948 became member of the Royal Musical Association. In 1955 he received the order of Commander of the British Empire in recognition of his services to music and the hon. degree of D. Litt. from Birmingham Univ. In his writings Blom combined an enlightened penetration of musical esthetics with a literary capacity for presenting his subjects and stating his point of view in a brilliant journalistic manner. In his critical opinions he never concealed his disdain for some composers of great fame and renown, such as Rachmaninoff. In 1946 he was entrusted with the preparation of a newly organized and greatly expanded edition of *Grove's Dictionary of Music and Musicians,* which was brought out under his editorship in 1954, in 9 vols., and to which Blom himself contributed hundreds of articles and translated entries by foreign contributors. In his adamant determination to make this edition a truly comprehensive work, he insisted on the inclusion of complete lists of works of important composers and exact dates of performance of operas and other major works. In 1946 Blom published his first lexicographical work *Everyman's Dictionary of Music,* which was reissued in an amplified edition by Jack Westrup in 1971. His other books include: *Stepchildren of Music* (1923); *The Romance of the Piano* (1927); *A General Index to Modern Musical Literature in the English Language* (1927; indexes periodicals for the years 1915–26); *The Limitations of Music* (1928); *Mozart* (1935); *Beethoven's Pianoforte Sonatas Discussed* (1938); *A Musical Postbag* (collected essays; 1941); *Music in England* (1942; revised edition, 1947); *Some Great Composers* (1944); *Classics, Major and Minor with Some Other Musical Ruminations* (London, 1958).

Blomberg, Erik, Swedish composer; b. Järnskog, May 6, 1922. He studied with Erland von Koch and Gunnar Bucht; later went to Uppsala where he became a music teacher.

WORKS: 5 symphonies: No. 1, *4 dramatiska skisser* (1966), No. 2, *3 studier i melodik* (1968), No. 3,

Associationskedjor (1971), No. 4 (1973) and No. 5 (1974); *3 Orchestral Fragments* (1968); *Dialog* for piano and orch. (1969); *Debatt* for wind orch. (1970); *Vila i rörelse* for string orch. (1970); *Vom Tod* for soloists, chorus and instruments (1970); *Die allerbeste Gabe* for soloists, chorus and orch. (1972); *Kompriment I-XIII* for various instrumental formations (1971–75); 3 string quartets; *4 Miniatures* for string trio (1966); 3 piano sonatas (1965, 1968, 1971).

Blomdahl, Karl-Birger, significant Swedish composer; b. Växjö, Oct. 19, 1916; d. Kungsängen (near Stockholm), June 14, 1968. He studied composition with Hilding Rosenberg and conducting with Thor Mann in Stockholm; in 1946 he traveled in France and Italy on a state stipend; in 1954–55 he attended a seminar at Tanglewood on a grant of the American-Scandinavian Foundation. Returning to Sweden, he taught composition at the Royal College of Music in Stockholm (1960–64); in 1964 he was appointed Music Director at the Swedish Radio. He was an organizer (with Bäck, Carlid, Johanson and Lidholm) of a "Monday Group" in Stockholm, dedicated to the propagation of an objective and abstract idiom as distinct from the prevalent type of Scandinavian romanticism. Blomdahl's early works are cast in a neo-Classical idiom, but he then turned to advanced techniques, including the application of electronic music. His Third Symphony, subtitled *Facetter (Facets)* utilizes dodecaphonic techniques. In 1959 he brought out his opera *Aniara,* which made him internationally famous; it pictures a pessimistic future when the remnants of the inhabitants of the Planet Earth, devastated by atomic wars and polluted by radiation, are forced to emigrate to saner worlds in the galaxy; the score employs electronic sounds, and its thematic foundation is derived from a series of 12 different notes and 11 different intervals.

WORKS: Trio for Oboe, Clarinet and Bassoon (1938); String Quartet No. 1 (1939); *Symphonic Dances* (Göteborg, Feb. 29, 1940); *Concert Overture* (Stockholm, Feb. 14, 1942); Suite for Cello and Piano (1944); Viola Concerto (Stockholm, Sept. 7, 1944); Symph. No. 1 (Stockholm, Jan. 26, 1945); Concerto Grosso (Stockholm, Oct. 2, 1945); *Vaknatten (The Wakeful Night),* theater music (1945); *3 Polyphonic Pieces* for piano (1945); String Trio (1945); Suite for Cello and Piano (1945); *Little Suite* for bassoon and piano (1945); Concerto for Violin and String Orch. (Stockholm, Oct. 1, 1947); Symph. No. 2 (1947; Stockholm, Dec. 12, 1952); *Dance Suite No. 1* for flute, violin, viola, cello and percussion (1948); String Quartet No. 2 (1948); *Pastoral Suite* for string orch. (1948); *Prelude and Allegro* for strings (1949); Symph. No. 3, *Facetter (Facets,* 1950; Frankfurt Festival, June 24, 1951); *Dance Suite No. 2* for clarinet, cello and percussion (1951); *I speglarnas sal (In the Hall of Mirrors),* oratorio of 9 sonnets from Erik Lindegren's "The Man Without a Road," for soli, chorus and orch. (1951–52; Stockholm, May 29, 1953); Chamber Concerto for Piano, Woodwinds and Percussion (Stockholm, Oct. 30, 1953); *Sisyfos,* choreographic suite for orch. (Stockholm, Oct. 20, 1954; produced as a ballet, Stockholm, April 18, 1957); Trio for Clarinet, Cello and Piano (1955); *Anabase* for baritone, narrator, chorus and orch. (Stockholm, Dec. 14, 1956); *Minotaurus,* ballet (Stockholm, April 5, 1958); *Aniara,* futuristic opera with electronic sound, after Harry Martinson's novel about an interplanetary voyage; libretto by Erik Lindegren (1957-59; Stockholm, May 31, 1959; numerous performances in Europe); *Fioriture* for orch. (Cologne, June 17, 1960); *Forma ferritonans* for orch. (Oxelösund, June 17, 1961); *Spel för åtta (Game for Eight),* ballet (Stockholm, June 8, 1962; also a choreographic suite for orch. 1964); *Herr von Hancken,* comic opera (Stockholm, Sept. 2, 1965); *Altisonans,* electronic piece from natural sound sources (1966); *....resan i denna natt (....the voyage in this night),* cantata, after Lindegren, for soprano and orch. (Stockholm, Oct. 19, 1966). At the time of his death, Blomdahl was working on an opera *The Saga of the Great Computer,* incorporating electronic and concrete sounds, and synthetic speech.

BIBLIOGRAPHY: Gunnar Bucht, ed., *"Facetter" av och om Karl-Birger Blomdahl* (Stockholm, 1970; contains a complete catalogue of works and dates of first performances); R. K. Inglefield, "Karl-Birger Blomdahl: A Portrait," *Musical Quarterly* (Jan. 1972).

Blon, Franz von, German composer; b. Berlin, July 16, 1861; d. Seilershof, Oct. 21, 1945. He studied in Berlin; was active as conductor. He wrote the operettas *Die Amazone* (1903) and *Die tolle Prinzess* (1913), and much instrumental music of a light variety, particularly waltzes and marches.

Blondeau, Pierre-Auguste-Louis, French violist and composer; b. Paris, Aug. 15, 1784; d. there, 1865. He studied at the Paris Cons. with Baillot, Gossec and Méhul; won the Prix de Rome in 1808 with his cantata, *Maria Stuart;* was violist in the Grand Opéra Orch. until 1842. He wrote an opera, *Alla fontana;* a ballet; 3 overtures; church music; chamber music; piano pieces and songs; also a number of theoretical works.

Bloomfield, Fannie. See **Zeisler, Fannie Bloomfield.**

Blow, John, great English composer and organist; b. Newark-on-Trent, Nottinghamshire, Feb. (baptized 23rd), 1648/9; d. Westminster (London), Oct. 1, 1708. In 1660-61 he was a chorister at the Chapel Royal, under Henry Cooke; he later studied organ with Christopher Gibbons. His progress was rapid, and on Dec. 3, 1668 he was appointed organist of Westminster Abbey. In 1679 he left this post and Purcell, who had been Blow's student, became his successor. After Purcell's untimely death in 1695, Blow was reappointed, and remained in Westminster Abbey until his death; he was buried there, in the north aisle. He married Elizabeth Bradcock in 1673; she died in 1683 in childbirth, leaving five children. Blow held the rank of Gentleman of the Chapel Royal from March 16, 1673/4; on July 13, 1674, he succeeded Humfrey as Master of the Children; was Master of the Choristers at St. Paul's (1687-1702/3). He held the honorary Lambeth degree of Mus. Doc., conferred on him in 1677 by the Dean of Canterbury. Still as a young chorister of the Chapel Royal, Blow began to compose church music; in collaboration with Humfrey and William Turner, he wrote the *Club Anthem* ("I will always give thanks"); at the behest of Charles II, he made a two-part setting of Herrick's "Goe, perjur'd man." He wrote many secular part-songs, among them an ode for New Year's Day 1681/82, "Great sir, the joy of all our hearts", an ode for St. Cecilia; 2 anthems for the coronation of James II; *Epicedium for Queen Mary* (1695) and *Ode on the Death of Purcell* (1696). Blow's collection of 50 songs, *Amphion Anglicus,* was published in 1700. His best known work is *Masque for the Entertainment of the King: Venus and Adonis,* written about 1685; this is his only complete score for the stage, but he contributed separate songs for numerous dramatic plays. Purcell regarded Blow as "one of the greatest masters in the world." 14 large works by Blow, anthems and harpsichord pieces, have been preserved; 11 anthems are printed in Boyce's *Cathedral Musick* (1760-78). Selected anthems are publ. in *Musica Britannica 7.* The vocal score of his masque *Venus and Adonis* was published by G. E. P. Arkwright in the Old English Edition (No. 25; 1902); the complete score was published by the Editions de l'Oiseau Lyre, as edited by Anthony Lewis (Paris, 1939).

BIBLIOGRAPHY: G. E. P. Arkwright's introduction to 'Six Songs by Dr. John Blow' in the Old English Edition (No. 23; 1900); H. W. Shaw's "John Blow, Doctor of Music," in the *Musical Times* (Oct.-Dec. 1937; also separately, London, 1943); id., "Blow's Use of the Ground Bass," in *Musical Quarterly* (Jan. 1938); id., "John Blow's Anthems," *Music & Letters* (Oct. 1938); H. L. Clarke, "John Blow; a Tercentenary Survey," *Musical Quarterly* (July 1949); R. McGuinness, *English Court Odes 1660-1820* (Oxford, 1971).

Blum, Robert, important Swiss composer; b. Zürich, Nov. 27, 1900. He studied at the Zürich Cons. with Andreae, Jarnach and others; in 1924 he took some lessons with Busoni. Upon his return to Switzerland, he devoted himself to choral conducting and teaching. In 1943 he was appointed prof. at the Music Academy in Zürich. In his own compositions he cultivates polyphonic music in the traditional style enhanced by modern harmonies and occasionally dissonant contrapuntal lines.

WORKS: the opera *Amarapura* (1926); the oratorio *Kindheit Jesu* (1936); many sacred choral works and psalms for voice and orch.; 6 symphonies (1924, 1926, 1935, 1959, 1961, 1969); *Passionskonzert* for organ and string orch. (1943); *Seldwyla-Symphonie* (1968); 4 *Partite* for orch. (1929, 1935, 1953, 1967); Concerto for Orch. (1955); *Overture on Swiss Themes* (1944); *Christ ist erstanden,* orchestral variations (1962); *Lamentatio angelorum* for chamber orch. (1943); Viola Concerto (1951); Oboe Concerto (1960); Concerto for Wind Quintet (1962); Triple Concerto for Violin, Oboe, Trumpet and Chamber Orch. (1963); Flute Quartet (1963); Sonata for Flute and Violin (1963); *Concertante Symphonie* for wind quintet and chamber orch. (1964); *Divertimento* on a 12-tone row for 10 instruments (1966); *Le tombe di Ravenna* for 11 woodwind instruments (1968); Quartet for Clarinet and String Trio (1970); String Quartet (1970); numerous songs, organ pieces and arrangements of old vocal compositions.

Blume, Clemens, German music scholar; b. Biller-
beck, Jan. 31, 1862; d. Königstein, April 8, 1932. He
studied theology; then taught it at the Catholic Univ.
in Frankfurt. He was regarded as an outstanding authority on texts of medieval Latin hymns. His books
include *Cursus Sanctus Benedicti* (liturgic hymns of
the 6th to 9th centuries; 1908); *Guide to Chevalier's
"Repertorium Hymnologicum"* (1911); *Analecta hymnica medii aevi* (his standard work; 1896–1922; vols.
1–48, co-ed. with C. M. Dreves; some vols. with H. M.
Bannister). A selection from this valuable source book
of hymnological research was extracted as *Ein Jahr-
tausend lateinischer Hymnendichtung* (2 vols., 1909).
Blume also published *Unsere liturgischen Lieder* (Pustet, 1932).

Blume, Friedrich, pre-eminent German musicologist
and editor; b. Schlüchtern, Jan. 5, 1893; d. there, Nov.
22, 1975. He was the son of a Prussian government
functionary; first studied medicine in Eisenach (1911);
then philosophy in Munich, and music in Munich and
Berlin. During World War I he was in the German
army; was captured by the British and spent three
years in a British prison camp. In 1919 he resumed his
studies at the Univ. of Leipzig, where he presented his
dissertation *Studien zur Vorgeschichte der Orchester-
suite im 15. und 16. Jahrhundert* (1921). He was appointed lecturer (1923) and then privatdozent (1925)
at the Univ. of Berlin; published the treatise *Das monodische Prinzip in der protestantischen Kirchenmusik* (1925). Further writings: *Die Kultur der Abtei Reichenau* (1925); *Die evangelische Kirchenmusik* in
Bücken's *Handbuch der Musikwissenschaft* (1931);
"Hermann Abert und die Musikwissenschaft," *Abert-
Festschrift* (1928) and *Abert's Gesammelte Schriften
und Vorträge* (1929), both edited by Blume. He prepared a collected edition of works by M. Praetorius
(20 vols. in 155 installments; 1928–40); also edited a
Passion by Demantius, *Sacri concerti* by Schütz; piano sonatas of Wilhelm Friedemann Bach, and *Geistliche Musik am Hofe des Landgrafen Moritz;* published minor studies on Mozart's piano concertos, on
the works of Josquin des Prez (1929), and on Haydn's
string quartets (1931). He was general editor of the
valuable collection of old polyphonic music *Das Chorwerk* (until 1939, 50 vols.; includes works of Pierre de
la Rue, Demantius, Josquin des Prez, Purcell, etc.). In
1943 he was entrusted with the preparation of the encyclopedia *Die Musik in Geschichte und Gegenwart,*
which began appearing in 1949. Almost immediately
after its completion in 1967, Blume undertook the
publication of an extensive Supplement, containing
numerous additional articles and corrections of ascertainable errors; its publication was continued after
Blume's death by his daughter, Ruth Blume.
BIBLIOGRAPHY: A. A. Abert and W. Pfannkuch,
Festschrift Friedrich Blume zum 70. Geburtstag (Kassel, 1963); G. Feder, "Friedrich Blume zum 80. Geburtstag," and G. Henle, "Zum 80. Geburtstag von
Friedrich Blume," in *Haydn Studien* (Jan. 1973).

Blumenfeld, Felix, Russian composer and conductor;
b. Kovalevka, near Kherson, April 19, 1863; d. Moscow, Jan. 21, 1931. He studied piano in Elizabethgrad;
then went to St. Petersburg, where he was a pupil in

composition of Rimsky-Korsakov; upon graduation in
1885 he joined the staff of the Cons. and taught there
until 1905, and again from 1911 to 1918; from 1895 to
1911 he was conductor at the Imperial Opera in St.
Petersburg; he was also guest conductor in the Russian repertoire in Paris during the "Russian seasons"
in 1908. He was a pianist of the virtuoso caliber; was
also active as an accompanist for Chaliapin and other
famous singers. From 1918 until 1922 he was prof. of
piano at the Cons. of Kiev, and from 1922 to his death
taught at the Moscow Cons. Among his piano students was Vladimir Horowitz. As a composer, Blumenfeld excelled mainly in his piano pieces and songs,
many of them published by Belaiev. He also wrote a
symphony entitled *To the Beloved Dead,* a string
quartet, and some other pieces.

Blumenfeld, Harold, American composer; b. Seattle,
Oct. 15, 1923. He studied at the Eastman School of
Music in Rochester with Bernard Rogers, and at Yale
Univ. with Paul Hindemith; also took courses in conducting with Leonard Bernstein at Tanglewood. In
1951 he became prof. at Washington Univ. in St.
Louis. His music is functional; he particularly excels
in writing for the stage. Among his works is an opera
Amphitryon 4, after Molière (1962); *The Road to Salem,* television opera (1969); also *Miniature Overture*
(1952); *Expansions* for woodwind quintet (1965), etc.

Blumenschein, William Leonard, German-American
composer and choral conductor; b. Brensbach, Germany, Dec. 16, 1849; d. Dayton, Ohio, March 27, 1916.
He studied at the Leipzig Cons. with Reinecke
(1869–72); then emigrated to the U.S. and settled in
Dayton, Ohio where he conducted several choral societies. He published some 50 piano pieces in an effective salon style, about 60 anthems and sacred choruses.

Blumenthal, Jacob, German pianist; b. Hamburg, Oct.
4, 1829; d. London, May 17, 1908. He studied music in
Hamburg and Vienna; in 1846 went to Paris where he
became a student of piano with Herz and in composition with Halévy. In 1848 he settled in London, where
he became the court pianist to Queen Victoria. He
composed a number of melodious piano pieces in a
fashionable salon style.

Blumer, Theodor, German conductor and composer;
b. Dresden, March 24, 1881; d. Berlin, Sept. 21, 1964.
He studied at the Dresden Cons. and was active as a
pianist, and from 1925 to 1931 as a conductor of the
Dresden radio. From 1931 to 1942 he conducted radio
broadcasts in Leipzig and in 1952 moved to Berlin. He
wrote several light operas, among them *Der Fünf-
Uhr-Tee* (Dresden, 1911) and *Trau schau wem!;* 3
symphonies; several overtures, and a considerable
amount of chamber music, including duo sonatas,
trios, quartets, quintets and sextets, as well as a
goodly amount of songs.

Blumner, Martin, German choral conductor and composer; b. Fürstenberg, Mecklenburg, Nov. 21, 1827; d.
Berlin, Nov. 16, 1901. He studied philosophy and
mathematics at Berlin Univ.; then music with Sieg-

fried Dehn. In 1847 he became a member of the Berlin Singakademie; appointed associate conductor (1853) and chief conductor (1876). He composed the oratorios *Abraham* (1860) and *Der Fall Jerusalems* (1874); the cantatas *Columbus* (1852), *In Zeit und Ewigkeit* (1885), and *Festival Cantata* (1891); a *Te Deum* in 8 parts; motets; psalms; etc.

BIBLIOGRAPHY: E. Dryander, *Zum Gedächtnis Martin Blumner* (Berlin, 1901).

Blüthner, Julius (Ferdinand), celebrated German piano maker; b. Falkenhain, near Merseburg, March 11, 1824; d. Leipzig, April 13, 1910. In 1853 he founded his establishment at Leipzig with three workmen; by 1897 it had grown to a sizable company, producing some 3,000 pianos yearly. Blüthner's specialty was the "Aliquotflügel," a grand piano with a sympathetic octave-string stretched over and parallel with each unison struck by the hammers. He was awarded many medals for his contributions to the advancement of piano construction. He was co-author, with H. Gretschel, of *Der Pianofortebau* (1872; 3d ed. revised by R. Hannemann, Leipzig, 1909).

Boatwright, Howard, American violinist and composer; b. Newport News, Virginia, March 16, 1918. He studied composition with Hindemith at Yale Univ.; then taught music theory there (1938–64). In 1964 he was appointed Dean of the Music School at Syracuse Univ. He gave many concerts in Europe and America, mostly in the program of old music, skillfully arranged for performance; his wife, the soprano **Helen Boatwright,** was often an associate artist. He wrote numerous pieces of chamber music, including *Serenade* for 2 string instruments and 2 wind instruments (1952); a clarinet quartet (1958); several works of sacred music, including *The Passion According to St. Matthew* (1962). His vocal works based on English and American folksongs are justly appreciated.

Boatwright, McHenry, black American baritone; b. Tenile, Georgia, Feb. 29, 1928. He studied at the New England Cons. in Boston; made his concert debut in 1956; sang in London in 1962; was soloist with the N.Y. Philharmonic, Philadelphia Orch. and other orchestras in the U.S. He created the central role in Gunther Schuller's opera *The Visitation* (Hamburg, Oct. 12, 1968).

Boccherini, Luigi, famous Italian composer; b. Lucca, Feb. 19, 1743; d. Madrid, May 28, 1805. He was a pupil of Abbate Vannucci, and later studied in Rome (1757); returned to Lucca for a time as cellist in the theater orchestra. He then undertook a concert tour with the violinist Filippo Manfredi; the high point of their success was in Paris, when they appeared at the Concerts Spirituel. So popular was Boccherini as a performer that his compositions were solicited by the leading Paris publishers; his first publications were 6 string quartets and 2 books of string trios. In 1769 Boccherini received a flattering invitation to the Madrid court, and became chamber composer to the Infante Luis, and, after Luis' death (1785), to King Carlos III. From 1787 he was also court composer to Friedrich Wilhelm II of Prussia, an amateur cello player. In this

capacity, Boccherini was in Germany for a time; after the king's death (1797), he returned to Madrid. In 1800 he enjoyed the patronage of Napoleon's brother, Lucien Bonaparte, French ambassador to Madrid. Boccherini's last years were spent in ill health and poverty. He was buried in Madrid; in 1927 his remains were transferred to Lucca and reinterred with great solemnity. Boccherini was an exceptionally prolific composer of chamber music. The list includes 20 chamber symphonies; 2 octets; 16 sextets; 125 string quintets; 12 piano quintets; 18 quintets for strings and flute (or oboe); 102 string quartets; 60 string trios; 21 violin sonatas; 6 cello sonatas; also 4 cello concertos. He further wrote 2 operas; a Christmas cantata; a Mass; etc. A full catalogue was compiled by L. Picquot in his monograph on Boccherini (Paris, 1851); a more recent catalogue is by Yves Gérard (1969). His music is marked by natural melody and fluency of instrumental writing, if not by originality of style. He had profound admiration for the music of Haydn; indeed, so close is Boccherini's style to Haydn's that the affinity gave rise to the saying "Boccherini is the wife of Haydn."

BIBLIOGRAPHY: D. M. Cerù, *Cenni intorno alla vita e le opere di Luigi Boccherini* (Lucca, 1864); H. M. Schletterer, *Boccherini* (Leipzig, 1882); G. Malfatti, *Luigi Boccherini nell' arte, nella vita e nelle opere* (Lucca, 1905); R. Sondheimer, "Boccherini e la sinfonia in do maggiore," *Rivista Musicale Italiana* (1920); C. Bouvet, "Boccherini inconnu," *Revue de musicologie* (Nov. 1929); Georges de Saint-Foix, "La Correspondance de Boccherini avec I. Pleyel," *Revue de Musicologie* (Feb. 1930); L. Parodi, *Luigi Boccherini* (1930); A. Bonaventura, *Boccherini* (Milan, 1931); Yves Gérard, *Thematic, Bibliographical and Critical Catalogue of the Works of Luigi Boccherini* (London, 1969); G. de Rothschild, *Luigi Boccherini* (Paris, 1962; London, 1965).

Bochsa, Robert-Nicolas-Charles, celebrated French harpist; b. Montmédy, Meuse, Aug. 9, 1789; d. Sydney, Australia, Jan. 6, 1856. He first studied music with his father; played in public at the age of seven; wrote a symphony when he was nine, and an opera *Trajan* at fifteen. He then studied with Franz Beck in Bordeaux, and later at the Paris Cons. with Méhul and Catel (1806). His harp teachers were Nadermann and Marin. Of an inventive nature, Bochsa developed novel technical devices for harp playing, transforming the harp into a virtuoso instrument. He was the court harpist to Napoleon, and to Louis XVIII. He wrote 8 operas for the Opéra-Comique (1813–16); several ballets, an oratorio, and a great number of works for the harp; also a Method for harp. In 1817 he became involved in some forgeries, and fled to London to escape prison. He became very popular as a harp teacher in London Society; organized a series of oratorio productions with Sir George Smart (1822). He was also the first professor of harp playing at the Academy of Music in London, but lost his position when a story of his dishonest conduct became widely known. However, he obtained a position as conductor of the Italian Opera at the King's Theatre (1826–32). Another scandal marked Bochsa's crooked road to success and notoriety when he eloped with the soprano singer Ann

Bishop, the wife of Sir Henry Bishop. He gave concerts with her in Europe, America, and Australia, where he died.

BIBLIOGRAPHY: Arthur Pougin, "Un Musicien voleur, faussaire et bigame," *Le Ménestrel* (Jan. 19 to March 9, 1907); J. B. Weidensaul, "Bochsa: A Biographical Sketch," *American Harp Journal* (Fall 1970).

Bockelmann, Rudolf, German baritone; b. Bodenteich, April 2, 1892; d. Dresden, Oct. 9, 1958. He studied singing with Oscar Lassner in Leipzig; appeared as a baritone at the Neues Theater (1921–26); at the Stadttheater in Hamburg (1926–32), and at the Staatsoper in Berlin (1932–45). After World War I he settled in Hamburg as a singing teacher. He also sang with the Chicago Opera (1930–31); was particularly noted for his interpretation of Wagnerian baritone roles. His notes on performance were published as "Die Rolle des Hans Sachs," *Sammelbände der Robert-Schumann-Gesellschaft II/1966* (Leipzig, 1967).

Böckh, August, German authority on Greek literature and music; b. Karlsruhe, Nov. 24, 1785; d. Berlin, Aug. 3, 1867. He studied philology at the Univ. of Halle; received his doctorate with the treatise *De harmonice veterum* (1807). In 1811 he became professor at the Univ. of Berlin, a position which he retained until his death, 56 years later. He edited the works of Pindar with an introduction *De metris Pindari* from which modern research on old Greek music received a new impetus.

BIBLIOGRAPHY: M. Hoffmann, *A. Böckh* (Leipzig, 1901); G. Lehmann, *Theorie und Geschichte der griechischen Harmonik in der Darstellung durch August Böckh* (Würzburg, 1935).

Boda, John, American composer; b. Boyceswille, Wisconsin, Aug. 2, 1922. He studied at the Eastman School of Music in Rochester, N.Y.; in 1946 joined the faculty of Florida State Univ. at Tallahassee. His *Sinfonia* was first performed in Knoxville, Tenn., on Dec. 6, 1960.

Bodanzky, Artur, famous Austrian conductor; b. Vienna, Dec. 16, 1877; d. New York, Nov. 23, 1939. He studied at the Vienna Cons., and later with Zemlinsky. He began his career as a violinist at the Vienna Opera. In 1900 he received his first appointment as conductor, leading an operetta season in Budweis; in 1902 he became assistant to Mahler at the Vienna Opera; conducted in Berlin (1905) and in Prague (1906–9). In 1909 he was engaged as music director at Mannheim. In 1912 he arranged a memorial Mahler Festival, conducting a huge ensemble of 1,500 vocalists and instrumentalists. He conducted *Parsifal* at Covent Garden, London, in 1914; his success there led to an invitation to conduct the German repertory at the Metropolitan Opera House; he opened his series with *Götterdämmerung* (Nov. 18, 1915). From 1916 to 1931 he was director of the Society of Friends of Music in New York; in 1919 he also conducted the New Symph. Orch. He made several practical arrangements of celebrated operas (*Oberon, Don Giovanni, Fidelio,* etc.) which he used for his productions with

the Metropolitan Opera. His style of conducting was in the Mahler tradition, with emphasis on climactic effects and contrasts of light and shade.

Bode, Rudolf, German acoustician and theorist of rhythmic gymnastics; b. Kiel, Feb. 3, 1881; d. Munich, Oct. 7, 1970. He studied physiology and philosophy at the Univ. of Leipzig, and music theory at the Leipzig Cons. After attending the Dalcroze Institute of Eurhythmics in Hellerau, he formulated a system of 'rhythmic gymnastics.' In 1911 Bode founded a school in Munich with courses embodying his body theories, intended to achieve perfect physical and mental health. He publ. a number of books and essays on the subject: *Der Rhythmus und seine Bedeutung für die Erziehung* (Jena, 1920); *Ausdruckgymnastik* (Munich, 1922; in English as *Expressions-Gymnastic,* N.Y., 1931); *Musik und Bewegung* (Kassel, 1930); *Energie und Rhythmus* (Berlin, 1939). He also wrote a manual of piano study as a rhythmic muscular action, *Rhythmus und Anschlag* (Munich, 1933).

Bodenschatz, Erhard, German theologian and music editor; b. Lichtenberg, 1576; d. Gross-Osterhausen, near Querfurt, 1636. He was a pupil of Calvisius in Pforta; then studied theology in Leipzig. In 1600 he became cantor in Schulpforta; in 1603 was pastor in Rehausen, and in 1608, in Gross-Osterhausen, where he remained until his death. He publ. several valuable collections of motets and hymns; particularly important is *Florilegium Portense* in 2 parts, of which the first was publ. in Leipzig in 1603 (1st ed. with 89 motets; 2nd ed. in 1618 with 120 motets); 2nd part (Leipzig, 1621) contained 150 motets, all by contemporary composers. There have been several reprints. He also publ. *Florilegium selectissimorum hymnorum* in 4 vols. (Leipzig, 1606). Bodenschatz's own compositions are not distinctive.

BIBLIOGRAPHY: Otto Riemer, *Erhard Bodenschatz und sein Florilegium Portense* (Leipzig, 1928).

Bodin, Lars-Gunnar, Swedish composer; b. Stockholm, July 15, 1935. He studied composition with Lennart Wenström (1955–59); attended the Darmstadt summer courses (1961); in 1972 became director of the electronic studio at the Stockholm Cons. In collaboration with the Swedish concrete poet and composer Bengt Emil Johnson, he produced a series of pieces described as "text-sound compositions."

WORKS: Brass Quartet (1960); *Arioso* for piano, percussion, cello, clarinet and trombone (1962); *Calendar Music* for piano (1963); *Semicolon* for piano and semaphoring chorus (1964); *My World Is Your World* for organ and tape (1966); ". . .from any point to any other point" for electronic sound (1968; also as a ballet, produced in Stockholm, Sept. 20, 1968); the electronic pieces *Place of Plays, Winter Events* (1967), *Toccata* (1969), *Traces I* and *II* (1970–71), *From the Beginning to the End* (1973), *Seeings (Earth, Sky, Winds)* (1973); the TV ballet, *Händelser och handlingar (Events and Happenings,* 1971); three compositions entitled *Dedicated to You* for organ and tape (1971).

Bodky, Erwin, German-American harpsichordist and music scholar; b. Ragnit, March 7, 1896; d. Lucerne, Switzerland, Dec. 6, 1958. He studied music in Berlin with Dohnányi and Juon at the Hochschule für Musik, and later took courses with Richard Strauss and Busoni at the Meisterschule für Komposition (1920-22). He subsequently taught at the Scharwenka Cons. in Berlin (1923-26) and other schools in Berlin. With the advent of the Nazi regime in 1933 he went to Amsterdam, where he taught until 1938, when he went to the U.S.; he taught at Longy School of Music in Cambridge, Mass. (1938-48); in 1949 was appointed prof. at Brandeis Univ. at Waltham. He was the founder of the Cambridge Society for Early Music. He published the valuable treatises, *Der Vortrag alter Klaviermusik* (Berlin, 1932) *Das Charakterstück* (Berlin, 1933) and *The Interpretation of J. S. Bach's Keyboard Works* (Cambridge, Mass., 1958).

Boehe, Ernst, German composer and conductor; b. Munich, Dec. 27, 1880; d. Ludwigshafen, Nov. 16, 1938. He studied with Rudolf Louis and Thuille in Munich; in 1907 was associate conductor, with Courvoisier, of the Munich Volkssymphoniekonzerte; from 1913-20 was court conductor at Oldenburg; then conducted concerts in Ludwigshafen. His works are of a programmatic type, the orchestration emphasizing special sonorities of divided strings, massive wind instruments, and various percussive effects; his tone-poems show a decisive Wagnerian influence, having a system of identification motifs. His most ambitious work was an orchestral tetralogy on Homer's *Odyssey,* under the general title *Odysseus' Fahrten,* comprising: *Odysseus' Ausfahrt und Schiffbruch* (Munich, Feb. 20, 1903; Philadelphia, Dec. 3, 1904), *Die Insel der Kirke, Die Klage der Nausikaa,* and *Odysseus' Heimkehr;* also the symph. poem *Taormina* (Essen, 1906; Boston Symph., Nov. 29, 1907).
    BIBLIOGRAPHY: Edgar Istel, "Ernst Boehe,"*Monographien moderner Musiker* (Leipzig, 1909).

Boekelman, Bernardus, Dutch pianist; b. Utrecht, Holland, June 9, 1838; d. New York, Aug. 2, 1930. He studied with his father and at the Leipzig Cons. with Moscheles, Richter, and Hauptmann. In 1864 he emigrated to Mexico; in 1866 settled in New York and then taught in various private schools. He published some piano pieces, edited the collection *Century of Music.* His analytical edition of Bach's *Well-Tempered Clavichord* and *2-Part Inventions* in colors (to indicate part-writing) is unique.

Boëllmann, Léon, French composer; b. Ensisheim, Alsace, Sept. 25, 1862; d. Paris, Oct. 11, 1897. He studied organ with Gigout; later was organ teacher in Paris. He left 68 published works, of which his *Variations symphoniques* for cello and orch. became part of the repertory of cello players. He wrote a symphony, *Fantaisie dialoguée* for organ and orch.; *Suite gothique* for organ; piano quartet; piano trio; cello sonata; *Rapsodie carnavalesque* for piano 4 hands; published a collection of 100 pieces for organ under the title *Heures mystiques.*
    BIBLIOGRAPHY: P. Locard, *L. Boëllmann* (Strasbourg, 1901).

Boëly, Alexandre Pierre François, French organist and composer; b. Versailles, April 19, 1785; d. Paris, Dec. 27, 1858. His father, a court musician, gave him his first instruction in music. Boëly studied piano and organ; occupied various positions as church organist in Paris. As a teacher he exercised a profound influence; Franck and Saint-Saëns owed much to him in the development of their style of organ writing.
    BIBLIOGRAPHY: A. Gastoué, "A Great French Organist A. Boëly and His Works," *Musical Quarterly* (July 1944); this article gives a list of works and a bibliography of the principal studies on Boëly; N. Dufourcq, "Le 'cas' Boëly," *L'Orgue* (April/June 1971).

Boelza, Igor, Russian composer and musicologist; b. Kielce, Poland, Feb. 8, 1904. He studied at the Kiev Cons.; taught there (1929-41). He was editor of the *Sovietskaya Musica* (1938-41); member of the board of the State Music Publishing House in Moscow (1941-48). He has written 5 symphonies, an overture, *Lyric Poem,* a piano concerto, an organ concerto, chamber music and songs. He published *Handbook of Soviet Musicians* (London, 1943); *Czech Opera Classics* (Moscow, 1951); *History of Polish Musical Culture* (Moscow, 1954); *History of the Czech Musical Culture* (Moscow, 1973).

Boepple, Paul, choral conductor and pedagogue; b. Basel, Switzerland, July 19, 1896; d. Brattleboro, Vermont, Dec. 21, 1970. He took courses at the Dalcroze Institute in Geneva, and adopted the Dalcroze System in his own method of teaching music; from 1918 to 1926 he was a member of the faculty of the Dalcroze Institute. In 1926 he emigrated to the U.S.; directed the Dalcroze School of Music in N.Y. (1926-32); then taught at the Chicago Musical College (1932-34) and at Westminster Choir School in Princeton (1935-38); subsequently he taught at Bennington College, Vermont. As a choral conductor, he gave numerous performances of modern works.

Boero, Felipe, Argentine opera composer; b. Buenos Aires, May 1, 1884; d. there, Aug. 9, 1958. He studied with Pablo Berutti; received a government prize for further study in Europe and attended the classes of Vidal and Fauré at the Paris Cons. (1912-14). Returning to Buenos Aires he became active as a teacher. Among his operas the following were produced at the Teatro Colón: *Tucumán* (June 29, 1918); *Ariana y Dionisios* (Aug. 5, 1920); *Raquela* (June 25, 1923); *Las Bacantes* (Sept. 19, 1925); *El Matrero* (July 12, 1929) and *Siripo* (June 8, 1937).

Boers, Joseph Karel, Dutch music scholar; b. Nimwegen, Aug. 4, 1812; d. Delft, Nov. 1, 1896. He was a pupil of Lübeck at The Hague Cons.; then was theater conductor in Holland and in France; in 1841 returned to Nimwegen as teacher and choral conductor; in 1853 settled in Delft as music director. He wrote an interesting *History of Musical Instruments in the Middle Ages;* also a complete bibliography of ancient and modern musical works produced in the Netherlands.

Boesmans, Philippe, Belgian composer; b. Tongeren, May 17, 1936. He studied composition with Froidebise and Pousseur; in his music he followed the abstract tenets of international modernism, with structural formulas determining the contents.

WORKS: *Etude I* for piano (1963); *Sonance I* for 2 pianos (1964); *Sonance II* for 3 pianos (1967); *Impromptu* for 23 instruments (1965); *Explosives* for harp and 10 instruments (1968); *Verticles* for orch. (1969); *Multiples* for 2 pianos and orch. (1974); *Element–Extensions* for piano and chamber orch. (1976).

Boësset, Antoine (Sieur de Villedieu), French composer of ballets; b. Blois, 1586; d. Paris, Dec. 8, 1643. He was court musician to Louis XIII, and wrote many *Airs du cour* for court performances; an English edition of these works was published in 1629 under the title *French Court Aires*; a number of these were reprinted by H. Expert in *Chants de France et d'Italie.*

Boetius (or **Boethius**), **Anicius Manlius Torquatus Severinus,** Roman philosopher and mathematician; b. Rome, c.480 A.D.; executed in 524 on suspicion of treason, by the Emperor Theodoric, whose counsellor he had been for many years. Boetius wrote a treatise in 5 books, *De Institutione Musica,* which was the chief source book for the theorizing monks of the Middle Ages; this treatise was published at Venice (1491; 1499), at Basel (1570), at Leipzig (1867), and in a German translation by Oscar Paul (Leipzig, 1872); a French translation, by Fétis, remains in MS. Whether the notation commonly called "Boetian" (using Latin indices to denote traditional Greek notation), is properly attributable to him, has been questioned for about three centuries (cf. Meibom, *Antiquae musicae auctores septem;* page 7 of introduction on Alypius). For a defense of its authenticity, see F. Celentano, "La Musica presso i Romani," *Rivista musicale italiana* (1913). In this connection see also H. Potizon, *Boèce, théoricien de la musique grecque* (Paris, 1961). L. Schrade has written several essays on Boetius: "Das propädeutische Ethos in der Musikanschauung des Boetius," *Zeitschrift für Geschichte der Erziehung und des Unterrichts* (1930); "Die Stellung der Musik in der Philosphie des Boetius," *Archiv für Geschichte der Philosophie* (1932); and "Music in the Philosophy of Boetius," *Musical Quarterly* (April 1947).

Boetticher, Wolfgang, German musicologist; b. Bad Ems, Aug. 19, 1914. He studied musicology at the Univ. of Berlin; received his Ph.D. in 1943. In 1948 he became prof. of musicology at Göttingen Univ. His interests range widely, from the Renaissance through Baroque, classical music and romantic music. He published *Robert Schumann, Einführung in Persönlichkeit und Werk* (Berlin, 1941); *Orlando di Lasso und seine Zeit* (2 vols.; Kassel, 1958); *Von Palestrina zu Bach* (Stuttgart, 1959); *Dokumente und Briefe um Orlando di Lasso* (Kassel, 1960). He further contributed individual articles on Mozart, Brahms, Chopin, Bruckner and other composers to various collections and *Festschriften.*

Bogatyrev, Anatoly, Soviet composer; b. Vitebsk, Aug. 13, 1913. He studied composition with Zolotarev at the Belorussian Cons. in Minsk, graduating in 1937; was instructor there from 1948. Bogatyrev wrote two patriotic operas, *In the Forests of Polesye* (Minsk, Aug. 28, 1939) and *Nadezhda Durova* (Minsk, Dec. 22, 1956); two symphonies (1946, 1947); cantatas *The Leningraders* (1942), *Belorussia* (1949), *Glory Be to Lenin* (1952); Cello Concerto (1962); Concerto for Double Bass and Orch. (1964). In 1957 he reconstructed from Tchaikovsky's sketches the 7th symphony in E-flat major.

Bogdanov-Berezovsky, Valerian, Soviet composer and musicologist; b. in the village of Starozhilovka, near St. Petersburg, July 17, 1903; d. Moscow, May 13, 1971. He studied with Maximilian Steinberg and Liapunov at the Leningrad Cons., graduating in 1927; taught there from 1945 to 1948, and was in charge of the artistic direction of the Leningrad Theater of Opera and Ballet from 1951 to 1962. He wrote the operas *The Frontier* (1941); *The Leningraders* (1943); *Nastasia Filippovna,* after Dostoevsky's novel *The Idiot* (1964); several ballets, including *The Seagull,* after Chekov (1959); 2 symphonies (1933, 1953); Piano Concerto; Violin Concerto; some chamber music; choruses. Bogdanov-Berezovsky was known chiefly as a critic and historian of Russian music, and wrote several monographs on Soviet composers and contributed numerous articles to Soviet journals.

BIBLIOGRAPHY: I. Gusin, *V. Bogdanov-Berezovsky* (Leningrad, 1966).

Boghen, Felice, Italian music editor; b. Venice, Jan. 23, 1869; d. Florence, Jan. 25, 1945. He studied with Martucci, Sgambati and Wolf-Ferrari; conducted orchestral concerts and theatrical productions in many Italian cities. He edited *Anciennes chansons de France; Fughe d'antichi Maestri italiani; Partite e Correnti;* and selected works of Nardini, Cimarosa, Frescobaldi, Porpora, Tartini, Pasquini, Alessandro Scarlatti, Bach, Clementi and Liszt; published numerous articles on piano playing and technique.

Boguslawski, Edward, Polish composer; b. Chorzów, Sept. 22, 1940. He studied composition with Szabelski in Katowice and with Haubenstock-Ramati in Vienna. In 1963 he joined the faculty of the State College of Music in Katowice. His music makes use of Impressionistic techniques.

WORKS: *Intonazioni I* for 9 instruments (1962); *Intonazioni II* for orch. (1967); *Apocalypse* for narrator, chorus and instruments (1965); *Signals* for orch. (1965–66); *Metamorphoses* for oboe, clarinet, 2 violins, viola and cello (1967); *Canti* for soprano and orch. (1967); Concerto for oboe, oboe d'amore, English horn, musette and orch. (1967–68); *Versions* for 6 instruments (1968); *Musica per Ensemble MW-2* for flute, cello and 2 pianos (1970); Trio for flute, oboe and guitar (1970); *Per Pianoforte* (1971); *Capriccioso-Notturno* for orch. (1972); *Impromptu* for flute, viola and harp (1972); *L'Être* for soprano, flute, cello and 2 pianos (1973); *Pro Varsovia* for orch. (1973–74); *Musica Notturna* for musette and piano (1974); *Evocations* for baritone and orch. (1974); *Divertimento* for chamber ensemble (1975); Concerto for oboe, soprano and orch. (1975–76).

Boháč, Josef, Czech composer; b. Vienna, March 25, 1929. After a preliminary course of music studies in Vienna, he went to Brno where he studied with Petrželka at the Brno Academy of Musical Arts; upon graduation he became active in the musical programming on the radio. His music follows the median line of Central European modernism, with occasional resort to serial methods.

WORKS: chamber opera, after Chekhov, *Námluvy* (The Proposal, 1967; Ustí nad Laben, Dec. 15, 1972); television opera, *Oči* (The Eyes, 1973; Prague television, Oct. 5, 1974); opera *Goya* (1972-77; Ostrava, 1977); Suite for string quartet (1953); Cello Sonata (1954); *Rhapsody* for orch. (1955); *Symphonic Prelude* (1964); *Sinfonietta Concertante* (1964-65; Prague, March 14, 1966); String Trio (1965); *Suita Drammatica* for strings and timpani (1969-70; Prague, March 23, 1974); *My Lute Sounds,* monodrama cycle of 12 songs on love, sickness, and death, for tenor and nonet (1971); *Southern Rainbow,* suite for orch. (1971); *Sonetti per Sonatori* for flute, bass clarinet, percussion and piano (1974; for the chamber group Sonatori di Praga); Piano Concerto (1974; Prague, March 29, 1976).

Bohlmann, Theodor Heinrich Friedrich, pianist; b. Osterwieck, Germany, June 23, 1865; d. Memphis, Tenn., March 18, 1931. He was a pupil of Eugene d'Albert and Moszkowski; made his début in Berlin in 1890; in the same year he emigrated to America and settled in Cincinnati as a teacher.

Böhm, Georg, German organist; b. Hohenkirchen, Thuringia, Sept. 2, 1661; d. Lüneburg, May 18, 1733. He studied at the Univ. of Vienna (1684); was in Hamburg in 1693; became organist at the Johanneskirche in Lüneburg (1698). His organ preludes and harpsichord pieces rank high among keyboard works of the time; undoubtedly Bach was influenced by Böhm's style of writing. A complete edition of Böhm's works was begun by Johannes Wolgast; vol. I, piano and organ works (Leipzig, 1927); vol. II, vocal works (Leipzig, 1932).

BIBLIOGRAPHY: J. Wolgast, *Georg Böhm* (Berlin, 1924); R. Buchmayer, "Nachrichten über das Leben Georg Böhms," *Programm-Buch des 4. Bachfestes* (1908); W. Wolffheim, "Die Möllersche Handschrift," *Bach-Jahrbuch* (1912).

Böhm, Joseph, violinist; b. Budapest, March 4, 1795; d. Vienna, March 28, 1876. He was a pupil of his father; at eight years of age he made a concert tour to Poland and St. Petersburg, where he studied for some years under Pierre Rode. His first concert at Vienna (1815) was very successful; after a trip to Italy, he was appointed (1819) violin professor at the Vienna Cons.; retired in 1848. He formed many distinguished pupils, including Joachim, Ernst, Auer, Hellmesberger (Sr.), Rappoldi and others.

Bohm, Karl, German pianist; b. Berlin, Sept. 11, 1844; d. there, April 4, 1920. He studied with Löschhorn; lived most of his life in Berlin. He wrote a number of piano pieces in the salon genre; also songs, of which *Still wie die Nacht* became popular.

Böhm, Karl, eminent Austrian conductor; b. Graz, Aug. 28, 1894. He studied musicology with Mandyczewski in Vienna; in 1917, at the age of 23, he was appointed conductor at the Graz City Theater; in 1921 he conducted the State Opera in Munich, and in 1931 in Hamburg. From 1934 to 1943 he was music director of the Dresden State Opera; in the last years of the raging war he conducted the Vienna Opera (1943-45). After the war he organized and conducted the German Opera Repertory at the Teatro Colón in Buenos Aires (1950-53); later on conducted opera performances in virtually every important opera house in Europe and America. He is also renowned as a symphonic conductor; his interpretations of the works of the modern German school are notable. He made his first American appearance with the Chicago Symph. Orch. on Feb. 9, 1956; conducted for the first time at the Metropolitan Opera, N.Y., in 1957; also conducted regularly at the Bayreuth Festivals beginning in 1962; in 1971 he led performances of the Vienna State Opera in Moscow. He conducted the world premieres of *Die Schweigsame Frau* (Dresden, 1935) and *Daphne* (Dresden, 1938) by Richard Strauss who dedicated the score of *Daphne* to him. He published *Begegnung mit Richard Strauss* (Munich, 1964) and a book of reminiscences, *Ich erinnere mich ganz genau* (Zürich, 1968).

Böhm, Theobald, German flutist and inventor of the 'Böhm flute'; b. Munich, April 9, 1794; d. there, Nov. 25, 1881. He was the son of a goldsmith and learned mechanics in his father's workshop; studied flute playing, achieving a degree of virtuosity that made him one of the greatest flute players of his time; he was appointed court musician in 1818; gave concerts in Paris and London. His system of construction marks a new departure in the making of woodwind instruments. To render the flute acoustically perfect, he fixed the position and size of the holes so as to obtain, not convenience in fingering, but purity and fullness of tone; all holes are covered by keys, whereby prompt and accurate 'speaking' is assured; and the bore is modified, rendering the tone much fuller and mellower. Böhm published *Über den Flötenbau und die neuesten Verbesserungen desselben* (Mainz, 1847; English transl. by W. S. Broadwood, London, 1882); *Die Flöte und das Flötenspiel* (Munich, 1871).

BIBLIOGRAPHY: Charles Welch, *History of the Boehm Flute* (London, 1883); V. Mahillon, *Etude sur le doigté de la flûte Boehm* (1885); R. Rockstro, *A Treatise on the Construction, the History and the Practice of the Flute* (London, 1890).

Böhme, Franz Magnus, German writer on music; b. Willerstedt, near Weimar, March 11, 1827; d. Dresden, Oct. 18, 1898. He was a pupil of Hauptmann and Rietz at Leipzig; taught at Dresden (1859-78) and at the Hoch Cons. in Frankfurt (1878-85); spent the remaining years of his life in Dresden.

WRITINGS: *Das Oratorium, eine historische Studie* (Leipzig, 1861; revised ed., Gütersloh, 1887, under the title *Geschichte des Oratoriums*); *Altdeutsches Liederbuch,* a collection of German folksongs of the 12th to 17th centuries (Leipzig, 1877; later editions,

1913 and 1925); *Aufgaben zum Studium der Harmonie* (Mainz, 1880); *Kursus in Harmonie* (Mainz, 1882); *Geschichte des Tanzes in Deutschland* (2 vols., Leipzig, 1886); *Volkstümliche Lieder der Deutschen im 18. und 19. Jahrhundert* (Leipzig, 1895); *Deutsches Kinderlied und Kinderspiel* (1897). He edited Erk's *Deutscher Liederhort* (3 vols., 1893–94; new ed., 1925); also published several books of sacred songs and male choruses.

Bohn, Emil, German music bibliographer; b. Bielau, near Neisse, Jan. 14, 1839; d. Breslau, July 5, 1909. He studied philology at Breslau, and then music; was organist of the Breslau Kreuzkirche and founder (1881) of the Bohn Choral Society.
WRITINGS: *Bibliographie der Musikdruckwerke bis 1700, welche auf der Stadtbibliothek . . . zu Breslau aufbewahrt werden* (1883); *Die musikalischen Handschriften des 16. und 17. Jahrhunderts in der Stadtbibliothek zu Breslau* (1890); *Die Nationalhymnen der europäischen Völker* (1908). He also published the annotated chronicle of his choral society: *Bohn'scher Gesangverein; 100 historische Konzerte in Breslau* (1905).

Bohn, Peter, German organist and teacher; b. Bausendorf, Nov. 2, 1833; d. Trier, June 11, 1925. He was organist and teacher at Trier from 1852–1905; prepared German translations of Franco's *Ars cantus mensurabilis* (1880); *Dialogus de musica* of Odo de Clugny (1880); Glareanus' *Dodecachordon* (2 vols., 1888–89); and *Der Einfluss des tonischen Akzents auf die melodische und rhythmische Struktur der gregorianischen Psalmodie* (from *Paléographie musicale*, Solesmes, 1894); also published *Das liturgische Rezitativ und dessen Bezeichnung in den liturgischen Büchern des Mittelalters* (1887), and *Philipp von Vitry* (1890).

Bohnen, Michael, German bass; b. Cologne, May 2, 1887; d. Berlin, April 26, 1965. He studied at the Cologne Cons.; sang at major opera houses in Germany, Spain and Sweden; made his American debut with the Metropolitan Opera on March 1, 1923, and created a leading part at the American performance of Krenek's opera *Jonny spielt auf* (Jan. 19, 1929); remained with the Metropolitan Opera until 1933; then returned to Germany, and was on the staff of the Berlin Opera until 1945.

Böhner, Ludwig, German composer; b. Töttelstedt, Gotha, Jan. 8, 1787; d. there, March 28, 1860. He studied with his father and with Johann Christian Kittel, a pupil of Bach. Having achieved considerable fame as pianist and composer, he failed to establish himself socially and economically, owing to his personal eccentricities. He wandered through Germany, often on foot, and worked irregularly as theatrical conductor and concert pianist. The claim he advanced that other composers plagiarized him, is supported by the fact that Weber had unintentionally borrowed one of the themes in *Der Freischütz* from Böhner's piano concerto. Böhner's life and character are understood to have inspired the figure of the eccentric genius, Kreis-

ler, in E. T. A. Hoffmann's *Capellmeister Kreisler*, and by the same token Schumann's *Kreisleriana*.
BIBLIOGRAPHY: K. F. Bolt, *J. L. Böhner. Leben und Werk* (Hildburghausen, 1940).

Bohnke, Emil, viola player and composer; b. Zdunska Wola, Poland, Oct. 11, 1888; d. Pasewalk, Pomerania, May 11, 1928 (in an automobile accident, en route from Berlin to Swinemunde). He studied at the Leipzig Cons.; then was violist in various chamber music groups. He wrote a violin concerto, a piano trio, a string quartet, and several violin sonatas.

Boieldieu, François-Adrein, celebrated French opera composer; b. Rouen, Dec. 16, 1775; d. Jarcy, near Grosbois, Oct. 8, 1834. His father was a functionary who at one time served as secretary to Archbishop Larochefoucauld; his mother had a millinery shop; the family was fairly prosperous until the Revolution; the parents were divorced in 1794. Young Boieldieu received excellent instruction from Charles Broche, organist and pupil of Padre Martini; stories of Broche's brutality and of Boieldieu's flight to Paris are fabrications not supported by any evidence. At the age of fifteen, Boieldieu became assistant organist to Broche at the church of St. André in Rouen. He began to compose piano pieces and songs; he was only 17 when his first opera *La fille coupable* (to his father's libretto) was successfully produced in Rouen (Nov. 2, 1793). The boy adapted himself to the revolutionary conditions, and composed partriotic works which were then in demand. His *Chant populaire pour la Fête de la Raison* for chorus and orch. was presented at the Temple of Reason (former cathedral) in Rouen on Nov. 30, 1793. His second opera, *Rosalie et Myrza* was produced in Rouen on Oct. 28, 1795. In August 1796 he set out for Paris where he was befriended by the composer Louis Jadin, and was accepted in the salon of the piano manufacturer Erard; he met Cherubini and Méhul; with the tenor Garat he made a tour of Normandy, revisiting Rouen. The material success of this tour was so satisfactory that Boieldieu was able to pay off all his debts. In Paris he found a publisher who printed some of his songs (*Le Ménestrel, S'il est vrai que d'être deux,* etc.), and piano sonatas (a complete edition of these sonatas was republished by G. Favre in 2 albums, 1944–1945). Boieldieu produced one opera after another at the Paris theaters: *La Famille suisse* (Feb. 11, 1797); *La Dôt de Suzette* (Sept. 5, 1797); *Zoraine et Zulnare* (May 10, 1798). As a sign of his growing recognition, Boieldieu was appointed prof. of piano at the Paris Cons. in 1798. His opera *Beniowski* was produced (June 8, 1800) with moderate success; but *Le Calife de Bagdad* (Sept. 16, 1801) received tremendous acclaim, and became one of Boieldieu's most enduring operas. On March 19, 1802, he married the dancer Clotilde Mafleurai, but her dissolute character made the marriage a failure. His opera *Ma tante Aurore* was produced on Jan. 13, 1803. In the meantime, Boieldieu received an invitation from Russia, and left in Oct., 1803 for St. Petersburg, his wife remaining in Paris. His contract guaranteed him a handsome salary of 4,000 rubles annually, his duties being to write operas for the Imperial theaters and supervise music at the court. The quality of his music written during his sojourn in Russia was not of the highest; the opera *La Jeune Femme colère* (St. Petersburg, April 18, 1805) was the most successful. A vaudeville, *Les Voitures versées* (St. Petersburg, Dec. 4, 1806) was revised and produced in Paris (April 29, 1820) as a comic opera with considerable success. Other operas staged in St. Petersburg were *Aline, reine de Golconde* (1804); *Un Tour de soubrette*; *Abderkan* (1805); *Télémaque dans l'isle de Calypso* (Dec. 28, 1806); *La Dame invisible* (1803); music to Racine's *Athalie* (1808) and *Rien de trop ou les deux paravents* (Dec. 25, 1810). In 1811, Boieldieu asked the Russian government to release him from further employment (despite his raise in salary to 5,000 rubles) and returned to Paris. His first act was to petition for a divorce, which was, however, rejected by the authorities. His estranged wife died in 1826, and a few weeks later Boieldieu married the singer Jenny Phillis, whom he had known in Russia. Once in Paris, Boieldieu arranged a revival of *Ma tante Aurore* and the first Paris production of *Rien de trop*. He regained the favor of the public with *Jean de Paris* (April 4, 1812) which achieved instant popularity. His next operas were *Le Nouveau Seigneur de village* (1813); *La Fête du village voisin* (March 5, 1816), and *Le Petit Chaperon rouge* (June 30, 1818; highly successful). In 1817 he was appointed professor of composition at the Paris Conservatory; resigned in 1826. In 1821 he was created Chevalier of the Legion of Honor. The culmination of his highly successful career was reached with the production of his great masterpiece *La dame blanche* (Dec. 10, 1825), which was hailed by the public and the press as the French answer and challenge to Rossini's rising fame in the operatic field. *La dame blanche* had 1000 performances in Paris alone from 1825 to 1862, and nearly 1700 performances before 1914; it also had numerous productions all over the world. At the height of his success, Boieldieu developed the first signs of a lung disease; his health deteriorated; a trip to Italy (1832) brought no improvement. His pecuniary circumstances were affected. Although he was offered his old position at the Cons., he could not teach because of his loss of voice. In 1833 he received a grant of 6,000 francs from the government of Louis Philippe, and retired to his country house at Jarcy, where he died. During the last years of his life he became interested in painting; his pictures, showing his considerable talent as a landscape artist, are preserved in the municipal museum at Rouen. Among his pupils were Fétis, Adam and Zimmerman. The historical position of Boieldieu is of great importance; he was one of the creators of French comic opera; he possessed melodic inventiveness and harmonic grace; in addition to facility in composition, he largely succeeded in attaining perfection of form and fine dramatic balance. Adopting the best devices of Italian operatic art, he nevertheless cultivated the French style which laid the foundation for the brilliant progress of French opera in the 19th century. Boieldieu wrote 40 operas in all, of which 8 are lost; he also collaborated with Cherubini in *La Prisonnière* (1799); with Méhul, Kreutzer and others in *Le Baiser et la quittance* (1803); with Cherubini, Catel and Isouard in *Bayard à Mézières*; with Kreutzer in *Les Béarnais, ou Henry IV en voyage* (1814); with Mme. Gail, pupil of

Fétis, in *Angéla, ou L'Atelier de Jean Cousin* (1814); with Hérold in *Charles de France, ou Amour et gloire* (1816); with Cherubini, Berton and others in *Blanche de Provence, ou La Cour des fées* (1821); with Auber in *Les trois Genres* (1824); with Berton and others in *La Marquise de Brinvilliers* (1831). His natural son, **Adrien-Louis-Victor Boieldieu** (b. Paris, Nov. 3, 1815; d. there, July 9, 1883; his mother was Thérèse Regnault, a singer) was also a composer; he wrote 2 operas: *Marguerite* (which had been sketched out but left incomplete by his father) and *L'Aïeule*.

BIBLIOGRAPHY: G. Héquet, *A. Boieldieu, sa vie et ses œuvres* (Paris, 1864); A. Pougin, *Boieldieu, sa vie es ses œuvres* (Paris, 1875); E. Neukomm, *Trois jours à Rouen, Souvenirs du centenaire de Boieldieu* (Paris, 1875); H. de Thannberg, *Le Centenaire de Boieldieu, anecdotes et souvenirs* (Paris, 1875); E. Duval, *Boieldieu, notes et fragments inédits* (1883); P. L. Robert, "Correspondance de Boieldieu," *Rivista Musicale Italiana* XIX and XXII (also separately, Rouen, 1916); G. de Saint-Foix, "Les Premiers Pianistes parisiens: Boieldieu," *La Revue Musicale* (Feb. 1926); G. Favre, "La Danseuse Clotilde Mafleurai, première femme d'Adrien Boieldieu," *La Revue Musicale* (Jan. 1940); G. Favre, *Boieldieu, sa vie, son œuvre* (part I, Paris, 1944; part II, Paris, 1945; an exhaustive work on the subject). See also F. Clément and Larousse, *Dictionnaire des opéras* (Paris, 1906); L. Augé de Lassus, *Boieldieu*, in the series *Les Musiciens célèbres* (Paris, 1908; contains catalogue of works); and Alfred Loewenberg, *Annals of Opera* (Cambridge, 1943; 2nd ed., 1955).

Bois, Rob du, Dutch composer; b. Amsterdam, May 28, 1934. He studied law after having had piano lessons as a child; was mainly audodidact as a composer. His works are strongly contrapuntal in texture, following the classical Flemish tradition but applying ultra-modern techniques, including serialism.

WORKS: Piano Concerto (1960, revised 1968); *Cercle* for piano, 9 winds and percussion (1963); Concertino for School Orch. (1963); *Simultaneous* for orch. (1965; Utrecht, Sept. 29, 1966); *Breuker Concerto* for 2 clarinets, 4 saxophones and 21 string players (1968); *A Flower Given to My Daughter* for orch. (1970); *Midas*, ballet (1970); *Le Concerto pour Hrisanide* for piano and orch. (1971; written for Rumanian virtuoso Alexandru Hrisanide); *Allegro* for strings (1973); *3 Pezzi* for orch. (1973); Suite No. 1 for orch. (1973); Violin Concerto (1975); *Vandaag is het morgen van gisteren* for narrator, soprano, youth choir, orch. and brass band (1975); *7 Pastorales:* No. 1 for oboe, clarinet and harp (1960, revised 1969); No. 2 for recorder, flute and guitar (1963, revised 1969); No. 3 for clarinet, bongos and double bass (1963, revised 1969); No. 4 for solo guitar (1963); No. 5 for string quartet (1964, revised 1966); No. 6 for piano (1964); No. 7 for recorder (1964); *Music* for solo flute (1961); *Bewegingen* for piccolo and piano (1961); Trio for Flute, Oboe and Clarinet (1961); *Rondeaux per deux* for piano and percussion (1962; second series, for piano 4-hands and percussion, 1964); *Spiel und Zwischenspiel* for recorder and piano (1962); *3 Pieces* for flute, oboe and cello (1962); *Chants et contrepoints* for wind quintet (1962); *Une façon de dire que les hommes de cent vingt ans ne chantent plus* for soprano, piano and 4 percussion instruments (1963); *Espaces à remplir* for 11 musicians (1963); Oboe Quartet (1964); *7 Bagatelles* for flute and piano (1964); *Ad libitum* for violin and piano (1965); *Pour faire chanter la polonaise* for flute, soprano and 3 pianos (1965); *Pour 2 Violins* (1966); *Words* for mezzo-soprano, flute, cello and piano (1966); String Trio (1967); *Musica per quattro* for horn, 2 trumpets and trombone (1967); *Beat Music* for 2 percussionists (1967); *Because Going Nowhere Takes a Long Time* for medium voice, flute and piano (1967; version for soprano, clarinet and piano, 1969); *Rounds* for clarinet and piano (1967); *Ranta Music* for percussionist (1968); *Music for a Sliding Trombone* (1968); *Musique d'atelier* for clarinet, trombone, cello and piano (1968); *Enigma* for flute, bass clarinet, piano and percussion (1969); *Symposion* for oboe, violin, viola and cello (1969); *Trio agitate* for horn, trombone and tuba (1969); *Réflexions sur le jour où Pérotin le Grand ressuscitera* for wind quintet (1969); *Polonaise* for a pianist and a percussionist (1971); *Fusion pour deux* for bass clarinet and piano (1971); *The Dog Named Boo Has a Master Called Lobo* for clarinet, violin and piano (1972); *Because It Is* for 4 clarinets (1973); *The Eighteenth of June, Springtime and Yet Already Summer* for 4 saxophones (1974); *Melody* for bass clarinet and string quartet (1974); *Inferno,* after Dante, for soprano, 2 violins, cello and harpsichord (1974); *Eine Rede* for soprano, clarinet, basset horn and bass clarinet (1974); Piano Sonatina (1960); *Voices* for piano (1964); *Just Like a Little Sonata* for piano (1964); *A Combination of Voices* for 2 pianos (1968); *New Pieces* for piano (1972); *Cadences* for piano (1975); songs.

Boise, Otis Bardwell, American organist; b. Oberlin, Ohio, Aug. 13, 1844; d. Baltimore, Dec. 2, 1912. He studied with Moscheles and Richter in Leipzig and with Kullak in Berlin. Returning to America in 1865, he occupied various posts as organist and teacher; eventually settled in Baltimore, where he taught at the Peabody Cons. Among his pupils were Ernest Hutcheson, Howard Brockway and Arthur Nevin. He publ. the textbooks *Harmony Made Practical* (N.Y., 1900) and *Music and its Masters* (N.Y., 1902).

Boismortier, Joseph Bodin de, French composer; b. Thionville (Moselle), Dec. 23, 1689; d. in Roissy-en-Brie, Oct. 28, 1755. He lived in Metz and Perpignan before settling in Paris in 1724. A prolific composer of instrumental music, he wrote more than 100 opus numbers; of these there are several for block flutes (i.e., recorders) and transverse flutes; 2 suites for clavecin; trio sonatas, among them one with the viola da gamba (1732; modern ed., Mainz, 1967); collections of pieces designed for amateurs (in the positive sense of this abused word), scored with a drone instrument, either the musette (a wind instrument), or vielle (string instrument), and publ. under such coaxing titles as "Gentillesses," or "Divertissements de campagne." Boismortier wrote also three ballet-operas, *Les Voyages de L'Amour* (1736); *Don Quichotte* (1743) and *Daphnis et Chloé* (1747), and a number of cantatas.
BIBLIOGRAPHY: H. Tribout de Morembert, "Bodin

de Boismortier; notes sur un musicien lorrain," *Revue de Musicologie* (1967); M. Pincherle, "A propos de Boismortier," *Journal Musical Français/Musica Disques* (Nov. 1968).

Boisselot, Xavier, French piano manufacturer; b. Montpellier, Dec. 3, 1811; d. Marseille, March 28, 1893. He studied with Fétis and Lesueur in Paris; received the Grand Prix de Rome in 1836; then went to Marseille where he joined the piano manufacturing company founded by his father.

Boito, Arrigo, important Italian poet and opera composer; b. Padua, Feb. 24, 1842; d. Milan, June 10, 1918. He studied at the Milan Cons. with Alberto Mazzucato and Ronchetti-Monteviti; his two cantatas, written in collaboration with Faccio, *Il 4 Giugno* (1860) and *Le Sorelle d'Italia* (1862) were performed at the Cons., and attracted a great deal of favorable attention; as a result, the Italian government granted the composers a gold medal and a stipend for foreign travel for two years. Boito spent most of his time in Paris, and also went to Poland to meet the family of his mother (who was Polish); he also visited Germany, Belgium, and England. He was strongly influenced by hearing new French and German music; upon his return to Milan he undertook the composition of his first and most significant large opera *Mefistofele,* which contains elements of conventional Italian opera, but also dramatic ideas stemming from Beethoven and Wagner. It was performed for the first time at La Scala (March 5, 1868). A controversy followed when a part of the audience objected to the unusual treatment of the subject and the music, and there were actual disorders at the conclusion of the performance. After the second production, the opera was taken off the boards, and Boito undertook a revision to effect a compromise. In this new version, the opera had a successful run in Italian cities; it was produced in Hamburg (1880); in London (in Italian) on July 6, 1880, and (in English) in Boston, on Nov. 16, 1880. It was retained in the repertory of the leading opera houses but its success never matched that of Gounod's *Faust.* Boito never completed his second opera *Nerone,* the composition of which took him more than half a century, from 1862 until 1916. The orchestral score was revised by Toscanini, and performed by him at La Scala on May 2, 1924. There are sketches for an earlier opera *Ero e Leandro,* but not enough material to attempt a completion. Boito's gift as a poet is fully equal to that as a composer. He publ. a book of verses (Turin, 1877) under the anagrammatic pen name of Tobia Gorrio; he wrote his own libretti for his operas and made admirable translations of Wagner's operas (*Tristan und Isolde, Rienzi*); wrote the libretti of *Otello* and *Falstaff* for Verdi (these libretti are regarded as his masterpieces); also for *Gioconda* by Ponchielli; *Amleto* by Faccio, etc. Boito also publ. novels. He held various honorary titles from the King of Italy; in 1892 he was appointed Inspector-General of Italian conservatories; was made honorary Mus. Doc. by Cambridge Univ. and Oxford Univ.; in 1912 he was made senator by the King of Italy.
BIBLIOGRAPHY: P. G. Molmenti, *Impressioni letterarie* (Milan, 1875); A. Boccardi, *Arrigo Boito* (Trieste,

1877); D. Mantovani, *Letteratura contemporanea* (Turin, 1893); R. Giani, *Il Nerone di A. Boito* (Turin, 1901); R. Barbiera, *A. Boito, inverso l'ideale* (Milan, 1905); M. Risolo, *Il primo Mefistofele di A. Boito* (Naples, 1916); C. Trevor, "Boito's Nero," *Musical Times* (June 1916); A. Lualdi, "A. Boito, un' anima," *Rivista Musicale Italiana* (1919); A. Pompeati, *A. Boito* (Florence, 1919); C. Ricci, *A. Boito* (Milan, 1919); F. Torrefranca, "A. Boito," *La Critica Musicale* (Nov./Dec. 1919); F. Torrefranca, "A. Boito," *Musical Quarterly* (Oct. 1920); G. M. Gatti, "Boito's Nero," *Musical Quarterly* (Oct. 1924); V. Gui, *Il Nerone di Arrigo Boito* (Milan, 1924); A. Bonaventura, *A. Boito; Mefistofele* (Milan, 1924); G. Cesari, "Note per una bibliografia delle opere di A. Boito," *Rassegna di Coltura* (March 1924); R. de Rensis, *Franco Faccio e Boito, documento* (Milan, 1934); F. Ballo, *A. Boito* (Turin, 1938); R. de Rensis, *A. Boito; aneddoti e bizzarrie poetiche e musicali* (Rome, 1942); P. Nardi, *Vita di Arrigo Boito* (Verona, 1942; 2nd ed., Milan, 1944; complete documented biography); Massimiliano Vajro, *Arrigo Boito* (Brescia, 1955); C. Orselli, "Arrigo Boito: un riesame," *Chigiana* (1968). Boito's letters were edited by R. de Rensis (Rome, 1932), who also edited Boito's articles on music (Milan, 1931).

Bok, Mary Louise Curtis, American patroness of music; b. Boston, Aug. 6, 1876; d. Philadelphia, Jan. 4, 1970. She inherited her fortune from Cyrus H. K. Curtis, founder of the Curtis Publishing Co. In 1924 she established in Philadelphia the Curtis Institute of Music and endowed it initially with a gift of $12.5 million in memory of her mother; the school had a faculty of the most distinguished American and European musicians, and it provided tuition exclusively on a scholarship basis; many talented composers and performers were its students. She was first married to Edward W. Bok in 1896; upon his death in 1930 she married Efrem Zimbalist, director of the Curtis Institute from 1941 to 1969. She purchased in England the famous Burrell Collection of Wagneriana and brought it to the U.S. Her honorary degrees include Hon. Dr. of Humane Letters, Univ. of Pennsylvania (1932), Hon. Mus. Doc., Williams College (1934), Order of Polonia Restituta (1932).

Bolck, Oskar, German composer; b. Hohenstein, March 4, 1837; d. Bremen, May 2, 1888. He studied at the Leipzig Cons. with Rietz and Moscheles; was active as theater conductor in various German towns and, as teacher, at Riga, where his opera *Pierre und Robin* was produced (1876). He wrote 2 other operas, *Gudrun* and *Der Schmied von Gretna Green*, both of which remain unperformed.

Bolcom, William, American pianist and composer; b. Seattle, May 26, 1938. He studied at the Univ. of Washington in Seattle with John Verrall; took a course in composition with Darius Milhaud at Mills College, Oakland, Calif. (1958–59), and continued to study with Milhaud in Paris (1959–61); also took a course in general esthetics with Olivier Messiaen; returning to America he studied advanced composition with Leland Smith at Stanford Univ. (1961–64). He subsequently occupied various teaching posts in Seattle and in N.Y. After absorbing a variety of techniques *sine ira et studio*, he began to experiment widely and wildly in serial thematics, musical collage, sophisticated plagiarism and microtonal electronics.

WORKS: He wrote 6 string quartets while still a teenager, a pop opera for actors and 11 instruments, entitled *Dynamite Tonite* (N.Y., Actors' Studio, Dec. 21, 1963); *Décalage* for cello and piano (1962); Octet, for flute, clarinet, bassoon, violin, viola, cello, double bass, piano (1962); several works each entitled *Session* for various instrumental ensembles and mandatory drum play (1965, 1967); *Dream Music* for percussion quartet (1967); *Oracles* for orch. (Seattle, May 2, 1965); several pieces entitled *Dream Music*; 14 piano rags (1967–70); *Dark Music* for kettledrums and cello (1970); *Frescoes* for 2 pianists, each doubling on a harmonium and harpsichord (first performed in Toronto, July 21, 1971 by Bruce Mather and Pierrette LePage); *Seasons* for guitar (N.Y., Jan. 9, 1976). He is also active as a pianist, recording and giving recitals of ragtime and, with his wife, singer **Joan Morris**, popular American songs from the 1890s–1930s. He published, with Robert Kimball, a book on the black-American song writing and musical comedy team Noble Sissle and Eubie Blake: *Reminiscing with Sissle and Blake* (N.Y., 1973).

Boldemann, Laci, Finnish-born Swedish composer; b. Helsinki, April 24, 1921; d. Munich, Aug. 18, 1969. He grew up in Germany; went to Sweden in 1939, but was forced to return to Germany for military service. His music is of a lyrical nature, showing the influence of Sibelius.

WORKS: the fairy-tale opera *Svart är vitt, sa kejsaren (Black Is White, Said the Emperor*; Stockholm, Jan. 1, 1965); the opera-musical *Dårskapens timme (Hour of Madness*; Malmö, March 22, 1968); an operatic scene, *Och så drömmer han om Per Jonathan (And He Dreams of Per Jonathan*; Stockholm, Nov. 29, 1969); *La Danza*, overture (1949–50); *Lieder der Vergänglichkeit,* cantata for baritone and strings (1951); *4 Epitaphs,* after Edgar Lee Masters, for soprano and strings (1952); Sinfonietta for Strings (1954); *Fantasia Concertante* for cello and orch. (1954); Piano Concerto (1956); *Notturno* for soprano and orch. (1958); Violin Concerto (1959); Symphony (Munich, Jan. 13, 1964); *John Bauer,* oratorio (1967); Trumpet Concerto (Malmö, Feb. 11, 1969); *Med bleck och med trä,* little overture for winds (1969); Violin Sonata (1950); *6 Small Pieces Without Pedal* for piano (1950); String Quartet (1950–57); *Canto elegiaco* for cello and piano (1962); about 50 songs.

Bolet, Jorge, brilliant Cuban-American pianist; b. Havana, Nov. 15, 1914; brother of the Cuban conductor **Alberto Bolet.** He studied piano at the Curtis Institute of Music in Philadelphia; made his American debut in New York in 1937 as a winner of the Naumburg Prize. He eventually established himself as one of the most brilliant modern virtuosos. In 1968 he joined the faculty of the School of Music of Indiana Univ. in Bloomington.

Bologna, Jacopo da. See **Jacopo da Bologna.**

Bölsche, Franz, German music editor; b. Wegenstedt, near Magdeburg, Aug. 20, 1869; d. Bad Oeynhausen, Oct. 23, 1935. He studied with Bargiel and Spitta in Berlin; became teacher of theory at the Cologne Cons. (1896–1931). He was an editor for the *Denkmäler deutscher Tonkunst,* and wrote the successful manual *Übungen und Aufgaben zum Studium der Harmonielehre* (Leipzig, 1911; 18th ed., 1938). Also composed a symphony, 4 overtures (*Tragödie der Menschen, Judith, Hero und Leander, Othello),* etc.

Bolzoni, Giovanni, Italian composer; b. Parma, May 14, 1841; d. Turin, Feb. 21, 1919. He studied at the Parma Cons.; was active as conductor in Perugia; director of the Liceo Musicale and theater conductor in Turin (1887). He composed the operas *Il Matrimonio civile* (Parma, 1870), *La Stella delle Alpi* (Savona, 1876), *Jella* (Piacenza, 1881); etc. A melodious minuet from one of his string quartets became a perennial favorite in numerous arrangements.

Bombardelli, Silvije, Croatian conductor and composer; b. Split, March 3, 1916. He studied violin in Belgrade; returning to Split in 1945 he organized an orchestra, and also conducted opera. In his music he applies modernistic procedures, including modified serial techniques.
WORKS: ballet *Stranac (The Stranger;* Split, Jan. 25, 1956); *Plameni Vjetar (The Flaming Wind)* for orch. and speaking chorus (Split, June 18, 1940); a symphony (Zagreb, Nov. 3, 1951); cantatas and choruses.
BIBLIOGRAPHY: K. Kovačević, *Hrvatski Kompozitori i Njihova Djela* (Zagreb, 1960).

Bomtempo, João Domingos, Portuguese pianist; b. Lisbon, Dec. 28, 1775; d. there, Aug. 18, 1842. He studied in Paris; lived there and in London until 1815 when he returned to Lisbon. He founded a Philharmonic Society in Lisbon; in 1833 became director of the Lisbon Cons. He wrote 6 symphonies, 4 piano concertos, 14 piano sextets, a piano quintet, and several piano sonatas; also an opera *Alessandro in Efesso.* He publ. a piano method (London, 1816).
BIBLIOGRAPHY: M. A. de Lima Cruz, *D. Bomtempo* (Lisbon, 1937).

Bon, Maarten, Dutch pianist and composer; b. Amsterdam, Aug. 20, 1933. He graduated from the Muzieklyceum in Amsterdam in 1954; studied piano with T. Bruins and Spaanderman, and composition with Baaren; then gave recitals with his wife, the violinist **Jeannelotte Hertzberger;** in 1971 was appointed pianist with the Dutch Radio Broadcasting Corporation. His compositions are whimsical: *Caprichoso y Obstinato* for solo flute (1965); *Disturbing the Peace,* improvisation for more or less 9 players (1968–69); *Let's Go Out for a Drive (and Pollute the Air),* improvisation for trombone, 3 pianists, and conductor (1970–74); *Free or Not* for 21 wind players (1972); *Sieben, jedenfalls sieben* for chamber ensemble (1976).

Bon, Willem Frederik, Dutch composer and conductor; b. Amersfoort, June 15, 1940. He studied clarinet, conducting and composition at the Cons. of Amster-

dam and The Hague. Since 1972 he has been conductor of the Eindhoven Baroque Ensemble and, since 1973, an assistant conductor of the Concertgebouw Orchestra in Amsterdam.
WORKS: 2 wind quintets (1963–66; 1969); Cello Sonata (1966); *Miniatures* for piano (1966); *Dialogues and Monologues* for piano and orch. (1968); Nocturnes for String Orch. (1968); *Sunphoneion I* for flute, vibraphone and piano (1968); *Variations on a Theme of Sweelinck* for chamber orch. (1969); *Sketches* for 13 instruments (1969); *Missa Brevis* for 4-voice choir and wind ensemble (1969); 2 symphonies: No. 1, *Usher Symphony,* after Edgar Allan Poe's short story (1968–70; originally intended as material for an opera); No. 2, *Les Prédictions* (1970); Sonata for Solo Bassoon (1970); Concerto for String Orch. (1970); *Games* for 6 winds, piano and string orch. (1970); *To Catch a Heffalump* for orch. (1971); *Riflessioni* for flute and harp (1971); *Circe,* prelude for orch. (1972); *Passacaglia in Blue* for 12 winds and double bass (1972); *Aforisms* for 15 strings (1972); *1999, 4 Prophesies of Nostradamus* for soprano and orch. (1973); Concerto for Oboe and Strings (1974).

Bona, Giovanni, cardinal; b. Mondovi, Oct. 12, 1609; d. Rome, Oct. 28, 1674. His tract *De divina psalmodia . . . tractatus historicus, symbolicus, asceticus* (Rome, 1653) contains valuable information on church music. A complete edition of his works was publ. in Rome in 1747.

Bona (or Buona), Valerio, Italian composer; b. Brescia, c.1560; date of death unknown, but he was still living in 1619. He was a Franciscan monk; maestro di cappella at the cathedrals of Vercelli (1591) and Mondovi, and at the Church of San Francesco, Milan (1596); musician at St. Francesco, Brescia (1611) and prefect at St. Fermo Maggiore, Verona (1614). He was a prolific composer in polyphonic style of sacred and secular vocal music (Masses, litanies, Lamentations, motets, madrigals, etc.), for much of which he used two choirs. Also a theorist, he publ. *Regole del contrapunto, et compositione brevemente raccolte da diuersi auttori* (Casale, 1595); *Esempii delli passagi delle Consonanze, et Dissonanze* (Milan, 1596); etc.

Bonanni, Filippo, Italian writer on music; b. Rome, Jan. 16, 1638; d. there, March 30, 1725. He was the author of the renowned manual *Gabinetto armonico pieno d'instromenti sonori, indicati, spiegati e di nuovo corretti ed accresciuti* (Rome, 1723, with 151 plates; 2nd ed. Rome, 1776).

di Bonaventura, Anthony, American pianist, brother of **Mario di Bonaventura;** b. Follensbee, West Virginia, Nov. 12, 1930. He was a child prodigy, who could play easy pieces on the piano as an infant; was soloist with the New York Philharmonic at the age of 13. He then enrolled at the Curtis Institute of Music in Philadelphia to study with Isabelle Vengerova. Upon graduation he played numerous engagements with the Philadelphia Orch., Vienna Symph. Orch., London Philharmonia, New York Philharmonic, and made appearances also with the Chicago, San Francisco, Baltimore, Cincinnati, Pittsburgh and Dallas symphonies, the London Royal Philharmonic, etc. He commissioned several composers to write special works for him, among them Luciano Berio, Milko Kelemen, Vincent Persichetti and Gÿorgi Ligeti. In 1974 he was appointed prof. of piano at Boston University.

Bonaventura, Arnaldo, Italian musicologist; b. Leghorn, July 28, 1862; d. Florence, Oct. 7, 1952. He studied law, violin and theory, but made musicology his career. He was prof. of history of music and librarian at the Royal Institute of Music until 1932; then became director of the Cons. and prof. of Music History and Esthetics.
WRITINGS: *Manuale di storia della musica* (Leghorn, 1898; 10th ed., 1920); *Elementi di Estetica musicale* (Leghorn, 1905; 3rd ed. 1926 as *Manuale di Estetica musicale*); *Dante e la musica* (Leghorn, 1904); *Storia degli stromenti musicali* (Leghorn, 1908; many other eds.); "La vita musicale in Toscana" (Florence, 1910 in *La Toscana al fine del Granducato*); *Niccolo Paganini* (1911; 3rd ed., 1925); *Saggio storico sul teatro musicale italiano* (Leghorn, 1913); *Storia e letteratura del pianoforte* (Leghorn, 1918); *I violinisti italiani moderni; Verdi* (Paris, 1923); *Bernardo Pasquini* (Rome, 1923); *Giacomo Puccini* (Leghorn, 1923); *Manuale di cultura musicale* (1924); *'Mefistofele' di Boito* (Milan, 1924); *Storia del violino, dei violinisti e della musica per violino* (Milan, 1925); *L'opera italiana* (1928); *Domenico del Mela* (1928); *Luigi Boccherini* (1931); *Musicisti livornesi* (1931); *Rossini* (1934); numerous essays in various journals. He was editor of works of J. Peri, B. Strozzi, Frescobaldi, da Firenze and others.

di Bonaventura, Mario, American conductor, educator, music publisher; b. Follensbee, West Virginia, Feb. 20, 1924. He studied violin in N.Y.; won an award of the N.Y. Philharmonic in Young Composers' Composition Competition in 1941. In 1947 he went to Paris where he became a scholarship student of Nadia Boulanger in composition and completed the piano accompaniment course at the Paris Cons. (1953). He studied conducting with Igor Markevitch at the Mozarteum in Salzburg and in Paris. As a laureate of the 1952 Besançon International Conducting Competition, he was chosen to conduct the orch. of the Paris Cons. at the Prix de Paris competition; he subsequently conducted film scores in France and wrote music arrangements for United Artists in Paris and London. In 1953 he was awarded the Lili Boulanger-Dinu Lipatti Memorial Prize in Composition. In 1954-56 he was staff pianist for the Pasdeloup Orchestra in Paris; wrote jazz arrangements for Django Reinhardt, guitarist, and various orchestral groups. Returning to the U.S. he was conductor of the Fort Lauderdale Symph. (1959-62) and prof. of music at Dartmouth College (1962-73); received an honorary doctor's degree at Dartmouth College. In 1963 he inaugurated an ambitious series of summer festivals at Dartmouth's Hopkins Center under the title "Congregation of the Arts," where 389 contemporary works were performed, during 7 summers, including 38 world premières. Among composers in residence were Zoltán Kodály, Frank Martin, Boris Blacher, Hans Werner Henze, Ernst Krenek, Witold Lutoslaw-

ski, Luigi Dallapiccola, Roberto Gerhard, Walter Piston, Roger Sessions, Carlos Chávez, Easley Blackwood, Elliott Carter, Aaron Copland, Henry Cowell, Ross Lee Finney, Alberto Ginastera, Peter Mennin and Vincent Persichetti. In 1968 Mario di Bonaventura produced and directed the 4th International Anton von Webern Festival; also initiated a program for promoting new music, which awarded 55 commissions to composers in 19 countries. As a conductor, he led orchestras in France, Germany, Russia, Poland, Hungary, Yugoslavia, Rumania and Israel, as well as in the U.S., during which he presented the world premières of 139 new works; composers who have dedicated works to him include Lutoslawski, Zsolt Durkó, Malipiero, Franco Donatoni, Alberto Ginastera and Boris Blacher. In 1974 di Bonaventura was appointed Vice President and Director of Publications of G. Schirmer/Associated Music Publishers, New York.

Bonavia, Ferruccio, eminent critic and composer; b. Trieste, Feb. 20, 1877; d. London, Feb. 5, 1950. He studied music in Trieste and Milan; went to England as a violinist (1898); became music critic of the *Manchester Guardian* and of the London *Daily Telegraph.* His compositions include a one-act opera, violin concerto, string octet, string quartet, songs, etc. He wrote a monograph on Verdi (London, 1930; 2nd ed., 1947); miniature biographies of Mozart (1938) and Rossini (1941); also a fanciful book of imaginary conversations, *Musicians in Elysium* (1949).

Bonawitz, Johann Heinrich, German conductor and composer; b. Dürkheim-on-Rhine, Dec. 4, 1839; d. London, Aug. 15, 1917. He studied at the Liège Cons. as a child; in 1852 his parents took him to America. He conducted an unsuccessful season of popular symphony concerts in N.Y. in 1872-73; then produced two of his operas, *The Bride of Messina* (Philadelphia, April 22, 1874) and *Ostrolenka* (Philadelphia, May 3, 1874). He composed two other operas, *Irma* and *Napoleon*; also wrote some sacred choral music. He eventually returned to Europe.

Bonci, Alessandro, Italian lyric tenor; b. Cesena (Romagna), Feb. 10, 1870; d. Viserba (near Rimini), Aug. 8, 1940. He studied with Carlo Pedrotti in Pesaro; made his début in 1896 at the Teatro Regio in Parma as Fenton in *Falstaff;* then sang at La Scala, and at St. Petersburg, Vienna, Berlin, Lisbon, Madrid, London, etc.; later made appearances in South America and Australia. In Dec., 1906, he made his New York début at the new Manhattan Opera House, where he was engaged for three seasons; made his début at the Metropolitan Opera as the Duke in *Rigoletto* (Nov. 22, 1907); was on the staff for three seasons. Later he made guest appearances at many European opera houses, and after his retirement taught voice privately in Milan. His was a lyric tenor of great charm, and he was one of the few Italian artists to achieve distinction as a singer of German lieder.

Bond, Carrie Jacobs, American composer of sentimental songs; b. Janesville, Wisconsin, Aug. 11, 1862; d. Glendale, Calif., Dec. 28, 1946. She was naturally gifted in music and painting, and improvised songs to her own words at the piano. She organized a music selling agency and published her own songs under the imprint Carrie Jacobs Bond and Son. Although deficient in musical training, she succeeded in producing sweet melodies in lilting rhythms with simple accompaniment that became extremely popular in America. Her first song was *Is My Dolly Dead?* This was followed by her greatest hit, *A Perfect Day,* and a series of other successful songs: *I Love You Truly, God Remembers When the World Forgets, Life's Garden* and many others. She published an autobiography, *The Roads of Melody* (1927) and an album of her poems with philosophical comments under the title, *The End of the Road.*

Bondeville, Emmanuel de, French composer; b. Rouen, Oct. 29, 1898. He studied organ in Rouen, and composition in Paris with Jean Déré. He was music director of the Eiffel Tower Radio Station (1935–49); managing director of the Opéra-Comique from 1949 to 1952; then joined the administration of the Grand Opéra. His works include 2 operas, both produced at the Opéra-Comique: *L'École des Maris* (June 19, 1935) and *Madame Bovary* (June 1, 1951); a symph. triptych to poems from Rimbaud's *Illuminations*: *Le Bal des pendus* (Paris, Dec. 6, 1930), *Ophélie* (Paris, March 29, 1933; also many performances abroad) and *Marine* (Paris, March 11, 1934); *Symphonie lyrique* (1957); *Symphonie chorégraphique* (1966); choral works and songs.

Bondon, Jacques, French composer; b. Boulbon (Bouches-du-Rhône), Dec. 6, 1927. He studied violin and painting in Marseille. In 1945 he went to Paris, where he took courses in composition with Kœchlin, Milhaud and Jean Rivier. After early experimentation with ultra-modern techniques he tergiversated to prudential modernism. He became associated with Martenot, and wrote a concerto for Ondes Martenot and orchestra (1955); also composed music for films and for the radio.
    WORKS: for orchestra: *La Coupole* (1954); *Le Taillis ensorcelé* (1954); *Suite indienne* (1958); *Musique pour un autre monde* (1962); *Concert de printemps* for trumpet, strings and percussion (1957); *Concerto de Mars* for guitar and orch. (Paris, Nov. 20, 1966); *Mélousine au rocher,* radio opera (Luxembourg, Oct. 30, 1969); *Le Soleil multicolore* for flute, harp and viola (1970); *Giocoso* for violin solo and string orch. (1970); *Lumières et formes animées* for string orch. (Paris, Oct. 6, 1970); opera, *Ana et l'Albatros* (Metz, Nov. 21, 1970); a science-fiction opera-ballet, *i. 330* (Nantes, May 20, 1975).
    BIBLIOGRAPHY: Jean Roy, *Musique française* (Paris, 1962; pp. 471–483); M.-J. Chauvin, "Entretien avec Jacques Bondon," *Courrier Musical de France* (Jan./April 1970).

Bonelli (real name **Bunn**), **Richard,** American baritone; b. Port Byron, N.Y., Feb. 6, 1887. He studied at Syracuse Univ., later with Jean de Reszke; made his operatic début as Valentine in *Faust* at the Brooklyn Academy of Music, N.Y., April 21, 1915; then sang in Europe at the Monte Carlo Opera, at La Scala, in Paris (with Mary Garden) and on tours throughout Ger-

many. He was a member of the Chicago Opera (1925–31) and of the Metropolitan Opera (début as Germont in *Traviata,* Dec. 1, 1932); retired in 1945.

Bonis, Mélanie (Mme. Albert Domange), French composer; b. Paris, Jan. 21, 1858; d. Sarcelles (Seine-et-Oise) March 18, 1937. She studied at the Paris Cons. with César Franck and Guiraud; wrote 22 chamber works (of which a Trio is still performed); 150 piano pieces; 27 choruses; also a Fantasy for piano and string orch. About 200 of her works are published.

Bonnet, Joseph, eminent French organist; b. Bordeaux, March 17, 1884; d. Ste. Luce-sur-Mer, Quebec, Aug. 2, 1944. He studied with his father, organist at Ste. Eulalie; at the age of 14 he was appointed regular organist at St. Nicholas, and soon after at St. Michel; entered the class of Guilmant at the Paris Cons. and graduated with the first prize. In 1906 he won the post of organist at St. Eustache over many competitors. After extensive tours on the continent and in England, he became organist of the Concerts du Conservatoire as successor to Guilmant (1911). He made his American début in New York (Jan. 30, 1917), followed by successful tours of the United States. He wrote many pieces for his instrument, and edited for publication all the works played in his series of New York concerts as *Historical Organ Recitals* (6 vols.); also publ. an anthology of early French organ music (N.Y., 1942).
    BIBLIOGRAPHY: H. B. Gaul, "Bonnet, Bossi, Karg-Elert. Three Aperçus," *Musical Quarterly* (July 1918).

Bononcini, Antonio Maria (not Marco Antonio as he is often listed), Italian opera composer, son of **Giovannia Maria** and brother of **Giovanni;** b. Modena, June 18, 1677; d. there, July 8, 1726. He studied with his father; his first success came with the production of his opera *Il trionfo di Camilla, regina dei Volsci* (Naples, Dec. 26, 1696). This opera was produced in many other theaters in Italy, sometimes under different titles, as *Amore per amore, La fede in cimento,* etc. It was presented in London (March 31, 1706) with great acclaim. In 1702 Bononcini was in Berlin; from 1704–1711 he was in Vienna where he produced the operas *Teraspo* (Nov. 15, 1704); *Arminio* (July 26, 1706); *La conquista delle Spagne di Scipione Africano* (Oct. 1, 1707); *La presa di Tebe* (Oct. 1, 1708); *Tigrane, re d'Armenia* (July 26, 1710). Returning to Italy, he produced the following operas in Milan: *Il tiranno eroe* (Dec. 26, 1715); *Sesostri, re di Egitto* (Feb. 2, 1716); and *Griselda* (Dec. 26, 1718). In his native town of Modena, he directed his operas *L'enigma disciolto* (Oct. 15, 1716); *Lucio Vero* (Nov. 5, 1716). Bononcini's last opera, *Rosiclea in Dania,* was staged in Naples (Oct. 1, 1721). He wrote 19 operas in all, and 3 oratorios. His most famous opera, *Il trionfo di Camilla,* has often been erroneously attributed to his brother; several songs from it were published in London by Walsh.
    BIBLIOGRAPHY: L. F. Valdrighi, *I Bononcini da Modena* (Modena, 1882); for details of his operatic productions see Loewenberg's *Annals of Opera* (1943; 2nd ed., 1955).

Bononcini, Giovanni (not Giovanni Battista, despite the fact that this name appears on some of his compositions), the best known composer of the Bononcini family; son of **Giovanni Maria;** b. Modena, July 18, 1670; d. Vienna, July 9, 1747 (buried July 11). His first teacher was his father; also studied with G. P. Colonna in Bologna, and took cello lessons from Giorgio. In 1687 he was a cellist in the chapel of San Petronio, Bologna; in the same year he became maestro di cappella at San Giovanni, in Monte. He published his first work *Trattenimenti da camera* for string trio in Bologna at the age of fifteen, followed in quick succession by a set of chamber concertos, 'sinfonie' for small ensembles, Masses, and instrumental duos (1685–91). In 1691 he went to Rome, where he produced his first opera *Serse* (Jan. 25, 1694), and shortly afterwards, another opera *Tullo Ostilio* (Feb., 1694). In 1698 he went to Vienna as court composer; there he brought out his operas *La fede pubblica* (Jan. 6, 1699) and *Gli affetti più grandi vinti dal più giusto* (July 26, 1701). He spent two years (1702–04) at the court of Queen Sophie Charlotte in Berlin; at her palace in Charlottenburg he produced, in the summer of 1702, the opera *Polifemo;* here he also presented a new opera *Gli amori di Cefalo e Procri* (Oct. 16, 1704). After the Queen's death (Feb. 1, 1705) the opera company was disbanded; Bononcini returned to Vienna and staged the following operas: *Endimione* (July 10, 1706); *Turno Aricino* (July 26, 1707); *Mario fuggitivo* (1708); *Abdolonimo* (Feb. 3, 1709) and *Muzio Scevola* (July 10, 1710). In 1711 Bononcini returned to Italy with his brother (who was also in Vienna). In 1719 he was in Rome where he produced the opera *Erminia*. In 1720 he received an invitation to join the Royal Academy of Music in London, of which Handel was director, and the Italian Opera Company connected with it. A famous rivalry developed between the supporters of Handel, which included the King, and the group of noblemen (Marlborough, Queensberry, Rutland, and Sunderland) who favored Bononcini and other Italian composers. Indicative of the spirit of the time was the production at the King's Theater of the opera *Muzio Scevola* with the first act written by Amadei, the second by Bononcini (he may have used material from his earlier setting of the same subject), and the third by Handel (April 15, 1721). By general agreement Handel won the verdict of popular approval; this episode may have inspired the well known poem published at the time ("Some say, compar'd to Bononcini, That Mynheer Handel's but a ninny, etc."). Other operas brought out by Bononcini in London were: *Astarto* (Nov. 19, 1720); *Crispo* (Jan. 10, 1722); *Farnace* (Nov. 27, 1723); *Calpurnia* (April 18, 1724) and *Astianatte* (May 6, 1727). Bononcini soon suffered a series of setbacks, first with the death of his chief supporter, Marlborough (1722), and then with the revelation that a madrigal he had submitted to the Academy of Music was an arrangement of a work by Lotti, which put Bononcini's professional integrity in doubt. To this was added his strange association with one Count Ughi, a self-styled alchemist who claimed the invention of a philosopher's stone, and who induced Bononcini to invest his earnings in his scheme for making gold. After his London debacle, Bononcini went to Paris where he was engaged as a cellist at the court of Louis XV. He was referred to in *Le Mercure de France* (Feb. 7, 1735) as the composer of 78 operas. In 1735 he was in Lisbon; in 1737, in Vienna where he produced the oratorio *Ezechia* (April 4, 1737) and a *Te Deum* (1740). Reduced to poverty, he petitioned the young Empress Maria Theresa for a pension, which was granted in Oct. 1742, giving him a monthly stipend of 50 florins, received regularly until his death on July 9, 1747 at the age of 77. This date, and the circumstances of his last years in Vienna, were first made known in the valuable paper by Kurt Hueber, *Gli ultimi anni di Giovanni Bononcini, Notizie e documenti inediti*, publ. by the Academy of Sciences, Letters and Arts of Modena (Dec., 1954). Among Bononcini's works, other than operas, are 7 oratorios (including *Ezechia*; all on various biblical subjects), and instrumental works published in London by Walsh: several suites for harpsichord; *Cantate e Duetti*, dedicated to George I (1721); Divertimenti for harpsichord (1722); *Funeral Anthem for John, Duke of Marlborough* (1722); *12 sonatas or chamber airs for 2 violins and a bass* (1732), etc. For further details regarding Bononcini's operas see Loewenberg's *Annals of Opera* (1943; 2nd ed., 1955).

Bononcini, Giovanni Maria, Italian composer; father of **Giovanni** and **Antonio Maria Bononcini;** b. Montecorone (Modena), Sept. 23, 1642; d. Modena, Oct. 19, 1678. He studied with Colonna in Bologna; as a very young man, he entered the service of Duke Francesco II, and was maestro di cappella at the churches of San Giovanni in Monte and San Petronio in Bologna. In 1668 he became a member of the celebrated Accademia Filarmonica there; then he returned to Modena; in 1671 he was a violinist in the court orchestra there; in 1674 was maestro di cappella at the Cathedral of Monte (Modena). He had 8 children, of whom the only two who survived infancy were Giovanni and Antonio Maria.

WORKS: Bononcini published 11 sets of instrumental works: *I primi frutti del giardino musicale* (Venice, 1666); *Varii fiori* (Bologna, 1669); *Arie, correnti, sarabande, gighe e allemande* (Bologna, 1671); *Sinfonia, allemande, correnti e sarabande* (Bologna, 1671); *Sonate* (Venice, 1672); *Ariette, correnti, gighe, allemande e sarabande* (Bologna, 1673); *Trattenimenti musicali* (Bologna, 1675); *Arie e correnti* (Bologna, 1678). Vocal Works: *Cantate da camara* for solo voice and 2 violins (Bologna, 1677); *Madrigali* for 5 voices (Bologna, 1678). A treatise, *Musico prattico* (Bologna, 1673; reprinted 1688, 1969; a German translation was publ. in Stuttgart, 1701).

BIBLIOGRAPHY: W. Klenz, *G. M. Bononcini of Modena; a Chapter in Baroque Instrumental Music* (Durham, N.C., 1962).

Bononcini, Marco Antonio. See **Bononcini, Antonio Maria.**

Bonporti, Francesco Antonio, Italian composer; b. Trento (baptized June 11), 1672; d. Padua, Dec. 19, 1748. He studied theology in Innsbruck and Rome; in 1695 returned to Trento; was ordained priest and served as a cleric at the Cathedral of Trento. He publ. 3 sets of 10 trio sonatas each (Venice, 1696, 1698 and

1703); 10 sonatas for violin and bass (Venice, 1707); 10 'concerti a 4' and 5 'concertini' for violin and bass; 6 motets for soprano, violin and bass. He also wrote 2 sets of minuets (50 in each set) which are lost. Four of his "Invenzioni" were mistaken for Bach's works and were included in the Bachgesellschaft edition (XLV, part 1, p. 172). Henry Eccles publ. the fourth of these pieces as his own, incorporating it in his violin sonata No. 11.

BIBLIOGRAPHY: G. Barblan, *Un musicista trentino, F. A. Bonporti* (Florence, 1940); Ch. Bouvet, "Un Groupe de compositions musicales de Bonporti publiées sous le nom de Bach, *Union Musicologique* (The Hague, 1921).

Bonsel, Adriaan, Dutch flutist and composer; b. Hilversum, Aug. 4, 1918. He studied at the Amsterdam Cons.; appeared as flute soloist in recital and with various orchestras.

WORKS: Suite for Flute and String Orch. (1946); *Folkloristic Suite* for orch. (1948); Clarinet concerto (1950); 2 symphonies (1956, 1957); Divertimento for Small Orch. (1957); *S. O. S.*, overture (1962); *Vrede-Oorlog-Vrede? (Peace-War-Peace?) Moto-perpetuo?* for orch. (1975); *Minneliederen*, 6 love songs for baritone, chorus and small orch. (1957); 2 wind quintets (1949, 1953); *Elegy* for solo viola (1961); *Concert Etudes* for solo flute (1963); *Musica* for flute, cello and piano (1971); *Anthriscus Sylvestris*, divertimento for 12 flutes (1974); Octet for Winds (1975).

Bontempi (real name **Angelini**), **Giovanni Andrea,** Italian composer and writer on music; b. Perugia, c. 1624; d. Brufa Torgiana, near Perugia, June 1, 1705. He was a choir boy at San Marco in Venice (1643); studied with Virgilio Mazzocchi; was maestro di cappella in Rome; then in Venice. He assumed the name Bontempi after his patron, Cesare Bontempi. In 1650 he entered the service of Johann Georg I of Saxony; in 1651 became head of the court chapel in Dresden; in 1680 he returned to Italy. His opera *Paride* (to his own libretto; Dresden, Nov. 3, 1662) was the first Italian opera produced in Dresden. Two later operas, both produced in Dresden, were *Apollo e Dafne* (in collaboration with Perandis; 1672) and *Giove e Io* (also with Perandis; 1673). He also composed an oratorio, *Martirio di San Emiliano;* published the treatises *Nova quatuor vocibus componendi methodus* (Dresden, 1660); *Tractus in quo demonstrantur occultae convenientiae sonorum systematis participati* (Bologna, 1690); *Historia musica, nella quale si ha piena cognitione della teorica e della pratica antica della musica harmonica secondo la dottrina de' Greci* (Perugia, 1695).

BIBLIOGRAPHY: G. B. Rossi Scotti, *Di Giovanni Andrea Bontempi di Perugia* (1878).

Bonvin, Ludwig, choral conductor and scholar; b. Siders, Switzerland, Feb. 17, 1850; d. Buffalo, Feb. 18, 1939. His musical training in early youth was irregular; as a musician he was chiefly self-taught; studied medicine in Vienna; entered the Jesuit novitiate in Holland (1874), where he became organist and choirmaster; continued his musical studies, especially of early sacred works. He settled in Buffalo, N.Y., as a

choral and orchestral director at Canisius College (1887-1907); then devoted himself exclusively to music scholarship; promulgated a theory of mensural rhythm in Gregorian chant. He published much sacred music, including 8 Masses; also a symphony; *Christmas Night's Dream* for string orch.; many pieces for organ, piano, violin, and voice; his works exceed 125 opus numbers.

WRITINGS: "Gregorian Accompaniment," *Musica sacra* (1931 and 1932); *Musical Accents in Gregorian Chant* (1932); "On Syrian Liturgical Chant," *Musical Quarterly* (Oct. 1918); "The 'Measure' in Gregorian Music," *Musical Quarterly* (Jan. 1929); etc.

BIBLIOGRAPHY: F. E. Bunse, "Ludwig Bonvin," *Musica sacra* (Jan. 1933).

Boom, Jan (Johannes) van, Dutch pianist and composer; b. Utrecht, Oct. 15, 1807; d. Stockholm, March 19, 1872. He began his career as a concert pianist at the age of 18; after a tour in Scandinavia, he settled in Stockholm, where he taught at the Royal Academy (1849-65). He composed piano pieces of the salon type.

Boone, Charles, American composer of the avant-garde; b. Cleveland, June 21, 1939. He studied with Karl Schiske at the Vienna Academy of Music (1960-61); took private lessons with Ernst Krenek and Adolph Weiss in Los Angeles (1961-63); attended Univ. of Southern Calif. (B.M., 1963) and San Francisco State College (M.A., 1968); served as chairman of the San Francisco Composers' Forum and coordinator of Mills College Performing Group and Tape Music Center. In his music he strives to create a sonic environment on purely structural lines, employing serial matrices, coloristic contrasts and spatial parameters of performing instruments, with resulting styles ranging from lyrical pointillism to static sonorism. He also avails himself of electronic resources.

WORKS: *Icarus* for flute solo (1964); *Song of Suchness* for soprano, flute, piccolo, viola, piano and celesta (1964); *Parallels* for violin and piano (1964); *Oblique Formation* for flute and piano (1965); *Starfish* for a small ensemble (1966); *The Yellow Bird* for orch. (1967); *Constant Comment* for stereophonic tape (1967); *Shadow* for oboe solo, tape and orch. (1968); *The Edge of the Land* for orch. (1968); *Not Now* for clarinet solo (1969); Quartet, for violin, clarinet, cello and piano (1970); *Zephyrus* for oboe and piano (1970); *Chinese Texts* for soprano and orch. (1970).

Booren, Jo van den, Dutch composer; b. Maastricht, March 14, 1935. He studied trumpet with Marinus Komst and composition with Kees van Baaren and Klaus Huber; was active as an orchestral trumpet player. In his music he pursues the goal of sonorous structuralism; some of his works bear ostentatiously abstract titles.

WORKS: Trio for Oboe, Clarinet and Bassoon (1960); Sonata for 3 Clarinets (1962); *Suite dionysienne* for English horn and string orch. (1963-64); *Estremi* for oboe, violin, viola and cello (1967); *Spectra* for wind quintet (1967); *Capriccio* for brass orch. (1968); *Spiel I* for oboe and electronic sound (1969); *Strofa I* for solo cello (1969); *Strofa II* for solo trumpet

(1970); *Strofa III* for solo horn (1972); *Equilibrio* for solo flute (1970); *Ballade* for solo oboe (1971); *Intrada Festiva* for 4 horns, 4 trumpets and 4 trombones (1971); *Akirob* for flute, violin and viola (1972); *Potpourri 1973* for brass quintet (1973); *Sinfonia Jubilata* for orch. (Tilburg, Oct. 3, 1975); *Birds,* a "story" for 5 flutes (1975).

Boosey & Hawkes, British music publishers. **Thomas Boosey** was a London book seller and a continental traveller since 1792. He was often asked to handle music, and in 1816 founded a music publishing house on Holles Street. On the continent he met eminent musicians of the time; he visited Vienna and negotiated about publication with Beethoven (who mentions Boosey's name in one of his letters to the Royal Philh. Society in London). Boosey's main stock consisted of Italian and French operas; he owned copyrights of Bellini, Donizetti and Verdi (until 1854); publ. inexpensive English editions of standard European works. In the 1820's he put his son, **Thomas,** in charge of musical publications. In 1846 the firm of Boosey & Sons began publishing band music; in 1855 (in conjunction with the flutist R. S. Pratten) the manufacture of improved flutes was begun; in 1868 the firm acquired Henry Distin's factory for musical instruments, and supplied band instruments for the British and Colonial armies. It was this development that eventually brought about the merger of Boosey and Hawkes. **William Henry Hawkes** was a trumpeter-in-ordinary to Queen Victoria. He established in 1865 a workshop of band instruments and an edition of concert music for orchestra and became a strong competitor of Boosey & Sons from 1885 on. Economic pressure forced the amalgamation of the two firms in 1930, combining valuable editions covering a whole century of music. A branch of Boosey & Sons had been established in New York (1892), discontinued in 1900 and re-established in 1906; after the merger, Boosey & Hawkes opened offices in New York, Chicago, and Los Angeles. In Canada, the business was inaugurated in 1913; the Editions Hawkes started a Paris branch in 1922; further affiliates were established in Australia (1933), India (1937), Argentine (1945), South Africa (1946), and Germany (1950). After World War II the factories for the manufacture of band instruments in London were greatly expanded; quantity production of wind instruments, harmonicas and drums enabled the firm to extend the market to all parts of the world. For a few years after World War II Boosey & Hawkes leased Covent Garden. In 1927 the firm acquired the American rights of Enoch & Sons; in 1943 the catalogue of Adolph Fürstner, containing all the operas of Richard Strauss, was bought for certain territories. In 1947, the Koussevitzky catalogue (Edition Russe de Musique and Edition Gutheil) was purchased, including the major output of Stravinsky, Prokofiev and Rachmaninoff. Other acquisitions include the copyrights of publications of Winthrop Rogers and Rudall Carte.

Boott, Francis, American composer; b. Boston, Mass., June 24, 1813; d. there, March 2, 1904. He was educated at Harvard (grad., 1831); lived for a time in Florence, Italy, where he studied music; returned to the U.S. in 1874, settling in Cambridge, Mass. In April, 1904, he bequeathed $10,000 to Harvard Univ. (which was increased through capital gains to $15,246 in 1960), the interest to form an annual prize for the best 4-part vocal composition written by a Harvard man. He was a prolific composer of secular and sacred songs, anthems, and chorales, many of which were included in the service book of King's Chapel, Boston. His songs *Here's a health to King Charles, When Sylvia sings,* and *Lethe* were once very popular.

Bopp, Wilhelm, German conductor and pedagogue; b. Mannheim, Nov. 4, 1863; d. Baden-Baden, June 11, 1931. He studied at the Leipzig Cons.; also took courses in conducting with Emil Paur at Mannheim; was teacher at the Mannheim Cons.; in 1907 moved to Vienna, where he became director of the Conservatorium der Musikfreunde.

Borch, Gaston Louis Christopher, composer and conductor; b. Guines, France, March 8, 1871; d. Stockholm, Sweden, Feb. 14, 1926. He studied in Paris with Massenet (comp.) and Delsart (cello); then with Svendsen in Copenhagen; conducted various organizations in Norway (1896–99); came to the U.S. in 1899 as cellist with the Thomas Orch. in Chicago; then played in the Pittsburgh Orch. (1903–06); conducted various orchestras in Switzerland, France, Belgium, Holland, and Germany. He composed 3 symph. poems: *Geneviève de Paris, Quo Vadis,* and *Frithjof;* made popular arrangements of standard classics for piano, violin, and cello. His one-act opera, *Silvio* (written as a sequel to *Cavalleria Rusticana*) was produced in Oslo, 1897. He published a *Practical Manual of Instrumentation* (Boston, 1918).

Borchard, Adolphe, French pianist and composer; b. Le Havre, June 30, 1882; d. Paris, Dec. 13, 1967. He studied at the Paris Cons. with Diémer and Lenepveu, where he won prizes for piano (1903) and composition (1905; 1907); toured extensively as a pianist, making his American début in 1910; later settled in Paris as director of various musical activities sponsored by the French government. He composed *Es Kual Herria (The Basque Country)* for piano and orch. (Paris, 1922); *En Marge de Shakespeare* for orch. (1923); *L'Élan* for orch. (1923); *Sept estampes amoureuses* for orch. (1927); numerous songs.

Borchers, Gustav, German vocal teacher; b. at Woltwiesche (Brunswick), Aug. 18, 1865; d. Leipzig, Jan. 19, 1913. He studied at the Leipzig Cons. (1887–89); then conducted various choral societies; in 1898 he founded a seminary for singing teachers, which later employed the methods of Jaques-Dalcroze ("rhythmical gymnastics") and Eitz ("Tonwort"); Borchers published a monograph on the "Tonwort" theory (1908).

Borck, Edmund von, talented German composer; b. Breslau, Feb. 22, 1906; killed in action near Nettuno, Italy, Feb. 16, 1944. He studied composition in Breslau (1920–26), and music history at the Univ. of Berlin; held several positions as opera conductor in Berlin and Frankfurt; then taught theory and composition in Berlin, until drafted into the Army in 1940. His progress as a composer was rapid; his early works indicated an original creative ability, and his death in combat was a great loss to German music. His style of composition is neo-classical, with strong contrapuntal structure; the rather austere and reticent mode of expression assumes in Borck's music a colorful aspect through a variety of melodic and rhythmic devices, often in a rhapsodically romantic vein.

WORKS: Concerto for Alto Saxophone and Orch. (1932); Violin Sonata (1932); *Orchesterstücke* (1933); *Ländliche Kantate* (1934); Concerto for Orch. (1936); Sextet for Flute and Strings (1936); *Kleine Suite* for unaccompanied flute (1938); *2 Fantasiestücke* for orch. (1940); Piano Concerto (1941); *Orphika,* 'an Apollonian transformation' for orch. (1941); an opera, *Napoleon* (Gera, 1942).

BIBLIOGRAPHY: K. Laux, "Edmund von Borck," in *Musik und Musiker der Gegenwart* (Essen, 1949); S. Borris, *Beiträge zu einer Musikkunde* (Berlin, 1948); K. H. Wörner, *Musik der Gegenwart* (Mainz, 1949).

Borde, Jean Benjamin de la. See **La Borde, Jean Benjamin de.**

Bordes, Charles, French choral conductor; b. Roche-Corbon, near Vouvray-sur-Loire, May 12, 1863; d. Toulon, Nov. 8, 1909. He studied piano with Marmontel; organ and composition with César Franck (1887–90). In 1890 he became maître de chapelle at St.-Gervais in Paris; in 1892 he established the Association des Chanteurs de St.-Gervais and presented with his church choir a series of regular concerts of French and Italian Renaissance music. In 1894, in association with Guilmant and d'Indy, he organized the Schola Cantorum, orginally for the purpose of training singers in the Palestrina style; at the same time he founded the *Tribune de St.-Gervais* as the official organ of the Schola Cantorum; the first issue appeared in Jan., 1895. In 1898 Bordes made a tour of France with his choir. In 1899 he founded a Schola Cantorum in Avignon; in 1905 he organized the Schola de Montpellier. His influence on musical culture in France, particularly in the field of old choral music, was considerable; in his numerous articles in French newspapers and magazines, and particularly in *La Grande Encyclopédie,* he disclosed profound scholarship. Bordes also took interest in folk music; in 1889 he was commissioned by the French government to make a study of Basque folksongs; he published 100 of these in *Archives de la tradition basque.*

WORKS: *Suite basque* for flute and string quartet (1888); *Danses béarnaises* (1888); *Rapsodie basque* for piano and orch. (1890); *Divertissement* for trumpet and orch. (1902); an opera, *Les Trois Vagues* (unfinished; MS in the library of the Paris Opéra); numerous arrangements of Basque songs. He edited several anthologies of old French music, published by the Schola Cantorum.

BIBLIOGRAPHY: *Charles Bordes, In memoriam* (Paris, Schola Cantorum, 1909); O. Séré, "Charles Bordes," in *Musiciens français d'aujourd'hui* (Paris, 1921); articles in the Aug. 1924 issue of *La Revue Musicale* (Paul Dukas, "Charles Bordes"; G. Samazeuilh, "Un Drame basque de Charles Bordes"; also a catalogue of works); F. P. Albert, *Charles Bordes à Ma-*

guelonne (Paris, 1926); René de Castera, "La Fondation de la Schola Cantorum," in *La Schola cantorum, 1925.*

Bordes-Pène, Léontine Marie, French pianist; b. Lorient, Nov. 25, 1858; d. Rouen, Jan. 24, 1924. She graduated with the first prize at the Paris Cons. in 1872; dedicated her concert career to propagandizing French music; she was the sister-in-law of Charles Bordes, and a friend of César Franck, Vincent d'Indy, etc. She suffered a paralytic stroke in 1890, and lived the rest of her life in Rouen.

BIBLIOGRAPHY: G. Samazeuilh, "Madame Bordes-Pène," *La Revue Musicale* (1924).

Bordier, Jules, French composer; b. Angers, Dec. 23, 1846; d. there, Jan. 29, 1896. He founded the concerts of the Association Artistique d'Angers in 1875; went to Paris (1894) as partner in the music publishing house of Baudoux & Cie. He composed a *Danse macabre* for violin; the operas *Nadia* (Brussels, 1887) and *Le Fiancé de la Mer* (Rouen, 1895); choruses.

Bordogni, Giovanni Marco, distinguished Italian tenor and singing teacher; b. Gazzaniga, near Bergamo, Jan. 23, 1789; d. Paris, July 31, 1856. He was a pupil of Simone Mayr; made his début at La Scala, Milan, in 1813. From 1819–33 he was engaged at the Théâtre des Italiens, Paris; later devoted himself to teaching. From 1820 (with occasional interruptions) he was prof. at the Paris Cons. His 36 vocalises, in 2 suites, have run through many editions; he also published several other sets.

Bordoni, Faustina. See **Hasse, Faustina.**

Borel-Clerc (real name **Clerc**), **Charles,** French composer of popular music; b. Pau, Sept. 22, 1879; d. Cannes, April 9, 1959. He studied music at first in Toulouse; at the age of 17 he went to Paris, where he studied the oboe at the Paris Cons. with Gillet, and composition with Lenepveu; then played oboe in various Paris orchestras. He wrote numerous operettas, music revues, and a great number of songs; his greatest success came with *La Matchiche* (1903), a song that became world-famous. His other celebrated songs are *C'est jeune et ça n'sait pas; Madelon de la Victoire* (1918; a sequel to the war song *Madelon* by Camille Robert); many chansonettes for Maurice Chevalier and other artists.

Boretz, Benjamin, American music critic, editor and occasional composer; b. New York, Oct. 3, 1934. He studied at Brooklyn College, at Brandeis Univ. and at Princeton Univ.; took courses in composition with Milton Babbitt, Irving Fine, Darius Milhaud and Roger Sessions. In 1964 he was appointed to the faculty of N.Y. Univ. In 1962 he founded a non-periodical publication, *Perspectives of New Music,* radiating potent charges of musical profundity. Among his works is a Concerto Grosso (1955); Divertimento for Chamber Orch. (1955); Violin Concerto (1957); String Quartet (1958); Brass Quintet (1963); and several "group variations" for the computer synthesizer.

Borgatti, Giuseppe, Italian tenor; b. Cento, March 19, 1871; d. Reno, Lago Maggiore, Oct. 18, 1950. He studied with Alessandro Busi in Bologna. He was engaged at La Scala in Milan and was particularly successful in Wagnerian roles. At the end of his career he became blind, but continued teaching activities.

Borgatti, Renata, Italian pianist, daughter of the tenor **Giuseppe Borgatti**; b. Bologna, March 2, 1894. She studied in Bologna and Munich; has appeared as soloist with major orchestras in Europe; has given programs of complete works of Debussy; also played all of Bach's *Well-tempered Clavier* over the BBC network in London. After World War II she taught in Switzerland and Italy.

Borge, Victor (real name **Borge Rosenbaum**), Danish pianist; b. Copenhagen, Jan. 3, 1909. He studied with his father, Bernhard Rosenbaum (1847–1932); then with V. Schioler. He developed a type of humorous piano concerts *sui generis* and appeared in Danish musical revues. In 1940, he settled in the U.S. and became extremely successful in his specialty on the radio and in television; in the autumn of 1953 he opened a series of daily recitals on Broadway, billed as "comedy in music," which ran for two and a half seasons, unprecedented in New York theatrical annals for a one-man show. In 1951 he was named "Funniest Man" in music.

Borghi, Adelaide, Italian mezzo-soprano; b. Bologna, Aug. 9, 1829; d. there, Sept. 28, 1901. Acting on the advice of Pasta, she trained herself for the stage; made her debut at Urbino (1846) in Mercadante's *Il Guiramento*; toured through Italy and to Vienna and Paris (1854–56); sang with the Grand Opéra in Paris (1856–59); appeared in London with great success (1860); then returned to Italy.

Borgioli, Dino, Italian stage-tenor, b. Florence, Feb. 15, 1891; d. there, Sept. 12, 1960. He made his début at the Teatro dal Verme, Milan, in 1918; then sang leading parts in various Italian opera houses, at Covent Garden Opera, London, and in Spain; in 1924 he joined Mme. Melba on her farewell tour of Australia; was then a member of La Scala, Milan, for several years; appeared in the U. S. from 1928–30. Later he settled in London as a vocal teacher.

Borgström, Hjalmar, Norwegian critic and composer; b. Oslo, March 23, 1864; d. there, July 5, 1925. He studied with Ursin, Svendsen and Lindeman; also at Leipzig, Berlin, Paris and London. In 1901 he returned to Oslo; was music critic of the *Aftenposten* from 1913.
WORKS: 2 operas, *Thora fra Rimol* and *Fiskeren*; 2 symphonies; symphonic poems *Hamlet, Jesus in Gethsemane, John Gabriel Borkman, Tanken*; *Reformation Cantata*, violin and piano concertos, chamber music, piano pieces, songs.

Bori, Lucrezia (real name **Lucrecia Borja y Gonzalez de Riancho**), lyric soprano; b. Valencia, Dec. 24, 1887; d. New York, May 14, 1960. She studied with Melchior Vidal; made her debut in Rome on Oct. 31, 1908, as Micaëla; then sang in Milan, Naples, and in 1910 in Paris as Manon Lescaut, with the Metropolitan Opera Co., then on a European tour. In 1911 she sang at La Scala; made her debut at the Metropolitan Opera House in New York as Manon Lescaut on Nov. 11, 1912, and sang there until the end of the season 1914–15. After a period of retirement, occasioned by a vocal affliction, she reappeared in 1919 at Monte Carlo as Mimi, returning to the Metropolitan in 1921 in the same role. Thereafter she appeared in New York with increasing success and popularity until the end of the 1935–36 season, when she retired permanently from opera.

Borisov, Lilcho, Bulgarian composer; b. Sofia, Nov. 1, 1925. He studied composition with Ghedini and clarinet at the Verdi Cons. in Milan, graduating in 1952.
WORKS: *Cosmic Scenes* for wind quartet (1958); Trio for clarinet, bassoon and piano (1958); Violin Sonata (1962); Clarinet Concerto (1966); *Scherzo* for clarinet and chamber orch. (1966); *6 Etudes* for 2 clarinets (1966); *Sonatina concertante* for violin and chamber orch.; Concerto for Violin and Chamber Orch. (1971); *5 Pieces* for violin and piano (1973).

Boŕkovec, Pavel, Czech composer; b. Prague, June 10, 1894; d. there, July 22, 1972. He originally studied philosophy and turned to composition rather late in life; took lessons with Jaroslav Kŕička and J. B. Foerster in 1919; in 1925–27 attended master classes of Josef Suk at the Prague Cons. From 1946 to 1964, he was on the faculty of the Academy of Musical Arts in Prague. His early works were in the manner of Dvoŕák and Suk; later he experienced the influence of neo-classicism and adopted the technique of dissonant counterpoint in the baroque framework; also cultivated topical subjects from the world of sports, exemplified by his symph. piece *The Start*.
WORKS: 2 operas: *The Satyr*, after Goethe's poem (1937–38; Prague, Oct. 8, 1942) and *Paleček* (*Tom Thumb*, 1945–47; Czech radio award, 1948; première, Prague, Dec. 17, 1958); a ballet, *Krysaŕ* (*The Pied Piper*, 1939; concert performance, Prague, Jan. 15, 1941; first stage performance, Oct. 8, 1942, along with *The Satyr*); *Stmívání* (*Twilight*), symph. poem (1920); 3 symphonies (1926–27, 1955, 1959); *The Start*, symph. allegro (1929; Prague, March 26, 1930; also performed at the Festival of the International Society for Contemporary Music in Liège, Sept. 6, 1930); 2 piano concertos (1931, 1949–50); Violin Concerto (1933); *Partita* for orch. (1936); Concerto Grosso for 2 violins, cello, orch. and piano (1941–42); 2 *Symphoniettas* (for chamber orch., 1944; 1963–68); Cello Concerto (1950–51); *Silentium Turbatum*, symph. movement for alto, orch. and electric guitar (Prague, Feb. 28, 1965); *Te Deum* for soli, chorus and orch. (1968); Piano Quartet (1922); 5 string quartets (1924, 1928, 1940, 1947, 1961–62); Solo Viola Sonata (1931); Wind Quintet (1932); 2 violin sonatas (1934, 1956); Nonet (1941–42); Violin Sonatina (1942); *Intermezzo* for horn and piano (1965); Suite for Piano (1930); Partita for Piano (1935); *2 Pieces* for piano (1941–42); a melodrama *Jen jedenkrát* (*Only Once*, 1921); *Stadion* (*The Stadium)* for voice, wind quintet and piano (1929); *Love Songs* after Goethe and Villon, for voice, and pi-

ano or small orch. (1932); *5 Songs*, to poems of Pasternak (1935); *6 Madrigals About Time* for chorus (1957).

BIBLIOGRAPHY: V. Holzknecht, *Hudební skupina Mánesa* (Prague, 1968).

Borland, John Ernest, English organist and writer on music; b. London, March 6, 1866; d. there, May 15, 1937. He was educated at Queen's College, Oxford, and at the Royal College of Music, London, and subsequently held positions as organist and music director at numerous churches. He was editor of *Musical News* (1895–1902); also prepared the music for the coronations of Edward VII, George V and George VI. His writings include *The Instruments of the Orchestra* and *Musical Foundations.*

Bornschein, Franz Carl, American composer; b. Baltimore, Feb. 10, 1879; d. there, June 8, 1948. He studied at the Peabody Cons. in Baltimore (1895–1902), and became teacher of violin and conductor of the student orchestra there in 1906.

WORKS: *The Phantom Canoe,* Indian suite for orch. (Baltimore, Nov. 24, 1916); *Onowa,* a cantata (1916); *The Sea God's Daughter,* symph. poem (Chicago, Feb. 10, 1924); *Old Louisiana,* symph. poem (1930); *The Willow Plate,* operetta (1932); *Leif Ericson,* symph. poem (Baltimore, Feb. 23, 1936); *Southern Nights,* symph. poem (Washington, March 1, 1936); *Moon over Taos* for flute, percussion, and string orch. (1939); some chamber music and vocal compositions.

Borodin, Alexander, celebrated Russian composer; b. St. Petersburg, Nov. 12, 1833; d. there, Feb. 27, 1887. He was the illegitimate son of a Georgian prince, Ghedeanov; his mother was the wife of an army doctor. In accordance with customary procedure in such cases, the child was registered as the lawful son of one of Ghedeanov's serfs, Porfiry Borodin; hence, the patronymic, Alexander Porfirievich. He was given an excellent education; learned several foreign languages, and was taught to play the flute. He played four-hand arrangements of Haydn's and Beethoven's symphonies with his musical friend M. Shtchiglev. At the age of 14 he tried his hand at composition; wrote a piece for flute and piano and a string trio on themes from *Robert le Diable.* In 1850 he became a student of the Academy of Medicine in St. Petersburg, and developed a great interest in chemistry; he graduated in 1856 with honors, and joined the staff as assistant prof.; in 1858 received his doctorate in chemistry; contributed several important scientific papers to the bulletin of the Russian Academy of Sciences; traveled in Europe on a scientific mission (1859–62). Although mainly preoccupied with his scientific pursuits, Borodin continued to compose. In 1863 he married Catherine Protopopova, who was an accomplished pianist; she remained his faithful companion and musical partner; together they attended concerts and operas in Russia and abroad; his letters to her from Germany (1877), describing his visit to Liszt in Weimar, are of great interest. Of a decisive influence on Borodin's progress as composer was his meeting with Balakirev in 1862; later he formed friendships with the critic Stassov, who named Borodin as one of the "mighty

Five" (actually, Stassov used the expression "mighty heap"), with Mussorgsky, and other musicians of the Russian National School. He adopted a style of composition in conformity with their new ideas; he particularly excelled in a type of Russian orientalism which exercised a great attraction on Russian musicians at the time. He never became a consummate craftsman, like Rimsky-Korsakov; although quite proficient in counterpoint, he avoided purely contrapuntal writing; his feeling for rhythm and orchestral color was extraordinary, and his evocation of exotic scenes in his orchestral works and in his opera *Prince Igor* is superb. Composition was a very slow process for Borodin; several of his works remained incomplete, and were edited after his death by Rimsky-Korsakov and Glazunov.

WORKS: OPERAS: *Prince Igor,* opera in 4 acts (begun in 1869, on the subject of the famous Russian medieval chronicle *Tale of Igor's Campaign;* completed posthumously by Rimsky-Korsakov and Glazunov; 1st perf. St. Petersburg, Nov. 4, 1890; London, June 8, 1914, in Russian; New York, Dec. 30, 1915, in Italian); an opera-farce *Bogatyry (The Valiant Knights,* anonymously produced in Moscow on Oct. 29, 1867; rediscovered in 1932, and produced in Moscow, Nov. 12, 1936, with a new libretto by Demian Biedny, to serve propaganda purposes in an anti-religious campaign, but two days later banned by the Soviet government for its mockery of Russian nationalism); sketches for the 4th act of an opera *Mlada,* each act of which was to be written by a different composer (never produced). ORCHESTRAL WORKS: Symph. No. 1 in E-flat (1862–67; St. Petersburg, Jan. 16, 1869); Symph. No. 2 in B minor (1869–76; St. Petersburg, March 10, 1877); Symph. No. 3 in A minor (1885–86; unfinished; two movements orchestrated by Glazunov); symph. sketch *In the Steppes of Central Asia* (1880); *Polovtzian Dances* from *Prince Igor* (perf. as an orchestral piece, St. Petersburg, March 11, 1879). CHAMBER MUSIC: String Quartet No. 1 in A (1877–79); String Quartet No. 2 in D (1881–87); *Serenata alla Spagnola,* 3rd movement of a quartet on the name B-la-f, for their publisher Be-la-ieff, by Borodin, Rimsky-Korsakov, Liadov, and Glazunov (1886); Scherzo for string quartet in the collective set *Les Vendredis.* A string trio (dated 1860) and a piano quintet were discovered in 1915. FOR PIANO: *Polka, Requiem, Marche funèbre,* and *Mazurka* in the series of paraphrases on the theme of the *Chopsticks Waltz* (includes variations by Borodin, other members of the Russian school, and Liszt; 1880); *Petite Suite,* comprising 7 pieces (*Au couvent, Intermezzo, Deux mazurkas, Rêverie, Sérénade, Nocturne;* 1885). VOCAL WORKS: *Sérénade de 4 galants à une dame* for a cappella male quartet (comical; no date); songs *Sleeping Princess* (1867), *The Princess of the Sea, The Song of the Dark Forest, The False Note, My Songs are full of venom* (1867–68), *The Sea* (1870), *From my tears* (1873), *For the shores of your distant country* (1881), *Conceit* (1884), *Arabian Melody* (1885), and *The Wondrous Garden* (1885).

BIBLIOGRAPHY: V. Stassov, *A. Borodin* (St. Petersburg, 1882; French transl. by A. Habets, in 2 vols., Paris, 1893); Rosa Newmarch, *Borodin and Liszt* (London, 1895); E. Braudo, *Borodin* (Moscow, 1922);

W. Kahl, "Die russischen Novatoren und Borodin," *Die Musik* (1923); G. Abraham, *Borodin, the Composer and His Music* (London, 1927); 2 vols. of Borodin's letters, edited by S. Dianin (Moscow, 1928, 1936); G. Abraham, "Prince Igor: An Experiment in Lyrical Opera," in the *Musical Quarterly* (Jan. 1931); M. Rinaldi, "Borodin," *Musica d'oggi* (1933); G. Khubov, *Borodin* (Moscow, 1933); N. Rimsky-Korsakov, *Memoirs of My Musical Life* (3rd to 5th eds., with preface and notes by A. Rimsky-Korsakov; Moscow, 1932–35); Y. Kremlev, *Borodin* (Leningrad, 1934); G. Abraham, *Studies in Russian Music* (London, 1935); M. D. Calvocoressi and G. Abraham, *Masters of Russian Music* (London and N. Y., 1936); D. Brook, *Six Great Russian Composers* (London, 1946); M. Ilyin and E. Segal, *Borodin* (Moscow, 1953); S. Dianin, *Borodin* (Moscow, 1955; in English, 1963); W. B. Ober, "Alexander Borodin, M. D. (1833–1887): Physician, Chemist, Composer," *New York State Journal of Medicine* (March 1967); L. Velluz, *Du laboratoire au Prince Igor, pages sur Borodine* (Paris, 1971); M. Smirnov, *The Piano Works of Composers Comprising "The Five"* (Moscow, 1971); G. Golovinsky, *The Chamber Music of Borodin* (Moscow, 1972).

Borovsky, Alexander, Russian-American pianist; b. Mitau, March 18, 1889; d. Waban, Mass., April 27, 1968. He first studied with his mother (a pupil of Safonov), then with A. Essipova at the St. Petersburg Cons., winning the Rubinstein Prize in 1912. He taught master classes at the Moscow Cons. from 1915–20; then went to Turkey, Germany, France and England and gave a number of piano recitals; was soloist with virtually all major European orchestras; he also made several successful tours in South America. In 1941 he settled in the U. S. and became prof. at Boston Univ. (1956).

Borowski, Felix, English-American composer and critic; b. Burton, England, March 10, 1872; d. Chicago, Sept. 6, 1956. He studied violin with his father, a Polish émigré; took lessons with various teachers in London, and at the Cologne Cons.; then taught in Aberdeen, Scotland. His early *Russian Sonata* was praised by Grieg; this provided impetus to his progress as a composer. In 1897 he accepted a teaching engagement at the Chicago Musical College; was its president in 1916–25. Subsequently he became active in musical journalism; in 1942 was appointed music editor of the *Chicago Sun*; also served as program annotator for the Chicago Symph. Orch., beginning in 1908. For 5 years he taught musicology at Northwestern Univ. (1937–42). Among his many musical works, the violin piece entitled *Adoration* became widely popular.
WORKS: *Boudour*, ballet-pantomime (Chicago, Nov. 25, 1919); *Fernando del Nonsensico*, satiric opera (1935); Piano Concerto (Chicago, 1914); *Allegro de Concert* for organ and orch. (Chicago, 1915); *Peintures* for orch. (Chicago, Jan. 25, 1918); *Le Printemps passionné*, symph. poem (Chicago North Shore Festival, Evanston, Ill., 1920); *Youth*, fantasy-overture (Chicago North Shore Festival, Evanston, Ill., May 30, 1923); *Ecce Homo*, symph. poem (New York, Jan. 2, 1924); *Semiramis*, symph. poem (Chicago, Nov. 13, 1925); 3 symphonies (I, Chicago, 1933; II, Los Angeles, 1936; III, Chicago, 1939); *The Little Match Girl* (after Andersen), for narrator and orch. (1943); *Requiem for a Child* (1944); *The Mirror*, symph. poem (Louisville, Nov. 27, 1954); 3 string quartets; many pieces for violin, organ, and piano; songs. Borowski revised G. P. Upton's *The Standard Operas* in 1928, and *The Standard Concert Guide* in 1930.

Borras de Palau, Juan, Catalan writer on music; b. Barcelona, Sept. 24, 1868; d. there, Jan. 29, 1953. He was a lawyer by profession; published numerous songs, some of which became popular; was for more than 50 years music critic of the *Correo Catalan*.

Børresen, Hakon, Danish composer; b. Copenhagen, June 2, 1876; d. there, Oct. 6, 1954. He studied with Svendsen; was awarded the Ancker scholarship for competition in 1901. He was president of the Danish Composers Society from 1924–49. Børresen's compositions include the operas *Den Kongelige Gaest* (Copenhagen, Nov. 15, 1919) and *Kaddara* (Copenhagen, March 16, 1921); a ballet *Tycho Brahes Dröm* (*Tycho Brahe's Dream*, Copenhagen, March 1, 1924); 3 symphonies; a violin concerto; chamber music; piano works; songs.

Borris, Siegfried, German composer; b. Berlin, Nov. 4, 1906. He studied piano as a child, and began to compose tentatively while still a schoolboy. He entered the Univ. of Berlin as a student of economics; in 1927 became a pupil of Paul Hindemith at the Berlin Musikhochschule; in 1933 he obtained a bachelor's degree in music at the Univ. of Berlin as a student of Arnold Schering, but with the advent of the Nazi regime he was compelled to abandon all his activities as a pianist or teacher. In 1945 he joined the staff of the Berlin Musikhochschule, and in 1967 became director of the composition class at the Julius Stern's Institute. Borris is a prolific composer; he describes his idiom of composition as "vitalism," which connotes a pragmatic type of harmony and counterpoint enlivened by dance-like rhythms; functional tonality is preserved without excluding modernistic dissonant combinations.
WORKS: *Frühlingsgesellen*, "liederspiel," to his own words (1951); *Die Rube*, fairy tale opera (1953); *Ruf des Lebens*, scenic cantata (1954); the radio operas, *Hans im Glück* (1947); *Hirolas und Gerline* (1948); a ballet, *Das Letzte Spiel* (1955); 5 symphonies (1940–53); Piano Concerto (1962); Organ Concerto (1965); Saxophone Concerto (1966); Horn Concerto (1967); Wind Quintet (1938); Wind Octet (1941); Octet, for clarinet, bassoon, horn and string quintet (1960); numerous Lieder, mostly to his own texts; piano pieces; choruses. As a pedagogue he published *Praktische Harmonielehre* (10th ed., Berlin, 1948); *Einführung in die Moderne Musik* (Halle, 1951); *Modern Jazz* (Berlin, 1962); also numerous articles in the musical press.

Bortkiewicz, Sergei, Russian pianist and composer; b. Kharkov, Feb. 28, 1877; d. Vienna, Oct. 25, 1952. He was a pupil of Liadov at the St. Petersburg Cons. (1896–9); later studied with Jadassohn in Leipzig. He made his début as a pianist in Munich, in 1902, and subsequently made concert tours of Germany, Australia, Hungary, France, and Russia. From 1904-14, he lived in Berlin, and taught at the Klindworth-Scharwenka Cons.; then went back to Russia; was in Vienna from 1920-29; in Berlin from 1929-34; and again in Vienna after 1934. His compositions include an opera, *Acrobats*; 2 symphonies; *Austrian Suite* and *Yugoslav Suite* for orch.; 4 piano concertos; violin concerto; cello concerto; piano pieces; songs. He was the author of the book *Die seltsame Liebe Peter Tschaikowskys und der Nadezhda von Meck* (1938).

Bortniansky, Dimitri, Russian composer; b. Glukhov, Ukraine, 1751; d. St. Petersburg, Oct. 10, 1825. He was a choirboy in the court chapel, where he attracted the attention of Galuppi, who was at the time conductor there; was sent to Italy where he studied with Galuppi and with other Italian masters in Venice, Bologna, Rome, and Naples (1769-79). In Italy Bortniansky produced his operas *Creonte* (Venice, 1776) and *Quinto Fabio* (Modena, 1779). In 1779 he returned to St. Petersburg and became director of vocal music at the court chapel (1796); as a conductor of the chapel choir he introduced radical reforms for improvement of singing standards; composed for his choir a number of sacred works of high quality, among them a Mass according to the Greek Orthodox ritual; 35 sacred concerti in 4 parts; 10 psalms in 8 parts; 10 concerti for double choir, etc. He also continued to compose for the stage; produced the comic operas in French, *Le Faucon* (Gatchina, Oct. 22, 1786) and *Le Fils rival* (Pavlovsk, Oct. 22, 1787). His sacred choral works are published in 10 vols., edited by Tchaikovsky.
BIBLIOGRAPHY: N. Findeisen, *History of Russian Music* (1929; vol. 2, pp. 260-76); B. Dobrohotov, *D. Bortniansky* (Moscow, 1950); A. Galkina, "About the Symphonism of Bortnjanskij," *Sovetskaja Muzyka* (Oct. 1973; in Russian).

Bortolotto, Mario, Italian physician and writer of music; b. Pordenone, Aug. 30, 1927. He published *Introduzione al lied romantico* (Milan, 1962) and *Fase seconda* (Milan, 1969) which aroused controversy; for polemical exchange that followed its publication see *Nuova Rivista Musicale Italiana* (Sept./Oct. 1969).

Börtz, Daniel, Swedish composer; b. Hässleholm, Aug. 8, 1943. He studied composition privately with Hilding Rosenberg; then with Blomdahl and Lidholm at the Royal Academy of Music in Stockholm; later attended seminars in electronic music at Utrecht. WORKS: a chamber opera, *Landskab med flod*, after Hesse (1972); 2 liturgical operas, *Muren—Vägen—Ordet* (1971-72) and *Den heliga Birgittas död och Mottagande i himmelen* (Lund, Oct. 7, 1973); *Intrada* for orch. (1964); 5 *Preludes* for flute (1964); *Il Canto dei Canti di Salomone* for soprano and instruments (1965); 4 *Monologhi: I* for cello (1965-66), *II* for bassoon (1966), *III* for violin (1967) and *IV* for piano and tape (1970); 2 string quartets (1966, 1971); *In memoriam di . . .* for orch. (Norrköping, May 29, 1969); *Voces* for 3 voices, tape and orch. (Stockholm, Sept. 19, 1968); *Josef K*, after Kafka, for narrator, 8 soli, chorus and orch. (1969; Swedish Radio, Oct. 8, 1970);

Night Winds for vocal quartet (1972); *Nightflies* for mezzo-soprano and chamber ensemble (1973); *Sinfonia I* (Göteborg, March 7, 1974).

Borwick, Leonard, English pianist; b. Walthamstow, Feb. 26, 1868; d. Le Mans, France, Sept. 15, 1925. He studied with Clara Schumann in Frankfurt; made his début there (1889); then in London (May 8, 1889); made a concert tour in America and Australia (1911); also played in Europe. His programs included classics and moderns; in the last years of his career he played much music of Debussy and Ravel; made a transcription for piano of Debussy's *L'après-midi d'un faune*.
BIBLIOGRAPHY: H. Plunket Greene, "L. Borwick," *Music & Letters* (1926).

Bos, Coenraad Valentyn, Dutch pianist and noted accompanist; b. Leiden, Dec. 7, 1875; d. Chappaqua, N. Y., Aug. 5, 1955. He was a pupil of Julius Röntgen at the Amsterdam Cons. (1892-95); later studied in Berlin. With two other countrymen, Jan van Veen (violin) and Jan van Lier (cello), he formed a trio in Berlin which enjoyed an enviable reputation during its active period (1896-1910). His masterly accompaniments on a tour with Ludwig Wüllner attracted more than ordinary attention, and made him one of the most celebrated accompanists both in Europe and the U. S., where he eventually settled. He was the accompanist of Julia Culp, Frieda Hempel, Helen Traubel, Fritz Kreisler, Ernestine Schumann-Heink, Pablo Casals, Elena Gerhard, Jacques Thibaud, Geraldine Farrar, and many others. He taught at the Juilliard School of Music from 1934-52; published (in collaboration with Ashley Pettis) a book *The Well-Tempered Accompanist* (1949).

Boschot, Adolphe, French music critic; b. Fontenay-sous-Bois, near Paris, May 4, 1871; d. Paris, June 1, 1955. He was music critic of *Echo de Paris* from 1910; of *Revue Bleue* from 1919; founded, with Théodore de Wyzewa, the Paris Mozart Society; was elected to the Institut de France in 1926, succeeding Widor as permanent secretary of the Académie des Beaux-Arts. His greatest work is an exhaustive biography of Berlioz in 3 volumes: *La Jeunesse d'un romantique, Hector Berlioz, 1803-31* (Paris, 1906); *Un Romantique sous Louis-Philippe, Hector Berlioz, 1831-42* (Paris, 1908); and *Crépuscule d'un romantique, Hector Berlioz, 1842-69* (Paris, 1913). For this work Boschot received a prize of the Académie. Other books are: *Le Faust de Berlioz* (1910; new ed. 1945); *Carnet d'art* (1911); *Une Vie romantique, Hector Berlioz* (an abridgement of his 3 vol. work, 1919; 27th ed., 1951; also in English. A definitive edition appeared in Quebec in 1965); *Chez les musiciens* (3 vols., 1922-26); *Entretiens sur la beauté* (1927); *La Lumière de Mozart* (1928); *Le Mystère musical* (1929); *La Musique et la vie* (2 vols., 1931-33); *Théophile Gautier* (1933); *Mozart* (1935); *La Vie et les œuvres d'Alfred Bruneau* (1937); *Musiciens-Poètes* (1937); *Maîtres d'hier et de jadis* (1944); *Portraits de Musiciens* (3 vols., 1946-50); *Souvenirs d'un autre siècle* (1947). Boschot translated into French the libretti of several of Mozart's operas. He was also prominent as a poet; publ. the collections *Poèmes dialogués* (1901) and *Chez nos poètes* (1925).

Boscovich, Alexander Uriah, significant Israeli composer; b. Klausenburg (Cluj), Transylvania, Aug. 16, 1907; d. Tel Aviv, Nov. 13, 1964. He studied in Budapest; later enrolled at the Vienna Academy where he studied piano with Victor Ebenstein and composition with Richard Stöhr; then went to Paris where he took courses with Paul Dukas and Nadia Boulanger; also had a few lessons in piano with Alfred Cortot. From 1930 to 1938 he was engaged as conductor at the State Opera in Cluj; in 1938 he emigrated to Palestine; taught at the Cons. of Tel Aviv (1945–64); wrote music criticism for the Israeli paper *Haaretz.*

WORKS: In his music he incorporates the quasi-oriental motives in the framework of Western music; in several of his works he makes use of authentic Jewish folksongs, adorning them with modernistic harmonies. In this manner he wrote his most popular piece *Chansons populaires juives* for orch. (Haifa, March 15, 1938; originally entitled *The Golden Chain*); Violin Concerto (1942); Oboe Concerto (1943); *Adonai Ro'i* (*The Lord Is My Shepherd*) for alto voice and orch. (1946); *Semitic Suite* for piano (1947; also for 2 pianos, and for orch.); *Piccola Suite* for flute, snare drum and string orch. (1956–57); *Psalm* for violin and piano (1957; contains thematic material from the violin concerto); *Cantico di ma'alot* (*Song of Ascent*) for orch. (1960); *Bal Yisrael* (*Daughter of Israel*), cantata for tenor, chorus and orch. (1960–61); *With Joy and Gladness* for 2 violins, with optional drum and triangle (1961); *Piece* for oboe and harpsichord (1961–62); *Lament* for violin or cello, and piano (1962); *Concerto da Camera* for violin and chamber ensemble (1962); *Ornaments* for flute and 4 orch. groups (1964).

BIBLIOGRAPHY: M. Brod and Y. Cohen, *Die Musik Israels* (Kassel, 1976, pp. 64–66).

Bösendorfer. Firm of piano makers at Vienna, specializing in concert grands; it was established by **Ignaz Bösendorfer** (b. Vienna, July 27, 1794; d. there, April 14, 1859) in 1828; later managed by his son Ludwig (b. Vienna, April 10, 1835; d. there, May 9, 1919). The firm, retaining its original name, was subsequently taken over by Carl Hutterstrasser (1863–1942). The Bösendorfer Saal (opened by Hans von Bülow in 1872, and used until 1913) was one of the finest chamber music concert halls in Europe.

Boskovsky, Willi, Austrian violinist and conductor; b. Vienna, June 16, 1909. He studied at the Vienna Academy of Music; in 1935 became violin instructor there. In 1939 he was appointed concertmaster of the Vienna Philharmonic; in 1948 he founded the Wiener Oktet, with which he toured widely. In 1955 he succeeded Clemens Krauss as conductor of "New Year Concerts" of the Vienna Philharmonic. In 1969 he became the principal conductor of the Vienna Strauss Orch., holding his violin relaxedly in his left hand à la Johann Strauss, and directing his group in an ingratiatingly authentic Viennese manner in flowing waltz time or rapid polka rhythm, as the case may be.

Bosmans, Henriette, Dutch pianist and composer; b. Amsterdam, Dec. 5, 1895; d. there, July 2, 1952. She studied piano with her mother at the Amsterdam Cons., and embarked on a career of a concert pianist.

In 1927 she took lessons in composition with Willem Pijper. In her own music she cultivated an agreeable neo-classical idiom, with coloristic éclat, suggesting the techniques and devices of French impressionism; wrote many songs to texts by French poets. In her instrumental works she particularly favored the cello (her father was a well-known cellist, but he died when she was a year old).

WORKS: Cello Sonata (1919), 2 cello concertos (1922, 1924), *Poem* for cello and orch. (1926); Violin Sonata (1918); Piano Trio (1921); String Quartet (1928); Concertino for Piano and Orch. (1928; performed at the Geneva Festival of the International Society for Contemporary Music, April 6, 1929); *Konzertstück* for flute and orch. (1929); *Konzertstück* for violin and orch. (1934); *Doodenmarsch* (*March of the Dead*) for narrator and chamber orch. (1946); piano pieces.

Bosquet, Emile, Belgian pianist; b. Brussels, Dec. 8, 1878; d. Uccle (Brussels), July 18, 1958. He studied with Tinel and Busoni; taught at the Cons. of Antwerp (1906–19) and in Brussels (from 1919); also made European tours. He published *La Musique de clavier* (Brussels, 1953).

Bosse, Gustave, music book publisher; b. Vienenburg (Harz), Feb. 6, 1884; d. Regensburg, Aug. 27, 1943. He founded his firm in 1912 at Regensburg; was the publisher of the *Zeitschrift für Musik* (since 1929) and *Deutsche Musikbücherei* (a collection of music books).

Bosseur, Jean-Yves, French composer; b. Paris, Feb. 5, 1947. He studied privately with Stockhausen and Pousseur. His music is marked by experimentalization without specific serial procedures. Among his works there is a symph. suite, *Un Arraché de partout* for brass, Hammond organ, 2 electric guitars, vibraphone, xylorimba, marimbaphone and percussion (Paris, March 22, 1968). He is also a prolific writer of articles on current music and musical life.

Bossi, Costante Adolfo, Italian composer; brother of **Marco Enrico Bossi;** b. Morbegno, Dec. 25, 1876; d. Milan, Jan. 4, 1953. He studied at the Milan Cons.; subsequently was prof. there (1914–41). He wrote an opera *La Mammola e l'eroe* (Milan, 1916); a Requiem (1920); numerous choruses and songs.

Bossi, Enrico (Marco Enrico), Italian composer; b. Salò, Brescia, April 25, 1861; d. at sea (en route from America to Europe), Feb. 20, 1925. Son and pupil of the organist **Pietro Bossi,** of Morbegno (1834–1896), he studied (1871–73) at the Liceo Rossini in Bologna, and at Milan (1873–81) under Sangali (piano), Fumagalli (organ), Campanari (violin), Boniforti (counterpoint), and Ponchielli (composition). He subsequently was maestro di cappella and organist at Como Cathedral (1881–89); then, until 1896, prof. of organ and harmony in the Royal Cons. San Pietro at Naples; prof. of advanced composition and organ at the Liceo Benedetto Marcello, Venice (1896–1902); and director of the Liceo Musicale at Bologna (1902–12). After a brief period of retirement from teaching, he was director of the Music School of the St. Cecilia Academy, Rome (1916–23); toured Europe, England and the U. S. as a pianist and organist.

WORKS: operas, *Paquita* (Milan, 1881), *Il Veggente* (Milan, 1890; rewritten and produced as *Il Viandante*, Mannheim, 1896), and *L'Angelo della notte*; *Intermezzi Goldoniani* for string orch.; *Concertstück* for organ and orch.; *Inno di Gloria*, for chorus and organ; *Tota pulchra*, for chorus and organ; *Missa pro Sponso et Sponsa* (Rome, 1896); *Il Cieco*, for solo, chorus and orch. (1897); *Canticum Canticorum*, biblical cantata; *Il Paradiso Perduto*, for chorus and orch. (Augsburg, 1903); *Surrexit pastor*, motet; *Giovanna d'Arco*, mystery play (Cologne, 1913); *Primavera classica*, for 5-part chorus a cappella; String Trio; Piano Trio, etc. He also wrote *Metodo di Studio per l'organo moderno* (in collaboration with G. Tebaldini; Milan, 1893).

BIBLIOGRAPHY: H. B. Gaul, "Bonnet, Bossi, Karg-Elert, Three Aperçus," *Musical Quarterly* (July 1918); E. Dagnino, *M. E. Bossi, Cenni biografici* (Rome, 1925); L. Orsini, *Fascicolo commemorativo* (Milan, 1926); G. C. Paribeni, L. Orsini and E. Bontempelli, *Marco Enrico Bossi: il compositore, l'organista, l'uomo* (Milan, 1934); F. Mompellio, *M. E. Bossi* (Milan, 1952; contains a complete list of works).

Bossi, Renzo, Italian conductor and composer; son of **Enrico Bossi;** b. Como, April 9, 1883; d. Milan, April 2, 1965. He studied in Venice and in Leipzig; took a course in conducting with Nikisch; conducted at various cities in Italy; in 1916 was appointed instructor at the Verdi Cons. in Milan.

WORKS: Operas, *Passa la ronda* (Milan, March 3, 1919), *Volpino il calderaio* (Milan, Nov. 13, 1925), *La Rosa Rossa* (Parma, Jan. 9, 1940); ballet, *Il trillo del diavolo* (1948); a symphony in 5 movements; violin concerto; many minor pieces for various instruments.

BIBLIOGRAPHY: His biographical data and a complete list of works are appended to F. Mompellio's monograph on his father (Milan, 1952). See also S. Pintacuda, *Renzo Bossi* (Milan, 1955).

Bostelmann, Otto, German-American composer; b. Hamburg, Aug. 22, 1907; settled in the U.S. in 1926. He studied with Wesley La Violette in Los Angeles; in 1957 organized the Bohemian Composers Group in Los Angeles. His works comprise 3 symphonies, 3 'crescendi' for orch.; much chamber music.

Bote & Bock, German music publishing firm established in Berlin in 1838 by **Eduard Bote** (retired 1847) and **Gustav Bock** (b. 1813; d. 1863); the directorship was assumed after Gustav Bock's death by his brother **Eduard Bock** (d. 1871), followed by his son **Hugo Bock** (b. Berlin, July 25, 1848; d. there, March 12, 1932) who handled the affairs of the firm for over sixty years. He acquired for the firm a great number of operas and operettas, and also a number of instrumental works by celebrated 19th-century composers. In 1904 Hugo Bock purchased the catalogue of Lauterbach & Kuhn of Leipzig, including the works of Max Reger (from op. 66 on). His successor was his son **Gustav Bock** (b. Berlin, July 17, 1882; d. July 6, 1953) who headed the firm until 1938, and again from

1947. The headquarters of the firm remained in Berlin; in 1948 a branch was formed in Wiesbaden. Apart from its musical publications, the firm publ. the *Neue Berliner Musikzeitung* (1847–96). A centennial volume was issued in 1938 as *Musikverlag Bote & Bock, Berlin, 1838–1938.*

Botstiber, Hugo, Austrian music scholar and writer; b. Vienna, April 21, 1875; d. Shrewsbury, England, Jan. 15, 1941. He was a pupil of R. Fuchs, Zemlinsky, H. Rietsch and Guido Adler; in 1896, assistant librarian of the Vienna Cons.; 1900, secretary of the Konzertverein there; and in 1905 secretary of the Akademie für Musik; was (until 1938) general secretary of the Vienna Konzerthaus-Gesellschaft; Knight of the Order of Franz Josef. He went to England in 1939. He edited the *Musikbuch aus Österreich* (1904–11); also organ compositions by Pachelbel, piano works of the Vienna masters, and waltzes of Johann Strauss for the *Denkmäler der Tonkunst in Österreich*; author of *Joseph Haydn und das Verlagshaus Artaria* (with Franz Artaria; Vienna, 1911); *Geschichte der Ouvertüre* (Leipzig, 1913); *Beethoven im Alltag* (Vienna, 1927); completed Pohl's biography of Haydn (vol. III, 1927); published a new edition of Kretzschmar's *Führer durch den Konzertsaal* (1932). Of special interest to American musicians is his article "Musicalia in der New York Public Library" in the bulletin of the Société Internationale de Musique (Oct. 1903), calling international attention for the first time to the important music collection of the New York Public Library.

Bott, Jean Joseph, German violinist and conductor; b. Kassel, March 9, 1826; d. New York, April 28, 1895. He studied with his father, the court musician **A. Bott,** and later with M. Hauptmann and L. Spohr; was court conductor at Meiningen (1852–57) and Hannover (1865); retired in 1878; settled in New York in 1885. He wrote 2 operas, a symphony, overtures, violin concertos, piano music, etc.

Botta, Luca, Italian tenor; b. Amalfi, Italy, April 16, 1882; d. New York, Sept. 29, 1917. He was a pupil of G. Vergine; made his operatic début as Turiddu in *Cavalleria Rusticana* (Naples, 1911); then sang in Malta, Turin, Mantua, Verona, Barcelona, Buenos Aires, and Milan; came to the U.S. in 1912 and sang with the Pacific Coast Opera Company in San Francisco; made his Metropolitan Opera House début as Rodolfo in *La Bohème* (New York, Nov. 21, 1914).

Bottée de Toulmon, Auguste, French writer on music; b. Paris, May 15, 1797; d. there, March 22, 1850. A lawyer by profession, he turned his attention to music, becoming a good amateur cellist; was the librarian of the Paris Cons. from 1831–48.

WRITINGS: *L'Art musical depuis l'ère chrétienne jusqu'à nos jours* (Paris, 1836); "De la chanson en France au moyen-âge," *L'Annuaire historique* (1836); "Notice biographique sur les travaux de Guido d'Arezzo," *Mémoires de la Société des Antiquaires de France* (1837); "Des instruments de musique en usage au moyen-âge," *L'Annuaire historique* (1838); *Observations sur les moyens de restaurer la musique religieuse dans les églises de Paris* (Paris, 1841); *Notice des manuscrits autographes de Cherubini* (Paris, 1843).

Bottenberg, Wolfgang, German-born Canadian composer; b. Frankfurt, May 9, 1930. He emigrated to Canada in 1958; studied music theory with R. A. Stangeland at the Univ. of Alberta, graduating in 1961; then with Scott Huston, J. Takács and P. Cooper at the Univ. of Cincinnati, obtaining his M.A. (1962) and M.D. (1970). Returning to Canada he taught music at the Acadia Univ., Wolfville, Nova Scotia (1965–73) and at the Univ. in Montreal. In his compositions he makes eclectic use of tonal, atonal and serial resources.

WORKS: Passacaglia for Orch. (1961, revised 1971); *Sinfonietta* (1961, revised 1969–70); Fantasia for Trumpet and Small Orch. (1966); *A Suite for Carols* for orch. (1963–67); *Ritual*, a satire-collage on commercial slogans and sounds, for chorus and small orch. (1970); *Fantasia Serena* for orch. (1973); Concerto for Organ and Small Orch. (1975); Quartet for Flute, 2 Clarinets and Bassoon (1960); Sonata for Flute and Clarinet (1960); Trio for Flute, Clarinet and Bassoon (1963); Trio for Flute, Clarinet and Piano (1964); Divertimento for 4 Flutes (1965); String Quartet (1968); *Variables* for narrator, wind quartet and string quartet (1969); Octet (1972); *Fa So La Ti Do Re* for soprano saxophone and string quartet (1972); songs; piano pieces.

Bottesini, Giovanni, Italian double-bass virtuoso, conductor and composer; b. Crema, Dec. 22, 1821; d. Parma, July 7, 1889. He studied double bass with Rossi at the Milan Cons. (1835–39); theory with Basili and Vaccai. He made his debut at a concert in his native town in 1840; in 1846 he went to Havana as a member of the orchestra there; he visited the U. S. in 1847; then was in England (1848) as a cello player in chamber music, producing a profound impression on the London music lovers. In 1853 he was again in America, where he conducted the New Orleans Opera; in 1856 was conductor at the Théâtre des Italiens in Paris; then toured in Russia and Scandinavia (1866–68). In 1871 he was invited by Verdi to conduct the world première of *Aida* in Cairo; in his last year of life he was appointed director of the Parma Cons. Bottesini was the first real virtuoso on the double bass and became a legendary paragon for the few artists who essayed this instrument after him; thus Koussevitzky was often described as the Russian Bottesini.

WORKS: He was a competent composer; wrote the operas *Cristoforo Colombo* (Havana, 1847), *L'Assedio di Firenze* (Paris, 1856), *Il Diavolo della notte* (Milan, 1858), *Marion Delorme* (Palermo, 1862), *Vinciguerra* (Paris, 1870), *Alí Babà* (London, Jan. 18, 1871), *Ero e Leandro* (Turin, Jan. 11, 1879), and *La Regina di Nepal* (Turin, 1880); the oratorio *The Garden of Olivet* (Norwich Festival, 1887); symphonies, overtures, quartets; effective pieces for double bass (*Carnevale di Venezia, Tarantella*, etc.). He published an excellent *Metodo completo per contrabasso*, in 2 parts, treating the double bass as an orchestral and as a solo instrument (an English adaptation of this method by F. Clayton was publ. in London, 1870).

BIBLIOGRAPHY: L. Escudier, *Mes souvenirs: les virtuoses* (Paris, 1868); C. Lisei, *G. Bottesini* (Milan, 1886); F. Warnecke, *Der Kontrabass* (Hamburg, 1909); A. Carniti, *In memoria di G. Bottesini* (Crema, 1922).

Bottje, Will Gay, American flutist and composer; b. Grand Rapids, Michigan, June 30, 1925. He studied composition with Vittorio Giannini at the Juilliard School of Music, N.Y. (1943–47); then went to Europe and took courses with Henk Badings in Holland and with Nadia Boulanger in Paris (1952–53); worked at the electronic studios at the Univ. of Utrecht (1962–63) and in Stockholm (1973). In the interim he was on the staff of the Univ. of Mississippi (1955–57); in 1957 went over to Southern Illinois Univ. in Carbondale, where he founded an electronic music laboratory in 1965. His music is highly experimental, both in its selection of instrumental combinations and an acrid dissonant idiom.

WORKS: opera, *Altgeld*, for 10 soloists, chorus, orch., dance, projections and tape (Southern Ill. Univ., Carbondale, March 6, 1968); a comic chamber opera, *Root!* (1971); 7 symphonies (1950–70); *Contrasts* for orch. (1949); *The Ballad Singer* for orch. (1951); Concerto for flute, trumpet, harp, strings and percussion (1955); Concertino for Piccolo and Orch. (1956); Theme and Variations for orch. (1958); Concerto for Trumpet, Trombone and Wind Instruments (1959); Piano Concerto (1960); Sinfonietta (1960); *Sinfonia Concertante* for brass quintet and wind instruments (1961); *Rhapsodic Variations* for viola, piano and strings (1962); *Duo-Sonatina* for 2 euphoniums and 14 winds (1969); *Metaphors* for wind ensemble and tape (1971); *Facets* for piano and wind instruments (1973); *Chiaroscuros* for orch. (1975); *Mutations* for small orch. (1977); Tuba Concerto (1977); *Diversions* for narrator, piano and wind quintet (1954); *What Is a Man?*, after Walt Whitman, for narrator, chorus, wind instruments and 2 pianos (1959); *Wayward Pilgrim*, after Emily Dickinson, for soprano, chorus and chamber orch. (1961); 3 string quartets (1950, 1959, 1962); Quintet for flute and strings (1954); *Fantasy Sonata* for viola and piano (1954); Wind Quintet (1957); *Recitativo, Arioso and Finale* for trombone and piano (1958); Trumpet Sonata (1959); Cello Sonata (1959); *Serenade* for nonet (1961); Quartet for saxophones (1963); Sextet for organ, brasses and percussion (1964); Suite for 6 violins (1964–65); *Fluctuations* for 5 clarinets (1966); Variations for brass quintet (1969); *Interplays* for horn, piano, harp and tape (1970); *Modalities I* for saxophone quartet and tape (1970) and *II* for clarinet and tape (1971); *Reflections* for flute, harp and tape (1971); *Triangles* for trumpet, trombone and tape (1971); *Incognitos* for 4 tubas (1972); *Modules I* for clarinet and piano (1973); *Modules II* for double bass and piano (1976); *Symbiosis* for flute, alto flute, clarinet, cello and tapes (1974); *3 Dimensions* for 5 cellos (1974); Concerto for Tuba and Piano (1974); *Cycles* for oboe and piano (1975); *Chaconne* for 5 guitars (1975); *Dances: Real & Imagined* for guitar and string quartet (1976); *Soundings* for oboe and harpsichord (1977); *Bandyings* for guitar and bassoon (1977); Piano Sonata (1958); songs.

Botto, Carlos, Chilean composer; b. Viña del Mar, Nov. 4, 1923. He studied in Valparaiso and later at the Santiago Cons. with Domingo Santa Cruz and Juan Orrego-Salas; in 1952 he was appointed to the faculty of the Chilean National Cons. of Music; in 1969 he became instructor of composition at the Catholic Univ. of Chile. His works are unpretentious in style; among them are String Quartet (1954); Fantasia for Viola and Piano (1962); brief piano pieces and songs.

Bottrigari, Ercole, Italian music theorist; b. Bologna (baptized Aug. 24), 1531; d. San Alberto, near Bologna, Sept. 30, 1612. He was an illegitimate son of the nobleman Giovanni Battista Bottrigari; studied mathematics and music in the house of his father; learned to sing and play several instruments; his house teacher was Bartolomeo Spontone. In 1551 he married a rich lady. In his residence he met many celebrated poets of the day, including Tasso. Having acquired profound learning in several scientific and artistic disciplines, he devoted much of his energies to theoretical musical subjects; published numerous papers, many of them of a polemical nature.
WRITINGS: *Il Patricio ovvero de' tetracordi armonici di Aristosseno* (Bologna, 1593); *Il Desiderio ovvero de' concerti di vari stromenti musicali* (Venice, 1594, without Bottrigari's name, but under the pseudonym **Alemanno Benelli,** anagram of the name of his friend, Annibale Melone; 2nd ed. with Bottrigari's name, Bologna, 1599; modern reprint of this edition, in 1924, with introduction and annotations by Kathi Meyer; 3rd ed., Milan, 1601, under the name of Melone); *Il Melone, discorso armonico* (Ferrara, 1602). He left translations of Boetius and other writers in MS, preserved in the library of the Liceo Musicale in Bologna.
BIBLIOGRAPHY: *Notizie biografiche intorno agli studii ed alla vita del Cavaliere Bottrigari* (Bologna, 1842); G. Gaspari, "Dei Musicisti Bolognesi al XVI secolo," in *Atti e Memorie* (Bologna, 1876).

Boucher, Alexandre-Jean, famous French violinist; b. Paris, April 11, 1778; d. there, Dec. 29, 1861. A brilliant violin virtuoso, he styled himself 'l'Alexandre des violons.' Boucher began his career at the age of 6, playing with the Concerts Spirituels in Paris; was soloist in the court of Charles IV of Spain (1787–1805); traveled extensively on the continent and in England. He wrote 2 violin concertos.
BIBLIOGRAPHY: G. Vallat, "Boucher, son temps, etc.," in *Etudes d'histoire* (1890).

Boucourechliev, André, Bulgarian-French music critic; b. Sofia, July 28, 1925. He studied in Paris and settled there; in 1964 traveled in the U.S. He publ. a biography of Schumann (Paris, 1957; N.Y., 1959), a pictorial biography of Chopin (N.Y., 1962), and a biography of Beethoven (Paris, 1963); became a music critic; also composed music in an advanced idiom. For Beethoven's bicentennial he wrote *Ombres, Hommage à Beethoven* for string orch. (Toulouse, June 8, 1970).

Boudreau, Robert Austin, American trumpeter and conductor; b. Bellingham, Mass., April 25, 1927. He studied trumpet with Georges Mager of the Boston Symph. and with William Vacchiano at the Juilliard School of Music, N.Y. He then taught music at Ithaca College (1951–52), Lehigh Univ. (1952–53) and at Duquesne Univ. (1955–57). In 1957 he founded in Pittsburgh the American Wind Symph. Orch., specializing in contemporary music; it commissioned works from Henk Badings, Henry Brant, Paul Creston, Alan Hovhaness, Somers, Weinzweig, Penderecki, and Mayuzumi; the performances take place aboard the *Point Counterpoint II,* a floating arts center that includes a theater and an art gallery.

Boughton, Rutland, English composer; b. Aylesbury, Jan. 23, 1878; d. London, Jan. 24, 1960. He studied at the Royal College of Music in London with Stanford and Walford Davies; without obtaining his diploma, he engaged in professional activity; was for a time a member of the orchestra at Haymarket Theatre, London; taught at Midland Institute, Birmingham (1904–11); also conducted a choral society there. He became a firm believer in the universality of arts on Wagnerian lines; formed a partnership with the poet Reginald Buckley; their book of essays, *The Music Drama of the Future,* expounding the neo-Wagnerian idea, was published in 1908. To carry out these plans, he organized stage festivals at Glastonbury, helped by his wife Christina Walshe. Boughton's opera, *The Immortal Hour,* was performed there on Aug. 26, 1914; his choral music drama, *The Birth of Arthur,* had a performance in 1920; these productions were staged with piano instead of an orchestra. After an interruption during World War I, Boughton tried to revive the Glastonbury festivals, but was unsuccessful. In 1927 he settled in the country in Gloucestershire. He continued to compose, however, and produced a number of stage works, as well as instrumental pieces, few of which have been performed. His ideas of universal art had in the meantime been transformed into concepts of socialist realism, with an emphasis on the paramount importance of folk music as against formal constructions.
WORKS: FOR THE STAGE: *The Birth of Arthur* (1909; Glastonbury, Aug. 16, 1920); *The Immortal Hour* (1913; Glastonbury, Aug. 26, 1914); *The Round Table* (Glastonbury, Aug. 14, 1916); *The Moon Maiden,* choral ballet for girls (Glastonbury, April 23, 1919); *Alkestis,* music drama (1922; Glastonbury, Aug. 26, 1922; Covent Garden, London, Jan. 11, 1924); *The Queen of Cornwall,* music drama after Thomas Hardy (Glastonbury, Aug. 21, 1924); *May Day,* ballet (1926); *The Ever Young,* music drama (1928; Bath, Sept. 9, 1935); *The Lily Maid,* opera (1934; Gloucester, Sept. 10, 1934); *Galahad,* music drama (1944); *Avalon,* music drama (1946). ORCHESTRAL WORKS: *The Skeleton in Armour,* symph. poem with chorus (1898); *The Invincible Armada,* symph. poem (1901); *A Summer Night* (1902); *Oliver Cromwell,* symph. (1904); *Love and Spring* (1906); *Midnight* (1907); *Song of Liberty* for chorus and orch. (1911); *Bethlehem,* choral drama (1915; his most successful work); *Pioneers,* after Walt Whitman, for tenor, chorus and orch. (1925); *Deirdre,* symph. (1927); Symphony in B minor (1937); Trumpet Concerto (1943). CHAMBER MUSIC: Violin Sonata (1921); Quartet for Oboe and Strings (1930); String Trio (1944); Piano Trio (1948); Cello Sonata

(1948); numerous choral works. He published several pamphlets and essays: *The Death and Resurrection of the Music Festival* (1913); *The Glastonbury Festival Movement* (1922); *Bach, the Master* (1930); *Parsifal: a Study* (1920); *The Nature of Music* (1930); *The Reality of Music* (1934).

BIBLIOGRAPHY: *The Self-Advertisement of Rutland Boughton* (anonymous pamphlet without date, c.1909); H. Antcliffe, "A British School of Music Drama: The Work of Rutland Boughton," *Musical Quarterly* (Jan. 1918); M. Hurd, *Immortal Hour: The Life and Period of Rutland Boughton* (London, 1962).

Bouhy, Jacques-Joseph-André, celebrated baritone; b. Pepinster, Belgium, June 18, 1848; d. Paris, Jan. 29, 1929. He studied at the Liège Cons.; then at the Paris Cons. He sang Escamillo in the first performance of *Carmen* (March 3, 1875); appeared at Covent Garden, London (April 22, 1882); in 1885 he went to New York as director of the N. Y. Cons. (until 1889); he was again in New York from 1904–07; then returned to Paris and settled there as a successful singing teacher.

Boulanger, Lili, talented French composer, sister of **Nadia Boulanger;** b. Paris, Aug. 21, 1893; d. Mézy (Seine-et-Oise), March 13, 1918. She studied composition with Paul Vidal at the Paris Cons. (1909–13); carried the Grand Prix de Rome (1913) with her cantata *Faust et Hélène* (first woman to gain this distinction). Her early death at the age of 24 was a great loss to the cause of French music. Her talent, delicate and poetic, continued in the tradition of *fin de siècle* French romanticism and incipient impressionism.

WORKS: She wrote, besides her prize-winning cantata, 2 symph. poems, *D'un soir triste* and *D'un matin de printemps*; music for Maeterlinck's play *La Princesse Maleine* from an unfinished opera; several choral works with orch.: *Soir sur la plaine*; *Hymne au soleil*; *La Tempête*; *Les Sirènes*; *Sous Bois*; *La Source*; *Pour les funerailles d'un soldat*; *3 Psaumes*; *Vieille prière bouddhique*; sacred chorus *Pie Jesu* for voice, strings, harp and organ; cycle of 13 songs to texts of Francis Jammes, *Clairières dans le ciel*; some flute pieces.

BIBLIOGRAPHY: C. Mauclair, "La Vie et l'œuvre de Lili Boulanger," *Revue Musicale* (Aug. 1921); P. Landormy, "Lili Boulanger," *Musical Quarterly* (Oct. 1930); R. Dumesnil, *Portraits de musiciens français* (Paris, 1938); E. Lebeau, *Lili Boulanger* (Paris, 1968).

Boulanger, Nadia, illustrious French composition teacher; sister of **Lili Boulanger;** b. Paris, Sept. 16, 1887. Both her father and grandfather were teachers at the Paris Cons.; her mother was Russian Countess Myshetskaya, a professional singer; it is from her that Nadia Boulanger received her Russian diminutive (for Nadezhda) name, and it was from her that she had her first music lessons. She entered the Paris Cons., where she studied organ with Guilmant and Vierne, and composition with Gabriel Fauré; she graduated with prizes in organ and theory; in 1908 she received 2nd Prix de Rome for her cantata *La Sirène*; she completed the composition of the opera by Raoul Pugno, *La Ville Morte*, left unfinished after his death; also composed cello music, piano pieces and songs; realiz-

ing that she could not compare with her sister Lili in talent as a composer, she devoted herself to teaching, and it is in that profession, often regarded as ancillary and uncreative, that she found her finest vocation. She was assistant in a harmony class at the Paris Cons. (1909–24); then was engaged as teacher at École Normale de Musique in Paris (1920–39); when the American Cons. was founded in 1921 at Fontainebleau, she joined its faculty as teacher in composition and orchestration; she also had a large class of private pupils from all parts of the world; many of them achieved fame in their own right; among Americans who went to Paris to study with her were Aaron Copland, Roy Harris, Walter Piston, Virgil Thomson, Elliott Carter, David Diamond, Elie Siegmeister, Irving Fine, Easley Blackwood, Arthur Berger, John Vincent and Harold Shapero; others were Igor Markevitch, Jean Françaix, Lennox Berkeley and Dinu Lipatti. Not all of her students were enthusiastic about her methods; some of them complained about the strict, and even restrictive, discipline she imposed on them; but all admired her insistence on perfection of form and accuracy of technique. Her tastes are far from the catholicity expected of teachers; she is a great admirer of Stravinsky, Debussy and Ravel, but has little appreciation of Schoenberg and the modern Vienna School. She visited the U.S. several times; played the organ part in Aaron Copland's Organ Symphony (which she advised him to compose) with the N.Y. Symph. Orch., under the direction of Walter Damrosh (Jan. 11, 1925), and was the first woman to conduct regular subscription concerts of the Boston Symph. Orch. (1938) and of the N.Y. Philharmonic (Feb. 11, 1939). During World War II she stayed in America; taught classes at Radcliffe College, Wellesley College and the Juilliard School of Music; returning to Paris in 1946, she took over a class in piano accompaniment at the Paris Cons.; continued her private teaching as long as her frail health permitted; her 90th birthday was celebrated in September, 1977, with sincere tributes from her many students in Europe and America.

BIBLIOGRAPHY: Alan Kendall, *The Tender Tyrant. Nadia Boulanger: A Life Devoted to Music* (London, 1977).

Boulez, Pierre, celebrated French composer and conductor; b. Montbrison, March 26, 1925. He studied theory with Olivier Messiaen at the Paris Cons., graduating in 1945; later took lessons with René Leibowitz, who initiated him into the procedures of serial music. In 1948 he became a theater conductor in Paris; made a tour of the U.S. with a French ballet group in 1952. In 1954 he organized in Paris a series of concerts named Domaine Musical, devoted mainly to avant-garde music. In 1963 he delivered lectures on music at Harvard Univ., and on May 1, 1964 made his American debut as conductor, in New York. In 1958 he went to Germany, where he gave courses at the International Festivals for New Music in Darmstadt. It was in Germany where he gained his experience as conductor of opera and symphony; he was one of the few Frenchmen to conduct Wagner's *Parsifal* in Germany, and in 1976 was engaged to conduct the *Ring* cycle in Bayreuth. His popularity as a conductor grew also in America. After having been a regular guest conductor of the Cleveland Orch., he was appointed in 1971 music director of the New York Philharmonic. In his program making he resolutely cultivated the works of the radical composers of Europe and America, and conducted more works of Schoenberg, Berg, Webern, Varèse and their followers, than all of his predecessors. This policy evoked the expected opposition on the part of many subscribers, but the management decided not to oppose Boulez in his choice of programs. Naturally, Boulez conducted symphonic works of the classics of old music, but he gave a relatively small place to such outspoken romanticists as Tchaikovsky. He distinguished himself by excellent presentations of French music of all periods. The termination of his appointment with the New York Philharmonic was announced for the season 1977–78, with Zubin Mehta selected as his successor. Despite his preoccupation with conducting, Boulez produced a body of works of great imagination and inventive power. In these works, he combines serial principles with constructions in which the contrasting sonorities determine the progress of each composition; in this respect he follows the precepts of Varèse.

WORKS: *Le Visage nuptial* for 2 solo voices, chorus and orch. (1946–50); *Le Soleil des eaux*, cantata (1948; revised 1965); *Symphonie concertante* for piano and orch. (1950); *Polyphonie X* for 18 solo instruments (Donaueschingen Music Festival, Oct. 6, 1951); *Le Marteau sans Maître*, cantata for contralto, flute, viola, guitar, vibraphone and percussion (International Festival of the Society for Contemporary Music, Baden-Baden, June 18, 1955); *Poésie pour pouvoir*, spatial work for 2 orchestras conducted by 2 synchronized conductors (Donaueschingen Festival, Oct. 19, 1958, under the direction of Boulez and Hans Rosbaud); *Pli selon pli* for voice and orch. (Cologne, June 13, 1960); *Figures, Doubles, Prismes* for orch. (Brussels, Dec. 13, 1964, composer conducting); *Éclat* for chamber orch. (Los Angeles, March 26, 1965, composer conducting); *Domaines* for solo clarinet and 21 instruments (1968); *Livre pour quatuor* for string quartet (1949; a version for string orch., *Livres pour cordes*, 1969); *. . . explosante/fixe . . .* for vibraphone, harp, violin, viola, cello, flute, clarinet, trumpet (N.Y., Jan. 5, 1973; employing electronic resources, including something called a Halaphone, run by a set of computers, governing the order of instrumental "explosions" and electronically altering the individual parts while the instrument plays a "fixed" continuity); *Rituel* for orch., oriental percussion and voice, subdivided into 15 sections, some of them aleatory, and dedicated to the memory of Bruno Maderna (1975); *Structures I* for 2 pianos (1951); *Structures II* for 2 pianos (1956–61); Piano Sonata No. 1 (1946); Piano Sonata No. 2, of truly transcendental difficulty (1948); Piano Sonata No. 3 (1957); *Sonatine* for flute and piano (1946). Boulez is a controversial writer on musical and socio-musical subjects; his anti-Schoenberg paper, pointedly entitled *Schoenberg est mort* (in English as "Schoenberg is Dead," *Score* 6 [1952]) produced vibrations of shock and dismay in the world of the musical avant-garde. Among his other writings are *Penser la musique aujourd'hui* (Paris, 1963; publ. in English as *Boulez on Music Today*, Cambridge, Mass., 1970); *Relevés d'apprenti* (Paris, 1967; English

translation as *Notes of an Apprenticeship*, N.Y., 1968).

BIBLIOGRAPHY: A. Goléa, *Rencontres avec Pierre Boulez* (Paris, 1958); V. M. Ames, "What Is Music?" *Journal of Aesthetics and Art Criticism* (Winter 1967); S. Borris, "Pierre Boulez—ein Komponistenporträt," *Musik im Unterricht* B/LIV/5 (1968); J. P. Derrien, "Pierre Boulez," *Musique en Jeu* (1970); M. Fink, "Pierre Boulez: A Selective Bibliography," *Current Musicology* 13 (1972); I. Stoianowa, "*Pli selon pli*, portrait de Mallarmé," *Musique en Jeu* (June 1973); Joan Peyser, *Boulez, Composer, Conductor, Enigma* (N.Y., 1976).

Boulnois, Joseph, French composer; b. Paris, Jan. 28, 1884; killed in battle at Chalaines, Oct. 20, 1918. He studied piano and composition at the Paris Cons.; later became church organist, and from 1909 was choir leader at the Opéra-Comique. He wrote an opera *L'Anneau d'Isis*, a *Symphonie funèbre*, a cello sonata, and various pieces for organ, piano and voice. His works remain mostly in MS. There has been a revival of interest in his music, which has resulted in some performances of his songs and choruses.

Boult, Sir Adrian Cedric, eminent English conductor; b. Chester, April 8, 1889. He studied at the Westminster School and at Christ Church, Oxford; received the degree of D. Mus. from Oxford Univ.; then went to Leipzig, where he studied conducting with Nikisch (1912–13); also took a course with Max Reger. He held a subsidiary position at Covent Garden in 1914; made his début as orchestral conductor with the Royal Philh. Society (1918); gave 4 concerts with the London Symph. Orch., in which he included *The Planets* by Holst and *London Symphony* by Vaughan Williams. In 1919 he became instructor in conducting at the Royal College of Music. In 1923 he conducted the Birmingham Festival Choral Society; in 1924 was engaged as conductor of the City of Birmingham Orch.; in 1930 obtained the post of mus. dir. and conductor of the BBC Symph. Orch. Under his direction this orchestra became one of the finest ensembles in England; in 1950 he was appointed conductor of the London Philharmonic Orch. He was guest conductor of the Boston Symph. and N. Y. Philh. in 1938–39. He was knighted in 1937. As conductor, Boult is objective in his emphasis upon primary musical values; he is equally proficient in the classical, romantic and modern repertories; he has given numerous performances of works by British composers. He is the author of *A Handbook on the Technique of Conducting* (Oxford, 1921; revised, London, 1968).

BIBLIOGRAPHY: Donald Brook, *International Gallery of Conductors* (Bristol, 1951; pp. 52–60).

Bourgault-Ducoudray, Louis-Albert, French composer; b. Nantes, Feb. 2, 1840; d. Paris, July 4, 1910. At the age of 18 he composed his first opera, *L'Atelier de Prague* (Nantes, 1859); was a pupil of Ambroise Thomas at the Paris Cons., taking the Grand Prix de Rome in 1862 with a cantata, *Louise de Mézières*. He founded an amateur choral society in Paris (1868); spent some time in research in Greece, after which he publ. *Souvenirs d'une mission musicale en Grèce, 30*

Mélodies populaires de Grèce et de l'Orient, and *Etudes sur la musique ecclésiastique grecque* (1877). He was appointed prof. of music history at the Paris Cons. in 1878. WORKS: 4 operas: *Thamara* (Paris Opéra, Dec. 28, 1891), *Michel Colomb* and *Bretagne* (not performed), *Myrdhin* (Nantes, March 28, 1912); for orch.: *Le Carnaval d'Athènes* (from his *Danses grecques,* originally for piano 4 hands); *Rapsodie Cambodgienne;* vocal works: *François d'Amboise,* cantata (1866); *Stabat mater* (1868); *La Conjuration des fleurs; Symphonie religieuse,* etc.; piano pieces; numerous songs, including *30 Mélodies populaires de la Basse-Bretagne,* with French translations (1885). BIBLIOGRAPHY: See M. Emmanuel, *Éloge funèbre de Louis-Albert Bourgault-Ducoudray* (Paris, 1911; with complete catalogue of works); M. Poté, "Bourgault-Ducoudray," *Bulletin de la Société Archéologie et Historique de Nantes* (1965).

Bourgeois, Loys (Louis), French composer; b. Paris, c.1510; d. there, c.1561. He was a follower of Calvin, with whom he lived (1545–57) in Geneva; then returned to Paris; was still living in 1561. He is renowned for having composed, or adapted, almost all the melodies the Calvinists sang to Marot's and Bèze's French versions of the Psalms. Clément Marot, poet in the service of Francis I as 'valet de chambre,' translated (1533–39) 30 psalms in metrical form, which found great favor with the court, who sang them to light melodies. However, the Sorbonne soon condemned them, and, in 1542, Marot had to flee to Geneva. The first edition of Calvin's Genevan Psalter, containing Marot's 30 psalms, his versifications of the Paternoster and Credo, 5 psalms of Calvin, and his versions of the Song of Simeon and Decalogue, was publ. at Geneva in 1542. 17 of the melodies, all but 3 of which were more or less altered, were adapted by Bourgeois from the earlier Strasbourg Psalter of Calvin (1539); 22 new ones were added. After arriving at Geneva, Marot added 19 other psalms and the Song of Simeon; these, together with the 30 previously publ., compose the so-called 'Cinquante Pseaumes,' which, with Marot's Décalogue, Ave and Graces (all with music), were added in the 1543 edition of the Psalter. By 1549, 17 of the melodies previously used were more or less altered by Bourgeois, and 8 others replaced; in 1551 he modified 4 and substituted 12 new tunes. Thus, several of the melodies are of later date than the psalms. On Marot's death, in 1544, Théodore de Bèze undertook completing the Psalter. In 1551 he added 34 psalms, in 1554 6 more, and in 1562 the remaining 60. Bourgeois composed, or adapted, the tunes to all except the last 40, they being set, supposedly, by Pierre Dubuisson, a singer. In 1557 Bourgeois left Geneva and severed his immediate contact with the work there, although he still continued his activity on the psalter. Claude Goudimel publ. harmonized editions of the Genevan Psalter after 1562, thereby creating the erroneous belief that he was the author of the melodies themselves. Bourgeois himself harmonized, and publ. in 1547, 2 sets of psalms in 4–6 parts, intended only for private use. His treatise, *Le droict chemin de musique,* etc. (Geneva, 1550), proposed a reform in the nomenclature of the tones to fit the solmisation-syllables, which was generally adopted in France (see Fétis, *Biographie des musiciens* vol. II, p. 42).

BIBLIOGRAPHY: Douen, *Clément Marot et le Psaultier Huguenot* (2 vols.; Paris, 1878–79); G. A. Crawford, "Clément Marot and the Huguenot Psalter," *Musical Times* (June/Nov. 1881); G. R. Woodward, "The Genevan Psalter of 1562," *Proceedings of the Mus. Assoc., session 44* (London, 1918); Sir Richard R. Terry, "Calvin's First Psalter," ibid., *session 57* (lecture; London, 1930); id., *Calvin's First Psalter* (London, 1932; contains a facsimile and transcription into modern notation of the 1539 Strasbourg Psalter); W. S. Pratt, *The Music of the French Psalter of 1562* (N.Y., 1939); P. A. Gaillard, *L. Bourgeois: sa vie, son œuvre comme pédagogue et compositeur* (Lausanne, 1948); P. Pidoux, "Loys Bourgeois Anteil am Hugenotten-Psalter," *Jahrbuch für Liturgik und Hymnologie* (1970).

Bourguignon, Francis de, Belgian composer; b. Brussels, May 29, 1890; d. there, April 11, 1961. He studied at the Brussels Cons. with Léon Dubois and Edgar Tinel (composition) and Arthur de Greef (piano); entered the Belgian Army and was wounded in 1915; was evacuated to England. After the war he made a tour as a pianist with Nellie Melba in Australia; went on concert tours in Canada, South America, Asia and Africa; circled the globe six times. In 1925 he returned to Brussels, and took a course in composition with Paul Gilson; with 7 other pupils of Gilson he formed the "Groupe des Synthétistes" with the proclaimed objective of promoting modern music. WORKS: chamber opera, *Le Mauvais pari* (1937), a ballet *La Mort d'Orphée* (1928), a radio play *Congo* (1936), an oratorio *La Nuit* (1945), the symph. poems *Le Jazz vainqueur* (1929) and *Oiseaux de nuit* (Paris, June 28, 1937), and the symph. suites *Puzzle* (1938) and *Juventus* (1941); Piano Concertino (1927); *2 esquisses sud-américaines* for orch. (1928); *Fête populaire,* symph. movement (1929); *Prelude and Dance* (1929); *Éloge de la Folie* for orch. (1934); Symphony (1934); *Fantasy on 2 Themes of Eugène Ysaÿe* for piano and orch. (1938); *Sinfonietta* (1939); *Berceuse* (1940); Suite for Viola and Orch. (1940); *Recuerdos: 2 impressions sud-américaines* (1943); Concerto Grosso (1944); Violin Concerto (1947); Piano Concerto (1949); *Récitatif et Ronde* for trumpet and orch. (1951); Concertino for Piano and Chamber Orch. (1952); 2-Piano Concerto (1953); *Ouverture martiale* (1960); String Trio; Piano Trio; 2 string quartets; Oboe Quintet; choral works; songs; and several piano suites including *Dans l'île de Pinang* (1925), *En Floride* (1927) and *2 Danses* (1939).

Bousquet, Georges, French conductor and music critic; b. Perpignan, March 12, 1818; d. St. Cloud, near Paris, June 15, 1854. He studied at the Paris Cons.; won the Prix de Rome (1838); conducted at the Opéra (1847) and at the Théâtre Italien (1849–51); wrote music criticism for *Le Commerce, l'Illustration,* and the *Gazette musicale.* He composed 3 operas, which were performed in Paris: *l'Hôtesse de Lyon* (Paris Cons., 1844); *Le Mousquetaire* (Opéra-Comique, 1844);

Tabarin (Théâtre-Lyrique, 1852); also a cantata; church music; chamber music.

Boutmy, Josse, Belgian organist and composer; b. Ghent, Feb. 1, 1697; d. Brussels, Nov. 27, 1779. He was a member of a musical family and received his training from his father, a church organist. In 1721 he went to Brussels where he became a teacher of the clavecin; also was organist at the Royal Chapel (from 1744). He published two books of clavecin pieces (Brussels, 1738; 1750); partial reprints are in volume V of *Monumenta Musicae Belgicae* (Antwerp, 1943), edited by Suzanne Clercx, with a biographical essay in Flemish and French.

Boutry, Roger, French pianist, conductor and composer; b. Paris, Feb. 27, 1932. He studied at the Paris Cons.; received first prize as pianist at the age of 16; first prize as conductor at 21; and the Premier Prix de Rome at 22. In 1963 he was awarded the Grand Prix Musical of the City of Paris. He embarked on a successful career as pianist; toured in Europe, Russia and Australia; as a conductor, he appeared with several orchestras in France; also conducted opera in Monte Carlo.
WORKS: Piano Concerto (1954); *Rapsodie* for piano and orch. (1956); *Ouverture-Tableau* for orch. (1959); *Divertimento* for saxophone and orch. (1964); *Concerto-Fantaisie* for 2 pianos and orch. (Paris, Feb. 16, 1967); *Intermezzi* for chamber orch. (1970); Quartet for Trombones; Flute Concerto; 2 sextets; *Pastels et Contours* for 5 harps; also didactic pieces for various instruments.

Bouvet, Charles, French musicologist; b. Paris, Jan. 3, 1858; d. there, May 22, 1935. He studied at the Paris Cons.; in 1903 founded a Bach Society; in 1919 was appointed archivist at the Paris Opéra; was general secretary of the French Musicological Society (1920–27).
WRITINGS: *Les Couperin* (Paris, 1919); *L'Opéra* (1924); *Massenet* (1929). He was the editor of works of Bonporti and Couperin; prepared for publication several collections of old French music.

Bouzignac, Guillaume, French composer of early seventeenth century; biographical data are lacking but several specimens of his music are extant. It is known that he was choir boy at Narbonne; in 1609 was the 'maître des enfants' at the Grenoble Cathedral. His creative period comprises the years 1610–40; he wrote a number of effective motets in the popular French style, distinguished by dramatic expression, as well as religious works. H. Quittard publ. several of these pieces in his paper "Un Musicien oublié du XVIIᵉ siècle," *Bulletin de la Société Internationale de Musique* (Paris, 1905).

Bovery, Jules (real name **Antoine-Nicolas-Joseph Bovy**), Belgian violinist and conductor; b. Liège, Oct. 21, 1808; d. Paris, July 17, 1868. He was employed in theater orchestras in France and Holland; eventually settled in Paris. He was the author of several operettas and semi-popular instrumental pieces in the salon style.

Bovy, Vina, operatic soprano; b. Ghent, Belgium, May 22, 1900. She studied piano and voice at Ghent Cons. (1915–17); made her début at the Théâtre de la Monnaie in Brussels; also appeared at the Opéra-Comique, Paris. After a series of operatic performances in Italy she was engaged by Toscanini at La Scala; later sang in Buenos Aires. She made her American début with the Metropolitan Opera as Violetta (Dec. 24, 1936). In 1938 she returned to Europe; in 1948 became managing director of the Ghent Opera.

Bovy-Lysberg, Charles-Samuel, Swiss pianist and composer; b. Lysberg, near Geneva, Feb. 1, 1821; d. Geneva, Feb. 15, 1873. He went to Paris and was one of the few young pianists to study with Chopin (1835). Returning to Switzerland he settled at Dardagny, near Geneva in 1848; taught piano at the Geneva Cons., and gave recitals in the French cantons. His opera, *La Fille du Carillonneur* was produced in Geneva in 1854; he also wrote a romantically inspired piano sonata *L'Absence*, but he became known chiefly by his effective salon pieces for piano (numbering about 130), among them *La Napolitaine, Le Réveil des oiseaux, Le Chant du rouet, Idylle, Les Ondines, Sur l'onde*, etc. His real name was Bovy, which he hyphenated it with Lysberg, the name of his birthplace.
BIBLIOGRAPHY: Pauline Long, "Charles-Samuel Bovy-Lysberg," *Schweizerisches Jahrbuch für Musikwissenschaft* III.

Bowen, Edwin York, English composer and pianist; b. London, Feb. 22, 1884; d. Hampstead, England, Nov. 23, 1961. He studied at the Royal Academy of Music, where he won the Erard and Sterndale Bennett scholarships; his teachers were Matthay (piano) and F. Corder (comp.). Upon graduation he was appointed instructor in piano there. A prolific composer, Bowen wrote 3 symphonies; 3 piano concertos; Violin Concerto; Viola Concerto; a Rhapsody for Cello and Orch.; several symph. poems (*The Lament of Tasso, Eventide*, etc.); orchestral suites; many practical piano pieces in miniature forms. Bowen was the author of a manual *Pedalling the Modern Pianoforte* (London, 1936).

Bowers, Robert Hood, American composer; b. Chambersburg, Pa., May 24, 1877; d. New York, Dec. 29, 1941. He studied in Chicago, Baltimore and Philadelphia; was active in radio and theatrical conducting; served for 16 years as recording director of the Columbia Phonograph Co. His compositions include *The Anniversary*, one-act opera; the operettas *The Red Rose* (N.Y., 1911), *Old English* (1924), *Oh Ernest* (1927), *Listen In* (1929), etc.

Bowles, Paul Frederic, American composer; b. New York, Dec. 30, 1910. He studied composition with Aaron Copland and Virgil Thomson. In 1941 he won a Guggenheim Fellowship and traveled to Spain and North Africa; eventually he settled in Tangiers. In 1949 he wrote a successful novel, *The Sheltering Sky,* which was acclaimed by the press as the revelation of an important literary talent, so that Bowles became known as primarily a writer. As a composer he is mainly interested in stage music.

WORKS: 3 operas: *Denmark Vesey* (1937), *The Wind Remains* (1943), and *Yerma* (1958), the last 2 to libretti by García Lorca; ballets, *Yankee Clipper* (1937), *The Ballroom Guide* (1937), *Sentimental Colloquy* (1944) and *Pastorela* (N.Y., 1947); many scores of incidental music for plays; also scores for documentary films. His orchestral pieces include *Danza mexicana* (1941), Concerto for 2 pianos, winds, and percussion (1947); *A Picnic Cantata* for women's voices, 2 pianos and percussion (N.Y., March 23, 1954); a number of pieces of chamber music, and many songs, mostly composed before 1950.

Bowman, Edward Morris, American organist; b. Barnard, Vt., July 18, 1848; d. New York, Aug. 27, 1913. He studied with William Mason in New York, and with Weitzmann in Berlin; was the first American to pass the examinations of the Royal College of Organists in London (1881). After his return to America he was active as organist, choir conductor and teacher in St. Louis and New York; was director of the music department at Vassar College (1891-95). In 1884, with 15 others, he founded the American College of Musicians and was its first president. He publ. the Bowman-Weitzmann *Manual of Musical Theory* (1877; a compilation of notes, from oral communications, of Weitzmann's principles and rules of harmony; later translated into German).

Boyce, William, celebrated English musician; b. London, Sept. 1711 (baptized Sept. 11); d. Kensington, Feb. 7, 1779. He was chorister in St. Paul's Cathedral under Charles King; then studied organ with Maurice Greene, the cathedral organist. After holding various positions as a tutor in private schools, he obtained an organist's post at St. Michael's, Cornhill; in 1758 he became an organist of the Chapel Royal. A victim of increasing deafness, he was compelled to abandon active musical duties after 1769. His main task consisted in composing sacred works; he also contributed incidental music to theatrical productions. He conducted the Festivals of the Three Choirs (Gloucester, Worcester, Hereford) in 1737, and was Master of the Royal Band in 1755. His magnum opus was the completion of the collection, *Cathedral Music* (3 vols., 1760-78; 2nd ed. 1788; later editions, 1844 and 1849; a facsimile of the 1788 ed. is available). This collection comprises morning and evening services, anthems and other church music by a number of British composers: Aldrich, Batten, Bevin, Blow, Bull, Byrd, Child, Clarke, Creyghton, Croft, Farrant, Gibbons, Goldwin, Henry VIII, Humfrey, Lawes, Locke, Morley, Mundy, Purcell, Rogers, Tallis, Turner, Tye, Weldon, Wise. Of his own music, there are remarkable instrumental works: 12 overtures (London, 1720; reprinted in *Musica Britannica*, vol. XIII); 12 sonatas for 2 violins and bass (London, 1745); 8 symphonies (London, 1750; modern edition by Constant Lambert); 10 voluntaries for organ (London, 1785). 2 overtures, edited by Lambert, and publ. under the titles *The Power of Music* and *Pan and Syrinx* are by John Stanley and not by Boyce. Stage works: *The Chaplet* (1749); *The Roman Father* (1750); *The Shepherd's Lottery* (1751); *Harlequin's Invasion* (with M. Arne, 1759); also incidental songs to Shakespeare's plays;

an Ode in Commemoration of Shakespeare (1757). Vocal works: *Lyra Britannica* (several books of songs and duets; 1745-55); 15 anthems (1780); a collection of anthems (1790); these were republished in Novello's edition of Boyce's church music in 4 vols.; various songs originally published in the anthologies *The British Orpheus, The Vocal Musical Mask,* and others. A considerable number of Boyce's songs still in MS are in the British Museum.

BIBLIOGRAPHY: D. A. Dawe, "New Light on William Boyce," *Musical Times* (Sept. 1968); John Hawkins, "Memoirs of Dr. William Boyce" (Intro. and notes by G. Beechey), *Musical Quarterly* (Jan. 1971); R. McGuinness, *English Court Odes 1660-1820* (Oxford, 1971).

Boyd, Charles N., American editor and writer on music; b. Pleasant Unity, Pa., Dec. 2, 1875; d. Pittsburgh, April 24, 1937. He was church organist and teacher of church music at the Western Theological Seminary (1903-37); director of the Pittsburgh Musical Institute (1915-37). He published *Lectures on Church Music* (1912).

Boyden, David D., American musicologist; b. Westport, Conn., Dec. 10, 1910; studied music at Harvard Univ. (A.B., 1932; M.A., 1938); in 1939 appointed to the staff of Univ. of California, Berkeley. He publ. *A Manual of Counterpoint* (1944); *The History and Literature of Music, 1750 to the Present* (1948); *An Introduction to Music* (1956); *The History of Violin Playing from its Origins to 1761* (London, 1965); *Catalogue of the Hill Collection of Musical Instruments in the Ashmolean Museum, Oxford* (London, 1969).

Boykan, Martin, American pianist and composer; b. New York, April 12, 1931. He studied composition with Walter Piston at Harvard Univ., and also with Copland and Hindemith. As a pianist, he developed a remarkable technique entirely adequate for the most demanding contemporary compositions. As a composer he writes mostly chamber music. His works include 2 string quartets (1949, 1967); Flute Sonata (1950); Duo for Violin and Piano (1951); Quintet for Flute, Piano and Strings (1953); *Chamber Concerto* (1970). In 1957 he was appointed to the faculty of Brandeis Univ.

Boyle, George F., American pianist and composer; b. Sydney, Australia, June 29, 1886; d. Philadelphia, June. 20, 1948. He received his early musical training from his parents; in 1905 went to Berlin where he took piano lessons with Busoni. He began his career as an accompanist. In 1910 he settled in the U.S.; taught piano at the Peabody Cons. in Baltimore (1910-22), and at the Curtis Institute in Philadelphia (1924-26); then taught privately. He was also a composer; wrote *Aubade* for orch. (St. Louis, March 5, 1916); Piano Concerto (Worcester Festival, Sept. 28, 1911); Cello Concerto (Washington, Feb. 7, 1918); 3 piano trios; Violin Sonata, Viola Sonata, Cello Sonata; about 100 piano pieces and 50 songs.

Bozay, Attila, Hungarian composer; b. Balatonfüzfö, Aug. 11, 1939. He studied in Budapest first at the Bartók Cons. (1954–57) and then at the Academy of Music with Ferenc Farkas (1957–62). In his music he makes use of modified serial techniques.

WORKS: opera, *Küngisz királynő (Queen Küngisz*, 1968–69); Duo for 2 Violins (1958); *Episodes* for bassoon and piano (1959); String Trio (1960, revised 1966); *Bagatelles* for piano (1961); *Papírszeletek (Slips of Paper)*, song cycle for soprano, clarinet and cello (1962); Wind Quintet (1962); *Ritornell* for solo violin (1963); *Kialtasok (Outcries)*, song cycle for tenor and chamber ensemble (1963); 2 string quartets (1964, 1971); Variations for Piano (1964); *Pezzo concertato* for orch. (1965); *Trapéz és korlát (Trapeze and Bars)*, cantata (1966); *Pezzo sinfonico* for orch. (1967); *Intervals* for piano (1969); *Formations* for solo cello (1969); *Sorozat (Series)* for chamber ensemble (1970); *Improvisations* for solo zither (1972); *Malom (Mill)* for wind instruments, portable organ and percussion (1973); *Pezzo concertato* No. 2 for zither and orch. (1974–75).

Božič, Darijan, Slovenian composer; b. Slavonski Brod, April 29, 1933. He studied composition with Škerjanc and conducting with Švara at the Music Academy of Ljubljana; upon graduation served as an opera conductor and artistic director of the Slovenian Philharmonic (1970–74). His music was at first influenced by jazz; later he adopted radical serial techniques.

WORKS: 3 operas: *Humoreske* (1958), *Spoštovanja vredna vlačuga* (1960) and *Ares Eros*; a musical happening, *Jago*; a dramatic collage, *Polineikes* (1966); 2 ballets: *Baletska jednočinka* (1957) and *Gluha okna* (1967); Piano Concerto (1956); Saxophone Concerto (1958); Trombone Concerto (1960); Trumpet Concerto (1961); Symph. (1964–65); *Audiostructures* for piano and orch.; *Audiospectrum* for orch. (1972); *Trije dnevni Ane Frank (Three Days of Anne Frank)* for 2 narrators, and synthetic sound (1963); *Gregora strniše* for narrator and 7 instruments (1965); *Kriki (Cries)* for narrator, brass quintet and tape (1966); *Requiem (to The Memory of a Murdered Soldier—My Father)*, sound collage for narrator, chorus, instruments and concrete sounds (1969); *Sonata in Cool I* for flute and piano (1961), *Sonata in Cool II* for clarinet and piano (1961); *Sonata in Cool III* for flute, bass clarinet and harp (1965); *Pop-art-music* for string quartet, piccolo and 2 metronomes (1969); *Audiogemi I-IV* for string quartet (1974).

Bozza, Eugène, French composer and conductor; b. Nice, April 4, 1905. He studied music at the Paris Cons.; received the Grand Prix de Rome in 1934. From 1939 to 1948 he was conductor of the Opéra-Comique in Paris; then moved to Valenciennes, where he was appointed director of the local conservatory.

WORKS: an opera, *Léonidas* (1947); a lyric drama *La duchesse de Langeais* (Lille, 1967); the ballets *Fête romaine* (1942) and *Jeux de plage* (1946); Symphony (1948); Violin Concerto (1938); Cello Concerto (1947); *Luciolles* for 6 clarinets; *Suite française* for 5 woodwind instruments; 3 pieces for 5 trombones and other compositions for unusual instrumental combinations.

Bradbury, William Batchelder, American music editor; b. York, Maine, Oct. 6, 1816; d. Montclair, N.J.,

Jan. 7, 1868. He studied with Lowell Mason; then went to Germany where he took courses with Hauptmann and Moscheles in Leipzig. Returning to America, he became active in various musical enterprises; from 1854–67 he was in business as maker of pianos. He edited some 50 collections of songs and instrumental pieces; one of these collections, *Fresh Laurels for the Sabbath School* (1867) reached the circulation of 1,200,000 copies; other collections were *Bradbury's Golden Shower of Sunday School Melodies; Bright Jewels for the Sunday School; Musical Gems for School and Home.* He was the author of well-known hymn tunes: *He leadeth me; Saviour, like a shepherd lead me;* etc.

Bradsky, Wenzel Theodor, Bohemian composer; b. Rakovnik, Jan. 17, 1833; d. there, Aug. 10, 1881. He studied in Prague; then was a choir singer in Berlin; in 1874 he was given the title of court composer by Prince Georg of Prussia, whose drama *Iolanthe* he set to music. He wrote the operas *Roswitha* (Dessau, 1860); *Das Krokodil* (1862); *Jarmila* (Prague, 1879); *Der Rattenfänger von Hameln* (Berlin, 1881); also many choruses and solo songs.

Braein, Edvard Fliflet, Norwegian composer; b. Kristiansund, Aug. 23, 1924; d. Oslo, April 30, 1976. He was of a musical family; his grandfather was an organist and choirmaster, and his father, **Edvard Braein** (1887–1957), was a composer, organist and conductor. E. F. Braein had his primary musical education at the Music Cons. in Oslo, studying conducting with Odd Grüner-Hegge and composition with Bjarne Brustad; played organ; later took private lessons with Jean Rivier in Paris (1950–51). Upon returning to Oslo, he conducted choirs and orchestras.

WORKS: an opera, *Anne Pedersdotter* (1971); *Serenade* for clarinet, violin, viola and cello (1947); *Concert Overture* (1948); 3 symphonies (1949–50, 1951–54, 1967); *Serenade* for orch. (1951–52); *Adagio* for strings (1953); *Capriccio* for piano and orch. (1956–57); Divertimento for Flute and Chamber Orch. (1959); *Symphonic Prelude* (1959); *Largo* for strings (1960–61); Divertimento for Clarinet, Violin, Viola and Cello (1962); *Little Overture* (1962); string trio (1964); *Ritmico e melodica* for orch. (1971); *Til Arendal*, overture (1972); *Havljom*, overture (1973); *Humoreske* for wind quintet (1973).

BIBLIOGRAPHY: B. Kortsen, *Contemporary Norwegian Orchestral Music* (Bergen, 1969); B. Kortsen, *Contemporary Norwegian Chamber Music* (Bergen, 1971).

Braga, Francisco, Brazilian composer; b. Rio de Janeiro, April 15, 1868; d. there, March 14, 1945. He played clarinet in military bands in Rio de Janeiro; at the age of 18 he composed an overture, which was played at the inauguration of the Society of Popular Concerts in Rio de Janeiro. He then went to Paris where he studied with Massenet; also traveled in Germany and Italy. Influenced mainly by Massenet and Mascagni, Braga wrote the opera *Jupira*, which was staged at Rio de Janeiro (March 20, 1899). From 1908 till 1933, he conducted symphonic concerts in Rio. His symph. works include the programmatic pieces *In-*

somnia, Cauchemar, Paysage, etc. Braga was the teacher of many Brazilian composers and contributed much to the musical culture of his country.

BIBLIOGRAPHY: biography by T. Gomes (Rio de Janeiro, 1937); *Exposição Comemorativa do Centenario do Nascimento de Francisco Braga* (Rio de Janeiro, 1968).

Braga, Gaetano, Italian cellist and composer; b. Giulianova, Abruzzo, June 9, 1829; d. Milan, Nov. 20, 1907. He studied at Naples Cons. with C. Gaetano (1841–52); made tours as a cellist in Europe and America; lived mostly in Paris and London. His *Leggenda valacca,* known in English as *Angel's Serenade,* originally written for voice with cello (or violin) obbligato attained tremendous popularity and was arranged for various instrumental combinations. Braga wrote several operas: *Alina* or *La spregiata* (1853), *Estella di San Germano* (Vienna, 1857), *Il Ritratto* (Naples, 1858), *Margherita la mendicante* (Paris, 1859), *Mormile* (La Scala, Milan, 1862), *Ruy Blas* (1865), *Reginella* (Lecco, 1871), *Caligola* (Lisbon, 1873); sacred choruses, and a valuable *Metodo di Violoncello.*

BIBLIOGRAPHY: V. Bindi, *Gaetano Braga: da ricordi della sua vita* (Naples, 1927); A. de Angelis, "Gaetano Braga," *Rivista Musicale Italiana* (June 1929).

Bragard, Roger, Belgian musicologist; b. Huy, Nov. 21, 1903. He studied philology at the Univ. of Liège; received his Ph.D. with a dissertation, *Les Sources du 'De Institutione Musica' de Boèce* (1926); then studied in Paris with Pirro (musicology) and Vincent d'Indy (composition). In 1931 he worked in various European libraries on problems of medieval music. In 1935 he became prof. of music history at the Cons. of Brussels. He publ. a number of valuable papers, among them, *Lambert de Sayve* (Liège, 1934); *Panorama de la musique belge du XIVᵉ au XVIIIᵉ siècle* (Brussels, 1938); *Boethiana* (Antwerp, 1945); *Histoire de la musique belge* (3 volumes, 1946; 1949; 1956); with F. De Hen, *Les instruments de musique dans l'art et l'histoire* (Brussels, 1967; Amer. ed., N.Y., 1968); etc.

Braga-Santos, Joly, Portuguese composer; b. Lisbon, May 14, 1924. He studied with Freitas-Branco; then went to Venice, Switzerland and Rome for further study. In 1961 he was appointed assistant conductor of the National Broadcasting Symph. Orch. in Portugal. He wrote 5 symphonies in 20 years (1946–66); Concerto for String Orch. (1950); an opera, *Merope* (1959); Viola Concerto (1960); Double Concerto for Violin, Cello and Orch. (1960); and *Trilogia das barcas,* opera (1969).

Braham (real name **Abraham**), **John,** renowned English tenor; b. London, March 20, 1774; d. there Feb. 17, 1856. He studied with Leoni in London, with Rauzzini in Bath, and with Isola in Genoa. He made his début at Covent Garden (April 21, 1787); then appeared at Drury Lane in 1796, in the opera *Mahmoud* by Storace. He was subsequently engaged to sing at the Italian Opera House in London. In 1798 he undertook an extensive tour in Italy; also appeared in Hamburg. Re-

turning to England in 1801, he was increasingly successful. Endowed with a powerful voice of 3 octaves in compass, he knew no difficulties in operatic roles. He was the original Huon in Weber's *Oberon* (1826). As a ballad writer he was very popular; he wrote much of the music for the operatic roles which he sang; often he added portions to operas by other composers, as in *The Americans* (1811), with its famous song *The Death of Nelson;* contributed incidental music to 12 productions. In 1831 he entered upon a theatrical business venture; he acquired the Colosseum in Regent's Park; in 1836 he had built the St. James's Theatre, but failed to recoup his investment and lost much of his considerable fortune. He made an American tour in 1840–42 despite the weakening of his voice with age; however, his dramatic appeal remained undiminished and he was able to impress the American public in concert appearances. He then returned to London; made his final appearance in 1852.

BIBLIOGRAPHY: J. Mewburn Levien, *The Singing of John Braham* (London, 1945).

Brahms, Johannes, one of the greatest masters of music; b. Hamburg, May 7, 1833; d. Vienna, April 3, 1897. His father, a double-bass player at the Hamburg Opera, was his first teacher; his subsequent instructor was one Otto Cossel; but the man who gave Brahms his first real appreciation of the art was Eduard Marxsen. He became proficient as a child pianist, and played at a public concert in Hamburg at the age of 14, including his own variations on a folk tune. He earned some money by playing in taverns; met the Hungarian violinist Reményi, and undertook a tour with him in Germany. Joseph Joachim heard Brahms and sent him to Liszt and Schumann. Liszt expressed his admiration for the Scherzo in E-flat minor and the piano sonatas which Brahms played for him, but their relationship never grew into a spiritual affinity. Much warmer was the reception by Schumann in Düsseldorf, and Brahms became a close friend of Robert and Clara Schumann. In a famous article 'Neue Bahnen' ('New Paths') in the *Neue Zeitschrift für Musik* Schumann saluted the 20-year-old Brahms as the coming genius of German music, appearing 'fully equipped, as Minerva sprang from the brain of Jupiter.' Schumann also arranged for the publication of Brahms's 3 piano sonatas and 3 sets of songs. It was only natural that Brahms had become a convinced follower of Schumann's ideals in music; a curious episode in his biography is the issuance of a manifesto (1860, signed by Brahms and Joachim), attacking the 'Music of the Future' as promulgated by Liszt and Wagner. In 1862 Brahms went to Vienna, where he conducted the concerts of the Singakademie (1863–64). The next 5 years he spent in various towns (Hamburg, Baden-Baden, Zürich, etc.); in 1868 he was again in Vienna; conducted orchestral concerts of the Gesellschaft der Musikfreunde from 1872 to 1875. After some travel in Germany, Brahms made his home in Vienna in 1878. Meanwhile, his fame as composer grew. In 1876 Cambridge Univ. tendered him the degree of Mus. Doc., but Brahms was reluctant to make the journey, and declined the honor. He accepted, however, the degree of *Dr. phil.* given him by Breslau Univ., and acknowledged it by composing the *Akademische Festouver-*

türe, with its rousing finale based on the German student song 'Gaudeamus igitur.' Other honors followed. In 1886 he was made a Knight of the Prussian 'Orde pour le mérite,' and elected a member of the Berlin Academy of Arts. In 1889 he was presented with the freedom of his native city, Hamburg, an honor which he particularly cherished. Meanwhile, his work at composition continued unabated. His first years in Vienna were extremely productive; he wrote several works of chamber music, a genre that he had enriched more than any composer after Beethoven. He also composed several sacred works, culminating in the creation of *Ein deutsches Requiem,* which was performed for the first time in its entirety at the Bremen Cathedral on Good Friday, April 10, 1868 (1st U.S. performance by the N.Y. Oratorio Society, March 15, 1877). Brahms conducted the Bremen performance himself; later added another movement in memory of his mother. This noble work marks the highest achievement in his vocal writing; the idea of writing an opera seemed natural, and it was not entirely alien to his mind (see Widmann's *Johannes Brahms in Erinnerungen*); but Brahms never made a practical beginning in composing for the theater. Some critics have suggested that he was committed to the role of a defender of 'absolute music' as an artistic ideal, and that the opposition of his friends and champions of Brahms to Wagner precluded his interest in writing for the stage. But Brahms himself was not hostile to Wagner; he studied his scores assiduously and expressed his admiration for some of Wagner's music. Brahms was not an innovator; but he was a master rather than a slave of established forms, and never hesitated to deviate from conventional lines when it suited his artistic purpose. Ever since Robert Schumann saluted the young Brahms as a coming genius of the age, a great responsibility to justify this prediction fell on Brahms. Many of his early admirers expected him to continue the tradition of romanticism as established by Schumann. However, Brahms chose to establish himself as the standard bearer of the glorious art of the past. His austerity of spirit was not broken by the blandishments of the Muse of Programs; his music proves that the classical forms were far from exhausted, even by the titanic Beethoven, and that further expansion was possible. It was in this mood that he approached the composition of his 1st Symphony in C minor, the symphony that Hans von Bülow so pointedly described as 'The Tenth,' thus placing Brahms in the direct line from Beethoven. It was also von Bülow who coined the phrase "Three B's of Music," Brahms being the third B after Bach and Beethoven. The themes for this work were present in the master's creative mind many years back; the famous horn solo of the last movement was inspired by a shepherd's horn call, and Brahms wrote it down in a letter to Clara Schumann dated Sept. 12, 1868. Brahms completed the score in 1876, when he was 43 years old; the 2nd Symphony followed in 1877; the 3rd Symphony was written in 1883; the Fourth in 1885. Thus, after a late beginning as a symphonic composer, Brahms completed all of his 4 symphonies within less than a decade. The chamber music he produced during this period (Piano Quartet, op. 60; String Quartet, op. 67; Piano Trio, op. 87; String Quintet, op. 88), the

great Violin Concerto, and the 2nd Piano Concerto, all are symphonic in design, grandeur of form, and fertility of thematic material. In his songs Brahms reveals himself as a master of the highest caliber, an equal of the great representatives of the art of the *Lied,* Schubert and Schumann. The gift of musical poetry is revealed in his handling of the words, in the perfection with which the mood of the poem is translated into melody. The piano accompaniment in the songs of Brahms is so closely knit with the melody that both seem to flow on together in one broad, deep current. His piano works, some of them of transcendent difficulty, add a new dimension to the technique of piano playing. Brahms himself was an unusual performer; despite his mastery of the keyboard he never became a popular virtuoso, and confined himself to the playing of his own music; those who heard him report the impression of solidity, sonority, and power. Brahms was doubtless one of the greatest contrapuntists of his time; the ingenuity and easy skill with which the separate thematic strains are combined without resulting in harmonic harshness, are truly astounding. Yet Brahms was not a musical scientist, a cerebral composer, as some of his critics described him. In Vienna, Brahms assimilated the poetic and sentimental expressiveness that marks the music of Schubert, Schumann, and such lesser Viennese composers as Johann Strauss. In his *Hungarian Dances* he shows his great feeling for folk rhythms; his settings of German folksongs are of the finest in the genre. Brahms was noted for his good nature, modesty and humor. He had no personal enemies, and in his mature years never participated in polemics, even when critical assaults from the Wagnerian camp transgressed the limits of the permissible (as in Hugo Wolf's violent criticisms). Brahms never married; he lived the simple life of a middle-class citizen, and enjoyed fairly good health until the last years of his life; he died of cancer of the liver. The appreciation of Brahms in the musical world at large grew after his death. In 1906 there was founded in Berlin the Deutsche Brahmsgesellschaft, with the aim of publishing books about the master. Numerous Brahms societies were also formed in other German and Austrian cities; in America the music of Brahms was received coldly at first, but soon was wholeheartedly accepted. The frequency of performances of his symphonies is not much below that of Beethoven's. The literature, biographical and analytical, dealing with Brahms, is increasing every year with new publications in many languages.

WORKS: FOR ORCH.: Serenade in D (op. 11; 1857–58); 2 piano concertos (I, op. 15, in D minor, 1854; II, op. 83, in B-flat, 1878–81); Serenade in A for small orch. (op. 16; 1857–60; revised and republ., 1875); *Variations on a Theme by Haydn* (op. 56a; 1873); 4 symphonies (I, op. 68, in C minor, 1855–76; II, op. 73, in D, 1877; III, op. 90, in F, 1883; IV, op. 98, in E minor, 1884–85); Violin Concerto in D (op. 77; 1878); *Akademische Festouvertüre* (op. 80; 1880); *Tragische Ouvertüre* (op. 81; 1880–81); Double Concerto in A minor for violin and cello (op. 102; 1887); Hungarian Dances (arrangements without opus no.).

CHAMBER MUSIC: 3 trios for violin, cello and piano (I, op. 8, in B, 1853–54; revised 1889; II, op. 87, in C, 1880–82; III, op. 101, in C minor, 1886); 2 string sextets (I, op. 18 in B-flat, 1860; II, op. 36, in G, 1864–65); 3 piano quartets (I, op. 25, in G minor, 1861; II, op. 26, in A, 1861; III, op. 60, in C minor, 1855–75); Piano Quintet in F minor (op. 34; 1864; after the Sonata for Two Pianos, 4 hands, op. 34a); 2 cello sonatas (I, op. 38, in E minor, 1862–65; II, op. 99, in F, 1886); Trio in E-flat for horn (or cello or viola), violin and piano (op. 40; 1865); 3 string quartets (I, op. 51, in C minor; II, in A minor: both op. 51; 1859–73; III, op. 67, in B-flat, 1875); 3 violin sonatas (I, op. 78, in G, 1878–79; II, op. 100, in A, 1886; III, op. 108, in D minor, 1886–88); 2 string quintets (I, op. 88, in F, 1882; II, op. 111 in G, 1890); Trio in A minor for clarinet, cello and piano (op. 114; 1891); Quintet in B minor for clarinet and strings (op. 115; 1891); 2 clarinet sonatas (I, in F minor; II, in E-flat; both op. 120; 1894); Movement in C minor in a violin sonata by Brahms, Schumann and Dietrich (1853).

VOCAL MUSIC: choral works: *Ave Maria,* for women's voices, organ and orch. (op. 12; 1858); *Funeral Hymn,* for chorus and wind orch. (op. 13; 1858); 4 Songs for women's voices, 2 horns and harp (op. 17; 1860); *Marienlieder,* for mixed chorus (7 songs; op. 22; 1859); 13th Psalm, for women's voices and organ (op. 27, 1859); 2 Motets for 5-part a cappella chorus (op. 29; 1860); *Lass dich nur nichts dauern,* for 4-part chorus with organ (op. 30; 1856); 3 Sacred Choruses for women's voices a cappella (op. 37; 1859–63); 5 *Soldatenlieder,* for 4-part male chorus a cappella (op. 41; 1861–62); 3 Songs for 6-part mixed chorus a cappella (op. 42; 1859–61); 12 Songs and Romances for women's voices a cappella (op. 44; 1859–63); *Ein deutsches Requiem* for soli, chorus and orch. (op. 45; 1857–68); *Rinaldo,* cantata for tenor, male chorus and orch. (after Goethe; op. 50; 1863–68); *Rhapsodie,* for alto, male chorus and orch. (after Goethe's *Harzreise;* op. 53; 1869); *Schicksalslied,* for chorus and orch. (op. 54; 1871); *Triumphlied,* for 8-part chorus and orch. (op. 55; 1870–71); 7 Songs for a cappella chorus (op. 62; 1874); 2 Motets for a cappella chorus (op. 74; 1863–77); *Nänie,* for chorus and orch. (after Schiller; op. 82; 1880–81); *Gesang der Parzen,* for 6-part chorus and orch. (after Goethe; op. 89; 1882); 6 Songs and Romances for 4-part a cappella chorus (op. 93a; 1883–84); *Tafellied,* for 6-part chorus with piano (op. 93b; 1884); 5 Songs for a cappella chorus (op. 104; 1888); *Deutsche Fest- und Gedenksprüche,* for a double a cappella chorus (op. 109; 1886–88); 3 Motets for 4- and 8-part a cappella chorus (op. 110; 1889); 13 Canons for women's voices and piano (op. 113; 1863–90); 14 *Volkskinderlieder,* with piano (without op. no.; 1858); 14 German Folksongs (2 vols.; without op. no.; 1864).

vocal quartets: publ. in sets, varying in number, as opp. 31, 64, 92, 103 (*Zigeunerlieder*), and 112; vocal duets as opp. 20, 28, 61, 66, and 75; songs for one voice with piano accomp. as opp. 3, 6, 7, 14, 19, 32, 33 (from Tieck's 'Magelone'), 43, 46–9, 57–9, 63, 69–72, 84–6, 91, 94–7, 105–7 and 121.

FOR KEYBOARD: organ works: 11 *Choralvorspiele* (2 vols.; op. 122; 1896; posth.); Fugue in A-flat minor (1856); *O Traurigheit,* Chorale, Prelude and Fugue in A minor (1856). Piano solos: 3 sonatas (I, op. 1, in C, 1852–53; II, op. 2, in F-sharp minor, 1852; III, op. 5, in F minor, 1853); Scherzo in E-flat minor (op. 4; 1851);

Variations on a Theme by Schumann (op. 9; 1854); 4 Ballades (op. 10; 1854); Variations in D: I, on Original Theme; II, on Hungarian Theme (op. 21; 1857); *Variations and Fugue on a Theme by Handel* (op. 24; 1861); *28 Variations [Studien] on a Theme by Paganini* (2 vols.; op. 35; 1862–63); 8 Pieces (2 vols.; op. 76; 1871–78); 2 Rhapsodies (op. 79; 1879); 7 *Fantasien* (2 vols.; op. 116; 1892); 3 *Intermezzi* (op. 117; 1892); 6 Pieces (op. 118; 1892); 4 Pieces (op. 119; 1892); 2 cadenzas to Beethoven's Piano Concerto in G (posth.). Piano duets: *Variations on a Theme by Schumann* (op. 23; 1861); 16 Waltzes (op. 39; 1865); *Liebeslieder,* waltzes with 4 voices (op. 52; 1868–69); *Liebeslieder* without voice parts (op. 52a; arranged 1874); *Neue Liebeslieder,* waltzes with 4 voices (op. 65; 1874); *Hungarian Dances* (4 vols.; without op. no.; 1852–69). For 2 pianos: Sonata in F minor (op. 34b; 1864; original version of piano quintet, op. 34); *Variations on a Theme by Haydn* (op. 56b; 1873).

WORKS WITHOUT OP. NO.: The song *Mondnacht* is without op. no., as are 7 vols. of German songs (I–VI: for solo voice; VII: for soli and small chorus). Brahms also wrote 5 *Songs of Ophelia,* for the actress Olga Precheisen, fiancée of his friend, Lewinsky. They were performed in 1873 in Prague, but were not publ. until 1935 (N.Y.); they are not included in Breitkopf & Härtel's collection ed. of Brahm's works. *Studien* for piano (5 vols.: I. Chopin's F minor Étude arranged in sixths; II, Weber's *Moto perpetuo;* III and IV, 2 arrangements of Bach's *Presto;* V. Bach's *Chaconne* [for left hand alone]); 51 Exercises for piano (7 books; 1890); Gluck's Gavotte in A arranged for piano; Joachim's Overture to *Henry IV* arranged for piano 4 hands. He also ed. piano works of Couperin for Chrysander's *Denkmäler der Tonkunst,* Schumann's *Presto Appassionato* and *Scherzo,* 3 posth. works of Schubert, including a transcription of *Ellens zweiter Gesang* (for soprano, women's chorus and wind instruments); provided accompaniments for an edition of vocal duets by Handel; amplified the figured bass of 2 violin sonatas by C. P. E. Bach; edited Mozart's *Requiem* for the complete edition of Mozart's works; and collaborated in the preparation of the complete edition of Chopin's works.

In 1924 a copy from the original score of a Trio in A, presumably written by Brahms when he was about 20 years old (see letter to R. Schumann, 1853), was discovered in Bonn; it was edited and published by E. Bücken and K. Hasse. See E. Bücken, "Ein neuaufgefundenes Jugendwerk von J. B.," *Die Musik* (Oct. 1937); Fr. Brand, "Das neue B.-Trio," ibid. (Feb. 1939).

A Thematic Catalogue was publ. by N. Simrock (Berlin, 1897; new augmented ed., prepared by J. Braunstein, N.Y., 1956; rev. by D. M. McCorkle, N.Y. 1973). In 1926–28 Breitkopf & Härtel publ. a collection of Brahms's entire works.

BIBLIOGRAPHY: BIOGRAPHY: M. Kalbeck, *Johannes Brahms* (8 vols., Berlin, 1904–14; the standard work); H. Deiters, *J. B. Eine Charakteristik* (Leipzig, I [1880], II [1898]; both in Waldersee's *Sammlung mus. Vorträge*); H. Reimann, *J. B.* (Berlin, 1897; 6th ed. 1922); A. Dietrich, *Erinnerungen an J. B. in Briefen, besonders aus seiner Jugendzeit* (Leipzig, 1898); J. Widmann, *J. B. in Erinnerungen* (Berlin, 1898; 3d ed. 1910). This and the preceding in Engl. translations by

Hecht as *Recollections of J. B.* (London, 1899); F. May, *The Life of J. B.* (2 vols., London, 1905); J. Erb, *B.* (London, 1905); H. Antcliffe, *B.* (ib., 1905); H. Imbert, *J. B.: sa vie et son œuvre* (Paris, 1906); G. Henschel, *Personal Recollections of J. B.* (Boston, 1907); W. Pauli, *J. B.* (Berlin, 1907); R. von Perger, *B.* (Leipzig, 1908); H. C. Colles, *B.* (London, 1908); R. von der Leyen, *J. B. als Mensch und Freund* (Berlin, 1908); J. Fuller-Maitland, *B.* (London, 1911); W. Thomas San Galli, *J. B.* (Munich, 1912); E. M. Lee, *B., the Man and His Music* (London, 1915); W. Niemann, *J. B.* (1920; in Engl., N.Y., 1929); Heinrich Reimann, *B.* (1920); Paul Landormy, *B.* (1920); G. Ophüls, *Erinnerungen an J. B.* (1921); W. Nagel, *J. B.* (1923); Jeffrey Pulver, *J. B.* (London, 1926; new ed. 1933); R. Specht, *J. B.* (1928; in Engl., 1930); J. F. Cooke, *J. B.* (Phila., 1928); M. Komorn, *J. B. als Chordirigent in Wien* (1928); G. Ernest, *J. B.* (1930); J. Ch. v. Sell, *J. B.* (1931); R. H. Schauffler, "B., Poet and Peasant," *Musical Quarterly* (1932); id., *The Unknown B., His Life, Character and Works* (N.Y., 1933); Brahms issue of the *Musical Quarterly* (April 1933; includes G. Adler, "J. B., His Personality, . . ."; Karl Geiringer, "B. as a Reader and Collector," and other articles); Karl Geiringer, *J. B.* (Vienna, 1933; new ed. 1935; in English, N.Y., 1936; 2d ed., N.Y., 1947); G. Adler, *J. B.* (1933); A. von Ehrmann, *J. B.: Weg, Werk und Welt*, with a supplementary volume containing complete thematic catalogue and bibliography of first editions (Leipzig, 1933); Ralph Hill, *B.* (London, 1933); Wm. Murdock, *B.* (with an analytical study of the complete piano works; London, 1933); J. Müller-Blattau, *B.* (Berlin, 1933); Ludwig Koch, *B. in Ungarn* (Budapest, 1933); R. Fellinger, *Klänge um B.* (Berlin, 1933); R. Hernried, *J. B.* (Leipzig, 1934); R. Lienau, *Erinnerungen an J. B.* (Berlin, 1935); Konrad Huschke, *Frauen um B.* (Karlsruhe, 1937); Alfred Orel, *J. B.s Leben in Bildern* (Leipzig, 1937); L. Koch, *B.-Bibliografia* (Budapest, 1943); M. Goss and R. H. Schauffler, *B., the Master* (1943); K. Laux, *Der Einsame, J. B., Leben und Werk* (Graz, 1944); Walter und Paula Rehberg, *J. B., sein Leben und Werk* (Zürich, 1947); P. Latham, *B.* (London, 1948; rev. by Jack Westrup, London, 1975); A. Orel, *J. B., Ein Meister und sein Weg* (Vienna, 1950); F. Grasberger, *J. B., Variationen um sein Wesen* (Vienna, 1952; contains chronological and alphabetical list of works; also new photographs); Claude Rostand, *Brahms* (Paris, 1954); Hans Gál, *Johannes Brahms: Werk und Persönlichkeit* (Frankfurt, 1961; in English as *J. B.—His Work and Personality*, N.Y., 1963). For Brahms iconography see W. Müller, *Ein B.-Bilderbuch* (Vienna, 1905); and Maria Fellinger, *B.-Bilder* (Leipzig, 1911). Unclassifiable in Brahms literature is the book of mystic speculation, *Brahms Noblesse* by Frederic Horace Clark (Berlin, 1912; parallel German and English texts); see also Arthur M. Abell, *Talks With Great Composers* (N.Y., 1955); Y. Tienot, *B., son vrai visage* (Paris, 1968); F. Grasberger, "Das Jahr 1868," *Österreichische Musikzeitschrift* (April 1968); K. Dale, *B.: A Biography with a Survey of Books, Editions & Recordings* (London, 1970); Richard Heuberger, *Erinnerungen an J. B. Tagebuchnotizen aus den Jahren 1875-1897* (Tutzing, 1971); B. James, *B. A Critical Study* (N.Y., 1972); K. Geiringer and I. Geiringer, "The B. Library in the Gesellschaft der Musikfreunde, Wien," *Notes* (Sept. 1973).

CORRESPONDENCE: The 'complete' correspondence has been publ. by the Deutsche Brahmsgesellschaft in 16 vols. (Berlin; begun in 1906) as follows: I, II. Ed. by M. Kalbeck, *J. B. im Briefwechsel mit Heinrich und Elisabet von Herzogenberg* (1906); III. Ed. by W. Altmann, *J. B. im Briefwechsel mit Reinthaler, Bruch, Deiters, Heimsoeth, Reinecke, Rudorff, Bernhard und Luise Scholz* (1907); IV. Ed. by R. Barth, *J. B. im Briefwechsel mit J. O. Grimm* (1907); V, VI. Ed. by A. Moser, *J. B. im Briefwechsel mit Joseph Joachim* (1908); VII. Ed. by L. Schmidt, *J. B. im Briefwechsel mit Levi, Gernsheim sowie den Familien Hecht und Fellinger* (1910); VIII. Ed. by M. Kalbeck, *J. B. im Briefwechsel mit Widmann, Vetter, Schubring* (1915); IX–XII. Ed. by M. Kalbeck, *J. B. im Briefwechsel mit Peter J. Simrock u. Fritz Simrock* (1917); XIII. Ed. by J. Röntgen, *J. B. im Briefwechsel mit Th. W. Engelmann* (1918); XIV. Ed. by W. Altmann, *J. B. im Briefwechsel mit Breitkopf & Härtel, Senff, Rieter-Biedermann, Peters, Fritzsch und Lienau* (1920); XV. Ed. by E. Wolff, *J. B. im Briefwechsel mit Franz Wüllner* (1922); XVI. Ed. by C. Krebs, *J. B. im Briefwechsel mit Ph. Spitta* (1922) and *J. B. im Briefwechsel mit Otto Dessoff* (1922). Of these, vols. I and II appeared in English translation by Hannah Bryant (N.Y., 1909). Interesting letters of Brahms are found in *Clara Schumann, J. B.: Briefe aus den Jahren 1853–96*, ed. by B. Litzmann (in German and English; 2 vols., 1927); K. Stephenson, *J. B.s Heimatbekenntnis in Briefen an seine Hamburger Verwandten* (Hamburg, 1933); Otto Gottlieb-Billroth, *B. und Billroth im Briefwechsel* (Vienna, 1935); Karl Geiringer, "Wagner and B." (unpublished letters), *Musical Quarterly* (April 1936); R. Litterscheid, ed., *J. B. in seinen Schriften und Briefen* (Berlin, 1943); F. Callomon, "Some Unpublished B. Correspondence," *Musical Quarterly* (Jan. 1943).

CRITICISM, APPRECIATION: L. Köhler, *J. B. und seine Stellung in der Musikgeschichte* (Hannover, 1880); E. Krause, *J. B. in seinem Werken* (Hamburg, 1892); D. G. Mason, *From Grieg to Brahms* (New York, 1902); R. Barth, *J. B. und seine Musik* (Hamburg, 1904); G. Jenner, *J. B. als Mensch, Lehrer und Künstler* (Marburg, 1905); W. A. Thomas, *J. B. Eine musikpsychologische Studie* (Strasbourg, 1905); J. Knorr and H. Riemann, *J. B. Symphonien und andere Orchesterwerke erläutert* (Berlin, 1908); M. Burkhardt, *J. B.; ein Führer durch seine Werke* (Berlin, 1912); W. Hammermann, *J. B. als Liederkomponist* (Leipzig, 1912); E. Evans, *Historical, Descriptive and Analytical Account of the Entire Works of J. B.* (London; I, vocal works, 1912; II and III, chamber and orchestral music, 1933–35; IV, piano works, 1936); W. Nagel, *Die Klaviersonaten von J. B.* (Stuttgart, 1915); M. Friedländer, *B.s Lieder* (Berlin, 1922; in English, London, 1928); P. Mies, *Stilmomente und Ausdrucksstilformen im B.-schen Lied* (Leipzig, 1923); G. Ophüls, *B.-Texte* (3rd ed. Berlin, 1923); H. Meyer, *Linie und Form: Bach, Beethoven, Brahms* (Berlin, 1930); E. Markham Lee, *B.'s Orchestral Works*, in the Musical Pilgrim series (London, 1931); D. G. Mason, "B.'s 3rd Symphony," *Musical Quarterly* (July 1931); H. S. Drinker, *The Chamber Music of B.* (Philadelphia, 1932); A. Schering, "B. und seine Stellung in der Musikgeschichte des 19. Jahrhunderts," _Jahrbuch Peters_ (1932); H. C. Colles, _The Chamber Music of B._ (London, 1933); D. G. Mason, _The Chamber Music of B._ (N.Y., 1933); P. A. Browne, _B.: The Symphonies,_ in _Musical Pilgrim series_ (London, 1933); W. Blume, _B. in der Meininger Tradition_ (Stuttgart, 1933); K. Huschke, _J. B. als Pianist, Dirigent und Lehrer_ (Berlin, 1935); F. Brand, _Das Wesen der Kammermusik von B._ (Berlin, 1937); J. A. G. Harrison, _Brahms and His Four Symphonies_ (London, 1939); J. Fry, "B.'s Conception of the Scherzo in Chamber Music," _Musical Times_ (April 1943); C. Mason, "B.'s Piano Sonatas," _Music Review_ (1950); Arnold Schoenberg, "B. the Progressive," in _Style and Idea_ (N.Y., 1950); G. Jacob, "Schoenberg and B.'s Op. 25," _Music & Letters_ (1951); F. Grasberger, _J. B.: Variationen um sein Wesen_ (Vienna, 1952); J. P. Fairleigh, "Neo-Classicism in the Later Piano Works of B.," _Piano Quarterly_ (Winter 1966-67); W. Czesla, "Motivischen Mutationen im Schaffen von J. B.," in S. Kross and H. Schmidt, eds. _Colloquium amicorum: Joseph Schmidt-Görg zum 70. Geburtstag_ (Bonn, 1967); R. Klein, "Die konstruktiven Grundlagen der B.-Symphonien," _Österreichische Musikzeitschrift_ (May 1968); K. Reinhardt, "Motivisch-Thematisches im _Deutschen Requiem_ von B.," _Musik und Kirche_ (Jan. 1969); H.-W. Kulenkampf, "Warum ist B. berühmt? Provokation eines unzeitgemassen Themas," _Neue Zeitschrift für Musik_ (Sept. 1969); K. Blum, _Hundert Jahre "Ein deutsches Requiem"_ von _J. B._ (Tutzing, 1971); M. Harrison, _The Lieder of B._ (N.Y., 1972); E. Sams, _B. Songs_ (BBC Music Guide series; London, 1972); K. Stahmer, "Korrekturen am B. Bild," _Die Musikforschung_ (April-June 1972); R. Jacobson, _The Music of J. B._ (London, 1977).

Brăiloiu, Constantin, Rumanian ethnomusicographer; b. Bucharest, Aug. 25, 1893; d. Geneva, Dec. 20, 1958. He studied in Austria and Switzerland; in 1928 founded the Archive of Folklore in Bucharest; also was a member of ethnomusical organizations in Geneva and Paris.
WRITINGS: _Esquisse d'une méthode de folklore musical_ (Paris, 1930); _La Musique populaire roumaine_ (Paris, 1940); _Le Folklore musical_ (Zürich, 1948); _Le Rythme aksak_ (Paris, 1952); _La Rythmique enfantine_ (Brussels, 1956); "Outline of a Method of Musical Folklore" (trans. by M. Mooney; ed. by A. Briegleb and M. Kahane), _Ethnomusicology_ (Sept. 1970).
BIBLIOGRAPHY: T. Alexandra, "Constantin Brăiloiu," _Revista de etnografie şi foleor_ (1968); special Brăiloiu issue of _Cercetări de muzicologie_ II (1970); V. Cosma, _Muzicieni români_ (Bucharest, 1970; pp. 75-79).

Brailowsky, Alexander, noted Russian pianist; b. Kiev, Feb. 16, 1896; d. New York, April 25, 1976. After study with his father, a professional pianist, he was taken to Vienna in 1911 and was accepted by Leschetizky as a pupil; made his debut in Paris after World War I; presented a complete cycle of Chopin's works in Paris (1924), and repeated it there several times. He made a highly successful tour all over the world; made his American debut at Aeolian Hall, N.Y., Nov. 19, 1924; made a coast to coast tour of the U.S. in 1936; first gave the Chopin cycle in America during the 1937-38 season, in 6 recitals in New York.

Brain, Aubrey, French-horn player; b. London, July 12, 1893; d. there, Sept. 21, 1955. He studied at the Royal College of Music in London; joined the London Symphony Orch.; then played in the B.B.C. Symph. Orch.; retired in 1945. He was appointed prof. at the Royal Academy of Music in 1923, and held this position for 30 years. His father was also a horn player, as was his brother **Alfred,** and his son **Dennis Brain.**

Brain, Dennis, French-horn player; b. London, May 17, 1921; d. in an automobile accident in Hatfield, Hertfordshire, Sept. 1, 1957. He studied with his father, **Aubrey Brain;** was first horn player in the Royal Philharmonic; then joined the Philharmonia Orch.; participated in the Festivals at Lucerne and Amsterdam (1948). He rapidly acquired the reputation of a foremost performer on his instrument. Benjamin Britten's _Serenade_ for tenor, horn and strings was written for Dennis Brain.

Braine, Robert, American composer; b. Springfield, Ohio, May 27, 1896; d. (suicide) New York, Aug. 22, 1940. He studied at the Cincinnati College of Music; acted as radio conductor in New York. He composed three operas: _The Eternal Light_ (1924); _Virginia_ (1926); _Diana_ (1929); symph. pieces, _S.O.S._; _The House of Usher, The Raven_ for baritone and orch.; _Concerto in Jazz_ for violin and orch.; _Barbaric Sonata_ for piano; and many other piano pieces; also about 50 songs.

Braithwaite, Sam Hartley, English composer; b. Egremont, Cumberland, July 20, 1883; d. Arnside, Westmoreland, Jan. 13, 1947. He studied at the Royal Academy of Music; upon graduation joined its faculty as instructor. His compositions include _Military Overture;_ the tone poem _A Night by Dalegarth Bridge,_ etc.

Braithwaite, Warwick, British conductor; b. Dunedin, New Zealand, Jan. 9, 1898; d. London, Jan. 18, 1971. He studied at the Royal Academy of Music in London. Was conductor of the Cardiff Musical Society (1924-32); and of the National Orchestra of Wales (1928-31). He then conducted opera at Sadler's Wells, London (1933-43); also directed the Scottish Orchestra, Glasgow; toured in New Zealand in 1947. From 1949 he has conducted ballet at Covent Garden, London. He published _The Conductor's Art_ (London, 1952).

Brambach, Caspar Joseph, German composer; b. Oberdollendorf, near Königswinter, July 14, 1833; d. there, June 19, 1902. He studied composition at the Cologne Cons.; then taught there (1858-61); later was active as teacher and composer in Bonn (1861-69). He wrote many secular cantatas, among them _Trost in Tönen, Das Eleusische Fest, Die Macht des Gesanges, Prometheus,_ and _Columbus_ (awarded the $1,000 prize at the Milwaukee Festival; performed there July 23, 1886); also an opera _Ariadne;_ concert overture _Tasso;_ a piano concerto; piano sextet; string sextet; 2 piano quartets, and songs.

Brambach, Wilhelm, German musicologist, brother of **Caspar Joseph Brambach;** b. Bonn, Dec. 17, 1841; d. Karlsruhe, Feb. 26, 1932. He studied classical languages and musicology at the Univ. of Bonn; taught philology at the Univ. of Freiburg (1866–72); then was for 32 years librarian of the district library at Karlsruhe (1872–1904).

WRITINGS: *Das Tonsystem und die Tonarten des christlichen Abendlandes im Mittelalter* (Leipzig, 1881); *Die Musikliteratur des Mittelalters bis zur Blüte der Reichenauer Sängerschule* (Karlsruhe, 1883); *Hermanni Contracti musica* (Leipzig, 1884); *Die Verloren geglaubte 'Historia de Sancta Afra Martyri' und das 'Salve regina' des Hermannus Contractus* (Karlsruhe, 1892); *Gregorianische-bibliographische Lösung der Streitfrage über die Ursprung des Gregorianischen Gesangs* (Leipzig, 1895; 2nd ed., 1901).

Brambilla, Marietta, Italian contralto; b. Cassano d'Adda, June 6, 1807; d. Milan, Nov. 6, 1875. She was a member of a musical family; her four sisters were singers. She made her debut in London in 1827; then sang in Italy, Vienna, and Paris. She eventually settled in Milan as a teacher; published collections of vocalises.

Brambilla, Paolo, Italian composer; b. Milan, July 9, 1787; d. there, 1838. He wrote 4 operas, produced in Milan and Turin, and 6 ballets for La Scala. He was the father of **Marietta** and **Teresa Brambilla.**

Brambilla, Teresa, Italian opera singer, sister of **Marietta;** b. Cassano d'Adda, Oct. 23, 1813; d. Milan, July 15, 1895. She studied singing at the Milan Cons.; made her debut in 1831 and traveled through Europe, including Russia. Her appearances at La Scala were highly successful. After several seasons in Paris, she was engaged at the Teatro Fenice in Venice, where she created the role of Gilda in *Rigoletto* (March 11, 1851).

Brancaccio, Antonio, Italian composer; b. Naples, 1813; d. there, Feb. 12, 1846. He studied at Naples, and produced his first opera, *I Panduri,* during the carnival of 1843; his other operas included *L'Assedio di Constantina* (Venice, 1844); *Il Puntiglione* (Naples, 1845); *L'Incognita* (Venice, 1846); *Le Sarte calabresi* (Naples, 1847; posthumous); *Lilla* (Venice, 1848; posthumous).

Brancour, René, French music critic; b. Paris, May 17, 1862; d. there, Nov. 16, 1948. Educated at the Paris Cons., he became curator of the collection of music instruments there; in 1906 began a course of lectures on esthetics at the Sorbonne; also wrote newspaper criticism. A brilliant writer, he poured invective on the works of composers of the advanced school; his tastes were conservative, but he accepted French music of the Impressionist period. He wrote biographies of Félicien David (1911) and Méhul (1912) in the series of *Musiciens célèbres;* of Massenet (1923) and Offenbach (1929) in *Les Maîtres de la Musique.* Other books are *La vie et l'œuvre de Georges Bizet* (1913);

Histoire des instruments de musique (1921); *La Marseillaise et le Chant du départ,* etc.

Brand, Max, Austrian composer; b. Lwow, April 26, 1896; studied with Franz Schreker at the State Academy of Music in Vienna. He made use of the 12-tone method of composition as early as 1927, but did not limit himself to it in his later works. His most spectacular work was the opera, *Maschinist Hopkins,* to his own libretto, chosen as the best operatic work of the year by the Congress of German Composers, and first produced at Duisburg on April 13, 1929; it was later staged in 37 opera houses in Europe, including Russia; it marked the climactic point of the 'machine era' in modern music between the two wars. Brand was also active in the field of experimental musical films in the triple capacity of author, composer, and director. From 1933–38 he remained in Vienna; then went to Brazil; in 1940 arrived in the U.S., becoming an American citizen in 1945. In 1975 he returned to Austria.

WORKS: *Nachtlied* (from Nietzsche's *Also sprach Zarathustra)* for soprano and orch. (1922); 3 Songs to Poems by Lao-Tse (Salzburg Festival, 1923); *Eine Nachtmusik* for chamber orch. (1923); String Trio (1923); *Die Wippe,* ballet (1925); *Tragœdietta,* ballet (1926); 5 Ballads, a study in 12 tones (1927); *Maschinist Hopkins,* opera in 3 acts (1928); *The Chronicle,* scenic cantata for narrator, soli, chorus, and orch. (1938); *Piece for Flute and Piano,* in 12 tones (1940); *Kyrie Eleison,* study in 12 tones for chorus (1940; perf. by Villa-Lobos, Rio de Janeiro, 1940); *The Gate,* scenic oratorio, with narrator (N.Y., May 23, 1944); *The Wonderful One-Hoss Shay,* symph. rondo for orch., after Oliver Wendell Holmes (Philadelphia, Jan. 20, 1950); *Night on the Bayous of Louisiana,* tone poem (1953); *Stormy Interlude,* opera in one act, libretto by the composer (1955). About 1958 Brand became absorbed in electronic music; wrote *The Astronauts, an Epic in Electronics* (1962); *Ilian 1 & 2* (1966) and numerous pieces of music for modern plays.

Brandeis, Frederick, composer and pianist; b. Vienna, July 5, 1832; d. New York, May 14, 1899. He was a pupil of Carl Czerny; settled in the United States in 1849, where he was active as solo pianist, conductor, and organist. He wrote numerous pieces for military band; a *Romanza* for oboe and orch.; a ballade, *The Sunken Cloister* (1882); some chamber music and a variety of piano works and songs. His style of composition was entirely without distinction.

Brandl, Johann Evangelist, German composer; b. Kloster Rohr, near Regensburg, Nov. 14, 1760; d. Karlsruhe, May 25, 1837. He studied in various religious schools and monasteries as a youth; then decided to devote himself to music, and became proficient as an organist and violinist; was attached to the court of the Archduke of Baden as music director.

WORKS: the operas *Germania* (1800), *Triumph des Vaterherzens* (Karlsruhe, Jan. 15, 1811), *Omar der Gute* (Karlsruhe, Aug. 24, 1811), *Nanthild, das Mädchen von Valbella* (Karlsruhe, May 19, 1813); a "Grande Symphonie"; Bassoon Concerto; a number of string quartets and string quintets; many songs; oratorios; masses.

BIBLIOGRAPHY: O. Danzer, *J. E. Brandls Leben und Werke* (Leipzig, 1936); F. Leinert, *J. E. Brandl als Lieder- und Kammermusik Komponist* (Wolfenbüttel, 1937).

Brandt, Jobst vom (or **Jodocus de Brant**), German musician; b. Waltershofen, near Marktredwitz, Oct. 28, 1517; d. Brand, near Marktredwitz, Jan. 22, 1570. In 1530 he enrolled at Heidelberg Univ.; in 1548 had become Captain of Waldsassen and Administrator of Liebenstein. He was one of the most important composers of the Senfl school; his music is distinguished by deep feeling and a skillful use of counterpoint.
WORKS: 45 *Psalmen und Kirchengesänge* (Eger, 1572–73; preserved in the library of K. Proske); 55 vocal pieces in G. Forster's collection *Ein Auszug guter alter und neuer teutscher Liedlein* (III; Wittenberg, 1549, and IV–V, 1556). Reprints are in R. von Liliencron's *Deutsches Leben im Volkslied 1530;* in Jöde's *Chorbuch III;* in *Kaiserliederbuch für gemischten Chor;* in *Staatliches Jugendliederbuch;* in the *Chorsammlung für gemischten Chor des Arbeitsängerbundes;* in *Monatshefte für Musikgeschichte* (vol. 26); etc.

Brandt, Marianne (real name **Marie Bischoff**), Austrian contralto; b. Vienna, Sept. 12, 1842; d. there, July 9, 1921. She studied at the Vienna Cons. with Frau Marschner; then in Paris with Viardot-Garcia; made her operatic debut as Rachel in *La Juive* (Graz, Jan. 4, 1867); sang in Hamburg and at the Berlin Opera; in 1872 she appeared in London; made her American debut as Leonore at the Metropolitan Opera (New York, Nov. 19, 1884), and reappeared there during subsequent seasons of German opera. In 1890 she settled in Vienna as a singing teacher.
BIBLIOGRAPHY: La Mara, *Musikalische Studienköpfe* (Leipzig, 1902).

Brandt, Noah, American composer; b. N.Y., April 8, 1858; d. San Francisco, Nov. 11, 1925. He studied at the Leipzig Cons. with Ferdinand David (violin) and Jadassohn (theory); toured in Europe and the U.S. as a violinist; finally settled in San Francisco. He was the author of a light opera *Captain Cook* (San Francisco, Sept. 2, 1895); his other operas *Wing Wong* and *Daniel* were not produced.

Brandts-Buys, Jan, composer; b. Zutphen, Sept. 12, 1868; d. Salzburg, Dec. 7, 1933. He was a pupil of M. Schwarz and A. Urspruch at the Raff Cons. in Frankfurt; lived for a time in Vienna; later settled in Salzburg. His first opera, *Das Veilchenfest* (Berlin, 1909), met with opposition; a second opera, *Das Glockenspiel* (Dresden, 1913), was received more kindly, while a third, *Die drei Schneider von Schönau* (Dresden, April 1, 1916), was quite successful; subsequent operas were: *Der Eroberer* (Dresden, 1918), *Micarême* (Vienna, 1919), *Der Mann im Mond* (Dresden, 1922), and *Traumland* (Dresden, 1927). He also wrote a ballet, *Machinalität* (Amsterdam, 1928), 2 piano concertos; a *Konzertstück* for cello and orch.; chamber music; piano pieces and songs.

Brandukov, Anatol, eminent Russian cellist; b. Moscow, Dec. 22, 1856; d. there, Feb. 16, 1930. He studied cello at the Moscow Cons. with Fitzenhagen (1868–77), and also attended Tchaikovsky's classes in harmony. In 1878 he undertook a concert tour of Europe; lived mostly in Paris until 1906. His artistry was appreciated by Tchaikovsky, who dedicated his *Pezzo capriccioso* for cello and orch. to him; he enjoyed the friendship of Saint-Saëns and Liszt. In 1906 he returned to Moscow where he was prof. at the Philharmonic Institute; from 1921 to 1930 he taught cello at the Moscow Cons. He composed a number of cello pieces and made transcriptions of works by Tchaikovsky, Rachmaninoff and others.
BIBLIOGRAPHY: L. Ginsburg, *A. A. Brandukov* (Moscow, 1951).

Branscombe, Gena, Canadian educator, chorus leader and composer; b. Picton, Ontario, Nov. 4, 1881; d. New York, July 26, 1977. She attended the Chicago Musical College where she studied piano with Rudolf Ganz, and composition with Felix Borowski; then went to Berlin where she took a course with Engelbert Humperdinck. Returning to America she took conducting lessons with Frank Damrosch and Albert Stoessel. In 1935 she organized the Branscombe Chorale, a women's ensemble that she conducted until 1953. She composed mostly choral works, often to her own texts; of these the most notable are *Conventry's Choir, The Phantom Caravan, A Wind From the Sea, Youth of the World,* and *Pilgrims of Destiny,* a choral drama (1928–29). She also composed a symph. suite, *Quebec,* and some 150 songs. Amazingly energetic, she continued to be active until an improbable old age and at the time of her death she was working on her autobiography.

Brant, Henry Dreyfus, American composer of ultramodern music; b. Montreal, Canada, of American parents, Sept. 15, 1913. He learned the rudiments of music from his father, a violinist, who taught at McGill Univ. Conservatorium in Montreal (1926–29). In 1929 his family moved to New York, where Brant studied piano with James Friskin and composition with Leonard Mannes at the Institute of Musical Art; subsequently attended classes of Rubin Goldmark at the Juilliard School of Music (1933); also took private lessons with Wallingford Riegger, Aaron Copland and George Antheil. After absorbing a multitude of diverse techniques of composition, he became a teacher. He taught at Columbia Univ. (1945–52) and at the Juilliard School of Music (1947–54); in 1957 was appointed to the faculty of Bennington College, Vermont; held Guggenheim Fellowships in 1946 and 1955. In his own music, Brant is an audacious explorer, drawing without prejudice on resources ranging from common objects of American life, such as kitchen utensils and tin cans, to the outermost reaches of euphonious cacophony. He is a pioneer in the field of spatial music, in which the instruments are placed at specific points of space, on the stage and in the hall. Among his innovations are wordless texts in vocal parts, wherein arrangements of vowels and consonants are contrived to suggest the sounds of imaginary languages. Brant expounded the rationale of spatial music in his article "Space as an Essential Aspect of Musical Composition," in *Contemporary Composers on Contemporary Music*, ed. by E. Schwartz and B. Childs (N.Y., 1967). The catalogue of Brant's works is impressive in its variety.

WORKS: FOR ORCH.: Variations for Chamber Orch. (N.Y., Feb. 7, 1931); Symphony (1931); Double-Bass Concerto (1932); *Angels and Devils* for an ensemble of innumerable flutes (N.Y., Feb. 6, 1933); *Coquette Overture* (1935); *Whoopee in D major* (1938); *Fishermen's Overture* (1938); *Hommage aux Frères Marx* for solo tin whistle and 6 instruments (1938); Clarinet Concerto (1938); Violin Concerto (1940); Saxophone Concerto (1941); *Downtown Suite* (1942); Symphony in F (1942); Symphony in B-flat (1945); *Statesmen in Jazz* (1945); *Jazz Clarinet Concerto* (1946); *Promised Land Symphony* (1947); *Millennium I* for 8 trumpets, glockenspiel, chimes, and cymbal (1950); *Symphony for Percussion* (1952); *Stresses* for 2 synchronized orchestras (1953); *Signs and Alarms* for percussion ensemble (1953); *Antiphony I* for 5 synchronized orchestral groups, each with its own conductor (N.Y., Dec. 6, 1953); *Millennium II* for multiple brass and percussion (1954); *Conclave* (1955); *Labyrinth* for 2 synchronized orchestras (1955); *Encephalograms* (1955); *On the Nature of Things* (Bennington, Aug. 18, 1956); *Hieroglyphics* (Washington, D.C., March 8, 1957); *Millennium III* for percussion and brass ensemble (Bennington, June 20, 1957); *Quombex* for viola d'amore and music boxes (1960); *Atlantis* (Poughkeepsie, N.Y., Jan. 31, 1960); *Violin Concerto with Lights*, wherein patterns of light are interpreted musically and performed by 5 musicians manipulating push-buttons (N.Y., April 30, 1961); *Odyssey—Why Not?* for flutes and orch. (Lausanne, Switzerland, Feb. 13, 1966); *Chanticleer* for instruments (N.Y., March 9, 1968); *Verticals Ascending* for 2 separate instrumental groups (Pittsburgh, July 7, 1968); *Immortal Combat* for spatial band (N.Y., June 4, 1972); *Sixty* (New Haven, Conn., Feb. 22, 1974); *Grand Pianos Bash Plus Friends* for 6 pianos, 3 piccolos, trumpet, trombone and percussion (Riverdale, N.Y., Nov. 10, 1974); *Nomads* for wordless text, brass and percussion (Bennington, June 2, 1974); *American Debate* for spatial band (1976).

VOCAL WORKS: *Underground Cantata* (1946); *Behold the Earth*, a requiem-cantata (1951); *Ceremony* for voices to wordless texts and instruments (N.Y., April 3, 1954); *December* for speakers, chorus and instruments (N.Y., Dec. 15, 1954); *Grand Universal Circus* with singing and speaking parts (N.Y., May 19, 1956); *The Children's Hour* (1958); *Mythical Beasts* for mezzo-soprano and instruments (N.Y., Feb. 10, 1958); *Dialogue in the Jungle* for soprano, woodwind quintet, and brass quintet (1959; N.Y., May 25, 1964); *The Fire Garden* for soprano, chorus and instruments (1960); *Feuerwerk* for speaker, fireworks and mixed ensemble (1961); *Voyage Four* for wordless text and orch. (New Haven, Conn., Jan. 14, 1964); *Kingdom Come* for wordless text, stage orch., balcony orch., sirens, slide whistles, bells and buzzers (Oakland, Calif., April 14, 1970); *Vita de Sancto Hieronymo* for chorus and instruments (1973); *An American Requiem* (Mt. Lebanon, Pennsylvania, June 8, 1974); *Solomon's Gardens* (N.Y., March 23, 1974); *Homage to Ives* for baritone, and orch. with 3 conductors (Den-

ver, Feb. 21, 1975); *A Plan of the Air* for singers, percussion and brass (River Falls, Wisconsin, April 24, 1975); *Spatial Concerto* for piano and voices (1976); *American Weather* (1976); *Long Life*, chorus a cappella "for 84 angels" (for Nicolas Slonimsky's (84—1)th birthday (April 27, 1977).

CHAMBER MUSIC: *5 & 10¢ Store Music* for violin, piano and assorted hardware (1932); *Kitchen Music* for water glasses, bottles, tin can cello and tin can bass (1946); *Galaxy I* for clarinet, horn, vibraphone and chimes (1954); *Galaxy II* for percussion and wind instruments (1954); *Conversations in an Unknown Tongue* for strings (1958); *Millennium IV* for voice and 5 instruments (N.Y., March 2, 1964); *September Antiphonies* for 4 clarinets and 4 trumpets (1964); *Consort for True Violins* for violins in 8 sizes (1965); *Windjammer* for woodwind quintet (N.Y., May 3, 1969); *Crossroads* for 4 violins (1971; East Hampton, N.Y., May 17, 1975); *Divinity* for harpsichord and brass quintet (N.Y., March 15, 1973); *From Bach's Menagerie* for saxophone quartet (1974); *Prevailing Winds* for woodwind quintet (Brooklyn, Oct. 5, 1974); Piano Sextet (1976).

BIBLIOGRAPHY: S. Stuart, "Henry Brant's Grand Universal Circus," *Juilliard Review* III/3 (1956); P. Yates, "The American Experimental Tradition II," in *Twentieth Century Music* (1967).

Branzell, Karin Maria, Swedish contralto; b. Stockholm, Sept. 24, 1891; d. Altadena, California, Dec. 14, 1974. She studied in Stockholm with Thekla Hofer, in Berlin with Bachner, and in New York with Rosati; made her debut in Stockholm in 1911; from 1912–18 was a member of the Stockholm Royal Opera; from 1919–23 sang with the Berlin State Opera; made her American debut as Fricka in *Die Walküre* at the Metropolitan Opera (N.Y., Feb. 6, 1924). Possessing a voice of exceptional range, she occasionally sang soprano roles. She taught voice at several schools in N.Y. until 1969 when she moved to California.

Braslau, Sophie, American contralto; b. New York City, Aug. 16, 1892; d. there, Dec. 22, 1935. She studied voice with Buzzi-Peccia; made her debut at the Metropolitan Opera in *Boris Godunov* (Nov. 26, 1914); was a member of the Metropolitan company until 1921; in 1931 toured Scandinavia and Holland. A large collection of her programs, reviews, and biographical materials was given by the family to the Music Division of the N.Y. Public Library (1938).

Brassin, Leopold, pianist; b. Strasbourg, May 28, 1843; d. Constantinople, May, 1890. He studied music with his brother, Louis; was court pianist at Koburg; taught in the Bern Music School, and later in St. Petersburg and Constantinople; wrote concertos and many pieces for piano.

Brassin, Louis, French pianist; b. Aix-la-Chapelle, June 24, 1840; d. St. Petersburg, May 17, 1884. He was a pupil of Moscheles at the Leipzig Cons.; made concert tours with his brothers Leopold and Gerhard; taught at the Stern Cons., Berlin (1866); at the Brussels Cons. (1869–79); then at the St. Petersburg Cons. He published the valuable *École moderne du piano*;

composed 2 piano concertos, salon pieces for piano, and songs. His effective piano transcription of the Magic Fire music from *Die Walküre* is well known.

Braudo, Eugen, Russian music scholar; b. Riga, Feb. 20, 1882; d. Moscow, Oct. 17, 1939. He studied natural science and musicology in Moscow, St. Petersburg and Germany; in 1914 became professor at St. Petersburg Univ.; from 1924 taught at the Moscow Pedagogical Institute and at the Institute for Drama and Opera. He wrote a music history (1921-27; 3 vols.); published the monographs, *E. T. A. Hoffmann* (1921); *A. Borodin* (1922); *Nietzsche, Philosopher and Musician* (1922); *Beethoven* (1927); translated numerous books on music into Russian.

Brauel, Henning, German composer; b. Hannover, July 1, 1940. He studied piano and composition in Hannover, Salzburg, and Stuttgart; in 1968 he moved to Koblenz. His style is marked by structural cohesion within a framework of freely dissonant counterpoint. His works include *Symphonic Paraphrases on a Theme by Paganini* (1968); *Notturno* for bassoon and chamber orch. (1969); also 2 string quartets and other chamber music.

Braun, Carl, German bass; b. Meisenheim, Prussia, June 2, 1885; d. Hamburg, April 19, 1960. A pupil of H. Gausche and E. Robert-Weiss, he appeared frequently on the concert stage and in opera in Europe (1904–13), and sang leading roles at the Metropolitan Opera (1913–17) with great acclaim. Returning to Germany at the beginning of World War I, he sang principal parts at the Berlin State Opera and at Wagner Festivals in Bayreuth. He retired as a singer in 1939, and founded a theatrical agency in Berlin.

Braun, Peter Michael, German composer; b. Wuppertal, Dec. 2, 1936. He studied in Dortmund; later took courses in Cologne with Frank Martin, Bernd Alois Zimmermann and Herbert Eimert, and also in Detmold with Giselher Klebe. His musical style is governed by structural considerations; in his varied techniques he applies the resources of "organized sound" as formulated by Varèse, the theory of sets and devices of synthetic *musique concrète.* He wrote *Thesis-Medium* for piano (1960); *Monophonie* for electric guitar (1961-67); *Wind Sextet* (1961); *Transfer* for orch. (1968).

Braun, Wilhelm. See Brown, William.

Braunfels, Walter, German composer; b. Frankfurt, Dec. 19, 1882; d. Cologne, March 19, 1954. He studied piano in Vienna with Leschetizky and composition in Munich with L. Thuille. He became active both as an educator and a composer. From 1913-25 he lived near Munich; in 1925 he became a co-director of the Hochschule für Musik in Cologne. With the advent of the Nazi regime, he was compelled to abandon teaching; from 1933-37 he was in Godesberg; from 1937-45 in Überlingen. He excelled mainly as an opera composer; the following operas are notable; *Prinzessin Brambilla* (Stuttgart, March 25, 1909; revised in 1931); *Ulenspiegel* (Stuttgart, Nov. 9, 1913); *Die Vögel*

(after Aristophanes; Munich, Dec. 4, 1920; his most successful opera; given also in Berlin and Vienna); *Don Gil* (Munich, Nov. 15, 1924); *Der gläserne Berg* (Cologne, Dec. 4, 1928); *Galathea* (Cologne, Jan. 26, 1930); *Der Traum, ein Leben* (1937); *Die heilige Johanna* (1942); also a mystery play, *Verkündigung,* after Paul Claudel (1936). He further wrote 2 piano concertos; organ concerto; *Revelation of St. John* for tenor, double chorus and orch.; piano music and songs. He believed in the artistic and practical value of Wagnerian leading motives; in his harmonies, he was close to Richard Strauss, but he also applied impressionistic devices related to Debussy.

Bravničar, Matija, Slovenian composer; b. Tolmin, near Gorica, Feb. 24, 1897. He studied at Gorica; from 1915-18 was in the Austrian army; from 1919-45 was a violinist at the opera theater in Ljubljana; meanwhile he graduated from the Academy of Music in Ljubljana in 1933; since 1945, prof. of composition there. In 1949 he was elected president of the Slovenian Composers' Union; in 1953, president of the Yugoslav Composers' Union. In his works, Bravničar cultivates a neo-classical style, with thematic material strongly influenced by the melorhythmic inflections of Slovenian folk music. He has written an opera-farce in 3 acts, *Pohujšanje v dolini Sentflorjanski (Scandal in St. Florian's Valley;* produced in Ljubljana, May 11, 1930); the opera in 8 scenes, *Hlapec Jernej in jegova pravica (Knight Jernej and his Right;* Ljubljana, Jan. 25, 1941); *Hymnus Slavicus* for orch. (Ljubljana, May 14, 1932); overture *King Mattias* (Ljubljana, Nov. 14, 1932); *Antithèse symphonique* (Ljubljana, Feb. 9, 1948; also at Salzburg Festival, June 29, 1952); 3 symphonies (1947, 1951, 1959); Horn Concerto (1964); *Fantasia rapsodica* (1967); 2 wind quintets (1930, 1968); *Suonata in modo antico* for violin and piano (1953); many piano pieces.

Breazul, George, Rumanian musicologist; b. Oltenien, Sept. 26, 1887; d. Bucharest, Aug. 3, 1961. He studied at the Bucharest Cons. with Castaldi and Kiriac, and in Berlin with Hornbostel, Sachs, Stumpf, Schünemann and Johannes Wolf. Upon return to Bucharest he organized a phonograph archive; publ. numerous articles dealing with Rumanian folklore. A festschrift, in Rumanian, was publ. in his honor in 1966.

Brecher, Gustav, conductor and editor; b. Eichwald, near Teplitz, Bohemia, Feb. 5, 1879; d. Ostend, May, 1940. His family moved to Leipzig in 1889, and he studied there with Jadassohn. His first major work, the symph. poem *Rosmersholm,* was introduced by Richard Strauss at a Liszt-Verein concert in Leipzig (1896); made his debut as a conductor there (1897); was vocal coach and occasional conductor of operas in Leipzig (1898); conducted in Vienna (1901); served as first Kapellmeister in Olmütz (1902), in Hamburg (1903), and Cologne (1911-16); then went to Frankfurt (1916-24) and Leipzig (1924-33). He committed suicide with his wife aboard a boat off the Belgian coast while attempting to flee from the advancing Nazi troops. His compositions include a symph. fantasia *Aus unserer Zeit.* He was the author of several essays:

Über die veristische Oper; Analysen zu Werken von Berlioz und Strauss; and *Über Operntexte und Opernübersetzungen* (1911).

Brediceanu, Tiberiu, Rumanian composer; b. Lugoj, Transylvania, April 2, 1877; d. Bucharest, Dec. 19, 1968. He studied music mainly in Rumania; was a founder-member of the Rumanian Opera and National Theater in Cluj (1919) and the Society of Rumanian Composers in Bucharest (1920); later became director of the Astra Cons. in Brasov (1934–40) and director-general of the Rumanian Opera (1941–44). He publ. valuable collections of Rumanian songs and dances, including 170 Rumanian folk melodies, 810 tunes of the Banat regions and 1000 songs of Transylvania. WORKS: the operas *Poemul muzical etnografic* (1905; revised and retitled *Romania in port, joc si cintec,* 1929), *La şezătoare* (1908), *Seara mare,* lyric scene (1924), *Învierea,* a pantomime (1932), and *La seceriş* (1936); *4 Symphonic Dances* (1951); 2 Suites for violin and piano (1951); piano pieces; songs.

Bree, Jean Bernard van (Johannes Bernadus van), Dutch violinist and composer; b. Amsterdam, Jan. 29, 1801; d. there, Feb. 14, 1857. He was a pupil of Bertelmann; in 1819 played the violin in the orchestra of the Théâtre Français (Amsterdam); in 1829 became director of the Felix Meritis Society, and in 1840 founded the Cecilia Society; later became director of the Music School of the Society for the Promotion of Music. WORKS: the operas *Sappho* (in Dutch; Amsterdam, March 22, 1834); *Nimm dich in Acht* (in German; 1845); and *Le Bandit* (in French; The Hague, 1840); also 2 melodramas; several Masses; cantatas, overtures; chamber music; etc. BIBLIOGRAPHY: H. Beijermann, *Jean Bernard van Bree* (1857).

Brehm, Alvin, American composer; b. New York, Feb. 8, 1925. He studied at the Juilliard School of Music and Columbia Univ.; also took lessons with Wallingford Riegger. A professional double-bass player, Brehm participates in chamber music concerts in New York, whenever a difficult part for the instrument is in the score. Among his compositions, a Divertimento for Brass Trio is often performed. His "extended overture," *Hephaestus* (N.Y., Nov. 22, 1966), was favorably received. He also wrote a set of variations for unaccompanied cello, a piece for bassoon and percussion and a song cycle for voice and 10 instruments to poems of Garcia Lorca.

Brehme, Hans, German composer; b. Potsdam, March 10, 1904; d. Stuttgart, Nov. 10, 1957. He studied piano in Berlin with Wilhelm Kempff; taught at Stuttgart and elsewhere. A highly diligent composer, he wrote music in many genres; the idiom of his compositions is fundamentally classical, with a generous admixture of moderately modern harmonies. He wrote an opera *Der Uhrmacher von Strassburg* (1941); an operetta *Versiegelten Bürgermeister* (1944); 2 symphonies; 2 piano concertos; Flute Concerto; Sextet, for flute, clarinet, horn, violin, viola and cello; Clarinet Quintet, Saxophone Sonata; *Triptycon* for orch. on a theme by Handel (highly successful); several works for the accordian. BIBLIOGRAPHY: Karl Laux, *Musik und Musiker der Gegenwart* (Essen, 1949).

Breil, Joseph Carl, American composer; b. Pittsburgh, June 29, 1870; d. Los Angeles, Jan. 23, 1926. He studied voice in Milan and Leipzig, and for a time sang in various opera companies. He was the composer of one of the earliest motion picture scores, *Queen Elizabeth* (Chicago, 1912); wrote words and music for the comic operas *Love Laughs at Locksmiths* (Portland, Maine, Oct. 27, 1910); *Prof. Tattle* (1913); and *The Seventh Chord* (1913). His serious opera *The Legend* was produced by the Metropolitan Opera on March 12, 1919. His opera *Asra* (after Heine) had a single perf. in Los Angeles (Nov. 24, 1925). BIBLIOGRAPHY: E. E. Hipsher, *American Opera and Its Composers* (Philadelphia, 1927; pp. 87–90).

Breithaupt, Rudolf Maria, German pianist, pedagogue and music scholar; b. Brunswick, Aug. 11, 1873; d. Ballenstedt, April 2, 1945. He studied jurisprudence, philosophy and musicology before he began taking piano lessons with Teichmüller at the Leipzig Cons.; then went to Berlin and was appointed piano teacher at the Stern Cons. there. He published valuable studies on piano playing; *Die natürliche Klaviertechnik* (Leipzig, 1905; in French, Paris, 1923); *Die Grundlagen der Klaviertechnik* (Leipzig, 1906; in French, 1908; in English, 1909; in Russian, 1929); *Praktische Studien* (1916–21). He also published *Musikalische Zeit und Streitfragen* (Berlin, 1906).

Breitkopf & Härtel, important German firm of book and music publishers. As an established printing firm in Leipzig, it was bought in 1745 by **Bernhard Christoph Breitkopf** (b. Klausthal Harz, March 2, 1695; d. Leipzig, March 23, 1777). His son, **Johann Gottlob Immanuel** (b. Nov. 23, 1719; d. Jan. 28, 1794) entered the business in 1745; it was his invention which made the basis for the firm's position in the publication of music. In 1756 he devised a font with much smaller division of the musical elements and this greatly reduced the cost of printing chords (and hence piano music). The firm soon began to issue numerous piano reductions of popular operas for amateur consumption. The earliest music publications, such as the *Berlinische Oden und Lieder* (3 vols., 1756, 1759, 1763) were made by Johann Gottlob Immanuel Brietkopf himself, and bore the name *Leipzig, Druckts und Verlegts Johann Gottlob Immanuel Breitkopf;* from 1765 to 1777 the name appears as *Bernhard Christoph Breitkopf und Sohn;* from 1777–1787 (after Christoph's death) Gottlob Immanuel's name again appears alone; Immanuel's second son, **Christoph Gottlob** (b. Leipzig, Sept. 22, 1750; d. there April 4, 1800), joined the firm in 1787; from 1787 to 1795 publications were issued as "im Breitkopfischen Verlage" (or Buchhandlung, or Musikhandlung); in 1795 (the year after Immanuel's death) Christoph Gottlob took as his partner his close friend, **Gottfried Christoph Härtel** (b. Schneeburg, Jan. 27, 1763; d. near Leipzig, July 25, 1827); since 1795 the firm has been known as Breitkopf und Härtel, although no Breitkopf has been actively associated with the firm since Christoph Gottlob's death in 1800. Härtel's tremendous energy revitalized the firm. He added a piano factory; founded the important periodical *Allgemeine musikalische Zeitung* (1798; editor, J. F. Rochlitz); introduced pewter in place of the harder copper for engraving music; used Senefelder's new lithographic process for either title pages or music where suitable; issued so-called 'complete' editions of the works of Mozart, Haydn, Clementi and Dusek. The firm also began the practice of issuing catalogues with thematic indexes and keeping stocks of scores. From 1827–1835 **Florenz Härtel** was head of the firm; **Hermann Härtel** (b. Leipzig, April 27, 1803; d. there, Aug. 4, 1875) and his brother, **Raimund Härtel** (b. Leipzig, June 9, 1810; d. there, Nov. 9, 1888) together dominated the book business of Leipzig (and thus all Germany) for many years; the sons of two sisters of Raimund and Hermann, **Wilhelm Volkmann** (b. Halle, June 12, 1837; d. Leipzig, Dec. 24, 1896) and **Dr. Oskar von Hase** (b. Jena, Sept. 15, 1846; d. Leipzig, Jan. 26, 1921) succeeded them. After Wilhelm Volkmann's death, his son **Dr. Ludwig Volkmann** (1870–1947), headed the firm jointly with von Hase; von Hase's son, **Hermann** (1880–1945) entered the firm in 1904 and was a co-partner from 1910–14. Hermann von Hase published essays tracing the relation of J. Haydn, C. P. E. Bach, and J. A. Hiller to the firm; in 1915 he became a partner in the book business of K. F. Koehler. his brother **Dr. Hellmuth von Hase** (b. Jan. 30, 1891) became director of the firm in 1919. The old house was destroyed during the air bombardment of Dec. 4, 1943; it was rebuilt after the war. In 1950 Dr. Hase moved to Wiesbaden where he established an independent business, reclaiming the rights for the firm in West Germany. Important enterprises of the firm throughout its existence are editions of Bach, Beethoven, Berlioz, Brahms, Chopin, Gluck, Grétry, Handel, Haydn, Lassus, Liszt, Mendelssohn, Mozart, Palestrina, Schein, Schubert, Schumann, Schütz, Victoria, and Wagner. The German government supported the publication by Breitkopf and Härtel of the two series of *Denkmäler deutscher Tonkunst* (1892–1931 and 1900–1931). Other publications of the firm are: *Der Bär,* yearbook (since 1924); *Katalog des Archivs von Breitkopf und Härtel,* edited by Dr. F. W. Hitzig (2 vols., 1925–26); *Allgemeine musikalische Zeitung* (weekly; 1798–1848 and 1863–65); *Monatshefte für Musikgeschichte* (1869–1905); *Mitteilungen des Hauses Breitkopf und Härtel* (1876–1940; resumed in 1950); *Vierteljahrsschrift für Musikwissenschaft* (1869–1906); *Zeitschrift der Internationlen Musikgesellschaft* (monthly; Oct. 1899–Sept. 1914); *Sammelbände der Internationalen Musikgesellschaft* (quarterly; 1899–1914); *Korrespondenzblatt des Evangelischen Kirchengesangvereins für Deutschland* (monthly; 1886–1922); *Zeitschrift für Musikwissenschaft* (monthly; 1919–35); *Archiv für Musikforschung,* (1936–43).

BIBLIOGRAPHY: B. Brook, ed., *The Breitkopf Thematic Catalogue. . .1762–1787* (N.Y., 1966); R. Elvers, ed., *Breitkopf & Härtel 1719–1969. Ein historischer Überblick zum Jubiläum* (Wiesbaden, 1968); I. Hempel, ed., *Pasticcio auf das 250jahrige Bestehen des Verlages B. & H.* (Leipzig, 1968); Hase, O. von, *B. & H.*

Gedenkschrift und Arbeitsbericht (3 vols.: I, 1542–1827; II, 1828–1918; III, 1918–1968; Wiesbaden, 1968); R. Elvers, "B. & H.s Verlagsarchiv," *Fontes Artis Musicae* (Jan.–Aug. 1970).

Brema, Marie (real name **Minny Fehrman**), English mezzo-soprano of German-American parentage; b. Liverpool, Feb. 28, 1856; d. Manchester, March 22, 1925. She studied singing with Georg Henschel, and made her debut in London on Feb. 21, 1891, under the name of Bremer (her father being a native of Bremen). She particularly excelled in Wagnerian roles, which she performed at the Metropolitan Opera in N.Y. (1895–96), and took part in the Bayreuth Festivals (1896–97). Returning to England, she taught singing at the Royal College of Music in Manchester.

Brendel, Alfred, Austrian pianist; b. Wiesenberg, Moravia, Jan. 5, 1931. He was a piano student of Edwin Fischer and Eduard Steuermann, and took courses in composition with Michl. He began his artistic career in 1948 giving recitals and appearing with orchestras all over the world. His repertory is unusually comprehensive, both in classical and modern music. From 1960 he gave annual master courses in piano in Vienna.

Brendel, Karl Franz, German writer on music; b. Stolberg, Nov. 26, 1811; d. Leipzig, Nov. 25, 1868. He studied piano with Wieck; entered the Schumann circle and became editor of the *Neue Zeitschrift für Musik* (1845–56); then was co-editor (with R. Pohl) of the monthly *Anregungen für Kunst, Leben und Wissenschaft* (1856–61). He was later appointed professor of music history at the Leipzig Cons.; was one of the founders (1861), of the Allgemeiner deutscher Musikverein. In his articles, he championed Wagner and Liszt.

WRITINGS: *Grundzüge der Geschichte der Musik* (1848); *Geschichte der Musik in Italien, Deutschland und Frankreich von den ersten christlichen Zeiten bis auf die Gegenwart* (1852; 7th ed., edited by Kienzl, 1888; new augmented ed., edited by R. Hövker, 1902, and reissued in 1906); *Die Musik der Gegenwart und die Gesamtkunst der Zukunft* (1854); *Franz Liszt als Sinfoniker* (1859); *Die Organisation des Musikwesens durch den Staat* (1865); *Geist und Technik im Klavierunterricht* (1867); also many newspaper articles, published as *Gesammelte Aufsätze zur Geschichte und Kritik der neueren Musik* (1888).

Brenet, Michel (real name **Marie Bobillier**), French musicologist; b. Lunéville, April 12, 1858; d. Paris, Nov. 4, 1918. After living in Strasbourg and Metz, she made her home in Paris from 1871.

WRITINGS: *Historie de la symphonie à orchestre depuis ses origines jusqu'à Beethoven* (1882); *Grétry, sa vie et ses œuvres* (1884); *Deux pages de la vie de Berlioz* (1889); *Jean d'Okeghem* (1893); *La Musique dans les processions* (1896); *Sébastien de Brossard* (1896); *La Musique dans les couvents de femmes* (1898); *Claude Goudimel* (1898); *Notes sur l'histoire du luth en France* (1899); *Les Concerts en France sous l'ancien régime* (1900); *Additions inédites de Dom Jumilhac à son traité* (1902); *La Jeunesse de Rameau*

(1903); *Palestrina* (1906, in *Les Maîtres de la Musique*; 3rd ed. 1910); *La Plus Ancienne Méthode française de musique* (1907); *Haydn* (1909, in *Les Maîtres de la Musique*; in English, 1926); *Les Musiciens de la Sainte-Chapelle: documents inédits* (1910); *Musique et musiciens de la vieille France* (1911); *Handel* (1912, in *Musiciens célèbres*); *La Musique militaire* (1917); *Dictionnaire pratique et historique de la musique* (posthumous; completed by A. Gastoué, Paris, 1926); valuable essays and articles in the *Grande Encyclopédie*, *Rivista Musicale Italiana*, and the *Musical Quarterly*.

BIBLIOGRAPHY: L. de la Laurencie, "Michel Brenet," *Bulletin de la Société française de Cologne* (1919, no. 4).

Brenta, Gaston, Belgian composer; b. Brussels, June 10, 1902; d. there, May 30, 1969. He studied music theory with Paul Gilson; in 1925, he and seven other pupils of Gilson formed the Belgian "Groupe des Synthétistes," advocating a more modern approach to composition. From 1931 he was associated with the Belgian Radio, and from 1953 to 1967 he was musical director of the French Services there. His music follows the traditions of cosmopolitan romanticism, with exotic undertones.

WORKS: opera *Le Khâdi dupé* (Brussels, 1929); 2 radio dramas: *Aucassin et Nicolette* (1934) and *Heracles* (1955); 3 full ballets: *Zo'har* (1928); *Florilège de Valses* (1940), *Candide* (1955) and a ballet *Le Bal Chez la Lorette* (1954), which forms a part of *Les Bals de Paris*, a large ballet consisting of passages contributed by several Belgian composers; an oratorio *La Passion de Notre-Seigneur* (1949). He also wrote *Variations sur un Thème Congolais* for orch. (1926); Nocturne for Orch. (1934); *Arioso et Moto Perpetuo* for orch. (1940); *War Music* for orch. (1946); Symphony (1946); *In Memoriam Paul Gilson* for orch. (1950); *Farandole Burlesque* for orch. (1951); 2 piano concertos (1952, 1968); Concertino for trumpet, strings and timpani (1958); *Saxiana*, concertino for saxophone, strings, timpani and piano (1962); *Airs variés pour de belles écouteuses (Various Tunes for Beautiful Listeners)* for bassoon and string orch. (1963); *Pointes sèches de la belle Époque* for piano and string orch. (1964); *Matinée d'été (Summer Morning)* for orch. (1967); *Marche Barbare* for piano (1926); *Impromptu* for piano (1926); *Étude de Concert* for piano (1931); String Quartet (1939); *Melopée* for violin and piano (1945); *Le Soldat Fanfaron (The Boastful Soldier)*, suite for quintet (1952); Concertino for 5 winds, double bass, piano and percussion (1963); songs, choruses.

Brent-Smith, Alexander, English composer; b. Brookthorpe, Gloucestershire, Oct. 8, 1889; d. there, July 3, 1950. After the completion of his studies, he devoted himself to a pedagogical career. His works consist mainly of choral pieces and concertos for various instruments.

Bresgen, Cesar, German composer; b. Florence (of German parents), Oct. 16, 1913. He studied composition with Haas in Munich; in 1939 he went to Salzburg where he taught at the Mozarteum. After the war he devoted himself mainly to teaching. In his compositions he cultivates the spirit of pragmatic communication; his musical fairy tales and school operas have become widely known; among them the most successful are *Der Igel als Brautigam* (1950); *Brüderlein Hund* (1953); *Der Mann im Mond* (1958); short operas *Die Freier* (1936); *Dornröschen* (1939); *Das Urteil des Paris* (1943); *Paracelsus* (1943); scenic cantatas *Der ewige Arzt* (1955); *Salzburger Passion* (1966); Chamber Concerto for 8 Solo Instruments (1934); Concerto for 2 Pianos (1936); Chamber Concerto for guitar and small orch. (1962); Wind Quintet (1964); numerous choral works for school performance. Bresgen has published articles and valuable collections of Austrian folk songs.

BIBLIOGRAPHY: D. Larese, *Cesar Bresgen* (Amriswil, 1968).

Breslaur, Emil, German music teacher and writer on music; b. Kottbus, May 29, 1836; d. Berlin, July 26, 1899. He studied at the Stern Cons. in Berlin (1863–67); taught at Kullak's Academy (1868–79); from 1863 was choirmaster at the Berlin Reformed Synagogue. A music teachers society founded by him in 1879 developed in 1886 into the Deutscher Musiklehrer-Verband. He was editor of the *Klavierlehrer*, and the author of several important works on piano playing: *Die technischen Grundlagen des Klavierspiels* (1874); *Führer durch die Klavierunterrichts-Literatur* (1887); *Zur methodischen Übung des Klavierspiels*; *Der entwickelnde Unterricht in der Harmonielehre*; *Über die schädlichen Folgen des unrichtigen Übens*. He also composed choral works, piano pieces, and songs.

Bresnick, Martin, American composer; b. New York, Nov. 13, 1946. He studied with Arnold Franchetti at the Hartt College of Music in Hartford, Conn. and with Leland Smith and John Chowning at Stanford Univ.; received a Fulbright Fellowship for study in Vienna (1969–70); there he took courses in composition with Gottfried von Einem and Friedrich Cerha.

WORKS: Trio for 2 Trumpets and Percussion (1966); String Quartet (1968); *PCOMP*, a computer composition (Vienna, April 8, 1970); *Ocean of Storms* for orch. (1970); also music for films, including a computer score for the film *Pour* (Praque, March 5, 1970).

Bressler-Gianoli, Clotilde, operatic contralto, b. Geneva (of Italian parents), June 3, 1875; d. there, May 12, 1912. She received her vocal training at the Milan Cons. with Sangiovanni, and made her operatic debut at the age of 19 at Geneva in *Samson et Dalila*. She later appeared at La Scala, the Opéra-Comique in Paris, and at numerous other European opera houses. She sang in the U.S. with the San Carlo Co. at New Orleans and N.Y., the Manhattan Opera House (1906–08) and the Metropolitan Opera (1909–10). Her best roles were Carmen and Mignon.

Bret, Gustave, French organist and composer; b. Brignoles, Aug. 30, 1875; d. Fréjus, April 16, 1969. He studied with Widor and d'Indy in Paris; wrote music criticism. He composed mostly church music.

Bretan, Nicolae, remarkable Rumanian composer; b. Năsăud, April 6, 1887; d. Cluj, Dec. 1, 1968. He studied at the Cons. of Cluj, composition and singing with Farkas and violin with Gyémánt (1906–08); then at the Musikakademie in Vienna (1908–09) and at the Magyar Királyi Zeneakademia in Budapest (1909–12) with Siklos (theory) and Szerémi (violin). His primary career was that of an opera singer, performing baritone parts at the opera houses in Bratislava, Oradea and Cluj between 1913 and 1944, also acting as a stage director. At the same time he suprisingly asserted himself as a composer of operas and lieder in an effective veristic manner, marked by a high degree of professional expertise and considerable originality.

WORKS: the 1-act operas *Luceafărul (The Evening Star;* in Rumanian; translated by the composer into Hungarian and German; Cluj, Feb. 2, 1921); *Golem* (in Hungarian; translated by the composer into Rumanian and German; Cluj, Dec. 23, 1924); *Eroii de la Rovine* (in Rumanian; Cluj, Jan. 24, 1935); *Horia* (in Rumanian; also translated into German by the composer; Cluj, Jan. 24, 1937); *Arald,* one-act opera in Rumanian (1939); *Requiem;* a mystery play, *An Extraordinary Seder Evening* (in Hungarian; also translated into English); about 230 songs, *Mein Liederland,* to Rumanian, Hungarian and German words.

Bretón y Hernández, Tomás, Spanish opera composer; b. Salamanca, Dec. 29, 1850; d. Madrid, Dec. 2, 1923. As a youth he played in restaurants and theaters; was graduated from Madrid Cons. (1872); conducted at the Madrid Opera; in 1901 joined the faculty of the Madrid Cons. A fertile composer, he contributed greatly to the revival of the zarzuela. He was at his best in the 1-act comic type *(género chico).* Among his operas and zarzuelas (all produced in Madrid) are: *Los Amantes de Teruel* (1889); *Juan Garín* (1892); *La Dolores* (1895); *El Domingo de Ramos* (1896); *La Verbena de la Paloma* (1894); *Raquel* (to his own libretto; Jan. 20, 1900); *El Caballo del señorito* (1901); *Farinelli* (1903); *Tabaré* (1913). He also wrote an oratorio, *Apocalipsia* (Madrid, 1882) and works for orch.: *Escenas Andaluzas;* Funeral March for Alfonso XII; Violin Concerto, etc.

BIBLIOGRAPHY: Angel S. Salcedo, *Tomás Breton: su vida y sus obras* (1924).

Breuer, Hans (real name **Johann Peter Joseph**), German tenor; b. Cologne, April 27, 1868; d. Vienna, Oct. 11, 1929. He was a pupil of Iffert and Stolzenberg at the Cologne Cons. (1890–92); made his operatic debut in 1896 as Mime at Bayreuth, and appeared regularly there until 1914. He made his Metropolitan Opera debut in *The Flying Dutchman* (New York, Jan. 6, 1900); then became a member of the Vienna Opera.

Breuning, Moritz Gerhard von, Austrian writer on music; b. Vienna, Aug. 28, 1813; d. there, May 6, 1892. He was a son of Beethoven's friend Stephan von Breuning; wrote *Aus dem Schwarzspanierhause* (Vienna, 1874; new ed., with additions by Kalischer, Berlin, 1907; 1970).

Bréval, Lucienne (stage name of **Bertha Schilling**), opera singer; b. Männedorf, Switzerland, Nov. 4, 1869; d. Paris, Aug. 15, 1935. She studied piano in Lausanne and Geneva, and then voice at the Paris Cons.; made her debut at the Paris Opéra as Selika in *L'Africaine* (Jan. 20, 1892) and was then engaged as principal dramatic soprano; made appearances in the U.S. (1900–02); then settled in Paris.

BIBLIOGRAPHY: *Le Monde Musical* (Sept. 1935).

Brevik, Tor, Norwegian composer; b. Oslo, Jan. 22, 1932. He studied violin, viola and music theory at the Cons. in Oslo, and in Sweden. He founded Youth Chamber Orchestra in Oslo (1958); was active as a music critic. He wrote an opera, *Da kongen kom til Spilliputt* (1973); *Adagio and Fugue* for string orch. (1958); *Overture* (1958); Serenade for Strings (1959); *Chaconne* for Orch. (1960); Concertino for Clarinets and Strings (1961); *Music* for solo violin (1963); *Canto Elegico* for orch. (1964); *Contrasts* chamber ballet (1964); *Elegy* for soprano, viola, double bass and percussion (1964); Divertimento for Wind Quintet (1964); *Adagio Religioso* for solo horn (1967); String Quartet (1967); Chamber Concerto for Strings (1967); *Music for 4 strings* (1968); *Intrada* for orch. (1969); *Romance* for violin and orch. or piano (1972); *Andante Cantabile* for violin and strings (1975).

Bréville, Pierre-Onfroy de, French composer; b. Barle-Duc, Feb. 21, 1861; d. Paris, Sept. 23, 1949. He studied at the Paris Cons. with Théodore Dubois (1880–82); late with César Franck; was professor of counterpoint at the Schola Cantorum; wrote music criticism for *La Revue Internationale de Musique,* and *Mercure de France.*

WORKS: an opera, *Eros Vainqueur* (Brussels, March 7, 1910); overture to Maeterlinck's drama *La Princesse Maleine,* and incidental music to his *Sept Princesses;* the orchestral suites *Nuit de décembre* and *Stamboul;* rondels; motets; liturgical choral compositions; piano pieces; songs; etc. He completed (with d'Indy and others) Franck's unfinished opera *Ghiselle;* wrote a monograph *Sur les chansons populaires françaises* (1901).

Brewer, Sir Alfred Herbert, English organist and composer; b. Gloucester, June 21, 1865; d. there, March 1, 1928. He studied at the Royal College of Music with Parratt, Stanford and Bridge; became organist of several churches, and director of musical societies. His compositions include many sacred cantatas (*Emmaus, The Holy Innocents, A Song of Eden,* etc.), which were performed at festivals in Gloucester, Worcester, Hereford, Cardiff and Leeds; patriotic odes, such as *England, my England;* organ pieces, songs, etc. He was knighted in 1926.

BIBLIOGRAPHY: See H. Brewer, *Memories of Choirs and Cloisters* (London, 1931).

Brewer, John Hyatt, American organist and composer; b. Brooklyn, N.Y., Jan. 18, 1856; d. there, Nov. 30, 1931. He studied organ and composition with Dudley Buck; was active as organist and music director of numerous local churches and musical societies. He was a prolific vocal composer; wrote the cantatas (for women's voices) *Hesperus, The Sea and the Moon, Herald of Spring,* etc.; and (for men's voices) *Birth of*

Love, *The Dunderberg,* etc.; also quartets, anthems, glees, and choruses.

Brian, Havergal, English composer of extraordinary fecundity and longevity; b. Dresden, Staffordshire, Jan. 29, 1876; d. Shoreham-by-Sea, Sussex, Nov. 28, 1972. He studied violin, cello and organ with local teachers; left school at 12 to earn his living and help his father who was a potter's turner. At the same time he taught himself elementary music theory, and also learned French and German without an instructor. In1904 he engaged in musical journalism, and continued to write on music until 1949. For years he was regarded in England as a harmless eccentric possessed by symphonic ambitions; although he wrote 32 symphonies (the numbering varies even in his own authorized catalogue), of which the last 7 were written after the age of 90, performances were few and far between. Then a few English writers discovered Havergal Brian and wrote articles about his unique eminence, and performances were given of some of his works. Brian's style of composition continued the line of romantic expressiveness and architectural formidability, with a modest admixture of modernistic devices, as exemplified by the ominous whole-tone scales in his opera *The Tigers,* to illustrate the aerial attacks on London by the Zeppelins during World War I.

WORKS: operas: *The Tigers,* to his own libretto (1916–18), *Turandot,* to a German libretto after Schiller (1951), *The Cenci,* after Shelley (1953), *Doktor Faust,* after Goethe (1956), *Agamemnon,* after Aeschylus, to an English libretto (1957); an oratorio, *The Vision of Cleopatra* (1908); Violin Concerto (1935; London, June 20, 1969); Cello Concerto (1964); 5 English suites for orch. (1899–1953); a concert overture entitled *For Valour* (1902); *Concerto for Orchestra* (1964) and *Legend: Ave atque Vale* (1968). His 32 symphonies are: No. 1, *The Gothic,* for vocal soloists, chorus, 4 mixed choirs, children's choir, 4 brass bands, and very large orch. (1919–22; first performed in London, June 24, 1961, with a semi-amateur group; first professional performance, London, Oct. 30, 1966); No. 2 (1931); No. 3 (1932); No. 4, *Das Siegeslied,* a setting of Psalm 68 in the Lutheran version, for soprano, double chorus and orch., with a German text (1933; London, July 3, 1967); No. 5, *Wine of Summer,* for baritone solo and orch. (1937; London, Dec. 11, 1969); No. 6, *Sinfonia Tragica* (1948; London, Sept. 21, 1966); No. 7, (1948; London, March 13, 1968); No. 8 (1949; London, Feb. 1, 1954); No. 9 (1951; London, March 22, 1958); No. 10 (1954; London, Nov. 3, 1958); No. 11 (1954; London, Nov. 5, 1959); No. 12 (1957; London, Nov. 5, 1959); No. 13 (1959); No. 14 (1960; London, May 10, 1970); No. 15 (1960); No. 16 (1960); No. 17 (1961); No. 18 (1961; London, Feb. 26, 1962); No. 19 (1961); No. 20 (1962); No. 21 (1963; London, May 10, 1970); No. 22, *Symphonia Brevis* (1965); No. 23 (1965); No. 24 (1965); No. 25 (1966); No. 26 (1966); No. 27 (1966); No. 28 (1967); No. 29 (1967); No. 30 (1967); No. 31 (1968); No. 32 (1968; London, Jan. 28, 1971). The Havergal Brian Society, in London and in Oak Park, Michigan, was formed to promote performances and recordings of Brian's works.

BIBLIOGRAPHY: R. Nettel, *Ordeal by Music: The Strange Experience of Havergal Brian* (London, 1945); R. L. E. Foreman, ed., *Havergal Brian, A Collection of Essays* (London, 1969); M. MacDonald, *Havergal Brian: Perspective on the Music* (London, 1972).

Briard, Etienne, type-founder at Avignon, active early in the 16th century. In his engraving he employed round note heads instead of the ordinary angular ones, and separate notes instead of ligatures. Peignot holds that another printer, Granjon, used these methods prior to Briard (see his *Dictionnaire de la bibliologie,* supp., p. 140); in any case, Briard's characters are much better formed and more easily read. Schmidt's *Ottaviano Petrucci* contains a facsimile of them. The *Liber primum missarum Carpentras* (works of Eleazar Genet, called "Il Carpentrasso"), printed with them at Avignon in 1532, is in the library of the Paris Conservatory.

BIBLIOGRAPHY: K. Meyer, "Music Printing, 1473–1934," *Dolphin* (N.Y., 1935).

Briccetti, Thomas, American composer; b. Mt. Kisco, N.Y., Jan. 14, 1936. He studied music in New York, then took residence in Indianapolis. His major work is an overture, *The Fountain of Youth* (1972).

Briccialdi, Giulio, Italian flutist; b. Terni, Papal States, March 2, 1818; d. Florence, Dec. 17, 1881. A precocious musician, he held an appointment with the St. Cecilia Academy at Rome at the age of 15; made concert tours in England and America; after 1842 lived chiefly in London. He wrote an opera, *Leonora de' Medici* (Milan, Aug. 11, 1855); many compositions for flute; also a method for flute.

Bricken, Carl Ernest, American pianist and composer; b. Shelbyville, Kentucky, Dec. 28, 1898. He studied piano with Alfred Cortot in Paris and with Hans Weisse in Vienna. Returning to America he taught piano in New York, Chicago and at the Univ. of Wisconsin in Madison. From 1944 to 1948 he was conductor of the Seattle Symph. Orch. His compositions include a symphony (1935) and several pieces of competent and agreeable chamber music, as well as piano pieces. In 1964 he relinquished his musical career and devoted himself to painting.

Brico, Antonia, American pianist and conductor; b. Rotterdam, June 26, 1902. She moved to California in 1906 and studied at the Univ. of California in Berkeley, graduating in 1923; then went to Berlin where she took lessons in conducting with Karl Muck at the State Academy of Berlin; also studied piano with Sigismund Stojowski. She gave piano recitals in Europe and America, but her prime interest was in conducting. Overcoming many difficulties, she organized a special concert with the Berlin Philharmonic on Jan. 10, 1930, which aroused considerable curiosity, women conductors having been a rare species at the time. Returning to America, she obtained an engagement with the Los Angeles Philharmonic at the Hollywood Bowl (Aug. 1, 1930); also arranged a few concerts in New York, which she had to finance out of her own resources. After some disheartening experiences (a famous male singer on whom the management counted for public success refused to appear at the last moment), she sought opportunity in Europe; gave concerts in Finland and received a commendation from Sibelius for her conducting of his music. About 1949 she became associated with Albert Schweitzer, visiting his hospital in West Africa; he gave her some suggestions about performances of Bach. Eventually she settled in Denver as piano teacher; to satisfy her unquenchable thirst for orchestral conducting, she managed to lead concerts of the community orchestra there. In 1974 she produced an autobiographical film called simply "Antonia" in which she eloquently pleaded for equality of sexes on the conducting podium; it was nominated for an Academy Award, and on the strength of it, she was able to obtain several bona fide orchestral engagements.

Bridge, Frank, distinguished English composer; b. Brighton, Feb. 26, 1879; d. Eastbourne, Jan. 10, 1941. He studied violin at the Royal College of Music; then composition with Stanford. He played the viola in the Joachim Quartet (1906) and later in the English String Quartet; won the gold medal of the Rajah of Tagore. His professional employment was as conductor of the Marie Brema Opera at the Savoy Theatre, London (1910–11); then conducted at Covent Garden during the seasons of Raymond Roze and Beecham; he also appeared as a symph. conductor at the Promenade Concerts. In 1923 he made a U.S. tour and conducted his own works in Rochester, Boston, Detroit, Cleveland and New York; he made two subsequent visits to the U.S., in 1934 and 1938. As a composer he received a belated recognition towards the end of his life, and posthumously; although he wrote a great deal of music, particularly for small instrumental combinations, his name never figured prominently in the constellation of modern English composers who came to the fore in the first decades of the century. His chamber music is eminently practical, designed for easy performance; however, there is no concession to popular taste in his works. As a teacher he enjoyed a great reputation among English musicians; among his pupils was Benjamin Britten.
WORKS: *The Christmas Rose,* children's opera (1919–29); *Isabella,* symph. poem (1907); *Dance Rhapsody* (1908); *Dance Poem* (1909); incidental music to *The Hunchback* (1910); *The Sea,* orchestral suite (1910–11; Promenade Concerts, London, Sept. 24, 1912); *Summer,* symph. poem (1914); *2 Poems* (after Richard Jeffries, 1915); *Lament* for string orch. (in memory of the victims of the sinking of the Lusitania; 1915); *Phantasm* for piano and orch. (1931); *Rebus,* overture (1940); *3 Novelettes* for string quartet (1904); Piano Quintet (1906); *3 Idylls* for string quartet (1906); String Quartet in E minor (1906; received a Bologna prize); *Miniatures* for piano trio (1906); *Phantasie Trio,* for piano (1908); *An Irish Melody (Londonderry Air)* for string quartet (1908); *Phantasie Quartet,* for piano, violin, viola and cello (1910); String Sextet (1912); Cello Sonata (1913–17); String Quartet in G minor (1915); *Sally in Our Alley* and *Cherry Ripe* for string quartet (1916); *Sir Roger de Coverly* for string quartet (1922; also arranged for orch.); Trio No. 2 for piano, violin and cello (1929); 4th String Quartet

(1937, dedicated to Mrs. E. S. Coolidge; performed at the Berkshire Festival, 1938); Violin Sonata (1904); Cello Sonata (1916–17); violin pieces; viola pieces; cello pieces; much piano music, including a sonata (1922–25); *4 Characteristic Pieces* (1915); *Arabesque* (1915); *3 Sketches* (1906); suite, *A Fairy Tale* (1917); *2 capriccios* (1903; 1916); organ pieces; vocal music including *A Prayer* for chorus and orch. (London, 1919); *Blow out, you Bugles* for tenor and orch. (1918); about 100 fine songs, which attained great popularity throughout the world.
BIBLIOGRAPHY: *Musical Times* (Feb. 1919); *Monthly Musical Record* (April 1930), Herbert Howells, "Frank Bridge," *Music & Letters* (1941). The Frank Bridge Trust, London, issues publications and promotes performances of Bridge's music.

Bridge, Sir John Frederick, English organist, conductor and composer; b. Oldbury, near Birmingham, Dec. 5, 1844; d. London, March 18, 1924. At the age of 14 he was apprenticed to John Hopkins, organist of Rochester Cathedral; later studied under John Goss; was principal organist at Westminster Abbey (1882–1918); took the degree of Mus. Doc. at Oxford in 1874 with his oratorio, *Mount Moriah;* then taught harmony and organ at various music schools, including the Royal College of Music (from 1883); was conductor of the Highbury Philh. Society (1878–86), the Madrigal Society, and the Royal Choral Society (1896–1922); also served as chairman of Trinity College of Music. He was knighted in 1897.
WORKS: the cantatas *Boadicea* (1880); *Rock of Ages* (1885); *Callirrhoë* (1888); and *The Lobster's Garden Party or The Selfish Shellfish* (1904); a dramatic oratorio, *The Repentance of Nineveh* (Worcester, 1890); concert overture, *Morte d'Arthur* (1896); choral ballades. He published primers on counterpoint, canon, organ accompaniment and other subjects; also *A Course of Harmony* (with Sawyer; 1899); *Samuel Pepys, Lover of Music* (1903); an autobiography, *A Westminster Pilgrim* (1918); *12 Good Musicians from John Bull to Henry Purcell* (1920); *The Old Cryes of London* (1921); *Shakespearean Music in the Plays and Early Operas* (1923); edited selected motets of Orlando Gibbons (1907).

Bridge, Joseph Cox, English organist and composer, brother of **John Frederick Bridge;** b. Rochester, Aug. 16, 1853; d. St. Albans, March 29, 1929. He studied with his brother and with John Hopkins; from 1877–1925 was organist of Chester Cathedral; in 1879 he revived the Chester Triennial Music Festival and became its conductor until 1900; also founded (1883) and conducted for 20 years the Chester Musical Society; from 1908 was professor of music at Durham Univ.
WORKS: an oratorio, *Daniel* (1885); the cantatas *Rudel* (1891) and *Resurgam* (1897); *Evening Service with orch.* (1879); *Requiem Mass* (1900); an operetta, *The Belle of the Area;* Symphony (1894); String Quartet; Cello Sonata; anthems, organ music, piano pieces, songs.

Bridgetower, George Auguste Polgreen, mulatto violinist; b. Biala, Poland, Feb. 29, 1780; d. London, Feb.

29, 1860 (on his 80th birthday). His father was an Abyssinian; his mother of Polish extraction. He studied with Giornovichi, and as a youth was in the retinue of the Prince of Wales in Brighton. He played in the violin section of the Haydn-Salomon London Concerts in 1791. His name is historically important because of his association with Beethoven; he gave the first performance, from manuscript, of the *Kreutzer Sonata*, with Beethoven himself at the piano, in Vienna on May 17, 1803. Beethoven spelled his name Brischdower.

BIBLIOGRAPHY: Betty Matthews, "George Polgreen Bridgetower," *Music Review* (Feb. 1968).

Briegel, Wolfgang Carl, German organist and composer; b. Königsberg, 1626; d. Darmstadt, Nov. 19, 1712. He was a court cantor in Gotha in 1650; court kapellmeister in Darmstadt (1671–1709). He wrote a great number of sacred works; also some vocal music for the stage.

BIBLIOGRAPHY: K. F. Hirschmann, *W. C. Briegel* (Giessen, 1936); Elisabeth Noack, *W. C. Briegel: ein Barock-Komponist in seiner Zeit* (Berlin, 1963); idem, *Musikgeschichte Darmstadts vom Mittelalter bis zur Goethezeit* (Mainz, 1967).

Brînduş, Nicolae, Rumanian composer; b. Bucharest, April 16, 1935. He studied at the Bucharest Cons. with Zeno Vancea, Alfred Mendelsohn, Tudor Ciortea and Anatol Vieru; in 1969 he became instructor there. In his music, he experiments with novel sonorities.

WORKS: *Balada lui Pintea Viteazul (The Ballad of Pintea the Brave)* for tenor, chorus and orch. (1964); *3 Pieces for orch.* (1964); *Music* for chamber orch. (1964); Concerto for piano, percussion and orch. (1964); *Strigoii (The Ghosts),* lyric poem for soloists, 3 choral-instrumental ensembles and tape (1966); *Mărturie (The Witness),* cantata for mezzo-soprano, chorus, 2 orch. groups, percussion, organ and piano (1967); *Domnişoara Hus (Miss Hus),* cantata for 3 basses and 3 instrumental groups (1968); *Phtora I,* symph. cycle for any group of instruments over a given minimum scoring (1968); *Inscripţie (Inscription)* for small orch. and tape (1969); *Match (Phtora II)* for 2 percussionists and 4 instruments or instrumental groups (1969); *Cantus firmus (Phtora III)* for electric organ or piano, and any number of different instruments (1970); *Idéophonie, Psaume XIII (Phtora IV)* for 2-5 antiphonal groups of 5 combined instrumentalists and voices (1970); *Soliloque (Phtora V)* for tape and small ensemble (1971); *Antiphonie* for a minimum of 18 string instruments (1971); *Vos vassales les symétries* for 4 trombones, 4 double basses, 4 string quartets, 4 wind instruments and 4 choral groups (1971); *Vagues* for piano, percussion, clarinet, violin, viola and cello (1972).

Brinsmead, John, English piano maker; b. Wear Giffard, Devon, Oct. 13, 1814; d. London, Feb. 17, 1908. He founded his piano factory in London in 1836. In 1863 his sons, **Thomas** and **Edgar,** were admitted to partnership; in 1900 the firm was incorporated and assumed its permanent title, John Brinsmead & Sons, Ltd. In 1868 they patented an improvement in piano construction, "Perfect Check Repeater Action." In 1908, upon the death of John Brinsmead, the controlling interest was purchased by W. Savile, a director of J. B. Cramer & Co. Edgar Brinsmead (d. Nov. 28, 1907) wrote a *History of the Pianoforte* (1868; revised and republished, 1879).

Bristow, George Frederick, American composer; b. Brooklyn, N.Y., Dec. 19, 1825; d. New York, Dec. 13, 1898. He was the son of **William Richard Bristow** (b. England, 1803; d. 1867), who was a well known conductor in New York. George Bristow was first active as a violinist; played in the orch. of the Olympic Theater in New York (1836); and in the N.Y. Philh. Society (from 1842); was organist at several churches; also conducted the Harmonic Society (1851–62) and later the Mendelssohn Union; from 1854 he was a teacher in the New York public schools. Bristow was one of the earliest American composers to write operatic and chamber music. He was a militant champion of music by Americans, and made frequent pronouncements urging musical organizations to perform American works.

WORKS: opera *Rip Van Winkle* (N.Y., Sept. 27, 1855); unfinished opera *Columbus* (overture performed by the N.Y. Philh., Nov. 17, 1866); oratorios: *Praise to God* (N.Y. Harmonic Society, March 2, 1861); *Daniel* (N.Y., Dec. 30, 1867); cantatas: *The Great Republic* (Brooklyn Philh. Society, May 10, 1879); *Niagara,* for soli, chorus, and orch. (Manuscript Society, Carnegie Hall, N.Y., April 11, 1898); Symphony in D minor, written for the French conductor Jullien (Jullien's concert, N.Y. Philh., March 1, 1856); Symphony in F-sharp minor (N.Y. Philh., March 26, 1859); *Arcadian Symphony* (N.Y. Philh., Feb. 14, 1874); overture *Jibbenainosay* (Harlem Philh., N.Y., March 6, 1889); 2 string quartets; organ pieces; piano pieces; songs; also publ. a *New and Improved Method for Reed or Cabinet Organ* (N.Y., 1888).

BIBLIOGRAPHY: J. T. Howard, *Our American Music* (4th ed., N.Y., 1965); G. Chase, *America's Music* (2d. ed., N.Y., 1966).

Britain, Radie, American composer; b. Amarillo, Texas, March 17, 1903. She studied piano at the American Cons. in Chicago (B.M., 1924); then went to Germany where she studied music theory in Munich. She excels in writing for chorus; several of her choral compositions were awarded prizes of the National Federation of Music Clubs, the National League of American Penwomen and other organizations dedicated to the appreciation of artistic works by American women.

WORKS: *A Heroic Poem* for orch., inspired by Lindbergh's flight to Paris in 1927 (won a prize at the Hollywood Bowl Contest; first performed in Rochester, N.Y., March 3, 1932); *Light,* dedicated to Edison (received first prize in the National Contest for Women Composers in 1935; first performed in Chicago, Nov. 29, 1938); *Ubiquity,* music drama (1937); *Southern Symphony* (Chicago, March 4, 1940); Fantasy for Oboe and Orch. (1941); *Cactus Rhapsody* for orch. (1945); *Happyland,* operetta (1946); *Carillon,* short opera (1952); *The Spider and the Butterfly,* children's operetta (1953); *Radiation* for orch. (1955); *Cowboy Rhapsody* for orch. (1956); *Minha Terra* for orch. (1958); *Kuthara,* chamber opera (1960); *Cosmic Mist Symphony* (1962); *Chipmunks* for woodwinds, harp and percussion (1964); 2 string quartets; several song cycles, including *Translunar Cycle,* celebrating the lunar landing of 1969, and dedicated to the National Aeronautics and Space Administration.

Britt, Horace, cellist; b. Antwerp, June 18, 1881; d. Austin, Texas, Feb. 3, 1971. He studied at the Paris Cons. with Jules Delsart (cello) and Albert Lavignac (harmony); was later a private pupil of André Caplet; made his American debut with the Chicago Symph. Orch. (1907); then toured extensively in the U.S. with Georges Barrère and Carlos Salzedo; was co-founder of the Barrère-Britt Concertino, a chamber music group organized in 1937.

Britten, Sir Benjamin, famous English composer; b. Lowestoft, Suffolk, Nov. 22, 1913; d. Aldeburgh, Dec. 4, 1976. He played the piano and improvised at a very early age; then took lessons in composition with Frank Bridge; in 1930 entered the Royal College of Music in London, where he studied piano with Arthur Benjamin and Harold Samuel, and composition with John Ireland. His *Fantasy Quartet* for oboe and strings was performed at the Festival of the International Society for Contemporary Music in Florence on April 5, 1934, when he was only 20 years old. He became associated with the theater and the cinema; wrote a number of documentary films. He was in the U.S. at the outbreak of World War II; returned to England in the spring of 1942; was exempt from military service as a conscientious objector. After the war he organized the English Opera Group (1947) and in 1948 founded the Aldeburgh Festival, in collaboration with Eric Crozier and the singer Peter Pears, devoted mainly to short opera productions by English composers; many of Britten's own works were performed at the Aldeburgh Festivals, often under his own direction; he also had productions at the Glyndebourne Festival. In harmony with the modern *zeitgeist,* Britten reduced the orchestral contingent to 12 performers in most of his operas, and virtually eliminated the chorus. This economy of means made it possible for small opera groups and university workshops to perform Britten's works; yet he succeeded in using a rich spectrum of modern techniques, ranging from simple triadic progressions, often in parallel motion, to ultrachromatic dissonant harmonies; upon occasion he applied dodecaphonic procedures, with thematic materials based on 12 different notes. A characteristic feature in Britten's operas is the inclusion of orchestral interludes, which become miniature symphonic poems in an impressionistic vein related to the dramatic action of the work. The cries of seagulls in Britten's most popular and musically most important opera, *Peter Grimes,* are striking in their surrealistic imagery. Britten was equally successful in treating tragic subjects, such as *Peter Grimes* and *Billy Budd,* as in comedy, exemplified by his *Albert Herring,* mystical and occult evocations, as in *The Turn of the Screw,* and patriotic themes, as in *Gloriana,* composed for the coronation of Queen Elizabeth II. A work apart is his educational score *Let's Make an Opera.* Conscious of his connection with the English musical past, Brit-

ten composed "realizations" of Gay's *Beggar's Opera* and of Purcell's *Dido and Aeneas.* He also wrote modern "parables" for church performance, and produced a modern counterpart of a medieval English miracle play *Noye's Fludde.* Among his other works, perhaps the most remarkable is *War Requiem,* a profound tribute to the dead of many wars. In June 1976 Britten was elevated to the peerage of Great Britain by the Queen, and became a Lord, the first composer to be so honored.

WORKS: OPERAS: first opera, *Paul Bunyan,* produced at Columbia Univ., N.Y., May 5, 1941, but was later withdrawn and not repeated until 1976. His first great operatic success was with *Peter Grimes* (London, June 7, 1945) which was originally commissioned by the Koussevitzky Foundation; it was performed at the Berkshire Music Festival in 1946; numerous performances followed in Europe and America. Subsequent operas were: *The Rape of Lucretia* (Glyndebourne, July 12, 1946); *Albert Herring* (Glyndebourne, June 20, 1947); *The Beggar's Opera,* a new "realization" (Cambridge, May 24, 1948); *The Little Sweep,* or *Let's Make an Opera,* "an entertainment for young people" with optional audience participation (Aldeburgh, June 14, 1949); *Billy Budd,* after Melville (London, Dec. 1, 1951); *Gloriana* (on the subject of Elizabeth and Essex; first performance during Coronation Week, June 8, 1953, at Covent Garden, in the presence of Queen Elizabeth II); *The Turn of the Screw,* after Henry James (Venice, Sept. 14, 1954); *Noye's Fludde,* one-act opera (Aldeburgh, England, June 18, 1958); *A Midsummer Night's Dream* (Aldeburgh, June 11, 1960); arrangement, with Imogen Holst, of Purcell's *The Fairy Queen* (London, 1970); a television opera *Owen Wingrave,* after Henry James (May 16, 1971; simultaneous production by the BBC and its affiliated stations and the NET Opera Theater in New York); *Death in Venice,* after Thomas Mann (Aldeburgh, June 16, 1973). A ballet, *The Prince of the Pagodas* (London, Jan. 1, 1957).

CANTATAS AND OTHER VOCAL WORKS: *Hymn to the Virgin* (1930); *A Boy Was Born* (1933); *Friday Afternoons* for children's voices (1934); *Ballad of Heroes* (1939); *A Ceremony of Carols,* for treble voices and harp (Aldeburgh, June 14, 1942); *Hymn to St. Cecilia* (BBC, Nov. 28, 1942); *Rejoice in the Lamb,* festival cantata (1943); *Festival Te Deum* (1945); *St. Nicolas,* cantata (Aldeburgh, July 24, 1948); *Spring Symphony,* for soloists, chorus and orch. (Amsterdam, July 14, 1949); *Nocturne,* suite of songs with orch. to English poems (Leeds, England, Oct. 16, 1958); *Missa Brevis* for boys' voices and organ (London, July 22, 1959); *Cantata Academica* (Basel, July 1, 1960); *War Requiem* to the texts of the Latin Requiem Mass and 9 poems of the British poet Wilfred Owen, for chorus, soloists and orch. (one of Britten's finest creations; first performed at the rebuilt Coventry Cathedral on May 30, 1962, obtaining instant recognition; first American performance by the Boston Symph. Orch. in Tanglewood, July 27, 1963); *Cantata Misericordium* (for the centenary of the International Red Cross; Geneva, Sept. 1, 1963); *Cantata Phaedra* (1970); *Sacred and Profane* for 5 solo voices, based on anonymous medieval poems (Aldeburgh, Sept. 14, 1975). Church parables: *Curlew River* (Aldeburgh,

England, June 13, 1964); *The Burning Fiery Furnace* (Aldeburgh, June 9, 1966); *The Prodigal Son* (Aldeburgh, June 10, 1968); ballad after Brecht, *Children's Crusade* (St. Paul's Cathedral, London, May 19, 1969). Songs: *7 Sonnets of Michelangelo* (1940); *Winter Words* (1953); *6 Songs from the Chinese* for voice and guitar (1958); *6 Hölderlin Fragments* (1958); *Songs and Proverbs of William Blake* (1965); *The Poet's Echo* (1965). Furthermore Britten published folksong arrangements in several installments; made arrangement with Peter Pears, of Purcell's *Harmonia Sacra* and *Orpheus Britannicus*.

FOR ORCH.: *Sinfonietta* (1932); *Simple Symphony* for strings (1925; revised in 1934); *Variations on a Theme by Frank Bridge* for strings (1937); *Canadian Carnival* (1939); *Sinfonia da Requiem* (N.Y. Philharmonic, March 29, 1941); *Scottish Ballad* for 2 pianos and orch. (Cincinnati, Nov. 29, 1941); *Les Illuminations* for voice and strings (London, Jan. 30, 1940); *Diversions on a Theme* for piano (left hand alone) and orch. (Philadelphia, Jan. 16, 1942, Paul Wittgenstein soloist); *Serenade* for tenor, horn and string orch. (London, Oct. 15, 1943); *The Young Person's Guide to the Orchestra,* variations and fugue on a theme by Purcell (originally, music for film "The Instruments of the Orchestra," 1945); *Divertimento,* for chamber orch. (Basel, Jan. 24, 1952); *Cello Symphony,* for cello and orch. (written for the Soviet cellist Rostropovitch, and first performed by him with Britten conducting, in Moscow, March 12, 1964); Suite for Harp (Aldeburgh, June 24, 1969).

CHAMBER MUSIC: *Fantasy Quartet* for oboe, violin, viola and cello (1932); Suite for Violin and Piano (1935); 3 string quartets (1941, 1945, 1976); *Six Metamorphoses,* after Ovid, for oboe solo (1951); "new realizations" of some works by Purcell (*The Golden Sonata* for 2 violins, cello and piano, etc.); Cello Sonata (1961); Suite for Cello Solo (1964); *Gemini Variations* for flute, violin and 4-hand piano (1965); Second Suite for Cello Solo (1968). With Imogen Holst he wrote *The Story of Music* (London, 1958) and *The Wonderful World of Music* (Garden City, N.Y., 1968).

BIBLIOGRAPHY: A whole literature has arisen about Benjamin Britten. A voluminous compendium, *Benjamin Britten: A Commentary on His Works from a Group of Specialists,* was published under the editorship of Donald Mitchell and Hans Keller (London, 1953); other biographical publications are E. W. White, *Benjamin Britten* (London, 1948; new revised edition 1970); *Tribute to Benjamin Britten on his 50th Birthday,* a collection of articles (London, 1963); Imogen Holst, *Britten* (London, 1966); Michael Hurd, *Benjamin Britten* (London, 1966); Percy M. Young, *Britten* (London, 1966); Patricia Howard, *The Operas of Benjamin Britten* (N.Y., 1969); A. Kendall, *Benjamin Britten* (1973).

Brixi, Franz Xaver, Bohemian composer of church music; b. Prague, Jan. 2, 1732; d. there, Oct. 14, 1771. He was a pupil of Segert in Prague; held several positions as church organist. He wrote a great number of sacred works: 105 Masses, 263 offertories and anthems; 6 oratorios; 3 organ concertos, etc.

BIBLIOGRAPHY: O. Kamper, *Franz Xaver Brixi* (Prague, 1926); V. Novák, "Šimon a František Brixi

. . . ," in *Zprávy Bertramky, jubilejní výtisk ke 40. výročí založení Mosartovy obce* (1967); idem, "Zur Katalogisierung von Werken der Familie Brixi," *Die Musikforschung* (July/Sept. 1969).

Brkanović, Ivan, Croatian composer; b. Škaljari, near Kotor, Dec. 27, 1906. He studied composition in Zagreb, and in 1937 took a course at the Scola Cantorum in Paris. Returning to Zagreb he was active as music teacher; from 1954 to 1957 he conducted the Zagreb Philharmonic, and from 1957 to 1962 was prof. at the Music Academy in Sarajevo. In his music he represented the national style of Croatia, making use of typical folksong patterns and rhythmic figures.

WORKS: the operas *Equinox* (Zagreb, Oct. 4, 1950) and *Zlato Zadra* (*The Gold of Zadar;* Zagreb, April 15, 1954); a ballet, *Heloti* (Zagreb, March 17, 1963); 5 symphonies (1935, 1946, 1947, 1948, 1949); *Sarajevska Suita* for orch. (Zagreb, Jan. 20, 1958); cantata, *Bosnanska sjeéanja* (*Souvenirs of Bosnia;* 1961); a number of choral works and songs.

BIBLIOGRAPHY: K. Kovačević, *Hrvatski Kompozitori i Njihova Djela* (Zagreb, 1960).

Broadwood & Sons, oldest keyboard instrument manufactory in existence; established in London in 1728 by the Swiss harpsichord maker **Burkhard Tschudi,** or **Shudi** (b. Schwanden, Switzerland, March 13, 1702; d. London, Aug. 19, 1773). **John Broadwood** (b. Cockburnspath, Scotland, 1732; d. London, 1812), a Scotch cabinet maker, was Shudi's son-in-law and successor; in 1773 he began to build square pianos modeled after Zumpe's instruments; in 1780 he marketed his own square pianos, which he patented in 1783; in these, he dispensed with the old clavichord arrangement of the wrest-plank and tuning-pins and transformed the harpsichord pedals into damper and piano pedals; another important invention came in 1788, when he divided the long bridge, which until then had been continuous. Broadwood's improvements were soon adopted by other manufacturers. In 1794 the range of the keyboard was extended to six octaves. John Broadwood's sons, **James Shudi Broadwood** (b. London, Dec. 20, 1772; d. there, Aug. 8, 1851) and **Thomas Broadwood,** were admitted to the firm in 1795 and 1807 respectively, and the business was then carried on under the name of John Broadwood & Sons. Beethoven received a Broadwood piano in 1817. **Henry John Tschudi Broadwood** (d. Feb. 8, 1911), great-grandson of the founder, patented the so-called 'barless' grand piano; he became a director of John Broadwood & Sons, Ltd., established in 1901, with W. H. Leslie as chairman. In 1925 the firm moved to new quarters in New Bond Street. Members of the Broadwood family are still active in its affairs.

BIBLIOGRAPHY: W. Dale, *Tschudi, the Harpsichord Maker* (London, 1913).

Broche, Charles, French organist and composer; b. Rouen, Feb. 20, 1752; d. there, Sept. 30, 1803. In 1771 he went to Paris; then to Italy and studied with Padre Martini in Bologna. In 1777 he returned to Rouen as organist of the cathedral. Among his pupils was Boieldieu. Broche publ. 3 piano sonatas (1782) and wrote some music for organ.

235

BIBLIOGRAPHY: G. Favre, "Un Organiste de la Cathédrale de Rouen, Charles Broche," *Revue de Musicologie* (1937).

Brockway, Howard A., American composer and pianist; b. Brooklyn, Nov. 22, 1870; d. New York, Feb. 20, 1951. He studied in Berlin (1890–95); returning to the U.S., he settled in N.Y. as a teacher and concert pianist; from 1903–10 taught at the Peabody Cons. in Baltimore.

WORKS: *Sylvan Suite* for orch. (Boston, April 6, 1901); Symphony in D (Berlin, Feb. 23, 1895; Boston, April 6, 1907, Karl Muck cond.); *Moment musical* for violin and piano; many character pieces for piano (*Moods, Dance of the Sylphs,* etc.). He wrote piano accompaniments for 2 albums of Kentucky songs which were publ. as *Lonesome Tunes* (N.Y., 1916) and *20 Kentucky Mountain Songs* (Boston, 1920).

Brod, Max, significant Czech-born writer and composer; b. Prague, May 27, 1884; d. Tel Aviv, Dec. 20, 1968. In Prague he associated himself with Kafka and other writers of the New School, and himself published several psychological novels. He studied music at the German Univ. in Prague and became a music critic in various Czech and German publications. In 1939 he emigrated to Tel Aviv, where he continued his literary and musical activities. Among his compositions are *Requiem Hebraicum* (1943); *2 Israeli Peasant Dances* for piano and small orch. (Tel Aviv, April 24, 1947); several piano suites and 14 song cycles. He wrote an autobiography, *Streitbares Leben* (Munich, 1960) and a book on music in Israel (Tel Aviv, 1951).

Broder, Nathan, American musicologist and editor; b. New York, Dec. 1, 1905; d. there, Dec. 16, 1967. He studied at the College of the City of New York. In 1945 he became associate editor of the *Musical Quarterly;* from 1946 to 1952 he was lecturer in music at Columbia Univ.; from 1959–62, adjunct prof. of music there. In 1956 he received a Guggenheim Fellowship grant; received a Ford Foundation grant for research in 1961. From 1963 until his death he was music editor of W. W. Norton & Co.; also in 1963–64, President of the American Musicological Society. He published a monograph on Samuel Barber (N.Y., 1954); edited Mozart's piano sonatas and fantasies (Bryn Mawr, 1956); compiled *The Collector's Bach* (Philadelphia, 1958); was co-editor (with Paul Henry Lang) of *Contemporary Music in Europe* (N.Y., 1965).

Brodsky, Adolf, distinguished Russian violinist; b. Taganrog, Russia, April 2, 1851; d. Manchester, England, Jan. 22, 1929. He studied at the Vienna Cons. (1860–63); returning to Russia he took violin lessons with Laub in Moscow (1873–75) and succeeded as prof. at the Moscow Cons. In 1881 he made a highly successful European tour, and in Vienna gave the world premiere of Tchaikovsky's Violin Concerto, which Tchaikovsky in gratitude dedicated to him, after it had been rejected by Auer as unplayable. From 1883 to 1891 Brodsky was prof. of violin at the Leipzig Cons.; there he organized the Brodsky Quartet (with Hugo Becker, Hans Sitt and Julius Klengel), which enjoyed an international reputation in Europe. From 1891 to 1894 Brodsky was in New York as concertmaster of the N.Y. Symph. Orch. In 1895 he settled in Manchester, England, where he taught at the Royal College of Music, and became its director, a post which he held until his death. In England he changed the spelling of his first name to Adolph.

Brodsky, Vera. See **Lawrence, Vera Brodsky**

Broekman, David, Dutch-born American conductor; b. Leyden, May 13, 1902; d. New York, April 1, 1958. He studied with Van Anrooy in The Hague; came to the U.S. in 1924 as music editor for M. Witmark & Sons; then went to Hollywood as composer of film scores. He eventually settled in New York, developing energetic activity as conductor of ultra-modern music. He wrote 2 symphonies (Hollywood Bowl, 1934; Cincinnati Symph., 1934); motion picture scores (*All Quiet on the Western Front; The Phantom of the Opera,* etc.); published a book, *The Shoestring Symphony* (N.Y., 1948), describing the life of a composer in Hollywood.

Brogi, Renato, Italian composer; b. Sesto Fiorentino, Feb. 25, 1873; d. San Domenico di Fiesole, Florence, Aug. 25, 1924. He studied music in Florence; then at the Milan Cons.; won the Steiner Prize in Vienna with his opera *La prima notte* (Florence, Nov. 25, 1898). He also composed the operas *L'Oblio* (Florence, Feb. 4, 1890) and *Isabella Orsini* (Florence, April 24, 1920); the operettas *Bacco in Toscana* and *Follie Veneziane* (both produced in Florence, 1923); a violin concerto; a string quartet; a piano trio; songs.

Brogue, Roslyn, American composer; b. Chicago, Feb. 16, 1919. She studied languages at the Univ. of Chicago and music at Radcliffe College (Ph.D., 1947). In 1944 she married her private student, Ervin Henning.

WORKS: Trio for Oboe, Clarinet and Bassoon (1946); *Suite* for small orch. (1947); *Suite for Recorders* (1949); Piano Quartet (1949); String Quartet (1951); Trio for Violin, Clarinet and Piano (1953); many songs with varied instrumental accompaniments. Her music follows dodecaphonic precepts.

Broman, Natanael, Swedish pianist and composer; b. Kolsva, Dec. 11, 1887; d. Stockholm, Aug. 27, 1966. He studied in Stockholm and later in Berlin. From 1925 to 1951 he was in charge of the music division of the Stockholm Radio. He was highly regarded as a pianist. In his compositions he follows the neo-romantic trend with a strong undertow of Scandinavian melos. He composed a symph. poem, *Fritiof och Ingeborg* (1912); some violin pieces, and a number of songs.

Broman, Sten, eminent Swedish composer, conductor and music critic; b. Uppsala, March 25, 1902. He studied at the German Music Academy in Prague, attending a master class in violin playing with Henri Marteau; subsequently studied musicology with Curt Sachs in Berlin. From 1929 to 1951 he played the viola in various Swedish string quartets; from 1946 to 1966 was conductor of the Philharmonic Society in Malmö. He was an influential music critic; served as chairman of the Swedish section of the International Society for Contemporary Music from 1933 to 1962. A prolific composer, he wrote 8 symphonies and a number of chamber music pieces. In his idiom he followed a median line of Scandinavian romanticism, but beginning about 1960 he adopted serial techniques and later experimented with electronic sound.

WORKS: *Choral Fantasia* for orch. (1931); *Gothic Suite* for strings (1932); a ballet, *Malmö Dances* (1952); 8 symphonies: No. 1, *Sinfonia ritmica* (Malmö, March 20, 1962); No. 2 (Stockholm, Nov. 16, 1963); No. 3 (Malmö, April 27, 1965); No. 4 (1965; Detroit, Nov. 17, 1966); No. 5, with soprano solo (Stockholm, April 19, 1968); No. 6, with taped organ sounds (Lund, Sweden, Oct. 13, 1970); No. 7, with electronic sound (Stockholm, May 5, 1972); No. 8 (Stockholm, April 5, 1975); *Sententia crevit* for orch. and concrete sound tape (Lund, June 13, 1968); *Musica Cathedralis* for soprano, bass, 3 choruses, tape, orch. and 2 organs (Lund, April 4, 1973); *Canon* for piano (1929); 3 string quartets (1929, 1933, 1970); Duo for Violin and Viola (1932); 3 suites for viola and piano (1935, 1937, 1942); Sextet for Strings, Percussion and Piano (1963); Septet for Percussion, Celesta and Piano (1968); Concerto for Brass (Malmö, Nov. 11, 1971); film music.

Brons, Carel, Dutch composer; b. Groningen, Jan. 1, 1931. He studied piano, organ and composition; in 1954 became engaged on the Radio Holland; in 1959 was appointed music director of the Hilversum Radio.

WORKS: *Balletto* for wind quintet (1961); *Dialogues I* for oboe and piano (1962) and *II* for flute and harp (1967); 2 string quartets (1962, 1969); *Inventions* for organ (1963); *Serenata I* for solo flute (1963), *II* for oboe, clarinet and bassoon (1964) and *III* for 4 clarinets (1974); *Mutazione* for wind quintet (1964); *Reflecties* for organ (1965); *Varianten* for organ (1965) and orch. (1966); *Imaginations I-III* for piano (1966, 1966, 1974); *Monologue I* for solo oboe (1967), *II* for solo flute (1967), *III* for solo clarinet (1968), *IV* for solo bassoon (1968) and *V* for solo trumpet (1970); *Prisms* for organ (1967); *Epitaphium* for orch. (1967); *Astrabikon* for organ (1968); *Music* for strings (1969); *Litany* for organ (1971).

Bronsart von Schellendorf, Hans, German pianist and composer; b. Berlin, Feb. 11, 1830; d. Munich, Nov. 3, 1913. He studied piano with Kullak in Berlin and took lessons with Liszt in Weimar. In 1897 he undertook a concert tour through Germany, France and Russia; from 1860 to 1867 he was active as conductor in Leipzig, Dresden and Berlin. In his compositions he followed the romantic trend in Schumann's tradition. His most successful was his youthful piano trio, his first opus number (1856); some of his piano pieces retained their popularity for a brief while. He also wrote a dramatic tone poem *Manfred,* for chorus and orch., to his own text (Weimar, Dec. 1, 1901); 2 programmatic symphonies and choruses. In 1861 he married the pianist Ingeborg Starck (1840–1913).

Bronsart von Schellendorf, Ingeborg (*née* Starck), pianist and composer; b. (of Swedish parents) St. Petersburg, Aug. 24, 1840; d. Munich, June 17, 1913. She studied piano with Liszt at Weimar; in 1861 she mar-

ried **Hans Bronsart von Schellendorf.** She composed 3 operas: *König Hjarne* (Berlin, 1891); *Jery und Bätely* (Weimar, 1873); *Die Sühne* (Dessau, 1909); also piano concertos, piano sonatas, salon pieces, violin pieces, cello pieces and songs.

Brooks, John Benson, American jazz pianist and composer; b. Houlton, Maine, Feb. 23, 1917. He attended John Cage's classes of modern music at the New School for Social Research, N.Y., and became immersed in dodecaphonic and aleatory lore. Moreover, he read books on astrology, numerology and epistemology. Using the techniques of horoscopes, ink-blot tests and extrasensory perception as catalytic agents to the imagination, he developed an individualized method of serial composition; by analogy with the principle of indeterminacy, he postulated that velocity of musical particles and their temporary positions at a given point cannot be both precisely determined, and followed this idea in his improvisations, with *ostinatos* as departures from randomness. He composed an *Alabama Concerto* and a number of jazz songs.

Broome, William Edward, Canadian organist and composer; b. Manchester, England, 1868; d. Toronto, Canada, May 10, 1932. He studied piano and organ with Dr. Roland Rogers at Bangor Cathedral in Wales (1876–90), was church organist in Bangor (1883–90); went to Canada and became organist in Montreal (1894–1905) and Toronto. He won prizes at Welsh National Festivals for his dramatic cantata *The Siege of Cardiff Castle* (1908) and other works; published much church music, including a *Hymn of Trust.*

Broqua, Alfonso, Uruguayan composer; b. Montevideo, Sept. 11, 1876; d. Paris, Nov. 24, 1946. He studied with Vincent d'Indy at the Schola Cantorum in Paris, where he settled. His works are characterized by a fine feeling for exotic material, which he presents in the brilliant manner of French modern music.

WORKS: opera, *Cruz del Sur* (1918); *Thelen at Nagouëy,* Inca ballet (1934); *Isabelle,* romantic ballet (1936); *Tabaré,* poetic cycle for soli, women's chorus and piano or orch. (1908); *Poema de las Lomas,* triptych for piano (1912); Piano Quintet; *3 Cantos del Uruguay,* for voice, flute and 2 guitars (1925); *Cantos de Parana,* for voice and guitar (1929); *Evocaciones Criollas,* 7 pieces for guitar (1929); *3 Préludes Pampéens,* for piano (1938; also in orchestral version).

Broschi, Carlo. See Farinelli.

Brosig, Moritz, German church composer; b. Fuchswinkel, Upper Silesia, Oct. 15, 1815; d. Breslau, Jan. 24, 1887. He studied with Franz Wolf, the cathedral organist at Breslau, and succeeded him in 1842. He wrote 4 grand and 3 short instrumental Masses; 7 books of graduals and offertories; 20 books of organ pieces; an *Orgelbuch,* a *Choralbuch,* a *Modulationstheorie* (1865), and a *Harmonielehre* (1874; 4th ed. 1899 as *Handbuch der Harmonielehre und Modulation,* ed. by Thiel); also *Über die alten Kirchenkompositionen und ihre Wiedereinführung* (1880). Leuckart publ. a selection of his works in 5 volumes.

Brossard, Noël-Matthieu, French writer on music; b. Chalons-sur-Saône, Dec. 25, 1789; date of death unknown. He was a judge; became interested in music; published *Théorie des sons musicaux* (Paris, 1847), a treatise on the variability of tones according to modulation (he reckoned 48 distinct tone-degrees within the octave).

Brossard, Sébastien de, French composer; b. Dompierre, Orne, 1655 (baptized Sept. 12); d. Meaux, France, Aug. 10, 1730. He studied theology at Caen (1670–76); was then in Paris (1678–87); in 1687 he went to Strasbourg; in 1689 became 'maître de chapelle' at the Strasbourg Cathedral; in 1698 received a similar post at the Cathedral of Meaux; in 1709 he became canon there. His fame rests upon the authorship of what was erroneously regarded as the earliest dictionary of musical terms; it was in fact preceded by many publications: the medieval compilation *De musica antica et moderna* (c.1100), the last section of which is a vocabulary of musical terms (to be found in Lafage's *Essais de dipthérographie musicale* vol. I, pp. 404–7), by Joannes Tinctoris' *Terminorum musicae diffinitorium* (c.1475), and Janowka's *Clavis ad thesaurum magnae artis musicae* (1701), to none of which Brossard had access, however. The title of Brossard's own volume is *Dictionnaire de musique, contenant une explication des termes grecs, latins, italiens et français les plus usités dans la musique, etc.* (Paris, 1703; 2nd ed. 1705; there is also an Amsterdam reprint, marked 6th edition, but this designation is erroneous; English translation by Grassineau, 1740). Brossard also wrote *Lettre à M. Demotz sur sa nouvelle méthode d'écrire le plain-chant et la musique* (1729); a considerable variety of church music, including a *Canticum Eucharisticum* on the Peace of Ryswick (1697; new edition by F. X. Mathias); motets; etc. He brought out several volumes of *Airs sérieux et à boire*. His library of manuscripts was acquired by Louis XV in 1724, and formed the nucleus of the music collection of the Bibliothèque Nationale.

BIBLIOGRAPHY: M. Brenet, *Sébastien de Brossard* (Paris, 1896); also E. Lebeau, "L'Entrée de la collection musicale de Sébastien de Brossard à la Bibliothèque du Roi," *Revue de Musicologie"* (Dec. 1950).

Brosses, Charles de, French magistrat and scholar; b. Dijon, Feb. 17, 1709; d. Paris, May 7, 1777. He first studied law, but later turned to science and literature, subjects on which he published several valuable dissertations; contributed the article "Musique" to the *Encyclopédie méthodique.* He was the first president of the parliament of Burgundy, and member of the Académie des Belles-Lettres (1758).

BIBLIOGRAPHY: H. Mamet, *Le Président Charles de Brosses, sa vie et ses ouvrages* (Lille, 1874); Cunisset-Carnot, "La Querelle de Voltaire et du président Charles de Brosses," *Revue des Deux Mondes* (Feb. 15, 1888).

Brott, Alexander, Canadian conductor, violinist and composer; b. Montreal, March 14, 1915. He studied piano, violin and composition at the McGill Cons. in Montreal (1928–35); then composition with Bernard Wagenaar, and conducting at Juilliard in New York (1935–39). In 1939 he returned to Montreal, where he was engaged as concertmaster and assistant conductor of the Montreal Symph. Orch. (1945–58). In his music he follows the romantic tradition, with impressionistic harmonies imparting an aura of modernity.

WORKS: a ballet *Le Corriveau* (1966); for orch.: *Oracle* (1938); *War and Peace* (1944); *Concordia* (1946); *From Sea to Sea,* suite (1947); Concerto for Violin and Chamber Orch. (Montreal, March 7, 1950); *Delightful Delusions* (1950); *Prelude to Oblivion* for chamber orch. (1951); *Fancy and Folly* (1953); *Scherzo* (1954); *Analogy in Anagram* (1955); *Israel* for chorus and orch. (1956); *Arabesque* for cello and chamber orch. (1957); *The Vision of Dry Bones* for baritone, piano and strings (1958); *3 Astral Visions* for strings (1959); *Spheres in Orbit* (1960); *Martlet's Muse* (1962); *Circle, Triangle, 4 Squares* for string orch. (1963); *Profundium Praedictum* for double bass or viola or cello, and string orch. (1964); *Centennial Celebration* for narrator, female chorus and strings (1967); *Paraphrase in Polyphony* (Montreal, Nov. 3, 1967; variants based on a recently unearthed 10-bar canon written by Beethoven in 1825); *The Young Prometheus* (1969; 12 preludes and fugues based on Beethoven sketches); *Accent* for narrator and strings (1970); *The Emperor's New Clothes* for narrator and orch. (Kingston, Ontario, Feb. 21, 1971); *Seven Minuets, Six Canons,* after Beethoven (1971); *Kinderscenen,* after Schumann (1972); *H.B.S.* (1975); Quintet for Recorder and String Quartet (1940); String Quartet (1941); Suite for Piano (1941); *Critic's Corner* for String Quartet and Percussion (1950); *5 Miniatures* for 8 players (1950); *Vignettes en Caricature* for piano (1952); *Sept for Seven* for narrator, string, trio, clarinet, saxophone and piano (1955); *3 Acts for 4 Sinners* for saxophone quartet (1961); *Mutual Salvation Orgy* for brass quintet (1962); *World Sophisticate* for soprano, brass quintet and percussion (1962); *Berceuse* for saxophone quartet (1962); *3 on a Spree* for flute, oboe and harp (1963); *Pristine Prisms in Polychrome* for violin (1966); *Mini-Minus* for clarinet, bassoon, trumpet, trombone, violin, double bass and percussion (1968); *Spasms for Six* for 6 percussionists (1971); *Saties-Faction* for string quartet (1972); *Tout de Suite* for cello (1972); choral works with piano.

Brouillon-Lacombe, Louis. See **Lacombe, Louis.**

Brounoff, Platon, Russian conductor and composer; b. Elizavetgrad, May 10, 1863; d. New York, July 11, 1924. He studied at the St. Petersburg Cons. (1890) with Rimsky-Korsakov. In 1891 he went to the U.S., where he was conductor of The Modern Symph. Orch., Russian Choral Society, and People's Male Chorus in New York.

WORKS: opera, *Ramona*; music dramas *Xilona* and *Titanic*; *Angel,* cantata for 2 solo voices, chorus and orch.; *The Glory of God,* oratorio; *Russia,* festival overture (N.Y., 1897); orchestral suites *Flower Garden* (1897), *Russian Village,* and *Palestine* (1908); piano pieces; collections of Russian and Jewish folk songs. He was the author of *Ten Commandments of Piano Practice* (publ. privately, 1910).

Brower, Leo, Cuban composer of the avant-garde; b. Havana, March 1, 1939. At the time of the Cuban Revolution he was in the United States, where he studied with Persichetti and Stephan Wolpe at the Juilliard School of Music and with Isadore Freed at the Hartt College in Hartford. Returning to Cuba, he occupied various important posts on Havana Radio and in the music division of the film industry; also was given a grant by the Cuban government to travel as concert guitar player. In his own compositions he follows the most advanced trends in contemporary music including pop art and multimedia productions. WORKS: He has written three pieces under the title *Sonograma,* one for prepared piano (1963), one for orchestra (1964), one for two pianos (1968); his other works of the ultra-modern type are *2 Conceptos del tiempo* for 10 players (1965); *Tropos* for orch. (1967); *Cantigas del tiempo nuevo* for actors, voices, piano, harp and percussion and *Hexahedron* for 6, or a multiple of 6, players (1969); other works are *El reino de este mundo* for woodwind quintet (1968); *Homage to Mingus* for jazz combo and orch. and *Conmutaciones* for prepared piano and 2 percussionists (1966).

Brown, Earle, innovative American composer; b. Lunenburg, Mass., Dec. 26, 1926. He studied mathematics and engineering at Northeastern Univ. in Boston; later took lessons in the Schillinger System of composition with Roslyn Brogue Henning. In 1952 he moved to New York; in 1965 he received a Guggenheim Fellowship; in 1968–70 he taught composition at the Peabody Conservatory in Baltimore. In his seminal work *25 Pages* (1953), he introduced the concepts of "open end" composition in which the performer is free to select the order of notated fragments; each page can be played upside down at will. In much of his music, Brown was impressed by abstract expressionism in painting and the mobile constructions of modern sculpture, as well as the poetic applications of surrealism and neo-Dadaism. As a reflection of these ideas, he built as early as 1952 a model of musical space "relative to conceptual mobility and transformation of events in arbitrary, unstable time." Brown was one of the first composers to introduce "time notation" in which the duration of each section is indicated in seconds; sometimes the performer is given freedom to exercise his own "time sense perception." WORKS: *3 Pieces* for piano (1951); *Perspectives* for piano (1952); *Music* for violin, cello and piano (1952); *Folio,* a set of 3 works, each composed for any number of instruments and bearing the titles of the chronology of composition: *November 1952,* subtitled *Synergy, December 1952* and *1953*; *25 Pages* for any number of pianos, up to 25 (1953); *Octet I* for 8 spatially directed magnetic tapes (1953); *Indices* for chamber orch. (1954); *Pentathis* for flute, bass clarinet, trumpet, trombone, harp, piano, violin, viola, cello (1957); *Hodograph* for flute, piano, celesta, bells, vibraphone and marimba (1959); *Available Forms I* for 18 musicians, playing determinate instruments (Darmstadt, Sept. 8, 1961); *Light Music* for electric lights, electronic equipment and variable numbers of instruments (1961); *Available Forms II* for 98 musicians, all playing determinate instruments, and directed by 2 conductors (1962); *Novara* for flute, bass clarinet, trumpet, piano, 2 violins, viola, cello (1962); *From Here* for 20 musicians and 4 optional choruses (1963); *Times Five* for 5 instruments and magnetic tape (1963); *Corroboree* for 3 pianos (1964); *String Quartet* (1965); *9 Rarebits* for 1 or 2 harpsichords (1965); *Event: Synergy II* for chamber orch. (1967–68); *Syntagm III* for 8 instruments (1970); *New Piece* for 18 instruments (1971); *Time Spans* for orch. (1972); *Sign Sounds* for chamber ensemble (1972); *Centering* for violin and 10 instruments (1973); *Cross Sections and Color Fields* for orch. (1973–75).

Brown, Eddy, American violinist; b. Chicago, July 15, 1895; d. Abano Terme, Italy, June 14, 1974. He was given his first lessons in violin playing by his father; then was taken to Europe, and studied in Budapest with Jenö Hubay. He won a violin competition at the age of 11 playing the Mendelssohn Concerto in Budapest. He then proceeded to London, and eventually to Russia where he became a pupil of Leopold Auer. Returning to the U.S. in 1915, he made several transcontinental tours; was a soloist with the New York Philharmonic, Chicago Symphony Orch., Philadelphia Orch. and Boston Symph. Orch. In 1922 he founded the Eddy Brown String Quartet; in 1932 he became president of the Chamber Music Society of America which he organized. He became active in educational programs over the radio; was music director of the Mutual Broadcasting System (1930–37) and of station WQXR (1936–55). From 1956 to 1971 he was artistic coordinator of the Cincinnati College and Conservatory of Music.

Brown, Howard Mayer, American musicologist; b. Los Angeles, April 13, 1930. He studied at Harvard Univ. with Walter Piston (composition), Otto Gombosi (musicology) and others (B.A., 1951; M.A., 1954; Ph.D., 1959); continued his study in Vienna (1951–53); held a Guggenheim Fellowship in Florence (1963–64). He taught at Wellesley College (1958–60); in 1960 he was appointed to the faculty of the Univ. of Chicago. WRITINGS: *Music in the French Secular Theater, 1400–1550* (Cambridge, Mass., 1963); *Instrumental Music Printed Before 1600: A Bibliography* (Cambridge, Mass., 1965).

Brown, James Duff, British music bibliographer; b. Edinburgh, Nov. 6, 1862; d. London, March 1, 1914. He was librarian of the Clerkenwell Library of London from 1888; co-author (with Stephen S. Stratton) of the valuable reference work *British Musical Biography: A Dictionary of Musical Artists, Authors and Composers born in Great Britain and its Colonies* (1897). He also published a *Biographical Dictionary of Musicians* (1886); *Guide to the Formation of a Music Library* (1893); *Characteristic Songs and Dances of All Nations* with historical notes and a bibliography (in collaboration with Moffat, 1901); and *Subject Classification* (1908). His *Manual of Library Economy* was publ. in several editions (3d ed., London, 1920).

Brown, Dr. John, English writer; b. Rothbury, Northumberland, Nov. 5, 1715; d. (suicide) Newcastle-on-Tyne, Sept. 23, 1766. He became vicar of Great Horkesley, Essex, in 1754, and of St. Nicholas', Newcastle, in 1758. He is the author of *Dissertation on the Rise, Union, and Power, the Progressions, Separations and Corruptions of Poetry and Music, to which is prefixed The Cure of Saul, A Sacred Ode* (London, 1763). A revised edition was publ. in 1764 as *The History of the Rise and Progress of Poetry, through its Several Species* (in French, Paris, 1768; in German, Leipzig, 1769; in Italian, 1772).

Brown, Merton, American composer; b. Berlin, Vermont, May 5, 1913. He studied both piano and violin; moved to N.Y. in 1935 and took piano lessons with Ann Hull, and studied composition privately with Wallingford Riegger (1939–42) and with Carl Ruggles (1943–45). From 1949 to 1967 he lived in Rome; then returned to America, and settled in Boston. His music is set in dissonant counterpoint of great density without negating the lyrical flow of melody.
    WORKS: *Consort for 4 Voices* scored for 2 pianos (N.Y., April 21, 1947); Piano Sonata (1948); *Chorale for Strings* (1948); *Duo in 3 Movements* for violin and piano (1956); *Concerto breve per archi* (Naples, Italy, Jan. 23, 1960); *Metamorfosi per piano* (1965); *Dialogo* for cello and piano (1970); *Concertino* for string orch. (1974); *Divertimento* for piano 4-hands (1975); *5 Pieces* for clarinet and piano (1976); *Psalm 13* (1976).

Brown, Nacio Herb, American composer of popular songs; b. Deming, New Mexico, Feb. 22, 1896; d. San Francisco, Sept. 28, 1964. He was a clothier and later a real-estate agent; learned a little about music in a Musical Arts High School in Los Angeles, where he began producing songs that seemed to be blessed with a dollar sign. Among his greatest hits were *Singin' in the Rain* (1929), made famous by Judy Garland in her movie *Little Nellie Kelly* (1940), and *Temptation,* glorified by Bing Crosby in the screen musical *Going Hollywood* (1933).

Brown, Rayner, American composer; b. Des Moines, Iowa, Feb. 23, 1912; studied at the Univ. of Southern California, obtaining his M. Mus. in 1946; became active as church organist in Los Angeles.
    WORKS: 3 symphonies (1952, 1957, 1958); Concerto for Organ and Orchestra (1959); Piano Quartet (1947); String Quartet (1953); 2 woodwind quintets (1955, 1957); Brass Quintet (1957); 2 flute sonatas (1944, 1959); 3 fugues for 5 flutes (1952); Trio for Flute, Clarinet and Viola (1957); 12 sonatinas for organ; piano sonata, etc.

Brown, William, flute player and composer, who settled in America in the middle of the 18th century. He gave a concert on the flute in Baltimore on Jan. 30, 1784; then went to Philadelphia, where he participated in numerous benefit concerts; in 1785 he established a series of Subscription Concerts in New York and Philadelphia (with Alexander Reinagle and Henri Capron). He composed *3 Rondos for the Pianoforte or Harpsichord* (dedicated to Francis Hopkinson). He was probably a German: may be identical with Wilhelm Braun of Kassel.
    BIBLIOGRAPHY: J. D. Apell, *Galerie der vorzüglichsten Tonkünstler und merkwürdigen Musikdilettanten in Kassel* (1806); J. T. Howard, *Our American Music* (4th ed.; N.Y., 1965); Carl Engel, "Introducing Mr. Brown," *Musical Quarterly* (Jan. 1944).

Browne, John Lewis, organist and composer; b. London, May 18, 1864; d. Chicago, Oct. 23, 1933. He was a pupil of his father, William Browne, a noted organist; later studied with S. P. Warren (1884) and F. Archer (1887); settling in America, he was active as organist in San Francisco, Atlanta, Philadelphia, and Chicago; during his career he gave more than 500 organ recitals. He designed an organ for Medinah Temple in Chicago, and inaugurated it with the first performance of Felix Borowski's *Allegro de Concert,* commissioned for the occasion.
    WORKS: an opera, *La Corsicana* (received an honorable mention in the Sonzogno Competition in 1902; first performed in Chicago on Jan. 4, 1923); an ode, *The Granite Walls Rise Fair* (1911); *Missa Solemnis* (1913); many songs.
    BIBLIOGRAPHY: E. E. Hipsher, *American Opera and Its Composers* (Philadelphia, 1927; pp. 93–97).

Browning, John, brilliant American pianist; b. Denver, May 22, 1933. He made his professional debut as a wunderkind at the age of 10; then studied in Los Angeles, with Lee Pattison; went to New York where he enrolled at the Juilliard School of Music as a student of Rosina Lhévinne. He received the Steinway Centennial Award in 1954 and the Leventritt Award in 1955. In 1956 he received second prize at Queen Elisabeth Competition in Brussels. He attracted favorable attention as soloist in the world première of the piano concerto by Samuel Barber, which he played with the Boston Symph. Orch. at Lincoln Center, New York, Sept. 24, 1962. From then on he established himself as a virtuoso pianist of a superior caliber.

Brownlee, John (full name **John Donald Mackensie Brownlee**), American baritone; b. Geelong, Australia, Jan. 7, 1900; d. New York, Jan. 10, 1969. He sang in an amateur choral group at Geelong College, when the famous prima donna Melba heard him and advised him to study singing seriously. He went to Paris to study, and made his operatic debut there in 1926; on June 26, 1926 he sang in Covent Garden in London in *La Bohème,* at Melba's farewell appearance in opera. He was a member of the staff at the Paris Opéra (1927–36); then joined the Metropolitan Opera in New York, making his debut there in *Rigoletto* on Feb. 17, 1937. In 1953 he abandoned his operatic career and in 1956 was appointed director of the Manhattan School of Music in New York.

Brubeck, Dave (David), American pianist and jazz improviser; brother of **Howard Brubeck;** b. Concord, California, Dec. 6, 1920. He played piano in jazz bands as a boy; then took lessons with Milhaud at Mills College, and with Schoenberg in Los Angeles. During World War II he was assigned to a band in Europe; after demobilization, he organized a highly successful band of his own. In his half-improvised compositions he employs a contrapuntal idiom combining elements of jazz with baroque textures. He wrote the oratorio *Truth Has Fallen* for the opening of the new Midland, Michigan, Center for the Arts, May 1, 1971. In the

1970s he drafted into his band his three rock-musician sons, **Darius** (named after Darius Milhaud), b. San Francisco, June 14, 1947 (plays acoustic and electric keyboards); **Chris,** b. Los Angeles, March 19, 1953 (trombone, bass, keyboards); and **Danny,** b. Oakland, Cal., May 5, 1955 (percussion).

Brubeck, Howard, American composer, brother of **David Brubeck;** b. Concord, California, July 11, 1916. After studying with Darius Milhaud and others, he devoted himself to teaching; was chairman of the Music Department at Palomar Jr. College in La Mesa, California.
WORKS: *Elizabethan Suite* for chamber orch. and women's chorus (1944); *California Suite* for orch. (1945); *Overture to the Devil's Disciple* (1954); *Four Dialogues* for jazz combo and orchestra (San Diego, Aug. 1, 1956); *The Gardens of Versailles,* suite for orch. (1960); Woodwind Quintet (1950); choruses; piano pieces; arrangements for jazz combo and orch. on David Brubeck's themes.

Bruch, Max, celebrated German composer; b. Cologne, Jan. 6, 1838; d. Friednau, near Berlin, Oct. 2, 1920. His mother, a professional singer, was his first teacher. He afterwards studied theory with Breidenstein in Bonn; in 1852 he won a scholarship of the Mozart Foundation in Frankfurt for four years, and became a pupil of Ferdinand Hiller, Reinecke, and Breuning. At the age of fourteen, he brought out a symphony at Cologne, and at 20 produced his first stage work, *Scherz, List und Rache,* adapted from Goethe's Singspiel (Cologne, Jan. 14, 1858). Between 1858 and 1861 he taught music in Cologne; also made prolonged visits to Berlin, Leipzig, Dresden and Munich; in 1863 he was in Mannheim, where he produced his first full-fledged opera. *Die Loreley* (April 14, 1863), to the libretto by Geibel, originally intended for Mendelssohn. About the same time he wrote an effective choral work *Frithjof,* which was presented with great success in various German towns, and in Vienna. In 1865 Bruch became a musical director of a concert organization in Koblenz; there he wrote his First Violin Concerto (G minor), which became a great favorite among violinists. In 1870 he went to Berlin; his last opera, *Hermione,* based on Shakespeare's *The Winter's Tale,* was produced at the Berlin Opera on March 21, 1872. In 1880 he accepted the post of conductor of the Liverpool Philharmonic, and remained in England for three years; in 1883 he visited the U.S. and conducted his choral work *Arminius* in Boston. From 1883–1890 he was music director of an orchestral society in Breslau; in 1891 he became professor of composition at the Musikhochschule in Berlin, retiring in 1910. Bruch was married to the singer **Clara Tuczek** (d. 1919). The Univ. of Cambridge conferred upon him the honorary degree of Mus. Doc. (1893); the French Academy elected him corresponding member; in 1918 the Univ. of Berlin gave him the honorary degree of Dr. phil. Bruch's music, although imitative in its essence and even in its melodic and harmonic procedures, has a great eclectic charm; he was a master of harmony, counterpoint and instrumentation; he was equally adept at handling vocal masses. He contributed a great deal to the development of the secular oratorio, using soloists, chorus and orchestra. In this genre he wrote *Odysseus, Arminius, Das Lied von der Glocke* and *Achilleus;* also *Frithjof* for baritone, female chorus and orch.; *Normannenzug* for baritone, male chorus and orch.; and several other works for various vocal ensembles. Among his instrumental works, the so-called *Scottish Fantasy* for violin and orch. (1880) was extremely successful when Sarasate (to whom the work was dedicated) performed it all over Europe; but the most popular of all works by Bruch is his *Kol Nidrei,* a Hebrew melody for cello and orch., composed for the Jewish community of Liverpool in 1880; its success led to the erroneous assumption that Bruch himself was Jewish (he was, in fact, of a clerical Protestant family). His Concerto for 2 Pianos and Orch. was commissioned by the American duo piano team Ottilie and Rose Sutro; when they performed it for the first time (Philadelphia Orch., Stokowski conducting, 1916) they drastically revised the original. In 1971 the authentic version was discovered in Berlin, and was given its first performance by Nathan Twining and Mer Berkofsky with the London Symph., Antal Dorati conducting, on May 6, 1974.
BIBLIOGRAPHY: Fritz Gysi, *Max Bruch* (Zürich, 1922); Hans Pfitzner, *Meine Beziehungen zu Max Bruch; persönliche Erinnerungen* (Munich, 1938); D. Kaemper, *Max Bruch-Studien. Zum 50. Todestag des Komponisten* (Cologne, 1970); Jacques Voois, "The Case of the Disappearing Double Piano Concerto," *Symphony News* (June 1974).

Bruchollerie, Monique de la, French pianist; b. Paris, April 20, 1915; d. there, Dec. 15, 1972. She studied with Isidor Philipp; graduated from the Paris Cons. at the age of 13; toured widely as a concert pianist; also was active as a teacher. In 1964 she made a bold proposal to modernize the piano as a performing instrument by constructing a crescent-shaped keyboard to facilitate simultaneous playing in high treble and low bass. She further proposed to install electronic controls enabling the pianist to activate a whole chord by striking a single key. See *Time* Magazine for April 30, 1965.

Bruči, Rudolf, Serbian composer; b. Zagreb, March 30, 1917. He studied in Vienna with Uhl; returning to Serbia, became teacher and opera conductor in Novi Sad. In his works he employs polytonal and atonal devices, culminating in free dodecaphony.
WORKS: *Maskal,* symph. suite (1955); Concerto for Orch. (Belgrade, Nov. 25, 1959); *Čovek je vidik bez kraja,* cantata (Belgrade, Dec. 21, 1961); *Srbija,* cantata (Belgrade, May 24, 1962); *Sinfonia lesta* (received the Grand Prix at the Queen Elisabeth of Belgium Competition in Brussels, 1965); *Sinfonietta* for strings (1965); *Salut au monde,* oratorio (1967).

Bruck (or **Brouck**), **Arnold von** (known also as **Arnold de Bruges** and **Arnoldo Flamengo**), Flemish composer; b. Bruges, c.1470; d. Linz, 1554. He studied with H. Finck in Salzburg; was in the service of the Hapsburgs in Vienna (1514); in 1529 was music director in the court of Kaiser Ferdinand I. Many of his motets, hymns and German part-songs are preserved in collections of the 16th century; reprints have been published in *Denkmäler der Tonkunst in Österreich* 72 (37.ii) and 99, R. Eitner in *Publikationen älterer Musik* (vol. 2), A. Schering in *Geschichte der Musik in Beispielen* (no. 110), J. Wolf in *Denkmäler deutscher Tonkunst* (vol. 34), Otto Kade in A. W. Ambros' *Geschichte der Musik* (vol. 5), C. G. Winterfeld in *Der evangelische Kirchengesang*, and A. T. Davison and W. Apel, *Historical Anthology of Music* (no. 111b).

Brucken-Fock, Emil von, Dutch composer; brother of **Gerard von Brucken-Fock;** b. Koudekerke, Oct. 19, 1857; d. Aerdenhout, Jan. 6, 1944. He conducted a military band and wrote music criticism in Utrecht; influenced by Wagner he composed the music drama *Seleneia.* He also wrote many songs.

Brucken-Fock, Gerard von, Dutch pianist and composer; brother of **Emil von Brucken-Fock;** b. Koudekerke, Dec. 28, 1859; d. Heemstede, Aug. 15, 1935. He studied with Friedrich Kiel and W. Bargiel. He wrote two symphonies, an oratorio *De Wederkomst van Christus,* a violin sonata, etc. Some of his piano preludes and songs have acquired considerable popularity in Holland.

Brückler, Hugo, German song composer; b. Dresden, Feb. 18, 1845; d. there, Oct. 4, 1871. He studied at the Dresden Cons.; published 2 groups of songs, both based on Scheffel's poem, *Trompeter von Säckingen (Songs of Young Werner by the Rhine* and *Margaret's Songs);* also *Sieben Gesänge* (posthumous; selected and edited by Adolf Jensen); a ballad, *Der Vogt von Tenneberg* (posthumous, edited by Reinhold Becker); *Nordmännersang; Marsch der Bürgergarde.*
BIBLIOGRAPHY: R. Musiol, *Hugo Brückler* (Dresden, 1896).

Bruckner, Anton, famous Austrian composer; b. Ansfelden, Sept. 4, 1824; d. Vienna, Oct. 11, 1896. A son of a village schoolmaster, he became an orphan early in life; chiefly by his own efforts he learned to play the organ, so that he was able to obtain an appointment as cathedral organist in Linz (1856) in competition with many rivals. As opportunity offered, he studied composition with Kitzler and Sechter. In 1867 he succeeded Sechter as court organist in Vienna, and also became instructor of organ and harmony at the Vienna Cons. In 1875 he received the post of lecturer on music at Vienna Univ.; in 1891 the Univ. gave him the title of *Dr. phil.* He traveled to France (1869) and to England (1871) and established himself as a great virtuoso on the organ. Recognition of the importance of Bruckner as a composer came slowly; in his symphonic works, he attempted to transplant the methods of Wagner to instrumental music. It was only many years after his death that his greatness as a symphonist was widely conceded.
WORKS: He discarded his two early symphonies; one in F minor (1863; discovered and perf. at Klosterneuburg, March 18, 1923); one in D minor (1864; revised 1869; perf. Klosterneuburg, Oct. 12, 1924; this symphony was marked by Bruckner as No. 0). The nine symphonies acknowledged by Bruckner and given in most catalogues are: No. 1 in C minor (1866;

Linz, May 9, 1868, under Bruckner's direction; revised 1877–91); No. 2 in C minor (1872; Vienna, Oct. 26, 1873, under Bruckner; two revisions between 1875 and 1877); No. 3 in D minor (1873; dedicated to Wagner; Vienna, Dec. 16, 1877, under Bruckner; 2 revisions, 1877 and 1888); No. 4 in E-flat, surnamed 'Romantic' (1874; Scherzo and Finale revised, 1878–80; Vienna, Feb. 20, 1881, under Richter); No. 5 in B-flat (1875–77; revised 1878; Graz, April 8, 1894, under Schalk); No. 6 in A (1879–81; Adagio and Scherzo perf. Vienna, Feb. 11, 1883, under W. Jahn; complete perf., posthumous, Feb. 26, 1899, under Mahler); No. 7 in E (1881–83; Leipzig, Dec. 30, 1884, under Nikisch); No. 8 in C minor, surnamed 'Apocalyptic' (1884–87; revised 1890; Vienna, Dec. 18, 1892, under Richter); No. 9 in D minor (1895–96; the Finale remained unfinished; perf. posthumously by Löwe, Vienna, Feb. 11, 1903, with Bruckner's *Te Deum* substituted for the Finale). Other works are Overture in G minor (left in sketches; comp. 1861–63), publ. in an album in 1949, along with several military marches by Bruckner; *Requiem* in D minor (St. Florian, March 13, 1849); *Missa Solemnis* in B-flat (St. Florian, Sept. 14, 1854); the choral works: *Germanenzug* (1863); *Abendzauber* (1878); *Helgoland* (1893); 3 Masses (1864; 1866; 1871); *Te Deum* (1881; revised 1884 perf. with orch., Vienna, Jan. 10, 1886); 105th Psalm (Vienna, Nov. 13, 1892); String Quintet in F, etc. For a complete list of works with dates of comp., see the exhaustive article by F. Blume in *Die Musik in Geschichte und Gegenwart* (vol. II, pp. 342–383). A new monumental edition of Bruckner's symphonies in their original orchestration (without revisions made by Löwe and Schalk in the first prints) under the editorship of Robert Haas and Alfred Orel was publ. under the auspices of the National Library in Vienna and the International Bruckner Society; other works are included in the complete edition of 22 volumes. A new critical edition, ed. by L. Nowak, was begun in 1953 and has reached 20 vols. The International Bruckner Society in Vienna publ. *Bruckner-Blaetter* (1929–37 and 1939) and the *Int. Bruckner Ges. Mitteilungsblatt.* The Bruckner Society of America, founded in 1931, publishes a journal *Chord and Discord;* it awarded Bruckner medals to Toscanini, Koussevitzky and others for performances of Bruckner's music. The Brucknerbund für Oberösterreich issues *Zeitschrift Brucknerland,* and additional publications come from Société Française Anton Bruckner.
BIBLIOGRAPHY: BIOGRAPHY: F. Brunner, *B.* (Linz, 1895); R. Louis, *A. B.* (Munich, 1905; new ed. 1917); Leon Funtek, *Bruckneriana* (Leipzig, 1910); F. Gräflinger, *A. B.; Bausteine zu seiner Lebensgeschichte* (Munich, 1911; new ed. 1927); M. Morold, *A. B.* (Leipzig, 1912; 2nd ed., 1920); Ernst Decsey, *A. B.* (1920); F. Gräflinger, *A. B.; Sein Leben und seine Werke* (1921); Erich Schwebsch, *A. B.* (Stuttgart, 1921; new ed. 1927); H. Tessmer, *A. B.* (Regensburg, 1922); K. Grunsky, *A. B.* (Stuttgart, 1922); Max Auer, *A. B.* (1923); Ernst Kurth, *A. B.* (2 vols., 1925); A. Orel, *A. B.; Das Werk; Der Künstler; Die Zeit* (1925); F. Klose, *Meine Lehrjahre bei Bruckner* (1927); F. Grüninger, *B.* (1930; new ed. 1950); G. Engel, *The Life of A. B.* (N.Y., 1931); Robert Haas, *A. B.* (Potsdam, 1934); A. Orel, *A. B. in Bildern* (Leipzig, 1936); August Göllerich and Max

Auer, *A. B.* (4 vols., 1922-37; fundamental biogr. source); E. Schwanzara, *Bruckners Stamm- und Urheimat* (Berlin, 1937); K. Laux, *A. B. Leben und Werk* (Leipzig, 1940); W. Wolff, *A. B.; Rustic Genius* (N.Y., 1942); L. Van Vassenhove, *A. B.* (Brussels, 1942); P. Raabe, *Wege zu Bruckner* (Regensburg, 1944); A. Machabey, *La Vie et l'œuvre d'A. Bruckner* (Paris, 1945); D. Newlin, *Bruckner, Mahler, Schoenberg* (N.Y., 1947); H. F. Redlich, *Bruckner and Mahler* (London, 1955); W. Abendroth, *Bruckner: Eine Bibliographie* (Munich, 1958); E. Doernberg, *The Life and Symphonies of Anton Bruckner* (London, 1960); H. H. Schönzeler, *Bruckner* (N.Y., 1970); D. Watson, *Bruckner* (1975).

ANALYSIS: A. Halm, *Die Symphonie A. B.s* (1914); A. Orel, *Unbekannte Frühwerke Bruckners* (1921); Kurt Singer, *Bruckners Chormusik* (1924); M. Auer, *B. als Kirchenmusiker* (1927); Fr. Munch, *La musique religieuse de B.* (Paris, 1928); H. A. Grunsky, *Formenwelt und Sinngefüge in den B. Sinfonien* (2 vols., 1931); E. Wellesz, "A. B. and the Process of Musical Creation," *Musical Quarterly* (1938); A. Maecklenburg, "Hugo Wolf and A. B.," ibid. (1938); H. Unger, *A. B. und seine 7. Sinfonie* (Bonn, 1944); Ilmari Krohn, *Anton Bruckners Sinfonien: eine Untersuchung über Formenbau und Stimmungsgehalt* (Helsinki, 1955); R. Simpson, *The Essence of Bruckner* (Philadelphia, 1968).

CORRESPONDENCE: Letters of Bruckner are contained in Gräflinger's monograph on Karl Waldeck, Bruckner's pupil and successor as Linz Cathedral organist (Linz, 1911); G. Bosse's *Deutsche Musikbücherei* (vols. 49 and 55); and in A. Orel, *Bruckner-Brevier; Briefe, Dokumente, Berichte* (Vienna, 1953).

Brugnoli, Attilio, Italian composer; b. Rome, Sept. 7, 1880; d. Bolzano, July 10, 1937. He studied piano and composition at the Naples Cons. with Paolo Serrao (grad., 1900); won the Rubinstein Prize in Paris (1905); taught at the conservatories of Parma (1907-21), and Florence (1921-37). His compositions include a Piano Concerto (1905); Violin Concerto (1908); piano suite, *Scene Napolitane* (1909); several songs; piano pieces; also a pedagogic work, *Dinamica pianistica* (Milan, 1926).

Bruhns, Nicolaus, German violinist, organist and composer; b. Schwabstedt, 1665; d. Husum, March 29, 1697. He studied with Buxtehude in Lübeck; was organist in Copenhagen, and from 1689 in Husum. He was also an experienced violinist. He wrote 12 church cantatas, and a number of organ pieces.

BIBLIOGRAPHY: H. Kölsch, *Nicolaus Bruhns* (Kassel, 1958).

Brüll, Ignaz, Austrian pianist and composer; b. Prossnitz, Moravia, Nov. 7, 1846; d. Vienna, Sept. 17, 1907. He studied in Vienna with Epstein (piano) and Dessoff (composition); subsequently made extended recital tours; eventually settled in Vienna, where he was professor of piano at the Horak Institute (1872-78). He was an intimate friend of Brahms, who greatly valued his advice.

WORKS: operas, *Die Bettler von Samarkand* (1864); *Das goldene Kreuz* (Berlin, Dec. 22, 1875; his most successful opera), *Der Landfriede* (Vienna, Oct. 4, 1877), *Bianca* (Dresden, Nov. 25, 1879), *Königin Marietta* (Munich, 1883), *Gloria* (Hamburg, 1886), *Das steinerne Herz* (Vienna, 1888), *Gringoire* (Munich, March 19, 1892), *Schach dem Könige* (Munich, 1893), *Der Husar* (Vienna, 1898; very successful), *Rübezahl* (unfinished); a ballet, *Ein Märchen aus der Champagne* (1896); an overture, *Im Walde*; 3 serenades and a dance suite for orch.; two piano concertos, violin concerto, piano pieces; songs.

BIBLIOGRAPHY: H. Schwarz, *Ignaz Brüll und sein Freundeskreis* (1922); also many references in the biographies of Brahms.

Brumby, Colin, Australian composer; b. Melbourne, June 18, 1933. He graduated from the Melbourne Univ. Cons. of Music in 1957; studied in London with Alexander Goehr and John Carewe (1963). He lectured at the Brisbane Teacher's Training College (1959-64) and in 1964 became a Senior Lecturer at the Univ. of Queensland. His music is medium modern, with liberal application of avant-garde techniques.

WORKS: *Aegean Suite* for flute and strings (1957); *Mediterranean Suite* for strings (1958); *4 Antiphons* for organ (1961); *Partite* for clarinet and strings (1961); *Pantos* for flute and strings (1963); *Fibonacci Variations* for orch. (1963); Wind Quintet (1964); *Antithesis* for strings (1964); *Chance Piece* for piano (1965); *Stabat Mater Speciosa*, a Christmas cantata (1965); Trio for Flute, Clarinet and Horn (1965); *Doubles* for wind quartet (1965); *Diversion* for horn and orch. (1966); *Realisations* for piano and orch. (1966); *Antipodea* for orch. (1966); *Bunyip*, ballet (1967); *French Suite* for 6 horns (1967); *Gilgamesh*, cantata for narrator, chorus, brass and percussion (1967); String Quartet (1968); *3 Italian Songs* for high voice and string quartet (1968); *Charlie Bubbles' Book of Hours* for soli, chorus, tape and orch. (1969); *Five Days Lost* for narrator and orch. (1969); *Bring Out Your Christmas Masks* for narrator, soli, chorus, tape and orch. (1969); *The Seven Deadly Sins*, opera (1970); Violin Concerto (1970); Concerto for Horn and Strings (1971); *A Ballade for St. Cecilia*, cantata (1971); *Celebrations and Lamentations* for narrators, soli, chorus and orch. (1971); *Litanies of the Sun*, symph. suite (1971); *Doubles* for piano (1972); Viola Concertino (1972); *Ishtar's Mirror*, opera (1972); *This is the Vine* for soli, chorus and orch. (1972; Melbourne, Feb. 24, 1973); several children's operettas; songs and choral pieces; piano pieces.

Brumel, Antoine, celebrated Flemish (or French) contrapuntist, contemporary of Josquin des Prez; b. 1460; d. after 1520. He was a chorister at the Cathedrals of Notre Dame, Chartres (1483), and Laon (1497); was a pupil of Okeghem; from 1498-1500 was choirmaster and canon at Notre Dame in Paris; then was in the service of Prince Sigismund Cantelmus of Sora at Lyons; in 1505 was engaged at the court of Alfonso I, Duke of Ferrara; nothing further is known of his life. The precise birth and death dates, 1475-1520, often given in music histories, are not supported by unimpeachable documentary evidence; nor is it known whether Brumel was Flemish or French. Five of his Masses in 4 parts, and the *Missa super Dringhs* in 6 parts, were published by Petrucci (1503 and 1508), as well as many motets (1502–14); other Masses can be found in the collections of A. Antiquus (1516); J. Ott (1539), and Petrejus (1539); portions of Brumel's Masses are included in *Fragmenta missarum;* Henri Expert published his Mass *De beata Virgine* in *Maîtres Musiciens* (vol. 9); other pieces are in Maldeghem's *Trésor.* A. Schering published the *Benedictus* from the *Missa super Dringhs* in his *Geschichte der Musik in Beispielen* (no. 64); further portions of Masses are to be found in K. E. Roediger's *Die geistlichen Musikhandschriften der Universitäts-Bibliothek Jena* (Jena, 1935). A complete edition of his works was begun by A. Carapetyan in 1951 in Rome (the American Institute of Musicology). Some of Brumel's correspondence was published by E. Van der Straeten in *La Musique au Pays-Bas* (vol. 6). Masses, motets, magnificats, etc., in MS, are at Munich, Vienna, Bologna, Basel and Milan.

BIBLIOGRAPHY: *Monatshefte für Musikgeschichte* (XVI/2); A W. Ambros, *Geschichte der Musik* (III, p. 244); P. Wagner, *Geschichte der Messe* (I, p. 175); F. J. Fétis, *Biographie des Musiciens* (II, p. 95); A. Pirro, "Dokumente über Antoine Brumel, Louis van Pullaer und Crispin van Stappen," *Zeitschrift für Musikwissenschaft* (March 1929); J. Delport, *Revue Liturgique et Musicale* XIV (Paris, 1930–31); Ch. van den Borren, *Études sur le XVᵉ siècle musical* (Antwerp, 1941); Gustave Reese, *Music in the Renaissance* (N.Y., 1954).

Brun, Alphonse, German-Swiss violinist; b. Frankfurt, Oct. 25, 1888; d. Bern, March 27, 1963. He studied in Zürich and Berlin; in 1912 settled in Bern, where he organized a renowned string quartet; also was active as teacher.

Brun, Fritz, Swiss composer and conductor; b. Lucerne, Aug. 18, 1878; d. Grosshöchstetten, Switzerland, Nov. 29, 1959. He studied in Lucerne and at Cologne; then lived in Berlin, in London and in Dormund; finally settled in Bern, where he taught at the Cons. and conducted the Bern Symph. Orch. He wrote 10 symphonies, much chamber music and choruses.

BIBLIOGRAPHY: *Kleine Festgabe für Fritz Brun* (Bern, 1941).

Brün, Herbert, Israeli composer; b. Berlin, July 9, 1918. In 1936 he emigrated to Palestine, where he studied composition in Jerusalem with Stefan Wolpe; later took courses at Columbia Univ. in New York. In 1950 he settled in Tel Aviv. In 1963 he joined the faculty of the Univ. of Illinois, and in 1969–70 taught composition at Ohio State Univ. In his works he explores the potentialities of computers as a catalytic factor for modern composition.

WORKS: The titles of his works often suggest paradoxical logic; among them are 3 string quartets (1953, 1957, 1961); *Mobile* for orch. (1958); *Futility* for electronic sounds, and voice on tapes (1964); *Gestures for 11* for chamber ensemble (1964); *Sonoriferous Loops* for an instrumental ensemble and tape (1964); a group of works for varying ensembles under the provocative title *Non sequitur* (1966); Trio for Trumpet, Trombone and Percussion (1966); *Mutatis mutandis* for "interpreters" (1968); Nonet (1969).

Brune, Adolf Gerhard, composer; b. Bakkum, near Hannover, June 21, 1870; d. Chicago, April 21, 1935. He studied piano with his father; came to the U.S. in 1889 and was organist in Peoria, Ill.; settled in Chicago in 1894; studied piano with Liebling and composition with Ziehn there, then taught piano and composition at Chicago Musical College (1898–1917). He wrote 3 symphonies and the symph. poems, *Lied des Singschwans* and *Evangeline.*

Bruneau, Alfred (Louis-Charles-Bonaventure-Alfred), French opera composer; b. Paris, March 3, 1857; d. there, June 15, 1934. In 1873 he entered the Paris Cons., where he was a pupil of Franchomme; won the first cello prize in 1876; later studied harmony with Savard and composition with Massenet; in 1881 he won the Prix de Rome with his cantata *Sainte-Geneviève.* He was music critic for *Gil Blas* (1892–95); then for *Le Figaro* and *Le Matin;* from 1903–04 was first conductor at the Opéra-Comique in 1900 he was made a member of the "Conseil Supérieur" at the Cons. and in 1909 succeeded Reyer as Inspector of music instruction. He made extensive tours of Russia, England, Spain and the Netherlands, conducting his own works. He was made a knight of the "Légion d'Honneur" in 1895; received the title "Commandeur de St.-Charles" in 1907; became a member of the Académie des beaux Arts in 1925. His role in the evolution of French opera is of great importance; he introduced realistic drama on the French musical stage, working along parallel lines with Zola in literature. He used Zola's subjects for his most spectacular opera, *L'Ouragan,* and also for the operas *Messidor* and *L'Enfant-Roi.* In accordance with this naturalistic trend, Bruneau made free use of harsh dissonance when it was justified by the dramatic action of the plot.

WORKS: operas (most of them produced in Paris at the Opéra-Comique): *Kérim* (June 9, 1887), *Le Rêve* (June 18, 1891), *L'Attaque du Moulin* (Nov. 23, 1893), *Messidor* (Feb. 19, 1897), *L'Ouragan* (April 29, 1901), *L'Enfant-Roi* (March 3, 1905), *Naïs Micoulin* (Monte Carlo, Feb. 2, 1907), *La Faute de l'Abbé Mouret* (March 1, 1907), *Les Quatre Journées* (Dec. 25, 1916), *Le Roi Candaule* (Dec. 1, 1920), *Angelo, tyran de Padoue* (Jan. 16, 1928), *Virginie* (Jan. 7, 1931); ballets: *L'Amoureuse leçon* (Feb. 6, 1913) and *Les Bacchantes* (after Euripides; Oct. 30, 1912); other works: the overtures *Ode héroïque* and *Léda;* symph. poem, *La Belle au Bois dormant;* symph. poem with chorus, *Penthésilée;* a requiem; *Lieds de France* and *Chansons à danser* (both to poems by C. Mendès); *Les Chants de la Vie* (to poems by H. Bataille, F. Gregh, etc.); *Le Navire* for voice and orch.; pieces for various combinations of string and wind instruments. he published *Musiques d'hier et de demain* (1900); *La Musique français* (1901); *Musiques de Russie et musiciens de France* (1903; German transl. by M. Graf in *Die Musik,* Berlin, 1904); *La vie et les œuvres de Gabriel Fauré* (1925); *Massenet* (1934).

BIBLIOGRAPHY: A. Hervey, "Alfred Bruneau," in *Living Masters of Music* (London, 1907); O. Séré in *Musiciens d'aujourd'hui* (Paris, 1911); J. Tiersot, *Un*

Demi-siècle de musique française (1918); A. Boschot, *La Vie et les œuvres d'Alfred Bruneau* (Paris, 1937); for detailed lists of performances see A. Loewenberg, *Annals of Opera* (1943; new ed., 1955).

Brunelli, Antonio, Italian theorist and contrapuntist of the late 16th and early 17th centuries. He was a pupil of G. M. Nanini; served as maestro di cappella and organist at San Miniato, Tuscany, through 1606; then held the same posts at the Cathedral of Prato until 1610, and in Florence from 1614–16, where he was also maestro de cappella to the Grand Duke of Tuscany. Between 1605 and 1621 he published motets, canzonette, psalms, madrigals, requiems, etc.; also a ballet, which has been reprinted by Eitner. Some of his works also appeared in J. Donfried's *Promptuarium Musicum* (1623). He published the theoretical pamphlets *Regole utilissime per li scolari che desiderano imparare a cantare, . . . con la dichiarazione de tempi, proporzioni et altri accidenti che ordinariamente s'usono* (Florence, 1606; one of the first published methods for voice); *Esercizi ad 1 e 2 voci* (Florence, 1607); and *Regole et dichiarazioni de alcuni contrappunti doppii . . . con diversi canoni sopra un solo canto fermo* (Florence, 1610).

Brunetti, Domenico, Italian composer; b. Bologna, later part of 16th century. He was organist at the Church of S. Domenico about 1609; was maestro di cappella at the Bologna Cathedral (1620); founded (with F. Bertacchi) at Bologna the Accademia dei Filoschici (1633), which later was absorbed into the Accademia Filarmonica. Publ. *Euterpe* (Venice, 1606); *Varii Concentus unica, voce, duabus, tribus, quatuor vel pluribus cum gravi et acuto ad Organum* (Venice, 1609); *Canticum Deiparae Virginis Octies iuxta singulos Rhytmorum Sacrorum . . .* (Venice, 1621). Several of his compositions (motets, madrigals, etc.) were publ. in contemporary collections (1611–26) of A. Schadeo, G. Donfried, A. N. di Treviso, F. Sammaruco, Z. Zanetti, and G. P. Biandrà.

Brunetti, Gaetano, Italian violinist and composer; b. probably in Fano, 1744; d. in Culminal de Oreja, near Madrid, Dec. 16, 1798. He studied with Nardini, and in about 1762 went to Madrid; in 1767 was appointed violinist in the Royal Chapel in Madrid, remaining in this post until his death. He composed many works for the Spanish Court, and also for the Duke of Alba; Boccherini, who was in Madrid during the same years as Brunetti, was also favored by the Court and the aristocracy, but there was apparently no rivalry between them as commissions were plentiful.
WORKS: Brunetti's productivity was astounding; he wrote 32 symphonies, 6 overtures, numerous dances for orch.; 12 sextets, 72 quintets, 50 quartets, 30 trios; 67 for violin and basso continuo; 23 divertimenti for violin, viola and cello; also an opera *Jason,* produced in Madrid on Oct. 4, 1768. The Library of Congress in Washington has a large collection of Brunetti's manuscripts.
BIBLIOGRAPHY: J. Subirá, *La música en la casa de Alba* (Madrid, 1927); Alice Belgray, *Gaetano Brunetti, an Exploratory Bio-bibliographical Study* (Univ. of Michigan, 1970).

Bruni, Antonio Bartolomeo, Italian violinist and composer; b. Cuneo, Jan 28, 1759; d. there, Aug. 5, 1821. He studied with Pugnani in Turin; in 1781 went to Paris as a theater orch. conductor. There he wrote 18 operas, of which the most successful were *Célestine* (Paris, Oct. 15, 1787), *Claudine* (Paris, March 6, 1794), and *La Rencontre en voyage* (Paris, April 28, 1798). He also wrote music for the violin; publ. a violin method and a viola method (the latter reprinted in 1928).
BIBLIOGRAPHY: G. Cesari, H. Closson, L. de La Laurencie, A. Della Corte, and C. Zino, *Antonio Bartolomeo Bruni, musicista cuneese* (Turin, 1931).

Brunold, Paul, French pianist, organist and writer on music; b. Paris, Oct. 14, 1875; d. there Sept. 14, 1948. He was a pupil of Marmontel (piano) and Lavignac (theory) at the Paris Cons.; later studied with Paderewski. In 1915 he became organist at St. Gervais, in Paris. With H. Expert, he edited the *Anthologie des maîtres français du clavecin des XVIIe et XVIIIe siècles;* with A. Tessier he bought out a complete edition of Chambonnière's works; he also edited 2 volumes of works by Dieupart for the Lyre-Bird Press of Paris (*6 Suites pour clavecin* and *Airs et Chansons*). He published the book *Histoire du grand orgue de l'Église St. Gervais à Paris* (1934).

Brunswick, Mark, American composer; b. New York, Jan. 6, 1902; d. London, May 26, 1971. He studied theory of composition with Rubin Goldmark in New York (1918–23); then took lessons with Ernest Bloch in Cleveland and with Nadia Boulanger in Paris (until 1929); later lived in Vienna. Returning to New York in 1937 he taught at various schools; was member of the music department of the College of the City of New York from 1946 to 1967.
WORKS: *2 Movements* for string quartet (1925); *Lysistrata* for mezzo-soprano, women's chorus and orch. (1930); Fantasia for Viola (1932); Symphony in B-flat (Minneapolis, March 7, 1947); Quartet for Violin, Viola, Cello and Double Bass (1957); Septet, for wind quintet, viola and cello (1958); 5 Madrigals for chorus, viola, cello and double bass (1958–66); also *Eros and Death,* a choral symph. to texts from Greek and Roman poetry (1932–54). He left an unfinished opera, *The Master Builder,* after Ibsen.

Bruscantini, Sesto, Italian baritone; b. Porto Civitanova, Dec. 10, 1919. He studied with Luigi Ricci in Rome; made his operatic debut at La Scala in Milan in 1949. In 1951 he joined the Glyndebourne Festivals, where he distinguished himself in the operas of Mozart and Rossini, particularly in the buffo parts.

Brusilovsky, Evgeny, Soviet composer; b. Rostov-on-the-Don, Nov. 12, 1905. He studied composition with Maximilian Steinberg at the Leningrad Cons., graduating in 1931. In 1933 he was commissioned by the Leningrad Union of Soviet Composers to go to Kazakhstan to help organize local musical activities there. He settled at Alma-Ata, the capital of Kazakhstan; wrote operas and ballets in the folk-like idiom, using native instruments.
WORKS: the operas (all produced in the Alma-Ata

Opera House): *Kyz-Zhibek* (1934); *Altynastyk (Seed of Gold,* 1940); *Guardia, alga! (Forward, Guardians!* 1942); *Dudaray* (1953); *The Heirs* (1964); several ballets; 7 symphonies (1931, 1933, 1944, 1957, 1965, 1966, 1969); Piano Concerto (1947); Trumpet Concerto (1965); Cello Concerto (1969); works for folk instruments; arrangements of Kazakhstan songs; piano pieces.

BIBLIOGRAPHY: A. Kelberg, *Evgeny Brusilovsky* (Moscow, 1959).

Brusselmans, Michel, Belgian composer; b. Paris, of Belgian parents, Feb. 12, 1886; d. Brussels, Sept. 20, 1960. He studied with Huberti, Tinel and Gilson at the Brussels Cons.; won the Agniez Prix in 1914 for his symph. poem, *Hélène de Sparte.* In 1922 he became editor for the Paris music publisher Jamin, and spent most of his life in France. His music is romantic in inspiration and programmatic in content.

WORKS: 3 ballets: *Les Néréides* (1911), *Kermesse flamande* (1912), and *Les Sylphides* (on themes of Chopin); an oratorio *Jésus* (1936); a *Psaume LVI* for soprano, chorus and orch. (1954); 3 symphonies (1924; 1934; *Levantine,* 1956–57); *Ouverture fériale* (1908); *Scènes Breugheliennes* for orch. (1911); *Télémaque a gaulus* for chamber orch. (1923); *Esquisses flamandes* for orch. (1927); *Légende du gapeau* for horn, and orch. or piano (1930); *Rhapsodie flamande* for orch. (1931); *Scènes provençales* for orch. (1931); *Suite phrygienne* for orch. (1932); *Suite d'après les Caprices de Paganini* for orch. (1936); *Suite Divertissement* for orch. (1937); *Rhapsodie* for horn and orch. (1938); Organ Concerto (1938); *Ouverture héroïque* (1942); Sinfonietta (1954); Violin Sonata (1915); Cello Sonata (1916); *Prelude and Fugue* for 8 winds (1923); *Visages de Paris* for piano (1946); songs.

Brustad, Bjarne, Norwegian composer; b. Oslo, March 4, 1895. He studied at the Cons. in Oslo; then took violin under Carl Flesch in Berlin (1915–16). From 1919 to 1922 he was violinist in the Oslo Philh. Orch.; 1928–43, was first viola. He also has conducted orchestras in Oslo; in 1951, received a government life pension. Brustad's music is romantic in its evocations, and traditional in form.

WORKS: an unperformed opera, *Atlantis* (1945); 2 suites for orch. (1920; ballet music, 1952); 4 violin concertos: No. 1 (1922), No. 2 (1927), No. 3 (unfinished), No. 4 (1961); *Atlantis,* symph. poem (1923; withdrawn); Concertino for Viola and Chamber Orch. (1932); Rhapsody for Violin and Orch. (1933); Concerto Grosso for orch. (1938); *Variations sérieuses,* on a theme by Corelli, for orch. (1945); 9 symphonies: No. 1 (1948), No. 2 (1951), No. 3 (1953), No. 4 (1957), No. 5 (1967), No. 6 (1970), No. 7 (1971), No. 8 (1972), No. 9 (1973); *Overture* (1950); Concerto for clarinet and String Orch. (1970); 3 string quartets (1919, 1929, 1959); *Capricci* for violin and viola (1931); Partita for Solo Viola (1931); *Eventyr-Suite (Fairytale-Suite)* for solo violin (1932); *Kinderspiele* for piano (1934; orchestrated, 1955); 3 sonatas for solo violin (1935, 1956, 1957); Trio No. 1 for clarinet, violin and viola (1938); *Fanitull Suite* for solo violin (1946); Trio No. 2, Serenade, for clarinet, violin and bassoon (1947); Violin Sonata (1950); Divertimento for Solo Flute (1958).

Bruyck, Karl Debrois van, Austrian writer on music; b. Brünn, March 14, 1828; d. Waidhofen, Aug. 5, 1902. Originally a law student in Vienna, he turned to music in 1850. He published *Technische und ästhetische Analyse des Wohltemperierten Klaviers* (Leipzig, 1867; 3rd ed. 1925); and *Die Entwicklung der Klaviermusik von J. S. Bach bis R. Schumann* (1880).

Bruynèl, Ton, Dutch composer of electronic music; b. Utrecht, Jan. 26, 1934. He studied piano at the Utrecht Cons.; then worked in the studio for electronic music at the State Univ. of Utrecht; in 1957 organized a private electronic music studio. Most of his compositions involve instruments in combination with electronics, and some require theatrical visualizations.

WORKS: *Resonance I,* theater piece (ballet) in collaboration with Japanese-American sculptor Chinkichi Tajiri and American painter Sam Middleton (1960–62); *Reflexes* for Birma drum (1961); *Resonance II,* theater piece in collaboration with the Dutch poet Gerrit Kouwenaar (1963); *Relief* for organ and 4 soundtracks (1964); *Mobile* for 2 soundtracks (1965); *Milieu* for 2 soundtracks and organ (1965–66); *Arc* for organ and 4 soundtracks (1966–67); *Mekaniek* for wind quintet and 2 soundtracks (1967); *Decor,* a ballet score (1967); *Signs* for wind quintet, 2 sountracks and video projection (1969); *Ingredients* for piano and soundtracks (1970); *Intra I* for bass clarinet and soundtrack (1971); *Elegy* for female voice and 2 soundtracks (1972); *Looking Ears* for bass clarinet, grand piano and soundtracks (1972); *Phases* for 4 soundtracks (Utrecht, Jan. 10, 1975); *Soft Song* for oboe and 2 soundtracks (1975); *Dialogue* for bass clarinet and soundtracks (1976).

Bruzdowicz, Joanna, Polish composer; b. Warsaw, May 17, 1943. She studied music theory with Sikorski at the Warsaw State School of Music; then went to Paris, where she took lessons with Nadia Boulanger and Messiaen; worked there with the "Groupe de Recherches Musicales." Eventually she went to live in Belgium.

WORKS: 2 operas, *The Penal Colony,* after Kafka (Tours, 1972) and *Les Troyennes,* after Euripides (Saint-Denis, France, 1973); a ballet, *Le Petit Prince,* after Saint-Exupéry (Brussels, Dec. 10, 1976); *Sketches from the Harbor,* cycle for mezzo-soprano, flute and percussion (1967); *Esquisses* for flute, piano, viola and cello (1969); *Jour d'ici et d'ailleurs* for narrator, chorus and instruments (1971); *Épisode* for piano and 13 instruments (1973); *Epitaph* for harpsichord and tape (1973); *Esitanza* for piano, 4-hands (1973); *Le Beau Danube bleu* for 2 pianos and tape (1973–74); Piano Concerto (1974); Symphony (1975); Violin Concerto (1975–76).

Bryant, Allan, American composer; b. Detroit, July 12, 1931. He attended Princeton Univ.; then went to Germany, where he worked at the electronic studio in Cologne. Returning to the U.S. he wrote music with multimedia resources designed for theatrical representation. His works include *Quadruple Play* for amplified rubber bands utilizing contact microphones and coordinated with an audio controlled lighting system (1966); *Impulses* for a variety of percussion, con-cussion and discussion sounds (1967); *Bang-Bang* for loud instruments including an amplified circular violin (1967); *X-es Sex,* an intersexual happening with boots and balloons (1967); also political works, e.g. *Liberate Isang Yun* (1967) for a multimillion-decibel electronic sound calculated to reach the ears of the South Korean abductors of the dissident Korean composer Isang Yun from West Berlin (he was liberated in 1969 yielding to the tremendous acoustical pressure of the Bryant piece).

Bryennius, Manuel, Byzantine writer on music, who flourished about 1320. His chief work, *Harmonicorum libri 3,* published in parallel Greek and Latin texts by Johannes Wallis in *Operum mathematicorum vol. 3* (Oxford, 1699), gives a comprehensive account of Greek music theories.
BIBLIOGRAPHY: R. Westphal, *Griechische Rhythmik und Harmonik* (Leipzig, 1867).

Bryson, (Robert) Ernest, English composer; b. Liverpool, March 31, 1867; d. St. Briavels, Gloucestershire, April 20, 1942. He was engaged in trade, and music was his avocation. He wrote 2 symphonies; several orchestral sketches, and an opera, *The Leper's Flute,* which was produced in Glasgow on Oct. 15, 1926.

Bucchi, Valentino, Italian composer; b. Florence, Nov. 29, 1916; d. Rome, May 9, 1976. He studied composition with Frazzi and Dallapiccola, and music history with Torrefranca at the Univ. of Florence, graduating in 1944; subsequently held teaching posts at the Florence Cons. (1945–52 and 1954–57), at the Cons. of Venice (1952–54) and at the Cons. of Perugia (1957–58); was music director of the Accademia Filarmonica Romana (1958–60) and artistic director of the Teatro Comunale in Bologna (1963–65); from 1969 he was musical consultant for Radio Italiano.
WORKS: operas *Il Giuoco del Barone* (Florence, Dec. 20, 1944), *Il Contrabasso,* after Chekhov (Florence, May 20, 1954), *Una notte in Paradiso* (Florence, May 11, 1960), and *Il coccodrillo* (Florence, May 9, 1970); the ballets *Racconto Siciliano* (Rome, Jan 17, 1956), and *Mirandolina* (Rome, March 12, 1957); *Ballata del Silenzio* for orch. (1951); *Concerto in rondo* for piano and orch. (1957); *Concerto lirico* for violin and strings (1958); *Concerto grottesco* for double bass and string orch. (1967); String Quartet (1956); Concerto for Clarinet Solo (1969); *Ison* for cello solo (1971); *Colloquio corale* for narrator, vocal solo, chorus and orch. (1971), etc. He also made arrangements of medieval madrigal and mystery plays. In his works he continued the national Italian tradition of the musical theater; in his instrumental music he attempts to modernize the polyphony of the Renaissance, along the lines established by Malipiero.

Bucci, Mark, American composer; b. New York, Feb. 26, 1924. He studied with Jacobi and Giannini at the Juilliard School of Music and with Copland at the Berkshire Music Center, Tanglewood; adopted a pragmatic method of composition in a strong rhythmic style, in modern but tonal harmonies, particularly effective in his stage works.
WORKS: one-act operas, *The Boor* (after Chekhov,

N.Y., Dec. 29, 1949), *The Dress* (N.Y., Dec. 8, 1953), *Sweet Betsy from Pike* (N.Y., Dec. 8, 1953), *The Thirteen Clocks* (N.Y., Dec. 29, 1953), *Tale for a Deaf Ear* (Tanglewood, Aug. 5, 1957), *The Hero* (Educational Television, N.Y., Sept. 24, 1965). His *Concerto for a Singing Instrument* was first performed as a *Concerto for Kazoo* by the N.Y. Philharmonic, Leonard Berstein conducting, on March 26, 1960, with Anita Darian as kazoo virtuoso.

Bucharoff (real name **Buchhalter**), **Simon,** Russian-American pianist and composer; b. Berditchev, April 20, 1881; d. Chicago, Nov. 24, 1955. He settled in America as a youth; studied piano with Paolo Gallico in N.Y., and later with Julius Epstein and Emil Sauer in Vienna. He occupied various teaching posts; lived principally in Chicago and Hollywood.
WORKS: operas, *A Lover's Knot* (Chicago Opera, Jan. 15, 1916), *Sakahra* (Frankfurt, Nov. 8, 1924; revised in 1953), *Jewel, Wastrel*; several symph. poems *(Reflections in the Water; Drunk; Doubt; Joy Sardonic,* etc.); published *The Modern Pianist's Textbook* (N.Y., 1931).
BIBLIOGRAPHY: E. E. Hipsher, *American Opera and Its Composers* (Philadelphia, 1927; pp. 93–97).

Bücher, Karl, German economist and writer on music; b. Kirchberg, near Wiesbaden, Feb. 16, 1847; d. Leipzig, Nov. 12, 1930. As professor of economics at the Leipzig Univ. (1892–1916), he became interested in the correlation between social conditions among primitive peoples and music; he published a book *Arbeit und Rhythmus* (1896), in which the origin of music is traced to natural rhythmic exertions during manual labor, with group singing in unison as a natural expedient for team-work. The book aroused a great deal of controversy, and went through several printings; 6th edition was published in 1924.
BIBLIOGRAPHY: Lotte (Bucheim) Stratil-Sauer, *Volksliedhaftes unter Büchers deutschen Arbeitsliedern* (Leipzig, 1931); also Bücher's memoirs, *Lebenserinnerungen* (1919).

Buchmayer, Richard, German pianist and music editor; b. Zittau, April 19, 1856; d. Tams (Salzburg), May 24, 1934. He studied at the Dresden Cons.; later taught piano there. In his recitals he presented many unknown works by old masters. In 1903 he discovered, in the municipal library of Lüneburg, some valuable manuscripts of 17th century organ and piano works, throwing new light on the subject of organ tablatures. The results of these studies were publ. in *Sammelbände der Internationalen Musik-Gesellschaft, Bach-Jahrbuch* (1908), *Signale,* etc. He edited Ch. Ritter's cantata *O sanctissime sponse, Jesu* and G. Böhm's cantata *Mein Freund ist mein;* also 5 volumes of piano and organ works of the 17th century (1927).

Buchner, Hans, German organist; b. Ravensburg, Württemberg, Oct. 26, 1483; d. probably in Constance, mid-February 1538. His father was an organist in Ravensburg, and gave Buchner his first instruction. After a period of study in Vienna, he obtained the post of organist at the Cathedral of Constance (1512). His magnum opus is a *Fundamentum,* a manual for composition and improvisation on the organ (1551).

Buchner, Philipp Friedrich, German organist; b. Wertheim, Sept. 11, 1614; d. Würzburg, March 23, 1669. He was a chorister in Frankfurt; in 1634 became church organist there; from 1641 he traveled in Poland and Italy; in 1647 he was in Mainz. His *Concerti ecclesiatici* were published in 2 books (Venice, 1642; 1644); he also wrote instrumental music for violins, violas and cembalo.

Bucht, Gunnar, Swedish composer; b. Stockholm, Aug. 5, 1927. He studied musicology at Uppsala Univ. (1947-53); concurrently took lessons in theory with Blomdahl (1947-51); later studied composition in Germany with Orff (1954), in Italy with Petrassi (1954-55), and in Paris with Max Deutsch (1961-62). He taught at the Stockholm Univ. (1965-69); was also employed in diplomatic service as cultural attaché at the Swedish Embassy in Bonn (1970-73). His music retains traditional forms, while adopting diverse modern techniques.
WORKS: an opera, *Tronkrävarna,* after Ibsen (*The Pretenders,* 1961-64; Stockholm, Sept. 10, 1966); an opera-oratorio, *Jerikos murar (The Walls of Jericho,* 1966-67; reworked as an electronic piece, 1970); 7 symphonies: No. 1 (1952; Swedish Radio, Dec. 6, 1953); No. 2 (1953; unperformed); No. 3 (1954; Swedish Radio, April 17, 1955); No. 4 (1957-58; Stockholm, April 3, 1959); No. 5 (1960; Stockholm, Jan. 14, 1962); No. 6 (1961-62; Stockholm, Nov. 20, 1963); No. 7 (1970-72; Norrköping, March 26, 1972); *Introduction and Allegro* for string orch. (1950); *Meditation* for piano and orch. (1950); Cello Concerto (1954); *Symphonic Fantasy* for orch. (1955); *Divertimento* for Orch. (1955-56); *Dagen svalnar (The Day Cools)* for soprano and orch. or piano (1956); *Envar sin egen professor* for tenor, chorus and orch. (1957); *La fine della diaspora,* after Quasimodo's "Auschwitz," for chorus and orch. (1958; Stockholm, Oct. 4, 1963); *Couplets et Refrains* for orch. (1960); *Dramma per Musica* for orch. (1963; symph. intermezzo from second act of opera *Tronkrävarna); Strangaspel* for strings (1965); *Eine lutherische Messe* for soloists, mixed and children's choruses and orch. (1972-73); *Winter Organ* for orch. (1974); *Music for Lau* for children's chorus, wind orch., percussion, double basses and tape (1974-75); *Theme and Variations* for piano (1949); String Quintet (1949-50); 2 piano sonatas (1951, 1959); 2 string quartets (1951, 1959); *5 Bagatelles* for string quartet (1953); Sonata for Piano and Percussion (1955); *Hommage à Edith Södergran* for mixed chorus (1956); *Kattens öron* for narrator, saxophone, double bass and percussion (1959); *Hund skenar glad (Dog Runs Happy),* chamber cantata for voice, female chorus and 8 instruments (1961); *Ein Wintermärchen* for voice and instrumental ensemble (1962); *6 arstidssånger (Season Songs)* for voice and piano (1965); *Symphonie pour la musique libérée* for tape (1969).

Büchtger, Fritz, German composer; b. Munich, Feb. 14, 1903. He studied composition with Beer-Walbrunn and general theory of music with Wolfgang von Waltershausen. He became actively involved in the propa-ganda for modern music between the two wars. Being an Aryan, he was able to remain unmolested during the Nazi period, but was compelled to write and conduct only nationalistically permissible music. In his works he excels in the application of modern techniques, including dodecaphony, to religious or other solemn subjects.
WORKS: two oratorios after the Apocalypse, *Der weisse Reiter* (1948) and *Das gläserne Meer* (1953); *The Resurrection* for chorus and orch. (1954); *Die Verklärung,* chamber oratorio (1957); *Christmas Oratorio* (1959); *Die Traumstadt* for 5 choruses (1961); *John the Baptist,* oratorio for baritone, chorus and orch. (1962); *Concerto for String Orch.* (1950); *Concerto for Orch.* (1957); Violin Concerto (1963); 3 string quartets (1948, 1958, 1967); *Strukturen* for 4 woodwinds and strings (1968); and several song cycles.

Buck, Dudley, American organist, composer and teacher; b. Hartford, Conn., March 10, 1839; d. Orange, N.J., Oct. 6, 1909. He studied piano with W. J. Babcock; later at the Leipzig Cons. with Plaidy and Moscheles (piano), Hauptmann (comp.) and J. Rietz (instrumentation) and later in Paris. Returning to America in 1862 he held posts as church organist in Hartford, Chicago, Boston, Brooklyn and elsewhere. He was one of the first American composers to achieve general recognition for his church music and sacred and secular cantatas.
WORKS: comic opera *Deseret, or a Saint's Affliction* (N.Y., Oct. 11, 1880); grand opera *Serapis;* symph. overture *Marmion* (1880); a Canzonetta and Bolero for violin and orch.; organ music: *Grand Sonata; Triumphal March; Impromptu and Pastorale; Rondo-Caprice; At Evening; Four Tone Pictures;* various transcriptions and sets of variations; also 18 *Pedal-phrasing Studies* (2 books). He wrote *Illustrations in Choir-Accompaniment, with Hints on Registration,* a valuable handbook for organists and students.

Buck, Dudley, Jr., American tenor, son of the preceding; b. Hartford, Conn., April 4, 1869; d. Fairfield, Conn., Jan. 13, 1941. He was a pupil of Vannucini in Florence, Stockhausen in Frankfurt, J. de Reske in Paris, Shakespeare and Randegger in London; made his debut as Turidu in *Cavalleria Rusticana* in Sheffield, England, Sept. 8, 1895. Until 1899 he appeared frequently throughout Great Britian in opera, oratorio and concert; then returned to the U.S. and was active as a singing teacher in N.Y.; eventually settled in Chicago, where he was affiliated with the Columbia School of Music.

Buck, Sir Percy Carter, English organist; b. London, March 25, 1871; d. there, Oct. 3, 1947. He studied at the Guildhall School and Royal College of Music; subsequently served as church organist. From 1901-27 he was music director at Harrow School; later taught at the Universities of Dublin, Glasgow, London and Sheffield. His works include an overture for orch., *Cœur de Lion;* String Quartet; Piano Quintet; sonatas, piano pieces, etc. He was the author of *Ten Years of University Music in Oxford* (1894; with Mee and Woods); *Unfigured Harmony* (1911); *Organ Playing*

(1912); *First Year at the Organ* (1912); *The Organ: A Complete Method for the Study of Technique and Style; Acoustics for Musicians* (1918); *The Scope of Music* (Oxford, 1924); *Psychology for Musicians* (London, 1944); also was editor of the introductory volume and volumes I and II of the 2nd edition of the *Oxford History of Music.*

Bücken, Ernst, eminent German musicologist; b. Aachen, May 2, 1884; d. Overath, near Cologne, July 28, 1949. He studied with Sandberger in Munich; also with Courvoisier; *Dr. phil.,* 1912 with a thesis on Anton Reicha; in 1920 became a member of the staff from 1945 lived in Overath.

WRITINGS: *München als Musikstadt* (1923); *Der heroische Stil in der Oper* (1924); *Führer und Probleme der neuen Music* (1924); *Musikalische Characterköpfe* (1925); "Frage des Stilverfalls," in Kroyer Festschrift (1933); *Deutsche Musikkunde* (1935); *Die Musik der Nationen* (1937); *Robert Schumann* (Cologne, 1940); *Kulturgeschichte der deutschen Musik* (1942); editor of the monumental *Handbuch der Musikwissenschaft* in 10 vols., begun in 1927, he contributed 3 vols.: *Die Musik des 19. Jahrhunderts bis zur Moderne* (1928); *Musik des Rokokos und der Klassik* (1929); and *Geist und Form im musikalischen Kunstwerk* (1929); compiled the collection *Musiker-Briefe* (1940).

Buckner, Milt (Milton), American jazz pianist; b. St. Louis, July 10, 1915. He played in Lionel Hampton's band; popularized the 'locked-hands' technique of parallel block chords; perfected the rigid rhythmical patterns in the blues style; was the first to use the Hammond organ in jazz.

Buczynski, Walter, Canadian composer and pianist; b. Toronto, Dec. 17, 1933. He studied music theory at the Cons. of Toronto; took lessons in composition with Darius Milhaud in Paris in the summer of 1956, and also with Nadia Boulanger (1960 and 1962). He studied piano mainly in Warsaw, Poland, where he has ethnic roots. Returning to Canada in 1962, he was appointed teacher of piano and theory at the Cons. of Toronto. His own music is influenced by the modern Polish school of composition; the titles of his works are in the spirit of aggressive modernism.

WORKS: chamber opera *From the Buczynski Book of the Living* for soprano, tenor, clarinet, piano and percussion (1972); Piano Trio (1954); Suite for Wind Quintet (1955); Divertimento, for violin, cello, clarinet and bassoon (1957); *Mr. Rhinoceros and His Musicians* for narrator, soprano and baritone (Canadian Radio, Dec. 25, 1965); *Do Re Mi* for soprano, tenor, 2 actors and instrumental ensemble (Canadian Radio, Dec. 13, 1967); *Two-and-a-Half Squares in a Circle* for flute, violin, cello and strings (1967); *4 Movements* for piano and strings (1969); *Zeroing In No. 1* for speaking voice, prepared piano and tape (1971); *Zeroing In No. 2 (Distraction and Then)* for orch. groups in the audience and on-stage strings (1971); *Zeroing In No. 3* for string quartet and orch. (1973); *Zeroing In No. 4 (Innards and Outards)* for soprano, flute, piano, and orch. (1972); *Zeroing In No. 5 (Dictionary of Mannerisms)* for piano (1972); *Three Against Many* for

flute, clarinet, bassoon, and orch. (1973); *27 Pieces for a 27-Minute Show* for piano (1973); Concerto for Violin, Cello and Orch. (1975); *Olympics '76* for brass quintet (1976); *The Tales of Nanabozho* for narrator and wind quintet (1976); songs; piano pieces for young people; piano pieces for adults; piano pieces for diverse ages.

Budashkin, Nicolai, Russian composer; b. Lubakhovka, in Kaluga region, Aug. 6, 1910, of a peasant family. After working as a blacksmith, he went to Moscow and took a course with Miaskovsky at the Moscow Cons. He specializes in music for Russian popular instruments in symphonic combinations; he wrote 2 concertos for domra and orch. (1944; 1947); Concert Variations for Balalaika with Orch. on a Russian folksong (1946), and works for ensembles consisting entirely of such instruments. His early *Festive Overture* (1937) has achieved considerable success in Russia.

Budd, Harold, American composer; b. Los Angeles, May 24, 1936. He studied composition, acoustics and esthetics with Gerald Strang and Aurelio de la Vega at San Fernando Valley State College, California (B.A., 1963) and at the Univ. of Southern California with Ingolf Dahl (M. Mus., 1966); in 1968 he was appointed to the faculty of the California Institute of the Arts. In the interim he earned his living as a jazz musician.

WORKS: His compositions are mostly for mixed media, some of them modular, capable of being choreographed one into another; some are mere verbalizations of the mode of performance in a frequently benumbing, stultifying, mesmerizing or fantasist manner. These works are *Analogies from Rothko* for orch. (1964); *The Sixth This Year* for orch. (1967); *September Music* (1967); *November* (1967; displayed as a painting at the Museum of Contemporary Crafts in New York); *Black Flowers,* a 'quiet chamber ritual for 4 performers,' to be staged in semi-darkness on the threshold of visibility and audibility (1968); *Intermission Piece,* to be played at random with the "amplitude spectrum barely audible" during intermission, with the audience "physically or conceptually, absent" (1968; Hartford, Conn., Jan. 28, 1970); *One Sound,* for string quartet glissando (1968); *Mangus Colorado* for amplified gongs (1969; Buffalo, Feb. 4, 1970); *Lovely Thing* for piano, telling the player to "select a chord—if in doubt call me (in lieu of performance) at 213–662–7819 for spiritual advice" (first performed, Memphis, Tenn., Oct. 23, 1969); *Lovely Thing* for strings (1969); *California 99* (1969); *The Candy-Apple Revision* (1970).

Bughici, Dumitru, Rumanian composer; b. Jassy, Nov. 14, 1921. After completing a course of elementary music at the Jassy Cons. he went to Leningrad, where he studied at the Cons. with Salmanov and Schnitke (1950–55). Returning to Rumania, he was appointed to the faculty of the Bucharest Cons.

WORKS: 2 ballets: *Lupta Luminii cu întunericul (Light and Darkness Wrestling,* (1965), and *Energie* (1965); Violin Concerto (1955); a symph. poem, *Evocare (Evocation,* 1956); *Poem concertant* for cello and orch. (1957); 3 sinfoniettas: No. 1, *Tinereţii (Youth,*

1958); No. 2 (1962); No. 3, *Musică de concert* (1969); *4 Choreographic Pictures* for orch. (1959); *Heroic Poem, Filimon Sîrbu* for orch. (1959); *Poemul primăverii (Spring Poem)* for violin and orch. (1960); 3 symphonies: No. 1, *Simfonia-Poem* (1960–61); No. 2, *Simfonia-coregrafică* (1964, revised 1967); No. 3, *Ecouri de Jazz (Jazz Echoes*, 1966); *Poemul bucuriei (Poem of Joy)* for orch. (1962); *Bolero* for orch. (1963); *Monumentul (The Monument)* for orch. (1964); *Partită* for orch. (1965); *Dialoguri dramatica* for string orch. and flute (1967); *Omagiu* for orch. (1967); *Baladă concertantă* for violin and orch. (1969); Sonata for String Orch. (1970); *Melodie, Ritm, Culoare (Melody, Rhythm, Color)*, a jazz concerto for orch. (1970); *Sinfonietta da camera* for strings, flute, oboe and percussion (1971); *Poem Iubirii (Poem to Love)* for orch. (1971); *File de letopiset (Chronicle Pages)*, symphony in 6 pictures (1972); *Symphonic Fantasia*, in jazz rhythm, for orch. (1973–74); Cello Concerto (1974); Concerto for Trumpet and Orch., in jazz rhythm (1975); *Symphonia 1907* (1975–76); Suite for Violin and Piano (1953); *Scherzo* for cello and piano (1954); 4 string quartets: No. 1 (1954); No. 2 (1968); No. 3, *Plaiurile copilăriei (Realm of Childhood*, 1971); No. 4 (1976–77); *Fantasia* for trumpet and piano (1960); *Divertimento* (Trio No. 1) for violin, cello and piano (1961); Violin Sonata (1963); *Mic (Small) Divertissement* for violin, viola, cello, piano, clarinet and percussion (1967) Sonata for Solo Violin (1968); *Fantasia Quartet* (1969); *Miniatures* for brass quintet (1975); Trio No. 2 for violin, cello and piano (1977). He published (in Rumanian) the books, *The Suite and the Sonata* (1965), *The Musical Forms: Lied, Rondo, Variations, and Fugue* (1969) and *Dictionary of Musical Forms and Genera* (1976).

Bühler, Franz, German composer; b. Schneidheim, near Nördlingen, April 12, 1760; d. Augsburg, Feb. 4, 1823. He was a Benedictine monk at Donauwörth; choral conductor at Botzen (1794) and at Augsburg Cathedral (1801); wrote an opera *Die falschen Verdachte*; an oratorio, *Jesus, der göttliche Erlöser*; sonatas and preludes for organ; also several theoretical pamphlets.

Buhlig, Richard, American pianist; b. Chicago, Dec. 21, 1880; d. Los Angeles, Jan. 30, 1952. He studied in Chicago, and in Vienna with Leschetizky (1897–1900); made his début in recital in Berlin (1901); then toured Europe and the U.S. (American début with the Philadelphia Orchestra in N.Y., Nov. 5, 1907). In 1918 he was appointed teacher of piano at the Institute of Musical Arts, N.Y.; later returned to Europe; eventually settled in Los Angeles as performer and teacher.

Buketoff, Igor, American conductor; b. Hartford, Conn., May 29, 1915. He studied music at the Juilliard School in New York (1939–42). In 1943 he began his conducting career; appeared as guest conductor in America and in Europe; in 1959 conducted concerts in Russia under the auspices of the State Dept. Cultural Exchange Program. A musician of searching interests, he conducted programs of works of classical and modern music outside the common repertory, exhibiting a fine understanding of the various styles represented in these programs. In 1968 he became director of the St. Paul Opera Association.

Bukofzer, Manfred F., eminent German-American musicologist; b. Oldenburg, March 27, 1910; d. Oakland, California, Dec. 7, 1955. He studied at the Hoch Cons. in Frankfurt, and at the Univs. of Heidelberg, Berlin and Basel (Dr. phil., 1936); also took courses with Hindemith in Berlin. He lectured in Basel (1933–39); also at the Univs. of Oxford and Cambridge. In 1939 settled in the U.S.; became a naturalized citizen in 1945. He taught at Western Reserve Univ. in Cleveland (1940–41). In 1941 he became a member of the faculty of Univ. of California, Berkeley; a year before his untimely death was appointed chairman of the Music Dept. His numerous publications are distinguished by originality of historical and musical ideas coupled with precision of factual exposition; having mastered the English language, he was able to write brilliantly in British and American publications; he was also greatly esteemed as teacher.

WRITINGS: *Geschichte des englischen Diskants und des Fauxbourdons* (Strasbourg, 1936; very valuable); "Über leben und Werke von John Dunstable," *Acta musicologica* (1936); "Hegels Musikästhetik," in reports of *Deuxième Congrès d'Esthétique et de Science de l'Art* (Paris, 1937); "Kann die 'Blasquintentheorie' zur Erklärung primitiver Tonsysteme beitragen?" in *Anthropos* (1937); many other articles and important reviews in various magazines; also "Allegory in Baroque Music," *Journal of the Warburg Institute* (1939); *Sumer Is Icumen In: A Revision* (Berkeley, 1944), placing the date of this famous canon later than the generally accepted year 1240; *Music in the Baroque Era* (N.Y., 1947); *Studies in Medieval and Renaissance Music* (N.Y., 1950). He was also editor of the complete works of Dunstable (1954, Vol. VIII of *Musica Britannica*).

BIBLIOGRAPHY: David D. Boyden "In Memoriam: Manfred F. Bukofzer," *Musical Quarterly* (July 1956; contains a complete list of Bukofzer's writings).

Bull, John, famous English organist and contrapuntal composer; b. Somersetshire, England, c.1562; d. Antwerp, March 12 or 13, 1628. He was a pupil of William Blitheman in the Chapel Royal; organist of Hereford Cathedral, 1582; later also Master of the Children; 1585, member of the Chapel Royal, becoming organist in 1591, on the death of his master; 1586, Mus. Bac.; 1592, Mus. Doc., Oxon. In 1596, he was appointed, on Queen Elizabeth's recommendation, prof. of music at Gresham College, a post resigned on his marriage, 1607. In 1611 he was in the service of Prince Henry, and left the country two years later, becoming one of the organists to the Archduke at Brussels. In 1617 he became organist of the cathedral of Notre Dame at Antwerp. He was acquainted with the great organist and composer Sweelinck and, with him, exerted a marked influence on the development of contrapuntal keyboard music. 200 compositions are attributed to John Bull; a list is given in Ward's *Lives of the Gresham Professors* (1740); exercises and variations for the virginals, some canons, a sacred madrigal, and an anthem, were printed in the following collections: the *Fitzwilliam Virginal Book* (45; modern ed. by J. A.

Fuller-Maitland and W. Barclay Squire, London, 1899), *Benjamin Cosyn's Virginal Book* (23), *Will. Forster's Virginal Book* (3), Leighton's *The Tears or Lamentacions of a Sorrowfull Soule;* in *Parthenia* (pieces for virginals by Bull, Byrd, and Gibbons; new ed. by Margaret H. Glyn, London, 1927), and others. The complete keyboard works appear in *Musica Britannica* XIX (ed. Thurston Dart, 1963; rev. 1970). The conjecture put forward by some writers, notably by Leigh Henry in his book, *Dr. John Bull* (London, 1937), that Bull was the author of *God Save the King,* does not have a scintilla of evidence.
BIBLIOGRAPHY: Ch. Van den Borren, *Les Origines de la musique de Clavecin en Angleterre* (1913); Hugh Miller, "John Bull's Organ Works," *Music & Letters* (Jan. 1947); W. Mellers, "John Bull and English Keyboard Music," *Musical Quarterly* (July and Oct. 1954).

Bull, Ole Bornemann, famous Norwegian violinist; b. Bergen, Feb. 5, 1810; d. Lyso, near Bergen, Aug. 17, 1880. He received his first instruction in violin playing from a Danish teacher named Paulsen, but he soon struck out on a method of this own, ignoring academic study. In order to be able to play unbroken chords on all four strings, he used an almost level bridge and a flat fingerboard. At the age of nine he was admitted to a local orchestra. Later he was sent by his father to Christiania (Oslo) to study theology, but university training was not for him; for a time he conducted a musical society; in 1829 he went to Kassel, and applied to Spohr for instruction, but Spohr was highly critical of his playing, and he returned to Norway in considerable disillusion. There he gave a series of concerts; in 1831 he went to Paris, where he heard Paganini for the first time, and became determined to emulate the great Italian virtuoso. In this he succeeded only as far as eccentricity was concerned. In 1836–37 he played 274 concerts in England and Ireland; in 1840 he performed Beethoven's *Kreutzer Sonata* with Liszt at the piano. He made five tours in the U.S., playing popular music and his own compositions on American themes (*Niagara, Solitude of the Prairies, To the Memory of Washington,* etc.) and a number of his arrangements of Norwegian folksongs. He had a strong conviction that Norway should form its own national art, but the practical applications of his patriotism were failures. In 1845 he started a theatrical enterprise in Bergen to promote national drama and music, but the project did not succeed, and was abandoned after a few seasons. In 1852 he purchased a large piece of land (125,000 acres) in Pennsylvania for a Norwegian settlement, but his lack of business acumen made him a victim of an easy swindle; subsequent lawsuits drained his last resources. The settlement was planned on socialist lines, and was given the name Oleana, thus establishing a personal connection with the name of its unlucky founder. Despite these reverses and eccentricities for which Ole Bull was notorious, he became a great national figure, revered in Norway for his passionate love of his native land. Some of his compositions have been published (*La Preghiera d'una madre, Variazioni di brauvra, Polacca guerriera, Notturno,* etc.); their musical value is nil.

BIBLIOGRAPHY: J. Lie, *Ole Bulls breve i utdreg* (Copenhagen, 1881); Sara C. Bull, (his second wife), *Ole Bull: A Memoir* (Boston, 1883; German ed., Stuttgart, 1886); O. Vik, *Ole Bull* (Bergen, 1890); C. A. Aarvig, *Den unge Ole Bull* (Copenhagen, 1935); A. Björndal, *Ole Bull og Norsk folkemusik* (Bergen, 1940); M. B. Smith, *The Life of Ole Bull* (Princeton, 1943); Z. Hopp, *Eventyret om Ole Bull* (Bergen, 1945); Ola Linge, *Ole Bull* (Oslo, 1953); I. Bull, *Ole Bull Returns to Pennsylvania* (N.Y., 1961).

Bullard, Frederick Field, American song composer; b. Boston, Sept. 21, 1864; d. there, June 24, 1904. He studied with Rheinberger at Munich; returned to Boston and became a music teacher; published about 40 songs, hymns and anthems.

Bülow, Hans Guido von, German pianist, conductor, and writer of great versatility and high attainments; b. Dresden, Jan. 8, 1830; d. Cairo, Egypt, Feb. 12, 1894. At the age of nine his teachers were Friedrich Wieck (piano) and Max Eberwein (theory). He studied law at the Univ. of Leipzig, and took a music course with Moritz Hauptmann. He then lived in Stuttgart, where he made his début as a pianist, playing Mendelssohn and Raff with the local orchestra. In 1850 he was in Berlin, where he joined the democratic groups and fell under the influence of Wagner's musical ideas. Shortly afterwards he went to Zürich, and became closely associated with Wagner, who was there in exile. After a year in Switzerland, where he was theater conductor, he went to Weimar to study with Liszt. In 1852 he published a collection of songs; wrote for the *Neue Zeitschrift für Musik;* in 1853 he made a tour through Germany and Austria as pianist; in 1855 he succeeded Kullak as head of the piano department at the Stern Cons. in Berlin, retaining this post until 1864. In the meantime he married Liszt's daughter Cosima (1857); in 1863 he received the honorary degree of Dr. from the Univ. of Jena. In 1864 he was called by Ludwig II of Bavaria to Munich as court pianist and conductor; the king, who was Wagner's great admirer and patron, summoned Wagner from exile to Munich; Hans von Bülow became Wagner's ardent champion and the best conductor of his music. He gave the first performances of *Tristan und Isolde* at the Court Opera in Munich on June 10, 1865 and the *Meistersinger* on June 21, 1868. A personal tragedy developed when Cosima abandoned him in 1869 for Wagner, whom she married the following year. Hans von Bülow went to live in Florence, where he remained until 1872. Despite his understandable bitterness towards Wagner, he continued to conduct Wagner's music; his growing admiration for Brahms cannot be construed as the result of his pique against Wagner. It was von Bülow who dubbed Brahms "the third B of music." He resumed his career in 1872 with world-wide piano tours; won triumphant successes in England and Russia; gave 139 concerts during his American tour in 1875–76; revisited America in 1889 and 1890. An important chapter in his career was his employment as conductor in Meiningen (1880–85). He married a Meiningen actress, Marie Schanzer, in 1882. After 1885 he conducted concerts in Hamburg and Berlin. He continued his untiring professional activities until 1893, when a lung ailment forced him to seek a cure in Egypt; he died shortly after his arrival in Cairo. Both as pianist and conductor, Hans von Bülow demonstrated his profound knowledge and understanding of the music he performed; as conductor he insisted on minute accuracy, but was able to project considerable emotional power. He was one of the first conductors to dispense with the use of the score. His memory was fabulous; it was said that he could memorize a piano concerto without the aid of an instrument, while on a journey. The mainstay of his repertoire was classical and romantic music, but he was hospitable towards composers of the new school; in Boston, he gave the world première of Tchaikovsky's First Piano Concerto; he encouraged the young Richard Strauss, and gave him his first position as conductor. He wrote a number of works, but they are entirely without enduring merit; on the other hand, as a writer and journalist, von Bülow was exceptionally brilliant; he was particularly apt at coining phrases, and his wit was legendary among musicians.

WORKS: music to Shakespeare's *Julius Caesar*; a symphonic ballad, *Des Sängers Fluch*; a symphonic "mood picture," *Nirwana*; *4 Charakterstücke* for orch.; piano pieces; songs; also masterly transcriptions of the prelude to Wagner's *Meistersinger* and the whole of *Tristan und Isolde*, of Berlioz' overtures to *Le Corsaire* and *Benvenuto Cellini*. His critical editions of Beethoven's sonatas and of Cramer's études attest his excellent editorial ability.

BIBLIOGRAPHY: E. Zabel, *Hans von Bülow* (Hamburg, 1894); Th. Pfeiffer, *Studien bei Hans von Bülow* (Berlin, 1894; 6th ed., 1909); R. Sternfeld, *Hans von Bülow* (Leipzig, 1894); Vianna da Motta, *Nachtrag zu den Pfeifferschen "Studien bei Hans von Bülow"* (Leipzig, 1895); W. Altmann, *Chronik des Berliner philharmonischen Orchesters, 1882-1901; zugleich ein Beitrag zur Beurteilung Hans von Bülows* (Berlin, 1902); G. Fischer, *Hans von Bülow in Hannover* (Hanover, 1902); H. Reimann, *Hans von Bülow: sein Leben und sein Wirken* (Berlin, 1909); C. Krebs, *Meister des Taktstocks* (1919); R. Du Moulin-Eckart, *Hans von Bülow* (1921); Marie von Bülow, *Hans von Bülow in Leben und Wort* (1925); Th. W. Werner, *Hans von Bülow in 75 Jahre Opernhaus Hannover* (1927); Walter Damrosch, "Hans von Bülow and the 9th Symphony," *Musical Quarterly* (April 1927); Ludwig Schemann, *Hans von Bülow im Lichte der Wahrheit* (Regensburg, 1935). Hans von Bülow's writings were published by his widow, Marie von Bülow, under the title *Briefe und Schriften Hans von Bülows* (8 vols., Leipzig, 1895-1908; vol. III, republished separately in 1936, contains selected essays, while the other volumes contain letters); selected letters in English translation were published by C. Bache, *The Early Correspondence of Hans von Bülow* (London, 1896); F. Rösch, *Musikästhetische Streitfragen; Streitlichter zu den ausgewählten Schriften von Hans von Bülow* (Leipzig, 1897); La Mara, *Briefwechsel zwischen Franz Liszt und Hans von Bülow* (Leipzig, 1898); E. Förster-Nietzsche and P. Gast, *Friedrich Nietzsches gesammelte Briefe* (Berlin, 1905; vol. III contains the correspondence between Nietzsche and von Bülow); von Bülow's letters to Wagner, Cosima, Klindworth, Bechstein, and Daniela, edited by R. DuMoulin-Eckart

(Munich, 1927; English transl., N.Y., 1931); W. M. Freitag, "An Annotated Biography of Hans von Bülow in the Harvard College Library," *Harvard Library Bulletin* (July 1967).

Bulthaupt, Heinrich, German dramatist and writer on music; b. Bremen, Oct. 26, 1849; d. there, Aug. 21, 1905. He studied jurisprudence at Göttingen, Leipzig and Berlin; spent some time in Kiev with private teachers, and then made an extensive trip in the Orient. In 1879 he was appointed librarian of the Municipal Library at Bremen. Besides his purely literary work, he wrote libretti for Rubinstein, Eugene d'Albert and others. His most important work dealing with music is *Dramaturgie der Oper* (2 vols.; Leipzig, 1887; 2nd ed., 1902). He also wrote a biography of Carl Loewe (1898) and *Richard Wagner als Klassiker* (1899).

Bumbry, Grace (Ann), black American singer; b. St. Louis, Jan. 4, 1937. She sang in church choirs as a child; in 1955 went to Northwestern Univ. to study voice with Lotte Lehmann, and continued her lessons with her in California. She made her professional debut in London in 1959; then made a spectacular appearance as Amneris at the Paris Opéra. In 1962 she appeared as Carmen with a French operatic troupe visiting Japan. Her greatest triumph came when she was selected by Wieland Wagner to sing Venus in *Tannhäuser* at the Bayreuth Festival (July 23, 1961), the first Afro-American to sing this role. She subsequently performed this role several times, including an appearance with the Lyric Opera of Chicago in 1963.

Bunger, Richard Joseph, American pianist and composer; b. Allentown, Penn., June 1, 1942. He studied at Oberlin College Cons. (B. Mus., 1964) and the Univ. of Illinois (M. Mus. 1965). In 1973 he was appointed to the faculty of Calif. State College, Dominguez Hills. He became absorbed in the modern techniques of composition, particularly in the new resources of prepared piano; published an illustrated volume *The Well-Prepared Piano* (1973), with a forward by John Cage; also evolved a comprehensive notational system "Musiglyph" which incorporates standard musical notation and musical graphics, indicating special instrumental techniques. He is the inventor of a "Bungerack," a music holder for the piano, particularly convenient for scores of large size.

Bungert, August, German composer; b. Mülheim, Ruhr, March 14, 1845; d. Leutesdorf, Oct. 26, 1915. He studied piano and composition at Cologne and Paris; lived mostly in Berlin. An ardent admirer of Wagner, Bungert devoted his life to the composition of a parallel work to Wagner's *Ring*, taking Homer's epics as the source of his libretti. The result of this effort was the creation of two operatic cycles: *The Iliad* comprising (1) *Achilleus*, (2) *Klytemnestra*; and *The Odyssey*, a tetralogy. The *Iliad* was never completed for performance, but all four parts of the *Odyssey* were performed in Dresden: *Kirke* (Jan. 29, 1898); *Nausikaa* (March 20, 1901); *Odysseus' Heimkehr* (Dec. 12, 1896, prior to premières of parts I and II); *Odysseus' Tod*

(Oct. 30, 1903). There were also subsequent productions in other German cities, but everywhere Bungert's operas were received without enthusiasm, and the evident ambition to emulate Wagner without comparable talent proved his undoing. Among other works are the programmatic score *Zeppelins erste grosse Fahrt;* several symphonic overtures; *Symphonia Victrix;* a *German Requiem;* many songs. His most successful work was a comic opera, *Die Studenten von Salamanka* (Leipzig, 1884); he also wrote a mystery play, *Warum? woher? wohin?* (1908); incidental music to Goethe's *Faust,* etc.

BIBLIOGRAPHY: F. A. Geissler, "August Bungert," *Musik* (Dec. 1907); M. Chop, *August Bungert, ein deutscher Dichterkomponist* (Leipzig, 1916).

Bunin, Vladimir, Russian composer; b. Scopin, Riazan district, July 24, 1908; d. Moscow, March 23, 1970. He studied at the Moscow Cons. with A. Alexandrov, graduating in 1938. In his music, Bunin follows the traditions of Russian classicism. He wrote 2 symphonies (1943, 1949); *Poem About Lenin* for orch. (1969); Violin Concerto (1953); Piano Concerto (1965); many piano pieces and songs.

Bunnett, Edward, English organist and composer; b. Shipdham, Norfolk, June 26, 1834; d. Norwich, Jan. 5, 1923. He was a chorister at Norwich Cathedral; then occupied various posts as organist; served as conductor of the Norwich Musical Union. He produced several cantatas at Norwich Festivals: *Rhineland* (1872); *Lora* (1876); and *De Profundis* (1880); also wrote numerous organ pieces. His *Nunc Dimittis* (1867) was for many years performed in English churches.

Bunning, Herbert, English conductor and composer; b. London, May 2, 1863; d. Thundersley, Essex, Nov. 26, 1937. He studied music with John Farmer at Harrow. After graduating from Oxford, he entered the army and served with the Queen's Own Hussars (1884); continued his musical studies in Milan with Vincenzo Ferroni and others (1886–91); upon his return to London, was appointed conductor of the Lyric Theatre (1892).

WORKS: an opera, *Princess Osra* (Covent Garden, London, July 14, 1902); 2 overtures: *Mistral* (1897), and *Spring and Youth* (1897); an Italian scena, *Ludovico il Moro* (1892); also *Shepherd's Call,* intermezzo for horn and strings (1893); *Village Suite* for orch. (1896); *Sir Launcelot and Queen Guinevere* for tenor and orch. (1905); incidental music to *Robin Hood* (1906); songs.

Bunting, Edward, historiographer of Irish music; b. Armagh, Feb. 1773; d. Dublin, Dec. 21, 1843. He played organ at Belfast; then moved to Dublin. He published 3 collections of old Irish airs in 1796, 1809 and 1840; these were reprinted in 2 vols. in 1969 under the title *The Ancient Music of Ireland;* many of these were published for the first time; the first volume contained songs by O'Conolan and O'Carolan; the second included piano arrangements and a discussion of the Irish, British and Egyptian harps; the third contained a long dissertation on the history of Irish popular music. Bunting collected his material from old singers

and harpers; his publications, therefore, have the value of authenticity.

Buonamente, Giovanni Battista, Italian composer who flourished in the first half of the 17th century; d. Assisi, 1643. He was maestro di cappella at the Austrian court in Vienna (1626); in Prague (1627); and at the Franciscan monastery in Assisi (1636). His importance in music history rests on his sonatas for violin, some of the earliest examples of this form; he published 7 books of such works in Venice between 1626 and 1637; also wrote trio sonatas for 2 violins and bass.

BIBLIOGRAPHY: A. Moser, *Geschichte des Violin-Spiels* (Berlin, 1923); Paul Nettl, "G. B. Buonamente," *Zeitschrift für Musikwissenschaft* (1927).

Buonamici, Giuseppe, Italian pianist; b. Florence, Feb. 12, 1846; d. there, March 17, 1914. He first studied with his uncle, Giuseppe Ceccherini; then at the Munich Cons. with Hans von Bülow and Rheinberger (1868–70); in 1873 returned to Florence where he was active as a teacher and choral conductor. He published a compilation of the technical figures found in Beethoven's piano music, in the form of daily studies; edited the *Biblioteca del Pianista* and the complete Beethoven sonatas; also published piano pieces of his own.

Buongiorno, Crescenzo, Italian composer; b. Bonito, Province of Avellino, 1864; d. Dresden, Nov. 7, 1903. He studied with Serrao at the Naples Cons.; later settled in Dresden.

WORKS: 4 operas: *Etelka* (Naples, 1887); *Das Erntefest* (Leipzig, 1896); *Das Mädchenherz* (Kassel, 1901); and *Michel Angelo und Rolla* (Kassel, 1903); also 12 operettas, including *Abukadabar* (Naples, 1889); *Circe e Calipso* (Turin, 1892); and *La nuova Saltarella* (Trieste, 1894).

Buononcini. See **Bononcini.**

Burada, Theodor, Rumanian violinist and folklorist; b. Jassy, Oct. 3, 1839; d. there, Feb. 17, 1923. He studied in Rumania and at the Paris Cons. His significance lies in his pioneer work connected with Rumanian folklore and codifying folk melodies and popular ballads. He also wrote some violin music.

Burbure, de Wesembeek, Léon-Philippe-Marie, Belgian music scholar; b. Termonde, Aug. 16, 1812; d. Antwerp, Dec. 8, 1889. A scion of an aristocratic family, he studied law at the Univ. of Ghent; he also received an excellent musical education at home with private teachers. In 1846 he settled at Antwerp, and became the keeper of Archives at the Cathedral. He made a profound study of materials on old music accessible to him, and published a number of valuable monographs dealing with the Renaissance music guilds of Antwerp, on lute-makers, etc. He also composed some 200 works, including an opera, 25 orchestral pieces, numerous choral works, etc.

WRITINGS: *Aperçu sur l'ancienne corporation des musiciens instrumentistes d'Anvers, dite de St. Job et de Ste. Marie-Madeleine* (Brussels, 1862); *Recherches sur les facteurs de clavecins et luthiers d'Anvers, depuis le XVIᵉ jusqu'au XIXᵉ siècle* (Brussels, 1869); *Notice sur Charles-Louis Hanssens* (Brussels, 1872); *Charles Luython (1550-1620), compositeur de musique de la Cour impériale* (Brussels, 1880); *Les œuvres des anciens musiciens belges* (Brussels, 1882). BIBLIOGRAPHY: F. A. Gevaert, *Notice sur le Chevalier Léon de Burbure* (Brussels, 1893).

Burck (real name **Moller**), **Joachim à,** German church composer; b. Burg, near Magdeburg, 1546; d. Mühlhausen, Thuringia, May 24, 1610. In 1563 he settled in Mühlhausen; became organist at the Protestant Church of St. Blasius in 1566.
WORKS: *Harmoniae sacrae* (5 books of motets; Nuremberg, 1566); *Die deutsche Passion* (Wittenberg, 1568); *Crepundia sacra* (4 books; Mühlhausen, 1578); several books of motets, odes and German songs, reprinted in various collections.
BIBLIOGRAPHY: A. Prüfer, *Untersuchungen über den aussernkirchlichen Kunstgesang in den evangelischen Schulen des 16. Jahrhundert* (Leipzig, 1890); R. Jordan, *Aus der Geschichte der Musik in Mühlhausen* (Mühlhausen, 1905).

Burco, Ferruccio, precocious Italian conductor; b. Milan, April 5, 1939; killed in an automobile accident near Ostuni, April 27, 1965. Phenomenally gifted, he was trained by his mother, a singer, and on May 30, 1943, at the age of 4, conducted an orchestra in Milan, by memorizing gestures to give cues. With his father acting as his manager, he was exhibited throughout Italy; in 1948 he was brought to the U.S. and conducted a concert at Carnegie Hall, N.Y.; also led sympathetic symphonic groups in Philadelphia, Detroit, Boston, Chicago, Los Angeles and San Francisco. At a special opera performance at the Triborough Stadium at Randalls Island in New York, he conducted *Cavalleria rusticana,* with his mother singing the role of Santuzza. During his American tour he weighed only 82 pounds. His subsequent development failed to do justice to his fantastic beginnings, and at the time of his death he was the leader of an itinerant provincial Italian band.

Burette, Pierre-Jean, French writer on music; b. Paris, Nov. 21, 1665; d. there, May 19, 1747. A physician by profession, he had an interest in musical subjects; was the author of the valuable treatise, *La Musique et la danse des anciens,* dealing mainly with the problems of Greek music. It was publ. in the *Mémoires de l'Académie des Inscriptions* (Nos. 1-17).

Burgess, Anthony, celebrated British novelist, author of *A Clockwork Orange* and other imaginative novels, who began his career as a professional musician; b. Manchester, England, Feb. 25, 1917. He played piano in jazz combos in England, at the same time studying classical compositions without a tutor. Despite his great success as a novelist, he continued to write music, and developed a style of composition that, were it not for his literary fame, would have earned him a respectable niche among composers. His music is refreshingly rhythmical and entirely tonal, but not without quirky quartal harmonies and crypto-atonal melodic flights.
WORKS: 3 symphonies (1937; 1956, subtitled *Sinfoni Melayu,* and based on Malaysian themes; 1975); *Sinfonietta* for jazz combo (1941); symph. poem, *Gibraltar* (1944); *Song of a Northern City* for piano and orch. (1947); *Partita* for string orch. (1951); *Ludus Multitonalis* for recorder consort (1951); Concertino for Piano and Percussion (1951); *Cantata for Malay College* (1954); Concerto for Flute and Strings (1960); Passacaglia for Orch. (1961); Piano Concerto (1976); Cello Sonata (1944); 2 piano sonatas (1946, 1951); incidental music for various plays; songs.

Burgin, Richard, American violinist and conductor; b. Warsaw, Oct. 11, 1892. He studied at the St. Petersburg Cons. with Auer; played at the age of 11 with the Warsaw Philharmonic; toured America as a concert violinist in 1907. He was concertmaster of the Helsingfors Symph. Orch. (1912–15) and of the Oslo Symph. Orch. (1916–19). In 1920 he emigrated to the U.S.; was appointed concertmaster of the Boston Symph. in 1920, and in 1927 became its assistant conductor. He also conducted the New England Cons. Orch.; for many years was instructor in conducting at the Berkshire Music Center, Tanglewood. In 1967 he went to Tallahassee, Florida, where he continued his activities as conductor and teacher. He is the husband of the violinist **Ruth Posselt,** whom he married on July 3, 1940.

Burgmüller, Johann August Franz, German organist and conductor; b. Magdeburg, April 28, 1766; d. Düsseldorf, August 21, 1824. He was of a clerical family; having received a good education, he became a teacher and then a traveling theatrical conductor; he founded a musical society in Düsseldorf, and enjoyed a considerable reputation among musicians as a scholar. His two sons, **Johann Friedrich Franz** and **Norbert,** were both musicians.

Burgmüller, Johann Friedrich Franz, German composer of piano music; b. Regensburg, Dec. 4, 1806; d. Beaulieu, near Paris, Feb. 13, 1874. He was the son of **Johann August Franz Burgmüller,** and brother of **Norbert;** having settled in Paris, he adopted a light style to satisfy the demands of Parisian music lovers, and wrote numerous pieces of salon music for piano; he also published several albums of piano studies that have become standard works.

Burgmüller, Norbert, German composer; son of **Johann August Franz** and brother of **Johann Friedrich Franz;** b. Düsseldorf, Feb. 8, 1810; d. Aachen, May 7, 1836. He was extremely gifted, and composed music since his early childhood. After study at home, he took lessons with Spohr; wrote many songs and a symphony. His second symphony remained incomplete at the time of his death at the age of 26; Schumann, who thought highly of him, orchestrated the third movement, a scherzo; in this form, the symphony had many performances in Europe and America, and Burgmüller was mourned by musicians as another Schubert. The point of coincidence was that his unfinished symphony was in the same key as that of Schubert.

BIBLIOGRAPHY: H. Eckert, *Norbert Burgmüller* (Augsburg, 1932).

Burgstaller, Alois, German tenor; b. Holzkirchen, Sept. 21, 1871; d. Gmund, April 19, 1945. He studied watch making until he met Cosima Wagner, who urged him to take up singing. After appearing in minor roles, he made his debut as Siegfried at Bayreuth in 1896. He was engaged at the Metropolitan Opera for the seasons 1903–08, making his American debut in *Die Walküre* (N.Y., Feb. 12, 1903); sang Parsifal at its first American performance (Dec. 24, 1903). In 1908 he returned to Germany.

Burian, Emil František, Czech composer; b. Pilsen, June 11, 1904; d. Prague, Aug. 9, 1959. He grew up in a musical family; his father, **Emil Burian** (1876–1926), was an operatic baritone; his uncle, **Karl Burian,** was a famous tenor. He studied with Foerster at the Prague Cons. From his first steps in composition, he adopted an extreme modernistic method—an eclectic fusion of jazz, Czech folk art and French Impressionism; was also active as a film producer, dramatist, poet, jazz singer, actor, piano accompanist, and journalist. In 1927 he organized a 'voice band' that sang according to prescribed rhythm but without a definite pitch; his presentation of the voice band at the Siena Fest. of the International Society for Contemporary Music (Sept. 12, 1928) aroused considerable interest, and achieved further notoriety through his association with his Dada theater in Prague (1933–41, 1945–49). During World War II Burian was put in a concentration camp by the Nazis, but survived and returned to active life. WORKS: fairy-tale opera, *Alladina and Palomid,* after Maeterlinck (1923); a one-act musical drama *Before Sunrise* (Prague, 1925); an opera buffa *Mister Ipokras* (1925; Prague, 1926; reworked into the opera farce *I Beg Your Pardon;* Prague, 1956); a jazz opera *Bubu from Montparnasse* (1927); an opera *Maryša* (Brno, April 16, 1940; his most important work); an operatic parody *The Emperor's New Clothes* (1947); a musical comedy *Lovers from the Kiosk* (1935); a singspiel *Opera from the Pilgrimage* (Prague, 1956); 4 ballets: *The Bassoon and the Flute* (1925; Prague, 1929), *Wooden Soldiers* (1926), *The Manège* (1927), and *The Motorcoach* (1927; Prague, 1928); a cantata, *May,* for harp, 2 pianos, kettledrums, solo voice and chorus (1946); *Suita Poetica* for orch. in 5 separate movements (1925, 1947, 1950, 1951, 1953); *Cocktails,* song cycle for voice and jazz orch. (1926); Suite for Oboe and String Orch. (1928); *Reminiscence,* symph. suite (1929–36); a symphony, *Siréna* (1947; music used in film of the same title); Symphony No. 2, with solo piano (1948); Accordian Concerto (1949); *Overture to Socialism* (1950); Trio for Flute, Viola and Cello (1924); *From Youth,* string sextet (1924); Duo for Violin and Cello (1925); *Requiem* for voice band and jazz band (1927); 8 string quartets (1927, 1929, 1940, 1947, 1947, 1948, 1949, 1951); Variations for Wind Quintet (1928); *Of Warm Nights,* suite for violin and piano (1928); *Passacaglia* for violin and viola (1929); *4 Pieces* for wind quintet (1929); Wind Quintet (1930);

Suite for Cello and Piano (1935); *Children's Songs* for voice and nonet (1937); *Sonata Romantica* for violin and piano (1938); *Lost Serenade* for flute and piano (1940); Duo for Violin and Piano (1946); Fantasie for Violin and Piano (1954); *American Suite* for 2 pianos (1926); *Piano Sonata* (1927); *Echoes of Czech Dances* for piano (1953); *Piano Sonatina* (1954); songs; film music. He also wrote the monographs *Polydynamika* (1926), *Modern Russian Music* (1926), *Jazz* (1928), *Almanack of the Burian Brothers* (1929), *Emil Burian* (1947) and *Karel Burian* (1948).

Burian, Karl, celebrated heroic tenor; b. Rusinov, near Rakovnik, Jan. 12, 1870; d. Senomaty, Sept. 25, 1924. He studied with F. Piwoda; made his debut in Brno (1891); then sang in Germany and Russia. In 1898 he was engaged to sing Parsifal at Bayreuth, and was extremely successful, becoming a favorite in Wagnerian roles. He sang the part of Herod in *Salome* at its world première in Dresden (Dec. 9, 1905). He made his American debut as Tannhäuser on Nov. 30, 1906, at the Metropolitan Opera; remained on the staff until 1911; then became a member of the Vienna Opera. In America he used the name **Karl Burrian.**

BIBLIOGRAPHY: E. F. Burian, *Karl Burian* (Prague, 1948).

Burk, John N., American writer on music; b. San José, Calif., Aug. 28, 1891; d. Boston, Sept. 6, 1967. He graduated from Harvard Univ. (A.B., 1916). In 1934 he succeeded Philip Hale as program annotator of the Boston Symphony Orch. He edited Philip Hale's Boston Symphony program notes (1935); annotated *Letters of Richard Wagner,* from the Burrell Collection (N.Y., 1950). He is the author of the books, *Clara Schumann, A Romantic Biography* (N.Y., 1940), and *The Life and Works of Beethoven* (N.Y., 1943).

Burkhard, Paul, Swiss operetta composer; b. Zürich, Dec. 21, 1911; d. Tösstal, Sept. 6, 1977. He studied at the Cons. in Zürich; was a conductor at a theater in Zürich (1939–44); conducted the Zürich Radio studio orch. (1944–57).

WORKS: an overture, *Der Schuss von der Kanzel* (1947); several operettas that enjoy considerable success in Switzerland: *Hopsa* (1935, revised 1957), *Dreimal Georges* (1936), *Der schwarze Hecht* (1939; revived under a new title, *Feuerwerk,* 1950), *Tic-Tac* (1942), *Casanova in der Schweiz* (1944), *Die kleine Niederdorfoper* (1954), *Die Pariserin* (1957); the fairytale operas *Die Schneekönigin* (1964) and *Bunbury* (1966); a Christmas opera *Ein Stern geht auf aus Jaakob* (1970).

Burkhard, Willy, significant Swiss composer; b. Évillard sur Bienne (Leubringen bei Biel), April 17, 1900; d. Zürich, June 18, 1955. He studied with Teichmüller and Karg-Elert in Leipzig (1921), Courvoisier in Munich (1922–23) and Max d'Ollone in Paris (1923–24). Returning to Switzerland, he taught at the Bern Cons. (1928–33) and at the Zürich Cons. (1942–55). His music is neo-classical in form and strongly polyphonic in structure; his astringent linear idiom is tempered by a strong sense of model counterpoint.

WORKS: an opera, *Die Schwarze Spinne* (*The Black Spider*, 1947–48; Zürich, May 28, 1949; revised 1954); the oratorios *Das Gesicht Jesajas* (*The Vision of Isaiah*, 1933–35; Basel, Feb. 18, 1936; his masterpiece) and *Das Jahr* (*The Year*, 1940–41; Basel, Feb. 19, 1942); the cantatas, with strings or orch.: *Biblischen Kantate* (1923), *Till Ulenspiegel* (1929), *Vorfrühling* (1930), *Spruchkantate* (1933), *Genug ist nicht genug* (1938–39; Basel, June 11, 1940); *Lob der Musik* (1939), *Cantate Domino* (1940), *Heimatliche Kantate* (1940), *Psalmen-Kantate* (1952) and several chamber and a cappella cantatas. Other vocal works include *Te Deum* for chorus, trumpet, trombone, kettledrum and organ (1931); *Das ewige Brausen* for bass and chamber orch. (1936); *Psalm 93* for chorus and organ (1937); *Kreuzvolk der Schweiz* for chorus and organ (1941); *Magnificat* for soprano and strings (1942); *Cantique de notre terre* for soli, chorus and orch. (1943); *Mass* for soprano, bass, chorus and orch. (1951; Zürich, June 28, 1951); *Psalm 148* for chorus and instruments (1954); for orch.: *Ulenspiegel Variations* (1932); *Fantasy* for strings (1934); *Small Serenade* for strings (1935); *Concerto for Strings* (1937); *Toccata for Strings* (1939); *Laupen-Suite* for orch. (1940); *Concertino for Cello and Strings* (1940); *Violin Concerto* (1943; Zürich, Jan. 26, 1946); *Symphony in One Movement* (1944); *Organ Concerto* (1945); *Hymne* for organ and orch. (1945); *Concertante Suite* (1946); *Piccola sinfonia giocosa* for small orch. (1949); *Fantasia mattutina* (1949); *Toccata, for 4 winds, percussion and strings* (1951; Zürich, Dec. 7, 1951); *Sonata da camera* for strings and percussion (1952); *Viola Concerto* (1953); *Concertino for 2 Flutes, Harpsichord and Strings* (1954); *String Trio* (1926); *String Quartet* (1929); *Fantasie for Organ* (1931); *Piano Trio* (1936); *Violin Sonatina* (1936); *Suite for 2 Violins* (1937); *Solo Viola Sonata* (1939); *Piano Sonata* (1942); *String Quartet in One Movement* (1943); *Serenade for 8 Instruments* (1945); *Romance* for horn and piano (1945); *Violin Sonata* (1946); *Cello Sonata* (1952); *Serenade* for flute and clarinet (1953); *Choral-Triptychon* for organ (1953); *Suite for Solo Flute* (1954–55); *6 Preludes* for piano (1954–55).

BIBLIOGRAPHY: Ernst Mohr, *Willy Burkhard: Leben und Werk* (Zürich, 1957); S. Burkhard and F. Indermühle, *Willy Burkhard (17. April 1900–18. Juni 1955) Werkverzeichnis* (issued by the Willy Burkhard Gesellschaft; Liebefeld, 1968); E. Schmidt, " 'Ahnung einer neuen Weltordnung'—Willy Burkhard," in U. von Brück, ed., *Credo musicale. . . . Festgabe zum 80. Geburtstag des . . . Professor D. Dr. h.c. Rudolf Mauersberger* (Berlin, 1969).

Burkhardt, Max, German music analyst and composer; b. Löbau, Sept. 28, 1871; d. Berlin, Nov. 12, 1934. He studied at the Leipzig Cons.; received his degree of *Dr. phil.* with the dissertation *Beiträge zum Studium des deutschen Liedes* (1897); then was a choral conductor in Cologne; in 1906 settled in Berlin as teacher and writer. He publ. several useful music guides: *Führer durch Richard Wagners Musikdramen* (Berlin, 1909; 3rd ed. 1913); *Führer durch die Konzertmusik* (Berlin, 1911; analyzes 1,500 works); *Johannes Brahms: Ein Führer durch seine Werke* (Berlin, 1912). He also wrote the operas *König Drosselbart* (Cologne,

1904) and *Das Moselgretchen* (Schwerin, 1912); choral works and a series of *Lautenlieder* with lute accompaniment.

Burlas, Ladislav, Slovak composer; b. Trnava, April 3, 1927. He studied general musical subjects at the Bratislava Univ. (1946–51) and composition with A. Moyzes at the Bratislava Cons. and at the Academy of Music there, graduating in 1955; then taught music theory at the Comenius Univ. in Bratislava; He published the monographs on J. L. Bella (Bratislava, 1953) and on A. Moyzes (Bratislava, 1956).

WORKS: *Symphonic Triptych* (1957); *Epitaph* for orch. (1958); *Bagatelles* for string orch. (1960); *Planctus* for string orch. (1968); *Concertino for Percussion and Winds* (1971); *Wedding Songs* for soloists, chorus and orch. (1955); *The Miner's Cantata* (1955); *The Singing Heart*, string sextet (1960); *Sonata for Solo Violin* (1968); *Music for string quartet* (1968–69); *String Quartet No. 2, in memory of Prokofiev* (1973); choruses; songs.

Burleigh, Cecil, American composer and teacher; b. Wyoming, N.Y., April 17, 1885. He studied in Berlin with Witek (violin) and Leichtentritt (comp.); returning to the U.S., he taught at various American colleges; in 1921, settled as violin teacher at the Univ. of Wisconsin. He has composed more than 100 works, among them 3 violin concertos (1915, 1919, 1928); a "trilogy of symphonies" (*Creation, Prophecy* and *Revelation*); and descriptive violin pieces (4 *Rocky Mountain Sketches*, 4 *Prairie Sketches*, 5 *Winter Evening Tales*, 6 *Nature Studies*, etc.; also a *Skeleton Dance*).

Burleigh, Henry Thacker, black American baritone and songwriter; b. Erie, Pa., Dec. 2, 1866; d. Stamford, Conn., Sept. 12, 1949. He studied at the National Cons., New York. In 1894 he became baritone soloist at St. George's Church, N.Y.; retired in 1946 after 52 years of service. He gained wide popularity as a songwriter. On May 16, 1917, the National Association for the Advancement of Colored People awarded him the Spingarn Medal for highest achievement by an American citizen of African descent during the year 1916.

BIBLIOGRAPHY: "In Retrospect . . . Harry T. Burleigh (1866–1949)," *Black Perspective in Music* (Sept. 1974).

Burmeister, Joachim, German poet and musician; b. Lüneburg, 1564; d. Rostock, May 5, 1629. He settled in Rostock in 1586, and obtained a master's degree at Rostock Univ. He published in Rostock the following treatises: *Hypomnematum Musicae Poeticae* (1599); *Musicae Practicae sive artis canendi ratio* (1601); wrote several sacred songs, which were published in 1601.

BIBLIOGRAPHY: Martin Ruhnke, *Joachim Burmeister*, (Kassel, 1955); C. Palisca, "Ut oratoria musica: The Rhetorical Basis of Musical Mannerism," in *The Meaning of Mannerism* (Hanover, N.H., 1972).

Burmeister, Richard, German composer and pianist; b. Hamburg, Dec. 7, 1860; d. Berlin, Feb. 19, 1944. He studied with Liszt at Weimar, Rome and Budapest, accompanying him on his travels; later taught at the

Hamburg Cons., at the Peabody Institute in Baltimore, Dresden Cons. (1903–06), and Klindworth-Scharwenka Cons. in Berlin (1907–25). Burmeister also made extensive concert tours of Europe and the U.S. His works include the symph. fantasy *Die Jagd nach dem Glück;* a piano concerto; *The Sisters* (after Tennyson) for alto with orch.; a romanza for violin and orch.; songs; piano pieces. He also rescored Chopin's F minor Concerto, Liszt's *Mephisto Waltz* and 5th Rhapsody (with new orchestral accompaniment), and Weber's *Konzertstück* for piano and orch.

Burmester, Willy, German violinist; b. Hamburg, March 16, 1869; d. there, Jan. 16, 1933. He studied with his father, and with Joachim in Berlin; from 1886, made frequent concert tours throughout Europe and America. He composed a Serenade for string quartet and double bass, and smaller virtuoso pieces; was the author of *Fünfzig Jahre Künstlerleben* (1926; in Danish, 1928).

Burney, Charles, celebrated English music historian; b. Shrewsbury, April 7, 1726; d. Chelsea, April 12, 1814. He was a pupil of Edmund Baker (organist of Chester Cathedral), of his eldest half-brother James Burney, and, from 1744–47, of Dr. Arne in London. In 1749 he became organist of St. Dionis-Backchurch, and harpsichord player at the subscription concerts in the King's Arms, Cornhill; resigned these posts in 1751, and, until 1760, was organist at King's Lynn, Norfolk, where he planned and began work on his *General History of Music.* He returned to London in 1760; received the degrees of Mus. Bac. and Mus. Doc. from Oxford Univ. in 1769. Having exhausted such material as was available in London for his *History of Music,* he visited France, Switzerland and Italy in 1770, and Germany, Holland and Austria in 1772, consulting the libraries, attending the best concerts of sacred and secular music, and forming contacts with the leading musicians and scholars of the period (Gluck, Hasse, Metastasio, Voltaire, etc.). The immediate result of these journeys was the publication of *The Present State of Music in France and Italy,* etc. (1771, in diary form) and *The Present State of Music in Germany, the Netherlands,* etc. (1773). His *General History of Music* appeared in 4 volumes (1776–89; new ed. by Frank Mercer in 2 vols. with "Critical and Historical Notes," London and N.Y., 1935), the first volume concurrently with the complete work of his rival, Sir John Hawkins. From 1806 he received a government pension. Other publications: *La musica che si canta annualmente nelle funzioni della settimana santa nella Cappella Pontificia, composta de Palestrina, Allegri e Bai* (1771; a book of sacred works with Burney's preface); *An Account of the Musical Performances in Westminster Abbey . . . in Commemoration of Handel* (1785); *Memoirs of the Life and Writings of the Abate Metastasio* (3 vols., 1796); the articles on music for Rees's *Cyclopedia;* etc. He composed, for Drury Lane, music to the dramas *Alfred* (1745), *Robin Hood,* and *Queen Mab* (1750), and *The Cunning Man* (1765), text and music adapted from *Le Devin du village* by Rousseau; also sonatas for piano and for violin; violin and harpsichord concertos, cantatas, flute duets, etc.

BIBLIOGRAPHY: Burney's daughter, Frances Burney (b. King's Lynn, Norfolk, June 13, 1752; d. London, Jan. 6, 1840), wrote the novel *Evelina,* and *Memoirs of Dr. Burney* (publ. in 3 vols., 1832); cf. A. R. Ellis, *Early Diary of Frances Burney* (2 vols., 1889); C. Hill, *The House in St. Martin Street, being Chronicles of the Burney Family* (London, 1906); L. M. Isaacs, "A Friend of Dr. Johnson," *Musical Quarterly* (Oct. 1915); C. Ricci, *Burney, Casanova e Farinelli in Bologna* (Milan, 1920); C. H. Glover, *Dr. Charles Burney's Continental Travels, 1770–72* (compiled from Burney's journals and other sources; London, 1927); P. A. Scholes, *The Great Dr. Burney* (a definitive biography; Oxford, 1948); Roger Lonsdale, *Dr. Charles Burney: a Literary Biography* (London, 1965); G. Stefani, "Musica, chiesa, società negli scritti dé Ch. Burney," *Nuova Rivista Musicale Italiana* (Jan.-Feb. 1971); J. C. Kassler, "Burney's *Sketch of a plan for a public music-school,*" *Musical Quarterly* (April 1972).

Burr, Willard, American composer; b. Ravena, Ohio, Jan. 17, 1852; d. Boston, May 12, 1915. He studied with August Haupt in Berlin; then settled in Boston as teacher. He wrote numerous works for piano, such as a suite *From Shore to Shore;* also anthems and art songs.

Burritt, Lloyd, Canadian composer; b. Vancouver, British Columbia, June 7, 1940. He studied with J. Coulthard and C. Hultberg at the Univ. of British Columbia, graduating in 1963 (M.M., 1968); then with G. Jacob and H. Howells in London at the Royal College of Music; later attended classes in conducting with Schuller, Leinsdorf and Bernstein at the Berkshire Music Center, Tanglewood (summers of 1965, 1966). Upon completing his studies he was appointed music director of the Argyle School in North Vancouver. His music is modernistic in harmony, and he is apt to use some audacious effects in his audio-visual works, with correspondingly dramatic titles.

WORKS: Symphony (1964); *3 Autumn Songs* for mezzo-soprano, piano and orch. (1965); *Assassinations* for orch. and tape (Vancouver, Dec. 1, 1968); *Hollow Men,* after T. S. Eliot, for chorus, orch. and tape (1968); *Landscapes,* after T. S. Eliot, for soprano, alto and tape (1968); *Acid Mass,* after T. S. Eliot, for chorus, dancers and film (1969); *Electric Tongue I* for orch. and tape (Vancouver, May 30, 1969; a version *II* included a direct telephone call by the conductor from London to Vancouver); *Cicada* for orch. and tape (1970); *New York* for orch. and tape (1970); *Overdose* for orch. and tape (1971); *Electric Chair* for saxophone, actress and tape (1971); *Rocky Mountain Grasshopper* for chorus, wind orch. and 2 tapes (1971); *Memo to RCCO* (Royal College of Canadian Organists) for organ and tape (1972); *Memo to NFBC* (National Film Board of Canada) for keyboard and tape (1972); *Spectrum* for strings and tape (1973); *David* for soli, chorus, orch. and tape (1977); several scores for theatrical plays.

Burrowes, John Freckleton, English composer; b. London, April 23, 1787; d. there, Mar. 31, 1852. He was a pupil of William Horsley; was organist of St. James' Church, Piccadilly, for many years. He wrote works for flute and other instruments, and made arrangements for operas. His 2 manuals *Thorough-Bass Primer* and *The Pianoforte Primer* were very successful and went through many editions before they became obsolete.

Burt, Francis, English composer; b. London, April 28, 1926. He studied at the Royal Academy of Music with Howard Ferguson (1948–51) and at the Hochschule für Musik in Berlin with Boris Blacher (1951–54); was awarded the German Mendelssohn Scholarship; went for further study to Rome; in 1956 he received a stipend from the Fondation européenne de la Culture; from 1957 lived mostly in Vienna.
WORKS: String Quartet (1953); *Iambics* for orch. (1955); *Music for two pianos* (1955); *The Skull,* cantata for tenor and orch. (1956); *Duo* for clarinet and piano (1956); *Bavarian Gentians* for vocal quartet and piano (1957); *Espressione orchestrale* (1959); *Volpone,* opera after Ben Jonson (Stuttgart, June 2, 1960); *The Golem,* ballet (1962); *Fantasmagoria* for orch. (1963); one-act opera, *Barnstable, or Someone in the Attic* (Stuttgart, Nov. 30, 1969).

Burtius (also known as **Burci** or **Burzio**), **Nicolaus,** Italian theorist; b. Parma, c.1445; d. there, after 1518. He studied with J. Gallicus; received first clerical Orders in Parma in 1472; then studied ecclesiastical law in Bologna; in 1487 he published *Musices Opusculum,* which was one of the earliest printed books on music, containing mensural notes printed from wood blocks. In this work Burtius supports the Guidonian system opposing the innovations introduced by Ramos de Pareja.

Burton, Frederick Russell, American writer on music; b. Jonesville, Mich., Feb. 23, 1861; d. Lake Hopatcong, N.J., Sept. 30, 1909. He was a graduate of Harvard Univ. (1882); then went to New York where he was active as music teacher. He made a study of Indian music, and publ. *Songs of the Ojibway Indians* (1903; later expanded into *American Primitive Music,* publ. posthumously, 1909).

Bury, Edward, Polish composer and conductor; b. Gniezno, Sept. 18, 1919. He studied composition with Sikorski and conducting at the Warsaw Cons. (1937–44); from 1945 to 1954 he taught at the Cracow Cons. He published 2 books on conducting, *Podstawy techniki dyrygowania* (*The Principals of Conducting Technique,* Cracow, 1961) and *The Technique of Reading Scores* (Cracow, 1971).
WORKS: *Czech Fantasy* for piano and orch. (1948); *Little Suite* for orch. (1950); *Triptych* for orch. (1952); Violin Concerto (1954); *Concert Overture* (1954); *Suita giocosa* for orch. (1956); *Maski* (The Masks), fantastic suite for orch. (1957); 6 symphonies: No. 1, *Symfonia Wolności* (*Freedom Symphony,* 1960), No. 2 *for 6 concertante instruments and orch.* (*1962*), No. 3, *Mówi Prezydent John F. Kennedy* (President Kennedy Speaks) for male speaker, women's speaking chorus, mixed chorus and orch. (1964), No. 4, *de timpani a tutti,* for solo bass, chorus, tape and orch. (1966–67), No. 5, *Bohaterska* (*Heroic,* 1969) and No. 6, *Pacem in terris,* to a text from the encyclical of Pope John

XXIII, for narrator, church bells and orch. (1972); *The Millennium Hymn* for chorus and orch. (1965); chamber music; piano pieces; choruses.

Busby, Thomas, English writer on music; b. Westminster, Dec., 1755; d. London, May 28, 1838. He was a chorister in London; then studied with Battishill (1769–74); served as church organist at St. Mary's, Newington, Surrey, St. Mary Woolnoth, and Lombard Street. He obtained the degree of Mus. Doc. from Cambridge Univ. in 1801. In collaboration with Arnold, he published *Complete Dictionary of Music* (1801); he then published *A Grammar of Music* (1818) and *A General History of Music* (2 vols., compiled from Burney and Hawkins; London, 1819; repr. 1968). In 1825 he brought out a set of 3 little volumes entitled *Concert Room and Orchestra Anecdotes of Music and Musicians, Ancient and Modern,* a compilation of some topical value, even though many of the stories are apocryphal. He also published *A Musical Manual, or Technical Directory* (1828). His anthology of sacred music *The Divine Harmonist* (1788) is valuable. His own compositions (oratorios and odes) are imitative of Handel. A melodrama, *Tale of Mystery,* with Busby's music was produced at Covent Garden, Nov. 13, 1807.
BIBLIOGRAPHY: K. G. F. Spence, "The Learned Doctor Busby," *Music & Letters* (April 1956).

Busch, Adolf, distinguished violinist (brother of **Hermann** and **Fritz Busch**); b. Siegen, Westphalia, Aug. 8, 1891; d. Guilford, Vermont, June 9, 1952. He studied at the conservatories of Cologne and Bonn; was concertmaster of the Vienna Konzertverein; then taught at the Musikhochschule in Berlin. In 1919 he organized the internationally known Busch Quartet and the Busch Trio (with his younger brother Hermann Busch, and his son-in-law Rudolf Serkin). Recordings and publications are issued by the Bruder-Busch Gesellschaft.

Busch, Carl, Danish-American conductor and composer; b. Bjerre, March 29, 1862; d. Kansas City, Dec. 19, 1943. He studied at the Royal Cons. in Copenhagen with Hartmann and Gade; then went to Paris; in 1887 settled in Kansas City, where he was active as conductor and teacher. From 1912 to 1918 he was conductor of the Kansas City Symph.; also conducted his own works with various orchestras in the U.S., Denmark and Germany.
WORKS: *The Passing of Arthur* (after Tennyson) and *Minnehaha's Vision,* for orch.; *Elegy,* for string orch.; cantatas: *The Four Winds, King Olaf, The League of the Alps, America,* etc.; many compositions for violin; songs.

Busch, Fritz, notable German conductor (brother of **Hermann** and **Adolph Busch**); b. Siegen, Westphalia, March 13, 1890; d. London, Sept. 14, 1951. He studied at the Cologne Cons. with Steinbach, Boettcher, Uzielli and Klauwell; then was active as conductor at Riga, Russia (1909), Gotha (1911), Aachen (1912), at the Stuttgart Opera (1918), and at the Dresden Opera (1922). He left Germany in 1933, and made frequent appearances as symphonic conductor in Europe; conducted opera in South America (1942–45) and at the Metropolitan Opera, N.Y. (1945–50). He wrote an autobiography *Aus dem leben eines Musikers* (Zürich, 1949; publ. in English under the title *Pages from a Musician's Life*, London, 1953). Recordings and publications are issued by the Bruder-Busch Gesellschaft.

Busch, William, English pianist and composer; b. London, June 25, 1901; d. Woolacombe, Devon, Jan. 30, 1945. Of German origin, he received his education in America and England; then studied in Germany with Leonid Kruetzer (piano) and Hugo Leichtentritt (theory). He made his debut in London (Oct. 20, 1927). His music shows competent craftsmanship; among his works are a piano concerto (1939); cello concerto (1941); piano quartet (1939); and pieces for piano solo.

Buschkötter, Wilhelm, German conductor; b. Höxter, Westphalia, Sept. 27, 1887; d. Berlin, May 12, 1967. He studied cello and conducting in German provincial towns; from 1926–37 was conductor at the radio station in Cologne; then was in Stuttgart and Dortmund (1937–39) and in Berlin (1945–49). In 1950 he returned to his post at the Western German Broadcasting Corporation.

Bush, Alan Dudley, notable English composer; b. Dulwich, Dec. 22, 1900. He studied piano with Matthay and composition with Corder at the Royal Academy of Music in London; also took private piano lessons with Artur Schnabel and composition with John Ireland. In 1929 he went to Berlin and took courses in musicology and philosophy. Returning to England, he was on the staff of the Royal Academy of Music, from 1925 till 1955. In 1935 he joined the Communist Party; in 1936 he organized in London the Workers' Music Association, remaining its president for 40 years. His early works contain some radical modernistic usages, but in accordance with his political views on art, he adopted the precepts of socialist realism, demanding a tonal idiom more easily appreciated by audiences. He made numerous trips to Russia and to the countries of the Socialist bloc; several of his works had their first performance in East Germany.
    WORKS: He wrote several operas on historical subjects dealing with social revolt: *Wat Tyler* (awarded a prize at the Festival of Britain in 1951, but not performed in England; its first production took place in concert form on the Berlin Radio, to a German libretto, on April 3, 1952); *The Men of Blackmoor* (Weimar, Nov. 18, 1956); *Guayana Johnny* (Leipzig, Dec. 11, 1966); *Joe Hill,* on the subject of the execution of the labor agitator Joe Hill in Salt Lake City on Nov. 19, 1915 (East Berlin, Sept. 29, 1970). Other works include Piano Concerto, with baritone solo and male chorus in the finale (1938); Symph. No. 1 (London, July 24, 1942, composer conducting); *Fantasia on Soviet Themes* for orch. (London, July 27, 1945); *English Suite* for string orch. (London, Feb. 9, 1946); *The Winter Journey,* cantata (Alnwick, Dec. 14, 1946); children's operetta, *The Press Gang* (Letchworth, March 7, 1947); *Piers Plowman's Day* for orch. (Prague Radio, Oct. 16, 1947); Violin Concerto (London, July 16, 1948); Symph. No. 2, subtitled *Nottingham* (Nottingham, June 27, 1949); *Song of Friendship*

for bass voice, chorus and band (London, Nov. 6, 1949); *Defender of the Peace* for orch. (Vienna Radio, May 24, 1952); cantata *The Ballad of Freedom's Soldier* (1953); *Byron Symphony* for chorus and orch. (1960); *Time Remembered* for chamber orch. (1969); *Scherzo* for wind instruments and percussion (1969) *Suite of Six* for string quartet (1975). A *Tribute to Alan Bush* was published by the Worker's Music Association for his 50th birthday (1950). He published an autobiography *In My Seventh Decade* (London, 1971).

Bush, Geoffrey, English organist, composer and pedagogue; b. London, March 23, 1920. He studied at Oxford Univ.; received his B.M. degree in 1940 and D.M. in 1946; upon graduation was active mainly as an organist, a teacher and music journalist. In 1952 he was appointed to the staff of the Univ. of London.
    WORKS: a puppet opera, *The Spanish Rivals* (1948); *A Summer Serenade* for chorus and instruments (1949); Trio for Oboe, Bassoon and Piano (1952); a children's opera *The Blind Beggar's Daughter* (1954); Symph. No. 1 (1954); one-act opera, *If the Cap Fits* (1957); Symph. No. 2 (1957); Concerto for Light Orch. (1958); *Dialogue* for oboe and piano (1960); Concerto for Piano, Trumpet and Strings (1962); Wind Quintet (1963); opera, *The Equation* (1968). He published *Musical Creation and the Listener* (London, 1954; revised 1967).

Busi, Alessandro, Italian composer; b. Bologna, Sept. 28, 1833; d. there, July 8, 1895. He was a conductor of the Communal Theater in Bologna and taught at the Bologna Liceo. His works include a choral symphony, *Excelsior; In alto mare* for chorus and orch.; many ballads for voice and piano; etc.
    BIBLIOGRAPHY: L. Torchi, *Commemorazione di Alessandro Busi* (Bologna, 1896).

Busnois (properly **De Busne**), **Antoine,** celebrated 15th-century contrapuntist; b. probably at or near Béthune, France; d. Bruges, Nov. 6, 1492. In 1467 he was chapel singer to Charles the Bold of Burgundy; in 1476 he was in Mons. Several of his works are still extant. They include 7 chansons in early publications of Petrucci's (1501–03), the MS Masses *L'Homme armé, O crux lignum* and a *Regina coeli* in the Papal Chapel at Rome, and some magnificats, motets and chansons in other libraries. In his *In hydraulis quondam Pythagoras* (*Denkmäler der Tonkunst in Österreich,* vol. 14/15; formerly vol. 7); he professed to be a pupil of Okeghem.
    BIBLIOGRAPHY: Ch. van den Borren, *Études sur le XVᵉ siècle musical* (Antwerp, 1941); full bibl. in *Die Musik in Geschichte und Gegenwart.*

Busoni, Ferruccio Benvenuto, distinguished Italian-German pianist and composer; b. Empoli, near Florence, April 1, 1866; d. Berlin, July 27, 1924. His father was a clarinet player; his mother, Anna Weiss, a good pianist; her father was a German. Busoni was brought up musically by his parents, and at eight gave a public piano recital in Trieste. At the age of ten he played in Vienna, in a program that included his own piano pieces. The following year the family moved to Graz, where he took lessons with W. A. Remy (Dr. W. Mayer). In Graz Busoni conducted his own *Stabat Mater*; he was then twelve years old. At 15 he was elected a member of the Reale Accademia Filarmonica; he performed his oratorio, *Il Sabato del Villaggio*, in Bologna (1883); went to Leipzig (1886); was for a season (1888–89) piano instructor at the Helsingfors Cons.; in 1890 he gave concerts and taught in Moscow, where he married Gerda Sjöstrand; received the Rubinstein Prize for his *Konzertstück* for piano and orch. In 1891 he accepted an offer to teach at the New England Cons. in Boston; appeared as pianist with the Boston Symph. Orch.; in 1893 he returned to Europe; made successful tours in Belgium, Denmark, and Italy; in 1894 he settled in Berlin. His fame as a pianist was now world-wide; he made triumphant tours of European countries, including Russia; in 1901–11 he gave concerts in the U.S. with great acclaim; he also conducted concerts of little known or seldom heard music (Berlin, 1905–07); taught at Vienna Cons.; in 1913 was director of the Liceo Musicale in Bologna; from 1915–20 he was in Zürich; returned to Berlin in 1920 and remained there until his death. In 1913 he received the order of Chevalier de la Légion d'Honneur, which had theretofore been bestowed on only two Italians: Rossini and Verdi. Busoni's virtuosity as pianist was distinguished by an element of tone color that gave it an orchestral quality; he particularly excelled in contrapuntal voice-leading, which he projected with extraordinary clarity and precision. His piano transcriptions of Bach's organ works are extremely effective and faithful to the spirit of the music. His edition of Bach's *Well-Tempered Clavier*, with its penetrating annotations, is valuable to students, even though not all Bach scholars would accept Busoni's interpretation of the ornaments; he also edited the piano works of Liszt for Breitkopf & Härtel. Busoni was a believer in new ideas, in music and in general esthetics; his *Entwurf einer neuen Ästhetik der Tonkunst* (Trieste, 1907; English transl. by Th. Baker, N.Y., 1911) abounds in interesting suggestions; other writings are *Versuch einer organischen Klaviernotenschrift* (Leipzig, 1910) and *Von der Einheit der Musik* (collected papers; Berlin, 1922). He applied his novel ideas in some of his works, particularly in the *Fantasia contrappuntistica*, where he used special scales and arpeggios.

WORKS: the operas *Die Brautwahl* (Hamburg, April 12, 1912), *Arlecchino*, *Turandot* (Zürich, May 11, 1917), *Doktor Faust* (unfinished; completed by Philipp Jarnach; performed posthumously, Dresden, May 21, 1925); for orch.: 2 symph. suites (1888; 1895); *Lustspielouvertüre* (1897); *Turandot Suite* (1904); *Nocturne symphonique* (1912); *Tanzwalzer* (1920); Piano Concerto, with male chorus finale (1904); *Indianische Fantasie* for piano and orch. (1913); *Romanza e scherzoso* (1921); Violin Concerto (1897); Clarinet Concerto (1919); 2 string quartets (1880; 1889); 2 violin sonatas (1890; 1898); for piano: *Una festa di villaggio* (6 characteristic pieces, 1882); *Tre pezzi nello stilo antico* (1882); *Macchiette medioevali* (1883); *Zwei Tanzstücke* (1914); 6 sonatinas; *10 Variations on Chopin's Prelude in C minor* (1922); *Fantasia contrappuntistica* (1910; also a version for 2 pianos, 1922); a number of liturgical songs; also songs to German, Italian and English words.

BIBLIOGRAPHY: H. Leichtentritt, *Ferruccio Busoni* (Leipzig, 1916); Hugo Leichtentritt, "Ferruccio Busoni as a Composer," *Musical Quarterly* (Jan. 1917); Gisella Selden-Goth, *Ferruccio Busoni* (Vienna, 1922); Augusta Cottlow, "My Years with Busoni," *The Musical Observer* (June 1925); Jakob Wassermann, *In Memoriam Ferruccio Busoni* (1925); Paul Bekker, *Klang und Eros* (1931); S. Nadel, *Ferruccio Busoni* (1931); E. J. Dent, *Ferruccio Busoni, A Biography* (Oxford, 1933); G. M. Gatti, "The Stage Works of Ferruccio Busoni," *Musical Quarterly* (July 1934); A. Santelli, *Busoni* (Rome, 1939); G. Guerrini, *Ferruccio Busoni, la vita, la figura, l'opera* (Florence, 1944); also an article on him in a special issue of *Rassegna Musicale* (Jan. 1940). Collections of Busoni's letters are published by F. Schnapp, *Briefe an seine Frau* (Zürich, 1935; English transl. by R. Ley, London, 1938); Gisella Selden-Goth, *25 Busoni Briefe* (Vienna, 1937); see also P. Rosenfeld, "Busoni in His Letters," *Musical Quarterly* (April 1939); O. Wessely, "Fünf unbekannte Jugendbriefe von Ferruccio Benvenuto Busoni," in H. Wegener, *Musa—Mens—Musici. In Gedenken an Walther Vetter* (Leipzig, 1969); Heinz Meyer, *Die Klaviermusik Ferruccio Busonis* (Zürich, 1969); H. H. Stuckenschmidt, *Ferruccio Busoni, Zeittafel eines Europäers* (Zürich, 1967; in English, *Ferruccio Busoni, Chronicle of a European*, London, 1970); H. Kosnick, *Busoni. Gestaltung durch Gestalt* (Regensburg, 1971).

Busschop, Jules-Auguste-Guillaume, French composer; b. Paris, Sept. 10, 1810; d. Bruges, Belgium, Feb. 10, 1896. He was entirely self-taught, and became successful as a composer of motets, cantatas etc., including the prize-cantata *Le Drapeau belge* (1834) and a *Te Deum* (Brussels, 1860). He also wrote a symphony, several overtures, military music, etc.

Busser, Henri-Paul, French composer and organist; b. Toulouse, Jan. 16, 1872; d. Paris, Dec. 30, 1973, at the age of 101. After primary musical studies in his native town he went to Paris, where he studied with Guiraud at the Paris Cons.; also took private lessons with Gounod, Widor, and César Franck. He won Second Premier Prix de Rome in 1893 with his cantata *Antigone*. A year before he was appointed organist at St. Cloud; later served as choirmaster of the Opéra-Comique; in 1902 appointed conductor of the Grand Opéra, a post which he held for 37 years until his resignation in 1939; was reappointed after the war in 1946, and served his term until 1951. He also was for several years president of the Académie des Beaux Arts. He taught composition at the Paris Cons. from 1930 until 1948. During his long career as conductor, he led several important productions, including the third performance of Debussy's opera *Pelléas et Mélisande*. His centennial was grandly celebrated in January, 1972 with performances of his works by the leading Paris Orchestras and by an exhibition of his manuscripts at the Opéra. In 1958 he married the French opera singer **Yvonne Gall** (1885–1972).

WORKS: *Daphnis et Chloë*, a scenic pastorale (Opéra-Comique, Paris, Dec. 14, 1897, composer conducting); the operas *Colomba* (Nice, Feb. 4, 1921), *Les Noces corinthiennes* (Paris, May 10, 1922), *La Carosse du Saint Sacrement* (1936), *Diafoirus 60* (Lille, 1963),

La Vénus d'Ille (Lille, 1964); ballets, La Ronde des Saisons (1905), Le Vert Galant (Paris, 1951), Gayarni (1963); Le Sommeil de l'Enfant Jésus for violin and orch.; A la Villa Medicis, symph. suite for orch.; Minerva, concert overture for orch.; Hercule au Jardin des Hespérides, symph. poem; Suite funambulesque for small orch.; A la Lumière (Poème lyrique); Suite brève for small orch.; Messe de Noël for 4 voices with organ or orch.; Pièce de Concert for harp with orch.; Appassionato for alto with orch.; Marche de Fête for orch.; Hymne à la France for tenor with orch.; Impromptu for harp with orch.; several preludes and fugues for organ on themes by Gounod, Massenet, A. Thomas, etc. He completed and arranged for performance Bizet's unfinished opera Ivan le Terrible; published a Précis de composition (Paris, 1943) and a volume of memoirs De Pelléas aux Indes Galantes (Paris, 1955).

Bussler, Ludwig, German music theorist and pedagogue; b. Berlin, Nov. 26, 1838; d. there, Jan. 18, 1900. His father was the painter, author, and privy councillor Robert Bussler; his maternal grandfather was the famous tenor singer, Karl Bader. He studied with Dehn, Grell and Wieprecht; then taught theory at the Ganz School of Music in Berlin (1865) and at the Stern Cons. (from 1879); was also active as a conductor at various Berlin theaters. In 1883 he became the music critic for the National-Zeitung. His eminently practical writings are: Musikalische Elementarlehre (1867; 3rd ed., 1882; English transl. N.Y., 1895; also in Russian); Der strenge Satz (1877); Harmonische Übungen am Klavier (1877; in English, N.Y., 1890); Kontrapunkt und Fuge im freien Tonsatz (1878); Musikalische Formenlehre (1878; English edition, N.Y., 1883); Praktische musikalische Kompositionslehre: Part I, Lehre vom Tonsatz (1878); Part II, Freie Komposition (1879); also Instrumentation und Orchestersatz (1879); Elementar-Melodik (1879); Geschichte der Musik (1882, six lectures); Modulationslehre (1882); Lexikon der musikalischen Harmonien (1889).

Bussotti, Sylvano, Italian composer of the avantgarde; b. Florence, Oct. 1, 1931. He studied violin; at the age of 9 was enrolled in the Cherubini Cons. in Florence, where he studied theory with Roberto Lupi, and also took piano lessons with Luigi Dallapiccola, while continuing his basic violin studies. In 1957 he went to Paris, where he studied privately with Max Deutsch. He became active as a theatrical director; also exhibited his paintings at European galleries. As a composer he adopted an extreme idiom, in which verbalization and pictorial illustrations are combined with aleatory discursions within the framework of multimedia productions. Many of his scores look like abstract expressionist paintings, with fragments of musical notation interspersed with occasional realistic representations of human or animal forms. WORKS: Memoria for baritone, chorus and orch. (1962); Fragmentations for harp (1962); and La Passion selon Sade, his crowning achievement, which makes use of theatrical effects, diagrams, drawings, surrealistic illustrations, etc., with thematic content evolving from a dodecaphonic nucleus, allowing great latitude for free interpolations, and set in an open-end

form in which fragments of the music are recapitulated at will, until the players are mutually neutralized. The unifying element of the score is the recurrent motive D-Es-A-D-E, spelling the name De Sade, interwoven with that of B-A-C-H. The first production of La Passion selon Sade took place in Palermo on Sept. 5, 1965. His grand opera Lorenzaccio, in 23 scenes, employing a multitude of performers which required 230 costumes, all designed by Bussotti himself, was produced at the opening of the Venice Festival of Contemporary Music on Sept. 7, 1972. Among Bussotti's other conceits is 5 Pieces for David Tudor (1959), in which the dedicatee wears thick gloves to avoid hitting single and potentially melodious tones on the keyboard. Among his other works of various descriptions are 3 pieces for puppet theater, Nottetempolunapark (1954), Arlechinbatocieria (1955), Tre mascare in gloria (1956); 7 Fogli for various instrumental combinations (1959); Phrase à trois for string trio (1960); Torso for voices, speaker and instrumentalists (1960–63); La Partition ne peut se faire que dans la violence for orch. (1962); I semi di Gramsci for quartet and orch. (1967); Tableaux vivants for 2 pianos (1965); Rara requiem to words in several languages (1969).

Bustabo, Guila, American violinist; b. Manitowoc, Wisconsin, Feb. 25, 1919. She was a child prodigy; played at a benefit concert in Chicago at the age of 4; at the age of 10 was soloist with the New York Philharmonic, performing a Wieniawski concerto (Nov. 2, 1929). She studied with Louis Persinger in New York and with Enesco and Hubay in Europe. From 1964 to 1970 she was on the faculty of the Cons. at Innsbruck, Austria.

Bustini, Alessandro, Italian composer; b. Rome, Dec. 24, 1876; d. there, June 23, 1970. He studied at the Santa Cecilia Academy with Sgambati (piano), Renzi (organ) and Falchi (composition), graduating in 1897. He was subsequently appointed to the faculty of Santa Cecilia, and was its president from 1952 to 1964. His works, all written in the traditional Italian manner, include the opera Maria Dulcis (Rome, April 15, 1902); 2 symphonies (1899 and 1909); Le tentazioni, a symph. poem (1914); Le stagioni for violin and chamber orch. (1934); 2 string quartets; songs; piano works.

Buths, Julius, German pianist; b. Wiesbaden, May 7, 1851; d. Düsseldorf, March 12, 1920. He was a pupil of his father; later of Hiller in Cologne and Kiel in Berlin; conducted the "Cecilia" at Wiesbaden (1871–72); traveled to Milan and Paris (1873–74); conducted in Breslau (1875–79) and in Elberfeld (1879–90); from 1890–1908 was music director at Düsseldorf, and conducted several Rhine music festivals; in 1902 was appointed director of the Düsseldorf Cons. He wrote a piano concerto; a piano quintet; a string quartet; a piano suite; etc.

Butler (real name **Whitwell**), **O'Brien,** Irish composer; b. Cahersiveen, Ireland, c.1870; d. May 7, 1915 (lost on the Lusitania). He began his musical studies in Italy, then became a pupil of C. V. Stanford and W.

Parratt at the Royal College of Music in London; later traveled extensively, and spent some time in India, where he wrote an opera *Muirgheis,* the first opera to be written to a libretto in the Gaelic language; it was produced in Dublin, Dec. 7, 1903. Other compositions include a sonata for violin and piano (on Irish themes) and songs.

Butt, Clara, English contralto; b. Southwick, Sussex, Feb. 1, 1873; d. Worthsloke, Oxford, Jan. 23, 1936. She studied with J. H. Blower at the Royal College of Music, later with Bouhy in Paris and Etelka Gerster in Berlin; made her debut as Ursula in Sullivan's *Golden Legend* (London, Dec. 7, 1892); then appeared with great success at the festivals at Hanley and Bristol. She was heard twice in the U.S. (1899 and 1913); made a world tour with her husband, **R. Kennerly Rumford,** a noted baritone (1913-14). Several composers wrote works especially for her (Elgar, *Sea-Pictures*; F. Cliff, *Triumph of Alcestis,* H. Bedford, *Romeo and Juliet*; etc.). In 1920 she was made Dame of the British Empire.
BIBLIOGRAPHY: W. Ponder, *Clara Butt* (London, 1928).

Butterley, Nigel, Australian composer; b. Sydney, May 13, 1935. He began piano lessons at the age of four; studied at the New South Wales State Cons. with Noel Nickson and Raymond Hanson (1952-55); then in London with Priaulx Rainier (1962). From 1955 to 1972 he was music adviser to the Australian Broadcasting Commission.
WORKS: *Diversion* for brass quintet (1958); *Canticle of David* for strings (1960); *Oboe Sonatina* (1960); *The Tell-Tale Heart,* after Poe, a ballet for 2 pianos and percussion (1961); *Laudes (Praises)* for flute, clarinet, horn, trumpet, violin, viola, cello and piano (1963); *String Quartet* (1965); *Canticle of the Sun* for 3 amateur instrumental groups (1965); *The White-Throated Warbler* for recorder and harpsichord (1965); *In the Head the Fire,* a "radio tableau" for narrator, tenor, baritone, chorus, winds, piano, organ and percussion (Italia Prize, 1966); *Interaction,* an "improvisation" for painter and orch. (1967; expanded into a television film); Variations, for wind quintet, piano and recorded piano (Canberra, Sept. 30, 1967); *Meditations of Thomas Traherne* for orchestra and recorder ensemble (1968); *Carmina* for voice and wind quintet (1968); Violin Concerto (1968-70); *Pentad* for 27 wind instruments (1969); *Refractions* for wind quintet and 28 string instruments (1969); *Explorations* for piano and orch. (Sydney, May 2, 1970, in the presence of Queen Elizabeth II); *Voices* for wind quintet (1972); *First Day Covers,* a "philharmonic philatelia" for narrator and orch. (1972); *Fire in the Heavens* for orch. (1973); *The Four Elements* for orch. (1973); *Watershore,* after Walt Whitman, for 4 narrators, improvising group, 3 cellos and piano roll (1977).

Butterworth, George Sainton Kaye, talented English composer; b. London, July 12, 1885; killed in the battle of Pozières, Aug. 5, 1916. He inherited his love for music from his mother, a singer, Julia Wigan; learned to play organ at school in Yorkshire; then studied piano at Eton. He later entered Trinity College, Oxford;

then engaged in music teaching and writing music criticism; also became an ardent collector of folksongs, and prepared material for Vaughan Williams's *London Symphony.* He made several arrangements of folksongs and wrote an orchestral piece, *The Banks of Green Willows,* on folk themes (London, March 20, 1914). He enlisted in the British army at the outbreak of World War I. He wrote *Six Songs from 'A Shropshire Lad'* (1911); 11 folksongs from Sussex (1912); *On Christmas Night* for mixed chorus (1912); *Cherry Tree,* a prelude for orch. (1912); *Love Blows as the Wind Blows* for baritone and string quartet (1914).

Butting, Max, German composer; b. Berlin, Oct. 6, 1888; d. there, July 13, 1976. He studied organ in Berlin and composition in Munich. Returning to Berlin he was a successful teacher, but in 1933 was deprived of his various positions for political reasons, being the former editor of a Socialist publication. He was able to return to his professional activities after the end of the war. In 1948 he was appointed lecturer in the music division of the East Berlin Radio; in 1968 he received an honorary doctor's degree from the Univ. of Berlin.
WORKS: an opera, *Plautus im Nonnenkloster* (Leipzig, Oct. 3, 1959); 10 symphonies (1923-63); *Sinfonietta with banjo* (1929); Flute Concerto (1950); *Symphonic Variations* (1953); Sinfonietta op. 100 (1960); Piano Concerto (1965); *Legende* for orch. (1966); *Triptychon* for orch. (1967); *Concert Overture* (1973); 10 string quartets (1914-71); String Quintet (1916); Quintet for Violin, Viola, Cello, Oboe and Clarinet (1921); Wind Quintet (1925); Piano Trio (1947); String Trio (1952); numerous minor pieces of chamber music; a considerable number of piano pieces, choruses and songs. His music is animated by polyphonic purposefulness and is marked by rhythmic vitality and lyric meditation. Since many of his works were destined for amateur performances, Butting shunned modernistic involvements; however in his 9th and 10th symphonies he applied dodecaphonic structures.
BIBLIOGRAPHY: Dietrich Brennecke, *Das Lebenswerk Max Buttings* (Leipzig, 1973).

Buttstett, Franz Vollrath, German composer, grandson of **Johann Heinrich Buttstett;** b. Erfurt, April 2, 1735; d. Rotenburg, May 7, 1814. He was a member of a musical family; received his education at home; was active as organist in Weckersheim from 1756, and went to Rotenburg in 1767. He wrote cantatas and instrumental sonatas.
BIBLIOGRAPHY: Hans Kern, *Franz Vollrath Buttstett: eine Studie zur Musik des Spätbarock* (Würzburg, 1939).

Buttstett, Johann Heinrich, German organist and composer; b. Bindersleben, near Erfurt, April 25, 1666; d. Erfurt, Dec. 1, 1727. He studied with Johann Pachelbel; occupied posts as organist in various churches in Erfurt. In 1713 he published an album of keyboard pieces, *Musikalische Klavier-Kunst;* also wrote 5 Masses and 36 chorale preludes. His *Harmonia aeterna* is a polemical pamphlet directed against Mattheson.

BIBLIOGRAPHY: E. Ziller, *Der Erfurter Organist, Johann Heinrich Buttstett* (Halle, 1934).

Buttykay, Akos, Hungarian pianist and composer; b. Halmi, July 22, 1871; d. Debrecen, Oct. 26, 1935. He studied at the Budapest Cons.; in 1894 went to Weimar for further courses in piano playing. He toured in Central Europe as a pianist; in 1907 settled in Budapest as piano teacher at the Musik Academy. He wrote several operettas which were modestly successful at their productions in Budapest: *The Flying Greek* (Budapest, Oct. 19, 1905); *Pompom* (1907); *Cinderella* (Budapest, Oct. 26, 1912); *A Love Storm* (Budapest, Feb. 6, 1920); 2 symphonies (1900, 1902); *Magyar Suite* for orch. (1900); *Magyar Rhapsody* for orch. (1931); Violin Sonata (1908); *Capriccio* for violin and piano (1928); many songs.

Buus, Jacques (Jachet de or **van Paus; Jacobus Bohusius),** Flemish contrapuntist; b. probably in Bruges; d. Vienna, late July, 1565. His first publications were 2 French songs, published in Lyons in 1538. In 1541 he went to Italy and was engaged as assistant organist at San Marco in Venice; he may have studied with Willaert there. He published in Venice 2 books of instrumental *Canzoni francese* (1543; 1550); 2 books of *Ricercari* (1547; 1549); and 1 book of *Motetti* (1549); his madrigals were published in various collections of the period; reprints are in Kinkeldey's *Orgel und Klavier in der Musik des 16. Jahrhunderts* (1910; p. 245 ff.) and Riemann's *Musikgeschichte in Beispielen* (No. 40).
BIBLIOGRAPHY: G. Sutherland, "The Ricercari of Jacques Buus," *Musical Quarterly* (Oct. 1945).

Buxtehude, Dietrich, famous organist and composer; b. Oldesloe (Holstein), c.1637; d. Lübeck, May 9, 1707. His father, **Johann Buxtehude** (1602–1674), an organist of German extraction, was active in Holstein, then under Danish rule. Despite diligent research, no documented information has been discovered to shed any light on Dietrich Buxtehude's early years. It is to be assumed that he studied with his father. He held a post as organist in Helsingborg, in 1657; was in Helsingör in 1660. On April 11, 1668, he was elected as successor to the famous organist Franz Tunder at the St. Mary Church in Lübeck; according to custom in such successions, he married Tunder's daughter (Aug. 3, 1668). In 1673 he established his celebrated musical services, the *Abendmusiken*, made up of organ music and concerted pieces for chorus and orch., held annually on the five Sundays before Christmas from 4 to 5. Handel journeyed to Lübeck (1703) with the apparent intention of securing Buxtehude's post after his retirement or death, but the notorious marriage clause which would have compelled him to marry one of Buxtehude's five daughters deterred him from further negotiations. In 1705 Bach traveled on foot 200 miles from Arnstadt to Lübeck to hear Buxtehude; it is presumed that Bach, too, declined the Lübeck post because of the marriage clause. There can be no doubt that Buxtehude exercised profound influence on Bach, both as organist and composer. A complete edition of Buxtehude's organ works was publ. by Spitta (2 vols., 1875–76) and by Josef Hedar (3 vols., 1952); a com-

plete edition of his vocal music ed. by W. Gurlitt *et al.*, is in 8 vols. (1927–58). The instrumental works are in vol. 11 of *Denkmäler deutscher Tonkunst*; and Abendmusiken and church cantatas are in vol. 14; 19 newly discovered keyboard suites by Buxtehude were brought out by E. Bangert (Copenhagen, 1942).
BIBLIOGRAPHY: H. Jimmerthal, *Buxtehude* (Lübeck, 1877); C. Stiehl, *Die Organisten an der Marienkirche und die Abendmusiken in Lübeck* (Leipzig, 1886); A Pirro, *Buxtehude* (Paris, 1913); S. E. A. Hagen, *Diderik Buxtehude* (Copenhagen, 1920); W. Stahl, *Franz Tunder und Dietrich Buxtehude* (Leipzig, 1926); W. Stahl, *Buxtehude* (Kassel, 1937); W. Buszin, "Buxtehude," *Musical Quarterly* (Oct. 1937); J. Hedar, *Buxtehude's Orgelwerke* (Stockholm, 1951). For a detailed list of editions and bibliographical minutiae, see *Die Musik in Geschichte und Gegenwart*.

Buzzi-Peccia, Arturo, song composer and teacher; b. Milan, Oct. 13, 1854; d. New York, Aug. 29, 1943. He emigrated to America in 1898 and lived mostly in New York as a vocal teacher. He published numerous songs and choral works; also a book, *How to Succeed in Singing* (1925).

Buzzolla, Antonio, Italian composer; b. Adria, March 2, 1815; d. Venice, March 20, 1871. He studied with his father, who was a conductor, and with Donizetti. After bringing out at Venice the operas *Ferramondo* (Dec. 3, 1836), *Mastino I della Scala* (1841), and *Gli Avventurieri* (May 14, 1842) he traveled in Germany and France; returned to Venice in 1847, where he produced 2 later operas: *Amleto* (Feb. 24, 1848) and *Elisabetta di Valois* (Feb. 16, 1850). In 1855 he was appointed maestro di cappella at San Marco, for which he subsequently wrote much sacred music. An opera in Venetian dialect, *La Puta onorata*, remained unfinished.
BIBLIOGRAPHY: A. Casellati, "Antonio Buzzolla," *Musica d'oggi* (July 1930)

Byrd (or **Byrde, Bird**), **William,** great English composer; b. probably in Lincolnshire, 1543; d. Stondon, Essex, July 4, 1623. Anthony Wood states that Byrd was "bred up to musick under Tallis" and there are other indirect indications that Byrd was Tallis's pupil. He was appointed organist of Lincoln Cathedral on Feb. 27, 1563, was married to Juliana Birley in 1568; early in 1570 he was elected a member of the Chapel Royal, but retained his post at Lincoln Cathedral until the end of 1572; he then assumed his duties, together with Tallis, as organist of the Chapel Royal. In 1575 the two were granted a patent by Queen Elizabeth for the exclusive privilege of printing music and selling music paper for 21 years; however, the license proved unprofitable, and they petitioned the Queen in 1577 to give them an annuity in the form of a lease; this petition was granted. In 1585, after the death of Tallis, the license passed wholly into Byrd's hands. The first publication of the printing press of Byrd and Tallis was the first set of *Cantiones sacrae* in 5 and 6 voices (1575), printed for them by Vautrollier and dedicated to the Queen; works issued by Byrd alone under his license were *Psalmes, Sonnets, and Songs of Sadness* *and Pietie* in 5 voices (1588; publ. by Thomas East; reprinted as vol. XIV by Fellowes, *English Madrigal School*); *Songs of Sundrie Natures* for 3–6 voices (1589; reprint in vol. XV of *English Madrigal School*); *Liber Primus Sacrarum Cantionum* for 5 voices (1589); *Liber Secundus Sacrarum Cantionum* (1591); also in 1591 appeared the famous collection of virginal music by Byrd, *My Ladye Nevells Booke* (42 pieces; modern edition publ. by Hilda Andrews, London, 1926; repr., N.Y., 1969). In 1593 Byrd moved to Stondon Place, near Ongar, Essex, and, owing to various litigations and disputes concerning the ownership of the property, did not publish anything until 1605, when he brought out the first book of *Gradualia*; 2 years later there followed the second book (both books republ. in *Tudor Church Music*, vol. 7). In 1611 the book of *Psalmes, Songs and Sonnets* was publ. (reprint in vol. XVI of *English Madrigal School*); in the same year Byrd contributed several pieces to *Parthenia*, a collection of virginal compositions by Byrd, Bull and Gibbons (newly ed. by Margaret H. Glyn; London, 1927); in 1614 he contributed 4 anthems to Leighton's *Teares or Lamentacions of a Sorrowful Soule*; separate numbers were publ. in various other collections (*Musica Transalpina*, 1588; Watson's *Italian Madrigales*, 1590; Barnard's *Selected Church Music*, 1641; Boyce's *Cathedral Music*); other music for virginals and organ in *Virginal Book of Queen Elizabeth, Fitzwilliam Virginal Book* (70 pieces), *Will. Forster's Virginal Book* (33 pieces), and *Benjamin Cosyn's Virginal Book* (2 pieces). New editions (besides those mentioned above): *Tudor Church Music* (vol. 2, English church music; vol. 9, Masses, cantiones and motets); psalms, sonnets and madrigals, by E. H. Fellowes (1920); a collected edition of Byrd's vocal works, also by Fellowes (7 vols., 1937–38); *Byrd Organ Book*, a collection of 21 pieces edited for piano from the virginal MSS by Margaret H. Glyn (London, 1923); 14 pieces for keyboard instruments, by J. A. Fuller-Maitland and W. Barclay Squire (London, 1923). A new publication of complete works, *The Byrd Edition*, ed. by P. Brett, was begun in 1968. A composer of great skill, Byrd was unsurpassed in versatility by any of his contemporaries; he excelled in all branches of composition, displaying his masterly technique equally well in ecclesiastical music, madrigal, solo song, chamber music and keyboard music.

BIBLIOGRAPHY: E. H. Fellowes, *English Madrigal Composers* (1921); E. H. Fellowes, *William Byrd: A Short Account of His Life and Work* (Oxford, 1923; 3rd ed., London, 1936); Margaret H. Glyn, *About Elizabethan Virginal Music and Its Composers* (London, 1924; revised ed., 1935); F. Howes, *William Byrd* (London, 1928); E. J. Dent, "William Byrd and the Madrigal," in the *Johannes Wolf Festschrift* (Berlin, 1929); J. A. Westrup, "William Byrd," *Music & Letters* (1943); W. Palmer, "Word-Painting and Suggestion in Byrd," *Music Review* (1952); W. Palmer, "Byrd and Amen," *Music & Letters* (1953); Fr. B. Zimmermann, "Advanced Tonal Design in the Part-Songs of William Byrd" in *Kongress Bericht* (Cologne, 1958); Th. Dart and Ph. Brett, "Songs by William Byrd in Manuscripts at Harvard, " *Harvard Univ. Bulletin* (1960); J. Kerman, "Byrd, Tallis and the Art of Imitation" in *Aspects of Medieval and Renaissance Music*, in the dedicatory volume for Gustave Reese (N.Y., 1966); H. Andrews, *The Technique of Byrd's Vocal Polyphony* (London, 1966); W. B. Gray, "Some Aspects of Word Treatment in the Music of William Byrd," *The Musical Quarterly* (1969). A list of Byrd's works was published by the Byrd Tercentenary Committee in London, 1923.

C

Caamaño, Roberto, Argentinian pianist and composer; b. Buenos Aires, July 7, 1923. He studied at the Conservatorio Nacional in Buenos Aires; toured South America as a concert pianist; from 1961 to 1964 he was artistic director of the Teatro Colón in Buenos Aires. In 1964 he was appointed prof. of composition of the Pontífica Universita Católica Argentina. He was the editor of a valuable compendium in 3 vols., *La Historia del Teatro Colón (1908–1968),* published in Buenos Aires in 1969, illustrated with color plates, drawings and photographs.

WORKS: *Magnificat* for chorus and orch. (1954); *Variaciones americanas* for orch. (1954); *Bandoneon Concerto* (1954); 2 Piano Concertos (1957, 1971); Piano Quintet (1962); 2 string quartets (1946, 1947); *Cantata para la Paz* (1966); *Tripartita* for wind orch. (1967).

Caba, Eduardo, Bolivian composer; b. Potosí, Oct. 13, 1890; d. La Paz, March 3, 1953. He was educated in Buenos Aires; then went to study with Turina in Spain; in 1942 he settled in La Paz. His ballets and other music are inspired by the pentatonic structure of certain Bolivian folksongs.

Cabanilles, Juan Bautista José, Spanish organist, and composer; b. Algemesí, province of Valencia, Sept. 4, 1644; d. Valencia, April 29, 1712. He studied for the priesthood at Valencia and probably received his musical training at the Cathedral there; was appointed organist of Valencia Cathedral, May 15, 1665 (succeeding J. de la Torre) and retained that post until his death; was ordained a priest on Sept. 22, 1668. He was the greatest of the early Spanish composers for organ, and the most prolific. He composed chiefly "tientos," remarkable for the ingenious use of the variation form (on liturgical or popular themes). A complete edition of his works, in 4 vols., has been edited by H. Anglès (Barcelona), 1927–56. The *Obras vocales* are ed. by J. Climent (Valencia, 1971).

BIBLIOGRAPHY: H. Anglès, "Orgelmusik der Schola Hispanica vom XV.–XVI. Jahrhundert." in *P. Wagner-Festschrift* (Leipzig, 1926); M. Bradshaw, "Juan Cabanilles: The Toccattas and Tientos," *Musical Quarterly* (April 1973).

Cabezón (Cabeçon), Antonio de, great Spanish organist and composer; b. Matajudíos, near Burgos, in 1510 (the exact date is unknown: see S. Kastner's letter to the editor of *Music & Letters* for April 1955); d. Madrid, March 26, 1566. He became blind in infancy; went to Palencia about 1521 to study with the cathedral organist García de Baeza and with Tomás Gómez. He was appointed organist to the court of the Emperor Charles V and Empress Isabel (1526); after her death, Cabezón entered the service of Prince Philip and accompanied him to Italy, Germany, the Netherlands (1548–51) and England (1554); he returned to Spain (1556) and remained court organist until his death. His keyboard style greatly influenced the development of organ composition on the continent and the composers for the virginals in England; Pedrell called him "the Spanish Bach." The series *Li-*

bro de cifra nueva (1557), which contains the earliest editions of Cabezón's works, was reprinted by H. Anglès in *La música en la corte de Carlos V* (1944). His son and successor at the court of Philip II, **Hernando** (b. Madrid; baptized Sept. 7, 1541; d. Valladolid, Oct. 1, 1602), published his instrumental works as *Obras de música para tecla, arpa y vihuela* (Madrid, 1578). This volume contains exercises in 2 and 3 parts, arrangements of hymn tunes, 4-part "tientos," arrangements of motets in up to 6 parts by Josquin and other Franco-Flemish composers, and variations on tunes of the day (*El Caballero,* etc.). Copies are in the British Museum, in Sir Percy Wyndham's Collection, at Brussels, Berlin, Madrid and Washington, D.C. A modern edition appears in *Hispaniae schola musica sacra* (F. Pedrell, 1898; 4 vols.). The Institute of Medieval Music has issued several volumes of Cabezón's *Collected Works* (C. Jacobs, ed.; N.Y., 1967–). A short MS work for 5 voices is in the Medinaceli Library, Madrid.

BIBLIOGRAPHY: Otto Kinkeldey, *Orgel und Klavier in der Musik des 16. Jahrhunderts* (1910); Willi Apel, "Early Spanish Music for Lute and Keyboard Instruments," *Musical Quarterly* (July 1934); S. Kastner, *Antonio de Cabezón* (Barcelona, 1952); T. Dart, "Cavazzoni and Cabezón," *Music & Letters* (Jan. 1955; a rebuttal to Dart's conjecture concerning the relationship of Cavazzoni and Cabezón is found in Knud Jeppesen's article in the summer 1955 issue of *Journal of the American Musicological Society;* special Cabezón issue of *Anuario musical* (Vol. XXI, 1966; publ. 1968); G. Bourligueux, "Antonio de Cabezón. Nota bibliográfia en su cuarto centenario," *Boletín de la Inst. Fernán González* (Jan.–June 1970).

Caccini, Francesca, daughter of **Giulio Caccini,** nicknamed "La Cecchina"; b. Florence, Sept. 18, 1587; d. about 1640. She was probably the first woman composer of operas. Her opera-ballet *La liberazione di Ruggiero dall'isola d'Alcina* was produced at a palace, near Florence, on Feb. 2, 1625, and a book of songs from it was publ. in the same year. A modern reprint, edited by Doris Silbert, was publ. in Northampton, Mass. (1945). Francesca Caccini wrote further a *Ballo delle zingare* (Florence, Feb. 24, 1615) in which she acted as one of the gypsies. Her sacred opera *Il martirio di Sant' Agata* was produced in Florence, Feb. 10, 1622.

BIBLIOGRAPHY: A. Bonaventura, "Il ritratto della Cecchina," *La Cultura musicale* (1922); D. Silbert, "F. Caccini called 'La Cecchina,'" *Musical Quarterly* (Jan. 1946); C. Raney, "Francesca Caccini's *Primo Libro,*" *Music & Letters* (Oct. 1967).

Caccini, Giulio, Italian composer called **Romano** because he lived mostly in Rome); b. Trivoli, c.1550; d. Florence, Dec. (buried Dec. 10), 1618. He was a pupil of Scipione della Palla in singing and lute playing. His first compositions were madrigals in the traditional polyphonic style, but the new ideas generated in the discussions of the artists and literati of the 'Camerata,' in the houses of Bardi and Corsi at Florence, inspired him to write vocal soli in recitative form (then termed 'musica in stile rappresentativo'), which he sang with consummate skill to his own accompaniment on the theorbo. These first compositions in a dramatic idiom were followed by his settings of separate scenes written by Bardi, and finally by the opera *Il combattimento d'Apolline col serpente* (poem by Bardi); next was *Euridice* (1600; poem by Rinuccini), and *Il rapimento di Cefalo* (in collaboration with others; first performed on Oct. 9, 1600, at the Palazzo Vecchio in Florence). Then followed *Le nuove musiche*, a series of madrigals for solo voice, with bass (Florence, 1602; new editions, Venice, 1607 and 1615; a modern edition of the 1602 publication, prepared by H. Wiley Hitchcock [Madison, Wisc., 1970], includes an annotated English trans. of Caccini's preface, realizations of the solo madrigals, airs, and the final section of *Il rapimento di Cefalo*, an introductory essay on Caccini, the music, the poetry, manuscripts, other editions, and a bibliography. A trans. of the preface is also available in O. Strunk, *Source Readings in Music History* [N.Y., 1950]). The song *Amarilli mia bella* from the first series became very popular. Caccini also published *Fuggilotio musicale* (Venice, 2nd ed., 1613; including madrigals, sonnets, arias, etc.). From 1565 Caccini lived in Florence as a singer at the Tuscan court. He was called, by abbate Angelo Grillo, the 'father of a new style of music'; Bardi said of him that he had 'attained the goal of perfect music.' But his claim to priority in writing vocal music in the 'stile rappresentativo' is not supported by known chronology. Caccini's opera *Il rapimento di Cefalo* was performed three days after Peri's path-breaking *Euridice*; the closeness in time of operatic productions by both Caccini and Peri is further emphasized by the fact that when Peri produced *Euridice* in Florence (1600), he used some of Caccini's songs in the score. Caccini later made his own setting of *Euridice* (1600), but it was not produced until Dec. 5, 1602. On the other hand, Caccini was undoubtedly the first to publish an operatic work, for his score of *Euridice* was printed early in 1601, before the publication of Peri's work of the same title.

BIBLIOGRAPHY: A. Ehrichs, *Giulio Caccini* (Leipzig, 1908); R. Marchal, "Giulio Caccini," *La Revue Musicale* (June 1925); F. Ghisi, *Alle fonti della monodia* (Milan, 1940); C. Morricone, "Considerazioni sul *Fuggilozio de Giulio Caccini*," *Rivista Italiana di Musicologia* (1968); L. Bianconi, "Giulio Caccini e il manierismo musicale," *Chigiana* XXV/5 (1968); H. W. Hitchcock, "Depriving Caccini of a Musical Pastime," *Journal of the American Musicological Society* (Spring 1972); idem, "A New Biographical Source for Caccini," ibid. (Spring 1973).

Cacioppo, George, American composer of the avantgarde; b. Monroe, Michigan, Sept. 24, 1927. He studied with Ross Lee Finney at the Univ. of Michigan; received his M.A. in composition in 1952; then worked in Tanglewood, studying with Leon Kirchner. In 1960 he attended classes of Roberto Gerhard, then a visiting prof. at the Univ. of Michigan. Cacioppo was a cofounder of the ONCE Festival concerts in Ann Arbor in 1960. His technique partakes of the Schoenbergian credo while studiously avoiding the chronic chromaticism of atonal writing. Verbalization is an integral part of all of his music; aleatory principles are expressed in 'open end' forms.

WORKS: *Pianopieces* for any number of pianos with their realizations on tape sounding synchronously or non-synchronously and lasting any practical, or impractical length of time; *Holy Ghost Vacuum, or America Faints,* for electric organ (Ann Arbor, March 29, 1966, composer at the manuals); *Time on Time in Miracles* for soprano, 2 horns, 2 trombones, cello, piano and percussion (1964); *Cassiopeia* for 2 pianos (1964).

Cadman, Charles Wakefield, American composer; b. Johnstown, Pa., Dec. 24, 1881; d. Los Angeles, Dec. 30, 1946. His great grandfather was Samuel Wakefield, the inventor of the so-called "Buckwheat Notation." Cadman studied organ with Leo Oehmler in Pittsburgh, and comp. with Emil Paur. He was especially interested in American Indian music; gave lecture recitals with the Indian mezzo-soprano Tsianina Redfeather.

WORKS: Dramatic: the opera *Shanewis* (*The Robin Woman*), his most successful work (Metropolitan Opera, March 23, 1918); *The Sunset Trail,* operatic cantata (Denver, Dec. 5, 1922); *The Garden of Mystery* (N.Y., March 20, 1925); *A Witch of Salem* (Chicago, Dec. 8, 1926); a radio play, *The Willow Tree* (NBC, October 3, 1933); Orchestral Works: *Thunderbird Suite* (Los Angeles, Jan. 9, 1917); *Oriental Rhapsody* (1917); *Dark Dancers of the Mardi Gras* (1933); *Suite on American Folktunes* (1937); symph. poem, *Pennsylvania* (Los Angeles, March 7, 1940); cantatas: *Father of Waters* (1928); *House of Joy; Indian Love Charm* for children's choir; *The Vision of Sir Launfal* for male voices, written for the Pittsburgh Prize Competition (1909); Piano Sonata; violin pieces; and about 180 songs, of which *At Dawning* acquired enormous popularity.

BIBLIOGRAPHY: E. E. Hipsher, *American Opera and Its Composers* (Philadelphia, 1934; pp. 99–110).

Caduff, Sylvia, Swiss conductor; b. Chur, Jan. 7, 1937. She studied at the Lucerne Cons., receiving a piano diploma in 1961; then attended Karajan's conducting classes at the Berlin Cons.; continued conducting studies with Kubelik, Matacio and Otterloo in Lucerne, Salzburg, and Hilversum (Holland); made her debut with the Tonhalle-Orch. of Zürich. She won first prize in the 1966 Dimitri Mitropoulos conducting competition in New York; as a result, she was an assistant conductor under Bernstein with the N.Y. Philharmonic (1966–67); taught orchestral conducting at the Bern Cons. (1972–77). In 1977 she became the first woman in Europe to be appointed a general music director when she took that position with the Orch. of the city of Solingen, Germany.

Cady, Calvin Brainerd, American music pedagogue; b. Barry, Illinois, June 21, 1851; d. Portland, Oregon, May 29, 1928. He studied at Oberlin College and at Leipzig Cons.; taught harmony and piano at Oberlin, the Univ. of Michigan, and the Chicago College of Music (1888–94); from 1907 he lectured on music at Columbia Univ. His teaching emphasized the understanding of music as a gateway to all liberal education. He published 3 vols. of a manual, *Musical Education* (1902–07).

Cafaro (Caffaro), Pasquale, Italian composer; b. San Pietro, in Galatina, Lecce, Feb. 8, 1716; d. Naples, Oct. 23, 1787. He became second master at the Naples Cons. della Pietà in 1759, and first master in 1771.
WORKS: the operas *Ipermestra* (Naples, Dec. 18, 1751), *La disfatta di Dario* (Naples, Jan. 20, 1756), *L'incendio di Troia* (Naples, Jan. 20, 1757), *L'Olimpiade* (Naples, Jan. 12, 1769), and *Antigono* (Naples, Aug. 13, 1770); 6 oratorios; 4 cantatas; a *Stabat Mater* in 2 parts, with organ.

Caffarelli (real name **Gaetano Majorano**), artificial soprano *(musico);* b. Bitonto, April 12, 1710; d. Naples, Jan. 31, 1783. A poor peasant boy, endowed with a beautiful voice, he was discovered by a musician, Domenico Caffarelli, who taught him, and later sent him to Porpora at Naples. In gratitude to his patron he assumed the name of Caffarelli. He studied for five years with Porpora, who predicted a brilliant career for him. Caffarelli became a master of pathetic song, and excelled in coloratura as well; read the most difficult music at sight, and was an accomplished harpsichord player. His debut at the Teatro Valle (Rome, 1724) in a female role (as was the custom for artificial soprani) was a triumph. In 1738 he sang in London, then in Paris and Vienna. His last public appearance took place on May 30, 1754 in Naples. He was in Lisbon during the earthquake of 1755; upon his return to Naples, he bought the dukedom of Santo-Durato with the fortune he had amassed during his career, and assumed the title of duke.

Caffi, Francesco, Italian music scholar; b. Venice, June 14, 1778; d. Padua, Jan. 24, 1874. After a period of study in Venice, he produced an allegorical drama, *L'armonia richiamata,* which was performed at the opening of the Istituto Filarmonico there (Aug. 20, 1811). In 1827 he moved to Milan; in 1840 to Rovigo. His most important work was a *Storia della musica sacra nella gia Cappella Ducale di San Marco in Venezia dal 1318 al 1797* (2 vols.; Venice, 1854–55; reprinted, 1931). This was the first part of an ambitious project dealing with music in Venice; the second part, *Storia della musica teatrale in Venezia durante la sua Repubblica* was completed by Caffi shortly before his death, but remained in MS. He further published monographs on Bonaventura Furlanetto (1820); Zarlino (1836); Lotti; Benedetto Marcello (in Cicogna's *Venetiani Iscritioni),* and on Giammateo Asola (Padua, 1862). Caffi's grandson, F. A. Salvagnini, wrote his biography (Rome, 1905).

Cage, John, American composer of ultra-modern tendencies; b. Los Angeles, Sept. 5, 1912. He studied piano with Fannie Dillon and Richard Buhlig in Los Angeles and with Lazare Lévy in Paris; returning to America he studied composition in California with Adolph Weiss and with Henry Cowell in New York; also attended Schoenberg's course at the Univ. of California, Los Angeles. He developed Cowell's piano technique, making use of tone clusters and playing directly on the piano strings, and initiated a type of procedure which he called "prepared piano." The "preparation" consists of placing on the piano strings a variety of objects, such as screws, copper coins, rubber bands and the like, which altered the tone color of individual keys. As a performer on the "prepared piano" John Cage attracted considerable attention at his concerts in America and Europe. Eventually the term and the procedure gained acceptance among many avant-garde composers and was listed as a legitimate innovative method in many music dictionaries. From 1937 to 1939 he was employed as an accompanist in a dance class at the Cornish School in Seattle, where he also organized a percussion group. He taught for a season at the School of Design in Chicago (1941–42); then moved to New York where he began his fruitful association with the dancer Merce Cunningham, for whom he wrote many special works. An even more important association was his collaboration with the pianist David Tudor, who was able to reify Cage's exotic inspirations, works in which the performer shares the composer's creative role. With the passing years Cage departed from the musical pragmatism of precise notation and definite ways of performance, electing instead to mark his creative intentions in graphic symbols and pictorial representations. He soon established the principle of indeterminacy in musical composition, borrowing the term from modern physics; in this sense no two performances of a composition can be identical. In the meantime he became immersed in the study of mycology, and acquired a formidable expertise in mushroom gathering; he even won a prize in Italy in competition with professional mycologists. He also became interested in chess and played demonstration games with Marcel Duchamps, the famous painter turned chessmaster, on chessboards designed by Lowell Cross to operate on aleatory principles with the aid of a computer and a system of laser rays. In his endeavor to achieve the ultimate in freedom of musical expression he produced a piece entitled *4'33",* "tacet, any instrument or combination of instruments," in 3 movements during which no sounds are intentionally produced. It was "performed" by David Tudor in Woodstock, N.Y., on Aug. 29, 1952, who sat at the piano playing nothing for the length of time stipulated in the title. This was followed by another "silent" piece *0'00",* an idempotent "to be performed in any way by anyone" presented for the first time in Tokyo, Oct. 24, 1962. Any sounds, noises, coughs, chuckles, groans and growls, produced by the captive listeners to silence, are automatically regarded as an integral part of the piece itself, so that the wise crack about the impossibility of arriving at a fair judgment of a silent piece since one cannot tell whose music is not being played is invalidated by the uniqueness of Cage's art. Cage is a consummate showman, and his exhibitions invariably attract music lovers and music haters alike, expecting to be outraged or exhilarated as the case may be. In many such public happenings he departs from musical, unmusical or even antimusical programs in favor of a free exercise of surrealist imagination, often instructing the audience to participate actively, as for instance going out in the street and bringing in garbage pails needed for percussion effects, with or without garbage. Cage is a brilliant writer, much influenced by the manner, grammar, syntax and glorified illogic of Gertrude Stein. He publ. a book of lectures entitled *Silence* (Middletown, Conn., 1961); *A Year from Monday* (Middletown, Conn., 1967); *Notations* (N.Y., 1969); and *M: Writings '67-'72* (Middletown, Conn., 1973). A detailed annotated catalogue of his works was publ. by Edition Peters (N.Y., 1962). In view of the indeterminacy of so many of Cage's works, such a catalogue can serve only as a list of titles and suggestions of contents. In order to eliminate the subjective element in composition, Cage resorts to a method of selecting the components of his pieces by dice throwing, suggested by the Confucian classic *I Ching,* an ancient Chinese oracle book; the result is a system of total serialism, in which all elements pertaining to acoustical pulses, pitch, noise, duration, relative loudness, tempi, combinatory superpositions, etc., are determined by previously drawn charts.

WORKS: Sonata for solo clarinet (1933); *Imaginary Landscape No. 1* for 2 variable speed phonograph turntables, muted piano and cymbal (1939); *A Valentine out of Season* for prepared piano (1944); one-act ballet, *The Seasons* for chamber orch. (N.Y., May 13, 1947); *Sonatas and Interludes* for prepared piano (1948); String Quartet (1950); Concerto for Prepared Piano and Chamber Orchestra (1951); *Imaginary Landscape No. 4* for 12 radios, 24 players and a conductor (1951); *Musical Changes* for piano, composed according to *I Ching* (1951); *Water Music* for pianist, radio receiver and drums (1952); *Music for Piano 4-84* for any number of pianists up to 84 (1953–56); *Winter-Music* for any number of pianists up to 20 (1957); *Concert* for piano and orch. (N.Y., May 15, 1958); *Fontana Mix,* an indeterminate composition played from 10 transparent sheets superimposed in various ways (N.Y., April 26, 1959); *Music for Amplified Toy Pianos* (Middletown, Conn., Feb. 25, 1960); *Cartridge Music* (Cologne, Oct. 6, 1960); *Atlas Eclipticalis* for orch. (Montreal, Aug. 3, 1961); *Cheap Imitation* for piano (a memorized impression of some of Erik Satie's music, 1969; also for 24 to 95 players, 1971); *Reunion* for electronic chessboard (Toronto, March 5, 1968); *Renga* with *Apartment House 1776* for two synchronized orchestral groups and 4 vocal soloists (Boston Symph. Orch., Sept. 29, 1976). With Lejaren Hiller, Cage created a multi-media event entitled *HPSCHD* ("harpsichord" in computer language, minus the vowels); it was first performed on the Urbana campus of the Univ. of Illinois on May 16, 1969, realized for 7 amplified harpsichords and a number of tapes, slides and films programmed by a computer, with 52 projectors and 52 channels of sound for the tapes. His 32 *Etudes Australes* for piano are based on the configurations of the stars of the Southern Hemisphere.

BIBLIOGRAPHY: R. Kostelanetz, ed. *John Cage* (a collection of essays; N.Y., 1970); Michael Nyman, *Experimental Music: Cage and Beyond* (London, 1974).

Cagnoni, Antonio, Italian composer; b. Godiasco, near Voghera, Feb. 8, 1828: d. Bergamo, April 30, 1896. He studied with Ray and Frasi at the Milan Cons. (1842–47), where 3 of his operas were produced while he was an undergraduate: *Rosalia di San Miniato* (1845), *I due Savojardi* (1846), and his most suc-

cessful work, *Don Bucefalo* (1847). From 1852–73 he was maestro di cappella in the cathedral of Vigevano; from 1873 in the cathedral of Novarra; from 1887 in Santa Maria Maggiore in Bergamo. From 1848–74 he brought out 15 operas in various Italian theaters.

Cahier, Mme. Charles (*née* **Sara Jane Layton-Walker**), distinguished American contralto; b. Nashville, Tennessee, Jan. 8, 1870; d. Manhattan Beach, California, April 15, 1951. She studied in Paris with Jean de Reszke and in Vienna with Gustav Walter. She made her operatic debut in Nice (1904); married Charles Cahier on March 30, 1905. She was engaged at the Vienna Hofoper, and made guest appearances at the Metropolitan Opera; toured Europe and America for many years as a concert artist; later she taught at the Curtis Institute of Music in Philadelphia. Her repertory included Carmen and Wagnerian contralto roles.

Cahn, Sammy, American song composer; b. New York, June 18, 1913. He played violin in variety shows and organized a dance band; in 1940 he went to Hollywood and wrote film scores. In 1955 he started a music publishing company. His tune *High Hopes* became J. F. Kennedy's campaign song in 1960. Among his film title songs were *Three Coins in the Fountain, Pocketful of Miracles* and *Come Blow Your Horn.*

Cahn-Speyer, Rudolf, Austrian conductor and musicologist; b. Vienna, Sept. 1, 1881; d. Florence, Dec. 25, 1940. He studied chemistry and music in Vienna; then in Leipzig and Munich; graduated from the Univ. of Munich in 1908 with the dissertation, *Franz Seydelmann als dramatischer Komponist* (Leipzig, 1909). He began conducting in Kiel (1908); subsequently conducted in Hamburg (1909–11); taught in Berlin; became conductor of the Budapest Volksoper (1913). In 1933 he left Germany to live in Italy. He published *Zur Opernfrage; das Wesen der Oper und ihre Entwickelung in der Gegenwart* (Leipzig, 1913); and *Handbuch des Dirigierens* (1919).

Caillet, Lucien, brilliant orchestral arranger; b. Dijon, France, May 22, 1891. He studied at the Dijon Cons. (grad., 1913); and with Paul Fauchet, Georges Caussade and Gabriel Pares; settled in the U.S. in 1916, living first in Pennsylvania and later in California. He made a new orchestral setting of Mussorgsky's *Pictures at an Exhibition* (1937), and of numerous other pieces. His own orchestral compositions include *Memories of Stephen Foster* (1935); *Strains from Erin* (1936); variations of the theme *Pop! Goes the Weasel* (1938); many scores for Hollywood motion pictures.

Caix d'Hervelois, Louis de, French viola da gamba player; b. Amiens, c. 1680; d. Paris, 1760. He studied with Sainte-Colombe; was active as a musician in the court of the Duc d'Orléans. His works include five volumes of *Pièces de viole* (1725–52) and two volumes of *Pièces pour la flûte* (1726; 1731). Some of these compositions have been edited by Karl Schroeder; various arrangements of his viola da gamba pieces have been made for contemporary instruments.

Caland, Elisabeth, Dutch-German piano teacher and music editor; b. Rotterdam, Jan. 13, 1862; d. Berlin, Jan. 26, 1929. She studied piano with Deppe in Berlin. Her piano manuals, most of which have gone through several editions, include the authoritative exposition of Deppe's method, *Die Deppesche Lehre des Klavierspiels* (Stuttgart, 1897; in English as *Artistic Piano-Playing*, 1903; also in French, Dutch and Russian); *Technische Ratschläge für Klavierspieler* (Magdeburg, 1897; also in English and Russian); *Die Ausnützung der Kraftquellen beim Klavierspiel* (Magdeburg, 1905); *Das künstlerische Klavierspiel in seinen physiologisch-physikalischen Vorgängen* (1910); *Praktische Lehrgänge für künstlerisches Klavierspiel* (Magdeburg, 1912); *Anhaltspunkte zur Kontrolle zweckmässiger Armbewegungen beim künstlerischen Klavierspiel* (1919).

Caldara, Antonio, Italian cellist and composer; b. Venice, 1670; d. Vienna, Dec. 26, 1736. He was a pupil of Legrenzi; lived in Rome, Milan, Bologna, Mantua and Madrid; on Jan. 1, 1716, he was appointed assistant choirmaster to J. J. Fux in Vienna. Caldara composed 87 operas and sacred dramas, 32 oratorios, about 30 Masses, other church music, chamber music, etc. A selection of his church music is reprinted in the *Denkmäler der Tonkunst in Österreich* 26 (formerly 13.i; ed. by Mandyczewski); other vocal works (cantatas, madrigals and canons) are in vol. 75 (formerly 39; ed. by Mandyczewski, with introduction and explanatory notes by Geiringer); *Dafne,* ed. by C. Schneider and R. John, is in vol. 91; further vocal works are reprinted in *Musique d'Église des XVIIᵉ et XVIIIᵉ siècles* (edited by Charles Pineau); a madrigal and 18 canons were edited by Geiringer in *Das Chorwerk* (1933); 28 three-part instrumental canons from Caldara's *Divertimenti Musicali* are in *Spielkanons* (Wolfenbüttel, 1928).
BIBLIOGRAPHY: A. Schering on Caldara's 32 oratorios, in his *Geschichte des Oratoriums* (1911); A. Gmeyner, dissertation on Caldara's 87 operas (Vienna, 1927); C. Gray, "Antonio Caldara (1670–1736)," *Musical Times* (March 1929); U. Kirkendele, *Antonio Caldara: sein Leben und seine venezianisch-römischen Oratorien* (Graz, 1966); R. Freeman, "La verità nella ripetizione," Musical Quarterly (April 1968); Mario Rinaldi, "Contributo alla futura biografia di Antonio Caldara," *Rivista Musicale Italiana* (Sept.–Oct. 1970).

Caldicott, Alfred James, English conductor and composer; b. Worcester, Nov. 26, 1842; d. near Gloucester, Oct. 24, 1897. He received Mus. Bac. degree at Cambridge (1878); was professor at the Royal College of Music in London (1883–1892). His works include the cantatas *The Widow of Nain* (1881) and *A Rhine Legend* for women's voices (1883); 13 operettas; numerous glees, especially the popular *Humpty Dumpty* (1878).

Caldwell, Sarah, remarkable American opera conductor; b. Maryville, Missouri, March 6, 1924. She learned to play violin at home and appeared at local events as a child; then enrolled as a psychology student at the Univ. of Arkansas. She undertook serious violin study at the New England Cons. in Boston with Richard Burgin, concertmaster of the Boston Symph. Orch.; also studied viola with Georges Fourel. In 1947 she was engaged by Boris Goldovsky, head of the opera dept. at the New England Cons. as his assistant, which proved a valuable apprenticeship for her. In 1952 she was engaged as head of the Boston Univ. opera workshop. In 1957 she formed her own opera company in Boston, called Opera Group; this was the beginning of an extraordinary career, in which she displayed her peculiar acumen in building up an operatic enterprise with scant musical and financial resources. In 1965 she changed the name of her enterprise to Opera Company of Boston, making use of a former vaudeville theater for her performances. In most of her productions she acts as producer, conductor, administrator, stage director, scenery designer and publicity manager. Among her productions were *La Traviata* and *Falstaff* by Verdi, *Benvenuto Cellini* by Berlioz, *Don Quichote* by Massenet, Bellini's *I Capuleti ed i Montecchi,* and several modern operas, among them Prokofiev's *War and Peace,* Schoenberg's *Moses and Aron,* Alban Berg's *Lulu,* Luigi Nono's *Intolleranza* and *Montezuma* by Roger Sessions. She was able to induce famous singers to lend their participation, among them Beverly Sills, Marilyn Horne, Tito Gobbi, Nicolai Gedda, Placido Domingo and others. Because of her imposing corpulence (circa 300 lbs.) she conducts performances sitting in a large armchair. Sober-minded critics heap praise on Sarah Caldwell for her musicianship, physical and mental energy, imagination and a sort of genius for opera productions. On Jan. 13, 1976 she became the first woman to conduct at the Metropolitan Opera (in a performance of *La Traviata*).

Calegari, Antonio, Italian composer and music theorist; b. Padua, Feb. 17, 1757; d. there, July 22, 1828. He was active as a composer in Padua, Venice and Paris; spent the last years of his life as organist of the Church of San Antonio in Padua. He brought out three operas in Venice: *Le Sorelle rivali* (1784), *L'Amor soldato* (1786), and *Il Matrimonio scoperto* (1789). He published a curious treatise on composition, *Gioco pittagorico musicale* (Venice, 1801), which was republished in Paris, during his residence there, as *L'Art de composer la musique sans en connaître les éléments* (1802). A *Sistema armonico* (1829) and a vocal method, *Modi generali del canto* (1836) were published posthumously.

Calkin, John Baptiste, English pianist, organist and composer; b. London, March 16, 1827; d. there, May 15, 1905. He studied music with his father; then was active as organist in several churches in London; also taught at the Guildhall School of Music. He wrote many sacred choruses and organ pieces.

Callaerts, Joseph, Belgian organist and composer; b. Antwerp, Aug. 22, 1838; d. there, March 3, 1901. He studied with Lemmens at the Brussels Cons.; was organist of the Jesuit College and later of the Antwerp Cathedral; from 1876 taught organ at the Music School in Antwerp. He composed a comic opera, *Le Retour imprévu* (Antwerp, 1889); a Symphony (1879);

a Piano Trio (1882); and sacred music, organ pieces and piano pieces.

Callas, Maria, celebrated American soprano; b. New York, Dec. 3, 1923; d. Paris, Sept. 16, 1977. Her real name was **Maria Anna Sofia Cecilia Kalogeropoulos;** her father was a Greek immigrant. The family went back to Greece when she was 13; she studied voice at the Royal Academy of Music in Athens with the Spanish soprano singer Elvira de Hidalgo, and sang Santuzza in the school production of *Cavalleria Rusticana.* She went back to N.Y. in 1945; auditioned for the Metropolitan Opera Co. and was offered a contract, but decided to go to Italy, where she made her operatic debut in the title role of *La Gioconda* (Verona, Aug. 3, 1947). She was encouraged in her career by the famous conductor Tullio Serafin, who engaged her to sing Isolde and Aida at various Italian productions. In 1951 she was accepted as a member of the staff of La Scala, Milan. She was greatly handicapped by her absurdly excessive weight (210 lbs); by a supreme effort of will she slimmed down to 135 pounds; with her classical Greek profile and penetrating eyes, she made a striking impression on the stage; in the tragic role of Medea in Cherubini's opera she mesmerized the audience by her dramatic representation of pity and terror. Some critics opined that she lacked a true *bel canto* quality in her voice and that her technique was defective in coloratura, but her power of interpretation was such that she was soon acknowledged to be one of the greatest dramatic singers of the century. Her personal life was as tempestuous as that of any prima donna of the bygone era. In 1949 she married the Italian industrialist Maneghini, who became her manager, but they separated 10 years later. Her romance with the Greek shipping magnate Aristotle Onassis was a recurrent topic of sensational gossip. Given to outbursts of temper, she made newspaper headlines when she walked off the stage following some altercation, or failed to appear altogether at scheduled performances, but her eventual return to the stage was all the more eagerly welcomed by her legion of admirers. Perhaps the peak of her success was her appearance as Norma at the Metropolitan Opera, N.Y., on Oct. 29, 1956; then again she quit the company as a result of disagreement with the management; but once more an accommodation was reached, and she sang Violetta (N.Y., Feb. 6, 1958); her last appearance with the Metropolitan Opera Co. was as Tosca in 1965, after which she abandoned the stage altogether. In 1971 she gave a seminar on opera at the Juilliard School of Music, and her magic worked even in the novel capacity as instructor; her classes were enthusiastically received by the students. In 1974 she went on a concert tour with the tenor Giuseppe di Stefano; then she returned to Europe. She died suddenly of a heart attack in her Paris apartment.

BIBLIOGRAPHY: E. Gara and R. Hauert, *Maria Callas* (Geneva, 1957; in English, London, 1958); E. Callas, *My Daughter Maria Callas* (as told to L. G. Blochman; N.Y., 1960); G. Jellinek, *Callas* (N.Y., 1960); M. T. Picchetti and M. Teglia, *El arte de María Callas* (Buenos Aires, 1969); S. Galatopoulos, *Callas—La Divina: Art That Conceals Art* (Elmsford,

N.Y., 1970); John Ardion, *The Callas Legacy* (analysis of recordings; N.Y., 1977).

Callaway, Paul (Smith), American organist, choirmaster and conductor; b. Atlanta, Illinois, Aug. 16, 1909. He attended Westminster College in Fulton, Missouri (1927–29); studied organ with Tertius Noble in N.Y. (1930–35), with Leo Sowerby in Chicago and with Marcel Dupré in Paris. He served as organist and choirmaster at St. Thomas's Chapel, N.Y. (1930–35); then at St. Mark's Chapel, Grand Rapids, Mich.; in 1939 he began his 38-year regime as principal organist and musical director of the Washington, D.C. National Cathedral, with an interruption during his service in the Army of the United States (1942–46). In 1941 he founded the Cathedral Choral Society; in 1962 was one of the founders of the College of Church Musicians at the Washington Cathedral, leaving it until 1969. He was also musical director of the Opera Society of Washington (1956–67) and directed the Lake George, N.Y., Opera Festival (1967–77); appeared as guest conductor of the National Symph. Orch., Washington; conducted the notable first performances at the Library of Congress of Menotti's work, *The Unicorn, the Gorgon, and the Manticore* (1956) and Dallapiccola's *Cinque Canti* (1956). Owing to his close affiliation with the Anglican Church, he was engaged to conduct the Cathedral Choir at Westminister Abbey, London, during the celebration of the 900th anniversary of the Abbey (1966). On Nov. 30, 1977 he was made an honorary Officer of the British Empire in ceremonies at the British Embassy in Washington. After his becoming Organist and Choirmaster Emeritus of the Washington Cathedral in 1977 he served on the faculty of the Univ. of Illinois at Carbondale, periodically returning to Washington to conduct the Cathedral Choral Society.

Callcott, John Wall, English organist and composer; b. London, Nov. 20, 1766; d. Bristol, May 15, 1821. Early in life he developed a particular talent for composing glees and catches; won three prize medals at a contest of the Catch Club of London (1785) for his catch *O Beauteous Fair;* a canon, *Blessed is He,* and a glee, *Dull Repining Sons of Care.* He received his Mus. Bac. from Oxford (1785) and his Mus. Doc. (1800); was a cofounder of the Glee Club (1787). During Haydn's visit to London in 1791 he took a few lessons with him and wrote a symphony in imitation of his style. In 1806 he was appointed lecturer at the Royal Institute. Shortly thereafter, his mind gave way from overwork on a projected biographical dictionary of musicians, just before he reached the quirky letter Q. He recovered, but not sufficiently to continue his work. In addition to numerous glees, catches and canons, he wrote *A Musical Grammar* (London, 1806), a standard elementary textbook that went through numerous editions in England and America. A 3-volume collection of glees, catches and canons, with a biographical memoir, was publ. posthumously by his son-in-law, William Horsley (London, 1824).

Calleja, Gómez Rafael, Spanish composer; b. Burgos, Dec. 23, 1874; d. Madrid, Feb. 7, 1938. He studied at the Madrid Cons.; subsequently conducted in Spain,

Portugal and South America. He composed about 300 revues and musical comedies, including *El Príncipe Carnaval, El Mozo Crúo,* etc.; published collections of folksongs from Santander, Galicia and Asturias.

Calligaris, Sergio, Argentinian-Italian pianist; b. Rosario, Jan. 22, 1941. He studied with Jorge Fanelli in Buenos Aires; in 1964 he went to the U.S. and became a student of Arthur Loesser at the Cleveland Institute of Music; then went to Italy where he took lessons with Guido Agosti at the Santa Cecilia Academy in Rome; in 1970-72 he taught at the California State Univ., Los Angeles; then returned to Italy, and in 1974 became an Italian citizen; also in 1974 he was appointed prof. of piano at the Cons. of San Pietro a Majella in Naples. His playing is distinguished by a romantic élan and virtuoso technique.

Callinet, François, French organ manufacturer; b. Ladoix, Bourgogne, Oct. 1, 1754; d. Rouffach, Alsace, May 21, 1820. He was apprenticed to K. Riepp in Dijon, and later worked with Joseph Rabiny, with whom he became associated in organ building in 1786. His two sons **Joseph** and **Claude-Ignace** and the latter's son **Louis-François** carried on the family trade; **Louis Callinet,** a nephew of the founder of the firm, joined Daublaine & Co., and continued organ manufacture.

Callinet, Louis, French organ manufacturer; b. in Weiler Ladoix, Bourgogne, April 19, 1786; d. Paris, Aug. 1, 1845; a nephew of **François Callinet** (1754-1820). He entered the partnership with Daublaine, who attended to the commercial interests of the firm known as Daublaine & Callinet, but broke with him and destroyed all instruments that he had built.

Calloway, Cab, American jazz singer; b. Rochester, N.Y., Dec. 25, 1907. He became a proponent of scat singing, characterized by nonsense syllabization and rapid glossolalia with the melodic line largely submerged under an asymmetric inundation of rhythmic heterophony. He led bands and appeared in the movies; also compiled a *Hepster's Dictionary,* listing jazz terms (1938), and published an informal autobiography, *Of Minnie the Moocher and Me* (N.Y., 1976).

Calvé, Emma, famous French soprano; b. Décazeville (Aveyron), Aug. 15, 1858; d. Millau, Jan. 6, 1942. She studied voice with Puget in Paris; made her operatic debut as Marguerite in Gounod's *Faust* in Brussels, Sept. 29, 1882; then sang at the Opéra-Comique in Paris. In 1892 she appeared at Covent Garden, London. She made her American debut at the Metropolitan Opera House on Nov. 29, 1893, and remained on its staff until 1897; her greatest role was that of Carmen. Subsequently she made sporadic, but successful, appearances in Europe and America; after 1910 she sang mainly in recitals. Calvé's biography was published in 1902 (A. Gallus, *Emma Calvé, Her Artistic Life*), and so great was the aura of her successes that her life was made the subject of a novel by Gustav Kobbé, *Signora, A Child of the Opera House* (N.Y., 1903). She publ. an autobiography, in English as *My Life* (N.Y., 1922); toward the end of her life she pub-

lished an additional volume of memoirs, *Sous tous les ciels j'ai chanté* (Paris, 1940). Forty of her letters, along with an extended biographical sketch, appear in A. Lebois, "Hommages à Emma Calvé (1858-1942)," *Annales, Faculté des Lettres de Toulouse* (Sept. 1967).

Calvisius, Sethus (real name **Seth Kallwitz**), theorist; son of a poor peasant at Gorsleben, Thuringia; b. Feb. 21, 1556; d. Leipzig, Nov. 24, 1615. He supported himself while studying in the Gymnasia of Frankenhausen and Magdeburg, and the Universities at Helmstadt and Leipzig. In Leipzig he became music director at the Paulinerkirche (1581); from 1582-92 he was cantor at Schulpforta, then cantor of the Thomasschule at Leipzig, and in 1594 became music director at the Thomaskirche and Nicolaikirche there. Calvisius was not only a musician, but a scholar of high attainments. His writings are valuable sources: *Melopoeia seu melodiae condendae ratio* (1582; 2nd ed. 1592); *Compendium musicae practicae pro incipientibus* (1594; 3d ed. as *Musicae artis praecepta nova et facillima,* 1612); *Harmoniae cantionum ecclesiasticarum a M. Luthero et aliis viris piis Germaniae compositarum 4 voc.* (1596); *Exercitationes musicae duae* (1600); *Auserlesene teutsche Lieder* (1603); *Exercitatio musicae tertia* (1611); *Biciniorum libri duo* (1612).
BIBLIOGRAPHY: K. Benndorf, "Sethus Calvisius als Musiktheoretiker," *Vierteljahrsschrift für Musikwissenschaft* (1894); R. Wustmann, *Musikgeschichte von Leipzig,* vol. I (1909); G. Pietzch, "Sethus Calvisius und Joh. Kepler," *Die Musikpflege* I/8 (1930).

Calvocoressi, Michel Dimitri, eminent writer on music; b. (of Greek parents) Marseilles, Oct. 2, 1877; d. London, Feb. 1, 1944. He studied music in Paris, but was mostly autodidact; also pursued the social sciences. In 1916 he settled in London. He wrote music criticism and correspondences for French and other journals. He mastered the Russian language and became an ardent propagandist of Russian music; made excellent translations into English and French of Russian and German songs. Among his books are *La Musique russe* (Paris, 1907); *The Principles and Methods of Musical Criticism* (London, 1923); *Musical Taste and How to Form It* (London, 1925); *Musicians' Gallery: Music and Ballet in Paris and London* (London, 1933); also monographs on Liszt (Paris, 1906), Mussorgsky (Paris, 1908), Glinka (Paris, 1911), Schumann (Paris, 1912), Debussy (London, 1941); a new extensive biography of Mussorgsky was posthumously published (London, 1946). With Gerald Abraham he published the valuable *Masters of Russian Music* (London, 1936).

Calzabigi, Ranieri di, Italian poet and music theorist; b. Leghorn, Dec. 23, 1714; d. Naples, July, 1795. In 1750 he went to Paris, and soon engaged in polemics regarding the relative merits of French and Italian operas; he lent energetic support to Gluck in his ideas of operatic reform. He wrote for Gluck the libretti of *Orfeo, Alceste,* and *Paride ed Elena.* In 1780 he returned to Italy. He published *Dissertazione su le poesie drammatiche del Sig. Abate Pietro Metastasio* (1755), a controversial work concerning Metastasio and Hasse.

BIBLIOGRAPHY: Heinrich Welti, "Gluck und Calzabigi," *Vierteljahrsschrift für Musikwissenschaft* (1891); Ghino Lazzeri, *La vita e l'opera letteraria di Ranieri Calzabigi* (1907); J.-G. Prod'homme, "Deux Collaborateurs italiens de Gluck," *Rivista Musicale Italiana* (1916); R. Haas, *Gluck in Durazzo* (1924); H. Hammelmann and M. Rose, "New Light on Calzabigi and Gluck," *Musical Times* (June 1969).

Cambert, Robert, the first French opera composer, preceding Lully; b. Paris c.1628; d. London, 1677. He was a pupil of Chambonnières. His first venture on the lyric stage was *La Pastorale,* written by Perrin and successfully produced at the Château d'Issy in 1659; it was followed by *Ariane, ou le Mariage de Bacchus* (rehearsed in 1661), and *Adonis* (1662; not performed; manuscript lost). Perrin having received, in 1669, letters patent for establishing the Académie royale de musique (the national operatic theater, now the Grand Opéra), brought out, in collaboration with Cambert, the opera, *Pomone* (1671); another, *Les Peines et les plaisirs de l'amour,* was written, but never produced, Lully having meantime had the patent transferred to himself. Cambert's disappointment drove him to London; he became a bandmaster, and died as Master of the Music to Charles II.
BIBLIOGRAPHY: A. Pougin, *Les Vrais Créateurs de l'opéra français, Perrin et Cambert* (Paris, 1881).

Cambini, Giovanni Giuseppe, Italian composer; b. Leghorn, Feb. 13, 1746; d. Bicêtre, Dec. 29, 1825. He was a pupil of Padre Martini, and a prolific composer of instrumental works, writing over 60 symphonies within a few years; also 144 string quartets; ballets, operas and oratorios. He died in an almshouse.
BIBLIOGRAPHY: D. L. Trimpert, *Die "Quatuors concertants" von Giuseppi Cambini* (Tutzing, 1967); H. Bol, "Een rivaal van Mozart te Parijs, G. G. Cambini (1746-1825)," *Mens en Melodie* (March 1968).

Cameron, Basil, English conductor; b. Reading, Aug. 18, 1884; d. London, June 26, 1975. He studied music in London with Tertius Noble and in Berlin with Joachim; also took a course in composition with Max Bruch. Returning to England he sought to obtain a conducting position by Germanizing his name as **Basil Hindenberg,** seeing that German conductors dominated the field in England, but changed it back to his real name when England went to war with Germany in 1914. He served in the British army and was wounded in action in 1918. He conducted the Hastings Municipal Orch. (1923-30); then was guest conductor of the San Francisco Symphony Orch.; from 1932 to 1938 he was conductor of the Seattle Symphony Orch.; during his tenure he played many new works by modern composers. He belongs to the category of "objective" conductors more interested in the music itself than in his individual communication, an attitude that in the end hampered his American success. He filled in a few engagements in Europe and eventually returned to London.

Cametti, Alberto, Italian musicologist; b. Rome, May 5, 1871; d. there, June 1, 1935. He studied at the Cons. della Accademia di S. Cecilia; was member of the commission appointed by Pope Pius X to investigate the condition of church music. In April, 1914, he publ. a full description and complete thematic catalogue in the *Rivista Musicale Italiana* (XXI, 2) of 43 compositions for 1-3 voices with basso continuo (chiefly arias) by Orazio Michi which he had discovered in various Italian libraries, and which prove Michi to have been one of the earliest and most important Roman masters of the monodic style.
WRITINGS: *Cenni biografici di G. P. da Palestrina* (Milan, 1894); *Il testamento di Jacobella Pierluigi* (1903); *Cristina di Suezia, l'arte musicale e gli spettacoli in Roma* (1911); *Documenti inediti su Luigi Rossi* (Leipzig, 1912); *Chi era l'Ippolita del cardinale di Montalto?* (1913); *L'accademia Filarmonica Romana, 1821-60* (1924); *I musici di Campidoglio dal 1524 al 1818* (1925); *La musica teatrale a Roma cento anni fa (1816-26)* (1928); *Dove fu sepolto il Palestrina?* (1929); *Bibliogr. delle opere di Costanzo Festa* (1931); biographical studies of Felice Anerio (1915), Giacomo Carissimi (1917), G. B. Costanzi (1924), Leonardo Vinci (1924), Ruggiero Giovanelli (1925), etc.; several valuable essays in *Rivista Musicale Italiana*: "Bellini a Roma" (1900); "Donizetti a Roma" (1904-07); "Mozart a Roma" (1907); "Frescobaldi a Roma" (1908); etc.

Camidge, Matthew, English organist; b. York, 1758; d. there Oct. 23, 1844; son of **John Camidge, Sr.,** whom he succeeded at Belfry Church in York (1799). He publ. *Cathedral Music; 24 Original Psalm- and Hymn-tunes;* piano sonatas and marches; a *Method of Instruction in Music by Questions and Answers,* etc.

Cammarano, Salvatore, Italian librettist; b. Naples, March 19, 1801; d. there, July 17, 1852. He wrote prose dramas, which were produced in Florence; after 1834 he devoted himself to writing opera libretti: Donizetti's *Lucia;* Pacini's *Reggente, Buondelmonte, Saffo, Merope,* etc.; Verdi's *Alzira, Battaglia di Legnano, Luisa Miller,* and *Il Trovatore.*
BIBLIOGRAPHY: T. Mantovani, "Salvatore Cammarano," *Musica d'oggi* (1926).

Camp, John Spencer, American organist and composer; b. Middletown, Conn., Jan. 30, 1858; d. Hartford, Conn., Feb. 1, 1946. After receiving an M.A. from Wesleyan Univ. (1881), he studied in New York with Dudley Buck and with Dvořák; was organist and choirmaster at various churches in Connecticut; helped found the American Guild of Organists. He wrote numerous pieces for choir, organ, piano, and orch.; also anthems and songs.

Campagnoli, Bartolommeo, renowned Italian violinist; b. Cento di Ferrara, Sept. 10, 1751; d. Neustrelitz, Germany, Nov. 6, 1827. He studied in Bologna with Dall'Occa and in Florence with Nardini; for several years gave concerts in Italy; became music director to the Duke of Kurland in Dresden, and made several successful concert tours with his service; from 1797-1818 was active as a violinist in Leipzig; then became maestro di capella at the Neustrelitz court. He composed 41 *Capricci per l'alto viola* (revised by E. Kreuz and A. Consolini as *Caprices pour le viola,*

1922); a violin concerto; études for violin; chamber music. He was the author of several pedagogic manuals for the violin: *Nouvelle méthode de la mécanique progressive du jeu de violon* (1791; in English, 1856), and *Metodo per violino* (1797; his chief work; publ., and reprinted in all European languages).

BIBLIOGRAPHY: G. Atti, *Biografia di B. Campagnoli* (Bologna, 1892).

Campana, Fabio, Italian singing teacher and composer; b. Leghorn, Jan. 14, 1819; d. London, Feb. 2, 1882. He studied in Bologna; produced the operas *Caterina di Guisa* (Leghorn, 1838); *Giulio d'Este* (Venice, 1841); *Vannina d'Ornano (Florence, 1842); Luisa di Francia* (Rome, 1844); then went to London, where he settled as a singing teacher. His opera *Almina* was staged in London at Her Majesty's Theatre (April 26, 1860); another opera *Esmeralda* was produced in St. Petersburg (Dec. 20, 1869); Patti sang the title role in its productions in Western Europe. He also wrote hundreds of songs.

Campanari, Giuseppe, Italian dramatic baritone, brother of **Leandro Campanari;** b. Venice, Nov. 17, 1855; d. Milan, May 31, 1927. He began his career as a cellist; played in the orch. of La Scala, and started to study singing; went to the U.S. in 1884, and played cello in the Boston Symph. Orch. until 1893, when he joined Hinrich's Opera Company in N.Y. as a baritone; made his debut (June 15, 1893) as Tonio in *Pagliacci;* after several years at the Metropolitan Opera he devoted himself to concert work and teaching.

Campanari, Leandro, Italian violinist and conductor; brother of **Giuseppe Campanari;** b. Rovigo, Oct. 20, 1857; d. San Francisco, April 22, 1939. He studied in Padua; attended the Milan Cons. graduating in 1877; after a tour of Europe, he came to the U.S. in 1881 and settled in Boston where he organized the Campanari String Quartet. He became a proficient conductor and was in charge of the Grand Orchestral Concerts at La Scala, Milan, from 1897 till 1905. In February 1907, he was engaged to complete the season of the Philadelphia Orchestra after the sudden illness of the regular conductor, Fritz Scheel. He failed to impress the orchestra or the audience and was not reengaged.

Campanini, Cleofonte, eminent Italian-American operatic conductor, brother of the famous tenor **Italo Campanini;** b. Parma, Sept. 1, 1860; d. Chicago, Dec. 19, 1919. He studied violin at the Parma Cons. and later at the Cons. of Milan; made his conducting début with *Carmen* at Parma (1883); conducted the first American performance of *Otello* at the Metropolitan Opera House (April 16, 1888), while his brother Italo was impresario. Between 1888 and 1906, he conducted in Italy, in England, and in South America. A larger field opened to him in 1906 when Hammerstein engaged him for the new Manhattan Opera House in New York. Differences with Hammerstein led him to resign in 1909. In the following year he was engaged as principal conductor of the newly formed Chicago Opera Co.; in 1913 he was appointed general director, which post he held until his death. Among opera conductors he occupied a place in the first rank; he

seemed to be equally at home in all styles of music. He introduced many new operas in the U.S., among them Massenet's *Hérodiade*, Debussy's *Pelléas et Mélisande*, Charpentier's *Louise*, Wolf-Ferrari's *Il Segreto di Susanna*, etc. On May 15, 1887, he married, in Florence, Eva Tetrazzini (sister of Luisa Tetrazzini).

Campanini, Italo, famous Italian tenor, brother of **Cleofonte Campanini;** b. Parma, June 30, 1845; d. Vigatto, near Parma, Nov. 14, 1896. In his early years he was an apprentice in his father's blacksmith shop; joined Garibaldi's army and was wounded in the Italian struggle for unification. Subsequently, he studied with Griffini and Lamperti; appeared at Bologna, in *Lohengrin* (Nov. 1, 1871), which started him on the road to fame. He made his London début as Gennaro in *Lucrezia Borgia* (May 4, 1872), and his American début, also as Gennaro, at the N.Y. Academy of Music (Oct. 1, 1873). He appeared in *Faust* at the opening of the Metropolitan Opera (Oct. 22, 1883); was briefly active as impresario; brought over his brother Cleofonte Campanini to conduct the American première of Verdi's *Otello* at the Metropolitan Opera (April 16, 1888).

Campbell, Aline, Pen name of **Merle Montgomery.**

Campbell-Tipton, Louis, American composer; b. Chicago, Nov. 21, 1877; d. Paris, May 1, 1921. He studied at Leipzig (1896–99) with Carl Reinecke and Gustav Schreck; returned to Chicago and was instructor of theory at the Chicago Musical College; then lived in Paris. He wrote chiefly for piano (*Sonata Heroic, Sea Lyrics, The Four Seasons*, Suite, Serenade, etc.), *Suite pastorale* for piano and violin; also a number of very effective songs.

Campbell-Watson, Frank, American music editor; b. New York, Jan. 22, 1898; studied at the Leipzig Cons. with Max Reger. Returning to the U.S., he held positions as editor with various publishing firms. He made transcriptions for string orch. of Bach, Reger, Mendelssohn and Albéniz. He was also the author of *University Course of Music Study* (1923); *Modern Elementary Harmony* (1930); edited *International Library of Music* (piano, 14 vols.; vocal, 12 vols.; violin, 14 vols.); *La Mejor Música del Mundo* (in Spanish, also in Portuguese, for piano, 14 vols.)

Campenhout, François van, Belgian composer, author of the Belgian national anthem; b. Brussels, Feb. 5, 1779; d. there April 24, 1848. Beginning as violinist in the Théâtre de la Monnaie, he studied singing under Plantade, and became a fine stage tenor, appearing in Belgium, Holland and France. He wrote 6 operas, 9 cantatas, etc. He is, however, chiefly remembered as the composer of *La Brabançonne*, which was written during the revolution of 1830, and eventually became the national anthem of Belgium.

Campion (Campian), Thomas, English physician; also poet, composer and dramatist; b. London, Feb. 12, 1567; d. there, March 1, 1620. He studied at Cambridge from 1581–85, residing at Peterhouse; nothing is recorded of his subsequent activities until 1602, when he first called himself Doctor of Physic, though no mention was made of any university or a degree; the only clue to his having studied medical science is made in an oblique reference of Philip Rosseter in 1601, in which he speaks of Campion's poetry and music as the 'superfluous blossoms of his deeper studies.' Campion was primarily a lyric poet; his music was to enhance the beauty of the poetry by supplying unobtrusive and simple harmonies; in this he differed from such contemporaries as John Dowland who contrived elaborate lute accompaniments.

WORKS: 3 songs (1596); *A Booke of Ayres, Set Foorth to be sung to the Lute Orpherian, and Base Violl* (1601; consists of 2 separate books, one by Campion and one by Rosseter; Campion wrote both the words and music for his half of the work); *First and Second Books of Airs* (1613?); *Third and Fourth Books of Airs* (1617?); songs for masques at the marriages of Sir James Hay (1607), Princess Elizabeth (1613), and Robert, Earl of Somerset (1613); songs for a masque at Caversham House (1613); *Songs of Mourning* (for Prince Henry; 1613; words by Campion, music by John Coperario); *A New Way for Making Foure Parts in Counterpoint* (1618; also in Playford's *Introduction to the Skill of Musick*, with additions by Christopher Simpson, 1655 and following years). Campion also publ. *Poemata*, a volume of Latin epigrams and elegiacs (1595; reprinted 1619), *Observations on the Art of English Poesie* (1602; condemns 'the vulgar and unartificial custom of riming'), etc. The 4 books of airs and the songs from Rosseter's *Books of Ayres* are reprinted in E. H. Fellowes, *English School of Lutenist Song-Writers*.

BIBLIOGRAPHY: A. H. Bullen, *Thomas Campion, Songs and Masques* (1903; includes comments on Campion's music by Janet Dodge); Percival Vivian's edition of the literary works of Thomas Campion (Oxford, 1909); Miles Kastendieck, *England's Musical Poet, Thomas Campion* (Oxford, 1938); W. R. Davis, ed. *The Works of Thomas Campion; Complete Songs, Masques, and Treatises* (Garden City, N.Y., 1967); S. J. London, "Thomas Campion, M.D. (1567-1620)," *New York State Journal of Medicine* (Dec. 1967); J. T. Irwin, "Thomas Campion and the Musical Emblem," *Studies in English Literature, 1500-1900* (Winter 1970); E. Lowbury, T. Salter, and A. Young, *Thomas Campion: Poet, Composer, Physician* (N.Y., 1970).

Campioni, Carlo Antonio, French-born Italian composer; b. Lunéville, France, Nov. 16, 1720; d. in Florence, April 12, 1788. He went to Florence in 1764, and was active there as music director and composer of church music. He also publ. instrumental works; among them 6 sonatas for two violins, which were fraudulently issued in Amsterdam as composed by Haydn, and were reprinted still under Haydn's name in Mainz in 1953. The very fact that these pieces could pass as Haydn's for two centuries obliquely testifies to Campioni as a highly competent composer.

Campo y Zabaleta, Conrado del, Spanish violinist and composer; b. Madrid, Oct. 28, 1879; d. there, March 17, 1953. He studied at the Madrid Cons.; later became its director.

WORKS: operas *El final de Don Alvaro* (1911), *La*

tragedia del beso (1915), *El Avapiés* (Madrid, March 8, 1919), *La Dama desconocida, La Culpa, Leonor Teller, Romeo y Julieta, Dies Irae, La Malquerida, Fantochines, La Flor del Agua* (most have been performed at the Madrid Opera House); symph. poems *La Divina Comedia, Granada, Airinos; Kasida,* an oriental fantasy; *Evocación Medieval* for chorus and orch.; 8 string quartets, of which the *Caprichos Románticos* (1908) is very well known in Spain and France.

Campos-Parsi, Hector, Puerto Rican composer; b. Ponce, Oct. 1, 1922. He studied at the New England Cons. in Boston, with Nadia Boulanger in Paris (1950-53) and with Copland at Tanglewood (summers, 1949, 1956); returning to Puerto Rico he developed energetic activities as composer, poet, journalist, music critic, educator, television commentator and concert manager.

WORKS: *Incidente,* ballet (1948); *Music for 3 violins* (1949); String Quartet (1950); *Versiculos* for viola unaccompanied (1950); *Melos,* ballet (1952); *Divertimento del Sur* for flute, clarinet and strings (1953); *Annunciation,* cantata (1954); *Juan Bobo,* ballet (1957); *Madrigales* for contralto and strings (1959); *Rapsodia elegiaca,* in memoriam Villa-Lobos (1960); *Duo Tragico* for piano and orch. (1965); Piano Sonata; *Petroglifos* for piano trio (1966); Sonatina for Violin and Piano; choruses; songs.

Campra, André, French opera composer; b. Aix (Provence) Dec. 4, 1660; d. Versailles, June 14, 1744. A pupil of Guillaume Poitevin, he was appointed maître de musique at the Toulon Cathedral at the age of 20; in 1681, maître de chapelle at Arles, and from 1683-94 at Toulouse Cathedral. He then went to Paris, where he was at first maître de chapelle at the Jesuit collegiate choir, and shortly after, at Notre Dame, an appointment which he held until the successful production of two operas (under his brother Joseph's name) induced him to choose a secular career. In 1722 he was made conductor of the Royal Orch. His operas had numerous performances in Paris, and he was regarded as a natural successor to Lully, until the advent of Rameau, whose genius eclipsed his efforts.

WORKS: operas: *L'Europe galante* (1697), *Le Carnaval de Venise* (1699), *Hésione* (1700), *Aréthuse, ou la vengeance de l'amour (1701), Tancrède* (1702), *Les Muses* (1703), *Iphigénie en Tauride* (1704), *Télémaque* (1704), *Alcine* (1705), *Le Triomphe de l'amour* (1705), *Hippodamie* (1708), *Les Fêtes vénitiennes* (1710; modern ed. with commentary by M. Lütolf, Paris, 1972); *Idoménée* (1712), *Les Amours de Mars et Venus* (1712), *Téléphe* (1713), *Camille* (1717), *Les Ages,* ballet-opera (1718), *Achille et Déidamie* (1735); several divertissements for the Versailles court; 3 books of *Cantates françoises* (1708, 1714, 1728); 5 books of motets (1695-1720); a Mass (1700); 2 books of psalms (1737-38).

BIBLIOGRAPHY: A. Pougin, *André Campra* (Paris, 1861); L. de La Laurencie, "Notes sur la jeunesse d'André Campra," *Sammelbände der Internationalen Musik-Gesellschaft* X/2 (1909); idem, "André Campra, musicien profane," *L'Année Musicale* (1913);

idem, *L'École française de violon de Lulli à Viotti* (1922–24).

Camps, Pompeyo, Argentine composer; b. Paraná, Oct. 27, 1924. After playing piano in bands in his native town, he settled in Buenos Aires in 1947; studied with Jaime Pahissa and adopted Pahissa's "intertonal system" of convertible counterpoint. In 1964 he modified this technique by incorporating serial procedures. He is also active as a music critic.
WORKS: *La Pendiente*, opera in 1 act (1959); *The Ballad of Reading Gaol* (1964) for men's choir, narrator and orch.; *Sinfónia para un Poeta* for baritone and orch. (obtained first municipal prize of Buenos Aires in 1967); *Tríptico Arcáico* for flute, viola, cello and guitar (1961); *Danzas* for percussion (1966); *Reflejos* for 13 brasses and percussion (1968); *Ciudad sin tregua* for string quartet (1974); songs; piano pieces.

Camussi, Ezio, Italian composer; b. Florence, Jan. 16, 1877; d. Milan, Aug. 11, 1956. He studied in Rome with Falchi and Sgambati; later with Massenet in Paris and at the Liceo Musicale, Bologna.
WORKS: operas: *La Dubarry* (Milan, Nov. 7, 1912), *I fuochi di San Giovanni* (Milan, 1920), *Il donzello, Scampolo* (Trieste, Feb. 22, 1925), *La principessa lontana, I Romanzeschi, Intermezzi giocosi* for puppet theater; for orch: *Baletto sinfonico, Pantomima romantica, Suita Romanesca, Intermezzi Goldoniani, Fantasticherie* for small orch., *Festival Miniature Overture, Scene medioevali* for violin and orch.; songs.

Cannabich, Christian, German composer; b. Mannheim, Dec. 28, 1731; d. Frankfurt, Jan. 20, 1798. He studied with Johann Stamitz in Mannheim; became a violinist in the Mannheim Orch. (1744); was sent by the Elector to Rome, where he studied with Jommelli (1753); returned to Mannheim and, after Stamitz's death (1757), became first violinist of the orch.; in 1774 was director of the instrumental music. Cannabich is usually credited with bringing the Mannheim Orch. to a degree of perfection theretofore never attained, particularly in the carefully graduated crescendo and diminuendo. He was also a prolific composer.
WORKS: some 90 symphonies; 3 violin concertos; 45 various pieces of chamber music; a Singspiel, *Azakia* (Mannheim, 1778); a melodrama, *Elektra* (Mannheim, 1781); 40 ballets. In *Denkmäler der Tonkunst in Bayern* appear a thematic index (vol. 4), a symphony and an overture (vol. 15), and a string quartet (vol. 27); H. T. David revised one of Cannabich's symphonies for an edition publ. by the N.Y. Public Library (1937).
BIBLIOGRAPHY: H. Hofer, *C. Cannabich* (Munich, 1921); R. Kloiber, *Die dramatischen Ballette von C. Cannabich* (Munich, 1928).

Cannon, Beekman Cox, American musicologist; b. Teaneck, N.J., Dec. 25, 1911. He studied at Yale Univ. (B.A., 1934; Ph.D., 1939). He served in the U.S. Navy during World War II, returning to teaching at Yale in 1946; received a Guggenheim Fellowship in 1950. He published a valuable monograph, *Johann Mattheson, Spectator in Music* (Yale Univ., 1947).

Cannon, Philip, English composer; b. Paris, Dec. 21, 1929, of English-French parentage. He was educated in England; studied composition with Imogen Holst; then at the Royal College of Music, London, with Gordon Jacob. He subsequently took lessons with Hindemith. After graduation from the Royal College, he was appointed lecturer on music at the Univ. of Sydney, Australia; in 1952 he joined the staff of the Royal College of Music, London. His style of composition is neo-romantic, but adheres to classical forms, preserving a clear sense of tonality.
WORKS: *Morvoren*, opera on a Cornish legend (London, July 15, 1964); 2 Rhapsodies for Piano (1943); String Quartet No. 1 (1944); String Trio (1945); Fantasia for String Quartet (1946); *In the Time of the Breaking of Nations*, after Thomas Hardy, for voice and piano quintet (1945); Sextet for Flute, Oboe and String Quartet (1946); Sinfonietta for chamber orch. (1947); *Symphonic Study: Spring* for orch. (1949); *Songs to Delight* for women's chorus and strings (1950); *Galop Parisien* for 2 pianos (1950); Sinfonietta for strings (1952); *Cinq Chansons de Femme* for soprano and harp (1952); *L'Enfant s'amuse*, suite for piano (1954); *Sonatine Champêtre* for piano (1959); Sonata for 2 pianos (1960); *Son of Science*, cantata for the Machine Age, for chorus, tenor, piano, percussion and strings (Aylesbury, Dec. 2, 1961); *Fanfare to Youth* for 8 trumpets (1963); String Quartet No. 2 (1964); *Kai-kaus (A Persian Suite)* for a chamber group (1965); *Lacrimae mundi* for piano trio (1974); *Son of Man* for chorus and orch. (Liverpool, June 26, 1975).

Cantelli, Guido, brilliant Italian conductor; b. Novara, April 27, 1920; d. in an airplane crash at Orly, near Paris, Nov. 24, 1956. He played in his father's military band as a boy; studied piano at the Cons. of Milan. After Italy withdrew from the war in 1943 he, among others, was sent to a German concentration camp in Stettin. After the end of the war he conducted opera at La Scala in Milan. By invitation of Toscanini, he was engaged to conduct the NBC Symph. Orch. in New York, making his debut on January 15, 1949 and producing an immediate impression of great excellence. Possessing an extraordinary memory, he conducted both rehearsals and performances of operatic and symphonic works without score. He lost his life flying to America to conduct a series of concerts with the New York Philharmonic.

Canteloube de Malaret, Marie-Joseph, French pianist, composer and writer on music; b. Annonay, near Tournon, Oct. 21, 1879; d. Grigny (Seine-et-Oise), Nov. 4, 1957. His name was simply Canteloube, but he added "de Malaret" after the name of his ancestral estate. He studied piano in Paris with Amélie Doetzer, a pupil of Chopin, and composition with Vincent d'Indy at the Schola Cantorum. He became an ardent collector of French folksongs and arranged and published many of them for voice with instrumental accompaniment. His *Chants d'Auvergne* (4 sets for voice with piano or orch., 1923–30) are frequently heard. Among his other albums, *Anthologie des chants populaires français* (4 sets, 1939–44) is a comprehensive collection of regional folksongs.

WORKS: 2 operas, *Le Mas* (1911–13; Paris Opéra, April 3, 1929), *Vercingetorix* (Paris Opéra, June 26, 1933); a symph. poem, *Vers la princesse lointaine* (1911); 3 symph. sketches, *Lauriers* (Paris, Feb. 22, 1931); *Pièces françaises* for piano and orch. (1935); *Poème* for violin and orch. (1937); and *Rustiques* for oboe, clarinet and bassoon (1946). He also published a biography of Vincent d'Indy (Paris, 1949).

Capdevielle, Pierre, French composer and pianist; b. Paris, Feb. 1, 1906; d. Bordeaux, July 9, 1969. He studied at the Paris Cons. with Gédalge and Vidal, and privately with d'Indy; composed an opera, *Les Amants captifs* (1947–50); the orchestral works *Incantation pour la mort d'un jeune spartiate* (1931), *Ouverture pour le pédant joué* (1943), and *Cantate de la France retrouvée* (1946); *Fille de l'homme*, lyric tragedy (Paris Radio, Nov. 9, 1967); 3 symphonies (1936, 1942, Chamber Symph., 1953); *Épaves retrouvées*, 4 symph. tableaux (1955); *Concerto del Dispetto* for piano and orch. (1959); Sonata concertante for trombone and piano (1963); *Sonatine pastorale* for flute and piano; a string quartet; etc.

Cape, Safford, American-Belgian choral conductor; b. Denver, June 28, 1906; d. Brussels, March 26, 1973. He studied in Europe, principally in Brussels, with Charles van den Borren, whose daughter he married. In 1933 he established in Brussels a music society, Pro Musica Antiqua, with which he gave numerous performances of choral and instrumental works by medieval and Renaissance composers.

Capell, Richard, English writer on music; b. Northampton, March 23, 1885; d. London, June 21, 1954. He was music critic for the London *Daily Mail* (1911–31) and for the *Daily Telegraph* (1928–33). From 1950 he edited *Music & Letters*. During World War II he was war correspondent in the French, Greek and Italian campaigns. He published *Schubert's Songs* (London, 1928), a biography of Gustav Holst (London, 1928), and *Opera* (London, 1930).

Capellen, George, German music critic; b. Salzuflen, Lippe, April 1, 1869; d. Hannover, Jan. 19, 1934. He studied philosophy and law at Tübingen, Göttingen and Berlin. He publ. "Harmonik und Melodik bei Richard Wagner," *Bayreuther Blätter* (1901); *Die musikalische Akustik als Grundlage der Harmonik und Melodik* (Leipzig, 1903); *Die Freiheit oder Unfreiheit der Töne und Intervalle als Kriterium der Stimmführung* (Leipzig, 1904); *Die Abhängigkeitsverhältnisse in der Musik* (Leipzig, 1904); *Die Zukunft der Musiktheorie* (Leipzig, 1905); *Ein neuer exotischer Musikstil* (Stuttgart, 1906); *Fortschrittliche Harmonie und Melodielehre* (Leipzig, 1908).

Capet, Lucien, distinguished French violinist; b. Paris, Jan. 8, 1873; d. there, Dec. 18, 1928. He studied at the Paris Cons.; in 1896–99 was concertmaster of the Lamoureux Orch.; from 1899 to 1903 taught violin at the Cons. of Ste. Cécile in Bordeaux. In 1904 he

founded the celebrated Capet Quartet, and played the first violin in it until 1921, specializing particularly in the later Beethoven quartets. In 1924 he was appointed director of the Institut de Violon in Paris. He composed *Le Rouet*, symph. poem; *Prélude religieux* for orch.; *Devant la mer* for voice and orch.; *Poème* for violin and orch.; 5 string quartets; 2 violin sonatas; 6 violin études. He published: *La Technique supérieure de l'archet* (Paris, 1916); *Les 17 Quatuors de Beethoven*; also a philosophical work, *Espérances.*

Caplet, André, French composer; b. Le Havre, Nov. 23, 1878; d. Paris, April 22, 1925. He studied violin in Le Havre, and played in theater orchestras there and in Paris; entered the Paris Cons. (1896) where he studied with Leroux and Lenepveu; in 1901 received the Grand Prix de Rome for his cantata *Myrrha*. His *Marche solennelle* for the centennial of the Villa Medicis was performed in Rome (April 18, 1903). He was active in France as a choral and operatic conductor; conducted the first performance of Debussy's *Le Martyre de St. Sebastien* (Paris, May 22, 1911); also conducted opera in the U.S. with the Boston Opera Co. (1910–14) and in London at Covent Garden (1912). He served in the French army during World War I; later continued his musical activities. Caplet's music is unequivocally Impressionistic, with a lavish use of whole-tone scales and parallel chord formations; he combined this Impressionism with neo-archaic usages and mystic programmatic ideas.

WORKS: oratorio, *Miroir de Jésus* (Paris, May 1, 1924); *Prières* for voice and chamber orch.; *The Masque of the Red Death* (after Poe) for harp and orch. (Paris, March 7, 1909; later arranged for harp and string quartet and retitled *Conte fantastique*; perf. Paris, Dec. 18, 1923); *Epiphanie* for cello and orch. (Paris, Dec. 29, 1923); Double Wind Quintet (Paris, March 9, 1901); *Messe des Petits de St. Eustache* (Paris, June 13, 1922); Sonata for Voice, Cello and Piano; Septet for Strings and 3 Female Voices; *Suite persane* for woodwind instruments; piano duets; piano pieces; minor choral works and songs. He left unfinished a *Sonata da chiesa* for violin and organ (1924) and *Hommage à Ste. Cathérine de Sienna* for organ and orch. He was a close friend of Debussy; recent discoveries show that he collaborated with Debussy on several of his orchestral works and even completed sections left unfinished by Debussy. His correspondence with Debussy was published in Monaco in 1957.

BIBLIOGRAPHY: M. Brillant, Roland-Manuel and Arthur Hoerée "André Caplet, musicien mystique," *La Revue Musicale* (July 1925); R. Dumesnil, *Portraits de musiciens français* (Paris, 1938).

Capocci, Gaetano, Italian organist, composer and teacher; b. Rome, Oct. 16, 1811; d. there, Jan. 11, 1898. He studied music with Valentino Fioravanti and organ with Sante Pascoli; at the same time he took courses in theology. In 1830 he was appointed organist and music director at the Santa Maria Church in Rome; was then organist at Santa Maria Maggiore (from 1839) and at S. Giovanni in Laterano (from 1855). He had numerous students, among them Margherita of Savoy, the future Queen of Italy. His chief merit as composer was a successful revival of the classical oratorio. He wrote the oratorios *Il Battista* (Rome, March 31, 1833) and *Assalonne* (Rome, Dec. 8, 1842); numerous sacred choruses and organ pieces.

Capoianu, Dumitru, Rumanian composer; b. Bucharest, Oct. 19, 1929. He studied at the Bucharest Cons. (1941–47, 1947–53) with Jora, Mendelsohn, Vancea, Andricu and Rogalski; from 1969 to 1973 he was music director of the Georges Enesco Philharmonic Orch.

WORKS: 2 suites for orch. (1953, 1954); *Divertissement* for string orch. and 2 clarinets (1956); Violin Concerto (1957); *Cosmos 60*, ballet scene (1960); *5 Songs of Transylvania* for female chorus, oboe and strings (1961); *Cinematographic Variations* for orch. (1965); *Steel*, ballet (1965); *Curtea domnească* (*The Princely Courtyard*), a "spectacle" of sound and light (1969); *Moto perpetuo* for solo violin or group of violins, and orch. (1972); Wind Quintet (1950); Viola Sonata (1952); 2 string quartets (1954, 1959); Trio for Violin, Viola and Cello (1968); film music.

Capoul, Joseph-Amédée-Victor, brilliant French tenor; b. Toulouse, Feb. 27, 1839; d. Pujaudran-du-Gers, Feb. 18, 1924. He studied voice at the Paris Cons.; made his debut at the Opéra-Comique on Aug. 26, 1861; then sang opera in London and New York. In 1897 he was appointed manager of the Grand Opéra in Paris.

BIBLIOGRAPHY: A. de Lassus, *Victor Capoul,* in *La Revue Musicale* (May 1906).

Capron, Henri, prominent American cellist and composer of French origin. He was a pupil of Gaviniés in Paris (1768); first appeared in Philadelphia in 1785; became active as manager (with Reinagle, William Brown, and Juhan) of subscription concerts in Philadelphia and N.Y.; played in the Old American Co. orchestra in N.Y., where he lived from 1788–92; 1794, settled permanently in Philadelphia and later was principal of a French boarding school. He wrote *New Contredances*; some songs.

BIBLIOGRAPHY: O. G. Sonneck, *Early Concert Life in America* (N.Y., 1907).

Capuana, Franco, Italian conductor; b. Fano, Sept. 29, 1894; d. Naples, Dec. 10, 1969. He studied in Naples; began his career as opera conductor in 1915; from 1930 to 1937 he was music director of the Teatro San Carlo in Naples. He specialized in Verdi and Wagner, and also produced a number of modern operas.

Carabella, Ezio, Italian composer of light operas and orchestral works; b. Rome, March 3, 1891; d. there, April 19, 1964. He studied at the Milan Cons. and at Santa Cecilia in Rome. He composed a number of singable operettas, among them *Bambù* (Florence, 1923), *La Linea del cuore* (Rome, 1924), *Il Candeliere* (Genoa, 1939), and incidental music to various comedies.

Caracciolo, Luigi, Italian composer and singing teacher; b. Andria (Bari), Aug. 10, 1847; d. London, July 22, 1887. He studied with Mercadante in Naples;

went to Dublin in 1878 where he taught singing; in 1881 settled in London. He wrote many popular songs, among them *Danza delle memorie, Un sogno fu!,* and *Rime popolari.*

Carafa de Colobrano, Michele Enrico, prolific composer of operas; b. Naples, Nov. 17, 1787; d. Paris, July 26, 1872. He was a son of Prince Colobrano, Duke of Alvito; began to study music at an early age. Though he became an officer in the army of Naples, and fought in Napoleon's Russian campaign, he devoted his leisure time to music, and after Waterloo adopted it as a profession. In 1827 he settled in Paris; succeeded Lesueur as a member of the Academy (1837); in 1840 was appointed professor of composition at the Paris Cons.

WORKS: operas: *Gabriella di Vergy* (Naples, July 3, 1816), *Ifigenia in Tauride* (Naples, June 19, 1817), *Berenice in Siria* (Naples, July 29, 1818), *Elisabetta in Derbyshire* (Venice, Dec. 26, 1818); the following operas were produced at the Opéra-Comique, Paris: *Jeanne d'Arc* (March 10, 1821), *Le Solitaire* (Aug. 17, 1822), *Le Valet de chambre* (Sept. 16, 1823), *L'Auberge supposée* (April 26, 1824), *Sangarido* (May 19, 1827), *Masaniello* (Dec. 27, 1827; on the same subject as Auber's *La Muette de Portici,* staged at the Paris Opéra two months later; yet Carafa's *Masaniello* held the stage in competition with Auber's famous opera for 136 nights), *La Violette* (Oct. 7, 1828), *Jenny* (Sept. 26, 1829), *Le Livre de l'ermite* (Aug. 11, 1831), *La Prison d'Edimbourg* (July 20, 1833); *Une Journée de la Fronde* (Nov. 7, 1833); *La Grande Duchesse* (Nov. 16, 1835); *Thérèse* (Sept. 26, 1838). He also composed ballets, cantatas and much church music.

Carapetyan, Armen, American musicologist of Armenian origin; b. Isfahan, Oct. 11, 1908. He studied philosophy in Paris and New York; musicology at Harvard Univ. In 1945 he organized the American Institute of Musicology, with headquarters in Rome and Cambridge, Mass.; edited valuable collections, among them *Corpus Mensurabilis Musicae, Corpus Scriptorum de Musica, Musicological Studies and Documents;* contributed numerous articles, mainly on the music of the Renaissance, to American and European periodicals.

Cardew, Cornelius, English composer of the extreme avant-garde; b. Winchcombe, Gloucester, May 7, 1936. He sang in the chorus at Canterbury Cathedral until puberty; then studied composition with Howard Ferguson at the Royal Academy of Music in London (1953–57); learned to play piano and cello. In 1957 he went to Cologne and worked at the electronic studio there as an assistant to Karlheinz Stockhausen (1958–60) whose *Carré* for 4 orchestras, 4 choruses and 4 conductors he helped to produce. Returning to England in 1960 he organized concerts of experimental music; in 1963–65 he was in Italy where he took lessons with Goffredo Petrassi in Rome. In 1967 he was appointed professor of composition at the Royal Academy of Music in London. In 1969, together with Michael Parsons and Howard Skempton, he organized the Scratch Orchestra, a heterogeneous group for performances of avant-garde music, militantly latitudinarian and disestablishmentarian. The activities of the group were disrupted on May Day 1971 when two of its members objected to the inherently bourgeois character of its programs and formed an ideological study group to subject the Scratch Orchestra to a proper Marxist revaluation, following the teachings of Mao Tsetung. Cardew himself joined the movement and criticized his own works as inimical to the interests of the working masses. In a book ominously entitled *Stockhausen Serves Imperialism* (London, 1974) he assailed his former close associates Stockhausen and John Cage. He also repudiated his own magnum opus *The Great Learning*, which was originally performed at the 1968 Cheltenham Festival, scored for non-singing chorus and organ to the texts of Ezra Pound's translation of Confucius; the chorus is admonished to play on tapped stones, to whistle, speak and shriek, but never to sing. In the revised version of the work, he rewrote the text, and appended to the title the slogan "Apply Marxism-Leninism-Mao Tsetung Thought in a living way to the problems of the present." This version was first performed by the Scratch Orchestra in the Promenade Concert in London on Aug. 24, 1972. His other works include a String Trio (1957); *Arrangement* for orch. (1960); *Volo Solo* for any instrument (1965); *Three Winter Potatoes* for piano solo scored for "matrices arranged around vocal sounds, triangles, newspapers, balloons, noise, desire, keyboard, with many people working" (Focus Opera Group, London, March 11, 1968); Cardew further published a number of polemical political essays, some of them devoted to a rather confusing confutation of Confucius. He also compiled a seminal manual, *Scratch Music* (London, 1970).

Cardus, Sir Neville, British writer on music and cricket; b. Manchester, April 2, 1889; d. London, Feb. 28, 1975. He studied singing, then turned to journalism; became an active contributor to the *Manchester Guardian*; wrote essays on numerous subjects, but primarily on cricket and music. He was cricket coach at Shrewsbury School (1912–16); from 1941–47 he was in Australia making broadcasts on music. Returning to England he became music critic for the *Manchester Guardian* in 1951. He received the Wagner Medal of the City of Bayreuth in 1963; was knighted in 1967. His literary style is quasi-Shavian in its colloquial manner and stubborn persuasion.
  WRITINGS: *A Cricketer's Book* (1921); *Autobiography* (1947); *Second Innings: More Autobiography* (1950); *Cricket All the Year* (1952); *A Composer's Eleven* (1958); *Sir Thomas Beecham: A Portrait* (1961); *The Playfair Cardus* (1963); *Gustav Mahler: His Mind and His Music*, Vol. I (1965); *The Delights of Music* (1966); *Full Score* (1970).

Carey, Bruce, Canadian choral conductor; b. Hamilton, Ontario, Nov. 16, 1876; d. there, May 8, 1960. He studied in London and Leipzig; returning to Canada he devoted himself to teaching in his hometown. In 1927 he conducted the "sesquicentennial choir" of Philadelphia and also directed other choral groups in America and in Canada.

Carey, Francis Clive Savill, English baritone; b. Sible Hedingham, Essex, May 30, 1883; d. London, April 30, 1968. He studied voice at the Royal College of Music in London; after graduation he dedicated himself to teaching; was also for a few years (1931–39) an opera producer in London. He made a world-wide tour as a member of the group known as the English Singers.

Carey, Henry, English writer for the theater; b. probably Yorkshire, c.1687; d. by suicide, London, Oct. 4, 1743. He was a natural son of Henry Savile, Lord Eland; studied music with Linnert, Roseingrave and Geminiani; settled in London about 1710, where he was active as poet, librettist, playwright and composer; wrote nine ballad-operas, of which *The Contrivances* (London, Aug. 5, 1729) achieved the greatest success. He wrote the words of the popular song *Sally in Our Alley* and composed a musical setting for it, but his setting was replaced in 1790 by the tune *What though I am a Country Lass*, which has since been traditionally sung to Carey's original poem; also popular was his intermezzo with singing, *Nancy, or The Parting Lovers* (1739). In 1737 he published a collection of 100 ballads, *The Musical Century*; also published *Six Cantatas* (1732) and *Three Burlesque Cantatas* (1741). Carey's claim to authorship of *God Save The King* was put forth by his son George Savile Carey (1743–1807) more than 50 years after his father's death, without any supporting evidence; many anthologies still list Carey's name as the author of the British National Anthem. For a complete account of this misattribution of the tune see P. A. Scholes, *God Save The Queen!* (London, 1954; Appendix I; pp. 284–88). Further discussion of the authorship of the British National Anthem is to be found in W. H. Cummings, *'God Save the King', the Origin and History of the Music and Words* (London, 1902); O. G. Sonneck, *Report on the Star-Spangled Banner* (1909); F. S. Boas and J. E. Borland, *The National Anthem* (London, 1916); J. A. Fuller-Maitland, "Facts and Fictions about *God Save the King,*" *Musical Quarterly* (Oct. 1916); E. A. Maginty, "*America:* The Origin of Its Melody," *Musical Quarterly* (July 1934).

Carissimi, Giacomo, Italian composer of sacred music; b. Marino, near Rome, baptized April 18, 1605; d. Rome, Jan. 12, 1674. From 1624–27 he was organist at the Cathedral of Tivoli; from 1628 to his death maestro di cappella in the Church of S. Apollinare, Rome. A prolific and original composer, he broke with the Palestrina tradition, devoting himself to perfecting the monodic style, as is evidenced by his highly developed recitative and more pleasing and varied instrumental accompaniments. His manuscripts were dispersed at the sale of the library of the German College, and many are lost, but a few printed works are still extant. There were publ. the 4 oratorios *Jephte* (his masterpiece), *Judicium Salomonis, Jonas, Balthazar;* 2 collections of motets *a* 2, 3 and 4 (Rome, 1664, 1667); Masses *a* 5 and 9 (Cologne, 1663, 1667); *Arie de camera* (1667); and separate pieces in several collections. The finest collection of his works is that made by Dr. Aldrich at Christ-Church College, Oxford. He also wrote a treatise, publ. only in German: *Ars cantandi, etc.* (Augsburg; 2d ed. 1692; 3d, 1696;

another ed. 1718). F. Chrysander publ. 4 oratorios (*Jephte, Judicium Salomonis, Balthazar, Jonas*) in *Denkmäler der Tonkunst* 2; *Jonas, Judicium Salomonis* and *Jephte* were also publ. in *I Classici della Musica Italiana*, No. 5 (Milan, 1919); vocal duets are reprinted in L. Landshoff's *Alte Meister des Bel canto* (1927); a motet was publ. in *Musique d'Église des XVIIe et XVIIIe siècles*, ed. by Ch. Pineau; *Six Solo Cantatas*, ed. with commentary by G. Rose (London, 1969). The complete works are being published by Istituto Italiano per la Storia della Musica (1951–). Claudio Sartori has compiled *Carissimi, catalogo delle opere attribuite* (1975).

BIBLIOGRAPHY: M. Brenet, "Les Oratorios de Carissimi," *Rivista Musicale Italiana* (1897); A. Schering, *Geschichte des Oratoriums* (Leipzig, 1911); A. Cametti, "Primo contributo per una biografia di Giacomo Carissimi," *Rivista Musicale Italiana* XXIV/3 (1917); F. B. Pratella, "G. Carissimi e i suoi oratori," *Rivista Musicale Italiana* XXIX/1 (1920); J. Loschelder, "Nuovi contributi a una biografia di G. Carissimi," *Archiv für Musikwissenschaft* (1940); G. Massenkeil, "Die Wiederholungsfiguren in den Oratorien Giacomo Carissimis," ibid. (Jan. 1956); E. Rosend, "Four Oratorios by Giacomo Carissimi," *Amor Artis Bulletin* (Feb. 1967); L. Bianci, *Carissimi . . . e l'oratorio musicale* (Rome, 1969).

Carl, William Crane, American organist; b. Bloomfield, New Jersey, March 2, 1865; d. New York, Dec. 8, 1936. He first studied in New York; in 1890 went to Paris where he studied with Guilmant; returning to America, he was engaged as organist of the Old First Presbyterian Church in N.Y., a post which he held until his death. He made seven tours to the Pacific coast and one to Alaska; was also active as a choral conductor in N.Y.; was a founder and served on the Council of the American Guild of Organists. He published *Masterpieces for the Organ*; *30 Postludes for the Organ*; 2 volumes of *Novelties for the Organ*; *Master Studies for the Organ*.

Carlid, Göte, Swedish composer; b. Högbo, Dec. 26, 1920; d. Stockholm, June 30, 1953. He was a philosophy student at the Univ. of Uppsala; then served as a municipal librarian in Enköping (1946–48) and Sollentuna (1948–50). As a composer, he was largely autodidact, but from the outset he adopted a modern idiom, making use of impressionistic and expressionistic techniques. His last works before his early death show a learned approach to the problems of new music.

WORKS: *Notturno* for string orch. (1945); *Small Pieces* for piano (1947); Piano Sonata (1948); *Quartetto elegiaco* for string quartet (1948); *3 Songs* for female voice, flute, clarinet and cello (1946–49); *A Little Tea Music* for flute, 2 clarinets and cello (1949); *Mass* for strings (1949); *Monologues* for piano (1944–50); *Triad* for saxophone and piano (1950); *Hymnes à la Beauté* for chorus and orch., to poems by Baudelaire (the only Swedish entry in the 1952 Salzburg Festival of the International Society for Contemporary Music); *The Music Bus* for soli, children's chorus and instruments (1952).

Carlstedt, Jan, Swedish composer; b. Orsa, June 15, 1926. He studied composition with Lars-Erik Larsson at the Royal Academy of Music in Stockholm (1948–52), and later in England (1952–53) and Italy (1954–55). Returning to Stockholm, he became active in furthering the cause of modern music; was a founder of the Society of Contemporary Music in Stockholm (1960).

WORKS: 4 string quartets (1951–52, 1966; 1967; 1972); 2 symphonies: No. 1 (1952–54, revised 1960; Stockholm, Oct. 4, 1961); No. 2, in memory of Martin Luther King (1968; New York, Dec. 20, 1970); String Trio (1955–56); Sonata for String Orch. (1956); Sonata for 2 Violins (1956); *12 Miniatures* for violin, clarinet and cello (1958); 8 Duets for 2 Violins (1958); Sinfonietta for Wind Quintet (1959); Sonata for Solo Violin (1959); *Ballata* for solo cello (1960); Divertimento for Oboe and String Trio (1962); Wind Quintet (1962); *Pentastomos* for wind quintet (1972–73).

Carmichael, Hoagy, American jazz pianist and composer; b. Bloomington, Indiana, Nov. 22, 1899. He played in various bands as a youth; later formed his own band with Benny Goodman and others. Although unable to read or write music, he composed a number of melodious songs of considerable sentimental impact; of these *Stardust* became famous. Other songs are *Lazy River, Rocking Chair, Georgia on My Mind*.

BIBLIOGRAPHY: H. Carmichael, *The Stardust Road* (N.Y., 1946); H. Carmichael and Stephen Longstreet, *Sometimes I Wonder: The Story of Hoagy Carmichael* (N.Y., 1965); A. Wilder, *American Popular Song* (N.Y., 1972).

Carmichael, Mary Grant, English pianist and composer; b. Birkenhead, 1851; d. London, March 17, 1935. She studied piano and composition in London; published a number of agreeable piano pieces and an operetta, *The Frozen Heart*.

Carner, Mosco, Austrian-English musicologist and conductor; b. Vienna, Nov. 15, 1904. He studied musicology with Guido Adler at the Vienna Cons. (Dr. Mus., 1928); was active conducting theater orchestras in Germany until 1933 when the advent of the Nazi regime forced him to emigrate. He settled in London and devoted himself mainly to musical journalism. He published a biography of Dvořák (London, 1941); *A Study of 20th-Century Harmony* (2 vols.; London, 1940–42); *Of Man and Music* (London, 1944); *The Waltz* (London, 1948); *Puccini: A Critical Biography* (London, 1958; revised 1974); *Alban Berg, the Man and his Work* (London, 1975).

Carney, Harry, black American jazz saxophonist, specializing on the baritone sax; b. Boston, April 1, 1910; d. New York, Oct. 8, 1974. He joined Duke Ellington's band in 1927 and remained with it until Ellington's death; Carney survived Ellington by only a few months. He was an innovator on his instrument, emphasizing the elements of pure sonority.

Carneyro, Claudio, Portuguese composer; b. Oporto, Jan. 27, 1895; d. there, Oct. 18, 1963. He studied composition with Lucien Lambert at the Oporto Cons. and later in Paris with Widor (1919–22) and Paul Dukas (1934); returning to Portugal, he taught composition at the Oporto Cons. (1922–58); was its director in 1955–58. In his music, he made ample use of authentic Portuguese motives, adorning them by sonorous impressionistic harmonies.

WORKS: *Pregões romarias e processões* for orch. (1928); *Memento* for string orch. (1933); *Cantarejo e dancara* for orch. (1938); *Pavana e gelharda* for string orch. (1939); *Catavento* for piano and chamber orch. (1942); *Portugalesas* for orch. (1949); *Khroma* for Viola and Orch. (1954); *Roda dos degredados* for violin and orch. (1960); *Bailadeiras* for orch. (1962); *Gradualis* for orch. (1962); Piano Quartet (1914); *Partita* for String Trio (1928–35); Violin Sonata (1929); String Quartet (1947); *Poemas em Prosa* for piano (1930–31); choruses; songs.

Carnicer, Ramón, Spanish composer; b. Tárrega, near Lérida, Oct. 24, 1789; d. Madrid, March 17, 1855. From 1818–20, conductor of the Italian Opera, Barcelona; 1828–30, of the Royal Opera, Madrid; 1830–54, professor of composition at Madrid Cons. One of the creators of Spanish national opera (the *zarzuela*), he composed 9 operas, wrote much church music, many symphonies, Spanish songs, etc.; also *Dulce Patria*, the national hymn of Chile.

Carolan, Turlough, Irish song composer; b. near Nobber, County Meath, 1670; d. near Kilronan, March 25, 1738. He was an itinerant harper, and improvised Irish verses and tunes; these were published in various 18th-century collections of Irish music; the number of his original tunes is about 220. He is also known under the name **O'Carolan.**
BIBLIOGRAPHY: D. O'Sullivan, *Carolan: The Life, Times and Music of an Irish Harper* (London, 1958).

Carol-Bérard, French composer and theorist; b. Marseilles, April 5, 1881; d. Paris, Dec. 13, 1942. He studied with Albéniz in Barcelona; then settled in Paris. His music, Impressionistic with an oriental flavor, remains largely unpublished. He evolved a theory of "chromophonie" (color in movement) and wrote several papers on the subject in *La Revue Musicale* and other publications. He also wrote poetry under the pseudonym **Olivier Realtor.**
WORKS: *Symphonie dansée*; *Symphonie des forces mécaniques* (in 3 movements: *Navire perdu*; *Gare Nocturne*; *L'Aéroplane sur la ville*, utilizing phonograph records of noises); *L'Oiseau des îles*, lyric piece in 2 acts (to his own words); three piano suites, *Egypte*, *d'une existence antérieure*, and *Extrême-Asie*; humorous piano pieces, *Les heures civiles et militaires*, *L'Elégie à jouer dans une cave*, and a number of songs to poems of Verlaine and Mallarmé.

Caron, Philippe, famous Burgundian contrapuntist of the 15th century, a pupil of Binchois or Dufay. O. J. Gombosi, in his monograph *Jacob Obrecht, eine stilkritische Studie* (Leipzig, 1925), groups Caron with composers of the Cambrai school interested in continuing Dufay's style; this work also contains a reprint of a 3-part chanson, *Vive Carloys*, MSS of which are in libraries at Rome and Florence. Other extant works include 4 Masses *a* 4 in the Papal Chapel, and a MS of 3 and 4 part chansons at Paris. Petrucci publ. a 5 part chanson, *Hélas que pourra deuenir*, in his *Odhecaton* (1501). The Institute of Medieval Music (Brooklyn, N.Y.) began issuing the complete works in 1971.

Caron, Rose (*née* **Meuniez**), French dramatic soprano; b. Monerville, Nov. 17, 1857; d. Paris, April 9, 1930. She entered the Paris Cons. in 1880, leaving in 1882 to study with Marie Sasse in Brussels, where her debut was made as Alice in *Robert le Diable* (1884). She sang two years at the Opéra, Paris, and again in Brussels, creating Lorance (in *Jocelyn*), Richilde, and Salammbô (1890); in 1890 she returned to the Paris Grand Opéra, where she sang Sieglinde (1893) and Desdemona (1894) in the first performances of *Walküre* and *Otello* in France; in 1898 she sang Fidelio at the Opéra-Comique. From 1900 she appeared almost exclusively on the concert stage; in 1902 appointed prof. of singing at the Paris Cons.
BIBLIOGRAPHY: H. de Curzon, *Croquis d'artistes* (Paris, 1898).

Carpani, Giuseppe, Italian writer, b. Villalbese, Jan. 28, 1752; d. Vienna, Jan. 22, 1825. He studied and practiced law in Milan, later abandoning it for a literary career and writing on music. He was editor of the *Gazzetta di Milano* (1792–96); the French invasion forced him to go to Venice and then to Vienna. A great admirer of Haydn, he published a monograph, *Le Haydine ovvero lettere su la vita e le opere del celebre Giuseppe Haydn* (Milan, 1812; enlarged ed., Padua, 1823). Stendhal printed a major part of this book as his own work, in French, under the pseudonym of Bombet (Paris, 1814); Carpani protested against this act of plagiarism in a pamphlet *Lettere dell'Autore delle Haydine* (Vienna, 1815), but Stendhal ignored the protest and republished his book in 1817, this time under the signature Stendhal. Carpani also wrote a monograph on Rossini, *Le Rossiniane* (Padua, 1824).

Carpenter, John Alden, American composer; b. Park Ridge, Chicago, Ill., Feb. 28, 1876; d. Chicago, April 26, 1951. He received his B.A. degree from Harvard Univ. in 1897; also studied music there with John K. Paine; entered his father's shipping supply business, and from 1909–36 was vice-president of the firm. During his earlier years in business he continued his musical studies with Edward Elgar in Rome (1906) and with Bernard Ziehn in Chicago (1908–12); was made a Knight of the French Legion of Honor (1921); received an honorary M.A. from Harvard Univ. (1922) and an honorary Mus. Doc. from Wisconsin Univ. (1933). After his retirement from business in 1936, he devoted himself entirely to composing; in 1947 was awarded the Gold Medal of the National Institute of Arts and Letters. From his musical contacts abroad he absorbed mildly modernistic and impressionistic techniques and applied them to his music based on American urban subjects, adding the resources of jazz rhythms. His first work in this American idiom was a "jazz pantomime," *Krazy Kat*, after a well-known cartoon series (1921); he then wrote a large-scale musical panorama, *Skyscrapers* (1926), performed as a ballet and an orchestral suite in America and abroad, attracting much critical comment as the first symphonic work descriptive of modern American civilization; as such, the score has historical significance.

WORKS: the ballets *Birthday of the Infanta* (Chicago Opera, Dec. 23, 1919); *Krazy Kat* (Chicago, Dec. 23, 1921); and *Skyscrapers* (Metropolitan Opera, N.Y., Feb. 19, 1926; Munich, 1928); an orchestral suite, *Adventures in a Perambulator* (Chicago, March 19, 1915); Concertino for Piano and Orch. (Chicago, March 10, 1916; revised 1947); Symph. No. 1, in C (Litchfield County Choral Union Festival, Norfolk, Conn., 1917; revised for the 50th anniversary of the Chicago Symph. and performed there, Oct. 24, 1940); *A Pilgrim Vision* for orch. (Philadelphia Nov. 23, 1920; for the tercentenary Mayflower Celebration); *Patterns* for piano and orch. (Boston, Oct. 21, 1932); *Sea-Drift*, symph. poem after Whitman (Chicago, Nov. 30, 1933; revised version, 1944); *Danza* for orch. (Chicago, 1935); Violin Concerto (1936; Chicago, Nov. 18, 1937); Symph. No. 2 (N.Y., Oct. 22, 1942); symph. poem, *The Anxious Bugler* (N.Y., Nov. 17, 1943); *The Seven Ages*, symphonic suite (New York, Nov. 29, 1945); *Carmel Concerto* for orch. (1948); *Song of Faith* for chorus and orch. (Washington Bicentennial Commission, 1932); *Song of Freedom* for chorus and orch. (1941); Violin Sonata (1912); String Quartet (Elizabeth Coolidge Festival, Wash., D.C., 1928); Piano Quintet (1934); songs: *Improving Songs for Anxious Children* (1904); *Gitanjali*, song cycle to poems by Tagore (1913; also arranged for voice and orch.); *Water Colors*, four Chinese songs with chamber orch. (1918); many other songs and piano pieces.

BIBLIOGRAPHY: Olin Downes, "J. A. Carpenter, American Craftsman" and Felix Borowski, "J. A. Carpenter," both in the *Musical Quarterly* (Oct. 1930); W. T. Upton, *Art-Song in America* (N.Y., 1930; pp. 197–213); M. Goss, *Modern Music Makers* (N.Y., 1952; pp. 34–47). *Modern Music Index*, ed. by W. Shirley, W. and C. Lichtenwanger (N.Y. 1977; pp. 39–40).

Carpentras (**Il Carpentrasso** in Italian; his real name was **Elzéar Genet**), composer and priest; b. Carpentras (Vaucluse), c.1470; d. Avignon, June 14, 1548. In 1508, leading singer in, and 1513–21 maestro di cappella of the Pontifical chapel in Rome; in 1521 he was sent to Avignon on negotiations connected with the Holy See; in 1524, made his last visit to Rome. Four volumes of his works (Masses, 1532; Lamentations, 1532; Hymns, 1533; Magnificats, 1537), printed at Avignon by Jean de Channey, are of great interest for being the first works to introduce Briard's new types, with round instead of diamond-shaped and square notes, and without ligatures; a complete copy is in the Vienna Staatsbibliothek, an incomplete one in the Paris Cons. library. His works, though severe and dignified in style, were highly esteemed by his contemporaries. A few motets are printed in Petrucci's *Motetti della Corona* (vol. I, 1514, and vol. III, 1519); other works in various contemporary collections.

BIBLIOGRAPHY: Quittard, "E Genet de Carpentras," *Tribune de St. Gervais* 7-9 (1899); Ch. Requin. "Elzéar Genet, dit il Carpentrasso," in the *Mémoires de l'Académie de Vaucluse* (1918); J. Tiersot, "Elzéar Genet, dit Carpentras et la chanson 'a lombre d'ung

buissonet'," *Bulletin de la Société française de musicologie* 3 (1918); C. A. Miller, "Jerome Cardan on Gombert, Phinot, and Carpentras," *Musical Quarterly* (July 1972).

Carr, Arthur, American pianist and composer; b. Pontiac, Michigan, Feb. 29, 1908. He studied theory with David Stanley Smith and Richard Donovan at Yale Univ.; piano with Bruce Simonds; composition with Halsey Stevens at the Univ. of S. Calif. (Mus. M., 1947). In 1942–46 he served as bandleader in the U.S. Army. His works include a symph. poem *Desire* (1932); a comic opera *Captain Jupiter* (1939); a *Celtic Rondo* for orch. (1941); *Thème varié* for string quartet; piano pieces; songs. He made several tours in America and in Europe as a pianist and accompanist.

Carr, Benjamin, composer and publisher; b. London, Sept. 12, 1768; d. Philadelphia, May 24, 1831. He studied music with Samuel Arnold and Charles Wesley; established himself as a composer in London. He went to America with his father and brother in 1793; settled in Philadelphia and established Carr's Musical Repository, one of the most important early American music stores and music publishing houses; the following year (1794) they opened branches in N.Y. and Baltimore. He was co-founder in 1820 of the Musical Fund Society in Philadelphia. A versatile musician, he was proficient as singer, pianist and organist, and was an influential figure in early American musical life.

WORKS: *Philander and Silvia*, a pastoral piece (London, Oct. 16, 1792); *The Archers, or Mountaineers of Switzerland*, a ballad opera, (N.Y., April 18, 1796); *Dead March for Washington* (1799); numerous songs and ballads. The N.Y. Public Library owns the only known copy of Carr's *Federal Overture* (Philadelphia, 1794), a medley of popular airs, including the first printing of *Yankee Doodle*.

BIBLIOGRAPHY: O. G. Sonneck, "Early American Concert Life," *International Music Quarterly* 6; Wm. Henry Richards, *Carr Geneology* (1931); Virginia L. Redway. "The Carrs, American Music Publishers," *Musical Quarterly* (Jan. 1932); John T. Howard, *Our American Music* (N.Y. 4th ed., 1965); J. Mates, *The American Musical Stage before 1800* (1962).

Carr, Frank Osmond, English composer; b. Yorkshire, Apr. 23, 1858; d. Uxbridge, Middlesex, Aug. 29, 1916. He received the Oxford degrees Mus. Bac. (1882) and Mus. Doc. (1891).

WORKS: composed the comic operas *The Rose of the Riviera* (1890), *Joan of Arc* (1891), *Blue-eyed Susan* (London, 1892), *In Town* (1892), *Morocco Bound* (1893), *Go Bang* (1894), *His Excellency* (1894, to a libretto by Gilbert), *Lord Tom Noddy* (1895), *The Clergyman's Daughter* (Birmingham 1896; subsequently performed in London under the title *My Girl*), etc.

Carr, Howard, English composer and conductor; b. Manchester, Dec. 26, 1880; d. London, Nov. 16, 1960. He was a conductor of light operas in London (1903–06) and in Australia (1906–08); after conducting in London, he again went to Australia in 1928; taught harmony and counterpoint at the Sydney Cons. until 1938, when he returned to London; then devoted himself to composing.

WORKS: the operettas *Under The Greenwood Tree* and *Master Wayfarer*; 2 symphonies; an orchestral suite, *The Jolly Roger*; *The Bush* for baritone solo, male chorus and orch.

Carranza, Gustavo Eduardo, Mexican-American pianist, teacher and composer; b. Mexico City, June 14, 1897; d. Fullerton, Calif., Nov. 1, 1975. He was in the U.S. from 1911 to 1914; returned to Mexico for a year in 1914 and studied composition with Julian Carrillo in Mexico City; settled in the U.S. permanently in 1915; studied piano for a short time in New York with Ethel Newcomb and Leopold Godowsky, while also pursuing intensive studies in philosophy. In 1930 he went to California; became a naturalized U.S. citizen in 1940.

WORKS: *Oriental Fantasy* for orch.; 2 piano concertos, surnamed respectively *Medieval* and *American*; *Humoresque on Chopsticks* for 2 pianos; and a large number of solo piano pieces, among them 5 sonatas; 24 concert etudes; 8 polonaises, 4 rhapsodies and several suites, most of them surnamed for a specific nationality. His style of composition is romantic, with a considerable infusion of exotic modalities.

Carraud, Michel-Gaston, French music critic and composer; b. Mée, near Paris, July 20, 1864; d. Paris, June 15, 1920. He studied with Massenet at the Paris Cons.; received the Premier Prix de Rome for his cantata *Cléopâtre*. He abandoned composition after 1905 and was mainly active as a music critic; published *La Vie, l'œuvre et la mort d'Albéric Magnard* (Paris, 1921).

Carré, Albert, French opera impresario; nephew of the librettist Michael Carré; b. Strasbourg, June 22, 1852; d. Paris, Dec. 12, 1938. He assumed the directorship of the theater at Nancy in 1884; 1885–90, of the Cercle at Aix-les-Bains. From 1898–1912 he was director of the Opéra-Comique, succeeding Carvalho.

Carreño, Inocente, Venezuelan composer; b. Porlamar, Dec. 28, 1919. He studied French horn, clarinet, piano and theory in Caracas; graduated in composition in 1946; subsequently became engaged in pedagogical work; also played the French horn in the Caracas Symph. Orch. and conducted choruses. His works include a symphonic poem, *El Pozo* (1946); *Margariteña*, suite for orch. (1954); Concerto for Horn and Strings (1958); *Sinfonieta Satírica* for 11 instruments (1965); *Dialogo* for flute and chamber orch. (1965); chamber music and choruses.

Carreño, Teresa (Maria Teresa), famous pianist; b. Caracas, Venezuela, Dec. 22, 1853; d. New York, June 12, 1917. As a child she studied with her father, an excellent pianist; driven from home by a revolution, the family settled in New York in 1862. At the age of eight she gave a public recital in New York (Nov. 25, 1862). She lived mainly in Paris from 1866 to 1870; then in England. She developed a singing voice and made an unexpected appearance in opera in Edinburgh as the Queen in *Les Huguenots* (May 24, 1872) in a cast that included Tietjens, Brignoli and Mario;

was again in the U.S. early in 1876, when she studied singing in Boston. For the Bolivar centenary celebration in Caracas (Oct. 29, 1885), she appeared as singer, pianist and composer of the festival hymn, written at the request of the Venezuelan government; hence the frequent but erroneous attribution to Carreño of the national hymn of Venezuela, *Gloria al bravo pueblo* (the music of which was actually composed in 1811 by J. Landaeta, and officially adopted as the Venezuelan national anthem on May 25, 1881). In Caracas she once again demonstrated her versatility when for the last three weeks of the season she conducted the opera company managed by her husband, the baritone **Giovanni Tagliapietra**. After these musical experiments she resumed her career as a pianist; made her German debut in Berlin, Nov. 18, 1889; in 1907 toured Australia. Her last appearance with an orchestra was with the N.Y. Philh. Society (Dec. 8, 1916); her last recital was in Havana (March 21, 1917). She impressed her audiences by the impetuous élan of her playing, and was described as "the Valkyrie of the piano." She was married four times: to the violinist **Emile Sauret** (June, 1873), to the baritone **Giovanni Tagliapietra** (1876), to **Eugène d'Albert** (1892–95), and to **Arturo Tagliapietra**, a younger brother of Giovanni (June 30, 1902). Early in her career, Teresa Carreño wrote a number of compositions, some of which were published: a string quartet; *Petite danse tsigane* for orchestra; 39 concert pieces for piano; a waltz *Mi Teresita* which enjoyed considerable popularity, and other small pieces. She was one of the first pianists to play MacDowell's compositions in public; MacDowell took lessons from her in New York. She was greatly venerated in Venezuela; her mortal remains were solemnly transferred from New York where she died and reburied in Caracas on Feb. 15, 1938.

BIBLIOGRAPHY: M. Milinowski, *Teresa Carreño* (New Haven, 1940). A. Marquez Rodriguez, *Esbozo biográfico de Teresa Carreño* (Caracas, 1953).

Carrillo, Julián, Mexican composer; b. Ahualulco, San Luis Potosí, Jan. 28, 1875; d. Mexico City, Sept. 9, 1965. He was of Indian extraction; lived mostly in Mexico City, where he studied violin with Pedro Manzano and composition with Melesio Morales. He graduated from the National Cons. in 1899 and received a government stipend for study abroad as a winner of the President Diaz Prize. He took courses at the Leipzig Cons. with Hans Becker (violin), Jadassohn (theory) and Hans Sitt (orchestration); played violin in the Gewandhaus Orch. under Nikisch. From 1902–04 he studied at the Ghent Cons., winning first prize as violinist. He returned to Mexico in 1905 and made numerous appearances as a violinist; also conducted concerts; was appointed general inspector of music and director of the National Cons. and held these posts until 1914. He visited the U.S. many times, and conducted his works in New York and elsewhere. During his years in Leipzig he wrote a symphony which he conducted there in 1902; at the same time he began experimenting with fractional tones; developed a theory which he named *Sonido 13*, symbolically indicating divisions beyond the 12 notes of the chromatic scale. He further devised a special number notation for quarter-tones, eighth-tones, and sixteenth-tones, and constructed special instruments for performance of his music in these intervals, such as a harpzither with 97 strings to the octave; his Concertino for Fractional Tones was perf. by Leopold Stokowski with the Philadelphia Orch. on March 4, 1927. Carrillo also publ. several books dealing with music of fractional tones, and edited a monthly magazine, *El Sonido 13*, in 1924-25.

WORKS: operas *Ossian* (1903), *Matilda* (1909), *Zultil* (1922); Symphony No. 1 (1901); Symphony No. 2 (1905); Symphony No. 3 (1948); 3 symphonies for fractional tones (1926); Triple Concerto for Violin, Flute, Cello and Orch. (1918); Concertino for Violin, Guitar, Cello, Piccolo and Harp in fractional tones, with orch. in normal tuning (1926); *Horizontes* for violin, cello, and harp in fractional tones, and orch. (1947; Pittsburgh, Nov. 30, 1951, Stokowski conducting); Concertino subtitled *Metamorfoseador Carrillo*, for piano in third-tones, and orch. (1950; Brussels, Nov. 9, 1958); Concerto for cello in quater- and eighth-tones, and orch. (1954; Brussels, Nov. 9, 1958); *Balbuceos* for piano in sixteenth-tones, and chamber orch. (Houston, Texas, March 18, 1960); 2 Concertos for violin in quarter-tones, and orch. (1963, 1964); chamber music: String Sextet (1902); Piano Quintet (1918); 4 atonal quartets (1928-48); *Preludio a Cristóbal Colón* for soprano with 5 instruments in fractional tones (Mexico City, Feb. 15, 1925); Sonata in Quarter-Tones for guitar (1925); also sonatas for string instruments in quarter tones with piano; *Mass for Pope John XXIII* for chorus a cappella (1962).

WRITINGS: an autobiography, *Julián Carrillo, su vida y su obra* (Mexico, 1945); *Leyes de metamórfosis musicales* (Mexico, 1949); several manuals of music theory.

Carrodus (real name **Carruthers**), **John Tiplady,** eminent English violinist; b. Keighley, Yorkshire, Jan. 20, 1836; d. London, July 12, 1895. He studied with his father, a local musician of considerable attainments; played in public as a child; then commenced serious study with Molique in London and in Stuttgart, where he joined the court orchestra, of which Molique was first violinist. Upon his return to England, Carrodus occupied various positions in theatrical orchestras; was appointed violin instructor at the Royal College of Music (1876); toured in South Africa in 1880. He published several pieces for the violin.

BIBLIOGRAPHY: A. Carrodus, *J. T. Carrodus, Violinist: a Life-Story* (London, 1897).

Carroll, Walter, English music pedagogue; b. Manchester, July 4, 1869; d. there, Oct. 9, 1955. He studied piano and theory privately; then at the Univ. of Manchester, obtaining his Mus. Doc. in 1900. He was on the faculty of the Manchester College of Music from 1893-1920 and musical adviser to the City of Manchester Education Committee from 1918-34. He specialized in methods of education for children; published a manual, *The Training of Children's Voices*, and various collections of children's songs.

Carruthers, John. See **Carrodus, John.**

Carse, Adam von Ahn, English composer and writer on music; b. Newcastle-on-Tyne, May 10, 1878; d. Great Missenden, Bucks., England, Nov. 2, 1958. He studied with F. Corder and Burnett at the Royal Academy of Music, London; from 1909-22 taught music at Winchester College; taught harmony and composition at the Royal Academy (1923-40). He assembled a collection of about 350 wind instruments, which he presented in 1947 to the Horniman Museum in London; published a catalogue of this collection in 1951.

WORKS: the symph. poems *The Death of Tintagiles* (London, 1902) and *In a Balcony* (Promenade Concerts, Aug. 26, 1905); Symphony in C minor (London, July 3, 1906); Symphony in G minor (London, Nov. 19, 1908; revised for the Newcastle Festival, 1909); orchestral suites: *The Merry Milkmaids* (1922) and *The Nursery* (1928); *Judas Iscariot's Paradise*, ballade for baritone solo, chorus and orch. (1922); two sketches for string orch. (1923); *Barbara Allen* for string orch.; *Norwegian Fantasia* for violin and orch.; *The Lay of the Brown Rosary*, dramatic cantata; numerous choruses; chamber music; piano pieces; songs.

WRITINGS: *Summary of the Elements of Music*; *Practical Hints on Orchestration*; *Harmony Exercises* (2 vols., 1923); *The History of Orchestration* (1925); *Orchestral Conducting* (1929); *Musical Wind Instruments* (London, 1939); *The Orchestra in the 18th Century* (Cambridge, 1940); *The Orchestra from Beethoven to Berlioz* (Cambridge, 1948); *The Orchestra* (London, 1948); *18th Century Symphonies* (London, 1951); *The Life of Jullien* (Cambridge, 1951).

Cartan, Jean, talented French composer; b. Nancy, Dec. 1, 1906; d. Bligny, March 26, 1932. He studied music with Marcel Samuel Rousseau; then with Paul Dukas at the Paris Cons. His works, composed within a brief period of six years, showed extraordinary promise, and his death at the age of 25 was mourned as a great loss to French music. He left a cantata *Pater Noster*, two string quartets, a Sonatina for Flute and Clarinet (International Festival for Contemporary Music, Oxford, July 25, 1931); piano pieces and several cycles of songs.

BIBLIOGRAPHY: A. Roussel, "Jean Cartan," *La Revue Musicale* (May 1932).

Carte, Richard D'Oyly, English impresario; b. London, May 3, 1844; d. there, April 3, 1901. He studied at Univ. College, London; wrote an opera *Dr. Ambrosias* and songs; later turned to music management; he represented, among others, Gounod, Adelina Patti and the tenor Mario. He then became interested in light opera and introduced in England Lecocq's *Giroflé-Girofla*, Offenbach's *Périchole* and other popular French operettas. His greatest achievement was the launching of comic operas by Gilbert and Sullivan; he commissioned and produced at the Royalty Theatre their *Trial by Jury* (1875) and then formed a syndicate to stage other productions of works by Gilbert and Sullivan at the London Opéra-Comique Theatre. Dissension within the syndicate induced him to build the Savoy Theatre (1881), which subsequently became celebrated as the home of Gilbert and Sullivan productions, with Carte himself as the leading "Savoyard." He successfully operated the Savoy Theatre until his death; the enterprise was continued by his wife (Helen Lenoir) until her death in 1913; and thereafter by his sons. In 1887 Carte attempted to establish serious English opera through the building of a special theater (now known as Palace Theatre), and the production in 1891 of Sullivan's grand opera *Ivanhoe* followed by commissions to other English composers (Hamish McGunn, F. H. Cowen, Goring Thomas) to write operas. D'Oyly Carte introduced many improvements in theatrical management, including the replacement of gaslight by electric illumination.

BIBLIOGRAPHY: F. Cellier and C. Bridgeman, *Gilbert, Sullivan and d'Oyly Carte* (London, 1914); Leslie Baily, the Gilbert and Sullivan Book (revised ed., London 1966).

Carter, Elliott Cook, Jr., outstanding American composer; b. New York, Dec. 11, 1908. After graduating from the Horace Mann High School in 1926 Carter entered Harvard Univ., majoring in literature and languages; at the same time studied piano at the Longy School of Music in Cambridge, Mass. In 1930 he devoted himself exclusively to music, taking up harmony and counterpoint with Walter Piston, and orchestration with Edward Burlingame Hill; also attended in 1932 a course given at Harvard Univ. by Gustav Holst. He obtained his M.A. in 1932, and then went to Paris where he studied with Nadia Boulanger at the École Normale de Musique, receiving there a *licence de contrepoint*; in the interim he learned mathematics, Latin and Greek. In 1935 he returned to America; was music director of the Ballet Caravan (1937–39); gave courses in music and also in mathematics, physics and classical Greek at St. John's College in Annapolis (1939–41); then taught at the Peabody Cons. in Baltimore (1946–48). He was appointed to the faculty of Columbia Univ. (1948–50) and also taught at Yale Univ. from 1958 to 1962. In 1962 he was the American delegate at the East-West Encounter in Tokyo; in 1963 was composer-in-residence at the American Academy in Rome, and in 1964 held a similar post in West Berlin. In 1967–68 he was Professor-at-Large at Cornell Univ. He held Guggenheim Fellowships in 1945 and 1950, and the American Prix de Rome in 1953. In 1965 he received the Creative Arts Award from Brandeis Univ. In 1953 he received first prize in the *Concours International de Composition pour Quatuor à Cordes* in Liège for his First String Quartet; in 1960 he received the Pulitzer Prize for his Second String Quartet, which also received the New York Music Critics Circle Award and was further elected as the most important work of the year by the International Rostrum of Composers. He again won the Pulitzer for his Third String Quartet in 1973. His reputation as one of the most important American composers grew with every new work he produced; Stravinsky was quoted as saying that Carter's Double Concerto was the first true American masterpiece. The evolution of Carter's style of composition is marked by his constant preoccupation with taxonomic considerations. His early works are set in a neo-classical style. He later absorbed the Schoenbergian method of composition with 12 tones; finally he developed a system of serial organization in which

all parameters, including intervals, metric divisions, rhythm, counterpoint, harmony and instrumental timbres, become parts of the total conception of each individual work. In this connection he introduced the term "metric modulation," in which secondary rhythms in a polyrhythmic section assume dominance expressed in constantly changing meters, often in such unusual time signatures as 10/16, 21/8, etc. Furthermore, he assigns to each participating instrument in a polyphonic work a special interval, a distinctive rhythmic figure and a selective register, so that the individuality of each part is clearly outlined, a distribution which is often reinforced by placing the players at a specified distance from one another.

WORKS: *Tom and Lily,* comic opera in one act (1934); Flute Sonata (1934); Tarantella for male chorus and orch. (1936); ballet, *The Ball Room Guide* (1937); *The Bridge,* oratorio (1937); *Madrigal Book* for mixed voices (1937); Concerto for English Horn (1937); ballet, *Pocahontas* (N.Y., May 24, 1939); *Heart Not So Heavy As Mine* for *a cappella* chorus (1939); Suite for Quartet of Alto Saxophones (1939); *The Defense of Corinth,* after Rabelais, for speaker, men's chorus, and piano 4 hands (Cambridge, Mass., March 12, 1942); Adagio for Viola and Piano (1943); Symph. No. 1 (Rochester, April 27, 1944); *The Harmony of Morning* for female chorus and small orch. (N.Y., Feb. 25, 1945); *Canonic Suite* for 4 clarinets (1945); *Warble for Lilac Time,* after Walt Whitman, for soprano and instruments (Yaddo, Sept. 14, 1946); Piano Sonata (1946); *The Minotaur,* ballet (N.Y., March 26, 1947); *Holiday Overture* for orch. (Baltimore, Jan. 7, 1948); Woodwind Quintet (N.Y., Feb 27, 1949); 8 pieces for 4 timpani (1949; Nos. 3 and 6 composed and added in 1966); Cello Sonata (N.Y., Feb. 27, 1950); String Quartet (1951); 8 Études and a Fantasy, for flute, oboe, clarinet and bassoon (N.Y., Oct. 28, 1952); Sonata for Flute, Oboe, Cello and Harpsichord (N.Y., Nov. 19, 1953); Variations for Orchestra (Louisville, April 21, 1956); Second String Quartet (1959); Double Concerto for Harpsichord and Piano with 2 Chamber Orchestras (N.Y., Sept. 6, 1961); Piano Concerto (Boston, Jan. 6, 1967); Concerto for Orchestra (N.Y. Philharmonic, N.Y., Feb. 5, 1970); String Quartet No. 3 (1971); Brass Quintet (1974); Duo for Violin and Piano (1974); *A Mirror on Which to Dwell* for soprano and 9 players, to a cycle of 6 poems by Elizabeth Bishop (N.Y., Feb. 24, 1976); *A Symphony of Three Orchestras* (N.Y., Feb. 17, 1977). See: Else Stone and Kurt Stone, editors, *The Writings of Elliott Carter. An American Composer Looks at Modern Music* (N.Y., 1977).

BIBLIOGRAPHY: A. Skulsky, "Elliott Carter," *American Composers Alliance Bulletin* (Summer 1953); Richard F. Goldman, "The Music of Elliott Carter," *Musical Quarterly* (April 1957); A. F. Edwards, III, and E. C., *Flawed Words and Stubborn Sounds* (N.Y., 1971); *Modern Music; an Analytical Index,* compiled by Wayne Shirley, W. and C. Lichtenwanger (N.Y., 1976; pp. 40–41).

Carter, Ernest Trow, American organist and composer; b. Orange, N.J., Sept. 3, 1866; d. Stamford, Conn., June 21, 1953. He studied piano with Mary Bradshaw and William Mason (1874–84); then composition in Berlin with Wilhelm Freudenberg, Otis Boise and others; returning to the U.S., he became organist and choirmaster at Princeton Univ. (1899–1901); settled in New York as arranger, conductor and composer. He received his B.A. from Princeton (1888); M.A., Columbia Univ. (1899).

WORKS: the operas *The Blonde Donna, or The Fiesta of Santa Barbara* (N.Y., Dec. 9, 1931) and *The White Bird* (Chicago, March 6, 1924; Osnabrück, Germany, Nov. 15, 1927); ballet pantomime, *Namba, or The Third Statue* (N.Y., April 22, 1933); *Symphonic Suite* for orch.; String Quartet; anthems, including *The Lord's Prayer* and *Out of the Depths*; male quartets; piano pieces; songs.

BIBLIOGRAPHY: E. E. Hipsher, *American Opera and Its Composers* (Philadelphia, 1927; pp. 113–17).

Cartier, Jean-Baptiste, French violinist and composer; b. Avignon, May 28, 1765; d. Paris, 1841. He was a pupil of Viotti; violinist at Grand Opéra (1791–1821); 1804, member of the Imperial Orch. under Paisiello; then of the Royal Orch. (1815–30). He composed 2 operas; 2 symphonies; sonatas, variations, duets and études for violin; published a manual, *L'Art du violon* (Paris, 1798, 1801, 1803; repr. N.Y., 1973), containing selections from eminent French, Italian and German masters of the 17th and 18th centuries.

Carulli, Ferdinando, Italian guitar player and composer; b. Naples, Feb. 20, 1770; d. Paris, Feb. 17, 1841. He went to Paris in 1818 and prospered there as a guitar teacher. He is generally regarded as the first guitarist to use his instrument for artistic performances; he published a method, *L'Harmonie appliquée à la guitarre* (Paris, 1825). His works number nearly 400 items, including concertos, quartets, trios, and duos, fantasias, variations and solos of all descriptions. In 1830 he composed a piece of program music for guitar entitled *Les Trois Jours*, descriptive of the days of the July 1830 revolution.

Caruso, Enrico, celebrated Italian tenor; b. Naples, Feb. 27, 1873; d. there, Aug. 2, 1921. He was the 18th child of a worker's family, his father being a machinist. All 17 children born before him died in infancy; two born after him survived. He sang Neapolitan ballads by ear; as a youth he applied for a part in *Mignon* at the Teatro Fondo in Naples, but was unable to follow the orchestra at the rehearsal and had to be replaced by another singer. His first serious study was with Guglielmo Vergine (1891–94); he continued with Vincenzo Lombardi. His operatic debut took place at the Teatro Nuovo, Naples, on Nov. 16, 1894 in *L'Amico Francesco*, by an amateur composer, Mario Morelli. In 1895 he appeared at the Teatro Fondo in *La Traviata, La Favorita* and *Rigoletto*; during the following few seasons he added *Aida, Faust, Carmen, La Bohème* and *Tosca* to his repertoire. The decisive turn in his career came when he was chosen to appear as leading tenor in the first performance of Giordano's *Fedora* (Teatro Lirico, Milan, Nov. 17, 1898), in which he made a great impression. Several important engagements followed. In 1899 and 1900 he sang in St. Petersburg and Moscow; between 1899 and 1903 he appeared in four summer seasons in Buenos Aires.

The culmination of these successes was the coveted opportunity to sing at La Scala; he sang there in *La Bohème* (Dec. 26, 1900), and in the first performance of Mascagni's *Le Maschere* (Jan. 17, 1901). At the Teatro Lirico in Milan he took part in the first performances of Franchetti's *Germania* (March 11, 1902) and Cilea's *Adriana Lecouvreur* (Nov. 6, 1902). In the spring season of 1902, he appeared (with Melba) in Monte Carlo, and was reengaged there for three more seasons. He made his London debut as the Duke in *Rigoletto* (Covent Garden, May 14, 1902) and was immediately successful with the British public and press. He gave 25 performances in London until July 28, 1902, appearing with Melba, Nordica and Calvé. In the season of 1902–03, Caruso sang in Rome and Lisbon; during the summer of 1903 he was in South America. Finally, on Nov. 23, 1903, he made his American debut at the Metropolitan Opera, in *Rigoletto*. After that memorable occasion, Caruso was connected with the Metropolitan to the end of his life. He traveled with various American opera companies from coast to coast; he happened to be performing in San Francisco when the 1906 earthquake nearly destroyed the city. He achieved his most spectacular successes in America, attended by enormous publicity. In 1907 Caruso sang in Germany (Leipzig, Hamburg, Berlin) and in Vienna; he was acclaimed there as enthusiastically as in the Anglo-Saxon and Latin countries. A complete list of his appearances is given in the appendix of his biography by Pierre Key and Bruno Zirato (Boston, 1922). Caruso's fees soared from two dollars as a boy in Italy in 1891 to the fabulous sums of fifteen thousand dollars for a single performance in Mexico City in 1920. He made recordings in the U.S. as early as 1902; his annual income from this source alone netted him one hundred and fifteen thousand dollars at the peak of his career. He excelled in realistic Italian operas; his Cavaradossi in *Tosca* and Canio in *Pagliacci* became models which every singer emulated. He sang several French operas; the German repertory remained completely alien to him; his only appearances in Wagnerian roles were three performances of *Lohengrin* in Buenos Aires (1901). His voice possessed such natural warmth and great strength in the middle register that as a youth he was believed to be a baritone. The sustained quality of his bel canto was exceptional and enabled him to give superb interpretations of lyrical parts. For dramatic effect, he often resorted to the "coup de glotte" (which became known as the "Caruso sob"); here the singing gave way to intermittent vocalization without tonal precision. While Caruso was criticized for such usages from the musical standpoint, his characterizations on the stage were overwhelmingly impressive. Although of robust health, he abused it by unceasing activity. He was stricken with a throat hemorrhage during a performance at the Brooklyn Academy of Music (Dec. 11, 1920), but was able to sing in N.Y. for the last time, Dec. 24, 1920. Several surgical operations were performed in an effort to arrest a pleurisy; Caruso was taken to Italy, but succumbed to the illness after several months of remission. He was known as a convivial person and a lover of fine food (a brand of macaroni was named after him). He possessed a gift for caricature; a collection of his drawings was published in New York in 1922 (2nd ed., 1951). His private life was turbulent; his liaison (never legalized) with Ada Giachetti, by whom he had two sons, was painfully resolved by court proceedings in 1912, creating much disagreeable publicity; there were also suits brought against him by two American women. In 1906, the celebrated "monkey-house case" (in which Caruso was accused of improper behavior toward a lady while viewing the animals in Central Park) threatened for a while his continued success in America. On Aug. 20, 1918, he married Dorothy Park Benjamin of New York, over the strong opposition of her father, a rich industrialist. Caruso received numerous decorations from European governments, among them the Order of Commendatore of the Crown of Italy; Légion d'honneur; and Order of Crown Eagle of Prussia. A fictional film biography, *The Great Caruso*, was made of his life in 1950.

BIBLIOGRAPHY: E. Caruso, *How to Sing* (London, 1913; German translation by A. Spanuth, *Wie man singen soll*, Berlin, 1914); J. H. Wagenmann, *E. C. und das Problem der Stimmbildung* (Altenburg, 1911); M. H. Flint, *C. and His Art* (N.Y., 1917); Pierre Key and Bruno Zirato, *E. C.* (Boston, 1922); Emil Ledtner, *Erinnerungen an C.* (1922); S. Fucito and B. J. Beyer, *C. and the Art of Singing* (N.Y., 1922); P. M. Marafioti, *C's Method of Voice Production* (N.Y., 1922; new ed., 1933); Dorothy B. Caruso and Mrs. T. Goddard, *Wings of Song; The Story of Caruso* (1928); C. Armin, *E. C.s Stimme und ihr Verhältnis zum Stauprinzip* (1929); Nicola Daspuro, *E. C.* (Milan, 1938); Eugenio Gara, *C., Storia di un Emigrante* (Milan, 1947); Dorothy Caruso, *E. C., His Life and Death* (N.Y., 1945); T. R. Ybarra, *C.: The Man of Naples and the Voice of Gold* (N.Y., 1953).

Carvalho, Eleazar, brilliant Brazilian conductor and composer; b. Iguatú (Ceará), July 28, 1912. His father was of Dutch extraction and his mother was part Indian. He studied in Fortaleza at the Apprentice Seaman's School; later joined the National Naval Corps in Rio de Janeiro and played tuba in the band. In 1941 he became assistant conductor of the Brazilian Symph. Orch. in Rio de Janeiro. In 1946 he went to the U.S. to study conducting with Koussevitzky at the Berkshire Music Center, and Koussevitzky invited him to conduct a pair of concerts with the Boston Symph. Orch. Carvalho demonstrated extraordinary ability and musicianship by leading all rehearsals and the concerts without score in a difficult program; his sense of perfect pitch is exceptional. He subsequently conducted a number of guest engagements with orchestras in America and in Europe. In 1963 he was appointed conductor of the St. Louis Symph. Orch.; during his tenure he introduced many modern works into his programs, much to the discomfiture of the financial backers of the orchestra; still, he lasted a few seasons in St. Louis. From 1969 to 1973 he was conductor of the Hofstra Univ. Orch. in Hempstead, N.Y., which offered him a more liberal esthetic climate; then returned to Brazil.

WORKS: 2 operas on Brazilian subjects: *Descuberta do Brasil* (Rio de Janeiro, June 19, 1939), and *Tiradentes* (Rio de Janeiro, Sept. 7, 1941, dealing with the exploits of a revolutionary dentist during the war

of liberation); *Sinfonia branca* (1943); symph. poems: *A Traicao* (1941), *Batalha Naval de Riachuelo* (1943), *Guararapes* (1945); 3 overtures; 2 trios; 2 string quartets; violin sonata; songs. He is the husband of the avant-garde composer and pianist **Jocy de Oliveira.**

Carvalho (real name **Carvaille**), **Léon,** distinguished French opera manager; b. Port-Louis, near Paris, Jan. 18, 1825; d. Paris, Dec. 29, 1897. He began his career as a singer; in 1853 married the French soprano **Marie Miolan;** from 1872–74, was manager of the Théâtre du Vaudeville; then stage-manager at the Grand Opéra; from 1875, director of the Opéra-Comique, succeeding du Locle. After the fire of 1887, in which 131 persons perished, he was arrested and sentenced to six months' imprisonment, but was acquitted on appeal, and reinstated in 1891. He not only produced acknowledged masterworks, but encouraged many young artists by bringing out new operas.

Carvalho-Miolan, Caroline-Marie-Félix, French dramatic soprano; b. Marseilles, Dec. 31, 1827; d. near Dieppe, July 10, 1895. She entered Paris Cons. at twelve; studied under Duprez; made her operatic debut Dec. 14, 1849 in *Lucia* at the Opéra-Comique, where she was engaged from 1849–55; 1856–67, sang at the Théâtre Lyrique, where she created the soprano parts in Gounod's *Faust, Roméo et Juliette, Mireille,* and Clapisson's *La Fanchonette;* 1868–1885, sang at the Opéra and at the Opéra-Comique; also appeared in London, Berlin, Brussels, St. Petersburg, etc.; retired in 1885. In 1853 she married **Léon Carvalho.**

BIBLIOGRAPHY: E. Accoyer-Spoll, *Mme. Carvalho* (Paris, 1885); H. de Curzon, *Croquis d'artistes* (Paris, 1898).

Carver, Robert, Scottish composer; b. 1487; d. after 1546. He was a Monk of Scone Abbey; developed a melismatic style of composition; wrote Masses on the medieval song *L'Homme armé* and many motets, one of them in 19 independent parts. He is regarded as an equal of Dunstable in melodic and rhythmic excellence. Vol. 1 of his collected works was publ. by the American Institute of Musicology, ed. by Denis Stevens, in 1959.

Cary, Annie Louise, celebrated American contralto; b. Wayne, Kennebec County, Me., Oct. 22, 1841; d. Norwalk, Conn., Apr. 3, 1921. She studied in Boston and Milan; made her operatic debut in Copenhagen as Azucena; studied under Mme. Viardot-Garcia at Baden-Baden; engaged at Hamburg, Stockholm, Brussels, London and St. Petersburg. Returning to the U.S., she continued her operatic career in New York theaters; was the first American woman to sing a Wagnerian role in the U.S. (Ortrud in *Lohengrin,* 1877). She married C. M. Raymond in 1882, and retired at the height of her powers. She appeared in concert or oratorio in all leading cities of America.

BIBLIOGRAPHY: G. T. Edwards, *Music and Musicians of Maine* (Portland, 1928; pp. 204–19).

Casabona, Francisco, Brazilian composer and pedagogue; b. São Paulo, Oct. 16, 1894. He studied in Brazil and in Italy; attended classes of Alessandro Longo (piano), Camillo de Nardis (theory) and Giovanni Barbieri (composition) at the Cons. of Naples. Returning to Brazil, he became prof. of the São Paulo Cons. In his music, Casabona follows an Italianate expressive style, excelling equally in vocal and instrumental works.

WORKS: comic operas *Godiamo la Vita* (Rome, 1917), and *Principessa dell'Atelier* (Naples, 1918); symph. poems *Nero* (1915), *Crepúsculo Sertanejo* (1926), and *Noite de São João* (1934); Sinfonia No. 1 (1937); Sinfonia No. 2 (1940); *La Fable d'Einstein* for orch. (1946); *Maracatú*, Afro-Brazilian dance (1964); Violin Sonata; piano pieces in the Brazilian idiom; choruses and songs.

Casadesus, François Louis, French conductor and composer; b. Paris, Dec. 2, 1870; d. Suresnes, near Paris, June 27, 1954. He studied at the Paris Cons.; conducted the Opéra and the Opéra-Comique on tour in France (1890-92); in 1895 conducted the Opéra on a European tour; was the founder and director (1918-22) of the American Cons. at Fontainebleau; later was active as radio conductor; wrote music criticism. A collection of valedictory articles was published in honor of his 80th birthday (Paris, 1950).

WORKS: the operas *Cachaprès* (Brussels, 1914), *La chanson de Paris* (1924), *Bertran de Born* (Monte Carlo, 1925), and *Messie d'Amour* (Monte Carlo, 1928); *Symphonie scandinave*; *Au beau jardin de France* for orch.; Symphony in E major; smaller compositions for orchestra; numerous songs.

Casadesus, Henri, French violinist, brother of the preceding; b. Paris, Sept. 30, 1879; d. Paris, May 31, 1947. He studied with Lavignac and Laforge in Paris; from 1910-17 was a member of the Capet Quartet; was a founder and director of the Société Nouvelle des Instruments Anciens, in which he played the viola d'amore; subsequently toured in the U.S., playing at the Elizabeth Sprague Coolidge Festivals, Library of Congress, Washington. Rare and ancient instruments collected by Casadesus are in the museum of the Boston Symphony Orchestra.

Casadesus, Jean, French pianist, son of **Robert** and **Gaby Casadesus;** b. Paris, July 7, 1927; d. in an automobile accident, near Renfrew, Ontario, Canada, Jan. 20, 1972. He studied piano with his parents; at the outbreak of World War II, he went to the U.S.; studied at Princeton Univ.; won the contest for young soloists held by the Philadelphia Orch. in 1946; appeared as soloist with the N.Y. Philh. and with major European orchestras; made tours of the U.S. and Canada.

Casadesus, Marius, French violinist, brother of **François Casadesus;** b. Paris, Oct. 24, 1892. He studied at the Paris Cons., graduating in 1914 with first prize in violin; after graduation he dedicated much of his time to reviving old string instruments, such as Quinton and Diskantgambe; was a founding member of the Société Nouvelle des Instruments Anciens (1920-40); also organized his own string quartet. He toured as soloist in Europe and America; for many years played sonata recitals with his nephew **Robert Casadesus.** He composed several works for violin and orch., some chamber music and songs, but his most notorious

contribution to violin literature was the so-called "Adelaide Concerto" for violin and orch., supposedly arranged by him from the violin and continuo parts composed by Mozart at the age of 10 for the eldest daughter of Louis XV, Adelaide (hence the nickname); it was first performed in Paris on Dec. 27, 1931 and acclaimed as a major discovery. But skepticism arose when Casadesus failed to produce either the manuscript or a photostatic copy of it. In 1977, in the course of a litigation for his copyright as the arranger, Casadesus admitted that the "Adelaide Concerto" was entirely his own work. For a detailed discussion of the whole subject, before the author's confession of his hoax, see "Misattributed Compositions" in Percy A. Scholes, *The Oxford Companion to Music.*

Casadesus, Robert, eminent French pianist and composer; b. Paris, April 7, 1899; d. there, Sept. 19, 1972. A scion of a remarkable musical family, he absorbed music at home from his earliest childhood. His uncles were **Henri** and **François Casadesus;** another uncle, **Marcel Louis Lucien** (1882-1917), was a cellist, and his aunt, **Rose,** was a pianist. He received his formal musical education studying piano with Diémer and composition with Leroux at the Paris Cons. In 1922 he embarked on a wide ranging tour as a concert pianist; after the outbreak of World War II he went to the U.S.; taught classes at various schools; appeared with his wife, **Gaby Casadesus,** in his Concerto for 2 Pianos with the N.Y. Philharmonic on Nov. 25, 1940. After the end of the war he taught at the American Cons. at Fountainebleau. He was a prolific composer; wrote 7 symphonies, of which the last was performed posthumously in New York on Nov. 8, 1972. He also wrote a Concerto for 3 pianos and string orch., which he performed for the first time with his wife Gaby and his son **Jean** in N.Y., July 24, 1965. As a pianist, Casadesus was distinguished for his Gallic sense of balance and fine gradation of tonal dynamics.

Casals, Pablo (Pau), famous Spanish cellist; b. Vendrell, Catalonia, Dec. 29, 1876; d. San Juan, Puerto Rico, Oct. 22, 1973. His father, an organist and piano teacher, gave him his first instruction in music. Casals studied violin until he was 12; then went to Barcelona, where he studied cello with José García; at the same time he studied harmony with José Rodoreda; his progress was amazingly rapid and soon he was able to assist his teacher in his classes. In 1891 he graduated from the Municipal School of Music and began his concert career. In 1894 he went to Madrid where he attracted the attention of Count Morphy, secretary to the Queen, and was given a stipend; also played at the court. He continued his musical studies with Tomás Bretón and assisted in the chamber music class of Jesús de Monasterio; in 1895 he went to Paris as cellist at the Paris Opéra; in 1897 he taught at the Paris Cons.; also organized a string quartet. The real beginning of his career dates from his appearance, in Lalo's Cello Concerto, with Lamoureux on Nov. 12, 1899. During these years he also gave concerts in various countries of western Europe; appeared in London in 1898; made successful tours through the U.S. in 1901-02, 1903-04, and 1914-17; played concerts in South America in 1903. In 1906 he married his pupil, the Portuguese cellist **Guilhermina Suggia** (divorced in 1912); 2 years later he married the American singer **Susan Metcalfe**. In 1919 he established himself in Barcelona as the leader of the Orquestra Pau Casals; the first concert took place on Oct. 13, 1920. He was also a member of the celebrated Cortot-Thibaud-Casals Trio. During the Civil War in Spain (1936–39) Casals was an ardent supporter of the Loyalist Government, and after its defeat he settled in the village of Prades in France, on the Spanish frontier; in 1950 he inaugurated there a summer series of chamber music concerts which attracted international attention. His fame as a master musician and virtuoso is legendary; as a cellist he had no superior and few, if any, equals. Casals has composed several cello pieces, of which *La Sardana*, for an ensemble of cellos (Zürich, Oct. 14, 1951), presents a certain interest from the technical viewpoint. His Christmas oratorio, *El Pesebre* (*The Manger*) was performed for the first time in Acapulco, Mexico, Dec. 17, 1960. He also wrote a choral work, *La visión de Fray Martín*. On Aug. 3, 1957, he took in marriage Marta Montañez, a cello student. After his death, she married the pianist Eugene Istomin (1976). In December 1976 the Spanish Government of King Juan Carlos issued a postage stamp in honor of Casals' 100th birthday.

BIBLIOGRAPHY: L. Littlehales, *Pablo Casals* (N.Y., 1929); A. Conte, *La Légende de Pablo Casals* (Perpignan, 1950); J.M. Corredor, *Conversations with Casals* (English trans. by André Mangeot; London, 1956); P. Moeschlin and A. Seiler, *Casals* (a book of pictures, with German text, publ. for 80th birthday (1956); P.C. and A. Kahn, *Joys and Sorrows: Reflections by Pablo Casals as Told to Albert E. Kahn* (N.Y., 1970; trans. as *Pablo Casals. Ma vie racontée à Albert E. Kahn*, Paris, 1970; Japanese trans., Tokyo, 1973); H.L. Kirk, *Pablo Casals. A Biography* (1974).

Casamorata, Luigi Fernando, composer and music editor; b. Würzburg, of Italian parents, May 15, 1807; d. Florence, Sept. 24, 1881. He studied law and music in Florence; became co-editor of the Florentine *Gazzetta Musicale* from its start (1842) and was the founder of Istituto Musicale in Florence (1860); published its history, *Origine, storia e ordinamento dell' Istituto musicale fiorentino*; also published *Manuale di armonia* (1876). His ballets and operas were unsuccessful, and he turned to instrumental and choral works, of which he wrote many.

Casanova, André, French composer; b. Paris, Oct. 12, 1919. He studied law as well as music; took lessons with René Leibowitz and others in Paris. His music is cast in a neo-classical framework, with some atonal deviations.

WORKS: Symph. No. 1 (1949); Symph. No. 2 for chamber orch. (1952; Nice, Feb. 20, 1971); Capriccio for Oboe and Chamber Orch. (1960); *Anamorphoses* for orch. (Strasbourg, June 21, 1963); Violin Concerto (1963); *La Clé d'argent*, lyric drama (1965); Trumpet Concerto (1966); *Le Bonheur dans le crime*, opera (1969); *Notturno*, ballet (Paris, June 20, 1972); Symph. No. 3, *Dithyrambe* (Paris, Feb. 13, 1973); *Récitatifs* for orch. (Nice, Feb. 2, 1974).

Casanovas, Narciso, Spanish composer; b. Sabadell, near Barcelona, Feb. 17, 1747; d. Montserrat, April 1, 1799. He was a member of the famous Catalan school of Montserrat; was ordained priest in 1763; served as organist at the Montserrat monastery. He wrote 5 motets, 13 psalms, several litanies, and many works for organ. His Sonata in F (in Haydn's style) is reprinted in J. Nin's *17 Sonates et pièces anciennes d'auteurs espagnols* (Paris, 1929).

Casavola, Franco, Italian composer; b. Modugno, July 13, 1891; d. Bari, July 7, 1955. He studied in Rome with Respighi; abandoned his academic pursuits, joined the futurist movement and composed music glorifying the mechanical age; also wrote futurist poetry. Among his works in this genre are a ballet, *Fantasia meccanica*, and *La danza dell'elica* for flute, clarinet, violin, percussion, wind machine and blasting machine. At a later period he changed his ideas and veered toward musical realism with romantic overtones. His operas *Il gobbo del califfo* (1929), *Astuzie d'amore* (1936), and *Salammbô* (1948) have been produced with some success; he also wrote 2 ballets, *L'alba di Don Giovanni* (1932) and *Il castello nel bosco* (1931).

Casella, Alfredo, outstanding Italian composer; b. Turin, July 25, 1883; d. Rome, March 5, 1947. He began to play the piano at the age of four and received his early instruction from his mother; in 1896 he went to Paris, and studied with Diémer and Fauré at the Paris Cons.; won first prize in piano in 1899. He made concert tours as pianist in Europe, including Russia; appeared as guest conductor with European orchestras; in 1912 conducted the Concerts Populaires at the Trocadéro; taught piano classes at the Paris Cons. from 1912–15; returned to Rome and was appointed professor of piano at Santa Cecilia, as successor to Sgambati. In 1917 he founded the Società nazionale di musica (later, the Società italiana di musica moderna; since 1923 as the Corporazione delle Musiche Nuove, Italian section of the International Society for Contemporary Music). On Oct. 28, 1921 he made his American debut with the Philadelphia Orch. in the triple capacity of composer, conductor and piano soloist; also appeared as guest conductor in Chicago, Detroit, Cincinnati, Cleveland and Los Angeles; was conductor of the Boston Pops in 1927–29, introducing a number of modern works, but failing to please the public. In 1928 he was awarded the first prize of three thousand dollars given by the Musical Fund Society in Philadelphia; in 1934 won the Coolidge Prize. In 1938 he returned to Italy, where he remained until his death. Apart from his activities as pianist, conductor and composer, he was a prolific writer on music, and contributed numerous articles to various publications in Italy, France, Russia, Germany and America; he possessed an enlightened cosmopolitan mind which enabled him to penetrate the musical cultures of various nations; at the same time he steadfastly proclaimed his adherence to the ideals of Italian art. In his music he applied modernistic techniques to the old forms; his style may be termed neo-Classical, but in his early years he cultivated extreme modernism.

WORKS: OPERAS: *La donna serpente* (Rome, March 17, 1932), *La favola d'Orfeo* (Venice, Sept. 6,

1932), *Il deserto tentato*, mystery in one act (Florence, May 6, 1937). BALLETS: *Il convento veneziano* (1912; perf. La Scala, Feb. 7, 1925), *La Giara*, 'choreographic comedy' after Pirandello (his most successful work; Paris, Nov. 19, 1924), *La Camera dei Disegni*, for children (Rome, 1940), *La Rosa del Sogno* (Rome, 1943). ORCHESTRAL WORKS: Symphony No. I in B minor (1905); Symphony No. II in C minor (1908–09); Symphony No. III, op. 63 (Chicago, March 27, 1941); Suite in C (1909); *Italia*, rhapsody based on folk themes (Paris, April 23, 1910); *Le Couvent sur l'eau*, symphonic suite based on the ballet *Il convento veneziano* (perf. Paris, April 23, 1914); *Notte di Maggio* for voice and orch. (Paris, March 29, 1914); *Elegia eroica* (Rome, Jan. 21, 1917); *Pagine di guerra* (1916); *Pupazzetti*, five pieces for puppets (1918); *Partita* for piano and orch. (N.Y., Oct. 29, 1925); *Scarlattiana* on themes by Scarlatti, for piano and orch. (N.Y., Jan. 22, 1927); *Concerto romano* for organ and orch. (N.Y., March 11, 1927); Violin Concerto in A minor (Moscow, Oct. 8, 1928); *Introduzione, Aria e Toccata* (Rome, April 5, 1933); Concerto for Trio and Orch. (Berlin, Nov. 17, 1933); Concerto (Amsterdam, 1937); *Paganiniana*, on themes by Paganini (Vienna, 1942). VOCAL WORKS: *L'Adieu à la vie*, cycle of 4 Hindu lyrics after Tagore's *Gitanjali* (1915; also for voice and orch., 1926); *4 Favole romanesche* (1923); *Ninna nanna popolare genovese* (1934); *3 Canti Sacri* for baritone and orch. (1943); *Missa solemnis pro pace* (1944). CHAMBER WORKS: *Barcarola e scherzo* for flute and piano (1904); 2 cello sonatas (1907; 1927); *Siciliana e burlesca* for flute and piano (1914; second version for piano trio, 1917); *5 Pezzi* for string quartet (1920); Concerto for String Quartet (1923–24; also arranged for string orch.); *Serenata* for clarinet, bassoon, trumpet, violin and cello (1927); *Sinfonia* for clarinet, trumpet, cello and piano (1932); Piano Trio (1933). FOR PIANO: many pieces, including the two series of stylistic imitations, *A la manière de . . .* : Wagner, Fauré, Brahms, Debussy, Strauss, Franck (1911), and (in collaboration with Ravel): Borodin, d'Indy, Chabrier, Ravel (1913); *Sonatina* (1916); *A notte alta* (1917; also for piano and orch., 1921); *11 Pezzi infantili* (1920); *Due ricercari sul nome Bach* (1932); *Three pieces for pianola* (1918). Casella orchestrated Balakirev's *Islamey*; edited Beethoven's sonatas and piano works of Albéniz; arranged Mahler's 7th Symphony for piano 4 hands. WRITINGS: *L'Evoluzione della musica* (publ. in Italian, French and English in parallel columns; 1919); *Igor Stravinsky* (1926; new ed., Milan, 1951); *'21 + 26'* (about Rossini, Tolstoy, Busoni, etc.; 1931); *Il Pianoforte* (1938); a manual of orchestration, *La tecnica dell'orchestra contemporanea* (completed by V. Mortari; Milan, 1950). In 1941 Casella published his memoirs, under the Title *I Segreti della Giara*; translated into English as *Music in My Time: The Memoirs of Alfredo Casella* (Oklahoma Univ. Press, 1955). BIBLIOGRAPHY: L. Cortese, *Alfredo Casella* (Genoa, 1935); G. M. Gatti, *Musicisti moderni d'Italia e di fuori* (Bologna, 1925); a special number of *Rassegna Musicale* in honor of Casella's 60th birthday (May–June 1943); G. M. Gatti, "In Memory of A. Casella," *Musical Quarterly* (July 1947); F. d'Amico & G. M. Gatti, eds., *Alfredo Casella* (Milan, 1958).

Casella, Pietro, Italian composer who flourished in the 13th century. He was a personal friend of Dante; long thought to be the earliest Italian madrigalist; however, this idea is now believed doubtful (see L. Ellinwood, "Origins of the Italian Ars Nova," *Papers of the American Musicological Society*, 1937; p. 30).

Cash, Johnny, American popular singer of partly Indian descent (¼ Cherokee); b. in a railroad shack near Kingsland, Arkansas, Feb. 26, 1932. He worked as a water boy in a farmer's family; sang Baptist hymns in church; at the age of 17 won five dollars at a local amateur talent contest. In 1950 he enlisted in the U.S. Air Force; served in Germany, returning to the U.S. in 1954. He learned to play the guitar while in the service; in 1955 began a series of appearances on the radio and various country circuits specializing in Country-Western music, and soon began to compose his own songs, both lyrics and tunes. He could never learn to read the notes, which was of no importance to his professional life. The subjects of his songs concern the miseries of common folks as well as prison life. His most popular songs are *Folsom Prison Blues* (inspired by his imprisonment overnight in El Paso on the charge of smuggling tranquilizer tablets from Mexico) and *I Walk the Line.*
BIBLIOGRAPHY: David Ewen, *All the Years of American Popular Music* (Englewood Cliffs, N.J., 1977; pp 574–76).

Casimiri, Raffaele Casimiro, Italian musicologist; b. Gualdo Tadino, Nov. 3, 1880; d. Rome, April 15, 1943. He studied in Padua; dedicated himself to musical journalism; also conducted church choirs in the provinces. He founded the ecclesiastical magazines *Psalterium* (1907) and *Sacri concentus*; also *Note d'Archivio* (1924). His specialty was polyphonic music of the time of Palestrina whose collected works he edited (1939–52). He contributed numerous articles to Italian publications; some of his findings on Palestrina have been disputed; his ingenious hoax, which he unveiled in *Note d'Archivio* of March 1924, claiming a discovery of a notebook of Palestrina establishing the date of Palestrina's birth, was deliberately contrived to confute his learned colleagues; he exposed it in a series of scurrilous letters. He also composed 2 oratorios, several Masses, motets and offertories.
BIBLIOGRAPHY: E. Dagnino, "R. Casimiri," *Rassegna Musicale* (April 1943).

Casini, Giovanni Maria, Italian organist and composer; b. Florence, Dec. 16, 1652; d. there, Feb. 25, 1719. He studied composition in Florence, and later in Rome with Matteo Simonelli and Bernardo Pasquini (organ). He became a priest and served as organist at the Cathedral of Florence from 1703–13. As a keyboard composer Casini represents the late Baroque style. As a theorist he was a follower of Nicolo Vicentino and Giovanni Battista Doni in their studies of the music of Greek antiquity.
WORKS: Existing publications of his works are: *Canzonette spirituali* (Florence, 1703); a collection of motets (in the style of Palestrina) in 4 voices, op. 1 (Rome, 1706); *Responsori per la Settimana Santa*, op. 2 (Florence, 1706); *Pensieri per l'organo*, op. 3 (Flor-

ence, 1714). There is also an oratorio by Casini (in manuscript), *Il viaggio di Tobia*. Modern reprints of 2 numbers from his op. 3 are found in L. Torchi's *L'Arte Musicale in Italia* (vol. III).

Cassadó, Gaspar, distinguished Spanish cellist, son of **Joaquín Cassadó;** b. Barcelona, Sept. 30, 1897; d. Madrid, Dec. 24, 1966. He studied cello with Casals; toured Europe; made his debut in America, in New York on Dec. 10, 1936; made another U.S. tour in 1949. He composed a cello sonata, a cello concerto and other pieces for his instrument. His *Catalonian Rhapsody* for orch. was performed by the N.Y. Philharmonic on Nov. 8, 1928. Cassadó also made arrangements for cello and orch. of a Mozart Horn Concerto and Weber's Clarinet Concerto.

Cassadó, Joaquín, Spanish organist and composer; b. Mataró, near Barcelona, Sept. 30, 1867; d. Barcelona, May 25, 1926. He served as a choir director and organist at several churches in Barcelona; wrote a comic opera *El Monjo Negro* (Barcelona, Jan. 24, 1920); *Hispania* for piano and orch.; church music.

Cassiodorus, Magnus Aurelius, historian, statesman and monk; b. Scyllacium (Squillace), Bruttii, c.485; d. Vivarese, Calabria, c.580. He was a contemporary of Boetius; held various civil offices under Theodoric and Athalaric until c.540, when he retired. He founded the monasteries of Castellum and Vivarium; at the latter he wrote his *De artibus ac disciplinis liberalium litterarum*; the section treating of music, *Institutiones musicae*, a valuable source, is printed in Gerbert's *Scriptores*, vol. I; a partial reproduction is to be found in Strunk's *Source Readings in Music History* (N.Y., 1950).

BIBLIOGRAPHY: A. Franz, *A. Cassiodorus* (1872); W. Brambach, *Die Musikliteratur des Mittelalters* (1883); H. Abert, "Zu Cassiodor," *Sammelbände der Internationalen Musik-Gesellschaft* III/3; H. Abert, *Die Musikanschauung des Mittelalters* (p. 132ff.; 1905); G. Pietzsch, *Die Klassifikation der Musik* (1929); G. Pietzsch, *Die Musik im Erziehungs- und Bildungsideal* (pp. 30ff.; 1932); G. Wille, *Musica Romana* (Amsterdam, 1967; pp. 700ff.).

Cassirer, Fritz, German conductor and writer on music; b. Breslau, March 29, 1871; d. Berlin, Nov. 26, 1926. He first studied philosophy (1889–92); then turned to music; was orchestral and operatic conductor in many German towns; also in London (1905–07). WRITINGS: *Edgar*, a poem (1894); "Beethovens Briefe," *Die Musik* (1909); *Helldunkle Weltgeschichte* (1920; pseudonym: **Friedrich Leopold**); *Beethoven und die Gestalt* (1925).

Cassuto, Alvaro, Portuguese conductor and composer; b. Oporto, Nov. 17, 1938. He studied violin and piano as a small child; then took courses in composition with Artur Santos and Lopes Graça. During the season 1960–61 he attended classes in new music in Darmstadt, Germany, with Ligeti, Messiaen and Stockhausen, and at the same time had instruction in conducting with Herbert von Karajan. He further studied conducting with Pedro de Freitas Branco in Lisbon and Franco Ferrara in Hilversum, The Netherlands. He served as an assistant conductor of the Gulbenkain Orch. in Lisbon (1965–68) and with Little Orch. in New York (1968–70). In 1970 he was appointed permanent conductor of the National Radio Orch. of Lisbon, and in 1975 was elected Music Director of the orchestra. In 1974 he was appointed Lecturer in Music and conductor of the Symphony Orch. of the University of California, Irvine. He also was guest conductor of numerous orchestras in Europe, South America, and the United States. In 1969 he received the Koussevitzky Prize in Tanglewood. A progressive-minded and scholarly musician, he amassed a large repertory of both classical and modern works, displaying a confident expertise. He is also a composer.

WORKS: *Sinfonia Breve No. 1* (Lisbon, Aug. 29, 1959, the first dodecaphonic work by a Portuguese composer); *Sinfonia Breve No. 2* (1960); *Variations for Orch.* (1961); *Permutations for 2 orchs.* (1962); *String Sextet* (1962); *Concertino for Piano and Orch.* (1965); *Cro (mo-no)fonia* for 20 string instruments (1967); *Canticum in Tenebris* for soloists, chorus and orch. (1968); *Evocations* for orch. (1969); *Circle* for orch. (1971); *In the Name of Peace*, one-act opera (1971); *Song of Loneliness* for 12 players (1972); *To Love and Peace*, symphonic poem (1973).

Castagna, Bruna, Italian contralto; b. Bari, Oct. 15, 1905. She studied in Milan; was engaged at the Teatro Colón in Buenos Aires for 3 seasons (1927–30); toured in Australia, Brazil, Egypt and Spain; made her debut at the Metropolitan Opera House in New York as Amneris in *Aida* on March 2, 1936 and remained on the Metropolitan Staff until 1940. She was particularly acclaimed as Carmen. She eventually went to live in Argentina.

Castagnone, Riccardo, Italian composer; b. Brunate, Como, Sept. 10, 1906. He studied piano, composition and conducting; was active mainly as an accompanist; in 1956 joined the Virtuosi di Roma as a cembalo player; also edited collections of Italian masters of the Baroque. He composed a *Sinfonia in Tre Tempi* (1940); 2 string quartets (1941–42); numerous piano pieces and songs.

Castaldi, Alfonso, Italian-born Rumanian composer; b. Maddalone, April 23, 1874; d. Bucharest, Aug. 6, 1942. He studied at the Cons. in Naples with Francisco Cilea and Umberto Giordano; then went to Rumania; from 1904 to 1940 he taught at the Bucharest Cons., was greatly esteemed as a pedagogue. He wrote several operas in an Italianate style; the symph. poems, *Thalassa* (1906) and *Marsyas* (1907); Symphony (1920); 3 string quartets; other chamber music; numerous choruses.

BIBLIOGRAPHY: Z. Vancea, *Creatia muzicală romaneâscă sec. XIX–XX* (Bucharest, 1968); V. Cosma, *Muzicieni romãni* (Bucharest, 1970; pp. 102–03, containing a complete list of works).

Castaldo, Joseph, American composer; b. New York, Dec. 23, 1927. He studied in New York; was a clarinetist; enrolled in the Santa Cecilia Academy in Rome.

Returning to the U.S. he took composition lessons with Giannini and Persichetti. Among his works are a string quartet; *Epigrams* for piano and orch.; *Flight*, a cantata; *Dichotomy* for woodwind quintet; *Epiphonia* for orch. In 1966 he was appointed President of the Philadelphia Music Academy.

Castan, Count Armand de. See **Castelmary.**

Castel, Louis-Bertrand, French acoustician, b. Montpellier, Nov. 11, 1688; d. Paris, Jan. 9, 1757. He became interested in Newton's observation on the correspondence, in proportionate breadth, of the 7 prismatic rays with the string-lengths required for the scale *re, mi, fa, sol, la, si, do;* acting upon this observation, he attempted the construction of a "Clavecin oculaire," to produce color-harmonies for the eye as the ordinary harpsichord produces tone-harmonies for the ear. His theory is explained in an essay, *Nouvelles expériences d'optique et d'acoustique* (1735; English transl., London, 1757).

Castelli, Ignaz Franz, Austrian opera librettist; b. Vienna, July 6, 1781; d. there, Feb. 5, 1862. He was employed as "Court Theater-Poet" at the Kärntnerthortheater in Vienna: was the founder and editor of the *Allgemeiner Musikalischer Anzeiger* (1829–40); he wrote numerous opera libretti; published a book of memoirs (1861; 4 vols.).

Castelmary (stage name of Count **Armand de Castan**), French baritone; b. Toulouse, Aug. 16, 1834; d. New York, Feb. 10, 1897, on the stage of the Metropolitan Opera House, just after the first act of *Martha.* He made his debut at the Paris Opéra (1864); remained there till 1870; then sang in London and New York; was particularly successful as Mephistopheles in *Faust.*

Castelnuovo-Tedesco, Mario, greatly significant Italian-American composer; b. Florence, April 3, 1895; d. Los Angeles, March 16, 1968. He studied at the Cherubini Institute with del Valle (piano) and Pizzetti (composition); he began to compose at an early age; his first organized composition, *Cielo di Settembre* for piano, revealed Impressionistic tendencies. He wrote a patriotic song, *Fuori i Barbari*, during World War I. He attained considerable eminence in Italy between the two wars, and his music was often heard at European festivals. Political events forced him to leave Italy; in 1939 he settled in the U.S. He became active as a film composer in Hollywood, but continued to write large amounts of orchestral and chamber music. His style is remarkably fluent and adaptable to the various moods evoked in his music, often reaching rhapsodic eloquence.
WORKS: OPERAS: *La Mandragola* (libretto by the composer, after Machiavelli, Venice, May 4, 1926; won the National Prize); *The Princess and the Pea*, after Andersen, overture with narrator (1943); *Bacco in Toscana*, dithyramb for voices and orch. (Milan, May 8, 1931); *Aucassin et Nicolette*, puppet show with voices and instruments (1938; first performed in Florence, June 2, 1952); *All's Well That Ends Well* after Shakespeare (1959); *Saul*, biblical opera (1960);

Il Mercante di Venezia, after Shakespeare's play *The Merchant of Venice*, to the composer's libretto in Italian (won first prize at the International Competition at La Scala, Milan; first performed at the Maggio Musicale, Florence, May 25, 1961); *The Importance of Being Earnest*, after Oscar Wilde, chamber opera (1962); *The Song of Songs*, scenic oratorio (Hollywood, Aug. 7, 1963); *Tobias and the Angel*, scenic oratorio (1965); BIBLICAL ORATORIOS: *Ruth* (1949) and *Jonah* (1951). FOR ORCH: *Cipressi* (Boston Symph., Koussevitzky cond., Oct. 25, 1940; originally for piano, 1921); Piano Concerto No. 1 (Rome, Dec. 9, 1928); Piano Concerto No. 2 (N.Y. Philh., Nov. 2, 1939, composer soloist); 3 violin concertos: *Concerto italiano* (Rome, Jan. 31, 1926), *The Prophets* (Jascha Heifetz and N.Y. Philh., Toscanini conducting, April 12, 1933), 3d Violin Concerto (1939); Cello Concerto (N.Y. Philh., Jan. 31, 1935, Piatigorsky soloist, Toscanini conducting); *Variazioni sinfoniche* for violin and orch. (N.Y. Philharmonic, April 9, 1930); overtures to Shakespeare's plays: *The Taming of the Shrew* (1930), *Twelfth Night* (1933), *The Merchant of Venice* (1933), *Julius Caesar* (1934), *A Midsummer Night's Dream* (1940), *Coriolanus* (1947), etc.; *Poem* for violin and orch. (1942); *The Birthday of the Infanta* (1942; New Orleans, Jan. 28, 1947); *Indian Songs and Dances*, suite (Los Angeles, Jan. 7, 1943); *An American Rhapsody* (1943); *Serenade for Guitar and Orch.* (1943); *Octoroon Ball*, ballet suite (1947); *Noah's Ark*, a movement for narrator and orch. from *Genesis*, a suite; other movements by Schoenberg, Stravinsky, Toch, Milhaud, Tansman, and N. Shilkret, who commissioned the work (Portland, Ore., Dec. 15, 1947). CHAMBER MUSIC: *Signorine: 2 Profili* for violin and piano (1918); *Ritmi* for violin and piano (1920); *Capitan Fracassa* for violin and piano (1920); *Notturno Adriatico* for violin and piano (1922); *I nottambuli* for cello and piano (1927); Cello Sonata (1928); 1st Piano Trio (1928); 1st String Quartet (1929); *Sonata quasi una fantasia* for violin and piano (1929); *The Lark* for violin and piano (1930); 1st Piano Quintet (1932); 2nd Piano Trio (1932); Toccata for Cello and Piano (1935); *Capriccio diabolico* for guitar (1935; later arranged as guitar concerto); Concertino for Harp and 7 Instruments (1937); *Ballade* for violin and piano (1940); Divertimento for 2 flutes (1943); Sonata for Violin and Viola (1945); Clarinet Sonata (1945); Sonatina for Bassoon and Piano (1946); 2nd String Quartet (1948); Quintet for Guitar and Strings (1950); Sonata for Viola and Cello (1950); Fantasia for Guitar and Piano (1950); *Concerto da camera* for oboe and strings (1950); Sonata for Violin and Cello (1950); 2nd Piano Quintet (1951). FOR PIANO: *English Suite* (1909); *Questo fu il carro della morte* (1913); *Il raggio verde* (1916); *Alghe* (1919); *I naviganti* (1919); *La sirenetta e il pesce turchino* (1920); *Cantico* (1920); *Vitalba e Biancospino* (1921); *Epigrafe* (1922); *Alt-Wien* (Viennese rhapsody, 1923); *Piedigrotta* (1924); *Le Stagioni* (1924); *Le danze del Re David* (1925); *3 poemi campestri* (1926); *3 corali su melodie ebraiche* (1926); Sonata (1928); *Crinoline* (1929); *Candide*, 6 pieces (1944); *6 canoni* (1950). SONGS: *Le Roy Loys* (1914); *Ninna-Nanna* (1914; very popular); *Fuori i barbari*, a patriotic song (1915); *Stelle cadenti* (1915); *Coplas* (1915); *Briciole* (1916); *3 fioretti di Santo Francesco*

(1919; also with orch.); *Girotondo de golosi* (1920); *Etoile filante* (1920); *L'Infinito* (1921); *Sera* (1921); *Due preghiere per i bimbi d'Italia* (1923); *1830*, after Alfred de Musset (1924); *Scherzi*, 2 series (1924–24); music to 33 Shakespeare songs (1921–25); *Indian Serenade* (1925); *Cadix* (1926); *3 Sonnets from the Portuguese*, after E. B. Browning (1926); *Laura di Nostra Donna* (1935); *Un sonetto di Dante* (1939); *Recuerdo* (1940); *Le Rossignol* (1942); *The Daffodils* (1944). FOR CHORUS: 2 madrigals *a cappella* (1915); *Lecho dodi*, synagogue chant for tenor, men's voices, and organ (1936); *Sacred Synagogue Service* (1943); *Liberty, Mother of Exiles* (1944). Numerous pieces for guitar including *Les Guitares bien temperées* (24 preludes and fugues for 2 guitars, 1962); 2 guitar concertos (1939, 1953); Concerto for 2 Guitars and Orch. (1962); 3rd String Quartet (1964); Sonatina for Flute and Guitar (1965); Sonata for Cello and Harp (1966).

BIBLIOGRAPHY: Guido M. Gatti, *Musicisti moderni d'Italia e di fuori* (Bologna, 1925); G. Rossi-Daria, "Mario Castelnuovo-Tedesco," *Chesterian* (Jan.–Feb. 1926); Roland von Weber, "Mario Castelnuovo-Tedesco," in David Ewen, ed., *The Book of Modern Composers* (N.Y., 1942; 3rd ed., 1961). Nick Rossi, *Complete Catalogue of Works by Mario Castelnuovo-Tedesco* (N.Y., 1977).

Castéra, René d'Avezac, French composer; b. Dax (Landes), April 3, 1873; d. Angoume (Landes), Oct. 8, 1955. He studied at the Schola Cantorum with Vincent d'Indy and Guilmant. In 1902 he founded the Edition Mutuelle for publication of works by French composers. He wrote an opera *Berteretche*, some symphonic pieces, a piano trio, a violin sonata, songs and character pieces for piano.

Castiglioni, Niccolò, Italian pianist and composer of avant-garde tendencies; b. Milan, July 17, 1932. He studied composition with Ghedini, Desderi and Margola at the Verdi Cons. in Milan, and piano with Gulda at the Mozarteum in Salzburg; also took composition lessons with Blacher. He began his career as a pianist; in 1966 emigrated to the U.S.; was composer in residence at the Center of Creative and Performing Arts at the State Univ. of N.Y. in Buffalo (1966–67); then was on the faculty of the Univ. of Michigan (1967) and Univ. of Washington at Seattle (1968–69); in 1970 he was appointed instructor at the Univ. of California in San Diego. In his music he follows a pragmatically modernistic line of composition, making use of any and all mannerisms of the neo-Classical, neo-Romantic and experimental resources while preserving a necessary minimum of communicable sound production.

WORKS: an opera, *Uomini e no* (1955); a radio opera, *Attraverso lo specchio* (*Through the Looking Glass*), after Lewis Carroll (1961; Italian Radio, Oct. 1, 1961); a chamber opera, *Jabberwocky*, after Lewis Carroll (1962); a 1-act opera, *Sweet*, for baritone, piano, bells and winds (Rome, 1968); an opera-triptych, *Three Mystery Plays* (Rome, Oct. 2, 1968; material made up of *Silence, Chordination* and *The Rise and Rebellion of Lucifer and Aria*); *Concertino per la notte di Natale* for strings and woodwinds (1952); Symph. No. 1 for soprano and orch., to a text by

Nietzsche (Venice, Sept. 15, 1956); Symph. No. 2 (1956–57; Italian radio, Nov. 23, 1957); *Canti* for orch. (1956); *Ouverture in Tre Tempi* (1957); *Elegia* for 19 instruments and soprano (1957); *Impromptus* for orch. (1957–58); *Inizio di Movimento* for piano (1958); *Movimento Continuato* for piano and 11 instruments (1958–59); *Sequenze* for orch. (1959); *Tropi* for 6 players (1959); *Apréslude* for orch. (1959); *Cangianti* for piano (1959); *Eine Kleine Weihnachtsmusik* (*A Little Christmas Music*) for chamber orch. (1959–60); *Disegni* for chamber orch. (1960); *Gymel* for flute and piano (1960); *Rondels* for orch. (1960–61); *Décors* for orch. (1962); *Consonante* for flute and chamber orch. (1962); *Synchromie* for orch. (1963); Concerto for Orch. (1963); *A Solemn Music I*, after Milton, for soprano and chamber orch. (1963); *Gyro* for chorus and 9 instruments (1963); *Caractéres* for orch. (1964); *Figure*, a mobile for voice and orch. (1965); *Alef* for solo oboe (1965); *Anthem*, composition in 5 strophes for chorus and orch. (1966); *Ode* for 2 pianos, wind instruments and percussion (1966); *Canzoni* for soprano and orch. (Naples, Oct. 18, 1966); *Carmina* for chamber ensemble (1967); *Sinfonia guerriere et amorose* for organ (1967); *Granulation* for 2 flutes and 2 clarinets (1967); *Masques* for 12 instruments, a bouillabaisse of polytonally arranged fragments of dimly remembered tunes by other composers (1967); *The New Melusine* for string quartet (1969); *La Chant du signe*, concerto for flute and orch. (1969); *Sinfonia in Do*, after Ben Jonson, Dante, Shakespeare and Keats, for chorus and orch. (1968–69; Rome, May 21, 1971).

Castil-Blaze. See **Blaze, François-Henri-Joseph.**

Castilla, Alberto, Colombian composer; b. Bogotá, April 9, 1883; d. Ibague, June 10, 1937. He studied engineering; was at one time connected with the government of Colombia. In 1898 he settled in Tolima, where he founded a music school. He wrote a number of songs, some of which achieved popularity. In 1954 the Colombian government issued a postage stamp in his honor.

Castillon, Alexis, French composer; b. Chartres, Dec. 13, 1838; d. Paris, March 5, 1873. He pursued a military career before turning to music. He studied with Victor Massé, and later took lessons with César Franck; was one of the founders of the Société Nationale de Musique. He composed mainly for chamber music groups; also wrote a Symphony, 2 overtures, a Mass and other religious music; his Piano Concerto was accepted for performance by Saint-Saëns, but was utterly unsuccessful.

Caston, Saul, American conductor; b. New York, Aug. 22, 1901. He studied at the Curtis Institute, Philadelphia, with Abram Chasins (piano), Scalero (composition) and Reiner (conducting); played trumpet in the Philadelphia Orch. (1918–45); taught trumpet at the Curtis Institute (1924–42); was associate conductor of the Philadelphia Orch. (1936–45); conductor of the Reading Symph. Orch. (1941–44); in 1945 was appointed conductor of the Denver Symph. Orch., retiring in 1960.

Castro, Jean (Juan) de, composer who flourished in the 16th century; b. probably in Liège about 1540; d. about 1611. From 1582–84 he was assistant choirmaster in Vienna; later, 1593–96, in Cleve, near Cologne.

WORKS: *Missae à 3* (Cologne, 1599); *Sacrae cantiones,* 5–8 parts (1571), *Sacrae cantiones,* 3 parts (1593 and 1596); in 5–8 parts (1588); *Tricinia sacra* (1574); *Bicinia sacra* (1594); *Chansons, Odes et Sonnets par P. Ronsard à 4–8 voix* (1576); *Cantiones sacra* (1591; repr. in *Denkmäler rheinischer Musik* 16, 1972); *Chansons, Stances, Sonnets et Epigrammes à 2 voix* (Antwerp, 1592); *Quintines, Sextines, Sonnets à 5 voix* (1594). Many of these works are of interest because of the exact rhythmical arrangement of the verses.

Castro, José María, Argentine composer and conductor; brother of **Juan José Castro;** b. Avellaneda, near Buenos Aires, Dec. 15, 1892; d. Buenos Aires, Aug. 2, 1964. He studied in Buenos Aires; then went to Paris, and like his brother, took a course with Vincent d'Indy. Returning to Argentina in 1930 he became conductor of the Orquesta Filharmónica in Buenos Aires; from 1933 to 1953 also led the Banda Municipal de la Ciudad de Buenos Aires.

WORKS: a ballet, *Georgia,* which he conducted for the first time at the Teatro Colón in Buenos Aires, on June 2, 1939; Concerto Grosso, his most successful work (Buenos Aires, June 11, 1933); Piano Concerto (Buenos Aires, Nov. 17, 1941); *Sinfonía de Buenos Aires* (1963); also Cello Concerto (1945); Violin Concerto (1953); 3 string quartets (1944, 1947, 1956); *Sonata poética* for violin and piano (1957); 6 piano sonatas, of which *Sonata de primavera* (1939) is notable, and 13 sonnets, *Con la patria adentro,* for tenor and orch. (1964).

Castro, Juan José, eminent Argentine composer and conductor; brother of **José María Castro;** b. Avellaneda, near Buenos Aires, March 7, 1895; d. in Buenos Aires, Sept. 3, 1968. After study in Buenos Aires he went to Paris where he took a course in composition with Vincent d'Indy. Returning to Argentina in 1929 he organized in Buenos Aires the Orquesta de Nacimiento, which he conducted; from 1930 he conducted opera at the Teatro Colón; also became the musical director of the Asociación del Profesorado Orquestal and Asociación Sinfónica, with which he gave first local performances of a number of modern works. In 1934 he received a Guggenheim Foundation grant; from 1951 to 1953 he was the principal conductor of the Victorian Symph. Orch. in Melbourne, Australia; in 1955 he returned to Argentina; from 1956 to 1959 he was conductor of the Orquesta Sinfónica Nacional in Buenos Aires; from 1959 to 1962 was director of the Cons. of San Juan, Puerto Rico. He was proficient in all genres of composition, but his works were rarely performed outside of South America, and he himself conducted most of his symphonic compositions.

WORKS: His most signal success on the international scene was the prize he received at the contest for the best opera at La Scala, Milan, for his opera *Prosperpina e lo Straniero* (in the original Spanish *Prosperina y el extranjero*), of which he conducted the first performance at La Scala in Milan on March 17, 1952; his other operas were *La Zapatera prodigiosa,* after García Lorca (Montevideo, Dec. 23, 1949); and *Bodas de Sangre,* also after Lorca (Buenos Aires, Aug. 9, 1956) and *Cosecha negra* (1961). Other works: the ballets, *Mekhano* (Buenos Aires, July 17, 1937); *Offenbachiana* (Buenos Aires, May 25, 1940); 5 symphonies: No. 1 (1931); *Sinfonía biblica,* for orch. and chorus (1932), *Sinfonía Argentina* (Buenos Aires, Nov. 29, 1936), *Sinfonía de los Campos* (Buenos Aires, Oct. 29, 1939), Symph. No. 5 (1956); *Dans le jardin des morts* (Buenos Aires, Oct. 5, 1924); *A una madre* (Buenos Aires, Oct. 27, 1925); *La Chellah,* symph. poem based on an Arabian theme (Buenos Aires, Sept. 10, 1927); *Allegro, Lento y Vivace* (1931); *Anunciación, Entrada a Jerusalem, Golgotha* (Buenos Aires, Nov. 15, 1932); *Corales Criollos,* symph. poem (1953; won first prize at the Caracas Music Festival, 1954); *Epitafio en ritmos y sonidos* for chorus and orch. (1961); *Negro* for soprano and orch. (1961); *Suite introspectiva* (1961; Los Angeles, June 8, 1962); Violin Concerto (1962); Violin Sonata (1914); Cello Sonata (1916); String Quartet (1942); 2 Piano Sonatas (1917, 1939); *Corales Criollos* No. 1 and No. 2 for piano (1947); songs.

Castro, Ricardo, Mexican composer and pianist; b. Durango, Feb. 7, 1864; d. Mexico City, Nov. 28, 1907. He studied with Melesio Morales in Mexico; in 1883 he appeared as pianist at the New Orleans Cotton Exposition. In 1902 he went to Europe and presented concerts of his works in Paris; he was soloist in his own piano concerto in Antwerp (Dec. 28, 1904). Returning to Mexico, he produced an opera *La Leyenda de Rudel* (Nov. 8, 1906). He composed three more operas (*Atzimba, Satán vencido* and *La Rousalka*), 2 symphonies (1883; 1887) and a number of piano pieces.

Castro, Washington, Argentine composer; brother of **José María** and **Juan José Castro;** b. Buenos Aires, July 13, 1909. He studied cello; in 1947 devoted himself mainly to conducting and teaching.

WORKS: *Sinfonía primaveral* (1956); Piano Concerto (1960); *Sinfonía breve* for strings (1960); Concerto for orch. (1963); *Rhapsody* for cello and orch. (1963); *3 Pieces* for orch. (1970); 3 string quartets (1945, 1950, 1965); piano pieces; songs.

Castrucci, Pietro, Italian violinist; b. Rome, 1679; d. Dublin, Feb. 29, 1752. He was a pupil of Corelli; came to London (1715) as leader of Handel's opera orch. He was a fine player on the "violetta marina," a stringed instrument invented by himself, and resembling the viola d'amore in tone. In *Orlando,* Handel wrote an air accompanied on two "violette marine" "per gli Signori Castrucci" (Pietro, and **Prospero,** his brother). Castrucci published violin concertos, and 2 books of violin sonatas.

Catalani, Alfredo, greatly talented Italian composer; b. Lucca, June 19, 1854; d. Milan, Aug. 7, 1893. He studied music with his father, a church organist; in 1871 went to Paris where he attended classes of Bazin. Returning to Italy he studied at the Milan Cons.

with Bazzini and Fortunato Magi; in 1888 he became the successor of Ponchielli as prof. of composition at the Milan Cons. It was in Milan that he became acquainted with Boito who encouraged him in his composition; he also met young Toscanini who became a champion of his music. Catalani was determined to create a Wagnerian counterpart in the field of Italian opera, and he selected for his libretti fantastic subjects suitable for dramatic action. After several unsuccessful productions he finally achieved his ideal in his last opera *La Wally;* he died of tuberculosis the year after its production.

WORKS: his operas include *La Falce* (Milan, July 19, 1875); *Elda* (Turin, Jan. 31, 1880; revised and produced under the title *Loreley,* Turin, Feb. 16, 1890), *Dejanice* (Milan, March 17, 1883), *Edmea* (Milan, Feb. 27, 1886), *La Wally* (Milan, Jan. 20, 1892); he further composed *Sinfonia a piena orchestra* (1872); *Il Mattino,* romantic symphony (1874); *Ero e Leandro,* symph. poem (Milan, May 9, 1885); a number of piano pieces and songs.

BIBLIOGRAPHY: D. L. Pardini, *Alfredo Catalani* (Lucca, 1935); J. W. Klein, "Alfredo Catalani," *Musical Quarterly* (July 1937); A. Bonaccorsi, *Alfredo Catalani* (Turin, 1942); Carlo Gatti, *Alfredo Catalani* (Milan, 1953); J. W. Klein, "Toscanini and Catalani—a Unique Friendship," *Music & Letters* (July 1967).

Catalani, Angelica, Italian soprano; b. Sinigaglia, May 10, 1780; d. Paris, June 12, 1849. She was taught at the convent of Santa Lucia di Gubbio in Rome; made her operatic debut at the Teatro la Fenice, Venice (1795); then sang at La Pergola, Florence (1799) and at La Scala, Milan (1801). In 1801, while engaged at the Italian Opera in Lisbon, she married M. Valabrègue, an attaché of the French embassy; subsequently gave highly successful concerts in Paris and London. From 1814–17 she undertook, without signal success, the management of the Théâtre des Italiens in Paris; then resumed her singing career, appearing in major European cities and at provincial festivals until 1828, when she retired to her country home near Florence. She won great acclaim for her commanding stage presence, wide vocal range, and mastery of the *bravura* singing style.

Catel, Charles-Simon, French composer and music pedagogue; b. l'Aigle, Orne, June 10, 1773; d. Paris, Nov. 29, 1830. He studied in Paris with Gossec and Gobert at the École Royale du Chant (later merged with the Cons.); served as accompanist and teacher there (1787); in 1790 was accompanist at the Opéra and assistant conductor (to Gossec) of the band of the Garde Nationale. In 1795, on the establishment of the Conservatoire, he was appointed professor of harmony, and commissioned to write a *Traité d'Harmonie* (published in 1802; a standard work at the Conservatoire for twenty years thereafter). With Gossec, Méhul and Cherubini, he was made an inspector of the Cons., resigning in 1814; named a member of the Academy in 1815. As a composer, Catel was at his best in his operas, written in a conventional but attractive style of French stage music of the time.

WORKS: operas, performed at the Paris Opéra and at the Opéra-Comique: *Sémiramis* (May 3, 1802); *L'Auberge de Bagnères* (April 16, 1807); *Les Artistes par occasion* (Feb. 24, 1807); *Les Bayadères,* his most successful work (Paris Opéra, Aug. 8, 1810); *Les Aubergistes de qualité* (June 17, 1812); *Bayard à Mézières* (Feb. 12, 1814); *L'Officier enlevé* (May 4, 1819); also several symphonies and chamber works.

BIBLIOGRAPHY: See J. Carlez, *Catel; Étude biographique et critique* (Caen, 1895); F. Hellouin and J. Picard, *Un Musicien oublié: Catel* (Paris, 1910).

Catelani, Angelo, Italian music historian; b. Guastalla, March 30, 1811; d. San Martino di Mugnano, Sept. 5, 1866. He studied piano with Asioli and harmony with M. Fusco; also at the Naples Cons. (1831) and privately with Donizetti and Crescentini; conducted at the Messina opera (1834), at Correggio (1837); appointed maestro di cappella at the cathedral and court of Modena (1838); from 1859 served as assistant librarian of the Este Library. He composed three operas, of which one was successfully produced; then turned to writing on music.

WRITINGS: "Notizie su padre Aaron e su Nicola Vicentino," *Gazzetta musicale di Milano* (1851); *Epistolario di autori celebri in musica* (1852–4); *Bibliografia di due stampe ignote di Ottaviano Petrucci da Fossombrone* (1858); *Della vita e delle opere di Orazio Vecchi* (1858); *Della vita e delle opere di Claudio Merulo da Correggio* (1860); *Delle opere di Alessandro Stradella* (1866).

Catoire, Georgy Lvovitch, Russian composer of French descent; b. Moscow, April 27, 1861; d. there, May 21, 1926. While a student of mathematics at the Univ. of Berlin, he took lessons in piano with Klindworth and in composition with Rüfer; later studied with Liadov in St. Petersburg; lived in Moscow and devoted himself to composing; also taught composition at the Moscow Cons.

WORKS: Symphony in C minor; symph. poem, *Mtsÿri;* Piano Concerto; cantata, *Russalka;* three poems of Tiutchev for female voices with piano; String Trio; String Quartet; String Quintet; 4 Preludes for Piano; violin sonata, *Poème;* Piano Quartet; Piano Quintet; many songs. He also published a manual on harmony (2 vols. 1924, 1925).

BIBLIOGRAPHY: V. Belaiev, *G. Catoire* (in Russian and German; Moscow, 1926).

Caturla, Alejandro García, Cuban composer; b. Remedios, March 7, 1906; assassinated at Remedios, Nov. 12, 1940. He studied with Pedro Sanjuán in Havana; then with Nadia Boulanger in Paris (1928); was founder (1932) and conductor of the Orquesta de Conciertos de Caibarién (chamber orchestra) in Cuba; served as district judge in Remedios. His works have been performed in Cuba, Europe and the U.S. In Caturla's music, primitive Afro-Cuban rhythms and themes are treated with modern techniques and a free utilization of dissonance.

WORKS: suite of three Cuban dances: *Danza del Tambor, Motivos de Danzas, Danza Lucumí* (Havana, 1928; also performed in Barcelona, Seville and Bogotá); *Bembé* for fourteen instruments (Paris, 1929); *Dos Poemas Afro-Cubanos,* for voice and piano (Paris, 1929; also arranged for voice and orch.); *Yam-*

bo-O, Negro liturgy for chorus and orch. (Havana, 1931); *Rumba*, for orch. (1931); *Primera Suite Cubana* for piano and eight wind instruments (1930).

BIBLIOGRAPHY: Alejo Carpentier, *Música en Cuba* (Havana, 1946); Otto Mayer-Serra, *Música y músicos de Latino-América* (Mexico, 1947); Adolfo Salazar, "La obra musical de Alejandro Caturla," *Revista Cubana* (Jan. 1938); Nicolas Slonimsky, "Caturla of Cuba," *Modern Music* (Jan. 1940); R. Nodal Consuegra, "La figure de Alejandro García Caturla en la musica cubana," *Exilo* (Summer 1971).

Cauchie, Maurice, French musicologist; b. Paris, Oct. 8, 1882; d. there, March 21, 1963. He was first a physicist and chemist; after 1917 devoted himself exclusively to music; specialized in the study of French music of the 16th and 17th centuries. He edited *Deux chansons à 5 voix de Clément Janequin* (1925); *Quinze chansons françaises du XVIᵉ siècle à 4 et 5 voix* (1926); *Trente chansons de Clément Janequin* (1928); the collected works of Clément Janequin; wrote *La Pratique de la musique* (1948); numerous essays in French magazines on Okeghem, Attaingnant, Janequin, Cléreau, Costeley, Boesset, Couperin, Gluck, Beethoven, etc.; compiled a thematic index of the works of François Couperin (1949).

Caudella, Edoardo, Rumanian violinist and composer of Italian origin; b. Jassy, June 3, 1841; d. there, April 11, 1924. He studied in Berlin and in Paris, where he took violin lessons with Vieuxtemps. Returning to Rumania he taught at the Cons. of Jassy. He wrote 2 violin concertos; 4 operas: *Olteanca* (Jassy, March 8, 1880); *Hatmanul Baltag* (Bucharest, March 1, 1884); *Fata razesului* (Bucharest, March 2, 1893); *Petru Raresch* (Bucharest, Nov. 14, 1900).

BIBLIOGRAPHY: Z. Vancea, *Creaţia muzicală romaneâscă sec. XIX–XX* (Bucharest, 1968).

Caurroy, Eustache du. See **Du Caurroy, François-Eustache.**

Cavaccio, Giovanni, Italian composer; b. Bergamo, 1556; d. there, Aug. 11, 1626. He was maestro di cappella at the Cathedral of Bergamo (1581–1604) and at Santa Maria Maggiore in Bergamo from 1604 till his death. Among his published works are collections of madrigals (1585, 1597, etc.); Psalms (1585); a Requiem (Milan, 1611); and a collection of keyboard pieces, *Sudori Musicali* (Venice, 1626). Music by Cavaccio was included in a publication of Psalms dedicated to Palestrina (1592), and pieces by him were printed in Bonometti's *Parnassus Musicus*. A *Canzon francese per organo* and a toccata are reprinted in L. Torchi, *L'Arte Musicale in Italia* (vol. III.)

Cavaillé-Coll, Aristide, celebrated French organ builder; b. Montpellier, Feb. 4, 1811; d. Paris, Oct. 13, 1899. His father, Dominique Hyacinthe (1771–1862), was also an organ builder. Aristide went to Paris in 1833; built the organ at St.-Denis, and thereafter many famous organs in Paris (St.-Sulpice, Madeleine, etc.), the French provinces, Belgium, Holland and elsewhere. He invented the system of separate wind chests with different pressures for the low, medium,

and high tones; also the "flûtes octaviantes." He publ. *Etudes expérimentales sur les tuyaux d'orgues* (report for the Académie des Sciences, 1849) and *Projet d'Orgue monumental pour la Basilique de Saint-Pierre de Rome* (1875).

BIBLIOGRAPHY: A. Peschard, *Notice biographique sur A. Cavaillé-Coll et les orgues électriques* (Paris, 1899); C. and E. Cavaillé-Coll, *A. Cavaillé-Coll; ses origines, sa vie, ses œuvres* (Paris, 1928); M. Vanmackelberg, 'L'Esthétique d'Aristide Cavaillé-Coll," *L'Orgue* (July-Sept. 1968).

Cavalieri, Emilio del, Italian composer; b. c.1550; d. Rome, March 11, 1602. He was a nobleman who served as Inspector-General of Art and Artists at the Tuscan court in Florence. He was one of the 'inventors' and most ardent champions of the monodic style, or 'stile recitativo,' which combines melody with accompanying harmonies. His chief work, *La Rappresentazione di anima e di corpo* (published by A. Guidotti, Rome, 1600, with explanatory preface; reprints: L. Guidiccioni-Nicastro, Leghorn, 1911; Munich, 1921), once regarded as the first oratorio, is really a morality play set to music; other dramatic works (*Il Satiro*, 1590; *Disperazione di Filene*, 1590; *Giuoco della cieca*, 1595) exemplify in similar manner the beginnings of modern opera form. In all of Cavalieri's music there is a *basso continuato* with thoroughbass figuring; the melodies are also crudely figured. A facsimile edition of the libretto for *La Rappresentazione* was published by D. Alaleona (Rome, 1912); a facsimile edition of the orchestral score is to be found in Mantica's *Collezione di prime fioriture del melodramma italiano* (Rome, 1912).

BIBLIOGRAPHY: D. Alaleona, "Su E. Cavalieri," *Nuova Musica* (Florence, 1905); Henry Prunières, "Une lettre inédite d'Emilio de Cavalieri," *Revue Musicale* (1923); U. Rolandi, "Emilio de Cavalieri," *Rivista Musicale Italiana* (1929); B. Becherini, "La musica nelle Sacre Rappresentazioni fiorentini," *Rivista Musicale Italiana* (1951); T. Antonicek, "Emilio de'Cavalieri und seine *Rappresentazione di anima e di corpo*," *Österreichische Musikzeitschrift* (Aug. 1969).

Cavalieri, Katharina, Austrian soprano of Italian descent; b. Währing, near Vienna, Feb. 19, 1760; d. Vienna, June 30, 1801. She studied with Salieri; sang with great success at the Italian Opera and then at the German Opera in Vienna. Although she never sang outside of Vienna, a passage in one of Mozart's letters, describing her as "a singer of whom Germany might well be proud," procured for her deserved recognition. She retired in 1793. Mozart wrote for her the role of Constanze in *Die Entführung*, and the aria 'Mi tradi' in *Don Giovanni*.

Cavalieri, Lina, Italian dramatic soprano; b. Viterbo, Dec. 25, 1874; d. Florence, Feb. 8, 1944. As a young woman she was renowned for her beauty, and became the cynosure of the Paris boulevardiers when she appeared at the Folies-Bergère. During her Russian trip in 1900, she married Prince Bariatinsky, who persuaded her to abandon vaudeville and engage in an operatic career. After a few singing lessons with Maddalena Mariani-Masi, she sang in opera in St. Petersburg and Warsaw. In 1906 she was engaged to sing at the Metropolitan Opera in New York, where she was praised for her dramatic performances as Tosca and Mimi. In 1907, after a Russian divorce from her aristocratic first husband, she contracted a lucrative marriage with the American millionaire Winthrop Chandler, but left him in a week precipitating a sensational scandal that, given the mores of the time, caused the Metropolitan Opera to break her contract. In 1909 she returned to New York for guest appearances at the Manhattan Opera House. In 1913 she married the French tenor Lucien Muratore; in 1919 she abandoned him, and opened a beauty salon in Paris. She then married her 4th husband Paolo D'Arvanni and went to live at her Villa Cappucina near Florence. Her life ended tragically, when both she and her last husband were killed during an air raid in 1944. She was the subject of an Italian film under the telling title *La Donna più bella dello mondo* with Gina Lollabrigida in the role of Lina Cavalieri.

Cavalli, Pier Francesco, celebrated Italian composer of operas; b. Crema, Feb. 14, 1602; d. Venice, Jan. 17, 1676. His father (whose real name was **Gian Battista Caletti-Bruni**) was maestro di cappella at Crema; his protector was a Venetian nobleman, Federigo Cavalli and, according to the prevailing fashion, he took the latter's name. Francesco Cavalli studied music in Venice; sang at San Marco under Monteverdi (1617); was appointed second organist there (1640); then first organist (1655) and finally maestro di cappella (1668). He composed prolifically; wrote forty-one operas; three operas achieved outstanding success and were performed repeatedly in Italian theaters: *Giasone* (Venice, Jan. 5, 1649); *Serse* (Venice, Jan. 12, 1654; chosen to be presented at the marriage festivities of Louis XIV of France, in 1660); *Ercole Amante* (written for the inauguration of the hall of the Tuileries, and performed there Feb. 7, 1662). Cavalli also composed a Requiem and much church music.

BIBLIOGRAPHY: L. Galvani, *I teatri musicali di Venezia nel secolo XVII* (1878); H. Kretzschmar, "Die venezianische Oper und die Werke Cavallis und Cestis," *Vierteljahrsschrift für Musikwissenschaft* (Leipzig, 1892); Taddeo Wiel, *F. Cavalli* (Venice, 1914); Egon Wellesz, "Cavalli und der Stil der venezianischen Oper von 1640-1660," *Studien zur Musikwissenschaft* (1913); H. Prunières, *Cavalli et l'opéra vénitien au XVIIe siècle* (Paris, 1931), A. Loewenberg, *Annals of Opera* (2nd ed., 1955); G. Crain, "Francesco Cavalli and the Venetian Opera," *Opera* (June 1967); R. J. Leppard, "Cavalli's Operas," *Proc. of the Royal Musical Assoc.* (1966/67); F. Bussi, "La produzione sacra di Cavalli e i suoi rapporti con quella di Monteverdi," *Rivista Italiano di Musicologica* II/2 (1967); H. Powers, "L'Erismena travestita," in *Studies in Music History* (Princeton, N.J., 1968); D. Swale, "Cavalli: the *Erismena* of 1655," *Miscellanea Musicologica* 3 (1968); Judith Glover, *Cavalli* (N.Y., 1977).

Cavazzoni, Girolamo, Italian organist and composer; b. Urbino, c.1520; d. Venice, 1560. He was a son of **Marco Antonio Cavazzoni** and godson of Cardinal Pietro Bembo. His *Intavolatura cioè Ricercari, Can-*

zoni, Hinni, Magnificati (Venice, 1542) contains the first examples of the polyphonic ricercar of the 16th century. His organ ricercars, though related to the motet, differ from it in their extension of the individual sections by means of more numerous entries of the subject and more definite cadences between sections. The two canzonas from the same work mark the beginnings of an independent canzona literature for the keyboard. Reprints of Cavazzoni's works are found in L. Torchi, *L'Arte Musicale in Italia* (vol. III); Tagliapietra, *Antologia di Musica* (vol. I); Davison and Apel, *Historical Anthology of Music;* and Schering, *Geschichte der Musik in Beispielen.*

BIBLIOGRAPHY: C. Sartori, "Precisazioni bibliografiche sulle opere di Girolamo Cavazzoni" *Rivista Musicale Italiana* (1940).

Cavazzoni (also called **da Bologna** and **detta d'Urbino**), **Marco Antonio,** Italian composer and singer, father of **Girolamo Cavazzoni**; b. Bologna, c.1490; d. c.1570 (the date appearing on his will is April 3, 1569). He went to Urbino about 1510 and became acquainted with Cardinal Pietro Bembo; then became a musician in the private chapel of Pope Leo X (1515). In Venice (1517) he was employed by Francesco Cornaro, nephew of the Queen of Cyprus. Back in Rome (1520) he was again in the employ of Pope Leo X. From 1522-24 and from 1528-31 he was in Venice, and in 1536-37 was organist at Chioggia. From 1545-59 he was a singer at San Marco (Venice) where Adriaen Willaert was maestro di cappella. As a youth, Cavazzoni wrote a Mass *Domini Marci Antonii,* so named because he derived its theme from the solmization syllables of his Christian names. His most important work is a collection of keyboard pieces, *Recerchari, motetti, canzoni, Libro I* (Venice, 1523). The ricercars are toccata-like rather than contrapuntal, and the motets and canzonas are instrumental transcriptions of vocal pieces. Modern reprints (with biographical notes) are found in Benvenuti's *I Classici musicali italiani* (Milan, 1941) and in K. Jeppesen, *Die italienische Orgelmusik am Anfang des Cinquecento* (Copenhagen, 1943).

BIBLIOGRAPHY: T. Dart, "Cavazzoni and Cabezón" (suggesting a conjecture that Marco Antonio may have been a brother of Cabezón, the latter being a possible Spanish form of Cavazzoni's name) *Music & Letters* (Feb. 1955); a rebuttal to this by Jeppesen appears in *Journal of the American Musicological Society* (Summer 1955) together with a final postscript by Dart.

Cavos, Catterino, Italian-Russian composer; b. Venice, Oct. 30, 1775; d. St. Petersburg, May 10, 1840. He studied with Francesco Bianchi; his first work was a patriotic hymn for the Republican Guard, performed at the Teatro Fenice (Sept. 13, 1797); he then produced a cantata *L'eroe* (1798). In 1799 he received an invitation to go to Russia as conductor at the Imperial Opera in St. Petersburg. He was already on his way to Russia when his ballet *Il sotterraneo* was presented in Venice (Nov. 16, 1799). He remained in St. Petersburg for the rest of his life. His Russian debut as a composer was in a collaborative opera *Russalka* (adapted from *Das Donauweibchen* by F. Kauer). This was followed by the operas *The Invisible Prince* (1805), *Three Hunchback Brothers* (1808), and several ballets. His most significant work was *Ivan Susanin*, which he conducted at the Imperial Theater on Oct. 30, 1815. The subject of this opera was used 20 years later by Glinka in his opera *A Life for the Tsar*; the boldness of Cavos in selecting a libretto from Russian history provided the necessary stimulus for Glinka and other Russian composers. (Cavos conducted the première of Glinka's opera.) His subsequent operas were also based on Russian themes: *Dobrynia Nikitich* (1818) and *The Firebird* (1822). Cavos was a notable voice teacher; among his pupils were several Russian singers who later became famous.

BIBLIOGRAPHY: R. Aloys Mooser, "Un musicista veneziano in Russia: Catterino Cavos," *Nuova Rivista Musicale Italiana* (Jan.–Feb. 1969).

Cazden, Norman, American composer; b. New York, Sept. 23, 1914. He studied piano with Ernest Hutcheson and composition with Bernard Wagenaar at the Juilliard School of Music in New York; later took courses at the City College of N.Y. and at Harvard Univ. where he was a student of Walter Piston. In 1948 he received his Ph.D. at Harvard Univ. with the dissertation *Musical Consonance and Dissonance.* He began his career as a pianist, and was active as piano teacher at various colleges and universities. In 1968 he joined the faculty of the Univ. of Maine at Orono. At various times he made trips of exploration to collect folk music in New York state. His compositions reflect the neo-classical trends.

WORKS: Concerto for 10 Instruments (1937); *3 Chamber Sonatas* for clarinet and viola (1938); Quartet for Clarinet and Strings (1939); Horn Sonata (1941); Flute Sonata (1941); Symphony (1948); *3 Ballads* for orch. (1949); Suite for Brass Sextet (1951); Quintet for Oboe and Strings (1960); *Woodland Valley Sketches* for orch. (1960); *Adventure* for orch. (1963); *Elizabethan Suite No. 1* for brass quintet (1965); Chamber Concerto for Orch. (1965); Woodwind Quintet (1966); Piano Trio (1969); Sonata for English Horn and Piano (1974); Six Preludes and Fugues for piano (1974); numerous other piano pieces.

BIBLIOGRAPHY: *Composers of the Americas*, Vol. 15 (Washington, 1969).

Cebotari, Maria, soprano; b. Kishinev, Bessarabia, Feb. 10, 1910; d. Vienna, June 9, 1949. She studied in Germany; made her debut in Dresden as Mimi; 1947–48, toured widely in Europe. During her brief career she was greatly admired.

BIBLIOGRAPHY: A. Mingotti, *Maria Cebotari, Das Leben einer Sängerin* (Salzburg, 1950).

Ceccato, Aldo, Italian conductor; b. Milan, Feb. 18, 1934. He studied at the Cons. of Milan, and at the Academy of Music in Berlin. In 1969 he won first prize in the International Competition of Italian Radio for young conductors. He made his American debut with the N.Y. Philharmonic on Nov. 5, 1970 with excellent success. From 1973 to 1977 was conductor of the Detroit Symphony Orchestra.

Ceely, Robert, American composer; b. Torrington, Conn., Jan. 17, 1930. He studied composition at the New England Cons. in Boston (B. Mus., 1954) and at Mills College (M.A., 1961); in 1965 he was appointed to the faculty of the New England Cons.

WORKS: String Trio (1953); *Music for 10 Instruments* (1963); *Strati* for magnetic tape (1963); *Logs,* a duet for double basses (1968); *Modules* for 7 instruments (1968); *Spectrum* for chamber ensemble and tape (1969); *Hymn* for double bass and cello (1970); *Slide Music* for 4 trombones (1975); *Rituals* for 40 flutes (1976); *Roundels* for wind ensemble (1977).

Cehanovsky, George, Russian baritone; b. St. Petersburg, April 14, 1892. He entered the Russian Navy during World War I and sustained a severe wound in a Naval encounter. After the war he studied singing with his mother who was a professional singer, and made his debut as Valentin in Gounod's *Faust* in Petrograd in 1921. In 1923 he emigrated to the U.S.; at first sang with various opera companies, and in 1926 was engaged by the Metropolitan Opera, with which he remained until 1958, the longest stretch of any member of the Metropolitan staff. He filled in 78 different roles during his career at the Metropolitan, all of them in *comprimario* parts, e.g. Wagner in *Faust,* Morales in *Carmen,* Sharpless in *Madama Butterfly,* and the second policeman in *Jonny spielt auf.* In 1956 he married the German soprano **Elisabeth Rethberg.**

Čelanský, Ludvík Vítězslav, Czech conductor and composer; b. Vienna, July 17, 1870; d. Prague, Oct. 27, 1931. He studied at the Prague Cons.; then conducted theater orchestras in Pilsen and Zagreb. Returning to Prague, he organized the Czech Philharmonic Orch. (1901) and led it for several seasons; also conducted opera and concerts abroad.

WORKS: an opera, *Camille* (Prague, Oct. 23, 1897); a symph. trilogy, *Adam, Noë, Moïse* (1915–19); church music; songs.

BIBLIOGRAPHY: A valedictory brochure, ed. by V. Balthasar, was publ. in honor of his 50th birthday (Prague, 1920).

Celibidache, Sergiu, Rumanian conductor; b. Roman, June 28, 1912. He earned his living as a youth by playing in nightclubs in Berlin and in Paris. In 1939 he enrolled at the Univ. of Berlin, studying mathematics and philosophy, and simultaneously took courses in musicology and conducting with Fritz Stein and Tiessen at the Berlin Cons. In 1945 he was suddenly thrust into the position of conductor of the Berlin Philharmonic when the regular conductor Furtwängler was temporarily removed on suspicion of collaboration with the Nazi regime. When Furtwängler was reinstated he took the Berlin Philharmonic on an American tour (1948), with Celibidache as his assistant. Subsequently Celibidache conducted in London and in Sweden; in 1970 he was engaged as conductor of the Stuttgart Radio Orchestra. Celibidache devotes much of his time to composition; he wrote 4 symphonies, a Piano Concerto and various other works. As a conductor he enjoys the reputation of a determined professional, intent on clarity and expressiveness of orchestral playing, without projecting his personality on the music he conducts. This impersonal artistry, admired by many, precluded, however, his ascent to the summits on the conductorial world.

Celis, Frits, Belgian conductor and composer, b. Antwerp, April 11, 1929. He studied composition at the Flemish Cons. in Antwerp, and harp at the Brussels Cons.; then attended the summer conducting course at the Mozarteum in Salzburg (1949-51) and similar courses at the Hochschule für Musik in Cologne (1953-54). He then became conductor of Théâtre de la Monnaie in Brussels (1954-59) and also conducted in Czechoslovakia, Holland, France and Spain. In 1960 he was appointed to the faculty of the Flemish Cons. of Antwerp. His compositions are all written in a *laissez faire* manner sparingly seasoned with atonality. WORKS: *Music* for strings (1951); Violin Sonata (1951); string trio *De Geestelijke bruiloft* for voice, and piano or chamber orch. (1958); Cello Sonata (1963); *Elegie* for orch. (Antwerp, Dec. 8, 1967); *3 Symphonic Movements* (1969); *Intrada and Toccata* for oboe and piano (1972); *Episodes* for viola and harpsichord (1973); *Variazioni* for chamber orch. (1974); choruses; songs.

Cellier, Alfred, English conductor and composer; b. (of French parents) London, Dec. 1, 1844; d. there, Dec. 28, 1891. He was a chorister at St. James' Chapel Royal; studied music with Thomas Helmore; in 1866 conductor at Belfast of the Ulster Hall concerts and the Philharmonic; from 1871-75 at the Prince's Theatre, Manchester; from 1877-79 at the London Opéra-Comique, and (with Sullivan) at the Promenade Concerts in Covent Garden. He then spent some years in America and Australia, returning to London in 1887. WORKS: light operas: *Charity Begins at Home* (London, 1870); *The Foster Brothers* (London, June 17, 1873); *The Sultan of Mocha* (Manchester, Nov. 16, 1874); *The Tower of London* (Manchester, Oct. 4, 1875); *Nell Gwynne* (Manchester, Oct. 16, 1876); *Dora's Dream* (London, Nov. 17, 1877); *The Spectre Knight* (London, Feb. 9, 1878); *Bella Donna or The Little Beauty and the Great Beast* (Manchester, April 27, 1878); *After All* (London, Dec. 16, 1878); *In the Sulks* (London, Feb. 21, 1880); *The Masque of Pandora*, after Longfellow (Boston, Mass., Jan. 10, 1881); *The Carp* (London, Feb. 11, 1886); *Dorothy* (London, Sept. 25, 1886); *Mrs. Jarramie's Genie* (London, Feb. 14, 1888); *Doris* (London, April 20, 1889); *The Mountebanks* (London, Jan. 4, 1892); also a setting of Gray's *Elegy*, written for the Leeds Festival (Oct. 10, 1883); a symphonic suite; many popular songs.

Ceremuga, Josef, Czech composer; b. Ostrava-Kunčice, June 14, 1930. He studied composition with Řídký at the Music Academy in Prague and advance harmony with Alois Hába (1950-53); did postgraduate study with Dobiáš (1953-56). He then became a member of the staff of the Academy; later was lecturer on the music for the cinema (1960-73). His own music reflects the modern Russian style, with broad neo-Romantic melos sharpened by euphonious dissonances. WORKS: a ballad-opera, *Juraj Ćup*, after Čapek (1958-60; Prague, April 27, 1963); 3 symphonies (1952, 1968, 1975); Violin Concerto (1955); *3 Sym-*

phonic Frescoes (1958-59); Piano Concerto (Teplice, Jan. 21, 1963); *Hommage aux étudiants*, overture (1964); *Concerto da camera* for wind quintet and string orch. (1970-71); 3 string quartets (1956, 1961, 1973); Piano Trio (1960); Cello Sonata (1957); Viola Sonata (1961); *4 Pictures* for clarinet and accordion (1961); 2 wind quintets (1964, 1967); songs.

Cererols, Joan, Catalan composer; b. Martorell, Sept. 9, 1618; d. Montserrat, Aug. 28, 1676. In 1636 he entered the Monastery of Montserrat; studied organ and violin there. He wrote a great number of sacred vocal works. The Monastery of Montserrat publ., in its series *Música Instrumental*, his Psalms and Vespers (vol. I, 1930), Masses (vol. II, 1931) and villancicos (vol. III, 1932), edited by Dom David Pujol.

Cerha, Friedrich, Austrian composer of the avant-garde; b. Vienna, Feb. 17, 1926. He studied violin with Vasa Prihoda and composition with Alfred Uhl at the Vienna Music Academy (1946-51); also attended courses in musicology and philosophy at the Univ. of Vienna (1946-50). Upon graduation, he became active in the modernistic movement as a violinist, conductor and composer. In 1958 he organized (with Kurt Schwertsik) the Vienna concert ensemble "die reihe," devoted to new music. In 1960 he became director of the electronic-music studio and a lecturer at the Vienna Academy, becoming a prof. in 1969. His music pursues the aim of "atomization of thematic materials" as a means toward total integration of infinitesimal compositional quantities, with minimal variations of successive temporal units. WORKS: *Deux éclats en reflexion* for violin and piano (1956); *Formation et solution* for violin and piano (1956-57); *Espressioni fondamentali* for orch. (1956-57; Berlin, Nov. 17, 1960); *Relazioni fragili* for harpsichord and chamber orch. (1957; Vienna, May 16, 1960); *Enjambements* for 6 players (1959; Paris, March 7, 1962); *Fasce* for orch. (1959; fair-copied in 3 stages, 1967-68, 1972-73 and 1975; Graz, Oct. 8, 1975); *Intersecazioni I* (1959-61) and *II* (1959-73; Graz, Oct. 16, 1973) for violin and orch.; *Mouvements I-III* for chamber orch. (1960); *Spiegel I-VII* for orch., some movements with tape (1960-61; fair-copied 1961-71; first complete performance of the entire 80-minute score, Graz, ISCM Fest., Oct. 9, 1972); *Exercises* for baritone, narrator and chamber ensemble (1962-67); *Elegie* for piano (1963); *Phantasme 63* for organ (3 players) and chamber orch. (1963); *Symphonien (Symphonies)* for winds and timpani (1964); *Catalogue des Objets Trouvés* for chamber orch. (1968-69; West Berlin, Oct. 1, 1970); *Verzeichnis* for chorus a cappella (1969); *Langegger Nachtmusik I* and *II* for orch. (1969, 1970); *Curriculum* for 12 winds (1972); symph. (1975); *Double Concerto* for violin, cello and orch. (1975).

Černohorsky, Bohuslav. See **Czernohorsky, Bohuslav.**

Černušák, Gracian, Czech music lexicographer; b. Ptení, near Prostějov, Moravia, Dec. 19, 1882; d. Brno, Oct. 13, 1961. He studied music in Prague; then was active as music teacher in Brno from 1919 to 1939 and again from 1945 to 1953; from 1945 to 1955 he also taught at the Univ. of Brno. He edited the *Hudební slovník naučný* (1937–40) and also prepared articles for the Czech music dictionary *Československý hudební slovník* (Prague, 1963–65). He contributed many entries on Czech composers to the 5th ed. of *Grove's Dictionary* (1954).

Černý, Ladislav, Czech viola player and composer; b. Pilsen, April 13, 1891; d. Prague, July 13, 1975. He studied violin at the Prague Cons.; then played viola at the opera in Ljubljana (1916–21); returning to Prague, he organized a string quartet; from 1952 was professor at the Prague Music Academy. Hindemith dedicated his Sonata for Solo Viola to him.

Cerone, Domenico Pietro, Italian tenor and music theorist; b. Bergamo, c.1566; d. Naples, 1625. In 1592 he went to Spain and became a singer in the court choir; later appointed teacher of plainsong to the clergy of the church of the Annunciation at Naples; from 1610 until his death sang in the Royal Chapel Choir there. He published the manual *Regole per il canto fermo* (Naples, 1609), and *El Melopeo y Maestro, tractado de música teórica y práctica* (Naples, 1613). This treatise, written in Spanish, numbers 1160 pages, containing a compendium of early music theory; it is divided into 22 books and 849 chapters; its pedantic exposition and inordinate length were the main target of Eximeno's satirical novel *Don Lazarillo Vizcardi*; Book XII is published in English in O. Strunk's *Source Readings in Music History* (N.Y., 1950); in the U.S., copies of the entire work are to be found in the Library of Congress, the N.Y. Public Library, the Hispanic Society of N.Y., and the Sibley Music Library, Rochester, N.Y.
BIBLIOGRAPHY: F. Pedrell, *P. Antonio Eximeno* (1920); G. Pannain, *L'Oratorio dei Filippini* (1934); Ruth Hannas, "Cerone, Philosopher and Teacher," *Musical Quarterly* (Oct., 1935), and "Cerone's Approach to the Teaching of Counterpoint," *Papers of the American Musicological Society* (1937); A. Howell, "Symposium on Seventeenth-century Music Theory," *Journal of Music Theory* (1972).

Cerreto, Scipione, Italian composer, lutenist and theorist; b. Naples, 1551; d. there, c.1632. He published two theoretical works containing valuable information on the music and musical instruments of his time: *Della prattica musica vocale e strumentale* (Naples, 1601), and *Arbore musicale* (Naples, 1608); a third work, *Dialogo harmonico*, remained unpublished (two forms, 1628 and 1631).

Certon, Pierre, French contrapuntist; b. c.1510; d. Paris, Feb. 22, 1572. He was a pupil of Josquin des Prez; was choirmaster of the Sainte-Chapelle in Paris (about 1532); composed Masses, motets, psalms, Magnificats, and 4-part chansons, which were printed in the collections of Ballard, Attaingnant, Susato, Phalèse and others between 1527 and 1560. Reprints of his Masses (*Sur le pont d'Avignon; Adjuva me; Regnum mundi*) are to be found in H. Expert's *Monuments de la musique française au temps de la Renais-*sance, vol. 2 (1925); 10 chansons in vol. 82 of *Das Chorwerk.*
BIBLIOGRAPHY: M. Brenet, *Les Musiciens de la Sainte-Chapelle* (Paris, 1910); a biographical account and bibliography, by A. Agnel, are included in the reprint *Pierre Certon: Chansons polyphoniques publiée par Pierre Attaingnant; livre I (1533–39)* (Paris, 1967).

Cervantes (Kawanag), Ignacio, Cuban pianist and composer; b. Havana, July 31, 1847; d. there, April 29, 1905. He studied with Gottschalk (1859–61) and at the Paris Cons. (1866–68), with Alkan and Marmontel; in 1870 returned to Cuba; in 1898 went to Mexico; also visited the U.S. He was one of the pioneers of native Cuban music; in his *Danzas Cubanas* for piano he employs Cuban rhythms in an effective salon manner; also wrote an opera, *Maledetto* (1895), and some orchestral pieces.
BIBLIOGRAPHY: E. Sánchez de Fuentes, *Ignacio Cervantes Kawanag* (Havana, 1936); Alejo Carpentier, *La música en Cuba* (Mexico, 1946).

Červený, Wenzel Franz, inventor of brass instruments; b. Dubeč, Bohemia, Sept. 27, 1819; d. Königgrätz, Jan. 19, 1896. He was a good performer on most brass instruments when he was only twelve years old; learned his trade with Bauer, a music instrument maker in Prague; worked at various times in Brünn, Bratislava, Vienna and Budapest; in 1842 established his own shop at Königgrätz. He invented the following instruments: Cornon (1844), Contrabass (1845), Phonikon (1848), Baroxiton (1853), Contrafagotto in metal (1856), Althorn obbligato (1859), Turnerhorn, Jägerhorn, army Trombones (1867), and Primhorn (1873). After the success of the Primhorn, he created the complete Waldhorn quartet, which he considered his greatest achievement. Then followed the Subcontrabass and the Subcontrafagotto, and finally an entire family of improved Cornets ("Kaiserkornette") and the "Triumph" Cornet. His "roller" cylinder-mechanism is an invention of the greatest importance. He also improved the Euphonion, the Russian Signal-horns, the Screw-drum and the church kettledrums. His instruments took first prizes at exhibitions in Europe and America.

Cervetti, Sergio, Uruguayan composer; b. Dolores, Nov. 9, 1940. He studied in Uruguay; then went to the U.S. and attended classes of Ernst Krenek and Stefan Grove at the Peabody Cons. (1963–67). In 1970, he was appointed teacher at the N.Y. Univ. of the Arts.
WORKS: String Trio (1963); Piano Sonata (1964); 5 *Sequences* for flute, horn, cello, electric guitar, piano and percussion (1966); *Orbitas* for orch. (1967); *El Carro de Heno* for small chorus and orch. (1967); *Zinctum* for String Quartet (Washington, June 24, 1968); *Dies Tenebrarum* for electric organ, 3 percussionists, male chorus and strings (1968); *Pulsar* for brass sextet (1969); *Prisons No. 1* for singers, dancers, pantomime, 2 trombones, electric organ, electric guitar, double bass and percussion (1969); *Prisons No. 2* for speaking chorus, orch. and tape (1970–71); *Peripetia* for 20–100 singers and instrumentalists (1970); *Cocktail Party* for amplified instruments and any number of invitations (Malmö, Sweden, Nov. 9, 1970); *Plexus*

for small orch. (Washington, May 18, 1971); *4 Fragmentos de Pablo Neruda* for soprano, oboe, guitar, cello and percussion (1970); *Raga I* for ensemble; *Raga II* for trombone and tape (both 1971); *Graffiti* for speaking chorus, orch. and tape (1971); *. . . from the earth. . .* for ensemble (1972).

Cervetto (real name **Bassevi**), **Giacomo,** Italian cellist; b. c.1682; d. London, Jan. 14, 1783. He settled in London in 1728, where he was a player and then manager of the Drury Lane Theatre; wrote some chamber music. He lived to be 100 years old. His son, **James Cervetto** (b. London, 1747; d. there, Feb. 5, 1837), was a cellist, too, and also lived to a very old age. He composed several cello pieces.

Cesana, Otto, American composer; b. Brescia, Italy, July 7, 1899. He came to the U.S. as a young man; studied music with Julius Gold in California; became active as a film composer in Hollywood; later was engaged as music arranger for several radio programs. A prolific composer, he wrote 6 symphonies, 6 concertos (for clarinet, trumpet, trombone, piano, 2 pianos, 3 pianos), a ballet, *Ali Baba and the 40 Thieves;* also a jazzy piece entitled *Swing Septet,* which was performed in Indianapolis, Jan. 23, 1942. He is the author of several manuals, among them *Course in Modern Harmony* (1939), *Course in Counterpoint* (1940) and *Voicing the Modern Dance Orchestra* (1946).

Cesari, Gaetano, Italian musicologist; b. Cremona, June 24, 1870; d. Sale Marasino, Oct. 21, 1934. He studied musicology in Germany; was a pupil of Mottl, Sandberger and Kroyer at the Univ. of Munich. Returning to Italy he was employed as teacher, music critic and librarian. He published several valuable essays on Italian music, among them "Musica e musicisti alla Corte Sforzesca," published in the *Rivista Musicale Italiana* (1922), a monograph *Amilcare Ponchielli nell' arte del suo tempo* (Cremona, 1934), and in collaboration with A. Luzio, published the important source book *I copialettere di Verdi* (1913).

Cesi, Beniamino, Italian pianist and pedagogue; b. Naples, Nov. 6, 1845; d. there, Jan. 19, 1907. He studied music with his father; then was a pupil of the celebrated pianist Thalberg; after a European tour he was piano instructor at the Royal Collegio in Naples (1866–85), and at the St. Petersburg Cons. (1885–91). In 1895 he returned to the Cons. of Naples where he taught until his death. His 2 sons, **Napoleone** and **Sigismondo,** were both pianists whom he trained for a concert career; among other pupils were Martucci, Cilea and A. Longo. He published a valuable *Metodo per pianoforte,* and also wrote an opera, *Vittor Pisani.*
BIBLIOGRAPHY: A. Longo, "Beniamino Cesi," *L'Arte Pianistica* (Jan. 1914).

Cesti, Marc' Antonio (baptismal name **Pietro**), renowned dramatic composer; b. Arezzo, Aug. 5, 1623; d. Florence, Oct. 14, 1669. As a boy, he entered the Minorite monastic order; was probably a pupil of Carissimi at Rome in 1640–45; later was maestro di cappella to Ferdinand II de' Medici, at Florence; 1660, tenor singer in the Papal choir; 1666–68, assistant Ka-

pellmeister to the Emperor Leopold I, at Vienna; then returned to Florence.
WORKS: His first opera, *Orontea* (Venice, Jan. 20, 1649), was much applauded; other dramatic ventures were also successful; *Cesare amante* (Venice, 1651); *Argia* (Innsbruck, 1655); *Dori* (Florence, 1661; selections printed in vol. XII of *Publikationen der Gesellschaft für Musikforschung; Il Principe generoso* (Vienna, 1665; authorship disputed); *Tito* (Venice, Feb. 13, 1666); *Nettuno e Flora festeggianti* (Vienna, July 12, 1666); *Il Pomo d'oro* (Vienna, 1667; published in its entirety in *Denkmäler der Tonkunst in Österreich,* 6, 9 [3.ii, 4.ii]); *Semiramide* (Vienna, June 9, 1667); *Le disgrazie d'Amore* (Vienna, 1667); *Argene* (Vienna, 1668); *Genserico* (Venice, Jan. 31, 1669). Cesti wrote numerous cantatas which are preserved in various European libraries; his dramatic flair was reflected in the theatrical forms of his cantatas; he also wrote madrigals, songs, etc. A. Schering's *Geschichte der Musik in Beispielen* contains an aria from *Argia* (No. 203); H. Riemann's *Kantaten-Frühling* (Leipzig, 1912; no. 9), F. Vatielli's *Antiche cantate d'amore* (Bologna, 1920; no. 8), and G. Adler's *Handbuch* (2nd ed. 1930; p. 439ff.)
BIBLIOGRAPHY: H. Kretzschmar, "Die venezianische Oper und die Werke Cavallis and Cestis," *Vierteljahrsschrift für Musikwissenschaft* (1892); E. Wellesz, "Ein Bühnenfestspiel aus dem 17. Jahrhundert," *Sämmelbande der Internationalen Musik-Gesellschaft* XV (1913; p. 134ff.); F. Coradini, "Padre A. Cesti, Nuove notizie biografiche," *Rivista Musicale Italiana* (July 1923); very valuable for biographical documentation; A. Sandberger, in the bulletin of the "Union Musicologique" (1925; pp. 121–73); P. Nettl, "Ein verschollenes Tournierballett von M. A. Cesti," *Zeitschrift für Musikwissenschaft* (April 1926); A. Tessier, "L'Orontée de Lorenzani et l'Orontea du Padre Cesti," *La Revue Musicale* IX/8 (1928); W. Holmes, "Giacinto Andrea Cicognini's and Antonio Cesti's Orontea (1649)," in W. Austin, ed. *New Looks at Italian Opera* (Ithaca, N.Y., 1968); T. Antonicek, "Zum 300. Todestag Antonio Cestis," *Oesterreichische Musikzeitschrift* (Oct. 1969); D. H. Shock, "Costuming for *Il Pomo d'Oro,*" *Gazette des Beaux-Arts* (April 1967); T. Antonicek, "Antonio Cesti alla corte di Vienna," *Nuova Rivista Musicale Italiana* (March/April 1970); W. C. Holmes, "Cesti's *L'Argia:* an Entertainment for a Royal Convert," *Chigiana* (1969/70).

Cezar, Corneliu, Rumanian composer; b. Bucharest, Dec. 22, 1937. He studied composition at the Bucharest Cons., with Tudor Ciortea, Mihail Jora, Alfred Mendelsohn and Anatol Vieru. After graduating he was active mainly as a piano teacher.
WORKS: opera, after Brecht, *Galileo Galilei* (1962; Bucharest, Dec. 16, 1964); Piano Sonata (1959); Quartet for Flute, Violin, Viola and Bassoon (1959); *Cronika* for orch. and tape (Bucharest, Feb. 1, 1968); a piece to a Polynesian text, *Taaroa,* for narrator, 2 prepared pianos, carillon on tape and clarinet (1968); and numerous scores of incidental music for the theater.

Chabrier, (Alexis-) Emmanuel, famous French composer; b. Ambert, Puy de Dôme, Jan. 18, 1841; d. Paris, Sept. 13, 1894. He studied law in Paris; later harmony with Semet and Hignard, and piano with Édouard Wolff. He served in the government from 1862; at the same time cultivated his musical tastes; with Duparc, Vincent d'Indy and others he formed a private group of music lovers, and was an enthusiastic admirer of Wagner. He began to compose in earnest, and produced two light operas: *L'Étoile* (Paris, Nov. 28, 1877) and *Une Éducation manquée* (Paris, 1879). In 1879 he went to Germany with Duparc to hear Wagner's operas; returning to Paris he published some piano pieces; then traveled to Spain; the fruit of this journey was his most famous work, the rhapsody *España* (1883), which produced a sensation when performed by Lamoureux in 1884. Another work of Spanish inspiration was the *Habanera* for piano (1885). In the meantime he served as chorus master for Lamoureux; this experience developed his knowledge of vocal writing; he wrote a brief cantata for mezzo-soprano and women's chorus, *La sulamite* (1884), and his two operas *Gwendoline* (Brussels, April 10, 1886) and *Le Roi malgré lui* (Opéra-Comique, Paris, May 18, 1887); another opera *Briséis* remained unfinished. In his operas Chabrier attempted a grand style; his idiom oscillated between passionate Wagnerianism and a more conventional type of French stage music; although these operas enjoyed a *succès d'estime*, they never became popular, and Chabrier's place in music history is secured exclusively by his *España*, and piano pieces such as *Bourée fantasque* (1891; orchestrated by Felix Mottl); his *Joyeuse Marche* for orch. (originally entitled *Marche française*, 1888) is also popular. Other works are *Ode à la musique* for voices and orch. (1890); *Dix pièces pittoresques* for piano (1880; four of them orchestrated and performed as *Suite pastorale*); *Trois valses romantiques* for two pianos (1883); songs.

BIBLIOGRAPHY: O. Séré, *E. Chabrier*, in *Musiciens français d'aujourd'hui* (Paris, 1911); René Martineau, *E. Chabrier* (Paris, 1911); G. Servières, *E. Chabrier* (Paris, 1912); A. Cortot, "L'œuvre pianistique de E. Chabrier," *La Revue musicale* (Oct. 1926); Joseph Desaymard, *Chabrier d'après ses lettres* (Paris, 1934); J.-G. Prod'homme, "Chabrier in His Letters," *Musical Quarterly* (Oct. 1935); Francis Poulenc, *Emmanuel Chabrier* (Paris, 1961); Rollo Myers, *Emmanuel Chabrier and His Circle* (London, 1969); F. Robert, *Emmanuel Chabrier. L'Homme et son œuvre* (Paris, 1970); R. Delage and F. Durif, "Emmanuel Chabrier en Espagne," *Revue de Musicologie* LVI/2 (1970).

Chadwick, George Whitefield, eminent American composer; b. Lowell, Mass., Nov. 13, 1854; d. Boston, April 4, 1931. He first studied music with Eugene Thayer in Boston; then became head of the music department at Olivet College in Michigan (1876); from 1877–78 studied at the Leipzig Cons. with Reinecke and Jadassohn; his graduation piece was an overture to *Rip Van Winkle*, which he conducted with the Leipzig Cons. Orch. on June 20, 1879; then studied organ and composition at Munich under Rheinberger; in 1880 returned to Boston as organist of the South Congregational Church and teacher of harmony and composition at the New England Cons.; in 1897 succeeded Faelten as director. He received the honorary degree of M.A., from Yale, and an honorary LL.D.

from Tufts College in 1905; received the Gold Medal of the Academy of Arts and Letters in 1928; for several seasons was conductor of the Worcester Music Festival; also head of music festivals in Springfield and Worcester, Mass.; was a member of the Boston Academy of Arts and Letters. Chadwick was one of the leading American composers; usually regarded as a pillar of the "Boston Classicists," he was actually an ardent romanticist; his musical style was formed under the influence of the German programmatic school; his harmonies are Wagnerian, his orchestration full and lush.

WORKS: FOR THE STAGE: the comic operas *The Quiet Lodging* (privately performed, Boston, 1892) and *Tabasco* (Boston, Jan. 29, 1894); *Judith*, lyric drama (Worcester Festival, Sept. 26, 1901); *The Padrone* (1915), opera; *Love's Sacrifice*, pastoral operetta (1916; Chicago, Feb. 1, 1923); incidental music to *Everywoman* (N.Y. and London, 1911). FOR ORCH.: 3 symphonies: I, in C (1882); II, in B-flat (Boston Symph., Dec. 11, 1886); III, in F (Boston Symph., Oct. 20, 1894); the overtures *Rip Van Winkle, Thalia, The Miller's Daughter, Melpomene* (Boston, Dec. 24, 1887; also arranged for piano 4 hands), *Adonais* (Boston, Feb. 3, 1900), *Euterpe* (Boston Symph., April 23, 1904; composer cond.), and *Anniversary Overture* (Norfolk Festival, 1922); Serenade in F for string orch.; *A Pastoral Prelude* (Boston, 1894); Sinfonietta in D (Boston, Nov. 21, 1904); the symphonic poems *Cleopatra* (Worcester Festival, 1905) and *Angel of Death* (N.Y., 1919); *Symphonic Sketches*, suite (*Jubilee, Noël, Hobgoblin*, and *A Vagrom Ballad*; Boston Symph., Feb. 7, 1908); Theme, Variations and Fugue for Organ and Orch. (Boston, 1908; arranged by J. Wallace Goodrich for organ solo); *Suite symphonique* (Philadelphia, 1911; first prize of the National Federation of Music Clubs); *Aphrodite*, symph. fantasy (Norfolk Festival, 1912); *Tam O'Shanter*, symph. ballad (Norfolk Festival, 1915). CHORAL WORKS: *Dedication Ode* (1886) for soli, chorus and orch.; *Lovely Rosabelle*, ballad for solo, chorus and orch. (Boston, 1889); *The Pilgrims* for chorus and orch. (Boston, 1891); *Ode for the Opening of the Chicago World's Fair*, for chorus with piano or orch. (1892); *Phoenix Expirans*, for soli, chorus and orch. (Springfield Festival, 1892); *The Lily Nymph*, cantata (1893); *Lochinvar*, for baritone and orch. (Springfield Festival, 1897); *Noël*, Christmas pastoral for soli, chorus and orch. (Norfolk Festival, 1908); *Aghadoe*, ballad for alto and orch.; numerous sacred works: *Ecce jam noctis* (Yale, 1897); *The Beatitudes; Jubilate*; etc.; many choruses for men's, women's, and mixed voices; also school choruses. CHAMBER MUSIC: 5 string quartets (I, in G minor; II, in C; III, in D; IV, in E minor; V, in D minor); Piano Quintet (1888); violin and cello pieces; etc. He composed about 100 songs with piano, organ or orch. (*Allah, Ballad of the Trees and Masters, The Danza, Before the Dawn*, etc.). ORGAN WORKS: *10 Canonic Studies for Organ* (1885); *Progressive Pedal Studies for Organ* (1890); miscellaneous pieces (*Requiem, Suite in Variation Form*, etc.); also numerous piano pieces. He was the author of *Harmony, A Course of Study* (Boston, 1897; revised ed., 1922) and *Key to the Textbook on Harmony* (Boston, 1902); was co-editor of *A Book of Choruses for High Schools and Choral Societies* (N.Y., 1923).

BIBLIOGRAPHY: For a full list of works, dates of composition, performance and publication, see C. Engel, "G. W. Chadwick," *Musical Quarterly* (July 1924); also A. L. Langley, "Chadwick and the New England Conservatory," *Musical Quarterly* (Jan. 1935).

Chaffin, Lucien Gates, American organist and composer; b. Worcester, Mass., March 23, 1846; d. New York, May 26, 1927. He studied at Brown Univ. (graduated, 1867); was active as a language teacher; studied music in Boston with Eugene Thayer; was organist in various churches in Boston, Buffalo and N.Y.; was music editor of the Buffalo *Express* (1879–83) and the N.Y. *Commercial Advertiser* (1884–90); lectured on music and contributed articles to various musical publications. He composed a cantata, *Holy Night*; many pieces for organ and piano; songs; made numerous arrangements for church of works by Grieg, Cornelius, Poldini, etc.; published a manual, *Song-writing and Song-making* (N.Y., 1923).

Chaikovsky. See **Tchaikovsky.**

Chailley, Jacques, French musicologist; b. Paris, March 24, 1910. He studied comp. with Nadia Boulanger, Delvincourt and Busser; musicology with Pirro; taught at the Paris Cons. and at the Sorbonne.
WRITINGS: *Histoire musicale du moyen âge* (Paris, 1950; new ed. 1969); *La Musique mediévale* (Paris, 1951); *Précis de Musicologie* (Paris, 1958); *40,000 ans de musique* (Paris, 1961; translated into English under the title *40,000 Years of Music: Man in Search of Music*, N.Y., 1964); *La Musique et le signe* (Lausanne, 1967); *Expliquer l'harmonie* (Lausanne, 1967); *"La Flûte enchanteé," opéra maçonnique* (Paris, 1968; Engl. trans., N.Y. 1971); *"L'Art de la fugue" de J. S. Bach. Étude critique des sources* (Paris; I, 1971, II, 1972); *"Carnaval" de Schumann* (Paris, 1971).

Chailly, Luciano, Italian composer; b. Ferrara, Jan. 19, 1920. He studied in Bologna and then with Renzo Bossi in Milan; in 1948 took courses with Hindemith in Salzburg. In 1962 he was appointed head of the Rome Television. He composes in a communicative neo-classical idiom with some dodecaphonic incrustations and electronic effects.
WORKS: operas *Ferrovia Sopraelevata* (Bergamo, Oct. 1, 1955), *Il Canto del Cigno* (Bologna, Nov. 16, 1957), *Una Domanda di matrimonio*, after Chekhov (Milan, May 22, 1957), *La Riva delle Sirti* (Monte Carlo, March 1, 1959), *Procedura penale* (Como, Sept. 30, 1959), *Il Mantello*, surrealist opera (Florence, May 11, 1960), *Era probita* (Milan, March 5, 1963), *L'Idiota*, after Dostoyevsky (Rome, Feb. 14, 1970); also music for television.

Chaix, Charles, French-born composer and pedagogue; b. Paris, March 26, 1885; d. Thônex, near Geneva, Feb. 16, 1973. He studied music at the École Niedermeyer in Paris; in 1904 he went to Geneva, where he studied with Otto Barblan at the Geneva Cons., graduating in 1908. He subsequently joined its staff (1910–1914); served in the French army during World War I, returning to Geneva after Armistice. He combined his pedagogical activities with service as a church organist; also conducted advanced classes in counterpoint at the Cons. of Lyon, France. He retired from teaching in 1961. His works include 2 symphonies (1914, 1928); Piano Quintet (1941); String Quartet (1948); also choral works. He publ. a treatise on harmony, *Éléments d'écriture musicale* (Geneva, 1935).

Chajes, Julius, Polish pianist and composer; b. Lwow, Dec. 21, 1910. He studied piano with Richard Robert and Hedwig Rosenthal in Vienna; composition with Hugo Kauder; in 1933 won a prize at the International Contest for pianists in Vienna; in 1937 came to the U.S.; in 1940 became director of music at the Jewish Community Center in Detroit.
WORKS: *Fantasy* for piano and orch. (Vienna Radio, Oct. 9, 1928, composer soloist); Cello Concerto (Karlsbad, Aug 5, 1932); Piano Concerto (Vienna Radio, Nov. 25, 1953; Detroit Symph., Dec. 17, 1953, composer soloist); *Scherzo* (Detroit, Jan 11, 1970); several cantatas on biblical subjects; String Quartet; Piano Trio; Piano Sonata (1958).

Chaliapin, Feodor, celebrated Russian bass; b. Kazan, Feb. 13, 1873; d. Paris, April 12, 1938. He was of humble origin; at the age of 10 he was apprenticed to a cobbler; at 14 he got a job to sing in a chorus in a traveling opera company; his companion was the famous writer Maxim Gorky, who also sang in a chorus; together they made their way through the Russian provinces, often forced to walk the railroad tracks when they could not afford the fare. Chaliapin's wanderings brought him to Tiflis, in the Caucasus, where he was introduced to the singing teacher Dimitri Usatov (1847–1913) who immediately recognized Chaliapin's extraordinary gifts and taught him free of charge, helping him besides with board and lodgings. In 1894 Chaliapin received employment in a summer opera company in St. Petersburg and shortly afterwards he was accepted at the Imperial Opera during the regular season. In 1896 he sang in Moscow with a private opera company and produced a great impression by his dramatic interpretation of the bass parts in Russian operas. He also gave numerous solo concerts, which were sold out almost immediately; young music lovers were willing to stand in line all night long to obtain tickets. Chaliapin's first engagement outside Russia was at La Scala, Milan, in 1901, where he sang the role of Mefistofele in Boito's opera of that name; he returned to La Scala in 1904 and again in 1908. On Nov. 20, 1907 he made his American debut at the Metropolitan Opera as Mefistofele; then sang Mephistophélès in Gounod's *Faust* on Jan. 6, 1908; sang Leporello in Mozart's *Don Giovanni* on Jan. 23, 1908. He did not return to America until 1921, when he sang one of his greatest roles, that of the Czar Boris in *Boris Godunov* (Dec. 9, 1921). He sang in Russian opera roles in Covent Garden, London, in 1913; returned to Russia in 1914, and remained there during World War I and the Revolution. He was given the rank of "People's Artist" by the Soviet Government, but this title was withdrawn after Chaliapin emigrated in 1922 to Paris, where he remained until his death, except for appearances in England and America. The critical attitude toward Chaliapin in Russia on account of his emigration changed when he was recognized as a great Russian artist who elevated the art of Russian opera to the summit of expressive perfection; numerous articles were published in the Russian language dealing with Chaliapin's life and career. He was indeed one of the greatest singing actors of all time; he dominated every scene in which he appeared, and to the last he never failed in his ability to move audiences, even though his vocal powers declined considerably during his last years. He was especially famed for his interpretation of the role of Boris Godunov in Mussorsgky's opera; both dramatically and vocally he created an imperishable image. He was equally great as Mephistophélès in *Faust* and in the buffo roles of Don Basilio in *The Barber of Seville* and Leporello in *Don Giovanni*. He also played the title role in a film version of *Don Quixote*. His last American recital took place in New York on March 3, 1935.

BIBLIOGRAPHY: F. Chaliapin, *Pages from My Life* (N.Y., 1926); M. Yankovsky, *Chaliapin* (Leningrad, 1972); V. Drankov, *The Character of Chaliapin's Talent* (Leningrad, 1973).

Chamberlain, Houston Stewart, English writer on music; b. Portsmouth, Sept. 9, 1855; d. Bayreuth, Jan. 9, 1927. He received his earliest education at Versailles, and then studied at Cheltenham College, Gloucester. Because of ill health he was obliged to abandon his intention of following a military career (his father was a British admiral), and in 1870 he went to Stettin. His association with Prof. Kuntze there filled him with enthusiasm for Germanic culture and civilization, to the study of which he devoted many years. The results of these studies he published in a remarkable work, *Die Grundlagen des 19. Jahrhunderts* (Munich, 1899-1901; 10th ed. 1914; English translation by Lord Redesdale, London, 1910). The years 1879-81 he spent in Geneva, studying science at the Univ. (taking his degree with the dissertation *Recherches sur la sève ascendante*) and music with A. Ruthardt. During his residence at Dresden (1885-9) he began his activities as contributor to various German, French and English journals, writing with equal facility in three languages. From 1889-1908 he lived in Vienna. In 1908 he married Wagner's daughter, Eva, then lived in Bayreuth. Chamberlain was one of the most ardent apostles of Wagner's art, and he was also the chief protagonist of Wagner's ideas of German supremacy which Chamberlain presented in a simplified and vulgar manner combined with pseudo-scientific speculation and spiced with heavy doses of anti-Semitism. As early as 1923, Chamberlain was attracted to Hitler, but he did not live to see the full flowering of the Nazi millennium. Chamberlain's books on Wagner are of value as a reflection of the time, even though biographical sections are incomplete and out of focus.

WRITINGS: *Das Drama Richard Wagners* (Leipzig, 1892; 6th ed., 1921; French translation 1894; English translation 1915); *Richard Wagner. Echte Briefe an F. Praeger* (Bayreuth, 1894; 2d ed. 1908); *Richard Wagner* (Munich, 1896; 9th ed. 1936; English translation 1897; French translation 1899); *Die ersten 20 Jahre der Bayreuther Bühnenfestspiele* (Bayreuth,

1896); *Parsifalmärchen* (Munich, 1900; 3rd ed. 1916); *Lebenswege meines Denkens*, autobiography (1919).

BIBLIOGRAPHY: L. von Schroeder, *Houston Stewart Chamberlain* (1918); Anna Chamberlain (his first wife, married 1878, divorced 1908), *Meine Erinnerungen an Houston Stewart Chamberlain* (1923).

Chambers, Stephen A. See **Hakim, Talib Rasul.**

Chambonnières, Jacques Champion (called **Champion de Chambonnières**), French clavecinist and composer, b. between 1601 and 1611; d. Paris, April 1672. He was first chamber musician to Louis XIV, and the teacher of the elder Couperins, d'Anglebert, Le Bègue, Hardelle and others. Considered the founder of the French clavecin school, he was famed throughout Europe and his style strongly influenced that of contemporary German composers, among them Froberger. Two books of his clavecin pieces were printed (Paris, 1670; repr. of *Les Pièces de Clavessin* in the series *Monuments of Music ... in Facsimile*, Paris, 1967). Chambonnières complete works were publ. by Brunold & Tessier (Paris, 1925; repr. with English trans. and new preface, 1961).

BIBLIOGRAPHY: H. Quittard, "Chambonnières," *Revue Internationale de Musique* 12 (1898); idem., "Un Claveciniste français du XVIIe siècle: Jacques Champion de Chambonnières," *Tribune de St. Gervais* (1901); B. Huys, "Jacques Champion de Chambonnières, humanist, klavicinist en komponist," *Vlaams Muziektijdschrift* (Oct. 1972); G. B. Sharp, "Gaultier and Chambonnières. Two French Tercentenaries," *Musical Times* (Dec. 1972).

Chaminade, Cécile, French composer and pianist; b. Paris, Aug. 8, 1857; d. Monte Carlo, April 13, 1944. She was a pupil of Lecouppey, Savard and Marsick; later studied composition with Benjamin Godard. She became successful as a concert pianist; wrote a great number of agreeable piano pieces, in the salon style, which acquired enormous popularity in France, England and America; her more serious works much less successful. She made her American debut playing the piano part of her *Concertstück* with the Philadelphia Orch. (Nov. 7, 1908); also wrote a lyric symphony, *Les Amazones* (Antwerp, 1888); two orchestral suites; 2 piano trios; more than 200 piano pieces in a romantic style, including *Étude symponique, Valse-Caprice, Les Sylvains, La Lisonjera, Arabesque, Impromptu, Six Airs de ballet*, etc.; numerous songs.

Chamlee, Mario (real name **Archer Cholmondeley**), American lyric tenor; b. Los Angeles, May 29, 1892; d. there, Nov. 13, 1966. He made his operatic debut as the Duke in *Rigoletto* (San Francisco Opera, 1917); from 1917-19 served with the U.S. Army in France; married the soprano **Ruth Miller** on Oct. 2, 1919; first appeared with the Metropolitan Opera as Cavaradossi in *Tosca* (Nov. 22, 1920); made extensive concert tours of the U.S. In 1940 settled in Hollywood as a voice teacher.

Champagne, Claude, Canadian composer; b. Montreal, May 27, 1891; d. there, Dec. 21, 1965. He studied violin, piano and composition in Montreal; then went to Paris where he took courses in composition with Gédalge, Koechlin and Laparra (1921–29). Returning to Canada he joined the staff of McGill Univ. in Montreal (1932–41). From 1942 to 1962 he served as associate coordinator at the Cons. of Quebec. In his music he follows the modern French tradition.

WORKS: *Hercule et Omphale,* symph. poem (1918; Paris, March 31, 1926); *Prelude et Filigrane* for piano (1918); *Suite Canadienne* for chorus and orch. (Paris, Oct. 20, 1928); *Habanera* for violin and piano (1929); *Danse villageoise* for violin and piano (1929; also orchestrated); *Quadrilha brasiliera* for piano (1942); *Images du Canada français* for chorus and orch. (1943; Montreal, March 9, 1947); *Évocation* for small orch. (1943); *Symphonie gaspésienne* (1945); Piano Concerto (1948; Montreal, May 30, 1950); String Quartet (1951); *Paysanna* for small orch. (1953); *Suite Miniature* for flute, cello and harpsichord (1958); *Altitude* for chorus and orch. with Ondes Martenot (Toronto, April 22, 1960); *Concertino Grosso* for string orch. (1963); organ pieces; songs.

Champein, Stanislas, French composer; b. Marseilles, Nov. 19, 1753; d. Paris, Sept. 19, 1830. He studied under Peccico and Chavet in Paris; at 13 he became maître de musique at the Collegiate Church at Pignon, for which he wrote a Magnificat, a Mass, and psalms; in 1770 he went to Paris, where some sacred works, and two operettas, made his name known. Up to 1792 he produced 22 operas, the best of which were *La Mélomanie* (1781); *Les Dettes* (1787); and *Le Nouveau Don Quichotte* (1789). From 1793–1804 he filled a government position; continued to compose for the stage, but without success; spent the last years of his life in poverty; a pension, arranged for him through the efforts of Boieldieu and Scribe, came only 18 months before his death. Though one of the best known stage composers of his time, Champein's works are wholly forgotten.

Champion, Jacques. See **Chambonnières, Jacques Champion.**

Chanler, Theodore Ward, American composer; b. Newport, Rhode Island, April 29, 1902; d. Boston, July 27, 1961. He studied in Boston with Hans Ebell (piano) and with Arthur Shepherd (composition); then at the Cleveland Institute of Music with Ernest Bloch; later went to England where he took courses at Oxford Univ. (1923–25); also studied with Nadia Boulanger in Paris. He returned to America in 1933. His music, mostly in smaller forms, is distinguished by a lyrical quality; his songs are particularly expressive; he employed the modern idiom of polytonal texture without overloading the harmonic possibilities; the melody is free, but usually within tonal bounds.

WORKS: 2 song cycles, *Epitaphs* (1937); *Pas de Trois,* ballet; *Ann Gregory,* for chorus; *Joyful Mystery,* fugue for two pianos; *The Children,* song cycle; Violin Sonata (1927); *Five Short Colloquies,* piano suite (1936); *The Pot of Fat,* chamber opera (Cambridge, Mass., May 8, 1955).

Chanot, François, French violin maker; b. Mirecourt, March 25, 1788; d. Rochefort (Charente-Maritime), Nov. 12, 1825. He was the son of an instrument-maker; became a naval engineer, was retired on half-pay, and during his forced inactivity constructed a violin on the principle that the vibratory power would be increased by preserving the longitudinal woodfibers intact as far as possible. Thus his violin had no bouts, but slight incurvations like a guitar; the sound holes were almost straight, and the belly nearly flat; the strings were attached to the edge of the belly, instead of to a tailpiece. The violin was submitted to the Academy, whose report after testing it rated it equally with those of Stradivari and Guarneri; despite this evaluation, Chanot's violin never became popular. His brother, a *luthier* at Paris, manufactured a number of them, but gave it up when a few years had demonstrated their unpractical character.

Chantavoine, Jean, French writer on music; b. Paris, May 17, 1877; d. Mussy-sur-Seine, July 16, 1952. He studied the history of music with Friedländer in Berlin (1898; 1901–2); from 1903–20 was music critic of *Revue Hebdomadaire* and *Excelsior* (1911–21); from 1921–23 lived in Wiesbaden as a member of the International Commission for the Rhine Province; in 1923 was appointed General Secretary of the Paris Cons.

WRITINGS: He edited the biographical series *Les Maîtres de la Musique,* to which he contributed the monographs on Beethoven (1906) and Liszt (1910; 3rd ed., 1913); publ. *Musiciens et Poètes* (Paris, 1912; contains an account of Liszt's early opera, *Don Sanche,* the score of which was found by Chantavoine); *De Couperin à Debussy* (1921); *Les Symphonies de Beethoven* (1932); *Petit guide de l'auditeur de musique* (Paris, 1947); *Mozart dans Mozart* (1948).

Chapí y Lorente, Ruperto, Spanish composer of light opera; b. Villena, near Alicante, March 27, 1851; d. Madrid, March 25, 1909. He studied at the Cons. of Madrid; received a stipend from the Spanish Academy for further study in Rome (1874); wrote some operas (*La hija de Jefte, La hija de Garcilaso,* etc.), but discovered that his talent found more suitable expression in the lighter zarzuela, in which form his first success was won with *La Tempestad* (1882); his work is noted for elegance, grace and exquisite orchestration; of one of his last zarzuelas (*La Revoltosa*), Saint-Saëns remarked that Bizet would have been proud to sign his name to the score. His last zarzuela, *Margarita la Tornera* (Madrid, Feb. 24, 1909) was produced shortly before his death. Chapí y Lorente wrote 155 zarzuelas and 6 operas. In 1893 he founded the Sociedad de Autores, Compositores y Editores de Música.

BIBLIOGRAPHY: A. S. Salcedo, *Ruperto Chapí, su vida y sus obras* (Madrid, 1929).

Chapman, William Rogers, American choral conductor; b. Hanover, Mass., Aug. 4, 1855; d. Palm Beach, Florida, Mar. 27, 1935. He was a chorus leader and conductor in New York; founder and conductor of the Apollo (male voices) and Rubinstein (female voices) Clubs, and from 1903 conductor of the annual Maine Festival at Bangor and Portland; wrote church music, choral works, piano pieces, songs, etc.

Chappell & Co., London music publishers, concert agents, and piano manufacturers. Founded in 1810 by Samuel Chappell, J. B. Cramer (the pianist), and F. T. Latour. Cramer retired in 1819, Latour in 1826, and S. Chappell died in 1834, when his son **William** (1809–88) became the head of the firm. In 1840 he established the Musical Antiquarian Society, for which he edited Dowland's songs; he also edited and publ. *A Collection of National English Airs* (2 vols., 1838–39), later enlarged as *Popular Music of the Olden Time* (2 vols., 1855–59; revised by H. E. Wooldridge and publ. in 2 vols., 1893); he left an unfinished *History of Music* (vol. I, London, 1874). His brothers, **Thomas Patey** (1819–1902) and **S. Arthur** (1834–1904), were respectively the founder and manager of the Monday and Saturday Popular Concerts. In 1897 the partnership became a limited comany, and Thomas was succeeded by his son, **T. Stanley** (d. 1933), as board chairman; later, William Boosey became managing director. In 1929 the firm was acquired by **Louis Dreyfus.** The American branch, under the direction of **Max Dreyfus,** brother of Louis, has publ. the songs and musical comedies of Richard Rodgers, Jerome Kern, Cole Porter, Harold Arlen, and other popular composers.

Chapple, Stanley, English conductor; b. London, Oct. 29, 1900. He studied at the Royal Academy of Music; became accompanist with the British National Opera Co. (1918–21); musical director of the Vocalion Gramophone Co. (1924–29) and opera conductor at the Guildhall School of Music (1935–39). He had, meanwhile, been making annual summer appearances in the U.S. (1929–39) and was assistant conductor at the Berkshire Music Center (1939–47). In 1948 he became director of the School of Music at the Univ. of Washington in Seattle.

Chapuis, Auguste, French composer; b. Dampieresur-Salon (Haute-Saône), April 20, 1858; d. Paris, Dec. 6, 1933. He studied at the Paris Cons. with Dubois, Massenet and César Franck, winning first prize for organ playing. He was active as a church organist in Paris; in 1894 was appointed prof. of harmony at the Paris Cons. He wrote several operas which were produced without much success: *Enguerrande* (1892); *Les Demoiselles de Saint-Cyr* (1921); *Tancred* (1898); several oratorios and dramatic cantatas; numerous choruses and several pieces of chamber music. He also published a harmony manual, *Traité d'harmonie théorique et pratique.*

Char, Friedrich Ernst (Fritz), German composer and conductor; b. Cleve, May 3, 1865; d. Velden, Sept. 21, 1932. He studied with Wüllner at Cologne (1883–86); then held various posts as opera conductor. He wrote the text and music of a successful romantic opera *Der Schelm von Bergen* (Zwickau, 1895); cantata *Spielmann;* Piano Concerto; numerous piano pieces; song cycles.

Charles, Ernest, American composer; b. Minneapolis, Minn., Nov. 21, 1895. He studied voice with Charles Wood; began his career as a singer; after several years in New York as a producer of radio programs, he settled in Hollywood in 1953. He composed many anthems and religious songs which became popular.

Charles, Ray, black American jazz singer and pianist; b. Albany, Georgia, Sept. 23, 1930. His real name was **Ray Charles Robinson,** but he changed it to avoid confusion with the boxer Sugar Ray Robinson. He lost his sight in childhood; he was educated at the St. Augustine School for the Blind in Florida, where he learned to play clarinet and alto saxophone. His style of performance incorporates 'soul music' of Gospel songs, syncopated urban sound and country balladry. He was twice arrested on narcotics charges (1955 and 1961) but rehabilitated himself. In 1964 he made a world tour.

Charpentier, Gustave, famous French opera composer; b. Dieuze, Lorraine, June 25, 1860; d. Paris, Feb. 18, 1956. He studied at the Paris Cons. (1881–87), where he was a pupil of Massart (violin), Pessard (harmony) and Massenet (composition). He received the Grand Prix de Rome in 1887 with the cantata *Didon.* Charpentier evinced great interest in social problems of the working classes, and in 1900 formed the society "L'oeuvre de Mimi Pinson," devoted to the welfare of the poor, which he reorganized during World War I as an auxiliary Red Cross society. He owes his fame to one amazingly successful opera *Louise,* a "roman musical" to his own libretto (his mistress at the time was also named Louise, and like the heroine of his opera, was employed in a dressmaking shop), which was produced at the Opéra-Comique in Paris on Feb. 2, 1900. The score is written in the spirit of naturalism and includes such realistic touches as the street cries of Paris vendors. Its success was immediate and it entered the repertory of opera houses all over the world; its first American production, at the Metropolitan Opera in N.Y., took place on Jan. 15, 1921. Encouraged by this success Charpentier wrote a sequel under the title *Julien* (June 4, 1913), but it failed to arouse interest comparable to that of *Louise.* Nor did Charpentier in his very long life (he lived to be 95) succeed in producing any other memorable scores. He wrote an orchestral suite *Impressions d'Italie* (1892), a cycle of songs *Les fleurs du mal* to Baudelaire's words, etc.

BIBLIOGRAPHY: O. Séré, "Gustave Charpentier," *Musiciens français d'aujourd'hui* (Paris, 1911); André Homonet, *Louise* (Paris, 1922); Marc Delmas, *Gustave Charpentier et le lyrisme français* (Paris, 1931); K. O'D. Hoover, "Gustave Charpentier, *Musical Quarterly* (July 1939).

Charpentier, Jacques, French composer; b. Paris, Oct. 18, 1933. He studied piano with Maria Cerati-Boutillier; lived in Calcutta (1953–54), where he made a study of Indian music; prepared a valuable thesis "Introduction à l'étude de la musique le l'Inde." Upon return to Paris he studied composition with Tony Aubin and musical analysis with Messiaen at the Paris Cons. In 1954 he was appointed organist at the church of St-Benoit-d'Issy; in 1966 was named chief inspector of music of the French Ministry of Cultural Affairs, and in 1975 was made Inspector General of the Secretariate of State for Culture; traveled to Brazil and the

U.S.S.R.; in 1974 was named official organist of the organ of St. Nicolas du Chardonnet in Paris. Several of his works are based on Hindu melorhythms.

WORKS: Violin Concerto (1953); *4 Psaumes de Toukaram* for soprano and orch. (1957); 4 symphonies: No. 1, *Symphonie brève*, for string orch. (1958); No. 2, *Sinfonia Sacra*, for string orch. (1965); No. 3, *Shiva Nataraja (Shiva—the King of the Dance*, 1968; Paris, March 2, 1969); No. 4, *Brasil*, in homage to Villa-Lobos (1973); Concerto for Ondes Martenot and Orch. (1959); Concertino, *Alla Francese*, for Ondes Martenot, strings and percussion (1959-60); *Tantum Ergo* for 4 voices and orch. (1962); Octuple Concerto for 8 Winds and Strings (1963); *La Croisade des pastoureaux*, oratorio (1964); *Prélude pour la Genèse* for string orch. (1967); *Récitatif* for violin and orch. (1968); Concerto No. 1 for Organ and Strings (1969), No. 2 for Guitar and Strings (1970), No. 3 for Harpsichord and Strings (1971), No. 4 for Piano and Strings (1971), No. 5 for Saxophone and strings (1975), No. 6 for Oboe and Strings (1975), and No. 7 for Trumpet and Strings (1975); *Musiques pour un Zodiaque*, oratorio (1971); 2 string quartets (1955, 1956); Piano Quintet (1955); Quartet for Ondes Martenot (1958); *Suite Karnatique* for solo Ondes Martenot (1958); *Prelude and Allegro* for bass saxophone and piano (1959); *Lalita* for Ondes Martenot and percussion (1961); *Pour Diane* for horn and piano (1962); *Pour Syrinx* for flute and piano (1962); *Mouvement* for flute, cello and harp (1965); *Gavambodi 2* for saxophone and piano (1966); *Pour le Kama Soutra* for percussion ensemble (1969); *Pour une Apsara* for 2 harps (1970); *Esquisses* for flute and piano (1972); *Tu dors mais mon coeur veille* for solo violin (1974); *Une Voix pour une autre* for 2 female voices, flute, clarinet and percussion (1974); *Prélude* for Harpsichord (1975); Toccata for Piano (1954); *Études Karnatique* for piano, in 4 cycles (1957-61); *Messe* for organ (1964); *Repons* for organ (1968).

Charpentier, Marc-Antoine, significant French composer; b. Paris, c.1636; d. there, Feb. 24, 1704. While he studied painting in Italy, his admiration for Carissimi's music led him to take up serious musical study with him. He then returned to Paris and was appointed maître de chapelle to the Dauphin, but lost the post through Lully's opposition. This episode so embittered Charpentier against Lully that he totally eschewed Lully's style, often to the detriment of his own compositions. He was appointed maître de chapelle and music teacher to Mlle. de Guise; then intendant to the Duke of Orleans; maître de chapelle of the Jesuit collegial church and monastery; and maître de chapelle of Sainte-Chapelle, a post which he held until his death. He composed 16 operas and lesser works for the stage; several 'tragédies spirituelles' for the Jesuits; Masses, motets, pastorales, drinking songs, etc. It has been claimed that Charpentier was Lully's superior in learning, if not in inventive power. Reprints: in *Musique d' Église des XVIIe et XVIIIe siècles* (ed. by Pineau); H. W. Hitchcock, ed. *Judicum Salomonis* (New Haven, Conn., 1964); *Medée* (facs. of Paris ed., 1694; Ridgewood, N.J., 1968); D. Launay, ed. *Te Deum*, in *Le Pupitre* 13 (Paris, 1969); C. de Nys, ed.

Mass for soloists, double chorus and orch. (London, 1971).

BIBLIOGRAPHY: H. Quittard, "Notes sur un ouvrage inédit de Marc-Antoine Charpentier," *Zeitschrift der Internationalen Musikgesellschaft* (May 1905); M. Brenet, *Les Musiciens de la Sainte-Chapelle* (1910); L. de La Laurencie, "Un Opéra inédit de Marc-Antoine Charpentier, *La Descente d'Orfée*," *La Revue de Musicologie* 31; C. Crussard, *Un Musicien français oublié, Marc-Antoine Charpentier* (Paris, 1945); H. Wiley Hitchcock, "The Latin Oratorios of Marc-Antoine Charpentier," *Musical Quarterly* (Jan. 1955); R. W. Lowe, *Marc-Antoine Charpentier et l' Opéra de College* (Paris, 1966); T. Käser, *Die Leçon (sic)* de Ténèbres *im 17. und 18. Jahrhundert unter besonderer Berücksichtigung der einschlägigen Werk von M.-A.C.* (Bern, 1966); G. Massenkeil, "M.-A.C. als Messenkomponist," in S. Kross and H. Schmidt, eds. *Colloquium amicorum* (Bonn, 1967); L. M. Ruff, "M.-A.C.'s *Régles de composition*," *Consort* 24 (1967); H. W. Hitchcock, "On M.-A.C.," *Amor Artis Bulletin* (Feb. 1968); idem., "M.-A.C. and the Comédie-Francçaise," *Journal of the American Musicological Society* (Summer 1971); idem., "Problémes d'edition de la musique de M.-A.C. pour *Le Malade imaginaire*," and "Deux 'nouveaux' manuscrits de M.-A.C.," *Revue de Musicologie* (1972); R. B. Petty," C.'s Mass *Assumpta est Maria*," *Music Analysis* (Summer 1972); H. W. Hitchcock, "Some Aspects of Notation in an *Alma Redemptoris Mater* (c.1670) by M.-A.C. (d.1704)," in E. Borroff, ed. *Notations and Editions* (Dubuque, 1974).

Charpentier, Raymond, French composer and music critic; b. Chartres, Aug. 14, 1880; d. Paris, Dec. 27, 1960. He studied composition with André Gédalge; from 1921 to 1946 he was music director of the Comédie Française; then was active on the French radio. Beginning in 1908 he wrote music criticism for various journals. As a composer he wrote some 20 scores of incidental music for the plays produced at the Comédie Française and a comic opera *Gérard et Isabelle* (Paris, 1912); also several symphonic overtures; 2 string quartets, a wind quartet, a viola sonata, piano pieces and songs to texts by Ronsard and Baudelaire.

Chase, Gilbert, eminent American musicologist; b. Havana, Cuba (of American parents), Sept. 4, 1906. He studied at Columbia Univ. and at the Univ. of North Carolina at Chapel Hill; also studied piano. From 1929 to 1935 he lived in Paris and was active as music correspondent for British and American music periodicals. In 1935 he returned to the U.S.; from 1940-43 he was consultant on Spanish and Latin American music at the Library of Congress in Washington; simultaneously was active in an advisory capacity to musical radio programs. From 1951 to 1953 he was Cultural Attaché at the American Embassy in Lima, and from 1953 to 1955 served in the same capacity in Buenos Aires. He then became Director of the School of Music at the Univ. of Oklahoma (1955-57); from 1958 to 1960 was Cultural Attaché in Belgium; from 1960 to 1966 was Prof. of Music and Director of Latin American Studies at Tulane Univ. in New Orleans; in 1965 he became editor of the *Year-*

book of *Inter-American Musical Research.* In 1963 he organized the First Inter-American Conference on Musicology in Washington. In 1955 the Univ. of Miami bestowed upon him the title Honorary Doctor of Letters.

WRITINGS: *The Music of Spain* (N.Y., 1941; new ed. 1959; in Spanish, Buenos Aires, 1943); *A Guide to the Music of Latin America* (Washington, 1962); *America's Music: From the Pilgrims to the Present* (N.Y., 1955; new rev. ed., 1966; very valuable; also translated into German, French, Portuguese and Spanish); *Introducción a la musica americana contemporánea* (Buenos Aires, 1958).

Chasins, Abram, brilliant American pianist and composer; b. New York, Aug. 17, 1903. He studied piano with Ernest Hutcheson and composition with Rubin Goldmark at the Juilliard School of Music; later enrolled as a piano student of Josef Hofmann at the Curtis Institute of Music in Philadelphia; from 1926 to 1935 he taught piano there. In the summer of 1931 he took a course in musical analysis with Donald Tovey in London. In 1941 he was appointed music consultant of the Radio Station WQXR in New York; in 1946 became its musical director, retaining this post until 1965. From 1972 to 1977 he was musician-in-residence at the Univ. of Southern California, Los Angeles; and director of the University radio station KUSC, which he reorganized as a medium for broadcasting classical and modern music. Chasins began his career as a pianist-composer in 1926; on Jan. 18, 1929 he was the soloist in his own Piano Concerto with the Philadelphia Orch., Ossip Gabrilowitsch conducting, and was again the soloist in his 2nd Piano Concerto with the Philadelphia Orch. on March 3, 1933 under the direction of Leopold Stokowski. In 1976 he received the award of the National Federation of Music Clubs for "outstanding service to American Music during the Bicentennial Year." He composed more than 100 piano pieces; his *3 Chinese Pieces* were particularly popular; Josef Lhévinne, Josef Hofmann and other famous pianists included them in their repertory. An orchestral version of *3 Chinese Pieces* became the first work by an American composer to be conducted by Toscanini (N.Y. Philharmonic, April 8, 1931). He also wrote 24 Preludes for Piano (1928), which are often used as teaching pieces. Chasins published several readable books: *Speaking of Pianists* (N.Y., 1958), *The Van Cliburn Legend* (N.Y., 1959), *The Appreciation of Music* (N.Y., 1966) and *Music at the Crossroads* (N.Y., 1972). In 1978 he became engaged on a biography of Leopold Stokowski, under the title, *Stoki, the Incredible Apollo.*

Chaumet, William, French composer; b. Bordeaux, April 26, 1842; d. Gajac, Gironde, Oct., 1903. He wrote several operas: *La Coche* (1865), *Le Péché de M. Géronte* (1873), *Hérode* (1885) and an operetta *La Petite Maison* (1903); also chamber music.

Chaun, František, Czech composer and painter; b. Kaplice, Jan. 26, 1921. He turned to music rather late in life; took occasional lessons in music theory with J. Feld and K. Slavický. As an accomplished painter, he

applies art techniques, at least nominally, to his musical compositions in a strikingly modern manner.

WORKS: *Fantasy* for orch. (1960); *Serenade for an Elderly Lady* for orch. (1962); *Sinfonietta Concertante* for bassoon, strings and piano (1963); *Kafka Trilogy* for orch. in 3 parts composed separately: *Proměna* (*The Metamorphosis,* 1968), *Zámek* (*The Castle,* 1964) and *Proces* (*The Trial,* 1967; Prague, Nov. 26, 1968); *Ghiribizzo* for piano and orch. (1969); *Sinfonietta buffa* (1970); *Hommage à Dubuffet,* double concerto for violin, cello, strings, 2 oboes and 2 horns (1970; Prague, March 4, 1971); *Pět obrázků* (*Five Pictures*) for orch. (1971; Prague, March 24, 1974); *150,000,000,* Cantata (1963); Trio for flute, violin and piano (1955); *Scherzino* for violin and piano (1960); *Divertimento* for 9 wind instruments (1961); *Pesante* for violin and bassoon (1962); Quartet for flute, oboe, cello and bassoon (1963); Trio for clarinet, horn and double bass (1963); *Serenata rabbiosa* for violin and 4 double basses (1964); *Adventures of Violin and 9 Instruments* (1969); Duo for viola and double bass (1969); *Ulysses,* string quartet (1970); *Fuga solemnis,* collage for 6 violins and 2 violas (1970); *Prelude, Improvisation and Scherzo* for piano (1955); *Variations on Scales* for piano (1960); songs.

Chausson, Ernest, distinguished French composer; b. Paris, Jan. 20, 1855; d. Limay, near Mantes, June 10, 1899 (in a bicycle accident). He studied with Massenet at the Paris Cons.; then took private lessons with César Franck, and began to compose. The influence of Wagner as well as that of Franck determined the harmonic and melodic elements in Chausson's music; but despite these derivations, he succeeded in establishing an indivudal style, tense in its chromaticism and somewhat flamboyant in its melodic expansion. The French character of his music is unmistakable in the elegance and clarity of its structural plan. He was active in musical society in Paris and was secretary of the Société Nationale de Musique. He composed relatively little music; possessing private means, he was not compelled to seek employment as a professional musician.

WORKS: operas: *Les Caprices de Marianne* (1800), *Hélène* (1885), *Le Roi Arthus* (perf. posthumously, Brussels, Nov. 30, 1903); incidental music to *La Légende de Sainte Cécile* (Paris, Jan. 25, 1892); for orch.: *Viviane,* symph. poem (1883); *Solitude dans les bois* (1886); Symphony in B-flat major (Paris, April 18, 1898; still in the repertoire); *Poème* for violin and orch. (Concerts Colonne, Paris, April 4, 1897; very popular among violinists); *Poème de l'amour et de la mer* for voice and orch. (1882-92); *Chanson perpetuelle* for voice and orch. (1898); for chorus: *Hymne védique* (1886; with orch.); *Chant nuptial* for women's voices and piano (1887); Piano Trio; Piano Quartet; String Quartet (unfinished); songs: *Chansons de Miarka* to words by Jean Richepin; *Serres chaudes* to words by Maeterlinck; *Deux poèmes* to words by Verlaine; etc.

BIBLIOGRAPHY: O. Séré, *Musiciens français d'aujourd'hui* (Paris, 1911); Special issue of *La Revue Musicale* (Dec. 1925; includes a catalogue of his works); H. Oulmont, *Musique de l'amour: Ernest Chausson et la "bande à Franck"* . . . (1935); J. P. Barricelli and

Leo Weinstein, *Ernest Chausson* (a centennial biography; Norman, Okla., 1955); Jean Gallois, *Ernest Chausson: l'Homme et son oeuvre* (Paris, 1967); L. Davies, *César Franck and His Circle* (Boston, 1970).

Chauvet, Charles-Alexis, French organist and composer; b. Marines (Seine-et-Oise), July 7, 1837; d. Argentan (Orne), Jan. 28, 1871. He studied organ and composition at the Paris Cons.; in 1869 he was appointed to the important post of chief organist at the Trinité in Paris. He published numerous organ works and piano pieces adaptable for teachers, students and performers.

Chavanne, Irene von, Austrian contralto; b. Graz, April 18, 1868; d. Dresden, Dec. 26, 1938. She studied at the Vienna Cons.; in 1885 joined the Dresden Court Opera. She was praised for the volume and range of her voice.

Chavarri, Eduardo Lopez, Spanish composer; b. Valencia, Jan. 31, 1871; d. there, Oct. 28, 1970. He was a pupil of F. Pedrell; taught and conducted at the Valencia Cons.; founded a chamber orchestra there. His compositions include *Acuarelas valencianas* for string orch.; *Rapsodía valenciana* for piano and orch.; *Concerto español* for piano and string orch.; *Leyenda* for chorus and orch.; *Quarteto hispano*; quartets for four violins; *Andaluza* for cello and piano; *Leyenda del Castillo Moro* for piano; piano pieces; songs. He published a music history (2 vols.; 3rd ed., 1929); *Música popular española* (1927; 2nd ed., 1940); *Chopin* (Valencia, 1950); *Folklore musical español* (Madrid, 1955).

Chávez, Carlos, distinguished Mexican composer and conductor; b. Calzada de Tacuba, near Mexico City, June 13, 1899; d. Mexico City, Aug. 2, 1978. He studied piano as a child with Pedro Luis Ogazón. He studied harmony with Juan B. Fuentes and Manuel Ponce. He began to compose very early in life; wrote a symphony at the age of 16; made effective piano arrangements of popular Mexican songs and also wrote many piano pieces of his own. His first important work was a ballet on an Aztec subject, *El Fuego Nuevo*, which he wrote in 1921, commissioned by the Secretariat of Public Education of Mexico. Historical and national Mexican subject matter remained the primary source of inspiration in many works of Chávez, but he rarely resorted to literal quotations from authentic folk melodies in his works; rather he sublimated and distilled the melorhythmic Mexican elements resulting in a *sui generis* style of composition. In 1922–23 he traveled in France, Austria and Germany and became acquainted with the modern developments in composition. The influence of this period of his evolution as a composer is reflected in the abstract titles of his piano works, such as *Aspectos, Energía, Unidad*. Returning to Mexico, he organized and conducted a series of concerts of new music, giving first Mexican performances of works by Stravinsky, Schoenberg, Satie, Milhaud and Varése. From 1926 to 1928 he lived in New York. In the summer of 1928 he organized the Orquesta Sinfónica de Mexico, of which he remained the principal conductor until 1949. Works of modern music occupied an important part in the program of this orchestra, including 82 first performances of works by Mexican composers, many of them commissioned by Chávez; Silvestre Revueltas was among those encouraged by Chávez to compose. During his tenure as conductor Chávez engaged a number of famous foreign musicians as guest conductors, as well as numerous soloists. In 1949 the orchestra was renamed Orquesta Sinfónica Nacional and remains a permanent institution. Chávez served as director of the Conservatorio Nacional de Música from 1928 to 1935 and was general director of the Instituto Nacional de Bellas Artes in 1946 to 1952. Beginning from 1936 Chávez conducted a great number of concerts with major American orchestras, and also conducted concerts in Europe and South America. Culturally, Chávez maintained a close connection with progressive artists and authors of Mexico, particularly the painter Diego Rivera; his *Sinfonía Proletaria* for chorus and orch. reflects his political commitment. In 1958–59 Chávez was Charles Eliot Norton Lecturer at Harvard Univ.; these lectures were published in book form under the title, *Musical Thought* (Cambridge, 1960); Chávez also published a book of essays *Toward a New Music* (N.Y., 1937). A detailed catalogue of his works in 3 languages, Spanish, English and French, was published in Mexico City in 1971.

WORKS: OPERA, *Panfilo and Lauretta*, first produced in English (N.Y., May 9, 1957; then revised and produced in a Spanish version as *El Amor propiciado*, Mexico City, Oct. 28, 1959; still later retitled *The Visitors*); BALLETS, *El fuego nuevo* (1921; Mexico City, Nov. 4, 1928); *Los cuatro soles* (1926; Mexico City, July 22, 1930); *Caballos de Vapor* (1926; first produced in English under the title *HP*, i.e. *Horsepower*, Philadelphia, March 31, 1932); *Hija de Colquide* (*Daughter of Colchis*; presented by Martha Graham under the title *Dark Meadow*, N.Y., Jan. 23, 1946); *Antígona* (Mexico City, Sept. 20, 1940; originally conceived as incidental music for Sophocles' *Antigone*, 1932). FOR ORCH.: *Sinfonía* No. 1 (1915); *Cantos de Méjico* for Mexican orch. (1933); *Sinfonía de Antígona*, derived from his ballet, *Antígona* (Mexico City, Dec. 15, 1933); *Obertura Republicana* (Mexico City, Oct. 18, 1935); *Sinfonía India* (1935; broadcast Jan. 23, 1936; also Boston Symph. Orch., April 10, 1936, composer conducting); Concerto for 4 Horns (Coolidge Festival, Washington, D.C., April 11, 1937; composer conducting); Piano Concerto (1938–40; world première, N.Y. Philh., Jan. 1, 1942); *Cuatro Nocturnos*, for voice and orch. (1939); *Xochipilli Macuilxochitl*, for ensemble of traditional Indian instruments (N.Y., May 16, 1940; composer conducting); *Toccata* for percussion instruments (Mexico City, Oct. 31, 1947); Violin Concerto (Mexico City, Feb. 29, 1952); Symph. No. 3 (1951; Caracas, Dec. 11, 1954, composer conducting; N.Y. Philh., Jan. 26, 1956); Symph. No. 4 (*Sinfonía romantica*; Louisville, Feb. 11, 1953; composer conducting); Symph. No. 5, for strings (Los Angeles, Dec. 1, 1953, composer conducting); Symph. No. 6 (N.Y., May 7, 1964); Symph No. 7 (unfinished); *Resonancias* for orch. (Mexico City, Sept. 18, 1964); *Elatio* for orch. (Mexico City, July 15, 1967); *Discovery* for orch. (Aptos, California, Aug. 24, 1969); *Clio,* symph. ode (Houston, Texas, March 23, 1970); CHORAL WORKS: *Tierra Mojada,* for chorus, oboe, and English horn (Mexico City, Sept. 6, 1932); *El Sol* for chorus and orch. (Mexico City, July 17, 1934); *Sinfonía Proletaria (Llamadas)* for chorus and orch. (Mexico City, Sept. 29, 1934); *La Paloma Azul,* for chorus and chamber orch. (1940); *Prometheus Bound,* cantata (1956). CHAMBER MUSIC: Piano and String Sextet (1919); String Quartet No. 1 (1921); Sonatina for Violin and Piano (1924); Sonatina for Cello and Piano (1924); *Energía* for 9 instruments (1925; Paris, June 11, 1931); Sonata for Horns (1930); String Quartet No. 2 (1932); *3 Espirales* for violin and piano (1934); String Quartet No. 3 (1944); Concerto for Violin and Orch. (1948); 4 pieces under the generic title *Soli* (No. 1 for oboe, clarinet, trumpet and bassoon, 1933; No. 2 for wind quintet, 1961; No. 3 for bassoon, trumpet, viola, timpani and orch., 1965; No. 4 for brass trio, 1966); 3 instrumental pieces, under the generic title *Invention* (No. 1, for piano, 1958; No. 2 for string trio, 1965; No. 3, for harp, 1967), introducing an inductive method of thematic illation in which each musical phrase is the logical consequent of the one immediately preceding it; *Fuga HAG,C* for violin, viola, cello and double bass (1964); Variations for Violin and Piano (1969). FOR PIANO: Sonata No. 1 (*Sonata Fantasía;* 1917); *Berceuse* (1920); *7 Madrigals* (1921–22); *Polígonos* (1923); Sonata No. 2 (1919); *Aspectos I and II* (1923); Sonatina (1924); Sonata No. 3 (1928); *Blues* (1928); *Fox* (1928); *Paisaje* (1930); *Unidad* (1930); 10 Preludes (1937); Sonata No. 4 (1941); *Fugas* (1942); *4 Études* (1949); *Left Hand Inversions of 5 Chopin Etudes* (1950); Sonata No. 5 (1960); Sonata No. 6 (1961); *Estudio a Rubinstein,* in minor seconds (1974); *5 Caprichos* (1975–76). VOICE AND PIANO: *3 Exágonos* (1923); *Inutil epigrama* (1923); *Otros tres exágonos* (1924); *3 Poemas* (1938); *La casada infiel* (1941). Also, *3 Pieces for Guitar* (1923); *Upingos* for oboe solo (1957).

BIBLIOGRAPHY: H. Weinstock, "Carlos Chávez," *Musical Quarterly* (Oct. 1936); R. G. Morillo, *Carlos Chávez, vida y obra* (Buenos Aires, 1960); Rodolfo Halffter, compiler, *Carlos Chávez, Catálogo Completo de sus obras* (Mexico City, 1971).

Chaynes, Charles, French composer; b. Toulouse, July 11, 1925. He studied violin at the Cons. of Toulouse; later took courses in harmony and counterpoint with Jean and Noël Gallon, and composition with Milhaud and Rivier at the Paris Cons. He received the Premier Grand Prix de Rome in 1951 and stayed at the Villa Medicis in Rome to compose; returned to France in 1955; in 1964 was appointed program director on the French Radio. In his music he makes use of "chromatic totality" which extends into free dodecaphony and aleatory usages.

WORKS: Concerto No. 1 for String Orch. (1953); a dramatic overture, *Ode Pour une Mort Tragique* (1954); Symphony (1955); Trumpet Concerto (1958); Violin Concerto (1958; Paris, March 14, 1961); *4 Illustrations pour la flûte de jade* for solo flute, strings, harp and percussion (1960); Concerto for Piano and Chamber Orch. (1961); Concerto No. 2 for Orch. (1961); *3 Études linéaires* for 13 instruments and percussion (1963); *Commentaires concertants* for violin and orch. (1964); *Expressions contrastées* for orch.,

piano and percussion (Strasbourg Festival, June 23, 1966); Concerto for Organ, Strings and Percussion (1966); *Transmutations* for orch. (1971); *Peintures noire* for orch. (1975); Flute Sonatina (1951); Violin Sonata (1952); *Serenade* for wind quintet (1954); *Quadretti italiani* for violin and piano (1957); *Réflexes* for violin and piano (1963); *Concordances* for piano and percussion (1967); *Irradiations* for violin, cello and harpsichord (1968); *Interférences* for cello and piano (1972); *Tarquinia,* 3 fresques for Ondes Martenot, piano and percussion (1973); *Joutes* for organ and harpsichord (1975); *Capriccio* for piano (1954); *Substances convergentes* for piano (1964); *M'zab,* suite for piano (1972); *Par ces chemins du coeur,* suite for soprano and orch. (1953); a chamber cantata *Joie aux âmes* (1962); *Alternances* for alto and piano (1965); *4 Poèmes de Sappho* for soprano and string trio (1968).

Chélard, Hippolyte-André, French composer; b. Paris, Feb. 1, 1789; d. Weimar, Feb. 12, 1861. He studied with Fétis, and Gossec at the Paris Cons.; won the Grand Prix de Rome in 1811; in Rome he studied with Baini, and then took lessons in Naples with Paisiello. Returning to Paris, he produced the opera *Macbeth* (to a libretto by Rouget de Lisle) on June 29, 1827 with meager success. He was much more fortunate in Germany as an opera composer; in Munich he produced a German version of *Macbeth,* a new opera *Mitternacht* (June 19, 1831), and a German version of his French opera *La Table et le logement* under the title *Der Student* (Feb. 19, 1832). These were followed by another German opera, *Die Hermannsschlacht.* In 1840 he was appointed court conductor at Weimar where he brought out 2 comic operas, *Der Scheibentoni* (1842) and *Die Seekadetten* (1844). He also wrote a symphonic poem in 8 movements entitled *La Symphonéide* (1848).

Chelius, Oskar von (pen name **Siegfried Berger**), German composer; b. Mannheim, July 28, 1859; d. Munich, June 12, 1923. Pupil in Mannheim of E. Steinbach, in Kassel of Reiss, in Leipzig of Jadassohn; made his career in the army, rising to the rank of major general in 1911.

WORKS: He wrote the operas *Haschisch* (Dresden, 1897) and *Die vernarte Prinzess* (Wiesbaden, 1905); symph. poem, *Und Pippa tanzt;* Requiem for Chorus and Orch.; Psalm 121; Violin Sonata; piano pieces; songs; etc.

Chelleri (real name **Keller**), **Fortunato,** Italian composer and choral director; b. Parma, May, 1690; d. Kassel, Dec. 11, 1757. He studied music with his uncle, F. M. Bassani, who was maestro di cappella at Piacenza Cathedral. His first opera, *Griselda* (Piacenza, 1707), was followed by fifteen more, written for various Italian stages. He settled in Kassel in 1725 as court music director, and remained there until his death, except for brief journeys to London (1726) and Stockholm (1731). Besides his operas, he wrote an oratorio *Dio sul Sinai* (1731); overtures; church music, etc. He published a volume of cantatas and arias (London, 1726), and a collection of 'Lessons' for harpsichord (London, 1750), containing two piano sonatas (really suites).

Chemin-Petit, Hans, German composer; b. Potsdam, July 24, 1902. Both his father and grandfather were professional musicians. He studied cello with Hugo Becker and composition with Paul Juon; upon graduation was active mainly as a cello player. In 1929 he was appointed to the staff of the Berlin Hochschule für Musik; then taught at the Akademie der Künste in Berlin; in 1968 was appointed director of its music department. In his music he adheres to the median line of neo-Classicism.

WORKS: chamber operas *Der gefangene Vogel* (1927), *Lady Monika* (1930), *König Nicolo* (1962), *Die Komödiantin* (1968); and *Die Rivalinnen* (1970); 2 symphonies (1932, 1949); Cello Concerto (1932); Concerto for Organ, Strings and Kettledrums (1963); 2 sonatas for recorder (1958, 1960); several cantatas, church music and piano pieces. He published a collection of choral arrangements of German folk songs (Berlin, 1949).

Chenoweth, Wilbur, American pianist, organist and composer; b. Tecumseh, Nebraska, June 4, 1899. He studied piano with Sigismund Stojowski and Alexander Lambert in N.Y.; organ and comp. with Pietro Yon. In 1938 he moved to Los Angeles.

WORKS: He composed numerous effective piano pieces (*Concert Waltz*; *Cortege*); choruses (*Of the Father's Love Begotten*; *God of Comfort*; *Noel, Noel, Bells are Ringing*; *Rise, Men Courageous*); songs (*Vocalise, The Arrow and The Song*). Among his works in larger forms is *Fiesta* for piano and orch. (also for two pianos).

Cherbuliez, Antoine-Élisée, Swiss musicologist; b. Mulhouse, Alsace, Aug. 22, 1888; d. Zürich, Oct. 15, 1964. He studied science at the Univ. of Strasbourg and took private organ lessons with Albert Schweitzer. He studied music with his grandfather Adolphe Koekkert in Geneva, and took courses at the Zürich Cons. From 1913 until 1916 he studied privately with Max Reger in Jena. He served for a time as an organist; in 1923 was appointed instructor in musicology at the Univ. of Zürich. He wrote some chamber music and choruses, but devoted his energies mainly to writing. He published *Gedankliche Grundlagen der Musikbetrachtung* (Zürich, 1924); *Zum problem der religiösen Musik* (Basel, 1924); *Die Anwendung der Sievers'schen Theorien auf die musikalische Interpretation* (Zürich, 1925); *Peter Cornelius* (Zürich, 1925); *J. S. Bach* (Zürich, 1926); *Die Schweiz in der deutschen Musikgeschichte* (Zürich, 1926; a valuable and extensive account of Swiss music history); biographies of Handel, Haydn, Chopin, Grieg, Verdi and Tchaikovsky; monographs on Mozart, Beethoven and Brahms; many articles for musical journals.

Cherepnin. See **Tcherepnin.**

Cherkassky, Shura, Russian pianist; b. Odessa, Oct. 7, 1911. He was a pupil of his mother; then studied with Josef Hofmann at the Curtis Institute in Philadelphia. He played all over the world; was at his best in the Romantic repertory; made his home in France.

Cherney, Brian, Canadian composer; b. Peterborough, Ontario, Sept. 4, 1942. He studied composition with Weinzweig and Dolin, and piano at the Univ. of Toronto, graduating in 1964 (M.M., 1967); had short periods of study at Columbia Univ. and at the international summer courses for new music in Darmstadt; taught at the Univ. of Victoria (1971–72) and since 1972 at McGill Univ. in Montreal. His music is determined by structural factors, and is largely atonal; visually it is drawn in graphic notation.

WORKS: 2 sets of *Variations* for orch. (1962, 1967); *2 Songs* for soprano and chamber orch. (1963); Violin Concerto (1964); *6 Miniatures* for oboe and strings (1968); *Mobile IV* for soprano and chamber ensemble (1970); *7 Images* for 22 players (1971); Violin Sonata (1961); *3 Pieces* for string quartet (1961); *Suite* for solo oboe (1962); Quintet for saxophone and string quartet (1962); *Interlude and Variations* for wind quintet (1965); *Suite* for viola and piano (1965); Wind Quintet (1965); 2 string quartets (1966, 1970); *Mobile II* for solo cello (1968); *Kontakion (Quiet Music for 11 Players)* (1969); *Mobile IIIa* for solo oboe (1970); *Notturno* for flute, oboe, clarinet, bassoon, horn and piano (1974); *Tangents* for solo cello, tape, piano, double bass and piano (1975); *Chamber Concerto* for viola and 10 players (1975); *Fantasy* for piano (1966); Piano Sonata (1966); *Interludes, Shapes and Patterns* for piano (1968); *6 Miniatures* for piano (1968); *Jest* for piano (1968).

Cherubini, Luigi (full baptismal name **Maria Luigi Carlo Zenobio Salvatore**), famous Italian composer; b. Florence, Sept. 14, 1760; d. Paris, March 13, 1842. As a young child he studied music with his father, cembalist at the Pergola Theater; his subsequent teachers were Bartolomeo and Alessandro Felici; then Bizarri and Castrucci; in 1777 he was sent by Duke Leopold II of Tuscany (the future Emperor Leopold III) to Milan to perfect himself in counterpoint under Sarti. At thirteen he had already written a Mass, and a stage-intermezzo for a society theater; at fifteen he composed another intermezzo, *Il Giuocatore;* during his years of study with Sarti he confined himself to contrapuntal work and church music; in 1780, *Quinto Fabio* (perf. at Alessandria della Paglia) opened the series of his dramatic works; its cool reception spurred him to renewed study, and *Armida* (Florence, 1782), *Adriano in Siria* (Leghorn, 1782), *Messenzio* (Florence, 1782), *Quinto Fabio* (revised; Rome, 1783), *Lo sposo di tre e marito di nessuna* (Venice, 1783), *Idalide* (Florence, 1784), and *Alessandro nelle Indie* (Mantua, 1784) received public approbation. Invited to London in the autumn of 1784, he brought out 2 operas, *La finta principessa* (1785), an opera buffa which had fair success, and *Giulio Sabino* (1786), which was less fortunate; Cherubini held the position of Composer to the King for one year, and in July, 1786, went to Paris for a one-year visit; in 1788 he brought out *Ifigenia in Aulide* at Turin; then settled permanently in Paris. His first French opera, *Demofoonte* (Grand Opéra, 1788), was a failure owing to his attempt to adapt his style of flowing melody to the ill-turned style of Marmontel, the librettist. Next year Léonard, the Queen's hairdresser, obtained a license to establish Italian opera in a little playhouse called the Théâtre de la Foire de St.-Germain; and here Cherubini conducted, until 1792, the best works of Anfossi, Paisiello and Cimarosa. During this period he developed, inspired by the text of his opera *Lodoiska* (Théâtre de Monsieur, 1791), a new dramatic style destined to work a revolution on the French stage; the increased breadth and force of the ensemble numbers, the novel and rich orchestral combinations, and the generally heightened dramatic effect were initiated or expanded by a host of composers of the French school: Méhul, Berton, Lesueur, Grétry. Cherubini's next operas, *Eliza ou le voyage au mont St.-Bernard* (1794), and *Médée* (1797), were hampered by poor libretti. In 1795 Cherubini was appointed one of the Inspectors of the new Conservatoire. Composing steadily, he brought out *L'Hôtellerie portugaise* (1798), *La Punition* (1799), *La Prisonnière* (1799; pasticcio, with Boieldieu), and in 1800, at the Théâtre Feydeau, *Les Deux Journées* (perf. In London, 1801, as *The Water-carrier*; in Germany as *Der Wasserträger*), his greatest operatic work. Cherubini had fallen into disfavor with Napoleon, whose opinion in musical matters he had slighted; but after the success of *Les Deux Journées*, he was able to produce at the Grand Opéra *Anacréon, ou l'amour fugitif* (1803), and the ballet *Achille à Scyros* (1804), neither of which, however, had good fortune. At this juncture Cherubini was invited to write an opera for Vienna; *Faniska*, brought out in 1807 at the Kärnthnerthor Theater, was an overwhelming success; so much so that a Vienna critic who ventured the prophecy that Beethoven's *Fidelio* would one day be equally esteemed, was laughed at. Returning to Paris after the French occupation of Vienna, Cherubini wrote *Primmalione* for the Italian opera at the Tuileries (1808), but did not win the Emperor's favor, and retired for a time to the château of the Prince of Chimay, where he occupied his leisure with botanizing. The request to write a Mass for the church of Chimay turned the current of his thoughts; he composed the celebrated 3-part Mass in F, the success of which was so marked that Cherubini thenceforward devoted more time to sacred than dramatic composition, though he did bring out *Le Crescendo* (1810), *Les Abencérages* (Opéra, April 6, 1813), *Bayard à Mézières* (1814), *Blanche de Provence* (1821) and *Ali Baba* (Opéra, July 22, 1833). On a visit to London, in 1815, he wrote for the Philharmonic Society a symphony, an overture, and a Hymn to Spring. In this year he lost his place in the Cons. during the troublous times of the Restoration, but was recompensed by his appointment as superintendent of the Royal Chapel, succeeding Martini. In 1816 he was made prof. of composition at the Cons., and its director in 1821; he retired in 1841. Cherubini was one of the great modern masters of counterpoint, and his scores, particularly in his admirable sacred music, bear witness on every page to his skill and erudition. As an opera composer, his main failing was the undue musical prolongation of scenes in which swifter dramatic action would have been preferable.

WORKS: His own catalogue of his works, *Notice des manuscrits autographes de la musique composée par feu M.-L.-C.-Z.-S. Cherubini* (publ. 1843; repr. London, 1967), includes 15 Italian and 14 French operas; (an uncatalogued, newly discovered opera, *Don Pistacchio*, was performed at Dresden, Nov. 27, 1926); a ballet; 17 cantatas and 'occasional' vocal works with orch.; many detached airs, romances, nocturnes, duets, etc.; 14 choruses; 4 sets of solfeggi (over 160 numbers); 11 Solemn Masses, 2 Requiems, many detached Kyries, Glorias, Credos, etc.; a Credo in 8 parts with organ; an oratorio (Florence, 1777); motets, hymns, graduals, etc., with orch.; a *Magnificat*, a *Miserere*, a *Te Deum* (each with orch.); 4 litanies, 2 Lamentations, 20 antiphons; etc.; for orch.: a symphony, an overture, 11 marches, 11 dances, etc.; chamber music: 6 string quartets, a String Quintet; a Sonata for 2 Organs; for piano: 6 sonatas, a grand fantasia, a minuet, a chaconne; etc. Cherubini's *Cours de Contrepoint et de Fugue* was prepared for publication by his pupil Halévy. It appeared in a German translation by Stöpel (1835-36), in English translation by J. Hamilton (1837) and C. Clarke (1854). Two new German editions were prepared by G. Jensen (1896) and R. Heuberger (1911).

BIBLIOGRAPHY: A. Bottée de Toulmon, *Notice des manuscrits autographes de Cherubini* (Paris, 1843); E. Bellasis, *Cherubini. Memorials Illustrative of His Life* (London, 1874; new augmented ed., Birmingham, 1912); F. J. Crowest, *Cherubini* (London and N.Y., 1890); M. E. Wittmann, *Cherubini* (Leipzig, 1895); M. Q. L'Épine, *Cherubini* (Lille, 1913); R. Hohenemser, *L. Cherubini Sein Leben und seine Werke* (Leipzig, 1913); H. Kretzschmar, "Über die Bedeutung von Cherubini's Ouvertüren und Hauptopern für die Gegenwart," *Peters Jahrbuch* (1906); L. Schemann, *Cherubini* (Berlin, 1925); O. A. Mansfield, "Cherubini's String Quartets," *Musical Quarterly* (1929); H. Mersmann, *Kammermusikführer* (analysis; 1932); P. Espil, *Les Voyages de Cherubini ou l'enfance de Mozart* (Bayonne, 1946); G. Confalonieri, *Prigionia d'un artista: il romanzo di Luigi Cherubini* (2 vols., Milan, 1948; A. Damerini, ed. *Luigi Cherubini nel II centenario della nascita* (Florence, 1962); Basil Deane, *Cherubini* (London, 1965); A. L. Ringer, "Cherubini's *Médée* and the Spirit of French Revolutionary Opera," in G. Reese and R. J. Snow, eds., *Essays in Music in Honor of Dragan Plamenac* (Pittsburgh, 1969).

Cheslock, Louis, American composer; b. London, England, Sept. 9, 1898. He was brought to the U.S. as an infant; studied music at the Peabody Cons. in Baltimore: violin with Van Hulsteyn and Gittelson, composition with Strube; became violin instructor there in 1916, composition instructor in 1922; in 1952 was appointed chairman of the department of theory. He was a violinist in the Baltimore Symph. Orch. (1916–37); also served as guest conductor. Cheslock writes in a neo-romantic style, rooted in traditional music, but not without excursions into modern techniques, including a modified application of dodecaphonic principles.

WORKS: a one-act opera, *The Jewel Merchants* (Baltimore, Feb. 26, 1940); a Symphony (1932); the tone poems for orch.: *Cathedral at Sundown, 'Neath Washington Monument,* and *At the Railway Station* (Chicago, April 29, 1923); ballet, *Cinderella* (Baltimore, May 11, 1946); oratorio, *The Congo* (Akron, Ohio, Oct. 30, 1942); Violin Concerto (Baltimore, Feb. 25, 1926); *Rhapsody in Red and White (An American*

Divertissement) for orch. (1950); string quartet (1957); piano pieces; published *Introductory Study on Violin Vibrato* (Baltimore, 1931); edited *H. L. Mencken on Music* (N.Y., 1961).

Chevé, Émile-Joseph-Maurice, French music theorist; b. Douarnenez, Finistère, May 31, 1804; d. Fontenay-le-Comte, Aug. 26, 1864. A physician of great merit, he became a zealous advocate of Pierre Galin's method of musical instruction explained in Galin's *Exposition d'une nouvelle méthode pour l'enseignement de la musique* (1818; 3rd ed. 1831), which attained considerable popularity; married **Nanine Paris** (d. 1868) and collaborated with her in a *Méthode élémentaire de musique vocale* (Paris, 1844; later ed. 1863; German translation by F. T. Stahl, 1878), in the preface to which he 'exposes' and attacks the 'defective' methods of the Conservatoire. He and his wife also published a *Méthode élémentaire d'harmonie* (with Galin; Paris, 1846); and Mme. Chevé wrote a *Nouvelle théorie des accords, servant de base à l'harmonie* (Paris, 1844). He published a long series of essays and articles by which he vainly sought to draw out the professors of the Conservatoire. Acrimonious polemics raged for years, and numerous pamphlets were issued in Paris by adherents and foes of the Chevé method.

BIBLIOGRAPHY: A. Pagés, *La Méthode musicale Galin-Paris-Chevé* (Paris, 1860); A. L. Montandon, *École Galin-Paris-Chevé; Problème musical, historique, pédagogique, prophétique* (Paris, 1861); O. Comettant, *Les Musiciens, les philosophes et les gaités de la musique en chiffres* (Paris, 1870).

Chevillard, Camille, French composer and conductor; b. Paris, Oct. 14, 1859; d. Chatou (Seine-et-Oise), May 30, 1923. He studied piano with Georges Mathias; was chiefly self-taught in composition. In 1897 he became assistant conductor of the Lamoureux Concerts; in 1898 succeeded Lamoureux as conductor after having married his daughter; from 1913 was conductor at the Grand Opéra.

WORKS: for orch. (all performed in Paris): *Ballade symphonique* (Feb. 23, 1890); *Le Chêne et le roseau* (March 8, 1891); *Fantaisie symphonique* (Oct. 21, 1894); also an *Étude chromatique* for piano; a Piano Quintet, Piano Quartet, Piano Trio; a String Quartet; Violin Sonata; Cello Sonata; songs with orch., *L'Attente* and *Chemins d'Amour.*

BIBLIOGRAPHY: R. Rolland, *Musiciens d'aujourd'hui* (1908); O. Séré, "Camille Chevillard," in *Musiciens français d'aujourd'hui* (Paris, 1911); R. Dumesnil, *Portraits des musiciens français* (Paris, 1938).

Chevreuille, Raymond, Belgian composer; b. Brussels, Nov. 17, 1901; d. Montignies-le-Tilleul, May 9, 1976. He took a course in harmony at the Brussels Cons., but was largely self-taught in composition. From 1936 to 1959 he was employed as a sound engineer at the Belgian Radio. His style of composition embodies distinct elements of French impressionism, with its searing melodies and rich harmonies within a framework of emancipated tonality, often verging on polytonal syncretism.

WORKS: chamber opera *Atta Troll* (1952); 4 ballets: *Jean et les Argayons* (1934), *Cendrillon* (1946), *La bal chez la portière* (1954) and *Spéléomagie*, miniature ballet for TV (1959); 2 symph. radio plays: *D'un diable de briquet* (1950; Prix Italia, 1950) and *L'Élixir du révérend père Gaucher* (1951); 9 symphonies: No. 1 (1939); No. 2, *Symphonie des souvenirs*, with soloists and chorus optional (Brussels, Nov. 23, 1945); No. 3 (Brussels, June 25, 1952); No. 4, *Short Symphony* (1952); No. 5, *Symphonie printanière* (1954); No. 6 (1957); Symphony for Chamber Orch. (1958); No. 7 (1964); No. 8 (1970); *Petite Suite* for orch. (1931); 3 piano concertos (1937, 1952, 1968); *Mouvements symphoniques* (1938); 2 cello concertos (1940, 1965); 3 violin concertos (1941, 1953, 1965); *Burlesque* for cello and orch. (1941); Concerto for Oboe, Clarinet, Bassoon and Orch. (1943); Double Concerto for Piano, Saxophone or Viola, and Orch. (1946); *Divertissement* for orch. (1946; extract from ballet *Cendrillon*); Concerto for Orchestra (1947); *Divertissement for Chamber Orch.* (1948); *Barbe-Bleu (Bluebeard)* for orch. (1949); Horn Concerto (Brussels, July 12, 1950); Trumpet Concerto (1954); *Récréation de Midi* for string orch. (1955); *Mouvements*, suite for brass (1956); *Carnaval à Ostende*, symph. suite (1959); *Presto Giocoso* for orch. (1961); Concerto Grosso for 2 Trumpets and Orch. (1961); Concerto for Flute and Chamber Orch. (1961); *Bruegel, peintre des humbles*, symph. suite (1963); Concerto for Clarinet, String Orch. and Percussion (1968); *2 Airs* for orch. (1971); 6 string quartets (1930, 1934, 1934, 1939, 1943, 1945); Piano Trio (1936); String Trio (1937); Piano Quartet (1938); Cello Sonata (1941); *Divertissement* for wind quintet (1942); *Musiques Lilliputiennes* for 4 flutes (1942); Quartet for 4 Cellos (1942); Piano Sonatina (1943); Suite for Piano (1944); Variations for Violin and Piano (1946); *Récit et Air Gai* for clarinet and piano (1950); 5 Bagatelles for String Quartet (1952); Serenade for Wind Quintet (1958); Viola Sonatina (1959); *Recitatif et Marche* for double bass and piano (1961); Wind Quartet (1964); Trio for Flute, Viola, and Double Bass or Piano (1961); Clarinet Quintet (1968); *Prelude, Scherzando et Marche* for horn and piano (1968); Clarinet Sonatina (1970); several cantatas: *Le Fléau* (1930), *Le cantique de soleil* (1941), *L'Éléphant et le papillon* (1941), *La dispute des orgues* (Brussels, Jan. 10, 1942), *Évasions* (1942) and *Saisons* (1943); *Prière pour les condamnés à mort* for narrator and orch. (Brussels, Oct. 14, 1945); *Assonances* for narrator and chamber orch. (1962); *Rhapsody* for female voice and chamber orch. (1969).

Chiari, Giuseppe, Italian composer of extreme avantgarde tendencies; b. Florence, Sept. 26, 1926. He studied piano; organized a group 'Musica e Segno' in association with Sylvano Bussotti; participated in the festival 'Fluxus' in Wiesbaden (1962), in avantgarde manifestations in New York (1964) and at the Centre de Musique in Paris (1965). Eventually he returned to Florence, where he owned a clothing store. In his productions he follows the most latitudinarian and disestablishmentarian trends of metadadaistic fragmentationarianism both in tonal and verbal structures. He publ. *Musica senza contrappunto*, a varitype anthology of disjected observations (Rome, 1969). In it he launched the slogan 'Musica gestuale,' which deals with audio-visual and tactile events, volitional as well as aleatory. His works include: *Intervalli* for piano (1956); *Per arco* for cello (1962); *Teatrino* for actor-pianist, rubber dolls, alarm clocks and a handsaw (1963); *Don't Trade Here* for action theater (1965).

Chiaromonte, Francesco, Italian musician of versatile attainments; b. Castrogiovanni, Sicily, July 26, 1809; d. Brussels, Oct. 15, 1886. He studied with Raimondi in Palermo and with Donizetti in Naples; began his musical career as a singing teacher, but was arrested for revolutionary activities in 1848 and after serving two years in prison was banished from Naples. He then proceeded to Paris, where he was employed as an opera chorus-master; then went to Brussels in 1871 and was appointed prof. at the Brussels Cons. He produced several operas and oratorios; also publ. a valuable *Méthode de Chant.*

Chickering, Jonas, American piano-maker; b. New Ipswich, N.H., April 5, 1798; d. Boston, Dec. 8, 1853. In 1818 he was apprenticed to John Osborn, a Boston piano-maker; 1823, founded (with James Stewart) the firm of Stewart & Chickering; from 1829, known as Chickering & Mackay (John Mackay, d. 1841); later, as Chickering & Sons. Jonas Chickering pioneered in the development of the upright piano, and the full metal plate for square and grand pianos. His son and successor, **Col. Thomas E. Chickering** (b. Boston, Oct. 22, 1824; d. there, Feb. 14, 1871) was named Chevalier of the Legion of Honor in addition to taking the first prize for pianofortes at the Paris Exposition of 1867. His three sons and their successors carried on the factory, which was famous for quality and high rate of production, until 1908, when it became part of the American Piano Co., and the factory was moved from Boston to East Rochester, N.Y. Later, the firm became a subsidiary of the Aeolian American Corp.
BIBLIOGRAPHY: R. G. Parker, *A Tribute to the Life and Character of Jonas Chickering* (Boston, 1854); *The Commemoration of the Founding of the House of Chickering* (Boston, 1904).

Chignell, Robert, English composer; b. Romsey, Hants, May 8, 1882; d. London, Feb. 27, 1939. He won a scholarship to the Royal College of Music, where his teachers were G. Garcia (voice) and Sir C. V. Stanford (composition); later continued vocal studies with C. W. Clark; was soloist with the Sheffield Choir on its world tour.
WORKS: operas *Romeo and Juliet, Herode, Aucassin and Nicolette*; two symph. poems: *Serenade humoresque* for orch.; *The Jackdaw of Reims, Sunrise and Sunset,* and *The Monks of Bangor* for chorus and orch.; about 250 songs.

Chihara, Paul, American composer of Japanese descent; b. Seattle, July 9, 1938. After the outbreak of the war, his family was relocated, among many other Japanese-Americans, to Minadoka, Idaho. He studied piano as a child; took courses in English literature at the Univ. of Washington (B.A., 1960) and at Cornell Univ. (M.A., 1961); then went to Europe, where he studied composition with Nadia Boulanger in Paris (1962–63); and with Ernst Pepping in West Berlin

(1965–66); in the interim he obtained his A.M.D. at Cornell Univ. (1965). From 1966 till 1976 he was on the music faculty of the Univ. of California, Los Angeles; traveled to Japan for research in 1967. In his music he utilizes advanced forms of serial techniques, occasionally extending them to aleatory procedures. In his choral compositions he follows the time-honored polyphonic methods of the Renaissance.
WORKS: Viola Concerto (1963); String Quartet (1965); *Tree Music* for 3 violas and 3 trombones (1966); *Branches* for 2 bassoons and percussion (1966); *Magnificat* for treble voices (1966); The 90th Psalm, a choral cantata (1966); Nocturne for 24 solo voices (1966); *Redwood* for viola and percussion (1967); *Willow, Willow* for bass flute, tuba and percussion (1968); *Rain Music,* a tape collage using brewery noises, commissioned by Rainier Breweries in Seattle (1968); *Forest Music* for orch. (1968; Los Angeles, May 2, 1971); *Driftwood* for violin, 2 violas and cello (1969); *Logs XVI* for amplified string bass and magnetic tape (1970); *Ceremony I* for Oboe, 2 Cellos, Double Bass, and Percussion (1971); *Ceremony II* for Flute, 2 Cellos, and Percussion (1972); *Ceremony III* for small orch. (1973); *Ceremony IV* for orch. (1974); *Ceremony V, Symphony in Celebration* (Houston, Sept. 8, 1975); *Grass,* Concerto for Double Bass and orch. (1971; Oberlin, Ohio, Cons., April 14, 1972); *Wild Song* for cello and orch. (1972). *Missa Carminum* for chorus a cappella (Los Angeles, Jan. 15, 1976).

Child, William, English organist and composer of sacred music; b. Bristol, 1606; d. Windsor, March 23, 1697. He was a boy chorister at Bristol Cathedral under Elway Bevin; in 1632 was in Windsor as organist at St. George's Chapel (jointly with J. Mundy) and then in London at the Chapel Royal; from 1643–60 he apparently lived in retirement, devoting himself to composition; in 1660 he was appointed chanter at the Chapel Royal, and a member of the King's private band. He received his Mus. Bac. in 1631 or 1639; his Mus. Doc. from Oxford in 1663.
WORKS: Child published psalms (1639; later editions 1650 and 1656), services, anthems, compositions in "Court Ayres," canons, catches, etc. (included in collections of Arnold Boyce, Hilton, Playford and others); also instrumental works. Numerous services, anthems (including *O Lord, grant the King a long life*), a motet (*O bone Jesu*), and chants exist in manuscript.
BIBLIOGRAPHY: F. Hudson; W. R. Large, "William Child—a New Investigation of Sources," *Music Review* (Nov. 1970).

Childs, Barney, American composer; b. Spokane, Washington, Feb. 13, 1926. He studied sporadically and intermittently with Leonard Ratner, Carlos Chávez, Aaron Copland and Elliott Carter; obtained a B.A. degree in English from the Univ. of Nevada, (1949); M.A. from Oxford Univ. as a Rhodes Scholar (1955); and Ph.D. at Stanford Univ., both in English and in music (1959). He taught English at the Univ. of Arizona (1956–65); was Dean of Deep Springs College (1965–69). In 1969–71 he taught theory at Wisconsin College Cons. in Milwaukee. Not overly concerned with public tastes and current fashions of cosmopolitan styles in music, he cultivates indeterminate structures.

WORKS: 2 symphonies (1954, 1956); 7 string quartets (1951–68); 5 wind quintets (1951–69); Violin Sonata (1950); Sonata for Solo Clarinet (1951); *Concerto da camera* for trumpet and woodwinds (1951); Trio for Flute, Oboe, and Clarinet (1952); Quartet for Clarinet and Strings (1953); Sonata for Bassoon and Piano (1953); *Four Involutions* for solo English horn (1955); *Five Considerations* for solo French horn (1955); 7 *Epigrams* for soprano and clarinet (1955); Concerto for English Horn, Strings, Harp and Percussion (1955); 2nd Violin Sonata (1956); Quartet for Bassoons (1958); Sonata for Solo Oboe (1958); Brass Trio (1959); Flute Sonata (1960); Sonata for Solo Trombone (1961); 6 pieces under the generic title *Interbalances* (1941–64) for various groups; *Take 5* for 5 instruments (1962); *Stances* for flute and silence (1963); Quartet for Flute, Oboe, Double Bass and Percussion (1964); *Music for Double-bass and Friend* (1964); 6 *Events* for band (1965); *Music for Piano and Strings* (1965); *Jack's New Bag* for 10 players (1966); *The Golden Bubble* for contrabass sarrusophone and percussion (1967); Nonet (1967); *Operation Flabby Sleep* for any instruments (1968); *Music for 6 Tubas* (1969); *Keet Seel* for chorus a cappella (1970); Concerto for Clarinet and Orch. (1970).

Chilesotti, Oscar, Italian music historiographer; b. Basano, July 12, 1848; d. there, June 20, 1916. He was a graduate in law of Padua Univ.; was also a good flutist and cellist; self-taught in harmony. He lived in Milan where he wrote regularly for the *Gazzetta Musicale.*
WRITINGS: *Biblioteca di Rarità musicali* (Milan, 1883; 9 vols.), containing transcriptions from little known works of the early 17th century, and (vol. IV) *Arianna* by Benedetto Marcello; *I nostri Maestri del passato* (Milan, 1882), biographical notes on the greatest Italian musicians, from Palestrina to Bellini; *Di G. B. Besardo e del suo 'Thesaurus Harmonicus'* (Milan, 1886; French ed. 1901); *Sulla lettera critica di B. Marcello contra A. Lotti* (Bassano, 1885); *Sulla melodia popolare del cinquecento* (Milan, 1889); *Lautenspieler des 16. Jahrhunderts* (Leipzig, 1891); *L'evoluzione nella musica, appunti sulla teoria di H. Spencer* (Turin, 1911); etc. He publ. in modern notation Roncalli's *Capricci armonici* on the Spanish guitar (Milan, 1881); and translated Schopenhauer's *Aphorismen* and *Die Welt als Wille und Vorstellung* into Italian.
BIBLIOGRAPHY: V. Fedeli, "Il Dr. O. Chilesotti," *Rivista Musicale Italiana* XXIII/3-4 (1916).

Chiriac, Mircea, Rumanian composer; b. Bucharest, May 19, 1919. He studied harmony with Otescu and Jora at the Bucharest Cons. (1936–45); in 1966 was appointed to its faculty. He wrote a ballet *Iancu Jianu* (1962); a symph. tableau, *Bucureştii de altadata* (*Bucharest of Old Times;* 1957); *Symphonic Triptych* (1971); *Divertissement* for string orch. (1972); and some chamber music.

Chisholm, Erik, Scottish composer; b. Glasgow, Jan. 4, 1904; d. Rondebosch, South Africa, June 8, 1965. He first studied music in Glasgow; then in London and in

Edinburgh with Donald Tovey (composition) and Puishnov (piano); received his Mus. Bac. in 1932, and his Mus. Doc. from Edinburgh Univ. in 1934. In 1940 joined the Carl Rosa Opera Company as conductor; in 1943 toured with the Anglo-Polish Ballet; later went to the Far East; organized the Singapore Symph. Orch., and conducted 50 concerts in Malaya; in 1946 was appointed Professor of Music and Director of the South African College of Music at Cape Town Univ.; also conducted operas in South Africa. His book, *The Operas of Leoš Janáček,* was publ. posthumously (N.Y., 1971).
WORKS: the operas *The Feast of Samhain* (1941), *The Inland Woman* (Cape Town, Oct. 21, 1953), *Dark Sonnet* (after O'Neill's drama *Before Breakfast;* Cape Town, Oct. 20, 1952); *Simoon* (after Strindberg; 1953); *Dark Sonnet* and *Simoon* were later combined with a third short opera, *Black Roses* (libretto by the composer), to form a trilogy entitled *Murder in Three Keys* (performed at the Cherry Lane Theater, Greenwich Village, N.Y., July 6, 1954); ballets: *The Pied Piper of Hamelin* (1937), *The Forsaken Mermaid* (1940), *The Earth Shapers* (1941), *The Hoodie* (1947); for orch.: *Straloch Suite* (1933); Symphony No. 1 (1938); Symphony No. 2 (1939); *The Adventures of Babar* (with narrator, 1940); *Piobaireachd* Concerto for piano and orch. (1940); *Pictures from Dante* (1948); *Hindustani* Concerto for piano and orch. (Cape Town, Nov. 22, 1949); Violin Concerto (Cape Town Festival, March 18, 1952); Concerto for Orchestra (Cape Town, March 29, 1952); chamber music: Double Trio for Clarinet, Bassoon, Trumpet, Violin, Cello and Double bass; choral works, songs, piano pieces. Chisholm's style of composition is marked by considerable complexity; elements of oriental scale formations are notable.

Chladni, Ernest Florens Friedrich, eminent acoustician; b. Wittenberg, Nov. 30, 1756; d. Breslau, April 3, 1827. At first a student and professor of law at Wittenberg and Leipzig, he turned to physics, and made highly important researches in the domain of acoustics. He discovered the 'Tonfiguren' (tone-figures; i.e., the regular patterns assumed by dry sand on a glass plate set in vibration by a bow); invented the Euphonium (glass-rod harmonica) and Clavicylinder (steel-rod keyboard harmonica). To introduce his ideas and inventions, he made long journeys and delivered many scientific lectures.
WRITINGS: His earlier publications, *Entdeckungen über die Theorie des Klanges* (1787), *Über die Longitudinal-schwingungen der Saiten und Stäbe,* and a series of minor articles in various periodicals, were followed by the important works *Die Akustik* (1802; 2nd ed., 1830; French translation, 1809); *Neue Beiträge zur Akustik* (1817); *Beiträge zur praktischen Akustik* (1821); *Kurze Übersicht der Schall-und Klanglehre* (1827).
BIBLIOGRAPHY: W. Bernhardt, *Dr. E. Chladni, der Akustiker* (Wittenberg, 1856).

Chlubna, Osvald, Czech composer; b. Brno, July 22, 1893; d. there, Oct. 30, 1971. He studied composition with Janáček in Brno (1914–15) and later at the Brno branch of the Master School of the Prague Cons. (1923–24); taught in Brno at the Cons. (1919–35) and at the Janáček Academy of Music (1953–59). His music is marked by rhapsodic élan; many of his works reflect national events. In 1948 he completed Janáček's unfinished symph. poem, *Dunaj (The Danube,* 1923–28).

WORKS: 8 operas: *Pomsta Catullova (Catullus' Revenge,* 1917; Brno, Nov. 30, 1921); *Aladina and Palomid,* after Maeterlinck (1921–22; Brno, May 31, 1925); *Nura* (1930; Brno, May 20, 1932); *Freje pana z Heslova (The Love Affairs of the Squire of Heslov,* 1939–40; Brno, Jan. 28, 1949); *Jiří of Kunštát and Poděbrady* (1941–42); *Kolébka (The Cradle,* 1952; Brno, 1953); *Eupyros* (1962); *Rytíř Jan z Linhartic (Knight Jan von Linhartic,* 1967); a scenic mystery play, *V den počátku (The Day of Beginning,* 1935; Brno, Jan. 24, 1936); 7 cantatas: *České vzkříšení (The Czech Resurrection,* (1943), *My Land Is Beautiful* (1955); *In the Name of Life* (1959), *The Eternal Vigils of Life and Death* (1964), *Only Once* (1967; chamber cantata), and *Leonydas* and *The Death of Caesar* (1968; 2 chamber cantatas); symph. poems: *Distance and Dreams* (1916), *Before I Grow Silent* (1918); *2 Fairy Tales* (1920); *A Song of Longing* (1922), *From Hills, Mountains and Forests* (1934), *Nature and Man* (a trilogy including the separate works *Spring, Summer Serenade* and *Carnival of Autumn,* 1949–53) and *This Is My Land* (a cycle including the separate works *The Fountains of Brno, The Abyss of Macocha, Pernštejn Castle, Moravian Slovakia* and *Brno Portals and Frescoes,* 1956–62); a sinfonietta (1924); 3 symphonies: No. 1, *Symphony of Life and Love* (1927); No. 2, *Brno Symphony* (1946); No. 3 (1960); Fantasy for Viola and Orch. (1936); Piano Concerto (1937); Cello Concerto (1938); Violin Concerto (1950); *Andante* for violin and small orch. (1951); 5 string quartets (1925; 1928; 1933; 1963; 1969); Sonata for Violin and Cello (1925); Wind Quintet (1936); Violin Sonata (1948); Cello Sonata (1948); Fantasy for String Trio (1953); Etudes for Oboe and Harp (1969); Etudes for Bass Clarinet (1969); Etude for Harpsichord and 12 Strings (1970); Viola Sonatina (1970); *Frescoes* for solo violin (1970); 5 Nocturnes for Piano (1933); Sonata-Fantasy for Piano (1959); *Elegies* for piano (1968); choruses; songs.

Cholmondeley, Archer. See **Chamlee, Mario.**

Chop, Max (pen name **Monsieur Charles**), German writer; b. Greuzen, Thuringia, May 17, 1862; d. Berlin, Dec. 20, 1929. A law student turned musician, he published several books of songs and ballades, 3 piano concertos, a piano trio, and 2 orchestral suites; lived from 1885–88 in Berlin as a writer of musical feuilletons; then, until 1902, in Neu-Ruppin as music critic and editor of the *Märkische Zeitung*; in 1902 he was again in Berlin; from 1920 until his death, was editor-in-chief of *Die Signale*. An ardent admirer of August Bungert, he published his detailed biography (Berlin, 1915); also analyses of his music dramas, and, was (from 1911) the editor of *Der Bund,* the official organ of the Bungert Association. He published *Zeitgenössische Tondichter* (2 vols., 1888–90, each containing 12 sketches); analyses of Liszt's symphonic poems, Wagner's music dramas, etc.; a sketch of August Bungert in volume III of *Monographien moderner Musiker*

(1903); *Vademecum für den Konzertsaal* (1904, et seq.); biographies of Delius (1907) and Rezniček (1920); *Führer durch die Musikgeschichte* (Berlin, 1912).

Chopin, (François-) Frédéric, an incomparable composer for piano; b. Zelazowa Wola, near Warsaw, in all probability, March 1, 1810, the date given by Chopin himself in his letter of acceptance of membership in the Polish Literary Society in Paris in 1833 (but the date, Feb. 22, 1810 is contained in the certificate of baptism); d. Paris, Oct. 17, 1849. His father, Nicolas Chopin, teacher in the Warsaw gymnasium, was a native of Marainville, Alsace, who went to Warsaw as a teacher of French; his mother, Justine Kryzanowska, was Polish. Frédéric was brought up in his father's private school, among sons of the Polish nobility. His musical education was entrusted to the Bohemiam pianist, Albert Zwyny and the Director of the Warsaw School of Music, Joseph Elsner. At the age of seven he played in public a piano concerto by Gyrowetz, and improvisations. His first attempts in composition were dances (Polonaises, Mazurkas and Waltzes); but he publ. (1825) as op. 1 a Rondo, and as op. 2 Variations on *Là ci darem la mano,* with orch. While a youth, he traveled in Europe, visiting Danzig, Dresden, Leipzig and Prague. In 1829, already a composer of eminent individuality and a finished performer, he set out for Vienna, Munich and Paris. His concert in Vienna, on Sept. 11, 1829 elicited high praise (see the Leipzig *Allgemeine Musikalische Zeitung,* Nov. 18, 1829, pp. 757–8). His first concert in Paris was given at Pleyel's house, before an invited audience of musicians, in 1831. His reception was so cordial that he made Paris his home for life. He was destined never to revisit Poland. Despite Kalkbrenner's finding fault with his fingering, and despite the dictum of Field that Chopin's talent was "of a sick chamber order," Chopin made a deep and lasting impression, not merely on Parisian society, of which he soon became the declared favorite, but on men like Liszt, Berlioz, Meyerbeer, Bellini, Adolphe Nourrit, Balzac and Heine, to whose intimacy he was admitted as a cherished and equal companion. From the beginning he taught the piano; his instruction was eagerly sought, chiefly by members of the French and Polish aristocracy; von Lenz (see below) gives a charming glimpse of Chopin the teacher. Chopin also gave yearly concerts to the musical *élite,* and played frequently in Parisian salons; but had an unconquerable aversion to miscellaneous concert-giving. His compositions took precedence over all else in the pianistic world. In 1839, Schumann wrote, reviewing some of Chopin's Preludes (op. 28), Mazurkas (op. 33), and Waltzes (op. 34): "Er ist und bleibt der kühnste and stolzeste Dichtergeist der Zeit" [He is indeed the boldest and proudest poetic spirit of the time] (*Neue Zeitschrift für Musik,* 1839). His position, both in society and the world of art, was assured; the devotion of his pupils and admirers bordered on fanaticism. The Paris critics found a Shakespearian epithet for him: "the Ariel of the piano."

In 1837 Liszt introduced Chopin to George Sand (Mme. Dudevant); their mutual attraction led to a deep companionship, marked by a paradoxical contrast. While George Sand was an energetic person, involved in social affairs and holding radical views, Chopin was a poet confined within his inner world; it has been said that she was the masculine and he the feminine partner in their liaison. They spent the winter of 1838–39 on the island of Majorca, where she attended to him, when he was already ailing, with tender devotion; but she portrayed Chopin in her novel *Lucrézia Floriani* under the guise of a weakly Prince Karol. Soon friction developed between them, and they parted in 1847. Chopin by that time suffered from the advanced stage of tuberculosis; nevertheless he undertook a concert tour in Great Britain in 1848; then returned to Paris to die. He was buried at Père Lachaise, between Cherubini and Bellini.

Chopin represents the full liberation of the pianoforte from traditional orchestral and choral influences—its authoritative assumption of a place as a solo instrument *per se*. Chopin's music, as none before, breathes the piano-spirit, incarnates the piano-soul, revels in the pure piano-tone, and illustrates the intrinsic piano-style, without seeking "orchestral" effects, tonal or technical. Not requiring of the piano the sonority of an orchestra, he may have seemed "effeminate" beside the titanic Liszt; yet his works, more especially the scherzos, ballades, preludes, nocturnes, and even the concertos (pianistically considered), mark a boundary in piano effect which has never been surpassed. In the small forms he chose there lies a world of originality in constructive ingenuity, in melody and melodic ornament, in harmonic progressions and arpeggiated figuration, of national melancholy or proud reminiscence, of tender or voluptuous sentiment and poetic reverie. His playing was notable for flawless accuracy and remarkable brilliancy and technique, sensuous charm in touch and tone, and a peculiar flexibility in the tempo (*rubato*) which was at times almost exaggerated. He was a most exquisite interpreter of his own works, but did not much care to play other piano music; all in all, a remarkably self-centered composer-pianist. A complete edition of Chopin's works in 14 volumes, edited by Liszt, Brahms, Bargiel, Franchomme, Reinecke and Rudorff, was publ. by Breitkopf & Härtel. Other excellent editions are those of Chopin's personal pupil, C. Mikuli, of Ignaz Friedman, of E. Ganche, of R. Joseffy (with introductions by J. G. Huneker), of Paderewski and Cortot. Innumerable editions of Chopin's works by categories have been brought out by virtually every large music publishing firm. A definitive edition of collected works in 26 vols. was initiated by Paderewski in collaboration with Joseph Turczynski and Ludwik Bronarski in 1940, and completed in 1954. A new "National Edition", in 36 vols., was begun in 1967 under the Editorship of J. Ekier.

WORKS: WITH OPUS NUMBERS: for piano with orch.: Variations on *Là ci darem la mano* (op. 2); 2 concertos (E minor, op. 11; F minor, op. 21); *Grand Fantasy on Polish Airs* (op. 13); *Krakowiak*, concert-rondo (op. 14); Grand Polonaise (op. 22). For piano with other instruments: *Introduction et Polonaise*, for piano and cello (op. 3); Piano Trio in G minor (op. 8); Cello Sonata (op. 65); Rondo in C for 2 pianos (op. 73). For piano solo: Rondos (opp. 1, 5, 16); Sonatas (opp. 4, 35, 58); Mazurkas (opp. 6, 7, 17, 24, 30, 33, 41, 50, 56,

59, 63, 67, 68); Nocturnes (opp. 9, 15, 27, 32, 37, 48, 55, 62, 72); Études (opp. 10, 25); Valses (opp. 18, 34, 42, 64, 69, 70); Scherzos (opp. 20, 31, 39, 54); Ballades (opp. 23, 38, 47, 52); Polonaises (opp. 26, 40, 44, 53, 61, 71); Preludes (opp. 28, 45); Impromptus (opp. 29, 36, 51); Fantasies (opp. 49, 61, 66); Grand Variations on *Je vends des Scapulaires* (op. 12); *Boléro* (op. 19); *Tarentelle* (op. 43); *Concert-Allegro* (op. 46); *Berceuse* (op. 57); *Bacarolle* (op. 60); 3 *Écossaises* and *Marche funèbre* (op. 72). For voice and piano: *17 Polish Songs* (op. 74; ed. with English text, N.Y.). WORKS WITHOUT OPUS NO.: *Duo concertant* in E, on themes from *Robert le Diable*, for piano and cello; 3 Études (F minor, A-flat, D-flat); 3 Mazurkas (G, B-flat, D); Mazurkas in C; in A minor (No. 2 in "Notre Temps"); in A minor, à Gaillard; in A and F; Fantasy in G-flat minor; Fantasy in B minor; Fantasy in G-flat; Var. No. VI from the *Hexaméron* (variations on the march from Bellini's *I Puritani*, the other variations being by Liszt, Thalberg, Pixis, Herz and Czerny); Valse in E; Valse in E minor; Polonaise (for Countess Victoire Skarbek); Polonaise (for Adalbert Zywny); Variations on the air, *Der Schweizerbub*; Polonaise in G-sharp minor; Polonaise in G-flat (authenticity doubtful); Polonaise in B-flat minor (*Farewell to Wilhelm Kolberg*); Nocturne in C-sharp minor (publ. as Adagio in 1875); Valse in E-flat and Valse in A-flat (from MSS found in possession of family of J. Elsner); Prelude in A-flat; Mazurka in F-sharp (authenticity doubtful).

Breitkopf & Härtel published a *Thematisches Verzeichniss der im Druck erschienenen Kompositionen von Fr. Chopin* (Leipzig, 1870); a second, augmented edition (1888) contains also a complete list of books written about Chopin up to 1888. Another thematic catalogue was publ. by F. Ch. Listy and H. Opienski (Warsaw, 1937). More current is J. E. M. Brown, *Chopin: An Index of His Works in Chronological Order* (London, 1960; 2d ed., N.Y., 1973). For a listing of manuscripts, see A. Hedley, *Catalogues des manuscrits de Frédéric Chopin* (Cracow, 1971).

BIBLIOGRAPHY: M. Karasowski, *F. Chopin Sein Leben, seine Werke u. Briefe* (2 vols., Dresden, 1877; in English, London, 1879; 3rd ed. 1938); J. Schucht, *F. Chopin und seine Werke* (Leipzig, 1879); A. Niggli, *F. Chopins Leben und Werke* (Leipzig, 1879); A. Audley, *Chopin, sa vie et ses œuvres* (Paris, 1880; largely drawn from Karasowski); F. Niecks, *F. Chopin as a Man and Musician* (2 vols., London, 1888; German translation by W. Langhans, Leipzig, 1890; a standard work); Ch. Willeby, *F. F. Chopin* (London, 1892); J. G. Huneker, *Chopin, the Man and His Music* (N.Y., 1900; new ed. 1925; very sympathetic, excellent analyses of the works); George Sand, *Histoire de Ma Vie* (5 vols., Paris, 1902–04); J. C. Hadden, *Chopin* (London, 1903; rev. ed. 1934); F. Hoesick, *Chopin* (Warsaw, 1904; 2nd ed., augmented to 3 vols., as *Chopin's Life and Works*, Warsaw, 1910–11; 3rd ed., in 2 vols., 1927; rev. and enlarged, 4 vols., Cracow, 1967–68); H. Leichtentritt, *F. Chopin* (Berlin, 1905); E. Poirée, *Chopin* (Paris, 1906); E. Redenbacher, *Chopin* (Leipzig, 1911); A. Weissmann, *Chopin* (Berlin, 1912); E. Ganche, *F. Chopin. Sa vie et ses œuvres* (Paris, 1913); Bernard Scharlitt, *Chopin* (1919); V. M. Gibert, *Chopin, sus obras* (in Spanish, 1920); Ad. Hillman, *Chopin* (1920); Henri Bidou, "Chopin," in *Les Maîtres de la Musique* (1926);

Z. Jachimecki, *Chopin* (Cracow, 1927; in French, 1930); G. de Pourtalès, *Chopin ou le poète* (French, German and English, 1927); Paul Landormy, "Chopin," *Musical Quarterly* (1929); Martial Douël "Chopin and Jenny Lind," *Musical Quarterly* (1932); Maurice Princet, *Chopin* (Paris, 1932); Basil Maine, *Chopin* (London 1933); G. Mariotti, *Chopin* (Florence, 1933); Leopold Binental, *Chopin* (Paris, 1934); Wm. Murdoch, *Chopin and His Life* (London, 1934); Ed. Ganche, *Voyages avec F. Chopin . . . illustrations et documents inédits* (Paris, 1934); John F. Porte, *Chopin, the Composer and His Music* (N.Y., 1935); Paul Egert, *Chopin* (Potsdam, 1936); Angelo Geddo, *Chopin* (Brescia, 1936); R. Koczalski, *F. Chopin* (Cologne, 1936); L. Bronarski, *Etudes sur Chopin* (3 vols., Lausanne, 1944) and *Chopin et l'Italie* (Lausanne, 1947); A. Hedley, *Chopin* (London, 1947); P. Leclerq, *Chopin et son époque* (Liège, 1947); K. Stromenger, *F. Chopin* (Warsaw, 1947); André Gide, *Notes sur Chopin* (Paris, 1948; English translation, N.Y., 1949); A. E. Cherbulliez, *F. Chopin, Leben und Werk* (Zürich, 1948); N. Slonimsky, "Chopiniana, Some Materials for a Biography," *Musical Quarterly* (Oct. 1948); B. E. Sydow, "O Date Urodzenia Fr. Chopina," *Ruch Muzyczny* 10 (1948), in which the author argues in favor of acceptance of Chopin's birth date as March 1, 1810, and publishes (for the first time) a facsimile of Chopin's letter to the Polish Literary Society of Paris, giving this date; M. Glinski, "Kiedy Urodzil Sie Chopin? *Ruch Muzyczny* 19 (1948), in which the author attempts to prove that Chopin was born on March 1, 1809. A. Cortot, *Aspects de Chopin* (Paris, 1949; in English as *In Search of Chopin*, London, 1951); T. Mayzner, *F. Chopin* (Berlin, 1949); W. Rehberg, *Chopin, sein Leben und seine Werke* (Zürich, 1949); H. Weinstock, *Chopin, the Man and His Music* (N.Y., 1949; in German as *Chopin, Mensch und Werk*, Munich, 1950); C. Wierzynski, *The Life and Death of Chopin* (N.Y., 1949; contains lurid correspondence with Potocka, which has since been proved spurious); R. Bory, *La Vie de F. Chopin par image* (Geneva, 1951); A. Cœuroy, *Chopin* (Paris, 1951); *Portret Fryderyka Chopina* (45 plates and annotations to Chopin's portraits; edited by M. Idzikowski and B. Sydow; Cracow, 1952); *Chopin w Kraju* (a lavish folio of portraits, music in facsimile, etc., Warsaw, 1955); A. Hedley, *Chopin* (London, 1957); I. Belza, *Fryderyk F. Chopin* (Moscow, 1960); J. M. Grenier, *Chopin* (Paris, 1964); J. Iwaszkiewicz, *Chopin* (Parigi, 1966).

CORRESPONDENCE: The earliest edition of selected letters is contained in Karasowski's biography; M. Karlowicz, *Souvenirs inédits de F. Chopin* (Paris, 1904); G. Petrucci, *Epistolario di F. Chopin* (Rocca San Casciano, 1907); B. Scharlitt, *F. Chopins gesammelte Briefe* (Leipzig, 1911); F. Hoesick, *Chopiniana* (vol. I, Correspondence, in Polish, Warsaw, 1912); H. Opienski, *Chopin; Collected Letters* (translated from the original Polish and French with a preface and editorial notes by E. L. Voynich; N.Y., 1931); complete edition of Chopin's letters (collected by H. Opienski) and documents, translated by S. Danysz, with index of works (Paris, 1933; preface by Paderewski); *Correspondance générale de F. Chopin* (3 vols.; translated into French and annotated by B. E. Sydow, Paris, 1953; vol. I appeared under the title *Correspondance;*

L'Aube, 1816-31); A. Hedley, *Selected Correspondence of Chopin* (London, 1962); A. Czartowski and Z. Jezewska, *Fryderyk Chopin* (3d ed., Warsaw, 1967); K. Kobylánska, ed. *Korespondencja Fryderyka Chopin z rodziną* (Warsaw, 1972).

CRITICISM; ANALYSIS: F. Liszt, *F. Chopin* (Paris, 1845; English translation by W. Cooke, London, 1877; also by J. Broadhouse, London, 1901; German translation by La Mara, Leipzig, 1880; reprinted in vol I. of F. Liszt's *Gesammelte Schriften*, Leipzig, 1910); W. von Lenz, in *Die grossen Pianoforte-Virtuosen* (Berlin, 1872; English translation, N.Y., 1899); J. Kleczinski, *F. Chopin. De l'interprétation de ses œuvres* (Paris, 1880; English translation, augmented by N. Janotha, as *Chopin's Greater Works*, London, 1896; German translation as *Chopins grössere Werke*, Leipzig, 1898); E. Gariel, *F. Chopin. La tradición de su música* (Mexico, 1895); G. C. Johnson, *A Handbook to Chopin's Works* (N.Y. 1905); H. Opienski, *Chopin as Creator* (in Polish; Warsaw, 1912); E. Stillman Kelley, *Chopin the Composer* (N.Y. 1913; a scholarly analysis); Ed. Ganche, *Dans le souvenir de Fr. Chopin* (1925); Helena Windakiewiczowa, *Die Urtypen Chopin'scher Melodik in der polnischen Volksmusik* (Cracow, 1926); Seweryn Barbag, *Über die Lieder von Fr. Chopin* (Lwow, 1927); H. Leichtentritt, *Analyse von Chopins Klavierwerken* (2 vols., 1921-22); J. P. Dunn, *Ornamentation in the Works of Chopin* (London, 1921; new ed. 1930); G. Abraham, *Chopin's Musical Style* (Oxford, 1939); E. Lopez Chavarri, *Chopin* (Valencia, 1950); Jan Holcman, *The Legacy of Chopin* (N.Y., 1954); Z. Lissa, ed. *The Book of the First International Musicological Conference Devoted to the Works of Frederick Chopin, Warsaw 16-22 February 1960* (Warsaw, 1963); A. Gauthier, *Chopin* (Paris, 1967); A. Walker, ed. *Frederic Chopin: Profiles of the Man and the Musician* (N.Y., 1967); Z. Lissa, ed. *Studia nad twórczóciq Fryderyka Chopina* (Cracow, 1970); the Norton Critical Score edition of the Preludes (N.Y., 1973) contains much valuable background, analysis, and commentary. Journals devoted to Chopin studies are *Rocznik chopinowski/Annales Chopin* (Warsaw, 1956) and *Chopin Jahrbuch* (Vienna).

For comprehensive bibliographies, see B. E. Sydow, *Bibliografia F. F. Chopin* (Warsaw 1949), and K. Michalowski, *Bibliografia chopinowska 1849-1969* (Cracow, 1970).

Chorbajian, John, American composer; b. New York, June 2, 1936. He studied composition with Vittorio Giannini at the Manhattan School of Music, obtaining his M.M. in 1959. Subsequently he became active as a teacher of piano and music theory in New York.

WORKS: Violin Sonata (1956); *Antigone*, one-act opera (1959); *The Magic of Music*, scene for mime with orchestra (1960); *The Crucifixion*, cantata for mixed chorus and orch. (1962); *The Swing* for children's chorus, flute and piano (1966); numerous choral pieces.

Chorley, Henry Fothergill, English writer on music; b. Blackley Hurst, Lancashire, Dec. 15, 1808; d. London, Feb. 16, 1872. He was at various times active as a dramatist, translator, art critic, poet, novelist and journalist; from 1831-68 was music critic of the London *Athenaeum.* During his extensive travels he heard all the best music of the day and met many musical celebrities; a partisan of Mendelssohn and Spohr, he was intolerant towards new musical ideas and attacked Chopin, Schumann and particularly Wagner, with extraordinary violence.

WRITINGS: *Music and Manners in France and Germany* (London, 1844; 3 vols.); *Modern German Music* (1854; 2 vols.); *Thirty Years' Musical Recollections* (1862, 2 vols.; abridged American edition, N.Y., 1926); an interesting *Autobiography, Memoir and Letters* (1873, 2 vols.; edited by H. G. Hewlett); *National Music of the World* (1880; edited by Hewlett; 3rd edition, 1912); *Handel Studies* (1859); a novel, *A Prodigy: a Tale of Music* (1866, 3 vols.).

Choron, Alexandre Étienne, French music editor and theorist; b. Caen, Oct. 21, 1771; d. Paris, June 28, 1834. A student of languages, and passionately fond of music, he took interest in music theory and through it in mathematics, which he studied till the age of 25; then, by several years' serious application to the Italian and German theorists, he acquired a thorough knowledge of the theory and practice of music. Becoming (1805) a partner in a music publishing firm, he devoted his entire fortune to editing and publishing classic and theoretical works and compositions, meanwhile contributing new works of his own. In 1811 he became a corresponding member of the Academie Française; he was entrusted with the reorganization of the maîtrises (training schools for church choirs), and was appointed conductor of religious festivals. In 1816, director of the Paris Opéra; reopened the Conservatoire (closed in 1815) as the École Royale de Chant et de Déclamation. Losing his directorship (1817) because he favored new works by unknown authors, he established, with a very moderate subsidy, the Institution de musique classique et religieuse, for which he labored indefatigably until the July Revolution (1830).

WRITINGS: *Principes d'accompagnement des écoles d'Italie* (1804); *Principes de composition des écoles d'Italie* (1808; 3 vols.; 2nd edition, 1816, 6 vols.); *Dictionnaire historique des musiciens* (1810–11, 2 vols.; with Fayolle); *Méthode élémentaire de musique et de plainchant* (1811); Francœur's *Traité général des voix et des instruments d'orchestre* (1813); translations of Albrechtsberger's *Gründliche Anweisung zur Komposition* and *Generalbassschule* (1814, 1815; new edition, 1830; English translation by A. Merrick, 1835), and of Azopardi's *Musico prattico* (1816); *Méthode concertante de musique à plusieurs parties* (written for his Conservatory, 1818; new edition, 1833); *Méthode de plainchant* (1818); *Manuel complet de musique vocale et instrumentale, ou Encyclopédie musicale* (1836–39; 6 vols. letter press and 5 vols. plates; with Lafage).

BIBLIOGRAPHY: L. E. Gautier, *Eloge de Choron* (Caen, 1845); H. Réty, *Notice historique sur Choron et son école* (Paris, 1873); J. Carlez, *Choron, sa vie et ses travaux* (Caen, 1880); G. Vauthier, *Choron sous l'Empire* (Poitiers, 1909).

Chotzinoff, Samuel, American pianist and music critic; b. Vitebsk, Russia, July 4, 1889; d. New York, Feb. 9, 1964. He was brought to America as a child; studied piano with Oscar Shack and music theory with Daniel Gregory Mason at Columbia Univ., graduating in 1912. He subsequently became an expert accompanist; toured with Zimbalist and Heifetz. In 1925 he turned to music criticism; served as music critic of the *N.Y. World* (1925–30) and the *N.Y. Post* (1934–41). He then occupied various teaching and administrative positions; was for several years music director of the National Broadcasting Company. He wrote a novel on Beethoven's life entitled *Eroica;* a book of reminiscences, *A Lost Paradise* (1955) and a monograph, *Toscanini, An Intimate Portrait* (N.Y., 1956). His autobiographical *Days at the Morn* and *A Little Night Music* were published posthumously in 1964.

Chou, Wen-chung, remarkable Chinese-American composer; b. Cheefoo, June 29, 1923 (corresponding to May 16, 1923, according to the lunar calendar in the Chinese Year of the Bear). He studied at the National Univ. of Chungking (1941–45); then went to the U.S.; took private lessons with Varèse in New York and with N. Slonimsky in Boston; then entered Columbia Univ., where he was a student of Otto Luening (M.A., 1954). In 1957 he received a Guggenheim Fellowship. In 1964 he joined the faculty of Columbia Univ. as teacher of composition. His music combines Chinese elements of structure and scale formation with free dissonant counterpoint related to the theory of "organized sound" of Varèse.

WORKS: *Landscapes* for orch. (San Francisco, Nov. 19, 1953); *7 Poems of T'ang Dynasty* for tenor, 7 wind instruments, piano and percussion (N.Y., March 16, 1952); *And the Fallen Petals,* a triolet for orch. (Louisville, Feb. 9, 1955); *In the Mode of Shang,* for chamber orch. (N.Y., Feb. 2, 1957); *Metaphors* for wind instruments (1960–61); *Cursive* for flute and piano (1963); *Riding the Wind* for wind ensemble (1964); *Pien* for piano, wind instruments and percussion (1966); *Yun* for wind instruments, 2 pianos and percussion (1969). In 1968 Chou Wen-chung completed Varèse's unfinished work *Nocturnal* for voices and instruments.

Chouquet, Adolphe-Gustave, French writer on music; b. Le Havre, April 16, 1819; d. Paris, Jan. 30, 1886. He lived in America as a music teacher from 1840–60; then in Paris. He twice won the Prix Bordin: in 1864 for a history of music from the 14th to 18th centuries, and in 1868 for *Histoire de la musique dramatique en France depuis ses origines jusqu'à nos jours* (published, 1873). From 1871, was custodian of the collection of instruments in the Conservatory; in 1875 he published a catalogue of them (2nd edition, 1884; supplemented by L. Pillaut, 1894; 1899; 1903).

Christiani, Adolf Friedrich, German pianist; b. Kassel, March 8, 1836; d. Elizabeth, N.J., Feb. 10, 1885. He went to London in 1855; then to America, teaching in Poughkeepsie, Pittsburgh, Cincinnati and New York. He wrote a theoretical work, *The Principles of Musical Expression in Pianoforte-playing* (N.Y., 1886; German ed. Leipzig, *Das Verständnis im Klavierspiel*).

Christiansen, Fredrik Melius, Norwegian-American choral conductor; b. Eidsvold, April 1, 1871; d. Northfield, Minn., June 1, 1955. He emigrated to the U.S. in 1888; studied at the Northwestern Cons. of Music; then went to Germany where he took courses at the Leipzig Cons. (1897–99). Returning to America, he served as director of the School of Music at St. Olaf's College, in Northfield, Minn.; organized the important group, the St. Olaf's Lutheran Choir there. He published several useful choral collections: *St. Olaf Choir Series* (6 vols., 1920); *Young Men's Choral Assembly for Schools* (1936); edited *50 Famous Hymns for Women's Voices* (1914) and published *Practical Modulation* (1916).

BIBLIOGRAPHY: L.N. Bergmann, *Music Master of the Middle West* (Minneapolis, 1944).

Christiansen, Olaf, American choral conductor, son of **Fredrik Melius Christiansen**; b. Minneapolis, Aug. 12, 1901. He succeeded his father as director of the music school at St. Olaf's at Northfield, Minn., in 1955.

Christie, Winifred, English pianist; b. Stirling, Feb. 26, 1882; d. London, Feb. 8, 1965. She was the second wife of the Hungarian pianist Emanuel Moór and made loyal propaganda for the Moór Duplex Piano, consisting of a double keyboard with a coupler between the two manuals. She was not successful in her task.

Christoff, Boris, eminent Bulgarian bass-baritone; b. Plovdiv, May 18, 1914. He studied law, and at the same time sang in a chorus in Sofia. A private stipend enabled him to go to Rome where he studied voice with Stracciari. In 1946 he made a successful debut in a solo recital in Rome, and in 1947 sang at La Scala, Milan. He excelled particularly in the role of Boris Godunov, which he sang in Russia; his interpretation recalled that of Chaliapin; he made his American debut in that role at the San Francisco Opera House on Sept. 25, 1956 with great acclaim. His operatic repertory includes about 40 parts in 6 languages.

BIBLIOGRAPHY: A monograph on Christoff by O. Deikowa was published in Bulgarian (Sofia, 1966); see also Fr. Barker, *Voice of the Opera: Boris Christoff* (London, 1951); G. Lauri Volpi, *Voci parallele: Boris Christoff* (Milan, 1953).

Christoff, Dimiter, Bulgarian composer; b. Sofia, Oct. 2, 1933. He studied composition with Goleminov at the Bulgarian State Cons. (1951–56); and later taught there. Like so many other Bulgarian composers, he utilized in his music the rich motivic resources and asymmetrical rhythmic figures of Balkan folksongs; however, these usages are not literal in his compositions, which are modernistic in their technique.

WORKS: Piano Concerto (1955); Sinfonietta for string orch. (1956); *Poem* for orch. (1957); 3 symphonies (1959, 1964, 1968); *Overture* (1961); *Symphonic Episodes* (1962); Violin Concerto (1966); *Chamber Suite* for flute, piccolo, and chamber orch. (1966); Cello Concerto (1969; Sofia, March 10, 1971); *Concert Miniatures* for orch. or piano (1970); *Overture with Fanfares* (1973); *Suite* for wind quintet (1953); *2 Dances* for trumpet and piano (1960); Solo Cello Sonata (1965); Concerto for 3 small drums and 5 instru-

ments (1967); String Quartet (1970); Quartet for flute, viola, harp and harpsichord (1972); 4 piano sonatas (1962, 1974, 1974, 1974); choruses; songs. He published six theoretical works, including *Hypothesis about the Polyphonic Structure* (Sofia, 1970) and *The Composer and the Public Spirit* (Sofia, 1975).

Christopher, Cyril (Stanley), English organist and composer; b. Oldbury, Worcestershire, June 23, 1897. He studied organ with Alfred Hollins; held numerous posts as church organist and choral conductor; also taught music theory at the Birmingham School of Music. He wrote mainly for chorus; among his instrumental works are a Fantasy-Trio for Clarinet, Violin and Piano (1939); Trio for Oboe, Bassoon and Piano (1954); Oboe Sonata (1956); Serenade for Wind Instruments, Cello and Double Bass (1967), and 2 short symph. poems *Midsummer Night* and *The Lone Shore.*

Christoskov, Peter, Bulgarian composer and violinist; b. Sofia, March 8, 1917. He studied violin at the Bulgarian State Cons. in Sofia, graduating in 1936; then went to Berlin where he continued his violin studies; returning to Bulgaria, he was appointed head of the instrumental department of the Bulgarian State Cons. In his own works he often applies the asymmetrical rhythms of Bulgarian folksongs, using dissonant harmonies for coloristic effects.

WORKS: *Moto Perpetuo* for string orch. (1956); 2 violin concertos (1958, 1961); Concerto for Orch. (1964); *Children's Album* for violin and chamber orch. (1966); Aria and Toccata for violin and orch. (1967); *Concerto-Improvisation* for Cello and Orch. (1970); Piano Concerto (1972); *Symphonic Sketches* (1973); *Concerto-Poem* for Cello and Orch. (1973).

Christou, Jani, remarkable Greek composer; b. Heliopolis, Egypt, Jan. 8, 1926, to Greek parents; d. in an automobile accident, with his wife, near Athens, on his 44th birthday, Jan. 8, 1970. He studied at Victoria College, Alexandria; then took courses in philosophy under Wittgenstein at King's College in Cambridge, England (M.A., 1948); concurrently studied composition with Hans Redlich in Letchworth (1945–48); then enrolled in the summer courses of the Accademia Musicale Chigiana in Siena (1949–50); during the same period he attended Karl Jung's lectures on psychology in Zürich. Christou returned to Alexandria in 1951; then lived on his family estate on the island of Chios. He evolved a system of composition embracing the totality of human and metaphysical expression, forming a "philosophical structure" for which he designed a surrealistic graphic notation involving a "psychoid factor," symbolized by the Greek letter psi; aleatory practices are indicated by the drawing of a pair of dice; a sudden stop, by a dagger, etc. His score *Enantiodromia (Opposed Pathways)* for orch. (1965, revised 1968; first performed in Oakland, Calif., Feb. 18, 1969), in such a graphic notation, is reproduced in the avant-garde publication *Source 6* (1969). His notation also includes poetry, choreographic acting, special lighting, film and projection meant to envelope the listener on all sides. At his death he left sketches for a set of 130 multi-media compositions of a category he called *Anaparastasis* ("proto-performances, meant to revive primeval rituals as adapted to modern culture"). His other works include *Phoenix Music* for orch. (1948–49); Symph. No. 1 (1950; London, April 29, 1951); *Latin Mass* for chorus, brass and percussion (1953; posthumous, Athens, Sept. 26, 1971); *David's Psalms* for baritone, chorus and orch. (1953); *6 Songs* for voice and piano, to poems by T. S. Eliot (1955, orchestrated 1957); Symph. No. 2 for chorus and orch. (1954–58; uses an adapted version of the *Latin Mass* as its finale); *Gilgamesh*, oratorio (1958); *Patterns and Permutations* for orch. (1960; Athens, March 11, 1963); Symph. No. 3 (1959–62); Toccata for Piano and Orch. (1962); *The 12 Keys* for mezzo-soprano and chamber ensemble (1962); *The Breakdown*, opera (1964); *Tongues of Fire*, Pentecost oratorio (1964; English Bach Festival, Oxford, June 27, 1964); *Mysterion*, oratorio for soli, 3 choirs, actors, orch. and tape, to ancient Egyptian myths (1965–66); *Praxis for 12* for 11 strings and pianist-percussionist-conductor (1966; Athens, April 18, 1966; an alternate version exists, titled simply *Praxis*, for 44 strings and pianist-percussionist-conductor); *Oresteia*, unfinished "super-opera," after Aeschylus (1967–70). Performable works from the cycle *Anaparastasis* are: *The Strychnine Lady* for female viola player, 2 groups of massed strings, brass, percussion, tapes, metal sheet, sound-producing objects and toys, a red cloth and 5 actors (Athens, April 3, 1967); *Anaparastasis I (Astron)* for baritone and instrumental ensemble (Munich, Nov. 12, 1968); *Anaparastasis III (The Pianist)* for actor, variable instrumental ensemble and 3 stereo tapes (Munich, Nov. 13, 1969); *Epicycle* for variable instrumental ensemble that may take a chiliad or a hebdomad, a nanosecond or a quindecillion of non-zero moments to perform (concise version, Athens, Dec. 15, 1968; extended version, Athens, Dec. 20, 1968); stage music for *The Persians* (1965), *The Frogs* (1966) and *Oedipus Rex* (1969).

Christov, Dobri, noted Bulgarian composer; b. Varna, Bulgaria, Dec. 14, 1875; d. Sofia, Jan. 23, 1941. He was first a school teacher; then pupil of Dvořák at Prague; spent the greater part of his career as director and teacher of composition of the Sofia Conservatory. He composed orchestral suites based on folk tunes; an overture, *Jvailo*; the ballad, *Zar Samuil*; 50 Bulgarian choral songs; also edited Bulgarian folksongs.

Christy, Edwin P., American minstrel show promoter and performer; b. Philadelphia, 1815; d. New York, May 21, 1862. About 1842 he founded the Christy Minstrels, which played a decisive role in the formation of a typical American variety show, consisting of songs, comic skits and short plays and parodies. He opened his enterprise in Buffalo; in 1846 he introduced his troupe in N.Y. and played there for 10 years. It was Christy who had Stephen Foster write his most famous "Ethiopian" songs for him; as was common in his time, Christy appropriated the authorship of these songs, but was decent enough to give Foster credit when the songs became greatly popular. Christy became mentally deranged and ended his life by jumping out of a window.

Chrysander, Karl Franz Friedrich, eminent German music historian and critic; b. Lübtheen, Mecklenburg, July 8, 1826; d. Bergedorf, Sept. 3, 1901. He received his *Dr. Phil.* from Rostock Univ.; from 1868–71 and 1875–82, was editor of the *Allgemeine musikalische Zeitung*, contributing many articles (sketch of history of music printing, 1879; papers on the Hamburg opera under Keiser, Kusser, et al., 1878–79); from 1885 he edited (with Spitta and Adler) the *Vierteljahrsschrift für Musikwissenschaft*. He also edited two *Jahrbücher für musikalische Wissenschaft* (1863; 1867), with important papers by various writers. He published two pamphlets, *Über die Molltonart in Volksgesängen* and *Über das Oratorium* (1853); *Händels biblische Oratorien in geschichtlicher Entwicklung* (1896; 4th ed. 1922); he also edited *Bachs Klavierwerke* (1856), shared in the editing of the *Denkmäler der Tonkunst* (5 vols., 1869–71), and was co-editor of *Allgemeine deutsche Biographien*. Together with G. Gervinus he founded, in 1856, the Deutsche Händelgesellschaft for the purpose of publishing a complete edition of Handel's works from the original MSS, but before long the other members lost interest, and Chrysander and Gervinus alone constituted the society. At their own expense they set up a little printing shop at Bergedorf, near Hamburg; in 1859 King George of Hannover granted Chrysander an annual subvention of 1000 thaler, which, after the annexation of Hannover by Prussia in 1866, was continued by the Prussian government. After the death of Gervinus in 1871, Chrysander, with the assistance of one printer and one engraver, continued work on the project until volume 100 (the last) was completed in 1894. During the preparation of this monumental edition he made several protracted visits to London to study Handel's autograph scores and others, in the possession of V. Schölcher, containing corrections and remarks in Handel's own hand. Of the latter he subsequently acquired 80 volumes for the music library at Hamburg. The enormous amount of biographical material Chrysander had collected led him to begin a life of Handel, of which he wrote two volumes and half of a third, bringing the life down to 1740 (Leipzig, 1858–67). Max Seiffert undertook the responsible task of completing Chrysander's work. This publication is regarded as the definitive edition of Handel's works; it is valuable both for its emphasis on word-tone relations, and for its faithful restoration of the original ornamentation of arias, and the original orchestration.

BIBLIOGRAPHY: J. Schaeffer, *F. Chrysander in seinen Klavierauszügen zur deutschen Händel-Ausgabe* (Leipzig, 1876); W. Weber, *Erläuterungen von Händels Oratorien in Chrysanders neuer Übersetzung und Bearbeitung* (3 vols.; Augsburg, 1898–1902); H. Kretzschmar," "Fr. Chrysander," *Jahrbuch Peters* (1902); E. Bernoulli, *Oratorientexte Händels* (1905); B. Baselt, "Beiträge zur Chrysander-Forschung," *Händel-Jahrbuch* (1969/70).

Chrysanthos of Madytos, learned Greek cleric and music theorist; b. in Madytos, Turkey (hence, known as "of Madytos") about 1770; d. in Bursa, Turkey, about 1843. He was Bishop of the Greek Orthodox Church in Constantinople, and taught at the music school of the Patriarchate there from 1815 to 1821. He subsequently served as Bishop in Durazzo, in Smyrna, and finally in Bursa, where he died. He undertook the reform of the post-Byzantine music notation by reducing the number of neumes and interval indexes; also revived the division of scales into the ancient Greek modes; diatonic, chromatic and enharmonic. He publ. two manuals in the Greek language: *Introduction into the Theory and Practice of Church Music* (Paris, 1821) and *Great Music Instruction* (Trieste, 1832).

Chueca, Federico, Spanish composer of zarzuelas; b. Madrid, May 5, 1846; d. there, June 20, 1908. He was a medical student; organized a band at the Univ. of Madrid; also conducted theater orchestras. He began to compose for the stage in collaboration with Valverde who helped him to harmonize and orchestrate his melodies. Thanks to his prodigious facility, he wrote a great number of zarzuelas, of which *La Gran Via,* produced in Madrid (July 2, 1886), became his greatest success, obtaining nearly 1000 performances in Madrid alone; it has also been performed many times in Latin America and the U.S. The march from his zarzuela *Cadiz* served for a time as the Spanish national anthem; dances from his *El año pasado por agua* and *Locuras madrileñas* also enjoyed great popularity. Chueca is regarded as one of the creators of the "género chico" (light genre) of Spanish stage music.
BIBLIOGRAPHY: M. Zurita, *Historia del género chico* (Madrid, 1920); J. Delito y Piñuela, *Origen y Apogeo del género chico* (Madrid, 1949).

Chvála, Emanuel, Czech critic and composer; b. Prague, Jan. 1, 1851; d. there, Oct. 28, 1924. He was mainly active as a critic; he published articles in Czech and in German dealing with Czech music, of which *Ein Vierteljahrhundert böhmischer Musik* (1887) was a pioneer work. He was also the composer of an opera, *Zaboj,* written in 1907, and produced in Prague on March 9, 1918.

Chwatal, Franz Xaver, Bohemian pianist and pedagogue; b. Rumburg, June 19, 1808; d. Elmen, June 24, 1879. He settled in Magdeburg as piano teacher; published a great number of piano pieces; his two piano methods were much used.

Chybinski, Adolf, eminent Polish musicologist; b. Cracow, March 29, 1880; d. Poznan, Oct. 31, 1952. He studied at the Univ. of Cracow; later in Munich with Sandberger and Kroyer; also with Thuille (1905–7); *Dr. phil.,* Munich, 1908. In 1912, instructor at Lwow Univ.; 1921, professor there; from 1916 also professor of theory at the Cons.; 1924, music counselor for the Polish State Art Dept.
WRITINGS (mostly in Polish): *Wagner's Meistersinger* (1908); *The Organ Tablatures of Joh. v. Lublin* (2 vols., 1911–14); *J. S. Bach* (2 vols., 1913); *Music Instruments of the Tatra* (1924–27); *Cracovian Music in the 17th Century* (Tarnov, 1928); *Musical Relations between Poland and France in the 16th Century* (Poznan, 1929); *Dictionary of Ancient Polish Musicians Before 1800* (in Polish; Cracow, 1949). He also translated German music books into Polish (Hausegger's *Musik als Ausdruck*); edited *Publications de Musique*

Ancienne Polonaise (17th vol. published in Warsaw, 1938; contains Bartolomei Perkiel's *Missa Pulcherrima ad instar Praenestini*).

Ciamaga, Gustav, Canadian electronic composer; b. London, Ontario, April 10, 1930. He studied music theory with Weinzweig and Beckwith at the Univ. of Toronto (1953–56); studied composition and musicology with Arthur Berger, Harold Shapero and Irving Fine at Brandeis Univ.; in 1963 he was appointed to the music faculty at the Univ. of Toronto, where he is director of its electronic music studio. His electronic scores include: *Ottawa 1967* (1966); *Curtain Raiser* (1969); *One-Part Invention* (1965); 8 *Two-Part Inventions* (1965–70); *Ragamuffin Nos. 1* and 2 (1967); he wrote several scores of computer music, among them *Canon for Stravinsky* (1972); for voice, instruments and tape he composed *Solipsism While Dying* (1972).

Ciccolini, Aldo, Italian pianist; b. Naples, Aug. 15, 1925. He studied with Paolo Denza at the Naples Cons.; in 1949 he was the winner of the Long-Thibaud prize in Paris. He toured in France, Spain and South America; on Nov. 2, 1950, he made his American debut with Tchaikovsky's Concerto No. 1 (N.Y. Philharmonic). He has since appeared with several major orchestras in the U.S., and has also continued his concerts in Europe. In 1971 he was appointed prof. at the Paris Cons. Ciccolini possesses a virtuoso technique combined with a lyrical sense of phrasing.

Ciconia, Jean (Johannes), Walloon theorist and composer; b. Liège, c.1335; d. Padua, between Dec. 11 and Dec. 24, 1411. Little is known about his life; he was in Italy from 1358 to 1367; was in Liège from 1372 until 1401. In 1402 he went to Padua where he was a canon. A treatise by him entitled *De proportionibus musicae,* which he completed shortly before his death, is extant. Several of his musical compositions are preserved in Italian libraries; modern reprints are in the *Denkmäler der Tonkunst in Österreich* (vols. VII and XXXI). Ciconia's significance lies in his early use of musical devices that did not become current until much later; he applies the technique of French isorhythmic style as well as canonic imitation.
BIBLIOGRAPHY: Suzanne Clercx, *Johannes Ciconia de Leodio* (Amsterdam, 1953); see also her addendum, "Question de Chronologie," *Revue belge de Musicologie* (1955).

Cifra, Antonio, Italian composer; b. probably near Terracina, 1584; d. Loreto, Oct. 2, 1629. He was a choirboy in the church of San Luigi, Rome; 1594–96, pupil of B. Nanini; also studied with Palestrina; 1609, maestro di cappella at the Collegio Germanico, Rome; 1609–22 and from 1626, maestro at Santa Casa di Loreto; 1623–25, at San Giovanni in Laterano, Rome. A prolific composer, he is considered one of the best of the Roman school; he published (between 1600 and 1638) 5 books of motets; 3 of psalms; 5 of Masses; 10 sets of *concerti ecclesiastici* (over 200 numbers); many more motets and psalms (in 2–12 parts); antiphons; litanies; madrigals; *ricercari; Scherzi ed arie a 1, 2, 3 e 4 voci, per cantar del clavicembalo, etc.*

BIBLIOGRAPHY: article by A. Cametti, in *Rivista Musicale Italiana* XXI (1915).

Cigna, Gina, French soprano; b. Paris, March 6, 1900. She studied at the Paris Cons.; made her operatic debut at La Scala, Milan, in 1929; sang at the Metropolitan Opera, N.Y., in 1937 (debut as Aida, Feb. 6, 1937). After a few more performances in N.Y., she returned to Europe, and settled in Milan as a voice teacher. From 1953 to 1957 she taught at the Royal Cons. in Toronto.

Cikker, Ján, eminent Slovak composer; b. Banská Bystrica, July 29, 1911. He studied composition at the Prague Cons. with Jaroslav Křička and Vítězslav Novák; also took a course in conducting with Felix Weingartner in Vienna. In 1951 he was appointed Prof. of composition at the Bratislava Cons. An exceptionally prolific composer, Cikker is distinguished particularly in his works for the musical theater; his operas enjoyed greatly merited success in their productions in Czechoslovakia and Germany. In his music he has developed an idiom deeply rooted in the melorhythmic patterns of Slovak folksongs, while his harmonic and contrapuntal treatment is marked by effective modernistic devices, making use of unresolved dissonances and atonal melodic patterns.
WORKS: 6 operas: *Juro Jánošík* (1950–53; Bratislava, Nov. 10, 1954), *Beg Bajazid (Prince Bajazid;* Bratislava, Feb. 16, 1957), *Mr. Scrooge,* after Dickens' *A Christmas Carol* (1958–59; produced in a German version under the title, *Abend, Nacht und Morgen,* Kassel, Oct. 5, 1963), *Vzkriesenie (Resurrection),* after Tolstoy's novel (1961; Prague, May 18, 1962; written in a highly tense, atonal and Romantically expressive modern idiom), *Hra o láske a smrti (A Play About Love and Death),* after Romain Rolland (1967; Munich, Aug. 1, 1969), and *Coriolanus,* after Shakespeare (1972; Prague, March 21, 1974); Symphony in C (1930); *Epitaph,* symph. poem (1931); *Symphonic Prologue* (1934); *Capriccio* for orch. (1936); *Spring Symphony* (1937); Sinfonietta (1940; instrumentation of his piano sonatina); a cantata *Cantus Filiorum* (1940); the symphonic trilogy *About Life: Léto (Summer,* 1941), *Vojak a matka (The Soldier and the Mother,* 1943) and *Ráno (Morning,* 1944–46); Piano Concertino (1942); *Slovak Suite* for orch. (1942); *The Bucolic Poem,* ballet music (1944); *Spomienky (Recollections)* for 5 wind instruments and string orch. (1947); *Dupák,* folk dance for chamber orch. (1950); *Dramatic Fantasia* for orch. (1957); *Orchestrálne štúdie k činohre (Orchestral Studies on a Drama,* 1965); *Hommage à Beethoven* for orch. (1970); *Variations on a Slovak Folk Song* for orch. (1971; also for piano); *Epitaph (Over an Old Trench),* symph. poem (1973); *Symphony 1945* (1974–75; Bratislava, May 22, 1975); 2 string quartets (1935); Piano Sonatina (1933); 3 Etudes *(Tatra Mountain Streams)* for piano (1954); *What Children Told Me* for piano (1957); film music.

Cilèa, Francesco, Italian opera composer; b. Palmi, Calabria, July 26, 1866; d. Varazze, Nov. 20, 1950. He studied at the Naples Cons. (1879–89) with Cesi (piano) and Serrao (composition); taught piano there (1890–92); then harmony at the Istituto Musicale in Florence (1896–1904); was head of the Palermo Cons. (1913–16); director of the Majella Cons., Naples (1916–35). He was a member of the Reale Accademia Musicale in Florence (1898) and a knight of the Order of the Crown of Italy (1893).
WORKS: the operas *Gina* (Naples, Feb. 9, 1889), *La Tilda* (Florence, April 7, 1892), *L'Arlesiana* (after Daudet; Milan, Nov. 27, 1897; later revised from 4 to 3 acts and produced in Milan, Oct. 22, 1898), *Adriana Lecouvreur,* after Scribe (his most famous opera; Milan, Nov. 6, 1902; Covent Garden, Nov. 8, 1904; Metropolitan Opera, Nov. 26, 1906), *Gloria* (La Scala, April 15, 1907); *Poema Sinfonico* for solo, chorus and orch. (Genoa, July 12, 1913); Piano Trio (1886); Cello Sonata (1888); Variations for Violin and Piano (1931); piano pieces; songs.
BIBLIOGRAPHY: Ettore Moschino, *Sulle opere di Francesco Cilèa* (Milan, 1932); C. P. Gaianus, *Francesco Cilèa e la sua nuova ora* (Bologna, 1939); T. d'Amico, *Francesco Cilèa* (Milan, 1960).

Cima, Giovanni Paolo, Italian organist and composer; b. Milan, c.1570; d. during the first half of the 17th century. In 1609 he was organist at the cathedral of Milan. Publications of his works, including *Concerti ecclesiastici* and motets, appeared between 1598 and 1622. His *Partito di Ricercari e Canzoni alla francese* (Milan, 1606) is a keyboard collection with an appendix containing rules for tuning keyboard instruments. The *Canzoni alla francese* of this collection are specially written for keyboard, and the *ricercari* are highly developed in their use of imitation. A modern reprint of a *Ricercare per organo* is contained in L. Torchi's *L'Arte Musicale in Italia* (vol. III).

Cimadoro, Giovanni Battista, Italian composer; b. Venice, 1761; d. Bath, England, Feb. 27, 1805. After early successes in Italy, where he produced an opera *Pimmaglione (Pygmalion;* Venice, Jan. 26, 1790), he settled in London; several arias from *Pygmalion* were published in London, and acquired considerable popularity. While in England, he used the shortened form of his name, **Cimador.**

Cimara, Pietro, Italian conductor; b. Rome, Nov. 10, 1887; d. Milan, Oct. 1, 1967. He was educated at the Accademia Santa Cecilia; made his debut as conductor in 1916 in Rome. In 1927 he began conducting at the Metropolitan Opera; remained at this post for 30 years. He composed numerous songs, published in Italy and America.

Cimarosa, Domenico, eminent Italian composer; b. Aversa, near Naples, Dec. 17, 1749; d. Venice, Jan. 11, 1801. The son of a poor mason and early orphaned, he attended the charity school of the Minorites; his first music teacher was Polcano, organist of the monastery. His talent was so marked that in 1761 he obtained a free scholarship to the Conservatorio di Santa Maria di Loreto, where he was taught singing by Manna and Sacchini, counterpoint by Fenaroli, and composition by Piccinni. In 1770 his oratorio *Giuditta* was performed in Rome; in 1772, having graduated from the Conservatory, he produced his first opera, *Le Stravaganze del Conte,* at Naples, with moderate success. But with *La finta parigina*, given next season at the Teatro Nuovo, Naples, he was fairly launched on a dramatic career singularly free from artistic reverses. His ease and rapidity of composition were phenomenal; in 29 years he wrote nearly 80 operas. His fame grew steadily, eventually rivaling that of Paisiello. In 1778 Cimarosa brought out *L'Italiana in Londra* in Rome, and lived, until 1781, alternately in Rome and Naples; following the custom of the period, he wrote one opera after another specially for the city in which it was to be performed. His speed of composition was such that during the year 1781 he brought out two operas in Naples, one in Rome, and two in Turin. His works became known far beyond the bounds of Italy; they were performed not only by Italian opera troupes in all European capitals, but also by foreign opera companies, in translation. After Paisiello's return from St. Petersburg, where he had served from 1776–85 as court composer, his post was offered to Cimarosa. He accepted, and set out for St. Petersburg in the autumn of 1787. His journey there was like a triumphant procession; at the courts of Florence, Vienna and Warsaw, he was overwhelmed with attentions; and he arrived in St. Petersburg, Dec. 2, 1787, wayworn and suffering from the wintry weather, but confident of success. Here he produced three operas, and during the three years of his stay wrote various other compositions for the court and nobility, including a ballet, *La felicità inaspettata* (Feb. 24, 1788) and a dramatic cantata, *Atene edificata* (June 29, 1788). But as Catherine the Great did not care for his choral works, he was replaced by Sarti, and in 1791 he left Russia; in the autumn of that year he arrived in Vienna, where Emperor Leopold engaged him at a salary of 12,000 florins as Kapellmeister. At Vienna, at the age of 42, he brought out his masterpiece, *Il Matrimonio segreto* (Feb. 7, 1792), the success of which eclipsed not only that of his former works but that of the works of all rivals, not excepting Mozart. It is probably the sole survivor, on the present-day stage, of all Cimarosa's dramatic works. Cimarosa remained long enough in Vienna to write two more operas; 1793 found him once more at home in Naples, where his *Matrimonio segreto* aroused unexampled enthusiasm, having 67 consecutive performances, the illustrious composer himself playing the cembalo for the first seven representations. In 1794 he visited Venice to bring out *Gli Orazi e Curiazi*; in 1796 and 1798 he was in Rome, periodically returning to Naples, and all the time actively engaged in operatic composition. In 1798, he was seriously ill at Naples; the year after, having openly taken part in the Neapolitan revolutionary demonstration on the entrance of the French army into the city, he was imprisoned for a number of days. He then went to Venice, and was at work on a new opera, *Artemisia*, when death suddenly overtook him. It was rumored abroad that he had been poisoned by order of Queen Caroline of Naples, as a dangerous revolutionist; the rumor was so persistent, and popular embitterment so great, that the Pope's personal physician, Piccioli, was sent to make an examination; according to his sworn statement, Cimarosa died of a gangrenous abdominal tumor.

Comedy opera was Cimarosa's *forte*: in his happiest moments he rivals Mozart; even in 'opera seria' many

of his efforts are worthy of a place in the repertory. The fluidity and fecundity of his melodic vein, his supreme command of form, and his masterly control of orchestral resources still excite astonishment and admiration. He was the peer of his great Italian contemporary, Paisiello.

WORKS: Of the 76 operas known as his, some of the finest are: *La finta parigina* (Naples, 1773); *Il Fanatico per gli antichi Romani* (Naples, 1777); *L'Italiana in Londra* (Rome, Dec. 28, 1778); *L'Infedeltà fedele* (Naples, July 20, 1779); *Caio Mario* (Rome, Jan., 1780); *Il convito di pietra* (Venice, Dec. 27, 1781); *Giannina e Bernardone* (Venice, Nov., 1781); *La ballerina amante* (Naples, 1782); *Artaserse* (Turin, Dec. 26, 1784); *Le Trame deluse* (Naples, Sept., 1786); *L'Impressario in angustie* (Naples, Oct., 1786); *Le vergine del sole* (St. Petersburg, Nov. 6, 1789); *Il Matrimonio segreto* (Vienna, Feb. 7, 1792); given in English with great success at the Metropolitan Opera in 1937); *Le astuzie femminili* (Naples, Aug. 16, 1794); *Orazi e Curiazi* (Venice, Dec. 26, 1796). He also produced three oratorios; several cantatas; Masses in four parts, with instrumental accompaniment; psalms, motets, Requiems, arias, cavatinas, solfeggi, and a great variety of other vocal works; 7 symphonies; cembalo sonatas (of which 32 were edited and published by F. Boghen, Paris, 1926).

BIBLIOGRAPHY: P. Cambiasi, *Notizie sulla vita e sulle opere di D. Cimarosa* (Milan, 1901); F. Polidoro, "La vita e le opere di D. Cimarosa," in *Atti del' Accademia Pontiniana* (1902); A. della Corte, *L'opera comica italiana nel 1700* (1925); R. Vitale, *D. Cimarosa* (Aversa, 1929); G. Biamonti, *Il matrimonio segreto* (Rome, 1930); M. Tibaldi Chiesa, *Cimarosa e il suo tempo* (Milan, 1939); Carl Engel, "A Note on Cimarosa's *Il matrimonio segreto*," *Musical Quarterly* (April 1947); A. Mooser, *Annales de la musique et des musiciens en Russie au XVIIIᵉ siècle* (Geneva, 1951; pp. 451–455); E. Ferrari Barassi, "Cimarosa clavicembalista," in *Scritti in onore di Luigi Ronga* (Milan, 1973).

Ciortea, Tudor, Rumanian composer; b. Braşov, Dec. 11, 1903. He studied composition with Joseph Jongen in Brussels and with Nadia Boulanger and Paul Dukas in Paris; returning to Rumania, he took a course with Otescu at the Bucharest Cons.; in 1949 he joined its staff. In his music he adopts the models of French impressionism; his songs to texts by Rumanian poets have a fine lyric quality.

WORKS: *Suită maramureşeană* for orch. (1949); Passacaglia and Toccata for orch. (1957); Concerto for String Orch. (1958); *Variaţiuni pe o temă de colind* for piano and orch. (1969); Clarinet Concerto (1973); Violin Sonata (1946); Cello Sonata (1946; revised 1958); 2 string quartets (1952, 1954); Piano Quintet (1957); Flute sonata (1959); octet, *The Adventures of Păcală* (1961; revised 1966); Clarinet Sonata (1962); *Canzona and Burlesque* for horn and piano (1962); Trumpet Sonata (1964); Brass Quintet (1970); *Danse tzigane* for piano (1927); *Suite on Themes of Tirnave* for piano (1948); 3 piano sonatas (1950, 1953, 1959); *3 Pieces* for piano (1955); Piano Sonatina (1960); *4 Songs from Maramures* for piano (1969); many songs, with diverse instruments.

Cipollini, Gaetano, Italian composer; b. Tropea, Cantanzaro, Feb. 28, 1851; d. Milan, Oct. 1, 1935. He was a pupil of Francesco Coppa; composed the effective melodrama in 3 acts, *Gennariello* (Milan, June 1, 1891); *Il piccolo Haydn,* lyric comedy (Como, Jan. 24, 1893); *Ninon de Lenclos,* lyric comedy (Milan, Dec. 3, 1895); a large number of *romanze* for voice; piano pieces. A five-act opera, *Simeta,* remained in MS.

Cipra, Milo, Croatian composer; b. Vares, Oct. 13, 1906. He studied composition with Bersa at the Zagreb Music Academy, graduating in 1933; taught there after 1941 and was its dean (1961-71). In his early composition he followed the national school, with thematic elements derived from folksong patterns of Croatia; then adopted a severe structural idiom, gradually increasing in modernity.
WORKS: 2 symphonies (1948, 1952); Sinfonietta (1934, revised 1946); *Dubrovački divertimento* for chamber orch. (1955-56); Concerto for strings (1956); *Sunčev put* (*Sun's Way*) for wind orch., piano, harp and percussion (1958-59); *3 susreta* (*Encounters*) for orch. (1961); *Epitaf* for orch. (1961); *Leda,* symph. pantomime (1965); 5 string quartets (1930, 1932, 1935, 1938, 1972); Piano Trio (1937); Violin Sonata (1944); Cello Sonata (1946); *Musica sine nomine* for 5 winds, piano and voice (1963); *Svitanje* (*Aubade*) for wind quintet (1965); Piano Sonata (1954); songs.

Cirino, Giulio, Italian bass; b. Rome, Feb. 15, 1880; d. there, Feb. 26, 1970. He made his opera debut in Rome in 1903; subsequently sang at La Scala in Milan; was on the roster of the Teatro Colón in Buenos Aires from 1909 to 1923; retired from the stage in 1935. He was particularly successful in buffo roles, in the Italian repertory; but he also sang in Wagner's operas.

Cisneros (née **Broadfoot**), **Eleanora de,** American contralto; b. New York, Nov. 1, 1878; d. there, Feb. 3, 1934. She studied singing in New York with Mme. Murio-Celli and later in Paris with Jean de Reszke. In 1901 she married Count Francesco de Cisneros of Havana, Cuba, and appeared professionally under this name. She enjoyed a brilliant career; sang in Italy between 1902 and 1914; and annually in London from 1903 to 1908. Between 1906 and 1911 she was the principal contralto singer at the Manhattan Opera, and later was a member of the Chicago Opera. In 1915 she toured Australia; then lived in Paris until 1929 when she returned to New York. See: (under De Cisneros) in Notable American Women (Cambridge, Mass., 1971, Vol. I).

Citkowitz, Israel, American composer; b. in Russia, Feb. 6, 1909; d. London, May 4, 1974. He was brought to the U.S. as a child; studied with Copland and Sessions in New York, and with Nadia Boulanger in Paris. He composed mainly for voice; his songs and choral works possess considerable expressive power.

Ciuciura, Leoncjusz, Polish composer; b. Grodzisk Mazowiecki, July 22, 1930. He studied with Szeligowski at the State College of Music in Warsaw. All of his works are essays in combinatorial permutation with optional instrumental or vocal additions, subtractions, multiplications or divisions.
WORKS: *Canti al fresco* for 9 female voices and instrumental ensemble (1961); *concertino de camera* for chamber orch. (1961); *Ornament* for flute, bassoon, clarinet and strings (1962); *Penetrations* for 4 orch. groups, 4 conductors and composer (1963); *Spirale I per uno,* for baritone and 36 percussion instruments (1964) and *Spirale II per uno e più,* for optional instrumental ensemble (1964); *Emergenza* for 3 orch. groups, 3 conductors and composer (1964); *Incidenti* for optional voices and instrumental ensemble (1964); *Per 5* for a group which would include any combination of flute, oboe, horn, bassoon and trumpet (1972); *Creatoria I* and *II* for optional solo voice or instrument or groups of instruments or voices (1975); *Music* for solo flute and 8 instruments (1976).

Ĉiurlionis, Mikolajus, Lithuanian composer; b. Varena, Oct. 4, 1875; d. Pustelnik near Warsaw, April 23, 1911. He studied composition with Noskowski, and at the Leipzig Cons. with Carl Reinecke, and Jadassohn. From 1902 till 1909 he was active in Warsaw as a choral conductor. His music reflects the Germanic romantic tendencies, but he also developed interesting theories of so-called "tonal ground formations" anticipating the serial methods of Schoenberg and Hauer. Ĉiurlionis was also a remarkable painter in an abstract expressionist manner; many of his paintings carry musical titles, such as "Prelude and Fugue," "Spring Sonata," etc. His musical works include the symph. poems *In the Forest* (1901) and *The Ocean* (1907); cantata *De profundis* (1899); String Quartet; numerous piano pieces and songs.
BIBLIOGRAPHY: V. Ĉiurlionytė-Karužiene et al., M. K. Ĉiurlionis. Bibliografia (Vilnius, 1970); J. Ĉiurlionytė, *Atsiminimai apie M. K. Ĉiurlionis* (Vilnius, 1970); V. Landsbergis, *Spring Sonata. The Creative Activity of M. K. Ĉiurlionis* (Leningrad, 1971).

Civil, Alan, prominent English horn player; b. Northampton, June 13, 1929. His father and grandfather played horn. He studied with Aubrey Brain in London and with Willy von Stemm in Hamburg; played horn in the Royal Philharmonic Orch. in London (1952-55); was co-principal horn player with Dennis Brain in the Philharmonic Orch. (1955-57), becoming principal hornist upon Brain's untimely death; also played with the BBC Symph. Orch. and with several English chamber ensembles. All of his compositions include conspicuous horn parts: Symphony for brass and percussion (1950); Wind Quintet (1951); Wind Octet (1951); Horn Trio (1952) and *Suite* for 2 horns.

Claassen, Arthur, American conductor and composer; b. Stargard, Prussia, Feb. 19, 1859; d. San Francisco, March 16, 1920. He studied in Weimar; his compositions aroused Liszt's interests, and he wrote a number of pieces in a Lisztian manner. In 1884 he was engaged as conductor of the choral group Arion in Brooklyn, and held this post for 25 years. In 1914 he took over the Beethoven Choral Society, a male chorus organization, in San Antonio, Texas; he also was engaged as conductor of the San Antonio Philharmonic, which later became the San Antonio Symph.

Simultaneously he organized the Mozart Society in San Antonio, a women's chorus, which enabled him to conduct choral works with the San Antonio Symph.; he left San Antonio in 1919. Among his works are a symph. poem *Hohenfriedberg, Waltz-Idyll* for string orch., and many choruses, of which *Der Kamerad* got a prize at the New York Singing Festival.

Claflin, (Alan) Avery, American composer; b. Keene, N. H., June 21, 1898. He studied law and banking and pursued a business career. He also took music courses at Harvard Univ. and in Europe; attracted attention by his amusing choral piece, a fiscal madrigal entitled *Lament for April 15* (1955), to the text of an Internal Revenue tax form. Among his other works are the operas *Hester Prynne* (after *The Scarlet Letter* of Hawthorne), of which scene II of Act II was performed at Hartford on Dec. 15, 1934; *The Fall of Usher* (not performed); *La Grande Bretèche,* on Balzac's story (CBS radio, Feb. 3, 1957); *Uncle Tom's Cabin* (1961–64); 2 symphonies; *Teen Scenes* for strings (1955); *Pop Concert Concerto* for piano and orch. (1958); Piano Trio and other chamber music.

Clapp, Philip Greeley, American composer and pedagogue; b. Boston, Aug. 4, 1888; d. Iowa City, April 9, 1954. He studied piano with his aunt Mary Greeley James (1895–99); and violin with Jacques Hoffman in Boston (1895–1905); also took lessons in music theory with John Marshall (1905). He then entered Harvard Univ. studying music theory and composition with Spalding, Converse and Edward Burlingame Hill; received his B.A. (1908); M.A. (1909); and Ph.D. (1911). He also studied composition and conducting in Stuttgart with Max von Schillings (1910). He became a teaching fellow at Harvard (1911–12); was Mus. Dir. at Dartmouth College (1915–18); in 1919 he was appointed Director of the Music Dept. at the Univ. of Iowa, and remained at that post for the rest of his life. Clapp was a prolific composer and competent teacher; he was also a brilliant pianist, but did not dedicate himself to a concert career; he also appeared as conductor of his own works and was in charge of the university orchestra at Iowa City. His music is conceived in an expansive romantic idiom much influenced by the modern German style of composition, and yet introducing some advanced melodic and harmonic patterns, such as building harmonies in fourths. WORKS: 12 symphonies: No. 1 in E major (1910; first performed, Waterloo, Iowa, April 27, 1933, composer conducting); No. 2 in E minor (Boston Symphony, April 10, 1914, composer conducting); No. 3 in E-flat major (Boston Symph., April 6, 1917, composer conducting); No. 4 in A major (1919; revised 1941; not performed); No. 5 in D major (1926; revised in 1941; Iowa City, July 26, 1944, composer conducting); No. 6 in B major, subtitled *Golden Gate* (1926; San José, Calif., June 5, 1951); No. 7 in A major (Boston, March 22, 1931, composer conducting); No. 8 in C major (1930; revised in 1941; N.Y. Philharmonic, Mitropoulos conducting, Feb. 7, 1952); No. 9 in E-flat minor, subtitled *The Pioneers* (1931; Iowa City, July 16, 1939); No. 10 in F major, subtitled *Heroic* (1935; Iowa City, May 23, 1951, composer conducting); No. 11 in C

major (1942; revised in 1950; not performed); No. 12, B-flat major (1944; not performed). *Norge,* symph. poem with piano obbligato (Cambridge, Mass., Boston Symph., April 29, 1909), his most popular work; *Song of Youth,* symph. poem (1910); *Dramatic Poem with Solo Trombone* (Cambridge, Mass., April 24, 1912, composer conducting); *Summer,* orch. prelude (St. Louis, Jan. 16, 1914); *Overture to a Comedy* (1933); *A Highly Academic Diversion on Seven Notes* for chamber orch. (Iowa City, Feb. 17, 1933, composer conducting); *Fantasy on an Old Plain Chant* for cello and orch. (Iowa City, Jan. 17, 1940); Concerto for 2 Pianos (Iowa City, Dec. 20, 1945). Chamber Music: Violin Sonata (1909); String Quartet (1909); Suite for Brass Sextet (1938); Concerto Suite for 4 Trombones (1939); *Prelude and Finale* for woodwind quintet (1939); numerous choral works, among them *A Chant of Darkness* for chorus and orch. to the text by Helen Keller (1919; revised 1933; Iowa City, April 16, 1935, composer conducting); two operas: *The Taming of the Shrew* (after Shakespeare; 1948), and *The Flaming Brand,* libretto by the composer on the exploit of John Brown (1949–53), neither of which was ever performed, nor are likely to be performed in any foreseeable future century. All his manuscripts are in the Music Library of the Univ. of Iowa.

BIBLIOGRAPHY: Dorothy R. Holcomb, *Ph. G. Clapp* in *Books at Iowa* (Univ. of Iowa, 1972).

Clari, Giovanni Carlo Maria, Italian composer and choral director; b. Pisa, Sept. 27, 1677; d. there, May 16, 1754. He studied under Colonna at Bologna, where his opera *Il Savio delirante* was produced in 1695; from 1712–36 he was in Pistoia as maestro di cappella of the cathedral; then went to Pisa. His best known work is a collection of madrigals for 2 and 3 voices (1720; reprinted by Carli, Paris, 1825); also wrote Masses, psalms, a Requiem, other sacred music.

BIBLIOGRAPHY: E. C. Saville, "Liturgical Music of Giovanni Clari: an Annotated Index," *Fontes Artis Musicae* XV/1 (1968).

Claribel. Pen name of **Charlotte Barnard.**

Clark, Edward, English conductor; b. Newcastle-on-Tyne, May 10, 1888; d. London, April 29, 1962. He studied in Paris, Vienna, and in Berlin with Schoenberg. He led the orchestra for Diaghilev's London seasons (1924–26); was with the BBC (1927–36); in 1940 he founded the North Eastern Regional Orch. in Newcastle. In 1947 he was elected president of the International Society for Contemporary Music. He was married to the composer **Elizabeth Lutyens.**

Clark, Frederick Scotson, English clergyman, organist and composer; b. London, Nov. 16, 1840; d. there, July 5, 1883. He studied with Sergent in Paris and with E. J. Hopkins; also studied at the Royal Academy of Music in London with Bennett, Goss, Engel, Pettit and Pinsuti; received his religious education at Cambridge and Oxford; was organist of Exeter College, Oxford; took further music lessons in Leipzig and Stuttgart; returned to London in 1873, where he founded the London Organ School; was the representative English organist at the Paris Exposition of 1878.

WORKS: His organ compositions (15 marches, 48 voluntaries, 6 communions; offertories, improvisations, impromptus, etc.) are his best works; composed over 100 piano pieces; sacred vocal music; songs, etc. Clark also played and composed for the harmonium.

Clark, Melville, one of the pioneers of the player piano industry; b. Oneida Co., N.Y., 1850; d. Chicago, Nov. 5, 1918. In 1875 he established himself as an organ builder in Oakland, Calif.; moved to Chicago in 1880; in 1894 he also opened a piano factory, after he had become interested in pneumatic actions; his experiments leading to practical results which convinced him of the possibilities of the player piano, he sold his organ factory, and, in 1900, organized the Melville Clark Piano Co., of which he was president. In 1901 he patented and placed on the market the 88-note roll, utilizing the full compass of the piano, and thus gave the impetus to the phenomenal player piano industry which later developed. In 1911 he patented a recording mechanism, which aimed to reproduce the actual performance of great pianists. He also held many other important patents.

Clark, Melville Antone, nephew of the preceding, harpist and harp manufacturer; b. Syracuse, N.Y., Sept. 12, 1883; d. there, Dec. 11, 1953. He received his first instruction on the harp from his father; pupil of Van Veachton Rogers (1896–99) and of John Aptommas in London (1908). While on a tour of Great Britain in 1908 he acquired a small Irish harp, formerly the property of the poet Thomas Moore; by the application of acoustic principles he improved the model and succeeded in producing a small, portable harp (39 inches high) of considerable tone volume; founded the Clark Harp Manufacturing Co. at Syracuse, which turned out the first small Irish harps in 1913; on a tour of the U.S. with John McCormack (1913–14) the inventor demonstrated the possibilities of the new instrument; took out fourteen patents on improvements for the portable harp and developed a new method of pedaling the concert harp; played about 4,000 recitals in the U.S., Canada and England; was co-founder of the Syracuse Symph. Orch.; treasurer of the National Association of Harpists; president of the Clark Music Co. (1910).
WRITINGS: *How to Play the Harp, Romance of the Harp, Singing Strings.*

Clarke, Henry Leland, American musicologist and composer; b. Dover, New Hampshire, March 9, 1907. He studied piano and violin; then took courses at Harvard Univ. (M.A., 1929; Ph.D., 1947). In 1929 he went to Paris where he took composition lessons with Nadia Boulanger at the École Normale de Musique. Upon return to the U.S., he occupied himself mainly with teaching; was on the faculty of Westminster Choir College (1938–42), at the Univ. of California, Los Angeles (1947–58) and at the Univ. of Washington, Seattle (1958–77). As a composer, Clarke applies a number of interesting innovations, e.g. "Intervalescent Counterpoint" (with interval values constantly changing from one voice to another), "Lipophony" (with certain notes systematically omitted), "Word Tones" (whenever a word recurs, it is assigned to the same pitch) "Rotating Triskaidecaphony" (a 12-tone series returning to note 1 for the 13th note, with the next row starting and ending on note 2, etc.).
WORKS: *Danza de la Muerte,* a choreography for oboe and piano (1937); *Monograph* for orch. (1952); chamber opera, *The Loafer and the Loaf* (Stockbridge, Mass., July 1, 1954); *Nocturne* for viola and piano (1955); *Saraband for the Golden Goose* for orch. (1957); *Points West* for wind and percussion (1960); *Encounter* for viola and orch. (1961); *Lysistrata,* opera (1969); *A Game that Two Can Play* for Flute and Clarinet (1966); *Concatenata* for French Horn and Woodwind Quartet (1969); *Danza de la Vida* a choreography for Oboe and Piano (1975); *These Are the Times that Try Men's Souls,* for chorus, to the text of Thomas Paine (1976); *The Young Dead Soldiers* for chorus, to words by Archibald MacLeisch (1977); *Give and Take* for 2 keyboards (1977).

Clarke, Hugh Archibald, organist; b. near Toronto, Canada, Aug. 15, 1839; d. Philadelphia, Dec. 16, 1927. Pupil of his father, **James Paton Clarke;** was organist in several churches in Philadelphia; in 1875 was elected Professor of the Science of Music in the University of Pennsylvania; retired in 1925.
WORKS: Clarke composed music to Euripides' *Iphigenia in Tauris,* an oratorio, *Jerusalem* (1891), piano music and songs.
WRITINGS: He published a treatise on harmony and one on counterpoint, also textbooks for organ; a book of fiction *The Scratch Club* (1888); *Music and the Comrade Arts* (1900); *Highways and Byways of Music* (1901).

Clarke, James Hamilton Smee, English organist; b. Birmingham, Jan. 25, 1840; d. Banstead, July 9, 1912. He was apprenticed to a land surveyor 1855–61; then turned to music, and in 1866 became organist to Queen's College, Oxford. In 1872 he succeeded Sullivan as organist of St. Peter's, South Kensington; was conductor of the D'Oyly Carte company on tour (1878); and also at the Lyceum Theatre, writing music for dramas given by Henry Irving. In 1893, first conductor of the Carl Rosa company.
WORKS: He published about 400 works, including music to *Hamlet, Merchant of Venice* and *King Lear;* the sacred cantata *Praise;* 8-part anthem, *The Lord is my light;* 2 symphonies; 6 overtures; organ music.

Clarke, James Paton, Scottish organist; b. 1808; d. Toronto, Aug. 27, 1877. In 1829 he was the leader of psalmody in St. George's Church in Glasgow; in 1834 became organist of St. Mary's Episcopal chapel, succeeding Thomas Macfarlane; emigrated to Canada in 1835 and became a farmer; went to Toronto about 1845. In 1846 took his Mus. Bac. degree at King's College with the 8-part anthem *Arise, O Lord God, forget not the poor.*
BIBLIOGRAPHY: H. Kallmann, "James Paton Clarke—Canada's Mus. Bac.," *Cahiers Canadiens de Musique* (Spring–Summer 1970).

Clarke, Jeremiah, English composer and organist; b. London, c.1673; d. there (suicide), Dec. 1, 1707. He was a chorister in the Chapel Royal; in 1700 was made

Gentleman Extraordinary of the Chapel Royal; in 1704 was appointed joint organist (with Croft) there. A hopeless love affair caused Clarke to take his own life.

WORKS: He composed (with others) the operas *The World in the Moon* (1697) and *The Island Princess* (1699); wrote incidental music to several plays; was the first composer to set Dryden's *Alexander's Feast* to music (for St. Cecilia's Day, Nov. 22, 1697); also wrote a cantata, an ode, anthems, songs, etc. He was the real author of the famous *Trumpet Voluntary*, erroneously ascribed to Purcell, and popularized by Sir Henry Wood's orchestral arrangement.

BIBLIOGRAPHY: C. L. Cudworth, "Some New Facts about the Trumpet Voluntary," *Musical Times* (Sept. 1953); T. F. Taylor, "Jeremiah Clarke's Trumpet Tunes: Another View of Origins," *Musical Quarterly* (July 1970); R. McGuinness, *English Court Odes 1660-1820* (Oxford, 1971).

Clarke (Clarke-Whitfield), John, English organist and composer; b. Gloucester, Dec. 13, 1770; d. Holmer, near Hereford, Feb. 22, 1836. He studied organ at Oxford with Philip Hayes; received his B. Mus. degree in 1793; was church organist at Ludlow, Armagh and Dublin; in 1799 he became choirmaster of Trinity and St. John's College in Cambridge; from 1820 to 1832 he was organist at the Hereford Cathedral. He was stricken with paralysis; was forced to resign his post, and was an invalid for the rest of his life.

WORKS: an oratorio *The Crucifixion and the Resurrection* (Hereford, 1822); four volumes of cathedral services and anthems (1805); 12 glees (1805); 12 songs; a *Selection of Single and Double Chants*; etc. He also edited the *Vocal Works of Handel* (1809, 17 vols.) with piano accompaniment.

Clarke, Rebecca, English composer and viola player; b. Harrow, Aug. 27, 1886. She studied composition at the Royal College of Music with Sir Charles Stanford. She was originally a violinist, but specialized later as a viola player. In 1916 she went to the U.S., in 1923 returned to England; in 1928 formed the English Ensemble, a piano quartet, and toured with it in Europe. She began to compose seriously after her arrival in the U.S. during World War I; won second prize in the Coolidge competition at the Berkshire Festival of 1919 with a viola sonata; other works include a Piano Trio (1921); *Chinese Puzzle* for violin and piano (1922); Rhapsody for Cello and Piano (1923); also three *Irish Country Songs* for violin and cello. Her music is quite advanced in modern technique, touching the fringes of atonality in melodic outline; impressionistic influences are also felt. She was still actively at work in New York in 1978.

BIBLIOGRAPHY: the entry on her chamber music in Cobbett's *Cyclopedic Survey of Chamber Music* (1929).

Clarke, Robert Coningsby, English song composer; b. Old Charlton, Kent, March 17, 1879; d. Walmer, Kent, Jan. 2, 1934. He studied with Sir John Frederick Bridge at Westminster Abbey; then served as church organist at Oxford. He wrote a number of popular ballads and piano pieces.

Clarke, William Horatio, American organist; b. Newton, Mass., March 8, 1840; d. Reading, Mass., Dec. 11, 1913. He was church organist in Boston; retired in 1887 to his estate in Reading, Mass., where he built a chapel of music, Clarigold Hall, containing a large 4-manual organ with 100 stops.

Clarus, Max, German composer; b. Mühlberg, March 31, 1852; d. Braunschweig, Dec. 6, 1916. He studied with his father, who was a municipal music director, and with Löschhorn in Berlin. He became a theatrical conductor, traveling in Germany, Austria and Hungary; composed mostly for the stage and for chorus.

WORKS: the operas (all produced in Braunschweig) *Des Königs-Rekrut* (1889); *Ilse* (1895; quite successful at the time); fairy operas *Der Wunschpeter* (1910) and *Der Zwerg Nase* (1912); also several ballets (*Opium-Träume*, etc.) and *Die Wacht vor Samoa* for baritone solo, male chorus and orch.; also numerous a cappella choruses.

Claudin le Jeune. See **Le Jeune, Claudin.**

Claussen, Julia (*née* **Ohlson**), dramatic mezzo-soprano; b. Stockholm, June 11, 1879; d. there, May 1, 1941. She studied at the Royal Academy of Music in Stockholm (1897–1902); then in Berlin with Prof. Friedrich. She made her debut as Leonora in *La Favorita* at the Stockholm Opera (Jan. 19, 1903); was engaged there from 1903 until 1912; made her debut at Covent Garden, London, in 1914; was a member of the Chicago Opera Company during World War I. She made her first appearance at the Metropolitan Opera House as Dalila on Nov. 23, 1917, and remained in the company until 1932; in 1934 she returned to Stockholm as a teacher at the Royal Academy of Music. After her death a memorial fund for vocal scholarships was established in Stockholm.

Clavé, José Anselmo, Spanish choral leader; b. Barcelona, April 21, 1824; d. there, Feb. 24, 1874. He was inspired by the success of the 'orpheons' in France, and organized male singing societies in Spain on a similar scale. At the first singing festival in Barcelona in 1860 he conducted a chorus of 200 voices; in 1864 he augmented his ensemble to 2,000 singers, representing 57 organizations. Some of his songs and choruses, especially composed for his festivals, enjoyed great popularity.

BIBLIOGRAPHY: J. Subirá, *El Músico-poeta Clavé* (Madrid, 1924); T. Caballé y Clós, *J. A. Clavé y su tiempo* (Barcelona, 1949).

Clay, Frédéric, composer; b. (of English parents) Paris, Aug. 3, 1838; d. Great Marlow, near London, Nov. 24, 1889. He studied with Molique at Paris and with Hauptmann in Leipzig.

WORKS: His early operettas, *The Pirate's Isle* (1859) and *Out of Sight* (1860), were performed privately in London; his first operetta to be produced at Covent Garden was *Court and Cottage* (1862); other light dramatic works subsequently performed at Covent Garden included *Constance* (1865); *Ages Ago* (1869); *The Gentleman in Black* (1870); *Happy Arcadia* (1872); *Cattarina* (1874); *Princess Toto* (1876);

Don Quixote (1876). He also composed two cantatas, *The Knights of the Cross* (1866) and *Lalla Rookh* (1877; including the well-known aria *I'll sing thee songs of Araby*).

BIBLIOGRAPHY: W. S. Gilbert, *Gilbert before Sullivan* (ed. and intro. by J. W. Stedman; Chicago, 1967).

Clemens, Charles Edwin, American organist; b. Plymouth, England, March 12, 1858; d. Cleveland, Ohio, Dec. 26, 1923. He studied at the Royal College of Music in London; as a boy played organ in churches; served as organist of the English Church in Berlin (1889–1896); settled in Cleveland as organist at St. Paul's Church (1896–1911); also taught at Western Reserve Univ.

WRITINGS: He published two manuals: *Pedal Technique* (1894) and *Modern School for the Organ* (1903).

Clemens, Hans, German tenor; b. Bicken-Gelsenkirchen, Germany, July 27, 1890; d. Montrose, Colorado, Aug. 25, 1958. After successful appearances in Germany and at Covent Garden, London, he came to the U.S.; made his New York debut at the Metropolitan Opera House in *The Flying Dutchman* (Nov. 1, 1930); appeared also in other Wagnerian roles; was particularly effective as David in *Die Meistersinger,* a role which he sang more than 100 times. In 1938 he settled in Los Angeles as a vocal teacher.

Clemens (Clement), Jacobus, called "Clemens non Papa," eminent Netherlandish contrapuntist; b. Ypres, c.1510; d. Dixmude, c.1556 (death date is surmised from the fact that vol. 1 of *Novum et insigne opus musicum,* publ. in 1558, contains the motet *Nanie,* composed by Jacob Vaet on Clemens' death). The exact meaning of "non Papa" is not clear; it was once thought to mean "not the Pope," to distinguish the composer from Clement VII; but a more recent interpretation suggests that "non Papa" was intended to differentiate Clemens from a poet also living in the town of Ypres, named Jacobus Papa. His teachers are not known; he was in France for a time; returned in 1540 to the Netherlands and settled in Bruges; in 1545 he went to Antwerp; later lived in Dixmude, where he was buried.

WORKS: 15 Masses, numerous motets, chansons, etc., publ. by Phalèse (Louvain, 1555–80); 4 books of *Souterliedekens a 3,* i.e., psalms set to popular Netherlandish tunes, publ. by T. Susato (Antwerp, 1556–57); and many miscellaneous pieces in collections of the period. Reprints are to be found in K. Proske's *Musica divina* (vol. II); R. J. van Maldeghem's *Trésor musical,* and F. Commer's *Collectio operum musicorum Batavorum.* El. Mincoff-Marriage republished the text of the *Souterliedekens* (The Hague, 1922); a selection of 15 of these pieces, with music, was edited by W. Blanke (Wolfenbüttel, 1929).

BIBLIOGRAPHY: J. Schmidt, "Die Messen des Clemens non Papa," *Zeitschrift für Musikwissenschaft* (1926); K. P. Bernet Kempers, "Zur Biographie des Clemens non Papa," ibid. (1927); K. P. Bernet Kempers, *J. Clemens non Papa und seine Motetten* (Augsburg, 1928). A complete ed. of his works was begun in Amsterdam (1953) under the editorship of K. P. Bernet Kempers.

Clément, Edmond, French tenor; b. Paris, March 28, 1867; d. Nice, Feb. 24, 1928. Pupil of Warot at the Paris Cons. in 1887; first prize, 1889; debut at Opéra-Comique, Nov. 29, 1889, as Vincent in Gounod's *Mireille.* His success was instantaneous, and he remained there until 1910 with frequent leave for extended tours; sang in the principal theaters of France, Belgium, Spain, Portugal, England and Denmark; 1909–10 at the Metropolitan Opera House; 1911–13, with the Boston Opera Co. His voice was a light tenor of very agreeable quality, with a range of two octaves. He created the chief tenor parts in the following operas (all at the Opéra-Comique): Bruneau's *L'Attaque du Moulin* (1893), Saint-Saëns' *Phryne* (1893), Cui's *Le Flibustier* (1894), Godard's *La Vivandière* (1895), Dubois' *Xavière* (1895), Hahn's *L'Île du Rêve* (1898), Erlanger's *Le Juif polonais* (1900), Saint-Saëns *Hélène* (1904), Dupont's *La Cabrera* (1905), Vidal's *La Reine Fiammette* (1908).

Clément, Félix, French writer on music; b. Paris, Jan. 13, 1822; d. there, Jan. 23, 1885. He devoted himself especially to historical studies; filled several positions as organist and teacher, and finally became organist and choirmaster at the Church of the Sorbonne. In 1849 the government chose him to direct music of the 13th century at the Sainte-Chapelle; published in score as *Chants de la Sainte-Chapelle,* in the same year (3d ed. 1875). He was active in establishing the Institution for Church Music.

WRITINGS: *Méthode complète du plain-chant* (1854; 1872); *Histoire générale de la musique religieuse* (1860); *Les Musiciens célèbres depuis le XVIe siècle* (1868; 4th ed. 1887); *Dictionnaire lyrique, ou histoire des opéras* (1869, 4 supplements up to 1881; new augm. ed. by A. Pougin, 1897 and 1904, under the title *Dictionnaire des opéras*); *Méthode d'orgue, d'harmonie et d'accompagnement* (1874; 2d ed. 1894); *Histoire de la musique depuis les temps anciens jusqu'à nos jours* (1885); etc.

Clement, Franz, Austrian violinist and composer; b. Vienna, Nov. 17, 1780; d. there, Nov. 3, 1842. He learned to play the violin as a child, and at the age of ten went to London where he appeared as a soloist at concerts directed by Salomon and Haydn. Returning to Vienna, he continued his successful career; was conductor at the Theater an-der-Wien (1802–11); made a tour in Germany and Russia (1813–18); participated in the concerts of the famous singer Angelica Catalani. He was greatly esteemed as violinist and musician by his contemporaries; Beethoven wrote his violin concerto for him, and Clement gave its first performance in Vienna (Dec. 23, 1806). He wrote 6 concertos and 25 concertinos for violin, as well as numerous technical studies.

BIBLIOGRAPHY: Robert Haas, "The Viennese Violinist Franz Clement," *Musical Quarterly* (Jan. 1948).

Clement, Jacobus. See **Clemens, Jacobus.**

Clementi, Aldo, Italian composer of avant-garde tendencies; b. Catania, May 25, 1925. He took piano lessons as a child in Catania and later was a piano pupil of Pietro Scarpini in Siena; subsequently studied composition with Alfredo Sangiorgi, a pupil of Schoenberg, in Catania (1945–52) and with Petrassi in Rome (1952–54); then attended summer courses in new music at Darmstadt (1955–62). After an initial period of writing music in a neo-Baroque manner, he adopted serial techniques, employing rhythmic indeterminacy and dense, clustered sonics.

WORKS: *Tre piccoli pezzi* for flute, oboe and clarinet (1955); Sonata for trumpet, guitar, and piano (1955); *Due studi* for trumpet, violin, and piano (1956); *Concertino in forma di Variazioni* for 9 instruments (1956); *Tre studi* for chamber orch. (1956–57; Darmstadt, July 27, 1957); *Composizione No. 1* for piano (1957); *Episodi* for orch. (1958); *Ideogrammi No. 1* for 16 instruments; *Ideogrammi No. 2* for flute and 17 instruments (both 1959); *Triplum* for flute, oboe, and clarinet (1960); *Sette Scene* for chamber orch. (1961); *Informel 1* for 12 percussion and keyboard instruments (1961), *2* for 15 players (1962) and *3* for orch. (1961–63; Palermo, Oct. 2, 1963); *Collage 1,* a 1-act "musical action" for the stage, for chamber ensemble and visuals (1961), *2* for tape (1962) and *3, Dies Irae,* for tape (1966–67); *Intavolatura* for harpsichord (1963); *Variante A* for chorus and orch. (1964; Rome, April 6, 1974) and *B* for orch. (1964; Venice Fest., Sept. 12, 1964); *Reticolo: 11* for 11 instruments (1966); *Silben* for female voice, clarinet, violin and 2 pianos (1966); Concerto for wind orch. and 2 pianos (1967; Venice Fest., Sept. 12, 1970); *Reticolo: 4* for string quartet (1968); *B.A.C.H.* for piano (1970); Concerto for piano and 7 instruments (1970; Venice Festival, Sept. 10, 1972); *Reticolo: 12* for 12 strings (1970); *Silbenmerz* (1971); *Replica* for harpsichord (1972); *Manualiter* for organ (1973); *Blitz,* "musical action" for chamber ensemble (1973); *Sinfonia da camera* (1974; Milan, April 22, 1974); Concerto for piano, 24 instruments and carillons (1975); *Reticolo: 3* for 3 guitars (1975); *Clessidra* for 11 instruments (1976).

Clementi, Muzio, celebrated pianist and composer; b. Rome, Jan. 23, 1752; d. at his country-seat at Evesham, England, March 10, 1832. His father, a goldsmith, was a devoted amateur of music, and had his son taught carefully, from early years, by Antonio Buroni, maestro di cappella in a Roman church. From 1759 the organist Condiceli gave him lessons in organ playing and harmony. So rapid was their pupil's progress that when but nine he obtained a position as organist, in competition with other and maturer players. Until fourteen years of age he pursued his studies in Italy, G. Carpani (composition) and Sartarelli (voice) being his next instructors. At a piano concert which Clementi gave in 1766, an English gentleman named Beckford was so delighted with his talent that he obtained the father's permission to educate the boy in England. Clementi lived and studied till 1770 in his patron's house in Dorsetshire; then, a thoroughly equipped pianist and musician, he took London by storm. In 1773 his op. 2 (3 piano sonatas dedicated to Haydn, and warmly praised by C. P. E. Bach) was published; they may be considered as finally establishing the form of the piano sonata. From 1777–80 he conducted, as cembalist, the Italian Opera. In 1781 he began a pianistic tour, giving concerts at Paris, Strasbourg, Munich and Vienna; here, on Dec. 24, 1781, he met Mozart in 'friendly' rivalry (Mozart's letters make no pretense of concealing his dislike of the 'Italian' composer and player); though the palm of final victory was awarded to neither, yet Clementi tacitly admitted, by changing from a mechanically brilliant to a more suave and melodious piano style, the musical superiority of Mozart. In Vienna his opp. 7, 9, and 10 were published by Artaria. Excepting a concert season at Paris, in 1785, Clementi now remained in London for 20 years (1782–1802). He not only made his mark, and incidentally amassed quite a fortune, as a teacher, pianist and composer, but also (after losses through the failure of Longman & Broderip, the instrument makers and music sellers) established, with John Longman, a highly successful piano factory and publishing house (now Collard & Collard). With his pupil Field, Clementi set out for St. Petersburg in 1802, passing through Paris and Vienna; their tour was attended by brilliant success, and Field was so well received in St. Petersburg that he accompanied his master no further. Clementi resided for several years alternately in Berlin, Dresden and St. Petersburg; then, after visiting Vienna, Milan, Rome and Naples, he again settled in London. The businessman in Clementi now gained the upper hand; he no longer played in public, but devoted himself to composition and the management of his prosperous mercantile ventures. He never again went far from London, except during the winter of 1820–21, which he spent in Leipzig. As a teacher Clementi trained many distinguished musicians: Field, Cramer, Moscheles, Kalkbrenner, Alexander Klengel, Ludwig Berger, Zeuner, even Meyerbeer, all owed much to his instruction.

WORKS: His compositions include symphonies (which failed in competition with Haydn's), and overtures for orchestra; 106 piano sonatas (46 with violin, cello, or flute); 2 duos for 2 pianos; 6 4-hand duets; fugues, preludes and exercises in canon form, toccatas, waltzes, variations, caprices, *Points d'orgue* . . . (op. 19); an *Introduction à l'art de toucher le piano, avec 50 leçons,* etc. (Engl. trans., London, 1801; repr. N.Y., 1973); by far the greater part of which are wholly forgotten. But his great book of études, the *Gradus ad Parnassum* (publ. 1817), is a living reminder that he was one of the greatest of piano teachers. Bülow's excellent selection of 50 of these études has been outdone by several later complete eds. (German, Italian, English), including that of Vogrich, arranged progressively (N.Y., 1898). The Library of Congress, Wash., D.C., acquired, largely through the efforts of Carl Engel, numerous MSS by Clementi, including 4 symphonies (almost complete); other fragments are in the British Museum. The first 2 of these symphonies were restored and edited for publication by Alfredo Casella, who performed them (using Clementi's original instrumentation) for the first time (No. 1, Turin, Dec. 13, 1935; No. 2, Rome, Jan. 5, 1936). The *Collected Works* (5 vols.; Leipzig, 1802–05) are now available in reprint (N.Y., 1973). Pietro Spada revised edited Symphonies Nos. 1–4 and 2 symphonies, op. 18.

BIBLIOGRAPHY: Giov. Froio, *Muzio Clementi, la sua vita, le sue opere e sua influenza sul progresso dell' arte* (Milan, 1876); O. Chilesotti, *I nostri maestri del passato* (Milan, 1882); F. Clément, *Les Musiciens célèbres depuis le XVI siècle* (Paris, 1878); J. S. Shedlock, *The Pianoforte Sonata* (London, 1895); M. Unger, *Muzio Clementis Leben* (Leipzig, 1914); G. C. Paribeni, *Muzio Clementi nella vita e nell'arte* (1921); A. Longo, "Gradus ad Parnassum" (analysis), *Arte pianistica* (1922); G. de Saint-Foix, "Muzio Clementi," *Musical Quarterly* (July 1923); idem, "Les Symphonies de Clementi," *Revue de Musicologie* (1924); idem, "Clementi, a Forerunner of Beethoven," *Musical Quarterly* (Jan. 1931); A. Stauch, *Muzio Clementis Klaviersonaten im Verhältnis zu den Sonaten von Haydn, Mozart, Beethoven* (dissertation, Cologne, 1929); A. Casella, "Muzio Clementi et ses symphonies," *Revue Musicale* (March 1936); H. Simon, "The Clementi Manuscripts at the Library of Congress," *Musical Quarterly* (Jan. 1942); A. W. Tyson, *Thematic Catalogue of the Works of Muzio Clementi* (Tutzing, 1967); E. Badura-Skoda, "Clementi's *Musical Characteristics* opus 19," in H. C. R. Landon and R. Chapman, eds. *Studies in Eighteenth-Century Music* (London, 1970); J. Bloch, "A Forgotten Clementi Sonata," *Piano Quarterly* (Fall 1972); L. Plantinga, "Clementi, virtuosity, and the 'German Manner,'" *Journal of the American Musicological Society* (Fall 1972). The Clementi-Archiv, in the Netherlands, issues the *Blätter aus dem Clementi-Archiv.*

Clemm, John (Johann Gottlob), German-American organ builder; b. Dresden, 1690; d. Bethlehem, Pa., May 5, 1762. Clemm reputedly learned organ making from A. Silbermann, probably while serving the Moravian Church settlement at Herrnhut, Saxony. He came to America with a group of Schwenkfelders in 1735, became a Separatist, and settled in Philadelphia in 1736. His first known organ was installed in Trinity Church, New York, in 1741. Subsequently, he assisted the Swedish-American organ builder, Hesselius, in Philadelphia. He reunited with the Moravians and moved to Bethlehem, Pa. (1756–58). There he continued his work with his assistant, David Tannenberg until his death. His descendants were important music dealers and publishers in Philadelphia up to 1879. His son, **John Clemm, Jr.,** was the first organist at New York's Trinity Church.
BIBLIOGRAPHY: A. H. Messiter, *History of the Choir and Music of Trinity Church* (N.Y., 1907); Donald M. McCorkle, "The Moravian Contribution to American Music," *Music Library Association Notes* (Sept. 1956).

Cleonides, a Greek writer on music; lived in the first half of the 2nd century, A.D. His treatise *Eisagoge harmonike (Introductio harmonica),* based on the theories of Aristoxenus, was for a long time ascribed to the mathematician Euclid, because it had been published under Euclid's name by Pena (Paris, 1557) and Meibom (Amsterdam, 1652), although it had been printed with the real author's name by Valla (Venice, 1497). A new critical edition was published by K. von Jan in *Musici Scriptores Graeci.* There is a French translation by Ruelle (1896). For an English translation of the *Introductio harmonica* see Strunk's *Source Readings in Music History* (N.Y., 1950).

Clérambault, Louis Nicolas, French composer and organist; b. Paris, Dec. 19, 1676; d. there, Oct. 26, 1749. He studied with André Raison; was organist at various Paris churches. He was a successful composer of theatrical pieces for the court: *Le Soleil vainqueur* (Paris, Oct. 21, 1721); *Le Départ du roi* (1745); etc. He also wrote a number of solo cantatas, in which genre he excelled; composed much organ music; some of his organ works are republished in Guilmant's *Archives des maîtres de l'orgue.* His son, **César François Nicolas Clérambault** (1700–1760), was also an organist and composer.

Clercx, Suzanne, Belgian musicologist; b. Houdeng-Aimeries, June 7, 1910. She studied at the Univ. of Liège, obtaining a doctorate in art history and archeology (1939); studied musicology with Charles van den Borren; was librarian at the Brussels Cons. (1941–49).
WRITINGS: She published a number of valuable treatises on Belgian music, among them H. J. de Croes (Brussels, 1940); *Grétry* (1944); *La baroque et la musique* (1948); *Pierre van Maldere* (1948); edited Boutmy's clavecin works in vol. V of *Monumenta Musicae Belgicae* (Antwerp, 1943); contributed historical articles to various musicological magazines.

Cléreau, Pierre, 16th-century French composer. Virtually nothing is known about his life, except that he was a chorister in Toul as a youth. However, many of his sacred works and 3-part chansons have been preserved. The following are extant: 4 Masses (Paris, 1554); *Missa pro mortuis* (Paris, 1554); 2 books of odes to Ronsard's words (Paris, 1566; several reprints).
BIBLIOGRAPHY: G. Thibault and L. Perceau, *Bibliographie des chansons de Ronsard mises en musique au XVIe siècle* (Paris, 1941).

Clérice, Justin, opera composer; b. Buenos Aires, Oct. 16, 1863; d. Toulouse, Sept. 9, 1908. He left Argentina as a young boy and spent most of his life in Paris, studying at the Paris Cons. with Delibes and Pessard (1882). He wrote many comic operas, most of which were performed in Paris: *Figarella* (June 3, 1889); *Le 3e Hussards* (March 14, 1894); *Pavie* (Jan. 28, 1897); *L'Ordre de l'empereur* (March 3, 1902); etc. His most successful comic opera *Le Meunier d'Alcala* was first performed in Portuguese (Lisbon, April 11, 1887); he also wrote an operetta *Phrynette* (1895); a pantomime, *Léda* (1896); a ballet-opera *Au temps jadis* (Monte Carlo, 1905).

Cleva, Fausto, Italian conductor; b. Trieste, May 17, 1902; d. Athens (collapsed while conducting), Aug. 6, 1971. He studied in Milan; began his conducting career as a youth; in 1920 emigrated to the U.S.; became an American citizen in 1931. He was chorusmaster and later conductor of the Metropolitan Opera until 1942; then was conductor of the San Francisco Opera Co. (1942–44 and 1949–55); then again with the Metropolitan Opera. In 1971 he was presented with a gold cigarette case by the directors of the Metropolitan Opera on the occasion of his 50th anniversary as a regular member, since the age of 18, of the Metropolitan conducting staff.

Cleve, Halfdan, Norwegian composer and pianist; b. Kongsberg, Oct. 5, 1879; d. Oslo, April 6, 1951. He studied with his father, an organist, and with Winter-Hjelms in Oslo; continued his studies in Berlin with O. Raif and with Scharwenka brothers (1899–1903). He made his debut as pianist in Berlin (1902); returned to Oslo in 1910, and settled as pianist and teacher.
WORKS: 5 piano concertos (1902, 1904, 1906, 1910, 1916); Piano Quintet; Violin Sonata; Ballade for Cello and Piano; many piano pieces and songs.

Cliburn, Van (Harvey Lavan, Jr.), brilliant American pianist; b. Shreveport, Louisiana, July 12, 1934; studied piano with his mother; then with Rosina Lhévinne at the Juilliard School of Music, N.Y., graduating in 1954. He made his debut with the Houston Symph. Orch. at the age of 13; appeared with the N.Y. Philharmonic in 1954; toured as a concert pianist in the U.S. He became suddenly famous when he won the Tchaikovsky Prize in Moscow in 1958, the first American to score such a triumph in Russia, where he became a prime favorite. Upon his return to New York he received a hero's welcome in a street parade. In 1964 he made his debut as orchestral conductor. His playing combines a superlative technique with a genuine romantic sentiment; this style is particularly effective in the music of Tchaikovsky and Rachmaninoff.
BIBLIOGRAPHY: A. Chasins: *The Van Cliburn Legend* (N.Y., 1959).

Clicquot, French family of organ builders of whom the earliest was **Robert Clicquot,** builder of the organ in the Versailles Chapel for Louis XIV (1711), and organs in the cathedrals of Rouen (1689) and Saint-Quentin (1703). His sons **Jean-Baptiste** (b. Paris, Nov. 3, 1678; d. there, 1744) and **Louis-Alexandre** (b. c.1680; d. Paris, Jan. 25, 1760) were his helpers. The most renowned of the family was **François-Henri Clicquot** (b. 1732; d. Paris, May 24, 1790), who constructed the great organ of Versailles Cathedral (installed Oct. 31, 1761) and the organ of St. Sulpice, with 5 manuals, 66 stops and a 32-ft. pedal (1781).
BIBLIOGRAPHY: F. Raugel, *Les Grandes Orgues des églises de Paris* (Paris, 1927); N. Dufourcq, *Les Clicquot* (Paris, 1942).

Cliffe, Frederick, English organist and composer; b. Bradford, Yorkshire, May 2, 1857; d. London, Nov. 19, 1931. He studied with his father, and showed such a precocious musical talent that at the age of eleven he performed his duties as organist at Wyke Parish Church; then was organist of the Bradford Festival Choral Society (1873–76); at the same time he continued his studies with Arthur Sullivan, Prout, Stainer and Franklin Taylor, as a scholarship student. In 1883 he joined the staff of the Royal College of Music, a post which he kept until his death.
WORKS: Symphony No. 1 (London, April 20, 1889); Symphony No. 2 (Leeds, 1892); tone poem, *Cloud and Sunshine* (1890); Violin Concerto (1896);

Ode to the North-East Wind for chorus and orch. (1905); church music.

Clifton, Chalmers, American conductor; b. Jackson, Miss., April 30, 1889; d. New York, June 19, 1966. He studied at the Cincinnati College of Music; then at Harvard with E. B. Hill, Walter Spalding and W. C. Heilman; further in Paris with Vincent d'Indy and Gédalge. Returning to America he conducted the Cecilia Society of Boston (1915–17); enlisted in the U.S. Army, and served in the Intelligence Service. He was active in the Federal Music Project in New York (1935–39); served in advisory capacity with various musical organizations.

Clippinger, David Alva, American choral conductor; b. Ohio, Sept. 2, 1860; d. Chicago, Feb. 20, 1938. He studied voice in London with William Shakespeare; then settled in Chicago where he conducted the Madrigal Club; edited the *Musical Monitor* and *Western Musical Herald;* publ. numerous manuals on the voice: *Systematic Voice Training* (1910); *The Head Voice and Other Problems* (1917); *Collective Voice Training* (1924); *Fundamentals of Voice Training* (1929); *Sight-Singing Based on Rhythmic-Melodic-Harmonic Ear Training* (1931).

Clokey, Joseph Waddell, American organist; b. New Albany, Indiana, Aug. 28, 1890; d. Covina, California, Sept. 14, 1960. He studied at Miami Univ. (B.A., 1912) and at the Cincinnati Cons. of Music (grad., 1915); from 1915–26 taught theory of music at Miami Univ.; from 1926–39 taught organ at Pomona College, Claremont, Calif.; from 1939–46 was dean of the School of Fine Arts at Miami Univ.; retired and lived in Claremont, Calif. He wrote much music for schools.
WORKS: the short operas *The Pied Piper of Hamelin* (Miami Univ., May 14, 1920); *The Nightingale* (after Andersen; Miami Univ., Dec. 12, 1925); *Our American Cousin* (Claremont, Calif., March 2, 1931); the sacred cantatas *The Vision; When The Christ Child Came; For He is Risen; We Beheld His Glory; Adoramus Te; Christ is Born;* organ pieces; songs. He published the manuals *Plainsong* (Boston, 1934) and *In Every Corner Sing: an Outline of Church Music for the Layman* (N.Y., 1945).
BIBLIOGRAPHY: E. E. Hipsher, *American Opera and Its Composers* (Philadelphia, 1927; pp. 122–25).

Closson, Ernest, Belgian writer on music; b. St. Josse ten Noode, near Brussels, Dec. 12, 1870; d. Brussels, Dec. 21, 1950. He was self-taught in music; occupied various posts as archivist; was assistant curator for the collection of music instruments at the Cons. of Brussels (1896); then taught at Brussels Cons. (1912); at the Cons. of Mons (1917); retired in 1935. From 1920–40 he was music critic of *L'Indépendance Belge.* In some of his writings he used the pen name Paul Antoine.
WRITINGS: *Siegfried de Wagner* (1891); *Edvard Grieg* (1892); *La Musique et les arts plastiques* (1897); *Chansons populaires des provinces belges* (1905; anthology with introduction and notes); *20 Noëls français anciens* (1911); *Le Manuscrit dit des basses-danses de la Bibliothèque de Bourgogne* (1912); *Notes*

sur la chanson populaire en Belgique (1913); *Esthétique musicale* (1921); *L'Élément flamand dans Beethoven* (1928; second ed., 1946; in English, London, 1936); "Grandfather Beethoven," *Musical Quarterly* (1933). Of his essays in various publications, "L'Instrument de musique comme document ethnographique," in *Guide musical* (1902), and "Le Dix-Neuvième Siècle et l'époque contemporaine," "Le Folklore" and "La Facture instrumentale," in *La Musique en Belgique du moyen-âge à nos jours* (1950) deserve mention. A collection, *Mélanges Closson*, dedicated to him (1948) contains a complete list of his writings.

Clough-Leighter, Henry, American music editor and composer; b. Washington, D.C., May 13, 1874; d. Wollaston, Mass., Sept. 15, 1956. He began to play piano as a child; then studied organ with G. Walter; held various positions as church organist. In 1901 he settled in Boston; was associate editor with Oliver Ditson & Co. (1901–08) and with the Boston Music Co. (1908–21); from 1921–56, editor-in-chief with E. C. Schirmer, Inc., Boston. He composed several cantatas and a number of other choral works; edited numerous music collections.

Cluer, John, English publisher and engraver of music; d. London, 1728; he claimed to be the inventor of engraving on tin plates. He set up his shop in London about 1715. He engraved and published Handel's operas, *Giulio Cesare, Tamerlano, Scipione,* and others; also Handel's *Suites de pièces de clavecin* and an 8vo collection of operatic arias.

BIBLIOGRAPHY: F. Kidson, *British Music Publishers, Printers and Engravers* (London, 1900).

Clutsam, George H., Australian pianist and composer; b. Sydney, Sept. 26, 1866; d. London, Nov. 17, 1951. As a young pianist, he made tours of Australia, India, China and Japan; settled in London in 1889 and became a professional accompanist; gave concerts with Melba (1893). From 1908 until 1918 he was a music critic of *The Observer* in London; at the same time wrote music for the stage.

WORKS: the operas *The Queen's Jester* (1905), *A Summer Night* (London, July 23, 1910), *After a Thousand Years* (1912), *König Harlekin* (Berlin, 1912); also several musical comedies: *Gabrielle, Lavender, The Little Duchess* (Glasgow, Dec. 15, 1922). His greatest popular success was the production of *Lilac Time*, an arrangement of Heinrich Berté's operetta *Das Dreimäderlhaus*, based on Schubert's melodies; Clutsam's version in English was first staged in London on Dec. 22, 1922, and had many revivals. Another theatrical medley, arranged from Chopin's melodies, was Clutsam's musical comedy *The Damask Rose* (London, June 17, 1929).

Cluytens, André, Belgian conductor; b. Antwerp, March 26, 1905; d. Neuilly, near Paris, June 3, 1967. He studied piano at the Antwerp Cons.; and received first prize at graduation. His father, conductor at the Théâtre Royal in Antwerp, engaged him as a choral coach; afterwards André Cluytens conducted opera there (1927–32); was theater conductor in Toulouse from 1932–35; in 1935 appointed opera conductor in Lyon; in 1949 became conductor of the Société des Concerts du Conservatoire de Paris, also conducting at the Opéra-Comique. He was subsequently appointed musical director of the Paris Opéra as well. He made appearances with major European orchestras in 1950–55, with ever increasing prestige. On Nov. 4, 1956, he made his American debut in Washington as guest conductor of the Vienna Philharmonic.

BIBLIOGRAPHY: B. Gavoty, *André Cluytens* in the series *Les Grands interprètes* (Geneva, 1955).

Cluzeau-Mortet, Luis, Uruguayan composer; b. Montevideo, Nov. 16, 1889; d. there, Sept. 28, 1957. He studied piano and theory with his maternal grandfather, who was the first Uruguayan to receive a prize at the Paris Cons. Cluzeau-Mortet played piano and the viola in radio bands in Montevideo and composed industriously. His music is marked by romantic influences, with occasional excursions into prudential modernism. All of his orchestral works were first performed by the Radio orch. SODRE, in Montevideo, of which he was a member.

WORKS: *Llanuras* (Oct. 14, 1944); *Rancherío* (Aug. 2, 1947); *Artigas* (Aug. 13, 1955); *Sinfonía del Este* (unfinished; a movement *La Laguna negra* was played on Aug. 16, 1958, as a posthumous act of homage); *Fantasía Concerto* for piano and chamber orch.; *4 Ritmos criollos* for string quartet; *Bagatelas criollas* for 4 flutes; songs and piano pieces. A complete catalogue of his works is found in Vol. 14 of the series *Compositores de América* (Washington, D.C., 1968).

Coates, Albert, eminent English conductor, b. St. Petersburg, Russia (of an English father and a mother of Russian descent), April 23, 1882; d. Milnerton, near Cape Town, Dec. 11, 1953. He went to England for his general education; enrolled in the science classes of Liverpool Univ., and studied organ with an elder brother who was living there at the time. In 1902 he entered the Leipzig Cons., studying cello with Klengel, piano with Robert Teichmüller, and conducting with Artur Nikisch; served his apprenticeship there and made his debut as conductor in Offenbach's *Les Contes d'Hoffmann* at the Leipzig Opera. In 1906 he was appointed (on Nikisch's recommendation) as chief conductor of the opera house at Elberfeld; in 1910 he was a joint conductor at the Dresden Opera (with Schuch); then at Mannheim (with Bodanzky). In 1911 he received the appointment at the Imperial Opera of St. Petersburg, and conducted many Russian operas. From 1913 he conducted in England, specializing in Wagner and the Russian repertoire; was a proponent of Scriabin's music. In 1920 he made his American debut as guest conductor of the N.Y. Symph. Orch.; from 1923–25 he led conducting classes at the Eastman School of Music in Rochester, N.Y.; also conducted the Rochester Symph. Orch. and appeared as guest conductor with other American orchestras. Subsequent engagements included a season at the Berlin State Opera (1931) and concerts with the Vienna Philharmonic (1935). In 1946 he settled in South Africa where he conducted the Johannesburg Symph. Orch. and taught at the Univ. of South Africa at Cape Town. Coates was a prolific composer, but his operas and other works had few performances (usually conducted by himself).

WORKS: symph. poem, *The Eagle* (Leeds, 1925; unsuccessful); the operas *Assurbanipal* (planned for performance in Moscow in 1915, but abandoned in view of wartime conditions); *Samuel Pepys* (produced in German, Munich, Dec. 21, 1929); *Pickwick* (London, Nov. 20, 1936); and *Tafelberg se Kleed* (English title, *Van Hunks and the Devil*; produced at the South African Music Festival in Cape Town, March 7, 1952).

Coates, Eric, English composer and viola player; b. Hucknall, Nottinghamshire, Aug. 27, 1886; d. Chichester, Dec. 21, 1957. He took instruction at the Royal Academy of Music with Tertis (viola) and Corder (composition). He was a member of the Hambourg String Quartet with which he made a tour of South Africa (1908); was first violist in Queen's Hall Orch. (1912-18). In 1946 he visited the U.S. conducting radio performances of his works; in 1948 toured in South America. He gives a detailed account of his career in his autobiography *Suite in Four Movements* (London, 1953). As a composer, Eric Coates specialized in semi-classical works for orch. His Valse Serenade *Sleepy Lagoon* (1930) attained enormous popularity all over the world, and was published in numerous arrangements; his *London Suite* (1933) was equally successful; its *Knightsbridge* movement became one of the most frequently played marches in England and elsewhere. He further wrote an orch. suite *Four Centuries* (1941) tracing typical historical forms and styles in 4 sections (*Fugue, Pavane, Valse,* and *Jazz*); *Three Elizabeths* for orch.; a great number of songs and instrumental pieces.

Coates, John, English tenor; b. Girlington, Yorkshire, June 29, 1865; d. Northwood, Middlesex, Aug. 16, 1941. He studied with his uncle, J. G. Walton, at Bradford; sang as a small boy at a Bradford church; began serious study in 1893 and took lessons with William Shakespeare in London. He sang tenor parts in Gilbert & Sullivan operettas, making his debut at the Savoy Theatre in *Utopia Limited* (1894); toured in the U.S. with a Gilbert & Sullivan company. He made his debut in grand opera as Faust at Covent Garden (1901); also sang Lohengrin in Cologne and other German cities with considerable success; later sang nearly all the Wagner parts in English with the Moody-Manners Co., Carl Rosa Co., and with Beecham (1910); from 1911-13 he toured with Quinlan's opera company in Australia and South Africa. He served in the British Army during World War I; in 1919, returned to London, devoting himself chiefly to teaching; also gave recitals of songs by English composers.

Cobbett, Walter Wilson, English patron of music; b. London, July 11, 1847; d. there, Jan. 22, 1937. He was a businessman and amateur violinist. An ardent enthusiast, he traveled widely in Europe and met contemporary composers. He was particularly active in promoting the cause of British chamber music, and arranged a series of Cobbett Competitions; also commissioned special works and established a Cobbett Medal for services to chamber music; the recipients included Thomas Dunhill (1924), Mrs. E. S. Coolidge

(1925), and A. J. Clements (1926). Among composers who received the Cobbett commissions and awards were Frank Bridge, York Bowen, John Ireland, Vaughan Williams, James Friskin, Waldo Warner and Herbert Howells. Cobbett edited the extremely valuable *Cyclopaedic Survey of Chamber Music* (2 volumes; Oxford, 1929; a Supplement was published in London, 1957).

Cocchi, Gioacchino, Italian composer; b. Padua, c.1715; d. Venice, 1804. He was teacher at the Conservatorio degli Incurabili in Venice; lived in London, 1757-63, writing operas; returned to Venice in 1773.

WORKS: His first opera was *Adelaide* (Rome, 1743); others were *Elisa* (1744); *Baiazette* (1746); *La Maestra* (Naples, 1747); *Arminio* (1749); *La Gismonda* (1750); *Semiramide riconosciuta* (1753); *Demofoonte* (1754); *Demetrio, re di Siria* (London, Nov. 8, 1757); *Zenobia* (London, 1758); *Ciro riconosciuto* (London, 1759); *La clemenza di Tito* (London, 1760); and *Tito Manlio* (London, 1761). He excelled in opera buffa and was also proficient in secular cantatas.

Coccia, Carlo, Italian opera composer; b. Naples, April 14, 1782; d. Novara, April 13, 1873. He studied with Paisiello; in 1808 went to Rome; in 1820 to London, where he became conductor of the Italian Opera. While there he produced his own opera *Maria Stuarda* (London, 1827) which was fairly successful. He returned to Italy in 1828; revisited London in 1833 and finally settled in Novara. Coccia wrote 37 operas in all; two of them especially, *Clotilda* (Venice, June 8, 1815), and *Caterina di Guise* (Milan, Feb. 14, 1833), had some success at the time.

Cochlaeus (real name **Dobnek**), **Johannes,** German music theorist; b. Wendelstein, near Nuremberg, Jan. 10, 1479; d. Breslau, Jan. 10, 1552. He studied philosophy at the Univ. of Cologne (1504); in 1509 became prof. there. In 1510 he taught history and geography in Nuremberg. From 1515 he traveled in Italy; obtained the degree of doctor of theology in Ferrara (1517); then was ordained priest in Rome; subsequently held various ecclesiastical posts in Germany; during the last seven years of his life he was at the Breslau Cathedral. Cochlaeus opposed Luther at the councils of Worms and Augsburg. He published numerous theological papers; was also the author of the treatise *Musica* (Cologne, 1507; enlarged ed. under the title *Tetrachordum musices,* Nuremberg, 1511 and 6 later editions).

BIBLIOGRAPHY: M. Spahn, *J. Cochlaeus* (Berlin, 1898).

Cocks & Co., London firm of music publishers, founded 1823 by **Robert Cocks;** his sons, **Arthur Lincoln Cocks** and **Stroud Lincoln Cocks,** became partners in 1868. Upon the death of the original founder (1887), **Robert Macfarlane Cocks** became the proprietor and carried on the business until 1898, when he retired and transferred the house to Augener and Co. The catalogue of publications comprised 16,000 numbers.

Cockshott, Gerald Wilfred, English composer; b. Bristol, Nov. 14, 1915. He took courses in English literature at the Univ. of Bristol; was head of the English Dept. at Whittingehame College, Brighton (1948–64) and at Ifield Grammar School, Crawley, Sussex (from 1965). He studied composition privately with Vaughan Williams; became active primarily as a writer on musical subjects. His music is transparently tonal and is impressed with melorhythms of English folksongs, but its simplicity is of a sophisticated nature.

WORKS: one-act operas *Apollo and Persephone* (1952), and *A Faun in the Forest* (1958); Symph. in B minor (1949); *Serenade* for flute and string orch. (1952); *Maddermarket Suite* for orch. (1953); Divertimento for Orch. (1960); *3 Pieces on Appalachian Folk Tunes* for cello and piano (1962); Duo for Clarinet and Bassoon on a Handel theme (1964); songs; carols; choruses; numerous arrangements of American, English, French-Canadian, Danish and Dutch songs.

Coclico, Adrianus Petit, Flemish musician and theorist; b. in Flanders c.1500; d. Copenhagen in 1563 (of plague). He was a disciple of Josquin; held a teaching post at the Univ. of Wittenberg (1545); then was in Frankfurt-on-the-Oder (1546), in Königsberg (1547) and in Nuremberg (1550). In 1555 he was in Wismar; was compelled to leave Germany when a charge of bigamy was made against him; he settled in Copenhagen in 1556 as organist of the court chapel. He was the author of the important tracts *Compendium musices* (1552; reproduced in facsimile [Kassel, 1955] in the series of Documenta Musicologica, ed. by M. Bukofzer; Engl. trans., A. Seay, Translations Series 5 [Colorado Springs, 1973]); and *Musica reservata* (1552).
BIBLIOGRAPHY: M. Van Crevel, *Adrianus Petit Coclico* (The Hague, 1940); G. Reese, *Music in the Renaissance* (N.Y., 1954).

Coelho, Ruy, eminent Portuguese composer; b. Alcaçer do Sal, March 3, 1891. He studied piano and composition in Lisbon; in 1910 he went to Germany where he took lessons in composition with Engelbert Humperdinck, Max Bruch, and Schoenberg (1910–13); subsequently took a course at the Paris Cons. with Paul Vidal; returning to Portugal he was active as a concert pianist; also wrote music criticism in the *Diario de Noticias*.
WORKS: As a composer he devoted himself mainly to opera. Most of these were produced at the Lisbon Opera: *Inês de Castro* (Jan. 15, 1927); *Belkiss* (June 9, 1928); *Entre gestas* (1929); *Tá-Mar* (June 16, 1937); *Don João IV* (Dec. 1, 1940); *Rosas de todo o Ano* (May 30, 1940); *A Rosa de Papel* (Dec. 18, 1947); *Auto da Barca do Inferno* (Jan. 15, 1950); *Inês Pereira* (1952); *O Vestido de Novia* (Jan. 4, 1959); *Orfeu em Lisboa* (1963); *A Bela Dama sem Pecado* (*Beautiful Lady Without Sin*; 1968); *Auto da Barca da Gloria* (1970); also *Serão da Infanta, Vagabundo, Soror Mariana,* and *Cavaleiro das maôs irresistiveis.* Ballets: *A Princesa dos Sapatos de ferro* (1912); *Rainha santa* (1926); *A Feira* (1930); *Dom Sebastião* (1943); *Arraial na Ribeira* (1951); *Fatima,* oratorio (1960); *Oratorio da Paz* (1967). Orchestral works: *5 Sinfonias camoneanas* (1912, 1917, 1943, 1951, 1957); *Nun Alvares,* symph. poem (1922); *Suite Portuguesa No. 1* (1926) and *No. 2* (1928); *Petites Symphonies* Nos. 1 and 2 (1928, 1932); *Sinfonia d'alem Mar* (1969); Piano Concerto No. 1 (1909); Piano Concerto No. 2 (1948); Violin Sonata No. 1 (1910); Violin Sonata No. 2 (1924); Piano Trio (1916); *Cançôes de Saudade e Amor* for voice and piano (1917); songs.

Coenen, Franz, Dutch violinist; b. Rotterdam, Dec. 26, 1826; d. Leyden, Jan. 24, 1904. A pupil of his father, an organist; then of Vieuxtemps and Molique. After tours as concert violinist with Henri Herz, and in South America with E. Lübeck, he settled in Amsterdam; until 1895 he was director in the Cons.

Coenen, Johannes Meinardus, Dutch bassoonist and conductor; b. The Hague, Jan. 28, 1824; d. Amsterdam, Jan. 9, 1899. Pupil at the Cons. there, of Lübeck; 1864, conductor at the Grand Dutch Theater, Amsterdam; then at the Palais d'Industrie. The Palais Orch., which he founded, became world famous. He retired in 1896.

Coenen, Willem, pianist, brother of **Franz Coenen**; b. Rotterdam, Nov. 17, 1837; d. Lugano, March 18, 1918. He traveled in South America and the West Indies; taught, gave concerts, and composed in London (1862–1909); then retired and lived near Lugano. He wrote an oratorio, *Lazarus* (1878); published piano music and songs; many cantatas, Masses, etc., remain in MS.

Coerne, Louis Adolphe, American composer; b. Newark, N.J., Feb. 27, 1870; d. Boston, Sept. 11, 1922. He studied violin with Kneisel and composition at Harvard Univ. with J. K. Paine (1888–90); then went to Germany where he took courses with Rheinberger in Munich. Returning to America, he became the first recipient of the degree of Ph.D. in music given by an American university, with the thesis *The Evolution of Modern Orchestration* (1905; publ. N.Y., 1908); then occupied teaching positions at Harvard Univ., Smith College, Univ. of Wisconsin, etc.
WORKS: opera *Zenobia* (1902; produced in Bremen, Germany, Dec. 1, 1905); for orch.: *Hiawatha,* symph. poem (1893); *Romantic Concerto* for violin and orch.; *Beloved America,* patriotic hymn for male chorus and orch.; many part songs; *Swedish Sonata* for violin and piano; 3 piano trios in canon. Most of his manuscript works are in the Boston Public Library.

Cœuroy, André (real name **Jean Belime**), distinguished French music critic; b. Dijon, Feb. 24, 1891; studied in Paris at the École Normale Supérieure, and with Max Reger in Germany. He was in the French army in World War I, and was taken prisoner. He continued his musical activities in the German prison camp, organizing instrumental bands and giving lectures on Wagner and other composers. After his release, he taught languages in Paris; lectured on French music in the U.S. (1930–31). He was a founder and associate editor of *La Revue Musicale* (1920) and wrote music criticisms in various French newspapers. His musical works include several pieces for clarinet; also a clarinet quintet. His writings are valuable for the originality of presentation as well as scholarship and accuracy.

WRITINGS: *La Musique française moderne* (Paris, 1921); *Essais de musique et littérature comparées* (1923); *Weber* (1924); *Le Jazz* (in collaboration with A. Schaeffner, 1926); *Le Phonographe* (1927); *Panorama de la musique contemporaine* (1928); *Panorama de la Radio* (in collaboration with J. Mercier, 1929); *Histoire de la musique avec l'aide du disque* (in collaboration with R. Jardillier, 1931); *La Musique et le peuple* (1942); *Histoire générale du jazz* (1943); *Les Lieder de Schubert* (1948); *R. Schumann* (1949); *La Musique et ses formes* (1950); *Chopin* (1951); *Dictionnaire critique de la musique ancienne et moderne* (Lausanne, 1956).

Cogan, Philip, Irish composer; b. Cork, 1748; d. Dublin, Feb. 3, 1833. He was a chorister at Cork; in 1772 went to Dublin where he occupied various posts as church organist. He acquired great renown as a teacher and performer; Michael Kelly and Thomas Moore were his pupils. Cogan wrote numerous pieces for the harpsichord and the piano, two piano concertos, and two comic operas: *The Ruling Passion* (Dublin, Feb. 24, 1778), and *The Contract* (Dublin, 1782; revived under the title, *The Double Stratagem,* 1784). In some of his piano works he incorporated Irish rhythms, and is therefore regarded as a pioneer composer of instrumental music in Ireland.

Cohan, George M. (Michael), celebrated American composer of popular songs; b. Providence, July 3, 1878 (Cohan, himself, believed that he was born on July 4, but the discovery of his birth certificate proves July 3 to be correct); d. New York, Nov. 5, 1942. He was a vaudeville performer and had a natural talent for writing verses and simple melodies in the ballad style. His greatest song, *Over There,* became sweepingly popular during World War I. A congressional medal was given to him for this song.

BIBLIOGRAPHY: W. Morehouse, *George Michael Cohan, Prince of the American Theater* (N.Y., 1943).

Cohen, Harriet, distinguished English pianist; b. London, Dec. 2, 1895; d. there, Nov. 13, 1967. She studied piano with her parents; then took an advanced course in piano playing with Matthay; made her first public appearance as a solo pianist at the age of 13. She then engaged in a successful career in England, both as a soloist with major orchestras and in chamber music concerts. She made a specialty of old keyboard music, but also played many contemporary compositions; Vaughan Williams, Arnold Bax and other English composers wrote special works for her. In 1938 she received the Order of Dame Commander of the British Empire in appreciation of her services. She published a book on piano playing. *Music's Handmaid* (London, 1936; 2nd ed., 1950). Her memoirs, *A Bundle of Time,* were published posthumously (London, 1969).

Cohen, Jules-Émile-David, French composer; b. Marseilles, Nov. 2, 1835; d. Paris, Jan. 13, 1901. He studied at the Paris Cons., piano with Marmontel, organ with Benoist and composition with Halévy, and carried

first prizes in each of these courses. He then served as instructor of choral singing at the Paris Cons.; in 1877 was engaged as chorusmaster at the Grand Opéra. He produced several operas, none too successful, among them *Les Bleuets* (Paris, Oct. 23, 1867), and *Dea* (Paris, April 30, 1870); also wrote 3 cantatas; several Masses; symphonic and chamber music; some 200 songs and 200 piano pieces.

Cohn, Arthur, American composer, conductor and publishing executive; b. Philadelphia, Nov. 6, 1910. He studied at the Combs Cons. of Music in Philadelphia (1920–28), and with William F. Happich; also studied violin with Sascha Jacobinoff (1930–31); in 1933–34 he studied composition at the Juilliard School of Music with Rubin Goldmark. Returning to Philadelphia, he was appointed Director of the Edwin A. Fleisher Collection at the Free Library of Philadelphia (1934–52); also served as executive director of the Settlement Music School in Philadelphia (1952–56). From 1942 to 1965 he conducted the Symphony Club of Philadelphia; also Germantown Symph. Orch. (1949–55), the Philadelphia Little Symphony (1952–56), and in 1958 was appointed conductor of the Haddonfield, New Jersey, Symph. Orch.; made guest appearances at Children's Concerts with the Philadelphia Orch. From 1956 to 1966 he was head of symphonic and foreign music at Mills Music Co., and from 1966 to 1972 held a similar position with the MCA Music. In 1972 he was appointed Director of Serious Music at Carl Fischer.

WORKS: 6 string quartets between 1928 and 1945; *5 Nature Studies* (1932); *Retrospections,* for string orch. (Phila., April 3, 1935); *Music for Brass Instruments* (1935); Suite for Viola and Orch. (1937); *Machine Music* for 2 pianos (1937); 4 Preludes for String Orch. (N.Y., May 26, 1937); *4 Symphonic Documents* (1939); *Music for Ancient Instruments* (1939; awarded first prize in a contest of the American Society of Ancient Instruments); Quintuple Concerto for 5 Ancient Instruments with a Modern Orch. (1940); Concerto for Flute and Orch. (1941); Variations for Clarinet, saxophone and String Orch. (1945); *Music for Bassoon,* unaccompanied (1947); *Kaddish* for orch. (1964). Perhaps the most remarkable of his works is *Quotations in Percussion* for 103 instruments handled by 6 players (1958). He published *The Collector's Twentieth-Century Music in the Western Hemisphere* (N.Y., 1961); *Twentieth-Century Music in Western Europe* (N.Y., 1965); *Musical Quizzical* (77 puzzles; N.Y., 1970; dedicated "to the most sagacious and needle-witted musician I know").

Cohn, Heinrich. See **Conried, Heinrich.**

Colasse, Pascal, French opera composer; b. Rheims, Jan. 22, 1649; d. Versailles, July 17, 1709. He was a pupil of Lully, who entrusted him with writing out the parts of his operas from the figured bass and melody. Later Colasse was accused of appropriating scores thrown aside by his master as incomplete. In 1683 he was appointed Master of the Music; in 1696, royal chamber musician. He was a favorite of Louis XIV, and obtained the privilege of producing operas at Lille, but the theater burned down; his opera *Polyxène* *et Pyrrhus* (1706) failed, and his mind became disordered. Of 10 operas, *Les Noces de Thétys et Pélée* (1689) was his best. He also composed songs, sacred and secular.

Colburn, George, American composer and conductor; b. Colton, N.Y., June 25, 1878; d. Chicago, April 18, 1921. He studied violin and singing at the American Cons. of Music in Chicago; then taught there (1903–15); conducted at Ravinia Park in 1913; from 1915 was director of municipal music at Winona, Minnesota. He wrote several symph. poems and scores for theatrical plays: *Masque of Montezuma* (1912); *Masque of Demeter and Persephone* (1913); *Anthony and Cleopatra* (1914); etc.; also some chamber music (Piano Quartet, etc.).

Cole, Nat "King" (**Nathaniel Adams Coles**), black American pianist and singer; b. Montgomery, Alabama, March 17, 1917; d. Santa Monica, Cal., Feb. 15, 1965. He worked as jazz pianist in Los Angeles night clubs; in 1939 formed the original King Cole Trio (piano, guitar, bass); then turned to singing. He was the first Negro artist to acquire a sponsor on a radio program; also had a brief series on television. He created a distinct style of velvet vocalization and satin softness in the rendition of intimate, brooding and sentimental songs. His appeal was universal; his tours in South America, Europe, the Middle East and Orient attracted great multitudes of admirers who knew him by his recordings. The sole exception was his native state; at his concert in Birmingham, Alabama, on April 10, 1956, he was attacked by six white men and suffered a minor back injury.

Cole, Rossetter Gleason, American composer; b. Clyde, Mich., Feb. 5, 1866; d. Lake Bluff, Ill., May 18, 1952. He studied music with C. B. Cady; in 1890 went to Germany where he studied composition with Max Bruch in Berlin, and organ with Middleschulte. Returning to America in 1892 he occupied various posts as teacher and organist in Wisconsin, Iowa and Illinois; lived mostly in Chicago.
WORKS: *The Maypole Lovers,* opera (1931; a suite from it was performed by the Chicago Symph. Orch., Jan. 9, 1936); *Hiawatha's Wooing* for narrator and orch. (1904); *King Robert of Sicily* for narrator and orch. (1906); *Ballade* for cello and orch. (Minneapolis, 1909); *Symphonic Prelude* (Chicago, March 11, 1915); *Pioneer Overture* (composed for the Centenary of the state of Illinois; performed by the Chicago Symph. Orch., composer conducting, March 14, 1919); *Heroic Piece* for organ and orch. (Chicago, Feb. 11, 1924); cantatas, *The Passing of Summer* (1902); *The Broken Troth* (1917); *The Rock of Liberty* (1920); Violin Sonata; several organ pieces; piano pieces (*From a Lover's Notebook, In Springtime, Sunset in the Hills,* etc.); songs (*Lilacs, Love's Invocation,* etc.). In 1896 he married the pianist **Fannie Louise Gwinner.**

Cole, Sidney Robert, English organist and music educator; b. London, Oct. 21, 1865; d. there, Nov. 28, 1937. He studied at the Royal College of Music; later was examiner there. In 1902 he went to Australia, settling as a teacher in Melbourne. He returned to England in 1932. His numerous compositions for organ, chorus, and piano, almost all in manuscript, are preserved in the library of the British Music Society in Melbourne.

Cole, Ulric, American composer and pianist; b. New York, Sept. 9, 1905. She studied with Goetschius and Rubin Goldmark (composition) and Josef Lhévinne (piano). She wrote two piano concertos; a piano quintet; two violin sonatas and many piano pieces. She was the soloist in the première of her Divertimento for Piano and String Orchestra with the Cincinnati Symph. (March 31, 1939).

Coleman, Ornette, black American jazz alto saxophonist and composer; b. Ft. Worth, Texas, March 9, 1930. He was autodidact; served his apprenticeship playing in carnival and 'rhythm and blues' bands. His own studies of harmony and theory led him to develop a distinctive style in which the improvisational melodic line is independent of the pre-assigned harmonic scheme. He also writes concert music in a respectable modernistic idiom.
BIBLIOGRAPHY: A. B. Spellman, *Black Music. Four Lives in the Bebop Business* (N.Y., 1966; pp. 77–1950); E. Jost, "Zur Musik Ornette Colemans," *Jazzforschung* (1970).

Coleridge-Taylor, Samuel, British composer of African descent (his father was a native of Sierra Leone; his mother English); b. London, Aug. 15, 1875; d. Croydon, Sept. 1, 1912. Studied violin at the Royal Academy of Music (1890); won composition scholarship (1893); studied under Stanford until 1896. In 1903 he founded at Croydon an amateur string orch. which was very successful; later he added professional woodwind and brass; appointed violin teacher at the Royal Academy of Music (1898); conductor of the London Handel Society (1904–12); later lived as composer and teacher in Croydon. Made three concert tours of the U.S. in 1904, 1906 and 1910, conducting his own works. From the very beginning his compositions showed an individuality that rapidly won them recognition, and his short career was watched with interest.
WORKS: a three-act opera, *Thelma*; the operettas *Dream Lovers* and *The Gitanos*; for soli, chorus and orch.: the successful trilogy *The Song of Hiawatha,* including *Hiawatha's Wedding Feast* (London, 1898); *The Death of Minnehaha* (North Staffordshire, 1899); *Hiawatha's Departure* (Albert Hall, 1900); the entire trilogy was first performed in Washington, D.C. (Nov. 16, 1904, composer conducting); *The Blind Girl of Castel Cuille* (Leeds, 1901); *Meg Blane* (Sheffield, 1902); *The Atonement* (Hereford, 1903); *Kubla Khan* (Handel Society, London, 1906); *Endymion's Dream,* one-act opera (Brighton, England, Feb. 3, 1910); *A Tale of Old Japan* (London Choral Society, 1911); for orch.: Ballade for Violin and Orch.; Symphony in A minor (London, 1896); *Legend* for Violin and Orch.; Ballade in A minor (Gloucester Festival, 1898); *African Suite*; Romance for Violin and Orch.; *Solemn Prelude* (Worcester, 1899); *Scenes from an Everyday Romance,* suite (London Phil. Society, 1900); *Idyll* (Gloucester Festival, 1901); *Toussaint l'Ouverture,* concert overture (Queen's Hall Symphony Concerts,

London, Oct. 26, 1901); *Hemo Dance*; *Ethiopa Saluting the Colours*, concert march; *4 Novelletten* for string orch.; *Symphonic Variations on an African Air* (London, June 14, 1906, composer conducting); *Bamboula*, rhapsodic dance (Norfolk Festival, Conn., 1910); Violin Concerto in G minor (Norfolk Fest., Conn., 1911); *Petite suite de concert*; incidental music to Phillips' *Herod* (1900), *Ulysses* (1902), *Nero* (1906), *Faust* (1908); etc.; chamber music: Piano Quintet; Nonet for Piano, Strings and Woodwind (1894); *Fantasiestücke* for string quartet (1895); Clarinet Quintet; String Quartet; Violin Sonata; vocal works: *Zara's Earrings*, rhapsody for voice and orch.; *Land of the Sun*, part song; *In Memoriam*, 3 rhapsodies for voice and piano; *The Soul's Expression*, 4 songs for contralto and orch.; *Sea Drift*, rhapsody for chorus; services, anthems, solo songs; for piano: *Silhouettes*; *Cameos*; *Scènes de ballet*; etc. Also other compositions for violin, organ, and arrangements.

BIBLIOGRAPHY: M. Byron, *A Day with Samuel Coleridge-Taylor* (1912); *Golden Hours ·with Samuel Coleridge-Taylor* (1913); W. C. B. Sayers, *Samuel Coleridge-Taylor, His Life and Letters* (1915); Mrs. Samuel Coleridge-Taylor, *Samuel Coleridge-Taylor, A Memory Sketch* (1942).

Colgrass, Michael (Charles), American composer; b. Chicago, April 22, 1932. He studied at the Univ. of Illinois (Mus.B., 1956); attended classes at the Berkshire Music Center in Tanglewood (1952–54). His principal teachers were Darius Milhaud, Lukas Foss, Wallingford Riegger and Ben Weber. A percussion player by profession, he was employed in various ensembles in N.Y. In his own music, percussion plays a significant melorhythmic role. He also studied theater arts, including special techniques of the Commedia dell' Arte of the Piccolo Teatro of Milan and physical training for actors at the Polish Theater Laboratory; wrote drama and poetry. He received the Guggenheim Fellowship Awards in 1964 and 1968; won the Pulitzer Prize in 1978.

WORKS: *Chamber Music* for 4 drums and string quartet (1954); Percussion Quintet (1955); Divertimento for 8 Drums, Piano and Strings (1960); Rhapsody for Clarinet, Violin and Piano (1962); *Light Spirit* for flute, viola, guitar and percussion (1963); *Sea Shadow* for orch. (1966); *As Quiet As* for orch. (1966); *New People*, song cycle for mezzo-soprano, viola and piano (1969); *The Earth's a Baked Apple* for chorus and orch. (1969); *Letter From Mozart*, a collage for piano and orch. (N.Y., Dec. 3, 1976); *Best Wishes, U.S.A.* for black chorus, white chorus, jazz band, folk instruments, 4 vocalists and orch. (1976); *Concertmasters*, concerto for 3 violins and orch. (1976). *Dejà vu*, concerto for 4 percussionists and orch. (1978; received the Pulitzer Prize).

Collaer, Paul, Belgian pianist and writer on music; b. Boom, June 8, 1891. He studied science at the Univ. of Brussels; then became interested in music; organized concerts; became director of the Brussels Radio and promoted performances of modern music.

WRITINGS: *Stravinsky* (1930); *J. S. Bach* (1936); *Signification de la musique* (1943); *Darius Milhaud* (1947); *La Musique moderne* (1955); *A History of Modern Music* (amplified edition of *La Musique moderne*, N.Y., 1963); *Ozeanien* (Leipzig, 1965); *Amerika; Eskimo und indianische Bevölkerung* (Leipzig, 1967); with A. van der Linden, *Atlas historique de la musique* (Paris, 1960); *La Musique Populaire Traditional en Belgique* (Brussels, 1974).

Collard, a family of pianoforte makers in London. M. Clementi, in partnership with John Longman, bought out the music publishers Longman & Broderip in 1798. Longman left to establish his own enterprise and Clementi entered into a new partnership including himself, Banger, F. A. Hyde, F. W. Collard and Davis; after several changes, the firm was known as Clementi, Collard & Collard (1823); following Clementi's death in 1832, it has been known as Collard & Collard. While Clementi undoubtedly played an important part in the success of the business, it was Collard's patented inventions which gave the pianofortes their distinctive character, and established the firm's reputation in that field.

Colles, Henry Cope, eminent British music scholar; b. Bridgnorth, Shropshire, April 20, 1879; d. London, March 4, 1943. He studied at the Royal College of Music with Parry (music history), organ with Walter Alcock, and theory with Walford Davies. Subsequently he received a scholarship at Worcester College, Oxford, to study organ; then entered Oxford Univ., obtaining his B.A. (1902), Mus. Bac. (1903) and M.A. (1907); honorary Mus. Doc. (1932). In 1905 he became music critic of *The Academy*; from 1906-19 was music critic of *The Times*; in 1919 was appointed teacher of music history and criticism at the Royal College of Music; was also music director of Cheltenham Ladies' College; in 1923, became member of the board of professors at the Royal College of Music. He was the editor of the third and fourth editions of *Grove's Dictionary of Music and Musicians* (1927-29 and 1939-40).

WRITINGS: *Brahms* (1908; in German, 1913); *The Growth of Music, a Study in Music History for Schools* (3 vols., 1912-16; 3rd ed., prepared by Eric Blom, 1956); *Voice and Verse, a Study in English Song* (1928); *The Chamber Music of Brahms* (1933); *English Church Music* (1933); *The Royal College of Music; a Jubilee Record, 1883-1933* (1933); *On Learning Music* (1940); *Walford Davies* (London, 1942). His *Essays and Lectures* were published posthumously in 1945. Articles: "Some Music Instruction Books of the 17th Century," in *Proceedings of the Music Academy* (1928-29); "Wagner," in D. Ewen's *From Bach to Stravinsky* (1933); "Sibelius," in *Great Contemporaries* (1933). Colles revised and added chapters to Sir Hubert Parry's *Evolution of the Art of Music* (new ed. 1930); edited vol. VII of *Oxford History of Music* (1934).

Collet, Henri, French music critic and composer; b. Paris, Nov. 5, 1885; d. there, Nov. 23, 1951. He was a pupil of J. Thibaut and Barès in Paris; then studied Spanish literature with Menéndez Pidal in Madrid, continuing his music studies under Olmeda. He coined the title 'Les Six Français' for a group of young French composers comprising G. Auric, L. Durey, A. Honegger, D. Milhaud, F. Poulenc and G. Tailleferre.

WORKS: (compositions mostly in Spanish style): *El Escorial*, symph. poem; *Danses castillanes* for orch.; *Gitanerías* for orch.; *La Cueva di Salamanca*, orchestral intermezzo; *Impressions (Vers Burgos)* for string quartet; *Rhapsodie castillane* for viola and orch.; *Romería castellana* for woodwinds; Piano Quintet; String Quartet; *Trio castillan; Sonata castillane* for violin and piano; many songs (based on texts by F. James and on Spanish folk themes).

WRITINGS: *Un tratado de Canto de órgano (siglo XVIº) MS. en la Biblioteca Nacional de Paris* (Madrid, 1913); *Le Mysticisme musical espagnol au XVIe siècle* (Paris, 1913); a biography of Victoria, in *Maîtres de la musique* (Paris, 1914); *Albéniz et Granados* (1926); *Samson et Dalila* (guide to Saint-Saëns's opera; 1926); "La Renaissance musicale en Espagne au XIXe siècle," in *Encyclopédie du Conservatoire; L'Essor de la musique espagnole au XXe siècle* (1929); also historical essays in *Bulletin Hispanique* and *L'Année Musicale*.

Collette, Buddy, black American jazz flutist and composer; b. Los Angeles, Calif., Aug. 6, 1922. He studied composition with Ernest Kanitz. He played flute with Henry Mancini, Quincy Jones and Benny Carter bands; appeared at the San Remo Festival, Italy, in 1962. He favors the West Coast jazz style in an eloquently cool technique; his song *Blue Sands* has become a jazz standard.

Collier, Ronald, Canadian composer; b. Coleman, Alberta, July 3, 1930. He played trombone in a school band in Vancouver (1943–49); studied composition privately with Gordon Delamont in Toronto (1951); later studied with Hall Overton in N.Y. He was a trombonist in several orchestras, including the Toronto Symph.; then formed his own jazz group, and was the first jazz composer to receive a Canada Council grant (1965); in 1971 became composer in residence at Humber College in Toronto.

WORKS: for jazz orch., include a ballet, *Aurora Borealis* (1967); music for a television drama, *Silent Night, Lonely Night* (1965); *Cambodian Suite* (1959); *The City*, with narrator-singer (1960); *Requiem for JFK* (1964); *Bonjour Canada Opening* (1967); *The Carnival*, with narrator-singer and solo flugelhorn (1969); *Celebration*, with solo piano (in collaboration with Duke Ellington, 1972); *Humber Suite* (1973); chamber pieces for jazz ensemble; *Invention Nos. 1* and *2* (1955); *Opus for Quintet* (1956); *Stratford Adventure* (1956); *Jazz Ballet* (1960); *2 Shades of Blue* (1962); *Impressions* (1963); *Hear Me Talkin' to Ya*, with narrator and singer (1964); *Walkin' Out* (1965). He also wrote a *Lyric for Trumpet* for trumpet and concert band (1970) and *Waterfront, Night Thoughts* for flute and piano (1965).

Collingwood, Lawrance Arthur, English composer; b. London, March 14, 1887. He studied at the Guildhall School and later at Exeter College. In 1912 he went to Russia where he entered the St. Petersburg Cons., studying with Glazunov, Wihtol, Steinberg and Tcherepnin; he remained there until the Revolution; returned to England (1918), where he became active as opera conductor. He conducted his own opera, *Macbeth*, at the Old Vic Theatre on April 12, 1934; his second opera *The Death of Tintagiles* was produced in concert form in London on April 16, 1950. His two piano sonatas were published in Russia. He has written many other instrumental works and has edited Breton folksongs.

BIBLIOGRAPHY: C. H. Glover, "Lawrance Collingwood," *Musical Quarterly* (April 1926).

Colobrano, Michele Enrico Carafa de. See **Carafa de Colobrano, Michele Enrico.**

Colonna, Giovanni Paolo, eminent composer of church music; b. Bologna, June 16, 1637; d. there, Nov. 28, 1695. He studied organ with Filipuzzi in Bologna; composition in Rome with Carissimi, Benevoli and Abbatini. In 1659 he became organist at San Petronio, Bologna; appointed maestro di cappella in 1674. He was several times elected President of the Accademia Filarmonica.

WORKS: composed mostly church music, but also wrote several operas, *Amilcare di Cipro* (1692) and others, and thirteen oratorios, *La profezia d'Eliseo* (1686), and others. Church works: *Motetti* for 2 and 3 voices (1681); three books of *Salmi brevi* for eight voices and organ (1681, 1686, 1694); *Motetti sacri a voce sola con due violini e bassetto di viola* (1681); *Litanie con le quattro antifone della B. Vergine* for 8 voices (1682); *Messe piene* for 8 voices with organ (1684); *Messa, salmi e responsori per li defonti* for 8 voices (1685); *Compieta con le tre sequenze dell' anno* for 8 voices (1687); *Sacre lamentazioni della settimana santa* for solo voice (1689); *Messa e salmi concertati* for 3 and 5 voices with instruments (1691); *Psalmi ad vesperas* for 3–5 voices (1694); many other church works are also extant in MS.

BIBLIOGRAPHY: L. Frati, "Per la storia della musica in Bologna nel secolo XVII," *Rivista Musicale Italiana* (1925); A. Schnoebelen, "Performance Practices at San Petronio in the Baroque," *Acta Musicologica* (Jan./June 1969).

Colonne, Édouard (real name **Judas**), French conductor and violinist; b. Bordeaux, July 23, 1838; d. Paris, Mar. 28, 1910. He studied at the Paris Cons. under Girard and Sauzay (violin) and with Elwart and Ambroise Thomas (composition). In 1873 he founded the 'Concerts National' (which later became famous as 'Concerts du Châtelet'; then 'Concerts Colonne') at which he brought out the larger works of Berlioz, and many new orchestral scores by contemporary German and French composers. In 1878 he conducted the official Exposition concerts; was conductor at the Grand Opéra in 1892; appeared frequently as visiting conductor in London, also in Russia, Portugal and with the New York Philharmonic (1905).

Coltrane, John William, remarkable black American jazz musician, a virtuoso on the tenor saxophone, whose theory and practice stimulated the creation of sophisticated jazz performance which came to be known as "the new black music"; b. Hamlet, North Carolina, Sept. 23, 1926; d. Huntington, Long Island, N.Y., July 17, 1967. He studied at the Ornstein School of Music in Philadelphia; played in the bands of Dizzy

Gillespie, Johnny Hodges, Miles Davis and Thelonious Monk. He enhanced the resources of his style by studying ancestral African and kindred Asian music, absorbing the mystical trends of these ancient cultures.

BIBLIOGRAPHY: C. O. Simpkins, *Coltrane: A Biography* (N. Y., 1975); J. C. Thomas, *Chasin' the Trane: The Music and Mystique of John Coltrane* (N. Y., 1975); Bill Cole, *John Coltrane* (N.Y., 1976).

Combarieu, Jules (-Léon-Jean), eminent French music historian; b. Cahors, Lot, Feb. 4, 1859; d. Paris, July 7, 1916. *Docteur ès lettres*; prof. of history of music at the Collège de France.

WRITINGS: *Les Rapports de la poésie et de la musique considérées du point de vue de l'expression* (1893; dissertation); "L'Influence de la musique allemande sur la musique française," *Jahrbuch Peters* (1895); *Études de philologie musicale*: 1. *Théorie du rhythme dans la composition moderne d'après la doctrine antique* (1896; critique and simplification of Westphal); 2. *Essai sur l'archéologie musicale au XIXe siècle et le problème de l'origine des neumes* (1896; these two latter were awarded prizes by the Académie); 3. *Fragments de l'Enéide en musique d'après un manuscrit inédit* (1898); *Eléments de grammaire musicale historique* (1906); *La Musique: ses lois, son évolution* (1907; numerous eds.; in English, 1910); *Histoire de la musique des origines au début du XXe siècle* (3 vols., Paris, 1913–19; an authoritative work; 8th ed. of vol. I, 1948; 6th ed. of vol. II, 1946; new ed. of vol. III, 1947).

Combe, Édouard, Swiss conductor and composer; b. Aigle, Sept. 23, 1866; d. Lausanne, Nov. 19, 1942. He studied in Paris; served as musical secretary to the conductor Lamoureux; was for a season a conductor in Cairo, Egypt (1895–96). In 1896 was appointed to the staff of the Geneva Cons.; from 1902–14 he taught music history in Lausanne. He contributed numerous articles on music to the *Gazette musicale de la Suisse Romande* and other music journals. He composed a symphonic poem *Les Alpes*, several overtures and marches.

Combs, Gilbert Raynolds, American organist; b. Philadelphia, Jan. 5, 1863; d. there, June 14, 1934. His father, a distinguished organist, was his first teacher. He originally studied medicine but made such progress in music, that he decided to become a professional musician. He studied violin and cello as well as organ; in 1885 founded his own conservatory in Philadelphia. He published a number of piano pieces; also wrote a *Dramatic Symphony*; compiled the manuals *The Science of Piano Playing* and *Introductory Steps to the Science of Piano Playing.*

Comes, Juan Bautista, Spanish composer; b. Valencia, Feb. 29, 1568; d. there, Jan. 5, 1643. He studied with Juan Peréz; became choirmaster at the Cathedral of Lérida; was at the Royal College in Valencia (1605–13); in 1619 was called by Philip III to Madrid; from 1629 again in Valencia. He left 216 works, sacred (Masses, psalms, litanies, etc.) and secular (villancicos, tonadas), most of them in manuscript, preserved at the Escorial. 2 volumes of selected numbers were published in Madrid in 1888.

BIBLIOGRAPHY: Manuel Palau, *La Obra del Músico Valenciano Juan Bautista Comes* (Valencia, 1943).

Comettant, Jean-Pierre-Oscar, French music critic and composer; b. Bordeaux, April 18, 1819; d. Montvilliers, near Le Havre, Jan. 24, 1898. He entered the Paris Cons. in 1839 and studied with Elwart and Carafa; developed considerable proficiency as composer of semi-popular songs and marches; also published piano transcriptions of famous operas, variations and fantasias. From 1852 till 1855 he lived in America, where he continued to write salon music. Returning to France, he became the musical *feuilletoniste* for *Le Siècle*, and a contributor to various musical journals; founded (with his wife, a singer) an Institut musical (1871).

WRITINGS: *Histoire d'un inventeur au 19e siècle: Adolphe Sax, ses ouvrages et ses luttes* (Paris, 1860); *Portefeuille d'un musicien; Musique et musiciens* (1862); *La musique, les musiciens et les instruments de musique chez les différents peuples du monde* (1869); *Les musiciens, les philosophes et les gaîtés de la musique en chiffres* (1870); *François Planté* (1874); *Les compositeurs illustres de notre siècle* (1883); *La Norvège musicale à Paris* (1889); *Histoire de cent mille pianos et d'une salle de concert: Histoire de la Maison Pleyel, Wolff et Cie* (1890); *La Musique de la Garde Républicaine en Amérique* (1894); etc.

Comissiona, Sergiu, Rumanian conductor; b. Bucharest, June 16, 1928. He studied violin and theory in Bucharest; conducting with Constantin Silvestri. He was one of the principal conductors of the Rumanian State Opera and the Bucharest Philharmonic; subsequently was music director of the Haifa Symph. Orch. (1959–64); was guest conductor with the London Philharmonic (1960–63), the Stockholm Philharmonic (1964–66), Berlin Radio Symph. Orch. (1965–67); also was guest conductor with major symphony orchestras in the U.S. In 1969 he was appointed musical director and conductor of the Baltimore Symph. Orch. He was an Israeli citizen (1959–76). On July 4, 1976 he became a U.S. citizen. Symbolically, the ceremony was held at Fort McHenry in Baltimore Harbor, site of the battle which inspired the writing of *The Star-Spangled Banner*.

Commer, Franz, German music historian; b. Cologne, Jan. 23, 1813; d. Berlin, Aug. 17, 1887. Pupil of Leibl and Josef Klein at Cologne; in 1828, organist of the Carmelite Church and chorister at the cathedral. In 1832 he went to Berlin to study with A. W. Bach (organ) and A. B. Marx and Rungenhagen (composition). Commissioned to arrange the library of the Royal Institute for Church Music, he pursued historical researches, and edited the following important collections of old music: *Collectio operum musicorum Batavorum saeculi XVI.* (12 volumes); *Musica sacra XVI, XVII. saeculorum* (28 volumes); *Collection de compositions pour l'orgue des XVIe, XVIIe, XVIIIe siècles* (in 6 parts); and *Cantica sacra* of the 16th–18th cent. (2 volumes). He was the founder (1844, with Küster and Kullak) of the Berlin Tonkünstlerverein;

wrote incidental music to the *Frogs* (Aristophanes) and *Electra* (Sophocles); Masses, cantatas and choruses.

Commette, Edouard, French organist; b. Lyon, April 12, 1883; d. there, April 21, 1967. He had his first appointment as church organist at Lyon in 1900; in 1956 was still active in this capacity; from 1928 he made recordings of the music of Bach. He wrote 34 organ works, and made many transcriptions for organ; also composed an opera and a symphony.

Compère, Loyset (real name **Louis**), important composer of the Flemish School; b. c.1450; d. St. Quentin, Aug. 16, 1518. He was a chorister in St. Quentin; then a singer in the chapel of the Duke of Milan (1474–75); in 1486 was singer in the service of Charles VIII of France; was subsequently canon of St. Quentin. He was greatly esteemed by his contemporaries.
WORKS: Not many of his works are extant; they include pieces in collections published by Petrucci (21 vocal works in 3, 4 and 5 parts, in *Odhecaton, Canti B,* and *Canti C*), Petrejus and Rhaw; Masses, motets, a Magnificat and chansons in MS. The motet *Omnium bonorum,* in which Compère mentions several Franco-Flemish composers beginning with Dufay and concluding with himself, was published from the Trent Codex 91 in vol. 14/15 (formerly 7) of *Denkmäler der Tonkunst in Österreich.* The *Opera Omnia,* in 6 vols., was edited by L. Finscher, and publ. as no. 15 of the *Corpus Mensurabilis Musicae* series of the American Institute of Musicology, Dallas, Texas.
BIBLIOGRAPHY: O. Gombosi, "Ghizeghem und Compère; Zur Stilgeschichte der burgundischen Chanson," in *Adler-Festschrift* (Vienna, 1930); J. Delporte, "L'École polyphonique franco-flamande; Louis Compère," *Revue Liturgique et Musicale* (July–Aug. 1932); L. Finscher, *Loyset Compère (c. 1450–1518); Life and Works* (Rome, 1964).

Concone, Giuseppe, Italian singing teacher and composer; b. Turin, Sept. 12, 1801; d. there, June 1, 1861. From 1832 until 1848 he lived in Paris where he became a popular singing teacher. His collection of solfeggi in 5 volumes *(50 Lezioni, 30 Esercizi, 25 Lezioni, 15 Vocalizzi, and 40 Lezioni per Basso)* became a standard work for singing teachers, showing no signs of obsolescence and continuing much in use all over the world. He also wrote an opera, *Un episodio del San Michele,* which was produced in Turin in 1836.

Cone, Edward T., American composer; b. Greensboro, N.C., May 4, 1917. He studied at Princeton Univ. (A.B., 1939) with Roger Sessions; was in the U.S. Army (1942–45); received a Guggenheim Fellowship in 1947; then appointed to the faculty of Princeton Univ. Among his works are a cantata *The Lotos Eaters* (1939–47); Clarinet Quintet (1941); 2 string quartets; Rhapsody for Viola and Piano; 2 violin sonatas; many piano pieces. Wrote *Musical Form and Musical Performance* (N.Y., 1968), and many articles.

Confalonieri, Giulio, Italian pianist and writer on music; b. Milan, May 23, 1896; d. there, June 29, 1972. He studied at the Univ. of Milan and Cons. of Bologna;

lived for some years in London; returned to Milan where he settled as teacher and music critic. He wrote an opera, *Rosaspina* (Bergamo, 1939); edited works by Cimarosa and Cherubini; published a comprehensive biography of Cherubini under the title: *Prigionia di un artista: il romanzo di Luigi Cherubini* (2 volumes; Milan, 1948).

Conforti (Conforto), Giovanni Luca, Italian theorist; b. Mileto (Calabria), c.1560; date of death unknown. He entered the Papal Choir in 1580 and remained there until Oct. 31, 1585, when he returned to Mileto; was chorister at the Papal Chapel again from Nov. 1, 1591. According to Baini, he was the first of his period to restore the 'trillo.'
WRITINGS: *Breve et facile maniera d'essercitarsi ad ogni scolaro . . . a far passaggi . . .* (Rome, 1593; facsimile ed., with translation, edited by Johannes Wolf, Berlin, 1922) and *Passaggi sopra tutti li salmi . . .* (Venice, 1607; contains a set of vocal ornamentations to be used in the singing of the Psalms employed on Sundays and holidays throughout the year).

Confrey, Zez (Edward Elezear), American pianist and composer of light music, especially of a style known as "novelty piano"; b. Peru, Ill., April 3, 1895; d. Lakewood, N.J., Nov. 22, 1971. He studied at the Chicago Musical College and privately with Jessie Dunn and Frank Denhart. He appeared as piano soloist, along with George Gershwin, at Paul Whiteman's concert "Experiment in Modern Music" (1924), at which Gershwin's *Rhapsody in Blue* was premiered.
WORKS: *Kitten on the Keys* (1921; his most popular piece); *Stumbling* (1922); *Dizzy Fingers, Valse Mirage,* and *Three Little Oddities* (1923); *Concert Etude* (1922); *Buffoon* (1930); *Grandfather's Clock* (1933); *Oriental Fantasy* (1935); *Ultra Ultra* (1935); *Rhythm Venture* (1936); *Della Robbia* (1938); *Champagne,* etc.

Connolly, Justin Riveagh, English composer; b. London, Aug. 11, 1933. He studied composition with Peter Racine Fricker at the Royal College of Music in London; held a Harkness Fellowship at Yale Univ. (1963–65); was instructor in music theory there in 1965–66. Returning to London, he joined the faculty of his alma mater; was also at various times engaged as conductor. He associates himself with the avant-garde; has been greatly influenced by new American methods, particularly the theory of combinatoriality of Milton Babbitt and the practice of metrical modulation of Elliott Carter; since 1968 he has made use of electronic sound.
WORKS: His works are often arranged in sets unified by a generic title and a numerical rubric; they include several *Triads* (i.e., trios): *Triad I* for trumpet, viola and piano; *Triad II* for double bass, piano and percussion; *Triad III* for oboe, viola and cello; *Triad IV* for flute, two percussion instruments and recorded sounds; *Triad V* for clarinet, viola and cello. Another set bears the general title *Obbligati: I* for 13 players; *II* for flute, clarinet, violin, cello and electronics; *III* for 20 players. Other works: *Poems of Wallace Stevens: I* for soprano and 7 players; *II* for soprano, flute and piano; *III* for soprano, piano and electronics. 2 compositions entitled *Tesserae: I* for oboe and harpsichord; *II*

for flute and piano; *Phases-Phrases* for 48 solo players; *Antiphonies* for 36 players; *Cinquepaces* for brass quintet; *M-piriform* (with reference to the piriform muscle of the thigh) for soprano, flute, violin and electronic instruments. He also wrote an overture *Rebus* for the 95th birthday of Havergal Brian in 1971, constructed on rhythmic figures of 5 and 19 units as factors of 95.

Conradi, August, German opera composer; b. Berlin, June 27, 1821; d. there, May 26, 1873. Pupil of Rungenhagen (composition). Organist of the "Invalidenhaus" in 1843; went in 1846 to Vienna, and brought out a symphony with marked success; was for years an intimate friend of Liszt at Weimar; then conducted in Stettin, Berlin, Düsseldorf, Cologne, and (from 1856) again in Berlin.
WORKS: operas (all produced in Berlin): *Rübezahl* (1847); *Musa, der letzte Maurenfürst* (1855); *Die Braut des Flussgottes* (1850); *Die Sixtinische Madonna* (1864); *Knecht Ruprecht* (1865); *So sind die Frauen; Im Weinberge des Herrn* (1867); *Das schönste Mädchen im Städtchen* (1868); also vaudevilles, farces, 5 symphonies, overtures, string quartets, etc. He arranged many popular potpourris.

Conried (real name **Cohn**), **Heinrich,** Austro-American operatic impresario; b. Bielitz, Austria, Sept. 13, 1848; d. Meran, Tyrol, April 27, 1909. He started as an actor in Vienna; in 1877 he managed the Bremen Municipal Theater; came to the U.S. in 1878 and took over the management of the Germania Theater in New York; then was in charge of various theatrical enterprises; from 1892 was director of the Irving Place Theater, N.Y., which he brought to a high degree of efficiency. From 1903 till 1908 he was the manager of the Metropolitan Opera and was instrumental in engaging numerous celebrated artists, including Caruso. During his first season he gave the first American production of *Parsifal*, despite the heated controversy regarding the rights of Wagner's heirs; his decision to produce the opera *Salomé* by Richard Strauss in 1907 also aroused a storm of protests. Conried resigned in 1908 because of dissension within the management of the Metropolitan Opera, and retired in Europe. He was decorated by several European governments; received an honorary M.A. from Harvard Univ.
BIBLIOGRAPHY: M. J. Moses, *Heinrich Conried* (N.Y., 1916).

Constant, Franz, Belgian composer and pianist; b. Montignies-le-Tilleul, Nov. 17, 1910. He studied music at the Charleroi Academy of Music and at the Brussels Cons., with M. Maas, L. Jongen, Bourguignon and Absil; in Paris studied with Tomasi. He became a concert pianist and formed a successful duo with his wife, **Jeanne Pellaerts.** In 1947 he was appointed to the faculty of the Brussels Cons. As a composer, he pursues the ideal of blending the modalities of the classical Belgian School with coloristic harmonies.
WORKS: a cantata, *Jeanne de Naples* for soprano, narrator, children's voices, speaking and singing choruses and orch. (1972); Rhapsodie for Violin and Orch. (1962); Saxophone Concerto (1963); Trumpet Concerto (1965); Sinfonietta for Flute, Oboe and String Orch. (1968); Fantasia for Saxophone and Orch. (1969); Concertino for Flute and String Orch. (1970); Violin Concerto (1971); Rhapsodie for Orch. (1973); *Expressions* for violin, piano and strings (1973); Clarinet Concertino (1975); *Allegro* for trumpet and piano (1959); *4 Séquences* for 4 saxophones (1962); *Impressions* for 4 clarinets (1964); Flute Sonata (1967); *Triade* for voice, saxophone, piano and percussion (1967); *Evocation* for flute and piano (1969); *Suo tempore* for violin and piano (1969); *Dialogue* for clarinet and piano (1970); *Sonatine picturale* for clarinet and piano (1970); *Couleur provençale* for horn and piano (1970); *Pour la guitare I* and *II* (1971); *5 Miniatures* for violin, flute and piano (1971); Piano Quartet (1971); Divertissement for Bassoon and Piano (1972); *Rythme et expression* for violin, saxophone, piano and percussion (1972); *Musique à deux* for flute and guitar (1973); *Histoires du dimanche* for children's chorus, and piano, or ensemble of 11 instruments (1973); *Marée* for oboe and piano (1973); 2 piano sonatinas (1950, 1960); Toccata for Piano (1952); *Sonatine française* for 2 pianos (1960); *Paysages* for piano (1965); *Nuances* for piano (1972); *Arcanes* for piano (1974); songs.

Constant, Marius, Rumanian-born French composer and conductor; b. Bucharest, Feb. 7, 1925. He graduated from the Bucharest Cons. in 1944; then went to Paris where he studied conducting with Fournet and composition with Messiaen, Nadia Boulanger and Honegger (1945–49); he was director of the *Ballets de Paris* of Roland Petit (1956–66); was founder, president and music director of "Ars Nova" (1963–71), a Parisian ensemble for new music; in 1967 he was guest lecturer at Stanford Univ.; in 1970 gave lectures in Hilversum, Holland. His early compositions are impressionistic; later he adopted serial and aleatory procedures, particularly in multi-media productions.
WORKS: an improvised opera, *La Serrure* (The Lock, 1969) and *Le Souper*, opera for baritone and vocal orch. (1969); the ballets *Joueur de flûte* (The Flute Players, 1952), *Haut-Voltage* (1956), *Cyrano de Bergerac* (1960), *Éloge de la folie* (with soprano, 1966), *Paradise Lost* (1967) and *Candide* (1970; Hamburg, Jan. 24, 1971; material reworked for a concert piece with solo harpsichord, 1971); *Le Jeu de Sainte Agnes*, "ecclesiastical action" on a 14th-century manuscript, for 6 singers, 5 actors, 1 dancer, Hammond organ, electric guitar, trombone and percussion (Besançon, Sept. 6, 1974); *Chants de Maldoror* for narrator, dancer-conductor, 23 improvising instrumental soloists, and 10 cellos (1962); Piano Concerto (1954); *24 Préludes* for orch. (1957); Concerto for tuba and string orch. (1958); *Concert Music* for saxophone and 11 instruments (1960); *Turner*, 3 essays for orch. (1961); *Chaconne et marche militaire* for orch. (1967); *5 Chants et une vocalise* for dramatic soprano and orch. (1968); *Winds* for 13 winds and double bass (1968); *Traits*, based on the 1930s game of surrealist poets, "exquisite corpse," for 6 to 25 musicians (1969); *Equal* for 5 percussionists (1969); *14 Stations* for 92 percussion instruments (1 player) and 6 instrumentalists (1969–70); *Candide* for amplified harpsichord and orch. (1971); *Strings* for strings (1972); *Faciebat Anno 1973* for 24 violins and orch. (Paris, July 19, 1973);

Piano Personnage for piano and chamber ensemble (Paris, Jan. 15, 1974); *For Clarinet* for solo clarinet (1974).

Constantinescu, Dan, Rumanian composer; b. Bucharest, June 10, 1931. He studied with Martian Negrea, Theodor Rogalski and Mihail Jora at the Bucharest Cons.; later joined its staff as instructor in music theory. He wrote *Divertissement in a Classical Style* for string orch. (1954); *Toma Alimos,* ballad for orch. (1955); *Partita for Orch.* (1957); Concerto for Piano and String Orch. (1963); Chamber Symphony (1968); *Sinfonia Concertante* for orch. (1970); Concerto for 2 Pianos and Orch. (1972); Trio for Violin, Clarinet and Piano (1964); Cello Sonata (1964); Clarinet Sonata (1965); Variations for Piano and String Trio (1966); String Quartet (1967); songs. His works are written in a compact neo-Classical idiom, with occasional melodic excursions into atonality.

Constantinescu, Paul, eminent Rumanian composer; b. Ploesti, July 13, 1909; d. Bucharest, Dec. 20, 1963. He studied composition at the Bucharest Cons. with Castaldi, Cuclin and Jora; then went to Vienna where he took courses with Schmidt and Joseph Marx. He was first engaged as a violinist in his native town of Ploesti (1927–34); then taught at the Academy for religious music in Bucharest (1933–41). In 1941 he was appointed prof. at the Bucharest Cons., and retained this post until his death.
WORKS: two operas, *O noapte furtunoasă* (Bucharest, Oct. 25, 1935; revised 1950 and produced in Bucharest, May 19, 1951), and *Pană Lesnea Rusalim* (Bucharest, June 27, 1956), enjoyed excellent success; 5 ballets: *Nunta în Carpaţi* (1938), *Spune, povesteste, spune* (1947), *Pe malul Dunării* (1947), *Tîrg pe muntele Găina* (1953), and *Înfrăţire* (1959); 2 Byzantine oratorios: *Patimile şi Învierea Domnului* (1946, revised 1948) and *Naşterea Domnului* (1947); Violin Sonatina (1933); *Burlesque* for piano and orch. (1937); Sinfonietta (1937); Symphony (1944, revised 1955); Concerto for String Quartet (1947); Piano Concerto (1952); *Rapsodie olteneasca* for orch. (1956); Violin Concerto (1957); Harp Concerto (1960); *Sinfonia Ploieşteană* (1961); Concerto for Violin, Cello, Piano and Orch. (1963; posthumous, Bucharest, Dec. 28, 1963); piano pieces; songs and choruses. His biography, by V. Tomescu was published in Bucharest in 1967.

Conti, Carlo, Italian composer and pedagogue; b. in Arpino, Oct. 9, 1796; d. Naples, July 10, 1868. An industrious composer, he wrote 11 operas and much church music. But his distinction lies principally in his excellence as a teacher. Conti was appointed "maestrino" at the Cons. of Naples about 1820; in 1846 he was named prof. of counterpoint (Rossini called him "the best Italian contrapuntist of his day.") Among Conti's famous pupils was Bellini.

Conti, Francesco Bartolomeo, Italian composer; b. Florence, Jan. 20, 1681; d. Vienna, July 20, 1732. He was court theorbist (from 1701) and court composer (from 1713); wrote about 40 stage works to Italian and German texts, of which the finest were *Clotilda* (Vi-enna, 1706) and *Don Chisciotte in Sierra Morena* (after Cervantes; Vienna, 1719); also 9 oratorios, 14 secular cantatas, and songs.
BIBLIOGRAPHY: C. Fruchtman and E. Fruchtman, "Instrumental Scoring in the Chamber Cantatas of Francesco Conti," in J. W. Pruett, *Studies in Musicology* (Chapel Hill, N.C., 1969).

Contilli, Gino, Italian composer; b. Rome, April 19, 1907. He studied at the S. Cecilia Academy in Rome with Respighi. Since 1942, was teaching composition at the Liceo Musicale in Messina.
WORKS: Toccata for Piano (1933); 2 concertos for orch. (1936, 1942); *Sinfonia italiana* (1938); Violin Sonata (1947); *La notte,* lyric suite for voice and small ensemble (1950); *In Lunam,* cantata (1957, Italian Radio, Nov. 20, 1964); *Espressioni sinfoniche* for orch. (1958; Venice, Sept. 21, 1960); *Offerta musicale* for soprano and 5 instruments (1959); *Immagini sonore* for soprano and 11 instruments (1964); *Preludi* for orch. (1966).

Conus, Georgi, Russian composer and theorist; b. Moscow, Sept. 30, 1862; d. there, Aug. 29, 1933. He studied at the Moscow Cons. with Taneyev and Arensky; from 1891–99 he taught there; from 1902, professor at the music school of the Philharmonic Society. He developed an original theory of metric analysis and published a brief outline of it; also wrote several symph. works, piano pieces, and songs.

Conus, Julius, Russian violinist and composer; brother of **Georgi Conus**; b. Moscow, Feb. 1, 1869; d. Malenki, Ivanov District, Jan. 3, 1942. He studied at the Moscow Cons.; later taught violin there. He was a friend of Tchaikovsky and was greatly esteemed in Moscow musical circles. His Violin Concerto, first performed by him in Moscow in 1898, has retained its popularity in Russia.

Conus, Sergei, Russian pianist and composer, son of **Julius Conus**; b. Moscow, Oct. 18, 1902. He studied music with his father, with his uncle, Leo Conus, and with Oskar Riesemann. In 1920 he went to Paris where he studied piano with Cortot and Isidor Philipp; then lived in Serbia, Bulgaria and Poland. He was again in France from 1937 to 1949, and in Morocco from 1949 to 1959; in 1959 settled in America; taught piano at the Boston Cons. His compositions are mostly for piano (24 Preludes, many miniatures, a Piano Concerto); he also wrote a symphony. His style is characteristically Russian, closely resembling that of Rachmaninoff.

Converse, Charles Crozat, American composer; b. Warren, Mass., Oct. 7, 1832; d. Englewood, N.J., Oct. 18, 1918. He studied at the Leipzig Cons. with Richter, Hauptmann and Plaidy (1855–59). Upon his return to America he was a practicing lawyer at Erie, Pa.; then lived in Highwood, N.J.
WORKS: He composed a number of patriotic overtures and cantatas, among them *American Concert Overture* on 'Hail, Columbia' (1869); *God for us,* an American hymn (1887), etc.; also vocal quartets, music for strings, 2 symphonies, 2 oratorios, etc. His

hymn *What a Friend we have in Jesus* was widely sung. In his writings he used the pen name **Karl Redan.** A man of many interests, he wrote articles on philosophical and philological subjects; proposed the use of the genderless pronoun of the third person, "thon," which has been incorporated in several dictionaries.

Converse, Frederick Shepherd, distinguished American composer; b. Newton, Mass., Jan. 5, 1871; d. Westwood, Mass., June 8, 1940. He graduated from Harvard Univ. (1893); studied music in Boston with Carl Baermann and Chadwick (1894–96); then in Munich at the Royal Academy of Music with Rheinberger, graduating in 1898. Returning to Boston, he taught harmony at the New England Cons. (1899–1901); was instructor of composition at Harvard Univ. (1901–07). He was vice-president of the Boston Opera Co. (1911–14); served as Captain in the U.S. Army (1917–19); was dean of the New England Cons. (1930–38); Mus. Doc., Boston Univ. (1933); member of the American Academy of Arts and Letters (1937). His early works reflect the influence of academic German training; later he began to apply more advanced harmonies; in his *Flivver Ten Million*, written to glorify the ten millionth Ford car, he adopted a frankly modern idiom, modeled after Honegger's *Pacific 231*.

WORKS: OPERAS: *The Pipe of Desire* (Boston Opera, Jan. 31, 1906; first American opera to be produced by the Metropolitan Opera Company, March 18, 1910; won David Bispham medal); *The Sacrifice* (Boston, March 3, 1911); *Sinbad the Sailor* (1913; not performed); *The Immigrants* (1914; not performed). Oratorios: *Job*, dramatic poem for soli, chorus and orch. (Worcester Festival, Oct. 2, 1907; also in Hamburg, Nov. 23, 1908; first American oratorio to be heard in Germany); *Hagar in the Desert*, dramatic narrative for low voice and orch. (written for Mme. Schumann-Heink; sung by her in Hamburg, 1908); cantatas: *The Peace Pipe* (1914); *The Answer of the Stars* (1919); *The Flight of the Eagle* (1930); other vocal works: *La belle dame sans merci*, ballade for baritone with orch. (1902); psalm, *I Will Praise Thee, O Lord* (1924). FOR ORCH.: symphonies, one in D minor, not numbered (performed in Munich on July 14, 1898); No. 1 (Boston, Jan. 30, 1920); No. 2 (Boston, April 21, 1922); No. 3 (1936); No. 6 (posthumously performed by the Indianapolis Symph. Orch., Nov. 7, 1940); concert overture, *Youth; Festival of Pan* (Boston, Dec. 21, 1900); *Endymion's Narrative* (1901; Boston, April 9, 1903); *Night* and *Day*, two poems for piano and orch. (Boston, Jan. 21, 1905); overture, *Euphrosyne* (Boston, 1903); orchestral fantasy, *The Mystic Trumpeter* (Philadelphia, March 3, 1905; many subsequent performances); symph. poem, *Ormazd* (St. Louis, Jan. 26, 1912); symph. poem, *Ave atque Vale* (St. Louis, Jan. 26, 1917); Fantasia for Piano and Orch. (1922); *Song of the Sea* (Boston, April 18, 1924); *Elegiac Poem* (Cleveland, Dec. 2, 1926); fantasy, *Flivver Ten Million* (Boston, April 15, 1927); *California*, festival scenes (Boston, April 6, 1928); symph. suite, *American Sketches* (Boston, Feb. 8, 1935). CHAMBER MUSIC: 3 string quartets; Violin Sonata; Cello Sonata; Piano Trio; also a violin concerto with piano accompaniment (1902); *Valzer Poetici* for piano 4 hands;

Scarecrow Sketches (excerpts from the Photo-Music-Drama *Puritan Passions*, commissioned by the Film Guild of New York, 1923; originally for piano; orchestrated and performed, Boston, Dec. 18, 1923); piano pieces and songs.

Conyngham, Barry, Australian composer; b. Sydney, Aug. 27, 1944. He studied composition in Sydney with Peter Sculthorpe; then went to Japan where he had some training in ultramodern music with Toru Takemitsu. He was employed as a jazz pianist and wrote film music for the Australian exhibit at Expo '70 in Osaka, Japan. He also wrote a number of scores for multi-media presentations and for sophisticated children in progressive Australian schools.

WORKS: *5 Windows* for orch. (1969); *Three* for a string quartet and 2 percussionists (1969); *Crisis: Thoughts in a City* for string orch. and percussion (1969); *Edward John Eyre* for actors, female voice, wind quintet, and string orch. (1970); *Ice Carving* for a lot of violins (1970); *Water . . . Footsteps . . . Time . . .* for piano, harp, electric guitar, tamtam and orch. (1970); *Five* for wind quintet (1971); *Six* for 6 solo percussion players, and wind instruments (1971).

BIBLIOGRAPHY: James Murdoch, *Australia's Contemporary Composers* (Melbourne, 1972).

Cooke, Arnold, English composer; b. Gomersal, Yorkshire, Nov. 4, 1906. He studied in Berlin with Hindemith; then at the Royal School of Music in Manchester and at Trinity College, London.

WORKS: Piano Concerto (1943); Concerto for String Orch. (1947); Symph. No. 1 (1949); Clarinet Concerto (1955); Oboe Sonata (1957); Violin Concerto (1958); Clarinet Sonata (1959); Suite for 3 Clarinets (1959); *Jabez and the Devil*, ballet (1961); Clarinet Quintet (1962); Symph. No. 2 (1963); *Variations on a Theme of Dufay* for orch. (1966); Symph. No. 3 (1967); Piano Quintet (1970); 2 overtures; 2 string quartets; Quintet, for harp, flute, clarinet, violin and cello; Quartet for Flute, Violin, Viola, Cello; Piano Quartet; Oboe Quartet; Piano Trio; Violin Sonata; Cello Sonata.

Cooke, Benjamin, English organist and composer; b. London, 1734; d. there, Sept. 14, 1793. He studied with Pepusch, whom he succeeded in 1752 as conductor at the Academy of Ancient Music; in 1757 he became choirmaster (after Gates), in 1758 lay vicar, and in 1762, organist of Westminster Abbey; Mus. Doc., Cambridge (1775) and Oxford (1782); organist of St. Martin-in-the-Fields, 1782; in 1789 he resigned the Academy conductorship in favor of Arnold. His best works are in the form of glees, canons and catches, for which he took several Catch Club prizes (*Collection of 20 Glees, Catches, and Canons for 3–6 voices in score*, London, 1775; *9 Glees and 2 Duets*, 1795). He also wrote odes, instrumental concertos, church music, pieces for organ and harpsichord, etc., and added choruses and accompaniments to Pergolesi's *Stabat Mater* (1759) and Galliard's *Morning Hymn* (1772) for the Academy of Ancient Music. His son **Robert** (b. Westminster, 1768; d. Aug. 13, 1814) became organist of St. Martin-in-the-Fields after his father's death in 1793, and on the death of Dr. Arnold, in 1802, was appointed organist and choirmaster of Westminster Abbey; ended his life by drowning himself in the Thames. He published a collection of glees in 1805.

Cooke, Deryck, English musicologist; b. Leicester, Sept. 14, 1919; d. London, Oct. 26, 1976. He studied piano privately and composition at Cambridge Univ. with Patrick Hadley and Robin Orr, earning his B.A. in 1940, M.A. in 1943, and Mus.B. in 1947. From 1947 to 1959 he was a member of the music staff of the BBC; after 1959, devoted most of his time to writing on music and broadcasting. He attracted considerable attention by his scholarly and congenial arrangement of Mahler's unfinished Tenth Symphony, which he completed using authentic fragments from Mahler's sketch; this version was approved by Alma Mahler, the composer's widow. It was first performed at a BBC Henry Wood Promenade Concert in the Albert Hall, London, on Aug. 13, 1964. Cooke published *The Language of Music* (London, 1959) and *Mahler 1860-1911* (BBC centenary booklet, 1960); contributed Part I to vol. X of the *New Oxford History of Music.*

Cooke, James Francis, eminent American writer on music and composer; b. Bay City, Mich., Nov. 14, 1875; d. Philadelphia, March 3, 1960. He was educated in Brooklyn and studied music with R. H. Woodman and W. H. Hall; went to Germany in 1900, and continued his studies with Meyer-Obersleben and H. Ritter. As editor of the *Etude* for 40 years (1908–49), he brought it to a high degree of popularity by promoting special features (columns dealing with performance and technique; simple arrangements of classics, etc.). He composed a number of successful piano pieces (*White Orchids, Moon Mist, Ballet Mignon, Sea Gardens, Italian Lake Suite*), and songs.

WRITINGS: *A Standard History of Music* (Phila., 1910); *Great Pianists on Piano Playing* (4th ed. 1914); *Mastering the Scales and Arpeggios* (1913); *Musical Playlets for Children* (1917); *Great Singers on the Art of Singing* (1921); *Great Men and Famous Musicians* (1925); *Young Folks' Picture-History of Music* (1925); *Light, more Light* (1925); *Johannes Brahms* (1928); *Claude Debussy* (1928); *Musical Travelogues* (1934); *How to Memorize Music* (1947); many non-musical works, including plays and poems.

Cooke, Thomas Simpson, English composer and singing teacher; b. Dublin, 1782; d. London, Feb. 26, 1848. A pupil of his father and Giordani; conducted theater orchestras in Dublin; was then for years an opera singer (tenor) and assistant conductor at Drury Lane, London, assistant conductor of the Philharmonic, and (1846) leader of the Concerts of Ancient Music. His versatility as an instrumentalist was displayed when, at one of his benefit concerts at Drury Lane, he performed on the violin, flute, clarinet, bassoon, horn, cello, double bass and piano. Also taught at the Royal Academy of Music; an esteemed singing teacher (Sims Reeves was his pupil), and the author of two vocal treatises, *Singing exemplified in a series of Solfeggi* and *Singing in Parts* (London, 1842). He composed nearly 20 operas for Drury Lane.

Cooley, Spade (Donnell), American country fiddler, once renowned as 'King of Western Swing'; b. in a storm cellar under a shack near Saddle Paddle Creek, Oklahoma, Dec. 17, 1910; d. Oakland, Cal., Nov. 23, 1969, while on a furlough from the Calif. State Medical Facility at Bakersfield, the minimum security state prison where he was confined from 1961 for the murder of his wife Ella Mae. Cooley was one-quarter Cherokee Indian; he joined the cowboy star Roy Rogers in Hollywood in his act, and acquired the nickname 'Spade' after a spectacular poker game during which he filled several successive flushes in spades. He replenished his financial resources from these winnings and went into the real estate business. He is credited with the authorship of the song *Shame, Shame on You.*

Coolidge, Elizabeth Sprague (Mrs. Frederick Shurtleff Coolidge), American music patron and accomplished composer; b. Chicago, Oct. 30, 1864; d. Cambridge, Mass., Nov. 4, 1953. In 1918 she established at Pittsfield, Mass. the Berkshire Festivals of Chamber Music, held annually under her auspices, which were later transferred to Washington, D.C. She was the sponsor of the Elizabeth Sprague Coolidge Foundation in the Library of Congress, created in 1925 for the purpose of producing concerts, music festivals, awarding prizes, etc., under the administration of the Music Division of the Library. Numerous modern composers, including Loeffler, Schoenberg, Malipiero, Bartók, Casella, Stravinsky, Prokofiev, Piston, and Hanson, have written works commissioned for it. The Auditorium of the Library, including its organ, is also a gift of Mrs. Coolidge. In 1932 she founded the Elizabeth Sprague Coolidge Medal "for eminent services to chamber music," which is awarded annually to one or more persons; its recipients have included Adolfo Betti, Walter W. Cobbett, Carl Engel, and E. T. Rice. She also initiated performances of modern and classical chamber music throughout the U.S. and Europe. Her sponsorship of the appearances of artists in the U.S. and abroad (the Pro Arte, Coolidge, Roth Quartets, etc.) was an important factor in the musical life of the U.S. In recognition of her many cultural contributions she was made honorary M.A. (Yale Univ., Smith College, Mills College), L.D. (Mt. Holyoke College), Mus. Doc. (Pomona College), LL.D. (Univ. of California). She received the Cobbett Medal and various foreign decorations.

Cools, Eugène, French composer; b. Paris, March 27, 1877; d. there, Aug. 5, 1936. He studied at the Paris Cons. with Gédalge, Fauré and Widor; won the Prix Crescent for his symphony (1906); was assistant of Gédalge at the Cons. (1907–23); taught at the École Normale de Musique (1919); was music critic for *Le Monde Musical;* in 1928 he was appointed editor-in-chief for Max Eschig, Paris music publisher.

WORKS: two operas, *Le Jugement de Midas* (1922) and *Kymris*; opera buffa, *Beaumarchais* on themes by Rossini; operettas: *Magda, Les Violettes de la Malmaison,* and *Ravioli*; symph. poem *La Mort de Chénier; Hamlet,* symph. suite; *Deux pièces russes* for orch. (most of these pieces are also available in piano arrangements); Piano Quintet; String Quartet; Violin

Sonata; Flute Sonata; about 80 songs; many piano pieces.

Coombs, Charles Whitney, American organist and composer; b. Bucksport, Maine, Dec. 25, 1859; d. Orange, N.J., Jan 24, 1940. He studied piano and composition in Germany; was organist of American Church in Dresden (1887–91); returned to America, and took charge of the music in the Church of the Holy Communion, N.Y., holding the position till 1908; at St. Luke's, 1908–28; retired in 1928. He was made honorary Mus. Doc. by Syracuse Univ. (1922).

WORKS: cantatas: *The Vision of St. John, Hymn of Peace, The First Christmas, The Ancient of Days, The Sorrows of Death; Song of Judith,* motet for soprano and baritone soli and chorus; a number of sacred songs, anthems, etc.; about 75 secular songs.

Cooper, Emil, Russian conductor; b. Kherson, Dec. 20, 1877; d. N.Y., Nov. 16, 1960. He studied at the Odessa Cons., then went to Vienna where he took lessons in violin with Joseph Hellmesberger; later studied in Moscow with Taneyev. At the age of 22 he began to conduct at the Kiev Opera. In 1909 he conducted the Russian Ballet and Opera with the Diaghilev troupe in Paris. He then conducted in Moscow; in 1923 he went abroad; in 1929 he conducted the Chicago Civic Opera; in 1944–50 was on the staff of the Metropolitan Opera Co.; then became musical director of the Montreal Opera Guild; subsequently lived in New York.

Cooper, George, English organist; b. London, July 7, 1820; d. there, Oct. 2, 1876. His father was an organist, and he served his apprenticeship at an early age; played organ when he was thirteen at St. Benet Church; five years later became assistant organist at St. Paul's; in 1856, appointed organist of the Chapel Royal. An able performer, he did much to elevate the public taste, especially by his playing of Bach's organ works. He published *The Organist's Assistant,* selections from classical authors; *The Organist's Manual; Organ Arrangements* (3 volumes); *Classical Extracts for the Organ; Introduction to the Organ;* also songs.

Cooper, Kenneth, highly talented American harpsichordist; b. New York, May 31, 1941. He studied harpsichord playing with Sylvia Marlowe at the Mannes College of Music, New York; also took harpsichord lessons with Fernando Valenti; then entered Columbia Univ. (B.A., 1962; M.A., 1964; Ph.D. in Musicology, 1971). He subsequently developed an energetic schedule of teaching; was instructor of music at Barnard College (1967–71), lecturing on all academic music subjects; at Brooklyn College, as adjunct assistant prof. (1971–73); in 1975 was appointed prof. of harpsichord at the Mannes College of Music, N.Y. A man of latitudinarian and panoramic faculties, Kenneth Cooper encompasses a 360° range of activities, specializing in playing piano and harpsichord, improvisation, authentication of performing usages of the Baroque, translation from musically important languages (Italian, German) and, last, not least, revivification of ragtime. He has published a number of scholarly articles dealing with the Baroque period; directed stage performance of neglected operas by Handel and gave concerts of Bach's music at midnight; he has further commissioned works for harpsichord to composers of the avant-garde; played recitals in England, at the Salzburg Festival; traveled as a concert artist in Russia, Rumania and Greece under the auspices of the U.S. Dept. of State; made frequent appearances with his wife, soprano **Josephine Mongiardo,** whom he married in 1969.

Cooper, Martin, English music critic; b. Winchester, Jan. 17, 1910. He studied at Oxford (B.A., 1931); then took courses with Egon Wellesz in Vienna (1932–34); was music critic for the *London Mercury* (1935–38); and the *Daily Herald* (1946–50); in 1954 he became music critic of the *Daily Telegraph.* He was editor of the *Musical Times* from 1953 till 1956. He is the author of several valuable monographs, on Gluck (1935), Bizet (1938) and on Opéra-Comique (1949); edited *The Concise Encyclopedia of Music and Musicians* (London, 1958; 3rd revised edition, 1975); *The Modern Age, 1890–1960* (London, 1964).

Cooper, Paul, American composer; b. Victoria, Illinois, May 19, 1926. He studied at the Univ. of Southern California under Ernest Kanitz and Roger Sessions (M.A. 1953; D.M.A. 1956); was a private student of Nadia Boulanger in Paris (1953–54). Upon return to the U.S., he held the posts of prof. of music at the Univ. of Michigan (1955–67), composer-in-residence at the Univ. of Cincinnati (1968–74), and at Rice Univ. in Houston (1974). He held two Guggenheim fellowships (1965, 1972).

WORKS: FOR ORCH.: Sinfonia for strings (1952); 4 symphonies (1954; 1956; *Lamentations,* for strings, 1971; 1973); Overture (1953); Concerto for Orchestra (1966); Violin Concerto (1967); *A Shenandoah* (for the centennial of Charles Ives, 1974). Wind ensemble: Sinfonia (1958); Concerto for Winds, Percussion and Piano (1968); *Liturgies* (1969); *Antiphons* for oboe and winds (1973). CHAMBER MUSIC: 5 string quartets (1953; 1954; 1959; 1964; *Umbrae,* 1973); *Canonic Variations* for wind quintet (1960); Viola Sonata (1961); Concerto for Harpsichord and Organ (1962); Violin Sonata (1962); Cello Sonata (1962); Sonata for Flutes and Piano (1963); Double-Bass Sonata (1964); *Concert for Two* for cello and piano (1965); *Concert for Four* for flute, oboe, harpsichord and double bass (1965); *Concert for Five* for wind quintet (1965); *Epitaphs* for alto flute, harp, and double bass (1969); *Soliloquies* for violin and piano (1970); *Chimera,* piano quartet (1972); *Variants II* for viola and piano (1972); *Aegina Music* for violin, cello and piano (1973). PIANO MUSIC: 2 sonatas (1949, 1963); *3 Small Sonatas* (1953); *Momentos* (1957); *Partimento* (1967); *Cycles* (1969). Organ music: Concerto for Antiphonal Organs (1954); Toccata (1959); *Variants I* (1971). CHORAL MUSIC: *Missa Brevis* (1954); *Chorales of Nativity* (1954); *4 Madrigals* (1956); *Genesis II* (1969); *Credo* for double chorus and orch. (1970); *?* for boys' chorus (1972); *Cantigas* for double chorus and orch. (1972). He publ. a textbook, *Perspectives in Music Theory* (1973).

Coopersmith, Jacob Maurice, American musicologist; b. New York, Nov. 20, 1903; d. Washington, May

345

12, 1968. He attended N.Y. Univ. (B.S., 1929), Columbia Univ. (M.A., 1930), Harvard Univ. (Ph.D., 1932), also studied organ with Samuel A. Baldwin and Dr. A. M. Richardson; won the Schepp Foundation Scholarship (Harvard, 1930–31), John K. Paine Traveling Fellowship (1932), Charles E. Ditson Traveling Fellowship (1933), Juilliard Foundation Grant (1934); was connected as a librarian with various radio stations. In 1949 he was appointed Senior Music Cataloger at the Library of Congress; has published many articles relating to Handel, and an edition of *Messiah* based on the original sources.

BIBLIOGRAPHY: M. Picker, "Jacob Maurice Coopersmith," *Journal of the American Musicologal Society* (Fall 1969); G. Reese, "Jacob Maurice Coopersmith," *Notes* (Dec. 1969).

Coperario (John Cooper, an Englishman who Italianized his patronymic after study in Italy), famous lutenist and viola-da-gamba player; b. c.1575; d. London, 1626. He went to Italy about 1600 and upon his return to England became an acknowledged authority in the field of instrumental and vocal music, patterned closely on the Italian model. He became teacher of music of the children of James I, and of Henry and William Lawes. His improvisations on the organ were greatly admired. He wrote a set of 'Fancies' for organ, and a set for viols; music for 2 masques; songs (*Funeral Teares*, 1606; *Songs of Mourning*, 1613, etc.). Two of his anthems are included in Leighton's *Teares of Lamentations*; numerous works for string instruments, with organ, are in the Christ Church library at Oxford; compositions for viols are preserved at the Royal College of Music, London, and other works in the British Museum. His treatise *Rules How to Compose* (c.1610) was published in facsimile in Los Angeles, 1951, with an introduction by the editor, Manfred Bukofzer.

BIBLIOGRAPHY: J. Pulver, in the *Monthly Musical Record* (April 1927); J. Pulver, in his *Biographical Dictionary of Old English Music and Instruments* (2nd ed. 1927); Ernst Hermann Meyer, *Die mehrstimmige Spielmusik des 17. Jahrhunderts in Nord und Mitteleuropa* (Kassel, 1934); G. Dodd, "Coperario or Bull?" and "The Coperario-Lupo Five-part Books at Washington," *Chelys* (1969).

Copland, Aaron, a greatly distinguished and exceptionally gifted American composer; b. Brooklyn, Nov. 14, 1900. He was educated in Boys' High School in Brooklyn; began to study piano with Victor Wittgenstein and Clarence Adler as a young child. In 1917 he took lessons in harmony and counterpoint with Rubin Goldmark in New York, and soon began to compose. His first published piece *The Cat and the Mouse* for piano (1920), subtitled *Scherzo Humoristique*, shows the influence of Debussy. In 1921 he went to Paris where he studied composition and orchestration with Nadia Boulanger. Returning to America in 1924 he lived mostly in New York; he became active in many musical activities, not only as a composer but also as a lecturer, pianist and organizer in various musical societies. He attracted the attention of Serge Koussevitzky who gave the first performance of his early score *Music for the Theater* with the Boston Symphony Orchestra in 1925; then engaged Copland as soloist in his Concerto for Piano and Orchestra in 1927; the work produced a considerable sensation because of the jazz elements incorporated in the score, and there was some subterranean grumbling among the staid subscribers to the Boston Symphony concerts. Koussevitzky remained Copland's steadfast supporter throughout his tenure as conductor of the Boston Symphony Orch., and later as the founder of the Koussevitzky Music Foundation. In the meantime, Walter Damrosch conducted in New York Copland's Symphony for Organ and Orchestra, with Nadia Boulanger as soloist. Other orchestras and their conductors also performed his music, which gained increasing recognition. Particularly popular were Copland's works based on folk motives; of these the most remarkable are *El Salón México* (1936) and the American ballets *Billy the Kid* (1938), *Rodeo* (1942) and *Appalachian Spring* (1944). A place apart is occupied by Copland's *Lincoln Portrait* (1942) for narrator and orchestra, with the texts arranged by the composer from speeches and letters of Abraham Lincoln; this work has had a great many performances, with the role of the narrator performed by such notables as Adlai Stevenson and Eleanor Roosevelt. His patriotic *Fanfare for the Common Man* (1942), achieved tremendous popularity and continued to be played on various occasions for decades; Copland incorporated it *in toto* into the score of his Third Symphony. He was for many years a member of the board of directors of League of Composers in New York; with Roger Sessions he organized the Copland-Sessions Concerts (1928–31), and was also a founder of the Yaddo Festivals (1932), and of the American Composers' Alliance (1937); also a participant in such organizations as the Koussevitzky Music Foundation, the Composers Forum, the Cos Cob Press, etc. He was head of the composition department at the Berkshire Music Center at Tanglewood from 1940 to 1965, and from 1957 to 1965 was Chairman of the Faculty. He has lectured extensively and has given courses at the New School for Social Research and at Harvard Univ. (1935 and 1944); was the Charles Eliot Norton Lecturer at Harvard in 1951–52. He is the recipient of many awards: Guggenheim Fellowship (1925–27); RCA Victor award of five thousand dollars for his *Dance Symphony*; Pulitzer Prize and New York Music Critics Circle Award for *Appalachian Spring* (1945); New York Music Critics Circle Award for the Third Symphony (1947); Oscar award for the film score *The Heiress* from the Academy of Motion Picture Arts (1950); Gold Medal for Music from the American Academy of Arts and Letters (1956); Presidential Medal of Freedom (1964); Howland Memorial Prize of Yale Univ. (1970); was also decorated with a Commander's Cross of the Order of Merit in West Germany; elected honorary membership of the Accademia Santa Cecilia, Rome. He holds numerous honorary doctor's degrees: Princeton Univ. (1956); Brandeis Univ. (1957); Wesleyan Univ. (1958); Temple Univ. (1959); Harvard Univ. (1961); Rutgers Univ. (1967); Ohio State Univ. (1970); New York Univ. (1970); Columbia Univ. (1971); also York Univ., England (1971). He has published the following books: *What to Listen for in Music* (N.Y., 1939; translated into German, Italian, Spanish, Dutch, Arabic and Chinese); *Our New Music* (N.Y., 1941); *Music and Imagination,* a collection of lectures delivered at Harvard in 1951–52 (Cambridge, Mass., 1952); *Copland on Music* (N.Y., 1960); *The New Music 1900–1960,* revised and enlarged edition (N.Y., 1968). About 1955 Copland developed a successful career as a conductor and has led major symphony orchestras in Europe, the United States, South America and Mexico; he also traveled to Russia under the auspices of the State Department. As a composer, Copland makes use of a broad variety of idioms and techniques, tempering dissonant textures by a strong sense of tonality. He enlivens his musical textures by ingenious applications of syncopation and polyrhythmic combinations; but in such works as Piano Variations he adopts an austere method of musical constructivism. He uses a modified 12-tone technique in his Piano Quartet (1950) and an integral dodecaphonic idiom in the score of *Connotations* (1962). A chronological list of his works was published by Boosey & Hawkes in 1960.

WORKS: THEATER MUSIC: *Grohg,* ballet in one act (1923; not performed; material incorporated into *Dance Symphony*); *The Second Hurricane,* a play-opera for high school (N.Y., April 21, 1937); *Billy the Kid,* ballet (Ballet Caravan Co., Chicago, Oct. 16, 1938; N.Y., May 24, 1939); *Sorcery to Science,* music for a puppet show (1939); *Rodeo,* ballet in one act (Ballet Russe de Monte Carlo, N.Y., Oct. 16, 1942); *Appalachian Spring,* ballet (Martha Graham Ballet, Washington, D.C., Oct. 30, 1944); *The Tender Land,* opera (N.Y., April 1, 1954); *Dance Panels* in 7 movements, ballet (Munich, Dec. 3, 1963).

FILM MUSIC: *The City* (1939); *Of Mice and Men* (1939); *Our Town* (1940); *North Star* (1943); *The Cummington Story* (1945); *The Red Pony* (1948); *The Heiress* (1949; received an Academy Award, 1950); incidental music to plays: *Miracle at Verdun* (1931), *The Five Kings* (1939), *Quiet City* (1939).

ORCHESTRAL: *Music for the Theater* (N.Y., League of Composers, Nov. 28, 1925, Koussevitzky conducting); Symphony for Organ and Orch. (N.Y., Jan. 11, 1925), Damrosch conducting; revised version without organ designated as First Symphony, 1928); *A Dance Symphony* (1922–25; Victor Talking Machine Co. Competition Prize; perf. by Stokowski and Philadelphia Orch., April 15, 1931); Concerto for Piano and Orch. (Boston Symph., Jan. 28, 1927, composer soloist, Koussevitzky conducting); *Symphonic Ode* (written for the 50th anniversary of the Boston Symph. and performed by Koussevitzky and the Boston Symph., Feb. 19, 1932; revised for the 75th anniversary of the Boston Symph. and rededicated to the memory of Koussevitzky; Boston Symph. under Munch, Feb. 3, 1956); *Short Symphony* (Mexico, Nov. 23, 1934, Chávez conducting; *Statements* (1933–35; first complete perf., N.Y. Philh., Jan. 7, 1942); *El Salón México* (Mexico City, Aug. 27, 1937, Chávez conducting); *Music for Radio* (CBS Symph. Orch., July 25, 1937; subtitled *Saga of the Prairie*); *An Outdoor Overture* (N.Y., Dec. 16, 1938); *John Henry,* railroad ballad (CBS, March 5, 1940); *Our Town,* orchestral suite from the film (CBS, June 9, 1940); *Quiet City,* suite from the film, for trumpet, English horn and strings (N.Y., Jan. 28, 1941); *Billy the Kid,* suite from the ballet (Boston

Symph., Jan. 30, 1942); *Lincoln Portrait* for speaker and orch. (commissioned by André Kostelanetz and perf. by him with the Cincinnati Orch., May 14, 1942; highly successful; numerous subsequent performances by many orchestras in America and Europe); *Music for Movies,* instrumental suite (N.Y., Feb. 17, 1943); *Fanfare for the Common Man* for brass and percussion (Cincinnati, March 12, 1943); *Letter from Home* (broadcast, Oct. 17, 1944); *Variations on a Theme by Eugene Goossens* (with 9 other composers; Cincinnati, March 23, 1945); *Appalachian Spring,* suite from the ballet (première, N.Y. Philh., Oct. 4, 1945; simultaneous performances next day by the Boston Symph. and Cleveland Orchestra; Copland's most popular orchestral work; received the Pulitzer Prize for 1945); *Danzón Cubano* (originally for 2 pianos, 1942; orchestral version, Baltimore Orch., Feb. 17, 1946); Third Symphony (in memory of Mme. Natalie Koussevitzky; Boston Symph., Oct. 18, 1946); Concerto for Clarinet, String Orch., Harp and Piano (Benny Goodman and NBC Symph., Fritz Reiner conducting, N.Y., Nov. 6, 1950); *The Red Pony,* suite from the film (Houston, Nov. 1, 1948); *Connotations* for orch., written entirely in the 12-tone technique (first performed, as a commissioned work, in Philharmonic Hall, Lincoln Center, N.Y., at its inauguration, Sept. 23, 1962); *Music for a Great City,* symph. suite descriptive of life in New York City (London, May 26, 1964; composer conducting the London Symph.); *Inscape* for orch., commissioned by the N.Y. Philharmonic (first performance at the Univ. of Mich., Ann Arbor, Sept. 13, 1967, Leonard Bernstein conducting the N.Y. Philharmonic).

VOCAL: Choral: *What Do We Plant?* for high-school chorus (1939); *Lark* for mixed chorus (1939); *Las Agachadas* for mixed chorus (1942); *In the Beginning* for mezzo-soprano and chorus (commissioned for Harvard Symposium; perf. at Harvard Univ., May 2, 1947). Songs: *Twelve Poems of Emily Dickinson* (1948–50); *Old American Songs* for voice and orch. (2 sets, 1950, 1952).

CHAMBER MUSIC: *Nocturne* and *Ukelele Serenade* for violin and piano (1926); *Lento Molto* and *Rondino* for string quartet (1928; also for string orch.); *As it fell upon a day* for soprano, flute and clarinet (1928); *Vitebsk,* trio for piano, violin and cello, on a Jewish theme (League of Composers, N.Y., Feb. 16, 1929); Sextet, for clarinet, piano and string quartet, arranged from *Short Symphony* (1933; N.Y., Feb. 26, 1939); Violin Sonata (1943); Quartet for Piano and Strings (Coolidge Festival, Washington, D.C., Oct. 29, 1950); Nonet for strings (1960; Georgetown, D.C., Mar. 2, 1961). For piano: *The Cat and the Mouse* (1919); Passacaglia (1922); Piano Variations (1930); two pieces for children: *Sunday Afternoon Music* and *The Young Pioneers* (1936); Piano Sonata (first performed by the composer; Buenos Aires, Oct. 21, 1941); Piano Fantasy (1957). For organ: *Episode* (1941).

BIBLIOGRAPHY: Paul Rosenfeld, *An Hour with American Music* (Philadelphia, 1929; pp. 126–143); Theodore Chanler, "Aaron Copland," in H. Cowell, ed., *American Composers on American Music* (Stanford, 1933); Arthur Berger, "The Music of Aaron Copland," *Musical Quarterly* (Oct. 1945); Arthur Berger, *Aaron Copland* (first full-length biography, N.Y.,

1953); Julia Smith, *Aaron Copland* (N.Y., 1955; a lengthy biographical study, written as a doctoral thesis); E.T. Cone, "Conversation with Aaron Copland," *Perspectives of New Music* (Spring/Summer 1968); C.O. Peare, *Aaron Copland. His Life* (N.Y., 1969); D. Hamilton, "Aaron Copland: a Discography of the Composer's Performances," *Perspectives of New Music* (Fall/Winter 1970); special issue of *Tempo*, devoted to Copland on the occasion of his 70th birthday (Winter 1970/71).

Coppet, Edward J. de, American patron of art and founder of the Flonzaley Quartet; b. New York, May 28, 1855; d. there, April 30, 1916. A man of wealth and refined artistic tastes, he engaged various artists for private quartet performances at his residence. When he realized that constant practice was indispensable for the attainment of a perfect ensemble, he commissioned A. Pochon, in 1902, to find four men of the highest artistic standing who were willing to devote all their time to quartet playing. In the summer of the following year Adolfo Betti, Alfred Pochon, Ugo Ara, and Ivan d'Archambeau (1st violin, 2nd violin, viola and cello, respectively) began to practice at Flonzaley, de Coppet's summer residence near Lausanne, Switzerland; in the spring of 1904 they made their first European tour, arousing admiration by the perfection of their ensemble; on Dec. 5, 1905, they gave their first public concert in America (Carnegie Chamber Music Hall, N.Y.) with overwhelming success. They then appeared regularly in America and Europe. After de Coppet's death, his son, **André,** continued the original policy until 1929, when the quartet disbanded.
BIBLIOGRAPHY: D. G. Mason, "Edward J. de Coppet," *Musical Quarterly* (Oct. 1916); E. T. Rice, "The de Coppet Music Room in New York and Switzerland," *Musical Quarterly* (Oct. 1937).

Coppola, Piero, Italian conductor and composer; b. Milan, Oct. 11, 1888; d. Lausanne, March 13, 1971. He studied at the Milan Cons., graduating in 1910; conducted at La Scala and in Brussels (1912–13); in 1914 was in London; from 1915–19, in Scandinavia; then settled in Paris. He wrote 2 operas, *Sirmione* and *Nikita* (1914); a Symphony (Concerts Pasdeloup, Paris, Nov. 13, 1924, composer conducting); *La Ronde sous la Cloche* (1924); symphonic dances; vocal works.

Coppola, Pietro Antonio (Pierantonio), Italian composer; b. Castrogiovanni, Sicily, Dec. 11, 1793; d. Catania, Nov. 13, 1877. For a short time he studied at the Naples Cons.; then began to compose operas, which obtained sufficient success to enable his friends and admirers to present him as a rival to Rossini.
WORKS: From the time he was 19, he produced one opera after another, but without much success until he composed *La Pazza per amore* (Rome, Feb. 14, 1835). This was his fifth opera and became popular all over Europe (presented in Paris under the title *Eva*). From 1839–43, and again from 1850 till 1871, he was conductor of the Lisbon Royal Opera. His other operas were: *Gli Illinesi* (Turin, Dec. 26, 1835); *Enrichietta di Baienfeld* (Vienna, June 29, 1836); *La Bella Celeste degli Spadari* (Milan, June 14, 1837); *Gio-*

vanna prima di Napoli (Lisbon, Oct. 11, 1840); *Il folletto* (Rome, June 18, 1843). He also wrote church music, notably a *Salve Regina* which was highly regarded. His son published his biography (1899).

Coquard, Arthur, French composer and music critic; b. Paris, May 26, 1846; d. Noirmoutier, Vendée, Aug. 20, 1910. He took private lessons with César Franck (1862–66); was music critic for *Le Monde* and *Echo de Paris.*
WORKS: *L'Epée du roi* (Angers, 1884); *Le Mari d'un jour* (Paris, 1886); *L'Oiseau bleu* (Paris, 1894); *La Jacquerie* (Paris, 1895); *Jahel* (Lyons, 1900); *La Troupe Joilicoeur* (Paris, May 30, 1902); an oratorio, *Jeanne d'Arc*; published *De la musique en France depuis Rameau* (Paris, 1892) which received a prize from the Académie des Beaux-Arts.
BIBLIOGRAPHY: N. Dufourcq, *Autour de Coquard, Franck et d'Indy* (Paris, 1952).

Corder, Frederick, English composer and eminent teacher of composition; b. London, Jan. 26, 1852; d. there, Aug. 21, 1932. Pupil at Royal Academy of Music; in 1875 won the Mendelssohn Scholarship; studied with Ferdinand Hiller at Cologne (1875–78); became conductor of Brighton Aquarium Concerts in 1880, and greatly improved their quality; from 1886, professor of composition at the Royal Academy of Music and, from 1889, also curator. In 1905 he founded the Society of British Composers. He was remarkably successful as a teacher, many prominent British composers having been his pupils; a zealous apostle of Wagner, he and his wife made the first English translation of the *Ring of the Nibelung, Meistersinger* and *Parsifal* for the original scores published by Schott; was also contributor to *Grove's Dictionary.*
WORKS: operas *Morte d'Arthur* (1877); *Nordisa* (Liverpool, Jan. 26, 1887; Drury Lane, London, May 4, 1887); *Ossian* (1905); the operettas *Philomel* (an operatic satire, 1880); *A Storm in a Teacup* (1880); *The Nabob's Pickle* (1883); *The Noble Savage* (1885); the cantatas *The Cyclops* (1881); *The Bridal of Triermain* (Wolverhampton Festival, 1886); *The Blind Girl of Castel-Cuillé* (1888); *The Sword of Argantyr* (Leeds Festival, 1889). For orch.: *Evening on the Sea Shore* (idyll, 1876); *Im Schwarzwald* (suite, 1876); *Ossian* (overture, 1882); *Nocturne* (1882); *Prospero* (overture, 1885); *Roumanian Suite* (1887); *Pippa Passes* (orchestral poem, 1897); *A Fairy Tale* (1913); incidental music to *The Tempest* (1886), *The Termagant* (1898), *The Black Tulip* (1899); *Dreamland*, ode for chorus and orch. (1883); *Roumanian Dances* for violin and piano (1883); *The Minstrel's Curse*, ballad for declamation with orch. (1888); *True Thomas*, musical recitation (1895); *The Witch's Song* (1904); *Elegy* for 24 violins (1908); *Empire Pageant Masque* (1910); *The Angels*, biblical scene for 6 choirs (1911); *Sing unto God*, 50-part motet (1912).
WRITINGS: *Exercises in Harmony and Musical Composition* (1891); *The Orchestra and How to Write for It* (1895; 2nd ed. 1902); *Modern Composition* (1909); *Musical Encyclopaedia* (1915); *History of the Royal Academy of Music* (1922).
BIBLIOGRAPHY: *Musical Times* (Nov. 1913).

Corder, Paul, English composer; son of **Frederick Corder;** b. London, Dec. 14, 1879; d. there, Aug. 6, 1942. He entered the Royal Academy of Music in 1895, studied piano with Oscar Beringer and Tobias Matthay, composition with his father; studied violin, viola, horn, clarinet, etc. Appointed professor of harmony and composition at Royal Academy of Music, 1907; elected Associate of Royal Academy of Music in 1905.

WORKS: two operas, *Grettir the Strong* and *Rapunzel* (finished 1917; *The Moon Slave,* terpsichorean fantasy; *Cyrano de Bergerac,* overture; *Dross,* music drama without words; op. 8, *Morar,* a 'Gaelic fantasy'; *The Dryad,* ballet; *Prelude and Fugue; Sea-Songs; 2 Choral Songs; Heroic Elegy;* many piano works (*Transmutations, 9 Preludes, Passacaglia,* etc.); songs.

Cordero, Roque, Panamanian composer; b. Panama, Aug. 16, 1917. He first studied in Panama; then came to the U.S. (1943); studied with Krenek in Minneapolis and with Stanley Chapple (conducting) at the Berkshire Music Center.

WORKS: *Capriccio Interiorano* for band (1939); Piano Concerto (1944); Symph. No. 1 (1947); *8 Miniatures* for orch. (1948); *Rapsodia campesina* for orch. (1949); Quintet for Flute, Clarinet, Violin, Cello, and Piano (1949); Symph. No. 2 (1956); *5 Mensajes breves* for orch. (1959); 2 string quartets (1969, 1968); Cello Sonata (1962); Violin Concerto (1962); Symph. No. 3 (1965); *Sonata breve* for piano (1966); *Circunvoluciones y moviles* for 57 players (1967); *Permutaciones 7* for 7 instrumentalists (1967); *Paz, Paix, Peace* for 4 trios and harp (1969); *Variations and Theme for Five,* for woodwind quartet and horn (1975).

Cordon, Norman, American baritone; b. Washington, N.C., Jan. 20, 1904; d. Chapel Hill, N.C., March 1, 1964. He attended the Fishburne Military School; later studied at the Univ. of N.C. and at the Nashville (Tenn.) Cons. of Music; voice student of Gaetano de Lucas and Hadley Outland; in 1933 made his debut at the Civic Opera, Chicago, of which he was a member until 1936; in 1936 became a member of the Metropolitan Opera; also appeared with the San Francisco Opera and Cincinnati Summer Opera.

Corelli, Arcangelo, famous Italian violinist and composer; b. Fusignano, near Imola, Feb. 17, 1653; d. Rome, Jan. 8, 1713. His violin teacher was G. Benvenuti in Bologna; he learned counterpoint with Matteo Simonelli. Little is known of his early life; about 1671 he went to Rome where he was a violinist at the French Church (1675); in the beginning of 1679, he played in the orch. of the Teatro Capranica; Rome remained his chief residence to the end of his life, except for visits to Modena (1689–90) and Naples (1702). There is no substance to the story that in 1672 he went to Paris and was driven out by the intrigues of Lully; biographers mention also his stay at the court of the Elector of Bavaria in Munich about 1680, but there is no documentary evidence for this stay. Equally unfounded is the story that while he was in Naples, a mediocre violinist, Giuseppe Valentini, won the favor of the Roman public so that Corelli returned to Rome a broken man and died shortly afterwards. Quite contrary to these fanciful legends, Corelli enjoyed respect, security, and fame. In Rome he had a powerful protector in Cardinal Benedetto Panfili; later he lived in the palace of Cardinal Pietro Ottoboni, conducting weekly concerts which were attended by the élite of Roman society. One of Corelli's admirers was Queen Christina of Sweden, who lived in Rome at the time. Among his pupils were Baptiste Anet, Geminiani, Locatelli, and Giovanni Somis. Corelli was famous as a virtuoso on the violin and may be regarded as the founder of modern violin technique; he systematized the art of proper bowing, and was one of the first to use double stops and chords on the violin. His role in music history is very great despite the fact that he wrote but few works; only six opus numbers can be definitely attributed to him. His greatest achievement was the creation of the concerto grosso. Handel, who as a young man met Corelli in Rome, was undoubtedly influenced by Corelli's instrumental writing. Corelli was buried in the Pantheon in Rome.

WORKS: 12 *Sonate a tre, due violini e violone o arcileuto col basso per l'organo,* op. 1 (Rome, 1681; dedicated to Queen Christina of Sweden); 12 *Sonate da camera a tre, due violini e violone o cembalo,* op. 2 (Rome, 1685); 12 *Sonate a tre, due violini e violone o arcileuto, col basso per l'organo,* op. 3 (Rome, 1689); 12 *Sonate a tre,* op. 4 (Rome, 1694; in Amsterdam as *Balleti da camera*); 12 *Sonate a violino e violone o cembalo,* op. 5 (Rome, 1700; later arranged by Geminiani as *Concerti grossi;* the 12th sonata of op. 5 is *La Follia,* the celebrated set of variations for violin); *Concerti grossi con due violini e violoncello di concertino obbligati, e due altri violini, viola, e basso di concerto grosso ad arbitrio che si potranno raddoppiare,* op. 6 (Amsterdam, 1714). All these were variously reprinted at the time; an important edition is by Pepusch (London, opp. 1–4 and op. 6); Joachim and Chrysander issued the "complete works" in 1888–91 (London; opp. 1–6); a new critical edition has been started at the Musikwissenschaftlichen Institut der Universität Basel (1976–   ).

BIBLIOGRAPHY: C. Piancastelli, *In onore di Corelli* (Bologna, 1914); A. Einstein in *Sammelbände der Internationalen Musik-Gesellschaft* IX (p. 414ff.); F. T. Arnold, "A Corelli Forgery" (about a forged Antwerp ed. of 1693), in *Proceedings of the Musical Association* (London, 1921); A. Moser, in *Archiv für Musikwissenschaft* I (p. 358ff.); A. Moser, in *Zeitschrift für Musikwissenschaft* I (p. 287ff.) and III (p. 415ff.); A. Cametti, "Corelli à Saint-Louis des Français à Rome," *Revue Musicale* (Jan. 1922); F. Vatielli, "Il Corelli e i maestri bolognesi del suo tempo," *Arte e vita musicale a Bologna* (1927); A. Toni, "Arcangelo Corelli, cenni biografici," *Bolletino bibliografico musicale* (1927); H. Engel, *Das Instr.-Konzert* (Leipzig, 1932); M. Pincherle, *Corelli* (Paris, 1933; completely revised ed., 1954; English transl., N.Y., 1956); C. Sartori, "Le 44 edizioni italiane delle sei opere di Corelli" (listing full titles of original editions and reprints), *Rivista Musicale Italiana* (Jan.-March 1953); M. Rinaldi, *Arcangelo Corelli* (Milan, 1953; a comprehensive biography, bibliography, and catalogue of works); Bernhard Paumgartner, detailed article in *Die Musik in Geschichte und Gegenwart;* D. D. Boyden, "The Corelli

'Solo' Sonatas and Their Ornamental Additions . . .,'' *Musiqua Antiqua* III (Bydgoszcz, 1972); D. Libby, "Interrelationships in Corelli," *Journal of the American Musicological Society* (Summer 1973).

Corelli, Franco, Italian tenor; b. Ancona, April 8, 1923. He learned to sing by imitating great voices on the phonograph; advanced rapidly in his career after a modest debut in Spoleto in 1952. He sang at La Scala, Milan, in 1953; made his first appearance at the Metropolitan Opera in New York on Jan. 27, 1961; thenceforth made successful tours all over the world.

Coria, Miguel Angel, Spanish composer; b. Madrid, Oct. 24, 1937. He studied at the Cons. of Madrid, and later took a course in electronic music in Utrecht, Holland. Returning to Spain, he organized the ultra-modern studio 'Alea' promoting aleatory and electronic music.
WORKS: *Imágenes* for flute, oboe, vibraphone, violin and viola (1963); *Vértices* for small ensemble (1964); *Volúmenes* for small ensemble (1967); *Joyce's Portrait* for chamber orch. (1968); several pieces for small ensemble under the generic name *Lúdica.*

Corigliano, John, American violinist; b. New York, Aug. 28, 1901; d. Norfolk, Conn., Sept. 1, 1975. He studied with Leopold Auer in New York; gave violin recitals; in 1935 he was appointed assistant concert master of the New York Philharmonic, and in 1943 concertmaster; he resigned his position in 1966.

Corigliano, John, American composer; son of the violinist John Corigliano; b. New York, Feb. 16, 1938. He studied at Columbia Univ. with Otto Luening (B.A., 1959), with Vittorio Giannini at the Manhattan School of Music, and privately with Paul Creston. He was subsequently employed as script writer for radio station WQXR in New York and as assistant director for musical television shows there; later he was in charge of the music section at WBAI. He held the Guggenheim Fellowship in 1968–69. His style of composition shows a fine capacity for lyrical expression, and an incisive sense of rhythm, in the generic tradition of Béla Bartók and Prokofiev. Despite the dissonant freedom of his polyphonic writing, his music retains a firm tonal anchorage.
WORKS: *Kaleidoscope* for two pianos (1959); *Pastorale* for cello and piano (1958); *Fern Hill* for chorus and orch. to words by Dylan Thomas (N.Y., Dec. 19, 1961); Violin Sonata (1963; received first prize in the Spoleto Festival Competition of 1964); *The Cloisters*, a cycle of songs (1965); *Elegy* for orch. (San Francisco, June 1, 1966); *Tournaments Overture* (1967); Piano Concerto (San Antonio, Texas, April 5, 1968, Hilde Somer soloist); *Poem in October* for tenor and 8 instruments (1969); Oboe Concerto (N.Y., Nov. 9, 1975); *Poem on His Birthday* for baritone, chorus, and orch. (Washington, April 24, 1976); Clarinet Concerto (N.Y., Dec. 6, 1977). Incidental music for Molière's *Le Malade imaginaire*, Sheridan's *The Rivals*, Sophocles' *Oedipus Rex*, Brecht's *Galileo*; also special scores for the New York Shakespeare Festival of 1970. He arranged Bizet's *Carmen* for singers, rock and pop groups, Moog Synthesizer and instruments, issued on record under the title *The Naked Carmen.*

Cornelis, Evert, Dutch conductor and pianist; b. Amsterdam, Dec. 5, 1884; d. Bilthoven, Nov. 23, 1931. Pupil of de Pauw at the Amsterdam Cons.; in 1904, won organ prize; conductor at the Amsterdam opera (1908); assistant conductor of the Concertgebouw Orch. (1910–19); from 1922 conductor of the orch. at Utrecht, later choral director at Rotterdam; conductor of the Netherlands Bach Society (1927); toured Europe, Dutch East Indies, Australia, etc., as guest conductor. He pioneered extensively for modern music.

Cornelius, Peter, important German composer and writer; b. Mainz, Dec. 24, 1824; d. there, Oct. 26, 1874. A nephew of the painter Peter von Cornelius, he at first embraced the profession of an actor; but after an unsuccessful debut he changed his mind, studied theory with Dehn at Berlin (1845–52), and then joined Liszt's following in Weimar as a champion of Wagner, contributing frequent articles to the *Neue Zeitschrift für Musik*. His masterpiece, the opera, *Der Barbier von Bagdad*, was produced at Weimar (Dec. 15, 1858) under the direction of Liszt, who resigned his position there because of hostile demonstrations while he was conducting the opera. In 1859 Cornelius went to Wagner at Vienna, and followed him to Munich (1865), where he was appointed reader to King Ludwig II, and professor of harmony and rhetoric at the Royal Music School. A second opera, *Der Cid*, was produced at Weimar on May 21, 1865; a third, *Gunlöd* (from the Edda), remained unfinished (completed by Lassen and produced at Weimar, May 6, 1891). *Der Barbier von Bagdad* was revived at Karlsruhe on Feb. 1, 1884, in a drastically altered version by F. Mottl. Cornelius published *Lieder-Cyclus* (op. 3); duets for soprano and baritone (op. 6); *Weihnachtslieder* (op. 8); *Trauerchöre* for male chorus (op. 9). A volume of *Lyrische Poesien* was issued in 1861. Cornelius wrote the libretti of his operas, and was a fine translator. A complete edition of his works was issued by Breitkopf & Härtel (1905–06): I, Songs; II, Choruses; III, *Der Barbier von Bagdad*; IV, *Der Cid*; V, *Gunlöd* (completed and orchestrated by W. von Baussnern); his literary works were also published by Breitkopf & Härtel (1904–05); I, II, Letters and pages from his diary, edited by his son, **Carl**; III, Essays on music and art, edited by E. Istel; IV, Complete poems, collected and edited by A. Stern.
BIBLIOGRAPHY: A. Sandberger, *Leben und Werke des Dichtermusikers Peter Cornelius* (Leipzig, 1887); E. Istel, *Peter Cornelius* (Leipzig, 1904); Max Hasse, *Peter Cornelius und sein Barbier von Bagdad* (exposing Mottl's transcription, 1904); E. Sulger-Gebing, *Peter Cornelius als Mensch und Dichter* (Munich, 1908); Max Hasse, *Der Dichtermusiker Peter Cornelius* (2 volumes, Leipzig, 1923); Carl Maria Cornelius, *Peter Cornelius, der Wortund Tondichter* (2 volumes, Regensburg, 1925); A. E. Cherbuliez, *Peter Cornelius* (Zürich, 1925); E. Istel, "Peter Cornelius," *Musical Quarterly* (July 1934); Paul Egert, *Peter Cornelius* (Berlin, 1940); W. Konold, "Peter Cornelius und die Liedästhetic der Neudeutschen Schule," *International Review of Music Aesthetics and Sociology* I/2 (1970).

Cornell, John Henry, American organist and writer on music; b. New York, May 8, 1828; d. there, March 1, 1894. He studied in New York, Germany and England; was organist in several N.Y. churches (1848, St. John's Chapel; 1868–77, St. Paul's Church; 1877–82, Old Brick Church). His sacred compositions were highly esteemed.

WRITINGS: *Primer of Modern Musical Tonality; Practice of Sight-Singing; Theory and Practice of Musical Form* (after L. Bussler); *Easy Method of Modulation; Manual of Roman Chant; Congregational Tune Book; The Introit Psalms as prescribed by the First Prayer book of Edward VI, set to Original Chants* (N.Y., 1871).

Corner, Philip, American composer; b. New York, April 10, 1933. He studied piano; began composing autogenetically at 13, gestated a 3-minute piano piece in 9 months, learned to play the trombone. In 1955 he went to Paris where he took a course in musical philosophy with Olivier Messiaen; spent a year in Korea studying Oriental calligraphy in order to apply it to the needs of graphic music notation. In 1958 he turned to serial music, but mitigated its stern doctrines by aleatory indeterminacy; he often composes works after their first performances to avoid the stigma of premeditation. The titles of his compositions show a surrealistic flavor: *Passionate Expanse of the Law, Certain Distilling Processes, Expressions in Parallel, Air Effect,* and *Music Reserved Until Now.* In his *Punishment Piece,* using the naked strings of a grand piano, musical material is determined by tossing spotted transparent paper on the manuscript. In 1965 he composed a timeless piece for indefinitely prolonged chanting on a single note. In 1968 he verbalized a work with the injunction: "One anti-personnel type CBU bomb will be thrown into the audience," publ. in *Source 6* (1969), but never performed.

Coronaro, Gaetano, Italian violinist and composer; b. Vicenza, Dec. 18, 1852; d. Milan, April 5, 1908. He studied with Faccio at the Milan Cons. and briefly in Germany; upon returning, producing a choral work, *Un Tramonto* (Milan, 1873); was for several years professor of harmony in the Milan Cons. He wrote the operas *La Creola* (Bologna, 1878), *Malacarne* (Brescia, 1894), and *Un curioso accidente* (Turin, 1903); also some instrumental music.

Coronaro, Gellio Benvenuto, Italian pianist and composer; b. Vicenza, Nov. 30, 1863; d. Milan, July 26, 1916. He was eight years old when he made his debut as pianist; at thirteen, was theater conductor at Marosteca, and chorus master at fifteen; in 1882 he entered the Liceo Rossini at Bologna, where his teachers were Busi, Parisini and Mancinelli; graduated in 1883, winning the first prize with a 1-act opera, *Jolanda,* which was produced at the Cons. (Milan, 1883). Other works: 1-act dramatic sketch *Festa a Marina* (took 1st Sonzogno Prize in 1892); operetta *Minestrone Napoletano* (Messina, 1893); 2-act opera *Claudia* (Milan, 1895); *Bertoldo* (Milan, 1910); also wrote 2 Masses, String Quartet, songs, piano pieces, etc.

Correa de Arauxo, Francisco, one of the most important Spanish organists of the Renaissance; b. Seville, c.1576; d. Segovia, Oct. 31, 1654. He held the posts of organist at the Church of San Salvador in Seville (1599–1636); at the Cathedral of Jaen (1636–40) and at Segovia (from 1640 until his death). His *Facultad orgánica* (originally publ. in Alcaláde Henares, 1626) contains 70 pieces for organ in tablature (most of them his own compositions), reproduced in the series *Monumentos de la Música española,* edited by Santiago Kastner (Madrid, 1950).

BIBLIOGRAPHY: The biography by Charles Jacobs, *Francisco Correa de Arauxo* (The Hague, 1973) contains errors pointed out by Robert Stevenson in the *Journal of the American Musicological Society* (Spring 1975). See also Robert Stevenson, "Francisco Correa de Arauxo" *Revista Musical Chilena* (Jan.-March 1968).

Correa de Azevedo, Luis Heitor, Brazilian musicologist; b. Rio de Janeiro, Dec. 13, 1905. He studied at the Instituto Nacional de Música in Rio de Janeiro; in 1932 was appointed librarian there; in 1939 became prof. of national folklore; in 1943 organized the "Centro de Pesquisas folklóricas" at the Escuela Nacional de Música. He published numerous valuable studies on Brazilian music: *Escala, Ritmo e Melodia na Música dos Indios Brasileiros* (Rio de Janeiro, 1938); *Relação das Operas de Autores Brasileiros* (Rio de Janeiro, 1938); *A Música Brasileira e seus Fundamentos* (Washington, D.C., 1948); *Música e Músicos do Brasil* (Rio de Janeiro, 1950); *150 Años de Música no Brasil* (Rio de Janeiro, 1956); *La Musique en Amérique latine* (Paris, 1957); several informative articles in Brazilian, French and American magazines. From 1947 to 1965 he was in charge of the music division of Unesco in Paris; in 1967–68 he gave lectures at the Newcomb College of Tulane Univ., Louisiana.

Corri, Domenico, Italian composer; b. Rome, Oct. 4, 1744; d. London, May 22, 1825. He was a pupil of Porpora in Naples; in 1781 went to Edinburgh as opera conductor. His attempt to organize his own opera company and a publishing firm there was a failure, and he sought better fortune in London (1790). There he engaged in various enterprises as publisher, composer and impresario. His opera, *The Travelers, or Music's Fascination,* was given at Drury Lane on Jan. 22, 1806 with little success. He published four music manuals in English: *A Complete Musical Grammar* (1787); *A Musical Dictionary* (1798); *The Art of Fingering* (1799); and *The Singer's Preceptor* (1810). His daughter, **Sophia Giustina,** a talented pianist and singer, married Dussek; his sons, **Montague Corri** (1784–1849) and **Haydn Corri** (1785–1860), were also musicians.

BIBLIOGRAPHY: P. J. Revitt, "Domenico Corri's 'New System' for Reading Thorough-Bass," *Journal of the American Musicological Society* (Spring 1968).

Corsi (Corso), Giuseppe (called **Celano** after his birthplace), Italian composer; b. May 1630; d. May 1690. He served as maestro di cappella at Santa Maria Maggiore, Rome (1659–61); at the Lateran Palace chapel (1661–65); at Santa Casa di Loreto (1668–75);

then returned to Rome, but, because of his dissemination of books placed on the Church Index, was persecuted and forced to leave (1678); from 1681, at the court of the Duke of Parma. Among his pupils were Jacopo Perti (at Parma) and Petronio Franceschini. He published *Motetti a 2, 3 e 4 voci* (Rome, 1667), *Miserere a 5*, and *Motetti a 9*; various other vocal works, in MS, are preserved in the library of the Liceo Musicale and the Archivio Musicale di S. Petronio at Bologna. Several of his works appeared in collections of the time. He is mentioned in Giuseppe Pitoni's *Guida armonica.*

Corsi, Jacopo, a Florentine nobleman and patron of art; b. Florence, July 17, 1560; d. there, 1604. In his palace, as in that of his friend Bardi, were held the memorable meetings of the 'Camerata' in which Peri, Caccini, Emilio del Cavaliere, Galilei, the poet Rinuccini and others took part, leading to the creation of the earliest operas. Corsi was a good musician, a skillful player on the harpsichord and a composer; he wrote the concluding two numbers of the first opera *Dafne* by Peri, which was performed at his home in 1598; these settings are preserved in the library of the Brussels Cons.; publ. in Solerti's *Albori del Melodramma* (Milan, 1905).

Corso, Giuseppe. See **Corsi, Giuseppe.**

Corte, Andrea della. See **Della Corte, Andrea.**

Corteccia, Francesco Bernardo, b. Florence, July 27, 1502; d. there, June 7, 1571. Organist, in 1531, of the Church of S. Lorenzo at Florence; 1539-71, maestro di cappella to Duke Cosimo the Great.
WORKS: wedding music (for the Duke), 9 pieces, *a 4, 6,* and *8* (Venice, 1539); 3 books of madrigals (1544, 1547, 1547); *Responsoria et lectiones* (1570); 32 hymns *a 4*; *Canticorum liber primus* (1571); many others have been destroyed. His musical intermezzi to stage works (e.g., to Francesco d'Ambra's *Il furto*, 1544) are noteworthy in the development of opera.
BIBLIOGRAPHY: O. G. Sonneck's articles in the *Musical Antiquary* (1911) and in his *Miscellaneous Studies in the History of Music* (N.Y., 1921); A. C. Minor and B. Mitchell, eds., *A Renaissance Entertainment. Festivities for the Marriage of Cosimo I, Duke of Florence, in 1539* (Columbia, Mo., 1968).

Cortés, Ramiro, American composer of Mexican extraction; b. Dallas, Texas, Nov. 25, 1933. He studied with Henry Cowell in New York and at the Univ. of Southern California with Halsey Stevens and Ingolf Dahl. From 1956 to 1958 he was in Rome on a Fulbright Fellowship Award; there he studied with Petrassi. Returning to America in 1959 he had sessions with Roger Sessions at Princeton Univ.
WORKS: *Elegy* for flute and piano (1952); *Divertimento* for Flute, Clarinet and Bassoon (1953); *Piano Quintet* (1953); *Piano Sonata* (1954; awarded Steinway Centennial prize); *Sinfonia Sacra* for orch. (1954; received George Gershwin Memorial Award; N.Y. Philharmonic, April 9, 1955; revised in 1959); *Night Music* for chamber orch. (1954; received first prize of Broadcast Music Incorporated Awards); *Yerma,*

symph. portrait after a play by García Lorca (1955); *Xochitl* for orch. (1955; Hollywood, April 22, 1956); Chamber Concerto for Cello Solo and 12 Wind Instruments (1958; first prize of Broadcast Music Incorporated Awards); Symphony (1953-58); *Sinfonia breve* (1955-58); String Quartet (1958); Piano Trio (1959); *Prometheus*, opera in one act (1960); *The Eternal Return* for orch. (1963; revised 1965); Violin Concerto (1965); Wind Quintet (1967-68); *Hommage to Jackson Pollack* for solo viola (1968); *Charenton*, suite for chamber orch. (1968-71); *Movements in Variation* for orch. (1972).

Cortese, Luigi, Italian pianist and composer; b. Genoa, Nov. 19, 1899; d. there, June 10, 1976. He studied music in Genoa with Emiliano Perotti and Mario Ferrari. He then took lessons with Gédalge in Paris and with Casella in Rome. He developed a multifarious activity as music critic, composer, pianist and teacher. In 1939 he was named curator of the City Archives in Genoa; from 1951 to 1964 he was director of the Istituto Musicale in Genoa.
WORKS: He was a prolific composer; his opera *Prometeo* was performed in Bergamo on Sept. 22, 1951; another opera *La notte veneziana* was produced on the Turin Radio in 1955. He further wrote several scores of incidental music for plays and an oratorio *David* (1938); he composed a Symphony (1953-56); Violin Concerto (1961); Horn Sonata (1955); Cello Sonata (1960); numerous piano pieces and songs. He published the monographs *Alfredo Casella* (Genoa, 1935); *Il Bolero di Ravel* (1944) and *Chopin* (1949).

Cortesi, Francesco, Italian composer; b. Florence, Sept. 11, 1826; d. there, Jan. 3, 1904. He studied at Bologna under Rossini and others; became a conductor and a composer of many light stage works; settled in Florence about 1880 as a singing master and was appointed head of the vocal department in the government music school. Many celebrated singers were his pupils.
WORKS: operas: *Il Trovatore* (Trieste, 1852; then at Florence, as *La Schiava*); *Almina* (Rome, 1859); *La Dama a servire* (Ancona, 1859); *La Colpa del cuore* (Florence, 1870); *Mariulizza* (Florence, 1874); *L'Amico di casa* (Florence, 1881); all fairly successful.

Cortolezis, Fritz, German composer and conductor; b. Passau, Feb. 21, 1878; d. Bad Aibling, Bavaria, March 13, 1934. Studied in Munich with H. Bussmeyer (piano) and with L. Thuille (composition) from 1899-1902; was répétiteur at the opera in Schwerin (1903); chorus master at the National Theater in Berlin (1904); first conductor in Regensburg (1905) and in Nuremberg (1906); upon Mottl's recommendation he was appointed conductor of the court opera in Munich; was engaged by Beecham in 1911 for the Wagner and Strauss performances in London; in 1912 first conductor at the Kurfürstenoper in Berlin; then in Karlsruhe (1913-24) and at the Breslau Opera (1925-28).
WORKS: operas: *Rosemarie* (Bremen, 1919); *Das verfemte Lachen* (Rostock, 1924); *Der verlorene Gulden* (Breslau, 1928).

Cortot, Alfred (Denis), famous French pianist; b. (of a French father and a Swiss mother) Nyon, Switzerland, Sept. 26, 1877; d. Lausanne, June 15, 1962. He was a pupil at the Paris Cons., and studied with Decambes, Rouquou and Diémer; he won the first prize for piano in 1896; the same year he made his debut in Paris, playing Beethoven's C minor Concerto at one of the Colonne concerts, and won signal success; he went to Bayreuth (1898) and studied Wagner's works with J. Kniese, and acted as répétiteur at the festivals from 1898–1901. Returning to Paris, he began a most active propaganda for the works of Wagner; on May 17, 1902, he conducted the French première of *Götterdämmerung* at the Théâtre du Château d'Eau, and in the same year established the Association des Concerts A. Cortot, which he directed for two years, educating the public to an appreciation of Wagner; in 1904 he became conductor of the orchestral concerts of the Société Nationale and of the Concerts Populaires at Lille (till 1908). In 1905, together with Jacques Thibaud (violin) and Pablo Casals (cello), he formed a trio, which soon gained a great European reputation. He founded, with A. Mangeot, the École Normale de Musique (1919), and became its director, also giving a summer course in piano interpretation there annually; gave many lecture recitals and appeared as guest conductor with various orchestras.
WRITINGS: articles on the piano works of Debussy, Fauré, Franck, Chabrier in the *Revue Musicale* (1920–26); published a new working edition of Chopin's Preludes and Études; also published *Principes rationnels de la technique pianistique* (French and English, Paris, 1928; American ed., Boston, 1930); *La musique française de piano* (vol. I, 1930; English translation, London, 1932; vol. II, 1932); *Cours d'interprétation* (vol. I, Paris, 1934; in English, London, 1937); *Aspects de Chopin* (Paris, 1949; English, *In Search of Chopin*, London, 1951). The publication of a classified catalogue of Cortot's library, entitled *Bibliothèque Alfred Cortot*, edited by F. Goldbeck and A. Fehr with preface by H. Prunières, was begun in 1936.
BIBLIOGRAPHY: Bernard Gavoty, *Alfred Cortot* (Paris, 1977).

Cosma, Viorel, Rumanian musicologist; b. Timişoara, March 30, 1923. He studied composition with Mihail Jora, Ion Dumitrescu, Paul Constantinescu, Theodor Rogalski; musicology with Zeno Vancea. He was active as a choral conductor and teacher; then devoted himself mainly to music criticism; publ. several valuable monographs on Rumanian musicians (Ciprian Porumbescu, Ion Ivanovici, and others). He compiled a uniquely useful biographical dictionary of Rumanian composers and musicologists, *Muzicieni Români* (Bucharest, 1965; revised and augmented edition, 1970).

Cossetto, Emil, Croatian composer; b. Trieste, Oct. 12, 1918. He studied in Zagreb. His compositions, based mostly on patriotic themes, include *Borbena Kantata (Cantata of the Struggle,* 1947), inspired by the wartime resistance in Yugoslavia; *Zagreb Cantata* (Zagreb, May 7, 1950); *Konjanik,* a 'cavalcade' for men's voices and orch. (Zagreb, Dec. 9, 1957); numerous choruses.

Cossmann, Bernhard, German cellist; b. Dessau, May 17, 1822; d. Frankfurt, May 7, 1910. He was a pupil of Espenhahn and Drechsler; also of Theodor Müller and Kummer (in Dresden); member of the Grand Opéra Orch., Paris (1840); London (1841); Opéra-Comique, Paris (till 1846); Gewandhaus, Leipzig (1847–48), as solo cellist, also studying composition under Hauptmann; at Weimar with Liszt (in 1850); professor at Moscow Cons. (1866); lived at Baden-Baden (1870–78); thereafter, professor of cello at Frankfurt Cons.

Cossotto, Fiorenza, Italian contralto; b. Crescentino, Vercelli, near Turin, April 22, 1935. She studied at the Turin Cons.; sang at La Scala as a student; at the Vienna State Opera, in Covent Garden, London, in Paris, in South America, and in Russia. She made her American debut in 1964 at the Lyric Opera in Chicago; was soloist in Verdi's *Requiem* in N.Y. with the orchestra of the Teatro alla Scala during its American visit in 1967. In 1968 she sang Amneris at her Metropolitan Opera debut. Among her most successful roles was that of Santuzza in *Cavalleria Rusticana.* She is married to the Italian bass Ivo Vinco.

Costa, Sir Michael (properly **Michele**), eminent conductor and opera composer; b. Naples, Feb. 4, 1806; d. Hove, England, April 29, 1884. He studied with his maternal grandfather, **Giacomo Tritto,** and with his father, **Pasquale Costa** (a composer of church music and pupil of L. Leo). He then studied at the Naples Cons. with Crescentini (singing) and Zingarelli (composition). His operas *Il Sospetto funesto* (Naples, 1826), *Il Delitto punito* (1827), *Il Carcere d'Ildegonda* (Naples, 1828), and *Malvina* (Naples, 1829) were well received; when Zingarelli was commissioned to write a psalm *Super Flumina Babilonis* for the Music Festival of Birmingham, England, he sent Costa to conduct it. When Costa arrived in Birmingham, the directors of the Festival refused to accept him as conductor owing to his extreme youth, but offered to pay him a similar fee for performance as tenor in Zingarelli's psalm and in other works. He was compelled to accept, but his debut as a singer was disastrous. Despite this setback, he decided to remain in England, in which he was encouraged by Clementi who was impressed by Costa's scoring of a Bellini aria. In 1830 Costa was engaged as "maestro al cembalo" at the King's Theatre in London; in 1832 he became musical director; and in 1833, director and conductor. During this time he produced three of his ballets, *Kenilworth* (1831), *Une heure à Naples* (1832), and *Sir Huon* (1833, for Taglioni). In 1846 he became conductor of the Philharmonic and of the new Italian Opera; in 1848, of the Sacred Harmonic Society. From 1849 he was the regular conductor of the Birmingham Festivals; from 1857, of the Handel Festivals. He was knighted in 1869; was appointed "director of the music, composer, and conductor" at Her Majesty's Opera in 1871. He produced two operas in London: *Malek Adel* (May 18, 1837; a revision of *Malvina*) and *Don Carlos* (June 20, 1844).

Costeley, Guillaume, French organist; b. probably at Pont-Audemer (Normandy), 1531; d. Évreux, Feb. 1, 1606. The theory that he was an Irishman named Costello who settled in France as well as the theory that he was of Scottish extraction have been discarded. He was court organist to Charles IX of France. In 1571 he became the first annually elected "prince" or "maître" of a society organized in honor of St. Cecilia, which, beginning in 1575, awarded a prize each year for a polyphonic composition. Costeley excelled as composer of polyphonic chansons; his *Musique,* a book of such works for 4-6 voices, appeared in 1570. Modern editions of some of those for 4 voices are in H. Expert, *Maîtres Musiciens de la Renaissance française* (volumes III, XVIII, XIX); an example for 5 voices in Cauchie's *Quinze chansons.*
BIBLIOGRAPHY: M. Cauchie, "Documents pour servir à une biographie de Guillaume Costeley," *Revue de Musicologie* (May 1926).

Cotapos, Acario, Chilean composer; b. Valdivia, April 30, 1889; d. Santiago, Nov. 22, 1969. He studied music in Santiago; in 1916 went to New York where he took lessons with 10 teachers, among them Ernest Bloch. He lived in France until 1936; then went to Spain to work in defense of the Loyalists during the Spanish Civil War; in 1939 he returned to Chile. An experimenter by nature, he adopted an advanced quasi-serial technique of monothematic mottoes of 8 or more notes. He wrote a music drama *Voces de Gesta* (1933); several symphonic preludes; a string quartet; *Sonata Fantasia* for piano (1924); songs; piano pieces.

Čotek, Pavel, Czech composer; b. Fryšava, March 12, 1922. He studied at the Prague Cons. and the Janáček Academy in Brno; then was active as a choirmaster and music critic.
WORKS: *Concertino Grosso* for oboe, clarinet, horn and strings (1964); *Symphonic Etudes* (1965); Concerto for 2 Solo Percussionists and Orch. (Olomouc, Oct. 22, 1968); *Responsoria* for organ and orch. (1969); *3 Romantic Compositions* for horn and piano (1954); *Dance Suite* for wind quintet (1955); Suite for Violin and Piano (1958); *3 Compositions* for flute and piano (1962); Violin Sonata (1962); *Portrait of a Bird,* melodrama for 2 narrators, flute, viola, bass clarinet, celesta and harp (1963); *Chamber Music* for string quartet and percussion (1963); *5 Short Movements* for clarinet and piano (1964-69); *Wind Music* for piccolo, trumpet, bass trumpet, bass trombone and piano (1970); *Agoge* for viola and piano (1973); choruses; songs.

Cottlow, Augusta, American pianist; b. Shelbyville, Ill., April 2, 1878; d. White Plains, N.Y., April 11, 1954. She received her first instruction from her mother; appeared in public as a child; went to Berlin in 1896 to study with Busoni; played concerts in Germany, England, and Russia. In 1912 she married Edgar E. Gerst of Berlin; returned to America in 1917. She publ. a memoir, "My Years with Busoni," *Musical Observer* (June 1925).

Cotton, John (or **Johannis Cottonis;** also **Joannes Musica, Johannes filius Dei,** and **Johannes of Afflighem**), an early music theorist (11th to 12th century); probable author of the treatise *Epistola ad Fulgentium* (printed by Gerbert in *Scriptores,* vol. II), a valuable work on music describing the modal system of the time and a phase of the development of organum. Six MS copies are preserved: in Leipzig, Paris, Antwerp, the Vatican Library, and two in Vienna. Various theories have been advanced concerning its authorship. In the copies at Antwerp and Paris the author is referred to as Cotton or Cottonius, while two others give the author's name as 'Joannes Musica.' In an anonymous work, *De script. eccles.,* quoted by Gerbert, there is a reference to a certain Joannes, an erudite English musician; the dedication of this volume, 'Domino et patri sua venerabili Anglorum antistiti Fulgentio,' adds further strength to the contention that the author of the *Epistola* was English. However, J. Smits van Waesberghe identifies him with the Flemish theorist Johannes of Afflighem, author of the treatise *De Musica cum tonario* (reprinted Rome, 1950). Other sources suggest that Cotton is also one Johannes filius Dei.
BIBLIOGRAPHY: L. Ellinwood, "John Cotton or John of Afflighem?" *Notes* (Sept. 1951); J. Smits van Waesberghe's reply in *Musica Disciplina* (1952; pp. 139-53); J. Pulver, "John Cotton," *Musical Times* (Oct. 1933); E. F. Flindell, "Johannis Cottonis, Corrigenda et Addenda," *Musica Disciplina* XXIII (1969).

Cottrau, Teodoro, Italian composer of Neapolitan ballads; b. Naples, Nov. 27, 1827; d. there, March 30, 1879. His father **Guillaume Louis Cottrau** (b. Paris, Aug. 9, 1797; d. Naples, Oct. 31, 1847) was also a composer of Neapolitan canzonettas (some of them used by Liszt in his piano work *Venezia e Napoli*), as was his brother **Giulio Cottrau** (b. Naples, Oct. 29, 1831; d. Rome, Oct. 25, 1916). Teodoro Cottrau was the composer of the perennial favorite *Santa Lucia* (1850).

Coulthard, Jean, Canadian pianist and composer; b. Vancouver, Feb. 10, 1908. She studied piano with her mother; went to London to study composition with Vaughan Williams (1929-30); had lessons at various times and at various places with Arthur Benjamin (1939), Milhaud (1942), Bartók (1944), Wagenaar (1945, 1949); Nadia Boulanger (1955) and Gordon Jacob (1965-66). In 1947 she joined the staff of the newly created department of music at the Univ. of British Columbia. In her music she rarely strays from conventional usages, but it is not devoid of occasional modernistic whimsicalities.
WORKS: *Canadian Fantasy* for orch. (1939); *Excursion,* ballet (1940); *Ballade (A Winter's Tale)* for string orch. (1940); *Song to the Sea,* overture (1942); *Music on a Quiet Song* for flute and strings (1946); Symph. No. 1 (1950-51); *Nightwind,* song cycle for mezzo-soprano and orch. or piano (1951); *Rider on the Sands* for orch. (1953); *A Prayer for Elizabeth* for strings (1953); *Music for St. Cecilia* for strings, organ and tape (1954, revised 1969); Violin Concerto (1955-59); *The Devil's Fanfare: 4 Bizarre Dances,* ballet for violin, piano and 3 dancers (1958-60); Fantasie for Piano, Violin and Chamber Orch. (1960-61); *Musenade* for string orch. (1961); *The Bird of Dawning*

Singeth All Night Long for violin, 9 strings and harp (1962); Piano Concerto (1963, revised 1967); *Endymion* for orch. (1964); *Symphonic Ode* for cello and orch. (1965); *This Land,* choral symph., with tape (1966–67); *Pastorale Cantata* for narrator, chorus, brass quintet and organ (1967); *2 Visionary Songs* for soprano, flute and strings (1970); *Kalamalka (Lake of Many Colors)* for orch. (1974); *Canadian Mosaic* for orch. (1974); Piano Quintet (1932); 2 violin sonatinas (1945); Cello Sonata (1947); Oboe Sonata (1947); Piano Sonata (1947–48); *3 Shakespearean Sonnets* for soprano and string quintet (1948); 2 string quartets (1948; 1953, revised 1969); 2 violin sonatas (*Duo Sonata,* 1952; *Correspondence,* 1964); Piano Quartet (1957); *Sonata Rhapsody* for viola and piano (1962); Divertimento for Wind Quintet and Piano (1968); *The Pines of Emily Carr* for narrator, contralto, string quintet, piano and timpani (1969); *12 Essays on a Cantabile Theme,* String Octet (1972); *The Birds of Lansdowne* for violin, cello, piano, and bird songs on tape (1972); *4 Prophetic Songs* for contralto, flute, cello and piano (1975); piano pieces; songs.

Couperin, a renowned family of French musicians. Its musical prominence dates from the three sons of **Charles Couperin,** merchant and organist of Chaume, in the department of Brie (now part of the department of Seine et Marne), and his wife, Marie Andry. The eldest of these, **Louis,** established the family in Paris, where it remained until the extinction of the male line in 1826. He was also the first of his name to hold the post of organist at St.-Gervais, Paris. He was followed in this position by his youngest brother, **Charles; François le Grand,** son of Charles, and the family's most illustrious representative; **Nicolas,** son of **François** (called **Sieur de Crouilly**); **Armand-Louis,** son of **Nicolas;** and by the two sons of Armand-Louis, **Pierre-Louis,** and **Gervais-François.** The following articles, arranged alphabetically, give the individual histories of the members of the Couperin family.

Couperin, Armand-Louis (son of **Nicolas**), b. Paris, Feb. 25, 1727; d. there, Feb. 2, 1789. His virtuosity on the organ was extraordinary; in 1748, succeeded his father as organist at St.-Gervais; was also organist to the King (1770–89), and held appointments at St.-Barthélemy, Ste.-Marguerite, the Ste.-Chapelle, St.-Jean-en-Grève, etc. He was one of the four organists of Notre-Dame. He died a violent death, having been knocked down by a runaway horse. His compositions include sonatas, a trio, motets, and other church music. His wife, **Elisabeth-Antoinette** (*née* **Blanchet;** b. Paris, Jan. 14, 1729), was also a remarkable organist and clavecinist, still playing in public at the age of 81 (in 1810). She was the daughter of **Blanchet,** the famous clavecin maker, and sister-in-law to **Pascal Joseph Taskin,** the court instrument keeper under Louis XV.

Couperin, Charles, b. Chaumes, April (baptized, April 9), 1638; d. Paris, 1679. He succeeded his brother Louis as organist at St.-Gervais in 1665. He married Marie Guérin (Feb. 20, 1662), and is principally remembered as being the father of the celebrated **François le Grand.**

BIBLIOGRAPHY: C. Bouvet, "Quelques précisions biographiques sur Charles Louis Couperin," *Revue de musicologie* (Paris, 1930).

Couperin, François (Sieur de Crouilly), b. Chaumes, c.1631; d. Paris, after 1708. He was a pupil of Chambonnières in harmony and clavecin playing; active as music teacher and organist. His daughter, **Marguerite Louise** (b. Paris, 1676; d. Versailles, May 30, 1728), was a well-known singer and harpsichordist. She was a fellow member of the Chambre du roi with her cousin, **François le Grand,** who wrote for her the verset *Qui dat nivem,* and other pieces.

Couperin, François, surnamed **le Grand** on account of his superiority in organ playing, the most illustrious member of a distinguished family, and one of the greatest of early French composers; b. Paris, Nov. 10, 1668; d. there, Sept. 11, 1733. He was the son of **Charles Couperin,** who was his first teacher; later pupil of Jacques-Denis Thomelin, organist of the King's chapel; in 1685 he became organist of St.-Gervais, which post he held until his death; on Dec. 26, 1693, after a successful competition, he succeeded Thomelin as organist of the Chapelle Royale, receiving the title of 'organiste du roi'; in 1701 he was appointed 'claveciniste de la chambre du roi, et organiste de sa chapelle', and in 1717 he received the title 'Ordinaire de la musique de la chambre du roi'; also made chevalier of the Order of Latran; he was music master to the Dauphin and other members of the royal family, and ranked high in the favor of Louis XIV, for whom he composed the *Concerts royaux,* which, during 1714–15, were played in Sunday concerts in the royal apartments. He married Marie-Anne Ansault (April 26, 1689) from whom he had two daughters: **Marie-Madeleine** (b. Paris, March 9, 1690; d. Montbuisson, April 16, 1742), who became organist of the Abbey of Montbuisson, and **Marguerite-Antoinette** (b. Paris, Sept. 19, 1705; d. there, 1778), who became a talented clavecin player; from 1731–33, she substituted for her father as 'claveciniste' to the king, being the first woman to hold this position (cf. C. Bouvet, "Les Deux d'Anglebert et Marguerite-Antoinette Couperin," *Revue de Musicologie,* 1928); there were also two sons, **Nicolas-Louis** (b. July 24, 1707), who died young, and **François-Laurent,** born c.1708. Famed as an organist, Couperin also acquired a high reputation for his remarkable ability as a performer on the clavecin.

WORKS: His compositions may be conveniently divided into three categories: those written for the church, those for the king, and those for the general public. More than half of his creative life was taken up with the religious compositions of the first two periods. These include *Pièces d'orgue consistantes en deux Messes* (1690, a total of 42 pieces), formerly attributed to his uncle, **François de Crouilly,** and, indeed, published under the latter's name in vol. 5 of *Archives des maîtres de l'orgue,* ed. by Guilmant, but now established, through the researches of A. Tessier and P. Brunold, as the early work of **Couperin le Grand;** motets; *Elévations; Leçons de Ténèbres;* etc. Couperin's last and most prolific period was concerned exclusively with instrumental works, and in this field he achieved his greatest and most enduring distinction. In 1713, 1716, 1722 and 1730, he published the 4 volumes of his *Pièces de clavecin,* consisting of about 230 pieces or 27 'Ordres' or Suites, each suite being a series of dance forms, programmatic in title and content (*La Majestueuse, La Nanette, Les Petits Moulins à Vent, Le Carillon de Cythère, Les Barricades Mystérieuses, Les Tic-Toc-Choc ou les Maillotins,* etc.). In 1716 he published an expository work pertaining to the execution of his clavecin pieces, *L'Art de toucher le clavecin,* which attained wide celebrity, and which influenced the keyboard style of Couperin's great contemporary, J. S. Bach. Couperin also introduced the trio sonata to France, his first works in this form being an imitation of Corelli. Later, in 1726, he publ. 4 sonatas, *Les Nations,* described as 'Sonades' or 'Suites de symphonies en trio', three of which are partial reworkings of earlier pieces. They are composed alternately in the strict primitive form, *sonata de chiesa,* and the more flexible composite of dance forms, *sonata de camera.* The last of the series, *L'Impériale,* perhaps represents his most mature and inspired style. Living at a time during which the rivalry between French and Italian music reached its climax, Couperin sought to adapt the new Italian forms to his own personal, and essentially French, style. In his *Les Goûts Réunis* (1724), a series of concerted pieces with strings very similar in form and spirit to the *Pièces de Clavecin,* one finds titles such as *Sicilienne* and *Ritratto dell' Amore,* and finally, as a closing number, a grand sonata *Le Parnasse ou l'Apothéose de Corelli.* In the following year he published an *Apothéose de Lully,* in which the rivals, Lully and Corelli, are made to unite for the furtherance of art. Couperin's style of composition was based on the *basso continuo,* the most important voices usually being the uppermost, carrying the melody, and the bass. Nevertheless, his music sometimes attains considerable complexity (on occasion requiring as many as three harpsichordists for its proper execution). His melodic invention, particularly in his use of the rondeau, was virtually inexhaustible, his themes swift and expressive. An outstanding feature was his inventive mode of ornamentation, in the 'gallant style' of the period. In 1933 the Lyrebird Press in Paris published a "complete" ed. of Couperin's works, in 12 volumes, under the chief editorship of Maurice Cauchie, assisted by P. Brunold, A. Gastoué, A. Tessier and A. Schaeffner. The contents are as follows: Vol. I, Didactic works: *Règle pour l'accompagnement* and *L'Art de toucher le clavecin;* Vols. II–V, the 4 books of *Pièces de clavecin;* Vol. VI, *Pièces d'orgue consistantes en deux Messes;* Vols. VII–X, chamber music, including *Concerts royaux, Les Goûts réunis ou Nouveaux concerts à l'usage de toutes les sortes d'instruments de musique, Les Nations, Le Parnasse ou l'Apothéose de Corelli, Apothéose de Lully, Pièces de violes avec la basse chiffrée,* and *Sonades inédites;* Vols. XI–XII, secular vocal music and religious music I and II. More recent editions are in *Le Pupitre* series, vols. 8 (*Leçons de tenebres*), 21–24 (*Pièces de clavecin,* books 1–4), 45 (*Neuf motets*), and 51 (*Pièces de violes*); also separate editions of *Pièces de clavecin,* ed. by M. Cauchie (1968–72) and by K. Gilbert (1969–72).

BIBLIOGRAPHY: H. Quittard, *Les Couperins* (Paris, 1913); C. Bouvet, *Une Dynastie de musiciens français: Les Couperins* . . . (Paris, 1919); L. de La Laurencie, *L'École française de violon de Lully à Viotti* (1922–24); Joan Llongueras, *Couperin o la Gracia* (1925); A. Tessier, *Couperin* (Paris, 1926); J. Tiersot, *Les Couperins* (Paris, 1926); J. Tiersot, "Two Centuries of a French Musical Family—The Couperins," *Musical Quarterly* (July 1926); P. Brunold, *Le Grande Orgue de St.-Gervais à Paris* (Paris, 1934); M. Riemann, *Untersuchungen zur Formgeschichte der französischen Klavier-Suite* . . . (1940; repr. Regensburg, 1968); P. Brunold, *François Couperin* (English transl., Monaco, 1949); M. Cauchie, *Thematic Index of Couperin* (Monaco, 1949); W. Mellers, *François Couperin and the French Classical Tradition* (London, 1950); M. Antoine, "Autour de François Couperin," *Revue de Musicologie* (Dec. 1952); P. Citron, *Couperin* (Paris, 1956); *Mélanges François Couperin. Publiés à l'occasion du Tricentenaire de sa Naissance* (Paris, 1968); V. Schwarz, "F. C. und seine Zeit. Zum 300 Geburstag des Meisters," *Österreichische Musikzeitschrift* (Nov. 1968); T. Dart, "On Couperin's Harpsichord Music," *Musical Times* (June 1969); N. Dufourcq, "F. C., musicien de la terre, de la ville, de l'église, de la cour," *XVIIe siècle* 82 (1969); F. Neumann, "Couperin and the Downbeat Doctrine for Appoggiaturas," *Acta Musicologica* (Jan.–June 1969); M. Pincherle, "F. C. et la conciliation des 'goûts' français et italien," *Chigiana* XXV/5 (1968); N. Dufourcq, "*Les Baricades mistérieuses* de F. C.," *Recherches sur la Musique Française* XIII (1973).

Couperin, Gervais-François (2nd son of **Armand-Louis**), b. Paris, May 22, 1759; d. there, March 11, 1826. Succeeded his brother, **Pierre-Louis,** as organist at St.-Gervais in 1789, also taking over his other appointments. He composed sonatas, variations, etc. He was the last of the Couperins to serve as organist at St.-Gervais, although his daughter, **Céleste** (b. 1793; d. Belleville, Feb. 14, 1860), played there at the time of her father's death. She was a teacher of singing and piano at Beauvais for about ten years.

BIBLIOGRAPHY: C. Bouvet, "La fin d'une dynastie d'artistes: Gervais-François Couperin et sa fille," *Revue de Musicologie* (1926).

Couperin, Louis, b. Chaumes, c.1626; d. Paris, Aug. 29, 1661. Went to Paris with Chambonnières, whose pupil he was; c.1650, became organist of St.-Gervais, a post in which he was succeeded, without interruption, by descendants and members of the Couperin family until 1826; from 1656, violinist and violist in the orchestras of the court ballets, and musician of the 'Chambre du roi'. Composed *Pièces de clavecin, Carillons* for organ, also violin pieces, etc. He was one of the earliest of French composers for the harpsichord in the new harmonic style employing the *basso continuo,* possibly being preceded only by his teacher, Chambonnières. The Lyrebird Press in Paris published a 'complete' edition of his works, ed. by P. Brunold. His *Pièces de clavecin* is publ. as vol. 18 of *Le Pupitre.*

BIBLIOGRAPHY: A. Pirro, "Louis Couperin," *Revue de musicologie* (1930).

Couperin, Nicolas (son of **François de Crouilly**), b. Paris, Dec. 20, 1680; d. there, July 25, 1748. In 1733 he succeeded his cousin, **François le Grand,** as organist at St.-Gervais.

Couperin, Pierre-Louis (called '**M. Couperin l'aîné** or '**Couperin fils**'), son of **Armand-Louis;** b. Paris, Mar. 14, 1755; d. there, Oct. 10, 1789. He was organist to the King, later at Notre-Dame, St.-Jean, St.-Merry, and at St.-Gervais (succeeded his father early in 1789; he died eight months later). Some of his compositions were publ. in contemporary collections; others are in MS.

Courboin, Charles Marie, American organist; b. Antwerp, April 2, 1884; d. New York, April 13, 1973. He studied at the Cons. of Brussels with J. Blockx and A. Mailly; in 1904 emigrated to the U.S.; made several transcontinental tours of the U.S. and Canada, and two European tours; in 1919 he played the organ in the first performance of Widor's *6th Symphony* (dedicated to Courboin) with the Philadelphia Orch. under Stokowski. He designed 144 important organs in the U.S., among them Wanamaker's in New York.

Courtois, Jean, French contrapuntist in the first half of the 16th century, was maître de chapelle at Cambrai Cathedral in 1539, when a 4-part motet of his, *Venite populi terrae,* was performed before Charles V of Spain. Many of his motets, psalms and songs appeared in publications of the period (printed at Paris, Lyons, Antwerp, Nuremberg, etc.); H. Expert reprinted some of his songs in *Les Maîtres musiciens de la Renaissance française.* Masses, motets and songs in MS are in the Munich State Library and the library at Cambrai.

Courvoisier, Karl, violinist; b. Basel, Nov. 12, 1846; d. Liverpool, Jan. 31, 1908. He studied with David and Röntgen at Leipzig Cons. (1867–69), and Joachim in Berlin (1869–70). In 1885 he settled in Liverpool as a teacher. He published *Die Violintechnik* (1878; English transl. by H. E. Krehbiel, *The Techniques of Violin Playing;* 2nd ed., N.Y., 1896); *École de la velocité* for violin and *Méthode de violon* (text in German, English and French; London, 1892).

Courvoisier, Walter, Swiss composer and conductor; b. Riehen, near Basel, Feb. 7, 1875; d. Locarno, Dec. 27, 1931. He first studied medicine (M.D., 1900), later music with Thuille in Munich (whose son-in-law he became); taught composition at the Academy of Music, Munich (1910–30).

WORKS: operas *Lanzelot und Elaine* (Munich, 1917), *Die Krähen* (Munich, 1921); the oratorio *Totenfeier;* chamber music; piano pieces; about 150 songs.

Coussemaker, Charles-Edmond-Henri de, French music scholar; b. Bailleul, Nord, April 19, 1805; d. Bourbourg, Jan. 10, 1876. He studied music as a child; his main profession was the law. While studying law at the Univ. of Paris, he took private lessons with Pellegrini in singing and Anton Reicha in harmony. He continued his studies with Lefebvre in Douai, after becoming a practicing lawyer. At this time (1831–35) he

found leisure to compose music of the most varied description, all of which, with the exception of a few *romances* and two sets of songs, is unpublished, and apparently lost. His interest in history and archaeology led him to the study of the authentic documents of music; he was also influenced by the scholarly articles in *La Gazette et Revue Musicale* (then edited by Fétis). During successive terms as judge in Hazebrouck, Dunkerque and Lille, he continued to accumulate knowledge of musical documentation; he assembled a vast library; 1075 items in his library are listed in the *Catalogue des livres, manuscrits et instruments de musique du feu M. Charles Coussemaker* (Brussels, 1877; issued for an auction).

WRITINGS: a great number of valuable treatises and collections: *Mémoire sur Hucbald* (Paris, 1841); *Notice sur les collections musicales de la bibliothèque de Cambrai . . .* (1843); "Essai sur les instruments de musique au moyen-âge," in Dindron, *Annales archéologiques,* illustrated; *Histoire de l'harmonie au moyen-âge* (1852); *Trois chants historiques* (1854); *Chants populaires des Flamands de France* (1856); *Drames liturgiques du moyen âge* (1860); *Les Harmonistes des XIIᵉ et XIIIᵉ siècles* (1865); a great work, intended for a supplement to Gerbert, entitled *Scriptorum de musica medii œvi nova series* (4 vols., 1864–76; new ed. Graz, 1908; anastatic reprint, 1931, by *Bolletino Bibliografico Musicale*); *L'art harmonique aux XIIᵉ et XIIIᵉ siècles* (1865); *Oeuvres complètes d'Adam de la Halle* (1872); etc.

BIBLIOGRAPHY: A. Desplanque, *Étude sur les travaux d'historie et d'archéologie de M. Edmond de Coussemaker* (Paris, 1870); R. Debevere, "Edmond de Coussemaker (1805–1876), een belangrijk frans-vlaming," *Ons Erfdeel* XII/2 (1968).

Coverly, Robert, Portuguese composer of light music; b. Oporto, Sept. 6, 1864; d. there, Sept. 19, 1944. He studied in London and New York; composed a great number of effective marches and songs, of which *The Passing Regiment,* a military march for band, achieved great popularity.

Coward, Sir Henry, English choral conductor; b. Liverpool, Nov. 26, 1849; d. Sheffield, June 10, 1944. He was apprenticed to be a cutler but attended classes of solfeggio. He organized a choral group at Sheffield and became its conductor. After a period of hard study, he obtained the B.Mus. degree at Oxford (1889), and later D.Mus. (1894). He organized spectacular choral festivals in Sheffield, in which thousands of choristers participated; gave concerts with his chorus in Germany (1906); in 1908 he presented 16 concerts in Canada with members of the Sheffield Choral Union, headed by him. A world tour followed in 1911, which included the U.S., Canada, Australia and South Africa. Coward was the leader of choral groups at Leeds and Glasgow; acted as a judge at Competition Festivals. He was knighted in 1926. He composed several cantatas and other choral works; edited a collection of Methodist hymns (1901); published *Choral Technique and Interpretation* (1914); *Reminiscences* (1919).

BIBLIOGRAPHY: J. A. Rodgers, *Dr. Henry Coward, The Pioneer Chorus-master* (London, 1911).

Coward, Sir Noel, British playwright and author of musical comedies; b. Teddington, Middlesex, Dec. 16, 1899; d. Port Maria, Jamaica, March 25, 1973. At the age of eleven, he appeared on the stage, and was associated with the theater ever since, in the triple capacity of actor, playwright and producer. Having had no formal education in music, he dictated his songs to a musical amanuensis. Among the musical comedies for which he wrote both words and music are *This Year of Grace* (N.Y., Nov. 7, 1928); *Bitter Sweet* (London, July 18, 1929); *Conversation Piece* (London, Feb. 16, 1934); *Pacific 1860* (London, Dec. 19, 1946); *Ace of Clubs* (London, July 7, 1950); *After the Ball*, to Wilde's *Lady Windermere's Fan* (London, June 10, 1954). 51 songs from his musical plays are published in the *Noel Coward Song Book* (N.Y., 1953) with the author's introduction. He also published an autobiography, *Present Indicative* (London, 1937); 2nd vol. *Future Indefinite* (London, 1954). He was knighted in 1970.

BIBLIOGRAPHY: Cole Lesley (Noel Coward's valet-companion), *Remembered Laughter* (N.Y., 1976).

Cowell, Henry Dixon, innovative American composer; b. Menlo Park, Calif., March 11, 1897; d. Shady, N.Y., Dec. 10, 1965. He studied with Charles Seeger; then took courses with Erich von Hornbostel in Berlin and with R. Huntington Woodman; studied piano with Richard Buhlig. Cowell toured Europe five times playing his own piano works; the U.S., twelve times; appeared as a soloist in his Piano Concerto with the Conductorless Orchestra, N.Y., April 26, 1930, and with the Havana Philharmonic (Dec. 28, 1930). As a young man he devised and developed the technique of "tone clusters" produced by striking the piano keys with forearm, palm or fist, embodying these devices in his piano concerto and in many of his other works. He also pioneered in playing the piano by plucking the strings directly under the lid, playing glissando, or sounding the strings with a variety of objects. In collaboration with Leon Theremin he invented the Rhythmicon, an instrument allowing the accurate and simultaneous production of sixteen different rhythms, from 1 to 16 beats to a given unit of measure, the component tones being parts of the overtone series. Cowell held teaching positions at Stanford Univ., the New School for Social Research in New York, Univ. of Southern California, Mills College, Peabody Conservatory of Music in Baltimore, Columbia Univ., etc.; was recipient of the Guggenheim Fellowship (1930–31). He wrote some 800 works of various descriptions; championed serious new music in the U.S. and abroad; founded the *New Music Quarterly* (1927) for publication of ultra-modern music; was also an organizer of the Pan-American Association of Composers. In 1951 Cowell was elected member of the National Academy of Arts and Letters. In 1956 he undertook a world tour with his wife, the ethnomusicologist Sidney Cowell. He used motives collected during his travels in several of his works.

WORKS: OPERA, *O'Higgins of Chile* (1949); FOR ORCH.: Symph. No. 1 (1918); No. 2, *Anthropos* (1939); No. 3, *Gaelic Symphony* (1942); No. 4, *Short Symphony* (Boston, Oct. 24, 1947); No. 5 (Washington, Jan. 5, 1949); No. 6 (1951; Houston, Nov. 14, 1955);

No. 7, (Baltimore, Nov. 25, 1952); No. 8, for chorus and orch. (Wilmington, Ohio, March 1, 1953); No. 9 (1953); No. 10, for chamber orch. (1953); No. 11, subtitled *Seven Rites of Music* (Louisville, May 29, 1954); No. 12 (Houston, Mar. 28, 1960); No. 13, surnamed *Madras Symphony* (Madras, India, Mar. 3, 1959); No. 14 (Washington, April 27, 1961); No. 15 (N.Y., Nov. 5, 1962); No. 16, *Icelandic Symphony* (Reykjavik, Mar. 21, 1963); No. 17 (1963); No. 18 (1964); No. 19 (Nashville, Tenn., Oct. 18, 1965); No. 20 (1965); *Synchrony* (Paris, June 6, 1931); *Rhythmicana*, for rhythmicon and orch. (1931); *Shipshape Overture* (1939; also for band); *Old American Country Set* (Indianapolis, Feb. 28, 1940); *Ancient Desert Drone* (1940); *Shoonthree* (1940); *Pastoral and Fiddler's Delight* (N.Y., July 26, 1940, Stokowski conducting); *Tales of the Countryside*, for piano and orch. (his most successful work; Atlantic City, May 11, 1941, Cowell soloist, Stokowski conducting); *Concerto piccolo*, for piano and orch. (1942); *Celtic Set* (1943; also for band); *Hymn and Fuguing Tune*, Nos. 1–8 (1943–47; based on the fuguing tunes of Billings; very successful); *United Music* (1944); *Big Sing* (1945); *Festival Overture*, for double orch. (1946); *Ongaku* for orch. (1957); Antiphony for 2 orchestras (1958); Percussion Concerto (1958); Accordion Concerto (1960); Harmonica Concerto (1960); Koto Concerto No. 2 (1965); Harp Concerto (1965); Concerto for Koto and Orch. (N.Y., Dec. 18, 1964). FOR BAND: *Animal Magic* (1944); *Grandma's Rumba* (1945); *Fantaisie* (U.S. Military Acad. Band, West Point, N.Y., May 30, 1952); etc. CHAMBER ORCH.: *Symphonietta* (1928); *Irish Suite* (1929); *Polyphonica* for 12 instruments (1930); *Exultation* for 10 string instruments (1930); *Competitive Sport* (1931); *Steel and Stone* (1931); *Heroic Dance* (1931); *4 Continuations* (1933); *6 Casual Developments* for five instruments (1935).

CHAMBER MUSIC: *Ensemble* for 2 violins, viola, 2 cellos and two thundersticks (1925); *Seven Paragraphs* for trio (1926); Quartet (1927); Suite for Violin and Piano (1927); *Movement* for string quartet (1934); *Mosaic Quartet* for strings (1935); *United Quartet* for strings (1936); *Chrysanthemums*, for soprano, 2 saxophones and 4 strings (1937); *Sarabande*, for oboe, clarinet and percussion (1937); *Trickster Coyote*, for flute and percussion (1942); *Action in Brass*, for five instruments (1943); *Two Bits*, for flute and piano (1944); Violin Sonata (1945); *Tall Tale*, for brass sextet (1947); Piano Trio (1965).

CHORAL WORKS: *The Thistle Flower*, for women's voices (1928); *The Coming of Light* (1939); *Fire and Ice*, for male voices and band (1942); *American Muse* (1943); *To America* (1946); *The Road to Tomorrow* (1947); *Afternoon, Evening, Night, Morning* (1947); numerous piano pieces with fanciful titles, mostly with the application of tone clusters (*Amiable Conversation; Fabric; Dynamic Motion; Advertisement*; etc.); songs: *Where She Lies, The Birthing of Manaunaun*, etc.; 2 ballets, *The Building of Banba* (1922); *Atlantis* (1926).

WRITINGS: *New Musical Resources* (N.Y., 1930); ed., *American Composers on American Music* (1933); *Charles Ives and His Music* (N.Y., 1955; in collaboration with his wife, Sidney Cowell).

BIBLIOGRAPHY: N. Slonimsky, "Henry Cowell," in

American Composers on American Music (1933); Hugo Weisgall, "The Music of Henry Cowell," *Musical Quarterly* (Oct. 1959); Oliver Daniel, "Henry Cowell," *Stereo Review* (Dec. 1974).

Cowen, Sir Frederic Hymen, English composer; b. Kingston, Jamaica, Jan. 29, 1852; d. London, Oct. 6, 1935. His evident talent for music caused his parents to take him to England to study at the age of four. He was a pupil of Benedict and Goss in London; studied at Leipzig under Hauptmann, Moscheles, Reinecke, Richter, Plaidy (1865–66); in Berlin under Kiel (1867–68); conductor of the London Philharmonic (1888–92) succeeding Sullivan; again from 1900–07; musical director of the Melbourne Centennial Exhibition (1888–89); conductor of the Liverpool Philharmonic from 1896–1913; Sir Charles Hallé's successor as conductor of the Manchester Concerts (1896–99); conducted Handel Triennial Festival (Crystal Palace, 1903–12); Cardiff Festival (1902–10). He received the degree Mus. Doc. from Cambridge (hon. c.1900) and Edinburgh (1910); knighted in 1911.
WORKS: 4 operas, *Pauline* (London, Nov. 22, 1876), *Thorgrim* (London, April 22, 1890), *Signa* (London, June 30, 1894), *Harold, or the Norman Conquest* (London, June 8, 1895); oratorios: *The Deluge* (1878), *St. Ursula* (1881), *Ruth* (1887), *The Veil* (Cardiff Festival, Sept. 20, 1910; his most successful work); cantatas. For orch.: 6 symphonies: 1 in C minor (1869); 2 in F minor (1872); 3 in C minor, *Scandinavian* (1880); 4 in B-flat minor, *Welsh* (1884); 5 in F (1887); 6 in E, *Idyllic* (1897); 3 suites: *The Language of Flowers, In the Olden Time, In Fairyland*; Sinfonietta; Piano Concerto; 4 overtures; *Of Life and Love*, fantasy. Chamber music: 2 piano trios; 2 string quartets; piano pieces; over 250 songs; etc. He published his memoirs as *My Art and My Friends* (London, 1913), and an amusing glossary of musical terms, *Music as is wrote* (London, 1915); also, for the Masterpieces of Music series, books (with biography and music) on Haydn, Mozart, Mendelssohn and Rossini.
BIBLIOGRAPHY: *Musical Times* (Nov. 1898).

Cowles, Walter Ruel, American composer; b. New Haven, Conn., Sept 4, 1881; d. Tallahassee, Florida, Dec. 8, 1959. He graduated from Yale Univ. (B.A. 1906; Mus. Bac. 1907); studied with Horatio Parker; then at the Schola Cantorum, Paris; was instructor of piano at Yale Music School (1911–19); professor of Theory of Music at Florida State College for Women (1930–1951); won the Steinert prize for composition at Yale. He composed a piano concerto; a piano trio; songs and piano pieces.

Crabbé, Armand, Belgian baritone; b. Brussels, April 23, 1883; d. there, July 24, 1947. He studied with Désiré Demest at the Brussels Cons. (1902–04); was engaged at the Théâtre de la Monnaie in Brussels where he created the role of the Friar in Massenet's *Jongleur de Nôtre-Dame* (also sung by him for the first time at Covent Garden, New York, Boston, etc.). In 1908 he joined Hammerstein's Manhattan Opera, N.Y.; then was with the Chicago Grand Opera (1910–11); returning to Europe, he settled in Brussels as a voice teacher. He wrote an opera *Les Noces d'or* (in collaboration with Auguste Maurage).

Craft, Marcella, American lyric soprano; b. Indianapolis, Aug. 11, 1880; d. Riverside, California, Dec. 12, 1959. She studied with Charles Adams in Boston (1897–1900) and with F. Mottino in Milan (1901–05); made her debut in Italy; sang in Germany until the outbreak of World War I, when she returned to the U.S.; subsequently appeared with the San Carlo Opera Co.; settled at Riverside, California, as a singing teacher.

Craft, Robert, American conductor and brilliant writer on music; b. Kingston, N.Y., Oct. 20, 1923. He studied at the Juilliard School of Music and the Berkshire Music Center. He took courses in conducting with Monteux. During World War II he was in the U.S. Army Medical Corps. In 1947 he conducted the New York Brass and Woodwind Ensemble. A decisive turn in his career was his encounter with Stravinsky whom he greatly impressed by his precise knowledge of Stravinsky's music; gradually he became Stravinsky's closest associate. He was also instrumental in persuading Stravinsky to adopt the 12-tone method of composition, a momentous turn in Stravinsky's creative path. He collaborated with Stravinsky on 6 volumes of a catechumenical and discursive nature: *Conversations with Igor Stravinsky* (N.Y., 1959); *Memories and Commentaries* (N.Y., 1960); *Expositions and Developments* (N.Y., 1962); *Dialogues and a Diary* (N.Y., 1963); *Themes and Episodes* (N.Y., 1967); *Retrospections and Conclusions* (N.Y., 1969). Resentful of frequent referral to him as a musical Boswell, Craft insists that his collaboration with Stravinsky was more akin to that between the Goncourt brothers, both acting and reacting to an emerging topic of discussion, with Stravinsky evoking his ancient memories in his careful English, or fluent French, spiced with unrestrained discourtesies toward professional colleagues on the American scene, and Craft reifying the material in an analeptic bulimia of quaquaversal literary, psychological, physiological and culinary references in a flow of finely ordered dialogue.

Cramer, Johann Baptist, famous German pianist and pedagogue, eldest son of **Wilhelm Cramer;** b. Mannheim, Feb. 24, 1771; d. London, April 16, 1858. He was brought to London as an infant, and throughout his life regarded it as his home. He received a fine musical education, first from his father, then from Clementi (1779–81) and C. F. Abel (1785). He began to travel as a concert pianist in 1788; visited Vienna where he met Haydn and Beethoven; in later years (1832–45) spent considerable time as teacher in Munich and Paris, finally returning to London. His greatest work is his piano method *Grosse Praktische Pianoforte Schule* (1815) in 5 parts, the last of which, *84 Studies* (op. 50; later revised and publ. as op. 81, including *16 nouvelles études*) is famous in piano pedagogy. Hans von Bülow made a selection of fifty studies from this collection, later revised and annotated in collections of 52 and 60; Henselt issued a different selection with accompaniment of 2nd piano; other editions of Cramer's studies are by Coccius, Riemann, Pauer, Lack, and Lickl; *100 Progressive Etudes* are also well known. Apart from his pedagogic collections, Cramer wrote 7 piano concertos; 105 piano sonatas; Piano Quartet; Piano Quintet, and numerous piano pieces of the salon type, but all these are quite forgotten, while his piano studies, with those of Czerny, have maintained their value for more than a century. In 1824, together with R. Addison and T. F. Beale, Cramer established a music publishing house (now J. B. Cramer & Co., Ltd.), of which he was director until 1842; in 1845 Addison retired and was succeeded by W. Chappell, the firm then becoming Cramer, Beale & Chappell; after Cramer's death in 1858, and Chappell's retirement in 1861, G. Wood became Beale's partner; about 1862 the firm began to devote much attention to the manufacture of pianos; on Beale's death in 1863, Wood became sole director, continuing it successfully until his death in 1893, although devoting more consideration to piano manufacture than to music publishing. His two nephews succeeded him. In 1897 the firm became a limited company.

BIBLIOGRAPHY: J. Pembaur, *Die 84 Etüden von J. B. Cramer; Anleitung zu gründlichem Studieren und Analysieren derselben* (Leipzig, 1901); Th. Schlesinger, *J. B. Cramer und seine Klavier-Sonaten* (Munich, 1928); P. F. Ganz, "Johann Baptist Cramer and His Celebrated Etudes," *Clavier* (Feb. 1967); H. Goldschmidt, "Beethovens Anweisungen zum Spiel der Cramer-Etüden," in H. A. Brockhaus and K. Niemann, *Bericht über den Int. Beethoven-Kongress 10.–12. Dezember 1970* (Berlin, 1971).

Cramer, Wilhelm, German violinist; b. Mannheim, June 1746 (baptized June 2, 1746); d. London, Oct. 5, 1799. He received his musical training from his father Jacob Cramer (1705–77) who was a violinist in the Mannheim Orchestra and also studied with Johann Stamitz and Cannabich; from 1757–72 he was a member of the Mannheim Orchestra. In 1772 he went to London, where he became a successful violinist and conductor. He was leader of the orch. of the Anacreontic Society during its most prestigious years (1773–91), and was the father of **Johann Baptist Cramer.** He wrote 6 string quartets, 6 violin sonatas and other string music.

Cranz, August, music publishing firm in Hamburg, founded 1813 by August Heinrich Cranz (1789–1870). His son **Alwin** (b. 1834; d. Vevey, Apr. 10, 1923), who succeeded him in 1857, bought the firm of C. A. Spina of Vienna in 1876, and in 1886 the firm of C. A. Böhme of Hamburg. Alwin's son, **Oskar** (pen name **Anton Toska**; d. Boston, Aug. 24, 1929), entered as partner in 1896. In 1897 the firm removed to Leipzig. Branches were established in Vienna (1876), Brussels (1883), and London (1896).

Cras, Jean Emile Paul, French composer; b. Brest, May 22, 1879; d. there, Sept. 14, 1932. He was an officer in the French Navy, reaching the rank of Vice-Admiral; he grew up in a musical atmosphere and when still a child began to compose; took lessons with Henri Duparc. Under the influence of Duparc's style, Cras composed a number of miniatures in an impressionistic vein; he was at his best in lyrical songs and instrumental pieces.

WORKS: an opera *Polyphème* (Paris, Opéra-Comique, Dec. 28, 1922) which won the Prize of the City of Paris; *Journal de Bord*, a symphonic suite (1927); *Légende* for cello and orch. (1929); Piano Concerto (1931); for voice and orch.: *L'offrande lyrique* (1920); *Fontaines* (1923); *Trois Noëls* (1929); many pieces of chamber music, a number of songs.

BIBLIOGRAPHY: René Dumesnil, "Jean Cras," in *Portraits de musiciens français* (Paris, 1938; pp. 153–60).

Crawford, Robert M., baritone and conductor; b. Dawson, Yukon Territory, Canada, July 27, 1899; d. New York, March 12, 1961. Studied at Princeton Univ., and also took courses at the Juilliard Graduate School and at the American Cons. at Fontainebleau, France. Returning to the U.S., he held various posts as choral teacher and conductor; was in charge of the Newark Symph. Orch. and Chautauqua Orch. (1933); composed several orchestral suites and songs, of which the most popular is *The U.S. Air Force* ("off we go . . .").

Crawford, Ruth Porter, remarkable American composer; b. East Liverpool, Ohio, July 3, 1901; d. Chevy Chase, Maryland, Nov. 18, 1953. She studied composition with **Charles Seeger,** whom she later married; her principal piano teacher was Henriot Levy. She dedicated herself to teaching and collecting American folksongs; still as a very young person she taught at the School of Musical Arts in Jacksonville, Florida (1918–21); then gave courses at the American Cons. in Chicago (1925–29) and at Elmhurst College of Music, Illinois (1926–29). In 1930 she received a Guggenheim Fellowship. She became known mainly as a compiler of American folksongs; she published *American Folk Songs for Children* (1948), *Animal Folk Songs for Children* (1950) and, *American Folk Songs for Christmas* (1953). Her own compositions, astonishingly bold in their experimental aperçus and insights, often anticipated many techniques of the future avant-garde; while rarely performed during her lifetime, they had a remarkable revival in the subsequent decades.

WORKS: Violin Sonata (1926), Suite for Piano and Woodwind Quintet (1927; performed for the first time in Cambridge, Mass., Dec. 14, 1975); *4 Diaphonic Suites* for various instruments (1930); *3 Songs* for contralto, oboe, percussion and piano, to words by Carl Sandburg (*Rat Riddles; Prayers of Steel; In Tall Grass;* performed at the Amsterdam Festival of the International Society for Contemporary Music, June 15, 1933); String Quartet (1931, containing a slow movement anticipating the "static" harmonies and "phase shifts"); *Sacco and Vanzetti* for chorus (Workers' Olympiad, 1933); *Risselty Rosselty* for small orch. (1941); Suite for Wind Quintet (1952); several sets of piano pieces; *2 Ricercari* for voice and piano (*Sacco, Vanzetti; Chinaman, Laundryman;* 1932).

BIBLIOGRAPHY: Charles Seeger, "Ruth Crawford" in Henry Cowell's symposium, *American Composers on American Music* (Stanford, 1933).

Creatore, Giuseppe, band conductor; b. Naples, June 21, 1871; d. New York, Aug. 15, 1952. He studied at the Naples Cons. with Nicola d'Arienzo and Camillo de Nardis. In 1900 he came to the U.S., organized his own band and toured from coast to coast and in Canada. In 1906 he returned to Italy, where he established a band which he brought to America for a tour. He then settled in N.Y. and was active as impresario of various opera companies which, however, were not successful; conducted band concerts during summer seasons in various U.S. cities.

Crécquillon (Créquillon), Thomas, Franco-Flemish contrapuntist; b. probably in Ghent; d. Béthune, 1557. It is known that he was maître de chapelle at Béthune in 1540; was court musician to Charles V of Spain between 1544–47; later was canon at Namur, Termonde and Béthune. His works, which rank with the best of that period, consist of 16 Masses in 4 and 5 parts, 116 motets, *cantiones,* and 192 French *chansons* in 4, 5 and 6 parts. Reprints appear in Commer's *Collectio operum musicorum Batavorum saeculi XVI* and Maldeghem's *Trésor musical.* For a complete list of his works (published mostly between 1545 and 1636) and a detailed bibliography, see the article on him in *Die Musik in Geschichte und Gegenwart.*

Crescentini, Girolamo, one of the last and finest of the Italian artificial mezzo-sopranos; b. Urbania, near Urbino, Feb. 2, 1762; d. Naples, April 24, 1846. He studied singing with Gibelli at Bologna, and made a highly successful debut at Rome in 1783; subsequent successes in other European capitals earned him the surname of "Orfeo Italiano." He sang at Leghorn, Padua, Venice, Turin, London (1786), Milan and Naples (1788–89). Napoleon, having heard him in 1805, decorated him with the Iron Crown, and engaged him from 1806–12; Crescentini then retired from the stage and left Paris, on account of vocal disorders induced by the climate; in 1816 he became professor of singing in the Royal Cons., Naples. Cimarosa wrote his *Orazi e Curiazi* for him. Crescentini published several collections of *Ariette* (Vienna, 1797), and a *Treatise on Vocalization in France and Italy,* with vocal exercises (Paris, 1811).

Creser, William, English organist and composer; b. York, Sept. 9, 1844; d. London, March 13, 1933. He was taught by his father, in whose choir (at St. John's Church) he sang; studied later with G. A. Macfarren (organ and composition); as early as 1856 he occasionally acted as Sir J. Barnby's substitute at Holgate Road Church; appointed organist at Holy Trinity, Micklegate, in 1859, and later succeeded Barnby; then filled various other positions; organist at the Chapel Royal, St. James' (1891–1902); from 1902 examiner of Trinity College of Music, in which capacity he made frequent visits to musical institutions throughout the British colonies; Mus. Bac., Oxonian, 1869; Mus. Doc., Oxonian, 1880. His wife (*née* **Amelia Clarke**) was a well known mezzo-soprano.

WORKS: an oratorio, *Micaiah;* the cantatas *Eudora* (Leeds, 1882); *The Sacrifice of Freia* (Leeds, 1889); *The Golden Legend; Tegner's Drapa;* a Mass; 2 Psalms; *Old English Suite* for orch.; String Quartet; Piano Trio; Violin Sonata; organ music.

Crespin, Regine, French soprano; b. Marseilles, Feb. 23, 1927. She studied pharmacology; then began taking voice lessons with Suzanne Cesbron-Viseur and Georges Jouatte in Paris. She made her debut at the Opéra-Comique as Tosca in 1951 and then sang at the Paris Opéra. She later acquired a European reputation as one of the best Wagnerian singers; she sang Kundry in *Parsifal* at the Bayreuth Festivals (1958–61); appeared also at La Scala, Milan, at Covent Garden in London, and on Nov. 19, 1962 made her American debut with the Metropolitan Opera in N.Y., in the role of Marschallin in *Der Rosenkavalier;* she remained on the staff of the Metropolitan through 1971; sang the parts of Elsa in *Lohengrin,* Sieglinde in *Die Walküre,* and Amelia in *Un Ballo in Maschera.* Her sonorous, somewhat somber voice suits dramatic parts excellently.

Creston, Paul (real name **Joseph Guttoveggio**), distinguished American composer; b. New York, Oct. 10, 1906. He studied piano with Randegger and Déthier and organ playing with Yon; he was essentially autodidact in composition. He adopted the name Creston, an anglicized version of his high school nickname Crespino, a role he acted in a play. He began to compose tentatively at the age of 8, but he did not compose his full-fledged opus 1, *Five Dances* for piano until he was 26. In 1938 he obtained a Guggenheim Fellowship, and in a few years advanced to the front ranks of American composers, with an impressive catalogue of major works. He filled various jobs as a theater organist for silent movies; then obtained the post of organist at St. Malachy's Church in New York (1934–67); concurrently he taught at the New York College of Music (1963–67). From 1968–75 he was prof. of music at Central Washington State College. In 1976 he moved to San Diego, Calif. He has written more than 100 major compositions, including 5 symphonies and 15 concertos for various instruments, as well as 35 other symphonic works, chamber music for various instrumental combinations, choral works, piano pieces and songs. His music is characterized by engaging spontaneity, with strong melodic lines and full-bodied harmonies; his instrumental writing is highly advantageous for virtuoso performance. He published two books *Principles of Rhythm* (New York, 1964) and *Creative Harmony* (New York, 1970). In his theoretical writings, he militates against the illogic of binary meters and proposes to introduce such time signatures as 6/12 or 3/9; some of these metrical designations he uses in his own works.

WORKS: 5 symphonies: No. 1 (N.Y., Feb. 22, 1941; received N.Y. Music Critics' Circle Award); No. 2 (N.Y., Feb. 15, 1945; highly successful); No. 3 (Worcester Festival, Oct. 27, 1950); No. 4 (Washington, Jan. 30, 1952); No. 5 (Washington, April 4, 1956).

OTHER WORKS FOR ORCH.: Partita for Flute, Violin and Strings (1937); *Threnody* for orch. (1938); *Two Choric Dances* for woodwinds, piano, percussion and strings (1938); Concertino for Marimba and Orch. (1940); *Prelude and Dance* for piano, strings and orch. (1941); *Pastorale and Tarantella* for piano, strings and orch. (1941); Saxophone Concerto (1941; N.Y., Jan. 27, 1944); *A Rumor,* symph. sketch (N.Y., Dec. 13, 1941); *Dance Variations* for soprano and orch. (1942); *Frontiers* for orch. (Toronto, Oct. 14, 1943); *Poem* for harp and orch. (1945); Fantasy for Trombone and Orch. (Los Angeles, Feb. 12, 1948); Piano Concerto (1949); Concerto for 2 Pianos and Orch.

(1951; Montevallo, Alabama, Nov. 18, 1968); *Walt Whitman*, symph. poem (1952); *Invocation and Dance* for orch. (Louisville, May 15, 1954); *Dance Overture* (1954); *Lydian Ode* (1956); Violin Concerto No. 1 (1956; Detroit, Jan. 14, 1960); *Toccata* (1957); *Pre-Classic Suite* for orch. (New Orleans, April 3, 1958); Accordion Concerto (1958); *Janus* for orch. (Denver, July 17, 1959); Violin Concerto No. 2 (Los Angeles, Nov. 17, 1960); *Corinthians XIII*, symph. poem (Phoenix, March 30, 1964); *Choreografic Suite* for orch. (1966); *Pavane Variations* for orch. (La Jolla, Calif., Aug. 21, 1966); *Chthonic Ode*, an "homage to Henry Moore" (Detroit, April 6, 1967); *The Psalmist* for contralto and orch. (1967); *Anatolia (Turkish Rhapsody)* for symphonic band (1967); *Thanatopsis* for orch. (1971).

CHAMBER MUSIC: Suite for Saxophone and Piano (1935); String Quartet (1936); Suite for Viola and Piano (1937); Suite for Violin and Piano (1939); Sonata for Saxophone and Piano (1939); Suite for Flute, Viola and Piano (1952); Suite for Cello and Piano (1956); Concertino for Piano and Woodwind Quintet (1969); *Ceremonial* for percussion ensemble (1972); *Rapsodie* for saxophone and organ (1976).

CHORAL WORKS: *Three Chorales from Tagore* (1936); *Requiem Mass* for tenor, bass and organ (1938); *Missa Solemnis* (1949); *Isaiah's Prophecy*, a Christmas oratorio (1961); *The Northwest* for chorus and orch. (1969); *Hyas Illahee* for chorus and orch. (Shreveport, Louisiana, March 14, 1976); liturgical vocal works with piano or organ accompaniment; piano pieces (*5 Little Dances, 5 Inventions*, etc.).

BIBLIOGRAPHY: Henry Cowell, "Paul Creston," *Musical Quarterly* (Oct. 1948).

Crist, Bainbridge, American composer; b. Lawrenceburg, Indiana, Feb. 13, 1883; d. Barnstable, Mass., Feb. 7, 1969. He studied piano and flute; later law at the George Washington Univ. (LL.B.); was a lawyer in Boston for six years (until 1912), continuing his music as an avocation; went to Europe to complete musical training (theory with P. Juon in Berlin and C. Landi, London, and singing with William Shakespeare); taught singing in Boston (1915–21) and Washington, D.C. (1922–23); returned to Europe (1923) and spent four years in Florence, Paris, Lucerne and Berlin; then came back to the U.S. and settled in Washington.

WORKS: FOR THE STAGE: *Le Pied de la Momie*, choreographic drama in 2 scenes (1915; Bournemouth Festival, England, 1925); *Pregiwa's Marriage*, a Javanese ballet in 1 scene (1920); *The Sorceress*, choreographic drama (1926). FOR ORCH.: *Egyptian Impressions*, suite (Boston Pops, June 22, 1915); *Abhisarika*, for violin and orch. (1921); *Intermezzo* (1921); *Chinese Dance* (1922); *Arabian Dance* (1922); *Nautch Dance* (1922); *Dreams* (1924); *Yearning* (1924); *Nocturne* (1924); *An Old Portrait* (1924); *La Nuit revécue* (1933; Radio City, N.Y., March 8, 1936); *Vienna 1913* (1933); *Frivolité* (1934); *Hymn to Nefertiti* (1936); *Fête espagnole* (1937); *American Epic 1620*, tone poem (Washington, D.C., Feb. 28, 1943). FOR VOICE AND ORCH.: *A Bag of Whistles* (1915); *The Parting*, poem (1916); *Rhymes* (1917); *O Come Hither!* (1918); *Drolleries* (1920); *Colored Stars*, a suite of 4 songs (1921); *Remember* (1930); *The Way That Lovers Use* (1931);

Noontime (1931); *Evening* (1931); *By a Silent Shore* (1932). Choral works for mixed, male and female voices; piano pieces; songs. He is author of *The Art of Setting Words to Music* (N.Y., 1944).

BIBLIOGRAPHY: J. T. Howard, *Bainbridge Crist* (N.Y., 1929); W. T. Upton, *Art-Song in America* (N.Y., 1930; pp. 236–49).

Cristofori, Bartolommeo, celebrated Italian instrument maker; b. Padua, May 4, 1655; d. Florence, Jan. 27, 1731. He was the inventor of the first practical piano as opposed to the clavichord (which also employs a type of hammer action), although two-keyed instruments called Piano e Forte are known to have existed in Modena in 1598, and a four-octave keyboard instrument shaped like a dulcimer, with small hammers and no dampers, dating from 1610, is yet in existence. He was a leading maker of clavicembali in Padua; about 1690 went to Florence, where he was instrument maker to Ferdinando de' Medici; on the latter's death in 1713, he was made custodian of the court collection of instruments by Cosimo III. According to an article by Maffei (published 1711, *Giornale dei Letterati d'Italia*), Cristofori had up to that year made three "gravecembali col piano e forte," these having, instead of the usual jacks plucking the strings with quills, a row of little hammers striking the strings from below. The principle of this hammer action was adopted, in the main, by Gottfried Silbermann, the Streichers, and Broadwood (hence called the "English action"). Following the designation by its inventor, the new instrument was named *Piano-forte*. A piano of Cristofori's make is in the possession of the N.Y. Metropolitan Museum of Art.

BIBLIOGRAPHY: F. Casaglia, *Per le onoranze a Bartolommeo Cristofori* (1876).

Crivelli, Giovanni Battista, Italian composer of the Lombardy school; b. Scandiano, Modena; d. Modena, 1682. He was organist at Reggio Cathedral; then maestro di cappella to the court of Ferrara; at the electoral court at Munich (1629–34); at the court of Francesco I at Modena (1651); at the Church of Santa Maria Maggiore, Bergamo (1642–48, and again in 1654). He published *Motetti concertati* (1626; 3rd ed. 1635) and *Madrigali concertati* (1626; 2nd ed. 1633).

Croce, Giovanni, eminent Venetian composer; b. Chioggia (hence surnamed "il Chiozzotto"), c.1560; d. Venice, May 15, 1609. He was a pupil of Zarlino; chorister at San Marco, where he succeeded Donato as maestro di cappella in 1603.

WORKS: Sonatas *a* 5 (1580); 2 volumes of motets *a* 8 (1589, 1590; volume II reprinted 1605 with organ bass; both volumes with organ bass in 1607); 2 volumes of madrigals *a* 5 (1585, 1588); *Triacca musicale* (caprices, or humorous songs in Venetian dialect, *a* 4–7; went through 4 editions—1596, 1601, 1607, 1609, and was his most popular and famous work; it includes the contest between the cuckoo and the nightingale, judged by the parrot); madrigals *a* 5–6 (1590–1607); *Cantiones sacrae a* 8, with basso continuo for organ (1622; a 2nd volume was published in 1623); *Canzonette a* 4 (1588; new editions, 1595, 1598); Masses *a* 8 (1596); Lamentations *a* 4 (1603,

1605) and *a* 6 (1610); *Magnificats a* 6 (1605), Vesper psalms *a* 8 (1589), etc. Younge printed some of Croce's madrigals in his *Musica Transalpina* (1588), and a selection of his church music was published with English words as *Musica sacra, Penetentials for 6 voyces*, in London in 1608. Modern reprints include 3 Masses published at Regensburg in 1888, 1891 and 1899, and other works in Proske's *Musica Divina*, Haberl's *Repertorium*, Torchi's *L'Arte musicale in Italia*, Bäuerle's *12 Hymnen und Motetten alter Meister*, and the publications of the Motet Society (London).

BIBLIOGRAPHY: F. X. Haberl, "Giovanni Croce," in *Kirchenmusikalisches Jahrbuch* (1888); L. Torri, in *Rivista Musicale Italiana* (1900); Denis Arnold, "Giovanni Croce and the Concertato Style," *Musical Quarterly* (Jan. 1953).

Croes, Henri-Jacques de, Belgian composer; b. Antwerp, Sept. 19, 1705; d. Brussels, Aug. 16, 1786. Violinist and assistant conductor at St.-Jacques, Antwerp; in 1729, musical director to the Prince of Thurn and Taxis, at Regensburg. He went to Brussels in 1749, conducted the choir of the Royal Chapel until 1755, and was then appointed maître de chapelle to Charles of Lorraine.

WORKS: Masses, motets, anthems and other church music; also symphonies, sonatas, etc.

BIBLIOGRAPHY: S. Clercx, *Henri-Jacques de Croes, Compositeur et Maître de Musique* (Brussels, 1940).

Croft (or **Crofts**), **William,** English organist and composer; b. Nether Ettington, Warwickshire (baptized) Dec. 30, 1678; d. Bath, Aug. 14, 1727 (buried in Westminster Abbey). A chorister in the Chapel Royal, under Dr. Blow; Gentleman of Chapel Royal, 1700, and (with J. Clarke) joint organist in 1707. Succeeded Blow as organist of Westminster Abbey, Master of the Children, and Composer of the Chapel Royal (1708).

WORKS: *Musica sacra*, 30 anthems *a* 2–8, and a burial service in score (1724; in 2 volumes; the first English work of church music engraved in score on plates); *Musicus apparatus academicus* (2 odes written for his degree of Mus. Doc., Oxon., 1713); overtures and act tunes for several plays; violin sonatas; flute sonatas, etc.

BIBLIOGRAPHY: F. G. E., "Dr. William Crofts," *Musical Times* (Sept. 1900); A. R. Carpenter, "William Croft's Church Music," *Musical Times* (March 1971).

Crooks, Richard (Alexander), American tenor; b. Trenton, N.J., June 26, 1900; d. Portola Valley, Calif., Sept. 29, 1972. He studied voice for five years with Sydney H. Bourne and also took lessons with Frank La Forge; boy soprano soloist in N.Y. churches, later tenor soloist; after war service made debut with the N.Y. Symph. Orch. under Damrosch in 1922; gave concerts in London, Vienna, Munich, Berlin and in the U.S. (1925–27); made his American debut as Cavaradossi with the Philadelphia Grand Opera Co. (Nov. 27, 1930); debut as Des Grieux at the Metropolitan Opera (Feb. 25, 1933); toured Australia (1936–39); gave concerts from coast to coast in the U.S. and Canada, ap-

peared in recitals, as orchestral soloist, and in festivals.

Crosby, Bing (real name **Harry Lillis**), celebrated American vocalist and song stylist; b. Tacoma, Washington, May 3, 1903; d. while playing golf at La Moraleja golf course outside Madrid, Spain, Oct. 14, 1977. He was a drummer in school bands; intermittently attended classes in law at Gonzaga Univ., Spokane, Wash.; when he became famous, the school gave him an honorary degree of Doctor of Music. In 1926 he went to Los Angeles where he filled engagements as a singer. He made his mark on the radio, and his success grew apace; he used his limited vocal resources to advantage by a cunning projection of deep thoracic undertones. He never deviated from his style of singing, unpretentious, sometimes mock-sentimental and invariably communicative; he became a glorified crooner. Apart from his appearances in concert and with bands, he also made movies; his series with Bob Hope, beginning with *Road to Morocco*, made in 1942, with their invariable girl companion Dorothy Lamour, became classics of the American cinema. He continued his appearances until the last months of life. The origin of his nickname Bing is in dispute; it was either derived from the popular comic strip "The Bingville Bugle," or from his habit of popping a wooden gun in school, shouting "Bing! Bing!" In 1953 he published his autobiography under the title *Call Me Lucky*. His brother **Bob Crosby** is a bandleader; Bing Crosby's four sons of his first marriage are also crooners.

BIBLIOGRAPHY: Ted Crosby, *The Story of Bing Crosby* (N.Y., 1937; 2nd ed., 1946); Barry Ulanov, *The Incredible Crosby* (N.Y., 1947); Charles Thompson, *Bing* (N.Y., 1976).

Crosby, John, American opera impresario; b. New York, July 12, 1926. He studied violin and piano with his mother. Upon graduating from high school he was drafted into the U.S. Army in 1944, serving in the infantry as a corporal; he played various instruments in the dance band of his regiment; after the end of the war he played trombone and double bass in dance orchestras. He then entered Yale Univ. where he studied composition with Hindemith, receiving his B.A. in music in 1950. In 1951 he took courses in conducting at Columbia Univ. with Rudolph Thomas; later he attended conducting seminars in Maine under Pierre Monteux. In 1956 Crosby persuaded his father, an affluent lawyer, to give him enough money to build an outdoor opera house in Santa Fe, New Mexico. He inaugurated the Santa Fe Festival in the summer of 1957, producing a season of classical and modern operas. The theater burned down in 1967, but Crosby collected enough money to build a new fireproof building for his enterprise, which eventually became known as the Santa Fe Opera. Crosby was able to persuade Stravinsky to conduct a performance of his opera *The Rake's Progress*; Hindemith was engaged to conduct his own opera *Neues vom Tage*. Weather has been an uncertain factor through the Santa Fe seasons, and once or twice a cloudburst forced the postponement of a performance. In 1975 he took over the presidency of Opera America, a cartel coordinating 43 opera companies; in 1976 he became president of the Manhattan School of Music.

BIBLIOGRAPHY: Winthrop Sargeant, "A Miracle in the Desert" *New Yorker* (Aug. 1, 1975).

Cross, Lowell Merlin, American composer and electro-musicologist; b. Kingsville, Texas, June 24, 1938. He studied mathematics and music at Texas Technological College, graduating in 1963; then entered the Univ. of Toronto, Canada, obtaining his M.A. in musicology in 1968; attended classes of Marshall McLuhan in environmental technology there; took a course in electronic music with Myron Schaeffer and Gustav Ciamaga. In 1970 he served as resident programmer for Experiments in Art and Technology at Expo '70 in Osaka, Japan, and guest consultant in electronic music at the National Institute of Design in Ahmedabad, India; in 1971 was engaged as Artist-in-Residence at the Center for New Performing Arts, Univ. of Iowa. Eschewing any preliminary serial experimentation, Cross espoused a cybernetic totality of audio-visual, electronic and theatrical arts.

WORKS: *4 Random Studies* for tape (1961); *0.8 Century* for tape (1962); *Eclectic Music* for flute and piano (1964); *Antiphonies* for tape (1964); *After Long Silence* for soprano and quadraphonic tape (1964); *3 Etudes* for tape (1965); *Video I* and *Video II* for variable media, including tape, audio system, oscilloscope and television (1965–68); *Musica Instrumentalis* for acoustical stereophonic instruments, monochrome and polychrome television (1965–68); *Video III* for television and a phase-derived audio system (1968); *Reunion* for an electronic chess board constructed by Cross and first demonstrated in Toronto, March 5, 1968, the main opponents in the chess game being the painter Marcel Duchamp and John Cage (Duchamp won readily); *Electro-Acustica* for instruments, a laser deflection system, television and a phase-derived audio system (1970–71). The notation of his audio-visual compositions consists of color photographs of television images resulting from the programmed manipulation of sound-producing mechanisms in the acoustical space. (See his technical paper, *Audio/Video/Laser*, publ. in *Source*, Sacramento, Calif., No. 8, 1970.) He compiled a valuable manual, *A Bibliography of Electronic Music* (Toronto, 1967). As a pioneer in astromusicology, he created the selenogeodesic score *Lunar Laser Beam* (broadcast as a salutatory message on Nicolas Slonimsky's 77th birthday, April 27, 1971, purportedly via Leningrad, the subject's birthplace, the Sea of Tranquillity on the moon and the Ciudad de Nuestra Señora Reina de Los Angeles in California). As director of the Video/Laser Laboratory at the Univ. of Iowa, Cross was responsible for the production of Scriabin's *Prometheus* by the Iowa Univ. orch., conducted by James Dixon, with color projections coordinated with the "color organ" *(luce)* as prescribed in the score (Iowa City, Sept. 24, 1975).

Cross, Ronald, American musicologist; b. Fort Worth, Texas, Feb. 18, 1929. He studied at Guilmant Organ School in N.Y., at Centenary College of Louisiana and at N.Y. Univ. (Ph.D., 1961). In 1955 he received a Fulbright Fellowship to travel in Italy. In 1959 he was appointed to the faculty of Notre Dame

College of Staten Island. He wrote a number of choral pieces; also chamber music; edited the collected works of Matthaeus Pipelare; contributed articles to musicological journals.

Crosse, Gordon, English composer; b. Bury, Lancashire, Dec. 1, 1937. He studied at Oxford Univ. where he took courses in music history with Egon Wellesz; did postgraduate work in medieval music. In 1962 he went to Rome where he attended the classes of Goffredo Petrassi at the Santa Cecilia Academy. Returning to England, he taught at Birmingham Univ. (extramurally); in 1969 was appointed to the music department of Essex Univ. His absorption in the studies of old music, in combination with an engrossment in modern techniques determine the character of his own compositions.

WORKS: *Concerto da camera* for violin and orch. (Violin Concerto No. 1, 1962; London, Feb. 18, 1968); *Carol* for flute and piano (1962); *Meet My Folks*, a multi-child presentation for voices, instruments and adults (1964); Symphonies for Chamber Orch. (Birmingham, Feb. 13, 1965); *Purgatory*, opera after Yeats (Cheltenham, July 7, 1966); *Ceremony* for cello and orch. (London, Aug. 4, 1966); *The Grace of Todd*, 1-act opera (Aldeburgh, June 7, 1967); *The Demon of Adachigahara* for speaker, adolescent chorus, mime and instruments (1968); Concerto for Chamber Orch. (Budapest, July 3, 1968); Violin Concerto No. 2 (Oxford, Jan. 29, 1970); *The History of the Flood* for children's voices and harp (London, Dec. 6, 1970); *Wheel of the World*, "entertainment" based on Chaucer's *Canterbury Tales* for actors, children's chorus, mixed chorus and orch. (Aldeburgh Festival, June 5, 1972); *Ariadne* for solo oboe and 12 players (Cheltenham Festival, July 11, 1972); *The Story of Vasco*, opera (London, March 13, 1974); *Celebration* for chorus (London, Sept. 16, 1974); *Holly from the Bongs*, opera (Manchester, Dec. 9, 1974); *Potter Thompson*, children's opera (London, Jan. 9, 1975); Symph. No. 2 (London, May 27, 1975); *Epiphany Variations: Double Variations for Orchestra* (N.Y., March 18, 1976); sacred and secular choruses.

Crossley, Ada (Jessica), Australian mezzo-soprano; b. Tarraville, Gippsland, March 3, 1874; d. London, Oct. 17, 1929. She was a pupil of Fanny Simonson (voice) in Melbourne; having sung in several churches, she made her concert debut with the Melbourne Philharmonic Society in 1892; came to London in 1894, studied with Santley, and later with Mme. Marchesi in Paris; made her London debut at Queen's Hall on May 18, 1895; her success was so emphatic that she sang by command five times before Queen Victoria within the next two years; appeared as soloist at all important English festivals; her tour of Australia in 1904 was a succession of triumphs; also made successful tours of the U.S. and South Africa.

Crotch, William, eminent English composer; b. Norwich, July 5, 1775; d. Taunton, Dec. 29, 1847. His extraordinary precocity may be measured by the well authenticated statement (Burney's paper, "Account of an Infant Musician," in the *Philosophical Transactions* of 1779), that when two and a half years old he played on a small organ built by his father, a master carpenter. In Oct. 1779, he was brought to London, and played in public. At the age of eleven he became assistant to Dr. Randall, organist of Trinity and King's Colleges at Cambridge; at fourteen, composed an oratorio, *The Captivity of Judah* (performed in 1789); he then studied for the ministry (1788–90); returned to music, he was organist of Christ Church, Oxford; graduated as Mus. Bac., Oxon., in 1794 (Mus. Doc., 1799); in 1797 succeeded Hayes as professor of music in the University, and organist of St. John's College. He lectured in the Music School (1800–04), and in the Royal Institution, London (1804, 1805, 1807; and again from 1820); was appointed Principal for the new Royal Academy of Music in 1822.

WORKS: 2 oratorios, *Palestine* (1812), and *The Captivity of Judah* (1834; a different work from his juvenile oratorio of the same name); 10 anthems; 3 organ concertos; piano sonatas; an ode, *Mona on Snowdown calls*; a glee, *Nymph, with thee*; a motet, *Methinks I hear the full celestial choir* (these last 3 were very popular); other odes; other glees, fugues; also wrote *Elements of Music Composition* (1812; 1833; 1856); *Practical Thorough-bass*; etc. A complete list of his compositions appeared in *Musical News* (April 17 and 24, 1897). The Crotch Society of London, England promotes research and performances.

Crouch, Frederick Nicholls, English conductor and composer; b. London, July 31, 1808; d. Portland, Maine, Aug. 18, 1896. He studied with Bochsa (cello), and entered Royal Academy of Music in 1822 (teachers: Crotch, Attwood, Howes, Lindley and Crivelli). At the age of nine he was cellist in the Royal Coburg Theater; played in Queen Adelaide's private band till 1832; was a teacher and singer in Plymouth, and cellist in various theaters. He went to New York in 1849; was in Philadelphia in 1856 as conductor of Mrs. Rush's Saturday Concerts; served in the Confederate Army, and settled in Baltimore, as a singing teacher.

WORKS: 2 operas; many collections of songs, some being original (among these latter the well-known *Kathleen Mavourneen*). Cora Pearl, the famous Parisian courtesan of the second Empire, was his daughter.

Crowest, Frederick J., English writer on music; b. London, Nov. 30, 1850; d. Edgbaston, June 14, 1927. He joined the editorial staff of Cassell, Petter & Galpin in 1886; held various editorial positions; in 1901 was appointed general manager and editor of Walter Scott Publishing Co., Ltd.; retired in 1917.

WRITINGS: *The Great Tone Poets* (1874); *Book of Musical Anecdote* (1878; 2 volumes; revised edition, 1902, as *Musicians' Wit, Humour and Anecdote*); *Phases of Musical England* (1881); *Musical History and Biography in the Form of Question and Answer* (1883); *Advice to Singers* (many editions); *Musical Groundwork*; "Cherubini" (in Great Musicians Series); *Dictionary of British Musicians* (1895); *The Story of British Music* (vol. I, 1895); *Catechism of Musical History* (many editions); *Story of Music* (1902; in America as *Story of the Art of Music*); *Verdi: Man and Musician* (1897); *Beethoven* (1899).

Crüger, Johann, noted German composer of church music; b. Grossbreese, near Guben, April 9, 1598; d. Berlin, Feb. 23, 1662. A student of divinity at Wittenberg in 1620, he had received thorough musical training at Regensburg under Paulus Homberger. He then traveled in Austria and Hungary; spent some time in Bohemia and Saxony before settling in Berlin. His fame rests on the composition of many fine chorales (*Jesu, meine Freude; Jesu, meine Zuversicht; Nun danket alle Gott*, etc.), which were originally published in the collection *Praxis pietatis melica* (Berlin, 1644; reprinted in 45 editions before 1736). In addition he published the following collections: *Neues vollkömmliches Gesangbuch Augspurgischer Konfession . . .* (1640); *Geistliche Kirchenmelodeyen . . .* (1649); *Dr. M. Luthers wie auch andrer gottseliger christlicher Leute Geistliche Lieder und Psalmen* (1657); *Psalmodia sacra . . .* (1658); the valuable theoretical works *Synopsis musica* (1630; enlarged 1634); *Praecepta musicae figuralis* (1625); and *Quaestiones musicae practicae* (1650).

BIBLIOGRAPHY: E. Fischer-Krückeberg's articles: "Johann Crüger als Musiktheoretiker," *Zeitschrift für Musikwissenschaft*, XII; "Johann Crügers Choralbearbeitungen," ibid., XIV; "Johann Crüger und das Kirchenlied des 17. Jahrhundert," *Monatsschrift für Gottesdienst und kirchliche Kunst*, XXXIV, 2; Otto Brodde, *Johann Crüger, sein Weg und sein Werk* (Leipzig, 1936); E. C. G. Langbecker, *J. Crügers Choral-Melodien* (Berlin, 1835).

Crumb, George, innovative American composer; b. Charleston, West Virginia, Oct. 24, 1929. He studied at the Mason College of Music in Charleston, at the Univ. of Illinois in Urbana, (M.M., 1953), at the Univ. of Michigan, where he was a student in composition of Ross Lee Finney (D.M.A., 1959); also took a course with Boris Blacher at the Hochschule für Musik in Berlin (1955–56). He received grants from the Rockefeller (1965), Guggenheim (1967), and Coolidge Foundations (1970); received the National Institute of Arts and Letters Award in 1967, and the Pulitzer Prize in 1968. He was a member of the faculty at the Univ. of Colorado (1959–65); in 1965 was appointed to the staff of the School of Music of the Univ. of Pennsylvania. He was visiting composer at Tanglewood in the summer of 1970. In his music he preserves the external formalities of traditional music, suggesting Baroque procedures, but he makes revolutionary changes in his technical resources, demanding from the performers an exceptional precision and subtlety of interpretation, exploiting the extreme instrumental registers and making use of outlandish effects in the vocal part, including tongue clicks, explosive shrieks, hissing and whispering, as well as singing fractional intervals. In his *Makrokosmos I* for piano he instructs the pianist to shout at specified bars of the music. His musical notation often emulated the symbolic designs affected by some composers of the Middle Ages and the Renaissance; particularly intriguing is his use of circular or spiral staves for recurring motives, as exemplified in *Makrokosmos* and *Star-Child*.

WORKS: String Quartet (1954); Sonata for Solo Cello (1955); *Variazioni* for orch. (1959); *Night Music I* for soprano, piano and percussion (1963); *Four Noc-*

turnes (Night Music II) for violin and piano (1964); *Madrigals*, Book I for soprano, vibraphone and double bass (1965); *Madrigals*, Book II for soprano, alto flute and percussion (1965); *Eleven Echoes of Autumn 1965* for violin, alto flute, clarinet and piano (1966); *Echoes of Time and The River: Four Processionals for Orchestra* (Chicago, May 26, 1967; received the Pulitzer Prize for 1968); *Songs, Drones and Refrains of Death* for baritone, electric guitar, electric double bass, electric piano and percussion, to poems by Federico García Lorca (1968); *Madrigals*, Book III for soprano, harp and percussion (1969); *Madrigals*, Book IV for soprano, flute, harp, double bass and percussion (1969); *Night of the Four Moons* for alto flute, banjo, electric cello and percussion (1969); *Black Angels: 13 Images from the Dark Land* for electric string quartet (1970); *Ancient Voices of Children* for soprano, boy soprano and 7 instrumentalists, to words by Federico García Lorca (Coolidge Festival of Chamber Music, Washington, Oct. 31, 1970; highly acclaimed); *Lux Aeterna for 5 Masked Musicians* for soprano, bass flute, sitar, and 2 percussion players (1971); *Vox Balaenae (Voice of the Whale)* for flute, cello and piano (1973); *Makrokosmos I* for piano (1972); *Makrokosmos II* (1973); *Makrokosmos III*, subtitled *Music for a Summer Evening* for 2 amplified pianos and percussion (1974); *Star-Child* for orch., soprano solo, children's chorus, a large percussion ensemble, and a carillon of bell ringers, multi-antiphonally scored and demanding the coordinating service of 4 conductors (first performed by the N.Y. Philharmonic, under the general direction of Pierre Boulez, May 5, 1977).

Cruz, Ivo, Portuguese conductor and composer; b. Corumbá, Brazil, May 19, 1901. He was taken to Portugal as a child; studied law at Lisbon Univ. (1919–24); then went to Munich, where he studied composition and conducting with Richard Mors and August Reuss (1925–30); took courses in musicology at Munich Univ.; returned to Portugal in 1931; organized a choral society in Lisbon; founded the Lisbon Philharmonic Orch. in 1937 and was its conductor until 1971; from 1938 to 1971 served as director of the National Cons. of Music in Lisbon. His music cultivates Portuguese themes.

WORKS: a ballet, *Pastoral (Poemas de Amor e Saudade)*, with optional female chorus (1942); orchestral suite, *Nocturnos da Lusitania* (1928); 2 "Portuguese" piano concertos, subtitled "Symbolic Poems": No. 1, *Coimbra* (1945); No. 2, *Lisboa* (1946); *Sinfonia de Amadis* (1952); *Idilio de Miraflores* for orch. (1952); *Sinfonia de Quelez* (1964); the song cycles with orch.: *Triptico* (1941) and *Os Amores do Poeta* (1942); Violin Sonata (1922). For piano: *Aguarelas* (1921), *Homenagens* (Homages, 1955); *Caleidoscopio* (1957). Songs: *Cancões perdidas* (1923), *Baladas lunaticas* (1944), *Cancões profanas* (1968) and *Cancões sentimentais* (1972).

Csiky, Boldizsár, Rumanian composer; b. Tîrgu-Mureş, Oct. 3, 1937. He studied with Demian, Toduţa and Jodál at the Cons. in Cluj (1956–61). In his music he applies dissonant sonorism, striving for coloristic effects.

WORKS: a chamber opera *Görög Ilona* (1966); *Octombrie*, cantata (1960); *Purtătorii de Făclii*, cantata (1961); *Overture* (1960); *Sinfonia* (1960); *Cîntec de Vitejie* for chamber orch. (1971); *Recitativo, Adagio and Fugue* for flute and piano (1958); 2 piano sonatas (1960, 1964); choruses; songs.

Ctesibius, inventor of the hydraulis. He flourished between 246 and 221 B.C., and is known in literature as Ctesibius of Alexandria. The weight of evidence collected by H. G. Farmer tends to demonstrate that the first hydraulis was indeed constructed by Ctesibius.

BIBLIOGRAPHY: P. Tannery, "Athénée sur Ctesibius et l'hydraulis," *Revue des Études Grécques* (1896); H. G. Farmer, *The Organ of the Ancients* (London, 1931).

Cubiles, José, Spanish pianist and conductor; b. Cadiz, May 15, 1894; d. Madrid, April, 1971. He studied in Paris with Diémer; gave concerts in Europe; returning to Spain, he devoted himself mainly to teaching.

Cuclin, Dimitri, prolific Rumanian composer; b. Galatz, April 5, 1885. He studied with Castaldi and others at the Bucharest Cons.; in 1907 went to Paris where he took courses with Widor and later with Vincent d'Indy at the Schola Cantorum. Returning to Rumania he taught violin at the Bucharest Cons. (1918–22). From 1924 to 1930 he was in America as violin teacher at the Brooklyn College of Music; from 1930 to 1948 he taught composition at the Bucharest Cons., remaining in Rumania and devoting himself mainly to composition, continuing unabashedly to write music until he was 90 years old.

WORKS: 20 symphonies: No. 1 (1910); No. 2 (1938); No. 3 (1942); No. 4 (1944); No. 5, with soloists and chorus (1947); No. 6 (1948); No. 7 (1948); No. 8 (1948); No. 9 (1949); No. 10, with chorus (1949); No. 11 (1950); No. 12, with soloists and chorus (1951); No. 13 (1951); No. 14 (1952); No. 15 (1954); No. 16, subtitled *Triumph of Peace* (1959); No. 17 (1965); No. 18 (1967); No. 19 (1971); No. 20 (1972); 5 operas: *Soria* (1911), *Traian Şi Dochia* (1921), *Agamemnon* (1922), *Bellérophon* (1924) and *Meleagridele;* Violin Concerto (1920); Piano Concerto (1939); *Rumanian Dances* for orch. (1961); Clarinet Concerto (1968); 3 string quartets (1914, 1948, 1949) and numerous other chamber works; piano pieces; sacred choruses and songs.

Cudworth, Charles, British librarian and musicologist; b. Cambridge, Oct. 30, 1908; d. there, Dec. 26, 1977. He served at the Music Division of the Library of Cambridge Univ. from 1943 on; in 1957 was appointed Curator of the Pendlebury Library of Music there; in 1965 was elected Fellow of the Univ. College at Cambridge; in 1968 was visiting prof. of the Univ. of Southern California, Los Angeles. His specialty was the music of the 18th century. He published a *Thematic Index of 18th-Century English Overtures and Symphonies* (London, 1953) and contributed numerous valuable articles to British and American music journals.

Cuénod, Hugues-Adhémar, Swiss tenor; b. Corseaux-sur-Vevey, June 26, 1902. He studied voice in Lausanne, Basel, Geneva and Vienna. After a long sojourn in Paris, he toured the U.S. (1937–39); during the war he taught at the Geneva Cons. (1940–46); then resumed his career as an opera singer; he appeared at La Scala, Milan, in 1951, and at Covent Garden in London in 1954. He attracted attention as performer of the leading part in the world première of Stravinsky's opera *The Rake's Progress* in Venice and also in Stravinsky's subsequent vocal works, *Threni* (1958) and *A Sermon, a Narrative and a Prayer* (1962). Then he turned almost exclusively to Baroque music; founded an "Ensemble baroque" in Lausanne; eventually settled in Vevey.

Cugat, Xavier, Spanish-American band leader; b. Barcelona, Jan. 1, 1900. As a youth he came to the U.S.; studied violin with Franz Kneisel; played at concerts with Caruso; became a cartoonist for the *Los Angeles Times.* In 1928 he organized a dance orch.; led a combo with his niece, the actress Margo, as a dancer. In 1933 he was engaged as band leader of the Hotel Astoria in N.Y.; played numerous engagements at hotels and night clubs, achieving popularity by his astute arrangements of Latin American dances; invented a congat (a crossbreed of bongos and a conga). He was married to the singers Carmen Castillo (1929–45), Lorraine Allen (1946–50) and Abbe Lane (1952–63). He publ. an autobiography, *The Rumba is My Life* (N.Y., 1949).

Cugley, Ian, Australian composer; b. Melbourne, June 22, 1945. He studied with Peter Sculthorpe and Peter Maxwell Davies at the Univ. of Sydney (1963–66); in 1967 was appointed to the faculty of the Univ. of Tasmania; also was percussionist in the Tasmanian Symphony Orch.; organized a contemporary music ensemble, Spectrum. His music represents a curious polarization of techniques, in which starkly primitive melorhythms enter a tangential relationship with total serialism.

WORKS: Variations for Flute, Oboe and Horn (1963); *Adagio* for 4 horns or string quartet (1964); *Pan, the Lake* for flute, horn, cello, strings and percussion, including 8 Indonesian Kulintang gongs (1965); Prelude for Orch. (1965); Sonata for Flute, Viola and Guitar or Harp (1966); *Canticle of All Created Things* for chorus, harp and percussion (1966); *Canticle II* (*In Cenerem Reverteris*) for soli, chorus and orch. (1967); *5 Variants* for string orch. (1968); *3 Pieces* for chamber orch. (1968); *The Six Days of Creation*, cantata (1969); *Chamber Symphony* for 11 wind instruments (1971); *Aquarelles* for piano (1972); *Sonata Movement* for violin and piano (1972); Violin Concerto (1973); numerous works for school orchestras; 3 electronic studies (1967–72); sacred music.

Cui, César, Russian composer, one of the group of the "Five"; b. Vilna, Jan. 18, 1835; d. Petrograd, March 26, 1918. He was the son of a soldier in Napoleon's army who remained in Russia, married a Lithuanian noblewoman and settled as a teacher of French in Vilna. Cui learned musical notation by copying Chopin's mazurkas and various Italian operas; then tried his hand at composition on his own. In 1849 he took lessons with Moniuszko who was in Vilna at the time. In 1850

he went to St. Petersburg, where he entered the Engineering Academy in 1851. After graduation in 1857 he became a topographer and later an expert in fortification. He participated in the Russo-Turkish war of 1877; in 1880 he became prof. at the Engineering Academy and was tutor in military fortification to the Czar Nicholas II. In 1856 Cui met Balakirev, who helped him master the technique of composition. In 1858 he married Malvina Bamberg; for her he wrote a scherzo on the theme *BABEG* (for the letters in her name) and *CC* (his own initials). In 1864 he began writing music criticism in the St. Petersburg *Vyedomosti* and later in other newspapers, continuing as music critic until 1900. Cui's musical tastes were conditioned by his early admiration for Schumann; he opposed Wagner, against whom he wrote vitriolic articles; he attacked Strauss and Reger with even greater violence. He was an ardent propagandist of Glinka and the Russian National School, but was somewhat critical towards Tchaikovsky. He published the first comprehensive book on Russian music, *Musique en Russie* (Paris, 1880). Cui was grouped with Rimsky-Korsakov, Mussorgsky, Borodin and Balakirev as one of the 'Mighty Five'; the adjective in his case, however, is not very appropriate, for his music lacks grandeur; he was at his best in delicate miniatures, e.g., *Orientale*, from the suite *Kaleidoscope*, op. 50.

WORKS: 6 operas produced in St. Petersburg: *The Mandarin's Son* (1859; Dec. 19, 1878); *The Prisoner of the Caucasus* (1859; rewritten 1881; prod. Feb. 16, 1883); *William Ratcliff* (Feb. 26, 1869); *Angelo* (Feb. 13, 1876); *The Saracen* (Nov. 14, 1899); *The Captain's Daughter* (1911). Other operas: *Le Flibustier* (Opéra-Comique, Paris, Jan. 22, 1894); *Mam'zelle Fifi* (Moscow, Nov. 16, 1903); *Matteo Falcone* (Moscow, 1908). *A Feast in Time of Plague*, written originally as a dramatic cantata, was produced as a 1-act opera (Moscow, Nov. 23, 1901). Children's operas: *The Snow Giant; Little Red Ridinghood; Puss in Boots; Little Ivan the Fool.* Orchestral works: *Tarantella* (1859); *Marche solennelle* (1881); *Suite miniature; Suite concertante* for violin and orch., (1883); *2 Morceaux* for cello and orch.; Suite No. 2 (1887); Suite No. 4, *À Argenteau* (1887); Suite No. 3, *In Modo populari;* 3 Scherzos (op. 82). Chamber music: 3 string quartets 1893; 1913); *5 Little Duets* for flute and violin; violin pieces: *2 Miniatures;* Violin Sonata; *Petite Suite; 12 Miniatures* (op. 20); *Kaleidoscope*, 24 numbers; *6 Bagatelles* (op. 51); many songs; piano pieces; choruses. Cui contributed a number to a set of Variations on 'Chopsticks' (with Borodin, Liadov and Rimsky-Korsakov). In 1914–16 Cui completed Mussorgsky's opera *The Fair at Sorotchinsk.* A volume of his *Selected Articles* (1864–1917) was published in Leningrad in 1953.

BIBLIOGRAPHY: Louise Mercy-Argenteau, *César Cui, Esquisse critique* (Paris, 1888); N. Findeisen, "C. A. Cui", *Russian Musical Gazette*, 1894; A. Koptyayev, "César Cui as Composer for the Pianoforte," *Russian Musical Gazette*, 1895; P. Weimarn, *César Cui as Song-writer* (St. Petersburg, 1896); *Musical Festival in Honor of C. A. Cui*, a symposium (St. Petersburg, 1910); G. Abraham, *Studies in Russian Music* (N.Y. and London, 1935); M. D. Calvocoressi and G. Abraham, *Masters of Russian Music* (N.Y., 1936);

M. Smirnov, *The Piano Works of Composers Comprising "The Five"* (Moscow, 1971); E. Guglielmi, "César Cui e l'Ottocento musicale russo," *Chigiane* XXV/5 (1968). See also the biographical note in the Appendix to Cui's *Musique en Russie* (1880).

Culbertson, Alexander (Sascha), violinist; b. Bessarabia, Aug. 10, 1894; d. N.Y., April 16, 1944. He received his first instruction on the violin from Zuckovsky, and at the age of nine entered the Rostov Cons.; pupil of Sevčik in Prague (1905-08); made his debut at Vienna (1908); toured Europe with extraordinary success (1908-14); joined the American Army (1918); debut in the U.S. (1919); gave concerts throughout the U.S. (1919-27); returned to Europe, residing in Paris as performer and teacher (1927-37); finally settled in N.Y. as a teacher.

Culp, Julia, Dutch contralto; b. Groningen, Oct. 6, 1880; d. Amsterdam, Oct. 13, 1970. She first studied violin as a child; then became voice pupil of Cornelia van Zanten at the Amsterdam Cons. (1897), and later of Etelka Gerster in Berlin; made formal debut in Magdeburg in 1901; her tours of Germany, Austria, the Netherlands, France, Spain and Russia were highly successful from an artistic standpoint, establishing her as one of the finest singers of German lieder. Her American debut took place at N.Y., Jan. 10, 1913; for many years, she visited the United States every season. In private life Mme. Culp was the wife of Erich Merten; in 1919 she married an Austrian industrialist, Willy Ginzkey; lived in Czechoslovakia; after his death (1934) she returned to Amsterdam.

Culwick, James C., English organist and composer; b. W. Bromwich, Staffordshire, April 28, 1845; d. Dublin, Oct. 5, 1907. He was a pupil of T. Bedsmore; assistant organist at Lichfield Cathedral and organist at various churches until 1881, when he was appointed to the Chapel Royal at Dublin, where he remained till his death; also professor of piano and theory at Alexandra College, and conductor of the Harmonic Society and Orpheus; Mus. Doc. *(honoris causa)* from Dublin Univ., 1893. He wrote a dramatic cantata, *The Legend of Stauffenberg* (1890); piano pieces (suite, ballade, sonatina, etc.); several anthems and church services.
WRITINGS: *Rudiments of Music* (1880; 2nd edition 1882); *The Study of Music and Its Place in General Education* (1882); *The Works of Sir R. Stewart* (1902).

Cumberland, Gerald (real name **C. F. Kenyon**), English critic and writer; b. Eccles, May 7, 1881; d. Southsea, June 14, 1926. He was music critic of the *Manchester Courier* (1909-12), of the *Daily Citizen* (1921-25), and of various American papers; publ. books and pamphlets: *How to Memorize Music*; *Set Down in Malice* (1918); *Written in Friendship* (1923); *Imaginary Conversations With Great Composers* (1924).

Cumberworth, Starling, American composer; b. Remson Corners, Ohio, July 25, 1915. He studied at the Cleveland Institute of Music with Herbert Elwell and Arthur Shepherd; than at Yale Univ. with Quincy Porter and Paul Hindemith (M.M., 1948) and at the Eastman School of Music, Rochester, with Bernard Rogers and Howard Hanson (Ph.D., 1956). In 1956 he joined the staff of the Cleveland Music School Settlement. Among his works are an opera *Home Burial* (1955); 2 string quartets; Suite for Oboe and Piano; Suite for Flute and Piano; Violin Sonata; Trio for Violin, Clarinet and Piano.

Cummings, William Hayman, English singer and music antiquarian; b. Sidbury, Devonshire, Aug. 22, 1831; d. London, June 6, 1915. He was a chorister in London at St. Paul's and at the Temple Church; organist of Waltham Abbey (1847); tenor singer in the Temple, Westminster Abbey and Chapel Royal; professor of singing at the Royal Academy of Music (1879-96); in 1882, appointed conductor of the Sacred Harmonic Society; precentor of St. Anne's, Soho (1886-98); principal of Guildhall School of Music (1896-1900); received an honorary degree of Mus. Doc. from the Univ. of Dublin (1900). He was a cultivated singer and a learned antiquarian; was instrumental in founding the Purcell Society, and edited its first publications; was the author of a biography of Purcell (in the Great Musicians Series; London, 1882); also published a *Primer of the Rudiments of Music* (1877), and a *Biographical Dictionary of Musicians* (1892); contributed to *Grove's Dictionary*. His library of 4,500 volumes contained many rare autographs. He composed a cantata, *The Fairy Ring* (1873), sacred music, glees, part songs, etc.

Cundell, Edric, English composer; b. London, Jan. 29, 1893; d. there, March 19, 1961. He was first a horn player; then a pianist; taught at Trinity College (1914); was conductor of the Westminster Orchestral Society (1920) and of the Stock Exchange Orch. (London, 1924). In 1935, he founded the Edric Cundell Chamber Orch.; in 1938, succeeded Sir Landon Ronald as director of the Guildhall School of Music; in 1949 received the order of Commander of the British Empire.
WORKS: He wrote a symphony; the symph. poems, *Serbia* (1919) and *The Tragedy of Deirdre* (1922); *Sonnet, Our Dead* for tenor and orch. (1922); Piano Concerto; Piano Quartet, String Sextet, String Quartet, Rhapsody for Viola and Piano; miscellaneous piano pieces (*Valse Fantastique*; *The Water Babies*, etc.); songs.

Curci, Giuseppe, Italian composer; b. Barletta, June 15, 1808; d. there, Aug. 5, 1877. He studied in Naples with Zingarelli and Crescentini; became a singing teacher; composed several operas: *Il Proscritto* (Turin, 1837); *Don Desiderio* (Venice, 1837); etc.; traveled in Germany and Austria; taught voice in Paris (1848-56), where his opera, *Il Baccelliere* was produced; then returned to his native town. He published a manual, *Il bel canto.*

Curran, Pearl Gildersleeve, American composer; b. Denver, Colorado, June 25, 1875; d. New Rochelle, N.Y., April 16, 1941. She studied music privately; published about 40 songs, many of them to her own texts. The most successful include *Dawn*; *Life*; *Rain*; *Nursery Rhymes*; *Nocturne.*

Curry, Arthur Mansfield, American composer and pedagogue; b. Chelsea, Mass., Jan. 27, 1866; d. Atlanta, Georgia, Dec. 30, 1953. He studied with Franz Kneisel (violin) and Edward MacDowell (composition); taught at the New England Cons. (1915–39).

WORKS: orchestral overture *Blomidon* (Worcester, 1902); the symph. poem *Atala* (after Chateaubriand; Boston Symph., April 21, 1911, composer conducting); *The Winning of Amarac,* Celtic legend for narrator, women's chorus and orch. (Boston, 1934); choruses for men's, women's and mixed voices; piano pieces and many songs (*Before Night, The Fiddler of Dooney,* etc.).

Curschmann, Karl Friedrich, German composer; b. Berlin, June 21, 1804; d. Langfuhr, near Danzig, Aug. 24, 1841. Originally a law student, he devoted himself to music, studying with Hauptmann and Spohr at Kassel, where his one-act opera *Abdul and Erinnieh* was produced (Oct. 29, 1828). His songs possess a fine poetic quality; a collection of 83 lieder and 9 duets and trios was published posthumously in 2 volumes (Berlin, 1871). He was also a noted singer, and gave concerts in Germany and Italy.

BIBLIOGRAPHY: G. Meissner, *Karl Friedrich Curschmann* (Bautzen, 1899).

Curti, Franz (Francesco), German composer; b. Kassel, Nov. 16, 1854; d. Dresden, Feb. 6, 1898. He studied medicine; became a dentist by profession; at the same time took music courses in Dresden with Kretschmer and Schulz-Beuthen. He wrote several operas: *Hertha* (Altenburg, 1887); *Reinhardt von Ufenau* (Altenburg, 1889); *Erlöst* (Mannheim, 1894); melodrama, *Schneefried* (Mannheim, 1895); 1-act Japanese fairy opera *Lili-Tsee* (Mannheim, 1896; New York, 1898); *Das Rösli vom Säntis* (Zürich, 1898); also a cantata *Die Gletscherjungfrau;* music to *Die letzten Menschen,* by W. E. Kirchbach; songs. A catalogue of his works appeared in 1898.

Curtin, Phyllis, American soprano; b. Clarksburg, West Virginia, Dec. 3, 1922. She studied with Olga Avierino in Boston; sang with the New England Opera Co.; was a member of the N.Y. City Opera; made successful appearances at the Teatro Colón in Buenos Aires (1959) and at the Vienna State Opera (1960–61). She made her debut with the Metropolitan Opera Co. on Nov. 4, 1961. Among her most successful roles is Salome; she also sang leading parts in first performances of several American operas.

Curtis, Natalie, American writer on folk music; b. New York, April 26, 1875; d. Paris, Oct. 23, 1921. She studied with Arthur Friedheim, with Busoni in Berlin, Alfred Giraudet in Paris, and Julius Kniese at the "Wagner-Schule" in Bayreuth; returning to the U.S., she became an ardent investigator of songs, legends and customs of the North American Indians. She was married to Paul Burlin of New York (July 25, 1917).

WRITINGS: *Songs of Ancient America* (1905); *The Indian's Book* (1907; containing over 200 songs of 18 different tribes); songs from *A Child's Garden of Verse: Negro Folk Songs* (4 volumes, 1918–19, collected in the South and recorded for the Hampton Institute, Virginia); *Songs and Tales from the Dark Continent* (1920).

Curtiss (née **Kirstein**), **Mina,** American writer; b. Boston, Oct. 13, 1896. She was educated at Smith College (M.A., 1918); was associate professor of English literature there (1920–34). Apart from her literary publications, she has contributed articles to the *Musical Quarterly;* wrote *Bizet and his World* (N.Y., 1958). In 1977 she published a memoir *Other People's Letters.*

Curwen, Rev. John, b. Heckmondwike, Yorkshire, Nov. 14, 1816; d. Manchester, May 26, 1880. In 1844 he was pastor at Plaistow, Essex. Becoming interested in Miss S. A. Glover's 'Tonic Sol-fa' system of teaching, he labored to improve it; established the Tonic Sol-Fa Association and the *Tonic Sol-Fa Reporter* in 1853, and the Tonic Sol-Fa College in 1875, having resigned his pastorate in 1867 to devote himself entirely to propagating the system. His numerous publications relate chiefly to Tonic Sol-Fa (issued by Novello).

BIBLIOGRAPHY: J. S. Curwen, *Memorials of John Curwen* (London, 1882). In 1863 Curwen founded the firm of John Curwen & Sons, publishers of works for school use, choral music, etc., also of the periodicals the *Musical News and Herald* (weekly) and the *Sackbut* (monthly; discontinued in 1934). In 1923 the business merged with F. & B. Goodwin.

Curwen, John Spencer, son of the **Rev. John Curwen;** b. Plaistow, Sept. 30, 1847; d. London, Aug. 6, 1916. Pupil of his father and G. Oakey; later of G. A. Macfarren, Sullivan and Prout at the Royal Academy of Music. Like his father, he became an active promoter of the Tonic Sol-Fa system; President of the Tonic Sol-Fa College in 1880; frequent contributor to the *Tonic Sol-Fa Reporter* and its continuation, the *Musical Herald.* Published *Studies in Worship Music* (1880), and a 2nd series in 1885; *Memorials of John Curwen* (1882); *Musical Notes in Paris* (1882); etc.

Curzon, Clifford, English pianist; b. London, May 18, 1907. Studied at the Royal Academy of Music, and later with Tobias Matthay in London, Artur Schnabel in Berlin, and Wanda Landowska in Paris. He made his American debut in New York on Feb. 26, 1939, and continued playing concerts in the U.S. In 1958 he was nominated Commander of the British Empire. He held the degree of D. Mus. *honoris causa* from Leeds Univ. in 1970.

Curzon, Emanuel-Henri-Parent de, French music critic and writer; b. Le Havre, July 6, 1861; d. Paris, Feb. 25, 1942. He was keeper of the government archives at Paris until 1926; music critic on the *Gazette de France* (1889–1918); contributor to the *Guide musical, Bulletin de la Société de l'histoire du théâtre,* etc.

WRITINGS: *Les Dernières Années de Piccini à Paris* (1890); *La Légende de Sigurd dans l'Edda; L'Opéra d'E. Reyer* (1890); *Musiciens du temps passé* (1893); *Croquis d'artistes* (1898); *Les Lieder de Schubert* (1899); "Biographie critique de Franz Schubert", *Revue des Études Historiques* (1899); *État sommaire des pièces et documents concernant la musique* (1899); *Guide de l'amateur d'ouvrages sur la musique* (1901); *Felipe Pedrell et 'Les Pyrénées'* (1902); *Les Lie-*

der de Beethoven (1905); *Essai de bibliographie mozartienne* (1906); *Grétry, biographie critique* (1907); *L'Évolution lyrique au théâtre* (1908); *Meyerbeer, biographie critique* (1910); *Documents inédits sur le 'Faust' de Gounod* (with A. Soubies; 1912); *La Vie artistique aux XVIIe et XVIIIe siècles; "*La Musique," *Bibliothèque française* (1914); *Mozart, biographie critique* (1914); "Rossini, biographie," (in *Les Maîtres de la Musique* (1920); *L'Œuvre de R. Wagner à Paris et ses interprètes* (1920); *A. Thomas* (1921); *G. Fauré* (1923); *E. Reyer* (1924); *Jean Elleviou* (1930); *Cosima Wagner et Bayreuth* (1930); *Berlioz, l'homme et le musicien* (1932); "Les Opéras-comiques de Boieldieu" (*Revue Musicale,* Nov. 1933); "Les Archives anciennes de l'Opéra-Comique, Paris," *Le Ménestrel* (1934). Translations: *Lettres complètes de Mozart* (1888, 1898); *Écrites de Schumann sur la musique et les musiciens* (1894, 1898); *Hoffmann: Fantaisies dans la manière de Callot* (1891); also several German, Italian, and Spanish opera libretti.

Cusins, Sir William George, English organist; b. London, Oct. 14, 1833; d. Remonchamps (Ardennes), Aug. 31, 1893. He was a choirboy of the Chapel Royal (1843); pupil of Fétis, in Brussels Cons. (1844), and of Bennett, Potter Lucas and Sainton, at the Royal Academy of Music (1847). Took the King's Scholarship in 1847 and 1849; in the latter year he was appointed organist of the Queen's private chapel, and became violinist in the Italian Opera orch. In 1851 he was a professor at Royal Academy of Music; succeeded Bennett (1867–83) as conductor of the Philharmonic, and also became conductor of the Royal Band in 1870; succeeded Bennett as examining professor at Queen's College (1875); professor at Trinity College and professor of piano at Guildhall School of Music (1885); knighted in 1892.

WORKS: *Royal Wedding Serenata* (1863); 2 concert overtures, *Les Travailleurs de la mer* (1869) and *Love's Labour's Lost* (1875); an oratorio, *Gideon* (Gloucester Festival, 1871); piano concerto; septet for wind and double bass; piano pieces; songs.

Custer, Arthur, American composer; b. Manchester, Conn., April 21, 1923. He studied composition with Paul Pisk at the Univ. of Redlands, Calif., and with Philip Bezanson at the Univ. of Iowa; after graduation, he took a course of studies in composition with Nadia Boulanger. Subsequently he held numerous teaching jobs; also served as music consultant to the U.S. Information Agency in Madrid (1960–62). In 1970 he was appointed Director of the Arts in the Education Project of the Rhode Island Council on the Arts.

WORKS: Sextet for Woodwinds and Piano (1959); *Colloquy* for string quartet (1961); *Sinfonia de Madrid* (Madrid, April 28, 1962); *Cycle* for a heterogeneous ensemble (1963); Concertino for Second Violin and Strings, in reality being his String Quartet No. 2 (1964); *Two Movements* for wind quintet (1964); *Permutations* for violin, clarinet and cello (1967); Concerto for Brass Quintet (1968); *Rhapsodality Brass!* for orch. (1969); *Interface I* for string quartet and two recording engineers, being (minus affectation) his String Quartet No. 3 (1969) and a thing entitled *Rhapsodality Brown!* for piano (1969); *Parabolas* for trombone and percussion (1969); *Parabolas* for viola and piano (1969). He also contributed a number of informative articles on American and Spanish music to various music journals.

Cutler, Henry Stephen, American organist and hymn writer; b. Boston, Oct. 13, 1824; d. there, Dec. 5, 1902. He studied in Germany; returning to the U.S. he held posts as church organist in Boston, New York and Philadelphia. His anthem, *The Son of God Goes Forth to War,* is well known.

Cuvillier, Charles, French composer of light opera; b. Paris, April 24, 1877; d. there, Feb. 14, 1955. He studied with Massenet at the Paris Cons.; then became interested in the theater; his first operetta, *Avant-hier matin,* was produced at the Théâtre des Capucines in Paris (1905); at the same theater, Cuvillier produced *Son Petit Frère* (1907); *Algar* (1909); *Les Muscadines* (1910) and *Sapho* (1912). His most successful operetta *La Reine s'amuse* was first staged in Marseilles (1912); was revised and produced in Paris as *La Reine joyeuse* (Nov. 8, 1918) and in London as *Naughty Princess* (1920). His other operettas were *La Fausse ingénue* (Paris, 1918); *Bob et moi* (1924); *Boufard et ses filles* (Paris, 1929), etc. Cuvillier was also active in musical administration as director of music at the Odéon in Paris. The waltz from *La Reine joyeuse* has retained its popularity in numerous arrangements.

Cuyler, Louise, American musicologist; b. Omaha, March 14, 1908. She studied at the Eastman School of Music at Rochester, N.Y., (B.M., 1929; Ph.D., 1947) and at the Univ. of Michigan (M.M., 1931), where she was a member of the staff from 1929 to 1975, with wartime leave (1942–45) for service with the American Red Cross in the Pacific. She contributed a number of informative papers to various scholarly publications, among them, "Mozart's Quartets Dedicated to Haydn" in the memorial volume for Curt Sachs (N.Y., 1965); "Music in Biographies of Emperor Maximilian" in the Festschrift for Gustave Reese (N.Y., 1966); also edited music: Isaac's *Choralis Constantinus,* Part III (Ann Arbor, Mich., 1950); *Five Polyphonic Masses of Heinrich Isaac* (Ann Arbor, Mich., 1956).

Cuzzoni, Francesca, celebrated Italian soprano; b. Parma, c.1700; d. Bologna, 1770. She studied with Lanzi; sang in Venice; was engaged at the Italian opera in London, making her debut as Teofane in Handel's opera, *Ottone* (Jan. 12, 1723). She made a profound impression on London opera lovers, and was particularly distinguished in lyric roles; but later her notorious rivalry with Faustina Bordoni nearly ruined her career. Following some appearances in Venice, she returned to London (1734); after several seasons she went to Holland, where she became impoverished and was imprisoned for debt. Eventually, she returned to Bologna, where she subsisted by making buttons.

Czernohorsky (Černohorsky), Bohuslav, Bohemian composer; b. Nimburg, Feb. 16, 1684; d. Graz, July 1, 1742. A Minorite monk, he was choirmaster at San Antonio, Padua, and organist at Assisi (Tartini was one of his pupils). Returning to Bohemia, he was Kapellmeister at the Teinkirche, Prague and (1735) at St. Jacob's (Gluck was among his pupils). Many MSS were lost at the burning of the Minorite monastery (1754). An offertory *a 4* and several organ fugues and preludes were published by O. Schmid in *Orgelwerke altböhmischer Meister*; 5 organ fugues have been edited by K. Pietsch; a *Regina Coeli* for soprano, organ and cello obbligato, and a motet, *Quem lapidaverunt*, are also extant; *Composizioni per organo* comprise vol. 3 of *Musica antiqua Bohemica* (Prague, 1968). The contrapuntal skill of Czernohorsky's fugal writing is remarkable; Kretzschmar described him as "the Bach of Bohemia"; Czech writers refer to him as "father of Bohemian music" despite the fact that Czernohorsky never made thematic use of native rhythms or melodies.

BIBLIOGRAPHY: O. Schmid, *Die böhmische Altmeisterschule Czernohorskys* (1900); A. Hnilička, *Porträte* (1922); Z. Culka, "Varhanní skladby Bohuslava Matěje Černohorského?" *Hudební Věda* V/4 (1968).

Czerny, Carl, celebrated Austrian pianist, composer and pedagogue; b. Vienna, Feb. 20, 1791; d. there, July 15, 1857. He was of Czech extraction (Czerny means black in Czech), and his first language was Czech. He received his early training from his father Wenzel Czerny, a stern disciplinarian who never let his son play with other children and insisted on concentrated work. Czerny had the privilege of having studied for three years with Beethoven, whose association with Czerny in subsequent years became a close one. Czerny also received advice as pianist from Hummel and Clementi. He made trips to Leipzig (1836); visited Paris and London (1837) and Italy (1846); with these exceptions he remained all his life in Vienna. His self-imposed daily schedule for work was a model of diligence; he denied himself any participation in the social life of Vienna and seldom attended opera or concerts. Very early in life he demonstrated great ability as a patient piano teacher. He was only 15 when Beethoven entrusted to him the musical education of his favorite nephew. When Czerny himself became a renowned pedagogue many future piano virtuosi flocked to him for lessons, among them Liszt (whom he taught without a fee), Thalberg, Theodore Kullak, Döhler, Jaëll and Ninette Belleville-Oury. Despite the heavy teaching schedule, Czerny found time to compose a fantastic amount of piano music, 861 opus numbers in all, each containing many individual items; these included not only piano studies and exercises for which he became celebrated, but also sonatas, concertos, string quartets, Masses and hymns. In addition, he made numerous piano arrangements of classical symphonies, including all of Beethoven's, and wrote fantasies for piano on the themes from famous operas of the time. So dedicated was he to his chosen work, that he renounced all thoughts of marriage (but a secret confession of his platonic adoration of an unnamed female person was found among his manuscripts); in this wistful deprivation, Czerny's fate paralleled Beethoven's. For a century there has been a fashion among musical sophisticates to deprecate Czerny as a pathetic purveyor of manufactured musical goods; his contemporary John Field, the originator of the genre of piano nocturnes, described Czerny as a "Tintenfass"—an inkpot. A quip was circulated that Czerny hated children, and that he published his voluminous books of piano exercises to inflict pain on young pianists. Of late, however, there has been a change of heart towards Czerny as a worthy composer in his own right. Stravinsky expressed his admiration for Czerny, and modern composers have written, with a half-concealed smile, pieces "à la manière de Czerny." Czerny was unexpectedly revealed to be a musician of imaginative fancy and engaging pedantic humor, as for instance, in his brobdingnagian arrangement of Rossini's Overture to *William Tell* for 16 pianists playing 4-hands on 8 pianos, pieces for three pianists playing 6-hand on a single keyboard, etc. Obsessed by an idea of compassing all musical knowledge at once, he published an *Umriss der ganzen Musikgeschichte* (Mainz, 1851), and also a volume in English entitled *Letters to a Young Lady on the Art of Playing the Pianoforte from the Earliest Rudiments to the Highest State of Cultivation* (the young lady in the title was never identified). Of his studies the most famous are *Schule der Geläufigkeit*, op. 299, and *Schule der Fingerfertigkeit*, op. 740; others are *Die Schule des Legato und Staccato*, op. 335; *40 Tägliche Studien*, op. 337, *Schule der Verzierungen*, op. 355, *Schule des Virtuosen*, op. 365, *Schule der linken Hand*, op. 399, etc. His Sonata, op. 7 was popular; among his piano transcriptions to be mentioned is *Fantaisie et Variations brilliantes* on an aria from Persiani's opera *Ines de Castro*. Czerny's autobiography, *Erinnerungen aus meinem Leben*, was edited by W. Kolneder (Baden-Baden, 1968; publ. in part in English in the *Musical Quarterly,* July 1956).

Czibulka, Alphons, Hungarian bandmaster and composer; b. Szepes-Várallya, Hungary, May 14, 1842; d. Vienna, Oct. 27, 1894. Originally a pianist, he became Kapellmeister at the Karltheater, Vienna, in 1865; bandmaster of the 17th regiment, and later of the 25th regiment at Prague; finally settled in Vienna, where he brought out the operetta *Pfingsten in Florenz* (Dec. 20, 1884); other stage works are *Der Glücksritter* (1887); *Gil Blas* (Hamburg, 1889); *Der Bajazzo* (Vienna, 1892); *Signor Annibale* (1893).

Cziffra, György, Hungarian pianist; b. Budapest, Sept. 5, 1921. His musical education was interrupted by World War II when he was in the Hungarian Army. He played in cafes and cabarets before engaging on a serious career as a concert pianist. After the abortive Hungarian revolt of 1956 he went to Paris; made numerous successful tours in Europe. He is most successful in the romantic repertory, which he interprets in a peculiarly free manner, often disregarding the tradition in favor of coloristic and rhythmic effects.

Czyz, Henryk, Polish conductor and composer; b. Grudziadz, June 16, 1923. He studied conducting and composition in Poznan; was conductor of the Cracow Philharmonic until 1971, when he was appointed conductor of the Düsseldorf Symphony. He wrote an opera *Bialowlosa* (1962), several orchestral works and film music.

D

Dachs, Joseph, pianist and pedagogue; b. Regensburg, Sept. 30, 1825; d. Vienna, June 6, 1896. He studied in Vienna with Czerny and Sechter; in 1861 was appointed professor of piano at the Vienna Cons.; he had numerous distinguished pupils, among them Vladimir de Pachmann, Laura Rappoldi, and Isabelle Vengerova. He also gave concerts which were well received in Vienna.

Daffner, Hugo, German composer and musicologist; b. Munich, June 2, 1882; perished in the concentration camp in Dachau, Oct. 9, 1936. He studied composition with Thuille and musicology with Sandberger and Kroyer at the Royal Academy in Munich; received his degree of Dr. phil. in 1904; subsequently took private lessons with Max Reger. He conducted at the Munich opera house from 1904–06; was active as music critic in Königsberg and Dresden. After World War I he decided to study medicine, and obtained the degree of Doctor of Medicine in 1920; in 1924 he went to live in Berlin as a practicing physician. He became a victim of the Nazi program of extermination of Jews.
WORKS: 3 operas: *Macbeth, Truffaldino, Der eingebildeste Kranke* (after Molière); 2 symphonies; 2 string quartets; 2 piano trios; 2 piano quintets, and various other pieces. He published several monographs, including his dissertation *Die Entwicklung des Klavierkonzerts bis Mozart* (Leipzig, 1908); edited writings by Nietzsche and C. P. E. Bach.

Dahl, Ingolf, distinguished composer; b. Hamburg, Germany (of Swedish parents), June 9, 1912; d. Frutigen, near Bern, Switzerland, Aug. 7, 1970. He studied composition at the Cons. of Cologne and musicology at the Univ. of Zürich. Came to the U.S. in 1935; settled in California (1938), where he became active as conductor and composer; appointed assistant professor at the Univ. of Southern California (1945); received Guggenheim Fellowship (1952). He taught at the Berkshire Music Center, Tanglewood, in the summers of 1952–55. As composer, he adhered to an advanced polyphonic style in free dissonant counterpoint.
WORKS: *Andante and Arioso* for flute, clarinet, oboe, horn and bassoon (1942); *Music for Brass Instruments* (1944); *Concerto a tre* for clarinet, violin, and cello (1946); Duo for Cello and Piano (1946); Divertimento for Viola and Piano (1948); Concerto for Saxophone and Wind Orch. (1949); *Symphony Concertante* for 2 clarinets and orch. (1953); *Sonata Seria* for piano (1953); *The Tower of Saint Barbara*, symphonic legend (Louisville, Jan. 29, 1955); Piano Quartet (1957); *Sonata Pastorale* for piano (1960); *Serenade* for 4 flutes (1960); *Sinfonietta* for concert band (1961); Piano Trio (1962); *Aria Sinfonica* (Los Angeles, April 15, 1965); *Elegy Concerto* for violin and small orch. (1963; completed by Donal Michalsky, 1971); *Duo Concertante* for flute and percussion (1966); *Sonata da camera* for clarinet and piano (1970); *Intervals* for string orch. (1970).

Dahl, Viking, Swedish composer; b. Osby, Oct. 8, 1895; d. Stockholm, Jan. 1, 1945. He studied at the Malmö and Stockholm Conservatories; later in Paris and London with Vidal, Viñes and Ravel; studied dancing with Isadora Duncan.
WORKS: The ballets *Oriental Suite* (Stockholm, 1919) and *Maison des fous* (Paris, 1920); *Pastorale* for oboe and orch.; chamber music; many songs.

Dahms, Walter, German music critic; b. Berlin, June 9, 1887; d. Lisbon, Oct. 5, 1973. He studied with Adolf Schultze in Berlin (1907–10), then engaged in music criticism; also composed some minor piano pieces and songs. About 1935 he went to Lisbon, Portugal, where he changed his name to **Gualtério Armando,** and continued to publish books on music in the German language, but for some unfathomable reason he persistently denied his identity. The reasons for his leaving Germany are obscure; he was not a Jew (in fact he wrote some anti-Semitic articles, directed against Schoenberg and others as early as 1910), and presumably had nothing to fear from the Nazi government, unless he regarded it as unduly liberal. A clue to his true identity was the synonymity of his first names in German (Walter) and in Portuguese (Gualtério).
WRITINGS: *Schubert* (Berlin, 1912); *Schumann* (1916); *Mendelssohn* (1919); *Die Offenbarung der Music; eine Apotheose Friedrich Nietzsches* (Munich, 1921); *Music des Südens* (1923), *Paganini* (Berlin, 1960); *Liszt* (Berlin, 1961); and *Wagner* (Berlin, 1962).

Dalayrac, Nicolas, French composer; b. Muret (Haute-Garonne), June 8 (baptized June 13), 1753; d. Paris, Nov. 26, 1809. (He signed his name d'Alayrac, but dropped the nobiliary particle after the Revolution.) His early schooling was in Toulouse; returning to Muret in 1767 he studied law and played violin in a local band. He then entered the service of Count d'Artois as his Guard of Honor, and at the same time took lessons in harmony with François Langlé at Versailles; he also received some help from Grétry. In 1781 he wrote 6 string quartets; his first theater work was a one-act comedy, *L'Eclipse totale* (Paris, March 7, 1782). From then on, he devoted most of his energies to the theater. He wrote 56 operas; during the revolution he composed patriotic songs for special occasions. He also enjoyed Napoleon's favors later on. During his lifetime, and for some three decades after his death, many of his operas were popular not only in France but also in Germany, Italy and Russia; then they gradually disappeared from the active repertoire, but there were several revivals even in the 20th century. Dalayrac's natural facility enabled him to write successfully in all operatic genres. The list of his operas produced in Paris (mostly at the Opéra-Comique) includes the following: *Nina* (May 15, 1786; one of his most successful operas); *Sargines* (May 14, 1788); *Les Deux Petits Savoyards* (Jan. 14, 1789); *Raoul, Sire de Créqui* (Oct. 31, 1789); *La Soirée orageuse* (May 29, 1790); *Camille* (March 19, 1791); *Philippe et Georgette* (Dec. 28, 1791); *Ambroise* (Jan. 12, 1793); *Adèle et Dorsan* (April 27, 1795); *Marianne* (July 7, 1796); *La Maison isolée* (May 11, 1797); *Gulnare* (Jan. 9, 1798); *Alexis* (Jan. 24, 1798); *Adolphe et Clara* (Feb. 10, 1799); *Maison à vendre* (Oct. 23, 1800; many revivals); *Léhéman* (Dec. 12, 1801); *L'Antichambre* (Feb. 26,

1802); *La Jeune Prude* (Jan. 14, 1804); *Une Heure de mariage* (March 20, 1804); *Gulistan* (Sept. 30, 1805); *Deux mots* (June 9, 1806); *Koulouf* (Dec. 18, 1806); *Le Poète et le musicien* (posthumous, Paris, May 30, 1811).
BIBLIOGRAPHY: R. C. G. de Pixérécourt, *Vie de Dalayrac* (includes a complete list of his operas; Paris, 1810); A. Fourgaud, *Les Violons de Dalayrac* (1856); G. Cucuel, *Les Créateurs de l'opéra-comique français* (Paris, 1914).

Dalberg, Johann Friedrich Hugo, German pianist, composer and writer on music; b. Herrnsheim, near Worms, May 17, 1760; d. there, July 26, 1812. He studied theology; became a canon in Trier; was also counsellor to the Elector of Trier at Coblenz. He traveled in Italy (1775) and England (1798); gave private concerts as pianist. Although he was not a professional musician, his compositions and particularly his writings reveal considerable musical culture. He published many vocal works; set to music Schiller's *Ode an die Freude* (1799); also wrote songs to English and French texts.
WRITINGS: *Blicke eines Tonkünstlers in die Musik der Geister* (Mannheim, 1787); *Vom Erfinden und Bilden* (Frankfurt, 1791); *Untersuchungen über den Ursprung der Harmonie* (Erfurt, 1800); *Die Äolsharfe, ein allegorischer Traum* (Erfurt, 1801); etc.; translated Jones's *The Musical Modes of the Hindus* (1802).

D'Albert, Eugène. See **Albert, Eugène d'**.

Dalcroze, Émile Jaques. See **Jaques-Dalcroze, Émile**.

Dale, Benjamin James, English composer; b. Crouch Hill, July 17, 1885; d. London, July 30, 1943. He studied at the Royal Academy of Music with F. Corder; was organist at St. Stephen's Ealing; then taught composition at the Royal Academy of Music.
WORKS: an overture, *The Tempest* (1902); Piano Sonata in D minor (1905; was frequently performed); suites for piano and viola (1907); *Before the Paling of the Stars*, for chorus and orch. (1912); *Songs of Praise*, for chorus and orch. (1923); *Rosa mystica* and *Cradle Song* for mixed chorus; 2 songs (after Shakespeare) for voice with viola obbligato; Sextet for Violas; Violin Sonata; piano pieces; songs; etc. His last work was *The Flowing Tide* for large orch., completed in 1943, from sketches made in 1924. For analysis of his chamber music, see Cobbett's *Cyclopedic Survey of Chamber Music* (London, 1929, I, 310-13).

D'Alembert, Jean le Rond. See **Alembert, Jean le Rond d'**.

D'Alheim, Marie. See **Olénine d'Alheim, Marie**.

D'Alheim, Pierre, French journalist; b. Laroche (Yonne), Dec. 8, 1862; d. Paris, April 11, 1922. In 1893 he married the singer **Marie Olénine** and organized her concerts in Moscow and in Paris. He became a propagandist of Russian music; published a book on Mussorgsky (Paris, 1896), and translated into French the libretti of *Boris Godunov* and *Khovanshchina* and Mussorgsky's songs.

Dall'Abaco, Evaristo Felice. See **Abaco, Evaristo Felice dall'**.

Dall'Abaco, Joseph. See **Abaco, Joseph Marie Clément dall'**.

Dallapiccola, Luigi, distinguished Italian composer; b. Pisino, Istria, Feb. 3, 1904; d. Florence, Feb. 19, 1975. He went to school in Trieste and later in Graz; in 1921 moved to Florence where he took courses at the Cherubini Cons., studying piano with Ernesto Consolo (graduated, 1924) and composition with Vito Frazzi (graduated, 1931). In 1934 he was appointed to the faculty of the Cherubini Cons. As a composer, Dallapiccola became interested from the very first in the melodic application of atonal writing; in 1939 he adopted the dodecaphonic method of Schoenberg, with considerable innovations of his own (e.g., the use of mutually exclusive triads in thematic structure and harmonic progressions). He particularly excelled in his handling of vocal lines in a difficult modern idiom. He visited London in 1946, and traveled on the continent; was engaged as instructor at the Berkshire Music Center in Tanglewood, Mass., in the summers of 1951 and 1952; taught several courses in American colleges: at Berkshire Music Center (1951), Queens College, N.Y. (1956, 1959), the Univ. of California, Berkeley (1962), Dartmouth College (summer, 1969).
WORKS: FOR THE STAGE: *Volo di notte*, opera after St.-Exupéry (Florence, May 18, 1940); *Il prigioniero*, opera (1944-48; radio première, Dec. 4, 1949; stage première, Florence, May 20, 1950); *Marsia*, ballet in one act (Venice, Sept. 9, 1948); *Odysseus*, opera (Berlin, Sept. 29, 1968, to a German libretto; in Italian, Milan, 1969). INSTRUMENTAL WORKS: Partita, for orch. (Florence, Jan. 22, 1933); *Piccolo concerto*, for piano and chamber orch. (1939-41); *Sonatina Canonica*, for piano (1943); *Ciaconna, Intermezzo e adagio*, for solo cello (1945); *Tartiniana*, for violin and orch., on Tartini's themes (Bern, March 4, 1952); Variations for Orch. (Louisville, Oct. 2, 1954); *Piccola Musica notturna* (1954; Hannover, June 7, 1954); *Tartiniana seconda* for violin and piano (1955-56); *Dialoghi* for cello and orch. (Venice, Sept. 17, 1960); *Three Questions with Two Answers* for orch. (1962; New Haven, Conn., Feb. 5, 1963); VOCAL WORKS: 2 Songs from the *Kalevala*, for two soloists, chamber chorus, and chamber orch. (1931); 3 Studies for Soprano and Chamber Orch. (Venice Festival, 1932); *Estate*, for male chorus a cappella (1932); *La Mort de Roland*, for voices and small orch. (1934); Rhapsody, for voice and chamber orch. (1934); *Cori di Michelangelo* in 3 sets (1933-36); *3 Laudi*, for soprano and chamber orch. (Venice Festival, 1937); transcription of Monteverdi's *Il Ritorno di Ulisse in Patria* (1942); *Liriche greche*, for soprano and instruments (3 sets; 1942-45); *3 poemi*, for voice and instruments (1949); *Job, sacra rappresentazione* (Rome, Oct. 31, 1950); *Goethe-Lieder*, for voice and three clarinets (1953); *Canti di Liberazione* for mixed chorus and orch. (Cologne, Oct. 28, 1955); *Concerto per la notte di Natale dell anno* for soprano and chamber orch. (Tokyo, Oct. 11, 1957); *Requiescant* for chorus, children's voices and orch. (1957-58; Hamburg, Nov. 17, 1959); *Preghiere* (*Prayers*) for baritone and chamber orch. (Berkeley, Calif., Nov. 10, 1962);

Parole di San Paolo for voice and instruments (Washington, Oct. 30, 1964); *Sicut umbra* for mezzo-soprano and 12 instruments (Washington, Oct. 30, 1970). *Commiato* for soprano and chamber ensemble (Murnau, Austria, Oct. 15, 1970). A complete catalogue of his works is publ. in the March 1976 issue of *Tempo*. An autobiographical fragment, "The Genesis of the *Canti di Prigionia* and *Il Prigioniero*," appears in the *Musical Quarterly* (July 1953). A collection of Dallapiccola's own essays is publ. under the title *Appunti, incontri, meditazioni* (Milan, 1970).

BIBLIOGRAPHY: G. M. Gatti, "Luigi Dallapiccola," *Monthly Musical Record* (Feb. 1937); Domenico de Paoli, "An Italian Musician: Luigi Dallapiccola," *Chesterian* (July 1938); "Nota bio-bibliografica," *Rassegna Musicale* (1950); Hans Nathan, "The Twelve-Tone Compositions of Luigi Dallapiccola," *Musical Quarterly* (April 1958); L. Pinzauti, "A colloquio con Luigi Dallapiccola," *Nuova Rivista Musicale Italiana* (Sept.-Oct. 1967); *Revue Musicale de Suisse Romande* (July-Aug. 1975), a special issue devoted to Dallapiccola.

Dal Monte, Toti, Italian coloratura soprano; b. Mogliano, near Treviso, June 27, 1893; d. Pieve di Soligo, Treviso, Jan. 26, 1975. Her original name was Antonietta Meneghelli. She studied piano and singing; made her operatic debut at La Scala, Milan, in 1916; made her first American appearance at the Metropolitan Opera House in New York in *Lucia di Lammermoor*, Dec. 5, 1924; toured Australia in 1929. After the end of her operatic career about 1950, she devoted herself to teaching.

Dalmorès, Charles, French dramatic tenor; b. Nancy, Jan. 1, 1871; d. Hollywood, Calif., Dec. 6, 1939. After taking first prizes at the local Cons. for solfeggio and French horn at 17, he received from the city of Nancy a stipend for study at the Paris Cons., where he took first prize for horn at 19; played in the Colonne Orch. (2 years) and the Lamoureux Orch. (2 years); at 23, professor of horn playing in Lyons Cons. His vocal teacher was Dauphin, the bass singer; his debut as tenor took place on Oct. 6, 1899 at Rouen; later he sang at the Théâtre de la Monnaie, Brussels; 7 seasons at Covent Garden; at the Manhattan Opera House, N.Y. (1906–10; debut as Faust, Dec. 7, 1906); then was with the Chicago Opera Co. (1910–18). His repertoire was large, and included Wagnerian as well as French operas; in Chicago he sang Tristan and the title role in the first performance of *Parsifal* to be presented there.

d'Alvimare, Martin-Pierre. See **Dalvimare, Martin-Pierre.**

Dalvimare (real name **d'Alvimare**), **Martin-Pierre,** French harpist and composer for harp; b. Dreux (Eure-et-Loire), Sept. 18, 1772; d. Paris, June 13, 1839. In 1800 he was harpist at the Paris Opéra; harpist to Napoleon, 1806; harp teacher to the Empress Josephine (1807); retired to his estate at Dreux in 1812. He wrote several sonatas for harp and violin; duets for two harps, for harp and piano, and for harp and horn; fantasies, variations, etc.

Damase, Jean-Michel, French composer and pianist; b. Bordeaux, Jan. 27, 1928. He studied with Delvincourt at the Paris Cons.; received the Grand Prix de Rome in 1947; made his U.S. debut April 20, 1954, in N.Y., as pianist-composer.

WORKS: ballets: *Le Saut du Tremplin* (Paris, 1944); *La Croqueuse de Diamants* (Paris, 1950); for orch.: *Interludes* (Nice, 1948); Rhapsody for Oboe and String Orch. (Paris Radio, 1948); Piano Concerto (Cannes, 1950); Violin Concerto (Paris, Dec. 22, 1956); Second Piano Concerto (Paris, Feb. 6, 1963); chamber music: Quintet for Violin, Viola, Cello, Flute and Harp (1947); Trio for Flute, Harp and Cello (1949); piano pieces and songs; an opera, *Colombe* (Bordeaux, May 5, 1961); *Eurydice*, an opera (Bordeaux Festival, May 26, 1972). A list of works and bibliography is publ. in C. Chamfray, "Jean-Michel Damase, *Courrier Musical de France* 18 (1967).

Dambois, Maurice, Belgian cellist; b. Liège, March 30, 1889; d. there, Nov. 12, 1969. He studied at the Cons. there (1899–1905) and won many prizes (piano, harmony, chamber music, fugue, cello); debut at 12 with Saint-Saëns' A minor Concerto; toured Germany (1905), England (1906–08), France, Portugal, and the Netherlands; appointed director of the Académie de Musique at Liège (1910), and professor of cello at the Brussels Cons. (1912). After the outbreak of the war he went to England (until 1916); went to the U.S. in 1917 with Ysaÿe; American debut New York, April 21, 1917, followed by successful tours. In 1926 he settled in Brussels, and resumed his post as prof. of cello at the Cons., retaining it for 30 years.

Damcke, Berthold, German conductor; b. Hannover, Feb. 6, 1812; d. Paris, Feb. 15, 1875. He was a pupil of Alexander Schmitt and F. Ries at Frankfurt; 1837, conductor of Potsdam Philharmonic Society, and of the Choral Union for operatic music (grand concerts, 1839–40); active in St. Petersburg (1845), Brussels (1855), Paris (1859). He was a friend and devoted admirer of Berlioz. He revised and edited, with F. Pelletan, Gluck's two *Iphigénies*; composed oratorios, part songs, piano pieces.

BIBLIOGRAPHY: *Berthold Damcke, Etude biographique et musicale* (Paris, 1895, anonymous).

Damerini, Adelmo, Italian musicologist; b. Carmignano, near Florence, Dec. 11, 1880; d. there, Oct. 12, 1976. He studied with Edgardo Binelli and Giannotto Bastianelli. He held teaching positions at the American Methodist Institute in Rome, at the Palermo Cons. and at the Cons. Boito in Parma; from 1933 till 1962 was prof. at the Cons. of Florence. He publ. *Origine e svolgimento della sinfonia* (Pistoia, 1919); *Classicismo e romanticismo nella musica* (Florence, 1942); with G. Roncaglia, *Volti musicale di Falstaff* (Siena, 1961); *Luigi Cherubini nel II centenario della nascita* (Florence, 1962).

Damoreau, Laure-Cinthie (*née* **Montalant;** first known as '**Mlle. Cinti**'), noted French operatic soprano; b. Paris, Feb. 6, 1801; d. Chantilly, Feb. 25, 1863. She studied at the Paris Cons.; made her debut in 1819 at the Théâtre Italien; later was engaged at the Opéra

(1826–35). Rossini wrote leading roles for her in *Le siège de Corinthe* and *Mosè*, as did Auber, during her engagement (1835–43) at the Opéra-Comique (*Domino noir*, *L'Ambassadrice*, etc.). Retiring from the stage, she made concert tours to England, Holland, Russia, and (with Artôt, the violinist) to the U.S. and Havana (1843). She was professor of singing at the Paris Cons. from 1834–56; then retired to Chantilly. Her husband was an actor at Brussels. She published an *Album de romances*, and a *Méthode de chant*.

Da Motta, José Vianna, noted Portuguese pianist; b. on Isle St. Thomas, Portuguese Africa, April 22, 1868; d. Lisbon, May 31, 1948. His family returned to Lisbon when he was a year old; he studied with local teachers; gave his first concert at the age of 13; then studied piano in Berlin with Xaver Scharwenka and composition with Philipp Scharwenka. In 1885 he went to Weimar, where he became a pupil of Liszt; also took lessons with Hans von Bülow in Frankfurt (1887). He then undertook a series of concert tours throughout Europe (1887–88), the U.S. (1892–93; 1899) and South America (1902). He was in Berlin until 1915; then became director of the Geneva Cons. In 1919 he returned to Lisbon and was appointed director of the Lisbon Cons., retiring in 1938. At the height of his career he was greatly esteemed as a fine interpreter of Bach and Beethoven. He was also the author of many articles in German, French and Portuguese; wrote *Studien bei Bülow* (1896); *Betrachtungen über Franz Liszt* (1898); *Die Entwicklung des Klavierkonzerts* (as a program book to Busoni's concerts); essays on Alkan; critical articles in the *Kunstwart*, *Klavierlehrer*, *Bayreuther Blätter*, etc.

WORKS: He was a prolific composer; among his works are *Die Lusiaden*, for orch. and chorus; String Quartet; many piano pieces, in some of which (e.g., the 5 *Portuguese Rhapsodies* and the Portuguese dance *Vito*) he employs folk themes with striking effect.

BIBLIOGRAPHY: F. Lopes Graça, *Vianna da Motta; subsidios para una biographia* (Lisbon, 1949).

Damrosch, Frank, German-American choral conductor, son of **Leopold Damrosch**; b. Breslau, June 22, 1859; d. New York, Oct. 22, 1937. He studied with Bruckner, Jean Vogt, and von Inten and composition with his father and Moszkowski. 1882–85, conductor of Denver (Colo.) Chorus Club, and (1884–85) Supervisor of Music in public schools, also organist at different churches; 1885–91, chorusmaster and assistant conductor at Metropolitan Opera House; till 1887 conductor of the Newark Harmonic Society; 1892, organized the People's Choral Union, an enterprise for the popularization of choral singing, for which he publ. in 1894 *Popular Method of Sight Singing*; 1897–1905, was Supervisor of Music in N.Y. City Public Schools; conducted the Oratorio Society (1898–1912). In 1893 he founded the "Musical Art Society," a chorus of 60 trained voices for the performance of a cappella music, which he conducted till 1920. In 1905 he established an exemplary organization, the splendidly equipped Institute of Musical Art, which, in 1926, became affiliated with the Juilliard School of Music; retained his position as dean until his retirement in 1933. He received the degree of Mus. Doc. (*honoris*

causa) from Yale Univ. in 1904; publ. vocal numbers (songs, choruses); also wrote *Some Essentials in the Teaching of Music* (N.Y., 1916) and *Institute of Musical Art, 1905–26* (N.Y., 1936).

BIBLIOGRAPHY: E. T. Rice, "A Tribute to Frank Damrosch," *Musical Quarterly* (April 1939); L. P. and R. P. Stebbins, *Frank Damrosch* (1945).

Damrosch, Leopold, eminent German-American conductor and violinist; b. Posen, Oct. 22, 1832; d. New York, Feb. 15, 1885. He studied with Ries, Dehn, and Böhmer; took the degree of *Dr. med.* (M.D.) at Berlin University in 1854, but then, against his parents' wishes, embraced the career of a musician; he appeared at first as a solo violinist in several German cities, later as a conductor at minor theaters, and in 1855 procured, through Liszt, the position of solo violinist in the Grand Ducal Orch. at Weimar. While here he was intimate with Liszt and many of his most distinguished pupils, and won Wagner's lifelong friendship; in Weimar, too, he married the singer **Helene von Heimburg** (b. Oldenburg, 1835; d. N.Y., Nov. 21, 1904). In 1858–60, Damrosch was conductor of the Breslau Philh. Concerts; gave up the post to make tours with von Bülow and Tausig; organized the Breslau Orchestral Society in 1862. Besides this, he founded quartet *soirées,* and a choral society; conducted the Society for Classical Music, and the theater orch. (for 2 years); and frequently appeared as a solo violinist. In 1871 he was called to N.Y. to conduct the "Arion Society," and made his debut, on May 6, 1871, as conductor, composer, and violinist. In N.Y. his remarkable capacity as an organizer found free scope; besides bringing the "Arion" to the highest pitch of efficiency and prosperity, he founded the "Symphony Society" in 1878, the latter's concerts succeeding those of the Thomas Orch. at Steinway Hall. In 1880 Columbia College conferred on him the degree of Mus. Doc.; in 1881 he conducted the first great Music Festival held in N.Y., with an orch. of 250 and a chorus of 1,200; in 1883 he made a highly successful western tour with his orch.; in 1884–85 he organized a German Opera Co., and, together with Anton Seidl, conducted a season of German opera at the Metropolitan Opera House presenting Wagner's *Ring des Nibelungen, Tristan und Isolde* and *Die Meistersinger* for the first time in the U.S. He composed 7 cantatas; Symphony in A; music to Schiller's *Joan of Arc*; marches for orch.; 3 violin concertos; several pieces for violin and orch., and for solo voice and orch.; choruses for mixed voices and male voices; duets; many songs.

BIBLIOGRAPHY: E. T. Rice, "Personal Recollections of Leopold Damrosch," *Musical Quarterly* (July 1942).

Damrosch, Walter Johannes, famous German-American conductor, composer, educator; son of **Leopold Damrosch;** b. Breslau, Jan. 30, 1862; d. New York, Dec. 22, 1950. He studied harmony with his father, also with Rischbieter and Draeseke in Dresden; piano with von Inten, Boekelmann and Max Pinner in the U.S.; and conducting with his father and with Hans von Bülow. He was conductor of the N.Y. Oratorio Society (1885–98) and of the N.Y. Symphony Society

(1885–1903); assistant conductor of German opera at the Metropolitan Opera House (1885–91); organized the Damrosch Opera Co. (1894) which he directed for five seasons, giving German opera (chiefly Wagner) in the principal cities of the U.S.; among the artists whom he first brought to the U.S. were Mmes. Klafsky, Gadski and Ternina; on March 3, 1886 he presented *Parsifal* in New York, in concert form for the first time in America; from 1900–02 he conducted Wagner's operas at the Metropolitan Opera House; then was conductor of the N.Y. Philharmonic Society (1902–03); in 1903 the N.Y. Symphony Society was reorganized with Damrosch as its regular conductor, a post he held until 1927; again conducted the Oratorio Society (1917); organized at the request of General Pershing the American Expeditionary Force bands and founded schools for bandmasters in Chaumont, France (1918); conducted a concert by the N.Y. Symphony Society Orch. in the first chain broadcast over the network of the newly organized NBC (Nov. 15, 1926); appointed musical adviser to NBC (1927, retired 1947); conductor of the NBC Symph. Orch. in a weekly series of music appreciation hours for the schools and colleges of the U.S. and Canada (1928–42). He conducted many famous works for the first time in the U.S. (Brahms' 3rd and 4th symphonies; Tchaikovsky's 4th and 6th symphonies, etc.); was U.S. delegate at the Paris International Music Congress (1937). Mus. Doc. *honoris causa*, Columbia Univ. (1914), Princeton Univ. (1929), Brown Univ. (1932), Dartmouth College (1933), N.Y. Univ. (1935); awarded the David Bispham medal (1929) and the gold medal of the National Institute of Arts and Letters (1938).

WORKS: the operas *The Scarlet Letter* (Damrosch Opera Co., Boston, Feb. 10, 1896); *Cyrano de Bergerac* (Metropolitan Opera House, Feb. 27, 1913; revised in 1939); *The Man Without a Country* (Metropolitan Opera House, May 12, 1937); *The Opera Cloak*, one-act opera (N.Y. Opera Co., Nov. 3, 1942); comic opera, *The Dove of Peace* (Philadelphia, Oct. 15, 1912). Other works: *Manila Te Deum* (N.Y., 1898); *An Abraham Lincoln Song* (N.Y., 1936); incidental music to Euripides' *Iphigenia in Aulis* and *Medea* (Berkeley, Calif., 1915), and to Sophocles' *Electra* (N.Y., 1917); Violin Sonata; *At Fox Meadow* (1899); *Dunkirk*, a setting of R. Nathan's poem, for baritone, solo, male chorus, and chamber orch. (NBC broadcast, May 2, 1943; many songs, including *Death and General Putnam* (1936), *Danny Deever*, etc. He published an autobiography, *My Musical Life* (N.Y., 1923; 2nd edition 1930); co-editor, with Gartlan and Gehrkens, of the Universal School Music Series.

BIBLIOGRAPHY: W. J. Henderson, "Walter Damrosch," *Musical Quarterly* (Jan. 1932); Gretchen Damrosch Finletter, *From the Top of the Stairs* (reminiscences of Walter Damrosch's daughter; Boston, 1946).

Dan, Ikuma, Japanese composer; b. Tokyo, April 7, 1924. He studied at the Tokyo Music Academy with K. Shimofusa and S. Moroi; taught at the Tokyo Music School (1947–50); has been active as a film music director and composer and, since 1967, presented pop music concerts on television.

WORKS: 5 operas: *Yûzuru* (*The Twilight Crane*, 1950–51; Tokyo, Jan. 30, 1952; revised 1956), *Kikimimi-zukin* (*The Listening Cap*, 1954–55; Tokyo, March 18, 1955), *Yang Kwei-fei* (1957–58; Tokyo, Dec. 11, 1958), *Chanchiki* (*Cling-Clang*, 1961–63), and *Hikarigoke* (1972; Osaka, April 27, 1972); *Symphonic Poem* (1948); 5 symphonies (1949–50, 1955–56, 1959–60, 1964–65, 1965); *Sinfonia Burlesca* (1953; Tokyo, Jan. 26, 1959); a dance suite for orch., *The Silken Road* (1953–54; Tokyo, June 23, 1955); *Journey Through Arabia*, symph. suite (1958); *Olympic Games Overture* (1964); *Festival Overture* (1965); *Japanese Poem* No. 1 for orch. (1967; Tokyo, Sept. 25, 1967; Arthur Fiedler conducting); *Hymn to the Sai-kai* for chorus and orch. (1969); *A Letter from Japan* No. 2 for orch. (1969); *Rainbow Tower* for orch. (1970); String Trio (1947); Piano Sonata (1947); String Quartet (1948); Divertimento for 2 Pianos (1949); *Futari Shizuka*, dance drama for flute, percussion and string ensemble (1961); Concerto Grosso for Harpsichord and String Ensemble (1965); choruses.

Dana, William Henry, American music pedagogue; b. Warren, Ohio, June 10, 1846; d. there, Feb. 18, 1916. He studied at Kullak's Academy of Music in Berlin and at the Royal Academy of Music, London (1881). He was a founder of the American Music Teachers' National Association. He published several manuals: *Practical Thorough-bass* (1873), *Orchestration* (1875), *Instrumentation for Military Bands* (1876), *Practical Harmony* (1884); composed a *De profundis* for soli, chorus and orch.; motets, songs, piano pieces.

Danbé, Jules, French violinist and composer; b. Caen, Nov. 16, 1840; d. Vichy, Nov. 10, 1905. He was a pupil at the Paris Cons.; 2nd director of the Cons. concerts till 1892; conductor at the Opéra-Comique (1877–98); from 1899 until his death, conductor at the Théâtre Lyrique, where he successfully revived Gluck's *Iphigénie en Tauride* after a long period of neglect.

Danckert, Werner, German musicologist; b. Erfurt, June 22, 1900; d. Krefeld, March 5, 1970. He studied natural science and mathematics at Jena, then musicology in Leipzig with Riemann; was assistant in musicology to G. Becking at Erlangen Univ. (1922); instructor at Jena Univ. (1926–29); in Weimar (1929–31); in Erfurt (1932–37); in Berlin (1937–39); in Graz (1943–45); in Krefeld (since 1950). Author of *Geschichte der Gigue* (Leipzig, 1924); *Ursymbole melodischer Gestaltung* (Kassel, 1932); *Das europäische Volkslied* (Berlin, 1939); *Claude Debussy* (Berlin, 1950); articles in various musical journals.

Danckerts, Ghiselin, Flemish contrapuntist and theorist; b. Tholen, Zeeland; entered the Papal Chapel in Rome as chorister in 1538; pensioned in 1565. He published (1559) two books of motets for 4–6 voices; single motets are included in Augsburg collections of 1540 and 1545. His ingenuity in counterpoint is demonstrated in the so-called 'Chessboard Canon' for 4 voices with alternating black and white notes. His autograph MS, pronouncing judgment on the theoretical dispute between Vincentino and Lusitano on the nature of ancient modes, is in the Vatican Library in Rome.

Dancla, Arnaud, French cellist; brother of **Jean-Baptiste-Charles Dancla**; b. Bagnères-de-Bigorre, Jan. 1, 1819; d. there, Feb. 1, 1862; author of a method for cello; composed études, duos, and melodies for his instrument.

Dancla, (Jean-Baptiste-) Charles, French violinist and composer; b. Bagnères-de-Bigorre, Dec. 19, 1817; d. Tunis, Nov. 9, 1907. He entered the Paris Cons. in 1828, his teachers being Baillot (violin), Halévy, and Berton. In 1834, he was a violinist in the Opéra-Comique orch.; became renowned by his playing in the 'Société des Concerts,' and was appointed professor of violin at the Paris Cons. in 1857. His quartet *soirées* were famous. Besides four symphonies, he composed some 130 works for violin; 14 string quartets; 4 piano trios.
WRITINGS: *Méthode élémentaire et progressive pour le violon*; *École du mécanisme*; *L'École de la mélodie*; *École de l'expression*; and (with Panseron) *L'Art de moduler sur le violon*; also books of essays, *Les Compositeurs chefs d'orchestre* (1873), and *Miscellanées musicales* (1876).
BIBLIOGRAPHY: *Charles Dancla, Notes et souvenirs* (Paris, 1893; 2nd edition 1898; contains catalogue of works).

Dancla, Léopold, French violinist; brother of the preceding; b. Bagnères-de-Bigorre, June 1, 1823; d. Paris, April 29, 1895. He was a pupil of Baillot at the Paris Cons., taking first prize in violin in 1842. He wrote 3 string quartets, *airs variés*, fantasies and studies for the violin.

Danco, Suzanne, Belgian soprano; b. Brussels, Jan. 22, 1911. She studied at the Brussels Cons.; in 1936 won the International Bel Canto Prize at Venice; in 1948 was engaged as soloist at the Edinburgh Festival; also sang in Milan; in 1950 made her American debut. She has gained a fine reputation in Europe and America for her musicianly performances in opera (ranging from Mozart to Alban Berg) and in concert recitals (notably in Debussy's songs).

Dandara, Liviu, Rumanian composer; b. Miorcani, near Botoşani, Dec. 3, 1933. He studied with Paul Constantinescu, Ion Dumitrescu and Tudor Ciortea at the Bucharest Cons. (1953–59).
WORKS: 2 cantatas: *1907* (1957) and *Construcţii* (1969); *Sinfonietta lirica* (1958); *Ouverture solennelle* (1959); Suite for Orch. (1962); *Divertissement* for orch. (1964); *Expresii umane* for orch. (1968); *Spaţii*, stereophonic music for 32 instruments and amplifiers (1971); Piano Concerto (1972); *3 Slow Movements* for clarinet and piano (1963); *Ipostaze* for wind quartet (1966); Sonata for Solo Clarinet (1966); *Dialoguri cu axa timpului* for flute, violin, piano and percussion (1968); *Pentaedre per la "Musica Nova"*, quintet for clarinet, violin, viola, cello and piano (1969; "Musica Nova" is a Rumanian ensemble); *Bamba!* for wind instruments, or voices and percussion (1971); *Miniatures* for piano (1959); Piano Sonatina (1961); Toccata

for Piano (1965); *Sonata brevis* for piano (1966); *Quadriforium* for piano and tape (1970; variable timing); *Timpul suspendat* for tape (1971); *Imnurile verii*, 3 madrigals for double chorus, xylophone and vibraphone (1967); songs; film music.

Dandelot, Georges, French composer; son of the impresario **Arthur Dandelot** (1864–1943); b. Paris, Dec. 2, 1895; d. at St.-Georges de Didonne (Charente-Maritime), Aug. 17, 1975. He studied with Widor at the Paris Cons.; later took lessons with Dukas and Roussel. He was in the French Army during World War I, and received the Croix de Guerre for valor. In 1919 he became an instructor at the École Normale de Musique in Paris; in 1942, appointed prof. at the Paris Cons. Dandelot composed an oratorio *Pax* (first prize at the International Exposition in Paris, 1937); 2 operas, *Midas* (1947) and *L'Ennemi* (1948); the ballets *Le Souper de famine* (1943); *Le Jardin merveilleux* (1944); and *Pierrot et la rose* (1948); Symphony (1941); Piano Concerto (Paris, Jan. 7, 1934); *Concerto romantique* for violin and orch. (1944); chamber music; songs.

Dandrieu, Jean François, French composer; b. Paris, 1682; d. there, Jan. 17, 1738. He was organist at Saint-Merry, Paris, in 1704; published: *Livre de Sonates en Trio* (1705); *Livre de Sonates* for solo violin (1710); *Principes de l'accompagnement du Clavecin* (1718); *Pièces de clavecin* (3 albums, 1724); organ pieces, airs. His importance lies in his works for clavecin written in a style closely resembling Couperin's.
BIBLIOGRAPHY: P. Brunold, *Dandrieu* (Paris, 1954).

Daneau, Nicolas, Belgian composer; b. Binche, June 17, 1866; d. Brussels, July 12, 1944. He studied at the Ghent Cons. with Adolphe Samuel, graduating in 1892; won the Second Prix de Rome in 1895. He was director of the Cons. of Tournai (1896–1919), and of Mons (1919–31).
WORKS: *Linario*, lyric drama (Tournai, 1906); *Myrtis*, opera-idyll (Tournai, 1910); *Le Sphynx*, opera; *La Brute*, lyric drama. For orch.: *Villes d'Italie*; *Adima et Hevah*; *Arles*; *Mardi-Gras*; *Petite Suite*. Chamber music: Suite for Violin and Piano; String Quartet; Piano Quintet. His daughter, **Suzanne Daneau** (b. Tournai, Aug. 17, 1901), was his pupil. She has written orchestral works, chamber music, and piano pieces, mostly based on native folk songs.
BIBLIOGRAPHY: L. J. Beatrice, *Daneau; Histoire d'une famille d'artistes* (Brussels, 1944).

Danhauser, Adolphe-Léopold, French composer and teacher; b. Paris, Feb. 26, 1835; d. there, June 9, 1896. He studied at the Paris Cons. with Halévy and Reber; won 1st prize in harmony (1857); 1st prize in fugue (1859); Second Prix de Rome (1862); was Chief Inspector of Instruction in Singing, in the Communal Schools, Paris and professor of solfeggio at the Cons. He wrote *Théorie de la musique*; published *Soirées orphéoniques*, a collection of 3-part choruses for equal voices. He composed *Le Proscrit*, musical drama with choruses, which was produced (1866) in a religious institution at Auteuil; a 3-act opera, *Maures* *et Castillans* (not performed). His *Solfège des solfèges* (3 volumes; translated into English and Spanish) is still in use throughout the U.S. and South America.

Daniel, Oliver, American music critic and editor; b. De Pere, Wisconsin, Nov. 24, 1911. He was editor of the American Composers' Alliance (1951–54); in 1954 became Director of the Concert Music Administration of Broadcast Music, Inc. He was co-founder, with Leopold Stokowski, of the Contemporary Music Society in 1952; represented the U.S. at the International Music Council of Unesco. He edited the collections, *The Harmony of Maine, Down East Spirituals* and *The Music of William Billings.*

Daniel, Salvador (real name **Francisco Daniel**), also known as **Salvador-Daniel,** French composer and political revolutionary; b. Bourges, Feb. 17, 1831; killed during the Paris Commune, May 23, 1871. For a brief time he was director of the Paris Cons. under the Commune. He taught music in an Arab school in Algiers; studied native folksongs of North Africa; wrote a valuable book *La Musique arabe* (Algiers, 1863), published in English as *The Music and Musical Instruments of the Arabs* (London, 1915).

Daniel-Lesur. See **Lesur, Daniel.**

Daniélou, Alain, French musicologist; b. Paris, Oct. 4, 1907. He devoted himself to the study of Asian and African music; lived mostly in India; lectured at the Univ. of Benares (1949–54); was director of research in Madras (1954–56), at the Institute of Indology in Pondichery (1956–59); in 1959 was appointed instructor at the École Française d'Extrême Orient in Paris; from 1960, member of the International Music Council of Unesco.
WRITINGS: *Northern Indian Music* (2 vols.; Calcutta, 1949, 1953); *Traité de musicologie comparée* (Paris, 1959); supervised numerous phonograph recordings of Asian music.

Daniels, Mabel Wheeler, American composer; b. Swampscott, Mass., Nov. 27, 1878; d. Boston, March 10, 1971. She studied at Radcliffe College (B.A. *magna cum laude,* 1900) and with Chadwick in Boston; then with Thuille in Munich; director of the Radcliffe Glee Club (1911–13); Hon. M.A., Tufts College, 1933; Hon. Mus. Doc., Boston Univ., 1939. As a composer she excelled in vocal writing; her instrumental pieces are cautiously modernistic.
WORKS: operetta, *The Court of Hearts* (Cambridge, Jan. 2, 1901; she sang the part of Jack of Hearts); operatic sketch, *Alice in Wonderland Continued* (Brookline, Mass., May 20, 1904). Vocal works with orch.: *The Desolate City* (1913); *Peace with a Sword* (Handel and Haydn Society, Boston, 1917); *Songs of Elfland* (St. Louis Symph. Orch., Feb. 2, 1924); *The Holy Star* (1928); *Exultate Deo* (for the 50th anniversary of Radcliffe College; Boston, May 31, 1929); *Song of Jael,* cantata for dramatic soprano, mixed voices and orch. (Worcester Festival, Oct. 5, 1940); *A Psalm of Praise* (composed for the 75th anniversary of the founding of Radcliffe College; Cambridge, Dec. 3, 1954; Boston Symph. Orch., April 27,

1956); also a choral cycle for women's voices, *In Springtime* (1910); 3-part women's choruses with piano and 2 violins: *Eastern Song* and *The Voice of My Beloved* (Prize of National Federation of Music Clubs, 1911); sacred choruses a cappella (*The Christ Child, Salve festa dies,* etc.); duets; part songs. For orch.: *Deep Forest,* prelude for small orch. (Barrère Little Symph., N.Y., June 3, 1931; rescored for full orch., 1934; Boston Symph., April 16, 1937, Koussevitzky conducting); *Pirates' Island* (Harrisburg Symph., Feb. 19, 1935). Chamber music: *Pastoral Ode* for flute and strings (1940); *Three Observations* for oboe, clarinet and bassoon (1943); *Digressions* for strings, a ballet (Boston, 1947). She is the author of a lively book, *An American Girl in Munich* (Boston, 1905).

Danjou, Jean-Louis-Félix, French music teacher; b. Paris, June 21, 1812; d. Montpellier, March 4, 1866. He studied organ with François Benoist at the Paris Cons.; then played organ at various churches from 1830; was organist at Notre Dame from 1840 till 1847. With his essay *De l'état de l'avenir du chant ecclésiastique* (1844) he became the pioneer in the movement for reforming plain chant; and his journal *Revue de la Musique Religieuse, Populaire et Classique* (1845–49) showed profound erudition gained by assiduous historical research. He was the discoverer (1847) of the celebrated 'Antiphonary of Montpellier.' He labored to promote organ building in France; made a special study of organ manufacture in Germany and Holland; entered into partnership with the organ builders Daublaine & Callinet of Paris, but lost his entire capital, gave up music, and in 1849 became a political journalist in Marseilles and Montpellier.

Dankevich, Konstantin, eminent Ukrainian composer; b. Odessa, Dec. 24, 1905. He studied with Zolotarev, at the Odessa Cons., graduating in 1929. In 1942 he was artistic director of the Red Army Ensemble of Songs and Dance in Tbilisi. From 1944 to 1953 he was prof. of composition at the Odessa Cons.; in 1953 he was appointed to the faculty of the Kiev Cons. In his works he successfully presents the motives of Ukrainian and Russian folksongs. He first attracted attention by his opera *Bogdan Khmelnitzky* (Moscow, June 15, 1951) on a subject from Ukrainian history; the opera was attacked for its libretto and its unsuitable music, and Dankevich revised the score, after which it gained favorable notices in Russia. He also wrote the opera *Nazar Stodolya* (Kharkov, May 28, 1960). His most popular score is *Lileya,* a ballet, produced in 1939 and retained in the repertory of Russian theater. Other works include 2 symphonies (1937, 1945), several overtures and patriotic choruses, including *Poem of the Ukraine* (1960) and the ideological cantata to his own words, *The Dawn of Communism Has Risen Over Us* (1961). A monograph on Dankevich was published in the Ukrainian language in Kiev in 1959.

Danks, Hart Pease, American song composer; b. New Haven, Conn., April 6, 1834; d. Philadelphia, Nov. 20, 1903. He studied at Saratoga Springs with Dr. L. E. Whiting; in 1851 moved to Chicago, where he became a photographer, and also sang bass in church. In 1864 he settled in New York and developed energetic activity as a prolific composer of sacred hymns and popular songs; published a total of about 1,300 separate numbers; also compiled books of church anthems; wrote two operettas: *Pauline, or the Belle of Saratoga* (1872) and *Conquered by Kindness* (1881). Among his sacred songs the most popular was *Not Ashamed of Christ* (1873); in the light genre, his greatest successes were the songs *Don't be angry with me, darling* and *Silver threads among the gold.*

BIBLIOGRAPHY: G. L. Howe, *A Hundred Years of Music in America* (Chicago, 1889, pp. 98–99).

Dannreuther, Edward George, pianist and music scholar; b. Strasbourg, Nov. 4, 1844; d. London, Feb. 12, 1905. He went with his parents in 1849 to Cincinnati, where he was taught by F. L. Ritter; then studied at the Leipzig Cons. with Richter, Moscheles, and Hauptmann (1859–63). On April 11, 1863, he made his debut in London, playing Chopin's Concerto in F minor. He introduced into England the piano concertos of Liszt, Grieg, and Tchaikovsky. In 1872 he founded the London Wagner Society, conducting its concerts (1873–74); was an active promoter of the Wagner Festival (1877); appointed professor at the Royal Academy of Music in 1895. An indefatigable champion of the new composers, he was equally active on behalf of the older masters; the chamber music concerts that he gave at his home (1874–93) were famous. Dannreuther visited the U.S. several times.

WRITINGS: "Richard Wagner and the Reform of the Opera," *Monthly Musical Record* (1872; separately, London, 1904); *Richard Wagner, His Tendencies and Theories* (London, 1873); *Musical Ornamentation* (2 vols., London, 1893–95; a valuable work, despite some misapprehensions exposed by later investigations); *The Romantic Period* (vol. VI of the Oxford History of Music, London, 1905; 3rd ed. 1931). He transl. into English several of Wagner's literary works: *Wagners Briefe an einen französischen Freund* (1873); *Das Kunstwerk der Zukunft* (1873); *Beethoven* (1880); *Über das Dirigieren* (1885; 4th ed., 1940).

Dannreuther, Gustav, American violinist, brother of **Edward;** b. Cincinnati, July 21, 1853; d. New York, Dec. 19, 1923. He studied at the Hochschule für Musik, Berlin, under de Ahna and Joachim (violin), and Heitel (theory); then lived in London; in 1877 he joined the Mendelssohn Quintette Club of Boston, traveling through the U.S., Canada and Newfoundland. From 1882–84 he was director of the Buffalo Philh. Society (a chamber music organization), and, during this period gave 60 concerts. In 1884 he founded the Beethoven String Quartet of N.Y. (renamed Dannreuther Quartet in 1894). From 1907 he taught violin at Vassar College.

Danzi, Franz, German composer and teacher; b. Mannheim, June 15, 1763; d. Schwetzingen, April 13, 1826. He studied with his father, **Innocenz Danzi,** a cellist; then with Abbé Vogler. He joined the court orch. on its removal to Munich in 1778; became assistant Kapellmeister in 1798; Kapellmeister at Stuttgart (1807–12), where he was the teacher of Carl Maria von Weber; then at Karlsruhe.

WORKS: *Cleopatra* (1780); *Azakia* (1780); *Der Triumph der Treue* (Munich, 1781); *Die Sylphe* (1782); *Der Kuss* (1799); *Die Mitternachtsstunde* (1801); *Der Quasi-Mann; Iphigenia in Aulis* (1807); *Turandot* (Karlsruhe, 1817); oratorios, cantatas; Masses; the 128th Psalm for chorus and orch.; symphonies, quintets, quartets, concertos, sonatas. He was an excellent singing teacher, and wrote vocal exercises of practical value.

BIBLIOGRAPHY: E. Reipschläger, *Schubaur, Danzi und Poissl als Opernkomponisten* (Rostock, 1911); M. Herre, *Franz Danzi* (Munich, 1924).

Da-Oz, Ram, German-born Israeli composer; b. Berlin, Oct. 17, 1929. He came to Palestine as a child in 1934; studied oboe and piano at the Cons. in Tel Aviv, and composition with André Hajos at the Music Academy there; he lost his eyesight during the Israeli war for independence.

WORKS: *Von Trauer und Trost* for orch. (1960); concerto for violin and string orch. (1961); *Dmuyoth umassechot (Changing Phantoms),* movements for chamber ensemble (1967); *Improvisation on a Song* for 10 instruments (1968); *Quartet* for narrator and small orch. (1970); *Rhapsody on a Jewish Yemenite Song* for piano and strings (1971); *3 Romances* for violin and small orch. (1975); 4 string quartets (1955–70); violin sonata (1960); string trio (1961); *Suite* for harpsichord, flute, oboe and cello (1963); piano trio (1963); *Dialogue* for 2 clarinets (1965); *Illumination* for solo violin (1966); *4 Miniatures* for recorders and piano (1975); *3 Snacks* for brass quartet (1977); songs; for piano solo: 2 sonatas (1955; *Movimenti quasi una sonata,* 1963), *5 Contrasts* (1958), *Capriccio* (1960), *8 Little Pictures* (1962), *Aspects* (1969), *Bells* (1973) and *Mood Ring* (1976).

Da Ponte, Lorenzo, famous librettist; b. Ceneda, near Venice, March 10, 1749; d. New York, Aug. 17, 1838. His real name was **Emanuele Conegliano;** he was of a Jewish family; was converted to Christianity at the age of 14, and assumed the name of his patron, Bishop of Ceneda, Lorenzo da Ponte. He then studied at the Ceneda Seminary; in 1774 obtained a post as prof. of rhetoric at Treviso, but was dismissed for insubordination two years later. He then went to Venice where he led an adventurous life, and was banished in 1779; subsequently lived in Austria and in Dresden; in 1782 he settled in Vienna and became official poet to the Imperial Theater; met Mozart and became his friend and librettist of his most famous operas, *Le Nozze di Figaro, Don Giovanni* and *Così fan tutte.* From 1792 to 1798 he was in London; traveled in Europe; then went to New York in 1805. After disastrous business ventures, with intervals of teaching, he became interested in various operatic enterprises. In his last years he was teacher of Italian at Columbia College. He published *Memorie* (4 vols., N.Y., 1823–27; English transls., London, 1929; Philadelphia, 1929).

BIBLIOGRAPHY: A. Marchesan, *Della vita e delle opere di Lorenzo da Ponte* (Treviso, 1900); J. L. Russo, *Lorenzo da Ponte, Poet and Adventurer* (N.Y., 1922); A. Fitzlyon, *The Libertine Librettist* (London, 1955).

Daquin, Louis-Claude, French organist and composer; b. Paris, July 4, 1694; d. there, June 15, 1772. He was a pupil of Marchand; at 6 played on the clavecin before Louis XIV; at 12 became organist at St.-Antoine, where his playing attracted crowds of curious listeners. From 1727 until his death he was organist at St.-Paul, winning the position in competition with Rameau. He published a book of *Pièces de clavecin* (1735; contains the celebrated piece *Le Coucou*); selections reprinted in Expert's *Les Maîtres du clavecin*; also revised by Brunold in 1926; a collection of *Noëls pour l'orgue ou Le Clavecin* (reprinted by Guilmant in *Archives des Maîtres de l'Orgue*), and a cantata, *La Rose*.

D'Aranyi, Yelly. See **Aranyi, Yelly.**

D'Archambeau, Iwan. See **Archambeau.**

Darcy, Robert, French-born Belgian cellist and composer; b. Paris, Nov. 10, 1910; d. Schaerbeek, near Brussels, June 6, 1967. He obtained the Premier Prix in cello at the Lyons Cons. (1928); studied composition with Francis Bousquet and Paul Vidal; played the cello in orchestras in Paris and Brussels. Mobilized in 1939, he was taken prisoner of war in June, 1940; while in captivity, he organized a prisoners' orchestra; returned to Belgium, becoming a citizen in 1949. His style is rooted in neo-classicism with an admixture of atonal elements.
WORKS: *Scherzo* for orch. (1923); *Rêverie* for orch. (1931); *7 Sketches* for small orch. (1933); Suite for Wind Orch. (1935); Suite for String Orch. (1936); Concerto for 4 Cellos and Wind Orch. (1936); *Piece* for 2 cellos and orch. (1937); Fantasie for Cello and Orch. (1937); *3 Marines* for orch. (1939); Concerto for 4 Saxophones and Orch. (1939); *Danses Mosanes* for orch. (1943); Trumpet Concerto (1948); Piano Concerto (1951); Symphony (1953); Concerto for Orch. (1965); 3 quartets for 4 cellos (1935–37); 3 string quartets (1936–1950); *Caprice* for wind quintet (1936); Sextet for Winds (1937); *6 Pieces* for 4 cellos (1937); Trio for Oboe, Clarinet and Bassoon (1938); Quartet for 4 Saxophones (1938); Bassoon Sonata (1948); *Piece* for wind quintet (1962); songs.

Dargomyzhsky, Alexander, outstanding Russian composer; b. in the government of Tula, Feb. 14, 1813; d. St. Petersburg, Jan. 17, 1869. From 1817 he lived in St. Petersburg; his teacher was Schoberlechner. At 20 he was a brilliant pianist; from 1831–35 he held a government position, but then devoted himself exclusively to music, studying assiduously for 8 years; visited Germany, Brussels, and Paris in 1845; at Moscow (Dec. 17, 1847) produced an opera *Esmeralda* (after Victor Hugo's *Notre-Dame de Paris*) with great success (excerpts published in piano score, Moscow, 1948). From 1845–55 he published over 100 minor works (vocal romances, ballads, airs, and duos; waltzes, fantasies, etc.); on May 16, 1856 he brought out his best opera, *Russalka*, at St. Petersburg (vocal score, with indications of instruments, published at Moscow, 1937); in 1867, an opera-ballet, *The Triumph of Bacchus* (written in 1845; performed in Moscow, Jan. 23, 1867); a posthumous opera *Kamennyi Gost*

(*The Stone Guest*, after Pushkin's poem of the same title) was scored by Rimsky-Korsakov and produced at St. Petersburg on Feb. 28, 1872; of *Rogdana*, a fantasy-opera, only a few scenes were sketched. At first a follower of Rossini and Auber, Dargomyzhsky gradually became convinced that dramatic realism with nationalistic connotations was the destiny of Russian music; he applied this realistic method in treating the recitative in his opera *The Stone Guest* and in his songs (several of these to satirical words). His orchestral works (*Finnish Fantasia, Cossack Dance, Baba-Yaga,* etc.) enjoyed wide popularity. In 1867 he was elected President of the Russian Music Society.
BIBLIOGRAPHY: N. Findeisen, *A. S. Dargomyzhsky: His Life and Work* (Moscow, 1902); S. B. Fried, *A. S. Dargomyzhsky* (St. Petersburg, 1913); A. N. Drosdov, *A. S. Dargomyzhsky* (Moscow, 1929); M. Pekelis, *Alexander Dargomyzhsky and His Circle* (2 vols., Moscow, 1966, 1973).

Darke, Harold Edwin, English organist and composer; b. London, Oct. 29, 1888; d. Cambridge, Nov. 28, 1976. He studied organ with Parratt and composition with Stanford at the Royal College of Music in London; from 1916 to 1966 he served as organist at St. Michael's Church, Cornhill, London. He wrote several cantatas and other sacred music, as well as organ pieces and songs.

Darnton, Charles, English composer and organist; b. Islington, Oct. 10, 1836; d. London, April 21, 1933. He was almost entirely self-taught; was organist of St. Jude's Church, Canonbury (1860–67), Park Chapel, Camden Town (1867–91), Gospel Oak, Hampstead (1892–1901); composed 90 anthems (prize anthem; *I will sing of the mercies of the Lord*, London, 1897); many other sacred works; operettas; piano pieces, etc.

Darnton, Christian, English composer; b. near Leeds, Oct. 30, 1905. He took piano lessons at 4, and began to compose at 9; studied with F. Corder, Sr., at the Brighton School of Music, then with H. Craxton (piano) at the Matthay School, London; pupil of Benjamin Dale in composition; studied (1923–26) with Charles Wood (composition) and G. Rootham (theory) at Cambridge; with G. Jacob at the Royal College of Music (1927); with M. Butting in Berlin (1928–29); gave a concert of his works at Grotrian Hall, London (1927).
WORKS: 3 symphonies; 2 piano concertos; *5 Orchestral Pieces* (Warsaw Festival, April 14, 1939); author of *You and Music* (1940).
BIBLIOGRAPHY: A. Rawsthorne, "Christian Darnton," *Monthly Musical Record* (Jan. 1939).

Darré, Jeanne-Marie, French pianist; b. Givet, July 30, 1905. She studied with Marguerite Long and Isidor Philipp in Paris; after numerous concerts in France and elsewhere in Europe, she made a successful series of tours in the U.S., appearing with major American orchestras. A virtuoso in a grand manner, she produced a sensation by playing several piano concertos on a single night.

Darrell, Robert Donaldson, American writer on music; b. Newton, Mass., Dec. 13, 1903; studied at the New England Cons. of Music; contributed to the *Phonograph Monthly Review* and became its editor and publisher in 1930; received a Guggenheim Fellowship in 1939. He published valuable compilations, *Gramophone Shop Encyclopedia of Recorded Music* (1936) and *Schirmer's Guide to Books on Music and Musicians* (annotated bibliography of books in English available in print; N.Y., 1951); also *Good Listening* (N.Y., 1953).

Dart, Thurston, eminent English musicologist; b. London, Sept. 3, 1921; d. there, March 6, 1971. He studied at the Royal College of Music and simultaneously took courses in mathematics at the Univ. of London. In 1947 he was appointed lecturer in music at Cambridge Univ.; he specialized in Old English music, and made important contributions to various music journals. He was editor of the *Galpin Society Journal* (1948-58), and Secretary of the documentary edition *Musica Britannica* (1949-64); from 1964 was prof. at King's College at the Univ. of London. His magnum opus was *The Interpretation of Music* (London, 1954, 1958, 1967; published in German, under the title *Practica musica,* Bern, 1959; and in Swedish, Stockholm, 1964). He was also an expert performer on the harpsichord, the virginals, and other old keyboard instruments.

Darvas, Gábor, Hungarian composer; b. Szatmárnémeti, Jan. 18, 1911. He studied at the Liszt Academy in Budapest with Kodály; lived in Chile (1939-48), where he was an assistant conductor to Erich Kleiber. He returned to Hungary in 1948; worked mainly on orchestral arrangements of classical compositions.
WORKS: *Harvest Festival* for orch. (1935); *Autumn Pastorale* for orch. (1936); *Symphonic Movement* (1937); *Improvisations symphoniques* for piano and orch. (1963); *Sectio Aurea* for 3 percussion groups and orch. (1964); *Medaille* for soprano, percussion, keyboard instruments and 2 loudspeakers (1965); *Der Turm* for soloists, chorus, percussion, 2 pianos and string orch. (1967); *Rotation 5* for 5 instrumental groups (1968); *Gyermekzene (Children's Music)* for soprano and 12 performers, 11 of whom play on child-sized instruments (1969); *Antiphon* for tape (1970).

Dārziņš, Emils, Latvian composer and writer on music; b. Lunpiebama, Nov. 3, 1875; d. Riga, Aug. 31, 1910. From 1898 to 1901 he was a pupil in composition of Rimsky-Korsakov at the St. Petersburg Cons. Returning to Latvia, he became active as a choral conductor and music critic while continuing to compose. He excelled particularly in vocal music; among his choral works, *Broken Pines* and *In the Faraway Land of Dreams* are best known. His style is marked by a fine mastery of old-fashioned Germanic romanticism, reflected through Slavic harmonic and melodic folkways. Among his symphonic pieces only his *Melancholy Waltz* survives. A program of his songs was presented in New York by the Latvian singer Janis Klavins on Jan. 25, 1976.

Dasch, George, American violinist and conductor; b. Cincinnati, Ohio, May 14, 1877; d. Chicago, April 12, 1955. He studied with Brockhoeven (theory) and L. Campanari (violin) at the Cincinnati College of Music; was a member of the Cincinnati Symph. Orch. (1895-98) and the Chicago Symph. Orch. (1898-1923); then organized his own string quartet. He was the conductor of the Chicago Civic Orch., the Joliet, Illinois, Symph. Orch. and the Evansville Philharmonic.

Daser (Dasser, Dasserus), Ludwig, German composer; b. Munich, c.1525; d. Stuttgart, March 27, 1589. He preceded Orlando di Lasso as Kapellmeister at Munich to Duke Albert V of Bavaria; held that post until 1559.
WORKS: published: Passion *a 4* (1578); motets in the *Orgeltabulaturbuch* of J. Paix.
BIBLIOGRAPHY: A. Sandberger, *Beiträge zur Geschichte der Beyerischen Hofkopelle I.* (1894); B. A. Wallner, *Musikalische Denkmäler der Steinätzkunst* (1912).

Dasser, Ludwig. See **Daser, Ludwig.**

Daublaine et Callinet, firm of Paris organ-builders; founded in 1838 as Daublaine et Cie. Daublaine was the business partner, Callinet the practical mechanician, Danjou, an intelligent and progressive theorist. After a quarrel in 1843, Callinet demolished the new work partly finished for the organ of St.-Sulpice, dissolved the partnership, and entered Cavaillé's workshops. The firm name became Ducroquet et Cie. in 1845; in 1855 it was succeeded by a limited company, later by 'Merklin, Schütze et Cie.' from Brussels; subsequently Merklin continued the business alone until his death in 1905. As a manufacturer of instruments, the firm no longer exists.

Dauney, William, British music historian; b. Aberdeen, Scotland, Oct. 27, 1800; d. Georgetown, British Guiana, July 28, 1843. In the Advocates' Library at Edinburgh he discovered what is now known as the "Skene MS," a collection of 114 English and Scottish dances, ballads and songs (written in tablature between 1614-20, containing the oldest known (and probably original) versions of *John Anderson my Jo, The Flowers of the Forest,* etc. Dauney transcribed these into modern notation, and publ. them, in 1838, as *Ancient Scottish Melodies from a MS. of the Reign of King James VI,* together with *An Introductory Enquiry Illustrative of the History of Music of Scotland.*

Dauprat, Louis-François, celebrated French horn player and composer for horn; b. Paris, May 24, 1781; d. there, July 16, 1868. Studied with Kenn at the Paris Cons.; joined the band of the Garde Nationale, and in 1799 the band of the Garde des Consuls, with which he passed through the Egyptian campaign. From 1801-05 he studied theory at the Cons. under Catel and Gossec, and studied again with Reicha from 1811-14; 1806-08 first horn at the Bordeaux Theater; succeeded Kenn in the Opéra orch., and Duvernoy (as *cor solo*), retiring in 1831. He was chamber musician to Napoleon (1811) and Louis XVIII (1816); in 1816 he was appointed prof. of horn in the Cons., resigning in 1842.

Dauriac, Lionel Alexandre, French psychologist and writer on music; b. Brest, Finistere, Nov. 19, 1847; d. Paris, May 26, 1923. He graduated from the École Normale Supérieure of Brest, 1867; *Docteur ès Lettres,* Paris, 1878 (with the dissertations *Des Notions de Matière et de Force dans les Sciences de la Nature* and *De Heraclito Ephesio*); held teaching positions in philosophy at Brest, Toulouse, and Montpellier; lecturer at the Sorbonne on musical psychology (1896–1903); Laureate of the Academy of Moral and Political Sciences (awarded Prix Gegner, 1916); 1st President of Paris section of International Music Society; from 1907, Honorary President. Besides many works dealing with philosophy, he publ. the following concerning music: *Introduction à la Psychologie du Musicien* (Paris, 1891), *La Psychologie dans l'opéra français* (Paris, 1897), *Essai sur l'esprit musical* (Paris, 1904), *Rossini, biographie critique* (Paris, 1905), *Le Musicien-poète Richard Wagner* (Paris, 1908), *Meyerbeer* (Paris, 1913).

Daussoigne-Méhul, Louis-Joseph, French composer; b. Givet, Ardennes, June 10, 1790; d. Liège, March 10, 1875. Nephew and foster-son of **Étienne-Nicolas Méhul.** Pupil of Catel and Méhul at the Cons.; took the Grand Prix de Rome in 1809; after writing 4 operas, which were rejected, he at length produced his 1-act *Aspasie* at the Grand Opéra (1820) with moderate success. He did still better with *Valentine de Milan,* a 3-act opera left unfinished by Méhul, which he completed. In 1827 he accepted the directorship of Liège Cons., which he retained, with great benefit to the school, until 1862. Daussoigne-Méhul was an associate of the Royal Academy, Brussels. He brought out a cantata with full orch. in 1828, and a choral symphony *(Une journée de la Révolution)* in 1834.

Dauvergne, Antoine, French composer and conductor; b. Clermont-Ferrand, Oct. 3, 1713; d. Lyons, Feb. 11, 1797. He received his first instruction from his father, went for further study to Paris, in 1739, and was appointed violinist in the Royal orch. (1741); 1755 appointed composer to the Royal orch.; 1762 conductor of "Concerts Spirituels," after 1769 active as conductor and manager of various enterprises, until his retirement to Lyons in 1790. He introduced into France the forms of the Italian intermezzo, substituting spoken dialogue for the recitative, and thus was the originator of a style that soon became typical of French dramatic composition. He wrote 15 operas, the first of which *(Les Troqueurs)* was produced at Paris in 1753, and is regarded as the first opéra-comique; wrote 2 books of symphonies, 12 sonatas for violin and basso continuo, etc.

Davenport, Francis William, English composer; b. Wilderslowe near Derby, April 9, 1847; d. Scarborough, April 1, 1925. He studied law at Oxford, but preferred music, and became the pupil (later son-in-law) of Sir G. A. Macfarren. In 1879, prof. at the Royal Academy of Music, and at the Guildhall School of Music in 1882.

WORKS: 2 symphonies; overture, *Twelfth Night;* 6 pieces for piano and cello; *Pictures on a Journey,* a series of piano pieces; part-songs and songs.

Davenport, Marcia (*née* **Abigail Gluck**), American writer on music; b. New York, June 9, 1903. She studied at Wellesley College and at the Univ. of Grenoble, France (graduated 1925). She has written successful novels, including one on a musical subject *(Of Lena Geyer,* based to some extent on the life of her mother **Alma Gluck,** 1936); a biography of Mozart (1932), and the memoirs, *Too Strong for Fantasy* (N.Y., 1967).

Davey, Henry, English musicologist; b. Brighton, Nov. 29, 1853; d. Hove, Sussex, Aug. 28, 1929. He entered Leipzig Cons. in 1874, devoting himself chiefly to theoretical studies; lived for several years in Brighton as teacher. Publ. *The Student's Musical History* (London, 1895; 2nd ed. 1921), a valuable work, the result of original research, and *History of English Music* (1921; repr. N.Y., 1969).

Davico, Vincenzo, Italian composer; b. Monaco, Jan. 14, 1889; d. Rome, Dec. 8, 1969. He studied in Turin, and later in Leipzig with Max Reger; graduated from the Leipzig Cons. in 1911; then he settled in Rome.

WORKS: the operas *La dogaressa* (Monte Carlo, Feb. 26, 1920) and *La Principessa prigioniera* (Bergamo, Sept. 29, 1940); ballets *L'agonia della rosa* (Paris, May 2, 1927), *Narciso* (San Remo, Feb. 19, 1935); oratorio, *La Tentation de Saint Antoine* (Monte Carlo, Dec. 15, 1921); *Requiem per la morte d'un povero* (1950); for orch.: *La Principessa lontana* (after Rostand's *Princesse lointaine;* won the Augusteo prize, 1911); *Poema erotico* (also won the Augusteo prize, 1913); *Polifemo,* symph. poem (Turin, 1920); *Impressioni dal mio diario di viaggio* (1949); piano pieces and numerous songs.

BIBLIOGRAPHY: G. Franchi, *Vincenzo Davico* (1924); Raymond Petit, *Les Mélodies de Vincenzo Davico* (Nice, 1925); Massimo Gaglione, "Vincenzo Davico," in his book *I giovani.*

David, Félicien-César, French composer; b. Cadenet, Vaucluse, Apr. 13, 1810; d. St.-Germain-en-Laye, Aug. 29, 1876. Of precocious talent, he was taught in the maîtrise of St.-Sauveur at Aix from 1818–25. He had a fine voice, and composed hymns, motets, and other music. He then studied in the Jesuit college for 3 years; became assistant conductor in the theater at Aix, and in 1829 maître de chapelle at St.-Sauveur; but a longing to widen his musical horizon drew him to Paris (1830), where he submitted specimens of compositions to Cherubini, and was admitted to the Cons., studying harmony with Reber and Millot, and counterpoint and fugue with Fétis. In 1831, when the meagre allowance given him by a rich and avaricious uncle had been withdrawn, he joined the socialistic movement of the St.-Simonists at Ménilmontant; here he composed a series of 4-part *hymnes* for men's voices (later publ. with the words, as the *Ruche harmonieuse*). On the dispersion of the society in 1833, David went to Marseilles with a group of the brotherhood, giving concerts on the way; they proceeded to Constantinople, Smyrna, and Egypt, where they finally dispersed; with an imagination stimulated by his long sojourn in the East, David returned alone to Paris in 1835. He now publ. a collection of *Mélodies orientales*; they met with small success, and he retired to the country, giving himself up to study and composition (2 symphonies, 24 small string quintets, 2 nonets for wind, romances, etc.). In 1838 his First Symphony was produced. On Dec. 8, 1844, he at last reaped the fruit of many years' study: his symphonic ode *Le Désert* was received at its first performance in the hall of the Cons. with 'delirious' applause, and a series of repeat performances were given to crowded houses at the Salle Ventadour for a month. The oratorio *Moïse au Sinai* followed in 1846, but, like a second symphonic ode, *Christophe Colomb* (Paris, March 7, 1847), and *L'Éden* (a 'mystery' in 2 parts, Grand Opéra, Aug. 25, 1848), met with a cool reception. However, his opera *La Perle du Brésil* (Théâtre-Lyrique, Nov. 22, 1851) was quite successful; a second, *Le Dernier Amour*, was rejected by the Grand Opéra and by the Théâtre-Lyrique; but the Grand Opéra accepted in 1859 as *Herculanum*, and for this opera the great state prize of 20,000 francs was awarded to David in 1867. *Lalla Roukh* (May 12, 1862) and *Le Saphir* (1865) were given at the Opéra-Comique (the former with great success, the latter with scarcely a 'succès d'estime'). David now abandoned dramatic composition, withdrawing his last opera, *La Captive*. In 1869 he was elected Académicien, taking Berlioz's chair, and succeeding him also as librarian of the Cons. Besides the above works, he wrote 12 melodies for cello; *Les Brises d'Orient*, piano pieces; *Les Minarets*, 3 piano pieces; *Les Perles d'Orient*, 6 melodies for voice and piano; etc.

BIBLIOGRAPHY: A. Azevedo, *Félicien David, Sa vie et son œuvre* (Paris, 1863); C. Bellaigue, "Félicien David," in *Études musicales et nouvelles silhouettes* (Paris, 1898); J.-G. Prod'homme, "Félicien David d'après sa correspondance inédite," in *Mercure Musical* II, III (1907); R. Brancour, *Félicien David* (Paris, 1911).

David, Ferdinand, German violinist and pedagogue; b. Hamburg, Jan. 19, 1810; d. near Klosters, Switzerland, July 18, 1873. From 1823–24 he studied with Spohr and Hauptmann at Kassel; played in the Gewandhaus, Leipzig, 1825; in 1827 became a member of the Königstadt Theater in Berlin. In 1829 he became the first violinist in the private string quartet of the wealthy amateur Baron von Liphardt of Dorpat, Russia, whose daughter he married. He remained in Russia until 1835, giving concerts in Riga, Moscow, and St. Petersburg with great acclaim. In 1836, at Mendelssohn's suggestion, he was appointed first violinist of the Gewandhaus Orch. in Leipzig, of which Mendelssohn was the conductor. They became warm friends; Mendelssohn had a great regard for him, and consulted him constantly while writing his Violin Concerto, and it was David who gave its first performance (Leipzig, March 13, 1845). When the Leipzig Cons. was established in 1843, David became one of its most important teachers; his class was regarded as the finishing school of the most talented violinists in Europe; among his pupils were Joachim and Wilhelmj. He published many valuable editions of violin

works by classical composers, notably *Die Hohe Schule des Violinspiels*, containing French and Italian masterpieces of the 17th and 18th centuries. His numerous violin exercises were still used by students. His pedagogical activities did not interfere with his concert career; he played in England in 1839 and 1841 with excellent success and was compared with Spohr as a virtuoso; also made occasional appearances on the continent.

WORKS: 5 violin concertos; many other pieces for violin; an opera *Hans Wacht* (Leipzig, 1852); 2 symphonies; string quartets and other chamber music. His violin pieces *Bunte Reihe* were transcribed for piano by Liszt.

BIBLIOGRAPHY: J. Eckardt, *Ferdinand David und die Familie Mendelssohn-Bartholdy* (Leipzig, 1888); A. Bachmann, "Ferdinand David," in *Les Grands Violinistes du passé* (Paris, 1913).

Dávid, Gyula, Hungarian composer; b. Budapest, May 6, 1913; d. there, March 14, 1977. He studied with Kodály at the Academy of Music in Budapest; won the Erkel Prize in 1952 and 1955 and the Kossuth Prize in 1957. His music is marked by a fashionable modernism, while retaining the traditional virtues of euphonious tonality.

WORKS: 4 symphonies (1947, 1957, 1960, 1970); Viola Concerto (1950); Sinfonietta (1960); *Felhőtlenég (Cloudless Skies)*, cantata (1964); Violin Concerto (1966); *Égö szavakkal (With Flaming Words)*, cantata (1969); Horn Concerto (1971); 5 wind quintets (1949; 1955; 1964; 1967; 1968); Flute Sonata (1955); Piano Sonata (1955); 2 string quartets (1962, 1974); *Miniatures* for brass sextet (1968); Violin Sonata (1968); Viola Sonatina (1969); Sonata for Violin Solo (1971); Piano Trio (1972); incidental music; songs and motets.

BIBLIOGRAPHY: J. Breuer, *Dávid Gyula* (Budapest, 1966).

David, Hans Theodore, American musicologist; b. Speyer, Palatinate, July 8, 1902; d. Ann Arbor, Mich., Oct. 30, 1967. He studied at various German universities; received the degree of Dr. phil. at Berlin (1928). In 1936 he emigrated to the U.S.; occupied various positions as researcher and librarian; headed dept. of musicology at Southern Methodist Univ. in Dallas, Texas; in 1950 was appointed to the faculty of the Univ. of Michigan. He published *J. S. Bach's Musical Offering, History, Interpretation and Analysis* (N.Y., 1945); ed., with A. Mendel, *The Bach Reader* (N.Y., 1945); co-author, with A. G. Rau, of *A Catalogue of Music of American Moravians* (Bethlehem, Pa., 1938); ed. Bach's *Art of Fugue, Musical Offering* and *Overture in the French Manner* (first version); *English Instrumental Music of the 16th and 17th Centuries*, etc. A biographical sketch is contained in the *Quarterly Journal of the Riemenschneider Bach Inst.* (July 1970).

David, Johann Nepomuk, outstanding Austrian composer; b. Eferding, Nov. 30, 1895; d. Stuttgart, Dec. 21, 1977. He studied with Joseph Marx at the Vienna Academy (1920–23); was organist in Wels, Upper Austria (1924–33); in 1934 was engaged as professor of composition at the Leipzig Cons., becoming its director in 1939. He was subsequently director at the Salzburg Mozarteum (1945–47). In 1947 he was appointed professor of composition at the Musikhochschule in Stuttgart, serving until 1963. David's music is severely polyphonic in its structure; almost all of his instrumental works are cast in forms influenced by the late Baroque; his mastery of counterpoint is revealed in his many choral pieces.

WORKS: For orch.: 8 symphonies (1936, 1938, 1941, 1948, 1951, 1954, 1956, 1965); Concerto Grosso for Chamber Orch. (1923); 2 Partitas (1935, 1940); 2 Concertos for string orch. (1949, 1950); Flute Concerto (1949); Violin Concerto (1952; Stuttgart Radio, April 25, 1954); *Sinfonia preclassica* (1953); *Sinfonia breve* (1955); 2nd Violin Concerto (1957); *Melancholia* for viola and chamber orch. (1958); *Sinfonia per archi* (1959); *Magische Quadrate*, a symph. fantasy on serial principles (1959); *Spiegelkabinett*, waltzes for orch. (1960); Organ Concerto (1965); *Variations on a Theme by Josquin* for flute, horn, and strings (1966); Concerto for violin, cello, and small orch. (1969); Chamber music: Clarinet Quintet (1924); 3 string quartets; Sonata for 3 Cellos (1962); several solo sonatas (for flute, for violin, for viola, for cello). Choral works: *Stabat Mater* in 6 parts (1927); *Mensch, werde wesentlich*, for men's voices; *Requiem chorale* for soloists, chorus and orch. (1956); oratorio, *Das Ezzolied*, for soli, chorus, and orch. (1957); many motets. Numerous organ works (*Chaconne, Ricercare, Fantasia super L'homme armé*, etc.); songs, piano pieces, etc. He is the author of a study of Mozart's *Jupiter Symphony* (2nd ed., 1956).

BIBLIOGRAPHY: H. H. Stuckenschmidt, articles in *Neue Zeitschrift für Musik* (Feb. 1932; Jan. 1937; Sept. 1938); K. H. Wörner, "J. N. David," in *Musik der Gegenwart* (Mainz, 1949); R. Klein, *J. N. David* (Vienna, 1964); H. H. Stuckenschmidt, *J. N. David* (Wiesbaden, 1965); R. Klein, "Neues von J.N.D.," *Österreichische Musikzeitschrift* (Nov. 1968); G. Sievers, ed. *Ex Deo nascimur. Festschrift zum 75. Geburtstag von J.N.D.* (Wiesbaden, 1970).

David, José, French composer, son of the singer **Léon David**; b. Sables-d'Olonne, Jan. 6, 1913. He entered the Paris Cons. in 1933; studied with Fauchet, Jacques de la Presle and Henri Busser; also took organ lessons with Marcel Dupré and music history with Maurice Emmanuel. He was mobilized in 1939 and served in the artillery regiment of the French Army during World War II. After the armistice he returned to Paris.

WORKS: *Impressions de Vendée* for piano (1944; also for orch.); *La Ballade de Florentin Prunier* for voice, violin, cello and piano (1947); *Symphonie* for Ondes Martenot and orch. (1948); ballet, *Jacquet le Prioux* (1950); Violin Sonata (1955); *Laudate Dominum* for 3 male voices and organ (1960); *2 Poems* for voice and piano (1973). He collaborated with Nicolas Obouhov in *Traité d'Harmonie Tonale et Atonale* (Paris, 1947).

David, Karl Heinrich, Swiss composer; b. St. Gall, Dec. 30, 1884; d. Nervi, Italy, May 17, 1951. He studied in Cologne and Munich; taught at the Basel Cons. (1910–14); then at Cologne and Berlin (1914–17); in 1918 returned to Switzerland. He was the editor of the *Schweizer Musikzeitung* in Zürich (1928–41).

WORKS: operas: *Aschenputtel* (Basel, Oct. 21, 1921); *Der Sizilianer* (Zürich, Oct. 22, 1924); *Jugendfestspiel* (Zürich, June 8, 1924); *Traumwandel* (Zürich, Jan. 29, 1928); *Weekend*, a comic opera (1933). Other works: Piano Concerto (1929); *Ballet* for orch. (1931); *Pezzo sinfonico* (1945); Concerto for Saxophone and String Orch. (1947); *Symphonie de la côte d'argent* (1948); *Mascarade*, overture (1950); *Andante and Rondo* for violin and chamber orch.; Two Pieces for Piano and 9 Woodwinds; Viola Suite; Piano Trio; Quartet for Saxophone, Violin, Cello, Piano (1946); Duet for Horn and Piano (1951); *Das hohe Lied Salomonis* for soprano, tenor, female chorus and orch.; songs.

David, Léon, French tenor; b. Sables-d'Olonne, Dec. 18, 1867; d. there, Oct. 27, 1962. He studied singing at the Cons. of Nantes and later at the Paris Cons.; made his debut at the Opéra-Comique in Paris in 1892; appeared subsequently in Brussels, Monte Carlo, Marseille, Bordeaux, Cairo, Lisbon, Bucharest, etc. He was prof. of singing at the Paris Cons. from 1924 to 1938.

David, Samuel, French composer; b. Paris, Nov. 12, 1836; d. there, Oct. 3, 1895. He studied at the Cons. with Halévy; won the Grand Prix de Rome (1858) for his cantata *Jephté*, and another prize for a work for male chorus and orch., *Le Génie de la terre*, performed by chorus of 6,000 singers (1859); professor at Collège de Sainte-Barbe (1861); music director in Jewish synagogues of Paris (1872). He wrote several operas, 4 symphonies, choruses, and songs.

Davidenko, Alexander, Russian composer; b. Odessa, April 1, 1899; d. Moscow, May 1, 1934. He organized, with Belyi, the Procoll (Production Collective of Composers) in Russia in 1925; wrote workers' songs. His most important work is the opera *1905* (written in 1929–33, with Boris Schechter); another opera, *Down the Cliff*, was left incomplete.

BIBLIOGRAPHY: M. Koval, "At the Side of Alexander Davidenko," *Sovietskaia Muzyka* (Feb. 1967); N. Martynov, ed., *Alexander Davidenko* (Leningrad, 1968).

Davidov, Carl, outstanding Russian violoncellist; b. Goldingen, Latvia, March 15, 1838; d. Moscow, Feb. 26, 1889. He studied cello in Moscow with Heinrich Schmidt and in St. Petersburg with K. Schuberth; in 1859 he went to Leipzig where he studied theory of composition with Hauptmann. In 1860 at the age of 22 he was appointed instructor at the Leipzig Cons. In 1862 he returned to Russia; from 1862 till 1887 was prof. of the St. Petersburg Cons., and acting director from 1876 to 1887. He made several European tours, during which he played recitals with Anton Rubinstein, Saint-Saëns and Liszt. Davidov was also a reputable composer; he wrote 4 cello concertos; a fantasy on Russian songs for cello and orch.; symph. poem, *The Gifts of the Terek River*; String Quartet; String Sextet; Piano Quintet; songs; publ. a cello method

(Leipzig, 1888; Russian ed., supervised by L. Gins-burg, Moscow, 1947).

BIBLIOGRAPHY: V. Hutor, *Carl Davidov und seine Art das Violoncell zu behandeln* (Moscow, 1899); S. Ginsburg, *Carl Davidov* (Moscow, 1950).

Davidovsky, Mario, Argentinian composer; b. Buenos Aires, March 4, 1934. He studied there with Ernesto Epstein and others; went to the U.S. in 1958; held two consecutive Guggenheim Fellowships (1960–62); worked in the electronic music center of Columbia Univ. and Princeton Univ. In 1971 he was appointed a prof. at the City College of N.Y. His method of composition tends towards mathematical parameters; his series of *Synchronisms* derives from the numerical coordinates of acoustical elements; electronic sound is integral to most of Davidovsky's output.

WORKS: String Quartet No. 1 (1954); Clarinet Quintet (1956); Nonet (1957); Concerto for Strings and Percussion (1957); String Quartet No. 2 (1958); *Suite Sinfónica para el Payaso* (1958); *Serie Sinfónica* (1959); *Planos* for orch. (1961); *2 Studies* for electronic sound (1961, 1962); *Contrasts* for strings and electronic sound (1962); *Inflexions* for 14 instruments (1965); 7 pieces under the generic title, *Synchronisms*: No. 1–6 for different instrumental groups (1963–70), and No. 7 for orch. and tape (1974; N.Y. Philharmonic, Dec. 4, 1975); *Chacona* for piano trio (1972); a cantata-opera, *Scenes from Shir Hashirim*, for 4 voices and chamber ensemble (1975–76). His *Synchronisms No. 6* for piano and electronic sound was awarded the 1971 Pulitzer Prize.

Davidson, Harold Gibson, American pianist and composer; b. Low Moor, Virginia, Feb. 20, 1893; d. Glendale, California, Dec. 14, 1959. He studied at the Cincinnati Cons.; taught at several schools; settled in California. His music is of an experimental nature, exemplified by such titles as *Auto Accident* and *Hell's Bells* (for percussion); *Two Minor Disturbances and One Major Calamity*, piano suite; *Legend of the Flying Saucers*, etc.

Davies, Ben (Benjamin) Grey, Welsh tenor; b. Pontardawe, near Swansea, S. Wales, Jan. 6, 1858; d. Bath, England, March 28, 1943. He studied at the Royal Academy of Music under Randegger, winning the bronze, silver, and gold medals, for best declamatory English singing; debut at Birmingham, Oct. 11, 1881, in *The Bohemian Girl.* He made several American tours beginning in 1893.

Davies, Fanny, English pianist; b. Guernsey, June 27, 1861; d. London, Sept. 1, 1934. She studied at the Leipzig Cons. with Reinecke and Paul (piano) and Jadassohn (theory) from 1882–83, and at the Hoch Cons., Frankfurt, with Clara Schumann (1883–85); also was a pupil of Scholz in fugue and composition. Her London debut took place at the Crystal Palace, Oct. 17, 1885; then she made successful tours in England, Germany, France, and Italy.

Davies, Sir Henry Walford, eminent English organist, educator and composer; b. Oswestry, Sept. 6, 1869; d. Wrington, Somerset, March 11, 1941. He was a pupil of Sir Walter Parratt at the Park Chapel in Windsor, where he also served as organist (1885–90); then held positions as organist at Christ Church, Hampstead (1891–98), at the Temple Church (1898–1923) and at St. George's Chapel Windsor (1924–32). Between 1924 and 1934 he led the novel broadcasting series "Music Lessons in Schools." He was knighted in 1922; was appointed Master of the King's Musick in 1934. He composed mostly sacred choruses.

WORKS: choruses: *The Temple* (1902), *Lift up Your Hearts* (1906); *Five Sayings of Jesus* (1911); *Heaven's Gate* (1916); *Men and Angels* (1925); *Christ in the Universe* (1929); also wrote several orchestral overtures: *Dedication Overture* (1893); *Festal Overture* (1910); and many works for school performance, including *A Children's Symphony* (1927), *London Calling the Schools* for piano, orch. and radio announcer (1932); *Conversations* for piano and orch. (London, Oct. 14, 1914); 2 violin sonatas (1894, 1896); *Peter Pan* for string quartet (1909); numerous part songs. He publ. *The Musical Outlook in Wales* (London, 1926); *The Pursuit of Music* (London, 1935); *Music and Worship* (with Harvey Grace, London, 1935).

BIBLIOGRAPHY: H. C. Colles, *Walford Davies, A Biography* (London, 1942).

Davies, Peter Maxwell, English composer; b. Manchester, Sept. 8, 1934. He studied at the Royal Manchester College of Music; in 1957 went to Rome to study with Goffredo Petrassi; from 1959–62 he was Director of Music at Cirencester Grammar School; in 1962 went to the U.S. and studied with Roger Sessions at Princeton Univ. In his music he effects a non-eclectic synthesis of disparate styles and idioms, ranging from Renaissance polyphony to serial organization; in some of his works he also applies precepts of controlled improvisation.

WORKS: Sonata for Trumpet and Piano (1955); *5 Pieces* for piano (1956); *Alma Redemptoris Mater* for wind sextet (1957); *St. Michael*, sonata for 17 wind instruments (1957); *Prolation* for orch. (1958); *Ricercar and Doubles* for 8 instruments (1959); *5 Motets for a cappella Chorus* (1959); *O Magnum Mysterium*, cycle of carols and instrumental sonatas (1960); String Quartet (1961); *Te Lucis ante Terminum*, cycle of carols with instrumental sonatas (1961); *Leopardi Fragments*, settings for soprano, contralto and chamber ensemble (1961); *Sinfonia* for chamber orch. (1962); *2 Fantasias on In nomine of John Taverner* for orch. (1962; 1964); *Veni sancte Spiritus* for soloists, chorus and orch. (1962); *Shakespeare Music*, a set of dances for 11 instruments (1963); *5 Motets for Voices, Chorus and Instruments* (1964); *Revelation and Fall* for soprano and chamber orch. (1965–66); *Antechrist* for chamber ensemble (1967); *L'Homme armé* for chamber ensemble and speaker (1968); *Worldes Blis* for orch. (London, Aug. 28, 1969); *Eight Songs for a Mad King* (George III) for voice and instruments (London, April 22, 1969); *Vesalii Icones*, for solo cello, wind instruments and piano, in 14 movements, after 14 anatomical drawings by Vesalius (London, Dec. 9, 1969); *From Stone to Thorn* for soprano and chamber ensemble (1971); *Blind Man's Buff* for soprano, dancer, mime, and small ensemble (1972); *Hymn to*

St. Magnus for soprano and chamber ensemble (1972); *Ave Maria Stella* for instruments (1974); *Miss Donnithorne's Maggot* for soprano and 6 instruments (1975); *A Stone Litany* for mezzo-soprano and orch. (London, March 7, 1975). In 1972 he fashioned materials from John Taverner's *In Nomine* into an opera entitled *Taverner*, produced at Covent Garden, July 12, 1972.

BIBLIOGRAPHY: R. Henderson, "Peter Maxwell Davies," *Musical Times* (Oct. 1961); many articles on individual works in the journal *Tempo.*

Davis, Colin, English conductor; b. Weybridge, Surrey, Sept. 25, 1927. He played the clarinet in various orchestras in London; at the same time did national service in the Household Cavalry. He studied academic musical subjects at the Royal College of Music in London, but was entirely autodidact in conducting, which he learned from printed manuals. He showed his mettle in 1952 when he was called upon to lead a concert performance of *Don Giovanni* unexpectedly for the suddenly indisposed Otto Klemperer, and displayed fine fettle again as a substitute for the ailing Sir Thomas Beecham in 1960 at the Glyndebourne Festival. Rapidly advancing in his career, he became assistant conductor of the BBC Scottish Orch. in Glasgow (1957–59); then was principal conductor at Sadler's Wells Opera in London. In 1967 he was appointed chief conductor of the BBC Symph. Orch., and in 1971 musical director of the Royal (Covent Garden) Opera. He made his entrance on the American scene with the Minneapolis Symph. Orch. in 1961, and subsequently conducted concerts with the New York Philharmonic, the Boston Symph., the Philadelphia Orch., the Los Angeles Philharmonic, etc. In 1968 he made his Metropolitan Opera debut in New York in a performance of Benjamin Britten's *Peter Grimes*; also appeared as guest conductor in major musical centers on the continent, including Russia, and in Canada. In 1965 he was created Commander of the Order of the British Empire. A scholar as well as a musician, Davis impresses his audiences and professional critics by the clarity of his interpretations.

Davis, Ivan, American pianist; b. Electra, Texas, Feb. 4, 1932. He studied piano with Silvio Scionti at North Texas State Univ. in Denton and later at the Academy of St. Cecilia in Rome with Carlo Zecchi. He also took private lessons with Vladimir Horowitz beginning in 1961. He obtained first prizes at Busoni Competition in Bolzano (1958), at Casella Competition at Naples (1958), and at the Franz Liszt Competition in New York (1960). He appeared as soloist with the N.Y. Philharmonic, Boston Symphony Orch., Philadelphia Orch., Chicago Symphony, London Symphony, Concertgebouw in Amsterdam, etc. In 1970 he was artist in residence at the Univ. of Miami at Coral Gables, Florida.

Davis, John David, English composer and music teacher; b. Birmingham, Oct. 22, 1867; d. Estoril, Portugal, Nov. 20, 1942. He studied music at Frankfurt and Brussels; returned to England in 1889; taught in various schools in Birmingham; in 1905, was appointed prof. of composition at the Guildhall School

of Music in London. He wrote an opera on a Russian subject, *The Zaporogue Cossacks*, which was produced in Birmingham on May 7, 1895; also a concert overture *Germania*; 2 string quartets; 2 violin sonatas; piano pieces and songs.

Davis, Miles Dewey, American jazz trumpeter and innovative band leader; b. Alton, Illinois, May 25, 1926. He played trumpet as a youth; studied at Juilliard in 1945; left in 1946 to be a full-time musician, working with Charlie Parker, Coleman Hawkins, Benny Carter and Billy Eckstein. His bebop style was modified in 1948–50 as a band he led (which included such an "untypically jazz" instrument as the French horn, played by Gunther Schuller) developed a "cool" style, a lyrical, understated manner that contrasted significantly with the frantic "hot" approach of bebop. His penchant for innovation again showed itself in 1958 as his album "Kind of Blue" introduced a style of jazz based on modal patterns, a major trend for the following decade. Meanwhile, in the 1960s and '70s he embarked upon Electronic jazz ("Bitches Brew," 1970) and the fusion style of jazz-rock.

Davison, Archibald Thompson, eminent American music educator; b. Boston, Oct. 11, 1883; d. Brant Rock, Cape Cod, Mass., Feb. 6, 1961. He studied at Harvard Univ. (B.A., 1906; M.A., 1907; Ph.D., 1908); took lessons in organ with Widor in Paris. Returning to America, he was organist and choirmaster of Harvard Univ. (1910–40); conducted the Harvard Glee Club (1912–33) and the Radcliffe Choral Society (1913–28); he was professor of music at Harvard until his retirement in 1954. He held numerous honorary degrees, including those of Mus. Doc. at Williams College and Oxford Univ.; Fellow of the Royal College of Music, London; Litt. D. from Washington Univ. (1953) and L.H.D. from Temple Univ. (1955). He wrote a musical comedy, *The Girl and the Chauffeur*, upon his graduation from Harvard (performed in Boston, April 16, 1906) and the overtures *Hero and Leander* (1908) and *Tragic Overture* (1918). His greatest achievement was as an educator and popularizer of musical subjects: his lectures on music appreciation were broadcast and enjoyed considerable success among radio listeners. He was associate editor with Thomas W. Surette, of a multi-volume collection of vocal and instrumental pieces, Concord Series, for which he made numerous arrangements.

WRITINGS: *Music Education in America* (1926); *Protestant Church Music in America* (1920; enlarged ed., 1933); *Harvard University Hymn Book* (with E. C. Moore, 1926); *Choral Conducting* (1945); edited with W. Apel, *Historical Anthology of Music* (Cambridge, Mass., 2 vols., 1946; revised ed., 1949); *Bach and Handel: the Consummation of the Baroque in Music* (Cambridge, Mass., 1951); *Church Music; Illusion and Reality* (Cambridge, Mass., 1952). A dedicatory volume, *Essays on Music in Honor of A. T. Davison by His Associates,* was published at Cambridge in 1957.

Davison, James William, renowned English music critic; b. London, Oct. 5, 1813; d. Margate, March 24, 1885. Editor of the *Musical Examiner* (1842–44) and the *Musical World* (1844–85); contributor to the *Sat-*

urday Review, Pall Mall Gazette, and *Graphic;* was the influential critic of *The Times* (1846–79). In 1860 he married his pupil, **Arabella Goddard.** He wrote the analytical program books for the Popular Concerts and the Hallé recitals; composed a few songs, several piano pieces, and a dramatic overture (for piano duet) to *Fortunatus,* a fairy tale. His memoirs were published by H. Davison as *From Mendelssohn to Wagner* (1912).

Davy, John, English song composer and violinist; b. Upton-Helions, near Exeter, Dec. 23, 1763; d. London, Feb. 22, 1824. He studied at Exeter, and then settled in London, where he played the violin at Covent Garden. He wrote the music to a number of plays: *A Pennyworth of Wit* (London, April 18, 1796); *Alfred, the Great,* a 'grand historical ballet' (London, June 4, 1798); etc. "The Bay of Biscay, O!", one of the songs from his incidental music to a play, *Spanish Dollars,* was extremely popular.

Dawson, Ted, Canadian composer; b. Victoria, British Columbia, April 28, 1951. He studied violin, viola and piano at the Victoria Cons. (1964–68); then took courses in music theory with Cherney and Komorous at the Univ. of Victoria (1968–72) and in composition with Hambraeus and electronic music with Alcides Lanza at McGill Univ. in Montreal (1973–74); subsequently engaged in teaching. WORKS: *Pentad* for string quartet (1971); *Concerto Grosso I* for quadraphonic tape, or amplified viola, amplified bassoon, trombone, percussion and stereo tape (1973–74); *Concerto Grosso II* for 5 instrumental soloists and orch. (1973); *Chameleon* for solo amplified viola (1974); *Chameleon* for solo amplified flute (1974–75); *The Clouds of Magellan* for 3 slide projectors, computerized dissolver, synchronization tape, and quadraphonic audiotape (1976–77); *Binaries in Lyrae* for 4 dancers, 2 amplified percussion ensembles, amplified piano, and lights (1977–78); *Megatherium* for 2 amplified pianos, synthesizer, and audiotape (1977–78).

Dawson, William Levi, American composer; b. Anniston, Alabama, Sept. 26, 1898. At the age of 13, he ran away from home to enter Tuskegee Institute; later played trombone on the Redpath Chautauqua Circuit; graduated from Tuskegee Institute in 1921; later studied with Carl Busch in Kansas City and at the American Cons. in Chicago. He received his M.A. in 1927. He played first trombone in the Chicago Civic Orch. (1926–30); then conducted the Tuskegee Choir. Among his works is a Negro folk symphony in 3 movements (Philadelphia Orch., Stokowski conducting, Nov. 16, 1934).

Day, Major Charles Russell, English writer on music; b. Horstead, Norwich, in 1860; d. Paardeberg, South Africa, Feb. 18, 1900. He was a soldier in the British army from 1880; served in India, later in South Africa where he was killed in battle. His chief work was *Music and Musical Instruments of Southern India and the Deccan* (London, 1891); also published *A Descriptive Catalogue of the Musical Instruments Recently Exhibited at the Royal Military Exhibition, London,* *1890* (London, 1891), and papers and pamphlets on national and military music. BIBLIOGRAPHY: A. J. Hipkins, in the *Musical Times* (April 1900).

Dayas, William Humphreys, American organist and teacher; b. New York, Sept. 12, 1863; d. Manchester, England, May 3, 1903. He studied piano with Joseffy; then went to Germany, and was one of Liszt's last pupils at Weimar; also studied there with Kullak, Haupt, Ehrlich, and Urban. He was piano teacher in Helsingfors Cons. (1890); taught in Düsseldorf (1894), Wiesbaden and Cologne; returned for a while to N.Y., and then settled in Manchester (1896), where he taught at the Music College.

De Ahna, Heinrich Karl Hermann, Austrian violinist; b. Vienna, June 22, 1835; d. Berlin, Nov. 1, 1892. He studied in Vienna with Mayseder and at the Prague Cons. with Mildner; made his debut as violinist at the age of 12, at Vienna, London, etc. He settled in 1862 in Berlin as a member of the Royal Orch., becoming its concertmaster in 1868.

Deák, Csaba, Hungarian-born Swedish composer; b. Budapest, April 16, 1932. He studied clarinet and composition in Budapest (1949–56); came to Sweden in 1957 and took lessons in composition with Hilding Rosenberg. In 1971 he was appointed to the staff of the Univ. of Göteborg. In his music he applies a modified type of dodecaphonic techniques. WORKS: a chamber opera, *Fäderna (The Ancestors)* for 3 singers, percussion and tape (Stockholm, Oct. 16, 1968); *Rondo* for piano (1957); *Jubilemus Salvatori,* chamber cantata (1958); Sonatina for Solo Clarinet (1958); 2 string quartets (1959, 1967); *Duo Suite* for flute and clarinet (1960); *Danaiderna* for narrator and chorus (1964); Wind Quintet (1965); *Klarinettofoni* for electronically altered clarinets (1968); *I 21* for winds, percussion and double bass (1969); an electronic ballet, *Etyd om våren (Spring Étude,* 1970); Trio for Flute, Cello and Piano (1971); *Ska vi göra musik?* for children's voices, cello, percussion and tape (1972); *Andante and Rondo* for wind quintet (1973); *Piri* for chorus and percussion (1973); music for theater productions.

Deakin, Andrew, English publisher and bibliographer; b. Birmingham, April 13, 1822; d. there, Dec. 21, 1903. While serving his apprenticeship as a printer, he taught himself music; established a publishing house in Birmingham, and held several positions as organist. His chief work is *Outlines of Musical Bibliography* (Birmingham, 1899), a catalogue of works on music printed in England from the 15th to the 18th century.

Dean, Winton, English musicologist; b. Birkenhead, March 18, 1916. He studied at King's College, Cambridge (B.A., 1938; M.A., 1941). Although he had no professional training in music, he became interested in musical biography. WRITINGS: monograph on Bizet in the Master Musicians series (London, 1948); also biographies on Handel, Franck, and Puccini; *Handel and the Opera Seria* (Berkeley, 1969).

Debain, Alexandre-François, the inventor of the harmonium; b. Paris, 1809; d. there, Dec. 3, 1877. He established a factory of pianos and organs in Paris (1834), and after long experimentation with free reeds patented his 'harmonium' in 1840. He also invented the 'antiphonel' and the 'harmonichorde' and improved the accordion.

De Boeck, Auguste, Belgian composer; b. Merchtem, near Brussels, May 9, 1865; d. there, Oct. 9, 1937. He studied composition with Paul Gilson; De Boeck taught organ (1893–1902) and harmony (1920–30) at the Brussels Cons. and was director of the Cons. at Mechelen (1920–30); also taught organ at the Antwerp Cons. (1909–21).
WORKS: 5 operas: *Théroigne de Méricourt* (1901), *Winternachtsdroom* (*Le Song d'une nuit d'hiver,* 1903), *De Rijndevergen* (*Les Gnomes du Rhin,* 1906), *Reinaert le Renard* (1909) and *Francesca* (*La route d'Émeraude,* 1921); 3 ballets: *Assepoes* (*Cendrillon,* 1895), *De Nachtvlinder* (*La Phalène,* 1896) and *La Tentation du Poète* (1929); *Rhapsodie Dahoméenne* for orch. (1893); Symphony (1896); *Fantaisie sur deux airs flamande* for orch. (1923); Violin Concerto (1925); various pieces for piano; songs, etc.

Debussy, Claude (Achille-Claude), great French composer; b. St.-Germain-en-Laye, Aug. 22, 1862; d. Paris, March 25, 1918. Mme. de Fleurville, a pupil of Chopin, prepared him for the Cons. at Paris, where he was admitted at the age of 10. Here he continued his study of piano with Marmontel, and won the second prize in 1877; in the solfeggio class of Lavignac he won the medal three years in succession (1874; 1875; 1876). Émile Durand was his teacher in the harmony class (1876–80); he received no awards there. After his graduation in 1880, Debussy was recommended to Mme. Nadezhda von Meck, Tchaikovsky's patroness, as a household pianist to teach piano to her children and play four hands with them. She summoned him to Switzerland, where she was traveling (he was not quite 18 at the time), and took him to Italy and Russia; he stayed with her family in Moscow and at her country estate in the summer of 1881, and again in 1882. There he had an opportunity to acquaint himself with the music of Borodin and Mussorgsky, which was to influence him greatly in the subsequent period of his creative activity. Although he played Tchaikovsky's scores for Mme. von Meck (including the manuscript of the 4th Symphony, dedicated to her) Debussy did not evince great interest in Tchaikovsky's works. Another influence in his youth was Mme. Vasnier, an excellent singer, whom he met during the years he was preparing for the Grand Prix (1881–4); he spent much of his time at the Vasnier residence at Ville-d'Avray; the first of his *Fêtes galantes,* on poems of Verlaine, as well as some other works, is dedicated to her. In the composition class of Guiraud he won a prize for counterpoint and fugue in 1882; the next year he was the winner of the second Prix de Rome, and finally, in 1884, he won the much coveted Grand Prix with his cantata *L'Enfant prodigue.* From the Villa Medici in Rome he sent as the fruit of the first year a fragment of a choral work, *Zuleïma* (after Heine's *Almanzor*),

which he later destroyed; he also worked on a composition for the stage, *Diane au bois,* which he had begun in Paris, but this was never finished. The second year he wrote *Printemps,* a symphonic suite, which found no favor with the jury at the Academy. This did not prevent Debussy from following the path on which he had struck out, and, returning to Paris, he composed another cantata, *La Damoiselle élue,* even more advanced; at this time (1887) he also visited London. The work of the last year in Rome (1888) was a *Fantaisie* for piano and orch. The customary performance of the "envois de Rome" never took place; the committee refused to put *Printemps* on the program, and Debussy insisted that either all or none be produced. At about that time Debussy became an intimate of a group of French poets of the symbolist school, and was particularly fascinated by Mallarmé; he also made a visit to Bayreuth (1888), where he heard *Parsifal;* he repeated this visit in 1889; in that year he also became greatly interested in Oriental music which was presented at the Paris Exposition, and acquired a taste for exotic musical colors. His early enthusiasm for Wagner soon frittered away, and he became actually antagonistic to Wagner's ideas. Contacts with the Impressionist movement, added to the influence of modern French poetry, contributed to Debussy's mature style, in which formal structure becomes less important, while mood, atmosphere, and color assume special significance. His *Ariettes oubliées* (1888) to Verlaine's words, and *Cinq poèmes* (1890) to Baudelaire's verses, are the first revelations of this new style. He wrote *Petite suite* for piano 4 hands (1889; arranged for orch. by H. Busser); in 1890 he began *Suite bergamasque* for piano, which includes the most celebrated single piece by Debussy, *Clair de lune* (the title is from Verlaine's poem, which also contains the word 'bergamasque,' adopted by Debussy); it is interesting to observe that in the framework of a classical suite, Debussy applies his novel methods of musical coloring. The year 1892 marked the beginning of the composition of his orchestral *Prélude à l'Après-midi d'un faune* (after Mallarmé; Paris, Dec. 23, 1894) and his only opera *Pelléas et Mélisande.* Debussy continued his productive work; he wrote a String Quartet (1893; designated as *Premier Quatuor,* although it was the only quartet he wrote); the song volumes *Proses lyriques* (1894), and *Chansons de Bilitis* to poems of Pierre Louÿs (1898), the latter being one of his most poetic invocations; another work, also entitled *Chansons de Bilitis,* for two flutes, two harps, and celesta was performed semiprivately (Paris, Feb. 7, 1901), in the form of a mimomelodrama. Debussy's major composition at the turn of the century was *Trois Nocturnes* for orch. (the first two, *Nuages* and *Fêtes,* were performed in Paris, Dec. 9, 1900; the third, *Sirènes,* for orch. and wordless choir of women's voices, was performed with the others on Oct. 27, 1901). On Oct. 19, 1899, Debussy married Rosalie Texier. (The *Nocturnes* are dedicated to her under the affectionate name "Lily-Lilo.") However, in 1904 he eloped with Mme. Emma Bardac, the wife of a banker; Rosalie shot herself in despair, but recovered; the divorce followed on Aug. 2, 1904, and Debussy finally married Mme. Bardac. A daughter born to this marriage ("Chouchou," to whom Debussy dedicated his *Children's Corner*) died at the age of fourteen on July 14, 1919. *Pelléas et Mélisande* was produced at the Opéra-Comique on April 30, 1902, after many difficulties, among them the open opposition of Maeterlinck, on whose play the opera was based. Mary Garden sang Mélisande, arousing admiration as well as wonderment as to the reason why an American singer with imperfect French enunciation should have been selected; Maeterlinck's own choice for the part was his mistress, Georgette Leblanc. The opera was attacked violently by some critics for its decadent character, and for many years was a center of musical controversy. Performances followed but slowly; it was produced at the Manhattan Opera House, N.Y., on Feb. 19, 1908; at Covent Garden, London, on May 21, 1909; at the Metropolitan Opera House, N.Y. on March 21, 1925. At various times it was reported that Debussy had completed other dramatic works; in fact, the Metropolitan Opera House even announced its acquisition of the rights for the production of *Le Diable dans le beffroi, La Chute de la maison Usher,* and *La Légende de Tristan*; two versions of Debussy's libretto for *La Chute de la maison Usher* are in existence, but nothing is known of any music for these works beyond mention of it in correspondence or conversations. *La Mer,* his next important composition, was completed at Eastbourne, England, in March 1905; it was first performed by Chevillard in Paris, Oct. 15, 1905. Then followed the orchestral suite *Images,* of which *Ibéria* (1908), descriptive of a Spanish fiesta, with guitar-like strumming on the violins, was the most successful. On Dec. 18, 1908, Harold Bauer played the first performance, at the Cercle Musical in Paris, of Debussy's *Children's Corner*; an orchestration by Caplet was performed in Paris on March 25, 1911. In 1908 Debussy conducted *La Mer* and *Prélude à l'Après-midi d'un faune* in London; in 1909 he appeared there again to conduct the *Nocturnes*; following this he filled various engagements as conductor in Paris, Vienna, and Budapest (1910), Turin (1911), Moscow and St. Petersburg (1913), and The Hague, Amsterdam, and Rome (1914). Diaghilev produced his ballet, *Jeux,* in Paris, May 15, 1913. Debussy contemplated an American tour with the violinist Arthur Hartmann in 1914, but abandoned the idea because of illness; thereafter his health failed rapidly owing to cancer, and, after two operations, he finally succumbed. Debussy's last appearance in public was on May 5, 1917, when he played (with Gaston Poulet) the piano part of his Violin Sonata.

Debussy is regarded as the creator and chief protagonist of musical Impressionism, despite the fact that he deprecated the term and denied his role in the movement. This, however, cannot alter the essential truth that, like Monet in painting and Mallarmé in poetry, Debussy created a style peculiarly sensitive to musical mezzotint from a palette of half-lit delicate colors. To accomplish the desired effect, Debussy introduced many novel technical devices. He made use of the Oriental pentatonic scale for exotic evocations, and of the whole-tone scale (which he did not invent, however; samples of its use are found in Glinka and Liszt); he emancipated dissonance, so that unresolved discords freely followed one another; he also revived the archaic practice of consecutive perfect intervals (particularly fifths and fourths). In Debussy's formal constructions, traditional development is abandoned and the themes themselves are shortened and rhythmically sharpened; in instrumentation, the role of individual instruments is greatly enhanced and the dynamic range subtilized. These applications aroused intense criticism on the part of traditionalists; a book, *Le Cas Debussy* (1910), gave expression to this opposition; see also N. Slonimsky, *Lexicon of Musical Invective,* N.Y., 1953.

WORKS, PUBLISHED: FOR THE STAGE: *Pelléas et Mélisande,* opera (1892–1902); *Le Martyre de Saint Sébastien,* music to the mystery play by d'Annunzio, for soli, chorus, and orch. (1911); *Jeux,* ballet (1912); *Khamma,* ballet (1912).

CHORAL WORKS: *Printemps,* for women's voices (1882); *Invocation,* for men's voices (1883); *L'Enfant prodigue,* cantata (1884); *La Damoiselle élue,* for soli, chorus and orch. (1887–8); *Trois Chansons de Charles d'Orléans,* for unaccompanied chorus (1908); *Ode à la France,* for solo, chorus, and orch. (1916–17).

FOR ORCH.: *Printemps,* symph. suite (1886–7); *Fantaisie* for piano and orch. (1888–9); *Prélude à l'Après-midi d'un faune* (1892–4); *Nocturnes* (1893–9); *La Mer,* 3 symph. sketches: 1. *De l'aube à midi sur la mer,* 2. *Jeux de vagues,* 3. *Dialogue du vent et de la mer* (1903–05); incidental music to Shakespeare's *King Lear* (1904); *Danse sacrée* and *Danse profane,* for harp and strings (1904); *Images: Gigues, Ibéria, Rondes de Printemps* (1906–12).

CHAMBER MUSIC: String Quartet (1893); *Rapsodie* for saxophone and piano (1903–05; also with orchl. accomp.); *Première rapsodie* for clarinet and piano (1909–10); *Petite pièce* for do. (1910); *Syrinx,* for flute alone (1912); Cello Sonata (1915); Sonata for Flute, Viola and Harp (1915); Violin Sonata (1916–17).

FOR PIANO SOLO: *Danse bohémienne* (1880); *Deux Arabesques* (1888); *Rêverie, Ballade, Danse, Valse romantique, Nocturne* (1890); *Suite bergamasque* (1890–1905); *Mazurka* (1891); *Pour le piano* (1896–1901); *Estampes* (1903); *D'un cahier d'esquisses* (1903); *Masques* (1904); *L'Isle joyeuse* (1904); *Images,* 1st series (1905); *Images,* 2nd series (1907); *Children's Corner* (1906–8); *Hommage à Haydn* (1909); *La Plus que lente* (1910); *Douze préludes* (1st book, 1910; 2nd book, 1910–13); *La Boîte à joujoux,* children's ballet (1913); *Berceuse héroïque pour rendre hommage à S.M. le Roi Albert Ier de Belgique et à ses soldats* (1914); 2 books of *Douze études* (1915).

FOR PIANO DUET: one movement of a *Symphonie en si* (1880; intended for orch.); *Triomphe de Bacchus* (1881); *Petite suite* (1889); *Marche écossaise sur un thème populaire* (1891; also for orch.); *Six épigraphes antiques* (1914).

FOR 2 PFS.: *Lindaraja* (1901); *En blanc et noir* (1915). 60 songs to texts by Verlaine, Bourget, Villon, Baudelaire, Louÿs, Girod, Mallarmé, and others. Various arrangements and orchestrations. Also *Masques et Bergamasques,* scenario for a ballet written in 1910.

WORKS, UNPUBLISHED: FOR THE STAGE: *Rodrigue et Chimène,* opera (unfinished; 1891–92); *F.E.A. (Frères en art),* 3 scenes of a play (1900; with René Peter); *Le Diable dans le beffroi* (orchestral sketch for scene 1; 1903); 2 versions of a libretto for *La Chute de la mai-*

son Usher (after Poe; 1908–18). Choral works: *Daniel,* cantata (1880–4); *Le Gladiateur* (1883).

FOR ORCH.: *Intermezzo* (after a passage from Heine's *Intermezzo*; 1882; also arranged for piano duet); *Printemps* (1884; manuscript destroyed in fire, but an arrangement for violin and piano was publ.; in 1913 Henri Busser orchestrated it according to Debussy's indications, and the work thus restored was performed in Paris, April 18, 1913, with Busser conducting).

CHAMBER MUSIC: Trio in G for piano, violin, and cello (1880); *Chansons de Bilitis,* incidental music for Louÿs' poems, for 2 flutes, 2 harps, and celesta (1900).

SONGS: *Caprice* (1880); *Chanson espagnole* for 2 voices, *Rondel chinois, Romance, Aimons-nous, La Fille aux cheveux de lin, Eclogue* (1880–4); *Berceuse* for the play *La Tragédie de la mort* (1908). An Intermezzo for Cello and Piano was found by Gregor Piatigorsky in Paris, 1938.

WRITINGS: Debussy contributed numerous criticisms and essays to the *Revue Blanche, Gil Blas, Musica, Mercure de France, La Revue S.I.M.,* etc. Collected essays and criticisms publ. in various journals were issued as *Monsieur Croche, anti-dilettante* (Paris, 1923; English transl. 1928, 1948; new ed. with commentary by F. Lesure, Paris, 1971).

BIBLIOGRAPHY: L. Gilman, *D.'s 'Pelléas et Mélisande'* (N.Y., 1907); Mrs. F. Liebich, *C.-A. D.* (London, 1908); L. Laloy, *C. D.* (Paris, 1909); F. Santoliquido, *Il Dopo-Wagner, C. D. e R. Strauss* (Rome, 1909); G. Caillard and J. de Berys, *Le Cas D.* (Paris, 1910); G. Setaccioli, *D. è un innovatore?* (Rome, 1910); M. Rivière, *Études* (Paris, 1911); O. Séré, *Musiciens français d'aujourd'hui* (Paris, 1911); R. Rolland, *Musiciens d'aujourd'hui* (Paris, 1912); D. Chennevière, *D. et son œuvre* (Paris, 1913); C. Paglia, *Strauss, Debussy, e compagnia bella* (Bologna, 1913); G. Jean-Aubry, *La Musique française d'aujourd'hui* (Paris, 1916); E. Newman, "The Development of D.," *Musical Times* (May, Aug. 1918); G. Jean-Aubry, "Some Recollections of D.," *Musical Times* (May 1918; full list of comps. and writings); L. S. Liebich. "An Englishwoman's Memories of D.," *Musical Times* (June 1918); G. Jean-Aubry, "C. D.," *Musical Quarterly* (Oct. 1918); J.-G. Prod'homme, "C.-A. D.," *Musical Quarterly* (Oct. 1918); A. Lualdi, "C. D. La sua Arte e la sua Parabola," in *Rivista Musicale Italiana* XXV/2 (1918); Guido M. Gatti, "The Piano Works of C. D.," *Musical Quarterly* (July 1921); A. Cortot, *The Piano Music of C. D.* (1922); L. Fabian, *D.* (Munich, 1923); André Suarès, *D.* (Paris, 1923; new ed. 1936); E. Gianturco, *C. D.* (Naples, 1923); J. G. Palache, "D. as Critic," *Musical Quarterly* (July 1924); L. Perrachio, *L'opera pianistica di Cl. D.* (Milan, 1924); F. H. Shera, *D. and Ravel* (London, 1925); M. Emmanuel, *Pelléas et Mélisande* (Paris, 1926); Rient van Sant, *D.* (Hague, 1926); F. Gysi, *D.* (Zürich, 1926); M. Arconada, *En torno a D.* (Madrid, 1926); J. Durand, *Lettres de C. D. à son editeur* (Paris, 1927); Léon Vallas, *Les idées de D., musicien français* (Paris, 1927; in Engl., 1929); Ch. Koechlin, *D.* (Paris, 1927); J. Fr. Cooke, *D.* (Philadelphia, 1928); A. Coeuroy, *D.* (1930); M. Boucher, *D.* (1930); J. Lépine, *La Vie de C. D.* (1930); R. Peter, *D.* (1931; augmented ed., 1944); M. Dumesnil, *How to Play and Teach D.* (N.Y., 1932); Ernst Decsey, *D.*

(1933; new ed. 1936); Léon Vallas, *C. D. et son temps* (Paris, 1932; in English, London, 1933); Andreas Liess, *C. D. Das Werk in Zeitbild,* 2 vols. (Strasbourg, 1936); Ed. Lockspeiser, *D.* (London, 1936; revised 1951); id., "Mussorgsky and D.," *Musical Quarterly* (Oct. 1937); Oscar Thompson, *D., Man and Artist* (N.Y., 1937); H. F. Kölsch, *Der Impressionismus bei D.* (Düsseldorf, 1937); M. Dumesnil, *C. D., Master of Dreams* (N.Y., 1940); H. Strobel, *C. D.* (Zürich, 1940); R. Paoli, *D.* (Florence, 1941); *D.: Lettres à deux amis* (Paris, 1942); G. Schaeffner, *C. D. und das Poetische* (Bern, 1943); L. Laloy, *C. D.* (Paris, 1944); Léon Vallas, *C. D.* (Paris, 1944); *D.: Correspondance avec Pierre Louys* (Paris, 1945); *D.: Correspondance avec d'Annunzio* (Paris, 1948); Guy Ferchault, *C. D., musicien français* (Paris, 1948); Rollo H. Myers, *D.* (London, 1948); H. B. Harvey, *Claude of France; the Story of Debussy* (N.Y., 1948); W. Danckert, *C. D.* (Berlin, 1950); E. Robert Schmitz, *The Piano Works of C. D.* (N.Y., 1950); A. Gauthier, *D., documents iconographiques* (Geneva, 1952); A. Colea, *Pelléas et Mélisande, analyse poétique et musicale* (Paris, 1952); J. van Ackere, *Pelléas et Mélisande* (Brussels, 1952); Germaine and D. E. Inghelbrecht, *D.* (Paris, 1953); J. d'Almendre, *Les Modes grégoriens dans l'œuvre de C. D.* (Paris, 1953); Victor Seroff, *D., Musician of France* (N.Y., 1956); E. Vuillermoz, *D.* (Geneva, 1957); E. Lockspeiser, ed., *Lettres inédites à André Caplet, 1908–1914* (Monaco, 1957); J. L. Pasteur Vallery-Radot, *Tel était C. D.* (with letters to the author; Paris, 1958); Y. Tiénot & O. d'Estrade-Guerra, *D.: l'homme, son œuvre, son milieu* (Paris, 1961); M. Dietschy, *La Passion de C. D.* (Neuchâtel, 1962); *C. D., Revue Musical,* special issue 258 (1964); E. Lockspeiser, *D.: His Life and Mind* (2 vols.; London, 1962, 1965); F. Lesure, ed., "C. D., Textes et Documents inédits," a special issue of *Revue de musicologie* (1962); A. Goléa, *C. D.* (Paris, 1965); E. Weber, ed. *D. et l'évolution de la musique au XXᵉ siècle* (Paris, 1965); P. Young, *D.* (London, 1966); E. Hardeck, *Untersuchungen zu den Klavierliedern C. D.* (Regensburg, 1967); V. Jankélévitch, *La Vie et la mort dans la musique de D.* (Neuchatel, 1968); F. Dawes, *D.'s Piano Music* (London, 1969); W. W. Austin, ed., Norton Critical Score edition of *Prelude to "The Afternoon of a Faune"* (contains background, criticism, analysis; N.Y., 1970); S. Jarocinski, *D., impressionisme et symbolisme* (Paris, 1970; trans. from Polish); H. Barraud, *Les Cinq grands opéras* (includes analysis of *Pelléas;* Paris, 1972); S. Jarocinski, *D. Kronika życia, d ziela, epoki* (Cracow, 1973); A. B. Wenk, *C. D. and the Poets* (1976). A periodical, *Cahiers Debussy* began publ. in 1974, issued by the Centre de Documentation Claude Debussy, Saint Germain-en-Laye, France.

Decadt, Jan, Belgian composer; b. Ypres, June 21, 1914. He studied with Joseph Ryelandt at the Cons. of Ghent, and later with Jean Absil in Brussels. He was director of the music school in Harelbeke in 1945, and in 1957 was appointed a prof. of fugue at the Antwerp Cons. His musical style is marked by strong polyphonic structures with Impressionistic coloration.

WORKS: *Variations on "Sir Halewijn"* for orch. (1943); *Ballada op een boom (Ballade on a Tree)* for soprano, flute, oboe and string trio (1945); Piano Concerto (1953); Symph. No. 1 (1958), *Constant Permeke*, cantata (1963); *Monographie musicale d'un grand peintre* for orch. (Johannesburg, Nov. 17, 1964); *Concerto Overture* for flute, oboe, and string orch. (1964); Suite for trumpet and chamber orch. (1967); *Petite planète* for narrator, soprano, flute, viola, and cello (1967); *Concertante Fantasia* for oboe and piano (1970); *Introduction and Capriccio* for clarinet and piano (1972); Saxophone Concerto (1973); Quartet for saxophones (1974).

Dechevrens, Antoine, Swiss musicologist; b. Chêne, n. Geneva, Nov. 3, 1840; d. Geneva, Jan. 17, 1912. Entered Jesuit Order in 1861; prof. of theology and philosophy at Univ. of Angers; devoted himself to the study of the Gregorian chant and of neume notation. Publ. *Du rythme dans l'hymnographie latine* (1895); *Études de science musicale* (3 vols., Paris, 1898); *Composition musicale et composition littéraire* (Paris, 1910); also publ. a study on Chinese music in *Sammelbände der Internationalen Musik-Gesellschaft,* vol II.

Decoust, Michel, French composer; b. Paris, Nov. 19, 1936. He studied at the Paris Cons. with Olivier Messiaen and others; received Premier Second Grand Prix de Rome (1963). His works include *Mouvement* for strings and percussion (1964); *Études* for Flutes and Cellos (1966); *Polymorphée* for orch. (Royan, April 1, 1967); *Instants-Stabiles* for a chamber ensemble (1967); *Actions* for voice and piano with audience participation (Angers, April 18, 1972); *T' Ai* for double bass, electric guitar, percussion harpsichord and voice (Paris, Jan. 25, 1972); *Et, ée* for chorus and orch. (Paris, July 23, 1973).

Decreus, Camille, French pianist; b. Paris, Sept. 23, 1876; d. Fontainebleau, Sept. 26, 1939. He studied piano with Pugno at the Paris Cons.; had a successful career as a pianist; made tours in England and Germany; after several concerts as assisting artist and accompanist in the U.S. he settled in Washington as a private teacher in the family of Senator W. Clark; then returned to France. In 1924 he was appointed director of the American Cons. at Fontainebleau, a post which he held until his death.

Decsey, Ernst, German-Austrian writer on music; b. Hamburg, April 13, 1870; d. Vienna, March 12, 1941. He studied composition with Bruckner at the Vienna Cons.; then was active as music critic in Graz and in Vienna. He was the author of the standard biography of Hugo Wolf, in 4 vols. (Berlin, 1903–1906; several subsequent printings; abridged one-volume edition appeared in 1921); also wrote monographs on *Anton Bruckner* (Berlin, 1920); *Johann Strauss* (Stuttgart, 1924); *Franz Lehár* (Vienna, 1924); *Maria Jeritza* (Vienna, 1931) and *Debussy* (2 vols., Graz, 1936–49).

Deering (or **Dering**), **Richard,** English composer; b. Kent, c.1580; d. London, 1630 (buried March 22). Educated in Italy; returned to England as a well-known musician and practiced in London; 1610, took the degree of Mus. Bac. at Oxford; 1617, organist at the con-

vent of English nuns at Brussels; 1625, appointed organist to Queen Henrietta Maria.

WORKS: *Cantiones sacrae sex vocum cum basso continuo ad organum* (Antwerp, 1597); *Cantiones sacrae quinque vocum* (1617); *Cantica sacra ad melodium madrigalium elaborato senis vocibus* (Antwerp, 1618); *Cantiones sacrae quinque vocum* (1619); 2 books of *Canzonette* for 3 and 4 voices respectively (1620; author's name given as "Richardo Diringo Inglese"); *Cantica sacra ad duos et tres voces, composita cum basso continuo ad organum* (posthumous; London, 1662). Sir Frederick Bridge ed. and publ. an elaborate work of Deering's entitled *The Cryes of London.* Various other compositions (anthems, motets, viol music), in MS, are preserved in the libraries of the British Museum, Christ Church, Oxford, the Royal College of Music, Peterhouse, Cambridge, Durham Cathedral, etc.

BIBLIOGRAPHY: Jeffrey Pulver, *Biographical Dictionary of Old English Music* (1923; 2nd ed. 1927); E. H. Meyer, *Die mehrstimmige Spielmusik des 17. Jahrhunderts in Nord- und Mitteleuropa* (Kassel, 1934); P. Platt, "Deering's Life and Training," *Music & Letters* (Jan. 1952); E. Brennecke, "The Country Cryes of Richard Deering," *Musical Quarterly* (July 1956).

Defauw, Désiré, Belgian conductor and violinist; b. Ghent, Sept. 5, 1885; d. Gary, Indiana, July 25, 1960. He was a pupil of Johan Smit (violin); from 1914–18, leader of his own quartet (with L. Tertis, C. Woodhouse, E. Doehard); was professor at the Antwerp Cons.; later conductor of the Defauw Concerts in Brussels; also conductor of the Royal Cons. Orch. there and director of the National Institute of Radio; guest conductor with the NBC Symph. Orch. in N.Y. (1938); in Sept., 1940, he returned to the U.S.; was conductor of the Chicago Symph. Orch. (1943–47) and the Gary Symph. Orch. (1950–1958).

Deffés, Pierre-Louis, French composer, b. Toulouse, July 25, 1819; d. there, June 10, 1900. Pupil of Halévy at the Paris Cons., taking Grand Prix de Rome in 1847 for the cantata *L'Ange et Tobie.*

Defossez, René, Belgian composer and conductor; b. Spa, Oct. 4, 1905. He studied with his father, then at the Liège Cons. with Rasse; received the Belgian Prix de Rome in 1935 for his opera-cantata *Le Vieux Soudard.* He was then active as conductor; from 1936 to 1959 was conductor of the Théâtre Royal de la Monnaie in Brussels; in 1946 succeeded Defauw as prof. of conducting at the Brussels Cons. He was an inspector of state-subsidized music schools (1961–71). In 1969 he was elected a member of the Royal Belgian Academy.

WORKS: the operas *Le Subterfuge improvisé* (1938), *À chacun son mensonge, Les Surprises de l'amour, À chacun sa vérité* and *L'Amour est Roi* (1946); the opera-cantatas: *La Conversion de St. Hubert* (1933) and *Le Vieux Soudard* (1935); the oratorios: *Bê Pretimps d'amour* for soprano and orch. (1939) and *La Frise empourprée* for soprano and orch. (1939); the ballets: *Floriante* (1942), *Le Sens du Divin* (1947), *Le Rêve de l'Astronome* (1950), *Les Jeulx de France* (1959), *Le Regard* (1970; Charleroi, March 27, 1971); the ballet cantata: *Le Pêcheur et son âme,* after Wilde

(*The Fisherman and His Soul,* 1965); *Aquarium,* 3 symph. impressions (1927); *Images Sous-marines* for orch. (1930); *Symphonie wallonne* (1935); *Poème romantique* for string orch. (1935); *Amaterasu,* symph. legend, with solo soprano (1935); Variations for Piano and Orch. (1938); *Adagio et Scherzo* for flute and orch. (1941); *Recitativo et Allegro* for trumpet and orch. (1945); *Marche Funebre* for orch. (1946); *Minutes heureuses,* small suite for orch. (1947); Trombone Concerto (1948); *Marche Triomphale* for wind orch. (1950); Violin Concerto (1951); Piano Concerto (1956); 2-Piano Concerto (1963; revision of the piano concerto); *La Chasseur d'Images* for orch. (1966); *Aria et Moto Perpetuoso* for orch. (1968); *Duo Concertante* for trumpet, percussion and strings; *Concerto Romantique* for piano and orch.; *Mini-Symphonie; Le Culte sans paroles* for orch.; *Fantaisie* for orch.; *Sinfonietta de Printemps* (1975); 2 string quartets (1934, 1950); Ballad for Clarinet and Piano (1942); Wind Trio (1946); *4 églogues* for 4 flutes and 2 percussionists; *Petit Quartet* for violin, piano, saxophone and percussion (1973); *3 Farces* for piano (1937; orchestrated, 1942); Variations for Piano (1941); *Les Caprices de ma poupée* for 2 pianos (1950; revised for wind quartet, 1965); Piano Sonatina (1958); choruses; songs.

DeGaetani, Jan, remarkable American mezzo-soprano singer; b. Massillon, Ohio, July 10, 1933. She studied with Sergius Kagen at the Juilliard School of Music in New York; in 1973 was appointed prof. of voice training at the Eastman School of Music, Rochester, N.Y. She achieved distinction as a virtuoso vocalist in her performances of ultra-modern works requiring accurate rendition of unusual intervallic skips, and often quarter tones and other fractional intervals in addition to special effects such as percussive tongue-clicking and a variety of finely calibrated dynamic nuances. In this field she has become a unique phenomenon; several vocal works have been written specially for her by grateful modern composers. As a lieder singer, Jan DeGaetani excels in an analytical capacity to express the most minute vocal modulations of the melodic line, while parsing the words with exquisite intellectual penetration of the verbal meaning, so that even experienced music critics are rendered helpless in search of congenial superlatives to describe her artistry.

Degen, Helmut, German composer; b. Aglasterhausen, near Heidelberg, Jan. 14, 1911. He studied piano, composition and conducting at the Hochschule für Musik in Cologne; then took courses at the Univ. of Bonn with Schiedermair and Schrade; taught at the Cons. of Duisburg; after the war he taught music at Trossingen. WORKS: A prolific composer, he wrote three symphonies (1945, 1947, 1948); *Symphonisches Spiel I* (1956), *Symphonisches Spiel II* for violin, cello, piano and orch. (1957) and *Symphonisches Spiel III* (1960); Piano Concerto (1940); Organ Concerto (1943); Concertino for 2 Clarinets and Orch. (1944); Cello Concerto (1945); Concerto for Harpsichord and 6 Instruments (1945); *Triptychon* (1952); 2 string quartets (1941, 1950); Piano Trio (1943); Trio for Flute, Viola, and Clarinet (1950); Saxophone Sonata (1950); Nonet

for Wind Instruments and Strings (1951); 4 piano sonatas; numerous concert studies; choruses. His music is couched in a well-defined, neo-Classical idiom, with strong points of reference to Baroque forms. He also published a *Handbuch der Formenlehre* (Regensburg, 1957).

BIBLIOGRAPHY: K. Laux, *Musik und Musiker der Gegenwart* (Essen, 1949; pp. 57–64).

Degeyter, Pierre, b. Oct. 8, 1848; d. St. Denis, near Paris, Sept. 27, 1932. Originally a wood carver, he wrote the famous workers' song *Internationale* in 1888. The authorship was contested by his brother, **Adolphe,** a blacksmith (b. 1858; d. Lille, Feb. 15, 1917), but after 18 years of litigation the Paris Appellate Court decided in favor of Pierre.

Degner, Erich Wolf, German composer; b. Hohenstein-Ernstthal, April 8, 1858; d. Berka, near Weimar, Nov. 18, 1908. Studied at the Grand-ducal school of music at Weimar, and later at Würzburg; taught at Regensburg and Gotha; 1885, director of the music school at Pettau, Styria; 1888, instructor at the Grand-ducal music school at Weimar; 1891, director of the music school of the Styrian Music Society at Graz; in 1902 again in Weimar as director of the music school.

WORKS: Symphony for Organ and Orch.; *Maria und die Mutter,* for soli, chorus and orch.; pieces for piano; songs; publ. *Anleitung und Beispiele zum Bilden von Kadenzen* (1902).

BIBLIOGRAPHY: R. Mojsisowicz, *Erich Wolf Degner* (1909).

De Guide, Richard, Belgian composer; b. Basècles, March 1, 1909; d. Brussels, Jan. 12, 1962. He studied with Paul Gilson and Jean Absil; worked for the Institute National de Radiodiffusion (1938–45); was director of the music academy of Woluwé-St.-Pierre in Brussels (1946–61); also taught at the Liège Cons. (1950–53) and at the Mons Cons. (1961).

WORKS: *Mouvements symphoniques* (1938); *Illustration pour un Jeu de l'Oie* for voice, and piano or orch. (1939–41); *Concerto for 11* for winds and percussion (1940); 3 symphonies: No. 1 (1943); No. 2, with organ (1951); No. 3, for strings, harp and timpani (1957); *Vincti non devicti,* symph. poem (1948); piano concerto, *Le Téméraire* (1952); *Le Tombeau de Montaigne,* symph. suite (1955); a ballet *Les Danaïdes* (1956); *Hommage à Hindemith* for chamber orch. (1958); *Humoresque* for piano (1927); *Préludes* for organ (1942); Duo for 2 Trumpets (1944); Duo for 2 Violins (1945); *Speciosa miracula,* sextet for wind quintet and piano (1948); *Préludes and Toccata* for piano (1949); *2 nômes* for flute (1951); *Suite "Les caractères du trombone"* for trombone and piano (1958); *4 symptômes* for piano, left hand (1960). He wrote a monograph, *Jean Absil, vie et œuvre,* published posthumously (Tournai, 1965).

Dehn, Siegfried Wilhelm, famous German music theorist; b. Altona, Feb. 24, 1799; d. Berlin, April 12, 1858. Law student at Leipzig, 1819–25; also studied harmony and cello playing. He studied theory assiduously with Bernhard Klein in Berlin; and at Meyerbeer's insistence (1842) was appointed librarian of the music department of the Royal Library. From 1842–48 he was also editor of the *Caecilia*. Dehn was a profound theorist, and very successful as a teacher of theory, numbering among his pupils Anton Rubinstein and Glinka.

WRITINGS: *Theoretisch-praktische Harmonielehre* (Berlin, 1840; 2nd ed. Leipzig, 1860; his most important work); an *Analyse dreier Fugen aus J. S. Bachs Wohltemperiertem Clavier und einer Vokaldoppelfuge G. M. Buononcinis* (Leipzig, 1858); *Eine Sammlung älterer Musik aus dem 16. und 17. Jahrhundert* (Berlin; 12 books of vocal compositions a 4–10); a translation of Delmotte's work on Orlandus Lassus, *Biogr. Notiz über Roland de Lattre* (Vienna, 1837). A posthumous *Lehre vom Kontrapunkt, dem Kanon und der Fuge* (Berlin, 1859; 2nd ed. 1883) was edited by B. Scholz.

Deis, Carl, American pianist, music editor and composer; b. New York, March 7, 1883; d. there, July 24, 1960. He studied piano at home from early childhood under the guidance of his father who was a trombone player; then was a pupil at the National Cons. of Music and the New York College of Music. In 1906 he became a choral conductor and voice teacher at various private schools in New York, was engaged as organist at the Society for Ethical Culture (1919–1933). In 1917 he was appointed music editor of G. Schirmer, Inc.; retired in 1953. He wrote several attractive songs, among them *New Year's Day, The Flight of the Moon, Come Down to Kew, The Drums, Were I a Star,* etc.

Deiters, Hermann, German writer on music; b. Bonn, June 27, 1833; d. Koblenz, May 11, 1907. Studied jurisprudence in Bonn, where he took the degrees of *Dr. jur.* and *Dr. phil.* in 1858. Teacher in the gymnasia at Bonn (1858) and Düren (1869); director of gymnasia at Konitz (1874), Posen (1878), and Bonn (1883); 'Provincial-Schulrath' at Koblenz (1885); assistant in the Ministry of Public Worship, at Berlin (1890); retired in 1903, living thereafter in Koblenz. Deiters wrote many musical articles for the *Deutsche Musikzeitung,* for the *Allgemeine musikalische Zeitung,* and other journals. He contributed several music biographies to Meyer's *Konversations-Lexikon* (3d ed.); wrote a biography of Brahms in Waldersee's *Sammlung mus. Vorträge* (1882, 1898). His greatest achievement was his masterly translation into German of Thayer's *Life of Beethoven,* with critical comments by Deiters (Berlin, 1866–79, in 3 vols.; 2nd ed., with 2 additional vols., edited by Riemann, Berlin, 1910–11).

Dejdler, Rochus, Austrian composer; b. Oberammergau, Jan. 15, 1779; d. Vienna, Oct. 15, 1822. He wrote the music of the Passion play still in use at Oberammergau.

Dejoncker, Theodore, Belgian composer; b. Brussels, April 11, 1894; d. Asse, July 10, 1964. He studied with Gilson; in 1925, founded, with 7 other composers, the progressive "Groupe des Synthétistes."

WORKS: 3 symphonies: *Sinfonia la classica* (1939); *Symphonie burlesque* and *Symphonie romantique;* an overture, *Brutus; Prologue symphonique; Portrait de Bernard Shaw* for orch.; String Quartet; Saxophone Quartet; String Trio (1960).

De Jong, Conrad, American composer; b. Hull, Iowa, Jan. 13, 1934. He studied trumpet at North Texas State Univ. in Denton, Texas, majoring in music education; received his B.M. Ed. in 1954; later studied composition with Bernhard Heiden at Indiana Univ. in Bloomington, obtaining his M.M. in 1959. He was appointed to the music faculty of Wisconsin State Univ. at River Falls in 1959.

WORKS: *Unicycle* for harpsichord (1960); *3 Studies* for brass septet (1960); *Music for Two Tubas* (1961); *Essay* for brass quintet (1963); String Trio (1964); *Fun and Games* for any instrument with piano (1966); *Aanraking (Contact)* for solo trombone (1969); *Hist Whist* for soprano, flute, viola and percussion (1969); *Grab Gab* for tuba ensemble (1970); *Peace on Earth* for unison chorus and organ (1970).

De Jong, Marinus. See Jong, Marinus de.

De Koven, (Henry Louis) Reginald, American composer; b. Middletown, Conn., April 3, 1859; d. Chicago, Jan. 16, 1920. He was educated in Europe from 1870, taking his degree at St. John's College, Oxford, in 1879. Before this he studied piano under W. Speidel at Stuttgart, and after graduation studied there another year under Lebert (piano) and Pruckner (harmony). After a six-months' course in Frankfurt under Dr. Hauff (composition), he studied singing with Vannucini at Florence, and operatic composition under Genée in Vienna and Delibes in Paris. In 1902 he organized the Philh. Orch. at Washington, D.C., which he conducted for three seasons. He was music critic for the *Chicago Evening Post* (1889–90), *Harper's Weekly* (1895–97), *N.Y. World* (1898–1900 and 1907–12), and later for the *N.Y. Herald.*

WORKS: He wrote several successful operettas: *The Begum* (Philadelphia, Nov. 7, 1887); *Don Quixote* (Boston, Nov. 18, 1889); *Robin Hood* (his best-known work; Chicago, June 9, 1890; London, Jan. 5, 1891; the celebrated song, *O Promise Me,* was introduced into the score shortly after its first performance; it was originally publ. as a separate song in 1889); *The Fencing Master* (Boston, 1892); *The Knickerbockers* (Boston, 1893); *The Algerian* (Philadelphia, 1893); *Rob Roy* (Detroit, 1894); *The Tzigane* (N.Y., 1895); *The Mandarin* (Cleveland, 1896); *The Paris Doll* (Hartford, Conn., 1897); *The Highwayman* (New Haven, 1897); the following all had their premières in N.Y.: *The Tree Dragoons* (1899); *Red Feather* (1903); *Happyland* (1905); *Student King* (1906); *The Golden Butterfly* (1907); *The Beauty Spot* (1909); *The Wedding Trip* (1911); *Her Little Highness* (1913). A grand opera, *The Canterbury Pilgrims,* was produced at the Metropolitan Opera House on March 8, 1917; another opera, *Rip van Winkle,* was performed by the Chicago Opera Co. (Jan. 2, 1920). Besides these, he wrote some 400 songs and a piano sonata.

BIBLIOGRAPHY: Anna de Koven, *A Musician and his Wife* (N.Y., 1926).

Dela, Maurice, French-Canadian composer and organist; b. Montreal, Sept. 10, 1919. He studied composition with Champagne at the Montreal Cons. and orchestration with Leo Sowerby in Chicago. He subsequently became a church organist in the province of Quebec. His music is pragmatic in style and idiom, tending towards Baroque consistency, but energized by an injection of euphonious dissonance.

WORKS: Ballade for Piano and Orch. (1945); Piano Concerto (1946); *Ronde* for soprano, and small orch. or piano (1949); *Le Chat, la Bélette et le petit Lapin* for narrator and orch. (1950, revised 1965); *Les Fleurs de Glais* for narrator and orch. (1951); *Scherzo* for orch. (1953); *Adagio* for string orch. (1956); Piano Concertino (1962); *2 Esquisses* for orch. (1962); *Projection* for orch. (1966); 2 symphonies (1968, 1972); *3 Dances* for orch. (1971); *Triptyque* for orch. (1974); *Petite suite maritime* for wind instruments (1946); Suite for Flute, Cello and Piano (1953–54); 2 string quartets (1960, 1963); *Divertissement* for brass quintet (1962); *Miniatures* for 3 recorders (1968); *Hommage* for piano (1950); *2 Impromptus* for piano (1964); songs; arrangements of folksongs of Quebec province.

Delage, Maurice, French composer; b. Paris, Nov. 13, 1879; d. there, Sept. 19, 1961. He was engaged as a clerk in a maritime agency in Paris and in a fishery in Boulogne; in 1900 was in the army; then became interested in music and took lessons with Ravel. Subsequently he made voyages to the Orient, and was greatly impressed with Japanese art. His music reveals Oriental traits in subject matter as well as in melodic progressions. An ardent follower of Debussy's principles, Delage wrote music in a highly subtilized manner with distinctive instrumental colors. After 1920 he lived mostly in Paris.

WORKS: symph. poem, *Conte par la mer*; several songs with small orch.; *4 poèmes hindous* (1921); *Roses d'octobre* (1922); *Sept Haï-Kaï* (1923); *Trois chants de la Jungle* (1935); *Deux fables de La Fontaine* (1949); *In Morte* (1951); also a string quartet (1948).

Delalande, Michel-Richard, French organist and composer; b. Paris, Dec. 15, 1657; d. Versailles, June 18, 1726. He was the 15th child of a Paris tailor; was apprenticed as a boy chorister at the Saint-Germain Auxerrois; when his voice broke, he began to study organ playing in which he succeeded so well that Louis XIV entrusted him with giving keyboard lessons to the royal princesses. In 1683 he received the position of a "surintendant" of the Royal Chapel. In 1704 he became master of the Royal Chapel; in 1722, he was joined in this directorship by Campra, Bernier and Gervais.

WORKS: Delalande was the composer of excellent ballets, even though they yielded in quality to those of Lully; of these *Ballet de la jeunesse* (1686), *Le Palais de Flore* (1689); *Adonis* (1698), *Le Ballet des fées* (1699), *L'Hymen champestre* (1700), *Le Ballet de la paix* (1713) and *Les Folies de Gardenio* (1720) were produced at the court in Versailles. With Destouches, he wrote the ballet *Les Élements,* which was produced at the Tuileries Palace in Paris on Dec. 31, 1721. (Vincent d'Indy edited the score and published it in 1883.) Delalande wrote also 42 motets, which were published in 1729; and a number of "symphonies pour les soupers du roi" (intermezzos to be played at court dinners) and "symphonies de Noël" (instrumental interludes for performances at Christmas time at the court). 22 "Noëls" (arranged in a series of 4 "symphonies") by Delalande were edited by A. Cellier (Paris, 1937).

BIBLIOGRAPHY: N. Dufourck, ed., *Notes et références pour servir à une histoire de Michel-Richard Delalande* (Paris, 1957; contains a thematic catalogue).

De Lamarter, Eric, American organist, music critic and composer; b. Lansing, Michigan, Feb. 18, 1880; d. Orlando, Florida, May 17, 1953. He studied organ with Fairclough in St. Paul, Middleschulte in Chicago, and Guilmant and Widor in Paris (1901–02); then was organist of various churches in Chicago till 1936; assistant conductor of the Chicago Symph. Orch. from 1918–36; also conducted the Chicago Civic Orch. He was music critic of the *Chicago Record-Herald* (1908–09), *Chicago Tribune* (1909–10), and *Inter-Ocean* (from 1910); held teaching positions at the Chicago Musical College and Olivet College.

WORKS: ballet, *The Betrothal* (N.Y., Nov. 19, 1918); ballet suite, *The Black Orchid* (Chicago Symph. Orch., Feb. 27, 1931, composer conducting); 4 symphonies (1914; 1926; 1931; 1932); overture, *The Faun* (1914); *Serenade* for orch. (1915); overture, *Masquerade* (1916); *Fable of the Hapless Folktune,* for orch. (1917); 2 organ concertos (1920 and 1922); *Weaver of Tales,* for organ and chamber orch. (1926); ballet suite, *The Dance of Life* (1931); *The Giddy Puritan,* overture on two early New England tunes (1921; NBC, June 6, 1938; Chicago Symph., March 9, 1942); organ works; songs.

Delamont, Gordon, Canadian composer; b. Moose Jaw, Saskatchewan, Oct. 27, 1918. He studied trumpet and played in his father's band in Vancouver; played in dance orchestras; led his own dance band (1945–59). His works are all in the jazz idiom. For jazz orch. he wrote *Allegro and Blues* (1964), *Ontario Suite* (1965), *Centum* (1966), *Song and Dance* (1969), *Collage No. 3* (1969). He also wrote *3 Entertainments* for saxophone quartet (1970) and *Moderato and Blues* for brass quintet (1972); published books on harmony and arranging: *Modern Harmony Technique I and II* (N.Y., 1965), *Modern Arranging Technique* (N.Y., 1965) and *Modern Twelve-Tone Technique* (N.Y., 1973).

Delaney, Robert Mills, American composer; b. Baltimore, July 24, 1903; d. Santa Barbara, Cal., Sept. 21, 1956. He studied music in the U.S., later in Italy, then in Paris (1922–27) with Capet (violin) and Nadia Boulanger and Arthur Honegger (composition). He won the Guggenheim Fellowship in 1929; in 1933 he received a Pulitzer Prize for his music to Stephen Vincent Benét's *John Brown's Body.* He then occupied various teaching posts; settled in Santa Barbara, California.

WORKS: *Don Quixote Symph.* (1927); *John Brown's Song,* choral symph. (1931); *Night* (after William Blake) for chorus, string orch., and piano (1934);

Work 22, overture (1939); Symph. No. 1 (1942); *Western Star* for chorus and orch. (1944); 2 string quartets.

Delannoy, Marcel, French composer; b. La Ferté-Alais, July 9, 1898; d. Nantes, Sept. 14, 1962. He served in the French Army in World War I; then took lessons with Gédalge and Honegger. After a few years of instruction, he produced an effective stage work, *Poirier de Misère* (Paris, Feb. 21, 1927) which obtained excellent success. Other works are the ballet-cantata *Le Fou de la Dame* (in concert form, Paris, Nov. 9, 1928; stage production, Geneva, April 6, 1929); *Cinderella*, ballet (Chicago, Aug. 30, 1931; revised and performed as *La Pantoufle de vair* at the Opéra-Comique, Paris, May 14, 1935); a Symphony (Paris, March 15, 1934); *Ginevra*, comic opera in 3 acts (Paris, Opéra-Comique, July 25, 1942); *Arlequin radiophile*, chamber opera (Paris, April 1, 1946); *Puck*, fairy opera after Shakespeare (Strasbourg, Jan. 29, 1949); *Concerto de mai*, for piano and orch. (Paris, May 4, 1950); *Travesti*, ballet (Enghien-les-Bains, June 4, 1952); ballet, *Les Noces fantastiques* (Paris, Feb. 9, 1955); Symphony for Strings and Celesta (1952–54); *Le Moulin de la galette*, symph. poem (1958).

De Lara (real name **Cohen**), **Isidore,** English composer of operas; b. London, Aug. 9, 1858; d. Paris, Sept. 2, 1935. He began to study the piano at the age of 10 with H. Aguilar; also studied singing with Lamperti and composition with Mazzucato at the Milan Cons. He then went to Paris to study with Lalo; returning to London, he wrote one opera after another, and easily secured performances.

WORKS: *The Light of Asia* (1892); *Amy Robsart* (London, July 20, 1893); *Moina* (Monte Carlo, March 14, 1897); *Messalina* (Monte Carlo, March 21, 1899; his most successful work); *Sanga* (Nice, Feb. 21, 1906); *Solea* (Cologne, Dec. 12, 1907); *Les Trois Masques* (Marseilles, Feb. 24, 1912); *Naïl* (Paris, April 22, 1912); and *Les Trois Mousquetaires* (Cannes, March 3, 1921).

Delcroix, Léon Charles, Belgian composer; b. Brussels, Sept. 15, 1880; d. there, Nov. 14, 1938. He studied piano with J. Wieniawski, organ with A. Mailly, and composition with Théo. Ysaÿe in Brussels and Vincent d'Indy in Paris. He conducted theater orchestras in Belgium (1909–27); then devoted his entire time to composition.

WORKS: For the stage: *Ce n'était qu'un rêve* (1 act); *La Bacchante*, ballet (Ghent, 1912); *Le Petit Poucet*, opera (Brussels, Oct. 9, 1913); for orch.: a symphony *Le Roi Harald*, *Çunacépa*, *Soir d'été à Lerici*, *Le Val harmonieux*; *Rapsodie languedocienne*; *Marche cortège*; *Sérénade* for clarinet, piano, and orch.; *Elégie et Poème* for violin and orch.; many chamber music works (quartets, quintets, sonatas, etc.); piano works; church music (*Pie Jesu, Resurrexi, Ecce panis*); songs. He wrote a biography of his teacher, J. Wieniawski (Brussels, 1908).

Delden, Lex van, Dutch composer; b. Amsterdam, Sept. 10, 1919. He studied medicine at the Univ. of Amsterdam; then turned to music; wrote criticism in the Dutch newspapers. In composition, he was entirely autodidact; yet he wrote a number of works, including 8 symphonies.

WORKS: 3 oratorios: *De Vogelvrijheid (The Phoenix Bird*, 1956), *Anthropolis* (1962) and *Icarus*, a radiophonic oratorio, with tape (1963); 8 symphonies: No. 1, *De stroom, Mei 1940 (The Torrent, May 1940)* for soprano, chorus, 8 instruments and percussion (1952; alternate version with orchestral scoring, 1954; describes the destruction of Rotterdam at the beginning of World War II); No. 2, *Sinfonia Giocosa* (1953); No. 3, *Facetten (Facets*, 1955); No. 4 (1957); No. 5 (1959); No. 6 (1963); No. 7, *Sinfonia concertante*, for 11 winds (1964); No. 8, for string orch. (1964); *Allegretto* for orch. (1949); *Introduction and Allegro*, small concerto for violin, piano and orch. (1951); Harp Concerto (1951); *In memoriam* for orch. (1953); Trio for String Orch. (1954); *Tij en Ontij*, ballet music (1956); Trumpet Concerto (1956); 2-Oboe Concerto (1959); Piano Concerto (1960); *Piccolo Concerto* for 12 winds and percussion (1960); Concerto for 2 String Orchestras (1961); *Piccola Musica Concertata* for 3 trombones and string orch. (1963); Flute Concerto (1965); Concerto for Violin, Viola, Double Bass and Orch. (1965); Concerto for 2 Soprano Saxophones and Orch. (1967); *Musica Sinfonica* (1967); Concerto for Percussion, Celeste and String Orch. (1968); Organ Concerto (1973); *Rubáiyát* for soprano, tenor, chorus, 2 pianos and percussion (1947); *Het Spoorboekje (The Railway Timetable)* for a cappella chorus (1952; a setting of a number of sections from the regulations of Dutch railways); *Canto della guerra* for chorus and orch. (1967); Suite for Violin and Piano (1939); *Ballet* for flute, viola, bassoon and guitar (1946); Piano Sonata (1949); *Introduction and Dance (Judith)* for flute, clarinet, violin, viola, cello and piano (1950); Duo for Flute and Harp (1950); *Small Suite* for 12 harps (1951; in collaboration with Marius Flothuis); Saxophone Sonatina (1952); 2 string quartets (1954, 1965); 4 Pieces for Harp (1954); *Impromptu* for harp (1955); *Sonatina Eroica* for piano (1956); Quartet for Flute, Violin, Viola and Cello (1957); Solo Cello Sonata (1958); *Intrada and Dance* for 6 harps (1961); Concertino for 2 Harps (1962); Violin Sonata (1964); Fantasia for Harp and 8 Winds (1965); *Musica notturna a cinque* for 4 cellos and harp (1967); Piano Trio (1969); Quartet for Flute, Oboe, Violin and Cello (1970); *Sestetto* for 6 strings (1971); songs.

Deldevez, Édouard-Marie-Ernest, French conductor and composer; b. Paris, May 31, 1817; d. there, Nov. 6, 1897. He studied violin with Habeneck and music theory with Halévy and Berton at the Paris Cons. In 1859 he was appointed assistant conductor at the Grand Opéra and of the Conservatoire Concerts; taught orchestral playing at the Paris Cons. (1874–85).

WORKS: ballets: *Eucharis* (1944); *Paquita* (1946); *Vert-Vert* (1951, with Tolbecque); the operas *Samson* and *Le Violon enchanté*; 3 symphonies; chamber music; sacred choruses and songs.

WRITINGS: the monograph *Curiosités musicales* (1873); also *La Notation de la musique classique comparée à la notation de la musique moderne, et de l'exécution des petites notes en général*; *L'Art du chef d'orchestre* (1878); *La Société des Concerts de 1860 à 1885* (1887); *De l'exécution d'ensemble* (1888); and *Le*

Passé à propos du présent (1892), a continuation of his personal recollections publ. in 1890 as *Mes Mémoires.*

BIBLIOGRAPHY: Ch. Malherbe, "Notice sur Deldevez," *La Revue Internationale de Musique* (1899).

De Leone, Francesco B., American composer; b. of Italian parents in Ravenna, Ohio, July 28, 1887; d. Akron, Ohio, Dec. 10, 1948. He studied at Dana's Musical Institute, Warren, Ohio (1901–03), and at the Royal Cons. of Naples (1903–10); returned to the U.S. and established his home in Akron, where he founded the De Leone School of Music, and organized and directed the Music Dept. of the Univ. of Akron; also conducted the Akron Symph. Orch. He wrote the operas *Alglala* (Akron, O., May 23, 1924); *A Millionaire Caprice* (in Italian; Naples, July 26, 1910); *Cave Man Stuff,* operetta; *Princess Ting-Ah-Ling,* operetta; the sacred musical dramas *Ruth, The Prodigal Son, The Golden Calf* and *David; The Triumph of Joseph,* oratorio; pieces for symph. orch.: 6 *Italian Dances, Italian Rhapsody, Gibraltar Suite;* over 400 songs; piano pieces.

Delgadillo, Luis Abraham, Nicaraguan composer; b. Managua, Aug. 26, 1887; d. there, Dec. 20, 1961. He studied at the Milan Cons.; returning to Nicaragua, he became a band conductor and opened a music school, which later became a conservatory. His music is permeated with native rhythm and melos; virtually all of his output is descriptive of some aspect of Latin American culture and history.

WORKS: for orch.: *Sinfonia indigena* (1921); *Sinfonia mexicana* (1924); *Teotihuacan* (1925); *Sinfonia incaica* (1926; conducted by the composer in Caracas, May 20, 1927); *Sinfonia serrana* (1928); 12 short symphonies, all composed in one year (1953) and couched in different styles, from classical to modernistic; overtures in the styles of Debussy and Schoenberg (*Obertura Debussyana; Obertura Schoenbergiana,* 1955); 7 string quartets; church music; piano pieces in various forms.

Delibes, (Clément-Philbert-) Léo, famous French composer; b. St.-Germain-du-Val, Sarthe, Feb. 21, 1836; d. Paris, Jan. 16, 1891. He entered the Paris Cons. in 1848, Le Couppey, Bazin, Adam, and Benoist being his chief teachers. In 1853 he became accompanist at the Théâtre-Lyrique, and organist at the Church of St.-Jean et St.-François.

WORKS: His first stage-work was the 1-act operetta *Deux sous de charbon* (1855), followed by 12 more of the same class up to 1865, when he was appointed 2d chorusmaster at the Grand Opéra. He then tried his hand at ballet writing, and brought out the ballet *La Source* (produced later in Vienna as *Naila, die Quellenfee*) at the Opéra (Nov. 12, 1866); the next ballet, *Coppélia, ou la fille aux yeux d'émail* (Opéra, May 25, 1870) was triumphantly successful, and has held the boards ever since. *Sylvia, ou la nymphe de Diane* (June 14, 1876) was also successful. After resigning his post as chorusmaster, he succeeded Reber (1881) as professor of composition at the Cons.; in 1884, was elected as Massé's successor in the Académie. Delibes' dramatic music is distinguished by melodiousness, vivacity, and elegance of instrumentation. His stage-works also include the operas *Le Roi*

l'a dit (Opéra-Comique, May 24, 1873), *Jean de Nivelle* (March 8, 1880), *Lakmé* (April 14, 1883; his masterpiece); *Kassya* (1893; posthumous, completed by Massenet); he left some sketches for a 3-act opéra comique, *Le Roi des Montagnes.* Besides these, a cantata *Alger* (1856); choruses for men's and women's voices; and a collection of 15 Melodies with piano, in German Lied style.

BIBLIOGRAPHY: E. Guiraud, *Notice sur la vie et les œuvres de Léo Delibes* (Paris, 1896); O. Séré, *Musiciens français d'aujourd'hui* (2nd ed. Paris, 1911); H. de Curzon, *Léo Delibes* (Paris, 1927).

Delius, Frederick, significant English composer of German parentage; full baptismal names, **Fritz Albert Theodor;** b. Bradford, Jan. 29, 1862; d. Grez-sur-Loing, France, June 10, 1934. He showed musical abilities as a boy, and learned to play the piano and violin. His father, who was an export merchant, was eager to have his son take up a business career, but Delius preferred adventure; at the age of 22 he went to Florida, where he cultivated orange groves. In Florida he met the organist, Thomas F. Ward, who gave him a brief course of musical instruction. In 1886 he entered the Leipzig Cons. and studied there with Reinecke, Sitt, and Jadassohn. One of the great events of his life was his meeting with Grieg in Norway; Delius became his friend and admirer; the subsequent style of his music was largely molded by Grieg's influence. In 1888 he settled at Grez-sur-Loing, near Paris, where he remained for the rest of his life, except for a few short trips. In 1903 he married the painter Jelka Rosen; in 1922 an illness set in which gradually developed into paralysis; Delius became a complete invalid, and also went blind. During this period, Eric Fenby, the English composer, served as his amanuensis and wrote down music at the dictation of Delius, including complete orchestral scores. In 1929 Sir Thomas Beecham organized a festival of Delius' music in London and the composer was brought from France to hear it (6 concerts; Oct. 12 to Nov. 1, 1929). In the same year Delius was made Companion of Honour by George V and hon. Mus. Doc. by Oxford. In his music, Delius follows divergent lines of thought; basically a Romanticist, influenced by Grieg, he was at his best in evocative programmatic pieces in small forms (*On Hearing the First Cuckoo in Spring; North Country Sketches,* etc.); but he also could produce brilliant stylizations of folk rhythms of various strains (*Brigg Fair, Appalachia, A Song of the High Hills*); his *Mass of Life* is his only work drawn on a large scale, with philosophic implications; he was also fascinated by possibilities of tone painting (as in his orchestral nocturne, *Paris: the Song of a Great City*). In his harmonic idiom, Delius used tense chromatic progressions, often resulting in clashing dissonances; he also applied Impressionistic devices, particularly the whole-tone scale. His orchestral writing is always lucid, with emphasis on individual instrumental color.

WORKS: FOR THE STAGE: the operas *Irmelin* (1890–92; first performance Oxford, May 4, 1953, Beecham conducting); *The Magic Fountain* (1893); *Margot la Rouge* (1902); *Koanga* (Elberfeld, March 30, 1904); *Romeo und Julia auf dem Dorfe* (Berlin, Feb. 21, 1907; London, as *A Village Romeo and Juliet,* Feb.

22, 1910; contains *The Walk to the Paradise Garden*); *Fennimore und Gerda* (after Niels Lhyne by Jacobsen; Frankfurt, Oct. 21, 1919). FOR ORCH.: *Florida*, suite (1886-87); *Hiawatha*, tone poem (1888); *Paa Vidderne*, for narrator and orch., after Ibsen (1888); *Marche Caprice* and *Schlittenfahrt*, (1888); *Rhapsodic Variations* (unfinished, 1888); *Pastorale* for violin and orch. (1888); *Petite Suite* (1889); *Légendes*, for piano and orch. (unfinished, 1890); *Sur les Cimes*, tone poem after Ibsen (1892); *Legend*, for violin and orch. (1893); *Over the Hills and Far Away* (1895); *Norwegian Suite*, as entr'acte music to Heiberg's *Folkeraadet* (1897); Piano Concerto (1897; revised in one movement, 1906); *The Dance Goes On*, tone poem (1898); *Paris: the Song of a Great City* (1899); *Life's Dance*, tone poem (revision of *The Dance Goes On*; 1901; first performance, Berlin, Nov. 15, 1912); *Appalachia*, orchestral variations with final chorus (1902); *Brigg Fair*, English Rhapsody (Liverpool, Jan. 18, 1908); *In a Summer Garden*, symph. poem, dedicated to his wife (London Philh., Dec. 11, 1908); *A Dance Rhapsody* (Hereford Music Festival, Sept. 7, 1909); *Summer Night on the River* and *On Hearing the First Cuckoo in Spring* (Leipzig, Oct. 2, 1913; first English performance of both pieces, London Philh., Jan. 20, 1914, Mengelberg conducting); *North Country Sketches* (1913-14); *Short Piece* for string orch. (1915); Concerto for Violin and Cello with Orch. (1915-16); *A Dance Rhapsody*, No. 2 (1916); Violin Concerto (1916); *Eventyr*, symph. poem, subtitled *Once Upon A Time* (London Promenade Concerts, Jan. 11, 1919); incidental music to James Elroy Flecker's *Hassan* (1920); Cello Concerto (1921); *A Song of Summer* (dictated by Delius to Eric Fenby in France; London, Sept. 17, 1931); *Fantastic Dance* (London, 1934). VOCAL WORKS: *Sea Drift*, rhapsody for baritone solo, chorus, and orch. to poem by Walt Whitman (1903; first performance, Essen, May 24, 1906); *A Mass of Life*, for soloists, chorus, and large orch. (London, June 7, 1909, Beecham conducting); *Songs of Sunset* (1906-07); *On Craig Dhu*, for unaccompanied chorus (1907); *Midsummer Song*, for unaccompanied chorus (1908); *Wanderer's Song*, for unaccompanied men's chorus (1908); *A Song of the High Hills* (1911-12); *Requiem*, "to the memory of all young artists fallen in the war" (composed 1914-18; London, Royal Philh., March 23, 1922); *A Song Before Sunrise* (1918); *Cynara* and *Arabesk* (London, Delius Festival, Oct. 18, 1929); numerous songs (several with orch.). CHAMBER MUSIC: 2 string quartets (1893, 1916-17); 3 violin sonatas (1892), 1915, after 1928); Romance for Violin and Piano (1896); Cello Sonata (1917); etc.

BIBLIOGRAPHY: M. Chop, *Frederick Delius*, vol. II of *Monographien moderner Musiker* (Leipzig, 1907); *Musical Times* (March 1915); Ph. Heseltine, *Frederick Delius* (London, 1923; new ed., 1931); R. H. Hull, *Frederick Delius* (London, 1928); E. Blom, "Delius and America," *Musical Quarterly* (July 1929); Clare Delius, *Frederick Delius, Memories of My Brother* (London, 1935); E. Fenby, *Delius as I Knew Him* (London, 1936); A. Hutchings, *Delius, A Critical Biography* (London, 1948); Sir Thomas Beecham, *Frederick Delius* (London, 1959); Gloria Jahoda, *The Road to Samarkand: Frederick Delius and His Music* (N.Y., 1969); E. W. Fenby, *Delius* (London, 1971); W. Randel,

"Frederick Delius in America," *Virginia Magazine of History & Biography* (July 1971); Rachel Lowe, *Frederick Delius, 1862-1934*, a catalogue of the Music Archive of the Delius Trust (London, 1974); L. Carley, *Delius: The Paris Years* (1975).

Della Ciaia, Azzolino Bernardino, Italian organist and composer; b. Siena, March 21, 1671; d. Pisa, Jan. 15, 1755. He was an organist and also an experienced organ builder; constructed a large organ with 4 manuals and 100 stops for the St. Stephen Church in Pisa. He publ. *Salmi concertati* for 4 voices with instruments (Bologna, 1700); *Cantate de camera* (Lucca, 1701); *Sonate per cembalo* (Rome, 1727); much of his church music is extant in MS. He is regarded by some as an Italian originator of sonata form; his instrumental music, however, is more interesting for its florid ornamentation than for a strict formal development.

BIBLIOGRAPHY: Fausto Torrefranca, "L'impressionismo ritmico e le sonate del Della Ciaia" *Rivista dei Amici della Musica in Milano* (1913); F. Vatielli, "Una lettera biografica di A. Della Ciaia," *Critica Musicale* IV/8-9. Béla Bartók made a piano transcription of a keyboard sonata by Della Ciaia, in *XVIIth and XVIIIth Century Italian Cembalo and Organ Music Transcribed for Piano* (N.Y., 1930); Luigi Silva arranged *Toccata e Canzona* for cello and piano (1952). Alessandro Esposito edited and arranged Della Ciaia's *12 soggetti, 6 ricercari, messa* and *12 cembalo pieces* (Padua, 1956).

Della Corte, Andrea, eminent Italian musicologist; b. Naples, April 5, 1883; d. Turin, March 12, 1968. He was self-taught in music; devoted himself mainly to musical biography and analysis. He taught music history at the Turin Cons. (from 1926) and at the Univ. of Turin (from 1939). From 1919 till 1967 he was music critic of *La Stampa*.

WRITINGS: A prolific writer, he published *Paisiello* (Turin, 1922); *Saggi di Critica Musicale* (Turin, 1922); *L'Opera comica italiana del 1700* (2 vols., Bari, 1923); *Piccola Antologia settecentesca, XXIV pezzi inediti o rari* (Milan, 1925); *Disegno storico dell'Arte Musicale* (Turin, 5th ed., 1950); *Antologia della Storia della Musica* (2 vols., Turin, 1927-29; 4th ed., 1945); *Niccolò Piccinni* (Bari, 1928); *Scelta di Musiche per lo Studio della Storia* (Milan, 3rd ed., 1949); *La Vita musicale di Goethe* (Turin, 1932); *Vincenzo Bellini* (in collaboration with Guido Pannain, Turin, 1936); *Ritratto di Franco Alfano* (Turin, 1936); *Pergolesi* (Turin, 1936); *Un Italiano all'Estero: Antonio Salieri* (Turin, 1937); *Tre secoli di Opera Italiana* (Turin, 1938); *Verdi* (Turin, 1939); *Toscanini* (Vicenza, 1946; in French, Lausanne, 1949); *Satire e Grotteschi di Musiche e di Musicisti d'ogni tempo* (Turin, 1947); *Le sei più belle opere di Verdi: Rigoletto, Il Trovatore, La Traviata, Aida, Otello, Falstaff* (Milan, 1947); *Gluck* (Florence, 1948); *Baldassare Galuppi* (Siena, 1949); *Arrigo Serato* (Siena, 1949); *Storia della Musica* (3 vols.; in collaboration with Guido Pannain; Turin, 3rd ed.; 1952; 2nd ed. translated into Spanish, 1950); *L'interpretazione musicale e gli interpreti* (Turin, 1951); edited song textbooks for the Italian schools. With Guido M. Gatti, he compiled a valuable *Dizionario di musica* (1926; 6th ed., 1959).

Della Maria, Pierre-Antoine-Dominique, French opera composer; b. Marseilles, June 14, 1769; d. Paris, March 9, 1800. Son of an Italian mandolinist, he was remarkably precocious; played the mandolin and cello at an early age, and at 18 produced a grand opera at Marseilles. He then studied composition in Italy (for a time with Paisiello) and produced in Naples a successful opera, *Il Maestro di cappella* (1792). He went to Paris in 1796; obtaining a libretto *(Le Prisonnier)* from Duval, he set it to music in eight days, brought it out at the Opéra-Comique (Jan. 29, 1798), and was at once famous. Before his death he finished 6 more operas, 4 of which were produced during his lifetime; a posthumous opera, *La Fausse Duègne* (completed by Blangini), was produced at Paris in 1802; several church compositions are in MS.

Deller, Alfred, English countertenor; b. Margate, May 30, 1912. He studied voice with his father; began singing as a boy soprano, later developing the alto range. He sang in the choirs of the Canterbury Cathedral (1940–47) and at St. Paul's in London. In 1948 he formed his own vocal and instrumental ensemble, the Deller Consort, acting as conductor and soloist in a repertory of old English music. This unique enterprise led to a modest revival of English madrigals and other songs of the Renaissance.

Delle Sedie, Enrico, Italian baritone and singing teacher; b. Leghorn, June 17, 1822; d. Garennes-Colombes, near Paris, Nov. 28, 1907. His teachers were Galeffi, Persanola, and Domeniconi. After imprisonment as a revolutionist (1848), he resumed the study of singing and made his debut at Florence (1851) in Verdi's *Nabucco.* Until 1861 he sang in the principal Italian cities; was then engaged at the Théâtre des Italiens, Paris, and appointed professor of singing in the Cons.; was regarded as one of the best singing teachers in Paris. His basic manuals, *Arte e fisiologia del canto* (Milan, 1876; in French as *L'Art lyrique,* Paris, 1876) and *L'estetica del canto e dell'arte melodrammatica* (Milan, 1886) were published in N.Y. in English as *Vocal Art* (3 parts) and *Esthetics of the Art of Singing, and of the Melodrama* (4 vols.). A condensation (by the author) of both manuals was published in one volume as *A Complete Method of Singing* (N.Y., 1894).

Dellinger, Rudolf, German composer and conductor; b. Graslitz, Bohemia, July 8, 1857; d. Dresden, Sept. 24, 1910. Pupil of the Prague Cons.; played clarinet in the city orch. at Brünn, 2d conductor there in 1880; 1883 at the Carl Schulze Theater in Hamburg; from 1893 till death conductor at the Residenz-Theater in Dresden. He produced the operettas *Don Caesar* (Hamburg, March 28, 1885; highly popular), *Lorraine* (Hamburg, 1886), *Capitän Fracassa* (Hamburg, 1889), *Saint-Cyr* (Hamburg, 1891), *Die Chansonnette* (Dresden, 1894; Prague, 1895, as *Die Sängerin*), *Jadwiga* (Dresden, 1901), *Der letzte Jonas* (1910).

Dello Joio (properly **Dello Ioio**), **Norman,** American composer; b. New York, Jan. 24, 1913 (descended from a musical Italian family). He studied with his father, an organist in New York, and later with his godfather, Pietro Yon; then took lessons with Bernard Wagenaar and Hindemith. He won the Town Hall Composition Award for his *Magnificat* in 1942, and held a Guggenheim Fellowship in 1944–45 and again in 1945–46; taught at Sarah Lawrence College (1944–50). In 1957 he became a teacher at Mannes College of Music in N.Y., and in 1972 became Dean of Fine Arts at Boston Univ. He won the Pulitzer Prize in 1957 for his *Meditations on Ecclesiastes.*

WORKS: OPERAS: *The Triumph of St. Joan* (Sarah Lawrence College, Bronxville, May 9, 1950); *The Ruby* (Bloomington, Ind., May 13, 1955); *The Trial at Rouen* (NBC, April 8, 1956; a different work from *The Triumph of St. Joan*); *Blood Moon* (San Francisco, Sept. 18, 1961). BALLETS: *Prairie* (1942); *Duke of Sacramento* (1942); *On Stage!* (Cleveland, Nov. 23, 1945); *Wilderness Stair* (Martha Graham, New London, Conn., Aug. 13, 1948). FOR ORCH.: Concertinos: for piano and chamber orch. (1939); for flute and strings (1940); for harmonica and chamber orch. (1942); *Sinfonietta* (1941); *Magnificat* (1942); Concerto for 2 Pianos and Orch. (1942); *To a Lone Sentry* (1943); *Concert Music* (1944); *Ricercari* for piano and orch. (N.Y., Dec. 19, 1946, composer as soloist); Harp Concerto (N.Y., Oct. 20, 1947); *Variations, Chaconne, and Finale* (Pittsburgh, Jan. 30, 1948); *Serenade* (1948); Concertante for Clarinet and Orch. (1949); *New York Profiles* (1949); *Epigraph* (1951); symphonic suite in three movements from the opera *The Triumph of Saint Joan* (1951); *Epigraph* (1954); *Meditations on Ecclesiastes* for string orch. (1956; winner of the 1957 Pulitzer Prize); *Ballad of the 7 Lively Arts* for piano and orch. (1958); *Air Power,* symph. suite based on music to the television series (1958); *Fantasy and Variations* for piano and orch. (Cincinnati, March 9, 1962); *Antiphonal Fantasy on a Theme of Vincenzo Albrici,* for organ, brasses and strings (1966); *Homage to Haydn* for orch. (1969); *Lyric Fantasies* for viola and strings (1973); *Notes from Tom Paine* for piano and band (1975); *Satiric Dances* for band (1975); *Colonial Variants* (Philadelphia, May 27, 1976). CHAMBER MUSIC: Sextet for 3 Recorders and String Trio (1943); Trio for Flute, Cello, and Piano (1944); *Duo Concertante* for cello and piano (1945); *Variations* and *Capriccio* for violin and piano (1949). Piano works: 3 piano sonatas (1942; 1943; 1947); *Duo Concertante* for 2 pianos (1943); *Prelude: To A Young Musician* (1945); *Prelude: To a Young Dancer* (1946); *Two Nocturnes* for piano (1949). For voice: *Vigil Strange* (1942); *Mystic Trumpeter,* cantata (1943); *A Jubilant Song* (1946); *A Fable; Madrigal* (1947); *Psalm of David,* for chorus, brass, strings, and percussion (1950); *Song of Affirmation* for soloists, narrator, and orch. (1952); *Lamentation of Saul,* for baritone and orch. (1954); *To Saint Cecilia,* cantata for chorus and brass (1957); *Songs of Walt Whitman* for chorus and orch., or piano (1967); *Years of the Modern* for chorus, percussion and brass (1968); Mass, for Chorus, Brass and Organ (1968); *Songs of Abélard* for band and optional voice (1969); *Evocations* for chorus and orch. (Tampa, Florida, Oct. 2, 1970, composer conducting); Mass for Chorus, Cantor, Congregation, Organ and Brass Ensemble (1976).

BIBLIOGRAPHY: Edward Downes, "The Music of Norman Dello Joio," *Musical Quarterly* (April 1962).

Dell'Orefice, Giuseppe, Italian composer; b. Fara, Abruzzio Chietino, Italy, Aug. 22, 1848; d. Naples, Jan. 3, 1889. Pupil of Fenaroli and Miceli in Naples Cons.; from 1878, conductor in the San Carlo Theater, Naples; wrote the ballet, *I Fantasmi notturni* (Naples, 1872), and the operas *Romilda de' Bardi* (Naples, 1874), *Egmont* (Naples, 1878), *Il Segreto della Duchesa* (Naples, 1879) and *L'oasi* (Vicenza, 1886); also songs and piano pieces.

Delmar, Dezso, Hungarian-American composer; b. Timișoara, July 14, 1891. He studied piano with Béla Bartók and theory with Kodály at the Royal Academy of Music in Budapest, graduating in 1913; concurrently took courses in jurisprudence, obtaining a lawyer's degree. He served in the Austro-Hungarian Army in World War I; after demobilization, he devoted himself entirely to music. He came to the U.S. in 1922; lived in New York until 1929, then moved to Los Angeles; in 1946 settled in Sacramento, California, as a teacher of piano and theory. His works include a symphony (1949); *Hungarian Sketches* for orch. (1947); 3 string quartets, a string trio, a violin sonata, etc.; choral music; many piano pieces and songs. His works reflect the melorhythmic modalities of Hungarian folk music.

Del Mar, Norman, English conductor; b. London, July 31, 1919. He studied composition at the Royal College of Music, London, with R. O. Morris and Vaughan Williams, and also played the violin and the French horn in the student orch. He then studied conducting with Constant Lambert. During the war, he played in Royal Air Force bands, and visited the United States with the R.A.F. Symphony in 1944. After the war he organized the Chelsea Symphony Orch. in London; in 1948 he toured Germany with the Sadler's Wells Ballet Company. He also publ. the valuable monographs *Paul Hindemith* (London, 1957); *Richard Strauss, A Critical Commentary of His Life and Works* (2 vols., London, 1962, 1968); *Modern Music and the Conductor* (London, 1960; paperback ed., 1970).

Delmas, Jean-François, famous French dramatic bass; b. Lyons, April 14, 1861; d. St. Alban de Monthel, France, Sept. 29, 1933. Pupil of the Paris Cons., where he won the 1st prize for singing in 1886; debut at the Grand Opéra, 1886, as St.-Bris in *Les Huguenots*; then a regular member of the Opéra, idolized by the public, and unexcelled as an interpreter of Wagner, in whose works he created the principal bass parts at all the French premières; he created also the chief roles in Massenet's *Le Mage* (1891) and *Thaïs* (1894), Leroux's *Astarté* (1901), Saint-Saëns' *Les Barbares* (1901), Erlanger's *Le Fils de l'Étoile* (1904), etc.; besides an enormous French repertory, he also sang the operas of Gluck, Mozart, and Weber.
BIBLIOGRAPHY: H. Curzon, *Croquis d'artistes* (Paris, 1898).

Delmas, Marc-Jean-Baptiste, talented French composer; b. St. Quentin, March 28, 1885; d. Paris, Nov. 30, 1931; pupil of Vidal and Leroux; won the Prix de Rossini (1911), the Grand Prix de Rome (1919), the Chartier Prix for chamber music, the Prix Cressent and other awards for various compositions.
WORKS: OPERAS: *Jean de Calais* (1907), *Laïs* (1909), *Stéfano* (1910), *Cyrce* (1920; perf. 1927); *Iriam* (1921), *Anne-Marie* (1922), *Le Giaour* (1925).
ORCH. MUSIC: *Les Deux Routes* (1913); *Au pays wallon* (1914); *Le Poète et la fée* (1920); *Le Bateau ivre* (1923); *Penthésilée* (1922); *Rapsodie ariégeoise* for cello and orch.; chamber music; piano pieces. Author of the books *G. Bizet* (Paris, 1930) and *G. Charpentier et le lyrisme français* (1931).

Del Monaco, Mario, Italian tenor; b. Florence, July 27, 1915. His father was a government official; his mother, a singer. His family moved to Pesaro when he was a child; he studied at the Cons. there, and sang a part in an opera performance at the age of 13 in a theater at Mondalfo, near Pesaro. He began serious study at 19; made his professional debut in Milan on Jan. 1, 1941 as Pinkerton in *Madama Butterfly*. During World War II he was in the army. After the armistice, he was engaged to sing at La Scala. He produced a highly favorable impression, and was engaged to appear at Covent Garden, London; also made a successful tour in South America; sang at the Colón in Buenos Aires, in Rio de Janeiro, Mexico City. He made his American debut with the San Francisco Opera; was then engaged to sing at the Metropolitan Opera House, where he made his first appearance in *Manon Lescaut* (Nov. 27, 1950). He was a regular member of the Metropolitan Opera Company during subsequent seasons. His repertory in Italian and French roles is extensive.

Delna (real name **Ledan**), **Marie,** French contralto; b. Meudon, near Paris, April 3, 1875; d. Paris, July 23, 1932. She made her debut at the Opéra-Comique, June 9, 1892, as Didon in Berlioz's *Les Troyens;* sang there for 6 years with great success; from 1898–1901 at the Opéra; then again at the Opéra-Comique; in 1903 married a Belgian, A. H. de Saone, and retired temporarily from the stage; her reappearance at the Opéra-Comique, in 1908, was acclaimed with great applause; after that she was a prime favorite; in 1910 she sang Orfeo (in Gluck's opera) and Françoise in Bruneau's *L'Attaque du Moulin,* at the Metropolitan Opera House, making a deep impression; then returned to Paris, where she continued to sing at the Opéra-Comique for many years.

Del Tredici, David, American composer; b. Cloverdale, Calif., March 16, 1937. He studied composition with Seymour Shifrin at the Univ. of California at Berkeley (B.A., 1959); at Princeton Univ. with Roger Sessions (M.F.A., 1964); later joined the faculty of Harvard Univ. In his music he plies a modified dodecaphonic course in a polyrhythmic context, without necessarily eschewing tonality.
WORKS: *Six Songs* to texts of James Joyce for voice and piano (1959); String Trio (1959); *The Last Gospel* for amplified rock group, chorus and orch. (1967); *Syzygy* for soprano, horn, chimes and chamber ensemble (N.Y., July 7, 1968); a series of independent pieces, each based on a different episode of *Alice in Wonderland*, and scored for electronically amplified

soprano-narrator and orch. (or chamber group): *Pop-Pourri* (1968); a ballet sequence, *The Lobster Quadrille* (London, Nov. 25, 1969); *Vintage Alice* (1972); *Adventures Underground* (1973); *In Wonderland*, in 2 parts (1969–75); *Annotated Alice* (1976) and *The Final Alice* (Chicago, Oct. 7, 1976).

De Luca, Giuseppe, Italian baritone; b. Rome, Dec. 25, 1876; d. New York, Aug. 26, 1950. He studied music at Santa Cecilia in Rome; made his first professional appearance in Piacenza (1897) as Valentine in *Faust*; then sang in various cities of Italy; from 1902, chiefly in Milan at the Teatro Lirico and La Scala; he created the principal baritone role in the world première of Cilea's *Adriana Lecouvreur* and in *Madama Butterfly*. He made his American debut at the Metropolitan Opera as Figaro in *Il Barbiere di Siviglia*, on Nov. 25, 1915 with excellent success, immediately establishing himself as a favorite; on Jan. 28, 1916 he sang the part of Paquiro in the world première of *Goyescas* by Granados, at the Metropolitan Opera, of which he became a member until 1935; after a sojourn in Italy, he returned to the U.S. in 1940, and made a few more appearances at the Metropolitan, his vocal powers undiminished by age. He sang almost exclusively the Italian repertory; his interpretations were distinguished by fidelity to the dramatic import of his roles; he was praised by the critics for his finely graduated dynamic range and his mastery of bel canto.

Delune, Louis, Belgian composer and conductor; b. Charleroi, March 15, 1876; d. Paris, Jan. 5, 1940. He studied with Tinel at the Brussels Cons.; won the Belgian Prix de Rome with his cantata *La Mort du roi Reynaud* (1905); then traveled as accompanist for César Thomson. He lived many years in Paris, and wrote most of his works there; composed *Symphonie chevaleresque*; the opera *Tania*; a ballet, *Le Fruit défendu*, Piano Concerto, violin pieces, etc.

Del Valle de Paz, Edgardo, Italian writer on music; b. Alexandria, Egypt, Oct. 18, 1861; d. Florence, Italy, April 5, 1920. He studied at Naples Cons. under B. Cesi (piano) and P. Serrao (composition); made pianistic tours in Italy and Egypt; in 1893 he established the "Circolo Del Valle" at Florence, and from 1896–1914 was director of the journal *La Nuova Musica* and prof. in the Florence Cons. (from 1890). He publ. a *Scuola pratica del pianoforte,* adopted by several Italian music schools. His opera, *Oriana,* was produced at Florence (1907).

Delvaux, Albert, Belgian composer; b. Louvain, May 31, 1913. He studied first at the Cons. in Louvain and completed his studies with Joseph Leroy at the Liège Cons. He won a 3rd prize (1957, for *Esquisses*) and a 1st prize (1961, for *Sinfonia Burlesca*) in the Queen Elisabeth International Composition Competition in Brussels.
WORKS: *Héro et Léandre,* for soloists, chorus and orch. (1941); *5 Pieces* for string orch. (1942); *Scherzo* for Orch. (1942); *Symphonic Poem* (1943); *Symphonic Suite* (1948); Symphonic Variations (1948); *Sinfonietta* (1952); Concerto for Cello and Chamber Orch.

(1957); *Esquisses (Schetsen)* for chamber orch. (1956); *Concerto da Camera* for chamber orch. (1957); *Sinfonia Burlesca* (1960); *5 Bagatelles* for chamber orch. (1960); *Miniatures* for orch. (1960); Violin Concerto (1961); *Sinfonia concertante* for violin, viola and strings (1963); *Mouvement symphonique* (1966); Concerto for Flute, Oboe, Clarinet, Bassoon and Chamber Orch. (1967); *Sinfonia* (1969); Concerto for Violin, Cello and Strings (1970); *Introduction e Allegro* for strings (1971); 2 string trios (1939, 1961); Sonata for Flute, Oboe, Clarinet and Bassoon (1940); 4 string quartets (1943, 1945, 1955, 1961); Trio for Oboe, Clarinet and Bassoon (1948); Oboe Sonatina (1956); *5 Impromptus* for flute, oboe, clarinet and piano (1959); Violin Sonata (1962); *Sonata a Quattro* for 4 clarinets, or flute, oboe, clarinet and bassoon (1964); *Walliser Suite* for wind quintet (1966); *Cassazione* for violin, oboe, clarinet and cello (1966); *Andante e Scherzando* for violin and piano (1972); choruses.

Delvincourt, Claude, outstanding French composer; b. Paris, Jan. 12, 1888; d. in an automobile accident in Orbetello, province of Grosseto, Italy, April 5, 1954. He studied with Widor at the Paris Cons.; in 1913 received the Prix de Rome for his cantata, *Faust et Hélène* (sharing the prize with Lili Boulanger). He was in the French army in World War I and on Dec. 31, 1915 suffered a crippling wound. He recovered in a few years, and devoted himself energetically to musical education and composition. He was director of the Cons. of Versailles; in 1941 he was appointed director of the Paris Cons. His music is distinguished by strong dramatic and lyric quality; he was most successful in his stage works.
WORKS: *Offrande à Siva,* choreographic poem (Frankfurt, July 3, 1927); *La Femme à Barbe,* musical farce (Versailles, June 2, 1938); *Lucifer,* mystery play (Paris Opéra, Dec. 8, 1948); two orchestral suites from the film score *La Croisière jaune: Pamir* (Paris, Dec. 8, 1935) and *Films d'Asie* (Paris, Jan. 16, 1937). He also wrote *Ce Monde de rosée,* for voice and orch. (Paris, March 25, 1935); some chamber music (Trio for Oboe, Clarinet, and Bassoon; Violin Sonata, etc.); piano pieces.
BIBLIOGRAPHY: W. L. Landowski, *Claude Delvincourt* (Paris, 1948).

Demantius, Christoph, German composer; b. Reichenberg, Dec. 15, 1567; d. Freiberg, Saxony, April 20, 1643. Cantor at Zittau, about 1596; at Freiberg, 1604–43; prolific composer of sacred and secular music, he ranks with Hassler, M. and H. Prätorius, and Eccard. He wrote *Deutsche Passion nach Johannes* (1631; ed. and publ. by F. Blume, 1934); *Triades precum vespertinarum* (1602); etc. He was the author of an instruction book, *Isagoge artis musicae* (Nuremberg, 1605; 10th ed. 1671).

Demarest, Clifford, American organist and composer; b. Tenafly, N.J., Aug. 12, 1874; d. there, May 13, 1946. He was organist at Church of the Messiah, N.Y.; wrote 2 cantatas, *The Shepherds of Bethlehem* and *The Cross Victorious*; a *Pastoral Suite* for organ; *Rip van Winkle,* for organ (1925); about 30 anthems; songs, etc.; also published *Hints on Organ Accompaniment.*

Demarquez, Suzanne, French composer; b. Paris, July 5, 1899; d. there, Oct. 23, 1965. She studied at the Paris Cons.; composed chamber music including a sprithly *Sonatine* for flute and piano (1953). She published the valuable monographs *André Jolivet* (Paris, 1958); *Manuel de Falla* (Paris, 1963; in English, Philadelphia, 1968); *Hector Berlioz* (Paris, 1969).

Demény, Desiderius, Hungarian composer; b. Budapest, Jan. 29, 1871; d. there, Nov. 9, 1937. He was a pupil of V. Herzfeld and S. von Bacho; ordained priest at Gran, 1893; court chaplain (1897); on 3 different occasions he won the Géza Zichy Prize (with *Ungarische Tanzsuite, Festouvertüre,* and *Rhapsodie*); in 1902 he founded *Zeneközlöny,* an important Hungarian music journal.
WORKS: 8 Masses; *Hungarian Suite* for mixed chorus; *Scherzo* for male chorus; 2 *Bilder aus Algier; Serenata sinfonica;* an operetta, *Der sieghafte Tod;* several melodramas; many other choral and vocal works, including about 100 songs (mostly to German texts).

Demessieux, Jeanne, French organist; b. Montpellier, Feb. 14, 1921; d. Paris, Nov. 11, 1968. She studied at the Paris Cons. with Tagliafero and Dupré; played organ at the age of 12 at the Saint-Esprit Church in Paris; toured widely in Europe; in 1952 was appointed professor at the Cons. of Liège; made a highly successful debut in the U.S. (1953). She was regarded as one of the most brilliant improvisers on the organ.

Demian, Wilhelm, Rumanian composer and conductor; b. Brasov, June 22, 1910. He studied music in his home town (1925–28); then in Vienna (1929–33); from 1935 to 1940 conducted the Philh. in Cluj; after 1949 was also conductor of the Hungarian State Opera there. His music is marked by a distinct neo-classical idiom in the manner of the Modern German school. Among his works are an opera *Capcana* (1964); Symphony (1947); Piano Concertino (1953); Violin Concerto (1956); *Liberté,* cantata (1957); Oboe Concerto (1963); and the musical *Attention! On tourne!* (1972).

De Mol, Pierre, Belgian composer; b. Brussels, Nov. 7, 1825; d. Alost, July 2, 1899. He was a pupil at Brussels Cons.; took Grand Prix de Rome (1855); was first cellist at Besançon Theater and teacher at the Cons.; later director of the Cons. at Alost.
WORKS: 3 cantatas, *Les Chrétiens Martyrs, Le Dernier Jour d'Herculaneum, La Fête de Belsazar;* the oratorio *St. Cecilia;* a Mass; 12 string quartets; an opera, *Quentin Metsys.*

Demuth, Norman, English composer and writer on music; b. London, July 15, 1898; d. Chichester, England, April 21, 1968. He studied with Parratt and Dunhill at the Royal College of Music in London. As a youth he joined the British army in 1915. After the end of the war he played organ in London churches. Later he became a choral conductor; in 1930 became professor of composition at the Royal Academy of Music. His works are influenced mainly by French music; in later years he became better known as the author of many books and unorthodox essays on music.

WORKS: 5 symphonies (two of which are entitled *Symphonic Study*); *Threnody* for strings (1942); *Overture for a Joyful Occasion* (1946); Violin Concerto (1937); Saxophone Concerto (1938); Piano Concerto (1943); Piano Concerto for the Left Hand (1947); 3 violin sonatas; Cello Sonata; Flute Sonata; many piano pieces.
WRITINGS: *The Gramophone and How to Use It* (London, 1945); *Albert Roussel* (London, 1947); *Ravel* in the Master Musicians Series (London, 1947); *An Anthology of Musical Criticism* (London, 1948); *César Franck* (London, 1949); *Paul Dukas* (London, 1949); *The Symphony: its History and Development* (London, 1950); *Gounod* (London, 1950); *Vincent d'Indy* (London, 1951); *A Course in Musical Composition* (London, 1951); *Musical Trends in the 20th Century* (London, 1952); *Musical Forms and Textures* (London, 1953); *French Piano Music: A Survey with Notes on its Performance* (London, 1959); *French Opera; Its Development to the Revolution* (Sussex, 1963).

Dencke, Jeremiah, American Moravian minister, organist, and composer; b. Langenbilau, Silesia, Oct. 2, 1725; d. Bethlehem, Pa., May 28, 1795. In 1748 he became organist at Herrnhut, the center of the European Moravians; came to America (1761) and served the Moravian settlements in Pennsylvania in various capacities. During the Revolutionary War he was warden of the Bethlehem congregation. Dencke was apparently the first individual to compose vocal concerted church music in the Moravian settlements in Pennsylvania, and possibly the first to write such music in colonial America. He was an able composer. The earliest work he is known to have composed in America is a simple anthem for chorus, strings, and figured bass, written for a *Liebesmahl* (Love Feast; a service of spiritual devotion and earthly fraternalism, composed of hymn singing and a light meal of roll and beverage) on Aug. 29, 1765. His finest works are 3 sets of sacred songs for soprano, strings and organ, composed in 1767–68. The first, written for the annual festival of the 'choir' of small girls, is included in the first volume of the series *Music of the Moravians in America,* issued by the N.Y. Public Library in 1938. The other sets of solos were written for Christmas services. Dencke's compositions are listed in A. G. Rau and H. T. David, *A Catalogue of Music by American Moravians, 1742–1842* (Bethlehem, Pa., 1938).
BIBLIOGRAPHY: H. T. David, "Musical Life in the Pennsylvania Settlements of the *Unitas Fratrum,*" *Transactions of the Moravian Historical Society* (1942; repr. as Moravian Music Foundation Publication No. 6, Winston-Salem, N.C., 1959); "Recent Discoveries in the Foundation Archives," *Moravian Music Foundation Bulletin* (Spring-Summer 1974).

Dendrino, Gherase, Rumanian composer and conductor; b. Turnu-Măgurele, Sept. 16, 1901; d. Bucharest, Jan. 4, 1973. He studied with Kiriac and Castaldi at the Bucharest Cons. (1920–27); after holding various theater conducting posts, he was conductor of the State Operetta Theater in Bucharest. He wrote 4 light operettas: *Lăsați-mă să cînt* (1953), *Poveste pe strune și pe clape* (1955), *De luni pînă luni* (1958), and his particularly successful *Lysistrata* (Bucharest, Dec. 15, 1960); film music; popular music.

Denéréaz, Alexandre, Swiss composer and musicologist; b. Lausanne, July 31, 1875; d. there, July 25, 1947. He studied at Lausanne Cons. with Blanchet and at the Dresden Cons. with Draeseke and Döring; in 1896 was appointed professor at the Lausanne Cons.; also taught musicology at the Lausanne Univ., publ. an original theory of harmony.

WORKS: 3 symphonies; many symph. poems; cantatas; Concerto Grosso for Orch. and Organ; string quartets; organ works; a male chorus; music to René Morax's *La Dime.* Author, in collaboration with C. Bourguès, of *La Musique et la vie intérieure: histoire psychologique de l'art musical* (appendix entitled *L'Arbre généalogique de l'art musical;* 1919).

Dengremont, Maurice, Brazilian violinist; b. Rio de Janeiro, Brazil, Mar. 19, 1866, of French parents; d. Buenos Aires, Sept., 1893. As a child prodigy he attracted general notice in Europe in 1877, but his early death did not allow him to develop his gifts.

Denis, Didier, French composer; b. Paris, Nov. 5, 1947. He studied at the Paris Cons. with Henri Challan, Marcel Bitsch, Olivier Messiaen and Jean Rivier, graduating in 1968.

WORKS: Trio for Flute, Clarinet and Bassoon (1966); *Sagesse, Force, Beauté, l'Amour* for coloratura soprano, 12 instruments and 6 percussion (1967); *Cinq fois je t'aime* for speaker, soprano, and orch. (1968); *Fugue indoue* for two groups of percussion instruments (1968); *Chants de Tse Yeh* for piano and 12 instruments (1969); *Puzzle* for voice, Spanish guitar and percussion (1970).

Denisov, Edison, Soviet composer; b. Tomsk, April 6, 1929. He was named after Thomas Alva Edison by his father, an electrical engineer. He studied mathematics at Moscow Univ., graduating in 1951, and composition at the Moscow Cons. with Shebalin and Rakov (1951–56); in 1959 he was appointed to its faculty. An experimenter by nature, Denisov wrote instrumental works of an empirical genre; of these the most typical is *Crescendo e diminuendo* for harpsichord and 12 string instruments, with the score partly written out in graph notation (1965; first performed at the Zagreb Festival, Yugoslavia, on May 14, 1967, and two days later by the N.Y. Philharmonic Orch.). Other works include an opera, *Ivan the Soldier* (1959); Symphony in C (1955); *Sinfonietta on Tadzhik Themes* (1957); *Children's Suite* for chamber orch. (1958); *Musica* for 11 wind instruments and timpani (1961); a cantata, *Solnze Inkov (Sun of the Incas)* for soprano and 11 instruments to words by Gabriela Mistral (Leningrad, Nov. 30, 1964); Symphony for 2 String Orchestras and Percussion (1963); *Peinture (Painting)* for orch. (Graz, Austria, Oct. 30, 1970); *Chant d'automne,* after Baudelaire, for soprano and orch. (1971); Cello Concerto (1972; Leipzig, Sept. 25, 1973); Piano Concerto (1975); Flute Concerto (1975); Variations for Piano (1952); *Improvviso* for violin and piano (1953); Trio for Violin, Clarinet and Bassoon (1957); Sonata for 2 Violins (1958); *Canti di Catulli* for bass and 3 trombones

(1962); Concerto for Flute, Oboe, Piano and Percussion (1963); Violin Sonata (1963); *Italian Songs,* for soprano, flute, violin, horn and harpsichord (1964); *5 Geschichten vom Herrn Keuner,* after Brecht, for tenor and 7 instruments (1966); *Les Pleurs (The Tears),* after Russian folk texts, for soprano, piano and 3 percussionists (1966), which combines in its texture Russian modalities and dodecaphonic devices; *3 Pieces* for piano, four hands (1967); *3 Pieces* for cello and piano (1967); *Ode in Memory of Che Guevara* for clarinet, piano and percussion (1968); *Romantic Music* for oboe, violin, viola, cello and harp (1968); String Trio (1969); *Silhouettes* for flute, 2 pianos and percussion (1969); Wind Quintet (1969); *D-S-C-H* for clarinet, trombone, cello and piano (1969), thematically derived from the initials of Dmitri Shostakovich in German spelling (D,Es,C,H); *Pyenye ptits (Singing of the Birds)* for prepared piano and tape (1969); Saxophone Sonata (1970); Cello Sonata (1971); Piano Trio (1971); *La Vie en rouge* for voice, flute, clarinet, violin, cello and piano (1973); piano pieces; songs.

Dennée, Charles (Frederick), American pianist and pedagogue; b. Oswego, N.Y., Sept. 1, 1863; d. Boston, April 29, 1946. He studied at the New England Cons., Boston; piano with A. D. Turner, and composition with S. A. Emery; also studied piano with Hans von Bülow during the latter's last visit to the U.S. (1889–90); in 1883 he was appointed teacher of piano at the New England Cons.; an accident to his right wrist caused his retirement in 1897, after he had played almost 1100 recitals; subsequent devotion to teaching was fruitful, for many of his pupils held prominent positions on the faculties of various conservatories and music colleges. He was among the first to give illustrated lecture-recitals in the U.S. A selection of his essays was published as *Musical Journeys* (Brookline, Mass., 1938). Some of his teaching pieces achieved steady popularity with piano students; he also published a manual, *Progressive Technique.*

Denny, William D., American composer; b. Seattle, July 2, 1910. He studied at the Univ. of California (A.B., 1931; M.A., 1933); then in Paris with Paul Dukas (1933–35); later held the Horatio Parker Fellowship at the American Academy in Rome (1939–41). From 1942–45 he was instructor of music at Harvard and asst. prof. at Vassar; from 1945 teaching at the Univ. of California, Berkeley.

WORKS: *Concertino* for orch. (San Francisco, April 25, 1939; composer conducting); Symphony No. 1 (1939); *Sinfonietta* for strings (1940); *Overture* for strings (1945); *Praeludium* for orch. (San Francisco, Feb. 5, 1947); Symphony No. 2 (San Francisco, March 22, 1951, composer conducting); 3 string quartets; Viola Sonata; choral works.

Densmore, Frances, specialist in Indian music; b. Red Wing, Minnesota, May 21, 1867; d. there, June 5, 1957. She studied at Oberlin, Ohio, Cons. (hon. M.A., 1924); then took courses with Leopold Godowsky (piano) and J. K. Paine (counterpoint); began study of Indian music in 1893 at the World's Fair in Chicago, continuing privately until 1907 when she began systematic research for the Bureau of American Ethnology (Smithsonian Institution), including an exhaustive study of the Cheyenne, Arapaho, Maidu, Santo Domingo Pueblo, and New Mexican Indian tribes. She lectured extensively on Indian music, and published a number of books and articles on the subject.

WRITINGS: *Chippewa Music,* a collection of Indian songs in 2 vols. (1910-13); *Poems from Sioux and Chippewa Songs* (words only; 1917); *Tetom Sioux Music* (1918); *Indian Action Songs* (1921); *Northern Ute Music* (1922); *Mandan and Hidatfa Music* (1923); *The American Indians and Their Music* (1926; 2nd ed. 1936); *The Music of the Tule Indians of Panama* (1926); *Some Results of the Study of American Indian Music* (reprinted from the *Journal of the Washington Academy of Sciences* XVIII/ 14; 1928); *Pawnee Music* (1929); *Papago Music* (1929); *What Intervals do Indians Sing?* (reprinted from the *American Anthropologist,* April/June, 1929); *Yaman and Yaqui Music* (U.S. Bureau of American Ethnology, Bulletin 110; 1932); *Menominee Music* (ibid., Bulletin 102; 1932); *Cheyenne and Arapaho Music* (Southwest Museum, 1936); *Alabama Music* (Texas Folk-Lore Society, 1937); *Music of Santo Domingo Pueblo, New Mexico* (Southwest Museum, 1938); *Nootka and Quileute Music* (Washington, D.C., 1939); *Music of the Indians of British Columbia* (Washington, D.C., 1943); *Choctaw Music* (1943); *Seminole Music* (1956). The April 1956 issue of the magazine *Ethnomusicology* contains a complete bibliography of her writings up to 1955 (pp. 13–29). A Frances Densmore ethnological library has been established at Macalester College, St. Paul, Minn.

Densmore, John H., American composer; b. Somerville, Mass., Aug. 7, 1880; d. Boston, Sept. 21, 1943. He was educated at the Harvard Univ. (B.A., 1904); wrote operettas for the Hasty Pudding Club. His mature works (mostly for chorus) are distinguished by practical adaptability.

Dent, Edward Joseph, eminent English music scholar; b. Ribston, Yorkshire, July 16, 1876; d. London, Aug. 22, 1957. He was a pupil at Eton College of C. H. Lloyd, and at Cambridge of Charles Wood and Stanford; appointed professor of music at Cambridge (1926); Mus. Bac. (1899); Fellow King's College, Cambridge (1902); M.A. (1905); hon. Mus. Doc., Oxford (1931), Harvard (1936); was Raske-Orsted lecturer, Copenhagen (1935); Messenger lecturer, Cornell Univ. (1937). The International Society for Contemporary Music came into being in 1922 largely through his efforts; he was its president from 1922-38 and again in 1945; was also active in organizing an English section known as the British Music Society; president of the Société Internationale de Musicologie since 1931. He helped to produce various old English stage works, particularly those of Purcell (*Dido and Aeneas,* with Kurt Jooss, at Münster, Westphalia, in 1928); contributed to the *Encyclopaedia Britannica, Grove's Dictionary, Musical Antiquary* ("The Baroque Opera," 1910; "Italian Chamber Cantatas," 1911), *Athenaeum* (1919-24), Tilley's *Modern France* (chapter on French music, 1922), *Oxford History of Music* ("Social As-

pects of Mediaeval Music"), *Cobbett's Cyclopedia of Chamber Music* ("Italian Chamber Music of the 17th Century"), the *Musical Quarterly* ("The Relation of Music to Human Progress," 1928; "The Historical Approach to Music," 1937), *Acta musicologica* ("Music and Music Research," 1931), etc. Also author of *A. Scarlatti, His Life and Works* (London, 1905); *Mozart's Operas, a Critical Study* (London, 1913; revised ed., 1947); *Terpander, or Music and the Future* (1926); *Foundations of English Opera* (1928); *Ferruccio Busoni: a Biography,* the standard work (London, 1933); *Music of the Renaissance in Italy* (1934); *Handel* (1934); translated many opera librettos into English (Mozart, Wagner, Berlioz, Verdi, etc.), published editions of old English music, and revised *The Opera* by R. A. Streatfeild (London, 1932).

BIBLIOGRAPHY: L. Haward, "E. J. Dent: Bibliography," *Music Review* (Nov. 1946); Winton Dean, "Edward J. Dent: A Centenary Tribute," *Music and Letters* (Oct. 1976).

Denza, Luigi, Italian song composer; b. Castellammare di Stabia, Feb. 24, 1846; d. London, Jan. 26, 1922. He studied with Serrao and Mercadante at the Naples Cons. Besides the opera *Wallenstein* (Naples, May 13, 1876), which was not especially successful, he wrote about 600 songs (some in Neapolitan dialect), many of which won great popularity. In 1879 he settled in London; appointed professor of singing at the Royal Academy of Music (1898); Chevalier of the order of the Crown of Italy. His most famous song is *Funiculi-Funicula,* which was used (under the mistaken impression that it was a folksong) by Richard Strauss in *Aus Italien.*

Denzler, Robert, Swiss conductor and composer; b. Zürich, March 19, 1892. He studied with Volkmar Andreae in Zürich; from 1912–15 was active as choral conductor in Lucerne; then held posts as conductor at the Municipal theater in Zürich (1915-27); Berlin Opera (1927-32), and again in Zürich (1934-47). He wrote a choral symphony, Piano Concerto, several instrumental suites, and songs.

Deppe, Ludwig, famous German piano pedagogue; b. Alverdissen, Lippe, Nov. 7, 1828; d. Bad Pyramont, Sept. 5, 1890. He was a pupil of Marxsen at Hamburg in 1849, later of Lobe at Leipzig. He settled in Hamburg in 1857 as a music teacher, and founded a singing society, of which he was the conductor till 1868. Went to Berlin in 1874, and from 1886-88 was court conductor; also conducted the Silesian Musical Festivals established by Count Hochberg in 1876. He wrote a symph.; 2 overtures, *Zriny* and *Don Carlos;* published *Zwei Jahre Kapellmeister and der Kgl. Oper in Berlin.*

BIBLIOGRAPHY: Amy Fay, "Deppe as Teacher," in her book, *Music Study in Germany* (1897); H. Klose, *Deppesche Lehre des Klavierspiels* (Hamburg, 1886); Elisabeth Caland, *Die Deppesche Lehre des Klavierspiels* (Stuttgart, 1897; in English as *Artistic Piano Playing,* 1903).

Déré, Jean, French composer; b. Niort, June 23, 1886; d. Sainte Suzanne (Mayenne), Dec. 6, 1970. He studied at the Paris Cons. with Caussade, Diémer, and Widor; won the 2nd Prix de Rome (1919). Among his works are the symph. poem *Krischna,* incidental music for Marlowe's *Faustus, 3 Esquisses* for piano and orch., chamber music, piano pieces, songs.

De Rensis, Raffaello, Italian music critic; b. Casacalenda, Campobasso, Feb. 17, 1879; d. Rome, Nov. 3, 1970. He founded the weekly magazine *Musica* in 1908; wrote music criticism in daily newspapers. He publ. a number of monographs: *Il Cantore del popolo, B. Gigli* (Rome, 1934); *F. Faccio e Verdi* (Milan, 1934); *Ottorino Respighi* (Turin, 1935); *E. Wolf-Ferrari* (Milan, 1937); *A. Boito* (Florence, 1942); *U. Giordano e R. Leoncavallo* (Siena, 1949); *F. Cilèa* (Palmi, 1950); also a collection of essays, *Musica vista* (Milan, 1960).

De Reszke, Edouard, famous bass, brother of the tenor, **Jean de Reszke,** and of the soprano, **Josephine de Reszke;** b. Warsaw, Dec. 22, 1853; d. Garnek, Poland, May 25, 1917. He studied with an Italian teacher, Ciaffei, in Warsaw; also was trained by his older brother, Jean. He then went to Italy where he continued his study with various teachers. His professional debut was at the Théâtre des Italiens in Paris when he sang Amonasro in *Aida* under Verdi's direction (April 22, 1876). He continued to make appearances in Paris for two seasons, and later sang at La Scala, Milan. From 1880–84 he sang in London with extraordinary success. He made his American debut in Chicago as the King in *Lohengrin* (Nov. 9, 1891); then as Frère Laurent in *Roméo et Juliette* at the Metropolitan Opera House, N.Y. (Dec. 14, 1891); his brother Jean made his N.Y. debut as Roméo at the same performance. His greatest role was that of Méphistophélès in *Faust;* he sang this part at the 500th performance of the opera at the Paris Opéra (his brother Jean sang the title role) on Nov. 4, 1887; and he selected this part also for his last appearance in America (March 21, 1903). He then retired and lived on his country estate near Warsaw.
BIBLIOGRAPHY: H. Klein, "E. de Reszke: The Career of a Famous Basso," *Musical Times* (July 1917).

De Reszke, Jean (Jan Mieczislaw), celebrated tenor, brother of **Edouard De Reszke;** b. Warsaw, Jan. 14, 1850; d. Nice, April 3, 1925. His mother gave him his first singing lessons. He sang at the Warsaw Cathedral as a boy; then went to Paris, where he studied with Sbriglia. He was first trained as a baritone, and made his debut in Venice (1874) as Alfonso in *La Favorita* under the name of **Giovanni di Reschi.** He continued singing in Italy and France in baritone parts; his first appearance as tenor took place in Madrid on Nov. 9, 1879, in *Robert le Diable.* He created the title role of Massenet's *Le Cid* at the Paris Opéra (Nov. 30, 1885) and became a favorite tenor there. He appeared at Drury Lane, London, as Radames on June 13, 1887 (having previously sung there as baritone in 1874); he then sang at Covent Garden (until 1900). On Nov. 9, 1891, he made his American debut in Chicago with the Metropolitan Opera Co. as Lohengrin; he remained with the Metropolitan Opera for eleven seasons. In order to sing Wagnerian roles, he learned

German and made a sensationally successful appearance as Tristan (New York, Nov. 27, 1895). His farewell appearance at the Metropolitan Opera House was in *Lohengrin* (March 29, 1901). The secret of his success rested not so much on the power of his voice (some baritone quality remained in his singing to the end) as on the controlled interpretation, musical culture, and fine dynamic balance. When he retired from the stage in 1902, settling in Paris as voice teacher, he was able to transmit his method to many of his students, several of whom later became famous on the opera stage.
BIBLIOGRAPHY: Clara Leiser, *Jean de Reszke and the Great Days of Opera* (London, 1933; P. G. Hurst, *Jean de Reszke: 40 Years of Opera, 1874–1914* (London, 1958).

De Reszke, Josephine, Polish soprano, sister of **Jean** and **Edouard de Reszke;** b. Warsaw, June 4, 1855; d. there, Feb. 22, 1891. She studied at the St. Petersburg Cons.; first appeared in public under the name of **Giuseppina di Reschi** at Venice in 1874; sang Marguerite in Gounod's *Faust* (Aug. 1, 1874) with her brother Jean as Valentin; then was engaged at the Paris Opéra, where she made her debut as Ophelia in *Hamlet* by Ambroise Thomas (Paris, June 21, 1875); later sang in Madrid and Lisbon; appeared as Aida in Covent Garden, London, on April 18, 1881; her career was cut short by her death at 35.

Dering, Richard. See **Deering, Richard.**

De Rose, Peter, American composer of popular music; b. N.Y., March 10, 1900; d. there, April 24, 1953. After desultory musical education, he formed a radio team, 'The Sweethearts of the Air,' with May Singhi Brown, whom he married. He gained fame with a piano piece entitled *Deep Purple;* it was introduced in an orchestral version by Paul Whiteman (N.Y., May 10, 1934) and subsequently converted into a saccharine ballad with lachrymose lyrics, which became a commercial hit. Other lucrative songs by De Rose are *The Lamp is Low* (derived from a malformed fragmentation of Ravel's *Pavane*) and *As Years Go By,* a sentimentalized misinterpretation of Brahms' *Hungarian Dance No. 4.*

Desderi, Ettore, Italian composer; b. Asti, Dec. 10, 1892; d. Florence, Nov. 23, 1974. He studied with Luigi Perrachio at the Turin Cons. and then with Franco Alfano in Bologna. From 1933–41 he was a director of the Liceo Musicale in Alessandria; from 1941–51, teacher of composition at the Milan Cons. From 1951 to 1963 he was director of the Cons. of Bologna.
WORKS: *Intermezzi all' Antigone,* for orch. (1924); *Job,* biblical cantata (1927); *Sinfonia Davidica,* for soli, chorus, and orch. (1929); Violin Sonata; Cello Sonata; many choral works. He published *La Musica Contemporanea* (Turin, 1930) and numerous magazine articles in Italian and German publications.
BIBLIOGRAPHY: A. Bonacorsi, "Ettore Desderi," *Il Pianoforte* (July 1926); Mario Rinaldi, *Ettore Desderi* (Tivoli, 1943); a festive volume *A Ettore Desderi nel suo 70 compleanno* (Bologna, 1963).

De Segurola, Andrés, Spanish bass; b. Valencia, March 27, 1874; d. Barcelona, Jan. 22, 1953. He studied with Pietro Farvaro; sang at the Teatro Liceo in Barcelona; made his American debut at the Metropolitan Opera as Alvise in *La Gioconda* (Nov. 15, 1909). For twenty years (1931-51) he lived in Hollywood as teacher; then returned to Spain.

Deshevov, Vladimir, Russian composer; b. St. Petersburg, Feb. 11, 1889; d. there (Leningrad), Oct. 27, 1955. He studied with Steinberg and Liadov at the Cons. there. Many of his themes are drawn from folk sources. Among his works are the revolutionary operas *The Red Hurricane* (Leningrad, Oct. 29, 1924), *Ice and Steel,* based on the Kronstadt rebellion of 1921 (Leningrad, May 17, 1930), and *The Hungry Steppe,* which has to do with socialist distribution of land in Uzbekistan.

Deslandres, Adolphe-Édouard-Marie, French composer; b. Batignolles, Monceaux, Jan. 22, 1840; d. Paris, July 30, 1911. He was a pupil of Leborne and Benoist at the Paris Cons.; 1862 appointed organist at Ste.-Marie. He wrote the operas *Dimanche et lundi* (1872), *Le Chevalier Bijou* (1875), *Fridolin* (1876); *Ode à l'harmonie; La Banque brisée;* a patriotic dirge, *Les Sept Paroles;* many sacred choruses.

Des Marais, Paul, American composer; b. Menominee, Michigan, June 23, 1920; was taken to Chicago as an infant; studied there with Leo Sowerby; then with Nadia Boulanger in Cambridge, Mass., and with Walter Piston at Harvard Univ. (B.A., 1949; M.A., 1953). He received the Lili Boulanger prize (1947-48); Boott prize in composition from Harvard Univ. (1949); John Knowles Paine Traveling Fellowship (1949-51); joined the staff of Univ. of California, Los Angeles, in 1960; received the Institute of Creative Arts Award there in 1964-65. His early music was oriented toward neoclassicism, with pandiatonic excrescences in harmonic structures; in 1959 he evolved a decaphonic idiom using series of no more than 10 notes, while preserving a free, not necessarily non-tonal, style of writing.
WORKS: Mass a cappella (1949); 2 piano sonatas (1947; 1952); *Theme and Changes* for harpsichord (1953); Motet for Mixed Voices, Cellos and Double Basses (1959); *Psalm 121* for chorus a cappella (1959); *Capriccio* for 2 pianos, percussion and celesta (1962; Los Angeles, March 18, 1963); *Epiphanies,* chamber opera with intervening film sequences (1964-68). In 1970-73 he held the Thorne Music Fund award to enable him to work on his project on the sounds produced by underwater mammals as a foundation of musico-marine electronic and acoustical works.

Desmarets, Henri, important French composer; b. Paris, 1661; d. Lunéville, Sept. 7, 1741. He was regarded as one of the most skillful musicians during the reign of Louis XIV. His first stage work produced was the opera *Didon* (Paris, Sept. 11, 1693); there followed (all at Paris) *Circé* (Oct. 1, 1694); *Les Amours de Momus,* ballet (May 25, 1695); *Venus et Adonis,* serious opera (March 7, 1697; *Les Fêtes galantes,* ballet (May 10, 1698); *Iphigénie en Tauride,* opera (May 6, 1704); etc. His personal life was stormy and included an abduction, for which he was sentenced to death *in absentia,* prompting him to flee France. He was then musician to Philip V of Spain, and intendant of music to the Duke of Lorraine at Lunéville. He was able to return to France in 1722 after his marriage to the abducted woman was recognized as valid by the French courts.
BIBLIOGRAPHY: M. Brenet, "Desmarets, un compositeur oublié du 17ᵉ siècle," *Le Ménestrel* 39-40 (1883).

Desmond, Paul, American jazz alto saxophonist; b. San Francisco, Nov. 25, 1924; d. N.Y., May 30, 1977. His real name was **Paul Emil Breitenfeld;** he picked up his professional name from a telephone book at random. He gained the rudiments of music from his father who played the organ for silent movies; Desmond played the clarinet in the school orchestra; then switched to the alto saxophone. He made rapid strides towards recognition and modest fame when he joined the Dave Brubeck Quartet, and continued with it until it was disbanded in 1967. He wrote some pieces for the Brubeck Quartet of which "Take Five," a jazz composition in $5/4$ meter, was adopted as their song signature, and became popular.

Desormière, Roger, brilliant French conductor; b. Vichy, Sept. 13, 1898; d. Paris, Oct. 25, 1963. He studied at the Paris Cons.; conducted the Swedish Ballet in Paris (1924-25) and the Ballets Russes (1925-29), and later at La Scala, Covent Garden, and in Monte Carlo; was at the Opéra-Comique (1936-44); at the Grand Opéra (1945); conducted the BBC in London (1946-47). In 1950 he was stricken with aphasia and other disorders, and was compelled to give up his career.

Despalj, Pavle, Croatian composer; b. Blato na Korčuli, June 18, 1934. He studied with Šulek in Zagreb; played violin in the Zagreb Philharmonic; also did some conducting; made symph. arrangements of Bach's works. As a composer, he deployed a nonatonal quasi-serialistic modus of composition, while outwardly adhering to classical forms.
WORKS: *Variations* for chamber orch. (1957); Violin Concerto (1960); Concerto for Alto Saxophone and String Orch. (1963).

Des Prez, Josquin, the greatest of the Franco-Flemish contrapuntists; b. c.1440 in Hainault or Henegouwen (Burgundy); d. Condé-sur-Escaut, as provost of the Cathedral Chapter, Aug. 27, 1521. His name was variously spelled: *Després, Desprez, Deprés, Depret, Deprez, Desprets, Dupré,* and by the Italians *Del Prato* (Latinized as *a Prato, a Pratis, Pratensis*), etc.; while Josquin (contracted from the Flemish Jossekin, "little Joseph") appears as *Jossé, Jossien, Jusquin, Giosquin, Josquinus, Jacobo, Jodocus, Jodoculus,* etc. His epitaph reads *Jossé de Prés.* However, in the motet *Illibata Dei Virgo* (contained in vol. 9 of the Josquin edition), of which the text is quite likely of Josquin's authorship, his name appears as an acrostic, thus: *I,*

O, S, Q, V, I, N, D[es], P, R, E, Z; this seems to leave little doubt as to its correct spelling. Few details of Josquin's early life are known. He was a boy-chorister of the Collegiate Church at St.-Quentin, later becoming canon and choirmaster there; possibly a pupil of Okeghem, whom he greatly admired (after Okeghem's death, in 1495, he wrote *La Déploration de Johan Okeghem*); 1475, at the Court of Duke Galeazzo Maria Sforza, Milan, as chorister; 1486-94, singer in the Papal choir under the Popes Innocent VIII and Alexander VI; he was also active, for various periods, in Florence, where he met the famous theorist Pietro Aron, in Modena, and in Ferrara (where Isaac was also). Later Josquin returned to Burgundy, finally settling in Condé-sur-Escaut. As a composer he was considered by contemporary musicians and theorists to be the greatest of his period, and he had a strong influence on all those who came into contact with his music or with him, personally, as a teacher; Adriaan Petit Coclicus, one of Josquin's distinguished pupils (publ. a Method in 1552, entitled *Compendium musices*, based on Josquin's teaching), terms him 'princeps musicorum.' His works were sung everywhere, and universally admired; in them he achieves a complete union between word and tone, thereby fusing the intricate Netherlandish contrapuntal devices into expressive and beautiful art forms. Two contrasting styles are present in his compositions. Some are intricately contrapuntal, displaying the technical ingenuity characteristic of the Netherlands style; others, probably as a result of Italian influence, are homophonic.

WORKS: Masses: (in Petrucci's Lib. I, Venice, 1502): *L'Omme armé*; *La sol fa re mi*; *Gaudeamus*; *Fortunata desperata*; *L'Omme armé, sexti toni*;—ibid. II, 1505): *Ave Maris stella*; *Hercules, dux Ferrarae*; *Malheur me bat*; *Lami Baudichon*; *Una musque de Buscaya*; *Dung aultre amor*;—ibid. III, 1514): *Mater patris*; *Faysans regrets*; *Ad fugam*; *Di dadi*; *De Beata Virgine*; *Sine nomine* (these 3 books republished by Junta, Rome, 1526);—(in Graphäus' *Missae III*): *Pange lingua*; *Da pacem*; *Sub tuum praesidium*; some of these are scattered in other collections, and fragments are found in still others; several more Masses are in MS at Rome, Munich, and Cambrai. Motets were publ. by Petrucci (8 in the *Odhecaton*, 1501; others in his books of motets); by Peutinger (*Liber selectarum cantionum*, 1520), and others of the period. His French chansons were published by T. Susato (1545), P. Attaignant (1549), and Du Chemin (1553). A complete edition of Josquin's works was issued (1921-69; 55 vols.) by the Vereeniging voor Nederlandsche Muziekgeschiedenis under the general editorship of A. Smijers, M. Amlonowycz, and W. Elders.

BIBLIOGRAPHY: E. Van der Straeten, *La Musique aux Pays-Bas avant le XIXe siècle*, VI (Brussels, 1882); F. de Ménil, *Les Grands musiciens du Nord: Josquin de Prés* (Paris, 1897); A. Schering, *Die niederländische Orgelmesse im Zeitalter des Josquin* (Leipzig, 1912); A. Gastoué, "J. des Prés, ses precurseurs et ses emules," *La Tribune de St. Gervais* (1921; pp. 201-23); T. W. Werner, "Anmerkungen zur Kunst Josquins und zur Gesamt-Ausgabe seiner Werke," *Zeitschrift für Musikwissenschaft* VII (1924); O. Ursprung, "Josquin Des Prez; Eine Charakterzeichnung," *Bulletin of the Union Musicologique* VI/1 (1926); A. Smijers, in *Proceedings of the Musical Association, Session 53* (London, 1926-27), pp. 95-116; E. E. Lowinsky, *Secret Chromatic Art in the Netherlands Motet* (N.Y., 1946); C. van den Borren, *Geschiedenis van de muziek in de Nederlanden* (Antwerp, 1948); M. Antonowitsch, *Die Motette "Benedicta Es" von Josquin Des Prez* (Utrecht, 1951); G. Reese, *Music in the Renaissance* (N.Y., 1954); C. Sartori, article in *Annales Musicologiques* (discusses birth date; 1956); H. Osthoff, *Josquin Desprez* (2 vols.; Tutzing, 1962, 1965); W. Elders, *Studien zur Symbolik in der Musik der alten Niederländer* (Bilthoven, 1968); idem.; "Das Symbol in der Musik von Josquin des Prez," *Acta Musicologica* (July-Dec. 1969). The International Josquin Festival Conference was held in N.Y. on June 21-25, 1971; reports appear in *Journal of the American Musicological Society* (Fall 1971), *Die Musikforschung* (Oct.-Dec. 1971), and *Current Musicology* 14 (1972). Papers presented at the Conference are published under the editorship of Edward Lowinsky (London, 1976).

Dessau, Bernhard, German violinist; b. Hamburg, March 1, 1861; d. Berlin, April 28, 1923. He studied violin with Joachim and Wieniawski; held various posts as concertmaster in Germany and Holland; in 1906 was appointed professor at the Berlin Cons. He was a prolific composer; his Violin Concerto 'im alten Stil' was widely known.

Dessau, Paul, German composer; b. Hamburg, Dec. 19, 1894. He studied at the Klindworth Cons. in Berlin and later in Hamburg; in 1913 became coach at the Hamburg Opera; then conducted in Cologne (1919-23), Mainz (1924), and Berlin (1925-33). In 1933, with the advent of the Nazi regime, he was compelled to leave Germany, and traveled in various European cities; also in Palestine; in 1939 he arrived in New York, where he remained until the end of the war. In 1948, he returned to Berlin and resumed his active participation in German musical life, aligning himself with the developments in East Germany. He has written much music for the theater and motion pictures; *Lanzelot und Sanderein* (Hamburg, 1918); two operas for children, *Das Eisenbahnspiel* (1932) and *Tadel der Unzuverlässigkeit* (1932); symph. triptych, *In Memoriam Bertolt Brecht* (1957); *Symph. Variations* on themes of J. S. Bach and C. P. E. Bach (1963); *Puntila*, opera (East Berlin, Nov. 15, 1966); *Geschäftsbericht*, "minimal opera" of 600 seconds duration (Leipzig, April 29, 1967); *Meer der Stürme*, symph. poem (East Berlin, Oct. 14, 1967); *Lenin* for orch. with a choral finale (1970); 5 string quartets (1932, 1943, 1946, 1948, 1955); Suite for Saxophone and Piano (1935); *Guernica* for piano (1938); numerous dance pieces for various instrumental combinations; cantatas, among them, *5. März 1953, 21 uhr 50* (day and hour of Stalin's death); *Appell der Arbeiterklasse* (1961); *Requiem für Lumumba* (1963); *Armeebefehl No. 13* (1967); numerous choruses to texts dealing with international disarmament and proletarian solidarity. His opera *Das Verhör des Lukullus* was presented at the Berlin State Opera on March 17, 1951 as a propaganda performance against military dictatorship, but it was severely criticized in East German newspapers and was taken out of the repertory.

BIBLIOGRAPHY: F. Hennenberg, *Dessau-Brecht; musikalische Arbeiten* (Berlin, 1963); idem, *Paul Dessau; eine Biographie* (Leipzig, 1965); Paul Dessau, *Musikarbeit in der Schule* (Berlin, 1968); F. Hennenberg, "Paul Dessaus politische Chorkantaten 1944–1968," in H. A. Brockhaus and K. Niemann, eds. *Sämmelbande zur Musikgeschichte der Deutschen Demokratischen Republic* (Berlin, 1969).

Dessauer, Joseph, composer; b. Prague, May 28, 1798; d. Mödling, near Vienna, July 8, 1876. He studied piano with Tomaschek and composition with Dionys Weber in Prague. He wrote several operas: *Lidwina* (Prague, 1836); *Ein Besuch in Saint-Cyr* (Dresden, May 6, 1838; his best work); *Paquite* (Vienna, 1851); *Domingo* (1860); and *Oberon* (not performed); also wrote overtures, string quartets, piano pieces, etc.

Dessoff, Felix Otto, German conductor; b. Leipzig, Jan. 14, 1835; d. Frankfurt, Oct. 28, 1892. He studied at the Leipzig Cons. with Moscheles, Hauptmann, and Rietz; then was theater conductor in various German cities (1854–60). In 1860 he became a conductor of the Vienna Opera; also conducted the Vienna Philharmonic Orch., and taught at the Vienna Cons. From 1875–81 he occupied similar posts at Karlsruhe; in 1881 he became opera conductor in Frankfurt. He was greatly esteemed for his musicianship by his many celebrated friends; his correspondence with Brahms was published by the Brahms Society. He also wrote chamber music (Piano Quintet; Piano Quartet, etc.).

Dessoff, Margarethe, Austrian choral conductor; b. Vienna, June 11, 1874; d. Locarno, Switzerland, Nov. 19, 1944. She was educated at the Frankfurt Cons.; taught there from 1912–17. She organized a madrigal singing group, and traveled with it in Germany (1916–21). In 1922 she settled in America, where she presented interesting programs of choral music (gave the first complete performance in New York of Vecchi's *L'Amfiparnaso*, 1933). In 1936 she went to Switzerland, where she remained until her death. The leadership of Dessoff Choir, which she established in N.Y., was taken over in 1936 by Paul Boepple.

Destinn (real name **Kittl**), **Emmy,** famous dramatic soprano; b. Prague, Feb. 26, 1878; d. Budějovice (Bohemia), Jan. 28, 1930. She first studied the violin; her vocal abilities were revealed later by Mme. Loewe-Destinn, whose second name she adopted as a token of appreciation. She made her debut as Santuzza in Berlin (1898) and was engaged at the Berlin Opera as a regular member. She then specialized in Wagnerian operas and became a protegée of Cosima Wagner in Bayreuth; because of her ability to cope with difficult singing parts Richard Strauss selected her for the title role in the Berlin and Paris premières of his *Salome*. She made her London debut at Covent Garden on May 2, 1904, as Donna Anna; her success in England was spontaneous and unmistakable and she continued to sing opera in England until the outbreak of World War I. She made her American debut in *Aida*

with the Metropolitan Opera Co., Toscanini conducting on Nov. 16, 1908, and remained with the company until 1914. She returned to America after World War I to sing *Aida* at the Metropolitan Opera House (Dec. 8, 1919); retired in 1921. For a few years, following World War I, she used her Czech name, **Ema Destinnová,** but dropped it later on. Her voice was a pure soprano of great power; she was a versatile singer; her repertory included some 80 parts.

BIBLIOGRAPHY: L. Brieger-Wasservogel, *Emmy Destinn und Maria Laiba* (1908); A. Rektorys, *Ema Destinnová* (Prague, 1936); M. Martínová, *Zivot Emy Destinnová* (Pilzen, 1946).

Destouches, André-Cardinal, French operatic composer; b. Paris, April, 1672 (baptized April 6); d. there, Feb. 7, 1749. After attending a Jesuit school in Paris, he went as a boy to Siam with his teacher, the missionary Gui Tachard (1686). He returned to France in 1688; served in the Royal Musketeers (1692–96) and later took lessons from André Campra, contributing 3 airs to Campra's opera-ballet *L'Europe Galante* (1967). After this initiation, Destouches produced his first independent work, *Issé,* a "heroic pastorale" in 3 acts (Fontainebleau, Oct. 7, 1697); its popularity was parodied in several productions of a similar pastoral nature (*Les Amours de Vincennes,* by P. F. Dominique, 1719; *Les Oracles* by J. A. Romagnesi, 1741). Among his other operas, the following were produced in Paris: *Amadis de Grèce* (March 25, 1699); *Omphale* (Nov. 10, 1700), and *Callirhoé* (Dec. 27, 1712). With Delalande, he wrote the ballet, *Les Elements,* which was produced at the Tuileries Palace in Paris on Dec. 31, 1721. In 1713 Louis XIV appointed him superintendent of the Paris Opéra; in 1728, he became director of the Académie Royale de Musique, retiring in 1730. A revival of *Omphale* in 1752 evoked Baron Grimm's famous *Lettre sur Omphale* inaugurating the so-called "Guerre des Bouffons" between the proponents of the French school, as exemplified by Destouches, and Italian opera buffa.

BIBLIOGRAPHY: K. Dulle, *A. C. Destouches* (Leipzig, 1908); A. Tessier, "Correspondance d'A. C. Destouches et du Prince Antoine 1er de Monaco," *La Revue Musicale* (Dec. 1926–May 1927); D. R. B. Kimbell, "The Amadis Operas of Destouches and Handel," *Music & Letters* (Oct. 1968).

Destouches, Franz (Seraph) von, German composer; b. Munich, Jan. 21, 1772; d. there, Dec. 10, 1844. He was a pupil of Haydn in Vienna in 1787; was appointed music director at Erlangen (1797); then was second concertmaster at the Weimar theater (1799); later becoming first concertmaster and director of music (1804–08); in 1810 was professor of theory at Landshut Univ.; then conductor at Homburg (1826–42); retired to Munich in 1842.

WORKS: *Die Thomasnacht,* an opera (Munich, Aug. 31, 1792); *Das Missverständniss,* an operetta (Weimar, April 27, 1805); a comic opera, *Der Teufel und der Schneider* (1843; not performed); incidental music to Schiller's version of Gozzi's *Turandot* (1802); Schiller's *Die Braut von Messina* (1803); *Die Jungfrau von Orleans* (1803); *Wilhelm Tell* (1804); Kotzebue's *Die Hussiten vor Naumburg* (1804); and Zacharias

Werner's play, *Wanda, Königin der Sarmaten* (1808); also a Piano Concerto; piano sonatas; fantasias; variations for piano; Piano Trio; Clarinet Concerto; a Mass; an oratorio *Die Anbetung am Grabe Christi.*
BIBLIOGRAPHY: Ernst von Destouches, *Franz von Destouches* (Munich, 1904).

Destranges, Louis Augustin Etienne Rouillé, French music critic; b. Nantes, March 29, 1863; d. there, May 31, 1915. He publ.: *L'Œuvre théatrale de Meyerbeer* (1893); *L'Évolution musicale chez Verdi* (1895); *Les Femmes dans l'œuvre de Richard Wagner* (1899); *Consonances et dissonances* (1906).

Deswert, Jules, Belgian cellist and composer; b. Louvain, Aug. 15, 1843; d. Ostend, Feb. 24, 1891. He studied with Servais at the Brussels Cons.; became prof. at the Hochschule in Berlin (1869-73). He was in Leipzig in 1881, and in 1888 was appointed director of the Ostend Music School and professor at the Ghent and Bruges Cons. He wrote two operas, *Die Albigenser* (Wiesbaden, Oct. 1, 1878); *Graf Hammerstein* (Mainz, 1884); a symphony, *Nordseefahrt*; 3 cello concertos; romances, fantasias, duos, and solo pieces for cello.

Déthier, Édouard, Belgian violinist, brother of **Gaston-Marie Déthier**; b. Liège, April 25, 1886; d. New York, Feb. 19, 1962. He studied at the Liège Cons. (1895-1901); then at the Brussels Cons. (1901-02); subsequently taught there (1902-04). He settled in the U.S. in 1906, appearing in recitals with the principal orchestras; taught at the Institute of Musical Art, and at the Juilliard Graduate School.

Déthier, Gaston-Marie, Belgian organist, brother of **Édouard Déthier**; b. Liège, April 18, 1875; d. New York, May 26, 1958. He studied at the Liège Cons. and later with Guilmant in Paris; came to the U.S. in 1894; was organist at St. Francis Xavier's, New York; taught at the Institute of Musical Art; in 1915, gave a series of successful sonata recitals as a pianist, with his brother, the violinist.

Detoni, Dubravko, Croatian pianist and composer; b. Križevci, Feb. 22, 1937. He graduated in piano from the Zagreb Academy of Music in 1960; studied with Alfred Cortot in Siena (1960-61); then took lessons in composition with Šulek at the Azgreb Academy, graduating in 1965; had advanced studies with Bacewicz and Lutoslawski at the experimental studio of the Polish Radio in Warsaw (1966-67) and with Stockhausen and Ligeti in Darmstadt. He was the founder and artistic leader of ACEZANTEZ, the Ensemble of the Center for New Tendencies in Zagreb. His music rejects all established formulas and seeks new conceptions in sound through serial, aleatory and musical-theater resources.
WORKS: *Passacaglia* for 2 piano and strings (1962); *Musica a cinque* for orch. (1962); *Tri koralne predigre* for piano (1963); *Preobrazbe (Transfigurations)* for orch. (1963; Zagreb, June 7, 1965); *Dramatski prolog* for orch. (1965); *Quatorze moments do-décaphoniques* for piano (1966); *Stravaganze* for wind quintet (1966); *Likovi i plohe (Forms and Surfaces)* for chamber orch. (1967; Graz, Austria, Sept.

26, 1968); *Phonomorphia 1* for electronic and concrete sounds (1967), *2* for piano and tape (1968) and *3* for voices, instrumental ensemble and tape (1969); *Šifre* for piano and 4 loudspeakers (1967); *Grafika I* for organ (1968), *II* for chamber ensemble (1968), *III* for vocal ensemble, 6 flutes, Ondes Martenot, organ and piano (1969), *IV* for ad lib. chamber ensemble (1971) and *V,* instrumental "theater" for chamber ensemble (1972; Graz, Oct. 14, 1973); *Assonanze No. 1* for cello and piano (1968); *Assonanze No. 2* for cello and orch. (1971); *Elucubrations* for piano and orch. (1969; Zagreb, Jan. 7, 1970); *Forte-Piano, Arpa, Crescendo* for 2 pianos and percussion (1969); *Notturni* for 4 vocal groups, 4 instrumental ensembles, organ and tape (1970); *d,* scene for harpsichord and electronic instruments (1971); *Einflüsse* for 2 cellos and orch. (1971); *Monos 1-3,* cycle for variable orchestration (1970-72); *Music, or Tract about the Superfluous* for narrating actor, organ, piano, percussion, clarinet and orch. (1973); *Fable,* synthetic music (1973); *10 Beginnings* for string quartet (1973); *Dokument 75* for chamber ensemble (1975); *Fragment 75* for chamber ensemble (Graz, Oct. 11, 1975).

Dett, R. (Robert) Nathaniel, distinguished Negro composer and writer; b. Drummondville, Quebec, Canada, Oct. 11, 1882; d. Battle Creek, Michigan, Oct. 2, 1943. He studied at the Oberlin Cons., Columbia Univ., Harvard Univ., Eastman School of Music, and Howard Univ. (Mus. Doc., 1924). He held teaching posts at various colleges in Tennessee, Missouri, Virginia, Texas and North Carolina.
WORKS: an oratorio, *The Ordering of Moses* (Cincinnati, May 7, 1937); numerous choruses on religious texts; piano suite *In the Bottoms* (1913; contains the popular *Juba Dance),* etc. He also publ. *Religious Folk Songs of the Negro* (1926) and *The Dett Collection of Negro Spirituals,* in 4 vols. (1936). His piano works were reprinted in 1973 (Evanston, Ill.), with introductory articles by Dominique-René de Lerma and Vivian Flagg McBrier.
BIBLIOGRAPHY: V. F. McBrier, *R. Nathaniel Dett, His Life and Works* (Washington, D.C., 1977); 3 articles repr. in *Black Perspective in Music* (Spring 1973): M. Stanley, "R. N. Dett, of Hampton Institute," *Musical America* (July 1918); R. Nathaniel Dett, "From Bell Stand to Throne Room," *Etude* (Feb. 1934); D.-R. de Lerma, "Dett and Engel: A Question of Cultural Pride," *Your Musical Cue* (Nov. 1970).

Dettmer, Roger (Christian), American music critic; b. Cincinnati, Aug. 2, 1927. He practiced piano, clarinet and drums before puberty; precociously produced, directed and starred in a school pageant-drama at ten; then took up music seriously at the Univ. of Cincinnati (1945-47), at Columbia Univ. (1948) and Univ. of Michigan (B.A., 1950); also studied composition privately with Vittorio Giannini. He composed sundry pieces for piano and other instruments, mostly in B-flat major, but destroyed the manuscripts. Relieved of the composing itch, he engaged in musical journalism. He was music editor of *Chicago Today* (1969-74); also contributed articles to various European publications.

Deutsch, Otto Erich, eminent Austrian musicologist; b. Vienna, Sept. 5, 1883; d. there, Nov. 23, 1967. He studied literature and history of art at the Univ. of Vienna and in Graz; was for a season the art critic of the Vienna periodical *Zeit* (1908–09); then became a book publisher; was librarian of the important collection of Anthony van Hoboken in Vienna (1926–35). In 1939 he emigrated to England and settled in Cambridge; in 1947 he became a British subject, but returned to Vienna in 1951.

WRITINGS: *Schubert-Brevier* (Berlin, 1905); *Beethovens Beziehungen zu Graz* (Graz, 1907); *Franz Schubert: Die Dokumente seines Lebens und Schaffens* (in collaboration, first with Ludwig Scheibler, then with Willi Kahl and Georg Kinsky), planned as a comprehensive work in 3 volumes containing all known documents, pictures, and other materials pertaining to Schubert, arranged in chronological order, with a thematic catalogue (Munich, 1913; vol. II, part I, publ. in English in a translation by Eric Blom, London, 1946, as *Schubert: A Documentary Biography*; American ed., N.Y., 1947, under the title *The Schubert Reader: A Life of Franz Schubert in Letters and Documents*; catalogue of Schubert's works, prepared by Deutsch for an English ed., in collaboration with Donald R. Wakeling, publ. as *Schubert: Thematic Catalogue of all his Works in Chronological Order*, London, 1951); *Franz Schuberts Briefe und Schriften* (Munich, 1919; 4th ed., enlarged and annotated, Vienna, 1954; English transl., London, 1928); *Schuberts Tagebuch*, a facsimile ed. (Vienna, 1928); *Handel: A Documentary Biography* (N.Y., 1954); edited the series *Musikalische Seltenheiten* (Vienna, 1921); contributed numerous articles of bibliographical and biographical nature on Mozart, Haydn, Beethoven, Schumann, etc. to German, English, and American music publications. A Festschrift, *Otto Erich Deutsch zum 80. Geburtstag*, was publ. in Vienna in 1963.

Devčić, Natko, Croatian composer; b. Glina, June 30, 1914. He studied piano and composition at the Zagreb Music Academy, graduating in 1939; after the war he studied with Joseph Marx in Vienna (1949–50) and Jean Rivier in Paris (1953); attended courses led by Boulez at Darmstadt (summer, 1965) and researched the potentialities of electronic sound with Davidowsky at the Columbia-Princeton Electronic Studio in N.Y. (1966–67). His early works are based on folklore resources; later on, he experimented with advanced techniques.

WORKS: an opera, *Labinska Vještica* (*The Witch of Labin*; Zagreb, Dec. 25, 1957); a ballet, *Dia . . .* (Zagreb, May 20, 1971); *Scherzo* for orch. (1936); *Nocturne* for orch. (1941; revised 1956); *Istarska suite* (*Istrian Suite*) for orch. (Zagreb, Dec. 8, 1948); symph. (1953); *Balada* for piano and orch. (1953); concertino for violin and chamber orch. (1958); *Prolog* for winds and percussion (1965); *Fibula* for 2 orch. (Zagreb, May 12, 1967); Concerto for voice, Ondes Martenot, and chamber ensemble (Graz, Austria, Oct. 23, 1969); *Panta Rei* (*All Things Change*, a motto of Heraclitus) for piano and orch. (1973); *Entre nous* for orch. (Zagreb, March 26, 1975); *Kantata o bezimenima* (*Cantata About a Nameless One*) for chamber chorus and 12 instruments (1959); *Ševa* (*The Lark*), cantata (Zagreb, March 30, 1960); *Igra riječi* (*Play of Words*) for 2 narrators, chorus, instrumental ensemble and tape (1969; Zagreb, May 9, 1969); *8 Minutes* for piano and chamber ensemble (1965); *Odrazi* (*Reflections*) for chamber ensemble (1965); *Micro-tune* for viola and piano (1971); *Sonata-Fantasy* for piano (1940); *Koraci* (*Steps*), 5 movements for piano (1962); *Micro-suite* for piano (1965); *Structures transparentes* and *Structures volantes* for solo harp (1966, 1971); *Columbia 68* for tape (1968).

BIBLIOGRAPHY: K. Kovačević, *Hrvatski Kompozitori i Njihova Djela* (Zagreb, 1960).

Devienne, François, versatile French musician; b. Joinville, Haute-Marne, Jan. 31, 1759; d. in the insane asylum at Charenton, Sept. 5, 1803. A flutist and bassoonist, member of the band of the Gardes Suisses, bassoonist at the Théâtre de Monsieur (1788), and prof. at the Paris Cons., he was an extraordinarily prolific composer of peculiar importance from the impulse which he gave to perfecting the technique of wind instruments.

WORKS: 12 operas; many concerted pieces for various wind instruments with orch.; overtures; concertos, quartets, trios, sonatas, etc., for flute, piano, and other instruments; *Douze suites d'harmonies à 8 et 12 parties*; numerous romances, chansons, etc.; also a valuable *Méthode de flûte* (Paris, 1795), which went through several editions.

De Vito, Gioconda, Italian violinist; b. in Martina Franca (Lecce), July 26, 1907. She studied at the Liceo Musicale in Pesara, graduating in 1921; then taught at the Bari Cons. From 1946–53 she gave concerts in England. She married David Bicknell, English record company executive, in 1949.

De Vocht, Lodewijk, Belgian conductor and composer; b. Antwerp, Sept. 21, 1887; d. 's Gravenzel, near Antwerp, March 27, 1977. He studied with Gilson and Mortelmans at the Royal Flemish Cons. in Antwerp; played the violin in the newly formed orch. of the Société des Concerts Nouveaux (1903) and became its conductor in 1921; conducted the choir of the Antwerp Cathedral (1912–50); for more than half a century led the Chorale Caecilia that he had founded (1915–68) and the Association des Concerts of the Antwerp Cons. (1935–53); taught music at the Flemish Cons. (1921–53). His own compositions are in a Romantic style.

WORKS: 3 symphonies (No. 1, with chorus, 1932); Violin Concerto (Antwerp, May 20, 1944); Cello Concerto (1955); Concerto for Recorder and Orch. (1957); *Primavera*, pastoral poem for soprano, tenor, chorus and orch. (1963–65); *Scaldis aeterna*, cantata (1966); several symph. poems, among them *Sortilèges des bois;* Wind Trio (1955); *Tylliederen*, 7 ballads for baritone, and guitar or piano (1968); *Suite champêtre* for guitar (1971–73); many choruses; 2 piano sonatas; Preludes and Fugues for organ.

Devreese, Frédéric, Belgian conductor and composer, son of **Godefroid Devreese;** b. Amsterdam, June 2, 1929. He studied first at the Cons. in Malines, then took courses in composition from Poot and conducting from Defossez at the Brussels Cons.; subsequently studied with Pizzetti at the Santa Cecilia Academy in Rome (1952–55). Returning to Belgium, he became associated with the Flemish Television, as program director.

WORKS: an opera that won the 1964 Prix Italia, *Willem van Saeftinghe* (Brussels TV, Sept. 28, 1964; first stage performance, Antwerp, Nov. 21, 1964); a TV opera, *De vreemde ruiter* (1966); 2 ballets: *Mascarade* (1955; Aix-les-Bains, France, 1956) and *L'Amour de Don Juan* (1973); 3 piano concertos (1949, 1952, 1955–56); Violin Concerto (1951); Symphony (1953); *Mouvement lent* for string orch. (1953); *Recitativo et Allegro* for trumpet and orch. (1959); *Mouvement vif* for string orch. (1963); *Evocation*, suite for orch. (1967); Divertimento for String Orch. (1970); *Complainte* for cello or oboe, and piano (1951); Quintet for Flute, Clarinet, Bassoon, Piano and Percussion (1957); *Ensorbeelden*, suite for brass quintet (1972).

Devreese, Godefroid, Belgian conductor and composer; b. Kortrijk, Jan. 22, 1893; d. Brussels, June 4, 1972. He studied at the Brussels Cons. with Ysaÿe and César Thompson (violin), and Rasse and Gilson (composition); was a conductor of the Antwerp Opera (1919–20); violinist with the Concertgebouw Orch., Amsterdam (1925–30); director of the Cons. of Malines (1930–58) concurrently giving courses at the Brussels Cons. (1944–59).

WORKS: a ballet, *Tombelène* (1927); *Poème heroïque* for orch. (1923); *Symphonic Variations on a Popular Scottish Theme* (1923); Concertino for Cello and Chamber Orch. (1926); *In memoriam* for orch. (1928); 2 violin concertos (1936, 1970); Piano Concerto (1938); 4 symphonies: No. 1, *Gothique* (1944); No. 2, *Goethe*, with chorus (1952); No. 3, *Sinfonietta* (1962); No. 4 (1965–66); Rhapsodie for Clarinet and orch. (1948); *Allegro* for trumpet and orch. (1950); Suite for orch. (1953); Sinfonietta for String Orch. (1962); *6 Variations on a Popular Theme* for string orch. (1963); *Capriccio* for violin and string orch. (1963); *Stabat Mater* for soprano, chorus and orch. (1965); *Te Deum* for chorus and orch. (1967; posthumous, Brussels, March 30, 1973); Violin Sonata (1924); Cello Sonata (1926); String Quartet (1937); Piano Trio (1950); *Scherzo de concert* for piano (1921); *Danse lente* for piano (1924); 7 piano sonatinas (1944–45); Piano Sonata (1945); songs.

Devrient, Eduard, German writer on musical subjects; b. Berlin, Aug. 11, 1801; d. Karlsruhe, Oct. 4, 1877. Pupil of Zelter; began his career as a baritone at the Royal Opera in 1819, but after the loss of his voice went over to the spoken drama, without losing his interest in music; he was the author of the text to Marschner's *Hans Heiling*, and also created the title role (1833). His chief work is *Geschichte der deutschen Schauspielkunst* (5 vols., 1848–74); his works concerning music are *Briefe aus Paris* (1840, about Cherubini) and *Meine Erinnerungen an Felix Mendelssohn-Bartholdy und seine Briefe an mich* (Leipzig, 1869). Within weeks after its publication, Wagner issued a polemical pamphlet entitled *Herr Eduard Devrient und Sein Styl* (Munich, 1869) under the pseudonym Wilhelm Drach, violently attacking Devrient for his literary style. Devrient's book was publ. in English in the same year (London, 1869; 3rd ed., 1891).

Devries, Herman, American bass; b. New York, Dec. 25, 1858; d. Chicago, Aug. 24, 1949. He studied in Paris; 1879, debut at the Paris Opéra as the Grand Inquisitor in *L'Africaine;* 1880–88, at the Opéra-Comique; then appeared in Brussels, Marseilles, Aix-les-Bains, and Vichy; debut at the Metropolitan Opera Dec. 17, 1898, appearing through that season; established his own studio in Chicago in 1900; was music critic of the *Chicago American;* composed various songs and several pieces for piano and orch.

Deyo, Felix, American composer and pianist; b. Poughkeepsie, N.Y., April 21, 1888; d. Baldwin, N.Y., June 21, 1959. He studied piano with his mother **Mary Forster Deyo** (1857–1947); at the Brooklyn Cons. of Music; after graduation, he taught there (1911–39). In 1939 he became director of the Baldwin, L.I., Cons. of Music; wrote 3 symphonies: *A Lyric Symphony* (Babylon, L.I., Dec. 8, 1949); *An Ancient Symphony* and *A Primeval Symphony*; also 2 piano sonatas, a violin sonata, and numerous piano pieces of a programmatic nature (*Flight of the Dodo Bird*, etc.). His wife **Asta Nygren Deyo** (1898–1953) was a piano teacher.

Deyo, Ruth Lynda, American pianist (second cousin of **Felix Deyo**); b. Poughkeepsie, N.Y., April 20, 1884; d. Cairo, March 4, 1960. She studied piano with William Mason and Teresa Carreño; comp. with MacDowell; made her debut at the age of 9 at the World's Columbian Exposition in Chicago (1893); concert debut in Berlin (March 23, 1904); subsequently played with major orchestras in the U.S. and in Europe; appeared in recitals with Kreisler and Casals. In 1925 she settled in Egypt and devoted herself mainly to composition. In 1930 she completed the full score of a large opera on Egyptian themes, *The Diadem of Stars* (libretto by her husband Charles Dalton; unperformed). The Prelude to this opera was perf. by Stokowski with the Philadelphia Orch. (April 4, 1931).

Dezède (Deziades, De Zaides), Nicolas, opera composer; b. in Slovenia, c.1740; d. Paris, Sept. 11, 1792. He was active in Paris, where over 15 of his stage works were produced, including *Julie* (1772), *Le Stratagème découvert* (1773), *Cécile* (1781), *Blaise et Babet* (1783), *Alexis et Justine* (1785), *Alcindor* (1787). The overture of his opera *Blaise et Babet* and a Finale, for piano, figured frequently on early American concert programs.

BIBLIOGRAPHY: O. G. Sonneck, *Early Concert-Life in America*, Leipzig, 1907; A. Pougin, *Dezède* (Paris, 1862).

D'Hoedt, Henri-Georges, Belgian composer; b. Ghent, June 28, 1885; d. Brussels, May 14, 1936. He was a student of Emile Mathieu and Leo Moeremans; became director of the Cons. at Louvain in 1924, serving until his death. He was one of the first Belgian composers to depart from late 19th-century Romanticism and come under the influence of French Impressionism.

WORKS: an opera *Klaas au Pays de Cocagne* (*Klaas in t'Luilekkerland*; Antwerp, 1926); a satirical symph. study, *Les Brèves Chroniques de la vie bourgeoise* (1934); *Narcisse* for orch.; *L'Ile de Cythère* for chorus and orch.; *La Vocation de Siddartha*, symph. trilogy; *Dionysos*, symph. poem; *Poème pantagruélique* for orch.; chamber music.

Diabelli, Anton, Austrian composer and publisher; b. Mattsee, n. Salzburg, Sept. 5, 1781; d. Vienna, April 8, 1858. He was a choir boy in the monastery at Michaelbeurn, and in Salzburg Cathedral; studied for the priesthood at the Munich Latin School, but continued his musical work, submitting his compositions to Michael Haydn, who encouraged him. On the secularization of the Bavarian monasteries, Diabelli, who had already entered that at Raichenhaslach, embraced the career of a musician, went to Vienna (where Joseph Haydn received him kindly), taught piano and guitar for a living, and in 1818 became a partner of Cappi, the music publisher, assuming control of the firm (Diabelli & Co.) in 1824. He published much of Schubert's music, but underpaid the composer, and complained that he wrote too much. In 1852 he sold his firm to C. A. Spina. A facile composer, Diabelli produced an opera, *Adam in der Klemme* (Vienna, 1809; one performance), Masses, cantatas, chamber music, etc., which are consigned to oblivion; his sonatinas are still used for beginners. His name was immortalized through Beethoven's set of 33 variations (op. 120) on a waltz theme by Diabelli.

Diack, John Michael, British vocal pedagogue; b. Glasgow, June 26, 1869; d. London, Feb. 2, 1946. He lived in London as head of the publishing house of Paterson Sons & Co.; published valuable pedagogic works: *Vocal Exercises on Tone-Placing and Enunciation* (1920); *Song Studies* (1920); *Five Minutes Daily Exercises on Vocal Technique* (Glasgow, 1920); *Tone Color and Interpretation* (1926); edited *New Scottish Orpheus* (2 volumes; 200 songs); *The Burns Song Book* (50 songs); and choral works of Bach and Handel.

Diaghilev, Sergei, creator and director of the famous Russian Ballet; b. Gruzino, in the Novgorod district, March 31, 1872; d. Venice, Aug. 19, 1929. He was associated with progressive artistic organizations in St. Petersburg, but his main field of activity was in western Europe. He established the Ballet Russe in Paris; he commissioned Stravinsky to write the ballets *The Firebird*, *Petrouchka*, and *Le Sacre du Printemps*; also commissioned Prokofiev, Henri Sauguet, Milhaud, Poulenc, Auric, and other composers of the younger generation. Ravel and Manuel de Falla also wrote works for Diaghilev. The great importance of Diaghilev's choreographic ideas lies in the complete abandonment of the classical tradition; in this respect Diaghilev was the true originator of the modern dance.

BIBLIOGRAPHY: Diaghilev issue of *La Revue Musicale* (Dec. 1930); *The Russian Ballet* (London, 1931); C. W. Beaumont, *Sergei Diaghilev* (London, 1933); A. L. Haskell, *Diaghilev, His Artistic and Private Life* (London, 1935); V. Kamenev, *Russian Ballet through Russian Eyes* (London, 1936); Serge Lifar, *Serge Diaghilev: his Life, his Work, his Legend* (London, 1940); C. W. Beaumont, *The Diaghilev Ballet in London, A Personal Record* (London, 1940); S. L. Grigoriev, *The Diaghilev Ballet* (London, 1953); Richard Buehle, *In Search of Diaghilev* (N.Y., 1956); Boris Kochno, *Diaghilev and the Ballets Russes* (N.Y., 1970).

Diamond, David, outstanding American composer; b. Rochester, N.Y., July 9, 1915. He studied composition with Bernard Rogers at the Eastman School of Music in his hometown (1930-34); then took courses with Roger Sessions in New York. In 1936 he went to Paris where he studied with Nadia Boulanger and became associated with the most important musicians and writers of the time. Returning to New York, he devoted his time exclusively to composition; various grants and awards enabled him to continue his work in relative financial prosperity. He received the Juilliard Publication Award for his *Psalm* (1937), 2 Guggenheim Fellowships (1938, 1941), American Academy in Rome award (1942), Paderewski Prize (1943), and a grant of one thousand dollars from the National Academy of Arts and Letters (1944). His early music is marked by a great complexity of harmonic writing, with the sense of tonality clearly present; the element of rhythm, often inspired by natural folklike patterns, is very strong in all of his works. In his later symphonies he adopted a modified dodecaphonic method of composition, while keeping free of doctrinaire serialism. His instrumental and vocal writing is invariably idiomatic, which makes his music welcome to performers and audiences alike.

WORKS: 8 symphonies: No. 1 (N.Y., Dec. 21, 1941); No. 2 (Boston, Oct. 13, 1944); No. 3 (1945; Boston, Nov. 3, 1950); No. 4 (Boston, Jan. 23, 1948); No. 5 (1947-64; N.Y., April 28, 1966); No. 6 (Boston, March 8, 1957); No. 7 (N.Y., Jan. 26, 1962); No. 8 (N.Y., Oct. 26, 1961, prior to Symphony No. 7); 3 violin concertos: No. 1 (N.Y., March 24, 1937); No. 2 (Vancouver, Feb. 29, 1948); No. 3 (N.Y., April 1, 1976); *Hommage à Satie* (1934); *Threnody* (1935); *Psalm*, for orch. (Rochester, Dec. 10, 1936); 1st suite from ballet *Tom* (1936); *Variations on an Original Theme* (1937; Rochester, April 23, 1940); *Elegy in Memory of Maurice Ravel* for brass, harp, and percussion (Rochester, April 28, 1938); *Heroic Piece* (Zürich, July 29, 1938); Cello Concerto (1938; Rochester, April 30, 1942); *Concert Piece* (N.Y., May 16, 1940); Concerto for Chamber Orch. (Yaddo, N.Y., Sept. 7, 1940, composer conducting); *Rounds* for string orch. (Minneapolis, Nov. 24, 1944; his most successful work); *Romeo and Juliet* (N.Y., Oct. 20, 1947); *The Enormous Room*, after E. E. Cummings (Cincinnati, Nov. 19, 1949); *Timon of Athens*, symph. portrait after Shakespeare (Louisville, 1949); Piano Concerto (1949; April 28, 1966); *Ahavah* for narrator and orch. (Washington, Nov. 17, 1954); *Diaphony* for brass, 2 pianos, timpani, and organ (N.Y., Feb. 22, 1956); *Sinfonia concertante* (Rochester, March 7, 1957); *World of Paul Klee*, orch. suite (Portland, Oregon, Feb. 15, 1958). Chamber music: Partita for Oboe, Bassoon, and Piano (1935); Concerto for String Quartet (1936); String Trio (1937); Quintet for Flute, String Trio, and Piano (1937); Piano Quartet

(1938); Cello Sonata (1938); 4 string quartets (1940, 1943, 1946, 1951); Violin Sonata (1945); *Canticle for Perpetual Motion* for violin and piano (1947); Chaconne for Violin and Piano (1947); Quintet for Clarinet, 2 Violas, and 2 Cellos (1951); Piano Trio (1951); Nonet for 3 Violins, 3 Violas, and 3 Cellos (1962). Vocal music: *This is the Garden*, chorus a cappella (1935); *3 Madrigals*, after James Joyce, for chorus a cappella (1937); *Young Joseph*, after Thomas Mann, for women's chorus and string orch. (1944); *L'Âme de Claude Debussy*, extracts from Debussy's letters to Jacques Durand (1949); *The Midnight Meditation*, cycle of 4 songs (1950); *This Sacred Ground* for chorus, male voice and orch. (Buffalo, Nov. 17, 1963); *A Secular Cantata*, to texts from James Agee's *Permit Me Voyage* (N.Y., Feb. 5, 1977). For piano: Sonatina (1935); Concerto for 2 Pianos (1941); *Album for the Young* (1946); Sonata (1947).

Dianda, Hilda, Argentinian composer; b. Córdoba, April 13, 1925. She studied in Europe with Scherchen and Malipiero; in 1958–62 worked at the Radiodiffusion Française in Paris. Upon returning to Argentina she devoted herself to composition and organization of concerts of ultra-modern music.

WORKS: 3 string quartets (1947, 1960, 1962); Concertante for Cello and Chamber Orch. (1952); Trio for Flute, Oboe and Bassoon (1953); Wind Quintet (1957); *Díptico* for 16 instruments (1962); *Núcleos* for string orch., 2 pianos and percussion (1964); works for various ensembles under the generic titles *Resonancias* and *Ludus* (1964–69).

Dianin, Sergei, Russian writer on music; b. St. Petersburg, Dec. 26, 1888; d. in the village of Davidovo, Vladimir district, Oct. 26, 1968. A son of Borodin's assistant in chemistry, he became a mathematician by profession; having access to Borodin's archives, he published 4 vols. of Borodin's letters (Moscow, 1928, 1936, 1949, 1950) and a biography *Borodin, Life, Materials, Documents* (Moscow, 1955; 2nd ed., 1960; in English, London, 1963).

Dianov, Anton, Russian composer; b. Moscow, Feb. 19, 1882; d. there, March 25, 1939. He was a pupil of the Moscow Cons., graduating in 1912; in 1920 became director of the Music School in Moscow. He wrote effective piano pieces, music for violin and piano (*Lyrische Fragmente*), and many songs.

Diaz (de la Peña), Eugène (-Émile), French composer, son of the celebrated painter; b. Paris, Feb. 27, 1837; d. Coleville, Sept. 12, 1901. He was a pupil of Paris Cons. (Halévy, Reber); produced the comic opera *Le Roi Candaule* (Paris, 1865) and won the government prize for the opera *La Coupe du roi de Thulé* (Paris, Jan. 10, 1873), which, however, proved a complete failure.

BIBLIOGRAPHY: A. Jullien, *Airs variés* (Paris, 1877; pp. 202–10).

Diaz, Rafaelo, American tenor; b. (of Spanish-American parents) San Antonio, Texas, 1884; d. New York, Dec. 12, 1943. He studied music in Berlin; voice in Italy; made his opera debut with the Boston Opera Co., Dec. 6, 1911; was a member of the Metropolitan Opera Co. from 1918 to 1936; then sang mostly in concerts.

Dibdin, Charles, English composer; b. Dibdin, near Southampton (bapt. March 4), 1745; d. London, July 25, 1814. 1756–59, chorister at Winchester Cathedral; took lessons there from Kent and Fussell, but was chiefly self-taught in composition; at 15 went to London, was engaged at Covent Garden as a singing actor, and soon began to write for the stage. His first piece, *The Shepherd's Artifice*, was produced at his benefit performance, at Covent Garden, on May 21, 1764. He was engaged at Birmingham, 1763–65, and at Covent Garden again till 1768, when he went over to Drury Lane. Falling out with Garrick, he went to France in 1776, remaining there until 1778, when he was appointed composer to Covent Garden, having up to that time brought out 8 operas. 1782–84, manager of the newly erected Royal Circus (later the Surrey Theatre). After the failure of certain theatrical enterprises, and a projected journey to India, he commenced a series of monodramatic "table-entertainments," of which song was a principal feature, and which were extremely popular from 1789 to 1805; in these Dibdin appeared as author, composer, narrator, singer, and accompanist. He then built and managed a small theater of his own, opened in 1796; he retired in 1805 on a pension, which was withdrawn for a time, but subsequently restored. Dibdin also composed numerous sea songs which were very popular at the time. He publ. *The Musical Tour of Mr. Dibdin* (1788), *History of the Stage* (1795, 5 vols.), *Professional Life* (1803, 4 vols.), and various novels.

BIBLIOGRAPHY: E. R. Dibdin, *A Charles Dibdin Bibliography* (Liverpool, 1937). His grandson, **Henry Edward Dibdin** (b. London, Sept. 8, 1813; d. Edinburgh, May 6, 1866), was an organist, harpist, and teacher, who compiled the collection *The Standard Psalm Tune Book* (1851).

di Bonaventura, Anthony and **Mario.** See **Bonaventura.**

Di Capua, Eduardo, Italian composer of Neapolitan ballads; b. Naples, 1864; d. there, 1917. He earned his living by playing in small theaters and cafés in and around Naples, and later in the cinemas; also gave piano lessons. His most famous song was *O Sole mio* (1898); its popularity was immense, and never abated. Other celebrated songs were *Maria Mari* (1899); *Torna maggio* (1900); *Canzona bella*, etc. Di Capua sold these songs to publishers outright, and so did not benefit by their popularity. He died in extreme poverty.

Dichter, Misha, American pianist; b. in Shanghai, China, of Russian parents, Sept. 27, 1945. He was raised in Los Angeles; at the age of 15 he won a contest of the Music Educators National Conference, Western Division. He subsequently appeared as soloist with young symphonic groups. He entered the Univ. of California, Los Angeles, where he enrolled in a master class conducted by Rosina Lhévinne; later joined her class at the Juilliard School of Music in

New York. In 1966 he entered the Tchaikovsky piano competition in Moscow and won 2nd prize, with great popular acclaim among Russian audiences. This marked the beginning of a highly successful career, with numerous appearances in America and in Europe. Dichter's natural predilections lie in the romantic repertory; his playing possesses a fine emotional appeal.

Dick, Marcel, Hungarian-American violinist and composer; b. Miskolcz, Hungary, Aug. 28, 1898. He came from a musical family; the famous Hungarian violinist Eduard Reményi was his great-uncle. He studied violin with Joseph Bloch and composition with Kodály. He was first violist in the Vienna Symph. Orch. (1924–27), and was also a member of the Kolisch Quartet and of the Rosé Quartet. In 1934 he went to the U.S.; was first violist of the Cleveland Orch. (1943–49); in 1948 appointed head of the department of theory of the Cleveland Institute of Music. He wrote a symphony (Cleveland, Dec. 14, 1950) and a symphony for 2 string orchestras (1964); also some chamber music and songs.

Dickinson, Clarence, American composer; b. Lafayette, Ind., May 7, 1873; d. New York, Aug. 2, 1969. He studied music with Weidig in Chicago; then went to Germany where he took courses with Riemann; further had piano lessons with Moszkowski; moved to Paris where he became a pupil of Guilmant in organ playing and with Pierné in composition. Returning to America in 1909, he settled in New York as church organist; from 1912–1945 he served as Director of Sacred Music at the Union Theological Seminary; also made lecture tours in the U.S., Canada, France, England and Spain. He composed the operas *The Medicine Man* and *Priscilla*; numerous organ pieces and songs; edited the collections *Historical Recitals for Organ* (50 numbers), *Book of 80 Amens,* and *Book of 40 Antiphons*. He also published *Excursions in Musical History* (1917); *Troubadour Songs* (1920); *Technique and Art of Organ Playing* (1921).

Dickinson, Edward, American music historian; b. W. Springfield, Mass., Oct. 10, 1853; d. Oberlin, Ohio, Jan. 25, 1946. He studied organ with Eugene Thayer at the New England Cons.; also traveled to Germany and attended classes with Spitta in Berlin. From 1883–1892 he was director of music at Elmira College; and in 1893 was appointed prof. of music history at Oberlin College. He publ. *Music in the History of the Western Church* (1902); *The Study of the History of Music* (1905); *The Education of a Music Lover* (1911); *Music and the Higher Education* (1915); *The Spirit of Music* (1925).

Dickinson, George Sherman, American music educator; b. St. Paul, Minn., Feb. 9, 1888; d. Chapel Hill, North Carolina, Nov. 6, 1964. He studied at Oberlin College (B.A., 1909); at the Oberlin Cons. of Music (Mus. Bac., 1910); and at Harvard Univ. (M.A., 1912); also studied with Kaun and Juon in Berlin (1913–14). He taught at the Oberlin Cons. from 1910–22, and was a member of the faculty of Vassar College from 1922–39. He wrote *The Growth and Use of Harmony*

(Vol. 4 of *Fundamentals of Musical Art*; 1927); *Classification of Musical Compositions* (1938); and *The Pattern of Music* (1939).

Dickinson, Helen Adell, Canadian-American author; b. Port Elmsley, Ont., Canada, Dec. 5, 1875; d. Tucson, Arizona, Aug. 25, 1957. She studied at Queen's Univ. in Kingston, Canada (M.A., 1895) and at Heidelberg Univ. (Ph.D., 1901); in 1904 she married Clarence Dickinson. She published *Metrical Translation of 150 Ancient Carols* (1930); *A Book of Antiphons* (1919); *The Coming of the Prince of Peace: A Nativity Play of Ancient Christmas Carols* (1919); and *A Treasury of Worship* (1926).

Dickinson, Peter, English composer; b. Lytham St. Annes, Lancashire, Nov. 15, 1934. Of a musical family, he studied piano and began to compose early in life. He entered the Univ. of Cambridge; after obtaining his M.A. Degree in music there, he went to the U.S. on a Rotary Foundation Fellowship, and studied with Bernard Wagenaar at the Juilliard School of Music, N.Y. (1958–60). Returning to England, he became lecturer at the College of St. Mark and St. John, London. In his music he combines the esoteric techniques of serialism with pragmatic considerations for performance.

WORKS: *Postlude on Adeste Fideles* for organ (1954); *Jesus Christ is Risen Today* for chorus a cappella (1955); *Sonatina for Flute and Piano* (1955); *4 W. H. Auden Songs* for voice and piano (1956); *Variations for Piano* (1957); *5 Blake Songs* for tenor, horn, clarinet and bassoon (1957); *String Quartet* (1958); *Air* for solo flute (1958); *Monologue* for string orch. (1959); *A Dylan Thomas Song Cycle* for baritone and piano (1959); *Study in Pianissimo* for organ (1959); *Fantasia for Solo Violin* (1959); *Vitalitas,* ballet (1960); *Violin Sonata* (1961); *4 Duos for Flute and Cello* (1962); *Trio for Flute, Oboe and Harpsichord* (1962); *5 Forgeries* for piano duet (1963); *5 Diversions* for keyboard instruments (1963); *Carillon* for organ (1964); *The Judas Tree,* a musical drama for speakers, singers, chorus and chamber orch. (London, May 27, 1965); *Outcry* for chorus and orch. (Leamington, May 10, 1969); *Diversions* for small orch. (Leamington, Nov. 23, 1969); *Transformations: Homage to Satie* for orch. (Cheltenham, July 3, 1970); *Organ Concerto* (Gloucester Cathedral, Aug. 22, 1971); *Concerto for Strings, Percussion and Electronic Organ* (Birmingham, Jan. 22, 1971).

BIBLIOGRAPHY: R. Norrington, "Peter Dickinson," *Musical Times* (Feb. 1965).

Diderot, Denis, illustrious projector and editor of the celebrated "Encyclopédie"; b. Langres, Oct. 5, 1713; d. Paris, July 30, 1784. In his work *Mémoirs sur différents sujets de mathématiques* (The Hague, 1748) are the essays "Des principes d'acoustique" and "Projet d'un nouvel orgue," the latter being an impracticable idea for a new kind of barrel organ.

Di Domenica, Robert, American composer and flutist; b. New York, March 4, 1927. He graduated in music education from New York University in 1951; then studied composition privately with Wallingford Riegger; also took flute lessons with Harold Bennett (1949-55). He performed as a flutist with the Metropolitan Opera, and various orchestral groups and also with the Modern Jazz Quintet. He taught flute privately in N.Y.; in 1969 he was appointed to the faculty of the New England Cons. in Boston; in 1976 became Dean there.

WORKS: an opera *The Balcony* (1972); Flute Sonata (1957); Sextet for Piano, Flute, Oboe, Clarinet, Horn and Bassoon (1957); Piano Sonatina (1958); Quartet for Violin, Flute, Horn and Piano (1959); *4 Movements* for piano (1959); Quartet for Flute, Violin, Viola and Cello (1960); *The First Kiss of Love* for soprano and piano (1960); String Quartet (1960); Symphony (1961; first complete perf., Boston, Nov. 15, 1972); *Variations on a Tonal Theme* for solo flute (1961); Concerto for Violin and Chamber Orch. (1962; N.Y., April 15, 1965); Wind quintet (1969); Piano Concerto (1963); Concerto for Wind Quintet, Strings and Timpani (1964); Quintet for Clarinet and String Quartet (1965); Trio for Flute, Bassoon and Piano (1960); Violin Sonata (1966); *Saeculum Aureum* for flute, piano and tape (1967); *Music* for flute and string orch. (1967); Saxophone Sonata (1968); *11 Short Pieces* for piano (1973); *Improvisations* for piano (1974); *4 Short Songs* for soprano, flute, clarinet, violin, viola, cello and piano (1975); *Songs from Twelfth Night* for tenor, flute, viola da gamba and harpsichord (1976); *Black Poems* for baritone, piano and tape (1976).

Didur, Adamo, famous Polish basso; b. Sanok, Galicia, Dec. 24, 1874; d. Katowice, Poland, Jan. 7, 1946. He studied with Wysocki and Emerich; in 1894 made his operatic debut in Rio de Janeiro, thereafter appearing at the La Scala Opera, Milan, at the Warsaw Opera, in Moscow, St. Petersburg, Barcelona, Madrid, London, and Buenos Aires; in 1907-08 appeared with the Manhattan Opera Co.; in 1908, made his debut as Méphistophélès at the Metropolitan Opera House, of which he was a leading member until 1932.

Didymus, a grammarian of Alexandria; b. 63 B.C. The number of his works was estimated by Seneca at 4,000; he wrote a tract on music, now known only by an epitome of Porphyry's, and some quotations by Ptolemy. In his system the octave of the diatonic genus is formed by two precisely similar tetrachords; and in all 3 species of tetrachord (diatonic, chromatic, enharmonic) the ratio for the interval of the major third is 4:5. He also recognized the difference between the major and minor whole tone; this difference ($9/8:10/9 = 81:80$) is, therefore, rightly termed the "comma of Didymus." Salinas and Doni have written on his musical system.

Diémer, Louis, distinguished French pianist; b. Paris, Feb. 14, 1843; d. there, Dec. 21, 1919. Pupil of Marmontel at the Cons., taking 1st piano prize in 1856; also of Ambroise Thomas and Bazin for composition, taking 1st harmony prize, 2d organ prize, and 1st prize for fugue. Played with great success at the Alard, Pasdeloup, and Cons. concerts; succeeded Marmontel (1887) as piano prof. at Cons. The immense success of his series of historical recitals, in 1889, determined him to make a specialty of early mu-

sic, and led to the establishing of the "Société des anciens instruments." Widor, Saint-Saëns, Lalo, and others wrote pieces for him which he played at the Colonne and Lamoureux Concerts. He edited a number of old French keyboard pieces; his collection, *Clavecinistes français*, was publ. posthumously in 1928.

Dienel, Otto, German organist; b. Tiefenfurth, Silesia, Jan. 11, 1839; d. Berlin, March 7, 1905; studied music in Berlin at the Royal Institute for Church Music, and at the Royal Academy. Teacher of music; organist at the Marienkirche, Berlin. He wrote compositions for organ, and choruses; author of *Die moderne Orgel* (1889, 2nd ed., 1891).

Diepenbrock, Alphons, eminent Dutch composer; b. Amsterdam, Sept. 2, 1862; d. there, April 5, 1921. He learned to play violin and piano in his childhood. In 1880 he entered the Univ. of Amsterdam, where he studied classical philology; received his Dr. phil. in 1888; then taught academic subjects at the grammar school at 's-Hertogenbosch (1888-94); then abandoned his pedagogical activities and devoted himself primarily to music; studied works of the Flemish School of the Renaissance, and later perused the scores of Berlioz, Wagner and Debussy. Despite this belated study, he succeeded in developing a rather striking individual style of composition, in which Wagnerian elements curiously intertwine with impressionistic modalities. However, he had difficulty in putting the results into definite shape, and he left more than 100 incomplete manuscripts at his death. His Catholic upbringing led him to concentrate mainly on the composition of sacred choral music; he wrote no symphonies, concertos or instrumental sonatas.

WORKS: *Stabat Mater* for men's chorus; *Missa in Die festo* for tenor, male chorus and organ (1890-91); *Les Elfes,* for soprano, baritone, women's chorus and orch. (1896); *Te Deum* for soloists, double chorus and orch. (1897); *2 Hymnen an die Nacht,* after Novalis, one each for soprano and contralto, with orch. (1899); *Vondel's Vaart naar Agrippine* (Vondel's *Journey to Agrippina*) for baritone and orch. (1902-03); *Im grossen Schweigen,* after Nietzsche, for baritone and orch. (Amsterdam, May 20, 1906); *Hymne aan Rembrandt,* for soprano, women's chorus and orch. (1906); incidental music to Verhagen's mythical comedy, *Marsyas of De betooverde Bron* (*Marsyas* or *The Enchanted Well,* 1909-10); *Die Nacht,* after Hölderlin, for mezzo-soprano and orch. (1910-11); *Lydische Nacht,* for baritone and orch. (1913); incidental music to Aristophanes' *The Birds* (1917; a concert overture from this music is fairly popular); incidental music to Goethe's *Faust* (1918); incidental music to Sophocles' *Electra* (1920); numerous choruses and songs. A collection of Diepenbrock's writings, *Verzamelde Geschriften,* edited by Eduard Reeser, was published in Utrecht (1950); a catalogue of his works was issued in Amsterdam in 1962. Eduard Reeser brought out *Brieven en documenten* (letters and documents of Diepenbrock; 2 vols.; Amsterdam, 1962-67); he also wrote "Some Melodic Patterns in the Music of Alphons Diepenbrock," in *Composers' Voice 3* (1976/1; pp. 16-25).

Dieren, Bernard van, important composer and writer; b. Rotterdam, Dec. 27, 1884; d. London, April 24, 1936. After studying in Germany and Holland, he settled in 1909 in London as music correspondent of the *Nieuwe Rotterdamsche Courant;* later devoted his time exclusively to composing. His works show radical tendencies.

WORKS: *6 Sketches* for piano (1911); 4 string quartets (1912; 1917, performed at the Donaueschingen Music Festival in 1920; 1919; 1923, performed at the Frankfurt International Music Festival in 1925); Symph. for Soli, Chorus, and Orch. on Chinese Texts (1914); *Diaphony* for baritone and chamber orch. on 3 Shakespearean sonnets; *Overture to an Ideal Comedy* (1916); *Les Propous des Beuveurs,* introit for orch. (after Rabelais; London, 1921); *Sonata Tyroica* for violin and piano (1927); many songs (also with string quartet and chamber orch.). Author of a book on the modern sculptor, Jacob Epstein (1920); and a collection of essays, *Down Among the Dead Men* (London, 1935).

BIBLIOGRAPHY: E. Davis, "B. van Dieren," *Musical Quarterly* (April 1938); G. Grouse, "Bernard van Dieren—Three Early Songs in Relation to His Subsequent Development," *Music Review* (May 1968).

Diet, Edmond-Marie, French dramatic composer; b. Paris, Sept. 25, 1854; d. there, Oct. 30, 1924. Pupil of César Franck and Guiraud; produced the operas *Stratonice* (1887), *Le Cousin Placide* (1887), *Fleur de Vertu* (1894), *La Revanche d'Iris* (1905); also ballets and pantomimes (*Scientia,* 1889; *La Grève; Masque rose; M. Ruy-Blas,* 1894; *La Belle et la Bête,* 1895; *L'Araignée d'or,* 1896; *Rêve de Noël,* 1896; *Watteau,* 1900 (with Pujet), and the 3-act operetta *Gentil Crampon* (Paris, 1897); besides songs, and church music.

Diether, Jack, Canadian-American musicologist; b. Vancouver, British Columbia, Feb. 26, 1919. He was educated at the Univ. of British Columbia; served in the Canadian Army and Air Force during World War II. In 1955 he settled in the U.S.; was employed at Pickwick Bookshop in Hollywood and at G. Schirmer's Music Store in N.Y. In the meantime he wrote for music magazines, concentrating on the clarification of obscure periods in the lives and works of Bruckner and Mahler; contributed valuable articles to the organ of the Bruckner Society of America, *Chord and Discord,* of which he became the editor in 1969; wrote annotations for orchestra programs and for phonograph records. His valuable article "Notes on Some Mahler Juvenilia," *Chord and Discord* 3/1 (1969) settles some moot questions regarding Mahler's early development.

Dietrich, Albert Hermann, German conductor; b. Forsthaus Golk, n. Meissen, Aug. 28, 1829; d. Berlin, Nov. 19, 1908. Pupil of J. Otto in Dresden and Moscheles and Rietz at Leipzig (1847-51); studied with Schumann at Düsseldorf (1851-54). From 1855-61, concert conductor, and from 1859 municipal music director, at Bonn; from 1861, at Oldenburg; retired in 1890 and lived in Berlin; made Royal Prof. in 1899. He was one of Schumann's best pupils. Wrote *Erinnerungen an Johannes Brahms in Briefen, besonders aus seiner Jugendzeit* (Leipzig, 1898; in English, 1899).

Dietrich (or Dieterich), Sixtus, composer; b. Augsburg, c.1492-94; d. St. Gall, Switzerland, Oct. 21, 1548. Boy chorister at Constance, 1504-06; 1508-09, studied in Freiburg; 1517, choirmaster in Constance, becoming chaplain in 1522; 1540 and 1544, in Wittenberg. He was one of the most important early Protestant composers of sacred music. A book of Magnificats (1535), and 2 collections of antiphons *a 4* (1541 and 1545), were published separately; motets, songs, etc., are scattered through various German collections printed 1536-68; 5 pieces are in Glareanus' *Dodecachordon* (1547). Reprints have been publ. in the *Denkmäler deutscher Tonkunst* 34, and by H. Zenck (13 hymns).

BIBLIOGRAPHY: H. Zenck, *S. Dietrich, Ein Beitrag zur Musik und Musikanschauung im Zeitalter der Reformation* (Leipzig, 1928).

Dietsch, Pierre-Louis-Philippe, French conductor; b. Dijon, March 17, 1808; d. Paris, Feb. 20, 1865. Pupil of Choron and the Paris Cons.; 1830, maître de chapelle at St.-Eustache, and later at Ste.-Madeleine; 1860-3, conductor at the Opéra; composer of 25 Masses and other sacred music. He would have been forgotten long ago, were his name not connected with that of Wagner. In 1842 he brought out at the Opéra *Le Vaisseau Fantôme,* written on Wagner's original sketch of *Der fliegende Holländer,* and in 1861 he conducted (most incompetently) the notorious three Paris performances of *Tannhäuser.* See references to Dietsch in Wagner's *Mein Leben* (vols. I and III).

Dietz, Max, Austrian musicologist; b. Vienna, Apr. 9, 1857; d. there, Aug. 5, 1928. Having obtained his degree (*Dr. phil.*) from the Univ. of Vienna, he spent some time in France in research work, the result of which he publ. in his *Geschichte des musikalischen Dramas in Frankreich während der Revolution bis zum Direktorium* (1885), a most valuable contribution to the history of opera; in 1886 he established himself as docent of musicology at the Univ. of Vienna; edited several Masses, a *Stabat Mater* and Requiem by Emperor Leopold I (1891), and *Recitativi e Duetto fra l'anima e Gesù Cristo* by A. de Liguori (1895).

Dieupart, François, French violinist and harpsichordist; b. c.1670; d. c.1740. He went to London in 1700; was maestro al cembalo, for several years, of Handel's operas, and d. in London almost destitute. Publ. *6 Suites de clavecin . . . composées et mises en concert pour un violon et une flûte, avec basse de viole et un archiluth.* Bach copied two of Dieupart's clavecin suites, and used various themes in his own *English Suites.* The Lyrebird Press of Paris publ. 2 vols. of Dieupart's works, ed. by P. Brunold (vol. I, *6 Suites pour clavecin;* vol. II, *Airs et Chansons*).

Dijk, Jan van, Dutch pianist and composer; b. Oostzaan, June 4, 1918. He studied composition with Willem Pijper in Rotterdam (1936-46); gave piano recitals; taught at the Brabant Cons. in Tilburg since its founding in 1955, and at the Royal Cons. in The Hague since 1961. A prolific composer, he wrote hundreds of works, not counting orchestrations of piano pieces by classical composers. He also produced music in the

31-tone system devised by Dutch physicist Adriaan Fokker.

WORKS: the operas *Flying Dutchman* (1953) and *Protesilaos and Laodamia* (1968); Dance Suite for Orch. and Jazz Combo (1961); Concertino for Flute, Piano, Percussion and Strings (1938); 3 sinfoniettas (1940, 1952, 1956); *Cassatio* for strings and piano obbligato (1943); 4 symphonies (1944, 1947, 1948, 1951); *Capriccio* for viola and orch. (1946); 4 piano concertinos (1948–49, 1953, 1966, 1966); Concertino for 2 Pianos and String or Wind Orch. (1949); *Suite pastorale* for oboe, English horn and small orch. (1953); 3 *Suites da Sonar* (1954, 1955, 1958); *Cortège en Rondeau* for orch. (1955); Saxophone Concertino (1956); Toccata for String Orch. (1957); Concertino for Recorder and Chamber Orch. (1958); Serenade for Winds, Percussion and Piano (1959); 4 *Bagatelles* for orch. (1960); Concertino for Accordion and String Orch. (1960); *17 Projections* for orch. (1962); Double-Bass Concerto (1962); *Salon symphonique* (1963); Concerto for Piano, 4-Hands, and Small Orch. (1963); *Contrasts* for orch. and jazz combo (1964); *Décorations et décompositions* for orch. (1964); *Duetto accompagnato* for saxophone, trombone and string orch. (1964); 2 serenades for small orch. (1966; 1970); *Jardin public*, divertimento for flute and orch. (1967); Triple Concerto for Flute, Recorder, Harpsichord and Orch. (1968); *Makedonski*, suite for chamber orch. (1969); 2 *Résumés* for piano and small orch. (1970); *Touch after Finish* for trumpet, organ, piano and strings (1971); *Fantaisie* for double-bass and orch. (1972); *About* for orch. (1973); *Kleine Concertante* for 2 flutes and chamber orch. (1974); *Affiche pour le Réouverture du magasin* for orch. (1974); *Accomplishement* for small orch. (1975); *Sinfonia e Fughetta* for orch. (1976); *Parties sur l'amitié* for orch. (1977). Vocal works: *Jaergetijde* for chorus and orch. (1944); *Het masker van den Rooden Dood (The Mask of the Red Death)*, after Edgar Allan Poe, for narrator and chamber orch. (1952); *Zwartbaard* for male chorus and orch. (1953); *De Kommandeur* for soloists, narrator, boys' chorus, and string quartet or string orch. (1958); *Heer en Knecht*, cantata (1963); *Coornhert*, cantata (1964); *Quodlibet* for chorus and orch. (1967); *Pros romaious*, cantata (1968); *Ars Vivendi* for chorus and orch. (1977). Chamber music: 5 string quartets (1940, 1941, 1942, 1965, 1974); Divertimento for Clarinet, Viola and Cello (1941); Septet (1949–50); Piano Trio (1950); Divertimento for 2 Violins and Cello (1951); Duo for Cello and Piano (1953); Cello Sonatina (1953); Violin Sonatina (1953); Saxophone Sonata (1953); Sonatina for Violin and Piano (1954); Serenade for Trumpet and Horn (1955); Suite for 2 Flutes and Piano (1957); 2 sonatas for solo flute (1961, 1966); *Musica Sacra I* for 2 violins, viola and organ (1966), *II* for flute, cello and piano (1968) and *III* for clarinet, violin and piano (1975); *Musique à trois* for flute, recorder and harpsichord (1967); Solo Violin Sonata (1968); *Quintetto* for mandolin, bass clarinet, percussion, organ and piano (1969); 4 *Caprices* for accordion (1969); *Pet* for flute, saxophone, trumpet, violin and double bass (1973); *Concertino à 3* for flute, violin and viola (1975). For piano: Sonata (1942); 18 sonatinas (1944–74); *Rondino* (1955); Sonatina for 4 Hands (1956); 2 *Kantieks* (1964, 1976); *Couple* (1969); *Something for 2 Piano Players* (1969); *Partita piccola* (1970); *Alba Communis* (1973); *3 Inventions* (1976). His 31-tone pieces include *7 Pieces* for organ (1948); *Musica per organo trentunisono I* for 31-tone organ (1950–51) and *II*, 7 pieces for 31-tone organ (1957); Concertino for Trombone, Violin and Cello (1961).

Diller, Angela, American pianist and pedagogue; b. Brooklyn, N.Y., Aug. 1, 1877; d. Stamford, Conn., April 30, 1968. She studied music at Columbia Univ. with Edward MacDowell and Percy Goetschius; also with Johannes Schreyer in Dresden; 1899–1916, head of the theory department, Music School Settlement, N.Y.; 1916–21, in charge of the normal work, David Mannes School; then director of the Diller-Quaile School of Music, N.Y.; on the faculty of the Univ. of Southern Calif. (1932), Mills College (1935), New England Cons. (1936 and 1937); co-founder, with Margarethe Dessoff, of the Adesdi Chorus and A Cappella Singers of New York; edited with E. Quaile, K. Stearns Page, and Harold Bauer, many educational music works. In 1953 she received a Guggenheim Fellowship award. She publ. *First Theory Book* (1921); *Keyboard Harmony Course* (4 books; 1936, 1937, 1943, 1949), and *The Splendor of Music* (1957).

Dilling, Mildred, American harpist; b. Marion, Ind., Feb. 23, 1894; studied with Louise Schellschmidt-Koehne, later in Paris with Henriette Renié. After her Paris debut she played in N.Y. (1913) with the Madrigal Singers of the MacDowell Chorus; appeared in Europe with Yvette Guilbert and the de Reszkes, in the U.S. with Alma Gluck and Frances Alda; toured the U.S. and Great Britain many times. She publ. *Old Tunes for New Harpists* (1934); *Thirty Little Classics for the Harp* (1938).

Dillon, Fannie Charles, American pianist; b. Denver, Colo., March 16, 1881; d. Altadena, Calif., Feb. 21, 1947. She studied at Claremont College, Pomona, Calif. and in Berlin (1900–08) with Godowsky and Hugo Kaun, later in N.Y. with Rubin Goldmark; debut as pianist in 1908; taught at Pomona College (1910–13), and from 1918 in Los Angeles High Schools.

WORKS: *Celebration of Victory* (1918); *The Cloud* (1918); *A Letter From the Southland*; *Mission Garden*; *The Alps* (1920); *Chinese Symph. Suite*; etc.; many piano pieces (*Birds at Dawn*, etc.); songs; anthems.

Dillon, Henri, French composer; b. Angers, Oct. 9, 1912; d. in Indo-China, in combat, July 9, 1954. He studied at the Military School in St.-Cyr; was in the army during World War II. He was largely self-taught in music, and adopted a classical style of composition, derived mainly from the melodic patterns of French folksongs.

WORKS: Cello Concerto (1949); Violin Concerto (1949); Viola Concerto (1952); Concerto for 2 Trumpets and Orch. (1953); *Arlequin*, divertimento for string orch. (1949); *Cassation* for 12 wind instruments (1953); Sonata for Saxophone and Piano (1949); Violin Sonata (1952); Concerto for 2 Pianos (Paris, Dec. 15, 1952); Piano Sonata (1953); various works for piano.

Dima, Gheorghe, Rumanian composer; b. Brasov, Oct. 10, 1847; d. Cluj, June 4, 1925. Pupil of Giehne in Karlsruhe, Uffmann in Vienna, Thieriot in Graz, and at the Leipzig Cons. (Richter, Jadassohn, and Reinecke); directed musical societies and church choirs in Sibiu and Brasov; also taught music in those cities.

WORKS: *La Mère d'Etienne le Grand,* oratorio; *Voilà la hora qui tourne,* for mixed chorus and orch.; *Salvum fac regem,* for voices and orch., etc.

Dimov, Bojidar, Bulgarian composer; b. Lom, Jan. 31, 1935. He studied composition with Veselin Stoyanov in Sofia and with Karl Schiske in Vienna. In 1968 he settled in Cologne, where he founded a group for promotion of new music, called "Trial and Error." His own compositions follow the experimental method symbolized by the name of this group, striving to obtain a pragmatic modern style and technique.

WORKS: *Incantations I–III* for soprano and chamber orch. (1963–69); *Komposition I* for piano (1963); *Komposition II* for string quartet (1964); *Komposition III* for orch. (1967–68); *Continuum,* subtitled *Trauerminuten für Dana Kosanova,* for chamber orch., commemorating a 15-year old Czech girl student killed in the course of the Soviet invasion of Czechoslovakia in 1968 (Graz, Oct. 25, 1969); *Raumspiel* for piano and chamber orch., a work of spatial music (1969); *Symphonies* for voice and chamber orch. (1970); *Dual* for 7 instruments (1971).

Dimov, Ivan, Bulgarian composer; b. Kazanlak, Dec. 13, 1927. He studied composition with Goleminov at the Bulgarian State Cons., graduating in 1953; then went to Moscow where he took courses in advanced composition at the Moscow Cons.

WORKS: 2 operas, *They Have Stolen the Council* (1966) and *The Emigrant* (1973); a ballet, *Laughter of Africa* (1966); *Pieces* for oboe and piano (1955); *Kardjalii,* dance drama for orch. (1959); Violin Concertino (1961); *Dramatic* Poem for orch. (1964); String Quartet in 2 parts (1971); *Miniatures* for piano (1973); choruses; songs.

D'Indy, Vincent. See **Indy, Vincent d'.**

Dinicu, Grigoras, Rumanian composer of light music; b. Bucharest, April 3, 1889; d. there, March 28, 1949. A member of a family of musicians, he studied violin with Carl Flesch, who taught at the Bucharest Cons., in 1902. At his graduation in 1906, Dinicu played a violin piece of his own based on popular Rumanian rhythms, *Hora Staccato.* Jascha Heifetz made a virtuoso arrangement of it in 1932. Subsequently Dinicu played in hotels, restaurants, night clubs and cafés in Bucharest and in Western Europe. Apart from *Hora Staccato* he composed numerous other pieces of light music in the gypsy and Rumanian manner.

BIBLIOGRAPHY: Viorel Cosma, *Figuri de Lautari* (Bucharest, 1960; pp. 189–229).

Dippel, Andreas, dramatic tenor and impresario; b. Kassel, Germany, Nov. 30, 1866; d. Hollywood, May 12, 1932. From 1882–87 he was employed in a banking house at Kassel, meanwhile beginning vocal study with Frau Zottmayr, a well-known singer at the court

theater; was engaged at the Bremen Stadttheater (1887–92); made his American debut at the Metropolitan Opera, N.Y. (Nov. 26, 1890); then sang at Covent Garden, London, in Munich, and at Bayreuth. His repertory included nearly 150 roles; he was particularly successful in Wagner's operas. In 1908 he became administrative manager of the Metropolitan Opera House; in 1910 he assumed control of the Chicago Opera Company; was its manager till 1913; then organized his own company, specializing in light opera.

Diruta, Girolamo, celebrated Italian organist; b. Deruta, province of Perugia, 1550; date of death unknown. He was a pupil, in Venice, of Zarlino, Costanzo Porta, and Claudio Merulo, the last of whom mentions the fact with pride in the preface of Diruta's *Il Transilvano.* In 1574, Diruta was in the Minorite monastery at Correggio; then church organist in Venice (1582–93); at the cathedral of Chioggia (1597); and at Agobbio (Gubbio) Cathedral (1609–12). His *Il Transilvano* is a valuable treatise on organ playing, the first work to treat the organ and its playing technique as distinct and separate from the clavier. It is in 2 parts, in dialogue form: *Dialogo sopra il vero modo di sonar organi e istromenti da penna* (Venice, 1593; further editions, 1597, 1609, 1612, 1625); *Dialogo diviso in quattro libri . . . il vero modo e la vera regola d'intavolare ciascun canto* (Venice, 1609; 2nd ed., 1622). Dannreuther, in his *Musical Ornamentation,* gives a thorough analysis of Diruta's system of ornamentation. Volume III of L. Torchi's *L'Arte Musicale in Italia* contains a ricercare and 2 toccatas for organ by Diruta.

BIBLIOGRAPHY: F. Briganti, *Il primo libro dei Contrapunti di Girolamo Diruta* (Perugia, 1951).

Distler, Hugo, important German composer; b. Nuremberg, June 24, 1908; d. (suicide) Berlin, Nov. 1, 1942. He studied at the Leipzig Cons. with Grabner and Martienssen. In 1931 he became a church organist at Lübeck; then was teacher at an ecclesiastical school in Spandau (1933–37); taught at Stuttgart (1937–40); from 1940 he was in Berlin. His early training and his connection with church music determined his style as composer; his music is marked by a strong sense of polyphony. He wrote but few works, mostly chamber music and choral pieces: Concerto for Cembalo and String Orch. (1938); the cantatas *An die Natur* (1933); *Das Lied von der Glocke* (1937); and *Lied am Herde* (1940). His oratorio *Die Weltalter* (1942) remained unfinished. Distler's works have been heard in frequent performances since his death.

BIBLIOGRAPHY: Karl Laux, *Musik und Musiker der Gegenwart* (Essen, 1949); L. G. Palmer, *Hugo Distler and His Church Music* (St. Louis, 1967); U. Herrmann, *Hugo Distler—Rufer und Mahner* (Berlin, 1972).

Di Stefano, Giuseppe, Italian tenor; b. Catania, July 24, 1921. He studied in Milan; sang at La Scala (1946–47); made a successful debut at the Metropolitan Opera, N.Y., in 1948 with numerous re-engagements; also appeared in Mexico (1952). He is equally adept in lyric and dramatic roles; besides his Italian repertoire, he performed leading tenor parts in French and Russian operas.

Ditson, Oliver, American music publisher; founder of the firm of Oliver Ditson & Co.; b. Boston, Oct. 20, 1811; d. there, Dec. 21, 1888. He established himself as a music seller and publisher in Boston in 1835; became a partner of G. H. Parker, his employer, under the firm name of Parker & Ditson; carried on the business in his own name (1842–57), when J. C. Haynes joined the firm, then changed to O. Ditson & Co. His eldest son, **Charles,** took charge of the N.Y. branch **(Ch. H. Ditson & Co.)** in 1867, the business being continued until his death. A Philadelphia branch, opened in 1875 by **J. Edward Ditson** as **J. E. D. & Co.,** was in existence until 1910. A branch for the importation and sale of instruments, etc., was established at Boston in 1860 as John C. Haynes & Co. On Oliver Ditson's death, the firm of O. Ditson & Co. was reorganized as a corporation, with J. C. Haynes as President (d. May 3, 1907); from 1907 until his death, on May 14, 1929, Charles H. Ditson managed the business; he was succeeded by H. H. Porter. In 1931 Theo. Presser Co., of Philadelphia, took over the management of the firm; its catalogue embraced about 52,000 titles. Publishers of the *Musical Record* (a monthly periodical) from 1878–1903, the *Musician* from 1896–1918, and several library series. The music house Lyon & Healy was founded by Oliver Ditson in Chicago, 1864, as a western branch. BIBLIOGRAPHY: W. A. Fisher, *Notes on Music in Old Boston* (Boston, 1918); W. A. Fisher, *One Hundred and Fifty Years of Music Publishing in the U.S.* (Boston, 1933).

Dittersdorf, Karl Ditters von, eminent Austrian violinist and composer; b. Vienna, Nov. 2, 1739; d. at Castle Rothlhotta, near Neuhaus, Bohemia, Oct. 24, 1799. At first taught by König and Ziegler, he became a favorite of Prince Joseph of Hildburghausen, who had him thoroughly trained by Trani (violin) and Bono (composition). He played in the prince's orch. till its dissolution in 1759, and then in the court theater at Vienna; accompanied Gluck on his Italian journey (1761), winning great fame as a violinist, and, on his return trip to Vienna, defeating the renowned Lolli. As Kapellmeister (1764–69) to the Bishop of Gross-Wardein, Hungary (succeeding Michael Haydn), he composed industriously (his first opera, *Amore in musica,* 1767; various oratorios, and much orchestral and chamber music). After traveling for a short time, he was appointed Kapellmeister to the Prince-Bishop of Breslau, Count von Schaffgotsch, at Johannesburg in Silesia, where he had a small theater built, for which he wrote several pieces; though his best operas (*Doktor und Apotheker, Betrug durch Aberglauben, Liebe im Narrenhaus, Hieronymus Knicker,* and *Rotkäppchen*) were composed during visits to Vienna. In 1770 the Pope bestowed on Dittersdorf the Order of the Golden Spur; in 1773 he was ennobled by the Emperor ('von Dittersdorf'). On the decease of the Prince-Bishop (1795), Dittersdorf, who had been very prodigal of his means while at the zenith of his popularity, lived on a small pension, in straitened circumstances, until a friend, Baron von Stillfried, took him into his castle, Rothlhotta. Of his 28 operas only one, *Doktor und Apotheker* (Vienna, July 11, 1786), still survives; despite the vein of jovial humor, bright and fluent melody, and easy and correct style, they were eclipsed by Mozart's genius. Yet Dittersdorf may well be regarded as a worthy precursor of Mozart in national dramatic composition.

WORKS: several oratorios and cantatas; 12 symphonies for orch. on Ovid's *Metamorphoses* (Vienna, 1785). Of these 12, only 6 are now extant, and have been republished (1899) by Reinecke Bros., Leipzig; they are remarkable specimens of early program music. The same firm also republished 2 other symphonies; the overture to *Esther* (oratorio); a short ballet; and the Divertimento *Il combattimento dell'umane passioni.* 41 MS symphonies; a Concerto grosso, for 11 concerted instruments, with orch.; 12 violin concertos; numerous string quartets (the best were edited by the Müller brothers, and publ.); 12 divertissements for 2 violins and cello; 12 4-hand sonatas for piano; 72 preludes, for piano; etc. A selection of his instrumental works was publ. in the *Denkmäler der Tonkunst in Österreich* 46 (23.ii).

WRITINGS: "Briefe über Behandlung italienischer Texte bei der Composition," *Allgemeine musikalische Zeitung* (Leipzig, 1799), and an autobiography (Leipzig, 1801; edited by Spazier; reprinted by E. Istel, Leipzig, 1909; English transl. by A. D. Coleridge, London, 1896; new edition as *Lebensbeschreibung, seinem Sohn in die Feder diktiert,* Leipzig, 1940).

BIBLIOGRAPHY: C. Krebs, *Dittersdorfiana* (Berlin, 1900; with thematic catalogue); K. M. Klob, *3 musikalische Biedermänner* (Ulm, 1911); K. Holl, *Karl Ditters von Dittersdorfs Opern für das wiederhergestellte Johannisberger Theater* (Heidelberg, 1913); L. Riedinger, "Dittersdorf als Opernkomponist," *Studien zur Musikwissenschaft* II (1914); Gertrude Rigler, "Die Kammermusik Dittersdorfs," ibid. XIV (1927).

Divitis (de Ryche, le Riche), Antonius (Antoine), celebrated French (or Flemish) contrapuntist of late 15th and early 16th centuries; b. Louvain, c.1475; d. probably after 1526, in which year he is mentioned as very likely being at St. Peter's in Rome as Antonius Richardus. He was singer and choirmaster at St. Donatien in Bruges (Brugge) from 1501–04; from 1504–05, choirmaster at St. Rombaut in Malines; then was in the service of Philippe le Beau in Brussels; chapel singer to Louis XII (1506–15).

WORKS: motets and chansons are scattered in collections, e.g., *Motetti de la corona* (1514), and others printed by Rhaw, Attaignant, etc. At Cambrai is a MS Mass; at Munich, 2 Credos and a Salve Regina *a* 5; at Rome, *Quem dicunt homines* for 4 voices.

BIBLIOGRAPHY: G. van Doorslaer, "Antonius Divitis," *Tijdschrift der Vereeniging voor Nederlandsche Muziekgeschiedenis,* XIII, 1 (1929).

Dixon, Dean, black American conductor; b. New York, Jan. 10, 1915; d. Zürich, Switzerland, Nov. 3, 1976. He showed a musical talent as a child, and began to take violin lessons. At the age of 17 he organized at his High School in the Bronx a group which he called the Dean Dixon Symphony Orchestra. Eleanor Roosevelt became interested in him and helped him to obtain a guest appearance with the N.Y. Philharmonic at the Lewisohn Stadium on Aug. 10, 1941, making him the first of his race to conduct the N.Y. Philharmonic. Encouraged, he entered the conducting class of Albert Stoessel at the Juilliard School of Music; also enrolled in academic classes at Teachers College, Columbia Univ. receiving an M.A. In 1944 Dixon founded the American Youth Orch., which had but a limited success. He decided to try his fortunes abroad, and in 1949 left for Europe; conducted orchestras in Sweden, where he was especially appreciated, in Germany, France, Italy and Spain. He also filled several engagements in Japan and Australia. Returning briefly to the U.S. in 1970, he was guest conductor for a series of N.Y. Philharmonic summer concerts in Central Park; then went back to Europe and settled in Switzerland. Although he underwent open-heart surgery in 1975, he resumed his career, conducting in Belgium and elsewhere, shortly before suffering a fatal stroke.

Dixon, James, American conductor; b. Estherville, Iowa, April 26, 1928. He studied at the Univ. of Iowa (B.M., 1952; M.M., 1956); was conductor of the U.S. 7th Army Symphony Orch. in Germany (1951–54); Univ. of Iowa Symph. Orch. in Iowa City (1954–59); New England Cons. Symph. Orch. in Boston (1959–61). In 1962 he returned to the Univ. of Iowa Symph. Orch. as its permanent conductor; since 1965, served as conductor of the Tri-City Symph. Orch. in Davenport, Iowa and Rock Island, Illinois. In addition, he was associate conductor of the Minneapolis Symph. Orch. (1961–62); guest conductor with the National Orch. of Greece in Athens (1955, 1959, 1961); Norddeutscher Rundfunk (1963); Westdeutscher Rundfunk (1964); Tanglewood (1965); Chicago Civic Symph. (1967) and Chicago Symph. Orch. (1972). He was recipient of the Gustav Mahler Medal in 1963. As an interpreter, he follows the style of Mitropoulos, under whose influence he began his career, combining precision of rhythmic flow with expressive shaping of melodic phrases.

Dizi, François-Joseph, famous French harpist; b. Namur, France, Jan. 14, 1780; d. Paris, Nov., 1847. He set out for London when only 16; lost his harp on the way, but went on without it, and introduced himself to Érard, who gave him a harp, and obtained pupils for him. Besides winning fame as a concert player, and as a harpist at the principal theaters, he invented the "perpendicular harp" (which was unsuccessful), and composed sonatas, romances, variations, studies, etc., for harp; also publ. an *École de Harpe, being a Complete Treatise on the Harp* (London, 1827). In 1830 he went to Paris, and established a harp factory with Pleyel, which did not do well. There he was appointed harp teacher to the royal princesses.

Dlabacz, Gottfried Johann, Bohemian music scholar; b. Brod, July 17, 1758; d. Prague, Feb. 4, 1820. He was librarian and choirmaster of the Premonstratensian monastery in Prague; publ. a valuable reference work, *Allgemeines historisches Künstlerlexikon für Böhmen* (3 vols., 1815–18), and contributed articles to Riegger's *Statistik von Böhmen.*

Dlugoszewski, Lucia, American composer; b. Detroit, June 16, 1931. She studied piano, and concurrently attended classes in physics at Wayne State Univ. (1946–49). Fascinated with mathematical aspects of music, she began to study with Edgar Varèse whose works illuminated this scientific relationship for her. Accordingly, in her own works she emphasizes the sonorific element of music; inspired by the example of Varèse's *Ionisation,* she invented or perfected a number of percussion instruments; one of her inventions is the timbre piano, in which she makes use of bows and plectra on the piano strings. In 1960 she joined the Foundation for Modern Dance, as teacher and composer.

WORKS: Her dance scores include *Openings of the Eye* for flute, percussion and timbre piano (1958); *8 Clear Places* for percussion ensemble (1958–61); *Geography of Noon* for new percussion instruments (1964); *Dazzle on a Knife's Edge* for timbre piano and orch. (1966); *Agathlon Algebra* for timbre piano and orch. (1968); and a series of works for various instrumental combinations under the title *Lords of Persia.* Other works are: *50 Transparencies* "for everyday sounds" (1951), *Arithmetic Points* for orch. (1955), *Instants in Form and Movements* for timbre piano and chamber orch. (1957); *Delicate Accidents in Space* for rattle quintet (1959); *Archaic Aggregates* for timbre piano, ladder harps, tangent rattles, unsheltered rattles and gongs (1961); *4 Attention Spans* for orch. (1964); several pieces entitled *Beauty Music,* and *Music for the Left Ear in a Small Room* and other bafflingly and provocatively yclept productions.

Doane, William Howard, American hymn writer; b. Preston, Conn., Feb. 3, 1832; d. South Orange, N.J., Dec. 24, 1915. He served as a clerk and later entered manufacturing business. He composed more than 2000 gospel songs and a Christmas cantata, *Santa Claus.* His hymn *Pass Me Not* was popular.

BIBLIOGRAPHY: R. G. McCutchan, *Our Hymnody* (N.Y., 1937).

Döbber, Johannes, German composer; b. Berlin, March 28, 1866; d. there, Jan. 26, 1921. Pupil in Stern Cons. of R. Radecke, L. Bussler (composition), and C. Agghazy (piano). He taught the first piano class in Kullak's Cons.; became Kapellmeister at Darmstadt; then was at Coburg-Gotha as tutor in music to Princess Beatrice: teacher and music critic of the *Volkszeitung* in Berlin (1908).

WORKS: the operas *Die Strassensängerin* (Gotha, 1890); *Der Schmied von Gretna-Green* (Berlin, 1893); *Dolcetta* (Brandenburg, 1894); *Die Rose von Genzano* (Gotha, 1895); *Die Grille* (Leipzig, 1897); *Die drei Rosen* (Coburg, 1902); *Der Zauberlehrling* (Brunswick, 1907); *Die Franzosenzeit* (Berlin, 1913); song-play, *Fahrende Musikanten* (Magdeburg, 1917); the operettas *Die Millionenbraut* (Magdeburg, 1913) and *Des Kaisers Rock* (Berlin, 1915); also a symphony, piano pieces; over 60 songs; quartets, duets, etc.

Dobiáš, Václav, Czech composer b. Radčice, near Semily, Sept. 22, 1909. He studied violin; then enrolled in the Prague Cons., where he was a student of Novák in composition. He also took instruction in the music of quarter-tones with Alois Hába and produced 3 works in this system: Suite for Piano (1939), *Lento* for 3 harps (1940) and Concerto for Violin and Chamber Orch. (1941). After 1945 he became involved in the political problems of music education; in conformity with the ideology in Eastern Europe, he began to write music for the masses in the manner of Socialist Realism; in 1958 he was elected to the Central Committee of the Communist Party of Czechoslovakia and was deputy to the National Assembly (1960–69).

WORKS: Chamber Symphony (1939); 2 numbered symphonies (1943; 1956–57); Sinfonietta (1946–47, revised 1962); Sonata, for piano, wind quintet, strings and timpani (1947); *The Grand Procession*, symph. poem (1948); *Jubilee Overture* (1964); the cantatas, *Stalingrad* (1945), *The Order No. 368* (1946) and *Build Up Your Country and Strengthen Peace*, also known as *The Czech Polka* (1947–50); *Praho Jediná (Only Prague)*, song cycle for lower voice and orch. (1960–61); numerous mass songs; 4 string quartets (1931, 1936, 1938, 1942); Violin Sonata (1936); Cello Sonata (1939); Suite for Cello and Piano (1942); *Říkadla (Rhymes)*, nonet (1938); *Pastoral Wind Quintet* (1943); *4 Nocturnes* for cello and piano (1944); *Quartettino* for string quartet (1944); *Dance Fantasy* for nonet (1948); *Of Native Land*, nonet (1952); for piano: Rondo (1931), 2 sonatas (1931; 1940); *Little Suite* (1937), *3 Toccatas* (1941) and 3 sonatinas (1945–46).

Dobos, Kálmán, Hungarian composer; b. Szolnok, July 22, 1931. He became nearly blind at the age of 14, but pursued studies of music at the Academy of Music in Budapest, graduating in 1957; later he worked on the Hungarian State Radio. He composed a Cello Sonata (1956); Symphony (1957); Piano Sonata (1957); an a cappella *Missa Brevis* (1957); *Adagio and Fugue* for string quartet (1959); *2 Movements* for piano trio (1960); *Musica da Camera* for violin and piano (1962); String Trio (1963); *Villanások (Flashes)* for soprano and piano trio (1963); *3 Hungarian Dances* for orch. (1964); *Meditation* for piano (1964); *Sound Phenomena* for orch. (1968); *Manifestations* for string quartet, piano and percussion (1969); *Belső mozdulatok (Inner Movements)* for clarinet, piano and percussion (1970); *Ringató (Rocking)* for piano (1972); *Vetületek (Projections)* for orch. (1973).

Dobronić, Antun, Croatian composer; b. Jelsa, Island of Hvar, April 2, 1878; d. Zagreb, Dec. 12, 1955. He studied music with Novák in Prague; then returned to Yugoslavia; in 1921 was appointed professor at the Cons. of Zagreb. He wrote many stage works, among them the operas *Ragusean Diptych; The Man of God; Mara; Dubrovnički triptihon* (1925); *Udovica Rozlinka* (1934); *Rkac* (1938); *Goran* (1944); the ballet, *The Giant Horse*; 8 symphonies; the symph. poems *Au long de l'Adriatique* (1948); *Les Noces* (1949); chamber music in the national style, including a piano quintet subtitled *Bosnian Rhapsody*; 5 string quartets; also choruses and songs. Dobronić is the author of "A Study of Yugoslav Music," *Musical Quarterly* (Jan. 1926).

Dobrowen, Issay, Russian conductor; b. Nizhny-Novgorod, Feb. 27, 1891; d. Oslo, Dec. 9, 1953. His real name was **Barabeichik;** his orphaned mother was adopted by Israil Dobrovel; Issay Dobrowen changed his legal name Dobrovel to Dobrowein, and later to Dobrowen. He studied at the Nizhny-Novgorod Cons. as a small child (1896–1900); then entered the Moscow Cons. and studied with Igumnov (piano) and Taneyev (composition); went to Vienna for additional study with Leopold Godowsky (piano). Returning to Moscow, he became conductor of the Moscow opera; in 1922 he led the Dresden State Opera in the German première of Mussorgsky's opera, *Boris Godunov*; in 1924 he conducted opera in Berlin; during the season 1927–28 he conducted opera in Sofia, Bulgaria. In 1931 he made his American debut; conducted the San Francisco Symph. Orch.; was guest conductor with the Minneapolis Symph. Orch., Philadelphia Orch., and the N.Y. Philh. However, he was received indifferently by American audiences, and returned to Europe. He was a regular conductor of the Budapest opera from 1936–39; at the outbreak of World War II he went to Sweden, where he won his greatest successes, as conductor of both opera and symphony, at the Stockholm Opera and the Philh. of Göteborg. In 1948 he conducted at La Scala, Milan. On frequent occasions Dobrowen acted as stage director as well as conductor in German, Italian, and Swedish opera houses. He was a prolific composer; wrote several piano concertos and pieces for piano solo, in a Romantic vein; also an orchestral fairytale, *1001 Nights* (Moscow, May 27, 1922).

Dobrowolski, Andrzej, Polish composer; b. Lwów, Sept. 9, 1921. He studied organ, singing, clarinet, theory and composition at the State College of Music in Cracow (1947–51); in 1954 joined the faculty of the Warsaw State College of Music. His music is a paradigm of modern structuralism and textural abstraction.

WORKS: *Symphonic Variations* (1949); *Overture* (1950); Oboe Concerto (1953); *Popular Overture* (1954); Trio for Oboe, Clarinet and Bassoon (1954); Symph. No. 1 (1955); *8 Studies* for oboe, trumpet, bassoon and double bass (1959); *Music No. 1* for tape (1962); *Music for strings and 4 groups of wind instruments* (1964); *Music for tape and solo oboe* (1965); *Music for strings, 2 groups of wind instruments, and 2 loud speakers* (1966); *Music for orch.* (1968–69); *Krabogapa* for clarinet, trombone, cello and piano (1969); *Music No. 2* for orch. (1970); *Music for tape and solo piano* (1972); *Music for solo tuba* (1972); *Music No. 3* for orch. (1972–73); *Music No. 4* for orch. (1974); *Music for chorus, 2 groups of winds, double bass and percussion* (1975).

Dobrzynski, Ignacy Felix, Polish pianist; b. Romanov, Volhynia, Feb. 15, 1807; d. Warsaw, Oct. 10, 1867. Son of a violinist, **J. Dobrzynski** (1777–1841); he was taught by his father, then by Elsner, being a fellow pupil and close friend of Chopin; on subsequent pianistic tours (1845–46) to Leipzig, Dresden, and Berlin, he had great success. For a time he conducted the opera in Warsaw, where he finally settled. He wrote an opera *Monbar or The Filibuster* (Warsaw, 1861); *Symphonie caractéristique*; string sextet, 2 string quintets, 2 string quartets; piano trio; violin sonata; a nocturne for violin and piano, *Les Larmes*; mazurkas for piano; songs. His son **Bronislaw Dobrzynski** publ. a monograph on him (Warsaw, 1893).

Doche, Joseph-Denis, French composer; b. Paris, Aug. 22, 1766; d. Soissons, July 20, 1825. He was a chorister at the cathedral of Meaux; then was organist at Coutances in Normandy. He played string instruments in a theater orchestra in Paris from 1794 till 1810; then became conductor, retiring in 1823. He wrote numerous successful vaudevilles; also operas: *Point du bruit* (Oct. 25, 1802); *Les Deux Sentinelles* (Sept. 27, 1803), and others.

Dodds, Baby (real first name **Warren**), black American drummer, brother of **Johnny Dodds;** b. New Orleans, Dec. 24, 1898; d. Chicago, Feb. 14, 1959. He played on showboats; joined the King Oliver Creole Band. He was praised by the cognoscenti as a rhythmician of versatile gifts. His autobiography 'as told to Larry Gara' was publ. posthumously in Los Angeles, 1959.

Dodds, Johnny, black American jazz clarinetist; b. New Orleans, April 12, 1892; d. Chicago, Aug. 8, 1940. He was a member of the King Oliver Creole Jazz Band with Louis Armstrong; played in the Hot Five; advanced to Hot Seven; excelled in the blues style. In his last years he formed the Johnny Dodds Washboard Band.
BIBLIOGRAPHY: G. E. Lambert, *Johnny Dodds* (N.Y., 1961).

Dodge, Charles, American composer; b. Ames, Iowa, June 5, 1942. He studied composition with Philip Benzanson at the Univ. of Iowa (B.A., 1964); with Darius Milhaud at Aspen Summer School (1961); Gunther Schuller and Arthur Berger at the Berskshire Music Center in Tanglewood (1964) and with Jack Beeson, Chou Wen-chung, Otto Luening, and Vladimir Ussachevsky at Columbia Univ. (M.A., 1966). He subsequently was on the faculty of Columbia and Princeton Univ., teaching electronic music; received numerous commissions, grants and awards, including one from the Koussevitzky Foundation in 1969. He composes in an empirical manner, following serial ideas; in most of his works he makes use of electronic media.
WORKS: *Folia* for 7 instruments and percussion (1963); *Rota* for orch. (1966); *Changes* for electronic tape with the aid of a digital computer storing a succession of numbers made audible by an analog converter (first performed at the Coolidge Festival, Washington, Oct. 31, 1970); *Palinode* for computerized tape and orch. (N.Y., Feb. 7, 1977).

Doebler, Curt, German composer of sacred music; b. Kottbus, Jan. 15, 1896; d. Berlin, June 19, 1970. He studied organ with A. Dreyer. From 1919–32 he was organist and choral leader at the Catholic Church in Charlottenburg; after occupying various positions as organist and teacher elsewhere, he returned to Charlottenburg (1950). In his music Doebler attempts to establish a modern style based on Palestrina's polyphony. His numerous choruses a cappella enjoy considerable renown in Germany.

Doenhoff, Albert von, American pianist; b. Louisville, Ky., March 16, 1880; d. New York, Oct. 3, 1940. He studied at the Cincinnati College of Music and then in N.Y. with Rafael Joseffy; made his professional debut in N.Y. on March 8, 1905; subsequently developed a successful career as a concert pianist. He published many pieces for piano (*Arabesque, Revery,* etc.); also pedagogical material (*Three Modern Etudes for the Virtuoso;* Six Special Studies Adapted to Small Hands, etc.); edited and revised numerous editions of classics for G. Schirmer, Inc.

Doflein, Erich, German musicologist; b. Munich, Aug. 7, 1900. He studied with Weismann, Auerbach, and Praetorius, and later with Kaminski; was music instructor in Freiburg-im-Breisgau (1924–41); taught in Breslau (1941–44); was prisoner of war in Russia (1944–46). After his return to Germany he taught at the Musikhochschule in Freiburg-im-Breisgau, retiring in 1965; he prepared modern editions of 6 sonatas by Boismortier (in 2 books, 1960); concertos by Fr. Durante (1967), etc.

Döhler, Theodor, Italian pianist and composer; b. Naples, April 20, 1814; d. Florence, Feb. 21, 1856. He was a pupil of Julius Benedict at Naples and of Czerny (piano) and Sechter (composition) at Vienna. In 1831 he became pianist to the Duke of Lucca, lived for a time in Naples, made brilliant pianistic tours from 1836–46 in Germany, Italy, France, Holland, and England; in 1843 went to Copenhagen, thence to Russia, and in 1846 to Paris; settled in Florence in 1848. In 1846 the Duke, his patron, ennobled him, and he married a Russian countess. He wrote an opera *Tancreda* which was performed posthumously in Florence in 1880; many piano pieces; nocturnes; tarantellas; *12 Études de concert; 50 Études de salon;* variations, fantasias and transcriptions.

Dohnányi, Christoph von, German-born conductor, grandson of **Ernst von Dohnányi;** b. Berlin, Sept. 8, 1929. He studied jurisprudence; then went to America, where he began taking lessons with his grandfather, who by then was living in New York. Returning to Germany, he was chorusmaster in Frankfurt (1952–57); subsequently was active as music director and conductor in Lübeck (1957–63) and in Kassel (1963–66); from 1964 to 1969 he was principal conductor with the Cologne Radio; in 1968 was appointed music director of the municipal theaters in Frankfurt; also conducted opera in Munich and Berlin, and was guest conductor of the Berlin Philharmonic. He soon achieved the reputation of one of the most competent opera and symphony conductors; made numerous appearances as an opera conductor in America. Contrary to the conservative traditions of his grandfather, Christoph von Dohnányi is passionately devoted to the cause of modern music; he is invariably selected to lead world premières of significant works, e.g., operas by Henze.

Dohnányi, Ernst von, noted Hungarian pianist and composer; b. Pressburg (Bratislava), July 27, 1877; d. New York, Feb. 9, 1960. He studied with his father, Friedrich von Dohnányi, prof. of mathematics and amateur cellist, and Karl Forstner, then at the Budapest Academy of Music, with Stefan Thomán (piano) and Hans Koessler (composition). After graduation in 1897, he studied during the summer with Eugen d'Albert. His first independent piano recital was at Berlin on Oct. 1, 1897, followed by a concert tour to Cologne, Dresden, Frankfurt, Vienna, etc. He appeared as pianist in London on Oct. 24, 1898; then made several successful tours in the U.S. He was prof. of piano at the Hochschule für Musik in Berlin from 1908 till 1915; then settled in Budapest, where he became director of the Cons. (1919) and conductor of the Budapest Philh. He was also guest conductor throughout Europe. He was director of the Hungarian Academy and President of the Budapest Philh. Orch. until 1945; then went to Austria, after losing both his sons in the war; toured in England and U.S. (1948–49); was briefly teaching in Tucumán, Argentina (1949); in the autumn of 1949, he went to the U.S. and became professor of piano and composition at Florida State University at Tallahassee. Dohnányi's music represents the last flowering of the Hungarian Romantic era. His chief inspiration came from Brahms (who praised Dohnányi's early works); the element of form is strong and the traditional harmonic structure remains unshaken, but this conservatism does not exclude flashes of musical wit.

WORKS: Symphony in F (not numbered; won the Hungarian Millennium Prize in 1896); op. 1, Piano Quintet in C minor; op. 2, Overture *Zrinyi* (shared the prize with the symph. in 1896); op. 3, *5 Klavierstücke*; op. 4, Variations for Piano; op. 5, Concerto for Piano and Orch. in E minor (won Bösendorfer Prize in Vienna, 1899); op. 6, Passacaglia, for piano; op. 7, String Quartet; op. 8, Sonata for Cello and Piano; op. 9, Symphony No. 1 (Manchester, England, Jan. 30, 1902); op. 10, Serenade, in C, for violin, viola, and cello; op. 11, *4 Rhapsodien* for piano; op. 12, *Konzertstück* for cello and orch.; op. 13, *Winterreigen* (10 bagatelles for piano); op. 14, 6 songs; op. 15, String Quartet; op. 16, *Im Lebenslenz* (6 songs); op. 17, *Humoresken in Form einer Suite*, for piano; op. 18, *Der Schleier der Pierrette* (pantomime; Dresden, 1910); op. 19, Suite in F-sharp minor, for orch.; op. 20, *Tante Simona* (1-act opera; Dresden, Jan. 20, 1913); op. 21, Sonata for Violin and Piano; op. 22, Concerto for Piano and Orch.; op. 23, *3 Stücke für Klavier*; op. 24, Suite for Piano; op. 25, Variations on a Nursery Song, for piano and orch. (1913; Berlin, Feb. 17, 1914, composer soloist; his most popular work); op. 26, 2nd Piano Quintet; op. 27, Violin Concerto; op. 28, 6 Concert Studies; op. 29, Variations on a Hungarian Folksong for Piano; op. 30, an opera, *The Tower of the Voivod* (Budapest, March 19, 1922; in German, Düsseldorf, 1926); op. 31, Festival Overture; op. 32, *Ruralia Hungarica* for piano (also for orch.) in 7 movements (Budapest, Nov. 17, 1924, composer conducting); *Szegedin Mass* (1930); a comic opera, *Der Tenor* (Budapest, Feb. 9, 1929); Symphony No. 2 (1944; London, Nov. 23, 1948; radically revised, and perf. in the new version, Minneapolis, March 15, 1957); 6 piano pieces (1945); Piano Concerto No. 2 (1946); 12 etudes for piano (1950); Violin Concerto No. 2, scored for orch. without violins (San Antonio, Jan. 26, 1952); Concertino for Harp and

Orch. (1952); *American Rhapsody* for orch. (Athens, Ohio, Feb. 21, 1954, composer conducting).

BIBLIOGRAPHY: Victor Papp, *Ernst von Dohnányi* (Budapest, 1927); also an autobiographical pamphlet, *Message to Posterity* (Jacksonville, Florida, 1960).

Doire, René, French composer and conductor; b. Evreux, June 13, 1879; d. Paris, July 9, 1959. He studied in Rouen and later in Paris with Widor and Vincent d'Indy; then was engaged as bandleader in the casinos of various French spas. He composed a one-act opera *Morituri* (1903); a cycle of songs, *Reflets de Jeunesse* for voice and piano, or orch. (1902); *Vision d'Espagne* for violin and orch. (1916); Violin Sonata (1918); *Dramatico* for piano and orch. (1923); songs.

Doktor, Paul, Austrian-American violist; b. Vienna, March 28, 1919. He studied with his father, **Karl Doktor,** violinist of the renowned Busch String Quartet; graduated as a violinist at the State Academy of Music in Vienna in 1938, but subsequently changed to viola, and in 1942 received the first prize for viola at the International Music Competition in Geneva. He left Vienna in 1938; from 1939–47 was solo violist of the Lucerne Orch.; emigrated to the U.S. in 1947. He edited several collections of viola music for G. Schirmer, Inc. (*Solos for the Viola Player*, Schubert's Arpeggione Sonata, 2 sonatas by Brahms, Mozart's Duets for violin and viola, etc.). In 1953 he was appointed to the faculty of the Mannes College of Music in New York.

Dolega-Kamieński. See **Kamieński, Lucian.**

Doles, Johann Friedrich, German composer; b. Steinbach, April 23, 1715; d. Leipzig, Feb. 8, 1797. He was a student of theology in Leipzig; then became a pupil of Bach (1740–44), who recommended him for the post of cantor at Freiberg, Saxony. In 1756 he became cantor at the St. Thomas School in Leipzig; was also director of the St. Thomas Church until 1789, when he resigned owing to old age. He wrote a great number of sacred works, a full list of which is given in *Die Musik in Geschichte und Gegenwart.*

BIBLIOGRAPHY: H. Banning, *J. F. Doles: Leben und Werke* (Leipzig, 1939).

Doležálek, Jan Emanuel, Czech musician; b. Chotěboř, May 22, 1780; d. Vienna, July 6, 1858. He studied music in Vienna with Beethoven's teacher, Albrechtsberger, and through him came to know Beethoven himself. It is owing chiefly to this association that Doležálek's name is known in music history. He arranged a number of Czech songs, and published a collection of them.

Dolin, Samuel, Canadian composer; b. Montreal, Aug. 22, 1917. He studied piano in Montreal and Toronto; later took lessons in composition with Weinzweig and Krenek. In 1945 he was appointed to the faculty of the Toronto Cons.; was active in various musical organizations; served as president of the Canadian League of Composers (1969–73).

WORKS: an opera *Casino* (*Greed*) (1966–67); *Drakkar*, "an entertainment" for narrator, mezzo-soprano,

2 baritones, 2 dancers, chamber ensemble, 2 synthesizers and amplifiers (1972; Toronto, Feb. 17, 1973); Sinfonietta (1950; the *Scherzo* movement is often played as a separate piece); Serenade for Strings (1951); 3 symphonies (1956, 1957, 1976); *Isometric Variables* (*Bassooneries in Free Variations*) for bassoon and strings (1957); Sonata for String Orch. (1962); Fantasy for Piano and Chamber Orch. (1967); Piano Concerto (1974); Violin Sonatina (1954); Violin Sonata (1960); *Portrait* for string quartet (1961); *Barcarolle* for violin and piano (1962); Concerto Grosso (*Georgian Bay*) for percussion, accordion and tape (1970); Sonata for Solo Accordion (1970); *Marchbankantata* for baritone, chorus, piano and synthesizer (1971); Mass for 6 voices, congregation and organ (1972); 3 sonatas: solo violin, solo flute, and solo cello, each with tape (all 1973); *Ricercar* for solo guitar (1974); *Adikia* for 1 to 5 accordions in any combination, and tape (1975); *4 Miniatures* for piano (1943); 3 Preludes for Piano (1949); Piano Sonata (1950); *Little Toccata* for piano (1959); Piano Sonatina (1959); Variation for 2 Pianos (1967); *If* for piano (1972); choruses; songs.

Dolmetsch, Arnold, English music antiquarian; b. Le Mans, Maine, France, Feb. 24, 1858; d. Haslemere, Surrey, Feb. 28, 1940. While apprenticed in his father's piano factory he learned to play both piano and violin, making such marked progress on the latter instrument that his father sent him to Brussels, where he became a pupil of Vieuxtemps; after completing his studies he went to Dulwich, was appointed instructor of violin at the College, and soon won a reputation as teacher. From his earliest years he had shown a decided predilection for the music of Bach and the old masters; when by chance he became the possessor of a well preserved viola d'amore, he did not rest until he had mastered the instrument; gradually he acquired the same skill on all the members of the viol family. He then gave up his large class of violin pupils and devoted his entire time to lecturing and giving recitals on the old instruments. In his quest for old music he found in the British Museum MSS of almost forgotten English composers (Simon Ives, Matthew Locke, Thomas Tomkins, John Jenkins, etc.). To become an authoritative interpreter of all this music he found it necessary to extend his investigations to the virginal, spinet, harpsichord, and clavichord. He began by collecting old books, in which those instruments were described by contemporary authorities; the mechanical skill he had acquired in his father's shop he turned to account in repairing the instruments he collected, and before long he was acknowledged as an authority on old music and instruments; he was not only a connoisseur and skilled workman, but also a masterly performer on every instrument in his large collection; with his wife and a pupil, **Kathleen Salmon,** he established the Dolmetsch Trio, devoted exclusively to the performance of old music on the original instruments. A tour of the U.S. in 1902 attracted so much attention that Chickering & Sons, of Boston, placed their factory and a force of their best workmen at Dolmetsch's disposal. The beginning was made with the restoration of a virginal by Hans Ruckers (1620); then a number of stringed and keyed instruments were built after the best models extant. The interest excited by the revival of these instruments induced several other artists (Wanda Landowska, Fuller-Maitland, the brothers Casadesus, etc.) to give recitals on them. From 1902–09 Dolmetsch lived in Boston, supervising the construction of his instruments and concertizing; after that, he resided in England. In 1925 he founded at Haslemere, Surrey, annual historical chamber music festivals, where the works were played (many by himself) on modern reconstructions of the original historic instruments (clavichord, harpsichord, viols, recorders, etc.). The Dolmetsch Foundation, a society for the purpose of cultivating old music and making his ideas more widely known, was founded by his friends in 1928.

WRITINGS: *Select English Songs and Dialogues of the 16th and 17th Centuries* (2 vols., 1912) and *The Interpretation of the Music of the 17th and 18th Centuries* (London, 1915; new ed., 1944).

BIBLIOGRAPHY: R. Donington, *The Work and Ideas of Arnold Dolmetsch* (Haslemere, 1932); Percy Grainger "Arnold Dolmetsch, Musical Confucius," *Musical Quarterly* (April 1933); M. Dolmetsch, *Personal Recollections of Arnold Dolmetsch* (London, 1957); M. Campbell, *Dolmetsch: The Man and His Work* (1975).

Dolukhanova, Zara, Russian mezzo-soprano of Armenian extraction; b. Moscow, March 5, 1918. She studied with private teachers; joined the Moscow Radio staff in 1944; was awarded the Lenin Prize in 1966. A lyric singer, she excels in the romantic Russian repertoire. In 1959 she made her first American tour, enjoying great acclaim; she toured America again in 1970.

Domaniewski, Boleslaus, Polish pianist; b. Gronówek, Russian Poland, July 16, 1857; d. Warsaw, Sept. 11, 1925. He studied at the St. Petersburg Cons.; from 1890 to 1900 taught at the Cons. of Cracow; in 1900 he became director of the Warsaw Cons. His piano method, *Vademecum pour le pianiste*, enjoyed considerable popularity.

Domingo, Placido, Spanish operatic tenor; b. Madrid, Jan. 21, 1941. He went to Mexico at the age of 9 with his parents who were performers of Spanish zarzuelas; took part in these performances still as a child, learned to play the piano and soon developed a pleasing baritone voice from which he changed to a fine tenorino. He studied operatic parts, accompanying himself at the piano. His first important engagement was in Tel Aviv, where he was engaged as an opera singer for 2 years. He then went to America; made his debut at the Metropolitan Opera House in New York as Turiddu in *Cavalleria Rusticana,* Aug. 9, 1966. In quick succession he sang Canio in *Pagliacci,* Cavaradossi in *Tosca,* Pinkerton in *Madama Butterfly,* Manrico in *Il Trovatore,* Alfredo in *La Traviata,* Rhadames in *Aida* and Don José in *Carmen.* He also sang in Hamburg, Milan and other European cities. Addicted to precise statistics he calculated the number of his appearances from 1966 to April 1977 at the Metropolitan Opera as 108, and the total of his appearances since his very first engagement up to the same terminal date as 1209 in 74 roles. His voice possesses a liquidity that is the essence of bel canto; he excels particularly in lyric parts in Italian operas, but he has also essayed Wagnerian roles.

Dominiceti, Cesare, Italian composer; b. Desenzano, July 12, 1821; d. Sesto di Monza, June 20, 1888. He studied in Milan, where all his operas were brought out; lived for a long time in Bolivia, made a fortune there, and, some years after his return to Italy, was appointed prof. of composition at Milan Cons. He wrote the operas, *Due mogli in una* (Milan, June 30, 1853), *La maschera* (Milan, March 2, 1854), *Morovico* (Milan, Dec. 4, 1873), *Il lago delle fate* (Milan, May 18, 1878), and *L'ereditiera* (Milan, Feb. 14, 1881).

Dommer, Arrey von, German musicographer; b. Danzig, Feb. 9, 1828; d. Treysa, Feb. 18, 1905. A theological student, he turned to music, and in 1851 became the pupil of Richter and Lobe (composition), and Schallenberg (organ) at Leipzig. He taught music at Leipzig, and went to Hamburg in 1863. He publ. *Elemente der Musik* (1862); *Musikalisches Lexikon* (1865; a revised ed. of Koch's); *Handbuck der Musikgeschichte* (1867; 2d ed., 1878; 3d ed., entirely rewritten and brought up to date by A. Schering, 1914).

Donalda, Pauline (real name **Lightstone,** translated by her father from Lichtenstein when he became a British subject), dramatic soprano; b. Montreal, March 5, 1882; d. London, Oct. 22, 1970. She received her first musical training at Royal Victoria College, Montreal, and then was a private pupil of Duvernoy in Paris; made her debut as *Manon* (Massenet) at Nice, Dec. 30, 1904; the next year she appeared at La Monnaie, Brussels, and Covent Garden; 1906-07, at the Manhattan Opera House, N.Y.; then chiefly at Opéra-Comique. From 1923-37 she had a singing school in Paris; 1937, returned to Montreal. In 1938 she presented her valuable music library (manuscripts, autographs, and music) to McGill Univ. Her stage name was taken in honor of Sir Donald Smith (later Lord Strathcona), who endowed the Royal Victoria College and was her patron.

Donati (Donato), Baldassare, famous Italian composer of motets and madrigals; b. Venice, c.1530; d. there, 1603. He was choirmaster of the so-called "small choir" at San Marco, Venice, from 1562-65; this was disbanded by Zarlino when he was appointed maestro di cappella in 1565, and Donati became a simple chorister; appointed maestro di canto to the Seminario Gregoriano di San Marco (1580); in 1590, he succeeded Zarlino as maestro di cappella. His compositions are distinguished by their well-defined rhythm and originality. Extant works include *Canzoni Villanesche alla Napoletana* (1550-58), several books of madrigals for 4 parts (1550-68), a volume of madrigals for 5-6 parts (1553; new eds., 1557, 1560), a volume of motets for 5-8 parts (1597), etc.

Donati, Ignazio, Italian composer; b. Casalmaggiore, c.1570; d. Milan, Jan. 21, 1638. He was maestro di cappella at the Urbino Cathedral (1612-16), then at Ferrara (1616-18); at Casalmaggiore (1618-23); at Nova-

ra and Lodi (1626-30). In 1631 he became maestro di cappella at the cathedral of Milan. He publ. 8 books of *concerti ecclesiastici,* 7 books of motets, Masses, and psalms.

Donati, Pino, Italian composer; b. Verona, May 9, 1907; d. Rome, Feb. 24, 1975. He studied violin; then took composition lessons with G. C. Paribeni. He wrote two operas: *Corradino lo Svevo* (Verona, April 4, 1931) and *Lancillotto del Lago* (Bergamo, Oct. 2, 1938); also chamber music.

Donato, Anthony, American violinist and composer; b. Prague, Nebraska, March 8, 1909. He studied at the Eastman School of Music in Rochester, N.Y., with Hanson, Rogers, and Royce; obtained the degrees of M. Mus. (1937) and Ph.D. (1947). He was a violin teacher at Drake Univ. (1931-37), Iowa State Teachers College (1937-39); the Univ. of Texas (1939-46); Northwestern Univ. (1947-77).
WORKS: 2 symphonies (1944; 1945); opera, *The Walker Through Walls* (Evanston, Illinois, Feb. 26, 1965, composer conducting); *March of the Hungry Mountains* for chorus and orch. (1949); *Solitude in the City* for narrator and instruments (1954); *Centennial Ode* for orch., commissioned by the Nebraska State Centennial (Omaha, Dec. 11, 1967); *Improvisation* for orch. (Kansas City, May 3, 1969); 3 string quartets (1941, 1947, 1951; the *Andante* from String Quartet No. 1 is also arranged for string orch.); 2 violin sonatas (1938, 1949); *Pastorale and Dance* for 4 clarinets (1947); Sonatina for 3 trumpets (1949); Sonata for Horn and Piano (1950); Piano Trio (1959); Sonata for Clarinet and Piano (1966); *Discourse* for flute and piano (1969); many choral works and piano teaching pieces. He publ. *Preparing Music Manuscript* (Englewood Cliffs, New Jersey, 1963).
BIBLIOGRAPHY: *Composers of the Americas,* vol. 15 (Washington, 1969).

Donatoni, Franco, Italian composer; b. Verona, June 9, 1927. He studied with Desderi in Milan, with Liviabella in Bologna and Pizzetti at the Accademia Nazionale di Santa Cecilia in Rome, graduating in 1953. He was then instructor at the Cons. of Bologna, at the Verdi Cons. in Milan, at the Verdi Cons. in Turin and, since 1970, at the Accademia Musicale Chigiana in Siena. In his music he adopts a system of serial techniques, while retaining a fairly strict Baroque structure.
WORKS: String Quartet (1950); Viola Sonata (1952); Concerto for Bassoon and Strings (1952); Concertino for strings, brass, and percussion (1952); *Sinfonia* for strings (1953); Overture (1953); *Divertimento I,* for violin and orch. (1954); *5 Pieces for 2 pianos* (1954); *La Lampara,* a ballet (1956); *Quartetto II* for string quartet (1958); *Serenata* for soprano and 16 instruments, to words by Dylan Thomas (1959); *Strophes* for orch. (Radio Rome, Jan. 30, 1960); *Movimento* for harpsichord, piano and 9 instruments (1959); *Sezioni (Sections)* for orch. (1960; Hamburg Radio, May 14, 1962); *Quartetto III* for 4-track tape (1961); *Puppenspiel I,* study for stage music, for orch. (Palermo, Oct. 8, 1962); *Per Orchestra* (1962; Warsaw Autumn Festival, Sept. 24, 1963); *Quartetto IV* for

string quartet (1963; an aleatory work); *Asar* for 10 string instruments (1964); *Black and White* for 37 string instruments (1964); *Divertimento II*, for string orch. (1965); *Puppenspiel II* for flute and orch. (Valdagno, Sept. 17, 1966); *Souvenir*, subtitled *Kammersymphonie*, for 15 instruments (Venice Festival, Sept. 12, 1967); *Etwas ruhiger im Ausdruck* for flute, clarinet, violin, cello and piano (1968; the title is taken from an expression mark in bar 8 of the 2nd of Schoenberg's *5 Piano Pieces*, op. 23); *Black and White No. 2*, exercises for 10 fingers for keyboard instrument (1968); *Orts (Souvenir No. 2)* for 14 instruments with optional lecturer (1969); *Solo* for 10 string instruments (1969); *Doubles II* for orch. (Rome, June 13, 1970; as a ballet, Venice, Jan. 15, 1971); Lied for 13 instruments (1972); *Voci* for orch. (1972–73; Rome, Feb. 3, 1974); *Lumen* for 6 instruments (1975); *Diario 1976* for 4 trombones and 4 trumpets (1976); *Ash* for 8 instruments; 4 works under the generic title *Estratto (Extract)*: No. 1 for piano (1969); No. 2 for harp, harpsichord, and piano (1970); No. 3 for piano and 8 wind instruments (1975); No. 4 for 8 instruments (1975).

Donaudy, Stefano, composer; b. (of French father and Italian mother) Palermo, Feb. 21, 1879; d. Naples, May 30, 1925. Pupil at Cons. of Palermo of G. Zuelli, 1896–1900; wrote the operas *Folchetto* (Palermo, 1892); *Scampagnata* (Palermo, 1898); *Theodor Körner* (Hamburg, Nov. 27, 1902); *Sperduti nel buio* (Palmero, April 27, 1907); *Ramuntcho* (Milan, March 19, 1921); *La Fiamminga* (Naples, April 25, 1922); a symph. poem, *Le Rêve de Polysende*; *Douze airs de style ancien* for voice and piano; and numerous piano pieces.

Donfrid, Johannes, German editor of church music; b. Veringenstadt, 1585; d. Rottenburg, Aug. 4, 1650. He was rector of a school, and cantor at St. Martin's Church in Rottenburg. His most important publication is the *Promptuarium musicum* (3 vols., Strasbourg, 1622–27), containing sacred works by various composers; a collection of songs *Viridarium Musico-Marianum* (Strasbourg, 1627) and *Corolla Musica,* including 37 Masses (Strasbourg, 1628).

Doni, Antonio Francesco, Italian writer; b. Florence, May 16, 1513; d. Monselice, near Padua, in Sept., 1574. For several years he was a member of the Servite fraternity in Florence; after leaving it in 1539, he led a wandering life as a lay priest. He publ., besides various non-musical treatises, a *Dialogo sulla musica* (1544; includes a list of 17 composers living in Venice at the time, with works of each), and a *Libraria* (Venice, 2 vols., 1550–51), containing a description of all published and unpublished musical books in Italian, known at the time, as well as a list of the music academies then in existence and details of their foundation.

Doni, Giovanni Battista, Italian music theorist, b. 1594; d. Florence, Dec. 1, 1647. He studied literature and philosophy at Bologna and Rome; from 1613–18 he was a law student at Bourges, France, and took his degree at Pisa. In 1621 he accompanied Cardinal Corsini to Paris, where he zealously prosecuted his literary and antiquarian studies; went to Rome in 1622, at

the invitation of Cardinal Barberini, who was passionately fond of music, and with whom he traveled. In the intervals of his profound study of ancient music, he found time to construct the "Lira Barberina" or "Amphichord," a species of double lyre, which he dedicated to Pope Urban VIII. Recalled to Florence in 1640 by deaths in his family, he settled there, married the next year, and accepted a professorship of elocution offered him by the Grand Duke. His criticism and discussions of the earliest operas are very valuable, and were publ. for the first time by A. Solerti in *Origini del melodramma. Testimonianze dei contemporanei* (Turin, 1903).

WRITINGS: *Compendio del trattato de' generi e de' modi della musica* (Rome, 1635); *Annotazioni* on the above (Rome, 1640); *De praestantia musicae veteris libri tres* (Florence, 1647); and several essays in manuscript (some still extant in the library of Sta. Cecilia, Rome).

BIBLIOGRAPHY: A. M. Blandini, *Commentarium de vita et scriptis G. B. Doni* (Florence, 1755); F. Vatielli, *La Lira Barberina di G. B. Doni* (Pesaro, 1909).

Donington, Robert, distinguished English musicologist; b. Leeds, May 4, 1907. He studied at Queen's College, Oxford (B.A., 1930); later became associated with Arnold Dolmetsch in the latter's workshop in Haslemere. He studied the technique of old instruments and contributed to the revival of Elizabethan instruments as player in the English Consort of Viols. He also edited the music magazine, *The Consort*. Later he studied with Wellesz, and adopted the 12-tone method of composition in his works (string quartet and small pieces).

WRITINGS: *The Work and Ideas of Arnold Dolmetsch* (Haslemere, 1932); *A Practical Method for the Recorder* (with Edgar Hunt; 2 vols.; Oxford, 1935); *The Instruments of Music* (London, 1949); *The Interpretation of Early Music* (N.Y., 1963); *Wagner's Ring and Its Symbols* (London, 1963).

Donizetti (real name **Ciummei**), **Alfredo,** b. Smyrna, Sept. 2, 1867; d. Rosario, Argentina, Feb. 4, 1921. He studied (1883–89) at Milan Cons. under Ponchielli and Dominiceti; then settled in Argentina. He wrote the operas *Nama* (Milan, 1890) and *Dopo l'Ave Maria* (Milan, 1896); also piano pieces, and songs.

Donizetti, Gaetano, one of the brilliant triumvirate (Donizetti, Rossini, and Bellini) of Italian opera composers in the first half of the 19th century; b. at Bergamo, Nov. 29, 1797; d. there, April 8, 1848. His father, a weaver by trade, later obtained a position in the local pawnshop and desired that his son should become a lawyer. But Donizetti's inclinations were towards art; besides being strongly attracted to music, he studied drawing. His father finally allowed him to enter the Bergamo school of music; his teachers were Salari (voice), Gonzales (piano), and J. S. Mayr (harmony). In 1815 he enrolled in the Bologna Liceo Filarmonico, here completing his contrapuntal studies under Pilotti and Padre Mattei. From his earliest attempts at composition Donizetti was determined to write operas. His first opera was *Il Pigmalione*, which was not produced; but he gained production with his next opera *Enrico di Borgogna* (Venice, 1818). Two operas—*Una Follia* (1818) and *I piccoli, Virtuosi ambulanti* (1819)—intervened before the success of *Il Falegname di Livonia* (Venice, 1819; given at first as *Pietro il Grande, Czar delle Russie*). However, *Le Nozze in villa* (Mantua, 1820) was a failure. At least a year before his next successful opera, *Zoraide di Granata* (Rome, Jan. 28, 1822), he was exempted from military service thanks to the intercession of an influential noblewoman. In seven years, between 1822 and 1829 he produced no fewer than 23 operas, none of which left a lasting impression. But with the next production, *Anna Bolena* (Milan, 1830), Donizetti established himself as a master of the musical theater. Written for Pasta and Rubini, after the Italian fashion of adapting roles for singers, its vogue was more than local; in 1831 it was produced in London, with the bass Lablache as Henry VIII. There followed *L'Elisir d'amore* (Milan, 1832), the tragic *Lucrezia Borgia* (La Scala, Milan, 1833), and the immensely popular *Lucia di Lammermoor* (Naples, 1835). Donizetti's life was now spent in traveling from place to place, bringing out opera after opera. He visited Paris in 1835, and produced *Marino Faliero* at the Théâtre des Italiens. In May, 1837, he succeeded Zingarelli as director of the Naples Cons. On July 30, 1837, he suffered a grievous loss when his wife died after 9 years of happy marital life. The censor's veto prevented the production of *Poliuto* (written for Nourrit after Corneille's *Polyeucte*), in Naples, and Donizetti decided to go to France. He produced at the Opéra-Comique in Paris the highly successful *La Fille du régiment* (1840), and, at the Grand Opéra, *Les Martyrs*, a revision of the forbidden *Poliuto* (1840). His next opera, *La Favorite* (1840), made a veritable sensation at its production at the Grand Opéra. After this series of Paris successes, Donizetti went back to Italy, where he produced *Adelia* (Rome, 1841) and *Maria Padilla* (Milan, 1841). His next travels took him to Vienna, where his new opera *Linda di Chamounix* evoked such enthusiasm that the Emperor conferred on him the titles of Court Composer and Master of the Imperial Chapel. In the interim, Donizetti composed a *Miserere* and an *Ave Maria* for the Austrian Court Chapel, in a severe purity of style. After the production of *Don Pasquale* (Paris, 1843), Donizetti had reached the height of his fame and prosperity; but he began to suffer from nervous fatigue and circulatory disturbance. The last opera produced in his lifetime was *Caterina Cornaro* (Naples, 1844); in 1845 he had a paralytic stroke from which he never recovered. Posthumous works were *Rita*, produced in 1860, *Gabriella di Vergy* (1869) and *Le Duc d'Albe* (1882). Besides operas, Donizetti wrote many songs, ariettas, duets, and canzonets; 7 Masses, one being a Requiem; cantatas; vespers, psalms, motets; 12 strings quartets; and piano music.

WORKS: a list of Donizetti's opera follows: *Il Pigmalione* (1817; not produced in Donizetti's lifetime, but had a modern revival in Bergamo, Oct. 13, 1960); *Enrico di Borgogna* (Venice, Nov. 14, 1818); *Una follia* (Venice, Dec. 15, 1818); *Pietro il Grande, Czar delle Russie*, better known under the title *Il Falegname di Livonia* (Venice, Dec. 26, 1819); *Le nozze in villa* (Mantua, Jan. 23, 1821); *Zoraide di Granata* (Rome, Jan. 28, 1822); *La zingara* (Naples, May 12,

1822); *La lettera anonima* (Naples, June 29, 1822); *Chiara e Serafina* (Milan, Oct. 26, 1822); *Alfredo il Grande* (Naples, July 2, 1823); *Il Fortunato inganno* (Naples, Sept. 3, 1823); *L'aio nell' imbarazzo* (Rome, Feb. 4, 1824); *Emilia di Liverpool* (Naples, July 28, 1824); *I voti dei Sudditi*, cantata (Naples, March 6, 1825); *Alahor di Granata* (Palermo, Jan 7, 1826); *Elvida* (Naples, July 6, 1826); *Olivo e Pasquale* (Rome, Jan. 7, 1827); *Gli esiliati in Siberia*, commonly known as *Otto Mesi in due ore* (Naples, May 13, 1827); *Il borgomastro di Saardam* (Naples, Aug. 19, 1827); *Le convenienze ed inconvenienze teatrali* (Naples, Nov. 21, 1827); *L'esule di Roma* (Naples, Jan. 1, 1828); *Alina, Regina di Golconda* (Genoa, May 12, 1828); *Gianni di Calais* (Naples, Aug. 2, 1828); *Il paria* (Naples, Jan. 12, 1829); *Elisabetta al Castello di Kenilworth* (Naples, July 6, 1829); *I pazzi per progetto* (Naples, Feb. 7, 1830); *Il diluvio universale* (Naples, Feb. 28, 1830); *Il ritorno desiderato*, cantata, which may be identical with *Il fausto Ritorno* (Naples, may have been performed in Aug., 1830 as a ceremonial piece to celebrate the return of Francesco I and Isabella Maria from Spain); *Imelda de' Lambertazzi* (Naples, Aug. 23, 1830); *Anna Bolena* (Milan, Dec. 26, 1830); *Francesca di Foix* (Naples, May 30, 1831); *La romanziera e l'uomo nero* (Naples, date cannot be established); *Fausta* (Naples, Jan. 12, 1832); *Ugo, conte di Parigi* (Milan, March 13, 1832); *L'elisir d'amore* (Milan, May 12, 1832); *Sancia di Castiglia* (Naples, Nov. 4, 1832); *Il furioso all'isola di San Domingo* (Rome, Jan. 2, 1833); *Parisina* (Florence, March 17, 1833); *Torquato Tasso* (Rome, Sept. 9, 1833); *Lucrezia Borgia* (Milan, Dec. 26, 1833); *Rosmonda d'Inghilterra* (Florence, Feb. 26, 1834); *Maria Stuarda* (Naples, Oct. 18, 1834); *Gemma di Vergy* (Milan, Dec. 26, 1834); *Marino Faliero* (Paris, March 12, 1835); *Lucia di Lammermoor* (Naples, Sept. 26, 1835); *Belisario* (Venice, Feb. 4, 1836); *Il campanello di notte* (Naples, June 1, 1836); *Betly* (Naples, Aug. 24, 1836); *L'assedio di Calais* (Naples, Nov. 19, 1836); *Pia de' Tolomei* (Venice, Feb. 18, 1837); *Roberto Devereux*, known also as *Il Conte d'Essex* (Naples, Oct. 29, 1837); *Maria di Rudenz* (Venice, Jan. 30, 1838); *Gianni di Parigi* (Milan, Sept. 10, 1839); *La Fille du régiment* (Paris, Feb. 11, 1840); *Les Martyrs* (Paris, April 10, 1840); *La Favorite* (Paris, Dec. 2, 1840); *Adelia* (Rome, Feb. 11, 1841); *Maria Padilla* (Milan, Dec. 26, 1841); *Linda di Chamounix* (Vienna, May 19, 1842); *Don Pasquale* (Paris, Jan. 3, 1843); *Maria di Rohan* (Vienna, June 5, 1843); *Dom Sébastien, roi de Portugal* (Paris, Nov. 13, 1843); *Caterina Cornaro* (Naples, Jan. 12, 1844); *Rita, ou Le Mari battu* (1840; Paris, May 7, 1860; posthumously produced); *Il Duca d'Alba* (1840; Rome, March 22, 1882; posthumously produced).

BIBLIOGRAPHY: F. Cicconetti, *Vita di Donizetti* (Rome, 1864); F. Alborghetti and Galli, *Donizetti e S. Mayr* (Bergamo, 1875); Ch. Malherbe, *Catalogue biographique di la Section française à l'exposition de Bergame* (Paris, 1897); E.C. Verzino, *Le opere di G. Donizetti, contributo alla loro storia* (Milan, 1897); Ippolito Valetti, *Donizetti* (Rome, 1897); Adolfo Calzado, *Donizetti e l'opera italiana in Spagna* (Paris, 1897); A. Gabrielli, *Gaetano Donizetti* (Turin, 1904); A. Cametti, *Donizetti a Roma, con lettere e documenti inediti* (Milan, 1907); C. Caversazzi, *Donizetti* (Bergamo, 1924); G. Donati-Petteni, *Donizetti* (Milan, 1930); G. Gavazzeni, *G. Donizetti* (Milan, 1935); Gino Monaldi, *G. Donizetti* (Turin, 1938); G. Zavadini, *G. Donizetti; vicende della sua vita e catalogo* (Bergamo, 1941); A . Fraccaroli, *Donizetti* (Milan, 1944); G. Barblan, *L'opera di Donizetti nell' eta romantica* (Bergamo, 1948); G. Zavadini, *Donizetti: vita, musiche, epistolario* (Bergamo, 1948; consists largely of Donizetti's correspondence, 1019 pp.); Lea Bossi, *Donizetti* (Brescia, 1956); H. Weinstock, *Donizetti and the World of Opera in Italy, Paris and Vienna in the First Half of the 19th Century* (N.Y., 1964); G. Barblan, "Lettura di un'opera dimenticata: *Pia de' Tolomei* di Donizetti," *Chigiana* XXIV/4 (1967); P. Rattalino, "Il processo compositivo nel *Don Pasquale*," *Nuova Rivista Musicale Italiana* (Jan–April 1970); J. D. Freeman, "Donizetti in Palermo and *Alahor in Granata*," *Journal of the American Musicological Society* (Summer 1972); John Allitt, *Donizetti and the Tradition of Romantic Love* (1975). The Donizetti Society, London, issues an annual journal and a quarterly newsletter.

Donizetti, Giuseppe, Italian bandmaster and composer; brother of **Gaetano Donizetti;** b. Bergamo, Nov. 9, 1788; d. Constantinople, Feb. 10, 1856. In 1832 he was summoned by the Sultan of Turkey to take charge of Turkish military bands. He accepted, and successfully accomplished the task of introducing Western instruments and modernizing the repertory. The sultan richly rewarded him with honors and money, and Donizetti remained in Constantinople to the end of his life.

Donner, Henrik Otto, Finnish composer; b. Tampere, Nov. 16, 1939. He studied composition at the Sibelius Academy in Helsinki with Nils-Eric Fougstedt and Joonas Kokkonen; then attended seminars in electronic music in Bilthoven, Holland; also took private lessons with Ligeti. For some years he earned his living as a jazz trumpeter in Helsinki; staged "happenings," with free improvisation on pre-programmed themes. WORKS: *3 Pieces* for flute and piano (1962); *Cantata Profana* (1962); *Ideogramme I* for flute, clarinet, trombone, percussion and 12 radios (1962); *Ideogramme II* employing 20 musicians, a tape recording, and renting a promenade room (1963); *For Emmy* for 3 female voices and an amplified chamber ensemble (1963); *Kinetique* for jazz band and chamber ensemble (1964); *Moonspring, or Afforderung zum . . . or Symphony 1,* subtitled "Hommâge à Ives," for strings, guitar, harp and Hammond organ (1964); *6 Bagatelles* for string quartet (1965); *Gilbert,* a musical (1965); *To Whom It May Concern* for orch. with jazz drums (1966); *XC* for soprano, chorus and chamber orch., on a text by Ezra Pound (1969); *String Quartet No. 1,* with baritone solo, on a text of Lenin (1970); *In the Afternoon* for viola (1971); *Notte* for guitar (1971); *Etyd för sommarvind (Etude for Summer Wind)* for male chorus (1971); music for films.

Donostia, José Antonio de, Basque composer and student of folklore; b. San Sebastián, Jan. 10, 1886; d. Lecároz, Navarra, Aug. 30, 1956. Donostia is his Basque name, corresponding to Dominus Sebastia-

nus, or San Sebastián, his religious name; full family name, José Antonio Zulacia y Arregui. He attended the Capuchin College in Lecaroz (Navarra); at the age of 16 entered the Franciscan Order; ordained priest. He studied organ and violin with various teachers; composition with Eugène Cools in Paris. He lived many years in France; also traveled in South America; was compelled to leave Spain during the civil war of 1936–39. He was one of the founders of the Instituto Español de Musicología, and corresponding member of the Academia de Bellas Artes in Madrid. His chief accomplishment is the collection of more than 1,000 Basque folksongs which he wrote down and transcribed during his methodical journeys through the Basque countryside; 493 of these are publ. in his Basque Cancionero, *Euskel Eres-Sorta* (1912); also publ. *De la música popular vasca; Como canta el vasco,* etc. He wrote several cantatas (*La vie profonde de Saint François d'Assise; Les trois miracles de Sainte Cécile; La quête héroïque de Graal); Préludes basques* for piano; many motets and other sacred choruses; *Itinerarium mysticum* for organ (3 vols., based on Gregorian themes); compiled a bibliography of Basque folk music.

Donovan, Richard Frank, American organist and composer; b. New Haven, Conn., Nov. 29, 1891; d. Middletown, Conn., Aug. 22, 1970. He studied music at Yale Univ. and at the Institute of Musical Art in N.Y. (M.B., 1922); also took lessons in organ playing with Widor in Paris. Returning to America, he served as organist in several N.Y. churches; from 1923–28 he was on the faculty of Smith College; in 1928 he was appointed to the School of Music at Yale University; was professor of theory there from 1947 to 1960. He conducted the New Haven Symph. Orch. from 1936 till 1951; was also organist and choirmaster of Christ Church in New Haven. As a composer, he adopted a modern polyphonic style in his choral works, while his instrumental scores often reveal impressionistic traits. WORKS: for orch., *Smoke and Steel,* symph. poem (1932); *Symphony for Chamber Orch.* (1936); *New England Chronicle,* overture (1947); *Passacaglia on Vermont Folk Tunes* (1949); *Symphony in D* (1956); *Epos* (1963); chamber music; *Wood-Notes* for flute, harp, and strings (1925); *Sextet* for wind instruments and piano (1932); *Piano Trio No. 1* (1937); *Serenade for Oboe, Violin, Viola and Cello* (1939); *Terzetto* for two violins and viola (1950); *Woodwind Quartet* (1953); *Soundings* for trumpet, bassoon and percussion (1953); *Music for Six* (1961); *Piano Trio No. 2* (1963); choral works: *Fantasy on American Folk Ballads* for men's voices and piano (1940); *Mass for Unison Voices* with organ, 3 trumpets and timpani (1955); *Forever, O Lord* for chorus a cappella (1965); 2 suites for piano and numerous organ works. BIBLIOGRAPHY: Alfred Frankenstein, "Richard Donovan," *American Composers Alliance Bulletin* (1956); *Composers of the Americas,* Vol. 15 (1969).

Dont, Jakob, Austrian violinist, teacher, and composer; b. Vienna, March 2, 1815; d. there, Nov. 17, 1888; son of the cellist, **Joseph Valentin Dont** (b. Georgenthal Bohemia, April 15, 1776; d. Vienna, Dec.

14, 1833); pupil of Böhm and Hellmesberger (Sr.) at Vienna Cons.; joined the orch. of the Hofburgtheater in 1831, and the court orch. in 1834. He taught in the Akademie der Tonkunst and the Seminary at St. Anna; Leopold Auer was his pupil. From 1873 he was professor at the Vienna Cons. His book of violin studies, *Gradus ad Parnassum,* is widely known; he published altogether some 50 works.

Door, Anton, Austrian pianist; b. Vienna, June 20, 1833; d. there, Nov. 7, 1919. He was a pupil of Czerny (piano) and Sechter (composition). He gave successful concerts in Germany; after a tour in Sweden (1856-57) he went to Russia, where he taught at the Moscow Cons. (1864). In 1869 he returned to Vienna and became professor of the advanced piano class at the Vienna Cons., a post that he held for 32 years (1869-1901).

Doorslaer, George van, Belgian music scholar; b. Malines, Sept. 27, 1864; d. there, Jan. 16, 1940. He studied medicine; music was his avocation. In association with Charles van den Borren he began a detailed study of old Belgian music; became particularly interested in the history of the carillon.
WRITINGS: *Le Carillon et les carilloneurs de la Tour Saint-Rombaut, à Malines* (1893); *Les Waghevens, fondeurs de cloches* (1908); *Le Carillon, son origine et son développement* (1911); numerous papers on Philippe de Monte, whose works he edited. For a complete list of publications see Albert van der Linden's article in *Die Musik in Geschichte und Gegenwart.*

Dopper, Cornelis, eminent Dutch composer and conductor; b. Stadskanaal, near Groningen, Feb. 7, 1870; d. Amsterdam, Sept. 18, 1939. He studied at the Leipzig Cons.; returning to Holland, he became assistant conductor of the Concertgebouw Orch. in Amsterdam (1908), and was associated with that orchestra until 1931. He also traveled as opera conductor in America (1906-08).
WORKS: four operas: *Het blinde meisje von Castel Cuille* (1892), *Het Eerekruis* (Amsterdam, 1894), *Fritjof* (1895), *Willem Ratcliff* (1901); the ballet, *Meidevorn,* with soli and chorus; 8 symphonies: No. 1, *Diana,* ballet symph. (1896); No. 2 (1903; finished after the 3rd); No. 3, *Rembrandt* (1892; later rewritten); No. 4, *Symphonietta* (1906); No. 5, *Symphonia Epica* with chorus and soli (1914); No. 6, *Amsterdam* (1912); No. 7, *Zuiderzee;* No. 8; other orchestral works: a symphonic rhapsody, *Paris;* 5 suites; Divertimento; *Ciaconna gotica,* symph. variations (his best known work; Concertgebouw, Amsterdam, Oct. 24, 1920, composer conducting); Concertino for Trumpet and 3 Kettledrums; Cello Concerto; 2 overtures; chamber music: String Quartet; Violin Sonatas; Cello Sonata; Scherzo for Woodwinds and Piano. Many choral works; songs; piano pieces.
BIBLIOGRAPHY: Sem Dresden, *Het Muziekleven in Nederland sinds 1880* (Amsterdam, 1923).

Doppler, Albert Franz, Austrian composer and conductor; b. Lwów, Oct. 16, 1821; d. Baden, near Vienna, July 27, 1883. He studied music with his father; played first flute in the Pest Opera Orch.; in 1858 settled in Vienna as ballet conductor at the Court Opera; taught flute at the Vienna Cons. from 1865. His first opera *Benjowsky* was well received in Budapest (Sept. 29, 1847) and had several revivals under the title *Afanasia;* the following operas were also produced in Budapest: *Ilka* (Dec. 29, 1849); *Wanda* (Dec. 16, 1856); *Two Hussars* (March 12, 1853); his last opera, *Judith,* was produced in Vienna (Dec. 30, 1870). He also wrote 15 ballets.

Doppler, Árpád, Hungarian pianist, son of **Karl Doppler;** b. Pest, June 5, 1857; d. Stuttgart, Aug. 13, 1927. He went to Stuttgart as a young man and studied there; was engaged to teach in N.Y. and spent three years there (1880-83); later returned to Stuttgart and taught at the Cons. He publ. a number of salon pieces for piano; also wrote a comic opera, *Caligula* (Stuttgart, 1891).

Doppler, Karl, Austrian composer and conductor; brother of **Albert Franz Doppler;** b. Lwów. Sept. 12, 1825; d. Stuttgart, March 10, 1900. Like his father and his brother, he became an excellent flute player; gave concerts in all major cities of Europe. He was then appointed as court Kapellmeister in Stuttgart, and held this position for 33 years (1865-98). He wrote an opera and pieces for the flute.

Doran, Matt, American composer; b. Covington, Kentucky, Sept. 1, 1921. He studied at the Univ. of Southern California with Ernst Toch; also took courses in composition with Hanns Eisler and Gail Kubik in Los Angeles, and orchestration with Caillet. His works include 2 one-act operas, *The Committee* (produced in Corpus Christi, Texas, May 25, 1955) and *Marriage Counselor* (Los Angeles, March 12, 1977), 2 symphonies; Double Concerto for Flute, Guitar and Strings (Los Angeles, May 21, 1976); Flute Concerto (1953); Horn Concerto (1954); String Quartet; Woodwind Quintet; Clarinet Sonata; Flute Sonata; Suite for Flute and Percussion; Quartet for Cellos; Sonatine for 2 Violins; Suite for Flute and Percussion; Trio for Oboe, Violin and Viola; many songs and piano pieces.

Dorati, Antal, distinguished Hungarian-American conductor and composer; b. Budapest, April 9, 1906. He studied composition with Bartók and Kodály and also attended classes in conducting; from 1923 to 1925 he took courses at the Univ. of Vienna. He made his debut as an opera conductor in Budapest at the age of 18; was on the staff of the Budapest Opera (1924-28); then conducted at the Dresden Opera (1928-29) and at the Münster State Opera (1929-32). As the political situation, both racially and artistically, darkened in Central Europe in 1933, Dorati went to France, where he conducted the Ballet Russe de Monte Carlo, which he took over to Australia. He made his American debut with the National Symph. Orch. in Washington (1937); settled in the U.S. in 1940, and became a naturalized American citizen in 1947. In America he held with great distinction the posts of symphony conductor and music director of the Dallas Symph. Orch. (1945-49) and Minneapolis Symph. Orch. (1949-60);

then was engaged as chief conductor of the BBC Symph. Orch., London (1962–66), and of the Stockholm Philharmonic (1966–70); subsequently was conductor of the National Symph. Orch. in Washington, D.C. (1970–77). In 1977 he was engaged as conductor and music director of the Detroit Symph. Orch. Simultaneously, he also held the position of principal conductor of the London Philharmonic. Through the years he has acquired the reputation of an orchestra builder able to handle not only the music but also the musicians; not only the public, but also the business management. Dorati is an active composer; among his works are String Quartet; String Octet; Oboe Quintet; *Divertimento* for Orch.; a ballet, *Graduation Ball,* arranged from the walzes of Johann Strauss; dramatic cantata, *The Way of the Cross* (Minneapolis, April 19, 1957); Symphony (Minneapolis, March 18, 1960); Piano Concerto (1974; Washington, Oct. 28, 1975); Cello Concerto (Louisville, Kentucky, Oct. 1, 1976).

Doret, Gustave, Swiss composer; b. Aigle, Sept. 20, 1866; d. Lausanne, April 19, 1943. He received his first instruction at Lausanne; studied violin with Joachim in Berlin; then entered the Paris Cons. as pupil of Marsick (violin) and Dubois and Massenet (composition); conductor of the 'Concerts d'Harcourt' and of the 'Société Nationale de Musique' in Paris (1893–95); conductor of the concerts at the National Exposition at Geneva (1896); conductor of the Saint-Saëns Festival at Vevey (1913); at the Opéra-Comique (1907–9); also appeared at visiting conductor in Rome, London, and Amsterdam. Doret was a member of the commission for editing Rameau's collected works. In his music Doret cultivated the spirit of Swiss folksongs; his vocal writing is distinguished by its natural flow of melody.
WORKS: the operas *Les Armaillis* (Paris, Oct. 23, 1906; an enlarged version, Paris, May 5, 1930); *Le Nain du Hasli* (Geneva, Feb. 6, 1908); dramatic legend, *Loÿs* (Vevey, 1912), *La Tisseuse d'Orties* (Paris, 1926); *Voix de la Patrie,* cantata (1891); an oratorio, *Les Sept Paroles du Christ* (1895); *La Fête des Vignerons* (1905); incidental music to Shakespeare's *Julius Caesar* and to plays by René Morax: *Henriette, Aliénor, La Nuit des quatre-temps, Wilhelm Tell, Davel* (all produced at Mézières); several pieces for orchestra: String Quartet; Piano Quintet; about 150 songs. Books: *Musique et musiciens* (1915); *Lettres à ma nièce sur la musique en Suisse* (1919); *Pour notre indépendance musicale* (1920); *Temps et Contretemps* (1942).
BIBLIOGRAPHY: J. Dupérier, *Gustave Doret* (Paris, 1932).

Dörffel, Alfred, German music editor; b. Waldenburg, Jan. 24, 1821; d. Leipzig, Jan. 22, 1905. He went to Leipzig at the age of 14, and studied with G. W. Fink and K. G. Müller. Mendelssohn and Schumann became interested in his musical education; in 1845 Schumann recommended him as arranger to Breitkopf & Härtel. In 1861 he opened a circulating library in Leipzig; it was later purchased by C. F. Peters and became the nucleus of the *Musikbibliothek Peters* at Leipzig. The fame of the *Edition Peters* is in large measure due to Dörffel's careful editorship. He pub-

lished a catalogue of his library (1861; with supplement, 1890); a German translation of Berlioz's *Traité d'Instrumentation* (1863, authorized by Berlioz himself; 4th ed., 1888); *Führer durch die musikalische Welt* (1868); *Geschichte der Gewandhauskonzerte 1781–1881* (Leipzig, 1884; a very valuable compilation, with commentary, of programs given by the Gewandhaus orch. for 100 seasons); a thematic catalogue of Bach's instrumental works and of Schumann's complete works. (1871).

Dorfmann, Ania, Russian-American pianist; b. Odessa, July 9, 1899; studied with Isidor Philipp in Paris; toured in Europe (1920–26); settled in America in 1936; made her first American appearance in a Town Hall recital in N.Y. (Nov. 27, 1936); played with the NBC Symph. Orch. under Toscanini (Dec. 2, 1939); also appeared in recitals.

Dorian, Frederick (real name **Friedrich Deutsch**), eminent musicologist; b. Vienna, July 1, 1902. He studied at the Univ. of Vienna with Guido Adler (*Dr. phil.,* 1925); also a graduate of the State Academy of Music in Vienna and a pupil of the Schönberg Seminar in Vienna; conducted operatic, concert, and broadcast performances in Austria, Germany, Italy, and the U.S.; was music critic of the *Berliner Morgenpost* (1930–33), the *Frankfurter Zeitung* (in Paris, 1934) and the *Neues Wiener Journal;* then came to the U.S.; in 1936 he was appointed prof. of music at the Carnegie Institute of Technology in Pittsburgh; he became an American citizen in 1941.
WRITINGS: "Die Fugenarbeit in den Werken Beethovens," *Studien zur Musikwissenschaft* (1927; under the name Friedrich Deutsch); *Hausmusik alter Meister* (3 vols.; Berlin, 1933); *The History of Music in Performance* (N.Y., 1942; also publ. in Japanese, Tokyo, 1964; and in Braille Edition, Division for the Blind, The Library of Congress, Washington, D.C., 1965); *The Musical Workshop* (N.Y., 1947; in Spanish, Buenos Aires, 1961; in French, Paris, 1962); *Commitment to Culture* (Pittsburgh, 1964).

Doring, Ernest Nicholas, American specialist in violins; b. New York, May 29, 1877; d. Fort Worth, Texas, July 9, 1955. He studied violin in Chicago; in 1894 he joined the violin maker John Friedrich of N.Y. and remained with the firm for 33 years (until 1927). In 1933 he moved back to Chicago; was manager of the rare violin dept. of the Wurlitzer Co. In 1938 he began publishing the magazine *Violins and Violinists.* Author of *How Many Strads?* (Chicago, 1945) and *The Guadagnini Family of Violin Makers* (Chicago, 1949).

Döring, (Carl) Heinrich, German piano pedagogue; b. Dresden, July 4, 1834; d. there, March 26, 1916. He was a pupil at the Leipzig Cons. (1852–55) and studied with Hauptmann, Lobe, Plaidy, and Richter: in 1858 joined the staff of the Dresden Cons. He published the piano collection, *Die Grundpfeiler des Klavierspiels* in 3 parts: *Praktische Studien und Übungsstücke für das polyphone Klavierspiel; Technische Hülfs- und Bildungsmittel; Rückblicke auf die Geschichte der Erfindung des Hammerklaviers im 18. Jahrhundert* (Dresden, 1898).

Dorn, Alexander (Julius Paul), son of **Heinrich Dorn;** prolific composer; b. Riga, June 8, 1833; d. Berlin, Nov. 27, 1901. He studied with his father; traveled as pianist and choral conductor; spent 10 years in Egypt (1855-65); then settled in Berlin, where he taught piano at the Hochschule. He wrote more than 400 compositions, including Masses and operettas; also a number of salon pieces for piano.

Dorn, Heinrich (Ludwig Egmont), German composer, conductor and pedagogue; b. Konigsberg, Nov. 14, 1800; d. Berlin, Jan. 10, 1892. He was a law student at Königsberg in 1823, but studied music diligently, continuing in Berlin under L. Berger (piano), Zelter, and B. Klein. After teaching in Frankfurt, he became Kapellmeister of the Königsberg Theater in 1828; in 1829, music director (and Schumann's teacher) at Leipzig, where he met young Wagner; music director at the Cathedral of St. Peter's in Riga (1831-42); Kapellmeister and city music director at Cologne (1843), where he founded (1845) the Rheinische Musikschule (which became the Cologne Cons. in 1850); 1844-47, conducted the Lower Rhenish Music Festivals. From 1849-69 he was court Kapellmeister at the Royal Opera, Berlin; was pensioned, with the title of "Royal Professor," and busied himself with teaching and musical criticism.
WORKS: the operas *Die Rolandsknappen* (Berlin, 1826), *Der Zauberer* (Berlin, 1827), *Die Bettlerin* (Königsberg, 1828), *Abu Kara* (Leipzig, 1831), *Das Schwärmermädchen* (Leipzig, 1832), *Der Schöffe von Paris* (Riga, 1841), *Die Musiker von Aix-la-Chapelle* (1848), *Artaxerxes* (Berlin, 1850), *Die Nibelungen* (Berlin, March 27, 1854; anticipating Wagner in the operatic treatment of the subject, but, despite initial successes, failing completely in the end), *Ein Tag in Russland* (Berlin, 1857; comic), *Der Botenläufer von Pirna* (Mannheim, March 15, 1865), an operetta; *Gewitter bei Sonnenschein* (Dresden, 1865); the ballet *Amors Macht* (Leipzig, 1830); *Missa pro defunctis* (Berlin, 1851); cantatas, symphonies, orchestral pieces (*Siegesfestklänge*, 1866); piano music; songs. He published an autobiography, *Aus meinem Leben*, with a collection of various essays (7 vols., 1870-86).
BIBLIOGRAPHY: W. Neumann, *Die Componisten der neueren Zeit,* IV (Kassel, 1854); Adam Rauh, *Heinrich Dorn als Opernkomponist* (Munich, 1939).

Dorsey, Jimmy (James), American clarinet and saxophone player, brother of **Tommy Dorsey;** b. Shenandoah, Pa., Feb. 29, 1904; d. N.Y., June 12, 1957. He played clarinet in school bands, and at one time led a band of his own; later joined his brother's group, rapidly climbing the ladder of commercial success, epitomized in the film *The Fabulous Dorseys* (1947).

Dorsey, Tommy (Thomas), American trombonist and band leader, brother of **Jimmy Dorsey;** b. Mahoney Plains, Pa., Nov. 19, 1905; d. Greenwich, Conn., Nov. 26, 1956. He played trumpet and other instruments in school bands; then took up the trombone and developed a virtuoso technique using a unique method of convex breathing that enabled him to maintain miraculously long passages *legato*. His brother regularly played the clarinet and alto saxophone in his band

from 1953 on. A film *The Fabulous Dorseys* (1947) bears eloquent testimony to the brothers' fame.

Dostal, Nico, Austrian composer of light music; b. Korneuburg, Nov. 25, 1895. He was brought up in a musical family; his uncle, **Hermann Dostal** (1874-1930), was a composer of celebrated military marches. Dostal studied in Linz and Vienna; specialized in arrangements of popular music, and began to compose on his own much later in life. Eventually he went to Salzburg to live.
WORKS: numerous successful operettas: *Clivia* (Berlin, 1933), *Die Vielgeliebte* (Berlin, 1934), *Prinzessin Nofretete* (Cologne, 1935), *Extrablätter* (Bremen, 1937), *Monika* (Stuttgart, 1937), *Die Flucht ins Glück* (Stuttgart, 1940), *Manina* (Berlin, 1942), *Zirkusblut* (Bielefeld, 1951), *Dr. Eisenbart* (Nuremberg, 1952), *Rhapsodie der Liebe* (Nuremberg, 1963).

Dotzauer, (Justus Johann) Friedrich, famous German cellist; b. Hässelrieth, near Hildburghausen, June 20, 1783; d. Dresden, March 6, 1860. Pupil of Heuschkel (piano), Gleichmann (violin), and Rüttinger (composition) at Hildburghausen, and of Hessner for cello; he took further lessons of Kriegck at Meiningen, where he played in the court orch. (1801-05); then was a member of the Leipzig orch. (1806-11). He joined the Dresden orch. in 1811; became first cellist in 1821 and was pensioned in 1852. Among his pupils were Karl Schubert, Drechsler, Kummer, and his own son, **K. L. Dotzauer.**
WORKS: opera, *Graziosa* (Dresden, 1841); symphonies, overtures, Masses and, more especially, cello concertos; sonatas, variations, exercises for cello.

Dotzauer, Karl Ludwig (Louis), German cellist; b. Dresden, Dec. 7, 1811; d. Kassel, July 1, 1897. He studied with his father, **Friedrich Dotzauer;** from his youth to his death, for 67 years, he was cellist of the court orch. in Kassel (1830-1897).

Doubrava, Jaroslav, Czech composer; b. Chrudim, April 25, 1909; d. Prague, Oct. 2, 1960. He studied privately with Otakar Jeremiáš (1931-37); was active mainly in the musical theater. He wrote the operas *A Midsummer Night's Dream,* after Shakespeare (1942-49; completed by Jiří Jaroch, 1966; posthumous première, Opava, Dec. 21, 1969), *Lazy John* (1952), *Balada o lásce* (*Ballad of Love,* 1959-60; completed by Jan Hanuš; posthumous première, Prague, June 21, 1962); 3 ballets: *The Tale of the Pea* (1935), *King Lavra* (1951), *Don Quixote* (1954-55); 3 symphonies: No. 1, with chorus (1938-40); No. 2, *Stalingrad* (1943-44); No. 3 (1956-58); an oratorio, *The Message* (1939-40); *Ballad About a Beautiful Death* for women's chorus and orch. (1941); the symph. marches, *Partisan March* and *Festive March* (1945); *Autumn Pastorale* (1960; fragment of his unfinished *Fourth Symphony,* arranged by Otmar Mácha); Piano Sonatina (1937); 2 violin sonatas (1942, 1958); Sonata for Solo Violin (1942); Piano Sonata (1948-49); piano pieces for children; song cycles.

Dougherty, Celius, American pianist and composer; b. Glenwood, Minnesota, May 27, 1902. He studied piano and composition at the Univ. of Minnesota with Donald Ferguson, and later at the Juilliard School with Rubin Goldmark (comp.) and Josef Lhévinne (piano). He became a highly successful accompanist and toured with many celebrated singers. He published a number of songs some of which became popular in recitals (*Weathers, Song for Autumn, Five American Sea-Chanties*). He also wrote an opera *Many Moons*, based on a story of James Thurber, which was first performed at Vassar College on Dec. 6, 1962.

Douglas, Clive, Australian composer; b. Rushworth, Victoria, July 27, 1903; d. Brighton, Victoria, April 30, 1977. He studied at the Melbourne Cons. (1929–34; D. Mus., 1958); was attached to the Australian Broadcasting Commission as a resident staff conductor in various cities (1936–66); taught at the Melbourne Cons. (1953–66). His music draws on indigenous Australian subjects and melorhythmic patterns; some abstractions suggesting serial techniques are found in his chamber music.

WORKS: 4 operas: *The Scarlet Letter*, after Hawthorne (1927–28), *Ashmadai* (1935), *Kaditcha* (1937–38) and the opera-trilogy, *Eleanor* (1940–43); 3 symphonies: *Jubilee*, 1951, *Namatjira*, 1956, 1963; the symph. poems *Carwoola* (1939) and *Sturt 1829* (1952); *Symphonic Fantasy* (1938); *Festival of Perth*, sinfonietta (1961); *Symphonic Variations* (1961); *Divertimento No. 2* for 2 pianos and chamber orch. (1962); *3 Frescoes* for orch. (1969); *Pastoral* for orch. (1970); *Discourse* for strings (1971); *The Hound of Heaven* for baritone, chorus and orch. (1932–33); *Terra Australis* for narrator, soprano, chorus and orch. (1959); 2 string quartets (1933, 1935); *Divertimento No. 1* for wind quintet (1962–63).

Dounias, Minos, musicologist; b. Cetate, Rumania, Sept. 26, 1900, of Greek parents; d. Athens, Oct. 20, 1962. He studied violin; musicology at the Univ. of Berlin with Abert and Schering; publ. a dissertation, *Die Violinkonzerte Giuseppe Tartinis* (Berlin, 1935). In 1936 he settled in Athens as music critic.

Dounis, Demetrius Constantine, Greek-American violinist and teacher; b. Athens, Dec. 7, 1886; d. Los Angeles, Aug. 13, 1954. He studied violin with Ondriček in Vienna and simultaneously enrolled as a medical student at the Univ. of Vienna; made several tours as a violinist in Europe, including Russia; after World War I he was appointed professor at the Salonika Cons. He then lived in England and eventually settled in America; established his N.Y. studio in 1939; went to Los Angeles in 1954. He originated the technique of the "brush stroke" in which the bow is handled naturally and effortlessly.

WRITINGS: numerous manuals, including: *The Artist's Technique of Violin Playing*; *The Absolute Independence of the Fingers*; *Advanced Studies for the Development of the Independence of the Fingers in Violin Playing on a Scientific Basis*; *The Development of Flexibility*, etc.

BIBLIOGRAPHY: V. Leland, *Dounis Principles of Violin Playing* (London, 1949).

Dowland, John, eminent lutenist and composer; b. Ireland, possibly in County Dublin, Dec. 1562; d. London, Jan. 21, 1626. He went to England c.1578; was in Paris in the service of Sir Henry Cobham (1580–83); then returned to England and married; Mus. Bac. (Oxford, 1588); went to Germany, where he was patronized by the Duke of Brunswick (1594); traveled on the continent (1594–1595) visiting Wolfenbüttel, Kassel, Nuremberg, Genoa, Florence and Venice. He subsequently returned to England for a short stay, then went to Dublin, where, it appears, he took up residence in Trinity College; appointed lutenist to the King of Denmark Christian IV (1598); lived at Elsinore, except for a time in 1601, until 1609, returning then to England; in 1612 he was lutenist to Lord Walden; later became one of the 6 lutenists in the service of Charles I. As a leader of the English school of lutenist-composers, Dowland brought about many innovations, chiefly in the structure of the song; among other things, he indulged in elaborate chromatic developments, and treated the accompanying part or parts as separate entities, obtaining, in them, harmonic effects quite modern even to present-day hearers.

WORKS: *The First Booke of Songes or Ayres of foure partes, with Tableture for the Lute* (1597); *The Second Booke of Songes or Ayres of 2. 4. and 5. partes* (1600); *The Third Booke of Songes or Ayres* (1603); *Lachrymae, or, Seven Teares, figured in seaven passionate Pavans . . . set forth for the Lute, Viols, or Violins, in five partes* (1605); songs in *A Musicall Banquett* (1610), ed. by his son Robert; *A Pilgrimes Solace . . . Musicall Harmonie of 3. 4. and 5. partes . . . with Lute and Viols* (1612); and a translation of Ornithoparcus' *Micrologus* (1609; repr. in English and Latin by the American Musicological Soc. and the Music Library Assoc., ed. by G. Reese and S. Ledbetter, N.Y., 1973). *The Collected Lute Music*, transcribed and ed. by D. Poulton and B. Lam, was publ. in 1974; other reprints are in *Musica Britannica* (vol. 6, *Ayres for 4 voices*), *The English Lute-Songs* (formerly known as *The English School of Lutenist Song Writers*), ed. by E. H. Fellowes et al. (vols. 1/2, 5/6, 10/11, 12/14; the 3 books of songs, *A Pilgrimes Solace*, 3 songs from *A Musicall Banquett*). The *Lachrymae*, transcribed into modern notation, were publ. by Peter Warlock (Oxford, 1927).

BIBLIOGRAPHY: O. Becker, *Die englischen Madrigalisten W. Bird, Th. Morley und J. Dowland* (Leipzig, 1901); E. H. Fellowes, *The English Madrigal Composers* (Oxford, 1921); Peter Warlock, *The English Ayre* (London, 1926); Cecil Hill, "John Dowland," *Musical Times* (Nov. 1963); P. Brown, "Influences on the Early Lute Songs of John Dowland," *Musicology* 3 (1968–69); V. Reed, "Doleful Dowland," *English Language Notes* (Sept. 1968); D. Poulton, *John Dowland* (London, 1972).

Dowland, Robert, English composer and lute player; son of **John Dowland**; b. London, 1591; d. there, Nov. 28, 1641. He remained in London after his father went to Denmark; in 1626, succeeded his father as lutenist to Charles I. He publ. *Varietie of Lute Lessons* (1610); edited *A Musicall Banquett*, a collection of English,

French, Spanish, and Italian airs (repr. in *The English Lute Songs*, vol. 20).

Downes, Edward (Thomas), English conductor; b. Aston (Birmingham), June 17, 1924. He studied at the Univ. of Birmingham (1941-44) taking B.A. in music; and at the Royal College of Music, London (1944-46), studying horn, theory and composition. In 1948 was awarded the Carnegie Scholarship which he used for taking a course in conducting with Hermann Scherchen. His first professional post as conductor was with the Carl Rosa Opera (1951); in 1952 he became a staff conductor of Covent Garden Opera in London, with which he conducted every work in the repertory, including the complete Ring of the Nibelung cycle; in 1969 he left the Covent Garden staff as a regular member in order to devote himself to symphonic conducting, but continued to fill in occasional opera engagements. He conducted the world première of Richard Rodney Bennett's opera *Victory* (April 13, 1970). He also conducted the world premières of Havergal Brian's 14th and 21st symphonies with the London Symph. Orch. on May 10, 1970.

Downes, Edward O. D. (Olin Davenport), American music critic and lecturer, son of **Olin Downes**; b. Boston, Aug. 12, 1911. He studied at Columbia Univ. (1929-30), Univ. of Paris (1932-33), Univ. of Munich (1934-36, 1938); Ph.D., Harvard Univ. (1958). Under the tutelage of his father, he entered the career of a music critic; wrote for the *N.Y. Post* (1935-38), the *Boston Transcript* (1939-41) and the *N.Y. Times* (1955-58); was program annotator for the N.Y. Philharmonic (1960-74); from 1958 acted as quizmaster for the Metropolitan Opera broadcasts. He was lecturer in music at Wellesley College (1948-49), Harvard Univ. (1949-50), Univ. of Minnesota (1950-55), and (from 1966) at Queens College.
WRITINGS: *Verdi, the Man and his Letters* (translation of correspondence, N.Y., 1942); *Adventures in Symphonic Music* (N.Y., 1943); co-edited J. C. Bach's opera *Temistocle* (Vienna, 1965); and *Perspectives of Musicology* (N.Y., 1972); contributed a great number of articles on a variety of subjects to music periodicals.

Downes, Olin, eminent American music critic; b. Evanston, Ill., Jan. 27, 1886; d. New York, Aug. 22, 1955. He began study of music at an early age, later student of Dr. L. Kelterborn (piano, music history, and analysis), Carl Baermann (piano), Homer Norris and Clifford Heilman (harmony), and J. P. Marshall (harmony and music appreciation); 1906-24, music critic of the *Boston Post*; in 1924 appointed music critic of the *New York Times*; held this post until his death. He was awarded Order of the Commander of the White Rose, Finland (1937); hon. Mus. Doc., Cincinnati Cons. of Mus. (1939).
WRITINGS: *The Lure of Music* (1918); *Symphonic Broadcasts* (1931); *Symphonic Masterpieces* (1935). He edited *Select Songs of Russian Composers* (1922); compiled and annotated *Ten Operatic Masterpieces, From Mozart to Prokofiev* (1952). A selection from his writings was publ. in 1957 under the title *Olin Downes on Music*, edited by his widow, Irene Downes.

Downey, John, American composer; b. Chicago, Oct. 5, 1927. He studied music theory with Leon Stein at De Paul Univ. in Chicago (1945-49) and advanced composition with Alexander Tcherepnin, Krenek, and Rieti at the Chicago Musical College of Roosevelt Univ. (M.M., 1951); went to Paris and took private lessons with Nadia Boulanger, Milhaud and Honegger (1952-58); returning to the U.S. he was appointed in 1964 to the music faculty of the Univ. of Wisconsin in Milwaukee.
WORKS: *La Joie de la Paix* for orch. (1956); *Chant to Michelangelo* for orch. (1958); Concerto for Harp and Chamber Orch. (1964); a ballet, *Ageistics* (1967); *Jingalodeon* for orch. (1968); *Prospectations III-II-I* for 3 simultaneous youth orchestras (1970); *Almost 12* for wind quintet, strings and percussion (1970); *Symphonic Modules Five* for orch. (1972); *Fantasy* for bassoon and orch. (1978); String Trio (1953); Violin Sonata (1954); Wind Octet (1954); 2 string quartets (1964, 1975); *Eartheatrics* for 8 percussionists (1967); *Tabu* for solo tuba (1967); *Ambivalences I* for any chamber combination (1972); *What If?*, after E. E. Cummings, for chorus, brass octet, timpani and 3 gongs (1973); *A Dolphin* for high voice, flute, viola, piano and percussion (1974); *Crescendo* for 13 percussionists (1976); *High Clouds and Soft Rain* for 24 flutes (1977); a ballet for tape, *Earthplace* (1973); 2 piano sonatas (1949, 1951); *Adagio Lyrico* for 2 pianos (1953); *Eastlake Terrace* for piano (1959); *Edges* for piano (1960); *Pyramids* for piano (1961); *Ambivalences II* for piano (1973); choruses; songs.

Doyen, Albert, French composer; b. Vendresse (Ardennes), April 3, 1882; d. Paris, Oct. 22, 1935. He studied composition with Widor at the Paris Cons. In 1917 he established the choral society Fêtes du Peuple, and subsequently conducted more than 200 concerts. Among his works are a symphony, an ode in memory of Zola, a string quartet, a piano trio, a violin sonata, and numerous choral compositions.

Draeseke, Felix (August Bernhard), significant German composer; b. Coburg, Oct. 7, 1835; d. Dresden, Feb. 26, 1913. He studied privately with Julius Rietz in Leipzig; became a friend of Liszt and Wagner, and an ardent champion of the New German School. In 1864 he went to Switzerland; taught at the Cons. of Lausanne (1864-74) and later in Geneva. In 1876 he returned to Germany and became prof. at the Dresden Cons. A Wagnerian in his youth, he was regarded as a radical, but he never accepted the modern tendencies of the 20th century, which he attacked in his pamphlet *Die Konfusion in der musik* (1906), directed chiefly against Richard Strauss. He was a prolific composer, but his works are virtually unknown outside Germany. A Draeseke society was formed in Germany in 1931, and issued sporadic bulletins.
WORKS: 6 operas: *König Sigurd* (1853-57; only a fragment performed, in Meiningen, 1867; *Herrat* (1879; Dresden, March 10, 1892), *Gudrun* (Hannover, Jan. 11, 1884), *Bertrand de Born* (1894), *Fischer und Kalif* (Prague, April 15, 1905), *Merlin* (perf. posthumously, Gotha, May 10, 1913); choral trilogy *Christus* (his major work), consisting of a prelude, *Die Geburt des Herrn*; I. *Christi Weihe*, II. *Christus der Prophet*,

III. *Tod und Sieg des Herrn* (produced on its entirety in Dresden and Berlin, 1912); Symph. in G (1872); Symph. in F (1876); *Symphonia Tragica* (1886); *Symphonia Comica* (1912); sacred and secular choruses; many songs; Piano Concerto; Violin Concerto; 3 string quartets; Quintet for Piano, Violin, Viola, Cello, and Horn; Clarinet, Sonata, etc. A complete list of works is found in H. Stephani's article on Draeseke in *Die Musik in Geschichte und Gegenwart*. Draeseke's theoretical publications include: *Anweisung zum kunstgerechten Modulieren* (1875); *Zur Beseitigung des Tritonus* (1876); a versified *Lehre von der Harmonia* (1885); *Der gebundene Stil: Lehrbuch für Kontrapunkt und Fugue* (Hannover, 1902).

BIBLIOGRAPHY: H. Platzbecker, *Felix Draeseke*, in vol. III of *Monographien moderner Musiker* (Leipzig, 1909); E. Röder, *Felix Draeseke* (2 vols.; Dresden, 1930; Berlin, 1935).

Draga, George, Rumanian composer; b. Bîrsa-Aldeşti, April 26, 1935. He studied with Vancea, Vieru and Ion Dumitrescu at the Bucharest Cons. (1957–63); in 1963 became editor of the periodical *Muzica*.

WORKS: Piano Sonata (1962); Clarinet Sonata (1963); *Se construieşte lumea noastră*, cantata (1963); Symphony (1965); *Cantata festiva* (1967); Concert Music for orch. (1968); String Quartet (1968); *Eterofonii* for strings, brass and percussion (1969); Concert Overture (1969); Prelude for Orch. (1971).

Draghi, Antonio, Italian composer of operas and oratorios; b. Rimini, 1635; d. Vienna, Jan. 16, 1700. He was a singer in Venice; in 1658 he settled in Vienna, and was appointed 'Hoftheater-Intendant' to Leopold I in 1673, also Kapellmeister to the empress. From 1661–99 he produced 67 operas, 116 festival plays ("feste teatrali") and serenades, 32 oratorios, 11 cantatas, 2 Masses, etc. Reprints are in the *Denkmäler der Tonkunst in Österreich* 46 (23.i; 2 Masses, a Stabat Mater, and 2 hymns), and in A. Schering's *Geschichte der Musik in Biespielen*, no. 226 (an opera scene).

BIBLIOGRAPHY: M. Neuhaus, "A. Draghi," *Studien zur Muzikwissenschaft* I (1913).

Draghi, Giovanni Battista, Italian harpsichordist; lived in London from 1667–1706, was organist to the queen in 1677; also music teacher to Queens Mary and Anne. He wrote the music to Dryden's ode *From Harmony*, and (with Locke) to Shadwell's *Psyche* and d'Urfey's *The Wonders in the Sun, or The Kingdom of Birds* (London, 1706); also many songs, and instructive harpsichord lessons.

Drăgoi, Sabin, eminent Rumanian composer and folklorist; b. Selişte, June 18, 1894; d. Bucharest, Dec. 31, 1968. He studied with Novák and Ostrčil in Prague (1920–22); from 1924 to 1942 taught at the Timişoara Cons.; then was prof. at the Cluj Cons. (1942–46); director of the Folklore Institute of Bucharest (1950–64) and prof. of folklore at the Bucharest Cons. (1950–52).

WORKS: the operas *Năpasta* (*Disaster*, 1927; Bucharest, May 30, 1928; revised 1958; Bucharest, Dec. 23, 1961), *Kir Ianulea* (1937; Cluj, Dec. 22, 1939), *Horia* (1945), and *Păcală* (1956; Brasov, May 6, 1962); an

oratorio *Povestea bradului* (1952); 3 cantatas *Slăvită lumină* (1937), *Mai multă lumină* (1951) and *Cununa* (1959); *3 Symphonic Tableaus* (1922); *Divertissement Rustic* for orch. (1928); *Divertissement sacru* for chamber orch. (1933); Piano Concerto (1941); Concertino for Tarogato and Orch. (1953); *7 Popular Dances* for orch. (1960); *Suită tătară* for small orch. (1961); *Suită lipovană* for small orch. (1962); Violin Sonata (1949); String Quartet (1952); *Dixtour* for winds, strings and piano (1955); *50 Colinde* for piano (1957); *10 Miniatures* for piano (1960); *12 Miniatures* for piano (1968); songs; film music.

Dragon, Carmen, American conductor of light music; b. Antioch, Calif., July 28, 1914. He studied in Los Angeles; organized and conducted orchestral groups; made adipose arrangements of popular works; filled engagements at the Hollywood Bowl and other open-air places, supplying desirable musical fare for the listening pleasure of contented people.

Dragonetti, Domenico, noted Italian double bassist; b. Venice, April 7, 1763; d. London, April 16, 1846. The "Paganini of the contra-basso" was self-taught, excepting a few lessons from Berini, bassist at San Marco, whom he succeeded in 1782; he had already played in the orchestras of the Opera buffa and Opera seria for 5 years, and composed concertos with double-bass parts impracticable for anyone but himself. He appeared at London in 1794; with the cellist Lindley, his close friend for 52 years, he played at the Antient Concerts and the Philharmonic. As late as 1845, his virtuosity still unimpaired, he led the double basses, at the unveiling of the Beethoven monument in Bonn, in the C minor Symphony. To the British Museum he left a remarkable collection of scores, engravings, and old instruments; to San Marco, his favorite cello (a Gasparo da Salò).

BIBLIOGRAPHY: F. Caffi: *Vita di D. Dragonetti* (Venice, 1846).

Drake, Earl R., American violinist and composer; b. Aurora, Ill., Nov. 26, 1865; d. Chicago, May 6, 1916. He studied violin in Chicago, and later with Joachim in Berlin. He was head of the violin department in Gottschalk Lyric School, Chicago (1893–7); organized his own school of music in Chicago in 1900.

WORKS: *The Blind Girl of Castel-Cuille*, opera and ballet (Chicago, Feb. 19, 1914); *The Mite and the Mighty*, light opera (Chicago, 1915); *Dramatic Prologue* for orch.; *Ballet* for orch.; *Gypsy Scenes* for violin and orch.; pieces for violin and piano (*Polish Dance*, *Mazurka*, *An Alpine Farewell*, etc.)

BIBLIOGRAPHY: E. E. Hipsher, *American Opera and Its Composers* (Philadelphia, 1934, pp. 162–164).

Drangosch, Ernesto, Argentinian pianist and composer; b. Buenos Aires, Jan. 22, 1882; d. there, June 26, 1925. He studied in Buenos Aires with Alberto Williams and Aguirre, and in Berlin with Max Bruch, Humperdinck, and Ansorge; later toured Europe and America as pianist; returned to Buenos Aires (1905), and founded his own conservatory. His piano pieces have been published.

Dranishnikov, Vladimir, Russian conductor; b. St. Petersburg, June 10, 1893; 1893; d. Kiev, Feb. 6, 1939. He studied at the St. Petersburg Cons. with Mme. Essipoff (piano), Steinberg, Liadov, and Wihtol (composition); and Nicolas Tcherepnin (conducting). He was employed as a rehearsal pianist at the St. Petersburg Imperial Opera (1914–18); in 1918 became conductor there, earning great esteem for his professional skill, in both the classical and modern repertory; he conducted the first Soviet performance of Alban Berg's *Wozzeck,* and of numerous Soviet operas; in 1930 he was appointed conductor of the Kiev Opera. He also wrote symphonic works and choruses.

Drdla, Franz, Bohemian composer and violinist; b. Saar, Moravia, Nov. 28, 1868; d. Gastein, Sept. 3, 1944. After 2 years at the Prague Cons. he studied at the Vienna Cons. under Hellmesberger (violin) and Krenn (composition), winning 1st prize for violin and the medal of the Gesellschaft der Musikfreunde; for several years violinist in the orch. of the Hofoper; then made successful tours of Europe; 1923–25, lived in the U.S.; then in Vienna and Prague. His pieces for violin and piano have won enormous popularity, especially *Souvenir, Vision,* and the first Serenade in A (dedicated to, and played by, Jan Kubelik); he also composed 2 operettas, *Das goldene Netz* (Leipzig, 1916) and *Die Ladenkomtesse* (Prague, 1917).

Drechsler, Joseph, Austrian composer; b. Wällisch-Birken, Bohemia, May 26, 1782; d. Vienna, Feb. 27, 1852. A pupil of the organist Grotius at Florenbach; chorusmaster and Kapellmeister (1812) at the Vienna court opera, then conductor in the theaters at Baden (near Vienna) and Pressburg; returning to Vienna, he became organist of the Servite church, in 1816 precentor at St. Ann's, in 1823 Kapellmeister at the University church and the Hofpfarrkirche; from 1822–30 he was also Kapellmeister at the Leopoldstadt Theater, and from 1844 Kapellmeister at St. Stephen's.
WORKS: 6 operas, and about 30 operettas, vaudevilles, and pantomimes; a Requiem, 10 other Masses, 3 cantatas, offertories, etc.; string quartets, organ fugues, piano sonatas, other piano music, songs, etc.; a method for organ, and a treatise on harmony. He reëdited Pleyel's *Piano School,* and publ. a theoretico-practical guide to preluding.
BIBLIOGRAPHY: C. Preiss, *Joseph Drechsler* (Graz, 1910).

Dregert, Alfred, German conductor; b. Frankfurt-am-Oder, Sept. 26, 1836; d. Elberfeld, March 14, 1893. He studied with Hans von Bülow in Berlin; after a brief concert career, devoted himself to opera conducting; also led choral societies.

Drejsl, Radim, Czech composer; b. Dobruska, April 29, 1923; d. (suicide) Prague, April 20, 1953. He studied piano at the Prague Cons. and then took composition with Bořkovec at the Academy of Musical Arts in Prague (1946–50); was musical director of the Vít Nejedlý Army Artistic Ensemble from 1949 until his death.
WORKS: 2 suites for piano (1945, 1946); 2 piano sonatas (1946, 1947); Flute Sonatina (1947); Bassoon Sonatina (1948); *Spring* for wind quintet (1948); Symphony for Strings (1948); Piano Concerto (1948–49); *Dožínková Suite (Harvest Home Suite)* for oboe or English horn, and piano (1949–50); military marches; choruses; songs.

Dresden, Sem, notable Dutch composer; b. Amsterdam, April 20, 1881; d. The Hague, July 30, 1957. He studied first in Amsterdam with Zweers; then went to Berlin where he took a course in composition with Hans Pfitzner (1903–05). Returning to Holland, he was active as a choral conductor; from 1919 to 1924 taught composition at the Amsterdam Cons.; then became its director (1924–37); subsequently was director of The Hague Cons. (1937–40). From 1914 till 1926 he led the Motet and Madrigal Society in Amsterdam. As a composer, Sem Dresden was influenced primarily by German neo-romanticism, but his harmonic idiom reveals some impressionistic usages; in many of his works there is a distinctive strain of Dutch melodic rhythms.
WORKS: an opera *François Villon* (1956–57, piano score only; orchestrated by Jan Mul and presented posthumously at the Holland Festival in Amsterdam, June 15, 1958); an operetta, *Toto* (1945); the oratorios *Saint Antoine* (1953) and *St. Joris* (1955); *Carnival Cantata* for soprano, male chorus and orch. (1954); *Chorus Tragicus* for chorus, 5 trumpets, 2 bugles and percussion (1927); *4 Vocalises* for mezzo-soprano and 7 instruments (1935); *O Kerstnacht* for chorus and strings (1939); *Chorus Symphonicus* for soprano, tenor, chorus and orch. (1943–44; revised 1955); *Psalm 99* for chorus, organ and 4 trombones (1950); *Psalm 84* for soprano, tenor, chorus and orch. (1954); *De Wijnen van Bourgondië (The Wines of Burgundy)* for chorus and orch. (1954); *Catena Musicale* for soprano, solo woodwind quartet, solo string trio and orch. (1956); and *Rembrandt's "Saul and David"* for soprano and orch. (1956). For orch.: Theme and Variations (Amsterdam, March 29, 1914); 2 violin concertos (1936, 1942); *Symphonietta* for clarinet and orch. (1938); Oboe Concerto (1939); Piano Concerto (1942–46); Flute Concerto (1949); *Dansflitsen (Dance Flashes)* for orch. (The Hague, Oct. 20, 1951); Organ Concerto (1952–53). Chamber music: 3 sextets (1910, 1913, 1920); 2 piano trios (1902, 1942); Violin Sonata (1905); Trio for 2 Oboes and English Horn (1912); 2 cello sonatas (1916, 1942); Sonata for Flute and Harp (1918); String Quartet (1924); Solo Violin Sonata (1943); Suite for Solo Cello (1943–47); piano pieces; organ pieces; choruses; songs. He was the author of *Het Muziekleven in Nederland sinds 1880* (Amsterdam, 1923); co-editor of the new edition of van Milligen's *Music History,* and with Worp and Milligen of *Algemeene Muziekleer* (1931); *Stromingen en Tegenstromingen in de Muziek* (Haarlem, 1953).
BIBLIOGRAPHY: P. F. Sanders, *Moderne Nederlandsche Componisten* (The Hague, 1930); C. Backers, *Nederlandse Componisten van 1400 tot op onze Tijd* (The Hague, 1949); J. Wouters, "Sem Dresden," *Sonorum Speculum* 25 (Winter 1965).

Dresel, Otto, German pianist and composer; b. Geisenheim, Dec. 20, 1826; d. Beverly, Mass., July 26, 1890. He was a pupil of Hiller at Cologne, and Mendelssohn at Leipzig. He went to N.Y. as concert pianist and teacher in 1848; revisited Germany, but settled in Boston in 1852, where for some 15 years he was very influential in introducing German music to the American public. He published only a few songs and piano pieces.

Dressel, Erwin, German composer; b. Berlin, June 10, 1909; d. there, Dec. 17, 1972. He studied with Wilhelm Klatte and Paul Juon in Berlin; then was active as conductor and arranger. Among his works are the comic operas *Armer Columbus* (1928), *Der Kuchentanz* (1929), *Die Zwillingsesel* (1932), *Die Laune der Verliebten* (1949) and *Der Bär* (1963); 4 symphonies; Oboe Concerto (1951); Clarinet Concerto (1961), Saxophone Concerto (1965); Viola Concerto (1969); 2 string quartets; String Trio; songs; piano pieces.

Dreves, Guido Maria, German music historian; b. Hamburg, Oct. 27, 1854; d. Mitwitz, near Kronach, June 1, 1909. He entered the Jesuit Order; lived in Vienna and Würzburg. For distinguished service to the cause of hymnology and medieval music, the Univ. of Munich made him *Dr. phil. (honoris causa).*
WRITINGS: co-editor, with C. Blume and H. M. Bannister, of the great *Analecta hymnica medii aevi* (53 vols., 1886–1911); *Cantiones Bohemicae* (1886); *Die Hymnen des Johannes von Jenstein* (1886); *Aurelius Ambrosius, der Vater des Kirchengesanges* (1893); *Psalteria rhythmica* (1901); *Die Kirche der Lateiner in ihren Liedern* (1908).

Drew, James, American composer; b. St. Paul, Minn., Feb. 9, 1929. He studied at Tulane Univ. (M.A., 1964); and at Washington Univ. (1964–65); also took private lessons in N. Y. with Wallingford Riegger and Edgar Varèse (1956–59). He subsequently was member of the music faculty at Northwestern Univ. (1965–67), Yale Univ. (1967–73) and Louisiana State Univ. (1973–76). In 1976–77 he taught at the California State College in Fullerton. Drew's style in composition is built on flexible techniques, both polythematic and monothematic, often deriving from varying elements of instrumental Klangfarbe; sometimes literal repetition of whole sections is used for emphasis. The stylistic sources of his music can be found in the works of Scriabin and Varèse. A professional pianist, he often appears as soloist in programs of contemporary music, including jazz. A polymath in his vocations and avocations, Drew drew the Downbeat International Jazz Critics Award in the New Star Category in 1961. Among his works are Passacaglia for Orch. (1957); *Indigo Suite* for piano, double bass and percussion (1959); *Divisiones* for 6 percussionists (1962); Piano Trio (1962); *Polifonica I* for flute, clarinet, oboe, string quartet and piano (1963); *The Lute in the Attic* for voice, flute, clarinet, cello and 3 gongs (1963); *4 Pieces* for string quartet (1964); *Contrappunto* for orch. (1965); *Collage* for wind instruments (1966); *Polifonica II* for flute and percussion (1966); Symph. No. 1 for chamber orch. (1968); *Symphonies* for orch., chorus and 3 conductors (1969); *October Lights* for orch. (New Haven, Oct. 18, 1969); *Violino Grande Concerto* for violino grande and orch. (1970); *Metal Concert* for percussion (N.Y., Feb. 2, 1971); Symph.

No. 2 (Norfolk, Virginia, Aug. 20, 1971); *Almost Stationary* for piano trio (1971); *Gothic Lights* for brass ensemble (1972); Concerto for Percussion (N.Y., March 21, 1973); *Tango* for cello solo (1973); *West Indian Lights* for orch. (Tanglewood, Aug. 9, 1973); *Epitaphium pour Stravinsky* for 3 trombones, horn, tuba, and piano (Atlanta, Feb. 14, 1974); *Crucifixus Domini Christi*, a dramatic stage work (Baton Rouge, Jan. 30, 1975); *The Fading of the Visible World*, oratorio (1975); *Suspense Opera* for voices and chamber ensemble (1975); *Metal Assemblage* for wind orch. (1976); Symph. No. 3 (1977); Violin Concerto (1977); String Quartet No. 2 (1977); *Dr. Cincinnati*, a dramatic entertainment for actors, dancers, singers, instrumentalists, magnetic tape segments (1977).

Dreyer, Johann Melchior, German organist and composer; b. Röttingen, Württemberg, June 24, 1747; d. Ellwangen, March 22, 1824. He studied in Ellwangen, where he became church organist; wrote chiefly church music, adopting a modern homophonic style. Among his published works are *6 Missae breves et rurales ad modernum genium* (1790); *24 Hymni brevissimi ad vesperas* (1791); *Sehr kurze und leichte Landmessen* (1793); *Deutsche Messe* (1800), etc.; also organ music.

Dreyfus, George, German-born Australian composer, bassoonist and conductor; b. Wuppertal, July 22, 1928. His family succeeded in leaving Germany in 1939, settling in Australia. He studied clarinet and then bassoon at the Melbourne Univ. Cons.; played the bassoon in various Australian orchestras; founded the Dreyfus Chamber Orch. in Melbourne. His music is pragmatically constructed and designed for performance by any competent instrumentalists or vocalists.
WORKS: opera for 8 characters and chamber orch., *Garni Sands* (1965–66; Sydney, July 12, 1972); opera, *The Gilt-Edged Kid* (1970; Melbourne, April 11, 1976); a 12-minute opera for children's choruses, *Song of the Maypole* (1968); school opera, *The Takeover* (1969); a ballet, *The Illusionist* (1965); Trio for flute, clarinet and bassoon (1956); *Galgenlieder* for baritone, flute, clarinet, bassoon and violin (1957); *Songs Comic and Curious* for baritone, flute, oboe, clarinet, horn and bassoon (1959); *Wilhelm Busch Lieder* for high voice and wind trio, to words from a famous German children's book (1959); *Music in the Air* for baritone, flute, viola and percussion (1961); *From Within Looking Out* for soprano, flute, viola, vibraphone and celeste (1962); *The Seasons* for flute, viola, vibraphone and percussion (1963); *Ned Kelly Ballads*, 3 folksongs for folk singer, 4 horns and rhythm section (1963); Wind Quintet (1965); *Music for Music Camp* for orch. (1967); 2 symphonies (1967, 1976); *Jingles*, 5 pieces for orch. (1968; a potpourri of styles from Mahler, Stravinsky, rock and roll, ballads and the Tijuana Brass); Wind Quintet (No. 2), after the notebook of J. G. Noverre (1968); *Reflections in a Glass-House*, an image of Captain James Cook, for narrator, children's chorus and orch. (1969); Sextet for didjeridu and wind quintet (1971); *MO* for baritone and string orch. (1971); *. . . and more Jingles*, 5 further pieces for orch. (1972); *The Grand Aurora Australis Now Show* for

orch. (1973); *Old Melbourne* for bassoon and guitar (1973); *Hallelujah for Handel* for orch. (1976); *Kaffeekonzert* for soprano and piano trio (1977); *Terrigal* for chorus and orch. (1977); Concerto for Bassoon and Strings (1978); film and television scores.

Dreyschock, Alexander, brilliant Bohemian pianist; b. Zack, Oct. 15, 1818; d. Venice, April 1, 1869. A student of Tomaschek, he acquired a virtuoso technique and was regarded as a worthy rival of Liszt in technical dexterity. At 8 he was able to play in public; toured North Germany (1838); spent two years in Russia (1840–42); visited Brussels, Paris, and London, then Holland and Austria. In 1862 he was called to St. Petersburg to act as professor in the newly founded Cons. In 1868, he went to Italy, where he died. His astounding facility in playing octaves, double sixths, and thirds, and performing solos with the left hand alone cast a glamour about his performance; he reached the zenith of his fame about 1850.
WORKS: an opera, *Florette, oder die erste Liebe Heinrichs des IV.*; an overture for orch.; Rondo for Orch.; String Quartet; 140 piano pieces of the salon type.

Dreyschock, Felix, German pianist, son of **Raimund Dreyschock;** b. Leipzig, Dec. 27, 1860; d. Berlin, Aug. 1, 1906. He studied under Grabau, Ehrlich, Taubert, and Kiel; gave successful concerts, and was professor at the Stern Cons., Berlin. His piano pieces are well-written and effective; he also published a violin sonata and songs.

Dreyschock, Raimund, Bohemian violinist, brother of **Alexander Dreyschock;** b. Zack, Bohemia, Aug. 20, 1824; d. Leipzig, Feb. 6, 1869. Pupil of Pixis, Prague; concertmaster at the Gewandhaus concerts (1850–69) and violin teacher in the Cons. at Leipzig. His wife **Elizabeth** (b. Cologne, 1832; d. there, July, 1911) was a contralto singer who founded and managed a vocal academy in Berlin.

Drieberg, Friedrich von, German music historian and composer; b. Charlottenburg, Dec. 10, 1780; d. there, May 21, 1856. He served in the Prussian Army until 1804 when he went to Paris to study composition with Spontini; also traveled to Vienna. He produced 2 operas, *Don Cocagno* (Berlin, 1812) and *Der Sänger und der Schneider* (Berlin, Nov. 23, 1814), but became known mainly through his speculative publications concerning Greek music, promulgating theories and conclusions that were utterly unfounded. However, they were published and seriously discussed if only in refutation. These are *Die mathematische Intervallenlehre der Griechen* (1818); *Aufschlüsse über die Musik der Griechen* (1819); *Die praktische Musik der Griechen* (1821); *Die pneumatischen Erfindungen der Griechen* (1822); *Wörterbuch der griech. Musik* (1835); *Die griechische Musik, auf ihre Grundgesetze zurückgeführt* (1841); *Die Kunst der musikalischen Composition . . . nach griechischen Grundsätzen bearbeitet* (1858).

Driessler, Johannes, German composer; b. Friedrichsthal, near Saarbrücken, Jan. 26, 1921. He studied organ and theory with Karl Rahner at the Cons. of Saarbrücken. Already at the age of 13 he filled a regular position as church organist. In 1946 he was engaged as instructor at the Music Academy in Detmold; in 1960 became its director. He devoted himself mainly to choral composition, in which he attained such an outstanding practical craft that his works entered the active repertory of both sacred and secular institutions in Germany.
WORKS: choral: *Sinfonia sacra* (1948), *Dein Reich komme* (1949), *Cantica nova* (1950), *Triptychon* (1950), secular oratorio *Gaudia Mundana* (1951), *De profundis* (1952), oratorio *Der Lebendige* (1956), oratorio *Der grosse Lobgesang* (1959), 2 *Concerti sacri* (1961), lyric opera *Claudia amata* (1952); 3 symphonies with subtitles of spiritual connotations: No. 1, *Dum spiro spero* (1964); No. 2, *Dum ludo laudo* (1966); No. 3, *Amo dum vivo* (1969); works for chamber ensembles and numerous teaching pieces.

Drigo, Riccardo, Italian composer and conductor; b. Padua, June 30, 1846; d. there, Oct. 1, 1930. He studied music in Venice; conducted opera in Venice and Milan. In 1879 he was engaged to conduct the Italian opera in St. Petersburg; in 1886 became permanent ballet conductor of the Imperial Theater there; conducted first performances of Tchaikovsky's ballets, *The Sleeping Beauty* and *The Nutcracker.* After Tchaikovsky's death, Drigo edited the score of the ballet *Swan Lake* and orchestrated a number of Tchaikovsky's piano pieces. Drigo's own ballets, melodious and easy to listen to, also enjoyed excellent success in Russia. Particularly popular was his ballet *Les Millions d'Arlequin (Harlequin's Millions),* which includes the famous *Serenade* for a soulful cello solo and the ingratiating *Valse Bluette.* Drigo conducted the first performance of this ballet in St. Petersburg, Feb. 10, 1900. From 1914–1916 he was in Italy; from 1916–1920 he was again in St. Petersburg, finally returning to Italy and remaining there until his death.
BIBLIOGRAPHY: S. Travaglia, *Riccardo Drigo, l'uomo e l'artista* (Padua, 1929).

Drinker, Henry S., Jr., American music scholar and translator; b. Philadelphia, Sept. 15, 1880; d. Merion, Pennsylvania, March 9, 1965. He was by profession a lawyer. He translated the texts of all the Bach cantatas and of the complete vocal works of Brahms and Schumann; author of *The Chamber Music of Johannes Brahms* (Philadelphia, 1932). He founded the Drinker Library of Choral Music, which he eventually donated to the Free Library of Philadelphia.

Drobisch, Moritz Wilhelm, German scholar; b. Leipzig, Aug. 16, 1802; d. there, Sept. 30, 1896. 1826 prof. extraordinary of mathematics, and 1842 prof. ordinary of philosophy, at Leipzig Univ. Besides various works on mathematics and philosophy, he wrote several valuable essays on musical subjects.
WRITINGS: *Über die mathematische Bestimmung der mus. Intervalle* (1846), *Über mus. Tonbestimmung und Temperatur* (1852), *Nachträge zur Theorie der mus. Tonverhältnisse* (1855), "Über ein zwischen Altem und Neuem vermittelndes Tonsystem," *Allege-*

meine Musikalische Zeitung (1871). *Über reine Stimmung und Temperatur der Töne* (1877).

Drouet, Louis Francois-Philippe, famous French flute player and composer; b. Amsterdam, April 14, 1792; d. Bern, Sept. 30, 1873. He studied at the Paris Cons. At the age of 16 was appointed solo flutist to King Louis of Holland, and at 19 became solo flutist to Napoleon; after Napoleon's defeat, he played the flute with fine impartiality for King Louis XVIII. In 1817 he went to London, and subsequently made concert tours across Europe. In 1840 he was appointed Kapellmeister at Coburg; in 1854 he visited America for a few months; then lived in Gotha and Frankfurt before going to Switzerland, where he died. He composed mainly for the flute; among his works are 10 flute concertos; 2 fantasias for flute and piano; 3 trios for 3 flutes; numerous sonatas and variations for flute and assorted instruments. Drouet is credited with the arrangement of the French popular air *Partant pour la Syrie,* supposedly sung for him by Queen Hortense of Holland.

Drozdov, Anatol, Russian pianist, pedagogue and writer on music; b. Saratov, Nov. 4, 1883; d. Moscow, Sept. 10, 1950. He studied piano at the St. Petersburg Cons., graduating in 1909; then engaged in teaching; was prof. of piano at the conservatories of Ekaterinoder (1911–16), Saratov (1918–20) and Moscow (1920–24). He published a number of articles in the Russian music journals; also composed 2 piano sonatas and other piano pieces and chamber music.

Drozdowski, Jan, Polish pianist; b. Cracow, Feb. 2, 1857; d. there, Jan. 21, 1918. He studied at the Vienna Cons. with Dachs and Epstein; also took lessons with Bruckner. In 1889 he was appointed prof. of piano at the Cracow Cons. and retained that post till his death. He publ. a piano method, *Systematic School of Pianoforte Technique* (1887; German ed., Munich, 1889, under the pseudonym **Jan Jordan**).

Druckman, Jacob, outstanding American composer; b. Philadelphia, June 26, 1928. He took private lessons in composition as a youth with Louis Gesensway in Philadelphia; played jazz trumpet as a teenager. Then entered the Juilliard School of Music in N.Y. and studied with Bernard Wagenaar, Vincent Persichetti, and Peter Mennin (B.S., 1954; M.S., 1956); also in Tanglewood with Aaron Copland (1949, 1950). In 1954–55 he enrolled at the École Normale de Musique in Paris where he studied with Tony Aubin. In 1957 he was appointed instructor in the department of Literature and Materials of Music at the Juilliard School; from 1967 he was also an associate at the Columbia-Princeton Electronic Music Center; taught at Brooklyn College from 1972 to 1974; in 1975 was appointed prof. at Yale Univ. He held Guggenheim grants in 1957 and 1968. In 1972 he received the Pulitzer Prize for music for his orchestral work *Windows.* In his music he happily combines the strict elements of polyphonic structure, harking back to Palestrina, with modern techniques of dissonant counterpoint, while refusing to adhere to any doctrinaire system of composition. In his orchestration he makes use of a plethora of per-

cussion instruments, including primitive drums; electronic sonorities also have an increasing importance in his works.

WORKS: *Violin Concerto* (1956); *4 Madrigals* for chorus (1959); *Dark Upon the Harp* for mezzo-soprano, brass quintet and percussion (1962); *Antiphonies* for 2 choruses (1963); *The Sound of Time* for soprano and orch. (1965); *Animus I* for trombone and tape (1966); *Incenters* for 13 players (1968); *Animus II* for mezzo-soprano, percussion and tape (1969); *Animus III* for clarinet and tape (1969); *Windows* for orch. (Chicago Symph. Orch., May 16, 1972); *Lamia* for soprano and orch. (1974); *Valentine* for doublebass solo (1975); *Chiaroscuro* for orch. (1976); 2 string quartets; other chamber music; songs.

Drysdale, Learmont, Scottish composer; b. Edinburgh, Oct. 3, 1866; d. there, June 18, 1909. Pupil of the Royal Academy of Music, and winner of the Lucas prize for composition (1890). He composed the orchestral overtures *Tam O'Shanter* (1891; awarded prize by Glasgow Society of Musicians) and *Herondean* (1894); also an opera, *The Red Spider* (1898), and some choral works.

Dubensky, Arcady, Russian-American violinist and composer; b. Viatka, Russia, Oct. 15, 1890; d. Tenafly, New Jersey, Oct. 14, 1966. He studied violin at the Moscow Cons. with Jan Hřimaly and composition with Ilyinsky, graduating in 1909; was a violinist at the Moscow Opera (1910–19); then left Russia; played in hotels and restaurants in Constantinople (1920); settled in the U.S. in 1921; was a member of the N.Y. Symph. Orch., and then of the N.Y. Philharmonic Orch., retiring in 1953. His music is conservative in its idiom; however, an impression of originality is created by his adroit use of unusual combinations (such as a quartet for double basses, a fugue for 18 violins, suite for 9 flutes, etc.).

WORKS: *Romance with Double Bass,* after Chekhov, comic opera (N.Y., Oct. 31, 1936); *Russian Bells,* symph. poem (N.Y., Dec. 29, 1927, composer conducting); *Prelude and Fugue* (1932; Boston Symph. Orch., Koussevitzky conducting, April 12, 1943); *Tom Sawyer,* overture (for Mark Twain's centennial, Philadelphia, Nov. 29, 1935); *Political Suite* for orch. (*Russian Monarchy, Nazi and Fascist, Communist;* N.Y. radio broadcast, Sept. 17, 1936); *Fantasy on a Negro Theme* for tuba and orch. (Indianapolis, 1938); *Stephen Foster,* symph. suite (Indianapolis, Jan. 31, 1941); *Trumpet Overture,* for 18 toy trumpets and 2 bass drums (N.Y., Dec. 10, 1949); *Trombone Concerto* (1953); *Gossips* for strings (Philadelphia, Nov. 24, 1928); *Fugue for 18 Violins* (his most successful work; Philadelphia, April 1, 1932, Stokowski conducting); *Prelude and Fugue for 4 Bassoons* (Brooklyn, Feb. 16, 1947); *Suite for 9 Flutes,* including a piccolo and basset horn (N.Y., Jan. 26, 1936, composer conducting); other chamber works for various combinations of instruments.

Dubinsky, Vladimir, Russian cellist; b. Russia, Sept. 10, 1876; d. Syracuse, N.Y., Jan. 10, 1938. He studied cello at the Cons. of Moscow; emigrated to the U.S. in 1905, and became cellist with the Tollefsen Trio in N.Y., where he lived for many years as a teacher.

Dubois, Léon, Belgian conductor and composer; b. Brussels, Jan. 9, 1859; d. Boitsfort, Nov. 19, 1935. He won the Prix de Rome at the Brussels Cons. in 1885; conducted opera at the Théâtre de la Monnaie (1892–97); was director of the Louvain Music School (1899–1912); then director of the Brussels Cons. (1912–26). He wrote the operas, *Son Excellence ma femme* (1884), *La Revanche de Sganarelle* (1886), and *Edénie* (Antwerp, 1912); a ballet *Smylis* (Brussels, 1891); the mimodrama *La Mort* (Brussels, 1894); chamber music.

Dubois, (Clément-François) Théodore, eminent French organist and composer; b. Rosnay, Marne, Aug. 24, 1837; d. Paris, June 11, 1924. He entered the Paris Cons. in 1853, working under Marmontel (piano), Benoist (organ), Bazin and Ambroise Thomas (composition), graduating (1861) as recipient of the Grand Prix de Rome with the cantata *Atala*, after having taken first prizes in all departments. Returning to Paris, he became *maître de chapelle* at Sainte-Clothilde and then succeeded Saint-Saëns, in 1877, as organist at the Madeleine. In 1871 he was made harmony prof. at the Paris Cons., succeeding Elwart; in 1891 became professor of composition; in 1894 was elected to the chair in the Academy left vacant by Gounod's death; in 1896 he succeeded Ambroise Thomas as director of the Paris Cons.; retired, 1905. WORKS: the comic operas *La Guzla de l'émir* (Paris, April 30, 1873) and *Le Pain bis, ou la Lilloise* (Opéra-Comique, Feb. 26, 1879); *Aben Hamet* (produced in Italian, Théâtre du Châtelet, Dec. 16, 1884); "idylle dramatique," *Xavière* (Opéra-Comique, Nov. 26, 1895); the ballet *La Farandole* (Paris Opéra, Dec. 14, 1883); 2 oratorios; *Les Sept Paroles du Christ* (1867), *Le Paradis perdu* (1878; won the City of Paris prize); several cantatas (*L'Enlèvement de Proserpine, Hylas, Bergerette, Les Vivants et les morts, Délivrance*); Masses and other church music; many orchestral works: *Marche heroïque de Jeanne d'Arc; Fantaisie triomphale,* for organ and orch.; *Hymne nuptiale; Méditation-Prière* for strings, oboe, harp, and organ; *Concerto-Capriccio,* for piano; 2nd Piano Concerto; a Violin Concerto; 2 symphonic poems, *Notre Dame de la Mer* and *Adonis; Symphonie française* (1908); *Fantasietta* (1917); piano pieces (*Chœur et danse des lutins; 6 poèmes sylvestres*); pieces for organ and for harmonium; a cappella choruses; etc. Dubois published a practical manual, *Traité de contrepoint et de fugue* (1901), a standard work at the Paris Cons.
BIBLIOGRAPHY: M. Widor, *Notice sur la vie et les travaux de Théodore Dubois* (Paris, 1924).

Dubois, Pierre-Max, French composer; b. Graulhet (Tarn), March 1, 1930. He studied at the Cons. in Tours, obtaining a prize in piano at the age of 15; later studied composition with Darius Milhaud at the Paris Cons. His works include *Impressions foraines* for orch. (1951); *Divertissement* for saxophone and orch. (1952); *Sérénades* for bassoon and orch. (1953); *Capriccio* for violin and orch. (1954); *Concertstück* for saxophone and piano (1955); Violin Concerto (Strasbourg, June 20, 1957); Cello Concerto (1958); Concerto for Saxophone and String Orch. (1959); Symph.

No. 1, subtitled *Drame pour Epidaure* (1960); *Le Docteur OX,* ballet-bouffe, after Jules Verne (Lyon, Feb. 23, 1964); Quartet for 4 French Horns (1961); Quartet for 4 Flutes (1961); Quartet for 4 Trombones (1961); *Concerto italien* for 2 pianos and orch. (1962); Concerto for Violin, Piano and Orch. (Besançon, Sept. 15, 1963); Quartet for 4 Clarinets (1962); Symph. No. 2 (*Symphonie-Sérénade*) for strings (1964); *Musique pour un Western,* for orch. (1964); *Cover Girls,* a choreographic spectacle (1965); *Concerto ironico* for bassoon and orch. (1968); Concertino for 4 Saxophones and Orch. (1969); *Beaujency concerto* for clarinet and orch. (1969); *Sinfonia militaire* (1969).

Dubrovay, László, Hungarian composer; b. Budapest, March 23, 1943. He studied in Budapest at the Academy of Music, graduating in 1966; then attended classes of Stockhausen in Germany; was a repetiteur with the Hamburg State Opera (1971–72). In his music he experiments with mathematically conceived forms.
WORKS: *5 Pieces* for bassoon and piano (1967); *6 Duos* for violin and percussion (1968); *Verificazione* for orch. (1969); String Quartet (1969); Brass Quintet (1969); *Succession* for orch. (1973); *E-Trio* for violin, percussion and synthesizer (1974); *Sequence* for flute and synthesizer (1974); *Magic Square* for violin and cimbalom (1975); A^2 for violin, cello, piano, percussion and synthesizer (1975); *Geometrum 1* for tape (1975); *Geometrum 2* for string quartet or 4 string instruments (1976); *Interferences* for 2 cimbaloms (1976); *Numberplay No. 1* for 20 instruments (1976); *Numberplay No. 2* for chorus (1977); *Oscillations No. 1* for electric organ and synthesizer; *Oscillations No. 2* for cello, cimbalom, electric organ and synthesizer; *Oscillations No. 3* for piano and synthesizer (1976–77); *Matuziáda Nos. 1–4* for 4 flutes (1976–77); *Caput* for chorus, electric organ, and phase shifter (1977).

Dubuc, Alexander, Russian pianist, composer, and teacher; b. Moscow, March 3, 1812; d. there, Jan. 8, 1898. He was a pupil of John Field, about whom he published a volume of memoirs; professor at the Moscow Cons. (1866–72). He wrote piano pieces, songs, and a work on piano technique (1866).

Du Cange, Charles Du Fresne, Sieur, French scholar; b. Amiens, Dec. 18, 1610; d. Paris, Oct. 23, 1688. He belonged to the famed group of 17th-century French writers who established the precepts of modern historical criticism; he is important to musicology because he included definitions of Latin musical terms in his lexicographies. The most valuable of his many works are the *Glossarium ad scriptores mediae et infimae latinitatis* (Paris, 1678, 3 vols.; 1733–36, 6 vols.; 1840–50, 7 vols. 1883–87, 10 vols.) and the *Glossarium ad scriptores mediae et infimae graecitatis* (Lyons, 1688; Breslau, 1889). Almost all his works are preserved in the Bibliothèque Nationale in Paris.
BIBLIOGRAPHY: H. Hardouin, *Essai sur la vie et sur les ouvrages de Du Cange* (Amiens, 1849); L. J. Feugère, in the *Journal de l'Instruction Publique* (Paris, 1852).

Du Caurroy, François-Eustache, Sieur de St.-Frémin; French composer; b. Beauvais, Feb. (baptized Feb. 4), 1549; d. Paris, Aug. 7, 1609. He was a member of the French nobility; his father was "procureur du roi." He entered the Royal Chapel as singer in 1569; in 1575 received a prize for a chanson, *Beaux yeux;* in 1578 he was "sous-maître"; in 1599 became superintendent of "la musique du roi." Influenced by Le Jeune, he began to compose "musique mesurée"; advanced in the favor of the court, receiving honors and awards; held the ecclesiastical titles of canon at the Ste. Chapelle of Dijon, Ste. Croix of Orleans, and other provincial posts. His greatest work was a collection *Meslanges de la musique,* containing psalms, "chansons mesurées," noëls, in 4, 5, and 6 voices (posthumously published, Paris, 1610; some specimens reprinted in Expert's *Maîtres musiciens,* vol. XIII). Other works: *Missa pro defunctis;* 2 vols. of *Preces ecclesiasticae;* instrumental *Fantaisies* for 3, 4, 5, and 6 parts (Paris, 1610; several numbers published separately by Expert); 5 vols. of his works in score are in the Bibliothèque Sainte-Geneviève in Paris.
BIBLIOGRAPHY: M. Th. Luillier, *Note sur quelques artistes-musiciens dans la Brie* (1870); N. Dufourcq, "À propos d'Eustache Du Caurroy," *Revue de Musicologie* (Dec. 1950); F. Lesure, "La Carrière et les fonctions de Du Caurroy," *Revue de Musicologie* (1952).

Ducis (Duch), Benedictus, distinguished composer of the 16th century; b. probably near Constance, c.1490; d. Schalckstetten, near Ulm, 1544. He may or may not be identical with **Benedictus de Opitiis,** who was organist at the Antwerp Cathedral (1514–16) and organist at the Chapel Royal in London (1516–22). It is known for a certainty that Benedictus Ducis was in Vienna c.1515; probably studied there; in 1532 he applied for a pastorate at Ulm (under the name **Benedict Duch**), but failed to obtain it. In 1533 he succeeded in receiving a pastorate at Stubersheim, near Geislingen; in 1535 he became pastor at Schalckstetten and remained there till his death. Benedictus Ducis has been confused by many writers with Benedictus Appenzeller; the long list of Ducis's works given by Fétis is spurious; Barclay Squire, in *Sammelbände der Internationalen Musik-Gesellschaft* (Jan. 1912) brought conclusive evidence that a considerable number of these works must be attributed to Benedictus Appenzeller. Two works by Ducis were published in facsimile by M. Nijhoff (The Hague, 1925); 10 sacred motets are repr. in the *Denkmäler deutscher Tonkunst,* vol. XXXIV (ed. by Joh. Wolf).
BIBLIOGRAPHY: F. Spitta, "Benedictus Ducis," *Monatsschrift für Gottesdienst und Kirchliche Kunst* (Jan.-March 1913); Charles Van den Borren, "Benedictus de Opitiis," *Musica sacra* (Sept. 1927); D. Bartha, *Benedictus Ducis und Appenzeller* (Wolfenbüttel, 1930).

Duckles, Vincent Harris, American musicologist and librarian; b. Boston, Sept. 21, 1913. He studied at Columbia Univ. and at the Univ. of Calif., Berkeley (Ph.D., 1953); in 1947, appointed Head of the Music Library, Univ. of Calif., at Berkeley; prof. of music there, 1960. He specializes in 17th-century English song literature; music bibliography; history of musical scholarship. He has held 2 Fulbright Fellowships (1950, Cambridge; 1957, Univ. of Göttingen); a Grant-in-Aid from the American Council of Learned Societies (1964, Florence). He publ. a valuable manual, *Music Reference and Research Materials: An Annotated Bibliography* (N.Y., 1964; 3rd ed., 1974).

Ducloux, Walter, Swiss-American conductor; b. Kriens, Switzerland, April 17, 1913. He studied at the Univ. of Munich (1932–35) and at the Academy of Music in Vienna (1935–37); was assistant to Toscanini at the Lucerne Festivals (1938–39); came to America and conducted opera in N.Y. (1940–42); became bandleader in the U.S. Army (1943–46); then was active in California and in Texas as opera conductor.

Dudarova, Veronica, Russian conductor; b. Baku, Dec. 5, 1916. She studied piano in Leningrad and took a course in conducting at the Moscow Cons. with Leo Ginsburg, graduating in 1947. In the same year became associate conductor of the Moscow State Orch. She is one of the foremost women conductors of the Soviet Union.

Dufallo, Richard, American clarinetist and conductor; b. East Chicago, Indiana, Jan. 30, 1933. He studied at the American Cons. of Music in Chicago; played clarinet as a youngster. Subsequently he studied composition with Lukas Foss at the Univ. of Calif., Los Angeles; in 1957 he joined the Improvisation Chamber Ensemble organized by Foss, and showed an exceptional talent for controlled improvisation in the ultra-modern manner. In 1965 he joined Lukas Foss as Associate Conductor of the Buffalo Philharmonic. He also was guest conductor with the Pittsburgh Symph. Orch.; attended a conducting seminar with William Steinberg and a course in conducting with Pierre Boulez in Basel in the summer of 1969. In 1967 he went to Japan and other Asian countries as Assistant Tour Conductor with the N.Y. Philharmonic.

Dufau, Jenny, French soprano, b. Rathau, Alsace, July 18, 1878; d. Pau, France, Aug. 29, 1924. Pupil of Etelka Gerster in Berlin (1901–5); studied subsequently with Mme. Marchesi, P. Vidal, A. Selva, and G. Benvenuti; sang at Berlin Opera (1910–11); from 1911, was with Chicago Opera Co.; later, appeared in vaudeville.

Dufay, Guillaume, chief representative of the Burgundian school, and famed particularly for his 3-part chansons, Masses, and motets; b. probably at Hainault, c.1400; d. Cambrai, Nov. 27, 1474. The last name is pronounced du-fah-ee, in 3 syllables, as indicated by the way he set his name to music in *Ave regina caelorum,* asking for the Lord's mercy: "Miserere tui labentis *Du-fa-y.*" He was a choirboy at the Cathedral of Cambrai, where he received an excellent training; his teachers were Loqueville and Grenon. He was in Rimini and Pesaro (1419–26); then returned to Cambrai, where he was chapel master (1426–28); then member of the Papal Chapel in Rome (1428–33); in the service of the Duke of Savoy (1433); again in Cambrai (1434); entered again the Papal Chapel (1435–37; not in Rome, however, but in Florence and Bologna);

was again in Savoy (1438–44); studied jurisprudence at the Univ. of Turin, obtaining the degree "Baccalarius in decretis" (c.1445). In 1445 he settled at Cambrai, holding the important position of canon at the cathedrals of Cambrai and Mons. Under these fortunate circumstances, which enabled him to live in comfort, he spent the rest of his life, greatly esteemed by both the Church authorities and musicians; he was described by Compère as "the moon of all music, and the light of all singers." Dufay wrote music in almost every form practiced in his time, and was successful in each. A complete list of works, including MS sources and approximate dates of composition, is found in Charles E. Hamm's *A Chronology of the Works of Guillaume Dufay* (1964). The *Opera Omnia* (issued by the American Inst. of Musicology, Rome 1947–50; 1st ed. by Guillaume de Van, continued by Heinrich Bessler) also contains valuable commentary.

BIBLIOGRAPHY: F. X. Haberl, "Wilhelm du Fay," *Bausteine für Musikgeschichte*, Vol. I (Leipzig, 1885); H. Besseler, "Studien zur Musik des Mittelalters," *Archiv für Musikwissenschaft* (June 1925); Charles Van den Borren, *Guillaume Dufay; son importance dans l'évolution de la musique au XVe siècle* (Brussels, 1926); K. Geiringer, "Dufay's 'Gloria ad modum tubae'," *Zeitschrift für Musikwissenschaft* (Jan. 1927); K. Dèzes, "Das Dufay zugeschriebene 'Salve Regina' eine deutsche Komposition," *Zeitschrift für Musikwissenschaft* (Feb. 1928); H. Besseler, *Die Musik des Mittelalters und der Renaissance*, in Bücken's Handbuch der Musikwissenschaft series (1931–34); Charles Van den Borren, "Guillaume Dufay, Light of the 15th Century," *Musical Quarterly* (July 1935); H. Besseler, "Neue Dokumente zum Leben und Schaffen Dufays," *Archiv für Musikwissenschaft* (Sept. 1952); D. Plamenac "An Unknown Composition by Dufay?" *Musical Quarterly* (April 1954); chapter 2 in Gustave Reese, *Music in the Renaissance* (N.Y., 1954); H. Besseler's article in *Die Musik in Geschichte und Gegenwart* incorporates new documentary discoveries on Dufay's life (many of them made by Besseler himself); C. Van den Borren, "Dufay and His School," in D. A. Hughes and G. Abraham, *Ars Nova and the Renaissance* (London, 1960); Charles E. Hamm, *A Chronology of the Works of Guillaume Dufay Based on a Study of Mensural Practice* (Princeton, N.J., 1964); L. Treitler, "Tone System in the Secular Works of Guillaume Dufay," *Journal of the American Musicological Society* (1965); A. E. Planchart, "Guillaume Dufay's Masses: Notes and Revisions," *Musical Quarterly* (Jan. 1972); F. Otterbach, *Kadenzierung und Tonalität im Kantilenensatz Dufays* (1974). A Dufay Quincentennial Conference was held at Brooklyn College on Dec. 6–7, 1974; a compilation of the papers read at the Conference was published in 1976 (ed. by Allan Atlas).

Dufourcq, Norbert, French organist and music historian; b. St. Jean-de-Braye (Loiret), Sept. 21, 1904. He studied with Gastoué; in 1941, appointed professor of music history at the Paris Cons. He has written numerous valuable books dealing with the organ in France and other subjects: *Documents inédits relatifs à l'orgue français* (1934–35; 2 vols.); *Esquisse d'une histoire de l'orgue en France du XIIIe au XVIIIe siècle* (1935); *Les Clicquot, facteurs d'orgue* (1942); *J. S.*

Bach, génie allemand? génie latin? (1947); *J. S. Bach, le maître de l'orgue* (1948); *César Franck* (1949); *Le Clavecin* (1949); *La Musique française* (1949); *La Musique d'orgue française de Jehan Titelouze à Jehan Alain* (1949); *Autour de Coquard, Franck et Vincent d'Indy* (1952); *Nicolas Lebègue* (1954); contributor to and editor of *La Musique des Origines à Nos Jours* (Paris, 1946; new ed., 1956); edited *Larousse de la Musique* (2 vols.; Paris, 1957).

Dufranne, Hector, French baritone; b. Mons, Belgium, Oct. 25, 1870; d. Paris, May 3, 1951. He made his debut as Valentine in *Faust* at La Monnaie, Brussels, Sept. 9, 1896; at Opéra-Comique, Paris, on June 18, 1900. Sang with the Manhattan Opera House, N.Y. (1908–10), and with the Chicago Opera Co. (1910–22).

Dugan, Franjo, Croatian composer and organist; b. Krapinica, Sept. 11, 1874; d. Zagreb, Dec. 12, 1948. He studied music with Max Bruch in Berlin, and also attended classes in mathematics. He settled in Zagreb as church organist; taught at the Zagreb Cons.; publ. manuals on orchestration and musical form; also many organ pieces.

Dugazon, Louise Rosalie, famous opera singer; b. Berlin, June 18, 1755; d. Paris, Sept. 22, 1821. She was brought up in the atmosphere of the theater; her father, F. J. Lefebvre, was a French dancer at the Berlin Opera; she herself began her career as a ballet dancer; then she became a singer, encouraged mainly by Grétry, who thought highly of her talent. She made her debut in Paris in Grétry's opera *Sylvain* (June 19, 1774); in 1775 she married an actor who used the professional name Dugazon; although they were soon separated, she adopted this name for her professional appearances. She sang mostly at the Opéra-Comique; created some 60 new roles; her last public appearance was at the Paris Opéra on Feb. 29, 1804. She was greatly admired by her contemporaries, and her name became a designation of certain types of operatic parts ("jeune Dugazon"; i.e., an ingénue).

BIBLIOGRAPHY: H. and A. Leroux, *La Dugazon* (Paris, 1926).

Duggan, Joseph Francis, Irish pianist and composer; b. Dublin, July 10, 1817; d. London, 1900. He was engaged at the Italian Opera, N.Y.; taught in Philadelphia, Baltimore, and Washington; then lived in London; became professor of singing in the Guildhall School of Music. He wrote 2 successful operas, *Pierre* (London, 1853) and *Leonie* (London, 1854); 2 symphonies; 6 string quartets, numerous piano pieces; also published *The Singing Master's Assistant* and transls. of Albrechtsberger's *Science of Music* (Philadelphia, 1842) and Fétis' *Counterpoint and Fugue.*

Duhamel, Antoine, French composer; b. Paris, July 30, 1925, a son of the famous writer, Georges Duhamel. He studied with René Leibowitz and from the very first began to compose in the dodecaphonic technique; has written a quintet for piano and wind instruments; also published a book, *L'Opéra depuis Wagner* (Liège, 1950).

Duiffoprugcar (properly **Tieffenbrucker**), **Gaspar,** Bavarian viol maker; b. Tieffenbrugg, Bavaria, 1514 (date established by Dr. Coutagne of Lyons, in his work *Gaspar Duiffoproucart et les luthiers lyonnais du XVIᵉ siècle*, Paris, 1893); d. Lyons, Dec. 16, 1571. Long reputed to be the first maker of violins; but Vidal, in his *Les Instruments à archet*, states that all the so-called Duiffoprugcar violins are spurious, having been made by Vuillaume, who in 1827 conceived the idea of making violins after the pattern of a viola da gamba by Duiffoprugcar. Apparently, the latter learned his trade in Italy, the usual spellings of his name showing it to be Italianized rather than Gallicized; he settled in Lyons in 1553, and was naturalized in 1559.

Dukas, Paul, famous French composer; b. Paris, Oct. 1, 1865; d. there, May 17, 1935. From 1882–88 pupil at the Cons. of G. Mathias (piano), Th. Dubois (harmony), and E. Guiraud (composition); won 1st prize for counterpoint and fugue in 1886, and Second Prix de Rome with a cantata *Velléda* (1888); music critic of the *Revue Hebdomadaire* and *Gazette des Beaux-Arts*; also contributor to the *Chronique des Arts, Revue Musicale*, etc.; 1906, Chevalier Légion d'Honneur; 1910–12, prof. of the orch. class at the Cons.; 1918, elected Debussy's successor as member of the *Conseil de l'enseignement supérieur* there; 1927, appointed prof. of composition at the Paris Cons.; also taught at the École Normale de Musique; assisted in the revising and editing of Rameau's complete works for Durand of Paris. Although he was not a prolific composer, he wrote a masterpiece of modern music in his orchestral scherzo *L'Apprenti Sorcier*; his opera *Ariane et Barbe-Bleue* is one of the finest French operas in the Impressionist style. Shortly before his death he destroyed several manuscripts of his unfinished compositions.
WORKS: 3 overtures: *King Lear* (1883), *Götz von Berlichingen* (1884), *Polyeucte* (1891); Symph. in C (Paris, Jan. 3, 1897); *L'Apprenti Sorcier* (May 18, 1897; his most famous work); opera, *Ariane et Barbe-Bleue* (Opéra-Comique, May 10, 1907); a ballet, *La Péri* (Paris, April 22, 1912); *Villanelle* for horn and piano (1906); for piano: Sonata in E-flat minor; *Variations, interlude et finale* on a theme by Rameau; *Prélude élégiaque.* Together with Saint-Saëns he completed Guiraud's opera *Frédégonde.*
BIBLIOGRAPHY: O. Séré, *Musiciens français d'aujourd'hui* (1911; revised ed. Paris, 1921); G. Samazeuilh, *Paul Dukas* (Paris, 1913); G. Jean-Aubry, *La Musique français d'aujourd'hui* (1916). V. d'Indy, *E. Chabrier et Paul Dukas* (1920); A. Cœuroy, *La Musique française moderne* (1922); A. Cortot, *La Musique française de piano;* I. Schwerke, "Paul Dukas," *Musical Quarterly* (1928); G. Samazeuilh, *Paul Dukas musicien français* (Paris, 1936); Dukas issue of the *Revenue Musicale* (May-June 1936). See also *Les Écritis de Paul Dukas sur la musique* (Paris, 1948).

Duke, John, American pianist and composer; b. Cumberland, Maryland, July 30, 1899. He studied at the Peabody Cons. in Baltimore with G. Strube (composition) and H. Randolph (piano); later studied in Europe with Schnabel and Nadia Boulanger. From 1923 to 1967 he taught piano at Smith College.
WORKS: String Trio (1937); Concerto for Piano and Strings (1938); *Carnival Overture* (1941); Piano Trio (1943); 1-act opera, *Captain Lovelock* (N.Y., Feb. 20, 1956); String Quartet (1969); *6 Song Settings of Emily Bronte's Poems* (1970); many songs.

Duke, Vernon. See **Dukelsky, Vladimir**

Dukelsky, Vladimir (pen name as composer of light music: **Vernon Duke**), versatile composer of both 'serious' and popular music; b. Oct. 10, 1903, in the railroad station of the village Parfianovka (during his mother's trip to Pskov); d. Santa Monica, Calif., Jan. 16, 1969. He was a pupil at the Kiev Cons. of Glière and Dombrovsky; left Russia in 1920 and went to Turkey, coming to the U.S. shortly afterward; later lived in Paris and London; settled in N.Y. in 1929 (naturalized 1936); lieutenant in Coast Guard (1939–44); went back to France (1947–48), but then returned to U.S. to live in N.Y. and Hollywood. He began to compose at a very early age; was introduced to Diaghilev, who commissioned him to write a ballet *Zéphyr et Flore,* the production of which put Dukelsky among the successful group of ballet composers. Another important meeting was with Koussevitzky, who championed Dukelsky's music in Paris and in Boston. In the U.S. Dukelsky began writing popular music; many of his songs, such as *April in Paris,* have enjoyed great popularity. At George Gershwin's suggestion, he adopted the name Vernon Duke for popular music works; in 1955 he dropped his full name altogether, and signed both his serious and light compositions as Vernon Duke.
WORKS: FOR THE STAGE: *Zéphyr et Flore* (Paris, Jan. 31, 1925); *Demoiselle Paysanne,* opera in 2 acts (1928); *Le Bal des blanchiseuses,* ballet (Paris, Dec. 19, 1946); *Souvenir de Monte Carlo,* ballet (1949–56); FOR ORCH.: Piano Concerto (1924; not orchestrated); 3 symphonies (No. 1, Paris, June 14, 1928; No. 2, Boston, April 25, 1930; No. 3, Brussels Radio Orch., Oct. 10, 1947); *Ballade* for piano and small orch. (1931); *Dédicaces,* for soprano, piano, and orch. (Boston Symph., Dec. 16, 1938); Violin Concerto (Boston, March 19, 1943); Cello Concerto (Boston, Jan. 4, 1946); *Ode to the Milky Way* (N.Y., Nov. 18, 1946); CHORAL MUSIC: *Dushenka,* duet for women's voices and chamber orch. (1927); *Epitaph* (on the death of Diaghilev), for soprano solo, chorus and orch. (Boston Symph., April 15, 1932); *The End of St. Petersburg,* oratorio (Schola Cantorum, N.Y., Jan. 12, 1938); *Moulin-Rouge,* for mixed chorus (1941); CHAMBER MUSIC: Trio (Variations) for Flute, Bassoon and Piano (1930); Etude for Bassoon and Piano (1932); *Capriccio Mexicano,* for violin and piano (1933); *3 Pieces* for woodwind (1939); Violin Sonata (1949); String Quartet (1956); SONGS: *The Musical Zoo* (20 songs to Ogden Nash's lyrics, 1946); *A Shropshire Lad,* song cycle (1949); FOR PIANO: Sonata (1927); *Surrealist Suite* (1944); *Souvenir de Venise* (1948); *Serenade to San Francisco* (1956). He wrote songs in the following musical comedies: *The Show is On, Garrick Gaieties, Walk a Little Faster, Three's a Crowd, Americana, Ziegfeld Follies, Cabin in the Sky,* etc.; added 2 ballets

and several songs to *Goldwyn Follies,* unfinished film score by George Gershwin (1937). He published an amusing autobiography, *Passport to Paris* (Boston, 1955) and a polemical book *Listen Here! A Critical Essay on Music Depreciation* (N.Y., 1963). See Igor Stravinsky, "A Cure for V.D.," in the unperiodical magazine *Listen* (Sept. 1964), a curiously undignified polemical incursion.

Dulcken, Ferinand Quentin, pianist and composer; b. London, June 1, 1837; d. Astoria, L.I., Dec. 10, 1901. He was the son of **Luise Dulcken,** and nephew of **Ferdinand David**; was a pupil of Moscheles and Gade at the Leipzig Cons.; also received encouragement from Mendelssohn. He subsequently taught at the Warsaw Cons., and also at Moscow and St. Petersburg; made many concert tours in Europe as pianist with Wieniawski, Vieuxtemps, and others. In 1876 he emigrated to America and gave concerts with Reményi; settled in N.Y. as teacher and composer. He publ. nearly 400 piano pieces of the salon type and also some vocal works.

Dulcken (*née* **David**), **Luise,** pianist; sister of **Ferdinand David**; b. Hamburg, March 29, 1811; d. London, April 12, 1850. She was taught by C. F. G. Schwencke and Wilhelm Grund; played in public (in Germany) when 11 years of age. She married in 1828, and went to London, where she met with brilliant success as a pianist and teacher. Queen Victoria was one of her many pupils.

Dulichius (Dulich, Deilich, Deulich), Philippus, German composer and music theorist; b. Chemnitz, Dec. 18 (baptized 19th), 1562; d. Stettin, March 24 (buried on March 25), 1631. He studied at the Univ. of Leipzig; there is no evidence that he went to Italy and studied with Gabrieli, although this assertion appears in his biographies. He was cantor in Stettin from 1587 until his death.
WORKS (EXCLUSIVELY VOCAL): *Novum opus musicum duarum partium continens dicta insigniora ex evangeliis* (Stettin, 1599); *Centuriae octonum et septenum vocum harmonias sacras laudibus sanctisimae Triados consecratas continentes* (4 parts, Stettin 1607). R. Schwartz published 7 choruses from the *Centuriae* (1896); the complete *Centuriae* are published in the *Denkmäler deutscher Tonkunst* (XXXI, XLI).
BIBLIOGRAPHY: R. Schwartz, "Philippus Dulichius," *Monatsschrifte für Gottesdienst und kirchliche Kunst* (1896).

Du Locle, Camille Théophile Germain du Commun, French librettist; b. Orange, Vacluse, July 16, 1832; d. Capri, Oct. 9, 1903. He was secretary of the Opéra under Perrin's direction; later, director of the Opéra-Comique. He commissioned Bizet to compose *Carmen;* was also instrumental in the preparation of the libretto for Verdi's opera *Aida.*

Dülon, Friedrich Ludwig, blind German flutist; b. Oranienburg, near Potsdam, Aug. 14, 1769; d. Würzburg, July 7, 1826. He was taught by his father (flute) and Angerstein (theory); in 1783 his concert travels began, and extended all over Europe. In 1793–94 he was chamber musician at the St. Petersburg court (gave first concert in St. Petersburg on March 30, 1793); then settled (1823) in Würzburg. He wrote an autobiography: *Dülons des blinden Flötenspielers Leben und Meinungen, von ihm selbst bearbeitet* (Zürich, 2 vols., 1807–08, ed. by Wieland).

Dumesnil, Maurice, French-American pianist; b. Angoulême, Charente, April 20, 1886; d. Highland Park, Michigan, Aug. 26, 1974. He studied at the Paris Cons. with Isidor Philipp, graduating in 1905. He received personal coaching from Debussy in playing Debussy's piano works, and was subsequently considered as an authority on the subject. He published *How to Play and Teach Debussy* (1933); and *Claude Debussy, Master of Dreams* (1940). Apart from his principal occupation as piano teacher, he was also active as conductor in Mexico (1916–20); eventually settled in N.Y.

Dumesnil, René, French writer; b. Rouen, June 19, 1879; d. Paris, Dec. 24, 1967. He studied literature at the Sorbonne; was active as a literary critic. Besides his publications dealing with literature, he wrote a number of books on music.
WRITINGS: *Le Rythme musical* (1921; 2nd augmented ed., 1949); *Le Monde des musiciens* (1924); *Le Don Juan de Mozart* (1927); *Musiciens romantiques* (1928); *Richard Wagner* (1929); *La Musique contemporaine en France* (1930); *Le Livre du disque* (with P. Hemardinquer; 1931); *Histoire illustrée de la musique* (1934); *Portraits de musiciens français* (1938); *La Musique romantique française* (1944); *La Musique en France entre les deux guerres* (Geneva, 1946); *L'Envers de la musique* (Paris, 1949); *Histoire illustrée du théâtre lyrique* (Paris, 1953; received the Grand Prix for musical literature); *Richard Wagner* (Paris, 1954; a much larger work than his first Wagner book of 1929).

Dumitrescu, Gheorghe, Rumanian composer, brother of **Ion Dumitrescu;** b. Oteşani, Dec. 28, 1914. He studied with Cuclin, Perlea and Jora at the Bucharest Cons. (1934–41); was active as a violinist; served as director at the National Theater in Bucharest (1935–46); was composer-counselor for the Armatei artistic ensemble (1947–57); in 1951 was appointed prof. at the Bucharest Cons. His music is marked by a vivacious quality typical of the operetta style.
WORKS: an operetta, *Tarsiţa şi Roşiorul* (1949); 5 operas: *Ion Vodă cel Cumplit* (*Ion Voda the Terrible,* 1955), *Decebal* (1957), *Răscoala* (1959), *Fata cu garoafe* (1961), and *Meşterul Manole* (1969); the oratorios: *Tudor Vladimirescu* (1950), *Griviţa noastră* (1963), *Zorile de aur* (1964), *Din lumea cu dor în cea fără dor* (1966) and *Pămînt dezrobit* (1968); numerous cantatas and other vocal-symphonic works; 4 symphonies: No. 1 (1945); No. 2, *A Republicii,* with chorus (1962); No. 3 (1965); No. 4 (1970); *Poem rustic* for orch. (1939); *Poemul amurgului* for orch. (1941); *Suită pitorească* for orch. (1942); *4 Symphonic Frescoes* (1943); *Suită primaverii* for orch. (1944); Cello Concerto (1947); *Suită cîmpenească* for orch. (1963); 2 piano sonatas (1938, 1939); Viola Sonata (1939); Violin Sonata (1939); Piano Quintet (1940); songs; choruses.

Dumitrescu, Ion, Rumanian composer, brother of **Gheorghe Dumitrescu;** b. Oteşani, June 2, 1913. He studied conducting with Perlea and composition with Cuclin at the Bucharest Cons. (1934–41); was a composer and conductor at the National Theater in Bucharest (1940–47); has taught at the Bucharest Cons. since 1944. He writes in classical forms with undertones of Rumanian folk music.

WORKS: 3 suites for orch. (1938, 1940, 1944); *2 Pieces* for orch. (1940); *Poeme* for cello and orch. (1940); Symph. No. 1 (1948); *Symphonic Prelude* (1952); Concerto for String Orch. (1956); Suite from the film "Muntele Retezat" (1956); *Sinfonietta* (1955–57); Piano Sonata (1938); *Suite în stil vechi* for viola and piano (1939); Piano Sonatina (1940); *2 Pieces* for piano (1942); String Quartet No. 1 (1949; transcribed for string orch., 1961); film music; songs.

Dumler, Martin G., American composer; b. Cincinnati, Dec. 22, 1868; d. there, Oct. 19, 1958. He studied at the Cincinnati College of Music (graduated 1901); was subsequently vice-president of the board of trustees; also president of the Bruckner Society. His compositions are chiefly settings of sacred texts.

Dumont (Du Mont), Henri (Henry), significant Belgian-French composer of motets; b. Villers l'Evèque, near Liège, 1610; d. Paris, May 8, 1684. He served as a chorister at Maestricht, and was ordained priest at Liège; then was organist at St. Paul's Church in Paris (1640–1663); maître de chapelle at the French court (1663–83); concurrently was maître de la musique for the Queen of France (1673–81).

WORKS: *5 Messes Royales en plain-chant* (Paris, 1699; 4th edition, 1701); 5 books of *Meslanges,* containing polyphonic choral works (only books 2 and 3 are extant, published in 1657 and 1661); 5 books of motets in 2, 3 and 4 voices (1652–86). Two of his organ pieces are found in *Les Maîtres français de l'orgue,* edited by F. Raugel (Paris, 1939); 4 motets are reproduced in *Anthologie du motet latin polyphonique en France,* edited by D. Launay (Paris, 1963).

BIBLIOGRAPHY: H. Quittard, *Un Musicien en France au XVIIᵉ siècle, Henri Dumont* (Paris, 1906); A. Gastoué, *Les Messes Royales de Henri Dumont* (Paris, 1912).

Dunayevsky, Isaak, Soviet composer of popular songs; b. Lokhvitza, near Poltava, Jan. 30, 1900; d. Moscow, July 25, 1955. He began to study piano as a child; then entered the Kharkov Cons. and studied violin with Joseph Achron. He devoted himself mainly to popular music; some songs from his operettas and film scores have become famous. At one time he experimented with jazz rhythms. He received many honors from the Soviet government; in 1941 he won the first Stalin Prize for his music to the film *The Circus.*

BIBLIOGRAPHY: L. Danilevitch, *Isaak Dunayevsky* (Moscow, 1947); A. Tchernov, *Isaak Dunayevsky* (Moscow, 1961).

Dunbar, Rudolph, black conductor and composer; b. British Guiana, April 5, 1907. He played as a child in a local military band. In 1919 came to the U.S. and entered the Juilliard School of Music, graduating in 1928. He made his London debut as conductor on April 26, 1942, and in Paris on Nov. 18, 1944.

Duncan, William Edmondstoune, English composer and writer on music; b. Sale, Cheshire, April 22, 1866; d. there, June 26, 1920. He studied at the Royal College of Music with Parry and Stanford; then acted as music critic and correspondent of British and American music magazines. He wrote an opera *Perseus* (1892); a setting of Milton's sonnet *To a Nightingale* for soprano and orch. (1895), etc.; also publ. several books on music: *Schubert* (1905; 2nd ed., 1934; in Spanish, Buenos Aires, 1942); *The Story of Minstrelsy* (1907); *A History of Music* (1908); *The Story of the Carol* (1911); *Encyclopedia of Musical Terms* (1914); *Ultra-Modernism in Music* (1917).

Dunham, Henry Morton, American organist; b. Brockton, Mass., July 29, 1853; d. Brookline, Mass., May 4, 1929. He studied at the New England Cons.; was organist at various churches in and around Boston; taught at the New England Cons. for 52 years (1876–1929). His works include 3 organ sonatas, marches, preludes, fugues, passacaglias, and other organ music; also numerous arrangements. He published: *Organ School* (in 4 books); *A System of Technique for Piano; The Choir Manual; Hymn Music.* His autobiography, *The Life of a Musician, Woven into a Strand of History of the New England Conservatory of Music* was published posthumously (N.Y., 1931).

Dunhill, Thomas Frederick, English composer; b. London, Feb. 1, 1877; d. Scunthorpe, Lincolnshire, March 13, 1946. He entered the Royal Academy of Music in 1893, and studied with Franklin Taylor (piano) and Stanford (theory); in 1905 appointed prof. at Royal Academy of Music; in 1907 he founded the "Concerts of British Chamber-Music," which he conducted until 1916.

WORKS: the operas *The Enchanted Garden* (London, 1927), *Tantivy Towers* (London, Jan. 16, 1931), *Happy Families* (Guildford, Nov. 1, 1933); ballet, *Gallimaufry* (Hamburg, Dec. 11, 1937); *Phantasy* for String Quartet; Piano Quintet; Quintet for Violin, Cello, Clarinet, Horn, and Piano; Quintet for Horn and String Quartet; Piano Quartet; Viola Sonata, 2 violin sonatas; *The Wind among the Reeds,* song cycle for tenor and orch.; violin pieces; compositions for cello. He published: *Chamber Music* (a treatise for students, 1912); *Mozart's String Quartets* (2 vols., 1927); *Sullivan's Comic Operas* (1928); *Sir Edward Elgar* (1938).

Duni, Egidio Romoaldo, Italian composer of opera; b. Matera, Feb. 9, 1709; d. Paris, June 11, 1775. He first studied in the Cons. "della Madonna di Loreto," under Durante; then in the Cons. "della Pietà de' Turchini." His first opera, *Nerone* (Rome, May 21, 1735), was a popular success. He went to London (1737) and Holland (1738); in 1739 he returned to Italy; in 1745 he was maestro di cappella at S. Nicolo di Bari, in Naples; became tutor at the Court of Parma, where, encouraged by the Duke, he began composing French operettas, one of which, *Le Caprice amoureux ou Ninette à la cour* (Parma, 1756) was so well received that Duni decided to try his fortune in Paris, where he brought out light and frivolous stage pieces which suited the prevailing taste; he is regarded by some music historians as a founder of French opéra-bouffe. He wrote about 15 Italian operas, and 20 in French.

Dunkley, Ferdinand (Luis), organist and composer; b. London, July 16, 1869; d. Waldwick, N.J., Jan. 5, 1956. He was a pupil at the Royal Academy of Music of Parry, Bridge, Martin, Gladstone, Sharpe, and Barnet; organist of St. Jude's, London (1885–87) and of St. Aubyn's, London (1888–93). In 1893 he was engaged as Director of Music at St. Agnes' School, Albany, N.Y.; was organist at Temple Sinai, New Orleans (1924–34); in 1934 appointed prof. at Loyola Univ., New Orleans. He made his last public appearance on his 82nd birthday when he gave an organ recital.
WORKS: *The Wreck of the Hesperus,* ballade for soli, chorus, and orch.; the choral works, *Praise the Lord* (1919), *Green Branches* (1919), *God is my strong salvation* (1921), *Street Cries* (1924), *Blessed is the man* (1937); etc.

Dunlop, Isobel, Scottish violinist and composer; b. Edinburgh, March 4, 1901; d. there, May 12, 1975. She studied with Tovey and Dyson; gave concerts presenting her own works.

Dunn, James Philip, American composer; b. New York, Jan. 10, 1884; d. Jersey City, N.J., July 24, 1936. He studied at the College of the City of N.Y. (B.A., 1903); then at Columbia Univ. with MacDowell, and subsequently with Cornelius Rybner. He was then active as teacher and church organist in N.Y. and elsewhere. As a composer, he attracted attention by his symph. poem descriptive of Lindbergh's transatlantic flight *We* (N.Y., Aug. 27, 1927). He also wrote an *Overture on Negro Themes* (N.Y., July 22, 1922), some chamber music and organ pieces.
BIBLIOGRAPHY: John Tasker Howard, *James Philip Dunn* (N.Y., 1925).

Dunn, John, English concert violinist; b. Hull, Feb. 16, 1866; d. Harrogate, Dec. 18, 1940. He received his first instruction from his brother, who was conductor of the Hull Theatre Orch.; then was a pupil at the Leipzig Cons. of Schradieck (violin) and Jadassohn (theory); toured England and Germany. He wrote a violin concerto and a spate of short violin pieces; publ. *Manual of Violin Playing* (London, 1898).

Dunn, John Petri, Scottish pianist and writer on music; b. Edinburgh, Oct. 26, 1878; d. there, Feb. 4, 1931. He studied in London with Matthay; toured Europe as accompanist of Jan Kubelik in 1904; later was professor at the Stuttgart and Kiel Conservatories; 1914, returned to Great Britain; was prof. of music at the Edinburgh Univ. from 1920 until his death.
WRITINGS: *Ornamentation in the Works of Chopin* (London, 1921); *A Student's Guide for Orchestration* (London, 1928); *The Basis of Pianoforte Playing* (London, 1933).

Dunstable (Dunstaple), John, English composer; b. probably at Dunstable, Bedfordshire, between 1380

and 1390; d. Dec. 24, 1453; buried in St. Stephen's Walbrook, London. He was the most important English composer of the early 15th century, rivalling his contemporaries Binchois and Dufay; also astrologer and mathematician. From April 28, 1419, to May 1440 he was canon of Hereford Cathedral and prebendary of Putson Minor; for some time he was in the service of John, Duke of Bedford; the Duke, as Regent of France, represented King Henry V in Paris for a number of years, and probably took his musicians with him. Practically nothing further is known of Dunstable's life. Much of his music is contained in the six MSS discovered by F. X. Haberl in the library of the cathedral of Trent in 1884 ('Trent Codices'). The *Complete Works* are published as vol. VIII of *Musica Britannica,* ed. by M. F. Bukofzer (London, 2d ed., rev., 1970). An examination of these compositions reveals not only the existence of a highly developed art in England early in the 15th century, antedating the full flowering of the Burgundian school (Binchois, Dufay), but also Dunstable's most important contributions to the music of the period in making use of the declamatory motet (in which the rhythm of the spoken word largely governs the musical rhythm) and, apparently, introducing the motet with double structure (which provided the predominant technique of Mass composition in the 15th century).
BIBLIOGRAPHY: C. Stainer, "Dunstable and the Various Settings of *O Rosa Bella,*" *Sammelbände der Internationalen Musik-Gesellschaft* II/1; H. Riemann, *Handbuch der Musikgeschichte* (Leipzig, 1907, II, 1, p. 106 ff.); R. von Ficker, in Adler's *Studien zur Musikwissenschaft* (VII and XI; on the 'Trent Codices'); Ch. Van den Borren, "The Genius of Dunstable," *Proceedings of the Musical Association* (London, 1921); Dom Anselm Hughes, in *Laudate* (1936); M. Bukofzer, *John Dunstable and the Music of His Time,* in the *Proceedings of the Musical Association* (London, 1938); idem, "Über Leben und Werke von Dunstable," *Acta musicologica* 8; idem, "John Dunstable; a Quincentenary Report," *Musical Quarterly* (Jan. 1954); R. L. Greene, "John Dunstable; a Quincentenary Supplement," *Musical Quarterly* (July 1954); E. Kovarik, "A Newly Discovered Dunstable Fragment," *Journal of the American Musicological Society* (Spring 1968).

Dunstan, Ralph, English composer and writer on music; b. Carnon Downs, Truro, Nov. 17, 1857; d. London, April 2, 1933. Mus. Doc. Cambridge, 1892. He edited *A Manual of Music* (1918); *A Cyclopedic Dictionary of Music* (1925); *Composer's Hand Book*; composed church music (21 Masses, anthems), cantatas, and songs for school use.

Duparc, Henri, one of the chief innovators in the domain of French song; b. Paris, Jan. 21, 1848; d. Mont-de-Marsan, Feb. 12, 1933. He studied with César Franck, who regarded him as his most talented pupil. Duparc suffered from a nervous affliction, which forced him to abandon his composition and seek rest in Switzerland. He destroyed the manuscript of his Cello Sonata, and several symphonic suites; of his instrumental works only the symphonic poems *Aux Étoiles* (performed in Paris on April 11, 1874) and *Lénore* (1875) survive, in addition to a suite for 6 piano pieces, *Feuilles volantes*. His songs, to words by Baudelaire and other French poets, are distinguished by exquisitely phrased melodies arranged in fluid modal harmonies; among the best are: *Invitation au voyage, Extase, Soupir, Sérénade, Chanson triste, La Vague et la cloche, Phidilé, Elégie, Testament, Lamento* and *La Vie antérieure.*

BIBLIOGRAPHY: Guy Ferchault, *Henri Duparc* (Paris, 1944); S. Northcote, *The Songs of Henri Duparc* (London, 1949).

Dupin, Paul, prolific French composer; b. Roubaix, Aug. 14, 1865; d. Paris, March 6, 1949. He worked in a factory; then was a menial clerk, but turned to music against all odds; took some lessons with Émile Durand, and then proceeded to compose with fanatic compulsion; somehow he managed to have more than 200 works actually published. Of these, the most original were about 500 canons for 3–12 voices, and 40 string quartets titled *Poèmes;* he wrote much other chamber music; some pretty piano pieces with fanciful titles such as *Esquisse fuguées, Dentelles,* etc.; he even wrote a grand opera, *Marcelle,* which he later hopefully renamed *Lyszelle* for exotic effect. He was much admired in Paris for his determination to succeed, but his works were rarely performed.

BIBLIOGRAPHY: R. Rolland, "Paul Dupin," *Bulletin Français de la S.I.M.* (Dec. 15, 1908); C. Koechlin, "Dupin," *Revue Musicale* (Jan. 1923); P. Ladmirault, *Les Chœurs en canon de Paul Dupin; notice biographique et analytique* (Paris, 1925).

Dupont, Gabriel, French composer; b. Caen, Mar. 1, 1878; d. Vésinet, Aug. 2, 1914. Pupil of his father, the organist at the Cathedral; later, of Gédalge; then of Massenet and Widor at the Paris Cons.; won the 2nd Prix de Rome in 1901. In a contest conducted in 1903 by Sonzogno, the publishing house in Milan, his opera *La Cabrera* was selected, along with 2 others, to be performed and judged by the public (237 works were submitted); it was produced at Milan on May 17, 1904, with great success, thereby winning for Dupont the prize of 50,000 lires; other operas: *La Glu,* libretto by Jean Richepin (Nice, Jan. 24, 1910); *La Farce du Cuvier* (Brussels, March 21, 1912); *Antar* (1913; the outbreak of war in 1914 prevented its planned production, and the opera was staged posthumously at the Paris Opéra on March 14, 1921); also *Les Heures dolentes,* for orch. (4 pieces from a suite of 14 compositions for piano, 1903–05); *Poèmes d'automne,* for piano; the symph. poems *Hymne à Aphrodite,* and *Le Chant de la destinée; Poème* for piano quintet; many other piano pieces; etc.

BIBLIOGRAPHY: M. Léna, "Gabriel Dupont, Souvenirs," and H. Collet, "Antar," in *Le Ménestrel* (March 18, 1921); E. Vuillermoz, "Antar de Gabriel Dupont à l'Opéra," *Revue Musicale* (April 1921); M. Dumesnil, "Gabriel Dupont, Musician of Normandy," *Musical Quarterly* (Oct. 1944).

Dupont, Pierre, French song writer; b. Rochetaillée, near Lyons, April 23, 1821; d. St. Etienne, July 25, 1870. The son of a laborer, and himself uneducated, he attracted attention by his political and rustic ditties, of which he wrote the words, and then sang the airs to Reyer, who put them into shape. His political songs (*Le Pain, Le Chant des ouvriers,* etc.) created such disturbances that he was banished in 1851, but pardoned in 1852. His song, *Les Bœufs,* enjoyed some popularity.

Duport, Jean-Louis, famous French cellist; b. Paris, Oct. 4, 1749; d. there, Sept 7, 1819. Made his public debut at the "Concert Spirituel" (1768); joined his brother, Jean Pierre, in Berlin at the outbreak of the Revolution; returning in 1806, he became musician to Charles IV, the ex-king of Spain, at Marseilles; returned to Paris in 1812, where he was soon regarded as the foremost French cellist. He wrote 6 cello concertos; sonatas, duos, airs variées, 9 nocturnes (for harp and cello), etc. His *Essai sur le doigté du violoncelle et la conduite de l'archet, avec une suite d'exercises,* is still a standard text-book, and practically laid the foundations of modern cello virtuosity.

Duprato, Jules-Laurent, French composer; b. Nîmes, Aug. 20, 1827; d. Paris, May 20, 1892. He studied with Leborne at the Paris Cons.; 1848, won the Prix de Rome. He composed operettas, cantatas, songs, etc.; also recitatives for Hérold's *L'Illusion* and Balfe's *The Bohemian Girl.*

BIBLIOGRAPHY: F. Clauzel, *Jules Duprato* (1896).

DuPré, Jacqueline, English cello player; b. Oxford, Jan. 26, 1945. The Gallic name of her family dates back to the Norman times. Both her parents were musicians; her mother even wrote a ballet score. Jacqueline DuPré studied cello at the Guildhall School of Music in London and later with Paul Tortelier in Paris, in Switzerland with Casals, and with Rostropovitch in Moscow. She owns the famous 'Davidov cello' made by Stradivarius in 1712. She made her American debut in N.Y. on May 14, 1965 with electrifying success, playing Elgar's Cello Concerto, eliciting rapturous reviews from the critics. On June 15, 1967 she married the Israeli pianist **Daniel Barenboim.** In 1972 she was stricken with multiple sclerosis and was obliged to give up her public appearances.

Dupré, Marcel, celebrated French organist and composer; b. Rouen, May 3, 1886; d. Meudon, near Paris, May 30, 1971. He was a pupil of his father **Albert Dupré,** also an organist; he then entered the Paris Cons. (1904) and studied with Guilmant, Diémer, and Widor, winning 1st prizes for organ (1907) and for fugue (1909); in 1914 he won the Grand Prix de Rome for the cantata *Psyché.* He was interim organist at Notre-Dame in 1916; in 1920 he gave at the Paris Cons. a cycle of 10 recitals of Bach's complete organ works, playing from memory. On Nov. 18, 1921, he made his N.Y. debut, followed by a transcontinental tour of 94 recitals given in 85 American cities; a second U.S. tour in 1923 included 110 concerts; he made his tenth tour of the U.S. in 1948. In 1939 he gave 40 concerts in Australia on his world tour. He had, meanwhile, been appointed prof. of organ at the Paris Cons. in 1926; in 1934 he succeeded Widor as organist at St. Sulpice; he became general director of the American Cons. in Fontainebleau in 1947 and was appointed director of the Paris Cons., in succession to Delvincourt,

in 1954. Dupré wrote his first work, the oratorio *La Vision de Jacob*, at the age of 14; it was performed on his 15th birthday at his father's house in Rouen, in a domestic production assisted by a local choral society. Most of his organ works are products of original improvisations. Thus *Symphonie-Passion*, first improvised at the Wanamaker organ in Philadelphia (Dec. 8, 1921), was written down much later and performed in its final version at Westminster Cathedral, London (Oct. 9, 1924). Similarly, *Le Chemin de la Croix* was improvised in Brussels (Feb. 13, 1931) and performed in a definitive version in Paris the following year (March 18, 1932). Among pre-composed works there are symphonies for organ: No. 1 (Glasgow, Jan. 3, 1929) and No. 2 (1946); Concerto for Organ and Orch. (Groningen, Holland, April 27, 1938, with Dupré as soloist); *Psalm XVIII* (1949); 76 chorales and several a cappella choruses; also numerous "verset-préludes." He is the author of a *Traité d'improvisation à l'orgue* (1925) and *Méthode d'orgue*.
BIBLIOGRAPHY: R. Delestre, *L'Œuvre de Marcel Dupré* (Paris, 1952); B. Gavoty, *Marcel Dupré* (Monaco, 1955).

Duprez, Louis-Gilbert, French tenor; b. Paris, Dec. 6, 1806; d. there, Sept. 23, 1896. His fine boy-voice gained him admission to Choron's Institute; after diligent vocal and theoretical study, he made his debut as Count Almaviva at the Odéon, in 1825. Dissatisfied with the results, he subjected himself to a long course of training in Italy, and in 1836 succeeded Nourrit at the Opéra. He was appointed prof. of lyrical declamation at the Cons. in 1842, but resigned in 1850 to establish a vocal school of his own, which flourished. He published the vocal methods, *L'Art du chant* (1845) and *La Mélodie, études complémentaires vocales et dramatiques de l'Art du chant* (1846); also wrote *Souvenirs d'un chanteur* (1880).
BIBLIOGRAPHY: A. A. Elwart, *Duprez, sa vie artistique* (Paris, 1838).

Dupuis, Albert, outstanding Belgian composer; b. Verviers, March 1, 1877; d. Brussels, Sept. 19, 1967. He studied piano, violin and flute at the Music Academy in Verviers; later entered the classes of Vincent d'Indy at the newly created Schola Cantorum in Paris (1897); returned to Belgium in 1899 and later won the Belgian Prix de Rome with his cantata *La Chanson d'Halewyn* (Brussels, Nov. 25, 1903; arranged and performed as a 3-act opera, Antwerp, Feb. 14, 1914). He became director of the Verviers Cons. in 1907, retiring in 1947. His other operas, the largest body of lyrical works by a Belgian composer, include *Bilitis* (Verviers, 1899), *Jean Michel* (1901–02; Brussels, March 5, 1903), *Martille* (1904; Brussels, March 3, 1905); *Fidélaine* (Liège, 1910), *Le Château de la Grande Bretèche* (Nice, 1913), *La Passion* (Monte Carlo, April 2, 1916; over 150 performances in Europe), *La Captivité de Babylone* (Biblical drama), *La Barrière* (Verviers, 1920), *La Délivrance* (Lille, 1921), *Le Sacrifice* (Antwerp, 1921), *La Victoire* (Brussels, 1923), *Ce n'était qu'un rêve* (Antwerp, 1935), *Hassan*, oriental fairy tale (Brussels, 1938), *Un Drame sous Philippe II* (Brussels, Jan. 18, 1938); the oratorios: *Les Cloches nuptiales* (1899), *Oedipe à Colone*, and *Psalm 118*; the

ballets: *Rêve d'enfant*, after Schumann (1951), *Au temps jadis* (1952) and *Evocations d'Espagne* (1954); the cantatas: *Vers le progrès, Pour la Paix, La Gileppe*, and a *Cantata jubilaire* for Belgian independence; 2 symphonies (1904, 1922–23); *Fantaisie rhapsodique* for violin and orch. (1906); *Poème Oriental* for cello and orch. (1924); *Hermann et Dorothée*, overture; Cello Concerto (1926); *Epitaphe* for orch. (1929); *Aria* for viola and orch. (1933); Piano Concerto (1940); *Caprice rhapsodique* for orch. (1941); Violin Concerto (1944); *Caprice* for flute and orch.; *Solo de concours* for horn and orch. and for trombone and orch.; *Valse Joyeuse* for orch.; *La Navarraise* for orch.; 2 concertinos for timpani and orch.; Violin Sonata (1904); String Quartet; 2 piano trios; Piano Quartet; *Scherzo* for solo horn; Variations for Solo Horn; *5 Pièces paradoxales* for piano; many other works for piano; choruses; songs; etc. In 1955 he was awarded a prize by the Société des auteurs lyriques de Paris for his creative output.
BIBLIOGRAPHY: J. Dor, *Albert Dupuis* (Liège, 1935).

Dupuis, Sylvain, Belgian conductor; b. Liège, Oct. 9, 1856; d. Bruges, Sept. 28, 1931. Pupil of the Liège Cons., winning the Prix de Rome in 1881; teacher of counterpoint there; conductor of the singing society *La Légia*; established in 1888 the *Nouveaux Concerts Symphoniques*; appointed 1st cond. at Théâtre de la Monnaie in Brussels, 1900, and conductor of the *Concerts Populaires*; from 1911 director of the Cons. at Liège.
WORKS: 2 operas, *Cour d'Ognon* and *Moïna*; 3 cantatas, *La Cloche de Roland, Camoëns*, and *Chant de la Création*; a symphonic poem, *Macbeth*; Concertino for Oboe and Orch.; 2 suites for orch.; pieces for violin; choruses.

Durand, Émile, French composer; b. St.-Brieuc, Feb. 16, 1830; d. Neuilly, May 6, 1903. While still a student at the Paris Cons., he was appointed (1850) teacher of an elementary singing class, and in 1871 prof. of harmony. He publ. *Traité d'harmonie* and *Traité de composition musicale*; also wrote several light operas.

Durand, Marie-Auguste, French organist and publisher; b. Paris, July 18, 1830; d. there, May 31, 1909. Organ pupil of Benoist; in 1849, organist at St. Ambroise, then at Ste.-Geneviève, St.-Roch, and (1862–74) St. Vincent de Paul. He also occupied himself with music criticism and composition (his Chaconne and *Valse* for piano are especially popular). In 1870 he entered into partnership with Schönewerk (acquiring Flaxland's music publishing business), the firm then being known as Durand & Schönewerk; when his son, **Jacques** (b. Paris, Feb. 22, 1865; d. Bel-Ébat, Aug. 22, 1928), replaced Schönewerk in 1891, the title became Durand & Fils. The house is now known as Durand & Cie.; it has made a specialty of publishing works of the outstanding French composers (Joncières, Lalo, Massenet, Debussy, Saint-Saëns, Chausson, Ravel, and many others), and has also brought out French editions of Wagner's *Tannhäuser*, *The Flying Dutchman*, and *Lohengrin*, as well as several editions of old masters, including a complete critical edition of Rameau, ed. by Saint-Saëns.

WRITINGS: by Jacques Durand: *Cours professionel à l'usage des employés du commerce de musique* (2 vols., 1923); *Quelques souvenirs d'un éditeur de musique* (2 vols., 1924-25). *Lettres de Cl. Debussy à son éditeur* (Paris, 1927).

Durante, Francesco, celebrated Italian church composer and noted teacher; b. Frattamaggiore, near Naples, March 31, 1684; d. Naples, Sept. 30, 1755. He studied in Rome with Pitoni and, under the guidance of his uncle, D. Angelo, at the Cons. di Sant' Onofrio, where he taught in 1710-11; then became maestro at the Cons. di Santa Maria di Loreto, and at the Cons. dei Poveri di Gesù Cristo from 1728-39, and again at Sant' Onofrio from 1745 until his death. After Alessandro Scarlatti, and with Leo, Durante ranks as one of the founders and a chief representative of the 'Neapolitan school' of composition. He devoted himself almost exclusively to sacred music, in which the breadth, vigor, and resourcefulness of his style are more in evidence than marked originality. He was a very great teacher; his pupils, Duni, Traetta, Vinci, Jommelli, Piccinni, Guglielmi, Pergolesi, Paisiello, and others, took almost complete possession of the European lyric stage during the latter half of the 18th century. The library of the Paris Cons. contains a rich collection of his works.

WORKS: 13 Masses, and fragments of Masses; 16 psalms, 19 motets, several antiphons and hymns; 12 madrigals; 6 harpsichord sonatas, etc. His *Lamentations of Jeremiah* and a *Pastoral Mass* are in the Vienna Library (in MS). The libraries of the Naples and Bologna Cons. also possess MSS of Durante. Karmrodt of Halle printed a grand Magnificat (with additional accompaniments by Robert Franz); Breitkopf & Härtel published 12 *duetti da Camera;* H. Schletterer ed. a selection of his keyboard pieces; other reprints of keyboard pieces are publ. by A. Diversi in *Arte antica e moderna* (vol. I; 3 studies), F. Boghen in *Antichi maestri italiani* (4 fugues, 3 toccatas), A. Longo in *Biblioteca d'oro* (vol. II; *Aria danzante*), G. Tagliapietra in *Antologia di musica antica e moderna* (vol. XI), M. Vitali in *Composizioni scelte* (vol. II). A. Diversi publ. a 4 voiced *Christe eleison* in his *Biblioteca mus. Sacra.* Concertos for orch. are printed in *Le Pupitre* 26.

BIBLIOGRAPHY: R. Fiammano, "F. Durante," *Musica d'oggi* (Aug.-Sept. 1936); V. de Rubertis, *Dos Bajetes de Francesco Durante, erroneamente interpretados por Fétis y de Nardis* (Buenos Aires, 1947), which reproduces in facsimile Durante's birth registry (confirming the date as March 31, 1684).

Durey, Louis, French composer; b. Paris, May 27, 1888. He studied music with Léon Saint-Requier (1910-14); became known as a member of "Les Six," a group of young French composers dedicated to modern music, the other five being Darius Milhaud, Arthur Honegger, Georges Auric, Francis Poulenc, and Germaine Tailleferre. Durey wrote music fashionable during a wave of anti-Romanticism, proclaiming the need of constructive simplicity in modern dress, with abundant use of titillating discords. Although he

was the oldest of "Les Six," he wrote the least quantity of music; most of his works are in miniature forms. Durey's esthetical code was radically altered in 1936 when he joined the French Communist Party. During the German occupation of France he was active in the Resistance, for which he wrote anti-Fascist songs. In 1948 he was elected Vice-President of the Association française des musiciens progressives; in 1950 he became the music critic of the Paris Communist newspaper *L'Humanité.* He subscribed to the tenets of the Prague Manifesto of 1948 which called upon progressive musicians to initiate a "democratization of musical forms," to abandon artistic individualism and to write music derived from national folksongs. In 1961 he received the Grand Prix de la musique française.

WORKS: *Le Navire* for voice and orch., to words by André Gide (1916); *Le Bestiaire* for voice and 12 instruments, after Apollinaire (1919); *Le Printemps au fond de la mer* for voice and wind instruments, to a text by Jean Cocteau (1920); *L'Occasion,* lyric drama after Mérimée (1928); *Fantaisie concertante* for cello and orch. (1947); *3 Poèmes de Paul Eluard* for voice and orch. (1952); *Trio-Serenade* for Violin, Viola, and Cello, in memory of Béla Bartók (1955); overture, *Île-de-France* (1955); Concertino for Piano, 16 wind instruments, Double Bass and Timpani (1956); *10 Chœurs de métiers* for chorus, 2 flutes, clarinet, violin, celesta, and piano (1957); *3 Polyphonies vocales et intrumentales* for vocal quartet and 8 instruments (1963); *Mouvement symphonique* (1964); *Les Soirées de Valfère* for wind instruments (1964); *Cantate de la rose et de l'amour* for soprano and strings (1965); Sinfonietta (1966); *4 Octophonies* for 8 string instruments (1966); *Dilection* for strings (1969); *Obsession* for wind instruments, harp, double bass and percussion (1970); political cantatas, *Paix aux hommes par millions,* to words by Mayakovsky (1949); *La longue marche,* after Mao Tse-tung (1949); 3 string quartets; numerous solo songs; piano pieces.

BIBLIOGRAPHY: F. Robert, *Louis Durey, L'aîné des Six* (Paris, 1968).

Durkó, Zsolt, Hungarian composer; b. Szeged, April 10, 1934. He studied composition at the Academy of Music at Budapest with Ferenc Farkas (1955-60) and at the Santa Cecilia Academy in Rome with Petrassi (1961-63). Many of his works have scientific connotations, at least in their titles; but some are rooted in Hungarian melorhythmic patterns.

WORKS: *11 Pieces* for string quartet (1962); *Episodi sul tema B-A-C-H* for orch. (1962-63); *Organismi* for violin and orch. (1963-64); *Psicogramma* for piano (1964); *Una Rapsodia Ungherese (A Hungarian Rhapsody)* for 2 clarinets and orch. (1964-65); *Improvisations* for wind quintet (1965); *Dartmouth Concerto* for soprano and chamber orch. (1966); 2 string quartets (1966, 1969); *Fioriture* for orch. (1966); *Altimara* for chorus and orch. (1967-68); *Cantilene* for piano and orch. (1968); *Symbols* for horn and piano (1968-69); *Colloïdes* for flute, piccolo, bassoon, string quartet and 5 alto voices (1969); *Quartetto d'Ottoni* for 2 trumpets, trombone, and tuba or second trombone (1970); Concerto for 12 Flutes and Orch. (1970); *2 Iconographies:* No. 1, for 2 cellos and harpsichord

(1970) and No. 2, for horn and chamber ensemble (1971); *Fire Music* for flute, clarinet, piano and string trio (1970–71); Cantata No. 1 (1971); Cantata No. 2 (1972); *Assonance* for organ (1972); *Halotti beszéd (Funeral Oration),* oratorio (1972); *Colloïdes* for flute, chamber ensemble and 3 contraltos (1975); *Turner Illustrations* for solo violin and 14 instruments (1976); an opera, *Moses* (Budapest, May 15, 1977).

Durme, Jef van. See **Van Durme, Jef**.

Dürrner, Ruprecht Johannes Julius, German conductor and composer; b. Ansbach, Bavaria, July 15, 1810; d. Edinburgh, June 10, 1859. Pupil of Friedrich Schneider at Dessau; from 1831–42, cantor at Ansbach, then studied under Mendelssohn and Hauptmann at Leipzig, and settled in Edinburgh as a conductor and vocal teacher. His choruses and quartets for male voices won great favor.

Duruflé, Maurice, French organist and composer; b. Louviers, Eure, Jan. 11, 1902. He studied organ with Guilmant, Tournemire, and Louis Vierne; took a course in composition with Paul Dukas, graduating with first prizes in all subjects. In 1930 he became organist of the church of St. Etienne-du-Mont in Paris. In 1943 he was appointed prof. of the Paris Cons. He composed a number of sacred works and organ pieces. His best known compositions are a Requiem (1947) and a Mass (1967).

Dushkin, Samuel, American violinist; b. Suwalki, Poland, Dec. 13, 1891; d. N.Y., June 24, 1976. He was brought to America as a child and was adopted by the composer Blair Child who gave him primary musical education. He studied violin with Leopold Auer in N.Y. and later took several lessons with Fritz Kreisler. He made his European debut as a violinist in 1918, and subsequently toured widely in Europe and America. In 1928 he became associated with Stravinsky and helped him in solving the technical problems in the violin part of his Violin Concerto, and was the soloist in the first performance of this work in Berlin on Oct. 23, 1931, with Stravinsky conducting. He also gave the first performance of Stravinsky's *Duo Concertant* for violin and piano, with Stravinsky playing the piano part (Berlin, Oct. 28, 1932). He recounted the details of his collaboration with Stravinsky in his article "Working with Stravinsky" published in the Merele Armitage collection, *Stravinsky* (N.Y., 1936).

Dussek (Dusík), Franz, Bohemian pianist; b. Chotěborky, Bohemia, Dec. 8, 1731; d. Prague, Feb. 12, 1799. He studied with Wagenseil at Vienna; settled in Prague, 1763, winning fame as a teacher and performer; was a close friend of Mozart. He published several sonatas (1773, 1774, 1799), a Piano Concerto; symphonies, concertos, quartets, trios.

Dussek (Dusík), Jan Ladislav, outstanding composer; b. Čáslav (Tschaslau), Bohemia, Feb. 12, 1760; d. St.-Germain-en-Laye, March 20, 1812. At first a boy soprano at the Minorite church, Iglau, he was taught music by Father Špinar, while attending the Jesuit college; was organist at the Jesuit church in Kutten-

berg for 2 years, and while studying theology at Prague Univ. found time to get a thorough musical training so that after graduation he obtained, through Count Männer, his patron, the post of organist at the church of St.-Rimbaut, Mechlin. Thence he went to Bergen-op-Zoom, and (1782) to Amsterdam; then spent a year at The Hague, and in 1783 studied under C. P. E. Bach at Hamburg; won renown as a pianist and as a performer on Hessel's "harmonica" in Berlin (1784) and St. Petersburg, then accepting an appointment from Prince Radziwill, with whom he lived in Lithuania for over a year. He played before Marie Antoinette in 1786, at Paris; soon went to Italy, and returned to Paris in 1788, whence the Revolution drove him to London. Here he married **Sofia Corri,** a singer, in 1792, and undertook a music business with his father-in-law; but his careless habits, and love of luxury and ease, ill fitted him for commercial pursuits; the enterprise failed, and he fled to Hamburg in 1800 to escape his creditors. Here he appears to have stayed about 2 years, giving concerts and teaching. In 1802 he gave a concert at Prague, and paid a visit to his father at Čáslav; he then entered the service of Louis Ferdinand of Prussia, whose heroic death in battle (1806) inspired one of Dussek's finest pieces, *Elégie harmonique* for piano. Afterwards, he was briefly attached to the Prince of Isenburg (1806–8); then went to Paris as chapel master to Prince Talleyrand. Dussek's significance in music history is unjustly obscured; he was a master craftsman; some canonic devices in his piano sonatas are remarkable for their skill; his piano writing had both brilliance and science; there are some idiomatic harmonies that presage Schumann and Brahms. He was a virtuoso at the keyboard; with Clementi he shares the honor of having introduced the "singing touch." A composer of amazing industry, Dussek wrote 12 piano concertos, 14 piano trios, 3 string quartets, a piano quartet, piano quintet (some interchangeable with flute), 53 violin sonatas (some interchangeable with flute), about 40 piano sonatas, 9 sonatas for piano four-hands, a number of sets of variations, dances, etc., for piano, as well as topical pieces on world events (*The Sufferings of the Queen of France; The Naval Battle and Total Defeat of the Dutch Fleet by Admiral Duncan,* etc.). He also wrote an opera, *The Captive* (London, 1798); incidental music to Sheridan's play *Pizarro* (London, 1799); publ. a piano method. His *Collected Works* were publ. in Leipzig in 1813–17 (12 vols.; repr. in 6 vols., N.Y., 1973).

BIBLIOGRAPHY: L. Schiffer, *Johann Ladislaus Dussek: seine Sonaten und seine Konzerte* (Leipzig, 1914; repr. N.Y., 1973); H. Truscott, "Dussek and the Concerto," *Music Review* (Feb. 1955).

Dustmann (*née* **Meyer**), **Marie Luise,** dramatic soprano; b. Aix-la-Chapelle, Aug. 22, 1831; d. Charlottenburg (Berlin), March 2, 1899. Made her debut in Breslau (1849); after this she was engaged at Kassel (under Spohr), at Dresden (1853), Prague (1854), and Vienna (1857). In 1858 she married a book dealer, Dustmann, and adopted her married name professionally.

Dutilleux, Henri, talented French composer; b. Angers, Jan. 22, 1916. He studied at the Paris Cons. with

H. Busser and with Jean and Noël Gallon; won first Grand Prix de Rome in 1938; subsequently was active on the Paris radio. He has developed a modernistic style which incorporates many procedures of Impressionism. His instrumental works have had numerous performances in France, England, and America; his most impressive work is a symphony (Paris, June 7, 1951; also performances in Germany, England, and America). Other works: *Les Hauts de Hurle-Vent*, symph. suite; *Symphonie de danses; Salmacis,* ballet; *Sarabande,* for orch. (1941); Sonatine for Flute and Piano (1943); *La Giole,* for voice and orch. (1944); *La Princesse d'Elide,* incidental music to Molière's play (1946); Piano Sonata (1946–48); *Monsieur de Pourceaugnac,* incidental music to Molière's play (1948); *Le Loup* (Paris, March 18, 1953); Symphony No. 2 (Boston, Dec. 11, 1959); *Cinq métaboles* for orch. (Cleveland, Jan. 14, 1965); *Tout un monde lointain* for cello and orch. (Aix-en-Provence, July 25, 1970); *Timbres, espace, mouvement* for orch. (Washington, D.C., Jan. 10, 1978); chamber music; piano pieces; film music and songs.

Dutoit, Charles, Swiss conductor; b. Lausanne, Oct. 7, 1936. He studied violin, viola, piano and percussion at the Cons. of Lausanne, and continued his studies at the Academy of Music in Geneva. He then took courses at the Accademia Musicale Chigiana in Siena and at the Cons. Benedetto Marcello in Venice; also attended a summer session in conducting at the Berkshire Music Center in Tanglewood, Mass. Returning to Switzerland, he joined the Lausanne Chamber Orch. as violist. He made his debut as conductor with the Bern Symph. Orch. in 1963, and showed his expertise in giving a competent performance of Stravinsky's *Le Sacre du Printemps.* In 1964 he was appointed conductor and assistant music director of the Bern Symph. Orch.; in 1967 became conductor and artistic director of the Radio-Zürich Orch.: at the same time filled in engagements as guest conductor of the Vienna Opera. He then embarked on a worldwide tour conducting in South America, South Africa, Japan, Australia, England, Canada and Israel. In 1975 he was appointed the regular conductor of the Göteborg Orch. in Sweden and in 1977 became music director of the Montreal Symph. Orch., while continuing his guest appearances on the five continents.

Duvernoy, Charles, French clarinetist; b. Montbéliard, 1776; d. Paris, Feb. 28, 1845. He came to Paris in 1810, and was first clarinet at the Théâtre de Monsieur and the Feydeau, retiring in 1824. Till 1802 he was also prof. at the Cons. He wrote several clarinet sonatas and clarinet duets.

Duvernoy, Henri-Louis-Charles, French composer; son of **Charles;** b. Paris, Nov. 16, 1820; d. there, Jan., 1906. Pupil of Halévy and Zimmermann at Paris Cons., in 1848 appointed prof. there. Publ. (with Kuhn) *Nouveaux choix de psaumes et de cantiques* (1848); *Solfège des chanteurs* (1855); *Solfège à changements de clefs* (1857); and *Solfège artistique* (1860); also some 100 light piano pieces.

Duvernoy, Victor-Alphonse, French pianist and composer; b. Paris, Aug. 30, 1842; d. there, March 7, 1907. He was a pupil of Bazin and Marmontel at the Paris Cons., taking the first prize for piano (1855). In 1869 he founded, together with Léonard, Stiehle, Trombetta, and Jacquard, a series of chamber music concerts; he devoted his time otherwise to composing and teaching, and held a professorship in the Cons. For some 11 years, musical critic of the *République française;* Chevalier of the Legion of Honor, and an officer of public instruction.
  WORKS: As a dramatic composer he produced the 3-act opera *Sardanapale* (Liège, 1892); the "scène lyrique" *Cléopâtre* (at the Concerts Colonne), and the 4-act opera *Hellé* (Grand Opéra, 1896). His symph. poem *La Tempête,* produced at the Concerts Colonne, won the City of Paris prize in 1880; he also wrote a ballet, *Bacchus* (1902); an overture, *Hernani;* much piano music.

Duvosel, Lieven, Belgian composer; b. Ghent, Dec. 14, 1877; d. Sint-Martens-Latem, Belgium, April 20, 1956. He studied in Antwerp and Paris; lived for a time in Berlin (where Nikisch and R. Strauss performed his works), later in The Hague and in Haarlem.
  WORKS: His most representative work is the symph. cycle in 5 parts, *Leie:* 1. *De Morgen;* 2. *De Leie;* 3. *De Liefde aan de Leie;* 4. *Kerstnacht (Christmas);* 5. *Het Leieland.* Other compositions: 3 symphonies; the symph. poem, *Den Avond (Evening); Wereldwee (World's Grief);* many cantatas; male and mixed chor.; songs; and the earlier works *Vers la Lumière, La Charité,* and *La Tristesse et la Consolation.*
  BIBLIOGRAPHY: F. van Durme, *Lieven Duvosel* (Antwerp, 1943); E. Collumbien, *Lijst der werken van Duvosel* (Ghent, 1950).

Dux, Claire, soprano; b. Bydgoszcz, Poland, Aug. 2, 1885; d. Chicago, Oct. 8, 1967. She studied voice with Teresa Arkel in Berlin; made operatic debut in Cologne in 1906; 1911–18, member of the Berlin State Opera (debut in *La Bohème* with Caruso); 1912–14, sang at Covent Garden, London; 1918–21, member of the Royal Opera, Stockholm; came to the U.S. in 1921 and joined the Chicago Civic Opera Co. in 1923; toured the U.S.; then retired. She was married to Ch. Swift of Chicago, where she settled.

Dvarionas, Balis, Lithuanian composer; b. Leipaia, June 19, 1904; d. Vilnius, Aug. 23, 1972. He studied at the Leipzig Cons. with Teichmüller (piano) and Karg-Elert (composition). In 1926 he went to Kaunas and taught piano there; 1933 he became prof. at the Lithuanian Cons. in Vilna; also conducted the Lithuanian Philharmonic Orchestra there. Among his works are a Symphony (1947); a Violin Concerto (1948; received a State Prize); 2 piano concertos (1958; 1962); opera, *Dalia* (1959); many choral works. He wrote the music for the national anthem of the Lithuanian Soviet Socialist Republic (1950).

Dvořáček, Jiří, Czech composer; b. Vamberk, June 8, 1928. He studied organ at the Prague Cons. (1943–47); entered the Prague Academy and studied composition with Řídký and Dobiáš (1949–53); in 1953 joined its faculty, becoming a senior lecturer in 1967. He represents a median course of Central European modernism. WORKS: opera, *The Island of Aphrodite* (1967; Dresden, Feb. 13, 1971); Symph. (1953); *Symphonic Suite* for orch. (1958); *Overture* (1958); *Inventions* for trombone, and string orch. or piano (1961); *Concertante Suite* for orch. (1962); *Ex Post*, symph. movement for piano and orch. (1963); *Quattro Episodi*, sinfonietta for orch. (1970); *Sonata capricciosa* for violin and piano (1956); *Meditations for Clarinet* for clarinet and percussion (1964); *3 Miniatures* for 2 trumpets and trombone (1966); *Due per Duo*, 2 rondos for horn and piano (1969); *Dialogues* for flute and piano (1973); Brass Quintet (1973); *April Sketches*, variations for piano (1955); *Etudes*, 3 compositions for piano (1959); *Sonatina di bravura* for piano (1960); choruses; songs.

Dvořák, Antonin, famous Bohemian composer; b. Mühlhausen, Sept. 8, 1841; d. Prague, May 1, 1904. His father, an innkeeper, wished him to enter the butcher's trade; but he, having learned to play the violin from the village schoolmaster, left home at the age of 16 and entered the Prague Organ School, studying under Pitzsch and earning a precarious livelihood as a violinist in a small orchestra. For about a decade (1861–71), he played the viola in the orchestra of the National Theater in Prague. It was not until 1873 that he brought out an important work, a *Hymnus* for mixed chorus and orch., which was performed on March 9 of that year and attracted wide notice; in 1875 he was awarded the Austrian State Prize for Symph. in E-flat (performed in Prague by Smetana in 1874), and he received that stipend repeatedly thereafter. He then devoted himself to composition with increasing success, becoming the most celebrated of Czech national composers. Liszt, Brahms, and Hans von Bülow, by securing performances and publication of his work, did much to obtain for his compositions the vogue they deservedly enjoy. In 1873 Dvořák gave up playing in orchestras, when he was appointed organist at St. Adalbert's Church in Prague. His fame as composer spread and numerous pupils flocked to him; finally, a professorship in composition at the Prague Cons. was offered him. In 1884 he was invited to conduct his *Stabat Mater* in London. It was received with such enthusiasm that in the fall of the same year Dvořák conducted it at the Worcester Festival, and was commissioned to write a new work for the Birmingham Festival of 1885 (*The Spectre's Bride*). The following year (1886) he visited England again to direct his oratorio *St. Ludmila* at the Leeds Festival; in 1891 he was made hon. Mus. Doc. by Cambridge and hon. Dr. Phil. by the Czech Univ. in Prague. In 1892 he accepted an invitation to head the National Cons. in N.Y. It was in America that he wrote his most celebrated work, the Symphony *From the New World* (first performed by the N.Y. Philh., Dec. 15, 1893); the themes seemed to reflect Negro spirituals, but Dvořák denied any conscious design in this approximation. The work, though, by proposing the use of Negro themes—or Negro-like themes—in symphonic music, had an enormous impact on American musical nationalism. He discussed the idea further in an article,

"Music in America," *Harper's New Monthly Magazine* (Feb. 1895), stating that although Americans have accomplished marvels in most fields of endeavor, in music they are decidely backward and are content to produce poor imitations of European music; the way to salvation, he suggests, is in the development of a national style, a style based on the melodies of Negroes and Indians. This proposal was greeted with enthusiasm by one segment of America's musical world, but by another, fearing a musical miscegenation, it was rejected with disdain. The controversy that ensued raged for more than 2 decades. Upon returning to Prague in 1895 he resumed his professorship at the Cons.; was appointed its artistic director in 1901. He was the first musician to be made a life member of the Austrian House of Lords. A composer of singular versatility and fecundity, the most prominent characteristics of his music are an inexhaustible, spontaneous melodic invention, rhythmic variety, free employment of national folk tunes, and an intensity of harmony which, in his finest works, has an electrifying effect, though sometimes bordering on the crude. His musical style was eclectic; the conflicting influences of Brahms and Wagner occasionally effected an inner incompatibility; however, his very lack of startling originality, combined with an uninhibited emotionalism, contributed to the lasting success of his music.

WORKS: OPERAS (all first performed at Prague): *The King and Collier* (op. 14, 1871; Nov. 24, 1874; revised 1874, 1887); *The Blockheads* or *The Pig-Headed Peasants* (op. 17; 1874; Oct. 2, 1881); *Vanda* (op. 25; April 17, 1876); *The Peasant a Rogue* (op. 37; Jan. 27, 1878); *Dimitrij* (op. 64; Oct. 8, 1882; revised 1883, 1894); *The Jacobin* (op. 84; Feb. 12, 1889; revised 1897); *The Devil and Kate* (op. 112; Nov. 23, 1899); *Rusalka* (op. 114; March 31, 1901; Dvořák's best opera; many revivals; very popular in Eastern Europe); *Armida* (op. 115; March 25, 1904).

FOR ORCH.: 7 published symphs.: op. 60, in D (1880); op. 70, in D minor; op. 76, in F (originally op. 24; 1875, 1887); op. 88, in G (1889); op. 95, in E minor (*From the New World*, 1893); in E-flat (originally op. 10, 1873; posthumous); in D minor (originally op. 13, 1874; posthumously, 1912); 2 discarded symphs.: in C minor, *The Bells of Zlonice* (originally op. 3, 1865; discovered in Prague, 1936) and in B-flat (originally op. 4, 1865); the symph. poems *The Watersprite* (op. 107; 1896); *The Midday Witch* (op. 108; 1896); *The Golden Spinningwheel* (op. 109; 1896); *The Wood Dove* (op. 110; 1896); *Heroic Song* (op. 111; 1897); various overtures: *Amid Nature*, op. 91 (1891); *Carnival*, op. 92 (1891); *Othello*, op. 93 (1891–92); etc.; *Slavonic Rhapsodies* (op. 45) and *Dances* (opp. 46, 72); *Romance* for violin and orch., op. 11 (1873); Piano Concerto in G minor, op. 33 (1876); Violin Concerto in A minor, op. 53 (1879–80); Cello Concerto in B minor, op. 104 (1895); other compositions. Choral works: *Stabat Mater*, op. 58 (1876–77); cantata, *The Spectre's Bride*, op. 69 (1884); oratorio, *St. Ludmila*, op. 71 (1885–86; amplified and performed as an opera, *Svatá Ludmila*, Prague, Nov. 30, 1901); Psalm 149, op. 79 (1879, 1887); Mass in D, op. 86 (1887, 1892); Requiem, op. 89 (1890); cantata, *The American Flag*, op. 102 (1892); *Te Deum*, op. 103 (1892); numerous other works.

CHAMBER MUSIC: String Sextet, 3 string quintets, 2 piano quintets, Piano Quartet, 13 string quartets, 5 piano trios, etc. Songs, vocal duets, piano pieces, etc. A complete edition of Dvořák's works under the general editorship of O. Šourek was begun in Prague in 1955 and continued after Šourek's death (1956) by a committee of Czech scholars.

BIBLIOGRAPHY: J. Zubatsky, *Antonin Dvořák, biographische Skizze* (Leipzig, 1886; in English by W. H. Hadow in *Studies in Modern Music*, 2nd series, London, 1895; 2nd ed. 1904); D. G. Mason, *From Grieg to Brahms* (N.Y., 1902); V. Joss, *Antonin Dvořák* (1903); K. Hoffmeister, *Antonin Dvořák* (in English by R. Newmarch, London, 1928); O. Šourek, *Antonin Dvořák* (in Czech, 4 vols., Prague 1916-33; in German as *Dvořák, Leben und Werk*, 1 vol., abridged by Paul Stefan from the original work, Vienna, 1935; in English, N.Y., 1954); O. Šourek, *Dvořáks Werke: Ein vollständiges Verzeichnis in chronologischer, thematischer und systematischer Anordnung* (Berlin, 1917); H. Sirp, *Antonin Dvořák* (Potsdam, 1939); P. Stefan, *Antonin Dvořák* (N.Y., 1941); A. Robertson, *Antonin Dvořák* (London, 1945); J. Van Straaten, *Slavonic Rhapsody, the Story of Antonin Dvořák* (N.Y., 1948); H. Boese, *Zwei Urmusikanten: Smetana, Dvořák* (Zürich, 1955; contains bibl.); J. Burghauser, *Antonin Dvořák: Thematic Catalogue, Bibliography, and Survey of Life and Work* (in Czech, German and English, Prague, 1960); A. Hetschko, *Antonín Dvořák* (Leipzig, 1965); J. Clapham, *Antonín Dvořák: Musician and Craftsman* (N.Y., 1966); Gervase Hughes, *Dvořák: His Life and Music* (N.Y., 1967); I. Spector, "Dvořák's American Period," *Illinois Quarterly* (Feb. 1971); L. Davis, "Dvořák and American Music," in J. Riedel, *A Tribute to Donald N. Ferguson* (Minneapolis, 1972); W. Beyer and E. Kapst, *Antonin Dvořák. Zur Ästhetik seines sinfonischen Schaffens* (Leipzig, 1973); M. Kantor and H. Pinsker, "Musical Expression and Psychopathology," *Perspectives in Biology and Medicine* (Winter 1973). The Dvořák Society of Epsom, England, issues a journal.

Dwight, John Sullivan, American music critic, and editor of *Dwight's Journal of Music;* b. Boston, Mass., May 13, 1813; d. there, Sept. 5, 1893. He graduated from Harvard in 1832, and was one of the founders and most active members of the Harvard Musical Association. After studying for the ministry, he, in 1840, took charge of the Unitarian Church at Northampton, Mass. His literary and socialistic proclivities, however, gained the mastery; he gave up his pastorate, and entered the ill-starred Brook Farm Community as a teacher of German music and the classics. Returning to Boston in 1848, after the failure of the socialistic experiment, he devoted himself to literature, founded the journal in 1852, and remained its editor-in-chief until its discontinuance in 1881. A prominent feature in this periodical were the valuable historical essays of A. W. Thayer. The entire journal is available in reprint (N.Y., 1968). Dwight also published the excellent *Translations of Select Minor Poems from the German of Goethe and Schiller, with Notes.*

BIBLIOGRAPHY: George Willis Cooke, *J. S. Dwight, Brook-Farmer, Editor, and Critic of Music* (Boston, 1898); Cooke's ed. of Dwight's correspon-

dence with George William Curtis (Boston, 1898); Edward N. Waters, "J. S. Dwight, first American Critic of Music," *Musical Quarterly* (Jan. 1935).

Dyer, Louise (Mrs. Louise B. M. Hanson), patroness of music and publisher; b. Melbourne, Australia, July 16, 1890; d. Monaco, Nov. 9, 1962. She established in Monaco an important publishing enterprise, L'Oiseau-Lyre (The Lyre-Bird Press), financing it entirely out of her own resources. The Lyre-Bird Press has issued a great number of unpublished or obscure works of medieval and Renaissance French music.

Dyer-Bennet, Richard, American ballad singer; b. Leicester, England, Oct. 6, 1913; emigrated to the U.S. in 1925; became naturalized citizen, 1935. He studied voice with Cornelius Reid, and guitar playing with José Rey De La Torre. He made his concert debut in N.Y. in 1944; also sang in night clubs. In 1970 he joined the State Univ. of N.Y. at Stony Brook as instructor in theatre arts dept. He acquired popularity mainly as a singer of English and American ballads, but he was also praised for his performance of Schubert song cycles, especially *Die schöne Müllerin* in his own translation under the title "The Lovely Milleress."

Dykema, Peter, American music pedagogue; b. Grand Rapids, Michigan, Nov. 25, 1873; d. Hastings-on-Hudson, N.Y., May 13, 1951. He studied law at the Univ. of Michigan (M.L., 1896); then took lessons in singing and in music theory at the Institute of Musical Art in N.Y. (1911-12); later supplemented his musical education in Germany; returning to America he held numerous teaching positions in high schools in Illinois and Indiana; from 1913-24 was on the faculty of the Univ. of Wisconsin; from 1924-39 was prof. of music education at Teacher's College, Columbia Univ. He published a number of music handbooks for schools, among them: *Twice 55 Community Songs* (6 vols., 1919-27); *School Music Handbook* (1931; revised ed., by Hannah M. Cundiff, Boston, 1955); *Singing Youth* (1935); *Golden Key Orchestral Series* (1937); *Modern Band Training Series* (with N. Church, 1938); *The Teaching and Administration of High School Music* (with K. W. Gehrkens, Boston, 1941).

Dykes, Rev. John Bacchus, English hymn-tune writer; b. Kingston-upon-Hull, England, March 10, 1823; d. in an asylum at Ticehurst, Sussex, Jan. 22, 1876. He was educated at Cambridge, was ordained minor canon and precentor at Durham Cathedral in 1849; took the degree of Mus. Doc. in 1861; in 1862 became Vicar of St. Oswald, Durham. He composed numerous anthems and part-songs.

BIBLIOGRAPHY: J. T. Fowler, *Life and Letters of John Bacchus Dykes* (London, 1897).

Dylan, Bob (real name **Robert Zimmerman**), American folk singer; b. Duluth, Minnesota, May 24, 1941. He adopted the name Dylan out of admiration for the poet Dylan Thomas. Possessed by wanderlust he rode freight trains across the country; played guitar and crooned in the coffee houses of N.Y. He also improvised songs to his own lyrics. His nasalized country-type semi-Western style and his self-haunted soft guitar strumming captured the imagination not only of untutored adolescents but also of certified cognoscenti in search of convincing authenticity. In 1966 he broke his neck in a motorcycle accident which forced him to interrupt his charismatic career for two years. In 1970 he was awarded an honorary doctorate from Princeton Univ., the first such honor given to a popular singer innocent of all academic training. A group of militants in the Students for a Democratic Society adopted the name "Weathermen" after a line from Dylan's song *Subterranean Homesick Blues,* "You don't need a weatherman to know which way the wind blows." The Weathermen claimed credit for several bombings in New York City during 1969 and 1970.

BIBLIOGRAPHY: Daniel Kramer, *Bob Dylan* (N.Y., 1967); Bob Dylan, *Tarantula* (N.Y., 1971).

Dyson, Sir George, English composer; b. Halifax (Yorkshire), May 28, 1883; d. Winchester, Sept. 28, 1964. He studied at the Royal College of Music in London; was its musical director from 1937-1952. He was knighted in 1941. His works include a Symphony (1937), a Violin Concerto (1943), an oratorio, *Quo Vadis* (1949); Suite for Small Orch.; *3 Rhapsodies* for string quartet; piano pieces; numerous pedagogic pieces and songs. His cantata *The Canterbury Pilgrims,* to words modernized from Chaucer's *Canterbury Tales* is his best known work; the overture to it was extracted in 1946, and performed separately under the title *At the Tabard Inn.* He further composed numerous sacred choruses; published the books *The New Music* (1924); *The Progress of Music* (1932), and a candid autobiography, *Fiddling While Rome Burns; A Musician's Apology* (London, 1954).

Dzegelenok, Alexander, Russian composer; b. Moscow, Aug. 24, 1891; d. there, Jan. 31, 1969. He studied at the Philharmonic Institute in Moscow with Koreshchenko. He composed an orchestral suite *Egypt;* also *Hiawatha* for voice and instruments; piano pieces and songs.

Dzerzhinsky, Ivan, Russian composer; b. Tambov, April 9, 1909. He studied composition with Boris Asafiev at the Leningrad Cons. (1932-34); then dedicated himself to the task of forming a distinctive style of Soviet opera according to the tenets of Socialist Realism. Possessing a facile gift of flowing folklike melody he produced a romantically patriotic opera *Quiet Flows the Don,* to a libretto from the novel by the Soviet writer Sholokhov; its production in Leningrad, on Oct. 22, 1935, was extremely successful, and became a model of the genre after Stalin personally congratulated him on his achievement. However, a sequel to this opera, *Soil Upturned* (Moscow, Oct. 23, 1937) was less successful. There followed the operas *The Tempest* (after Ostrovsky, 1940); *The Blood of the People* (Leningrad, Jan. 21, 1942); *The Blizzard* (after Pushkin, 1946); *Nadezhda Svetlova* (Orenburg, Sept. 8, 1943); and *A Man's Destiny* (Moscow, Sept. 30, 1961). He further wrote 3 piano concertos (1932, 1934, 1945); numerous piano pieces and songs.

BIBLIOGRAPHY: O. M. Tompakova, *Essays on the Life and Work of Ivan Dzerzhinsky* (Lenigrad, 1964).

E

Eames, Emma, famous soprano; b. of American parentage in Shanghai, China, Aug. 13, 1865; d. N.Y., June 13, 1952. Her mother, who was her first teacher, took her to America as a child; she then studied with Clara Munger in Boston and with Mme. Marchesi in Paris. She made her operatic debut at the Grand Opéra, March 13, 1889, as Juliette in Gounod's *Roméo et Juliette*. She subsequently sang in Covent Garden, London, and on Nov. 9, 1891 made her debut at the Metropolitan Opera House, N.Y., as Elsa in *Lohengrin*. She remained with the Metropolitan Opera until 1908, appearing as Marguerite in *Faust*, Desdemona in *Otello*, Elisabeth in *Tannhäuser*, Aida, Tosca and Donna Anna in *Don Giovanni*. From 1923 to 1936 she made her home intermittently in Paris and Bath, Maine; in 1936 she settled in N.Y., where she remained until her death. She received the Jubilee Medal from Queen Victoria, and was decorated by the French Academy with the order of Les Palmes académiques. Her emotional life was turbulent; she married the painter Julian Story in 1891 but they were separated in the midst of a widely publicized scandal; in 1911 she married the baritone **Emilio de Gogorza,** but left him too. She publ. an autobiography, *Some Memories and Reflections* (N.Y., 1927).

Eames, Henry Purmort, American pianist and music educator; b. Chicago, Sept. 12, 1872; d. Claremont, Calif., Nov. 25, 1950. After completing preliminary music education in the U.S., he went to Europe where he took piano lessons with Clara Schumann and Paderewski; after a career as a concert pianist, he devoted himself to teaching; was on the faculty at the Univ. of Nebraska (1898–1908), and eventually at the American Cons. in Chicago (1923–28). He then settled in California where he taught at Scripps College, Claremont. He was also a composer; wrote for chorus, voice and piano.

Earhart, Will, American music educator; b. Franklin, Ohio, April 1, 1871; d. Los Angeles, April 23, 1960. From 1900 to 1912 he was school supervisor in various localities in Ohio and Indiana; in 1912 he went to Pittsburgh where he lectured on music education at the Univ. of Pittsburgh and at the Carnegie Institute of Technology. He published a number of books on musical education, among them: *Music in the Public Schools* (1914); *Music in Secondary Schools* (with O. McConathy; 1917); *Music to the Listening Ear* (1932); *The Meaning and Teaching of Music* (1935); and *Elements of Music Theory* (with Ch. N. Boyd; 2 vols. 1938); edited *Art Songs for High Schools* (1910); *The School Credit Piano Course* (with others; 1918).
BIBLIOGRAPHY: C. V. Buttelman, ed., *Will Earhart: Teacher, Philosopher, Humanitarian* (Washington, 1962).

Easdale, Brian, English composer; b. Manchester, Aug. 10, 1909; studied at the Royal College of Music in London (1925–33). He became interested in theatrical music; wrote 3 operas, *Rapunzel* (1927), *The Corn King* (1935), and *The Sleeping Children* (1951); incidental music to Shakespeare's plays and several film scores, of which the most successful was *The Red Shoes*. Other works include a Piano Concerto and several orchestral pieces of a descriptive nature (*Dead March; The Phoenix; Bengal River*, etc.); also a *Cavatina* for brass ensemble (1961).

East (Easte, Este), Thomas, English music printer and publisher of Elizabethan madrigals; b. London, c.1535; d. there, Jan. 1609. He received his license as printer in 1565; his first musical publication was Byrd's collection *Psalmes, Sonets and Songs of Sadnes and Pietie* (1587); he was also the assignee of Byrd's patent for printing music paper and musical compositions. In 1592 he brought out *The Whole Booke of Psalmes, with their wonted tunes as they are sung in Churches, composed in four parts*, containing harmonizations by Allison, Blancks, Cavendish, Cobbold, Dowland, Farmer, Farnaby, Hooper, Johnson, and Kirbye; republished in 1594 and 1604; reprinted in score by the Musical Antiquarian Society (1844). This collection is of historical significance, for it was the first to be printed in score rather than in separate part-books; also for the first time, the tunes were designated by specific names, such as "Kentish," "Cheshire," etc. Other works printed by East are Yonge's *Musica Transalpina* (1588), Byrd's *Songs of Sundrie Natures* (1589), Watson's *Madrigals* (1590), Byrd's *Cantiones Sacrae* (2 books, 1589, 1591), Morley's *Canzonets* (1593), Mundy's *Songs and Psalmes* (1594), Kirbye's *Madrigals* (1596), Wilbye's *Madrigals* (1598), Dowland's *Ayres* (1600), Bateson's *Madrigals* (1603), Michael East's *Madrigals* (1604), Pilkington's *Songs or Ayres* (1604), Byrd's *Gradualia* (1605), Youll's *Canzonets* (1607). East's presumed son **Michael East** (c.1580–c.1648) was a composer; his set of madrigals was publ. by Thomas East in 1604. He served as organist at Lichfield Cathedral; received the degree of B. Mus. at Cambridge (1606); he published six sets of vocal pieces (madrigals, anthems, etc.) and a set of instrumental works (1638).
BIBLIOGRAPHY: F. Kidson, *British Music Publishers* (London, 1900); E. H. Fellowes, *The English Madrigal Composers* (London, 1921; 2nd ed., 1948).

Eastman, George, American industrialist; b. Waterville, N.Y., July 12, 1854; d. (suicide, when he learned he had cancer), Rochester, March 14, 1932. Eastman made important and far-reaching contributions to the cause of education; invested immense sums in scientific institutions, particularly the Univ. of Rochester, which includes the Eastman Theater and School of Music (one of the leading music schools of the U.S.). This alone he endowed with $3,500,000
BIBLIOGRAPHY: Carl W. Ackerman, *George Eastman* (1930).

Easton, Florence, operatic soprano; b. Middlesbrough-on-Tees, Yorkshire, Oct. 24, 1884; d. N.Y., Aug. 13, 1955. She studied singing at the Royal Academy of Music in London and with Elliott Haslam in Paris. Made her debut at Covent Garden in 1903; in 1906 she married the tenor **Francis Maclennan** (divorced in 1929); her second husband was Stanley Rogers. She toured the U.S. with the Savage Grand

Opera; then was engaged at the Berlin Opera (1907–13) and at Hamburg (1913–15). She was with the Chicago Opera (1915–17); from 1917 to 1929 she was a member of the Metropolitan Opera Company; after a sojourn in Europe, she reappeared meteorically on leap-year day in 1936 at the Metropolitan Opera as Brünnhilde in *Die Walküre.*

Eaton, John, American composer; b. Bryn Mawr, Pa., March 30, 1935. He received his A.B. and M.F.A. degrees from Princeton Univ., where he studied composition with Milton Babbitt, Edward Cone and Roger Sessions; subsequently held three American Prix de Rome awards and two Guggenheim grants. In his works he avails himself of all resources of modern music, including serial techniques, microtones and electronic media. In several of his scores he makes use of the Syn-Ket (a portable electronic synthesizer built by the Roman sound engineer named Ketoff) and of the Syn-Mill (an electric generator based on a design of Robert Moog and built specially for Eaton by Edward Miller).

WORKS: three operas: *Ma Barker* (1957), *Heracles* (Turin, Italy, Oct. 10, 1968); *Myshkin,* opera after Dostoyevsky's novel, *The Idiot* (Bloomington, Indiana, April 23, 1973); *Holy Sonnets of John Donne* for orch. and soprano solo (1957); Piano Variations (1958); Trumpet Sonata (1958); String Quartet (1959); *3 Epigrams* for clarinet and piano (1960); *Concert Music for solo clarinet* (1961); *Concert Piece* for magnetic tape and jazz ensemble (1962); *Soliloquy* for Syn-Ket (1967); *Vibrations* for woodwinds with quarter-tone scordatura (1967); *Thoughts on Rilke* for solo soprano, Syn-Ket and Syn-Mill (1967); *Concert Piece* for Syn-Ket and orch. (Berkshire Music Center, Tanglewood, Mass., Aug. 9, 1967); Duet for Syn-Ket and Moog Synthesizer (1968); Mass for soprano, clarinet, 3 Syn-Kets, Moog synthesizer and Syn-Mill, commissioned by the Koussevitzky Foundation, and first performed at the Coolidge concert at the Library of Congress in Washington on Oct. 31, 1970.

Eaton, Louis, American violinist, b. Waltham, Mass., Feb. 24, 1872; d. Hartford, Conn., May 4, 1927. He studied violin with Loeffler and Bernard Listemann and piano with **Jessie Downer** (b. Middlebury, Vermont, Nov. 17, 1872; d. Hartford, Conn., Nov. 22, 1936) whom he married in 1899. In 1915 they settled in Hartford as teachers. With the cellist Arthur Hadley, they formed the Downer-Eaton Trio, which presented first American performances of a number of chamber works.

Ebel, Arnold, German composer and choral conductor; b. Heide, Holstein, Aug. 15, 1883; d. Berlin, March 4, 1963. He studied at Berlin Univ.; also took private lessons with Max Bruch; from 1909 was active in Berlin as organist, choral conductor, and teacher; served as president of the German Composers' Association (1920–33 and again from 1949). He wrote numerous piano pieces and songs; also a *Sinfonietta giocosa* for orch.

Eben, Petr, Czech composer; b. Žamberk, Jan. 22, 1929. He studied composition with Bořkovec at the Prague Academy (1948–54); upon graduation he taught musicology at the Charles Univ. in Prague. In his own composition he follows the traditions of Central European classicism, with modern techniques adding zest to old forms.

WORKS: Organ Concerto, subtitled *Symphonia Gregoriana* (1954); Piano Concerto (1961); *Vox clamantis,* symph. movement for 3 trumpets and orch. (1969); an oratorio, *Apologio Sokratus,* based on the Greek text of Plato's defense of Socrates, for alto, baritone, children's chorus, mixed chorus, and orch. (1961–67); 2 cantatas: *The Lover's Magic Spell,* small cantata for solo female voice and chorus (1957) and *Bitter Earth* for baritone, chorus and organ (1959); *Ballads* for soloists, chorus and orch. (1956); Oboe Sonata (1950); *Suite Baladica* for cello and piano (1955); *Duetti* for 2 trumpets (1956); *Sonatina semplice* for violin or flute, and piano (1957); *Ordo Modalis* for oboe and harp (1964); Wind Quintet (1965); *Fantasia Verpertina* for trumpet and piano (1967); *Variations on a Chorale* for brass quintet (1969); Trio for Oboe, Bassoon and Piano (1970); *Okna* (*Windows*) for trumpet and organ (1976); Piano Sonata (1950); *Love and Death* for chorus to folk texts (1958); *Ubi Caritas et Amor,* antiphon (1964); songs, among them *Písně nelaskavé* (*Loveless Songs*) for contralto and 6 violas (1963).

Eberhardt, Siegfried, German violin pedagogue; b. Frankfurt, March 19, 1883; d. Zwickau, June 29, 1960; son of the violinist and pedagogue **Goby Eberhardt** (1852–1926). He studied violin with Dessau at the Stern Cons. in Berlin, and then with Serato; was teacher of violin at the Stern Cons. (1908–35); then lived in Halle and Lübeck; in 1953 moved to Zwickau.

WRITINGS: *Der beseelte Violinton* (with Carl Flesch; Dresden, 1910; 4 eds.; also in English); *Treffsicherheit auf der Violine* (1911; 22 eds.; also in English, French, and Swedish); *Virtuose Violintechnik* (1920); *Paganinis Geigenhaltung* (1921); *Die Lehre der organischen Geigenhaltung* (1922); *Der Körper in Form und Hemmung* (Munich, 1926); *Wiederaufstieg oder Untergang der Kunst der Geigen* (1956).

BIBLIOGRAPHY: K. Schröter, *Flesch-Eberhardt, Naturwidrige oder natürliche Violintechnik?* (1924).

Eberl, Anton Franz Josef, Austrian pianist and composer; b. Vienna, June 13, 1765; d. there, March 11, 1807. On Feb. 27, 1787, he produced the opera *La Marchande de modes;* this was followed by the opera *Die Zigeuner* (1793). His symphonies and piano music were praised by Mozart and Gluck. He made a concert tour with Mozart's widow in 1795; lived in St. Petersburg from 1796 to 1799; revisited Russia in 1801; gave concerts there on Dec. 8, 15, and 28, 1801, presenting the first performances in Russia of Haydn's *The Creation;* returned to Vienna early in 1802; traveled through Germany in 1806. Besides 3 more operas, he wrote a cantata, symphonies, piano concertos, much chamber music, many piano works (especially sonatas), songs, etc.

BIBLIOGRAPHY: Fr. J. Ewens, *Anton Eberl* (Dresden, 1927; with thematic catalogue); R. Haas, "Anton Eberl," *Mozart-Jahrbuch 1951* (Salzburg, 1953).

Eberlin (Eberle), Johann Ernst, German composer; b. Jettingen, Bavaria, March 27, 1702; d. Salzburg, June

19, 1762. From 1729, cathedral organist and choirmaster at Salzburg; from 1749, court Kapellmeister to the Prince-Archbishop there.

WORKS: *Der Blutschwitzende Jesus* (in *Denkmäler der Tonkunst in Österreich* 55[28.i]; *XI Toccate e Fughe per l'organo* (Augsburg, 1747; several reprints); fugues and toccatas (in Commer's *Musica sacra*); 2 motes (publ. by Schott); 2 sonatas (publ. by Haffner); 5 pieces in L. Mozart's *Der Morgen und der Abend* (Augsburg, 1759). In MS: 13 oratorios in Regensburg (Proske's Library); an offertory and Miserere (Berlin Library); a volume of organ pieces (Royal Institute for Church Music, Berlin); other works in the Vienna Library (a 4-voiced Mass with organ motets, cantatas, etc.), the Munich Library (18 Masses and other pieces), and in the libraries of Kremsmünster and Salzburg (37 Masses with orch., 75 oratorios, 43 psalms with orch., 3 Te Deums, etc.).

BIBLIOGRAPHY: Robert Haas, "Eberlins Schuldramen und Oratorien," in *Studien zur Musikwissenschaft* (1921); C. Schneider, *Geschichte der Musik in Salzburg* (Salzburg, 1935); K. A. Rosenthal, "Mozart's Sacramental Litanies and Their Forerunners," *Musical Quarterly* (Oct. 1941).

Eberwein, Carl, German composer; b. Weimar, Nov. 10, 1786; d. there, March 2, 1868. He was a member of a musical family; after a study of general subjects at the Weimar Hochschule he received an appointment as a court musician at the age of 16. He then studied with Zelter in Berlin; returning to Weimar, he held the posts of chamber musician (1810–18); music director of the Weimar town church (1818–26); and conductor of Weimar opera (1826–49). He was a friend of Goethe, who often mentions him, and for whom he composed some songs.

WORKS: the operas *Die Heerschau, Der Graf zu Gleichen,* and *Der Teppichhändler;* several cantatas written for various state occasions; some chamber music, and a great number of songs with piano accompaniment.

BIBLIOGRAPHY: W. Bode, *Goethes Schauspieler und Musiker* (1912, with autobiographical sketch of Eberwein); H. J. Moser, *Goethe und die Musik* (Leipzig, 1949).

Eberwein, Traugott Maximilian, German composer, brother of **Carl Eberwein**; b. Weimar, Oct. 27, 1775; d. there, Dec. 2, 1831. He played the violin in the Weimar court orch. as a very young man; like his brother, he was a protégé of Goethe, and wrote two operas, *Claudine von Villa Bella* (1815) and *Der Jahrmarkt von Plundersweilen* (1818), to texts by Goethe; he further composed church music and instrumental concertos.

Eccard, Johannes, eminent German composer; b. Mühlhausen, 1553; d. Berlin, 1611. He was a pupil (1571–74) of Orlandus Lassus in Augsburg; director of J. Fugger's private orch. at Augsburg (1577); in 1578 he moved to Königsberg, as a member of the Prussian chapel; in 1580 became its assistant conductor, and in 1604, chief conductor. In 1608 he was called to Berlin to serve as court musician to the Elector. He was an important composer of sacred music.

WORKS: published (with Burgk): *Odae sacrae* (1574) and *Crepundia sacra* (in 2 parts, 1578); his own works include *Neue deutsche Lieder mit 4 und 5 Stimmen,* dedicated to J. Fugger (1578); *Neue geistliche und weltliche Lieder mit 4 und 5 Stimmen* (1589: ed. in score by R. Eitner, in *Publikationen älterer Musik,* vol. 25); *Geistliche Lieder auf den Choral mit 5 Stimmen,* 51 songs (2 parts, 1597; ed. by Teschner and Fr. von Baussnern, 1928); *Preussische Festlieder auf das ganze Jahr für 5–8 Stimmen* (posthumous in 2 parts, 1642–44; ed. by Teschner, 1858); also occasional songs (many in the Königsberg Library).

BIBLIOGRAPHY: C. von Winterfeld, *Der evangelische Kirchengesang* . . . , I and II; A. Mayer-Reinach, "Zur Geschichte der Königsberger Hofkapelle," *Sammelbände der internationalen Musik-Gesellschaft;* H. E. Brinckmann, "Neue Forschungen zum Leben der grossen Mühlhauser Musiker," in the *Armin Tille Festschrift* (Weimar, 1930); H. Heckmann, "Johannes Eccards Gelegenheitskompositionen," in M. Ruhnke, ed. *Festschrift Bruno Stäblein* (Cassel, 1967).

Eccles, Henry, English violinist; b. London, c.1670; d. Paris, c.1742; brother of **John Eccles;** a member of the King's Band (1689–1710), and then of the French court orch. In 1720 he published under his own name 12 violin solos, adaptations of works by Giuseppe Valentini and others.

Eccles, John, English violinist and composer; b. London, c.1668; d. Kingston, Surrey, Jan. 12, 1735. He was the son and pupil of the violist **Solomon Eccles** (1618–1683). He became a member of the Queen's Band in 1694, and Master of it in 1700. He was active as a composer for the theater from about 1681; in 1694 wrote music for *Don Quixote* (with Purcell); in 1700, for Congreve's *The Judgment of Paris* and *The Way of the World;* 1710, publ. a collection of his own songs (about 100), which enjoyed wide popularity. He also publ. 3 volumes of 'Theatre Music' (c.1700). In all, he wrote music for 12 masques and 56 pieces of incidental music for the stage.

BIBLIOGRAPHY: John Jeffreys, *The Eccles Family* (Enfield, 1951).

Echaniz, José, Cuban pianist; b. Havana, June 4, 1905; d. Pittsford, N.Y., Dec. 30, 1969. He studied piano in Havana; appeared as soloist with major American orchestras, receiving praise for his brilliant interpretations. In 1944 he joined the staff of the Eastman School of Music in Rochester. He also served as conductor of the Grand Rapids Symph. Orchestra.

Eckard (Eckardt, Eckart), Johann Gottfried, German composer of keyboard music; b. Augsburg, Jan. 21, 1735; d. Paris, July 24, 1809. He was a copper engraver by profession and learned music in his spare time. In 1758 he was taken to Paris by the piano manufacturer J. A. Stein, and remained there. He acquired a great facility as pianist, and gave successful concerts in Paris. In the preface to his album of six sonatas he states that his task was to compose music suitable for any keyboard instrument, but the indications of dynamics in the manuscript show that he had mainly the then novel piano in view. Mozart admired Eckard's works, and there are traits in Mozart's keyboard music of the Paris period that may be traced to Eckard's usages. A complete edition of Eckard's works for piano, ed. by Eduard Reeser and annotations by J. Ligtelijn, has been publ. (Amsterdam, 1956).

Eckardt, Hans, German musicologist, authority on Japanese music; b. Magdeburg, Oct. 10, 1905; d. Berlin, Feb. 26, 1969. He studied philology in Leipzig, Berlin, Paris, and Heidelberg (1925–29); musicology with Sachs, Hornbostel, and Schünemann. From 1932 to 1945 he was in Kyoto, Japan, as director of the Japanese-German Research Institute of Cultural History. In 1948 he settled in Heidelberg. He contributed articles on music of Asia to *Die Musik in Geschichte und Gegenwart*; wrote several papers in Japanese for *Monumenta Nipponica.*

Eckelt, Johann Valentin, German organist; b. Werningshausen, near Erfurt, May (baptized 8th), 1673; d. Sondershausen, Dec. 18, 1732. From 1696 he was organist at Wernigerode; from 1703, at Sondershausen.
WORKS: *Experimenta musicae geometrica* (1715); *Unterricht, eine Fuge zu formieren* (1722); *Unterricht, was ein Organist wissen soll.* His MS Passion, cantatas, and organ works are of interest. His valuable library was acquired by E. L. Gerber, and utilized by the latter in the compilation of his dictionary.
BIBLIOGRAPHY: E. Jacobs, "Der Orgelspieler und Musikgelehrte J. V. Eckelt," *Vierteljahrsschrift für Musik-Wissenschaft* (1893).

Eckerberg, Sixten, Swedish conductor, pianist and composer; b. Hjältevad, Ingatorp, Sept. 5, 1909. He studied at the Stockholm Cons. (1927–32); received a Jenny Lind stipend to study conducting with Weingartner in Basel (1932–34); also was a piano pupil of Emil Sauer in Vienna and of Isidor Philipp in Paris. In 1937 he was appointed conductor of the Göteborg Symphony Orchestra.
WORKS: 3 symphonies (1941; 1944; 1965); *Sommarmusik* for orch. (1941); *Sub luna,* symph. poem (1942); 3 piano concertos (1943, 1949, 1971); *Visione* for orch. (1961); Piano Concertino (1962); *Triologi* for voice, flute and percussion (1969); *La danza della vita* for orch. (1970); Nocturne for Alto and Orch. (1970–71); *Promenade Suite* for winds and percussion (1971); *Sagan om asarna* for orch. (1971); Serenade for Orch. (1972); *Skogssuset* for orch. (1973); *Ånger,* musical after Maupassant (1972; Radio Sweden, July 22, 1975); Cello Concerto (1974); chamber music; piano pieces. He published an autobiography, *Musiken och mitt lif* (Stockholm, 1970).

Eckert, Karl Anton Florian, German composer and conductor; b. Potsdam, Dec. 7, 1820; d. Berlin, Oct. 14, 1879. At the age of 6 he was considered a prodigy; the poet F. Förster became interested in him and sent him to the best teachers; he studied piano with Rechenberg and Greulich, violin with Botticher and Ries, and composition with Rungenhagen. At 10 he wrote an opera, *Das Fischermädchen*; at 13, an oratorio, *Ruth.* After study (for a time at Leipzig under Mendelssohn) he went to the U.S. with Henriette Sontag; was then conductor of the Italian opera in Paris (1852); in 1853

appointed conductor and mus. director of the Vienna Opera; from 1860–67 held a similar post in Stuttgart; he was in Baden-Baden from 1867–69; then was called to Berlin to succeed Heinrich Dorn as director of the Berlin Opera. He wrote four operas, several oratorios, and a cello concerto which had little success; his songs, however, proved more popular; of these the *Swiss Echo Song* is the best known.

Eckhard, Jacob, one of early German organists in America; b. Eschwege (Hesse), Nov. 24, 1757; d. Charleston, S.C., Nov. 10, 1833. He came to the U.S. in 1776 and settled in Richmond, Va. In 1786 he was organist of St. John's Lutheran Church in Charleston; in 1809 received the post of organist at St. Michael's Episcopal Church. He published a hymn book (printed in Boston, 1816); wrote two patriotic naval songs, *The Pillar of Glory* and *Rise, Columbia, Brave and Free.*
BIBLIOGRAPHY: G. W. Williams, "Jacob Eckhard and His Choirmaster's Book," *Journal of the American Musicological Society* (Spring 1954).

Eckhardt-Gramatté, Sonia (Sophie-Carmen), violinist, pianist and composer; b. Moscow, Jan. 6, 1902; d. Stuttgart, Dec. 2, 1974, in a traffic accident while visiting Europe. She received early piano training from her mother, a former student of Anton Rubinstein; was taken to Paris where she studied violin and piano at the Cons. there. She made her concert debut in Berlin at the age of 11 on the piano and violin, playing Beethoven sonatas for each instrument; later took violin lessons with Bronislaw Huberman; after World War I, she toured Europe as a duo-pianist with Edwin Fischer. In 1920 she married the painter Walter Gramatté; they lived in Barcelona from 1924 until his death in 1929. In 1934 she returned to Germany and married the art critic Ferdinand Eckhardt, adding his name to that of her first husband in her patronymic. She took additional courses in composition with Max Trapp (1936–42). In 1953 she moved to Winnipeg, Canada. Her own compositions are marked by impressive craftsmanship.
WORKS: 2 piano concertos (1925; 1946); 2 symphonies (1939; *Manitoba,* 1969–70); *Capriccio Concertante* for orch. (1940); Concertino for String Orch. (1947); *Markantes Stück* for 2 pianos and orch. (1946–50); Triple Concerto for Trumpet, Clarinet, Bassoon, Strings and Timpani (1949); Bassoon Concerto (1950); 2 violin concertos (1951, 1952); Concerto for Orchestra (1953–54); *Symphony-Concerto* for piano and orch. (1966–67); 4 suites for solo violin (1922–68); 6 piano suites (1923–52); Concerto for Solo Violin (1925); 10 *Caprices* for solo violin (1924–34); *6 Caprices* for piano (1934–36); 3 string quartets (1938; 1943; 1962–64); 2 Duos for 2 Violins (1944); Duo for Viola and Cello (1944); Duo for 2 Cellos (1944); Wind Quartet (1946); 2 string trios (1947); *Ruck-Ruck Sonata* for clarinet and piano (1947); Wind Trio (1947); *Duo Concertante* for flute and violin (1956); *Duo Concertante* for cello and piano (1959); Wind Quintet (1962–63); Nonet (1966); Piano Trio (1967); Woodwind Trio (1967); Concerto for Viola da Gamba and Harpsichord (1971); *Fanfare* for 8 brasses (1971).

Eckstein, Pavel, Czech musicologist; b. Opava, April 27, 1911. He studied jurisprudence at Charles Univ. in Prague, graduating in 1935; received his musical education there. During the German occupation (1941–45) he was in a concentration camp in Lodz, Poland, but survived and returned to Prague where he became active as organizer of music festivals, editor and writer on music.

Eckstine, Billy (William Clarence), black American jazz singer and bandleader; b. Pittsburgh, July 8, 1914. He worked in night clubs as a crooner; formed a band of his own in 1944, proselytizing for bebop, in association with such bop figures as Dizzy Gillespie and Miles Davis; later became successful as a balladeer of "cool" jazz.

Écorcheville, Jules, French writer on music; b. Paris, July 17, 1872; d. Feb. 19, 1915 (fell in battle at Perthesles-Hurlus). He was a pupil of César Franck, 1887–90; student of literature and art history in Paris and (1904–05) Leipzig; *Docteur ès lettres* (Paris, 1906); editor of *La Revue Musicale S.I.M.* and writer on the history and esthetics of music. WRITINGS: *De Lully à Rameau: 1690–1730, l'Esthétique musicale* (1906); *Corneille et la musique* (1906); *Actes d'état civil des musiciens insinués au Châtelet de Paris de 1539 à 1650* (1907); *Catalogue du fonds de musique ancienne de la Bibliothèque Nationale* (thematic list of 10,000 items, to be completed in 10 vols.; only 8 vols. were publ.); "Un Livre inconnu sur la danse" (F. de Lauze's *Apologie de la danse,* 1623), in *Riemann-Festschrift,* 1909; also edited *Vingt suites d'orchestre du XVIIᵉ siècle français* (1906; facsimile and transcription). BIBLIOGRAPHY: *Le Tombeau de Jules Écorcheville: suivi de lettres inédites* (Paris, 1916).

Eddy, Clarence, distinguished American organist; b. Greenfield, Mass., June 23, 1851; d. Chicago, Jan. 10, 1937. He studied with Dudley Buck in N.Y.; in 1871 he went to Berlin to study piano with Loeschhorn. He made frequent tours in America and Europe; appeared at the Vienna Exposition of 1873; at the Philadelphia Centennial in 1876; gave a series of 100 organ recitals in Chicago (1879) with completely different programs; appeared at the Chicago Columbian Exposition in 1893, etc. He wrote many pieces for organ; publ. *The Church and Concert Organist* (2 vols., 1882–85); *The Organ in Church* (1887); *A Method for Pipe Organ* (1917); and translated K. A. Haupt's *Theory of Counterpoint and Fugue* (1876).

Eddy, Nelson, popular American baritone; b. Providence, R.I., June 29, 1901; d. Miami Beach, Florida, March 6, 1967. He studied voice with W. Vilonat in N.Y.; then in Dresden and Paris; was for 4 years a member of the Philadelphia Opera Co.; then sang on the radio with sensational success; also acted in musical films.

Edelmann, Jean-Frédéric, Alsatian musician of considerable accomplishments and a tempestuous and tragic life; b. Strasbourg, May 5, 1749; executed on the guillotine in Paris, on July 17, 1794. He studied law, matriculating from the Univ. of Strasbourg in 1770. He went to Paris in 1774 where he became a successful music teacher; among his students was the opera composer Méhul. It was Edelmann who in his teaching and in his compositions made the piano a fashionable instrument in Paris. He joined the Jacobins during the Revolution, and this proved his undoing when the Revolution took a more violent turn. WORKS: His keyboard pieces are in the manner of Couperin; he affected suggestive subtitles, such as *La Coquette* and *La Caressante.* He also wrote an oratorio *Esther,* which was performed at the Concert Spirituel in Paris on April 8, 1781; on Sept. 24, 1782 the Paris Opéra presented two of Edelmann's lyric dramas, *Feu* and *Ariane dans l'isle de Naxos.* Many of his keyboard works were publ. in his lifetime; of these there are two albums of *Six Sonates pour le clavecin* (Paris, 1775 and 1777); *Divertissements pour le clavecin* (1776); *Sinfonie pour le clavecin,* accompanied by 2 violins, 2 horns and cello ad libitum (1776); *4 quatuors* for clavecin, 2 violins and viola (1781); *4 sonates* for clavecin and violin (1782); Concerto for Clavecin, 2 Violins, 2 Oboes, 2 Horns and Bass ad libitum (1782); *4 sonates en quatuor* for clavecin, 2 violins and bass (1784); *3 concerts* for clavecin, 2 violins and viola (1785); *4 Divertissements* for clavecin, 2 violins and viola (1786); *Airs pour clavecin ou le forte piano* (1788). A thematic catalogue of Edelmann's works is published by Rita Benton in *Fontes Artis Musicae,* XI/2 (1964). BIBLIOGRAPHY: Vogeleis, *Bausteine und Quellen zu einer Geschichte der Musik im Elsass* (Strasbourg, 1911); G. de Saint-Foix, "Les premiers pianistes parisiens: J. F. Edelmann," *La Revue Musicale* (June 1924); Rita Benton, "Jean-Frédéric Edelmann, A Musical Victim of the French Revolution," *Musical Quarterly* (April 1964).

Eder, Helmut, Austrian composer; b. Linz, Dec. 26, 1916. He studied at the Bruckner Cons. in his home town; was drafted into the army during World War II; after the end of the war, he resumed his musical studies, taking composition lessons with Carl Orff and Johann Nepomuk David. In 1950, he joined the staff of his alma mater in Linz, and proceeded to modernize its curriculum, establishing an electronic studio and organizing a series of disturbing avant-garde concerts. In 1967 he was appointed to the faculty of the Music Academy at the Mozarteum in Salzburg, and quieted down. WORKS: the operas *Oedipus* (1960), *Der Kardinal* (1965) and *Die Weisse Frau* (1968), the television opera *Konjugation 3* (1969); the ballets *Moderner Traum* (1957), *Anamorphase* (1963) and *Infahrten des Odysseus* (1969); 3 symphonies (1952, 1960, 1962); String Quartet (1948); Trio for Flute, Clarinet, and Bassoon (1952); Concerto for Piano, 15 Wind Instruments, Double Basses, and Percussion (1952); Partita for 2 Guitars (1954); Piano Concerto (1958); *Concerto semiserio* for 2 pianos and orch. (1962); *Concerto a dodici* for strings (1963); Violin Concerto (1964); Oboe Concerto (1966); *Syntagma* for orch. (1967); *Nil admirari* for chamber orch. (1967); *L'Homme armé* for organ and orch. (1969); *Septuagesima instrumentalis* for wind quintet (1969); *Metamorphosen* for orch. (1970); choruses; songs.

Edmunds, Christopher, English organist and composer; b. Birmingham, Nov. 26, 1899. He studied with Bantock; was organist at Aston; and from 1945 to 1957 was prof. at the Birmingham School of Music. He wrote an opera *The Blue Harlequin*; 2 symphonies and chamber music.

Edmunds, John, American composer and music scholar; b. San Francisco, June 10, 1913. He studied with Rosario Scalero at the Curtis Institute and with Walter Piston at Harvard Univ., where he received his M.A. Working on various fellowships he did valuable work in editing songs by Purcell; solo cantatas by Alessandro Scarlatti and Benedetto Marcello; then was in charge of the Americana Collection in the Music Division of the N.Y. Public Library. In 1970 he was appointed prof. of music at Louisiana State Univ. in Baton Rouge. He published several hundred songs of his own composition.

Edson, Lewis, American musician; b. Bridgewater, Mass., Jan. 22, 1748; d. Woodstock, N.Y., 1820. Originally a blacksmith by trade, he became very active as a music teacher. He went to N.Y. in 1776; moved to Woodstock in 1817. He compiled (with Thomas Seymour) *The New York Collection of Sacred Music*; composed the hymn tunes *Bridgewater, Lenox, Greenfield,* and others.

Edwards, Clara, American musician of varied accomplishments as singer, pianist and song composer; b. Mankato, Minnesota, April 18, 1887; d. New York, Jan. 17, 1974. She studied voice in Vienna; returned to America in 1914 and became active as a singer and pianist. She wrote a number of songs to her own words, among them, *By the Bend of the River* and *Into the Night*; also composed music for children's plays and animated cartoons.

Edwards, Henry John, English composer; b. Barnstaple, Devon, Feb. 24, 1854; d. there, April 8, 1933. He received his first instruction from his father, organist of the Barnstaple Parish Church; from 1874–76 studied with H. C. Banister (harmony), G. Macfarren (composition), and S. Bennett (piano and orchestration); at Oxford he took degrees of Mus. Bac. (1876) and Mus. Doc. (1885); succeeded his father in 1886; also conducted Barnstaple Music Festival Society, and Exeter Oratorio Society (1896–1921); retired in 1926. He wrote 2 oratorios, *The Ascension* (Exeter Festival, 1888) and *The Risen Lord* (Exeter Festival, 1906); a cantata, *The Epiphany* (1891); motets, etc.

Edwards, Henry Sutherland, English writer on music; b. Hendon (London), Sept. 5, 1829; d. London, Jan. 21, 1906. For many years he was critic of the *St. James Gazette;* among his numerous books the following are the most important: *The Russians at Home* (1861); *History of the Opera from its Origin in Italy to the Present Time* (1862; 2nd ed. published in same year as *History of the Opera, from Monteverdi to Donizetti); Life of Rossini* (1869; in condensed form in *Great Musicians Series,* 1881); *The Lyric Drama* (2 vols., 1881); *Famous First Representations* (1886); *The Prima Donna* (2 vols., 1888).

Edwards, Julian, operetta composer; b. Manchester, England, Dec. 11, 1855; d. Yonkers, N.Y., Sept. 5, 1910. He was a pupil in Edinburgh of Sir H. Oakeley, and in London of Sir George Macfarren; conducted the Royal English Opera Co. (1877) and the English Opera at Covent Garden (1883); came to U.S. in 1888, settling in Yonkers and devoting himself entirely to composition. Some of his comic operas achieved more than average success; among them, *Victoria* (Sheffield, March 6, 1883); *Jupiter* (N.Y., April 14, 1892); *Friend Fritz* (N.Y., Jan. 26, 1893); *King Rene's Daughter,* lyric drama (N.Y., Nov. 22, 1893); *Madeleine* (N.Y., July 31, 1894); *The Goddess of Truth* (N.Y., Feb. 26, 1896); *Brian Boru,* romantic Irish opera (N.Y., Oct. 19, 1896); *The Wedding Day* (N.Y., April 8, 1897); *The Patriot* (1907; N.Y., Nov. 23, 1908; revived, July 24, 1975, at the Newport, Rhode Island, Music Festival; the libretto deals with an attempted assassination of George Washington).

Edwards, Richard, English composer; b. Somersetshire, near Yeovil, c.1522; d. London, Oct. 31, 1566. He studied at Oxford (M.A. in 1547); was (from 1561) master of the children of the Chapel Royal. With these choirboys he presented in 1565 his musical play *Damon and Pithias* (publ. in 1571). Edwards is best known for his madrigal 'In going to my naked bed,' written about 20 years before the period when the madrigal became popular in England (this piece is reprinted by Fellowes in *The English Madrigal School* 36).

Edwards, Ross, Australian composer; b. Sydney, Dec. 23, 1943. He studied at the New South Wales State Cons. (1959–62); privately with Richard Meale (1963) and Peter Sculthorpe (1965); at the Univ. of Adelaide with visiting composers Peter Maxwell Davies and Sandor Veress (1966–69).

WORKS: *Chamber Symphony* (1962); Piano Sonata (1962); *2 Pieces* for piano (1962); Wind Quintet No. 1 (1963); Trio for Flute, Harp and Viola (1965); *Music for flute and tape* (1965); Wind Quintet No. 2 (1965); Sextet for Flute, Clarinet, Horn, Harp, Viola, and Cello (1966); Sonata for Wind Quintet, Violin, Viola, Cello and Harp (1967); 3 string quartets (1968, 1969, 1972); Étude for Orch. (1969; Sydney, April 3, 1971); *Monos I* for cello (1970); *II* for piano (1970), *III* for violin (1971); *Choros* for piano and orch. (1971); *Kan-Touk* for female voice, harp, 2 pianos, 2 percussion and tape (1973); *Antiphon* for chorus, 3 trumpets, 3 trombones, organ and tam-tams (1973).

Eeden, Jean-Baptiste van den, Belgian composer; b. Ghent, Dec. 26, 1842; d. Mons, April 4, 1917. Pupil of the Cons. at Ghent and Brussels, winning at the latter the 1st prize for composition (1869) with the cantata *Faust's laatste nacht.* In 1878, appointed director of Mons Cons., succeeding Huberti.

WORKS: The operas *Numance* (Antwerp, Feb. 2, 1897) and *Rhena* (Brussels, Feb. 15, 1912); oratorios *Brutus, Jacqueline de Bavière, Jacob van Artevelde,*

Le Jugement dernier, and the dramatic scene for 3 voices *Judith*; 2 cantatas, *Het Woud* and *De Wind*; symph. poem, *La Lutte au XVIe siècle*; *Marche des esclaves*, etc.; also choruses and songs.

BIBLIOGRAPHY: Paul Bergmans, "Notice sur Jean van den Eeden," in the annual publ. of the Académie Royale (Brussels, 1924; pp. 375–436; contains a complete catalogue of works); M. Delsaux, *Jean van den Eeden et son œuvre* (Mons, 1925).

Effinger, Cecil, American composer; b. Colorado Springs, July 22, 1914. He studied violin and oboe; then went to Paris where he attended classes in composition with Nadia Boulanger. Returing to America he was first oboist in the Denver Symph. Orch.; then served as bandmaster in the U.S. Army in France (1942–45). Beginning with 1936, he taught music at the Univ. of Colorado, in Boulder, retaining this post in 1977. In his own music, he maintains a median modern style, making use of polytonal and atonal procedures, without abandoning the basic sense of tonality. Effinger is the inventor of a practical music typewriter patented in 1955 under the name "Musicwriter."

WORKS: an opera *Cyrano de Bergerac* (Univ. of Colorado; Boulder, Colorado, July 21, 1965); a children's opera *Pandora's Box* (1962); 5 symphonies (1946–58); 2 sinfoniettas (1945, 1958); Piano Concerto (1946); a Choral Symphony (Denver, Dec. 2, 1952); cantata, *The St. Luke Christmas Story* (1953); *Symphonie concertante* for harp, piano and orch. (1954); *Tone Poem on the Square Dance* for orch. (1955); oratorio *The Invisible Fire* (1957); *Trio concertante* for trumpet, horn, trombone and chamber orch. (1964); 4 string quartets (1943, 1944, 1948, 1963); Viola Sonata (1944); Suite for Cello and Piano (1945); *Pastoral* for oboe and strings (1948); *Landscape* for brass and strings (1966); Violin Concerto (1970); *The Long Dimension* for baritone, chorus, and orch., (1970); *A Cantata for Easter* (1971); *Quiet Evening* for flute, marimba, and strings (1972); *This We Believe*, oratorio (1975); *Capriccio* for orch. (1975); a music drama *The Gentleman Desperado and Miss Bird* (1976).

Egenolff, Christian, an early German music printer; b. July 26, 1502; d. Frankfurt, Feb. 9, 1555. He published 2 collections of 4-part songs, *Gassenhawerlin* and *Reuterliedlin* (1535; facsimile ed. publ. by Moser, Augsburg, 1927) which are of decided value.

BIBLIOGRAPHY: H. Grotefend, *Christian Egenolff* (Frankfurt, 1881).

Egge, Klaus, prominent Norwegian composer; b. Gransherad, Telemark, July 19, 1906. He studied piano with Nils Larsen and composition with Fartein Valen; after a brief period of further instruction at the Hochschule für Musik in Berlin, he became engaged in organizational work in Norway; was president of the Society of Norwegian composers from 1945. In 1949 he received the State Salary of Art (a government life pension for outstanding artistic achievement). His style of composition is conditioned by Scandinavian modalities, within a framework of euphonious and resonantly modernistic harmonies. He likes to sign his scores with the notes E-g-g-e of his name, a motto which also serves him occasionally as a basic theme.

WORKS: 3 piano concertos: No. 1 (Oslo, Nov. 14, 1938); No. 2 (Oslo, Dec. 9, 1946); No. 3 (Bergen, April 25, 1974); *Sveinung Vreim* for soli, chorus and orch. (Oslo, Dec. 1, 1941); *Fjell-Norig* (*Mountainous Norway*) for voice and orch. (Oslo, Oct. 1, 1945); *Noregsonger* (*The Norway Song*) for chorus and orch. (Oslo, May 2, 1952); 5 symphonies: No. 1, *Lagnadstonar* (*Sounds of Destiny*: Oslo, Oct. 4, 1945); No. 2, *Sinfonia Giocosa* (Oslo, Dec. 9, 1949); No. 3, commissioned by the Louisville Orch. (Louisville, Kentucky, March 4, 1959); No. 4, *Sinfonia seriale sopra B.A.C.H— E.G.G.E* (Detroit, March 28, 1968); No. 5, *Sinfonia dolce quasi passacaglia* (Oslo, Sept. 27, 1969); *Elskhugskvaede* (*Love Song*) for voice, and strings (1942); *Draumar i stjernesno* (*Starsnow Dreams*), 3 songs for soprano and orch. (1943); *Fanitullen* (*Devil's Dance*), ballet (Oslo, 1950); *Tårn over Oslo*, overture (1950); Violin Concerto (Oslo, Nov. 5, 1953); Cello Concerto (Oslo, Sept. 9, 1966); Violin Sonata (1932); 2 piano sonatas: No. 1, *Draumkvede* (*Dream Vision*, 1933) and No. 2, *Patética* (1955); String Quartet (1933; revised 1963); 3 Fantasies for Piano in the rhythms of Norwegian dances, Halling, Springar and Gangar (1939); Wind Quintet (1939); Piano Trio (1941); *Duo concertante* for violin and viola (1950); choruses and songs.

Eggebrecht, Hans Heinrich, eminent German music scholar; b. Dresden, Jan. 5, 1919. He attended high school in Schleusingen, of which his father was superintendent; was drafted into the army during World War II, through which he went unscathed, and undertook earnest music study in Weimar; passed an examination in musicology in 1948, under the guidance of H. J. Moser and R. Münnich; from 1949–51 assisted W. Vetter in the seminar on music history at the Univ. of Berlin; from 1951–55 was working on a dictionary of musical terminology and related subjects at Freiburg-im-Breisgau. In 1961 he succeeded W. Gurlitt as prof. of music at the Univ. there. He publ. a number of valuable articles in German music journals; his most signal accomplishment is the completion of the volume on musical terms and historical subjects (*Sachteil*) for the 12th edition of Riemann's *Musik Lexikon* (Mainz, 1967), in which he settles many debatable points of musical terminology. His separate monographs include *Studien zur musikalischen Terminologie* (Mainz, 1955); *J. S. Bach* (Darmstadt, 1970); *Heinrich Schütz, Musicus poeticus* (Göttingen, 1959); *Beethoven und der Begriff der Klassik* (Vienna, 1971).

Eggen, Arne, Norwegian composer; b. Trondheim, Aug. 28, 1881; d. Baerum, near Oslo, Oct. 26, 1955. He studied in Oslo and in Leipzig; toured Norway and Sweden giving organ recitals; from 1927 to 1945 was president of the Society of Norwegian Composers. In 1934 he received the Norwegian State Salary of Art (a government life pension).

WORKS: 2 operas: *Olav Liljekrans*, after Ibsen (1931–40; Oslo, 1940) and *Cymbeline*, after Shakespeare (1943–48; Oslo, 1951); Symphony (Oslo, 1920); *King Olav*, oratorio (1930); Chaconne for Organ

(1918); 2 violin sonatas; Piano Trio; many songs and choral works.

Eggen, Erik, Norwegian composer and musicologist (brother of **Arne Eggen**); b. Trondheim, Nov. 17, 1877; d. Ringsaker, June 7, 1957. He was a school teacher in southern Norway (1906–13); then devoted himself to the study of folk music; composed *Norsk Rapsodi* for orch., a cantata, and choral works, mostly in a folksong vein; published a monograph on Grieg (1911).

Egghard, Julius (pen name of **Count Hardegen**), Austrian pianist; b. Vienna, April 24, 1834; d. there, March 23, 1867. He was a pupil of Czerny and became a concert pianist; wrote a number of piano pieces in salon style, which were extremely popular.

Egidi, Arthur, German organist and composer; b. Berlin, Aug. 9, 1859; d. there, June 3, 1943. He studied in Berlin; taught at Hoch's Cons. in Frankfurt (1885–92); then was organist and choral conductor in Berlin. He composed mostly for the organ; publ. a collection of reprints of works by old German masters under the title *Musikschätze der Vergangenheit.*

Egk, Werner, significant German composer; b. Auchsesheim, near Donauwörth, May 17, 1901. His original name was **Mayer,** and the rumor had it that he took the name EGK as a self-complimentary acronym for "ein grosser (or even ein genialer) Komponist." Egk himself rejects this frivolous suspicion, offering instead an even more fantastic explanation that Egk is a partial acronym of the name of his wife Elisabeth Karl, with the middle guttural added "for euphony." He studied piano with Anna Hirzel-Langenhan and composition with Carl Orff in Munich, where he made his permanent home. Primarily interested in theater music, he wrote several scores for a Munich puppet theater; was also active on the radio; then wrote ballet music to his own scenarios and a number of successful operas. He was also active as opera conductor and music pedagogue. He conducted at the Berlin State Opera from 1938 to 1941, and was head of the German Union of Composers from 1941 to 1945. He was commissioned to write music for the Berlin Olympiad in 1936 for which he received a Gold Medal. He also received a special commission of 10,000 marks from the Nazi Ministry of Propaganda. The apparent favor that Egk enjoyed during the Nazi reign made it necessary for him to stand trial before the Allied Committee for the de-Nazification proceedings in 1947; it absolved him of political taint. As a composer, Egk continued the tradition of Wagner and Richard Strauss, without excluding, however, the use of acidulous harmonies, based on the atonal extension of tonality. The rhythmic investiture of his works is often inventive and bold.
WORKS: Piano Trio (1922); Passacaglia for Strings (1923); String Quartet (1924); String Quintet (1924); radio opera *Columbus* (Munich, July 13, 1933; 1st stage performance, Frankfurt, Jan. 13, 1942); *Die Zaubergeige,* opera in 3 acts (Frankfurt, May 19, 1935); *Olympische Festmusik,* for orch. (Berlin Olympiad, Aug. 1, 1936); cantatas *Natur-Liebe-Tod* and *Mein Vaterland* (both performed at Göttingen, June 26, 1937);

Peer Gynt, opera (Berlin, Nov. 24, 1938, composer conducting; highly successful despite the inevitable comparisons with Grieg); *Joan von Zarissa,* ballet (Berlin, Jan. 20, 1940); *La Tentation de Saint Antoine* for contralto and string quartet (Baden-Baden, May 18, 1947); Piano Sonata (1947); *Abraxas,* ballet (Baden-Baden radio, Dec. 7, 1947; stage performance, June 6, 1948, in Munich); *Circe,* opera after Calderón (Berlin, Dec. 18, 1948, composer conducting); *Französische Suite,* after Rameau, for orch. (Munich, Jan. 28, 1950); *Ein Sommertag,* ballet (Berlin, June 11, 1950); *Allegria,* suite for orch. (Baden-Baden radio, April 25, 1952); *Die chinesische Nachtigall,* ballet after Andersen (Munich, May 6, 1953); *Chanson et Romance,* for coloratura soprano and chamber orch. (Aix-en-Provence, July 19, 1953); *Irische Legende,* opera after Yeats (Salzburg, Aug. 17, 1955); *Der Revisor,* opera after Gogol (Schwetzingen, May 9, 1957); *Variations on a Caribbean Theme* for orch. (Baden-Baden, Jan. 18, 1960); *Die Verlobung in San Domingo,* opera (Munich, Nov. 27, 1963); *17 Days & 4 Minutes,* burlesque opera (Stuttgart, June 2, 1966); *Casanova in London,* ballet (Munich, Nov. 23, 1969); *Moria* for orch. (Nuremberg, Jan. 12, 1973).

Egli, Johann Heinrich, Swiss composer; b. Seegraben, near Zürich, March 4, 1742; d. Zürich, Dec. 19, 1810. He studied voice, violin, piano and composition; diligently perused theoretical works by Kirnberger and Carl Philip Emanuel Bach. He composed mainly sacred choruses; publ. several song collections, among them *Lieder der Weisheit und Tugend* (Zürich, 1790); also publ. arrangements of Swiss folksongs, *Schweizerlieder* (Zürich, 1787).
BIBLIOGRAPHY: A. Nef, *Das Lied in der deutschen Schweiz* (Zürich, 1909).

Ehlert, Louis, German composer, conductor and writer on music; b. Königsberg, Jan. 13, 1825; d. Wiesbaden, Jan. 4, 1884. In 1845 he entered the Leipzig Cons., where he studied with Mendelssohn and Schumann; then took music courses in Vienna and Berlin, where he lived from 1850 to 1863. He visited Italy; conducted the "Società Cherubini" in 1869; from 1869 to 1871 taught piano at Tausig's school for advanced pianists; then was active in Meiningen and Wiesbaden mainly as a piano teacher. He wrote a great many piano pieces, and also a *Frühlingssinfonie* and a *Requiem für ein Kind.* His collection of essays, *Aus der Tonwelt* (Berlin, 1877) was published also in English under the title *From the Tone World* (N.Y., 1885); he also wrote an entertaining volume *Briefe über Musik an eine Freundin* (Berlin, 1859), which was issued in an English translation as *Letters on Music, to a Lady* (Boston, 1870).

Ehmann, Wilhelm, German musicologist; b. Freistatt, Dec. 5, 1904. He studied at the Univ. of Freiburg and in Leipzig; taught musicology at the Univ. of Innsbruck (1940); served in the German Navy (1943–45). In 1948, he became director of the Westphalian church music school.
WRITINGS: *Das Schicksal der deutschen Reformationsmusik* (Göttingen, 1935); *Adam von Fulda* (Berlin, 1936); *Die Chorführung* (2 vols., Kassel, 1949; 2nd

ed., 1950); *Erziehung zur Kirchenmusik* (Gütersloh, 1951); *Erbe und Auftrag musikalischer Erneuerung* (Kassel, 1951); *Das Chorwesen in der Kulturkrise* (Regensburg, 1952); *Kirchenmusik, Vermächtnis und Aufgabe* (Darmstadt, 1958); *Alte Musik in der neuen Welt* (Darmstadt, 1961).

Ehrenberg, Carl Emil Theodor, German conductor and composer; b. Dresden, April 6, 1878; d. Munich, Feb. 26, 1962. He studied with Draeseke at the Dresden Cons. (1894–98); from 1898 on was engaged as conductor in Germany; in 1909–14 conducted concerts in Lausanne, Switzerland; in 1915–18 was opera conductor in Augsburg; conducted concerts in Bad Homburg (1918–22); then became conductor at the Berlin State Opera (1922–24). Subsequently he devoted himself mainly to teaching; was prof. at the Cologne Hochschule für Musik (1924–35) and at the Akademie der Tonkunst in Munich (1935–45).

WORKS: two operas *Und selig sind* (1904) and *Anneliese* (after a tale by Hans Christian Andersen, 1922); several overtures, 2 symphonies; Sinfonietta; Cello Concerto; 4 string quartets; Piano Trio; Wind Quartet; String Trio; Violin Sonata; many choruses; songs; piano pieces.

Ehrlich, Abel, German-born Israeli composer; b. Cranz, Sept. 3, 1915. He studied music in Germany; then studied at the Music Academy of Zagreb (1934–38). He went to Palestine in 1939 and studied composition with Solomon Rosowsky at the Jerusalem Academy of Music (1939–44); attended the summer courses in new music led by Stockhausen, Nono and others at Darmstadt (1959, 1961, 1963, 1967). In Israel he has taught in various schools, since 1964 at Tel-Aviv Academy. Until 1955 he based his music on Middle Eastern themes and folklore; since then he has developed a personal amalgam of traditional Jewish cantillation and modern serialism.

WORKS: *Immanuel Haromi* (1970) and *Carolus-Music* (1975); *arpmusic* for baritone, mime, 8 instruments and electro-acoustics, a tribute to the surrealist sculptor Hans Arp (1971); 6 string quartets (1947, 1947, 1952, 1962, 1967, 1969); *Bashrav* for solo violin (1953); *A Game of Chess* for winds, percussion, piano and double bass (1957); *The Towers and the Shadows* for narrator, singers and instruments (1960); *Testimony* for 2 flutes (1961); *The Writing of Hezekiah* for soprano, violin, oboe and bassoon (1962); 4 wind quintets (1966–70); *Radiations* for piano (1967); *And Though Thou Set Thy Nest Among the Stars* for orch. (1969); *Music for solo cello* (1970); *Evolution* for orch. (1970); *The Answer* for tenor, flute, and saxophone (1970); *Deliver Them that are Drawn unto Death* for string orch. (1970); Trio for Violins (1970); *Improvisations with a Game in Hell* for string trio (1970); Trio for Horn; Cello and Percussion (1970); *The Unicorn* for 12 singers, 3 percussionists and 3 oboes (1971); *Seven Minutes* for strings (1971); *Seeing* . . . for singer, violin and cello (1971); *Divertimento,* for oboe, clarinet, 2 horns and strings (1971); *Job 7, 11–16* for baritone, chorus and orch. (1971); *Ne subito* . . . for chorus and orch. (1971); *Comedy* for orch. (1971); Trio for Violin, Flute and Bassoon (1971); Trio for Horn, Violin and Piano (1972); Piano Sonata (1973); *Music for violin, cello, piano and 2 tape recorders* (1974); *Diario* for solo flute (1975); *A Vision of God* for 8 groups, each consisting of soprano, alto, violin and viola (1975); *Personal Boxes* for soprano and instruments (1976); *Many Wonders* for soprano and wind quintet (1977); *Sonnets,* after Shakespeare, for soprano, baritone, chorus, oboe, violin and viola (1977).

Ehrlich, (Alfred) Heinrich, Austrian pianist and writer on music; b. Vienna, Oct. 5, 1822; d. Berlin, Dec. 29, 1899. He was a pupil of Henselt and Thalberg (piano), and of Sechter (composition). For several years he lived at Hannover as court pianist; then at Wiesbaden (1855–57), London, Frankfurt, and Berlin. He was a piano teacher at the Stern Cons. from 1864 to 1872 and again from 1886 to 1898. He was also music critic of the *Berliner Tageblatt.*

WRITINGS: *Schlaglichter und Schlagschatten aus der Musikwelt* (1872), *Für den Ring des Nibelungen gegen Bayreuth* (1876), *Wie übt man am Klavier?* (1879; 2nd ed. 1884; English translation as *How to Practice on the Piano*; 2nd ed., 1901); *Die Musikästhetik in ihrer Entwickelung von Kant bis auf die Gegenwart* (1881); *Lebenskunst und Kunstleben* (1884); *Wagnersche Kunst und wahres Christentum* (1888); *Aus allen Tonarten* (1888); *Musikstudium und Klavierspiel* (1891); *Dreissig Jahre Künstlerleben* (1893); *Berühmte Klavierspieler der Vergangenheit und Gegenwart* (1893; in English as *Celebrated Pianists of the Past and Present Time,* 1894); *Berühmte Geiger der Vergangenheit und Gegenwart* (1893; in English as *Celebrated Violinists, Past and Present,* 1897); *Die Ornamentik in Beethovens Sonaten* (1896); *Die Ornamentik in Beethovens Klavierwerken* (1896; in French and English, 1898); also the novels *Abenteuer eines Emporkömmlings* (1858), *Kunst und Handwerk* (1862), *Vier Noveletten aus dem Musikantenleben* (1881).

Ehrling, Sixten, Swedish pianist and conductor; b. Malmö, April 3, 1918. He studied piano and composition at the Stockholm Cons.; conducting with Albert Wolff in Paris, and in 1941 with Böhm in Dresden. In 1944 he became conductor of the Royal Opera in Stockholm; also appeared as piano soloist with major European orchestras. From 1953 to 1960 he was on the staff of the Stockholm Opera and from 1963 to 1973 was music director and conductor of the Detroit Symph. Orch.; in 1973 was appointed head of the orchestral conducting class at the Juilliard School of Music, N.Y.; from 1974 to 1976 was principal conductor of the Göteborg, Sweden, Symph. Orch. In 1978 he became adviser and principal guest conductor of the Denver Symph. Orch.

Eibenschütz, José, German conductor; b. Frankfurt, Jan. 8, 1872; d. Sülzhayn, Harz, Nov. 27, 1952. He studied at Hoch's Music School in Frankfurt; in 1894 was appointed orchestral conductor in Åbo, Finland; there he remained until 1905; subsequent positions as conductor: Görlitz (1905–08); Hamburg Philh. Orch. (1908–21); Oslo Philh. (1921–27); North German Radio (1928). From 1938–46 he conducted in Scandinavia and in Russia; returned to Germany in 1946.

Eichberg, Julius, German violinist and composer; b. Düsseldorf, June 13, 1824; d. Boston, Jan. 19, 1893. His first teachers were J. Fröhlich (at Würzburg) and J. Rietz (at Düsseldorf); he then (1843–45) attended the Brussels Cons. (Fétis, Meerts, and Bériot); in 1846 was appointed prof. of violin and composition at the Geneva Cons.; in 1856 came to New York; settled in Boston in 1859 as director of the Museum Concerts (till 1866). He also became director of the Boston Cons., superintendent of music in the public schools; founded the Eichberg School for Violin.

WORKS: light operas, *The Doctor of Alcantara* (Boston, April 7, 1862); *The Rose of Tyrol* (1865); *The Two Cadis* (Boston, March 5, 1868); studies, duets, and characteristic pieces for violin; trios and quartets for strings; songs.

Eichborn, Hermann, German composer, writer and inventor; b. Breslau, Oct. 30, 1847; d. Gries, near Bozen, April 15, 1918. He studied jurisprudence; then became interested in music and took organ lessons with the organist of the Breslau Cathedral. His income from a wine-brewing business in Gries enabled him to devote himself to writing and the invention of instruments. He also supported a local orch. which performed several of his works. In 1882 he patented his invention of the soprano French horn in F, which he called Oktav Waldhorn, and which was adopted in many Silesian bands.

WORKS: Sonata for Waldhorn and Piano; *Rondo brillant* for Waldhorn and orch.; *Trompeters Berglied,* an "echo piece" for 2 trumpets; *Trompeter blas! Nur ein Spass!* for 2 trumpets and orch., and several operettas. He publ. numerous pamphlets on instruments: *Die Trompete in alter und neuer Zeit* (Leipzig, 1881, new ed., Wiesbaden, 1968); *Das alte Clarinblasen auf Trompeten* (Leipzig, 1894); *Die Dämpfung beim Horn* (Leipzig, 1897); *Militarismus und Musik* (Leipzig, 1909).

Eichheim, Henry, American composer and violinist; b. Chicago, Jan. 3, 1870; d. Montecito, near Santa Barbara, Cal., Aug. 22, 1942. He received his elementary musical training from his father, **Meinhard Eichheim,** a cellist in the Theodore Thomas Orch.; then studied with C. Becker and L. Lichtenberg at the Chicago Musical College. After a season as violinist in the Thomas Orch. in Chicago, he was a member of the Boston Symph. Orch. (1890–1912); then devoted himself to concert work and composition. He made four trips to the Orient (1915, 1919, 1922, 1928) and collected indigenous instruments, which he subsequently used in his orchestral music. All of his works are on oriental subjects.

WORKS: *Oriental Impressions,* or *The Story of the Bell* (Boston Symph., March 24, 1922, composer cond.); *The Rivals,* ancient Chinese legend, ballet (Chicago, Jan. 1, 1925; an an orch. piece, under the title *Chinese Legend,* Boston Symph., April 3, 1925, composer cond.); *Malay Mosaic* (International Composers' Guild, N.Y., March 1, 1925); *Impressions of Peking* and *Korean Sketch* for chamber orchestra and a group of oriental instruments (Venice Festival of the International Society for Contemporary Music, Sept. 3, 1925); *Burma,* symph. poem (Neighborhood Playhouse Co., N.Y., March 16, 1926, as incidental music for a play; Chicago Symph. Orch., Feb. 18, 1927, composer cond.); *Java* (Philadelphia Orch., Nov. 8, 1929, composer cond.; contains a 'gamelan' section, with 45 instruments); *Bali* (Philadelphia Orch., Stokowski cond., April 20,1933, at a Youth Concert); also a Violin Sonata (1934) and other chamber music. The harmonic idiom of these works is derived from Debussy and Scriabin.

Eichner, Ernst, German composer and bassoon virtuoso; b. Arolsen, Hesse, Feb. 1740 (baptized Feb. 15, 1740); d. Potsdam, 1777; concertmaster at the court of Pfalz-Zweibrücken; went to Paris in 1770, and after a very successful season in London (1773) was appointed member of the orch. of Prince Frederick William of Prussia.

WORKS: 31 symphonies (thematic catalogue in *Denkmäler der Tonkunst in Bayern,* 13–formerly 7.ii); piano concertos; piano trios; piano sonatas; duets for violin and viola; quartets for flute, violin, viola, and cello; quintets for flute and string quartet. A Symphony in D was published by Riemann in *Denkmäler der Tonkunst in Bayern,* 15 (formerly 8.ii); some chamber music in volumes 27, 28 (15, 16); a Symph. in F (1772) was revised for violin and piano by R. Sondheimer in 1923.

BIBLIOGRAPHY: A. Volk, *Ernst Eichner* (Cologne, 1943); Marianne Reissinger, *Die Sinfonien Ernst Eichners* (Wiesbaden, 1970).

Eijken, Jan Albert van. See **Eyken, Jan Albert van.**

Eilers, Albert, German bass singer; b. Cöthen, Dec. 21, 1830; d. Darmstadt, Sept. 4, 1896. He studied at the Cons. of Milan; made his opera debut in Dresden (1854); sang at the German Theater in Prague (1858–65). In 1876 Wagner selected him to sing the part of the giant Fasolt at Bayreuth. In 1882 he became a member of the Darmstadt Opera. He wrote a fairly successful comic opera *Die Johannisnacht* (Koblenz, 1889).

Eimert, Herbert, German music theorist; b. Bad Kreuznach, April 8, 1897; d. Düsseldorf, Dec. 15, 1972. He studied at the Cons. and Univ. of Cologne (musicology and philosophy); became interested in new musical techniques and publ. several essays on the subject, among them *Atonale Musiklehre* (Leipzig, 1924) and *Lehrbuch der Zwölftontechnik* (Wiesbaden, 1950).

Einem, Gottfried von, outstanding Austrian composer; b. Bern, Switzerland (where his father was attached to the Austrian Embassy), Jan. 24, 1918. He went to Germany as a child; studied at Plön, Holstein; then was opera coach at the Berlin Staatsoper. In 1938 he was arrested by the German Gestapo, and spent 4 months in prison. After his release he studied composition with Boris Blacher in Berlin (1942); was later in Dresden (1944); eventually settled in Salzburg. In 1953 he visited the U.S. His main interests are in the field of modern opera. Having absorbed the variegated idioms of advanced technique, Einem has produced a number of successful short operas and ballets; in his music he emphasizes the dramatic element by dynamic and rhythmic effects; his harmonic idiom is terse and strident; his vocal line often borders on atonality, but remains singable.

WORKS: OPERAS: *Dantons Tod* (Salzburg, Aug. 6, 1947); *Der Prozess (The Trial;* after Kafka; Salzburg Festival, Aug. 17, 1953); *Der Zerrissene* (Hamburg, Sept. 17, 1964); *Der Besuch der alten Dame* (after Dürrenmatt's play; Vienna, May 23, 1971); *Kabale und Liebe,* after Schiller (Vienna, Dec. 17, 1976). BALLETS: *Prinzessin Turandot* (Dresden State Opera, Feb. 5, 1944); *Pas de cœur* (Munich, July 22, 1952); *Rondo vom goldenen Kalb* (Hamburg, Feb. 1, 1952); *Medusa* (1957; revised, 1971). FOR ORCH. *Capriccio* (1943); *Orchestra Music* (1948); Serenade for double string orch. (1949–50); *Meditations* (Lousiville, Nov. 6, 1954); Piano Concerto (1956); *Symphonic Scenes* (1956–57); *Ballade* (1958); *Das Stundenlied,* after Brecht, for chorus and orch. (Hamburg, March 1, 1959); *Von der Liebe,* lyrical fantasies for high voice and orch. (1961); *Philadelphia Symphony* (Vienna, Nov. 14, 1961; Philadelphia, Nov. 9, 1962); Violin Concerto (1966; Vienna, May 31, 1970); *Hexameron* (1969; Los Angeles, Feb. 19, 1970); *Bruckner Dialog* (1971); *Rosa Mystica* for voice and orch. (1972); *An die Nachgeborenen* for soloists, chorus, and orch. (N.Y., Oct. 24, 1975).

Einstein, Alfred, pre-eminent German musicologist; b. Munich, Dec. 30, 1880; d. El Cerrito, Calif., Feb. 13, 1952. A member of a family of scholars (Albert Einstein was his cousin), he first studied law, then turned to music and took courses with Sandberger and Beer-Walbrunn at the Univ. of Munich; Dr. phil., 1903 (thesis: *Zur deutschen Literatur für Viola da Gamba;* Leipzig, 1905); 1918–33, editor of the *Zeitschrift für Musikwissenschaft;* lived in Munich until 1927 as music critic of the *Münchner Post;* 1927–33, influential critic of the *Berliner Tageblatt;* in 1933 he left Germany; lived in London and Italy (near Florence); in 1938 settled in the U.S.; taught at Smith College (retired, 1950); naturalized as American citizen, March 2, 1945.

WRITINGS: Revised editions of Riemann's *Musiklexikon* (9th ed., 1919; 10th ed., 1922; 11th enlarged ed., 1929); *Neues Musiklexikon* (German ed. of A. Eaglefield-Hull's *Dictionary of Modern Music and Musicians,* 1926); *Geschichte der Musik,* with *Beispielsammlung zur älteren Musikgeschichte* (1917–18; 4th ed., 1930); new edition (3rd) of Köchel's *Mozart Verzeichnis* (Leipzig, 1937; very valuable; reprint ed. with numerous corrections, Ann Arbor, 1947); *A Short History of Music* (London, 1936; N.Y., 1937; 2nd ed., 1938; 3d ed., 1947; trans. of *Geschichte der Musik); Gluck* (London, 1936). He contributed a great many valuable papers to the publications of the International Music Society and to other learned editions, to Festschrifte, Jahrbücher, etc.; his articles for the *Musical Quarterly* are especially notable: "The Madrigal" (Oct. 1924), "Dante, on the Way to the Madrigal" (Jan. 1939; also "A Supplement," Oct. 1939), etc. He also prepared a modern ed. of Andrea Antico's publication of 1517, *Canzoni, Sonetti, Strambotti, et Frottole* (Northampton, Mass., 1941); ed. a collection, *The Golden Age of the Madrigal* (N.Y.,

1942). His writings in America (publ. in English transl. from his original German) include: *Greatness in Music* (N.Y., 1941; German ed., *Grösse in der Musik,* Zürich, 1951); *Mozart; His Character, His Work* (N.Y., 1945); *Music in the Romantic Era* (N.Y., 1947; German ed., *Die Romantik in der Musik,* Vienna, 1950); *The Italian Madrigal,* in 3 vols. (Princeton, 1949; of fundamental importance); *Schubert: A Musical Portrait* (N.Y., 1950); *Essays on Music* (N.Y., 1956; posthumous). A profound scholar, Einstein was also a brilliant journalist, with a vivid, richly metaphorical style, capable of conveying to the reader an intimate understanding of music of different eras.

Eisenberg, Maurice, outstanding cellist; b. Königsberg, Feb. 24, 1900; d. while teaching a cello class at the Juilliard School of Music in N.Y., Dec. 13, 1972. He was brought to the U.S. as a child; studied violin; then, at the age of 12, took up the cello. He played as a youth in café orchestras, and studied at the Peabody Cons. in Baltimore; was a cellist of the Philadelphia Orch. (1917–19); then joined the N.Y. Symphony (under Walter Damrosch). He went to Europe in 1927 and studied in Berlin with Hugo Becker; in Leipzig with Julius Klengel; in Paris with Alexanian; and in Spain with Casals; then taught at the École Normale in Paris (1930–37); returning to the U.S., he gave a concert in N.Y. (Dec. 27, 1937) with excellent success; then appeared with major symph. orchestras; taught at various colleges; publ. a book *Cello Playing of Today* (1957).

Eisenberger, Severin, Polish pianist; b. Cracow, July 25, 1879; d. New York, Dec. 11, 1945. He studied with Leschetizky in Vienna; was prof. at the Cracow Cons. from 1914–21; lived several years in Vienna, and later came to the U.S. He played as soloist with the Cincinnati Symph. Orch. in 1935, and gave recitals in Cleveland and elsewhere in the U.S.

Eisfeld, Theodor, German conductor; b. Wolfenbüttel, April 11, 1816; d. Wiesbaden, Sept. 2, 1882. He conducted at the Wiesbaden court theater (1839–43); then in Paris. He occasionally visited Italy; took lessons with Rossini at Bologna; became an honorary member of the Academy of St. Cecilia. From 1848–66, he lived in New York; he conducted the N.Y. Philharmonic for several years, and the Harmonic Society from its foundation; established quartet *soirées* in 1851 with Noll, Reyer, and Eichhorn, joined also by Otto Dresel as pianist. Till 1865 he alternated with Bergmann in conducting the Philharmonic Concerts at New York; retired to Wiesbaden in 1866.

Eisler, Hanns, remarkable German composer; b. Leipzig, July 6, 1898; d. Berlin, Sept. 6, 1962. He studied at the Academy of Music, Vienna; pupil of Arnold Schoenberg in composition; won the Music Prize of the City of Vienna (1924); was in Berlin until 1932; came to the U.S. in 1933; lectured on music at the New School for Social Research, N.Y.; was musical assistant to Charlie Chaplin in Hollywood (1942–47); left the U.S. under the terms of "voluntary deportation" in 1948, on account of his radical political past; then lived in Vienna and in Berlin. Under Schoenberg's influence, he adopted the 12-tone method of composition; most of his symph. works are in this advanced style. However, he demonstrated his capacity for writing simple songs for use of choral ensembles; several of his choruses for workers and for the Red Army have become popular in Russia. Eisler was the author of the music of the national anthem of the German Democratic Republic, *Auferstanden aus Ruinen*, adopted in 1949 edition of his collected works was initiated by the German Academy of the Arts in East Berlin in connection with the Hanns Eisler Archive in 1968, in 3 vols. I, Vocal music; II, Instrumental music; III, Writings and Documents.

WORKS: opera, *Johannes Faustus* (East Berlin, March 11, 1953); about 40 scores of incidental music, to plays by Brecht (*Rote Revue; Die Rundköpfe und die Spitzköpfe; Galileo Galilei; Die Tage der Kommune*, etc.), by Ernst Toller (*Feuer aus der Kesseln*), by Feuchtwanger (*Kalkutta, 4. Mai*), Shakespeare, Schiller, Aristophanes; about 40 film scores (*Der Rat der Götter; Die Hexen von Salem; Trübe Wasser*, etc.); cantatas (*Tempo der Zeit; Die Massnahme; Kalifornische Ballade*, etc.); several cantatas to texts by Brecht (*Die Weissbrotkantate; Kantate im Exil; Kriegskantate; Kantate auf den Tod eines Genossen*, etc.); *Deutsche Symphonie* for soli, 2 speakers, chorus, and orch. (Paris, June 25, 1937); 6 orch. suites (Nos. 2-6 from film scores; 1930-34); *Kliene Symphonie* (1931-32); *5 Orchestral Pieces* (1938); *Kammersinfonie* (1940); *Rhapsody* for orch. and soprano (1940); *Ernste Gesänge* for baritone and string orch. (1962); chamber music: 2 nonets (1939); 2 septets (1941-47); *Divertimento* for wind quintet (1923); *14 Arten, den Regen zu beschreiben* for flute, clarinet, violin, cello, and piano (1947); String Quartet (1941); Quintet for Flute, Clarinet, Violin, Cello, and Piano (1941-44); Sonata for Flute, Oboe, and Harp (1935); Duo for Violin and Cello (1925); Violin Sonata (1937); 3 piano sonatas (1922, 1923, 1943); piano albums for children; numerous choruses, mass songs, among them several to Brecht's words (*Das Einheitsfrontlied*, etc.). He published a book, *Composing for the Films* (N.Y., 1947).

BIBLIOGRAPHY: Hanns Eisler, *Reden und Aufsätze* (Leipzig, 1961); I. Nestyev, *Hanns Eisler and His Songs* (Moscow, 1962); N. Notowicz, *Hanns Eisler Quellennachweise* (Leipzig, 1966).

Eisler, Paul, Austrian pianist and conductor; b. Vienna, Sept. 9, 1875; d. New York, Oct. 16, 1951. He was a pupil of Bruckner at the Vienna Cons.; conducted in Riga, Vienna, and at the Metropolitan Opera in New York; made numerous tours as accompanist for Caruso, Ysaÿe, and other celebrated artists; composed several operettas (*Spring Brides; The Sentinel; The Little Missus; In the Year 1814*).

Eisma, Will, Dutch violinist and composer; b. Sungailiat, island of Bangka, Indonesia, May 13, 1929. He learned violin from his father; then studied theory with Kees van Baaren at the Rotterdam Cons. (1948-53); in 1959-61 he took a course with Petrassi at the Accademia Santa Cecilia in Rome; also studied electronic music in Bilthoven. He was employed as an orchestral violinist with the Rotterdam Philharmonic

(1953-59) and since 1961 with the Hilversum Radio Chamber Orch., where he joined a group of avant-garde musicians, Instrumental Circuitry Ensemble. In his works he cultivates a strong polyphonic idiom in an uncompromisingly dissonant counterpoint, while the titles reflect preoccupations with structural abstractions.

WORKS: 3 orchestral concertos (1958, 1959, 1960); Concerto for 2 Violins and Orch. (1961); *Taurus* for orch. (1963); *Volumina* for orch. (1964); *Diaphora* for 15 strings, harpsichord, marimbaphone and percussion (1964); *Pages from Albion Moonlight* for 2 mezzo-sopranos, baritone, chorus and orch. (1968); *5 Roses for Diana* for 16 amplified winds (1969); *Orchestral Music with Voice* for soloists, chorus and orch. (1969); *Vanbridge Concerto* for horn player (on 2 different horns, and tuba) and orch. (Einhoven, Nov. 18, 1970); *Little Lane*, concerto for oboe and orch. (Hilversum, Feb. 15, 1974); *Le Choix du costume est libre*, concerto for solo string trio and chamber orch. (1974); Duo for Violin and Viola (1956); *Concert Piece* for violin and piano (1956); Septet (1959); Sonata, for clarinet, horn, violin, viola and cello (1959); Solo Flute Sonatina (1959); Violin Sonatina (1960); 4 Duos for Violins (1961); String Quintet (1961); 2 Madrigals for Violin and Piano (1962); *Diaphonia* for oboe, violin, viola and cello (1962); *Archipel* for string quartet (1964); *Affairs II* for recorder and harpsichord (1964), and *III* for oboe, clarinet and bassoon (1965); *Fontemara* for wind quintet (1965); *World Within World* for oboe, violin, viola and cello (1966); *Klein protokol* for violin and cello (1966); *Non-lecture IV* for solo violin (1967); *Hot Powdery Stones* for solo alto recorder (1968); *Because It Is* for oboe, harpsichord and percussion (1968); *Non-lecture III* for solo viola (1970); *Gezang XXIII* for violin and percussion (1970); *La Sonorité Suspendue*, string trio (1970); *If . . .* for wind and string quartets (1970); *Non-lecture II* for solo saxophone (1971); *Le Gibet* for baritone, 7 instruments and live electronics (1971); *The Light of the Cold Still Moon* for cello and piano (1972); *10 Flutes and Tape* (1973); *Collected Papers II* for solo instrument, percussion and synthesizer (1973-74); *Concert à vapeur* for violin, tape and synthesizer (1974); *Helena Is Coming Later* for 2 violins, viola, cello and synthesizer (1975); *Le Cheval Mort* for mezzo-soprano, bass clarinet, piano, percussion, 2 synthesizers and tape (1976); tape pieces; songs.

Eitler, Esteban, Austrian-Chilean composer; b. Bolzano, Tyrol, June 25, 1913; d. São Paulo, Brazil, June 25, 1960. He studied at the Univ. of Budapest; left Europe in 1936; went to Buenos Aires, where he was associated with modernist music groups; in 1945 he settled in Santiago, Chile.

WORKS: *Microsinfonia Politonal* (1943) for full orch. and *Policromia* (1950) for string orch.; *Serie Boliviana* for flute and string orch. (1941); Concertino for Piano and 11 Instruments (1947); Concertino for Horn and 11 Instruments (1949); Wind Quintet (1945); Quartet for Piccolo, Flute, Trumpet, and Saxophone (1945); Quartet for Flute, Violin, Viola, and Cello (1950), etc.

Eitner, Robert, eminent German musicologist; b. Breslau, Oct. 22, 1832; d. Templin, Feb. 2, 1905. A pupil of M. Brosig; settled (1853) in Berlin as a teacher, and gave concerts (1857-59) of his own compositions. He established a piano school in 1863, and published a *Hilfsbuch beim Klavierunterricht* (1871). He devoted himself chiefly to musical literature, and especially to researches concerning works of the 16th and 17th centuries. One of the founders of the Berlin *Gesellschaft für Musikforschung,* he edited its *Monatshefte für Musikgeschichte* from 1869 till his death; also the *Publikationen älterer praktischer und theoretischer Musikwerke.*
WRITINGS: "Verzeichnis neuer Ausgaben alter Musikwerke aus der frühesten Zeit bis zum Jahr 1800," *Monatshefte* (1871); *Bibliographie der Musiksammelwerke des 16. und 17. Jahrhunderts* (with Haberl, Lagerberg, and Pohl); "Verzeichnis der gedruckten Werke von Hans Leo Hassler und Orlandus de Lassus," *Monatshefte* (1873-74); "S. G. Staden's 'Seelewig,'" *Monatshefte* 1881); *Die Oper von ihren ersten Anfängen bis 1750* (3 vols., 1881-85); *Quellen und Hilfswerke beim Studium der Musikgeschichte* (1891); *Buch- und Musikaliendrucker nebst Notenstecher* (1904; as supplement to *Monatshefte*). His principal work is the great *Biographisch-bibliographisches Quellenlexikon der Musiker und Musikgelehrten der Christlichen Zeitrechnung bis zur Mitte des 19. Jahrhunderts* (10 vols., Leipzig, 1899-1904; additions and corrections published from 1913-16 in a quarterly, *Miscellanea Musicae Bio-bibliographica,* ed. by H. Springer, M. Schneider, and W. Wolffheim; reprinted, N.Y., 1947). Among Eitner's compositions (several of which were published) are a biblical opera *Judith,* an overture, a piano Fantasia on Themes from *Tristan und Isolde;* songs.

Eitz, Karl Andreas, German singing teacher; b. Wehrstadt, near Halberstadt, June 25, 1848; d. Eisleben, April 18, 1924. He originated a new system of solmisation ("Tonwortmethode"), somewhat similar to the English tonic sol-fa system; it is widely used in German music schools.
WRITINGS: *Das mathematisch-reine Tonsystem* (1891); *100 geistliche Liedweisen in Tonsilben gesetzt* (1893); *Deutsche Singfibel* (1899); *Tonwort-Wandtafel* (1907); *Bausteine zum Schulgesangunterricht im Sinne der Tonwortmethode* (Leipzig, 1911; 2nd ed., edited by F. Bennedik, 1928).
BIBLIOGRAPHY: G. Borchers, *Karl Eitz* (1908); O. Messmer, *Die Tonwortmethode von Karl Eitz* (Würzburg, 1911); F. Bennedik, *Historische und psychologisch-musikalische Untersuchungen über die Tonwortmethode von Eitz* (Langensalza, 1914); M. Koch, *Kurzgefasste Einführung in das Eitzsche Tonwort* (1925); F. Bennedik and A. Strube, *Handbuch für den Tonwortunterricht* (1926); R. Junker and R. M. Breithaupt, *Tonwort-Klavierschule* (1933); W. Stolte, *Carl Eitz in seiner Bedeutung für Wissenschaft und Schule* (Detmold, 1951).

Ek, Gunnar, Swedish organist, cellist and composer; b. Åsarum, Blekinge, June 21, 1900. He studied organ, cello and composition at the Stockholm Cons.; was cellist in the Swedish film industry orch. (1928-37); from 1942 was an organist in Lund.
WORKS: 3 symphonies (1928, revised 1942; 1932; 1936); *Swedish Fantasy* for orch. (1935); Fantasy for Violin and Orch. (1939); Piano Concerto (1944); *Doomsday Cantata* (1946); *Dig vare lov och pris, o Krist,* choral fantasy for chorus, organ and strings (1950; Malmö, Dec. 13, 1964); *Fantasy, Fugue and Coda* for strings (1963); Suite for Organ (1966); *Dorisk Suite* for strings and 5 winds (1966, revised 1968-69); *Variations on a Chorale Theme* for strings (1969); Wind Octet (1970); Concertino for Strings (1971); songs.

Ekier, Jan, Polish pianist and composer; b. Cracow, Aug. 29, 1913. He studied composition with K. Sikorski and piano with Z. Drzewiecki; became a concert pianist; taught piano at the State College of Music in Warsaw. Among his works are *Highland Suite* for chamber orch. (1936); *Variations and Fugue* for string quartet (1937); Piano Concerto (1949); and *Melodies in Color* for mixed chorus and orch., to words from folk songs in Polish, Russian, German, French and English (1951).

Eklund, Hans, Swedish composer; b. Sandviken, July 1, 1927. He studied at the Royal Academy of Music in Stockholm with Lars-Erik Larsson (1949-52); then went to Berlin where he took lessons with Ernst Pepping (1954). His music follows a tradition of neo-Classicism; most of his instrumental works are set in Baroque forms.
WORKS: radio opera, *Moder Svea (Mother Svea)* for soloists, chorus, trumpet and strings (Swedish Radio, Oct. 7, 1972); Variations for Strings (1952); *Symphonic Dances* (1954); 6 numbers of *Musica da camera:* No. 1, for cello and chamber orch. (1955); No. 2, *Art Tatum in Memoriam,* for trumpet, piano, percussion and strings (1956); No. 3, for violin and chamber orch. (1957); No. 4, for piano and orch. (1959); No. 5, Fantasia, for cello and string orch. (1970); No. 6, for oboe and chamber orch. (1970); 3 symphonies: No. 1, *Sinfonia seria* (1958); No. 2, *Sinfonia breve* (1964); No. 3, *Sinfonia Rustica* (1967-68); *Music for Orchestra* (1960); *Bocetos españoles* for chamber orch. (1961); *Songs from Stahl,* cantata (1961); *Variazioni brevi* for orch. (1962); *Introduzione-Versioni e Finale* for strings (1962-63); *Facce* for orch. (1964); *Toccata* for Orch. (1966); *Interludio* for orch. (1967); *Primavera* for strings (1967); *Pezzo elegiaco* for cello, percussion and strings (1969); *Introduction and Allegro* for harpsichord and string orch. (1972); Concerto for Trombone, Winds and Percussion (1972); *Hjalmar Branting in memoriam* for orch. and narration (1973); 3 string quartets (1954, 1960, 1964); *Little Serenade* for violin, clarinet and double bass (1954); Solo Violin Sonata (1956); *Improvisata* for wind quintet (1958); *Canzona and Dance* for solo violin (1962); Piano Trio (1963); *4 Pieces for Solo Clarinet* (1963); *Invocazione* for chorus, piano and percussion (1963); *4 Temperamenti* for 4 clarinets (1963); *Zodinai* for flute, 2 clarinets, bassoon and piano (1966); *Per Violincello* (1967); *Sommarparafras* for wind quintet (1968); Toccata and Fugue for Piano (1971); *Notturno,* 3 pieces for piano

(1972); *5 Bagatelles* for solo oboe (1973); *4 Pieces* for solo bassoon (1973).

Ekman, Karl, Finnish pianist and conductor; b. Kaarina, near Åbo, Dec. 18, 1869; d. Helsinki, Feb. 4, 1947. He studied in Helsinki (1889–92); 1892–95, pupil of H. Barth in Berlin and A. Grünfeld in Vienna; 1895, piano teacher at, 1907–11 director of, the Helsinki Cons.; 1912–20, conductor of the orch. at Åbo. He arranged Swedish and Finnish folksongs, and edited a piano method; published a biography of Sibelius (Stockholm, 1935; English transl., 1936). His wife **Ida** (b. Helsinki, April 22, 1875; d. there, April 14, 1942); a concert singer, studied in Helsinki, Paris, and Vienna; she distinguished herself by her performances of Sibelius' songs.

El-Dabh, Halim, Egyptian composer; b. Cairo, March 4, 1921; studied agriculture, and graduated from Cairo Univ. as an agrarian engineer (1945); then became interested in Egyptian musical instruments and composition; in 1950 received a Fulbright Fellowship for music study in America; took courses at the New England Cons. in Boston and at the Berkshire Center, Tanglewood, Mass. (with Irving Fine and Copland). Most of his music is derived from authentic Egyptian melodies and rhythms, but the contrapuntal and harmonic accoutrements are of a Western modern type. WORKS: 3 symphonies (1952–56); Concerto for an Egyptian Drum with String Orch. (1955); *Tahmela*, symph. poem (Cairo, Jan. 22, 1960); *Ballet of Lights* (*Cairo, Before the Sphinx,* July 23, 1960); and *Opera Flies,* on the story of the Kent State Univ. killings of 1969, the "flies" in the title being an ironically bitter reference to the student victims (Washington, May 5, 1971); String Quartet (1951); Sextet for Wind Instruments and Percussion (1952); songs, and music for drums (for which he devised his own system of notation).

Elewijck, Xavier Victor van, Belgian music scholar; b. Brussels, April 24, 1825; d. in the insane asylum at Zickemont, April 28, 1888. He was the author of several monographs: *Discours sur la musique religieuse en Belgique* (1861); *Mathias van den Gheyn* (1862); and *De l'état actuel de la musique en Italie* (1875).

Elgar, Sir Edward (William), eminent English composer; b. Broadheath, near Worcester, June 2, 1857; d. Worcester, Feb. 23, 1934. He received his musical education from his father, who was organist at St. George's Roman Catholic Church in Worcester for 37 years. At an early age he assisted his father at the organ, and took part in the rehearsals and concerts at the Worcester Glee Club; in 1879 he took a few violin lessons in London from Adolf Pollitzer; in the same year, he accepted an appointment as bandmaster at the County Lunatic Asylum in Worcester; he also played in Stockley's orch. in Birmingham; in 1882, was appointed conductor of the Worcester Amateur Instrumental Society; in 1885 succeeded his father as organist at St. George's. After his marriage (1889) to a daughter of Sir Henry Roberts, he tried his fortune in London but found conditions unfavorable, and settled in Malvern (1891), where he remained for 13 years. He

went to Hereford in 1904, and later to London, until 1920, when he returned to Worcester, following the death of his wife. The first composition of Elgar that had a public performance was an orchestral intermezzo (Birmingham, Dec. 13, 1883); his first signal success was with the concert overture *Froissart* (Worcester Festival, Sept. 9, 1890). His cantata *The Black Knight* was produced by the Festival Choral Society in Worcester (April 18, 1893) and was also heard in London, at the Crystal Palace (Oct. 23, 1897); the production of his cantata *Scenes From the Saga of King Olaf* at the North Staffordshire Festival (Oct. 30, 1896) attracted considerable attention; from then on, Elgar's name became familiar to the musical public. There followed the cantata *Caractacus* (Leeds Festival, Oct. 5, 1898), and Elgar's masterpiece, the oratorio *The Dream of Gerontius* (Birmingham Festival, Oct. 3, 1900). In the meantime, Elgar gave more and more attention to orchestral music. On June 19, 1899, Hans Richter presented the first performance in London of Elgar's *Variations on an Original Theme* (generally known as *Enigma Variations*). This work consists of fourteen sections, each marked by initials of fancied names of Elgar's friends; in later years, Elgar issued cryptic hints as to the identities of these persons, which were finally revealed. Elgar also stated that the theme itself was a counterpoint to a familiar tune, but the concealed subject was never discovered; various guesses were advanced in the musical press from time to time; a contest for the most plausible answer to the riddle was launched in America by the *Saturday Review* (1953) with dubious results. It is most probable that no such hidden theme existed, and that Elgar, who had a stately sense of humor, indulged in harmless mystification. The success of the *Enigma Variations* was followed by the production of Elgar's *Pomp and Circumstance* marches (1901–30), the first of which became Elgar's most famous piece through a setting to words by Arthur Christopher Benson, used by Elgar in the *Coronation Ode* (1902), and then published separately as *Land of Hope and Glory;* another successful orchestral work was the *Cockaigne Overture* (London, June 20, 1901). Elgar's two symphonies, written in close succession in 1908 and 1910, received respectful attention in England, but never became popular elsewhere. His Violin Concerto, first performed by Fritz Kreisler (London, Nov. 10, 1910), was more successful; there was also a Cello Concerto (London, Oct. 26, 1919). The emergence of Elgar as a major composer about 1900 was all the more remarkable since he had no formal academic training. Yet he developed a masterly technique of instrumental and vocal writing. His style of composition may be described as functional romanticism; his harmonic procedures remain firmly within the 19th-century tradition; the formal element is always strong, and the thematic development logical and precise. Elgar had a melodic gift, which asserted itself in the earliest works such as the popular *Salut d'amour;* his oratorios, particularly *The Apostles,* were the product of Elgar's fervent religious faith (he was a Roman Catholic); however he avoided archaic usages of Gregorian chant; rather, he presented the sacred subjects in a communicative style of secular drama. Elgar's stature in England is very great. During his lifetime he was a recipient of many honors. He was knighted in 1904. He received honorary degrees of Mus. Doc. from Cambridge (1900), Oxford (1905), Aberdeen (1906); also an LL.D., from Leeds (1904). During his first visit to the U.S. in 1905 he was made Doctor of Music of Yale Univ.; in 1907 he received the same degree from the Univ. of Pennsylvania. He received the Order of Merit in 1911; was made K. C. V. O. in 1928 and a baronet in 1931; was appointed Master of the King's Musick in 1924, succeeding Sir Walter Parratt. Although he was not a proficient conductor, he appeared on various occasions with orchestras in his own works; during his second visit to the U.S. he conducted his oratorio *The Apostles* (N.Y., 1907); also led the mass chorus at the opening of the British Empire Exhibition in 1914.

WORKS: ORATORIOS: op. 29, *The Light of Life* (Worcester, 1896); op. 38, *The Dream of Gerontius* (Birmingham, 1900); op. 49, *The Apostles* (Birmingham, 1903); op. 51, *The Kingdom* (Birmingham, 1906). CANTATAS: op. 25, *The Black Knight* (1893); op. 30, *Scenes From the Saga of King Olaf* (1896); op. 33, *The Banner of St. George* (1897); op. 35, *Caractacus* (1898); op. 44, *Coronation Ode* (Sheffield, 1902); op. 69, *The Music Makers* (Birmingham, 1912). CHORAL WORKS WITH ORCH.: op. 23, *Star of the Summer Night* (1892); op. 27, *Scenes from the Bavarian Highlands* (1896); op. 80, *The Spirit of England* (1916).

FOR ORCH.: op. la, *The Wand of Youth*, suite in 7 movements (subtitled *Music to a Child's Play*, written at the age of 12 and orchestrated 37 years later; London, Queen's Hall Orch., Dec. 14, 1907); op. 1b, 2nd suite, *The Wand of Youth* (1908); op. 7, *Sevillana*; op. 10, *Three Pieces (Mazurka, Sérénade mauresque, Contrasts)*; op. 12, *Salut d'amour* (Crystal Palace, London, Nov. 11, 1889); op. 15, *Two Pieces (Chanson du Matin, Chanson du soir)*; op. 19, *Froissart*, overture (1890); op. 20, *Serenade*, for string orch. (1892); op. 32, *Imperial March*, for Queen Victoria's Diamond Jubilee (1897); op. 36, *Enigma Variations* (1899); op. 39, *Pomp and Circumstance*, 4 military marches (1901–07; a 5th composed in 1930); op. 40, *Cockaigne*, overture (1901); op. 43, *Dream Children*, two pieces for small orch. (London Symph. Orch., March 8, 1905, composer conducting); op. 47, *Introduction and Allegro*, for strings (London, March 8, 1905); op. 50, *In the South*, overture (1904); op. 55, Symphony No. 1 (Manchester, Dec. 3, 1908); op. 58, *Elegy* for strings (1909); op. 61, Violin Concerto (London, Nov. 10, 1910); op. 63, Symphony No. 2 (London, May 24, 1911); op. 65, *Coronation March* (1911); op. 68, *Falstaff*, symph. study (1913); op. 70, *Sospiri*, for string orch., harp, and organ (1914); op. 75, *Carillon*, for recitation with orch. (1914); op. 76, *Polonia*, symph. prelude (1915); op. 77, *Une Voix dans le désert*, for recitation with orch. (1915); op. 79, *Le Drapeau belge*, for recitation with orch. (1917); op. 85, Cello Concerto (1919); op. 87, *Severn Suite* for brass band (1930); *Nursery Suite* for orch. (1931); incidental music for *Grania and Diarmid* (op. 42); a masque, *The Crown of India* (op. 66, 1912); *The Starlight Express* (op. 78, 1915); music for Laurence Binyon's and J. M. Harvey's play, *King Arthur* (London, 1923).

CHAMBER MUSIC: op. 6, Quintet for Wind Instruments; op. 8, String Quartet (MS destroyed); op. 9,

Violin Sonata; op. 82, Violin Sonata in E minor (MS destroyed); op. 83, String Quartet in C minor (1918); op. 84, Piano Quintet (1919). Organ works: op. 14, Voluntaries; op. 28, Sonata in G; also choruses and solo songs.

BIBLIOGRAPHY: R. J. Buckley, *Sir Edward Elgar* (London, 1904; new ed., 1925); E. Newman, *Elgar* (London, 1906); D. G. Mason, "A Study of Elgar," *Musical Quarterly* (April 1917); J. F. Porte, *Sir Edward Elgar* (London, 1921); J. H. Shera, *Elgar's Instrumental Works* (London, 1931); J. F. Porte, *Elgar and His Music* (London, 1933); B. S. Maine, *Elgar, His Life and Works* (2 vols., London, 1933); A. J. Sheldon, *Edward Elgar* (London, 1933); A. H. Fox-Strangways, "Elgar," *Music & Letters* (Jan. 1934); R. C. Powell, "Elgar's Enigma," ibid. (July 1934); special Elgar issue, ibid. (Jan. 1935); C. Barber, "Enigma Variations," ibid. (April 1935); William H. Reed, *Elgar as I Knew Him* (London, 1936; new ed. 1973); Mrs. Richard Powell, *Edward Elgar: Memories of a Variation* (London, 1937; 2nd ed., 1947); William H. Reed, *Elgar* (London, 1939; contains a complete list of works); W. R. Anderson, *Introduction to the Music of Elgar* (London, 1949); Diana McVeagh, *Edward Elgar, His Life and Music* (London, 1955); Percy Young, *Elgar, O. M.* (London, 1955; new ed., 1973); idem, ed. *Letters of Edward Elgar and Other Writings* (London, 1956); idem, ed. *Letters to Nimrod from Edward Elgar* (London, 1965); M. Kennedy, *Portrait of Elgar* (London, 1968); M. Hurd, *Elgar* (London, 1969); R. Fiske, "The Enigma: a Solution," *Musical Times* (Nov. 1969); E. Sams, "Elgar's Cipher Letter to Dorabella," ibid. (Feb. 1970); idem, "Variations on an Original Theme (Enigma)," ibid. (March 1970); I. Parrott, *Elgar* (London, 1971). The Elgar Society in Northwood, Middlesex, England, publishes the *Elgar Society Newsletter* triennually.

Elías, Alfonso de, Mexican composer, father of **Manuel Jorge Elías;** b. Mexico City, Aug. 30, 1902. He studied piano with José Velasquez, orchestration with Gustavo Campa, and composition with Rafael Tello at the National Cons. of Mexico (1915–27); was subsequently active as a pianist and conductor; taught at the Universidad Autónoma of Mexico from 1958 and at the National Cons. from 1963. His music is cast in a romantic idiom, much in the manner of Tchaikovsky, and contains few concessions to modern usages.

WORKS: ballet, *Las Biniguendas de Plata* (1933; concert version, Mexico City, Nov. 21, 1940); *El Jardín encantado*, symph. triptych (1924); 3 symphonies (1926, 1934, 1968); *Variaciones sobre un tema Mexicano (Las Mañanitas)* for orch. (1927); the symph. poems *Leyenda Mística del Callejón del Ave María* (1930) and *Cacahuamilpa* (1940); *Tlalmanalco*, suite for clarinet, bassoon, trumpet, piano and strings (1936); 2 string quartets (1930, 1961); Violin Sonata (1932); *6 Pieces* for string quartet, *Suite Antiqua* for 4 recorders (or 2 flutes and 2 clarinets), *5 Pieces* for violin and piano, and *4 Pieces* for cello and piano (all 1937–66); Organ Sonata (1963); piano pieces; commemorative Masses for soloists, organ and strings; motets. A complete list of his works through 1972 is found in *Composers of the Americas*, Vol. 18 (Washington, 1972).

Elías, Manuel Jorge de, Mexican composer, son of **Alfonso de Elías;** b. Mexico City, June 5, 1939. He received his early musical training from his father; he then entered the Autonomous National Univ. of Mexico and the National Cons., where he studied piano, organ, flute, violin and cello (1959–62); in Mexico City he also attended courses by visiting lecturers, on *musique concrète* given by Jean-Etienne Marie (1967), and on new music by Stockhausen (1968); had lessons in conducting with Herrera de la Fuente (1968–72); attended a class in electronic music at Columbia Univ., N.Y. (1974); then traveled to Belgium and enrolled in a workshop in opera and ballet conducting with Edgar Doneux in Brussels (1974–75); returning to Mexico, he founded in 1976 the Institute of Music of the Univ. of Veracruz. His music is hedonistically pragmatic and structurally precise, but allows interpolation of aleatory passages.

WORKS: *Pequeños Corales* for chorus a cappella (1954–57); *Suite Romántica,* 10 pieces for piano (1954–56); *Suite de Miniaturas* for wind quartet (1957); *Sonata Breve* for piano (1958); *Estampas Infantiles,* suite for strings (1959); Sinfonietta (1958–61); *Vitral No. 1* for chamber orch. (1962), *No. 2* for chamber orch. and tape (1967) and *No. 3* for orch. (Mexico City, Nov. 7, 1969); *Fantasía* for solo cello (1962); *Elegía* for solo clarinet (1962); *Divertimento* for percussion (1963); a ballet, *Jahel,* for 2 pianos (1964); *Aforismo No. 1,* *Pájaros perdidos,* for chorus a cappella (1963); *Aforismo No. 2* for flute and tape (1968); *Guanajuato,* overture-divertimento for orch. (1964); *Impresiones sobre una Estampa Colonial,* divertimento for orch. (1965); *Microestructuras* for piano (1965); *Ciclos elementarios* for wind quartet (1965); *Speculamen* for 2 violins, 2 violas, 3 cellos and double bass (1967); *Elegía heroica,* symph. poem (1967); *Memento* for recorder, chorus, strings and narrator (1967); string quartet No. 1 (1967); *Música nupcial* for contralto, and brass or strings (1967); *Aforismo* for solo flute (1968); 2 solo violin sonatas (1968, 1969); *Pro Pax* for tape (1968); *Nimyé* for solo flute (1969); 3 *Quimeras* for 2 pianos (1969, 1973, 1974); 3 *Kaleidoscopios* for organ (1969, 1973, 1974); *Sonante (Sonority) No. 1* for piano (1971), *No. 2* for solo clarinet (1970), *No. 3* for trumpet, trombone and horn (1970; version for orch., 1974), *No. 4* for orch. (Mexico City, March 26, 1971), *No. 5* for orch. (Mexico City, Nov. 24, 1972), *No. 6, Homenaje a Neruda,* for string orch. (1973) and *No. 7* for orch. (Brussels, Dec., 1974); *Parametros I* for synthesizer (1971); *Ludus* for 3 choruses (1972–73); *Concertante No. 1* for violin and orch. (1973); *Música domestica* for recorder and percussion (1973); *Sine Nomine* for string quartet and piano (1975); *Jeux* for horn, trumpet and bassoon (1975); *Obertura-Poema* for soloists, chorus, organ and wind orch. (1975); *Preludio* for solo violin (1975); *To Play Playing* for solo flute (1976); *Preludio* for solo guitar (1976); *Preludio* for solo viola (1976); further choruses; songs. For a list of his works through 1969, see *Composers of the Americas,* Vol. 15 (Washington, 1969).

Elías, Salomon (Salomonis), French monk at Sainte-Astère, Périgord. He wrote in 1274 a treatise *Scientia artis musicae* (printed by Gerbert, *Scriptores,* vol. III), of value as the first practical work giving rules for improvised counterpoint.

BIBLIOGRAPHY: E. T. Ferand, *Die Improvisation in der Musik* (Zürich, 1938); idem, "The 'Howling in Seconds' of the Lombards," *Musical Quarterly* (July 1939).

Eliasson, Anders, Swedish composer; b. Borlänge, April 3, 1947. He studied in Stockholm with Ingvar Lidholm and Soderholm. His music emphasizes the structural elements in freely dissonant texture.

WORKS: *In Medias* for solo violin (1970); *Kantillation* for mezzo-soprano and organ (1970); a string quartet, *Melos* (1970); *Picnic* for wind quintet (1972); *Tider* for mezzo-soprano, trombone, cello, electric organ, marimba, vibraphone and percussion (1972); *Glasdans* for orch. (1973; Swedish Television, Jan. 9, 1974); *Inför logos (In the Presence of Logos),* after Kafka, for chorus and tape (1973); *Quo Vadis* for mezzo-soprano, electric organ and tape (1973); a church opera, *En av oss (One of Us,* 1974); *Disegno della pioggia* for piano 4-hands, cello and xylophone (1974); *Disegno* for string quartet (1975); *Disegno* for 6 brasses (2 trumpets, horn, 2 trombones and tuba, 1975); several electronic pieces.

Elizalde, Federico, Spanish composer; b. Manila, Philippine Islands (of Spanish parents), Dec. 12, 1908. He entered the Madrid Cons. as a child and received the first prize as a pianist at the age of 14. Later he went to California, and studied law at Stanford Univ. At the same time he took lessons with Ernest Bloch. He was subsequently active as conductor of hotel orchestras in England; also visited Germany. Returning to his native islands, he became conductor of the Manila Symphony Orch. (1930); then conducted in Paris and Spain. On April 23, 1936, he conducted his *Sinfonia Concertante* at the Festival of the International Society for Contemporary Music in Barcelona. He was in France during World War II; in 1948 he assumed the post of president of the Manila Broadcasting Co., but continued his travels in both hemispheres. His music is influenced mainly by Manuel de Falla; beginning with dance-like works in the Spanish vein, Elizalde has gradually changed his style toward neo-classicism. He wrote the opera *Paul Gauguin* for the centennial of Gauguin's birth (1948); Violin Concerto (1943); Piano Concerto (1947); much chamber music.

Elkan, Henri, American conductor and music publisher; b. Antwerp, Nov. 23, 1897; studied viola and piano at the conservatories of Antwerp (1914) and Amsterdam (graduated 1917); in 1920 came to the U.S.; played the viola in the Philadelphia Orch. (1920–28); was conductor of the Philadelphia Grand Opera Co. (1928–36) and of the Philadelphia Ballet Co. (1926–39). In 1926 he founded the Henri Elkan Music Publ. Co. in Philadelphia; it became the Elkan-Vogel Music Publ. Co. in 1928, when Adolphe Vogel, a cellist in the Philadelphia Orch., joined Elkan; the partnership was dissolved in 1952; in 1956 he formed a publ. firm under his own name, specializing in works by American and Latin American composers.

Elkus, Albert (Israel), American composer and teacher; b. Sacramento, California, April 30, 1884; d. Oakland, California, Feb. 19, 1962. He studied piano with Hugo Mansfeldt in San Francisco, and later with Harold Bauer and Josef Lhévinne; went to Vienna where he took lessons in conducting with Franz Schalk and counterpoint with Karl Prohaska; then took courses with Robert Fuchs and Georg Schumann in Berlin. Returning to the U.S. he taught at the Dominican College in San Rafael, California (1924–31); was on the faculty of the San Francisco Cons. (1923–25 and 1933–37); was its director from 1951 to 1957; he also taught at Mills College in Oakland, California (1929–44). Among his compositions are *Concertino on Lezione III of Ariosto* for cello and string orch. (1917); *Impressions from a Greek Tragedy* (San Francisco, Feb. 27, 1921); a chorus for men's voices, *I Am the Reaper* (1921).

Elkus, Jonathan, American conductor, pedagogue and composer; son of **Albert Elkus;** b. San Francisco, Aug. 8, 1931. He started his musical career as a bassoon player; was bassoonist in the California National Guard (1949–57); enrolled at Stanford Univ., studying composition with Ernst Bacon and Leonard Ratner (M.A., 1954); then took a course with Darius Milhaud at Mills College, Oakland, in 1957. He served as conductor of the University Bands at Lehigh Univ. in Bethlehem, Pennsylvania (1957–73); concurrently taught music courses there (1965–73); after 1973 he was engaged mainly as music editor and band arranger. His compositions are directed mainly at high school and college workshops. WORKS: OPERAS: *Tom Sawyer* (San Francisco, May 22, 1953); *The Outcasts of Poker Flat* (Lehigh Univ., April 16, 1960); *Treasure Island,* after R. L. Stevenson (1961); *The Mandarin* (N.Y., Oct. 26, 1967); *Helen in Egypt* and *Medea* (Milwaukee, Nov. 13, 1970); FOR BAND: *Camino Real* (1955); *The Apocalypse* (1974); *Chiaroscuro* (1977); CHAMBER MUSIC: *Five Sketches* for 2 clarinets and bassoon (1954); *Triptych* for 4 bassoons and mezzo-soprano (1962); *The Charmer* for clarinet, trombone and piano (1972); choruses and songs. He arranged for band *Decoration Day* by Charles Ives, Wagner's *Siegfried's Funeral March* and numerous college songs and popular tunes. He published a monograph, *Charles Ives and the American Band Tradition: A Centennial Tribute* (Univ. of Exeter, England, 1974).

Ella, John, English writer on music; b. Leicester, Dec. 19, 1802; d. London, Oct. 2, 1888. He studied violin in London; then enrolled as a harmony student at the Royal Academy of Music; in 1827 went to Paris to study with Fétis. Returning to London, he played in theater orchestras; in 1845 established The Musical Union, presenting morning concerts of chamber music, and was its director until 1880; in 1850 opened a series of "Music Winter Evenings" which continued until 1859. For these organizations he wrote analytical program notes, of excellent quality for the time. He was a contributor of reviews and music articles to the *Morning Post,* the *Musical World,* and the *Athenaeum.* WRITINGS: *Lectures on Dramatic Music Abroad and at Home* (1872); *Musical Sketches Abroad and at Home* (3 eds.: 1861, 1869, 1878); *Record of the Musical Union* (1845–80); *Personal Memoir of Meyerbeer* (1868); and other publications.

BIBLIOGRAPHY: John Ravell, "John Ella," *Music & Letters* (Jan. 1953).

Ellberg, Ernst Henrik, Swedish composer and pedagogue; b. Söderhamn, Dec. 11, 1868; d. Stockholm, June 14, 1948. He studied violin and composition at the Stockholm Cons., and was teacher there from 1904 to 1933; among his pupils were Hilding Rosenberg, Dag Wiren, and Gunnar de Frumerie. He wrote an opera, *Rassa,* which received a prize; several ballets and concert overtures, and some chamber music.

Ellegaard, France, Danish pianist; b. Paris (of Danish parents), Oct. 10, 1912. She studied at the Paris Cons. (1922–33), then toured in Germany, France, and England. In 1949 she married the Finnish painter Birger Carlstedt. In 1969 she was appointed prof. at the Sibelius Academy in Helsinki.

Eller, Louis, Austrian violinist; b. Graz, June 9, 1820; d. Pau, July 12, 1862. He studied with Hysel; from 1836 made tours in central Europe; traveled to Spain and Portugal with Gottschalk. He wrote several effective pieces for the violin: *Valse diabolique, Menuet sentimental,* etc.

Ellert, Laurence B., American music editor; b. Louisville, Jan. 3, 1878; d. Washington, D.C., Oct. 25, 1940. He attended Georgetown Univ.; 1900–02, was director of the Mandolin Club there; studied piano and harmony privately; in 1902 entered the music business; 1919, associated with the sales dept. of G. Schirmer, Inc.; 1920, general manager of Willis Music Co., Cincinnati; 1923, again in N.Y. as director of publication for the Boston Music Co. and Willis Music Co., specializing in educational music.

Ellerton, John Lodge (real name **John Lodge**), English poet and prolific composer; b. Chester, Jan. 11, 1801; d. London, Jan. 3, 1873. An Oxford graduate, he studied counterpoint under Pietro Terziani at Rome, where he composed 7 Italian operas; lived for some time in Germany, where he wrote 2 German operas. Besides his operas, he wrote an oratorio, *Paradise Lost;* 6 symphonies, 4 concert overtures, 3 quintets, 44 string quartets, 3 string trios, 8 trios for various instruments, 13 sonatas, 61 glees, 83 vocal duets, songs.

Elleviou, Jean, French operatic tenor; b. Rennes, June 14, 1769; d. Paris, May 5, 1842. He made his debut in Monsigny's *Déserteur* at the Comédie Italienne in Paris in 1790, and sang there until 1813. The revival of interest in the works of Grétry in 1801 was largely due to his influence and excellent interpretations; Méhul wrote his *Joseph* (1807) and Boieldieu his *Jean de Paris* (1812) for him.

BIBLIOGRAPHY: E. H. P. de Curzon, *Jean Elleviou* (Paris, 1930).

Ellicott, Rosalind Frances, English composer; b. Cambridge, Nov. 14, 1857; d. London, April 5, 1924.

She studied at the Royal Academy of Music (1875–76), and later with Thomas Wingham (1885–92); she received several commissions to write works for the Gloucester and Cheltenham Festivals; among them were the cantatas *Radiant Sister of the Dawn* (Cheltenham, 1887) and *Elysium* (Gloucester, 1889). She retired from active musical work in 1900.

Elling, Catherinus, Norwegian composer and folklorist; b. Oslo, Sept. 13, 1858; d. there, Jan. 8, 1942. He studied music with native teachers; then in Leipzig (1877–78) and Berlin (1886–96). In 1908 a subvention was granted him by the state for the pursuit of his studies of Norwegian folksongs, on which he published various essays; he also wrote biographies of Ole Bull, Grieg, Svendsen, and Kjerulf, and published a book, *Norsk folkemusik* (Oslo, 1922). He composed an opera, *Kosakkerne* (1897); an oratorio, *The Prodigal Son;* Symphony; incidental music to *A Midsummer Night's Dream;* chamber music, and many songs.

Ellington, Edward Kennedy (known as **Duke Ellington**), black American pianist, bandleader, and composer; one of the most remarkable musicians of jazz; b. Washington, D.C., April 29, 1899; d. New York, May 24, 1974. He played ragtime as a boy; he worked with various jazz bands in Washington during the 1910s and early '20s, and in 1923 went to N.Y. where he organized a "big band" (originally 10 pieces) that he was to lead for the next half-century, a band that revolutionized the concept of jazz: no longer was jazz restricted to small combos of 4–6 "unlettered" improvisers; with the Ellington band complex arrangements were introduced requiring both improvising skill and the ability to read scores; eventually these scores were to take on the dimensions and scope of classical compositions while retaining an underlying jazz feeling. In the early days his chief collaborator in composition and arrangements was trumpeter James "Bubber" Miley; baritone saxophonist Harry Carney, another arranger, was with the band from its inception until Ellington's death; from 1939 the main collaborator was pianist-composer Billy Strayhorn. Ellington possessed a social elegance and the gift of articulate verbal expression that inspired respect, and he became known as "Duke" Ellington. He was the only jazz musician to receive an honorary degree from Columbia University (1973). He was also the recipient of the Presidential Medal of Freedom on his 70th birthday at the White House in 1969. He made several European trips under the auspices of the State Department; toured Russia in 1970 and also went to Latin America, Japan, and Australia. So highly was he esteemed in Africa that the Republic of Togo issued in 1967 a postage stamp bearing his portrait. Since Duke's death, his band has been led by his son **Mercer Ellington** (b. Washington, D.C., March 11, 1919). WORKS: more than 1,000 compositions, including *East St. Louis Toodle-Oo* (pronounced "toad-lo; 1926), *Black and Tan Fantasy* and *Creole Love Song* (1927), *Mood Indigo* (1930), *Sophisticated Lady* (uses a whole-tone scale; 1932), *Diminuendo and Crescendo in Blue* (1937), *Black, Brown and Beige* (a tonal panorama of Negro history in America; 1943), *Liberian Suite* (1948), *My People,* commissioned for the 100th

anniversary of the Emancipation Proclamation (1963), *First Sacred Concert* (1st perf. Grace Cathedral, San Francisco, 1965), *Second Sacred Concert* (1st perf. St. John the Divine, N.Y., 1968), *The River* (ballet, 1970). He published a book, *Music Is My Mistress* (Garden City, N.Y., 1973).

BIBLIOGRAPHY: B. Ulanov, *Duke Ellington* (N.Y., 1946); P. Gammond, *Duke Ellington, His Life and Music* (London, 1958); S. Dance, *The World of Duke Ellington* (N.Y., 1970); Derek Jewell, *Duke, A Portrait of Duke Ellington* (N.Y., 1977). The Duke Ellington Society, in N.Y., promotes lectures, performances, and scholarships.

Ellinwood, Leonard Webster, American musicologist; b. Thomaston, Conn., Feb. 13, 1905. He studied at Aurora College, Illinois and at the Eastman School of Music in Rochester, N.Y., where he received the degrees of M.M. and Ph.D. He subsequently held a number of teaching positions until 1939 when he became cataloguer at the Library of Congress in Washington. He compiled *Musica Hermanni Contracti* (Rochester, N.Y., 1936); edited works of Francesco Landini (1939) and *The History of American Church Music* (N.Y., 1953); also contributed to the Episcopal songbook *The Hymnal Companion* (1951).

Ellis (real name **Sharpe**), **Alexander John,** English writer on musical science; b. Hoxton (London), June 14, 1814; d. Kensington, Oct. 28, 1890. He studied at Trinity College, Cambridge, graduating in 1837; his subjects were mathematics and philology; he also studied music; was elected Fellow of the Royal Society (1864) and was President of the Philological Society; publ. valuable papers in the *Proceedings of the Royal Society:* "On the Conditions . . . of a Perfect Musical Scale on Instruments with Fixed Tones" (1864), "On the Physical Constitutions and Relations of Musical Chords" (1864), "On the Temperament of Instruments with Fixed Tones" (1864), and "On Musical Duodenes; or, The Theory of Constructing Instruments with Fixed Tones in Just or Practically Just Intonation" (1874). Papers containing new theories, etc., for the Musical Association are as follows: "The Basis of Music" (1877), "Pronunciation for Singers" (1877), and "Speech in Song" (1878). He was awarded a silver medal for his writings on musical pitch for the *Proceedings of the Society of Arts* (1877, 1880, and 1881; publ. separately, 1880–81; and in summary form in the Appendix to the 2nd ed. of his transl. of Helmholtz's *Lehre von den Tonempfindungen* under the title, *On the Sensations of Tone, as a Physiological Basis for the Theory of Music;* 1st ed., 1875; 6th ed., 1948); also wrote "Tonometrical Observations, or Some Existing Non-harmonic Scales" (Royal Society, 1884), and "On the Musical Scales of Various Nations" (Society of Arts, 1885).

Ellis, Don, American trumpet player, arranger and composer; b. Los Angeles, July 25, 1934. He studied composition at Boston Univ. with Gardner Read and later at the Univ. of Calif., Los Angeles, with John Vincent. He took trumpet lessons with 7 teachers in Boston, N.Y. and Los Angeles; was first trumpet player with the National Symph. Orch., Washington;

then with numerous bands in Boston and N.Y.; subsequently formed his own band. In his compositions and arrangements he boldly introduces nonbinary meters and asymmetrical rhythms. His major work is *Contrasts for Two Orchestras and Trumpet* (1965).

Elman, Mischa, remarkable Russian violinist; b. Talnoy, Jan. 20, 1891; d. New York, April 5, 1967. At the age of 6 he was taken by his father to Odessa where he became a violin student of Fidelmann, and a pupil of Brodsky. His progress was extraordinary, and when Leopold Auer heard him play in 1902, he immediately accepted him in his class at the St. Petersburg Cons. In 1904 he made his debut in St. Petersburg with sensational acclaim; his tour of Germany was equally successful; in 1905 he appeared in England where he played the Glazunov Violin Concerto. In 1908 he made his American debut and was hailed as one of the greatest virtuosos of the time; he played with every important symphony orch. in the U.S.; with the Boston Symph. alone he was a soloist at 31 concerts. In the following years he played all over the world, and, with Jascha Heifetz, became a synonym of violinistic prowess. His playing was a quintessence of romantic interpretation; his tone was mellifluous, but resonant; he excelled particularly in the concertos of Mendelssohn, Tchaikovsky, and Wieniawski; but he could also give impressive performances of Beethoven and Mozart. He published several violin arrangements of classical and romantic pieces, and he also composed some playable short compositions for his instrument. His father published a sentimental book, *Memoirs of Mischa Elman's Father* (N.Y., 1933).

Elmore, Robert Hall, American organist and composer; b. Ramapatnam, India, Jan. 2, 1913 (of American parentage); studied organ with Pietro Yon, composition with Harl McDonald, and at the Univ. of Pennsylvania (graduated 1937; Mus. Bac.); from 1936, organ teacher at the Clarke Cons. of Music, Philadelphia. He wrote a tone poem, *Valley Forge* (Philadelphia Orch., April 9, 1937, Stokowski cond.), an Organ Concerto, String Quartet, many sacred songs and cantatas; secular songs, etc.

Eloy, Jean-Claude, French composer; b. Mont-Saint-Aignan (Seine-Maritime), June 15, 1938. He studied in Paris with Darius Milhaud and in Basel with Pierre Boulez. From his earliest works he adopted the advanced techniques of serialism; his main influences are Boulez, Varèse and Webern; there is an extreme miniaturization in his instrumental music. He composed *Équivalences* (1963) and *Faisceaux-Diffractions* (1970), both for chamber orch.; also *Shanti* (Tibetan for "good fortune"), electronic work lasting 2½ hours without interruption, probably the longest uninterrupted piece ever composed (London, April 6, 1975).

Elsenheimer, Nicholas J., German music educator; b. Wiesbaden, June 17, 1866; d. Limburg a. d. Lahn, July 12, 1935. He was a pupil of his father; took degree of LL.D. at Heidelberg; studied under G. Jacobsthal in Strasbourg. In 1890 he went to America; taught at the Cincinnati College of Music (1890–1906); after 1907 taught in N.Y.; then went back to Germany.

Elsner, Joseph, noted Polish composer, teacher of Chopin; b. Grottkau, June 29, 1769 (of German descent); d. Warsaw, April 18, 1854. He studied violin, voice, and organ at Grottkau, Breslau, and Vienna. In 1791 he became concertmaster of the Brünn Opera Theater; then was Kapellmeister at Lemberg (from 1792). He was Chopin's teacher at Warsaw, and founded a school there for organists which later became the Warsaw Cons. His autobiography (1840–49), written in German, was published posthumously in a Polish translation (1855; new ed., Cracow, 1957).

WORKS: 32 operas, including *King Wladislaw* (Warsaw, April 3, 1818), duo-dramas, and musical plays, of which 2 were produced in German at Lemberg (*Die seltenen Brüder,* 1794; *Der verkleidete Sultan,* 1796) and the rest in Warsaw; 17 Masses; several ballets; sacred and secular choral works; 8 symphonies; 11 string quartets; 2 piano quartets; 3 violin sonatas (a number of these works were published by Breitkopf & Härtel and by French and Polish publishers). He also published 2 treatises on the vocal treatment of Polish texts (Warsaw, 1818). A medal was struck in his honor on his 80th birthday (1849).

BIBLIOGRAPHY: F. Hoesick, *From Elsner's Memoirs* (Warsaw, 1901, in Polish); J. Reiss, *Joseph Elsner* (Katowice, 1936).

Elson, Arthur, American writer on music; son of **Louis C. Elson;** b. Boston, Nov. 18, 1873; d. New York, Feb. 24, 1940. He studied with J. K. Paine at Harvard Univ. and at the New England Cons. of Music; received fundamental training from his father. He was a graduate of Harvard and of the Mass. Institute of Technology.

WRITINGS: *A Critical History of the Opera* (1901; new edition, 1926, as *A History of Opera*); *Orchestral Instruments and Their Use* (1902; new ed., Boston, 1930); *Woman's Work in Music* (1903; new ed., 1931); *Modern Composers of Europe* (1905; new ed., 1922); *Music Club Programs from All Nations* (1906; new ed., 1928); *The Musician's Guide* (1913); *The Book of Musical Knowledge* (1915; new ed., N.Y., 1934); *Pioneer School Music Course* (1917).

Elson, Louis Charles, American music historian; b. Boston, Mass., April 17, 1848; d. there, Feb. 14, 1920. He studied voice with Kreissmann at Boston and music theory with Karl Gloggner Castelli in Leipzig. Returning to Boston, he was for many years music editor of the *Boston Advertiser;* in 1880 became lecturer on music history at the New England Cons.; was also editor-in-chief of the *University Encyclopedia of Music* (10 vols., 1912). In his music criticism he attacked the modernists with vicious eloquence, reserving the choicest invective for Debussy; he called *La Mer,* "Le Mal de Mer," and said that the faun of *L'Après-midi d'un faune* needed a veterinary surgeon.

WRITINGS: *Curiosities of Music* (1880); *History of German Song* (1888); *The Theory of Music* (1890; revised by F. Converse, 1935); *European Reminiscences* (Chicago, 1891; new ed., Philadelphia, 1914); *The*

Realm of Music (1892); *Great Composers and Their Work* (1898); *The National Music of America and Its Sources* (1899; new ed., revised by Arthur Elson, 1924); *Famous Composers and Their Works* (with Philip Hale; new series, Boston, 1900); *Shakespeare in Music* (1901); *History of American Music* (N.Y., 1904; 2nd ed., 1915; revised ed. by A. Elson, 1925); *Music Dictionary* (1905); *Pocket Music Dictionary* (1909; many reprints); *Folk Songs of Many Nations* (1905); *Mistakes and Disputed Points in Music* (1910); *Woman in Music* (1918); *Children in Music* (1918).

El-Tour, Anna, Russian soprano; b. Odessa, June 4, 1886; d. Amsterdam, May 30, 1954. She studied at the St. Petersburg Cons. (voice with Mme. von Hecke; piano with Essipova). From 1913–20, she taught in Moscow; then left Russia; from 1922–25 was in Berlin; 1925–48, taught at the Conservatoire International de Paris. After 1948, she was professor of singing at the Amsterdam Cons. She traveled widely in the Far East; gave recitals in Israel in 1953.

Elvey, Sir George (Job), English organist and composer; b. Canterbury, March 27, 1816; d. Windlesham, Surrey, Dec. 9, 1893. He was a chorister at Canterbury Cathedral; studied with Skeats, Potter, and Dr. Crotch at the Royal Academy of Music. From 1835 until 1882 he served as organist and master of the boys at St. George's Chapel, Windsor; Mus. Bac., Oxford (1838); Mus. Doc. (1840); knighted in 1871.

WORKS: 2 oratorios, which were moderately successful: *The Resurrection and Ascension* (London, Dec. 2, 1840) and *Mount Carmel* (London, June 30, 1886); also many pieces of church music; glees, part-songs; organ pieces. His widow publ. a memoir, *Life and Reminiscences of George J. Elvey* (London, 1894).

Elvey, Stephen, English organist and composer, brother of **Sir George Elvey;** b. Canterbury, June 27, 1805; d. Oxford, Oct. 6, 1860. He was a chorister of Canterbury Cathedral, and a pupil of Skeats there; in 1830 he became organist of New College, Oxford; Mus. Bac. (1831); Mus. Doc. (1838). He was Choragus at Oxford from 1848 until his death. He wrote mostly church music, and publ. a successful handbook, *The Psalter, or Canticles and Psalms, Pointed for Chanting, upon a New Principle* (London; 6 eds. to 1866).

Elwart, Antoine-Aimable-Élie, French writer on music and composer; b. Paris, Nov. 18, 1808; d. there, Oct. 14, 1877. A chorister at St.-Eustache when 10 years old, he was apprenticed at 13 to a mechanic, but ran away, and joined a small theater orch. as violinist. From 1825–34 he studied at the Paris Cons., taking the Grand Prix de Rome in 1834; taught at the Paris Cons. from 1836 to 1871. Among his pupils were Gouvy, Grisar, and Weckerlin.

WORKS: an opera, *Les Catalans* (Rouen, 1840); an "oratorio-symphonie" *Noé, ou le déluge universel* (Paris, 1845); oratorio, *La Naissance d'Ève* (Paris, 1846); *Les Noces de Cana,* a mystery; *Ruth et Booz,* a vocal symphony; Masses, cantatas, a Te Deum, a Miserere, and other church music; symphonies, overtures, chamber music, etc. He is better known by his musico-literary works: *Duprez, sa vie artistique, avec une biographie authentique de son maître A. Choron* (1838), *Théorie musicale* (*Solfège progressif,* etc., 1840), *Feuille harmonique* (1841), *Le Chanteur accompagnateur* (1844), *Traité de contrepoint et de la fugue, Essai sur la Transposition, Études élémentaires de musique* (1845), *L'Art de chanter en chœur, L'Art de jouer impromptu de l'alto-viola, Solfège de jeune âge, Le Contrepoint et la fugue appliqués au style idéal, Lutrin et Orphéon* (theoretical and practical vocal studies), *Histoire de la Société des Concerts du Conservatoire* (1860; 2d ed. 1863), *Manuel des aspirants aux grades de chef et de souschef de musique dans l'armée française* (1862), *Petit manuel d' instrumentation* (1864), *Histoire de concerts populaires* (1864). His projected complete ed. of his own compositions (1867–70) reached only vol. III.

Elwell, Herbert, American composer and music critic; b. Minneapolis, May 10, 1898; d. Cleveland, April 17, 1974. He studied at the Univ. of Minnesota; then took courses with Ernest Bloch in N.Y. and Nadia Boulanger in Paris in 1926–27; held a fellowship at the American Academy in Rome. Returning to the U.S. he held a post as teacher of composition at the Cleveland Music Institute; from 1932 to 1964 served as music critic for the Cleveland *Plain Dealer.*

WORKS: His most successful work was the ballet *The Happy Hypocrite,* after Max Beerbohm (an orchestral suite drawn from the score was performed in Rome on May 21, 1927, with Elwell himself conducting); *Introduction and Allegro* for orch. (N.Y., July 12, 1942); *I Was With Him,* cantata for male chorus, tenor solo, and 2 pianos (Cleveland, Nov. 30, 1942); *Blue Symphony,* for voice and string quartet (Cleveland, Feb. 2, 1945); *Lincoln: Requiem Aeternam,* for chorus and orch. (Oberlin, Feb. 16, 1947); *Pastorale,* for voice and orch. (Cleveland, March 25, 1948); *Ode* for orch. (1950); *The Forever Young,* for voice and orch. (Cleveland, Oct. 29, 1953); 2 string quartets; Piano Sonata, Violin Sonata, etc.

Elwes, Gervase, English tenor; b. Billing Hall, near Northampton, Nov. 15, 1866; d. Boston, Mass., Jan. 12, 1921. He began his career as a diplomat; while stationed in Vienna (1891–95) he studied singing; during his sojourn in Paris he took voice lessons with Bouhy, and soon achieved competence as a concert singer. He made a tour of Germany in 1907 and two tours in the U.S. (1909 and 1921; died on his 2nd tour; killed by train in the railroad station in Boston). He excelled in oratorio; sang Elgar's *Dream of Gerontius* about 150 times. Winifred and Richard Elwes published an impassioned family monograph, *Gervase Elwes: The Story of His Life* (London, 1935).

Emerson, Luther Orlando, American composer and conductor; b. Parsonsfield, Maine, Aug. 3, 1820; d. Hyde Park, Mass., Sept. 29, 1915. He was a competent composer of church music, a popular conductor of the early musical conventions, and a compiler of numerous successful collections of songs and hymn tunes: *The Romberg Collection* (1853), *The Golden Wreath* (1857, Sunday-school music), *The Golden Harp* (1860), *The Sabbath Harmony* (1860), *The Harp of Ju-*

dah (1863), *Merry Chimes* (1865), *Jubilate* (1866), and *The Chorus Wreath.*

Emery, Stephen Albert, American music teacher, writer, and composer; b. Paris, Maine, Oct. 4, 1841; d. Boston, April 15, 1891. His first teacher was H. S. Edwards, of Portland; in 1862 he went to Leipzig, where he studied with Plaidy, Papperitz, Richter, and Hauptmann. He returned to Portland in 1864; went to Boston in 1866; taught at the New England Cons. there from 1867. He publ. 2 textbooks, *Foundation Studies in Piano Playing* and *Elements of Harmony* (1879; several later editions).

Emery, Walter, English organist and writer; b. Tilshead, Wiltshire, June 14, 1909; d. Salisbury, June 24, 1974. He studied organ at the Royal Academy of Music in London; then was engaged as church organist; in 1937 became an associate of Novello & Co. in the editorial dept.; publ. several valuable books and pamphlets: *The St. Matthew Passion: its Preparation and Performance* (with Sir Adrian Boult; London, 1949); *Bach's Ornaments* (London, 1953); commentaries on Bach's organ works, etc.

Emmanuel, Maurice, eminent French music scholar; b. Bar-sur-Aube, May 2, 1862; d. Paris, Dec. 14, 1938. He received primary education in Dijon; sang in the church choir in Beaune; then studied at the Paris Cons. (1880–87) with Savard, Dubois, Delibes, and Bourgault-Ducoudray; then specialized in the musical history of antiquity under Gevaert in Brussels; also studied ancient languages at the Sorbonne; Licencié ès Lettres (1887); Docteur ès Lettres (1895) with the theses *De saltationis disciplina apud Graecos* (publ. in Latin, Paris, 1895) and *La Danse grecque antique d'après les monuments figurés* (Paris, 1896; in English as *The Antique Greek Dance after Sculptured and Painted Figures,* N.Y., 1916). He was prof. of art history at the Lycée Racine and Lycée Lamartine (1898–1905); maître de chapelle at Ste.-Clotilde (1904–07); in 1907 he succeeded Bourgault-Ducoudray as prof. of music history at the Paris Cons., and held this post for 30 years; edited vols. 17 and 18 of the complete works of Rameau; also Bach's works in Durand's edition of the classical masters.

WRITINGS: *Histoire de la langue musicale* (2 vols.; Paris, 1911; new ed., 1928); *Traité de l'accompagnement modal des psaumes* (Lyons, 1912); *La Polyphonie sacrée* (with R. Moissenet; Dijon, 1923); *Pelléas et Mélisande de Claude Debussy* (Paris, 1926); *César Franck* (Paris, 1930); *Antonin Reicha* (Paris, 1937); also articles in the *Revue Musicale, Musical Quarterly,* etc.

WORKS: an opera, *Salamine* (Paris, June 28, 1929); opéra-bouffe, *Amphitryon* (Paris, Feb. 20, 1937); 2 symphonies (1919; 1931); 2 string quartets and other chamber music; 6 piano sonatinas; vocal music (much of it published).

BIBLIOGRAPHY: special issue of the *Revue Musicale* devoted to Maurice Emmanuel (1947).

Emmett, Daniel Decatur, American composer of *Dixie* and other popular songs; b. Mt. Vernon, Ohio, Oct. 29, 1815; d. there, June 28, 1904. He began his career as drummer in military bands; then joined the Virginia Minstrels, singing and playing the banjo; later was a member of Bryant's Minstrels. He wrote the lyrics and the music of *Dixie* in 1859, and it was performed for the first time in New York on April 4, 1859; upon publication, the popularity of the song spread, and it was adopted as a Southern fighting song during the Civil War (even though Emmett was a Northerner). His other songs, *Old Dan Tucker, The Road to Richmond, Walk Along,* etc., enjoyed great favor for some years, but were eclipsed by *Dixie.*

BIBLIOGRAPHY: Ch. B. Galbreath, *Daniel Decatur Emmett* (Columbus, Ohio, 1904); R. B. Harwell, *Confederate Music* (Chapel Hill, N.C., 1950); Hans Nathan, "Dixie," *Musical Quarterly* (Jan. 1949); H. O. Wintermute, *Daniel Decatur Emmett* (Mount Vernon, Ohio, 1955); Hans Nathan, *Dan Emmett and the Rise of Early Negro Minstrelsy* (Norman, Oklahoma, 1962).

Enacovici, George, Rumanian composer; b. Focşani, May 4, 1891; d. Bucharest, Jan. 26, 1965. He studied at the Bucharest Cons. with Kiriac and Castaldi (1905–12); studied composition, with d'Indy, and violin at the Schola Cantorum in Paris (1914–18); taught violin at the Bucharest Cons. (1919–54) and was concertmaster of the Bucharest Philh. (1920–21) and the Bucharest Radio Orch. (1928–33). He was a founder-member of the Society of Rumanian Composers (1920).

WORKS: *Intermezzo* for string orch. and harp (1912); *Poem* for violin and orch. (1920); *Suite in a Rumanian Style* for orch. (1928); *Symphonic Episode* (1933); *Rapsodie română* for orch. (1934); *Amfitrita,* symph. poem with violin obbligato (1940); *Arlequinada,* capriccio for 2 violins and chamber orch. (1941); *Symphony* (1954); *Violin Concerto* (1956); 3 string quartets; *Violin Sonata; Piano Sonata;* minor pieces in various genres.

Encina, Juan del, Spanish poet and composer; b. Salamanca, July 12, 1468; d. León, late in 1529. He was the son of a shoemaker of Salamanca named Juan de Fermoselle; became chorister at Salamanca Cathedral; studied music under his elder brother, Diego de Fermoselle, and under Fernando de Torrijos; took his degree in law at Salamanca Univ., where he enjoyed the favor of the chancellor, Don Gutiérrez de Toledo. About 1492 he entered the household of the 2nd Duke of Alba, for whom he wrote a series of pastoral eclogues that form the foundation of the Spanish secular drama. These eclogues included 'villancicos,' or rustic songs, for which Encina composed the music. He went to Rome in 1500; on May 12, 1500, was appointed canon at the Cathedral of Salamanca; from Feb. 2, 1510 until 1512, he was archdeacon and canon of Málaga; on May 2, 1512, he again went to Rome; his *Farsa de Plácida e Vittoriano* was performed there in the presence of Julius II on Jan. 11, 1513. In 1517, he was 'subcollector of revenues to the Apostolic Chamber'; in 1519, appointed prior of León, and that same year made a pilgrimage to Jerusalem, where he was ordained a priest. He described his sacred pilgrimage in *Tribagia o Via Sacra de Hierusalem* (Rome, 1521). After the death of Leo X in 1521, Encina returned to Spain and spent his last years as prior at León. Besides being the creator of the Spanish drama, Encina was the most important Spanish composer of the reign of Ferdinand and Isabella; he cultivated with notable artistry a type of part-song akin to the Italian "frottola," setting his own poems to music. Sixty-eight of these songs are preserved in the valuable *Cancionero musical de los siglos XV y XVI,* ed. by F. A. Barbieri (Madrid, 1890; new ed., in 3 vols., by H. Anglès, 1947, 1951, 1953). No religious music by Encina is known to exist.

BIBLIOGRAPHY: E. Diaz-Jiménez, *Juan del Encina en León* (Madrid, 1909); R. Mitjana, *Estudios sobre algunos músicos españoles del siglo XVI* (Madrid, 1918); R. Espinosa Maeso, "Nuevos datos biográphicos de Juan del Encina," *Boletín de la Royal Academia Española* (1921); J. Subirá, *La música en la Casa de Alba* (1927); F. Pedrell, *Cancionero musical popular español* (new ed., 2 vols., Barcelona, 1936); J. P. Wichersham Crawford, *Spanish Drama Before Lope de Vega* (revised ed., Philadelphia, 1937); G. Chase, "Origins of the Lyric Theater in Spain," *Musical Quarterly* (July 1939); G. Chase, "Juan del Encina, Poet and Musician," *Music & Letters* (Oct. 1939); C. Terni, "Juan del Encina," *Chigiana* (1968).

Enckhausen, Heinrich Friedrich, German organist and composer; b. Celle, Aug. 28, 1799; d. Hannover, Jan. 15, 1885. He studied with Aloys Schmitt in Berlin, succeeding him as court organist. He wrote an opera *Der Savoyard* (Hannover, 1832) and sacred music; publ. a book of chorales.

Ende, Heinrich vom, German music publisher; b. Essen, Aug. 12, 1858; d. Cologne, Jan. 20, 1904. He published popular manuals on music, such as *Schatzkästlein;* also composed a considerable number of male choruses (*Das Kätzchen; Es ist ein Brünnlein geflossen,* etc.), songs, and piano pieces.

Enesco (Enescu), Georges, foremost Rumanian composer and violinist; b. Liveni-Virnaz, Aug. 19, 1881; d. Paris, May 4, 1955. He began to play violin when only 4 years old, taking lessons with a Rumanian gypsy violinist, Nicolas Chioru; then studied with the violinist and composer, Caudella; from 1888–93 he was a pupil at the Vienna Cons. under Hellmesberger (violin) and R. Fuchs (theory), winning first prize in violin and harmony (1892); 1894–99 he studied at the Paris Cons. with Marsick (violin), Fauré and Massenet (composition); won second *accessit* for counterpoint and fugue (1897) and first prize for violin (1899); at the same time he studied cello, organ, and piano, attaining more than ordinary proficiency on all these instruments. His talent for composition manifested itself very early, his first efforts dating from his student days in Vienna; on June 11, 1897, when he was not quite sixteen, he presented in Paris a concert of his own works (a string quintet, piano suite, violin sonata, and songs), which attracted the attention of Colonne, who produced the following year the youthful composer's op. 1, *Poème roumain.* On March 8, 1903, he conducted in Bucharest the first performances of his two *Rumanian Rhapsodies,* the first of which was to become his most enduring work. He was appointed court violinist to the Queen of Rumania; gave master

classes in violin interpretation at the École Normale de Musique; among his pupils was Yehudi Menuhin. In 1912 he offered an annual prize for Rumanian composers (won by Jora, Enacovici, Stan Golestan, Otescu, and others); then toured Europe; first visited the U.S. in 1923, making his debut as conductor, composer, and violinist in a N.Y. concert of the Philadelphia Orch. (Jan. 2, 1923); returned to the U.S. in 1937, and conducted the N.Y. Philh. on Jan. 28, 1937, and several subsequent concerts with remarkable success; reengaged in 1938 and conducted the N.Y. Philh. in 14 concerts; appeared twice as a violinist; also conducted two concerts of Rumanian music at the N.Y. World's Fair (May, 1939). The outbreak of World War II found Enesco in Rumania, where he lived on his farm in Sinaia, near Bucharest. He remained there through the war years; in 1946 he came again to the U.S. to teach in N.Y. On Jan. 21, 1950, on the 60th anniversary of his first public appearance at the age of 8, he played a farewell concert in N.Y. in the multiple capacity of violinist, pianist, conductor, and composer, in a program comprising Bach's Double Concerto (with his pupil, Yehudi Menuhin), his Violin Sonata (playing the piano part with Menuhin), and his *First Rumanian Rhapsody* (conducting the orch.). He then returned to Paris; in July 1954 he suffered a stroke, and became an invalid for his remaining days. In homage to his accomplishment in Rumanian music, his native village was renamed Enescu and a street in Bucharest was also named after him. Periodical *Enescu Festivals* and international performing contests were established in Bucharest in 1958. Enesco had an extraordinary range of musical interests. His compositions include artistic stylizations of Rumanian folk strains; his style was neo-romantic, but he made occasional use of experimental devices, such as quarter tones in his opera, *Œdipe.* He possessed a fabulous memory and was able to play complete symphonic works without the scores.

WORKS: LYRIC TRAGEDY, *Œdipe* (1931; Paris, Grand Opéra, March 10, 1936; Bucharest, posthumous production, Sept. 22, 1958); FOR ORCH.: 3 early symphonies, unnumbered (1895, 1896, 1898); Symph. No. 1 (Paris, Jan. 21, 1906); No. 2 (Bucharest, March 28, 1915); No. 3 (1918; Bucharest, May 25, 1919); Symph. No. 4 (1934; unfinished); Symph. No. 5, with tenor and women's chorus (1941; unfinished); *Ballad* for violin and orch. (1895); *Tragic Overture* (1895); Violin Concerto (1896; Paris, March 26, 1896, at a Paris Cons. concert); Fantasy for Piano and Orch. (1896; Bucharest, March 26, 1900); *Rumanian Poem* (1897; Paris, Feb. 9, 1898); *Pastorale* (1899; Paris, Feb. 19, 1899); *Rumanian Rhapsody No. 1* (1901) and *No. 2* (1902; both performed for the first time in Bucharest, March 8, 1903, Enesco conducting); *Symphonie concertante* for cello and orch. (1901; Paris, March 14, 1909); Suite No. 1 (1903; Paris, Dec. 11, 1904); Suite No. 2 (1915; Bucharest, March 27, 1916, Enesco conducting); Suite No. 3, *Villageoise* (1938; N.Y. Philharmonic, Feb. 2, 1939, Enesco conducting); *Concert Overture on Popular Rumanian Themes* (1948; Washington, D.C., Jan. 23, 1949, Enesco conducting); *Symphonie de chambre* (1954; Paris, Jan. 23, 1955); *Vox maris,* symph. poem (1955; posthumous, Bucharest, Sept. 10, 1964). CHAMBER MUSIC: *Ballad* for violin and piano (1895); Piano

Quintet (1895); Violin Sonata No. 1 (1897); *Nocturne et Saltarelle* for cello and piano (1897); Cello Sonata No. 1 (1898); Violin Sonata No. 2 (1899); *Aubade* for string trio (1899); Octet for 4 Violins, 2 Violas and 2 Cellos (1900); *Intermezzo* for strings (1903); *Allegro de concert* for harp and piano (1904); *Dixtuor* for wind instruments (1906); *Au soir*, nocturne for 4 trumpets (1906); *Legenda* for trumpet and piano (1906); *Konzertstück* for viola and piano (1906); Piano Quartet No. 1 (1909); String Quartet No. 1 (1920); Violin Sonata No. 3 "in popular Rumanian character" (1926); Cello Sonata No. 2 (1935); Piano Quintet No. 2 (1940); *Impressions d'enfance* for violin and piano (1940); Piano Quartet No. 2 (1944); String Quartet No. 2 (1951). FOR PIANO: *Variations on an Original Theme* for 2 pianos (1899); 2 suites for piano solo: No. 1, *Dans le style ancien* (1897); No. 2 (1903); *Pièces impromptues* (1915–16); 3 sonatas (1924, 1927, 1934). VOCAL WORKS: *La Vision de Saul*, cantata (1895); *L'Aurore*, cantata (1898); *Waldgesang* for chorus (1898); many songs to words by the Queen of Rumania, who wrote poetry in German under the pen name Carmen Sylva, among them *Armes Mägdlein* (1898), *Der Schmetterlingskuss* (1898), *Schlaflos* (1898), *Frauenberuf* (1898), *Sphynx* (1898), *Königshusarenlied* (1899), *Ein Sonnenblick* (1901), *Regen* (1903), *Entsagen* (1907), *Morgengebet* (1908); also several cycles of songs to French texts.
BIBLIOGRAPHY: B. Gavoty, *Les Souvenirs de Georges Enesco* (Paris, 1955); G. Balan, *George Enescu* (Bucharest, 1962); B. Kotlyarov, *George Enescu* (Moscow, 1965); M. Voicana, et al., ed., *George Enescu*, a symposium (2 vols., Bucharest, 1971). A complete list of works and extensive bibliography is found in Viorel Cosma, *Muzicieni Romăni* (Bucharest, 1970).

Engel, Carl, German musical historiographer; b. Thiedenwiese, near Hannover, July 6, 1818; d. by suicide, London, Nov. 17, 1882. He studied organ with Enckhausen at Hannover and piano with Hummel at Weimar. After residing in Hamburg, Warsaw, and Berlin, he went to Manchester, England, in 1846, and in 1850 to London. There he became an influential writer, and an authority on musical history and musical instruments.
WRITINGS: *The Pianist's Handbook* (1853), *Piano School for Young Beginners* (1855), *Reflections on Church Music* (1856); his lifework began with *The Music of the Most Ancient Nations, Particularly of the Assyrians, Egyptians, and Hebrews* (1864), followed by *An Introduction to the Study of National Music* (1866); *Musical Instruments of all Countries* (1869); *Catalogue of the Special Exhibition of Ancient Musical Instruments* (2d ed., 1873); *Descriptive Catalogue of the Musical Instruments in the South Kensington Museum* (1874); *Musical Myths and Facts* (1876); *The Literature of National Music* (1879); *Researches into the Early History of the Violin Family* (1883). Among his unpublished MSS is a large history of the musical instruments of the world (4 quarto vols. with over 800 illustrations).
BIBLIOGRAPHY: Carl Engel, "Some Letters to a Namesake," *Musical Quarterly* (July 1942); Gustave

Reese, "More About the Namesake," in *A Birthday Offering to Carl Engel* (N.Y., 1943).

Engel, Carl, distinguished American musicologist and writer on music; b. Paris, July 21, 1883; d. New York, May 6, 1944. He was a great-grandson of **Josef Kroll,** founder of Kroll's Etablissement in Berlin, and grandson of **J. C. Engel,** who made the 'Kroll Opera' famous. Carl Engel was educated at the Universities of Strasbourg and Munich; studied composition in Munich with Thuille. He came to the U.S. in 1905 and established himself as editor, musicologist, librarian, and publisher. He was editor and musical advisor of the Boston Music Co. (1909–21); chief of the Music Division of the Library of Congress (1922–34); president of G. Schirmer, Inc. (1929–32); in 1939 became editor of the *Musical Quarterly;* from 1934 again president of G. Schirmer, Inc., and honorary consultant in musicology for the Library of Congress; U.S. delegate to the Beethoven Centenary, Vienna, 1927; U.S. representative of the International Society of Musicology; first chairman of the Committee on Musicology, American Council of Learned Societies; president of the American Musicological Society (1937–38); honorary member of the Harvard Musical Association; Fellow of the American Academy of Arts and Letters; honorary Mus. Doc., Oberlin College (1934); Chevalier of the Légion d'Honneur (1937); recipient of the Elizabeth Sprague Coolidge medal 'for eminent services rendered to chamber music' (1935). A writer with a brilliant style and of wide learning, Carl Engel contributed valuable essays to the *Musical Quarterly* (*Views and Reviews;* articles on Chadwick, Loeffler, etc.); publ. two collections of essays: *Alla Breve, from Bach to Debussy* (N.Y., 1921); *Discords Mingled* (N.Y., 1931). Carl Engel was also a composer; his music was in the French tradition, in an impressionistic vein; his songs, particularly his settings of poems by Amy Lowell, were often sung (the best known among them is *Sea-Shell*); other works include *Triptych* for violin and piano; *Perfumes,* for piano (an album of 5 pieces); *Presque Valse* for piano was publ. posthumously.
BIBLIOGRAPHY: G. Reese, ed., *A Birthday Offering to Carl Engel* (N.Y., 1943); Harold Bauer, "Carl Engel," *Musical Quarterly* (July 1944); G. Reese, "A Postscript" (ibid.); H. Putnam and E. S. Coolidge, "Tributes to Carl Engel," *Musical Quarterly* (April 1945).

Engel, David Hermann, German organist and composer; b. Neuruppin, Jan. 22, 1816; d. Merseburg, May 3, 1877. He studied in Breslau; in 1848 became organist at Merseburg; wrote a comic opera *Prinz Carneval* (Berlin, 1862); publ. a *Beitrag zur Geschichte des Orgelbauwesens* (1855).

Engel, Gabriel, American writer, violinist, and composer; b. Beregszasz, Hungary, May 4, 1892; d. Vergennes, Vermont, Aug. 1, 1952. He was the author of *The Life of Anton Bruckner* (N.Y., 1931) and *Gustav Mahler—Song-Symphonist* (N.Y., 1932); also editor of *Chord and Discord,* the magazine of the Bruckner Society of America. During the last 15 years of his life he was engaged in the rare books business.

Engel, Gustav Eduard, German music critic and singing teacher; b. Königsberg, Oct. 29, 1823; d. Berlin, July 19, 1895. He was music critic of the *Vossische Zeitung* from 1861; taught singing at Kullak's Academy from 1862; among his pupils was Lola Beeth. He publ. *Sängerbrevier* (daily vocal exercises, 1860), *Ästhetik der Tonkunst* (1884), and other books and articles.

Engel, Hans, eminent German musicologist; b. Cairo, Egypt, Dec. 20, 1894; d. Marburg, May 15, 1970. He studied in Munich with Klose and Sandberger; after receiving his *Dr. phil.* at the Univ. of Munich, he occupied teaching posts at Königsberg and Marburg. He publ. *Die Entwicklung des deutschen Klavierkonzertes von Mozart bis Liszt* (Leipzig, 1927); *Carl Loewe* (Greifswald, 1934); *Franz Liszt* (Potsdam, 1936); *Deutschland und Italien in ihren musikgeschichtlichen Beziehungen* (Regensburg, 1944); *J. S. Bach* (Berlin, 1950); *Musik der Völker und Zeiten* (Hannover, 1952). He was the editor of works by Marenzio, Joh. Fischer, Torelli; also of *Denkmäler der Musik in Pommern.*

Engel, Joel, Russian writer on music; b. Berdiansk, April 16, 1868; d. Tel Aviv, Palestine, Feb. 11, 1927. He studied at Kharkov; later with Taneyev and Ippolitov-Ivanov in Moscow. In 1922 he went to Berlin, where he organized a publishing house for propaganda of Jewish music; issued a collection of Jewish folksongs in 3 vols. His publications in the Russian language are: *Pocket Music Dictionary* (Moscow, 1913); *Essays on Music History* (Moscow, 1911); *In the Opera* (1911).

Engel, Johann Jakob, German musician and writer; b. Parchim, Mecklenburg, Sept. 11, 1741; d. there, June 28, 1802. He was tutor to the Crown Prince (later Friedrich Wilhelm III); publ. an interesting essay, *Über die musikalische Malerei* (1780).

Engel, Lehman (actually **A. Lehman**), American composer and conductor; b. Jackson, Miss., Sept. 14, 1910. He studied at the Cincinnati College of Music and at the Juilliard Graduate School, N.Y., where he took courses with Rubin Goldmark; also had private sessions with Sessions. After graduation (1934) he devoted himself chiefly to theater conducting; toured with musical comedy troupes; conducted many premières of modern operas; was founder and conductor of the Madrigal Singers (1936–39), with which he presented early American music and works of the polyphonic masters. As a composer, Engel is at his happiest in theater music; his choral writing is expert.
    WORKS: OPERAS: *Pierrot of the Minuet* (Cincinnati, April 3, 1928), *Malady of Love* (N.Y., May 27, 1954), *The Soldier* (N.Y., Nov. 25, 1956; concert version); *Golden Ladder,* a musical (Cleveland, May 28, 1953). BALLETS: *Phobias* (N.Y., Nov. 18, 1932), *Ceremonials* (N.Y., May 13, 1933), *Transitions* (N.Y., Feb. 19, 1934), *The Shoebird* (Jackson, Miss., April 20, 1968). Incidental music to Shakespeare's plays: *Hamlet* (1938), *Macbeth* (1941), *Julius Caesar* (1955), *The Tempest* (1960); also music to plays by contemporary authors. FOR ORCH.: 2 symphonies (1939, 1945); Violin Concerto (1945); Viola Concerto (1945); *The Creation,* for narrator and orch. (1947); *Overture Jackson* (Jackson, Miss., Feb. 13, 1961). CHAMBER MUSIC: Cello Sonata (1945); Violin Sonata (1953). FOR CHORUS: *Rain* (1929); *Rest* (1936); *Chansons innocentes* (1938); *Let Us Now Praise Famous Men* (1955). He published an autobiography, *This Bright Day* (N.Y., 1956; new ed., 1974); an instruction book, *Planning and Producing the Musical Show* (N.Y., 1957; revised, 1966); *The American Musical Theater: A Consideration* (N.Y., 1967); edited the collection, *Three Centuries of Choral Music: Renaissance to Baroque* (N.Y., 1939–56). A detailed list of Lehman Engel's works for the theater is found in Walter Rigdon, ed. *Who's Who of the American Theater* (N.Y., 1966).

Engelke, Bernhard, German musicologist; b. Brunswick, Sept. 2, 1884; d. Kirchbarkau, near Kiel, May 16, 1950. He studied at Halle with H. Abert and at Leipzig Univ. with Riemann (Dr. phil. 1908 for his dissertation on J. F. Fasch). In 1912 he went to Magdeburg as teacher and choirmaster at the Cathedral; in 1925 he settled in Kiel. He published numerous articles in music journals dealing mainly with German church music and musicians.

Engelmann, Hans Ulrich, German composer; b. Darmstadt, Sept. 8, 1921. He had piano lessons while in high school; after the end of the disrupting war, he took courses in composition with Wolfgang Fortner in Heidelberg (1945–49); in 1948–50 he attended the classes of René Leibowitz and Ernst Krenek in Darmstadt; enrolled at the Univ. of Frankfurt (1946–52) in the classes of musicology (with Gennrich and Osthoff) and philosophy (with Adorno); in 1952, received his Dr. phil. with a thesis on Béla Bartók's *Mikrokosmos* (publ. Würzburg, 1953). Parallel to these pursuits, he took courses in architecture. In 1949 he held a Harvard Univ. stipend at the Salzburg Seminar in American Studies; was active in radio programming, composition for films and for the theater; spent a season in Iceland (1953–54); then was theater composer in Darmstadt (1954–61). In 1969 he was appointed instructor at the Musikhochschule in Frankfurt. His early works are impregnated by chromaticism with an impressionistic tinge; rhythmically his music is affected by jazz techniques. Under the influence of Leibowitz and Krenek he adopted the 12-tone method of composition, expanding it into a sui generis "field technique" of total serialism, in which rhythms and instrumental timbres are organized systematically. In his theater music he utilizes aleatory devices, musique concrète, and electronic sonorities.
    WORKS: *Klangstück* for violin and piano (1947); Concerto for Cello and String Orch. (1948); *Doktor Fausts Höllenfahrt,* chamber opera (Hamburg, Jan. 11, 1951); *Orchester-Fantasie* (1951); String Quartet (1953); *Komposition in 4 Teilen* (1953; his first work in the 12-tone technique); Partita for 3 Trumpets, Percussion and Strings (1953); *Integrale* for saxophone and piano (1954); *Strukturen* for chamber orch. (1954); *Atlantische Ballade* for voices, strings and percussion (1955); *Die Mauer,* dramatic cantata, after Langston Hughes (radio production, Hamburg, Oct. 4, 1955; stage première, Darmstadt, March 21, 1960);

Metall, "chronicle" for soloists, chorus and orch. (1958); *Permutazioni* for flute, oboe, clarinet and bassoon (1959); *Ezra Pound Music* for chamber orch. (1959); *Der Verlorene Schatten,* opera (1960); *Trias* for piano, orch. and magnetic tape (1962); *Noche de Luna,* ballet (Lübeck, June 1, 1965); *Duplum* for 2 pianos (1965); *Manifest vom Menschen,* oratorio (1966); *Capricciosi* for orch. (1967); *Der Fall Van Damm,* radio opera (Cologne, June 7, 1968); *Sinfonies* for orch. (1968); *Ophelia,* music for action theater (Hannover, Feb. 1, 1969); *Drei Kreise* for orch. groups (1970).

Englert, Giuseppe Giorgio, Italian organist and composer; b. Fiesole, near Florence, July 22, 1927. He studied composition with Willy Burkhard at the Zürich Cons. (1945–48); in 1949 went to Paris, where he took organ lessons with André Marchal (1949–56), became his assistant as organist of the St. Eustache Church (1957–62); in 1970 he was appointed a lecturer at the Univ. of Paris at Vincennes.
WORKS: *Rime serie* for wind quintet (1958–61); *Au Jour ultime liesse,* cantata for voice and 6 instruments (1961–63); *Les Avoines folles* for string quartet (1962–63); *Aria* for timpani and 13 instruments (1965); *La joute des lierres* for string quartet (1965–66); *Tarok,* musical game for 3–6 string instruments (1967); *Vagans animula* for organ and tape (1969); *Maquillage,* theatrical composition for voice, scenic apparatus and tape (1967–71); *Cantus plumbeus* for organ (1972); *Non pulsando* for organ (1972); *Caracol* for 15 instruments (1974).

English, Granville, American composer; b. Louisville, Kentucky, Jan. 27, 1895; d. New York, Sept. 1, 1968. He was educated at the Chicago Musical College (Mus. Bac., 1915).
WORKS: *Ugly Duckling,* cantata (1924); *Among the Hills,* orchestral scherzo (Oklahoma City, March 9, 1952); *Mood Tropicale,* for orch. (Baltimore, Feb. 5, 1955); *Evenings by the Sea,* symphonic poem (Port Washington, Long Island, N.Y., Jan. 20, 1956); *Song of the Caravan* for male chorus (1937); piano pieces; violin pieces; songs.

Englund, Einar, Finnish composer; b. Ljugarn, Gotland, Sweden, June 17, 1916. He studied at the Sibelius Academy in Helsinki (1933–45); in 1949 he took a course in composition with Aaron Copland in Tanglewood. Returning to Finland, he became a teacher at the Sibelius Academy.
WORKS: Piano Quintet (1941); Symph. No. 1 (1946); *Epinaka,* symph. poem (1947); Symph. No. 2 (1948); *The Great Wall of China,* symph. suite from incidental music to Max Frisch's play (1949); Cello Concerto (1954); Piano Concerto No. 1 (1955); *Odysseus,* symph. suite (1959); *Sinuhe,* symph. suite from the ballet (1965); Chaconne for Chorus, Trombone and Double Bass (1969); *Introduzione e Capriccio* for violin and piano (1970); Symph. No. 3, *Cholecystitis* (Helsinki, May 12, 1972); Piano Concerto No. 2 (1974); music for numerous radio plays and films.

Enna, August, eminent Danish composer; b. Nakskov, May 13, 1860; d. Copenhagen, Aug. 3, 1939. He was partly of German and Italian blood; his grandfa-

ther, an Italian soldier in Napoleon's army, married a German girl, and settled in Denmark. Enna was brought to Copenhagen as a child, and went to school there. He learned to play piano and violin; had sporadic instruction in theory; later became a member of a traveling orch. and played with it in Finland (1880). Upon his return to Copenhagen, he taught piano and played for dancers; in 1883 he conducted a theater orch.; and wrote his first stage work *A Village Tale,* which he produced in 1883. After these practical experiences, he began to study seriously; took lessons with Schjorring (violin), Matthesson (organ) and Rasmussen (composition) and soon published a number of piano pieces, which attracted the attention of Niels Gade, who used his influence to obtain a traveling fellowship for Enna; this made it possible for Enna to study in Germany (1888–89) and acquire a complete mastery of instrumental and vocal writing.
WORKS: He followed the German Romantic School, being influenced mainly by Weber's type of opera, and by Grieg and Gade in the use of local color; the first product of this period was his most successful work, in the opera *Heksen* (*The Witch*) produced in Copenhagen (Jan. 24, 1892), then in Germany. Enna's other operas also enjoyed a modicum of success; these are *Cleopatra* (Copenhagen, Feb. 7, 1894); *Aucassin and Nicolette* (Copenhagen, Feb. 2, 1896); *The Match Girl,* after Andersen (Copenhagen, Nov. 13, 1897); *Lamia* (Antwerp, Oct. 3, 1899); *Ung Elskov* (first produced in Weimar, under the title *Heisse Liebe,* Dec. 6, 1904); *Princess on the Pea,* after Andersen (Aarhus, Sept. 15, 1900); *The Nightingale,* also after Andersen (Aarhus, Sept. 15, 1900); *The Nightingale,* also after Andersen (Copenhagen, Nov. 10, 1912); *Gloria Arsena* (Copenhagen, April 15, 1917); *Comedians,* after Victor Hugo's *L'Homme qui rit* (Copenhagen, April 8, 1920); *Don Juan Mañara* (Copenhagen, April 17, 1925). He further wrote the ballets: *The Shepherdess and the Chimney Sweep* (Copenhagen, Oct. 6, 1901); *St. Cecilia's Golden Shoe* (Copenhagen, Dec. 26, 1904); *The Kiss* (Copenhagen, Oct. 19, 1927); also a violin concerto, two symphonies; an overture *Hans Christian Andersen;* choral pieces.

Enríquez, Manuel, Mexican composer and violinist; b. Ocotlán, June 17, 1926. He studied violin with Camarena and composition with Bernal Jiménez at the Guadalajara Cons. (1942–50); then went to New York and took lessons in composition with Peter Mennin and violin with Ivan Galamian at the Juilliard School of Music (1955–57); also had private theory lessons with Stefan Wolpe and attended the Columbia-Princeton Electonic Music Center (1971). Returning to Mexico, he was concertmaster of the Guadalajara Symph. Orch.; later supervised music courses at the Institute of Fine Arts in Mexico City. In 1975 he went to France under a special commission from the Mexican government. As a composer, he follows the median line of cosmopolitan modernism, making use of a severe constructivist idiom, employing graphic optical notation.
WORKS: *Suite* for violin and piano (1949); 2 violin concertos (1955, 1966); Symph. No. 1 (1957); 3 string quartets (1959, 1967, 1974); *Preámbulo* for orch. (1961); Sonatina for solo cello (1962); *Divertimento*

for flute, clarinet and bassoon (1962); *4 Pieces* for viola and piano (1962); *Obertura Lírica* for orch. (1963); *Pentamúsica* for wind quintet (1963); *Tres Formas Concertantes* for violin, cello, clarinet, bassoon, horn, piano and percussion (1964); Violin Sonata (1964); *Tres Invenciones* for flute and viola (1964); *Módulos* for 2 pianos (1965); *Transición* for orch. (1965); *Poema* for cello and small string orch. (1966); *Ego* for female voice, flute, cello, piano and percussion (1966); *Trayectorias* for orch. (1967); *Ambivalencia* for violin and cello (1967); *Si Libet* for orch. (1968); *5 Plus 2* for flute, viola, trombone, piano, and percussion, with actress and director (1969); *Concierto para 8* (1969); *Ixamatl* for orch. (1969); *Díptico I* for flute and piano (1969); *Díptico II* for violin and piano (1971); *Presagios* for piano (1970); *Móvil I* for piano (1969); Piano Concerto (1971); *El y Ellos* for solo violin and orch. ensemble (1973).

Enriquez de Valderrabano, Enrique, Spanish 16th-century lutenist; native of Peñaranda de Duero. He wrote the tablature book *Libro de música de vihuela, intitulado Silva de Sirenas* (Valladolid, 1547), containing transcriptions for vihuela (large 6-stringed guitar) of sacred and secular vocal works (some arranged for 2 vihuelas), also some original pieces.
BIBLIOGRAPHY: G. Morphy, *Les Luthistes espagnols du XVIᵉ siècle* (1902); J. B. Trend, *Luis Milán and the Vihuelistas* (1925); W. Apel, "Early Spanish Music for Lute and Keyboard Instruments," *Musical Quarterly* (July 1934).

Enthoven, Emil, Dutch composer; b. Amsterdam, Oct. 18, 1903; d. New York, Dec. 26, 1950. He studied composition with Johan Wagenaar in Utrecht, and at the age of 15 wrote an adolescent but well-crafted symphony, which Mengelberg performed with the Concertgebouw Orch. in Amsterdam (1918). But this precocious success was not a manifestation of enduring talent; his later works lacked originality. Soon he abandoned composition altogether and took up jurisprudence; for a time he lectured on political science at the Univ. of Leiden; in 1939 emigrated to America and settled in N.Y.

Entremont, Philippe, French pianist; b. Rheims, June 6, 1934. Both his parents were professional musicians and teachers, and he received his first training from them. He subsequently studied piano with Marguerite Long; then entered the Paris Cons.; won 1st prize in solfège at 12; 1st prize in chamber music at 14, and 1st prize in piano at 15. In 1951 he was the winner of the Belgian State Competition in Brussels. He then toured in Europe; on Jan. 5, 1953, he made his American debut with the National Orch. Association in N.Y.; appeared also as soloist with other American orchestras.

Eppert, Carl, American composer; b. Carbon, Ind., Nov. 5, 1882; d. Milwaukee, Oct. 1, 1961. He studied in Chicago and in Germany; founder and conductor of the Civic Symph. Orch. in Milwaukee (1923–26).
WORKS: 7 symphonies; *Escapade,* for orch. (Indianapolis, Jan. 3, 1941); symph. fantasy, *Traffic* (NBC orch., May 8, 1932); 2 symphonic poems: *City Shadows* and *Speed* (both performed at Rochester,

Oct. 30, 1935); *Two Symphonic Impressions* (Chicago, Feb. 13, 1941; received 1st prize in the Chicago Symph. Orch. Golden Jubilee in 1940–41).

Epstein, David M., American composer; b. New York, Oct. 3, 1930. He was educated at the New England Cons. of Music (M. Mus., 1953); at Brandeis Univ. (M.F.A., 1954) and Princeton Univ. (Ph.D., 1968); also studied composition privately with Darius Milhaud, and conducting with Max Rudolf, Izler Solomon and George Szell; appeared as conductor with the Cleveland Orch. and in Europe. In 1965 he was appointed prof. of music at the Massachusetts Institute of Technology in Cambridge, Mass.
WORKS: *Movement* for orch. (1953); *Excerpts from a Diary,* song cycle (1953); Piano Trio (1953); *The Seasons,* song cycle, to poems by Emily Dickinson (1956); Symphony (1958); Piano Variations (1961); String Trio (1964); *Sonority-Variations* for orch. (1968); music for films.

Epstein, Julius, Austrian pianist; b. Agram, Croatia, Aug. 7, 1832; d. Vienna, March 1, 1926. He was a pupil at Agram of Ignaz Lichtenegger, and at Vienna of Anton Halm (piano) and Johann Rufinatscha (composition). From 1867 to 1901 he was prof. of piano at the Vienna Cons.; one of the editors of Breitkopf & Härtel's monumental edition of Schubert's works. Among his pupils were Gustav Mahler and Ignaz Brüll.
BIBLIOGRAPHY: H. Schuster, *J. Epstein; Ein tonkünstlerisches Charakterbild zu seinem 70. Geburts-Feste* (Vienna, 1902).

Epstein, Peter, German musicologist; b. Strasbourg, Nov. 12, 1901; d. Breslau, June 9, 1932. He studied in Frankfurt, in Berlin, and at the Univ. of Breslau. He published catalogues of church music manuscripts of the Library of the City of Frankfurt (1926; in collaboration with C. Süss), and of musical instruments in the Breslau Museum (1932); edited Schutze's *St. Luke Passion* (1930).

Epstein, Richard, Austrian pianist, son of **Julius Epstein;** b. Vienna, Jan. 26, 1869; d. New York, Aug. 1, 1919. He was a pupil at the Vienna Cons. of his father and R. Fuchs (composition); prof. of piano at the Vienna Cons.; lived in London (1904–14); then in New York. He excelled as an accompanist, in which capacity he was frequently heard with such artists as Sembrich, Fremstad, Culp, Gerhardt, Destinn, Elman, Kreisler, and as assisting artist with famous chamber music organizations (Joachim, Rosé, Bohemian Quartets, etc.).

Érard, Sébastien, famous maker of pianos and harps; b. Strasbourg, April 5, 1752; d. in his château, La Muette, near Paris, Aug. 5, 1831. His family name was originally Erhard; his father was a cabinetmaker by trade, and in his shop Sébastien worked until he was 16, when his father died. He was then engaged by a Paris harpsichord maker, who dismissed him "for wanting to know everything"; under a second employer his ingenuity made a stir in the musical world, and the invention of a 'clavecin mécanique' (described by Abbé Roussier, 1776) made him famous. The

Duchess of Villeroy became his patroness, and fitted up in her home a workshop for Érard, in which (1777) he finished the first piano forte made in France. In the meantime, his brother, **Jean-Baptiste,** joined him, and they founded an instrument factory in the Rue Bourbon. Their growing success led to a conflict with the fan-makers' guild (to which the brothers did not belong), which tried to prevent them from working. But the Érards obtained a special 'brevet' from Louis XVI for the manufacture of 'forté-pianos' and this enabled them to continue their trade unmolested. In the following years, Érard invented the 'piano organisé' with two keyboards, one for piano and the other for a small organ; he also became interested in the harp, and invented the ingenious double-action mechanism, perfected in 1811. From 1786-96 he was in London; returning to Paris, he made his first grand piano, and employed the English action until his invention, in 1809, of the repetition action, which is regarded as his supreme achievement. An 'orgue expressif,' built for the Tuileries, was his last important work. His nephew, **Pierre Érard** (1796-1885), succeeded him; he published *The Harp in its present improved state compared with the original Pedal Harp* (1821), and *Perfectionnements apportés dans le mécanisme du piano par les Érards depuis l'origine de cet instrument jusqu'à l'exposition de 1834* (1834). Pierre's successor was his wife's nephew, **Pierre Schäffer** (d. 1878); the firm is still the leading French manufacturer of pianos and harps.

BIBLIOGRAPHY: F. Fétis, *Notice biographique sur Sébastien Érard* (Paris, 1831).

Eratosthenes, Greek philosopher; b. Cyprene, c.276 B.C.; d. Alexandria, Egypt, c.194 B.C. He wrote on numerous subjects, chiefly mathematics, and was custodian of the Alexandria library. The *Catasterismi,* attributed to Eratosthenes, contain scattered notes on Greek music and instruments, especially the "lyra" (German transl. by Schaubach, 1795; Bernhardy publ. in 1822 an ed. of the original text). His work on music is lost; Ptolemy quotes his division of the tetrachord.

Erb, Donald, American composer; b. Youngstown, Ohio, Jan. 17, 1927. He played the trumpet in dance bands and in the U.S. Navy; attended Kent State Univ. (B.S., 1950), the Cleveland Institute of Music (M.M., 1953) and Indiana Univ. (D.M., 1964); was a member of the music faculty at the Cleveland Institute of Music (1953-61), at Indiana Univ. (1961-64), at Bowling Green State Univ. (1964-65), at Case Institute of Technology (1965-67); composer-in-residence with the Dallas Symph. Orch. (1968-69); held fellowships and awards from Ford Foundation (1962-63), Guggenheim (1965-66); and National Council on the Arts (1967-68); in the summer of 1968 he headed the composition workshop at the Centennial Alaska Festival. His music combines classical structural elements with ultramodern serial and aleatory techniques.

WORKS: *Dialogue* for violin and piano (1958); String Quartet No. 1 (1960); *Spacemusic* for symphonic band (1963); *Hexagon* for 6 instruments (1963); *Antipodes* for string quartet and 4 percussion instruments (1963); *Symphony of Overtures* (Indiana Univ., Bloomington, Feb. 11, 1965); Trio for Violin, Electric Guitar and Cello (1966); Concerto for Solo Percussion and Orch. (Detroit, Dec. 29, 1966); *Reconnaissance* for violin, string bass, piano, percussion and 2 electronic setups (1967); *Christmas Music* for orch. (Cleveland, Dec. 21, 1967); *The Seventh Trumpet* for orch. (Dallas, April 5, 1969); *Basspiece* for string bass and 4 tracks of prerecorded string bass (1969); *Klangfarbenfunk I* for orch., rock band and electronic sounds (Detroit, Oct. 1, 1970); Cello Concerto (Rochester, N.Y., Nov. 4, 1976).

Erb, John Lawrence, American music pedagogue and author; b. Reading, Pa., Feb. 5, 1877; d. Eugene, Oregon, March 17, 1950. He studied at the Metropolitan College of Music in New York; then was director of the Wooster, Ohio, Cons. (1905-13) and of the School of Music, Univ. of Illinois (1914-21); was lecturer at the American Institute of Applied Music, N.Y. (1921-24); from 1923 at Connecticut College for Women. He published *Brahms,* a biography (1895; 1905; revised ed., London, 1934); *Hymns and Church Music* (1911); *Elements of Harmony* (1911); *Elementary Theory* (1911); *Music Appreciation for the Student* (1926); *Select Songs for the Assembly* (1931). He also composed songs, piano pieces, organ music, anthems, and music for pageants.

Erb, John Warren, American music educator and composer; b. Massillon, Ohio, April 17, 1887; d. Pittsburgh, July 2, 1948. He studied in Berlin with Xaver Scharwenka, Siegfried Ochs, and Felix Weingartner, and in the U.S. with Stillman Kelley. After completing his musical education, he occupied various teaching positions in small colleges and music clubs; wrote some pieces for chorus, etc.

Erb, Marie Joseph, Alsatian composer and organist; b. Strasbourg, Oct. 23, 1858; d. Andlau, July 9, 1944. He studied at first in Strasbourg; then (1875-80) in Paris, under Saint-Saëns, Gigout, and Loret, at the "École de musique classique"; returned to Strasbourg as teacher of piano and organ, and organist in the Johanniskirche (Roman Catholic) and at the Synagogue.

WORKS: the operas (all first performed in Strasbourg, unless otherwise noted) *Der Letzte Ruf* (1895), *Der glückliche Taugenichts* (1897), *Abendglocken* (1900), *Eifersüchtig* (Leipzig, 1901), *Der Riese Schletto* (1901), *Der Zaubermantel* (1901), *Die Vogesentanne* (1904), *Der Heimweg* (ballet-opera, 1907), *Prinzessin Flunkerli* (1912); Symphony in G; 3 violin sonatas; Cello Sonata; 2 string quartets; String Trio; Octet for Wind and Strings; *Sonata liturgica* (1919); *Suite liturgique; Danses et pièces alsaciennes* (1924 and 1925); 8 Masses; organ pieces; pieces for piano (2 and 4 hands); songs; also 2 vols. of Alsatian folksongs.

BIBLIOGRAPHY: *Marie Joseph Erb, sa vie et son œuvre,* ed. by P. de Bréville (Strasbourg, 1948).

Erbach, Christian, German organist and composer; b. Hesse, 1570; d. Augsburg, 1635 (buried, June 14, 1635). He was the successor of Hassler as town organist in Augsburg (1602); in 1625 became organist of the cathedral there. He publ. 3 books of *Modi sacri* (1600, 1604, 1611; under varying titles) for 4-10 voices; several works by him are included in contemporary collections; 12 motets are in A. B. Gottron, *Christian Erbach* (Mainz, 1943).

Erbse, Heimo, German composer; b. Rudolstadt (Thuringia), Feb. 27, 1924. He studied in Weimar, and in Berlin with Boris Blacher; in 1957 moved to Salzburg.

WORKS: Sonata for 2 pianos (1951); *Capriccio* for piano, strings, and percussion (1952); Piano Trio (1953); 12 *Aphorismen* for flute, violin, and piano (1954); *Sinfonietta glocosa* (1955); *Dialog* for piano and orch. (1955); *Tango-Variationen* for orch. (1958); *Julietta*, opera semi-seria (Salzburg, Aug. 17, 1959); Wind Quartet (1961); Piano Concerto (1962); Symphony (1964); comic opera, *Herr in Grau* (1966); *5 Songs* for baritone and orch. (1969).

Erdmann, Eduard, Latvian pianist and composer; b. Tsezis (Wenden), March 5, 1896; d. Hamburg, June 21, 1958. He studied in Riga; then went to Berlin, where he studied piano with Konrad Ansorge (1914–17) and composition with Heinz Tiessen (1915–18). From 1925–35 he was prof. at the Cologne Cons.; active as concert pianist (1935–50); in 1950, appointed prof. of piano at the Hochschule für Musik in Hamburg. He wrote 4 symphonies; piano pieces; songs.

Erdmannsdörfer, Max von, German conductor; b. Nuremberg, June 14, 1848; d. Munich, Feb. 14, 1905. He studied at the Leipzig Cons. (1863–67), and in Dresden (1868–69). From 1871 to 1880 he was court conductor at Sondershausen; then was active in Vienna, Leipzig, and Nuremberg. In 1882 he was engaged as conductor of the Imperial Musical Society in Moscow; in 1885 became prof. at the Moscow Cons. His symphonic concerts in Moscow were of great importance to Russian music; he introduced many new works by Russian composers, and his influence was considerable in the Moscow musical circles, despite the mediocrity of his conducting. Returning to Germany, he became conductor of the Bremen Philharmonic Concerts (until 1895); in 1897 he settled in Munich.

Erede, Alberto, Italian conductor; b. Genoa, Nov. 8, 1908. He studied at the Milan Cons. (piano, cello, theory); then in Basel with Weingartner (conducting). He conducted opera in England (1934–39); in 1954 was engaged as guest conductor at the Metropolitan Opera in N.Y.; from 1958 to 1962 was general music director of the German Opera Theater in Düsseldorf; in 1961 became conductor of the Göteborg, Sweden, Orchestra.

BIBLIOGRAPHY: L. Rognoni, *Alberto Erede* (Arzignano, 1954).

Erhardt, Otto, German opera director; b. Breslau, Nov. 18, 1888; d. near Buenos Aires, Jan. 18, 1971. He studied violin; took courses in music and art at Breslau, Munich, Oxford, and London. He played violin in various orchestras (1908–11); then became a stage director; acted in this capacity with the Stuttgart Opera (1920–27); at the Dresden Opera (1927–32); directed the festivals at Salzburg (1933–36). In 1938 he went to

Buenos Aires, where he was stage director at the Teatro Colón; subsequently divided his time between South America, Europe, and the U.S. He published a book, *Die Operndichtung der deutschen Romantik* (Breslau, 1911); also a biography of Richard Strauss (Buenos Aires, 1950, in Spanish; German ed., 1953).

Erickson, Robert, American composer; b. Marquette, Mich., March 7, 1917. He studied music with Wesley La Violette at the Chicago Cons.; with Ernst Krenek at Hamline Univ. in St. Paul (B.A.), and in 1950, attended a seminar in composition under Roger Sessions at the Univ. of Calif., Berkeley; in 1966 held a Guggenheim Fellowship. In 1967 he was appointed prof. of composition at the Univ. of Calif., San Diego. In his music he explores electronic and serial techniques.

WORKS: *Introduction and Allegro* for orch. (Minneapolis, March 11, 1949); Piano Sonata (1948); String Quartet No. 1 (1950); Piano Trio (1953); Divertimento for flute, clarinet and strings (1953); Fantasy for Cello and Orch. (1953), String Quartet No. 2 (1956); Variations for Orch. (1957); Duo for Violin and Piano (1959); *Chamber Concerto* (1960); Toccata for Piano (1962); Concerto for Piano and 7 Instruments (1963); *Sirens and Other Flyers* for orch. (1965); *Piece for Bells and Toy Pianos* (1965); *Ricercar a 5* for trombone and tape (1966); *Scapes*, a 'contest for 2 groups' (1966); *Birdland* for electronic tape (1967); *Ricercar a 3* for solo double bass and electronic tape (1967); *Cardenitas*, dramatic aria for singer, mime, conductor, 7 musicians and stereophonic prerecorded tape (1968); *Pacific Sirens*, for instruments and tape (1969); *General Speech* for trombone (1969).

Erk, Ludwig (Christian), German music scholar and educator; b. Wetzlar, Jan. 6, 1807; d. Berlin, Nov. 25, 1883. He received good training in music from his father, **Adam Wilhelm Erk** (1779–1820), who was organist at Wetzlar. His further studies were under André in Offenbach and Spiess in Frankfurt. In 1826 he became prof. at the seminary in Mörs, where he taught until 1835; from 1836 to 1840 he was instructor in liturgical singing at Berlin, and conducted a choir. In 1852, he founded the "Erk Gesangverein" for mixed voices. During his years as conductor of choral societies, he became interested in folksongs, and accumulated a great collection of authentic materials on the subject; also published songbooks for schools, which attained considerable popularity; some of these were written jointly with his brother **Friedrich Erk,** and his brother-in-law, **Greef.** He also published *Die deutschen Volkslieder mit ihren Singweisen* (1838–45); *Volkslieder, alte und neue* (1845–46); *Deutscher Liederhort* (folksongs; vol. 1 publ. 1856; MS of the remainder was bought—with the rest of his valuable library—for the Royal Hochschule für Musik, Berlin; continued and ed. by Magnus Böhme, and publ. in 4 vols., 1894); *Mehrstimmige Gesänge* (1833–35); *Volksklänge* (1851–60); *Deutscher Liederschatz* (1859–72); *Vierstimmige Choralgesänge der vornehmsten Meister des 16. and 17. Jahrhunderts* (1845); *J. S. Bachs mehrstimmige Choralgesänge und geistliche Arien* (1850–65); *Vierstimmiges Choralbuch für evangelische Kirchen* (1863); *Choräle für Männer-*

stimmen (1866); *Methodischer Leitfaden für den Gesangunterricht in Volksschulen* (1834, Part I).

BIBLIOGRAPHY: *Chronologisches Verzeichnis der musikalischen Werke und literarischen Arbeiten von Ludwig Erk* (compiled by a group of friends; Berlin, 1867); K. Schultze, *Ludwig Erk* (Berlin, 1876); H. Schmeel, *Ludwig Erk, ein Lebensbild* (Giessen, 1908).

Erkel, Franz (Ferenc), the creator of Hungarian national opera; b. Gyula, Hungary, Nov. 7, 1810; d. Pest, June 15, 1893. He was taught by his father; at 24 became director of the Kaschau opera troupe, and went with it to Pest, where he was appointed conductor at the National Theater on its opening in 1837. He was the founder and director of the Budapest Philharmonic Concerts (1853), and first prof. of piano and instrumentation at the National Musical Academy. His numerous songs, in the national vein, became very popular. He composed the Hungarian National Hymn (1845).

WORKS: operas (all first presented in Budapest): *Báthory Mária* (Aug. 8, 1840); *Hunyady László* (Jan. 27, 1844; first truly national Hungarian opera; given almost 300 performances in the first 50 years); *Erzsébet* (May 6, 1857); *Kúnok* (1858); *Bánk-Bán* (March 9, 1861; highly successful in Hungary); *Sarolta*, comic opera (June 26, 1862); *Dózsa György* (April 6, 1867); *Brankovics György* (May 20, 1874); *Névtelen hosök* (Nov. 30, 1880); *István király* (March 14, 1885); music for plays; *Festival Overture*, for orch. (1887); many songs and anthems. A symposium of essays on Erkel was published in *Zenetudományi Tanulmányok* (Budapest, 1954, II) under the editorship of B. Szabolcsi.

BIBLIOGRAPHY: K. Abrányi, *Franz Erkel* (Budapest, 1895); F. Scherer, *Franz Erkel* (Gyula, 1944).

Erkin, Ulvi Cemal, Turkish composer; b. Istanbul, March 14, 1906. He studied in Paris with Isidor Philipp (piano) and Nadia Boulanger (composition) from 1925–30; graduated from the École Normale de Musique (1930), and returned to Turkey. He taught piano at the State Cons. in Ankara, and was its director from 1949 to 1951.

WORKS: *Bayram*, tone poem (Ankara, May 11, 1934); Piano Concerto (1942); Symph. No. 1 (Ankara, April 20, 1946); Symph. No. 2 (1948–51); Violin Concerto (Ankara, April 2, 1948); String Quartet (1936); Piano Quintet (1943); Piano Sonata (1946); *Kelaglan*, ballet music (1950); *Concertante Symphony* for piano and orch. (1966); *Symphonie Piece* (1969); songs; piano pieces.

Erlanger, Camille, French composer; b. Paris, May 25, 1863; d. there, April 24, 1919. He was a pupil of the Paris Cons. under Delibes, Durand, Matthias; in 1888, took the Grand Prix de Rome for his cantata *Velléda*. He earned fame with his opera *Le Juif polonais* (Paris, April 11, 1900), which has remained in active repertory; other operas are: *Kermaria* (Paris, Feb. 8, 1897); *Le Fils de l'étoile* (Paris, April 20, 1904); *Aphrodite* (Paris, March 27, 1906); *Bacchus triomphant* (Bordeaux, Sept. 11, 1909); *L'Aube rouge* (Rouen, Dec. 29, 1911); *La Sorcière* (Paris, Dec. 18, 1912); *Le Barbier de Deauville* (1917); *Forfaiture* (performed posthumously at the Opéra-Comique in 1921). He also wrote

several symphonic poems (*Maître et serviteur*, after Tolstoy, etc.) and a French Requiem.

d'Erlanger, Baron Frédéric, member of the family of bankers; composer and opera director; b. Paris, May 29, 1868; d. London, April 23, 1943. In 1897 he assumed the pseudonym **Regnal,** formed by reading backward the last six letters of his name. He lived in London, where, for many years, he was one of the directors of the Covent Garden Opera.

WORKS: the operas, *Jehan de Saintre* (Aix-les-Bains, Aug. 1, 1893); *Inez Mendo* (London, July 10, 1897, under the pseudonym Regnal); *Tess*, after Thomas Hardy (Naples, April 10, 1906); *Noël* (Paris, Dec. 28, 1910; Chicago, 1913); Piano Quintet; String Quartet; Violin Concerto (London, March 12, 1903, Kreisler soloist); Violin Sonata; *Andante* for cello and orch.

d'Erlanger, Rodolphe, French musicologist, specialist in Arab studies; b. Boulogne-sur-Seine, June 7, 1872; d. Sidi-bou-Sadi, Tunisia, Oct. 29, 1932. He went to Tunis in 1910, and began a thorough study of the theory and history of Arabian music, The result was a series of publications of primary importance, most of them issued posthumously, including a monumental work in 6 volumes under the general title *La Musique arabe* (Paris, 1930–1959).

Erlebach, Philipp Heinrich, important German composer; b. Esens, East Frisia, July 25, 1657; d. Rudolstadt, April 17, 1714. He was Hofkapellmeister at Rudolstadt from at least 1681. His style was strongly influenced by that of Lully. He wrote orchestral suites (6 overtures publ. 1693); suites for violin, viola da gamba and continuo (1694), one of which was reprinted by Einstein in *Zur deutschen Literature für Viola da Gamba* (1905); cantatas; sacred and secular songs, including *Harmonische Freude* (2 parts: 1697, 1710; reprinted by Kinkeldey in vol. 46/47 of the *Denkmäler deutscher Tonkunst*); organ works; etc. Examples from his *Gottgeheiligte Singstunde* (1704) are printed in M. Friedlaender's *Das deutsche Lied im 18. Jahrhundert* (1902).

Erlebach, Rupert, English composer; b. London, Nov. 16, 1894. He studied at the Royal Academy of Music with Stanford and Vaughan Williams. As a composer, he makes considerable use of English folk material.

WORKS: *Before Dawn, Aubade, A Memory, High Noon, Lark's Song at Evening*; for orch.: Rhapsody for Cello and Orch.; *Folksong Poems* for string orch.; Rhapsody for Flute, Oboe, Violin, Viola, and Cello; *Moods* for string quartet; *Legends* for violin and piano; Sonata for Violin and Piano; 2 sonatas for cello and piano (one, *Folksong Sonata*); piano pieces; organ pieces; songs; choral works.

Ermatinger, Erhart, Swiss composer; b. Winterthur, Feb. 16, 1900; d. Arnhem, July 14, 1966. He studied at the Zürich Cons. with Jarnach, then at the Berlin Hochschule; 1922–23, chorus master at the Zürich Opera; later a private teacher there; 1925–26, teacher of theory at the Freiburg Univ.; lived in Berlin, then in Holland. He wrote an opera, *Gijsbrecht van Amstel*

(1947); 3 symphonies, 2 string quartets, songs; publ. a book *Bildhafte Musik: Entwurf einer Lehre von der musikalischen Darstellungskunst* (Tübingen, 1928).

Ernesaks, Gustav, Estonian composer; b. Chariu, Dec. 12, 1908. He studied composition at the Tallinn Cons. with Arthur Kapp; then was active as a choral conductor. He wrote the music drama *Tormida Rand* (*Stormy Coast*; Tallinn, Sept. 29, 1949), and a comic opera *Bridegrooms* (1960); also many choruses in Estonian.

Ernst, Alfred, French writer and critic; b. Périgueux, April 9, 1860; d. Paris, May 15, 1898. A pupil of the École Polytechnique, he abandoned science for art; was a passionate admirer and defender of Wagner. Besides many contributions to musical journals, he published *L'Œuvre dramatique de Berlioz* (1884), *Richard Wagner et le drame contemporain* (1887), *L'Art de Richard Wagner, l'œuvre poétique* (1893; a projected 2nd vol. on *l'œuvre musicale* remained unfinished); *Étude sur 'Tannhäuser,'* analysis and thematic guide (1895; with E. Poirée). He translated *Die Meistersinger* and *Der Ring des Nibelungen* into French.

Ernst, Heinrich Wilhelm, violinist and composer; b. Brünn, May 6, 1814; d. Nice, Oct. 8, 1865. He was a pupil of Böhm (violin) and Seyfried (composition) in Vienna, with further study under Mayseder; 1832–38, lived in Paris. From 1838 to 1850 he was almost continually on concert tours; then settled in London (1855). His works for violin are brilliant and effective; the *Élégie,* the Concerto in F-sharp minor (new ed. by Marteau, 1913), and *Carnaval de Venise,* are a few of the most celebrated.
BIBLIOGRAPHY: A. Heller, *Heinrich Wilhelm Ernst im Urteile seiner Zeitgenossen* (Brünn, 1904).

Erös, Peter, Hungarian conductor; b. Budapest, Sept. 22, 1932. He studied piano with Lajos Hernadi, composition with Zoltán Kodály, conducting with Lászlo Somogyi and chamber music with Leo Weiner. After the abortive revolution in Hungary in 1956, he emigrated to Holland. There he served as assistant to Otto Klemperer at the Holland Festival of 1958; from 1958–61 was assistant to Ferenc Fricsay working with the Deutsche Grammophon Gesellschaft; in 1960 attended the master classes at Bayreuth. His subsequent professional engagements were: assistant conductor of the Concertgebouw Orch. in Amsterdam (1960–65); chief conductor of the Malmö Symph. Orch. (1966–68); Permanent Guest Conductor of the Melbourne Symph. (1969–70). In 1972 he was appointed music director and conductor of the San Diego Symph. Orch.; was active as conductor of the West Australian Symph. Orch. of the Australian Broadcasting Commission. He was also a guest conductor of orchestras all over the world.

Erpf, Hermann, German musicologist; b. Pforzheim, April 23, 1891; d. Stuttgart, Oct. 17, 1969. He studied at Heidelberg and with Riemann at Leipzig; was in the army (1914–18); teaching at Pforzheim (1919–23); at the Univ. of Freiburg (1923–25); assistant director at the Academy of Speech and Music in Münster (1925–27); in charge of the Folkwangschule in Essen (1927–43). In 1943–45, and again in 1952, director of the Hochschule für Musik in Stuttgart.
WRITINGS: *Entwicklungszüge in der zeitgenössischen Musik* (Karlsruhe, 1922); *Studien zur Harmonie- und Klangtechnik der neueren Musik* (Leipzig, 1927); *Harmonielehre in der Schule* (Leipzig, 1930); *Vom Wesen der neuen Musik* (Stuttgart, 1949); *Neue Wege der Musikerziehung* (Stuttgart, 1953); *Gegenwartskunde der Musik* (Stuttgart, 1954). He composed a Mass, numerous cantatas, 3 string quartets, and piano music.

Erskine, John, American educator and writer on music; b. New York, Oct. 5, 1879; d. there, June 1, 1951. He studied piano with Carl Walter; composition with MacDowell; then took up an academic and literary career, becoming highly successful as a novelist and essayist. He was educated at Columbia Univ. (B.A., 1900; M.A., 1901; Ph.D., 1903; LL.D., 1929); prof. of English there (1909–37); then prof. emeritus. In 1923 he resumed piano study under Ernest Hutcheson; played as soloist with the N.Y. Symph. Orch., the Baltimore Civic Orch.; was president of the Juilliard School of Music, N.Y. (1928–37); president of the Juilliard Music Foundation from 1948 until his death. He was editor of *A Musical Companion* (1935). He received the degree of Mus. Doc. from Rollins College, Florida (1931), Cornell College, Iowa (1935); also Litt. D. from Amherst College (1923) and the Univ. of Bordeaux, France (1929). Erskine was an Officer of the French Legion of Honor. He published books on music, including *Is there a Career in Music?* (N.Y., 1929); *Song Without Words; The Story of Felix Mendelssohn* (1941); *The Philharmonic-Symphony Society of N.Y., Its First Hundred Years* (N.Y., 1943); *What is Music?* (Philadelphia, 1944); *The Memory of Certain Persons* (Philadelphia, 1947); *My Life as a Teacher* (N.Y., 1948); *My Life in Music* (N.Y., 1950).

Ertel, (Jean) Paul, German pianist and composer; b. Posen, Jan. 22, 1865; d. Berlin, Feb. 11, 1933. He studied with L. Brassin (piano) and later took lessons with Liszt; also studied law; was music critic of the *Berliner Lokal Anzeiger* and editor of *Deutscher Musikerzeitung* (1897–1905). He wrote several symph. poems in a general Lisztian vein (*Der Mensch, Die nächtliche Heerschau,* etc.); many ballads for voice and instruments; violin sonata and other chamber music.

Escher, Rudolf, Dutch composer; b. Amsterdam, Jan. 8, 1912. He studied harmony, violin and piano at the Toonkunst Cons. in Rotterdam (1931–37); was a student in composition of Pijper (1934); worked in the electronic music studios in Delft (1960) and in Utrecht (1961). He wrote monographs on Debussy (1938) and Ravel (1939); was a program annotator for the Concertgebouw Orch. in Amsterdam (1955–62); in 1962 was appointed to the faculty of the Institute for Musical Science at the Utrecht Univ. His music is very much influenced by the modern French school.
WORKS: *Sinfonia in memoriam Maurice Ravel* (1940); *Musique pour l'esprit en deuil (Music for the Soul in Mourning)* for orch. (1941–43); Passacaglia for

Orch. (1945); *Protosilaos en Laodamia,* musical comedy for mezzo-soprano, tenor, baritone and orch. (1946–48); Concerto for String Orch. (1947–48); *Hymne du grand meaulnes* for orch. (1950–51; after a novel by Fournier); *Nostalgies,* 4 songs for tenor and chamber orch. (1951); *Chants du désir* for mezzo-soprano or piano (1951–52); Piano Concerto (1952); 2 symphonies (1953–54; 1958, revised 1964); *Summer Rites at Noon* for 2 facing orchestras (1962–68); *Univers de Rimbaud,* first cycle, for tenor and orch. (1969–70); Trio for Oboe, Clarinet and Bassoon (1942); *Sonata Concertante* for cello and piano (1943); Sonata for 2 Flutes (1944); Sonata for Solo Cello (1945); Solo Flute Sonata (1949); Violin Sonata (1950); *Le Tombeau de Ravel,* sextet for flute, oboe, violin, viola, cello and harpsichord (1952); *Air pour charmer un lézard* for solo flute (1953); String Trio (1959); Wind Quintet (1966–67); *Monologue* for solo flute (1970); Solo Clarinet Sonata (1973); Sinfonia for 10 Instruments (1976); Piano Sonata (1935); Passacaglia for Organ (1937); *Arcana Misae Dona,* suite for piano (1944); Piano Sonatina (1951); *Lettre du Mexique* for baritone and piano; *Strange Meeting,* after Wilfred Owen, for baritone and piano (1952); *Le Vrai Visage de la paix,* after Eluard, for a cappella chorus (1953); *Songs of Love and Eternity,* after Emily Dickinson, for a cappella chorus (1956); *Ciel, air et vents,* after Ronsard, for a cappella chorus (1957); *3 Poems,* after Auden, for chamber chorus (1975); incidental music: *De poort van Isthar* for chorus and orch. (1947) and *De Perzen (The Persians),* after Aeschylus (1963).

Eschig, Max, French music publisher; b. Opava, now Czechoslovakia, May 27, 1872; d. Paris, Sept. 3, 1927. He settled in Paris and founded a publishing firm under his name in 1907, prospering continually and forming an impressive catalogue of modern works by Ravel, Manuel de Falla, and many other French, Spanish, and English composers.

Eschmann, Johann Karl, Swiss pianist and pedagogue; b. Winterthur, April 12, 1826; d. Zürich, Oct. 27, 1882. He studied in Leipzig with Moscheles, and also had some lessons with Mendelssohn. He then settled in Zürich as a piano teacher; publ. a valuable manual *Wegweiser durch die Klavierliteratur* (Zürich, 1879; 8th ed., 1914), and *100 Aphorismen aus dem Klavierunterricht* (2nd ed., 1899).

Escobar, Luis Antonio, Colombian composer; b. Villapinzón, near Bogotá, July 14, 1925. He studied music at the Bogotá Cons.; then took courses with Nicolas Nabokov at the Peabody Cons. in Baltimore and with Boris Blacher in Berlin. He returned to Bogotá in 1953, and received the post of prof. at the Cons. WORKS: *Sinfonía Cero* (1955); *Sinfonía X* (1955); Piano Concerto (1959); *Juramento a Bolívar* for male chorus and orch. (1964); *Little Symphony* (Washington, May 7, 1965); a flute concerto; 2 string quartets; 2 violin sonatas; 2 sonatas and 3 sonatinas for piano, etc. His style is brisk and terse in the modern manner; but there is in his music also a melorhythmic pattern of Spanish-American dances.

Escobar-Budge, Roberto, Chilean composer; b. Santiago, May 11, 1926. He studied composition with René Amengual and Alfonso Letelier; was active as a music critic.
WORKS: Wind Quintet (1957); *Diferencias Sinfónicas* for orch. (1962); *Los Bisontes,* symph. suite (1964); Nonet (1965); *Cuarteto Estructural* for strings (1965); *Sinfonía Valparaíso* (1967); *Incógnita* for harpsichord, trumpet, bassoon, cello and percussion (1967); choruses; piano pieces.

Escobedo, Bartolomé, Spanish composer of the 16th century; b. Zamora, c.1515; d. in Nov. 1563 as canon at Segovia; from 1536–41, and again from 1545–54, singer in the Papal Choir at Rome. He was a judge in the famous dispute between Nicola Vicentino and Vincento Lusitano (1551) over the qualities of Greek modes. He composed 2 Masses and a number of motets.

Escot, Pozzi, Peruvian-born American composer of French parentage; b. Lima, Oct. 1, 1933. She studied with the Belgian-born Peruvian composer Andrés Sás; in 1953 emigrated to the U.S., where she took courses in composition with William Bergsma at the Juilliard School of Music in New York and with Philipp Jarnach at the Hochschule für Musik in Hamburg (1957–61); subsequently appointed to the faculty of Wheaton College in Massachusetts. Her musical idiom follows the tenets of modern structural formalism with modified serial procedures.
WORKS: 3 piano sonatinas (1950, 1951, 1952); 4 string quartets (1951; 1954; 1965; *Credo,* with soprano, 1958); 3 symphonies (*Little Symphony,* 1952–1953; Symphony for Strings, 1955; 1957); *And Here I Rest,* cantata (1958); *3 Poems of Rilke* for narrator and string quartet (1959); *3 Movements* for violin and piano (1960); *Differences, Group I and II* for piano (1961, 1963); *Lamentus* for soprano, 2 violins, 2 cellos, piano and 3 percussionists (Madrid, Oct. 22, 1964); *Cristos* for 3 violins, alto flute, double-bassoon and percussion (1963); *Visione* for solo double bass, flute, saxophone, soprano, "ghost" speaker, and percussion (N.Y., Nov. 20, 1964); *Sands . . .* for 9 double basses, 17 violins, 5 different saxophones, electric guitar and 4 bass drums of varying sizes (Caracas, May 6, 1966); *Interra* for piano, tape, spotlights and simultaneous slide projections (1968–69); *Ainu* for 20 vocal soloists (1970–71); *Fergus Are* for organ (1974–75). She is the co-author of a book, *Sonic Design: The Nature of Sound and Music* (N.Y., 1976).

Escudier, Léon, French music journalist; b. Castelnaudary, Aude, Sept. 17, 1816; d. Paris, June 22, 1881. He was a brother and partner of **Marie Escudier,** b. Castelnaudary, June 29, 1809; d. Paris, April 18, 1880. In 1838, the brothers began publishing the periodical *La France musicale* and soon afterwards established a music shop. Industrious writers, they issued jointly the following works: *Études biographiques sur les chanteurs contemporains* (1840), *Dictionnaire de musique d'après les théoriciens, historiens et critiques les plus célèbres* (1844, 2 vols.; reprinted in 1854 as *Dictionnaire de musique, théorique et historique*); *Rossini, sa vie et ses œuvres* (1854); *Vie et aventures des* *cantatrices célèbres, précédées des musiciens de l'Empire, et suivies de la vie anecdotique de Paganini* (1856). Léon broke up partnership with his brother in 1862, retaining the music business; he established a new paper, *L'Art musical,* which continued to appear until Sept. 27, 1894. Marie retained the publishing and editorial rights to *La France Musicale,* which ceased publ. in 1870.

Eshpai, Andrei, Soviet composer, son of **Yakov Eshpai;** b. Kozmodemiansk, May 15, 1925. He studied with Aram Khatchaturian in Moscow; during the war he acted as a translator from German. In his music he makes use of folk motives of the Mari nation from which he descended.

WORKS: 3 symphonies (1959, 1962, 1964); *Symphonic Dances* (1951); *Hungarian Melodies* for violin and orch. (1952); 2 piano concertos (1954; 1972); 2 violin sonatas (1966; 1970); Concerto for Orch., with solo trumpet, vibraphone, piano, and double bass (1967); *Festival Overture* for chorus, 12 violins, 8 cellos, 6 harps, 4 pianos, and orch. (1970).

Eshpai, Yakov, Russian composer of Mari extraction; b. near Zvenigorodsk, Oct. 29, 1890; d. Moscow, Feb. 20, 1963. He studied violin and singing in Kazan, and later at the Moscow Cons. He publ. important collections of national songs of the Ural region, particularly of the Mari ethnic group; also wrote vocal and instrumental music on native themes.

Eslava y Elizondo, Miguel Hilarión, Spanish composer and scholar; b. Burlada, Navarra, Oct. 21, 1807; d. Madrid, July 23, 1878. He was a choirboy at the Cathedral of Pamplona; studied organ and violin; in 1827 he went to Calahorra, where he studied with Francisco Secanilla; at the age of 21 he was appointed music director at the Cathedral of Burgo de Osma, where he was ordained a priest. In 1832 he became music director at Seville; in 1847 he obtained the appointment as chapel master to Queen Isabella in Madrid; in 1854 he became prof. at the Madrid Cons. He also edited a periodical, *Gaceta musical de Madrid* (1855–56). He wrote 3 operas with Italian texts: *Il Solitario del Monte Selvaggio* (Cádiz, 1841), *La tregua di Ptolemaide* (1842), and *Pietro il crudele* (1843); his fame rests, however, not on his musical compositions, but on his great collection in 10 vols., *Lira sacro-hispana* (Madrid, 1869), an anthology of Spanish sacred music from the 16th to the 19th centuries, including some of Eslava's own works (Requiem, *Te Deum,* etc.). He also publ. a *Método de solfeo* (1846) and *Escuela de Armonía y Composición* (1861).

BIBLIOGRAPHY: G. Chase, "Miguel Hilarión Eslava," *Musical Quarterly* (Jan. 1938).

Espagne, Franz, German music editor; b. Münster, April 21, 1828; d. Berlin, May 24, 1878. He studied with Dehn; after Dehn's death, he became head of the Music Dept. of the Royal Library in Berlin; edited new classical editions (works by Palestrina, Beethoven, and others).

Espinosa, Guillermo, Colombian conductor; b. Cartagena, Jan. 9, 1905. He studied music in Milan and in Berlin. After appearing as guest conductor in Italy, Switzerland, Denmark, and France, he returned to Colombia, and in 1936 founded the National Symph. Orch. at Bogotá, which he led for ten years. In 1947, he settled in Washington, D.C., as an official of the Division of Music in the Pan American Union; in 1953, succeeded Charles Seeger as chief; retired in 1975.

BIBLIOGRAPHY: F. C. Lange, "Guillermo Espinosa y la Sinfónica Nacional," *Bolletín Latino-Americano de Música* (1938).

Esplá, Oscar, Spanish composer; b. Alicante, Aug. 5, 1886; d. Madrid, Jan. 6, 1976. He at first studied engineering and philosophy; then turned to music, traveling and studying for some years in Germany. He was the first president of the Junta Nacional de Música under the Spanish Republic (1934) and in 1936 was director of the Madrid Cons.; then lived in Brussels and Paris; eventually returned to Spain.

WORKS: *La Bella durmiente,* opera (Vienna, 1909); *La Balteira,* opera (1939); the ballets *Ciclopes de Ifach* and *El contrabandista;* orchestral works: *Suite levantina; El Sueño de Eros, Don Quixote, Ambito de la Danza, Las Cumbres;* scenic cantata, *Nochebuena del diablo; Sonata del Sur,* for piano and orch. (1936–43); *Sinfonía Aitana* (Madrid, Oct. 31, 1964); String Quartet (1947); piano pieces; songs. He publ. the books *El arte y la musicalidad* and *Las actividades del espíritu y su fundamento estético.*

BIBLIOGRAPHY: A. Iglesias, *Oscar Esplá* (Madrid, 1960).

Esposito, Michele, Italian composer and conductor; b. Castellamare, near Naples, Sept. 29, 1855; d. Florence, Nov. 23, 1929. He studied at the Cons. San Pietro at Naples with Cesi (piano) and Serrao (theory); for a time he gave piano concerts in Italy; from 1878–82 was in Paris; in 1882 he was engaged as piano teacher at the Irish Academy of Music in Dublin; he organized the Dublin Orch. Society in 1899 and conducted it until 1914, and again in 1927. He held the honorary degree of Mus. Doc. of Trinity College, Dublin.

WORKS: He composed several works on Irish subjects: Irish operetta, *The Post Bag* (London, Jan. 27, 1902); incidental music for *The Tinker and the Fairy* (Dublin, 1910); *Suite of Irish Dances* for orch.; 2 Irish Rhapsodies; several arrangements of Irish melodies. He received first prizes for his cantata *Deirdre* (Irish Festival, Dublin, 1897); *Irish Symphony* (Irish Festival, Dublin, 1902); also wrote 2 string quartets, 2 violin sonatas, cello sonatas, etc.

Esser, Heinrich, German composer; b. Mannheim, July 15, 1818; d. Salzburg, June 3, 1872. He studied in Vienna with Lachner and Sechter. In 1847 he became conductor of the Vienna Opera, succeeding Otto Nicolai; in 1869 retired and lived in Salzburg. He was a competent opera conductor; he also had a modicum of success as opera composer; 3 of his operas were performed: *Sitas* (Mannheim, 1839); *Thomas Riquiqui* (Frankfurt, 1843); and *Die zwei Prinzen* (Munich, 1844); also numerous vocal works; 5 symphonies; arrangements of Bach's organ works; a string quartet.

BIBLIOGRAPHY: *Lichte eines zeitgenössischen*

Briefwechsels (1902); Karl-Josef Müller, *Heinrich Esser als Komponist* (Mainz, 1969).

Essipoff (Essipova), Anna, famous Russian pianist and pedagogue; b. St. Petersburg, Feb. 13, 1851; d. there, Aug. 18, 1914. She was a pupil of Leschetizky, and married him in 1880 (divorced 1892). She made her debut in St. Petersburg; subsequently made long concert tours throughout Europe and in America; her distinguishing artistic quality was a singing piano tone and "pearly" passage work. From 1870 to 1885 she gave 669 concerts. In 1893 she was engaged as prof. of piano at the St. Petersburg Cons., and continued to teach there until the last years of her life. Many famous pianists and composers, Prokofiev among them, were her students.

Esteban, Julio, noted pianist and pedagogue; b. Shanghai (of Spanish parentage), March 18, 1906; in 1907 was taken to Spain; gave concerts in Spain from 1919 to 1924; in 1925 went to Manila, where he taught at the Cons. of Music of the Univ. of the Philippines until 1947, when he was appointed director of the Cons. of Music at the Univ. of Santo Tomás there. He traveled through the Orient; gave concerts in Hong Kong and in Japan in 1952; also played for the U.N. troops in Korea. In 1955 he left Manila and joined the faculty of the Peabody Cons. in Baltimore.

Estes, Charles E., American organist; b. Somersworth, New Hampshire, Aug. 28, 1882; d. Dover, New Hampshire, Sept. 16, 1968. He studied at Dartmouth College with Charles S. Morse and at Teachers College, Columbia Univ.; also with Widor in Paris (1917–18) and Seth Bingham in New York (1924–25); was head of the music department of the Robert College in Constantinople, from 1910 to 1917, and again from 1926 to 1947. In 1948 he returned to America and served as organist at the First Paris Church, Dover, New Hampshire.

Esteve, Pablo, Catalonian composer; b. c.1730, probably in Barcelona; d. Madrid, June 4, 1794. He went to Madrid about 1760; was maestro di cappella to the Duke of Osuna; in 1778 appointed official composer for the municipal theaters of Madrid. He composed over 300 tonadillas, and some zarzuelas. His song, *El jilguerito con pico de oro,* has been arranged for soprano and orch. by Joaquín Nin.
    BIBLIOGRAPHY: F. Pedrell, *Teatro lírico español anterior al siglo XIX;* J. Nin, *Les Classiques espagnols du chant* (2 vols.; Paris, 1926); J. Subirá, *Tonadillas teatrales inéditas* (Barcelona, 1932; contains score of Esteve's *Los signos del año*).

Estévez, Antonio, Venezuelan composer; b. Calabozo, Jan. 3, 1916. He studied composition in Caracas with Vicente Emilio Sojo; played the oboe in the Caracas Symph. Orch. At the age of 50 he became interested in electronic music and obtained a scholarship from the Venezuelan National Institute of Culture and Fine Arts to study electronic techniques in Paris.
    WORKS: *Suite Llanera* for orch. (1942); *Cantata Criolla* for voices and orch. (1954); choruses; piano pieces and a group of electronic works under the title *Cosmovibrafonía* (1968).

Estrada, Carlos, Uruguayan composer and conductor; b. Montevideo, Sept. 15, 1909; d. there, May 7, 1970. He studied in Paris with Roger-Ducasse and Henri Busser (composition); conducting with Philippe Gaubert. Returning to Montevideo, he was associated with the State Radio (1940–54) and later became Director of the National Cons. in Montevideo (1954–68). He wrote 2 symphonies (1951; 1967); chamber music and effective piano pieces. A complete list of his works is found in Vol. 16 of *Composers of the Americas* (Washington, D.C., 1970).

Estrada, Garcia Juan Agustín, Argentine composer; b. Buenos Aires, Nov. 8, 1895. He studied law; then went to Paris, where he took lessons in composition with Jacques Ibert. Returning to Argentina, he became a municipal judge.
    WORKS: *Tres aires argentinos* for orch. (Paris, Feb. 28, 1929); an opera, *La Cuarterona* (Buenos Aires, Aug. 10, 1951); and a number of songs.

Etler, Alvin Derald, American oboist and composer; b. Battle Creek, Michigan, Feb. 19, 1913; d. Northampton, Mass., June 13, 1973. He studied at the Univ. of Illinois, Western Reserve Univ. and Yale Univ. (Mus. B., 1944); was oboist in the Indianapolis Symph. Orch. (1938–40); taught at Yale (1942–46); at Cornell (1946–47); from 1947–1949 was on the staff of the Univ. of Illinois; and in 1949 he took a teaching position at Smith College. He held two Guggenheim Fellowships (1941, 1942).
    WORKS: *Triptych* for orch. (1961); Concerto for Wind Quintet and Orch. (Tokyo, Oct. 18, 1962); Brass Quintet (1962); String Quartet No. 1 (1963); String Quartet No. 2 (1965); Concerto for String Quartet and Orch. (1967); 2 sinfoniettas; Woodwind Quintet; Suite for Oboe, Violin, Viola and Cello; Sonata for Oboe, Clarinet, and Viola, etc.

Ett, Kaspar, German organist and composer; b. Eresing, Jan. 5, 1788; d. Munich, May 16, 1847, where from 1816, he was court organist at St. Michael's Church. He was active in reviving the church music of the 16th–17th centuries; his own sacred compositions (of which but a few graduals and *cantica sacra* were printed) follow these early works in style. He composed 273 separate works; a complete enumeration is given by F. Bierling, *Kaspar Ett* (1906).
    BIBLIOGRAPHY: K. F. E. von Schafhäutl, "Erinnerungen an Kaspar Ett," *Kirchenmusikalisches Jahrbuch* (1891).

Ettinger, Max, German composer and conductor; b. Lemberg (Lwow), Dec. 27, 1874; d. Basel, July 19, 1951. He studied in Berlin and Munich; was active as conductor in Munich (1900–20), Leipzig (1920–29), and Berlin (1929–33). In 1938 he went to Switzerland, where he remained until his death.
    WORKS: operas, *Judith* (Nuremberg, 1921); *Der eifersüchtige Trinker,* after Boccaccio (Nuremberg, 1925); *Juana* (Nuremberg, 1925); *Clavigo,* after Goethe (Leipzig, 1926); *Frühlings Erwachen* (Leipzig,

1928); oratorio, *Weisheit des Orients*, after Omar Khayyam (Nuremberg, 1924); *Jewish Requiem* (1947); also chamber music and songs.

Euclid, the famous Greek geometer, lived at Alexandria about 300 B.C. He is the reputed author of a treatise on music, *Katatomè kanonos (Sectio canonis)*, following the theories of Pythagoras (new critical ed. by K. von Jan in *Musici scriptores graeci*). For another treatise long ascribed to Euclid, see the entry on Cleonides.

Eulenburg, Ernst, German music publisher; b. Berlin, Nov. 30, 1847; d. Leipzig, Sept. 11, 1926. He studied at the Leipzig Cons.; established, in 1874, in Leipzig the publishing house bearing his name; after his acquisition of Payne's *Kleine Partitur-Ausgabe* (1892) he enormously increased the scope of that publication so that large orchestral scores could be included. His son, **Kurt Eulenburg** (b. Berlin, Feb. 22, 1879), joined the firm in 1911; upon his father's death in 1926 he became the sole owner. He enlarged the number of editions in miniature score and included the original text ("Urtext") of some of Mozart's works, edited by Einstein, Blume, Kroyer, and others. In 1939 he went to Switzerland. On Sept. 28, 1939 he opened a new company in London with a branch in Zürich. He settled in London in Nov., 1945.

Euler, Leonhardt, famous scientist; b. Basel, April 15, 1707; d. St. Petersburg, Oct. 18, 1783. He was prof. of mathematics at St. Petersburg (1730) and Berlin (1741); published several important works on musical theory and acoustics, chief among them being the *Tentamen novae theoriae musicae* (1739). Euler was the first to employ logarithms to explain differences in pitch.
BIBLIOGRAPHY: Schulz-Euler, *Leonhardt Euler* (Frankfurt, 1907); also Treubner's ed. of Euler's *Opera omnia*, series 3, vol. I (1926).

Euting, Ernst, English musicologist; b. London, Feb. 7, 1874; d. Berlin, April 21, 1925. From 1892–96 he attended the Hochschule für Musik in Berlin, then devoted himself to musicology at the Univ. there, and became Dr. phil. with the thesis *Zur Geschichte der Blasinstrumente im 16. und 17. Jahrhundert* (1899); in the same year he founded the *Deutsche Instrumenten-bau-Zeitung*, of which he was the editor; also edited the *Zeitschrift of the Internationale Musik-Gesell-schaft* (1902–03).

Evangelisti, Franco, Italian composer of avant-garde convictions; b. Rome, Jan. 21, 1926. He studied in Rome, and with Genzmer, in Darmstadt; experimented with electronic music in the studios of Cologne and Warsaw.
WORKS: *4!* for violin and piano (1954); *Variazioni* for orch. (1955); *Incontri di fasce sonore* for magnetic tape (1957); *Ordini* for orch. (1958); *Campi integrati* for magnetic tape (1959); *Proporzioni* for flute solo (1960); *Aleatorio* for chamber orch. (1960); *Spazio a 5* for voices and percussion (1961); *Random or not Random* for orch. (1962).

Evans, David Emlyn, Welsh music editor and composer; b. near Newscastle Emlyn, Wales, Sept. 21, 1843; d. London, April 19, 1913. He was established in business at Cheltenham, but devoted his leisure hours to music; took part in many Welsh music festivals (Eisteddfodau), his works invariably winning prizes; after the Eisteddfod at Wexham in 1876, where he carried off all four prizes, he voluntarily withdrew from further competitions, but frequently acted as judge; at the National Eisteddfod in London, 1887, he was awarded a prize for his *Biography of Welsh Musicians*; for many years he was editor of *Y Cerddor (The Musician)*. His chief work is *Alawon Fy Ngwlad* (2 vols., 1896), a collection of 500 Welsh airs in piano arrangements; his publ. comps. include 2 cantatas, *The Christian's Prayer* and *The Fairy-tribe*, many glees, anthems, and part-songs.

Evans, Edwin, Sr., English organist and writer; b. London, 1844; d. there, Dec. 21, 1923. An assiduous and thorough scholar, he publ. basic analytic volumes on Beethoven and Brahms: *Beethoven's 9 Symphonies, fully described and analyzed* (London, 1923–24), and the remarkable 4-vol. edition (1581 pages; over 1000 mus. examples), *Historical, Descriptive and Analytical Account of the Entire Works of Johannes Brahms:* vol. I, vocal music (1912); vol. II, chamber and orchestral music up to op. 67 (1933; reprinted, 1950); vol. III, chamber and orchestral music from op. 68 to the end (1935; reprinted, 1949); vol. IV, piano works (1936; reprinted, 1950). Vols. II, III, and IV were publ. posthumously. He also wrote *Accompaniment of Plainchant* (1911); *Wagner's Teachings by Analogy* (1915); *How to Compose; How to Accompany at the Piano* (London, 1917); *Method of Instrumentation* (vol. I, *How to Write for Strings*); *Technics of the Organ* (London, 1938); transl. Wagner's *Oper und Drama;* made organ arrangements of operatic overtures.

Evans, Edwin, Jr., English writer on music; son of **Edwin Evans, Sr.**; b. London, Sept. 1, 1874; d. there, March 3, 1945. He studied for a business career; was engaged in telegraphy, railroads, and finance from 1889 to 1913; then devoted himself exclusively to musical pursuits. He was music critic of the *Pall Mall Gazette* (1914–23) and other London papers; was one of the founders of the International Society for Contemporary Music (1922); in 1938 was elected its president, retaining this post until his death. He wrote *Tchaikovsky* (London, 1906; revised ed., 1935); *The Margin of Music* (London, 1924); *Music and the Dance* (posthumous; London, 1948).

Evans, Geraint, Welsh baritone; b. Pontypridd, South Wales, Feb. 16, 1922. He studied in Hamburg and Geneva; was associated with the Glyndebourne Festivals from 1949 to 1961; appeared in San Francisco in 1959, and also sang at La Scala in Milan in 1960 and at the Vienna Opera in 1961. He distinguished himself particularly in the roles of Figaro, Leporello, and Papageno.

Evans, (given names **Ian Ernest Gilmore Green) Gil,** Canadian jazz pianist and bandleader; b. Toronto,

May 13, 1912. He went to California as a youth and had a band of his own in Stockton (1933–38); then moved to N.Y.; made arrangements of popular songs utilizing non-jazz instruments; became a proponent of cool jazz, and since 1949 has collaborated frequently with Miles Davis in such albums as *Birth of the Cool, Miles Ahead,* and *Sketches of Spain.* He has also made arrangements for other groups and has recorded his own albums *(The Individualism of Gil Evans).* Moving toward increasingly complex modernity, he applies polyharmonic and polyrhythmic procedures in his arrangements.

Evett, Robert, American composer; b. Loveland, Colorado, Nov. 30, 1922; d. Takoma Park, Maryland, Feb. 3, 1975. He studied with Roy Harris in Colorado Springs; settled in Washington.
WORKS: Cello Concerto (1954); Variations for Clarinet and Orch. (1955); Piano Concerto (1957); Symph. No. 1 (1960); Concerto for Harpsichord and Orch. (Washington, April 25, 1961); Sonata for Cello and Harpsichord (1955); Viola Sonata (1958); Piano Quartet (1961); Sonata for Oboe and Harpsichord (1964); Symph. No. 2, subtitled *Billy Ascends* for voices and orch., to the text by Melville (Washington, May 7, 1965); *The Windhover,* a concerto for bassoon and orch. (5th Inter-American Music Festival, Washington, May 20, 1971); songs; piano pieces.

Evseyev, Sergei, Russian composer and pedagogue; b. Moscow, Jan. 24, 1893; d. there, March 16, 1956. He studied piano with Medtner as a youth; then entered the Moscow Cons. where he continued to study piano with Goldenweiser and also attended classes in composition with Taneyev; upon graduation, he devoted himself to teaching music theory at the Moscow Cons., where he introduced a special seminar in modern harmony; he also taught a course of specific Russian folksong polyphony; furthermore, he conducted classes in musical education by correspondence on an experimental basis (1936–41).
WORKS: 3 symphonies (1925, 1933, 1943); 2 piano concertos (both in 1932); Clarinet Concerto (1943); 2 string quartets (1935, 1945); *Dramatic Sonata* for cello and piano (1941), and many piano pieces (most of them influenced by Medtner).

Ewald, Victor, Russian composer; b. St. Petersburg, Nov. 27, 1860; d. Leningrad, April 26, 1935. He studied engineering; from 1895 to 1915 was prof. at the Institute of Civil Engineering. Music was his avocation; he played the cello and the French horn; took part in Belaieff's quartet evenings and wrote a number of chamber music works; of these, his brass quintet is still popular. After the Revolution he continued to work in his primary profession as a civil engineer and instructor; also was active as an ethnomusicologist and participated in the expeditions in the North of European Russia collecting folksongs. His daughter **Zinaida** (1894–1942) continued his work in folklore and publ. several collections of Russian songs, in collaboration with her husband **Evgeny Gippius** (b. 1903).

Ewen, David, prolific American writer on music; b. Lwow, Poland, Nov. 26, 1907; came to the U.S. in 1912. He attended the College of the City of New York; studied music theory with Max Persin; was enrolled as a student at the Music School Settlement and at Columbia Univ. He was music editor of *Reflex Magazine* (1928–29) and *The American Hebrew* (1935); was active briefly as publisher (1946–49); in 1965 joined the music faculty of the Univ. of Miami which awarded him in 1974 the honorary degree of Doctor of Music. In all probability, Ewen has published more books on music and edited more reference publications than anyone in the 20th century; (80 at the last count in 1977). Some of his publications have been translated into 17 languages.
WRITINGS (not including revisions published with the amplificatory modifier "New"): *The Unfinished Symphony* (1931); *Hebrew Music* (1931); *Wine, Women, and Waltz* (1933); *Composers of Today* (1934); *The Man with the Baton* (1936); *Composers of Yesterday* (1937); *Men and Women Who Make Music* (1939); *Musical Vienna* (with Frederic Ewen; 1939); *Living Musicians* (1940); *Pioneers in Music* (1941); *Music Comes to America* (1942; revised, 1947); *Dictators of the Baton* (1943; revised, 1948); *Men of Popular Music* (1944; revised, 1952); *Music for the Millions* (1944; revised, 1946, 1949; published under title *Encyclopedia of Musical Masterpieces,* 1950); *American Composers Today* (revised ed., 1949); *The Story of Irving Berlin* (1950); *The Story of Arturo Toscanini* (1951; in Italian, Milan, 1952); *Fun with Musical Games and Quizzes* (with Slonimsky, 1952); *The Complete Book of 20th Century Music* (1952); *European Composers Today* (1953); *The Story of Jerome Kern* (1953); *The Milton Cross Encyclopedia of Great Composers and Their Music* (with Milton Cross, 1953); *Encyclopedia of the Opera* (1955); *A Journey to Greatness, George Gershwin* (1956; rewritten in 1970 under the title *George Gershwin: His Journey to Greatness);* *Panorama of American Popular Music* (1957); *Complete Book of the American Musical Theater* (N.Y., 1958; extremely valuable; brought up to date as *The New Complete Book of the American Musical Theater,* 1970); *Encyclopedia of Concert Music* (N.Y., 1959); *The World of Jerome Kern* (N.Y., 1960); *Leonard Bernstein* (N.Y., 1960; revised 1967); *History of Popular Music* (N.Y., 1961); *The Story of America's Musical Theater* (N.Y., 1961; revised 1969); *Ewen's Lighter Classics in Music* (N.Y., 1961); *David Ewen Introduces Modern Music* (N.Y., 1962; revised in 1969); *The Book of European Light Opera* (N.Y., 1962); *Popular American Composers* (N.Y., 1962); *The Complete Book of Classical Music* (N.Y., 1963); *The Life and Death of Tin Pan Alley* (N.Y., 1964); *American Popular Songs: From the Revolutionary War to the Present* (N.Y., 1966); *Great Composers: 1300–1900* (N.Y., 1966); *The World of 20th-Century Music* (N.Y., 1968); *Composers Since 1900* (N.Y., 1969); *Great Men of American Popular Songs* (N.Y., 1970); *Composers of Tomorrow's Music* (N.Y., 1971); *New Encyclopedia of the Opera,* a radical revision of *Encyclopedia of the Opera* (1971); *Popular American Composers;* First Supplement (N.Y., 1972); *Mainstreams of Music* (in 4 vols. N.Y., 1972, 1973, 1974, 1975); *All the Years of American Popular Music* (Englewood Cliffs, N.J., 1977). He also publ. a number of books for young people (on Gershwin, Bernstein, Haydn, Irving Berlin,

Toscanini, Johann Strauss, Jerome Kern, Richard Rodgers and Cole Porter). He rewrote, revised and expanded the *Milton Cross Encyclopedia of Great Composers* (N.Y., 1960). Revised editions of *The Book of Modern Composers*, originally publ. in 1943, appeared as *The New Book of Modern Composers* in 1960 and 1967. He further edited *From Bach to Stravinsky* (1933) and *The World of Great Composers* (Englewood Cliffs, N.J., 1962).

Excestre, William, English singer and composer who flourished c.1390–1410. He was clerk of the Chapel Royal in 1393, and received a prebend in St. Stephen's, Westminster, in 1394. He was one of the composers whose music is contained in the *Old Hall Manuscript;* a Gloria, a Credo, and a Sanctus (all for 3 voices) are extant.

Eximeno (y Pujades), Antonio, one of the most important Spanish writers on music; b. Valencia, Sept. 26, 1729; d. Rome, June 9, 1808; entered the Company of Jesus at the age of 16; became prof. of rhetoric at the Univ. of Valencia; 1764, appointed prof. of mathematics at the military academy in Segovia. When the Jesuits were expelled from Spain in 1767 he went to Rome, and in 1768 began to study music. In 1774 he publ. *Dell' origine e delle regole della musica colla storia del suo progresso, decadenza e rinnovazione* (Rome; Spanish transl. by Gutierrez, 1776, 3 vols.), in which he protested against pedantic rules and argued that music should be based on the natural rules of prosody. His theories were strongly controverted, especially by Padre Martini; in answer to the latter, Eximeno publ. *Dubbio di Antonio Eximeno sopra il Saggio fondamentale, pratico di contrappunto del Maestro Giambattista Martini* (Rome, 1775). His dictum that the national song should serve as a basis for the art-music of each country was taken up by Pedrell and led to the nationalist movement in modern Spanish music. Eximeno also wrote a satirical musical novel, *Don Lazarillo Vizcardi,* directed against the theories of Pietro Cerone (publ. by Barbieri, 1872–73, 2 vols.).

BIBLIOGRAPHY: F. Pedrell, *Padre Antonio Eximeno* (Barcelona, 1921).

Expert, Henry, eminent French music editor; b. Bordeaux, May 12, 1863; d. Tourettes-sur-Loup (Alpes-Maritimes), Aug. 18, 1952. He attended a Jesuit school in Bordeaux; went to Paris in 1881 and studied with César Franck and Eugène Gigout; taught at the École Nationale de Musique Classique, and lectured at the École des Hautes Études Sociales; from 1909, deputy-librarian of the Paris Cons.; chief of the library in 1921; founder (1903, with Maury) of the 'Société d'études musicales et concerts historiques,' also of the choral society 'Chanterie de la Renaissance' (1924). In 1933 he retired. His life work was the editing and publication of Franco-Flemish music of the 15th and 16th centuries, in six parts: I. *Les Maîtres-Musiciens de la Renaissance française* (works by Orlando di Lasso, Goudimel, Costeley, Janequin, Brumel, La Rue, Mouton, Fevin, Mauduit, Claude Le Jeune, Regnart, Du Caurroy, Gervaise, and Attaingnant's collection of chansons, all in modern notation, with facsimiles, etc.;

23 vols. publ., 1894–1908); II. *Bibliographie thématique* (2 vols., catalogue of publications of Attaingnant); III. *Les Théoriciens de la musique au temps de la Renaissance* (works of Michel de Menhou); IV. 2 vols. of music by Antoine de Bertrand; V. *Commentaires;* VI. *Extraits des Maîtres Musiciens* (selected single compositions, arranged for modern use; a large number have been publ., including works by some composers not found in Part I, viz.: Bertrand, Bonnet, Certon, De La Grotte, Gardanne, Josquin des Prez, Le Heurteur, Le Pelletier, Passereau, Thoinot-Arbeau). In 1924 Expert began the publication of a new series of French music of the 16th century entitled *Monuments de la musique française au temps de la Renaissance* (with scores in modern notation), of which 10 vols. were published; these contain works by Le Jeune, in 2 vols. (*Octonaires de la vanité et inconstance du monde*), Certon (3 Masses), Le Blanc (*Airs de plusieurs musiciens*), Bertrand, in 4 vols. (*Amours de P. de Ronsard*), Goudimel (*Messes à 4 voix*), L'Estocart (*Octonaires de la vanité du monde*). Expert also edited *Chansons mondaines des XVIIe et XVIIIe siècles français* (80 songs), *Airs français des XVIe et XVIIe siècles,* (Boesset, Guedron, Tessier, Lambert), *Florilège du concert vocal de la Renaissance* (1928–29), in 8 parts (Janequin, Lassus, Costeley, Bonnet, Le Jeune, Mauduit), *Les Maîtres du clavecin des XVIIe et XVIIIe siècles* (Dandrieu, Daquin, Corrette), *Amusements des Maîtres français du XVIIIe siècle* (Chédeville, J. Aubert, Baton), *Répertoire de musique religieuse et spirituelle* (Campra, Charpentier, Dumont, Lully, Bernier, Couperin le Grand, Clérambault, Lalande, Rameau, etc.), *La Fleur des musiciens de P. de Ronsard* (1923), instrumental *Fantaisies* by Le Jeune and Du Caurroy; and *Le Pseautier huguenot du XVIe siècle* (the Huguenot Psalter; 1902). He contributed the chapter on the music of France during the 16th century to Lavignac's *Encyclopédie de la Musique.*

Eybler, Joseph, Austrian composer; b. Schwechat, near Vienna, Feb. 8, 1765; d. Schönbrunn, July 24, 1846. He studied with Albrechtsberger in Vienna; was a friend of Haydn and Mozart; in 1792, became choirmaster at the Carmelite Church; was tutor to the princes in 1810, and first court Kapellmeister in 1824, on Salieri's retirement. He composed symphonies, concertos, quartets, sonatas, etc.; also 2 oratorios, 32 Masses, a Requiem, 7 *Te Deums,* and 30 offertories.

BIBLIOGRAPHY: Hildegard Herrmann, *Joseph Eybler* (thematic catalogue, 1976).

Eyken (Eijken), Jan Albert van, Dutch organist; b. Amersfoort, April 26, 1823; d. Elberfeld, Sept. 24, 1868. He studied at the Leipzig Cons., and afterwards at Dresden with Schneider. In 1848, he became organist of the Remonstrantenkerk, Amsterdam; in 1853, of the Zuyderkerk, and teacher at the music school in Rotterdam; in 1854, he became organist at Elberfeld. His organ pieces (150 chorales with introductions, 25 preludes, a toccata and fugue on B–A–C–H, 3 sonatas, variations, transcriptions, etc.) are well and favorably known.

Eymieu, Henry, French composer and writer on music; b. Saillans, Drôme, May 7, 1860; d. Paris, March 21, 1931. He studied law; then turned to music, taking lessons with Widor; settling in Paris, he wrote for *Le Ménestrel* and other musical publications; publ. *Études et biographies musicales* (Paris, 1892); composed a great variety of piano pieces, songs, and duets for piano and violin (58 published opus numbers in all); also produced a stage piece, *Un Mariage sous Néron* (Paris, 1898), and an oratorio, *Marthe et Marie* (Asnières, 1898).

Eyser, Eberhard, Polish-born Swedish violinist, violist and composer; b. Kwidzyn (Marienwerder), East Prussia, Aug. 1, 1932. He studied at the Music Academy in Hannover (1952-57); also attended seminars of Alois Hába in Prague, Hauer in Vienna, and of Xenakis. In 1961 he became a violist in the Royal Opera House Orch. in Stockholm.

WORKS: FOR THE STAGE: two 1-act operas: *Carmen 36,* after Strindberg, for 2 singing voices, 1 speaking voice, chamber orch. and tape (1972; Umeå, Nov. 5, 1975) and *Kalifens son* (1970-73); two chamber operas, after Strindberg: *Molonne* (Stockholm, Oct. 27, 1970) and *Sista resan* (*Last Voyage*), after Strindberg, for 2 voices, clarinet and tape (1972-73; Vadstena, July 24, 1974); a miniature opera, *Hjärter Kung eller Trägen vinner,* for 9 voices and instrumental ensemble (1973; Vadstena, June 6, 1973); 3 "operettinas": *I, Drömmen om mannen* (*Dream of Man*) for 7 voices, small girls' chorus and chamber orch. (1972), *II* for 2 voices a cappella (1971) and *III* for 4 voices and 2 pianists on 1 piano (1971). His other works include Toccata for Orch. (1957); *Iberian Suite* for chamber orch. (1957); *Serenata spagnola* for English horn and string quartet (1959); *Capriccio svedese* for 12 solo strings (1964); *Metastrophý* for orch. (1965); *Podema* for string quartet (1969); *Capriccio 68* for orch. (1968); *Colludo* for 3 to 8 string and wind instruments (1971); concertino for horn and chamber orch. (1971); *Constructo* for optional instrumental ensemble (1971); *Solo* for double bass (1971); Sonata, for bass clarinet, cymbal and piano (1972); *Petite Nocturne* for double bass, harpsichord and string orch. (1972); Sonata for Solo Bassoon (1973); Serenade for Flute, Viola and Cello (1973); *Stochasta 57-74* for winds and percussion (1974); *Symphonie orientale* for chamber orch. (1974); Passacaglia for Solo Cello (1974); *Ottoletto* for 8 clarinets (1975); *Circus Overture* for 12 winds, percussion and double bass (1976).

Eysler, Edmund S., Austrian operetta composer; b. Vienna, March 12, 1874; d. there, Oct. 4, 1949. He produced a great number of stage works; in 1915 he wrote no fewer than four operettas (*Leutnant Gustl, Der grosse Gabriel, Ein Tag im Paradies, Die oder Keine*). His most successful operetta was *Bruder Straubinger* (Vienna, Feb. 20, 1903; over 100 performances in that year). Other successful operettas: *Pufferl* (Vienna, April 13, 1905); *Künstlerblut* (1906); *Das Glückschweinchen* (1908); *Der unsterbliche Lump* (1910); *Das Zirkuskind* (1911); and *Die goldene Meisterin* (Vienna, Sept. 13, 1927).

BIBLIOGRAPHY: R. Prosl, *Edmund Eysler* (Vienna, 1947).

Ezaki, Kenjiro, Formosan-born Japanese composer; b. Tainan, Oct. 27, 1926. He studied at the Nihon Univ. in Tokyo (1953-57); also in the U.S. at the Univ. of Illinois Experimental Music Studio, and with Ussachevsky at the Columbia-Princeton Electronic Music Center. Returning to Japan, he operated his own electronic music studio in Tokyo; in 1971 he was appointed to the faculty of the Univ. of Tokyo. He uses electronic sound in many of his works.

WORKS: *Discretion* for a female voice (1961); *Concretion* for string trio (1962); *Dim Light* for chorus and 6 instruments (1962); *Contention* for soprano and guitar (1963); *Presage* for orch., in mobile configuration (1964); *Omen* for modified orch. (1964); Piano Trio (1964); *Pharos No. 1* and *No. 2* for chorus, flute, clarinet, oboe and piano (1965); *Music I* and *II* for guitar and tape (1967, 1971); *Ensemble* for a piano and 2 playback devices (1967); *Composition 5* for flute, 2 guitars, cello, percussion and soprano (1968); *Musicronics No. 1* for piano, percussion and tape (1968); *Zamuzara,* ballet music for tape (1968); *Requiem 1970* for soprano and tape (1969); *Computer Music No. 1* (1969; composed on the FACOM 270-30 computer); *Liaison* for 12-channel tape (1971).

F

Faber, Heinrich (known as **Magister Henricus Faber**), German theorist; b. Lichtenfels, c.1500; d. Ölsnitz, Saxony, Feb. 26, 1552. He entered the Univ. of Wittenberg in 1542; received the degree of Master of Liberal Arts in 1545; was then rector of the school of St. George's Monastery near Naumburg; in 1551 was appointed lecturer at Wittenberg Univ.; then was rector at Ölsnitz. He publ. *Compendiolum musicae pro incipientibus* (1548; reprinted many times and also issued in German transl. as *Musica, Kurtzer Inhalt der Singkunst*, 1572; edited by Adam Gumpelzhaimer and publ. as *Compendium musicae pro illius artis tironibus*, 1591). Faber further publ. *Ad Musicam practicam introductio* (1550); a *Musica poetica* remains in manuscript.

Fabini, Eduardo, Uruguayan composer; b. Solís del Mataojo, May 18, 1882; d. Montevideo, May 17, 1950. He studied violin in Montevideo, and later in Europe with César Thomson at the Brussels Cons., winning first prize; then gave concerts as a violinist in South America, and in the U.S. (1926); eventually returned to Montevideo, and was active there as composer and educator.
WORKS (all first performed in Montevideo): the ballets *Mburucuyá* (April 15, 1933) and *Mañana de Reyes* (July 31, 1937); symph. poem *Campo* (April 29, 1922); overture, *La Isla de los Ceibos* (Sept. 14, 1926); *Melga sinfónica* (Oct. 11, 1931); Fantasia for Violin and Orch. (Aug. 22, 1929); choral works; piano pieces; songs. His music is inspired entirely by South American folklore; the idiom is mildly modernistic, with lavish use of whole tone scales and other external devices of impressionism.

Fabricius, Johann Albert, eminent bibliographer; son of **Werner Fabricius**; b. Leipzig, Nov. 11, 1668; d. Hamburg, April 30, 1736. A learned man, he was professor of elocution; publ. important books of reference, valuable to musicology for the information they contain on musical topics: *Thesaurus antiquitatum hebraicarum* (1713, 7 vols.); *Bibliotheca latina mediae et infimae aetatis* (1712–22; 2nd ed., 1734; 6 vols.); *Bibliotheca graeca sive notitia scriptorum veterum graecorum* (1705–28, 14 vols.).

Fabricius, Werner, German composer; b. Itzehoe, April 10, 1633; d. Leipzig, Jan. 9, 1679. He studied with Thomas Selle and Heinrich Scheidemann in Hamburg; then took courses in law in Leipzig, where he also served as organist of the Nicolaikirche and Paulinerkirche.
WORKS: publ. a collection of pavanes, allemandes, etc., for viols and other instruments, under the title *Deliciae harmonicae* (Leipzig, 1656); *Geistliche Lieder* (Jena, 1659); *Geistliche Arien, Dialogen, Concerten, etc.* (Leipzig, 1662); motets, etc.

Faccio, Franco, Italian composer and conductor; b. Verona, March 8, 1840; d. near Monza, July 21, 1891. His first teacher was G. Bernasconi; from 1855–64 he studied at Milan Cons.; Arrigo Boito was his fellow pupil and friend; they wrote together a patriotic music drama, *Le Sorelle d'Italia,* which was produced by the students, and served together under Garibaldi in 1866. His first opera was *I profughi fiamminghi* (La Scala, Nov. 11, 1863); this was followed by the Shakespearian opera *Amleto,* for which Boito wrote the libretto (Genoa, May 30, 1865). In 1866–68 Faccio made a tour in Scandinavia as symphonic conductor; in 1868 he became prof. at Milan Cons., and in 1871 succeeded Terziani as conductor at La Scala; on April 25, 1886, he conducted for the 1000th time there. His performances of Verdi's operas were regarded as most authentic; he gave the world première of *Otello* at La Scala (1887).
BIBLIOGRAPHY: R. de Rensis, *Franco Faccio e Verdi* (Milan, 1934).

Fachiri, Adila, Hungarian violinist; grandniece of **Joachim;** sister of **Yelly d'Aranyi;** b. Budapest, Feb. 26, 1886; d. Florence, Dec. 15, 1962. She studied with Joachim, and received from him a Stradivarius violin. In 1909 she settled in London, where she married Alexander Fachiri, a lawyer. She appeared many times with her sister in duets; on April 3, 1930, the sisters gave in London the first performance of Holst's Concerto for 2 Violins, written especially for them.

Faelten, Carl, pianist and teacher; brother of **Reinhold Faelten;** b. Ilmenau, Thuringia, Dec. 21, 1846; d. Readfield, Maine, July 20, 1925. He studied in Frankfurt, and profited by advice from Raff. From 1878–82 he taught at the Hoch Cons. in Frankfurt; then was engaged at the Peabody Inst., Baltimore (1882–5); at the New England Cons., Boston (1885–97); was its director from 1890 until 1897, when he founded the Faelten Pianoforte School in Boston.
WORKS: *The Conservatory Course for Pianoforte* (1888); *Fundamental Training Course for Pianoforte* (in collaboration with his brother, Reinhold Faelten; 1895); also *Technische Übungen* for piano; *30 Characteristic Studies* (transcribed for piano from the violin sonatas of Bach); *30 Instructive Pieces* by G. F. Handel; transcriptions of 6 songs by Schubert; etc.

Faelten, Reinhold, pianist and teacher, brother of **Carl Faelten;** b. Illmenau, Thuringia, Jan. 17, 1856; d. Worcester, Mass., July 17, 1949. A pupil of Klughard and Gottschalk at Weimar; taught in Frankfurt, Baltimore and Boston; founded, in 1897, with his brother Carl Faelten, the Faelten Pianoforte School in Boston. Jointly with his brother, he wrote several books on the Faelten method: *100 Ear-training Exercises; Keyboard Harmony;* also a *Transposition System.*

Fagan, Gideon, South African conductor and composer; b. Somerset West, Cape Province, Nov. 3, 1904. He studied in Cape Town with W. H. Bell and later in London at the Royal College of Music, where his teachers were Vaughan Williams and Kitson. He began to conduct at the age of 18, mainly for the theater and cinema. He returned to South Africa in 1949; was Head of Music of the Johannesburg Radio from 1963 to 1966; then was a lecturer at Capetown Univ. He composed 2 symphonies, an orchestral suite on South African folk tunes, choruses and piano pieces.

Fago, Nicola, Italian composer, called "Il Tarantino" after his place of birth; b. Taranto, Feb. 26, 1677, d. Naples, Feb. 18, 1745. He was a pupil of Provenzale at the Conservatorio della Pietà in Naples (from 1693); he became his assistant in 1697 and his successor in 1705. From 1704 to 1708 he was maestro di cappella at the Cons. di Sant' Onofrio; from 1709 to 1731, maestro di cappella at the Tesoro di San Gennaro; retired on a modest pension in 1740. He was the teacher of Leonardo Leo, Francesco Feo, Jommelli, and Sala. His son **Lorenzo Fago** (b. Naples, Aug. 13, 1704; d. there, April 30, 1793), an organist and composer, was his successor at the Tesoro di San Gennaro (1731–66 and 1771–80), and taught at the Cons. della Pietà dei Turchini for 56 years (1737–93) until his death.

WORKS: 4 operas: *Radamisto* (1707), *Astarto* (1709), *La Cassandra indovina* (1711), and *Lo Masillo* (1712); 2 oratorios, *Faraone sommerso* and *Il monte fiorito;* a *Te Deum* and other sacred music, much of it still preserved in the archives of Naples, Paris and London.

BIBLIOGRAPHY: E. Faustini-Fasini, *Nicola Fago, Il Tarantino e la sua famiglia* (Taranto, 1931).

Fahrbach, Philipp, Austrian conductor; b. Vienna, Oct. 26, 1815; d. there, March 31, 1885. He was a pupil of Lanner; conducted his own orch. for years, and then a military band. His dances (over 150 works) were very popular. His three brothers, his son, and his nephews were all active as band musicians.

BIBLIOGRAPHY: P. Fahrbach, *Alt-Wiener Erinnerungen* (the composer's memoirs, publ. on the 50th anniversary of his death, 1935); O. Schneider, "Die Fahrbachs; eine Wiener Musikerfamilie der Strauss-Zeit," *Österreichische Musikzeitschrift* (Jan. 1967).

Faignient, Noë, Flemish 16th century contrapuntist; b. c.1540; d. c.1595 in Antwerp. His compositions, written in the style of Orlando di Lasso, consist of 2 sets of chansons, madrigals, and motets for 4, 5 and 6 voices (1568; 1569). Two of his madrigals are included in Maldeghem's *Trésor musical.*

Fain, Sammy, American composer of popular music; b. New York, June 17, 1902. He moved to California as a youth and wrote music for films. Gifted with a simple talent for facile tunes he wrote several hit songs, among them *When I Take My Sugar to Tea, Dear Hearts and Gentle People,* and *Love Is a Many-Splendored Thing.*

Fairchild, Blair, American composer; b. Belmont, Mass., June 23, 1877; d. Paris, April 23, 1933. He studied composition with J. K. Paine and Walter Spalding at Harvard Univ. (B.A., 1899); then took courses with Giuseppe Buonamici in Florence. From 1901 till 1903 he was attaché in the American embassies in Turkey and Persia. From 1905 he lived mostly in Paris, where he continued his musical studies with Charles Widor. Influenced by his travels in the Orient, and fascinated by the resources of exotic melos and rhythm, he wrote a number of pieces for orch., for piano, and many songs in a pseudo-oriental manner; despite the imitative qualities of his music, Fairchild must be regarded as one of the few Americans who tried to transplant exotic folkways, both in subject matter and in melodic turns.

WORKS: symph. poems *East and West* (1908); *Légende* for violin and orch. (1911); *Taminch,* symph. sketch after a Persian legend (1913); *6 chants nègres* for piano (also orchestrated and performed by the Boston Symph. Orch., Dec. 6, 1929); *12 Indian Songs and Dances* for piano; Violin Sonata; 5 sets of *Stornelli Toscani* for piano; song cycles, among them *Persian Folk Songs, 5 Sea Prayers,* etc.

BIBLIOGRAPHY: W. T. Upton, *Art-Song in America* (N.Y., 1930; pp. 169–76); W. T. Upton, "Our Musical Expatriates," *Musical Quarterly* (Jan. 1928).

Fairclough, George Herbert, American organist and composer; b. Hamilton, Canada, Jan. 30, 1869; d. Saratoga, Calif., March 27, 1954. He studied at Toronto Cons. (1887–90); then went to Berlin, where he took organ lessons at the Hochschule für Musik with Karl Heinrich Barth and with Bargiel. Returning to America he served from 1900 until 1937 as organist at St. John's Episcopal Church, St. Paul; concurrently taught organ at the Univ. of Minnesota (1917–37); then retired. He composed a number of organ works and some sacred music.

Fairlamb, James Remington, American composer; b. Philadelphia, Jan. 23, 1838; d. Ingleside, N.Y., April 16, 1908. As a youth he played organ in several Philadelphia churches; in 1858 went to Paris; studied piano there with Marmontel. While in Europe, he was appointed by Abraham Lincoln as American Consul at Zürich (1861) and stayed in Zürich until 1865, when he returned to the U.S. He organized an amateur opera company with which he brought out his 4-act grand opera *Valérie, or Treasured Tokens* (Philadelphia, Dec. 15, 1869). From 1872–98 he was church organist in Philadelphia, Jersey City, and New York. Besides *Valérie,* he wrote another grand opera *Lionello* (which was never performed) and two light operas: *Love's Stratagem* and *The Interrupted Marriage;* some 50 of his choral works and nearly 150 songs and organ pieces are published. He was one of the founders of the American Guild of Organists.

Faisst, Immanuel Gottlob Friedrich, German composer; b. Esslingen, Württemberg, Oct. 13, 1823; d. Stuttgart, June 5, 1894. He studied theology at Tübingen, and also learned to play the organ; subsequently took lessons with Dehn in Berlin. He became active as choral conductor and organist; organized a society for classical church music (1847) in Stuttgart, where he settled. He was the founder of the *Schwäbischer Sängerbund* (1849); with Lebert, Stark, Brachmann, and others he established the Stuttgart Cons. (1857); became its director in 1859. He received a *Dr. phil.* at Tübingen Univ. for his essay *Beiträge zur Geschichte der Klaviersonate* (*Cäcilia,* 1846; repr. in the *Neues Beethovenjahrbuch* 1, 1924). He was the editor (with Lebert) of the famous edition of classical piano works, *Instruktive ausgewählte classische Werke,* publ. by Cotta; also (with Stark) of *Elementar- und*

Chorgesangschule (2 vols.; Stuttgart, 1880–82). Faisst was a prolific composer; a number of his songs, ballads, choral works, etc., were publ. during his lifetime, but then were completely forgotten. He also publ. several school manuals on harmony.

Faith, Percy, American conductor and arranger of popular music; b. Toronto, Canada, April 7, 1908; d. Los Angeles, Feb. 9, 1976. He studied with Louis Waizman and Frank Wellman at the Toronto Cons.; played piano in movie theaters and in dance bands. In 1931 he joined the Canadian Broadcasting Corporation and conducted the radio orchestra in popular programs of Canadian music; in 1940 moved to the United States to fill a conducting post for the NBC Carnation Contented Hour; in 1950 he became music director of Columbia Records and made more than 45 albums of his own. He composed numerous film scores for Hollywood movies and in 1955 won an Academy Award nomination for "Love Me or Leave Me." An amiably disposed composer of music "for listening pleasure," he described his goal as "satisfying the millions of devotees of that pleasant American institution known as the quiet evening at home, whose idea of perfect relaxation is the easy chair, slippers and good music."

Falabella Correa, Roberto, Chilean composer; b. Santiago, Feb. 13, 1926; d. there, Dec. 15, 1958. Paralyzed by polio since childhood, Falabella was educated at home; studied privately with Lucila Césped (1945–46), Alfonso Letelier (1949–50), Gustavo Becerra (1952), Miguel Aguilar and Esteban Eitler (1956–57). His music is classical in form, romantic in content, and modernistic in technique.
    WORKS: a chamber opera, *Epitafios fúnebres* (1952); a miniature opera, *Del diario morir* (1954); 2 piano sonatas (1951, 1954); *Dueto* for flute and violin (1952); *Preludios episódicos* for piano (1953); a ballet, *El Peine de oro* (1954); *Palimpsestos* for contralto, bassoon, horn and percussion (1954); Violin Sonata (1954); Cello Sonata (1954); *Impresiones* for piano (1955); Symph. No. 1 (1955); 2 Divertimenti for Strings (1955); *Emotional Studies* for piano (1957; also for orch., 1957); a ballet, *Andacollo,* for voices, piano and percussion (1957); String Quartet (1957); *Retratos* for piano (1957); *La Lámpara en la tierra,* cantata for baritone and orch. (1958; Santiago, Oct. 21, 1960).

Falchi, Stanislao, Italian composer; b. Terni, Jan. 29, 1851; d. Rome, Nov. 14, 1922. He studied in Rome with C. Maggi and S. Meluzzi; in 1877 he became a teacher at Santa Cecilia; from 1902 till 1915 was its director. Among his pupils were A. Bonaventura, A. Bustini, V. Gui, B. Molinari, L. Refice, and F. Santoliquido. He wrote the operas *Lorhelia* (Rome, Dec. 4, 1877), *Giuditta* (Rome, March 12, 1887), and *Il Trillo del diavolo* (Rome, Jan. 29, 1899); also a *Requiem* for the funeral of Victor Emmanuel II (Jan. 17, 1883).

Falcon, Marie-Cornélie, remarkable French dramatic soprano; b. Paris, Jan. 28, 1814; d. there, Feb. 25, 1897. She was a pupil of Bordogni and A. Nourrit; made her debut at the Paris Opéra on July 20, 1832, as Alice in *Robert le Diable.* She sang at the Paris Opéra with brilliant success until 1837, when, though still a very young woman, she unaccountably lost her voice. After many attempts to regain her vocal powers, including quack medicines and bogus treatment of all sorts, she was forced to abandon the stage, and retired to her villa near Paris; she lived another sixty years. Despite the brevity of her active career, her singing of such roles as Valentine in *Les Huguenots* and Rachel in *La Juive* became a lengendary memory, so that the description "Falcon type" was applied to singers who excelled in her roles.

Falconieri, Andrea, Italian composer and lutenist; b. Naples, 1586; d. there, July 29, 1656. He was in the service of the house of Farnese at Parma; studied with Santino Garsi there until 1614; in 1615 was in Florence; 1616, in Rome; 1619, again in Florence; 1620–21, at the court of Modena; then traveled in Spain and France; 1629–35, again at Parma; from 1639, maestro di cappella at the royal court, Naples; 1642, in Genoa; 1650, in Naples. His *Libro Primo di Villanelle a 1, 2 e 3 voci* (with alphabetical tablature for Spanish guitar) was publ. at Rome, 1616 (reprinted by Gardano at Venice); various other books followed, the *Libro V delle Musiche* appearing in 1619; probably one of his last works was the valuable instrumental collection *Primo Libro di Canzone, Sinfonie, Fantasie, Capricci per Violini e Viole, overo altri Strumenti a 1, 2 e 3 voci con il basso continuo* (Naples, 1650). Reprints: arias (2 books) in the *Raccolta nazionale delle musiche italiane;* in A. Parisotti's *Arie antiche* and *Piccolo album di musica antica;* in L. Torchi's *Eleganti canzoni ed arie italiane del secolo XVII;* and *L'arte musicale in Italia* (vol. VII); *17 Arie a una voce,* ed. by G. Benvenuti; *2 Villanelle a 3,* ed. by C. Sabatini; 4 songs in *La Flora,* ed. by Knud Jeppesen (Copenhagen, 1949). L. Valdrighi, *Atti* (1883; p. 488); L. Torchi, in *Rivista Musicale Italiana* (1898; p. 65).

Falk, Richard, German-American opera conductor; b. Moringen, April 29, 1878; d. New York, March 3, 1949. He studied at the Leipzig Cons. with Jadassohn and Riemann; conducting with Nikisch. After graduation in 1908 he began to conduct theater orchestras in Berlin and other German cities; in 1939 he settled in the U.S. He adapted and produced a number of 18th-century Italian operas.

Falkner, Donald Keith, English bass; b. Sawston, Cambridge, March 1, 1900. He was a chorister at New College School in Cambridge; then served in the Royal Navy during World War I. It was only after the end of the war that he began to study singing seriously, taking lessons with Plunkett Greene in London, Lierhammer in Vienna, and also in Paris, with Dossert. He was particularly successful in modern English and Elizabethan songs. He taught voice at the Royal College of London (1935–39) and at Cornell Univ. in Ithaca, N.Y. (1950–60); then returned to the Royal College as Director of Music.

Fall, Fritz (Frederick), nephew of **Leo Fall;** b. Vienna, July 25, 1901; d. Washington, D.C., Nov. 24, 1974. He studied at the Vienna Academy; was opera conductor in Austria, Germany, and Czechoslovakia (1925–37); in 1937 he went to America; 1938–42, conducted and taught in Tyler, Texas; during World War II was with the Office of Strategic Services of the U.S.; 1945–48, with the Allied Military Government in Europe; from 1948, teaching and conducting (Dept. of Agriculture Symph. Orch.) in Washington, D.C. He changed his first name from Fritz to Frederick after becoming an American citizen.

Fall, Leo, Austrian composer of light opera; b. Olmütz, Feb. 2, 1873; d. Vienna, Sept. 15, 1925. His father was a military bandmaster, and it was from him that Leo Fall received his training in practical music making; then he took up academic courses at the Vienna Cons. with Johann Fuchs and others. For some years he was theater conductor in Berlin, Hamburg, and Cologne, but lived for most of his life in Vienna. His operettas are typical Viennese products, lighthearted, romantic, and melodious. Although they never reached the height of international success obtained by such masters of the genre as Lehár, at least one of them, *Die Dollarprinzessin* (Vienna, Nov. 2, 1907), was famous for many years. The list of his operettas includes also *Der fidele Bauer* (Mannheim, July 27, 1907), *Eternal Waltz* (London, Dec. 22, 1911), *Die Rose von Stambul* (Vienna, Dec. 2, 1916), and *Mme. Pompadour* (Vienna, March 2, 1923). His operetta *Der Rebell*, a failure at its first production (Vienna, Nov. 29, 1905), was revised and staged under the new title *Der liebe Augustin* (Berlin, Feb. 3, 1912), scoring excellent success.

BIBLIOGRAPHY: W. Zimmerli, *Leo Fall* (Zürich, 1957).

Falla, Manuel de, one of the greatest Spanish composers; b. Cádiz, Nov. 23, 1876; d. Alta Gracia, in the province of Córdoba, Argentina, Nov. 14, 1946. He studied with J. Tragó (piano) and F. Pedrell (composition) in Madrid; composed some zarzuelas, which he later discarded. His opera, *La Vida breve*, won the prize awarded by the Academia de Bellas Artes, Madrid, in 1905; in that year he also won the Ortiz y Cussó Prize for pianists. In 1907 he went to Paris, where he became friendly with Debussy, Dukas, and Ravel, who aided and encouraged him. Under their influence he adopted the principles of impressionism without, however, giving up his personal and national style; in 1914, returned to Spain and in 1921 made his home in Granada, frequently touring Europe as conductor of his own works. In May, 1938, he was made President of the Instituto de España. In 1939, at the end of the Spanish Civil War, he went to Argentina; after conducting a few concerts of his music in Buenos Aires, he withdrew to the small locality of Alta Gracia, where he lived the last years of his life in seclusion. His art is rooted both in the folksongs of Spain and in the purest historical traditions of Spanish music. Up to 1919 his works were cast chiefly in the Andalusian idiom, and his instrumental technique was often conditioned by effects peculiar to Spain's national instrument, the guitar. In *El Retablo de Maese Pedro* he turns to the classical tradition of Spanish (especially Castilian) music; the keyboard style of his Harpsichord Concerto shows, in the classical lucidity of its

writing, a certain kinship with Domenico Scarlatti (who lived in Spain for many years). De Falla taught composition privately, his most gifted pupils being Ernesto Halffter and Joaquín Nin-Culmell.

WORKS: the opera *La Vida breve* (Nice, April 1, 1913; Metropolitan Opera, N.Y., March 7, 1926); *El Retablo de Maese Pedro*, for marionettes and singers (performed in Madrid, in concert form, March 23, 1923; a private stage performance was given in the salon of Princesse de Polignac, in Paris, on June 25, 1923; first public stage performance, Paris, Nov. 13, 1923, under the composer's direction); the ballets *El Amor brujo* (Madrid, April 15, 1915; a tremendously effective work; numerous performances as an orchestral suite) and *El Sombrero de tres picos* (London, July 22, 1919; very successful); *Noches en los jardines de España* for piano and orch. (1909–15; Madrid, April 9, 1916); Concerto for Harpsichord (or Piano), Flute, Oboe, Clarinet, Violin, and Cello, written at the suggestion of Wanda Landowska (Barcelona, Nov. 5, 1926; composer conducting; Wanda Landowska soloist); *Homenajes*, in 4 parts: 1. *Pour le Tombeau de Debussy* (originally for guitar, 1920); 2. *Fanfare pour Arbós* (1933); 3. *Pour le Tombeau de Paul Dukas* (originally for piano, 1935); 4. *Pedrelliana* (1938; first performance of the entire suite, Buenos Aires, Nov. 18, 1939, composer conducting); for piano: *4 pièces espagnoles: Aragonesa, Cubana, Montañesa, Andaluza; Fantasia Bética;* songs: *Trois mélodies* (1909); *Siete canciones populares españolas* (1914; very popular); *Psyché*, for voice, flute, harp, violin, viola, and cello (1924); *Soneto a Córdoba* for voice and harp (1927). A posthumous opera, *La Atlántida*, begun in 1928 and based on M. J. Verdaguer's Catalan poem, was completed by Ernesto Halffter and produced at La Scala, Milan, on June 18, 1962. De Falla's writings on music were collected and edited by F. Sopeña and publ. as *Escritos sobre música y músicos* (Buenos Aires, 1950); another collection, in German transl. and edited by J. Grunfeld, is *Spanien und die neue Musik. Ein Lebensbild in Schriften, Bildern Erinnerungen* (Zürich, 1968).

BIBLIOGRAPHY: G. Jean-Aubry, "Manuel de Falla," *Musical Times* (April 1917); M. Castelnuovo-Tedesco, in "Il pianoforte" (Jan. 1923); E. Istel, "Manuel de Falla," *Musical Quarterly* (Oct. 1926); Roland-Manuel, *Manuel de Falla* (Paris, 1930); J. B. Trend, *Manuel de Falla and Spanish Music* (N.Y., 1929; new ed., 1934); G. Chase, "Falla's Music for Piano Solo," *Chesterian* (1940); Jaime Pahissa, *Vida y obra de Manuel de Falla* (Buenos Aires, 1947; also publ. in English, London, 1954); J. M. Thomas, *Manuel de Falla en la Isla* (Palma, 1947); J. Jaenisch, *Manuel de Falla und die spanische Musik* (Freiburg, 1952); Kurt Pahlen, *Manuel de Falla und die Musik in Spanien* (Olten, 1953); Suzanne Demarquez, *Manuel de Falla* (Paris, 1963; also in English, Philadelphia, 1968); J. J. Vinegra and Lasso de la Vega, *Vida intima de Manuel de Falla* (Cadiz, 1966); A. Saeardia, *Vida y Obra de Manuel de Falla* (Madrid, 1967).

Faller, Nikola, Croatian conductor and composer; b. Varaždin, April 22, 1862; d. Zagreb, Feb. 28, 1938. He studied with Bruckner in Vienna and with Massenet in Paris. He was active as opera conductor in Split and Zagreb; composed choral works and dances.

Famintsyn, Alexander, Russian critic and composer; b. Kaluga, Nov. 5, 1841; d. Ligovo, near St. Petersburg, July 6, 1896; studied with Jean Vogt in St. Petersburg, and then with Hauptmann and Richter in Leipzig. He taught music history at the St. Petersburg Cons. (1865–72); translated into Russian the textbooks *Allgemeine Musiklehre* by Marx and *Harmonielehre* by Richter. However he soon abandoned his teaching activities and devoted himself chiefly to music criticism, taking a very conservative attitude; he indulged in frequent polemics against the Russian composers of the National School; Mussorgsky caricatured Famintsyn in his satirical song *The Classicist* and in a section of his burlesque *Rayok*. Famintsyn's publications on Russian instruments are valuable; he publ. essays on the gusli (1890) and the domra (1891). He was also a composer; his opera *Sardanapal* was produced in St. Petersburg on Dec. 5, 1875, but without any success; his other opera, *Uriel Acosta* (1883), was not performed. He further wrote a Piano Quintet, String Quartet, and some songs.

Fanciulli, Francesco, Italian conductor and composer; b. Porto San Stefano, July 17, 1850; d. New York, July 17, 1915. He studied in Florence; after some years as opera conductor in Italy, he came to America (1876) and earned his living as organist and theatrical conductor; in 1893 he succeeded Sousa as conductor of the Marine Band in Washington; was then bandmaster of the 71st Regiment, N.Y. (1898–1904); after that conducted his own band. He wrote an opera, *Priscilla*, which was produced in Norfolk, Virginia, on Nov. 1, 1901.

Fanelli, Ernest, French composer; b. Paris, June 29, 1860; d. there, Nov. 24, 1917. He played drums in orchestras as a small boy; entered the Paris Cons. in 1876, in the class of Delibes. He worked as a copyist and music engraver for many years; in 1912 he applied to Gabriel Pierné for work, submitting the score of his own symph. poem *Thèbes* as a specimen of his handwriting. This score, composed by Fanelli as early as 1883, seemed to anticipate the instrumental and harmonic usages of Debussy and other composers of impressionist music, and Pierné decided to perform it as a curiosity; he conducted it at the Colonne concert in Paris (March 17, 1912), and the novelty created a mild sensation in French musical circles; other works by Fanelli (*Impressions pastorales; L'Effroi du Soleil; Suite rabelaisienne,* etc.), all written before 1893, were also found interesting. However, the sensation proved of brief duration, and the extravagant claims for Fanelli's talent collapsed.
BIBLIOGRAPHY: M.-D. Calvocoressi, "An Unknown Composer of Today," *Musical Times* (April 1912).

Faning, Eaton, English conductor and composer; b. Helston, Cornwall, May 20, 1850; d. Brighton, Oct. 28, 1927. He studied at the Royal Academy of Music, London, with Sterndale Bennett and Arthur Sullivan, winning the Mendelssohn Scholarship (1873) and the Lucas medal (1876); received Mus. Bac., Cambridge (1894) and Mus. Doc. (1899). From 1878 he taught piano at the Royal Academy of Music; in 1885 became music director at Harrow School (until 1901); thereafter occupied various educational posts, and was a member of examination boards. He wrote a symphony, some chamber music, and several operettas. An account of his career is found in the *Musical Times* of Aug. 1901.

Fano, Guido Alberto, Italian composer and writer on music; b. Padua, May 18, 1875; d. Tauriano di Spilimbergo (Udine), Aug. 14, 1961. He studied with Pollini in Padua and Martucci in Bologna; at the same time he took courses in law; became *Dr. juris* of Bologna Univ. in 1898. In 1900 he was appointed teacher of piano at the Liceo Musicale in Bologna; was director of the Cons. of Parma (1905–11); then taught piano at Naples (1912–17), Palermo (1917–21), and Milan (1921–38). He wrote an opera *Iuturna;* a symph. poem *La Tentazione di Gesù;* also publ. several books: *Pensieri sulla musica* (Bologna, 1903); *Nella vita del ritmo* (Naples, 1916); *Lo studio del pianoforte* (3 vols.; Milan, 1923–34).

Fara, Giulio, Italian writer on music and composer; b. Cagliari, Sardinia, Dec. 3, 1880; d. Pesaro, Oct. 9, 1949. He studied singing and composition; became instructor in public schools of Sardinia; collected Sardinian folksongs and used some of them in his own compositions, notably in the opera *Elia.* He publ. a biography of Rossini (1915) and a collection of essays *L'anima musicale d'Italia* (1921); contributed to the *Rivista Musicale Italiana* and other Italian publications. His collection of Sardinian songs was publ. by Ricordi (1924).

Farinelli (real name **Carlo Broschi**), celebrated Italian artificial soprano; b. Andria, Jan. 24, 1705; d. Bologna, Sept. 16, 1782. He adopted the name Farinelli to honor his benefactor Farina. He was a student of Porpora; sang in Naples with great success, achieving fame as 'il ragazzo' (the boy). At the age of 16 he sang in Rome in Porpora's opera *Eomene;* his fame spread in Italy and abroad. In 1727 he met the famous castrato singer Bernacchi in Bologna; in a singing contest with him, Farinelli acknowledged defeat, and persuaded Bernacchi to give him lessons to achieve virtuosity in coloratura. He visited Vienna in 1724, 1728, and 1731. In 1734 he was sent by Porpora to London to join the Italian opera there. He made his London debut on Oct. 27, 1734, in *Artaserse* by Hasse, appearing with Senesino and Cuzzoni; he remained in London for two years, amassing a fortune; he then went to Paris, and in 1737 to Madrid, where he attained unparalleled success as court singer to King Philip V; his duty was to sing several arias every night to cure the king's melancholy. His influence on the ailing monarch, and on the Queen, was such that he was able to command considerable funds to engage famous performers at the Madrid court. When his voice began to fail, he undertook to serve as impresario, decorator, and stage director. He continued to enjoy the court's favor under Philip's successor, Ferdinand VI, but at the accession to the Spanish throne of Carlos III in 1759,

Farinelli was dismissed. He went back to Italy in possession of great wealth; he assembled his family in a palatial villa which he built near Bologna, and spent his last 20 years of life in contentment.

BIBLIOGRAPHY: G. Sacchi, *Vita del Cavaliere Don Carlo Broschi, detto Farinelli* (Venice, 1784); J. Desastre, *G. Broschi* (Zürich, 1903); G. Monaldi, *Cantanti evirati celebri* (Rome, 1919); F. Haböck, *Die Gesangskunst der Kastraten* (Vienna, 1923); R. Bouvier, *Farinelli, le chanteur des rois* (Paris, 1943).

Farinelli, Giuseppe, prolific Italian composer; b. Este, May 7, 1769; d. Trieste, Dec. 12, 1836. In 1785 he entered the Cons. della Pietà dei Turchini at Naples, his teachers being Barbiello, Fago, Sala, and Tritto; his first opera, *Il Dottorato di Pulcinella,* produced in 1792, was followed by 50 or 60 others, not original, but in very happy imitation of Cimarosa's style and chiefly comic. From 1810-17 he lived at Turin; then went to Trieste as organist at the Cathedral of San Giusto. He also wrote several oratorios, cantatas, 5 Masses, 2 Te Deums, and other church music.

Farjeon, Harry, English composer; b. Hohokus, N.J. (of English parents), May 6, 1878; d. London, Dec. 29, 1948. He was a son of the English novelist B. L. Farjeon, and grandson of the famous actor Joseph Jefferson. He was educated in England, taking music lessons with Landon Ronald and John Storer; then studied composition with Corder at the Royal Academy of Music; won the Lucas Medal and other prizes. In 1903 he became an instructor there.

WORKS: the opera *Floretta* (1899) and 2 operettas, *The Registry Office* (1900) and *A Gentleman of the Road* (1902), all performed in London; Piano Concerto (1903); *Hans Andersen Suite* for small orch. (London, 1905); 2 song cycles, *Vagrant Songs* and *The Lute of Jade.* The score of a symph. poem *Summer Vision* (regarded by the composer as his best work) was sent to Germany shortly before World War I and was lost.

Farkas, Edmund, Hungarian composer; b. Puszta-Monostor, 1851; d. Klausenburg, Sept. 1, 1912. He studied engineering at the Univ. of Budapest; then took courses at the Budapest Academy of Music with Erkel, Volkmann, and others. Upon graduation he was appointed director at the Klausenburg Cons. There he organized an orchestra, established a musical journal, and promoted national Hungarian music.

WORKS: the operas (first performed in Budapest) *Bayadere* (Aug. 23, 1876), *Valentin Balassa* (Jan. 16, 1896), *The Inquest* (Oct. 5, 1900), and *The World of Kurucz* (Oct. 26, 1906); several symph. poems in a romantic vein (*Dusk, Storm,* etc.); church music; 5 string quartets; several piano pieces in the Hungarian style; publ. (in Hungarian) several papers on school music.

Farkas, Ferenc, Hungarian composer; b. Nagykanizsa, Dec. 15, 1905. He began to study piano as a child; took courses with Leo Weiner and Albert Siklós at the Academy of Music in Budapest (1923-28); a state scholarship enabled him to study with Respighi at the Cons. of St. Cecilia in Rome (1929-31); later was engaged as conductor of incidental music to films in Vienna and Copenhagen (1933-35). Returning to Hungary, he was a music teacher at the municipal school in Budapest (1935-41); from 1941 to 1944 he taught at the Cons. of Kolozsvár (Cluj); in 1949, appointed prof. of composition at the Academy of Music in Budapest. In 1950 he was awarded the Kossuth Prize and in 1960 the Erkel Prize.

WORKS: FOR THE STAGE: *The Magic Cupboard,* comic opera (1938-42; Budapest, April 22, 1942; also a separate overture, 1952); *The Sly Students,* ballet (1949); *Csinom Palkó,* musical play (1950, revised 1960); *Vidróczki,* opera (1964); *Piroschka,* musical comedy (1967); *Story of Noszty Junior with Mari Tóth,* musical comedy (1971); *Panegyricus,* ballet with narrator and chorus (1972). FOR ORCH: Fantasy for Piano and Orch. (1929); Divertimento (1930); Harp Concertino (1937, revised 1956); *Dinner Music* for chamber orch. (1938); *Rhapsodia Carpathiana* (1940); *Marionette's Dance Suite* (1941); *Musica Pentatonica* for string orch. (1945); Prelude and Fugue (1947; originally titled *Musica Dodecatonica*); Piano Concertino (1948); *Lavotta,* suite (1951); Symphony (1951-52); *Scherzo Sinfonico* (1952); *Symphonic Overture* (1952); *Sketches from the Bükk* (1955); *Piccola Musica di Concerto* for string orch. (1961); *Trittico Concertato* for cello and string orch. (1964); *Gyász és vígasz* (*Planctus et Consolationes,* 1965); *Concerto all'Antica* for baryton (viola da gamba) and string orch. (1965); *Serenata concertante* for flute and string orch. (1967). CHORAL AND OTHER VOCAL: *Cantata Lirica* (1945), *Cantus Pannonicus,* cantata to the Latin verses of the 15th-century Hungarian archbishop Janus Pannonius (1959; Budapest, April 3, 1959); *Laudatio Szigethiana,* oratorio (1967) and other works for voice and/or chorus and orch. CHAMBER WORKS: 3 violin sonatinas (1930, 1931, 1959); String Quartet (1970-72) and other chamber pieces; for piano: Sonata (1930), Toccata (1945), *Correspondences* (1957), *Hybrids* (1957) and *3 Monograms* (1962); *Naptár (Calendar)* for soprano, tenor, and piano or chamber ensemble (1956) and other songs; incidental music.

Farley, Carole Ann, American soprano; b. LeMars, Iowa, Nov. 29, 1946. She studied at Indiana Univ.; then with Marianne Schech at the Hochschule für Musik, Munich, and with Cornelius Reid, N.Y. She made her debut in Linz, Austria, in 1969; married José Serebrier. Her singing of the title role in Alban Berg's *Lulu* at the Metropolitan Opera, N.Y., in 1977 placed her at the foremost rank of musicianly artists and singing intellectuals. She also appeared as Lulu in Cologne. Other roles are: Manon, Donna Anna, Mimi, Violetta.

Farmer, Henry George, eminent musicologist; authority on Oriental music; b. Birr, Ireland, Jan. 17, 1882; d. Law, Lanarkshire, Dec. 30, 1965. He studied piano and violin, and as a boy joined the Royal Artillery Orch. in London, playing the French horn at its concerts. He then studied philosophy and languages at Glasgow Univ. An extremely prolific writer, he publ. a number of original works, dealing with such varied subjects as military music and Arabic musical theories. He was the founder and conductor of the Glasgow Symph. Orch. (1919-43); wrote several overtures and some chamber music.

WRITINGS: *Memoirs of the Royal Artillery Band* (1904); *The Rise and Development of Military Music* (1912); *The Arabian Influence on Musical Theory* (1925); *Byzantine Musical Instruments in the 9th Century* (1925); *The Arabic Musical MSS. in the Bodleian Library* (1926); *A History of Arabian Music to the 13th Century* (1929); *Music in Medieval Scotland* (1930); *Historical Facts for the Arabian Musical Influence* (1930); *The Organ of the Ancients* (1931); *Studies in Oriental Musical Instruments* (1931); *An Old Moorish Lute Tutor* (1931); *Al-Farabi's Arabic-Latin Writings* (Glasgow, 1934); *Turkish Instruments of Music in the 17th Century* (1937); *New Mozartiana* (1938); *Sa'adyah Gaon on the Influence of Music* (1943); *A History of Music in Scotland* (London, 1947); *Music Making in the Olden Days* (1950); *Military Music* (1950); *Oriental Studies, Mainly Musical* (London, 1953); *The History of the Royal Artillery Band* (1954); *British Bands in Battle* (London, 1965).

Farmer, John, Elizabethan madrigal composer, active from 1591 to 1601. In 1595 he was organist at the Christ Church Cathedral in Dublin; in 1599 he left Dublin and went to London. Among his madrigals the best known are *Fair Phyllis I saw sitting all alone, You pretty flowers,* and *A little pretty bonny lass,* included in his *First Set of English Madrigals to Foure Voices* (London, 1599; reprinted in vol. 8 of E. H. Fellowes' *English Madrigal School*). He contributed a 6-part madrigal *Fair Nymphs, I heard one telling* to *The Triumphes of Oriana,* and several canticles and hymns to Thomas East's *Whole Booke of Psalmes* (1592). Extant MSS are in the Christ Church Library and Music School at Oxford, and in the British Museum. Farmer was also the author of *Divers and sundry waies of two parts in one* (London, 1591).
BIBLIOGRAPHY: E. H. Fellowes, *The English Madrigal Composers* (1921; 2nd ed., 1948).

Farmer, John, English composer; b. Nottingham, Aug. 16, 1836; d. Oxford, July 17, 1901. He studied at the Leipzig Cons. and later at Coburg; then lived in Switzerland, returning to England in 1862; taught at Harrow School (1862–85). He composed an oratorio *Christ and His Soldiers* (1878); a fairy opera *Cinderella* (1882); comic cantata *Froggy Would A-wooing Go* (1887); settings of nursery rhymes for chorus and orch.; church music; chamber music; a piano quintet, and other chamber music.

Farnaby, Giles, English composer; b. probably in Cornwall, c.1565; d. London, Nov. 1640 (buried, Nov. 25, 1640). He graduated from Oxford in 1592, receiving the degree of B.Mus.; later moved to London, where he remained until his death.
WORKS: *Canzonets to Fowre Voyces* (1598; includes an added madrigal for 8 voices, one of the few such works in the English school; reprint by E. H. Fellowes, in vol. 20 of the *English Madrigal School*); vocal religious works in various collections, and motets, psalms, etc.; more than 50 virginal pieces in the Fitzwilliam Virginal Book (ed. by J. A. Fuller-Maitland and W. Barclay Squire, London, 1899); a madrigal, *Come, Charon,* is in MS at the Royal College of Music;

part of another is in the British Museum. Farnaby's son, Richard Farnaby, was also a gifted composer.
BIBLIOGRAPHY: E. H. Fellowes, *The English Madrigal Composers* (1921; 2nd ed., 1948).

Farnam, W. Lynnwood, Canadian-American organist; b. Sutton, Quebec, Jan. 13, 1885; d. New York, Nov. 23, 1930. He studied with his mother and local teachers; came to America in 1904; was organist at several churches in N.Y. and Boston.

Farnsworth, Charles Hubert, music educator; b. Cesarea, Turkey, Nov. 29, 1859; d. Thetford, Vt., May 22, 1947. He studied organ in Worcester, Mass.; held various positions as organist; was head of the music dept. at Colorado Univ. (1888–1900); then was on the faculty at Teachers College, Columbia Univ. (1900–25); retired and lived in Vermont. He publ. several pamphlets on music education; among them, *The Why and How of Music Study* (1927); *Short Studies in Musical Psychology* (N.Y., 1930). An appreciation of his work was publ. in the *Musician* (1933).

Farrant, John, English organist and composer, active in the 16th century; he served as organist at the Ely Cathedral (1567–72); then was lay clerk at Salisbury, and subsequently organist at the Salisbury Cathedral (1587–92); he was briefly organist at Hereford (1593). Contemporary records testify to his intractable temper, which resulted in physical clashes with the dean of the Salisbury Cathedral, and led to his expulsion there. As a composer Farrant is chiefly distinguished for his Service in D minor (misattributed in a 19th-century ed. to Richard Farrant). His son, also named **John Farrant** (baptized Salisbury, Sept. 28, 1575; d. there, 1618), was a chorister at the Salisbury Cathedral in 1585, and organist there from 1598 till 1616. Another John Farrant, possibly related to the preceding, was organist at Christ Church, Newgate, London; he was the author of a Magnificat; this work, sometimes referred to as 'Farrant in G minor' is often confused with Richard Farrant's Service in A minor.

Farrant, Richard, English composer; b. c.1530; d. Windsor, probably Nov. 30, 1580. He was a Gentleman of the Chapel Royal during the reign of Edward VI; then became master of the choristers (1564) at St. George's Chapel, Windsor; also served as a lay clerk and organist there. Beginning with 1567 Farrant presented a play annually before the Queen. In 1569 he returned to the Chapel Royal. Farrant wrote mainly church music; his Cathedral Service in A minor and 2 anthems, *Hide not Thou Thy Face* and *Call to Remembrance,* are regarded as the most beautiful examples of English sacred music of the 16th century. A Service in D minor was published as that by Richard Farrant, but this was a misattribution, the real author being John Farrant of Salisbury. Several of Richard Farrant's works are in the British Museum and at Durham Cathedral.

Farrar, Ernest Bristow, English organist and composer; b. London, July 7, 1885; d. in the battle of the Somme, France, Sept. 18, 1918. He studied at the Royal College of Music with Stanford and Parratt;

served as organist of the English Church in Dresden (1909); then at various churches in England (1910–14). His orch. suite *English Pastoral Impression* won the Carnegie Award; he further wrote the orch. pieces *The Open Road, Lavengro, The Forsaken Merman,* and *Heroic Elegy;* also *3 Spiritual Studies* for strings; variations on an old English sea song, for piano and orch.; the cantatas *The Blessed Damozel* and *Out of Doors;* chamber music (*Celtic Suite* for violin and piano, etc.); songs; preludes for organ, etc.

Farrar, Geraldine, celebrated American soprano; b. Melrose, Mass., Feb. 28, 1882; d. Ridgefield, Conn., March 11, 1967. She studied music with Mrs. J. H. Long of Boston; at 17, she went to Europe; took lessons with Emma Thursby in N.Y., with Trabadello in Paris and Graziani in Berlin; made a successful debut at the Berlin Opera on Oct. 15, 1901, as Marguerite, under the direction of Karl Muck; then studied with Lilli Lehmann. She sang at the Monte Carlo Opera for three seasons (1903–06). Her career in Europe was well established before her American debut as Juliette at the Metropolitan Opera (Nov. 26, 1906); she remained on the staff for 16 years; made her farewell appearance in *Zaza* on April 22, 1922, but continued to sing in concert; gave her last public performance at Carnegie Hall in 1931; then retired to Ridgefield, Conn. Her greatest success was *Madama Butterfly,* which she sang with Caruso in its American première at the Metropolitan on Feb. 11, 1907; subsequently sang this part in America more than 100 times. Her interpretation of Carmen was no less remarkable. She also appeared in silent motion pictures between 1915 and 1919; her film version of Carmen aroused considerable interest. On Feb. 8, 1916, she married the actor Lou Tellegen, from whom she was subsequently divorced. She made adaptations of pieces by Kreisler, Rachmaninoff, and others, for which she published the lyrics. She wrote an autobiography, *Such Sweet Compulsion* (N.Y., 1938; reprinted in 1970).
BIBLIOGRAPHY: H. T. Finck, *Success in Music* (N.Y., 1909); Ed. Wagenknecht, *Geraldine Farrar: An Authorized Record of Her Career* (Seattle, 1929); Oscar Thompson, *The American Singer* (N.Y., 1937).

Farrell, Eileen, brilliant American soprano; b. Willimantic, Connecticut, Feb. 13, 1920. Her parents were vaudeville singers; she received her early vocal training with Merle Alcock in N.Y., and later studied with Eleanor McLellan. In 1940 she sang on the radio; in 1947–48 made a U.S. tour as a concert singer; toured South America in 1949. Her song recital in N.Y. on Oct. 24, 1950, was enthusiastically acclaimed and secured for her immediate recognition. She was soloist in Beethoven's Ninth Symphony with Toscanini and the NBC Symph. Orch.; also appeared many times with the N.Y. Philharmonic. In 1958 she joined the San Francisco Opera Co. and in 1959 became a member of the Lyric Opera of Chicago. On Dec. 6, 1960, she made a successful debut with the Metropolitan Opera Co., N.Y., in Gluck's *Alcestis.* Her voice is remarkable for its projective power and indefatigability.

Farrenc, Aristide, French flutist and music editor; b. Marseilles, April 9, 1794; d. Paris, Jan. 31, 1865. He studied flute; went to Paris in 1815, and studied at the Cons.; at the same time was engaged as second flutist at the Théâtre Italien. In 1821 he established a music shop and printing press; publ. French editions of Beethoven; also composed music for the flute. He married **Louise Dumont,** a talented musician in her own right. He diligently collected material for the rectification of existing biographies, but generously turned it over to Fétis for use in the 2nd edition of his great work, of which Farrenc also read proofs. Jointly with Fétis's son, Edouard, he began the publication of *Trésor des pianistes* (23 vols., 1861–72; repr. N.Y., 1977, foreword by Bea Friedland), a collection of piano music from the 16th century to Mendelssohn, with historical notes; it was continued after his death by his wife. From 1854 he contributed papers to *La France Musicale* and other journals.

Farrenc (*neé* **Dumont**), **Louise,** French pianist and composer; b. Paris, May 31, 1804; d. there, Sept. 15, 1875. She studied music with Reicha; in 1821 married **Aristide Farrenc,** but was not entirely eclipsed by his acknowledged eminence. While most female composers of her time hardly ever rose above the level of barely tolerable salon music, she actually labored and produced works of such competence that they might well have been written by Onslow or some other male contemporary. Her three symphonies had respectable performances: No. 1 in Brussels, Feb. 23, 1843; No. 2 in Paris, May 3, 1846; No. 3 in Paris, April 22, 1849; the latter received an accolade in the prestigious, and definitely male-oriented *Gazette Musicale,* which conceded that "she revealed, alone among her sex in musical Europe, genuine learning, united with grace and taste." She also wrote a Piano Concerto; 30 études in all major and minor keys for piano; 4 piano trios; a Cello Sonata; 2 violin sonatas; 2 piano quintets; a Sextet and a Nonet for winds and strings; one of her overtures (1840), was reviewed by Berlioz, who remarked that it was orchestrated "with a talent rare among women." Louise Farrenc was a brilliant pianist; she taught piano at the Paris Cons. from 1842 till 1872, the only woman ever to hold a permanent position as an instrumentalist there in the 19th century. Her daughter **Victorine** (1827–1859) was also a talented pianist whose promising career was cut short by an early death. After the death of her husband in 1865, Louise Farrenc assumed the editorship of the monumental collection *Le Trésor des pianistes* begun by him.
BIBLIOGRAPHY: Bea Friedland, "Louise Farrenc, Composer, Performer, Scholar," *Musical Quarterly* (April 1974).

Farrow, Norman D., Canadian baritone; b. Regina, May 6, 1916. He studied at the Juilliard School of Music and at N.Y. Univ.; took voice lessons with Mack Harrell and others; was one of the organizers of the Bach Aria Group; he toured as soloist with choral ensembles; in 1960 he was engaged as artist-in-residence at Southern Methodist Univ. in Dallas.

Farwell, Arthur, American composer and music educator; b. St. Paul, Minn., April 23, 1872; d. New York, Jan. 20, 1952. He studied at the Mass. Inst. of Technology, graduating in 1893; then studied music with Homer Norris in Boston, Humperdinck in Berlin, and Guilmant in Paris. He was lecturer on music at Cornell Univ. (1899-1901); in 1909 was on the editorial staff of *Musical America;* then directed municipal concerts in N.Y. City (1910-13); was director of the Music School Settlement in N.Y. (1915-18); in 1918 he went to California; lectured on music there; was acting head of music dept. at the Univ. of Calif., Berkeley (1918-19); in 1919 he founded the Santa Barbara Community Chorus, which he conducted until 1921; was first holder of composers' fellowship of the Music and Art Association of Pasadena (1921-25); taught music theory at Michigan State College in East Lansing (1927-39); eventually settled in N.Y. Farwell was a pioneer in new American music, and tirelessly promoted national ideas in art. He contributed to various ethnological publications. From 1901-11 he operated the Wa-Wan Press (Newton, Mass.), a periodical publication (quarterly 1901-07; monthly 1907-11) that printed piano and vocal music of "progressive" American composers of the period, the emphasis being on works that utilized indigenous (Negro, Indian, and cowboy) musical materials (repr. N.Y., 1970, under direction of Vera Brodsky). Disillusioned about commercial opportunities for American music, including his own, he established at East Lansing, Mich., in April 1936, his own lithographic handpress, with which he printed his music, handling the entire process of reproduction, including the cover designs, by himself. WORKS: His works are mostly based on American subjects. For orch.: *Symbolistic Study No. 3,* after Walt Whitman (1905; revised, 1922; Philadelphia Orch., March 30, 1928); *Pageant Scene* (1913); *The Gods of the Mountain* (Minneapolis Symph. Orch., Dec. 13, 1929); music for pageants, including Percy MacKaye's *Caliban by the Yellow Sands* (N.Y., May 1916; written for the Shakespeare tercentenary); *Pilgrimage Play* (Hollywood, 1921); *Symph. Song on 'Old Black Joe'* (Hollywood, 1923); *Symph. Hymn on 'March! March!';* also *The Hako* for string quartet (1922); *Violin Sonata* (1928); *Concerto for 2 Pianos and String Orch.,* a version of *Symbolistic Study No. 6* (1931; won first prize of the National Federation of Music Clubs Competition; broadcast by CBS, May 28, 1939); numerous school choruses, and vocal compositions; piano pieces (many of them arranged for various instrumental ensembles); several collections of American Indian melodies and folksongs of the South and West; arrangements of Indian melodies (*Dawn,* a fantasy on Indian themes, in various versions, dated between 1901 and 1926, is characteristic of these works). BIBLIOGRAPHY: Brice Farwell *et al. Guide to the Music of Arthur Farwell and to the Microfilm Collection of His Work* (Briarcliff Manor, N.Y., 1971).

Fasch, Johann Friedrich, German composer; b. Buttelstadt, near Weimar, April 15, 1688; d. Zerbst, Dec. 5, 1758. He studied with Kuhnau at Leipzig, and later (1713) with Graupner and Grunewald at Darmstadt; in 1721 he went to Lukaveč, Bohemia, as Kapellmeister to Count Morzin; after 1722, Kapellmeister at Zerbst. A catalogue of his works, compiled in 1743, enumerates 7 complete series of church cantatas, 12

Masses, 69 overtures, 21 concertos (for violin, flute, oboe, etc.), some of which have been printed in modern editions. Many scores are preserved in MS in the libraries of Darmstadt, Dresden, Leipzig, and Brussels; in the archives of the Thomasschule at Leipzig are the parts of five orchestral suites of Fasch in the handwriting of J. S. Bach, who entertained a very high opinion of the works of his contemporary. Hugo Riemann published 5 trio sonatas and a quartet in *Collegium Musicum* and 2 orchestral suites in Breitkopf & Härtel's *Orchesterbibliothek;* a Violin Concerto in D was ed. by A. Hoffmann (Wolfenbüttel, 1961). Fasch's autobiography appeared in vol. III of F. W. Marpurg's *Historisch-kritische Beyträge zur Aufnahme der Musik* (Berlin, 1754-78).

BIBLIOGRAPHY: J. A. Hiller, *Lebensbeschreibungen berühmter Musikgelehrten und Tonkünstler neuerer Zeit* (Leipzig, 1784); B. Engelke, *Johann Friedrich Fasch, sein Leben und seine Tätigkeit als Vokalkomponist* (Leipzig, 1908); B. Engelke, "Johann Friedrich Fasch, Versuch einer Biographie", *Sammelbände der Internationalen Musik-Gesellschaft* (1909); C. A. Schneider, *J. Fr. Fasch als Sonatenkomponist* (Münster, 1936); G. Küntzel, "Die Instrumentalkonzerte von Johann Friedrich Fasch," *Die Musikforschung* (Oct.-Dec. 1969); D. A. Sheldon, "Johann Friedrich Fasch: Problems in Style Classification," *Musical Quarterly* (Jan. 1972).

Fasch, Karl Friedrich Christian, German composer, son of **Johann Friedrich Fasch;** b. Zerbst, Nov. 18, 1736; d. Berlin, Aug. 3, 1800. He learned to play the violin and harpsichord as a child; studied all musical subjects with Hertel at Strelitz. At the age of 15, he joined the violinist Franz Benda as his accompanist and at the age of 20 he was recommended by Benda as harpsichordist to Frederick the Great, jointly with C. P. E. Bach. He also taught music and composed contrapuntal pieces of considerable ingenuity and complexity. He was conductor at the Berlin Opera (1774-76). In 1790 he organized a choral society, which led to the foundation of the famous Singakademie. Fasch was greatly admired by musicians for his contrapuntal skill; the renown of his name was still strong in the first part of the 19th century; in 1839, 6 vols. of his sacred works were publ. by the Singakademie.

BIBLIOGRAPHY: C. F. Zelter, *Biographie von Karl Friedrich Christian Fasch* (Berlin, 1801); M. Blummer, *Geschichte der Berliner Singakademie* (Berlin, 1891); G. Schünemann, *Die Singakademie zu Berlin* (Regensburg, 1941).

Fattorini, Gabriele, Italian composer; b. Faenza in the latter part of the 16th century; date of death unknown. He was maestro di cappella at Faenza, and possibly in Venice. His compositions include *Sacri Concerti a due voci* (Venice, 1600; further editions, 1602, 1608); *Completorium Romanum* (Venice, 1602); motets, madrigals, etc. Several of his works appeared in contemporaneous collections between 1605 and 1622 (Bodenschatz, Donfried, Diruta, etc.). Two of his *Ricercare* for organ are in vol. III of Torchi's *L'Arte Musicale in Italia.* Banchieri mentions Fattorini in his *Conclusioni del suono dell'Organo* (Lucca, 1591; Bologna, 1609). For bibliographical details, see F. Ghisi's article on Fattorini in *Die Musik in Geschichte und Gegenwart*.

Fauchet, Paul Robert, French composer; b. Paris, June 27, 1881; d. there, Nov. 12, 1937. He studied at the Paris Cons., and later taught harmony there; also was the maître de chapelle of the Saint-Pierre de Chaillot in Paris. He wrote a number of sacred works, but is remembered mainly for his *Symphonie* for band, the earliest example of a classical symphony written for the medium (1936); its *Scherzo* is profusely enmeshed with whole-tone scales.

Fauchey, Paul, French composer; b. Paris, March 18, 1858; d. there, Nov. 15, 1936. He was active in the theater as chorus master and then began to compose light operas, of which *La Carmagnole* (Paris, 1897) was quite popular for a time.

Faulkes, William, English organist and composer; b. Liverpool, Nov. 4, 1863; d. there, Jan. 25, 1933. He studied with W. Dawson and H. Dillon-Newman; from 1886 he was active in Liverpool as organist and teacher; composed mostly for organ; publ. several albums of organ pieces.

Fauré, Gabriel-Urbain, great French composer; b. Pamiers (Ariège), May 12, 1845; d. Paris, Nov. 4, 1924. His father was a provincial inspector of primary schools; noticing the musical instinct of his son, he took him to Paris to study with Louis Niedermeyer; after Niedermeyer's death in 1861, Fauré studied with Saint-Saëns, from whom he received a thorough training in composition. In 1866 he went to Rennes as organist at the church of Saint-Sauveur; returned to Paris on the eve of the Franco-Prussian war in 1870, and volunteered in the light infantry. He was organist at Notre-Dame de Clignancourt, Saint-Honoré d'Eylau, and Saint-Sulpice; in 1877 became second organist at the Madeleine; in 1896 he was appointed chief organist there, and prof. of composition at the Paris Cons. He was an illustrious teacher; among his students were Ravel, Enesco, Koechlin, Roger-Ducasse, Laparra, Florent Schmitt, Louis Aubert, and Nadia Boulanger. In 1905 he succeeded Théodore Dubois as director; resigned in 1920, when growing deafness and ill health made it impossible for him to continue to direct the Conservatory. From 1903 till 1921 Fauré wrote occasional music reviews in *Le Figaro* (publ. as *Opinions Musicales;* posthumous, Paris, 1930); he was elected member of the Académie des Beaux Arts in 1909; Commander of the Légion d'honneur in 1910. Fauré's stature as composer is undiminished by the passage of time. He developed a musical idiom all his own; by subtle application of old modes he evoked the aura of eternally fresh art; by using unresolved mild discords and special coloristic effects in his instrumental music he anticipated the procedures of impressionism; in his piano works he shunned virtuosity in favor of the classical lucidity of the French masters of the clavecin; the precisely articulated melodic line of his songs is in the finest tradition of French vocal music. Several of his works (significantly, those of his early period) have entered the general repertory: the great Requiem, First Violin Sonata, *Elégie* for cello and piano; songs (*Ici-bas, Les roses d'Ispahan, Clair de lune, Au cimetière,* etc.).

WORKS: FOR THE STAGE: *Caligula,* incidental music to a play by A. Dumas, Jr. (Paris, Nov. 8, 1888); *Shylock,* after Shakespeare (Paris, Dec. 17, 1889); *Pelléas et Mélisande,* after Maeterlinck (London, June 21, 1898; often performed as an orchestral suite); *Prométhée,* lyric tragedy (Béziers, Aug. 27, 1900); *Le Voile du bonheur,* incidental music for Clemenceau's play (Paris, Nov. 4, 1901); *Pénélope* (Monte Carlo, March 4, 1913); *Masques et bergamasques,* stage music (Monte Carlo, April 10, 1919). FOR ORCH: symphony in D minor (Paris, March 15, 1885); Suite (1875; only one movement, *Allegro symphonique,* was publ.); *Pavane* (1887); Ballade for Piano and Orch. (1881); Romance for Violin and Orch. (1882); *Fantaisie* for piano and orch. (1919). CHORAL WORKS: *Cantique de Jean Racine* for mixed chorus, harmonium, and string quartet (1873); *Les Djinns* for chorus and orch. (1875); *La Naissance de Vénus* for soli, chorus, and orch. (1882); *Messe de Requiem* for soli, chorus, organ, and orch. (1887); *Tantum ergo* for solo voice and chorus (1890); offertories and other church music. CHAMBER MUSIC: 2 violin sonatas (1879; 1886); 2 piano quartets (1879; 1886); 2 piano quintets (1906; 1921); 2 cello sonatas (1918; 1922); Piano Trio (1923); String Quartet (1924); *Elégie* for cello and piano (1883); *Sérénade* for cello and piano (1908); also *Fantaisie* for flute and piano (1898). PIANO WORKS: 13 nocturnes, 13 barcarolles, 5 impromptus, 4 waltzes, etc.; 96 songs: 4 to words by Victor Hugo; 4 after Théophile Gautier; 3 after Baudelaire; 16 after Paul Verlaine (including the cycle *La Bonne Chanson*), etc.

BIBLIOGRAPHY: O. Séré, *Musiciens français d'aujourd'hui* (Paris, 1911); L. Vuillemin, *Gabriel Fauré et son œuvre* (Paris, 1914); the special Fauré issue of *La Revue Musicale* (Oct. 1922); Aaron Copland, "Gabriel Fauré; a Neglected Master," *Musical Quarterly* (Oct. 1924); Alfred Bruneau, *La Vie et les œuvres de Gabriel Fauré* (Paris, 1925); Charles Koechlin, *Gabriel Fauré* (Paris, 1927; English transl., London, 1945); Ph. Fauré-Fremiet, *Gabriel Fauré* (Paris, 1929); G. Servières, *Gabriel Fauré* (Paris, 1930); Paul Landormy, "Gabriel Fauré," *Musical Quarterly* (July 1931); V. Jankélévitch, *Gabriel Fauré et ses mélodies* (Paris, 1938; enlarged ed., 1951); G. Faure, *Gabriel Fauré* (Paris, 1945); Claude Rostand, *L'Oeuvre de Gabriel Fauré* (Paris, 1945); Norman Suckling, *Fauré* (in the Master Musicians Series; London, 1946); G. Samazeuilh, *Musiciens de mon temps* (Paris, 1947); Max Favre, *Gabriel Faurés Kammermusik* (Zürich, 1948); Ph. Fauré-Fremiet, ed., *Fauré, Lettres intimes* (Paris, 1951); E. Vuillermoz, *Gabriel Fauré* (Paris, 1960; in English, Philadelphia, 1969); Florent Schmitt's article on Fauré's chamber music in *Cobbett's Cyclopedia of Chamber Music;* the article by Fauré's son, Philippe Fauré-Fremiet, in *Die Musik in Geschichte und Gegenwart,* contains a very extensive bibliography about Fauré.

Faure, Jean-Baptiste, famous French baritone; b. Moulins, Allier, Jan. 15, 1830; d. Paris, Nov. 9, 1914. He was a choirboy at the Madeleine and other Paris churches; entered the Paris Cons. at the age of 21;

after a short period of study he made his debut at the Opéra-Comique, in Massé's opera *Galathée* (Oct. 20, 1852); from 1861–76 he was on the staff of the Paris Opéra; his farewell appearance was in *Hamlet* by Ambroise Thomas (May 13, 1876), the role that he created in 1868. Subsequently he sang in concerts, appearing with enormous success in Vienna and in London. He was particularly impressive in dramatic roles in Meyerbeer's operas and also in Gounod's *Faust*, as Mephistophélès. He also wrote a number of songs, of which several became fairly successful (*Crucifix, Les Rameaux*, etc.).

BIBLIOGRAPHY: H. de Curzon, "Jean-Baptiste Faure," *Musical Quarterly* (April 1918); H. de Curzon, *Jean-Baptiste Faure* (Paris, 1923).

Favarger, René, French pianist; b. Dun-sur-Auron, Cher, Feb. 25, 1815; d. Etretat, Aug. 3, 1868. He was successful as a teacher in Paris and in London; composed a number of salon pieces for piano.

Favart, Charles-Simon, French librettist; b. Paris, Nov. 13, 1710; d. Belleville, near Paris, March 12, 1792. He published satirical plays as a youth; after a successful performance of one of his vaudevilles at the Opéra-Comique, he was appointed stage manager there; in 1758 he became its director. He wrote about 150 plays used for operas by Duni, Philidor, and Gluck; he was also the author of *Les Amours de Bastien et Bastienne* (1753), used by Mozart in a German version for his early opera (1768).

Fay, Amy, American pianist; b. Bayou Goula, Louisiana, May 21, 1844; d. Watertown, Mass., Feb. 28, 1928. She studied in Berlin with Tausig and Kullak; then became a pupil of Liszt in Weimar. She publ. a vivid book of impressions *Music-Study in Germany* (Chicago, 1881), which went through more than 20 printings, and was translated into French and German.

Fay, Maud, American soprano; b. San Francisco, April 18, 1879; d. there, Oct. 7, 1964. She studied in Dresden; became a member of the Munich Opera (1906–16); appeared in Covent Garden, London, in 1910, and with the Thomas Beecham Opera Co. in 1914. After the outbreak of World War I she returned to America; sang with the Metropolitan Opera in 1916; also appeared with the Chicago Opera Co. She was particularly distinguished in Wagnerian roles.

Fayolle, François-Joseph-Marie, French writer on music and literature; b. Paris, Aug. 15, 1774; d. there, Dec. 2, 1852. A man of brilliant faculties, he was equally proficient in mathematics and poetry; also studied harmony and cello; after 1814 he lived in London; returned to Paris in 1830; he died in an almshouse. He contributed a number of articles to Fétis's *Biographie Universelle*; together with Choron, he publ. a *Dictionnaire historique des musiciens* (Paris, 1810–11); his other writings on music include *Notices sur Corelli, Tartini, Gaviniès, Pugnani et Viotti* (Paris, 1810); *Sur les drames lyriques et leur exécution* (Paris, 1813) and *Paganini et Bériot* (Paris, 1830).

Fayrfax, Robert, English composer; b. Deeping Gate, Lincolnshire, April, 1464 (baptized April 23); d. London, Oct. 24, 1521. He was a Gentleman of the Chapel Royal in 1496, and organist at St. Alban's Abbey and at King's Chapel (1497–98); B.A., Cambridge (1501); Mus. Doc., Cambridge (1504); Mus. Doc., Oxford (1511; with his Mass, *O quam glorifica*). In 1520 was the leader of the Royal Singers in France. 32 works of Fayrfax are extant: 6 Masses (4 are in the Oxford Music School Collection); 2 *Magnificats*, 13 motets, 9 part songs, 2 instrumental pieces. Sacred and secular vocal works of Fayrfax appear in the *Fairfax Book* (British Museum MS Add. 5465) and in other British MSS; lute arrangements of several sacred compositions and an instrumental piece for 3 parts are in the British Museum. Reprints of some of his compositions are in J. Stafford Smith's *Musica Antiqua* (1912).

BIBLIOGRAPHY: J. Pulver, "Robert Fayrfax," *Musical News* (Feb. 10, 1917); Dom Anselm Hughes, "An Introduction to Fayrfax," *Musica Disciplina* (1952).

Feather, Leonard, British-American writer on music, expert on jazz; b. London, Sept. 13, 1914. He studied at St. Paul School in London; in 1935 he came to the U.S.; naturalized in 1948. He held various jobs as an arranger, lyricist, advisor for jazz festivals, radio commentator and lecturer; specialized in the field of jazz and folk music; publ. *Inside Be-bop* (N.Y., 1949); a compendious *Encyclopedia of Jazz* (N.Y., 1955), which he supplemented by *New Encyclopedia of Jazz* (1960); and *Encyclopedia of Jazz in the 60's* (1966). He makes his home in Hollywood.

Fechner, Gustave Theodor, German music theorist; b. Gross-Särchen, Niederlausitz, April 19, 1801; d. Leipzig, Nov. 18, 1887. He was prof. of physics at Leipzig from 1834. He publ. *Repertorium der Experimentalphysik*, in which musical phenomena are treated; also *Elemente der Psychophysik* (1860, 2 vols.), and *Vorschule der Aesthetik* (1870, 2 vols.), valuable as establishing a basis of musical esthetics.

Fedeli, Vito, Italian composer; b. Fogligno, June 19, 1866; d. Novara, June 23, 1933. He was a pupil of Terziani in Rome; was director of the Cons. at Novara from 1904.

WORKS: The operas *La Vergine della Montagna* (Reggio-Calabria, Sept. 6, 1897) and *Varsovia* (Rome, Dec. 15, 1900); several Masses a cappella; also pieces for orch. He contributed valuable historical articles to the *Rivista Musicale Italiana* and the *Zeitschrift der Internationalen Musik-Gesellschaft;* also wrote a book, *Giacomo e Gaudenzio Battistini* (1932).

BIBLIOGRAPHY: G. Bustico, *Bibliografia di un musico novarese, Vito Fedeli* (1925).

Federhofer, Helmut, Austrian musicologist; b. Graz, Aug. 6, 1911. He studied piano with Anatol Vietinghoff-Scheel in Graz; musicology with Alfred Orel and Robert Lach at the Univ. of Vienna, graduating in 1936. He also took private lessons in composition with Alban Berg. In 1937–44 he was State Librarian; from 1945–62, prof. at the Univ. of Graz. In 1962 he was appointed Director of the Musicologist Institute at the Gutenberg Univ. of Mainz, Germany. In the same year he joined the staff of *Acta Musicologica*. His publications range widely covering the history of Austrian court music, biographical data of little-known composers of the Renaissance and abstruse points of old and new music theory. He also edited works of Renaissance composers.

Federici, Vincenzo, Italian dramatic composer; b. Pesaro, 1764; d. Milan, Sept. 26, 1826. He became an orphan at 16; lived in Turin, where he produced his first opera *L'Olimpiade* (Dec. 26, 1789). He then made his way to London, where he became cembalist at the Italian Opera; returned to Italy in 1802; in 1814 he became teacher of harmony at the Milan Cons.

Federlein, Gottfried H., American organist, son of **Gottlieb Federlein;** b. New York, Dec. 31, 1883; d. there, Feb. 26, 1952. He studied with his father; then with Goetschius; in 1915 became organist at Temple Emanu-El in New York. He published a number of anthems and organ pieces.

Federlein, Gottlieb (Heinrich), organist and vocal pedagogue; b. Neustadt-an-der-Aisch, near Nuremberg, Nov. 5, 1835; d. Philadelphia, April 29, 1922. He studied with Rheinberger in Munich; was active as organist and singing teacher in New York; published numerous songs and a manual, *Practical School of Voice Culture* (N.Y., 1880).

Fedorov, Vladimir, music librarian and historian; b. near Tchernigov, Aug. 18, 1901. He studied at the Univ. of Rostov; emigrated to Turkey in 1920; then settled in Paris, where he studied art, archeology, and music; took lessons with Gédalge and Vidal; later took additional courses in Germany. In 1933 he became librarian at the Sorbonne; later took a post in the music division of the Bibliothèque Nationale in Paris (1946–66). He publ. *Moussorgsky, biographie critique* (Paris, 1935) and numerous articles on a variety of musical subjects in French magazines; also compiled catalogues of music libraries; composed several piano works.

Fehr, Max, Swiss musicologist; b. Bülach, near Zürich, June 17, 1887; d. Winterthur, April 27, 1963. He studied at the Univ. of Zürich with Eduard Bernoulli. In 1917 he became librarian, and in 1923, president, of the Allgemeine Musikgesellschaft of Zürich. WRITINGS: *Spielleute im alten Zürich* (Zürich, 1916); *Die Meistersinger von Zürich,* a satirical novelette (Zürich, 1916); *Unter Wagners Taktstock* (Winterthur, 1922); *Geschichte des Musikkollegiums Winterthur, I. Teil: 1629–1830* (1929); *Richard Wagners Schweizer Zeit,* in 2 vols. (Aarau, 1934; 1953); *Die Familie Mozart in Zürich* (Zurich, 1942).

Feicht, Hieronim, Polish musicologist; b. Mogilno, near Poznan, Sept. 22, 1894; d. Warsaw, March 31, 1967. He was a theological student; then studied composition with Wallek-Walewski in Cracow and with Soltys in Lwow, where he also studied with Chybinski. From 1952–1964 he was prof. of music history at the Univ. of Warsaw. He publ. important essays on Polish music: *Musik-historische Bemerkungen über*

die Lemberger Handschriften des Bogarodzica-Liedes (Poznan, 1925); *Wojciech Debolecki, ein polnischer Kirchenkomponist aus der I. Hälfte des 17. Jahrhunderts* (Lwow, 1926). In 1964, a *Festschrift* was publ. in his honor on his 70th birthday.

Feinberg, Samuel, eminent Russian pianist and composer; b. Odessa, May 26, 1890; d. Moscow, Oct. 22, 1962. He graduated in 1911 from the Moscow Cons.; from 1922 was prof. of piano and composition there. Feinberg was well known in Russia as an excellent pianist and teacher; he was also a competent composer of piano music; he wrote 12 piano sonatas; 3 piano concertos (1931, 1944, 1947); numerous small piano pieces, some chamber music and songs. His book, *Piano Playing as an Art,* was publ. posthumously (Moscow, 1965).
BIBLIOGRAPHY: V. Belaiev, *Samuel Feinberg* (1927; in Russian and German).

Felciano, Richard, American composer; b. Santa Rosa, California, Dec. 7, 1930. He studied with Darius Milhaud at Mills College; subsequently took courses with Milhaud at the Paris Cons. In 1958–59 he took private lessons with Luigi Dallapiccola in Florence. He holds a Ph.D. from the Univ. of Iowa (1959). He was the recipient of the Guggenheim Fellowship in 1969 and two fellowships from the Ford Foundation (1964; 1971–73). He is also the holder of the American Academy of Arts and Letters Award (1974). In 1967 he was appointed Resident Composer at the National Center for Experiments in Television in San Francisco. At the same time he was also on the music faculty of the Univ. of California at Berkeley. WORKS: an opera *Sir Gawain and the Green Knight* (1964); *Four Poems from the Japanese* for 5 harps, women's voices and percussion (1964); *Contractions,* theatrical mobile for woodwind quintet (1965); *Mutations* for orch. (1966); *Aubade* for string trio, harp and piano (1966); *Glossolalia* for organ, baritone, percussion and tape (1967); *Spectra* for piccolo, flute, alto flute, and double bass (1967); *Noosphere I* for alto flute and tape (1967); *Noosphere II* for electronic tape (1967); *Trio* for speaker, screen and viewer, a videotape (1968); Quintet for Piano, Strings and Electronic Tape (1970); *Lamentations for Jani Christou* for 12 instruments and electronic tape (1970); *Soundspace for Mozart* for flute, electronics and tape (1970); *Galactic Rounds* for orch. (1972); *Chod* for violin, violoncello, double bass, piano, percussion, electronics (1975).

Feld, Jindřich, Czech composer; b. Prague, Feb. 19, 1925. He studied violin with his father and took composition with Hlobil at the Prague Cons. (1945–48), with Řidký at the Prague Academy of Music (1948–52); also studied musicology at Charles Univ. (1945–52). During the academic year 1968–69 he was visiting prof. at the Univ. of Adelaide in Australia; returning to Prague, he was appointed to the staff of the Prague Cons. His early music is in a neo-Baroque manner, but he soon adopted a variety of modern techniques. WORKS: a children's opera, *Postácká opera (The Postman's Tale),* after Capek (1956); *Divertimento* for string orch. (1950); *Furiant* for orch. (1950); Concerto for Orch. (1951, revised 1957); *Comedy Overture* (1953); Flute Concerto (1954; Czech Radio, Oct. 26, 1956); *Rhapsody* for violin and orch. (1956); Concerto in C for chamber orch. (1956–57); Cello Concerto (1958); Bassoon Concerto (1958–59); *May 1945*, dramatic overture (1959–60); Suite for Chamber String Orch. (1960–61); *Thuringian Ouverture* (1961); *3 Frescoes* for orch. (Prague, Feb. 21, 1964); *Concert Music* for oboe, bassoon and orch. (1964); *Serenata giocosa* for chamber orch. (1966); *Concert Piece* for horn and orch. (1966); Symph. No. 1 (Prague, Jan. 23, 1969); *Dramatic Fantasy* for orch. (1968–69); Oboe Concerto (1970); Piano Concerto (1973); Suite for Clarinet and Piano (1948–49); 4 string quartets (1949, 1952, 1962, 1965); 2 wind quintets (1949, 1968); Sonatina for 2 Violins (1952–53); *2 Compositions* for cello and piano (1954–55); Viola Sonata (1955); *Rhapsody* for violin and piano (1956); Flute Sonata (1957); *Chamber Suite* for nonet (1960); String Trio (1961); Trio for Flute, Violin and Cello (1963); *Capriccio* for wind quartet and guitar (1964); Suite for Solo Accordion (1965); *4 Intermezzos* for accordion (1967); *Miniatures* for violin, guitar and accordion (1967–68); Brass Quintet (1969–70); *Concertante Suite* for bass clarinet and piano (1971); Cello Sonata (1972); Prelude and Toccata for 2 pianos (1960); Piano Sonata (1971–72); *Rhapsody* for organ (1963); *3 Inventions* for chamber chorus (1966); *Mockery of Names* for women's chorus, oboe, clarinet, bass clarinet, ocarina, double bass, piano and percussion (1974); many educational pieces for various instruments.

Feldbusch, Eric, Belgian cellist and composer; b. Grivegnée, March 2, 1922. He studied cello at the Liège Cons. (1934–39); later took courses in composition with Quinet and Legley (1947–48). He divided his time between concert activity as a cellist and teaching; was director of the Cons. of Mons (1963–72); in 1973 was appointed director of the Brussels Cons.

Works: an opera *Orestes* (1969); a ballet *El Diablo Cojuelo* (1972); *Variations sur un air connu* for orch. (1955); *Contrastes* for orch. (1956); *5 Brief Pieces* for string orch. and piano (1957); *Les Moineaux de Baltimore,* suite for orch. (1958; also as a radio play); *Adagio* for string orch. (1958); *Adagio* for 3 cellos and string orch. (1960); *Mosaïque* for string orch. (1961); *Overture* for string orch. (1961); *Shema Israël* for string orch. (1962); *Choral* for a group of wind instruments (1963); *3 Poems de Federico García Lorca* for voice and orch. (1964); *Ode à des enfants morts* for orch. (1965–66); Violin Concerto (1967); *Fantaisie-Divertissement* for orch. (1967); *Cantique des Cantiques* for soprano and orch. (1970); *Piccola musica* for string orch. (1971); *Kadisch* for baritone, solo violin and strings (1974); *Aquarelles* for wind quintet (1947); Sonata for Violin and Cello (1955); *Cadence and Allegro* for cello and piano (1956); Violin Sonata (1957); *3 Pièces* for viola, cello and oboe (1957); Duo for Violin and Piano (1958); 4 string quartets (1955, 1958, 1963, 1971); *Mosaïque* for solo cello (1958); Piano Trio (1958); Duo for Flute and Piano (1959); *Variations extra-formelles* for cello and piano (1959); Trio for Flute, Violin and Cello (1961); Duo for Flute and Viola (1963); Septet, for soprano, 2 violins,

double bass, flute, trumpet and percussion (1969); *Arabesques* for piano; *3 Movements* for piano; *Dicht am Flüsschen,* variations for piano (1960); incidental music for theater plays.

Felderhof, Jan, Dutch composer; b. Bussum, near Amsterdam, Sept. 25, 1907. He studied theory of composition with Sem Dresden at the Amsterdam Cons. In 1934 he was appointed to its faculty; during intervening years taught at the music school in Bussum (1944–54) and at the Utrecht Cons. (1956–67). He composed a radio opera *Vliegvuur* (*Wildfire,* 1959–64; Dutch radio, Nov. 10, 1965); a cantata *Tot wien zullen wij henengaan* (*To Whom Shall We Make Our Way,* 1935–41); *Music* for 15 winds and percussion (1930); *5 Dance Sketches* for orch. (1930); 2 sinfoniettas (1932, 1962); Suite for Flute and Small Orch. (1933); *Rhapsodie* for oboe and small orch. (1937); Symphony (1949); *Ouverture* (1955); Concerto for Flute, String Orch. and Percussion (1955); *Omaggio* for orch. (1974); *Complimento* for string orch. (1975); 3 violin sonatas (1932, 1939, 1965); 4 string quartets (1932, 1936, 1938, 1957); Suite for Flute and Piano (1933); String Trio (1934); Cello Sonata (1935); Piano Trio (1936); Divertimento for Brass Quartet (1950); Violin Sonatina (1953); *Rondo* for oboe, clarinet and bassoon (1960); Trio for 3 Different Clarinets (1968); Suite for Flute, Oboe and Piano (1974); 5 piano sonatinas (1933–62); piano and organ pieces; songs. All of these works have an agreeable veneer of simple musicality, and all are excellently written for the instruments.

Feldman, Ludovic, Rumanian composer; b. Galati, June 6, 1893. He studied violin in his home town; then at the Bucharest Cons. and with Frantisek Ondricek at the Vienna Cons. (1911–13). He was a violinist with the Bucharest Philharmonia and at the State Opera (1926–40). Then, after a long career as a violinist, he began to study composition with Mihail Jona; wrote numerous works for orch. and chamber groups, adopting a fairly modern idiom within a classical framework.

Works: Symphony (1947); 5 suites for orch. (1948, 1949, 1951–52, 1960, 1960); *Fantaisie concertante* for cello and orch. (1949); *Poeme concertant* for violin and orch. (1951); *8 Scenes de ballet* (1952); Ballade for Violin and Orch. (1952); Concerto for Flute and Chamber Orch. (1952); *Ode solennelle* for orch. (1954); *6 Symphonic Pieces* (1956); Concerto for 2 String Orchestras, Celesta, Piano and Percussion (1958); *Rapsodie dobrogeană* for orch. (1960); *5 Symphonic Pieces* (1961); Sinfonietta (1962); *Sonata concertante* for cello and chamber orch. (1964); *3 Symphonic Images* (1965); *Symphonic Variations* (1966); *De profundis* for orch. (1967); Chamber Symphony (1969); *Suite de concert* for bassoon and orch. (1969); *Ombres et lumières* for orch. (1969); *Alternances,* symph. triptyque (1970); Symphony for 15 Instruments (1970); *Sinfonia concertante* for string orch. (1971); 2 suites for violin and piano (1947, 1948); 2 viola sonatas (1953, 1965); String Trio (1955); String Quartet (1957); Wind Quintet (1957); Violin Sonata (1963); Cello Sonata (1963–66); *3 Concert Pieces* for string quartet and percussion (1968); piano pieces; songs.

Feldman, Morton, American composer of the avant-garde; b. New York, Jan. 12, 1926. He studied piano with Vera Maurina-Press and composition with Wallingford Riegger and Stefan Wolpe. Profoundly impressed by the abstract expressionism of modern painting, he evolved a congenial set of musical concepts and introduced an element of predetermined indeterminacy into the performance of his music. Accordingly, he indicates only an approximation of the notes to be played in a musical 'action,' specifying the instrumental range (high, medium, low) and the number of notes per time unit in any voluntary or involuntary rhythmic distribution. He uses graphic optical notation optionally, transcribing it into traditional score for practical performance.

WORKS: His works include several sets of instrumental pieces, with subsets designated by Roman numerals: *Durations I-V; Extensions I-V; Projections I-V; Vertical Thoughts I-V; Intermissions I-VI; Structures I-II; Intervals* for baritone and instruments; *Eleven Instruments* for 11 instruments; *Two Instruments* for cello and French horn; pieces for piano solo, piano 3 hands, piano 4 hands, 2 pianos, 4 pianos; *Last Pieces* for piano solo; *Numbers* for 9 instruments; *Journey to the End of the Night* for soprano and 4 wind instruments; ballet *Ixion;* cantata, *The Swallows of Salangan* for mixed chorus and 16 instruments; *The Straits of Magellan* for 7 instruments; *Atlantis* for chamber orch.; *De Kooning* for piano, violin, cello, French horn and percussion; *For Franz Kline* for soprano, violin, cello, French horn, chimes and piano; *Rabbi Akiba* for soprano and 10 instruments; *Mme. Press Died Last Week at 90* (St. Paul de Vence, July 20, 1970, Lukas Foss conducting); *The Viola in My Life* for viola and 6 instrumentalists (1970).

Felix, Hugo, Austrian composer of operettas; b. Vienna, Nov. 19, 1866; d. Hollywood, Aug. 24, 1934. He produced several operettas in Vienna: *Husarenblut* (1894); *Das Kätzchen* (1892), etc.; and several in Berlin (*Madame Sherry,* 1902, etc.). After World War I he settled in America; wrote an operetta with an English text, *The Sweetheart Shop* (Chicago, 1920); also incidental music to Otis Skinner's *Sancho Panza,* and other plays.

Felix, Václav, Czech composer; b. Prague, March 29, 1928. He studied composition with Bořkovec and Dobiáš at the Prague Academy of Arts and Music (1949–53); then theory with K. Janeček (1953–56), obtaining a Ph.D. in philosophy. From 1961 to 1976 he was on the staff of the Prague Academy, as prof. of composition. His own music follows the golden mean of agreeable Central European modernism.

WORKS: 2 comic operas, *What Matures Men* (1966) and *The Timid Casanova* (1975); *Concerto Romantico* for violin, clarinet or viola, harp and string orch. (1953); *Fantasy* for clarinet and orch. (1959); *Concertant Variations* for orch. (1962); *Suite for String Orch.* (1969); *Joyful Prelude* for orch. (1971); *Symph. for Mezzo-Soprano and Orch.* (1974); an oratorio, *Legend About Lenin* (1956); 2 cantatas: *Scientific Songs* (1963) and *Where Do the Months Come From* (1965); 2 double-bass sonatinas (1951, 1970); Duo for Violin and Cello (1962); 3 piano trios (1955, 1956, 1962); Cello Sonata (1960); String Trio (1961); *The Story of Snow White,* quintet for harp and string quartet (1963); 2 violin sonatinas (1963, 1968); *Sonata a tre* for violin, viola and harp (1967); *Sonata da Requiem* for horn or bass clarinet, and piano (1969); *Terzetto* for oboe, clarinet and bassoon (1971); Wind Quintet (1972); Brass Quintet (1972); Trio for Violin, Horn and Piano (1973); *Open House,* chamber cantata for contralto, tenor and piano (1961); Piano Sonata (1950); 3 piano sonatinas (1969); choruses, songs. He also published monographs on Vít Nejedlý (Prague, 1968) and Václav Kálik (Opava, 1973).

Fellegara, Vittorio, Italian composer; b. Milan, Nov. 4, 1927. He studied at the Cons. of Milan; received his diploma in composition in 1951. In 1960 he was appointed to the staff of the Istituto Musicale in Bergamo. He has written a number of works in an effective neo-Baroque manner, following the models of Casella and Malipiero, among them a ballet *Mutazioni* in four choreographic sections (1963); *Sinfonia* (1957); *Serenata* for chamber orch. (1960); and a cantata to words by Lorca, *Requiem di Madrid* (1958).

Fellerer, Karl Gustav, German musicologist; b. Freising, July 7, 1902. Studied musicology in Munich with Sandberger, and in Berlin with Abert, Wolf, and Sachs; 1927, docent at the Univ. of Münster; 1929–31 editor of the *Kirchenmusikalisches Jahrbuch;* 1931, prof. in Freiburg, Switzerland; 1939, succeeded Theodor Kroyer as prof. of music history at the Univ. of Cologne; retired in 1970.

WRITINGS: *Beiträge zur Musikgeschichte Freisings von den ältesten Zeiten bis zur Auflösung des Hofes 1803* (1926); *Der Palestrinastil und seine Bedeutung in der vokalen Kirchenmusik des 18. Jahrhunderts* (1928); *Die Deklamationsrhythmik in der vokalen Polyphonie des 16. Jahrhunderts* (1928); *Orgel und Orgelmusik* (1929); *Grundzüge der Geschichte der katholischen Kirchenmusik* (1930; 2d ed., 1949); *Palestrina* (1929); *Beiträge zur Choralbegleitung und Choralverarbeitung in der Orgelmusik des ausgehenden 18. und beginnenden 19. Jahrhunderts* (1932); *Das deutsche Kirchenlied in Ausland* (1935); *Puccini* (1937); *Grieg* (1942); *Deutsche Gregorianik im Frankenreich* (1941); *Die Musik im Wandel der Zeiten und Kulturen* (1948); *Die Messe* (1951); *Einführung in die Musikwissenschaft* (Hamburg, 1956). Edited *Beiträge zur Musikgeschichte der Stadt Essen* (Cologne, 1955); *Beiträge zur Geschichte der Musik am Niederrhein* (Cologne, 1956). A *Festschrift* was publ. to honor him on his 60th birthday (Regensburg, 1962).

Fellowes, Rev. Edmund Horace, eminent English musicologist and editor; b. London, Nov. 11, 1870; d. Windsor, Dec. 20, 1951. He attended Winchester and Oriel Colleges, Oxford; studied music with P. C. Buck, Fletcher, and L. Straus; Mus. Bac., Oxford (1896); hon. Mus. Doc., Dublin Univ. (1917), Oxford (1938), and Cambridge (1950); 1897–1900, precentor at Bristol Cathedral. 1900, canon; 1923–27, conductor at St. George's Chapel, Windsor Castle; 1918, librarian at St. Michael's College, Tenbury; 1927–29, toured the U.S. and Canada with the Choir of St. George's Chapel and Choristers of Westminster Abbey; also lectured on old English music at various universities; 1932–33, lecturer on music, Liverpool Univ. He ed. the valuable collections *The English Madrigal School*, including the works of Thomas Morley, Orlando Gibbons, John Wilbye, John Farmer, Thomas Weelkes, William Byrd, Henry Lichfild, John Ward, Thomas Tomkins, Giles Farnaby, Thomas Bateson, John Bennet, George Kirbye, etc. (36 vols., 1913–36), and *The English School of Lutenist Songwriters*, containing the collected works of John Dowland, Thomas Campion, Thomas Ford, Francis Pilkington, Robert Jones, etc. (32 vols.; 1920–32); co-editor of the Carnegie edition, *Tudor Church Music*, including works of White, Tallis, Taverner, Byrd, Gibbons (10 vols.; 1919–47); editor of collected works of William Byrd (20 vols.; 1937–50); 11 fantasies for strings by Orlando Gibbons (1925); songs of Fletcher and Beaumont; etc.

WRITINGS: *English Madrigal Verse* (1920; 2nd ed., 1931); *The English Madrigal Composers* (1921; 2nd ed., 1948); *William Byrd, A Short Account of his Life and Work* (1923; 2nd ed., 1928); *Orlando Gibbons* (1925; 2nd ed., 1951); *The English Madrigal* (London, 1925); *Windsor Castle, St. George's Chapel and Choir* (1927); *Repertory of English Cathedral Music* (in collaboration with C. H. Stewart, 1930); *The Catalogue of the Manuscripts at St. Michael's College, Tenbury* (1934); *William Byrd* (1936; an entirely different book from the monograph of 1923, and much larger in scope; 2nd ed., 1948); *Westminster Abbey and Its Music; Organists and Masters of the Choristers of St. George's Chapel in Windsor Castle* (1939); *English Cathedral Music from Edward VI to Edward VII* (1941; rev., 1945). He wrote an autobiography *Memoirs of an Amateur Musician* (London, 1946). Fellowes was a composer of church music; in his early years he wrote many anthems, *Morning and Evening Service*, songs, and a string quartet.

Felsenstein, Walter, Austrian opera director; b. Vienna, May 30, 1901; d. East Berlin, Oct. 8, 1975. He studied music in Graz; was opera intendant in Mannheim (1924–25); Basel (1927–29); Freiburg-im-Breisgau (1929–32); Cologne (1932–34); Frankfurt (1934–36); Zürich (1938–40) and in Berlin (1940–47). In 1947 he became director of the Komische Oper in East Berlin, bringing it to a high point of excellence. He visited the U.S. in the spring of 1971 on a lecture tour illustrated by films of his productions.

BIBLIOGRAPHY: *The Music Theater of Walter Felsenstein. Collected Articles Speeches and Interviews* by Felsenstein and Others, translated and edited by Peter Paul Fuchs (N.Y., 1975).

Felsztyn (Felstin, Felstinensis, Felsztynski), Sebastian von, notable Polish theorist and composer; b. Felsztyn, Galicia, c.1490; d. c.1543. He studied (1507–09) at the Univ. of Cracow (bachelor's degree); chaplain at Felsztyn, later at Przemysl; then provost in Sanok. He wrote a compendium on Gregorian chant and mensural music, publ. in several editions (1515, 1519, 1522, 1534, 1539) as *Opusculum utriusque musicae tam choralis quam etiam mensuralis.* He further publ. a practical manual for church singing, *Directiones musicae ad cathedralis ecclesiae Premisliensis usum* (Cracow, 1543); edited St. Augustin's *Dialogus*

de musica (with comments), and composed a volume of hymns, *Aliquot hymni ecclesiastici vario melodiarum genere editi* (Cracow, 1522; partly lost). His significance as composer lies in the fact that he was the first Polish musician to employ consistent 4-part writing; one selection for 4 voices is reprinted in Surzynski's *Monumenta musices sacrae in Polonia* (vol. II).

BIBLIOGRAPHY: A. Chybinski, *The Relationship of Polish and West-European Music of the 15th and 16th Centuries* (1909; in Polish); A. Chybinski, *The Mensural Theory in Polish Musical Literature of the 1st Half of the 16th Century* (1911); S. Lobaczewska, *Sebastian Felsztyn as Composer* (1928). See also Zofia Lissa's article in *Die Musik in Geschichte und Gegenwart.*

Felumb, Svend Christian, Danish composer; b. Copenhagen, Dec. 25, 1898; d. there, Dec. 16, 1972. He studied in Copenhagen with L. Nielsen and Bruce, and in Paris with Blenzel and Vidal; from 1924 till 1947 he was oboist in the Danish Royal Orch.; from 1947–1962 he conducted the Tivoli Orch. He was the founder of the Society "Ny Musik" in Copenhagen and a leader of the movement for modern national Danish music.

Fenaroli, Fedele, Italian music theorist; b. Lanciano, April 25, 1730; d. Naples, Jan. 1, 1818. He studied with his father, who was a church organist; then went to Naples, where he became a pupil of Francesco Durante and Leonardo Leo at the Cons. of Santa Maria di Loreto; in 1762 became second master there, and in 1777 the first; also taught at the Cons. della Pietà. He trained many famous musicians (Cimarosa, Conti, Mercadante, Zingarelli, etc.); his theoretical manuals were highly regarded, not only in Italy, but in France; he publ. *Partimento ossia Basso numerato* (Rome, 1800); *Studio del contrappunto* (Rome, 1800); *Regole musicali per i principianti di cembalo* (Naples, 1775). He was a prolific composer of church music, which, however, did not sustain its initial renown; composed two oratorios, *Abigaille* (1760) and *L'arca nel Giordano.*

BIBLIOGRAPHY: T. Consalvo, *La teoria musicale del Fenaroli* (1826); G. de Napoli, "F. Fenaroli nel secondo centenario della nascita," *Musica d'oggi* (March, 1930).

Fenby, Eric, English composer; b. Scarborough, April 22, 1906. He studied piano and organ; after a few years as organist in London, he went (1928) to Grez-sur-Loing, France, as amanuensis for Frederick Delius, taking down his dictation note by note, until Delius' death in 1934. Two years later he publ. his experiences in a book entitled *Delius as I Knew Him.* Because of the beneficent work he undertook, he neglected his own compositions; however he wrote some pleasant music for strings.

Fendler, Edvard, German-American conductor; b. Leipzig, Jan. 22, 1902. He studied conducting with G. Brecher; composition with Leichtentritt; conducted in Germany, France, and Holland (1927–41); conductor of the National Symphony Orch., Ciudad Trujillo, Dominican Republic (1942–44); then was in the U.S.

(1945–47); conductor of the National Symph. Orch. in San José, Costa Rica (1948–49); returned to the U.S. in 1949; from 1952 till 1970 he was conductor of the Mobile, Alabama, Symph. Orch.

Fennell, Frederick, American band conductor; b. Cleveland, July 2, 1914. He began conducting during the summers of 1931-33 at the National Music Camp, Interlochen, Mich.; went on to study at the Eastman School of Music, Rochester, N.Y. (B.M., 1937, M.M., 1939); then served on its faculty as conductor of the Little Symphony and Symphony Band (1939–65). In 1952 he founded the Eastman Wind Ensemble with which he made numerous record albums; he was also guest conductor at the Boston Pops. In 1965 he was appointed conductor-in-residence of the Univ. of Miami School of Music at Coral Gables, Florida; also made European tours with the School Orchestra of America (1965, 1966) and produced a series of specially recorded concerts at the Library of Congress, using 19th-century band instruments and music (1972, 1973, 1977). He is the recipient of an honorary Mus. D. degree from the Univ. of Oklahoma City; in 1958 was made an Honorary Chief by the Kiowa Indian Tribe. He published *Time and the Winds* (Kenosha, Wis., 1954) and *The Drummer's Heritage* (Rochester, N.Y., 1957).

Feo, Francesco, celebrated Italian composer; b. Naples, 1691; d. there, Jan. 18, 1761. He was a pupil of Fago at the Cons. della Pietà from 1704; his first opera was *Amor tirannico* (Naples, Jan. 18, 1713); then followed *La forza della virtù* (Naples, Jan. 22, 1719), *Teuzzone* (Naples, Jan. 20, 1720), *Siface, re di Numidia* (Naples, Nov. 4, 1720), *Andromaca* (Rome, Feb. 5, 1730), and *Arsace* (Turin, Dec. 26, 1740). He also wrote pieces for special occasions, including a serenade for the marriage of Charles of Bourbon, King of the Two Sicilies, to Princess Maria Amalia of Poland (1737) and a piece for the Spanish King's birthday (1738). Feo spent most of his life in Naples; was first maestro di cappella at the Cons. of Sant' Onofrio (1723–39); then at the Cons. dei Poveri di Gesù Cristo (1739–43). Most of his works (150 in all) are extant in manuscript at Naples.

Ferand, Ernst Thomas, Hungarian music scholar; b. Budapest, March 5, 1887; d. Basel, May 29, 1972. He studied at the Budapest Academy of Music, graduating in 1911; then collaborated with Jaques-Dalcroze in Dresden-Hellerau and Geneva; taught at Fodor Cons. of Music, Budapest (1912–19) and at Dalcroze School in Hellerau (1920–25); directed the Hellerau-Laxenburg College in Vienna (1925–38). In 1938 he emigrated to the U.S. and taught at the New School for Social Research in New York (1939–65); then went to Basel. He publ. a textbook on harmony in Hungarian (Budapest, 1914); *Die Improvisation in der Musik* (Zürich, 1939); an anthology of improvised music, *Die Improvisation in Beispielen aus neun Jahrhunderten abendländischer Musik* (Cologne, 1956); contributed valuable articles to music magazines.

Ferchault, Guy, French musicologist; b. Mer (Loiret-Cher), Aug. 16, 1904. He studied philosophy and music; held teaching positions in music education in Orléans (1941), Poitiers (1942–49), Tours (1948–51), and Roubaix (since 1952). He published a monograph on Henri Duparc (Paris, 1944); *Les Créateurs du drame musical* (Paris, 1944); *Faust, une légende et ses musiciens* (Paris, 1948); *Claude Debussy, musicien français* (Paris, 1948); *Richard Wagner* (Paris, 1955).

Fere, Vladimir, Russian composer and ethnomusicologist; b. Kamyshin, in the Saratov district, May 20, 1902; d. Moscow, Sept. 2, 1971. He studied piano with Goldenweiser and composition with Glière and Miaskovsky at the Moscow Cons. (1921–29). In 1936 he went to Frunze, Kirghizia; composed (in collaboration with Vlasov) a number of operas based on native folk motives; all these operas were first produced in Frunze: *Golden Girl* (May 1, 1937); *Not Death but Life* (March 26, 1938); *Moon Beauty* (April 15, 1939); *For People's Happiness* (May 1, 1941); *Patriots* (Nov. 6, 1941); *Son of the People* (Nov. 8, 1947); *On the Shores of Issyk-Kul* (Feb. 1, 1951); *Toktogul* (July 6, 1958); *The Witch* (1965); *One Hour Before Dawn* (1969). He furthermore wrote several symphonic pieces on Kirghiz themes; numerous choruses; also chamber music.

Ferenczy, Oto, Slovak composer; b. Brezovice, March 30, 1921. He studied philosophy, esthetics and musicology at the Comenius Univ. in Bratislava; is mainly self-taught in composition. In 1954 he joined the staff of the Bratislava Academy of Music and Dramatic Arts; in 1962 was appointed its rector. His music is entrenched well within the inoffensive idiom of Central European neo-Classicism; it is expertly crafted.
WORKS: a comic opera, *Nevšedná humoreska* (*An Uncommon Humoresque*, 1966–67); *Merry-Making*, dance suite for orch. (1951); *Hurbanovská*, overture (1952); *Serenade* for harp, flute, clarinet, bassoon and string orch. (1955); *Capriccio* for piano and orch. (1957); *Elegy* for orch. (1957); *Finale* for orch. (1958); *Partita* for chamber orch. (1963–65); *Symphonic Prologue* (1975); *The Star of the North*, cantata (1960); *Music* for 4 string instruments (1947, revised 1973); Concerto for 9 Instruments (1949); String Quartet (1962); Violin Sonata (1964); Concertino for 12 Instruments (1965); piano pieces; choruses; solo songs.

Ferguson, Donald Nivison, American music educator; b. Waupun, Wisconsin, June 30, 1882. Since 1913, teaching music at the Univ. of Minnesota. He is the author of *History of Musical Thought* (N.Y., 1935; revised, 1948; 3rd ed., 1959); *A Short History of Music* (N.Y., 1943); *Piano Music of Six Great Composers* (N.Y., 1947); *Masterworks of the Orchestral Repertoire* (Minneapolis, 1954); *Music as Metaphor; The Elements of Expression* (Minneapolis, 1960); *Image and Structure in Chamber Music* (Minneapolis, 1964); *The Why of Music* (Minneapolis, 1969).

Ferguson, Howard, British composer and music editor; b. Belfast, Oct. 21, 1908. He studied composition with R. O. Morris at the Royal College of Music in London; piano with Harold Samuel. From 1948 to 1963 he was prof. at the Royal Academy of Music in

London. His music is neo-Classical in its idiom; in some of his compositions he makes use of English, Scottish and Irish folksongs.

WORKS: *Chauntecleer,* a ballet (1948); Piano Concerto (London Philharmonic, May 29, 1952, Myra Hess, soloist); Octet, for clarinet, horn, string quartet and double bass (1933); the cantatas *Amore langueo* (1956); and *The Dream of the Road* (1959); 2 violin sonatas; piano pieces. He edited many old keyboard works, among them those by Purcell (1964) and Blow (1965); also the anthologies *Style and Interpretation* (4 vols., 1963–64), *Early French Keyboard Music* (2 vols., 1966); *Early Italian Keyboard Music* (2 vols., 1968); *Early German Keyboard Music* (2 vols., 1970); *Early English Keyboard Music* (1971).

Fernandez, Oscar Lorenzo, Brazilian composer; b. Rio de Janeiro, Nov. 4, 1897; d. there, Aug. 26, 1948. He studied music at the Instituto Nacionale de Musica, and appeared as composer, conductor, and pianist in his own works in Brazil and other Latin American countries. He won several prizes. In 1925 he became prof. at the Instituto Nacionale, and organized a choral society there. In his music he adopted a strongly national style, derived from Brazilian folksongs, without, however, actual quotation.

WORKS: Opera, *Malazarte* (Rio de Janeiro, Sept. 30, 1941, composer conducting); ballet on Inca themes, *Amayá* (Rio de Janeiro, July 9, 1939); suite for orch. *Imbapará* (Rio de Janeiro, Sept. 2, 1929); suite for orch. *Reisado do pastoreio* (Rio de Janeiro, Aug. 22, 1930; the last movement of this suite, *Batuque,* a Brazilian dance, became popular); Violin Concerto (1942); Symphony (performed posthumously by the Boston Symph. Orch., Eleazar de Carvalho conducting, Feb. 25, 1949); also a number of chamber music compositions: *Trio Brasileiro* (1924); Suite for Flute, Oboe, Clarinet, Bassoon, and Horn (Rio de Janeiro, Sept. 20, 1927); several piano works; songs. A complete bibliography of magazine articles on Fernandez is found in Vasco Mariz, *Dicionario Bio-Bibliografico Musical* (Rio de Janeiro, 1948).

Fernández Arbós, Enrique. See **Arbós, Enrique Fernández.**

Fernández Bordas, Antonio, eminent Spanish violinist; b. Orense, Jan. 12, 1870; d. Madrid, Feb. 18, 1950. He studied at the Madrid Cons. with Jesús de Monasterio, and at the age of 11, won first prize for violin students; gave concerts in England, France, and other European countries; returning to Spain he became prof. of violin at the Madrid Cons.; in 1921 he was elected director.

Fernández Caballero, Manuel, Spanish composer; b. Murcia, March 14, 1835; d. Madrid, Feb. 20, 1906. He was a precocious musician; learned to play violin, piano, and the piccolo as a child, and at the age of 7, played in a school band. He then studied violin with Soriano Fuertes in Murcia; in 1850 he entered the Madrid Cons., where his teachers were Eslava and Pedro Albéniz; in 1856 he received first prize in composition; then conducted various orchestras and became interested in theatrical composition. During his career as conductor and composer, he wrote more than 200 zarzuelas, several of which attained great popularity: *Los Dineros del Sacristan* and *Los Africanistas* (Barcelona, 1894); *El cabo primero* (Barcelona, 1895); *La Rueda de la Fortuna* (Madrid, 1896); *Los Estudiantes* (Madrid, 1900). He also wrote sacred music.

Fernström, John (Axel), Swedish conductor and composer; b. in I-Chang, Hupei, China (the son of a Swedish missionary), Dec. 6, 1897; d. Hälsingborg, Oct. 19, 1961. He studied first at the Cons. in Malmö, then took violin lessons in Copenhagen, where he also studied with P. Gram (1923–30). He took courses in conducting at Sonderhausen, Germany, and later settled in Hälsingborg.

WORKS: An exceptionally prolific composer, he wrote three operas: *Achnaton* (1931); *Isissystrarnas bröllop* (1942) and *Livet en dröm* (1946); 12 symphonies: No. 1 (1920); No. 2 (1924); No. 3, *Exotica* (1928); No. 4 (1930); No. 5 (1932); No. 6 (1938); No. 7, *Sinfonietta in forma di sonata de chiesa* (1941); No. 8, *Amore studiorum* (1942); No. 9, *Sinfonia breve* (1943); No. 10, *Sinfonia discrète* (1944); No. 11, *Utan mask* (1945); No. 12 (1951); *Symphonic Variations* (1930); 2 violin concertos (No. 2, 1952); Chaconne for Cello and Orch. (1936); Clarinet Concerto (1936); Viola Concerto (1937); Concertino for Flute, Female Chorus and Small Orch. (1941); Bassoon Concerto (1946); Cello Concertino (1949); *Ostinato* for strings (1952); Mass for Soli, Chorus and Orch. (1931); *Stabat Mater* for soli, chorus and strings (1936); *Songs of the Sea,* suite for soprano and strings (1943); *Den mödosamma vägen,* profane oratorio (1947); 8 string quartets: (1920, 1925, 1931, 1942, 1945, 1947, 1950, 1952); many other chamber works; songs and choral works. He publ. an autobiographical book *Confessions* (1946).

Ferrabosco, Alfonso, Italian composer; son of **Domenico Ferrabosco;** b. Bologna, Jan. (baptized Jan. 18), 1543; d. there, Aug. 12, 1588. He went to England as a youth; in 1562 he was in the service of Queen Elizabeth; went back to Italy in 1564; and was again in England from 1564 to 1569. He lived in France for some time, and married a woman from Antwerp; after another sojourn in England (1572–78) he was in Turin in the service of the Duke of Savoy, whom he accompanied to Spain (1585); eventually he returned to Bologna. The historical position of Alfonso Ferrabosco is important for the influence of Italian music that he brought to the court of Queen Elizabeth. Some of his madrigals are found in Young's *Musica transalpina* (London, 1588, 1597), Morley's *Madrigals to Five Voyces* (London, 1598), Pevernage's *Harmonia celesta* (1593) and other collections up to 1664; further compositions appear in collections of P. Phalèse (1583, 1591, 1593), A. Morsolina (1588), G. B. Besardo (1603), etc. MSS are in the Bodleian Library and Music School at Oxford, British Museum, St. Michael's College, Tenbury, and Royal College of Music Library.

BIBLIOGRAPHY: G. E. P. Arkwright, "Un compositore italiano alla corte di Elisabetta, Alfonso Ferrabosco di Bologna," *Rivista Musicale Italiana* (1897); S. Cordero di Pamparato, *Musici alla Corte di Carlo Emanuele I di Savoia* (Turin, 1930); A. Einstein, *The Italian Madrigal* (Princeton, 1949); see also J. Kerman, "Master Alfonso and the English Madrigal," *Musical Quarterly* (April 1952).

Ferrabosco, Alfonso, Italian-English composer; natural son of the preceding; b. Greenwich, England, c.1575; d. there, March (buried March 11), 1628. He was educated in England, and remained there after his father returned to Italy in 1578. He was supported from the funds of the English Court; was one of the King's Musicians for the Violins from about 1602 until his death. During the last year of his life he was made Composer of the King's Music; also Composer of Music in Ordinary to the King. He was highly regarded as composer of the music for masques of Ben Jonson, of whom he was a close friend: *The Masque of Blackness* (1604–05), *The Masque of Hymen* (1605–06), *The Masque of Beauty* (1607–08), *The Masque for Lord Haddington's Marriage* (1607–08), and *The Masque of Queens* (1608–09). In 1609 he publ. a vol. of *Ayres* (dedicated to Prince Henry) and a book of *Lessons for 1, 2 and 3 Viols;* also contributed 3 compositions to Leighton's *Teares or Lamentacions* (1614). MSS are in libraries of the British Museum, the Music School and Church, Oxford, and the Royal College of Music. His works for viols demonstrate extraordinary ability in contrapuntal writing, while preserving the rhythmic quality of the dance forms (pavans, etc.) and the free ornamental style of the fantasies.

BIBLIOGRAPHY: G. E. P. Arkwright, "Notes on the Ferrabosco Family," *Musical Antiquary* (July 1912); G. Livi, "The Ferrabosco Family," ibid. (April 1913).

Ferrabosco, Domenico Maria, Italian composer; b. Bologna, Feb. 14, 1513; d. there, Feb. 1574. He was maestro di cappella at San Petronio in Bologna; in 1546 he was at the Vatican, returning to Bologna in 1548; was again at the Vatican from 1550 until 1555. He is chiefly known as a composer of madrigals; his book of 45 madrigals, *Il Primo libro de' Madrigali a 4 voci,* was publ. by Gardano in 1542; Gardano also publ. motets (1554) and other madrigals (1557) by Ferrabosco; some madrigals and a 4-voiced canzona, the latter in lute tablature, appeared in 1584 (publ. by Scotto).

Ferrara, Franco, Italian conductor; b. Palermo, July 4, 1911. He studied piano, violin, organ and composition at the Cons. of Palermo and Bologna; made his debut as conductor in Florence in 1938; in 1959 went to Holland, where he gave courses in conducting with the Holland Radio Philharmonic. Among his students was Edo de Waart.

Ferrari, Benedetto, Italian opera composer, called "Della Tiorba" from his proficiency on the theorbo; b. Reggio, 1597; d. Modena, Oct. 22, 1681. He studied music in Rome; in 1637 he proceeded to Venice; there he wrote the libretto of *Andromeda* (music by Francesco Manelli), which was the first opera that was publicly performed anywhere; it was produced at the Teatro Tron di San Cassiano, early in 1637; he then produced in Venice four operas to his own libretto: *Armida* (Feb. 1639); *Il pastor regio* (Jan. 23, 1640); *La ninfa avara* (1641); *Il principe giardiniero* (Dec. 30, 1643). In 1645 he went to Modena, where he remained until 1651, at the ducal court; from 1651–53 he was in Vienna; then returned to Modena, where he produced an opera *Erosilda* (1658); he also wrote two cantatas *Premo il giogo delle Alpi* and *Voglio di vita uscir* (reprinted in Riemann's *Kantatenfrühling,* 1912).

Ferrari, Carlotta, Italian composer of operas; b. Lodi, Jan. 27, 1837; d. Bologna, Nov. 23, 1907. She studied with Strepponi and Mazzucato at the Milan Cons.; then devoted herself to the composition of operas to her own librettos. The following operas were produced: *Ego* (Milan, 1857), *Sofia* (Lodi, 1866) and *Eleanora d'Armorea* (Cagliari, 1871).

Ferrari, Domenico, Italian composer and violinist; b. Piacenza, c.1722; d. Paris, 1780. He studied with Tartini; traveled as a concert violinist, obtaining great success; in 1753 he joined the orch. of the Duke of Württemberg in Stuttgart; in 1754 he went to Paris, where he became extremely successful; he excelled as a virtuoso; his employment of passages in octaves, and particularly of harmonics, was an innovation at the time. He wrote several sets of violin sonatas and also trio sonatas, which were published.

Ferrari, Gabrielle, French pianist and composer; b. Paris, Sept. 14, 1851; d. there, July 4, 1921. She studied at the Milan Cons. and later in Paris, where she had lessons with Gounod. She wrote a number of effective piano pieces (*Rapsodie espagnole, Le Ruisseau, Hirondelle,* etc.) and songs (*Larmes en Songe, Chant d'Exil, Chant d'Amour,* etc.); finally ventured to compose operas, producing *Le Dernier amour* (Paris, June 11, 1895), *Sous le masque* (Vichy, 1898), *Le Tartare* (Paris, 1906), and *Le Cobzar,* which proved to be her most successful opera (Monte Carlo, Feb. 16, 1909; several subsequent revivals).

Ferrari, Giacomo Gotifredo, Italian composer; b. Rovereto, Tyrol (baptized April 2), 1763; d. London, Dec. 1842. He studied piano at Verona with Marcola and theory with Marianus Stecher at the Monastery of Mariaberg, Switzerland. He then went to Naples, where he studied with Latilla. There he met Chevalier Campan, household master for Marie Antoinette; he was then appointed as court musician at the Tuileries. He arrived in Paris in 1787; after the Revolution he went to London, where he settled as a singing teacher. He produced in London the operas *I due Svizzeri* (May 14, 1799), *Il Rinaldo d' Asti* (March 16, 1802), *L'eroina di Raab* (April 8, 1813), and *Lo sbaglio fortunato* (May 8, 1817); he also wrote two ballets and several instrumental works (4 septets; 2 piano concertos, etc.).

WRITINGS: *Concise Treatise on Italian Singing* (1818); *Studio di musica pratica, teorica* (1830), and a book of reminiscences, *Anedotti piacevoli ed interresanti* (London, 1830, in Italian; contains some vivid recollections of Haydn and other celebrities; new ed., Palermo, 1920).

BIBLIOGRAPHY: D. G. Fino, *Giacomo Gotifredo Ferrari, musicista roveretano* (Trent, 1928); G. de Saint-Foix, "A Musical Traveler," *Musical Quarterly* (Oct. 1939).

Ferrari, Gustave, Swiss pianist and composer; b. Geneva, Sept. 28, 1872; d. there, July 29, 1948. He studied at the Geneva Cons., and later in Paris. In 1900 he went to London, where he remained for many years. From 1917 till 1925 he conducted operetta in America; then returned to Europe and toured with Yvette Guilbert, as her accompanist in a repertory of French folksongs; later on he gave song recitals himself, singing with his own accompaniment folksongs of France and French Canada; also lectured on the subject, and edited collections of French folk music. As a composer, he wrote mostly incidental music for the stage; composed a cantata for the Rousseau Festival (Geneva, 1912); *The Wilderness,* a Greek dance ballad (London, 1915); other choral works; a song cycle *Le Livre pour toi.*

Ferrari-Fontana, Edoardo, Italian operatic tenor; b. Rome, July 8, 1878; d. Toronto, Canada, July 4, 1936. As a young man he served in the Italian consulate in South America; also studied singing. Returning to Italy in 1908; he sang in operetta; given a chance to appear as Tristan in Turin (Dec. 23, 1909), he scored a signal success, and in a few years became well known as a principal Italian tenor in Wagner's repertory. He sang in America during the 1913–14 season of the Boston Opera Co. and with the Metropolitan Opera in New York, and later at the Chicago Opera. In 1926 he settled in Toronto as a singing teacher. He was married (June 26, 1912) to **Margarete Matzenauer,** but was separated from her after a few years.

Ferrari-Trecate, Luigi, Italian composer; b. Alessandria, Piedmont, Aug. 25, 1884; d. Rome, April 17, 1964. He studied with Antonio Cicognani at the Cons. of Pesaro, and also with Mascagni. Subsequently he was engaged as a church organist; was prof. of organ playing at the Liceo Musicale in Bologna (1928–31); in 1931 was appointed director of the Parma Cons. He wrote several operas which had considerable success: *Pierozzo* (Alessandria, Sept. 15, 1922); *La Bella e il mostro* (Milan, March 20, 1926); *Le astuzie di Bertoldo* (Genoa, Jan. 10, 1934); *Ghirlino* (Milan, Feb. 4, 1940); *Buricchio* (Bologna, Nov. 5, 1948); *L'Orso Re* (Milan, Feb. 8, 1950); *La capanna dello Zio Tom* (*Uncle Tom's Cabin*; Parma, Jan. 17, 1953); also wrote music for a marionette play *Ciottolino* (Rome, Feb. 8, 1922).

Ferrata, Giuseppe, Italian-American composer; b. Gradoli, Romagna, Jan. 1, 1865; d. New Orleans, March 28, 1928. At the age of 14 he won a scholarship to study at Santa Cecilia in Rome, where he took courses with Sgambati and Terziani, graduating in 1885; than had the good fortune of benefiting from the last lessons that Liszt gave; in 1892 came to the U.S.; taught at Tulane Univ. in New Orleans. He wrote a symphony, a piano concerto, a string quartet, numerous songs, to Italian and English texts (*Night and the Curtains Drawn, A Song of Thanksgiving, On Music, Alla musa,* etc.); piano pieces (*Humoresque, A Wave, An Eagle, Leonard Serpent, Serenade triste*); compiled a book of scales and *Esthetic Exercises of Technique.*

Ferrer, Mateo, Catalan composer; b. Barcelona, Feb. 25, 1788; d. there, Jan. 4, 1864. A highly gifted musician, he was famous for his improvisations on the organ. He was organist at the Barcelona Cathedral for 52 years from 1812 until his death. His Sonata (1814), printed by Joaquín Nín in his collection, *16 Sonates anciennes d'auteurs espagnols* (Paris, 1925), shows a certain affinity with early Beethoven.

Ferrer, Rafael, Spanish conductor; b. St.-Celoni, near Barcelona, May 22, 1911. He studied with Luis Millet and Enrique Morera (composition) and Eduardo Toldrá (violin). He played the violin in various orchestras in Spain; then devoted himself mainly to conducting. He specializes in Spanish music, and has revived many little-known works of Granados, Turina, and other Spanish composers.

Ferrero, Willy, precocious Italian conductor; b. Portland, Maine, May 21, 1906; d. Rome, March 24, 1954. He was taken to Italy in his infancy; as a child of six he conducted a performance at the Teatro Costanzi in Rome; at the age of eight he conducted symphony concerts in European capitals with sensational success, and was the object of extravagant praise as a phenomenal musician. World War I interrupted his career; he continued to conduct operas and concerts in Italy, but failed to fulfill the extraordinary promise of his early youth. He received an excellent academic education; studied at the Vienna Academy (graduated in 1924); composed a symph. poem, *Il Mistero dell' aurora,* and some chamber music.

BIBLIOGRAPHY: Alberto de Angelis, "Willy Ferrero," *Noi e il Mondo* (Rome, 1919).

Ferretti, Dom Paolo, eminent Italian musicologist; b. Subiaco, Dec. 3, 1866; d. Bologna, May 23, 1938. He studied theology at the Benedictine College of San Anselmo in Rome; then taught in Malta, Genoa, and Parma; was abbot of the Benedictine Monastery of San Giovanni in Parma; in 1922 was appointed by Pope Pius XI director of the Pontifical Institute of Sacred Music. During the summers of 1925, 1927, and 1928 he taught courses in Gregorian chant at the Pius X School of Liturgical Music in New York. The importance of his investigations lies in a scholarly analysis of the rhythmic treatment and especially the forms of Gregorian chant. He publ. *Principii teorici e practici del Canto Gregoriano* (Rome, 1905); *Il Cursus metrico e il Ritmo delle melodie del Canto Gregoriano* (Rome, 1913); *Estetica gregoriana* (Rome, 1934; also in French, Tournai, 1938).

Ferri, Baldassare, celebrated artificial soprano; b. Perugia, Dec. 9, 1610; d. there, Nov. 18, 1680. At the age of 11 he was choirboy to Cardinal Crescenzio in Orvieto, in whose service he remained until 1625, when he entered the service of Prince Ladislaus of Poland in Warsaw, remaining with him until 1655, with some interruptions for trips to Italy. From 1655 he was in Vienna at the court of Ferdinand III; appeared briefly in London (1671); then returned to Italy. His success at the various courts, and with the public in several countries, must have been great, for he accumulated a fortune. According to contemporary accounts (e.g., A.

Bontempi, *Historia Musica,* 1695), he possessed a phenomenal voice.

BIBLIOGRAPHY: G. Conestabile, *Notizie biografiche di Baldassare Ferri* (Perugia, 1846).

Ferrier, Kathleen, remarkable English contralto; b. Higher Walton, Lancashire, April 22, 1912; d. London, Oct. 8, 1953. She studied piano; for a time made her living as a telephone operator; began studying voice at the age of 25. Having appeared as a soloist in *Messiah* at Westminster Abbey in 1943, she rapidly advanced to the first rank among English singers. She sang the title role in the première of Britten's *Rape of Lucretia* (Glyndebourne, 1946); made two highly successful tours in the U.S. in 1947–48 and in 1950–51. Towards the end of her brief career she acquired in England an almost legendary reputation for vocal excellence and impeccable musical taste, so that her death (of cancer) was mourned by musicians as a national calamity.

BIBLIOGRAPHY: N. Cardus, *Kathleen Ferrier, a Memoir* (London, 1954), Charles Rigby, *Kathleen Ferrier* (London, 1955).

Ferris, William, American organist, choral conductor and composer; b. Chicago, Feb. 26, 1937. He studied composition with Alexander Tcherepnin at the De Paul Univ. School of Music (1955–60) and took private lessons with Leo Sowerby in Chicago (1957–62). In 1960 he founded the William Ferris Chorale, specializing in the music of the Renaissance and that of 20th-century composers. He served as organist of Holy Name Cathedral in Chicago (1954–58, 1962–64); director of music at Sacred Heart Cathedral in Rochester, N.Y. (1966–71); in 1973 he joined the faculty of the American Cons. of Music in Chicago. His compositions are mostly liturgical.

WORKS: *Concert Piece* for trumpet, horn and string orch. (1960); *October–November,* symph. movement (1962; Rochester, Nov. 6, 1968); *Concert Piece* for organ and string orch. (1963; Boston Symph., Worcester, Mass., Nov. 19, 1967); *Celebrations,* overture (1966); Trio for Flute, Bassoon and Piano (1957); String Trio (1958); Piano Sonata (1976). Vocal works: *De Profundis* (Fordham Univ. Nov. 22, 1964); *Ed e Subito Sera* (Rochester, Nov. 6, 1968); *Durobrivae,* music for tenors, basses, 5 brasses and kettledrums (1970); *A Canticle of Celebration* for chorus, brasses and kettledrums (1971); *Make We Joy,* cantata (Chicago, Dec. 12, 1976); *A Song of Light,* cantata (Chicago, Oct. 11, 1977); numerous works for chorus and organ; a cappella choruses; songs.

Ferroni, Vincenzo Emidio Carmine, Italian composer and educator; b. Tramutola, Feb. 17, 1858; d. Milan, Jan. 10, 1934. He studied at the Paris Cons. (1876–83) with Savard and Massenet; in 1888 returned to Italy, where he became prof. of composition at the Milan Cons., succeeding Ponchielli; resigned in 1929. He wrote 3 operas: *Rudello* (Milan, 1892), *Ettore Fieramosca* (Como, 1896), and *Il Carbonaro* (Milan, 1900); 2 symphonies, a symph. poem, *Risorgimento,* and many works in smaller forms.

Ferroud, Pierre-Octave, French composer; b. Chasselay, near Lyons, Jan. 6, 1900; d. near Debrecen, Hungary (killed in an automobile accident), Aug. 17, 1936. He attended the Univ. of Lyons, and studied there and in Strasbourg with Erb, Ropartz, Witkowski, and Florent Schmitt; in 1923 settled in Paris, where he developed varied activities as composer, music critic, and adviser for radio broadcasting. He first attracted attention with the performance of a ballet *Le Porcher* (Ballets suédois, Paris, Nov. 15, 1924); there followed the symph. poem *Foules* (Paris, March 21, 1926); an operatic sketch, *Chirurgie,* after Chekhov (Monte Carlo, March 20, 1928); and a symphony in A (Paris, March 8, 1931, Monteux conducting; also at the Prague Festival of the International Society for Contemporary Music, Sept. 6, 1935); other works are the ballets, *Jeunesse* (Paris, April 29, 1933) and *Vénus ou L'équipée planétaire* (1935); Cello Sonata (1933); *Andante cordial* for violin, cello, and piano; Trio for Oboe, Clarinet, and Bassoon (1934); also several song cycles and piano pieces. Ferroud's music is distinguished by an adroit application of contrapuntal methods to compositions of essentially popular style; his chief influence was Florent Schmitt, about whom he wrote a book, *Autour de Florent Schmitt* (Paris, 1927).

BIBLIOGRAPHY: René Dumesnil, *Pierre-Octave Ferroud, Revue Musicale* (Oct.-Nov. 1931).

Fesca, Alexander Ernst, German pianist and composer, son of **Friedrich Ernst Fesca;** b. Karlsruhe, May 22, 1820; d. Brunswick, Feb. 22, 1849. He studied with his father, and later with Taubert. He was extremely successful as a concert pianist in 1839; in 1841 he became chamber musician to Prince Fürstenberg; settled in Brunswick in 1842, where he brought out his operas *Der Troubadour* (July 25, 1847) and *Ulrich von Hutten* (1849); he also wrote a piano sextet, 2 piano trios, a violin sonata, and many songs, some of which became popular. His early death at the age of 28 was regretted by many admirers who believed that he was a composer of uncommon talent.

Fesca, Friedrich Ernst, German composer; b. Magdeburg, Feb. 15, 1789; d. Karlsruhe, May 24, 1826. He studied violin; made a debut in his own violin concerto; in 1806 he joined the orch. of the Duke of Oldenburg; in 1808 he obtained a similar position at the Westphalian court at Kassel; in 1813 he was in Vienna; in 1814 became a member of the Karlsruhe Orch. He was a prolific composer of chamber music (20 quartets and 5 quintets); also wrote 2 operas, *Cantemire* (1819) and *Omar und Leila* (1823); 3 symphonies, 4 overtures, etc.

Fesch, Willem de, Flemish organist; b. Alkmaar, Aug. 25, 1687; d. London, Jan. 3, 1761. He was organist at Antwerp; in 1731 went to London, where he produced his oratorios *Judith* (1733) and *Joseph* 1745).

BIBLIOGRAPHY: F. van den Bremt, *Willem de Fesch, Nederlands Componist en Virtuoos* (Louvain, 1949).

Festa, Costanzo, Italian composer; b. Rome, c.1480; d. there, April 10, 1545. He was a singer in the Pontifical Chapel from about 1517. He was a composer of much importance, being regarded as a forerunner of Palestrina, whose works were strongly influenced by those of Festa; was the first important Italian musician who successfully fused the Flemish and Italian styles, melodically and harmonically. He may well be considered one of the first, if not the first, of the native Italian madrigalists. The earliest known publ. work of his appeared in 1519. Of his numerous compositions, many sacred works were publ. in various collections from 1513 till 1549; a *Te Deum a 4* (publ. in Rome, 1596) is still sung in the Vatican on solemn festivals. A complete list of Festa's works, together with reprints, is found in A. Cametti's "Per un precursore del Palestrina; il compositore piemontese Costanzo Festa," *Bollettino Bibliografico Musicale* (April 1931); publication of a complete edition of his works was begun in 1940 by the Istituto Italiano per la Storia della Musica Sacra in Rome.

Festing, Michael Christian, English violinist; b. London, c.1680; d. there, July 24, 1752. He was a pupil of Richard Jones and Geminiani. In 1735 he joined the king's private band and became first violin in an amateur group called the Philh. Society; 1737, appointed director of the Italian Opera; 1742, conductor at Ranelagh Gardens. In 1738 he established, with Dr. Greene and others, the "Society of Musicians," for the maintenance of impoverished musicians and their families. He wrote numerous solos and concertos for violin; 18 sonatas for violins and bass; cantatas; songs.

Fétis, Édouard-Louis François, Belgian music editor; son of **Francois-Joseph Fétis**; b. Bouvigne, near Dinant, May 16, 1812; d. Brussels, Jan. 31, 1909. He edited his father's *Revue musicale* (1833–35); was for years librarian of the Brussels Library. He publ. *Les Musiciens belges* (1848) and *Les Artistes belges à l'étranger* (1857–65), and compiled a catalogue of his father's library. His brother, **Adolphe-Louis-Eugène Fétis** (b. Paris, Aug. 20, 1820; d. there, March 20, 1873), was a pupil of his father, and of Herz (piano); lived in Brussels and Antwerp, and from 1856 in Paris as a music teacher. He composed music for piano and harmonium.

Fétis, François-Joseph, erudite Belgian musical theorist, historian, and critic; b. Mons, March 25, 1784; d. Brussels, March 26, 1871. He received primary instruction from his father, an organist at the Mons cathedral; learned to play the violin, piano, and organ when very young, and in his ninth year wrote a concerto for violin with orch.; as a youth was organist to the Noble Chapter of Sainte-Waudru. In 1800 he entered the Paris Cons., where he studied harmony with Rey and piano with Boieldieu and Pradher; in 1803 he visited Vienna, there studying counterpoint, fugue, and masterworks of German music. Several of his compositions (a symphony, an overture, sonatas and caprices for piano) were published at that time. In 1806 Fétis began the revision of the plainsong and entire ritual of the Roman Church, a vast undertaking completed, with many interruptions, after 30 years of patient research. A wealthy marriage in the same year enabled him to pursue his studies at ease for a time;

but the fortune was lost in 1811, and he retired to the Ardennes, where he occupied himself with composition and philosophical researches into the theory of harmony; in 1813, he was appointed organist for the collegiate church of St.-Pierre at Douai. In 1818 he settled in Paris; in 1821 became prof. of composition at the Paris Cons.; in 1824 his *Traité du contrepoint et de la fugue* was publ. and accepted as a regular manual at the Cons. In 1827 he became librarian of the Cons., and in the same year founded his unique journal *La Revue Musicale,* which he edited alone until 1832; his son edited it from 1833 until 1835, when its publication ceased. Fétis also wrote articles on music for *Le National* and *Le Temps.* In 1828 he competed for the prize of the Netherlands Royal Institute with a treatise *Quels ont été les mérites des Néerlandais dans la musique, principalement aux XIVe-XVIe siècles . . . ;* Kiesewetter's essay on the same subject won the prize, but Fétis' paper was also printed by the Institute. In 1832 he inaugurated his famous series of historical lectures and concerts. In 1833 he was called to Brussels as maître de chapelle to King Leopold I, and Director of the Cons.; during his long tenure of the latter position, for nearly 40 years, the Cons. flourished as never before. He also conducted the concerts of the Academy, which elected him a member in 1845. Fétis was a confirmed believer in the possibility of explaining music history and music theory scientifically; in his scholarly writings he attempted a thorough systematization of all fields of the art; he was opinionated and dogmatic, but it cannot be denied that he was a pioneer in musicology. He published the first book on music appreciation, *La Musique mise à la portée de tout le monde* (Paris, 1830; numerous reprints and transls. into English, German, Italian, Spanish, Russian); further pedagogical writings are: *Solfèges progressifs* (Paris, 1837); *Traité complet de la théorie et de la pratique de l'harmonie* (Brussels, 1844). As early as 1806 Fétis began collecting materials for his great *Biographie universelle des musiciens et bibliographie générale de la musique* in 8 vols. (Paris, 1833–44; 2nd ed., 1860–65; supplement of 2 vols., 1878–80; edited by A. Pougin). This work of musical biography was unprecedented in its scope; entries on composers and performers whom Fétis knew personally still remain prime sources of information. On the negative side are the many fanciful accounts of composers' lives taken from unreliable sources; in this respect Fétis exercised a harmful influence on subsequent lexicographers for a whole century. His *Histoire générale de la musique,* in 5 vols., only goes as far as the 15th century (Paris, 1869–76); this work exhibits Fétis as a profound scholar, but also as a dogmatic philosopher of music propounding opinions without convincing evidence to support them. Of interest are his *Esquisse de l'histoire de l'harmonie considerée comme art et comme science systématique* (Paris, 1840); *Notice biographique de Nicolo Paganini* (Paris, 1851; with a short history of the violin); *Antoine Stradivari* (Paris, 1856; with a commentary on bowed instruments); reports on musical instruments at the Paris Expositions of 1855 and 1867, etc. Fétis was also a composer; between 1820 and 1832 he wrote 7 operas, serious and light, for the Opéra-Comique; composed church music, 3 string quartets, 3 string quintets, 2 symphonies, and a flute concerto. His valuable library of 7,325 vols. was acquired after his death by the Bibliothèque Royale of Brussels; a catalogue was publ. in 1877.

BIBLIOGRAPHY: K. Gollmick, *Fétis als Mensch, Kritiker, Theoretiker und Komponist* (Berlin, 1852); L. Alvin, *Notice sur François-Joseph Fétis* (Brussels, 1874); R. Wangermée, *F.-J. Fétis, musicologue et compositeur* (Brussels, 1951).

Feuermann, Emanuel, Austrian cello virtuoso; b. Kolomea, Galicia, Nov. 22, 1902; d. New York, May 25, 1942. He studied with Anton Walter in Vienna and with Julius Klengel in Leipzig; taught at the Cologne Cons. at the age of 16; then toured Europe and the U.S.; from 1930–33 he was prof. at the Berlin Hochschule für Musik; in 1934 went to Vienna. He made his American debut with the N.Y. Philharmonic, Jan. 2, 1935; also gave chamber music concerts with Schnabel and Hubermann. He owned a rare Stradivarius cello.

Fevin, Antoine de, French composer; b. probably in Arras, 1474; d. Blois, Jan. 1512. He was a younger contemporary of Josquin des Prez, whose style he emulated. He composed 12 Masses, 6 of which were printed in collections by Petrucci (1515) and Antico (1516); also 29 motets, 3 *Magnificats*, and Lamentations (publ. by Montanus in 1549). 3 works by Fevin are in the archives of Toledo Cathedral (cf. F. Rubio Piqueras, *Música y músicos toledanos*, 1923). 6 motets were printed in Petrucci's *Motetti della corona* (1514), and some French chansons in various collections. Fevin's Mass *Mente tota* is reprinted in Expert's *Maîtres musiciens* (vol. 5); a 6-voice motet and parts of Masses are in Eslava's *Lira sacro-hispana*; a 4-voice *Kyrie* in Burney's *General History of Music* (vol. 2); the Mass *Ave Maria* and *Benedictus et Hosanna* in Delporte's *Collection de Polyphonie classique*; several motets reprinted by B. Kahmann (Amsterdam, 1951).

BIBLIOGRAPHY: P. Wagner, in *Geschichte der Messe* (vol. I); J. Delporte, *Revue Liturgique et Musicale* (Jan.-Feb. 1935).

Fevin, Robert, composer; a native of Cambrai, probably a relative of **Antoine Fevin.** He was maestro di cappella to the Duke of Savoy at the beginning of the 16th century. One Mass, *Le Vilain jaloux,* probably by Robert Fevin, was printed by Petrucci as by Antoine Fevin; another, on *La sol fa re mi,* is in the Munich Library.

Février, Henri, French opera composer; b. Paris, Oct. 2, 1875; d. there, July 6, 1957. He studied at the Cons. with Fauré, Leroux, Messager, Pugno, and Massenet; composed the operas *Le Roi aveugle* (Paris, May 8, 1906), *Monna Vanna* (Paris, Jan. 13, 1909), *Gismonda* (Chicago, Jan. 14, 1919; Paris, Oct. 15, 1919), *La Damnation de Blanche-Fleur* (Monte Carlo, March 13, 1920), *La Femme nue* (Monte Carlo, March 23, 1929); the operettas *Agnès, dame galante* (1912), *Carmosine* (1913), *Île désenchantée* (Paris, Nov. 21, 1925), etc. Février wrote the monograph, *André Messager; mon maître, mon ami* (Paris, 1948).

Ffrangcon-Davies, David Thomas (real name **David Thomas Davis;** the surname Ffrangcon was taken from the Nant-Ffrangcon mountain range near his birthplace), prominent British baritone; b. Bethesda, Caernarvon, Dec. 11, 1855; d. London, April 13, 1918. He was ordained a priest in 1884, but later left the church to take up a musical career; studied singing with Richard Latter, Shakespeare, and Randegger in London; made his concert debut in Manchester (Jan. 6, 1890); stage debut at Drury Lane Theatre (April 26, 1890). From 1896–98, he sang in festivals throughout the U.S. and Canada; then lived in Berlin (1898–1901); from 1903, professor of singing at the Royal College of Music, London. After a nervous breakdown in 1907 he gave up public singing. His book, *The Singing of the Future* (London, 1905; preface by Elgar), was republished by his daughter, Marjorie Ffrangcon-Davies, as Part II of *David Thomas Ffrangcon-Davies, His Life and Book* (London, 1938; introduction by Ernest Newman).

Fiala, George, Russian-born Canadian composer; b. Kiev, March 31, 1922. He took piano lessons at the music school for gifted children in Kiev; then studied composition at the Kiev Cons. with Revutsky, Liatoshinsky and others (1939–41). When the Germans occupied Kiev in 1942, he went to Berlin, where he continued his studies despite wartime difficulties; also took courses in conducting with Furtwängler. In 1945 he moved to Belgium, where he became a student of Léon Jongen at the Brussels Cons. In 1949 he emigrated to Canada; settled in Montreal; became a Canadian citizen in 1955. Besides his activities as a composer, pianist and teacher, he also became music producer with the Russian section of the Radio-Canada International. His compositions still retain traces of Russian and Ukrainian modalities; the settings are formally in a classical vein.

WORKS: Piano Concerto (1946); *Autumn Music* for orch. (1949); Symph. in E minor (1950); Concertino for Solo Piano, Trumpet, Timpani and Strings (1950); *Suite Concertante* for oboe and strings (1956); *Introduction and Fugato* for English horn and strings (1961); *Capriccio* for piano and orch. (1962); *Shadows of Our Forgotten Ancestors,* symph. poem (1962); *Divertimento Concertante* for violin and orch. (1965); *Eulogy,* in memory of President Kennedy, for orch. (1965); *Canadian Credo* for chorus and orch. (1966); *Montréal,* symph. suite (1968); *Musique Concertante* for piano and orch. (1968); *Serenade Concertante* for cello and strings (1968); *Sinfonietta Concertata* for solo free bass accordion, harpsichord and strings (1971); *Overture Burlesque* (1972); *5 Ukrainian Songs* for voice and orch. (1973); Violin Concerto (1973); Symph. No. 4, *Ukrainian* (1973); *Ukrainian Suite* for cello and piano (1948); Wind Quintet (1948); Trio for Oboe, Cello and Piano (1948); Woodwind Octet (1948); 2 saxophone quartets (1955, 1961); String Quartet (1956); Quartet for 4 Cellos (1957); Piano Quartet (1957); Violin Sonatina (1959); Cello Sonata (1969); Violin Sonata (1969); *Musique à Trois* for string trio (1970); Saxophone Sonata (1970); *Duo Sonata* for violin and harp (1971); *Sonata Fantasia* for cello and piano (1971); *Sonata da Camera* for soprano saxophone and free bass accordion (1971); *Musique à quatre* for string quartet (1972); *Concertino Canadese* for 4 harps (1972); *Sonata Breve* for clarinet and harp (1972); 8 piano sonatas (No. 7, 1947; No. 8, 1970); *10 Postludes* for piano (1947, revised 1968); *Australian Suite* for piano (1963); *3 Bagatelles* for piano (1968); 2-Piano Sonata (1970).

Fibich, Zdenko, significant Czech composer; b. Seboriče, Dec. 21, 1850; d. Prague, Oct. 15, 1900. He studied first in Prague, then at the Leipzig Cons. with Moscheles (piano) and Richter (theory). Upon his return to Prague, he occupied the posts of conductor of the National Theater (1875–78) and director of the Russian Church choir (1878–81). From then on, he continued to live in Prague, devoting himself mainly to composition. In his music, he was greatly influenced by Wagner, and applied quasi-Wagnerian methods even when treating national Bohemian subjects. His main distinction was a gift of facile melody, and he was at his best in his short pieces, such as *Poème*, op. 41, no. 6, for piano, which has become extremely popular through many arrangements for various instrumental combinations.
WORKS: operas (produced at Prague): *Bukovin* (April 16, 1874); *Blaník* (Nov. 25, 1881); *Nevěsta Messinska* (*The Bride of Messina;* March 28, 1884; very popular); *Bouře* (*The Tempest;* March 1, 1895); *Hédy* after Byron's *Don Juan* (Feb. 12, 1896); *Sarka* (Dec. 28, 1897); *Pad Arkuna* (*The Fall of Arkun;* produced posthumously, Nov. 9, 1900; his most important work); music to the dramatic trilogy *Hippodamia* by Vrchlický, a sequence of 3 scenic melodramas with actors reciting to orchestral accompaniment: (1) *Namluvy, Pelopovy* (*The Wooing of Pelops,* Feb. 21, 1890); (2) *Smír Tantaluv* (*The Atonement of Tantalus,* June 2, 1891); (3) *Smrt Hippodamia* (*Hippodamia's Death,* Nov. 8, 1891). For orch.: 3 symphonies: No. 1 (1883); No. 2 (1893); No. 3, in E minor (1898); symphonic poems: *Othello* (1873); *Zaboj, Slavoj a Ludek* (1873); *Toman a lesni panna* (*Toman and the Wood Nymph;* 1875); *Bouře* (*The Tempest;* 1880); *Vesna* (*Spring;* 1881); *Vigiliae,* for small orch. (1883); *V Podvečer* (*At Twilight;* 1893); a choral ballad, *Die Windsbraut;* melodramas: *Stědry Den* (*Christmas Day;* 1875); *Vodnik* (*The Water Sprite;* 1883); *Hákon* (1888); *Věčnost* (*Eternity;* 1878); *Spring Romanza* for chorus and orch. (1880); 2 string quartets; piano quartet; *Romance* for violin and piano; piano pieces; songs; choruses. He also published a method for piano.
BIBLIOGRAPHY: C. L. Richter, *Zdenko Fibich* (Prague, 1899); Zd. Nejedlý, *Fibich* (Prague, 1900); O. Hostinský, *Erinnerungen an Fibich* (1909); J. Bartoš, *Zdenko Fibich* (1913); A. Rektorys, *Zdenko Fibich* (2 vols., Prague, 1952).

Ficher, Jacobo, Argentinian composer; b. Odessa, Jan. 14, 1896. He studied violin with Stolarsky and Korguev in Odessa and composition with Kalafati and Steinberg at the St. Petersburg Cons., graduating in 1917. In 1923 he left Russia and emigrated to Argentina; earned his living by playing the violin in theater orchestras in Buenos Aires. His music is characterized by a rhapsodic fluency on development and a rich harmonic consistency. A prolific composer, he wrote for the stage, for orchestra and for voice; he particularly excelled in chamber music.
WORKS: CHAMBER OPERAS: *The Bear* (1952) and *Proposal in Marriage* (1955), both after Chekhov; the ballets *Colombina de Hoy* (1933), *Los Invitados* (1933), *Golondrina* (1942); 8 symphonies (1932, 1933, 1940, 1946, 1947, 1956, 1959, 1964); *Sulamita,* symph. poem (Buenos Aires, July 20, 1929); *Obertura patetica* (Buenos Aires, May 17, 1930); Violin Concerto (1942); 3 piano concertos (1945, 1954, 1960); Flute Concerto (1965); CHAMBER MUSIC: 4 string quartets (1927, 1936, 1943, 1952); Piano Quintet (1961); Piano Trio (1967); 3 violin sonatas (1929, 1945, 1959); *Suite en estilo antiguo* for woodwind quintet (1930); Sonata for Viola, Flute and Piano (1931); Sonatina for Saxophone, Trumpet and Piano (1932); Piano Trio (1935); Flute Sonata (1935); Clarinet Sonata (1937); Oboe Sonata (1940); Cello Sonata (1943); Sonata for Flute and Clarinet (1949); Sonata for Flute, Oboe and Bassoon (1950); Viola Sonata (1953); 8 piano sonatas; several sets of piano pieces (including 2 groups of effective "fables," descriptive of animals).
BIBLIOGRAPHY: B. Zipman, *Jacobo Ficher* (Buenos Aires, 1966).

Fickenscher, Arthur, American composer and pianist; b. Aurora, Ill., March 9, 1871; d. San Francisco, April 15, 1954. He studied at the Munich Cons.; toured the U.S. as accompanist to famous singers, among them Bispham and Schumann-Heink. From 1920 till 1941 he was head of the Music Dept. of the Univ. of Virginia, Charlottesville. In 1947 he settled in San Francisco. A musician of an inquisitive mind, he elaborated a system of pure intonation; contrived the "Polytone," an instrument designed to play music in which the octave is subdivided into 60 tones; publ. an article, "The Polytone and the Potentialities of a Purer Intonation," *Musical Quarterly* (July 1941).
WORKS: His major work was the *Evolutionary Quintet,* evolved from a violin sonata and an orchestral scherzo written in the 1890's; the manuscripts were burned in the San Francisco earthquake and fire of 1906; the musical material was then used from memory for a quintet for piano and strings, in 2 movements; the second movement, entitled *The Seventh Realm,* became a separate work. He also wrote *Willowwave and Wellowway* for orch. (1925); *The Day of Judgment,* for orch. (1927; Grand Rapids, Feb. 10, 1934); *Out of the Gay Nineties,* for orch. (Richmond, Va., Dec. 4, 1934, composer conducting); *Variations on a Theme in Medieval Style* for string orch. (1937); *Dies Irae,* for chamber orch. (1927); *The Chamber Blue,* a mimodrama for orch., soli, women's chorus, and dancers (Univ. of Virginia, April 5, 1938); a large choral work, with orch. *The Land East of the Sun and West of the Moon* (after William Morris).

Ficker, Rudolf von, distinguished German musicologist; b. Munich, June 11, 1886; d. Igls, near Innsbruck, Aug. 2, 1954. From 1905–1912 he studied at the Univ. of Vienna with Adler (musicology), and in Munich with Thuille and Courvoisier (composition). He held various teaching posts before his appointment as prof. at the Univ. of Munich (1930). He was a specialist in early Gothic music.

WRITINGS: "Die Musik des Mittelalters und ihre Beziehungen zum Geistesleben," *Vierteljahrsschrift für Literaturwissenschaft und Geistesgeschichte* (1925); "Polyphonic Music of the Gothic Period," *Musical Quarterly* (Oct. 1929); "Agwillare, a Piece of Late Gothic Minstrelsy," *Musical Quarterly* (April 1936); "Probleme der modalen Notation," *Acta Musicologica* (1946). He edited vol. XXVII, 1 (4th selection from the Trent Codices; in collaboration with A. Orel) and vol. XXXI (5th selection) in the *Denkmäler der Tonkunst in Österreich;* likewise the *Sederunt principes* of Pérotin (1930).

Fiedler, Arthur, highly popular American conductor; b. Boston, Dec. 17, 1894. He studied with his father, **Emanuel Fiedler,** a violinist of the Boston Symphony Orch.; after graduating from high school in Boston, he went to Berlin, where he studied with Willy Hess. He returned to the U.S. in 1914, and soon joined the Boston Symph. as viola player; in 1929 he organized the Esplanade Concerts in Boston, playing light and classical music outdoors; in 1930 he was appointed conductor of the Boston Pops, a series of summer concerts. Adroitly combining music of popular appeal with movements from classical symphonies and occasional modern works, and employing soloists, Fiedler built an eager audience in Boston; traveled with his especially assembled orchestra all over the U.S., and in Europe. In 1976 he received the Presidential Medal of Freedom.

BIBLIOGRAPHY: R. Moore, *Fiedler, The Colorful Mr. Pops* (Boston, 1968); C. G. Wilson, *Arthur Fiedler, Music for the Millions* (N.Y., 1968).

Fiedler, Max, German conductor; b. Zittau, Dec. 31, 1859; d. Stockholm, Dec. 1, 1939. He was a piano pupil of his father, and studied the organ and theory with G. Albrecht; attended the Leipzig Cons. (1877–80). In 1882, appointed teacher at the Hamburg Cons.; in 1903 director; in 1904 he succeeded Barth as conductor of the Hamburg Philharmonic Society. Although he had won an enviable reputation as a concert pianist, he soon abandoned that career and rapidly won distinction as a conductor. He was guest conductor of the N.Y. Philharmonic Orchestra during the season of 1905–06; in 1907, conducted the London Symph. Orch. The climax of his career was the prestigious appointment as conductor of the Boston Symphony Orchestra, the position he held from 1908 to 1912. In 1934 he conducted in Sweden. He composed a symphony, a piano quintet and a string quartet, a *Lustspiel* overture, piano pieces, and songs.

BIBLIOGRAPHY: G. Degmek, *Max Fiedler; Werden und Werken* (Essen, 1940).

Field, John, remarkable Irish pianist and composer; b. Dublin, July 26, 1782; d. Moscow, Jan. 23, 1837. His father was a violinist; his grandfather, an organist; it was from his grandfather that he received his first instruction in music. He then had lessons with Clementi, and was also employed in the salesrooms of Clementi's music establishment in London. In 1802 he followed Clementi to Paris, and in 1803 to St. Petersburg, where Field settled as a teacher and performer. After many concert tours in Russia, he returned to England temporarily, and performed his Concerto in E-flat with the London Philharmonic (Feb. 27, 1832); he continued a European tour in 1833, playing in Paris, in Switzerland, and in Italy. He was stricken with an ailment at Naples, and remained in a hospital for nine months; at the end of his resources, he was persuaded by a friendly Russian family to return to Moscow. On the way, he was able to give a concert in Vienna with extraordinary success; but the combination of alcoholism and general ill health led to his death two years after arrival in Moscow. Field's historical position is of importance, even though his music in itself does not reveal a great original talent. He was undoubtedly a precursor of Chopin in his treatment of piano technique; he was also the originator of keyboard nocturnes. He greatly developed the free fantasias and piano recitative, while following the basic precepts of classical music. Like Chopin after him, Field wrote mainly for the piano; he composed 7 piano concertos; 4 sonatas; 18 nocturnes; polonaises and other pieces, also a quintet for piano and strings and 2 divertimenti for piano, strings, and flute.

BIBLIOGRAPHY: F. Liszt, *Über John Fields Nocturnes* (Hamburg, 1859; also in vol. IV of Liszt's *Gesammelte Schriften*, Leipzig, 1882); H. Dessauer, *John Field, sein Leben und seine Werke* (Langensalza, 1912); Wm. H. Grattan Flood, *John Field of Dublin* (Dublin, 1920); E. von Tideböhl, "Reminiscences of John Field," *Monthly Musical Record* (1923); E. Blom, "John Field," *Chesterian* (1930); A. Nikolaev, *John Field* (Moscow, 1960); Patrick Piggott, *The Life and Music of John Field* (London, 1973).

Fields, James, American pianist; b. Los Angeles, Nov. 1, 1948. He studied piano with Ethel Leginska and Victor Aller; appeared in public as a child. In 1965 he won a debut grant of the Young Musicians Foundation in California, which catapulted him into a promising concert career.

Fielitz, Alexander von, German conductor and composer; b. Leipzig, Dec. 28, 1860; d. Bad Salzungen, July 29, 1930. He was of Slavic origin; his mother was Russian. He studied piano with Julius Schulhoff and composition with Kretschmer in Dresden; in conducting he profited by the advice of Nikisch. He conducted opera in various German towns; a nervous disorder caused him to take a prolonged rest in Italy (1887–97); then he settled in Berlin as a teacher. From 1905–08 he was in Chicago, where he organized an orch. and conducted it for a season; in 1908 he returned to Berlin as teacher and later director (1916) at Stern's Cons. He wrote a number of songs and piano pieces; his song cycle *Eliland* and his songs based on Tuscan folk music were quite popular; he also wrote 2 operas, *Vendetta* (Lübeck, 1891) and *Das stille Dorf* (Hamburg, March 13, 1900).

Figner, Nicolay, celebrated Russian tenor; b. Nikiforovka, in the Kazan government, Feb. 21, 1857; d. Kiev, Dec. 13, 1919. He was a lieutenant in the Russian Navy before his voice was discovered; then he studied diligently in Milan; in 1887 he returned to Russia and was engaged as a tenor at the Imperial Theater in St. Petersburg. He was the favorite tenor of

Tchaikovsky and was selected to sing the leading role in the première of *The Queen of Spades;* his interpretation of Lensky in *Eugene Onegin* was also famous. In 1889 he married the Italian soprano **Medea Mei,** who wrote a book of memoirs (St. Petersburg, 1912) in which she described their careers.

BIBLIOGRAPHY: *Nicolay Figner: Recollections, Letters, Materials* (Leningrad, 1968).

Figueredo, Carlos, Venezuelan composer; b. Valencia, Aug. 15, 1910. He studied with Vicente Emilio Sojo at the Caracas School of Music graduating in 1947. In 1948 he entered the diplomatic service as a cultural attaché at the Venezuelan Embassy in Paris, consul in Copenhagen, and then in Madrid. However, he did not abandon music; he wrote 4 competent symphonies (1947, 1948, 1951, 1953), some acceptable chamber music and tolerable choruses.

Figulus (real name **Töpfer**), **Wolfgang,** German writer on music; b. Naumburg, c.1525; d. Meissen, Sept. 1589. He studied in Leipzig; 1549–51, cantor at the Thomasschule in Leipzig; 1551–58, at the Fürstenschule in Meissen. He wrote *Elementa musicae* (1555; many other editions); revised Martin Agricola's *Deutsche Musica* (1560); publ. a book of motets, *Precationes* (Leipzig, 1553); *Cantiones sacrae* (1575); and *Hymni sacri et scholastici* (revised by his son-in-law, Friedrich Birck, 1604); a collection of Christmas songs, containing works of his own, of Martin Agricola and others, was publ. posthumously in two books (1594 and 1605).

Figuš-Bystrý, Villiam, Slovak composer; b. Banská Bystrica, Feb. 28, 1875; d. there, May 11, 1937. He spent many years in collecting Slovak folk melodies, which he publ. in 5 vols. (1906–15) for voice and piano; also publ. a collection of 1000 arranged for piano only (1928). He further wrote an opera, *Detvan* (Bratislava, Aug. 1, 1928); a cantata *Slovenská Piesen* (1913); an orchestral suite *From My Youth;* Piano Quartet; Piano Trio; 3 sonatines for violin and piano; violin pieces; piano works; choruses and songs.

Filev, Ivan, Bulgarian composer and conductor; b. Kazanluk, June 22, 1941. He studied conducting with Iliev and composition with Goleminov and Raichev at the Bulgarian State Cons. in Sofia, graduating in 1968. He is currently conductor of the National Opera in Rousse.

WORKS: 2 piano concertinos (1963, 1967); String Quartet (1964); *Music for Strings, Winds and Piano* (1966); Symphony for String Orch. (1967); *5 Pieces for Orch.* (1967); Rondo for String Orch. (1968); Prelude and Fugue for Orch. (1968); *Symphonic Forms* (1970); Concerto for Orch. (1973).

Filiasi, Lorenzo, Italian composer; b. Naples, March 25, 1878; d. Rome, July 30, 1963. He studied at the Cons. di S. Pietro a Majella with Nicola d'Arienzo. His first success came with the opera *Manuel Menendez,* which won the Sonzogno Competition Prize in 1902, and was produced in Milan (May 15, 1904); his other operas were *Fior di Neve* (La Scala, April 1, 1911), *Messidoro* (1912), etc. He also wrote a pantomime,

Pierrot e Bluette (1895); a choral work with orch., *La preghiera del marinaio italiano; Visioni romantiche* for orch.; violin pieces and many songs.

Filippi, Filippo, Italian composer and critic; b. Vicenza, Jan. 13, 1830; d. Milan, June 25, 1887. He studied law at Padua, taking his degree in 1853. In 1852 he began his career as a music critic with a warm defense of Verdi's *Rigoletto;* from 1858 till 1862 was editor of the *Gazzetta Musicale,* and in 1859 music critic of the newly founded *Perseveranza.* He publ. a collection of essays on great musicians, *Musica e Musicisti* (Milan, 1876); as a zealous Wagnerite he wrote a pamphlet, *Riccardo Wagner* (in German, as *Richard Wagner: eine musikalische Reise in das Reich der Zukunft,* 1876); also publ. a monograph *Della vita e delle opere di Adolfo Fumagalli* (Milan, 1857); composed a string quintet, 9 string quartets, piano trio; piano pieces, songs.

Filke, Max, German composer; b. Steubendorf-Leobschütz, Silesia, Oct. 5, 1855; d. Breslau, Oct. 8, 1911. He studied with Brosig in Breslau and with Haberl at the Kirchenmusikschule in Regensburg (1877); then with Piutti at the Leipzig Cons. (1880); was engaged as choirmaster at Straubing (1881) and conductor of the "Sängerkreis" at Cologne (1890); then became director at the Cathedral in Breslau and prof. at the institute for church music there. His numerous compositions for the church assign him a distinguished position among composers of sacred music.

Filleul, Henry, French composer; b. Laval, May 11, 1877; d. Saint-Omer, May 1, 1959. He studied at the Paris Cons. with Lavignac and Casadesus; in 1908 became director of the École nationale de musique at St. Omer, France.

WORKS: *Le Jugement de Triboulet,* comic opera (1923); oratorios: *Le Christ vainqueur* (1925), *Le Miracle de Lourdes* (1927); *Les Doulces Joyes de Nostre Dame* (1928); *Jeanne d'Arc* (1929); *Eva* (1931); *Variations symphoniques sur un thème languedocien* (1939); *Fantaisie concertante* for piano and orch. (1950); Cello Concerto; violin pieces with organ; motets; male choruses; etc.

BIBLIOGRAPHY: *Hommage à Henri Filleul* (St. Omer, 1952).

Fillmore, Henry (full name **James Henry Fillmore, Jr.**), American bandleader and composer; b. Cincinnati, Feb. 3, 1881; d. Miami, Florida, Dec. 7, 1956. His paternal grandfather was August Damerin Fillmore (second cousin of President Millard Fillmore); his father James Henry Fillmore and his uncles Fred A. and Charles M. Fillmore were the founders of the Cincinnati music publishing firm of Fillmore Bros. Co. Henry Fillmore was educated at the Miami, Ohio, Military Institute, and later at the Cincinnati College of Music. As a bandmaster, he led the Syrian Shrine Band of Cincinnati to national prominence in the period 1920–26, making several transcontinental tours; in 1915 he founded the Fillmore Band, which was one of the earliest bands to make regular radio broadcasts (1927–34). In 1938 he moved to Miami, Florida, where he conducted bands at the Orange Bowl. He is best known, however, as the composer of numerous popular marches (*Americans We, Men of Ohio, His Honor*, et al.), second only to Sousa's in their tuneful liveliness. He was also the leading proponent of the "trombone smear," a humorous effect of the trombone glissando. He used numerous pseudonyms in his published pieces (**Al Hayes, Harry Hartley, Ray Hall, Gus Beans, Henrietta Moore, and Harold Bennett**, under which name he published the popular *Military Escort March*). He was also a compiler of sacred songs and tunebooks. In 1956 he received an honorary Dr. Mus. degree from the Univ. of Miami, Florida.

Fillmore, John Comfort, American music educator; b. New London, Conn., Feb. 4, 1843; d. there, Aug. 15, 1898. He was a pupil of G. W. Steele at Oberlin College, Ohio; then at Leipzig Cons. (1865–67). He was director of the music department at Oberlin College (1867); at Ripon College, Wis. (1868–78); at Milwaukee College for Women (1878–84). He founded (1884) the Milwaukee School of Music, of which he was the director until 1895, when he took charge of the School of Music of Pomona College, Claremont, Calif.
WRITINGS: *Pianoforte Music: Its History, with Biographical Sketches and Critical Estimates of its Greatest Masters* (Chicago, 1883); *New Lessons in Harmony* (1887); *Lessons in Music History* (1888); *A Study of Omaha Indian Music* (with Alice C. Fletcher and F. La Flesche, 1893).

Filtz, Anton, talented German composer; b. Eichstätt, Sept. 1733 (baptized, Sept. 22, 1733); d. Mannheim, March (buried March 14), 1760. He was a pupil of J. Stamitz; from 1754, first cellist in the Mannheim Orch. He belongs to the school of Mannheim Symphonists, early practitioners of classic instrumental style. That his works must have enjoyed great popularity seems to be proved by the numerous reprints issued at London and Amsterdam, pirated from the original Paris editions. He was exceptionally prolific; in the span of his brief life he completed 41 symphonies, many trio sonatas, string trios, sonatas for violin, cello, flute, etc., and concertos for various instruments. Riemann publ. 4 symphonies by Filtz in *Denkmäler der Tonkunst in Bayern* (4 and 13; formerly 3.i and 7.ii); 2 trios (ibid., 27; formerly 15); and one in *Collegium Musicum.*

Finagin, Alexei, Russian musicologist; b. St. Petersburg, March 16, 1890; d. there (Leningrad), Feb. 4, 1942. He publ. *Russian Folksongs* (Petrograd, 1923); *Fomin: His Life and Works* (in vol. 1 of *Music and Musical Life of Old Russia*; Leningrad, 1927); contributed to various periodicals.

Finck, Heinrich, German composer; b. Bamberg, 1445; d. in the Schottenkloster, Vienna, June 9, 1527. He was in the service of 3 Polish kings: Johann Albert (1492), Alexander (1501), and Sigismund (1506); was in Cracow from at least 1491; 1492, visited Budapest, Vienna, and Torgau, but returned to Poland; 1510–13, Kapellmeister to Duke Ulrich at Stuttgart; then at the court of Maximilian I, in Augsburg; 1520, appointed composer of the cathedral chapter at Salzburg; 1525–26, Hofkapellmeister to Ferdinand I at Vienna,

where he was succeeded by his pupil Arnold von Bruck.
WORKS: *Schöne auserlesene Lieder des hochberühmten Heinrich Finckens* (Nuremberg, 1536; reprinted in R. Eitner's *Publikationen*, vol. VIII); other songs publ. by Salblinger (1545) and by Rhaw (1542). Reprints are to be found in Blume's *Das Chorwerk* (hymns ed. by R. Gerber; the *Missa in summis*), in A. W. Ambros' *Geschichte der Musik* (vol. 5), in the *Denkmäler der Tonkunst in Österreich* (72; formerly 37.ii), in H. J. Moser's *Kantorei der Spätgotik.*
BIBLIOGRAPHY: H. Riemann, in *Kirchenmusikalisches Jahrbuch* (1897); P. Wagner, in *Geschichte der Messe* (I, 275).

Finck, Henry Theophilus, American music critic and editor; b. Bethel, Missouri, Sept. 22, 1854; d. Rumford Falls, Maine, Oct. 1, 1926. He was brought up in Oregon; then entered Harvard Univ., where he studied with J. K. Paine. After graduation in 1876 he went to Germany; studied comparative psychology in Berlin and Vienna, and published a book *Romantic Love and Personal Beauty* (1887), propounding a theory that romantic love was unknown to the ancient nations. He was music critic for the *Nation* magazine from 1881 to 1924; music editor of the *N.Y. Evening Post.* Finck was a brilliant journalist; in his books on music he stressed the personal and psychological elements.
WRITINGS: *Chopin, and Other Musical Essays* (1889); *Wagner and His Works* (N.Y., 1893; reprinted 1968); *Pictorial Wagner* (1899); *Songs and Song Writers* (1900); *Grieg and His Music* (1909); *Success in Music and How It Is Won* (1909); *Massenet and His Operas* (1910); *Richard Strauss* (1917); *My Adventures in the Golden Age of Music* (1926). He edited *50 Master Songs* (1902), *50 Schubert Songs* (1903), and *50 Grieg Songs* (1909).

Finck, Hermann, German composer, great-nephew of **Heinrich Finck**; b. Pirna, Saxony, March 21, 1527; d. Wittenberg, Dec. 28, 1558. He was educated at the court chapel of King Ferdinand of Bohemia; studied at Wittenberg Univ. (1545); then taught music there (1554); was appointed organist in 1557. His major work is the treatise *Practica musica*, publ. by Rhaw (1556), and subdivided into 5 parts. Some of Hermann Finck's works are reprinted by Eitner in his *Publikationen* (vol. VIII, 1879).

Findeisen, Nicolai, Russian music historian and editor; b. St. Petersburg, July 24, 1868; d. there, Sept. 20, 1928. He studied with Nikolai Sokolov; in 1893 he founded the *Russian Musical Gazette* and remained its editor until it ceased publication in 1917. His writings include monographs on Verstovsky (1890), Serov (1900), Dargomyzhsky (1902), Anton Rubinstein (1905), and Rimsky-Korsakov (1908); he published a series of brochures and books on Glinka; the first volume of a projected large biography, *Glinka in Spain*, appeared in 1896; a catalogue of Glinka's manuscripts, letters, and portraits was publ. in 1898; he also edited Glinka's correspondence (1908). His major achievement was the extensive history of Russian music up to the year 1800, publ. in two vols. (partly posthumously) in Leningrad (1928–29) under the title

Sketches of Music in Russia from the most Ancient Times Until the End of the 18th Century.

Findeisen, Otto, composer of operettas and theater conductor; b. Brünn, Dec. 23, 1862; d. Leipzig, Jan. 23, 1947. He conducted in Magdeburg from 1890, and produced two of his operettas there: *Der alte Dessauer* (1890) and *Hennigs von Treffenfeld* (1891). Other light operas were: *Frau Holle* (Berlin, 1904); *Kleopatra* (Hamburg, 1897); *Der Spottvogel* (Bremen, 1898); *Der Sühneprinz* (Leipzig, 1904); *Sonnenguckerl* (Vienna, 1908); *Meister Pinkebank* (Vienna, 1909), etc.

Fine, Irving, remarkable American composer; b. Boston, Dec. 3, 1914; d. there, Aug. 23, 1962. He studied with Walter Piston at Harvard Univ. (B.A., 1937; M.A., 1938) and with Nadia Boulanger in Cambridge, Mass. (1938) and in France (1939); also took a course in choral conducting with A. T. Davison. He was assistant prof. of music at Harvard (1947–50); in 1950 appointed prof. at Brandeis Univ.; also a member of the faculty at the Berkshire Music Center in Tanglewood, Mass. He was at first influenced by Stravinsky and Hindemith, and adopted a cosmopolitan style of composition in which contrapuntal elaboration and energetic rhythm were his main concerns; later on, however, he developed a distinctive style of his own with a lyrical flow of cohesive melody supported by lucid polyphony.
WORKS: Violin Sonata (1946); *Toccata concertante* for orch. (1947); Partita for Wind Quintet (1948); suite, *Alice in Wonderland* for chorus and orch. (1949); String Quartet (1950); Nocturne for Strings and Harp (1951); Fantasy for String Trio (1952); several ingenious piano pieces for children, and his capital work, *Symphony 1962* (Boston Symph. Orch., March 23, 1962).

Fine, Vivian, American composer; b. Chicago, Sept. 28, 1913. She studied piano in N.Y. with Abby Whiteside, and composition with Ruth Crawford and Roger Sessions. She was active mainly as a piano teacher; in 1964 was appointed to the faculty of Bennington College. In her music, she adopts a cheerful neo-classical manner of composition, with a considerable injection of modernistic elements.
WORKS: 2 ballets, *The Race of Life* (1938) and *Alcestis* (1960); a one-act stage work, *A Guide to the Life Expectancy of a Rose* for voices and 5 instruments (1957; N.Y., Feb. 7, 1959); *The Great Wall of China* for violin, flute, cello and piano, to the text of Kafka (1948); Concertino for Piano and Orch. (1944); *Capriccio* for oboe and string trio (1946); Divertimento for Cello and Percussion (1951); Violin Sonata (1952); String Quartet (1957); Duo for Flute and Viola (1961); Chamber Concerto for Cello and 6 Instruments (1966); Quintet for String Trio, Trumpet and Harp (1967); *Meeting for Equal Rights: 1866,* a cantata (N.Y., May 20, 1976).

Fink, Christian, German organist and composer; b. Dettingen, Aug. 9, 1822; d. Esslingen, near Stuttgart, Sept. 5, 1911. He studied at the Leipzig Cons.; became organist there (1856–60); in 1863 was appointed church organist at Esslingen; published numerous organ works. He was greatly esteemed in Germany; his choral works and organ pieces were often performed.

Fink, Gottfried Wilhelm, German writer on music and editor; b. Sulza, Thuringia, March 7, 1783; d. Leipzig, Aug. 27, 1846. He studied music and theology in Leipzig; wrote the criticism in the *Allgemeine Musikalische Zeitung* from 1808; in 1827 he became editor of this influential publication (until 1841); also contributed articles on music and musicians to various German encyclopedias. His extensive music history remain in MS. Among his publications are the collections of German songs, *Musikalischer Hausschatz* (Leipzig, 1843) and *Die deutsche Liedertafel* (Leipzig, 1846). For a complete list of his writings, see the article by W. Boetticher in *Die Musik in Geschichte und Gegenwart.*

Finke, Fidelio Fritz, outstanding German composer; b. Josefsthal in Northern Bohemia, Oct. 22, 1891; d. Dresden, June 12, 1968. He studied with Vitězlav Novák at the Prague Cons.; later was composition teacher there (1915–1920); in 1920 he became supervisor of German music schools in Czechoslovakia, and teacher of composition at the German Academy of Music in Prague. He was subsequently director of the State Music Academy in Dresden (1946–51); in 1951 was appointed prof. of composition at the Hochschule für Musik in Leipzig. As a composer he followed the evolutionary path from the neo-Classicism of Brahms and Max Reger to the structural concepts of the New Vienna School.
WORKS: the operas *Die Jakobsfahrt* (Prague, 1937), *Der schlagfertige Liebhaber* (1950–53), and *Der Zauberfisch* (Dresden, June 3, 1960); *Das Lied der Zeit,* choreographic poem (1946); numerous pieces of chamber music, including 8 suites for various ensembles; Divertimento for Chamber Orch. (1964); a number of choruses; Toccata for Piano Left-Hand; organ works and songs.
BIBLIOGRAPHY: D. Härtwig, *Fidelio F. Finke. Leben und Werk* (Leipzig, 1970).

Finney, Ross Lee, distinguished American composer and teacher; b. Wells, Minnesota, Dec. 23, 1906. He studied at the Univ. of Minnesota with Donald Ferguson; also took cello lessons. He received a Bachelor of Arts degree in 1927 from Carleton College. In 1928 he went to Paris where he took lessons with Nadia Boulanger; returning to America he enrolled at Harvard Univ. where he attended the classes of Edward Burlingame Hill. For some 20 years (1929–48) he also had sporadic sessions with Sessions who advised him on modern techniques. He taught at Smith College from 1929 to 1947; concurrently he was on the faculty of Mt. Holyoke College (1938–40). During his sabbatical year in 1931 he went to Vienna where he took private lessons with Alban Berg in advanced composition; in 1937 he took a course in composition and musicology with Francesco Malipiero in Venice. In the interim he also taught composition at the Hartt School of Music in Hartford, Conn. (1941–42) and at Amherst College (1946–47). During the last year of World War II he served with the Office of Strategic Services in Paris;

he was slightly injured when he stepped on a land mine near the front and received the Purple Heart and Certificate of Merit. His professional career was facilitated by two Guggenheim Fellowships (1937, 1947) and a Pulitzer traveling fellowship (1937). In 1948 he was appointed composer-in-residence at the Univ. of Michigan in Ann Arbor, where he also was chairman of the Dept. of Composition; furthermore he established there an electronic music laboratory. Because of his wide-ranging background of studies, comprising strict Baroque structures in neo-classical forms, modern but tonal harmonies and the 12-tone technique, Finney's own music is marked by a catholicity of style and idiom, which paradoxically results in the formation of an individual manner of writing.

WORKS: 4 SYMPHONIES: No. 1, subtitled *Communiqué* (1942); No. 2 (Ann Arbor, Michigan, May 8, 1960); No. 3 (Philadelphia, March 6, 1964); and No. 4 (1972); Violin Concerto (1933); *Barbershop Ballad* for orch. (C.B.S., Feb. 6, 1940); *Overture for a Drama* (Rochester, N.Y., Oct. 28, 1941); *Hymn, Fuguing and Holiday* for orch. (1943); Piano Concerto No. 1 (1948); Variations for Orch. (1957; Minneapolis, Dec. 30, 1965); Concerto for Percussion and Orch. (1965); *Symphony Concertante* (1967); Piano Concerto No. 2 (1968); Violin Concerto No. 2 (Dallas, March 31, 1976); *Concerto for Strings* (N.Y., Dec. 5, 1977); CHAMBER MUSIC: 8 string quartets (1931–1960); 2 piano trios (1938, 1954); Piano Quartet (1948); 2 piano quintets (1953, 1961); String Quintet (1958); *Divertissement* for clarinet, violin, cello and piano (1964); 2 viola sonatas; 2 cello sonatas; 3 violin sonatas; 4 piano sonatas; CHORAL PIECES: *Pilgrim Psalms* (1945); *Spherical Madrigals* a cappella (1947); *Still Are New Worlds* for narrator, chorus, orch. and tape (1963); *Nun's Priest's Tale* for chorus, soloists, narrator, folksong singer with electric guitar, and orch. (1965); and *The Martyr's Elegy* for tenor, chorus and orch. (1966); several song cycles. He edited Geminiani's 12 sonatas for violin and piano (Northampton, Mass., 1935); wrote *The Game of Harmony* (N.Y., 1947).

BIBLIOGRAPHY: Paul Cooper, "The Music of Ross Lee Finney," *Musical Quarterly* (Jan. 1967).

Finney, Theodore Mitchell, American music educator and historian; brother of **Ross Lee Finney;** b. Fayette, Iowa, March 14, 1902. He studied at the Univ. of Minnesota; then at the American Cons. at Fontainebleau (1926) and in Berlin (1927–28). He was a member of the viola section in the Minneapolis Symph. Orch. (1923–25); then assistant prof. of music at Carleton College (1925–32) and lecturer at the Smith College Summer School (1930–38). In 1936 he was appointed head of the music department at Pittsburgh Univ. He publ. a practical college textbook, *A History of Music* (N.Y., 1935; revised ed., 1946); also *Hearing Music, A Guide to Music* (N.Y., 1941); *We Have Made Music* (essays; Pittsburgh, 1955); and some scholarly articles in music journals.

Fino, Giocondo, Italian composer; b. Turin, May 2, 1867; d. there, April 19, 1950. He studied Oriental languages and theology; concurrently took music lessons with Giovanni Bolzoni; he remained in Turin practically all his life. He wrote the operas *La festa del gra-*

no (Turin, 1910), and *Campana a gloria* (Turin, 1916); several stage works in the Piedmont dialect; biblical cantata, *Noemi e Ruth* (Bergamo, 1908); ballets, pantomimes, choral works; chamber music and piano pieces.

Finzi, Gerald, English composer; b. London, July 14, 1901; d. Oxford, Sept. 27, 1956. He studied composition with R. O. Morris; his first important work was *Severn Rhapsody* for chamber orch. (1924); its contemplative manner of writing and simplicity of harmonic expression remain characteristic of Finzi's music; its materials are often related to the songs of the English countryside. Other works: *Introit* for violin and orch. (1935); *Farewell to Arms* for tenor and chamber orch. (1945); Concerto for Clarinet and Strings (1949); *Intimations of Immortality* for tenor, chorus, and orch. (1950); Cello Concerto (1955); several groups of choral pieces.

Fiocco, Jean-Joseph, Belgian composer, second son of **Pietro Antonio Fiocco** (of the first marriage); b. Brussels, Dec. 1686 (baptized Dec. 15); d. there, March 30, 1746. He succeeded his father as music master at the ducal chapel, and held this post for 30 years (1714–44); wrote 5 oratorios, 8 psalms, 9 Requiems, motets, etc. Two copies of his *Sacri concentus* for 4 voices and 3 instruments are known to exist; most of his other works are lost.

BIBLIOGRAPHY: Christiane Stellfeld, *Les Fiocco* (Brussels, 1941).

Fiocco, Joseph-Hector, Belgian composer, seventh child of **Pietro Antonio Fiocco** (of his second marriage); b. Brussels, Jan. 1703; d. there, June 22, 1741. He was music master of the cathedral of Antwerp from 1731–37; then at Ste.-Gudule in Brussels until his death. He wrote numerous sacred works, published in *Monumenta Musicae Belgicae* (vol. III); also wrote *Pièces de Clavecin* (two suites of 12 pieces each).

BIBLIOGRAPHY: Christiane Stellfeld, *Les Fiocco* (Brussels, 1941).

Fiocco, Pietro Antonio, Italian composer; b. Venice, c.1650; d. Brussels, Sept. 3, 1714. He traveled to Germany, then settled in Brussels, marrying a Belgian lady in 1682; she died in 1691, and Fiocco remarried in 1692. He was music master of the ducal chapel in Brussels; in 1694 he established an opera enterprise; wrote special prologues for the operas of Lully; also wrote music for the court; his pastoral play *Le Retour du Printemps* was produced in 1699. A collection of his sacred concertos was published in Antwerp (1691). Among his instrumental works only a *Sonate à quatre* is extant. Two of his sons, **Jean-Joseph** and **Joseph-Hector** became professional musicians.

BIBLIOGRAPHY: Christiane Stellfeld, *Les Fiocco,* (Brussels, 1941).

Fioravanti, Valentino, Italian composer; b. Rome, Sept. 11, 1764; d. Capua, June 16, 1837. He studied in Rome with Jannaconi and with Sala and Fenaroli in Naples. Returning to Rome in 1782, he began his career as a prolific composer of operas. He visited Naples quite often; was in Paris in 1807; succeeded his teacher, Jannaconi, as maestro di cappella at St. Peter's in Rome in 1816; during his last period he wrote much church music.

WORKS: His earliest work, an intermezzo, was *Le avventure di Bertoldino* (Rome, 1784); he produced a comic opera *Gl' inganni fortunati* in Naples (1786); there followed *Il furbo contro al furbo* (Venice, Dec. 29, 1796). His greatest success was achieved by his comic opera *Le Cantatrici Villane*, first produced in Naples (1799) and then in Venice in a new version under the title *Le Virtuose ridicole* (Dec. 28, 1801); there were performances all over Europe, including Russia; the opera was particularly in favor with German audiences (under the title *Die Dorfsängerinnen*); other operas were: *La capricciosa pentita* (Milan, Oct. 2, 1802) and *I virtuosi ambulanti* (Paris, Sept. 26, 1807); Fioravanti produced 77 operas in all between 1784 and 1824. His autobiographical sketch was reprinted by G. Roberti in *La Gazzetta musicale* (1895).

Fioravanti, Vincenzo, Italian composer, son of **Valentino Fioravanti;** b. Rome, April 5, 1799; d. Naples, March 28, 1877. He studied with his father, and also with his father's teacher, Jannaconi; he also took lessons with Donizetti. He wrote a number of operas in the Neapolitan dialect; only a few of them (translated into conventional Italian) were produced outside Italy. He composed about 40 operas in all.

Fiorillo, Dante, American composer; b. New York, July 4, 1905. He studied the cello, and later began to compose without formal instruction. He held Guggenheim Fellowships in composition for four successive years (1935–39). Extraordinarily prolific, he wrote 12 symphonies; 11 string quartets; piano quintets and trios; piano sonatas; choral music. He vanished from the public world c.1950.

Fiorillo, Federigo, violinist and composer; b. Brunswick, Germany (baptized June 1), 1755; date and place of death unknown. He was taught by his father, **Ignazio Fiorillo;** he traveled as violinist and conductor; was in Riga (1782–84); in 1785 he went to Paris, where he participated in the Concert Spirituel; in 1788 he was in London, where he played the viola in Salomon's quartet. He probably remained in London until about 1815; then he was in Amsterdam and again in Paris. He was a prolific composer for violin and various combinations of string instruments; but he is known chiefly through his useful collection, *Études de Violon,* comprising 36 caprices, which were frequently reprinted.

Fiorillo, Ignazio, Italian composer, father of **Federigo Fiorillo;** b. Naples, May 11, 1715; d. Fritzlar, near Kassel, 1787. He studied with Durante and Leo in Naples; composed his first opera *Mandane* at the age of 20 (Venice, 1736). Other operas were: *Artimene* (Milan, 1738), *Partenope nell' Adria* (Venice, 1738), and *Il Vincitor di se stesso.* (Venice, 1741). He traveled as a theater conductor; was appointed court conductor at Brunswick (1751); in 1762 he received a similar post at Kassel, retiring in 1780. He wrote a number of German operas in Brunswick, and 3 Italian operas in Kassel. An oratorio, *Isacco,* a Requiem, and other church works are also noteworthy.

Fiqué, Karl, German organist; b. St. Magnus, near Bremen, April 17, 1867; d. Brooklyn, N.Y., Dec. 7, 1930. After studying at the Leipzig Cons. with Carl Reinecke he emigrated to the U.S. (1887) and settled in Brooklyn, where he served as church organist and lectured at the Brooklyn Institute of Arts and Sciences (1897–1915). He married the soprano **Katherine Noack** (d. 1940). He wrote 2 comic operas in German: *Priesewitz* (Brooklyn, 1893) and *Der falsche Mufti* (N.Y., 1901); a string quartet, several choral works, and numerous piano pieces. Shortly before his death, he finished an operetta, *Merry Madrid.*

Firkušný, Rudolf, brilliant Czech pianist; b. Napajedla, Feb. 11, 1912. He studied piano at the Brno Cons., and Janáček, impressed by his musical talent as a wunderkind, gave him lessons in music theory; in 1928 he entered the Prague Cons., studied piano with Bilém Kurz, graduating as soloist in his own piano concerto at the age of 17. He then engaged on a European tour. He made his American debut in N.Y., January 13, 1938; in America he also took piano lessons with Schnabel, who was in N.Y. at the time. After the occupation of Czechoslovakia by the Germans, he definitely settled in New York in 1940. He subsequently revisited his liberated country, and gave concerts in Prague and Brno; also undertook concert tours in South America. He was also a member of the faculty of the Juilliard School of Music in N.Y. Firkušný represents the modern school of Central European art of piano playing at its best, successful in both classical and modern works; one of his outstanding accomplishments was his authentic renditions of the complete pianistic oeuvre of Janáček. As a composer, besides his early piano concerto, he wrote chamber music, and a number of virtuoso pieces for piano.

Fischer, Carl, music publisher; b. Buttstädt, Thuringia, Dec. 7, 1849; d. New York, Feb. 14, 1923. He studied music in Gotha; entered a partnership in an instrument manufacturing business with his brother **August Emil Fischer** in Bremen. In 1872 he went to New York and opened a music store at 79 East 4th Street; in 1923 the store was moved to 62 Cooper Square. He secured the rights for republishing orchestral scores and parts by German composers, eventually becoming one of the most important of American music publishing firms. From 1907 to 1931 the firm published a monthly periodical, the *Musical Observer,* edited by Gustav Sänger; in 1923 the business was incorporated and Carl Fischer's son **Walter S. Fischer** (b. New York, April 18, 1882; d. there, April 26, 1946) became president; after his death, Frank H. Connor (1903–77) was elected president; upon his death he was succeeded by his son. In 1909 the firm established a branch in Boston, which was expanded in 1960 through the purchase of the Charles Homeyer Music Co. of Boston; in 1935 a branch was also opened in Los Angeles, and in 1969 one in San Francisco. In 1947 the firm occupied a new building in N.Y. at 165 West 57th Street, which also housed a concert hall. The catalogue of the firm is representative of all genres of musical composition; early acquisitions were works by composers living in America, including Rachmaninoff and Ernest Bloch; in the last quarter of the century, the firm published a number of instrumental and vocal works by composers of the avant-garde, including some in graphic notation.

Fischer, Edwin, eminent Swiss pianist; b. Basel, Oct. 6, 1886; d. Zürich, Jan. 24, 1960. He studied with Hans Huber in Basel and with Martin Krause in Berlin; then taught at the Stern Cons., Berlin (1905–14); between 1926 and 1932 he was also engaged as conductor in Lübeck, Munich and Berlin. In 1942 he returned to Switzerland. He was renowned as one of the most intellectual pianists of his time and a distinguished pedagogue. He also published several valuable books on music: *J. S. Bach* (Potsdam, 1945); *Musikalische Betrachtungen* (Wiesbaden, 1949; in English as *Reflections on Music*, London, 1951); and *Beethovens Klaviersonaten* (Wiesbaden,1956).
BIBLIOGRAPHY: B. Gavoty, *Edwin Fischer* (Geneva, 1954).

Fischer, Emil, German operatic bass singer; b. Brunswick, June 13, 1838; d. Hamburg, Aug. 11, 1914. He received his vocal training entirely from his parents, who were opera singers; made his debut in Graz in 1857; then was with the Danzig Opera (1863–70); in Rotterdam (1875–80) and with the Dresden Opera (1880–85); then went to America; made his debut with the Metropolitan Opera Co. on Nov. 25, 1885, and remained on the staff for more than 20 years. He sang in public for the last time at the age of 71; lived mostly in N.Y. as vocal teacher; returned to Germany shortly before his death. He was particularly famous for his Wagnerian roles; his greatest impersonation was Hans Sachs in *Die Meistersinger.*

Fischer, Erich, German music editor and composer; b. Kreuzlingen, April 8, 1887. He studied musicology in Berlin at the Univ. under Kretzschmar, Stumpf, and Friedländer; received his Dr. phil. in 1909 with the dissertation *Über die Musik der Chinesen;* in 1914, he founded in Berlin the "Musikalische Hauskomödien," a society for the performance of little-known music by German composers, arranged as Singspiele with new words; for this venture he organized his own company of singers.

Fischer, Frederick, German conductor; b. Munich, May 25, 1868; d. St. Louis, April 17, 1931. He studied at the Royal Academy of Music in Munich; then came to the U.S., where he conducted the California Opera Co.; in 1904 he settled in St. Louis and was assistant conductor of the St. Louis Symph.; also guest conductor of the Boston People's Orch., choral societies, etc.; wrote music to the pageant *Missouri 100 Years Ago,* choral works, and songs.

Fischer, Jan, Czech composer; b. Louny, Sept. 15, 1921. He studied at the Prague Cons. (1940–45) and took lessons in composition from Řídký at the Master Class there (1945–48). His music occupies the safe ground of Central European Romanticism, not without some audacious exploits in euphonious dissonance.
WORKS: 5 operas: *Ženichové* (*Bridegrooms,* 1956; Brno, Oct. 13, 1957), *Romeo, Julie a tma* (*Romeo, Juliet and Darkness,* 1959–61; Brno, Sept. 14, 1962), *Oh, Mr. Fogg,* (comic chamber opera after Jules Verne's *Around the World in 80 Days,* 1967–70; Saarbrücken, June 27, 1971), *Miracle Theater,* radio opera (1970); and *Decamerone,* chamber opera (1975–76); a ballet, *Eufrosyne* (1951; Pilsen, 1956); *Pastoral Sinfonietta* (1944); Violin Concerto (1946); *Essay* for jazz orch. and solo piano (1947); *Popular Suite* for wind orch. and piano (1950); *Dance Suite* for orch. (1957); *Fantasia* for piano and orch. (1953); Symph. No. 1, *Monothematic* (1959); Clarinet Concerto (1965); *Obrazy I* (*Pictures I*) and *Obrazy II* for orch. (1970, 1973); Harp Concerto (1972); Flute Sonata (1944); Suite for Wind Sextet (1944); Suite for English Horn and Piano (1945); *Ballada* for string quartet and clarinet (1949); Piano Quintet (1949); *Ut stellae* for soprano, 2 pianos, flute, bass clarinet, percussion and tape (1966); *Amoroso* for clarinet and piano (1970); Wind Quintet (1971); *4 Studies* for solo harp (1971).

Fischer, Johann Caspar Ferdinand, German composer of keyboard music; b. c.1665; d. Rastatt, Aug. 27, 1746. He served as house musician to the Margrave of Baden (1696–1716).
WORKS: During his lifetime he publ. the following: *Le Journal du printemps,* op. 1 (airs and ballet numbers in the style of Lully; 1696; reprinted in the *Denkmäler deutscher Tonkunst* X/1); *Les Pièces de clavecin,* op. 2 (1696; reprinted 1698, under the title *Musikalisches Blumen-Büschlein*); *Vesper Psalms,* op. 3 (1701); *Ariadne musica neo-organoedum,* op. 4 (1715; contains 20 preludes and fugues for organ in 20 different keys, thus foreshadowing Bach's *Well-Tempered Clavier*); *Litaniae Lauretanae,* op. 5 (1711); also *Musikalischer Parnassus* (9 keyboard suites named after the 9 Muses; Augsburg, 1738); and *Blumenstrauss* (a series of 8 preludes and fugues in 8 church modes). His *Sämtliche Werke für Klavier und Orgel,* ed. by E. V. Werra, were publ. in Leipzig, 1901.
BIBLIOGRAPHY: For discussion of Fischer's influence on Bach, see Max Seiffert, *Geschichte der Klavier-Musik,* vol. 1 (Berlin, 1899); also R. Opel, "Fischers Einfluss auf Bach," *Bach-Jahrbuch* (1910).

Fischer, Joseph, music publisher; b. Silberhausen, Germany, April 9, 1841; d. Springfield, Ohio, Nov. 24, 1901. He emigrated to the U.S. as a youth, and established the firm of J. Fischer & Bro. in Dayton, Ohio (1864) with his brother **Ignaz Fischer;** in 1875 the firm moved to N.Y. Joseph Fischer was succeeded at his death by his sons **George** and **Carl;** the sons of George Fischer, **Joseph** and **Eugene,** became proprietors of the firm in 1920. During its early years, J. Fischer & Bro. specialized in music for the Roman Catholic Church, but later expanded their activities to include instrumental music by contemporary composers, organ works, and also light opera.

Fischer, Ludwig, German bass singer; b. Mainz, Aug. 18, 1745; d. Berlin, July 10, 1825. He sang in Mainz, Mannheim, and Vienna, and with great success in

Paris (1783) and Italy; from 1788 till 1815 was in Berlin. Mozart wrote the part of Osmin, in *Die Entführung aus dem Serail,* for Fischer.

Fischer, Michael Gotthard, German organist and composer; b. Alach, near Erfurt, June 3, 1773; d. Erfurt, Jan. 12, 1829. He was a pupil of Kittel; also concert conductor and teacher in the seminary at Erfurt. He wrote about 50 organ pieces; symphonies, concertos, chamber music, piano pieces, motets, chorales, concertos, etc.; publ. an *Evangelisches Choral-Melodienbuch.*

Fischer, Wilhelm, eminent Austrian musicologist; b. Vienna, April 19, 1886; d. Innsbruck, Feb. 26, 1962. He studied with Guido Adler at the Univ. of Vienna; received his Dr. phil. degree with the dissertation *Zur Entwicklungsgeschichte des Wiener klassischen Stils* (1915); was prof. at the Univ. of Innsbruck from 1928 to 1938; was deprived of his position after the Anschluss, and was employed during the war as a metal worker. In 1948 he returned to the Univ. In 1948 he was elected President of the Central Institute of Mozart Research at the Mozarteum in Salzburg. In 1956 he was presented a Festschrift on the occasion of his 70th birthday. He published numerous essays on Mozart and other classical composers; among his most important writings, apart from his dissertation on the classical style of Vienna, are *Zur Geschichte des Fugenthemas* (Leipzig, 1925) and *Beethoven als Mensch* (Regensburg, 1928).

Fischer, William Gustavus, American hymn tune writer; b. Baltimore, Oct. 14, 1835; d. Philadelphia, Aug. 13, 1912. He sang in a Baltimore German church; was a bookbinder by trade and a choral conductor by avocation; then entered the retail piano business and, under its imprint, Gould & Fischer, printed a number of Sunday-school leaflets. Of his songs, *Coming to the Cross,* first sung at a National Camp meeting at Hamilton, Mass., June 22, 1870, is the best known.

BIBLIOGRAPHY: R. G. McChutchan, *Our Hymnody* (N.Y., 1937).

Fischer-Dieskau, Dietrich, outstanding German baritone; b. Berlin, May 28, 1925. He studied piano as a child, but at the age of 16 took voice lessons with Hermann Weissenborn. In 1943 he was drafted into the German Army and was made a prisoner of war by the English during the Italian campaign. Returning to Berlin in 1947 he resumed his voice studies with Weissenborn. In 1947 he also made his debut as baritone soloist in the Brahms *Requiem.* This was followed by numerous appearances in song recitals, during which he sang the complete Lieder of Schubert. He also appeared in opera, singing a great variety of parts of both the classical and modern repertory, including *Wozzeck.* He made his American debut in N.Y. on May 2, 1955, obtaining immediate acclaim. His singing is distinguished both by a superlative technique and an intellectual quality peculiarly fitting the German repertory. He also published several books, among them *Auf den Spuren der Schubert-Lieder* (Wiesbaden, 1971; in English translation under the title *Schubert, A Biographical Study of His Songs,*

London, 1976); and *Wagner & Nietzsche* (1974; in English, N.Y., 1976).

Fischhof, Joseph, Austrian pianist; b. Butschowitz, Moravia, April 4, 1804; d. Vienna, June 28, 1857. He studied piano with Anton Halm in Vienna; then became a private teacher there, with growing success, and in 1833 was appointed prof. in the Vienna Cons. He published many piano pieces (rondos, variations, fantasias, dances, marches, etc.) and a *Versuch einer Geschichte des Klavier-Baus* (Vienna, 1853). He gathered a remarkable collection of musical MSS, including one of Bach's *Wohltemperierte Clavier,* and authentic materials for a Beethoven biography collected by Hotschewar (the guardian of Beethoven's nephew); these MSS were given, after Fischhof's death, to the Berlin State Library.

Fišer, Luboš, outstanding Czech composer; b. Prague, Sept. 30, 1935. He studied composition with Hlobil at the Prague Cons. (1952–56) and then with Hlobil again and Bořkovec at the Prague Academy of Music. In 1971 he was a composer-in-residence with the American Wind Symphony Orch. in Pittsburgh. His music is highly dramatic and thoroughly modern, employing sharp contrasts and occasionally using techniques of collage, allowing aleatory interpretation.

WORKS: chamber opera *Lancelot* (1959–60; Prague, May 19, 1961); a musical *Dobrý voják Švejk* (*The Good Soldier Schweik,* Prague, 1962); a ballet, *Changing Game* (1971); Suite for Orch. (1954); String Quartet (1955); Sextet for Wind Quintet and Piano (1956); 5 piano sonatas (1955–74); 2 symphonies (1956, 1958–60); *Ruce (The Hands),* sonata for violin and piano (1961); *Symphonic Fresco* (1962–63); *Chamber Concerto* for piano and orch. (1963); *Relief* for organ (1964); *15 Prints after Dürer's Apocalypse* for orch. (1964–65; Prague, May 15, 1966; his most successful work); *Caprichos,* for vocalists and chorus, after a text drawn from Goya's paintings (1966); *Pietà* for chamber ensemble (1967); Requiem (Prague, Nov. 19, 1968); *Riff* for orch. (1968); *Lament over the Destruction of the City of Ur,* after Ur-Sumerian tablets, for soprano, baritone, 3 narrators, mixed choruus, children's and adults' speaking choruses, 7 timpani and 7 bells (1969); *Double* for orch. (1969); *Crux* for violin, timpani and bells (1970); *Report* for wind orch. (1971; commissioned by the American Wind Symph. Orch.); *Kreutzer Etude* for chamber orch. (1974).

Fisher, William Arms, American music editor and publisher; b. San Francisco, April 27, 1861; d. Boston, Dec. 18, 1948. He studied theory with Horatio Parker; singing with William Shakespeare in London. When Dvořák came to New York in 1892 Fisher became his pupil. In 1897 he settled in Boston as editor and director of music publication for O. Ditson & Co.; was its vice-president from 1926–37; then retired. He edited several vocal albums, among them *60 Irish Folksongs* (Boston, 1915) and *Ye Olde New England Psalm Tunes* (Boston, 1930). He wrote the words *Goin' Home* to the melody of the slow movement of Dvořák's *New World Symphony,* a setting that became enormously popular.

WRITINGS: *Notes on Music in Old Boston* (1918); *The Music that Washington Knew* (1931); *One Hundred and Fifty Years of Music Publishing in the U.S.* (1933); *Music Festivals in the U.S.* (1934).

Fissot, Alexis-Henri, French pianist and composer; b. Airaines (Somme), Oct. 24, 1843; d. Paris, Jan. 28, 1896. He entered the Paris Cons. as a child of nine, and studied piano with Marmontel, organ with Benoist, and composition with Ambroise Thomas till 1860, taking successively all first prizes. He then taught piano at the Paris Cons. (from 1887). He wrote many effective piano pieces: *12 Préludes, 2 Ballades, 3 Feuillets d'Album, 12 Pièces de Genre,* etc.

Fistoulari, Anatole, Russian conductor; b. Kiev, Aug. 20, 1907. He studied with his father, the opera conductor **Gregory Fistoulari;** as a child prodigy, he conducted Tchaikovsky's Sixth Symph. at the age of 8; in 1920 went to Rumania and Germany; was in Paris as ballet conductor in 1933; later toured with the Ballet-Russe de Monte Carlo in the U.S. (1937). He was in the French Army in 1939; in 1940 made his way to London, where he settled as orchestral and theatrical conductor.

Fitelberg, Gregor, eminent Polish conductor and composer; b. Dvinsk, Latvia, Oct. 18, 1879; d. Katowice, June 10, 1953. He studied at the Warsaw Cons. with Barcewicz and Noskowski; then played the violin in the Warsaw Philharmonic; became its concertmaster, and eventually (1908) conductor. After the outbreak of World War I he went to Russia as conductor of symphony concerts; in 1921 he went to Paris; conducted performances of Diaghilev's Russian Ballet; in 1923 he returned to Poland; in 1940 he was in Buenos Aires, after fleeing Warsaw via Vienna, Italy, and Paris; from 1942–45 he was in the U.S.; in 1947 he went back to Poland, and became conductor at the Polish Radio. At his symphonic concerts he gave many performances of works by Polish composers; was one of the best interpreters of Szymanowski. In 1951 the Polish government awarded him a state prize. Fitelberg was also a composer; he wrote 2 symphonies (1903; 1906); a Polish Rhapsody for Orch. (1913); a symph. poem *In der Meerestiefe* (1913), and some chamber music; his Violin Sonata received the Paderewski prize in 1896.

Fitelberg, Jerzy, talented Polish composer; son of **Gregor Fitelberg;** b. Warsaw, May 20, 1903; d. New York, April 25, 1951. He received his musical education mainly from his father; then took courses in the Hochschule für Musik in Berlin. In 1933 he went to Paris; in May 1940 he came to the U.S., where he remained until his death. In 1936 he received an Elizabeth Sprague Coolidge award for his string quartet, which was performed at the Coolidge Festival of Chamber Music in Washington (1937); his orchestral and chamber music was often performed in Europe; much of it was published. His works are couched in the neo-Classical style, and are cosmopolitan in thematic substance; they are distinguished by energetic rhythm and strong contrapuntal texture; only a few of his compositions reflect Polish melos

WORKS: 3 suites for orch. (1926–30); Concerto for String Orch. (1928; arrangement of the Second String Quartet); Violin Concerto No. 1 (Vienna Festival of the International Society for Contemporary Music, June 20, 1932); Violin Concerto No. 2 (Paris Festival, June 22, 1937); *The Golden Horn* for string orch. (1942); Nocturne for Orch. (N.Y. Philh., March 28, 1946, Rodzinski conducting); Octet for Wind Instruments; 5 string quartets; Sonata for 2 Violins and 2 Pianos; Sonatina for 2 Violins; *3 Polish Folksongs* for women's voices (1942).

BIBLIOGRAPHY: Emilia Elsner, "Jerzy Fitelberg," *Chesterian* (Sept.-Oct. 1939).

Fitzgerald, Ella, black American jazz singer; b. Newport News, Virginia, April 25, 1918. She began singing in small clubs in Harlem in the early 1930s; discovered by Chick Webb (one of Harlem's most popular musicians) in 1935, she joined his band; upon his death in 1939, she became its leader; in 1942 she became a freelance singer and has since worked with most major jazz musicians and groups. She is particularly adept at scat singing and improvising, frequently creating new melodies over given harmonies much in the manner of a jazz instrumentalist. Stylistically, she is equally at ease in swing and bebop; developing, over the years, a superlative blend of musicianship, vocal ability, and interpretive insight, she has achieved a popularity and respect rarely acquired by jazz singers.

Fitzwilliam, Viscount Richard, wealthy British collector of paintings, engravings, books, and musical MSS; b. Richmond, Surrey, Aug. 1745; d. London, Feb. 4, 1816. He bequeathed his library to the Univ. of Cambridge. The musical MSS include especially valuable works: the immensely important *Fitzwilliam Virginal Book* (often wrongly termed *Virginal Booke of Queen Elizabeth*), anthems in Purcell's hand, sketches by Handel, and many early Italian compositions. Vincent Novello edited and publ. 5 vols. of the Italian sacred music as *The Fitzwilliam Music* (London, 1825); J. A. Fuller-Maitland and A. H. Mann made a complete catalogue of it (1893). The entire contents of the *Fitzwilliam Virginal Book* were edited and published by J. A. Fuller-Maitland and William Barclay Squire (2 vols., Leipzig and London, 1894–99; facsimile reprint, N.Y., 1954).

BIBLIOGRAPHY: E. W. Naylor, *An Elizabethan Virginal Book* (London, 1905).

Fiume, Orazio, Italian composer; b. Monopoli, Jan. 16, 1908. He studied piano and theory in Palermo and Naples; was later a student of Pizzetti (composition) and Molinari (conducting) in Rome. He taught harmony at the Cons. of Parma (1941–51), at Milan (1951–59), Pesaro (1959–60) and in 1961 became director of the Cons. of Trieste. His music follows the tradition of expansive Italian romanticism. He wrote an opera *Il Tamburo di panno* (Rome, April 12, 1962); 2 concertos for orch. (1945, 1956); cantata *Ajace* (1940); songs.

Fizdale, Robert, American pianist; b. Chicago, April 12, 1920. He studied with Ernest Hutcheson at the

Juilliard School of Music; formed a piano duo with Arthur Gold; they made a professional debut at the New School for Social Research in 1944, in a program devoted entirely to the music for prepared pianos by John Cage. They toured widely in the U.S., Europe and South America; works were written specially for them by Samuel Barber, Milhaud, Poulenc, Auric, Virgil Thomson, Norman Dello Joio and Ned Rorem.

Flackton, William, English organist and composer; b. Canterbury, March, 1709; d. there, Jan. 5, 1798. He was organist at Faversham from 1735-52; wrote church music; also 6 'overtures' for harpsichord; 6 sonatas for 2 violins and cello; 3 cello sonatas and 3 viola sonatas; a song *The Chase* (with a horn obbligato).

Flagello, Nicolas, American composer of Italian extraction; b. New York, March 15, 1928. He studied piano, violin, cello and oboe; obtained his M.M. from the Manhattan School of Music in 1950; then went to Italy where he took lessons with Ildebrando Pizzetti at the St. Cecilia Academy in Rome; received his Mus. D. degree there in 1956. Returning to the U.S., he joined the staff of the Manhattan School of Music. He toured as accompanist to Tito Schipa, Richard Tucker and other singers; played violin, viola and oboe in various orchestras; in 1960-61 served as assistant conductor at the Chicago Lyric Opera. His music exhales an uninhibited lyrical sentiment in the finest Italianate tradition and is animated in rapid passages by an impetuous flow of kinetic energy; his contrapuntal and harmonic lines are invariably lucid. Flagello writes in a modern idiom with a prudential application of non-toxic dissonances.
WORKS: *Lyra* for 6 brass instruments (1945); *Beowulf*, symph. poem (1949); Piano Concerto No. 1 (1950); *Mirra*, opera in 3 acts (1953); *The Wig*, one-act opera (1953); Piano Concerto No. 2 (1955); Violin Concerto (1956); *Rip Van Winkle*, children's operetta (1957); *Missa sinfonica* for orch. without voices (1957); *The Sisters*, one-act opera (1958); N.Y., Feb. 23, 1961); Concerto for String Orch. (1959); *The Judgment of St. Francis*, one-act opera (1959; N.Y., March 18, 1966); Divertimento for Piano and Percussion (1960); *Capriccio* for cello and orch. (1961); *Burlesca* for flute and guitar (1961); Piano Concerto No. 3 (1962); Concertino for piano, brass and timpani (1963); Violin Sonata (1963); *Lautrec*, ballet suite (1965); Symphony No. 1 (1967; N.Y., April 23, 1971); *Passion of Martin Luther King* for soloists, orch. and chorus (1968); *Te Deum for Mankind* for chorus (1968); *The Piper of Hamelin*, children's opera to Flagello's own libretto (1970).

Flagg, Josiah, American bandmaster, b. Woburn, Mass., May 28, 1737; d. c.1795. He organized and drilled the first regular militia band of Boston (most probably the first group of that nature in America); on June 29, 1769, presented its first concert and on Oct. 28, 1773, gave a "final Grand Concert" at Faneuil Hall with about 50 players. Subsequently he settled in Providence and served there as lieutenant colonel during the Revolution; little is known of his other activities. He publ. *A Collection of the best Psalm Tunes in 2, 3 and 4 parts . . . To which is added some Hymns and Anthems, the Greater part of them never before printed in America* (introduced the anthem to the English colonies; 1764; engraved by Paul Revere) and *Sixteen Anthems . . . To which is added a few Psalm Tunes* (1766). Flagg was the first in America to establish a connection between sacred and secular music. That he was an educated practical musician and was acquainted with European music is evidenced by the type of programs he conducted.
BIBLIOGRAPHY: O. G. Sonneck, *Early Concert Life in America* (Leipzig, 1907); *Dictionary of American Biography*, vol. VI (N.Y., 1931).

Flagler, Isaac Van Vleck, American organist; born Albany, N.Y., May 15, 1844; d. Auburn, N.Y., March 16, 1909. He studied with H. W. A. Beale at Albany, Edouard Batiste in Paris, and others. He was organist and music director of various churches; co-founder of the American Guild of Organists. He published *The Organist's Treasury, Flagler's New Collection of Organ Music,* and *Flagler's New Collection for Choirs and Soloists.*

Flagstad, Kirsten, famous Norwegian soprano; b. Hamar, Norway, July 12, 1895; d. Oslo, Dec. 7, 1962. She studied with her mother (coach at the Oslo Opera) and with Ellen Schytte-Jacobsen in Oslo; in 1912 she made her debut there at the National Theater as Nuri in d'Albert's opera *Tiefland;* then sang in oratorio, operettas, and musical comedies in Oslo; from 1928-30 was engaged at the Storm Theater at Göteborg; from 1931-32, again at the National Theater; in 1933 and 1934, appeared at the Bayreuth Festival. On Feb. 2, 1935, she made a very successful debut at the Metropolitan Opera as Sieglinde in *Die Walküre,* and sang Isolde (her most celebrated role), Brünnhilde, Elizabeth, Elsa and Kundry in her first season there; appeared at Covent Garden, London, as Isolde, on May 18, 1936. She also sang with the San Francisco Opera (1935-38), Chicago City Opera (1937), and made numerous guest appearances through the U.S. and Australia. In 1941 she returned to Norway; in 1951 she reappeared at the Metropolitan Opera in N.Y. singing Isolde and Brünhilde.
BIBLIOGRAPHY: *The Flagstad Manuscript* (an autobiography narrated to Louis Biancolli, N.Y., 1952).

Flament, Édouard, French composer, conductor, and bassoon virtuoso; b. Douai, Aug. 27, 1880; d. Bois-Colombes (Seine), Dec. 27, 1958. He studied at the Paris Cons. with Bourdeau (bassoon), Lavignac, Caussade, and Lenepveu (composition). After graduation (1898), he played the bassoon in the Lamoureux Orch. (1898-1907) and in the Société des Instruments à Vent (1898-1923); conducted opera and concerts in Paris (1907-12), Algiers (1912-14), Marseilles (1919-20), summer concerts at Fontainebleau (1920-22); then with the Diaghilev Ballet in Monte Carlo, Berlin, London, Spain (1923-29). In 1930 he became conductor at the Paris Radio.
WORKS: An exceptionally prolific composer, he wrote between 1894 and 1957 some 175 opus numbers, including the operas *La Fontaine de Castalie, Le Cœur de la Rose, Lydéric et Rosèle;* 8 symphonies;

Oceano Nox, symph. poem; *Variations radio-pho-niques;* 5 piano concertos; *Concertstück* for bassoon and orch; Divertimento for 6 Bassoons; Quintet for 5 Bassoons; Quartet for 4 Bassoons; 3 string quartets; Violin Sonata, Viola Sonata, 2 cello sonatas, etc.; about 180 film scores. Few of his works are publ.; most of the larger ones remain unperformed.

Flammer, Harold, American music publisher; b. New York, Sept. 19, 1889; d. Bronxville, N.Y., Oct. 23, 1939. He studied at Princeton Univ. (Litt. B., 1911). In 1913 he entered G. Schirmer, Inc.; 1917, established Harold Flammer, Inc.; 1929–34, Vice-President and Business Manager of G. Schirmer; 1934, re-established own firm. During the years 1932–36 he was at various times treasurer, president, and vice-president of Music Publ. Association of the U.S. He published piano compositions, songs, and many song texts and translations.

Flanagan, William, American composer; b. Detroit, Aug. 14, 1923; d. New York, Aug. 31, 1969 (found dead in his apartment, a victim of an overdose of barbiturates). He studied composition at the Eastman School of Music, Rochester, N.Y., with Burrill Phillips and Bernard Rogers; then at the Berkshire Music Center in Tanglewood with Arthur Honegger, Arthur Berger and Aaron Copland; also, in N.Y., with David Diamond. Concurrently, he became engaged in musical journalism; was a reviewer for the *N.Y. Herald Tribune* (1957–60). His style of composition is characterized by an intense pursuit of an expressive melodic line, projected on polycentric but firmly tonal harmonies.
WORKS: one-act opera *Bartleby,* after Melville's short story (1952–57; N.Y., Jan. 24, 1961); *A Concert Ode for Orch.* (1951; Detroit, Jan. 14, 1960); *A Concert Overture* (N.Y., Dec. 4, 1959); *Divertimento for Classical Orchestra* (1948; Toledo, Ohio, Jan. 9, 1960); *Notations* for large orch. (1960); *Chapter from Ecclesiastes,* for mixed chorus and string quintet (N.Y., March 21, 1963); *Narrative for Orchestra* (Detroit, March 25, 1964); *Divertimento for String Quartet* (1947); Chaconne for Violin and Piano (1948); Passacaglia for Piano (1947); Piano Sonata (1950); song cycles. He wrote background music for Edward Albee's plays *The Sandbox* (1961) and *The Ballad of the Sad Café* (1963).
BIBLIOGRAPHY: articles on Flanagan in the *Bulletin of the American Composers Alliance* (Sept. 1961).

Flaxland, Gustave-Alexandre, French music publisher; b. Strasbourg, Jan. 26, 1821; d. Paris, Nov. 11, 1895. He studied at the Paris Cons.; founded a music publishing business in 1847, and, by acquiring copyrights of compositions of Schumann and Wagner, made it prominent. He sold his firm to Durand et Schönewerk in 1870, and commenced making pianos.

Flecha, Mateo, Spanish composer; b. Prades, Tarragona, 1530; d. Solsona, Lérida, Feb. 20, 1604. He received his musical education from his uncle, also named **Mateo Flecha** (1481–1553); was chamber musician at the courts of Charles V and Philip II; from about 1575 he was in Prague; returned to Spain in 1599. He publ. a book of madrigals in Venice (1568), and a collection *Las Ensaladas* (Prague, 1581) containing 'ensaladas' (quodlibets, comic songs) by his uncle, and some by himself. This collection was brought out in a modern edition by Higinio Anglés, with an introductory essay on the Flechas (Barcelona, 1954).

Fleck, Henry T., American music educator; b. Buffalo, N.Y., April 28, 1863; d. Rockaway Beach, Long Island, N.Y., Sept. 6, 1937. He studied music with Wüllner at Cologne; upon returning to the U.S., he organized in N.Y. the Euterpe Choral Society (1889) and the Harlem Philharmonic Society (1890), which he conducted till 1901; also established free concerts of chamber music in N.Y. From 1901 until his death he was prof. of music at Hunter College, N.Y.

Flégier, Ange, French composer; b. Marseilles, Feb. 25, 1846; d. there, Oct. 8, 1927. He studied first at the Cons. of Marseilles and then at the Paris Cons. (1866–69), returning to Marseilles in 1870. He wrote *Fatima,* comic opera; *Ossian,* lyric poem for soli, chorus, and orch.; *Françoise de Rimini,* cantata; miscellaneous orch. pieces (*Valse du rêve, Badinage, Habanera, Manuet, Berceuse, Mignardise,* etc.); many songs, of which *Le Cor* is the best known.

Fleischer, Anton, Hungarian conductor and composer; b. Makó, May 30, 1891; d. Budapest, Oct. 30, 1945. He studied in Budapest with Kodály; 1913–15, first conducted at the Budapest Municipal Theater; conducted at the Budapest Opera (1915) and taught at the National Cons. from 1918; won the Hungarian State Prize with his symph. on Oscar Wilde's *The Nightingale and the Rose* (1915).

Fleischer, Oskar, eminent German musicologist; b. Zörbig, Nov. 2, 1856; d. Berlin, Feb. 8, 1933. He studied philology at Halle (1878–83); then musicology in Berlin under Spitta. In 1892 he became *privatdozent* at the Univ. of Berlin; promoted to professorship in 1895. He was a founder and first president of the Internationale Musik-Gesellschaft (1899); together with Johannes Wolf edited its publications, the *Zeitschrift* and *Sammelbände,* until 1904. In 1892 he represented the Prussian government at the Vienna Exhibition, of which he publ. an exhaustive report, *Die Bedeutung der internationalen Musik- und Theaterausstellung in Wien für Kunst und Wissenschaft der Musik* (Leipzig, 1894).
WRITINGS: *Führer durch die königliche Sammlung alter Musikinstrumente* (Berlin, 1892); *Musikinstrumente aus deutscher Urzeit* (1893); *W. A. Mozart* (1899); *Führer durch die Bachausstellung* (Berlin, 1901); *Neumen-Studien* (4 vols., 1895, 1897, 1904, 1923; the 3rd. vol. with facsimiles of late Byzantine notation; the 4th entitled *Die germanischen Neumen als Schlüssel zum altchristlichen und gregorianischen Gesang).* He also wrote short biographies of the masters of music in *Grosse Männer* (1922–23); contributed valuable articles to various German music journals.

Fleisher, Edwin A., American patron of music; b. Philadelphia, July 11, 1877; d. there, Jan. 9, 1959. He studied at Harvard Univ. (B.A., 1899). He founded a Symphony Club in Philadelphia (1909) and engaged conductors to rehearse an amateur orch. there; at the same time he began collecting orchestral scores and complete sets of parts, which became the nucleus of the great Edwin A. Fleisher Collection presented by him to the Free Library of Philadelphia. A partial catalogue of the collection was publ. in 1935, 2nd vol. in 1945, supplement in 1956.

Fleisher, Leon, American pianist; b. San Francisco, July 23, 1928 (of Russian immigrant parents). He played in public as a small child; then was sent to Europe where he had regular piano lessons with Artur Schnabel at Lake Como, Italy (1938–39). At the age of 16 he was soloist with the N.Y. Philharmonic (Nov. 4, 1944); subsequently developed a brilliant career as a concert pianist; in 1952 he won 1st prize at the international competition for pianists in Brussels. In 1964 his right hand became inoperative, owing to some intractable psychosomatic ailment; yet he did not abandon his concerts but learned piano works written for left hand alone including those originally commissioned by Paul Wittgenstein, the pianist who had lost his right arm in World War I; performed left-hand concertos by Ravel, Prokofiev and a quintet for strings and piano, left-hand by Franz Schmidt. Fleisher found another outlet for his musical talent in conducting, which he first learned with Pierre Monteux in San Francisco and at the conducting school established by Monteux in Hancock, Maine; he also profited by advice from George Szell. In 1974 he became resident conductor of the Baltimore Symph. and also led a community orchestra in Annapolis; taught at the Peabody Cons. in Baltimore; filled in guest appearances with the New Jersey Symph. and the Los Angeles Chamber Orchestra.

Fleming, Robert, Canadian pianist and composer; b. Prince Albert, Saskatchewan, Nov. 12, 1921; d. Ottawa, Nov. 28, 1976. He studied piano with Arthur Benjamin and composition with Herbert Howells at the Royal College of Music in London (1937–39); served in the Canadian Air Force during World War II; after the end of the war he continued his musical education at the Toronto Cons. with Healey Willan and others. He subsequently joined the National Film Board of Canada in 1946 and was its musical director from 1958 to 1970; wrote music for some 250 films.
WORKS: the ballets *Chapter 13* (1950) and *Shadow on the Prairie* (1951); 3 puppet plays; *Around the House,* suite for orch. (1942); *Rondo* for orch. (1942); *6 Variations on a Liturgical Theme* for string orch. (1946); *Kaleidoscope* for small orch. (1949); *Red River Country* for small orch. (1953); *Hymn to War* for baritone and strings (1954); *Recollections* for violin and strings (1954); *Summer Suite* for orch. (1957); *Suite Short and Simple* for piano and strings (1959); Piano Concerto (1963); *3 Contrasts* for school orch. (1964); *Concerto '64* for piano and orch. (1964); Tuba Concerto (1966); *4 Fantasias on Canadian Folk Themes* for orch. or symph. band. (1966); Divertimento for Organ, 2 Oboes and Strings (1970); *Hexad* for small

orch. (1972); *Our Mind Was the Singer,* cycle for baritone and orch. (1972); *3 Scenarios* for symph. band (1974); *Of a Timeless Land* for contralto and orch. (1974); *Bella Bella Sonatina* for violin and piano (1943); Violin Sonata (1944); *Colors of the Rainbow* for wind quartet, string quartet and harp (1962); *Maritime Suite* for wind quartet, string quartet and harp (1962); *3 Miniatures* for brass quintet (1962); *Go for Baroque* for flute, oboe and harpsichord (1963); *3 Dialogues* for flute or oboe, and piano or harpsichord (1964); *A Quartet for Strings* (1969); *Threo* for soprano saxophone and piano (1972); piano pieces; choruses.

Flesch, Carl, celebrated violinist and pedagogue; b. Moson, Hungary, Oct. 9, 1873; d. Lucerne, Switzerland, Nov. 14, 1944. He was a violin pupil of Grün at the Vienna Cons. (1886–89), then of Souzay and Marsick at the Paris Cons. (1890–94). From 1897 to 1902 he was prof. at the Cons. in Bucharest; from 1903–08 prof. at the Cons. in Amsterdam. From 1924 till 1928 Flesch was head of the violin dept. of the Curtis Institute in Philadelphia; then divided his time between the U.S. and Germany; in 1933 he went to England; and then to Switzerland. He issued the standard pedagogic work for violin *Die Kunst des Violinspiels* in 2 vols. (Berlin, 1923; new edition, 1954), which was translated into English (Boston, 1924–30), Italian (Milan, 1953), Polish (Cracow, 1964), and Russian (vol. 1, Moscow, 1964); also wrote *Das Klangproblem im Geigenspiel* (Berlin, 1931; in English, N.Y., 1934). His manuscript work, *Die Hohe Schule des Violin-Fingersatzes* was publ. first in Italian (Milan, 1960), then in English, as *Violin Fingering, Its Theory and Practice* (N.Y., 1966). His *Erinnerungen eines Geigers* were published posthumously (Freiburg-im-Breisgau, 1960), and appeared previously in English translation, edited by Hans Keller and C. F. Flesch, under the title *The Memoirs of Carl Flesch* (London, 1957). Carl Flesch published new editions of Kreutzer's Etudes, Mozart's violin sonatas (with Schnabel), 20 etudes of Paganini, and the violin concertos of Beethoven, Mendelssohn and Brahms.

Fleta, Miguel, Spanish tenor; b. Albalate, Dec. 28, 1893; d. La Coruna, May 30, 1938. He studied in Barcelona; made his debut in Trieste Nov. 14, 1919. After a successful career in Europe, Mexico and South America, he came to the U.S. in 1923 and sang with the Metropolitan Opera; returned to Spain in 1926.

Fleta, Pierre, French tenor, son of **Miguel Fleta;** b. Villefranche-sur-Mer, July 4, 1925. He studied with his mother, **Louise Pierrick-Fleta,** a member of La Scala; then sang as a boy soprano at Cannes; went to London, where he was engaged as a professional singer before making his opera debut in Barcelona in 1949. He made a concert tour in the Middle East in 1951; then was engaged as first tenor at the Théâtre de la Monnaie in Brussels (1952). He has also developed a repertory of French, Italian, Spanish, and English folksongs.

Fletcher, Alice C., American ethnologist; b. Cuba (of American parents), March 16, 1838; d. Washington,

D.C., April 6, 1923. She devoted her life to the study of North American Indians, among whom she lived for a number of years; 1896, became vice-president of American Association for the Advancement of Science; president of American Anthropological Society (1903) and American Folk Lore Society (1905). She is the author of *Indian Story and Song from North America* (1900); *A Study of Omaha Indian Music* (1903); *Indian Games and Dances* (1915); numerous articles in the *Journal of American Folk Lore*, etc.

BIBLIOGRAPHY: *Dictionary of American Biography*, vol. VI (N.Y., 1931).

Fletcher, Grant, American composer and conductor; b. Hartsburg, Ill., Oct. 25, 1913. He studied at the Univ. of Michigan; then in Toronto with Healey Willan; in Rochester with Bernard Rogers and Howard Hanson; in Cleveland with Herbert Elwell. From 1945-48 he was conductor of the Akron, Ohio, Orch. In 1970 he was appointed to the staff of the Arizona State Univ. at Tempe.

WORKS: *The Crisis*, after Thomas Paine, for chorus and orch. (1945); *An American Overture* (Duluth, April 23, 1948); *A Song for Warriors* (on Yugoslav themes, Rochester, Oct. 25, 1945); *Panels from a Theater Wall* (Rochester, April 27, 1949); Symphony No. 1 (Rochester, April 24, 1951); an opera, *The Sack of Calabasas* (1964; excerpts performed in Phoenix, Arizona, April 6, 1964); *Glyphs* for orch. (1968); *Diaphony* for symph. band (1968); *Uroboros* for a percussion ensemble (1969); Symph. No. 2 (1970); *Quadra* for percussion ensemble (1976); 2 books of nocturnes for piano (1935); 4 American dance pieces for piano (1944); 5 string quartets; several choral works; songs.

Fletcher, Percy E., English composer; b. Derby, Dec. 12, 1879; d. London, Sept. 10, 1932. He went to London in 1899 as conductor at various theaters there; he composed many works in a light, melodious style, including the orchestral pieces *Woodland Pictures, Sylvan Scenes, Parisian Sketches, Three Frivolities*, the overture *Vanity Fair;* also a short sacred cantata, *Passion of Christ.*

Fleury, André, French organist and composer; b. Neuilly-sur-Seine, July 25, 1903. He studied with his father; later with Gigout, Marcel Dupré, and Louis Vierne. In 1930 he became organist at St. Augustin, Paris; in 1943 he was appointed prof. of organ playing at the École Normale de Musique; after World War II he taught at the Cons. of Dijon. Fleury wrote 2 symphonies for organ and numerous other works for his instrument.

Fleury, Louis, eminent French flutist; b. Lyons, May 24, 1878; d. Paris, June 11, 1925. He studied at the Paris Cons.; from 1905 until his death was head of the famous Société Moderne d'Instruments à Vent, also (1906) of the Société des Concerts d'Autrefois, with which he gave concerts in England; made appearances with Melba and Calvé. Debussy composed *Syrinx* for unaccompanied flute for him. He edited much old flute music, including sonatas and other pieces by Blavet, Naudet, Purcell, J. Stanley, etc., and contrib-

uted to French and English periodicals ("Souvenirs d'un flûtiste," *Le Monde Musical*, etc.).

Flodin, Karl, Finnish composer; b. Wasa (Vaasa), July 16, 1858; d. Helsinki, Nov. 30, 1925. He studied music with Faltin in Helsinki (1877-83), and with Jadassohn at the Leipzig Cons. (1890-92). In 1908 he went to Buenos Aires as music critic on a German paper there; returned to Finland in 1921. He publ. numerous essays on Finnish music (in Finnish and German); wrote a biography of Martin Wegelius (1922); composed a *Cortège* for horn and orch., as well as incidental music to various plays; publ. some 80 piano pieces. He was married to the singer **Adée Leander** (1873-1935).

Floersheim, Otto, editor and composer, b. Aix-la-Chapelle, March 2, 1853; d. Geneva, Switzerland, Nov. 30, 1917. He was a pupil of Ferdinand Hiller at Cologne; went to New York in 1875, became editor of the *Musical Courier* in 1880, and from 1894-1904 was manager of its Berlin branch. As a music journalist and a man of musical affairs, he was very influential in America; he was also a composer of competently put together piano pieces and songs in a German romantic vein.

Flood, (William Henry) Grattan, Irish organist and music historian; b. Lismore, Nov. 1, 1859; d. Enniscorthy, Aug. 6, 1928. He served as a church organist in Dublin; achieved recognition as a writer on Irish music and musicians. He published *History of Irish Music* (1895; 4th ed. 1927); *Story of the Harp* (1905); *Story of the Bagpipe* (1911); *W. Vincent Wallace, a Memoir* (1912); *John Field of Dublin* (Dublin, 1920); *Introductory Sketch of Irish Musical History* (1921); *Early Tudor Composers* (1925); *Late Tudor Composers* (1929); was the editor of *Songs and Airs of O'Carolan, Moore's Irish Melodies, Armagh Hymnal,* and *The Spirit of the Nation.*

Floquet, Étienne Joseph, French composer; b. Aix-en-Provence, Nov. 23, 1748; d. Paris, May 10, 1785. After studying in his native town, he went to Paris; there he wrote the opera-ballet *L'Union de l'Amour et des arts,* produced with great success at the Académie Royale de Musique (Sept. 7, 1773); his second opera *Azolan, ou Le Serment indiscret* (Nov. 22, 1774, also at the Académie), was a fiasco. Floquet then went to Italy, where he perfected his knowledge by studying with Sala in Naples and with Martini in Bologna. Returning to Paris, he had two operas performed at the Académie: *Hellé* (Jan. 5, 1779) and *Le Seigneur bienfaisant* (Dec. 14, 1780). He also wrote a comic opera *La Nouvelle Omphale* (Comédie-Italienne, Nov. 22, 1782). In an attempt to challenge Gluck's superiority, Floquet wrote the opera *Alceste* on the same subject as Gluck's famous work, but it was never produced.

BIBLIOGRAPHY: A. Pougin, *Étienne-Joseph Floquet* (Paris, 1863); F. Huot, *Étude biographique sur Étienne-Joseph Floquet* (Aix, 1903).

Florence (real name **Houghton**), **Evangeline,** American soprano; b. Cambridge, Mass., Dec. 12, 1873; d. London, Nov. 1, 1928. She studied with Henschel and

Lilli Lehmann. She made her debut in London, in 1892, and carried on her entire concert career in England.

Flores, Bernal, Costa Rican composer; b. San José, July 28, 1937. After acquiring the rudiments of music in Costa Rica he came to the U.S. and enrolled at the Eastman School of Music in Rochester (M.M., 1962; Ph.D. 1964). Returning to Costa Rica, he became prof. at the Cons. of San José.
WORKS: Symph. No. 1 for Strings (1965); Symph. No. 2 (1966); Concerto for Piano, Percussion and Orch. (1963); Clarinet Concerto (1968); piano pieces; songs.

Floridia, Pietro, Italian composer; b. Modica, Sicily, May 5, 1860; d. New York, Aug. 16, 1932. He studied in Naples with Cesi (piano) and Lauro Rossi (composition); while at the Naples Cons. he published several piano pieces which became quite popular. On May 7, 1882, he brought out in Naples a comic opera *Carlotta Clepier.* From 1888 to 1892 he taught at the Cons. of Palermo; then lived in Milan. In 1904 he emigrated to the U.S.; taught at the Cincinnati College of Music (1906–08); in 1908 settled in N.Y.; in 1913 organized and conducted an Italian Symph. Orch. there. His music (mostly for the stage) is written in a competent manner, in the style of the Italian verismo.
WORKS: the operas *Maruzza* (Venice, Aug. 23, 1894); *La Colonia libera* (Rome, May 7, 1899); *Paoletta* (Cincinnati, Aug. 29, 1910); also *The Scarlet Letter* (1902; not produced) and *Malia* (completed in 1932; not produced). Floridia edited a valuable collection in 2 vols., *Early Italian Songs and Airs* (Philadelphia, 1923).

Florimo, Francesco, Italian musician and historian; b. S. Giorgio Morgeto, Calabria, Oct. 12, 1800; d. Naples, Dec. 18, 1888. In 1817 he entered the Collegio di Musica at Naples; Furno, Elia, Zingarelli, and Tritto were his teachers; from 1826–51 he was librarian there. He was Bellini's closest friend; in 1876 he escorted the latter's remains from Paris to Catania, and publ. the pamphlet "Trasporto delle ceneri di Bellini a Catania"; composed *Sinfonia Funebre per la morte di Bellini;* founded the "Bellini Prize," a competition open to Italian composers not over 30.
WRITINGS: His chief work is *Cenno storico sulla scuola musicale di Napoli* (Naples, 1869–71, 2 vols.; republ. 1880–84, in 4 vols., as *La scuola musicale di Napoli e i suoi Conservatori,* a complete musical history of Naples and its conservatories, their teachers and pupils, etc.; despite numerous errors, it remains an extremely valuable guide; *Riccardo Wagner ed i Wagneristi* (Naples, 1876); *Bellini, memorie e lettere* (Florence, 1882); an *Album Bellini* (Naples, 1886), containing opinions by many eminent musicians on Bellini's works; and a *Metodo di canto,* adopted by the Paris Cons. and described as "magistrale" by Rossini. Florimo was also an excellent singing teacher.
BIBLIOGRAPHY: G. Megali, *Francesco Florimo* (Naples, 1901).

Florio, Caryl (real name **William James Robjohn**), organist; b. Tavistock, Devon, Nov. 3, 1843; d. Morgan-town, S.C., Nov. 21, 1920. He left England at the age of 14 and settled in N.Y.; was engaged as a singer and organist at various churches in N.Y., Baltimore, Indianapolis, etc.; conducted choral societies in N.Y.; eventually settled in Asheville, N.C. He wrote two operas to his own texts: *Guilda* (1879); and *Uncle Tom's Cabin* (1882); several operettas; the cantatas *Song of the Elements* (1872) and *Bridal of Bethlehem;* two symphonies; Quintet for Piano and 4 Saxophones (the first work written for such an ensemble); Piano Concerto; 4 violin sonatas, and 2 piano sonatas.

Flosman, Oldřich, Czech composer; b. Plzeň, April 5, 1925. He studied composition with Janeček at the Prague Cons. and with Bořkovec at the Prague Academy, graduating in 1950. In his music he follows the neo-Romantic tradition of the Czech school of composition, with the strong formal design and an animating rhythmic pulse; the influence of Prokofiev's lyrical dynamism is much in evidence.
WORKS: a pantomine, *Pierrot and Columbine* (1957); the ballets *The Woman Partisan* (1959), *The Taming of the Shrew* (1960) and *Maska (The Mask,* 1968); the cantatas *Tři zastavení (3 Stoppings,* 1960), *Count Sámo* (1970) and *Moments of Victory,* for male chorus and chamber ensemble (1972); Double Concerto for Harp, Clarinet and Orch. (1950); Clarinet Concerto (1954); Bassoon Concertino (1956); 2 violin concertos (1958, 1972); *Dances* for harp, and string quartet or string orch. (1961); *Cuban Overture* (1962); 2 symphonies (1964, 1974); *3 Studies* for strings and piano (1965); *Concertante Music* for wind quintet and chamber orch. (1965); Sonata for Soprano and Strings (1967); Flute Concerto (1969); Horn Concerto (1970); *Fugues for Strings* (1970); *Fires on the Hills,* symph. prelude (1973); 2 wind quintets (1948, 1962); *Bagatelles* for winds and piano (1950); Sonatina for Clarinet and Piano (1952); *Jesenik Suite* for Viola and piano (1956); 3 string quartets (1956, 1963, 1966); *Dreaming About a Violin* for violin and piano (1962); *Romance and Scherzo* for flute and harp (1962); Nonet No. 2 (1967); Sonata for Wind Quintet and Piano (1970); *Chamber Music* for flute, oboe, violin, viola and cello (1971); Sonata for Violin, Cello and Piano (1971); *Letters to You,* 4 songs for soprano, flute and piano (1973); *Motýli zde nežijí (Butterflies Don't Live Here Any Longer);* piano sonata inspired by the film about children's drawings from a Nazi concentration camp (1961); *4 Fugues* for piano (1967); *5 Madrigals* for chorus a cappella (1965).

Flothuis, Marius, eminent Dutch composer; b. Amsterdam, Oct. 30, 1914. He received his rudimentary musical education at home from his uncle, who taught him piano; then had piano lessons with Arend Koole and studied music theory with Brandts-Buys. He took academic courses at the Univ. of Amsterdam, and musicology at the Univ. of Utrecht (1934–37); he served as assistant manager of the Concertgebouw Orch. After the occupation of Holland by the Germans in 1940 he was dismissed from his job (his wife was half-Jewish). On Sept. 18, 1943, he was arrested by the Nazis on the charge of hiding Jews, and transported to the concentration camp in Vught, Holland, and a year later to a German labor camp. His liberation came on May 4, 1945, in a forest near Schwerin; he returned to Amsterdam and was reinstated at his managerial job at the Concertgebouw. From 1955 till 1974 he was artistic director of the Concertgebouw. In 1974 he was appointed prof. of musicology at the Univ. of Utrecht. In his works he adopts the motivic method of melodic writing and its concomitant form of variations in freely dissonant counterpoint and largely neo-Classical format. Dissatisfied with his youthful works, he destroyed his manuscripts dating before 1934, including some perfectly acceptable symphonic pieces.

WORKS: *4 Songs* for soprano, and small orch. or piano (1937–38); Concertino for Small Orch. (1940); *Sonnet* for mezzo-soprano and small orch. (1939–40); *Small Overture* for soprano and orch. (1942); *Dramatic Overture* (1943–46); Flute Concerto (Utrecht, Dec. 19, 1945); *2 Sonnets* for mezzo-soprano and orch. (1945); Concerto for Horn and Small Orch. (1945); *Valses sentimentales* for small orch. (1946; also for piano, 4 hands); Concerto for Piano and Small Orch. (1946–48); *To an Old Love* for mezzo-soprano and orch. (1948); *4 Trifles* for high voice and small orch. (1948–50); *Capriccio* for wind orch. or string orch. (1949); Concerto for Violin and Small Orch. (1950; Utrecht, Jan. 14, 1952); Fantasia for Harp and Small Orch. (1953; Amsterdam, May 26, 1955); *Sinfonietta concertante* for clarinet, saxophone and small orch. (1954–55; Amsterdam, June 2, 1955); *Concert Overture* (1955); *Rondo festoso* for orch. (Amsterdam, July 7, 1956); Clarinet Concerto (1957); *Symphonic Music* for orch. (1957); *Spes Patriae,* sinfonietta for small orch. (1962); *Espressioni cordiali,* 7 bagatelles for string orch. (1963); *Canti e Giouchi (Songs and Games)* for wind quintet and string orch. (1964); *Celdroom,* radiophonic scene for speakers, chorus and orch. (1964); *Hymnus* for soprano and orch. (1965); Concertino for Oboe and Small Orch. (1968); *Fantasia quasi una cantate* for 12 strings, harpsichord and soprano (1968); *Per Sonare ed Ascoltare,* 5 canzonas for flute and orch. (1971); *Cantata Silesiana* for chorus, flute, string quartet and harpsichord (1946); *Love and Strife,* cantata for contralto, flute, oboe d'amore, viola and cello (1948–49); *Een Amsterdams Lied,* cantata for solo soprano and baritone, flute, clarinet, 2 violins, viola, cello, double bass and piano (1951); *Negro Lament,* after Langston Hughes, for contralto, saxophone and piano (1953); *Odysseus and Nausikaa,* madrigal for soprano, contralto, tenor, baritone and harp (1958–60); Solo Cello Sonata (1937–38); Nocturne for Flute, Oboe and Clarinet (1941); Quintet for Flute, Oboe, Clarinet, Bass Clarinet and Bassoon (1941–42); *Sonata da camera* for flute and piano (1943); *2 Pieces* for guitar (1944); *Aria* for trumpet and piano (1944); *Aubade* for solo flute (1944); *3 Pieces* for 2 horns (1945); *Ronde champêtre* for flute and harpsichord (1945); Solo Violin Sonata (1945); Sonatina for Horn, Trumpet and Trombone (1945); Partita for Violin and Piano (1950); *Pour le tombeau d'Orphée* for solo harp (1950); *Trio Serio* for piano trio (1950–51); *Sonata da Camera* for flute and harp (1951); *Small Suite* for 12 harps (1951; in collaboration with Lex Van Delden); String Quartet (1951–52); *Small Suite* for oboe, trumpet, clarinet or saxophone, and piano (1952); Divertimento for Clarinet, Bassoon, Horn, Vio-lin, Viola and Double Bass (1952); *4 Invenzioni* for 4 horns (1963); Partita for 2 Violins (1966); Concertino for Oboe, Violin, Viola and Cello (1967); *Allegro Vivace* for 2 harps (1969); *Caprices Roumains* for oboe and piano (1975); *Adagio* for piano 4 hands and percussion (1975); *Romeo's Lament* for solo horn (1975); Sonata for Flute and Alto Flute (1975); Suite for Piano (1937–38); *Divertimento on a Theme of Kees Stokvis* for 2 pianos (1946); *6 Moments Musicaux* for piano (1946–47); *5 Epigrams and a Capriccio* for piano (1970); songs.

BIBLIOGRAPHY: "Marius Flothuis on Himself," *Key Notes* (Amsterdam, 1976).

Flotow, Friedrich von, famous German opera composer; b. Teutendorf, April 26, 1812; d. Darmstadt, Jan. 24, 1883. He was a scion of an old family of nobility, tracing its ancestry to the 13th century; received his first music lessons from his mother; then was a chorister in Güstrow. At the age of 16 he went to Paris, where he studied piano with J. P. Pixis and composition with Reicha. After the revolution of 1830, he returned home; but went to Paris again the following year; there he met Auber, Rossini, and Meyerbeer, and resolved to devote himself to opera. He associated himself with the influential composer Grisar, and contributed several arias and other numbers to Grisar's productions; his first independent work in Paris was the opera *Le Naufrage de la Méduse* (1839); then followed *L'Esclave de Camoëns;* also a ballet *Lady Henriette* (1844). He achieved his decisive success with the romantic opera *Alessandro Stradella,* based on the life of the composer Stradella; it was staged first in Hamburg (1844), and was produced subsequently in Paris and elsewhere with excellent success. Three years later, the production of his opera *Martha* (Vienna, 1847) established him as a celebrity; in this opera, Flotow demonstrated his ability to combine the German romantic spirit with Parisian elegance; the libretto (and some of the music) was elaborated from his early ballet *Lady Henriette,* with a setting in Queen Anne's England; an authentic Irish tune, *The Last Rose of Summer,* is used in the score as a recurrent theme, lending a certain nostalgic charm to an otherwise incongruous story. Flotow's aristocratic sympathies made it psychologically difficult for him to remain in Paris after the revolution of 1848; he subsequently lived in Schwerin, where he held the post of intendant of court music (1855–63); traveled in Austria and Italy, and revisited Paris (then under the Second Empire); in 1880 he retired and lived near Darmstadt.

WORKS: OPERAS: *Pierre et Catherine* (Schwerin 1835); *Serafine* (Royaumont, Oct. 30, 1836); *Le Comte de Saint-Mégrin* (Royaumont, June 10, 1838); *Le Naufrage de la Méduse* (with Grisar and Pilati; Paris, May 31, 1839; in German as *Die Matrosen,* Hamburg, Dec. 23, 1845); *L'Esclave de Camoëns* (Paris, Dec. 1, 1843); *Alessandro Stradella* (Hamburg, Dec. 30, 1844); *L'Âme en peine* (or *Leoline;* Paris, June 29, 1846); *Martha* (Vienna, Nov. 25, 1847; his greatest success); *Sophia Catharina,* or *Die Grossfürstin* (Berlin, Nov. 19, 1850); *Indra* (a revision of *L'Esclave de Camoëns,* with a German libretto; Vienna, Dec. 18, 1852); *Rübezahl* (Frankfurt, Nov. 26, 1853); *Albin,* or

Der Pflegsohn (Vienna, 1856; revived under the title *Der Müller von Meran,* Königsberg, Jan. 15, 1860); *Pianella* (Schwerin, Dec. 27, 1857); *La Veuve Grapin* (Paris, Sept. 21, 1859); *Naida* (St. Petersburg, Dec. 11, 1865); *Zilda* (Paris, May 28, 1866); *Am Runenstein* (Prague, April 13, 1868); *L'Ombre* (Paris, July 7, 1870); also separate numbers for Grisar's operas *Lady Melvil* (1838) and *L'Eau merveilleuse* (1839). BALLETS: *Lady Henriette* (Paris, Feb. 22, 1844); *Die Libelle* (Schwerin, Aug. 8, 1856); *Die Gruppe der Thetis* (Schwerin, Aug. 18, 1858); *Tannkönig* (Schwerin, Dec. 22, 1861); *Der Königsschuss* (Schwerin, May 22, 1864). INSTRUMENTAL MUSIC: *Trio de salon* for piano, violin, and cello (1850); Violin Sonata (1861); *Chants du soir* for cello and piano (1845); Études for Piano 4-Hands (1872); a piano concerto in MS.
BIBLIOGRAPHY: G. von Flotow, *Beiträge zur Geschichte der Familie von Flotow* (Dresden, 1844); W. Neumann, *Friedrich von Flotow* (Kassel, 1855); F. von Flotow, "Erinnerungen aus meinem Leben" (in Lewinsky's *Vor den Coulissen,* Berlin, 1882); R. Swoboda, *Friedrich von Flotows Leben; von seiner Witwe* (Leipzig, 1892); B. Bardi-Poswiansky, *Flotow als Opernkomponist* (Königsberg, 1927).

Flower, Sir Newman, English publisher and writer on music; b. Fontmell Magna, Dorset, July 8, 1879; d. Dorset, March 12, 1964. He joined the firm of Cassel & Co. in 1906; purchased it in 1927. As an avocation, he became deeply interested in music; publ. an extensive biography, *G. F. Handel* (1923; revised ed., 1947); *Sir Arthur Sullivan, His Life and Letters* (with Herbert Sullivan; 1927; revised ed., 1950); *Franz Schubert* (1928; revised ed., 1949); also publ. a volume of memoirs, *Just as It Happened* (1950). He was knighted in 1938.

Floyd, Carlisle, American opera composer; b. Latta, South Carolina, June 11, 1926; studied at Syracuse Univ. with Ernst Bacon; obtained a M. Mus. degree there; also took private lessons with Rudolf Firkušný. In 1947 he joined the staff of the School of Music, Florida State Univ., Tallahassee. His musical drama in 2 acts and 10 scenes, *Susannah,* was produced there (Feb. 24, 1955); it was later staged at the City Center, N.Y. (Sept. 27, 1956); received the Music Critics Circle of New York Award as the best opera of the year. Floyd's other works include *Slow Dusk,* a musical play in one act (1949); *Fugitives,* a musical drama in 3 acts (1951); the operas: *Wuthering Heights* (Santa Fe, July 16, 1958); *The Passion of Jonathan Wade* (N.Y., Oct. 11, 1962); *The Sojourner and Mollie Sinclair* (Raleigh, N. Carolina, Dec. 2, 1963); *Markheim* (New Orleans, March 31, 1966); *Of Mice and Men,* after John Steinbeck's novel (Seattle, Jan. 22, 1970); and *Bilby's Doll,* for the Bicentennial (Houston, Feb. 29, 1976). He further wrote *Lost Eden* for 2 pianos (ballet; 1952); and *Pilgrimage,* a cycle of 5 songs (1955), and other vocal and instrumental pieces.

Flury, Richard, Swiss composer; b. Biberist, March 26, 1896; d. Solothurn, Switzerland, Dec. 23, 1967. He studied musicology in Basel, Bern, and Geneva, then theory and composition with Kurth, Hubert, Lauber, and Marx; conducted orchestras and choral societies in Switzerland (Zürich, Bern and Solothurn); taught at the Solothurn Canton School.
WORKS: operas: *Eine florentinische Tragödie* (1926), *Die helle Nacht* (1932), *Casanova e l'Albertolli* (1937); ballet *Die alte Truhe;* several festival music scores; 8 symphonies: No. 1 (1923), *Fastnachts-Symphonie* (1928), *Tessiner Symphonie* (No. 2, 1936), *Waldsymphonie* (1942), *Bucheggbergische Symphonie* (No. 3, 1946), No. 4 (1950), No. 5 (1952), No. 6 (1953); 6 symph. overtures; 3 violin concertos (1933, 1940, 1944); 2 piano concertos (1927, 1943); chamber music: Oboe Sonata (1926), 2 cello sonatas (1937, 1941), 4 string quartets (1926, 1929, 1938, 1940), Piano Quintet (1948); 7 piano sonatas; *50 romantische Stücke* for piano; 24 preludes for piano; 15 military marches and other music for band; choruses; about 150 songs. He wrote an autobiography, *Lebenserinnerungen* (1950; with a list of works).

Foch (real name **Fock**), **Dirk,** composer and conductor; b. Batavia, Java (where his father was Governor General of the Dutch East Indies), June 18, 1886; d. Locarno, Switzerland, May 24, 1973. He studied in Holland and Germany; began his career in Sweden; conducted the Göteborg Symph. Orch. (1913–15); was guest conductor of the Concertgebouw in Amsterdam and of the orch. at The Hague (1917–19). He made his American debut as conductor with a specially assembled orch. at Carnegie Hall, N.Y., April 12, 1920; also conducted orchestral groups in the U.S., and in Vienna.
WORKS: *Ein hohes Lied* (5 fragments from the Bible), for recitation and orch. (Amsterdam, 1931); a musical pageant in the style of the medieval mystery plays, *From Aeon to Aeon;* 3 ballades for piano (1913); a cycle of songs from the Chinese (1921); *Java Sketches* for piano (1948).

Fodi, John, Hungarian-born Canadian composer; b. Nagyteval, March 22, 1944. He came to Canada as a child; studied music theory with Lorne Betts in Hamilton; then went to Toronto where he took courses in composition with Weinzweig and Beckwith at the Toronto Cons. (1966–70); also studied composition with Anhalt and Pedersen at McGill Univ. in Montreal (1970–71). Fodi's own compositions partake of multifarious techniques of ultra-modern music; the titles alone point to a preoccupation with abstract textures and mathematical processes, e.g. *Contrasts Four, Pi, Divisions, Signals, Segments* and even *Erro.*
WORKS: 6 string quartets (1963; 1963; 1965; *Fantasia,* 1967; *Ch'ien,* 1969; *Concerto a Quattro,* 1973); *Movement* for wind quintet and string quartet (1964); *Prelude* for small orch. (1964); Piano Sonata (1964–66); Symphony (1964–66); *Contrasts Four* for piano (1964–66); *Chamber Symphony* for flute, horn, piano and string quartet (1967); *Polyphony* for 2 woodwinds and 2 strings (1967); *7 Fantasias* for solo flute (1968); *Tettares* for percussion quartet (1968); *Pi* for trombone and piano (1968); Harpsichord Sonata (1968); *Signals* for soprano saxophone, tenor saxophone, trombone, percussion and piano (1969); *Divisions I* for piano (1970), *II* for piano and harpsichord (1972), *III* for solo viola (1971) and *IV* for solo guitar (1974–77); *Symparanekromenoi* (Greek polynome;

translatable as *Those Who, for Some Cause or Another, Are Living Lives that Are Spiritually or Mentally Entombed and Isolated*) for orch. (1969–71; first complete perf., Toronto, July 25, 1974); *Segments* for piano (1971); *Variations I* for flute, clarinet, percussion and 3 strings (1972) and *II* for wind quintet (1975); Concerto for viola and 2 wind ensembles (1972); *Erro* for organ (1974); *An Investigation*, graphic score for oboe, organ, viola and percussion, in any combination (1974); *Iz Ist in der Werlt Wol Schin* for high voice and viola (1975); *Dragon Days* for orch. (1974–76); *Partimento: Here the Forsaken Virgin Rests . . .* for flute, oboe, cello, piano, electric organ, spinet and percussion (1976); Trio for flute, viola and harpsichord (1976–77); *Capriccio* for solo double bass (1977); *Patrem Omnipotentem* for flute, trombone, viola, cello piano and percussion (1977); 5 pieces for tape.

Fodor, Eugene, American violinist; b. Turkey Creek, Colorado, March 5, 1950, of Hungarian-Italian extraction. (His great-great-grandfather founded the Fodor Cons. in Hungary.) He studied violin with Harold Wippler in Denver; in 1967 he went to N.Y. and studied with Galamian; later took lessons in the master class of Jascha Heifetz at the Univ. of Southern California. In 1972 he won the Paganini Competition in Genoa, Italy. In 1974 he shared second prize with two Soviet violinists (no 1st prize was awarded) at the Tchaikovsky Violin Contest in Moscow. Returning to America, he was given the honors of the State of Colorado, and on Sept. 12, 1974 played at a state dinner at the White House for the premier of Israel, Rabin.

BIBLIOGRAPHY: *Current Biography* (April 1976).

Foerster, Adolph Martin, American composer; b. Pittsburgh, Pa., Feb. 2, 1854; d. there, Aug. 10, 1927. He owed his first musical training to his mother; studied at the Leipzig Cons. with Richter; then returned to Pittsburgh, where he was active as a teacher of singing and piano. He composed *Dedication March* for the opening of Carnegie Music Hall in Pittsburgh (Nov. 7, 1895); symph. poem *Thusnelda*; Violin Concerto; 2 piano trios; 2 piano quartets; 2 string quartets; numerous piano works; songs.

Foerster, Josef Bohuslav, significant Czech composer; b. Prague, Dec. 30, 1859; d. Nový Vestec, near Stará Boleslav, May 29, 1951. He was the son of the Czech organist, **Josef Förster** (1833–1907). He studied organ and was for several years organist of St. Adelbert's Church in Prague; conducted choruses; wrote music criticism. He married the opera singer **Berta Lauterer** in 1888; when she was engaged to sing at the Municipal Theater of Hamburg in 1893, Foerster followed her, and became prof. of the Hamburg Cons. and also music critic of the *Hamburger Nachrichten*. Subsequently his wife was engaged by Mahler for the Vienna Court Opera (1903), and Foerster obtained a position at the New Cons. in Vienna. In 1918, he returned to Prague, where he held teaching positions; taught composition at the Prague Cons.; was president of the Czech Academy (1931–39); in 1945, he received the honorary title of National Artist of the

Republic of Czechoslovakia. He continued to teach privately and to compose almost to the end of his very long life; many Czech composers of the 20th century were his students. Foerster wrote in every genre; his music is suffused with lyric melos, and reveals characteristic national traits in his treatment of melodic and rhythmic material. His harmonic idiom represents the general style of central European romanticism, stemming from Dvořák, and ultimately from Wagner and Brahms.

WORKS: operas (all first performed in Prague): *Deborah* (Jan. 27, 1893), *Eva* (Jan. 1, 1899), *Jessica* (April 16, 1905), *Nepřemoženi (The Conquerers;* Dec. 19, 1918), *Srdce (The Heart;* Nov. 15, 1923), *Bloud (The Simpleton;* Feb. 28, 1936); incidental music for Shakespeare's plays *Love's Labour's Lost, Twelfth Night,* and *Julius Caesar,* and for Strindberg's *Journey of Fortunate Peter;* 4 Masses; oratorio *St. Venceslas* (1928); cantata *May* (1936); a cantata on the subject of the Thirty Years' War (1940); cantata entitled *1945,* written to celebrate the liberation of Czechoslovakia; 5 symphonies (1888, 1893, 1895, 1905, 1929); symph. poems *My Youth* (1900) and *Enigma* (1909); symph. suite *Cyrano de Bergerac* (1903); *Solemn Overture* (1907); 2 violin concertos (1911, 1926); Cello Concerto (1931); *Capriccio* for flute and small orch. (1940); 4 string quartets (1882, 1893, 1907, 1944); 3 piano trios (1883, 1894, 1921); String Quintet (1886); Wind Quintet (1909); Nonet for string and wind instruments (1931); 2 violin sonatas (1889, 1892); *Sonata quasi una fantasia* for violin and piano (1943); Suite for Viola and Piano (1940). He publ. a book of memoirs, *Poutník v Cizině* (Prague, 1947; in German as *Der Pilger,* 1955).

BIBLIOGRAPHY: Z. Nejedlý, *J. B. Foerster* (Prague, 1910); J. Bartoš, *J. B. Foerster* (Prague, 1923); a symposium, *J. B. Foerster,* by various Czech writers, was publ. for his 90th birthday (Prague, 1949).

Fogg, Eric, English organist and composer; b. Manchester, Feb. 21, 1903; d. London, Dec. 19, 1939. He studied organ with his father; composition with Granville Bantock. He was active as organist in Manchester; then was music director with the British Broadcasting Corporation. He wrote an overture to the *Comedy of Errors* (1922); *Poem* for cello and piano; Suite for Violin, Cello, and Harp; songs (*Love and Life, The Little Folk,* etc.); piano pieces; choral works; etc.

Foggia, Francesco, Italian composer; b. Rome, 1604; d. there, Jan. 8, 1688. He was a pupil of A. Cifra; served at several German courts; returning to Rome, he was maestro di cappella at the Lateran (1636–61); at San Lorenzo in Damaso (1661), and, from 1677, at Santa Maria Maggiore. A prolific and masterly composer, he continued the traditions of the Roman School. He wrote the oratorios *David fugiens a facie Saul* and *San Giovanni Battista* (1670); numerous Masses a cappella (also a few with organ); litanies, motets, etc.

Fogliani (Fogliano), Ludovico, Italian theorist; b. Modena, 2d half of 15th cent.; d. there, 1538. Famous for his book *Musica theorica . . .* (Venice, 1529), in which he preceded Zarlino in declaring the correct proportion of the major third to be 4:5, and in distinguishing between the major and minor (greater and lesser) semitones. In Petrucci's *Frottole* (1504–08) are some specimens of his compositions.

Fogliano, Giacomo, Italian theorist and composer, brother of **Ludovico Fogliani;** b. Modena, 1468; d. there, April 10, 1548. He was chorister in the Papal Chapel in Rome (1513–14); later was choirmaster of the Modena Cathedral. He published *Musica Theorica* (Venice, 1529), of importance for the problem of tuning compatible organs in fifths and thirds.

BIBLIOGRAPHY: J. Barbour, *Tuning and Temperament* (East Lansing, Michigan, 1953).

Foldes, Andor, Hungarian pianist; b. Budapest, Dec. 21, 1913. He was given piano lessons by his mother as a child, and at the age of 8 already played a Mozart concerto with the Budapest Philharmonic. From 1922 to 1932 he was a pupil of Dohnányi at the Liszt Academy of Music in Budapest; in 1933 he received the Liszt Prize, and in 1934 began his first European tour as a concert pianist. In 1939 he went to New York, and became a naturalized American citizen in 1948; then he returned to Europe; lived in Germany and in Switzerland. In 1969 he toured India and Japan; also gave concerts in Argentina and South Africa. Apart from the regular piano repertory, Foldes played almost all piano works by Bartók. With his wife, **Lili Foldes,** he published an entertaining booklet, *Two on a Continent* (N.Y., 1947); he further published a lively piano manual, *Keys to the Keyboard* (N.Y., 1948), which was translated into German, Hungarian, Italian, Spanish, Norwegian, Polish, Dutch, Japanese and Korean.

Foley, Allan James, Irish bass; b. Cahir, Tipperary, Ireland, Aug. 7, 1835; d. Southport, England, Oct. 20, 1899. He was a pupil of Bisaccia in Naples. Following a widely spread fashion among English opera singers, he changed his name to an Italian-sounding homonym "Foli," and made a career as **"Signor Foli."** He sang all over Europe, in America, Russia, Australia and South Africa.

Folville, Juliette Éugénie-Émilie, Belgian composer; b. Liège, Jan. 5, 1870; d. Dourgne, France, Oct. 28, 1946. She studied piano with her father, then violin with César Thomson. When she was only 17, her *Chant de Noël* was performed at the Liège Cathedral. In 1898 she was appointed professor at the Liège Cons. After the outbreak of World War I in 1914, she lived in Bournemouth, England; later returned to the Continent. She wrote an opera, *Atala* (Lille, 1892); miscellaneous pieces for piano, violin and organ; choruses.

Fomin, Evstignei, one of the earliest Russian national composers; b. St. Petersburg, Aug. 16, 1761; d. there, April 27, 1800. He was sent to Bologna to study with Padre Martini; returned to St. Petersburg in 1785; then became singing teacher and operatic coach at the theatrical school there. He composed about 10 operas, including *Novgorod Hero Vassily Boyeslavitch*

(St. Petersburg, Dec. 8, 1786); *Yamshchiki (Coachmen;* St. Petersburg, Jan. 13, 1787); *Orpheus and Eurydice* (St. Petersburg, Jan. 13, 1792), and *The Americans* (St. Petersburg, Feb. 19, 1800; the title refers to the Russians in Alaska; vocal score publ. in 1893; the opera was revived in a performance at Moscow, Jan. 17, 1947). A number of other operas were erroneously attributed to Fomin, among them the popular *Miller, Wizard, Cheat, and Marriage-Broker,* produced in Moscow on Jan. 31, 1779, the music of which was actually written by an obscure violinist named Sokolovsky.

BIBLIOGRAPHY: A. Finagin, "E. Fomin," in the collection, *Music in Old Russia* (Leningrad, 1927); N. Findeisen, "The Earliest Russian Operas," *Musical Quarterly* (July 1933); A. Rabinovich, *Russian Opera Before Glinka* (Moscow, 1948; pp. 50–57 and 85–105); B. Dobrokhotov, *Evstigney Fomin* (Moscow, 1968).

Fongaard, Björn, Norwegian composer; b. Oslo, March 2, 1919. He studied at the Oslo Cons. with Bjarne Brustad; later took a course in advanced techniques with Karl Andersen. He also began to experiment with fractional intervals. His total output numbers 340 polyphonic studies in tonality, 12 piano sonatinas, 44 experimental piano pieces, and much instrumental music. Fascinated by science, he wrote a symph. poem, *Uran 235,* glorifying the energy of the fissionable isotope (1963); *Galaxies* for three specially designed quarter-tone guitars (1966); *Kosmos* for strings and percussion (1968). Other works are: *Orafoni* for male speaking chorus, strings and percussion (1964); *Orchestra Antiphonalis* (1968); Sonata for a Single Tam-Tam, electronically metamorphosed (1968); *Vision* for strings (1968). Fongaard is renowned as a guitar virtuoso and is professor of guitar playing at the Cons. of Oslo.

Fonseca, Julio, Costa Rican composer; b. San José, Costa Rica, May 22, 1885; d. there, June 22, 1950. He received elementary musical training at home, from his father, a military band musician. A government grant enabled him to pursue serious study in Europe, at the Cons. of Milan and in Brussels. Returning to Costa Rica, he became active as a teacher at music schools in San José and a church organist. His works consist mostly of pleasant salon music for piano and effective band pieces, much of it based on native folk rhythms, such as his band pieces, *Suite tropical* (1934) and *Gran Fantasia sinfónica sobre motivos folklóricos* (1937).

Fontanelli, Alfonso, Italian madrigal composer; b. Reggio Emilia, Feb. 15, 1557; d. Rome, Feb. 11, 1622. He was in the service of Duke Alfonso II of Este in Ferrara (1588–97) and of his successor, Cesare II, until 1601, when he left the court to save himself from prosecution for a suspected complicity in the assassination of his second wife's lover. However, he was again in the service of the Estes in 1605, when he was in Rome as emissary of the Duke of Modena; in 1608 he was in Modena; in 1612–13, at the Spanish court. He took holy orders in 1621. He was a friend of Gesualdo, Prince of Venosa, and may have been influenced by him in his madrigals. He published anonymously 2 books of madrigals in 5 voices: *Primo libro* (Ferrara, 1595; reprint, Venice, 1603); *Secondo libro* (Venice, 1604; reprints 1609 and 1619). He was greatly esteemed by his contemporaries; Orazio Vecchi contributed an introduction to the 1603 ed. of his *Primo libro,* praising him for the inventiveness and dignity of his music.

BIBLIOGRAPHY: F. Vatielli, *Il Principe di Venosa e Leonora d'Este* (Milan, 1941); A. Einstein, *The Italian Madrigal* (Princeton, 1949; vol. 2, p. 703).

Fontyn, Jacqueline, Belgian composer; b. Antwerp, Dec. 27, 1930. She studied piano with Marcel Maas in Brussels (1935–48); then took lessons in composition with Marcel Quinet and with Max Deutsch in Paris; also attended courses at the Akademie für Musik und darstellende Kunst, in Vienna and at the Chapelle Musicale Reine Elizabeth in Brussels (1956–59). She taught at the Royal Flemish Cons. in Antwerp (1963–70) and at the Brussels Cons. Her music has won numerous international prizes. She was married to the Belgian composer **Camille Schmit.**

WORKS: a ballet, *Piedigrotta* (1958); 2 cantatas: *La trapéziste qui a perdu son coeur* for mezzo-soprano and chamber orch. (1953) and *Psalmus Tertius* for baritone, chorus and orch. (1959); *Petite Suite* for orch. (1951); *Divertimento* for strings (1953); *Danceries* for orch. (1956); *Prelude and Allegro* for orch. (1957); *Mouvements concertants* for 2 pianos and strings (1957); *2 Estampies* for orch. (1961); *Digressions* for chamber orch. (1962); *6 Ebauches (6 Sketches)* for orch. (1964); *Digressions* for cello, and chamber orch. or piano (1964); *Galaxie* for 17 instruments (1965); Piano Concerto (1969); *Colloque* for chamber orch. (1970); *Pour onze cordes (For 11 Strings,* 1971); *Evoluon* for orch. (1973); *Per Archi* for 11 strings (1973); Flute Sonata (1952); *Danceries* for violin and piano (1953); Wind Quintet (1954); Piano Trio (1956); String Quartet (1958); *Mosaïci* for 4 clarinets (1965); *Musica a quattro* for violin, viola or clarinet, cello and piano (1966); *Mosaïques* for clarinet and piano (1967); *Dialogues* for saxophone and piano (1969; an adaptation of *Digressions* for cello and chamber orch.); Nonet (1969); *Filigrane* for flute and harp (1970); *6 Climats* for cello and piano (1972); *Strophes* for violin and piano (1972); *2 Impromptus* for piano (1950); *Capriccio* for piano (1954); Ballade for Piano (1963); *Mosaïci* for piano (1964); *Spirales* for 2 pianos (1972); *Digitale* for harpsichord (1973); choruses; songs.

Foote, Arthur, eminent American composer; b. Salem, Mass., March 5, 1853; d. Boston, April 8, 1937. He studied piano with a local teacher in Salem; in 1870 he entered Harvard Univ., studying composition with J. K. Paine; he received the A.M. degree in 1875 (the first such degree in music given in America). He also studied organ with B. J. Lang. In 1876 he attended the Wagner Festival in Bayreuth. In 1878 he became organist in the Boston First Unitarian Church, a post that he held until 1910. In 1881 he organized in Boston a series of chamber music concerts which continued until the end of the century; he was frequently pianist with the Kneisel Quartet (1890–1910), performing several of his own works. For 50 years, from 1883, he

was a successful teacher in Boston. He was a member of the Music Teachers National Association; a founding member of the American Guild of Organists, and its president from 1909–12; also member of the National Institute of Arts and Letters and Fellow of the American Academy of Arts and Sciences. His music is distinguished by a fine lyrical feeling, in a romantic tradition.

WORKS: Many of his orchestral works were presented for the first time by the Boston Symphony Orchestra: overture, *In the Mountains* (Feb. 5, 1887; also performed at the Paris Exposition, July 12, 1889); Suite for Strings in D, op. 21 (Nov. 23, 1889); symphonic prologue, *Francesca da Rimini* (Jan. 24, 1891); Suite in D minor, op. 36 (March 7, 1896); Suite for Strings in E, op. 63 (April 16, 1909). Of these, the Suite for Strings in E is particularly popular. Other works include: Serenade in E for strings, op. 25; *4 Character Pieces* after Omar Khayyám, op. 48, for orch.; Cello Concerto; *A Night Piece* for flute and strings; the cantatas (for chorus and piano or orchestra): *The Farewell of Hiawatha,* for men's voices, op. 11; *The Wreck of the Hesperus,* op. 17; *The Skeleton in Armor,* op. 28. Chamber music: 3 string quartets, 2 piano trios, Violin Sonata, Piano Quartet, Piano Quintet, Cello Sonata, various pieces for instruments with piano accompaniment; more than 100 songs, of which the following are the best known: *The Night Has a Thousand Eyes; I Know a Little Garden Path; Constancy; In Picardie; Ashes of Roses;* also vocal quartets; church music.

WRITINGS: He was the author of several manuals: *Modern Harmony in its Theory and Practice* (jointly with W. R. Spalding, 1905; reprinted, 1936; revised in 1959; republished as *Harmony,* 1969); *Some Practical Things in Piano-Playing* (1909); *Modulation and Related Harmonic Questions* (1919); also transl. Richter's *Treatise on Fugue;* ed. vol. 9 of *The American History and Encyclopedia of Music* (1908–10). His autobiography was privately printed by his daughter, Katharine Foote Raffy (Norwood, Mass., 1946). See also his article "A Bostonian Remembers," *Musical Quarterly* (Jan. 1937).

Foote, George, American composer; b. Cannes, France, of American parents, Feb. 19, 1886; d. Boston, March 25, 1956. He studied with E. B. Hill at Harvard Univ.; then in Berlin with Koch and Klatte. Upon his return to the U.S. he was a member of the staff in the Music Dept. of Harvard Univ. (1921–23) and president of the South End Music School in Boston (until 1943).

WORKS: *Variations on a Pious Theme* for orch. (Boston Symph., Feb. 11, 1935); *In Praise of Winter,* symph. suite (Boston Symph., Jan. 5, 1940); *98th Psalm,* for chorus and organ (1934); religious pantomime, *We Go Forward* (1943); Trio for Flute, Harp, and Violin; other chamber music.

Forbes, Elliot, American choral conductor and music educator; b. Cambridge, Mass., Aug. 30, 1917. He studied at Harvard Univ. (B.A., 1941; M.A., 1947); also took courses at Mozarteum in Salzburg (1937). He subsequently joined the staff of the Music Dept. of Princeton Univ. (1947–57). In 1958 he was appointed prof. of Harvard Univ. and conductor of the Harvard Glee Club and Radcliffe Choral Society; conducted the Harvard Glee Club in a tour around the world in 1961 and the Harvard-Radcliffe Chorus in a North American tour in 1964. In 1965 he taught at the Berkshire Music Center in Tanglewood. He is the editor of the revision of Thayer's *Life of Beethoven* (Princeton, 1964), of *Harvard-Radcliffe Choral Music* and the *Harvard Song Book* (Boston, 1965).

Forbes, Henry, English composer; b. London, 1804; d. there, Nov. 24, 1859. He studied with Sir George Smart in London, and with Moscheles and Hummel in Germany; was engaged as church organist and publ. a collection of psalm tunes, *National Psalmody* (1843). His opera *The Fairy Oak* was produced in London (Oct. 18, 1845) with considerable success.

Ford, Ernest, English conductor and composer, b. London, Feb. 17, 1858; d. there, June 2, 1919. He was a pupil of Arthur Sullivan in the Royal Academy of Music and of Lalo in Paris; for some years conductor at the Royal English Opera House (where he conducted the première of Sullivan's *Ivanhoe* in 1891), then at the Empire Theatre; 1897–1908, Royal Amateur Orch. Society; from 1916, prof. of singing at Guildhall School of Music; Fellow of the Royal Academy of Music from 1899. He wrote operas; operettas; motet, *Domine Deus* (for 250th anniversary of Harvard Univ.); songs, duets, etc.; published a *Short History of Music in England* (1912).

Ford, Thomas, English composer and lutenist; b. c.1580; d. Nov. (buried Nov. 17), 1648. He was appointed musician to Prince Henry in 1611, and to Charles I in 1626. He was especially successful in the "ayre," a type of composition developed by Dowland, in which melodic prominence is given to the upper voice. These "ayres" appear in alternative settings, either as solo songs with lute accomp. or as 4-part a cappella songs. He wrote *Musicke of Sundrie Kindes* (1607; 1st part contains 11 ayres); 2 anthems in Leighton's *Teares;* canons in Hilton's *Catch that catch can;* and the famous madrigal, *Since first I saw your face.* MSS are at Christ Church, Oxford, and at the British Museum.

Fordell, Erik, Finnish composer; b. Kokkola, July 2, 1917. He studied at the Sibelius Academy and the Helsinki Institute of Church Music. He is unquestionably the most prolific Finnish composer of symphonies, of which he wrote 25 in 20 years: No. 1 (1949); No. 2 (1949); No. 3 (1952); No. 4 (1955); No. 5 (1955); No. 6 (1955); No. 7 (1955); No. 8 (1955); No. 9 (1955); No. 10 (1956); No. 11 (1957); No. 12 (1957); No. 13 (1957); No. 14 (1958); No. 15 (1961); No. 16 (1955, revised 1961); No. 17 (1966); No. 18 (1958, revised 1966); No. 19 (1967); No. 20 (1968); No. 21 (1968); No. 22 (1969); No. 23 (1969); No. 24 (1969); No. 25 (1969); also an unnumbered *Nature Symphony* (1970–71); 2 violin concertos (1955; 1959); 4 piano concertos (1961; 1962; 1962; 1962); Horn Concerto (1956); *Oratorium Profanum* (1968); *Trilogy* for orch. (1969); *Symphonic Trilogy* (1970); 8 suites for strings; 5 cantatas; 4 wind quintets; 7 string quartets; Violin Sonata; Flute Sonata; songs; choral music; piano pieces.

Forkel, Johann Nikolaus, erudite German music historian; b. Meeder, near Coburg, Feb. 22, 1749; d. Göttingen, March 20, 1818. He was a chorister at Lüneburg (1762–66) and at Schwerin (1766). In 1769 he began the study of law in Göttingen, supporting himself by teaching music. He served as a church organist; in 1778 was appointed as music director at the Univ. of Gottingen.

WRITINGS: *Über die Theorie der Musik, sofern sie Liebhabern und Kennern derselben nothwendig und nützlich ist* (1774); *Musikalischkritische Bibliothek* (Gotha, 1778–79, 3 vols.); *Über die beste Einrichtung öffentlicher Concerte* (1779); *Genauere Bestimmung einiger musikalischer Begriffe* (1780); *Musikalischer Almanach für Deutschland* (1782, 1783, 1784, and 1789); *Allgemeine Geschichte der Musik* (Leipzig, 1788 and 1801, 2 vols., covering the period up to 1550; his materials for later times went to the publisher Schwickert); *Allgemeine Literatur der Musik, oder Anleitung zur Kenntniss musikalischer Bücher* (1792; important as the pioneer work of its class); *Über Johann Sebastian Bachs Leben, Kunst und Kunstwerke* (Leipzig, 1802; the first full biography of Bach, based on information supplied by Bach's sons; in English, London 1820; new transl., London, 1920, by Terry). Forkel's unique transcriptions, in modern notation, of Graphäus' *Missae XIII* (1539), and of the *Liber XV. missarum* of Petrejus (1538; Masses by Ockeghem, Obrecht, Josquin, and others), were engraved, and a proof pulled, but the invading French army melted down the plates for cannon balls. The proof sheets, corrected by Forkel, are in the Berlin Library. His publ. compositions include piano sonatas and songs; in MS are the oratorio *Hiskias;* 2 cantatas *Die Macht des Gesangs* and *Die Hirten an der Krippe zu Bethlehem;* symphonies, trios, choruses, etc.

BIBLIOGRAPHY: Heinrich Edelhoff, *J. N. Forkel* (Göttingen, 1935); W. Franck, "Musicology and Its Founder, J. N. Forkel," *Musical Quarterly* (Oct. 1949).

Formes, Karl Johann, German bass; b. Mülheim, Aug. 7, 1815; d. San Francisco, Dec. 15, 1889. He made his opera debut at Cologne, 1841; from 1843–48 he was engaged at Mannheim; 1852–57 at the Royal Italian Opera, London; in 1857 he made his first American tour; then divided his time between Europe and America. He wrote an autobiography, *Aus meinem Kunst- und Bühnenleben* (1888; in English, San Francisco, 1891).

Formes, Theodor, German tenor, brother of **Karl Formes;** b. Mülheim, June 24, 1826; d. Endenich, near Bonn, Oct. 15, 1874. He made his debut at Ofen (1846); then sang opera in Vienna (1848) and Berlin (1851–66); made a tour in America with his brother. He lost his voice temporarily; returned to the stage for a few years; then suffered a setback, became insane, and died in an asylum.

Fornerod, Aloys, Swiss violinist and composer; b. Montet-Cudrefin (Vaud), Nov. 16, 1890; d. Fribourg, Switzerland, Jan. 8, 1965. He studied violin and theory at the Cons. of Lausanne and at the Schola Cantorum in Paris. Returning to Switzerland, he was a member of the Lausanne Symph. Orch.; in 1954 he was appointed director of the Fribourg Cons. As a composer, he followed the French modern style, in the spirit of fin-de-siècle impressionism.

WORKS: *Geneviève,* one-act comic opera (Lausanne, May 20, 1954); *Te Deum* for soloists, chorus and orch. (1955); *Hymne à la Très Sainte Trinité* for chorus and brass (1961); *Le Voyage de printemps,* symph. suite (1943); Piano Concerto (1944); Violin Sonata (1925); Concerto for 2 Violins and Piano (1927); Cello Sonata (1934); choruses and songs. He publ. *Les Tendances de la musique moderne* (Lausanne, 1924); was for 40 years a critic in *La Tribune de Lausanne.*

Fornia-Labey, Rita (*née* **Newman**), American soprano; b. San Francisco, July 17, 1878; d. Paris, Oct. 27, 1922. She adopted the name Fornia from her native state of California; married J. P. Labey in 1910. She studied in Paris with Jean de Reszke; began her career as a coloratura soprano; then changed to mezzo-soprano. She made her debut in Germany; came to the U.S. in 1906 as a member of H. W. Savage's Opera Co.; from 1908–22 she was on the staff of the Metropolitan Opera; also made appearances at Covent Garden in London. She was particularly effective in Wagnerian roles.

Foroni, Jacopo, Italian conductor and composer; b. Verona, July 25, 1825; d. Stockholm, Sept. 8, 1858 (of cholera). He settled in Stockholm in 1849, and became court conductor there; was very successful at his public concerts, and also as a composer. He wrote several operas, among them *I Gladiatori* (Milan, Oct. 7, 1851). His opera *Advokaten Patelin,* performed posthumously in Stockholm (Dec. 4, 1858), was revived several times until 1926.

Forqueray, Antoine, French player on the viola da gamba; b. Paris, 1671; d. Nantes, June 28, 1745. He held an appointment as royal chamber musician to Louis XIV from 1690; publ. pieces for his instrument. His brother, **Michel Forqueray** (b. Paris, Feb. 15, 1681; d. Montfort l'Amaury, May 30, 1757), was a Paris organist; **Jean Baptiste Forqueray** (b. Paris, April 3, 1699; d. there, Aug. 15, 1782), son of **Antoine Forqueray,** was also a player on the viola da gamba; transcribed for the harpsichord some of his father's pieces; **Nicolas Gilles Forqueray** (b. Paris, Feb. 15, 1703; d. there, Oct. 23, 1761), another son of **Antoine,** was a church organist.

Forrest, Hamilton, American composer; b. Chicago, Jan. 8, 1901; he sang as a chorister in Chicago churches; studied with Adolf Weidig; has written mainly for the stage: operas *Yzdra* (1925; received the Bispham Memorial Medal of the American Opera Society of Chicago) and *Camille* (Chicago, Dec. 10, 1930, with Mary Garden in the title role); also ballet music and *Watercolors* for 14 wind instruments and harp.

Forrester, Maureen, Canadian contralto; b. Montreal, July 25, 1930. She studied piano and singing in Toronto, and made her concert debut in 1953 in Montreal. In 1956 she was soloist in Mahler's *Resurrection Symphony* in New York with Bruno Walter conducting, scoring a remarkable success. This led to numer-

ous appearances with major American orchestras. Subsequently she made extensive concert tours in Europe. Critics in America and in Europe invariably lauded her for the sensitive and artistic performances of German Lieder.

Forsell, John, famous Swedish baritone; b. Stockholm, May 6, 1868; d. there, May 30, 1941. He was in the Swedish army before embarking on his vocal studies. He made his debut in 1896 at the Stockholm Opera; sang there from 1896 to 1901, and again in 1903–09. He was on the roster of the Metropolitan Opera during the season of 1909–10. In 1924 he was appointed director of the Stockholm Opera, a post that he held until 1939; also taught singing at the Stockholm Cons. from 1924. A jubilee collection of essays, *Boken om J. Forsell,* was publ. on his 70th birthday (Stockholm, 1938).

Förster, Alban, German violinist; b. Reichenbach, Oct. 23, 1849; d. Neustrelitz, Jan. 18, 1916. He was a pupil at Reichenbach of R. Blume; later of Dresden Cons.; in 1871, court musician at Neustrelitz, also conducting the Singakademie; 1881, teacher in Dresden Cons., and cond. of the Liedertafel; 1882–1908, court Kapellmeister at Neustrelitz. He wrote a ballet *Träumerei in der Waldmühle* (Zwickau, 1896); orchestral and chamber music (string trios and quartets), violin music, instructive piano pieces, and songs.

Förster, August, German piano manufacturer; b. Löbau, July 30, 1829; d. there, Feb. 18, 1897. He founded a piano factory in Bohemia; also owned the Förster Saal in Berlin. His firm constructed the first quartertone piano with two manuals (1924).

Förster, Emanuel Aloys, German composer and theorist; b. Niederstein, Silesia, Jan. 26, 1748; d. Vienna, Nov. 12, 1823. After service in the Prussian Army, where he played the oboe in a band, he went to Vienna for a thorough course in music, eventually becoming a teacher himself, even though without a school position. He became friendly with Beethoven, who expressed esteem for him. Förster was a prolific composer; he wrote 48 string quartets, 5 oboe concertos, 10 violin sonatas, 21 piano sonatas, etc. His variations on arias from operas by Mozart, Sarti, and others enjoyed great popularity. He also publ. a manual, *Anleitung zum Generalbass* (1805; several later editions).

Forster, Georg, German composer and compiler of music; b. Amberg, c.1510; d. Nuremberg, Nov. 12, 1568. He sang at the Heidelberg chapel in 1521, matriculating in classical studies in 1528. In 1531 he undertook medical studies at Ingolstadt; in 1534, studied humanities in Wittenberg with Melanchthon. In 1544 he received his degree of doctor of medicine at Tübingen Univ.; then was medical practitioner in Amberg, Würzburg, Heidelberg, and Nuremberg (1544). He edited the valuable collection *Ein Auszug guter alter und neuer teutscher Liedlein* (in 5 parts; Nuremberg, 1539–56). Reprints are found in Jöde's *Das Chorbuch,* and Schering's *Geschichte der Musik in*

Beispielen (no. 88). Part II of the collection is published in R. Eitner's *Publikationen*, vol. 29.

BIBLIOGRAPHY: H. J. Moser in *Jahrbuch Peters* (1928; p. 45 ff.).

Förster, Joseph, Czech organist and composer; b. Osojnitz, Bohemia, Feb. 22, 1833; d. Prague, Jan. 3, 1907. He was organist in several churches in Prague, and prof. of theory at the Prague Cons. He wrote organ pieces, church music, and a treatise on harmony. He was the father of the celebrated Czech composer **Joseph Bohuslav Foerster.**

Forsyth, Cecil, English composer and writer on music; b. Greenwich, Nov. 30, 1870; d. New York, Dec. 7, 1941. He received his general education at Edinburgh Univ.; then studied at the Royal College of Music with Stanford and Parry. He joined the viola section in the Queen's Hall Orch.; also was connected with the Savoy Theatre, where he produced two of his comic operas, *Westward Ho!* and *Cinderella.* After the outbreak of World War I he went to N.Y., where he remained for the rest of his life. He composed a viola concerto and *Chant celtique* for viola and orch.; also songs, sacred music, and instrumental pieces. He was the author of a comprehensive manual *Orchestration* (N.Y., 1914; 2nd ed., 1935; reprinted, 1948); *Choral Orchestration* (London, 1920); also *Music and Nationalism* (London, 1911; a treatise on English opera); publ. (in collaboration with Stanford) *A History of Music* (London, 1916); and a collection of essays *Clashpans* (N.Y., 1933).

Forsyth, Josephine, American song composer; b. Cleveland, July 5, 1889; d. there, May 24, 1940. She was married to P. A. Meyers on April 29, 1928, and wrote a setting of the *Lord's Prayer* for her wedding. This setting later attained considerable popularity, and was sung for many years at Easter sunrise ceremonies at the Hollywood Bowl.

Forsyth, Malcolm, South African-born Canadian composer and trombonist; b. Pietermaritzburg, Dec. 8, 1936. He studied composition with Mátyás Seiber, Erik Chisholm and Stefans Grové, trombone and conducting at the Univ. of Cape Town (1959-63; M.M., 1966; D. Mus., 1972); further composition studies with Ronald Stevenson. He was a trombonist in the Cape Town Symph. Orch. (1960-67); in 1968 went to Canada and became trombonist with the Edmonton, Alberta, Symph. Orch.; also taught trombone and theory at the Univ. of Alberta; became a Canadian citizen in 1974. His music is highly colorful and rhythmic, making use of African folk tunes in a modern Western dressing.

WORKS: *Erewhon,* overture (1962); *Jubilee Overture* (1964); *Essay for Orchestra: 67,* variations on a groundbass for orch. (Cape Town, Dec. 15, 1967); 2 symphonies: No. 1 (1968-72; Cape Town, Sept. 4, 1972) and No. 2, *. . . a host of nomads . . .* (1976); *Sketches from Natal* for 2 oboes, 2 horns and strings (Edmonton, March 23, 1970); Piano Concerto (1973-75); 2 concertos grossos for brass quintet and orch.: No. 1, *Sagittarius* (1975; Banff, Alberta, Aug. 16, 1975) and No. 2, *Quinquefid* (1976-77); *Quartet 61*

for 4 trombones (1961); *Poem* for brass (1964-66); *Pastorale and Rondo* for 4 wind instruments and piano (1968-69); *Aphorisms* for brass (1969-71); *Music for Mouths, Marimba, Mbira and Roto-Toms* for chorus and percussion (1973); *Quartet 74* for 4 trombones (1974); *Salterello,* ballet score for brass quintet and tape (1976-77).

Fortlage, Karl, German theorist; b. Osnabrück, June 12, 1806; d. Jena, Nov. 8, 1881. He studied theology and philosophy; was prof. at Jena Univ. from 1846. In connection with his study of Greek philosophy, he became interested in the Greek musical system; publ. one of the earliest comprehensive works on the subject, *Das musikalische System der Griechen in seiner Urgestalt* (Leipzig, 1847).

Fortner, Wolfgang, important German composer; b. Leipzig, Oct. 12, 1907. He studied composition with Hermann Grabner at the Leipzig Cons. and musicology with Theodore Kroyer at the Univ. there. Upon graduation he was engaged as instructor in music theory at the Institute of Sacred Music in Heidelberg (1931); in 1954 he was engaged in a similar capacity at the Music Academy in Detmold, and in 1957 was appointed to the faculty of the Musikhochschule in Freiburg-im-Breisgau. Concurrently, he led the concerts of Musica Viva in Munich and also lecturer at the Academy of the Arts in West Berlin. In 1961 he was engaged to conduct a seminar at the Berkshire Music Center at Tanglewood; he visited the U.S. again in 1968. His music is marked by exceptional contrapuntal skills, with the basic tonality clearly present even when harmonic density reaches its utmost; occasionally Fortner makes use of melodic procedures of a dodecaphonic nature. He is equally expert in his works for the musical theater and purely instrumental compositions; the German tradition is maintained throughout, both in the mechanics of strong polyphony and audacious innovations.

WORKS: *Die Witwe von Ephesus* (Berlin, Sept. 17, 1952); *Der Wald* for voices, speaker and orch., after the play of García Lorca (Frankfurt, June 25, 1953; later revised as a lyric tragedy and produced under the title *Die Bluthochzeit* in Cologne, May 25, 1957; in 1963 he wrote another version of *Die Bluthochzeit*); also wrote another opera to a play by Lorca *In seinem Garten liebt Don Perlimplin Belison* (Schwetzingen, May 10, 1962). Further compositions are: the ballet *Die weisse Rose,* after Oscar Wilde's *The Birthday of the Infanta* (Berlin, April 28, 1951); Concerto for Strings (1932); *Sinfonia concertante* (1937); Symphony (1947); Organ Concerto (1932; revised as harpsichord concerto, 1935); Piano Concerto (1943); Violin Concerto (1947); Cello Concerto (1951); many choral works for various festive occasions; a cantata *Die Nachgeborenen* (1948); three string quartets; Suite for Saxophone after Sweelinck (1930); Serenade for Flute, Oboe, and Bassoon (1948); *Phantasie über B-A-C-H* for two pianos, 9 instruments and orch., based on a 12-tone row (1950); also *Triplum* for 3 pianos and orch. (International Festival for Contemporary Music, Prague, Oct. 4, 1967); *Immagini* for strings with optional sopranos (1967); *Marginalien* for orch. (1969).

BIBLIOGRAPHY: Karl Laux, "Wolfgang Fortner," in *Musik und Musiker der Gegenwart* (Essen, 1949); H. Lindlar, ed., *Wolfgang Fortner* (Rodenkirchen, 1960).

Foss, Hubert James, English writer on music; b. Croydon, May 2, 1899; d. London, May 27, 1953. He attended Bradfield College; 1921, became a member of the educational department of the Oxford Univ. Press and in 1924 founded the music department, of which he was head till 1941. He composed *Seven Poems by Thomas Hardy* for baritone, male chorus, and piano; instrumental pieces; songs. He was the author of *Music in My Time* (1933); *The Concertgoer's Handbook* (London, 1946); *Ralph Vaughan Williams* (London, 1950). His book, *London Symphony; Portrait of an Orchestra,* remained unfinished at his death, and was completed by Noël Goodwin (London, 1954).

Foss (real name **Fuchs**), **Lukas,** brilliant American pianist, conductor and composer; b. Berlin, Aug. 15, 1922. He studied piano and theory in Berlin with Julius Goldstein; with the advent of the Nazi government in 1933, his family moved to Paris, where he took piano lessons with Lazare Lévy, composition with Noël Gallon, chamber music with Marcel Moyse and orchestration with Felix Wolfes. He went to the U.S. in 1937 and enrolled at the Curtis Institute in Philadelphia, where he studied piano with Isabelle Vengerova, composition with Rosario Scalero, and conducting with Fritz Reiner; for several summers he was in Koussevitzky's conducting class at the Berkshire Music Center; in addition took a course in advanced composition with Hindemith at Yale Univ.; became a naturalized American citizen in 1942. He began to compose at a very early age, and was the youngest composer to be awarded a Guggenheim Fellowship (1945). His first public career, however, was that of a concert pianist and he elicited high praise for his appearances with the New York Philharmonic and other orchestras as a soloist. From 1944-1950 he was pianist of the Boston Symph. Orch.; then traveled to Rome on a Fulbright Fellowship (1950-52). From 1953 to 1962 he was prof. of composition at the Univ. of Calif. in Los Angeles, where he also established a chamber ensemble to teach the art of improvisation; he also taught at the Berkshire Music Center at Tanglewood. In 1963 he was appointed music director and conductor of the Buffalo Philharmonic Orch.; during his tenure there he introduced ultra-modern works much to the annoyance of some regular subscribers; he resigned his position there in 1970. In 1971 he became principal conductor of the Brooklyn Philharmonia; and from 1972 he conducted the Jerusalem Symphony Orch. He conducted numerous guest appearances with major symphony orchestras in America and Europe, including his own works; in 1960 he toured Russia under the auspices of the State Department; in 1965 he was music director of the American-French Festival of the N.Y. Philharmonic at Lincoln Center in New York; through the years he also conducted special concerts of modern music. As a composer Foss underwent a radical change of style and idiom; his early works are marked by romantic lyricism, which gave way to a strong neo-Classical technique; his later avatar adopts an entire vocabulary of modernistic innovations, with the fashionable aleatory element appearing in the form of "controlled improvisation." His earliest piano pieces were published when he was 15 years old; there followed an uninterrupted flow of compositions in various genres; he was fortunate in being a particular protégé of Koussevitzky, who conducted many of his works with the Boston Symphony. WORKS: incidental music to Shakespeare's play *The Tempest* (N.Y., March 31, 1940); *The Prairie,* cantata after Carl Sandburg's poem (N.Y., May 15, 1944; an orchestral suite from it was performed earlier by the Boston Symph. Orch., Oct. 15, 1943); Piano Concerto No. 1 (1944); *Symphony in G* (Pittsburgh, Feb. 4, 1945, composer conducting); *Ode* for orch. (N.Y., March 15, 1945); *Gift of the Magi,* ballet after O'Henry (Boston, Oct. 5, 1945); *Song of Anguish,* biblical solo cantata (1945; Boston, March 10, 1950); *Song of Songs,* biblical solo cantata (Boston, March 7, 1947); String Quartet (1947); *Recordare* for orch. (Boston, Dec. 31, 1948); Oboe Concerto (N.Y., radio première, Feb. 6, 1950); opera, *The Jumping Frog of Calaveras County* after Mark Twain (Bloomington, Indiana, May 18, 1950); Piano Concerto No. 2 (Venice, Oct. 7, 1951, composer soloist; revised, 1953; N.Y. Music Critics' Award, 1954); *A Parable of Death,* cantata after Rilke (Louisville, March 11, 1953); opera, *Griffelkin* (NBC television, Nov. 6, 1955); *Psalms* for voices and orch. (N.Y., May 9, 1957); *Symphony of Chorales,* based on Bach's chorales (Pittsburgh, Oct. 24, 1958); *Introductions and Goodbyes,* miniature opera (N.Y., May 6, 1960); *Time Cycle,* suite for soprano and orch. in 4 movements to texts by Auden, Housman, Kafka and Nietzsche with intercalative improvisations by a combo of clarinet, cello, percussion and piano (N.Y., Oct. 21, 1960; won the N.Y. Music Critics' Award); *Echoi* for piano, percussion, clarinet and cello (N.Y., Nov. 11, 1963); *Elytres* for 21 instruments (Los Angeles, Dec. 8, 1964); *Phorion* for electric guitar, electric piano and electric organ, with thematic material derived from Bach's E major Partita for Solo Violin (hence the title, *Phorion,* meaning "borrowed" in Greek; first performed, N.Y., April 27, 1967; later incorporated into *Baroque Variations,* consisting of *Largo* from Handel's Suite in E, Scarlatti's Sonata in E and *Phorion*); *Concert* for cello and orch. (N.Y., March 5, 1967, Rostropovich soloist); *Geod* (abbreviation of Geodesics), a musical action for orch. (Hamburg, Dec. 6, 1969, composer conducting); *MAP* (acronym for Men At Play), a musical play for 5 instrumentalists (1970); *Paradigm* for percussionist, electric guitar and 3 instruments (N.Y., March 19, 1970); Wind Quintet (1972); *Orpheus* for cello, or viola, or guitar with orch. (1972); *Divertissement* for string quartet (1972); *Ni bruit ni vitesse* for 2 pianos playing on the keys and 2 percussionists playing on piano strings (1973); *Folksong for Orchestra* (1976); *Quartet Plus,* for narrator and double string quartet (N.Y., April 29, 1977); *American Cantata* for tenor, soprano, 2 speakers, chorus and orch. (N.Y., Dec. 1, 1977).

Foster, Fay, American composer; b. Leavenworth, Kansas, Nov. 8, 1886; d. Bayport, N.Y., April 17, 1960.

She studied at the Munich Cons. with Schwartz (piano) and Jadassohn (composition); studied piano further with M. Rosenthal and Sophie Menter; won a prize at the International Waltz Competition (Berlin, 1910); 1st prize in American Composers' Contest (N.Y., 1913); made several tours as a pianist; eventually settled in N.Y. She wrote 3 operettas; over 100 songs (*The Americans Come!, My Journey's End,* etc.); piano studies, etc.

Foster, Lawrence, American conductor; b. Los Angeles, Oct. 23, 1941. He made his first conducting appearance with the Young Musicians Foundation Debut Orch. in 1960. At the age of 24 he was appointed assistant conductor of the Los Angeles Philharmonic Orch.; in 1966 received the Koussevitzky Memorial Conducting Prize at the Berkshire Music Festival in Tanglewood, Mass. In 1969 he became a regular guest conductor of the Royal Philharmonic Orchestra of London. In 1970 he was appointed conductor-in-chief of the Houston Symphony Orch. He is particularly notable for his dynamic interpretations of modern works, but has also been acclaimed for his precise and intelligent presentations of the Classical and Romantic repertory.

Foster, Muriel, English contralto; b. Sunderland, Nov. 22, 1877; d. London, Dec. 23, 1937. In 1896 she entered the Royal College of Music. She sang before Queen Victoria in 1900; in 1901 toured Canada with Mme. Albani. After her marriage to Ludwig Goetz, in 1906, she appeared infrequently in public.

Foster, Myles Birket, English organist; b. London, Nov. 29, 1851; d. there, Dec. 18, 1922. He was a pupil of Hamilton Clarke; later of Arthur Sullivan, Prout, and Westlake at the Royal Academy of Music; served as organist at the Foundling Hospital (1880–92); from 1888, Examiner of Trinity College, London, in which capacity he spent many years in Australia and South Africa. He publ. *Anthems and Anthem-Composers* (1901), *History of the London Philharmonic Society, 1813-1912* (1913), and pedagogic works.

Foster, Sidney, American pianist; b. Florence, South Carolina, May 23, 1917; d. Boston, Feb. 7, 1977. He began playing piano when he was 4 years old, and at the age of 10 was admitted to the Curtis Institute in Philadelphia, where he studied with Isabelle Vengerova and David Saperton. In 1940 he won the first Leventritt Foundation Award, which entitled him to an appearance as soloist with the New York Philharmonic. This was the beginning of a brilliant international career. In 1964 he played 16 concerts in Russia. He taught piano at Florida State Univ. (1949–51); in 1952 he joined the piano faculty of Indiana Univ. at Bloomington.

Foster, Stephen Collins, American composer of famous songs; b. Lawrenceville, Pa., July 4, 1826; d. New York, Jan. 13, 1864. He learned to play the flute as a child; publ. a song *Open thy Lattice, Love* at the age of 18. His father was a government worker and business man, active in politics; his brothers were engaged in commerce. About 1846 he went to Cincinnati as accountant for his brother Dunning. The total number of Foster's songs is 189, for most of which he wrote both words and music. Of these, *Old Folks at Home,* sometimes referred to as *Swanee Ribber* (from its initial line "Way down upon de Swanee ribber"), was published on Oct. 21, 1851, with the subtitle "Ethiopian Melody as sung by Christy's Minstrels." Christy's name was given as author, in consideration of a small sum of money received by Foster, whose name was not attached to the song until 1879, upon the expiration of the original copyright. About 40,000 copies of this song were sold during the year after publication. Foster was greatly encouraged, and, as he wrote to Christy, hoped to establish himself as "the best Ethiopian song writer." Of other songs, the most notable are *Oh! Susanna* (1848; became popular in the gold rush of 1849); *My Old Kentucky Home, Massa's in de Cold Ground, Jeanie with the Light Brown Hair, Old Black Joe, Nelly was a Lady, Laura Lee,* etc. The title page of *Beautiful Dreamer* (publ. 1864) bears the legend "the last song ever written by Stephen C. Foster. Composed but a few days previous to his death," but this maudlin claim (an appeal for sales) is false as the work was prepared for publication in 1862. It is not known which song was Foster's last. On July 22, 1850, Foster married Jane McDowell in Pittsburgh; they had a daughter, but the marriage was not happy. In 1853 Foster went to New York and stayed there for a year alone; in 1854 he was living in Hoboken, N.J.; went to New York again in 1860, while his wife remained with relatives. Foster died penniless at Bellevue Hospital; yet his earnings were not small; from 1849–1860 he received about $15,000 in royalties. Apart from the songs, Foster wrote 12 instrumental pieces in salon music style, and made numerous arrangements for flute, guitar, violin, etc. for the collection *Foster's Social Orchestra* (N.Y. 1854). He had some knowledge of instrumental writing; his harmonies, though simple, are adequate. The extant manuscripts are mostly in the Foster Hall Collection at the Univ. of Pittsburgh (dedicated on June 2, 1937); bibliographical bulletins are issued periodically by this organization. A one-penny stamp bearing Foster's picture was brought out by the U.S. post office in 1940. In 1915 W. R. Whittlesey and O. G. Sonneck publ. a *Catalogue of First Editions of S. Foster.* There are hundreds of reprints of Foster's songs, but almost all are in "improved" arrangements. A facsimile repr. of the original sheet music of 40 songs was publ., with valuable commentary by Richard Jackson, in N.Y., 1974.

BIBLIOGRAPHY: M. Foster (brother), *Biography, Songs and Musical Compositions of Stephen Foster* (1896; not always accurate); H. V. Milligan, *S. C. Foster* (N.Y., 1920); J. T. Howard, *Stephen Foster, America's Troubadour* (N.Y., 1934; new ed., 1953); idem, "Stephen Foster and His Publishers," ed., *Musical Quarterly* (Jan. 1934); J. T. Howard, *Newly Discovered Fosteriana* (N.Y., 1935); G. P. Jackson, *Stephen Foster's Debt to American Folk-Songs* (N.Y., 1936); R. Walters, *Stephen Foster: Youth's Golden Gleam* (Princeton, N.J., 1936); J. T. Howard, *The Literature on Stephen Foster* (Washington, D.C., 1944); Evelyn Foster Morneweck, *Chronicles of Stephen Foster's Family* (2 vols.; Pittsburgh, 1944); Otto Gombosi,

"Stephen Foster and 'Gregory Walker,'" *Musical Quarterly* (April 1944); F. Hodges, Jr., "Stephen Foster, Democrat," *Lincoln Herald* (June 1945; published separately, Pittsburgh, 1946); G. Chase, *America's Music* (2nd ed., N.Y., 1966); H. Wiley Hitchcock, "Stephen Foster," *HiFi/Stereo Review* (Jan. 1967); H. Wiley Hitchcock, *Music in the United States* (Englewood Cliffs, N.J., 1969; 2nd ed. 1974); W.W. Austin, *Susanna, Jeanie, and The Old Folks at Home: The Songs of Stephen Foster from His Time to Ours* (N.Y., 1975).

Fotek, Jan, Polish composer; b. Czerwinsk on the Vistula, Nov. 28, 1928. He studied composition with Wiechowicz at the State College of Music in Cracow and with Szeligowski at the State College of Music in Warsaw.

WORKS: *Opus concertante* for organ, piano and percussion (1959); *Gregorian Hymn* for chorus and orch. (1963); *A Cycle of Verses* for children's chorus and orch. (1963); *Trimorphie* for 3 flutes, harpsichord and piano (1966); *Epitasis* for orch. (1967); *Galileo,* musical drama (1969); *The Last War,* rhapsody for narrator, chorus and orch. (1971); *Cantata Copernicana* (1973); *Partita* for 12 bassoons and 3 double bassoons (1973).

Fougstedt, Nils-Eric, Finnish conductor and composer; b. Raisio (near Turku), May 5, 1910; d. Helsinki, April 4, 1961. He studied composition in Helsinki with Furuhjelm, in Italy with Carlo Felice Boghen, and in Berlin with Max Trapp. Upon return to Finland in 1932 he lectured in music theory at the Music Institute in Helsinki; was also active as conductor; led the Finnish Radio Orchestra from 1951 until his death.

WORKS: Piano Trio (1933); Divertimento for Wind Quintet (1936); Suite for Orch. (1936); Violin Sonata (1937); Violin Concertino (1937); 2 symphonies (1938, 1949); String Quartet (1940); Cello Concerto (1942); Piano Concerto (1944); *Tulukset (The Tinder Box),* cantata after Hans Christian Andersen (1950); *Trittico sinfonico* (1958); many choruses and songs.

Foulds, John Herbert, English composer; b. Manchester, Nov. 2, 1880; d. Calcutta, April 24, 1939. At the age of 14 he played in theater orchestras; 1900–10, member of the Hallé Orch.; then conducted stage music. In 1921 he became director of the Univ. of London Music Society. He experimented with quarter tones, and as early as 1898 wrote a string quartet using them.

WORKS: dramatic music: *Wonderful Grandmamma, The Whispering Well, Julius Caesar, Sakuntala, The Trojan Women, Debureau, The Fires Divine, The Vision of Dante;* for orch.: *Epithalamium; Music Pictures* (London, Sept. 5, 1912); *Celtic Suite;* incidental music to Bernard Shaw's *Saint Joan;* Cello Concerto; vocal works: *A World Requiem* for chorus (London, 1923), *Mood Pictures* for 3 voices, *The Easter Lover,* for alto and orch.; piano works; violin and vocal pieces; songs. He publ. *Music To-day: its Heritage from the Past, and Legacy to the Future* (London, 1934).

BIBLIOGRAPHY: M. MacDonald, *John Foulds: His Life in Music* (1975).

Fourdrain, Félix, French composer; b. Nice, Feb. 3, 1880; d. Paris, Oct. 23, 1923. He studied with Widor; wrote the operas *Echo* (Paris, 1906), *La Légende du point d'Argentan* (Paris, April 17, 1907), *La Glaneuse* (Lyons, 1909), *Vercingétorix* (Nice, 1912), *Madame Roland* (Rouen, 1913), *Les Contes de Perrault* (Paris, 1913), *Les Maris de Ginette, La Mare à diable, La Griffe;* the operettas *Dolly* (Paris, 1922), *L'Amour en Cage, Le Million de Colette, La Hussarde* (Paris, 1925); incidental music to Cain's *Le Secret de Polichinelle* (Cannes, 1922); *Anniversaire,* for orch.; many songs (*Le Papillon, Sérénades, Revanche d'amour, Pays des cours,* etc.).

Fourestier, Louis, French composer and conductor; b. Montpellier, May 31, 1892; d. Boulogne-Billancourt, Sept. 30, 1976. He studied at the Paris Cons. under Gédalge and Leroux; won the Rossini Prize in 1924 (for his cantata, *Patria*), the Grand Prix de Rome in 1925 (for the cantata, *La Mort d'Adonis*), and the Heugel Prize in 1927 (for the symph. poem *Polynice*); served as conductor at Marseilles and Bordeaux; 1938, appointed conductor at the Paris Opéra; 1947–48, was in the U.S. as guest conductor of the Metropolitan Opera.

Fouret, Maurice, French composer; b. St.-Quentin, Nov. 28, 1888; d. Paris, Jan. 22, 1962. He studied with Ravel, Charpentier and Busser. He composed several symph. poems on exotic subjects, among them *Aladdin* (Paris, Nov. 28, 1920), *Danse de Sita* (1922); the ballets *Le Rustre imprudent* (1931), *La Jeune Fille aux joues roses* (1934); a group of symph. suites inspired by Alsatian folklore; songs.

Fournier, Émile-Eugène-Alix, French composer; b. Paris, Oct. 11, 1864; d. Joinville-le-Pont, Sept. 12, 1897. He was a pupil of Delibes and Dubois at the Paris Cons.; took 2nd Grand Prix de Rome in 1891 and the Prix Cressent in 1892 for the 1-act opera *Stratonice* (Paris, 1892); publ. a number of songs.

Fournier, Pierre, famous French cellist; b. Paris, July 24, 1906. He studied cello with Paul Bazelaire and G. Hekking at the Paris Cons. He then taught at the École Normale de Musique and at the Paris Cons., until 1949, when he decided to devote himself entirely to his concert career, which took him all over the world, including South America, Japan, Australia, New Zealand and South Africa; he also made regular appearances in the U.S.; was praised for his natural bel canto quality on his instrument, as well as for his impeccable musical taste. Several composers wrote special works for him; he gave first performances of the cello concertos of Albert Roussel, Frank Martin, Bohuslav Martinů and Jean Martinon. He also possessed the entire repertoire of cello works of Bach, Beethoven and Brahms. In 1970 he settled in Switzerland where he holds summer courses in interpretation in Zürich.

BIBLIOGRAPHY: B. Gavoty, *Pierre Fournier* (Geneva, 1957).

Fournier, Pierre-Simon, French cutter and founder of music type; b. Paris, Sept. 15, 1712; d. there, Oct. 8, 1768. Instead of the lozenge-shaped types in the style of Hautin's (1525), Fournier introduced round-headed notes, described in his *Essai d'un nouveau caractère de fonte . . .* (1756); he also publ. a *Traité historique sur l'origine et le progrès des caractères de fonte pour l'impression de la musique* (Paris, 1765).

Fox, Charles Warren, American musicologist; b. Gloversville, N.Y., July 24, 1904. He studied psychology at Cornell Univ. (B.A., 1929; Ph.D., 1933); also took courses in musicology with Otto Kinkeldey there. In 1933 he was appointed instructor in psychology at the Eastman School of Music, Rochester; 1934, began teaching musicology as well. He contributes frequent articles to American music magazines (*Musical Quarterly, Journal of the American Musicological Society, Notes,* etc.).

Fox, Charlotte (*née* **Milligan**), b. Omagh, Ireland, 1860; d. London, Mar. 26, 1916. She was an enthusiastic musical amateur, specially interested in Irish music; in 1904 she founded the Irish Folk Song Society; in her will she left the Bunting MSS to Belfast Univ. She publ. *Annals of the Irish Harpers* (London, 1911); composed the well-known song *The Foggy Dew.*

Fox, Felix, pianist and teacher; b. Breslau, May 25, 1876; d. Boston, March 24, 1947. He studied at the Leipzig Cons. with Reinecke (piano) and Jadassohn (theory); then with Isidor Philipp in Paris, where he gave several recitals introducing works by MacDowell. In 1897 he returned to the U.S. and settled in Boston as pianist and teacher; in 1898 he established, with C. Buonamici, a piano school which enjoyed an excellent reputation; after Buonamici's death in 1920 it became the Felix Fox School of Pianoforte Playing; it was discontinued in 1935. Fox wrote many piano pieces; songs; made transcriptions of MacDowell's works; also edited numerous piano works.

Fox, Virgil, American organist; b. Princeton, Illinois, May 3, 1912. He studied with Wilhelm Middelschulte in Chicago and with Marcel Dupré in Paris. From 1946 to 1964 he was organist at Riverside Church in New York. He made a grand tour of European cathedrals giving special concerts there, including Westminster Abbey in London. Returning to America, he evolved an idiosyncratic type of performance in which he combined thorough knowledge of the Baroque style with romantic extravaganza; at his recitals he often apostrophizes the public in a curious mixture of lofty elevation and disarming self-deprecation. This mixture of high art and personal address contributed greatly to his popularity among the emancipated musical youth in America; he reciprocated by including whimsical offerings in his programs, such as the discordant arrangement of *America* by Charles Ives.

Fox-Strangways, Arthur Henry, English writer on musical subjects; b. Norwich, Sept. 14, 1859; d. Dinton, near Salisbury, May 2, 1948. He graduated from Oxford; 1893–1901, music director at Wellington College, London; 1911 to 1925, music critic of the *London Times,* later of the *Observer;* in 1920 he founded the quarterly magazine *Music & Letters,* of which he remained editor until 1936 (succeeded by Eric Blom).

He was a specialist on Indian music and wrote several books on the subject, including *The Music of Hindustan* (1914); also publ. a collection of essays, *Music Observed* (1936) and a biography of Cecil Sharp (1933). He contributed the article "Folk-Song" to the introductory vol. of the *Oxford History of Music* (1929).

BIBLIOGRAPHY: *Music & Letters* for Oct. 1939 (articles by Blom, Colles, Dent, Dyson, Vaughan Williams, etc.) and for July 1948.

Fracassi, Américo, composer; brother of **Elmérico Fracassi;** b. Lucito, Campobasso, Italy, Feb. 29, 1880; d. Goya, Argentina, Aug. 15, 1936. With his brother, he left his native Italy as a very young man and settled in Buenos Aires, where he taught various musical subjects at a music school. He composed some songs and piano pieces.

Fracassi, Elmérico, composer; brother of **Américo Fracassi;** b. Lucito, Campobasso, Italy, Dec. 19, 1874; d. Buenos Aires, Oct. 12, 1930. He was taken to Buenos Aires as a boy, but returned to Italy in 1890 for his musical training (Cons. of Naples, with Rossomandi and D'Arienzo); toured Europe twice as a concert pianist; 1904, appointed director (together with G. d'Andrea) of the Almagro Cons. in Buenos Aires. He composed 2 operas, *Finlandia* (Turin, 1914) and *Merletti di Burano;* Piano Concerto; Violin Sonata; piano studies; songs; and 4 Argentinian anthems, one of which, *Himno al Centenario,* won a prize from the Argentine Government.

Frackenpohl, Arthur, American composer; b. Irvington, N.J., April 23, 1924. He studied at the Eastman School of Music, Rochester, with Bernard Rogers; also with Milhaud at the Berkshire Music Center, and with Nadia Boulanger at Fontainebleau. In 1949 was appointed member of the faculty at the State Univ. Teachers' College, Potsdam, N.Y.

WORKS: Sonatina for Clarinet and Piano (1948); Brass Quartet (1949); Trio for Oboe, Horn, and Bassoon (1949); cantata, *A Child This Day Is Born* (1951); Suite for Strings (1953); *An Elegy on the Death of a Mad Dog* (1955); *Allegro Giocoso* for band (1955); *A Jubilant Overture* for orch. (1956); Variations for Tuba and Winds (1974); Duo for Clarinet and Percussion (1974).

Fradkin, Fredric, American violinist; b. Troy, N.Y., April 2, 1892; d. New York, Oct. 3, 1963. At the age of five he became a pupil of Schradieck; later studied with Max Bendix and Sam Franko in N.Y.; then went to Paris; studied at the Cons. there with Lefort, graduating in 1909 with first prize. He was concertmaster of the Bordeaux Opera Co.; then took instruction with Ysaÿe in Brussels. Returning to America, he made his debut as concert violinist in N.Y. on Jan. 10, 1911; then gave concerts in Europe; in 1918–19 he was concertmaster of the Boston Symph. Orch.; later settled in N.Y. as private teacher.

Fraemcke, August, German pianist and pedagogue; b. Hamburg, March 23, 1870; d. N.Y., Jan 18, 1933. He studied at the Hamburg Cons.; then at the Vienna

Cons., where he won the Beethoven Prize. In 1891 he emigrated to the U.S., and joined the staff of the N.Y. College of Music, in 1906 becoming its co-director. He was active in the Bohemian Club in N.Y. City.

Fraenkel, Wolfgang, German-American composer; b. Berlin, Oct. 10, 1897. He studied violin, piano and music theory at the Klindworth-Scharwenka Cons. in Berlin; at the same time practiced law; he was a judge in a Berlin court until the advent of the Nazi regime in 1933; was interned at the Sachsenhausen concentration camp, but released in 1939; went to Shanghai, China, where he was on the faculty of the National Cons. of Music; in 1947 settled in Los Angeles; earned his living for a time as a music copyist in film studios, but continued to compose.
WORKS: As a composer, Fraenkel attracted attention in 1965 when he received 1st prize at the International Competition of the City of Milan for his *Symphonische Aphorismen*. His other works include an opera *Der brennende Dornbusch* (1924–27); 3 string quartets (1924; 1949; 1960) of which No. 3 received the Queen Elisabeth Prize, and was performed at the Liège Festival of the International Society for Contemporary Music in 1962); Flute Concerto (1930); *Der Wegweiser*, cantata (1931); Cello Sonata (1934); Violin Sonata (1935); *Filippo* for speaker and orch. (1948); Sonata for Solo Violin (1954); *Variations and Fantasy on a Theme by Schoenberg* for piano (1954); *Frescobaldi*, transcription 5 of Frescobaldi's organ pieces for orch. (1957); viola sonata (1963); *Klavierstück* for magnetic tape and piano (1964); *Joseph* for baritone and orch., to a text by Thomas Mann (1968); *Missa Aphoristica* (1973); String Quintet with 2 cellos (1976). His complete works, both published and in manuscript, are deposited in the Moldenhauer Archives in Spokane, Washington.

Frager, Malcolm, American pianist; b. St. Louis, Jan. 15, 1935. He studied languages at Columbia Univ.; majored in Russian, graduating in 1957. He studied piano with Carl Friedberg in N.Y. (1949–55); received various prizes in the U.S. In 1960 he won the Queen Elisabeth of Belgium International Competition, which marked the beginning of his world-wide career; he was particularly successful in Russia.

Framery, Nicolas Étienne, French composer, writer on music, and poet; b. Rouen, March 25, 1745; d. Paris, Nov. 26, 1810. He composed the text and music for the comic opera *La Sorcière par hasard* (1768); its performance at Villeroy earned him the position of superintendent of music with the Count of Artois. The opera was played at the Comédie-Italienne (Paris, Sept. 3, 1783), but suffered a fiasco because of the antagonism against Italian opera generated by the adherents of Gluck. He also wrote librettos for Sacchini, Salieri, Paisiello, Anfossi, and other Italian composers; edited the *Journal de Musique* in Paris from 1770 till 1778, and *Calendrier Musical Universal* (1788–89); compiled, together with Ginguené and Feytou, the musical part of vol. I of *Encyclopédie méthodique* (1791; vol. II by Momigny, 1818); besides smaller studies, he wrote *De la nécessité du rythme et de la césure dans les hymnes ou odes destinées à la mu-*

sique (1796); transl. into French Azopardi's *Musico prattico* (*Le Musicien pratique*; 2 vols., 1786).
BIBLIOGRAPHY: J. Carlez, *Framery, littérateur-musicien* (Caen, 1893).

Françaix, Jean, talented French composer; b. Le Mans, May 23, 1912. He first studied at Le Mans Cons., of which his father was director; then at the Paris Cons. with Isidor Philipp (piano) and Nadia Boulanger (composition). In his music, Françaix associates himself with the neo-French school of composers, pursuing the twofold aim of practical application and national tradition; his instrumental works represent a stylization of classical French music; in this respect, he comes close to Ravel.
WORKS: operas, *La Main de gloire* (Bordeaux, May 7, 1950) and *La Princesse de Clèves* (1953; Rouen, Dec. 11, 1965); ballets: *Scuola di Ballo* (1933), *Les Malheurs de Sophie* (1935), *Le Roi nu*, after Andersen (Paris, June 15, 1936), *Le Jeu sentimental* (1936), *La Lutherie enchantée* (1936), *Verreries de Venise* (1938), *Le Jugement du fou* (1938), *Les Demoiselles de la nuit* (1948); *L'Apostrophe*, musical comedy in 1 act, after Balzac (Amsterdam, July 1, 1951); oratorio, *L'Apocalypse de St. Jean* (Paris, June 11, 1942); *Cantate de Méphisto* for bass solo and strings (Paris, Oct. 8, 1955); Symphony (Paris, Nov. 6, 1932); Concertino for Piano and Orch. (1934); Piano Concerto (Berlin, Nov. 8, 1936); *Musique de cour*, suite for flute, violin, and orch. (1937); *Le Diable boiteux*, musical dialogue for men's voices (1937); *Paris à nous deux*, lyric fantasy (Fontainebleau, Aug. 7, 1954); *Divertissement* for bassoon and string quartet (1944); *Invocation à la volupté* for baritone and orch. (1946); *Rapsodie* for viola and wind instruments (1946); *Cantate satirique*, after Juvenal, for 4 string instruments and piano 4 hands (1947); Wind Quintet (1948); *Variations sans thème* for cello and piano (1951); *Sonatine* for trumpet and piano (1952); *Ode à la gastronomie* for mixed chorus (1953); *L'Horloge de Flore*, suite for oboe and orch. (Philadelphia, March 31, 1961); Flute Concerto (Schwetzingen, May 13, 1967); Violin Concerto (1970); Quartet for English Horn, Viola and Cello (1971); *Cassazione per 3 orchestre* (1975).

Francescatti, Zino, brilliant violinist; b. Marseilles, Aug. 9, 1902. His father, a Frenchman of Italian extraction, was a violin pupil of Paganini; prodded by him, Zino Francescatti appeared in public as a violinist at the age of 5, and played the Beethoven Violin Concerto with an orchestra at 10. In 1927 he went to Paris, where he began teaching at the École Normale de Musique; also conducted occasional performances of the Paris symphonic organization "Concerts Poulet." Between 1931 and 1939 he made several world tours; in 1939 made his home in the U.S., appearing in concert recitals and as soloist with orchestras.

Franchetti, Alberto, Italian composer; b. Turin, Sept. 18, 1860; d. Viareggio, Aug. 4, 1942. He studied in Turin with Niccolò Coccon and Fortunato Magi; then with Rheinberger in Munich and with Draeseke in Dresden. He devoted his entire life to composition, with the exception of a brief tenure as director of the Cherubini Cons. in Florence (1926–28).

WORKS: operas: *Asrael* (Reggio Emilia, Feb. 11, 1888), *Cristoforo Colombo* (Genoa, Oct. 6, 1892), *Fior d'Alpe* (Milan, March 15, 1894), *Il Signor di Pourceaugnac* (Milan, April 10, 1897), *Germania* (his most successful opera; produced at La Scala, March 11, 1902; also had repeated performances in New York, London, Buenos Aires, etc.), *La figlia di Jorio* (Milan, March 29, 1906), *Notte di leggenda* (Milan, Jan. 14, 1915), *Giove a Pompei* (with Umberto Giordano; Rome, June 5, 1921), *Glauco* (Naples, April 8, 1922); Symphony (1886); symph. poems *Loreley* and *Nella selva nera*; *Inno* for soli, chorus, and orch. (for the 800th anniversary of the Univ. of Bologna); several pieces of chamber music and songs.

Franchi-Verney, Giuseppe Ippolito, Conte della Valetta, Italian composer and writer; b. Turin, Feb. 17, 1848; d. Rome, May 15, 1911. He studied jurisprudence, but gave up his career as a lawyer for music. He was one of the founders of the Società del Quartetto (1875); under the pen name of Ippolito Valetta he wrote for the *Gazzetta del Popolo;* later for *Il Risorgimento* and other papers. In 1889 he married the violinist **Teresina Tua.** Among his compositions (most of them in a Wagnerian vein) are a "lyric sketch" *Il Valdese* (Turin, 1885) and a ballet, *Il Mulatto* (Naples, 1896).

Franchomme, Auguste-Joseph, famous French cellist; b. Lille, April 10, 1808; d. Paris, Jan. 21, 1884. He studied at the Paris Cons. with Levasseur; then played cello in various opera houses. In 1846 he was appointed prof. at the Paris Cons. He was an intimate friend of Chopin; established evenings of chamber music in Paris with Hallé and Alard. He wrote cello pieces, mostly in variation form, and operatic potpourris.

Franck, César (-Auguste), great Belgian composer and organist; b. Liège, Dec. 10, 1822; d. Paris, Nov. 8, 1890. He studied first at the Royal Cons. of Liège with Daussoigne and others; at the age of 9 he won first prize for singing, and at 12 first prize for piano. As a child prodigy he gave concerts in Belgium. In 1835 his family moved to Paris, where he studied privately with Anton Reicha; in 1837 he entered the Paris Cons., studying with Zimmermann (piano), Benoist (organ), and Leborne (theory). A few months after his entrance examinations he received a special award of "grand prix d'honneur" for playing a fugue a third lower at sight; in 1838 he received the 1st prize for piano; in 1839, a 2nd prize for counterpoint; in 1840 1st prize for fugue; and in 1841 2nd prize for organ. In 1842 he was back in Belgium; in 1843 he returned to Paris, and settled there for the rest of his life. On March 17, 1843, he presented there a concert of his chamber music; on Jan. 4, 1846, his first major work, the oratorio *Ruth,* was given at the Paris Cons. On Feb. 22, 1848, in the midst of the Paris revolution, he married; in 1851 he became organist of the church of St.-Jean-St.-François; in 1853, maître de chapelle and, in 1858, organist at Ste.-Clotilde, which position he held until his death. In 1872 he succeeded his former teacher Benoist as prof. of organ at the Paris Cons. Franck's organ classes became the training school for a whole generation of French composers; among his pupils were Vincent d'Indy, Chausson, Bréville, Bordes, Duparc, Ropartz, Pierné, Vidal, Chapuis, Vierne, and a host of others, who eventually formed a school of modern French instrumental music. Until the appearance of Franck in Paris, operatic art dominated the entire musical life of the nation, and the course of instruction at the Paris Cons. was influenced by this tendency. By his emphasis on organ music, based on the contrapuntal art of Bach, Franck swayed the new generation of French musicians towards the ideal of absolute music. The foundation of the famous 'Schola Cantorum' by Vincent d'Indy, Bordes, and others in 1894 realized Franck's teachings. After the death of d'Indy in 1931, several members withdrew from the 'Schola Cantorum' and organized the 'École César Franck' (1938). César Franck was not a prolific composer; but his creative powers rose rather than diminished with advancing age; his only symphony was completed when he was 66; his remarkable Violin Sonata was written at the age of 63; his String Quartet was composed in the last year of his life. Lucidity of contrapuntal design and fulness of harmony are the distinguishing traits of Franck's music; in melodic writing he balanced the diatonic and chromatic elements in fine equilibrium. Although he did not pursue innovation for its own sake, he was not averse to using unorthodox procedures. The novelty of introducing an English horn into the score of his Symphony aroused some criticism among academic musicians of the time. Franck was quite alien to the Wagner-Liszt school of composition, which attracted many of his own pupils; the chromatic procedures in Franck's music derive from Bach rather than from Wagner.

WORKS: OPERAS: *Le Valet de Ferme* (1852); *Hulda* (1882–85; Monte Carlo, March 8, 1894); *Ghisèle* (unfinished; orchestration completed by d'Indy, Chausson, Bréville, Rousseau, and Coquard; 1st performance, Monte Carlo, April 6, 1896). ORATORIOS: *Ruth* (1845); *La Tour de Babel* (1865); *Les Béatitudes* (1869–79); *Rédemption* (1871; 2nd version 1874); *Rébecca* (Paris, March 15, 1881; produced as a 1-act sacred opera at the Paris Opéra, May 25, 1918). SYMPH. POEMS: *Les Éolides* (Paris, May 13, 1877); *Le Chasseur maudit* (Paris, March 31, 1883); *Les Djinns* (Paris, March 15, 1885); *Psyché* (Paris, March 10, 1888). OTHER WORKS FOR ORCH.: *Variations symphoniques* for piano and orch. (Paris, May 1, 1886); Symphony in D minor (Paris, Feb. 17, 1889). CHAMBER MUSIC: 4 piano trios (early works; 1841–42); *Andante quietoso* for piano and violin (1843); *Duo pour piano et violon concertants,* on themes from Dalayrac's *Gulistan* (1844); Quintet in F minor for Piano and Strings (1879); Violin Sonata (1886); String Quartet (1889). ORGAN WORKS: 6 *pièces* (Fantaisie; Grande pièce symphonique; Prélude, Fugue, and Variations; Pastorale; Prière; Finale); 3 *pièces* (Fantaisie; Cantabile; Pièce heroique); *Andantino;* 3 *Chorales;* an album of 44 *Petites pièces;* an album of 55 pieces, entitled *L'Organiste,* etc. SACRED MUSIC: *Messe solennelle* (1858); *Messe à trois voix* (1860); *Panis angelicus* for tenor, organ, harp, cello, and double bass; offertories, motets, etc.; 16 songs, among them *La Procession* (also arranged for voice and orch.). PIANO PIECES: 4 *fantai-*

sies; *Prélude, choral et fugue; Prélude, aria et final; Trois petits riens; Danse lente;* etc.

BIBLIOGRAPHY: A. Coquard, *C. Franck* (Paris, 1890; new ed., 1904); E. Destranges, *L'Œuvre lyrique de C. Franck* (Paris, 1896); G. Servières, *La Musique française moderne* (Paris, 1897); G. Derepas, *C. Franck; étude sur sa vie, son enseignement, son œuvre* (Paris, 1897); A. Meyer, *Les Critiques de C. Franck* (Orléans, 1898); P. Locard, *Les Maîtres modernes de L'orgue* (Paris, 1900); P. L. Garnier, *L'Héroïsme de C. Franck; psychologie musicale* (Paris, 1900); F. Baldensperger, *C. Franck, l'artiste et son œuvre* (Paris, 1901); D. G. Mason, *From Grieg to Brahms* (N.Y., 1904); R. Canudo, *C. Franck e la giovane scuola musicale francesa* (Rome, 1905); Ch. Van den Borren, *L'Œuvre dramatique de C. Franck* (Brussels, 1906); Vincent d'Indy, *C. Franck* (Paris, 1906; in English, London, 1910); Romain Rolland, "Le Renouveau," in *Musiciens d'aujourd'hui* (Paris, 1908); O. Séré, *Musiciens français d'aujourd'hui* (Paris, 1911); J. Rivière, *Études* (Paris, 1911); J. W. Hinton, *C. Franck, Some Personal Reminiscences* (London, 1912); May de Rudder, *C. Franck* (Paris, 1920); E. Closson, *C. Franck* (Charleroi, 1923); R. Jardillier, *La Musique de chambre de C. Franck* (Paris, 1929); M. Emmanuel, *C. Franck* (Paris, 1930); A. Cortot, *La Musique française de piano* (Paris, 1930); Ch. Tournemire, *C. Franck* (Paris, 1931); Thelma Lynn, *C. Franck: a Bio-bibliography* (N.Y., 1934); H. Haag, *C. Franck als Orgelkomponist* (Kassel, 1936); P. Kreutzer, *Die sinfonische Form César Francks* (Düsseldorf, 1938); M. Kunel, *La Vie de C. Franck* (Paris, 1947); John Horton, *César Franck* (London, 1948); N. Demuth, *C. Franck* (London, 1949); N. Dufourcq, *C. Franck: le milieu, l'œuvre, l'art* (Paris, 1949); L. Vallas, *La Véritable Histoire de C. Franck* (Paris, 1950; in English, London, 1951); Charlotte Taube, *César Franck und wir; eine Biographie* (Berlin, 1951); Nancy van der Elst, *Organist van de Sinte Clotilde* (Tilburg, 1953); E. Buenzod, *César Auguste Franck* (Paris, 1966); W. Mohr, *César Franck* (Tutzing, 1969); Laurence Davies, *César Franck and his Circle* (Boston, 1970); Wilhelm Mohr, in his book, *Cäsar Franck; ein deutscher Musiker* (Stuttgart, 1942), purports to prove that Franck was ethnically German; the same contention is advanced by R. Zimmermann in his similarly titled book, *Cäsar Franck; ein deutscher Musiker in Paris* (Aachen, 1942). A rebuttal is found in M. Monnikendam's biography, *César Franck* (Amsterdam, 1949), which presents documentary evidence that Franck was of Flemish and Walloon extraction.

Franck, Eduard, German pianist, pedagogue, and composer; b. Breslau, Oct. 5, 1817; d. Berlin, Dec. 1, 1893. At the age of 17 he studied with Mendelssohn; later he met Schumann and became his friend. These associations were the formative factor in the development of his career; he wrote piano pieces and songs in a romantic vein, closely adhering to the style of Mendelssohn and, to some extent, of Schumann. As a piano teacher, he enjoyed great renown. He taught in Cologne (1851-58), then in Bern (1859-67) and in Berlin (1867-78). Among his works are 2 piano concertos, 2 violin concertos, much chamber music, and numerous collections of piano pieces.

BIBLIOGRAPHY: R. Franck, *Musikalische und unmusikalische Erinnerungen* (Heidelberg, 1928).

Franck, Johann Wolfgang, German composer; b. Unterschwaningen, June (baptized June 17), 1644; d. c.1710. He was brought up in Ansbach, and served there as court musician from 1665 till 1679; produced 3 operas at the Ansbach court: *Die unvergleichliche Andromeda* (1675), *Der verliebte Föbus* (1678), and *Die drei Töchter Cecrops* (1679). On Jan. 17, 1679, in a fit of jealousy, he killed the court musician Ulbrecht, and was forced to flee. He found refuge in Hamburg with his wife Anna Susanna Wilbel (whom he married in 1666), and gained a prominent position at the Hamburg Opera; between 1679 and 1686 he wrote and produced 17 operas, most important of which was *Diokletian* (1682). His private life continued to be stormy; he deserted his wife and their ten children, and went to London, where he remained from 1690 to about 1695. The exact place and date of his death are unknown. In London he organized (with Robert King) a series of "Concerts of Vocal and Instrumental Music"; publ. 41 English songs. Other publications are: *Geistliche Lieder* (Hamburg, 1681, 1685, 1687, 1700; republished in 1856 by D. H. Engel, with new words by Osterwald; newly edited by W. Krabbe and J. Kromolicki in vol. 45 of the *Denkmäler deutscher Tonkunst;* 12 arrangements for 4 voices by A. von Dommer, publ. 1859; separate reprints by Riemann, Friedlaender, and others); *Remedium melancholiae* (25 secular solo songs with basso continuo; London, 1690); arias, etc.

BIBLIOGRAPHY: F. Zelle, *J. W. Franck, ein Beitrag zur Geschichte der äl testen deutschen Oper* (Berlin, 1889); A. Werner, "J. W. Francks Flucht aus Ansbach," *Sammelbände der Internationalen Musik-Gesellschaft* (XIV/2); W. Barclay Squire. "J. W. Franck in England," *Musical Antiquary* (July 1912); R. Klages, *J. W. Franck, Untersuchungen zu seiner Lebensgeschichte und zu seinen geistlichen Kompositionen* (Hamburg, 1937); G. Schmidt, *Die Musik am Hofe der Markgrafen von Brandenburg-Ansbach* (Munich, 1953).

Franck, Joseph, Belgian composer and organist, brother of **César Franck;** b. Liège, Oct. 31, 1825; d. Issy, near Paris, Nov. 20, 1891. He studied organ with Benoist at the Paris Cons., obtaining the 1st prize (1852); then was organist at the church of St. Thomas d'Aquin in Paris. He composed sacred music, piano works, and publ. several manuals on harmony, piano technique, and other pedagogical subjects.

Franck, Melchior, German composer; b. Zittau, c. 1579; d. Coburg, June 1, 1639. He went to Nuremberg in 1601 and in 1602 obtained the post of Kapellmeister at Coburg, where he remained to the end of his life. He was an excellent contrapuntist; composed sacred and secular vocal music, and exerted considerable influence on his contemporaries. Selections from his instrumental works, edited by F. Bölsche, comprise vol. XVI of *Denkmäler deutscher Tonkunst;* vol. XVII of the *Monatshefte für Musikgeschichte* contains a careful description of his printed works, also of MSS preserved in public libraries. Reprints of his sacred vocal works have been publ. by F. Commer, E. Mauersberger, F. Jöde; secular works in the *Staatliches Liederbuch, Kaiser-Liederbuch,* and other collections.

BIBLIOGRAPHY: Aloys Obrist, *Melchior Franck* (Berlin, 1892).

Franck, Richard, German pianist, son of **Eduard Franck;** b. Cologne, Jan. 3, 1858; d. Heidelberg, Jan. 22, 1938. He studied with his father in Berlin and also attended the Leipzig Cons. (1878–80). He was in Basel from 1880–83 and again from 1887 till 1900, and was active there as pianist and teacher. He later lived in Kassel, and finally in Heidelberg. He was highly regarded as an interpreter of Beethoven's sonatas; published a book of memoirs, *Musikalische und unmusikalische Erinnerungen* (Heidelberg, 1928).

Franckenstein, Clemens von, German composer; b. Wiesentheid, July 14, 1875; d. Hechendorf, Aug. 19, 1942. He spent his youth in Vienna; then went to Munich, where he studied with Thuille; later took courses with Knorr at the Hoch Cons. in Frankfurt. He traveled with an opera company in the U.S. in 1901; then was engaged as a theater conductor in London (1902–7). From 1912–18 and from 1924–34 was intendant at the Munich Opera. He wrote several operas, the most successful of which was *Des Kaisers Dichter* (on the life of the Chinese poet, Li-Tai Po), performed in Hamburg (Nov. 2, 1920) and elsewhere in Germany. Other operas are: *Griselda* (Troppau, 1898), *Fortunatus* (Budapest, 1909), and *Rahab* (Hamburg, 1911). He also wrote several orchestral works.

BIBLIOGRAPHY: W. Zentner, "Clemens von Franckenstein," *Zeitschrift für Musik* (1929; pp. 769–75).

Franco of Cologne, medieval theorist and practical musician. His identity is conjectural; there was a learned man known as Magister Franco of Cologne who flourished as early as the 11th century; several reputable scholars regard him as identical with the musical theorist Franco; against this identification is the improbability of the emergence of theories and usages found in Franco's writings at such an early date. The generally accepted period for his activities is the middle of the 13th century (from 1250 to about 1280). The work on which the reputation of Franco of Cologne rests is the famous treatise *Ars cantus mensurabilis.* Its principal significance is not so much the establishment of a new method of mensural notation as the systematization of rules that had been inadequately or vaguely explained by Franco's predecessors. The treatise is valuable also for the explanation of usages governing the employment of concords and discords. It was reprinted, from different MSS, in Gerbert's *Scriptores* (vol. III) and in Coussemaker's *Scriptores* (vol I). Gerbert attributes it to a Franco of Paris, a shadowy figure who may have been the author of a treatise and three summaries, all beginning with the words 'Gaudent brevitate moderni.' The *Ars cantus mensurabilis* is reproduced in English in O. Strunk's *Source Readings in Music History* (N.Y., 1950).

BIBLIOGRAPHY: O. Koller, "Versuch einer Rekonstruktion der Notenbeispiele zum 11. Kapitel von

Francos *Ars cantus mensurabilis,"* *Vierteljahrsschrift für Musikwissenschaft* VI (p. 242ff.); J. F. R. Stainer, "The Notation of Mensurable Music," *Proceedings of the Musical Association of London* 26 (1900); Hugo Riemann, *Geschichte der Musiktheorie* (Leipzig, 1898; p. 114ff.); Johannes Wolf, *Handbuch der Notationskunde* (vol. I, Leipzig, 1913); G. Reese, *Music in the Middle Ages* (N.Y., 1940; p. 288ff.); W. Apel, *The Notation of Polyphonic Music, 900–1600* (Cambridge, Mass., 1942; p. 310ff.); Y. Rokseth, *Polyphonies du XIIIe siècle* (Paris, 1948); F. Gennrich, *Franco von Köln, Ars Cantus Mensurabilis* (Darmstadt, 1955).

Franco, Johan, American composer; b. Zaandam, Holland, July 12, 1908. He studied at the Cons. of Amsterdam (1929–34); in 1936 he emigrated to America; in the U.S. Army during World War II; he wrote 5 symphonies (1933, 1939, 1940, 1950, 1958); symph. poem *Péripétie* (1935); Violin Concerto (Brussels, Dec. 6, 1939); *Serenata Concertante* for piano and chamber orch. (N.Y., March 11, 1940); symph. poem *Baconiana* (1941); Divertimento for Flute and String Quartet (1945); 5 string quartets (1931–53); 6 partitas for piano (1940–52); 8 toccatas for carillon (1953–58); *American Suite* for carillon (1952); *Saga of the Sea* for carillon (1970); numerous vocal works with orch. and chorus a cappella; many songs. In all his works Franco follows the ideal of cyclic construction, with classical symmetry governing not only the larger forms but separate sections of each individual work. His instrumental writing is invariably functional.

Francœur, François, French violinist; b. Paris, Sept. 28, 1698; d. there, Aug. 7, 1787. He was a member of the orch. of the Paris Opéra, a chamber musician to the king, and one of the '24 violons du roi' (1730). Conjointly with his inseparable friend François Rebel he was director of the Opéra (1751) and superintendent of the king's music (1760). He wrote 2 books of violin sonatas; produced 10 operas (in collaboration with Rebel).

Francœur, Louis-Joseph, French violinist, nephew of **François Francœur;** b. Paris, Oct. 8, 1738; d. there, March 10, 1804. He entered the orch. of the Paris Opéra at the age of 14; became its conductor at 27. During the Revolution he was imprisoned as a suspect, but released after the Thermidor coup d'état (1794) and was appointed director of the Paris Opéra. He wrote an act for the opera *Lindor et Ismène* (Paris, Aug. 29, 1766); publ. a treatise *Diapason général de tous les instruments à vent* (1772). The MS of his *Essai historique sur l'établissement de l'opéra en France* is preserved in the library of the Cons. in Paris.

François, Samson, French pianist; b. Frankfurt, son of the French consul there, May 18, 1924; d. Paris, Oct. 22, 1970. He received a prize at the Nice Cons. at the age of 11; studied in Paris with Alfred Cortot. He traveled widely as a concert pianist; made his American debut in 1947; played again in N.Y. in 1960 and 1961. In 1964 he made a concert tour of China. He was particularly noted for his interpretations of Debussy.

Frank, Alan, English music scholar; b. London, Oct. 10, 1910. He studied the clarinet, conducting, and composition. At the age of 17 he joined the staff of the Oxford Univ. Press; during the war was in the Royal Air Force. In 1947 he was appointed music editor of the Oxford Univ. Press, and in 1954 became head of the Music Department. In 1935 he married **Phyllis Tate**, the composer. He has published *The Playing of Chamber Music* (with George Stratton; London, 1935; 2nd ed., 1951); *Modern British Composers* (London, 1953); he is also co-author (with Frederick Thurston) of *A Comprehensive Tutor for the Boehm Clarinet* (London, 1939).

Frank, Claude, German-American pianist; b. Nuremberg, Dec. 24, 1925. In 1938 he moved to Paris, and in 1940 went to New York; there he took piano lessons with Artur Schnabel and composition with Paul Dessau (1941-44) who were then living in N.Y.; later studied composition with Norman Lockwood (1946-48); also attended classes in conducting under Koussevitzky in Tanglewood (1947). He taught at Bennington College (1948-55); eventually joined the staff of the Mannes School of Music in N.Y. A pianist of a grand envergure, he has earned merited encomiums for his sensitive interpretations of the classics.

Frank, Ernst, German conductor and composer; b. Munich, Feb. 7, 1847; d. Oberdobling, near Vienna, Aug. 17, 1889. He studied with M. de Fontaine (piano) and F. Lachner (composition); 1868, was conductor at Würzburg; 1869, chorus master at the Vienna Opera; 1872-77, conductor at Mannheim; 1877-79, at Frankfurt; 1879, at the Hannover court opera. He wrote the operas *Adam de la Halle* (Karlsruhe, 1880), *Hero* (Berlin, 1884), and *Der Sturm* (after Shakespeare; Hannover, 1887); completed H. Götz's opera *Francesca da Rimini* and produced it at Mannheim (1877). Frank was a friend of Brahms.
BIBLIOGRAPHY: A. Einstein, "Briefe von Brahms an E. Frank," *Zeitschrift für Musikwissenschaft* (April 1922).

Frankel, Benjamin, noted English composer; b. London, Jan. 31, 1906; d. there, Feb. 12, 1973. He worked as an apprentice watchmaker in his youth; then went to Germany to study music; returning to London, he earned his living by playing piano or violin in restaurants. It is only then that he began studying composition seriously. In the interim he made arrangements, played in jazz bands and wrote music for films; some of his film scores, such as that for "The Man in the White Suit," are notable for their finesse in musical characterization. In 1946 he was appointed to the faculty of the Guildhall School of Music and Drama in London. Frankel also took great interest in social affairs; was for many years a member of the British Communist Party and followed the tenets of Socialist Realism in some of his compositions.
WORKS: 7 symphonies: No. 1 (1952), No. 2 (Cheltenham, July 13, 1962), No. 3 (1965), No. 4 (London, Dec. 18, 1966), No. 5 (1967), No. 6 (London, March 23, 1969), No. 7 (London, June 4, 1970); *The Aftermath* for tenor, trumpet, harp and strings (1947); Violin Concerto (dedicated "to the memory of the 6 million,"

Stockholm Festival, June 10, 1956); Bagatelles for 11 Instruments (1959); *Serenata concertante* for piano trio and orch. (1961); *Overture for a Ceremony* (1970); Quintet for Clarinet and String Quartet (1953); 5 string quartets; Piano Quartet; *Pezzi pianissimi* for clarinet, cello and piano; 2 string trios; 2 sonatas for solo violin; *Sonata ebraica* for cello and harp; *Elégie juive* for cello and piano; Trio for Clarinet, Cello and Piano; songs.

Frankenstein, Alfred, American music critic; b. Chicago, Oct. 5, 1906. He studied at the Univ. of Chicago (graduated, 1932); played clarinet in the Civic Orch. of Chicago (1923-30); then turned to criticism and teaching; was lecturer on music at the Univ. of Chicago (1932-34); from 1934 to 1965, music critic of the *San Francisco Chronicle;* also from 1934, its art critic. He published a collection of essays, *Syncopating Saxophones* (Chicago, 1925), *A Modern Guide to Symphonic Music* (N.Y., 1967) and several books and essays on American art, and lectured on the subject at several colleges and universities. He was the first to publish the sketches of Victor Hartmann that inspired Mussorgsky's *Pictures at an Exhibition* (*Musical Quarterly,* July 1939); also brought out an illustrated edition of this score (1951).

Franklin, Aretha, black "soul" singer; b. Memphis, Tenn., March 25, 1942. Her father was a Baptist preacher; the family settled in Detroit where he established a pastorate; his church became a hearth of gospel songs and evangelical group singing. At 18 Aretha Franklin went to N.Y. where she quickly attracted attention; her singing at the Newport Jazz Festival in 1963 led to numerous important and lucrative engagements; the sales of her recordings skyrocketed to the million mark. In 1967 she toured Europe; in 1968 she made a sensation with her "soul" version of *The Star-Spangled Banner* at the ill-fated Democratic Convention in Chicago.

Franklin, Benjamin, the great American statesman; b. Boston, Jan. 17, 1706; d. Philadelphia, April 17, 1790. An amateur musician, he invented (1762) the "armonica," an instrument consisting of a row of glass discs of different sizes set in vibration by light pressure. A string quartet mistakenly attributed to him came to light in Paris in 1945, and was publ. there (1946). The parts are arranged in an ingenious "scordatura"; only open strings are used, so that the quartet can be played by rank amateurs. Franklin also wrote entertainingly on musical subjects; his letters on Scottish music are found in vol. VI of his collected works.
BIBLIOGRAPHY: O. G. Sonneck, *Suum cuique: Essays in Music* (N.Y., 1916); Lionel de la Laurencie, "Benjamin Franklin and the claveciniste Brillon de Jouy," *Musical Quarterly* (April 1923); "L'Harmonica de Benjamin Franklin," *Dissonances* (July-Aug. 1944); K. M. Stolba, "Benjamin Franklin y la musica," *Heterofonia* (July-Aug. 1971); M. E. Granander, "Benjamin Franklin's String Quartet," *Early American Literature* (Fall 1972); W. T. Marrocco, "The String Quartet Attributed to Benjamin Franklin," *Proceedings of the American Philosophical Society* (1972).

Franko, Nahan, American violinist and conductor; brother of **Sam Franko;** b. New Orleans, July 23, 1861; d. Amityville, N.Y., June 7, 1930. As a child prodigy he toured with Adelina Patti; then studied in Berlin with Joachim and Wilhelmj. Returning to America, he joined the orch. of the Metropolitan Opera; was its concertmaster from 1883–1905; was the first native-born American to be engaged as conductor there (1905–07).

Franko, Sam, American violinist; b. New Orleans, Jan. 20, 1857; d. New York, May 6, 1937 (from skull fracture as a result of a fall). He was educated in Germany; studied in Berlin with Joachim, Heinrich de Ahna, and Eduard Rappoldi. Returning to the U.S. in 1880, he joined the Theodore Thomas Orch. in N.Y., and was its concertmaster from 1884–91; in 1883 he toured the U.S. and Canada as soloist with the Mendelssohn Quintette Club of Boston. In order to prove that prejudice against native orchestral players was unfounded, he organized in 1894 the American Symphony Orchestra of 65 American-born performers; this orchestra he later used for his "Concerts of Old Music" (1900–09). In 1910 he went to Berlin and taught at Stern's Cons.; he returned to N.Y. in 1915 and remained there for the rest of his life. At the celebration of his 79th birthday (1936), he gave his valuable collection of music MSS to the Music Division of the N.Y. Public Library. He publ. for piano *Album Leaf* (1889); *Viennese Silhouettes* (a set of 6 waltzes, 1928), etc.; several violin pieces; practical arrangements for violin and piano of works by Bach, Chopin, Mendelssohn, Rimsky-Korsakov, etc.; also edited classical music albums. His memoirs were publ. posthumously under the title *Chords and Discords* (N.Y., 1938).

Franz, Robert, famous German song composer; b. Halle, June 28, 1815; d. there, Oct. 24, 1892. His family name was **Knauth;** his father, Christoph Franz Knauth, legally adopted the name Franz in 1847. The parents did not favor music as a profession, but Franz learned to play the organ and participated as an accompanist in performances in his native city. In 1835, he went to Dessau, where he studied with Friedrich Schneider; in 1837, he returned to Halle. He published his first set of songs in 1843; they attracted immediate attention and were warmly praised by Schumann. Shortly afterwards he received an appointment as organist at the Ulrichskirche in Halle, and also as conductor of the Singakademie there; later he received the post of music director at Halle Univ., which conferred on him the title of Mus. Doc. in 1861. The successful development of his career as a musician was interrupted by a variety of nervous disorders and a growing deafness, which forced him to abandon his musical activities in 1868. Liszt, Joachim, and others organized a concert for his benefit, collecting a large sum of money (about twenty-five thousand dollars); his admirers in America (Otto Dresel, S. B. Schlesinger, B. J. Lang) also contributed funds for his support.

WORKS: Franz was undoubtedly one of the finest masters of the German lied. He published about 350 songs; among those best known are *Schlummerlied,*

Die Lotosblume, Die Widmung, and *Wonne der Wehmuth.* He also wrote: 117th Psalm for double chorus a cappella; Kyrie for chorus a cappella and solo voices; Liturgy; arranged works by Bach (*St. Matthew Passion, Christmas Oratorio,* 10 cantatas, etc.) and Handel (*Messiah; L'Allegro, Il Penseroso, ed Il Moderato,* etc.). Published *Mitteilungen über J. S. Bachs Magnificat* (Leipzig, 1863); *Offener Brief an Ed. Hanslick über Bearbeitungen älterer Tonwerke, namentlich Bachscher und Händelscher Vokalwerke* (Leipzig, 1871); both were reprinted by R. Bethge as *Gesammelte Schriften über die Wiederbelebung Bachscher und Händelscher Werke* (Leipzig, 1910).

BIBLIOGRAPHY: F. Liszt, *R. Franz* (Leipzig, 1855; reprinted in *Gesammelte Schriften,* vol. IV, Leipzig, 1882); H. M. Schuster, *R. Franz* (Leipzig, 1874); La Mara, *R. Franz,* in vol. III of *Musikalische Studienköpfe* (Leipzig, 1868–82); publ. separately, 1911); W. Waldmann, *R. Franz; Gespräche aus zehn Jahren* (Leipzig, 1894); R. Procházka, *R. Franz* (Leipzig, 1894); W. Golther, *R. Franz und Arnold Freiherr Senfft von Pilsach; ein Briefwechsel 1861–89* (Berlin, 1907); R. Bethge, *R. Franz; ein Lebensbild* (Halle, 1908); H. Kleemann, "*R. Franz,*" *Musical Quarterly* (Oct. 1915); O. Lessmann, "Persönliche Erinnerungen an R. Franz," *Allgemeine musikalische Zeitung* (1915); S. E. Barbak, *Die Lieder von R. Franz* (Vienna, 1922); H. von der Pfordten, *R. Franz* (Leipzig, 1923); J. M. Boonin, *An Index to the Solo Songs of Robert Franz* (Hackensack, N.J., 1970).

Fränzl, Ferdinand, German violinist and composer, son of **Ignaz Fränzl;** b. Schwetzingen, May 24, 1770; d. Mannheim, Nov. 19, 1833. He studied with his father; later was a pupil in composition of F. X. Richter and Pleyel at Strasbourg, and of Mattei at Bologna. He entered the Mannheim court orchestra at the age of 12; in 1785 began to travel on concert tours with his father. He was appointed conductor of the Munich Opera in 1806, but continued his tours; retired in 1826; finally settled in Mannheim. As a master violinist he enjoyed great renown.

WORKS: A prolific composer, wrote 8 Violin Concertos; Double Concerto for 2 Violins; 6 operas; 9 string quartets; 6 string trios; symphonies, overtures, and songs.

BIBLIOGRAPHY: R. Würtz, "Ferdinand Fränzl," *Mannheimer Hefte* 2 (1967).

Fränzl, Ignaz, German violinist and composer, father of **Ferdinand Fränzl;** b. Mannheim, June 3, 1736; d. there, 1811. He entered the Mannheim court orchestra as a boy of 11, and was its conductor from 1790 to 1803. He made several concert tours with his son; composed symphonies and music for the violin, and also wrote for the stage. His Singspiel, *Die Luftbälle,* was produced in Mannheim with excellent success (April 15, 1787); he also wrote music for Shakespeare's plays.

BIBLIOGRAPHY: R. Würtz, "'. . . ein sehr solider Geiger'. Mozart und Ignaz Fränzl," *Acta Mozartiana* (Nov. 1969); idem, *Ignaz Fräzl* (Mainz, 1970).

Fraser, Norman, Chilean-born English pianist; b. Valparaiso, Nov. 26, 1904. He pursued his musical studies in Chile; in 1917 he went to England, and attended classes in the Royal Academy of Music in London; then took piano lessons with Isidor Philipp in Paris. He subsequently made several tours in South America as a representative of various British organizations. From 1954 to 1971 he was engaged as European Music Supervisor at the BBC; gave numerous joint recitals with his wife, **Janet Fraser,** British mezzo-soprano (b. Kirkealdy, May 22, 1911). In 1973 he settled at Seaford, England. He composed a number of attractive piano pieces, and also some chamber music.

Frazzi, Vito, Italian composer; b. San Secondo Parmense, Aug. 1, 1888; d. Florence, July 8, 1975. He studied organ at the Parma Cons.; also took courses in piano and theory. In 1912 he joined the staff of the Florence Cons. He wrote a music drama *Re Lear* after Shakespeare (Florence, 1939); an opera *Don Quixote* (Florence, April 27, 1952); several symph. poems; chamber music; orchestrated Monteverdi's stage works.

Freccia, Massimo, Italian conductor; b. Florence, Sept. 19, 1906. He studied at the Florence Cons. and later in Vienna with Franz Schalk. In 1933–35 he conducted the Budapest Symph. Orch.; was guest conductor at the Lewisohn Stadium in N.Y. in 1938–40; then was conductor of the Havana Philharmonic Orch. (1939–43); of the New Orleans Symph. Orch. (1944–52) and of the Baltimore Symph. Orch. (1952–59). He returned to Italy in 1959, and conducted the Rome Radio Orch., until 1963.

Frederick II (Frederick the Great), of Prussia; b. Berlin, Jan. 24, 1712; d. Potsdam, Aug. 17, 1786. He was an enlightened patron of music, a flute player of considerable skill, and an amateur composer. He studied flute with Quantz; in 1740, when he ascended the throne, he established a court orchestra and an opera house; Bach's son Karl Philipp Emanuel was his harpsichordist until 1767. In 1747 J. S. Bach himself was invited to Potsdam; the fruit of this visit was Bach's *Musical Offering,* written on a theme by Frederick II. A collection of 25 flute sonatas and 4 concertos by Frederick was publ. by Spitta (3 vols., Leipzig, 1889; repr. N.Y., 1967); other works were publ. in vol. XX of *Die Musik am preussischen Hofe.* Selections from different compositions were edited by Barge, G. Lenzewski, E. Schwarz-Reiflingen, H. Osthoff, G. Müller, G. Thouret, and others. Besides instrumental works, Frederick contributed arias to several operas: *Demofoonte* by Graun (1746); *Il re pastore* (1747; with Quantz and others); *Galatea ed Acide* (1748; with Hasse, Graun, Quantz, and Nichelmann), and *Il trionfo della fedelità* (1753; with Hasse and others).
BIBLIOGRAPHY: K. F. Müller, *Friedrich der Grosse als Kenner und Dilettant auf dem Gebiete der Tonkunst* (Potsdam, 1847); W. Kothe, *Friedrich der Grosse als Musiker* (Leipzig, 1869); G. Thouret, *Friedrichs des Grossen Verhältniss zur Musik* (Berlin, 1895); G. Thouret, *Friedrich der Grosse als Musikfreund und Musiker* (Leipzig, 1898); Karl von Forstner, *Friedrich der Grosse, Künstler und König* (Berlin, 1932); G. Müller, *Friedrich der Grosse, seine Flöten und sein Flötenspiel* (Berlin, 1932); G. M. Fitzgibbon,

"Of Flutes and Soft Recorders," *Musical Quarterly* (April 1934); John Bourke, "Frederick the Great as Music Lover and Musician," *Music & Letters* (Jan. 1947); C. Wolf, "Überlegungen zum *Thema Regium,*" *Bach-Jahrbuch* (1973). Frederick's correspondence with Algarotti was publ. by F. Förster (Berlin, 1837); correspondence between him and the margravine of Bayreuth is contained in chapter IV of Mary Burrell's *Thoughts for Enthusiasts at Bayreuth* (London, 1891).

Freed, Isadore, composer; b. Brest-Litovsk, Russia, March 26, 1900. He came to the U.S. at an early age; graduated from the Univ. of Pennsylvania in 1918 (Mus. Bac.); then studied with Ernest Bloch and with Vincent d'Indy in Paris; returned to the U.S. in 1934; held various teaching positions; in 1944 was appointed head of the music department at Hartt College of Music, Hartford, Conn.
WORKS: FOR THE STAGE *Vibrations,* ballet (Philadelphia, 1928); operas, *Homo Sum* (1930) and *The Princess and the Vagabond* (Hartford, May 13, 1948). For orch.: *Jeux de Timbres* (Paris, 1933); Symph. No. 1 (1941); *Appalachian Symphonic Sketches* (Chautauqua, July 31, 1946); *Festival Overture* (San Francisco, Nov. 14, 1946); Rhapsody for Trombone and Orch. (radio première, N.Y., Jan. 7, 1951); Symph. No. 2, for brass (San Francisco, Feb. 8, 1951, composer conducting); Violin Concerto (N.Y., Nov. 13, 1951); Cello Concerto (1952); Concertino for English Horn and Orch. (1953). CHAMBER MUSIC 3 string quartets (1931, 1932, 1937); Trio for Flute, Viola, and Harp (1940); *Triptych* for violin, viola, cello, and piano (1943); Passacaglia, for Cello and Piano (1947); Quintet for Woodwinds and Horn (Hartford, Dec. 2, 1949); Sonatina for Oboe and Piano (Boston, March 31, 1954); also choral works; piano and organ pieces; songs; co-editor of *Masters of Our Day* (contemporary educational material for piano; N.Y., 1936–37).
BIBLIOGRAPHY: E. Steinhauer, *A Jewish Composer by Choice, Isadore Freed: His Life and Work* (N.Y., 1961).

Freedman, Harry, Polish-born Canadian composer and oboist; b. Lodz, April 5, 1922. He was taken to Canada as an infant, and his family settled in Winnipeg in 1931. He studied composition with Weinzweig and oboe with Perry Bauman at the Toronto Cons. (1945–50); in the summer of 1950 he attended courses of Messiaen and Copland at the Berkshire Music Center in Tanglewood. In the interim he played the English horn in the Toronto Symph. Orch. (1946–70); in 1975 he was elected president of the Canadian League of Composers. His style of composition reflects various influences; he astutely applies serial techniques and electronic sound.
WORKS: the ballets *Rose Latulippe* (Stratford Festival, Aug. 16, 1966) and *Five Over Thirteen* (1969); 2 nocturnes for orch. (1949, 1975); *Matinée Suite* for orch. (1951–55); *Fantasia and Dance* for violin and orch. (1955, revised 1959); *Images,* symph. suite on 3 Canadian paintings (1957–58); Symphony (1954–60; Washington, April 23, 1961); *3 Poèmes de Jacques Prévert* for soprano and string orch. (1962); Chaconne for Orch. (1964); *A Little Symphony* (1966); *Armana* for orch. (1967); *Tangents,* symph. variations (Mon-

treal, July 21, 1967); *Klee Wych (The Laughing One)* for orch. (1970; Klee Wych is the Indian name for the artist Emily Carr); *Scenario* for saxophone, electric bass guitar and orch. (Toronto, May 29, 1970); *Graphic I (Out of Silence. . .)* for orch. and tape (1971; Toronto, Oct. 26, 1971); *Preludes for Orchestra,* orchestrated from Debussy (1971); *Tapestry* for small orch. (1973); Trio for 2 Oboes and English Horn (1948); Wind Quintet (1962); *The Tokaido* for chorus and wind quintet (1964); *3 Duets* for basses or cellos (1965); *Variations* for oboe, flute and harpsichord (1965); *Graphic II* for string quartet (1972); Quartet for Trombones, Bassoons or Cellos (1973); *Vignette* for clarinet and piano (1975); *Love and Age* for soprano, baritone, wind quintet and brass quintet (1975); *5 Rings* for brass quintet (1976); *Fragments of Alice* for soprano, alto, 8 instruments and percussion (1976); Suite for Piano (1951). He wrote many film scores; of these, *An Act of the Heart* was especially successful.

Freeman, Harry Lawrence, black American composer; b. Cleveland, Ohio, Oct. 9, 1869; d. New York, March 24, 1954. He studied theory with J. H. Beck and piano with E. Schonert and Carlos Sobrino; taught at Wilberforce Univ. (1902–04) and Salem School of Music (1910–13); organized and directed the Freeman School of Music (1911–22) and the Freeman School of Grand Opera (from 1923); conducted various theater orchestras and opera companies. In 1920 he organized the Negro Opera Co.; in 1930 received the Harmon Gold Award; conducted a pageant *O Sing a New Song,* at the Chicago World's Fair in 1934. He was the first black composer to conduct a symphony orchestra in his own work (Minneapolis, 1907), and the first of his race to write large operatic compositions. All his music is written in folksong style; his settings are in simple harmonies; his operas are constructed of songs and choruses in simple concatenation of separate numbers.

WORKS: the grand operas (all on Negro, Oriental, and Indian themes): *The Martyr* (Denver, 1893); *Valdo* (Cleveland, May 1906); *Zuluki* (1898); *African Kraal* (Wilberforce Univ., Chicago, June 30, 1903; with an all-Negro cast, composer conducting; revised 1934); *The Octoroon* (1904); *The Tryst* (N.Y., May 1911); *The Prophecy* (N.Y., 1912); *The Plantation* (1914); *Athalia* (1916); *Vendetta* (N.Y., Nov. 12, 1923); *American Romance,* jazz opera (1927); *Voodoo* (N.Y., Sept. 10, 1928); *Leah Kleschna* (1930); *Uzziah* (1931); *Zululand,* a tetralogy of music dramas: *Nada, The Lily* (1941–44; vocal score contains 2150 pp.), *Allah* (1947), and *The Zulu King* (1934); *The Slave,* ballet for choral ensemble and orch. (Harlem, N.Y., Sept. 22, 1932); songs (*Whither, If thou did'st love,* etc.).

BIBLIOGRAPHY: E. E. Hipsher, *American Opera and Its Composers* (Philadelphia, 1934; pp. 189–95).

Freer, Eleanor (*née* Everest), American composer; b. Philadelphia, May 14, 1864; d. Chicago, Dec. 13, 1942. She studied singing in Paris (1883–86) with Mathilde Marchesi; then took a course in composition with Benjamin Godard. Upon her return to the U.S., she taught singing at the National Cons. of Music, N.Y. (1889–91). On April 25, 1891, she married Archibald

Freer of Chicago; they lived in Leipzig from 1892–99; then settled in Chicago where she studied theory with Bernard Ziehn (1902–07). She publ. some light pieces under the name Everest still as a young girl, but most of her larger works were written after 1919.

WORKS: 9 operas, of which the following were performed: *The Legend of the Piper* (South Bend, Ind., Feb. 28, 1924), *The Court Jester* (Lincoln, Nebraska, 1926), *A Christmas Tale* (Houston, Dec. 27, 1929), *Frithiof* (Chicago, Feb. 1, 1931; in concert form); and *A Legend of Spain* (Milwaukee, June 19, 1931; in concert form); a song cycle (settings of Elizabeth Browning's entire *Sonnets from the Portuguese*); about 150 songs; piano pieces.

BIBLIOGRAPHY: She wrote an autobiography, *Recollections and Reflections of an American Composer* (Chicago, 1929); A. G. Foster, *Eleanor Freer and her Colleagues* (Chicago, 1927); E. E. Hipsher, *American Opera and Its Composers* (Philadelphia, 1927; pp. 196–204).

Freitas, Branco, Luiz de, Portuguese composer; b. Lisbon, Oct. 12, 1890; d. there, Nov. 26, 1955. He studied in Berlin with Humperdinck, later in Paris; wrote 3 symphonies, Cello Concerto, Ballade for Piano and Orch., an oratorio, organ works, chamber music, and songs.

Fremstad, Olive, famous dramatic soprano; b. Stockholm, March 14, 1871 (entered into the parish register as the daughter of an unmarried woman, Anna Peterson); d. Irvington-on-Hudson, N.Y., April 21, 1951. She was adopted by an American couple of Scandinavian origin, who took her to Minnesota; she studied piano in Minneapolis; came to New York in 1890 and took singing lessons with E. F. Bristol; then held several church positions; in 1892 she sang for the first time with an orch. (under C. Zerrahn) in Boston. In 1893 she went to Berlin to study with Lilli Lehmann; made her operatic debut in Cologne as Azucena in *Il Trovatore* (1895); sang contralto parts in Wagner's operas at Bayreuth during the summer of 1896; in 1897 made her London debut; also sang in Cologne, Vienna, Amsterdam, and Antwerp. From 1900 to 1903 she was at the Munich Opera. She made her American debut as Sieglinde at the Metropolitan Opera on Nov. 23, 1903. Subsequently she sang soprano parts in Wagnerian operas; at first she was criticized in the press for her lack of true soprano tones; however, she soon triumphed over these difficulties, and became known as a soprano singer to the exclusion of contralto parts. She sang Carmen with great success at the Metropolitan (March 4, 1906), with Caruso; her performance of Isolde under Mahler (Jan. 1, 1908) produced a deep impression; until 1914, she was one of the brightest stars of the Metropolitan Opera, specializing in Wagnerian roles, but also was successful in *Tosca* and other Italian operas. She sang Salomé at the first American performance of the Strauss opera (N.Y., Jan. 27, 1907) and in Paris (May 8, 1907). After her retirement from the Metropolitan, she appeared with the Manhattan Opera, the Boston Opera, the Chicago Opera, and in concerts; presented her last song recital in N.Y. on Jan. 19, 1920. In 1906 she married Edson Sutphen of N.Y. (divorced in 1911); in 1916 she married her accompanist, **Harry Lewis Brainard** (divorced in 1925). In Willa Cather's novel, *The Song of the Lark,* the principal character was modeled after Olive Fremstad.

French, Jacob, American composer of psalm tunes; b. Stoughton, Mass., July 15, 1754; d. Simsbury, Conn., May 1817. He was co-founder with William Billings of the Stoughton Music Society in 1774; fought at the battle of Bunker Hill in the Revolutionary War; was one of the few survivors of the Cherry Valley Massacre. After the war he became a singing teacher, retiring in 1814. He publ. *New American Melody* (1789), *Psalmodist's Companion* (1793), and *Harmony of Harmony* (1802).
BIBLIOGRAPHY: J. T. Howard, *Our American Music* (N.Y., 4th ed., 1965).

Freni, Mirella, Italian lyric soprano; b. Modena, Feb. 27, 1935. She studied voice with Ettore Campogalliani; first sang in public at the age of 10. She made her professional debut as Micaela in *Carmen* in Modena in 1956; in 1959 sang in Amsterdam; in 1961 appeared at Covent Garden in London; in 1963 sang the role of Mimi in *La Bohème* at La Scala in Milan. She made her American debut in this part with the Metropolitan Opera in New York on Sept. 29, 1965. Her roles include Susanna in the *Marriage of Figaro,* Marguerite in *Faust* and such "spinto" parts as Desdemona in *Otello.* In 1970 she joined the cast of the Paris Opéra and sang during its American tour in 1976.

Frere, Rudolph Walter Howard, English music scholar; b. Dungate, near Cambridge, Nov. 25, 1863; d. Mirfield, Yorkshire, April 2, 1938. He studied at Trinity College, Cambridge; was ordained curate in 1887; from 1923 to 1934 he was bishop of Truro. He specialized in plainsong, and contributed valuable articles on this subject to *Grove's Dictionary* and to the *Oxford History of Music.* Among his important publications are *Bibliotheca musica liturgica* (1901) and an introduction to *Hymns, Ancient and Modern* (1909). He edited the *Graduale Sarisburiense* (1893), *The Sarum Gradual* and the *Gregorian Antiphonale Missarum;* and, with John Stainer and H. B. Briggs, *A Manual of Plainsong* (1902); also *Pars antiphonarii* (1923); *Holy Week Services of the Church of England* (2nd ed., 1933).

Freschi, Giovanni Domenico, Italian composer; b. Bassano, Vicenza, c.1625; d. Vicenza, July 2, 1710. He was maestro di cappella at the Cathedral of Vicenza; publ. 2 Masses and a number of psalms (1660; 1673). In 1677, he went to Venice, remaining there for eight years; wrote 10 operas, which were successfully produced there, and a series of short pieces for an opera house in Piazzola near Padua. He also wrote two oratorios, *Giuditta* and *Il Miracolo del mago.*
BIBLIOGRAPHY: Paolo Camerini, *Piazzola* (Milan, 1925).

Frescobaldi, Girolamo, one of the greatest Italian organists and composers of the Renaissance; b. Ferrara, 1583 (baptized Sept. 9); d. Rome, March 1, 1643. He studied with Luzzasco Luzzaschi in Ferrara; served as

singer and organist at the Accademia di Santa Cecilia in Rome; in 1607 traveled to Brussels in the retinue of the Papal Nuncio; publ. his first work, a collection of 5-part madrigals in Antwerp in 1608, printed by Phalèse. Returning to Rome in the same year, he was appointed organist at St. Peter's as successor to Ercole Pasquini. He retained this all-important post until his death, with the exception of the years 1628 to 1634 when he was court organist in Florence. A significant indication of Frescobaldi's importance among musicians of his time was that Froberger, who was court organist in Vienna, came to Rome especially to study with Frescobaldi (1637–41). Frescobaldi's place in music history is very great; particularly as a keyboard composer he exercised a decisive influence on the style of the early Baroque; he enlarged the expressive resources of keyboard music so as to include daring chromatic progressions and acrid passing dissonances, "durezze" (literally "harshnesses"); in Frescobaldi's terminology "toccata di durezza" signified a work using dissonances; he used similar procedures in organ variations on chorale themes, "fiori musicali" (musical flowers). His ingenious employment of variations greatly influenced the entire development of Baroque music.
WORKS: *Fantasie a 2, 3 e 4* (Milan, 1608, Book I); *Ricercari e canzoni francese* (Rome, 1615); *Toccate e partite d'intavolatura di cembalo* (Rome, 1615); *Il 2° libro di toccate, canzoni, versi d'inni, magnificat, gagliarde, correnti ed altre partite d'intavolatura di cembalo ed organo* (Rome, 1616); *Capricci sopra diversi soggetti* (Rome, 1624); *Arie musicale a più voci* (Florence, 1630); *Fiori musicali di diverse compositioni toccate, Kirie, Canzoni, Capricci e Recercari in partitura* (Venice, 1935); *Canzoni alla francese* were publ. posthumously in Rome, 1945. A complete edition of organ and other keyboard works by Frescobaldi was issued in 5 volumes, edited by P. Pidoux in Kassel (1950–54); *Keyboard Compositions Preserved in Manuscripts,* No. 30 of Corpus of Early Keyboard Music (3 vols., 1968); selected organ works, in 2 volumes, were publ. in Leipzig in 1943–48; *Fiori musicale & Toccate e Partite* in 2 volumes were publ. in Rome in 1936–37; *Fiori musicale* were also brought out by J. Bonnet and A. Guilmant (Paris, 1922); *25 Canzoni, 7 Toccate & Correnti* were edited by F. Boghen (Milan, 1918); *Toccate, Ricercari, Canzoni,* etc. were issued by Casella in *I Classici della musica italiana* (Milan, 1919); numerous other editions of selected pieces are also available. A "complete works" edition is now in progress, under the auspices of the Comune di Ferrara and the Società Italiana di Musicologica; the 1st vol., issued in 1975, is of *Due messe a otto voci.*
BIBLIOGRAPHY: The literature is considerable; among the most important essays are N. Bennati, *Ferrara e Girolamo Frescobaldi* (Ferrara, 1908); L. Ronga, *G. Frescobaldi* (Turin, 1930); W. Apel, "Neapolitan Links between Cabezón and Frescobaldi," *Musical Quarterly* (Oct. 1938); A. Machabey, *G. Frescobaldi, la vie, l'œuvre* (Paris, 1952); Roland Jackson, "On Frescobaldi's Chromaticism and Its Background," *Musical Quarterly* (April 1971).

Frešo, Tibor, Slovak composer and conductor; b. Štiavnik, Nov. 20, 1918. He studied composition with

A. Moyzes and conducting with J. Vincourek at the Bratislava Cons., graduating in 1938; then studied with Pizzetti at the Santa Cecilia Academy in Rome (1939–42). Returning to Czechoslovakia he served as conductor of the Bratislava Opera (1942–49) and the Košice Opera (1949–52); in 1953 appointed director of the Slovak National Opera.

WORKS: a children's opera, *Martin and the Sun* (Bratislava, Jan. 25, 1975); 3 cantatas: *Stabat Mater* (1940), *Mother* (1959) and *Hymn to the Fatherland* (1961); *Little Suite* for orch. (1938); *Concert Overture* (1940); *Symphonic Prolog* (1943); the symph. poems *A New Morning* (1950) and *Liberation* (1955); *Little Concerto* for piano and orch.; *Meditation* for soprano and orch. (1942); *Song about Woman* for alto, narrator, children's and mixed choruses, and orch. (1975); String Quartet.

Freudenberg, Wilhelm, German composer and conductor; b. Raubacher Hütte, near Neuwied, March 11, 1838; d. Schweidnitz, May 22, 1928. He studied at the Leipzig Cons. with Moscheles and others; in 1870 he went to Wiesbaden where he was active as a choral conductor; in 1886 he settled in Berlin where he was a theater conductor and teacher; eventually went to Schweidnitz. He wrote several light operas: *Die Pfahlbauer* (Mainz, 1877), *Die Mühle im Wispertale* (Magdeburg, 1883), *Das Jahrmarktsfest zu Plundersweilen* (Bremen, 1908), etc.; also choruses, songs and chamber music.

Freund, John Christian, English-American music journalist; b. London, Nov. 22, 1848; d. Mt. Vernon, N.Y., June 3, 1924. He studied music in London and Oxford; in 1871 arrived in New York where he became the editor of the *Musical and Dramatic Times;* in 1890 began publishing a commercial magazine *Music Trades.* In 1898 he founded the weekly magazine *Musical America* and was its editor until his death. In his editorials he fulminated against the rival magazine *The Musical Courier,* and also wrote sharp polemical articles denouncing composers and music critics who disagreed with his viewpoint; in this respect he was a typical representative of the personal type of musical journalism of the time.

Freund, Marya, soprano; b. Breslau, Dec. 12, 1876; d. Paris, May 21, 1966. She first studied violin, taking lessons with Sarasate; then began to study singing; made successful appearances in Europe and America with symphony orchestras and in recital. Her career as a singer was mainly significant, however, not for the excellence of her performances in standard repertory, but for her devotion to modern music. She sang the principal vocal works by Schoenberg, Stravinsky, Ravel, Bloch, Milhaud, and many others; eventually settled in Paris as singing teacher.

Freundt, Cornelius, German composer; b. Plauen, 1535; d. Zwickau, Aug. 26, 1591. He was a cantor at Borna; in 1565, became organist at Zwickau, where he remained until his death. His compositions were designed for use in church and school; most of his sacred works remain in MS. Georg Göhler wrote a dissertation on him (Leipzig, 1896).

Frey, Adolf, German-American pianist; b. Landau, April 4, 1865; d. Syracuse, N.Y., Oct. 4, 1938. He studied with Clara Schumann, and served as court musician to Prince Alexander Friedrich of Hesse (1887–93), before emigrating to the U.S. From 1893 to 1913 he was the head of the piano dept. at the Univ. of Syracuse.

Frey, Emil, eminent Swiss pianist and composer; b. Baden, in the canton of Aargau, April 8, 1889; d. Zürich, May 20, 1946. He studied musical subjects with Otto Barblan at the Geneva Cons.; at the age of 15 was accepted as a student of Louis Diémer in piano and Widor in composition; in 1907 went to Berlin, and later to Bucharest where he became a court pianist. In 1910 he won the Anton Rubinstein prize for his piano trio in St. Petersburg; on the strength of this success he was engaged to teach at the Moscow Cons. (1912–17). Returning to Switzerland after the Russian Revolution, he joined the faculty of the Zürich Cons.; he continued his concert career throughout Europe and also in South America. He wrote 2 symphonies (the first with a choral finale), Piano Concerto, Violin Concerto, Cello Concerto, Swiss Festival Overture, Piano Quintet, String Quartet, Piano Trio, Violin Sonata, Cello Sonata, several piano sonatas, piano suites and sets of piano variations; publ. a piano instruction manual, *Bewusst gewordenes Klavierspiel und seine technischen Grundlagen* (Zürich, 1933).

Frey, Walter, Swiss pianist, brother of **Emil Frey;** b. Basel, Jan. 26, 1898. He studied piano with F. Niggli and theory with Andreae. From 1925 to 1958 he was, jointly with his brother, instructor in piano at the Zürich Cons.; concurrently evolved an active concert career in Germany and Scandinavia; specialized in modern piano music and gave first performances of several piano concertos by contemporary composers. He published (with Willi Schuh) a collection, *Schweizerische Klaviermusik aus der Zeit der Klassik und Romantik* (Zürich, 1937).

Fribec, Krešimir, Croatian composer; b. Daruvar, May 24, 1908. He studied in Zagreb; adopted a nationalistic style of composition; wrote mostly vocal music.

WORKS: *Povratak,* poem for baritone and orch. (1951); *Bijele Noći,* song cycle with orch. (1953); *Vibracije,* ballet pantomime (1955); the operas *Sluga Jernej* (Zagreb, Feb. 12, 1952); *Romeo and Juliet* (Zagreb, June 21, 1955); *Krvava Svadba* (*Blood Wedding;* 1956). See K. Kovačević, *Hrvatski Kompozitori i Njihova Djela* (Zagreb, 1960).

Fricker, Herbert Austin, English organist; b. Canterbury, Feb. 12, 1868; d. Toronto, Nov. 11, 1943. He studied organ with W. H. Longhurst, organist of Canterbury Cathedral; composition with Sir Frederick Bridge and Edwin Lemare. After filling posts as organist in Canterbury, Folkstone and Leeds, he moved to Toronto, Canada in 1917, and conducted the Mendelssohn Choir there. He composed sacred and secular choruses and organ pieces.

Fricker, Peter Racine, significant English composer; b. London, Sept. 5, 1920. He studied at the Royal College of Music and later with Matyas Seiber. In 1952, appointed musical director at Morley College in London. In 1964 he went to Santa Barbara, Calif., as visiting prof. at the Univ. of California; in 1970 he became chairman of the music department there.

WORKS: *Rondo scherzoso* for orch. (1948); Symph. No. 1 (1949; awarded the Koussevitzky prize; Cheltenham Festival, July 5, 1950); Symph. No. 2 (Liverpool, July 26, 1951); *Canterbury Prologue,* ballet (London, 1951); Concerto for Viola and Orch. (Edinburgh, Sept. 3, 1953); Piano Concerto (London, March 21, 1954); *Rapsodia Concertante* for violin and orch. (Cheltenham Festival, July 15, 1954); *Concertante* for 3 pianos, strings, and timpani (London, Aug. 10, 1956); *The Death of Vivien,* radio opera (1956); *A Vision of Judgment,* oratorio (Leeds, Oct. 13, 1958); *Comedy Overture* (1958); Toccata for Piano and Orch. (1959); Symph. No. 3 (London, Nov. 8, 1960); *O Longs Désirs,* song cycle for soprano and orch. (1964); Symph. No. 4, "In Memoriam Mátyás Seiber" (Cheltenham, Feb. 14, 1967); *3 Scenes for Orch.* (Santa Barbara, Feb. 26, 1967); *7 Counterpoints for Orch.* (Pasadena, Oct. 21, 1967); *Magnificat* for soloists, chorus and orch. (Santa Barbara, May 27, 1968); *The Roofs* for coloratura soprano and percussion (1970); chamber music: Wind Quintet (1947); *3 Sonnets of Cecco Angiolieri* for tenor, wind quintet, cello, and double bass (1947); String Quartet in One Movement (1948; Brussels Festival, 1950); *Prelude, Elegy and Finale* for strings (1949); Concerto for Violin and Chamber Orch. (1950); Violin Sonata (1950); *Concertante* for English horn and strings (1950); String Quartet No. 2 (1953); Suite for Recorders (1956); Cello Sonata (1957); Octet for wind and string instruments (1958); *Serenade No. 1* for 6 instruments (1959); *Serenade No. 2* for flute, oboe and piano (1959); *4 Dialogues* for oboe and piano (1965); *5 Canons* for 2 flutes and 2 oboes (1966); Fantasy for Viola and Piano (1966); *Concertante No. 4,* flute, oboe, violin and strings (Santa Cruz, Calif., Feb. 25, 1969); *Some Superior Nonsense* for tenor, flute, oboe and harpsichord (Santa Barbara, Feb. 26, 1969); *Serenade No. 3* for saxophone quartet (1969); *3 Arguments* for bassoon and cello (1969); Suite for Harpsichord (1957); *14 Aubades* for piano (1958); 12 Studies for Piano (1961); *Commissary Report* for men's voices (1965); *Refrains* for solo oboe (1968); *Paseo* for guitar (1969).

Fricsay, Ferenc, Hungarian conductor; b. Budapest, Aug. 9, 1914; d. Basel, Feb. 20, 1963. He received his early musical training from his father, a military bandleader; he was barely 6 years old when he was accepted as a pupil in the music class for beginners at the Budapest high school; as he grew up he took piano lessons with Bartók and composition with Kodály. He also learned to play almost all orchestral instruments. At the age of 15 he conducted a radio performance of his father's military band; in 1934 he became orchestral conductor at Szeged, and in 1936 conducted the opera there. In 1944 he returned to Budapest; in 1945 made his debut as conductor at the Budapest Opera. In 1947 he conducted at the Salzburg Festival; subsequently made a European tour as guest conductor; also toured South America. In 1949 he was engaged as conductor of the radio orchestra RIAS in the American sector of divided Berlin. On Nov. 13, 1953 he made a highly successful American debut with the Boston Symph. Orch.; in 1954 was engaged as conductor of the Houston Symphony Orch., but soon resigned owing to disagreement on musical policy with the management. He then settled in Switzerland, continuing to conduct occasional guest engagements, until his illness (leukemia) forced him to abandon all activities.

BIBLIOGRAPHY: Fr. Herzfeld, *Ferenc Fricsay. Ein Gedenkbuch* (Berlin, 1964).

Frid, Géza, Hungarian-born Dutch composer and pianist; b. Mármarossziget, Jan. 25, 1904. He studied composition with Kodály and piano with Bartók at the Budapest Cons. (1912–24); settled in Amsterdam in 1929, becoming a Dutch citizen in 1948. In 1964 he joined the faculty of the Cons. of Utrecht.

WORKS: an opera, *De zwarte bruid* (1959; Amsterdam, 1959); 2 ballets, *Luctor et Emergo* (1953), and *Euridice* (1961); *Podium-Suite* for violin and orch. (1928); Suite for Orch. (1929); Violin Concerto (1930); *Tempesta d'orchestra* (1931); Divertimento for string orch. or string quintet (1932); Symphony (1933); *Romance and Allegro* for cello and orch. (1935); *Abel et Cain,* symph. tableau for low voice and orch. (1938); *Schopenhauer Cantata* (1944); Nocturnes for flute, harp, and string orch. or string quintet (1946); *Paradou,* symph. fantasy (1948); *Variations on a Dutch Folk Song* for wind orch., or chorus and orch. (1950); *Fête champêtre,* suite of dances for string orch. and percussion (1951); *Hymne aan de Arbeid (Hymn to Labor)* for male chorus and orch. (1951); 2-Violin Concerto (1952); *Caecilia Ouverture* (1953); *Études symphoniques* (1954); *South African Rhapsody* for orch. or wind orch. (1954); *3 Romances* for soprano and orch. (1955); *Das Sklavenschiff* for tenor and baritone, male chorus, brass, percussion and piano (1956); Serenade for Chamber Orch. (1956); 2-Piano Concerto (1957); *Rhythmic Studies* for chamber orch., or 2 pianos (1959); Concertino for violin, cello, piano and orch. (1961); *Sinfonietta* for string orch. (1963); *7 pauken en een koperorkest,* concerto for 7 percussionists and brass orch. (1964; Amsterdam, May 14, 1965); *Ballade* for chorus and wind orch. (1965; version for chorus, string orch., piano 4 hands, and percussion, 1968); *4 Sketches* for wind orch. (1966); 3-Violin Concerto (The Hague, July 4, 1970); Concerto for 4 different clarinets (one soloist) and string orch. (1972); Toccata for orch. or 2 pianos (1973); 4 string quartets (1926, 1939, 1949, 1956); String Trio (1926); Serenade for Wind Instruments (1928); Cello Sonata (1931); Concerto for Piano and Mixed Chorus (1934); Solo Violin Sonata (1936); Viola Sonatina (1946); Piano Trio (1947); *20 Duos* for 2 violins (1951); *Frühlingsfeier* for soprano, alto, flute, clarinet, bassoon, horn, violin, viola, cello and piano (1952); Violin Sonata (1955); *12 Metamorphoses* for 2 flutes and percussion (1957); *Fuga* for 3 harps (1961); Sextet for wind quintet and piano (1965); *Dubbeltrio* for wind instruments (1967); *Chemins divers* for flute, bassoon and piano (1968; also arranged for 2 violins and piano); *Paganini Variations* for 2 violins (1969); *Houdt den Tijd!* for male chorus and percussion (1971); Duo for Violin and Piano (1972) *Caprices roumains* for oboe and piano (1975); *Sons Roumains* for flute, viola, harp and percussion (1975); *Little Suite* for saxophone and piano (1975); Piano Sonata (1929); *4 Etudes* for piano (1932); *Foxtrot* for 2 pianos (1975); songs; choruses.

Friderici, Daniel, German composer and theorist; b. Klein-Eichstedt, near Querfurt, 1584; d. Rostock, Sept. 23, 1638. He served as a choirboy; then studied music in Magdeburg; settled in Rostock, where he was cantor of St. Mary's Church from 1617 till his death. He died of pestilence. He publ. in Rostock a number of sacred and secular songs to German words, and a theoretical work, *Musica Figuralis oder neue Unterweisung des Singe Kunst* (1618; 6th ed., 1677).
BIBLIOGRAPHY: W. Voll, *Daniel Friderici* (Kassel, 1936).

Fried, Alexej, Czech composer and conductor; b. Brno, Oct. 13, 1922. He studied theory with Theodore Schaefer at the Brno Cons.; then took lessons in composition with Hlobil and Bořkovec at the Prague Academy, graduating in 1953. By that time he had considerable experience in the jazz field; in 1954 organized a dance orch. under his own name. Most of his music is in the "third-stream" manner, fusing jazz with classical styles.
WORKS: 4 musicals: *The Devil Passed Through the Town* (1956-67), *A Fete in Harlem* (1959); *Savage River* (1965), *Carnival in San Catarina* (1974); a ballet, *Peter and Lucia* (1965); Piano Trio (1951); *For a New Man*, symph. poem (1953); *Corrida*, dance metaphor for orch. (1965). His symphonic jazz works for large jazz band include *Akt (Nude Portrait)*, with solo trumpet and flute (1966); Jazz Clarinet Concerto (1970); *Souvenir* (1970); *Jazz Dance Etudes*, with solo clarinet, soprano saxophone and alto saxophone (1970); *Moravian Wedding* for orch. (1972); *Solstice*, concerto for 2 jazz bands (1973); Jazz Clarinet Concertino (1974); *Dialogue*, with 2 solo alto saxophones (1974); Concerto for Jazz Band (1976); jazz works for symph. orch. include a *Triple Concerto* for flute, clarinet, horn and orch. (1971), Concerto for Orch. (1974) and Concerto No. 2 for Clarinet and Orch. (1976).

Fried, Oskar, German conductor and composer; b. Berlin, Aug. 10, 1871; d. Moscow, July 5, 1941. He studied with Humperdinck in Frankfurt and Ph. Scharwenka in Berlin; played the horn in various orchestras until the performance of his choral work with orch., *Das trunkene Lied,* given by Karl Muck in Berlin (April 15, 1904), attracted much favorable attention; he continued to compose prolifically; wrote *Verklärte Nacht* for solo voices and orch.; *Andante und Scherzo* for wind instruments, 2 harps, and kettledrums; *Präludium und Doppelfuge* for string orch., etc. At the same time he began his career as conductor, achieving considerable renown in Europe; he was conductor of the Gesellschaft der Musikfreunde in Berlin (1907-10) and of the Berlin Symph. Orch. (1925-26); left Berlin in 1934 and went to Russia; became a Soviet citizen in 1940. For several years before his death he was conductor of the Tiflis Opera, in the Caucasus.

BIBLIOGRAPHY: Paul Bekker, *Oskar Fried* (Berlin, 1907); Paul Stefan, *Oskar Fried* (Berlin, 1911).

Friedberg, Carl, German pianist; b. Bingen, Sept. 18, 1872; d. Merano, Italy, Sept. 8, 1955. He studied piano at the Frankfurt Cons. with Kwast, Knorr, and Clara Schumann; also took a course in composition with Humperdinck; subsequently taught piano at the Frankfurt Cons. (1893-1904) and at the Cologne Cons. (1904-14). In 1914 he made his first American tour with excellent success; taught piano at the Institute of Musical Art in N.Y.; was a member of the faculty of the Juilliard School of Music, N.Y. Among his pupils were Percy Grainger, Ethel Leginska, Elly Ney, and other celebrated pianists.

Friedheim, Arthur, pianist; b. St. Petersburg (of German parents), Oct. 26, 1859; d. New York, Oct. 19, 1932. He was a pupil of Anton Rubinstein and Liszt, and became particularly known as an interpreter of Liszt's works. He made his first American tour in 1891; taught at the Chicago Musical College in 1897; then traveled; lived in London, Munich, and (after 1915) N.Y., as teacher and pianist; composed a piano concerto and many pieces for solo piano, as well as an opera, *Die Tänzerin* (Karlsruhe, 1897). His memoir, *Life and Liszt: The Recollections of a Concert Pianist,* was published posthumously (N.Y., 1961).

Friedlaender, Max, eminent German musicologist; b. Brieg, Silesia, Oct. 12, 1852; d. Berlin, May 2, 1934. He was first a bass; studied voice with Manuel García in London; appeared at the London Monday Popular Concerts in 1880. He returned to Germany in 1881 and took a course at Berlin Univ. with Spitta; obtained the degree of *Dr. phil.* at Rostock with the thesis *Beiträge zur Biographie Franz Schuberts* (1887); then was "Privatdozent" at Berlin Univ. in 1894, and prof. in 1903. He was Exchange Prof. at Harvard Univ. in 1911; lectured at many American universities and received the degree of LL.D. from the Univ. of Wisconsin; retired in 1932. He discovered the MSS of more than 100 lost songs by Schubert and publ. them in his complete edition (7 vols.) of Schubert's songs. Together with Johann Bolte and Johann Meier he searched for years in every corner of the German Empire in quest of folksongs still to be found among the people; some of these he publ. in a volume under the title *100 Deutsche Volkslieder* (1885); was editor of *Volksliederbuch für gemischten Chor* (1912); ed. songs of Mozart, Schumann, and Mendelssohn, Beethoven's "Scotch Songs," the first version of Brahms' *Deutsche Volkslieder* (1926), *Volksliederbuch für die deutsche Jugend* (1928), etc.
WRITINGS: *Goethes Gedichte in der Musik* (1896); *Gedichte von Goethe in Kompositionen seiner Zeitgenossen* (1896 and 1916); *Das Deutsche Lied im 18. Jahrhundert* (2 vols., 1902); *Brahms Lieder* (1922; in English, London, 1928); *Franz Schubert, Skizze seines Lebens und Wirkens* (1928).
BIBLIOGRAPHY: E. J. Dent, "Max Friedlaender," *Monthly Musical Record* (June 1934).

Friedman, Ignaz, famous Polish pianist; b. Podgorze, near Cracow, Feb. 14, 1882; d. Sydney, Australia, Jan.

26, 1948. He studied music theory with Hugo Riemann in Leipzig and piano with Leschetizky in Vienna. In 1904 he launched an extensive career as a concert pianist; gave about 2800 concerts in Europe, America, Australia, Japan, China and South Africa. In 1941 he settled in Sydney. He was renowned as an interpreter of Chopin; prepared an annotated edition of Chopin's works in 12 vols., published by Breitkopf & Härtel; also edited piano compositions of Schumann and Liszt for Universal Edition in Vienna. Friedman was himself a composer; he wrote a hundred or so pieces for piano in an effective salon manner, among them a group of *Fantasiestücke.*

Friedman, Ken, American avant-garde composer; b. New London, Conn., Sept. 19, 1939. He became associated with Richard Maxfield who initiated him into the arcana of modern music. Friedman developed feverish activities in intellectual and musical fields; edited ephemeral magazines; directed an underground radio program "Garnisht Kigele" in Mt. Carroll, Illinois; was a founder of the avant-garde group "Fluxus." As an avant-garde artist and designer he exhibited his products in Brno, Nice, Cologne, Copenhagen, Trieste and San Diego; staged happenings and audio-visual events in California, announcing himself as "The Truly Incredible Friedman." Most of his works are verbal exhortations to existentialist actions, e.g., *Scrub Piece* (scrubbing a statue in a public square), *Riverboat Brawl* (starting a brawl in a riverboat at Disneyland), *Goff Street* (a "theft event," transplanting a street sign), *Come Ze Revolution* (chanting pseudo-Greek songs), *Watermelon* (splitting a watermelon with a karate blow), etc. He also composed a *Quiet Sonata* (1969) for 75 truncated guitar fingerboards with no strings attached; realized for Nam June Paik his alleged *Young Penis Symphony* for 10 ditto, and had it performed in a hidden retreat, reportedly in Frisco.

Friedman, Richard, American composer; b. in New York, Jan. 6, 1944. He received his formal education in exact sciences, specializing in electronics. He worked at the Intermedia Electronic Music Studio at N.Y. Univ. (1966–68) in collaboration with Morton Subotnick; prepared electronic tape pieces, mostly of scientific inspiration: *Lumia Mix* (1967); *Crescent* (1967); and *To the Star Messenger* (1968), a melodrama depicting the discovery of the moons of Jupiter by Galileo. Another piece of the period was *Alchemical Manuscript* (1968), inspired by the arcane lore of the searchers for the philosopher's stone. In 1968 Friedman moved to California; worked with the Music Department of the radio station KPFA in Berkeley; arranged numerous broadcasts of electronic materials, notably *Serenade* for viola on tape and *Four-Pole Neuro-Magnet with Double Cross,* composed in 1970. Taking advantage of the techniques of amplification, Friedman was able to create a sound of an orchestra of violas with a single viola player. In most of his works he applies the avant-garde philosophy of tonal frugality, limiting his resources to a few notes. Apart from his radio work, he conducted information/media performances at the San Francisco Museum of Art under the general title 'Outside/Inside,' utilizing closed circuit television, inflatable structures and sculptures activated by light beams.

Friedrich II (der Grosse). See **Frederick II.**

Friemann, Witold, Polish composer; b. Konin, Aug. 20, 1889. He studied composition with Z. Noskowski and piano with A. Michalowski at the Warsaw Cons., graduating in 1910; then went to Germany, where he became a student of Max Reger in Leipzig. Returning to Poland, he taught classes at the Lwów Cons. (1921–29) and at the Katowice Military School of Music (1929–33); was head of the music section of the Polish Radio (1934–39); after World War II taught at a school for the blind in Laski.

WORKS: An exceptionally industrious composer, he wrote nearly a thousand works, including 3 operas (*Gewont, Kasia* and *Polish Folk Mystery Play*); 6 cantatas; 5 *Mazovia Suites* for soloists, chorus and orch. (1948, 1949, 1949, 1951, 1956); *Konrad Wallenrod,* symph. poem (1909); 3 symphonies: No. 1, *Slavonic* (1948), No. 2, *Mazovian* (1950) and No. 3 (1953); 24 concertos, including 5 for piano (No. 1, 1911; No. 2, 1951; No. 5, 1960); 3 for trombone (1969, 1969, 1970), 2 for viola (1952; with string orch., 1968), 2 for clarinet (1954, 1964), and one each for cello (*Lirico,* 1950), violin (1953–54), double bass (1967), 2 pianos (1960), flute (1963), oboe (*Lirico,* 1961), bassoon (*Eroico,* 1965–67), 2 bassoons (with string orch., 1968), horn (1966–68) and trumpet (1967); 600 works for piano; 3 string quartets (1933, 1946, 1953); 80 sonatas, suites, etc., for chamber combinations; songs.

Fries, Wulf (Christian Julius), German-American cellist and teacher; b. Garbeck, Jan. 10, 1825; d. Roxbury, Mass., April 29, 1902. As a cellist he played in Norway, at the Bergen theater orch. (from 1842), and at Ole Bull's concerts. In 1847 he went to Boston, where he became a founder member of the Mendelssohn Quintette Club, with A. Fries (1st violin), Gerloff (2nd violin), Edward Lehmann (1st viola), Oscar Greiner (2nd viola), and himself as cellist. He belonged to it for 23 years; also figured in the Musical Fund Society and the Harvard Musical Association; played in trios with Anton Rubinstein, and until 1901 took part in concerts in New England.

Frijsh, Povla (real name **Paula Frisch**), concert soprano; b. Aarhus, Denmark, Aug. 3, 1881; d. Blue Hill, Maine, July 10, 1960. She first studied piano and theory in Copenhagen with O. Christensen, later voice in Paris with Jean Périer; made her debut in Paris at the age of 19; appeared in concert and recital in Paris and briefly in opera in Copenhagen; made her American debut in 1915; gave many first performances of modern vocal music (Bloch's *Poèmes d'Automne,* Loeffler's *Canticle of the Sun,* songs by Griffes, etc.), and made a specialty of modern international song literature. She introduced Negro spirituals to Paris and Copenhagen.

Friml, Rudolf, famous Bohemian-American operetta composer; b. Prague, Dec. 2, 1879; d. Hollywood, Nov. 12, 1972. His original family name was **Frimel.** He was a pupil at Prague Cons. of Juranek (piano) and Foerster (theory and composition); toured Austria, England, Germany, and Russia as accompanist of Kubelik, the violinist, coming with him to the U.S. in 1900 and again in 1906; remained in the U.S. after the second tour; gave numerous recitals, appeared as soloist with several of the large symphony orchestras (played his piano concerto with the N.Y. Symph. Orch.), and composed assiduously; lived in New York and Hollywood, composing for motion pictures.

WORKS: the operettas *The Firefly* (Syracuse, Oct. 14, 1912), *High Jinks* (Syracuse, Nov. 3, 1913), *Katinka* (Morristown, N.Y., Dec. 2, 1915), *You're in Love* (musical comedy; Stamford, Conn., 1916), *Glorianna* (1918), *Tumble In* (1919), *Sometime* (1919), *Rose Marie* (N.Y., Sept. 2, 1924; very popular), *Vagabond King* (N.Y., Sept. 21, 1925; highly successful). In 1937 Metro-Goldwyn-Mayer made a film of *The Firefly*, the popular *Donkey Serenade* being added to the original score; also wrote a great number of piano pieces in a light vein.

Frimmel, Theodor von, Austrian writer on music; b. Amstetten, Dec. 15, 1853; d. Vienna, Dec. 25, 1928. He first studied medicine in Vienna; then became interested in art and maintained an art gallery; taught history of art at the Athenäum in Vienna. In 1908 he became editor of the *Beethoven-Jahrbuch.*

WRITINGS: *Beethoven und Goethe* (1883); *Neue Beethoveniana* (1887, with 9 authentic portraits of Beethoven; 2nd enlarged ed., 1889); *Beethovens Wohnungen in Wien* (1894); "Beethoven," in *Berühmte Musiker* (1901; 5th ed., 1919); *Beethoven Studien:* I. *Beethovens äussere Erscheinung* (1905), II. *Bausteine zu einer Lebensgeschichte des Meisters* (1906); *Beethoven im zeitgenössischen Bildnis* (Vienna, 1923); *Lose Blätter zur Beethoven-Forschung* (1911–28; 10 issues); *Beethoven-Handbuch* (2 vols., 1927).

Frisch, Paula. See **Frijsh, Povla.**

Frischenschlager, Friedrich, Austrian composer and musicographer; b. Gross Sankt Florian, Styria, Sept. 7, 1885; d. Salzburg, July 15, 1970. He studied music in Graz; in 1909 went to Berlin, where he studied musicology with Johann Wolf and Kretzschmar, and also attended Humperdinck's master classes in composition. In 1918 he was engaged as music teacher at the Mozarteum in Salzburg; remained there until 1945; also edited the bulletin of the Mozarteum. An industrious composer, he wrote the fairy-tale operas *Der Schweinehirt,* after Hans Christian Andersen (Berlin, May 31, 1913); *Die Prinzessin und der Zwerg* (Salzburg, May 12, 1927); and *Der Kaiser und die Nachtigall,* after H. Chr. Andersen (Salzburg, March 27, 1937); also several choral works; *Symphonische Aphorismen* for orch., and teaching materials for voice.

Friskin, James, American pianist and composer; b. Glasgow, March 3, 1886; d. New York, March 16, 1967. He studied with E. Dannreuther (piano) and Stanford (composition) at the Royal College of Music in London; then taught at the Royal Normal College for the Blind (1909–14). In 1914 he came to the U.S. In 1934 he gave 2 recitals in N.Y. consisting of the complete *Wohltemperierte Clavier* of Bach. In 1944 he married Rebecca Clarke. Among his works are *Phantasy-Quintet* for piano and strings, and a Violin Sonata. He published *The Principles of Pianoforte Practice* (London, 1921; new ed., N.Y., 1937); also (with Irwin Freundlich) *Music for the Piano* (N.Y., 1954).

Fritzsch, Ernst Wilhelm, German music publisher; b. Lützen, Aug. 24, 1840; d. Leipzig, Aug. 14, 1902. He was a pupil (1857–62) at Leipzig Cons.; lived several years in Bern, and in 1866 took over the music publishing firm of Bromnitz in Leipzig, carried on under his own name until 1903, then acquired by C. F. W. Siegel. Fritzsch publ. Wagner's *Gesammelte Schriften,* edited the *Musikalisches Wochenblatt* (from 1870), and in 1875 started the *Musikalische Hausblätter.* By publishing the works of rising composers (Rheinberger, Svendsen, Grieg, Cornelius), he promoted modern musical development. He was an excellent musician and for many years a member of the Gewandhaus Orchestra in Leipzig.

Froberger, Johann Jakob, famous German organist; b. Stuttgart, May 18, 1616; d. Héricourt, Haute-Saône, France, May 7, 1667. Shortly after 1630 he went to Vienna, where he entered the Institute of "Singer oder Canthoreyknaben"; there it was the custom to allow the choirboys, when their voices had changed and when they had attained a certain degree of musical scholarship, to serve as apprentices to famous masters of the time on stipends given by Emperor Ferdinand II. Froberger, however, did not apply for the subvention until late 1636, when it was refused him; thereupon, he held the position of 3rd organist at the court from Jan. 1 to Sept. 30, 1637. He then again applied with success, and was granted a stipend of 200 gulden; in Oct. of that year he left to study under Frescobaldi in Rome, remaining there for three and a half years. In March, 1641, he returned to Vienna, where he again was organist from 1641–45 and 1653–57; after this he made long concert tours (to Paris and London). Stories of his adventures in London, and of his appointment first as organ blower at Westminster Abbey and then as court organist to Charles II (first publ. by Mattheson, but not corroborated from any English sources) must be dismissed as apocryphal. He spent his last years in the service of the Duchess Sybille of Württemberg at her chateau near Héricourt. Although two collections of *toccate, canzoni,* and *partite* were publ. long after his death (1693 and 1696), there is internal evidence that the majority of these works were written before 1650. Thus Froberger must be regarded as the real creator of the keyboard suite as well as the master who definitely fixed the order of movements in the suite (*Allemande, Courante, Sarabande, Gigue*).

WORKS: organ toccatas, fantasias, canzoni, fugues, etc., of which 3 MS vols. are in the Vienna Library; in Berlin are 2 printed vols., *Diverse ingegnosissime, rarissime, et non maj più viste curiose partite di toccate, canzoni, ricercari, capricci,* etc. (1693; rep. at Mainz, 1695) and *Diverse curiose e rare partite musicali,* etc. (1696); also a vol. of suites de clavecin. Froberger's works, edited by G. Adler, are in *Denkmäler* der Tonkunst in Österreich (vols. 8, 13, 21; formerly vols. 4.i, 6.ii, 10.ii).

BIBLIOGRAPHY: A monograph on Froberger by Fr. Beier in Waldersee's *Sammlung musikalischer Vorträge* (Nos. 59 and 60); 2 letters from Duchess Sybille to Chr. Huygens concerning him, publ. by E. Schebek (Prague, 1874); a MS preface to Fuchs' thematic catalogue of Froberger's works (in the Berlin Library) throws some light on his career; A. W. Ambros, *Geschichte der Musik* (vol. IV, p. 463 ff.); E. Schebek, *Zwei Briefe über J. J. Froberger* (Prague, 1874); H. Riemann, *Handbuch der Musikgeschichte* (vol. II, 2; p. 364 ff.); A. Tessier, "Une Pièce inédite de Froberger," *Adler-Festschrift* (1930); K. Seidler, *Untersuchungen über Biographie und Klavierstil Johann Jakob Frobergers* (1930); G. B. Sharp, "J. J. Froberger (1616-1667): A Link between the Renaissance and the Baroque," *Musical Times* (Dec. 1967); H.-A. Timmerman, "Johann Jakob Froberger," *De Praestant* 16/3 (1967); G. Leonhardt, "Johann Jakob Froberger and His Music," *L'Organo* (Jan.-June 1968); U. Scharlau, "Neue Quellenfunde zur Biographie Johann Jakob Frobergers," *Die Musikforschung* (Jan.-March 1969); G. Beechey, "Johann Jakob Froberger," *Consort* (July 1972).

Froidebise, Pierre, important Belgian composer, organist and teacher; b. Ohey, May 15, 1914; d. Liège, Oct. 28, 1962. He began studies in harmony and organ playing with Camille Jacquemin (1932-35); then entered the classes at the Namur Cons. with René Barbier and at the Brussels Cons. with Moulaert and Léon Jongen. His chosen specialty was the history of organ music; he publ. in 1958 a monumental *Anthologie de la musique d'orgue des primitifs à la Renaissance.* But he also was deeply interested in the techniques of new music, particularly Schoenberg's method of composition with 12 tones; in 1949 he formed in Liège a progressive society under the name "Variation." As a teacher of composition in Liège, he attracted many students of the avant-garde, among them Henri Pousseur.

WORKS: 2 radio operas, *La Bergère et le ramoneur* and *La Lune amère* (both composed in 1957); *De l'aube à la nuit* for orch. (1934-37); *Antigona* for soli, chorus and orch. (1936); Violin Sonata (1938); *La Légende Saint-Julien l'Hospitalier,* symph. poem after Flaubert (1941); *3 Poèmes japonais* for voice and piano (1942-43); *5 Comptines* for voice and 11 instruments (1947; International Society for Contemporary Music Fest., Brussels, June 27, 1950); *Amercœur,* cantata for voice, wind quintet, and piano (1948); *Stèle pour sei Shonagon* for soprano and 19 instruments (1958; contains aleatory passages); *Justorum animae* and *Puer natus est* for chorus and orch.

Froment, Louis de, French conductor; b. Paris, Dec. 5, 1921. He studied at the Paris Cons.; won the Premier Prix de Direction d'Orchestre there (1948); conducted the orchestra of Radiodiffusion Française; was music director at the Casinos in Cannes, Deauville, and Vichy (1950-54); conducted at various festivals in France; toured in Germany, England, Sweden, Holland, Spain, Russia and South America.

Fromm, Andreas, German composer; b. Plänitz, near Wusterhausen, 1621; d. in the Strahov monastery, in Prague, Oct. 16, 1683. A son of a Lutheran pastor, he studied theology; in 1649, he became cantor in Stettin; he was subsequently in Rostock (1651), Wittenberg (1668), and Prague, where he turned to the Roman Catholic Church. His principal musical work was an 'actus musicus' *Die Parabel von dem reichen Mann und dem armen Lazarus* (1649); the opinion that it was the first German oratorio (cf. R. Schwartz, "Das erste deutsche Oratorium," *Jahrbuch der Musikbibliothek Peters 1899*) is discounted by later analysts. See Hans Engel's article in *Die Musik in Geschichte und Gegenwart.*

Fromm, Herbert, German-American composer; b. Kitzingen, Germany, Feb. 23, 1905. He studied privately with A. Reuss in Munich; was conductor at the Civic Theater in Bielefeld (1930) and at Würzburg (1931-33). He came to the U.S. in 1937; was organist at Temple Beth Zion, Buffalo (1937-41); since 1941, music director at Temple Israel in Boston. He published 12 choral works for the Hebrew service; also a Violin Sonata. His cantata *The Stranger* was performed in N.Y., March 12, 1957.

Frontini, Francesco Paolo, Italian composer; b. Catania, Aug. 6, 1860; d. there, July 26, 1939. He was a pupil of his father, **Martino Frontini,** who was also an opera composer, and of Lauro Rossi at Naples; was director of the Catania Cons. until 1923.

WORKS: the operas *Nella* (Catania, March 30, 1881), *Malia* (Bologna, May 30, 1893), *Il Falconiere* (Catania, Sept. 15, 1899); the oratorio *Sansone e Dalila* (Catania, Aug. 23, 1882); numerous choral pieces and songs. Ricordi published his collection of Sicilian songs *Eco di Sicilia* (1883) and of Sicilian dances *Antiche danze di Sicilia* (3 vols., 1936).

BIBLIOGRAPHY: G. C. Balbo, *Note critico-biografiche su F. P. Frontini* (Catania, 1905).

Froschauer, Johann, an Augsburg printer (end of 15th century), once thought to have been the first to print music with movable type, in Michael Keinspeck's *Lilium musicae planae* (1498); however, it is now known that wood blocks were employed for the music illustrations in that work; it also appears fairly certain that music printing with movable type preceded Froschauer's work.

Frost, Charles Joseph, English composer; b. Westbury-on-Trym, June 20, 1848; d. Brockley, Oct. 13, 1918. He was engaged as organist and choral leader in various provincial towns in England; was active also as a lecturer; he wrote a cantata *By the Waters of Babylon* (1876), much sacred music, and pieces for organ (55 hymn-tune voluntaries, 40 preludes, a sonata, etc.).

Frost, Henry Frederick, English organist and writer; b. London, March 15, 1848; d. there, May 3, 1901. He was a boy chorister at Windsor; was organist of the Chapel Royal (1865-91); then taught organ at the Guildhall School of Music (1880-88); also wrote for *The Athenaeum* and *The Standard.* He wrote a biography of Schubert for the Great Musicians Series; publ. *Savoy Hymn-tunes and Chants.*

Frotscher, Gotthold, German musicologist; b. Ossa, near Leipzig, Dec. 6, 1897; d. Berlin, Sept. 30, 1967. He studied in Bonn and Leipzig; was univ. instructor in Danzig (1924–32); professor at Berlin Univ. (1935–45). He wrote a valuable history of organ playing, *Geschichte des Orgelspiels und der Orgelkomposition* (2 vols., Berlin, 1935).

Frotzler, Carl, Austrian organist and composer; b. Stockerau, April 10, 1873; d. there, July 8, 1960. Of very precocious talent, he wrote a grand Mass at 14; then entered the Vienna Cons., where he studied with Franz Krenn. He later occupied various posts as organist: at the Pfarrkirche, Stockerau (1887–93); at Tosis, Hungary, as Kapellmeister to Count Nicolaus Esterhazy (1893–97); then lived in Linz; in 1938 was in Vienna; in 1953 lived in retirement in Stockerau.

Frugatta, Giuseppe, Italian pianist and composer; b. Bergamo, May 26, 1860; d. Milan, May 30, 1933. He studied with A. Bazzini (composition) and C. Andreoli (piano) at Milan Cons., where he became prof. He composed a number of effective piano pieces (*Polonaise de concert, Moments poétiques,* etc.). He published *Preparazione al 'Gradus ad Parnassum' di Clementi* (1913).

Früh, Armin Leberecht, German musical inventor; b. Mühlhausen, Thuringia, Sept. 15, 1820; d. Nordhausen, Jan. 8, 1894. He invented, in 1857, the 'Semeiomelodicon' (an apparatus for facilitating musical instruction, consisting of a series of note heads which, when pressed by the finger, produced tones of corresponding pitch); he traveled to introduce his invention to prominent musicians, and established a factory in Dresden in 1858, but soon failed.

Früh, Huldreich Georg, Swiss pianist and composer; b. Zürich, June 16, 1903; d. there, April 25, 1945. He studied piano with Walter Frey and music theory with Andreae at the Zürich Cons.; then became an instructor at the Volksklavierschule, and later joined the group of avant-garde musicians at the cabaret Cornichon. He wrote mainly theatrical pieces and songs on politically oriented radical subjects.

Frühbeck de Burgos, Rafael, Spanish conductor of German parentage; b. Burgos, Sept. 15, 1933. He studied violin and piano at the Bilbao Cons. and later at the Cons. of Madrid and at the Hochschule für Musik in Munich. In 1959 he was appointed musical director of the Bilbao Symph. Orch., the youngest musician to lead an orchestra in Spain. In 1962 he was appointed conductor of the Orquesta Nacional in Madrid. In the meantime he toured as guest conductor in the European music centers. In 1968–70 he was guest conductor with major orchestras in the United States; from 1974 to 1976 he was conductor of the Montreal Symphony Orchestra.

Frumerie, (Per) Gunnar (Fredrik) de, eminent Swedish composer; b. Nacka, near Stockholm, July 20, 1908. He enrolled at the Royal College of Music in Stockholm where he studied piano with Lundberg and composition with Ernst Ellberg; was a stipendiary of the Jenny Lind Foundation (1929–32) in Vienna where he took courses in piano with Emil von Sauer and composition with Erwin Stein; then went to Paris where he took piano lessons with Alfred Cortot and composition with Leonid Sabaneyev. After returning to Sweden, he was active as concert pianist; in 1945 was appointed to the piano faculty at the Royal College. As a composer, he adheres to the Scandinavian romantic tradition.

WORKS: an opera, *Singoalla* (Stockholm, March 16, 1940); a ballet, *Johannesnatten (The Night of St. John,* 1947); 2 piano concertos (1929, 1932); *Suite in an Ancient Style* for chamber orch. (1930); *En moder,* melodrama to text by Andersen (1932); Variations and Fugue for piano and orch. (1932); Violin Concerto (1936); Partita for String Orch. (1937); *Pastoral Suite* for flute and piano (1933); *Symphonic Variations* (1941); *Symphonic Ballad* for piano and orch. (1943–44) a cantata, *Fader vår (Our Father,* 1945); Divertimento for Orch. (1951); 2-Piano Concerto (1953); *8 Psalms* for chorus and orch. (1953–55); Concerto for Clarinet, String Orch., Harp and Percussion (1958; Trumpet Concerto (1959); Concertino for Oboe, String Orch., Harp and Percussion (1960); Flute Concerto (1969); Horn Concerto (1971–72); 2 piano trios (1932, 1952); 2 violin sonatas (1934, 1944); 2 piano quartets (1941; 1963); *Elegiac Suite* for cello and piano (1946); 2 piano sonatinas (1950); *Ballad* for piano (1965); *Circulus quintus,* 24 miniatures for piano (1965); 2 piano sonatas (1968); Suite for Wind Quintet (1973); a cappella choral works; solo songs.

Fry, William Henry, American composer and journalist; b. Philadelphia, Aug. 10, 1813; d. Santa Cruz, West Indies, Sept. 21, 1864. He was one of the most vociferous champions of American music and particularly opera on American subjects in the English language. Ironically, his own opera *Leonora* (performed in Philadelphia, June 4, 1845), for which he claimed the distinction of being the first grand opera by a native American composer, was a feeble imitation of Italian vocal formulas in the manner of Bellini, with a libretto fashioned from a novel by Bulwer-Lytton, *The Lady of Lyons. Leonora* ran for 16 performances before closing; a revival of some numbers in concert form was attempted in New York on Feb. 27, 1929, as a period piece, but was met with puzzled derision. Fry continued his campaign in favor of American opera in English, and composed three more operas, one of which, *Notre Dame de Paris,* after Victor Hugo, was produced in Philadelphia on May 3, 1864; two other operas, *The Bridal of Dunure* and *Aurelia the Vestal,* were not performed. He also wrote 4 symphonies, subtitled respectively, *Santa Claus, The Breaking Heart, Childe Harold* and *A Day in the Country,* as well as a symphonic poem *Niagara* (N.Y., May 4, 1854). Fry's various proclamations, manifestoes, and prefaces to published editions of his works, are interesting as the illustration of patriotic bombast and humbug that agitated American musicians in the mid-19th century.

BIBLIOGRAPHY: W.T. Upton, *The Musical Works*

of *William Henry Fry* (Philadelphia, 1946); idem, *William Henry Fry, American Journalist and Composer-Critic* (N.Y., 1954).

Frye, Walter, English composer of the 15th century; nothing is known regarding his life, but from indirect indications, it appears that he was attached to the court of Burgundy. Of his 3 Masses (in MS at the Royal Library in Brussels) two are without a Kyrie, a lack characteristic of the English school; his *Ave Regina* is an early example of the 'song motet.'
BIBLIOGRAPHY: M. Bukofzer, "An Unknown Chansonnier of the 15th Century," *Musical Quarterly* (Jan. 1942; reproduces a chanson by Frye); G. Reese, *Music in the Renaissance* (N.Y., 1954, pp. 92-95; contains Frye's *Ave Regina*); D. Plamenac, "A Reconstruction of the French Chansonnier in the Bibl. Colombina, Seville," *Musical Quarterly* (Oct. 1951).

Fryer, George Herbert, English pianist and pedagogue; b. London, May 21, 1877; d. there, Feb. 7, 1957. He studied at the Royal College of Music; then with Matthay in London and Busoni in Weimar. He made his debut as a pianist in London (Nov. 17, 1898); then traveled in Europe; in 1914 he made a tour in the U.S.; in 1915 gave recitals for the British Army in France; in 1917 returned to London; taught at the Royal College of Music (1917-47). He wrote miscellaneous pieces for piano; also publ. a book, *Hints on Pianoforte Practice* (N.Y., 1914).

Fryklöf, Harald Leonard, Swedish composer and teacher; b. Uppsala, Sept. 14, 1882; d. Stockholm, March 11, 1919. He studied theory with J. Lindegren at the Stockholm Cons. and piano with Ph. Scharwenka in Berlin. In 1911 he became prof. of harmony at the Cons. of Stockholm. With G. Sandberg, A. Hellerström, and H. Palm, he edited the choral series *Musica sacra* (1915); also publ. *Koralharmonisering-Kyrkotonarterna* (Choral Harmonizations-Church Modes; 1915); wrote a concert overture, songs, piano pieces.

Fryklund, Lars Axel Daniel, Swedish musicologist and specialist on musical instruments; b. Västerås, May 4, 1879; d. Hälsingborg, Aug. 25, 1965. He studied Romanic philology at the Univ. at Uppsala; taught at the Univ. of Hölsingborg (1921-44).
WRITINGS: *Swedish Instruments* (Uppsala, 1910), *African Instruments* (1915), *Study on the Pocket Violin* (1917), *Tromba Marina* (1919), *Viola d'amore* (1921).

Frysinger, J. Frank, American organist; b. Hanover, Pa., April 7, 1878; d. York, Pa., Dec. 4, 1954. He studied with F. W. Wolff in Baltimore (1887-95) and with E. S. Kelley (1898-1900); was organist at First Presbyterian Church at York, Pa., from 1909-11 and again from 1922-53; published about 200 works for organ; also piano pieces and songs.

Fuchs, Albert, German composer and pedagogue; b. Basel, Aug. 6, 1858; d. Dresden, Feb. 15, 1910. He studied with Selmar Bagge in Basel, and later at the Leipzig Cons. with Reinecke and Jadassohn (1876-79). He conducted oratorios in Trier (1880-83); then lived in Dresden; was subsequently director of the Wiesbaden Cons. (1889-98). In 1898 he joined the staff of the Dresden Cons.; was also conductor at the Schumann Singakademie (from 1901). He was a prolific composer, and publ. a number of choral works and songs; wrote 2 oratorios: *Selig sind, die in dem Herrn sterben* (1906) and *Das tausendjähriges Reich* (1908); several instrumental concertos; publ. *Taxe der Streichinstrumente* (1907; many reprints); edited an album of Italian songs of the early 18th century, and a collection of Italian arias.
BIBLIOGRAPHY: F. A. Seissler, *Albert Fuchs,* in vol. III of *Monographien moderner Musiker* (Leipzig, 1909).

Fuchs, Johann Nepomuk, Austrian composer; b. Frauenthal, Styria, May 5, 1842; d. Vöslau, near Vienna, Oct. 5, 1899. He studied with Sechter at Vienna; conducted the Pressburg Opera in 1864; held similar positions at Cologne, Hamburg, Leipzig, and at the Vienna Opera. In 1894 he succeeded Hellmesberger as director of the Vienna Cons. He produced the opera *Zingara* (Brünn, 1892) and several others.

Fuchs, Joseph, American violinist; b. New York, April 26, 1900. He studied violin with Franz Kneisel; was concertmaster of the Cleveland Orch. (1926-40); toured Europe in 1954, South America in 1957, and Russia in 1965; continued to appear in concerts in 1977.

Fuchs, Karl Dorius Johann, distinguished German music scholar; b. Potsdam, Oct. 22, 1838; d. Danzig, Aug. 24, 1922. He studied piano with Hans von Bülow, Weitzmann, and Kiel; took the degree of Dr. phil. at Greifswald, with the dissertation *Präliminarien zu einer Kritik der Tonkunst.* In 1868 he became teacher at the Kullak Academy in Berlin; then gave piano concerts in Germany. In 1874 he went to Danzig, where he was organist at the Petrikirche and music critic of the *Danziger Zeitung* (1887-1920); was also organist for many years at the Synagogue in Danzig, and wrote *Andachts-lieder für Tempel und Haus.* Fuchs was a friend of Nietzsche, with whom he corresponded.
WRITINGS: *Betrachtungen mit und gegen Arthur Schopenhauer* (1868); *Ungleiche Verwandte unter den Neudeutschen* (1868); *Virtuos und Dilettant* (Leipzig, 1871); *Die Zukunft des musikalischen Vortrags* (Danzig, 1884); *Die Freiheit des musikalischen Vortrags* (Danzig, 1885); *Praktische Anleitung zum Phrasieren* (Berlin, 1886, with Hugo Riemann; English transl., N.Y., 1892); *Künstler und Kritiker* (1898); *Takt und Rhythmus im Choral* (Berlin, 1911); *Der taktgerechte Choral, Nachweisung seiner 6 Typen* (Berlin, 1923). His letters were publ. by his son, Hans Fuchs in *Ostdeutsche Monatshefte* (Sept. 1923).

Fuchs, Lukas. See **Foss, Lukas.**

Fuchs, Robert, renowned Austrian composer and pedagogue; brother of **Johann Nepomuk Fuchs;** b. Frauenthal, Feb. 15, 1847; d. Vienna, Feb. 19, 1927. He studied at the Cons. of Vienna; from 1875 till 1912 was prof. of harmony there, and established himself as a teacher of historical importance; among his students were Gustav Mahler, Hugo Wolf and Schreker. His own compositions are, however, of no consequence, and there is no evidence that he influenced his famous pupils stylistically or even technically; the only pieces that were at all successful were his 5 serenades for string orch. He wrote also 3 symphonies, a Piano Concerto, 2 piano trios, 3 string quartets, 2 piano quartets, Piano Quintet, and numerous pieces for piano solo and for piano 4-hands.

BIBLIOGRAPHY: Anton Mayr, *Erinnerungen an Robert Fuchs* (Graz, 1934).

Fuchs, Viktor, Austrian-American opera singer and teacher; b. Vienna, Jan. 19, 1891; d. Los Angeles, Sept. 14, 1966. He studied voice with Franz Steiner; sang both tenor and baritone parts; made his operatic debut in Breslau in 1912. From 1918 he taught at the Vienna Cons. In 1938 he went to the U.S. and settled in Hollywood as a vocal teacher. He publ. a manual, *The Art of Singing and Voice Technique* (London, 1962).

Fučík, Julius, Czech composer of band music; b. Prague, July 18, 1872; d. Leitmeritz, Sept. 25, 1916. He was a bassoon player at the German Opera in Prague (1893) and later in Zagreb and Budapest; studied composition with Dvořák; was bandmaster of the 86th and 92nd Austrian regiments. He wrote a great number of dances and marches for band, including the immensely popular march, *Entrance of the Gladiators.*

Fuenllana, Miguel de, blind Spanish vihuela virtuoso and composer; b. Navalcarnero, Madrid, early in the 16th century; date of death unknown. He was chamber musician to the Marquesa de Tarifa, and later at the court of Philip II, to whom he dedicated (1554) his *Libro de música para vihuela, intitulado Orphenica Lyra.* From 1563, he was chamber musician to Queen Isabel de Valois, 3rd wife of Philip II. The *Libro* gives evidence of a high state of musical art in Spain during the 16th century; besides fantasias and other compositions for vihuela by Fuenllana and old Spanish ballads (such as the famous *Ay de mi, Alhama*), it contains arrangements for vihuela of works by Vásquez, Morales, P. and F. Guerrero, Flecha, Bernal, and several Flemish masters.

BIBLIOGRAPHY: H. Riemann, in *Monatshefte für Musikgeschichte* (1895); G. Morphy, *Les Luthistes espagnols* (Leipzig, 1902); A. Koczirz, "Die Gitarrekompositionen in Miguel de Fuenllana's Orphenica Lyra," *Archiv für Musikwissenschaft* (1922); H. Anglès, "Dades desconegudes sobre Miguel de Fuenllana, vihuelista," *Revista Musical Catalana* (April 1936).

Fuentes, Juan Bautista, Mexican composer; b. Guadalajara, Jalisco, March 16, 1869; d. Leon, Guanajuato, Feb. 11, 1955. He studied in Mexico City; then taught music in various schools there. He published the manuals *Teoría de la Música* (1899); *Tratado de Intervalos y Trasposición* (1909); *Método de Armonía* (1920); composed a number of piano pieces in a salon style; also some orchestral works, among them *Sinfonia Mexicana.*

Fuerstner, Carl, German-American pianist, conductor and composer; b. Strasbourg, June 16, 1912. He attended the Hochschule für Musik in Cologne (1930–34), studying composition and conducting; his teachers there were Hermann Abendroth, Walter Braunfels, Philipp Jarnach and Ernst Klussmann. Still as a student, he composed incidental music for theatrical plays. In 1939 he went to the U.S. as assistant conductor of the San Francisco Opera Co.; served as head coach of the opera dept. at the Eastman School of Music in Rochester, N.Y. and conducted the Rochester Civic Community Orch.; then was engaged as piano teacher at Brigham Young Univ. in Provo, Utah; toured as piano accompanist to many famous artists, among them the violinists Menuhin, Ricci, and Spivakovsky; the cellist Nelsova and the singers Martinelli, Kipnis, Traubel, Peerce, Siepi and Leontyne Price; conducted an impressive repertory of classical and modern operas with various operatic groups in America and in Europe. In 1963 he was appointed head coach of the opera dept. at Indiana Univ., Bloomington.

WORKS: *Concerto rapsodico* for cello and orch. (Rochester, May 11, 1947); *Metamorphoses on a Chorale Theme,* scored for 20 trombones, 2 tubas and percussion (Rochester, April 5, 1949); *Symphorama* for orch. (1960); *Overture,* and many more pieces for concert band, as well as transcriptions for band of various classical and romantic works. In 1973 Fuerstner was elected to the faculty of the International Summer Courses at the Mozarteum in Salzburg.

Fugère, Lucien, French baritone; b. Paris, July 22, 1848; d. there, Jan. 15, 1935. He began as a singer in cabarets; then sang in light opera; in 1877 joined the Opéra-Comique, and acquired a great following as a brilliant performer of the comic parts; his best roles were Figaro and Bartolo. He was also well known as a teacher; among his pupils was Mary Garden.

Führer, Robert (Johann Nepomuk), composer and organist; b. Prague, June 2, 1807; d. Vienna, Nov. 28, 1861. He studied with Johann Vitásek; was organist in provincial towns before succeeding his teacher as Kapellmeister at the Prague Cathedral in 1839. He became involved in fraudulent transactions and was dismissed from his post in 1845. He then held various positions as organist and choral conductor in Vienna, Salzburg, Munich, Augsburg, and Gmunden. A series of embezzlements and other criminal offenses perpetrated by him resulted in his dismissal from several of his positions, but he continued to compose and perform; in 1856 he was Bruckner's competitor for the organist's post in Linz, arousing great admiration for his skill, even though Bruckner was selected. He served a prison term in 1859, but was given full freedom to write music. He published numerous sacred works (32 Masses, 14 Requiems, 4 litanies, etc.) and many organ pieces; also handbooks on harmony and organ playing. Despite his notoriously dishonest acts and professional untrustworthiness (he publ. one of Schubert's Masses under his own name), he enjoyed a fine reputation for his musicianship.

Fukai, Shiro, Japanese composer; b. in Akita-City, April 4, 1907. He studied composition in Tokyo with M. Sugawara; among his works are the orchestral suite *Paradise* (Tokyo, Jan. 29, 1937); *Tropical Scene* (Tokyo, Jan. 14, 1943); a large choral work, *Prayer for Peace* (Tokyo, Aug. 15, 1949); a cantata, *Heiankyo* (1939); and the ballets *A City* (Tokyo, June 18, 1936), *Ocean* (Tokyo, Jan. 30, 1938), and *Distorted Letters ABC* (1955).

Fukushima, Kazuo, Japanese composer; b. Tokyo, April 11, 1930. Autodidact in composition, he became determined to effect an esthetic and idiomatic synthesis between the traditional Japanese style of court music and the serial organization of western modernism. In 1963 he received a traveling fellowship of the Japan Society of New York.
WORKS: *Kadha Hi-Haku (The Flying Spirit)* for chamber orch.; *Tsuki-shiro (The Moon Spirit)* for string orch.; *Hi-Kyo* for flute, strings and percussion; *3 Pieces from Chu-U* for flute and piano; etc.

Fuleihan, Anis, American pianist, conductor, and composer; b. Kyrenia, Cyprus, April 2, 1900; d. Palo Alto, Calif., Oct. 11, 1970. He studied there at the English School; came to the U.S. in 1915 and continued his study of the piano in New York with Alberto Jonás; toured the U.S., also the Near East, from 1919 to 1925; then lived in Cairo, returning to the U.S. in 1928; was on the staff of G. Schirmer, Inc. (1932–39); 1947, became prof. at Indiana Univ.; 1953, director of the Beirut Cons., Lebanon. In 1962 he went to Tunis under the auspices of the State Dept.; in 1963 organized the Orchestre classique de Tunis.
WORKS: an opera, *Vasco* (1960); for orch.: *Mediterranean Suite* (1922; Cincinnati, March 15, 1935); *Preface to a Child's Story Book* (1932); Symphony No. 1 (N.Y. Philharmonic, Dec. 31, 1936); Concerto No. 1 for Piano and String Orch. (Saratoga Springs, N.Y., Sept. 11, 1937, composer soloist); Concerto No. 2 for Piano and Orch. (N.Y., 1938); Fantasy for Viola and Orch. (1938); Violin Concerto (1930); *Fiesta* (Indianapolis Symph. Orch., Dec. 1, 1939); *Symphonie Concertante,* for string quartet and orch. (N.Y. Philharmonic, April 25, 1940); Concerto for 2 Pianos and Orch. (Hempstead, N.Y., Jan. 10, 1941); *Epithalamium* for piano and strings (Philadelphia, Feb. 7, 1941); Concerto for Theremin and Orch. (N.Y., 1945); *Invocation to Isis* (Indianapolis Symph. Orch., Feb. 28, 1941); *Three Cyprus Serenades* for orch. (Philadelphia Orch., Dec. 13, 1946, Ormandy cond.); Rhapsody for Cello and String Orch. (Saratoga Springs, Sept. 12, 1946); *Overture for Five Winds* (N.Y., May 17, 1947); *The Pyramids of Giza,* symph. poem (1952); Toccata for Piano and Orch. (1960); *Islands* symph. suite (1961); Piano Concerto No. 3 (1963); Cello Concerto (1963); Viola Concerto (1963); Violin Concerto No. 2 (1965); Symph. No. 2 (N.Y., Feb. 16, 1967); 5 string quartets; 11 piano sonatas; Horn Quintet; Clarinet Quintet; Violin Sonata; Viola Sonata; Cello Sonata; choral pieces, songs.

Fuller-Maitland, John Alexander, eminent English music scholar; b. London, April 7, 1856; d. Carnforth Lane, March 30, 1936. He studied at Westminster School and Trinity College in Cambridge (M.A., 1882); then took piano lessons with Dannreuther and W.S. Rockstro. He was the music critic of the *Pall Mall Gazette* (1882–84); of the *Manchester Guardian* (1884–89); lectured extensively on the history of English music; appeared as pianist with the Bach Choir and as performer on the harpsichord in historical concerts; contributed to the first ed. of *Grove's Dictionary* and edited the 'Appendix'; editor-in-chief of the 2nd ed. (1904–10); ed. of *English Carols of the 15th Century* (1887), *English Country Songs* (1893; with L. E. Broadwood), *Fitzwilliam Virginal Book* (1899; with W. Barclay Squire, his brother-in-law), 12 trio sonatas and *St. Cecilia Ode* of Purcell in the monumental edition of the Purcell Society, the piano works of Purcell's contemporaries (1921). Together with Clara Bell he translated Spitta's *Bach* (3 vols., 1884; 2nd ed., 1899); compiled the catalogue of the music division of the Fitzwilliam Museum (1893). He is the author of the following books: *Schumann* (1884); *Masters of German Music* (1894); *The Musician's Pilgrimage* (1899); *English Music in the 19th Century* (1902); *The Age of Bach and Handel* (vol. IV of *The Oxford History of Music,* 1902; new ed., 1931); *Joseph Joachim* (1905); *Brahms* (1911; in German, 1912); *The Concert of Music* (1915); *The "48"—Bach's Wohltemperiertes Clavier* (2 vols., 1925); *The Keyboard Suites of J.S. Bach* (1925); *The Spell of Music* (1926); *A Door-Keeper of Music* (1929); *Bach's Brandenburg Concertos* (1929); *Schumann's Concerted Chamber Music* (1929); *The Music of Parry and Stanford* (Cambridge, 1934).

Fumagalli, four brothers, natives of Inzago, Italy: **Disma,** b. Sept. 8, 1826; d. Milan, March 9, 1893. He was a pupil at, and from 1857 prof. in, Milan Cons. Prolific composer of piano music (over 250 numbers). **Adolfo,** b. Oct. 19, 1828; d. Florence, May 3, 1856, at the age of 27. Pianist, pupil of Gaetano Medaglia, and later of Angeleri and Ray at Milan Cons.; then undertook tours throughout Italy, France, and Belgium, earning the sobriquet of the "Paganini of the pianoforte." During his brief lifetime he publ. about 100 elegant and effective piano pieces, which obtained an extraordinary vogue. Filippo Filippi wrote a sketch, *Della vita e delle opere di Adolfo Fumagalli* (Milan, 1857). **Polibio,** b. Oct. 26, 1830; d. Milan, June 21, 1891. Pianist; composer for piano and for organ. **Luca,** b. May 29, 1837; d. Milan, June 5, 1908. He was a pupil of the Milan Cons.; played with great success in Paris (1860), and published salon music for piano; also produced an opera, *Luigi XI* (Florence, 1875).

Fumet, Dynam-Victor, French organist and composer; b. Toulouse, May 4, 1867; d. Paris, Jan. 2, 1949. He studied with César Franck and with Guiraud at the Paris Cons. At an early age he became involved in the political activities of French anarchists and was forced to leave school. For a time he earned his living as piano player in Paris night clubs; in 1910 became organist of St. Anne's Church in Paris. His music follows the precepts of French Wagnerism; the influence of Franck is also noticeable. Fumet wrote several orchestral works on mystic themes, among them *Magnetisme céleste* for cello and orchestra (1903); *Trois* *âmes* (1915); *Transsubstantiation* (1930); *Notre mirage, notre douleur* (1930). During the German occupation he wrote *La Prison glorifiée* (1943).

Fumi, Vinceslao, Italian conductor; b. Montepulciano, Tuscany, Oct. 20, 1823; d. Florence, Nov. 20, 1880. He conducted opera in various Italian cities; also in Constantinople, Montevideo, and Buenos Aires; finally at Florence. His compositions include the opera, *Atala* (Buenos Aires, 1862), a symphony, and other orchestral works. A collection of folksongs of all times and nations, which he undertook, remained unfinished.

Furno, Giovanni, Italian composer and pedagogue; b. Capua, Jan. 1, 1748; d. Naples, June 20, 1837. He studied at the Cons. di Saint Onofrio in Naples, and in 1775 became teacher of theory of composition there. Among his pupils were Bellini and Mercadante. He wrote two operas, sacred choral music and some instrumental pieces.

Fursch-Madi, Emma, operatic soprano; b. Bayonne, France, 1847; d. Warrenville, N.Y., Sept. 20, 1894. She studied at the Paris Cons.; her first opera engagement was in Paris as Marguerite. She visited America in 1874 with the New Orleans French Opera Co.; sang at Covent Garden (1879–81) and at the Metropolitan Opera, where her final appearance (Feb. 6, 1894) was as Ortrud in *Lohengrin.* She was married three times: to **Madi Manjour,** a violinist, to Henry Verié, and to M. Wurst.

Fürstenau, Moritz, German writer on music and flutist; b. Dresden, July 26, 1824; d. there, March 25, 1889. He was a member of the Dresden court orch. from 1842; librarian of the music section, Royal Library, from 1852; from 1858, flute teacher in the Cons.
WRITINGS: *Beiträge zur Geschichte der königlichsächs. musikalischen Kapelle* (1849); *Zur Geschichte der Musik und des Theaters am Hofe zu Dresden* (1861–62, 2 vols.; a supplement, by Dr. Hans van Brescius, entitled *Die königliche sächs. musikalische Kapelle von Reissiger bis Schuch, 1826–98,* was publ. at Dresden, 1898); *Die Fabrikation musikalischer Instrumente im königlich sächsischen Vogtland* (1876, with Th. Berthold); also essays and articles in musical journals.

Fürstner, Adolf, German publisher; b. Berlin, April 3, 1833; d. Bad Nauheim, June 6, 1908. He was a member of a family of merchants; although lacking in musical education he showed a keen understanding of commercial values of good music. He founded a music publishing firm under his own name in Berlin in 1868; in 1872 he acquired the catalogue of the Dresden firm of C. F. Meser, which owned several operas by Wagner and some works of Liszt; he subsequently purchased the rights of operas by Massenet, and later demonstrated his business acumen by securing *Pagliacci.* His firm distinguished itself as the earliest publisher of Richard Strauss. Fürstner was succeeded after his death by his son **Otto** (b. Berlin, Oct. 17, 1886; d. London, June 8, 1958); in 1933, Otto Fürstner was compelled to leave Germany; he went to England,

where he resumed his business and gradually won back the German rights to the original editions of the firm. After the death of Otto Fürstner, his widow **Ursula Fürstner** took over the ownership of the firm; in 1970, it was incorporated as Fürstner, London.

Furtwängler, Wilhelm, celebrated German conductor; b. Berlin, Jan. 25, 1886; d. Baden-Baden, Nov. 30, 1954. He grew up in Munich, where he studied music with Schillings, Rheinberger, and Beer-Waldbrunn; conducting with Mottl. His first appearances as conductor were in opera, at Zürich and Strasbourg; then in Lübeck (1911–15) and Mannheim (1915–19). From 1919–21, he conducted the Tonkünstler Orch. in Vienna; from 1920–22, the Staatskapelle, Berlin. In 1919 he became musical director of the Berlin State Opera. In 1922 he was appointed conductor of the Berlin Philharmonic as successor to Nikisch; he also conducted the Gewandhaus Orch. in Leipzig (until 1928) and at the Bayreuth Festivals (1931–32). He made a sensationally successful American debut with the N.Y. Philharmonic on Jan. 3, 1925, and led the orch. again in February 1926, and March, 1927. On April 17, 1932, he was awarded the Goethe Gold Medal. In 1933–34, he had several clashes with the Nazi Government on questions of policy, and on Dec. 4, 1934, resigned his posts at the Berlin Philharmonic, the State Opera, and the Reichsmusikkammer (of which he had been briefly deputy president). However, a few months later, he made an uneasy peace with the Nazi authorities and agreed to resume his post with the Berlin Philharmonic (April 25, 1935). In 1936 he was offered a contract as permanent conductor of the N.Y. Philharmonic, but declined when accusations were leveled at him as a former collaborator with the Nazi regime. He continued conducting in Germany during World War II; in 1945 he went to Switzerland. Returning to Germany in 1946, he was absolved from the charges of pro-Nazi activities (Dec. 17, 1946). He was tentatively engaged to conduct the Chicago Symph. Orch. in 1949, but the contract was cancelled when public opinion proved hostile. In Western Europe, however, Furtwängler was received most enthusiastically when he led the Berlin Philharmonic in guest appearances in England and France. He was to conduct the Berlin Philharmonic in its first American tour in 1955, but death intervened, and Herbert von Karajan was appointed his successor. Furtwängler was also a composer; he wrote 2 symphonies, a piano concerto, a *Te Deum,* and some chamber music; publ. a monograph, *Johannes Brahms und Anton Bruckner* (Leipzig, 1942); collections of essays, *Gespräche über Musik* (Zürich, 1948; in English as *Concerning Music,* London, 1953); *Ton und Wort* (Wiesbaden, 1954); and *Der Musiker und sein Publikum* (Zürich, 1954).
BIBLIOGRAPHY: R. Specht, *Wilhelm Furtwängler* (1922); A. Einstein, "Wilhelm Furtwängler," *Monthly Musical Record* (Jan. 1934); O. Schrenck, *Wilhelm Furtwängler* (1940); F. Herzfeld, *Wilhelm Furtwängler, Weg und Wesen* (Leipzig, 1941); Berta Geissmar, *Two Worlds of Music* (N.Y., 1946); Willy Siebert, *Furtwängler, Mensch und Künstler* (Buenos Aires, 1950); Curt Riess, *Furtwängler; Musik und Politik* (Bern, 1953). Newsletters and other publications are issued by the Wilhelm Furtwängler Society of Los An-

geles, Calif., the Société Wilhelm Furtwängler of Paris, France, and the Wilhelm Furtwängler Associates of Urawa City, Japan.

Furuhjelm, Erik Gustaf, Finnish composer; b. Helsinki, July 6, 1883; d. there, June 13, 1964. He studied violin; then took lessons in composition with Sibelius and Wegelius; continued his studies in Vienna with Robert Fuchs. From 1909 to 1935 he lectured in music theory at the Helsinki School of Music and from 1920 to 1935 served the school as assistant director. He founded the magazine *Finsk Musikrevy;* in 1916 he wrote the first book-length biography of Sibelius.
WORKS: Piano Quintet (1906); 2 symphonies (1906–11, 1925–26); *Romantic Overture* (1910); *Konzertstück* for piano and orch. (1911); *Intermezzo and Pastorale for Orch.* (1920–24); *Fem bilder (5 Pictures)* for orch. (1924–25); *Phantasy* for violin and orch. (1925–26); *Folklig svit (Rustic Suite)* for orch. (1939); *Solitude* for orch. (1940); String Quartet.

Fussan, Werner, German composer; b. Plauen, Dec. 25, 1912. He studied at the Hochschule für Musik in Berlin; served in the German Army during World War II; after the war he taught composition at the Cons. of Wiesbaden; in 1948 was appointed to the faculty of the Hochschule für Musik in Mainz.
WORKS: *Capriccio* for orch. (1949); Suite for Strings (1951); Concertino for Flute and Strings (1957); Concertino for Clarinet, Trumpet and Strings (1966); Wind Quintet (1948); String Trio (1953); other chamber music; *Tanzlieder,* cantata (1968); choruses and numerous teaching pieces for various instruments.

Futterer, Carl, Swiss composer; b. Basel, Feb. 21, 1873; d. Ludwigshafen, Nov. 5, 1927. He studied to be a lawyer; then began taking lessons in composition with Hans Huber; wrote operas and other works but kept them hidden until late in life. His comic opera *Don Gil mit den grünen Hosen* (1915) was produced in Freiburg-im-Breisgau in 1922; another opera *Der Geiger von Gmünd* (1917) was produced in Basel in 1921. He further wrote a Sinfonietta (1917); Octet (1921); Quartet for oboe, clarinet, horn and bassoon (1921); Trio for clarinet, cello and piano (1924); Piano Trio (1927); Violin Sonata (1927); Piano Concerto (1927).

Fux, Johann Joseph, Austrian composer and learned theorist; b. Hirtenfeld, Styria, 1660; d. Vienna, Feb. 13, 1741. Nothing definite is known concerning his teachers or course of study. In 1696 he was appointed organist at the Schottenkirche, Vienna; in 1698 he was made court composer; in 1704 Kapellmeister at St.

Stephen's, and assistant Kapellmeister to the court in 1713, succeeding Ziani as first Kapellmeister (the highest position attainable for a musician) in 1713. This office he held until his death, under 3 successive emperors, and received many tokens of imperial favor. Of his 405 extant works, the greatest and the most enduring is his treatise on counterpoint, *Gradus ad Parnassum,* published originally in Latin (Vienna, 1725), since then in German, Italian, French, and English (1791; part of the *Gradus ad Parnassum* was published in English as *Steps to Parnassus,* N.Y., 1943); Mozart and Haydn studied it; Cherubini and Albrechtsberger adopted its method, which was sanctioned by Piccini and Padre Martini. Vogler, however, condemned it (see introduction to Vogler's *Choral-System,* p. 1; Fröhlich's biography of Vogler, p. 18). Fux was well aware of the weakness of contemporary music practice and, in trying to arrive at a satisfactory remedy, disregarded the modern idiom already established when he was writing and chose, as the basis of his theory, the style of Palestrina. Although his presentation of that style is not very strong or even authentic, for, among other things, he could not have been very well acquainted with the main body of Palestrina's works because they were not commonly available at the time, the method is still valuable for its organization and the discipline it affords (cf. K. Jeppesen's *Counterpoint,* 1931; in English, N.Y., 1939).
WORKS: 18 operas; 10 oratorios; 29 partitas (among them the *Concentus musico-instrumentalis*); much sacred music: 50 Masses (the *Missa canonica* is a contrapuntal masterpiece), 3 Requiems, 2 *Dies irae,* 57 vespers and psalms, etc., and 38 "sacred sonatas." The Johann Joseph Fux Gesellschaft began issuing the Collected Works in 1959, a series that is still in progress; to date, 11 vols. have been publ.; in addition, a selection from his works is publ. in *Denkmäler der Tonkunst in Österreich* vols. 1, (1.i; 4 Masses), 3 (2.i; 27 motets), 19 (9.ii; 2 sacred sonatas, 2 overtures), 34/35 (17; the opera *Costanza e fortezza;* later ed. by G. P. Smith, Northampton, Mass., 1936), 47 (23. ii; the *Concentus musico-instrumentalist*), 85 (keyboard works).
BIBLIOGRAPHY: L. von Köchel, *Johann Joseph Fux* (Vienna, 1872; full biography and thematic catalogue of works); C. Schnabl, "Johann Joseph Fux, der österreichische Palestrina," *Jahrbuch der Leo Gesellschaft* (Vienna, 1895); H. Rietsch, "Der Concentus von Johann Joseph Fux," *Studien zur Musikwissenschaft* 4 (1912); A. Liess, *Johann Joseph Fux* (Vienna, 1948); J. H. Van den Meer, *Johann Josef Fux als Opernkomponist* (3 vols.; Bilthoven, 1961); E. Wellesz, *Fux* (London, 1965).

G

Gabold, Ingolf, German-born Danish composer; b. Heidelberg, March 31, 1942. He studied theory and music history at the Copenhagen Cons., and composition with Nørgaard at the Cons. in Århus. His stated goal is to "combine music with Jung's depth psychology."

WORKS: opera, *Seven Visions to Orpheus* for 4 singers, an actor, dancers and orch. (Danish television, Sept. 28, 1970); a television play, *Mod Vandmandens tegn (Towards Aquarius)* for soprano, bass, chorus and organ (Copenhagen, Nov. 11, 1973); *Für Louise* for soprano and chamber orch. (Copenhagen, Aug. 18, 1967); *Atlantis* for rock group and orch. (Danish Radio, Feb. 4, 1972); *Visione* for 4 vocal soloists and mixed chorus (1962); *Your Sister's Drown'd* for soprano and male chorus (1968; to a text from *Hamlet*); *Written in Sand* for chorus a cappella (1973).

Gabriel, Mary Ann Virginia, English composer; b. Banstead, Surrey, Feb. 7, 1825; d. London, Aug. 7, 1877. She studied with Pixis, Döhler, Thalberg, and Molique; married George E. March (1874), who wrote most of her libretti.

WORKS: 3 cantatas, *Evangeline* (Brighton Festival, Feb. 13, 1873), *Dreamland,* and *Graziella;* 6 operettas, *Widows Bewitched* (London, Nov. 13, 1867), *Grass Widows, Shepherd of Cornouailles, Who's the Heir?, Follies of a Night,* and *A Rainy Day;* piano pieces.

Gabrieli, Andrea, eminent Italian organist and composer; b. Venice, c.1510; d. there, 1586. He was a pupil of Adrian Willaert at San Marco and chorister there (1536); then traveled in Germany and Bohemia; was in Bavaria in 1562 and went to Frankfurt, to the coronation of Maximilian II, as court organist of Duke Albert V of Bavaria. In 1566 he returned to Venice and was appointed 2nd organist at San Marco; became 1st organist on Jan. 1, 1585, succeeding Merulo. He enjoyed a great reputation as organist (his concerts with Merulo, on 2 organs, were featured attractions). Among his pupils were his famous nephew, **Giovanni Gabrieli,** and Hans Leo Hassler. A prolific composer, he wrote a large number of works of varied description, many of which were published posthumously, edited by his nephew. His versatility is attested by the fact that he was equally adept in sacred music of the loftiest spirit, and in instrumental music, as well as in madrigals, often of a comic nature.

WORKS: *Sacrae cantiones* (37 motets, 1565); *Libro I di madrigali a 5 voci* (30 madrigals, 1566); *Libro II di madrigali a 5 voci* (28 madrigals, 1569); *Greghesche e justiniane* (15 numbers, 1571); *Primus Liber Missarum 6 vocum* (4 Masses, 1572); *Libro I di madrigali a 6 voci* (30 madrigals, 1574); *Libro di madrigali a 3 voci* (30 madrigals, 1575); *Ecclesiasticae cantiones a 4 voci* (58 motets, 1576); *Libro II de madrigali a 6 voci* (22 madrigals, 1580); *Psalmi Davidici a 6 voci* (7 psalms, 1583); *Sonate a 5 strumenti* (lost, 1586); *Concerti di Andrea et di Giovanni Gabrieli* (39 motets, 26 madrigals, 1587); *Edippo Tiranno* (choruses for Sophocles' *Oedipus*, performed in Vicenza in 1585, 1588); *Libro III di madrigali a 5 voci* (22 madrigals, 1589); *Madrigali et ricercari* (24 madrigals, 7 ricercars, 1589); *Intonazioni d'organo* (12 *intonazioni*, 1593); *Ricercari di Andrea Gabrieli* (13 ricercars, 1595); *Libro III de ricercari* (6 ricercars, 1 fantasia, 1 motet, 1 canzon, 2 madrigals, 1 capriccio on the *passamezzo antico*, 1596); *Mascherate di Andrea Gabrieli et altri* (3 *mascherate*, 3 madrigals, 1601); *Canzoni alla francese et ricercari* (4 canzoni, 7 ricercars, 1605); *Canzoni alla francese* (9 canzoni, one ricercar, 1605); and a large number of detached works in contemporary and later collections.—Modern editions: G. Benvenuti, *Istituzioni e monumenti dell' arte musicale italiana* (vols. I and II; vocal and instrumental pieces); L. Torchi, *L'arte musicale in Italia* (vols. II and III; 16 motets and pieces for organ); K. von Winterfeld, in *Joh. Gabrieli und sein Zeitalter* (1834; 2 vols. and a musical supplement); J. von Wasielewski, in *Geschichte der Instrumental-Musik im 16. Jahrhundert* (1878) and in the music supplement of *Die Violine im 17. Jahrhundert* (2nd ed., 1905); A. G. Ritter, *Geschichte des Orgelspiels im 14.–18. Jahrhundert* (1884; revised by Frotscher, 1933); G. d'Alessi, *Classici della musica italiana* (vol. VI); de la Moskowa, *Recueil des morceaux de musique ancienne* (1843); H. Riemann, *Alte Kammermusik* (8-voiced ricercar); O. Kinkeldey in *Orgel und Klavier in der Musik des 16. Jahrhunderts* (organ arrangements by Andrea Gabrieli of Orlando di Lasso's chanson, *Susanne un jour*); J. Wolf, in *Sing- und Spielmusik* (a *Canzona francese);* H. Bäuerle (*Missa Brevis,* 1932); W. Schöllgen (Easter Motet, 1932); A. Einstein, *Denkmäler der Tonkunst in Österreich,* vol. 77 (41; 3 madrigals in 6, 7, 8 voices, 1934); idem, in the musical supplement (no. 21) of *A Short History of Music* (N.Y., 1938); idem, in *The Golden Age of Music* (N.Y., 1942); idem, in *The Italian Madrigal* (vol. III, Princeton, 1949); A. Schering, *Geschichte der Musik in Beispielen* (no. 130); Davison and Apel, *Historical Anthology of Music* (vol. I, nos. 135, 136); Parish and Ohl, *Masterpieces of Music before 1750* (no. 21); *Das Chorwerk* 96 (3 motets). The *Opera Omnia,* edited by Denis Arnold, is being issued by the American Institute of Musicology; as of 1977, 6 vols. have appeared.

BIBLIOGRAPHY: G. Benvenuti, "Andrea e Giovanni Gabrieli e la musica strumentale in S. Marco," *Istituzioni e monumenti dell'arte musicale italiana* (vol. II); Ilse Zerr-Becking, *Studien zu Andrea Gabrieli* (Prague, 1933); G. Reese, *Music in the Renaissance* (N.Y., 1954); see also bibliography listed under Giovanni Gabrieli.

Gabrieli (Gabrielli), Domenico (called the "Menghino dal violoncello," Menghino being the diminutive of Domenico), Italian composer; b. Bologna, c.1650; d. there, July 10, 1690. An excellent cellist, he played in the orchestra of San Petronio, Bologna (1680–87); was a member of the Bologna Philharmonic Academy (1676); then became its president (1683). He was one of the earliest composers for cello solo.

WORKS: He produced 12 operas in Bologna, Venice, Modena, and Turin; his last opera, *Tiberio in Bi-*

sanzio, was performed posthumously in Lucca (Jan. 20, 1694). Other works: *Ricercari per violoncello solo* (1689; MS at the Liceo in Bologna); *Balletti, gighe, correnti e sarabande* for 2 violins, cello, and basso continuo (1684; 2nd ed., 1704); *Vexillum pacis* (motets for contralto with instrumental accompaniment; posthumous, 1695). L. Landshoff edited 3 *Arie* with instrumental obbligato (in *Alte Meister des Bel Canto,* 1912) and 2 cello sonatas (1930); A. Einstein printed a chamber cantata in the music supplement (no. 28) of his *A Short History of Music* (N.Y., 1938).

BIBLIOGRAPHY: E. Albini, "Domenico Gabrieli, il Corelli del violoncello," *Rivista Musicale Italiana* (1937).

Gabrieli, Giovanni, celebrated Venetian composer; nephew and pupil of **Andrea Gabrieli;** b. Venice, between 1554 and 1557; d. there, Aug. 12, 1612. He lived in Munich from 1575–79, taken to that court by Lassus. On Nov. 1, 1584 he was engaged to substitute for Merulo as 1st organist at San Marco in Venice; on Jan. 1, 1585, was permanently appointed as 2nd organist (his uncle meanwhile took charge of the 1st organ); retained this post until his death. As a composer, he stands at the head of the Venetian school; he was probably the first to write vocal works with parts for instrumental groups in various combinations, partly specified, partly left to the conductor, used as accompaniment as well as interspersed instrumental *sinfonie (Sacrae Symphoniae).* His role as a composer and teacher is epoch-making; through his innovations and his development of procedures and devices invented by others (free handling of several choirs in the many-voiced vocal works, 'concerted' solo parts and duets in the few-voiced vocal works, trio-sonata texture, novel dissonance treatment, speech rhythm, root progressions in fifths, use of tonal and range levels for structural purposes, coloristic effects) and through his numerous German pupils (particularly Schütz) and other transalpine followers, he gave a new direction to the development of music. His instrumental music helped to spark the composition of German instrumental ensemble music, which reached its apex in the symphonic and chamber music works of the classical masters. Of interest also is the fact that one of his ricercars, a 4-part work in the 10th tone (1595), is an early example of the "fugue with episodes" (reprinted in Riemann's *Musikgeschichte in Beispielen,* no. 52, Leipzig, 1913).

WORKS: Publications (very few) contain both sacred and secular vocal, as well as instrumental, works: *Concerti di Andrea et di Giovanni Gabrieli* (5 motets, 5 madrigals; 1587); *Intonazioni d'organo di Andrea Gabrieli et di Giovanni suo nepote* (11 *intonazioni;* 1593); *Sacrae Symphoniae Joannis Gabrielii* (42 motets, Mass, 12 instrumental *canzoni,* 3 sonatas; 1597); *Sacrarum Symphoniarum Continuatio* (9 motets, of which 5 are reprints; 1600); *Canzoni per sonare* (6 *canzoni;* 1608); *Sacrae Symphoniae Diversorum Autorum* (26 motets; 1613); *Sacrae Symphoniae, Liber II* (26 motets, Mass, 3 Magnificats; 1615); *Canzoni et Sonate* (15 *canzoni,* 5 sonatas; 1615); *Reliquiae Sacrorum Concentum* (1 Magnificat, 19 motets, of which 10 are reprints; 1615). Detached pieces in collections up to 1625: 25 more madrigals, 1 canticle,

Magnificats, motets, ricercars, toccatas, fantasias. Modern publications: G. Benvenuti publ. 3 secular vocal pieces in vol. I (1931) and G. Cesari, 13 *canzoni* and 2 *sonate* (from *Sacrae Symphoniae,* 1597) in vol. II (1932) of the *Istituzioni e monumenti dell'arte musicale italiana (Andrea e Giovanni Gabrieli e la musica strumentale in S. Marco);* K. von Winterfeld, *Johannes Gabrieli und sein Zeitalter* (1834; 2 vols. and a vol. of music supplements); Proske, Griesbacher, Commer, etc. (motets); J. von Wasielewski, *Geschichte der Instrumental-Musik im 16. Jahrhundert* (1878), and in the music supplement of *Die Violine im 17. Jahrhundert* (2nd ed., 1905); Riemann, *Alte Kammermusik (Sonata a 3 violini* and *Canzona a 8);* Torchi, *L'arte musicale in Italia* (vols. II, III); by H. Besseler, *Das Chorwerk* (vols. 10 and 67; 3 motets in each); A. Schering, *Geschichte der Musik in Beispielen* (nos. 130, 148); G. Tagliapietra *Antologia di musica antica e moderna per piano* (vol. II, 1931); A. Einstein (*Canzoni a 4,* 1933, Schott Antiqua; motet in the music supplement of his *Short History of Music,* no. 19, 1938; madrigal in *The Golden Age of the Madrigal,* 1942, no. 6); W. Danckert (*Sonata a 3 violini,* 1934); Davison and Apel, *Historical Anthology of Music* (vol. I, nos. 157, 173); F. Stein (*Sonata pian e forte,* 1931); J. F. Williamson (motet, 1932); G. W. Woodworth (3 motets, 1950–52); Bongiovanni (5 motets, 1954). Hans David has adapted several of Gabrieli's *canzoni* for modern use. An *Opera Omnia,* in 10 vols., ed. by Denis Arnold, is being issued by the American Institute of Musicology in its *Corpus Mensurabilis Musicae* series.

BIBLIOGRAPHY: A. G. Ritter, *Geschichte des Orgelspiels im 14.–18. Jahrhundert* (1884: revised by Frotscher, 1933): H. Leichtentritt, *Geschichte der Motette* (1908); O. Kinkeldey, *Orgel und Klavier in der Musik des 16. Jahrhunderts* (1910); G. S. Bedbrook, "The Genius of Giovanni Gabrieli," *Music Review* (Jan. 1947); G. Reese, *Music in the Renaissance* (N.Y., 1954); Denis Arnold, *Giovanni Gabrieli* (London, 1977).

Gabrielli, Caterina, famous soprano; b. Rome, Nov. 12, 1730; d. there, Feb. 16, 1796. She was known under the nickname 'La Coghetta' (that is, little cook, for her father was a cook in a Roman nobleman's palace). She made her debut at Venice in 1754; then went to Vienna, where she was hailed as a 'new star on the musical firmament' and was coached by Gluck and Metastasio; she sang many parts in the Vienna productions of Gluck's operas, up to 1761; made triumphant appearances in Milan, Turin, and Naples; then went to Russia (with Traetta) and sang in St. Petersburg with unfailing acclaim (1772–74). In 1775 she made her first appearance in London, arousing admiration among the cognoscenti; but she was also the object of common gossip related to her notoriously loose morals. She returned to Italy after only one season in London, and eventually settled in Rome.

Gabrielli, Domenico. See **Gabrieli, Domenico.**

Gabrielli, Nicolò, Italian composer; b. Naples, Feb. 21, 1814; d. Paris, June 14, 1891. He was a pupil of Buonamici, Conti, Donizetti, and Zingarelli at Naples

Cons.; from 1854 he lived in Paris. He wrote 22 operas and 60 ballets, produced at Naples, Paris, and Vienna.

Gabrilowitsch, Ossip, notable pianist and conductor; b. St. Petersburg, Feb. 7, 1878; d. Detroit, Sept. 14, 1936. From 1888–94 he was a pupil at the St. Petersburg Cons., studying piano with A. Rubinstein and composition with Navrátil, Liadov, and Glazunov; graduated as winner of the Rubinstein Prize, and then spent two years (1894–96) in Vienna studying with Leschetizky; then toured Germany, Austria, Russia, France, and England. His first American tour (debut Carnegie Hall, N.Y., Nov. 12, 1900) was eminently successful, as were his subsequent visits (1901, 1906, 1909, 1914, 1915, 1916). During the season 1912–13 he gave in Europe a series of six historical concerts illustrating the development of the piano concerto from Bach to the present day; on his American tour in 1914–15 he repeated the entire series in several of the larger cities, meeting with an enthusiastic reception. On Oct. 6, 1909, he married the contralto **Clara Clemens** (daughter of Mark Twain), with whom he frequently appeared in joint recitals. He conducted his first New York concert on Dec. 13, 1916; was appointed conductor of the Detroit Symph. Orch. in 1918. In 1928 and the following years he also conducted the Philadelphia Orch., sharing the baton with Leopold Stokowski, but still retaining his Detroit position.
BIBLIOGRAPHY: Clara Clemens, *My Husband Gabrilowitsch* (N.Y., 1938).

Gaburo, Kenneth, American composer; b. Somerville, New Jersey, July 5, 1926. He studied composition with Bernard Rogers at the Eastman School of Music, Rochester, N.Y. (M.M., 1949) and at the Univ. of Illinois, Urbana (D.M.A., 1962); then went to Rome where he studied with Goffredo Petrassi. Returning to America, he occupied teaching posts at Kent State Univ., Ohio (1949–50); at McNeese State College in Lake Charles, Louisiana (1950–54) and at the Univ. of Illinois, Urbana (1955–68); in 1968 was appointed to the faculty of the Univ. of California at San Diego. In 1967 he held a Guggenheim Fellowship. His music is quaquaversal.
WORKS: the operas *The Snow Queen* (Lake Charles, Louisiana, May 5, 1952), *The Widow* (Urbana, Illinois, Feb. 26, 1961); *Bodies,* abstract theater piece (1957); *The Dog-King,* a play with music (1959); *On a Quiet Theme* for orch. (1952); *4 Inventions* for clarinet and piano (1953); *Music for 5 Instruments* (1954); a set of *3 Ideas and Transformations* for strings (1955); String Quartet (1956); *Line Studies* for 4 instruments (1957); electronic score for the play *The Hydrogen Jukebox; Lingua I-IV,* a massive theater play exploring the structural properties of language in a musical context (1959); Viola Concerto (1959); *Antiphony I* for 3 string groups and electronic sound; *Antiphony II* for piano and electronic sound; *Antiphony III* for singers and electronic sound; *Antiphony IV* for piccolo, double bass, trombone and electronic sound; *Antiphony V* for piano and electronic sound; *Two* for mezzo-soprano, alto flute and double bass (1963); *Circumcision* for 3 groups of male voices (1964); *The Flow of E,* based on a synthesized vowel *E* and its electronic transformations (1965); *Inside,* a quartet for a single double bass player (1969); *Mouthpiece,* sextet for solo trumpet and 5 projection slides (1970).

Gabussi, Giulio Cesare, Italian composer; b. Bologna, 1555; d. Milan, Sept. 12, 1611. He was a pupil of Costanzo Porta; in 1582 he was called to Milan as singer and composer at the cathedral, and remained in that post until his death, with the exception of a brief stay in Poland in the service of Sigismund III (1604). He publ. 2 books of madrigals for 5 voices (Venice, 1580 and 1598); motets for 4 and 5 voices (Venice, 1586); *Te Deum* for 4 voices (Milan, 1598), etc. He was one of the first composers whose works in the Ambrosian ritual (litanies, etc.) appeared in print.

Gade, Axel Willy, Danish violinist, son of **Niels Gade;** b. Copenhagen, May 28, 1860; d. there, Nov. 9, 1921. He studied with his father and with Joachim; was active in Copenhagen as theater conductor and teacher. He wrote a violin concerto and an opera, *Venezias Nat* (Copenhagen, Jan. 18, 1919).

Gade, Jacob, Danish composer; b. Vejle, Nov. 29, 1879; d. Copenhagen, Feb. 21, 1963. He studied violin; was a member of the New York Symph. Orch. (1919–21); then returned to Copenhagen and was active there as conductor. Among his light compositions, *Jalousie* (1925) attained great popularity. He also wrote several symphonic poems (*Den sidste Viking, Leda and the Swan,* etc.).
BIBLIOGRAPHY: Karl Bjarnjof, *Tango Jalousie* (Copenhagen, 1969).

Gade, Niels (Wilhelm), Danish composer and founder of the modern Scandinavian school of composition; b. Copenhagen, Feb. 22, 1817; d. there, Dec. 21, 1890. He was the only child of an instrument maker; studied violin with a member of the Danish court band, and gave a concert in Copenhagen at the age of 16. He then took composition lessons with A. P. Berggreen; soon he began writing songs to German texts. At the age of 23, he wrote his overture, *Nachklänge von Ossian,* for which he was awarded a prize by the Copenhagen Musical Society. The work was performed in Copenhagen on Nov. 19, 1841, and was soon published; this early overture remained the most popular work of Gade, and endured in the orchestral repertory for many years. His next important work was Symphony in C minor. Gade sent this to Mendelssohn in Leipzig, and Mendelssohn performed it at a Gewandhaus concert on March 2, 1843. Subsequently Gade received a government stipend for travel in Germany; he went to Leipzig, where Mendelssohn accepted him as a friend, and let him conduct some of the Gewandhaus concerts. Gade's talent flourished in the congenial atmosphere; an ardent admirer of Mendelssohn and Schumann, he adopted a Romantic style in the prevalent Germanic spirit. After Mendelssohn's death in 1847, Gade assumed the conductorship of the Gewandhaus concerts, but on the outbreak of the Schleswig-Holstein war in the spring of 1848, he returned to Copenhagen. In 1850, he became chief conductor of the Copenhagen Musical Society; also was a cofounder of the Copenhagen Cons. in 1866. He visited

Birmingham in 1876 to conduct his cantata, *Zion*, at the festival there. In the same year, the Danish government granted him a life pension. In Denmark, his position as a prime musician was by then fully established; but he was accepted in Germany, too, as a master composer. Despite his adherence to the Germanic school, he infused elements of national Danish melodies into his works, and so led the way to further development of Scandinavian music.

WORKS: 8 symphonies (1841-71); overtures: *Nachklänge von Ossian* (1840), *Im Hochlande* (1844), *Hamlet* (1861), *Michelangelo* (1861); Violin Concerto (1880); cantatas: *Comala* (1846), *Elverskud* (1853), *The Holy Night* (1861), *At Sunset* (1865), *Kalanus* (1871), *Zion* (1873), *The Crusaders* (1873), *The Mountain Thrall* (1873), *Gefion* (1875), *Psyche* (1882), *Der Strom*, after Goethe's *Mahomet* (1889); chamber music: 2 string quintets, String Octet, Piano Trio, String Quartet, 3 violin sonatas, *Folk Dance* for violin and piano, *Pictures of the Orient* for violin and piano; for piano solo: *Spring Flowers*, *Aquarelles* (3 books), *Idylls*, 4 *Fantastic Pieces*, *Folk Dance*, Sonata in E minor; also 21 vocal works for various combinations, in the style of folksongs; incidental music for a play, *Mariotta*; ballet music, etc.

BIBLIOGRAPHY: Gade's autobiographical *Aufzeichnungen und Briefe*, ed. by Dagmar Gade (German transl., Basel 1893); C. Rubner, "Niels Wilhelm Gade, in Remembrance of the Centenary of His Birth," *Musical Quarterly* (Jan. 1917); C. Kjerulf, *Niels Wilhelm Gade* (Copenhagen, 1917); W. Behrend, *Gade* (Leipzig, 1917); W. Behrend, *Minder om Gade* (Copenhagen, 1930).

Gadsby, Henry Robert, English music teacher; b. Hackney, London, Dec. 15, 1842; d. Putney, Nov. 11, 1907. He was a chorister at St. Paul's from 1849 to 1858; organist at St. Peter's, Brockley; in 1884 succeeded Hullah as prof. of harmony at Queen's College, London; was prof. at the Guildhall School of Music from its foundation (1880) until his death. He wrote 3 symphonies, several overtures, songs, etc.

Gadski, Johanna (Emilia Agnes), celebrated German soprano; b. Anclam, June 15, 1872; d. Berlin, Feb. 22, 1932, as a result of an automobile accident. She studied voice with Frau Schroeder-Chaloupka at Stettin; made her opera debut at the age of 17 in Berlin; she then sang in Mainz, Bremen and Stettin. On March 1, 1895 she made her American debut with the Damrosch Opera Company in New York as Elsa in *Lohengrin*, and subsequently sang other Wagnerian roles, including Elisabeth, Eva, and Sieglinde. On Dec. 28, 1899 she appeared for the first time with the Metropolitan Opera Company, and established herself as a prime interpreter of dramatic parts, excelling in particular as Brünnhilde and Isolde. In the interim she sang at Covent Garden, London; in 1904-06 she made two transcontinental tours of the U.S., as a concert singer. In 1907 she returned to the Metropolitan Opera where she continued to appear until 1912. On Nov. 11, 1892 she was married to Lieutenant Hans Tauscher.

Gadzhibekov, Uzeir, Azerbaijan composer; b. Agdzhabedy, near Shusha, Sept. 17, 1885; d. Baku, Nov. 23, 1948. He studied in Shusha; then lived in Baku, where he produced his first opera on a native subject, *Leyly and Medzhnun* (Jan. 25, 1908). His comic opera *Arshin Mal Alan* (Baku, Nov. 27, 1913) had numerous performances; another opera *Kyor-Oglu (A Blind Man's Son)* was produced at the Azerbaijan Festival in Moscow (April 30, 1937).

Gaffurio, Franchino. See **Gaforio, Franchino.**

Gaforio (or **Gafori, Gafuri, Gaffurio**), **Franchino** (Latinized **Franchinus Gafurius;** often simply **Franchinus**), celebrated Italian theorist; b. Lodi, Jan. 14, 1451; d. Milan, June 24, 1522. He studied theology and music; lived in Mantua, Verona, and Genoa (1477); he formed an intimacy with the Doge Prospero Adorno (then in exile) and fled with him to Naples. There he met various distinguished musicians, and held public disputation with Johannes Tinctoris, Guarnier, and Hycart. The plague and the Turkish invasion compelled him to return to Lodi; he was choirmaster at Monticello for 3 years, made a short visit to Bergamo in 1483, and in 1484 became singer and master of the boys in Milan Cathedral, and first singer in the choir of Duke Lodovico Sforza. In 1485 he also founded a music school at Milan, which prospered.

WRITINGS: *Theoricum opus harmonicae disciplinae* (Naples, 1480; 2nd ed., Milan, 1492, as *Theorica musicae*; facsimile reprint, Rome, 1934); *Practica musicae Franchino Gaforio Laudensis . . . in IV libris* (Milan 1496; his magnum opus, with examples of mensural notation in block-print; other editions, 1497, 1502, 1508, 1512, 1522); *Angelicum ac divinum opus musicae materna lingua scriptum* (Milan, 1496); *De harmonia musicorum instrumentorum* (Milan, 1518, with biography of Gaforio by P. Meleguli); *Apologia Franchini Gafurii musici adversus Ioannem Spatarium et complices musicos Bononienses* (Turin, 1520; concerning the controversy between the Milanese and Bolognese schools). A complete ed. of his compositions, ed. by Lutz Finscher, was begun in 1955.

BIBLIOGRAPHY: E. Prätorius, *Die Mensuraltheorie des Franchino Gaforio und der folgenden Zeit bis zur Mitte des 16. Jahrhunderts* (Leipzig, 1905); G. Cesari, "Musica e Musicisti alla corte Sforzesca," *Rivista Musicale Italiana* (1922; with reprints); P. Hirsch, "Bibliographie der musikalischen Drucke des Franchino Gaforio," *J. Wolf-Festschrift* (1929); G. Zampieri, *Franchino Gaforio* (Milan, 1925); A. Careta, *Franchino Gafurio* (Lodi, 1951).

Gagliano, the name of a family of famous violin makers at Naples. **Alessandro,** who worked from 1695 to 1725, was a pupil of Stradivari, and he, as well as his sons **Nicola** (1695-1758) and **Gennaro** (1700-88), followed largely the Stradivari model. The instruments of **Ferdinando Gagliano** (c.1724-81), a son of **Nicola,** exhibit less skillful workmanship than those of the older members of the family.

Gagliano, Marco da, Italian opera composer; b. Gagliano, May 1, 1582; d. Florence, Feb. 25, 1643. He was a pupil of L. Bati; 1608, became maestro at S. Lorenzo in Florence; 1609 canon, and 1614 Apostolic Protonotary. In 1607 he founded the "Accademia degli Elevati." Gagliano was among the first composers to write in the "stile rappresentativo," which he developed further by ornamentation.

WORKS: *Dafne,* "opera in musica" (his most important work; first played at Mantua, 1608; published in Florence, 1608, and reprinted in shortened form by R. Eitner in vol. 10 of the *Publikationen älterer Musikwerke*); *La Flora,* opera (with Peri; Florence, 1628); *Due Messe, a 4, 5* (Florence, 1594); 6 vols. of madrigals *a 5* (1602–17); *Sacrae cantiones* (*I a 6,* with a Mass, 1614; *II a 1–6,* with basso continuo, 1622); *Musiche a 1, 2, e 3 voci* (Venice, 1615, with continuo).

BIBLIOGRAPHY: L. Piccianti, "Marco da Gagliano," *Gazzetta Musical di Milano* (1843–44); A. Solerti, *Musica alla Corte Medicea* (1905).

Gagnebin, Henri, Swiss composer and pedagogue; b. Liege (of Swiss parents), March 13, 1886; d. Geneva, June 2, 1977. He studied organ with Vierne and composition with Vincent d'Indy at the Schola Cantorum in Paris; served as church organist in Paris (1910–16) and in Lausanne (1916–25); was director of the Cons. of Geneva from 1925 to 1957. He published the books, *Entretiens sur la Musique* (Geneva, 1943) and *Musique, mon beau souci* (Paris, 1968).

WORKS: 4 Symphonies (1911, 1918–21, 1955, 1970); 3 *Tableaux symphoniques d'après F. Hodler* (1942); *Suite d'orchestre sur des Psaumes huguenots* for orch. (1950); Piano Concerto (1951); Clarinet Concerto (1971); Concerto for oboe, bassoon, and string orch. (1972); String Trio (1968); Wind Octet (1970); Brass Quintet (1970); Wind sextet (1971); other chamber music, including several string quartets; many organ pieces.

Gailhard, Pierre, French operatic singer; b. Toulouse, August 1, 1848; d. Paris, Oct. 12, 1918. He began his vocal studies in his native city, and entered the Paris Cons. in 1866. After one year of study under Révial he graduated in 1867, winning three first prizes. He made his debut at Opéra-Comique (Dec. 4, 1867) as Falstaff in Thomas' *Songe d'une nuit d'été;* on Nov. 3, 1871, he made his debut at the Opéra as Mephistopheles in Gounod's *Faust.* At the height of his powers and success he gave up the stage when, in 1884, he accepted, jointly with M. Ritt, the management of the famous institution; on the appointment of M. Bertrand as successor to Ritt, in 1892, he retired, but joined Bertrand the following year as co-director; after the latter's death, in 1899, he remained sole director till 1907. His administration was remarkably successful, considering both the novelties produced and the engagement of new singers (Melba, Eames, Bréval, Caron, Ackté, Alvarez, Saléza, Renaud, the two de Reszkes, etc.). Against violent opposition he introduced, and maintained in the repertory, *Lohengrin* (1895), *Walküre* (1893), *Tannhäuser* (1895; the first perf. after the notorious fiasco of 1861), *Meistersinger* (1897), *Siegfried* (1902).—His son, **André Gailhard** (b. Paris, June 29, 1885; d. Ermont, Val d'Oise, July 3, 1966), composed the operas *Amaryllis* (Toulouse, 1906), *Le Sortilège* (Paris, 1913), and *La Bataille* (Paris, 1931), and the cantata *La Sirène.*

Gaillard, Marius-François, French composer and conductor; b. Paris, Oct. 13, 1900; d. Evecquemont (Yvelines), July 23, 1973. He studied with Diémer and Leroux at the Paris Cons. He began his career as a pianist; then started a series of symphonic concerts in Paris, which he conducted from 1928 till 1949. He traveled all over the world, collecting materials of primitive music. His compositions follow a neo-Impressionist trend.

WORKS: for the stage: *La Danse pendant le Festin* (1924) and *Détresse,* ballet (1932); 3 symphonies; *Guyanes,* symph. suite (1925); *Images d'Epinal,* for piano and orch. (1929); Violin Sonata (1923); String Trio (1935); *Sonate baroque* for violin and piano (1950); Concerto classique for cello and orch. (1950); *Tombeau romantique* for piano and orch. (1954); *Concerto leggero* for violin and orch. (1954); Concerto agreste for viola and orch. (1957); Harp Concerto (1960); many songs and piano pieces.

Gaines, Samuel Richards, American vocal teacher; b. Detroit, April 23, 1869; d. Boston, Oct. 8, 1945. He studied composition with Goetschius and Chadwick; lived in Boston and Wellesley, Mass., as teacher. He won several national and international prizes for his choral compositions.

Gaisser, Dom Ugo Atanasio (Josef Anton) German music scholar; b. Aitrach, Dec. 1, 1853; d. Monastery Ettal, March 26, 1919. He specialized in the study of Byzantine church music, on which he wrote a number of important studies.

WRITINGS: *Guido von Arezzo oder St. Mauro* (Aix-la-Chapelle, 1889); review of Jacobsthal's "Die chromatische Alteration im liturgischen Gesänge der abendländischen Kirche," *Revue Bénédictine de Maredsous* (1897–98); "Le Système musicale de l'Église grecque d'après la tradition," *Rassegna Gregoriana* (Rome, 1901); *Les 'Hirmoi' de pâques dans l'office grec* (Rome, 1905).

Gaito, Constantino, Argentine composer; b. Buenos Aires, Aug. 3, 1878; d. there, Dec. 14, 1945. He studied in Naples with Platania; lived in Buenos Aires as a teacher; wrote the operas (all produced at Buenos Aires) *Caio Petronio* (Sept. 2, 1919), *Flor de Nieve* (Aug. 3, 1922), *Ollantay* (July 23, 1926), and *La Sangre de las Guitarras* (Aug. 17, 1932); the ballet, *La Flor de Irupé* (Buenos Aires, July 17, 1929); oratorio, *San Francisco Solano* (1940); Symph. poem *El ombú* (1924); songs, and piano pieces.

Gál, Hans, Austrian composer and music scholar; b. Brunn, near Vienna, Aug. 5, 1890. He studied at the Univ. of Vienna with Mandyczewski and Guido Adler; from 1919–29 he lectured at the Vienna Univ.; then went to Germany; was director of the Cons. of Mainz from 1929–33; returned to Vienna in 1933; after the advent of the Nazi government was compelled to leave Vienna in 1938, and settled in Edinburgh, where he became lecturer on music at the Univ. (1945-65), while continuing to compose.

WORKS: operas, *Der Arzt der Sobeide* (Breslau, 1919), *Die heilige Ente* (Düsseldorf, April 29, 1923), *Das Lied der Nacht* (Breslau, April 24, 1926), *Der Zau-*

berspiegel (Breslau, 1930; also as an orchestral suite), *Die beiden Klaas* (1933); 3 symphonies (1928, 1949, 1952); *A Pickwickian Overture* (1939); Violin Concerto (1931); Cello Concerto (1944); Piano Concerto (1947); *Idyllikon* for small orch. (1969); Triptych for orch. (1970); 2 string quartets (1916; 1929); String Trio (1931); Piano Quartet (1915); Piano Trio (1948); Violin Sonata (1921); numerous choral works, sacred and secular. He publ. a manual, *Anleitung zum Partiturlesen* (Vienna, 1923; in English under the title *Directions for Score-Reading*, 1924).

Galamian, Ivan, eminent American violinist and pedagogue; b. Tahrig, Persia, of Armenian parents; Feb. 5, 1902. He studied at the Moscow Philharmonic Institute, graduating in 1922; then went to Paris where he took private violin lessons with Lucien Capet (1923–24). He gave violin recitals in France and Germany; in 1930 emigrated to the U.S.; in 1944 was appointed to the staff of the Curtis Institute of Music in Philadelphia, and in 1946 joined the faculty of the Juilliard School, N.Y. In later years he taught privately in his own apartment in New York, and in the summer at the Meadowmount School in Westport, N.Y. Among his students were Pichas Zukerman, Jaime Laredo, Michael Rabin, Paul Zukofsky, and Itzhak Perlman. He publ. *Principles of Violin Playing and Teaching* (Englewood Cliffs, N.J., 1962); *Contemporary Violin Technique* (N.Y., 1966).

Galeotti, Cesare, Italian composer; b. Pietrasanta, June 5, 1872; d. Paris, Feb. 19, 1929. He studied piano with Sgambati and composition with Guiraud at the Paris Cons. Several of his symphonic works were performed in Paris; his opera *Anton* was staged at La Scala, Milan (Feb. 17, 1900). Another opera, *Dorisse,* was first given in Brussels (April 18, 1910).

Gales, Weston, American organist and conductor; b. Elizabeth, N.J., Nov. 5, 1877; d. Portsmouth, N.H., Oct. 21, 1939. He studied composition with Horatio Parker at Yale Univ. and organ with Gaston-Marie Déthier in N.Y.; held various posts as church organist in Boston; then took additional instruction with Widor and Vierne in Paris. Returning to America, he was active as choral conductor. In 1914, he organized the Detroit Symph. Orch.; conducted it until 1917.

Galilei, Vincenzo, celebrated writer on music, father of Galileo Galilei, the astronomer; b. Florence, c.1520; d. there, June (buried July 2), 1591. A skillful lutenist and violinist, and student of ancient Greek theory, he was a prominent member of the artistic circle meeting at Count Bardi's house; his compositions for solo voice with lute accompaniment may be regarded as the starting point of the monody successfully cultivated by Peri, Caccini, etc., the founders of the "opera in musica." A zealous advocate of Grecian simplicity, in contrast with contrapuntal complexity, he publ. a *Dialogo . . . della musica antica et della moderna* (Florence, 1581; to the 2nd ed. [1602] is appended a polemical *Discorso . . . intorno all' opere di messer Gioseffo Zarlino da Chioggia,* which had appeared separately in 1589); and *Fronimo. Dialogo . . .* (in 2 parts: Venice, 1568 and 1569; new ed. 1584); all of

considerable historical interest.—Vol. IV of *Istituzioni e Monumenti dell' Arte Musicale Italiana* (Milan, 1934), ed. by F. Fano, is devoted entirely to Galilei; it contains a large selection of music reprints from his *Fronimo. Dialogo* (lute transcriptions by Galilei and original compositions), *Libro d'intavolatura di Liuto* (1584), *Il Secondo Libro de Madrigali a 4 et a 5 voci* (1587), and a 4-part *Cantilena,* together with biographical details, list of works, notes about extant MSS, reprints, transcriptions, etc. His *Contrapunti a due voci* (1584) was edited by Louise Read (Northampton, Mass., Smith College Music Archives, vol. VIII, 1947).

BIBLIOGRAPHY: Otto Fleissner, *Die Madrigale Vincenzo Galileis und sein Dialogo della musica antica e moderna* (Munich, 1922).

Galin, Pierre, French music pedagogue; b. Samatan, Gers, 1786; d. Bordeaux, Aug. 31, 1821. He was teacher of mathematics at the Lycée in Bordeaux, and conceived the idea of simplifying music instruction by a method which he termed the "Méloplaste" and explained in his work *Exposition d'une nouvelle méthode pour l'enseignement de la musique* (1818; 2nd and 3rd eds., 1824 and 1831). The method attracted attention, and was energetically promoted by Chevé.

Galindo, Blas, Mexican composer; b. San Gabriel, Jalisco, Feb. 3, 1910. He studied harmony, counterpoint and fugue with Rolón, musical analysis with Huízar, composition with Chávez, and piano with Rodriguez Vizcarra at the National Cons. in Mexico City (1931–42); had special composition lessons with Aaron Copland at the Berkshire Music Center in Tanglewood, Mass. (1941–42); in 1934 he formed, together with Ayala, Contreras and Moncayo, the *Grupo de los Cuatro* for the presentation of modern music (disbanded after a few years). He was prof. of music and director of the National Cons. in Mexico City from 1947 till 1961; in 1955 became director of the orch. of the Mexican Institute of Social Security; was pensioned by the government in 1965 and devoted himself mainly to composition. In his music he stresses native elements, while adhering to classical forms; in his later works he made use of electronic sound.

WORKS: 7 BALLETS: *Entre sombras anda el fuego* (*Among Shadows Walks Fire;* Mexico City, March 23, 1940); *Danza de las fuerzas nuevas* (*Dance of the New Forces,* 1940); *El Zanate* (Mexico City, Dec. 6, 1947); *La Manda* (Mexico City, March 31, 1951); *El sueño y la presencia* (Mexico City, Nov. 24, 1951); *La Hija del Yori* (Mexico City, 1952); *El Maleficio* (Mexico City, Oct. 28, 1954). FOR ORCH.: *Sones de mariachi* (1940); 2 piano concertos: No. 1 (Mexico City, July 24, 1942); No. 2 (Mexico City, Aug. 17, 1962); *Nocturno* (1945); *Don Quijote* (1947); *Homenaje a Cervantes,* suite (1947); *Astucia* (1948); *Poema de Neruda* for string orch. (1948); *Pequeñas Variaciones* (1951); *Los signos del zodíaco* for small orch. (1951); 3 symphonies: No. 1, *Sinfonía breve,* for strings (Mexico City, Aug. 22, 1952), No. 2 (Caracas, March 19, 1957; shared 1st prize at the Caracas Festival) and No. 3 (Washington, April 30, 1961); *Obertura mexicana* (1953); flute concerto (1960; New Orleans, April 3, 1965); *4 Pieces* (1961; Mexico City, Nov. 15, 1963);

Edipo Rey (1961; incidental music for Sophocles' *Oedipus Rex*); Violin Concerto (1962; Mexico City, Sept. 13, 1970); *3 Pieces* for Clarinet and Orch. (1962); *Obertura* for organ and strings (1963); *3 Pieces* for Horn and Orch. (1963); Concertino for Electric Guitar and Orch. (1973; Mexico City, June 12, 1977); *En busca de un muro* (1973). FOR VOICE: *Jicarita* for voice and orch. (1939); *Primavera*, youth cantata for wind orch. and children's chorus (1944); *Arrullo* for voice, and small orch. or piano (1945); *La Montana* for chorus a cappella (1945); *A la Patria*, cantata (1946); *Tres canciones de la Revolución* for orch. and chorus (1953); *Homenaje a Juárez*, cantata with narrator (1957); *A la Independencia*, cantata (Mexico City, Nov. 24, 1960); *Quetzalcoatl* for orch. and narrator (1963); *Tríptico Teotihuacán* for wind orch., indigenous Mexican percussion instruments, chorus and soloists (Teotihuacán, Sept. 14, 1964); *Letanía erótica para la paz* for orch., organ, chorus, soloists, narrator and tape (1963–65; Mexico City, May 2, 1969); *La ciudad de los dioses (Luz y Sonido)* for orch., chorus and narrators (1965); *Homenaje a Rubén Dario* for narrator and string orch. (1966); choruses; songs. CHAMBER MUSIC: Suite for Violin and Cello (1933); Quartet for 4 Cellos (1936); *Bosquejos* for wind instruments (1937); *2 Preludes* for oboe, English horn and piano (1938); *Obra para orquesta mexicana* for indigenous instruments (1938); Sextet, for flute, clarinet, bassoon, horn, trumpet and trombone (1941); Violin Sonata (1945); Cello Sonata (1949); Suite for Violin and Piano (1957); Quintet for Piano and String Quartet (1960); *Tres sonsonetes* for wind quintet and electronic sound (1967); String Quartet (1970); *Titoco-tico* for indigenous percussion instruments (1971); *Tríptico* for strings (1974). FOR PIANO: *Llano Alegre* (1938); *5 Preludios* (1945); *7 Piezas* (1952); Sonata (1976); numerous small pieces. FOR ORGAN: *Estudio* (1971). A list of his works up to 1965 is found in *Composers of the Americas*, Vol. 11 (Washington, 1965).

Galkin, Elliott, American conductor and teacher; b. Brooklyn, Feb. 22, 1921. He served with the U.S. Air Force (1943–46); was stationed in France, and took courses at the Paris Cons. and the École Normale de Musique. Held the diploma as conductor there (1948). Returning to the U.S. he enrolled in Cornell Univ. (M.A., 1955; Ph.D., 1960); subsequently held various teaching positions. In 1964 he joined the faculty at Peabody Cons. in Baltimore; in 1962 became music editor of the *Baltimore Sun*. In 1977 he was appointed director of the Peabody Cons. of Music in Baltimore.

Galla-Rini, Anthony, American accordionist and composer; b. Manchester, Conn., Jan. 18, 1904. He learned music from his father, a bandmaster; toured the U.S. and Canada since the age of 6, playing accordion, cornet, mandolin, piccolo, oboe, French horn, contrabassoon, euphonium and sarrusophone, as well as several other instruments. He was the first accordionist to appear with an orchestra in a concerto of his own composition (Oklahoma City, Nov. 15, 1941); invented many technical improvements for his instrument; was the first to omit the fifth in the dominant-seventh row. In 1921 he introduced the 160-bass system in an extended left-hand range model. He publ. a number of transcriptions of classical and popular music for accordion.

Gallay, Jules, French cellist and music publisher; b. Saint-Quentin, 1822; d. Paris, Nov. 2, 1897. A wealthy amateur, he became a good cello player and a zealous student of *lutherie* in all its forms; publ. the following valuable pamphlets: *Les Instruments à archet à l'Exposition universelle de 1867* (Paris, 1867); *Les Luthiers italiens aux XVIIe et XVIIIe siècles, nouvelle édition du 'Parfait Luthier' (la Chélonomie) de l'abbé Sibire, suivie de notes sur les maîtres des diverses écoles* (Paris, 1869); a reprint of du Manoir's *Le Mariage de la musique avec la danse*, with historical introduction (Paris, 1870); *Les Instruments des écoles italiennes, catalogue précédé d'une introduction et suivi de notes sur les principaux maîtres* (Paris, 1872). As a member of the jury at Vienna, 1873, he edited the *Rapport sur les instruments de musique à archet* (Paris, 1875).

Gallenberg, Wenzel Robert, Austrian composer; b. Vienna, Dec. 28, 1783; d. Rome, March 13, 1839. He studied under Albrechtsberger; in 1803 he married Countess Giulietta Guicciardi (to whom Beethoven dedicated his Sonata Op. 27, No. 2). In Naples, shortly thereafter, he made the acquaintance of the impresario Barbaja; wrote numerous successful ballets for him, and from 1821–23 was his partner when Barbaja was director of opera in Vienna. He attempted the management of the Kärntnerthor-Theater in 1829, but failed, and was obliged to return to Italy, rejoining Barbaja. He wrote about 50 ballets; a sonata, marches, fantasies, etc., for piano. On one of his themes Beethoven wrote a set of variations.

Gallès, José, Catalan organist and composer; b. Casteltersol, Catalonia, 1761; d. Vich, 1836. He was for many years organist of the Vich Cathedral; was ordained priest. J. Nin published his piano sonata (1800) in the collection *17 Sonates et pièces anciennes d'auteurs espagnols* (Paris, 1929).

Galli, Amintore, Italian composer; b. Talamello, near Rimini, Oct. 12, 1845; d. Rimini, Dec. 8, 1919. He was a pupil of Mazzucato at Milan Cons. (1862–67); was musical editor for the publisher Sonzogno, and critic of *Il Secolo;* later edited *Il Teatro Illustrato* and *Musica Popolare.*
WORKS: the operas *Il Corno d'oro* (Turin, Aug. 30, 1876) and *David* (Milan, Nov. 12, 1904); oratorios *Espiazione* (after Moore's *Paradise and Peri*) and *Cristo al Golgota;* Goethe's *Totentanz* for baritone solo and orch.; String Quintet, etc. He published *Musica e Musicisti dal secolo X sino ai nostri giorni* (1871); *Estetica della musica* (1900); *Storia e teoria del sistema musicale* (1901); *Piccolo lessico di musica* (1902).

Galli-Curci, Amelita, brilliant Italian soprano; b. Milan, Nov. 18, 1882; d. La Jolla, Calif., Nov. 26, 1963. She studied in Milan and intended to be a pianist; graduated in 1903 from the Milan Cons., winning the 1st prize. She never took regular voice lessons, but acquired an excellent vocal technique by devising a unique method of self-instruction, listening to recordings of her own voice. She received advice from Mascagni and William Thorner. She made her debut in Rome as Gilda (1909), then sang in various opera houses in Italy and in South America (1910). She continued her successful career as an opera singer in Europe until 1915; after the entry of Italy into the war, she went to America; made a sensationally successful debut with the Chicago Opera Co. as Gilda (Nov. 18, 1916); she made her first appearance with the Metropolitan Opera as Violetta (Nov. 14, 1921); remained as a member of the Metropolitan until 1930; then gave concert recitals; eventually retired to California. She was married twice: to the painter, Luigi Curci (1910; divorced 1920), and to **Homer Samuels,** her accompanist.

BIBLIOGRAPHY: E. LeMassena, *Galli-Curci's Life of Song* (N.Y., 1945).

Galli-Marié, Célestine (*née* **Marié de l'Isle**), French dramatic mezzo-soprano; b. Paris, Nov., 1840; d. Vence, near Nice, Sept. 22, 1905. Her father, an opera singer, was her only teacher. She made her debut at Strasbourg (1859); sang in Toulouse (1860); and in Lisbon (1861). She sang the *Bohemian Girl* at Rouen (1862) with such success that she was immediately engaged for the Paris Opéra-Comique; made her debut there (1862) as Serpina in *La Serva padrona*. She created the roles of Mignon (1866) and Carmen (1875).

Galliard, Johann Ernst, German oboist and composer; b. Celle, c.1680; d. London, 1749. He was a pupil of A. Steffani at Hannover. A skillful oboist, he went to London, 1706, as chamber musician to Prince George of Denmark; succeeded Draghi as organist at Somerset House; 1713, played in the Queen's Theatre orch.; 1717 till 1736, engaged in writing music for the stage productions at Covent Garden and Lincoln's Inn Fields. He last appeared as an oboist probably in 1722.

WORKS: Besides the music to numerous plays, masques, and pantomimes, he wrote cantatas, a Te Deum, a Jubilate, anthems, soli for flute and cello, etc.; set to music the *Morning Hymn of Adam and Eve,* from Milton's *Paradise Lost.* He also made some translations.

BIBLIOGRAPHY: *Dictionary of National Biography* (London, 1921–22); S. Lincoln, "J. E. Galliard and *A critical discourse,"* *Musical Quarterly* (July 1967).

Gallico, Paolo, composer and pianist; b. Trieste, May 13, 1868; d. New York, July 6, 1955. At the age of 15, he gave a recital at Trieste; then studied at the Vienna Cons. under Julius Epstein, graduating at 18 with highest honors. After successful concerts in Italy, Austria, Russia, Germany, etc., he settled in N.Y. in 1892 as concert pianist and teacher; toured the U.S. frequently as pianist in recitals and as soloist with the principal orchestras. He won the prize of the National Federation of Music Clubs in 1921 with his dramatic oratorio *The Apocalypse* (performed by the N.Y. Oratorio Society, Nov. 22, 1922). His symphonic episode, *Euphorion,* was performed in Los Angeles (April 6, 1923), N.Y. and Detroit; his sextet was performed by the Society of the Friends of Music, N.Y. He also

wrote an opera, *Harlekin,* piano pieces, and songs. His son, Paul Gallico, is a well-known writer.

Gallignani, Giuseppe, Italian composer and writer on music; b. Faenza, Jan. 9, 1851; d. (suicide) Milan, Dec. 14, 1923. He studied at the Milan Cons.; was then choir leader at the Milan Cathedral; edited the periodical *Musica Sacra* (1886–94); was director of the Parma Cons. (1891–97); from 1897, director of the Milan Cons. He produced the operas *Il Grillo del focolare* (Genoa, Jan. 27, 1873), *Atala* (Milan, March 30, 1876), and *Nestorio* (Milan, March 31, 1888), which were unsuccessful; but his church music was greatly appreciated (particularly his Requiem for King Umberto I).

Gallo, Fortune, impresario; b. Torremaggiore, Italy, May 9, 1878; d. New York, March 28, 1963. He studied the piano in Italy; migrated to the U.S. in 1895; first directed the tours of a number of famous bands (1901–9), then founded the San Carlo Opera Co. (1909); in 1920, brought Anna Pavlova and her Ballet Russe to America; 1923, organized an opera season in Havana, Cuba; 1925, was director of the tour of Eleanora Duse; 1926 built and operated the Gallo Theater; 1928, made a film version of *Pagliacci;* presented performances of operetta in N.Y. and elsewhere.

Gallon, Jean, French composer and pedagogue; b. Paris, June 25, 1878; d. there, June 23, 1959. He studied piano with Diémer and theory with Lavignac and Lenepveu at the Paris Cons.; was chorus director of the Société des Concerts du Conservatoire (1906–14) and at the Paris Opéra (1909–14). From 1919 till 1949 he taught harmony at the Paris Cons. Among his pupils were Robert Casadesus, Marcel Delannoy, Henri Dutilleux, Olivier Messiaen, and Jean Rivier. He published harmony exercises for use at the Cons.; with his brother **Noël Gallon,** he composed several pieces of theater music, among them a ballet, *Hansli le Bossu* (1914); also some chamber music and songs.

Gallon, Noël, French composer; brother of **Jean Gallon;** b. Paris, Sept. 11, 1891; d. there, Dec. 26, 1966. He studied piano with I. Philipp and Risler, theory with Caussade and Lenepveu at the Paris Cons., and also with Rabaud. In 1910 he received 1st Prix de Rome. From 1920, on the faculty of the Paris Cons. as instructor in solfège, counterpoint, and fugue. As a composer, he was influenced by his brother, who was his first tutor in music; with him he wrote a ballet, *Hansli le Bossu* (1914); his own works comprise a few symph. pieces; Suite for Flute and Piano (1921); Quintet for Horn and Strings (1953); teaching pieces.

Gallus (also **Gallus Carniolus**), **Jacobus,** important Slovenian composer; b. Carniola (probably in Ribnica), between April 15 and July 31, 1550; d. Prague, July 24, 1591. His Slovenian name was **Petelin** (which means cockerel); its Germanic equivalent was **Handl,** or **Hähnel** (diminutive of Hahn, rooster); he published most of his works under the corresponding Latin name Gallus (rooster). As a master of polychoral counterpoint, Gallus was highly regarded in his time; he held several important positions as an organist and music director; was Kapellmeister to the Bishop of Olomouc and later was employed at the church St. Johannes in Vado in Prague. A number of his works were published during his lifetime. Of these there are several Masses: *Selectiores quaedam Missae* (Prague, 1580), containing 4 books of 16 Masses, from 4 to 8 voices; a modern edition by Paul A. Pisk was published in the *Denkmäler der Tonkunst in Österreich* (Vienna, 1935; reprinted in 1959, 1967 and 1969); 4 books of motets were published in Prague in 1586–91 under the title *Opus musicum*: first part (1586) from 4 to 8 voices (exact title, *Tomus primus musici operis harmonium quatuor, quinque, sex, octo et pluribus vocum*); 2nd and 3rd were published in 1587, and 4th in 1591; 5 additional motets were printed individually from 1579 to 1614. *Opus musicum* was reprinted in a modern edition by Emil Bezecny and Josef Mantuani in *Denkmäler der Tonkunst in Österreich* (Vienna, 1899, 1905, 1908, 1913, 1917, 1919; all reprinted again in 1959); *Moralia 5, 6 et 8 vocibus concinnata*, originally published in 1596, was reprinted in a modern edition by Dragotin Cvetko (Ljubljana, 1968) and Allen B. Skei (Madison, Wisconsin, 1970). His secular works include *Harmoniae morales* (Prague, 1589–90; modern edition by Dragotin Cvetko, Ljubljana, 1966) and *Moralia* (Prague, 1596). A motet by Gallus, *Ecce quomodo moritur justus*, was borrowed by Handel for his *Funeral Anthem*.

BIBLIOGRAPHY: Paul A. Pisk, "Die Parodieverfahren in den Messen des Jacobus Gallus," *Studien zur Musikwissenschaft* (1918; pp. 35–48); Allen B. Skei, "Jacob Handl's *Moralia*," *Musical Quarterly* (Oct. 1966); Allen B. Skei, "Jacob Handl's Polychoral Music," *Music Review* (May 1968); Dragotin Cvetko, *Jacobus Gallus, sein Leben und Werk* (Munich, 1972).

Gallus, Johannes (Jean le Cocq, Maître Jean, Mestre Jhan), Flemish contrapuntist; d. c.1543. He was maestro di cappella to Duke Ercole of Ferrara in 1534 and 1541. Many pieces were publ. in collections and in a vol. of motets printed by Scotto (1543). He was long confused with Jhan Gero.

Galpin, Rev. Francis William, English writer on music; b. Dorchester, Dorset, Dec. 25, 1858; d. Richmond, Surrey, Dec. 30, 1945. He graduated with classical honors from Trinity College, Cambridge, B.A. (1882), M.A. (1885); received his music education from Dr. Garrett and Sterndale Bennett; held various posts as vicar and canon (1891–1921); Hon. Freeman, Worshipful Company of Musicians (1905); wrote many articles on the viola pomposa and other old instruments in *Music & Letters* and *Monthly Musical Record* (1930–33). A Galpin Society was formed in London in 1946 with the object of bringing together all those interested in the history of European instruments and to commemorate the pioneer work of Galpin; it publishes, once a year, the *Galpin Society Journal* (1948–).

WRITINGS: *Descriptive Catalogue of the European Instruments in the Metropolitan Museum of Art, N.Y.* (1902); *The Musical Instruments of the American Indians of the North West Coast* (1903); *Notes on the Roman Hydraulus* (1904); *The Evolution of the Sackbut* (1907); *Old English Instruments of Music* (1910; new ed., London, 1932); *A Textbook of European Musical Instruments* (London, 1937); *The Music of the Sumerians, Babylonians and Assyrians* (1937); *The Music of Electricity* (1938). Galpin was the editor of the revised and augmented ed. of Stainer's *Music of the Bible* (1913).

Galston, Gottfried, Austrian-American pianist; b. Vienna, Aug. 31, 1879; d. St. Louis, April 2, 1950. He was a pupil of Leschetizky in Vienna, and of Jadassohn and Reinecke at the Leipzig Cons.; 1903–07, taught at Stern's Cons. in Berlin. On his extended concert tours he proved himself a player of keen analytical powers and intellectual grasp; 1902, toured Australia; then Germany, France, and Russia; 1912–13, America; toured Russia 11 times (last, in 1926); 1921–27, lived in Berlin; returned to the U.S. in 1927 and settled in St. Louis. He published a *Studienbuch* (1909; 3rd ed., Munich, 1920; analytical notes to a series of 5 historical recitals).

Galuppi, Baldassare, surnamed **Il Buranello** from the island of Burano, near Venice, on which he was born; Italian composer; b. Oct. 18, 1706; d. Venice, Jan. 3, 1785. He studied with his father, a barber and violin player; in 1722 he brought out at Vicenza an opera, *La fede nell'incostanza*, which attracted attention to his talent; he then studied under Lotti in Venice, and in 1729 produced his opera *Dorinda*. He cultivated comic opera with such success as to earn the title of "padre dell'opera buffa." He was also a distinguished player on the harpsichord. In 1740 he was appointed 'maestro del coro' at the Ospizio dei Mendicanti; 1741, visited London; 1748, returned to Venice, where he was 2nd maestro at San Marco; 1762–64, principal maestro there. From 1765 to 1768 he acted as maestro to the Russian court; taught many Russian singers and composers; Bortniansky, who later followed him to Venice, was one of his pupils. Galuppi wrote a prodigious amount of music, some 112 operas and 20 oratorios; also sacred music and 12 harpsichord sonatas.

BIBLIOGRAPHY: A. Wotquenne, "Baldassare Galuppi," *Rivista Musicale Italiana* (1899); F. Piovano, "Baldassare Galuppi, Note bio-bibliografiche," ibid. XIII/4 (1906), XIV/2 (1907), XV/2 (1908); A. della Corte, *L'opera comica italiana nel 1700* (1923); F. Raabe, *Baldassare Galuppi als Instrumentalkomponist* (Munich, 1926); F. Torrefranca, in *Rivista Musicale Italiana* XVIII; Ch. Van den Borren, ibid. XXX; W. Bollert, *Die Buffo-Opern Baldassare Galuppis* (Bottrop, 1935); A. della Corte, *Baldassare Galuppi; profilo critico* (Siena, 1948).

Galway, James, Irish flute virtuoso; b. Belfast, Dec. 8, 1939. His first instrument was the violin, but he soon began to study the flute. At the age of 14 he went to work in a piano shop in Belfast; a scholarship enabled him to go to London, where he continued to study flute and also took academic courses in music at the Royal College of Music and the Guildhall School of Music and Drama. He then received a grant to go to Paris to study with the celebrated flutist Jean-Pierre Rampal at the Paris Cons. His first professional job as a flutist was with the wind band at the Royal Shakespeare Theatre in Stratford on Avon. He subsequently played with the Sadler's Wells Opera Co., the Royal Opera House Orch. and the BBC Symph. Orch.; then was appointed principal flutist of the London Symph. Orch., and later with the Royal Philharmonic. As his reputation grew, he was engaged in 1969 by Herbert von Karajan as first flutist in the Berlin Philharmonic, a post he held until 1975. Abandoning his role as an orchestral flutist, he devoted himself to a career as a concert artist; in a single season 1975–76 he appeared as a soloist with all 4 major London orchestras; also toured in the U.S., Australia and the Orient as well as in Europe. He became successful on television, playing his 18-carat gold flute.

Gamba, Piero, precocious Italian conductor; b. Rome, Sept. 16, 1936. He received his musical training from his father, a violinist; at the age of nine he was given a chance to conduct an orchestra. Unlike so many child prodigies, he continued to develop his natural gifts, and in time became a conductor of high caliber; conducted concerts in 40 countries and 300 cities during twenty years of his active career. An enthusiastic press agent calculated that the name of Piero Gamba became known to one billion people (including 900,000,000 in China). In 1970 he was appointed conductor and music director of the Winnipeg Symph. Orch., Canada. Gamba is also a composer of various instrumental pieces; among them, a symph. poem, *Ombre della sera,* which he conducted for the first time in Winnipeg on Jan. 20, 1978.

Gamucci, Baldassare, Italian music scholar; b. Florence, Dec. 14, 1822; d. there, Jan. 8, 1892. He was a pupil of C. Fortini (piano) and L. Picchianti (composition). In 1849 he founded the Società Corale del Carmine, which later became the Scuola Corale, of the Music Institute at Florence. He published several monographs on composers, and didactic manuals.

Ganche, Édouard, French writer on music; b. Baulon (Ille-et-Vilaine), Oct. 13, 1880; d. Lyon, May 31, 1945. He studied with Imbert, Henry Expert, and others in Paris. He devoted his life to the study of Chopin and published *La Vie de Chopin dans son œuvre* (1909); *Frédéric Chopin, sa vie et ses œuvres* (1913). He was also the editor of the Oxford edition of Chopin's works (1932).

Gandolfi, Riccardo (Cristoforo Daniele Diomede), Italian composer; b. Voghera, Piedmont, Feb. 16, 1839; d. Florence, Feb. 5, 1920. He was a pupil of Carlo Conti at the Naples Cons., then of Mabellini in Florence; appointed inspector of studies at the Real Istituto di Musica in Florence (1869); chief librarian in 1889; pensioned in 1912. He began as a dramatic composer, then turned to the larger instrumental and vocal forms, and finally abandoned composition altogether, devoting himself to historical studies, which won him distinction.

WORKS: operas *Aldina* (Milan, 1863), *Il Paggio* (Turin, 1865), *Il Conte di Monreale* (Genoa, 1872), *Caterina di Guisa* (Catania, 1872); *Messa da Requiem;* a cantata, *Il Battesimo di S. Cecilia;* several overtures; chamber music.

WRITINGS: *Sulla relazione della poesia colla mu-sica melodrammatica* (1868); *Una riparazione a proposito di Francesco Landino* (1888); *Commemorazioni di W. A. Mozart* (1891); *Illustrazioni di alcuni cimeli concernanti l'arte musicale in Firenze* (1892); *Appunti di storia musicale* (1893); *Onoranze Fiorentine a G. Rossini* (1902).

Gange, Fraser, distinguished baritone; b. Dundee, Scotland, June 17, 1886; d. Baltimore, July 1, 1962. He studied there with his father; later was a pupil of Amy Sherwin in London; made his debut as a basso at the age of 16; toured England, Scotland, Australia, and New Zealand twice; taught singing at the Royal Academy of Music, London; 1923, came to the U.S. and made his American debut, N.Y. (Jan. 18, 1924); from 1932–46 prof. of voice at the Juilliard Summer School, N.Y.; from 1934 at Peabody Cons., Baltimore. His repertory includes 40 oratorios and more than 2000 songs; he presented in Baltimore a concert of songs on his 70th birthday in 1956.

Ganne, Louis Gaston, French composer; b. Buxières-les-Mines, Allier, April 5, 1862; d. Paris, July 13, 1923. He was a pupil of Th. Dubois, Massenet, and César Franck at the Paris Cons. He was conductor of the balls at the Opéra, and at the municipal Casino at Monte Carlo; wrote successful comic operas, ballets, and divertissements.

WORKS: operas: *Rabelais* (Paris, Oct. 25, 1892); *Les Colles des femmes* (Paris, 1893); *Les Saltimbanques* (Paris, Dec. 30, 1899); *Miss Bouton d'Or* (Paris, Oct. 14, 1902); *Hans le joueur de flûte* (his most successful operetta; Monte Carlo, April 14, 1906); *Les Ailes* (Paris, Sept. 1, 1910); the ballets *Au Japon* (1903; very successful), *Kermesse flamande* (1917); many orchestral dances, of which *La Czarine* and *La Tsigane* became favorites, and patriotic tunes, *La Marche Lorraine* and *Le Père de la Victoire,* immensely popular in France; about 150 piano pieces.

Gänsbacher, Johann, Austrian composer; b. Sterzing, Tyrol, May 8, 1778; d. Vienna, July 13, 1844. He studied with Abbé Vogler and Albrechtsberger in Vienna (1801); visited Prague, Dresden and Leipzig; then resumed study under Vogler, at Darmstadt (Weber and Meyerbeer were his fellow pupils). With Weber, he went to Mannheim and Heidelberg, and rejoined him later in Prague. In Vienna Gänsbacher also met Beethoven. He served in the war of 1813, led a roving life for several years, and finally (1823) settled in Vienna as Kapellmeister of the cathedral. Of his 216 compositions (Masses, requiems, etc., orchestral works, piano pieces, songs, etc.), only a small part has been published.

BIBLIOGRAPHY: C. Fischnaler, *Johann Gänsbacher* (Innsbruck, 1878).

Gantvoort, Arnold Johann, Dutch musician; b. Amsterdam, Dec. 6, 1857; d. Los Angeles, Calif., May 18, 1937. He came to America in 1876; gave private lessons, and taught in various colleges; in 1894, head of dept. for preparing public school music teachers, College of Music, Cincinnati. He published *Familiar Talks on the History of Music* (N.Y., 1913), and a series of public school music readers.

Ganz, Rudolph, distinguished pianist and conductor; b. Zürich, Feb. 24, 1877; d. Chicago, Aug. 2, 1972. He studied music assiduously, first as a cellist (with Friedrich Hegar) then as a pianist (with Robert Freund) in Zürich; he continued his piano study with his great-uncle **C. Eschmann-Dumur,** and also took composition lessons with Charles Blanchet at the Cons. of Lausanne; in 1897–98, he studied piano with F. Blumer in Strasbourg; and in 1899 took a course in advanced piano playing with Ferruccio Busoni in Berlin. He made his first public appearance at the age of 12 as a cellist, and at 16 as a pianist. In 1899, he was the soloist in Beethoven's *Emperor Concerto* and Chopin's E minor Concerto with the Berlin Philharmonic; and in May 1900 the Berlin Philharmonic performed his First Symphony. In 1901 he went to the U.S. and was engaged as prof. of piano at the Chicago Musical College; between 1905 and 1908 he made several tours of the U.S. and Canada, and in 1908–11, toured Europe, playing 16 different piano concertos. After 1912 he divided his time touring in Europe and America; in 1921 he added one more profession to his career, that of a symphonic conductor; from 1921–27 he was music director and conductor of the St. Louis Symphony; from 1938–1949 he conducted a highly successful series of Young People's Concerts with the N.Y. Philharmonic; concurrently, from 1929–54 he served as director of the Chicago Musical College. He played first performances of many important works by modern composers, including those of Ravel, Bartók, Busoni, and others. In July, 1900 he married **Mary Forrest,** an American concert singer. He was a highly successful pedagogue, and continued to teach almost to the time of his death at the age of 95. Besides the early symphony, he wrote a lively suite of 20 pieces for orch., *Animal Pictures* (Detroit, Jan. 19, 1933, composer conducting); Piano Concerto (Chicago Symph. Orch., Feb. 20, 1941, composer soloist); *Laughter—Yet Love, Overture to an Unwritten Comedy* (1950); solo piano pieces; and a couple of hundred songs to words in German, French, English, Swiss and Alsatian dialects. He published *Rudolph Ganz Evaluates Modern Piano Music* (N.Y., 1968).

Ganz, Wilhelm, German pianist; b. Mainz, Nov. 6, 1833; d. London, Sept. 12, 1914. He studied music with his father, Adolf Ganz (b. Mainz, Oct. 14, 1796; d. London, Jan. 11, 1870) and with Anschütz. He followed his father to London, where he appeared as pianist; in 1856 he became accompanist to Jenny Lind. In 1879 he organized the Ganz Orchestral Concerts in London, and gave 1st London performances of works by Liszt and Berlioz; many celebrated artists (Saint-Saëns, Pachmann, etc.) made their English debuts at his concerts. After the discontinuance of his enterprise, in 1883, he devoted himself mainly to teaching. He publ. *Memories of a Musician* (London, 1913).

Garaguly, Carl, Hungarian-Swedish violinist and conductor; b. Budapest, Dec. 28, 1900. He studied violin with Hubay in Budapest and with Marteau in Lichtenberg. He was then a violinist in the Berlin Philharmonic Orch.; in 1923 went to Sweden; from 1923–30 he was concertmaster of the Göteborg Orch.; then played the violin in the Stockholm Orch. From 1941 to 1953 he conducted the Stockholm Orch., and from 1953 to 1958 was conductor of the Bergen, Norway, Philharmonic. After 1960 he was active mainly as a guest conductor in Denmark and Holland.

Garant, Serge, Canadian composer; b. Quebec City, Sept. 22, 1929. He studied piano and clarinet in Sherbrooke and composition in Montreal with Claude Champagne. In 1951 he went to Paris to take a course in musical analysis with Messiaen. Returning to Canada in 1953, he worked as a pianist and music arranger; with the composers Morel and Joachim and pianist Jeanne Landry he organized in Montreal a modern group "Musique de notre temps" dedicated to the presentation of new European and American music; in 1967 he was appointed to the music faculty of the Univ. of Montreal. His music is constructed with formal precision from given thematic, metric and rhythmic elements, and developed along classical lines.

WORKS: *Musique* for saxophone and winds (1948–50); *Pièces* for 4 saxophones (1948); Piano Sonatina (1948); *2 Pièces pour piano* (1953, 1962); Piano Variations (1954); *Musique pour la mort d'un poète* for piano and strings (1954); *Nucléogame* for flute, oboe, clarinet, horn, trumpet, trombone, piano and tape (1955); *Canon VI* for 10 players (1957); a study on chance, *Pièces,* for string quartet (1958); *Asymétries* No. 1 for piano (1958) and No. 2 for clarinet and piano (1959); *Anerca (The Soul),* cycle for soprano and 8 instruments, to words of 2 Eskimo poems (1961, revised 1963); *Ouranos* for orch. (1963); *Ennéade* for orch. (1964); *Phrases I* for mezzo-soprano, piano, celesta and percussion (1967); *Phrases II* for 2 orch. (1968; members of the orchestra are instructed to recite texts from proclamations of Che Guevara); *Amuya* for 20 musicians (1968); *Jeu à Quatre* for 4 instrumental groups (1968); a group of 5 works based on mathematical proportions taken from the theme of Bach's *Musical Offering: Offrande I* for 19 musicians and prerecorded voice (1969; alternative title, *Cérémonial du corps;* Montreal, March 6, 1970); *Offrande II* for orch. (Toronto, July 29, 1970); *Offrande III* for 3 cellos, 2 harps, piano and 2 percussionists (1971); *Circuit I* for 6 percussionists (1972); *Circuit II* for 14 players (1972); *Circuit III* for 18 players (1973); *". . . chant d'amours,"* video work with chorus and solo cello (1975); *Rivages* for baritone and chamber ensemble (1976); songs, including *Cage d'oiseau* for soprano and piano (1962).

Garat, Pierre-Jean, famous French concert-singer and teacher; b. Ustaritz (Bas-Pyrénées), April 25, 1762; d. Paris, March 1, 1823. His talent was discovered early, and he studied theory and singing with Franz Beck in Bordeaux; his father wished him to become a lawyer, and sent him to the Univ. of Paris in 1782. However, Garat neglected his legal studies, and aided by the Count d'Artois, he was introduced to Marie Antoinette, whose special favor he enjoyed up to the Revolution. He earned his livelihood as a concert-singer; accompanied Rode, in 1792, to Rouen, where he gave numerous concerts before being arrested as a suspect during the Terror; subsequently he went to Hamburg; he returned to Paris in 1794, and sang (1795) at the Feydeau Concerts, where his triumphs speedily procured him a professorship of singing in the newly established Conservatory. For 20 years longer, his fine tenor-baritone voice, trained to perfection, made him the foremost singer on the French concert stage. Nourrit, Levasseur, and Ponchard were his pupils.

BIBLIOGRAPHY: Paul Lafond, *Garat* (Paris, 1899); B. Miall, *Pierre Garat, Singer and Exquisite; his Life and his World* (London, 1913); Isidoro de Fagoaga, *Pedro Garat, el Orfeo de Francia* (Buenos Aires, 1948).

Garaudé, Alexis de, French singer and composer; b. Nancy, March 21, 1779; d. Paris, March 23, 1852. He studied theory under Cambini and Reicha, and singing under Crescentini and Garat; was a singer in the royal choir from 1808–30 and prof. of singing in the Cons. from 1816–41. He publ. 3 string quintets, many ensemble pieces for violin, flute, clarinet, and cello, sonatas and variations for piano, a solemn Mass, vocalises, arias, duets, and songs; also a *Méthode de chant* (1809, op. 25; 2nd revised ed. as *Méthode complète de chant*, op. 40); *Solfège, ou méthode de musique; Méthode complète de piano;* and *L'Harmonie rendue facile, ou théorie pratique de cette science* (1835). He also arranged the vocal scores of Meyerbeer's *Le Prophète* and other operas.

Garay, Narciso, Panamanian violinist, composer, and diplomat; b. Panama, June 12, 1879; d. there, March 27, 1953. He studied at the Brussels Cons., graduating with a Premier Prix; later he attended courses at the Schola Cantorum in Paris. He published a violin sonata and a valuable treatise on Panamanian folk music, *Tradiciones y Cantares de Panama* (1930). He also occupied diplomatic posts and at one time was Minister of Foreign Affairs.

Garbousova, Raya, brilliant Russian cellist; b. Tiflis, Oct. 10, 1905. She studied at the Cons. there, graduating in 1923; later studied with Hugo Becker, Felix Salmond, and Pablo Casals. After many concerts in Europe, she settled in the U.S. (1927); appeared as soloist with major American orchestras.

Garbuzov, Nikolai, eminent Russian musicologist; b. Moscow, July 5, 1880; d. there, May 3, 1955. He studied with Koreshchenko and Kastalsky at the Moscow Philharmonic Institute; from 1921 to 1931 was director of the State Institute for Musicology; from 1923 to 1951 was instructor at the State Academy of the Arts, in the dept. of acoustics; publ. the manual *Musical Acoustics* (Moscow, 1940) and numerous articles in which he derived the laws of harmony from acoustical phenomena.

García Estrada. See **Estrada, García.**

García, Eugénie, wife and pupil of **Manuel García;** French soprano; b. Paris, 1818; d. there, Aug. 12, 1880. She sang for several years in Italian theaters, then (1840) at the Opéra-Comique, Paris; 1842 in London; finally, separated from her husband, she lived as a singing teacher in Paris.

García, Francisco Javier (Padre García, called in Rome "lo Spagnoletto"), Spanish composer of church music; b. Nalda, 1731; d. Saragossa, Feb. 26, 1809. He lived for some years in Rome as a student and singing teacher; in 1756 he was appointed maestro at Saragossa Cathedral. His works show a marked contrast to the fugal style prevailing before, being more natural and simple. Wrote an oratorio, *Tobia* (1773); the operas *La Finta Schiava* (Rome, 1754), *Pompeo Magno in Armenia* (Rome, 1755), *La Pupilla* (Rome, 1755), *Lo Scultore deluso* (Rome, 1756); Masses and motets, chiefly in 8 parts. His most noted pupil was Caterina Gabrielli.

García Mansilla, Eduardo, American-born French-Argentinian composer; b. Washington, March 7, 1870; d. Paris, May 9, 1930. He was in diplomatic service, and traveled widely; studied composition with Massenet, Saint-Saëns and Vincent d'Indy in Paris and with Rimsky-Korsakov in St. Petersburg. His opera *Ivan* was produced in St. Petersburg in 1905 and another opera, *La angelica Manuelite,* in Buenos Aires in 1917. He also wrote choruses.

García, Manuel del Popolo Vicente, famous Spanish tenor, singing teacher, and dramatic composer; b. Seville, Jan. 22, 1775; d. Paris, June 9, 1832. A chorister in Seville Cathedral at 6, he was taught by Ripa and Almarcha, and at 17 was already well known as a singer, composer, and conductor. After singing in Cadiz, Madrid, and Málaga, he proceeded (1806) to Paris, and sang to enthusiastic audiences at the Théâtre-Italien; in 1809, at his benefit, he sang his own monodrama *El poeta calculista* with extraordinary success. From 1811 to 1816 he was in Italy. On his return to Paris, his disgust at the machinations of Catalani, the manageress of the Théâtre-Italien, caused him to break his engagement and go to London (1817), where his triumphs were repeated. From 1819–24 he was again the idol of the Parisians at the Théâtre-Italien; sang as first tenor at the Royal Opera, in London (1824) and in 1825 embarked for New York with his wife, his son Manuel, and his daughter, Maria (Malibran), and the distinguished artists Crivelli *fils,* Angrisani, Barbieri, and de Rosich; from Nov. 29, 1825, to Sept. 30, 1826, they gave 79 performances at the Park and Bowery Theaters in New York; the troupe then spent 18 months in Mexico. Garcia returned to Paris, and devoted himself to teaching and composition. His operas, all forgotten, comprise 17 in Spanish, 18 in Italian, and 8 in French, besides a number never performed, and numerous ballets. A preeminently successful teacher, his 2 daughters, Mmes. Malibran and Pauline Viardot-Garcia, Nourrit, Rimbault, and Favelli were a few of his best pupils.

BIBLIOGRAPHY: G. Malvern, *The Great Garcías* (N.Y., 1958).

García, Manuel Patricio Rodriguez, distinguished Spanish vocal teacher, son of preceding; b. Madrid, March 17, 1805; d. London, July 1, 1906 (aged 101). He was intended for a stage singer; in 1825 went to New York with his father, but in 1829 adopted the vocation of a singing teacher (in Paris) with conspicuous success. An exponent of his father's method, he also carefully investigated the functions of the vocal organs; invented the laryngoscope, for which the Königsberg Univ. made him Dr. phil. In 1840 he sent to the Academy a *Mémoire sur la voix humaine,* a statement of the conclusions arrived at by various investigators, with his own comments. He was appointed prof. at the Paris Cons. in 1847, but resigned in 1848 to accept a similar position in the London Royal Academy of Music, where he taught uninterruptedly from Nov. 10, 1848 until 1895. Among Garcia's pupils were his wife, Eugénie, Jenny Lind, Henriette Nissen, and Stockhausen. His *Traité complet de l'art du chant* was publ. in 1847; English ed., 1870; revised ed. by Garcia's grandson **Albert Garcia,** as *Garcia's Treatise on the Art of Singing* (London, 1924). He also publ. (in English) a manual, *Hints on Singing* (London, 1894).

BIBLIOGRAPHY: M. Sterling Mackinlay, *Garcia, the Centenarian, and His Time* (Edinburgh, 1908); J. M. Levien, *The Garcia Family* (London, 1932); G. Malvern, *The Great Garcías* (N.Y., 1958).

García, Pauline Viardot-. See **Viardot-García, Pauline.**

Gardano, Antonio, one of the earliest and most celebrated Italian music-printers; b. c.1500; d. Venice, Oct. 28, 1569. From 1537 he reprinted many current publications as well as important novelties, and compositions of his own, e.g., *Motetti del frutto* (1538) and *Canzoni franzese* (1539). His works also appeared in various collections of the time. After 1571 his sons **Alessandro** and **Angelo** carried on the business till 1575, when they separated; the former later set up for himself in Rome (1582–91), while the latter remained in Venice till his death (1610); his heirs continued publishing under his name till 1677.

Garden, Mary, celebrated operatic soprano; b. Aberdeen, Scotland, Feb. 20, 1874; d. there, Jan. 3, 1967. She came to the United States as a child; lived in Hartford, Conn., and then in Chicago. She studied violin and piano; in 1893 she began the study of singing with Mrs. Robinson Duff in Chicago; in 1895 she went to Paris, where she studied with many teachers (Sbriglia, Bouhy, Trabadello, Mathilde Marchesi, and Lucien Fugère). Her funds, provided by a wealthy patron, were soon depleted, and Sybil Sanderson, the American soprano living in Paris, came to her aid and introduced her to Albert Carré, director of the Opéra-Comique. Her operatic debut was made under dramatic circumstances on April 10, 1900, when the singer who performed the title role of Charpentier's *Louise* at the Opéra-Comique was taken ill during the performance, and Mary Garden took her place. She revealed herself not only as a singer of exceptional ability, but also as a skillful actress. She subsequently sang in several operas of the general repertory; also created the role of Diane in Pierné's opera *La Fille de Tabarin* (Opéra-Comique, Feb. 20, 1901). A historic turning point in her career was reached when she was selected to sing Mélisande in the world première of Debussy's opera (Opéra-Comique, April 30, 1902). She also became the center of a raging controversy, when Maurice Maeterlinck, the author of the drama, voiced his violent objection to her assignment (his choice for the role was Georgette Leblanc, his common-law wife), and pointedly refused to have anything to do with the production. Mary Garden won warm praise from the critics for her musicianship, despite the handicap of her American-accented French. She remained a member of the Opéra-Comique; also sang at the Grand Opéra, and at Monte Carlo. She made her American debut as Thaïs at the Manhattan Opera House, N.Y. (Nov. 25, 1907), and presented there the first American performance of *Pelléas et Mélisande* (Feb. 19, 1908). She also undertook the performance of *Salome* at its 2nd production in N.Y. (Jan. 27, 1909). In 1910 she joined the Chicago Opera Co.; she became its impresario in the season 1921–22, during which the losses mounted to about one million dollars. She sang in the first American performances of Honegger's *Judith* (Chicago, Jan. 27, 1927), Alfano's *Resurrection* (1930), and Hamilton Forrest's *Camille* (1930), an opera she specially commissioned. After 1930 she made sporadic appearances in opera and concerts; in 1935, she gave master classes in opera at the Chicago Musical College; acted as technical adviser for opera sequences in motion pictures in Hollywood; in 1939 she returned to Scotland; made a lecture tour in the U.S. in 1947. With Louis Biancolli she wrote a book of memoirs, *Mary Garden's Story* (N.Y., 1951).

Gardes, Roger, French tenor; b. Paris, March 4, 1922; he sang in the chorus of the Opéra-Comique in 1950; in 1954, won first Grand Prix at a contest of tenors in Cannes, and was engaged as soloist at the Opéra-Comique (debut, Aug. 14, 1954, in *La Bohème*); subsequently sang tenor roles in *Lakmé, Eugene Onegin, Les Pêcheurs de Perles,* etc.

Gardiner, Henry Balfour, English composer; b. London, Nov. 7, 1877; d. Salisbury, England, June 28, 1950. He was a pupil of Iwan Knorr in Frankfurt; taught singing for a short time in Winchester, but then devoted his whole time to composition. He was also an ardent collector of English folksongs; his own compositions reflect the authentic modalities of the English countryside. He wrote a *Phantasy* for orch.; *English Dance;* Symphony in D; String Quintet; *News from Wydah,* for soli, chorus, and orch.; piano pieces; songs. His most successful piece was *Shepherd Fennel's Dance* for orchestra.

Gardiner, William, British writer on music; b. Leicester, March 15, 1770; d. there, Nov. 16, 1853. His father, a hosiery manufacturer, was an amateur musician from whom he acquired rudiments of music. During his travels on the continent on his father's business he gathered materials for a collection *Sacred Melodies* (1812–15) adapted to English words from works by Mozart, Haydn, and Beethoven. His book *The Music of Nature* (London, 1832) enjoyed a certain vogue; he also published memoirs, *Music and Friends, or Pleasant Recollections of a Dilettante* (3 vols.; I-II, London, 1838; III, 1853); *Sights in Italy, with some Account of the Present State of Music and the Sister Arts in that Country* (London, 1847).

Gardner, John Linton, English composer; b. Manchester, March 2, 1917. He studied organ at Exeter College, Oxford, with Sir Hugh Allen, Ernest Walker, R. O. Morris, and Thomas Armstrong (Mus. B., 1939). In 1946-52 he was opera coach at Covent Garden; in 1953 appointed instructor at Morley College; served as its director of music (1965-69); concurrently he taught at the Royal Academy of Music in London (from 1956). His style is characteristically fluent and devoid of attempts at experimentation; modernistic devices are used sparingly.

WORKS: operas, *The Moon and Sixpence,* after Somerset Maugham (London, May 24, 1957); the *Visitors* (Aldeburgh Festival, June 10, 1972); *Bel and the Dragon* (1973); *The Entertainment of the Senses* (London, Feb. 2, 1974); *Tobermoray* (1976); for orch. Symphony (Cheltenham, July 5, 1951); *A Scots Overture* (London, Aug. 16, 1954); Piano Concerto No. 1 (1957); *Sinfonia piccola* for strings (1974); *An English Ballad* (1969); *Three Ridings* (1970); Sonatina for strings (1974); chamber music: *Rhapsody* for Oboe and String Quartet (1935); Oboe sonata (1953); *Concerto da Camera* for 4 instruments (1968); *Chamber Concerto* for organ and 11 instruments (1969); sacred and secular choruses; piano pieces; songs.

Gardner, Samuel, American violinist and composer; b. Elizabethgrad, Russia, Aug. 25, 1891. He came early to the U.S. and studied violin with Felix Winternitz and Franz Kneisel; composition with Goetschius, and later with Loeffler in Boston. He was a member of the Kneisel String Quartet (1914); also played violin in American orchestras. From 1924 to 1941 he taught violin at the Institute of Musical Art in New York. He wrote a number of pleasant pieces: *Country Moods,* for string orch. (Staten Island Civic Symph. Dec. 10, 1946); a tone poem, *Broadway* (Boston Symph., April 18, 1930, composer conducting); also published *Essays for Advanced Solo Violin* (1960).

Gariel, Edoardo, Mexican music pedagogue; b. Monterey, Aug. 5, 1860; d. Mexico City, March 15, 1923. He studied with Marmontel in Paris; upon his return to Mexico he occupied various teaching jobs (1887-1908). In 1915 he visited the U.S. From 1916 to his death he was in charge of the School of Theater Arts in Mexico City. He published *Nuevo Sistema de Armonía basado en cuatro acordes fundamentales* (1916; also in English as *A New System of Harmony based on four fundamental chords*).

Garlandia, Johannes de, (sometimes called Johannes de Garlandia the Elder to distinguish him from a hypothetical Joh. Garlandia the Younger, proposed by H. Riemann on rather suppositional grounds), 13th-century writer on mathematics, theology, and alchemy; b. England, c.1195. He studied at Oxford, in 1217 went to Paris; joined the Crusade against the Albigenses; was probably still living in 1272. He is the supposed author of several tracts on music, among them the *De Musica Mensurabili Positio,* a valuable treatise on mensural music, 2 versions of which were printed by Coussemaker in his *Scriptores,* vol. I. There are altogether 4 works printed under his name in Gerbert and Coussemaker.

BIBLIOGRAPHY: H. Riemann, *Geschichte der Musiktheorie im 9.-19. Jahrhundert* (1898); L. J. Paetow, "The Life and Works of John of Garland," in *Memoirs of the Univ. of Calif.,* IV/2 (1927); G. Reese, *Music in the Middle Ages,* chap. 10 (N.Y., 1940).

Garner, Erroll, black American jazz pianist and composer; b. Pittsburgh, June 15, 1921; d. Los Angeles, Jan. 2, 1977. Completely untutored and unlettered, he composed tunes extemporaneously, singing and accompanying himself at the piano, with an amanuensis to put down the notes. He also played drums and slapbass. His nervous rubato style won acclaim from the cognoscenti and jazz aficionados. Incredibly precocious, he played regularly over the radio station KDKA in Pittsburgh at the age of 7 with a group called the Candy Kids; as an adolescent, he played piano on riverboats cruising the Allegheny River; then was a featured piano player in nightclubs and restaurants. He went to New York in 1944; formed his own trio in 1946. In 1948 he went to Paris; made further European tours in 1962, 1964, 1966 and 1969. His whimsical piano style especially appealed to French jazz critics who called him "The Picasso of the Piano" and, alluding to his digital dexterity, "The Man with 40 Fingers." In 1971 the Republic of Mali issued a postage stamp in his honor. Among his own songs, the plangent *Misty* became greatly popular; many of his other songs (he composed about 200 of them) reflect similar wistful moods, exemplified by such titles as *Dreamy, Solitaire,* and *That's My Kick.*

Garratt, Percival, English composer; b. Little Tew Grange, May 21, 1877; d. London, April 16, 1953. He studied in Vienna, Berlin, and at Marlborough College; toured Europe and South Africa; was accompanist of Clara Butt and Elman; composed many piano pieces (*Pageant Piece, Rondel, Night Piece, Arabesque, Helston Furry Dance, Mock Antiques,* and others); *Cherry-stones,* a children's musical play; *A Cartload of Villains,* 3-act pantomime.

Garreta, Julio, Catalan composer; b. San Feliu, March 12, 1875; d. there, Dec. 2, 1925. Entirely self-taught, he learned piano and composition. He wrote a great number of 'sardanas' (the Catalan national dance); a friendship with Casals stimulated several larger works; his *Impressions symphoniques* for string orch. were performed in Barcelona on Oct. 29, 1907. His *Suite Empordanesa* for orch. received first prize at the Catalan Festival in 1920. He also wrote a cello sonata, a piano sonata, and a piano quartet.

Garrett, George Mursell, English composer and organist; b. Winchester, June 8, 1834; d. Cambridge, April 8, 1897. A pupil of Elvey and Wesley, he was assistant organist at Winchester Cathedral (1851-54); organist of Madras Cathedral (1854-56); of St. John's College, Cambridge (1857); organist to the Univ., 1873, succeeding Hopkins. He took the degree of Mus. Bac. 1857, Mus. Doc. 1867; also received the degree of M.A. *propter merita* in 1878. From 1883, he was Univ. Lecturer on harmony and counterpoint; also Examiner in Music of Cambridge Univ. He wrote 5 cantatas, 4 services, and other church music.

Garrido, Pablo, Chilean composer and ethnomusicologist; b. Valparaíso, March 26, 1905. He studied theory with local teachers; in 1932 went to Paris to acquire further musical knowledge by direct contact with French musicians; returned to Chile in 1934 and settled in Santiago. He conducted concerts of Chilean music; gave lectures; taught at various musical institutions. He composed an opera, *La Sugestión* (Santiago, Oct. 18, 1961); the ballet *El Guerrillero* (1963); *Rapsodía chilena* for piano and orch. (1938); Piano Concerto (1950); *Fantasía antillana* for cello and orch. (1950); *13 x 13* for string quartet (1951); piano pieces and songs. He published a valuable monograph *Biografía de la Cueca* (Santiago, 1942).

Garrido-Lecca, Celso, Peruvian composer; b. Piura, March 9, 1926. He studied music theory with Andrés Sas and Rodolfo Holzmann in Lima; then went to Santiago, Chile, where he took courses in composition with Domingo Santa Cruz. In 1964 he received a Guggenheim Fellowship. In 1967 he was appointed to the faculty of the Univ. of Chile.
WORKS: Sinfonia (first performed at the Inter-American Music Festival in Washington, April 22, 1961); *Laudes* for orch. (1963); *Elegía a Machu Picchu* (1965; performed by the N.Y. Philharmonic, March 23, 1967); *Música* for 6 instruments and percussion (1957); Divertimento for Wind Quintet (1965); String Quartet (1963); *Antaras* for string nonet (1969); choruses; piano pieces; songs.

Garrison, Mabel, American coloratura soprano; b. Baltimore, Md., April 24, 1886; d. New York, Aug. 20, 1963. She was a pupil of W. E. Heimendahl and P. Minetti at Peabody Cons. (1909–11); then of O. Saenger in New York (1912–14), and of H. Witherspoon (1916). She made her debut as Filina *(Mignon)* in Boston, April 18, 1912; was a member of Metropolitan Opera from 1914–22; made a world tour; in 1933 she taught singing at Smith College; then retired.

Gaspari, Gaetano, Italian historiographer; b. Bologna, March 15, 1807; d. there, March 31, 1881. He entered the Liceo Musicale in 1820; took 1st prize in composition in 1827. He served as maestro di cappella at various churches; then devoted himself to historical research.
WRITINGS: *Ricerche, documenti e memorie risguardanti la storia dell'arte musicale in Bologna* (1867); *Ragguagli sulla cappella musicale della Basilica di S. Petronio in Bologna* (1869); *Memorie dell'arte musicale in Bologna al XVI secolo* (1875), etc.
BIBLIOGRAPHY: F. Parisini, *Elogio funebre del professore Gaetano Gaspari* (1882).

Gasparini, Francesco, Italian composer; b. Camaiore, n. Lucca, March 5, 1668; d. Rome, March 22, 1727. He was a pupil of Corelli and Pasquini in Rome, where he taught for a time; about 1700, became director of music at the Cons. della Pietà, Venice. In 1725 he was appointed maestro di cappella at the Lateran, Rome. Between 1702–23 he produced about 50 operas at Venice, Rome, and Vienna, with great success; he also wrote Masses, motets, cantatas, psalms, oratorios, etc. His chief work was a method of thorough-bass playing, *L'Armonico pratico al cimbalo* (Venice, 1708; 7th ed., 1802), used in Italy for nearly a hundred years. His most famous pupil was Benedetto Marcello.
BIBLIOGRAPHY: E. Celani, "Il primo amore di P. Metastasio," *Rivista Musicale Italiana* (1904).

Gasparo, da Salò (family name **Bertolotti**), Italian instrument maker; b. Polpenazzi, 1540 (baptized in Salò, May 20, 1540); d. Brescia, April (buried 14th), 1609. He came to Brescia in 1562, and settled there as a maker of viols, viole da gamba, and contrabass viols, which gained much celebrity; his violins were less valued. His pupils were his eldest son, **Francesco;** Giovanni Paolo Maggini, and Giacomo Lafranchini. Dragonetti's favorite double bass was an altered "viola contrabassa" of Gasparo's.
BIBLIOGRAPHY: V. M. Rhò-Guerriero, *Gasparo da Salò* (Rome, 1892); P. Bettoni, "Gasparo da Salò e l'invenzione del violino," *Commentari del Ateneo di Brescia* (1901); M. Butturini, *Gasparo da Salò: Studio critico* (Salò, 1901); G. Bignami, "Gasparo da Salò," *Musica d'oggi* (Feb. 1940); A. M. Mucchi, *Gasparo da Salò* (Milan, 1940).

Gasperini, Guido, Italian musicologist; b. Florence, June 7, 1865; d. Naples, Feb. 20, 1942. He was a pupil of Tacchinardi (composition) and Sbolci (cello); from 1902, librarian and teacher of music history at Parma Cons.; later, librarian at Naples Cons.; in 1908 he founded the Associazione dei Musicologi Italiani, one of the main purposes of which was the examination and cataloguing of all books on music and musical MSS in the Italian libraries; in 1909 it was affiliated with the Internationale Musik-Gesellschaft (as its Italian branch), and began the issue of a quarterly *Catalogo delle opere musicali . . . esistenti . . . nelle biblioteche e negli archivi pubblici e privati d'Italia*.
WRITINGS: *Storia della musica* (1899; a series of 10 lectures); *Dell' arte d'interpretare la scrittura della musica vocale del Cinquecento* (1902); *Storia della Semiografia musicale* (1905); *I caratteri peculiari del Melodramma italiano* (1913); *Musicisti alla Corte dei Farnesi;* "L'Art Italien avant Palestrina," *Mercure musical*, II, 6–8; *Noterelle su due liutiste al servizio di Casa Farnese* (1923).

Gassmann, Florian Leopold, important Austrian composer; b. Brüx, Bohemia, May 3, 1729; d. Vienna, Jan. 20, 1774. He learned to play the violin and harp from a local chorusmaster; but at the age of 13 ran away from home, and reached Italy; there is no corroboration for the claim that he became a student of Padre Martini in Bologna. After living in Venice in the service of Count Leonardo Veneri, he was called by the Austrian Emperor Francis I in 1764 as theater conductor in Vienna. In 1772 he succeeded Reutter as Court Kapellmeister, and founded the "Tonkünstler-Societät" for the relief of the widows and orphans of musicians. He was greatly esteemed as a teacher; among his students was Salieri. Gassmann's two daughters, **Maria Anna** (b. Vienna, 1771; d. there, Aug. 27, 1852) and **Therese Maria** (b. Vienna, April 1, 1774; d. there, Sept. 8, 1837) were opera singers. Gassmann was a remarkably prolific opera composer; he wrote about 25 operas, several of which were produced during his travels in Italy: *Achille in Sciro* (Venice, 1766), *Ezio* (Rome, 1770); his "dramma giocoso," *La Contessina,* was one of the earliest comic operas treating the social world of aristocrats and merchants. He further composed many cantatas, some 50 sacred works, numerous trio sonatas and quartets and about 50 "symphonien" in the concertante manner, some derived from the instrumental portions of his operas. Mozart greatly appreciated some of Gassmann's chamber music. One of the symphonies, in B minor, was edited by Karl Geiringer for Universal Edition (1933). *La Contessina* and a selection of Gassmann's sacred music are published in the *Denkmäler der Tonkunst in Österreich,* vols. 42–44 and 83 (former nos. 21.i and 45).

BIBLIOGRAPHY: R. Haas and G. Donath, "F. L. Gassmann als Opernkomponist," *Studien zur Musikwissenschaft* (1914); F. Kosch, "F. L. Gassmann als Kirchenkomponist" (ibid., 1927); E. Girach, *F. L. Gassmann* (Reichenberg, 1930).

Gassner, Ferdinand Simon, Austrian violinist; b. Vienna, Jan. 6, 1798; d. Karlsruhe, Feb. 25, 1851. In 1816, he was violinist at the National Theater in Mainz; 1818, he became music director at Giessen Univ., which in 1819 made him Dr. phil. and lecturer on music. In 1826 he joined the court orch. at Darmstadt, and afterwards became teacher of singing and chorusmaster at the theater. From 1822–35 he publ. the *Musikalischer Hausfreund* at Mainz; he edited (1841–45) the *Zeitschrift für Deutschlands Musikvereine und Dilettanten.* He wrote *Partiturkenntniss, ein Leitfaden zum Selbstunterricht* (1838; French ed. 1851, as *Traité de la partition*); and *Dirigent und Ripienist* (1846); contributed to the Supplement of Schilling's *Universallexikon der Tonkunst* (1842) and edited an abridgment of the entire work (1849). He composed 2 operas, several ballets, a cantata, songs, etc.

Gast, Peter. See **Köselitz, Heinrich.**

Gastaldon, Stanislas, Italian composer; b. Turin, April 7, 1861; d. Florence, March 7, 1939. At the age of 17 he began publishing nocturnes, *ballabili,* and other pieces for piano; was, for a number of years, music critic for the *Nuovo Giornale* in Florence. He wrote about 300 songs, some of which have had great vogue (*La musica proibita; Ti vorrei rapire; Frate Anselmo; Donna Clara);* he was fairly successful with his operas *Mala Pasqua* (Rome, 1890), *Il Pater* (Milan, 1894), *Stellina* (Florence, 1905), *Il Sonetto di Dante* (Genoa, 1909), *Il Reuccio di Caprilana* (Turin, 1913). He also wrote marches for military band; a piano fantasia, *La dansa delle scimmie;* etc.

Gastinel, Léon-Gustave-Cyprien, French composer; born Villers, near Auxonne, Aug. 13, 1823; d. Fresnes-les-Rurgis, Oct. 20, 1906. He was a pupil of Halévy at the Paris Cons., taking 1st Grand Prix de Rome for his cantata *Vélasquez* in 1846. A successful composer of operas, he produced *Le Miroir* (1853), *L'Opéra aux fenêtres* (1857), *Titus et Bérénice* (1860), *Le Buisson vert* (1861), *Le Barde* (Nice, 1896), and the ballet *Le Rêve* (Opéra, 1890) besides other stage works: *La Ker-*

messe, Eutatès, Ourania, and *La Tulipe bleue;* also 4 oratorios and 3 solemn Masses, orchestral compositions, chamber music, choruses, etc.

BIBLIOGRAPHY: F. Boisson, *Léon Gastinel* (1893).

Gastoldi, Giovanni Giacomo, Italian composer; b. Caravaggio; d. 1622. In 1581 he was a singer at the court of Mantua; contributed part of the score of *Idropica,* produced in Mantua on June 2, 1608. In 1609 he was maestro di cappella in Milan. A number of his works were publ.: 4 books of madrigals (1588, 1589, 1592, 1602); 4 books of canzonette (1592, 1595, 1596, 1597); many individual pieces are reproduced in contemporary collections. His 'balletti' (dance songs) are remarkable for their rhythmic vigor in folksong style.

BIBLIOGRAPHY: A. Einstein, *The Italian Madrigal,* vol. III (Princeton, 1949). See also Denis Arnold's article on Gastoldi in *Die Musik in Geschichte und Gegenwart.*

Gastoué, Amédée, French music scholar; b. Paris, March 13, 1873; d. there, June 1, 1943. He studied piano and harmony with A. Deslandres (1890), harmony with Lavignac (1891), then organ with Guilmant and counterpoint and composition with Magnard. From 1896–1905 he was editor of *Revue du Chant Grégorien;* in 1897 he began to contribute to the *Tribune de St.-Gervais,* became editor in 1904, and, on the death of Ch. Bordes (1909), editor-in-chief and director; he was prof. of Gregorian Chant at the Schola Cantorum from its foundation (1896); also music critic of *La Semaine Littéraire* in 1905; he was appointed advisory member of the Pontifical Commission of the Editio Vaticana in 1905. For many years he was organist and maître de chapelle at St.-Jean-Baptiste-de-Belleville, Paris, where he also gave concerts of works in the Palestrina style; lecturer at the Catholic Univ. and École des Hautes Etudes Sociales; Laureate of the Académie des Inscriptions et Belles-Lettres; commander of the Order of St. Gregory the Great; 1925, member of the Académie des Beaux Arts.

WRITINGS: *Cours théorique et pratique de plainchant romain grégorien* (1904); *Historie du chant liturgique à Paris* (vol. I: *Des Origines à la fin des temps carolingiens,* 1904); *Les Origines du chant romain, l'antiphonaire grégorien* (1907); *Catalogue des manuscrits de musique byzantine de la Bibliothèque Nationale de Paris et des bibliothèques publiques de France* (1907; with facsimiles); *Nouvelle méthode pratique de chant grégorien* (1908); *Traité d'harmonisation du chant grégorien* (1910); *L'Art grégorien* (1911); *La Musique de l'église* (1911); *Variations sur la musique d'église* (1912); *Musique et liturgie. Le Graduel et l'Antiphonaire romain* (Lyons, 1913); *L'Orgue en France de l'antiquité au début de la période classique* (1921); *Les Primitifs de la musique française* (1922); *Le Cantique populaire en France: ses sources, son histoire* (Lyons, 1924); *La Vie musicale de l'église* (1929); *La Liturgie et la musique* (1931); *Le Manuscrit de musique polyphonique du trésor d'Apt, XIVᵉ-XVᵉ siècles* (1936); *L'Église et la musique* (Paris, 1936). Gastoué edited several volumes of ecclesiastical music, collected from old sources, and wrote various articles on the subject.

Gatti, Guido, eminent Italian music critic and writer; b. Chieti, May 30, 1892; d. Grottaferrata, near Rome, May 10, 1973. He was editor of *La Riforma Musicale,* Turin (1913-15) and *Il Pianoforte,* Turin (1920-27), which changed its name in 1927 to *La Rassegna Musicale.*
WRITINGS: *Guida musicale della Giovanna d'Arco di Enrico Bossi; Biografia critica di Bizet* (1914); "Figure di musicisti francesi," *Biblioteca della Riforma musicale* (Turin, 1915); *Musicisti moderni d'Italia e di fuori* (Bologna, 1920; 2nd ed. 1925); *Le Barbier de Seville de Rossini* (Paris, 1925); *Debora e Jaele di I. Pizzetti* (1922); *Dizionario Musicale* (in collaboration with A. della Corte; 1925, 2nd ed. 1930; revised ed. 1952); *Ildebrando Pizzetti* (Turin, 1934; in English, London, 1951); contributed to *Grove's Dictionary;* wrote numerous articles for music magazines in Europe and America.

Gatti-Casazza, Giulio, Italian impresario; b. Udine, Feb. 3, 1868; d. Ferrara, Sept. 2, 1940. He was educated at the universities of Ferrara and Bologna, and graduated from the Naval Engineering School at Genoa; when his father, who had been chairman of the Board of Directors of the Municipal Theater at Ferrara, accepted a position in Rome in 1893, Gatti-Casazza abandoned his career as engineer and became director of the theater. His ability attracted the attention of the Viscount di Modrone and A. Boito, who, in 1898, offered him the directorship of La Scala at Milan. During the ten years of his administration the institution came to occupy the first place among the opera houses of Italy. From 1908-35 he was general director of the Metropolitan Opera, and the period of his administration was, both artistically and financially, the most flourishing in the history of the house; he vastly improved the orch., chorus, and all mechanical departments; one of his first suggestions to the Board of Directors was to offer a $10,000 prize for the encouragement of native operatic composers (won by Horatio Parker with *Mona,* 1912); the doors were opened to American composers (starting with Converse, Damrosch, and Herbert), and eminent foreign composers gladly accepted invitations to have the world première of new works take place at the Metropolitan (Humperdinck's *Königskinder,* Puccini's *Girl of the Golden West,* Granados' *Goyescas,* Giordano's *Madame Sans-Gêne,* etc.); the list of novelties produced is a long one, numbering 110 works; besides, there were noteworthy revivals of older works, e.g., Gluck's *Iphigénie en Tauride* (revised by Richard Strauss), etc. During this period, Giulio Setti was chorus master and set a high standard for the opera chorus. Gatti-Casazza procured the services of the best conductors available, bringing with him from La Scala such a master as Arturo Toscanini, and such able conductors as Polacco and Panizza. He resigned in 1935, Giulio Setti leaving with him, and went to Italy, where he lived in retirement. On April 3, 1910, Gatti-Casazza married the soprano **Frances Alda;** divorced in 1929; in 1930 he married Rosina Galli (d. April 30, 1940), première danseuse and ballet mistress.
BIBLIOGRAPHY: I. Kolodin, *The Metropolitan Opera, 1883-1935* (N.Y., 1936); Pitts Sanborn, *Metropol-*itan *Book of the Opera* (N.Y., 1937). Gatti-Casazza's *Memories of the Opera* was posthumously published in English in 1941.

Gatty, Nicholas Comyn, English composer; b. Bradfield, Sept. 13, 1874; d. London, Nov. 10, 1946. He was educated at Downing College, Cambridge (B.A., 1896; Mus. B., 1898); then studied with Stanford at the Royal College of Music; was organist to the Duke of York's Royal Military School at Chelsea; music critic of *Pall Mall Gazette,* 1907-14; also acted as assistant conductor at Covent Garden.
WORKS: the 1-act operas (all produced in London) *Greysteel* (1906), *Duke or Devil* (1909), *The Tempest* (April 17, 1920), *Prince Ferelon* (1921; received the Carnegie Award for this opera); *Macbeth,* 4-act opera (MS); *King Alfred and the Cakes;* Milton's *Ode on Time,* for soli, chorus, and orch.; *3 Short Odes;* Variations for Orch. on *Old King Cole;* piano concerto; piano trio; string quartet; waltzes for piano; songs.

Gatz, Felix Maria, German conductor; b. Berlin, May 15, 1892; d. Scranton, Pennsylvania, June 20, 1942. He studied at the Univs. of Berlin, Heidelberg, and Erlangen (Dr. phil., 1917), and conducting with Nikisch and Paul Scheinpflug; in 1922-23, he was conductor of the Lübeck Civic Opera; 1923-33, conductor of Bruckner Society series with Berlin Philh.; 1925-34, prof. of esthetics at State Academy of Music, Vienna. In 1934 he settled in the U.S.; 1934-36, prof. at Duquesne Univ., Pittsburgh; 1936-37, visiting prof. at N.Y. Univ.; from 1937 head of music and art dept. of the Univ. of Scranton, Pa.; he was also founder (1938) and conductor (1938-39) of the Scranton Orch.; publ. *Musik-Aesthetik grosser Komponisten* (Stuttgart, 1929), etc.

Gaubert, Philippe, renowned French conductor and composer; b. Cahors, July 3, 1879; d. Paris, July 8, 1941. He studied flute with Taffanel at the Paris Cons.; 1905, won second Prix de Rome; from 1919-38, was conductor of the Paris Conservatory concerts; 1920, first conductor at the Opéra, Paris.
WORKS: the operas *Sonia* (Nantes, 1913) and *Naïla* (Paris, April 7, 1927); a ballet, *Philotis* (Paris, 1914); the oratorio *Josiane* (Paris, Dec. 17, 1921); SYMPHONIC WORKS: *Rhapsodie sur des thèmes populaires* (1909), *Poème pastoral* (1911), *Le Cortège d'Amphitrite* (Paris, April 9, 1911); *Fresques,* symph. suite (Paris, Nov. 12, 1923); *Les Chants de la mer,* 3 symph. pictures (Paris, Oct. 12, 1929); Violin Concerto (Paris, Feb. 16, 1930); *Les Chants de la terre* (Paris, Dec. 20, 1931); *Poème romanesque,* for cello and orch. (Paris, Jan. 30, 1932); *Inscriptions sur les portes de la ville,* 4 symph. tableaux (Paris, Nov. 18, 1934); Symphony in F (Paris, Nov. 8, 1936); *Poème des champs et des villages* (Paris, Feb. 4, 1939); chamber music: *Médailles antiques,* for flute, violin, and piano; *Divertissement grec,* for flute and harp; *Sur l'eau,* for flute and piano; *Intermède champêtre,* for oboe and piano; Violin Sonata; songs; *Méthode complète de flûte,* in 8 parts (1923); many transcriptions for flute of works by Mozart, Beethoven, Lully, Rameau, etc.

Gaudimel, Claude. See **Goudimel, Claude.**

Gaul, Alfred Robert, English composer; b. Norwich, April 30, 1837; d. Worcestershire, Sept. 13, 1913. A chorister in the cathedral at 9, he was apprenticed to Dr. Buck; was organist at Fakenham, Birmingham, and Edgbaston; graduated (1863) as Mus. Bac., Cantab.; became conductor of the Walsall Philharmonic in 1887, then teacher and conductor at the Birmingham and Midland Institute, and teacher at King Edward's High School for Girls and at the Blind Asylum.
WORKS: An oratorio, *Hezekiah* (1861); several sacred cantatas, some of which *(Ruth* and *The Holy City)* are popular in the U.S.; Passion music; the 96th Psalm; an ode, *A Song of Life;* glees, vocal trios and duets, songs and part-songs, etc.

Gaul, Harvey Bartlett, American conductor and composer; b. New York, April 11, 1881; d. Pittsburgh, Dec. 1, 1945. He studied harmony, composition, and organ in New York with G. F. Le Jeune and Dudley Buck (1895); later (1906), in England, he studied composition with A. R. Gaul and Dr. Armes. In Paris he attended the Cons. and the Schola Cantorum; studied composition and orchestration with Vincent d'Indy, and organ with Widor, Guilmant, and Decaux (1910). He was conductor of the Pittsburgh Civic String Orch. and member of the faculty of Carnegie Institute, Pittsburgh. He composed many choruses *(Appalachian Mountain Melodies, Prayer of Thanksgiving,* etc.), chamber music, songs, organ pieces, etc.; won prizes in various competitions with his songs.

Gaultier, Denis, famous French lute player and composer; b. Marseilles, c.1600; d. Paris, late Jan. 1672. He was active as a composer from about 1625 or 1630; lutenist in Paris in 1626.
WORKS: *La Rhétorique des Dieux,* a collection of 69 compositions compiled between 1664–72 (facsimile reprint, together with transcription into modern notation, ed. by A. Tessier in *Publications de la Société Française de musicologie,* vols. VI, 1932, and VII, 1932–33); *Pièces de luth* (1669, publ.); *Livre de tablature* (publ. by his widow and Jacques Gaultier, 1672); many other MSS in the Berlin, Vienna, and Paris libraries. Much of his work is in the form of dance suites, each selection in the various groups bearing a descriptive title. As a composer Gaultier developed a type of ornamentation which influenced the keyboard style of Froberger and Chambonnières. Among his pupils were Mouton, DuFaux, Gallot, and others.
BIBLIOGRAPHY: O. Fleischer, "Denis Gaultier," *Vierteljahrsschrift für Musikwissenschaft,* II, 1 ff. (with transcription of *La Rhétorique,* 1886; also publ. separately, Leipzig, 1886); L. de la Laurencie, "Le Luthiste Gaultier," *Revue Musicale* (1924).

Gauthier, Eva, soprano; b. Ottawa, Canada, Sept. 20, 1885; d. New York, Dec. 26, 1958. She studied voice in Ottawa and at the Paris Cons. with Frank Buels and Jacques Bouhy, later with Schoen-René in Berlin; in 1909, she made her operatic debut as Micaela in Pavia, Italy; 1910, appeared at Covent Garden, London (Yniold in *Pelléas et Mélisande);* later devoted herself to a concert career; performed many works of contemporary composers; during her world tours she also made a study of Javanese and Malayan folksongs.

Gauthier-Villars, Henri (called **Willy**), French music critic; b. Villiers-sur-Orge, Aug. 10, 1859; d. Paris, Jan. 12, 1931. He was music critic for the *Revue des Revues,* writer for the *Revue Internationale de musique,* the *Écho de Paris* (over the signature "L'Ouvreuse du Cirque"), and other Paris papers. Several volumes of his numerous criticisms have been published: *Lettres de l'ouvreuse, Bains de sons, Rhythmes et rires, La Mouche des croches, Entre deux airs, Notes sans portées, La Colle aux quintes;* he also wrote a biography of Bizet (1912).

Gautier, Jean-François-Eugène, French composer; b. Vaugirard, near Paris, Feb. 27, 1822; d. Paris, April 1, 1878. He was a pupil of Habeneck (violin) and Halévy (composition) at the Paris Cons.; 1848, 3rd conductor at the Théâtre-Italien; also prof. of harmony at the Cons.; and in 1872 prof. of history. He composed 14 comic operas; an oratorio, *La Mort de Jesus;* a cantata, *Le 15 août;* an *Ave Maria;* etc.

Gavazzeni, Gianandrea, Italian composer and conductor; Bergamo, July 25, 1909. He studied at the Academy of Santa Cecilia in Rome (1921–24); then at the Milan Cons. (1925–31) where his principal teacher was Pizzetti. He then became engaged in musical journalism and in conducting; it was as conductor that he became mostly known in Italy and abroad; conducted concerts in England, Moscow, Canada (1965–67). He was music director of La Scala, Milan from 1965–1972; led the La Scala Opera in Moscow (1965) and in Montreal (1967); on Oct. 11, 1976, made his American debut at the Metropolitan Opera in New York.
WORKS: *Concerto Bergamasco* for orch. (1931); a scenic melodrama *Paolo e Virginia* (1932); a ballet, *Il furioso nell' Isola di San Domingo* (1933); several orchestral works and pieces of chamber music. He is also a prolific writer on music; among his publications are *Musicisti d'Europa* (Milan, 1954); *La casa di Arlecchino* (autobiographical; 1957); *Trent'anni di musica* (1958); *Le campane di Bergamo* (Milan, 1963); *I nemici della musica* (1965).

Gaviniès, Pierre, French violinist and composer; b. Bordeaux, May 11, 1728; d. Paris, Sept. 8, 1800. He learned to play the violin as a child in the workshop of his father, who was a lute maker. In 1734, the family moved to Paris. Gaviniès made his first public appearance in a Concert Spirituel at the age of 13; he reappeared at these concerts as a youth of 20; his success with the public was such that Viotti described him as "the French Tartini." From 1773 to 1777 he was director (with Gossec) of the Concerts Spirituels. When the Paris Cons. was organized in 1794, he was appointed professor of violin. His book of technical exercises *Les 24 Matinées* (violin studies in all the 24 keys) demonstrates by its transcendental difficulty that Gaviniès must have been a virtuoso; he attracted numerous pupils, and is regarded as the founder of the French school of violin pedagogy. His original works are of less importance; he wrote 3 sonatas for violin accompanied by cello (publ. posthumously; the one in F minor known as *Le Tombeau de Gaviniès);* his most celebrated piece is an air, *Romance de Gaviniès,* which has been publ. in numerous arrangements; he wrote further 6 sonatas for 2 violins and 6 violin concertos, and produced a comic opera, *Le Prétendu* (Paris, Nov. 6, 1760).

BIBLIOGRAPHY: C. Pipelet, *Éloge historique de Pierre Gaviniès* (Paris, 1802); L. de la Laurencie, *L'École française du violon* (Paris, 1923).

Gavoty, Bernard, French writer on music; b. Paris, April 2, 1908; studied philosophy and literature at the Sorbonne; also music at the Paris Cons. Under the nom de plume **Clarendon,** he wrote music criticism in *Le Figaro.* He publ. *Louis Vierne, le musicien de Notre-Dame* (Paris, 1943); *Jehan Alain, musicien français* (Paris, 1945); *Souvenirs de Georges Enesco* (Paris, 1955); also issued a series of de luxe publications, under the general title *Les Grands Interprètes* (Geneva, 1953, et seq.), containing biographies and photographs of Gieseking, Furtwängler, Menuhin, and many others.

Gavrilin, Valery, Russian Soviet composer; b. Vologda, Aug. 17, 1939. He studied with Evlakhov at the Leningrad Cons.; evolved a style of composition in which the melorhythmic patterns of old Russian folksongs are intertwined with modern street tunes, arranged in broad diatonic harmonies and diversified by sudden modulatory twists. His most successful pieces are for chorus; he also wrote an opera, *Family Album* (1969), and oratorios, among them *Letters from Soldiers* (1970); published 2 collections of piano pieces.

Gawronski, Adalbert, Polish pianist and composer; b. Seimony, near Vilna, April 27, 1868; d. Kowanónak near Poznan, Aug. 6, 1910. He studied with Noskowski at the Warsaw Music Institute and later, in Berlin and Vienna; then went to Russia, where he organized a music school in Orel, returning to Warsaw after a few years. He wrote 2 operas, *Marja* and *Pojata;* a symphony; 3 string quartets; piano pieces, songs, etc.

Gay, John, English librettist of *The Beggar's Opera;* b. Barnstaple, Devon, Sept. (baptized 16th), 1685; d. London, Dec. 4, 1732. The opera was brought out in London Jan. 29, 1728, and was immensely popular for a century, chiefly because of its sharp satire and the English and Scots folk melodies it used. It has had a number of successful revivals. The government disliked *The Beggar's Opera,* and forbade the performance of its sequel, *Polly,* the score of which was printed in 1729. When *Polly* was finally performed in 1777, it was a fiasco, because the conditions satirized no longer prevailed.

BIBLIOGRAPHY: *Dictionary of National Biography,* VII (repr. Oxford, 1921–22); C. E. Pearce, *Polly Peachum: the story of 'Polly' and 'The Beggar's Opera'* (London, 1923); W. E. Schultz, *Gay's Beggar's Opera* (New Haven, Conn., 1923); O. Sherwin, *Mr. Gay; being a Picture of the Life and Times of the Author of the Beggar's Opera* (N.Y., 1929); Cäcilie Tolksdorf, *John Gay's Beggar's Opera und Bert Brechts Dreigroschenoper* (Rheinberg, 1934); E. Gagey, *Ballad Opera* (N.Y., 1937).

Gay, Maria, Spanish contralto; b. Barcelona, June 10, 1879; d. New York, July 29, 1943. She studied sculpture and the violin and became a singer almost by chance, when Pugno, traveling in Spain, heard her sing and was impressed by the natural beauty of her voice. She sang in some of his concerts; also with Ysaÿe in Brussels; made her debut there as Carmen (1902), a role that became her finest. She then studied in Paris with Ada Adiny, and when she returned to the operatic stage made an international reputation. After tours in Europe, she made her American debut at the Metropolitan Opera as Carmen on Dec. 3, 1908, with Toscanini conducting. She sang with the Boston Opera Co. in 1910–12 and with the Chicago Opera Co. from 1913 to 1927, when she retired from the stage. She and her husband, the tenor **Giovanni Zenatello,** whom she married in 1913, settled in N.Y.

Gaynor, Mrs. Jessie Smith, American composer of children's songs; b. St. Louis, Feb. 17, 1863; d. Webster Groves, Missouri, Feb. 20, 1921. After studying piano with L. Maas and theory with A. J. Goodrich and A. Weidig, she taught in Chicago, St. Louis, and St. Joseph, Mo. Among her published works are: *Songs of the Child World* (2 books), *Playtime Songs,* etc. and a children's operetta, *The House That Jack Built.*

Gaztambide, Joaquín, Spanish composer; b. Tudela, Navarre, Feb. 7, 1822; d. Madrid, March 18, 1870. He studied at Pamplona and at the Madrid Cons. with Pedro Albéniz (piano) and Ramón Carnicer (composition). After a stay in Paris, he returned to Madrid as manager of several theaters and as conductor of the Cons. concerts; he became director of the "Concert Society" in 1868. He was best known, however, for his zarzuelas, the satiric musical productions which are identified with the Madrid stage. Gaztambide wrote 44 zarzuelas, many of which became popular; one, *El juramento,* first produced in 1858, was revived in Madrid in 1933. He took a zarzuela company to Mexico and Havana in 1868–69.

Gazzaniga, Giuseppe, Italian opera composer; b. Verona, Oct. 5, 1743; d. Crema, Feb. 1, 1818. He was a pupil of Porpora in Naples; after the production of his early opera *Il barone di Trocchia* there (1768), he traveled to Venice and to Vienna; his opera *Don Giovanni Tenorio* (Venice, Feb. 5, 1787) anticipated Mozart's *Don Giovanni;* he wrote 50 operas in all, several of which became quite popular at the time (*La locanda, L'isola di Alcina, La vendemmia, La moglie capricciosa,* etc.). Mozart's librettist, Lorenzo da Ponte, wrote the libretto of Gazzaniga's opera *Il finto cieco* (Vienna, Feb. 20, 1770).

Gebel, Georg (Jr.), German composer; b. Brieg, Silesia, Oct. 25, 1709; d. Rudolfstadt, Sept. 24, 1753. He studied with his father; was organist at St. Maria Magdalene, Breslau, and Kapellmeister to the Duke of Oels. In 1735 he joined Count Brühl's orch. at Dresden, where he met Hebenstreit, the inventor of the "Pantaleon," and learned to play that instrument. In 1747 he was appointed Kapellmeister to the Prince of Schwarzburg-Rudolfstadt. He was a precocious composer, and wrote a number of light operas (to German rather than Italian librettos, thus upholding the national tradition), and more than 100 symphonies, partitas, and concertos.

Gebhard, Heinrich, pianist, composer, and teacher; b. Sobernheim, July 25, 1878; d. North Arlington, N.J., May 5, 1963. As a boy of 8, he came with his parents to Boston where he studied with Clayton Johns; after a concert debut in Boston (April 24, 1896), he went to Vienna to study with Leschetizky. He gave first American performances of works by Vincent d'Indy; his most notable intepretation was Loeffler's work for piano and orch., *A Pagan Poem,* which he played nearly 100 times with U.S. orchestras. His own works are also in an Impressionistic vein: Fantasy for Piano and Orch. (N.Y. Philh., Nov. 12, 1925, composer soloist); symph. poem, *Across the Hills* (1940); Divertimento for Piano and Chamber Orch. (Boston, Dec. 20, 1927); String Quartet; *Waltz Suite* for two pianos; song cycle, *The Sun, Cloud and the Flower;* many piano pieces. He also arranged Loeffler's *A Pagan Poem* for two pianos. His book, *The Art of Pedaling,* was publ. posthumously with an introduction by Leonard Bernstein, who was one of his students (N.Y., 1963).

Gédalge, André, eminent French theorist, composer, and pedagogue; b. Paris, Dec. 27, 1856; d. Chessy, Feb. 5, 1926. He began to study music rather late in life, and entered the Paris Cons. at the age of 28. However, he made rapid progress, and obtained the 2nd Prix de Rome after a year of study (under Guiraud). He then elaborated a system of counterpoint, later published as a *Traité de la fugue* (Paris, 1901), which became a standard work. In 1905, Gédalge was engaged as prof. of counterpoint and fugue at the Paris Cons.; among his students were Ravel, Enesco, Koechlin, Roger-Ducasse, Milhaud, and Honegger. He also publ. *Les Gloires musicale du monde* (1898) and other pedagogic works. As a composer, Gédalge was less significant. Among his works are a pantomime, *Le Petit Savoyard* (Paris, 1891); an opera, *Pris au piège* (Paris, 1895), and 3 operas that were not performed: *Sita, La Farce du Cadi, Hélène;* he also wrote 3 symphonies, several concertos, some chamber music, and songs.
BIBLIOGRAPHY: "Hommage à Gédalge," *Revue Musicale* (March 1, 1926), containing articles by Koechlin, F. Schmitt, Honegger, Milhaud, and others.

Gedda, Giulio Cesare, Italian conductor and composer; b. in Turin, April 16, 1899; d. Callegno, near Turin, Sept. 7, 1970. He studied composition with Alfano in Turin; played cello and organ; began conducting in 1932; lived mostly in Turin. He wrote an opera *L'amoroso fantasma* (Turin, 1933); 2 Violin Concertos (1930, 1954); Viola Concerto (1940); Cello Concerto; Concerto for 4 saxophones (1952). He ended his days in a mental institution.

Gedda (real name **Ustinov**), **Nicolai,** noted Swedish tenor; b. Stockholm, July 11, 1925, of Russian-Swedish extraction. He studied in Stockholm, where he made his debut in 1952; in 1953 appeared in Paris and London; in 1957 was engaged by the Metropolitan Op-

era in N.Y.; sang the role of Anatol in Samuel Barber's opera *Vanessa* (1958); also appeared in Salzburg.

Gedzhadze, Irakly, Georgian composer; b. Mtskheta, Oct. 26, 1925. He studied with Matchavariani at the Cons. of Tbilisi; graduated in 1957. His works include the opera *Sunrise* (Tbilisi, Nov. 23, 1961); *Lake Palestomi,* symph. poem (1956); piano pieces.

Geehl, Henry Ernest, English composer; b. London, Sept. 28, 1881; d. Beaconsfield, Buckinghamshire, Jan. 14, 1961. A pupil of R. O. Morgan, he was appointed professor at Trinity College of Music, London, in 1919, and was still holding this post in 1954. He has written a symphony; a violin concerto; a piano concerto; pieces for brass band, including *Cornwall* and *Cornish Rhapsody;* pedagogic piano pieces; songs.

Gehot, Jean (also **Joseph**), Belgian violinist and composer; b. Brussels, April 8, 1756; d. in the U.S. about 1820. He went to London after 1780; there he publ. *A Treatise on the Theory and Practice of Music* (1784), *Art of Bowing the Violin* (1790), and *Complete Instructions for Every Musical Instrument* (1790). In 1792, he went to America; gave concerts in New York, where he presented his work, *Overture in 12 movements, expressive of a voyage from England to America.* He then played violin at the City Concerts in Philadelphia, under the management of Reinagle and Capron. However, he failed to prosper in America; most of his works were publ. in London, among them 17 string quartets, 12 string trios, and 24 'military pieces' for 2 clarinets, 2 horns, and bassoon.
BIBLIOGRAPHY: Some information on Gehot's life is found in J. R. Parker's "Musical Reminiscences," *Euterpiad* (Feb. 2, 1822). See also O. Sonneck, *Early Concert Life in America* (1907).

Gehrkens, Karl Wilson, American music educator; b. Kelleys Island, Ohio, April 19, 1882; d. Elk Rapids, Michigan, Feb. 28, 1975. After graduation from Oberlin College (B.A., 1905; M.A., 1912), he became prof. of school music at the Oberlin Cons. of Music in 1907; retired in 1942. He was editor of *School Music* from 1925 to 1934; co-editor, with Walter Damrosch and George Gartlan, of the *Universal School Music Series,* teachers' manuals for grade and high schools (1923–36), etc.
WRITINGS: *Music Notation and Terminology* (1914); *Essentials in Conducting* (1919); *An Introduction to School Music Teaching* (1919); *Fundamentals of Music* (1924); *Handbook of Musical Terms* (1927); *Twenty Lessons in Conducting* (1930); *Music in the Grade Schools* (1934); *Music in the Junior High School* (1936); with P. W. Dykema, *The Teaching and Administration of High School Music* (1941).

Geiringer, Karl, eminent Austrian-American music scholar and writer; b. Vienna, April 26, 1899. He studied musicology in Vienna with R. Stöhr, music history with Guido Adler, and in Berlin with Curt Sachs; from 1923–38 he was custodian of the archives and instrument collection of the Gesellschaft der Musikfreunde in Vienna; left Austria after the Anschluss and went to London, where he was guest lecturer at the Royal

College of Music (1939–40); then emigrated to the U.S.; from 1941–61 was professor at Boston Univ.; in 1962 was appointed to the faculty of the Univ. of California at Santa Barbara. WRITINGS: *Die Flankelwirbelinstrumente in der bildenden Kunst des 14.–16. und der 1. Hälfte des 17. Jahrhunderts* (dissertation, 1923): "Joseph Haydn" in Bücken's *Grosse Meister* (Potsdam, 1932); *Johannes Brahms* (Vienna, 1935; in English, London and N.Y., 1936; 2nd ed., 1947; also in Italian, Japanese, and Hebrew); *Musical Instruments, Their History in Western Culture* (London, 1943); *Haydn, a Creative Life in Music* (N.Y., 1946; also in Swedish, 1953); *The Bach Family* (N.Y., 1954; also in French, 1955; in Dutch, 1956); *Music of the Bach Family* (Cambridge, Mass., 1955); *Johann Sebastian Bach: The Culmination of an Era* (N.Y., 1966; in Swedish, 1969; in French, 1970). He edited Pergolesi's *Serva Padrona* and several little-known works by Haydn; arranged and publ. orch. works by Dittersdorf, Johann Christian Bach, Florian Gassmann, Michael Haydn, and others; also a collection of piano works, *Wiener Meister um Mozart und Beethoven* (Vienna, 1935). A Festschrift, *Studies in 18th century Music: A Tribute to Karl Geiringer on His 70th Birthday,* edited by H.C. Robbins Landon and Roger E. Chapman, was publ. in his honor (N.Y., 1970).

Geiser, Walther, Swiss composer and pedagogue; b. Zofingen, May 16, 1897. He studied violin with Hirt and composition with Suter at the Basel Cons.; then went to Berlin, where he took lessons with Busoni. After Busoni's death in 1924, he returned to Basel, and taught violin and composition at the Cons. until 1963. He composed 2 symphonies (1953, 1967); Violin Concerto (1930); *Concerto da camera* for 2 Solo Violins, Harpsichord, and string orch. (1957); Piano Concerto (1959); 2 flute concertos (1921, 1963); several choral works and solo piano pieces.

Geisler, Paul, German conductor and composer; b. Stolp, Aug. 10, 1856; d. Posen, April 3, 1919. He was a pupil of his grandfather, who was a conductor at Marienburg, and also of Constantine Decker. As a conductor, Geisler was associated with the Leipzig musical theater (1881), A. Neumann's traveling Wagner company (1882); for the following two years he was conductor at Bremen. He lived in Leipzig and Berlin for most of his career before going to Posen, where he became director of the Cons. He wrote much music for the stage; his other work, including two cyclic cantatas, symphonic poems, and incidental stage music, is mostly in manuscript.

Geistinger, Maria (Marie) Charlotte Cäcilia, Polish operetta singer; b. Graz, Styria, July 26, 1883; d. Rastenfeld, Sept. 29, 1903. She sang chiefly in Vienna, but also in Prague, Leipzig, Berlin, etc. In 1897 she made a successful appearance in New York.

Gelbrun, Artur, Polish-born Israeli composer; b. Warsaw, July 11, 1913. He studied at the Warsaw Cons.; then went to Italy where he took courses with Molinari and Casella at the Santa Cecilia Academy in Rome; from Rome he proceeded to Switzerland, where he studied composition with Willy Burkhard and conducting with Scherchen in Zürich. He was employed as an orchestral violinist in Zürich and Lausanne; in 1949 emigrated to Israel and joined the staff of the Academy of Music in Tel Aviv as prof. of conducting and composition. WORKS: a radiophonic oratorio, *Le Livre du feu* (1964; Jerusalem, 1966); 4 ballets: *Hedva* (1951; concert version, Ein-Gev, May 27, 1951); *Miadoux* (1966–67), *Prologue to Décameron* (1968); *King Solomon and the Hoopoes* (1976); Variations for Piano and Orch. (1955); *Prologue Symphonique* (1956); *5 Capriccios* for orch. (1957); 3 symphonies (1957, 1961, 1973); *Song of the River* for soprano and orch. (1959); Cello Concerto (1962); *Piccolo Divertimento* for youth orch. (1963); *Concerto-Fantasia* for flute, harp and string orch. (1963); Concertino for Chamber Orch. (1974); Sonatina for 2 violins (1944); String Trio (1945); *Esquisses* for narrator, flute and harp (1946); Sonatina for Solo Violin (1957); *5 Pieces* for Solo Cello (1962); *5 Pieces* for Solo Viola (1963); Partita for Clarinet Solo (1969); *Miniature* for solo bassoon (1969); String Quartet (1969); Wind Quintet (1971); Trio for trumpet, horn and trombone (1972); Piano Trio (1977); a number of piano pieces, choruses and songs.

Gelineau, Joseph, French composer of sacred music and editor; b. Champ-sur-Layon (Maine-et-Loire), Oct. 31, 1920. At age of 21 he entered the Order of Jesuits; studied organ and composition at the École César Franck in Paris; also obtained a doctorate in theology. He publ. *Chant et Musique dans le Culte Chrétien* (Paris, 1962); composed *Missa Plebs Sancta* (1960), psalms, etc.; translated and set to music the Psalmody of the Bible of Jerusalem.

Gelinek (properly **Jelinek**), **Joseph,** composer; b. Seltsch, near Beroun, Bohemia, Dec. 3, 1758; d. Vienna, April 13, 1825. He studied philosophy in Prague and at the same time took lessons in music with Segert; became a good pianist (Mozart praised him); ordained priest in 1786, but did not abandon music; went to Vienna and settled there as a piano teacher; in 1795, became music master to Prince Esterhazy. He was a prolific composer; 92 opus numbers are listed in a catalogue issued by André; his fantasias, variations, and dances for piano were quite successful.

Gellman, Steven, Canadian composer; b. Toronto, Sept. 16, 1948. He studied piano and composition with Samuel Dolin at the Royal Cons. in Toronto; then studied with Berio, Sessions and Persichetti at the Juilliard School of Music in N.Y. (1965–68), with Milhaud at Aspen, Colorado (summers 1965 and 1966) and with Messiaen at the Paris Cons. (1974–76). In 1976 he joined the faculty of the Univ. of Ottawa. He adopted an uncompromisingly modernistic idiom in most of his music, while safeguarding the formal design of classical tradition. WORKS: Piano Concerto (1964); *Mural* for orch. (1965); *Movement* for violin and orch. (1967); *Symphony in 2 Movements* (Ottawa, July 15, 1971); *Odyssey* for rock group, solo piano and orch. (Hamilton, Ontario, March 9, 1971); *Symphony II* (Toronto, Dec. 2, 1972); *Encore (Mythos I Revisited)* for orch. (1972);

Overture for Ottawa (1972); *Chori* for orch. (1974); *Animus-Anima* for orch. (Paris, April 28, 1976); *2 Movements* for string quartet (1963); *Soliloquy* for solo cello (1966); *After Bethlehem* for string quartet (1966); *Quartets: Poems of G.M. Hopkins* for voice, flute, cello and harp (1966–67); *Mythos II* for flute and string quartet (1968); *Sonate pour Sept* for flute, clarinet, cello, guitar, piano and 2 percussionists (1975); *Piano Sonata* (1964); *Fantasy for Piano* (1967); *Melodic Suite* for piano (1971–72).

Geminiani, Francesco, Italian violinist and writer; b. Lucca (baptized Dec. 5), 1687; d. Dublin, Sept. 17, 1762. He studied with Corelli in Rome and Alessandro Scarlatti in Naples; in 1706 returned to Lucca and played violin in the town orch. In 1714 he went to London, where he won a reputation as a teacher and performer; in 1731 he presented a series of subscription concerts in London; in 1733 he went to Dublin, where he established a concert hall and gave concerts; in 1734 he returned to London; in 1740 he was briefly in Paris; he was again in Paris for a longer period between 1749 and 1755, when he went back once more to London; in 1759 he settled in Dublin, where he was music master to Count Bellamont. Both in London and Dublin he was financially successful; besides music, he was interested in art, and bought and sold pictures. As a virtuoso, Geminiani continued the tradition established by his teacher, Corelli, and made further advances in violin technique by the use of frequent shifts of position, and by a free application of double-stops. In his compositions, he adopted the facile method of the Italian school; he excelled particularly in brisk allegro movements. During his years in England and Ireland he made a determined effort to please English tastes; his works are often extremely effective, but his inherent talents fell far short of Corelli's, and in music history he remains but a secondary figure. The claim that Geminiani was the author of the first published violin method, *The Art of Playing on the Violin,* which appeared anonymously in vol. V of Prelleur's *The Modern Musick Master* (London, 1730) is erroneous; upon examination it proves to be an edited republication of an earlier anonymous violin method titled *Volens Nolens,* originally published in London in 1695; perpetuating the misattribution, this text was later published under Geminiani's own name as *The Compleat Tutor for the Violin;* in 1751 a 3rd edition appeared under the original title, *The Art of Playing on the Violin;* it was subsequently translated into French (Paris, 1752) and German (Vienna, 1785); a facsimile edition of the original, prepared by D. D. Boyden, was issued in 1952. Boyden established the relevant facts in the matter in his paper "Geminiani and the First Violin Tutor" (*Acta Musicologica,* Feb. 1960). Apart from the question of authorship, *The Art of Playing on the Violin* is of historic importance because it sets forth the principles of violin playing, as formulated by Corelli, with many of the rules still in common use. Other papers and manuals, published under Geminiani's name, and assumed to be authentic, are: *Rules for Playing in a true Taste on the Violin, German Flute, Violoncello and Harpsichord* (London, 1745); *A Treatise on good Taste, being the second Part of the Rules* (London, 1749); *Guida Armonica o*

Dizionario Armonico being a Sure Guide to Harmony and Modulation (London, 1742; in French, 1756; in Dutch, 1756); *A Supplement to the Guida Harmonica* (London, 1745); *The Art of Accompaniament* [sic] *or a new and well digested method to learn to perform the Thorough Bass on the Harpsichord* (London, 1775); *The Art of Playing the Guitar or Cittra, Containing Several Compositions with a Bass for the Violoncello or Harpsichord* (London 1760); also compiled *The Harmonical Miscellany* (London, 1758). WORKS: (all instrumental) comprise: op. 1, 12 sonatas for violin and figured bass (1716); op. 2, 6 concerti grossi (1732); op. 3, 6 concerti grossi (1733); op. 4, 12 sonatas for violin and figured bass (1739); op. 5, 6 sonatas for cello and figured bass (1739); op. 6, 6 concerti grossi (1741); op. 7, 6 concerti gross (1746); also 12 string trios and arrangements of Corelli's works for various instrumental combinations. The concerti grossi have been publ. in modern editions by P. Mies (op. 2, no. 2), in *Musik im Haus* (1928); M. Esposito (op. 2, no. 2, arranged for string orch., London, 1927); H. J. Moser (op. 2, nos. 4, 5, 6, arranged for strings and piano) in *Das Musik-Kränzlein* (Leipzig, 1937); R. Hernried (op. 3, nos. 1–6, Leipzig, 1935). Violin sonatas have been publ. by: R. L. Finney (op. 1, nos. 1–12, Northampton, Mass., 1935); A. Moffat (op. 4, no. 8, Mainz, 1910; op. 4, no. 11, Berlin, 1899). BIBLIOGRAPHY: W. H. Grattan Flood, "Geminiani in England and Ireland," *Sammelbände der Internationalen Musik-Gesellschaft* (1910–11; pp. 108–12); A. Betti, *La Vita e l'arte di Francesco Geminiani* (Lucca, 1933); R. Hernried, "Geminiani's Concerti Grossi, op. 3," *Acta Musicologica* (1937; pp. 22–30).

Gemünder, August Martin Ludwig, violin maker; b. Ingelfingen, Württemberg, Germany, March 22, 1814; d. New York, Sept. 7, 1895. He established a shop at Springfield, Mass., in 1846; then moved to Boston, where he was joined by his brother **Georg** (b. April 13, 1816; d. Jan. 15, 1899), also a violin maker, a pupil of J. B. Vuillaume in Paris. In 1852, the brothers settled in New York, where they established themselves as the foremost manufacturers of musical instruments; between 1860 and 1890 they received numerous medals for excellence at expositions in Europe and America. After the death of August Gemünder, the business was continued by 3 of his sons, as August Gemünder & Sons. Georg Gemünder wrote an autobiographical sketch, with an account of his work, *Georg Gemünder's Progress in Violin Making* (1880, in German; 1881, in English). BIBLIOGRAPHY: *Dictionary of American Biography,* VII (N.Y., 1931).

Genée, (Franz Friedrich) Richard, German operetta composer; b. Danzig, Feb. 7, 1823; d. Baden, near Vienna, June 15, 1895. At first a medical student, he took up music, and studied under Stahlknecht at Berlin; was theater conductor (1848–67) at Riga, Cologne, Düsseldorf, Danzig, Amsterdam, and Prague; from 1868–78, conductor at the Theater an der Wien, Vienna, then retiring to his villa at Pressbaum, near Vienna. He wrote (some with F. Zell) several of his own libretti; he also wrote libretti for Strauss, Suppé, and Millöcker.

WORKS: Operettas: *Der Geiger aus Tirol* (1857), *Der Musikfeind* (1862), *Die Generalprobe* (1862), *Rosita* (1864), *Der schwarze Prinz* (1866), *Am Runenstein* (with Fr. von Flotow, 1868), *Der Seekadett* (1876), *Nanon* (1877), *Im Wunderlande der Pyramiden* (1877), *Die letzten Mohikaner* (1878), *Nisida* (1880), *Rosina* (1881), *Die Zwillinge* (1885), *Die Piraten* (1886), *Die Dreizehn* (1887).

Generali, (real name **Mercandetti**), **Pietro,** Italian opera composer; b. Masserano, Oct. 23, 1773; d. Novara, Nov. 3, 1832. He studied in Rome; began to compose sacred music at an early age, but soon turned to opera. He traveled all over Italy as producer of his operas and also went to Vienna and Barcelona. Returning to Italy, he became maestro di cappella at the Cathedral of Novara. He anticipated Rossini in the effective use of dynamics in the instrumental parts of his operas and was generally praised for his technical knowledge. He wrote about 50 stage works, both in the serious and comic genre, but none survived in the repertory after his death. The following were successful at their initial performances: *Pamela nubile* (Venice, April 12, 1804); *Le lagrime di una vedova* (Venice, Dec. 26, 1808); *Adelina* (Venice, Sept. 16, 1810); *L'impostore* (Milan, May 21, 1815); *I Baccanali di Roma* (Venice, Jan. 14, 1816; reputed to be his best work); *Il servo padrone* (Parma, Aug. 12, 1818); *Il divorzio persiano* (Trieste, Jan. 31, 1828).
BIBLIOGRAPHY: Piccoli, *Elogio del maestro Pietro Generali* (1833).

Genetz, Emil, Finnish choral composer; b. Impilahti, Oct. 24, 1852; d. Helsinki, May 1, 1930. He studied at the Dresden Cons. (1875–77); returning to Finland, he devoted himself chiefly to vocal music; many of his male choruses are well known and frequently sung in Finland.

Gennrich, Friedrich, German musicologist; b. Colmar, March 27, 1883; d. Langen (Hessen), Sept. 22, 1967. He studied Roman philology at the Univ. of Strasbourg; took courses in musicology with F. Ludwig. In 1921 he went to Frankfurt where he taught musicology at the Univ. He was regarded as a leading authority on music of the troubadours, trouvères, and Minnesinger.
WRITINGS: *Musikwissenschaft und romanische Philologie* (Halle, 1918); *Der musikalische Vortrag der altfranzösischen Chansons de geste* (Halle, 1923); *Die altfranzösiche Rotrouenge* (Halle, 1925); *Das Formproblem des Minnesangs* (Halle, 1931); *Grundriss einer Formenlehre des mittelalterlichen Liedes* (Halle, 1932; a comprehensive work); *Die Strassburger Schule für Musikwissenschaft* (Würzburg, 1940); *Abriss der frankonischen Mensuralnotation* (Nieder-Modau, 1946; 2nd ed., Darmstadt, 1956); *Abriss der Mensuralnotation des XIV. und der 1. Hälfte des XV. Jahrhunderts* (Nieder-Modau, 1948); *Melodien altdeutscher Lieder* (Darmstadt, 1954); *Franco von Köln, Ars Cantus Mensurabilis* (Darmstadt, 1955); *Die Wimpfener Fragmente der Hessischen Landesbibliothek* (Darmstadt, 1958); *Der musikalische Nachlass der Troubadours* (Darmstadt, 1960). He further contributed numerous papers to special publications on Romance literature.

Gentele, Goeran, brilliant Swedish opera manager; b. Stockholm, Sept. 20, 1917; killed in an automobile crash near Olbia, Sardinia, July 18, 1972. He studied political science in Stockholm, and art at the Sorbonne in Paris. He was first engaged as an actor, and then stage director at the Royal Drama Theater in Stockholm (1941–52); and at the Royal Opera (1952–63). In 1970 he became engaged as general manager of the Metropolitan Opera House in New York, effective June 1972; great expectations for his innovative directorship in America were thwarted by his untimely death during a vacation in Italy.

Genzmer, Harald, German composer; b. Bremen, Feb. 9, 1909. He studied piano and organ in Marburg; then took courses in composition with Hindemith in Berlin. He spent the war years in Berlin; from 1946–57 taught at the Hochschule für Musik in Freiburg-im-Breisgau; in 1957 he was appointed to the faculty of the Hochschule für Musik in Munich; Emeritus, 1974. A prolific composer, he writes music in a utilitarian manner adhering closely to classical forms, while allowing for dissonant counterpoint. He took interest in the electronic instrument Trautonium and wrote 2 concertos for it (1939, 1952).
WORKS: *Bremer Sinfonie* (1942); Symph. No. 1 (1957); Symph. No. 2 (1958); Piano Concerto (1948); Cello Concerto (1950); Flute Concerto (1954); Violin Concerto (1959); Viola Concerto (1967); Organ Concerto (1971); Oboe Concerto (1957); Harp Concerto (1965); and Trumpet Concerto in memory of the slain brothers Jack and Robert Kennedy (1968); much chamber music including 2 string quartets; Quartet for violin, viola, cello and double bass; 2 piano trios; Trio for harp, flute and viola; 3 violin sonatas, 2 flute sonatas, Sonata for viola solo; several works for piano and for organ; also cantatas and other choral works.

George, Earl, American pianist and composer; b. Milwaukee, Wisconsin, May 1, 1924. He studied at the Eastman School of Music in Rochester, N.Y., obtaining his Ph.D. in 1948. He has published a number of teaching pieces for piano under such fetching titles as *At Bedtime, Chicken Feed, Drifting Clouds, Hopscotch* and *Copy-Cat.*

Georges, Alexandre, French opera composer; b. Arras, Feb. 25, 1850; d. Paris, Jan. 18, 1938. He studied at the Niedermeyer School in Paris, and later became a teacher of harmony there. He occupied various posts as organist in Paris churches, and was a successful organ teacher. As a composer, he was mainly interested in opera; the following operas were produced in Paris: *Le Printemps* (1888); *Poèmes d'Amour* (1892); *Charlotte Corday* (March 6, 1901); *Miarka* (Nov. 7, 1905; his most successful work; revived and shortened, 1925); *Myrrha* (1909); *Sangre y sol* (Nice, Feb. 23, 1912). He also wrote the oratorios *Notre Dame de Lourdes, Balthazar, Chemin de Croix;* the symph. poems *Léila, La Naissance de Vénus, Le Paradis Perdu.* He wrote some chamber music for unusual combinations: *A la Kasbah* for flute and clarinet; *Kosaks* for violin and clarinet, etc. He is best known, however, for his melodious *Chansons de Miarka* for voice and piano (also with orch.). His arrangement of *Chansons champenoises à la manière ancienne,* by G. Dévignes, is also well known.

Georgescu, Corneliu-Dan, Rumanian composer; b. Craiova, Jan. 1, 1938. He studied at the Popular School for the Arts (1952–56) and with Ion Dumitrescu, Ciortea, Olah and Mendelsohn at the Bucharest Cons. (1956–61). Since 1962 he has been head of research at the Ethnography and Folklore Institute of the Rumanian Academy. His music employs folksong motives in a modern manner.

WORKS: Piano Sonata (1958); Trio for Flute, Clarinet and Bassoon (1959); *3 Pieces* for orch. (1959); *Motive maramureşene,* suite for orch. (1963; Bucharest, Dec. 3, 1967; *4* pieces for orch.: *Jocuri I* (1963); *II, Dialogue rythmique* (1964); *III, Danses solennelles* (1965); and *IV, Collages* (1966); Partita for Orch. (1966); a cycle of 4 pieces for various orchestral groupings: *Alb-negru* (1967), *Zig-Zag* (1967), *Continuo* (1968) and *Rubato* (1969); *Chorals I, II* and *III* for flute, violin, viola, cello and piano (1970).

Georgescu, Georges, Rumanian conductor; b. Sulina, Sept. 12, 1887; d. Bucharest, Sept. 1, 1964. He studied at the Bucharest Cons.; then took cello lessons with Hugo Becker in Berlin; returning to Rumania, he was conductor in Bucharest from 1919–38; in the interim also conducted guest appearances with European orchestras; during the seasons 1926–27 and 1960–61 he was guest conductor of the N.Y. Philharmonic.

Georgiades, Thrasybulos, Greek musicologist; b. Athens, Jan. 4, 1907. He studied piano in Athens; then went to Munich, where he took a course in musicology with Rudolf von Ficker (1930–35); also studied composition with Carl Orff. In 1955, settled in Munich. He contributed valuable papers to German music magazines on ancient Greek, Byzantine, and medieval music.

WRITINGS: *Englische Diskanttraktate aus der ersten Hälfte des 15. Jahrhunderts* (Würzburg, 1937); *Volkslied als Bekenntnis* (Regensburg, 1947); *Der griechische Rhythmus* (Hamburg, 1940); *Musik und Rhythmus bei den Griechen; Zum Ursprung der abendländischen Musik* (Hamburg, 1958); *Das musikalische Theater* (Munich, 1965); *Schubert, Musik und Lyrik* (Göttingen, 1967). His book on Greek music was publ. in English under the title *Greek Music, Verse, Dance* (N.Y., 1956).

Georgiadis, Georges, Greek pianist and composer; b. Salonika, Sept. 8, 1912. He studied piano and composition at the Cons. of Athens; in 1943 was appointed prof. of piano there. His music, in a traditional mold, is inspired chiefly by Greek folk resources.

WORKS: Symphony in E minor, surnamed *De la Paix* (1960); Concertino for Piano and Orch. (1959); two violin sonatas; songs; many piano pieces; incidental music for *Demeter and Persephone, Medea,* etc.

Georgii, Walter, German pianist and pedagogue; b. Stuttgart, Nov. 23, 1887; d. Tübingen, Feb. 23, 1967.

He studied piano in Stuttgart and music theory in Leipzig, Berlin and Hallé. From 1914 to 1945 he taught piano in Cologne; then went to Munich. He publ. several valuable books on piano playing: *Weber als Klavierkomponist* (Leipzig, 1914); *Geschichte der Musik für Klavier zu 2 Hände* (Zürich, 1941; revised ed., with added material on piano music for 1 hand, 3, 5 and 6 hands, 1950); *Klavierspielerbüchlein* (Zürich, 1953). He also published an anthology of piano music, *400 Jahre europäischer Klavier Musik* (Cologne, 1950).

Gérardy, Jean, Belgian cellist; b. Spa, Dec. 6, 1877; d. there, July 4, 1929. At the age of 5 he began to study the cello with R. Bellmann; he was a pupil of Massau at Liège Cons. from 1885–89. In 1888 he played as a student in a trio with Ysaÿe and Paderewski; he became noted as an ensemble player; with Ysaÿe and Godowsky, he formed a trio and toured the U.S. in 1913–14. Gérardy's instrument was a Stradivari, made in 1710.

Gerber, Ernst Ludwig, celebrated German lexicographer, son and pupil of **Heinrich Nikolaus Gerber;** b. Sondershausen, Sept. 29, 1746; d. there, June 30, 1819. He likewise studied law and music in Leipzig, becoming a skillful cellist and organist, in which latter capacity he became (1769) his father's assistant, and succeeded him in 1775. He was also a chamber musician. He was able to visit Weimar, Kassel, Leipzig, and other cities, and gradually gathered together a large collection of musicians' portraits; to these he appended brief biographical notices, and finally conceived the plan of writing a biographical dictionary of musicians. Though his resources, in a small town without a public library, and having to rely in great measure on material sent him by his publisher, Breitkopf, were hardly adequate to the task he undertook, his *Historisch-biographisches Lexikon der Tonkünstler* (Leipzig, 2 vols., 1790–92) was so well received, and brought in such a mass of corrections and fresh material from all quarters, that he prepared a supplementary edition, *Neues historisch-biographisches Lexikon der Tonkünstler* (4 vols., 1812–14). Though the former was intended only as a supplement to Walther's dictionary, and both are, of course, out of date, they contain much material still of value, and have been extensively drawn upon by more recent writers. He composed sonatas for piano, chorale preludes for organ, and music for wind band. The Viennese Gesellschaft der Musikfreunde purchased his large library.

Gerber, René, Swiss composer; b. Travers, June 29, 1908. He studied with Andreae in Zürich and with Nadia Boulanger and Paul Dukas in Paris. Upon his return to Switzerland he devoted himself to teaching; in 1947 was appointed director of the Cons. of Neuchâtel and was so until 1951.

WORKS: *3 Suites françaises* for orch. (1933–45); 2 sinfoniettas for string orch. (1949, 1968); 2 harp concertos (1931, 1969); 2 piano concertos (1933, 1966–70); Clarinet Concerto (1932); Flute Concerto (1934); Bassoon Concerto (1935–39); Trumpet Concerto (1939); Violin Concerto (1941); 3 string quartets (1947–70);

opera *Roméo et Juliette* (1957–61); *3 Visions espagnoles* for voice and small ensemble (1973).

Gerber, Rudolf, German musicologist; b. Flehingen, Baden, April 15, 1899; d. Göttingen, May 6, 1957. He attended the Universities of Halle and Leipzig, receiving his Dr. Phil. from the latter in 1925. He went as Abert's assistant to the Univ. of Berlin in 1926; in 1928, Gerber became professor at Giessen Univ.; he was head of the Music-Historical Institute there from 1937 to 1943, when he became a professor at Göttingen Univ. An authority on German music, he published the following: *Der Operntypus J. A. Hasses und seine textlichen Grundlagen* (Leipzig, 1925); *Das Passionsrezitativ bei H. Schütz* (Gütersloh, 1929); *Johannes Brahms* (Potsdam, 1938); *Christoph Willibald Gluck* (Potsdam, 1950); *Bachs Brandenburgische Konzerte* (Kassel, 1951). He was editor of the *Mozart-Jahrbuch*, III (1929); a collaborator in F. Blume's collected edition of Praetorius.

Gerbert, Martin, eminent German music scholar; b. Hornau, near Horb-on-Neckar, Aug. 12, 1720; d. St.-Blasien, May 13, 1793. A student in the Benedictine monastery at St.-Blasien, he joined the order in 1737, became a priest in 1744, then prof. of theology there; 1759–62, he made trips to Germany, France, and throughout Italy, collecting old MSS, particularly those on music history, of which he later made valuable use in his own works; also visited Padre Martini in Bologna, corresponding with him from 1761 until Martini's death in 1784; in 1764, he was elected Prince-Abbot of the monastery at St.-Blasien. His writings on music are *De cantu et musica sacra* (St.-Blasien, 1774, 2 vols.; from the beginnings of music to the 18th cent.), *Vetus liturgia alemannica* (1776, 2 vols.), *Monumenta veteris liturgiae alemannicae* (1777, 2 vols.), and *Scriptores ecclesiastici de musica sacra potissimum* (1784, 3 vols.; facsimile ed., Berlin, 1905; also reprinted in *Bolletino bibliografico musicale*, Milan, 1931); the first and last are still among the most valued sources for the study of music history, the last being one of the two great collections of treatises by theorists of the Middle Ages (for the other see **Coussemaker**).
BIBLIOGRAPHY: J. Bader, *Fürstabt Martin Gerbert* (Freiburg, 1875); Fr. Niecks, "Martin Gerbert: Priest, Prince, Scholar and Musican," *Musical Times* (Nov.-Dec. 1882); A. Lamy, *Martin Gerbert* (Rheims, 1898); A. Brinzinger, "Zu Martin Gerberts . . . 200jährigem Geburtsfest," *Neue Musik-Zeitung* (Sept. 2, 1920); G. Pfeilschifter, *Die Korrespondenz des Fürstabtes Martin Gerbert von St. Blasien* (vol. I, 1752–73; 1931); Eliz. Hegar, *Die Anfänge der neueren Musikgeschichtsschreibung um 1770 bei Gerbert, Burney and Hawkins* (Strasbourg, 1932).

Gerelli, Ennio, Italian conductor and composer; b. Cremona, Feb. 12, 1907; d. there, Oct. 5, 1970. He studied at the Cons. of Bologna; conducted ballet and opera in Italy; was on the staff of La Scala in Milan (1935–40); in 1961 he founded the Camerata di Cremona. He also wrote some chamber music.

Gerhard, Roberto, eminent Catalonian composer; b. Valls, near Tarragona (Spain), Sept. 25, 1896; d. Cambridge, England, Jan. 5, 1970. Although of Swiss parentage and nationality, he was prominently associated with the Catalonian musical movement. He studied piano in Barcelona with Granados (1915–16) and was the last composition student of Felipe Pedrell (1916–22). The currents of Central European music were already becoming apparent in his music even before he joined Schoenberg's master classes in Vienna and Berlin (1923–28). Gerhard held a brief professorship in Barcelona and served as head of the music department of the Catalan Library there until the defeat of the Republic in the Spanish Civil War; lived in Paris until June, 1939, then settled in England and became a British subject. He was a guest prof. of composition at the Univ. of Michigan in the spring of 1960 and at the Berkshire Music Center, Tanglewood, during the summer of 1962. In his music written in England, Gerhard makes use of serialistic procedures, extending the dodecaphonic principle into the domain of rhythms (12 different time units in a theme, corresponding to the intervallic distances of the notes in the tone row from the central note).
WORKS: an opera, *The Duenna*, after Sheridan's play (1945–47; performed in concert form, Wiesbaden, June 27, 1951); 5 ballets: *Ariel* (1934; ballet suite, Barcelona, April 19, 1936); *Soirées de Barcelona* (1936–38); *Don Quixote* (1940–41; London, Feb. 20, 1950); *Alegrías, Divertissement Flamenco* for 2 pianos (also an orch. suite, BBC radio, April 4, 1944); *Pandora* for 2 pianos and percussion (1943–44; also for orch., Cambridge, Jan. 26, 1944); 2 cantatas: *L'Alta Naixença del Rei en Jaume* (1931), and *The Plague* after Camus (London, April 1, 1964). He also wrote *Albade, Interludi i Dansa* for orch. (1936; London, June 24, 1938); a symphony, *Pedrelliana (Homenaje a Pedrell)*, based on themes from Pedrell's opera *La Celestina* (1941); Violin Concerto (1942; revised 1945 and 1949; Florence, Maggio Musicale, June 16, 1950); Concerto for Piano and Strings (1950); 5 numbered symphonies: No. 1 (1952–53; Baden-Baden, June 21, 1955); No. 2 (London, Oct. 28, 1959; revised in 1967–68 and retitled *Metamorphoses*); No. 3, *Collages*, for orch. and tape (London, Feb. 8, 1961); No. 4, *New York* (N.Y., Dec. 14, 1967); No. 5 (1969, unfinished); Concerto for Harpsichord, Strings and Percussion (1955–56); *Concerto for Orchestra* (Boston, Mass., April 25, 1965); *Epithalamion* for orch. (Valdagno, Italy, Sept. 17, 1966); *L'Infantament meravellós de Schahrazade*, song cycle for voice and piano (1918); Piano Trio (1918); *Dos Apunts* for piano (1922); *7 Hai-Kai* for voice, 4 winds and piano (1922–23); *2 Sardanas* for 11 instruments (1928); *6 cançons populars catalanes* for soprano and piano (1928; orchestrated in 1931, and performed in Vienna, June 16, 1932, Anton von Webern conducting); Wind Quintet (1928); *Cancionero de Pedrell*, 8 songs for soprano and chamber orch. (1941); *Capriccio* for solo flute (1949); *Impromptus* for piano (1950); Viola Sonata (1950); 2 string quartets (1950–55; 1961–62); *The Akond of Swat*, after Edward Lear, for voice and 2 percussionists (London, Feb. 7, 1956); Nonet for 4 woodwinds, 4 brass and accordion (1956); *Chaconne* for solo violin (1958); *Concert for 8* for flute, clarinet, guitar, mando-

lin, double bass, accordion, piano and percussion (London, May 17, 1962); *Hymnody* for 7 winds, percussion and 2 pianos (London, May 23, 1963); Cello Sonata (BBC Radio, Oct. 10, 1964); *Gemini* for violin and piano (1966; originally titled *Duo Concertante*); *Libra* for flute, clarinet, violin, guitar, piano and percussion (BBC Radio, Oct. 26, 1968); *Leo,* chamber symphony (Dartmouth College, Hanover, N.H., Aug. 23, 1969). He wrote an electronic sound track for a medical film, *Audiomobile No. 2 "DNA"* and electronic music to accompany a reading of García Lorca's *Lament for the Death of a Bullfighter;* incidental music to Shakespeare's plays *(Romeo and Juliet, Taming of the Shrew, Midsummer Night's Dream, King Lear);* film music; harmonizations of Catalan melodies, etc.

BIBLIOGRAPHY: Sept. 1956 issue of *The Score,* publ. on the occasion of Gerhard's 60th birthday, with articles by Donald Mitchell, Norman Del Mar, John Gardner, Roman Vlad, David Drew, Laurence Picken, and Roberto Gerhard himself; also the report on Gerhard (pp. 175–187) in Francis Routh's *Contemporary British Music: The Twenty-five Years from 1945 to 1970* (London, 1972).

Gerhardt, Elena, celebrated German lieder singer (mezzo-soprano); b. Leipzig, Nov. 11, 1883; d. London, Jan. 11, 1961. She studied at the Leipzig Cons. (1899–1903) with Marie Hedmont; toured Europe as a lieder singer with great success; made her English debut in London in 1906, and her American debut in New York, Jan. 9, 1912. In 1933 she settled in London as a teacher. She compiled *My Favorite German Songs* (1915), edited a selection of Hugo Wolf's songs (1932), and wrote her autobiography, *Recital* (London, 1953; preface by Dame Myra Hess).

Gericke, Wilhelm, noted Austrian conductor; b. Schwanberg, April 18, 1845; d. Vienna, Oct. 27, 1925. He studied with Desoff in the Vienna Cons.; then became Kapellmeister of the theater at Linz; in 1880, succeeded Brahms as conductor of the "Gesellschaftsconcerte." From 1884 to 1889 he held the prestigious post as conductor of the Boston Symph. Orch.; after 9 years of absence, he conducted it again in 1898–1906; then returned to Vienna. Gericke was a remarkably competent conductor and an efficient drillmaster.

BIBLIOGRAPHY: J. N. Burk, "Wilhelm Gericke: a Centennial Retrospect" *Musical Quarterly* (April 1945).

Gerlach, Theodor, German conductor and composer; b. Dresden, June 25, 1861; d. Kiel, Dec. 11, 1940. A student of Fr. Wüllner, Gerlach first attracted attention by an effective cantata, *Luthers Lob der Musica.* In 1886, he became conductor of the German Opera in Posen. After several other posts as conductor, he settled in Karlsruhe as director of the 'Musikbildungsanstalt.' He wrote an opera *Matteo Falcone,* to his own libretto, which was produced with considerable success in Hannover (1898); of greater interest are his experiments with 'spoken opera' employing inflected speech; of these, *Liebeswogen* was produced in Bremen on Nov. 7, 1903; later revised and produced un-

der the title *Das Seegespenst* in Altenburg, April 24, 1914; he applied the same principle, using the spoken word over an instrumental accompaniment in his *Gesprochene Lieder.* Also of interest is his early *Epic Symphony* (1891).

Gerle, Hans, German lutenist; b. Nuremberg, c.1500; d. there, 1570. He was well known in his time both as performer on the lute and manufacturer of viols and lutes. His works in tablature are of considerable historic value. They include *Musica Teusch auf die Instrument der grossen unnd kleinen Geygen, auch Lautten* (Nuremberg, 1532; 2nd ed., 1537; 3rd ed., under the title *Musica und Tabulatur,* 1546); *Tabulatur auff die Laudten* (Nuremberg, 1533); *Ein newes sehr künstlichs Lautenbuch* (Nuremberg, 1552; with pieces by Francesco da Milano, Ant. Rotta, Joan da Crema, Rosseto, and Gintzler). Reprints of his works have been ed. by W. Tappert in *Sang und Klang aus alter Zeit* (1906) and by H. D. Bruger in *Schule des Lautenspiels I/2,* and *Alte Lautenkunst I.*

BIBLIOGRAPHY: W. Tappert, "Die Lautenbücher des Hans Gerle," *Monatshefte für Musikgeschichte* (1886).

German, Sir Edward (real name **Edward German Jones**), English composer; b. Whitchurch, Feb. 17, 1862; d. London, Nov. 11, 1936. He began serious music study in Jan. 1880, under W. C. Hay at Shrewsbury; in Sept. he entered the Royal Academy of Music, studying organ (Steggall), violin (Weist-Hill and Burnett), theory (Banister), and composition and orchestration (Prout), graduating with a symphony; he was elected Fellow of the Royal Academy of Music in 1895. In 1888–89 he conducted the orch. at the Globe Theatre; here his incidental music to Richard Mansfield's production of *Kind Richard III* was so successful that Sir Henry Irving commissioned him to write the music to *Henry VIII* (1892). German was then abled to give up teaching and to devote himself entirely to composition. He was knighted in 1928; awarded the gold medal of the Royal Philh. Society in 1934.

WORKS: 2 SYMPHONIES; *Gypsy Suite* (1892); Suite in D minor (1895); English fantasia, *Commemoration* (1897); symph. poem, *Hamlet* (1897); symph. suite, *The Seasons* (1899); *Rhapsody on March-Themes* (1902); *Funeral March* in D minor for orch.; *Welsh Rhapsody* (1904); *Coronation March and Hymn* (1911); Theme and 6 Variations (1919); *The Willow Song* (1922); Serenade for Voice, Piano, Oboe, Clarinet, Bassoon, and Horn; *The Guitar; Bolero* for violin and orch.; incidental music to *Richard III* (1889), *Henry VIII* (1892), *As You Like It* (1896), *Much Ado About Nothing* (1898), *Nell Gwyn* (1900), *The Conqueror* (1905). OPERAS: *The Emerald Isle* (with Sullivan; 1901); *Merrie England* (London, April 2, 1902); *A Princess of Kensington* (1903); *Tom Jones* (London, April 17, 1908); *Fallen Fairies* (1909; the last libretto written by Sir W. S. Gilbert); operetta *The Rival Poets* (1901); many piano solos (incl. a suite) and duets; chamber music, organ pieces, etc.; Te Deum in F; patriotic hymn, *Canada;* intercessory hymn, *Father Omnipotent; Three Albums of Lyrics* (with Harold Boul-

ton); *The Just So Song Book* (words by Rudyard Kipling); other songs; etc.
BIBLIOGRAPHY: W. H. Scott, *Sir Edward German* (London, 1932).

Gernsheim, Friedrich, German composer and conductor; b. Worms, July 17, 1839; d. Berlin, Sept. 11, 1916. He studied at the Leipzig Cons. with Moscheles (piano) and Hauptmann (theory); then was in Paris (1855–61) for further studies. Returning to Germany, he became prof. at the Cologne Cons. (1865–74); then conducted choral concerts in Rotterdam (1874–80), subsequently taught at the Stern Cons. in Berlin (1890–97). His works are marked by a characteristic Romantic flair, as an epigone of Schumann; he was also influenced by Brahms, who was his friend. He wrote 4 symphonies, several overtures, a piano concerto, a violin concerto; 4 string quartets, 3 piano quartets, 2 piano trios, 1 string quintet, 3 violin sonatas, 2 cello sonatas, and numerous choral works, songs, and piano pieces, totalling to 92 opus numbers.
BIBLIOGRAPHY: K. Holl, *Friedrich Gernsheim, Leben, Erscheinung und Werk* (Leipzig, 1928).

Gero, Jhan (Jehan), Flemish composer who flourished in the 16th century; he was a fine madrigal writer, published 2 books of madrigals for 4 voices (1549); 2 books of madrigals for 3 voices (1553); and a book of madrigals for 2 voices (1541); he also wrote motets. He was at one time confused with **Johannes Gallus.**
BIBLIOGRAPHY: Alfred Einstein, *The Italian Madrigal,* vol. 1 (Princeton, 1949).

Gérold, Théodore, eminent Alsatian music scholar; b. Strasbourg, Oct. 26, 1866; d. Allenwiller, Feb. 16, 1956. He studied theology at the Univ. of Strasbourg, and musicology with Gustaf Jacobsthal. In 1890 he went to Frankfurt to study singing with Jules Stockhausen; then took courses at the Paris Cons. He received his Dr. phil. from the German Univ. of Strasbourg with a dissertation, *Zur Geschichte der französischen Gesangskunst;* was a lecturer on music at the Univ. of Basel from 1916 to 1918; returned to Strasbourg in 1919 to lecture on music at the new French Univ., from which in 1921 he received the degree of *Dr. ès lettres,* and in 1927, the degree of *Dr. en théologie.* He retired from the Univ. in 1937; occupied an ecclesiastical lecturing position in Allenwiller in 1951.
WRITINGS: *Le Manuscrit de Bayeux, chansons du XVe siècle; Kleine Sängerfibel* (Mainz, 1908); *Chansons populaires des XVe et XVIe siècles* (Strasbourg, 1913); *Les Psaumes de Clément Marot et leurs mélodies* (Strasbourg, 1919); *La musicologie médiévale* (Paris, 1921); *L'Art du chant en France au XVIIe siècle* (Strasbourg, 1921); *Schubert* (Paris, 1923); *J. S. Bach* (Paris, 1925); *Les Pères de l'église et la musique* (Paris, 1931); *La Musique au moyen âge* (Paris, 1932); *Histoire de la musique des origines à la fin du XIVe siècle* (Paris, 1936). Gérold transcribed into modern notation (with critical notes) the melodies of the 14th-century "drame provençal" *Le Jeu de Ste. Agnès,* ed. by A. Jeanroy (Paris, 1931).

Gerschefski, Edwin, American composer; b. Meriden, Conn., June 10, 1909. He studied piano with Bruce Simons at Yale Univ.; then went to London where he took a course for a season at the Tobias Matthay Piano School; he further had lessons with Artur Schnabel in Como, Italy. Returning to New York in 1935 he studied the Schillinger system of composition with Schillinger himself (1935–37). From then on he occupied various teaching posts; in 1960 was appointed to the faculty of the Univ. of Georgia. His works are of a pleasing modernistic type, showing knowledge and ability in handling instrumental and vocal idioms.
WORKS: Piano Quintet (1935); *Discharge in E* and *Streamline* for band (1935); 8 Variations for String Quartet (1937); Brass Septet (1938); cantata *Half Moon Mountain* for baritone, women's chorus and orch., after a story in *Time* magazine (Spartanburg, April 30, 1948); 100 Variations for Solo Violin (1952); Toccata and Fugue for Orch. (1954); Piano Trio (1956); Rhapsody for Violin, Cello and Piano (1963); 24 Variations for Cello (1963); *Celebration* for violin and orch. (1964); *Workout* for 2 violins and 2 violas (1970); *Suite* for horn solo (1976); choruses.

Gershfeld, David, Moldavian composer; b. Bobrinets, Aug. 28, 1911. He studied French horn and music theory in Odessa; then moved to Kishinev, where he produced two operas on Moldavian subjects: *Grozovan* (Kishinev, June 9, 1956) and *Aurelia* (Kishinev, April 26, 1959); also a Violin Concerto (1951) and a ballad for unaccompanied chorus, *Twenty-Six Commissars of Baku* (commemorating the Bolshevik representatives in Azerbaijan martyred by the British expeditionary force). In 1966 he moved to Sochi in the Caucasus.

Gershkovitch, Jacques, Russian conductor; b. Irkutsk, Siberia, Jan. 3, 1884; d. Sandy, Oregon, Aug. 12, 1953. He studied at the St. Petersburg Cons. with Rimsky-Korsakov, Glazunov, and Nicolas Tcherepnin. He graduated with honors, and received a scholarship to study in Germany under Artur Nikisch. Upon his return to Russia, he became director of the Irkutsk Cons.; after the Revolution, he joined the orch. of Pavlova's ballet troupe as flutist, and traveled with it to the Orient. He settled in Tokyo, where he organized special concerts for young people; after the earthquake of 1923, he went to the U.S.; conducted guest engagements with the San Francisco Symph.; then was in Portland, Oregon, where he founded the Portland Junior Symphony; he conducted it for 30 years until his death.

Gershwin, George, immensely gifted American composer; b. Brooklyn, N.Y., Sept. 26, 1898; d. Beverly Hills, Calif., July 11, 1937. His real name was **Jacob Gershvin,** according to birth registry; his father was an immigrant from Russia whose original name was Gershovitz. Gershwin's extraordinary career began when he was 16, playing the piano in music stores to demonstrate new popular songs. His studies were desultory; he took piano lessons with Ernest Hutcheson and Charles Hambitzer in N.Y.; he studied harmony with Edward Kilenyi and with Rubin Goldmark; later on, when he was already a famous composer of popular music, he continued to take private lessons; he studied counterpoint with Henry Cowell and with Wallingford Riegger; during the last years of his life, he applied himself with great earnestness to studying with Joseph Schillinger in an attempt to organize his technique in a scientific manner; some of Schillinger's methods he applied in *Porgy and Bess*. But it was his melodic talent and a genius for rhythmic invention, rather than any studies, that made him a genuinely important American composer. As far as worldly success was concerned, there was no period of struggle in Gershwin's life; one of his earliest songs, *Swanee*, written at the age of 19, became enormously popular (more than a million copies sold; 2,250,000 phonograph records). He also took time to write a lyrical *Lullaby* for string quartet (1920). Possessing phenomenal energy, he produced musical comedies in close succession, using the fashionable jazz formulas in original and ingenious ways. A milestone of his career was *Rhapsody in Blue*, for piano and jazz orchestra, in which he applied the jazz idiom to an essentially classical form. He played the solo part at a special concert conducted by Paul Whiteman at Aeolian Hall, N.Y., on Feb. 12, 1924. The orchestration was by Ferde Grofé, a circumstance that generated rumors of Gershwin's inability to score for instruments; this, however, was quickly refuted by his production of several orchestral works, scored by himself in a brilliant fashion. He played the solo part of his Piano Concerto in F, with Walter Damrosch and the N.Y. Symph. Orch. (Dec. 3, 1925); this work had a certain vogue, but its popularity never equalled that of the *Rhapsody in Blue*. Reverting again to a more popular idiom, Gershwin wrote a symphonic work, *An American in Paris* (N.Y. Philh., Dec. 13, 1928, Damrosch conducting). His *Rhapsody No. 2* was performed by Koussevitsky and the Boston Symph. on Jan. 29, 1932, but was unsuccessful; there followed a *Cuban Overture* (N.Y., Aug. 16, 1932) and Variations for Piano and Orch. on his song *I Got Rhythm* (Boston, Jan. 14, 1934, Gershwin soloist). In the meantime, Gershwin became engaged in his most ambitious undertaking: the composition of *Porgy and Bess*, an American opera in a folk manner, for Negro singers, after the book by Dubose Heyward. It was first staged in Boston on Sept. 30, 1935, and shortly afterwards in N.Y. Its reception by the press was not uniformly favorable, but its songs rapidly attained great popularity (*Summertime; I Got Plenty o' Nuthin'; It Ain't Neccessarily So; Bess, You Is My Woman Now*); the opera has been successfully revived in N.Y. and elsewhere; it received international recognition when an American company of Negro singers toured South America and Europe in 1955, reaching a climax of success with several performances in Russia (Leningrad, Dec. 26, 1955, and also Moscow); it was the first American opera company to visit Russia. Gershwin's death (of a brain tumor) at the age of 38 was mourned as a great loss to American art; memorial concerts have been held at Lewisohn Stadium, N.Y., on each anniversary of his death, with large attendance. His musical comedies include: numbers for *George White's Scandals* of 1920, 1921, 1922, 1923, and 1924; *Our Nell* (1922); *Sweet Little Devil* (1923); *Lady Be Good* (1924); *Primrose* (1924); *Tip Toes* (1925); *Song of the Flame* (1925);

135th Street (one-act, 1923; produced in concert form Dec. 29, 1925, Paul Whiteman conducting); *Oh Kay!* (1926); *Strike Up the Band* (1927); *Funny Face* (1927); *Rosalie* (1928); *Treasure Girl* (1928); *Show Girl* (1929); *Girl Crazy* (1930); *Of Thee I Sing* (1931; a political satire which was the first musical to win a Pulitzer Prize); *Pardon My English* (1932); *Let 'Em Eat Cake* (1933); for motion pictures: *Shall We Dance, Damsel in Distress, Goldwyn Follies* (left unfinished at his death; completed by Vernon Duke). A collection of his songs and piano transcriptions, *George Gershwin's Song Book*, was publ. in 1932; repr. as *Gershwin Years in Song* (N.Y., 1973).

BIBLIOGRAPHY: S. N. Behrman, "Troubadour," *The New Yorker* (May 1929); I. Goldberg, *George Gershwin, A Study in American Music* (N.Y., 1931); C. Engel, "George Gershwin's Song Book" in Views and Reviews of the *Musical Quarterly* (Oct. 1932); V. Thomson, "George Gershwin," *Modern Music* (Nov. 1935); F. Jacobi, "George Gershwin," *Modern Music* (Nov.-Dec. 1937); M. Armitage, editor, *George Gershwin*, a collection of articles (N.Y., 1938); O. Levant, *A Smattering of Ignorance* (N.Y., 1938); R. Chalupt, *George Gershwin, le musicien de la "Rhapsody in Blue"* (Paris, 1949); M. V. Pugliaro, *Rhapsodia in blu; l'arte e l'amore nella vita di George Gershwin* (Turin, 1951); D. Ewen, *A Journey to Greatness; George Gershwin* (N.Y., 1956; radically revised under the new title *George Gershwin, His Journey to Greatness*, 1970); M. Armitage, *George Gershwin, Man and Legend* (N.Y., 1958); E. Jablonski and L. D. Stewart, *The Gershwin Years* (N.Y., 1958); R. Kimball and A. Simon, *The Gershwins* (N.Y., 1973); C. Schwartz, *Gershwin* (includes extensive bibliography; N.Y., 1973).

Gershwin, Ira, one of the most talented American librettists and lyricists; brother of **George Gershwin;** b. New York, Dec. 6, 1896. He attended night classes at the College of the City of N.Y., wrote verses and humorous pieces for the school paper, and served as cashier in a Turkish bath of which his father was part owner. He began writing lyrics for shows in 1918, using the pseudonym **Arthur Francis.** His first full-fledged show as a lyricist was the musical comedy *Be Yourself*, for which he used his own name for the first time. He achieved fame when he wrote the lyrics for his brother's musical comedy *Lady, Be Good!* (1924). He remained his brother's collaborator until George Gershwin's death in 1937, and his lyrics became an inalienable part of the whole, so that the brothers George and Ira Gershwin became artistic twins like Gilbert and Sullivan, indissolubly united in some of the greatest productions of the music theater in America: *Strike Up The Band* (1930), *Of Thee I Sing* (1931), etc. and the culminating product of the brotherly genius, the folk opera *Porgy and Bess* (1935). Ira Gershwin also wrote lyrics for other composers, among them Vernon Duke (*The Ziegfeld Follies of 1936*), Kurt Weill (*Lady in the Dark*, and several motion pictures), and Jerome Kern (the enormously successful song *Long Ago and Far Away* from the film *Cover Girl*).

Gerstberger, Karl, German music scholar and composer; b. Neisse, Feb. 12, 1892; d. Bremen, Oct. 30,

1955. He studied in Cologne with Othegraven and in Munich with Courvoisier. In 1926 he gave a concert of his works in Berlin. In his music he endeavored to revive the spirit of Lutheran polyphony. He wrote choral works, lieder, a string quartet, 2 string trios, etc.; published a collection of essays, *Zum Schicksal der Musik.*

Gerster, Etelka, Hungarian dramatic soprano; b. Kaschau, June 25, 1855; d. Pontecchio, near Bologna, Aug. 20, 1920. She studied with Mathilde Marchesi in Vienna, then made her debut in Venice as Gilda in *Rigoletto,* Jan. 8, 1876. Her great success resulted in engagements in Berlin and Budapest in Italian opera under the direction of Carlo Gardini. She married Gardini on April 16, 1877, and continued her successful career, making her London debut on June 23, 1877 as Amina in *Sonnambula,* and her U.S. debut in the same role on Nov. 18, 1878 at the N.Y. Academy of Music. She returned to London for three more seasons (1878–80), then sang again in N.Y. in 1880–83 and in 1887. After retiring, she taught singing in Berlin, and in N.Y. at the Institute of Musical Art (1907). She wrote *Stimmführer* (1906; 2nd. ed., 1908).

Gerster, Ottmar, eminent German violinist, composer and pedagogue; b. Braunfels, June 29, 1897; d. Leipzig, Aug. 31, 1969. He studied theory of music with Bernhard Sekles at the Frankfurt Cons. (1913–16); then was mobilized during the last years of World War I; after the war studied violin with Adolf Rebner (1919–21); played the viola in string quartets (1923–27), and concurrently was concertmaster in the Frankfurt Symph. Orch. From 1927 to 1939 he taught violin and theory at the Folkwang-Schule in Essen; in 1940 was again in the army. After the end of that war he was on the faculty of the Musik-Hochschule in Weimar (1947–52) and in Leipzig (1952–62). His music is marked by melodious polyphony is a neo-Classical vein; in his operas he used folklike thematic material.

WORKS: the operas *Madame Liselotte* (Essen, 1933), *Enoch Arden* (Düsseldorf, 1936); *Die Hexe von Passau* (Düsseldorf, 1941); *Das Verzauberte Ich* (Wuppertal, 1949); *Der fröhliche Sünder* (Weimar, 1963); a ballet *Der ewige Kreis* (Duisburg, 1939); *Kleine Sinfonie* (1931); *Thüringer Sinfonie* (1952); *Leipziger Sinfonie* (1965); *Oberhessische Bauerntänze* for orch. (1937); Cello Concerto (1946); Piano Concerto (1956); Horn Concerto (1962); 2 string quartets (1923, 1954); String Trio (1957); *Ballade vom Manne Karl Marx (und der Veränderung der Welt)* baritone, solo, chorus, and orch. (1961); many other choruses, some to words of political significance; and songs.

BIBLIOGRAPHY: O. Goldhammer, *Ottmar Gerster* (Berlin, 1953).

Gerstman, Blanche, South African composer; b. Cape Town, April 2, 1910. She studied at the South African College of Music with W. H. Bell; in 1950 she went to London and took additional courses at the Royal Academy of Music. Returning to South Africa she played double bass in the municipal orch. of Cape Town.

Gertler, André, Hungarian violinist; b. Budapest, July 26, 1907. He studied with Hubay and Kodály; in 1928 settled in Belgium; in 1931 he formed the "Quatuor Gertler" in Brussels. He later taught at the Brussels Cons.; in 1964 he was appointed prof. of violin at the Hochschule für Musik in Hannover.

Gervaise, Claude, French composer of the 16th century. He was a viol player, chamber musician to François I and Henri II. He composed many dances and *chansons;* 6 vols. of his *Danceries à 4 et 5 parties* were published by Attaignant from about 1545 to 1556, but only 3 vols. remain; a selection of his dances is included in vol. 23 *(Danceries)* of *Les Maîtres Musiciens* ed. by H. Expert (1908). Several *chansons* by Gervaise appear in 16th century collections.

Gerville-Réache, Jeanne, French dramatic contralto; b. Orthez, March 26, 1882; d. New York, Jan. 15, 1915. She spent her childhood in Guadeloupe, French West Indies, where her father was governor. In 1898 she was sent to Paris to study singing with Mme. Viardot-Garcia. She sang at the Opéra-Comique in Paris between 1900 and 1903; went to New York, where she became a member of the Manhattan Opera Co. (1907–10); subsequently sang opera in Chicago, Boston, Philadelphia and Montreal. In 1908 she married Dr. Georges Rambaud, director of the Pasteur Institute in New York.

Gesensway, Louis, American violinist and composer; b. Dvinsk, Latvia, Feb. 19, 1906; d. Philadelphia, March 11, 1976. The family moved to Canada when he was a child; he studied violin; in 1926 he joined the Philadelphia Orchestra, remaining with it until 1971. He was also a prolific composer of some originality; he developed a system of "color harmony" by expanding and contracting the intervals of the diatonic scale into fractions, establishing a difference between enharmonically equal tones; such a scale in Gesensway's projection contained 41 degrees.

WORKS: for orch.: Flute Concerto (Philadelphia, Nov. 1, 1946); *the Four Squares of Philadelphia* for narrator and orch. (Philadelphia, Feb. 25, 1955); *Ode to Peace* (Philadelphia, April 15, 1960); *Commemoration Symphony* (1966–68; Philadelphia, Feb. 25, 1971); *A Pennsylvania Overture* (1972); Cello Concerto (1973); Chamber music: Concerto for 13 brass instruments (1942); Quartet for Clarinet and Strings (1950); Quartet for Oboe, Bassoon, Violin and Viola (1951); Sonata for Solo Bassoon; Duo for Oboe and Guitar (1959); Duo for Viola and Bassoon (1960); Duo for Violin and Cello (1970).

Gesualdo, Don Carlo, Prince of Venosa, lutenist and composer; b. Naples, c.1560; d. there, Sept. 8, 1613. Probably studied with Pomponio Nenna; 1590, his unfaithful wife and 1st cousin, Maria d'Avalos, and her lover were murdered at Gesualdo's orders; 1594, he was at the court of the Estensi in Ferrara, where he married his 2nd wife, Leonora d'Este, in that year; some time after the death of the Duke of Ferrara, in 1597, Don Carlo returned to Naples, where he remained till death. Living at the epoch when the 'new music' (the homophonic style) made its appearance, he was one of the most original musicians of the time. Like Rore, Banchieri, and Vincentino, he was a so-called 'chromaticist'; his later madrigals reveal a distinctly individual style of expression and are characterized by strong contrasts, new (for their time) harmonic progressions, and a skilful use of dissonance; he was a master in producing tone color through the use of different voice registers and in expressing the poetic contents of his texts. Publ. 6 vols. of madrigals *a* 5 (Genoa, 1585, each part separately; an edition in score was publ. by G. Pavoni, Venice, 1613). A complete ed. of his works was begun by the Istituto Italiano per la Storia della Musica (Rome), but only one vol. (2 books of madrigals) appeared (1942); a new edition of the 6 books of madrigals, edited by F. Vatelli and A. Bizzelli, was publ. 1956–58. A new edition of his works, in 10 vols. (6 books of madrigals, 3 vols. of sacred works, and 1 vol. of instrumental works, canzonettas, and psalms), edited by W. Weisman and G. E. Watkins, was publ. 1957–67.

BIBLIOGRAPHY: Ferd. Keiner, *Die Madrigale Gesualdos von Venosa* (diss., Leipzig, 1914); Cecil Gray and Philip Heseltine, *Carlo Gesualdo, Prince of Venosa, Musician and Murderer* (London, 1926); F. Vatielli, *Il Principe di Venosa e Leonora d'Este* (Milan, 1941); Glenn Watkins, *Gesualdo, the Man and His Music* (London, 1973).

Gevaert, François Auguste, eminent Belgian composer and musicologist; b. Huysse, near Audenarde, July 31, 1828; d. Brussels, Dec. 24, 1908. He was a pupil of Sommère (piano) and Mengal (composition) at Ghent Cons. (1841–47), taking the Grand Prix de Rome for composition; from 1843 he was also organist at the Jesuit church. He produced 2 operas in 1848, with some success; lived in Paris for a year (1849–50), and was commissioned to write an opera for the Théâtre-Lyrique; then a year in Spain, his *Fantasía sobre motivos españoles* winning him the order of Isabella la Católica; he also wrote a *Rapport sur la situation de la musique en Espagne* (Brussels, 1851). After a short visit to Italy and Germany, he returned to Ghent in 1852, and up to 1861 brought out 9 operas in quick succession. In 1857 his festival cantata *De nationale verjaerdag* won him the order of Léopold. In 1867 he was appointed chorus master at the Opéra, Paris; in 1870, the German investment caused him to return home, and from 1871 he was director of the Brussels Cons., succeeding Fétis. In this position he gave evidence of remarkable talent for organization. As conductor of the 'Concerts du Cons.' he exerted a far-reaching influence through his historical concerts, producing the works of all nations and periods. In 1873 he was elected member of the Academy, succeeding Mercadante; in 1907 he was created a baron.

WORKS: 12 operas; 3 cantatas; a *Missa pro defunctis* and *Super flumina Babylonis* (both for male chorus and orch.); overture *Flandre au lion;* ballads (*Philipp van Artevelde,* etc.); songs (many in the collection *Nederlandsche Zangstukken*). Even more important than Gevaert's compositions are his scholarly books: *Leerboek van den Gregoriaenschen Zang* (1856); *Traité d'instrumentation* (1863; revised and enlarged as *Nouveau traité de l'instrum.,* 1885; German translation by Riemann, 1887; Spanish by Neu-

parth, 1896; Russian by Rebikov, 1899); *Histoire et Théorie de la musique de l'antiquité* (2 vols., 1875, 1881); *Les Origines du chant liturgique de l'église latine* (1890; German translation by Riemann; threw new [for that time] light on the Gregorian tradition); *Cours méthodique d'orchestration* (2 vols., 1890; complement of *Nouveau traité*); *La Mélopée antique dans l'église latine* (1895; a monumental work); *Les Problèmes musicaux d'Aristote* (3 vols., 1899–1902; adopts the theories of Westphal, certain of which were later proved untenable); *Traité d'Harmonie théorique et pratique* (2 vols., 1905, 1907). Edited *Les Gloires de l'Italie* (a collection of vocal numbers from operas, oratorios, cantatas, etc., of the 17th and 18th centuries); *Recueil de chansons du XVe siècle* (transcribed in modern notation); *Vademecum de l'organiste* (classic transcriptions).

BIBLIOGRAPHY: F. Dufour, *Le Baron François Auguste Gevaert* (Brussels, 1909); E. Closson, *Gevaert* (Brussels, 1928).

Ghedini, Giorgio Federico, Italian composer; b. Cuneo, July 11, 1892; d. Nervi, March 25, 1965. He studied piano and organ with Evasio Lovazzano in Turin, cello with S. Grossi, and composition with G. Cravero; then at the Liceo Musicale in Bologna with M. E. Bossi, graduating in 1911. In 1918 he became instructor at the Liceo Musicale in Turin; from 1938–41, taught composition at the Cons. of Parma; in 1941, held a similar post at the Cons. of Milan; in 1951, was appointed its director.

WORKS: OPERAS: *Maria d'Alessandria* (Bergamo, Sept. 9, 1937); *Re Hassan* (Venice, Jan. 26, 1939); *La Pulce d'oro* (Genoa, Feb. 15, 1940); *Le Baccanti* (Milan, Feb. 21, 1948); *Billy Budd* (Venice, Sept. 7, 1949); *L'Ipocrita felice,* after Max Beerbohm's *The Happy Hypocrite* (Milan, March 10, 1956); *La Via della Croce* (Venice, April 9, 1961). FOR ORCH.: *Marinaresca e Baccanale* (Rome, Feb. 2, 1936); *Architecture* (Rome, Jan. 19, 1941); *Concerto dell'Albatro,* after Melville's *Moby Dick,* for narrator and small orch. (Rome, Dec. 11, 1945); Piano Concerto (1946); *Musica notturna* (1947); Concerto for 2 Pianos and Chamber Orch. (1947); Concerto for Violin and String Orch., subtitled *Il Belprato* (1947); Concerto for Flute, Violin, and Chamber Orch., subtitled *L'Alderina* (1951); Concerto for 2 Cellos and Orch., subtitled *L'Olmeneta* (1951); *Concentus Basiliensis* for violin and orch. (1954); Piano Quartet; Violin Sonata; several sacred choral works; songs; several transcriptions for modern performance of works by Monteverdi, Andrea Gabrieli, Giovanni Gabrieli, etc.

Gheluwe, Leon van, Belgian composer; b. Wanneghem-Lede, Sept. 15, 1837; d. Ghent, July 14, 1914. He studied in Ghent with Gevaert and others; became prof. at the Cons. of Ghent in 1869, and later was director of the École de Musique in Bruges. He wrote a Flemish opera *Philippine van Vlaanderen* (Brussels, 1876) and a number of songs.

Ghent, Emmanuel, American composer; b. Montreal, Canada, May 15, 1925. He studied bassoon and music theory at McGill Univ.; also took courses in psychology and psychoanalysis; eventually settled in New

York as a practicing psychiatrist. In 1964, with the aid of an engineer, he constructed the Polynome, a device capable of accurate reproduction of multiple rhythms by click signals transmitted to a performer's ear through a tiny earphone; applied this instrument in several compositions.

WORKS: *Movement* for wind quintet (1944); *3 Duos for Flutes* (1944); *Lament* for string quartet (1958); Quartet for Flute, Oboe, Clarinet and Bassoon (1960); *2 Duos* for flute and clarinet (1962); *Dance Movement* for trumpet and string quartet (1962); *Entelechy* for viola and piano (1963); *Triality I and II* for violin, trumpet and bassoon in conjunction with the Polynome (1964); *Dithyrambos* for brass quintet (1965); *Hex, an Ellipsis* for trumpet, 11 instruments and synchronized tape (1966); *Helices* for violin, piano and tape (1969). Electronic compositions include *Lady Chatterley's Lover* (1969); *L'Après-midi d'un Summit Meeting* (1970); *Our Daily Bread* (1970); *12 Electronic Highlights* (1970).

Gheorghiu, Valentin, Rumanian composer; b. Galatzi, March 21, 1928. He studied composition with Jora and Andricu at the Bucharest Cons.; then went to Paris where he studied piano with Lazare Lévy and harmony at the Paris Cons. (1937–39). His works include 2 symphonies (1949, 1956); Piano Concerto (1959); *Imagini din copilărie (Images of Youth),* suite for orch. (1961); *Burlesca* for piano and orch. (1964); String Quartet (1946); Piano Sonata (1946); Cello Sonata (1950); Piano Trio (1950); songs.

Gheyn, Matthias van den, Flemish organist and composer; b. Tirlemont, Brabant, April 7, 1721; d. Louvain, June 22, 1785. From 1741, organist at St. Peter's, Louvain, and from 1745, town "carillonneur"; he was celebrated in both capacities.

WRITINGS: *Fondements de la basse continue* (lessons and sonatinas for organ and violin); *6 Divertissements pour clavecin* (c.1760); also pieces for organ and for carillon.

BIBLIOGRAPHY: S. van Elewyck, *Matthias van den Gheyn* (Louvain, 1862).

Ghezzo, Dinu, Rumanian composer; b. Tusla, July 2, 1941. He studied music at the Bucharest Cons., graduating in 1966; then went to the U.S. where he enrolled at the Univ. of Calif., Los Angeles (Ph.D., 1973). In 1974 he was appointed to the faculty of Queens College. In 1976 he organized in N.Y. The New Repertory Ensemble, for the purpose of presenting programs of new music. His works are of a distinct modern character making use of electronic instruments. His compositions include Clarinet Sonata (1967); String Quartet (1967); *Segmenti* for clarinet, cello and piano (1968); *Music* for flutes and tapes (1971); *Kanones* for flutes, cello, harpsichord and tapes (1972); *Images* for bass flute, divider and Echoplex (1972); *Thalla* for piano, electric piano and 16 instruments (1974); Concertino for Clarinet and Winds (1975); *Ritualen* for prepared piano (1969); *Ritualen II* for prepared piano and tape (1970); *Cantos nuevos,* ballet (1977).

Ghiaurov, Nicolai, Bulgarian bass singer; b. Velimgrad, Sept. 13, 1929. He studied violin and piano in Bulgaria; then went to Moscow where he received his vocal training. He made his debut in Sofia as Don Basilio in *The Barber of Seville* in 1956; then appeared in Moscow (1958) and at La Scala in Milan (1959). He soon established himself as a fine singer; his quality of voice is that of basso cantante. He sang Méphistophèlès in *Faust* at his debut with the Metropolitan Opera in New York (Nov. 8, 1965).

Ghignone, Giovanni Pietro. See **Guignon, Jean-Pierre.**

Ghione, Franco, Italian conductor; b. Acqui, Aug. 28, 1886; d. Rome, Jan. 19, 1964. He studied violin with his father, organized a band which he later conducted. After study at the Parma Cons., he became assistant conductor to Toscanini at La Scala (1922–23). From 1937 to 1940 he was associate conductor of the Detroit Symph. Orch.

Ghis, Henri, French pianist and composer; b. Toulon, May 17, 1839; d. Paris, April 24, 1908. He studied at the Paris Cons. with Marmontel (piano); received 1st prize in 1854; also organ with Benoist (graduated in 1855). He became a fashionable piano teacher in Paris; many aristocratic ladies (to whom he dedicated his pieces) were his pupils. He was the first teacher of Ravel. He publ. salon music for piano: waltzes, mazurkas, polonaises, polkas, gavottes, caprices, etc., often with superinduced titles, as *Séduction, Menuet de la petite princesse, La Marquisette,* etc.; but his name is mostly known through his extremely popular arrangement of an old aria, which he publ. for piano as *Air Louis XIII* (1868); the actual melody was definitely not by Louis XIII; its authorship is unknown; in all probability it is an old French folksong.

Ghisi, Federico, Italian musicologist and composer; b. Shanghai, China (of Italian parents), Feb. 25, 1901. His father was a member of the diplomatic corps in China; the family returned to Italy in 1908, and settled in Milan. Ghisi studied music with Ghedini; in 1937, became instructor at the Univ. of Florence. He composed the operas *Il Dono dei Re Magi* (1959) and *Il Vagabondo e la guardia* (1960); *L'ultima visione,* oratorio after Plato's *Republic* (1968); published a number of valuable papers dealing with Italian music, among them *I Canti Carnascialeschi* (Florence, 1937); *Le Feste musicali della Firenze Medicea* (Florence, 1939); *Alle Fonti della Monodia* (Milan, 1940); edited collections of Italian Baroque works.

Ghislanzoni, Antonio, Italian writer and dramatic poet; b. Barco, near Lecco, Nov. 25, 1824; d. Caprino-Bergamasco, July 16, 1893. Intended for the church, his fine baritone voice led him to adopt the career of a stage singer (Lodi, 1846), which he speedily abandoned, however, for literary work. He became the manager of *Italia Musicale,* and was for years the editor of the Milan *Gazzetta Musicale,* to which he remained a faithful contributor till death. He wrote over 60 opera libretti, that of *Aida* being the most famous; publ. *Reminiscenze artistiche* (which contains an episode entitled *La casa di Verdi a Sant' Agata*).

BIBLIOGRAPHY: T. Mantovani, "Librettisti Verdiani, VI: Antonio Ghislanzoni," *Musica d'oggi* (March-April 1929).

Ghys, Joseph, Belgian violinist; b. Ghent, 1801; d. St. Petersburg, Aug. 22, 1848. A pupil of Lafont at Brussels Cons., he later taught in Amiens and Nantes, and, beginning in 1832, made concert tours in France, Belgium, Germany, Austria, and northern Europe. He wrote *Le Mouvement perpétuel* for violin with string quartet, a violin concerto, and other music for the violin.

Giacomelli, Geminiano, Italian composer; b. Piacenza, c.1692; d. Parma, Jan. 25, 1740. He studied with Capelli at Parma, and wrote his first opera, *Ipermestra,* in 1724. It was the first of 19 operas which he wrote for Venice, Parma, Naples, and other Italian towns; the most popular was *Cesare in Egitto* (Milan, 1735). He was maestro di cappella for the church of San Giovanni in Piacenza from 1727 to 1732; he held a similar post at Santa Casa in Loreto from 1738. His many church compositions include an oratorio, *La conversione di Santa Margherita,* and a setting of Psalm VIII for two tenors and bass.
BIBLIOGRAPHY: G. Tebaldini, *L'Archivio musicale della Cappella Lauretana* (Loreto, 1929); C. Anguissola, *Geminiano Giacomelli e Sebastiano Nasolini, musicisti piacentini* (Piacenza, 1935).

Gialdini, Gialdino, Italian conductor and composer; b. Pescia, Nov. 10, 1843; d. there, March 6, 1919. He was a pupil of T. Mabellini at Florence. His first opera, *Rosamunda* (prize opera in a competition instituted by the Pergola Theater, Florence), given in 1868 was unsuccessful; after producing 2 "opere buffe," *La Secchia rapita* (Florence, 1872) and *L'Idolo cinese* (1874), in collaboration with other musicians, he gave up opera writing, and devoted himself with success to conducting. Later he again turned to dramatic composition, producing the operas *I due soci* (Bologna, Feb. 24, 1892), *La Pupilla* (Trieste, Oct. 23, 1896), *La Bufera* (Pola, Nov. 26, 1910); these operas were successful. He also publ. *Eco della Lombardia,* a collection of 50 folksongs.

Gianettini (or **Zanettini**), **Antonio,** Italian composer; b. 1648; d. Munich, July 12, 1721. He was organist at San Marco, Venice (1676-86); produced 2 operas in Venice, winning a reputation that led to his appointment as maestro di cappella at the court of Modena; was organist at Modena from 1686 till 1721, except during 1695, when he brought out 3 operas in Hamburg. He moved to Munich with his family in May, 1721. He composed 6 operas; 6 oratorios; several cantatas; a Kyrie *a* 5; and Psalms *a* 4, with instruments (Venice, 1717).
BIBLIOGRAPHY: E. J. Luin, *Antonio Gianettini e la musica a Modena alla fine del secolo 17* (Modena, 1931).

Gianneo, Luis, Argentinian composer; b. Buenos Aires, Jan. 9, 1897; d. there, Aug. 15, 1968. He studied composition with Gaito and Drangosch. From 1923 to 1943 he taught at the Instituto musical in Tucumán; then was prof. of music at various schools in Buenos Aires. He was especially interested in the problems of musical education of the very young; in 1945 he organized and conducted the "Orquesta sinfónica juvenil argentina"; from 1955 to 1960 he was director of the Cons. of Buenos Aires.
WORKS: 3 symphonies (1938, 1945, 1963); *Turay-Turay,* symph. poem (Buenos Aires, Sept. 21, 1929); *Obertura para una comedia infantil* (1939); Sinfonietta (Buenos Aires, Sept. 20, 1943); Violin Concerto (Buenos Aires, April 13, 1944); *Variaciones sobre tema de tango* for orch. (1953); 4 string quartets; 2 piano trios; String Trio; Violin Sonata; Cello Sonata; teaching pieces for piano; 3 Piano Sonatas; songs.

Giannetti, Giovanni, Italian composer; b. Naples, March 25, 1869; d. Rio de Janeiro, Dec. 10, 1934. He studied in Naples, Trieste, and Vienna; 1912-13, director of the Liceo Musicale, Siena; 1915, in Rome, where (from 1920) he was musical director of the Teatro dei Piccoli with which he toured Europe and South America.
WORKS: Operas: *L'Erebo* (Naples, April 9, 1891), *Padron Maurizio* (Naples, Sept. 26, 1896), *Milena* (Naples, Nov. 15, 1897), *Il Violinaro di Cremona* (Milan, Nov. 23, 1898), *Don Marzio* (Venice, March 2, 1903), *Il Cristo alla festa di Purim* (Rio de Janeiro, Dec. 16, 1904), *Il Nazareno* (Buenos Aires, Jan. 20, 1911), *La Serenata di Pierrot,* pantomime (Rome, April 18, 1917), *Cuore e bautte* (Rome, June 5, 1918), and *Il Principe Re,* operetta (Rome, July 7, 1920).

Giannini, Dusolina, American soprano, sister of **Vittorio Giannini;** b. Philadelphia, Dec. 19, 1902. She received her earliest musical education at home; her mother was a violinist; her father, **Ferruccio Giannini** (1869-1948), was an Italian tenor who made one of the earliest phonograph recordings in 1896. She studied voice with Marcella Sembrich; made her concert debut in N.Y., March 14, 1920. In 1927 she made her operatic debut in Hamburg, and subsequently sang in opera in London, Berlin and Vienna. On Feb. 12, 1936, she appeared with the Metropolitan Opera in the role of Aida, and remained on its staff until 1940. She sang the part of Hester in the first performance of the opera *The Scarlet Letter,* by her brother, **Vittorio Giannini** (Hamburg, June 2, 1938).

Giannini, Vittorio, American composer, brother of **Dusolina Giannini;** b. Philadelphia, Oct. 19, 1903; d. New York, Nov. 28, 1966. Brought up in a musical family he showed a precocious talent. He was sent to Italy at the age of 10, and studied at the Cons. of Milan (1913-17). After returning to the U.S. he took private lessons with Martini and Trucco in New York; in 1925 he entered the Juilliard graduate school where he was a pupil of Rubin Goldmark in composition and with Hans Letz in violin; in 1932 he won the American Prix de Rome; went to Rome for a period of 4 years. Upon his return to New York he was appointed to the faculty of the Juilliard School of Music in 1939 as teacher of composition and orchestration; in 1941 he also became instructor in music theory; furthermore, he was appointed prof. of composition at the Curtis Institute of Music in Philadelphia in 1956. As a composer, Giannini was at his best in opera, writing music of fine emotional éclat, excelling in the art of bel canto and avoiding extreme modernistic usages; in his symphonic works he also continued the rich Italian tradition; these qualities endeared him with opera singers, but at the same time left his music out of the mainstream of the modern century.

WORKS: the operas: *Lucedia* (Munich, Oct. 20, 1934); *Flora* (1937); *The Scarlet Letter* (Hamburg, June 2, 1938); *Beauty and the Beast* (1938; concert version, CBS Radio, Nov. 24, 1938; stage première, Hartford, Connecticut, Feb. 14, 1946); *Blennerhasset*, radio opera (CBS Radio, Nov. 22, 1939); *The Taming of the Shrew* (his most appreciated opera; in concert form, Cincinnati Symph. Orch., Jan. 31, 1953; in color telecast, NBC opera theater, March 13, 1954); *The Harvest* (Chicago, Nov. 25, 1961); *Rehearsal Call*, opera buffa (N.Y., Feb. 15, 1962); *The Servant of Two Masters* (posthumous, N.Y., March 9, 1967); for orch.: Symphony, subtitled "In Memoriam Theodore Roosevelt" (1935; N.Y., NBC Orch., Jan. 19, 1936, composer conducting); I.B.M. Symph., commissioned for New York World's Fair (1939); 4 numbered symphonies: No. 1, *Sinfonia* (Cincinnati, April 6, 1951); No. 2 (St. Louis, April 16, 1956); No. 3 for band (1958); No. 4 (N.Y., May 26, 1960); 3 Divertimentos (1953, 1961, 1964); *Psalm 130, concerto for double bass and orch.* (Brevard, N.C., Aug. 9, 1963); *The Medead*, monodrama for soprano and orch. (Atlanta, Georgia, Oct. 20, 1960); Piano Concerto (1937); Organ Concerto (1937); Concerto for 2 Pianos (1940); several sacred works for chorus; *Canticle of the Martyrs* (commissioned for the 500th anniversary of the Moravian Church, 1957, at Winston-Salem, North Carolina); Concerto Grosso for Strings (1931); Piano Quintet (1931); Woodwind Quintet (1933); Piano Trio (1933); 2 violin sonatas (1926, 1945); Piano Sonata; many songs.

Giarda, Luigi Stefano, Italian cellist and composer; b. Cassolnuovo, Pavia, March 19, 1868; d. Viña del Mar, Chile, Jan. 3, 1953. He was a pupil at the Milan Cons.; teacher at the Padua music school (1893-97); instructor at the Royal Cons. in Naples (1897-1910); then went to Santiago, Chile, where he was vice-director of the Cons. of Santiago; also taught theory there.

WORKS: the operas *Reietto* (Naples, 1898) and *Giorgio Byron* (Santiago, Chile, 1910); symph. poems, *Loreley*; *La vida*; *Triptico* (*Civilization, War, Peace*) for 3 voices and orch.; concert pieces for cello and orch.; a string quartet; *Adagio* for 4 celli; 2 cello sonatas; Prelude and Scherzo for violin and cello.

Giardini, Felice de', Italian violinist and composer; b. Turin, April 12, 1716, d. Moscow, June 8, 1796. He was a chorister at the cathedral of Milan; studied singing with Paladini and violin with Somis. As a young man he played in various theater orchestras in Rome and Naples and often improvised cadenzas at the end of operatic numbers. He acquired popularity in Italy and made a tour in Germany (1748); then went to London (1750) where he made a series of successful appearances as a concert violinist. In 1752 he joined the Italian opera in London as concertmaster and conductor; he became its impresario in 1756, and was connected with the management, with interruptions, for several

more seasons, returning to the career of virtuoso and teacher in 1766. He conducted the "Three Choirs" festival (1770-76) and was concertmaster at the "Pantheon Concerts" (1774-80); also conducted other theater orchestras. From 1784-89 he was in Italy, but returned to London in 1789 and led three seasons of Italian opera, without financial success. In 1796 he was engaged as violinist in Russia and gave his initial concert in Moscow on March 24, 1796, but soon became ill, and died shortly afterwards. As a violinist he was eclipsed in London by Salomon and Cramer, but he left his mark on musical society there.

WORKS: among operas entirely by him were: *Rosmira* (April 30, 1757), *Siroe* (Dec. 13, 1763), *Enea e Lavinia* (May 5, 1764), and *Il re pastore* (March 7, 1765); he also wrote music for various pasticcios; also wrote several overtures, concertos, string quartets, and violin sonatas.

BIBLIOGRAPHY: R. A. Mooser, *Annales de la musique et des musiciens en Russie au XVIIIe: siècle* (Lausanne, 1951; vol. 2, p. 657f.).

Giazotto, Remo, Italian musicologist; b. Rome, Sept. 4, 1910. He studied piano at the Milan Cons. and later took a course in literature at the Univ. of Genoa; undertook a detailed study of the musical history of Genoa, and publ. a work of fundamental value, *La musica a Genova nella vita pubblica e privata dal XIII al XVIII secolo* (1952). He is also the author of a definitive biography of Tomaso Albinoni (Milan, 1945), containing newly discovered materials as well as a thematic catalogue. He further publ. a monograph, *Ferruccio Busoni, la vita nell' opera* (Milan, 1948).

Gibbons, Christopher, English organist and composer; b. London (baptized Aug. 22), 1615; d. there, Oct. 20, 1676. He was the son of **Orlando Gibbons;** pupil at the Chapel Royal; in 1638, he became organist at Winchester Cathedral; in 1660, he was appointed organist of the Chapel Royal, private organist to Charles II, and organist at Westminster Abbey. He received the degree of Mus. D. from Oxford in 1663, at the special request of the king. He wrote anthems and many string fantasies, now in MS in the British Library, Christ Church, Oxford, the Royal College of Music, Marsh's Library, Dublin, and Durham and Ely Cathedrals; some of his motets are in Playford's 'Cantica sacra' (1674). He also collaborated with Matthew Locke in the music for Shirley's masque, *Cupid and Death.*

Gibbons, Edward, English musician; b. Cambridge, 1568; d. probably Exeter, c.1650. The eldest living son of **William Gibbons,** who founded this musical family, he was the brother of **Ellis** and **Orlando.** He received a B. Mus. degree from both Oxford and Cambridge; after serving as a lay clerk at King's College, Cambridge, he became master of choristers in 1593, and kept the post until 1598, when he went to Exeter Cathedral, where he served for many years, with the titles of "priest-vicar" and succentor, though he remained a layman. Little of his music is in existence; a few of his compositions, all for the church, are in the

British Library, at Christ Church, Oxford, and in the Bodleian Library.

Gibbons, Ellis, English composer and organist, brother of **Edward** and **Orlando Gibbons;** b. Cambridge, 1573; d. May, 1603. The only compositions of his which are known to exist are two madrigals included by Morley in his collection *The Triumphs of Oriana* (*Long live fair Oriana* and *Round about her charret*).

Gibbons, Orlando, celebrated English composer and organist, brother of **Edward** and **Ellis Gibbons;** b. Oxford (baptized Dec. 25), 1583; d. Canterbury, June 5, 1625. He was taken to Cambridge as a small child; in 1596, he became chorister at King's College there; matriculated in 1598; composed music for various occasions for King's College (1602-3). On March 21, 1605, he was appointed organist of the Chapel Royal, retaining this position until his death. He received the degree of B. Mus. from Cambridge Univ. in 1606. In 1619 he became chamber musician to the King; in 1623, organist at Westminster Abbey. He conducted the music for the funeral of James I (1625); died of apoplexy 2 months later. His fame as a composer rests chiefly on his church music; he employed the novel technique of the 'verse anthem' (a work for chorus and solo voices, the solo passages having independent instrumental accompaniment, either for organ or strings); other works followed the traditional polyphonic style, of which Gibbons became a master. He was also one of the greatest English organists of the time.

WORKS: *Fantasies of 3 Parts . . . composed for viols* (1610; described on the title page as 'Cut in copper, the like not heretofore extant in England'; ed. by E. F. Rimbault in *Musical Antiquarian Society* vol. 9; new ed. by E. H. Fellowes, 1924); pieces for the virginal, in *Parthenia* (1611, 21 pieces of Gibbons, Byrd, and John Bull; repr. in *Musical Antiquarian Society* vol. 18; new ed. by Margaret H. Glyn, 1927); *The First Set of Madrigals and Mottets of 5 Parts* (London, 1612; repr. *Musical Antiquarian Society* vol. 3; new ed. by E. H. Fellowes in *The English Madrigal School* vol. 5, 1921); 9 Fancies, appended to *20 konincklijke Fantasien op 3 Fiolen* by Th. Lupo, Coperario, and Wm. Daman (Amsterdam, 1648); 2 anthems in Leighton's *Teares or Lamentacions of a Sorrowfull Soule* (the only sacred works by Gibbons publ. during his lifetime). A 'complete' ed. of all extant sacred compositions in *Tudor Church Music* 4; Gibbons's entire keyboard works were ed. by Margaret H. Glyn in 5 vols. (London, 1925); also *Musica Britannica* 20. Further new eds. follow: The madrigal *God give you good morrow* (from *The Cryes of London*, an early 17th cent. MS [in the Brit. Museum] containing 2 other sets of street cries likewise polyphonically treated by T. Weelkes and R. Deering, ed. by Sir Fred. Bridge (London, 1920); 2 Fantazias for string quartet or small string orch. and a pavan and galliard for string sextet or small string orch., ed. by E. H. Fellowes (London, 1925); 10 pieces from the virginal book of B. Cosyn, arranged for modern organ by J. A. Fuller-Maitland (London, 1925).

BIBLIOGRAPHY: E. H. Fellowes, *The English Mad-*

rigal Composers (1921); Margaret H. Glyn, *About Elizabethan Virginal Music and Its Composers* (1924); E. H. Fellowes, *Orlando Gibbons, a Short Account of His Life and Work* (1925); and *Orlando Gibbons and His Family* (1951).

Gibbs, Cecil Armstrong, English composer; b. Great Baddow near Chelmsford, Aug. 10, 1889; d. Chelmsford, May 12, 1960. He studied at Trinity College, Cambridge, and at the Royal College of Music in London; later became an instructor there; in 1934 he received the Cobbett Gold Medal for his services to British chamber music.

WORKS: the operas *The Blue Peter* (1924), *Twelfth Night* (1947), and *The Great Bell of Burley* (children's opera, 1949); 3 symphonies; *Spring Garland* for strings; Oboe Concerto; *Peacock Pie*, suite for piano and strings; Rhapsody for Violin and Orch.; *Essex Suite* for strings; several string quartets; a lyric sonata for violin and piano; Piano Trio; cantatas: *La Belle Dame sans Merci*, *The Lady of Shalott*, *Deborah and Barak*, *Before Daybreak*, *Odyssey*; also a Pastoral Suite for baritone, chorus, and orch. (1951). Gibbs has written more than 100 songs, many of them to poems of Walter de la Mare. His musical style adheres to the Romantic school; the influence of folk melodies and rhythms is also noticeable. See the entry on Gibbs in Cobbett's *Cyclopedic Survey of Chamber Music.*

Gibson, Archer, American organist; b. Baltimore, Dec. 5, 1875; d. Lake Mahopac, N.Y., July 15, 1952. He studied with his father, later with W. G. Owst (composition) and Harold Randolph (organ and piano); held various positions as church organist; wrote the cantatas *Emancipation* and *A Song to Music;* an opera, *Yzdra;* organ pieces; choral and orchestral arrangements.

Gideon, Miriam, American composer; b. Greeley, Colorado, Oct. 23, 1906. She studied piano with Hans Barth in N.Y. and with Felix Fox in Boston; then enrolled at Boston Univ. (B.A., 1926) and took courses in musicology at Columbia Univ. (M.A., 1946); studied composition privately with Lazare Saminsky and Roger Sessions. She served on the music faculty of Brooklyn College (1944-54) and was prof. of music at the City Univ. of N.Y. (1971-76); elected to the American Academy and Institute of Arts and Letters in 1975. She wrote music in all genres, in a style distinguished by its attractive modernism.

WORKS: an opera, *Fortunato* (1958), *The Adorable Mouse*, a French folk tale for narrator and chamber orch. (1960); *Lyric Piece* for string orch. (1941); *Symphonia Brevis* (1953); *Songs of Youth and Madness* for voice and orch. on poems of Friedrich Hölderlin (1977); String Quartet (1946); Viola Sonata (1948); *Fantasy on a Javanese Motive* for cello and piano (1948); Divertimento for Woodwind Quartet (1948); *Biblical Masks* for violin and piano (1960); Cello Sonata (1961); Suite for Clarinet and Piano (1972); *Fantasy on an Irish Folk Motive* for oboe, viola, bassoon and vibraphone (1975); *The Hound of Heaven,* to the poem by Francis Thompson, for voice, violin, viola, cello and oboe (1945); *Sonnets from Shakespeare* for voice, trumpet and string quartet (1950); *Sonnets* from "*Fatal Interview*," after Edna St. Vincent Millay, for voice, violin, viola and cello (1952); *The Condemned Playground* for soprano and instruments (1963); *Questions on Nature* for voice, oboe, piano, tamtam, and glockenspiel (1965); *Rhymes from the Hill,* after the *Galgenlieder* of Christian Morgenstern, for voice, clarinet, cello and marimba (1968); *The Seasons of Time,* after Japanese poetry, for voice, flute, cello and piano (1969); Clarinet Sonata (1973); *Nocturnes* for voice, flute, oboe, violin, cello, and vibraphone (1976); *Canzona* for piano (1945); *6 Cuckoos in Quest of a Composer* for piano (1953); Piano Sonata (1977); choruses and songs.

Gieburowski, Waclaw, eminent Polish musicologist; b. Bydgoszcz, Feb. 6, 1876; d. Warsaw, Sept. 17, 1943. He was a student of theology in Regensburg, where he also took courses in church music with Haberl; then in Berlin with Wolf and Kretzschmar and in Breslau with Otto Kinkeldey; obtained a doctorate with his dissertation *Die Musica Magistri Szydlowitae, ein polnischer Choraltraktat des 15. Jahrhunderts* (1913; publ. Poznán, 1915). He settled in Poznán as prof. of church music at the Univ.; in 1916 was appointed choir conductor at the Poznán cathedral; wrote church music. In 1928 he began the publication of the valuable series *Cantica Selecta Musices Sacrae in Polonia;* restored to use many sacred works by Polish composers of the Renaissance; published several treatises on this subject; also composed several sacred choral works.

Giegling, Franz, Swiss musicologist; b. Buchs, near Aarau, Feb. 27, 1921. He studied piano and theory at the Zürich Cons. with Cherbuliez; received his Ph.D. with the valuable dissertation, *Giuseppe Torelli, ein Beitrag zur Entwicklungsgeschichte des italienischen Konzerts* (1949); was music critic of the *Neue Zürcher Zeitung* (1949–55); contributed articles to *Die Musik in Geschichte und Gegenwart.*

Gielen, Michael, German conductor; b. Dresden, July 20, 1927. He received his musical training in Buenos Aires, where his father Josef Gielen, an operatic director, emigrated in 1939. Returning to Europe in 1951, he became assistant conductor at the Vienna State Opera, until 1960; then was principal conductor at the Royal Opera in Stockholm (1960–65); in 1969 appointed principal conductor of the Orchestre National de Belgique in Brussels. Gielen is also a composer; he wrote Variations for 40 Instruments (1959); *Pentaphonie* for piano, 5 soloists and 5 quintets (1960–63); and other chamber music.

Gieseking, Walter, distinguished pianist; b. Lyons, France, of German parents, Nov. 5, 1895; d. London, Oct. 26, 1956. He studied with Karl Leimer at the Hannover Cons., graduating in 1916; then served in the German army during World War I; began his concert career with extensive tours of Europe; made his American debut at Aeolian Hall, N.Y., Feb. 22, 1926, and after that appeared regularly in the U.S. and Europe with orchestras and in solo recitals. He became one of the most brilliant and musicianly pianists of his generation, capable of profound and intimate inter-

pretations of both classical and modern piano music. His dual German-French background enabled him to project with the utmost authenticity the piano masterpieces of both cultures. His playing of Debussy was remarkable; he was also an excellent performer of works by Prokofiev and other modernists. He composed some chamber music and made piano transcriptions of songs by Richard Strauss. He became the center of a political controversy when he arrived in the U.S. early in 1949 for a concert tour; he was accused of cultural collaboration with Nazi regime, and public protests forced the cancellation of his scheduled performances at Carnegie Hall. However, he was later cleared by an Allied court in Germany and was able to resume his career in America. He appeared again at a Carnegie Hall recital on April 22, 1953, and until his death continued to give numerous performances in both hemispheres. His autobiography *So Wurde ich Pianist* was publ. posthumously in Wiesbaden, 1963.

BIBLIOGRAPHY: B. Gavoty, *Gieseking,* in the series *Les grands interprètes* (Geneva, 1955).

Gigli, Beniamino, famous Italian tenor; b. Recanati, March 20, 1890; d. Rome, Nov. 30, 1957. He studied with Rosati in Rome; made his operatic debut in Rovigo, near Venice, in 1914, as Enzo in *La Gioconda;* then sang in many Italian cities. His first American appearance was as Faust in Boito's *Mefistofele* with the Metropolitan Opera (Nov. 26, 1920); he remained on its staff until 1932, and returned there for one season in 1938. He then went back to Italy, where he remained during World War II. He revisited the U.S. in 1955 and gave a series of concerts with considerable success despite his age. At the height of his career, he ranked among the best tenors in opera; he was particularly impressive in the lyric roles of Verdi's and Puccini's operas; he also sang in the German and French repertory; his interpretation of Lohengrin was acclaimed. His voice possessed great strength and a variety of expressive powers.

BIBLIOGRAPHY: R. Rosner, *Beniamino Gigli* (Vienna, 1929); R. de Rensis, *Il cantatore del popolo: Beniamino Gigli* (Rome, 1933; in German, Munich, 1936); D. Silvestrini, *Beniamino Gigli* (Bologna, 1937). Gigli's memoirs were publ. in English at London (1957).

Gigout, Eugène, French organ virtuoso and composer; b. Nancy, March 23, 1844; d. Paris, Dec. 9, 1925. He began music studies in the *maîtrise* of Nancy Cathedral; at 13 he entered the Niedermeyer School at Paris, in which he subsequently taught from 1863–85, and from 1900–5; for a time, pupil of Saint-Saëns. From 1863, Gigout was organist at the church of St.-Augustin; he won fame as a concert organist in France, England, Germany, Switzerland, Spain, and Italy; he was especially famous for his masterly improvisations. In 1885 he founded at Paris an organ school subsidized by the government, from which many excellent pupils graduated (Boëllmann, Fauré, Messager, A. Georges, A. Roussel, C. Terrasse, etc.); from 1911, prof. of organ and improvisation at the National Cons., Paris. He was also an esteemed writer on music and critic; Commander of the Order of Isabella la Católica; Officer of Public Instruction (from 1885); and Chevalier of the Legion of Honor (from 1895). As a composer he followed the severe style.

WORKS: For organ: *Cent pièces brèves* (Gregorian), *Album Grégorien* (3 vols., each containing 100 pieces exclusively in the church modes), *Rhapsodie sur des Noëls, Toccata, Scherzo, Prélude et Fugue* in B-flat, *Marche de Fête, Rhapsodie sur des Airs Catalans, Rhapsodie sur des Airs Canadiens, Poèmes Mystiques,* Piano Sonata in F; other pieces for piano (2 and 4 hands); sacred choruses, songs.

BIBLIOGRAPHY: *Hommage à Eugène Gigout* (Paris, 1923; contains a biographical sketch by Gabriel Fauré and catalogue of works).

Gilardi, Gilardo, Argentine (opera) composer; b. San Fernando, May 25, 1889; d. Buenos Aires, Jan. 16, 1963. He studied with Pablo Berutti, then devoted himself to teaching and composing. Two of his operas were produced at the Teatro Colón in Buenos Aires: *Ilse* (July 13, 1923); *La Leyenda de Urutaú* (Oct. 25, 1934). He also wrote Sinfonia Cíclico (1961), 3 piano trios, 2 string quartets, *Sonata Popular Argentina* for violin and piano (1939) and many dances and songs based on native melodies.

Gilbert, Henry Franklin Belknap, remarkable American composer; b. Somerville, Mass., Sept. 26, 1868; d. Cambridge, Mass., May 19, 1928. He studied at the New England Cons. and with E. Mollenhauer; 1889–92, pupil of MacDowell (composition) in Boston. Rather than do routine music work to earn his livelihood (he had previously been violinist in theaters, etc.), he took jobs of many descriptions, becoming, in turn, a real-estate agent, a factory foreman, a collector of butterflies in Florida, etc., and composed when opportunity afforded. In 1893, at the Chicago World's Fair, he met a Russian prince who knew Rimsky-Korsakov and gave him many details of contemporary Russian composers whose work, as well as that of Bohemian and Scandinavian composers which was based on folksong, influenced Gilbert greatly in his later composition. In 1895 he made his 1st trip abroad and stayed in Paris, subsequently returning to the U.S.; when he heard of the première of Charpentier's *Louise* he became intensely interested in the work because of its popular character, and, in order to hear it, earned his passage to Paris, in 1901, by working on a cattle-boat; the opera impressed him so that he decided to devote his entire time thereafter to composition. In 1902 he became associated with Arthur Farwell, whose Wa-Wan Press published Gilbert's early compositions. During this time (from 1903) he employed Negro tunes and rhythms extensively in his works. The compositions of his mature period (from 1915) reveal an original style, not founded on any particular native American material, but infused with elements from many sources, and are an attempt at 'unEuropean' music, expressing the spirit of America and its national characteristics.

WORKS: OPERA: *The Fantasy in Delft* (1915). FOR ORCH.: *Two Episodes* (Boston, Jan. 13, 1896); *Humoresque on Negro-Minstrel Tunes* (originally entitled *Americanesque,* 1903; Boston Pops, May 24, 1911); *Comedy Overture on Negro Themes* (1905; perf. at a

N.Y. municipal concert, Aug. 17, 1910; Boston Symph., April 13, 1911; also perf. by Glière, in Feodosia, Crimea, July 22, 1914, and in Odessa, Aug. 1, 1914); symph. poem, *The Dance in Place Congo* (1906; perf. as ballet at the Metropolitan Opera, N.Y., March 23, 1918); *Strife* (1910); *Negro Rhapsody* (Norfolk, Conn., Festival, June 5, 1913, composer conducting; symph. prologue for Synge's *Riders to the Sea* (1904; MacDowell Festival, Peterboro, N.H., Aug. 20, 1914; rev. version, N.Y. Philharmonic, Nov. 11, 1917); *American Dances* (1915); *Indian Sketches* (Boston Symph., March 4, 1921); Suite from *Music to Pilgrim Tercentenary Pageant* (Boston Symph., March 31, 1922); *Symphonic Piece* (Boston Symph., Feb. 26, 1926); *Nocturne,* a 'symphonic mood' after Walt Whitman (Philadelphia, March 16, 1928); Suite for Chamber Orchestra (commissioned by the E. S. Coolidge Foundation; first perf., Chamber Orch. of Boston, Slonimsky conducting, April 28, 1928); *To Thee, America,* a hymn for chorus and orch. (MacDowell Festival, Peterboro, N.H., Jan. 25, 1915); *Salammbô's Invocation to Tänith,* aria for soprano and orch. (N.Y., Elise Stevens, with the Russian Symph. Orch., March 10, 1906); an early string quartet. FOR PIANO: *Negro Episode, Mazurka, Scherzo, Two Verlaine Moods, The Island of the Fay* (also for orch.), *Indian Scenes, A Rag Bag, Negro Dances.* Songs: *Pirate Song,* after Stevenson; *Celtic Studies,* a cycle of 4 songs to poems by Irish poets; *The Lament of Deirdre; Faery Song; Two South American Gypsy Songs; Fish Wharf Rhapsody: Give me the Splendid Sun; The Owl; Orlamonde; Zephyrus; Homesick; Tell Me Where is Fancy Bred?; Croon of the Dew; Eight Simple Songs; Perdita; The Curl; School Songs;* also edited *100 Folksongs* (Boston, 1910); contributed articles to the *Musical Quarterly* ("The American Composer," April 1915; "The Survival of Music," July 1916; "Originality," Jan. 1919), and to other magazines.

BIBLIOGRAPHY: Arthur Farwell, "*Wanderjahre* of a Revolutionist," *Musical America* (April 10, 1909); "An American Composer's Triumph in Russia," *Current Opinion* (May 1916); E. C. Ranck, "The Mark Twain of American Music," *Theatre Magazine* (Sept. 1917); Olin Downes, "An American Composer," *Musical Quarterly* (Jan. 1918); "Gilbert, Henry," *Dictionary of American Biography* (vol. 7, N.Y., 1931); J. T. Howard, *Our American Music* (N.Y., 1939, and subsequent eds.); Olin Downes, "Henry Gilbert: Nonconformist," in *A Birthday Greeting to Carl Engel* (N.Y., 1943); E. Carter, "American Figure," *Modern Music* (1943); H. G. Sear, "H. F. Gilbert," *Music Review* (1944); Gilbert Chase, *America's Music* (N.Y., 1955; 2nd ed. 1966).

Gilbert, Jean (pen name of **Max Winterfeld**), German operetta composer; b. Hamburg, Feb. 11, 1879; d. Buenos Aires, Dec. 20, 1942. He studied with Scharwenka; was active as theater conductor in Hamburg and Berlin. In 1933 he left Germany, eventually settling in Buenos Aires.

WORKS: the operettas *Die keusche Susanne* (1910), *Polnische Wirtschaft* (1910), *Die Kino-Königin* (1911), *Püppchen* (1912), *Die Frau im Hermelin* (1918), *Die Braut des Lucullus* (1920), *Katja, die Tänzerin* (1922), *Das Weib im Purpur* (1923), *In der Jo-*

hannisnacht (1926), *Hotel Stadt Lemberg* (1929), *Das Mädel am Steuer* (1930). The song *Puppchen, du bist mein Augenstern,* from the operetta *Puppchen,* achieved immense popularity in Europe.

Gilbert, L. Wolfe, American songwriter; b. Odessa, Russia, Aug. 31, 1886; d. Beverly Hills, Calif., July 12, 1970. His family went to Philadelphia when he was an infant; at 14 he went to New York and sang in vaudeville, burlesque theaters and nightclubs; he also toured as an entertainer with John L. Sullivan, the prize fighter. In 1912 he wrote his first hit song, *Waitin' for the Robert E. Lee.* He settled in Hollywood in 1929, where he formed his own publishing company. He composed some 250 songs, of which several became perennial favorites: *Ramona* (written for a motion picture in 1927); *Peanut Vendor, Down Yonder,* and *Lucky Lindy,* inspired by Lindbergh's transatlantic flight of 1927.

Gilbert, Timothy, piano maker in Boston. After 1820 made several innovations of his own invention to improve the action of the piano. Brought out the organ-piano in 1847.

Gilbert, Sir William Schwenck, British playwright, creator with Sir Arthur Sullivan of the famous series of comic operas; b. London, Nov. 18, 1836; d. Harrow Weald, Middlesex, May 29, 1911 (of cardiac arrest following a successful attempt to rescue a young woman swimmer from drowning). He was given an excellent education (at Boulogne and at King's College, London) by his father, who was a novelist. After a routine career as a clerk, Gilbert drifted into journalism, contributing drama criticism and humorous verse to London periodicals. His satirical wit was first revealed in a theater piece, *Dulcamara* (1886), in which he ridiculed grand opera. He met Sullivan in 1871, and together they initiated the productions of comic operas which suited them so perfectly. Some plots borrow ludicrous situations from actual Italian and French operas; Gilbert's libretti, in rhymed verse, were none the less unmistakably English. This insularity of wit may explain the enormous popularity of the Gilbert & Sullivan operas in English-speaking countries, while they are practically unknown on the Continent. Despite the fact that the targets of Gilbert's ridicule were usually the upper classes of Great Britain, the operas were often performed at court. He was knighted in 1907. After 20 years of fruitful cooperation with Sullivan, a conflict developed, and the two severed their relationship for a time. A reconciliation was effected, but the subsequent productions fell short of their greatest successes. The most popular of the Gilbert & Sullivan operettas are *H.M.S. Pinafore* (1878); *The Pirates of Penzance* (1880); *Iolanthe* (1884); *The Mikado* (1885), and *The Gondoliers* (1889). A special theater, the Savoy, was built for the Gilbert & Sullivan productions in London in 1881 by the impresario Richard D'Oyly Carte.
BIBLIOGRAPHY: W. S. Gilbert, *Gilbert before Sullivan; Six Comic Plays,* ed. by J. W. Stedman (Chicago, 1967); J. W. Stedman, "From Dame to Woman: W. S. Gilbert and Theatrical Transvestism," *Victorian Studies* (Sept. 1970); see also entry under Sullivan.

Gilberté, Hallett, American song composer; b. Winthrop, Maine, March 14, 1872; d. New York, Jan. 5, 1946. He studied piano with J. Orth and C. Barmann and composition with E. Nevin in Boston. He wrote about 250 songs, some of which were quite successful *(Spanish Serenade, Mother's Cradle Song, In Reverie, Two Roses, Song of the Canoe, Ah, Love but a Day, Spring Serenade, Minuet La Phyllis, Moonlight and Starlight).*

Gilboa, Jacob, Czech-born Israeli composer; b. Košice, May 2, 1920. He grew up in Vienna and went to Palestine in 1938. He studied composition with Josef Tal in Jerusalem and Ben-Haim in Tel Aviv (1944–47); then traveled to Germany and attended courses of new music with Stockhausen, Pousseur, Alois Kontarsky and Caskel. His music represents a blend of oriental and Eastern Mediterranean idioms, basically lyrical, but technically ultra-modern.
WORKS: *7 Little Insects,* piano pieces for children (1955); *Wild Flowers,* 4 lyrical pieces for female voice, horn, harp and string orch. (1957); *Passing Clouds* for female voice, clarinet, cello and piano (1958); Violin Sonata (1960); *The Twelve Jerusalem Chagall Windows* for voices and instruments (1966); *The Beth Alpha Mosaic* for female voice, chamber ensemble and tape (1975; Chicago, Jan. 24, 1976); *Crystals* for flute, viola, cello, piano and percussion (1967); *Horizons in Violet and Blue,* ballet scene for 6 players (1970); *Pastels* for 2 prepared pianos (1970); *Thistles,* theater piece for singing and speaking voices, horn, cello, piano and percussion (1970); *Cedars* for orch. (1971); *From the Dead Sea Scrolls* for chorus, children's chorus, 2 organs, tape and orch. (1971; Hamburg, Jan. 11, 1972); *14 Epigrams for Oscar Wilde* for female voice, piano and tape (1973); *Bedu,* metamorphoses on a Bedouin call, for male voice, cello, flute and piano (1975); *5 Red Sea Impressions* for violin, piano, harp, electric guitar, organ and tape (1976).

Gilchrist, William Wallace, American composer; b. Jersey City, N.J., Jan. 8, 1846; d. Easton, Pa., Dec. 20, 1916. He studied organ with H. A. Clarke at the Univ. of Penna., which conferred on him the degree of Mus. Doc. in 1896. He was a choirmaster at various Philadelphia churches; from 1882, taught at the Philadelphia Music Academy. He formed the Mendelssohn Club and was its conductor later. He wrote cantatas, a Christmas oratorio, 2 symphonies, chamber music, church music, and songs.
BIBLIOGRAPHY: Sumner Salter, "Early Encouragement to American Composers," *Musical Quarterly* (Jan. 1932).

Gilels, Emil, outstanding Russian pianist; b. Odessa, Oct. 19, 1916. He studied at the Odessa Cons. with Yakov Tkatch and Berthe Ringold, graduating in 1935; then went to Moscow for advanced piano studies with Heinrich Neuhaus at the Moscow Cons. (1935–38). He made his first public appearance at the age of 13 in Odessa; in 1933 he received first prize at the Moscow competition; in 1936 he carried 2nd prize at the international piano competition in Vienna, and in 1938 won the first prize at the prestigious international competition in Brussels, which marked the highest point of his career; also in 1938 he was appointed prof. at the Moscow Cons. He made numerous appearances in concert recitals and as soloist with major orchestras of Europe, America and the Far East; he made his first American tour in 1955, and returned at regular intervals; in 1977 he toured the U.S. for the 12th time. His playing is distinguished by a quality of romantic intellectuality, with a fine understanding of the special pianistic sonorities. At several of his tours he played all five Beethoven piano concertos in succession.

BIBLIOGRAPHY: V. Delson, *Emil Gilels* (Moscow, 1959); S. Hentova, *Emil Gilels* (Moscow, 1967).

Giles, Nathaniel, English organist and composer of church music; b. Worcester, c.1558; d. Windsor, Jan. 24, 1633. A son of **Thomas Giles,** organist of St. Paul's Cathedral, London, he studied at Oxford; was organist at Worcester Cathedral from 1581 to 1585, when he became clerk, organist, and choirmaster at St. George's Chapel, Windsor; in 1596, he took over the same duties at the Chapel Royal; in 1597, became Gentleman and Master of the Children there. He wrote four services for the Church; a great number of anthems; several motets and a 5-part madrigal (incomplete or in MS). Some of his compositions are included in Leighton's *Teares or Lamentacions of a Sorrowfull Soule* (1614); a service and an anthem are in Barnard's *Church Music* (1641); Hawkins's *History of Music* contains Giles's *Lesson of Descant of thirty-eighte Proportions of sundrie Kindes*.

BIBLIOGRAPHY: J. Pulver, "Nathaniel Giles," *Monthly Musical Record* (Nov. 1933).

Gilibert, Charles, dramatic baritone; b. Paris, Nov. 29, 1866; d. New York, Oct. 10, 1910. He sang one season at the Opéra-Comique, and then went to the Théâtre de la Monnaie, Brussels, where he became a great favorite; 1900–03, member of the Metropolitan Opera; at his debut on Dec. 18, 1900, and throughout the entire season, he failed to make a decided impression, but on his appearance in the second season took the public by storm; 1906–10, at the Manhattan Opera House, N.Y.; he was then reengaged for the Metropolitan Opera, and was to have created Jack Rance in *The Girl of the Golden West,* but died just before the opening of the season. He was also a distinguished concert singer and interpreter of old French songs.

Gillespie, John Birks ("Dizzy"), American jazz trumpeter and bandleader; b. Cheraw, South Carolina, Oct. 21, 1917. He picked up the rudiments of music from his father; at the age of 18 he went to Philadelphia where he joined a local jazz band; in 1939 he became a member of the Cab Calloway orchestra, and in 1944 he was with the Billy Eckstine band. Soon he emerged as a true innovator in jazz playing, and was one of the founders of the style variously known as bebop, bop, and rebop. He received his nickname "Dizzy" because of his wild manner of playing, making grimaces and gesticulating during his performances. Gillespie is doubtless one of the greatest trumpeters in jazz history and practice, a true virtuoso on his instrument, extending its upper ranges, and improvising long passages at breakneck speed.

Gillet, Ernest, French composer; b. Paris, Sept. 13, 1856; d. there, May 6, 1940. He studied cello at the Paris Cons., and was for many years a cellist in the orch. of the Paris Opéra. He publ. a number of melodious pieces, of which *Loin du bal* for piano became a perennial drawing-room favorite, available also in numerous arrangements.

Gillette, James Robert, American organist and composer; b. Roseboom, N.Y., May 30, 1886; d. Lake Forest, Ill., Nov. 26, 1963. He studied music at Syracuse Univ.; taught at Wesleyan College, Macon, Ga., and at Carleton College, Northfield, Minn.; then was organist of the First Presbyterian Church, Lake Forest, Ill.

WORKS: *Pagan Symphony* for band; *Cabins,* an American rhapsody for orch.; 3 cantatas: *On Calvary's Cross; The Shepherd and His Lamb; The Resurrection According to Nicodemus;* 42 anthems for church use; 7 overtures for symphonic band; 40 organ pieces (*Chanson de Matin, Toccatina, Pastorale,* etc.). He publ. *The Organist's Handbook* (1928) and *The Modern Band in Theory and Practice* (1936).

Gillis, Don, American composer and arranger; b. Cameron, Missouri, June 17, 1912; d. Columbia, S.C., Jan. 10, 1978. He played trumpet and trombone in school bands; graduated from the Christian Univ. at Fort Worth, Texas, in 1936. From 1944 to 1954 he was producer director for the National Broacasting Co., and became associated with Toscanini, who was then conductor of the NBC Symph. Orch. Gillis acquired a facility for arranging, and also composed music on his own. In 1960 he became chairman of the division of Arts at Dallas Baptist College, Texas; later was composer-in-residence at the Univ. of South Carolina.

WORKS: 10 symphonies, supplementing them with an intercalatory work which he called *Symphony No. 5 1/2* and subtitled it "Symphony for Fun." It so amused Toscanini that he performed it in 1947 with the NBC Symphony; among his other orchestral works with similarly whimsical titles are *The Panhandle, Thoughts Provoked on Becoming a Prospective Papa,* etc. He also wrote several short operas to his own libretti, among them, *The Park Avenue Kids* (Elkhart, Indiana, May 12, 1957), *Pep Rally* (Interlochen, Michigan, Aug. 15, 1957), *The Libretto* (Norman, Oklahoma, Dec. 1, 1961), *The Gift of the Magi* (Forth Worth, Texas, Dec. 7, 1965), *The Legend of the Star Valley Junction* (N.Y., Jan. 7, 1969); patriotic pieces for orch., among them *The Alamo* (1947) and *The Secret History of the Birth of the Nation* with narrator and chorus (York, Pa., Nov. 14, 1976); 2 piano concertos; *Rhapsody* for trumpet and orch.; 6 string quartets; other chamber music.

Gillock, William L., American pianist and composer; b. Lawrence County, Missouri, July 1, 1917. He devoted himself mainly to teaching piano; published some 300 piano pieces under such engaging titles as *Autumn is Here, Happy Holiday,* and the *Prowling Pussy Cat.*

Gilman, Lawrence, renowned American music critic; b. Flushing, N.Y., July 5, 1878; d. Franconia, N.H., Sept. 8, 1939. He was self-taught in music; from

1901–13, music critic of *Harper's Weekly;* 1915–23, musical, dramatic, and literary critic of *North American Review,* from 1921, author of the program notes of the N.Y. Philh. and Philadelphia Orch. concerts; from 1923, music critic of *N.Y. Herald Tribune,* member of the National Institute of Arts and Letters.

WRITINGS: *Phases of Modern Music* (1904); *Edward MacDowell* (1905, in Living Masters of Music series; rev. and enlarged as *Edward MacDowell: A Study,* 1909); *The Music of To-Morrow* (1906); *Stories of Symphonic Music* (1907); *Aspects of Modern Opera* (1909); *Nature in Music* (1914); *A Christmas Meditation* (1916); "Taste in Music," *Musical Quarterly* (Jan. 1917); *Music and the Cultivated Man* (1929); *Wagner's Operas* (1937); *Toscanini and Great Music* (1938). He set to music 3 poems of W. B. Yeats *(The Heart of the Woman, A Dream of Death,* and *The Curlew).*

BIBLIOGRAPHY: Carl Engel, "Lawrence Gilman," *Musical Quarterly* (Jan. 1940).

Gil-Marchex, Henri, French pianist; b. St. Georges d'Éspérance (Isère), Dec. 16, 1894; d. Paris, Nov. 22, 1970. He studied at the Paris Cons., then with L. Capet and A. Cortot; toured Europe, Russia, and Japan, and performed modern works at various festivals in Europe. In 1956, he was director of the Cons. at Poitiers.

Gilmore, Patrick Sarsfield, American bandmaster; b. County Galway, Ireland, Dec. 25, 1829; d. St. Louis, Mo., Sept. 24, 1892. He went to Canada with an English band, but soon settled in Salem, Mass., where he conducted a military band. In 1859 in Boston he organized the famous 'Gilmore's Band.' As bandmaster in the Federal army at New Orleans (1864), he gave a grand music festival with several combined bands, introducing the novel reinforcement of strong accents by cannon shots. He won wide renown by the "National Peace Jubilee" (1869), and the "World's Peace Jubilee" (1872), two monster musical festivals held in Boston; in the former, Gilmore led an orch. of 1000 and a chorus of 10,000; in the latter, an orch. of 2000 and a chorus of 20,000; the orch. was reinforced by a powerful organ, cannon fired by electricity, anvils, and chimes of bells. After the second Jubilee, Gilmore went to New York, and, as a popular bandmaster, traveled with his men throughout the U.S. and Canada, and also (1878) to Europe. He also led bands or orchestras in various resorts in and near New York.

WORKS: Military music, dance music, many arrangements for band. Some of his songs were popular. He claimed to be the composer of *When Johnny Comes Marching Home* (1863), a song that remained a favorite long after the Civil War. The song bears the name of Louis Lambert as composer; this may have been one of Gilmore's many aliases—at any rate, he introduced the song and started it on its way to popularity.

BIBLIOGRAPHY: M. Darlington, *Irish Orpheus: the Life of Patrick Gilmore* (Philadelphia, 1950).

Gilse, Jan van, Dutch composer; b. Rotterdam, May 11, 1881; d. Oegstgeest, near Leyden, Sept. 8, 1944. He studied with Wüllner at the Cologne Cons.

(1897–1902) and with Humperdinck in Berlin (1902–03). He was a conductor of the Opera at Bremen (1905–08) and of the Dutch Opera at Amsterdam (1908–09); was music director of the City of Utrecht (1917–22). He lived again in Berlin (1922–33); then was director of the Utrecht Cons. (1933–37). His music is heavily imbued with German Romanticism.

WORKS: 2 operas: *Frau Helga von Stavern* (1911) and *Thijl* (1938–40; first complete perf., Amsterdam, Sept. 21, 1976; a symph. extract, *Funeral Music,* is often heard separately); *Concert Overture* (1900); 4 symphonies: No. 1 (1900–01); No. 2 (1902–03); No. 3, *Erhebung,* with soprano (1907); No. 4 (1914); No. 5 (1922–23; unfinished sketch only); *Eine Lebensmesse,* oratorio (1904); *Variaties over een St. Nicolaasliedje (Variations on a St. Nicholas Song)* for orch. or piano (1909); *3 Songs,* after Tagore's "Gitanjali," for soprano and orch. (1909); *3 Songs,* after Tagore's "Der Gartner," for soprano and orch. (1923); *3 Tanzkizzen (Dance Sketches)* for piano and small orch. (1926); *Der Kreis des Lebens,* oratorio (1928); *Prologus brevis* for orch. (1928); *Kleine Vals* for small orch. (1936); Nonet (1916); Trio for Flute, Violin and Viola (1927); songs.

Gilson, Paul, Belgian composer, critic, and educator; b. Brussels, June 15, 1865; d. there, April 3, 1942. He studied with Auguste Cantillon and Charles Duyck, took lessons from Gevaert; in 1889, he won the Belgian Prix de Rome with his cantata, *Sinai,* performed at Brussels in 1890. His subsequent works, both choral and orchestral, won him a foremost place among modern Flemish composers. In addition to his composing, he wrote numerous books and articles on music, and taught, beginning in 1899 as prof. of harmony at Brussels Cons.; in 1904, also on the faculty of Antwerp Cons.; in 1909, he left both posts to become musical inspector in the Belgian schools. He was also an important music critic: for *Soir* from 1906 to 1914, for *Le Diapason* from 1910 to 1914, and later for *Midi.* He was the founder of the *Revue Musicale Belge* (1924). In 1942, he published his memoirs, *Notes de musique et souvenirs.* He also publ. *Les Intervalles, Le Tutti orchestral, Quintes et octaves, Traité d'harmonie, Traité d'orchestre militaire.*

WORKS: CHORAL: *Inaugural Cantata* (for Brussels Exhibition, 1897); *Francesca da Rimini,* after Dante (Brussels, 1895); *Le Démon,* after Lermontov; *Que la lumière soit; Hymne à l'Art; Ludus pro Patria;* ballets: *La Captive* (Brussels, 1902), *Les Deux Bossus, Légende rhénane;* incidental music for E. Hiel's drama, *Alva;* operas: *Prinses Zonneschijn* (Antwerp, 1903), *Zeevolk* (Antwerp, 1904), *Rooversliefde (Les Aventuriers;* Antwerp, 1906), *Mater Dolorosa;* ORCH. WORKS: 3 symph. poems: *La Mer* (Brussels, 1892), *Italia, La Destinée;* 8 suites; *Danses écossaises; Rapsodie écossaise; Andante et presto sur un thème brabançon; Rapsodie canadienne;* 2 string quartets; String Trio; pieces for military band; choruses; piano pieces; instrumental pieces; songs.

Giltay, Berend, Dutch composer; b. Hilversum, June 15, 1910; d. Utrecht, March 21, 1975. He studied violin and viola with Dick Waleson and composition with Badings; was a violinist with the Hilversum Radio

Philh. and with various other Dutch orchestras. From 1963 to 1966 he attended courses in electronic music at the Utrecht Univ. and worked in Bilthoven at the Gaudeamus electronic studio.

WORKS: Violin Concerto (1950); *4 Miniatures* for viola and piano (1952); *Sonata a tre* for oboe, clarinet and bassoon (1953); Concerto for Viola and Chamber Orch. (1955); Wind Quintet (1956); Oboe Concerto (1956–57); *Sinfonia* (1956–57); String Quintet (1957); Horn Concerto; Concerto for Orch. (1960); 2 duos for 2 violins (1962, 1966); Divertimento for 5 Flutes (1963); *Scherzo* for 2 violins (1963); *6 Studi concertante* for solo viola (1963); *Phonolieten* for tape (1965); *Polychromie I* for tape (1966); and *II* for a solo trio of piccolo, flute and alto flute, 4 flutes or other instruments, and tape (1972); *Kurucz Változatok Zenekarra,* variations for orch. (1966–67); 2-Violin Concerto (1966–67); *Elegy* for alto flute and 4 flutes (1969); *Gossauer Symphonie* (Utrecht, Oct. 3, 1972); Trio, for 2 violins and cello (1971); *Kosmochromie 1* for 4 loudspeakers and orch. (Utrecht, Feb. 22, 1974); *Kosmochromie II* for string quartet, chamber orch. and tape (1974).

Giménez (Jiménez), Jerónimo, Spanish composer of zarzuelas; b. Seville, Oct. 10, 1854; d. Madrid, Feb. 19, 1923. He studied with Alard, Savard, and A. Thomas at the Paris Cons.; was conductor of Sociedad de Conciertos in Madrid. He wrote about 60 light operas *(género chico).*

Gimpel, Bronislaw, Polish violinist; b. Lwow, Jan. 29, 1911. He studied in Vienna with Flesch and Huberman. In 1929, he was concertmaster of the Radio Orch. in Königsberg; from 1931–36, in Göteborg; later toured as soloist in Europe and America.

Ginastera, Alberto, remarkable Argentinian composer; b. Buenos Aires, April 11, 1916. He studied piano as a child; then took courses at the National Cons. of Music in Buenos Aires with Athos Palma, José Gil and José André, graduating in 1938. In 1946–47 he traveled to the U.S. on a Guggenheim Fellowship. Returning to Argentina, he was appointed to the faculty of the National Cons. From his earliest steps in composition, Ginastera showed great sensitivity to the melodic and rhythmic resources of Argentine folk music, and he evolved a fine harmonic and contrapuntal idiom congenial with these patterns. His first significant work was the ballet *Panambí,* completed in 1937, in which Argentinian motives are presented in an effective Impressionistic vein; in 1938 he wrote his poetic song *Canción al árbol del olvido.* His ballet *Estancia,* inspired by scenes of rural Argentina, commissioned by the American Ballet Caravan of New York, was signally successful. There followed a group of pieces under the generic title *Pampeana,* based on the folkloric elements of the Argentenian pampas. In his *Cantata para América Mágica* he introduced distinctly modern procedures; the first performance of the work in 1961 was enthusiastically acclaimed at the Inter-American Music Festival in Washington. An entirely new departure in Ginastera's evolution was the composition of the opera *Don Rodrigo* (1964), in which he applied techniques of the avant-garde; this was followed by an opera of even a greater complex-ity, making use of serial procedures, *Bomarzo,* produced in Washington in 1967. His subsequent opera *Beatrix Cenci* (1971) concluded his operatic trilogy based on historical characters. Among instrumental works of this latest period, the most remarkable is the Second Piano Concerto (1972), commissioned by the pianist Hilde Somer; its serial structure is based on the famous dissonant chord in the finale of Beethoven's Ninth Symphony; the second movement of the concerto is written for left hand alone.

WORKS: OPERAS: *Don Rodrigo* (Buenos Aires, July 24, 1964), *Bomarzo* (Washington, May 19, 1967), *Beatrix Cenci* (Washington, Sept. 10, 1971); BALLETS: *Panambí* (Buenos Aires, July 12, 1940), *Estancia* (1941; Buenos Aires, Aug. 19, 1952); FOR ORCH: *Concierto Argentino* (Montevideo, July 17, 1941), *Sinfonia Porteña* (Buenos Aires, May 12, 1942); *Obertura para el Fausto criollo* (Santiago, Chile, May 12, 1944); *Sinfonia elegíaca* (Buenos Aires, May 31, 1946); *Ollantay* (Buenos Aires, Oct. 29, 1949); *Variaciones Concertantes* (Buenos Aires, June 2, 1953); *Pampeana No. 3,* symphonic pastoral (Louisville, Oct. 20, 1954); Piano Concerto No. 1 (Washington, April 22, 1961); Violin Concerto (N.Y., Oct. 3, 1963); Harp Concerto (Philadelphia, Feb. 18, 1965); *Concerto per corde* (Caracas, May 14, 1966); *Estudios sinfónicos* (Vancouver, Canada, March 31, 1968); Cello Concerto (Dartmouth College, Hanover, New Hampshire, July 7, 1968); Piano Concerto No. 2 (Indianapolis, March 22, 1973, Hilde Somer, soloist); *Glosses sobre temas de Pau Casals* for string orch. and string quartet "in Lontano" (San Juan, Puerto Rico, June 14, 1976); CHAMBER MUSIC: *Impresiones de la Puna* for flute and string quartet (1934); Duo for Flute and Oboe (1945); *Pampeana No. 1* for violin and piano (1947); String Quartet No. 1 (1948); *Pampeana No. 2* for cello and piano (1950); String Quartet No. 2 (1958); Piano Quintet (1963); String quartet No. 3, with soprano (1974); VOCAL WORKS: *Psalm 1950,* for chorus, boys' choir and orch. (Buenos Aires, April 7, 1945); *Cantata para América Mágica* for soprano and 53 percussion instruments (Washington, April 30, 1961); *Sinfonía Don Rodrigo* for soprano and orch. (1964); *Bomarzo,* cantata for narrator, voice and chamber orch. (Washington, Nov. 1, 1964); *Milena,* cantata for soprano and orch. (Denver, April 16, 1973); FOR PIANO: *Dances Argentinas* (1937); *Malambo* (1940); *12 American Preludes* (1944); *Suite de danzas criollas* (1946); Sonata (1952).

BIBLIOGRAPHY: Pola Suárez Urtubey, *Alberto Ginastera* (Buenos Aires, 1967).

Gingold, Josef, American violinist; b. Brest-Litovsk, Oct. 28, 1909. He came to the U.S. in 1920. He studied in New York, and later in Brussels with Eugène Ysaÿe. He gave 40 concerts in Belgium (1926–28); then returned to America. He was a member of the NBC Symphony Orch. under Toscanini (1937–44); concertmaster of the Detroit Symphony (1944–47), and concertmaster of the Cleveland Orch. (1947–69); then appointed to the faculty of Indiana Univ. in Bloomington.

Ginguené, Pierre Louis, French historian of literature and writer on music; b. Rennes, April 25, 1748; d. Paris, Nov. 16, 1816. He studied at Rennes College;

then went to Paris; was an original member of the Institute of France; served in government posts, then wrote extensively on the history of French and Italian literature. He was an ardent advocate of Piccini in the Gluck-Piccini controversy; his attacks on Gluck are contained in *Lettres et articles sur la musique, insérés dans les journaux sous le nom de Mélophile, pendant nos dernières querelles musicales, en 1780, 1781, 1782 et 1783* (Paris, 1783). He also wrote *Notice sur la vie et les ouvrages de Piccini* (Paris, 1800); contributed historical articles to the *Dictionnaire de musique* of the *Encyclopédie méthodique*.

BIBLIOGRAPHY: D. J. Garat, *Notice sur la vie et les ouvrages de P. L. Ginguené* (Paris, 1817).

Ginsburg, Lev, Russian music scholar, cellist and pedagogue; b. Mohilev, Jan. 28, 1907. He studied cello at the Moscow Cons., and music history with Konstantin Kuznetsov, graduating in 1931. In 1936 he was appointed to the faculty of the Moscow Cons. His specialty is history of string instrument playing in Russia. He publ. *History of the Art of Cello Playing* in 3 vols. (Moscow, 1950; 1957; 1965); *History of the Performances of Beethoven's Quartets in Russia* (Bonn, 1970); *Research Papers, Articles, Essays* (Moscow, 1971). He also published the monographs *Luigi Boccherini* (1938), *Karl Davydov* (1950), *Ferdinand Laub* (1950), *Anatoly Brandukov* (1951), *Pablo Casals* (1958), *Eugène Ysaÿe* (1959), *Mstislav Rostropovich* (1962), *Giuseppe Tartini* (1969); and numerous articles in the Soviet musical press.

Ginsburg, Semion, Russian musicologist and pedagogue; b. Kiev, May 23, 1901. He studied art history and musicology in Petrograd; in 1925 was appointed to the faculty of the Leningrad Cons.; in his scientific pursuits, he explored the sociological foundation of national musical resources. He publ. *Fundamentals of Musical Culture* (Leningrad, 1935); *Russian Music on the Threshold of the 20th Century* (Moscow, 1966).

Giordani, Giuseppe (called **Giordanello**), Italian composer; b. Naples, Dec. 9, 1743; d. Fermo, Jan. 4, 1798. He studied with Fenaroli at San Loreto Cons., Naples; Cimarosa and Zingarelli were fellow-students. His first opera, *Epponina*, was given in Florence in 1779. He continued to write operas for various Italian towns, but they were not outstanding and few of the 30-odd he wrote have survived. He also wrote several oratorios and church music. From 1791 until his death he was maestro di cappella at Fermo Cathedral. He is sometimes credited with *Il Bacio* and other operas and works produced in London by Tommaso Giordani; Giuseppe was not related to Tommaso, and never left Italy. The famous song, *Caro mio ben*, popularized in London by Pacchierotti, was probably written by Giuseppe.

Giordani, Tommaso, Italian composer; b. Naples, c.1730; d. Dublin, late Feb., 1806. His family, which included his father, **Giuseppe;** his mother, **Antonia;** his brother, **Francesco;** and his sisters, **Marina** and **Nicolina** (known later as **Spiletta** from one of her opera roles), together formed a strolling opera company, with the father as impresario and singer and the rest

of the family, except Tommaso, as singers. Tommaso was probably a member of the orch. and arranger of music. They left Naples about 1745 and moved northward, appearing in Italian towns, then in Graz (1748), Frankfurt (1750), and Amsterdam (1752). They made their London debut at Covent Garden, Dec. 17, 1753, and returned in 1756, at which time Tommaso first appeared as a composer, with his comic opera, *La comediante fatta cantatrice* (Covent Garden, Jan. 12, 1756). The Giordani company next went to Dublin, appearing there in 1764; Tommaso continued active both in Dublin and in London; he was conductor and composer at the King's Theatre, London, in 1769 and many following seasons, and in Dublin, where he lived after 1783, was conductor and composer at the Smock Alley and Crow Street theaters; he also taught piano between operas. In 1794, he was elected president of the Irish music fund. He played an important part in Irish music circles, and wrote altogether more than 50 English and Italian operas, including pasticcios and adaptations.

WORKS: *L'eroe cinese* (Dublin, 1766), *Il padre el il figlio rivali* (London, 1770), *Artaserse* (London, 1772), *Il re pastore* (London, 1778); *Il bacio* (London, 1782). He also wrote several cantatas, including *Aci e Galatea* (London, 1777); an oratorio, *Isaac* (Dublin, 1767); songs for the original production of Sheridan's *The Critic* (Drury Lane, London, Oct. 29, 1779); many Italian and English songs that were popular for a long time; concertos, string quartets, trios, many piano pieces.

Giordano, Umberto, Italian opera composer; b. Foggia, Aug. 28, 1867; d. Milan, Nov. 12, 1948. He studied with Gaetano Briganti at Foggia, and then with Paolo Serrao at Naples Cons. (1881–86). His 1st composition performed in public was a symph. poem, *Delizia* (1886); he then wrote some instrumental music. In 1888 he submitted a short opera, *Marina*, for the competition established by the publisher Sonzogno; Mascagni's *Cavalleria Rusticana* received 1st prize, but *Marina* was cited for distinction. Giordano then wrote an opera in 3 acts, *Mala Vita*, which was performed in Rome, Feb. 21, 1892; it was only partly successful; was revised and presented under the title *Il Voto* in Milan (1897). There followed a 2-act opera, *Regina Diaz* (Rome, Feb. 21, 1894), which obtained a moderate success. Then Giordano set to work on a grand opera, *Andrea Chénier*, to a libretto by Illica. The production of this opera at La Scala (March 28, 1896) was a spectacular success, which established Giordano as one of the best composers of modern Italian opera. The dramatic subject gave Giordano a fine opportunity to display his theatrical talent; but the opera also revealed his gift for lyric expression. *Andrea Chénier* was produced at the N.Y. Academy of Music shortly after its Milan première; a performance at the Metropolitan Opera House came considerably later (March 7, 1920). Almost as successful was his next opera, *Fedora* (Teatro Lirico, Milan, Nov. 17, 1898; Metropolitan Opera, Dec. 5, 1906), but it failed to hold a place in the world repertory after initial acclaim; there followed *Siberia*, in 3 acts (La Scala, Dec. 19, 1903). Two short operas, *Marcella* (Milan, Nov. 9, 1907) and *Mese Mariano* (Palermo, March 17, 1910), were hardly noticed and seemed to mark a decline in Giordano's dramatic gift; however, he recaptured the attention of the public with *Madame Sans-Gêne*, produced at a gala première at the Metropolitan Opera on Jan. 25, 1915, conducted by Toscanini, with Geraldine Farrar singing the title role. With Franchetti, he wrote *Giove a Pompei* (Rome, 1921); then he produced *La cena delle beffe* in 4 acts, which was his last signal accomplishment; it was staged at La Scala, Dec. 20, 1924, and at the Metropolitan, Jan. 2, 1926. He wrote one more opera, *Il Re* in 1 act (La Scala, Jan. 10, 1929). During his lifetime he received many honors, and was elected a member of the Accademia Luigi Cherubini in Florence and of several other institutions. Although not measuring up to Puccini in musical qualities or to Mascagni in dramatic skill, Giordano was a distinguished figure in the Italian opera field.

BIBLIOGRAPHY: G. C. Parabeni, *Madame Sans-Gêne di Umberto Giordano* (Milan, 1923); D. Cellamare, *Umberto Giordano: la vita e le opere* (Milan, 1949).

Giorni, Aurelio, pianist and composer; b. Perugia, Italy, Sept. 15, 1895; d. Pittsfield, Mass., Sept. 23, 1938. He studied piano with Sgambati at the Cons. of Santa Cecilia in Rome (1909–11); composition with Humperdinck in Berlin (1911–13); in 1915 he came to the U.S. where he remained; taught at Smith College, Philadelphia Cons. of Music, Hartford School of Music, and other music schools; in his last years, was a teacher in N.Y. He wrote a symph. poem, *Orlando furioso* (1926); *Sinfonia concertante* (1931); Symph. in D minor (1937); 3 trios; 2 string quartets; Cello Sonata; Violin Sonata; Piano Quartet; Piano Quintet; Flute Sonata; Clarinet Sonata; 24 concert études for piano; songs.

Giornovichi, Giovanni Mane, Italian violinist, probably of Croatian extraction (his real name was **Jarnowick**); b. Raguso or Palermo, c.1735; d. St. Petersburg, Russia, Nov. 23, 1804. He was a pupil of Antonio Lolli in Palermo; gave successful concerts in Europe; on the strength of his reputation, he was engaged as court musician to Catherine II, succeeding his teacher Lolli in that post. He was in Russia from 1789–91; then appeared in London (1791–94), Paris, Hamburg, and Berlin. He returned to Russia in 1803, and died there the following year. In his old age he abandoned the violin and devoted himself to playing billiards for money. Among his works are 22 violin concertos (17 extant); 3 string quartets; *Fantasia e Rondo* for piano. He was probably the first to introduce the 'romance' into the violin concerto as a slow movement, and helped to set the rondo as the finale.

BIBLIOGRAPHY: R. Aloys Mooser, *Annales de la musique et des musiciens en Russie au XVIIIᵉ siècle* (Geneva, 1950; vol. II, pp. 379–81); C. White, "The Violin Concertos of Giornovichi," *Musical Quarterly* (Jan. 1972; includes a concordance of editions).

Giorza, Paolo, Italian composer; b. Milan, Nov. 11, 1832; d. Seattle, May 5, 1914. He was especially known for his ballet music; wrote more than 40 ballets. He lived in New York, in London, and in San Francisco; in 1906 settled in Seattle.

Giovannelli, Ruggiero, Italian composer; b. Velletri, 1560; d. Rome, Jan. 7, 1625. On Aug. 6, 1583 he was nominated director of the cappella of San Luigi de' Francesi at Rome; later in the Collegium Germanicum; in 1594 he succeeded Palestrina as maestro at St. Peter's, and in 1599 joined the Pontifical Chapel. One of the most famous masters of the Roman School; of his works there have been printed 3 books of madrigals *a* 5 (1586, 1587, 1589; completely reprinted 1600); 2 of *Madrigali sdruccioli a* 4 (1585 [7th ed. 1613], 1589 [5th ed. 1603]); 2 books of motets *a* 5–8 (1589, 1604); *Canzonette* and *Villanelle a* 3 (1592, 1593); also scattered works in collections publ. from 1583–1620 (Scotto, Phalèse, Schadaeus, etc.). K. Proske's *Musica divina* contains a psalm (vol. III, 1859); L. Torchi's *L'Arte Musicale in Italia* includes a motet and psalm *a* 8 and a madrigal *a* 5 (vol. II). In the Vatican Library are many sacred works in MS. To Giovanelli was entrusted, by Pope Paul V, the preparation of a new ed. of the Gradual (1614, 1615, 2 vols.).

BIBLIOGRAPHY: C. Winter, *Ruggiero Giovannelli (c.1560–1625), Nachfolger Palestrinas zu St. Peter in Rom* (Munich, 1935).

Giovanni da Cascia (Johannes de Florentia), Italian 14th-century composer. According to his younger contemporary, Filippo Villani, in *Liber de civitatis Florentiae famosis civibus*, he was the initiator of the stylistic reform which spread from Florence shortly after 1300. He was organist and probably chorusmaster at Santa Maria del Fiore at Florence; lived at the court of Mastino II della Scala, Verona, from 1329–51. His compositions included madrigals, *ballate*, etc.; MSS may be found in libraries at Florence, Paris, and in the British Museum. In all, 28 works by Giovanni, in 2–3 parts, are known. The madrigal, *Agnel son bianco*, was edited and publ. by Johannes Wolf in *Sammelbände der Internationalen Musik-Gesellschaft* (1902; ex. 4); 2 other compositions were also edited and publ. by Wolf in his *Geschichte der Mensural-Notation* (pp. 61–64; Leipzig, 1904).

BIBLIOGRAPHY: J. Wolf, "Florenz in der Musikgeschichte des 14. Jahrhunderts," *Sammelbände der Internationalen Musik-Gesellschaft* (1902; pp. 609–10); H. Riemann, in *Handbuch der Musikgeschichte* (1922; p. 41); A. Morini, "Un celebre musico dimenticato, Giovanni da Cascia," *Bollettino della regia deputazione di storia patria per l'Umbria* (Perugia, 1926; p. 305 ff).

Gipps, Ruth, English pianist and composer; b. Bexhill-on-Sea, Sussex, Feb. 20, 1921. She studied at the Royal College of Music in London with Vaughan Williams, piano with Matthay. She began to compose very early in life and at the age of eight won a prize for a piano piece. Her works include 4 symphonies (1942, 1946, 1965, 1972); Clarinet Concerto; Oboe Concerto; Violin Concerto; Horn Concerto; Trio, for oboe, clarinet, and piano; Quintet, for oboe, clarinet, violin, viola, and cello; an oratorio, *The Cat* (1952); a bizarre piece entitled Leviathan for double bassoon and chamber orch. (London, Feb. 13, 1971). Apart from composition, she conducted the London Repertory Orch. and the Chanticleer Orch. In 1967 she was appointed a prof. at the Royal College of Music in London.

Giraldoni, Eugenio, famous Italian baritone; b. Marseilles, France, May 20, 1871; d. Helsinki, Finland, June 23, 1924. Both his parents were professional singers; his father, **Leone Giraldoni,** was a renowned baritone and his mother, **Carolina Ferni-Giraldoni,** a famous soprano. He made his debut in Barcelona as Don José in 1891; then sang in Buenos Aires and in Italy (at La Scala and other theaters); eventually settled in Russia.

Giraudet, Alfred-Auguste, dramatic basso and vocal pedagogue; b. Étampes, March 29, 1845; d. New York, Oct. 17, 1911. He studied with Delsarte; made his operatic debut at the Théâtre-Lyrique in Paris as Mephistopheles (1868); then sang at the Théâtre-Italien, Opéra-Comique, and at the Opéra; in 1883 he retired from the stage and devoted himself to teaching; eventually settled in New York.

Girdlestone, Cuthbert Morton, English music scholar; b. Bovey-Tracey, Sept. 17, 1895. He received his education at Cambridge Univ. and at the Sorbonne in Paris; was for 35 years (1926–61) prof. of French literature at King's College at Newcastle-on-Tyne. He publ. a valuable book on analysis of Mozart's piano concertos and a monograph on Rameau (both in French).

Giuliani, Mauro, Italian guitar virtuoso; b. Barletta, July 27, 1781; d. Naples, May 8, 1829. He was entirely self-taught; at the age of 19 undertook a highly successful tour in Europe; settled in Vienna in 1807, where he became associated with Hummel, Moscheles, and Diabelli; Beethoven became interested in him, and wrote some guitar music expressly for his performances. In 1833 he visited London, where he won extraordinary acclaim; a special publication, named after him *The Giulianiad* and devoted to reports about his activities, was initiated there, but only a few issues appeared in print. Giuliani publ. a number of guitar solos; he also perfected a new guitar with a shorter fingerboard ("la ghitarra di terza").
BIBLIOGRAPHY: *The Guitar Review* 18 (1955), containing a biographical sketch of Giuliani by Ph. J. Bone; also Thomas F. Heck, "Mauro Giuliani," *The Guitar Review* (1972).

Giulini, Carlo Mario, eminent Italian conductor; b. Barletta, May 9, 1914. He studied violin, viola and composition at the Conservatorio di Musica Santa Cecilia in Rome, receiving his diploma in 1939; took a course in conducting with Molinari at the Accademia Musicale, graduating in 1941. He was conductor of Radio Rome (1946–50), Radio Milano (1950–53); then was engaged as conductor of La Scala in Milan (1953–56). He then expanded his activities as a symphonic conductor of all major orchestras of Europe and America, achieving a fine reputation as a highly competent and inspiring orchestral leader. In 1978 he was appointed conductor and music director of the Los Angeles Philharmonic Orchestra.

Giulini, Giorgio, Italian composer; b. Milan, 1716; d. there, 1780. He was the author of several instrumental works of considerable merit.
BIBLIOGRAPHY: G. Cesari, "Giorgio Giulini, musicista," *Rivista Musicale Italiana* (1917).

Gladstone, Francis Edward, noted English organist; b. Summertown, near Oxford, March 2, 1845; d. Hereford, Sept. 6, 1928. He was a pupil of S. Wesley, 1859–64; filled positions as organist at Weston-super-Mare, Llandaff, Chichester, Brighton, London, and Norwich. After embracing the Catholic faith, he was choir director at St. Mary of the Angels, Bayswater, until 1894. In 1876 he took the degree of Mus. Bac., Cambridge; in 1879, Mus. Doc.; prof. of harmony and counterpoint at Royal College of Music, 1883–1910.
WORKS: An oratorio, *Philippi* (1883), much church music, an overture, some chamber music (all in MS); publ. organ pieces, *The Organ-Student's Guide* and *A Treatise on Strict Counterpoint* (1906). He also wrote an a cappella chorus, *In Paradisium,* for his own funeral and trained four monks to sing it.

Glanville-Hicks, Peggy, Australian composer and critic; b. Melbourne, Dec. 29, 1912. She studied composition with Fritz Hart at the Melbourne Cons.; in 1931 went to London where she took courses in piano with Arthur Benjamin, theory with R. O. Morris and C. Kitson at the Royal College of Music, composition with Vaughan Williams, orchestration with Gordon Jacob and conducting with Constant Lambert and Sir Malcolm Sargent. She obtained a traveling scholarship which enabled her to go to Paris for lessons with Nadia Boulanger and to Vienna where she took a course in musicology and advanced composition with Egon Wellesz. In 1939 she came to the U.S; from 1948 to 1958 she wrote music criticism for the *N.Y. Herald Tribune.* In 1957 she received a Guggenheim Fellowship; in 1959 she went to Greece, and made her residence in Athens. There she produced her opera *Nausicaa* to the text of Robert Graves (Athens, Aug. 19, 1961) which had a modicum of success. Her other operas are: *Caedmon* (1934); *The Transposed Heads* (Louisville, March 27, 1954); *The Glittering Gate* (N.Y., May 14, 1959); *Sappho* (1963). She wrote the ballets *Hylas and the Nymphs* (1937); *Postman's Knock* (1940); *The Masque of the Wild Man* (1958); *Saul and the Witch of Endor* (1959); *Tragic Celebration* (1966); *A Season in Hell* (1967); *Letters from Morocco* for voice and orch. to texts from actual letters she received from the composer Paul Bowles (N.Y., Feb. 22, 1953); *Sinfonia da Pacifica* (1953); *Tapestry* for orch. (1956); Piano Concerto (1936); Flute Concerto (1937); *Concertino da camera* for flute, clarinet, bassoon and piano (Amsterdam Festival, June 10, 1948); *3 Gymnopedies* for harp and other instruments (1953); *Etruscan Concerto* for piano and chamber orch. (N.Y., Jan. 25, 1956); *Concerto romantico* for viola and orch. (1957); *Concertino antico* for harps and string quartet; several other works inspired by ancient Greek modalities; choral pieces; songs. As a pragmatic composer of functional music with human connotations, Peggy Glanville-Hicks shuns the monopolistic fashion of mandatory dissonance but explores attentively the resources of folk music, making use of

Greek melos in her opera *Nausicaa,* Hindu rhythmic modes in the opera *The Transposed Heads* and allusions to non-Western modalities in *Letters from Morocco.*

Glareanus, Henricus (also **Heinrich Glarean;** real name **Heinrich Loris;** Latinized: **Henricus Loritus**), Swiss musical theorist and writer; b. Mollis, in the canton of Glarus, June, 1488; d. Freiburg, Baden, March 28, 1563. He studied with Rubellus at Bern, and later with Cochläus at Cologne, where he was crowned poet laureate by Emperor Maximilian I in 1512, as the result of a poem he composed and sang to the emperor. He first taught mathematics at Basel (1515); went to Paris, where he taught philosophy; returned to Basel where he stayed till 1529, when he settled in Freiburg. His first important work, *Isagoge in musicen,* publ. at Basel in 1516, dealt with solmization, intervals, modes, and tones. A still more important volume, the *Dodecachordon,* was publ. in 1547; in it, Glareanus advanced the theory that there are 12 church modes, corresponding to the ancient Greek modes, instead of the commonly accepted 8 modes. The 3rd part of the *Dodecachordon* contains many works by 15th- and 16th-century musicians. A copy of the *Dodecachordon,* with corrections in Glareanus' own handwriting, is in the Library of Congress, Washington, D.C. A German transl., with the musical examples in modern notation, was publ. by P. Bohn in vol. 16 of *Publikationen der Gesellschaft für Musikforschung* (Leipzig, 1888); English transl. and commentary by C. A. Miller in *Musicological Studies and Documents* 6 (1965); facsimile ed. in *Monuments of Music and Music Literature in Facsimile* 2/65 (N.Y., 1967). A complete index of Glareanus' works is contained in P. Lichtenthal's *Dizionario e bibliografia della musica,* IV, pp. 274–76 (Milan, 1826). J. L. Wonegger publ. *Musicae epitome ex Glareani Dodekachordo* (1557; 2nd ed., 1559; in German: *Uss Glareani Musik ein Usszug,* 1557).

BIBLIOGRAPHY: Biographies of Glareanus have been written by H. Schreiber (Freiburg, 1837) and O. F. Fritzsche (Frauenfeld, 1890); P. Spitta in *Vierteljahrsschrift für Musik-Wissenschaft* (vol. VII, p. 123 ff.); A. Schering, "Die Notenbeispiele in Glareanus Dodecachordon," *Sammelbände der Internationalen Musik-Gesellschaft* (1912); E. Refardt, *Musikerlexikon der Schweiz* (1928); E. Kirsch, "Studie zum Problem des Heinrich Loriti (Glarean)," *Festschrift A. Schering zum 60.sten Geburtstag* (Berlin, 1937).

Glasenapp, Carl Friedrich, music scholar, biographer of Wagner; b. Riga, Oct. 3, 1847; d. there, April 14, 1915. He studied philology at Dorpat; from 1875, headmaster at Riga. An ardent admirer of Wagner's art, he devoted his entire life to the study of the master's works, and was one of the principal contributors to the *Bayreuther Blätter* from their foundation. His great work is the monumental biography of Wagner, *Richard Wagners Leben und Wirken,* of which the first two vols. were publ. at Kassel and Leipzig (1876, 1877); after the 2nd enlarged ed. (1882) these were rewritten, and the entire work was issued at Leipzig as *Das Leben Richard Wagners* (I, 1813–43 [1894]; II, 1843–53 [1896]; III, 1853–62 [1899]; IV, 1862–72 [1904]; V, 1872–77 [1907]; VI, 1877–83 [1911]). Vols. I, II, and III appeared in English transl. (with amplifications) by W. A. Ellis (London, 1900, 1901, 1903), but after that Ellis continued the biography as an independent work. Though Glasenapp's work was considered the definitive biography in its time, its value is diminished by the fact that he published only materials approved by Wagner's family; as a result, it was superseded by later biographies. His other works on Wagner include: *Wagner-Lexikon* with H. von Stein (1883); *Wagner-Encyklopädie* (2 vols., 1891); *Siegfried Wagner* (1906); *Siegfried Wagner und seine Kunst* (1911), with sequels, *Schwarzschwanenreich* (1913) and *Sonnenflammen* (1919); he also edited *Bayreuther Briefe, 1871–73* (1907) and *Familienbriefe an Richard Wagner, 1832–74* (1907).

Glaser, Werner Wolf, German-born Swedish composer; b. Cologne, April 14, 1910. He studied composition with Jarnach in Cologne and with Hindemith in Berlin; was then active as choral conductor. In 1934 he left Germany; from 1934 till 1943 lived in Copenhagen, where he became director, jointly with Lyngby, of a music school. In 1943 he went to Sweden, and in 1945 headed a music school in Västerås. A man of wide interests, he studied modern art and literature; also investigated the potentialities of music therapy. A very prolific composer, he followed the neo-Classical line, influenced mainly by Hindemith.

WORKS: 3 chamber operas: *Kagekiyo* (1961), *Möten* (Västerås, Dec. 13, 1970) and *Cercatori* (1972); the opera buffa, *En naken kung (A Naked King),* based on H. C. Andersen (Göteborg, April 6, 1973); a ballet for chamber orch., *Les Cinq Pas de l'homme* (1973); 7 symphonies (1934; 1935; 1936; 1943; 1949; 1957; 1961); Chamber Symphony (1936); 3 concertos for orch. (1950–66); Flute Concerto (1934); *Trilogia* for orch. (1939; Swedish Radio, Sept. 18, 1971); *3 Pieces* for strings (1947); *Concerto della cappella* for winds, percussion and piano (1960); *Musica Sacra* for flute, clarinet, organ and strings (1960); *Le tre gradi* for strings (1961); Clarinet Concertino (1962); Concerto for Violin, Winds and Percussion (1962); *Capriccio III* for piano and orch. (1964); Violin Concerto (1964); *ASEA-Musik* for chorus and orch. (1965); Concerto for 20 Winds and Percussion (1966); *Transformations* for piano and orch. (1966); Oboe Concerto (1966); *Paradosso* for 2 string orchestras (1967); Horn Concerto (1969); *Canto* for saxophone and orch. (1970); *Concerto lirico* for soprano, piano, timpani and strings (1971); *Chamber Music* for winds and strings (1971). He also wrote 9 string quartets (1934–67); 7 piano sonatas (1933–36); *In memoriam Paul Klee* for violin (1961); *Capriccio I* for piano (1963) and *II* for viola and piano (1963); *Ordo meatus* for oboe d'amore solo (1968); *Capricci* for clarinet (1969); *Baroque cantata* for soprano, flute, viola d'amore and cello (1969); *Paysages sonores* for piano trio (1973); piano pieces; children's choruses; incidental music for the theater.

Glass, Louis Christian August, Danish composer; b. Copenhagen, March 23, 1864; d. there, Jan. 22, 1936. He was a pupil of his father, **Christian Hendrik** (1821–93), then at Brussels Cons. of J. de Zarembski and J. Wieniawski (piano) and J. Servais (cello); appeared both as pianist and cellist, but was more important as composer.

WORKS: 6 symphonies (the fifth: *Sinfonia svastica,* in C, op. 59); 2 overtures, *Der Volksfeind* and *Dänemark; Sommerliv,* suite for orch.; a dance poem, *Artemis* (Copenhagen, Oct. 27, 1917); *Fantasie* for piano and orch.; Concerto for Oboe and Orch.; String Sextet; Piano Quintet; 4 string quartets; Piano Trio; 2 violin sonatas; numerous works for piano.

Glass, Philip, American composer of the extreme avant-garde; b. Baltimore, Jan. 31, 1937. He studied flute at the Peabody Cons. in Baltimore and attended classes in the liberal arts at the Univ. of Chicago from 1952–56; subsequently went to New York where he took courses in composition with Vincent Persichetti at the Juilliard School of Music, obtaining his M.S. in 1962. In 1964 he went to Paris to study with Nadia Boulanger; there he met Ravi Shankar who initiated him into the recondite world of Indian music. In 1966 he traveled to India in order to become acquainted more fully with Indian modalities. Returning to New York in 1967 he organized an ensemble of electrically amplified wind instruments which became the chief medium of his own compositions. On April 13, 1968 he presented his first concert at Queens College, New York. In 1969 he traveled with his ensemble to Europe; made altogether 8 European tours between 1969 and 1975. In 1970 and 1973 Glass was again in India. In his compositions he amalgamates seemingly incongruous elements; abstract intervallic structures, Oriental modes and serial procedures, further diversified by aleatory devices. His productions, both in America and in Europe, became unexpectedly successful, particularly with young audiences, mesmerized by this mixture of rock realism with nebulous mysticism; these audiences were not deterred by the indeterminability and indeed interminability of the Glass productions, some lasting several hours of unremitting homophony; Satie-like mind-boggling titles proved an additional tantalizing attraction. The list of performed works follows: *Piece in the Shape of a Square* (N.Y., May 19, 1968); *Music in Fifths* (N.Y., Jan. 16, 1970); *Music with Changing Parts* (N.Y., Nov. 10, 1970); *Music for Voices* (N.Y., Nov. 10, 1972); *Music in 12 Parts* (first full performance, N.Y., June 1, 1974); *Another Look at Harmony* (N.Y., May 6, 1975); *North Star* for two voices and instruments (1975). Increasingly, Philip Glass incorporated theatrical elements, both dramatic and choreographic, into his productions, culminating in the "opera" by Robert Wilson, with a musical score by Glass, *Einstein on the Beach,* first produced at the Festival of Avignon, France, on July 25, 1976, and subsequently performed in Venice, Belgrade, Brussels, Paris, Hamburg, Rotterdam, and Amsterdam, finally reaching the stage of the Metropolitan Opera at Lincoln Center in New York on Nov. 21, 1976, where it proved something of a sensation of the season.

Glaz, Herta, Austrian contralto; b. Vienna, Sept. 16, 1908. She made her debut at the Breslau Opera in 1931, presaging a successful career, but in 1933 was forced to leave Germany. She toured Austria and Scandinavia as a concert singer; sang at the German Theater in Prague during the season 1935–36; in 1936 she took part in the American tour of the Salzburg Opera Guild; subsequently sang at the Chicago Opera (1940–42); on Dec. 25, 1942 she made her debut with the Metropolitan Opera in New York, and remained on its staff until 1956; then taught voice at the Manhattan Conservatory.

Glazunov, Alexander, notable Russian composer; b. St. Petersburg, Aug. 10, 1865; d. Neuilly-sur-Seine, March 21, 1936. Of a well-to-do family (his father was a book publisher), he studied at a technical high school in St. Petersburg, and also took lessons in music with a private tutor. As a boy of 15, he was introduced to Rimsky-Korsakov, who gave him weekly lessons in harmony, counterpoint, and orchestration. Glazunov made rapid progress and at the age of 16 completed his first symphony, which was performed by Balakirev on March 29, 1882 in St. Petersburg. So mature was this score that Glazunov was hailed by Stasov, Cui, and others as a rightful heir to the masters of the Russian National School. The music publisher Belaiev arranged for publication of Glazunov's works, and took him to Weimar, where he met Liszt. From that time Glazunov composed assiduously in all genres except opera. He was invited to conduct his symphonies in Paris (1889) and London (1896–97). Returning to St. Petersburg, he conducted concerts of Russian music. In 1899 he was engaged as instructor in composition and orchestration at the St. Petersburg Cons. He resigned temporarily during the revolutionary turmoil of 1905 in protest against the dismissal of Rimsky-Korsakov by the government authorities, but returned to the staff after a full autonomy was granted to the Conservatory by the administration. On Dec. 14, 1905, Glazunov was elected Director and retained this post until 1928 when he went to Paris. In 1929 he made several appearances as conductor in the U.S.; led his 6th Symphony with the Detroit Symph. Orch. (Nov. 21, 1929) and also conducted the Boston Symph. He was the recipient of honorary degrees of Mus. D. from Cambridge and Oxford Universities (1907). Although he wrote no textbook on composition, his pedagogical methods left a lasting impression on Russian musicians through his many students who preserved his traditions. His music is often regarded as academic; yet there is a flow of rhapsodic eloquence that places Glazunov in the Romantic school. He was for a time greatly swayed by Wagnerian harmonies, but resisted this influence successfully; Lisztian characteristics are more pronounced in his works. Glazunov was one of the greatest masters of counterpoint among Russian composers, but he avoided extreme polyphonic complexity. The national spirit of his music is unmistakable; in many of his descriptive works, the programmatic design is explicitly Russian *(Stenka Razin, The Kremlin,* etc.). His most popular score is the ballet *Raymonda.* The major portion of his music was written before 1906, when he completed his 8th Symph.; after that he wrote mostly for special occasions.

WORKS: incidental music to Grand Duke Konstantin Romanov's mystery play *The King of the Jews* (1914); ballets, *Raymonda* (1896; St. Petersburg, Jan. 19, 1898); *Ruses d'amour* (1898); *The Seasons* (1899).

FOR ORCH.: Symph. No. 1 (1881; St. Petersburg, March 29, 1882); 2 *Overtures on Greek Themes* (1881–85); 2 Serenades (1883); *Stenka Razin,* symph. poem (1884); *A la mémoire d'un héros* (1885); *Suite caractéristique* (1885); *Idyll* and *Rêverie orientale* (1886); Symph. No. 2 (1886; Paris, June 29, 1889, Glazunov conducting); *Une Pensée à Franz Liszt* for string orch. (1886); *Mazurka* (1887); *The Forest,* symph. poem (1888); *Mélodie and Sérénade espagnole* for cello and orch. (1888); *Marche des Noces* for large orch. (1889); *Une Fête slave,* symph. sketch (1890; from *Quatuor slave*); *The Sea, symph. fantasy* (1890); *Oriental Rhapsody* (1890); *The Kremlin,* symph. picture (1890); Symph. No. 3 (1891); *Printemps,* musical picture (1892); *Triumphal March* on the occasion of the famous Columbian Exposition in Chicago (1893); overture *Carnaval* (1894); *Chopiniana,* suite on Chopin's themes (1894); 2 *Valses de concert* (1894); Symph. No. 4 (St. Petersburg, Feb. 3, 1894, composer conducting); *Cortège solennel* (1894); *Scènes de ballet* (1894); *Fantaisie* (1895); Symph. No. 5 (1895); suite from the ballet *Raymonda* (1897); Symph. No. 6 (1896); *Pas de caractère,* on Slavic and Hungarian themes (1900); *Intermezzo romantico* (1901); *Chant du Ménestrel* for cello and orch. (1901; also for cello and piano); *Ouverture solennelle* (1901); *Marche sur un thème russe* (1901); Symph. No. 7 (St. Petersburg, Jan. 3, 1903); *Ballade* (1903); *From the Middle Ages,* suite (1903); *Violin Concerto* (1904; St. Petersburg, March 4, 1905, Leopold Auer, soloist; first performance outside Russia, London, Oct. 17, 1905, Mischa Elman, soloist); *Scène dansante* (1905); Symph. No. 8 (Dec. 22, 1906); *Le Chant du destin,* dramatic overture (1907); 2 Preludes: No. 1, *In Memory of V. Stasov* (1906); No. 2, *In Memory of Rimsky-Korsakov* (1908); *In Memory of Gogol* (1909); *Finnish Fantasy* (Helsingfors, Nov. 7, 1910, composer conducting); Piano Concerto No. 1 (1911); *Finnish Sketches* (1912); *Dance of Salomé,* after Oscar Wilde (1912); *Karelian Legend* (1914); Piano Concerto No. 2 (1917); *Concerto-Ballata* for cello and orch. (Paris, Oct. 14, 1933, composer conducting, Maurice Eisenberg, soloist); Saxophone Concerto (in collaboration with Sigurd Rascher; first performed by him in Nykoping, Sweden, Nov. 25, 1934). VOCAL WORKS: *Coronation Cantata* (1894); *Hymn to Pushkin* for female chorus (1899); cantata for women's chorus with 2 pianos, 8 hands (1900); *Memorial Cantata* (1901); 21 songs. CHAMBER MUSIC: 7 string quartets: No. 1 in D (1882); No. 2 in F (1884); No. 3 in G (*Quatuor Slave,* 1889); No. 4 in A (1899); No. 5 in D (1900); No. 6 in B-flat (1930); No. 7 in C (1931); 5 *Novelettes* for string quartet (1888); Suite for String Quartet (1894); String Quintet (1895); Suite for String Quartet (1929); *Pensée à Liszt* for cello and piano; *Rêverie* for French horn and piano; *In modo religioso* for 4 brass instruments; *Elegy* for viola and piano; *Oberek* for violin and piano. PIANO MUSIC: 2 sonatas (1898; 1899); *Barcarolle; Novelette;* Prelude and 2 Mazurkas; 3 Etudes; *Petite Valse;* Nocturne; *Grande Valse de Concert: 3 Miniatures; Valse de Salon; 3 Morceaux;* 2 *Impromptus;* Prelude and Fugue; Theme and Variations; Suite for 2 Pianos (1920); 4 Preludes and Fugues (1922). Glazunov also completed and orchestrated the overture to Borodin's *Prince Igor*

(from memory, having heard Borodin play it on the piano).

BIBLIOGRAPHY: A. W. Ossovsky, *Glazunov: His Life and Work* (St. Petersburg, 1907); M. Montagu-Nathan, *Contemporary Russian Composers* (N.Y., 1917); V. Belaiev, *Glazunov* (vol. 1, Petrograd, 1921); I. Glebov, *Glazunov* (Leningrad, 1924); M.D. Calvocoressi and G. Abraham, *Masters of Russian Music* (N.Y., 1936); Galina Fedorova, *Glazunov* (Moscow, 1947).

Gleason, Frederick Grant, American organist, composer and critic; b. Middletown, Conn., Dec. 17, 1848; d. Chicago, Dec. 6, 1903. He studied in Hartford with Dudley Buck, later at the Leipzig Cons., in Berlin, and in London. Upon return to the U.S., he was active as a church organist, teacher and music critic. He wrote 2 operas, *Otho Visconti* (posthumous production; Chicago, June 4, 1907) and *Montezuma;* 4 cantatas; a symph. poem, *Edris;* a piano concerto; 3 piano trios; organ and piano pieces; songs; 2 Episcopal church services.

BIBLIOGRAPHY: E. E. Hipsher, *American Opera and Its Composers* (Philadelphia, 1934; pp. 216–17).

Gleason, Harold, American organist and musicologist; b. Jefferson, Ohio, April 26, 1892; studied organ in California with Lemare, and in Paris with Bonnet; composition with Herbert Inch at the Eastman School; occupied positions as church organist in Pasadena (1911–15), N.Y. (1918), Rochester (1919–49); was head of the organ department at the Eastman School from 1921–53; professor of musicology there from 1932–55. He designed organs for the Eastman School; was active in educational organizations. He publ. a *Method of Organ Playing* (1937); *Examples of Music before 1400* (1942; 2nd ed., 1945); *Music Literature Outlines* (5 issues; 1949–55); *Music in America,* an anthology (in collaboration with W. T. Marrocco; N.Y., 1964); contributed papers to music magazines.

Glebov, Igor. Pen name of **Boris Asafiev.**

Glen, John, Scots collector of native music; b. Edinburgh, June 13, 1833; d. there, Nov. 29, 1904. His father **Thomas** (1804–73), the inventor of the 'Serpentcleide,' had established himself as a manufacturer of musical instruments, and the son succeeded to the business in 1866; he confined himself to the manufacture of bagpipes, of which he was soon recognized as the foremost manufacturer of Great Britain. He was equally noted for his research in Scottish music; compiled *The Glen Collection of Scottish Dance Music, Strathspeys, Reels and Jigs . . . containing an Introduction on Scottish Dance Music* (2 vols., 1891, 1895); vol. I contains 144, vol. II 148, tunes. His chief work is *Early Scottish Melodies: including examples from MSS. and early printed works, along with a number of comparative tunes, notes on former annotators, English and other claims, and Biographical Notices, etc.* (1900).

BIBLIOGRAPHY: *Musical Times,* Jan. 1905.

Glick, Srul Irving, Canadian composer; b. Toronto, Sept. 8, 1934. He studied composition with Weinzweig at the Univ. of Toronto (M.M., 1958); then attended classes of Darius Milhaud in Aspen, Colorado (summers 1956, 1957) and later took lessons with him in Paris (1959–60). Returning to Canada, he taught theory and composition at the Cons. in Toronto (1963–69). His catalogue of works contains scores of two distinct types: those of a traditional Hebraic nature, direct and recognizable, and those that are abstract, written in a highly advanced idiom.

WORKS: *Heritage,* dance symphony (Toronto, Dec. 9, 1967); *2 Essays* for orch. (1957); Sonata for String Orch. (1957); *Sinfonietta* (1958); *Sinfonia Concertante* No. 1, for string orch. (1961); *Sinfonia Concertante* No. 2, *Lamentations,* for string quartet and orch. (1972); *Suite hébraïque* for orch. (1961); *Dance Concertante No. 1* for small orch. (1963); *Symphonic Dialogues* for piano and orch. (Toronto, Dec. 20, 1964); *Pan,* sketch for orch. (1966); Symph. No. 1 for chamber orch. (Toronto, April 24, 1966); Symph. No. 2 for full orch. (Toronto, Jan. 24, 1969); *Gathering In,* a "symphonic concept" for strings (Montreal, March 26, 1970); *Psalm* for orch. (Hamilton, Oct. 17, 1971); *Symphonic Elegy* (Toronto, April 20, 1974); Violin Concerto, subtitled *Shir Hamaalot (Songs of Ascents;* Victoria, British Columbia, Nov. 14, 1976); *. . . i never saw another butterfly . . . ,* to a text of children's poems written in the Terezin concentration camp, for alto, and chamber orch. (1968); *Deborah (Flaming Star),* for narrator and brass quintet (1972); *Divertimento Sextet,* for flute, clarinet, bassoon and string trio (1958); Trio for Clarinet, Piano and Cello (1958–59); String Trio (1963); *Dance Concertante No. 2* for flute, clarinet, trumpet, cello and piano (1964); Sonata for jazz quintet (1964); Sonatina for jazz sextet (1965–66); *Divertissement for 7 Instruments and Conductor* (1968); *Suite hébraïque* No. 2 for clarinet, piano and string trio (1969); *Suite hébraïque* No. 3 for string quintet (1975); *Prayer and Dance* for cello and piano (1975); a number of piano pieces; songs; liturgical choruses for Hebrew services.

Glière, Reinhold, eminent Russian composer; b. Kiev, Jan. 11, 1875; d. Moscow, June 23, 1956. He studied violin with Hrimaly; entered the Moscow Cons., where he took courses with Arensky, Taneyev, and Ippolitov-Ivanov (1894–1900), graduating with a gold medal. In 1905 he went to Berlin, where he remained for 2 years; returning to Russia, he became active as a teacher; was appointed prof. of composition at the Kiev Cons., and was its director from 1914–20; then was appointed to the faculty of the Moscow Cons., a post he retained to the end of his life. He traveled extensively in European and Asiatic Russia, collecting folk melodies; conducted many concerts of his own works; he made his last tour a month before his death, conducting in Odessa, Kishinev, and other cities. He was an extremely prolific composer, and was particularly distinguished in symphonic works, in which he revealed himself as a successor of the Russian National School. He never transgressed the natural borderline of traditional harmony, but he was able to achieve effective results. His most impressive work is his 3rd Symph., surnamed *Ilya Murometz,* an epic description of the exploits of a legendary Russian hero. In his numerous songs Glière showed a fine lyrical talent. He wrote relatively few works of chamber music, most of them early in his career. In his opera, *Shah-Senem,* he made use of native Caucasian songs. Glière was the teacher of two generations of Russian composers; among his students were Prokofiev and Miaskovsky.

WORKS: OPERAS: *Shah-Senem* (Baku, May 4, 1934); *Leily and Medzhnun* (Tashkent, July 18, 1940); *Rachel,* one-act opera after Maupassant's *Mademoiselle Fifi* (Moscow, April 19, 1947); *Ghulsara* (Tashkent, Dec. 25, 1949); ballets: *Chrysis* (Moscow, Nov. 30, 1912); *Cleopatra* (Moscow, Jan. 11, 1926); *Red Poppy* (Moscow, June 14, 1927); *Comedians* (Moscow, April 5, 1931); *The Bronze Knight* (Leningrad, March 14, 1949). INCIDENTAL MUSIC: *King Oedipus* of Sophocles (1921); *Lysistrata* of Aristophanes (1923); *Marriage of Figaro* of Beaumarchais (1927). FOR ORCH.: Symph. No. 1 (Moscow, Jan. 3, 1903); Symph. No. 2 (Berlin, Jan. 23, 1908, Koussevitzky conducting); *The Sirens,* symph. poem (Moscow, Jan. 30, 1909); Symph. No. 3, *Ilya Murometz* (Moscow, March 23, 1912); *Two Poems* for soprano and orch. (1924); *Cossacks of Zaporozh,* symph. poem (1921; Odessa, Dec. 23, 1925); *Trizna,* symph. poem (1915); *For the Festival of the Comintern,* fantasy for wind orch. (1924); *March of the Red Army,* for wind orch. (1924); *Imitation of Jezekiel,* symph. poem for narrator and orch. (1919); Concerto for Harp and Orch. (Moscow, Nov. 23, 1938); *Friendship of Nations,* overture (1941); Concerto for Coloratura Soprano and Orch. (Moscow, May 12, 1943); *For the Happiness of the Fatherland,* overture (1942); *25 Years of the Red Army,* overture (1943); *Victory,* overture (Moscow, Oct. 30, 1945); Cello Concerto (Moscow, Feb. 18, 1947); Horn Concerto (Moscow, Jan. 26, 1952, composer conducting); he left an unfinished violin concerto. CHAMBER MUSIC: 5 string quartets (No. 4 won the Stalin Prize, 1948; No. 5 left unfinished at his death); 3 string sextets; 1 string octet. Other music: 20 pieces for violin and piano; 12 duos for two violins; Ballad for Cello and Piano; 4 pieces for double bass and piano; 8 pieces for violin and cello; 12 pieces for cello and piano; 10 duos for 2 cellos; miscellaneous pieces for different instruments. He also wrote about 200 songs and 200 piano pieces.

BIBLIOGRAPHY: Igor Boelza, *R. M. Glière* (Moscow, 1962). A 2-volume edition of articles and memoirs on Glière was published in Moscow in 1965, 1967.

Glinka, Mikhail, great Russian composer, often called "father of Russian music" for his pioneering cultivation of Russian folk modalities; b. Novosspaskoye, Govt. of Smolensk, June 1, 1804; d. Berlin, Feb. 15, 1857. A scion of a fairly rich family of landowners, he was educated in an exclusive school at St. Petersburg (1818–22); he also took private lessons in music; his piano teacher was a resident German musician, Carl Meyer; he also studied violin; when the famous pianist, John Field, was in St. Petersburg, Glinka had an opportunity to study with him, but he had only three lessons owing to Field's departure. He began to compose even before acquiring adequate training in theory. As a boy he traveled in the Caucasus; then stayed for a while at his father's estate; at 20 entered the

Ministry of Communications in St. Petersburg; he remained in government employ until 1828; at the same time, he constantly improved his general education by reading; he had friends among the best Russian writers of the time, including the poets Zhukovsky and Pushkin. He also took singing lessons with an Italian teacher, Belloli. In 1830 he went to Italy, where he continued irregular studies in Milan (where he spent most of his Italian years); he also visited Naples, Rome, and Bologna. He met Donizetti and Bellini. He became enamored of Italian music, and his early vocal and instrumental compositions are thoroughly Italian in melodic and harmonic structure. In 1833 he went to Berlin, where he took a course in counterpoint and general composition with the famous German theorist Dehn; thus he was nearly 30 when he completed his theoretical education. In 1834 his father died, and Glinka went back to Russia to take care of the family affairs. In 1835 he was married; but the marriage was unhappy, and he soon became separated from his wife, finally divorcing her in 1846. The return to his native land led him to consider the composition of a truly national opera on a subject (suggested to him by Zhukovsky) depicting a historical episode in Russian history, the saving of the first Tsar of the Romanov dynasty by a simple peasant, Ivan Susanin. (The Italian composer, Cavos, wrote an opera on the same subject 20 years previously, and conducted it in St. Petersburg.) Glinka's opera was produced in St. Petersburg on Dec. 9, 1836, under the Title, *A Life for the Tsar.* The event was hailed by the literary and artistic circles of Russia as a milestone of Russian culture, and indeed the entire development of Russian national music received its decisive creative impulse from Glinka's patriotic opera. It remained in the repertory of Russian theaters until the Russian Revolution made it unacceptable, but it was revived, under the original title, *Ivan Susanin,* on Feb. 27, 1939, in Moscow, without alterations in the music, but with the references to the Tsar eliminated from the libretto, the idea of saving the country being substituted for that of saving the Tsar. Glinka's next opera, *Ruslan and Ludmila,* after Pushkin's fairy tale, was produced on Dec. 9, 1842; this opera, too, became extremely popular in Russia. Glinka introduced into the score many elements of Oriental music; one episode contains the earliest use of the whole-tone scale in an opera. Both operas retain the traditional Italian form, with arias, choruses, and orchestral episodes clearly separated. In 1844, Glinka was in Paris, where he met Berlioz; he also traveled in Spain, where he collected folksongs; the fruits of his Spanish tour were two orchestral works, *Jota Aragonesa* and *Night in Madrid.* On his way back to Russia, he stayed in Warsaw for 3 years; the remaining years of his life he spent in St. Petersburg, Paris, and Berlin, where he died.

WORKS: OPERAS: *A Life for the Tsar; Ruslan and Ludmila;* sketches for 3 unfinished operas; *Chao-Kang,* a ballet (1828–31); incidental music for Kukolnik's tragedy, *Prince Kholmsky;* incidental music for the play, *The Moldavian Gypsy;* FOR ORCH.: *Andante Cantabile and Rondo;* a larghetto; 2 overtures; Symphony in B-flat; *Trumpet March* (1828); *Overture-Symphony on Russian Themes* (1834; completed in 1938 by V. I. Shebalin); *Valse* (1839); *Polonaise*

(1839); *Valse-Fantaisie* (1839); *Capricio brillante* on the *Jota Aragonesa* (1845; afterwards renamed *Spanish Overture No. 1); Summer Night in Madrid: Spanish Overture No. 2* (1848); *Kamarinskaya* (1848); symph. poem on Gogol's *Taras Bulba* (unfinished, part of first movement only; 1852); *Festival Polonaise* on a bolero melody (1855); CHAMBER MUSIC: Septet in E-flat (1824); 2 string quartets (1824, 1830); *Trio pathétique* (1827); 2 serenades (1832); Sonata for Piano and Viola (1825–28); about 40 piano numbers (5 valses, 7 mazurkas, nocturnes, etc.); much vocal music, including choral works, quartets, duets, arias, and about 85 songs with piano accompaniment, many set to poems by Pushkin and Zhukovsky.

BIBLIOGRAPHY: O. Comettant, *Musique et Musiciens* (Paris, 1862); C. Cui, *La Musique en Russie* (Paris, 1880); O. Fouque, *Glinka* (Paris, 1880); K. Albrecht, *Catalogue of Glinka's Vocal Works* (Moscow, 1891); P. Weimarn, *M. I. Glinka* (Moscow, 1892); L. Shestakova, *Glinka as He Was* (St. Petersburg, 1894); N. F. Findeisen, *M. I. Glinka* (St. Petersburg, 1896); N. F. Findeisen, *Glinka in Spain and the Spanish Folksongs Recorded by Him* (St. Petersburg, 1896); N. F. Findeisen, *Catalogue of the Musical Manuscripts, Letters, and Portraits of M. I. Glinka in the Manuscript Section of the Imperial Public Library in St. Petersburg* (St. Petersburg, 1898); V. Avenarius, *Glinka, the Creator of Russian Opera* (St. Petersburg, 1903); A. Pougin, *Essai historique sur la musique en Russie* (Paris, 1904); M. D. Calvocoressi, *Glinka* (Paris, 1913); M. Montagu-Nathan, *Glinka* (London, 1916); K. A. Kuznetzov, *Glinka and His Contemporaries* (1926); M. D. Calvocoressi and G. Abraham, *Glinka in Masters of Russian Music* (N.Y., 1936); D. Brook, *Six Great Russian Composers* (London, 1946); I. I. Martinov, *M. I. Glinka* (Moscow, 1947); A. Altayev, *M. I. Glinka* (Moscow, 1947); B. Asafiev, *Glinka* (Moscow, 1947); E. Kann-Novikova, *M. I. Glinka, New Materials and Documents* (Moscow, 1951); A. Orlova, *M. I. Glinka, Chronicle of Life and Work* (Moscow, 1952); P. G. Dippel, *Klingende Einkehr; Glinka und Berlin* (Berlin, 1953); A. Orlova, *Glinka in St. Petersburg* (Leningrad, 1970). Glinka's autobiographical sketch intended for inclusion in the *Biographie universelle des musiciens* by Fétis was publ. for the first time in *Muzikalnaya Letopis* in 1926; his collected letters, edited by N. Findeisen, were publ. in 1907.

Glinski, Mateusz, Polish musicologist; b. Warsaw, April 6, 1892; d. Welland, Ontario, Canada, Jan. 3, 1976. He studied at the Warsaw Cons. with Barcewicz (violin) and Statkowski (composition); then took courses in Leipzig with Max Reger, Riemann and Schering; also had lessons in conducting with Nikisch. He went to St. Petersburg in 1914; studied composition with Glazunov and Steinberg and conducting with Nicolas Tcherepnin. He conducted several concerts; also contributed articles on music to Russian periodicals. In 1918 he went to Warsaw; from 1924 to 1939 was editor of the Polish periodical *Muzyka.* At the outbreak of World War II he went to Rome, where he engaged in various activities as music critic and editor. In 1949 he established in Rome the Istituto Internazionale Federico Chopin. In 1956 he went to America; from 1959 to 1965 he taught at Assumption

Univ. in Windsor, Canada. In 1965 he established the Niagara Symph. Orch., which he conducted. His works include an opera, *Orlotko,* after Rostand's play *L'Aiglon* (1918-27); a symph. poem, *Wagram* (1932); several choral works, songs and piano pieces. He published, in Polish, a monograph on Scriabin (Warsaw, 1933) and numerous articles in the Polish periodicals. He also published an edition, *Chopin's Letters to Delfina Potocka* (Windsor, Canada, 1961), in which he subscribes to the generally refuted belief that these letters that came to light in 1945 are indeed genuine.

Globokar, Vinko, French composer of Slovenian descent; b. Anderny, July 7, 1935. He studied trombone in Ljubljana (1949-54); and at the Paris Cons. (1955-59); took composition lessons in Paris with René Leibowitz and with Luciano Berio. In 1965 he was appointed trombone instructor at the Cologne Musikhochschule. As a composer he follows the most modern ideas of serial music in aleatory distribution. His works include *Plan* for a Persian drum and 4 instruments (1965); *Fluide* for 9 brasses and 3 percussion instruments (1967); *Traumdeutung,* a "psychodrama" (Amsterdam, Sept. 7, 1968); *Étude pour folklore I* for 19 soloists (1968); *Étude pour folklore II* for orch. (1968); *Concerto Grosso* (Cologne, Nov. 6, 1970); *Airs de voyages vers l'interieur* for ensemble (Stuttgart, Nov. 3, 1972).

Glock, Sir William, English music critic; b. London, May 3, 1908. He studied at Caius College, Cambridge; then took piano lessons with Schnabel in Berlin. In 1949 he founded *The Score* magazine; edited it until 1961; from 1959 he was attached to the BBC; in 1964 he was created Commander of the Order of the British Empire; was knighted in 1970.

Glodeanu, Liviu, Rumanian composer; b. Dîrja, Aug. 6, 1938. He studied with Liviu Comes and Dorin Pop at the Cluj Cons. (1955-57) and at the Bucharest Cons. with Ion Dumitrescu, Martian Negrea, Alfred Mendelsohn and Tudor Ciortea (1957-61). He taught at the School of Arts there (1961-63); then was artistic adviser of the Philharmonic Orch. (1963-71).

WORKS: a radio opera *Zamolxe* (Bucharest Radio, Oct. 8, 1969); 4 cantatas: *The Young Dead Soldiers,* after MacLeish (1958), *Inscription on the Cradle* (1959), *Bright Horizons* (1960) and *Canata 1933* (1961); Concerto for String Orch. and Percussion (1959); Piano Concerto (1960); Flute Concerto (1962); Violin Concerto (1966); *Ulysses,* poem for soprano or tenor, and orch. or piano (1967); *Studies* for orch. (1967); *Ricercari* for orch. (1971); *Symphonies* for wind instruments (1971); Suite for children's chorus, winds and percussion (1961); *2 Madrigals* for chorus and percussion (1963); *Incantation* for chorus, flute, clarinet and percussion (1965); *Gloire* for children's chorus and percussion (1967); 2 piano sonatas (1958, 1963); Clarinet Sonata (1959); 2 string quartets (1959, 1970); *Inventions* for wind quintet and percussion (1963); Violin Sonatina (1963); *Melopée* for flute, clarinet, violin and tape (1971).

Glorieux, François, Belgian pianist and composer; b. Courtrai, Aug. 27, 1932. He studied at the Royal Cons.

in Ghent, graduating in 1953; concertized in the U.S., Canada, Latin America, Africa, Spain and the Middle East. His music, couched in a clear tonal idiom, reflects his preoccupation with exotic rhythms.

WORKS: the ballets *L'Énigme* and *Ritus Paganus* (1970); *Mouvements* for piano, brass and percussion (Brussels, Nov. 28, 1964); *Effects* for percussion, flute and piano (1966); *Rites* for 10 percussionists (1969); *Manhattan* for orch. (Antwerp, March 28, 1974); Piano Sonata and small piano pieces.

Glover, John William, Irish composer and conductor; b. Dublin, June 19, 1815; d. there, Dec. 18, 1899. He studied in Dublin, and was violinist in an orchestra there; in 1848, he became prof. of vocal music in the Normal Training School of the Irish National Education Board and also director of music in the Roman Catholic procathedral. He established the Choral Institute in 1851, and was noted for his promotion of choral music in Ireland. He edited Moore's *Irish Melodies* (1859).

WORKS: opera, *The Deserted Village,* after Goldsmith (London, 1880); 2 Italian operas to librettos by Metastasio; cantata, *St. Patrick at Tara* (1870); *Erin's Matin Song* (1873); ode to Thomas Moore, *One hundred years ago* (1879); also concertos, piano pieces, songs, church music.

Glover, Sarah Ann, English piano pedagogue; b. Norwich, Nov. 13, 1786; d. Malvern, Oct. 20, 1867. She was the originator of the tonic sol-fa system of notation, a method later modified and developed by John Curwen. She wrote: *Scheme for rendering Psalmody Congregational* (1835), *Manual of the Norwich Sol-fa System* (1845), and a *Manual containing a Development of the Tetrachordal System* (1850). She devised a pictorial chart called the "Norwich Sol-fa Ladder."

Glover, William Howard, English conductor and composer; b. London, June 6, 1819; d. New York, Oct. 28, 1875. He played the violin in the Lyceum Theater orch. in London; conducted opera in Manchester, Liverpool and London. In 1868 he came to New York, where he was conductor at Niblo's Garden until his death.

WORKS: opera, *Ruy Blas* (London, Oct. 21, 1861); operettas: *Aminta* (London, Jan. 26, 1852); *Once Too Often* (London, Jan. 20, 1862); *Palomita, or The Veiled Songstress* (publ. in N.Y., 1875); cantata, *Tam o' Shanter* (London, July 4, 1855, Berlioz conducting); overtures; piano music; songs.

Gluck, Alma (real name **Reba Fiersohn**), American soprano; b. Bucharest, Rumania, May 11, 1884; d. New York, Oct. 27, 1938. Her parents brought her to New York as a small child; she was educated in the public schools, the Normal School (now Hunter College), and Union College, Schenectady, N.Y. After her marriage to Bernard Gluck, she studied singing with Buzzi-Peccia; she was engaged for the Metropolitan Opera in 1909, and made her debut as Sophie in Massenet's *Werther* on Nov. 16, 1909. She became a favorite with the public, and sang more than 20 roles during her three years in opera. In 1912, she gave up opera for the concert stage; she also divorced Mr.

Gluck; she studied for a year with Marcella Sembrich in Berlin; returned to the U.S. in 1913 for many years of successful concert work; she was noted also as a recording artist. She married the violinist **Efrem Zimbalist** in 1914. She returned from retirement to give a concert at the Manhattan Opera House in 1925. Glimpses of her career are shown in *Of Lena Geyer*, a novel published by her daughter, **Marcia Davenport**.

Gluck, Christoph Willibald (Ritter von), renowned composer; b. Erasbach, near Weidenwang in the Upper Palatinate, July 2, 1714; d. Vienna, Nov. 15, 1787. His father was a forester at Erasbach until his appointment as forester to Prince Lobkowitz of Eisenberg about 1729. Gluck received his elementary instruction in the village schools at Kamnitz and Albersdorf near Komotau, where he was taught singing and instrumental playing. Some biographers refer to his study at the Jesuit college at Komotau, but there is no documentary evidence to support this contention. In 1732 Gluck went to Prague to complete his education, but it is doubtful that he took any courses at Prague Univ. He earned his living in Prague by playing violin and cello at rural dances in the area; also sang at various churches; there he had an opportunity to meet Bohuslav Černohorsky, who was chapelmaster at St. James' Church from 1735; it is probable that Gluck learned the methods of church music from him. He went to Vienna in 1736, and was chamber musician to young Prince Lobkowitz, son of the patron of Gluck's father. In 1737 he was taken to Milan by Prince Melzi; this Italian sojourn was of the greatest importance to Gluck's musical development. There he became a student of G. B. Sammartini and acquired a solid technique of composition in the Italian style. After 4 years of study, Gluck brought out his first opera *Artaserse*, to the text of the celebrated Metastasio; it was produced in Milan (Dec. 26, 1741) with such success that Gluck was immediately commissioned to write more operas. There followed *Demetrio* or *Cleonice* (Venice, May 2, 1742); *Demofoonte* (Milan, Dec. 26, 1742); *Il Tigrane* (Crema, Sept. 9, 1743); *La Sofonisba* or *Siface* (Milan, Jan. 13, 1744); *Ipermestra* (Venice, Nov. 21, 1744); *Poro* (Turin, Dec. 26, 1744); *Ippolito* or *Fedra* (Milan, Jan. 31, 1745). He also contributed separate numbers to several other operas produced in Italy. In 1745 Gluck received an invitation to go to London; on his way, he visited Paris and met Rameau. He was commissioned by the Italian Opera of London to write 2 operas for the Haymarket Theatre, as a competitive endeavor to Handel's enterprise. The first of these works was *La Caduta dei giganti*, a tribute to the Duke of Cumberland on the defeat of the Pretender; it was produced on Jan. 17, 1746; the second was a pasticcio, *Artamene*, in which Gluck used material from his previous operas; it was produced March 15, 1746. Ten days later, Gluck appeared with Handel at a public concert, despite the current report in London society that Handel had declared that Gluck knew no more counterpoint than his cook (it should be added that a professional musician, Gustavus Waltz, was Handel's cook and valet at the time). On April 23, 1746, Gluck gave a demonstration in London, playing on the 'glass harmonica.' He left London late in 1746 when he received an engagement

as conductor with Pietro Mingotti's traveling Italian opera company. He conducted in Hamburg, Leipzig, and Dresden; on June 29, 1747, he produced a 'serenata,' *Le Nozze d'Ercole e d'Ebe*, to celebrate a royal wedding; it was performed at the Saxon court, in Pillnitz. Gluck then went to Vienna, where he staged his opera, *Semiramide riconosciuta*, after a poem of Metastasio (May 14, 1748). He then traveled to Copenhagen, where he produced a festive opera, *La Contesa dei Numi* (March 9, 1749), on the occasion of the birth of Prince Christian; his next productions (all to Metastasio's words) were *Ezio* (Prague, 1750); *Issipile* (Prague, 1752); *La Clemenza di Tito* (Naples, Nov. 4, 1752); *Le Cinesi* (Vienna, Sept. 24, 1754); *La Danza* (Vienna, May 5, 1755); *L'innocenza giustificata* (Vienna, Dec. 8, 1755); *Antigono* (Rome, Feb. 9, 1756); *Il re pastore* (Vienna, Dec. 8, 1756). In 1750 Gluck married Marianna Pergin, daughter of a Viennese merchant; for several years afterwards he conducted operatic performances in Vienna. As French influence increased there, Gluck wrote several entertainments to French texts, containing spoken dialogue, in style of opéra comique; of these, the most successful were *Le Cadi dupé* (December, 1761) and *La Rencontre imprévue* (Jan. 7, 1764; performed also under the title *Les Pèlerins de la Mecque*), his most popular production in this genre). His greatest work of the Vienna period was *Orfeo ed Euridice* to a libretto by Calzabigi (in a version for male contralto; Oct. 5, 1762, with the part of Orfeo sung by the famous castrato, Gaetano Guadagni). Gluck revised it for a Paris performance, produced in French on Aug. 2, 1774, with Orfeo sung by a tenor. There followed another masterpiece, *Alceste* (Vienna, Dec. 16, 1767), also to Calzabigi's text. In the preface to *Alceste*, Gluck formulated his esthetic credo, which elevated the dramatic meaning of musical stage plays above the mere striving for vocal effects: "I sought to reduce music to its true function, that of seconding poetry in order to strengthen the emotional expression and the impact of the dramatic situations without interrupting the action and without weakening it by superfluous ornaments." Among other productions of the Viennese period were *Il Trionfo di Clelia* (Vienna, May 14, 1763); *Il Parnaso confuso* (Schönbrunn Palace, Jan. 24, 1765); *Il Telemacco* (Vienna, Jan. 30, 1765), and *Paride ed Elena* (Vienna, Nov. 30, 1770). The success of his French operas in Vienna led Gluck to the decision to try his fortunes in Paris, yielding to the persuasion of François du Roullet, an attaché at the French embassy in Vienna, who also supplied Gluck with his first libretto for a serious French opera, an adaptation of Racine's *Iphigénie en Aulide* (Paris, April 19, 1774). Gluck set out for Paris early in 1773, preceded by declarations in the Paris press by du Roullet and Gluck himself explaining in detail Gluck's ideas of dramatic music. These statements set off an intellectual battle in the Paris press and among musicians in general between the adherents of traditional Italian opera and Gluck's novel French opera. It reached an unprecedented degree of acrimony when the Italian composer Nicola Piccinni was engaged by the French court to write operas to French texts, in open competition to Gluck; intrigues multiplied, even though Marie Antoinette never wavered in her admiration for Gluck, who taught her singing and harpsichord playing, However, Gluck and Piccinni themselves never participated in the bitter polemics unleashed by their literary and musical partisans. The sensational successes of the French version of Gluck's *Orfeo* and of *Alceste* were followed by the production of *Armide* (Sept. 23, 1777), which aroused great admiration. Then followed Gluck's masterpiece, *Iphigénie en Tauride* (May 17, 1779), which established Gluck's superiority to Piccinni, who was commissioned to write an opera on the same subject, but failed to complete it in time. Gluck's last opera, *Echo et Narcisse* (Paris, Sept. 24, 1779), did not measure up to the excellence of his previous operas. By that time, Gluck's health had failed; he had several attacks of apoplexy, which resulted in a partial paralysis. In the autumn of 1779 he returned to Vienna, where he lived as an invalid for several more years. His last work was a *De profundis* for chorus and orchestra, written 5 years before his death. Besides his operas, he wrote several ballets, of which *Don Juan* (Vienna, Oct. 17, 1761) was the most successful; he further wrote a cycle of 7 songs to words by Klopstock, 7 trio sonatas, several overtures, etc. Breitkopf & Härtel publ. excellent editions of Gluck's most important operas; other operas are included in *Denkmäler der Tonkunst in Bayern* vol. 26 (14.ii) and *Denkmäler der Tonkunst in Österreich* vols. 44a, 60, and 82 (21.ii, 30.ii and 44); H. Gál edited a Sinfonia in G, identical with the overture to *Ipermestra*; the trio sonatas are found in Riemann's *Collegium musicum;* songs in Delsarte's *Archives du chant.* Wagner, while in Dresden (1842–49), made a complete revision of the score of *Iphigénie en Aulide;* this arrangement was so extensively used that a Wagnerized version of Gluck's music became the chief text for performances during the 19th century. A complete ed. of Gluck's works was begun by the Bärenreiter Verlag in 1951.

BIBLIOGRAPHY: F. J. Riedel, *Über die Musik des Ritters Christoph von Gluck* (Vienna, 1775); C. P. Coqueau, *Entretiens sur l'état actuel de l'opéra de Paris* (Paris, 1779; dialogue on the Gluck-Piccinni controversy); G. M. Leblond, *Mémoires pour servir à l'histoire de la révolution opérée dans la musique par M. le Chevalier Gluck* (Paris, 1781; German transl., 1823; 2nd ed., 1837); J. G. Siegmeyer, *Über den Ritter Gluck und seine Werke* (Berlin, 1837); E. Miel, *Notice sur Gluck* (Paris, 1840); A. Schmid, *Christoph Willibald Ritter von Gluck* (Leipzig, 1854); W. Neumann, *Christoph Willibald Gluck* (Kassel, 1855); J. Baudoin, *L'Alceste de Gluck* (Paris, 1861); A. B. Marx, *Gluck und die Oper* (Berlin, 1863); L. Nohl, *Gluck und Wagner* (Munich, 1870); G. Desnoiresterres, *Gluck et Piccinni* (Paris, 1875); A. Jullien, *La Cour et l'opéra sous Louis XVI* (Paris, 1878); E. Thoinan, *Notes bibliographiques sur la guerre musicale des Gluckistes et Piccinnistes* (Paris, 1878); H. Barbedette, *Gluck* (Paris, 1882); A. Reissmann, *Christoph Willibald von Gluck* (Berlin, 1882); K. H. Bitter, *Die Reform der Oper durch Gluck und Wagner* (Brunswick, 1884); H. Welti, *Gluck* (Leipzig, 1888); E. Newman, *Gluck and the Opera* (London, 1895); J. d'Udine, *Gluck* (Paris, 1906); J. Tiersot, *Gluck* (Paris, 1910); La Mara, *Gluck* (Leipzig, 1912; reprinted from *Musik Studienköpfe);* Ernst Kurth, "Die Jugendopern Gluck," *Studien zur Musikwissenschaft* I (1913); H. Berlioz, *Gluck and His Operas* (transl. from the French by Edwin Evans, Sr.; London, 1915); S. Wortsmann, *Die deutsche Gluck-Literatur* (Nuremberg, 1914); W. B. Squire, "Gluck's London Operas," *Musical Quarterly* (July 1915); J.-G. Prod'homme, "Gluck's French Collaborators," *Musical Quarterly* (April 1917); J.-G. Prod'homme, "Les Portraits français de Gluck," *Rivista Musicale Italiana* XXV, 1 (1918); M. Arend, *Gluck* (1921); W. Vetter, "Die Arie bei Gluck," *Zeitschrift für Musikwissenschaft* III (1921); R. Haas, "Die Wiener Ballet-Pantomime im 18. Jahrhundert und Glucks *Don Juan,*" *Studien zur Musikwissenschaft* X (1923); E. H. Müller, "Zwei unveröffentlichte Briefe Glucks an Carl August," *Die Musik* (Stuttgart, 1923); G. Scuderi, *Christoph Gluck: Orfeo* (Milan, 1924); R. Haas, *Gluck und Durazzo im Burgtheater* (Vienna, 1925); Paul Brück, "Glucks *Orpheus* und *Eurydike,*" *Archiv für Musikwissenschaft* VIII/4 (1926); Georg Kinsky, "Glucks Reisen nach Paris," *Zeitschrift für Musikwissenschaft* VIII; Georg Kinsky, *Glucks Briefe an Franz Kruthoffer* (Vienna, 1929); M. Cauchie, "Gluck et ses éditeurs parisiens," *Le Ménestrel* (1927); Th. Veidl, "Neues über Glucks Jugend," *Auftakt* VIII/3 (1928); Julien Tiersot, "Gluck and the Encyclopaedists," *Musical Quarterly* (July 1930); E. Istel, "Gluck's Dramaturgy," *Musical Quarterly* (April 1931); K. Huschke, "Gluck und seine deutsche Zeitgenossen," *Zeitschrift für Musikwissenschaft* (March 1933); L. de la Laurencie, *Gluck, Orphée: étude et analyse musicale* (Paris, 1934); D. F. Tovey, "Christoph Willibald Gluck and the Musical Revolution," in H. Foss, *The Heritage of Music,* vol. 2 (London, 1934); M. Cooper, *Gluck* (London, 1935); A. Einstein, *Gluck* (London, 1936); R. Tenschert, *Christoph Willibald Gluck (1714–1787); sein Leben in Bildern* (Leipzig, 1938); P. Landormy, *Gluck* (Paris, 1941); A. Della Corte, *Gluck* (Turin, 1942); W. Brandl, *Christoph Willibald Ritter von Gluck* (Wiesbaden, 1948); A. Della Corte, *Gluck e i suoi tempi* (Florence, 1948); J.-G. Prod'homme, *Gluck* (Paris, 1948); R. Gerber, *C. W. Ritter von Gluck* (Potsdam, 1950); R. Tenschert, *Christoph Willibald Gluck: der grosse Reformator der Oper* (Freiburg, 1951); A. A. Abert, *G. W. Gluck* (Munich, 1959); *The Collected Correspondence and Papers of C. W. Gluck* (London, 1962); Patricia Howard, *Gluck and the Birth of Modern Opera* (N.Y., 1964); W. Vetter, *Christoph Willibald Gluck* (Leipzig, 1964); D. Heartz, "From Garrick to Gluck: The Reform of Theatre and Opera in the Mid-Eighteenth Century," *Proceedings of the Royal Musical Association* (1967–68); G. Croll, "Gluckforschung und Gluck-Gesamtausgabe," in R. Baum and W. Rehm, eds. *Musik und Verlag* (Kassel, 1968); H. C. R. London, *Essays on the Viennese Classical Style* (N.Y., 1970); K. Hortschansky, "Arianna (1762)—ein Pasticcio von Gluck," *Die Musikforschung* (Oct.–Dec. 1971). A thematic catalogue was publ. by A. Wotquenne (Leipzig, 1904; German transl. with supplement by J. Liebeskind). See also C. Hopkinson, *A Bibliography of the Printed Works of C.W. von Gluck, 1714–1787* (2nd ed., N.Y., 1967).

Glyn, Margaret Henrietta, English musicologist; b. Ewell, Surrey, Feb. 28, 1865; d. there, June 3, 1946. She studied in London under Henry Frost and Yorke Trotter; became an authority on keyboard music of the Tudor period. She edited organ and virginal music by Byrd, Orlando Gibbons, John Bull, and other composers, and wrote the following books: *The Rhythmic Conception of Music* (1907); *Analysis of the Evolution of Musical Form* (1909); *About Elizabethan Virginal Music and Its Composers* (1924; 2nd ed., 1934); *Theory of Musical Evolution* (1924). She also composed a number of works for organ.

Gnazzo, Anthony J., American avant-garde composer; b. New Britain, Conn., April 21, 1936. He studied music theory at Brandeis Univ. (M.F.A., 1965; Ph.D., 1970); mathematics at the Univ. of Hartford (B.A., 1963); served in the U.S. Navy (1957–61); attended 21 Navy schools and took courses in technology, data processing and allied subjects; was instructor in electronic system design at the Univ. of Toronto (1965–66); lecturer in music at Mills College (1967–69); in 1969 appointed design consultant and equipment technician in the electronics laboratory at Calif. State College at Hayward; also worked as computer programmer. His compositions are notated in the form of geometric graphs with verbal instructions and rhetorical interjections, e.g. 'Music, is it? Eh? It IS!!! But! Music? Yes, Music!' His 'theater pieces' are graphic scenarios with action indicated by circles, curves and vectors. His *Canned Music* (1969) is a sticker inscribed, 'Caution—Caution—Caution—This Can Has Been Filled with Extremely Loud Sound for 45 Minutes! Open With Care!' He also designed a piece entitled *Four-Letter Words* in surrealistically drawn phallic shapes. Among his literary productions are intermittent dialogues and 'manifolds' for the theater, e.g. *Inevitably Plastic* (1969) and *Experience Counter Experience* (1970).

Gnecchi, Vittorio, Italian opera composer; b. Milan, July 17, 1876; d. there, Feb. 1, 1954. He studied at the Milan Cons. His opera, *Cassandra,* was performed at Bologna on Dec. 5, 1905; some years later, after the première of Richard Strauss's *Elektra,* there was considerable discussion when the Italian critic Giovanni Tebaldini pointed out the identity of some 50 themes in both *Cassandra* and *Elektra* ("Telepatia Musicale," *Rivista Musicale Italiana,* Feb.-March 1909). Gnecchi also wrote the operas *Virtù d'Amore* (1896) and *La Rosiera,* after a comedy by Alfred de Musset (given at Gera, Germany, Feb. 12, 1927; in Italian, at Trieste, Jan. 24, 1931).

BIBLIOGRAPHY: F. B. Pratella, *Luci ed ombre: per un musicista italiano ignorato in Italia* (Rome, 1933).

Gnessin, Mikhail, Russian composer; b. Rostov-on-the-Don, Feb. 2, 1883; d. Moscow, May 5, 1957. He studied at the St. Petersburg Cons. with Rimsky-Korsakov and Liadov from 1901–08; went to Germany in 1911; in 1914, returned to Rostov, where he composed, taught music, and interested himself in various socialist activities. He made a trip to Palestine in 1921 to study Jewish music; some of his subsequent work reflected this visit. After 1923, he composed and taught alternately in Moscow and Leningrad. In addition to his Jewish music, he composed a number of works in the Romantic vein.

WORKS: DRAMATIC MUSIC: *Balagan,* by Blok (1909); *The Rose and the Cross,* by Blok (1914); *Antigone,* by Sophocles (1909-15); *Phoenician Women,* by Euripides (1912-16); *Oedipus Rex,* by Sophocles (1914-15); *The Story of the Red-Haired Motele,* by Utkin (1926-29); *The Inspector-General,* by Gogol (1926); OPERAS: *Abraham's Youth* (1921-23) and *The Maccabees;* symph. movement for solo voices, chorus and orch.: *1905-1917* (1925); FOR VOICE AND ORCH.: *Ruth* (1909); *Vrubel* (1912); *The Conqueror Worm* (1913); FOR ORCH.: symph. fragment, *After Shelley* (1906-08); *Songs of Adonis* (1919); symph. fantasy, *Songs of the Old Country* (1919); suite, *Jewish Orchestra at the Town Bailiff's Ball* (1926); CHAMBER MUSIC: Requiem, in memory of Rimsky-Korsakov, for string quartet and piano (1913-14); *Variations on a Jewish Theme,* for string quartet (1916); *Azerbaijan Folksongs,* for string quartet (1930); *Adygeya,* for violin, viola, cello, clarinet, horn, and piano (1933); *Sonata-Fantasia* for piano, violin, viola, and cello (1945); Theme with Variations, for cello and piano (1955); several song cycles; piano pieces; arrangements of Jewish folksongs. He publ. *Reflections and Reminiscences of Rimsky-Korsakov* (Moscow, 1956).

BIBLIOGRAPHY: L. Sabaneyev, *Modern Russian Composers* (N.Y., 1927); A. Drozdov, *Gnessin* (Moscow, 1927; in Russian and German).

Gobbaerts, Jean-Louis, Belgian pianist and composer; b. Antwerp, Sept. 28, 1835; d. Saint-Gilles, near Brussels, May 5, 1886. He studied at the Brussels Cons. He wrote more than a thousand light piano pieces, some quite popular, using the pseudonyms "Streabbog" (Gobbaerts reversed), "Ludovic," and "Lévi." His *Little Fairy Waltz* was a favorite of President Harry S. Truman.

Gobbi, Tito, Italian baritone; b. Bassano del Grappa, Oct. 24, 1913. He studied law at Padua Univ., then took vocal lessons in Milan; made his opera debut at Rome in 1938; sang at La Scala in 1942; in 1947 began European tours; made his American debut in San Francisco in 1948; appeared at the Metropolitan Opera as Scarpia in *Tosca* on Jan. 13, 1956, obtaining a decisive success. His repertory contains some 100 roles.

Godard, Benjamin (Louis Paul), French composer; b. Paris, Aug. 18, 1849; d. Cannes, Jan. 10, 1895. He studied violin with Richard Hammer and later with Vieuxtemps, composition with Reber of the Paris Cons. He publ. his first work, a violin sonata, at the age of 16 and wrote several other chamber music pieces, obtaining the Prix Chartier. In 1878 he received a municipal prize for an orchestral work; in the same year he produced his first opera, *Les Bijoux de Jeannette.* His second opera was *Pedro de Zalamea* (Antwerp, Jan. 31, 1884), but it left little impact; then came his masterpiece, *Jocelyn,* after Lamartine's poem (Brussels, Feb. 25, 1888). The famous *Berceuse* from this opera became a perennial favorite, exhibiting Godard's lyric talent at its best. There followed the opera *Dante,* produced at the Opéra-Comique on Nov. 7, 1890. His opera, *La Vivandière,* was left unfinished at his death, and the orchestration was completed by Paul Vidal; it was staged posthumously in Paris on

April 1, 1895; another posthumous opera, *Les Guelphes,* was produced in Rouen (Jan. 17, 1902). Godard wrote 3 programmatic symphonies: *Symphonie Gothique* (1883), *Symphonie Orientale* (1884), and *Symphonie Légendaire* (1886); and a *Concerto Romantique* for violin and orch. (1876); he also wrote 3 string quartets, 4 violin sonatas, a cello sonata, and 2 piano trios; piano pieces, and more than 100 songs. A 2-volume collection of Godard's piano works was publ. by G. Schirmer (N.Y., 1895); another collection of piano pieces was edited by Paolo Gallico (N.Y., 1909).

BIBLIOGRAPHY: M. Clerjot, *Benjamin Godard* (Paris, 1902).

Goddard, Arabella, English pianist; b. St.-Servan, near Saint-Malo, France, Jan. 12, 1836; d. Boulogne, France, April 6, 1922. She began study with Kalkbrenner in Paris at the age of 6, made her first public appearance at the age of 14, in London at a Grand National Concert. After 3 years of study with the critic, J. W. Davison (whom she married in 1859), she made tours of Germany and Italy (1854–55); later toured the U.S., Australia, and India (1873–76). She wrote some piano pieces and a ballad.

Godfrey, Sir Dan (Daniel Eyers), English conductor; b. London, June 20, 1868; d. Bournemouth, July 20, 1939. He was the son of **Daniel Godfrey, Sr.;** studied at the Royal College of Music; was conductor of the London Military Band in 1890. In 1892, he settled in Bournemouth as conductor of the Winter Gardens orch.; founded the Symphony Concerts there in 1894, directed them until his retirement in 1934; he brought the concerts to a high level, and used all his efforts to promote the works of British composers. He was knighted in 1922 for his services to orchestral music. He wrote his memoirs, *Memories and Music* (1924).

Godfrey, Daniel Sr., English bandmaster; b. Westminster, Sept. 4, 1831; d. Beeston, near Nottingham, June 30, 1903. Pupil and Fellow of the Royal Academy of Music, in which he was prof. of military music. Bandmaster of the Grenadier Guards, 1856; traveled with his band in the U.S., 1872; retired in 1896. He wrote popular waltzes (*Mabel, Guards, Hilda,* etc.), and made many arrangements for military band.

Godfrey, George. See **Müller, Georg Gottfried.**

Godimel, Claude. See **Goudimel, Claude.**

Godowsky, Leopold, famous pianist; b. Soshly, near Vilna, Feb. 13, 1870; d. New York, Nov. 21, 1938. He played in public as a child in Russia; at 14, was sent to Berlin to study at the Hochschule für Musik, but after a few months there, proceeded to New York; gave his first American concert in Boston, Dec. 7, 1884; in 1885, played engagements at the N.Y. Casino; in 1886, toured Canada with the Belgian violinist Ovide Musin. He then went back to Europe; played in society salons in London and Paris, and became a protégé of Saint-Saëns. In 1890 he joined the faculty of the N.Y. College of Music; on May 1, 1891, married Frieda Saxe, and became an American citizen. He taught at the

Broad Street Cons. in Philadelphia (1894–95); was head of the piano dept. of the Chicago Cons. (1895–1900); then embarked on a European tour; gave a highly successful concert in Berlin (Dec. 6, 1900), and remained there as a teacher; from 1909–14, conducted a master class at the Vienna Academy of Music; made tours in the U.S. from 1912–14, and settled permanently in the U.S. at the outbreak of World War I. After the end of the war, he traveled in Europe, South America, and Asia as a concert pianist; his career ended in 1930 when he suffered a stroke. Godowsky was one of the outstanding masters of the piano; possessing a scientifically inclined mind, he developed a method of 'weight and relaxation'; applying it to his own playing, he became an outstanding technician of his instrument, extending the potentialities of piano technique to the utmost, with particular attention to the left hand. He wrote numerous piano compositions of transcendental difficulty, yet entirely pianistic in style; also arranged works by Weber, Brahms, and Johann Strauss. Particularly remarkable are his 53 studies on Chopin's Études, combining Chopin's themes in ingenious counterpoint; among his original works, the most interesting are *Triakontameron* (30 pieces; 1920; no. 11 is the well known *Alt Wien*), and *Java Suite* (12 pieces). He also wrote simple pedagogical pieces, e.g., a set of 46 *Miniatures* for piano four-hands, in which the pupil is given a part within the compass of 5 notes only (1918); edited piano studies by Czerny, Heller, Köhler, etc.; composed music for the left hand alone (*6 Waltz Poems, Prelude and Fugue,* etc.), and publ. an essay, "Piano Music for the Left Hand," *Musical Quarterly* (July 1935). Maurice Aronson publ. a musical examination paper, providing an analysis of Godowsky's *Miniatures* (N.Y., 1935).

BIBLIOGRAPHY: Leonard S. Saxe, "The Published Music of Leopold Godowsky," *Notes* (March 1957), containing an annotated list of original works, arrangements and editions.

Godron, Hugo, Dutch composer; b. Amsterdam, Nov. 22, 1900; d. Zoelmond, Dec. 6, 1971. He studied violin at the music school in Bussum and composition with Sem Dresden in Amsterdam (1921–22). He taught composition and harmony at music schools in Bussum, Hilversum and Utrecht; from 1939 to 1969 was active as a sound engineer in Hilversum and Amsterdam. His music is generally joyful, almost playful, in character.

WORKS: a radio fairy tale, *Assepoes (Cinderella)* (1946–47); Sinfonietta for small orch. (1932–33); 7 *Miniatures* for piano and strings (1933); Piano Concerto (1938–39); *Sérénade occidentale* for orch. (1942–48); *Amabile Suite* for clarinet, piano and strings (1943); Concerto Grosso for Clarinet and Small Orch. (1944–45); *Concert Suite* for piano and string orch. (1945–47); *Miniatuur Symphonie* (1949–50; orchestration of *Gardenia Suite* for piano); 2 orch. Polkas (1950–51, 1957–58); Suite for string orch. and harpsichord (1950); *Hommage à Chabrier* for orch. (1950–51); *Hommages classiques* for flute, piano and strings (1950); Concerto for Orch. (1953–54); *Variations traditionnelles* for small orch. (1954); *Promenades,* suite for orch. (1954–55); *4 Impressies* for chamber orch. (1956–57); *Aubade Gaude-*

amus, suite for piano, string orch. and percussion (1966–68); *Hommage à Bizet* for small orch. (1971); String Trio (1937); Serenade, for piano and wind quintet (1947); Sonatina, for flute, violin, viola and piano (1948); Piano Trio (1948); *Sonata facile* for cello and piano (1950); Divertimento for 2 violins and piano (1956); *Nouvelles* for piano trio (1963); *Quatuor Bohémien* for piano quartet (1970). He wrote several piano works, including *Mon Plaisir* (1937–38); *Suite Moderne* for 2 pianos (1941); Sonata for 2 Pianos (1944–45); *Escapades,* 12 pieces (1944); *Gardenia Suite* (1949); *Pastorale* for 2 pianos (1953); *3 Nocturnes* (1953); *Introduction and Rondo* (1955); *24 Chansonnettes* (1966).

Goeb, Roger, American composer; b. Cherokee, Iowa, Oct. 9, 1914. He studied agriculture at the Univ. of Wisconsin, graduating in 1936; played in jazz bands; then went to Paris where he took lessons with Nadia Boulanger. Returning to America in 1939, he obtained his Ph.D. at the Univ. of Iowa; subsequently occupied teaching posts at the Univ. of Oklahoma (1942–44); at the State Univ., Iowa (1944–45) and at the Juilliard School of Music (1947–50). He held 2 Guggenheim Fellowships (1950, 1952); he taught music at Stanford Univ. (1954–55), then became director of the American Composers Alliance (1956–62). Personal misfortunes (both his wife and his son died of multiple sclerosis) caused him to cease his professional activities and his composition. He retired to Rockville Centre, New York.
WORKS: 4 symphonies (1942, 1945, 1950, 1955); 2 sinfonias (1957, 1962); *5 American Dances* for string orch. (1952); 4 instrumental pieces each named *Concertant* (1948, 1950, 1951, 1951); 2 *Concertinos* for orch. (1949, 1956); Violin Concerto (1953); Piano Concerto (1954); *Declarations* for cello, flute, oboe, clarinet, bassoon, horn (1961); 2 *Divertimenti* for 2 flutes (1950); *Encomium* for woodwinds, brass and percussion (1958); *Iowa Concerto* for chamber orch. (1959); Quartet for Oboe and Strings (1964); Clarinet Quartet, for 4 clarinets (1948); Quintet for Trombone and Strings (1949); 3 string quartets, string trio, woodwind trio, woodwind quintet, piano quintet, brass septet. His style of composition reveals a thoroughly functional technique and highly competent instrumental facture.

Goedicke, Alexander, Russian pianist and composer; b. Moscow, March 4, 1877; d. there, July 9, 1957. Goedicke was a member of a musical family of German extraction; his father was an organist and a conservatory teacher. He entered the Moscow Cons. where he studied piano with Safonov, composition with Arensky; graduated in 1898. In 1900 he won the Rubinstein Prize for his pieces for violin at the international competition in Vienna; in 1909 he was appointed prof. of piano at the Moscow Cons.; he also taught organ playing.
WORKS: 4 operas to his own librettos: *Virineya* (1915); *At the Crossing* (1933); *Jacquerie* (1937) and *Macbeth* (1944); 3 symphonies (1903, 1905, 1922); Piano Concerto (1900); Violin Concerto (1951); Horn Concerto; Trumpet Concerto; Piano Quintet; 2 piano trios; String Quartet; numerous teaching pieces for pi-

ano; many arrangements of Russian songs. His 80th birthday was celebrated in Moscow at a gala banquet, a few months before his death.
BIBLIOGRAPHY: V. Yakovlev, *A. Goedicke* (Moscow, 1927; in Russian and German); K. Adzhemov, *A. Goedicke* (articles and reminiscences; Moscow, 1960).

Goehr, Alexander, English composer; son of **Walter Goehr;** b. Berlin, Aug. 10, 1932; studied at the Royal Manchester College of Music and at the Paris Cons. He began to compose prolifically from an early age, adopting a severe atonal style of polyphonic writing, tending toward integral serialism.
WORKS: Piano Sonata (1952); Fantasies for Clarinet and Piano (1955); Fantasia for Orch. (1955); *Narration,* to words of Blake, for voice and piano (1955); String Quartet (1958); *The Deluge,* cantata (1958); *Sutter's Gold,* cantata (1960); *Hecuba's Lament,* cantata (1960); Suite, for flute, clarinet, horn, violin, viola, cello and harp (1961); *Four Songs from the Japanese* for soprano and orch. (1961); Violin Concerto (1962); *Arden muss sterben,* opera (Hamburg, March 5, 1967); Symphony (London, May 9, 1970); *Triptych,* theater piece for actors, singers and instruments (*Naboth's Vineyard,* 1968; *Shadowplay,* after Plato's *Republic,* 1970; and *Sonata About Jerusalem,* 1970); Concerto for 11 Instruments (Brussels, Jan. 25, 1971).

Goehr, Walter, German conductor; b. Berlin, May 28, 1903; d. Sheffield, England, Dec. 4, 1960. He studied theory with Schoenberg; then became conductor of the Berlin Radio (1925–31). In 1933 he went to England; from 1946–49, was conductor of the BBC Theatre Orch.

Goepfart, Karl Eduard, German pianist, conductor, and composer; b. Weimar, March 8, 1859; d. there, Feb. 8, 1942. He studied with his father, Christian Heinrich Goepfart (1835–1890); also had lessons with Liszt. He toured as theater conductor in the U.S. and in Germany; wrote several operas of which only one, *Der Müller von Sans Souci* was produced (Weimar, 1907). He further wrote 2 symphonies, church music, and many songs.

Goepp, Philip Henry, American organist and writer on music; b. New York, June 23, 1864; d. Philadelphia, Aug. 25, 1936. He studied in Germany (1872–77); graduated from Harvard with honors in music in 1884; while there, he studied composition with J. K. Paine; graduated from the Univ. of Pennsylvania Law School in 1888, and practiced law until 1892. He then devoted himself to music in Philadelphia, as organist, teacher, and writer; from 1900 to 1921, he wrote the program notes for the Philadelphia Orch.; publ. *Annals of Music in Philadelphia* (1896); *Symphonies and Their Meaning* (3 vols., 1898, 1902, 1913); and composed pieces for piano and organ, a *Christmas Cantata* and an operetta, *The Lost Prince.*

Goethals, Lucien, Belgian composer; b. Ghent, June 26, 1931. He was taken to Argentina as a child; returning to Belgium in 1947 he studied with Rosseau at the Royal Cons. in Ghent (1947–56) and took courses at the Institute for Psycho-Acoustics and Electronic Music of the Ghent State Univ.; also worked in an electronic studio in Germany. In 1964 he organized the Belgian group "Spectra" devoted to promotion of new music. His own compositions explore the problems of modernistic constructivism.

WORKS: *Vensters,* an audio-visual play for 2 narrators, cello, piano, percussion, recorded sounds and film projections (Brussels, Sept. 16, 1967); *Hé,* audiovisual production for 10 instruments, tapes and film projections (1971; in collaboration with Herman Sabbe and Karel Goeyvaerts); *5 Impromptus* for chamber orch. (1959); *Dialogos* for string orch., wind quintet, 2 string quintets, percussion and tape (Ghent, Sept. 3, 1963); *Dialogos Suite* for chamber orch. (1963); *Sinfonia in Gris Mayor* for 2 orch., percussion and tape (Brussels, June 14, 1966); *Enteuxis* for string orch., oboe and flute (Ghent, Sept. 2, 1968); Violin Sonata (1959); *Rituele Suite* for wind quintet (1959); Sonata for Solo Guitar (1961); *Endomorfie I* for violin, piano and tape (1964); *Endomorfie II* for flute, oboe, clarinet, bassoon, 2 trumpets, trombone and tuba (1964); *Cellotape* for cello, piano, tape and contact microphone (1965); *Movimientos y Acciones* for flute, clarinet, string quartet, chromatic harp and percussion (1965); *Lecina* for mezzo-soprano, flute, violin and cello (1966); *Mouvement* for string quartet (1967); *Cascaras,* chamber cantata for mezzo-soprano, flute, clarinet, violin, cello and piano (1969); *Quebraduras* for piano quartet (1969); *Ensimismamientos* for violin, cello, bassoon, piano and tape (1969); *4 Pieces* for bass clarinet and piano (1970); *7 Soliloquies* for solo violin (1970); *Superposiciones* for violin, cello, bassoon and piano (1970); *Suma* for an undefined number of instruments and tape (1971); *3 paisajes sonores* for flute, oboe, cello, trombone, double bass and harpsichord (1973); *Llanto por Salvador Allende* for solo trombone (1973); *Difonium* for bass clarinet and tape (1974); *Diferencias* for 10 instruments (1974); *Fantasia and Humoreske* for 2 oboes and English horn (1975); *Triptiek* for violin and harpsichord (1975); *Fusion* for bass clarinet, piano and tape (1975); for piano: *Musica dodecafonica* (1957) and *Pentagoon* (1963); for organ: *Sinfonia* (1959) and *Klankstrukturen* (1962); several works for tape alone.

Goethe, Wolfgang von, the illustrious German poet; b. Frankfurt-am-Main, Aug. 28, 1749; d. Weimar, March 22, 1832. Although he could not comprehend Beethoven, and even snubbed him, he had ideas of his own on music (see *Briefwechsel zwischen Goethe und Zelter,* Berlin, 1833); Ferd. Hiller also shows this in his *Goethes musicalisches Leben* (Cologne, 1883). In recent years Goethe's attitude toward music has been made the subject of investigation by several scholars.

BIBLIOGRAPHY: K. Mendelssohn-Bartholdy, *Goethe und Felix Mendelssohn-Bartholdy* (Leipzig, 1871; in English, with additions, London, 2nd ed., 1874); A. Julien, *Goethe et la musique: ses jugements, son influence, les œuvres qu'il a inspirées* (Paris, 1880); J. W. von Wasielewski, *Goethe's Verhältnis zur Musik* (Leipzig, 1880; in Waldersee's *Sammlung mus. Vorträge*); H. Blaze de Bury, *Goethe et Beethoven* (Paris, 1892); W. Nagel, *Goethe und Beethoven* (Langensalza, 1902); W. Nagel, *Goethe und Mozart* (Langensalza 1904); J. Chantavoine, *Goethe musicien* (Paris, 1905);

J. Simon, *Faust in der Musik* (Berlin, 1906); E. Segnitz, *Goethe und die Oper in Weimar* (Langensalza, 1908); W. Bode, *Die Tonkunst in Goethes Leben* (2 vols., Berlin, 1912); W. Bode, *Goethes Schauspieler und Musiker: Erinnerungen von Eberwein und Lobe* (1912); H. Abert, *Goethe und die Musik* (1922); P. Frenzel, *R. Schumann und Goethe* (1926); H. John, *Goethe, und die Musik* (1928); E. Ludwig, *Goethe, the History of a Man* (1928; in English); W. Nohl, *Goethe und Beethoven* (1929); R. Rolland, *Goethe et Beethoven* (Paris, 1930; in English, N.Y. and London, 1931); W. Engelsmann, *Goethe und Beethoven* (1931); Goethe issue of *Revue Musicale* (1932); Goethe issue of the *Zeitschrift für Musikwissenschaft* (1932); A. della Corte, *La vita musicale di Goethe* (Turin, 1932); G. Kinsky, *Die Handschriften von Beethovens Egmont-Musik* (Vienna, 1933); F. Küchler, *Goethes Musikverständnis* (Leipzig, 1935); F. W. Sternfeld, *Goethe and Music* (N.Y., 1954); W. Gerstenberg, *Goethes Dichtung und die Musik* (Leipzig, 1966).

Goetschius, Percy, renowned American music teacher and pedagogue; b. Paterson, N.J., Aug. 30, 1853; d. Manchester, N.H., Oct. 29, 1943. He studied at Stuttgart Cons., and taught various classes there; also wrote music criticism. He returned to the U.S. in 1890; was on the faculty of Syracuse Univ. (1890–92) and at the New England Cons. of Music in Boston (1892–96). In 1905 he was appointed head of the dept. of music at the N.Y. Institute of Musical Art; retired in 1925. Goetschius was a product of the fossilized Germanic tradition; convinced that the laws of harmony as set by old German pedagogues were unalterable and inviolate, he stood in horror before any vestige of unresolved dissonances.

WRITINGS: He wrote many books on music pedagogy, among them: *The Material Used in Musical Composition* (Stuttgart, 1882; N.Y., 1889; 14th ed. 1913; a valuable contribution to teaching of harmony); *The Theory and Practice of Tone-relations* (Boston, 1892; 17th revised ed. 1917); *Models of Principal Musical Forms* (Boston, 1895); *Syllabus of Music History* (1895); *The Homophonic Forms of Musical Composition* (N.Y., 1898; 10th ed. 1921); *Exercises in Melody Writing* (N.Y., 1900; 9th ed. 1923); *Applied Counterpoint* (N.Y., 1902); *Lessons in Music Form* (Boston, 1904); *Exercises in Elementary Counterpoint* (N.Y., 1910; an attempt to blend the disciplines of harmony and counterpoint); *Essentials in Music History* (N.Y., 1914; jointly with Thomas Tapper); *The Larger Forms of Musical Composition* (N.Y., 1915); *Masters of the Symphony* (Boston, 1929); *The Structure of Music* (Philadelphia, 1934). He composed a number of pieces for piano; was joint editor of *The School Credit Piano Course* (1918–22).

BIBLIOGRAPHY: Arthur Shepherd, "Papa Goetschius in Retrospect," *Musical Quarterly* (July 1944).

Goetz, Hermann, German composer; b. Königsberg, Prussia, Dec. 7, 1840; d. Hottingen, near Zürich, Dec. 3, 1876. He studied at the Stern Cons. in Berlin from 1860–63, with von Bülow in piano, and H. Ulrich in composition. In 1863, he took the post of organist at Winterthur, Switzerland; then lived in Zürich; gave private lessons; conducted a singing society. His most famous work is the opera, *The Taming of the Shrew (Der Widerspenstigen Zähmung,)* based on Shakespeare's play, which was given in Mannheim, Oct. 11, 1874; it was then given in Vienna, in Berlin, Leipzig, and other German cities, and produced in an English version in London (Drury Lane Theatre, Oct. 12, 1878). His other works include the opera, *Francesca da Rimini* (Mannheim, Sept. 30, 1877; unfinished; 3rd act completed by Ernst Frank); incidental music for Widmann's play, *Die heiligen drei Könige* (Winterthur, Jan. 6, 1866); Symph. in F; chamber music; several pieces for piano, and 24 songs.

BIBLIOGRAPHY: A. Steiner, *Hermann Goetz* (Zürich, 1907); E. Kreuzhage, *Hermann Goetz: sein Leben und sein Werke* (Leipzig, 1916); G. R. Kruse, *Hermann Goetz* (1920).

Goetze, Walter W., German composer of light opera; b. Berlin, April 17, 1883; d. there, March 24, 1961. He began as a composer of popular ballads; then produced numerous operettas, among them *Der liebe Pepi* (1913); *Ihre Hoheit, die Tänzerin* (Stettin, May 8, 1919; highly popular; about 700 performances in Berlin alone); *Adrienne* (1926); *Der Page des Königs* (1933); *Akrobaten des Glücks* (1933); *Der goldene Pierrot* (Berlin, March 31, 1934; successful); *Sensation im Trocadero* (1936); *Liebe im Dreiklang* (1951).

Goetzl, Anselm, Bohemian composer; b. Karolinenthal, Aug. 20, 1878; d. Barcelona, Jan. 9, 1923 (while traveling). He studied with Winkler, Fibich, and Dvořák in Prague, and with Schalk and Adler in Vienna; came to the U.S. in 1913 as conductor of Dippel's Light Opera Co. He wrote 3 operettas, a piano quartet, 2 string quartets, a clarinet quintet, and songs.

Goeyvaerts, Karel, significant Belgian composer; b. Antwerp, June 8, 1923. He studied at the Antwerp Cons. (1943–47) and with Milhaud, Messiaen and Maurice Martenot in Paris (1947–501); received the Lily Boulanger Award in 1949. He taught music history at the Antwerp Cons. (1950–57); in 1970 he organized the Ghent Institute of Psycho-acoustics and Electronic Music (IPEM). Goeyvaerts is one of the pioneers of serialism, spatial music and electronic techniques. His works bear pointedly abstract titles with structural connotations; he also applies aleatory devices in audio-visual collages.

WORKS: *3 Lieder per sonare a venti-sei* for 6 solo instruments (1948–49); Sonata for 2 Pianos, op. 1 (1950–51); *Opus 2* for 13 instruments (1951); *Opus 3 aux sons frappés et frottés (with Striking and Rubbing Sounds)* for 7 instruments (1952); *Opus 4 aux sons morts (with Dead Sounds)* for tape (1952); *Opus 5 aux sons purs (with Pure Sounds)* for tape (1953); *Opus 6* for 180 sound objects (1954); *Opus 7 aux niveaux convergents et divergents (with Converging and Diverging Levels)* for tape (1955); *Diaphonie,* suite for orch. (1957); *Improperia,* cantata for Good Friday, for alto, double chorus and 6 instruments (1958); *Piece for 3* for flute, violin and piano (1960); *Jeux d'été* for 3 orch. groups (1961); *La Passion* for orch. (1962); *Cataclysme,* ballet for orch. and ad lib. narration (1963); *Piece* for piano with tape (1964); *Goathermala* for mezzo-soprano and flute (1966); *Parcours* for 2 to 6

violins (1967); *Mass in Memory of John XXIII* for chorus and 10 winds (1968); *Actief-Reactief* for 2 oboes, 2 trumpets and piano (1968); *Catch à quatre,* verbal composition for 4 wandering musicians (1969); *Al naar gelang* for 5 instrumental groups (1971); *Hé,* audio-visual production (1971; in collaboration with Herman Sabbe and Lucien Goethals); Piano Quartet, mobile composition for violin, viola, cello and tape (1972); *Belise dans un jardin (Belise in the Garden)* for chorus and 6 instruments (1972); *Nachklänge aus dem Theater* for tape (1972); *Op acht paarden wedden (To Bet on 8 Horses),* electronic mobile composition for 8 sound tracks (1973); *Landschap,* mobile composition for harpsichord (1973); *You'll Never Be Alone Anymore* for bass clarinet and electronics (1974).

Gogorza, Emilio Edoardo de, American baritone; b. Brooklyn, N.Y., May 29, 1874; d. New York, May 10, 1949. After singing as a boy soprano in England, he returned to the U.S. and studied with C. Moderati and E. Agramonte in N.Y.; he made his debut in 1897 with Marcella Sembrich in a concert; sang throughout the country in concerts and with leading orchestras. Beginning in 1925, was for several years instructor of voice at the Curtis Institute of Music, Phila. He married the American soprano, **Emma Eames,** in 1911.

Goh, Taijiro, Japanese composer; b. Dairen, Manchuria, Feb. 15, 1907; d. Shizuoka, July 1, 1970. He studied in Tokyo and organized a Society of Japanese Composers and created the Japan Women's Symphony Orch. (1963). In 1961 he founded the Japan Association for Promotion of Student Dormitory Songs; in 1966–68 he resided in the U.S. and Brazil. His music follows the European academic type of harmonic and contrapuntal structure.

WORKS: 3 operas: *Madame Rosaria* (1943), *Tsubaki saku koro (When Camellias Blossom,* 1949; unfinished) and *Tais* (1959; unfinished); a ballet, *Oni-Daiko (Devil Drummers,* 1956*);* 2 choreographic plays, *Koku-sei-Ya* and *Rashōmon* (both 1954); 8 symphonies: No. 1 (1925); No. 2 (1930); No. 3, *Kumo (Clouds,* 1938); No. 4 (1938); No. 5, *Nippon* (1939); No. 6, *Asia* (1939); No. 7, *Sokoku (Motherland,* 1942); No. 8, *Chō-jō Banri (The Long Wall,* 1945; only the first movement was completed); 3 violin concertos (1935; 1937; 1962); 2 piano concertos (1936; 1940); *Movement* for cello, temple blocks and orch. (1937); Theme and Variations for Orch. (1938); 2 overtures: *Otakebi (War Cry,* 1939) and *Over the Tan-Shan Southern Path* (1941); 3 symph. marches: *Eiyū (Hero,* 1940), *Taiiku (Gymnastics,* 1940) and *Akeyuku Azia (Asia Dawning,* 1942); *Shimpi-shu (Mysteries),* ballet suite (1942); *Nemuri no Serenâde (Serenade for Slumber)* for vocal solo and orch. (1944); *The Flow of the River Dalny* for chorus and orch. (1950); *Seija to Eiyū (The Saint and the Hero),* symph. dance piece (1961); *Brasil,* symph. poem with narration and chorus (1967); numerous short symph. works, including *Konchū (Insects,* 1941) and *Gekiryū (Torrent,* 1952); several pieces for vocal soloist or narrator, and orch.; Theme and Variations for String Trio (1933); 2 string quartets (1935, 1938); *Imayo* for cello and piano (1954); 5 piano sonatas (1915, 1919, 1920, 1927, 1927); *November in Manchuria,* rhapsody for piano (1926); Fantasy for Piano (1927); Variations for Piano (1931); *8 Chinese Dances* for piano (1941); *Katyusha,* choreographic poem for piano (1954); over 100 songs.

Göhler, (Karl) Georg, German conductor and composer; b. Zwickau, June 29, 1874; d. Lübeck, March 4, 1954. He was a pupil of Vollhardt at Zwickau; then studied at the Leipzig Univ. and Cons.; obtained his Dr. phil. with a dissertation on the 16th century composer Cornelius Freundt; he then pursued the career of chorus conductor; from 1913–15, conducted opera at Hamburg; in 1915, succeeded Furtwängler as conductor of symph. concerts in Lübeck; in 1922, he became conductor of the State Theater in Altenburg; also conducted symph. concerts in Halle. He wrote 5 symphonies; a clarinet concerto; 2 violin concertos; a cello concerto; *Quartetto enimmatico* for piano and strings (1940); a string trio (1942); more than 200 songs, and numerous choral works; also 24 bagatelles for piano. He edited works by Freundt, Hasse, Handel, Haydn, Schubert, Mozart, etc.; wrote numerous articles on various musical subjects. He was an admirer of Mahler and Bruckner and gave frequent performances of their symphonies.

Gold, Arthur, Canadian pianist; b. Toronto, Feb. 6, 1917. He studied with Josef and Rosina Lhévinne at the Juilliard School of Music; upon graduation, formed a piano duo with Robert Fitzdale; together they gave numerous concerts in Europe and America, in programs of modern music, including works specially written for them by such celebrated composers as Samuel Barber, Darius Milhaud, Francis Poulenc, Georges Auric and Virgil Thomson. Gold and Fitzdale also pioneered performances of works by John Cage for prepared piano.

Gold, Ernest, Austrian-American composer; b. Vienna, July 13, 1921. He studied piano and violin at home (his father was an amateur musician); in 1938 emigrated to the U.S.; studied harmony in N.Y. with Otto Cesana. He began writing songs in a popular vein; of these, *Practice Makes Perfect* became a hit. At the same time he composed in classical forms; to this category belong his *Pan American Symphony,* Piano Concerto, String Quartet and Piano Sonata. In 1946 he went to Hollywood as an arranger; took lessons with George Antheil; then was commissioned to write film scores; among them the following were very successful: *The Defiant Ones, On the Beach, Exodus* (Academy Award, 1960); *Judgment at Nuremberg* (1961); *It's a Mad, Mad, Mad World* (1963). In 1950 he married the singer **Marni Nixon.**

Gold, Julius, American musicologist and teacher; b. St. Joseph, Missouri, Feb. 18, 1884; d. Los Angeles, May 29, 1969. He studied at Chicago Musical College; then taught theory and composition at Drake Univ., Des Moines, Iowa (1910–14) and at Dominican College, San Rafael, Calif. (1930–34); later lived in Los Angeles.

Goldbach, Stanislaw, Czech composer; b. Strelce, near Brno, July 13, 1896. He studied with J. B. Foerster in Prague and Vincent d'Indy in Paris. He wrote

the symph. poems: *Cyrano de Bergerac* (1924), *New Icarus* (1928), *May Festival* (1931); Symphony (1932); and *Anna Karenina,* opera after Tolstoy (1928–30).

Goldbeck, Fred, Dutch-French music critic; b. The Hague, Feb. 13, 1902. After study with various teachers in several European countries, he settled in Paris in 1925 as music critic; contributed numerous articles to the *Revue Musicale* and many other publications; publ. a book, *The Perfect Conductor* (N.Y., 1951); edited the music magazine *Contrepoints* (1946–52).

Goldbeck, Robert, pianist and conductor; b. Potsdam, April 19, 1839; d. St. Louis, May 16, 1908. He studied in Paris; made his concert debut in London; came to New York in 1857, where he remained until 1867, when he founded a cons. in Boston. From 1880 to 1903 he lived variously in N.Y., Germany, St. Louis, Chicago, and London; in 1903 he returned to St. Louis. He publ. a textbook on harmony (1890) and a 3-volume *Encyclopedia of Music Education* (1903).

Goldberg, Albert, American music critic; b. Shenandoah, Iowa, June 2, 1898. He studied at the Chicago Musical College (1920–22); taught there (1924–26); appeared as pianist and conductor; was music critic of the *Chicago Herald Examiner* (1925–36) and of the *Chicago Tribune* (1943–46). In 1947 he was appointed to the staff of the *Los Angeles Times,* still writing for it in 1978.

Goldberg, Johann Gottlieb, remarkable German organist and harpsichord player; b. Danzig, baptized March 14, 1727; d. Dresden, April 13, 1756. When a child, he was brought to Dresden by his patron, Count Hermann Carl von Kaiserling; he studied with Wilhelm Friedemann Bach, and later with J. S. Bach (1742–43); in 1751, he became musician to Count Heinrich Brühl, a post he held till his death. His name is immortalized through the set of 30 variations written for him by Bach, and generally known as *Goldberg Variations.* Goldberg's own compositions include 2 concertos; 24 Polonaises; a sonata with minuet and 12 variations for clavier; 6 trios for flute, violin, and bass; a motet; a cantata; and a psalm.
BIBLIOGRAPHY: E. A. Dadder, *Johann Gottlieb Goldberg: Leben und Werke* (Bonn, 1923).

Goldberg, Szymon, eminent Polish violinist; b. Wloclawek, June 1, 1909. He studied with Carl Flesch in Berlin; became concertmaster of the Berlin Philharmonic, but was forced to leave in 1934 despite Furtwängler's defense of the Jewish members of the orchestra, and went to London, and in 1938 to America. He toured widely all over the world; on his tour in Asia, was interned in Java by the Japanese from 1941–45; after the end of the war he went to America; in 1953 became an American citizen; after 1970 lived mostly in London.

Goldberg, Theo, German composer; b. Chemnitz, Sept. 29, 1921. He studied in Berlin. He has composed the chamber operas *Minotauros* and *Schwere Zeiten für Engel* (Berlin, Sept. 20, 1952); a ballet, *Nacht mit*

Kleopatra (Karlsruhe, Jan. 20, 1952); several symphonic works. He eventually settled in Canada.

Golde, Walter, American pianist, vocal teacher and music educator; b. Brooklyn, Jan. 4, 1887; d. Chapel Hill, North Carolina, Sept. 4, 1963. He studied at Dartmouth College, Hanover, N.H., graduating in 1910; then went to Vienna, where he took vocal lessons as well as academic courses at the Vienna Cons. Returning to the U.S., he became a professional accompanist; played for Casals, Mischa Elman, Mary Garden and Melchior. From 1944 to 1948 he headed the voice dept. of Columbia Univ.; in 1953 he was appointed director of the Institute of Opera at the Univ. of North Carolina. He composed a number of attractive songs and piano pieces.

Goldenweiser, Alexander, Russian piano pedagogue; b. Kishinev, March 10, 1875; d. Moscow, Nov. 26, 1961. He studied piano with Pabst and composition with Arensky at the Moscow Cons.; in 1906 became prof. of piano there, holding this post for 55 years until his death. Two generations of Russian pianists were his pupils, among them Kabalevsky and Lazar Berman. As a pedagogue, he continued the traditions of the Russian school of piano playing, seeking the inner meaning of the music while achieving technical brilliance. He was a frequent visitor at Tolstoy's house near Moscow, and wrote reminiscences of Tolstoy (Moscow, 1922); published several essays on piano teaching; also composed chamber music and piano pieces.

Goldman, Edwin Franko, eminent American bandmaster; b. Louisville, Ky., Jan. 1, 1878; d. New York, Feb. 21, 1956. He was the nephew of **Sam Franko** and **Nahan Franko,** well-known conductors; was brought to N.Y., where he studied composition with Dvořák, and cornet with J. Levy and C. Sohst. He became solo cornetist of the Metropolitan Opera orch. when he was 17, remaining there for 10 years. For the next 13 years he taught cornet and trumpet; he formed his first band in 1911. In 1918, the Goldman Band outdoor concerts were inaugurated. His band was noted not only for its skill and musicianship but for its unusual repertory, including modern works especially commissioned for the band. Goldman was a founder and 1st president of the American Bandmasters' Association; received honorary Doc. Mus. degrees from Philips Univ. and Boston Univ., and medals and other honors from governments and associations throughout the world. He wrote more than 100 brilliant marches, of which the best known is *On the Mall;* also other band music; solos for various wind instruments; studies and methods for cornet and other brass instruments; several songs. He was the author of *Foundation to Cornet or Trumpet Playing* (1914); *Band Betterment* (1934); *The Goldman Band System* (1936).

Goldman, Richard Franko (son of **Edwin Franko Goldman**), American bandmaster and composer; b. New York, Dec. 7, 1910. He studied at Columbia Univ.; after graduation became an assistant of his father in conducting the Goldman Band; on his father's death, he succeeded him as conductor. In 1968 he was appointed director of the Peabody Cons. of Music in Baltimore. He has written many works for various ensembles: *A Sentimental Journey* for band (1941); 3 duets for clarinets (1944); Duo for Tubas (1948); Violin Sonata (1952); many arrangements for band. A progressive musician, Goldman has experimented with modern techniques, and his music combines highly advanced harmony with simple procedures accessible to amateurs. He has published 2 reference books, *The Band's Music* (1938) and *The Concert Band* (1946); also *Harmony of Western Music* (N.Y., 1965), as well as articles and reviews. He has been editor of the *Juilliard Review* since it was founded in 1953.

Goldmark, Karl, eminent Austro-Hungarian composer; b. Keszthely, Hungary, May 18, 1830; d. Vienna, Jan. 2, 1915. The son of a poor cantor, he studied at the school of the Musical Society of Sopron (1842–44); while there, his talent as a violinist resulted in his being sent to Vienna, where he studied with L. Jansa (1844–45), later at the Vienna Cons., as a pupil of Preyer (harmony) and Böhm (violin). He spent most of his life in Vienna, where the first concert of his compositions was given March 20, 1857. Landmarks in his career were the first performance of his *Sakuntala* overture by the Vienna Philh. on Dec. 26, 1865, and the première of his 1st opera, *Die Königin von Saba,* at the Vienna Opera on March 10, 1875; both were very successful.

WORKS: Operas (in addition to *Die Königin von Saba*): *Merlin* (Vienna, Nov. 19, 1886); *Das Heimchen am Herd,* based on Dickens' *The Cricket on the Hearth* (Vienna, March 21, 1896); *Die Kriegsgefangene* (Vienna, Jan. 17, 1899); *Götz von Berlichingen,* based on Goethe's play (Budapest, Dec. 16, 1902); *Ein Wintermärchen,* based on Shakespeare's *A Winter's Tale* (Vienna, Jan. 2, 1908). For orch.: 7 overtures: *Sakuntala, Penthesilea, Im Frühling, Der gefesselte Prometheus, Sappho, In Italien, Aus Jugendtagen;* symph., *Ländliche Hochzeit;* Symph.; symph. poem, *Zrinyi;* several instrumental concertos. Chamber music: 2 piano trios, Piano Quintet, Cello Sonata, Violin Sonata; piano pieces; songs and choral works. He publ. an autobiography, *Erinnerungen aus meinem Leben* (Vienna, 1922; in English as *Notes from the Life of a Viennese Composer,* N.Y., 1927).

BIBLIOGRAPHY: O. Keller, *Karl Goldmark* (1901); H. Schwarz, *Ignaz Brüll und sein Freundeskreis: Erinnerungen an Brüll, Goldmark und Brahms* (Vienna, 1922); L. Koch, ed., *Karl Goldmark* (Budapest, 1930; contains full bibliography); biographies in Hungarian by Kálmán (1930), Klempá (1930) and Várnai (1957).

Goldmark, Rubin, American composer and teacher, nephew of **Karl Goldmark;** b. New York, Aug. 15, 1872; d. there, March 6, 1936. He studied at the Vienna Cons. with A. Door (piano) and J. N. Fuchs (composition); from 1891–93, he was a student at the National Cons. in New York with Joseffy (piano) and Dvořák (composition). He went to Colorado Springs for his health in 1894; taught at the College Cons. there (1895–1901). Returning to New York in 1902, for the next 20 years he gave private lessons in piano and theory. In 1924, he was appointed head of the composition department of the Juilliard School, N.Y., and remained there until his death; among his pupils were Aaron Copland, Abram Chasins, Frederick Jacobi, and other American composers.

WORKS: for orch.: overture, *Hiawatha* (Boston, Jan. 13, 1900); tone poem, *Samson* (Boston, March 14, 1914); Requiem, suggested by Lincoln's Gettysburg Address (N.Y., Jan. 30, 1919); *A Negro Rhapsody* (his most popular work; N.Y., Jan. 18, 1923); Piano Quartet (Paderewski Prize, 1909; N.Y., Dec. 13, 1910); Piano Trio; *The Call of the Plains,* for violin and piano (1915); songs.

Goldovsky, Boris, Russian-American pianist and conductor; son of the violinist **Lea Luboshutz;** b. Moscow, June 7, 1908. He studied piano with his uncle **Pierre Luboshutz;** later in Berlin with Schnabel and Kreutzer, and in Budapest with Dohnányi. He appeared as soloist with the Berlin Philharmonic at the age of 13 in 1921; came to America in 1930; was director of the Opera Workshop at the Berkshire Music Center, Tanglewood (1942–62); founded the New England Opera Co. in 1946. A versatile musician, he translated opera librettos into singable English; presented popular radio talks on music; acted as moderator for Metropolitan opera broadcasts. A collection of his comments was publ. as *Accents on Opera* (N.Y., 1953); he also wrote *Bringing Opera to Life* (N.Y., 1968).

Goldsand, Robert, Austrian pianist; b. Vienna, March 17, 1911. He studied with A. Manhart, M. Rosenthal, Camillo Horn, and Joseph Marx. He played in public at the age of 10; then toured in Europe and South America; made his U.S. debut at Carnegie Hall, March 21, 1927; then was again in Europe, but settled permanently in the U.S. in 1939.

Goldschmidt, Adalbert von, Austrian composer; b. Vienna, May 5, 1848; d. there, Dec. 21, 1906. He studied at the Vienna Cons.; from his earliest efforts in composition, he became an ardent follower of Wagner. At the age of 22, he wrote a cantata, *Die sieben Todsünden* (Berlin, 1875); this was followed by a music drama, *Helianthus* (Leipzig, 1884), for which he wrote both words and music. A dramatic trilogy, *Gaea* (1889), was his most ambitious work along Wagnerian lines. He also brought out a comic opera, *Die fromme Helene* (Hamburg, 1897); wrote about 100 songs and a number of piano pieces.

BIBLIOGRAPHY: E. Friedegg, *Briefe an einen Komponisten: Musikalische Korrespondenz an Adalbert von Goldschmidt* (Berlin, 1909).

Goldschmidt, Berthold, German composer; b. Hamburg, Jan. 18, 1903. He studied at Hamburg Univ. and the Berlin State Academy of Music; after serving as assistant conductor of the Berlin State Opera (1926–27) and conductor of the Darmstadt Opera (1927–29), he went to England in 1940; conducted the Glyndebourne Opera in 1947. He has written 2 operas: *Der gewaltige Hahnrei* (Mannheim, Feb. 14, 1932) and *Beatrice Cenci* (1951; won a prize at the Festival of Britain); a ballet, *Chronica;* Symphony (1944); concertinos for violin (1933), cello (1933), harp (1949) and clarinet (1955); piano pieces.

Goldschmidt, Hugo, German writer on music; b. Breslau, Sept. 19, 1859; d. Wiesbaden, Dec. 26, 1920. He studied singing under Stockhausen at Frankfurt (1887–90); was co-director of the Scharwenka-Klindworth Cons. in Berlin (1893–1905).

WRITINGS: *Die italienische Gesangsmethode des 17. Jahrhunderts* (1890); *Der Vokalismus des neuhochdeutschen Kunstgesangs und der Bühnensprache* (1892); *Handbuch der deutschen Gegangspädagogik* (1896); *Studien zur Geschichte der italienischen Oper im 17. Jahrhundert* (2 vols., 1901, 1904; the 2nd vol. contains a reprint of Monteverdi's opera, *Incoronazione di Poppea;* reprint, 1967); *Die Lehre von der vokalen Ornamentik* (vol. I contains the 17th and 18th centuries to the time of Gluck; 1907); *Die Musikästhetik des 18. Jahrhunderts und ihre Beziehungen zu seinem Kunstschaffen* (Zürich, 1915; reprint, 1968).

Goldschmidt, Otto, German pianist; b. Hamburg, Aug. 21, 1829; d. London, Feb. 24, 1907. At first a pupil of Jakob Schmitt and F. W. Grund, then of Mendelssohn at the Leipzig Cons., and of Chopin at Paris (1848). In 1849 he played in London at a concert given by **Jenny Lind;** accompanied her on her American tour (1851), and married her at Boston, Feb. 5, 1852; from 1852–55 they lived in Dresden, from 1858 until her death (1887) in London. He founded the Bach Choir in 1875, and conducted it till 1885. He composed an oratorio, *Ruth* (Hereford, 1867); choral song, *Music,* for soprano and women's chorus (Leeds, 1898); piano music, including a concerto, piano studies, 2 duets for two pianos; was co-editor of *The Chorale Book for England,* a collection of hymns (1863).

Goldsmith, Jerry, American composer for films; b. Los Angeles, Feb. 10, 1929. He studied music at the Univ. of Southern California; became a staff composer with the Twentieth Century Fox Film Corporation; wrote the scores for *The Sand Pebbles, Freud, Planet of the Apes,* etc. He also wrote chamber music and vocal works.

Goldstein, Mikhail, Russian violinist and composer; b. Odessa, Nov. 8, 1917. He was a violin prodigy before entering the Moscow Cons., where he studied violin with Yampolsky, composition with Miaskovsky and conducting with Saradzev. During the war (1941–45) he was active in the Soviet Army entertainment corps. In 1946 he returned to Odessa. In 1948 he perpetrated a hoax by claiming the discovery of the 21st symphony allegedly written in 1810 by a mythical Russian musician Ovsianiko-Kulikovsky; a doctoral dissertation on it was written by the Soviet musicologist Valerian Dovzhenko. The work was widely performed in the Soviet Union and recorded. When Goldstein admitted his deception and declared that the symphony was in fact his own composition, he was attacked in the Soviet press as an impostor trying to appropriate an authentic work of historical importance. In eclipse as a result of this episode, Goldstein left Russia in 1964; lived in East Berlin; in 1967 went to Israel and taught violin at the Musical Academy in Jerusalem. In 1969 he settled in Hamburg, where he resumed his primary career as a concert violinist; contributed articles to various German publications. His works include, apart from the "Ovsianiko-Kulikov-sky" score, 4 symphonies (1934, 1936, 1944, 1945); 2 violin concertos (1936, 1939); Violin Sonata (1935); Sonata for Violin and Viola (1946); 12 Preludes for 2 Violins (1964); pedagogical pieces for violin.

Goleminov, Marin, Bulgarian composer; b. Kjustendil, Sept. 28, 1908. He studied music theory and violin at the Bulgarian State Cons. in Sofia (1927–31); then went to Paris and took courses in composition with Lioncourt and Le Flem (1931–34); from Paris he proceeded to Germany and enrolled in the class of composition with Joseph Haas at the Akadamie der Tonkunst in Munich (1938–39). After World War II he taught at the Bulgarian Cons. in Sofia. His music utilizes folk elements, particularly the asymmetrical rhythms of Bulgarian folk motives, in a fairly modern but still quite accessible idiom.
WORKS: 2 operas: *Ivailo* (1958; Sofia, Feb. 13, 1959) and *Zahari the Icon Painter* (1971; Sofia, Oct. 17, 1972); an operatic fairytale, *Zlatnata ptica (The Golden Bird,* 1961; Sofia, Dec. 20, 1961); 2 ballets: *Nestinarka* (1940; Sofia, Jan. 4, 1942) and *The Daughter of Kaloyan* (1973; Sofia, Dec. 23, 1973); an oratorio, *The Titan* (1972; Sofia, June 25, 1972); a cantata, *Father Paissy* (1966); *Night,* symph. poem (1932); Cello Concerto (1949–50); *Prelude, Aria and Toccata* for piano and orch. (1947–53); *Poem* for orch. (1959); Concerto for string quartet and string orch. (1963; Moscow, Feb. 11, 1964); 3 symphonies: No. 1, *Detska (Children's Symphony,* 1963), No. 2 (1967; Sofia, March 6, 1968) and No. 3, *Peace in the World* (1970; Sofia, April 21, 1971); Violin Concerto No. 1 (1968); *Aquarelles* for string orch. (1973); Piano Concerto (1975); *3 Miniatures* for soprano and chamber orch. 7 string quartets (1934; 1938; 1944; *Micro-quartet,* 1967; 1969; 1975; 1977); 2 wind quintets (1936, 1946); Trio for oboe clarinet and bassoon (1964); Solo Cello Sonata (1969); choruses; songs; incidental music. He published several teaching manuals and essays on Bulgarian music: *The Sources of Bulgarian Musical Composition* (Sofia, 1937); *Instrumentation* (Sofia, 1947); *Problems of Orchestration,* 2 vols., (Sofia, 1953; 2nd and 3rd editions, 1958, 1966); *Behind the Curtain of the Creative Process* (Sofia, 1971).

Golestan, Stan, Rumanian composer; b. Vaslui, May 26, 1872; d. Paris, April 22, 1956. He studied in Paris at the Schola Cantorum with Vincent d'Indy, Albert Roussel and Paul Dukas (1897–1903); remained in Paris; was engaged as a music critic, writing in *Le Figaro* and other publications. He maintained contact with Rumania, and most of his works derive thematically from Rumanian folk music; in 1915 he received the national Rumanian prize for composition.
WORKS: *La Dembovitza* for orch., based on Rumanian popular melodies (1902); Symphony (1910); *Rapsodie roumaine* for orch. (1912); *Rapsodie concertante* for violin and orch. (1920); *Concerto roumain* for violin and orch. (1933); *Concerto moldave* for cello and orch. (1936); *Sur les cîmes carpathiques* for piano and orch. (1940); *Serenade* for Cello and Piano (1909); *Poèmes et paysages* for piano solo (1922); 2 string quartets; *Ballade roumaine* for harp (1932); many

songs to French words, among them *Hora* (which received the Verley Prize, 1921).

Golitzin, Nikolai, Russian nobleman, a music amateur; b. St. Petersburg, Dec. 19, 1794; d. in Tambov district, Nov. 3, 1866. He was a talented cello player, but his name is remembered mainly by his connection with Beethoven, who dedicated to Golitzin the overture op. 124 and the string quartets ops. 127, 130, 132. Golitzin was also responsible for the first Russian performance of Beethoven's *Missa Solemnis* (1824).
BIBLIOGRAPHY: L. Ginzburg, "Beethoven und Nikolai Golitzin," *Beethoven Jahrbuch* (Bonn, 1962).

Göllerich, August, Austrian writer on music; b. Linz, July 2, 1859; d. there, March 16, 1923. He was a pupil of Liszt; studied composition with Bruckner; acquired Ramann's music school in Nuremberg in 1890, and established branches in Erlangen, Fürth, and Ansbach; from 1896, conductor of the Musikverein and director of the Cons. in Linz; his wife, **Gisela Pászthory-Voigt** (also a pupil of Liszt), supervised the other schools. He published *A. Reissmann als Schriftsteller und Komponist* (1884); *Beethoven* (1904); *Franz Liszt* (1908); guides to Liszt's *Graner Festmesse* and Wagner's *Ring des Nibelungen* (1897). His chief work, the biography of Bruckner (who himself selected him for this task), in 4 vols., was completed by Max Auer (1st vol., Regensburg, 1924; 2nd, 1928; remaining vols., 1932 and 1937).

Gollmick, Adolf, German pianist and composer; son of **Karl Gollmick;** b. Frankfurt, Feb. 5, 1825; d. London, March 7, 1883. He studied with his father and other teachers in Frankfurt; in 1844, he settled in London as a pianist and teacher. He composed 3 comic operas: *Dona Constanza, The Oracle, Balthasar;* 2 'operatic cantatas': *The Blind Beggar's Daughter of Bethnal Green* and *The Heir of Lynne;* also several symphonic works, piano pieces, and songs.

Gollmick, Karl, German composer and music theorist; b. Dessau, March 19, 1796; d. Frankfurt, Oct. 3, 1866. He was of a musical family; his father, **Friedrich Karl Gollmick** (1774–1852), was an opera tenor. He studied theology in Strasbourg; in 1817, he settled in Frankfurt, where he taught French and served as chorusmaster. He wrote mostly for piano; publ. potpourris, etc. His writings include *Kritische Terminologie für Musiker und Musikfreunde* (1833; 2nd ed., 1839); *Fétis als Mensch, Kritiker, Theoretiker und Komponist* (1852); *Handlexikon der Tonkunst* (1858), etc. He also wrote an autobiography (1866).

Golovanov, Nikolai, Russian conductor, composer and pedagogue; b. Moscow, Jan. 21, 1891; d. there, Aug. 28, 1953. He studied choral conducting with Kastalsky at the Synodal School in Moscow, graduating in 1909; then entered composition classes of Ippolitov-Ivanov and Vassilenko at the Moscow Cons. After graduation in 1914 he was engaged as assistant chorus conductor at the Bolshoi Theater in Moscow; was rapidly promoted and from 1948 until his death was chief conductor there; he also was director of the theatrical division of the Moscow Radio. He was awarded the Order of the Red Banner in 1935, and was 4 times recipient of the First Stalin Prize (1946, 1948, 1950, 1951). He wrote an opera *Princess Yurata;* Symphony; a symph. poem *Salome,* after Oscar Wilde; numerous piano pieces and songs.

BIBLIOGRAPHY: N. Anosov, "Nikolai Golavanov," *Sovietskaya Musica* (May 1951).

Golschmann, Vladimir, renowned French conductor; b. Paris, Dec. 16, 1893; d. New York, March 1, 1972. He studied violin and piano at the Schola Cantorum; as early as 1919 he organized the Concerts Golschmann in Paris, in programs featuring many first performances of modern works. In 1923 he conducted ballet in the U.S.; then was conductor of the Scottish Orch., Glasgow (1928-30). In 1931 he was engaged conductor of the St. Louis Symph. Orch., and held this post for more than a quarter of a century (1931-1958); from 1964-1970 was conductor of the Denver Symph. Orchestra; also appeared as guest conductor with other American orchestras.

Goltermann, Georg (Eduard), German cellist and composer; b. Hannover, Aug. 19, 1824; d. Frankfurt, Dec. 29, 1898. He studied cello in Munich, where he was also a pupil of Lachner in composition. After concert tours in 1850-52, he became music director at Würzburg; in 1853, he was appointed music director of the City Theater of Frankfurt. He composed a number of works for cello, including 6 concertos; sonatas with piano; *Morceaux caractéristiques; Danses allemandes; Elégie,* etc. He also wrote a symphony, 2 overtures, and songs.

Golther, Wolfgang, German writer; b. Stuttgart, May 25, 1863; d. Rostock, Dec. 14, 1945. He was prof. of Germanic philology at Rostock; beside works on this subject, he wrote several important books on the music of Richard Wagner: *Die Sage von Tristan und Isolde* (1887), *Die sagengeschichtlichen Grundlagen der Ringdichtung Richard Wagners* (1902), *Bayreuth* (1904), *Richard Wagner als Dichter* (1904; English translation, 1907), *Tristan und Isolde in den Dichtungen des Mittelalters und der neueren Zeit* (1907), *Zur deutschen Sage und Dichtung* (1911), *Parsifal und der Gral in deutscher Sage des Mittelalters und der Neuzeit* (1913; new ed., 1925); *Richard Wagner* (1926); edited Wagner's correspondence with the Wesendoncks; *Richard Wagner, Zehn Lieder aus den Jahren 1838-58* (1921). He wrote an opera, *Hassan gewinnt* (Rostock, 1929).

Golyscheff, Jefim (Jef), Russian composer and theorist; b. Kherson, Sept. 20, 1897; d. Paris, Sept. 25, 1970. He studied violin in Odessa and played in public as a child. In 1909, in the wake of anti-Jewish pogroms in Russia, he went to Berlin where he studied chemistry as well as music theory; at the same time he began to paint in the manner of abstract expressionism. Golyscheff played a historic role in the development of the serial methods of composition; his String Trio, written about 1914, and published in 1925, contains passages described by him as "Zwölftondauer-Komplexen," in which 12 different tones are given 12 different durations in the main theme. Both

as a painter and musician he was close to the Dada circles in Berlin, and participated in futuristic experiments. On April 30, 1919 he presented at a Dada exhibition in Berlin his *Anti-Symphonie,* subtitled *Musikalische Kreisguillotine (Musical Circular Guillotine),* with characteristic titles of its movements: 1) *Provocational Injections* 2) *Chaotic Oral Cavity, or Submarine Aircraft* 3) *Clapping in Hyper F-sharp Major.* On May 24, 1919 he appeared at a Berlin Dada soirée with a piece of his composition entitled *Keuchmaneuver (Cough Maneuver).* All this activity ceased with the advent of the Nazis in 1933. As a Jew, Golyscheff had to flee Germany; he went to Paris, but after the fall of France in 1940 was interned by the Vichy authorities. His life was probably spared because of his expertise as a chemist; he was also conscripted as a cement laborer. In 1956 he went to Brazil where he devoted himself exclusively to painting, and had several successful exhibitions in São Paulo. In 1966 he returned to Paris, where he remained until his death.

BIBLIOGRAPHY: H. Eimert, *Atonale Musiklehre* (Leipzig, 1924; reprinted under the title, *Zwölftontechnik,* Wiesbaden, 1954); D. Gojowy, "Jefim Golyscheff, der unbequeme Vorläufer," *Melos* (May-June 1975).

Gombert, Nicolas, Flemish composer; b. southern Flanders, possibly between Lille and St. Omer, c.1490; d. 1556. He was one of the most eminent pupils of Josquin des Prez, on whose death he composed a funeral dirge. The details of his early life are obscure and uncertain. He is first positively accounted for in 1526, when his name appears on the list of singers at the court chapel of Charles V that was issued at Granada in that year; the restless Emperor traveled continually throughout his extensive domain—Spain, Germany, and the Netherlands—and his retinue was obliged to follow him in his round of his courts at Vienna, Madrid, and Brussels; Gombert probably was taken into the service of the Emperor on one of the latter's visits to Brussels. He is first mentioned as 'maistre des enffans de la chapelle de nostre sr empereur' (master of the boys of the royal chapel) in a court document dated Jan. 1, 1529; he remained in the Emperor's employ until 1538-40, during which time he took an active part in the various functions of the court, composing assiduously. After his retirement from his post in the royal chapel, he seems to have returned to his native Netherlands (Tournai) and there continued to compose until his death. He held a canonship at Notre Dame, Courtrai, from June 23, 1537, without having to take up residence there, and was also a canon at the Cathedral of Tournai from June 19, 1534. Despite his many trips abroad and the natural influence of the music of other countries, Gombert remained, stylistically, a Netherlander. The chief feature of his sacred works is his use of imitation, a principle which he developed to a high state of perfection. The parts are always in motion, and pauses appear infrequently and, when they do occur, are very short. In his handling of the dissonance he may be regarded as a forerunner of Palestrina. His secular works, of which the earliest known printed examples (9 4-part chansons) are included in Attaignant's collection of 1529-49, are characterized by a refreshing simplicity and directness. Gombert's greatest contributions to the development of the 16th-century music lay in his recognizing the peculiarities of the Netherlandish polyphony and his developing and spreading it abroad. He wrote 11 Masses and about 250 motets and chansons, many of which appeared in contemporary (mostly Spanish) lute and guitar arrangements, a fact which shows the great vogue they had. Reprints have been publ. by F. Commer in *Collectio operum musicorum Batavorum* (1839 ff.) VIII (1 motet) and XII (2 chansons); A. Reissmann in *Allgemeine Geschichte der Musik* (1863; 1 chanson); R. J. v. Maldeghem in *Trésor musical* (1865 ff.) II (1 motet), XI (3 chansons), XII (1 motet), XIV (5 chansons), XVI (1 motet of doubtful authorship), XVII (1 chanson), XX (2 motets); R. Eitner in *Publikationen älterer praktischer . . . Musikwerke* III (1875; 2 chansons); A. W. Ambros in *Geschichte der Musik* V (3rd ed. 1911; 1 motet, revised by O. Kade); E. H. Wooldridge in *The Oxford History of Music* II (1905; 1 motet); Th. Kroyer in *Der vollkommene Partiturspieler* (1930; 10 Magnificat selections); A. Schering in *Geschichte der Musik in Beispielen* (1931; no. 102, portion of the Mass *Media vita*); a motet is in Attaignant's *Treize livres de motets* (Book I, pp. 167-75), reprinted by the Lyrebird Press (Paris, 1934). Gombert's *Opera omnia*, ed. by J. Schmidt-Görg, projected 12 vols., began publication in 1951 (American Institute of Musicology in Rome).

BIBLIOGRAPHY: D. von Bartha, "Probleme der Chansongeschichte im 16. Jahrhundert," *Zeitschrift für Musikwissenschaft* (Aug.-Sept. 1931); H. Eppstein, *Nicolas Gombert als Motettenkomponist* (Würzburg, 1935); J. Schmidt-Görg, "Die acht Magnifikat des Nicolas Gombert," *Gesammelte Aufsätze zur Kulturgeschichte Spaniens* V (1935; contains a *Magnificat secundi toni* and selections from other Magnificats); J. Schmidt-Görg, *Nicolas Gombert, Leben und Werk* (Bonn, 1938; contains bibliography of works, musical examples, etc.); C. A. Miller, "Jerome Cardan on Gombert, Phinot, and Carpentras," *Musical Quarterly* (July 1972).

Gombosi, Otto, eminent Hungarian musicologist; b. Budapest, Oct. 23, 1902; d. Natick, Mass., Feb. 17, 1955. He studied at the Academy of Music in Budapest; then at the Univ. of Berlin. From 1926–28 he edited the progressive Hungarian music periodical, *Crescendo*. In 1940 he came to the U.S.; was lecturer in music at the Univ. of Washington, Seattle; then taught at Michigan State College and at the Univ. of Chicago; in 1951, appointed prof. at Harvard Univ. He contributed numerous valuable papers to various periodicals, in Hungarian, German, Italian, and English; among his most important writings are *Jakob Obrecht* (Leipzig, 1925); *Tonarten und Stimmungen der antiken Musik* (Copenhagen, 1939); a treatise on V. Bakfark in *Musicologia Hungarica* (Budapest, 1935; contains Bakfark's 10 fantasias); "Studien zur Tonartenlehre des frühen Mittelalters," *Acta musicologica* (1938–39). He contributed the chapter on Hungarian music to G. Reese's *Music in the Renaissance* (N.Y., 1954).

Gomes, Antonio Carlos, Brazilian composer; b. (of Portuguese parents) Campinas, Brazil, July 11, 1836; d. Pará (Belém), Sept. 16, 1896. He was a pupil of his father, then of the Cons. in Rio de Janeiro, where he produced 2 operas, *Noite do Castello* (1861) and *Joanna de Flandres* (1863). The success of these works induced the Emperor Don Pedro II to grant him a stipend for further study in Milan; there he soon made his mark with a little humorous piece entitled *Se sa minga* (a song from this work, *Del fucile ad ago*, became popular), produced in 1867. After another piece in the same vein (*Nella Luna*, 1868), he made a more serious bid for fame with the opera *Il Guarany*, produced at La Scala on March 19, 1870, with brilliant success; this work, in which Amazon-Indian themes are used, quickly went the round of Italy, and was given in London (Covent Garden) on July 13, 1872. Returning to Rio de Janeiro, Gomes brought out a very popular operetta, *Telegrapho elettrico*. His other operas are *Fosca* (La Scala, Milan, Feb. 16, 1873), *Salvator Rosa* (Genoa, March 21, 1874), *Maria Tudor* (La Scala, Milan, March 27, 1879), *Lo Schiavo* (Rio de Janeiro, Sept. 27, 1889), and *Condor* (La Scala, Milan, Feb. 21, 1891). He wrote the hymn *Il saluto del Brasile,* for the centenary of American independence (1876); also the cantata *Colombo* for the Columbus Festival in 1892. In 1895 he was appointed director of the newly founded Cons. at Pará, but he died soon after arriving there. Besides his operas, he composed songs (3 books), choruses, and piano pieces.

BIBLIOGRAPHY: S. Boccanera Júnior, *Um artista brasileiro: in memoriam* (Bahia, 1904); H. P. Vieira, *Carlos Gomes: sua arte e sua obra* (São Paulo, 1934); I. Gomes Vaz de Carvalho, *A vida de Carlos Gomes* (Rio de Janeiro, 1935; Italian transl., Milan, 1935); R. Seidl, *Carlos Gomes, brasileiro e patriota* (Rio de Janeiro, 1935); L. F. Vieira Souto, *Antonio Carlos Gomes* (Rio de Janeiro, 1936); centenary issue of *Revista brasileira de musica* (1936); J. Prito, *Carlos Gomes* (São Paulo, 1936); R. Almeida, *Carlos Gomes* (Rio de Janeiro, 1937); M. de Andrade, *Carlos Gomes* (Rio de Janeiro, 1939); P. Cerquera, *Carlos Gomes* (São Paulo, 1944).

Gomes de Araújo, João, Brazilian composer; b. Pindamonhangaba, Aug. 5, 1846; d. São Paulo, Sept. 8, 1942. He studied at São Paulo and Milan; in 1905, became a teacher at São Paulo Cons., and remained there almost to the end of his long life.

WORKS: 4 operas: *Edmea; Carminosa* (Milan, 1888); *Maria Petrowna* (1904; São Paulo, 1929); *Helena* (São Paulo, 1910); also 6 symphonies, 6 Masses, vocal and instrumental works.

Gómez Calleja. See **Calleja, Gómez Rafael.**

Gómez, Julio, Spanish composer and musicologist; b. Madrid, Dec. 20, 1886; d. there, Dec. 22, 1973. He studied at the Madrid Cons. In 1911 he became director of the Archeological Museum in Toledo; later head of the music division of the National Library in Madrid, and librarian of the Cons. there. He wrote the comic opera *El Pelele* (1925); piano pieces, songs.

Gomezanda, Antonio, Mexican pianist and composer; b. Lagos, Jalisco, Sept. 3, 1894. He studied piano with Manuel M. Ponce; then went to Germany, where he took lessons in composition and conducting in Berlin. Returning to Mexico, he taught piano at the National Cons. (1921-29) and at the Univ. of Mexico (1929-32). Among his works are an "Aztec ballet," *Xiuhtzitzquilo,* which was produced in Berlin on Feb. 19, 1928; *Fantasia mexicana,* for piano and orch. (1923); piano pieces; songs.

Gomólka, Michal, Polish musician, son of **Mikolaj Gomólka;** b. Sandomierz, 1564; d. Jazlowiec, March 9, 1609. He was active as a band conductor at various palaces of Polish noblemen; little is known of his life, except that he enjoyed the favor of Polish aristocratic society.

Gomólka, Mikolaj (Nicolas), Polish composer; b. Sandomierz, about 1535; date of death unknown. He was a chorister at Cracow (1545), and then played trumpet and flute in the court orchestra. In 1566 he returned to his native town, where he married and served as a judge. His chief work was *Melodiae na psalterz polski* (Cracow, 1580), containing 150 melodies to words from the Psalms translated by the poet Jan Kochanowski; new edition was publ. by J. W. Reiss in 1923; several pieces are included in the anthology by Jachimecki and Lissa, *Music of the Polish Renaissance* (Warsaw, 1954).
BIBLIOGRAPHY: J. W. Reiss, *Melodye psalmowe M. Gomolki* (Cracow, 1912); A. Chybinski, *Slownik Muzykow Dawnej Polski* (Cracow, 1949); M. Perez, *Mikolaj Gomólka* (Warsaw, 1969).

Gondimel, Claude. See **Goudimel, Claude.**

González-Avila, Jorge, Mexican composer; b. Mérida, Yucatán, Dec. 10, 1925. In 1949 he moved to Mexico City; studied composition with Rodolfo Halffter, harmony with Blas Galindo, piano with Francisco Agea Hermosa and theory with Hernández Moncada at the National Cons. (1949-53); had a course in musical orientation with Jesús Bal y Gay in 1952, and a year later a similar course with Chávez at the National College. He devoted himself to teaching; in 1972 was appointed director of the Audiotranscription Division of the Centro Nacional de Investigación, Documentación y Información Musical (CENIDIM) of the National Institute of Fine Arts in Mexico City. He wrote an impressive quantity of piano pieces and some other instrumental music.
WORKS: *3 Inventions* for solo violin (1955); *Impromptus* for string quartet (1960); *Invention* for soprano, piano and orch. (1964); *Invention interpolar* for piano and orch. (1974); 2 sonata trios for flute, cello and piano (1965, 1977); *Solo Violin Sonata* (1966); *Suite for Solo Guitar* (1968); *2 Interludes* for violin and piano (1968); *Recitativo* for violin and piano (1969); *Inventions quasi Fantasia* for viola and piano (1970); *Invention concertante No. 1* for piano and orch. (1973); *Impromptu* for solo viola (1974); *2 Preludes* for horn and piano (1974); *Invention* for tuba and piano (1974); *Fantasia* for organ (1974); *Invention* for English horn, piano and orch. (1975); *Prelude and Invention* for string orch. (1976); *Violin Sonata* (1977); *Duo for Viola and Piano* (1977). For piano he composed 17 sonatas; 2 sonatinas (1975, 1976); 20 suites

(1953-75); 7 partitas (1953-73); 14 fantasias (1956-75); 8 studies (1959-76); 12 impromptus (1960-75); 16 preludes in 3 sets (1969-73); 2 *Symphonic Studies* (1970); 2 ballets (1973, 1975); 8 *Preludes and Inventions* (1974); 5 *Bagatelles* (1975); 24 *Inventions* (1959); 5 *Variation Studies* (1960); 77 *Miniature Studies* (1973); *Prelude and Invention* for 2 pianos (1975); 2-piano sonata (1977).

González-Zuleta, Fabio, Colombian composer; b. Bogotá, Nov. 2, 1920. He studied organ and composition at the Bogotá Cons.; after graduation became a member of its faculty; in 1957 was appointed its director.
WORKS: Symph. No. 1 (1956); Violin Concerto (1958); Symph. No. 2 (1959); Piano Trio (1955); Trio for Flute, Violin and Viola (1955); Suite for Wind Quintet (1956); Clarinet Sonata (1958); *Quintetto Abstracto* for wind instruments (1960); Sonata for Double Bass and Piano (1960).

Goodall, Reginald, English conductor; b. Lincoln, July 13, 1905. He studied piano with Arthur Benjamin and violin with W. H. Reed at the Royal College of Music in London; from 1936 to 1939 was assistant conductor at Covent Garden; then went to Germany, and was engaged as an assistant to Furtwängler at the Berlin Philharmonic; also led many operatic performances. He is regarded as a foremost interpreter of Wagner's music dramas; in 1973 he conducted the entire cycle of the *Ring of the Nibelung* at Sadler's Wells Opera in London.

Goodman (real name **Guttmann**), **Alfred,** German-American composer; b. Berlin, March 1, 1920. He studied at the Berlin Cons.; in 1939 went to England, and in 1940 settled in America; was in the U.S. Army during World War II. In 1946 he was arranger with several dance bands; at the same time he studied with Henry Cowell and Otto Luening at Columbia Univ., receiving his B.S. in 1952 and his M.A. in 1953. In 1960 he returned to Germany.
WORKS: *The Audition,* one-act opera (Athens, Ohio, July 27, 1954); 2 symphonies; choral and chamber music. He published a music lexicon, *Musik von A-Z* (Munich, 1971).

Goodman, Benny (Benjamin David), American clarinetist and jazz band leader; b. Chicago, May 30, 1909. He acquired a taste for syncopated music as a child by listening to phonographic recordings of ragtime; was playing professionally by the age of 12 (1921), and in 1926 was working with Ben Pollack, one of the leading Chicago jazz musicians of the period. In 1928, he went to New York as a clarinetist in various bands. In 1934 formed his own band, which became known nationwide from its weekly appearances on the "Let's Dance" radio program. Both as the leader of a large dance band and for his virtuoso performances in various jazz combos, Goodman was the best-known and most successful musician of the swing era; was called the King of Swing. He also played clarinet parts in classical works in concert and for records, appearing as soloist in Mozart's Clarinet Concerto with the N.Y. Philharmonic (Dec. 12, 1940), and recording works by Copland, Bartok, Stravinsky, Morton Gould, and

Leonard Bernstein. His autobiography, *The Kingdom of Swing,* was published in 1939; a biographical movie, *The Benny Goodman Story,* was made in 1955.

Goodrich, Alfred John, American music pedagogue; b. Chilo, Ohio, May 8, 1848; d. Paris, April 25, 1920. A self-taught musician, he became a teacher of theory at the Grand Cons., N.Y.; the Fort Wayne Cons., Ind.; director of the vocal department at the Beethoven Cons., St. Louis; member of music department, Martha Washington College, Abingdon, Va.; later lived in Chicago, Paris, and St. Louis as writer and teacher.
WRITINGS: *Music as a Language* (1880); *The Art of Song* (1888); *Complete Musical Analysis* (1889); *Analytical Harmony* (1894); *Theory of Interpretation* (1898; publ. by subscription); *Guide to Memorizing Music* (1904; revised ed., 1906); *Synthetic Counterpoint* (in MS).

Goodrich, (John) Wallace, American organist, conductor, and writer on music; b. Newton, Mass., May 27, 1871; d. Boston, June 6, 1952. He studied at the New England Cons. in Boston (organ with Dunham, composition with Chadwick); then in Munich with Rheinberger (1894–95) and with Widor in Paris. In 1896–97, he was coach at the Leipzig Municipal Theater. In 1897 he returned to Boston and became an instructor at the New England Cons.; he was appointed dean in 1907, and director in 1931, a post he held until 1942. He was organist of Trinity Church from 1902–09, and for the Boston Symph. Orch., from 1897–1909. He founded the Choral Art Society in 1902 and was its conductor until 1907; he was also, at various periods, conductor of the Cecilia Society, the Boston Opera Co., and the Worcester County Choral Association. He composed an *Ave Maria* for chorus and orch. (Munich, 1895) and other choral music; wrote *The Organ in France* (Boston, 1917) and translated A. Pirro's *J. S. Bach and His Works for the Organ* (1902) and d'Ortigue's *Méthode d'accompagnement du plain-chant* (1905).

Goodson, Katharine, English pianist; b. Watford, Hertfordshire, June 18, 1872; d. London, April 14, 1958. From 1886–92 she was a pupil of O. Beringer at the Royal Academy of Music, and from 1892–96 of Leschetizky in Vienna; debut in London at a Saturday Pop. Concert, Jan. 16, 1897, with signal success; then followed tours of England, France, Austria, and Germany, which established her reputation; her American debut, with the Boston Symph., took place Jan. 18, 1907; since then she made many tours of the U.S., also of Holland, Belgium, and Italy. In 1903 she married the English composer **Arthur Hinton.**

Goossens, Sir Eugene, outstanding English conductor and composer; b. London, May 26, 1893; d. there, June 13, 1962. A scion of a family of musicians of Belgian extraction, he was educated at the Bruges Cons., returning to England in 1906; he subsequently studied at the Liverpool College of Music (1906); then won a scholarship of the Royal College of Music in London (1907); studied violin with Rivarde, piano with Dykes, and composition with Charles Wood and Stanford; won the silver medal of the Worshipful Company of

Musicians; then played the violin in the Queen's Hall Orch. He was associated with Sir Thomas Beecham's operatic enterprises (1915–20); conducted a season of concerts with his own orch. in London (1921). In 1923 he was engaged as conductor of the Rochester, N.Y., Philharmonic Orch.; in 1931 he was appointed conductor of the Cincinnati Symph. Orch., remaining at that post until 1946. From 1947 to 1956 he was director of the New South Wales Cons. of Music at Sydney and conductor of the Sydney Symph. Orch.; he was knighted in 1955. Goossens belonged to a group of English composers who cultivated exotic themes with modernistic harmonies stemming from Debussy. He conducted his first orchestral piece, *Variations on a Chinese Theme,* at the age of 19 at the Royal College of Music in London (June 20, 1912); continued to write prolifically in all genres (opera, ballet, symphony, chamber music); his mature style became a blend of impressionistic harmonies and neo-classical polyphony; while retaining a clear tonal outline, Goossens often resorted to expressive chromatic melos bordering on atonality.
WORKS: *Variations on a Chinese Theme* for orch. (1911); *Miniature Fantasy* for string orch. (1911); Suite for Flute, Violin, and Harp (1914); *Five Impressions of a Holiday* for flute, cello, and piano (1914); symph. poem, *Perseus* (1914); symph. prelude, *Ossian* (1915); *Phantasy Quartet* for strings (1915); String Quartet No. 1 (1916); 2 sketches for string quartet: *By the Tarn* and *Jack o' Lantern* (1916); *Kaleidoscope,* suite of piano pieces in a humorous vein (1917–18); Violin Sonata No. 1 (1918); prelude to Verhaeren's *Philip II* (1918); *The Eternal Rhythm* for orch. (London, Oct. 19, 1920); *4 Conceits* for piano (1918); Piano Quintet (1919); *Lyric Poem* for violin and piano (1921; also arranged for violin and orch.); ballet *L'École en crinoline* (1921); *Silence* for chorus and piano (1922); incidental music to W. Somerset Maugham's *East of Suez* (1922); *Sinfonietta* (London, Feb. 19, 1923); String Sextet (1923); *Pastoral and Harlequinade* for flute, oboe, and piano (1924); Fantasy for Wind Instruments (1924); opera, *Judith* (1925; Covent Garden, June 25, 1929); *Rhythmic Dance* for orch. (Rochester, March 12, 1927); Concertino for Double String Orch. (1928); Oboe Concerto (London, Oct. 2, 1930; Leon Goossens, soloist); Violin Sonata No. 2 (1930); opera, *Don Juan de Mañara* (1934; Covent Garden, June 24, 1937); Symph. No. 1 (Cincinnati, April 12, 1940); 2nd String Quartet (1942); *Phantasy-Concerto* for piano and orch. (Cincinnati, Feb. 25, 1944, composer conducting; Iturbi, soloist); 2nd Symph. (BBC, Nov. 10, 1946); oratorio, *Apocalypse* (1951; Sydney, Nov. 22, 1954, composer conducting). Goossens is the author of *Overture and Beginners; A Musical Autobiography* (London, 1951).

Goossens, Leon, English oboist, brother of **Eugene Goossens;** b. Liverpool, June 12, 1897. He studied at the Royal College of Music; in 1913–24 was first oboist of the Queen's Hall Orch.; afterward played with the Royal Philharmonic Orch., the London Philharmonic Orch., and the Covent Garden Opera; held oboe professorships at the Royal College of Music and Royal Academy of Music; appeared in many countries, including the U.S., where he first performed with his brother, Eugene, in N.Y. in 1927.

Goovaerts, Alphonse Jean Marie André, Belgian musicologist; b. Antwerp, May 25, 1847; d. Brussels, Dec. 25, 1922. He was a member of a literary family; as a youth he became greatly interested in Flemish literature and in church music. He arranged and publ. a collection of Flemish songs (1868–74); composed several pieces of church music, and performed them with a chorus which he established in Antwerp; also made transcriptions for chorus of works by Palestrina and Flemish contrapuntists. He publ. several papers propounding a reform in church music, which aroused opposition from conservative circles *(La Musique de l'eglise,* 1876; in Flemish as *De Kerkmuziek);* also publ. a valuable book, *Histoire et bibliographie de la typographie musicale dans le Pays-Bas* (1880; awarded the gold medal of the Belgian Academy); a monograph on the Belgian music printer, Pierre Phalèse, and other studies relating to Flemish music.

Gorczycki, Gregor Gervasius, Polish composer; b. Cracow, c.1664; d. there, April 30, 1734. He was a student of theology at Prague Univ.; was ordained priest in Cracow in 1692; became chapel master at the Cracow Cathedral in 1698, retaining this position until his death. He was the composer of many excellent motets, hymns, psalms, and Masses in a polyphonic style, a cappella and with instrumental accompaniment, to Latin texts; several of them were reprinted in the Polish collections edited by Cichocki, Surzynski, Sowinski, and Chybinski.
BIBLIOGRAPHY: A. Chybinski, *G. G. Gorczycki* (Posen, 1927); also see Chybinski's *Slownik Muzykow Dawnej Polski* (Cracow, 1949) for a complete list of editions of Gorczycki's sacred works.

Gordeli, Otar, Georgian composer; b. Tbilisi, Nov. 18, 1928. He studied composition with Andrey Balantchivadze; later took courses at the Moscow Cons., graduating in 1955. In 1959 he was appointed instructor at the Cons. of Tbilisi. In his music he applies resources of native folk songs; his polyphonic structure is considerably advanced.
WORKS: Piano Concerto (1952); cantata, *The Seasons,* for narrator, boys' chorus and chamber orch. (1955); Concertino for Flute and Orch. (1958); *Festive Overture* (1959); *Georgian Dance* for orch. (1961); film music; jazz pieces.

Gordigiani, Luigi, Italian composer; b. Florence, June 21, 1806; d. Modena, May 1, 1860. He is chiefly known for his more than 300 songs for voice and piano; these *canzonette* and *canti populari* were based on Italian folk tunes; Gordigiani wrote the words for many himself. He also publ. a collection of songs based on Tuscan folk poems. Ricordi has publ. 67 songs in 2 vols. in the series 'Canti popolari italiani.' Other works by Gordigiani include 10 operas, 3 cantatas, a ballet, and an oratorio.

Gordon, Gavin Muspratt, Scottish singer and composer; b. Ayr, Nov. 24, 1901; d. London, Nov. 18, 1970. He studied at the Royal College of Music with Vaughan Williams; later was active as singer, film actor, and composer. He wrote several ballets: *A Toothsome Morsel* (1930); *Regatta* (1931); *The Scorpions of Ysit* (1932); *The Rake's Progress* (London, Sadler's Wells, May 20, 1935).

Gordon, Jacques, Russian violinist; b. Odessa, March 7, 1899; d. Hartford, Conn., Sept. 15, 1948. He studied at the Odessa Cons.; went to the U.S., and took courses at the Institute of Musical Art, N.Y., with Kneisel (violin) and Goetschius (theory). From 1918–21, was a member of the Berkshire String Quartet; in 1921 he founded the Gordon String Quartet. From 1921–30, he was concertmaster of the Chicago Symph. Orch., and violin teacher at the American Cons. in Chicago. He publ. some arrangements for violin.

Gordon, James Carel Gerhard, flute maker; b. Cape Town, May 22, 1791; d. (insane) Lausanne, c.1845. He was a son of a Dutch captain and a Swiss mother in South Africa. He joined the Swiss Guards of Charles X in Paris in 1814; at the same time, studied flute with Tulou; worked on improvements of its mechanism more or less at the same time as Böhm, so that the priority of the invention became a matter of insoluble controversy. He escaped with his life during the attack on the Swiss Guards in the Revolution of 1830; was pensioned and retired to Switzerland when his mind became deranged.
BIBLIOGRAPHY: C. Welch, *History of the Boehm Flute* (London, 1896); Percival R. Kirby, "Captain Gordon, The Flute Maker," *Music & Letters* (July 1957).

Górecki, Henryk Mikolaj, significant Polish composer; b. Czernica, Dec. 6, 1933. He studied composition with Boleslaw Szabelski at the Cons. of Katowice (1955–60); in 1968 was appointed to its faculty. In his music he makes use of the entire arsenal of modern techniques, while preserving the traditional formal design.
WORKS: *Toccata* for 2 pianos (1955); piano sonata (1956); *Pieśń o radości i rytmie* (*Song of Joy and Rhythm*) for orch. (1956); sonata for 2 violins (1957); concerto for 5 instruments and string quartet (1957); *Epitaph* for chorus and instrumental ensemble (1958); *5 Pieces* for 2 pianos (1959); Symph. No. 1, for string orch. and percussion (1959); *3 Diagrams* for solo flute (1959); *Monologhi* for soprano and 3 instrumental groups (1960); *Zderzenia* (*Collisions*) for orch. (1960); *Genesis,* cycle of 3 works: *Elementi* for string trio (1962), *Canti strumentali* for 15 performers (1962) and *Monodram* for soprano, metal percussion and 6 double basses (1963); *Chóros I* for 56 strings (1964); *Refren* (*Refrain*) for orch. (1965); *La Musiquette I* for 2 trumpets and guitar (1967); *La Musiquette II* for brass and percussion (1967); *La Musiquette III* for violas (1969); *La Musiquette IV* for clarinet, trombone, cello and piano (1970); *Muzyka Staropolska* (*Old Polish Music*), 3 pieces for orch. (Warsaw, Sept. 24, 1969); Symph. No. 2, (*Copernican Symphony*), for soprano, baritone, chorus and orch. (Warsaw, June 22, 1973); *Amen* for chorus a cappella (1975).

Gorin, Igor, Russian baritone; b. Grodek, Ukraine, Oct. 26, 1908. He studied at the Vienna Cons., graduating in 1930; sang at the Vienna Opera and the Czech State Opera; came to the U.S. in 1933; became a citizen in 1939. He wrote several songs, including *Lament, Caucasian Song, Lullaby Within My Dreams, Remembered Mornings, The Jumping Jack,* etc.

Gorini, Gino, Italian composer and pianist; b. Venice, June 22, 1914. He studied there at the Cons. Benedetto Marcello; received diplomas in piano (1931) and composition (1933); later studied composition with Malipiero; in 1940 was appointed prof. of piano at the Venice Cons.; made many tours in Italy and abroad, including two-piano team tours in Italy with Sergio Lorenzi.

WORKS: *Tre omaggi,* for orch. (1933); suite for piano and orch. (1934); Violin Concerto (1934); Symph. (1935); *Introduction and Arioso* for orch. (1937); *Concertino* for 7 instruments (1933); *Contrasti* for 5 instruments (1933); Divertimento for Chamber Orch. (1935); Piano Sonata (1936); String Quartet (1936); Cello Sonata (1939); Quintet for Piano and Strings (1939); *5 Studi* for 2 pianos, strings and timpani (1960); Concerto for Viola, Orch. and Piano (1968).

Goritz, Otto, German dramatic baritone; b. Berlin, June 8, 1873; d. Hamburg, April 11, 1929. He received his entire musical education from his mother, Olga Nielitz; debut, Oct. 1, 1895, as Matteo (*Fra Diavolo*) at Neustrelitz; his success led to an immediate engagement for 3 years; 1898-1900, at the Stadttheater in Breslau; 1900-3, at Stadttheater in Hamburg. On Dec. 24, 1903, he made his American debut at the Metropolitan Opera House as Klingsor in the first production of *Parsifal* outside Bayreuth. In 1924, returned to Germany, where he sang in opera in Berlin and Hamburg.

Gorney, Jay, American composer; b. Bialstok, Poland, Dec. 12, 1896; emigrated to U.S. as a child. He studied music at the Univ. of Michigan. Beginning in 1924 he wrote a number of scores and separate songs for Broadway. In 1933 he went to Hollywood. He composed the celebrated song, *Brother, Can You Spare a Dime?,* which became a musical symbol of the Depression era.

Gorno, Albino, pianist and composer; b. Casalmorano (Cremona), March 10, 1859; d. Cincinnati, Ohio, Oct. 29, 1945. He studied at the Milan Cons., where he took 3 gold medals, and where his opera, *Cuore e Patria,* was produced. He was accompanist to Adelina Patti on her American tour (1881-82); stayed and became head of the piano department and dean of faculty at the Cincinnati College of Music. He wrote a cantata, many pieces for piano, and songs.

Gorno, Romeo, pianist and teacher; brother of **Albino Gorno;** b. Cremona, Italy, Jan. 1, 1870; d. Cincinnati, Nov. 28, 1931. He studied in Milan with his father, later a pupil of the Cons. there; then went to the U.S. and joined his brother as prof. of piano at the Cincinnati College of Music.

Gorodnitzki, Sascha, Russian pianist; b. Kiev, May 24, 1905; brought to the U.S. as an infant. He studied at the Institute of Musical Art and the Juilliard Graduate School in New York; appeared as a child prodigy at 9; toured the U.S. and Canada in recitals; in 1930, won the Schubert Memorial Prize; appointed prof. of piano at the Juilliard Graduate School in 1932.

Gorter, Albert, German conductor and composer; b. Nuremberg, Nov. 23, 1862; d. Munich, March 14, 1936. He studied at the Royal Music School in Munich and in Italy; became assistant conductor of the Bayreuth festivals; then conducted in various German cities until 1925, when he settled in Munich. He wrote text and music of an opera, *Harold;* 3 comic operas, *Der Schatz des Rhampsinit* (Mannheim, 1894), *Das süsse Gift* (Cologne, 1906), and *Der Paria* (Strasbourg, March 31, 1908); 2 symph. poems; piano pieces, and songs.

Goss, Sir John, English organist and composer; b. Fareham, Hants, Dec. 27, 1800; d. London, May 10, 1880. A son of **Joseph Goss,** the Fareham organist, he became a child chorister of the Royal Chapel; then studied under Attwood. He was successively organist of Stockwell Chapel (1821), St. Luke's, Chelsea (1824), and St. Paul's Cathedral (1838-72). In 1856 he was appointed a composer to the Chapel Royal; he was knighted in 1872, and received the degree of Mus. Doc. from Cambridge Univ. in 1876. His music includes church services, anthems, chants, psalms, etc.; and some orchestral pieces; songs and glees. He edited a collection of hymns, *Parochial Psalmody* (1827); *Chants, Ancient and Modern* (1841); *Church Psalter and Hymnbook* (1856; with Rev. W. Mercer). He publ. *The Organist's Companion,* 4 vols. of voluntaries and interludes, and *An Introduction to Harmony and Thorough-bass* (1833; many editions).

Goss, John, English baritone; b. London, May 10, 1894; d. Birmingham, Feb. 13, 1953. He began to study music relatively late in life, and was active as a singer and a music editor. He gave a number of successful recitals in England and America, in variegated programs of unusual old and new songs. He edited an *Anthology of Song* (London, 1928) and a collection, *Ballads of Britain* (London, 1937); also publ. a novel, *Cockroaches and Diamonds* (1937).

Gossec, François-Joseph, significant Belgian composer; b. Vergnies, Jan. 17, 1734; d. Paris, Feb. 16, 1829. He showed musical inclinations at an early age, and was engaged as a chorister at the Cathedral of Antwerp; received some instruction in violin and organ playing there. In 1751 he went to Paris, and in 1754 joined a private musical ensemble of the rich amateur, La Pouplinière. There he wrote chamber music and little symphonies, in which he seems to have anticipated Haydn; several works for string quartet followed in 1759. After the death of La Pouplinière in 1762, Gossec became a member of the retinue of the Prince de Conti, and continued to compose for private performances. In 1760 he wrote a Requiem; then turned his attention to stage music; produced a one-act opera, *Le Faux Lord* (Paris, June 27, 1765); obtained a decisive success with another short opera, *Les Pêcheurs* (June 7, 1766); there followed the operas (performed at the Comédie-Italienne and at the Paris Opéra) *Toinon et Toinette* (June 20, 1767); *Le Double Déguisement* (Sept. 28, 1767); *Sabinus* (Feb. 22, 1774); *Alexis et Daphné* (Sept. 26, 1775); *La Fête du village* (May 26, 1778); *Thésée* (March 1, 1782); *Rosine* (July 14, 1786); several other operas *(Nictocris, La Fédération,* etc.) were not performed. In 1770 he organized a performing society, Concerts des Amateurs; became a director of the Concert Spirituel (1773); was also an associate director of the Paris Opéra (1780–85) and manager of the École Royale de Chant (1784); when this school became the Conservatoire in 1795, Gossec became one of the inspectors, and also taught composition there; he publ. a manual, *Exposition des principes de la musique* for use of the Conservatoire. In 1795 he became a member of the newly founded Institut de France. Gossec welcomed the French Revolution with great enthusiasm, and wrote many festive works to celebrate Revolutionary events, among them *L'Offrande à la Liberté* (1792); *Le Triomphe de la République* (1793); *Le Cri de vengeance* (1799), and numerous marches and hymns. During his long life, he saw many changes of regime, but retained his position in the musical world and in society throughout the political upheavals. He retired to Passy, then a suburb of Paris, at the age of 80. Gossec's historic role consists in his creation of a French type of symphonic composition, in which he expanded the resources of instrumentation so as to provide for dynamic contrasts; he experimented with new sonorities in instrumental and choral writing; his string quartets attained a coherence of style and symmetry of form that laid the foundation of French chamber music. In his choral works, Gossec was a bold innovator, presaging in some respects the usages of Berlioz; his *Te Deum,* written for a Revolutionary festival, is scored for 1200 singers and 300 wind instruments; in his oratorio, *La Nativité,* he introduced an invisible chorus of angels placed behind the stage; in other works, he separated choral groups in order to produce special antiphonal effects. Among reprints of Gossec's works are: Trio, in Riemann's *Collegium musicum* (Leipzig, 1909); String Quartet, op. 15, no. 2, in *Veröffentlichungen der Musiksammlung W. Höckner* (facsimile reprint; Leipzig, 1932); 2 symphonies, edited by S. Beck (N.Y., 1937); a symphony in Sondheimer's collection *Werke aus dem 18. Jahrhundert* (Berlin, 1922–39); a symphony for 10 instruments, in G. Cucuël, *Études sur un orchestre de XVIIIme siècle* (Paris, 1913); 3 works ed. by Barry Brook (Paris, 1962–63): Symphonie in D, op. III/6; Symphonie in E-flat, op. VIII/1; Symphonie concertante (du *Ballet de Mirza*).

BIBLIOGRAPHY: P. Hédouin, *Gossec, sa vie et ses ouvrages* (Paris, 1852); E. G. J. Gregoir, *Notice bibliographique sur M. Gossé, dit Gossec* (Paris, 1878); F. Hellouin, *Gossec et la musique française à la fin du XVIIIe siècle* (Paris, 1903); L. Dufrane, *Gossec* (Paris, 1927); F. Tonnard, *F. J. Gossec,* (Brussels, 1938); J. G. Prod'homme, *F.-J. Gossec* (Paris, 1949); Barry Brook, *La Symphonie française dans la moitié du XVIIIe siècle* (3 vols.; Paris, 1962); W. Thibaut, *François-Joseph Gossec, chantre de la Révolucion française* (Gilly, 1970).

Gostuški, Dragutin, Serbian composer; b. Belgrade, Jan. 3, 1923. He studied in Belgrade, where he was subsequently engaged as a music critic. His works include a symph. poem, *Belgrade* (Belgrade, June 11, 1951); *Concerto accelerato* for violin and orch. (Belgrade, Nov. 14, 1961); a fantastic ballet, *Remis* (1955; first stage performance, Zagreb, May 15, 1963); chamber music; piano pieces; songs.

Gotovac, Jakov, notable Yugoslav composer; b. Split, Oct. 11, 1895. He studied law in Zagreb, and music with Dobronić in Zagreb and Joseph Marx in Vienna. In 1923 he was appointed conductor of the Zagreb Opera. Gotovac is a prolific composer; his *Symphonic Kolo* (Zagreb, Feb. 6, 1927) is an effective national dance; his symph. poem *Guslar* (Zagreb, Oct. 7, 1940) is a musical portrait of a Croatian folk player. Gotovac wrote several operas, of which the comic opera *Ero s onoga svijeta* (Zagreb, Nov. 2, 1935) became popular; under the title *Ero der Schelm* it was performed in German, in Karlsruhe (April 3, 1938). His other operas are: *Morana* (Brno, Nov. 29, 1930); *Kamenik* (Zagreb, Dec. 17, 1946); the historic music drama *Mila Gojsalica* (Zagreb, May 18, 1952); *Stanac,* (Zagreb, Dec. 6, 1959); and *Dalmaro,* opera-legend (Zagreb, Dec. 20, 1964).

Gotthelf, Felix, German composer; b. Mönchen-Gladbach, near Düsseldorf, Oct. 3, 1857; d. Dresden, April 21, 1930. He studied music while working for his M.D. degree; became coach at the Stadttheater in Cologne in 1892; in 1893 was conductor in Kolberg; from 1893–98, devoted himself to composition in Bonn; lived in Vienna from 1898 to 1920, when he settled in Dresden.

Gottlieb, Jack, American composer; b. New Rochelle, N.Y., Oct. 12, 1930. He studied with Karol Rathaus at Queens College and Irving Fine at Brandeis Univ.; at the Berkshire Music Center in Tanglewood with Boris Blacher and Aaron Copland and at the Univ. of Illinois with Burrill Phillips and Robert Palmer (D.M.A., 1964). He was music director of Congregation Temple Israel in St. Louis (1970–73), and in 1973 was appointed composer-in-residence at the School of Sacred Music, Hebrew Union College, N.Y.

WORKS: Quartet for 3 Clarinets and Bass Clarinet (1952); String Quartet (1954); *Twilight Crane* for woodwind quintet (1961); *Pieces of Seven,* overture (Jacksonville, Florida, Oct. 23, 1962); Piano Sonata (1960); *Song of Loneliness,* cycle of 7 songs for baritone and piano (1962); *The Silent Flickers,* 12 diversions for piano 4-hands (1967); *4 Affirmations* for chorus and brass sextet (N.Y., April 17, 1976).

Gottschalg, Alexander Wilhelm, German organist and editor; b. Mechelrode, Feb. 14, 1827; d. Weimar, May 31, 1908. He studied with G. Töpfer, and succeeded him as court organist at his death (1870); also publ. a biography of him. Gottschalg's most important publication is the *Repertorium für die Orgel* (issued serially, from 1860), to which Liszt contributed. His memoirs of Liszt were published posthumously (1910).

Gottschalk, Louis Moreau, celebrated American pianist and composer; b. New Orleans, May 8, 1829; d. Rio de Janeiro, Dec. 18, 1869. He studied in Paris from 1841–46 (piano under Hallé and Stamaty; harmony under Maleden) and became the rage of the salons, winning praise from both Chopin and Berlioz. He made a successful tour through France, Switzerland, and Spain in 1852; returned to the U.S. in 1853 for a grand tour throughout the country, playing his own piano works and conducting his orchestral works at huge festivals; his popularity was phenomenal. The impresario Max Strakosch engaged Gottschalk for an even more extended tour throughout the U.S. Gottschalk died of yellow fever in Rio de Janeiro during his travels. His compositions are mostly for piano, or piano with other instruments, and are cast in both conventional Romantic idioms and in the more exotic Creole, Afro-Hispanic, and "Americanistic" patterns; about 300 works are currently known, but the existence of additional MSS is suspected.

WORKS: 2 operas, *Charles IX* and *Isaura de Salerno* (never performed); 2 symph. poems, *La Nuit des Tropiques* and *Montevideo: Grand Marcha solemne* for orch. (dedicated to the Emperor of Brazil); *Escenas campestres cubanas* for orch.; *Variations on Dixie's Land; The Dying Poet; Morte!!; The Last Hope* (these last 3 being his most popular works). *The Piano Works of Louis Moreau Gottschalk* (5 vols.; N.Y., 1969), ed. by V. L. Brodsky, is a collection of facsimiles of early editions; it contains a valuable essay by Robert Offergeld. Seven additional, previously unpublished piano pieces appear in *The Little Book of Louis Moreau Gottschalk*, ed. by Richard Jackson and Neil Ratliff (N.Y. 1976). A list of works comp. by Offergeld is publ. as *The Centennial Catalogue of the Published and Unpublished Compositions of Louis Moreau Gottschalk* (N.Y., 1970). Gottschalk's journals were translated from French and published in English under the title *Notes of a Pianist* (Philadelphia, 1881; reprinted, N.Y., 1964).

BIBLIOGRAPHY: O. Hensel, *Life and Letters of L. M. Gottschalk* (Boston, 1870; unreliable as to facts); L. R. Fors, *Gottschalk* (Havana, 1880); J. T. Howard, "L. M. Gottschalk," *Musical Quarterly* (Jan. 1932); C. F. Lange, "Vida y Muerte de Gottschalk, *Revista de Estudios Musicales* (Mendoze, Argentina, Aug. 1950; Dec. 1950; April 1951; Aug. 1951); V. Loggins, *Where the World Ends: The Life of Louis Moreau Gottschalk* (Baton Rouge, 1958); D. Thompson, "Gottschalk in the Virgin Islands," *Yearbook for Inter-American Music Research* (1970); C. F. Lange, "Louis Moreau Gottschalk," *Boletín Interamericano de Musica* (May 1970); L. Rubin, "Louis Moreau Gottschalk and the 1860–61 Opera Season in Cuba," *Inter-American Music Bulletin* (July-Oct. 1970).

Gotze, Emil, German tenor; b. Leipzig, July 19, 1856; d. Charlottenburg, Sept. 28, 1901. He studied in Dresden; then was engaged at the Dresden Opera. Owing to a throat ailment, he was forced to retire temporarily in 1885, but later resumed his career in Berlin.

Götze, Johann Nikolaus Konrad, German violinist; b. Weimar, Feb. 11, 1791; d. there, Feb. 5, 1861. He studied with Kreutzer in Paris; returning to Weimar, he became music director to the Grand Duke (1826–48). He played concerts in Germany and Austria; also wrote operas (some of which he produced in Weimar) and chamber music.

Götze, Karl, German composer; b. Weimar, 1836; d. Magdeburg, Jan. 14, 1887. A pupil of Töpfer and Gebhardi, later of Liszt; in 1855, chorusmaster at the Weimar opera; then theater conductor at Magdeburg, Berlin (1869), Breslau (1872), and Chemnitz (1875).

WORKS: the operas *Die Korsen* (Weimar, 1866); *Gustav Wasa, der Held des Nordens* (Weimar, 1868); *Judith* (Magdeburg, 1887); a symph. poem, *Eine Sommernacht;* piano pieces; songs.

Goudimel, Claude (his name was variously spelled in contemporary and later editions as **Gaudimel, Gaudiomel, Godimel, Gondimel, Goudmel, Gudmel,** etc.), celebrated French composer and theorist; b. Besançon, c.1510; killed in the St. Bartholomew massacre at Lyons, Aug. 27, 1572. In 1549 Goudimel was in Paris, where he publ. a book of chansons as a joint publisher with Du Chemin. He lived in Metz between 1557 and 1568; there he became a Huguenot; in 1568 he returned to Besançon, and then lived in Lyons, where he perished. It was long supposed that he lived in Rome, where he founded a school of music, but this assertion is totally lacking in foundation. It seems certain that Goudimel never visited Italy, and it is significant that none of his numerous works appeared in Roman publications. Most of his music was publ. by Du Chemin in Paris; other contemporary publishers were Adrien Le Roy and Robert Ballard, who publ. his complete Huguenot psalter in 1564 under the title *Les CL pseaumes de David, nouvellement mis en musique à quatre parties;* it was publ. in Geneva in 1565 as *Les Pseaumes mis en rime françoise par Clément Marot et Th. de Bèze, mis en musique à quatre parties;* it was reprinted in a facsimile edition in Kassel, 1935; a 1580 edition, also issued in Geneva, was republished by H. Expert in vols. 2–4 of *Les Maîtres Musiciens de la Renaissance* (1895–97). A German transl. of the psalms, with Goudimel's musical settings, first appeared in 1573; many reprints followed. Goudimel also composed 5 Masses, publ. by Du Chemin (1, 1554) and Le Roy and Ballard (4, 1558), together with other sacred music. Two 4-part motets were included in T. Susato's *Ecclesiasticarum cantionum* (Antwerp, 1553–55). Further reprints have been edited by R. J. v. Maldeghem in *Trésor musical* III (1867; 12-part *Salve Regina* and 2 4-part motets) and XI (1875; 3 3-part chansons); C. Bordes in *Anthologie des maîtres religieux primitifs* II (the Mass *Le bien que j'ay*) and III (4-part motet); K. von Winterfeld, A. Ebrard, H. Bellermann, etc. (psalms). Three Masses are in H. Expert's *Monuments de la musique française au temps de la renaissance* IX (1928); 9 psalms in P. Pidoux's *Collection de musique protestante* (1935). Publication of the Complete Works, under the direction of L. Dittmer and P. Pidoux (Inst. of Medieval Music), began in 1967.

BIBLIOGRAPHY: G. Becker, *Goudimel et son oeuvre* (1885); M. Brenet, *Claude Goudimel, Essai bio-bibliographique* (Besançon, 1898); H. Kling, "Les Compositeurs de la musique du Psautier Huguenot

Genevois," *Rivista Musicale Italiana* (1899); J. Tiersot, *Ronsard et la musique de son temps* (1901); G. R. Woodward, "The Genevan Psalter of 1562; set in 4-Part Harmony by Claude Goudimel in 1565," *Proceedings of the Musical Association* (London, 1918; pp. 167–89); E. H. Müller, "Claude Goudimel zum 350. Todestage," *Neue musikalische Zeitung* (1922; pp. 375–76); C. Schneider, *La Restauration du Psautier huguenot d'après les sources de 1562 et de 1565* (Neuchâtel, 1930); G. Thibault, *Bibliographie des éditions d'Adrien Le Roy et Robert Ballard* (Paris, 1955).

Goudoever, Henri Daniel van, Dutch cellist and composer; b. Utrecht, Nov. 12, 1898; d. The Hague, March 3, 1977. He studied cello privately; then attended classes in composition with Johan Wagenaar at the Utrecht Cons. (1913–16); completed his cello studies with Charles van Isterdael in Utrecht (1916–18) and with Gérard Hekking in Paris (1918–21). He traveled to the U.S. in the winter of 1921–22, where he appeared as soloist in some of his own works with the N.Y. Philh., under Mengelberg; was then first cellist with Mengelberg and the Amsterdam Concertgebouw (1922–24); then served as Kapellmeister in Coburg, Bavaria, at the behest of the exiled King Ferdinand of Bulgaria (1924–32); subsequently conducted the Utrecht Municipal Orch. (1932–37). In 1937 he abandoned music and became a disciple of Rudolf Steiner, founder of the Anthroposophical Society; traveled as a speaker and monitor of anthroposophy until his death. He composed *La Fête bleue,* symph. poem for cello and orch. (1917); *Sphynx,* a nocturne for orch. (1919); pieces for cello.

Gould, Glenn, Canadian pianist; b. Toronto, Sept. 25, 1932. He studied at the Royal Cons. of Music in Toronto with Alberto Guerrero (piano) and Leo Smith (composition); graduated at the age of 12, the youngest ever to do so. He made his debut at the age of 14 as soloist with the Toronto Symph. Orch.; first U.S. concert in Washington (Jan. 2, 1955); N.Y. debut one week later; first continental tour of the U.S. during the season 1956–57. European debut in Berlin as soloist with Berlin Philh. under Herbert von Karajan (April 28, 1957). In 1970 he started a series of documentary radio and television broadcasts from Canada, as programmer and interlocutor in interviews.

Gould, Morton, brilliant American composer and conductor; b. Richmond Hill, New York, Dec. 10, 1913. He studied at the Institute of Musical Art; later was a radio pianist and leader of a program of light orch. music. He has appeared as guest conductor with major American orchestras. His music emphasizes American themes; he freely employs advanced harmonic usages. In 1976 he made an extensive tour of Australia as guest composer-conductor.
    WORKS: A musical comedy, *Billion Dollar Baby* (1945); *3 American Symphonettes* (1933, 1935, 1937); *Chorale and Fugue in Jazz,* for two pianos and orch. (Youth Orch., N.Y., Jan. 2, 1936, Stokowski conducting); Piano Concerto (1937); Violin Concerto (1938); *Foster Gallery* (Pittsburgh, Jan. 12, 1940); *Spirituals* for orch. (N.Y., Feb. 9, 1941, composer conducting); *Latin American Symphonette* (Brooklyn, Feb. 22,

1941); *Cowboy Rhapsody* (1942); *American Concertette* (broadcast Aug. 23, 1943); 1st Symph. (Pittsburgh, March 5, 1943); *Symphony on Marching Tunes,* No. 2 (N.Y., June 4, 1944); Viola Concerto (1944); Concerto for Orch. (Cleveland, Feb. 1, 1945); *Harvest,* for harp, vibraphone, and strings (St. Louis, Oct. 27, 1945); *Minstrel Show* (Indianapolis, Dec. 21, 1946); 3rd Symph. (Dallas, Feb. 16, 1947; composer conducting); *Fall River Legend,* ballet (N.Y., April 21, 1948); 4th Symph. (for band; West Point, April 13, 1952, composer conducting); Concerto for Tap Dancer and Orch. (Rochester, Nov. 16, 1952, composer conducting); *Inventions* for 4 pianos and orch. (N.Y., Oct. 19, 1953); *Dance Variations* for 2 pianos and orch. (N.Y., Oct. 24, 1953); *Jekyll and Hyde Variations* for orch. (N.Y., Feb. 2, 1957); *Fiesta,* ballet (Cannes, France, March 17, 1957): *Declaration* for orch., chorus and 2 speakers (Washington, Jan. 20, 1957); *Venice* for double orch., and brass bands (Seattle, May 2, 1967); *Troubadour Music* for 4 guitars and orch. (1969); *Symphony of Spirituals* (Detroit, April 1, 1976); American Ballads (Queens, N.Y., April 24, 1976, composer conducting).

Gounod, Charles François, famous French composer; b. Paris, June 17, 1818; d. there, Oct. 18, 1893. His father, Jean François Gounod, was a painter, winner of the 2nd Grand Prix de Rome, who died when Gounod was a small child. His mother, a most accomplished woman, supervised his literary, artistic, and musical education, and taught him piano. He completed his academic studies at the Lycée St. Louis; in 1836, he entered the Paris Cons., studying with Halévy, Lesueur, and Paër. In 1837 he won the 2nd Prix de Rome with his cantata, *Marie Stuart et Rizzio;* in 1839 he obtained the Grand Prix with his cantata, *Fernand.* In Rome, he studied church music, particularly the works of Palestrina; composed there a Mass for 3 voices and orch., which was performed at the church of San Luigi dei Francesi. In 1842, during a visit to Vienna, he conducted a Requiem of his own; upon his return to Paris, he became precentor and organist of the Missions Etrangères; studied theology for two years, but decided against taking holy orders; yet he was often referred to as l'Abbé Gounod; some religious choruses were published in 1846 as composed by Abbé Charles Gounod. Soon Gounod tried his hand at stage music. On April 16, 1851, his first opera, *Sapho,* was produced at the Grand Opéra, with only moderate success; he revised it much later, extending it to four acts from the original three, and it was performed again on April 2, 1884; but even in this revised form it was unsuccessful. Gounod's second opera, *La Nonne sanglante,* in five acts, was staged at the Paris Opéra on Oct. 18, 1854; there followed a comic opera, *Le Médecin malgré lui,* after Molière (Jan 15, 1858), which also failed to realize Gounod's expectations. In the meantime, he was active in other musical ways in Paris; he conducted the choral society Orphéon (1852–60) and composed for it several choruses. Gounod's great success came with the production of *Faust,* after Goethe (Théâtre-Lyrique, March 19, 1859; performed with additional recitatives and ballet at the Opéra, March 3, 1869); *Faust* remained Gounod's greatest masterpiece, and indeed the most successful

French opera of the 19th century, triumphant all over the world without any sign of diminishing effect through a century of changes in musical tastes. However, it was widely criticized for the melodramatic treatment of Goethe's poem by the librettists, Barbier and Carré, and for the somewhat sentimental style of Gounod's music; in Germany, it is usually produced under the title *Margarete* or *Gretchen* to dissociate it from Goethe's work. The succeeding four operas, *Philémon et Baucis* (Paris, Feb. 18, 1860), *La Colombe* (Baden-Baden, Aug. 3, 1860), *La Reine de Saba* (Paris, Feb. 29, 1862), and *Mireille* (Paris, March 19, 1864), were only partially successful, but with *Roméo et Juliette* (Paris, April 27, 1867), Gounod recaptured universal acclaim. In 1870, during the Franco-Prussian War, Gounod went to London, where he organized "Gounod's Choir," and presented concerts at the Philharmonic and the Crystal Palace; when Paris fell, he wrote an elegiac cantata, *Gallia*, to words from the Lamentations of Jeremiah, which he conducted in London on May 1, 1871; it was later performed in Paris. He wrote some incidental music for productions in Paris: *Les Deux Reines*, to a drama by Legouvé (Nov. 27, 1872) and *Jeanne d'Arc*, to Barbier's poem (Nov. 8, 1873). In 1875, he returned to Paris; there he produced his operas *Cinq-Mars* (April 5, 1877), *Polyeucte* (Oct. 7, 1878), and *Le Tribut de Zamora* (April 1, 1881) without signal success. The last years of his life were devoted mainly to sacred works, of which the most important was *La Rédemption*, a trilogy, first performed at the Birmingham Festival in 1882; another sacred trilogy, *Mors et vita*, also written for the Birmingham Festival, followed in 1885. Gounod continued to write religious works in close succession, and produced (among many others) the following: *Te Deum* (1886); *La Communion des Saints* (1889); *Messe dite le Clovis* (1890); *La Contemplation de Saint François au pied de la croix* (1890); *Tantum Ergo* (1892). A *Requiem* (1893) was left unfinished, and was arranged by Henri Büsser after Gounod's death. One of Gounod's most popular settings to religious words is *Ave Maria*, adapted to the first prelude of Bach's *Well-Tempered Clavier*, but its original version was *Méditation sur le premier Prélude de Piano de S. Bach* for violin and piano (1853); the words were added later (1859). Other works are: 2 symphonies (1855); *Marche funèbre d'une Marionette* for orch. (1873); *Petite Symphonie* for wind instruments (1888); 3 string quartets; a number of piano pieces, and songs. Among his literary works were *Ascanio de Saint-Saëns* (1889); *Le Don Juan de Mozart* (1890; in English, 1895), and an autobiography, *Mémoires d'un Artiste* (publ. posthumously, Paris, 1896; in English translated by W. H. Hutchenson, *Autobiographical Reminiscences with Family Letters and Notes on Music*, N.Y., 1896).

BIBLIOGRAPHY: A. Peña y Goñi, *Impressiones y recuerdos; Charles Gounod* (Madrid, 1879); M. A. de Bovet, *Charles Gounod* (Paris, 1890); in English, London, 1891); L. Pagnerre, *Charles Gounod, sa vie et ses œuvres* (Paris, 1890); C. Saint-Saëns, *Charles Gounod et le Don Juan de Mozart* (Paris, 1893); T. Dubois, *Notice sur Charles Gounod* (Paris, 1894); P. Voss, *Charles Gounod: Ein Lebensbild* (Leipzig, 1895); H. Tolhurst, *Gounod* (London, 1905); P. L. Hillemacher,

Charles Gounod (Paris, 1906); C. Bellaigue, *Gounod* (Paris, 1910); J. G. Prod'homme and A. Dandelot, *Gounod: sa vie et ses œuvres*, in 2 vols., the standard biography (Paris, 1911); H. Soubiès and H. de Curzon, *Documents inédits sur le Faust de Gounod* (Paris, 1912); J. Tiersot, "Charles Gounod, a Centennial Tribute," *Musical Quarterly* (July 1918); J. G. Prod'homme, "Miscellaneous Letters by Gounod," *Musical Quarterly* (Oct. 1918); J. Tiersot, "Gounod's Letters," *Musical Quarterly* (Jan. 1919); C. Saint-Saëns, "Le Livret de Faust," *Monde Musical* (1914–19); R. d'Ollone, "Gounod et l'opéra comique," *Revue Musicale* (Nov. 1933); M. Cooper, "Charles Gounod and His Influence on French Music," *Music & Letters* (1940); P. Landormy, *Gounod* (Paris, 1942); P. Landormy, *Faust de Gounod: étude et analyse* (Paris, 1944); H. Wagener, "Die Messen Charles Gounods," *Kirchenmusikaliches Jahrbuch* 51 (1967; repr. in *Musica Sacra*, July-Aug. and Sept.-Oct. 1970); idem, "Charles François Gounod. Ein Beitrag zur Kirchenmusik des 19. Jahrhunderts," *Musica Sacra* (Jan. 1968); A. Lebois, "La Reine de Saba ou Amour et Franc-Maçonnierie," *Annales Publiées par la Faculté des Lettres de Toulouse. Littératures* (Oct. 1968).

Gouvy, Louis Théodore, prolific composer; b. Goffontaine, near Saarbrücken, July 5, 1819; d. Leipzig, April 21, 1898. The son of French parents, he graduated from the college at Metz; went to Paris to study law, but turned to music; presented a concert of his works in Paris in 1847; also made frequent trips to Germany, where his music was received with great favor.

WORKS: about 200 works, including an opera, *Der Cid*; 7 symphonies; Wind Nonet; Wind Octet; Sextet for Flute and Strings; Piano Quintet; String Quintet; 5 string quartets; 5 piano trios; numerous piano pieces in an ingratiating salon manner; songs.

BIBLIOGRAPHY: O. Klauwell, *L. T. Gouvy, Sein Leben und Seine Werke* (Berlin, 1902).

Gow, George Coleman, American music pedagogue; b. Ayer Junction, Mass., Nov. 27, 1860; d. Poughkeepsie, N.Y., Jan. 12, 1938. He studied music privately; graduated from Brown Univ. in 1884 and Newton Theological Seminary in 1889; then taught harmony and piano at Smith College for 6 years; from 1895 to 1932, he was professor of music at Vassar College. He wrote a textbook on notation and harmony, *The Structure of Music* (N.Y., 1895); composed organ pieces and songs.

Gow, Nathaniel, Scottish violinist, arranger, and music publisher; b. Inver, near Dunkeld, May 28, 1763; d. Edinburgh, Jan. 19, 1831. He played the trumpet in Scottish bands; then changed to violin. In 1788 he opened a music shop in Edinburgh; publ. numerous arrangements of Scotch tunes by his father and also his own arrangements of Scottish dances. He also led a band for various aristocratic assemblies. Among his original pieces there was an interesting instrumental composition, *Caller Herrin'*, based on a street vendor's cry.

BIBLIOGRAPHY: Henry G. Farmer, *History of Music in Scotland* (London, 1947; pp. 343–44).

Gow, Niel, Scottish violinist and composer; father of Nathaniel Gow; b. Strathbrand, Perthshire, March 22, 1727; d. Inver, near Dunkeld, March 1, 1807. He played Scottish reels on the violin, and as a young man earned his living by performing at social gatherings in Edinburgh and London. He publ. a number of "Strathspey Reels"; however, many of them were not original compositions but arrangements of old dance tunes.

BIBLIOGRAPHY: John Glen, *The Glen Collection of Scottish Dance Music* (Edinburgh, 1891).

Graben-Hoffmann, Gustav (properly **Gustav Hoffmann**), German composer; b. Bnin, near Posen, March 7, 1820; d. Potsdam, May 20, 1900. He studied with his father and with other teachers in Posen; then taught music in various localities in East Germany; in 1843, settled in Berlin; in 1850, he founded a Musikakademie für Damen; then went to Leipzig, where he studied composition with Moritz Hauptmann; in 1869, he returned to Berlin, where he taught singing. In the meantime, he composed industriously; wrote a number of songs, but was compelled to publ. them at his own expense, despite economic hardships; of these, *500,000 Teufel* had great vogue. He also publ. singing manuals, *Die Pflege der Singstimme* (1865); *Das Studium des Gesangs* (1872); *Praktische Methode als Grundlage für den Kunstgesang* (1874).

Grabert, Martin, German composer; b. Arnswalde (Neumark), May 15, 1868; d. Berlin, Jan. 23, 1951. He studied with Bellermann and Bargiel. In 1895 he settled in Berlin as church organist. He wrote some 80 op. numbers, mostly for chorus and for organ; a complete list of his works is given in Heinz Becker's article in *Die Musik in Geschichte und Gegenwart.*

Grabner, Hermann, Austrian composer and theorist; b. Graz, May 12, 1886; d. Bolzano, Italy, July 3, 1969. He took his degree in law at Graz Univ. in 1909; then studied music with Reger and Hans Sitt at the Leipzig Cons.; he became a lecturer in theory at Strasbourg Cons. in 1913; served in the German army in World War I; after the armistice taught at the Mannheim Cons.; in 1924 was appointed prof. of composition at Leipzig Cons.; from 1938–46, taught at the Hochschule für Musik in Berlin, and later at the Berlin Cons.

WRITINGS: *Regers Harmonik* in Würz's symposium on Reger (Munich, 1920); *Die Funktionstheorie Hugo Riemanns und ihre Bedeutung für die praktische Analyse* (Munich, 1923); *Allgemeine Musiklehre* (Stuttgart, 1924; 5th ed., 1949); *Lehrbuch der musikalischen Analyse* (Leipzig, 1925); *Der lineare Satz; ein Lehrbuch des Kontrapunktes* (Stuttgart, 1930); new rev. ed., 1950); *Handbuch der Harmonielehre* (Berlin, 1944); several short books of exercises for theory students. He also wrote an opera, *Die Richterin* (Barmen, May 7, 1930); *Perkeo Suite* and *Burgmusik* for wind orch.; Concerto for 3 Violins; organ pieces; songs; etc.

Grabovsky, Leonid, Ukrainian composer; b. Kiev, Jan. 28, 1935. He studied at the Kiev Cons. with Revutsky and Liatoshinsky, graduating in 1959. His music is marked by modern tendencies, making use of dissonant counterpoint and asymmetric polyrhythmic combinations.

WORKS: *Intermezzo* for orch. (1958); String Quartet (1958); *4 Ukrainian Songs* for chorus and orch. (1959); Sonata for Unaccompanied Violin (1959); *Symphonic Frescoes* (1961); two comic operas, after Chekhov, *The Bear* (1963) and *Marriage Proposal* (1964); Trio for Violin, Double Bass and Piano (1964); *Microstructures* for oboe solo (1964); *Constants* for 4 pianos, 6 percussion groups and solo violin (1964); *Little Chamber Music* No. 1 for 15 string instruments (1966); *Homeomorphia* I, II, III for one or two pianos (1968); *Ornaments* for oboe, viola and harp (1969); *Homeomorphia IV* for orch. (1970); *Little Chamber Music* No. 2 for oboe, harp and 12 solo string instruments (1971); *2 Pieces for String Orch.* (1972); *St. John's Eve,* symph. legend, after Gogol, for orch. (1976).

Grace, Harvey, English organist and writer on music; b. Romsey, Jan. 25, 1874; d. Bromley, Kent, Feb. 15, 1944. He studied with M. Richardson at Southwark Cathedral, London; was organist at various churches in London; directed the St. Cecilia Festivals; from 1918 to his death, he was editor of the *Musical Times* and wrote editorial articles for it under the name "Feste"; also edited *The New Musical Educator* (London, 1934).

WRITINGS: *French Organ Music, Past and Present* (N.Y., 1919); *The Complete Organist* (London, 1920; standard teaching manual; 4th ed., 1956); *The Organ Works of Bach* (London, 1922); *The Organ Works of Rheinberger* (London, 1925); *Ludwig van Beethoven* (London, 1927); *A Musician at Large* (collection of articles from the *Musical Times;* London, 1928; *A Handbook for Choralists* (London, 1928); also, with Sir Walford Davies, *Music and Worship* (London, 1935); composed 20 organ pieces; made 30 transcriptions from Bach, mostly for organ; edited Rheinberger's 20 sonatas for organ.

BIBLIOGRAPHY: obituary article, "Harvey Grace," Musical Times (March 1944).

Grad, Gabriel, Lithuanian composer; b. Retovo, near Kovno, July 9, 1890; d. Tel Aviv, Dec. 9, 1950. He studied in Ekaterinoslav and in Berlin; founded a Jewish music school in Kovno (1920–22); went to Palestine in 1924; since 1925, founder and director of the Benhetov Cons. in Tel Aviv. He wrote an opera, *Judith and Holofernes,* and about 250 other works, including chamber music, piano pieces, choruses, and songs, many of which are based on Jewish folk melodies.

Grädener, Hermann (Theodor Otto), German violinist and composer; son of **Karl Grädener;** b. Kiel, May 8, 1844; d. Vienna, Sept. 18, 1929. He studied at the Vienna Cons.; was violinist in the court orch. in Vienna; then taught theory at the Vienna Cons. (from 1874); in 1899 he became Bruckner's successor at Vienna Univ. He wrote 2 operas, *Der Richter von Zalamea* and *Die heilige Zita;* 2 symphonies; concertos for violin, for cello, and for piano; String Octet; String Quintet; Piano Quintet; 2 string quartets; *5 Impromp-*

tus for piano and strings; *5 Intermezzi* for violin and piano; Sonata for 2 Pianos, etc.

Grädener, Karl Georg Peter, German cellist and composer; b. Rostock, Jan. 14, 1812; d. Hamburg, June 10, 1883. He was music director at Kiel Univ. for 10 years; in 1851, established an academy for vocal music in Hamburg; after 3 years at the Vienna Cons. (1862–65) he returned to Hamburg, and became teacher at the Cons. there; was also co-founder and a president of the Hamburger Tonkünstlerverein. He wrote *System der Harmonielehre* (Hamburg, 1877); his articles in music periodicals were publ. as *Gesammelte Aufsätze* (Hamburg, 1872).
WORKS: 2 operas, *König Harald* and *Der Mullerin Hochzeit;* an oratorio, *Johannes der Täufer;* 2 symphonies; *Fiesco,* an overture; a piano concerto; *Romance* for violin and orch.; a string octet; 5 piano quintets; 3 string quartets; string trio; 2 piano trios; 3 violin sonatas; a cello sonata; many piano pieces.

Gradenwitz, Peter, German-Israeli musicologist; b. Berlin, Jan. 24, 1910; studied literature and philosophy at Berlin Univ.; composition with Julius Weismann and Josef Rufer. In 1934 he went to Paris; in 1935, to London; in 1936, settled in Tel Aviv, where he became active as writer, lecturer, and organizer of concerts; established Israeli Music Publications; also active on the radio.
WRITINGS: *Johann Stamitz* (Vienna, 1936); *The Music of Israel* (N.Y., 1949); *Wege zur Musik der Gegenwart* (Stuttgart, 1963); books in Hebrew: *Music History* (Jerusalem, 1939); *The World of the Symphony* (Jerusalem, 1945; 7th ed., 1953). *Music and Musicians in Israel* (Tel Aviv, 1959). Wrote a string quartet; *Palestinian Landscapes,* for oboe and piano; songs.

Gradstein, Alfred, Polish composer; b. Czenstochowa, Oct. 30, 1904; d. Warsaw, Sept. 9, 1954. He studied at the Warsaw Cons. (1922–25) and at the State Academy of Music in Vienna; from 1928–47 lived in Paris; then returned to Poland. He wrote mostly for piano; his Piano Concerto was publ. in 1932.

Graener, Paul, significant German composer; b. Berlin, Jan. 11, 1872; d. Salzburg, Nov. 13, 1944. He was a chorister at the Berlin cathedral; then studied piano with Veit and composition with Albert Becker. He then traveled in Germany as theater conductor. In 1896, he went to London where he taught at the Royal Academy of Music (1897–1902). He was then in Vienna as teacher at the Neues Konservatorium; subsequently directed the Mozarteum in Salzburg (1910–13); then lived in Munich; in 1920, he succeeded Max Reger as prof. of composition at the Leipzig Cons. (until 1924); was director of the Stern Cons. in Berlin (1930–34). He wrote music in all genres, and was fairly successful as an opera composer; in his style, he followed the Romantic movement, but also emphasized the folk element.
WORKS: OPERAS: *Don Juans letztes Abenteuer* (Leipzig, June 11, 1914); *Theophano* (Munich, June 5, 1918); *Schirin und Gertraude* (Dresden, April 28,

1920); *Hanneles Himmelfahrt* (Dresden, Feb. 17, 1927); *Friedemann Bach* (Schwerin, Nov. 13, 1931); *Der Prinz von Homburg* (Berlin, March 14, 1935); *Schwanhild* (Cologne, Jan. 4, 1941). For orch.: Symph.; *Romantische Phantasie; Waldmusik; Gothische Suite;* Piano Concerto; Cello Concerto. CHAMBER MUSIC: 6 string quartets; Piano Quintet; 3 violin sonatas. In several of his chamber music works, Graener attempted to carry out a definite programmatic design, while maintaining traditional form, as in his *Kammermusik-Dichtung* for piano trio.
BIBLIOGRAPHY: G. Graener, *Paul Graener* (Leipzig, 1922); P. Grümmer, *Verzeichnis der Werke Paul Graeners* (Berlin, 1937).

Graeser, Wolfgang, talented Swiss composer; b. Zürich, Sept. 7, 1906; d. (suicide) Nikolassee, June 13, 1928. He went to Berlin in 1921; studied violin with Karl Klingler, and quickly acquired erudition in general music theory; also made a serious study of various unrelated arts and sciences (mathematics, Oriental languages, painting). His signal achievement was an orchestration of Bach's *Kunst der Fuge* (performed at the Leipzig Thomaskirche by Karl Straube, June 26, 1927). He publ. a book, *Körpersinn* (Munich, 1927). A memorial symposium, *Wolfgang Graeser Gedächtnisheft,* was publ. in Munich shortly after his tragic death; See also H. Zurlinden, *Wolfgang Graeser* (Munich, 1935).

Graetzer, Guillermo, Austrian-Argentine composer; b. Vienna, Sept. 5, 1914. He studied in Vienna with Paul A. Pisk; in 1930 moved to Buenos Aires, devoting himself mainly to educational activities; also edited musical anthologies.
WORKS: *Concierto para Orquesta* (1939); *La Parábola* for orch. (1947); *Sinfonía Brevis* (1951); *Concierto de Cámara* (1953); Cello Concerto (1957); *Cantos de la eternidad* for orch. (1958); arrangements of folk dances of Argentina and Brazil for recorder and percussion (1968).

Graf, Herbert, Austrian opera stage director; son of **Max Graf;** b. Vienna, April 10, 1903; d. Geneva, April 5, 1973. He studied at the Univ. of Vienna with Guido Adler; received his Ph.D. in 1925. He then was stage director at the opera houses in Münster, Breslau, Frankfurt, and Basel. In 1934 he came to the U.S.; was associated with the Philadelphia Opera in 1934–35; in 1936 he was appointed stage director of the Metropolitan Opera; in 1949, became head of the opera dept. at the Curtis Institute, Philadelphia. He returned to Europe in 1960. He published *The Opera and Its Future in America* (N.Y., 1941) and *Opera for the People* (Univ. of Minnesota, 1951).

Graf, Max, Austrian music critic, b. Vienna, Oct. 8, 1873; d. there June 23, 1958. He studied at the Univ. of Vienna; taught music history and esthetics at the Staatsakademie für Musik; music critic of *Wiener Allgemeine Zeitung* (from 1900–20); in 1939 came to the U.S.; after World War II, returned to Vienna.
WRITINGS: *Deutsche Musik im 19. Jahrhundert* (1898); *Wagner-Probleme und andere Studien* (1900); *Die Musik im Zeitalter der Renaissance* (1905); *Die*

innere Werkstatt des Musikers (1910); *Legends of a Musical Past* (1945); *Composer and Critic* (1946); *Modern Music* (1946; also appeared in German as *Geschichte und Geist der modernen Musik* (Frankfurt, 1954); *From Beethoven to Shostakovitch* (N.Y., 1947).

Graffigna, Achille, Italian opera composer; b. S. Martino dall' Argine, near Mantua, May 5, 1816; d. Padua, July 19, 1896. He studied with Alessandro Rolla in Milan; wrote church music and theatrical cantatas; then devoted himself to opera; his *Ildegonda e Rizzardo* (La Scala, Milan, Nov. 3, 1841) was accepted with favor. In 1842 he went to Verona where he produced *Eleonora di San Bonifacio* (March 11, 1843); there followed *Maria di Brabante* (Trieste, Oct. 16, 1852); *L'assedio di Malta* (Padua, July 30, 1853); *Gli Studenti* (Milan, Feb. 7, 1857); *Veronica Cibo* (Mantua, Feb. 13, 1858; revised and produced at the Théâtre Italien, Paris, March 22, 1865, as *La Duchessa di San Giuliano); Il Barbiere di Siviglia* (Padua, May 17, 1879; intended as an homage to Rossini); *Il matrimonio segreto* (Florence, Sept. 8, 1883); *La buona figliuola* (Milan, May 6, 1886).

Graffman, Gary, talented American pianist; b. New York, Oct. 14, 1928. He studied with Isabelle Vengerova at the Curtis Institute of Music; made his 1st public appearance at the age of 10; won numerous prizes; was engaged as soloist with major American orchs. He made several European tours, beginning in 1950; then appeared regularly in recitals and as soloist with major orchestras all over the world, establishing himself as a virtuoso of the first rank.

Gräflinger, Franz, Austrian writer on music; b. Linz, Nov. 26, 1876; d. Bad Ischl, Austria, Sept. 9, 1962. He served as municipal accountant in Linz, and at the same time studied music; wrote criticism in local newspapers; then devoted his energies chiefly to Bruckner research; publ. two biographies of Bruckner (Munich, 1911; Regensburg, 1921) and *Liebes und Heiteres um Anton Bruckner* (Vienna, 1948); edited vol. I of Bruckner's *Gesammelte Briefe* (1924).

Grahn, Ulf, Swedish composer; b. Solna, Jan. 17, 1942. He studied composition under Hans Eklund at the Royal College of Music in Stockholm. In 1972 he visited the U.S., and served as an assistant at the electronic music studio at the Catholic University in Washington, D.C. In his music he cultivates unusual instrumental effects in a modern manner.
WORKS: *Musica da Camera* for chamber orch. (1964); *Fancy* for orch. (1965); *Lamento* for strings (1967); Symphony (1966–67); Trio for Flute, Oboe and Clarinet (1967); *Hommage à Charles Ives* for strings (1968); Concerto for Double Bass and Chamber Ensemble (1968); *Joy for Band* for winds (1969); *Ancient Music,* after Eliot's "The Hollow Men," for piano and chamber orch. (1970); *A Dream of a Lost Century* for flute, oboe, clarinet, strings and piano (1971); *Snapshots* for piano (1971); *Looking Forward To* for piano (1972); *Mirrors* for organ (1972); *This Reminds Me Of . . .* for flute, clarinet, horn, trombone and percussion (1972); Concerto for Vocalizing Soloists and Orch. (1973); *Soundscape I* for flute, English horn, bass

clarinet and percussion (1973); *The Wind of Dawn* for orch. and tape (1973); *Halloween* for solo clarinet (1974).

Grainger, Percy Aldridge, celebrated pianist and composer; b. Melbourne, Australia, July 8, 1882; d. White Plains, N.Y., Feb. 20, 1961. He received his early musical training from his mother; at the age of 10, appeared as pianist at several public concerts; then had lessons with Louis Pabst; in 1894, went to Germany, where he studied with Kwast in Frankfurt; also took a few lessons with Busoni. In 1900 he began his concert career in England; then toured South Africa and Australia. In 1906 he met Grieg, who became enthusiastic about Grainger's talent; Grainger's performances of Grieg's Piano Concerto were famous. In 1914, Grainger settled in the U.S., made a sensational debut in N.Y., Feb. 11, 1915; gave summer sessions at the Chicago Musical College from 1919 to 1931; was for one academic year chairman of the music dept. of N.Y. Univ. (1932–33). In 1935 he founded a museum in Melbourne, in which he housed all his manuscripts and his rich collection of musical souvenirs. After 1940 he lived mostly at White Plains, N.Y. He married Ella Viola Ström in 1928 in a spectacular ceremony staged at the Hollywood Bowl, at which he conducted his work, *To a Nordic Princess,* written for his bride. Grainger's philosophy of life and art calls for the widest communion of peoples and opinions; his profound study of folk music underlies the melodic and rhythmic structure of his own music; he made a determined effort to recreate in art music the free flow of instinctive songs of the people; he experimented with "gliding" intervals within the traditional scales and polyrhythmic combinations with independent strong beats in the component parts. In a modest way he was a pioneer of electronic music; as early as 1937 he wrote a quartet for electronic instruments, notating the pitch by zig-zags and curves. He introduced individual forms of notation and orchestral scoring, rejecting the common Italian designations of tempi and dynamics in favor of colloquial English expressions. An eccentric to the last, he directed that his skeleton, after the removal and destruction of the flesh, be placed for preservation and possible display in the Grainger Museum at the Univ. of Melbourne, but his request was declined and he was buried in an ordinary manner.
WORKS: FOR ORCH.: *Mock Morris* (1911); *Irish Tunes from County Derry* (1909); *Molly on the Shore; Shepherd's Hey; Colonial Song* (1913); *The Warriors* (music to an imaginary ballet; 1916); *English Dance,* for orch. and organ (1925); *Ye Banks and Braes o' Bonnie Doon* (1932); *Harvest Hymn* (1933); *Danish Folk-song Suite* (1937). FOR CHAMBER ORCH.: *The Nightingale and the 2 Sisters* (1931). FOR CHORUS AND ORCH.: *Marching Song of Democracy* (1916); *The Merry Wedding* (1916); *Father and Daughter; Sir Eglamore; The Camp; The March of the Men of Harlech; The Hunter in His Career; The Bride's Tragedy; Love Verses from 'The Song of Solomon'; Tribute to Foster* (1931). FOR CHORUS AND BRASS BAND: *I'm Seventeen come Sunday; We Have Fed Our Seas for a Thousand Years* (1912); *Marching Tune.* FOR A CAPPELLA CHORUS: *Brigg Fair; The Innuit; Morning Song in the Jungle; A Song of Vermland; At Twilight; Tiger-*

Tiger!; The Immovable Do; etc. All these are also issued in various arrangements. CHAMBER MUSIC: *Handel in the Strand* (1913); octet, *My Robin Is to the Greenwood Gone; Walking Tune,* for woodwind quintet; *Green Bushes* (1921); *Hill-Song No. 1* (1923); *Shallow Brown* (1924); *Hill-Song No. 2* (1929); *Spoon River* (1930); *Free Music for strings* (1935). FOR MILITARY BAND: *Children's March* (1918); march, *The Lads of Wamphrey; Lincolnshire Posy,* 6 folksongs from Lincolnshire, England; settings, in various combinations, of 20 of Kipling's poems (1911–38); 32 settings of British folksongs (1911–38); piano pieces, etc.

BIBLIOGRAPHY: C. Scott, "Percy Grainger, the Music and the Man," *Musical Quarterly* (July 1916); D. C. Parker, *Percy A. Grainger, a Study* (N.Y., 1918); C. W. Hughes, "Percy Grainger, a Cosmopolitan Composer," *Musical Quarterly* (April 1937); R. L. Taylor, *The Running Pianist* (N.Y., 1950); T. C. Slattery, *Percy Grainger: the Inveterate Innovator* (1974); *A Complete Catalogue of Works of Percy Grainger,* edited by Teresa Balough (Univ. of Western Australia, 1975); John Bird, *Percy Grainger* (London, 1976).

Gram, Hans, Danish-born American composer; b. Copenhagen, May 20, 1754; d. Boston, April 28, 1804. He studied philosophy at the Univ. of Copenhagen, and also had some training in music. About 1785 he went to America, and settled in Boston, where he became organist of the Brattle Street Church. He contributed various musical pieces to the *Massachusetts Magazine,* including a curious composition entitled *The Death Song of an Indian Chief* for voice, 2 clarinets, 2 horns and strings, which was published in the March 1791 issue; it was apparently the first orchestral score published in the U.S.; he also wrote *Sacred Lines for Thanksgiving Day* (1793) and some other vocal works for the same magazine. He was a co-editor of *The Massachusetts Compiler,* a rather progressive collection on Psalmody, which also contained a music dictionary.

BIBLIOGRAPHY: F. J. Metcalf, *American Writers and Compilers of Sacred Music* (N.Y., 1925).

Gram, Peder, Danish conductor and composer; b. Copenhagen, Nov. 25, 1881; d. there, Feb. 4, 1956. After graduating from Copenhagen Univ. he studied at the Leipzig Cons. with Sitt (theory) and Nikisch (conducting) from 1904–7. Returning to Copenhagen in 1908, he applied himself mainly to conducting; was chief conductor of the Danish Concert Society (1918–32); in 1937 became chief conductor of the Danish Radio Orch. His compositions include 2 symphonies; Violin Concerto; Cello Sonata; Wind Quintet; other chamber music; publ. books (in Danish) on modern music (1934) and harmonic analysis (1948).

Gramatges, Harold, Cuban composer; b. Santiago de Cuba, Sept. 26, 1918. He studied with José Ardévol and Amadeo Roldán in Havana; in 1942 went to the U.S. and took a summer course in composition with Aaron Copland at the Berkshire Music Center at Tanglewood. Returning to Havana, he founded, with several other modern Cuban composers, the *Grupo de Renovación Musical* (1943). From 1961 to 1964 he was a member of the Cuban Embassy in Paris. Once

again in Havana, he organized the music Dept. of the Casa de las Américas. In his own works he pursues the aim of enlightened functionalism in an effective modern style.

WORKS: *Invenciones* for chamber orch. (1941); ballet, *Icaro* (1943); *Mensaje al futuro* for wind orch. (1944); Symphony (1945); *Móvil* for 7 instruments (1969); Wind Quintet (1957); *La muerte del guerrillero* for speaker and orch. (1969).

Gramm, Donald John, American bass-baritone; b. Milwaukee, Feb. 26, 1927. He studied piano and organ at the Wisconsin College of Music (1935–44) and at the Chicago Mus. College (1944–49); also took voice lessons. Still a youth, he engaged on a concert career; gave recitals in Alaska and Canada; was soloist at the Hollywood Bowl; in 1960 made his operatic debut with the Santa Fe Opera Co.; in 1964 joined the staff of the Metropolitan Opera Co.; also appeared as soloist with the Boston Symph. Orch., Philadelphia Orch., Chicago Symph. Orch. His chief roles are Méphistophélès in *Faust,* Leporello in *Don Giovanni;* Figaro in *Nozze di Figaro;* Scarpia in *Tosca;* Falstaff in Verdi's opera; he also sang Moses in Schoenberg's *Moses und Aron* and Dr. Schön in Berg's *Lulu.*

Grammann, Karl, German composer; b. Lübeck, June 3, 1844; d. Dresden, Jan 30, 1897. He studied at the Leipzig Cons.; spent some years in Vienna; in 1885, settled in Dresden. As a youth, he wrote 2 operas, *Die Schatzgräber* and *Die Eisjungfrau,* which were not produced; the following operas were staged with some success: *Melusine* (Wiesbaden, 1875); *Thusnelda und der Triumphzug des Germanicus* (Dresden, 1881); *Das Andreasfest* (Dresden, 1882); 2 short operas, *Ingrid* and *Das Irrlicht* (Dresden, 1894). His last opera, *Auf neutralem Boden* was produced posthumously (Hamburg, 1901). He further wrote several cantatas, symphonies, string quartets, violin sonatas, and other chamber music works.

BIBLIOGRAPHY: F. Pfohl, *Karl Grammann. Ein Künstlerleben* (Berlin, 1910).

Granados, Eduardo, Spanish composer, son of **Enrique Granados;** b. Barcelona, July 28, 1894; d. Madrid, Oct. 2, 1928. He studied in Barcelona with his father; then at the Madrid Cons. with Conrado del Campo; taught at the Granados Academy in Barcelona; was also active as conductor; presented many works by his father. He wrote several zarzuelas, of which the first, *Bufon y Hostelero,* was performed with some success in Barcelona (Dec. 7, 1917); other stage works are: *Los Fanfarrones,* comic opera; *La ciudad eterna,* mystery play; *Los Cigarrales,* operatic sketch; also musical comedies (*Cocktails del Nuevo,* etc.).

Granados, Enrique, outstanding Spanish composer; b. Lérida, July 27, 1867; d. at sea, March 24, 1916 (victim of the sinking by a German submarine of the S. S. Sussex in the English Channel). He studied piano at the Barcelona Cons. with Pujol, winning first prize (1883); then studied composition at the Madrid Cons., with Pedrell (1884–87). He first supported himself by playing piano in restaurants and giving private concerts. He first attracted attention as a composer with an opera, *Maria del Carmen* (Madrid, Nov. 12, 1898); in 1900 he conducted a series of concerts in Barcelona; also established a music school, Academia Granados. He then wrote 4 operas which were produced in Barcelona with little success: *Picarol* (Feb. 23, 1901); *Follet* (April 4, 1903), *Gaziel* (Oct. 27, 1906), and *Liliana* (1911). He then undertook the composition of a work that was to be his masterpiece, a series of piano pieces entitled *Goyescas*, inspired by the paintings and etchings of Goya; his fame rests securely on these imaginative and effective pieces, together with his brilliant *Danzas españolas*. Later, Fernando Periquet wrote a libretto based on the scenes from Goya's paintings, and Granados used the music of his piano suite for an opera, *Goyescas*. Its première took place, in the presence of the composer, at the Metropolitan Opera in New York, on Jan. 28, 1916, with excellent success; the score included an orchestral *Intermezzo*, one of his most popular compositions. It was during his return voyage to Europe that he lost his life. Other works by Granados include an intermezzo to *Miel de la Alcarría* (1893); symph. poems, *La Nit del Mort* and *Dante; Suite Arabe; Suite Gallega; Marcha de los Vencidos; Serenata;* orch. suites, *Elisenda* and *Navidad;* Piano Trio; String Quartet; *Serenata* for 2 violins and piano; *Oriental* for oboe and strings; *Trova* for cello and piano; *Cant de les Estrelles* for chorus, organ, and piano. Piano works: *Danzas españolas* (4 vols.); *Goyescas:* (Part I) *Los Requiebros, Coloquio en la Reja, El Fandango del Candil, Quejas o la Maja y el Ruiseñor;* (Part II) *El Amor y la Muerte (Ballade), Epílogo (Serenade of the Spectre), El Pelele (Escena goyesca);* 6 Pieces on Spanish popular songs; *Valses poéticos; Cuentos para la Juventud; Marche Militaire* and *A la Cubana* (also arranged for orch.); *Deux danses caractéristiques: Danza gitana* and *Danza aragonesa;* songs: *Colección de Tonadillas, escritas en estilo antigua; Colección de Canciones amatorias.* Granados's music is essentially Romantic, with an admixture of specific Spanish rhythms and rather elaborate ornamentation.

BIBLIOGRAPHY: special Granados number of *Revista Musical Catalana* (June 15, 1916); G. Jean-Aubry, "Enrique Granados," *Musical Times* (Dec. 1916); E. Newman, "The Granados of the *Goyescas*" *Musical Times* (Aug. 1917); G. Boladeres Ibern, *Enrique Granados, Recuerdos de su vida y estudio crítico de su obra* (Barcelona, 1921); H. Collet, *Albéniz et Granados* (Paris, 1926); J. Subira, *Enrique Granados* (Madrid, 1926); E. L. Mason, "Enrique Granados," *Music & Letters* (1933); A. Livermore, "Granados and the Nineteenth Century in Spain," *Musical Review* (1946); F. Vicens, *Enrique Granados* (Barcelona, 1958).

Grancino, a family of violin makers, active in the 17th and early 18th centuries. **Andrea Grancino** established a workshop in Milan in 1646; his son, **Paolo,** worked in Milan between 1665 and 1692; he belonged to the Amati school, and several violins attributed to Amati are apparently the work of Paolo Grancino. Paolo's son, **Giovanni,** began making violins in 1677; he is reputed to be the best of the family. His 2 sons, **Giovanni Battista** and **Francesco,** were active between 1715 and 1746; their labels are marked **Fratelli Grancini.**

Grancino (Grancini), Michel Angelo, Italian composer; b. Milan, 1605; d. there, April 17, 1669. He was organist at the Paradiso Church in Milan as a youth of 17; then appointed organist at San Sepolcro (1624) and later at San Ambrogio (1628). In 1630 he became a maestro di cappella of the Milan Cathedral, and retained this post until his death. During his lifetime, he publ. some 20 volumes of his works, which included madrigals, motets, and *concerti sacri,* only a few of which are extant.

Grandert, Johnny, Swedish composer; b. Stockholm, July 11, 1939. He studied under Lidholm at the Royal College of Music in Stockholm (1959–64); also took music courses in Germany, Italy and America. The titles of his compositions betray a desire to puzzle and tantalize, but the music itself is not forbidding despite the application of startling effects.

WORKS: *Chamber Music* for chamber ensemble (1961); string quartet, *40, 2°* (1963); Nonet, for winds, euphonium and cello (1964); *86 T* for chamber ensemble (Stockholm, June 4, 1965); *Mirror 25* for chorus and orch. (Stockholm, Feb. 11, 1966; the score calls for a machine gun and the chorus is invited to belch at some points); *Ten an' Thirty* for chamber ensemble (1966); Octet, for 3 voices, flute, trombone, viola, double bass and harp (1966); *The D. of B.* for orch. (1967); *Barypet,* concerto for trumpet and baritone saxophone, with 16 flutes, percussion and strings (1968); *Prego I* for cello and horn (1968); *Non omesso* for chamber ensemble (1969); *Skorogovorka* (Russian word for a tongue twister) for wind orch. and percussion (Swedish Radio, April 18, 1971); *Non lo so* (*I do not know it* in Italian) for flute, cello and piano (1970); wind quintet, *Pour Philippe* (1970); *Pour Pjotr* for voice, piano, cello, clarinet and percussion (1971); 3 symphonies: No. 1 (1971); No. 2 (1972); No. 3, *Sinfonia Calamagrostis* (1972); Quartet for Recorders (1972); *Jerikos murar* for flute, slide flute, 3 bass recorders, 3 clarinets, 15 trombones, percussion, organ and strings (Norrtälje, Nov. 25, 1972).

Grandi, Alessandro, Italian composer; b. 1577; place of birth uncertain; d. Bergamo, 1630. He was maestro di cappella at Ferrara, first at the Accademia della Morte (1597–1604), then at the Accademia dello Spirito Santo (1604–1616); 1617, was a singer at San Marco, Venice; 1620, 2nd maestro di cappella at San Marco; in 1627, he went to Bergamo as maestro di cappella at Santa Maria Maggiore; he and his family died there in 1630 of the plague. He was one of the leading masters of Stile nuovo in Italy. His works include 3 books of *Cantade et arie* (Venice, 1620–29); 2 books of *Madrigali concertati* (Venice, 1615–22); several books of motets (Venice, 1610–29); other music in MS is at the Fitzwilliam Museum, Cambridge; Christ Church, Oxford; in Berlin and Vienna.

BIBLIOGRAPHY: Denis Arnold, "Alessandro Grandi, a Disciple of Monteverdi," *Musical Quarterly* (April 1957).

Grandjany, Marcel, French harpist; b. Paris, Sept. 3, 1891; d. New York, Feb. 24, 1975. He studied at the Paris Cons., winning 1st prize for harp (1905); made his Paris debut on Jan. 24, 1909; his American debut,

N.Y., Feb. 7, 1924; taught at the Fontainebleau Cons. (1921–35); in 1936 settled in N.Y.; became an American citizen in 1945. In 1938 he joined the staff of the Juilliard School of Music. He composed a *Poème symphonique* for harp, French horn, and orch., and several other works for harp; also songs to French texts. Published *First Grade Harp* Pieces (N.Y., 1964).

Grandjean, Axel Karl William, Danish composer; b. Copenhagen, March 9, 1847; d. there, Feb. 11, 1932. He began his career as an opera singer, but gave up the stage for teaching and composition; also conducted several choral societies in Copenhagen. He wrote the operas *Colomba* (Copenhagen, Oct. 15, 1882), *Oluf* (Copenhagen, April 7, 1894), and others; many choral works; also edited (for Holberg's bicentennial in 1884) a collection of incidental music written to Holberg's dramas.

Grandval, Marie Félicie Clémence de Reiset, French composer; b. Saint-Rémy-des-Monts (Sarthe), Jan. 21, 1830; d. Paris, Jan. 15, 1907. She studied composition with Flotow and Saint-Saëns; under various pen names she wrote the operas *Le Sou de Lise* (Paris, 1859); *Les Fiancés de Rose* (Paris, May 1, 1863); *La Comtesse Eva* (Paris, Aug. 7, 1864); *La Pénitente* (Paris, May 13, 1868); *Piccolino* (Paris, Jan. 5, 1869); *Mazeppa* (Bordeaux, 1892); the oratorio *St. Agnès* (Paris, April 13, 1876); *La Forêt,* lyric poem, for soli, chorus, and orch. (Paris, March 30, 1875); songs.

Granichstaedten, Bruno, Austrian operetta composer; b. Vienna, Sept. 1, 1879; d. New York, May 20, 1944. He began his career as a cabaret singer; in 1908 he turned to composing light opera; produced 16 stage works before 1930; of these, *Der Orlow* (Vienna, April 3, 1925) was the most successful; other operettas are *Bub oder Mädel, Auf Befehl der Kaiserin, Evelyne, Walzerliebe,* etc. In 1938 Granichstaedten left Austria and settled in the U.S.

Grant-Schaefer, George Alfred, American composer and teacher; b. Williamstown, Ontario, July 4, 1872; d. Chicago, May 11, 1939. He studied in Montreal, Chicago, and London; from 1896 to 1908 was organist and choirmaster in Chicago; in 1908–20 was head of vocal dept. of Northwestern Univ., Evanston, Illinois. He composed mostly for schools; also published a collection of French Canadian songs (Boston, 1925).

Gräsbeck, Gottfrid, Finnish composer; b. Turku, Feb. 15, 1927. He graduated with a philosophy degree from the Turku Academy; traveled on study trips to West Germany and America. Upon return to Finland, he taught at Turku; also founded his own concert agency. Among his works are *Toccata dodecafonica* for orch. (1959); Concerto for Orch. and Tape (1964); *Visan Från molnet (Song About the Cloud),* cantata for female chorus and orch. (1967); *Sinfonia da camera* (1969); *Lucia Musik* for solo voices, chorus, organ and orch. (1971); Sonata for Guitar (1974).

Grasse, Edwin, American violinist and composer; b. New York, Aug. 13, 1884; d. there, April 8, 1954. Blind from infancy, he dictated his compositions to an ac-

companist. He studied the violin with Carl Hauser in N.Y.; then went to Brussels for study with César Thomson; in 1899 entered the Brussels Cons., where he won 1st prize in 1900, and Diplôme de Capacité in 1901; toured Europe and America. His works include *American Fantasie* for violin and orch.; Violin Sonata and other violin pieces; organ pieces.

Grassi, Eugène, composer; b. Bangkok, Siam, July 5, 1881; d. Paris, June 8, 1941. He was born of French parents in Siam; went to France as a youth and studied with Vincent d'Indy; he revisited Siam in 1910–13 to collect materials on indigenous music; his works reflect this study as well as, in harmonic idiom, the influence of Debussy. Among his compositions, all with Oriental flavor, are *Le Revéil de Bouddha,* symph. poem (Paris, Feb. 20, 1920); *Poème de l'Univers* for orch. (Paris, April 9, 1922); *Les Sanctuaires* (Paris, March 25, 1926); also songs in the Impressionist manner.

Grassini, Josephina (Giuseppina), Italian contralto; b. Varese, April 8, 1773; d. Milan, Jan. 3, 1850. She made her debut as an opera singer in Milan in 1794; soon attained popularity on all leading Italian stages; in 1800 she sang in Milan before Napoleon, who took her with him to Paris, where she sang at national celebrations. She was in London from 1804–06; then returned to Paris and sang at the French court; she was noted for her beauty and her acting as well as her voice.

BIBLIOGRAPHY: P. Cambiasi, "Una famosa cantante varesina," *Gazzetta Musicale di Milano* (Feb. 20, 1902); A. Pougin, *Une cantatrice 'amie' de Napoléon: Giuseppina Grassini* (Paris, 1920); A. Gavoty, *La Grassini* (Paris, 1947).

Grau, Maurice, American operatic impresario; b. Brünn, Moravia, 1849; d. Paris, March 14, 1907. He was taken to the U.S. at the age of 5, and studied law at Columbia Univ. In 1872 he was a co-manager of the American tours of Anton Rubinstein; in 1873 he organized the Kellogg Opera Co.; was instrumental in bringing Offenbach to the U.S. In 1890 he presented a special season of 21 performances at the Metropolitan Opera House, with such famous artists as Adelina Patti, Emma Albani, Nordica, and Tamagno. From 1891 to 1897 the Metropolitan Opera was leased to the partnership of Abbey, Schoeffel and Grau, and upon Abbey's death, to the Maurice Grau Opera Co. (1898–1903). In 1903 Grau retired and went to Paris. The secret of Grau's success as an impresario was his perfect understanding of public taste in opera; he frankly subordinated the repertory to the favorite roles of the great European stars; he did not produce Wagner's operas until Wagnerian cycles presented by Damrosch had shown that American audiences were ripe for them. In fact, the growing popularity of Wagner contributed greatly towards the financial success of Grau's last seasons.

Graudan, Nikolai, Russian-American cellist; b. Libau, Sept. 5, 1896; d. Moscow, Aug. 9, 1964. He studied cello with Abbiate at the St. Petersburg Cons.; subsequently was instructor there; left Russia in 1922 and went to Germany; was first cellist of the Berlin Philharmonic (1926–35). In 1935 he went to London, and in 1938 to the U.S.; in 1939–44 was first cellist of the Minneapolis Orch.; in 1944–50 lived in New York; in 1950 settled in Los Angeles; gave duo recitals with his wife, the pianist Joanna Freudberg; was member of the Festival Quartet; taught at Black Mountain College, Santa Barbara Academy of the West, at Aspen and at the Univ. of California, Los Angeles. In 1964 he went to Moscow for a visit, and died there. He edited 6 Vivaldi cello sonatas with the realization of the keyboard part; arranged several Chopin pieces for cello and piano.

Graun, August Friedrich, German composer, brother of **Carl Henrich Graun;** b. Wahrenbrück, near Dresden, 1699; d. Merseburg, May 5, 1765. He was active as organist and cantor at Merseburg, where he settled in 1729. Only one of his works is preserved, *Kyrie et Gloria* for 4 voices with instruments.

Graun, Carl Heinrich, German composer; b. Wahrenbrück, near Dresden, May 7, 1704; d. Berlin, Aug. 8, 1759. He received his primary education at the Kreuzschule in Dresden (1713–20), where he studied with Grundig (voice) and Petzold (organ). He sang soprano in the town council choir; then began to study composition with Johann Christoph Schmidt. In 1725 he was engaged as operatic tenor at the Brunswick court; soon he began to compose operas for production at the court theater: *Sinilde* (Feb. 3, 1727), *Iphigenia in Aulis* (Aug. 16, 1728), *Polidorus* (1731), and *Scipio Africanus* (1732), all to German librettos. On June 14, 1733, he staged his first Italian opera, *Lo specchio della fedeltà* (also known under the title *Timareta*). In 1735 Graun was invited by Frederick the Great (then Crown Prince of Prussia) to Rheinsberg, as musical director; Graun gladly accepted, and followed Frederick to Berlin when he became king (1740). In Rheinsberg, Graun wrote a great number of cantatas, in the Italian style; in Berlin, his chief duty was to establish an Italian opera troupe, for which purpose he traveled to Italy in search of good singers. Upon his return to Berlin, Graun produced his first opera for his company, *Rodelinda* (Dec. 13, 1741); there followed *Cleopatra e Cesare* (Dec. 7, 1742), staged for the inauguration of the new opera house. He continued to compose operas with unfailing regularity for each season, 28 in all, among them *Artaserse* (Dec. 2, 1743), *Catone in Utica* (1744), *Alessandro nell' Indie* (1744), *Adriano in Siria* (1746), *Mitridate* (1750), and *Semiramide* (1754). Frederick the Great himself wrote the librettos (in French) for Graun's operas *Montezuma* (Berlin, Jan. 6, 1755; printed in *Denkmäler deutscher Tonkunst* 15) and *Merope* (March 27, 1756). In those years Graun enjoyed very high renown and royal favor; only Hasse approached him in public esteem. In his operas, Graun adhered to the Italian tradition, and was preoccupied chiefly with the requirements of the singing voice. During the last years of his life he wrote some excellent church music; his *Te Deum* commemorating Frederick's victory at the battle of Prague (1756) is regarded as one of the finest sacred works in Germany; even more renowned is Graun's Passion oratorio, *Der Tod Jesu* (1755), which was performed annually for a century. Graun's instrumental music displays a high degree of contrapuntal craftsmanship, as well as a facile melodic gift, but despite these qualities, it failed to sustain interest as well as his sacred works did. He wrote a Concerto Grosso for flute, violin, viola da gamba, cello, and strings; about 30 concertos for harpsichord; 6 flute concertos; 3 quintets for harpsichord and strings; about 35 trio sonatas; duets for various instruments, etc.

BIBLIOGRAPHY: A. Mayer-Reinach, *Carl Heinrich Graun als Opernkomponist* (Berlin, 1899); K. Mennicke, "Zur Biographie der Brüder Graun," *Neue Zeitschrift für Musik* (1904); K. Mennicke, *Hasse und die Brüder Graun als Sinfoniker* (Leipzig, 1906; with biography and complete thematic catalogues); B. Hitzig, "Briefe Carl Heinrich Grauns," *Zeitschrift für Musikwissenschaft* (1926).

Graun, Johann Gottlieb, German composer, brother of **Carl Heinrich Graun;** b. Wahrenbrück, near Dresden, 1703; d. Berlin, Oct. 27, 1771. He studied violin with Pisendel in Dresden and with Tartini in Padua. In 1726 he was appointed Kapellmeister in Merseburg, where he was the teacher of Wilhelm Friedemann Bach. In 1732 he became Konzertmeister for Crown Prince Frederick (later Frederick the Great) at Rheinsberg, and from 1741 held a similar position in the newly founded Royal Opera in Berlin, where his brother, Carl Heinrich, was Kapellmeister. His works include 100 symphonies, 20 violin concertos, 24 string quartets, and a number of sacred works. Only a few are published: 6 harpsichord concertos; 8 sonatas for 2 flutes and violin. Riemann reprinted 3 trio sonatas in *Collegium musicum* (1906). A complete list of works and editions is found in Werner Freytag's article on the Graun brothers in *Die Musik in Geschichte und Gegenwart.*

Graupner, Christoph (Johann Christoph), German composer; b. Kirchberg, Saxony, Jan. 13, 1683; d. Darmstadt, May 10, 1760. He studied music at the Thomasschule, Leipzig, with Kuhnau and Heinichen; then was in Hamburg as opera accompanist under Keiser (1706–09). In 1710 he became vice-Kapellmeister and in 1712, Kapellmeister, at Darmstadt, where he remained all his life. He was offered the post of cantor at the Thomasschule in 1722, but decided against acceptance, and the position was given to Bach. Graupner was an industrious worker, and was active in Hamburg as composer, conductor, and teacher; he engraved for publication several of his keyboard pieces. He produced 6 operas in Hamburg of which only 3 are extant: *Dido* (1707); *Der angenehme Betrug* (1707, with Keiser; publ. in *Denkmäler deutscher Tonkunst* 38); *L'amore ammalato* or *Antiochus und Stratonice* (1708). He wrote 3 operas in Darmstadt, of which *La costanza vince l'inganno* is preserved. He publ. for harpsichord 8 *Partien* (2 vols., 1718 and 1726), the *Monatliche Klavier-Früchte* (1722), and the *Vier Jahreszeiten* (1733); also a *Hessen-Darmstädttisches Choralbuch* (1728). The Darmstadt library contains a great number of MSS by Graupner, among them 44 concertos, 80 overtures, and 116 symphonies; 6 harpsichord sonatas, trio sonatas, and about 1300 sacred works. Selected examples from his cantatas are publ. in vols. 51–52 of *Denk-*

mäler deutscher Tonkunst. A projected edition of his works remains incomplete after only 4 vols. appeared (ed. by F. Noack, Kassel, 1955-57).

BIBLIOGRAPHY: W. Nagel, *Christoph Graupner als Sinfoniker* (Langensalza, 1912); F. Noack, *Christoph Graupners Kirchenmusiken* (Leipzig, 1916); F. Noack, *Musikgeschichte Darmstadts vom Mittelalter bis zur Goethezeit* (Mainz, 1967); A. Lindner, "Christoph Graupners Familie und Vorfahren," *Genealogie* XVII/9 (1968).

Graupner, Johann Christian Gottlieb, composer; b. Verden, near Hanover, Oct. 6, 1767; d. Boston, April 16, 1836. He was the son of the oboist, **Johann Georg Graupner,** and became himself an oboist in military bands. In 1788, he was in London, and played in Haydn's orchestra in 1791. About 1795, he emigrated to America, settling in Charleston, S.C.; played his Oboe Concerto there on March 21, 1795; early in 1797, he went to Boston; in 1800, he opened a music store; also taught piano, and all orchestral instruments, on which he was fairly proficient; publ. works by himself and other composers; he became an American citizen in 1808. In 1810, he organized the Boston Philharmonic Society, which was the first semiprofessional orchestra in Boston; it gave performances of Haydn's symphonies, presented *Messiah* in 1818 and Haydn's *Creation* in 1819; the orchestra continued its activity until Nov., 1824. In 1815, Graupner was a co-founder of a musical organization which became the Handel and Haydn Society of Boston, and which greatly influenced the development of choral music in New England. In view of these accomplishments, Graupner is referred to by some writers as the 'father of American orchestral music.' In 1806, he publ. *Rudiments of the art of playing the piano forte, containing the elements of music* (repr. 1819, 1825, and 1827). He was married to **Catherine Hillier,** a professional singer (1770-1821); on Dec. 30, 1799, she sang in Boston a Negro ballad; this fact led to erroneous reports that Graupner himself appeared as a blackface minstrel.

BIBLIOGRAPHY: O. G. Sonneck, *Early Concert Life in America* (1907); J. T. Howard, *Our American Music* (4th ed.; N.Y., 1965); H. E. Johnson, *Musical Interludes in Boston* (N.Y., 1943, chap. VI). Typescript copies of a memoir on Graupner, compiled by his granddaughter, Catherine Graupner Stone (1906), are available in the Library of Congress, N.Y. Public Library, and Boston Public Library.

Graveure, Louis (real name **Wilfred Douthitt**), concert singer; b. London, March 18, 1888; d. Los Angeles, April 27, 1965. He studied voice with Clara Novello-Davies; came to the U.S. and under his real name, Douthitt, sang the baritone part in the operetta, *The Lilac Domino,* in N.Y. on Oct. 28, 1914; in 1915 he reappeared in N.Y. as Louis Graveure (after his mother's maiden name) and became a popular concert artist, singing all types of music. On Feb. 5, 1928, he gave a concert in N.Y. as a tenor; from 1931-38, he was in Germany; 1938-40, in France; 1940-47, in England; in 1947, returned to the U.S.; taught in various music schools.

BIBLIOGRAPHY: "The Case of a Beardless Bari-

tone," in N. Slonimsky, *A Thing or Two about Music* (N.Y., 1948; pp. 220-21).

Gray, Alan, English organist and composer; b. York, Dec. 23, 1855; d. Cambridge, Sept. 27, 1935. He took degrees in law and music from Trinity College, Cambridge; was musical director of Wellington College (1883-92); 1892-1912, conductor of the Cambridge Univ. Musical Society; also organist at Trinity College (1892-1930). He wrote 5 cantatas, a *Coronation March;* chamber music; many organ works. He was also an editor for the Purcell Society.

Gray, Cecil, British writer on music; b. Edinburgh, May 19, 1895; d. Worthing, Sept. 9, 1951. He studied music with Healey Willan; in 1920, with Philip Heseltine (Peter Warlock), he edited a new magazine of music criticism, *The Sackbut;* later was music critic for the *Daily Telegraph* and the *Manchester Guardian;* wrote 3 operas (to his own texts) and other music.

WRITINGS: *A Survey of Contemporary Music* (1924); *Carlo Gesualdo, Prince of Venosa; Musician and Murderer* (in collaboration with Philip Heseltine; 1926); *The History of Music* (1928); *Sibelius* (1931); *Peter Warlock* (1934); *Sibelius: the Symphonies* (1935); *Predicaments, or Music and the Future* (1936); *The 48 Preludes and Fugues of Bach* (1938); *Contingencies* (N.Y., 1947); memoirs, *Musical Chairs or Between Two Stools* (London, 1948).

BIBLIOGRAPHY: R. Gorer, "The Music of Cecil Gray," *Musical Review* (Aug. 1947).

Gray, Donald, American publisher; b. New Rochelle, N.Y., May 25, 1903; d. Stamford, Conn., Oct. 21, 1969. He studied at Dartmouth College, graduating in 1924; joined the music publishing house founded by his father H. Willard Gray; succeeded him as president in 1951. He published many works by American composers, among them Aaron Copland, Leo Sowerby and Philip James.

Gray, Jerry, American bandleader, composer and arranger; b. Boston, July 3, 1915; d. Dallas, Texas, Aug. 10, 1976. He studied violin with Ondříček in Boston; at the age of 13, was concertmaster of the Boston Junior Symph. Orch.; then became a jazz band leader. He played in nightclubs and other locales of musical subculture; in 1936 joined the Artie Shaw Orch. as arranger; during World War II was arranger for the fabled Glenn Miller band, which he took over after Miller's death in a plane crash in 1944. He had his own radio show (1946-52); led dance orchestras; also wrote several songs that became popular, among them *Strings of Pearls.*

Graziani, Bonifazio, Italian composer of church music; b. Marino, 1605; d. Rome, June 15, 1664; held the post as maestro di cappella in Rome; composed much sacred music publ. in 1652-78.

Greatorex, Thomas, English organist, singer, and conductor; b. North Wingfield, Derby, Oct. 5, 1758; d. Hampton, near London, July 18, 1831. He was the son of an amateur organist; the family moved to Leicester in 1767. He studied with Dr. B. Cooke (1772); was befriended by Lord Sandwich and became musical director of his household for a time. He sang at the Concerts of Ancient Music in London (from 1776) and was organist at Carlisle Cathedral (1781–84). He then traveled in Holland, Italy, and France, and took lessons in Strasbourg with Pleyel. Settling in London, he became a highly popular singing teacher (in one week he gave 84 lessons at a guinea each). In 1793 he was appointed conductor of the Concerts of Ancient Music, a post which he held until his death, never missing a single concert. He assisted in the revival of the Vocal Concerts in 1801; from 1819 he was organist at Westminster Abbey; he conducted festivals throughout England, and was one of the founders of the Royal Academy of Music in London (1822). He published *A Selection of Tunes* (London, 1829); a collection *Parochial Psalmody* (1825); *12 Glees* (1832); anthems, psalms and chants, but it was as an organist that Greatorex was best known.

Greef, Arthur de, Belgian pianist and composer; b. Louvain, Oct. 10, 1862; d. Brussels, Aug. 29, 1940. He studied at the Brussels Cons. with L. Brassin (piano) and Gevaert (composition); then traveled as pianist in Europe; in 1885 he was appointed prof. of piano at the Brussels Cons., retaining that post until 1930.

WORKS: opera in Flemish, *De Marketenster* (Louvain, 1879); Symphony; Ballad for Strings; 2 piano concertos; 2 violin sonatas; *Quatre vieilles chansons flamandes* for piano; a number of piano études; songs.

BIBLIOGRAPHY: F. Rasse, "Notice sur Arthur de Greef," *Annuaire de l'Académie Royale de Belgique* (1949).

Green, John, American composer and conductor of popular music; b. New York, Oct. 10, 1908. He studied economics at Harvard Univ. (A.B., 1928); music theory with W. R. Spalding; piano with Ignace Hilsberg. He settled in Hollywood in 1942; became arranger for Guy Lombardo; wrote songs; among them, *Body and Soul* (1931) and *I Cover the Waterfront* (1933) became popular; conducted many motion picture scores and received Academy Awards for *Easter Parade* (1948), *An American in Paris* (1951) and *West Side Story* (1961); also arranged and conducted music for television. He was conductor of the Los Angeles Philharmonic Promenade Concerts (1959–63) and guest conductor of other orchestras in the U.S.

Green, L. Dunton (Louis Grein), Dutch music critic; b. Amsterdam, Dec. 22, 1872; d. Ruysselede, Belgium, Dec. 30, 1933. He studied music in Germany and in Paris; lived for many years in London; contributed numerous articles on modern composers to English, Italian, French, and American magazines.

Green, Ray, American composer; b. Cavendish, Missouri, Sept. 13, 1909. He studied composition with Ernest Bloch at the San Francisco Cons. (1927–33) and with Albert Elkus at the Univ. of California, at Berkeley (1933–35). In 1943 he entered the armed forces; from 1946 to 1948 was chief of music for the Veterans Administration; from 1948 to 1961 served as executive secretary of the American Music Center in New York; from 1961 on he devoted himself to music publishing and electronic music. His own compositions are often modal in harmonic settings; rhythmic animation is much in evidence in his pieces based on American rural songs.

WORKS: 2 symphonies (1945, 1953); *Sunday Sing Symphony* (1946); Violin Concerto (1952); *12 Short Sonatas* for piano (1949–70); many pieces for band derived thematically from regional American rhythms *(Kentucky Mountain Running Set, Jig Theme, Six Changes);* madrigals, choruses, rhapsodies, dance scores, hymn tunes; also published *Piano Books for Young People* in 6 vols. (1961).

Greenberg, Noah, American conductor and musicologist; b. New York, April 9, 1919; d. there, Jan. 9, 1966. He studied music privately; served in the U.S. Merchant Marine (1944–49); organized choruses in New York. In 1952 he founded the New York Pro Musica Antiqua, an organization specializing in Renaissance and Medieval music, performed in authentic styles and on copies of early instruments; revived medieval liturgical music dramas *The Play of Daniel* (1958) and *The Play of Herod* (1963); traveled with his ensemble in Europe in 1960 and 1963. It was primarily through the efforts of the N.Y. Pro Musica Antiqua that early music, formerly known only to musicologists, became a viable idiom available to modern audiences. Greenberg held a Guggenheim Fellowship in 1955 and the Ford Fellowship in 1960 and 1962.

Greene, Harry Plunket, Irish singer; b. near Dublin, June 24, 1865; d. London, Aug. 19, 1936. He studied in Florence with Vannuccini, and in London under J. B. Welsh and A. Blume; made his debut in *Messiah* at Stepney (Jan. 21, 1888) and soon became a popular concert artist. He made the first of several tours of the U.S. in 1893; also appeared in Canada. He was noted for his interpretations of Schumann and Brahms; publ. a valuable instruction book for singers, *Interpretation in Song* (London, 1912), a biography of Stanford (London, 1935), and a volume of musical reminiscences, *From Blue Danube to Shannon.*

Greene, Maurice, English organist and composer; b. London, 1695; d. there, Dec. 1, 1755. He served as a choirboy in St. Paul's Cathedral; became proficient as an organist; was appointed organist of St. Paul's in 1718. In 1727 he succeeded Croft as composer to the Chapel Royal; in 1730 he was Tudway's successor as prof. of music at the Univ. of Cambridge, receiving the title of Mus. Doc. In 1735 he became master of the King's Band of Music. Beginning in 1750, he accumulated and collated a great number of English sacred works; he willed this material to Boyce, who made use of it in his monumental collection, *Cathedral Music.*

WORKS: 2 oratorios, *Jephtha* (1737), and *The Force of Truth* (1744); 3 dramatic pastorals: *Love's Revenge* (1734), *The Judgment of Hercules* (1740), and *Phoebe* (1748); a collection of 12 English songs, *The Chaplet;* an album of 25 sonnets for voice with harpsichord and violin, *Spenser's Amoretti;* collected *40 Select Anthems in Score* (2 vols.; 1743); composed nu-

merous catches and canons, organ voluntaries, harpsichord pieces, etc.
BIBLIOGRAPHY: E. Walker, "The Bodleian MSS of Maurice Greene," *Musical Antiquarian* (April-July 1910).

Greenfield, Edward, English writer on music; b. Westcliff-on-Sea, Essex, July 30, 1928. He studied law at Cambridge Univ. (1949–52); joined the staff of the *Manchester Guardian* as phonograph record critic in 1955, and became its music critic in 1964. He was a regular broadcaster for BBC from 1957; contributed to the *Gramophone* and other music journals. He was joint author (with Denis Stevens and Ivan March) of the multi-volume *Stereo Record Guide.* He publ. a monograph, *Puccini: Keeper of the Seal* (London, 1958).

Gregh, Louis, French composer and music publisher; b. Philippeville, Algeria, March 16, 1843; d. St. Mesme (Seine-et-Oise), Jan. 21, 1915. He began his musical career with the production of a light opera, *Un Lycée de jeunes filles* (Paris, 1881), which won a decided success; this was followed by several other operettas, *Le Présomtif* (1884), *Le Capitaine Roland* (1895), and ballets. He then turned to publishing; the firm was continued by his son, **Henri Gregh,** who established it as Henri Gregh & Fils (1902); Henri Gregh's son, **André,** succeeded him as director in 1934.

Gregoir, Edouard (Georges Jacques), Belgian composer and writer on music; b. Turnhout, near Antwerp, Nov. 7, 1822; d. Wyneghem, June 28, 1890. He studied piano, and was a professional accompanist; in 1851, he settled in Antwerp.
WORKS: He was a prolific composer; wrote 154 works in all. His Flemish opera, *Willem Beukels,* was produced in Brussels (July 21, 1856); incidental music to various patriotic plays: *De Belgen in 1848*; *La Dernière Nuite du Comte d'Egmont,* etc.; symphonic oratorio, *Le Déluge* (1849); a historical symphony, *Les Croisades* (1846).
WRITINGS: *Essai historique sur la musique et les musiciens dans les Pays-Bas* (1861); *Histoire de l'orgue* (1865, with biographical notes on Belgian and Dutch organists and organ builders); *Galerie biographique des artistes-musiciens belges du XVIIIe et du XIXe siècles* (1862; 2nd ed., 1885); *Notice sur l'origine du célèbre compositeur Louis van Beethoven* (1863); *Les Artistes-Musiciens néerlandais* (1864); *Du chant choral et des festivals en Belgique* (1865); *Notice historique sur les sociétés de musique d'Anvers* (1869); *Recherches historiques concernant les journaux de musique depuis les temps les plus reculés jusqu'à nos jours* (1872); *Notice biographique d'Adrian Willaert*; *Réflexions sur la regénération de l'ancienne école de musique flamande et sur le théâtre flamand; Les Artistes-Musiciens belges au XIXe siècle; réponse à un critique de Paris* (1874); *Documents historiques relatifs à l'art musical et aux artistes-musiciens* (1872–76; 4 vols.); *Panthéon musical populaire* (1876–77; 6 vols.); *Notice biographique sur F. J. Gossé dit Gossec* (1878); *L'Art musical en Belgique sous les règnes de Léopold I et Léopold II* (1879); *Les Gloires de l'Opéra et la musique à Paris* (4 vols., 1880–3, vol. I embraces the period 1392–1750); *A.-E.-M. Grétry* (1883); *Souvenirs artistiques* (3 vols., 1888–9).

Gregoir, Joseph Jacques, Belgian pianist and composer, brother of **Edouard Gregoir;** b. Antwerp, Jan. 19, 1817; d. Brussels, Oct. 29, 1876. He studied with Henri Herz in Paris and with Rummel in Biebrich. He gave a number of successful piano recitals in Belgium, Germany, and Switzerland; wrote salon pieces for piano and several practical methods of piano playing; publ. duets for violin and piano in collaboration with Vieuxtemps; he also wrote an opera, *Le Gondolier de Venise* (1848).

Gregor, Čestmír, Czech composer; b. Brno, May 14, 1926. He studied composition with Kvapil at the Brno Cons.; in 1959, appointed music director of the Ostrava Radio.
WORKS: ballet, *Závrat* (*Vertigo,* 1963; Ostrava, May 9, 1964; ballet version of the *Choreographic Symphony*); *Joyous Overture* (1951); *No One is Alone,* rhapsody for piano and orch. (1955); *Prosím o slovo* (*May I Speak?*), overture (1956); *Tragic Suite* for chamber orch. (1957); *Concerto Semplice* for piano and orch. (1958); *Polyfonietta* for orch. (1961); *The Children of Daidalos,* symph. poem (1961); *Choreographic Symphony* (1963); *Prague Walker,* 2 nocturnes for 16 strings (1963); *Violin Concerto* (1965); *Symfonie Mého Města* (*Symphony of My Town,* 1970); *Sinfonietta* (1973); *Cello Concerto,* subtitled *Complimento alla musica di ogni giorno* (1974); *Overture Giocosa* (1975); *Sinfonia Notturna di Praga* (1976); *Trio for Flute, Viola and Bass Clarinet* (1959); *String Quartet* (1965); *Experiment* for piano (1946); *Sonata brevis* for piano (1946); *Tre Movimenti* for piano (1966); *Sonata in Tre Tempi* for piano (1966).

Gregor, Christian Friedrich, composer and hymnologist; b. Dirsdorf, Silesia, Jan. 1, 1723; d. Zeist, Holland, Nov. 6, 1801. As organist, music director, composer, and hymnologist, Gregor was the most important musician of the international Moravian Church (Unitas Fratrum) of the 18th century. Joining the Moravian Brethren in 1742, he soon assumed leading positions in its management: financial agent of Zinzendorf, member of Unity Elders Conference (1764–1801), and bishop (1789–1801). He made numerous business trips to Germany, Holland, England, Russia, and North America (Pennsylvania, 1770–72); while in Pennsylvania, he gave instruction in composition to Johann Friedrich Peter. During his stay at Herrnhut, Saxony, as organist, Gregor compiled the first hymnal published by the Moravians (*Choral-Buch, enthaltend alle zu dem Gesangbuche der Evangelischen Brüder-Gemeinen vom Jahre 1778 gehörige Melodien;* Leipzig, Breitkopf, 1784) and arranged the musical liturgies.
WORKS: 308 hymns (*Gesangbuch zum Gebrauch der evangelischen Brüder-Gemeinen;* Barby, 1778, et seq.), about 100 chorale tunes, and approximately 200 anthems and arias. The latter are preserved in MS in the Moravian Church Archives at Bethlehem, Pennsylvania, and Winston-Salem, North Carolina. Several of his anthems were republished frequently in 19th-century American tunebooks.

BIBLIOGRAPHY: *Historische Nachricht vom Brü-der-Gesangbuche des Jahres 1778, und von dessen Lieder-Verfassern* (Gnadau, 1835); J. Julian, *A Dictionary of Hymnology* (2nd ed. London, 1908; repr. N.Y., 1957).

Gregory I, "the Great"; b. Rome, 540; d. there, March 12, 604. He was pope from 590–604; celebrated in music history as reputed reformer of the musical ritual of the Roman Catholic Church. It is traditionally believed that by his order, and under his supervision, a collection was made in 599 of the music employed in the different churches; that various offertories, antiphons, responses, etc., were revised and regularly and suitably distributed over the entire year in an arrangement which came to be known as Gregorian Chant. While for centuries the sole credit for the codification, which certainly took place, had been ascribed to Gregory, investigations by such scholars as Gevaert, Riemann, P. Wagner, Frere, Houdard, Gastoué, Mocquereau, and others have demonstrated that some of Gregory's predecessors had begun this reform and even fixed the order of certain portions of the liturgy, and that the work of reform was definitely completed under some of his immediate successors. Evidence in favor of Gregory's leading part in the reform is marshaled in E. G. P. Wyatt's *Saint Gregory and the Gregorian Music* (1904); evidence against his participation is given in Paul Henry Lang's *Music in Western Civilization* (N.Y., 1941). See also G. Morin, *Les Véritables Origines du Chant grégorien* (Maredsous, 1890); W. Brambach, *Gregorianisch* (Leipzig, 1895); F. H. Duddin, *Gregory the Great* (2 vols., London, 1905); F. Tarducci, *Storia di S. Gregorius e del suo tempo* (Rome, 1909); P. C. Vivell, *Der gregorianische Gesang: eine Studie über die Echtheit der Tradition* (Graz, 1904).

Grein, Louis. See **Green, L. Dunton.**

Greissle, Felix, Austrian composer and editor; b. Vienna, Nov. 15, 1899. He studied there at the Univ. with Guido Adler, and privately with Schoenberg and Alban Berg; from 1925–37, he conducted the Cantata Association of the Vienna State Opera. In 1938 he went to N.Y.; became associated with various music publishers. He wrote the first published explanation of Schoenberg's method of composition with 12 tones (in the periodical *Anbruch,* 1925).

Greiter, Matthaeus, German poet and composer; b. Aichach, Bavaria, c.1490; d. Strasbourg, Dec. 20, 1550. He wrote the texts and melodies of Psalm-Lieder for Lutheran services, and settings, for 4 voices, of German songs. He also wrote a tract, *Elementale Musicum Inventuti* (1544).
BIBLIOGRAPHY: Th. Gérold, *Les Plus Anciennes Melodies de l'église protestante de Strasbourg et leurs auteurs* (Paris, 1928); E. E. Lowinsky, "Matthaeus Greiter's Fortuna; an Experiment in Chromaticism and in Musical Iconography," *Musical Quarterly* (Oct. 1956 and Jan. 1957).

Grell, Eduard August, German organist and composer; b. Berlin, Nov. 6, 1800; d. Steglitz, near Berlin,

Aug. 10, 1886. He studied organ with his father and theory with Zelter; at the age of 17, he became a member of the Singakademie and was connected with it for 59 years, until his death; he was director from 1853–76. Grell held the view that only vocal music was the true art; consequently, he wrote almost exclusively for voice. His works include a *Missa Solemnis* (in 16 parts a cappella); an oratorio, *Die Israelitin in der Wüste,* and other church music.
BIBLIOGRAPHY: H. Bellermann, *Biographie Grells* (Berlin, 1899); Bellermann also edited Grell's essays, *Aufsätze und Gutachten* (Berlin, 1887).

Grešák, Jozef, Slovak composer; b. Bardejov, Dec. 30, 1907. He had training in piano and organ, but was largely autodidact in composition; after his youthful opera *Prichod Slovákov* (*The Arrival of the Slovaks,* 1925) he had a hiatus in his work as a composer, and did not resume composition until much later with a ballet, *Radúz and Mahuliena* (1954–55), and an interesting ethnic work *The Emigrant Songs* for soloists, male chorus and orch. (1961). There followed a Piano Concerto (1963); *Concertino-Pastorale* for oboe, English horn, horn and orch. (1965); *Zemplin Variations* for soloists, chorus and orch. (1965); *Morceau I* for violin and orch. (1965); *Morceau II* for violin and piano (1968); *Rotors I* for piano (1966); *Rotors II* for orch. (1969); *Hexody* for clarinet and piano (1967); *Workers' Songs* for soloist, chorus and orch. (1971); *Amoebae,* overture (1971); an opera, *With Rosary* (1970–73); *Zuzanka Hraškovie,* monodrama for soprano, organ and orch. (1973; Bratislava, Jan. 15, 1975); and *Concertant Symfonietta* for orch. (1975; Košice, May 5, 1976).

Gresnich, Antoine-Frédéric, Belgian composer; b. Liège, March (baptized March 2), 1755; d. Paris, Oct. 16, 1799. He was a chorister at the St. Lambert Church in Liège, and studied in Naples under Sala. He made several trips to London, where he produced his operas *Demetrio, Alessandro nell'Indie, Donna di Cattiva Umore,* and *Alceste* with considerable success. He was in Lyons in 1789–93; his opera *L'Amour exilé de Cythère* was produced there in 1793. He then returned to Paris, where he died in poverty.

Gretchaninov, Alexander, Russian composer; b. Moscow, Oct. 25, 1864; d. New York, Jan. 3, 1956. He studied at the Moscow Cons. (1881–91) with Safonov (piano) and Arensky (composition); then entered the St. Petersburg Cons. as a pupil of Rimsky-Korsakov (1891–1903); prof. of composition at the Moscow Institute until 1922; then lived in Paris; visited the U.S., where he appeared with considerable success as guest conductor of his own works (1929–31); came to the U.S. again in 1939, settling in New York. He became an American citizen on July 25, 1946. He continued to compose until the end of his long life. A concert of his works was presented on his 90th birthday in Town Hall, New York (Oct. 25, 1954) in the presence of the composer. A complete catalogue of his works is appended to his autobiography, *My Life.* His music is rooted in the Russian national tradition; influences of both Tchaikovsky and Rimsky-Korsakov are in evidence in his early works; towards 1910 he attempted to inject some Impressionistic elements into his vocal compositions, but without signal success. His masterly sacred works are of historical importance, for he introduced a reform into Russian church singing by using nationally colored melodic patterns; in several of his Masses he employed instrumental accompaniment contrary to the prescriptions of the Russian Orthodox faith, a circumstance that precluded the use of these works in Russian churches. His *Missa Oecumenica* represents a further expansion towards ecclesiastical universality; in this work he makes use of elements pertaining to other religious music, including non-Christian. His instrumental works are competently written, but show less originality than his vocal music. His early *Lullaby* (1887) and the song, *Over the Steppes* still retain their popularity, and have been published in numerous arrangements.

WORKS: OPERAS: *Dobrinya Nikititch* (Moscow, Oct. 27, 1903), *Sister Beatrice* (Moscow, Oct. 25, 1912; suppressed after 3 performances as being irreverent), *The Dream of a Little Christmas Tree*, children's opera (1911), *The Castle Mouse*, children's opera (1921), *The Cat, the Fox, and the Rooster*, children's opera (1919), *Marriage*, comic opera after Gogol (1945–46; Berkshire Music Festival, Aug. 1, 1948); *Idylle forestière*, ballet divertissement for orch. (N.Y., 1925); incidental music to Ostrovsky's *Sniegurotchka* (Moscow, Nov. 6, 1900), A. Tolstoy's *Tsar Feodor* (Moscow, Oct. 26, 1898), and *Death of Ivan the Terrible* (1899). FOR ORCH.: Concert Overture in D minor (1892; St. Petersburg, March, 1893); *Elegy in Memory of Tchaikovsky* (1893; St. Petersburg, Dec. 31, 1898, Rimsky-Korsakov conducting); 5 symphonies (No. 1, 1893, St. Petersburg, Jan. 26, 1895; No. 2, 1909, Moscow, March 14, 1909; No. 3, 1920–23, Kiev, May 29, 1924; No. 4, 1923–24, N.Y., April 9, 1942; No. 5, 1936; Philadelphia, April 5, 1939); *Poème elégiaque* (Boston, March 29, 1946); *Festival Overture* (Indianapolis, Nov. 15, 1946); *Poème lyrique* (1948). VOCAL WORKS: *Liturgy of St. John Chrysostom* (Moscow, Oct. 19, 1898); *Laudate Deum* (Moscow, Nov. 24, 1915); *Liturgia Domestica* (Moscow, March 30, 1918); *Missa Oecumenica*, for soli, chorus, and orch. (Boston, Feb. 25, 1944); 84 choruses; 14 vocal quartets; 8 duets; 258 songs (some with orch.). CHAMBER MUSIC: 4 string quartets, 2 trios, Violin Sonata, Cello Sonata, 2 clarinet sonatas, 2 *Miniatures* for saxophone and piano. FOR PIANO: 2 sonatas (2nd in 1944); *Petits tableaux musicaux* (1947); etc. After the Revolution, Gretchaninov wrote a new Russian national anthem, *Hymn of Free Russia* (sung in N.Y. at a concert for the benefit of Siberian exiles, May 22, 1917) but it was never adopted by any political Russian faction. Gretchaninov wrote 201 op. numbers in all; op. 201 is a chorus a cappella, *Have Mercy O God.*

BIBLIOGRAPHY: He publ. a book of reminiscences, *My Life* (Paris, in Russian, 1934; in English, with additions and introduction by N. Slonimsky, N.Y., 1952; contains a complete catalogue of works). See also M. Montagu-Nathan, *Contemporary Russian Composers* (N.Y., 1917); J. Yasser, "Gretchaninov's 'Heterodox' Compositions," *Musical Quarterly* (July 1942).

Grétry, André Ernest Modeste, greatly significant French opera composer; b. Liège, Feb. 8, 1741; d.

Montmorency, near Paris, Sept. 24, 1813. His father was a violinist at the church of St. Martin in Liège; at the age of 9, Grétry was entered as chorister at the St. Denis Church, but was dismissed 2 years later. At 12, he began to study violin and singing; he learned music under Leclerc and the organist Nicolas Rennekin. At that time, an Italian opera company gave a season in Liège, and young Grétry thus received his first impulse towards dramatic music. Still his early works were instrumental; in 1758, he wrote 6 small symphonies; his next work was a Mass, which interested the ecclesiastical authorities; as a result, he was enabled (through the Canon du Harlez) to go to Rome (1759), where he entered the College de Liège, a school founded for the education of natives of Liège. There he studied diligently, and composed several church works, 6 string quartets, a flute concerto, and a light opera, *Le Vendemmiatrici*, which was produced in Rome in 1765. In 1766, he was in Geneva as a music teacher. He met Voltaire, who advised him to go to Paris; before his departure, he produced in Geneva a stage work, *Isabelle et Gertrude*, to a libretto by Favart, after Voltaire. He arrived in Paris in the autumn of 1767; he sought the patronage of aristocrats and diplomats; the Swedish ambassador, Count de Creutz, gave him the first encouragement by obtaining for him Marmontel's comedy, *Le Huron;* it was performed with Grétry's music at the Comédie-Italienne (Aug. 20, 1768). From then on, Grétry produced operas, one after another, without interruption even during the years of the French Revolution.

The merit of Grétry's operas lies in their melodies and dramatic expression. He was not deeply versed in the science of music; yet despite this lack of craftsmanship in harmony and counterpoint, he achieved fine effects of vocal and instrumental writing. His operas suffered temporary eclipse when Méhul and Cherubini entered the field, but public interest was revived by the magnificent tenor, Elleviou, in 1801. The changes in operatic music during the next 30 years caused the neglect of Grétry's works. Nevertheless, Grétry—"the Molière of music" as he was called—founded the school of French opéra comique, of which Boieldieu, Auber, and Adam have been such distinguished alumni. During his lifetime, he was greatly honored: he was elected a member of many artistic and learned institutions in France and abroad; the Prince-Bishop of Liège made him a privy councillor in 1784; a street in Paris was named for him in 1785; he was admitted to the Institut de France in 1795, as one of the first three chosen to represent the department of musical composition; in 1795 he was also appointed Inspector of the Paris Cons., but resigned in a few months; his bust was placed in the Grand Opéra foyer, and a marble statue in the entrance hall of the Opéra-Comique; Napoleon made him a Chevalier of the Legion of Honor in 1802, and granted him a pension of 4,000 francs in compensation for losses during the Revolution. Grétry bought 'L'Ermitage,' Rousseau's former residence at Montmorency, and lived there in retirement. He was married, and had several children, but survived them all. His daughter, **Lucille** (real name **Angélique-Dorothée-Lucie;** b. Paris, July 15, 1772; d. there, Aug. 25, 1790), was a gifted musician who died young; at the age of

13, with some assistance from her father, she composed an opera, *Le Mariage d'Antonio*, which was produced at the Opéra-Comique, July 29, 1786; her second opera, *Toinette et Louis*, was produced on March 23, 1787. Grétry's *Mémoires ou Essais sur la musique* were publ. in 1789 (reprinted in 1797 with 2 additional vols. edited by his friend, Legrand; in German, in 1800 at Leipzig, with critical and historical annotations by K. Spazier; in 3 vols. by Mass in 1829 and an enlarged edition by P. Magnette, Liège, 1914). In these essays, Grétry set forth his views on the paramount importance of the just declamation of every syllable set to music. He also wrote a *Méthode simple pour apprendre à préluder en peu de temps avec toutes les resources de l'harmonie* (1802); *De la Vérité*, an ardent avowal of Republican tenets, with remarks on the feelings and the best means of exciting and expressing them by music (1803), and *Réflexions sur l'art*, in 6 vols., were never published. During the last years of his life he wrote *Réflexions d'un Solitaire;* his friends did not think its publication was advisable; the MS was considered lost until C. Malherbe discovered it in 1908; it was publ. in 4 vols., ed. by L. Solvay and E. Closson, in Brussels and Paris, 1919–22. Besides his dramatic works, Grétry composed a *De Profundis, Confiteor,* a Requiem, an antiphon, motets, and a good deal of instrumental music. Under the auspices of the Belgian government, a complete ed. of his works was published in 1883–97, under the editorship of Gevaert and others.

WORKS: The list of his operas is long; they include: *Lucile* (Paris, Jan. 5, 1769); *Le Tableau parlant* (Paris, Sept. 20, 1769; very popular); *Les Deux Avares* (Fontainebleau, Oct. 27, 1770); *Sylvain* (Paris, Feb. 19, 1770); *L'Amitié à l'épreuve* (Fontainebleau, Nov. 13, 1770); *L'Ami de la maison* (Fontainebleau, Oct. 26, 1771); *Zémire et Azor* (Fontainebleau, Nov. 9, 1771); *Le Magnifique* (Paris, March 4, 1773); *La Rosière de Salency* (Fontainebleau, Oct. 23, 1773); *Céphale et Procris, ou L'Amour conjugal* (Versailles, Dec. 30, 1773); *La Fausse Magie* (Paris, Feb. 1, 1775); *Les Mariages samnites* (3 acts, from the 1-act opera of 1768; Paris, June 12, 1776); *Amour pour amour* (Versailles, March 10, 1777); *Matroco* (Chantilly, Nov. 12, 1777); *Le Jugement de Midas* (Paris, March 28, 1778); *Les Fausses Apparences, ou L'Amant jaloux* (Versailles, Nov. 20, 1778); *Les Événements imprévus* (Versailles, Nov. 11, 1779); *Aucassin et Nicolette, ou Les Moeurs du bon vieux temps* (Versailles, Dec. 30, 1779); *Andromaque* (Paris, June 6, 1780); *Émilie* (Paris, Feb. 22, 1781); *La Double Épreuve, ou Colinette à la Cour* (Paris, Jan. 1, 1782); *Le Sage dans sa retraite* (The Hague, Sept. 19, 1782); *L'Embarras de richesses* (Nov. 26, 1782); *La Caravane du Caire* (Fontainebleau, Oct. 30, 1783); *Théodore et Paulin* (Versailles, March 5, 1784); *Richard Cœur de Lion* (his greatest masterpiece; Paris, Oct. 21, 1784); *Panurge dans l'isle des lanternes* (Paris, Jan. 25, 1785); *Amphitrion* (Versailles, March 15, 1786); *Les Méprises par ressemblance* (Fontainebleau, Nov. 7, 1786); *Le Comte d'Albert* (Fontainebleau, Nov. 13, 1786); *Le Prisonnier anglois* (Paris, Dec. 26, 1787; with alterations in 1793 as *Clarice et Belton);* *Le Rival confident* (Paris, June 26, 1788); *Raoul Barbe-Bleue* (Paris, March 2, 1789); *Aspasie* (Paris, March 17, 1789); *Pierre le grand* (Paris, Jan. 13, 1790); *Guillaume Tell* (Paris, April 9, 1791); *Cécile et Ermancé, ou Les Deux Couvents* (Paris, Jan. 16, 1792); *A Trompeur, trompeur et demi* (Paris, Sept. 24, 1792); *Joseph Barra* (Paris, June 5, 1794); *Denys le tyran, maître d'école à Corinthe* (Paris, Aug. 23, 1794); *La Rosière républicaine, ou La Fête de la vertu* (Paris, Sept. 3, 1794); *Callias, ou Nature et patrie* (Paris, Sept. 18, 1794); *Lisbeth* (Paris, Jan. 10, 1797); *Anacréon chez Polycrate* (Paris, Jan. 17, 1797); *Le Barbier de village, ou Le Revenant* (Paris, May 6, 1797); *Élisca, ou L'Amour maternel* (Paris, Jan. 1, 1799); *Le Casque et les colombes* (Paris, Nov. 7, 1801); *Delphis et Mopsa* (Paris, Feb. 15, 1803).

BIBLIOGRAPHY: Comte de Livry, *Recueil de lettres écrites à Grétry, ou à son sujet* (Paris, 1809); A. J. Grétry (the composer's nephew), *Grétry en famille* (Paris, 1815); Gerlache, *Essai sur Grétry* (Liège, 1821); F. van Hulst, *Grétry* (Liège, 1842); L. de Saegher, *Notice biographique sur André Grétry* (Brussels, 1869); E. Gregoir, *André E. M. Grétry* (1883); M. Brenet, *Grétry* (Paris, 1884); C. Gheude, *Grétry* (Liège, 1906); H. de Curzon, *Grétry* (Paris, 1907); E. Closson, *Grétry* (Turnhout, 1907); P. Long des Clavières, *La Jeunesse de Grétry et ses débuts à Paris* (Besançon, 1921); P. Long des Clavières, "Les Ancêtres de Grétry," *Revue Musicale*, IV, 3 (1923); O. G. Sonneck, "Grétry," *Scheurleer-Festschrift* (1925); H. Wichmann, *Grétry und das musikalische Theater in Frankreich* (Halle, 1929); Romain Rolland, "Grétry," *Musiciens d'autrefois* (Paris, 1908; 2nd ed., 1925; English transl., London, 1915); J. E. Bruyr, *Grétry* (Paris, 1931); P. Lasserre, *Essay en 'Philosophie du gout musical'* (Paris, 1931); J. Sauvenier, *André Grétry* (Brussels, 1934); J. de Froidcourt, *43 Lettres inédites de Grétry à A. Rousselin, 1806–12* (Liège, 1937); Gérard-Gailly, *Grétry à Honfleur* (Paris, 1938); S. Clercx, *Grétry* (Brussels, 1944); G. de Froidcourt, *Grétry, Rouget de Lisle et la Marseillaise* (Liège, 1945); *La Correspondance générale de Grétry* (Brussels, 1962).

Grevillius, Nils, Swedish conductor; b. Stockholm, March 7, 1893; d. Mariefred, Sweden, Aug. 15, 1970. He studied there at the Academy of Music (1905–11), receiving 1st prize for the violin and the Prix Marteau; from 1911–14 was leader of the Royal Opera orch.; conducted the Swedish ballet season in Paris in 1922–23; then returned to Stockholm to conduct the Radio Orchestra.

Grey, Madeleine, French soprano; b. Villaines-le-Juhel, Mayenne, June 11, 1896. She made her debut in Paris in 1919 in the first performance of Fauré's *Mirages;* thereafter she was identified with modern French music; was chosen to present French art songs at 3 international festivals (Venice, 1930; Siena, 1932; Florence, 1934); also toured South America. She abandoned her career in 1952.

Grider, Rufus, American Moravian musician and historian; b. Bethlehem, Pennsylvania, 1817; date and place of death unknown (sometime after 1873 he wandered away from home and was never heard from again). Raised in the exceedingly rich musical culture of the American Moravians, Grider was a flutist in the Bethlehem orchestra and a leading tenor; he was also a poet, artist, and antiquarian. His claim to remembrance stems from his unique and detailed portrayal of Moravian musical life in *Historical Notes on Music in Bethlehem, Pennyslvania, from 1741 to 1871* (Bethlehem, 1873; repr. as Moravian Music Foundation Publication No. 4, Winston-Salem, 1957).

Grieg, Edvard Hagerup, celebrated Norwegian composer; b. Bergen, June 15, 1843; d. there, Sept. 4, 1907. The original form of the name was Greig. His great-grandfather, Alexander Greig of Scotland, emigrated to Norway about 1765, and changed his name to Grieg (see J. Russell Greig, "Grieg and His Scottish Ancestry," in Hinrichsen's *Music Year Book,* 1952). Grieg received his first instruction in music from his mother, an amateur pianist. At the suggestion of the Norwegian violinist, Ole Bull, young Grieg was sent to the Leipzig Cons. (1858), where he studied piano with Plaidy and Wenzel; later with Moscheles; theory with E. F. Richter, Moritz Hauptmann, and Reinecke. He became immersed in the atmosphere of German Romanticism, with the esthetic legacy of Mendelssohn and Schumann; Grieg's early works are permeated with lyric moods related to these influences. In 1863, he went to Copenhagen, where he took a brief course of study with Niels Gade. In Copenhagen, he also met the young Norwegian composer, Rikard Nordraak, with whom he organized the Euterpe Society for the promotion of national Scandinavian music, in opposition to the German influences dominating Scandinavian music. The premature death of Nordraak at the age of 23 (1866) left Grieg alone to carry on the project. After traveling in Italy, he returned to Norway, where he opened a Norwegian Academy of Music (1867), and gave concerts of Norwegian music; he was also engaged as conductor of the Harmonic Society in Christiania (Oslo). In 1867 he married his cousin, the singer, **Nina Hagerup.** At that time he had already composed his 2 violin sonatas and the first set of his *Lyric Pieces* for piano, which used Norwegian motifs. On April 3, 1869, Grieg played the solo part in the world première of his piano concerto, which took place in Copenhagen. Thus at the age of 25, he established himself as a major composer of his time. In 1874 he wrote incidental music to Ibsen's *Peer Gynt;* the two orchestral suites arranged from this music became extremely popular. The Norwegian government granted him an annuity of 1600 crowns, which enabled him to devote most of his time to composition. Performances of his works were given in Germany with increasing frequency; soon his fame spread all over Europe. On May 3, 1888, he gave a concert of his works in London; he also prepared recitals of his songs with his wife. He revisited England frequently; he received the honorary degree of Mus. Doc. from Cambridge (1894) and Oxford (1906). Other honors were membership in the Swedish Academy (1872), the French Academy (1890), etc. Despite his successes, Grieg was of a retiring disposition, and spent most of his later years in his house at Troldhaugen, near Bergen, avoiding visitors and shunning public acclaim. However, he continued to compose at a steady rate. His death, of heart disease, was mourned by all Norway; he was given a state funeral and his remains were cremated, at his own request, and sealed in the side of a cliff projecting at the fjord at Troldhaugen. Grieg's importance as a composer lies in the strongly pronounced nationalism of his music; without resorting to literal quotation from Norwegian folksongs, he succeeded in recreating their melodic and rhythmic flavor. In his harmony, he remained well within the bounds of tradition; the lyric expressiveness of his best works and the contagious rhythm of his dance-like pieces imparted a charm and individuality which contributed to the lasting success of his art. His unassuming personality made friends for him among his colleagues; he was admired by Brahms and Tchaikovsky. The combination of lyricism and nationalism in Grieg's music led some critics to describe him as "the Chopin of the North." He excelled in miniatures, in which the perfection of form and the clarity of musical line are remarkable; the unifying purpose of Grieg's entire creative life is exemplified by his lyric pieces for piano. He composed 10 sets of these pieces in 34 years, between 1867 and 1901. His songs, which he wrote for his wife, are distinguished by the same blend of romantic and characteristically national inflections. In orchestral composition, Grieg limited himself to symphonic suites, and arrangements of his piano pieces; in chamber music, his 3 violin sonatas, a cello sonata, and a string quartet are examples of fine instrumental writing.

WORKS: FOR ORCH.: *In Autumn,* concert overture (op. 11, 1865); *Two Elegiac Melodies* for string orch. (op. 34, based on songs from op. 33; *The Wounded One* and *The Last Spring*); Concerto in A minor for Piano and Orch. (op. 16, 1868); *Norwegian Dances* (op. 35, 1881); *Holberg Suite* for string orch. (op. 40, 1884–85); *Peer Gynt Suite* no. 1 (op. 46, 1876; includes *Morning, Aase's Death, Anitra's Dance, In the Hall of the Mountain King); Two Melodies* for string orch. (op. 53, 1891; based on songs from op. 21 and op. 23: *Norwegian* and *First Meeting); Peer Gynt Suite* no. 2 (op. 55, 1876; includes *The Abduction and Ingrid's Lament, Arab Dance, Peer Gynt's Homecoming, Solveig's Song); Sigurd Jorsalfar Suite* (op. 56, 1872); *Two Norwegian Melodies* for string orch. (op. 63, 1894–95; based on melodies from op. 17: *In the Style of a Folksong* and *Cowkeeper's Tune and Peasant Dance); Symphonic Dances* (1898), *Evening in the Mountains* for oboe, horn, and strings (arranged from op. 68, no. 4; 1898); *At the Cradle* for string orch. (arranged from op. 68, no. 5; 1898); *Funeral March in Memory of Rikard Nordraak* for military band (arranged from the piano solo written in 1866); *Lyric Suite* (arranged from piano solos, op. 54, 1891; includes *Shepherd Boy, Norwegian March, Nocturne, March of the Dwarfs).* CHAMBER MUSIC: Sonata in F for Violin and Piano (op. 8, 1865); Sonata in G minor for Violin and Piano (op. 13, 1867); String Quartet in G minor (op. 27, 1877–78); Sonata in A minor for Cello and Piano (op. 36, 1883); Sonata in C minor for Violin and Piano (op. 45, 1886–87); String Quartet in F (2 movements only; 1892). CHORAL WORKS: *At a Southern Convent's Gate* (op. 20, 1871); 2 songs from *Sigurd Jorsalfar* (op. 22, 1870); *Album for Male Voices* (op. 30, 1877); *Landsighting* (op. 31, 1872); *Scenes from 'Olav Trygvason'* (op. 50, 1873); *Ave Maris Stella* (no opus number); *Four Psalms* (op. 74, 1906); he also wrote *The Bewitched One* for baritone with strings and 2 horns (op. 32, 1878); and the ballad, *Bergliot* for declamation and orch. (op. 42, 1870–71). He wrote the incidental music for Björnson's *Sigurd Jorsalfar* (Christiania, April 10, 1872) and Ibsen's *Peer Gynt* (Christiania, Feb. 24, 1876), from which the suites so named were taken. FOR PIANO: piano solos: 4 pieces (op. 1, 1862); *Poetic Tone-Pictures* (op. 3, 1863); *Humoresker* (op. 6, 1865); Sonata in E minor (op. 7, 1865); *Funeral March in Memory of Rikard Nordraak* (1866); 10 sets of *Lyric Pieces* (Book 1, op. 12, 1867; Book 2, op. 38, 1883; Book 3, op. 43, 1884; Book 4, op. 47, 1888; Book 5, op. 54, 1891; Book 6, op. 57, 1893; Book 7, op. 62, 1895; Book 8, op. 65, 1896; Book 9, op. 68, 1898; Book 10, op. 71, 1901; among the most famous individual numbers of the *Lyric Pieces* are: *Butterfly, Erotik*, and *To Spring* in Book 3; *March of the Dwarfs* in Book 5); *Norwegian Dances and Songs* (op. 17, 1870); *Scenes from Peasant Life* (op. 19, 1872); *Ballad in the Form of Variations on a Norwegian Folksong* (op. 24, 1875); *Album Leaves* (op. 28, 1864, 1874, 1876, 1878); *Improvisations on Norwegian Folksongs* (op. 29, 1878); *Holberg Suite* (op. 40, 1884); *Norwegian Folk Melodies* (op. 66, 1896); *Norwegian Peasant Dances* (op. 72, 1902); *Moods* (op. 73, 1906); *6 Norwegian Mountain Tunes* (no opus number); 3 piano pieces (no opus number; nos. 2 and 3 written in 1898 and 1891); arrangements for piano solo of a number of his songs and orchestral works; original piano duets: *Norwegian Dances for 4 Hands* (op. 35, 1881); *Valses-Caprices* (op. 37, 1883); 2nd piano parts to 4 piano sonatas by Mozart (1877). SONGS: 25 sets of songs to German and Norwegian words; of these, *I Love Thee* attained enormous popularity. An edition of his works, in 20 vols., is projected by the Edvard Grieg Committee, Oslo.

BIBLIOGRAPHY: E. Closson, *Grieg et la musique scandinave* (Paris, 1892); D. G. Mason, *From Grieg to Brahms* (N.Y., 1902); G. Schjelderup, *Edvard Grieg, ghans vaerker* (Copenhagen, 1903); H. T. Finck, *Edvard Grieg* (N.Y., 1905; considerably enlarged and publ. as *Grieg and His Music*, 1909; new ed., 1929); E. M. Lee, *Edvard Grieg* (London, 1908); G. Schjelderup and W. Niemann, *Edvard Grieg: Biographie und Würdigung seiner Werke* (Leipzig, 1908); R. H. Stein, *Grieg* (Berlin, 1921); M. Beyer, *Edvard Grieg: Breve til Frants Beyer 1872–1907* (Christiania, 1923); P. de Stoecklin, *Edvard Grieg* (Paris, 1926); J. Röntgen, *Grieg* (The Hague, 1930); E. von Zschinsky-Troxler, *Edvard Grieg: Briefe an die Verleger der Edition Peters 1866–1907* (Leipzig, 1932); Y. Rokseth, *Grieg* (Paris, 1933); D. Monrad Johansen, *Edvard Grieg* (Oslo, 1934; in English, Princeton, N.J., 1938); K. G. Fellerer, *Edvard Grieg* (Potsdam, 1942); G. Abraham, ed., *Grieg, a Symposium* (London, 1948); J. Horton, *Grieg* (London, 1950); K. Dale, "Grieg Discoveries," *Monthly Musical Record* (Dec. 1954); H. J. Hurum, *I Edvard Griegs verden* (Oslo, 1960).

Grieg, Nina Hagerup, Norwegian singer, wife of **Edvard Grieg;** b. near Bergen, Nov. 24, 1845; d. Copenhagen, Dec. 9, 1935. Her father, Herman Hagerup, was a brother of Grieg's mother. She studied singing with Helsted; she met Grieg in Copenhagen, and married him on June 11, 1867. Her interpretations of Grieg's songs elicited much praise from the critics.

Griend, Koos van de, Dutch composer; b. Kampen, near Zwolle, Dec. 11, 1905; d. Amsterdam, Jan. 12, 1950. He studied in Amsterdam and in Berlin. Returning to Amsterdam in 1933, he developed energetic activities as pianist, conductor, and music critic. He wrote 2 symphonies, a cello concerto, and 3 string quartets; quartet for 4 horns.

Griepenkerl, Friedrich Konrad, German music editor; b. Peine, Dec. 10, 1782; d. Brunswick, April 6, 1849. He taught esthetics at Hofwyl, Switzerland, then settled in Brunswick as professor at the Carolinum there. He published a *Lehrbuch der Aesthetik* (1827); edited (ably) Bach's instrumental works.

Griepenkerl, Wolfgang Robert, German music theorist, son of preceding; b. Hofwyl, May 4, 1810; d. Brunswick, Oct. 16, 1868. He studied philosophy and literature at Berlin Univ.; taught art history at the Carolinum, Brunswick (1839) and at the Brunswick Cadet School (1840–47). He wrote the tragedies *Robespierre* (which inspired Litolff's well-known overture) and *Girondistes*. He also published *Das Musikfest, oder die Beethovener* (a novel, 1838; 2nd ed., 1841); *Ritter Berlioz in Braunschweig* (1843); *Die Oper der Gegenwart* (1847); and papers in *Neue Zeitschrift für Musik*.

BIBLIOGRAPHY: O. Sievers, *Robert Griepenkerl* (Brunswick, 1879); Th. W. Werner, "Wolfgang Robert Griepenkerls Schriften über Musik," *Zeitschrift für Musikwissenschaft* II (1920).

Griesbach, John Henry, English composer; b. Windsor, June 20, 1798; d. London, Jan. 9, 1875. He was of German descent; he studied cello with his father, and played in the court band. His major work was an oratorio, *Belshazzar's Feast* (1835; revised and performed as *Daniel*, London, June 30, 1854); also wrote a number of overtures and cantatas. He was an amateur scientist and wrote several papers dealing with acoustics which remained in manuscript.

Griesbacher, Peter, German theorist and church music composer; b. Egglham, March 25, 1864; d. Regensburg, Jan. 28, 1933. He studied theology; was ordained priest in 1886; was instructor at the Franciscan church in Regensburg (from 1894); edited various publications for Catholic church music; wrote 40 Masses, secular cantatas, and songs (about 250 op. numbers). He began as a composer in the strict style of contrapuntal writing; his later works, in which he applied modern harmonies to Gregorian melodies, aroused considerable opposition. He published several manuals: *Lehrbuch des Kontrapunkts* (1910); *Kirchenmusikalische Stilistik und Formenlehre* (3 vols., 1912–13); *Glockenmusik* (1926).

BIBLIOGRAPHY: M. Tremmel, *Peter Griesbacher* (Passau, 1935).

Griffes, Charles Tomlinson, outstanding American composer; b. Elmira, N.Y., Sept. 17, 1884; d. New York, April 8, 1920. He studied piano with a local teacher, Mary S. Broughton; also took organ lessons. In 1903, he went to Berlin, where he was a pupil of Gottfried Galston (piano), Rüfer and Humperdinck (composition). To eke out his living, he gave private lessons; also played his own compositions in public recitals. In 1907, he returned to the U.S., and took a music teacher's job at the Hackley School for Boys at Tarrytown, N.Y.; at the same time he continued to study music by himself; he was fascinated by the exotic art of the French Impressionists, and investigated the potentialities of oriental scales. He also was strongly influenced by the Russian school, particularly Mussorgsky and Scriabin. A combination of natural talent and determination to acquire a high degree of craftsmanship elevated Griffes to the position of a foremost American composer in the Impressionist genre; despite changes of taste, his works retain an enduring place in American music.

WORKS: His best are *The White Peacock* for piano (1917; also for orch., Philadelphia, Stokowski conducting, Dec. 19, 1919) and the tone poem, *The Pleasure Dome of Kubla Khan,* after Coleridge (Boston Symph. Orch., Nov. 28, 1919); others are *The Kairn of Koridwen,* dance drama for 5 woodwinds, celesta, harp, and piano (N.Y., Feb. 10, 1917); *Shojo,* Japanese pantomimic drama for 4 woodwinds, 4 muted strings, harp, and percussion (1917); *Poem* for flute and orch. (N.Y., Nov. 16, 1919); *2 Sketches on Indian Themes* for string quartet (1922); for piano: *3 Tone Pictures (The Lake at Evening, The Vale of Dreams,* and *The Night Winds;* 1915); *Fantasy Pieces (Barcarolle, Notturno,* and *Scherzo;* 1915); *Roman Sketches (The White Peacock, Nightfall, The Fountain of Acqua Paola,* and *Clouds,* 1917); Sonata in F (1921); vocal works: *These Things Shall Be,* for unison chorus (1917); songs to German texts (*Auf geheimen Waldespfade, Auf dem Teich,* etc.); songs to English words: *The First Snowfall, The Half-ring Moon, Evening Song; Tone Images (La Fuite de la lune, Symphony in Yellow,* and *We'll to the Woods,* and *Gather May;* 1915); *2 Rondels (Come, love, across the sunlit land* and *This book of hours;* 1915); *3 Poems (In a Myrtle Shade, Waikiki,* and *Phantoms;* 1916); *5 Poems of Ancient China and Japan (So-Fei gathering flowers, Landscape, The Old Temple, Tears,* and *A Feast of Lanterns;* 1917); *3 Poems (The Lament of Ian the Proud, Thy Dark Eyes to Mine,* and *The Rose of the Night;* 1918); *An Old Song Re-sung* (1920).

BIBLIOGRAPHY: W. T. Upton, "The Songs of Charles T. Griffes," *Musical Quarterly* (July 1923); M. Bauer, "Charles T. Griffes as I Remember Him," *Musical Quarterly* (July 1943); E. M. Maisel, *Charles Tomlinson Griffes* (N.Y., 1943; repr. with new preface by D. K. Anderson, N.Y., 1972).

Griffis, Elliot, American pianist and composer; b. Boston, Jan. 28, 1893; d. Los Angeles, June 8, 1967. He studied at Yale School of Music with Horatio Parker and at the New England Cons. with Chadwick; held numerous educational posts as teacher of piano and theory; appeared in recitals; eventually settled in Los Angeles. His music is set in ingratiatingly romantic colors. He also publ. several volumes of verse.

WORKS: *Paul Bunyan, Colossus,* symph. poem (1926–34); *Fantastic Pursuit,* for strings (1941); *Port of Pleasure,* one-act opera (Los Angeles, June 29, 1963); semiclassical piano pieces.

Grignon, Ricard Lamote de. See **Lamote de Grignon, Ricard.**

Grigoriu, Theodor, Rumanian composer; b. Galatzi, July 25, 1926. He studied violin with Enacovici at the Bucharest Cons. and composition with Jora; then went to Moscow where he had lessons with Khatchaturian and Golubev (1954–55).

WORKS: 2 cantatas: *Cantată pentru 23 August* (1951) and *Odă orașului meu (Ode to My City,* 1963; revised 1971); *Sinfonia cantabile* (1950, revised 1966); *Dans tătar,* choreographic piece for orch. (1953); *Theatrical Suite in the Classical Style* for chamber orch. (1956); *Symphonic Variations,* on a melody by Anton Pann, for orch. (1955; Bucharest, Jan. 21, 1956); Concerto for Double Chamber Orch. and Solo Oboe (1957); *Vis cosmic (Cosmic Dream),* symph. poem with vocalizing tenor or electronic instrument (1959; Bucharest, Oct. 28, 1965); *Hommage to Enesco* for 4 groups of violins (1960); *Melodic Infinită* for chamber string orch. (1969); *Elegie pontică,* to verses by Ovid, for bass-baritone, female chorus and chamber orch. (Bucharest, June 24, 1969); String Quartet (1943); Piano Trio (1943); *Pe Argeș în sus (The River Arges Flows On),* suite for string quartet (1953); choral music; songs; film music.

Grimm, Carl Hugo, American organist and composer; b. Zanesville, Ohio, Oct. 31, 1890. He studied music with his father; subsequently held positions as organist in Cincinnati; taught composition at the Cincinnati Cons. (1907–31).

WORKS: *Erotic Poem* for orch. (1927; received a prize of the National Federation of Music Clubs); *Thanatopsis* for orch. (1928); *Abraham Lincoln,* "character portrait" for orch. (1930); *Montana,* symph. poem (Cincinnati, March 26, 1943); *An American Overture* (Cincinnati, Feb. 15, 1946); Trumpet Concerto (1948); Symph. in F minor (1950); *Pennsylvania Overture* (1954); *Gothic Mass* (1970); *Byzantine Suite* for 10 instruments (1930); *Little Serenade* for wind quintet (1934); Cello Sonata (1945); many anthems, songs, and organ pieces; also works for multiple flutes (ensembles of 4, 8 and 12 flutes).

Grimm, Friedrich Melchior (Baron von), German writer; b. Regensburg, Sept. 25, 1723; d. Gotha, Dec. 19, 1807. He went to Paris in 1750 and remained there till the Revolution, frequenting literary and musical circles and taking an active part in all controversies; his "Lettre sur Omphale" in the *Mercure de France,* 1752, took the side of Italian opera in the 'guerre des bouffons' but some years later he upheld Gluck against the Italian faction supporting Piccinni. He edited the *Correspondance littéraire, philosophique et critique,* which offers important data on French opera (standard ed. in 16 vols., Paris, 1877–82). He befriended the Mozarts on their first visit to Paris (see the many references to him in E. Anderson, *Letters of Mozart and His Family,* London, 1938). He also wrote a satire on J. Stamitz, *Le Petit Prophète de Boehmisch-Broda;* it is reproduced in English in O. Strunk's *Source Readings in Music History* (N.Y., 1950).

BIBLIOGRAPHY: Carlez, *Grimm et la musique de*

son temps (1872); Jullien, *La Musique et les philosophes* (1873); E. Schérer, *Melchior Grimm* (1887); E. Hirschberg, *Die Encyklopädisten und die französische Oper im 18. Jahrhundert* (1903); H. Kretzschmar, "Die *Correspondance littéraire* als musikgeschichtliche Quelle," *Jahrbuch Peters* (1903); P. Nettl, *Der kleine Prophète de Boehmisch-Broda* (Esslingen, 1951).

Grimm, Heinrich, German composer; b. Holzminden, c.1593; d. Brunswick, July 10, 1637. He studied theology at the Univ. of Helmstedt; in 1619, became rector of the Magdeburg town school; in 1631, when the town was destroyed, he fled with his family to Brunswick, where he became a cantor at the church of St. Catherine; subsequently at St. Andrea's church (1632–37). He was an exponent of the concerted style, with thorough-bass, at that time still a novel technique in Germany. His extant works include Masses, psalms, Passions, and several pedagogical works; published *Unterricht, wie ein Knabe nach der alten Guidonischen Art zu solmisieren leicht angeführt werden kann* (Magdeburg, 1624) and *Instrumentum Instrumentorum* (1629); prepared a combined edition of *Melopoeia seu melodiae condendae ratio* by Calvisius and *Pleiades Musicae* by Baryphonus (Magdeburg, 1630).
BIBLIOGRAPHY: B. Engelke, *Magdeburgische Musikgeschichte* (1914); H. Lorenzen, *Der Cantor Heinrich Grimm; sein Leben und seine Werke mit Beitrag zur Musikgeschichte Magdeburgs und Braunschweigs* (Hamburg, 1940).

Grimm, Julius Otto, German composer; b. Pernau, Latvia, March 6, 1827; d. Münster, Dec. 7, 1903. He studied philosophy at the Univ. of Dorpat; then lived in St. Petersburg; in 1851, he went to Leipzig, where he studied with Moscheles and Hauptmann; there he formed a close friendship with Brahms and Joachim. In 1855, he went to Göttingen; in 1860, obtained a position as conductor in Münster. During 40 years of his life there, he presented some 1500 orchestral works, ranging from Bach to the modern Russian school. He wrote a symphony (1874); a suite for string orch. in canon form; several cycles of songs, and albums of piano pieces.
BIBLIOGRAPHY: F. Ludwig, *Julius Otto Grimm* (Leipzig, 1925); *Brahms im Briefwechsel mit J. O. Grimm* (Berlin, 1912).

Grimm, Karl, German cellist; b. Hildburghausen, April 28, 1819; d. Freiburg, Jan. 9, 1888. He was for half a century the first cellist at the Wiesbaden Opera; composed many cello pieces, some of which attained considerable popularity.

Grimm, Karl Konstantin Ludwig, German harpist; b. Berlin, Feb. 17, 1820; d. there, May 23, 1882. He enjoyed a considerable reputation as a harp soloist; also wrote various pieces for his instrument.

Grinblat, Romuald, Soviet composer; b. Tver, April 11, 1930. He studied at the Latvian Cons. in Riga; after graduation in 1955 he devoted himself to composition and teaching. His works include 4 symphonies (1955,

1957, 1964, 1967); *Youth Overture* (1958); Piano Concerto (1963); Flute Concerto (1970); Piano Quintet (1954); Nocturne for 17 Strings (1966); a ballet, *Rigonda* (1959); a children's opera, *Barber's Daughter* (1972); piano pieces; a curious work for voices, *Exercises in Phonetics* (1969).

Grisar, Albert, Belgian dramatic composer; b. Antwerp (of German-Belgian parentage), Dec. 26, 1808; d. Asnières, near Paris, June 15, 1869. He studied for a short time (1830) with Reicha in Paris. Returning to Antwerp, he brought out his opera *Le Mariage impossible* (Brussels, March 4, 1833), and obtained a government subsidy for further study in Paris. On April 26, 1836 he produced *Sarah* at the Opéra-Comique; then *L'An mille* (June 23, 1837), *La Suisse à Trianon* (March 8, 1838), *Lady Melvil* (Nov. 15, 1838, with Flotow), *L'Eau merveilleuse* (Jan. 31, 1839, with Flotow), *Le Naufrage de la Méduse* (May 31, 1839, with Flotow and Pilati), *Les Travestissements* (Nov. 16, 1839), and *L'Opéra à la cour* (July 16, 1840, with Boieldieu, Jr.). In 1840 he went to Naples for further serious study under Mercadante; returning to Paris in 1848, he brought out *Gilles ravisseur* (Feb. 21, 1848), *Les Porcherons* (Jan. 12, 1850), *Bonsoir, M. Pantalon* (Feb. 19, 1851), *Le Carillonneur de Bruges* (Feb. 20, 1852), *Les Amours du diable* (March 11, 1853), *Le Chien du jardinier* (Jan. 16, 1855), *Voyage autour de ma chambre* (Aug. 12, 1855); *Le Joaillier de St. James* (revision of *Lady Melvil;* Feb. 17, 1862); *La Chatte merveilleuse* (March 18, 1862), *Bégaiements d'amour* (Dec. 8, 1864), and *Douze innocentes* (Oct. 19, 1865). He left, besides, 12 finished and unfinished operas; also dramatic scenes, over 50 *romances,* etc. His statue (by Brackeleer) was placed in the vestibule of the Antwerp Theater in 1870.
BIBLIOGRAPHY: A. Pougin, *Albert Grisar* (Paris, 1870).

Grisart, Charles Jean Baptiste, French composer; b. Paris, Sept. 29, 1837; d. Compiègne, March 11, 1904. He is known for his light operas, the most popular of which were: *La Quenouille de verre* (1873), *Les Trois Margots* (1877), *Le Pont d'Avignon* (1878), *Les Poupées de l'Infante* (1881), *Le Bossu* (1888), *Le Petit Bois* (1893), *Voilà le roi!* (1894). He also wrote many piano pieces, Masses, *mélodies,* etc., and a quantity of transcriptions.

Griselle, Thomas, American composer; b. Upper Sandusky, Ohio, Jan. 10, 1891; d. Hollywood, Dec. 27, 1955. He studied at the Cincinnati College of Music; later took courses in Europe with Nadia Boulanger and Arnold Schoenberg; toured as accompanist of Alice Nielsen and other singers; in 1928, won the ten thousand dollar prize of the Victor contest for American composers with his *Two American Sketches.* In 1939, settled in Hollywood. He wrote a number of semipopular pieces, often with humorous intent, such as *A Keyboard Symphony* for 6 pianos (Providence, March 27, 1928); *Tutti-Frutti* and *Czerny Pilots a Flying Saucer* for piano, etc.

Grisi, Giuditta, Italian mezzo-soprano; b. Milan, July 28, 1805; d. Robecco d'Oglio, near Cremona, May 1,

1840. She was a niece of the famous contralto, Josephina Grassini; a cousin of the dancer, Carlotta Grisi, and the elder sister of the celebrated soprano, **Giulia Grisi**. She studied at the Milan Cons.; made her 1st appearance in Vienna in 1823; afterward sang with success in Italy and in Paris at the Théâtre-Italien under Rossini's management; retired in 1834 on her marriage to Count Barni. Bellini wrote for her the part of Romeo in *I Capuleti ed i Montecchi* (Venice, March 11, 1830); her sister sang Juliet.

Grisi, Giulia, celebrated Italian soprano; b. Milan, July 28, 1811; d. Berlin, Nov. 29, 1869. She studied with her sister, **Giuditta Grisi** and with Filippo Celli and Pietro Guglielmi, son of the composer; made her first appearance at 17 as Emma in Rossini's *Zelmira;* won the admiration of Bellini, who wrote for her the part of Juliet in *I Capuleti ed i Montecchi* (Venice, March 11, 1830); she sang in Milan until 1832; dissatisfied with her contract and unable to break it legally, she fled to Paris, where she joined her sister at the Théâtre-Italien; she made her Paris debut in the title role of Rossini's *Semiramide* (Oct. 16, 1832); her success was phenomenal, and for the next 16 years she sang during the winter seasons at the Théâtre-Italien. She made her London debut in Rossini's *La gazza ladra* (April 8, 1834), and continued to visit London annually for 27 years. With Rubini, Tamburini, and Lablache, she appeared in Bellini's *I Puritani* and other operas; when the tenor Mario replaced Rubini, Grisi sang with him and Tamburini; she married Mario (her second husband) in 1844; toured the U.S. with him in 1854; retired in 1861, and lived mostly in London, making occasional visits to the continent; on one such visit to Berlin, she died of pneumonia.

Griswold, Putnam, American bass; b. Minneapolis, Dec. 23, 1875; d. New York, Feb. 26, 1914. He studied with A. Randegger in London, with Bouhy in Paris, Stockhausen in Frankfurt, and Emerich in Berlin; sang at the Berlin Opera in 1904; in 1904–05 toured the U.S. with Savage's company, appearing in the English version of *Parsifal;* from 1906–11 was a popular singer at the Berlin Opera; made his Metropolitan Opera debut on Nov. 23, 1911, in the role of Hagen in *Götterdämmerung*. He was identified with the bass parts in Wagner's works until his death; German critics pronounced him the greatest foreign interpreter of these roles, and he was twice decorated by the Kaiser.

Grocheo, Johannes de (active in Paris about 1280), author of the treatise *Theoria* (c.1300), important as a source of information on secular music of the Middle Ages. It is printed in the original Latin with German transl. by J. Wolf in *Sammelbände der Internationalen Musik-Gesellschaft* (1899–1900; vol. I, pp. 69–130); emendations were provided by H. Müller (op. cit., vol. IV, pp. 361–68).

BIBLIOGRAPHY: Ernst Rohloff, *Studien zum Musiktraktat des Johannes de Grocheo* (Leipzig, 1930); also J. A. Westrup, *Medieval Song,* in *New Oxford History of Music* (London, 1954; vol. II, pp. 223–29); J. E. Maddrell, "*Mensura* and the Rhythm of Medieval Monodic Song," *Current Musicology* 10 (1970); H. Vanderwerf, "Concerning the Measurability of Medi-

eval Music," ibid.; J. E. Maddrell, "Grocheo and the Measurability of Medieval Music," ibid. 11 (1971); E. Rohloff, *Die Quellenhandschriften zum Musiktraktat des Johannes de Grocheo* (Leipzig, 1972).

Grofé, Ferde (Ferdinand Rudolph von), American composer, pianist, and arranger; b. New York, March 27, 1892; d. Santa Monica, California, April 3, 1972. He attended N.Y. and California public schools; studied music with Pietro Floridia; then was engaged as viola player in the Los Angeles Symphony Orch., at the same time working as popular pianist and conductor in theaters and cafés; joined Paul Whiteman's band in 1920 as pianist and arranger; it was his scoring of Gershwin's *Rhapsody in Blue* (1924) that won him fame. In his own works, Grofé successfully applied jazz rhythms, interwoven with simple ballad-like tunes; his *Grand Canyon Suite* (Chicago, Nov. 22, 1931, Paul Whiteman conducting) has become very popular. Other light pieces in modern vein include *Broadway at Night, Mississippi Suite, Three Shades of Blue, Tabloid Suite* (N.Y., Jan. 25, 1933), *Symphony in Steel* (N.Y., Jan. 19, 1937), *Hollywood Suite, Wheels Suite, New England Suite, Metropolis, Aviation Suite, San Francisco Suite* for orch. (San Francisco, April 23, 1960); *Niagara Falls Suite* for orch. (Buffalo, Feb., 1961), *World's Fair Suite* for orch. (N.Y., April 22, 1964); *Virginia City: Requiem for a Ghost Town,* symph. poem (Virginia City, Nevada, Aug. 10, 1968).

Gröndahl, Launy, Danish conductor and composer; b. Ordrup, near Copenhagen, June 30, 1886; d. Copenhagen, Jan. 21, 1960. He studied violin with Anton Bloch and Axel Gade, and theory with Ludolf Nielsen; later took music courses in Paris, Italy, Vienna, and elsewhere. Returning to Denmark, he became president of the Society of Young Musicians; then was appointed conductor of the Danish State Radio Orch., giving his first concert on Oct. 28, 1919.

WORKS: Symphony (1919); Violin Concerto (1917); Trombone Concerto (1924); Bassoon Concerto (1943); 2 string quartets; Violin Sonata; numerous piano pieces and songs.

Groningen, Stefan van, Dutch pianist and pedagogue; b. Deventer, Holland, June 23, 1851; d. Laren, March 25, 1926. He studied with Kiel in Berlin; gave concerts as a pianist; taught in various music schools in The Hague, Utrecht, and Leiden. He wrote mostly piano music, also a piano quartet.

Groot, Cor de, Dutch pianist and composer; b. Amsterdam, July 7, 1914. He studied composition with Sem Dresden at the Amsterdam Cons.; in 1936 won the international piano contest in Vienna; then gave concerts in Europe and America and made numerous recordings. He taught piano in The Hague; also served as librarian and archivist in Hilversum.

WORKS: Piano Concerto (1931); *Concerto Classico* for piano and orch. (1932); 2-Piano Concerto (1939); 2-Oboe Concerto (1939); Piano Concertino (1939); Clarinet Concerto (1940); Flute Concerto (1940); Violin Concerto (1940); Divertimento for Orch. (1949); *Wilhelmus ouverture* (1950); *Minuten Concerto* for piano and orch. (1950); *Ouverture energico* (1951); *Capriccio* for piano and orch. (1955); *Variations Imaginaires* for piano left hand and orch. (1960–62); Concertino for Clarinet and Small Orch. (1971); *"Bis" (Evocation)* for piano and orch. (1972); String Quartet (1947); Serenade for Oboe and Bassoon (1949); *Apparition* for violin and piano (1960); *2 Figures* for oboe and piano (1968); *Solitude* for cello and piano (1968); *Invocation* for cello and piano (1974); Piano Sonatina (1940); *Cloches dans le matin* for 1 or 2 pianos (1972).

Grosbayne, Benjamin, American conductor; b. Boston, April 7, 1893; d. Brookline, Mass., Jan. 24, 1976. He studied at Harvard Univ. (B.A., 1917) and at the New England Cons.; conducting with Monteux and Weingartner; was engaged as violinist and conductor with various opera companies in the U.S.; from 1931–38 was head of the Music Dept. of Brooklyn College. He publ. *Techniques of Modern Orchestral Conducting* (Cambridge, Mass., 1956).

Grosheim, Georg Christoph, German composer; b. Kassel, July 1, 1764; d. there, Nov. 18, 1841. He played viola in the court orch. at Kassel; edited a music magazine *Euterpe* in 1797–98; wrote biographical articles on composers, and corresponded with Beethoven. He composed 2 operas, *Titania* (1792) and *Das heilige Kleeblatt* (1793); also set the Ten Commandments for voices. His autobiography was published by G. Heinrichs (1926).

Grosjean, Ernest, nephew of **Jean Romary Grosjean;** French organist and composer; b. Vagney, Dec. 18, 1844; d. Versailles, Dec. 28, 1936. He studied in Paris with Boëly and Stamaty; was organist at Verdun Cathedral from 1868–1916; then organist at St. Antoine, Versailles; from 1888–1914 was editor of the *Journal des Organistes.* He wrote many works for organ and a *Théorie et pratique de l'accompagnement du plainchant.*

Grosjean, Jean Romary, French organist and composer; b. Epinal, Jan. 12, 1815; d. St. Dié, Feb. 13, 1888. He was organist at the St. Dié Cathedral from 1839; he publ. a 2-vol. collection of organ works, *Album d'un organiste catholique,* which included some of his own compositions; also edited a complete collection of noëls and folksongs of Lorraine.

Grossmann, Ferdinand, Austrian conductor; b. Tulln, July 4, 1887; d. Vienna, Dec. 5, 1970. He studied music in Linz; later took a course in conducting with Weingartner in Vienna. In 1923 he founded a Volkskonservatorium in Vienna; in 1946 organized the Chamber Chorus of the Vienna Academy of Music and toured with it in Europe and America. He was also a composer; wrote a *German Mass* a cappella (1952) and some chamber music.

Grosvenor, Ralph L., American organist and teacher; b. Grosvenor's Corners, N.Y., Dec. 5, 1893. He studied organ with Huntington Woodman in N.Y., composition with Ernest Bloch. He served in World War I, and remained in France after service, taking lessons in organ with Poillot and Moissenet. Upon his return to the

U.S., he occupied various organ positions in and around New York; also took vocal lessons, and appeared as tenor in local opera companies. He wrote a number of sacred choruses and semipopular songs (*My Desire, Wishing,* etc.).

Grosz, Wilhelm (Will), Austrian composer; b. Vienna, Aug. 11, 1894; d. New York, Dec. 9, 1939. He studied composition with Franz Schreker in Vienna; then lived in Berlin (1928–33). In 1933 he went to London; in 1938 went to New York. He wrote an opera, *Sganarell,* after Molière (Dessau, Nov. 21, 1925); *Der arme Reinhold,* a "danced fable" (Berlin, Dec. 22, 1928); a modern musical comedy *Achtung, Aufnahme!* (Frankfurt, March 23, 1930); *Jazzband,* for violin and piano (1924); Violin Sonata (1925); a song cycle, *Liebeslieder.* As Will Grosz, he wrote light songs.

Grout, Donald Jay, eminent American musicologist; b. Rock Rapids, Iowa, Sept. 28, 1902. He studied philosophy at Syracuse Univ. (A.B., 1923) and musicology at Harvard Univ. (A.M., 1931; Ph.D., 1939). He studied piano in Boston, and gave a solo recital there in 1932. In the interim he went to Europe where he took a course in French music of the Baroque period in Strasbourg and history of opera in Vienna. In 1935–36 he was visiting lecturer in music history at Mills College, California; from 1936 to 1942 he was on the staff of the music dept. at Harvard Univ.; from 1942–45 at the Univ. of Texas in Austin; from 1945 to 1970 was prof. of musicology at Cornell Univ. He held a Guggenheim Foundation grant in 1951. He served as President of the American Musicological Society (1961–63); in 1966 became Curator of the Accademia Monteverdiana in New York. He is the author of the valuable publications, *A Short History of Opera* (2 vols., N.Y., 1948; revised ed., 1965); and *A History of Western Music* (N.Y., 1960; 2nd ed., 1972). He is a member of the Editorial Board of Grove's *Dictionary of Music and Musicians* (6th ed., 1979). In his honor a Festschrift was issued, W. W. Austin, ed. *New Looks at Italian Opera: Essays in Honor of Donald J. Grout* (Ithaca, N.Y., 1968).

Grove, Sir George, eminent English musicographer; b. London, Aug. 13, 1820; d. there, May 28, 1900. He studied civil engineering; graduated in 1839 from the institution of Civil Engineers, and worked in various shops in Glasgow, and then in Jamaica and Bermuda. He returned to England in 1846, and became interested in music; without abandoning his engineering profession he entered the Society of Arts, of which he was appointed secretary in 1850; this position placed him in contact with the organizers of the 1851 Exhibition; in 1852 he became secretary of the Crystal Palace. He then turned to literary work; was an editor of the *Dictionary of the Bible;* traveled to Palestine in 1858 and 1861 in connection with his research; in 1865 he became director of the Palestine Exploration Fund. In the meantime, he accumulated a private music library; began writing analytical programs for Crystal Palace concerts; these analyses, contributed by Grove during the period 1856–96, established a new standard of excellence in musical exegesis. Grove's enthusiasm for music led to many important associations;

with Arthur Sullivan he went to Vienna in 1867 in search of unknown music by Schubert, and discovered the score of Schubert's *Rosamunde*. In 1868, he became editor of *Macmillan's Magazine;* in 1878, he visited America; he received many honors for his literary and musical achievements, among them the D.C.L., Univ. of Durham (1875); LL.D., Univ. of Glasgow (1885). In 1883 he was knighted by Queen Victoria. When the Royal College of Music was formed in London (1882), Grove was appointed director, and retained this post until 1894. His chief work, which gave him enduring fame, was the monumental *Dictionary of Music and Musicians*, which Macmillan began to publ. in 1879. It was first planned in 2 vols., but as the material grew, it was expanded to 4 vols., with an appendix, its publication being completed in 1889. Grove himself contributed voluminous articles on his favorite composers, Beethoven, Schubert, and Mendelssohn; he gathered a distinguished group of specialists to write the assorted entries. The 2nd ed. of Grove's *Dictionary* (1904–10), in 5 vols., was edited by Fuller-Maitland; 3rd ed. (1927–28), by H. C. Colles; an American supplement, first publ. in 1920, edited by W. S. Pratt and C. H. N. Boyd, was expanded and republished in 1928; 4th edition, also edited by H. C. Colles, was publ. in 5 vols., with a supplementary volume, in 1940. Eric Blom was entrusted with the preparation of an entirely revised and greatly enlarged 5th ed., which was publ. in 9 vols. in 1954; it became the largest music reference book in the English language; Grove's original articles on Beethoven, Schubert, and Mendelssohn were publ. separately in 1951, since their bulk was out of proportion even in this edition; revised articles on these composers were included instead. A new, 6th edition, under the editorship of Stanley Sadie, in 20 volumes, numbering some 15,000 pages, containing about 22,500 articles and over 3,000 illustrations, was announced for publication for 1979. Grove further publ. *Beethoven and His Nine Symphonies* (1896; new ed., 1948); contributed prefaces to Otto Jahn's *Life of Mozart* and Novello's *Short History of Cheap Music;* also numerous articles to the musical press.

BIBLIOGRAPHY: C. L. Graves, *The Life and Letters of Sir George Grove* (London, 1904); C. L. Graves, "George Grove: a Centenary Study," *Music & Letters* (1920).

Grové, Stefans, South African composer; b. Bethlehem, Orange Free State, July 23, 1922. He studied piano with his mother and his uncle; later with Cameron Taylor at the South African College of Music; then took courses with W. H. Bell in Cape Town and with Piston at Harvard Univ. (1953–54). In 1956, he was appointed instructor at the Peabody Cons., Baltimore. Grové's music is distinguished by clarity of formal presentation and a free flow of melodic line; the contrapuntal structure is often complex, but it is invariably cast within clearly outlined harmonies.

WORKS: Clarinet Sonata (1947); String Trio (1948); *Elegy* for string orch. (Cape Town, July 9, 1948); Duo for Violin and Cello (1950); ballet, *Die Dieper Reg* (1950); Piano Trio (1952); Trio for Oboe, Clarinet, and Bassoon (1952); Quintet, for flute, oboe, viola, bass clarinet, and harp (1952); Flute Sonata (1955);

Sinfonia Concertante (Johannesburg, Oct. 23, 1956); Quartet for Flute, Oboe, Clarinet, and Bassoon (1956); Violin Concerto (1960).

Groven, Eivind, Norwegian composer and musicologist; b. Lårdal, Telemark, Oct. 8, 1901. He studied at the Oslo Cons. (1923–25) and later in Berlin. In 1932 he was appointed a consultant on folk music for the Norwegian Radio; collected about 1800 Norwegian folk tunes, several of which he used as thematic foundation for his own compositions. In 1965 he patented an electronic organ, with special attachments for the production of non-tempered intervals.

WORKS: the symph. poems *Renaissance* (1935), *Historiske syner* (*Historical Visions*, 1936), *Fjelltonar* (*Tunes from the Hills*, 1938), *Skjebner* (*The Fates*, 1938), and *Bryllup i skogen* (*Wedding in the Wood*, 1939); 2 symphonies: No. 1, *Innover viddene* (*Toward the Mountains*, 1937; revised 1951) and No. 2, *Midnattstimen* (*The Midnight Hour*, 1946); *Hjalarljod*, overture (1950); Piano Concerto (1950); *Symfoniske slåtter* (*Norwegian Folk Dances*), 2 sets: No. 1 (1956) and No. 2, *Faldafeykir* (1967). Vocal music: *Brudgommen* (*The Bridegroom*) for soprano, 2 altos, tenor, chorus and orch. (1928–31); *Naturens tempel* (*The Temple of Nature*) for chorus and orch. (1945); *Ivar Aasen*, suite for soprano, bass, chorus and orch. (1946); *Soga om ein by* (*The Story of a Town*) for soprano, tenor, bass, chorus and orch. (1956); *Margjit Hjukse* for chorus and hardanger fiddle (1963); *Draumkaede* for soprano, tenor, baritone, chorus and orch. (1965); *Ved foss og fjord* (*By Falls and Fjord*) for male chorus and orch. (1966); among his many songs for solo voice, most scored with piano and later rescored with orch., are: *Moen* (*The Heath*, 1926; orch. 1934); *Neslandskyrkja* (*The Nesland Church*, 1929; orch. 1942); *Moderens korstegn* (*The Mother's Sign of the Cross*, 1930; orch. 1942); *På hospitalet om natten* (*In the Hospital at Night*, 1930; orch. 1946) and *Høstsanger* (*The Autumn Song*, orch. 1946). Chamber music: *Solstemning* (*Sun Mood*) for solo flute, or flute and piano (1946); *Balladetone* for 2 hardanger fiddles (1962) and *Regnbogen* (*The Rainbow*) for 2 hardanger fiddles (1962). His many theoretical studies include *Naturskalaen* (*The Natural Scale*, Skein, 1927), *Temperering og renstemning* (*Temperament and Non-tempered Tuning*, dealing with a new system of piano tuning according to natural intervals, Oslo, 1948; English trans., 1970); *Eskimomelodier fra Alaska* (*Eskimo Melodies from Alaska*, Oslo, 1955).

Grovlez, Gabriel (Marie), French conductor, writer, and composer; b. Lille, April 4, 1879; d. Paris, Oct. 20, 1944. He studied at the Paris Cons. under Diémer, Lavignac, Gédalge, and Fauré; won 1st prize in piano there (1899); then taught piano at the Schola Cantorum (from 1908); appointed conductor at the Paris Opéra in 1914; also conducted the Chicago Opera Co. (1921–22 and 1925–26).

WORKS: the operas *La Princesse au jardin* (Monte Carlo, 1920), *Psyché*, and *Cœur de rubis* (Nice, 1922); an opéra-bouffe, *Le Marquis de Carabas* (1925); 2 ballets, *Maïmouna* (Paris Opéra, April 25, 1921) and *Le Vrai Arbre de Robinson* (Chicago, 1921); symph. poems, *Madrigal lyrique*, *La Vengeance des fleurs*, *Le*

Reposoir des amants; Dans le jardin, for soprano, women's chorus, and orch.; Violin Sonata; Cello Sonata; more than 50 songs, and many piano pieces, including *Recuerdos, Deux études, A Child's Garden, Nocturne, Le Royaume puéril, Deux impressions,* and the sets, *Almanach aux images* and *London Voluntaries;* was an editor of Rameau's works; edited the collection, *Les Plus Beaux Airs de l'opéra français* (in 8 vols., Paris, 1924); publ. a book *L'Initiation à l'orchestration* (Paris, 1944).

Grua, Carlo Luigi Pietro, Italian composer; b. Florence, c.1665; date of death unknown. He was in Dresden from 1691 to 1694, first as singer in the electoral chapel, then as assistant Kapellmeister; his opera, *Camillo generoso,* was produced in Dresden in 1693; he next went to the Palatine court at Düsseldorf as assistant Kappellmeister; his opera, *Telegono,* was given there during the 1697 Carnival; he remained in Düsseldorf for a number of years, then went to Venice, where he produced 2 operas: *Il pastor fido* (1721) and *Romolo e Tazio* (1722).

Grua, Carlo Pietro, Italian composer; b. c.1695; place of birth uncertain; d. Mannheim, 1773 (buried April 11, 1773). He may have been a son or relative of Carlo Luigi Pietro Grua. He was Kapellmeister at Mannheim from about 1734 until his death; during this time, wrote 2 operas, *Meride* (1742) and *La clemenza di Tito* (1748); also 5 oratorios and a *Miserere.*

Grua, Francesco de Paula (or **Paolo**), Italian composer, son of **Carlo Pietro Grua;** b. Mannheim, 1753 (baptized Feb. 1, 1753); d. Munich, July 5, 1833. He studied with Holzbauer at Mannheim, then went to Bologna, where he was a pupil of Padre Martini, and to Parma, where he studied with Traetta. Returning to Mannheim, he became a member of the electoral orch.; in 1778, accompanied the court to Munich; became court conductor there in 1784. He wrote one opera, *Telemaco,* given at the Munich Carnival in 1780; also much church music, including 31 orchestral Masses.

Gruber, Franz Xaver, Austrian composer and organist; b. Unterweizburg, Nov. 25, 1787; d. Hallein, near Salzburg, June 7, 1863. He acquired fame as the composer of the Christmas carol, *Stille Nacht, Heilige Nacht.* Of a poor family, Gruber had to do manual work as a youth, but managed to study organ; by dint of perseverance he obtained, at the age of 28, his first position as church organist and schoolmaster at Oberndorf. It was there, on Christmas Eve, 1818, that a young curate, Joseph Mohr, brought him a Christmas poem to be set to music, and Gruber wrote the celebrated song.
BIBLIOGRAPHY: K. Weinmann, *Stille Nacht, Heilige Nacht* (Regensburg, 1918); J. Mühlmann, *Franz Xaver Gruber* (Salzburg, 1966); A. Schmaus and L. Kriss-Rettenbeck, *Stille Nacht, Heilige Nacht* (Innsbruck, 1967).

Gruber, Georg, Austrian conductor; b. Vienna, July 27, 1904. He studied music at the Vienna Univ.; received his Ph.D. in 1928. In 1930, he became conduc-

tor of the famous Vienna Choir Boys, and toured with them throughout Europe, South America, and the U.S. He also arranged for his choir folksongs and choral works of the Renaissance period. In 1953 he was appointed prof. of music at the Rhodes Univ. in Grahamstown, South Africa.

Gruenberg, Eugene, Austrian-American violinist; b. Lemberg, Oct. 30, 1854; d. Boston, Nov. 11, 1928. He studied violin with Heissler and ensemble playing with Hellmesberger at the Vienna Cons.; took a course in composition with Bruckner. He went to Leipzig, where he played the violin in the Gewandhaus Orch. In 1891 he emigrated to America and taught at the New England Cons. He published *The Violinist's Manual* (N.Y., 1897; revised ed., 1919, as *Violin Teaching and Violin Studies,* with a preface by Fritz Kreisler). Gruenberg composed a symphony, a violin sonata, and wrote a cadenza for Brahms's Violin Concerto.

Gruenberg, Louis, eminent American composer; b. near Brest Litovsk, Poland, Aug. 3, 1884; d. Los Angeles, June 9, 1964. He was brought to the U.S. as an infant; studied piano with Adele Margulies in N.Y.; then went to Berlin, where he studied with Busoni (piano and composition); in 1912 made his debut as pianist with the Berlin Philh.; intermittently took courses at the Vienna Cons., where he also was a tutor. In 1919 he returned to the U.S. and devoted himself to composing. He was one of the organizers and active members of the League of Composers (1923); became a champion of modern music, and one of the earliest American composers to incorporate jazz rhythms in works of symphonic dimensions (*Daniel Jazz, Jazzettes,* etc.); from 1933–36 he taught composition at the Chicago Mus. College; then settled in Santa Monica, Calif.
WORKS: His opera *The Emperor Jones,* to O'Neill's play (Metropolitan Opera, N.Y., Jan. 7, 1933), attracted a great deal of attention by its dramatic effects and novel devices, particularly in the use of percussion; it received the David Bispham medal. OTHER STAGE WORKS: *The Witch of Brocken* (1912); *The Bride of the Gods* (1913); *Dumb Wife* (1921); *Jack and the Beanstalk* (libretto by John Erskine; N.Y., Nov. 19, 1931); *Queen Helena* (1936); *Green Mansions,* radio opera (CBS, Oct. 17, 1937); *Volpone,* opera (1945); *The Miracle of Flanders,* mystery play (1950); *Anthony and Cleopatra,* opera (1940–1960). FOR ORCH.: 5 symphonies (No. 1, 1919; rev. in 1929; won the five thousand dollar RCA Victor prize in 1930; performed by Koussevitzky and the Boston Symph., Feb. 10, 1934); Nos. 2, 3, 4, 5 (1942–48); *Vagabondia* (1920); *The Hill of Dreams,* symph. poem (won Flagler prize; N.Y., Oct. 23, 1921); *Jazz Suite* (Cincinnati, March 22, 1929); *The Enchanted Isle,* symph. poem (Worcester Festival, Oct. 3, 1929); *Nine Moods* (1929); *Music for an Imaginary Ballet,* 2 sets (1929; 1944); *Serenade to a Beauteous Lady* (Chicago, April 4, 1935); 2 piano concertos; Violin Concerto (Philadelphia Orch., Dec. 1, 1944, Heifetz soloist); *Americana,* suite for orch. (1945). VOCAL WORKS: *Daniel Jazz,* for tenor and 8 instruments (N.Y., Feb. 22, 1925); *Creation,* for baritone and 8 instruments (N.Y., Nov. 27, 1926); *Animals*

and *Insects,* for voice and piano; *Four Contrasting Songs; A Song of Faith,* spiritual rhapsody for speaker, voices, chorus, orch. and a dance group (1952–62), etc.; also published 4 vols. of Negro spirituals. CHAMBER MUSIC: Suite for Violin and Piano (1914); 2 violin sonatas (1912; 1919); *Indiscretions* for string quartet (1922); *Diversions* for string quartet (1930); 2 string quartets (1937; 1938); *Jazzettes* for violin and piano (1926); 2 piano quintets (1929; 1937); *Poem in Form of a Sonatina* for cello and piano (1925); *4 Whimsicalities* for string quartet (1923). PIANO WORKS: *Jazzberries, Polychromatics, Jazz Masks, 6 Jazz Epigrams, 3 Jazz Dances,* etc.

Gruhn, Nora, English soprano; b. London, March 6, 1908. She studied at the Royal College of Music. She has sung with the Cologne Opera (1930–31), at Covent Garden (1931–34), and at Sadler's Wells (1946–48). She has appeared as Gretel in *Hänsel and Gretel* some 400 times in England.

Grumiaux, Arthur, Belgian violinist; b. Villers-Perwin, March 21, 1921. He studied at the Brussels Cons. and with Enesco; received the Vieuxtemps Prize in 1939. Since 1945, he has been giving concerts in Europe and teaching at the Brussels Cons.

Grümmer, Paul, German cellist; b. Gera, Feb. 26, 1879; d. Zug, Switzerland, Oct. 30, 1965. He studied in Leipzig and Berlin; in 1899 went to London as cellist at Covent Garden and a member of the Jan Kubelik string quartet; in 1913, he joined the Adolf Busch quartet; from 1926–33 he taught at the Musikhochschule, Cologne; from 1933–40, prof. at the Musikhochschule in Berlin; from 1940–45, at the Vienna Music Academy; since 1945, living in retirement at Zürich. He has written pedagogic works for the cello and has edited Bach's unaccompanied cello suites.

Grün, Jakob, violinist and teacher; b. Budapest, March 13, 1837; d. Baden, near Vienna, Oct. 1, 1916. He was a pupil of J. Böhm in Vienna and M. Hauptmann in Leipzig; in 1858 he became a member of the Weimar court orch.; went to Vienna in 1868, as concertmaster at the court opera; from 1877 till his retirement in 1909 he was prof. at the Vienna Cons.

Grund, Friedrich Wilhelm, German conductor and composer; b. Hamburg, Oct. 7, 1791; d. there, Nov. 24, 1874. He was brought up in a musical family, his father having been a theater conductor. He studied cello, but after a brief concert career, devoted himself mainly to conducting. In 1819, he founded in Hamburg the "Gesellschaft der Freunde des religiösen Gesanges," which later became the Hamburg Singakademie. In 1828, was engaged to lead the newly established Philharmonic Concerts, a post he held until 1862. In 1867 he organized (with Karl Grädener) the Hamburg Tonkünstlerverein. He wrote several operas, which were not performed; a cantata *Die Auferstehung und Himmelfahrt Christi;* some chamber music (Octet for Wind Instruments and Piano; Quintet for Oboe, Clarinet, Horn, Bassoon, and Piano; *Trio de Salon,* for piano 4 hands and cello); many piano

pieces, which enjoyed considerable success and were praised by Schumann.

Grunenwald, Jean-Jacques, French organist and composer of Swiss parentage; b. at Cran-Gevrier, near Annecy, Feb. 2, 1911. He studied organ with Dupré at the Paris Cons.; received 1st prize in 1935; composition with Henri Busser, obtaining another 1st prize in 1937. From 1936 to 1945 he was assistant of Dupré at the St.-Sulpice in Paris; in 1956 appointed organist at St.-Pierre-de-Montrouge. He was prof. at the Schola Cantorum in Paris from 1956 to 1961, and from 1961 to 1966 on the faculty of the Cons. of Geneva. Through the years he played more than 1500 concerts, presenting the complete organ works of Bach and César Franck. He also became famous for the excellence of his masterly improvisations rivaling those of his teacher Marcel Dupré. His compositions include *Fêtes de la lumière* for orch. (1937); Piano Concerto (1940); *Concert d'été* for piano and string orch. (1944); lyric drama *Sardanapale,* after Byron (1945–50); numerous sacred choruses and organ and piano pieces.

BIBLIOGRAPHY: A. Machabey, *Portraits de 30 musiciens français* (Paris, 1949, pp. 93–96).

Grünfeld, Alfred, Austrian pianist and composer; b. Prague, July 4, 1852; d. Vienna, Jan. 4, 1924. He studied in Prague, and later at Kullak's Academy in Berlin; settled in Vienna in 1873, and established himself there as a popular concert pianist and teacher; he also made tours in other European countries, including Russia. He composed an operetta, *Der Lebemann* (Vienna, Jan. 16, 1903) and the comic opera, *Die Schönen von Fogaras* (Dresden, 1907); made brilliant arrangements for piano of waltzes by Johann Strauss; also publ. piano studies and various other pieces (*Spanish Serenade, Hungarian Fantasy, Barcarolle, Impromptu,* etc.).

Grünfeld, Heinrich, renowned cellist, brother of **Alfred Grünfeld;** b. Prague, April 21, 1855; d. Berlin, Aug. 26, 1931. He studied at the Prague Cons.; went to Berlin in 1876, and taught cello at Kullak's Academy; also played chamber music with X. Scharwenka and G. Hollander. He publ. a book of memoirs, *In Dur und Moll* (Berlin, 1924).

Grunn, John Homer, American pianist and composer; b. West Salem, Wisconsin, May 5, 1880; d. Los Angeles, June 6, 1944. He studied piano with E. Liebling in Chicago and then at Stern's Cons. in Berlin; taught piano at the Chicago Mus. College (1903–07), then was in Phoenix, Arizona; in 1910, he settled in Los Angeles as piano teacher. He became especially interested in Indian music, and wrote a number of pieces based on Indian motives: ballets *Xochitl* and *The Flower Goddess* (both on Aztec subjects); *Hopi Indian Dance* for orch.; *Zuni Indian Suite* for orch.; many songs *(From Desert and Pueblo,* etc.).

Grünner-Hegge, Odd, Norwegian pianist, conductor and composer; b. Oslo, Sept. 23, 1899, d. there, May 11, 1973. He studied piano and composition in Oslo; then took courses in conducting with Weingartner. He was conductor of the Olso Philharmonic (1931–61) and of the Norwegian Opera there (1932–61); from 1923 to 1964 was a member of the board of the Society of Norwegian Composers (1923–64). He composed a Violin Sonata (1915); Piano Trio (1918, revised 1959) and piano pieces.

Grunsky, Karl, German music critic; b. Schornbach, March 5, 1871; d. Vaihingen, near Stuttgart, Aug. 2, 1943. He studied political science at the Univ. of Stuttgart; obtained his Ph.D. in 1893, and began a career as political journalist; also studied music; wrote music criticisms in Stuttgart and Munich papers.
WRITINGS: *Musikgeschichte des 19. Jahrhunderts* (Leipzig, 1902; 4th ed., in 2 vols., 1923); *Musikgeschichte des 17. Jahrhunderts* (Leipzig, 1905; 3rd ed., 1925); *Musikgeschichte des 18. Jahrhunderts* (Leipzig, 1905; 2nd ed., 1914); *Musikästhetik* (Leipzig, 1907; 4th ed., 1923); *Anton Bruckner* (Stuttgart, 1922); *Franz Liszt* (Leipzig, 1925); *Hugo Wolf* (Leipzig, 1928); *Der Kampf um deutsche Musik* (Stuttgart, 1933); *Richard Wagner* (Stuttgart, 1933); *Volkstum und Musik* (Esslingen, 1934). He publ. transcriptions for 2 pianos, 8 hands, of all the Bruckner symphonies; wrote program notes for the Bayreuth Festivals (1924); commentaries to performances of Bruckner's works, etc.; also *Die Technik des Klavierauszuges, entwickelt am dritten Akt von Wagners Tristan* (Leipzig, 1911; contains technical discussion of arranging).

Grunwald, Hugo, German-American pianist and teacher; b. Stuttgart, March 17, 1869; d. New York, Oct. 2, 1956. He studied music at the Stuttgart Cons.; emigrated in 1893 to the U.S., where he taught at the N.Y. College of Music. He was one of the founders, in 1905, of the Bohemian Club of New York.

Gruppe, Paulo Mesdag, American cellist; b. Rochester, N.Y., Sept. 1, 1891. He studied at The Hague Cons., then in Paris with J. Salomon; won a scholarship at the Paris Cons., where he studied with Casals; made his debut at The Hague in 1907, then toured Europe; in 1909 made his 1st appearance in the U.S.; was a member of the Letz Quartet and the Tollefsen Trio; in 1953 lived in New Haven; then in Mexico City. He publ. a book, *A Reasonable and Practical Approach to the Cello* (Univ. of Illinois, Urbana, Ill., 1964).

Grützmacher, Friedrich (Wihelm Ludwig), renowned German cellist; b. Dessau, March 1, 1832; d. Dresden, Feb. 23, 1903. He received his musical training from his father, a chamber musician at Dessau; at the age of 16, he went to Leipzig and produced such a fine impression that Ferdinand David secured for him the post of first cellist of the Gewandhaus Orch. (1849). In 1860, he went to Dresden, where he remained for more than 40 years, until his death, acting as teacher and chamber music player. Among his pupils were Hugo Becker and several other well known cellists. He wrote a cello concerto; *Hohe Schule des Violoncellspiels* (Leipzig, 1891); several books of cello studies, and numerous arrangements for cello of works by classical composers; also edited cello works by Beethoven, Mendelssohn, Chopin, and Schumann. His brother, **Leopold Grützmacher** (b. Dessau, Sept. 4,

1835; d. Weimar, Feb. 26, 1900), was also a cellist; he studied in Dessau, and later joined the Gewandhaus Orch. in Leipzig; after occupying various posts in theater orchestras, he settled in Weimar as teacher at the court chapel. He wrote 2 cello concertos and a number of salon pieces for his instrument. Leopold's son, **Friedrich** (b. Meiningen, July 20, 1866; d. Cologne, July 25, 1919), carried on the family tradition of cello playing; was a pupil of his father as well as of his uncle; was a member of various theater orchestras in Budapest and elsewhere; finally settled in Cologne as teacher at the Cons. there. He publ. a number of valuable cello collections and transcriptions.

Guadagni, Gaetano, famous male contralto; b. Lodi, c.1725; d. Padua, Nov., 1792. He began his career in Parma (1747); in 1748, he went to London, where he attracted the attention of Handel, who gave him contralto parts in *Messiah* and *Samson;* after many successful appearances in London, he sang in Dublin (1751–52); then went to Paris (1754) and to Lisbon (1755), where he studied with Gizziello. He then returned to Italy; in 1762, Gluck secured an engagement for him in Vienna to sing Orfeo in Gluck's opera. In 1769, Guadagni was again in London. In 1770 he sang in Munich; in 1772, he appeared in Venice; in 1776, he was summoned by Frederick the Great to Potsdam, receiving great acclaim; in 1777, he settled in Padua, where he continued to sing at churches. He was not only a fine singer but an excellent actor; also wrote various arias, one of which, *Pensa a serbarmi,* is preserved in the Bologna library.

Guadagnini, family of famous violin makers of Piacenza, Italy. **Lorenzo** (1695–1745) used the label "Laurentius Guadagnini, alumnus Antonius Stradivarius," and he may have studied with Stradivarius in Cremona shortly before the latter's death in 1737; certainly he followed Stradivarius's models in his violin making. Lorenzo's son, **Giovanni Battista** (b. Cremona, 1711; d. Turin, Sept. 18, 1786), received his training presumably from his father, and may have been with him at the shop of Stradivarius; he followed his father from Cremona to Piacenza in 1737; worked in Milan (1749–58); was in Parma (1759–71); then settled in Turin. His violins are regarded as the finest of the Guadagninis. His two sons, **Giuseppe** (1736–1805) and **Gaetano** (1745–1817), continued the family tradition and manufactured some good instruments, but failed to approach the excellence of their father's creations. Violin making remained the family's occupation through four more generations in Turin; the last representative, **Paolo Guadagnini,** perished in the torpedoing of an Italian ship, on Dec. 28, 1942.
BIBLIOGRAPHY: W. L. von Lütgendorff, *Die Geigen- und Lautenmacher vom Mittelalter bis zur Gegenwart* (Frankfurt, 1904); E. N. Doring, *The Guadagnini Family of Violin Makers* (Chicago, 1949).

Gualdo, Giovanni (John), Italian musician and wine merchant. He arrived in Philadelphia from London in 1767 and opened a store there; among other things, he sold instruments, taught violin, flute, guitar, and other instruments; also arranged music; presented concerts; the first of these, given in Philadelphia on Nov. 16,

1769, was devoted largely to Gualdo's own compositions, and may well be regarded as the earliest "composer's concert" in America. He died insane at the Pennsylvania hospital, Philadelphia, Dec. 20, 1771. His *6 easy evening entertainments for 2 mandolins or 2 violins with a thorough bass for the harpsichord or violincello* are in MS in the Library of Congress, Washington, D.C.; the printed op. 2, *6 Sonates for 2 German flutes with a thorough bass* (his name appears here as **Giovanni Gualdo da Vandero**) is in the British Museum. Copies of both sets are owned by the N.Y. Public Library.
BIBLIOGRAPHY: O. G. Sonneck, *Early Concert-Life in America* (Leipzig, 1907; pp. 70–74).

Guami, Francesco, Italian musician, brother of **Gioseffo Guami;** b. Lucca, c.1544; d. there, Jan. 30, 1602. He was trombonist at the court chapel in Munich (1568–80), and maestro di cappella at Baden-Baden (1580–88), at Venice (1593), and at Lucca (1598–1601). He wrote madrigals on the Venetian model, and some church music.
BIBLIOGRAPHY: L. Nerici, *Storia della Musica in Lucca* (1879).

Guami, Gioseffo (Giuseppe), Italian organist and composer; brother of **Francesco Guami;** b. Lucca, c.1540; d. there, 1612. He was organist at the court in Munich (1568–79), maestro di cappella at the court in Genoa (1585). From 1588–91 he was first organist at San Marco in Venice (while Giovanni Gabrieli was second organist); in 1591 he returned to Lucca as church organist. His surviving compositions include madrigals, motets, and toccatas; in his madrigals, he followed the Venetian school. Some of his Masses are reprinted in F. Commer's *Musica Sacra* (vols. 17 and 18); a toccata is included in L. Torchi's *L'Arte Musicale in Italia* (vol. 3).
BIBLIOGRAPHY: L. Nerici, *Storia della Musica in Lucca* (1879); G. Benvenuti (editor), *Istituzioni e Monumenti dell'Arte Musicale Italiana* vol. 1 (1931).

Guarino, Carmine, Italian composer; b. Rovigo, Oct. 1, 1893; d. Genoa, June 5, 1965. He studied violin and composition at the Cons. of Naples. His first opera *Madama di Challant,* set in a Verdian tradition, was produced there on March 9, 1927, attracting favorable comments. He was also the composer of the first Italian radio opera, *Cuore di Wanda* (Radio Italiano, Dec. 20, 1931). Other works for the stage comprise an operetta *Gaby* (San Remo, March 20, 1924); a musical fable, *Tabarano alla Corte di Nonesiste* (1931); one-act opera *Balilla* (Rome, March 7, 1935); one-act opera *Sogno di un mattino d'autunno* (Cluj, Rumania, March 30, 1936); and a ballet *El Samet, il silenzioso* (1958).

Guarneri, famous family violin makers in Cremona. The Italian form of the name was Guarnieri; Guarneri was derived from the Latin spelling, Guarnerius; the labels invariably used the Latin form. **Andrea,** head of the family (b. Cremona, c.1625; d. there, Dec. 7, 1698), was a pupil of Nicolo Amati; he lived in Amati's house from 1641 on; in 1653, after his marriage, he moved to his own house in Cremona and began making his own

violins, labeling them as 'Alumnus' of Amati and, after 1655, 'ex alumnis,' often with the additional words of 'sub titolo Sanctae Theresiae.' Andrea's son **Pietro Giovanni,** known as **Peter of Mantua** (b. Cremona, Feb. 18, 1655; d. Mantua, March 26, 1720), worked first at Cremona; then went to Mantua, where he settled; he also used the device 'sub titolo Sanctae Theresiae.' Another son of Andrea, **Giuseppe** (b. Cremona, Nov. 25, 1666; d. there, c.1740), worked in his father's shop, which he eventually inherited; in his own manufactures, he departed from his father's model and followed the models of Stradivarius. Giuseppe's son, **Pietro** (b. Cremona, April 14, 1695; d. Venice, April 7, 1762), became known as **Peter of Venice;** he settled in Venice in 1725, and adopted some features of the Venetian masters, Montagnana and Serafin. **Giuseppe Antonio,** known as **Giuseppe del Gesù,** from the initials I H S often appearing on his labels (b. Cremona, Aug. 21, 1698; d. there, Oct. 17, 1744), was a son of Giuseppe. He became the most celebrated member of the family; some of his instruments bear the label 'Joseph Guarnerius Andreae Nepos Cremonae' which establishes his lineage as a grandson of Andrea. His violins are greatly prized; only Stradivarius excelled him in the perfection of instrumental craftsmanship; he experimented with a variety of wood materials, and also made changes in the shapes of his instruments during different periods of his work. Paganini used one of his instruments.
BIBLIOGRAPHY: G. de Piccolellis, *Liutai antichi e moderni, genealogia degli Amati et dei Guarnieri* (Florence, 1886); Lütgendorff, *Die Geigen- und Lautenmacher vom Mittelalter bis zur Gegenwart* (Frankfurt, 1904; 4th ed., 1922, in dictionary form); H. Petherick, *Joseph Guarnerius, His Work and His Master* (London, 1906); A. Pougin, *Une Famille de grands luthiers italiens;* H. Wenstenberg, *Joseph Guarnerius del Gesù Abbildungen und Beschreibungen seiner Instrumente aus seinen drei Perioden* (Berlin, 1921); W. H. Hill, *Violin Makers of the Guarneri Family, 1626–1762: Their Life and Work* (London, 1931).

Guarnieri, Camargo Mozart, outstanding Brazilian composer; b. Tiété, state of São Paulo, Feb. 1, 1907. He studied piano and composition in São Paulo before going to Paris in 1938, where he took a course in composition with Charles Koechlin and conducting with Rühlmann. In 1942 and 1946 he visited the U.S. as conductor of his own works. His music is permeated with "Brasilidad," a syndrome that is Brazilian in its melody and rhythm; his *Dansa brasileira* is typical in its national quality.
WORKS: 4 symphonies (1944, 1946, 1952, 1963); 5 piano concertos (1936, 1946, 1964, 1967, 1970); 2 violin concertos (1940, 1953); *Overture concertante* (1943); *Dansa brasileira* for orch. (São Paulo, March 7, 1941; originally for piano, 1931); *Dansa negra* for orch. (1947); several symphonic suites; *Chôro* for violin and orch. (1951); *Chôro* for cello and orch. (1961); 3 string quartets, 6 violin sonatas, many songs and solo piano pieces.

Guastavino, Carlos, Argentinian composer; b. Santa Fé, Argentina, April 5, 1912. He studied chemistry; then turned to music, and took a course in composition with Athos Palma. He cultivates miniature forms, mostly for piano; of these, the suite *10 Cantilenas argentinas* (1958) and *Las presencias* radiate a certain melorhythmic charm. He also wrote choruses on Argentinian themes; many songs.

Guba, Vladimir, Ukrainian composer; b. Kiev, Dec. 22, 1938. He studied at the Kiev Cons. with Liatoshinsky; became interested in modern techniques of composition; applied the 12-tone method in his piano pieces *Deformation* and *Echo* (1961); also wrote a series of 30 piano pieces, *In the World of Childhood,* and a cycle of 24 piano pieces, *Sonorous Exhibits.*

Gudehus, Heinrich, German tenor; b. Altenhagen, near Celle, March 30, 1845; d. Dresden, Oct. 9, 1909. He first studied organ, and also taught school; then took up singing; made his debut in Berlin in Spohr's *Jessonda* (Jan. 7, 1871). After several engagements in various German towns, he sang Parsifal in Bayreuth (July 28, 1882) with excellent success; was with the Dresden Opera from 1880–90; appeared in London (1884) in Wagnerian roles; was with the German Opera in N.Y. (1890–91); then returned to Germany.

Gudmel, Claude. See **Goudimel, Claude.**

Gudmundsen-Holmgreen, Pelle, Danish composer; b. Copenhagen, Nov. 21, 1932. He studied theory and composition with Finn Höffding and Svend Westergaard at the Royal Danish Cons. in Copenhagen (1953–58); served as stage manager of the Royal Theater there (1959–64); taught composition at the Jutland Academy of Music in Aarhus (1967–73). He followed serial techniques; then experimented with "new simplicity" achieved through persistent repetition of notes and patterns; employed optical notation, in which the distance between notes in a score equals the "time span" between the playing of those notes.
WORKS: *Ouverture* for strings (1955); *Improvisations* for 10 instruments (1960); *Chronos* for 22 instrumentalists (1962); *Collegium Musicum Concerto* for chamber orch. (1964); *Mester Jakob (Frère Jacques)* for chamber orch. (1964); *Reprises (Recapitulations)* for 15 instrumentalists (1965); Symphony (1962–65; Danish Radio, Jan. 11, 1968); *5 Pieces* for orch. (1966); *Je ne me tairai jamais, jamais!* for 12 voices and 9 instruments (1966); *Repriser (Rerecapitulations)* for 13 instruments (1967); *Variations for Aunt Rix* for chamber orch. (1968); *Stykke for Stykke (Piece by Piece)* for chamber orch. (1968); *3 Movements* for string orch. and cowbells (1968); *Tricolore IV* for orch. (Copenhagen, Sept. 11, 1969; 3 previous *Tricolores* are unfinished); *5 Movements* for concert band (1969); *Catalogue and Coda* for concert band (1969); *Prelude and Fugue* for brass band (1969); *Spejl II (Mirror II)* for orch. (Copenhagen, Feb. 24, 1974); *Antiphony* for orch. (1974–77); 4 string quartets (1958; 1959; 1960; 1967); *In terra pax* for clarinet, piano and 2 percussionists (1961); *Canon* for 9 instruments ad lib. (1967); *Plateaux pour deux* for cello and percussion (1970); *Terrace,* in 6 stages, for wind quintet (1970); *Solo* for electric guitar (1972); *Spejl I* for violins and tape (1971–73); Septet (1975); *The Old Man* for 2 flutes, harp, viola and cello (1976); *Ritual Dances* for 6 per-

cussionists, or 5 percussionists and electric guitar (1976); Variations for Piano (1959); *Udstillingsbilleder (Pictures at an Exhibition)* for piano (1968); *Spejl III* for organ (1974); *5 Songs* for soprano, flute, violin and cello (1958); *3 Songs to Texts from Politiken* (a Danish newspaper) for contralto, violin, viola, cello, guitar and percussion (1967); *Songs Without* for mezzo-soprano and piano (1976); a cappella choruses, including *Examples* (1975).

Gueden, Hilde, Austrian soprano; b. Vienna, Sept. 15, 1917. Both her parents were musicians. She made her debut in operetta at the age of 16; in 1939 the family moved to Switzerland; in 1941 she sang Zerlina in Munich; in 1942, made her debut in Rome. In 1947 Gueden became a member of the Vienna State Opera; also appeared at La Scala, Milan. She made her American debut at the Metropolitan Opera in N.Y., on Nov. 15, 1951, as Gilda.

Guédron, Pierre, French composer; b. Châteaudun, 1565; d. Paris, 1621. He was a choirboy in the chapel of Cardinal de Guise and later sang in the royal chapel (1590). In 1601 he was appointed composer of the King's Music. He wrote ballets for the court, which included solo songs. Some of his airs are included in *Airs de Cour* (1615–18), and other contemporary collections. He is regarded as a precursor of Lully in the creation of French ballet music.
BIBLIOGRAPHY: H. Quittard, "L'Air de cour: Pierre Guédron," *Revue Musicale* (1905); H. Prunières, *Le Ballet de cour en France avant Benserade et Lully* (Paris, 1914); L. de la Laurencie, "Un Musicien dramatique du XVIIᵉ siècle français; Pierre Guédron," *Rivista Musicale Italiana* (1922).

Guénin, (Marie) Alexandre, French violinist and composer; b. Maubeuge, Feb. 20, 1744; d. Etampes, Jan. 22, 1835. He showed a precocious talent, and was sent to Paris for study with Gaviniès (violin) and Gossec (composition). In 1771 he joined the orchestra of the Paris Opéra; later was active as conductor in the Paris society called Concert Spirituel; taught at the École Royale de Chant. Several works were publ. in his lifetime: 6 symphonies; 6 violin duos; 6 string trios.
BIBLIOGRAPHY: L. de la Laurencie, *L'École française du violon* (Paris, 1922).

Guenther, Felix, pianist and writer on music; b. Trautenau, Austria, Dec. 5, 1886; d. New York, May 6, 1951. He studied at the Vienna Cons.; then at the Univ. of Berlin, obtaining his Ph.D. there in 1913. He emigrated to the U.S. in 1937; was connected with various music publishers in N.Y.; made arrangements and edited classical anthologies. He publ. *Weingartner* (Berlin, 1918), *Schuberts Lied* (Stuttgart, 1928), and *Mein Freund Schubert* (Hamburg, 1928).

Guéranger, Dom Prosper Louis Pascal, French ecclesiastic scholar; b. Sable-sur-Sarthe, April 4, 1805; d. Solesmes, Jan. 30, 1875. As abbot of the Benedictine monastery at Solesmes, his research and writings gave the impetus to and laid the foundations for scholarly investigations leading to the restoration of Gregorian melodies. Dom Guéranger and the Benedictines of Solesmes played a role of prime importance in the accomplishment of this work. He wrote *Institutions liturgiques* (3 vols., 1840–53; 2nd ed., 4 vols., 1878–85); *L'Année liturgique* (15 parts, 1840–1901; continued by Fromage); *Ste. Cécile et la Société Romaine* (1873; 8th ed., 1898).

BIBLIOGRAPHY: G. Guépin, *Prosper Guéranger* (Le Mans, 1876); *Bibliographie des Bénédictins de la Congrégation de France* (Solesmes, 1889); Chamard, *Guéranger et l'abbé Bernier* (Angers, 1901); P. Delatte, *Dom Guéranger, abbé de Solesmes* (2 vols., Paris, 1909).

Guerra-Peixe, César, Brazilian composer; b. Petropolis, March 18, 1914. He studied composition with H. J. Koellreuther; played violin in theater orchestras; arranged music for radio. As a composer, he plunged headlong into the torrent of dodecaphony, but about 1949 changed his orientation and returned to his Brazilian roots, nurtured by melorhythmic folksong resources. He wrote 2 symphonies (1946, 1960); pieces for guitar; miscellaneous chamber music.

BIBLIOGRAPHY: Vasco Mariz, "César Guerra-Peixe," in the compendium *Música brasileña contemporánea* (Rosario, Argentina, 1952).

Guerrero, Francisco, Spanish composer; b. Seville, 1528 (probably on St. Francis Day, Oct. 4); d. there, Nov. 8, 1599. He was a pupil of his brother, **Pedro,** and for a short time of Morales. In 1545, he became maestro di cappella of Jaén cathedral; in 1548, he went to Seville as cantor at the cathedral there. In 1554, he was offered a similar post at the cathedral of Malaga, but declined it. In 1556, he was in Lisbon; in 1567, in Cordova; in 1570, in Santander; in 1574 he went to Rome; in 1588, he was in Venice, whence he undertook a pilgrimage to Palestine. His account of his journey, *El viaje de Jerusalem que hizo Francisco Guerrero,* was publ. in 1611, and went through numerous editions. As a composer he was greatly appreciated by his contemporaries but the comparisons with Morales or Victoria overestimate his importance.

WORKS: *Sacrae cantiones vulgo moteta* (1555); *Psalmorum, Liber I, accedit Missa defunctorum* (1559; 2nd ed., with Italian title, 1584); *Canticum beatae Mariae quod Magnificat nuncupatur, per octo musicae modos variatum* (1563); *Liber I missarum* (1566; contains 9 Masses for 4–5 voices and 3 motets for 4–8 voices); *Motteta* (1570); *Missarum Liber II* (1582; contains 7 Masses and a *Missa pro defunctis);* *Liber vesperarum* (1584; includes 7 psalms, 24 hymns, 8 Magnificats, Te Deum, etc.); *Passio . . . secundum Matthaeum et Joannem more Hispano* (1585); *Canciones y villanescas espirituales* (1589); *Mottecta* (1589); *Missa Saeculorum Amen* (1597), etc. Reprints have been made by Eslava (2 *Passiones)* in *Lira sacrohispana* and by Pedrell in *Hispaniae schola musica sacra* (in vol. II: *Magnificat, Officium defunctorum,* Passions, antiphonals, etc.; in vol. VI: a *Falso bordone).* The *Libro de música para vihuela, intitulado Orphénica Lyra* of Miguel de Fuenllana contains some works by Guerrero arranged for vihuela. Two vols. of Guerrero's *Opera omnia* (unfinished), ed. by V. Garcia and M. Q. Garalda (1955–57), containing *Canciones y*

villanescas espirituales, comprise vols. 16 and 19 of *Monumentos de la música española.*

BIBLIOGRAPHY: R. Mitjana, *Francisco Guerrero, estudio crítico-biográfico* (Madrid, 1922); R. Stevenson, *Spanish Cathedral Music in the Golden Age* (Berkeley, Cal., 1961).

Guerrini, Guido, Italian composer; b. Faenza, Sept. 12, 1890; d. Rome, June 13, 1965. He was a pupil of Consolini (violin), and Toschi and Busoni (composition) at the Liceo musicale at Bologna; prof. of harmony there (1919–23); prof. of composition at Parma Cons. (1924–28); director of Cherubini Cons. in Florence (1928–44); director of Bologna Cons. (1944–50); in 1951 appointed director of the Santa Cecilia Cons. in Rome.

WORKS: operas: *Zalebi* (1915), *Nemici* (Bologna, Jan. 19, 1921), *La vigna* (Rome, March 7, 1935), *Enea,* after Virgil (Rome, Feb. 11, 1953); *Missa pro defunctis,* in memory of Marconi, for solo voices, chorus, and orch. (1939); *La città perduta,* biblical cantata (1942); *Tre liriche* for voice and orch. (1947); Cello Concerto (1914); *Canzonetta* for 4 saxophones (1938); *Arcadia,* for oboe and piano; piano quintet; 3 string quartets; *Le Suore,* 3 pieces for harp; vocal works, *Le fiamme su l'altare,* for voice, double string quartet, and 2 harps; songs. He also wrote the books: *Trattato di armonia complementare* (1922); *Origine, evoluzione e caratteri degli strumenti musicali* (1926); *Prontuario dei tempi e colori musicali* (1939); *F. Busoni, la vita, la figura, l'opera* (Florence, 1944); *Appunti d'orchestrazione* (1945); *A. Vivaldi,* (Florence, 1951); A catalogue of his works and an appreciation were publ. for his 70th birthday in Rome (1960).

Guerrini, Paolo, Italian music historian; b. Bagnolo Mella, near Brescia, Nov. 18, 1880; d. Brescia, Nov. 19, 1960. He specialized in Italian sacred music; edited the periodical *Brixia Sacra* (1910–25); in 1930, he began publication of the historical studies *Memorie storiche della Diocesi di Brescia;* served further as archivist and librarian in Brescia. In 1936, he was appointed canon of the Brescia cathedral. He revived and translated into Italian the music books of Cardinal Katschthaler *(Storia della musica sacra);* publ. *Storia della cappella musicale del Duomo di Brescia e del Duomo di Salò* and *Storia della musica sacra in Italia nei secolo XIX e XX.*

Guézec, Jean-Pierre, French composer; b. Dijon, Aug. 29, 1934; d. Paris, March 9, 1971. He enrolled at the Paris Cons. where he attended classes of Olivier Messiaen, Darius Milhaud and Jean Rivier; received Premier Prix in 1963; joined the faculty of the Paris Cons. in 1969.

WORKS: Concerto for violin and 14 instruments (1960); *Concert en Trois Parties* for 11 instruments (1961); *Suite pour Mondrian* for orch. (1962); *Architectures colorées* for 15 instruments (1964); *Ensemble multicolore 65* for 18 instruments (1965); *Formes* for orch. (1966); *Textures enchaînées* for 28 wind instruments (1967); *Assemblages* for 28 instruments (1967); String Trio (1968); *Reliefs polychromés* for chorus (1969); *Couleurs juxtaposées* for 2 percussion groups (1969); *Onze pour Cinz* for percussionists (1970).

Guglielmi, Pietro Alessandro, Italian composer; b. Massa di Carrara, Dec. 9, 1728; d. Rome, Nov. 18, 1804. He studied with his father, Jacob Guglielmi, and with Durante at the Cons. Santa Maria di Loreto at Naples. His 1st comic opera, *Lo solachianello 'mbroglione,* was performed at Naples in 1757; during the next 10 years, he wrote 24 operas, including *Il ratto della sposa* (Venice, 1765) and *La sposa fedele* (Venice, 1767), which were played all over Europe and became highly popular. He went to London in 1767; during his 5 years there, conducted and wrote several operas, among them *Ezio* (Jan. 13, 1770), in which his wife, **Lelia Achiapati,** sang. He returned to Italy in 1772; in 1793 was appointed maestro di cappella of San Pietro in Vaticano by Pope Pius VI and turned to church music; composed several oratorios, of which *Debora e Sisara* (1794) was regarded as his masterpiece. A detailed list of Guglielmi's operas is found in F. Piovano's articles on him and on his son in the *Rivista Musicale Italiana* (1905 and 1910).
BIBLIOGRAPHY: G. Bustico, *Pietro Guglielmi* (Massa, 1899); A. Della Corte, *L'Opera comica italiana nel settecento* (Bari, 1923).

Guglielmi, Pietro Carlo, Italian composer, son of **Pietro Alessandro Guglielmi;** b. Naples, c.1763; d. there, Feb. 28, 1817. After study at the Cons. di Santa Maria di Loreto at Naples, he went to Spain; his first operas were performed at Madrid in 1793 and 1794; then lived in Italy, producing operas in Naples, Florence, and Rome. He went to London in 1809; presented several operas at the King's Theatre; returned to Italy in 1810, and was appointed maestro di cappella to the Duchess Beatrice at Massa di Carrara. A list of his works, including some 40 operas, oratorios, and cantatas, was publ. by Francesco Piovano in the *Rivista Musicale Italiana* (1909–10).

Gui, Vittorio, Italian composer and conductor; b. Rome, Sept. 14, 1885; d. Florence, Oct. 16, 1975. He studied at the Liceo Musicale di Santa Cecilia in Rome; began his career as an opera conductor; then conducted in Parma, Naples, and at La Scala in Milan (1923); eventually settled in Florence. From 1947 to 1965 he conducted opera in England; was counsellor of Glyndebourne Festival Opera (1960–65).
WORKS: an opera, *Fata Malerba* (Turin, May 15, 1927); the symph. works *Giulietta e Romeo* (1902), *Il tempo che fu* (1910), *Scherzo fantastico* (1913), *Fantasia bianca* (1919; an orch. experiment making use of films), *Giornata di Festa* (1921); publ. a volume of critical essays, *Battute d'aspetto* (Florence, 1944).

Guidetti, Giovanni Domenico, Italian ecclesiastic scholar; b. Bologna, 1530 (baptized Jan. 1, 1531); d. Rome, Nov. 30, 1592. After taking holy orders, he went to Rome, where he became Palestrina's pupil and in 1575 was appointed "cappellano" (a clerical beneficiary) and chorister in the papal choir. From 1576 to 1581, he worked with Palestrina on a revised edition of the Gradual and Antiphonary, but this work being forestalled by the publication of Leichtenstein's edition (Venice, 1580) he obtained permission to publish the services for everyday use: *Directorium chori ad usum sacro-sanctae basilicae Vaticanae* (Rome,

1582, and several reprints); *Cantus ecclesiaticus passionis Domini Nostri Jesu Christi* (Rome, 1586); *Cantus ecclesiasticus officii majoris* (Rome, 1587; new ed., 1619); also publ. *Praefationes in cantu firmo* (Rome, 1588).

Guido d'Arezzo (known also as **Guido Aretinus**), famous reformer of musical notation and vocal instruction; b. c.997; d. Pomposa; date of death uncertain; May 17, 1050, often cited, is unfortunately without foundation. He received his education at the Benedictine abbey at Pomposa, near Ferrara. He left the monastery in 1025, as a result of disagreements with his fellow monks, who were envious of his superiority in vocal teaching; he was then summoned by Bishop Theobald of Arezzo to the cathedral school there; it was because of this association that he became known as Guido d'Arezzo. The assertions that he traveled in France and spent several years at the monastery of Saint-Maur des Fossés, near Paris (see, for example, Dom G. Morin in *Revue de l'art chrétien,* 1888) are not borne out by documentary evidence. Still more uncertain are the claims of his travels in Germany, and even in England. However this may be, his fame spread and reached the ears of Pope John XIX, who called him to Rome to demonstrate his system of teaching (1028). In his last years, he was a prior of the Camaldolite fraternity at Avellano. Guido's fame rests on his system of solmization, by which he established the nomenclature of the major hexachord Ut, Re, Mi, Fa, So, La, from syllables in the initial lines of the Hymn of St. John:
Ut queant laxis *Re*sonare fibris
*Mi*ra gestorum *Fa*muli tuorum,
*Sol*ve polluti *La*bii reatum,
Sancte Joannes.
No less epoch-making was Guido's introduction of the music staff of 4 lines, retaining the red *f*-line and the yellow *c*-line of his predecessors, and drawing between them a black *a*-line, above them a black *e*-line, and writing the plainsong notes (which he did *not* invent) in regular order on these lines and in the spaces:
New black line e———————
Old yellow line c———————
New black line a———————
Old red line   f
He also added new lines above or below these, as occasion required; thus, Guido's system did away with all uncertainty of pitch. Another invention credited to Guido is the so-called Guidonian hand, relating the degrees of the overlapping hexachords to various places on the palm of the left hand, a device helpful in directing a chorus by indicating manually the corresponding positions of the notes. Opinions differ widely as to the attribution to Guido of all these innovations; some scholars maintain that he merely popularized the already-established ideas and that somization, in particular, was introduced by a German abbot, Poncius Teutonicus, at the abbey of Saint-Maur des Fossés. Guido's treatises are *Micrologus de disciplina artis musicae* (publ. by A. Amelli, Rome, 1904; ed. by J. Smits van Waesberghe, 1955); *Regulae de ignoto cantu; Epistola de ignoto cantu* (publ. in English in Strunk's *Source Readings in Music History,* N.Y., 1950).

BIBLIOGRAPHY: L. Angeloni, *Sopra la vita, le opere ed il sapere di Guido d'Arezzo* (Paris, 1811); R. G. Kiesewetter, *Guido von Arezzo* (1840); G. Ristori, *Biografia di Guido Monaco d'Arezzo* (2nd ed., 1868); M. Falchi, *Studi su Guido Monaco di San Benedetto* (1882); J. Wolf, *Handbuch der Notationskunde* (vol. I); H. Wolking, *Guidos Micrologus de disciplina artis musicae und seine Quellen* (Emsdetten, 1930); J. Smits van Waesberghe, *De musico-paedogogico et theoretico Guidone Aretino eiusque vita et moribus* (in Latin; Florence, 1953); H. Oesch, *Guido von Arezzo* (Bern, 1954); J. Smits van Waesberghe, *Musikerziehung. Lehre und Theorie der Musik im Mittelalter.* Musikgeschichte in Bildern 3/3 (Leipzig, 1969); M. Huglo, "L'Auteur du *Dialogue sur la musique* attribué à Odon," *Revue de Musicologie* LV/2 (1969); D. Harbinson, "The Hymn *Ut queant laxis,*" *Music & Letters* (Jan. 1971).

Guignon, Jean-Pierre (Giovanni Pietro Ghignone), violinist and composer; b. Turin, Feb. 10, 1702; d. Versailles, Jan. 30, 1774. He went to Paris from Italy in his youth; was engaged as music tutor to the dauphin, and persuaded the king to revive and bestow on him the title of Roi des Violons et Ménétriers, which had last been used in 1695; every professional musician in France was required to join a guild and to pay a fee to Guignon as holder of the title; so much opposition was aroused by this requirement that parliament considered the case and deprived Guignon of this prerogative. He wrote several books of concertos, sonatas, and duos for violin.

Guilbert, Yvette, famous French *diseuse* and folk-song singer; b. Paris, Jan. 20, 1867; d. Aix-en-Provence, Feb. 2, 1944. She made her debut in Paris as an actress in 1885; in 1890 she began her career as a café singer; at first she sang popular songs in Paris; later, as she toured Europe and the U.S., where she first appeared in 1896, she became noted for her interpretations of French folksongs; she regarded herself as primarily an actress rather than a singer. She wrote her memoirs, *La Chanson de ma vie* (Paris, 1927) and *Autres temps, autres chants* (Paris, 1946).

Guillemain, Gabriel, French violinist and composer; b. Paris, Nov. 7, 1705; d. there (suicide), Oct. 1, 1770. He was a member of the king's orch. and gave concerts as a virtuoso. He was one of the first French composers to write violin sonatas with a developed clavichord accompaniment. He also wrote several ballets and instrumental music for various combinations.

BIBLIOGRAPHY: L. de la Laurencie, *L'École française de violon,* vol. II.

Guillou, Jean, French organist, pianist and composer; b. Angers, April 4, 1930. He began playing the piano and organ as a child; in 1952 he went to study with Dupré and Duruflé at the Paris Cons.; upon graduation he taught organ playing in Lisbon, Portugal (1955–58); then moved to Berlin where he was active as a concert pianist and organist (1958–63). Returning to France, he was appointed organist of the St. Eustache Church in Paris; since 1972 he has conducted annual master classes in Zürich. As a solo organist he has given concerts in Poland, Russia, Japan and the U.S.; he often concludes his concerts with improvisations on themes proposed by members of the audience. He has made numerous effective transcriptions for organ of works by Bach, Vivaldi, Mozart, and other classical composers; also a transcription of Stravinsky's *Petrouchka.* His own compositions are written in a neo-Baroque idiom.

WORKS: an oratorio *Le Jugement dernier* (1958; Cracow, June 16, 1968); 3 concertos for organ and orch.: *Inventions,* No. 1 (1956), No. 2 (1966; Leningrad, Oct. 10, 1972) and No. 3 (1967; Rouen, France, Jan. 16, 1972); *Triptyque* for strings (1957); 3 symphonies: *Judith* (No. 1), with soprano (1968; Paris, Feb. 25, 1971); No. 2, for strings (1971; Paris, Nov. 30, 1972); No. 3 (1974); Piano Concerto (1970); 5 *Colloques:* No. 1, for flute, oboe, violin and piano (1954); No. 2, for piano and organ (1960); No. 3, for oboe, harp, celesta, vibraphone, xylophone, timpani, percussion, 4 cellos and 2 double basses (1961); No. 4 for piano, organ and percussion (1965); No. 5 for piano and organ (1975); *Cantilia* for piano, harp, timpani and 4 cellos (1961); Oboe Quartet (1975); 2 Piano Sonatas (1967, 1975). For organ: 18 Variations (1954); Sinfonietta (1958); *Fantaisie* (1962); Toccata (1963); *Pour le Tombeau de Colbert* (1963); *Symphonie Initiatique* for 3 organs (1965; 1 live, 2 on tape); *Allen* (1966); 6 *Sagas* (1968); *La Chapelle des Abîmes* (1973); *Scènes d'énfants* (1973).

Guilmant, Alexandre (Félix), eminent French organist and composer; b. Boulogne, March 12, 1837; d. Meudon, near Paris, March 29, 1911. He studied organ with his father, Jean-Baptiste Guilmant (1793–1890); took harmony lessons with Gustave Carulli in Boulogne. In 1860, he took an advanced course in organ playing with Lemmens in Brussels. When still a child, he substituted for his father at the church of St.-Nicolas in Boulogne; at 20, he taught at Boulogne Cons. and conducted choral concerts. He then played organ in various churches in Paris, including St.-Sulpice (1863) and Notre Dame (1868); in 1871, he was appointed organist of Ste. Trinité, remaining at this post for 30 years. He was one of the founders of the Schola Cantorum (1894); in 1896, he was appointed prof. of organ at the Paris Cons.; also appeared as organ soloist with Paris orchestras and subsequently all over Europe and in the U.S. (1893–97). He was not only a virtuoso of the first rank, but a master in the art of improvisation; he formed a great school of students, among whom were René Vierné, Joseph Bonnet, Nadia Boulanger, Marcel Dupré, and the American organist, William Carl. He was a prolific composer of works for organ, which include 8 sonatas, 2 symphonies for organ and orch., 25 books of organ pieces, 10 books of *L'Organiste liturgiste;* there are also 3 Masses, psalms, vespers, motets, etc. Of greater importance than these are Guilmant's monumental editions of old masters: *Archives des maîtres de l'orgue* (Paris, 1898–1914; 10 vols.) and *École classique de l'orgue* (1898–1903); he also edited selected works of French composers performed at his historical concerts (1902–06); made numerous arrangements for organ of various classical works.

BIBLIOGRAPHY: *A la mémoire de Alexandre Guil-*

mant, by his friends of the Schola (Paris, 1911); A. Eaglefield-Hull,"The Organ Works of Guilmant," *Monthly Musical Record* (Oct.-Nov. 1914); N. Dufourcq, *La Musique d'orgue française* (Paris, 1949).

Guion, David (Wendell Fentress), American composer; b. Ballinger, Texas, Dec. 15, 1892. He studied piano with Leopold Godowsky in Vienna; returning to the U.S. in 1915, he occupied various teaching posts in Texas colleges; then lived in New York; finally settled in Pennsylvania. Guion devoted many years to collecting and arranging American folksongs; of these, *Turkey in the Straw, Arkansas Traveler,* and *Home on the Range,* in various transcriptions, have become extremely popular. His works for orch. include an African ballet suite, *Shingandi; Southern Nights Suite; Sheep and Goat Walking to the Pasture; Alley Tunes; Mother Goose Suite; Suite for Orch.* He also made many choral arrangements of American folksongs.

Guiraud, Ernest, French composer; b. New Orleans, June 23, 1837; d. Paris, May 6, 1892. He studied with his father, Jean Baptiste Guiraud; produced his 1st opera *Le Roi David,* in New Orleans at the age of 15. He then went to Paris, which was his home for the rest of his life; studied at the Paris Cons., with Marmontel (piano) and Halévy (composition); won the Grand Prix de Rome in 1859 with his cantata, *Bajazet et le joueur de flûte.* He stayed in Rome for 4 years; then returned to Paris, where his 1-act opera, *Sylvie,* was produced at the Opéra-Comique (May 11, 1864). He was appointed prof. at the Cons. in 1876; among his students were Debussy, Gédalge and Loeffler. He wrote the recitatives to Bizet's *Carmen* and completed the orchestration of Offenbach's *Contes d'Hoffmann.* His operas (all first performed in Paris) include *En prison* (March 5, 1869); *Le Kobold* (July 2, 1870); *Madame Turlupin* (1872); *Piccolino* (April 11, 1876, his most popular stage work); *Galante aventure* (March 23, 1882); *Frédégonde* (completed by Saint-Saëns; Dec. 18, 1895). He also wrote a ballet, *Gretna Green* (1873); 2 suites for orch.; *Arteveld,* an overture; a *Caprice* for violin and orch.; and a treatise on instrumentation.

Gulak-Artemovsky, Semyon, Ukrainian singer and composer; b. Gorodishche, Feb. 16, 1813; d. Moscow, April 17, 1873. He studied voice in Italy; sang at the Imperial Opera of St. Petersburg (1842–64); then lived in Moscow. His opera *Zaporozhets za Dunayem (A Cossack Beyond the Danube)* was produced in St. Petersburg on April 26, 1863, and subsequently acquired considerable popularity in Russia.
BIBLIOGRAPHY: L. Kaufman, *Semyon Gulak-Artemovsky* (Kiev, 1962; in the Ukrainian language).

Gulbins, Max, German organist and composer; b. Kammetschen, East Prussia, July 18, 1862; d. Breslau, Feb. 19, 1932. He studied at the Hochschule in Berlin; was organist at Elbing from 1900–08, then went to St. Elizabeth's in Breslau. He wrote, for men's chorus and orch., *Sturmlied, An das Vaterland,* and *Burggraf Friedrich von Nürnberg;* also organ pieces.

Gulbranson, Ellen (*née* **Norgren**), Swedish soprano; b. Stockholm, March 4, 1863; d. Oslo, Jan. 2, 1947. She sutdied at the Stockholm Cons., then with Mathilde Marchesi in Paris; returning to Stockholm, she made her concert debut in 1886; in 1896 she sang the part of Brünnhilde at Bayreuth, with great success; she also sang in Berlin, Paris, Moscow, Amsterdam, and London.

Gulda, Friedrich, Austrian pianist; b. Vienna, May 16, 1930. He studied piano in early childhood (1937–42) with Felix Pazofsky; then enrolled at the Vienna Music Academy as a piano student of Bruno Seidlhofer. At the age of 16 he won 1st prize at the International Pianists' Contest in Geneva, and immediately embarked on a concert career, giving recitals in Europe (1947–48), South America (1949) and the U.S., making a brilliant American debut in Carnegie Hall, N.Y., Oct. 11, 1950. He was praised by critics for his intellectual penetration of the music of Bach, Beethoven and Mozart; about 1955 he became intensely fascinated by jazz, particularly in its improvisatory aspect which he construed as corresponding to the freedom of melodic ornamentation in Baroque music. He often included jazz numbers (with drums and slap bass) at the end of his recitals; learned to play the saxophone, began to compose for jazz, and organized the Eurojazz Orchestra. As a further symptom of his estrangement from musical puritanism he returned the Beethoven Bicentennial ring given to him by the Vienna Music Academy (his old alma mater) in appreciation of his excellence in playing Beethoven's music, and gave a speech explaining the reasons for his action. He composed and performed jazz pieces, among them *The Veiled Old Land* for jazz band (1964); *The Excursion* for jazz orch. (1965, celebrating the flight of the American spaceship Gemini 4); *Concertino for Players and Singers* (1972). He further made a bold arrangement of Vienna waltzes in the manner of the blues; also composed a jazz musical *Drop-out oder Gustav der Letzte* (1970), freely after Shakespeare's *Measure for Measure;* publ. a book of essays, *Worte zur Musik* (Munich, 1971). He eventually made his home in Munich.
BIBLIOGRAPHY: Erich Jantsch, *Friedrich Gulda* (Vienna, 1953).

Gumbert, Ferdinand, German composer; b. Berlin, April 22, 1818; d. there, April 6, 1896. He was first trained by his father for book selling, but he pursued his musical studies, developing a particular interest in opera. After a short study of singing, he appeared at the Cologne Opera (1840–42); in 1842 he settled in Berlin as a voice teacher and also began to compose. His songs, written in a facile, eclectic style, enjoyed a considerable vogue. He produced several operettas in Berlin: *Der kleine Ziegenhirt* (Jan. 21, 1854), *Bis der Rechte kommt* (Nov. 20, 1856), etc.; publ. *Musik, Gelesenes und Gesammeltes* (Berlin, 1860).
BIBLIOGRAPHY: W. Neumann, *Ferdinand Gumbert* (Kassel, 1856).

Gumpeltzhaimer, Adam, German composer; b. Trostberg, c.1559; d. Augsburg, Nov. 3, 1625. He studied music with Father Jodocus Enzmüller at the monastery of St. Ulric in Augsburg; then became musician to the Duke of Württemberg; from 1581 to 1621 he was cantor at St. Anna, Augsburg.

WORKS: *Erster (zweiter) Teil des Lustgärtleins teutsch und lateinischer Lieder mit drei Stimmen* (1591 and 1611); *Erster (zweiter) Teil des Wirtzgärtleins 4 stimmiger geistlicher Lieder* (1594 and 1619); *Psalmus LI octo vocum* (1604); *Sacri concentus octonis vocibus modulandi cum duplici basso in organorum usum* (1601 and 1614; 2 parts); *10 geistliche Lieder mit 4 Stimmen* (1617); *2 geistliche Lieder mit 4 Stimmen; 5 geistliche Lieder mit 4 Stimmen zur der Himmelfahrt Jesu Christi; Newe teutsche geistliche Lieder mit 3 und 4 Stimmen* (1591 and 1594); *Das Inventar der Kantorei St. Anna in Augsburg* (compiled 1620–22; publ. in the edition of R. Schaal, Kassel, 1965). A number of Gumpeltzhaimer's motets have been reprinted in Bodenschatz's *Florilegium Portense*, Schadaeus's *Promptuarium* and Vintzius's *Missae*. O. Mayr edited a selection of his works in the *Denkmäler der Tonkunst in Bayern* 19 (10.ii).

BIBLIOGRAPHY: O. Mayr, *Adam Gumpeltzhaimer* (Munich, 1908).

Gumpert, Friedrich Adolf, German horn player; b. Lichtenau, April 27, 1841; d. Leipzig, Dec. 31, 1906. He studied with Hammann in Jena; from 1864, played 1st horn in the Gewandhaus Orch., Leipzig. He published valuable manuals for horn and other instruments: *Praktische Hornschule; a Solobuch* for horn (difficult passages from operas, symphonies, etc.); *Hornquartette* (2 books); *Hornstudien;* and orchestral studies for clarinet, oboe, bassoon, trumpet, and cello.

Gumprecht, Armand J., American organist and composer; b. Boston, Mass., June 26, 1861; d. Washington, D.C., March 13, 1943. He studied violin with C. Eichler, organ with J. Singenberger and S. B. Whitney; from 1891 to 1918, was prof. of music and organist at Georgetown Univ. He wrote 4 Masses, piano pieces, songs.

Gumprecht, Otto, German music critic; b. Erfurt, April 4, 1823; d. Meran, Feb. 6, 1900. He studied law in Halle and Berlin, but developed an interest in music, and began writing music criticism in 1849, continuing until 1889, when he suffered a stroke of paralysis.

WRITINGS: *Musikalische Charakterbilder* (1869); *Neue Charakterbilder* (1876); *Richard Wagner und der Ring des Nibelungen* (1873); *Unsere klassischen Meister* (2 vols., 1883–85) and *Neuere Meister* (2 vols., 1883); the last two are continuations of the *Charakterbilder;* he also edited 5 vols. of *Erlesene musikalische Meisterwerke.*

Gundry, Inglis, English composer; b. London, May 8, 1905. He studied law at Oxford Univ.; 1935 entered the Royal College of Music in London, where he took a music course with Vaughan Williams. In 1942 he was appointed Royal Marines Schoolmaster; then taught music history at London Univ. In 1960 he became music director of the Sacred Music Drama Society. He wrote the operas (all to his own librettos) *Naaman, the Leprosy of War* (1938); *The Return of Odysseus* (1941; revised in 1957); *The Partisans* (London, May 28, 1946); *Avon* (London, April 11, 1949);

The Logan Rock (Portchurno, Aug. 15, 1956); *The Prince of the Coxcombs* (London, Feb. 3, 1965); *The Three Wise Men* (London, Jan. 11, 1968); *The Prisoner Paul* (1969); a ballet *Sleep* (1943); *Symphonic Fantasy* for orch. (1948); the song cycles *The Black Mountains* (1956) and *The Year of the Firebird* (1957); he also arranged several old English music dramas.

Gungl, Joseph, famous Hungarian bandmaster and popular composer; b. Zsámbék, Dec. 1, 1810; d. Weimar, Jan. 31, 1889. He played the oboe in an artillery regiment in the Austrian army, and later became that band's conductor; he wrote a number of marches and dances, which became extremely popular; traveled with his band all over Germany. In 1843, he established his own band in Berlin; made an American tour in 1849; then returned to Europe and lived mostly in Munich and Frankfurt.

Gunn, Glenn Dillard, American pianist and music critic; b. Topeka, Kans., Oct. 2, 1874; d. Washington, D.C., Nov. 22, 1963. He studied at Leipzig Cons. with Carl Reinecke (piano); appeared as pianist in German cities; returning to the U.S. in 1900, he taught at the Chicago Mus. College (1901–05). In 1915 he founded the American Symph. Orch. of Chicago, the object of which was the performance of American works and the engagement of American soloists. He was music critic for the *Chicago Tribune* (1910–14) and the *Chicago Herald and Examiner* (1922–36); in 1940, was appointed music critic of the *Washington Times-Herald*. He publ. *A Course of Lessons on the History and Esthetics of Music* (1912) and *Music, Its History and Enjoyment* (1930).

Gunn, John, Scottish cellist and writer on music; b. Edinburgh, c.1765; d. there, c.1824. He went to London in 1790, where he taught cello and flute; returned to Edinburgh in 1795.

WRITINGS: *Forty Scotch Airs arranged as trios for flute, violin and violoncello; The Art of Playing the German Flute on New Principles; The Theory and Practice of Fingering the Violoncello* (London, 1793); *An Essay, Theoretical and Practical, on the Application of Harmony, Thorough-Bass, and Modulation to the Violoncello* (Edinburgh, 1801), and a valuable work, commissioned by the National Society of Scotland, *An Historical Inquiry respecting the Performance on the Harp in the Highlands of Scotland from the earliest Times until it was discontinued about the year 1734* (Edinburgh, 1807).

Gunsbourg, Raoul, Rumanian-French impresario; b. Bucharest, Dec. 25, 1859; d. Monte Carlo, May 31, 1955. After directing opera companies in Russia, he became the director of the Monte Carlo Opera; his first important production there was the stage version of *Damnation of Faust* by Berlioz (Feb. 18, 1893). He produced at Monte Carlo several of his own operas (he wrote the piano scores, and the orchestration was done by L. Jehin); of these *Le Vieil Aigle*, after Maxim Gorky's fable (Monte Carlo, Feb. 13, 1909), had a modicum of success.

Gura, Eugen, operatic baritone; b. Pressern, near Saatz, Bohemia, Nov. 8, 1842; d. Aufkirchen, Bavaria, Aug. 26, 1906. He studied in Vienna and in Munich; he sang in Munich (1865–67), Breslau (1867–70), Leipzig (1870–76), obtaining extraordinary success; then was in Hamburg (1876–83) and Munich (1883–95). He was particularly impressive in Wagnerian roles; his performance of Hans Sachs was greatly praised. He publ. *Erinnerungen aus meinem Leben* (Leipzig, 1905). His son, **Hermann Gura** (b. Breslau, April 5, 1870; d. Bad Wiessee, Bavaria, Sept. 13, 1944) was also a baritone; like his father, he specialized in Wagnerian roles; after a successful career as an opera singer in Germany, he settled in Berlin as voice teacher.

Guridi, Jesús, Spanish composer; b. Vitoria, Basque province of Alava, Sept. 25, 1886; d. Madrid, April 7, 1961. He studied in Madrid, at the Schola Cantorum in Paris, in Brussels (with Jongen), and in Cologne. He returned to Spain in 1909; became organist at Bilbao, where he remained until 1939; then moved to Madrid; appointed prof. of organ at the Madrid Cons. in 1944. During his 30 years in Bilbao, he promoted the cause of Basque folk music; publ. an album of 22 Basque songs. His zarzuelas make frequent use of Basque folk music; of these, *El caserío* (Madrid, 1926) attained enormous success in Spain; other stage works are *Amaya,* lyric drama in 3 acts (Bilbao, 1920), *La meiga* (Madrid, 1928), and *Mirentxu,* an idyll in 2 acts; he further wrote a symph. poem, *An Adventure of Don Quixote; Sinfonia pirenáica; Basque Sketches* for chorus and orch.; an orch. suite, *10 Basque Melodies* (very popular in Spain); a number of choral works a cappella on Basque themes; 4 string quartets; pieces for piano; various songs.
BIBLIOGRAPHY: J. M. de Arozamena, *Jesús Guridi* (Madrid, 1967).

Gurlitt, Cornelius, German composer; b. Altona, Feb. 10, 1820; d. there, June 17, 1901. He was a member of an artistic family; his brother, Louis Gurlitt, was a well-known landscape painter. He studied piano with Johann Peter Reinecke in Altona, and with Weyse in Copenhagen, where he went in 1840. In 1845, he made a journey through Europe; he met Schumann, Lortzing, Franz, and other eminent composers. In 1864 he was appointed organist of the Altona cathedral, retaining this post until 1898; also taught at the Hamburg Cons. (1879–87). He wrote an opera, *Die römische Mauer* (Altona, 1860); another opera, *Scheik Hassan,* was not performed. He further composed 3 violin sonatas, 3 cello sonatas, several cycles of songs, etc. He is chiefly remembered, however, by his numerous piano miniatures, in Schumann's style; a collection of these was publ. by W. Rehberg, under the title, *Der neue Gurlitt* (2 vols.; Mainz, 1931).
BIBLIOGRAPHY: Paul T. Hoffman, *Neues Altona* (Jena, 1929; vol. II).

Gurlitt, Manfred, German conductor and composer; b. Berlin, Sept. 6, 1890; d. Tokyo, April 29, 1972. He was of an artistic family; his grandfather was the well-known landscape painter Louis Gurlitt, whose brother was the composer **Cornelius Gurlitt.** He studied in Berlin with Humperdinck (composition) and

Karl Muck (conducting); rapidly progressed as a professional conductor; was a coach at the Berlin Opera (1908) and at the Bayreuth Festival (1911); theater conductor in Essen and Augsburg; conductor and music director at the Bremen Opera (1914–27); then at the Berlin Opera and on the German radio. After 1933, he was deprived of his position by the Nazi regime; in 1939 he settled in Japan, as teacher and conductor; organized the Gurlitt Opera Company in Tokyo.
WORKS: the operas *Die Heilige* (Bremen, Jan. 27, 1920), *Wozzeck* (Bremen, April 22, 1926; written almost at the same time as Alban Berg's *Wozzeck*), *Soldaten* (1929), *Nana* (1933), *Seguidilla Bolero* (1937), *Nordische Ballade,* and *Wir schreiten aus; Drei politische Reden* for baritone, men's chorus, and orch.; *Goya Symphony* (1950); *Shakespeare Symphony* (1954) for 5 solo voices and orch.; songs with orch.; concertos for piano, for violin, for cello; piano quartet, songs.

Gurlitt, Wilibald, German musicologist; b. Dresden, March 1, 1889; d. Freiburg-im-Breisgau, Dec. 15, 1963. He was a grand-nephew of the composer **Cornelius Gurlitt,** and a cousin of **Manfred Gurlitt.** He studied musicology at Heidelberg with P. Wolfrum and at the Leipzig Cons. with Hugo Riemann; received his Ph.D. in 1914 with a dissertation on Michael Praetorius; subsequently was assistant to Riemann. He served in World War I; was a war prisoner in France. After the Armistice he became a lecturer at the Univ. of Freiburg; was prof. of musicology there until 1937, when he was prevented by the Nazi regime from continuing his teaching; resumed his post in 1945. His investigations of the organ music of Praetorius led him to construct (in collaboration with Oscar Walcker) a "Praetorius organ" which was to reproduce the tonal quality of the period. This created the impetus for a new movement in Germany, the aim of which was to give performances of historic works played on contemporaneous instruments.
WRITINGS: *Burgundische Chanson und deutsche Liedkunst des 15. Jahrhunderts* (Basel, 1924); *François-Joseph Fétis* (Brussels, 1930); "Johannes Walter und die Musik der Reformationzeit," in *Luther-Jahrbuch* (Munich, 1933); *Johann Sebastian Bach, der Meister und sein Werk* (Berlin, 1936; 3rd ed., Basel, 1949; English transl., St. Louis, 1954). Among his many editions are organ works of Michael Praetorius; vol. 17 of the collected works of Praetorius; facsimile reprint of Praetorius' *De Organographia* (Kassel, 1929); a reprint of Johann Walter's *Lob und Preis der löblichen Kunst Musica* (Kassel, 1938); also new editions of 16 chansons by Gilles Binchois and 12 *Liebesgesänge* by Paul Fleming (Kassel, 1948). In 1952 he became editor of the *Archiv für Musikwissenschaft.* He also edited the first 2 vols. (1959; 1961) of the 12th edition of Riemann's *Musik-Lexikon.* For a complete list of his writings, see his autobiographical article in *Die Musik in Geschichte und Gegenwart.*

Gurney, Ivor, English song composer; b. Gloucester, Aug. 28, 1890; d. Dartford, Kent, Dec. 26, 1937. He was a chorister at Gloucester Cathedral; studied at the Royal College of Music in London with Stanford and Vaughan Williams; served in World War I, was wounded and gassed, and never recovered his physical and mental health; the 2 vols. of his war poems illustrate the turmoil of his inner life. After the Armistice, Gurney began to compose songs; 27 were publ. before his death, and several more were included in a 2-vol. edition of his melodies publ. posthumously. Gurney's gift was not for larger forms; he was at his best in his songs; he also wrote *5 Western Watercolors* and 5 Preludes for piano and some violin pieces. A memorial Gurney issue of *Music & Letters* with articles by Vaughan Williams, Walter de la Mare, and others, was publ. in 1938.

Gürsching, Albrecht, German oboist and composer; b. Nuremberg, Sept. 9, 1934. He studied composition in Stuttgart with Karl Marx and in Munich with Günter Bialas; was engaged as oboist in various ensembles. His works include a Concerto for Oboe, Viola and Strings (1961); *Rondo* for violin and string quartet (1963); 2 string quartets (1964); Quartet for Oboe and String Trio (1964); Symph. for Small Orch. (1964).

Gusikoff, Michel, American violinist and composer; b. New York, May 15, 1895. He studied violin with Franz Kneisel and composition with Percy Goetschius; made his debut in 1920; was concertmaster of the Philadelphia Orch., N.Y. Symphony Orch., and NBC Orch.; also associate conductor of the Pittsburgh Symph. Orch. He made violin arrangements of songs by Gershwin; also wrote an *American Concerto* for violin and orch.

Gutchë, Gene (real name **Romeo E. Gutsche**), American composer; b. Berlin, July 3, 1907. He studied in Germany, then went to the U.S., where he undertook additional academic work at the Univ. of Minnesota with Donald Ferguson and at the Univ. of Iowa with Philip Greeley Clapp (Ph.D., 1953); held two Guggenheim Fellowships (1961, 1964). His music is marked by a fairly advanced idiom and a neo-Romantic treatment of programmatic subject matter. In some of his orchestral works he applies fractional tones by dividing the strings into two groups tuned at slightly differing pitches.
WORKS: Symph. No. 1 (Minneapolis, April 11, 1950); Symph. No. 2 (1950–54); Symph. No. 3 (1952); *Rondo Capriccioso* (1953; N.Y., Feb. 19, 1960; with the application of fractional tones); Piano Concerto (Minneapolis, June 19, 1956); Cello Concerto (1957); Symph. No. 4 (1960; Albuquerque, March 8, 1962); Symph. No. 5 for strings (Chautauqua, July 29, 1962); *Timpani Concertante* (Oakland, Calif., Feb. 14, 1962); Violin Concerto (1962); *Genghis Khan,* symph. poem (Minneapolis, Dec. 6, 1963); *Rites in Tenochtitlán* for small orch. (St. Paul, Jan. 26, 1965); *Gemini* for orch., with microtones (Minneapolis, July 26, 1966); *Classic Concerto* for orch. (St. Paul, Nov. 11, 1967); *Epimetheus USA* for orch. (Detroit, Nov. 13, 1969); 4 string quartets; 3 piano sonatas; choruses.
BIBLIOGRAPHY: *Composers of the Americas,* vol. 15 (Washington, 1969).

Gutheil-Schoder, Marie, German mezzo-soprano; b. Weimar, Feb. 10, 1874; d. there, Oct. 4, 1935. She studied in Weimar, made her debut there in 1891; sang with the court opera until 1900, when she went to the Vienna Opera, becoming an outstanding singer-actress in such roles as Carmen, Elektra, Salome; in 1926 she was appointed stage director of the opera. She married the composer and conductor **Gustav Gutheil.**
BIBLIOGRAPHY: L. Andro, *Marie Gutheil-Schoder* (1923).

Guthrie, Woody (full name **Woodrow Wilson Guthrie**), American folk singer; b. Okemah, Oklahoma, July 14, 1912; d. New York, Oct. 3, 1967. His father was a prize fighter and a professional guitar player. The family suffered adversity during the depression; Woody Guthrie took to the road; performed in saloons and at labor meetings, improvising songs of social significance. Later he joined Pete Seeger and others in a group known as Almanac Singers; publ. the books *Bound for Glory* and *American Folksong.* Although not a trained singer, Guthrie acquired fame as an impassionate balladeer of disadvantaged Americans. Ignoring for the moment his freely professed radical convictions, the U.S. government bestowed upon him in 1966 an award of merit as "a poet of the American landscape." His career was cut short in 1957 when he contracted Huntington's chorea, which incapacitated him. His son **Arlo Guthrie** (b. New York, July 10, 1947) carried on Woody Guthrie's tradition as a folk singer; became famous for his ballad *Alice's Restaurant,* which is also the title of a motion picture in which he starred as himself, getting busted.

Gutiérrez, Gonzalo, Spanish organist and composer; b. about 1540; d. Granada, 1605. He was appointed organist at the Cathedral of Granada in 1569, and held this post until his death.
BIBLIOGRAPHY: José Lopez Calo, *La Música en la Catedral de Granada en el Siglo XVI* (Granada, 1963; vol. I, pp. 205–210; vol. II includes several of his works).

Gutiérrez Heras, Joaquín, Mexican composer; b. Tehuacán, Sept. 28, 1927. He attended classes in architecture at the National Univ. of Mexico and then studied composition with Blas Galindo and Rodolfo Halffter at the National Cons. of Mexico (1950–52). A scholarship from the French Institute of Mexico enabled him to go to Paris, where he took courses in composition with Messiaen, Rivier and Georges Dandelot at the Paris Cons. (1952–53); on a Rockefeller Foundation scholarship, he studied composition with Bergsma and Persichetti at the Juilliard School of Music in N.Y. (1960–61). Upon his return to Mexico, he gave radio lectures and taught music theory. As a composer, he professes a "voluntary lack of complexity."
WORKS: Divertimento for Piano and Orch. (1949); a satirical ballet, *El deportista* (1957); *Variations on a French Song* for piano or harpsichord (1958–60); *Chamber Cantata on Poems by Emilio Prados* for soprano, 2 flutes, harp and 4 strings (1961); a symph. scene *Los Cazadores* (*The Hunters,* 1962); Duo for Alto Flute and Cello (1964); *Sonata simple* for flute and piano (1965); Trio for Oboe, Clarinet and Bassoon (1965); *2 Pieces for 3 Brasses* (1967); *Night and Day*

Music for wind symph. orch. (1973); *De profundis* for a cappella chorus (1977); several scores for theater and film.

Gutman, Robert W., American writer on music; b. New York, Sept. 11, 1925. He studied at N.Y. Univ. (B.A., 1945; M.A., 1948); his principal teacher in musicology was Curt Sachs. In 1957 he was appointed to the faculty of the Univ. of the State of N.Y. He contributed essays to music magazines; publ. a searching and original biographical analysis of Wagner, *Richard Wagner: The Man, His Mind and His Music* (N.Y., 1968; German translation, Munich, 1970; French translation, 1971).

Gutmann, Adolph, German pianist; b. Heidelberg, Jan. 12, 1819; d. Spezia, Oct. 27, 1882. He lived mostly in Paris, where he studied with Chopin, and became a close friend of his. He publ. an album of *Études caractéristiques* which were quite popular in the 19th century, and much salon music for piano. He was also a successful performer whose virtuoso technique made him popular with audiences.

Gutsche, Romeo E. See **Gutchë, Gene.**

Guyonnet, Jacques, Swiss composer; b. Geneva, March 20, 1933. He studied at the Geneva Cons. (1950–58); had courses in new music with Boulez at the summer sessions held in Darmstadt (1958–61); in 1959 he founded the "Studio de Musique Contemporaine" in Geneva; in 1965 elected president of the Swiss section of the International Society for Contemporary Music.
WORKS: *Monades I* for chamber ensemble (1958); *Monades II-III* for orch. (1960, 1961); *Polyphonie I* for flute and piano (1961); *Polyphonie II* for 2 pianos (1959); *Polyphonie III* for flute, viola and 2 pianos (1964); *Chronicles* for piano (1964–71); *En trois Eclats!* for piano and chamber orch. (1964); *Stèle in memoriam J. F. Kennedy* for chamber orch. and tape (1964); *The Approach to the Hidden Man I* for solo cello and 6 instruments (1966), and *II* for mezzo-soprano, chamber orch. and electronic sound (1967); *7 Portes du Temps* for orch. (1966–69); *Entremonde,* ballet for flute, piano, 4 percussionists and tape (1967); *Let There Be Events!* for 17 instrumental soloists (1968–71); *Good Grief Jerry!* for soprano and chamber orch. (1970–71); *Modèles I-II* for any number of instrumental soloists (1970); *A Single R* for viola and chamber orch. (1971); *Le Chant remémoré* for 4 vocal soloists and orch. (1972); *Die Wandlung* for orch. (1973); *Les Enfants du Désert* for string orch. (1974); *Mémorial* for 4 trumpets and 4 trombones (1974).

Guyot, Jean, Flemish musician, also known under the names of **Jean de Chatelet** and **Johannes Castileti;** b. Chatelet (Hainaut) in 1512; d. Liège, March 11, 1588. He studied at the Univ. of Louvain, and received the degree of licencié-es-arts on March 22, 1537; in 1545 he was chaplain at St. Paul's in Liège; published his first motets in Antwerp in 1546; was later maître de chapelle at the Cathedral of St. Lambert in Liège; on Nov. 1, 1563, appointed music master at the Imperial Court in Vienna; he returned to Liège in Aug., 1564, and remained maître de chapelle at the Cathedral of St. Lambert to his death.
BIBLIOGRAPHY: C. Lyon, *Jean Guyot* (Charleroi, 1876).

Guy-Ropartz. See **Ropartz, Guy.**

Guzikov, Michal Jozef, famous performer on the xylophone; b. Szklow, Poland, Sept. 14, 1806; d. Aachen, Oct. 21, 1837. Of a Jewish musical family, he showed precocious talent; with four relatives he traveled all over Europe; his virtuosity on the xylophone was extraordinary, and elicited praise from the public as well as from celebrated musicians, among them Mendelssohn. Guzikov's programs consisted of arrangements of well-known works and also his own pieces; his most successful number was a transcription of Paganini's *La Campanella.*
BIBLIOGRAPHY: S. Schlesinger, *Josef Guzikov* (Vienna, 1936).

Gyrowetz, Adalbert, notable Austrian composer; b. Budweis, Bohemia, Feb. 19, 1763; d. Vienna, March 19, 1850. He studied organ with his father, a local choirmaster; then went to Prague, where he studied law; at the same time, began to compose band pieces and waltzes; he was befriended by Count Franz von Fünfkirchen, who was a music lover, and whose secretary he became. For the private orch. of Count von Fünfkirchen, Gyrowetz wrote 6 symphonies in Haydn's style; later, when he was in Vienna, he showed these works to Mozart, who encouraged him, and arranged for a performance of one of Gyrowetz's symphonies. From Vienna, he traveled through Italy; in Naples, he studied with Sala and Paisiello. In 1789, he went to Milan, Genoa, and finally to Paris, where several of his works were accepted by publishers. He then moved to London, where one of his pieces was performed at a Haydn concert (March 23, 1792). He was commissioned to write an opera, *Semiramide,* for the Pantheon Theatre, but before the announced performance, the opera building burned down, and with it perished the manuscript of *Semiramide.* After 3 years in London, he returned to the continent, eventually settling in Vienna (1793), where he became Kapellmeister at the Vienna Opera (1804–31). In Vienna, he enjoyed a great reputation as composer, and his name was often coupled with Beethoven's in public prints.
WORKS: He composed a number of operas, which were performed, one after another, at the Vienna Opera: *Selico* (Oct. 15, 1804); *Agnes Sorel* (Dec. 4, 1806); *Die Junggesellen-Wirtschaft* (June 18, 1807); *Die Pagen des Hertzogs von Vendome* (Aug. 5, 1808); *Der betrogene Betrüger* (Feb. 17, 1810); *Der Augenarzt* (his most successful opera; Oct. 1, 1811); *Das Winterquartier in Amerika* (Oct. 30, 1812); *Robert* (July 15, 1813); *Helene* (Feb. 16, 1816); *Aladin* (Feb. 7, 1819); *Der blinde Harfner* (Dec. 19, 1827); *Der Geburtstag* (Feb. 11, 1828); *Felix und Adele* (Aug. 10, 1831); also several operettas and *Singspiele.* In 1834, he produced in Dresden an opera, *Hans Sachs,* using essentially the same literary material as Wagner's *Meistersinger.* He further wrote a number of ballets; much church

music; some 60 symphonies; about 60 string quartets; 30 trios; about 40 violin sonatas, as well as piano pieces and songs. The historical reasons for the rapid decline of Gyrowetz's repute as a composer after his death are not easy to explain; attempted revivals of his music proved futile.

BIBLIOGRAPHY: Gyrowetz publ. his autobiography (Vienna, 1848); it was brought out in an annotated edition by Alfred Einstein (Leipzig, 1915); numerous references to Gyrowetz are found in the Haydn literature; see also K. Mey, "A. Gyrowetz und seine neu aufgefundene Hans Sachs-Oper," *Die Musik* (May 1903).

Gysi, Fritz, Swiss musicologist; b. Zofingen, Feb. 18, 1888; d. Zürich, March 5, 1967. He studied at the Basel Cons., at Zürich Univ., and at Berlin Univ.; in 1921 became lecturer in music at the Univ. of Zürich. He published the following books: *Mozart in seinen Briefen* (1921); *Max Bruch* (1922); *Claude Debussy* (1926); *Richard Wagner und die Schweiz* (1929); *Richard Strauss* (1934); *Hans Georg Nägeli* (1936).

H

Haan, Willem de, Dutch composer; b. Rotterdam, Sept. 24, 1849; d. Berlin, Sept. 26, 1930. He studied at the Leipzig Cons.; in 1876 became conductor in Darmstadt; in 1923 moved to Berlin. He wrote an opera *Die Kaiserstochter* (Darmstadt, Feb. 1, 1885) and much choral music.

Haapanen, Toivo, Finnish musicologist; b. Karvia, May 15, 1889; d. Asikkala, July 22, 1950. He studied music and philosophy at the Univ. of Helsinki; in 1925, appointed to its faculty. He specialized in bibliographical work and research in Finnish music of the Middle Ages.
WRITINGS: Catalogue of manuscripts of the Middle Ages in the library of the Univ. of Helsinki (I. *Missalia,* 1922; II. *Gradualia, Lectionaria missae,* 1925; III. *Breviaria,* 1932; also *The Neume Fragments in the Univ. Library at Helsinki* 1924); "Die Finnen," in Adler's *Handbuch.*

Haarklou, Johannes, Norwegian composer; b. Söndfjord, near Bergen, May 13, 1847; d. Oslo, Nov. 26, 1925. He studied at the Leipzig Cons.; then in Berlin with Haupt, Kiel, and Bungert; for 40 years (1880–1920) he was organist at the old Akers Church in Oslo; also conducted symphonic concerts there for 3 seasons. His 5 operas have not made their way beyond Norway, but among the works more generally known is an oratorio, *Skapelsen (The Creation,* 1891; Oslo, 1924). He further wrote 4 symphonies and *Olafs-Legende* for orch.; a violin sonata; piano pieces, choruses, and organ works.
BIBLIOGRAPHY: F. Benestad, *Johannes Haarklou, Mannen og verket* (Oslo, 1961).

Haas, Joseph, eminent German composer and pedagogue; b. Maihingen, March 19, 1879; d. Munich, March 30, 1960. He studied with Max Reger in Munich and with Karl Straube in Leipzig (organ). In 1911 he was appointed composition teacher at the Stuttgart Cons.; in 1921 became prof. at the Institute of Church Music in Munich. Through the long years of his pedagogical activities, Haas established himself as one of the most reputable teachers in Germany. At the time of his retirement in 1950, a Joseph Haas Society was organized in Munich, with the aim of issuing bulletins regarding his works. As a composer, Haas is equally estimable, but his music has failed to gain popularity outside his circle. He wrote more than 100 opus numbers.
WORKS: Operas, *Tobias Wunderlich* (Kassel, Nov. 24, 1937) and *Die Hochzeit des Jobs* (Dresden, July 2, 1944); oratorios, *Die heilige Elisabeth* (1931), *Christnacht* (1932), *Das Lebensbuch Gottes* (1934), *Das Lied von der Mutter* (1939), *Das Jahr in Lied* (1952), *Die Seligen* (Kassel, April 12, 1957), *Deutsche Kindermesse* (1958), *Marienkantate* (1959); *Variations on a Rococo Theme* for orch.; *Ouvertüre zu einem frohen Spiel* (1943); 2 string quartets (1908, 1919); Trio for 2 Violins and Piano (1912); many song cycles. He publ. a biography of Max Reger (Bonn, 1949); contributed articles to various publications.
BIBLIOGRAPHY: *Festgabe J. Haas* (a collection of articles by his students and colleagues on his 60th birthday, Mainz, 1939); a catalogue of works compiled by K. G. Fellerer (issued by the Haas Society, 1950; 2nd ed., 1953); K. Laux, *J. Haas* (Mainz, 1931; 2nd ed., 1954); special issue of the *Zeitschrift für Musik* on his 75th birthday, March, 1954). A collection of his speeches and articles was published posthumously, as *Reden und Aufsätze* (Mainz, 1964).

Haas, Monique, French pianist; b. Paris, Oct. 20, 1906. She studied at the Paris Cons. with Lazare Lévy; became greatly interested in modern music, and gave numerous concerts all over Europe in programs of 20th-century composers; also appeared with orchestras in modern concertos. She is married to the composer **Marcel Mihalovici.**

Haas, Pavel, Czech composer; b. Brno, June 21, 1899; put to death in the concentration camp at Auschwitz (Oswiecim), Poland, Oct. 17, 1944. He studied piano and composition in Brno; was a soldier in the Austrian army in World War I; after the Armistice, continued his study with Petřelka at the Brno Cons. (1919–21) and at the Master Class there with Janáček (1921–22). He tried to leave Czechoslovakia after its occupation by the Nazi hordes but the outbreak of World War II made it impossible; in 1941 he was placed in a concentration camp in Terezín; in Oct. 1944 was sent to Auschwitz and put to death there. He continued to compose in the concentration camp until he was sent to Auschwitz.
WORKS: an opera, *Šarlatán,* to his own libretto (*The Charlatan,* 1936; Brno, April 2, 1938); *Zesmutnělé Scherzo (Mournful Scherzo)* for orch. (1921); *Předehra pro rozhlas (Overture for Radio)* for orch., male chorus and narrator (1930); Symphony (1941; unfinished); *Studie* for string orch. (1943); Variations for Piano and Orch. (1944); a cantata, *Introduction and Psalm XXIX* (1931); 3 string quartets (1920, 1925, 1938); *Fata morgana,* piano quintet with tenor solo (1923); Wind Quintet (1929); Suite for Oboe and Piano (1939); Suite for Piano (1935); songs. His extant manuscripts are preserved in the Moravian Museum in Brno.

Haas, Robert Maria, distinguished Austrian musicologist; b. Prague, Aug. 15, 1886; d. Vienna, Oct. 4, 1960. He received his primary education in Prague; then studied music history in the universities of Prague, Berlin, and Vienna; received his Ph.D. at the Univ. of Prague for his dissertation *Das Wiener Singspiel* (1908). He then was assistant prof. at the Institute for Music History in Vienna (1908–09); from 1910 to 1914, he was engaged as theater conductor in various German cities; during World War I was in the Austrian army; in 1920 was appointed chief of the music division of the National State Library in Vienna; in 1923 became instructor at the Vienna Univ.; in 1929, appointed prof. there. Throughout this period he was active in various musical societies; contributed to many publications; was engaged in editorial work.
WRITINGS: *Gluck und Durazzo im Burgtheater* (Vienna, 1925); *Die Wiener Oper* (Vienna, 1926); *Wie-*

ner *Musiker vor und um Beethoven* (Vienna, 1927); *Die estensischen Musikalien* (Regensburg, 1927); *Mozart* (Potsdam, 1933; 2nd ed., 1950); *Bruckner* (Potsdam, 1934); *Bach und Mozart in Wien* (Vienna, 1951). He edited the symphonies of Bruckner, publ. by the International Bruckner Society (1935–45); for the *Denkmäler der Tonkunst in Österreich* edited the works of Umlauf, Gassmann, Eberlin, Monteverdi, Gluck, and Schenk.

Haase, Hans, German musicologist; b. Neumünster (Schleswig-Holstein), May 12, 1929. He studied with Friedrich Blume and Albrecht at the Univ. of Kiel (1950–55); from 1954 to 1958 was editorial contributor to *Die Musik in Geschichte und Gegenwart;* then did valuable work in the various archives and libraries; also wrote newspaper music criticism. He published the monographs *Jobst vom Brandt* (Kassel, 1967); *Heinrich Schütz* (Wolfenbüttel, 1972); and numerous valuable articles on German composers of the Reformation. He also became interested in applied psychology; lectured on this subject in Zürich and Vienna; publ. *Die harmonikalen Wurzeln der Musik* (Vienna, 1969) and *Aufsätze zur harmonikalen Naturphilosophie* (Graz, 1974).

Hába, Alois, notable Czech composer of microtonal music; b. Vizovice, Moravia, June 21, 1893; d. Prague, Nov. 18, 1973. He studied with Novák at the Prague Cons. (1914–15); then with Schreker at the Vienna Academy (1917–20) and the Hochschule für Musik in Berlin (1920–23). He became interested in the folk music of the Orient, which led him to consider writing in smaller intervals than the semitone. His first work in the quarter-tone system was the 2nd String Quartet (op. 7, 1920); in his 5th String Quartet (op. 15, 1923) he first applied the sixth-tones; in his 16th String Quartet (op. 98, 1967), he introduced the fifth-tones. He notated these fractional intervals by signs in modified or inverted sharps and flats. The piano manufacturing firm A. Förster constructed a quarter-tone piano for him (1925) and a sixth-tone harmonium (1927); other firms manufactured at his request a quarter-tone clarinet (1924) and trumpet (1931). From 1923 to 1953 Hába led a class of composition in fractional tones at the State Cons. in Prague, attracting a large number of students, among them his brother, **Karel,** the conductor Ančerl and the composers Dobiáš, Ježek, Kowalski, Kubín, Lucký, Ponc, Karel Reiner (who, along with E. Schulhoff, specialized in quarter-tone piano playing and premièred 10 of Hába's works), Seidel, Srnka and Susskind; Constantin Iliev of Bulgaria; Slavko Osterc of Yugoslavia; Necil Kâzim Akses of Turkey, and many others. Hába published an important manual of modern harmony, *Neue Harmonielehre des diatonischen, chromatischen, Viertel-, Drittel-, Sechstel-, und Zwölfteltonsystems* (*New Principles of Harmony of the Diatonic, Chromatic, Fourth-, Third-, Sixth-, and Twelfth-Tone Systems,* Leipzig, 1927), detailing new usages introduced by him in his classes; he further publ. *Harmonicke základy čtvrttónové soustavy* (*Harmonic Foundation of the Quarter-Tone System,* Prague, 1922) and *Von der Psychologie der musikalischen Gestaltung, Gesetzmässigkeit der Tonbewegung und Grundlagen*

eines neuen Musikstils (*On the Psychology of Musical Composition; Rules of Tonal Structure and Foundation of New Musical Style,* Vienna, 1925); also *Mein Weg zur Viertel- und Sechstetonmusik* (Düsseldorf, 1971). As a composer he cultivated a "non-thematic" method of writing, without repetition of patterns and devoid of development.

WORKS: OPERAS: *Matka* (*Mother,* 1927–29), in quarter tones, to his own text; it was first performed in Munich in a German version as *Die Mutter* on May 17, 1931, and subsequently produced in Czech (Prague, May 27, 1947); *Nová Země* (*The New Land,* 1934–36), written in the traditional tempered scale; never performed, except for the overture, played in Prague on April 8, 1936; *Přijd království Tvé* (*Thy Kingdom Come;* 1937–40, in fractional tones, to Hába's own text; unperformed); cantata, *Za mír* (*For Peace;* Prague, Nov. 1, 1950); FOR ORCH.: Overture (Berlin, Dec. 9, 1920); *Symphonic Fantasy* for piano and orch. (1921); *Cesta života* (*The Path of Life;* Winterthur, Switzerland, March 15, 1934); *Valašská suita* (Prague, Oct. 29, 1953); Violin Concerto (1955; Prague, Feb. 17, 1963); Viola Concerto (1955–57). CHAMBER MUSIC: the following are in the tempered scale: 4 nonets for wind and string instruments (1931, based on a 12-tone row; 1932, based on a 7-tone row; 1953; 1963); string quartets Nos. 1, 7, 8, 9, 13, and 15 (1919; 1951; 1951; 1952; *Astronautic,* 1961; 1964); Violin Sonata (1915); Fantasy for Flute or Violin, and Piano (op. 34, 1928; op. 34a, 1967, version for bass clarinet and piano); Sonata for Guitar Solo (1943); Sonata for Chromatic Harp (op. 59, 1944); Sonata for Diatonic Harp (op. 60, 1944); *Intermezzo and Preludium* for diatonic harp (1945); Suite for Solo Bassoon (1950; op. 69a, 1968, version for bass clarinet); Suite, quartet for bassoons (1951); *Fantasy* and *Fantasy and Fugue* for organ (both 1951); Solo Clarinet Sonata (1952); Suite for Solo Violin (op. 81a, 1955); Suite for Solo Cello (op. 81b, 1955); Suite for Solo Cymbalom (1960); Suite for Solo Bass Clarinet (op. 96, 1964); Suite for Solo Saxophone (1968); Suite for Bass Clarinet and Piano (1969); *Observations from a Journal* for narrator and string quartet (1970); Suite for Violin and Piano (op. 103, 1972; his last work); *Fugue Suite* for piano (1918); *Variations on a Canon by Schumann* for piano (1918); *2 Morceaux* for piano (1917–18; arranged for string orch. by R. Kubín, 1930); Piano Sonata (op. 3, 1918); *6 Pieces* for piano (1920); *4 Modern Dances* for piano (1927); *Toccata quasi una Fantasia* for piano (1931); *6 Moods* for piano (1971). Works in quarter-tones: string quartets Nos. 2, 3, 4, 6, 12 and 14 (1920, 1922, 1922, 1950, 1960, 1963); Fantasy for Solo Violin (1921); *Music* for solo violin (1922); Fantasy for Solo Cello (1924); Fantasy for Violin and Piano (op. 21, 1925); Suite No. 1, for clarinet and piano (1925); Fantasy for Viola and Piano (1926); Fantasy for Cello and Piano (1927); 2 Suites for Solo Guitar (1943, 1947); Suite No. 2, for solo clarinet (1943–44); Suite for Trumpet and Trombone (1944); Suite for 4 trombones (1950); Suite for Solo Violin (op. 93, 1961–62); 6 Suites for Piano (1922, revised 1932; 1922, revised 1932; 1923; 1924; 1925; 1959); 11 Fantasies for Piano (Nos. 1–10, 1923–26; No. 11, 1959); Piano Sonata (op. 62, 1947). Works in fifth-tones: String Quartet No. 16 (1967). Works in sixth-tones: String Quartets Nos. 5,

10 and 11 (1923, 1952, 1958); Duo for 2 Violins (1937); Suite for Solo Violin (op. 85a, 1955); Suite for Solo Cello (op. 85b, 1955); *6 Pieces* for harmonium (1928). He also wrote songs and choral pieces, many of them in the quarter-tone system.

BIBLIOGRAPHY: Jiří Vysloužil, *Alois Hába: život a dílo* (Prague, 1974).

Hába, Karel, Czech composer (brother of **Alois Hába**); b. Vizovice, Moravia, May 21, 1898; d. Prague, Nov. 21, 1972. He studied violin with Karel Hoffmann and Jan Mařák and music theory with V. Novák, J. Křička and J. B. Foerster at the Prague Cons.; also attended his brother's class in quarter-tone music (1924–27). He wrote only 3 pieces in quarter-tones, but he faithfully followed the athematic method of composing that was the cornerstone of Alois Hába's esthetics. Karel Hába was employed as violinist in the Czech Philh. Orch. (1929–36), a music critic and lecturer in music education at Charles Univ. (1950–63). He wrote *Violin Manual in the Quarter-tone System* (manuscript, 1927) and *Modern Violin Technique,* in 2 vols. (Prague, 1928).

WORKS: 4 operas: *Jánošík* (1929–32; Prague, Feb. 23, 1934; first operatic treatment of this famous historical Czech figure), *Stará historia* (The Old Story, 1934–37; unperformed), *Smolíček* (Prague, Sept. 28, 1950; a children's radio opera) and *Kalibův zločin* (Kaliba's Crime, 1957–61; Košice, May 16, 1968); a cantata, *To Those Who Build up Ostrava* (1950–51); Overture (1922); Violin Concerto (Prague, March 6, 1927); *Scherzo* for orch. (1928); Cello Concerto (Prague, Sept. 1, 1935); 2 symphonies (1947–48, 1953–54); *Brigand's Suite* for orch. (1955); Suite for Orch. (1963); 4 string quartets (1922, 1924, 1943, 1969); Trio for Violin, Cello and Quarter-tone Piano (1926); *3 Pieces* for violin and piano in quarter-tones (1927); Flute Sonatina (1927); Septet, for violin, clarinet, viola, horn, cello, bassoon, and piano (1928–29); Duo for Violin and Cello (1935); Piano Trio (1940); Wind Quintet (1944); *3 Inventions* for harp (1945); Nonet (1950); Trio for 2 Violins and Viola (1952); *15 Concert Etudes* for violin (1956); Sonatina for 3 Violins (1960); Sonatina for 3 Clarinets (1960); *3 Instructive Duos* for 2 violins (1968); 2 Suites for Piano (1920; 1929); Suite for Quarter-Tone Piano (1925); Piano Sonata (1942); choral pieces; songs.

Habeneck, François-Antoine, eminent French conductor and composer; b. Mézières, Jan. 22, 1781; d. Paris, Feb. 8, 1849. His father, a native of Mannheim and a member of a regimental band, taught him the violin. In 1800 Habeneck entered the Paris Cons., studying violin with Baillot. In 1806 Habeneck was appointed conductor of the student orchestra; in 1825, prof. of violin at the Cons., holding this post almost until his death. He was musical director of the Paris Opéra (1821–24); then its conductor (1824–46). In 1828 he founded the Société des Concerts du Conservatoire de Paris, comprising an orchestra of 80 musicians and a chorus of 80 singers. At his opening concert (March 9, 1828) he presented Beethoven's *Eroica;* subsequently gave concerts exclusively of Beethoven's works, culminating in the first Paris performance of the Ninth Symphony (March 27, 1831). Al-

though Habeneck retained many characteristics of an amateur in conducting (for instance, he used the violin part, with other instruments cued in, instead of a full score), he became a major influence in French musical life because of the excellence of his programs; his championing of Beethoven exercised a profound influence on French composers, among them Berlioz. As a composer he was not significant. With Isouard and Benincori, he wrote an opera *Aladin ou la Lampe merveilleuse* (Paris Opéra, Feb. 6, 1822); composed 2 violin concertos and other violin music; publ. *Méthode théorique et pratique de violon* (Paris, 1835).

Haberbier, Ernst, German pianist; b. Königsberg, Oct. 5, 1813; d. Bergen, Norway, March 12, 1869. He studied with his father, an organist; left home in 1832; went to Russia and became a court pianist in St. Petersburg in 1847; gave concerts in London in 1850; in 1852 appeared in Paris, where he scored a sensational success; in 1866 he settled in Bergen. He perfected what he considered a novel system of piano technique, dividing difficult passages between the two hands (however, this had been done by Scarlatti and Bach long before). He wrote a number of effective piano pieces, of which *Études-Poésies* (op. 53) are the best known.

Haberl, Franz Xaver, eminent German theorist, music editor, and historiographer; b. Oberellenbach, Lower Bavaria, April 12, 1840; d. Regensburg, Sept. 5, 1910. He studied in the Boys' Seminary at Passau, and took holy orders in 1862; 1862–67, cathedral Kapellmeister and musical director at the Seminary; 1867–70, organist at Santa Maria dell' Anima, Rome; 1871–82, cathedral Kapellmeister at Regensburg, where he founded, in 1875, a world-renowned school for church music. He was an authority on Catholic church music, past and present. In 1872 he assumed the editorship of the collection *Musica divina;* and edited the periodical *Musica sacra* in 1888. In 1876 he began to publish the *Cäcilienkalender,* the scope of which was greatly widened, until, after 1885, it was issued under the more appropriate name of *Kirchenmusikalisches Jahrbuch;* as such it has become one of the most important publications for historical studies concerning the church music of the 15th, 16th, and 17th centuries; Haberl continued as editor until 1907, when he resigned and was succeeded by Karl Weinmann. He founded a Palestrina Society in 1879, and (beginning with vol. X) was editor-in-chief of Breitkopf & Härtel's complete edition of Palestrina's works (33 vols., finished on the tercentenary of Palestrina's death, 1894), which he aided not only by his experience and learning, but also by rare manuscripts from his private collection. In 1899 he was elected President of the "Allgemeiner Cäcilienverein," and became editor of its official organ, *Fliegende Blätter für katholische Kirchenmusik.* In 1889 he was made Dr. theol. (*honoris causa*) by the University of Würzburg; in 1908 "Monsignore." Under his general supervision a new edition of the *Editio Medicea* (1614) of the plainchant melodies was issued, with papal sanction, at Regensburg (1871–81). When modern scholarship had proved that the original edition had not been published with papal sanction and had not been revised by Palestrina, that, in fact, it contained the old melodies in badly distorted and mutilated form, the papal sanction was withdrawn, the edition suppressed and replaced by a new *Editio Vaticana* in 1904. The result of this was that Haberl's books dealing with plainchant (which had been held in the highest esteem, and had passed through many editions) fell into desuetude. The books thus affected are: *Praktische Anweisung zum harmonischen Kirchengesang* (1864), *Magister Choralis* (1865; 12th ed., 1899; translated into English, French, Italian, Spanish, Polish, and Hungarian), *Officium hebdomadae sanctae* (1887, in German), *Psalterium vespertinum* (1888). His other writings, the value of which remains unimpaired, are *Bertalotti's Solfeggien* (1880), *Wilhelm Dufay* (1885), *Die römische 'Schola Cantorum' und die päpstlichen Kapellsänger bis zur Mitte des 16. Jahrhunderts* (1887), *Bibliographischer und thematischer Musikkatalog des päpstlichen Kapellarchivs im Vatikan zu Rom* (1888).

Habert, Johannes Evangelista, Bohemian organist, composer, and writer; b. Oberplan, Bohemia, Oct. 18, 1833; d. Gmunden, Sept. 1, 1896. He was organist at Gmunden from 1861; wrote sacred music and organ pieces; a complete edition of his works was published by Breitkopf & Härtel. He was founder and editor of the *Zeitschrift für katholische Kirchenmusik* (1868–83); publ. also *Beiträge zur Lehre von der musikalischen Komposition* (4 vols.; 1889 et seq.).
BIBLIOGRAPHY: A. Hartl, *Johannes Evangelista Habert, Organist in Gmunden* (Vienna, 1900).

Hackett, Charles, American tenor; b. Worcester, Mass., Nov. 4, 1889; d. New York, Jan. 1, 1942. He studied voice first in Boston, and then in Florence; made his opera debut in Genoa; then sang at La Scala, Milan; subsequently appeared in South America, London, Paris, etc. On Jan. 31, 1919, he made his American debut as the Count in *Il Barbiere di Siviglia* with the Metropolitan Opera Company; was a member of the Chicago Civic Opera (1923-33); in 1934 rejoined the Metropolitan Opera, and remained on its staff until his death.

Hackh, Otto (Christoph), German-American music teacher and composer; b. Stuttgart, Sept. 30, 1852; d. Brooklyn, Sept. 21, 1917. He studied at the Stuttgart Cons.; traveled as a concert pianist in Europe; in 1880 settled in New York; was head of the Grand Cons. there (1880-89); then taught piano privately. He publ. some 200 pieces for piano, in a modern salon style, and also many songs, some of which became extremely popular.

Hadden, James Cuthbert, Scottish writer on music; b. Banchory-Ternan, near Aberdeen, Sept. 9, 1861; d. Edinburgh, May 1, 1914. He studied organ in London; was organist in Aberdeen and Edinburgh; edited the *Scottish Musical Monthly* (1893-96); publ. several biographies: *Handel* (1888; new ed., 1904); *Mendelssohn* (1888; new ed., 1904); *George Thomson, the Friend of Burns* (1898); *Haydn* (1902); *Chopin* (1903); also *The Operas of Wagner; Their Plots, Music and History*

(1908); *Master Musicians* (1909); *Favorite Operas* (1910); *Composers in Love and Marriage* (1913); *Modern Musicians* (1914); edited *The Lays of Caledonia*, a collection of Scottish airs (Glasgow, 1883).

Hadley, Henry (Kimball), eminent American composer and conductor; b. Somerville, Mass., Dec. 20, 1871; d. New York, Sept. 6, 1937. He studied piano and violin with his father and then with S. Emery and G. W. Chadwick at the New England Cons. in Boston; in 1894, studied theory with Mandyczewski in Vienna. Returning to America, he became director of music at St. Paul's School, Garden City (1895-1902); toured various cities in Germany conducting his own works (1905-09); conducted at the Stadttheater in Mainz (1908-09) and brought out there his one-act opera *Safié*. In 1909 he was engaged as conductor of the Seattle Symph. Orch.; from 1911-15 he was conductor of the San Francisco Symph. Orch., and from 1920-27, associate conductor of the N.Y. Philharmonic Orch. In 1924 he again toured Europe; conducted symphonic concerts in Buenos Aires in 1927; was conductor of the Manhattan Symph. Orch. (1929-32) producing many American works. He was conductor at the opening concert of the Berkshire Festival at Stockbridge, Mass., in 1933. He traveled extensively; conducted his own works in Japan and Argentina; spent his last years mostly in New York. He received a Mus. D. from Tufts College (1925); was a member of the National Institute of Arts and Letters and the American Academy of Arts and Letters; and received the Order of Merit from the French government. Hadley occupied a position of prominence among American composers. In his style, he frankly adhered to programmatic writing. Although he shunned the unresolved dissonances of the ultra-modern school, he was not averse to using fairly advanced harmonies in an impressionist vein; he often applied exotic colors when the subject matter justified it. He was an excellent craftsman, both as composer and conductor, and contributed much to the growth of American music culture.
WORKS: A comic opera *Nancy Brown;* the grand operas *Safié* (Mainz, April 4, 1909), *Azora, The Daughter of Montezuma* (Chicago, Dec. 26, 1917), *Bianca* (N.Y., Oct. 18, 1918; composer conducting); *The Fire-Prince,* operetta (1917); *Cleopatra's Night* (N.Y., Jan. 31, 1920); *A Night in Old Paris* (1925); a festival play, *The Atonement of Pan* (San Francisco, Aug. 10, 1912); 5 symphonies: No. 1, *Youth and Life* (N.Y. Philharmonic, Dec. 2, 1897), No. 2, *The Four Seasons* (N.Y. Philharmonic, Dec. 20, 1901; won the Paderewski prize and one offered by the New England Cons.), No. 3 (Berlin Philharmonic, Dec. 27, 1907; composer conducting), No. 4, *North, East, South, West* (Norfolk, Conn., Festival, Jan. 6, 1911; composer conducting), No. 5, *Connecticut* (Norfolk, Conn., Festival, 1935); the overtures *Hector and Andromache, In Bohemia* (Boston Symph., Dec. 16, 1901), *Herod, Othello* (Philadelphia Orch., Dec. 26, 1919), *Youth Triumphant, Aurora Borealis* (1931), *Academic Overture*, and *Alma Mater* (1932); *The Enchanted Castle* (1933); the tone poems *Salome* (composed in 1905, before the production of *Salome* by Richard Strauss; publ. in 1906; performed by Muck and the Boston

Symph., April 12, 1907); *Lucifer* (Norfolk, Conn., Festival, June 2, 1914; composer conducting), *The Ocean* (N.Y. Philh., Nov. 17, 1921; composer conducting); an orchestral rhapsody, *The Culprit Fay* (Chicago Symph. at Grand Rapids, Mich., May 28, 1909; composer conducting; won a $1000 prize of the National Federation of Music Clubs); the orchestral suites *Oriental* (1903); *Ballet of the Flowers* (1925); *Suite ancienne* (1926); *Silhouettes, San Francisco* in 3 movements (Robin Hood Dell, July 17, 1932; composer conducting); *Streets of Pekin* (Tokyo, Sept. 24, 1930; composer conducting); *Scherzo Diabolique* for orch. "to recall a harrowing personal experience during a terrifying automobile ride at night, exceeding all speed limits" (Century of Progress Exposition, Chicago, Aug. 1934; composer conducting); incidental music to *The Daughter of Hamilcar* and *Audrey;* a *Konzertstück* for cello and orch. (1937); Piano Quintet (1920); 2 string quartets; 2 piano trios; Violin Sonata; Elegy for Cello and Piano; choral works with orch.: *In Music's Praise* (1899; won the Oliver Ditson Prize), *Merlin and Vivien, The Fate of Princess Kiyo, The Nightingale and the Rose, The Golden Prince, The Fairy Thorn, Ode to Music* (1917), *The New Earth* (1919), *Resurgam* (Cincinnati Music Festival, May 1923), *Mirtil in Arcadia* (Harrisburg, Pa., Festival, May 17, 1928), *Belshazzar* (1932); 6 ballads (*The Fairies; In Arcady; Jabberwocky; Lelawala, a Legend of Niagara; The Princess of Ys; A Legend of Granada);* many anthems; piano pieces and over 150 songs to German and English words. A Henry Hadley Foundation for the Advancement of American Music was organized in 1938.

BIBLIOGRAPHY: H. R. Boardman, *Henry Hadley, Ambassador of Harmony* (Emory Univ., Georgia, 1932); P. Berthoud, *The Musical Works of Dr. Henry Hadley* (N.Y., 1942).

Hadley, Patrick Arthur Sheldon, British composer; b. Cambridge, March 5, 1899; d. King's Lynn, Norfolk, Dec. 17, 1973. He studied at the Royal College of Music in London with Vaughan Williams and others (1922-25); in 1938 joined the music faculty at Cambridge Univ. He composed mostly vocal music; among his works are the cantatas *The Trees So High* (1931); *La Belle Dame sans merci* (1935); *Travelers* (1940); *The Hills* (1946); *Fen and Flood* (1956); *Connemara* (1958); *Cantata for Lent* (1960).

BIBLIOGRAPHY: W. Todds, *Patrick Hadley; a Memoir;* with a catalogue of works (London, 1974).

Hadow, Sir William Henry, English music educator; b. Ebrington, Gloucestershire, Dec. 27, 1859; d. London, April 8, 1937. He studied at Malvern College (1871-78) and Worcester College, Oxford (1878-82); M.A. (1888); Mus. B. (1890). He held various positions in English universities from 1885 till 1919; was knighted in 1918. He wrote a cantata, *The Soul's Pilgrimage;* a string quartet; 2 violin sonatas; a viola sonata; and a number of anthems. These however are of little significance; Hadow's importance lies in his books, written in a lively journalistic style. His book on Haydn, *A Croatian Composer* (London, 1897), claiming that Haydn was of Slavonic origin, aroused considerable controversy; modern research proves

the claim fanciful and devoid of foundation. Of more solid substance are his other writings: *Studies in Modern Music* (2 vols., 1892-95; 10th ed., 1921); *Sonata Form* (1896); *The Viennese Period* (vol. 5 of the Oxford History of Music, 1904); *Beethoven* (1917); *William Byrd* (1923); *Music* (in the Home Univ. Library, 1924; 3rd revised ed. by Sir George Dyson, 1949); *Church Music* (1926); *A Comparison of Poetry and Music* (1926); *Collected Essays* (1928); *English Music* (1931); *The Place of Music Among the Arts* (1933); *Richard Wagner* (1934). He edited songs of the British Islands (1903); was editor-in-chief of the *Oxford History of Music* (1901-05 and 1929); contributed articles to various British magazines and to the *Musical Quarterly* (Jan. 1915).

Hadzhiev, Parashken, Bulgarian composer; b. Sofia, April 14, 1912. He studied with his father, an opera conductor, and with Pantcho Vladigerov; later was a student in composition of Josef Marx in Vienna. Returning to Sofia, he was appointed prof. of the Sofia Cons. As a composer, he is at his best in music for the theater.

WORKS: musical fairly tale *There Was a Time* (Sofia, April 11, 1957); a comic opera *Lud gidia* (*Madcap;* Sofia, Nov. 15, 1959); a ballet *Silver Slippers* (Varna, March 20, 1962) and a tragic opera on a national Bulgarian subject, *Albena* (Varna, Nov. 2, 1962). Another opera, *A July Night,* was produced in Plovdiv, Feb. 16, 1965.

Hadzidakis, Manos, Greek composer; b. Xanthi, Macedonia, Oct. 23, 1925. He wrote piano pieces in an advanced idiom, recalling Prokofiev; then turned to film music. He is the composer of the famous theme song in the film released in America under the title *Never on Sunday.*

Haeffner, Johann Christian Friedrich, German composer; b. Oberschönau, near Suhl, March 2, 1759; d. Uppsala, Sweden, May 28, 1833. He was a pupil of Dierling at Schmalkalden; then studied at the Univ. of Leipzig, and served as proofreader for Breitkopf; then became conductor of a traveling opera troupe; in 1780 he arrived in Stockholm, where he became an organist at a German church. He produced at Stockholm several operas in the style of Gluck: *Electra* (1787), *Alkides* (1795), *Renaud* (1801), which had a favorable reception; in 1793 he was appointed court conductor; in 1808 he went to Uppsala, where he remained for the rest of his life, acting as organist of the cathedral and music director of the Univ. He took great interest in Swedish national music; publ. Swedish folksongs with accompaniment, and revised the melodies of the Geijer-Afzelius collection; edited a *Svenska Choralbok* (2 parts, 1819-21), in which he restored the choral melodies of the 17th century, and added preludes (1822); also arranged a collection of old Swedish songs in 4 parts (1832-33; he finished only 2 books).

Haesche, William Edwin, American music educator; b. New Haven, Conn., April 11, 1867; d. Roanoke, Va., Jan. 26, 1929. He studied violin with Bernhard Listemann and piano with Perabo; composition with Horatio Parker at Yale Univ. (Mus. Bac., 1897); taught orchestration at Yale Univ. (1903–22); in 1923 appointed violin teacher at Hollins College, Va., a post he held until his death. He was one of the organizers of the New Haven Symph. Orch., and was its concertmaster for 20 years. He wrote a symph. poem *Fridthjof and Ingeborg* (1897), *The Haunted Oak of Nannau*, for chorus and orch. (1902), and many violin pieces.

Hagel, Richard, German conductor; b. Erfurt, July 7, 1872; d. Berlin, May 1, 1941. He studied with his father; was an orch. violinist in Abo, Finland (1889), Koburg (1890), Meiningen (1892), and Sondershausen (1893); later undertook serious study at the Leipzig Cons. (1898–1900); conducted at the Leipzig Stadttheater (1900–09) and at Brunswick (1911–14). From 1919 till 1925 he conducted the Berlin Philharmonic; subsequently taught at various schools. He publ. *Die Lehre vom Partiturspiel* (Berlin, 1937).

Hageman, Maurits Leonard, Dutch violinist and composer; b. Zutfen, Sept. 25, 1829; d. Nijmegen, April 16, 1906. He studied with Bériot and Fétis at the Brussels Cons., graduating in 1852. After playing violin in the Italian Opera orch. at Brussels, he became a conductor at Groningen; then was director of the Cons. of Batavia, Java (1865–75) and conductor of the orch. there. Returning to Holland, he founded a music school in Leeuwarden. He wrote an oratorio *Daniel;* several other choral works; piano pieces; songs.

Hageman, Richard, distinguished American pianist, conductor and composer; b. Leeuwarden, Holland, July 9, 1882; d. Beverly Hills, Calif., March 6, 1966. He studied music with his father, **Maurits Hageman;** then took courses at the Brussels Cons. with Gevaert and Arthur de Greef. He held an auxilliary position as conductor at the Royal Opera in Amsterdam (1899–1903). After playing accompaniments for Mathilde Marchesi in Paris (1904–05), he came to the U.S. as accompanist for Yvette Guilbert in 1906; from 1905 until 1926 was on the conducting staff of the Metropolitan Opera; also conducted the summer opera at Ravinia Park in Chicago and taught voice at the Chicago Musical College. In 1938 he settled in Hollywood where he was engaged as composer of film music. He wrote 2 operas: *Caponsacchi* (1931; produced in Freiburg, Germany, as *Tragödie in Arezzo*, Feb. 18, 1932; at the Metropolitan Opera House, N.Y., Feb. 4, 1937; received the David Bispham Memorial Medal) and *The Crucible* (Los Angeles, Feb. 4, 1943). He achieved a lasting reputation mainly through his solo songs, of which *Do Not Go My Love* (to words by Rabindranath Tagore) and *At the Well* became extremely popular.

Hagen, Francis Florentine, American Moravian minister and composer; b. Salem, N.C., Oct. 30, 1815; d. Lititz, Pa., July 7, 1907. Served as teacher and minister in various Moravian congregations. He edited and compiled *Church and Home Organist's Companion* (several vols.). Wrote a number of anthems, in which a definite sense for distinguished popular melody is noticeable; also a cantata and an overture. His *Morning Star,* a Christmas carol, which, in Moravian communities, stood in continuous favor for almost a century, was reprinted in 1939. Another anthem is

included in the series *Music of the Moravians in America,* publ. by the N.Y. Public Library.

BIBLIOGRAPHY: A. G. Rau and H. T. David, *A Catalogue of Music by American Moravians* (Bethlehem, 1938).

Hagen, Friedrich Heinrich von der, German scholar; b. in the Ukraine, Feb. 19, 1780; d. Berlin, June 11, 1856, as prof. of German literature at the Univ. He publ. the valuable collection, *Minnesinger* (1838–56, in 5 vols.; in vol. III are *Minnegesänge* in notation according to the Jena Codex and other sources, with a treatise on the music of the Minnesinger); *Melodien zu der Sammlung deutscher, vlämischer und französcher Volkslieder* (1807; with Büsching).

Hagen, Theodor, writer on music; b. Hamburg, April 15, 1823; d. New York, Dec. 21, 1871. He lived in New York from 1854 as a teacher and critic; edited the *New York Weekly Review.* Under the *nom de plume* **Joachim Fels** he published *Civilisation und Musik* (1845).

Hagerup Bull, Edvard, Norwegian composer; b. Bergen, June 10, 1922. He studied composition in Norway with Bjarne Brustad and Ludvig Irgens Jensen; in 1947 went to Paris, where he took courses with Koechlin, Rivier, Messiaen and Milhaud; continued his studies in Berlin with Boris Blacher. His music bears a pleasing neo-Classical stamp.

WORKS: *Le Soldat de Plomb,* ballet suite (1948–49); Serenade for Orch. (1950); *Morceaux Rapsodiques,* divertimento for orch. (1950); 2 trumpet concertos (1950; 1960); *Sinfonia di Teatro,* symph. prelude (1950–51); *Petite Suite Symphonique* for small orch. (1951); *Escapades,* suite for orch. (1952); Divertimento for Piano and Orch. (1954); 5 symphonies: No. 1, *3 Mouvements Symphoniques* (1955); No. 2, *In modo d'una sinfonia* (1958–59); No. 3, *Sinfonia Espressiva* (1964); No. 4, *Sinfonia Humana* (1968); No. 5, *Sinfonia in memoriam* (1971–72); *3 Morceaux brefs* for saxophone and orch. (1955); *Cassation* for chamber orch. (1959); *Münchhausen,* ballet (1961); *Epilogue* for strings (1961); *Undecim Sumus* for chamber orch. of soloists (1962); *Dialogue* for flute, strings and piano (1965); *6 Epigrammes* for chamber ensemble (1969); Concerto for Flute and Chamber Orch. (1969); *Air Solennel,* symph. movement (1972); Clarinet Sonata (1951); *3 Bucoliques* for oboe, clarinet and bassoon (1953); Duo for Violin and Piano (1956); *Ad Usum Amicorum* for flute, violin, cello and piano (1957); *Marionettes sérieuses* for wind quintet (1960); *Quadrige* for 4 clarinets (1963); Sextet for Saxophone and Wind Quintet (1965); *Sonata Cantabile* for flute, violin, cello and piano (1966); *Concert* for trumpet, horn and trombone (1966); *Accents* for piano (1968); *Sonata con spirito* for piano quartet (1970).

Hägg, Gustaf Wilhelm, eminent Swedish organist and composer; b. Visby, Nov. 28, 1867; d. Stockholm, Feb. 7, 1925. Hägg was his mother's name which he legally adopted; his father's name was Peterson. Hägg was a remote relative of Jacob Adolf Hägg. He studied organ at the Stockholm Cons.; in 1893 he was appointed organist at the Klara Church in Stockholm, retaining this position for the rest of his life. In the interim he traveled for further study purposes in Germany and France (1897-1900). In 1904 he joined the staff of the Stockholm Cons., as teacher of harmony and organ playing. He enjoyed a distinguished reputation in Sweden as an organist, and gave numerous recitals in which he played the works of César Franck and other organ composers. He also composed 5 organ concertos and other organ pieces; several cantatas and songs. He arranged and published collections of Swedish songs (Stockholm, 1908), and an album *Songs of Sweden* (N.Y., 1909).

Hägg, Jacob Adolf, Swedish composer; b. Oestergarn, June 27, 1850; d. Hudiksvall, March 1, 1928. He was a remote relative of Gustaf Wilhelm Hägg. He studied at the Stockholm Cons.; then received a stipend to take courses with Gade in Denmark who exercised a decisive influence on his style of composition; he further studied piano with Anton Door in Vienna and music theory with Kiel in Berlin. Ambition to learn and relentless diligence in his studies upset his mental equilibrium so that he had to spend 15 years in a sanitarium (1880–95). He recovered but retired to the country, reducing his activity to a minimum. Despite this misadventure he was able to leave a considerable legacy of works, among them 5 symphonies, of which *Nordische Symphonie* (1870; revised in 1890) was the best known; 3 overtures; Cello Sonata; Piano Trio; String Quartet and other chamber music; piano pieces; and songs.
BIBLIOGRAPHY: *Jacob Adolf Hägg* (Leipzig, 1903).

Haggard, Merle Ronald, American song writer and popular singer; b. Bakersfield, Calif., April 6, 1937. He sang country music since early childhood; socially incorrigible, he escaped from two reform schools 7 times before being jailed for an abortive heist; in his autobiographical song he asks a rhetorical question: "Did you ever steal a quarter when you was 10 years old?" and after detailing his adult misdeeds, answers "I done it all." This ballad, for which he improvised both words and music, was his first great hit. His popularity grew; his recordings fetched top premiums, with individual albums reaching "gold" and "platinum" numbers in sales.

Haggin, Bernard H., American music critic; b. New York, Dec. 29, 1900. He was music critic of the *Brooklyn Daily Eagle* (1934-37) and of *The Nation* (1936-57). An aggressive writer who held unalterable opinions on musical matters, he adopted a polemical manner of personal journalism, disregarding all conventional amenities. He collected many of his articles in book form. He publ. *A Book of the Symphony* (N.Y., 1937); *Music on Records* (N.Y., 1938; 4th edition, 1946); *Music for the Man Who Enjoys Hamlet* (N.Y., 1944); *Music in The Nation* (N.Y., 1949; a collection of articles from the magazine *The Nation*); *The Listener's Musical Companion* (New Brunswick, N.J., 1956); *Conversations with Toscanini* (N.Y., 1959); *Music Observed* (N.Y., 1964; reprinted in 1974 under the title *35 Years of Music*); *The New Listener's Companion and Record Guide* (N.Y., 1967; new editions,

1968, 1971); *The Toscanini Musicians Knew* (N.Y., 1967); *A Decade of Music* (N.Y., 1973).

Hahn, Carl, American conductor; b. Indianapolis, Oct. 23, 1874; d. Cincinnati, May 13, 1929. A member of a musical family (his father played the flute; his brother was a violinist), he studied piano and cello. From 1909 to 1912 he conducted the Beethoven Society, a male chorus, in San Antonio, Texas; then lived in New York and Cincinnati. He wrote a number of choruses and songs, some of which are quite singable.

Hahn, Reynaldo, Venezuelan-born French composer; b. Caracas, Aug. 9, 1874; d. Paris, Jan. 28, 1947. His father, a merchant from Hamburg, settled in Venezuela about 1850; the family moved to Paris when Reynaldo Hahn was five years old. He studied singing and apparently had an excellent voice; a professional recording he made in 1910 testifies to that. He studied music theory at the Paris Cons. with Dubois and Lavignac and composition with Massenet who exercised the most important influence on Hahn's own music. He also studied conducting, achieving a high professional standard as an opera conductor. In 1906 he was invited to conduct at the Mozart Sesquicentennial Festival in Salzburg (other conductors were Mahler and Richard Strauss). In 1934 he became music critic of *Le Figaro*. He remained in France during the Nazi occupation at a considerable risk to his life, since he was Jewish on his father's side. In 1945 he was named a member of the Institut de France and Music Director of the Paris Opéra. Hahn's music is distinguished by a facile, melodious flow and a fine romantic flair. Socially, he was known in Paris for his brilliant wit. He maintained a passionate youthful friendship with Marcel Proust, who portrayed him as a poetic genius in his novel *Jean Santeuil*; their intimate correspondence was published in 1946.
WORKS: OPERAS: *L'Île du Rêve*, a "Polynesian idyll," after Pierre Loti (Opéra-Comique, Paris, March 23, 1898); *La Carmélite* (Opéra-Comique, Paris, Dec. 16, 1902); *Nausicaa* (Monte Carlo, April 10, 1919); *Fête triomphale* (Paris Opéra, July 14, 1919); *La Colombe de Bouddah* (Cannes, March 21, 1921); *Ciboulette*, light opera (Théâtre des Variétés, Paris, April 7, 1923); *Le Marchand de Venise*, after Shakespeare (Paris Opéra, March 25, 1935). OPERETTAS: *Miousic* (Paris, March 22, 1914); *Mozart*, after a play by Sascha Guitry (Paris, Dec. 2, 1925); *Brummel* (Paris, Jan. 20, 1931); *O mon bel inconnu* (Paris, Oct. 5, 1933); *Malvina* (Gaîté Lyrique, Paris, March 25, 1935); incidental music to Daudet's *L'Obstacle* (1890), Croisset's *Deux courtisanes* (1902); Racine's *Esther* (1905); Hugo's *Angelo* (1905); Hugo's *Lucrèce Borgia* (1911); Wolff's and Duvernois' *Le Temps d'aimer* (1926). BALLETS: *Fin d'amour* (1892); *Le Bal de Béatrice d'Este* (Paris, April 11, 1907); *La Fête chez Thérèse* (Paris, Feb. 16, 1910); *Medusa* (Monte Carlo, Dec. 24, 1911); *Le Dieu bleu* (Diaghilev's Ballet, Paris, May 14, 1912); *Le Bois sacré* (1912); two symphonic poems: *Nuit d'amour bergamasque* (1897) and *Promethée triomphant* (1911); a Christmas mystery, *La Pastorale de Noël* (1908). A lyric comedy *Le Oui des jeunes filles*, left unfinished at Hahn's death, was completed and orchestrated by Henri Busser and performed posthu-

mously at the Opéra-Comique in Paris on June 21, 1949. Hahn further wrote a Violin Concerto (Paris, Feb. 26, 1928); Piano Concerto (Paris, Feb. 4, 1931); Cello Concerto, Piano Quintet, String Quartet and a number of piano pieces, among them a suite, *Portraits des peintres,* inspired by poems of Marcel Proust. But his most signal accomplishment lies in his songs, such as *Les Chansons grises* (1891–92), written when he was still a conservatory student, *L'Heure exquise* and *Si mes vers avaient des ailes.* Hahn was a brilliant journalist. His articles were collected in the following publications: *Du Chant* (Paris, 1920); *Notes. Journal d'un Musicien* (Paris, 1933); *L'Oreille au guet* (Paris, 1937); and *Thèmes variés* (Paris, 1946).

BIBLIOGRAPHY: Daniel Bendahan, *Reynaldo Hahn. Su vida y su obra* (Caracas, 1973; profusely illustrated with photographs and musical examples); Bernard Gavoty, *Reynaldo Hahn: le musicien de la belle époque* (Paris, 1976).

Hahn, Ulrich. See **Han, Ulrich.**

Haibel, Petrus Jakob, Austrian composer; b. Graz, July 20, 1762; d. Djakovar, March 24, 1826. He was engaged in Vienna as a tenor; in 1806 he settled in Djakovar; there he married Sophie Weber, sister of Mozart's widow. He produced several stage works in Vienna, among them the ballet *Le nozze disturbate* (May 18, 1795), and a singspiel *Der Tyroler Wastl* (May 14, 1796), which became very popular. Other productions were *Der Papagei und die Gans* (May 25, 1799); *Tsching, Tsching, Tsching* (Feb. 6, 1802); *Der kleine Cesar* (July 25, 1804), etc.

Haieff, Alexei, Russian-American composer; b. Blagoveshchensk, Siberia, Aug. 25, 1914. He received his primary education at Harbin, Manchuria; in 1931 came to the U.S.; studied with Rubin Goldmark and Frederick Jacobi at the Juilliard School of Music in New York, and also took private piano lessons with Alexander Siloti, then resident in New York; during 1938–39 he studied with Nadia Boulanger in Paris. He held a Guggenheim Fellowship in 1946 and again in 1949; was a Fellow at the American Academy in Rome (1947–48); prof. at the Univ. of Buffalo (1962–68) and composer-in-residence at the Univ. of Utah (1968–71). In his music Haieff follows Stravinsky's type of neo-Classical writing, observing an austere economy of means, but achieving modernistic effects by a display of rhythmic agitation, often with jazzy undertones.

WORKS: the ballets *The Princess Zondilda and Her Entourage* (1946) and *Beauty and the Beast* (1947); 3 symphonies: No. 1 (1942); No. 2 (Boston, April 11, 1958; received the American International Music Fund Award); No. 3 (New Haven, April 11, 1961); Divertimento for Orch. (N.Y., April 5, 1946); Violin Concerto (1948); Piano Concerto (N.Y., April 27, 1952; received the Award of the N.Y. Music Critics Circle); Sonatina for String Quartet (1937); 3 *Bagatelles* for oboe and bassoon (1939); Serenade for Oboe, Clarinet, Bassoon and Piano (1942); *Eclogue* for cello and piano (1947); *La Nouvelle Héloise* for harp and string quartet (1953); Cello Sonata (1963); *Éloge* for chamber orch. (1967); *Caligula* for baritone and orch.,

after Robert Lowell (N.Y., Nov. 5, 1971); Sonata for 2 pianos (1945); Piano Sonata (1955); songs.

Haile, Eugen, German-American composer; b. Ulm, Feb. 21, 1873; d. Woodstock, N.Y., Aug. 14, 1933. He studied at the Stuttgart Cons.; emigrated to America in 1903. He wrote about 200 songs to German texts, some of them of excellent quality (*Herbst, Der Todesengel singt, Teufelslied, Soldaten kommen,* etc.). His musical setting to a spoken drama ('gesprochene Oper'), *The Happy Ending,* produced in New York on Aug. 21, 1916, is an interesting attempt to combine spoken words in the play with pitch inflections in the vocal parts, in the manner of Sprechstimme. His other opera *Harold's Dream* was produced in Woodstock on June 30, 1933. His wife, **Elise Haile,** was a singer; together they presented several concerts of his German songs in New York. A Eugen Haile Society was formed in New York in 1914 to organize further performances of his music.

Hainl, François, French cellist and conductor; b. Issoire, Nov. 16, 1807; d. Paris, June 2, 1873. After graduating as a cellist from the Paris Cons. with a first prize (1830), he went to Lyons, where he conducted theater music (1841–63); then conducted at the Paris Opéra (1863–72). He wrote an orch. fantasy on Rossini's *William Tell;* publ. a valuable account *De la musique à Lyon depuis 1713 jusqu'à 1852.*

Haitink, Bernard, eminent Dutch conductor; b. Amsterdam, March 4, 1929. He studied violin, and as a youth played in the Netherlands Radio Philharmonic Orch.; took lessons in conducting with Felix Hupka and Ferdinand Leitner. In 1957 he became the principal conductor of the Radio Philharmonic, and in 1961, associate conductor of the Amsterdam Concertgebouw; he conducted it on its American tour in 1961 and in 1962 led it on a tour in Japan. In the interim he made guest appearances in England, in Berlin, Vienna, and in Los Angeles. In 1968 he obtained the post of conductor with the London Philharmonic, while keeping his position in Amsterdam. In 1976 he made his debut as guest conductor with the New York Philharmonic, and was reengaged for several appearances in 1978. He conducted opera in Glyndebourne from 1972 on and made his first appearance at Covent Garden in 1977, in operas of Mozart and Wagner. In his interpretations, Haitink follows the venerated traditions of Mengelberg, without the latter's penchant for romantic rhetoric; like his predecessors at the Concertgebouw, Haitink cultivates in his programs the symphonies of Mahler and Bruckner, as well as cycles of Beethoven's symphonies. He was knighted in 1978 by Queen Elizabeth II of England in recognition of "his enormous contribution to the artistic life in England."

Haitzinger, Anton, Austrian tenor; b. Wilfersdorf, Liechtenstein, March 14, 1796; d. Vienna, Dec. 31, 1869. He studied in Vienna; made his opera debut in 1821; then sang in Prague, Frankfurt, Paris, and London; retired in 1850, and returned to Vienna. In his prime he enjoyed an excellent reputation, and was equally successful in the Italian and German repertory. He publ. a song, *Vergiss mein nicht,* and a manual of singing.

Hajdú, André, Hungarian-born Israeli composer; b. Budapest, March 5, 1932. He studied with Kodály, Szabó, Szervánszky and Kosá at the Budapest Music Academy; then took seminars in Paris with Milhaud and Messiaen (1956). For 2 years he taught at the Cons. in Tunis (1959–61); emigrated to Israel in 1966 and in 1967 became a teacher at the Tel Aviv Academy of Music. His music is folkloristic in its sources of inspiration, while the harmonic idiom is fairly advanced.
    WORKS: *Gypsy Cantata* (1956); *A Little Hell* for orch. (1960); *Babeliana* for orch. (1964); Piano Concerto (1968); *Ludus Paschalis* for 8 soloists, children's chorus, and 9 instruments (1970); *Terouath Melech,* Jewish rhapsody for clarinet and string orch. (1973); *Military Diary* (*The Art of the Canon*), 50 canons for different instrumental combinations (1976); *Stories About Mischievous Boys* for orch. (1976); *5 Sketches in a Sentimental Mood* for piano quartet (1976); *The Prophet of Truth and the Prophet of Deceit* for narrator and string orch. (1977).

Hajdú, Lóránt, Rumanian-born Hungarian composer; b. Bucharest, Aug. 12, 1937. He was brought to Budapest as an infant; he studied music with István Szelényi; also studied horn playing at the Budapest Cons.; later took courses in composition with Endre Szervánszky at the Academy of Music, graduating in 1965. He subsequently devoted himself to teaching. Among his works are Bagatelles for Piano (1955); Elegy for Horn and Piano (1958); Cello Sonata (1958); Piano Sonatina (1959); Horn Quartet (1960); Suite for 2 Horns and Piano (1962); 2 wind quintets (1965, 1973); Piano Concerto (1966); Violin Concerto (1967); Symph. No. 1 (1968); *10 Miniatures,* trio for winds (1970); Trumpet Sonata (1971); Piano Concertino (1972); *Oscillazione* for clarinet and piano (1972); Toccata for Piano (1972); *Scherzo-capriccio* for piano (1972).

Hajdu, Mihály, Hungarian composer; b. Orosháza, Jan. 30, 1909. He studied composition with Kodály at the Academy of Music in Budapest; in 1961 was appointed to its faculty.
    WORKS: an opera, *Kádár Kata* (1957; Budapest, 1959); *2 Scherzi* for piano (1931); Suite for Orch. (1934); 2 string quartets (1936, 1970); Piano Sonata (1940); Piano Sonatina (1952); Violin Sonata (1953); Variations and Rondo for cello and piano (1955); Piano Trio (1957); *A munka dicsérete* (*In Praise of Work*), symph. poem (1958); Trio for Winds (1958); Concertino for Cello and Strings (1966); Piano Concerto (1968); Cello Sonatina (1969); *Capriccio all'ongarese* for clarinet and orch. (1969); *8 Etudes* for string orch. (1970); *3 Pieces* for 2 pianos (1971); *30 Little Pieces* for cello and piano, or 2 cellos (1973).

Hakansson, Knut Algot, Swedish composer; b. Kinna, Nov. 4, 1887; d. Göteborg, Dec. 13, 1929. He studied philosophy and philology at the Univ. of Uppsala; later traveled in Germany. He wrote a ballet *Mylitta* (1918); several orchestral suites on Swedish themes; a string quartet, a string trio and other chamber music.

His most significant works are for chorus, many of them derived from the melodic patterns of Swedish folksongs.

Hakim, Talib Rasul, black American composer; b. Asheville, North Carolina, Feb. 8, 1940. His original name was **Stephen A. Chambers;** he changed it to Hakim in 1973 after conversion to Sufism, a precursory philosophy of Islam. He studied music at the Manhattan School of Music, New York College of Music and the New School for Social Research (1958–65), where his teachers included Starer, Sydeman, Overton, Feldman, Chou Wen-Chung, Wittenberg and the jazz saxophonist Ornette Coleman. He taught at Pace College in New York (1970–72) and since 1972 at Adelphi University. Hakim received a National Endowment for the Arts grant for 1973–74 and for 1975; received the ASCAP Composers' Award 3 times and the Bennington Composers' Conference Fellowship 4 times. He employs in his music a series of dissonant blocks of sound moving along in asymmetrical progressions.
    WORKS: *Mutations* for bass clarinet, trumpet, horn, viola and cello (1964); *Peace-Mobile* for wind quintet (1964); *Ode to Silence* for soprano and piano (1964); *Encounter* for wind quintet, trumpet and trombone (1965); *Four* for clarinet, trumpet, trombone and piano (1965); *A Piano Piece* (1965); *Shapes* for chamber orch. (1965); *Portraits* for flute, bass clarinet, piano and 3 percussionists (1965); *Titles* for wind quartet (1965); *Contours* for oboe, bassoon, horn, trumpet, cello and double bass (1966); *Inner-Sections* for flute, clarinet, trombone, piano and percussion (1967); *Roots and Other-things* for flute, oboe, clarinet, horn, trumpet, trombone, viola, cello and double bass (1967); *Sound-Gone,* "philosophical sketch" for piano (1967); *Currents* for string quartet (1967); *Quote-Unquote* for baritone, oboe, trumpet and 2 percussionists (1967); *Sound-Image* for female voices, brass, strings, and percussion (1969); *Placements* for piano and 5 percussionists (1970); *Set-three* for soprano, cello and piano (1970); *Visions of Ishwara* for orch. (N.Y., Oct. 10, 1970); *Reflections on the 5th Ray* for narrator and chamber orch. (1972); *Sketchy Blue-bop* for jazz band ensemble (1973); *Tone-Prayers* for chorus, piano and percussion (1973); *Re/Currences* for orch. (Washington, June 7, 1975); *Concepts* for orch. (1976); *Music* for soprano and 9 players (1977).

Halász, László, Hungarian-American conductor; b. Debrecen, June 6, 1905. He studied piano, theory and conducting at the Budapest Cons., graduating in 1929; toured Europe as a concert pianist (1928–31), but devoted himself mainly to conducting. After numerous conducting engagements in Budapest, Prague and Vienna, he emigrated to America in 1936; became a naturalized American citizen in 1943. He was conductor of the St. Louis Grand Opera (1939–42); in 1943 was appointed conductor and music director of the New York City Opera Co., where he established an audacious policy of producing modern operas, but became embroiled in personal difficulties with the management, and resigned in 1951. He then filled in engagements as an opera conductor in America, Spain and Brazil. From 1965 to 1968 he conducted the Eastman Philharmonic Orch. in Rochester, N.Y.; then was director of the Music College at Old Westbury campus of State Univ. of N.Y. (1968–71); in 1971 was appointed program director of music at the State Univ., N.Y., at Stony Brook.

Hale, Adam de la. See **Adam de la Halle.**

Hale, Philip, eminent American music critic; b. Norwich, Conn., March 5, 1854; d. Boston, Nov. 30, 1934. He took music lessons in his early youth, and as a boy played the organ in the Unitarian Church at Northampton, Mass.; went to Yale Univ. to study law, and was admitted to the bar in 1880. He then took organ lessons with Dudley Buck; subsequently went to Europe (1882–87), where he studied organ with Haupt in Berlin, and composition with Rheinberger in Munich and with Guilmant in Paris. Returning to America he served as church organist in Albany, Troy and Boston, but soon abandoned this employment for his true vocation, that of drama and music criticism. He was a forceful and brilliant writer; his articles were often tinged with caustic wit directed against incompetent performers and, regrettably, against many modern composers; he also disliked Brahms, and was credited with the celebrated but possibly apocryphal quip that the exits in the newly opened Symphony Hall in Boston should have been marked not "Exit in Case of Fire," but "Exit in Case of Brahms." Another verbal dart attributed to Philip Hale was his dismissal of a singer with a concluding sentence, "Valuable time was consumed." Hale was the music critic for the *Boston Home Journal* (1889–91), *The Boston Post* (1890–91), *The Boston Journal* (1891–1903), and for *The Boston Herald,* of which he was also drama editor (1904–33). He was also editor of the Boston *Musical Record* (1897–1901). From 1901 till 1933 he compiled the program books of the Boston Symph. Orch., setting a standard of erudition and informative annotation. He edited *Modern French Songs* for The Musician's Library (1904); was joint author with Louis C. Elson of *Famous Composers and Their Works* (1900). Hale was succeeded as the program annotator of the Boston Symph. by John N. Burk, who published a selection of Hale's articles under the title *Philip Hale's Boston Symph. Programme Notes* (N.Y., 1935; revised edition, 1939). Hale's voluminous archives and collections of newspaper articles are preserved in the Music Division of the Boston Public Library.

Hales, Hubert (James), English composer; b. Bradford, April 29, 1902; d. Cromer, England, July 13, 1965. He studied at Eton College and at King's College in Cambridge; subsequently devoted himself to teaching; occupied various posts as Director of Music in British schools and colleges. He wrote several works for orchestra, a string quartet and a number of piano pieces.

Halévy, Jacques-François-Fromental-Élie, celebrated French opera composer; b. Paris, May 27, 1799; d. Nice, March 17, 1862. He was a child prodigy. At ten he entered the Paris Cons. as an elementary pupil of Cazot. In 1810 he studied piano with Lambert; in 1811, harmony with Berton; and counterpoint for five years with Cherubini. At seventeen he competed for the Prix de Rome, winning the 2nd prize with his cantata *Les Derniers Moments du Tasse;* in 1817 he again won the 2nd prize with *La Mort d'Adonis;* in 1819 he gained the Grand Prix de Rome with his *Herminie.* He had previously composed an opera, *Les Bohémiennes* (never performed), published a piano sonata for 4 hands, and set to music the 130th Psalm in Hebrew, the De Profundis. During his stay in Italy he wrote another opera. In 1822, on his return to Paris, he made vain attempts to produce his grand opera *Pygmalion* and *Les Deux Pavillons* (comedy-opera). It was not until 1827 that he brought out a one-act comedy-opera, *L'Artisan,* at the Théâtre Feydeau; though with little success. The same year he succeeded Daussoigne as prof. of harmony and accompaniment at the Cons.; following Fétis as prof. of counterpoint and fugue in 1833, and taking a class of advanced composition in 1840. In 1827 he was engaged as the harpsichordist at the Italian Opera. In 1828, with Rifaut, he composed *Le Roi et le bâtelier* in honor of Charles X. On Dec. 9 of the same year *Clari* (with Malibran as prima donna) was a success at the Théâtre Italien; *Le Dilettante d'Avignon* was produced on Nov. 7, 1829; and on May 3, 1830 the grand ballet *Manon Lescaut.* Halévy was now appointed "chef du chant" at the Opéra, a post retained during 16 years. In 1831 *La Langue musicale* was produced at the Opéra-Comique; *La Tentation* (Paris, June 20, 1832; ballet-opera, with Gide), at the Opéra; *Les Souvenirs de Lafleur* (Opéra-Comique, March 4, 1833); and on May 16 of the same year a completion of Hérold's unfinished *Ludovic,* which proved very successful. On Feb. 23, 1835, the Paris Opéra produced Halévy's masterpiece, *La Juive,* which soon became one of the most spectacular successes of opera theaters throughout Europe and America. A few months later appeared *L'Éclair* (Dec. 16, 1835), a sparkling comedy-opera. To add to his growing reputation, Halévy was created Chevalier of the Legion of Honor. On the death of Reicha (1836) Halévy succeeded him as one of the three musical members of the Académie; and in 1854 was appointed Secretary for life. With *La Juive* Halévy attained not only the zenith of his powers, but also of his triumphs. *La Juive* was followed by *Guido et Ginevra* (March 5, 1838); *Les Treize* (April 15, 1839); *Le Shérif* (Sept. 2, 1839); *Le Drapier* (Jan. 6, 1840); *Le Guitarrero* (Jan. 21, 1841); *La Reine de Chypre* (Dec. 22, 1841); *Charles VI* (Feb. 3, 1843); *Le Lazzarone* (March 23, 1844); *Les Mousquetaires de la reine* (March 15, 1846). He collaborated with Adam, Auber, and Carafa in *Les Premiers Pas* for the inauguration of the National Opera (1847). His next productions were: *Le Val d'Andorre* (Nov. 11, 1848); *La Fée aux roses* (Oct. 1, 1849); *La Dame de Pique* (Dec. 28, 1850). On June 8, 1850, Halévy conducted in London an Italian opera, *La Tempesta.* He then produced in Paris *Le Juif errant* (April 23, 1852); *Le Nabab* (Sept. 1, 1853); *Jaguarita* (May 14, 1855); *L'Inconsolable* (under the nom de plume **Albert;** 1855); *Valentine d'Aubigny* (1856); *La Magicienne* (March 17, 1858). Besides his operas, Halévy wrote a piano sonata for 4 hands, *romances,* nocturnes, part-songs for men's voices; scenes from *Prometheus Unbound* (Paris, March 18, 1849); the cantatas *Italie* (1849) and *Les Plagues du Nil* (1859) and left the almost finished scores of two operas, *Vanina d'Ornano* (completed by Bizet) and *Le Déluge* (originally *Noé*, completed by Bizet; performed on April 5, 1885). In the Paris schools his *Leçons de lecture musicale* (Paris, 1857) was adopted as the textbook for singing. *Souvenirs et portraits* (1861) and *Derniers souvenirs et portraits* (1863) were collections of the funeral orations that, as Secretary of the Académie, he had delivered at the obsequies of deceased members. At the Paris Cons. he had many distinguished pupils, among them Gounod and Bizet (who married Halévy's daughter).

BIBLIOGRAPHY: Short biographies of Halévy were published by his brother Léon (1862), E. Monnais (1863), A. Catelin (1863), and A. Pougin (1865); see also Mina Curtiss, "F. Halévy," *Musical Quarterly* (April 1953).

Halffter, Cristóbal, significant Spanish composer and conductor (nephew of **Ernesto** and **Rodolfo**); b. Madrid, March 24, 1930. He studied composition with Conrado del Campo at the Cons. in Madrid (1947–51), then had private lessons with Alexandre Tansman in Paris. He taught at the Madrid Cons. (1960–67) and was associated with the Radio Nacional de Espana; traveled as conductor and lecturer in Europe; visited the U.S. in 1966. In his music, he adopted a radical modern idiom; evolved a modified technique of dodecaphonic writing, and explored electronic sound.

WORKS: an opera, *Don Quichotte* (Düsseldorf, 1970); a ballet, *Saeta* (Madrid, Oct. 28, 1955); *Scherzo* for orch. (1951); Piano Concerto (Madrid, March 13, 1954); *2 Movements* for timpani and strings (Madrid, June 26, 1957); Concertino for String Orch. (1956; expanded version of his First String Quartet); *5 Microformas* for orch. (1960); *Rhapsodia española de Albeniz* for piano and orch. (1960); Sinfonia for 3 Instrumental Groups (1963); *Sequencias* for orch. (1964; Madrid, June 16, 1964); *Lineas y puntos* for 20 winds and strings (1967; Donaueschingen, Oct. 22, 1967); *Anillos* for orch. (1967–68; performed as a ballet, Lyon, April 13, 1971); *Fibonaciana*, concerto for flute and string orch. (Lisbon, May 30, 1970); *Planto por las victimas de la violencia (Plaint for the Victims of Violence)* for chamber ensemble and tape (Donaueschingen, Oct. 17, 1971); *Requiem por la Libertad Imaginada* for orch. (1971); *Pinturas negras* for orch. and concertante organ (1972); *Procesional* for 2 pianos, winds and percussion (Strasbourg, June 8, 1974); *Tiempo para Espacios* for harpsichord and 12 strings (1974); Cello Concerto (1974; Granada, June 24, 1975); *Elegias a la Muerte de Tres Poetas Españoles* for orch. (1974–75); *Pourquoi* for 12 strings (1974–75). FOR VOICE: *Antifona Pascual a la Virgen (Regina Coeli)* for soprano, contralto and orch. (1951); *Misa Ducal* for chorus and orch. (Madrid, May 14, 1956); *In exspectatione resurrectionis Domini*, cantata (1962); *Brecht-Lieder* for voice and orch. (1967); *In memoriam Anaick* for child narrator, children's chrous and ad lib. instruments (1967); *Symposion* for baritone, chorus and orch. (1968); *Yes Speak Out Yes*, cantata, after a text by Norman Corwin, in honor of the 20th anniversary of the UN's declaration of human rights (New York, Dec. 12, 1968); *Noche pasiva*

del sentido for soprano, 2 percussionists and tapes (1971); *Gaudium et Spes* for 32 voices and tapes (1972); *Oracion a Platero* for narrator, chorus, children's chorus and 5 percussionists (1975). CHAMBER MUSIC: 2 string quartets: No. 1, *3 Pieces* (1955) and No. 2, *Memories, 1970* (1970); *3 Pieces* for solo flute (1959); Solo Violin Sonata (1959); *Codex* for guitar (1963); *Espejos (Mirrors)* for 4 percussionists and tape (1963); *Antiphonismoi* for 7 players (1967); *Oda* for 8 players (1969); *Noche Activa del Espiritu* for 2 pianos and electronics (1973). FOR PIANO: Sonata (1951), and *Formantes* for 2 pianos (1961).

Halffter, Ernesto, important Spanish composer; brother of **Rodolfo Halffter;** b. Madrid, Jan. 16, 1905. He studied composition with Manuel de Falla and Adolfo Salazar; as a young man he organized a chamber ensemble in Seville with which he presented works by contemporary Spanish composers. He first attracted attention of the music world with his *Sinfonietta* which was included in the program of the Oxford Festival of the International Society for Contemporary Music (July 23, 1931). At the outbreak of the Spanish Civil War in 1936, he went to Lisbon; returned to Madrid in 1960. In his music he continued the tradition of Spanish modern nationalism, following the stylistic and melorhythmic formations of his teacher Manuel de Falla; he also completed and orchestrated Falla's unfinished scenic cantata, *Atlántida*, which was first performed in Milan on June 18, 1962. His other significant works are *Fantaisie portugaise* for orch. (Paris, March 23, 1941); *Automne malade* for voice and orch.; *Suite ancienne* for wind instruments; chamber opera, *Entr'acte* (1964); ballet, *Fantasía galaica* (Milan, 1967); *Psalmen* for soloist, chorus and orch. (1967); Guitar Concerto (1968).

BIBLIOGRAPHY: A. Salazar, *La música contemporanea en España* (Madrid, 1930).

Halffter, Rodolfo, eminent Spanish-Mexican composer (brother of **Ernesto** and uncle of **Cristóbal**); b. Madrid, Oct. 30, 1900. He acquired a considerable technique of composition mainly by the study of classical works; received some instruction and advice from Manuel de Falla in Granada (1929). As a young man, he was a member of a group of Spanish composers promoting national Spanish music in a modern idiom. From 1934–36 he was a music critic of *La Voz*. During the Spanish Civil War, he occupied important positions in the cultural sections of the Loyalist government; was chief of the Music Section of the Ministry of Propaganda (1936) and then became a member of the Central Musical Council of the Spanish Republic (1937); after the Loyalist defeat, he fled to France and then to Mexico, where he settled in 1939 and became a naturalized citizen. In 1940 he founded the first Mexican company for contemporary ballet, "La Paloma azul"; founded the publishing house Ediciones Mexicanas de Música in 1946 and remains its manager; edited the journal *Nuestra Música* (1946–52); was director of the music department of the National Institute of Fine Arts (1959–64).

WORKS: His early music is influenced by Manuel de Falla and is imbued with Spanish melorhythms; he experimented with dodecaphonic structures; his *3 Ho-*

jas de álbum (1953) were the earliest pieces of 12-tone music published in Mexico. The scores of his opera buffa *Clavileño* (1934–36) and an *Impromptu* for orch. (1931–32) were lost when a bomb hit the house where he stayed on the Spanish border during the Civil War. His other works include 3 ballets: *Don Lindo de Almería* (1935; Mexico City, Jan. 9, 1940); *La Madrugada del Panadero* (*The Baker's Morning*, Mexico City, Sept. 20, 1940) and *Elena la Traicionera* (Mexico City, Nov. 23, 1945); Suite for Orch. (1924–28; Madrid, Nov. 5, 1930); *Obertura concertante* for piano and orch. (1932; Valencia, May 23, 1937); Divertimento for 9 Instruments (1935; Mexico City, Nov. 18, 1943); Violin Concerto (1939–40; Mexico City, June 26, 1942); an orchestral scoring of *Tres sonatas* of Antonio Soler (1951); *Obertura festiva* (Mexico City, May 25, 1953); *Tres Piezas* for string orch. (Mexico City, Aug. 10, 1955); *Tripartita* for orch. (Mexico City, July 15, 1960); *Diferencias* for orch. (Mexico City, Sept. 13, 1970); *Alborada* for orch. (Mexico City, May 9, 1976); *Giga* for solo guitar (1930); *Pastorale* for violin and piano (1940); *Tres Piezas breves* for solo harp (1944); String Quartet (1957–58); Cello Sonata (1960); *Tres Movimientos* for string quartet (1962); *8 Tientos* (*Fantasias*) for string quartet (1973). FOR PIANO: *Dos sonatas de El Escorial* (1928), *Preludio y fuga* (1932), *Danza de Ávila* (1936), *Pequeñas Variaciones Elegiacas* (1937), *Homenaje a Antonio Machado* (1944), 3 sonatas (1947, 1951, 1967), *11 Bagatelles* (1949), *Tres Hojas de álbum* (1953), *Música* for 2 pianos (1965), *Laberinto: Cuatro intentos de acertar con la salida* (*Labyrinth: 4 Attempts to Locate the Exit*, 1971–72), *Homenaje a Arturo Rubinstein* (1973) and *Facetas* (1976). FOR VOICE: *La nuez* for children's chorus (1944); *Tres epitafios* for chorus a cappella (1947–53), *Pregón para una Pascua pobre* for chorus, 3 trumpets, 2 tenor trombones, bass trombone and percussion (Mexico City, April 6, 1969) and the song cycles *Marinero en tierra* (1925), *Dos sonetos* (1940–46) and *Desterro* (1967).

Halič, Carl, distinguished violinist; b. Hohenelbe, Bohemia, Feb. 1, 1859; d. Berlin, Dec. 21, 1909. He was a pupil of Bennewitz at the Prague Cons., and of Joachim in Berlin. In 1884 he was appointed concertmaster of the court orch. at Weimar; in 1893 he obtained a similar post in Berlin; also appointed prof. at the Hochschule there; for a time he was a member of the Joachim Quartet, but later formed his own quartet (with Exner, Müller, and Dechert), which became famous. His tour of the United States (1896–97) was very successful. His pedagogic exercises for the violin, *Tonleiterstudien*, are still in use. In 1888 he married **Theresa Zerbst**, a fine soprano.

Hall, Charles King, English composer and writer; b. London, 1845; d. there, Sept. 1, 1895. He was organist at various London churches; pub. *A School for Harmonium*, and produced a number of operettas, some of which were successful in their day (*Foster Brothers, Doubleday's Will, A Tremendous Mystery, The Artful Automaton, A Strange House, A Christmas Stocking,* etc.).

Hall, John, English song writer; b. c.1529; d. c.1565. He was a surgeon by profession and a musician by avocation. A collection of 30 melodies and one song in 4 parts entitled *The Court of Vertu,* composed by him, is preserved.

Hall, Marie (Mary Paulina), English violinist; b. Newcastle-on-Tyne, April 8, 1884; d. Cheltenham, Nov. 11, 1956. As a small child, she gave performances with her father, an amateur harp player, her uncle (violin), her brother (violin), and her sister (harp), in the homes of music lovers in Newcastle, Malvern, and Bristol. Elgar heard her, and was impressed by her talent; he sent her to Wilhelmj in London for regular study; she also studied with Johann Kruse. At the age of 15 she won the first Wessely Exhibition at the Royal Academy of Music. She was recommended by Jan Kubelik to Ševčik in Prague (1901), from whom she received rigorous training; made her professional debut in Prague (1902); then played in Vienna. After a highly successful London concert (Feb. 16, 1903), she made her American debut as soloist with the New York Symphony, Walter Damrosch conducting (Nov. 8, 1905); toured Australia (1907) and India (1913). On Jan. 27, 1911 she married her manager Edward Baring, and settled in Cheltenham; continued to appear in concerts in England until 1955, with her daughter, **Pauline Baring,** as her accompanist.

BIBLIOGRAPHY: J. Cuthbert Hadden, "Marie Hall," in *Modern Musicians* (Edinburgh, 1913; pp. 176–83).

Hall, Pauline, Norwegian composer; b. Hamar, Aug. 2, 1890; d. Oslo, Jan. 24, 1969. She studied composition with Catharinus Elling in Oslo (1910–12) and later in Paris (1912–14) and Dresden. From 1934 to 1964 she served as music critic of *Dagbladet*. In her music, Pauline Hall follows the modern French ideal of classical clarity, seasoned with euphonious dissonance.

WORKS: *Verlaine Suite* for orch. (1929); *Circus Sketches,* orch. suite (1933); Suite for Wind Quintet (1945); *Little Dance Suite* for oboe, clarinet and bassoon (1958); *4 Tosserier* for soprano, clarinet, bassoon, horn and trumpet (1961); *Variations on a Classical Theme* for solo flute (1961); *Markisen* (*The Marquise*), ballet (1964).

Hall, Walter Henry, English-American organist and choral conductor; b. London, April 25, 1862; d. New York, Dec. 11, 1935. He studied at the Royal Academy of Music; settled in America in 1883; was organist at various churches in Pennsylvania before settling in New York; organist at St. James' (1896–1913). In 1893 he founded the Brooklyn Oratorio Society, which he led until his death; also conducted the Musurgia Society (1889–1906); was lecturer in music at Columbia Univ. (1909–30).

Hallberg, Björn Wilho, Norwegian-born Swedish composer; b. Oslo, July 9, 1938. He studied with Bjarre Brustad and Finn Mortensen; came to Sweden in 1962 where he studied with Lidholm, Bo Wallner and Blomdahl at the Royal College of Music in Stockholm; also took sporadic lessons with Ligeti. His own compositions are exploratory in techniques.

WORKS: an opera, *Evakueringen* (*The Evacuation,* 1969; Stockholm, Dec. 9, 1969); *Felder* for flute and percussion (Vienna Festival, June 17, 1961); String Quartet (1963); *Ur dagboken* (*From the Diary*) for percussion ensemble (1964); Études for Chamber Ensemble (1966); *Missa pro defunctis,* in memory of Dag Hammarskjöld, for soprano, chorus, tape and orch. (Stockholm, May 17, 1968); *Conversation/Vide* for 5 singers, 5 woodwinds, tape and loudspeakers (1968); *États* for soprano, flute, double bass, piano and percussion (1970); *Aspiration* for orch. (Östersund, July 11, 1971); *Novelletten* for orch. (1973); *Die Drohung,* ballet music for wind orch. (1973).

Halle, Adam de la. See **Adam de la Halle.**

Hallé, Sir Charles (real name **Karl Hallé**), renowned pianist and conductor; b. Hagen, Westphalia, April 11, 1819; d. Manchester, Oct. 25, 1895. Son of a local church organist, he revealed a musical talent as a child, and performed in public at the age of 4; at 15 he was sent to study music seriously with Rinck at Darmstadt; in 1836 he went to Paris, where he entered the friendly circle of Chopin, Liszt, and others. In 1846 he gave concerts of his own as a pianist in chamber music. After the Revolution of 1848, he went to England, settling in Manchester, where he conducted an orchestra, choruses, and opera. In 1857 he established subscription concerts with an orchestral ensemble of his own, which became famous as Charles Hallé's Orchestra, endured for a century, and eventually became an honored institution known as the Hallé Orchestra. Although his chief activities were connected with Manchester, he also conducted the London Popular Concerts; gave piano recitals; in 1861 he presented all of Beethoven's sonatas in 8 concerts, repeating this cycle in 2 successive seasons. From 1873 till 1893 he conducted the Bristol Festivals; in 1883 he became conductor of the Liverpool Philharmonic Society, as successor to Max Bruch. He was a champion of Berlioz in England, and gave several complete performances of Berlioz's *Damnation de Faust.* His first wife was Désirée Smith de Rilieu, his second wife the violinist **Wilma Neruda.** With her he made 2 Australian tours (1890 and 1891). He was knighted in 1888. He established a very high standard of excellence in orchestral performance, which greatly influenced musical life in England. He publ. a *Pianoforte School* (1873) and edited a *Musical Library* (1876).

BIBLIOGRAPHY: L. Engel, *From Handel to Hallé* (London, 1890); C. E. and M. Hallé, *Life and Letters of Sir Charles Hallé* (London, 1896); C. Rigby, *Sir Charles Hallé* (Manchester, 1952); C. B. Rees, *100 Years of the Hallé* (London, 1957).

Hallén, Andreas, notable Swedish composer; b. Göteborg, Dec. 22, 1846; d. Stockholm, March 11, 1925. He studied with Reinecke in Leipzig, Rheinberger in Munich, and Rietz in Dresden; upon his return to Sweden, conducted in Göteborg (1872–78 and 1883–84); then was conductor of the Philharmonic Concerts in Stockholm (1884–92) and of the Royal Opera (1892–97). From 1908 till 1919 he was prof. of composition at the Stockholm Cons.

WORKS: operas, *Harald der Viking* (Leipzig, Oct.

16, 1881), *Hexfällan* (Stockholm, March 16, 1896), *The Treasure of Waldemar* (Stockholm, April 8, 1899), *Walpurgis Night* (revised version of *Hexfällan;* Stockholm, March 15, 1902); choral works with orch. (*The Page and the King's Daughter, Dream-King and His Love, Goblin's Fate, Christmas Eve, Peace*); a *Missa solemnis* (Stockholm, 1923); symph. poems (*En Sommarsaga, Die Toteninsel, Sphärenklänge*); overtures.

BIBLIOGRAPHY: P. Vretblad, *Andreas Hallén* (Stockholm, 1918).

Haller, Michael, German church composer; b. Neusaat, Jan. 13, 1840; d. Regensburg, Jan. 4, 1915. He was educated at Matten monastery; took holy orders in 1864; appointed prefect of the Regensburg Cathedral Choristers' Institution.

WORKS: 14 Masses; psalms; litanies; a Te Deum; melodramas; string quartets; etc. He completed the third-choir parts of 6 compositions *a* 12 of Palestrina, which had been lost (vol. XXVI of the complete edition).

WRITINGS: *Vademecum für den Gesangsunterricht* (1876; 12th ed., 1910); *Kompositionslehre für den polyphonen Kirchengesang* (1891); *Modulation in den Kirchentonarten; Exempla polyphoniae ecclesiasticae* (in modern notation, with explanatory notes).

Hallgrimsson, Haflidi Magnus, Icelandic composer and cellist; b. Akureyri, Sept. 18, 1941. He graduated from the Icelandic Music Conservatoire in 1962; then studied at the Accademia Sancta Cecilia in Rome and the Royal Academy in London; also took private lessons with Alan Bush and P. M. Davies. Returning to Iceland, he was active as a cello player.

WORKS: 2 string quartets (1962, 1964); Fantasia for Solo Cello (1969); *Elegy* for mezzo-soprano, piano, celesta, flute and 2 cellos (1971); Duo for Viola and Cello (1972); *Hoa-Haka-Nana-Ia* for clarinet, strings and percussion (1972); 7 *Icelandic Folksongs* for cello and piano (1973); Divertimento for Harpsichord and String Trio (1974); 2 *Icelandic Folksongs* for mezzo-soprano, clarinet, flute, cello and piano (1974).

Hallnäs, Hilding, Swedish composer and organist; b. Halmstad, May 24, 1903. He studied at the Royal Academy of Music in Stockholm (1924–29). He subsequently served as church organist in Göteborg, where he was also active as a teacher. His works reflect the prevalent romantic style of Scandinavian music; in later compositions he applies modified serial techniques.

WORKS: He wrote 9 symphonies, but withdrew the first two and renumbered the others: No. 1, *Sinfonia pastorale* (1944; Göteborg, March 22, 1945); No. 2, *Sinfonia Notturna* (Göteborg, March 4, 1948); No. 3, *Little Symphony* for strings and percussion (Göteborg, Oct. 3, 1948); No. 4, *Metamorfose Sinfonische* (Göteborg, April 17, 1952; revised, 1960); No. 5, *Sinfonia aforistica* (Göteborg, Jan. 24, 1963); No. 6, *Musica intima* for strings and percussion (Malmö, Nov. 7, 1967); No. 7, *A Quite Small Symphony* for chamber orch. (Minneapolis, June 12, 1974). He further wrote 2 ballets, *Kärlekens ringdans* (*Love's Dance in the Round,* 1955–56) and *Ifigenia* (1961–63; also a suite);

Divertimento for Orch. (1937); 2 violin concertos (1945, 1965); *Symphonic Ballet Suite* (1955-56); Piano Concerto (1956); *Cantica Lyrica* for tenor, chorus and orch. (1957); 2 Concertos for Flute, Strings and Percussion (1957, 1962); Concerto for String Orch. and Percussion (1959); *Epitaph* for strings (1963); *Rapsodie* for chamber orch. and soprano (1963); *En Grekisk Saga* (*A Greek Saga*) for orch. (1967-68; dedicated to Melina Mercouri, Mikis Theodorakis and the Greek people); *Momenti bucolichi* for oboe and orch. (1969); *Horisont och linjespel* for string orch. (1969); *Triple Concerto* for violin, clarinet, piano and orch. (1972-73); 2 String Quartets (1949, 1967); Quintet for Flute, Oboe, Viola, Cello and Piano (1954); *Cantata* for soprano, flute, clarinet, cello and piano (1955); Violin Sonata (1957); piano trio, *Stanze sensitive* (1959); Piano Sonata (1963); organ sonata, *De Profundis* (1965); *24 Preludes* for guitar (1967); *Passionsmusik*, 15 pieces for organ (1968); *3 Momenti Musicali* for violin, horn and piano (1971); *Invocatio* for chorus and string quartet (1971); *Confessio*, trio for clarinet, cello and piano (1973); *Triptykon* for violin, clarinet and piano (1973).

Hallström, Ivar, significant Swedish composer; b. Stockholm, June 5, 1826; d. there, April 11, 1901. He studied jurisprudence at the Univ. of Uppsala; there he became a friend of Prince Gustaf who was himself a musical amateur; on April 9, 1847, jointly with Gustaf, he produced in Stockholm an opera, *The White Lady of Drottningholm;* later he became librarian to Prince Oscar; in 1861 he became a member of the Stockholm Academy of Music. His second opera, *Hertig Magnus,* was produced at the Royal Opera in Stockholm on Jan. 28, 1867, but had only 6 performances in all, purportedly because it contained more arias in minor keys (10, to be exact) than those in major (only 8). He then produced another opera, *The Enchanted Cat* (Stockholm, April 20, 1869), which was more successful. With his next opera *Den Bergtagna* (*The Bewitched One*), produced in Stockholm on May 24, 1874, he achieved his greatest success; it had repeated performances not only in Sweden, but also in Germany and Denmark. In this work Hallström made use of Swedish folk motifs, a pioneer attempt in Scandinavian operatic art. His next opera, *Vikingarna* (Stockholm, June 6, 1877), was but moderately successful; there followed *Neaga* (Stockholm, Feb. 24, 1885) to a libretto by Carmen Sylva (Queen Elisabeth of Rumania). He also wrote several ballets, cantatas, and arrangements of Swedish folksongs for piano.

Halm, August, German composer and writer; b. Gross-Altdorf, Württemberg, Oct. 26, 1869; d. Saalfeld, Feb. 1, 1929. A member of a family of scholars, he received an excellent general education; then studied theology at Tübingen. In 1892 he went to Munich, where he took courses with Rheinberger. Subsequently he devoted himself mainly to musical pedagogy; taught in various schools in Thuringia; conducted choral societies and also wrote music criticism. An August Halm Society was organized after his death. He was a prolific composer, but his music failed to take hold. He wrote 2 symphonies, which

were performed in Ulm and Stuttgart; a piano concerto; 8 string quartets; 2 suites for string trio, and a number of piano studies. He publ. *Harmonielehre* (Berlin, 1905); *Von zwei Kulturen der Musik* (Munich, 1913; 3rd ed., 1947); *Die Symphonien A. Bruckners* (Munich, 1914; 2nd ed., 1923); *Von Grenzen und Ländern der Musik* (Munich, 1916); *Einführung in die Musik* (Berlin, 1926); *Beethoven* (Berlin, 1927).

Halvorsen, Johan, Norwegian violinist and composer; b. Drammen, March 15, 1864; d. Oslo, Dec. 4, 1935. He studied violin with Lindberg at the Stockholm Cons.; was concertmaster of the Bergen Orch.; then went to Leipzig to study with Brodsky; subsequently studied with César Thomson in Belgium; returning to Norway in 1892, he became conductor of a theater orch. in Bergen; in 1899 was appointed conductor at the National Theater in Oslo. He was married to a niece of Grieg; this association was symbolic of his devotion to Grieg's art; his music reflects Grieg's influence very strongly. He wrote incidental music to Björnson's *Vasantasena* and *The King,* to Drachmann's *Gurre,* Eldegard's *Fossegrimen, Dronning Tamara,* and others. He further wrote 3 symphonies, a violin concerto, 2 Norwegian rhapsodies, several orchestral suites on Norwegian themes. His most popular works are the march, *Triumphant Entry of the Boyars,* and an arrangement of Handel's Passacaglia for violin and viola (or cello).

Halvorsen, Leif, Norwegian violinist and composer; b. Oslo, July 26, 1887; d. there, Dec. 28, 1959. He studied violin with local teachers; then went to St. Petersburg where he became a pupil of Leopold Auer. Upon his return to Norway, he served as concertmaster in the National Theater Orchestra of Oslo (1915-17), then was an opera conductor (1918-21); also led the Fredrikstad Singing Society (1925-47). He wrote much incidental music for theatrical plays; an orchestral suite, *Peasant's Legend;* piano pieces and songs.

Ham, Albert, English organist; b. Bath, June 7, 1858; d. Brighton, Feb. 4, 1940. He studied music in Dublin; in 1897 went to Canada, where he taught at the Toronto Cons. and served as a cathedral organist there. He wrote a number of choral works; his choral arrangements of the tune *Little Jack Horner* became very popular.

Hamal, Henri-Guillaume, Belgian organist and composer; b. Liège, Dec. 3, 1685; d. there, Dec. 3, 1752. As a youth he excelled in the various capacities of harpsichord player, singer, and cellist; was also a versatile composer of songs to texts in many languages. However, none of his works is preserved, and his reputation was transmitted mainly by members of his family. His son, **Jean-Noël Hamal** b. Liège, Dec. 23, 1709; d. there, Nov. 26, 1778), studied with his father and later served as chorus master at the Liège Cathedral; also traveled in Italy, where he acquired additional knowledge of composition. He wrote a great number of church works: 56 Masses, 32 cantatas, 5 oratorios, 179 motets, also operas, overtures, and numerous pieces for the harpsichord. **Henri Hamal** (b. Liège, July 20, 1744; d. there, Sept. 17, 1820), a nephew of

Jean-Noël Hamal, studied with him, and later in Italy. He was a chorusmaster at the Liège Cathedral for some time. He wrote much church music, of which 3 volumes are preserved in the Royal Library of Brussels.

BIBLIOGRAPHY: Louis de Lavalleye, *Les Hamal de Liège* (Liège, 1860); M. de Smet, *Jean-Noël Hamal, chanoine impérial et Directeur de la Musique de la Cathédrale Saint-Lambert de Liège: Vie et œuvre* (Brussels, 1959).

Hambourg, a family of musicians of Russian extraction. **Michael Hambourg,** pianist and teacher; b. Yaroslavl, in 1856; d. Toronto, Canada, June 18, 1916. He went to England in 1890; in 1911 moved to Toronto, Canada, where he established, with his son Boris, the Hambourg Conservatory of Music. **Boris Hambourg,** cellist, son of Michael Hambourg; b. Voronezh, Jan. 8, 1885; d. Toronto, Nov. 24, 1954. He studied cello with Hugo Becker in Frankfurt (1898–1903); in 1910 made an American tour, and in the following year went to Toronto, where he established, with his father, the Hambourg Conservatory. **Jan Hambourg,** violinist; b. Voronezh, Aug. 27, 1882; d. Tours, France, Sept. 29, 1947. He studied violin with Sauret and Wilhelmj in London, with Sevčik in Prague, and with Eugène Ysaÿe in Brussels. With his brothers Boris and Mark he established the Hambourg Trio; he died during a concert tour in France. **Mark Hambourg,** pianist; b. Bogutchar, June 12, 1879; d. Cambridge, England, Aug. 26, 1960. He studied piano with his father Michael Hambourg, and made his debut in Moscow at the age of 9; then went to Vienna to study with Leschetizky. He was highly successful as a concert pianist; traveled all over the world; played his 1000th concert on June 16, 1906. He toured with his brothers Boris and Jan in the U.S. in 1935; then returned to England. He published 2 piano manuals: *How to Play the Piano* (Philadelphia, 1922); *From Piano to Forte; a Thousand and One Notes* (London, 1931); and a book of memoirs, *The Eighth Octave* (London, 1951).

Hamboys, John. See **Hanboys, John.**

Hambraeus, Bengt, prominent Swedish composer, organist and musicologist; b. Stockholm, Jan. 29, 1928. He took organ lessons with Alf Linder (1944–48); then entered Uppsala Univ. (M. A. 1956); he also attended the summer courses of modern music at Darmstadt (1951–55). In 1957 he joined the music staff of the Swedish Broadcasting Corp.; in 1972 was appointed to the faculty of McGill Univ. in Montreal. His style of composition oscillates between modernistic constructivism based on strong dissonant polyphony and sonoristic experimentalism; he is regarded as a leader of the Swedish musical avant-garde.

WORKS: two chamber operas: *Experiment X*, making use of electronic sound (Stockholm, March 9, 1971) and a church opera, *Se människan* (Stockholm, May 15, 1972); 3 string quartets (1948–64); Concerto for Organ and Harpsichord (1947–51); *Diptychon* for flute, oboe, viola, celesta and harpsichord (1952); *Spectogram* for soprano and instrumental ensemble (1953); *Giuoco del Cambio* (*Play of Changes*) for 5 instruments and percussion (1952–54); *Antiphones en rondes* for soprano and 24 instruments (1953); *Crystal Sequence* for soprano choir and instrumental ensemble (1954); *Cercles* for piano (1955); a 5-work cycle of compositions: *Rota I* for 3 orchestras (Stockholm, May 27, 1964); *Rota II* for electronically modulated organ and bell sounds (1963); *Transit I* for tape (1963); *Transit II* for horn, piano, trombone and electric guitar (1963) and *Transfiguration* for orch. (1962–63; Swedish radio, Feb. 20, 1965); *Constellations I–III: I* for organ (1958); *II* for taped organ sounds (1959); *III* includes tape from *II*, plus new, superimposed live organ score (1961); *Introduzione—Sequenze—Coda* for 3 flutes, 6 percussion and amplifier (1958–59); *Segnali* for 7 string instruments (1956–60); *Notazioni* for harpsichord, 10 wind instruments, celesta and percussion (1961); *Mikrogram* for alto flute, viola, harp and vibraphone (1961); *Interferences* for organ (1962); *Responsorier* for tenor, chorus, 2 organs and church bells (1964); *Tetragon* (*Homenaje a Pablo Picasso*) for electronically modulated soprano and chamber ensemble (1965); *Klassiskt spel* (*Classical Play*), electronic ballet (1965); *Praeludium, Kyrie, Sanctus* for solo voice, 2 choruses, 2 organs and church bells (1966); *Motetum Archangeli Michaelis* for chorus and organ (1967); *Movimento—Monodia—Shogaku* for organ (1967); *Fresque Sonore* for electronically modulated soprano and chamber ensemble (1965–67); *Inventions II* for piano (1967–68); *Rencontres* for orch. (Swedish Radio, Aug. 8, 1971); *Pianissimo in due tempi* for 20 string instruments (1970–72); *Recit de deux* for soprano (vocalizing and playing percussion), flute and piano (1973). He published a book, *Om notskifter* (*On Notation*, Stockholm, 1970).

Hamel, Fred, German musicologist; b. Paris, Feb. 19, 1903; d. Hamburg, Dec. 9, 1957. He studied chemistry in Bonn and Berlin and musicology in Berlin and Giessen, graduating in 1930. He was then engaged mainly as a music critic; published a monograph on J. S. Bach: *Geistige Welt* (Göttingen, 1951) and contributed numerous articles to German magazines.

Hamel, Marie-Pierre, French organ builder; b. Auneuil, Oise, Feb. 24, 1786; d. Beauvais, July 25, 1879. He was from a family of jurists, and himself pursued a legal career; in 1817 he became a judge at Beauvais. Apart from his professional activities, he was from his childhood interested in music; he manufactured a small organ of 3 octaves at the age of 13, and successfully repaired an old organ in a neighboring village to the satisfaction of the church wardens. He later rebuilt the grand organ of the Cathedral of Beauvais (1826). He publ. several manuals and descriptions of organs in various French cities. Principal writings: *Rapport sur les travaux du grand orgue de l'Église de la Madeleine à Paris* (Paris, 1846); *Nouveau Manuel complet du facteur d'orgues* (Paris, 1849; 3 vols.; new ed. by Guédon, 1903; contains a history of organ building).

Hamelle, Jacques, French music publisher; in 1877 he acquired the publishing firm established by J. Maho in 1855. After Hamelle's death in 1917, the business was taken over by his sons. Among the principal composers represented in the catalogue are Franck, Saint-Saëns, Fauré, and Vincent d'Indy.

Hamerik (real name **Hammerich**), **Asger,** Danish composer; b. Copenhagen, April 8, 1843; d. Frederiksborg, July 13, 1923. He was a son of a prof. of divinity, who discouraged his musical interests; despite this opposition, he studied with Gade in Copenhagen and with Hans von Bülow in Berlin. He met Berlioz at Paris in 1864, and accompanied him to Vienna in 1866, studying orchestration. Hamerik was probably the only pupil that Berlioz had. He received a gold medal for his work *Hymne de la Paix,* at the contest for the Paris Exposition. His opera *Tovelille* was performed in Paris in concert form (May 6, 1865); another opera, *Hjalmar and Ingeborg,* was not performed in its entirety. In 1870 he visited Italy and produced his opera in Italian *La Vendetta* (Milan, Dec. 23, 1870). He then received an invitation to become director of the newly organized Peabody Cons. in Baltimore. He accepted, and remained in Baltimore for 26 years, until 1898, when he returned to Copenhagen. In Baltimore he wrote a number of symphonic works, which he conducted with the cons. orch.
    WORKS: *5 Nordic Suites* (1872–78); *Symphonie poétique* (1879); *Symphonie tragique* (1881); *Symphonie lyrique* (1885); *Symphonie majestueuse* (1888); *Symphonie sérieuse* (1892); *Symphonie spirituelle,* for string orch. (1895); and a choral symph. (No. 7).

Hamerik, Ebbe, Danish composer, son of **Asger Hamerik;** b. Copenhagen, Sept. 5, 1898; d. there, Aug. 11, 1951 (drowned in the Kattegat). He studied music with his father; was active mainly as conductor. He composed the operas *Stepan* (Mainz, Nov. 30, 1924); *Leonardo da Vinci* (Antwerp, 1939); *Marie Grubbe* (Copenhagen, May 17, 1940); and *Rejsekammeraten,* after Andersen (Copenhagen, Jan. 5, 1946); also 5 symphonies; 2 string quartets; piano pieces; songs.

Hamilton, Clarence Grant, American organist and music educator; b. Providence, R. I., June 9, 1865; d. Wellesley, Mass., Feb. 14, 1935. He studied piano with Arthur Foote in Boston and Matthay in London; composition with Chadwick. He occupied various positions as organist in and around Boston; taught at Wellesley College for many years (1904–34); wrote piano pieces and songs.
    WRITINGS: *Outlines of Music History* (1908; new ed., 1924); *Piano Teaching* (1910); *Sound and Its Relation to Music* (1911); *Music Appreciation, based upon Methods of Literary Criticism* (1920); *Piano Music, Its Composers and Characteristics* (1925); *Epochs in Musical Progress* (1926); *Touch and Expression in Piano Playing* (1927); *What Every Piano Pupil Should Know* (1928); *Ornaments in Classical and Modern Music* (1929).

Hamilton, Iain, remarkable Scottish composer; b. Glasgow, June 6, 1922. He was taken to London at the age of 7, and attended Mill Hill School; after graduation, he became an apprentice engineer but studied music at his leisure. He was 25 years old when he decidedly turned to music as his career; entered the Royal Academy of Music where he was a piano stu-

dent of Harold Craxton and composition student of William Alwyn; concurrently he attended the Univ. of London, obtaining his B. Mus. in 1950. He made astonishing progress as a composer, and upon graduation from the Royal Academy received the prestigious Dove Prize; other awards followed, among them the Royal Philharmonic Society's Prize for his Clarinet Concerto, the Koussevitzky Foundation Award for his Second Symphony, Edwin Evans Prize, Butterworth Award and Arnold Bax Gold Medal. From 1952 to 1960 he taught composition at Morley College in London, and during the same period conducted classes in musical analysis at the Univ. of London. In 1962 he received an appointment as prof. of music at Duke Univ., North Carolina; was resident composer and teacher at Tanglewood in the summer of 1962, and also taught at the Summer School of Music, Dartington Hall, England. In 1970 he received the honorary degree of D. Mus. at Glasgow Univ.; in 1971 he received a professorship at Lehman College, City Univ. of New York, but resigned precipitously after a single day because of unacceptable teaching conditions. Apart from his regular pedagogic activities, he has served as a music consultant on various committees, including the Music Advisory Panel of the British Broadcasting Corp. and the National Music Council. During the first two decades of his work as a composer he wrote mainly instrumental music, but beginning in 1966 he devoted himself primarily to the composition of operas, completing 5 opera scores within 10 years; of these, *The Catiline Conspiracy* is acknowledged as his masterpiece. Hamilton's style of composition is marked by terse melodic lines animated by a vibrant rhythmic pulse, creating the impression of kinetic lyricism; his harmonies are built on a set of peculiarly euphonious dissonances, which repose on emphatic tonal centers. For a period of several years he pursued a sui generis serial method, but soon abandoned it in favor of a free modern manner; in his operas he makes use of thematic chords depicting specific dramatic situations.
    WORKS: 6 OPERAS: *The Royal Hunt of the Sun,* to his own libretto from a play by Peter Shaffer (1966–68; orchestration completed in 1975; produced by the English National Opera in London, Feb. 3, 1977); *Agamemnon,* after Aeschylus (1967–69); *Pharsalia,* a dramatic commentary with a libretto by the composer from Lucan (1968); *The Catiline Conspiracy* to a text by the composer, based on Ben Jonson's play (produced at Stirling, Scotland, March 16, 1974); radio opera *Tamburlaine* (BBC, London, Feb. 14, 1977); *Anna Karenina* (1977–78). FOR ORCH.: *Variations on an Original Theme* for string orch. (1948); Symph. No. 1 (1948); Clarinet Concerto (1950); Symph. No. 2 (1951); Violin Concerto (1952); *Bartholomew Fair,* overture (1952); *Symphonic Variations* (1953); *Scottish Dances* (1956); *Sonata* for chamber orch. (1957); *Overture: 1912* (1957); Concerto for Jazz Trumpet and Orch. (1957); *Sinfonia for Two Orchestras* (1958); *Ecossaise* (1959); Piano Concerto (1960); *The Chaining of Prometheus* for wind instruments and percussion (1963); Concerto for Organ and Small Orch. (1964); *Circus* for 2 trumpets and orch. (1969); *Alastor* (1970); *Voyage* for horn and chamber orch. (1970); *Amphion* for violin and orch.

(1971); *Aurora* (1972). CHAMBER MUSIC: Quintet No. 1 for clarinet and string quartet (1948); String Quartet (1950); Quartet for Flute and String Trio (1951); *Variations* for unaccompanied violin (1951); *3 Nocturnes* for clarinet and piano (1951); Viola Sonata (1951); *Capriccio* for trumpet and string piano (1951); Clarinet Sonata (1954); Octet for Strings (1954); *Songs of Summer* for soprano, clarinet, cello and piano (1954); *Serenata* for violin and clarinet (1955); Piano Trio (1955); Cello Sonata No. 1 (1959); Sextet, for flute, 2 clarinets, violin, cello and piano (1962); *Sonatas and Variants* for 10 wind instruments (1963); Brass Quintet (1964); *Sonata Notturna* for horn and piano (1965); String Quartet No. 2 (1965); *Sonata for Five* for wind quintet (1966); Flute Sonata (1966); *Sea Music* (Quintet No. 2) for clarinet and string quartet (1971); *5 Scenes* for trumpet and piano (1971); Violin Sonata (1974); Cello Sonata No. 2 (1974); *The Alexandrian Sequence* for 12 instruments (1976). VOCAL WORKS: *The Bermudas* for baritone, chorus and orch. (1956); Cantata for Tenor and Piano (1957); *5 Love Songs* for voice and orch. (1957); *Nocturnal* for 11 solo voices (1959); *A Testament of War* for baritone and small ensemble (1961); *Dialogues* for coloratura soprano and small ensemble (1965); *Epitaph for this World and Time* for 3 choruses and 2 organs (1970); *Te Deum* for mixed chorus, wind instruments and percussion (1972); *To Columbus*, a setting of Walt Whitman's poem, for mixed chorus, 3 trumpets, 3 trombones and percussion, written for the U.S. Bicentennial (1976); organ pieces; 2 piano sonatas (1951; 1970); *Nocturnes with Cadenzas* for piano (1963); *Palinodes* for piano (1972); *A Vision of Canopus* for organ (1975).

Hamilton, James Alexander, English musician; b. London, 1785; d. there, Aug. 2, 1845. He was a son of a bookseller; his voluminous reading gave him a fine literary education. He developed a knack of transmitting knowledge acquired from music books to the public in an easy and attractive form; his numerous manuals went through several editions, but because of his intemperate habits, he was always in penury.
WRITINGS: *Modern Instructions for the Piano; Catechism of Singing; Catechism of the Rudiments of Harmony and Thoroughbass; Catechism of Counterpoint, Melody and Composition; A New Theoretical and Practical Musical Grammar;* a dictionary of musical terms; transl. Cherubini's *Counterpoint and Fugue.*

Hamlin, George, American tenor; b. Elgin, Ill., Sept. 20, 1868; d. New York, Jan. 20, 1923. He studied irregularly with various teachers; sang in oratorio; made his operatic debut in Victor Herbert's *Natoma* (Philadelphia, Dec. 15, 1911); among his chief parts were Cavaradossi in *Tosca* and Don José in *Carmen.*

Hamlisch, Marvin, American composer of popular music; b. New York, June 2, 1944. His father, an accordionist, trained him in music; he studied piano at the Juilliard School of Music and at Queens College; began writing songs at the age of 15. His first signal success came in 1974 when he won three motion picture Academy Awards for the music scores for the movies *The Way We Were* and *The Sting.* (For the

latter, his award was won for a score written mostly by others: piano music of Scott Joplin, composed 60–70 years earlier, and orchestrations by Gunther Schuller, adapted from 60-year-old stock arrangements.) In 1975 he wrote the score for the musical *A Chorus Line* which received the Pulitzer Prize for the play and a Tony award for the best musical score; Universal Pictures bought the cinema rights for $5,500,000. The Broadway production opened on July 25, 1975 to a chorus line of hosannas from otherwise sober-sided critics; a second Broadway production followed in 1976; an international touring company was started in Toronto in May 1976, and a national company began its cross-country tour a few days later.
BIBLIOGRAPHY: *Current Biography* (May 1976).

Hamm, Adolf, church organist and choral conductor; b. Strasbourg, March 9, 1882; d. Basel, Oct. 15, 1938. He studied with Straube in Leipzig; in 1906, settled in Basel, where he became chief organist at the cathedral; also organized the Bach Choir there; taught at the Basel Cons. Paul Sacher edited a memorial volume, *Adolf Hamm: Erinnerungsschrift* (Basel, 1942).

Hammer, Heinrich Albert Eduard, German-American violinist, conductor, and composer; b. Erfurt, Germany, Oct. 27, 1862; d. Phoenix, Arizona, Oct. 28, 1954. He studied violin with A. Pott, theory with H. Ritter; also took singing lessons with Mme. Viardot-Garcia in Paris. He then lived in Holland (1893–96) and Bochum (1897–1901); conducted the Lausanne Symph. Orch. (1901–05); in 1905 he organized a symph. orch. in Göteborg, Sweden. In 1908 he settled in America; conducted his own orch. in Washington, until 1921, when he went to California; lived mostly in Pasadena; continued to compose until the end of his long life; at the age of 90, married his pupil Arlene Hammer, who helped him to edit his autobiography. Among his works are a symphony; 3 American Indian Rhapsodies for orch.; symph. poem, *Sunset at Sea;* an orchestral ode, *Columbia Triumphant in Peace* (1915), and much church music.

Hammerich, Angul, Danish writer on music; brother of **Asger Hamerik** (whose real name was **Hammerich**); b. Copenhagen, Nov. 25, 1848; d. there, April 26, 1931. He studied cello; at the same time, occupied a post in the Dept. of Finance; wrote music criticism; taught musicology at the Univ. of Copenhagen. In 1898 he founded the Collection of Ancient Musical Instruments; was a founder of the Danish Musicological Society (1921).
WRITINGS: *Studies in Old Icelandic Music* (1900; Danish and German); *The Conservatory of Music at Copenhagen* (1892; in Danish); *Essay on the Music at the Court of Christian IV* (1892; in German, 1893); *On the Old Norse Lurs* (1893; in German, 1894); *Descriptive Illustrated Catalogue of the Historical Musical Museum of Copenhagen* (1909; in Danish; German transl. by E. Bobé, 1911); *Medieval Musical Relics of Denmark* (1912; in Danish; English transl. by Margaret Williams-Hamerik, 1912); *J. P. E. Hartmann, Biographical Essays* (1916); a history of Danish music to c.1700 (1921).

Hammerschlag, János, music critic and composer; b. Prague, Dec. 10, 1885; d. Budapest, May 21, 1954. He was taken to Budapest as a child and studied music and literature; as a young man, became a newspaper critic; also taught music history and conducted choral concerts at the Budapest Cons. (1919–47); led the Madrigal Society; publ. a book on Bach (Budapest, 1926); numerous other writings (in Hungarian and German) are listed in J. S. Weissmann's article on Hammerschlag in *Die Musik in Geschichte und Gegenwart.*

Hammerschmidt, Andreas, important composer of sacred music; b. Brüx, Bohemia, 1612; d. Zittau, Nov. 8, 1675. In 1626, his father took him to Freiberg, Saxony, and it was there that he received his education; studied music with Stephen Otto; in 1634, appointed organist at Freiberg, and in 1639, at Zittau, retaining this post until his death. A statue was erected to his memory there. His works for the Lutheran services are of great significance. He was one of the earliest composers to adopt the new Italian style of writing elaborate instrumental accompaniments to polyphonic vocal works.

WORKS: *Musikalische Andachten* (subtitled *Geistliche Concerten*) in 5 parts (1638; 1641; 1642; 1646; 1652); *Dialogi oder Gespräche zwischen Gott und einer gläubigen Seelen,* in 2 parts (Dresden, 1645; first part repr. in the *Denkmäler der Tonkunst in Österreich* 16 [8.i]); *Weltliche Oden oder Liebesgesänge,* in 2 parts (1642–43); *Musicalische Gespräche über die Sonntags- und Fest-Evangelia* (Dresden, 1655–56). Reprints by H. J. Moser in *Alte Meister des deutschen Liedes* and A. Schering in *Geschichte der Musik in Beispielen* (no. 194). Hugo Leichtentritt publ. a selection in vol. 40 of the *Denkmäler deutscher Tonkunst,* other reprints by Commer in *Musica sacra* (nos. 25/26); Oppenheimer, Sulzbach, etc.

BIBLIOGRAPHY: E. Steinhard, *Zum 300. Geburtstage Andreas Hammerschmidts* (Prague, 1914); G. Schünemann, "Beiträge zur Biographie Hammerschmidts," *Sammelbände der Internationalen Musik-Gesellschaft* (XII); F. Blume, *Das monodische Prinzip in der protestantischen Kirchenmusik* (Leipzig, 1925).

Hammerstein, Oscar, celebrated impresario; b. Stettin, Germany, May 8, 1846; d. New York, Aug. 1, 1919. At the age of 16 he ran away from home; spent some time in England; then went to America, where he worked in a New York cigar factory. Possessing an inventive mind, he patented a machine for shaping the tobacco leaves by suction; later edited a tobacco trade journal. At the same time, he practiced the violin; learned to write music, and dabbled in playwriting; in 1868 he produced in New York a comedy in German; he also wrote the libretto and music of an operetta, *The Kohinoor* (N.Y., Oct. 24, 1893). His main activity, however, was in management. He built the Harlem Opera House (1888), Olympia Music Hall (1895), and the Republic Theater (1900), and presented brief seasons of plays and operas there. In 1906 he announced plans for the Manhattan Opera House in New York, his crowning achievement. The enterprise was originally planned as a theater for opera in English, but it opened with an Italian company in Bellini's *Puritani*

(Dec. 3, 1906). Hammerstein entered into bold competition with the Metropolitan Opera, and engaged celebrated singers, among them Melba, Nordica, Tetrazzini, and Mary Garden; among spectacular events presented by him were the first American performances of 5 operas by Massenet, Charpentier's *Louise,* and Debussy's *Pelléas et Mélisande.* The new venture held its own for 4 seasons, but in the end Hammerstein was compelled to yield; in April, 1910, he sold the Manhattan Opera House to the management of the Metropolitan for $1,200,000, and agreed not to produce grand opera in New York for 10 years. He also sold to the Metropolitan (for $100,000) his interests in the Philadelphia Opera House built by him in 1908. (The texts of these agreements were published in full in the *Musical Courier* of March 29, 1911.) Defeated in his main ambition in America, Hammerstein transferred his activities to England. There he built the London Opera House, which opened with a lavish production of *Quo Vadis* by Nougès (Nov. 17, 1911). However, he failed to establish himself in London, and after a season there, returned to New York. In contravention of his agreement with the Metropolitan Opera, he announced a season at the newly organized America Opera House in New York, but the Metropolitan secured an injunction against him, and he was forced to give up his operatic venture.

BIBLIOGRAPHY: Vincent Sheean, *Oscar Hammerstein, I: The Life and Exploits of an Impresario* (with a preface by Oscar Hammerstein II; N.Y., 1956); J. F. Cone, *Oscar Hammerstein's Manhattan Opera Company* (Norton, Oklahoma, 1966).

Hammerstein, Oscar, II, American lyricist; grandson of the preceding; b. New York, July 12, 1895; d. Highland Farms, Doylestown, Penn., Aug. 23, 1960. He studied law at Columbia Univ., graduating in 1917; then became interested in the theater. He collaborated in the librettos for Friml's *Rose Marie* (1924) and Romberg's *The Desert Song* (1926); his greatest success as a lyricist came with the production of Jerome Kern's *Show Boat* (1926), including the celebrated song *Ol' Man River.* In 1943 he joined hands with the composer Richard Rodgers, and together they produced several brilliant musical comedies, with spectacular success: *Oklahoma!* (1943; Pulitzer Prize); *Carousel* (1945); *Allegro* (1947); *South Pacific* (1949; Pulitzer Prize, 1950); *The King and I* (1951); *Me and Juliet* (1953); *Pipe Dream* (1955); etc. His lyrics are characterized by a combination of appealing sentiment and sophisticated nostalgia, making them particularly well suited to the modern theater.

BIBLIOGRAPHY: Deems Taylor, *Some Enchanted Evenings: The Story of Rodgers and Hammerstein* (N.Y., 1953); David Ewen, *Richard Rodgers* (N.Y., 1957); Max Wilk, *They're Playing Our Song* (N.Y., 1973); Hugh Fordin, *Getting to Know Him, A Biography of Oscar Hammerstein II* (N.Y., 1977).

Hammond, John Hays, Jr., American organist and manufacturer of organs; b. San Francisco, April 13, 1888; d. New York, Feb. 12, 1965. He studied at Yale Univ. (B.S., 1910); devoted himself to the task of improving pipe organ mechanisms; invented a new type of reflecting modulator for pianos and a dynamic multiplicator for electrical recording; he also patented a gadget named "Pirafon," designed to combine in one unit a piano, a phonograph and a radio.

Hammond, Laurens, American manufacturer of keyboard instruments; b. Evanston, Ill., Jan. 11, 1895; d. Cornwall, Connecticut, July 1, 1973. He studied engineering at Cornell Univ.; then went to Detroit to work on the synchronization of electrical motor impulses, a principle which he later applied to the Hammond Organ, an electronic keyboard instrument resembling a spinet piano, which suggests the sound of the pipe organ. Still later he developed a new-fangled electrical device which he called the Novachord and which was designed to simulate the sound of any known or hypothetical musical instrument; he gave the first demonstration of the Novachord in the Commerce Department auditorium, Washington, D.C., on Feb. 2, 1939. In 1940 he introduced the Solovox, an attachment to the piano keyboard which enables an amateur player to project the melody in organ-like tones. A further invention, that proved attractive to dilettantes, was a "chord organ" which he introduced in 1950, and which is capable of supplying basic harmonies when a special button is pressed by the performer.

Hampton, Lionel, American jazz vibraphonist, drummer, pianist and band leader; b. Louisville, Kentucky, April 12, 1909. He played drums in Chicago night clubs; then moved to Los Angeles where he formed a band of his own. He was a pioneer in introducing the vibraphone, on which he is a virtuoso performer, to jazz, gaining nationwide prominence as a member of the Benny Goodman Quartet from 1936–40. From then on he usually led his own bands, most often playing vibes, but occasionally performing on other instruments; he is the originator of the 'trigger-finger' method of piano playing (2 forefingers drumming upon a single note *prestissimo*). Beginning in 1956 he made several successful European tours. In 1965 he gave up his big band and founded a sextet called Jazz Inner Circle.

Han (Hahn), Ulrich (Udalricus Gallus), German music printer; b. Ingolstadt, c.1425; d. Rome, after 1478. He is believed to be the first to print music with movable type, in his *Missale secundum consuetudinem curie romane* (Rome, 1476). In this work the double-process method was employed, i.e., 2 impressions were made; first, the lines of the staff were printed, following which the note forms (mostly square black heads with a stem at the right side) were superimposed over them.

BIBLIOGRAPHY: O. Kinkeldey, "Music and Music Printing in Incunabula," *Papers of Bibliographic Society of America* (1932).

Hanboys (or Hamboys), John, English music theorist of the 15th century. He was one of the first Englishmen on whom the degree of Mus. D. was conferred. He also held an ecclesiastic rank. His Latin treatise, *Summa super musicam continuam et discretam,* which describes the musical notation of his time, is printed by Coussemaker in his *Scriptores* (vol. 1, p. 416).

BIBLIOGRAPHY: J. Bale, *Illustrium Maioris Britanniae Scriptorum Catalogus* (1559; p. 617); J. Pulver, *Biographical Dictionary of Old English Music* (1923); J. Pulver, "The English Theorists, VI; John Hanboys," *Musical Times* (March 1934).

Hanchett, Henry Granger, American music pedagogue and inventor; b. Syracuse, N.Y., Aug. 29, 1853; d. Siasconset, Mass., Aug. 19, 1918. He studied at the N.Y. Homeopathic Medical College (M.D., 1884); at the same time he pursued pianistic studies with various teachers; held teaching positions in music schools in N.Y. and elsewhere; also was organist at many churches (1884–1898). In 1874, he obtained a patent for the sustaining piano pedal, now in use on all grand pianofortes. He publ. *Teaching as a Science* (1882), *The Art of the Musician* (1905), and *An Introduction to the Theory of Music* (1918); also wrote several church services and anthems.

Handel, George Frideric, illustrious composer; b. Halle, Feb. 23, 1685; d. London, April 14, 1759. This is the anglicized form of the name; the German (and original) form is Georg Friedrich Händel; other forms used in various branches of the family were Hendel, Hendeler, Händler, and Hendtler; the first spelling in England was Hendel; in France it is spelled Haendel. His father, a barber, afterwards surgeon and valet to the Prince of Saxe-Magdeburg, at the age of 61 married a second wife, Dorothea Taust, daughter of the pastor of Giebichenstein, near Halle. Handel was the second son of this marriage. At the age of 7, Handel was taken by his father on a visit to an elder stepbrother, valet at the court of Saxe-Weissenfels; here the boy gained access to the chapel and its organ. The Duke of Saxe-Weissenfels noticed the boy's eagerness in learning music and persuaded his father to give him a musical education. Although the father intended Handel to pursue a legal career, he made arrangements for music lessons with the organist of the cathedral of Halle, Friedrich Wilhelm Zachau. Under Zachau's efficient guidance, Handel practiced the oboe, harpsichord, and organ; also studied counterpoint and fugue. He was only 12 years old when he became assistant organist there; he composed 6 sonatas for 2 oboes and bass, and wrote a motet for every Sunday. That year (1697) his father died; in pious fulfillment of the parent's wishes, Handel entered the Univ. of Halle (1702) as a law student, but left school after a year and went to Hamburg. There he was engaged as 'violino di ripieno' by Reinhard Keiser, the director of the German Opera. In Hamburg he met Mattheson, and in his company made a journey to Lübeck (1703), seeking the position of organist, as successor to the aging Buxtehude. It was a custom for an incoming organist to marry the old organist's daughter, and this condition neither Mattheson nor Handel was willing to fulfill. Accordingly, they returned to Hamburg. Mattheson was apparently jealous of Handel's growing success, and annoyed by Handel's haughty manner. A violent quarrel occurred between the two in the course of a production of Mattheson's opera *Cleopatra.* Mattheson, who not only sang on the stage, but also directed from the harpsichord at the conclusion of his acting, asked Handel to take his place while he was on the stage. Handel refused to be a mere substitute, and would not give up his seat at the harpsichord. The story goes that a duel ensued, and shots exchanged; it was asserted even that Handel had a narrow escape, when a bullet hit his waistcoat button and was deflected. However, the conflict could not have been so vehement, since Mattheson remained Handel's friend and became his biographer. In the meantime, Handel made great progress as composer. He produced 2 operas at Hamburg, *Almira* (Jan. 8, 1705) and *Nero* (Feb. 25, 1705); he was also commissioned by Keiser's successor, Saurbrey, to write *Florindo und Daphne* (1708), an opera filling 2 evenings. In 1706, with 200 ducats saved from music teaching, Handel went to Italy, visiting Florence, Venice, Rome, and Naples. In Florence he brought out his first Italian opera, *Rodrigo* (1707); his next Italian opera, *Agrippina*, was produced in Venice (Dec. 26, 1709) with extraordinary success. In Rome he produced 2 oratorios, *La Resurrezione* (April 8, 1708) and *Il Trionfo del tempo e del disinganno* (1708), with the famous violin virtuoso Corelli as leader; and in Naples the serenata *Aci, Galatea e Polifemo* (July 19, 1708), remarkable for its bass solo for a voice of 2 octaves and a fifth in compass. He made the acquaintance of Domenico Scarlatti, with whom he vied at the harpsichord and organ, and he also met Alessandro Scarlatti. In 1710 Handel returned to Germany and became Kapellmeister to the Elector of Hannover, replacing Steffani, who had especially recommended him as successor. Late in that year Handel visited England; he produced his opera *Rinaldo* at the Haymarket Theatre on Feb. 24, 1711, with excellent success, even though the score was compounded of arias and other material composed at an earlier date. He then returned to Hannover, but in 1712 obtained a leave of absence and went again to London. The operas that he produced there, *Il Pastor fido* (Nov. 22, 1712) and *Teseo*, (Jan. 10, 1713), were much superior to *Rinaldo*, but failed to win comparable acclaim; but an ode for Queen Anne's birthday, performed at Windsor on Feb. 6, 1713, and a *Te Deum* and *Jubilate* in celebration of the Peace of Utrecht (1713) won him royal favor, with an annuity of £200. Encouraged, Handel tarried in London for a longer time than the leave of absence from Hannover entitled him. On Queen Anne's death, however, the Elector of Hannover became King George I of England. Handel, with his old patron on the English throne, decided to remain in England permanently; in 1727 he became a British subject. The story that George I was angry at Handel for his neglect of duty in Hannover, and that he was consequently cold to Handel in the first year of his reign, is to be regarded as a legend. All evidence points to continued favors bestowed on Handel by the King, who added another £200 to Handel's annuity. In 1716 Handel accompanied him on a visit to Hannover. On July 17, 1717, an aquatic fête on the Thames River was arranged by royal order. The King's boat was followed by a barge in which an orchestra of some fifty players was arrayed. It was Handel who was given the task of writing the music, and the King liked it so well that he ordered the playing to be repeated twice.

Whether Handel's music played then was completely or even partly identical with the score later published as *Water Musick* is a moot question. In 1717 Handel succeeded Pepusch as chapel master to the Duke of Chandos, for whom he wrote his first English oratorio, *Esther*, the secular cantata *Acis and Galatea,* and the so-called *Chandos Anthems.* Handel also served as music master to the daughters of the Prince of Wales, and wrote for Princess Anne his first collection of *Suite de pièces* (1720) for harpsichord (*The Lessons*), which includes the air with variations later known (even though the nickname is gratuitous) as *The Harmonious Blacksmith.* He was then appointed director of the new Royal Academy of Music, established chiefly for the production of Italian opera, and on April 27, 1720, successfully brought out his opera *Radamisto.* It was about then that the strife arose between Handel and the Italian composer Giovanni Bononcini, who enjoyed the support of a powerful group of the English aristocracy. The feud was immortalized by the poet John Byrom in verse ('Some say, compar'd to Bononcini, that Mynheer Handel's but a ninny,' etc.). Handel won a Pyrrhic victory when Bononcini was caught in an act of plagiarism and was compelled to leave England in disgrace; Handel's own operas failed to gain public honor even with the elimination of his chief rival. During this period Handel staged, with varying success, the following operas at the King's Theatre: *Floridante* (Dec. 9, 1721), *Ottone* (Jan. 12, 1723), *Flavio* (May 14, 1723), *Giulio Cesare* (Feb. 20, 1724), *Tamerlano* (Oct. 31, 1724), *Rodelinda* (Feb. 13, 1725), *Scipione* (March 12, 1726), *Alessandro* (May 5, 1726), *Admeto* (Jan. 31, 1727), *Riccardo Primo* (Nov. 11, 1727), *Siroe* (Feb. 17, 1728), and *Tolemeo* (April 30, 1728). In 1727 he wrote 4 grand anthems for the coronation of George II and Queen Caroline. In 1729, after a visit to Germany and Italy, Handel associated himself with Heidegger, the owner of the King's Theatre, and inaugurated the season with his opera *Lotario* (Dec. 2, 1729), followed by *Partenope* (Feb. 24, 1730), *Poro* (Feb. 2, 1731), *Ezio* (Jan. 15, 1732), *Sosarme* (Feb. 15, 1732), and *Orlando* (Jan. 27, 1733), when the partnership ended. In 1732, Handel gave a special and successful production of his revised oratorio *Esther*, followed by *Acis and Galatea.* In 1733 he brought out the oratorios *Deborah* (March 17) and *Athalia* (July 10) at Oxford, where he publicly played the organ, and excited as much admiration by his performance as by his works; he was offered the degree of Mus. Doc. (*honoris causa*). The same year, Handel undertook the sole management of opera, but his manners and methods, a quarrel with his principal singer, Senesino, and a raising of prices caused many of his chief subscribers to suspend their support and start a rival troupe, The Opera of the Nobility, with Porpora and later Hasse as composer and conductor. They took possession of the King's Theatre; Handel went first to Lincoln's Inn Fields, and then to Covent Garden, but in 1737 failed; the rival house also had to close. The operas of this period were *Il Pastor Fido* (revised version; preceded by a ballet, *Terpsicore,* 1734), *Ariodante* (Jan. 8, 1735), *Alcina* (April 16, 1735), *Atalanta* (May 12, 1736), *Arminio* (Jan. 12, 1737), *Giustino* (Feb. 16, 1737), and *Berenice* (May 18, 1737); the ode *Alexander's Feast* was also produced at Covent Garden (Feb. 19, 1736), and *Il Trionfo del tempo e della verità* (a revision of *Il Trionfo del tempo e del disinganno* of 1707) in 1737. A stroke of paralysis incapacitated one of his hands, and, by the urgent advice of his friends, he went to Aix-la-Chapelle for a rest; he returned to London in November, 1737, with improved health. Heidegger had meantime formed a new company from the ruins of the two, and for this venture Handel wrote several operas: *Faramondo* (Jan. 3, 1738), *Serse* (April 15, 1738), *Jupiter in Argos* (May 1, 1739), *Imeneo* (Nov. 22, 1740), and *Deidamia* (Jan. 10, 1741). This last date marks a decisive turning point: he now abandoned stage composition for the work to which he owes enduring fame—oratorio. In close succession, Handel produced the oratorios *Saul* (Jan. 16, 1739) and *Israel in Egypt* (April 4, 1739). There followed the *Ode for St. Cecilia's Day* (Nov. 22, 1739), and *L'allegro, il pensieroso, ed il moderato*, after Milton (Feb. 27, 1740). In 1741, at the invitation of the viceroy of Ireland, Handel visited Dublin, and produced his immortal *Messiah* on April 13, 1742. His cordial reception in Ireland greatly compensated for previous disasters. On his return to London, he again became the popular favorite. *Messiah* was followed by *Samson* (Feb. 18, 1743), the *Dettinger Te Deum, Semele* (Feb. 10, 1744), *Joseph and his Brethren* (March 2, 1744), and *Belshazzar* (March 27, 1745). Once more he became entangled in monetary troubles, but his creative strength was not impaired thereby. Soon his two works, *Occasional Oratorio* (Feb. 14, 1746) and *Judas Maccabaeus* (April 1, 1747) were brought out; then appeared *Joshua* (March 9, 1748), *Susanna* (Feb. 10, 1749), *Solomon* (March 17, 1749), *Theodora* (March 16. 1750), *The Choice of Hercules* (March 1, 1751), and *Jephtha* (Feb. 26, 1752). In 1750, retrieving his fortune for the third time, Handel revisited his native country. In 1751, during the composition of *Jephtha*, he was afflicted with failing eyesight, and underwent three unsuccessful operations for cataract, total blindness being the result. He continued his musical performances under the direction of his pupil John Christopher Smith, and accompanied his oratorios on the organ up to his death. On April 6, 1759, *Messiah* was given as the final performance of the season, Handel presiding at the organ; on the 14th, the Saturday between Good Friday and Easter, he died. He was buried in Westminster Abbey, where a magnificent monument by Roubiliac marks his grave.

Handel had a commanding presence, and his features were animated and dignified. His health was robust. Of fearless independence, he was of a choleric temperament and prone to furious outbreaks, but he was easily restored to good humor and possessed a fund of ready wit. His liberality and charitableness were renowned. He remained unmarried but enjoyed the company of women.

The grandeur and sustained power of Handel's oratorio style, the expressive simplicity of his melody, and the breadth and clarity of the harmonic structure form a wonderful artistic whole. He is unquestionably one of the "great masters." His *Messiah* took England, and after her the rest of the musical world, by storm. At the first London performance, when the grand "Hallelujah Chorus" rang out, the entire audience rose like one man, carried away by lofty enthusiasm—thus originating the custom of standing during this chorus. Mozart, Mendelssohn, Brahms, and others have provided additional accompaniments to several of his works. Handel was peculiarly fortunate in coming to England just as the ebb of English national stage music after the death of Purcell (from whom Handel learned much) was turning toward the flood of Italian opera. His own dramatic works, strongly influenced by Keiser in Hamburg and the two Scarlattis in Italy, are of the finest of the period, and the best of them bear comparison with his oratorios. Precisely contemporary with J. S. Bach, he was quite outside the latter's sphere of influence and no communication existed between them. Of purely instrumental compositions Handel wrote a considerable number: FOR HARPSICHORD: 3 sets of *Lessons;* 6 fugues; many minuets; a march; the *Forest Musick* (Dublin, 1742); short pieces. FOR ORCH.: *Water Musick* (1717); the *Fireworks Musick* (1749); 2 sets of 6 organ concertos each (1738 and 1740); *Concertone* in 9 parts, for 2 violins, cello, oboe, and string orch. (1741); Concerto for Trumpets and Horns; Concerto for Horns and Sidedrums. CHAMBER MUSIC: several trio sonatas for various instruments, a sonata for flute with bass, etc. He bequeathed many original manuscripts of his works to his amanuensis, John Christopher Smith; the latter's son, Handel's pupil, presented them to George III. They are now in the British Museum as a part of the King's Music Library, and comprise 32 vols. of operas, 21 of oratorios, 7 of odes and serenatas, 12 of sacred music, 11 of cantatas and sketches, and 5 of instrumental music. In the Fitzwilliam Collection at Cambridge are 7 vols. containing rough drafts, notes and sketches for various works; also a complete Chandos anthem, *O praise the Lord with one consent.*

An edition of Handel's works in 36 vols., by Arnold, was publ. by command of George III (1787–97), but it is incomplete and inaccurate. A monumental edition in 100 vols. was issued (1856–94) by the German Handel Society, under the editorship of Fr. Chrysander. J. M. Coopersmith collected and edited 10 vols. of unpublished material to complete this edition, brought out an authentic version of *Messiah* in vocal score, and also worked on a thematic index of the whole. In 1955 a new complete ed., The Hallische Händel-Ausgabe, was begun by Max Schneider and Rudolf Steglich for the Georg-Friedrich-Händel Gesellschaft in Halle. A thematic catalogue has been compiled by A. C. Bell, 1969.

BIBLIOGRAPHY: J. Mattheson, *Grundlage einer Ehrenpforte* (Hamburg, 1740; reprint, Berlin, 1910); J. Mainwaring, *Memoirs of the Late G. F. Handel* (London, 1760; German transl., with notes by Mattheson, 1761; French transl. by Arnauld and Suard, 1778); Ch. Burney, *An Account of the Musical Pantheon in Commemoration of Handel* (London, 1785); W. Coxe, *Anecdotes of G. F. Handel and J. C. Smith* (London, 1799); R. Clark, *Reminiscences of Handel* (London, 1836); K. E. Förstemann, *G. F. Händels Stammbaum* (Leipzig, 1844); W. H. Callcott, *A Few Facts in the Life of Handel* (London, 1850); H. Townsend, *An Account of Handel's Visit to Dublin* (Dublin, 1852); V. Schoelcher, *The Life of Handel* (London, 1857); A. E. Stothard, *Handel: His Life, Personal and Professional*

(London, 1857); Fr. Chrysander, *G. F. Händel* (Leipzig, 1858–67; the most elaborate biography, in 3 vols., bringing the chronology to 1740; the work remains incomplete; repr. 1919); M. Delany, *Autobiography of Mary Granville* (London, 1862; contains a detailed account of Handel's death); F. J. van Kempen, *G. F. Handel: Een Leven* (Leyden, 1868); J. Marshall, *Handel* (London, 1881); W. S. Rockstro, *Life of Handel* (London, 1883); J. O. Opel, *Mitteilungen zur Geschichte der Familie des Tonkünstlers Händel* (Leipzig, 1885); F. Volbach, *Handel* (Berlin, 1897; augmented ed., 1906); F. C. A. Williams, *Handel* (London, 1904); J. C. Hadden, *Life of Handel* (London, 1905); R. A. Streatfeild, *Handel* (London, 1909); Romain Rolland, *Handel* (Paris, 1910; English transl., N.Y., 1923); H. Davey, *Handel* (London, 1912); G. Thormälius, *G. F. Händel* (Stuttgart, 1912); M. Brenet, *Haendel* (Paris, 1912); Newman Flower, *G. F. Handel, His Personality and His Times* (London, 1923; new ed., 1947); Hugo Leichtentritt, *Händel* (Stuttgart, 1924); J. Fuller-Maitland and W. B. Squire, "Handel," in *Dictionary of National Biography*; H. J. Moser, *Der junge Händel und seine Vorgänger in Halle* (Halle, 1929); J. M. Coopersmith, "A List of Portraits, Sculptures, etc., of Handel," *Music & Letters* (1932); J. Müller-Blattau, *Händel* (Potsdam, 1933); E. J. Dent, *Handel* (London, 1934); Ch. F. Williams, *Handel* (London, 1935); Lore Liebeman, *G. F. Händel und Halle* (Halle, 1935); E. Müller, ed., *The Letters and Writings of G. F. Handel* (London, 1935); H. Weinstock, *Handel* (N.Y., 1946); P. M. Young, *Handel* (London, 1946); W. C. Smith, *Concerning Handel, His Life and Works* (London, 1949); A. E. Cherbuliez, *G. F. Händel: Leben und Werk* (Olten, 1949); G. Abraham, ed., *Handel: a Symposium* (Oxford, 1954); Otto Erich Deutsch, *Handel, A Documentary Biography* (N.Y., 1954; most valuable; reproduces in chronological order all pertinent contemporary documents and notices in the press); W. Serauky, *G. F. Händel: Sein Leben, sein Werk* (an extensive, multivolume biography; Kassel, 1956–58); E. Flessa, *Ombra mai fu: Die Händel Chronik des Christopher Smith* (Biberbach, 1958); P. Nettl, *G. F. Händel* (Berlin, 1958); J. M. Müller-Blattau, *G. F. Händel: Der Wille zur Vollendung* (Mainz, 1959); R. Friedenthal, *G. F. Händel in Selbstzeugnissen und Bilddokumenten* (Hamburg, 1959; 3rd ed., Reinbeck, 1967); M. Nicolescu, *Händel* (Bucharest, 1959); N. Flower, *G. F. Handel: His Personality and His Times* (London, 1959); W. Rockwitz and H. Steffens, *G. F. Händel, Persönlichkeit, Umwelt, Vermächtnis* (Leipzig, 1962); P. H. Lang, *G. F. Händel* (N.Y., 1965; highly valuable, both historically and biographically); M. Szentkuthy, *Händel* (Budapest, 1967); K. Sasse, *Bildsammlung; Hogarth-Grafik; Darsfellung zur Geschichte, Händelpfege und Musikkunde* (Halle, 1967); W. B. Ober, "Bach, Handel, and 'Chevalier' John Taylor, M.D., Opthalmiater," *N.Y. State Journal of Medicine* (June 1969); M. Foss, *The Age of Patronage: The Arts in England 1660–1750* (Ithaca, N.Y., 1971).

CRITICISM, APPRECIATION: J. M. Weissebeck, *Der grosse Musikus Händel im Universalruhme* (Nuremberg, 1809); H. Chorley, *Handel-Studies* (2 vols., London, 1859); G. Gervinus, *Händel und Shakespeare* (Leipzig, 1868); R. Franz, *Über Bearbeitungen älterer Tonwerke, namenlich Bachscher und Händelscher Vokalmusik* (Leipzig, 1871; reprinted by R. Bethge as *Gesammelte Schriften über die Wiederbelebung Bachscher und Händelscher Werke* (Leipzig, 1910); E. Frommel, *Händel und Bach* (Berlin, 1878); Fr. Chrysander, *Händels biblische Oratorien in geschichtlicher Betrachtung* (Hamburg, 1897); F. J. Crowest, "Handel and English Music," in Traill, *Social England*, vol. 5 (London, 1893–98); G. Vernier, *L'Oratorio biblique de Handel* (Cahors, 1901); J. A. Fuller-Maitland, *The Age of Bach and Handel* (Vol. IV of *The Oxford History of Music*; Oxford, 1902); J. Garat, *La Sonate de Handel* (Paris, 1905); S. Taylor, *The Indebtedness of Handel to Works by Other Composers* (Cambridge, 1906); J. R. Carreras, *El Oratorio musical desde su origen hasta nuestros días* (Barcelona, 1906); P. Robinson, *Handel and His Orbit* (London, 1908); A. Schering, *Geschichte des Oratoriums* (Leipzig, 1911); R. A. Streatfeild, "The Granville Collection of Handel MSS," *Musical Antiquary* (July 1911); W. J. Lawrence, "Handeliana; the Dublin Charitable Musical Society," *Musical Antiquary* (Jan. 1912); H. Abert, *Händel als Dramatiker* (Göttingen, 1921); E. Bairstow, *The Messiah* (London, 1928); F. Kahle, *Handels Cembalo-Suiten* (Berlin, 1928); F. Ehrlinger, *Händels Orgelkonzerte* (Erlangen, 1934); Hugo Leichtentritt, "Handel's Harmonic Art," *Musical Quarterly* (April 1935); Virginia L. Redway, "Handel in Colonial and Post-Colonial America," *Musical Quarterly* (April 1935); J. M. Coopersmith, "Handelian Lacunae," *Musical Quarterly* (April 1935); R. M. Myers, *Handel's Messiah, A Touchstone of Taste* (N.Y., 1948); J. Herbage, *Messiah* (N.Y., 1948); J. P. Larsen, *Handel's Messiah* (N.Y., 1957); A. Loewenberg, *Annals of Opera* (for a list of revivals of Handel's operas; Cambridge, 1943; new ed., 1955); W. Dean, *Handel's Dramatic Oratorios and Masques* (London, 1959); W. C. Smith and C. Humphries, *Handel: A Descriptive Catalogue of the Early Editions* (London, 1960; 2nd ed., 1970); H. B. Dietz, *Die Chorfuge bei G. F. Händel* (Tutzing, 1961); K. Sasse, *Handel-Bibliographie* (Leipzig, 1963; new edition, 1967; with supplement, 1969); H. Federhofer, *Unbekannte Kopien von Werken G. Fr. Handels* (Kassel, 1963); H. W. Shaw, *A Textual and Historical Companion to Handel's Messiah* (London, 1965); W. C. Smith, *A Handelian's Notebook* (London, 1965); John Tobin, *Handel's Messiah* (London, 1969); A. C. Bell, *Chronological Catalogue of Handel's Work* (Greenock, Scotland, 1969); W. Dean, *Handel and the Opera Seria* (Berkeley, Calif., 1969); A. Mann and J. M. Knapp, "The Present State of Handel Research," *Acta Musicologica* (1969); W. Meyerhoff, ed., *50 Jahre Göttinger Händel-Festspiele. Festschrift* (Kassel, 1970); S. Sadie, *Handel Concertos* (London, 1972). The *Händel-Jahrbuch*, publ. by the Georg-Friedrich-Händel-Gesselschaft, was issued from 1928–33, and resumed publication in 1955.

Handl, Jacob. See **Gallus, Jacob Handl.**

Handrock, Julius, German piano pedagogue and composer; b. Naumburg, June 22, 1830; d. Halle, Jan. 5, 1894. He publ. several collections of piano studies which have retained their popularity among teachers and students for many years (*Moderne Schule der*

Geläufigkeit; 50 Melodisch-technische Klavier-Etuden, etc.).

Handschin, Jacques, eminent Swiss musicologist; b. Moscow, April 5, 1886; d. Basel, Nov. 25, 1955. In 1905 he went to Basel where he studied mathematics and history; then moved to Germany, where he took a course in music with Max Reger in Munich and studied organ playing with Karl Straube in Leipzig; subsequently he also studied organ with Widor in Paris. Returning to Russia he was appointed prof. of organ playing at the St. Petersburg Cons. (1909–20). In 1921 he returned to Switzerland and established himself in Basel, where he taught musicology at the University, a post he occupied until the end of his life. He also served as church organist in Basel and Zürich. He was greatly esteemed for his ample erudition and the dignity of his analytical theories; he evolved philosophical principles of musical esthetics seeking the rational foundations of the art. He publ. *Der Toncharakter; eine Einführung in die Tonpsychologie* (Zürich, 1948; his most important work, setting down his principles of musical esthetics); *Musikgeschichte im Überblick* (Lucerne, 1948); contributed valuable articles to music journals. A memorial volume, *Jacques Handschin, Aufsätze und Bibliographie,* containing reprints of some 50 articles by Handschin, was publ. in Basel in 1957, ed. by Dr. Hans Oesch. See also *In Memoriam Jacques Handschin,* ed. by H. Anglès (Strasbourg, 1962).

Handy, W. C. (William Christopher), American black composer, "father of the blues"; b. Florence, Ala., Nov. 16, 1873; d. New York, March 28, 1958. His father and grandfather were ministers. In 1892 he was graduated from the Teachers' Agricultural and Mechanical College, Huntsville, Alabama; became a school teacher and also worked in iron mills; learned to play the cornet and was soloist at Chicago World's Fair (1893); became bandmaster of Mahara's Minstrels. From 1900–02 he taught at Agricultural and Mechanical College; then from 1903–21, conducted his own orchestra and toured the South. He received the award of the National Association for Negro Music, St. Louis (1937). On Jan. 1, 1954, he married his secretary, Irma Louise Logan. His famous song, *Memphis Blues* (publ. 1912; the second piece to be published as a "blues," and the first blues to achieve popularity), was originally written as a campaign song for the Mayor of Memphis, E. H. Crump (1909); this song, along with his more celebrated *St. Louis Blues* (1914), opened an era in popular music, turning the theretofore prevalent spirit of ragtime gaiety to ballad-like nostalgia, with the lowered 3rd, 5th and 7th degrees ("blue notes") as distinctive melodic traits. He followed these with more blues: *Yellow Dog, Beale Street, Joe Turner;* the march *Hail to the Spirit of Freedom* (1915); *Ole Miss,* for piano (1916); the songs, *Aunt Hagar's Children* (1920); *Loveless Love* (1921); *Aframerican Hymn;* etc. He publ. the anthologies *Blues: An Anthology* (also publ. as *A Treasury of the Blues;* N.Y., 1926; 2nd ed., 1949; 3rd ed., rev. by J. Silverman, 1972); *Book of Negro Spirituals* (N.Y., 1938); *Negro Music and Musicians* (N.Y., 1944); also *Negro Authors and Composers of the U.S.* (N.Y., 1936); wrote an autobiography, *Father of the Blues* (N.Y., 1941). A commemorative stamp showing Handy playing the trumpet was issued on May 17, 1969 in Memphis, Tennessee, the birthplace of his "blues."

Handy, Will. Pseudonym for the song-writing team Cole and Johnson Bros.; see **Johnson, J. Rosamond** and **Johnson, James Weldon.**

Hanff, Johann Nikolaus, German organist and composer; b. Wechmar, near Mühlhausen, 1665; d. Schleswig, 1711. He was organist in Eupin; later in Hamburg (1706–11). A few months before his death, he was appointed organist at the cathedral of Schleswig. He was a master of the chorale-prelude, and his works considerably influenced J. S. Bach's style in this form. Only six of his chorale-preludes are extant (publ. in 1907 by K. Straube in his 45 *Choralvorspiele alter Meister;* reprinted by E. White in *Masterpieces of Organ Music,* N.Y., 1949).

BIBLIOGRAPHY: Hans Schillings, *Tobias Eniccelius, Friedrich Meister, Nikolaus Hanff: ein Beitrag zur Geschichte der evangelischen Frühkantate in Schleswig-Holstein* (Kiel, 1934); H. J. Moser, *Die evangelische Kirchenmusik in Deutschland* (Berlin, 1954).

Hanfstängel, Marie, German soprano; b. Breslau, April 30, 1846; d. Munich, Sept. 5, 1917. She studied at Baden-Baden with Mme. Viardot-Garcia; made her debut as Agathe in *Der Freischütz* at the Théâtre Lyrique, Paris (Feb. 27, 1867). On the declaration of the Franco-Prussian war, she returned to Germany, and was engaged at the Stuttgart Opera. She sang at the Metropolitan Opera House in N.Y. (1884–86); then retired and lived mostly in Munich. She publ. *Meine Lehrweise der Gesangskunst* (1902).

Hanisch, Joseph, German organist and composer; b. Regensburg, March 24, 1812; d. there, Oct. 9, 1892. He studied with his father, and with Proske, with whom he went to Italy as an assistant (1834). In 1839 he became organist at the Regensburg Cathedral. He wrote *Missa auxilium Christianorum; Quatuor hymni pro festo corporis Christi;* contributed organ accompaniments to the *Graduale* and *Vesperale Romanum* (with Haberl); also composed pieces for organ solo. He was a master of improvisation, and was regarded as one of the greatest in this field in his time.

Hanke, Karl, German composer; b. Rosswalde, Silesia, c.1750; d. Flensburg, June 10, 1803. As a young man, he was sent to Vienna to pursue his music studies; there he briefly associated himself with Gluck, and profited by the master's advice. He then held the post of musical director in Brünn (1778–81), Warsaw (1781–83), and Hamburg (1784–86). In 1791 he settled in Flensburg, where he remained until the end of his life. He composed several pieces for the stage; his Singspiel *Der Wunsch mancher Mädchen* (1781), dedicated to Gluck, was performed on various occasions with some success; 2 albums of his songs were publ. in 1796–97.

BIBLIOGRAPHY: Alfred Einstein, "Ein Schüler Glucks," *Acta Musicologica* (1938).

Hannay, Roger, talented American composer; b. Plattsburg, N.Y., Sept. 22, 1930. He studied composition with F. Morris and Dika Newlin at Syracuse Univ. (1948–52), H. Norden at Boston Univ. (1952–53), with Bernard Rogers and Howard Hanson at the Eastman School of Music in Rochester, N.Y. (1954–56; Ph.D., 1956), and Lukas Foss and Aaron Copland at the Berkshire Music Center (1959); had sessions with Sessions and attended lectures by Elliott Carter at the Princeton Seminar for Advanced Studies (1960). He taught at various colleges; in 1966 joined the music faculty of the Univ. of North Carolina at Chapel Hill and organized the electronic music studio there (1970). An unprejudiced and liberal music maker, he makes use of varied functional resources, from neo-Classical pandiatonism to dodecaphony; resorts also to the device of "objets trouvés," borrowing thematic materials from other composers.

WORKS: 2 chamber operas: *2 Tickets to Omaha, The Swindlers* (1960) and *The Fortune of St. Macabre* (1964); *Requiem,* after Whitman's 'When Lilacs Last . . .' (1961); Cantata (1952); *The Inter-Planetary Aleatoric Serial Factory* for soprano solo, string quartet, rock band, actors, dancers, tapes, film and slides (1969); 4 symphonies: No. 1 (1953, revised 1973), No. 2 (1956); No. 3, "The Great American Novel," with chorus and tape-recorded sound (1976–77); No. 4, "American Classic" (1977); *Dramatic Overture,* an homage to Schoenberg (1955); *Lament* for oboe and strings (1957); *Symphony for Band* (1963); *Sonorous Image* for orch. (1968); *Sayings for Our Time,* to a text from the 'current news media,' for chorus and orch. (Winston-Salem, Aug. 2, 1968); *Fragmentation* for orch. or chamber orch. (1969); *Listen* for orch. (1971; Guilford College, N.C., July 7, 1973); *Celebration* for tape and orch. (N.Y., May 19, 1975); *Suite-Billings* for youth orch. (1975); *Rhapsody* for flute and piano (1952); Sonata for Brass Ensemble (1957); Divertimento for Wind Quintet (1958); *Concerto da Camera* for recorder, violin, viola, cello, harpsichord and soprano (1958, revised 1975); 4 string quartets: No. 1 (1962); No. 2, *Lyric* (1962); No. 3, *Designs* (1963); No. 4, *Quartet of Solos* (1974; comprised of the simultaneous performances of the 4 solo pieces *Grande Concerte, Second Fiddle, O Solo Viola* and *Concert Music*); *The Fruit of Love,* after St. Vincent Millay, for soprano, and piano or chamber orch. (1964, 1969); *Spectrum* for brass quintet (1964); *Structure* for percussion ensemble (1965, revised 1974); *Marshall's Medium Message* for mod-girl announcer and percussion quartet (1967); *America Sing!* for tape and visuals (1967); *Fantome* for viola, clarinet and piano (1967); *Live and in Color!* for mod-girl announcer, percussion quartet, 2 action painters, tape, films and slides (1967); *Confrontation* for tape and percussion (1969); *Squeeze Me* for chamber ens. and film (1970); *Tuonelan Joutsen,* vocalise for soprano, English horn and film (1972, after Sibelius' *Swan of Tuonela*); *Prophecy of Despair* for male chorus and percussion (1972); *Grande Concerte* for solo violin (1972); *Concert Music* for solo cello (1973); *Sphinx* for tape and trumpet (1973); *Four for Five* for brass quintet (1973); *O Solo Viola* for solo viola (1974); *Second Fiddle* for solo violin (1974); *Phantom of the Opera* for organ and soprano (1975); *Pied Piper* for tape and clarinet (1975); *Oh Friends!* for chamber wind ensemble and pitch percussion (1976); Suite for Piano (1954); *Abstractions* for piano (1962); Piano Sonata (1964); *Sonorities* for piano (1966); *The Episodic Refraction* for tape and piano (1971); choruses; songs.

Hannikainen, Ilmari, Finnish pianist and composer; b. Jyväskylä, Oct. 19, 1892; d. Kuhmoinen, July 25, 1955. A scion of a musical family (his father **Pekka Hannikainen** was conductor and composer), he studied in Helsinki; then took lessons with Alexander Siloti in St. Petersburg and with Alfred Cortot in Paris. Returning to Finland, he was active as piano teacher; with his brothers **Tauno** and **Arvo Hannikainen,** he organized a concert trio. He composed a folk opera *Talkoottanssit* (1930), a piano concerto, a piano quartet and many solo piano pieces.

Hannikainen, Pekka, Finnish conductor; b. Nurmes, Dec. 9, 1854; d. Helsinki, Sept. 13, 1924. He was the founding member of a musically important family in Finland; his sons **Ilmari, Tauno, Arvo** and **Väinö,** were respectively a pianist, a cellist, a violinist and a harpist.

Hannikainen, Tauno, Finnish cellist and conductor; b. Jyväskylä, Feb. 26, 1896; d. Helsinki, Oct. 12, 1968. A member of a prominent musical family in Finland (his father **Pekka Hannikainen** was a conductor and composer; his brother **Ilmari Hannikainen** was a pianist and composer), he studied in Helsinki, and took some cello lessons with Pablo Casals in Paris. Returning to Finland, he organized a trio with his two brothers **Arvo,** a violinist, and **Ilmari,** a pianist. He conducted the Symph. Orch. of Turku (1927–40); then went to America where he was the principal conductor of the Symph. Orch. of Duluth, Minnesota (1942–46), and assistant conductor of the Chicago Civic Symph. Orch. (1947–50); then returned to Finland where he was conductor of the City Orch. in Helsinki. He was married to the Finnish soprano **Anne Niskanen.**

Hannikainen, Väinö, Finnish harpist and composer; son of **Pekka Hannikainen;** b. Jyväskylä, Jan. 12, 1900; d. Kuhmoinen, Finland, Aug. 7, 1960. He studied in Helsinki and Berlin; from 1923–1957 was first harpist of the Helsinki Orch. He wrote several symphonic poems, a harp concerto, a harp sonata, some theater music and songs.

Hanon, Charles-Louis, French pianist and pedagogue; b. Renescure, near Dunkerque, July 2, 1819; d. Boulogne-sur-Mer, March 19, 1900. Next to Czerny, Hanon was the most illustrious composer of piano exercises embodied in his chef d'œuvre entitled *Le Pianiste-virtuose* which for over a century was the vademecum for many millions of diligent piano students all over the face of the musical globe; its validity as a book of exercises remains solid well into the 21st century. He further wrote a collection of 50 instructive piano pieces under the title *Méthode élémentaire de piano;* a useful compilation, *Extraits des chefs-*

d'œuvres des grands maîtres, as well as a selection of 50 ecclesiastical chants, *50 cantiques choisis parmi les plus populaires.* He also attempted to instruct uneducated musicians in the art of accompanying plainchant in a curious didactic publication *Système nouveau pour apprendre à accompagner tout plainchant sans savoir la musique.*

Hansen, (Emil) Robert, Danish cellist; b. Copenhagen, Feb. 25, 1860; d. Aarhus, July 18, 1926. He received his first instruction from his father, then studied with F. Neruda at the Copenhagen Cons., and with Fr. Grützmacher in Dresden; from 1877–89, member of the court orch. in Copenhagen. After a stay in London, he settled in 1891 in Leipzig, where he joined the Gewandhaus orch. and became prof. at the Cons. From 1918 he was conductor of the Symph. Orch. of Aarhus, Denmark.
WORKS: an opera, *Frauenlist* (Sondershausen, 1911), and an operetta, *Die wilde Komtesse* (Eisenach, 1913); Symphony; Symph. Suite for Strings and 2 Horns; Piano Concerto; Cello Concerto; Piano Quintet; String Quartet.

Hansen, Wilhelm, Danish music publishing firm founded in Copenhagen by Jens Wilhelm Hansen (1821–1904). His sons, **Jonas W. Hansen** (1850–1919) and **Alfred W. Hansen** (1854–1922), also played an active part in the business, which was eventually entrusted to the sons of Alfred, **Asger** (b. 1889) and **Svend** (b. 1890). A large proportion of published Scandinavian (Danish, Swedish, Norwegian) music is brought out by this firm; it has also bought other smaller firms, and publ. some of the works of Arnold Schoenberg. Branches have been established in Oslo, Stockholm, Frankfurt and London.

Hanslick, Eduard, greatly renowned music critic; b. Prague, Sept. 11, 1825; d. Baden, near Vienna, Aug. 6, 1904. He studied law at Prague and Vienna; took degree of Dr. jur. in 1849, qualifying himself for an official position. But he had already studied music under Tomaschek at Prague; from 1848–49 was music critic for the *Wiener Zeitung,* and soon adopted a literary career. His first work, *Vom Musikalisch-Schönen: ein Beitrag zur Revision der Aesthetik der Tonkunst* (Leipzig, 1854; in French, 1877; Spanish, 1879; Italian, 1884; English, 1891; Russian, 1895), brought him world-wide fame. Its leading idea is that the beauty of a musical composition lies wholly and specifically in the music itself; i.e., it is immanent in the relations of the tones, without any reference whatever to extraneous (non-musical) ideas, and can express no others. Such being his point of view through life, it follows logically that he could not entertain sympathy for Wagner's art; his violent opposition to the music-drama was a matter of profound conviction, not personal spite. On the other hand, he was one of the very first and most influential champions of Brahms. From 1855–64, Hanslick was music editor of the *Presse;* thereafter of the *Neue freie Presse;* he became lecturer on music history and esthetics at Vienna Univ., prof. extraordinary in 1861, and in 1870, full professor, retiring in 1895 (succeeded by Guido Adler). At the Paris Expositions of 1867 and 1878, and the Vienna

Exposition of 1873, Hanslick was a juror in the department of music. What gives his writings permanent value is the sound musicianship underlying their brilliant, masterly style. Yet, in music history, he is chiefly known as a captious and intemperate reviler of genius; Wagner caricatured him in the part of Beckmesser (originally, the name was to be Hans Lick).
WRITINGS: *Geschichte des Concertwesens in Wien* (1869); *Aus dem Concertsaal* (1870); a series begun with *Die moderne Oper* (1875) and followed by 8 more vols., giving a fairly comprehensive view of the development of opera from Gluck to 1900: II. *Musikalische Stationen* (1880); III. *Aus dem Opernleben der Gegenwart* (1884); IV. *Musikalisches Skizzenbuch* (1888); V. *Musikalisches und Litterarisches* (1889); VI. *Aus dem Tagebuch eines Musikers* (1892); VII. *Fünf Jahre Musik* (1896); VIII. *Am Ende des Jahrhunderts* (1899); IX. *Aus neuer und neuester Zeit* (1900); *Suite, Aufsätze über Musik und Musiker* (1885); *Konzerte, Komponisten und Virtuosen der letzten fünfzehn Jahre* (1886); *Aus meinem Leben* (2 vols., 1894). All these books passed through several editions. He also edited Th. Billroth's posthumous essay, *Wer ist musikalisch?* (1895; 4th ed., 1912); and wrote the commentary for the illustrated *Galerie deutscher Tondichter* (1873) and *Galerie französischer und italienischer Tondichter* (1874). A collection of Hanslick's articles in the *Neue freie Presse* was published in English transl. under the title, *Vienna's Golden Years of Music, 1850–1900* (N.Y., 1950).
BIBLIOGRAPHY: R. Schafke, *Eduard Hanslick und die Musikästhetik* (1922); S. Deas, *In Defense of Hanslick* (London, 1940).

Hanson, Howard, distinguished American composer; b. Wahoo, Nebraska, Oct. 28, 1896. His parents emigrated from Sweden to America in their youth; his Scandinavian ancestry plays an important part in Hanson's spiritual outlook. He studied at the Luther College in Wahoo; then went to New York, where he studied with Percy Goetschius at the Institute of Musical Art; also at Northwestern Univ. in Evanston, Ill., with P. C. Lutkin and Arne Oldberg; after graduation in 1916, he became instructor at the College of the Pacific in San José, Calif.; was its dean in 1919–21. In 1921, he won the American Prix de Rome; spent 3 years at the American Academy in Rome and composed several important works there. In 1924, he was appointed by George Eastman as director of the Eastman School of Music, Rochester, N.Y.; in 1925, began there a series of orchestral concerts featuring works by American composers. During the 4 decades of his leadership of the Eastman School of Music and his conductorship of the American Music Festivals, Hanson has contributed greatly to the cause of American musical education, as well as to that of American music. In 1932, he conducted programs of American music in Europe; also was guest conductor with major American orchestras in programs of American music, including his own works. In 1961–62 he conducted the Eastman School Philharmonia Orch. in Portugal, Spain, Switzerland, France, Luxembourg, Belgium, Sweden, Greece, Cyprus, Syria, Egypt, Lebanon, Turkey, Germany, Poland and Russia, under the auspices of the State Department. Hanson continued to be director of the Eastman School of Music until 1964 when he retired. In 1935, he was elected a member of the National Institute of Arts and Letters; in 1938, a fellow of the Royal Academy of Music in Sweden. He has furthermore been, at various times, president of the National Association of Schools of Music; president of the Music Teachers' National Association; president of the National Music Council; also active in various capacities for numerous music organizations. He holds honorary D. Mus. degrees from Syracuse Univ., Univ. of Nebraska, Northwestern Univ.; awarded the Pulitzer Prize for his 4th Symph. (1944); Ditson Award (1945); George Foster Peabody Award (1946), etc. His music is permeated with outspoken Romanticism; he pointedly entitled one of his symphonies *Romantic Symphony;* his profound kinship for Scandinavia is expressed in his *Nordic Symphony* and other works. An influence of Sibelius is notable in Hanson's broad lyrical passages, and in the sombre coloring of his instrumentation. In his strong and often asymmetrical rhythms, Hanson demonstrates a certain spirit of experimentation; his harmonies, frequently set at the tritone's distance of their tonics, stand on the borderline of pungent bitonality, but he never employs extreme modernistic effects. As a teacher he shaped the musical style of a generation of American composers.

WORKS: FOR THE STAGE: *California Forest Play of 1920,* for ballet and orch. (1920); *Merry Mount,* opera in 3 acts (1933; commissioned by the Metropolitan Opera; produced there, Feb. 10, 1934). FOR ORCH.: *Symph. Prelude* (1916); *Symph. Legend* (San Francisco, 1917); *Symph. Rhapsody* (Los Angeles, 1919); *Before the Dawn,* symph. poem (Los Angeles, 1920); *Exaltation,* a symph. poem for orch. with piano obbligato (San Francisco, 1920); Concerto for Organ, Strings, Harp, and Orch. (1921); Symph. No. 1 (*Nordic Symph.;* Rome, composer conducting, May 30, 1923; 1st American performance, Rochester, N.Y., March 19, 1924); *North and West,* symph. poem with choral obbligato (N.Y., 1923); *Lux Aeterna,* symph. poem with viola obbligato (Rome, 1923); *Pan and the Priest,* symph. poem with piano obbligato (London, 1926); Concerto for Organ and Orch. (Rochester, 1926); Symph. No. 2 (*Romantic Symph.;* commissioned for the 50th anniversary of the Boston Symph. Orch., Koussevitzky conducting, Nov. 28, 1930; very successful); Symph. No. 3 (NBC Symph., March 26, 1938, composer conducting); Symph. No. 4, subtitled *The Requiem* (Boston Symph., Dec. 3, 1943, composer conducting; won a Pulitzer Prize, 1944); *Serenade,* for flute, strings, harp, and orch. (1945); Piano Concerto (Boston, Dec. 31, 1948); Symph. No. 5 (*Sinfonia Sacra;* Philadelphia, Feb. 18, 1955); *Elegy in Memory of Serge Koussevitzky* (Boston, Jan. 20, 1956); *Summer Seascape* (New Orleans, March 10, 1959); Bold Island Suite (Cleveland, Jan. 25, 1962); *Dies Natalis* (1967). *Mosaics* for orch. (Cleveland, Jan. 23, 1958); Symph. No. 6 (N.Y., Feb. 29, 1968). CHORAL WORKS: *The Lament of Beowulf* (Ann Arbor Festival, 1926); *Heroic Elegy,* for chorus and orch., without words (for the Beethoven centenary, 1927); *3 Songs from 'Drum Taps'* (Whitman), for voices and orch. (1935); *Hymn for the Pioneers,* for men's voices (1938); *The Cherubic Hymn,* for chorus and orch. (1949); *How Excellent*

Thy Name, for chorus and piano (1952); *The Song of Democracy,* for soli, chorus, and orch. (Philadelphia, April 9, 1957); *Song of Human Rights,* cantata (Washington, Dec. 10, 1963); *New Land, New Covenant,* oratorio to words by Isaac Watts, T. S. Eliot, John Newton, the Bible and the Declaration of Independence (1976). *4 Psalms* for baritone, solo cello, string sextet (Washington, Oct. 31, 1964); *Streams in the Desert* for chorus and orch. (1969); Symph. No. 7, *A Sea Symphony,* after Walt Whitman, for chorus and orch. (Interlochen, Michigan, Aug. 7, 1977; for the 50th anniversary of the famous National Music Camp there). CHAMBER MUSIC: Piano Quintet (1916); *Concerto da camera,* for piano and string quartet (1917); String Quartet (1923); *Fantasia on a Theme of Youth,* for piano and strings (Northwestern Univ., Feb. 18, 1951). FOR PIANO: *Prelude and Double Fugue,* for 2 pianos (1915); *4 Poems* (1917–18); *Sonata* (1918); *3 Miniatures* (1918–19); *Scandinavian Suite* (1918–19); *3 Etudes* (1920); *2 Yuletide Pieces* (1920); songs. He published a manual, *Harmonic Materials of Modern Music: Resources of the Tempered Scale* (N.Y., 1960).

BIBLIOGRAPHY: E. Royce, "Howard Hanson," in Cowell's symposium *American Composers on American Music* (Stanford, 1933); B. C. Tuthill, "Howard Hanson," *Musical Quarterly* (April 1936); M. Alter, "Howard Hanson," *Modern Music* (Jan.-Feb. 1941).

Hanssens, Charles-Louis, Belgian cellist, conductor, and composer; b. Ghent, July 12, 1802; d. Brussels, April 8, 1871. As a child of 10 he played in the orch. of the National Theater, Amsterdam; was first cellist of the orch. in the Brussels theater (1824–27); then taught harmony at the Brussels Cons.; subsequently conducted French opera at the Hague and at Ghent. From 1848 to 1869 he was conductor at the Théâtre de la Monnaie, Brussels.

WORKS: 8 operas, ballets, symphonies, overtures, orchestral fantasies; Violin Concerto, Cello Concerto, Clarinet Concerto, several piano concertos; string quartets; *Symphonie concertante* for clarinet and violin; Masses, cantatas, a cappella choruses.

BIBLIOGRAPHY: L. de Burbure, *Notice sur Charles-Louis Hanssens* (Antwerp, 1872) and L. Bäwolf, *Charles-Louis Hanssens* (Brussels, 1895).

Hanuš, Jan, Czech composer; b. Prague, May 2, 1915. He studied composition privately with Jeremiáš, and conducting with Pavel Dědeček at the Prague Cons. He then devoted himself to editorial work in music publishing houses; was an assistant in preparing the complete critical edition of Dvořák's collected works; also completed the instrumentations of the unfinished operas *Tkalci* by Nejedlý and *Balada o lásce* by Doubrava. His own music is marked by lyrical romanticism, not without stringent dissonant textures.

WORKS: 4 operas: *Plameny* (*Flames,* 1942–44; Pilsen, 1956), *Sluha dvou pánů* (*Servant of 2 Masters,* 1958; Pilsen, 1959), *Pochodeň Prometheova* (*The Torch of Prometheus,* 1961–63; Prague, 1965) and *Pohádka jedné noci* (*The Story of One Night,* 1965–68); 2 ballets: *Sůl nad zlato* (*Salt Is Worth More Than Gold,* 1953) and *Othello* (1956); 2 cantatas: *The Country Speaks* (1940) and *The Song of Hope* (1945–48); *Rondo capriccio* for orch. (1937); 5 symphonies (with solo alto, 1942; 1951; 1957; 1960; 1965); *The Eulogy*, sinfonietta for soprano and orch. (1945); *Concertante Symphony* for organ, harp, tympani and strings (1954); *Petr a Lucie (Peter and Lucia)*, symph. fantasy (1955); *Overture*, after Walt Whitman's "The Bugler's Secret" (1961); Double Concerto for oboe, harp and orch. (1965); *Relay Race*, symph. allegro (1968); *Pražská nokturna (Prague Nocturne)* for chamber orch. (1972–73); Fantasy for String Quartet (1939); *Sonata-Rhapsody* for cello and piano (1941); *Suite to Paintings by Mánes* for violin and piano (1948); *A Year in Bohemia* for children's chorus, and piano or chamber orch. (1949–52); Serenade for Nonet (1953); Viola Sonatina (1958); *Suita Dramatica* for string quartet (1959); *3 Portraits from "Othello"* for violin and piano (1960); *Frescoes*, piano trio (1961); *Suita domestica* for wind quintet (1964); *Poselství (The Message)*, tryptich for baritone, chorus, 2 prepared pianos, electric guitar, percussion and tape (1969); *Musica concertante* for cello, piano, winds and percussion (1969–70); Concertino for 2 Percussionists and Tape (1972); *The Swallow*, concerto piccolo for chorus, flute and cello (1973); *Meditations* for piano (1938–39); Preludes for Piano (1949); *Suita Lyrica* for organ (1957); *Contemplazioni* for organ (1969); Canons for children's chorus (1971–72) and other choral works; songs.

Harasiewicz, Adam, Polish pianist; b. Chodziez, Western Poland, July 1, 1932. He studied with Kazimierz Mirski until 1950; then at the State School of Music in Cracow. He entered the Chopin Contest in 1949, but failed to win a prize. In March, 1955, he competed again, at the 5th International Chopin Contest in Warsaw, in which pianists of 27 countries took part, and won the first prize of 30,000 zlotys.

Harasowski, Adam, Polish pianist and writer on music; b. Delatyn, district of Stanisławów, Sept. 16, 1904. He was brought up in a musical family. He studied at the Cons. of Lwów with Adam Soltys (1923–29); also took private lessons in composition with Szymanowski during his frequent visits at Lwów. Concurrently he studied mechanical engineering, graduating from the Lwów Polytechnic in 1931, and subsequently earned his living mainly as an engineering draftsman. At the outbreak of World War II he went to England with the Polish Air Force, and remained with the Royal Air Force of Great Britain as Flight Lieutenant (1943–58); he retired in 1958 and devoted himself to journalism, both in Polish and in English; published *The Skein of Legends Around Chopin* (Glasgow, 1967); also compiled collections of Polish songs.

Haraszti, Émile, Hungarian musicologist; b. Nagyvárad, Nov. 1, 1885; d. Paris, Dec. 27, 1958. He studied composition and musicology in Vienna, Munich, Leipzig, Berlin and Paris. Returning to Budapest, he served as the music critic of the *Budapest Hirlap* (1908–30); then lectured on music at the Univ. of Budapest. In 1945 he went to Paris.
WRITINGS: *Wagner et la Hongrie* (Budapest, 1916); *La Musique hongroise* (Paris, 1933); *Béla Bartók, His Life and Works* (Oxford, 1938); *Un Centenaire romantique: Berlioz et la Marche Hongroise*

d'après des documents inédits (Paris, 1946); also contributed valuable studies to various magazines. His monograph on Liszt was publ. posthumously in Paris in 1967. A complete list of his writings is found in his autobiographical notice in *Die Musik in Geschichte und Gegenwart*.

Harbison, John, American composer; b. Orange, N.J., Dec. 20, 1938. He studied piano, violin, viola, and conducting; took courses in composition at Harvard Univ. (B.A., 1960) and at Princeton Univ. with Roger Sessions (M.F.A., 1963). In 1969 he was appointed assistant prof. of music at the Massachusetts Institute of Technology. His works include a *Sinfonia* for violin and double orch. (1963); *Confinement* for a chamber ensemble (1965); Violin Concerto (1967); Serenade for six players (1968); Piano Trio (1969); *Diotima* for orch. (Boston, March 10, 1977).

d'Harcourt, Eugène, French conductor and composer; b. Paris, May 2, 1859; d. Locarno, Switzerland, March 4, 1918. He studied at the Paris Cons. with Massenet, Durand and Savard (1882–86); then took courses in Berlin with Bargiel. In 1892 he built the "Salle d'Harcourt" in Paris where he presented 3 seasons of "Concerts éclectiques populaires." He wrote an unsuccessful opera *Le Tasse* (Monte Carlo, 1903), in addition to 3 unnecessary symphonies and some passable chamber music.

d'Harcourt, Marguerite, French folksong collector and composer; b. Paris, Feb. 24, 1884; d. there, Aug. 2, 1964. She studied composition with Vincent d'Indy and Maurice Emmanuel; composed 2 symphonies; *Rapsodie péruvienne* for oboe, clarinet, and bassoon; and many songs. With her husband, **Raoul d'Harcourt,** she publ. a valuable treatise *Musique des Incas et ses survivances* (Paris, 1925; 2 Vols.) based on materials gathered during their journeys in Peru; another valuable publication which she compiled was a collection of 240 songs, *Chansons folkloriques françaises au Canada* (Quebec, 1956).

Hardegg, Grad, Austrian pianist; b. Vienna, April 24, 1834; d. there, March 22, 1867. He was a piano pupil of Czerny, and composed a number of pieces of salon music which became popular.

d'Hardelot, Guy (Mrs. W. I. Rhodes, *née* **Helen Guy),** French song composer; b. 1858 at the Chateau d'Hardelot, Boulogne-sur-Mer; d. London, Jan. 7, 1936. She studied at the Paris Cons.; traveled with Emma Calvé in the U.S. in 1896; then married, and settled in London. She wrote many melodious songs: *Sans toi, Because* (very popular), *Tristesse*, etc.

Harding, A. A. (Albert Austin), American college bandmaster; b. Georgetown, Ill., Feb. 10, 1880; d. Champaign, Ill., Dec. 3, 1958. At 14 he began to play cornet, and then trombone and other wind instruments. After graduation from high school in Paris, Illinois, he conducted the local concert band. In 1902 enrolled as an engineering student at the Univ. of Illinois, acquiring his bachelor's degree in 1906. At the same time he developed many campus music contacts and in 1905 was made acting leader of the University Band; in 1907 he was appointed Director, a post he held until 1948. Harding was the first to succeed in raising college bands to a "symphonic" level in which oboes, saxophones, and other reed instruments supplied variety to the common brass-heavy contingent; thanks to this sonic enhancement, Harding was able to arrange orchestral works of the general repertory and perform them in a satisfactory musical manner; he was credited with 147 such transcriptions. John Philip Sousa, who greatly admired Harding, bequeathed to him and his band his own entire music library. Harding was a charter founder of the American Bandmasters Association in 1929 and was its President in 1937-38; Honorary Life President from 1956 until his death. He also was active in founding the College Band Directors Association, of which he was Honorary Life President from its founding in 1941.

BIBLIOGRAPHY: Calvin E. Weber, "Albert Austin Harding: Pioneer College Bandmaster," *Journal of Band Research* (Autumn 1966).

Harewood, 7th Earl of, George Henry Hubert Lascelles, British music editor and organizer; b. Cambridge, Feb. 7, 1923. He was educated at Eton and King's College, Cambridge, served as Capt., Grenadier Guards in World War II; wounded and taken prisoner in 1944. He was founder and editor of magazine *Opera* (1950-53); Chairman of the Music Advisory Committee, British Council from 1956; Artistic Director of the Edinburgh International Festival 1961-64; Chancellor, Univ. of York since 1962. He edited Kobbé's *Complete Opera Book* (1954).

Harker, F. Flaxington, organist and composer; b. Aberdeen, Scotland, Sept. 4, 1876; d. Richmond, Va., Oct. 23, 1936. While acting as assistant organist at the York Minster, he studied with T. Tertius Noble, who was organist there. In 1901 he came to the United States and served as organist in churches in Biltmore, N.C. and Richmond, Va. He wrote 2 cantatas, *The Star of Bethlehem* and *The Cross;* publ. Harker's Organ Collection (2 vols.; 27 works by modern masters of the organ).

Harline, Leigh, American composer; b. Salt Lake City, March 26, 1907; d. Long Beach, Calif., Dec. 10, 1969. He studied music at the Univ. of Utah; went to Los Angeles in 1928 when he became arranger for Walt Disney (1931-42); then worked as film music composer in Hollywood; his song *When You Wish Upon a Star* received an Academy Award in 1940.

Harling, William Franke, American composer; b. London, England, Jan. 18, 1887; d. Sierra Madre, Calif., Nov. 22, 1958. He was brought to the U.S. in infancy; filled various jobs as a church organist. Eventually settled in Hollywood. He wrote a one-act opera, *A Light from St. Agnes* (Chicago, Dec. 26, 1925); a "native opera with jazz," *Deep River* (Lancaster, Penn., Sept. 18, 1926; N.Y., Oct. 4, 1926); some instrumental music and more than 100 songs. He was also the composer of the march *West Point Forever.*

BIBLIOGRAPHY: E. E. Hipsher, *American Opera and Its Composers* (Philadelphia, 1927; pp. 250-56).

Harman, Carter, American music critic, recording-firm executive, and composer; b. Brooklyn, June 14, 1918. He studied with Roger Sessions at Princeton Univ. (1936-40); was a pilot in the U.S. Army Air Corps in the Burma-Indo-China theater in World War II (1942-45); then returned for further study at Columbia Univ. (1945-48). From 1947 to 1952 he was a music critic for the *N.Y. Times* and later music editor of *Time* magazine (1952-57); from 1958 to 1967 he lived in Puerto Rico, where he became president of the West Indies Recording Corp.; was location sound engineer for the film *Lord of the Flies,* and others. In 1967 Harman became producer and executive vice-president of Composers Recordings, Inc. in N.Y., devoted mainly to recording contemporary American music.

WORKS: a ballet *Blackface* (N.Y., May 18, 1947); children's operas *Circus at the Opera* (1951), *Castles in the Sand* (1952) and a group of 34 songs for children. In 1974 he began experiments with the total electronic synthesizing of nursery rhymes (with vocal parts accomplished by using a Sonovox and "artificial larynx") for an "entertainment" called *Alex and the Singing Synthesizer,* completed in 1977. He publ. *A Popular History of Music from Gregorian Chant to Jazz* (N.Y., 1956; revised 1968).

Harmat, Artur, Hungarian composer; b. Nyitrabajna (now Bojna, Czechoslovakia), June 27, 1885; d. Budapest, April 20, 1962. He studied at the Budapest Academy of Music and later took courses in Prague and Berlin. From 1920 to 1946 he was an inspector of singing in the Budapest schools; from 1924 to 1959 he was professor of religious music at the Budapest Academy. He wrote 2 valuable manuals on counterpoint (1947, 1956) and composed a great quantity of church music, based on the lines of Palestrina's polyphony.

WORKS: *Te Deum* for chorus and organ (1912-29); *Tu es Petrus* for chorus and orch. (1929); *Psalm 150* for chorus and instruments (1929); *De Profundis* for a cappella chorus (1932); *Szép Ilonka (Fair Helen),* a cantata (1954); Organ Sonata (1956).

Harmati, Sándor, Hungarian-American violinist; b. Budapest, July 9, 1892; d. Flemington, New Jersey, April 4, 1936. He studied at the Budapest Academy of Music; came to the U.S. in 1914 and became a member of the Letz Quartet (1917-21), then of the Lennox Quartet (1922-25); from 1925 to 1930 he was conductor of the Omaha Symph. Orch. He composed a symphonic poem, a string quartet and several works for the violin, as well as piano pieces and songs.

Harper, Heather, English soprano; b. Belfast, May 8, 1930. She studied piano at Trinity College, London; then began training for voice. She was engaged for television productions by the British Broadcasting Corporation; sang the responsible prime roles, among them Violetta (1956) and Mimi (1957). In 1967 she sang Elsa at the Bayreuth Festival, and in 1971 in Buenos Aires sang Marguerite; she also sang in modern operas, including *Peter Grimes.* In 1965 she was made a Commander of the British Empire.

Harraden, Samuel, English music scholar; b. Cambridge, 1821; d. Hampstead, July 17, 1897. He studied with Walmisley; in 1841, became organist at St. Luke's, Manchester; in 1846, went to India and settled in Calcutta, where he became organist at the Old Mission Church. He greatly influenced the musical life of Calcutta; founded the first glee club there; became an enthusiastic student of Hindu Music; was on the staff of the Hindu College of Music. In appreciation of his contribution to native art, he was made Mus. D. by the Bengal Royal Academy of Music.

Harrell, Mack, American baritone; b. Celeste, Texas, Oct. 8, 1909; d. Dallas, Jan. 29, 1960. He studied violin and voice at the Juilliard School of Music in N.Y.; after some concerts as a soloist he joined the staff of the Metropolitan Opera (1939–54); also taught voice at the Juilliard School (1945–56). He published a book, *The Sacred Hour of Song* (N.Y., 1938).

Harris, Augustus, celebrated English impresario; b. Paris, 1852; d. Folkestone, England, June 22, 1896. An actor by profession, he became a stage manager at Manchester in 1873. In 1879 he leased the Drury Lane Theatre in London; in 1887 took up promotion of Italian opera and secured control of Her Majesty's Theatre, Covent Garden, the Olympia, and various provincial stages. He introduced to the English public many of the most famous singers of his time, among them Melba, Maurel and the de Reszkes.

Harris, Charles K. (Kassell), American song composer; b. Poughkeepsie, N.Y., May 1, 1865; d. New York, Dec. 22, 1930. He played banjo and piano as a child, and soon began to write songs; went into business for himself at 18 and put out the shingle, "Banjoist and song writer/Songs written to order." He established his own publishing firms in Milwaukee and New York. His most spectacular success was the song *After the Ball* (1892); characteristically, he entitled his autobiography, *After the Ball: 40 Years of Melody* (N.Y., 1926).

Harris, Donald, American composer; b. St. Paul, Minnesota, April 7, 1931. He studied with Ross Lee Finney at the Univ. of Michigan (M.M., 1954); then went to Paris where he took courses with Nadia Boulanger and André Jolivet. Returning to the U.S. in 1967 he devoted himself to teaching and composing; served as vice president at the New England Cons. of Music, Boston (from 1971). In his music he follows the trends of the cosmopolitan avant-garde. His works include a symphony (1961); a string quartet (1965); *Ludus I* for 10 instruments (1966); Ludus II for 5 instruments (1973); *Charmes* for voice and orch., to texts of Paul Valéry (1976); other songs.

Harris, Roy, significant American composer; b. Lincoln County, Oklahoma, Feb. 12, 1898. His parents, of Irish and Scottish descent, settled in Oklahoma; in 1903 the family moved to California, where Roy Harris took music lessons with Henry Schoenfeld and Ar-

thur Farwell. In 1926 he went to Paris where he studied composition with Nadia Boulanger; was able to continue his stay in Paris thanks to two consecutive Guggenheim Fellowship Awards (1927, 1928). Upon return to the U.S. he lived in California and in New York; several of his works were performed and attracted favorable attention; his former teacher Arthur Farwell published an article in the *Musical Quarterly* (Jan. 1932) in which he enthusiastically welcomed Harris as an American genius. In his compositions, Harris has shown a talent of great originality, with a strong melodic and rhythmic speech that is indigenously American; he writes in a broad diatonic style, avoiding chromatic progressions of a merely decorative nature; in rhythm he cultivates asymmetrical constructions; his harmonies are triadic, often in bitonal combinations. In his chamber music he has developed a type of modal symbolism akin to Greek ethos, with each particular mode related to a certain emotional state; canonic and fugal procedures abound in most of his works. Instrumental music is the genre in which Harris particularly excels; he never wrote an opera or an oratorio, but has used choral masses in his symphonic works. He held numerous teaching positions: Westminster Choir School, Princeton (1934–35), Cornell Univ. (1941–43), Colorado College (1943–48); Utah State Agricultural College in Logan (1948–49), Peabody College for Teachers at Nashville, Tenn. (1949–51) and at Sewanee, Tenn. (1951); Pennsylvania College for Women (1951–56); Univ. of Southern Illinois (1956–57); Indiana Univ. (1957–60); Inter-American Univ., San Germán, Puerto Rico (1960–61); Univ. of California, Los Angeles (1961–73); in 1973 he was appointed composer-in-residence at Calif. State Univ., Los Angeles. He holds honorary Mus. Doc. degrees from Rutgers Univ. and the Univ. of Rochester, N.Y.; in 1942 he received the Elizabeth Sprague Coolidge Medal "for eminent services to chamber music." In 1936 he married the pianist **Johana Harris** (*née* Beula Duffey; b. Jan. 1, 1913 in Ottawa, Canada); she assumed her professional name Johana in honor of J. S. Bach; the single *n* is used owing to some esoteric numerologic considerations, to which Roy Harris is partial.

WORKS: FOR ORCH.: 15 symphonies: No. 1 (Boston, Jan. 26, 1934); No. 2 (Boston, Feb. 28, 1936); No. 3 (Boston, Feb. 24, 1939; his most famous and most frequently performed work; it was the first American symphony to be played in China, during the 1976 tour of the Philadelphia Orchestra, Ormandy conducting); No. 4, *Folksong Symphony,* with chorus (Cleveland, Dec. 26, 1940); No. 5 (Boston, Feb. 26, 1943); No. 6, *Gettysburg Address* (Boston, April 14, 1944); No. 7 (Chicago, Nov. 20, 1952); No. 8 (San Francisco, Jan. 17, 1962); No. 9 (Philadelphia, Jan. 18, 1963); No. 10, *Abraham Lincoln Symphony* for chorus, brass, 2 amplified pianos and percussion (Long Beach, Calif., April 14, 1965); No. 11 (N.Y., Feb. 8, 1968); No. 12 (partial performance, Milwaukee, Feb. 24, 1968); No. 13 (1969); No. 14 (1974); No. 15 (1978); Symphony for band (West Point, N.Y., May 30, 1952); *When Johnny Comes Marching Home,* symph. overture (Minneapolis, Jan. 13, 1935); *Farewell to Pioneers,* symph. elegy (Philadelphia, March 27, 1936); Concerto for 2 pianos and orch. (Denver, Jan. 21, 1947); *Kentucky Spring*

(Louisville, Kentucky, April 5, 1949); Piano Concerto (Louisville, Dec. 9, 1953); *Fantasy* for piano and orch. (Hartford, Conn., Nov. 17, 1954); *Epilogue to Profiles in Courage: J.F.K.* (Los Angeles, May 10, 1964); *These Times* for orch. with piano (1962); Concerto for amplified piano, wind instruments, and percussion (1968).

VOCAL WORKS: *Whitman Triptych* for women's voices and piano (1927); *A Song for Occupations*, after Whitman, for chorus a cappella (1934); *Symphony for Voices,* after Walt Whitman, for chorus a cappella (Princeton, May 20, 1936); *American Creed* for chorus and orch. (Chicago, Oct. 30, 1940); Mass for men's voices and organ (N.Y., May 13, 1948); *Canticle to the Sun* for coloratura soprano and chamber orch., after St. Francis (Washington, Sept. 12, 1961); *Jubilation* for chorus, brasses, and piano (San Francisco, May 16, 1964).

CHAMBER MUSIC: Concerto for Clarinet, Piano, and String Quartet (Paris, May 8, 1927); 3 String Quartets (1930, 1933, 1939); String Sextet (1932); Fantasy for Piano, Flute, Oboe, Clarinet, Bassoon, and Horn (Pasadena, Calif. April 10, 1932); Piano Trio (1934); Quintet for Piano and Strings (1936); *Soliloquy and Dance* for Viola and Piano (1939); String Quintet (1940).

FOR PIANO: Sonata (1929); *Variations on an Irish Theme* (1938); *Little Suite* (1938); *American Ballads* (1942).

BIBLIOGRAPHY: Arthur Farwell, "Roy Harris," *Musical Quarterly* (Jan. 1932); Henry Cowell, "Roy Harris," *American Composers on American Music* (Stanford, Calif., 1933); Walter Piston, "Roy Harris," *Modern Music* (Jan.-Feb. 1934); Nicolas Slonimsky, "Roy Harris," *Musical Quarterly* (Jan. 1947).

Harris, Victor, American song composer; b. New York, April 27, 1869; d. there, Feb. 15, 1943. He studied voice and organ; music theory with Fred K. Schilling, and conducting with Anton Seidl. He subsequently served as organist at various churches in N.Y., and was vocal coach at the Metropolitan Opera (1892–95); from 1902 to 1936 was conductor of the St. Cecilia Club, N.Y. He published about 150 songs, some of which enjoyed considerable popularity.

Harrison, Beatrice, English cellist; b. Roorke, India, Dec. 9, 1892; d. Smallfield, Surrey, March 10, 1965. She was brought to England in infancy; entered the Royal College of Music in London; won a prize at the age of 10; she was 14 when she made her first public appearance as a soloist with an orchestra (London, May 29, 1907); then went to Berlin where she took lessons with Hugo Becker; was the winner of the prestigious Mendelssohn Prize. She made several European tours, most of them in company with her sister, **May,** the violinist; toured the U.S. in 1913 and 1932.

Harrison, George, English rock singer; member of the celebrated group The Beatles; b. Liverpool, Feb. 25, 1943. Like his co-Beatles, he had no formal musical education and learned to play the guitar by osmosis and acclimatization. Not as extrovert as John Lennon, not as exhibitionistic as Paul McCartney, and not as histrionic as Ringo Starr, he was not as conspicuously projected into public consciousness as his comrades-

in-rock. Yet he exercised a distinct influence on the character of the songs that The Beatles sang. He became infatuated with the mystical lore of India; sat at the feet of a hirsute guru; introduced the sitar into his rock arrangements. He is the author of *Something,* one of the greatest successes of The Beatles. When the group broke up in 1970, Harrison proved sufficiently talented to impress his individual image in his own music; he also collaborated on songs of social consciousness with Bob Dylan.

BIBLIOGRAPHY: Hunter Davies, *The Beatles: The Authorized Biography* (N.Y., 1968); Ned Rorem, "The Beatles," *N.Y. Review of Books* (Jan. 18, 1968); G. Geppert, *Songs der Beatles. Texte und Interpretationen* (2nd ed., Munich, 1968); E. Davies, "The Psychological Characteristics of Beatle Mania," *Journal of the History of Ideas* (April-June 1969); P. McCabe and R. D. Schonfeld, *Apple to the Core: The Unmaking of the Beatles* (N.Y. 1972); F. Seleron, *Les Beatles* (Paris, 1972); W. Mellers, *Twilight of the Gods: The Music of the Beatles* (N.Y., 1973).

Harrison, Guy Fraser, American conductor; b. Guildford, Surrey, England, Nov. 6, 1894. He studied at the Royal College of Music, where he won an organ scholarship; served as an organist of the Episcopal Cathedral in Manila (1914–20); then emigrated to America; was organist of St. Paul's Cathedral in Rochester, N.Y. (1920–24); then was conductor of the Eastman Theater Orch. in Rochester (1924–49). In 1951 he was appointed conductor of the Oklahoma City Orch.; retired in 1972.

BIBLIOGRAPHY: Hope Stoddard, *Symphony Conductors of the U.S.A.* (N.Y., 1957).

Harrison, Jay, American music critic and editor; b. New York, Jan. 25, 1927; d. there, Sept. 12, 1974. He studied music with Philip James at New York University (A.B., 1948); was subsequently active mainly as music critic; was on the staff of the *N.Y. Herald Tribune* (1948–61); contributed articles to various music magazines. He collected a large number of valuable autograph letters by famous musicians, which he bequeathed to the Music Division of the Library of Congress.

Harrison, Julius Allen Greenway, English conductor and composer; b. Stourport, Worchestershire, March 26, 1885; d. London, April 5, 1963. He studied music with Granville Bantock; subsequently was active mainly as conductor; filled in engagements with the Beecham Opera Co., the Scottish Symph. Orch., the Handel Society, etc. In his music he makes competent use of English folksongs. He wrote an opera *The Canterbury Pilgrims* and an orchestral suite *Worcestershire Pieces*; cantatas, some chamber music and many songs.

Harrison, Lou, American composer of the avant-garde; b. Portland Oregon, May 14, 1917. After a period of study with Henry Cowell at the San Francisco State College he plunged headlong into the cross-currents of modern music. In 1941 he attended the classes of Schoenberg at the Univ. of California, Los Angeles; in 1943 moved to New York where he worked as a music critic for the *N.Y. Herald Tribune* (1945–48); for a while taught at the progressive Black Mt. College in North Carolina. He held two Guggenheim Foundation Awards (1952 and 1954); eked out his finances by accompanying modern dancers, and also performing himself as a dancer; at one time he was employed as a florist. He tried his luck as an instrument maker; invented two new principles of clavichord construction; built a Phrygian aulos, developed a process for direct composing on a phonograph disc; in 1938 proposed a theory in Interval Control, and in 1942 supplemented it by a device for Rhythm Control; also wrote plays and versified poematically. He was one of the earliest adherents to an initially small group of American musicians who promoted the music of Charles Ives, Carl Ruggles, Varèse and Cowell; he prepared for publication the Third Symphony of Charles Ives, which he conducted in its first performance in 1947. He visited the Orient in 1961, and fortified his immanent belief in the multiform nature of music by studying Japanese and Korean modalities and rhythmic structures. Returning to California, he taught at San José State College. Seeking new sources of sound production, he organized a percussion ensemble of multitudinous drums and such homely sound makers as coffee cans and flowerpots. He wrote texts in Esperanto for his vocal works.

WORKS: the opera, *Rapunzel* (N.Y., May 14, 1959); *Young Caesar*, a puppet opera (Aptos, Calif. Aug. 21, 1971); the ballet scores *Marriage at the Eiffel Tower* (1948), *Perilous Chapel* (1949); *Solstice* (1950); other works for dance; *Changing World, Johnny Appleseed, Almanac of the Seasons, Changing Moment, Omnipotent Chair, Praises for Hummingbirds and Hawks, Something to Please Everybody*, etc.; *Jepthah's Daughter*, "a theater kit" (Cabrillo College, March 9, 1963); FOR ORCH.: *Symphony on G* (1947–53; Oakland, California, Feb. 8, 1966); Suite for Solo Violin, Solo Piano and Orch. (N.Y., Jan. 11, 1952, composer conducting); *Simfony from Simfonies* in free style for orch. (1956); *Koncerto por la Violono kun perkuta orkestro* (title in Esperanto; N.Y., Nov. 19, 1959); *Suite for Simfoniaj Kordoj* (Esperanto for Suite for string orch.; 1960); *Nova Odo* for orch. (Seoul, Korea, 1963); 14 or more sinfonias for percussion orch.; *Recording Piece* for concert boobams, talking drums and percussion (1955); Mass, and other sacred works for chorus.

Harrison, May, British violinist; sister of **Beatrice Harrison**; b. Roorke, India, March, 1891; d. South Nutfield, Surrey, June 8, 1959. She attended the Royal College of Music in London; like her sister, she was a precocious talent; at the age of 10 she won a gold medal of the Royal College of Music against some 3,000 contestants. She then went to St. Petersburg where she took lessons with Leopold Auer; returning to England she made several concert tours, often in the company of her sister.

Harriss, Charles Albert Edwin, English composer and organist; b. London, Dec. 15, 1862; d. Ottawa, Ont., Aug. 1, 1929. As a boy he sang in a church choir at Wrexham, where his father was an organist; in 1883 the family went to Montreal, where he became a church organist. He wrote an opera *Torquil* (Montreal, 1896); a cantata *Daniel before the King* (1890); organ music; songs.

Harsányi, Tibor, Hungarian composer; b. Magyarkanizsa, Hungary, June 27, 1898; d. Paris, Sept. 19, 1954. He studied at the Budapest Academy of Music with Kodály; in 1923 he settled in Paris, where he devoted himself to composition. The melodic material of his music stems from Hungarian folk melos; his harmonic idiom is largely polytonal; the rhythms are sharp, often with jazz-like syncopation; the form remains classical.

WORKS: chamber opera *Les Invités* (Gera, Germany, 1930); radio opera *Illusion* (Paris, June 28, 1949); 4 ballets: *Le Dernier Songe* (Budapest, Jan. 27, 1920), *Pantins* (Paris, 1938), *Chota Roustaveli* (in collaboration with Honegger and A. Tcherepnin; Monte Carlo, 1945), and *L'Amour et la vie* (1951); a puppet show, *L'Histoire du petit tailleur* for 7 instruments and percussion (1939). FOR ORCH: *La Joie de vivre* (Paris, March 11, 1934, composer conducting); 2 divertissements (1940–41, 1943); Violin Concerto (Paris Radio, Jan. 16, 1947); *Figures et rythmes* (Geneva, Nov. 19, 1947, composer conducting); *Danses variées* (Basel, Feb. 14, 1950, composer conducting); Symphony (Salzburg Festival, June 26, 1952). CHAMBER MUSIC: Sonatina for Violin and Piano (1918); *3 Pieces* for flute and piano (1924); 2 string quartets (1918, 1935); Cello Sonata (1928); Nonet, for string and wind instruments (Vienna Festival, June 21, 1932); Rhapsody for Cello and Piano (1939); Picnic for 2 violins, cello, double bass, and percussion (1951); many piano pieces, among them, *5 études rythmiques* (1934), *3 pièces lyriques*, and albums for children. He also wrote several choral works, including *Cantate de Noël* for voices, flute, and strings (Paris, Dec. 24, 1945).

BIBLIOGRAPHY: J. S. Weissmann, "Tibor Harsányi," *Chesterian* (1952).

Harshaw, Margaret, American opera singer; b. Narbeth, Pa., May 12, 1912. She won an audition with the Metropolitan Opera as contralto in 1942, and appeared in the roles of Amneris, Azucena, etc.; in 1950, changed to soprano, and specialized in Wagnerian roles; her interpretations (both as soprano and contralto) soon placed her among the most celebrated singers of Wagner's operas; she sang Isolde, Elisabeth, and all three Brünnhildes. She married Oskar Leopold Eichna (Sept. 7, 1935).

Hart, Frederic Patton, American composer; b. Aberdeen, Washington, Sept. 5, 1894. He studied at the American Cons. in Chicago and at the Art Institute there; later took courses with Rubin Goldmark, Ernest Hutcheson, and at the Diller-Quaile School in N.Y. He taught at Sarah Lawrence College (1929–47) and at the Juilliard School of Music (1947–60); then settled in Los Angeles.

WORKS: an opera, *The Wheel of Fortune* (1943); an opera-ballet, *The Romance of Robot* (1937); chamber music; piano pieces; songs.

Hart, Fritz, English composer and conductor; b. Brockley, Kent, Feb. 11, 1874; d. Honolulu, July 9,

1949. He went to Australia in 1909 and settled there; director of the Melbourne Cons.; joint artistic director of the Melbourne Symph. Orch.; conducted both the Manila Symph. and the Honolulu Orch. (1931–36); settled in Honolulu in 1936 when appointed professor of music at the Univ. of Hawaii; retired in 1942.

WORKS: 16 operas, 2 operettas, a symph. and other orchestral works, chamber music; choral works, songs; etc.

Hart, James, English bass singer and composer; b. York, 1647; d. London, May 8, 1718. He was a singer in York Minister until 1670; then appointed Gentleman of the Chapel Royal and lay-vicar of Westminster Abbey; settled in London and composed songs publ. in *Choice Ayres, Songs and Dialogues* (1676–84), *The Theater of Musick* (1685–87), *Banquet of Musick* (1688–92), and other collections. He wrote *Adieu to the pleasures and follies of love* for Shadwell's operatic adaptation of *The Tempest* (1674), publ. as one of 6 "Ariel's Songs."

Hart, Lorenz, American lyricist; b. New York City, May 2, 1895; d. there, Nov. 22, 1943. He began as a student of journalism at Columbia Univ. (1914–17); then turned to highly successful theatrical writing. During his 18-year collaboration with Richard Rodgers, he wrote the lyrics for *Connecticut Yankee* (1927); *On Your Toes* (1936); *Babes in Arms* (1937); *The Boys from Syracuse* (1938); *I Married an Angel* (1938); *Too Many Girls* (1939); *Pal Joey* (1940); *By Jupiter* (1942). Some of their best songs (*Manhattan, Here in My Arms, My Heart Stood Still, Small Hotel, Blue Moon, Where or When, I Married an Angel*) are published in the album, *Rodgers & Hart Songs* (N.Y., 1951).
BIBLIOGRAPHY: S. Marx and J. Clayton, *Rodgers and Hart* (N.Y., 1976); D. Hart, *Thou Swell, Thou Witty: Life and Lyrics of Lorenz Hart* (N.Y., 1976).

Hart, Philip, English organist; date and place of birth unknown; d. London, July 17, 1749. He composed anthems, organ fugues, music for Hughes's *Old in Praise of Musick* (1703), and for *The Morning Hymn* from Milton's *Paradise Lost*, Book V (1729).

Hart & Sons, a firm of London violin makers, founded in 1825 by **John Hart.** His son, **John Thomas Hart** (b. Dec. 17, 1805; d. London, Jan. 1, 1874), a pupil of Gilkes, made a complete study of Cremonese and other violins of Italian make, establishing a reputation as an expert in his field. John Thomas's son, **George Hart** (b. London, March 23, 1839; d. near Newhaven, April 25, 1891), succeeded him. He was a good violinist himself; publ. valuable books, *The Violin: Its Famous Makers and Their Imitators* (London, 1875; French ed., Paris, 1886) and *The Violin and Its Music* (London, 1881). His sons, **George** and **Herbert Hart,** inherited the business.

Hart, Weldon, American composer; b. Place-Bear Spring, Tennessee, Sept. 19, 1911; d. East Lansing, Michigan, Nov. 20, 1957 (suicide). He studied music in Nashville, at the Univ. of Michigan, and at the Eastman School in Rochester, with Howard Hanson and Bernard Rogers, receiving his Ph.D., in 1946. He was head of the music dept. of Western Kentucky State College (1946–49) and director of the School of Music of the University of West Virginia (1949–57). In 1957 he was engaged as head of the Music Dept. of Michigan State Univ. at East Lansing; upon arrival there he became despondent over his inability to produce an impression with a concert of his works, and killed himself with carbon monoxide exhaust in his car. Yet his music, although not innovative, is well crafted. He wrote a *Sinfonietta* (1944); a symph. poem *The Dark Hills* (1939); Symphony (1945); Violin Concerto (1951); *3 West Virginia Folk Songs,* for chorus and orch. (1954); several violin pieces and choruses.

Harth, Sidney, American violinist; b. Cleveland, Oct. 5, 1929. He studied with Joseph Fuchs and Georges Enesco; was a recipient of the Naumburg prize in 1948; made his debut at Carnegie Hall, New York, in 1949; since then he has given numerous concerts in the U.S. and in Europe, often appearing with orchestras in duo violin concertos with his wife, **Teresa Testa Harth.** In 1973 he was appointed concertmaster of the Los Angeles Philharmonic; in 1976–1981 was associate conductor as well as concertmaster of the orchestra.

Harthan, Hans, German composer and pianist; b. Bavaria, Feb. 23, 1855; d. Glendale, California, March 14, 1936. He studied with Lachner and Rheinberger in Germany. In 1883 he obtained the post of professor of music in Odessa, Russia; in 1896 he went to Chile where he became director of the National Cons. of Music in Santiago. In 1903 he emigrated to the United States, eventually settling in California, the final destination of so many retiring European musicians. During his extended lifetime he wrote and published an astounding number of vocal and instrumental compositions, particularly for piano, expertly imitating the models of Schumann and Mendelssohn.

Hartig, Heinz, German composer; b. Kassel, Sept. 10, 1907; d. Berlin, Sept. 16, 1969. He studied piano at the Kassel Cons. and musicology at the Univ. of Vienna. Unable to hold a teaching post under the Nazi regime, he occupied himself by performances as harpsichord player; in 1948 he joined the Hochschule für Musik in Berlin. In his compositions he applies varied techniques of modern music, from neo-Classicism to serialism, with the formal unity achieved by the principle of free variations. He wrote a ballet, *Schwarze Sonne* (1958); chamber opera, *Escorial* (1961); *Immediate* for flute, clarinet, piano and 2 cellos (1966); *Concerto strumentale* for violin and orch. (1969).
BIBLIOGRAPHY: Wolfgang Burde, *Heinz Hartig* (Berlin, 1967).

Hartmann, Arthur, Hungarian-American violinist; b. Maté Szalka, Hungary, July 23, 1881; d. New York, March 30, 1956. He was brought to Philadelphia as a child and first studied with his father; then was a pupil of Loeffler (violin) and Homer Norris (composition). He made his debut in Philadelphia (1887) as a child prodigy; by the time he was 12, had played practically the entire modern violin repertory. He toured the

United States, Canada, Scandinavia; played in Paris in recitals with Debussy, and became his intimate friend. In 1939 he settled in New York; retired in 1954. He made numerous transcriptions and arrangements; discovered and edited 6 sonatas of Felice de' Giardini; wrote an essay on Bach's Chaconne which has been translated into 14 languages.

Hartmann, August Wilhelm, Danish organist and composer, son of **Johann Ernst Hartmann;** b. Copenhagen, Nov. 6, 1775; d. there, Nov. 15, 1850. He studied with his father; was first violinist in the Royal Chapel (1796–1817); then was appointed organist at the Garrison Church in Copenhagen. His organ works and other compositions are found in the Royal Library.

Hartmann, Carl, German tenor; b. Solingen, May 2, 1895; d. Munich, May 30, 1969. He studied in Cologne and Düsseldorf; made a successful debut in Elberfeld as *Tannhäuser* (1928), and then sang all over Germany, in Vienna, in Paris, and in Stockholm. In 1930 he toured the U.S. with Gadski's Opera Co., appearing in Wagnerian tenor roles; from 1937 to 1940 was a member of the Metropolitan Opera Co. in New York; then returned to Germany and lived mostly in Munich.

Hartmann, Eduard von, German writer on musical esthetics; b. Berlin, Feb. 23, 1842; d. Grosslichterfelde, near Berlin, June 5, 1906. He studied philophy; music was his avocation; he wrote numerous songs and even began writing an opera. In his philosophical essays, he proposed some plausible theories concerning the laws of musical esthetics; of chief importance in this respect are his publications *Deutsche Ästhethik seit Kant* (Berlin, 1886) and *Philosophie des Schönen* (Berlin, 1887), which contains the chapter "Idealismus und Formalismus in der Musikästhetik."

Hartmann, Emil, Danish composer, son of **Johann Peder Emilius Hartmann;** b. Copenhagen, Feb. 21, 1836; d. there, July 18, 1898. He received his early education from his father and from Niels Gade (who was his brother-in-law); was from 1861 till his death organist in various churches in Denmark. After Gade's death, he conducted a season of the Musical Society at Copenhagen (1891–92). WORKS: the operas *Elverpigen* (Copenhagen, Nov. 5, 1867), *Korsikaneren* (Copenhagen, April 7, 1873), *Ragnhild* (1896), *Det store Lod* (1897); the ballet *Fjeldstuen* (Copenhagen, May 13, 1859); 7 symphonies and other instrumental works.

Hartmann, Johan Peder Emilius, celebrated Danish composer; b. Copenhagen, May 14, 1805; d. there, March 10, 1900. He was the most famous of the Hartmann family in Denmark; grandson of **Johann Ernst Hartmann,** and son of **August Wilhelm Hartmann.** He studied law at the Univ. of Copenhagen, and for many years occupied a public position as a jurist (1828–70), but he was also profoundly interested in music; studied with his father and became his assistant as organist at the Copenhagen Cathedral (1843), remaining in that capacity until his death. He also taught at the

Cons. of Copenhagen (from 1827). In 1836 he was one of the organizers of the Danish Music Society; in 1868 was appointed its director. He was also co-director (with Niels Gade) of the new Copenhagen Cons., established in 1867. He spent almost his entire life in Denmark; the only extensive traveling he undertook was in 1836, when he visited Germany and France. He was greatly esteemed in Denmark. A Hartmann Scholarship was founded on the occasion of his 50th jubilee, and he received the 'Daneborg' order. Gade was his son-in-law.

WORKS: He was a prolific composer; wrote the operas *The Raven* (Copenhagen, Oct. 29, 1832), *The Corsairs* (Copenhagen, April 23, 1835), *Little Christina* (Copenhagen, May 12, 1846); the ballets *Valkyrien* (Copenhagen, Sept. 13, 1861), and *Thrymskviden* (Copenhagen, Feb. 21, 1868); a melodrama, *The Golden Horns* (1834); overtures; Violin Concerto; Flute Sonata; Violin Sonata; pieces for piano; songs. With Gade, he was a foremost representative of the Danish Romantic school of composition.

BIBLIOGRAPHY: W. Behrend, *J. P. E. Hartmann* (Copenhagen, 1895); A. Hammerich, *J. P. E. Hartmann* (Copenhagen, 1916); R. Hove, *J. P. E. Hartmann* (Copenhagen, 1934).

Hartmann, Johann Ernst, German-Danish composer and violinist, founder of the "Hartmann dynasty" of musicians active in Denmark; b. Glogau, Silesia, Dec. 24, 1726; d. Copenhagen, Oct. 21, 1793. He studied violin in Silesia, and held various posts as band violinist. In 1766 he settled in Copenhagen; became conductor of the Royal Orch. in 1768. Most of his manuscripts were lost in a fire (1794), but his violin method and a few instrumental works are extant. His chief claim to fame is the fact that the melody of the present national anthem of Denmark, *Kong Christian stod ved hojen Mast,* was used in the score he wrote for the melodrama *Fiskerne* (Copenhagen, Jan. 31, 1780), and was for a long time regarded as his own composition, although it may have been borrowed from some unknown source of folk origin. A study of this melody is included in Angul Hammerich's book, *J. P. E. Hartmann, Biographical Essays* (1916).

Hartmann, Karl Amadeus, outstanding German composer; b. Munich, Aug. 2, 1905; d. there, Dec. 5, 1963. He studied with Josef Haas at the Music Academy in Munich (1923–27) and later with Scherchen. He began to compose rather late in life; his first major work was a trumpet concerto, which was performed in Strasbourg in 1933. During the War he studied advanced musical composition and analysis with Anton von Webern in Vienna (1941–42). After the War he organized in Munich the society "Musica viva." He received a prize from the city of Munich in 1949; in 1952 was elected a member of the German Academy of Fine Arts and soon after became president of the German section of the International Society for Contemporary Music. Despite his acceptance of a highly chromatic, atonal idiom and his experimentation in the domain of rhythm (patterned after Boris Blacher's "variable meters"), Hartmann retained the orthodox form and structural cohesion of basic classicism. He was excessively critical of his early works, and discarded many of them, but some have been retrieved and performed after his death.

WORKS: a chamber opera, *Des Simplicius Simplicissimus Jugend* (1934–35; Cologne, Oct. 20, 1949; a revised, reduced scoring of the work was made in 1955 and retitled, *Simplicius Simplicissimus*); 8 symphonies: No. 1, *Versuch eines Requiems*, words by Walt Whitman, for soprano and orch. (*Attempt at a Requiem*, 1936–40; Vienna, June 22, 1957); No. 2, *Adagio* (1941–46; Donaueschingen, Sept. 10, 1950); No. 3 (1948–49; Munich, Feb. 10, 1950); No. 4, for string orch. (1946-47; Munich, April 2, 1948); No. 5, *Symphonie concertante*, for wind instruments, cellos and double basses (1950; Stuttgart, April 21, 1951; based on "variable meters"); No. 6 (1951–53; Munich, April 24, 1953); No. 7 (1958; Hamburg, March 15, 1959); No. 8 (1960–62; Cologne, Jan. 25, 1963); *Miserae* (Prague, Sept. 1, 1935); *Concerto Funebre* for violin and string orch. (1939, revised 1959; Braunschweig, Nov. 12, 1959); *Symphonischen Hymnen* (1942; Munich, Oct. 9, 1975); a symphonic overture; *China kämpft* (*China at War*, 1942; Darmstadt, July, 1947); Concerto for Piano, Winds and Percussion (Donaueschingen, Oct. 10, 1953); Concerto for Viola, Piano, Winds and Percussion (Frankfurt, May 25, 1956); *Gesangsszene*, on German texts of Jean Giraudoux's "Sodome et Gomorrhe," for baritone and orch. (1962–63, unfinished; Frankfurt, Nov. 12, 1964); *Kammerkonzert* for clarinet, string quartet and string orch. (Zürich, June 17, 1969); *Jazz-Toccata and -Fugue* for piano (1928); *Tanzsuite* for wind quintet (1931; Frankfurt, April 20, 1975); Piano Sonatina (1931); 2 string quartets (*Carillon*, 1933; 1945–46); *Burleske Musik* for 6 winds, percussion and piano (c.1933; Rotterdam, June 30, 1967); *Friede Anno 48*, after Gryphius, for soprano, chorus and piano (1937; Cologne, Oct. 22, 1968; the sections for soprano and piano also exist as a separate piece called *Lamento*, cantata for soprano and piano); *Kleines Konzert* for string quartet and percussion (version for string orch. and percussion, Braunschweig, Nov. 29, 1974).

Hartmann, Pater (real name **Paul Eugen Josef von An der Lan-Hochbrunn**), German conductor and composer; b. Salurn, near Bozen, Dec. 21, 1863; d. Munich, Dec. 5, 1914. He entered the Franciscan order at the age of 16; studied theology and music in various monasteries; then completed his musical studies with Josef Pembaur in Innsbruck; ordained priest in 1886; appointed organist at the Church of the Redeemer in Jerusalem (1893) and at the Church of the Holy Sepulchre (1894); in 1895 he was transferred to Rome as organist of the monastery Ara Coeli and director of the Scuola Musicale Cooperativa. From 1906 till his death he lived in the Franciscan monastery of St. Anna at Munich. During the season of 1906–07 he visited the United States, conducting some of his oratorios. His sacred music retains its importance in Germany.

WORKS: the oratorios *Petrus* (1900), *Franziskus* (1902), *Das letzte Abendmahl* (1904), *Der Tod des Herrn* (1905), *Septem ultima verba Christi in Cruce* (1908); a *Te Deum* (1913); Masses; organ works.

Hartmann, Thomas de, Russian composer; b. Khoruzhevka, Ukraine, Sept. 21, 1885; d. Princeton, N.J., March 26, 1956. He studied piano with Anna Essipova at the St. Petersburg Cons.; composition with Taneyev and Arensky. His first important work, the ballet *The Purple Flower*, was produced at the Imperial Theater in St. Petersburg in 1907 with Pavlova, Karsavina, Nijinsky, and Fokine. After the Revolution he went to the Caucasus; taught at the Tiflis Cons. (1919); then went to Paris, where he remained until 1951, when he settled in New York. His early music is in the Russian national style, influenced particularly by Mussorgsky; from about 1925, he made a radical change in his style of composition, adopting many devices of outspoken modernism (polytonality, etc.).

WORKS: *The Purple Flower*, ballet (St. Petersburg, Dec. 16, 1907; *Babette*, ballet (Nice, March 10, 1935); an opera, *Esther* (not performed); 4 symphonies (1915, 1944, 1953, 1955, the last unfinished); Cello Concerto (1935; Boston, April 14, 1938); Piano Concerto (1940; Paris, Nov. 8, 1942); Double Bass Concerto (1943; Paris, Jan. 26, 1945); Harp Concerto (1944); Violin Concerto (Paris, March 16, 1947); Flute Concerto (Paris, Sept. 27, 1950); *12 Russian Fairy Tales*, for orch. (Houston, April 4, 1955, Stokowski conducting); Violin Sonata (1937); Cello Sonata (1942); Trio, for flute, violin, and piano (1946); 3 song cycles to words by Verlaine, Proust, and James Joyce; other songs; piano pieces.

Hartog, Edouard de, Dutch composer; b. Amsterdam, Aug. 15, 1829; d. The Hague, Nov. 8, 1909. He studied in Germany with Hoch and Mme. Dulcken, and in Paris with Elwart. He lived many years in Paris, where he produced the opera *Le Mariage de Don Lope* (1865); another opera by him, *L'Amour et son Hôte*, was produced in Brussels (1873). He also wrote several symph. works, chamber music, and piano pieces.

Hartog, Jacques, Dutch composer and writer; b. Zalt-Bommel, Oct. 24, 1837; d. Amsterdam, Oct. 3, 1917. He studied with Ferdinand Hiller at Cologne; upon his return to Holland, he was appointed prof. at the Amsterdam School of Music, and held this post for many years (1886–1913). He publ. monographs (in Dutch) on Beethoven (1904), Mozart (1904), Haydn (1905), Mendelssohn (1909), Schumann (1910), Bach (1911), and Wagner (1913); translated into Dutch several German theory books; also wrote some orchestral and chamber music.

Harty, Sir Hamilton, eminent Irish conductor and composer; b. Hillsborough, County Down, Ireland, Dec. 4, 1879; d. Brighton, Feb. 19, 1941. He received his entire musical education from his father, an organist, and substituted for him as a child. At the age of 12, he was able to fill a position as organist at Magheracoll Church, County Antrim; then was church organist in Belfast and Dublin. In 1900 he went to London, where he was active as an accompanist; on July 15, 1904 he married the singer **Agnes Nicholls;** also began to compose seriously; his piano quintet won a prize in 1904. It was much later in life that he devoted himself to conducting; he was appointed conductor of the Hallé Orch. in Manchester in 1920, remaining at this post for 13 seasons; his programs showed fine discrimination in balancing classical and modern music. He conducted several works by British composers, and in appreciation of his work, he was knighted (1925). In 1931 he made his American debut; in subsequent seasons he conducted in Boston, Chicago, Cleveland, and also at the Hollywood Bowl. In 1934 he conducted in Australia.

WORKS: the most interesting is *Irish Symphony* (revised version, Manchester, Nov. 13, 1924); other works are *Comedy Overture* (1907); *Ode to a Nightingale*, after Keats, for soprano and orch. (1907); *With the Wild Geese*, a symph. poem (1910); *Violin Concerto* (1909); *The Mystic Trumpeter*, for baritone, chorus, and orch. (1913); *The Children of Lir*, poem for orch. (London, March 1, 1939); he made excellent arrangements of Handel's *Water Music* and *Fireworks Music* for modern orch.; also arranged *A John Field Suite*, from piano works by Field.

Harwood, Basil, English organist and composer; b. Woodhouse, Gloucestershire, April 11, 1859; d. London, April 3, 1949. He studied piano with J. L. Roeckel, organ with George Risely; also with Reinecke and Jadassohn at the Leipzig Cons. Returning to England, he occupied various posts as organist: at St. Barnabas Church, Pimlico (1883–87), Ely Cathedral (1887-92), Christ Church Cathedral, Oxford (1892–1909). He edited the *Oxford Hymn Book* (1908), and wrote a number of sacred works for chorus, and organ pieces (2 sonatas, Organ Concerto, Christmastide, *Dithyramb*, etc.); a cantata, *Ode on May Morning*, after Milton (Leeds Festival, 1913).

Harwood, Elizabeth, English operatic soprano; b. Kettering, May 27, 1938. She was a joint winner of the International Verdi Competition in 1963; then sang prime roles (Lucia di Lammermoor, Gilda, Manon) with the Scottish Opera and also proved herself as an excellent interpreter of soprano roles in modern operas.

Häser, August Ferdinand, German composer; b. Leipzig, Oct. 15, 1779; d. Weimar, Nov. 1, 1844. He was a member of a musical family; his 3 brothers and a sister were musicians. He was educated at the Thomasschule in Leipzig, and studied theology at the Leipzig Univ. In 1797 he went to Lemgo, Westphalia, where he taught mathematics in high school. He traveled in Italy from 1806–13; then returned to Lemgo. In 1817 he was engaged in Weimar as music teacher to Princess Augusta (the future German empress); also conducted the chorus at the Court Opera there; was church organist and teacher of Italian.

WORKS: 3 operas, which were performed in Weimar; an oratorio, *Die Kraft des Glaubens;* many sacred choruses, 4 overtures, several instrumental works in salon style. He publ. *Versuch einer systematischen Übersicht der Gesanglehre* (Leipzig, 1822); *Chorgesangschule für Schul- und Theaterchöre* (Mainz, 1831; in French as *Méthode pour apprendre à chanter en choeur à l'usage des écoles, des théâtres*).

Haskil, Clara, brilliant Rumanian pianist; b. Bucharest, Jan. 7, 1895; d. Brussels, Dec. 7, 1960. A precocious musician, she played in public at the age of 7; then entered the Paris Cons., where she studied piano with Cortot and won a first prize at the age of 14. Busoni heard her in Basel and invited her to study with him in Berlin. She played programs of Beethoven sonatas with Enesco, Ysaÿe and Casals; subsequently gave piano recitals and appeared as a soloist with major symphony orchestras in Europe and America. A muscular deficiency severely impeded her concert career; however, she continued playing concerts during periods of remission of her ailment. Music critics praised her fine musicianship and her penetrating interpretation of classical piano music.

BIBLIOGRAPHY: R. Wolfensberger, *Clara Haskil* (Bern, 1961); J. Spycket, *Clara Haskil*, with a preface by Herbert von Karajan (Paris, 1975).

Haslinger, Tobias, Austrian music publisher; b. Zell, March 1, 1787; d. Vienna, June 18, 1842. He went to Vienna in 1810 after studying music in Linz; was bookkeeper in Steiner's music establishment; later became partner and, after Steiner's retirement in 1826, sole proprietor. A gregarious and affable person, he made friends with many musicians, and was on excellent terms with Beethoven, who seemed to enjoy Haslinger's company; many letters to him from Beethoven are extant, among them the humorous canon *O Tobias Dominus Haslinger*. He was succeeded by his son **Carl Haslinger** (b. Vienna, June 11, 1816; d. there, Dec. 26, 1868). The latter studied with Czerny and became a brilliant pianist as well as an industrious composer; he publ. more than 100 works of various kinds. Continuing the tradition of his father, he publ. several symphonies, piano concertos, overtures, and other works by Beethoven, and later Liszt's Piano Concerto in E-flat; he was also the publisher of many Strauss waltzes. In 1875 the firm was bought from his widow by Schlesinger of Berlin (subsequently, R. & W. Lienau).

Hassard, John Rose Green, American journalist and music critic; b. New York, Sept. 4, 1836; d. there, April 18, 1888. He studied at St. John's College, Fordham; served as music critic of the *New York Tribune* (1868–84). His account of the Festival at Bayreuth in 1876 (later publ. as a pamphlet) was the fullest that appeared in any American newspaper.

Hasse (*née* **Bordoni**), **Faustina,** famous Italian mezzo-soprano, wife of **Johann Adolf Hasse;** b. Venice, c.1700; d. there, Nov. 4, 1781. She studied with Gasparini and Benedetto Marcello. She made her debut in 1716 in Pollarolo's opera *Ariodante,* and obtained such success that soon she was called the "New Siren." When she sang in Florence a few years later (1722), a special medal was issued in her honor; she was equally successful in Naples. She became a member of the court theater in Vienna in 1724, at a high salary. Handel heard her there, and engaged her for his opera enterprise in London, where she made her debut on May 5, 1726, winning high praise. She remained in London for 2 seasons; her quarrel with Francesca Cuzzoni in a competition for public attention resulted in her departure from England. She went back to Venice; in 1730, she married Hasse, and devoted her life thenceforth to his success, without abondoning her own career. From 1731 till 1763 they lived in Dresden; then in Vienna (until 1775), finally settling in Venice. According to Burney, she could sustain a note longer than any other singer; her trills were strong and rapid; her intonation perfect. Burney also praised her physical qualities.

BIBLIOGRAPHY: A. Niggli, "Faustina Bordoni-Hasse," in Waldersee's *Sammlung musikalischer Vorträge* (1880); G. M. Urbani de Gheltof, *"La Nuova Sirena" ed il "Caro Sassone"* (Venice, 1890); Margarete Högg, *Die Gesangskunst der Faustina Hasse und das Sängerinnenwesen ihrer Zeit in Deutschland* (Berlin, 1931). An interesting fictional biography is Elise Polko's *Faustina Hasse* (Leipzig, 1860; new ed., 1895).

Hasse, Johann Adolph, important German composer; b. Bergedorf, near Hamburg, March 25, 1699; d. Venice, Dec. 16, 1783. He received his first instruction in music from his father, a schoolmaster and organist. At the age of 18, he went to Hamburg and, at the recommendation of Ulrich König, the poet, was engaged by Keiser, director of the Hamburg Opera, as tenor; he sang there 4 seasons, and later was tenor at the Brunswick theater; it was there that Hasse first appeared as composer, with his opera *Antioco* (Aug. 11, 1721). He then went to Naples to study the craft of composition more thoroughly; there he was a pupil of Porpora and later of Alessandro Scarlatti, and brought out his 2nd opera *Tigrane* (Nov. 4, 1723). In 1725 he wrote a serenade for 2 voices which was performed by Farinelli and Vittoria Tesi, and this further promoted Hasse's career in Italy; there followed a successful production of his new opera *Sesostrate* (Naples, May 13, 1726). In 1727 he was appointed to the staff of the Scuola degl'Incurabili in Venice; there he wrote his *Miserere,* which enjoyed excellent success throughout Italy for many years afterwards. His ability to ingratiate himself with society, his affable manners and handsome appearance, contributed to his artistic success; he was often referred to as "il caro Sassone" (even though he was not a Saxon). In 1729 he met the famous singer **Faustina Bordoni,** and married her in Venice the following year. She sang the leading roles in many of his operas, and together they attained the highest positions in the operatic world. He wrote two operas for her: *Artaserse* and *Dalisa,* produced in Venice shortly after their marriage. In 1731 Hasse received an appointment as musical director of the Dresden Opera, with Faustina Hasse as prima donna; his first operatic production in Dresden was *Cleofide,* on Sept. 13, 1731, in which his wife scored a brilliant success. During frequent leaves of absence, they traveled in Italy, where Hasse produced the following operas: *Catone in Utica* (Turin, Dec. 26, 1731); *Caio Fabrizio* (Rome, Jan. 12, 1732); *Siroe, re di Persia* (Bologna, May 2, 1733); and *Tito Vespasiano* (Pesaro, Sept. 24, 1735). In Dresden, he produced *Senocrita* (Feb. 27, 1737), *Atalanta* (July 26, 1737), *Asteria* (Aug. 3, 1737), *Alfonso* (May 11, 1738), *Numa* (Oct. 7, 1741), *Arminio* (Oct. 7, 1745), *La Spartana generosa* (June 14, 1747), *Demofoonte* (Feb. 9, 1748); *Attilio Regolo* (Jan. 12, 1750), *Ciro riconosciuto* (Jan. 20, 1751), *Adriano in Siria* (Jan. 17, 1752), *Solimano*

(Feb. 5, 1753), *Artemisia* (Feb. 6, 1754), *L'Olimpiade* (Feb. 16, 1756), etc. In 1734 Hasse visited London, where he was offered the management of the opera company established in opposition to Handel; although his opera *Artaserse,* which he presented there (Nov. 10, 1734), was very successful, he decided not to challenge Handel's superiority, and returned to Dresden. Among other capital cities he visited during this period was Warsaw, where he produced *Il sogno di Scipione* (Oct. 7, 1958) and *Zenobia* (Oct. 7, 1761). His productions in Vienna were *Ipermestra* (Jan. 8, 1744), *Alcide al Bivio* (Oct. 8, 1760), *Il trionfo di Clelia* (April 27, 1762), *Egeria* (April 24, 1764), *Partenope* (Sept. 9, 1767), and *Piramo e Tisbe* (Nov., 1768). His last opera was *Ruggerio,* produced in Milan on Oct. 16, 1771.

Although Hasse was fortunate in his artistic life and never lacked the support of the public, he had to face strong rivalry on the part of the Italian composer Porpora, who was engaged by the Dresden court in 1747. Furthermore, Porpora's pupil, a young singer named Regina Mingotti, became a formidable competitor to Faustina Hasse, no longer in her prime. Hasse succeeded in maintaining his firm position in Dresden, and Porpora departed for Vienna in 1752. In 1760, during the siege of Dresden in the course of the Seven Years' War, Hasse's house was set afire by gunfire, and nearly all of his manuscripts perished. Hasse's vitality and determination overcame these challenges, and he never ceased to produce new works with astounding facility. His music did not break new paths in operatic art, but he was a master of singing melody in the Italian style, and a fine craftsman in harmony and instrumentation. *Pallido è il sole* and *Per questo dolce amplesso* from his opera *Artaserse* were the two airs that Farinelli sang every evening for 10 years to soothe the melancholy of the ailing Spanish King Philip. In addition to his operas, Hasse wrote 9 oratorios, 10 Masses, 3 Requiems, 10 psalms, 5 litanies, 22 motets, a Te Deum, and a Salve Regina (publ. in London in 1740, under the title *The Famous Salve Regina Composed by Signor Hasse*); also wrote instrumental concertos, string trios, sonatas, etc. An important collection of Hasse's MSS is in the Dresden Library. A selection of his works was publ. by A. Schering in the *Denkmäler deutscher Tonkunst* (vols. 20, 29/30) and by Otto Schmid in *Musik am sächsischen Hofe* (vols. 1, 2, 6, 7, 8); G. Göhler edited *10 ausgewählte Orchesterstücke* (1904). Other reprints are by Christian I. Latrobe in his *Selection of Sacred Music* (6 vols., 1806–26), by B. Engländer (keyboard sonatas; Leipzig, 1930), etc.; cantatas for solo female and orch. are in *Le Pupitre* 11. S. H. Hansell's *Works for Solo Voice of Johann Adolph Hasse* (Detroit, 1968) is a thematic index of 132 solo vocal works with orchestral or continuo accompaniment: cantatas, motets, and antiphons.

BIBLIOGRAPHY: W. H. Riehl, *Musikalische Charakterköpfe,* vol. 1 (6th ed., Stuttgart, 1879); K. Mennicke, "J. A. Hasse," *Sammelbände der Internationalen Musik-Gesellschaft* (1904); K. Mennicke, *Hasse und die Brüder Graun als Symphoniker* (Leipzig, 1906; with a thematic catalogue); W. Müller, *J. A. Hasse als Kirchenkomponist* (Leipzig, 1911; with a thematic catalogue of Hasse's sacred works); L. Kamiensky, *Die Oratorien von J. A. Hasse* (Berlin, 1911); B. Zeller, *Das Recitativo accompagnato in den Opern Hasses* (Halle, 1911); Rudolf Gerber, *Der Operntypus J. A. Hasses und seine textlichen Grundlagen* (Leipzig, 1925).

Hasse, Karl, German composer and musicologist; b. Dohna, near Dresden, March 20, 1883; d. Cologne, July 31, 1960. He studied with Kretzschmar and Riemann at the Univ. of Leipzig and with Straube and Nikisch at the Leipzig Cons.; later took courses at the Munich Academy with Reger and Mottl. He then held posts as choral conductor and organist in Heidelberg, Chemnitz, and Osnabrück and taught music in Cologne. He wrote a number of works for orch., chamber groups, organ, and voice, aggregating 120 opus numbers; publ. several books on Max Reger (Leipzig, 1921; Berlin, 1936; Leipzig, 1948; Dortmund, 1951); 3 books on Bach (Leipzig, 1925; Cologne, 1938; Leipzig, 1949); contributed numerous articles to German music magazines.

Hasse, Max, German musicologist; b. Buttelstedt, near Weimar, Nov. 24, 1859; d. Magdeburg, Oct. 20, 1935. He was music critic of the *Magdeburger Zeitung* from 1894 till 1927; publ. the basic works on Cornelius, *Peter Cornelius und sein Barbier von Bagdad* (1904) and *Der Dichter-Musiker Peter Cornelius* (2 vols., 1922–23); edited the complete works of Cornelius, in 5 volumes.

Hassell, Jon, American composer of the avant-garde; b. Memphis, Tenn., March 22, 1937. He was trained as a trumpet player; studied composition with Bernard Rogers at the Eastman School of Music in Rochester, N.Y. (B.M., 1969; M.M. 1970). Progressing away from traditional arts, he took courses in advanced electronic techniques with Karlheinz Stockhausen and Henri Pousseur in Cologne (1965–67); returning to the U.S., was composer-in-residence and performer at the Center for Creative and Performing Arts in Buffalo (1967–69). In 1969 he moved to New York City to pursue independent activities in music and in sculpture.
WORKS: *Music for Vibraphones* (1965); *Blackboard Piece with Girls and Loops* for 2 girls and 2 pitch-producing blackboards (N.Y., March 26, 1968); *Superball* for 4 players, with hand-held magnetic tape heads (Ithaca, Oct. 29, 1969); *Goodbye Music* for mixed media (Buffalo, May 4, 1969); also sound sculptures: *Map 1* and *Map 2* for hand-held magnetic playback heads, designed to explore potential sounds (exhibited in Buffalo, as sculptures, 1969); and *Elemental Warnings* (1969).

Hasselmans, Louis, French cellist and conductor; b. Paris, July 25, 1878; d. San Juan, Puerto Rico, Dec. 27, 1957. He was the son of a harpist and grandson of a conductor. He studied the cello with Jules Delsart at the Paris Cons., winning first prize at the age of 15, and theory with Lavignac and B. Godard. From 1893 to 1909 he was cellist in the Capet Quartet; made his debut as conductor in Paris in 1905; then conducted at the Opéra-Comique (1909–11); in Montreal (1911–13); was conductor of the Chicago Opera (1918–20) and was engaged as conductor of French operas at the Metropolitan Opera in New York (1921–36); then taught at Louisiana State Univ. in Baton Rouge (1936–48).

Hassler, Caspar, German composer; brother of **Hans Leo Hassler**; b. Nuremberg, Aug. (baptized, Aug. 17) 1562; d. there, Aug. 19, 1618. In 1586 he was appointed organist at the Lorenz-Kirche; also supervised the building of the organ in the Würzburg Cathedral. He wrote a number of organ pieces; edited several collections of sacred works by various authors.

Hassler, Hans Leo, celebrated German composer; b. Nuremberg, Oct. 25, 1564; d. Frankfurt, June 8, 1612. He studied with his father Isaak Hassler (1530–91), and from his earliest years became extremely proficient on the organ. In 1584 he went to Venice to study with Andrea Gabrieli. Hassler was the first notable German composer who went to Italy for musical study; however, he did not remain long in Venice; after a year there, he was recalled to Germany, where he obtained the post of chamber musician to Count Octavianus Fugger in Augsburg; following the latter's death in 1600, he became a leader of the town band in Nuremberg and also organist at the Frauenkirche there. On Jan. 1, 1602 he received the post of chamber organist to the Court of Rudolf II at Prague; this was an honorary position rather than an actual occupation, and Hassler appeared but infrequently, if at all, at the imperial court in Prague. At the time he was busily engaged in the manufacture and installation of musical clocks; his commercial pursuits led to numerous litigations with business rivals. In 1604 he took a leave of absence from Nuremberg and went to Ulm; in 1609 he became organist to the Elector of Saxony in Dresden, and in 1612 accompanied him to Frankfurt; but Hassler was weakened by tuberculosis and died shortly after arrival there. The style of Hassler's music is greatly influenced by his teacher Andrea Gabrieli, and the latter's nephew, Giovanni Gabrieli, with whom Hassler became friendly in Venice. Having absorbed the Italian techniques, Hassler applied his knowledge to the composition of strongly national German songs, and became one of the founders of national musical art in Germany.
WORKS: *Canzonette a 4* (Nuremberg, 1590); *Cantiones sacrae a 4–12* (Augsburg, 1591); *Neue teutsche Gesäng nach Art der welschen Madrigalien und Canzonetten a 4–8* (Augsburg, 1596); *Madrigali a 5–8* (Augsburg, 1596); 8 Masses *a 4–8* (Nuremberg, 1599); *Sacri concentus a 4–12* (Augsburg, 1601; 2nd ed., 1612); *Lustgarten neuer teutscher Gesäng, Balletti, Gailliarden und Intraden a 4–8* (Nuremberg, 1601; later editions, 1605, 1610; reprints in Eitner's *Publikationen älterer praktischer und theoretischer Musikwerke* vol. 15); *Psalmen und christliche Gesäng mit vier Stimmen auf die Melodien fugweis componirt* (Nuremberg, 1607); *Kirchengesänge, Psalmen und geistliche Lieder, auf die gemeinen Melodien mit vier Stimmen simpliciter gesetzt* (Nuremberg, 1608; 2nd enlarged ed., 1637); *Venusgarten oder neue lustige liebliche Tänz a 4–6* (with V. Haussmann; Nuremberg, 1615); numerous motets, litanies, and organ works in various contemporary collections. Reprints are in the *Denkmäler deutscher Tonkunst* (vols. 2, 7,

24/25); *Denkmäler der Tonkunst in Bayern*, vols. 7, 9, 20 (4.ii, 5.ii, 11.i); in Riemann's *Illustrationen zur Musikgeschichte* and *Musikgeschichte in Beispielen;* Schering's *Geschichte der Musik in Beispielen;* Leichtentritt's *Meisterwerke deutscher Tonkunst*, etc. R. von Saalfeld edited the psalms and sacred songs (1925); H. Bäuerle edited 2 Masses. A chronological list of Hassler's printed works was publ. by Eitner in the *Monatshefte für Musik-Geschichte* (1874). Publication of the *Collected Works*, ed. by C. Russell Crosby, was begun in 1961 (Wiesbaden).

BIBLIOGRAPHY: R. Schwartz, "Hans Leo Hassler unter dem Einfluss der italienischen Madrigalisten," *Vierteljahrsschrift für Musikwissenschaft* (1893); A. Sandberger, "Bemerkungen zur Biographie Hans Leo Hasslers und seiner Brüder," *Denkmäler der Tonkunst in Bayern* 8 (5.i); Hugo Leichtentritt, *Geschichte der Motette* (Leipzig, 1908; p. 293 ff.); P. Wagner, *Geschichte der Messe* (1914; p. 342 ff.); M. Seiffert, *Geschichte der Klaviermusik* (1899; p. 95 ff.); H. J. Moser, *Geschichte der deutschen Musik* (vol. I, pp. 493–504; 5th ed., 1930).

Hassler, Jakob, German organist and composer; brother of **Hans Leo Hassler;** b. Nuremberg, Dec., 1569 (baptized Dec. 18); d. Eger, between April and Sept., 1622. Like his famous brother, he enjoyed the patronage of the Fugger family; was enabled to go to Italy in 1590 to improve his musical education; upon his return to Germany, on his brother's recommendation, he received the honorary post of organist to Emperor Rudolf II in Prague. In 1611 he settled in Eger. He publ. a collection of Italian madrigals (Nuremberg, 1600) and a book of sacred works (Nuremberg, 1601). E. von Werra publ. several keyboard pieces by Jakob Hassler in the *Denkmäler der Tonkunst in Bayern* 7 (4.ii).

Hässler, Johann Wilhelm, German composer and pianist; b. Erfurt, March 29, 1747; d. Moscow, March 29, 1822. His father was a maker of men's headwear; he followed his father's trade, while studying organ with his uncle, Johann Christian Kittel. At the age of 14, he was able to earn his living as organist at an Erfurt church. After his father's death, in 1769, he maintained for some years a manufactory of fur muffs. A meeting in Hamburg with Carl Philipp Emanuel Bach gave him a fresh impetus toward continuing his musical activities. He gave concerts as pianist, and publ. several piano sonatas. On Feb. 8, 1779 he married his pupil, Sophie Kiel. In 1780 he opened public winter concerts in Erfurt; his wife appeared there as a singer and choral director. In 1789, he played in Berlin and Potsdam; in Dresden he took part in a contest with Mozart, as organist and pianist, without producing much impression either on Mozart himself or on the listeners. In 1790 he went to London, where he performed piano concertos under the direction of Haydn. In 1792 he went to Russia, where he remained for 30 years, until his death. In Moscow he became greatly renowned as pianist, composer, and particularly as teacher. Most of his works were published in Russia; these included sonatas, preludes, variations, fantasies, etc., and also pieces for piano, 4 hands. His style represents a transition between Bach and Beethoven,

without attaining a degree of the imagination or craftsmanship of either. However, his piano pieces in the lighter vein have undeniable charm. His Gigue in D minor was well known. His autobiography is included in Willi Kahl, *Selbstbiographien deutscher Musiker* (Cologne, 1948). See also W. Georgii, *Klavier-Musik* (Zürich, 1950); R.-A. Mooser, *Annales de la musique et des musiciens en Russie au XVIIIᵉ siècle* (Geneva, 1951; Vol. II, pp. 659–61).

Hastings, Thomas, American composer of hymntunes; b. Washington, Litchfield County, Conn., Oct. 15, 1784; d. New York, May 15, 1872. The family moved to Clinton, N.Y., when Hastings was 12; he became interested in practical music and was a leader of a village chorus. He collected hymns, which were later published in a collection, *Musica Sacra* (with S. Warriner, 1816). He moved to Utica in 1828 and was a member of a Handel and Haydn society there; he also edited a religious weekly publication, *The Western Recorder.* In 1832 he settled in New York, where he was connected with the Normal Institute, in association with Lowell Mason. He received the honorary degree of Doctor of Music from N.Y. Univ. (1858).

WRITINGS: Among his many publications were *Musical Reader* (1817); *Dissertation on Musical Taste* (in which he discourses on the superiority of German music; Albany, 1822; 2nd enlarged ed., 1853); *The Union Minstrel* (1830); *Spiritual Songs for Social Worship* (with Lowell Mason, 1831); *Devotional Hymns and Religious Poems* (1850); *History of Forty Choirs* (1854); and *Sacred Praise* (1856). His own hymn tunes have been estimated to number more than 1000, and, next to those of Lowell Mason, are regarded as the finest of his time in America. These include the tune to which the celebrated hymn *Rock of Ages* is sung; the words are by Augustus Toplady, and Hastings entitled his tune simply *Toplady* to honor the author of the words. Other well-known hymn tunes are *Retreat, Zion,* and *Ortonville.* He publ. many of his melodies under foreign-sounding names, and it is not always possible to ascertain their authorship.

BIBLIOGRAPHY: F. J. Metcalf, *American Writers and Compilers of Sacred Music* (N.Y., 1925); J. T. Howard, *Our American Music* (N.Y., 1939, and subsequent eds.); M. B. Scanlon, "Thomas Hastings," *Musical Quarterly* (April 1946); also the article on Hastings in *Dictionary of American Biography.*

Hastreiter, Helene, American dramatic contralto; b. Louisville, Ky., Nov. 14, 1858; d. Varese, Italy, Aug. 6, 1922. She sang as a child in a Chicago church; at the age of 22 went to Italy where she studied with the Lampertis (father and son) in Milan. She made her operatic debut there, and after several successful appearances in Italy was engaged by Col. Mapleson for his London season (1885). She then sang mostly in Italy; married Dr. Burgunzio there and lived in Genoa. Some of her leading operatic parts were Orfeo, Euridice, Dalila, Senta, and Ortrud.

Hatrík, Juraj, Slovak composer; b. Orkučany, May 1, 1941. He studied with Alexander Moyzes at the Bratislava Music Academy (1958–62); then taught esthetics and psychology of music there.

WORKS: Sinfonietta (1962); *Contrasts* for violin and piano (1963); *Canto responsoriale* for double chorus and 4 kettledrums (1964); *Čakanie (Waiting)* for narrator, flute, harp, strings and percussion (1965); *Monumento malincolico* for organ and orch. (1965); *Concertino in modo classico* for piano and orch. (1968); *Introspection* for soprano, flute, violin, cello, clarinet, horn and vibraphone (1968); *Domov sú ruky*, cantata (1968); *Sonata ciacona* for piano (1970); *Da Capo al Fine*, symph. poem (1975; Bratislava, Feb. 19, 1976); *Choral Fantasia* for accordian and chamber ensemble (1976).

Hatton, John Liptrot, British composer of light music; b. Liverpool, Oct. 12, 1809; d. Margate, Sept. 20, 1886. He acquired facility as pianist and singer, and appeared on the vaudeville stage as a musical comedian. He publ. a great number of songs, among which *Anthea* and *Good-bye, sweetheart, good-bye* became extremely popular. In 1832 he went to London; produced his operetta, *The Queen of the Thames*, there (Feb. 25, 1843). He then went to Vienna, where he staged his opera *Pascal Bruno* (March 2, 1844). For some of his numbers he used the punning pseudonym **Czapek** (genitive plural of the Hungarian word for hat). In 1848–50 he made an extensive American tour. Returning to England, he was musical director at the Princess's Theatre (1853–59); wrote music for several Shakespeare plays there; wrote a cantata *Robin Hood* (Bradford Festival, Aug. 26, 1856); a grand opera *Rose, or Love's Ransom* (London, Nov. 26, 1864), and a sacred drama *Hezekiah* (Dec. 15, 1877); edited collections of old English songs.

Hattstaedt, John James, American pianist and pedagogue; b. Monroe, Mich., Dec. 29, 1851; d. Chicago, Nov. 30, 1931. He studied in Germany; then taught piano in Detroit (1870–72), St. Louis (1872–73), and Chicago (1875–86). In 1886 he founded the American Cons. of Music in Chicago. He publ. a *Manual of Musical History*.

Hatze, Josip, Croatian composer; b. Split, March 21, 1879; d. there, Jan. 30, 1959. He studied with Mascagni in Italy. He belongs to a generation of Croatian composers entirely influenced by Italian music. He wrote the operas *Povratak* (*The Return*; Zagreb, March 21, 1911); *Adel i Mara* (Zagreb, March 1, 1933); many songs.

Haubenstock-Ramati, Roman, Polish composer of experimental music; b. Cracow, Feb. 27, 1919. He studied philosophy at the Univ. of Cracow; also took music lessons with Arthur Malawski and Josef Koffler. From 1947 to 1950 he was music director of Radio Cracow; then went to Israel where he was director of the State Music Library in Tel Aviv (1950–56). In 1957 he settled in Vienna where he was for a time employed by Universal Edition as the reader and adviser for publications of new music. In 1959 he organized in Donaueschingen the first exhibition of musical scores in graphic notation; he himself evolved a curious type of modern particella, in which the right-hand page

gives the outline of musical action for the conductor while the left-hand page is devoted to instrumental and vocal details. This type of notation combined the most advanced type of visual guidance with an *aide-memoire* of traditional theater arrangements. In 1967 he inaugurated a weekly seminar for avant-garde music in Bilthoven, Holland. In 1968 he gave lectures in Buenos Aires and in 1969 he conducted a seminar in Stockholm, Sweden. Several of his works bear the subtitle "Mobile" to indicate the flexibility of their architectonics.

WORKS: *Ricercari* for string trio (1950); *Blessings* for voice and 9 players (1952); *Recitativo and Aria* for cembalo and orch. (1954); *Papageno's Pocket-Size Concerto* for orch. and glockenspiel (1955); *Les Symphonies de timbres* for orch. (1957); *Chants et prismes* for orch. (1957); *Sequences* for violin and orch. in 4 groups (1958); *Interpolation*, a 'mobile' for flute solo (1958); *Liaisons*, a 'mobile' for vibraphone and marimbaphone (1959); *Petite musique de nuit*, a 'mobile' for orch. (1959); *Mobile for Shakespeare* for voice and 6 players (1960); *Credentials* or *Think, Think Lucky* for speech-voice and 8 players (1960); *Jeux* for 6 percussion groups (1961); *Vermutungen über ein dunkles Haus* for 3 orchestras (1963); *Amerika*, opera after Kafka's novel (Berlin, Oct. 8, 1966); an "anti-opera" *La Comédie* for 3 speakers and 3 percussionists (1969); several pieces under the generic name *Catch* (1969–71); *Multiple I-VI* for varying numbers of players arranged in multitudinous alternative versions (1969); *Alone* for trombone and a mime (1969). He published several papers dealing with graphic notation.

Haubiel, Charles, American composer; b. Delta, Ohio, Jan. 30, 1892. He first took piano lessons with his sister and played a piano recital at the age of 14 at the New York College of Music. He then went to Europe where he studied music theory with Alexander von Fielitz. Returning to America in 1913, he toured as associate artist with the Czech violinist Jaroslav Kocian. In 1917 he enlisted in the U.S. Army, from which he received his honorable discharge, as a 2nd Lieutenant, in 1919. In 1920 he joined the piano faculty of the Institute of Musical Art of N.Y. (Juilliard Foundation), where he taught for 10 years; in 1923 he became a faculty member of N.Y. Univ., where he remained until 1947. In 1935 he founded the Composer's Press, Inc., and was its president until 1966, when it was taken over by Southern Music Co. During his teaching years in N.Y. he also took piano lessons with Josef and Rosina Lhévinne, and studied composition with Rosario Scalero and orchestration with Modest Altschuler. In the 1960's he settled in Los Angeles. His music is marked by a fine craftsmanship in a neo-Romantic manner, not without a welcome infusion of coloristic harmonies.

WORKS: *Sunday Costs Five Pesos*, Mexican folk opera (Charlotte, North Carolina, Nov. 6, 1950); *Mars Ascending*, for orch. (1923); *Karma*, symph. variations (1928; revised in 1968 and retitled *Of Human Destiny*); *Rittrati* (*Portraits*) for orch. (Chicago, Dec. 12, 1935); *Suite Passacaglia* (Los Angeles, Jan. 31, 1936; originally for two pianos); *Symphony in Variation Form* (1937); *Vox Cathedralis*, for orch. (N.Y.,

May 6, 1938; originally for organ); *Miniatures,* for string orch. (N.Y., April 23, 1939); *American Rhapsody* for orch. (1948); *Pioneers,* symph. saga of Ohio (1946; revised, 1956); *Cryptics,* for bassoon and piano (1932); *Lodando la Danza,* for oboe, violin, cello, and piano (1932); *Echi classici,* for string quartet (1936); *In the French Manner* for flute, cello and piano (1942); String Trio (1943); Cello Sonata (1944); *Nuances,* for flute and piano (1947); *Shadows,* for violin and piano (1947); *Epochs* for violin and piano (1954); *Threnody for Love* for 6 instruments (1965); Trio for Clarinet, Cello and Piano (1969); *Cryptics* for cello and piano (1973); many choral works: *Sea Songs* (1931), *Vision of Saint Joan* (1941), *Jungle Tale* (1943), *Father Abraham* (1944), etc.; song cycle *Ohioana* (1966); for piano: suite, *Solari* (1932–34).

Haudebert, Lucien, French composer; b. Fougères, April 10, 1877; d. Paris, Feb. 24, 1963. He studied organ; then went to Paris, where he took lessons in composition with Fauré. He followed in his music the traditions of César Franck, preferring large sonorities and clear tonal harmonies. He stood aloof from modern developments in France and had little recognition even among traditional musicians, despite praise from Romain Rolland. His most effective work is the oratorio, *Dieu Vainqueur* (1916–22); other significant works are: the oratorio *Moïse* (1928); *Symphonie bretonne* (1936); *Symphonie française* (1941); *Voyage en Bretagne,* for orch. (1953); *Chants de la Mer,* for voices and orch. (1950); also chamber music, including a quartet for saxophones.

Hauer, Josef Matthias, significant Austrian composer and original theorist; b. Wiener-Neustadt, near Vienna, March 19, 1883; d. Vienna, Sept. 22, 1959. After attending a college for teachers, he became a public school instructor; at the same time he studied music. An experimenter by nature, with a penchant for mathematical constructions, he developed a system of composition based on "tropes," or patterns, which aggregated to thematic formations of 12 different notes. As early as 1912 he published a piano piece, entitled *Nomos* (*Law*), which contained the germinal principles of 12-tone music; in his theoretical publications he elaborated his system in greater details. These were: *Vom Wesen des Musikalischen* (Berlin, 1922); *Deutung des Melos* (Vienna, 1923); *Vom Melos zur Pauke* (Vienna, 1925), and finally *Zwölftontechnik* (Vienna, 1926), in which the method of composing in the 12-tone technique was illustrated with practical examples. Hauer asserted his priority in 12-tone composition with great vehemence; he even used a rubberstamp on his personal stationery proclaiming himself the true founder of the 12-tone method. This claim was countered, with equal vehemence, but with more justification, by Schoenberg; indeed, the functional basis of 12-tone composition in which the contrapuntal and harmonic structures are derived from the unifying tone row did not appear until Schoenberg formulated it and put it into practice in 1924. Hauer lived his entire life in Vienna, working as a composer, conductor and teacher. Despite its forbidding character, his music attracted much attention.

WORKS: the oratorios, *Wandlungen* (1928) and *Der Menschen Weg* (1937) to poems by Hölderlin; opera, *Salambo,* after Flaubert (1930); the singspiel *Die Schwarze Spinne* (1935; performed posthumously, Vienna, May 23, 1966); *Romantische Phantasie* for orch. (1925); *Sinfonietta* (1927); Violin Concerto (1928); Piano Concerto (1928); 8 orchestral suites; 7 dance fantasies; 2 dance suites for chamber ensemble; 6 string quartets; *Langsamer Walzer* for orch. (1953); *Labyrinthischer Tanz* for piano four-hands (1952); *Chinesisches Streichquartett* (1953); *Hausmusik* for piano four-hands (1958); Quintet, for clarinet, violin, viola, cello and piano; several sets of piano pieces entitled *Nomoi;* nearly 1000 pieces of all descriptions, each ostentatiously bearing the subtitle *Zwölftonspiel; Apokalyptische Fantasie* for orch. (1913; posthumous; Graz, Oct. 21, 1969).

BIBLIOGRAPHY: Willi Reich, "J. M. Hauer," *Die Musik* (May 1931); H. Picht, *J. M. Hauer, ein Vorkämpfer geistiger Musikauffassung* (Stuttgart, 1934); Monika Lichtensfeld, *Untersuchungen zur Theorie der Zwölftontechnik bei J. M. Hauer* (Regensburg, 1964); Walter Szmolyan, *Josef Matthias Hauer* (Vienna, 1965); J. Sengstschmid, "Anatomie eines Zwölftonspiele. Ein Blick in die Werkstalt Josef Matthias Hauers," *Zeitschrift für Musiktheorie* (April 1971); H. Schöny, "Die Vorfahren des Komponisten Josef Matthias Hauer," *Genealogie* (Aug. 1971).

Haug, Gustav, Swiss composer; b. in Strasbourg, Nov. 30, 1871; d. in St. Gallen, April 22, 1956. He studied at the Cons. of Strasbourg; then went to Switzerland and settled in St. Gallen, where he was active as a church organist and a voice teacher. As a composer he produced a number of singable choral anthems, several works for solo voices with orchestral accompaniment, and many songs to German texts.

Haug, Hans, Swiss composer; b. Basel, July 27, 1900; d. in Lausanne, Sept. 15, 1967. He studied piano with Egon Petri and Ernst Levy in Basel, and later with Busoni at the Munich Academy of Music. Returning to Switzerland he became choral conductor at the Municipal Theater in Basel (1928–34); from 1935–38 he conducted the orchestra of the Radio Suisse Romande and also taught at the Cons. of Lausanne, where he finally settled. As a composer, he was most successful in writing for the theater.

WORKS: the operas *Don Juan in der Fremde* (Basel, Jan. 15, 1930); *Madrisa* (Basel, Jan. 15, 1934); *Tartuffe* (Basel, May 24, 1937); *Le Malade imaginaire,* after Molière (Zürich, Feb. 8, 1947); *Der Spiegel der Agrippina* (1954); *Justice du roi* (1963); radio operas *Gardien vigilant* (1967); *Le Souper de Venise* (1967); an oratorio, *Michelangelo* (Solothurn, Feb. 28, 1943); operettas, *Barbara* (1938); *Gilberte de Courgenay* (1939); several radio operettas; the ballets, *L'Indifférent; Pan und Apollo;* incidental music for theatrical plays; numerous cantatas, including a humorous *Cantate gastronomique* for soli, chorus and orch.; a symphony (1948); *Capriccio* for wind instruments and piano (1957); Concertino for Flute and Small Orch. (1943); Concertino for Oboe, Viola and Small Orch.; Concertino for Piano and Orch.; Guitar Concerto (1952); 2 piano concertos (1938; 1962); Double Concerto for Oboe and Viola (1953); 3 string quartets;

Wind Quartet; Wind Quintet; *Kurze Musik* for cello and orch., etc.; also a curious symphonic poem entitled *Charlie Chaplin* (1930).

Hauk, Minnie (real name **Mignon**), celebrated American soprano; b. New York, Nov. 16, 1851; d. Triebschen, near Lucerne, Switzerland, Feb. 6, 1929. Her father was a German carpenter who became involved in the political events of 1848, emigrated to America and married an American woman; he named his daughter Mignon after the character in Goethe's *Wilhelm Meister*. The family moved to Atchison, Kansas, when Minnie was very young; her mother maintained a boarding house at a steamboat landing on the Missouri. In 1860 they moved to New Orleans; there Minnie Hauk began to sing popular ballads for entertainment. She made her operatic debut at the age of 14 in Brooklyn, in *La Sonnambula* (Oct. 13, 1866); then took lessons with Achille Errani of New York. On Nov. 15, 1867, she sang Juliette at the American première of Gounod's opera in N.Y. She attracted the attention of the rich industrialist Leonard Jerome, and the music publisher Gustave Schirmer, who financed her trip to Europe. She sang in opera in Paris during the summer of 1868; made her London debut at Covent Garden on Oct. 26, 1868; in 1870 she sang in Vienna. She sang the title roles in the first American performances of *Carmen* (N.Y. Academy of Music, Oct. 23, 1878) and Massenet's *Manon* (Dec. 23, 1885); appeared at the Metropolitan Opera during the season of 1890-91, but following a disagreement with the management, decided to organize her own opera group; with it, she gave the first Chicago performance of *Cavalleria Rusticana* (Sept. 28, 1891). She then settled in Switzerland with her husband Baron Ernst von Hesse-Wartegg, whom she had married in 1881; after his death she lived mostly in Berlin; lost her fortune in the depreciation of her holdings in Germany. In 1919, Geraldine Farrar launched an appeal to raise funds for her in America. Her autobiography, collated by E. B. Hitchcock, was publ. as *Memories of a Singer* (London, 1925).
  BIBLIOGRAPHY: Oscar Thompson, *The American Singer* (N.Y., 1937; pp. 93-118).

Haupt, Karl August, German organist; b. Kuhnau, Silesia, Aug. 25, 1810; d. Berlin, July 4, 1891. He studied with Dehn and others in Berlin; played in various Berlin churches and became famous for his masterly improvisations in the style of Bach. He was one of the experts consulted for the specifications in building the grand organ at the Crystal Palace in London. He had many distinguished pupils, including about 40 American organists. He publ. a valuable *Choralbuch* (1869); many other compositions for organ remain in manuscript.

Hauptmann, Moritz, eminent German theorist and composer; b. Dresden, Oct. 13, 1792; d. Leipzig, Jan. 3, 1868. His father was an architect and hoped to bring up his son in that profession; however, there was no parental opposition to music studies; he took lessons with Scholz (violin) and Morlacchi (composition) in Dresden; in 1811 he went to Gotha to study violin and composition with Spohr and became his lifelong friend. In 1812 he joined the Dresden Court orch. as violinist; in 1815 he became music teacher in the family of the Russian military governor of Dresden, Prince Repnin, and went with them to Russia, where he remained for 5 years. In 1820, he returned to Dresden; in 1822, Spohr engaged him as violinist in the court orch. at Kassel. In 1842, at Mendelssohn's recommendation, he was appointed cantor at the Thomasschule and prof. of composition at the Leipzig Cons., retaining these posts until his death. He became greatly renowned as a teacher of violin and composition. Among his pupils were Ferdinand David, Joachim, Hans von Bülow, Jadassohn, and Arthur Sullivan. A master of classical form, he was a polished composer, in the tradition of Spohr and Mendelssohn; the architectonic symmetry of his instrumental works and the purity of part-writing in his vocal music aroused admiration among his contemporaries; yet his music failed to endure, and rapidly went into decline after his death. He publ. about 60 works, among them 3 violin sonatas, 4 violin sonatinas, 2 string quartets, piano pieces, sacred works, and a number of lieder, a genre in which he excelled. His theoretical work, *Die Natur der Harmonik und Metrik* (Leipzig, 1853; 2nd ed., 1873; English transl., London, 1888), is an attempt to apply Hegel's dialectical philosphy to the realm of music. It exercised considerable influence on the later development of German theory of harmony; among other German scholars, Riemann was influenced by it. Hauptmann's other writings are: *Erläuterungen zu J. S. Bachs Kunst der Fuge* (Leipzig, 1841; 2nd ed., 1861); *Die Lehre von der Harmonik* (ed. by Oscar Paul; Leipzig, 1868); *Opuscula* (miscellaneous writings, edited by E. Hauptmann; Leipzig, 1874). His letters to Spohr and others were edited by F. Hiller (Leipzig, 1876). A. D. Coleridge publ. a selection, in English, of Hauptmann's correspondence as *Letters of a Leipzig Cantor* (1892).
  BIBLIOGRAPHY: O. Paul, *Moritz Hauptmann, eine Denkschrift zur Feier seines Siebzigjährigen Geburtstages am 13. October 1862* (Leipzig, 1862); Stephan Krehl, *Moritz Hauptmann; ein Dank- und Gedenkwort* (Leipzig, 1918); P. Rummenhöller, *Moritz Hauptmann als Theoretiker* (Wiesbaden, 1963).

Hauschka, Vincenz, gifted cellist and composer; b. Mies, Bohemia, Jan. 21, 1766; d. Vienna, Sept. 13, 1840. He was a pupil of his father, a school teacher; became chorister in Prague cathedral; studied composition with Zöger, cello with Christ. He was appointed cellist to Count Joseph von Thun in Prague (1782); made successful concert tours through Germany performing not only on the cello, but also on the baryton (a popular instrument at the time; Haydn wrote numerous works for it). He publ. 9 sonatas for cello; a book of vocal canons; in MS are several pieces for the baryton.

Hausegger, Friedrich von, Austrian musicologist; b. St. Andrä, Carinthia, April 26, 1837; d. Graz, Feb. 23, 1899. He was a pupil of Salzmann and Otto Desoff; also studied law and became a barrister at Graz. In 1872 he became a teacher of history and theory of music at the Univ. of Graz. He contributed to music periodicals.

WRITINGS: His *Musik als Ausdruck* (Vienna, 1885) is a valuable essay on musical esthetics. He also wrote *Richard Wagner und Schopenhauer* (1890); *Vom Jenseits des Künstlers* (1893); *Die künstlerische Persönlichkeit* (1897). After his death, his book, *Unsere deutschen Meister,* was ed. by R. Louis (1901); his *Gesammelte Schriften* were brought out by his son in 1939.

Hausegger, Siegmund von, Austrian conductor and composer; b. Graz, Aug. 16, 1872; d. Munich, Oct. 10, 1948. He was trained musically by his father, Friedrich von Hausegger. At the age of 16 he composed a grand Mass which he himself conducted; at 18, he brought out in Graz an opera, *Helfrid.* Richard Strauss thought well enough of Hausegger as composer to accept for performance his comic opera *Zinnober,* which he conducted in Munich on June 19, 1898. Hausegger began his own conducting career in Graz as a theater conductor in 1895; in 1897 he was guest conductor in Bayreuth; then led the Kaim Orch. in Munich (1899–1902) and the Museum Concerts in Frankfurt (1903–06). In 1910 he was appointed conductor of the Philharmonic Concerts in Hamburg. From 1920 to 1934 he was director of the Academy of Musical Art in Munich.

WORKS: *Dionysische Fantasie* for orch. (1899); symph. poems *Barbarossa* (1900) and *Wieland der Schmied* (1904); *Natursymphonie,* with a choral finale (1911); several works for chorus and orch.; symph. variations on a children's song, *Aufklänge* (1919), etc. He published a monograph, *Alexander Ritter, ein Bild seines Charakters und Schaffens* (Berlin, 1907); edited *R. Wagners Briefe an Frau Julie Ritter* (Munich, 1920), his father's correspondence with Peter Rosegger (Leipzig, 1924). His collected articles appeared under the title *Betrachtungen zur Kunst* (Leipzig, 1921).

Hauser, Miska, Austrian violinist; b. Pressburg (Bratislava), 1822; d. Vienna, Dec. 8, 1887. He studied with Kreutzer in Vienna, and traveled as a child prodigy in Europe; in 1853–58 made a grand tour of America and Australia. He wrote an operetta, *Der blinde Leiermann;* numerous violin pieces, of which his meretricious *Rapsodie hongroise* and *Lieder ohne Worte* enjoyed undeserved popularity; an *American Rhapsody* for violin and piano (1855). During his American tour he sent correspondence to the *Ostdeutsche Post* which was collected and publ. in 2 vols., *Aus dem Wanderbuch eines österreichischen Virtuosen* (Leipzig, 1858–59). *History of Music in San Francisco* (San Francisco, 1939) contains English translations of some of these reports, which are not devoid of interest.

Hausmann, Robert, German cellist; b. Rottleberode, Harz, Aug. 13, 1852; d. Vienna, Jan. 18, 1909. He studied cello with Theodore Müller in Berlin; was the cellist of the Hochberg quartet in Dresden (1872-76); then joined the Joachim quartet (1879), with which he remained until its dissolution after Joachim's death (1907).

Haussmann, Valentin. Five German musicians in direct lineal descent bore this name: **Valentin Hauss-**

mann I, the eldest, b. Nuremberg, 1484, composed chorales, and was a friend of Luther. His son, **Valentin Haussmann II,** was organist at Gerbstädt, and an industrious composer of motets, canzonets, and dances. A selection of his instrumental works was publ. by F. Bölsche in the *Denkmäler deutscher Tonkunst* (vol. 16). **Valentin Haussmann III,** son of the preceding, was organist at Löbejün, and an expert in organ construction. His son, **Valentin Haussmann IV,** b. Löbejün about 1647, occupied the posts of chapel musician to the Köthen Court. **Valentin Bartholomäus Haussmann V,** son of the preceding, b. Löbejün, 1678, became cathedral organist at Merseburg and Halle, and became burgomaster at Lauchstadt.

Hausswald, Günter, German musicologist; b. Rochlitz, March 11, 1908; d. Stuttgart, April 23, 1974. He studied piano with Max Pauer in Leipzig and composition with Karg-Elert; took courses in musicology with Theodor Kroyer and Grabner. Then he became a music teacher in Leipzig and Dresden (1933–45) and at the Univ. of Jena (1950–53); his merit lies chiefly in his informative monographs: *Johann David Heinichens Instrumentale Werke* (Dresden, 1937); *Heinrich Marschner* (Dresden, 1938); *Die deutsche Oper* (Cologne, 1941); *Mozarts Serenaden* (Leipzig, 1951); *Richard Strauss* (Dresden, 1953); *Dirigenten: Bild und Schrift* (Berlin, 1966); in 1951 he began publishing the valuable periodical accounts *Das neue Opernbuch.* He further supplied exemplary editions of works by Gluck, Heinichen, Telemann, Weber and others.

Havelka, Svatopluk, Czech composer; b. Vrbice, Silesia, May 2, 1925. He began composing as a child; studied violin, piano and harmony; took courses in history and philosophy at the Univ. of Prague; studied privately with K. B. Jirák; later was active as director of music programs at the Ostrava Radio (1949–51) and with the Army Artistic Ensemble in Prague (1951–54). His music follows the folkloric trends, with some sonoristic and generally modernistic deflections from the nationalistic formulae.

WORKS: *Mort et Redemption* for orch. (1944); *4 Baroque Songs* for medium voice and piano (1944), retitled *Růže Ran (Rose of Wounds)* and scored with instrumental accompaniment, 1974; Suite for Small Orch. (1947); *2 Pastorales* for orch. (1948; 1951); *4 Suites to Moravian Folk Texts* for narrator, soli, chorus and chamber orch. (1948, 1949, 1949, 1951); a cantata, *Spring* (1949); Symph. No. 1 (Prague, Nov. 5, 1956); a cantata, *Chvála světla* (In Praise of Light, Prague, May 4, 1960); *Heptameron,* subtitled *A Poem of Nature and Love,* for narrator, 4 soli and orch. (Prague, March 25, 1964); *Pěna (Foam),* to the poem of the same title by H. M. Enzensberger, for orch. (1965; Olomouc, Feb. 9, 1966); *Ernesto Ché Guevara,* symph. poem in memory of the fallen Cuban revolutionary (1969); a ballet *Pyrrhos* (1970); *Hommage à Hieronymus Bosch,* symph. fantasy (1974); nonet (1976); songs; film music.

Havemann, Gustav, German violinist; b. Güstrow, March 15, 1882; d. Schöneiche, near Berlin, Jan. 2, 1960. He studied with his father; then enrolled at the Berlin Hochschule für Musik where he was a pupil of

Joachim. As a youth he played in the court orchestra in Schwerin; then was concertmaster in Lübeck and Darmstadt and Hamburg. In 1911 he joined the faculty of the Leipzig Cons.; subsequently was concertmaster at the Dresden State Opera (1915–20); from 1920 to 1945 was professor at the Berlin Musik Hochschule. He was the first violinist in the prestigious Havemann String Quartet, which performed much modern music. He himself composed a Violin Concerto (1938) and a useful manual *Die Violintechnik bis zur Vollendung* (1928).

Havingha, Gerhardus, Dutch organist and theorist; b. Groningen, Nov. 15, 1696; d. Alkmaar, March 6, 1753. He studied with his father, a church organist at Groningen; then became an organist at various churches in Holland; publ. *Oorspronk en Voortgang der orgelen* (Alkmaar, 1727), an important source of organ history and practice in Holland. His suite for harpsichord (Amsterdam, 1725) was republ. by J. Watelet in 1951.

Hawel, Jan, Polish composer; b. Pszow, July 10, 1936. He studied composition and conducting at the Katowice State College of Music, graduating in 1967; then became a member of its faculty.
WORKS: *Profiles* for male chorus and orch. (1962); Symph. for Strings (1962); *Contrasts* for orch. (1964); *Constructions* for orch. (1965); Divertimento, for trombone, piano and percussion (1968); *Woodland Impressions* for narrator, chorus and orch. (1969); *Sinfonia concertante* for organ and orch. (1972); String Quartet (1971–72); *Stained Glass Windows* for piano (1972).

Hawes, William, English composer and conductor; b. London, June 21, 1785; d. there, Feb. 18, 1846. As a boy he was a chorister at the Chapel Royal (1793–1801); then violinist at Covent Garden (1802); became Gentleman of the Chapel Royal in 1805; vicar-choral and master of choristers at St. Paul's Cathedral (1812); master of the children of the Chapel Royal (1817); and lay-vicar of Westminster Abbey (1817–20). He was director of English opera at the Lyceum; it was at his suggestion that Weber's *Der Freischütz* was given for the first time in England (July 22, 1824); he contributed some airs of his own composition to this production. Subsequently, he adapted and produced many Italian, French, and German operas for the English stage; he wrote and staged several light operas, among them, *Broken Promises* (1825), *The Quartette, or Interrupted Harmony* (1828), *The Sister of Charity* (1829), etc. Some of his glees were popular. He edited the publication (in score) of the *Triumphes of Oriana* (1818), various collections of glees, etc.

Hawkins, Coleman (nicknamed **Bean** and **Hawk**), black American jazz tenor saxophonist; b. St. Joseph, Mo., Nov. 21, 1904; d. New York, May 19, 1969. He joined the Kansas City "Jazz Hounds" in 1921; from 1923–34 was a member of Fletcher Henderson's band in New York; his full tone and heavy vibrato became the standard for tenor saxophone, and he was considered the foremost performer on the instrument. In 1934–39 he worked in Europe; upon his return to the U.S. in 1939 he made his most influential recording, *Body and Soul;* departing from the usual paraphrase approach of swing improvisation, his extemporized solo became an inspiration to the new generation of jazz musicians and paved the way for bebop of the 1940s.

Hawkins, John, Canadian composer and pianist; b. Montreal, July 26, 1944. He studied piano at the Montreal Cons. (premier prix, 1967); composition with Anhalt at McGill Univ.; then attended a course in modern music given by Boulez in Basel, Switzerland (1969). Returning to Canada in 1970, he taught music theory at the Univ. of Toronto.
WORKS: *8 Movements* for flute and clarinet (1966); *3 Cavatinas* for soprano, violin, cello, vibraphone and celesta (1967); *Sequences for 2 Groups* for 18 instruments (1968); *Remembrances* for piano, harp, horn, trumpet and trombone (1968); Variations for Orch. (1969–70; Montreal, June 4, 1975); *Waves* for soprano and piano (1971); *Etudes* for 2 pianos (1974).

Hawkins, Sir John, eminent English music historian; b. London, March 30, 1719; d. there, May 21, 1789. He studied law while serving as a clerk, and soon was able to act as an attorney. An ardent devotee of music, he entered the musical society of the time and was on friendly terms with Handel; he also participated in literary clubs, and knew Samuel Johnson, Goldsmith, and others. A wealthy marriage (1753) enabled him to devote his leisure to literature and music. In the meantime, he progressed on the ladder of success in the legal profession. In 1761, he became a magistrate; in 1763, chairman of the Quarter Sessions; he was knighted in 1772. His first publication dealing with music was brought out anonymously: *An Account of the Institution and Progress of the Academy of Ancient Music* (1770). The culmination of 16 years of labor was his monumental *General History of the Science and Practice of Music,* publ. in 1776 in 5 vols., 4to, containing 58 portraits of musicians; it was reprinted in 1853 (2 vols.) and 1875 (3 vols.) by Novello, 8vo.; the 1875 edition was reprinted again, with posthumous notes by Hawkins, in 2 vols., edited by O. Wessely, in Graz, 1969. The first volume of Burney's *General History of Music* appeared at the same time as the 5 vols. of Hawkins; thus, Hawkins undoubtedly held priority for the first general history of music publ. in England; however, its reception was rather hostile; Burney himself derided Hawkins in an unpublished poem. Yet the Hawkins work contained reliable information, particularly dealing with musical life in London in the 18th century. Hawkins died of a paralytic stroke and was buried in Westminster Abbey.
BIBLIOGRAPHY: R. Stevenson, "'The Rivals'—Hawkins, Burney, and Boswell," *Musical Quarterly* (Jan. 1950); Percy A. Scholes, *Sir John Hawkins: Musician, Magistrate, and Friend of Johnson* (London, 1953; a definitive biography).

Hawley, Charles Beach, American organist; b. Brookfield, Mass., Feb. 14, 1858; d. Red Bank, N.J., Dec. 29, 1915. He studied organ at the Cheshire Military Academy; took composition lessons in New York with Dudley Buck; then served as organist in various churches; publ. some songs, showing a facile melodic invention.

Hay, Edward Norman, Irish composer and organist; b. Faversham, April 19, 1889; d. Belfast, Sept. 10, 1943. He studied organ with Koeller and Eaglefield-Hull; was organist of various churches in Ireland. He won the Feis Ceoil Prize in 1916 with his Cello Sonata on Irish folk tunes, the Cobbett Prize (1917) with his *Folksong Phantasy* for string quartet, and the Carnegie Award (1918) with his String Quartet in A. He also wrote the orchestral compositions *The Gilly of Christ, Dunluce* (1921), etc.; organ works and songs.

Hay, Frederick Charles, Swiss composer; b. Basel, Sept. 18, 1888; d. Langau, July 18, 1945. He was a medical student; then studied with Huber in Basel, and Widor in Paris and F. Schalk in Vienna; conducted the Univ. of Bern orch. (1912) and oratorio concerts in Geneva (1920–25); taught musicology at the Univ. of Geneva. He wrote the orchestral works *Heaven and Earth, Der Dom;* concertos for oboe, violin, piano, and viola; *Notturno, Intermezzo e Capriccio,* for piano and woodwind orch.; choral works; hymns, and piano pieces.

Hayasaka, Fumio, Japanese composer; b. Sendai-City, Aug. 19, 1914. He studied in Tokyo with Alexander Tcherepnin; won the Weingartner Prize (1938). He has been particularly successful in writing for Japanese motion pictures; wrote the score for the film *Rashomon,* the recipient of first prize at the International Festival in Venice (1952). Among his works are Overture in D major (Tokyo, March 17, 1940); Piano Concerto No. 1 (Tokyo, June 22, 1948); *The Ancient Dance* (Tokyo, May 15, 1939); *Yukara,* suite (Tokyo, June 9, 1955); etc.

Haydn, (Franz) Joseph, illustrious Austrian composer; b. Rohrau-on-the-Leitha, Lower Austria, March 31 (baptized April 1), 1732; d. Vienna, May 31, 1809. He was the second son of Matthias Haydn, a wheelwright, the sexton and organist of the village church and a fine tenor singer. His mother, Maria Koller, was a daughter of the market inspector, sang in the village choir, and had been cook in the household of Count Harrach, the lord of the village. Of their 12 children, 2 (Joseph and **Michael**) became musicians. On Sundays and holidays there was music at home, the father accompanying the voices on the harp, which he played by ear. At 5 years of age, Joseph Haydn's musical aptitude was noticed by a paternal cousin, Johann Matthias Frankh, a good musician and choral director at Hainburg. He took the boy home with him and gave him elementary instruction, taught him Latin, singing, the violin, and other instruments. Georg Reutter, musical director at St. Stephen's, Vienna, had his attention drawn to the boy's talent and engaged him as chorister for St. Stephen's, undertaking his further education. Haydn was 8 years of age when he went to Vienna. Besides the daily service, and 2 hours' choir practice, he studied religion, Latin, writing, and arithmetic. He also received instruction in singing, and on the violin and harpsichord, from Finsterbusch and Gegenbauer. Harmony and composition were supposed

to be taught by Reutter, who did not trouble himself about the matter. Still, unaided, Haydn applied himself assiduously to composition; though ridiculed by Reutter, he persisted, and spent a little money, begged from his father for the renewal of his clothing, in the purchase of Fux's *Gradus ad Parnassum* and Mattheson's *Vollkommener Kapellmeister,* the principles of which he labored to master. In 1748 his voice began to break, and he was supplanted by his brother **Michael,** who had joined him in 1745. Reutter made a practical joke which Haydn played on a fellow-student a pretext for punishment and dismissal. Some poor but kindhearted friends gave him shelter; he also obtained a few pupils, and a sympathetic Viennese tradesman lent him 150 florins; he was thus enabled to rent an attic room for himself, together with a rickety harpsichord. Here he could practice uninterruptedly; his chief sources of study were keyboard sonatas by C. P. E. Bach. He also diligently practiced the violin, but was (in his own words) 'no conjuror on any instrument, though able to play a concerto.' In the same house lived Metastasio, the poet, who taught him Italian, and recommended him as musical instructor to a Spanish family, the de Martinez, for their daughter Marianne. Through playing her accompaniments at the house of Porpora, her singing teacher, he became acquainted with that surly old master, and in the performance of various menial services gained his good will sufficiently to receive valuable instruction in composition from him, and a recommendation to the Venetian ambassador for a stipend, which was granted, of 50 francs a month. Haydn went with Porpora to the baths of Mannersdorf and made the acquaintance of Bonno, Wagenseil, Dittersdorf, and Gluck. Thus far he had composed sonatas, trios, and other instrumental music, a Mass and the Singspiel *Der krumme Teufel,* produced in 1752 at the Stadttheater (a satire on the lame Baron Affligio, official director of the court opera, and suppressed after the 3d representation but afterwards given in Prague, Berlin, and other cities). He received 25 ducats for this work, of which the libretto alone has been preserved. One of his sonatas earned the good graces of Countess Thun, who engaged him as harpsichordist and singing master. Haydn also met Baron Karl Josef Fürnberg, for whom he wrote his first string quartets. These two wealthy friends introduced him to Count Ferdinand Maximilian Morzin, who, in 1758, appointed Haydn "Musikdirector" and "Kammercompositeur" at Lukaveč, near Pilsen. In 1759 Prince Paul Anton Esterházy heard one of his symphonies and asked the Count to release Haydn to him. In 1761 Haydn entered his service as 2nd Kapellmeister at the Prince's estate in Eisenstadt, becoming 1st Kapellmeister in 1766. On Nov. 26, 1760, Haydn married Maria Anna, the eldest daughter of an early benefactor, Keller, a wigmaker. He was in love with the second daughter, but she entered a convent, and Haydn was induced to marry the sister. Of an extravagant, vixenish, incompatible temperament, she made their married life miserable. In 1762 the "great" Esterházy, Prince Nikolaus, succeeded his deceased brother, and under his *régime* the status of music and musicians was much improved. For the Prince's new palace at Esterház, besides the daily music, Haydn had to provide two weekly operatic performances and two formal concerts; while in his service, Haydn wrote some 80 symphonies, 43 quartets, numerous divertimenti, clavier works of all descriptions, and nearly all his operas, besides other instrumental and vocal comps. His music became known throughout Europe; in 1766 the official gazette alluded to him as 'our national favorite.' In 1780 he was elected member of the Modena Philharmonic Society; in 1784 Prince Henry of Prussia sent him a gold medal and his portrait; in 1785 he was commissioned to write a 'passione instrumentale,' *The Seven Last Words,* for the Cathedral of Cadiz; in 1787 King Friedrich Wilhelm II gave him a diamond ring; many other distinctions were conferred upon him. During his visits to Vienna, his friendship for Mozart developed. In 1790 Prince Nikolaus died, and his son Anton curtailed the chapel music, retaining Haydn, however, as Kapellmeister, and increasing his stipend of 1,000 florins by an additional 400. He was virtually independent; his time was his own, and he added to his income by the sale of his works. For some time he had received pressing invitations to visit London. He had settled in Vienna, when Salomon appeared with a tempting offer, and induced him to accompany him, although his friends, especially Mozart, tried to dissuade him. In 1791, he arrived in England, and remained there 18 months, fêted by royalty and the nobility. In July, Oxford Univ. conferred on him the honorary degree of Mus. D., and his best orchestral works, the "Salomon symphonies," were written during this and the following visit. In 1792 Haydn returned via Bonn to Frankfurt, for the coronation of Emperor Franz II; went then to Vienna, also visiting his native place to witness the unveiling of a monument created in his honor by Count Harrach, his mother's former employer. In that year, he gave Beethoven the lessons with which the latter was so dissatisfied. In 1794 he revisited London; his former triumphs were repeated, and though pressed by the King to make England his home, he returned to his native land in affluence, at the invitation of a new Prince, to reorganize the Esterházy chapel. But his fame, though great, was not yet at its zenith. In 1797 he composed *Gott erhalte Franz den Kaiser,* which became the Austrian National Anthem; in 1798, he wrote his immortal oratorio *Die Schöpfung (The Creation),* and in 1801, *Die Jahreszeiten (The Seasons).* But his health began to fail, and thenceforward he lived in retirement. Only once did he again appear in public, on March 27, 1808, at a special performance of *The Creation;* but he had to be carried out before the finish, friends and pupils, among whom was Beethoven, surrounding him to take leave. He lingered until 1809, when his end was hastened by the shock of the bombardment of Vienna by the French. He was buried in the Hundsthurm churchyard. As a result of some fantastic events, his skull became separated from his body before his reinterment at Eisenstadt in 1820, and after many peregrinations, was exhibited in the hall of the Society of Friends of Music in Vienna. It was finally reburied in Eisenstadt with the body on June 5, 1954, attended by official ceremony.

Although of unprepossessing personal appearance, stern, dignified in aspect, and laconic in speech, Haydn was of a humorous, agreeable, and amiable temperament. The religious side of his character is shown in the inscriptions of all his scores, with the motto "In Nomine Domini" and all ending with "Laus Deo" or "Soli Deo Gloria."

Haydn was the first great master of the new instrumental style which reached its highest development in the works of Beethoven. Since the publication of instrumental works by his Viennese predecessors, by the composers of the 'Mannheim school,' and by other early symphonists, Haydn can no longer be regarded as the 'Father of the symphony' or the 'Father of the modern orchestra.' But he availed himself of the forms and achievements of his predecessors, and his greater genius soon caused the earlier efforts to fall into undeserved oblivion. That his music accomplished this is the most eloquent tribute to its inherent power and greatness; it is not the mere creation of a new form that counts, but the artistic content. Haydn's position as the first 'great master' of the new instrumental style remains unshaken. His melodic vein is inexhaustible; the gaiety of 'Papa Haydn's' lighter music went straight to the hearts of the impressionable Viennese and lent new vivacity to European concert halls; in his moods of tenderness or of passion he is a worthy forerunner of Beethoven. And to all this must be added the marvelous fertility of his creative resources. The precise extent of Haydn's productivity will probably never be known.

WORKS: Many works are irretrievably lost; others, listed in various catalogues, may have never existed, or were duplications of extant works; some are of doubtful authenticity; several are definitely spurious. Thus, the celebrated *Toy Symphony* appears not to be a work by Haydn, but by Leopold Mozart. The authorship of the so-called Zittau Divertimenti, including the one in B-flat major with the *Chorale St. Antonii,* is also very doubtful. If Haydn was indeed not the author, then the *Variations on a Theme by Haydn* of Brahms, based on the *Chorale St. Antonii,* is a misnamed work. Two piano trios are now definitely known to be the works of Haydn's pupil Ignaz Pleyel, who was capable of imitating his master's style with amazing ingenuity. The generally accepted list of Haydn's authentic symphonies comprises 104 items; but see the monumental work *The Symphonies of Haydn* by H. C. Robbins Landon (1955) for particulars. Many of these symphonies bear descriptive titles, attached to them by publishers (only a few of them were authorized by Haydn himself, e.g., Nos. 6–8: *Le Matin, Le Midi,* and *Le Soir):* the *Abschiedssymphonie (Farewell Symphony;* performed by Haydn at Esterház in 1772 as a humorous and sad leave-taking when Prince Esterházy decided to disband the orchestra; this explanation of the origin of the Farewell Symphony, found in *Anedotti piacevoli ed interessanti* by G. G. Ferrari, 1830, is more plausible than the generally accepted one that the performance of the work was a hint that the orchestra needed a vacation); *La Chasse (The Hunt,* 1781); *L'Ours (The Bear,* 1786); *La Poule (The Hen,* 1786); *Oxford* (performed at Oxford in 1791, when Haydn was given an honorary degree); *Paukenschlag (Drumstroke,* 1791; known as *Surprise Symphony); Military Symphony* (1794); *Die Uhr (The Clock,* 1794); *Paukenwirbel (Drumroll,* 1795). The last of the 12 Salomon Symphonies (written for the London impresario Salomon) is known as the *London Symphony*; 6 symphonies written for performances in Paris are known as *Paris Symphonies*. Similarly distinctive titles are attached to some of Haydn's 82 string quartets: *Russian Quartets* (1781; known in Italian as *Gli scherzi*; the 2nd of the set, *The Joke*; 3d, *The Bird*; 5th, *How Do You Do?*); *Prussian Quartets* (1787; 5th of the set, *The Dream*; 6th, *The Frog*, or *The House on Fire*, or *The Row in Vienna*); *Razor Quartet* (1788; No. 2 of the set written for the Vienna merchant Johann Tost; *Lerchenquartett* (*Lark Quartet*; 1790; 5th of the Tost Quartets; also known as *Hornpipe Quartet*); *Quintenquartett* (*Quartet of the Fifths*, 1796–97; also known as *The Bell* or *The Donkey*; the minuet called *Hexenminuett*); *Kaiserquartett* (*Emperor Quartet*, 1796–97; contains variations on Haydn's hymn *Gott erhalte Franz den Kaiser*); *The Sunrise* (1796–97). Other instrumental works include about 15 piano concertos; 3 violin concertos; 2 cello concertos (the most celebrated one, in D major, has been ascribed, erroneously, to Anton Kraft); 2 horn concertos; trumpet concerto; flute concerto; 5 concertos for 2 liras with instruments; 8 *Notturni* for the King of Naples (1790); a *symphonie concertante* for oboe, violin, bassoon, cello, and orch. (1792); about 40 divertimenti; numerous string trios, and some 35 piano trios; 6 duets for violin and viola; a violin sonata; a great number of works for baryton, written for Prince Esterházy, who was a baryton player: 125 divertimenti for baryton with viola and cello, 6 duets for barytons, 6 sonatas for baryton and cello, 12 cassations for baryton with other instruments, 3 baryton concertos; about 60 piano sonatas (of which 8 are lost); various pieces for piano solo; 32 miscellaneous arrangements written for mechanical clocks.

VOCAL WORKS: Operas and Singspiele: *Der krumme Teufel* (1752) and *Der neue krumme Teufel* (1758); 4 Italian comedies, *La Marchesa Nespola*, *La vedova*, *Il dottore*, and *Il Sganarello* (all in 1762); *Acide*, opera seria (Eisenstadt, Jan. 11, 1763); *La cantarina*, opera buffa (Esterház, 1767); *Lo speziale*, opera buffa (Esterház, 1768); *Le pescatrici*, opera buffa (Esterház, Sept. 16, 1770); *L'infedeltà delusa*, burletta (Esterház, July 26, 1773); *L'incontro improviso* (Esterház, Aug. 29, 1775); *Il mondo della luna* (Esterház, Aug. 3, 1777); *La vera costanza* (Esterház, 1779); *L'isola disabitata* (Esterház, Dec. 6, 1779); *La fedeltà premiata* (Esterház, Oct. 15, 1780); *Orlando Paladino* (Esterház, 1782); *Armida* (Esterház, Feb. 26, 1784); *Orfeo ed Euridice* (originally entitled *L'anima del filosofo*; 1791; revised form, 1805); incidental music to various plays; several marionette operas. Oratorios: *Il ritorno di Tobia* (Vienna, April 2, 1775), *The Creation* (Haydn's most famous choral work; written to an English text by Lidley; translated into German and first performed, April 29, 1798 at the Schwarzenberg Palace in Vienna), and *The Seasons* (German text by Gottfried van Swieten after James Thomson; Vienna, April 24, 1801); several cantatas, numerous arias, etc.; *The Seven Last Words* (*Die Sieben Worte des Erlösers am Kreuze*; 1785; originally written for the Cadiz Cathedral as a suite of 7 instrumental sonatas with a concluding movement *Il terremoto*; then a series of accompanied recitatives were added; also arranged by Haydn in 1796 for solo voices, chorus, and orch.);

14 Masses (only 13 extant; one of them, *Missa Rorate coeli desuper*, in G major, long regarded as lost, was discovered by H. C. Robbins Landon in 1957); 2 Te Deums; a Stabat Mater; offertories; about 45 songs with piano accompaniment; 2 vocal duets, 4 vocal trios, and 9 vocal quartets with piano accompaniment; about 50 canons and rounds for 3–8 voices; arrangements of 150 songs of Scotland, publ. by Napier as *Selections of Original Scots Songs in Three Parts*, *the Harmony by Haydn*; arrangements of Scotch, Irish, and Welsh melodies in Thomson's *Select Melodies of Scotland, Ireland and Wales*; the hymn *Gott erhalte Franz den Kaiser*, which was the Austrian national anthem (until 1918).

REPRINTS AND INDEXES: A monumental edition of Haydn's works in about 80 volumes, prepared by G. Adler, H. Kretzschmar, E. Mandyczewski, M. Seiffert, and others, was begun in 1907 by Breitkopf & Härtel, but was interrupted twice by the two world wars; 4 vols. of symphonies (3 edited by E. Mandyczewski, the 4th by H. Schultz), 3 vols. of piano sonatas (ed. by Päsler); the oratorios *Die Schöpfung* and *Die Jahreszeiten* (Mandyczewski), and songs (Friedlaender) have appeared; an attempt to continue the publication was made by the Haydn Society of Boston in 1950, but it, too, failed. The Haydn Institute of Cologne (editors: J. P. Larsen and G. Feder) began a new complete edition in 1958, and as of 1977 have issued 50 vols. H. C. Robbins Landon edited all of the symphonies in a separate series, issued in miniature score between 1963–68. A comprehensive list of Haydn's works is found in J. P. Larsen's *Drei H. Kataloge in Faksimile* (Copenhagen, 1941); a descriptive catalogue of Haydn's symphonies, with exhaustive commentaries on their authenticity, chronology, and availability, is in H. C. Robbins Landon's *The Symphonies of H.* (London, 1955); see also his article "H. and Authenticity," in *Music Review* (May 1955). A complete thematic catalogue is Anthony Hoboken's *Thematisch-Bibliographisches Werkverzeichnis* (2 vols.; Mainz, 1957, 1971).

BIBLIOGRAPHY: BIOGRAPHY: Simon Mayr, *Brevi notizie istoriche della vita e delle opere di H.* (Bergamo, 1809); G. A. Griesinger, *Biographische Notizen über H.* (Leipzig, 1810); A. K. Dies, *Biographische Nachrichten über H.* (Vienna, 1810); G. Carpani, *Le Haydine* (Milan, 1812; 2nd augmented ed., Padua, 1823); Th. von Karajan, *H. in London* (Vienna, 1861); K. F. Pohl, *H.* (incomplete; 2 vols. relate the biography until 1790; Leipzig, 1875, 1882. A third vol., completing the biography, was publ. by Hugo Botstiber, 1927); A. Reissmann, *H.* (Berlin, 1879); L. Schmidt, *H.* (Berlin, 1898; new ed., 1914); La Mara, *H.*, in vol. IV of *Musikalische Charakterköpfe* (Leipzig, 1900; separate reprint, 1912); J. C. Hadden, *H.* (London, 1902; new ed., 1934); J. F. Runciman, *H.* (London, 1908); M. Brenet, *H.* (Paris, 1909; English trans., Oxford, 1926); A. Schnerich, *H. und seine Sendung* (Vienna, 1922); G. G. A. Fox, *H.* (London, 1929); Karl Geiringer, *H.* (Potsdam, 1932); K. Kobald, *H.* (Vienna, 1932); R. Tenschert, *H.* (Berlin, 1932); F. Amoroso, *H.* (Turin, 1933); E. F. Schmid, *H., Vorfahren und Heimat des Meisters* (Kassel, 1934); R. Tenschert, *H.: sein Leben in Bildern* (Leipzig, 1935); Karl Geiringer, *H., A Creative Life in Music* (N.Y., 1946); L. Nowak, *H.: Leben, Bedeutung und Werk* (Vienna, 1951); R. Sondheimer, *H., A Historical and Psychological Study Based on His Quartets* (London, 1951); Hans Rutz, *H.* (Munich, 1953); L. Nowak, *J. H.: Leben, Bedeutung, und Werk* (Zürich, 1959); H. Seeger, *J. H.* (Leipzig, 1961); Anthony Hoboken, *Discrepancies in H. Biographies* (Washington, D.C., 1962); G. A. Greisinger, *J. H.* (Madison, Wisconsin, 1963); H. C. Robbins Landon, *Das kleine Haydnbuch* (Salzburg, 1967); H. C. Robbins Landon, *Haydn in England 1791-1795* (vol. 3 of *Haydn: Chronicle and Works*, Bloomington, Ind., 1976).

CRITICISM, ANALYSIS, APPRECIATION: K. F. Pohl, *Mozart und H. in London* (Vienna, 1867); K. von Wurzbach, *H. und sein Bruder Michael* (Vienna, 1862); L. Wendschuh, *Über Haydns Opern* (Rostock, 1896); W. H. Hadow, *A Croatian Composer; Notes toward the Study of H.* (London, 1897; controversial; an attempt to prove Haydn's Slavic origin); H. E. Krehbiel, *Music and Manners in the Classical Period* (N.Y., 1898; contains Haydn's notes on his London visit); J. Hartog, *H., sijn broeder Michael en hunne werke* (Amsterdam, 1905); M. Puttmann, *H. als Vokalkomponist* (Langensalza, 1909); A. Schnerich, *Messe und Requiem seit H. und Mozart* (Vienna, 1909); H. Von Hase, *H. und Breitkopf & Härtel* (Leipzig, 1909); J. E. Engl, *Haydns handschriftliches Tagebuch aus der Zeit seines zweiten Aufenthalts in London* (Leipzig, 1909); F. Artaria and Hugo Botstiber, *H. und das Verlagshaus Artaria* (Vienna, 1909); A. Sandberger, *Zur Geschichte des H.schen Streichquartetts* (Munich, 1921); A. Sandberger, *Zur Entwicklungsgeschichte von Haydns Sieben Worte* (Munich, 1921); F. Blume, "Haydns Persönlichkeit in seinen Streichquartetten," *Jahrbuch der Musikbibliothek Peters* (1931); Ludwig Koch, *H. Bibliography of the Budapest City Library* (in German and Hungarian; Budapest, 1932); A. Hindenberger, *Die Motivik in H. Streichquartetten* (Turbenthal, 1935); Haydn issue of the *Musical Quarterly* (April 1932; contains articles by G. Adler, H. Botstiber, O. Strunk, G. de Saint-Foix, M. M. Scott, P. H. Lang, J. Muller, Karl Geiringer, and M. D. Herter Norton); Haydn issue of the *Zeitschrift für Musik* (April 1932); C. S. Smith, "Haydn's Chamber Music and the Flute," *Musical Quarterly* (July and Oct. 1933); A. Sandberger, "Neue Haydniana," *Jahrbuch der Musikbibliothek Peters* (1933); O. Strunk, "Notes on a Haydn Autograph," *Musical Quarterly* (April 1934; contains a chronological list of Haydn's late piano works); J. P. Larsen, "H. und das 'kleine Quartbuch,'" *Acta Musicologica* (1935; reply by A. Sandberger in the *Zeitschrift für Musik*, 1935); J. Frölich, *H., neu herausgegeben und eingeleitet von Adolf Sandberger* (Regensburg, 1936); J. P. Larsen, *Die H.-Überlieferung* (Copenhagen, 1939); D. Barth and M. Somfai, *H. als Opernkapellmeister* (Mainz, 1960); Alan Tyson and H. C. Robbins Landon, "Who Wrote H.'s Op. 3?" *Musical Times* (July 1964); Reginald Barrett-Ayres, *J. H. and the String Quartet* (London & N.Y., 1974); W. Koller, *Aus der Werkstatt der Wiener Klassiker: Bearbeitung Haydns* (Tutzing, 1975); B. Wackernagel, *J. H. frühe Klaviersonaten* (Tutzing, 1975); A. Hodgson, *The Music of J. H. The Symphonies* (Cranbury, N.J., 1977).

CORRESPONDENCE: W. Sandys and S. A. Forster, *History of the Violin* (contains Haydn's correspondence with W. Forster; London, 1864); Lady Wallace, *Letters of Distinguished Musicians* (London, 1867); J. C. Hadden, *G. Thomson, His Life and Correspondence* (London, 1898); H. C. R. Landon, *The Collected Correspondence and London Notebooks of J. H.* (London, 1959); D. Bartha, *J. H.: Gesammelte Briefe und Aufzeichungen* (Kassel, 1965).

BIBLIOGRAPHIES: A. Peter Brown, Carol V. Brown, & James T. Berkenstock, "Joseph Haydn in Literature: A Bibliography," *Haydn-Studien* (July 1974, Bd. III, Heft 3/4, pp. 173-352; an alphabetical list, chiefly by author, of 2285 books, monographs, periodical and *Festschrift* articles, and some unpublished dissertations, with full bibliographical information and indexes by names, topics, and works); A. Peter Brown & Carol V. Brown, "Joseph Haydn in Literature: A Survey," *Notes* (March 1975).

Special publications devoted to Haydn are the *Haydn Yearbook*, ed. by H. C. R. Landon (1962–); *Haydn-Studien* (Joseph Haydn Institute, Cologne, 1965–); and the *Haydn-Mozart Newsletter* (Haydn-Mozart Society, London).

Haydn, (Johann) Michael, Austrian composer, brother of **Franz Joseph Haydn**; b. Rohrau, Sept. 14, 1737; d. Salzburg, Aug. 10, 1806. He served as boy soprano at St. Stephen's Cathedral in Vienna (1745-55); his voice was remarkable for its wide range, reaching 3 octaves. He replaced his brother in solo parts, when a younger voice was required. He studied composition mainly by reading books on counterpoint, particularly *Gradus ad Parnassum* by Fux. In 1757 he became chapelmaster at Grosswardein; in 1762, musical director to Archbishop Sigismund at Salzburg. In 1768 he married the daughter of the organist Lipp, Maria Magdalena, an excellent soprano singer, who was praised by Mozart. The French occupation of Salzburg in 1800 deprived him of his property, but he was aided by his brother. His fortunes were mended somewhat by the handsomely rewarded commission of a Mass (the so-called *Theresienmesse*) which he received from the Empress Teresia, wife of the Emperor Francis II, and which was performed at Luxenburg Palace on Oct. 4, 1801. He opened a school of composition, and educated many distinguished pupils, including Reicha and Carl Maria von Weber. In 1833, Martin Bischofsreiter, a Benedictine monk, published *Partitur-Fundamente*, a collection of thoroughbass exercises written by Michael Haydn for his scholars. He composed a Mass and vespers for Prince Esterházy, who twice offered to make him assistant chapel master; but Haydn declined, hoping that the Salzburg chapel would be reorganized. A prolific composer, his best works were his sacred compositions, which his brother held in high esteem. Although he had advantageous offers for publication from Breitkopf & Härtel, he was reluctant to accept, so that most of his music remained in MS at the time of his death. He left some 400 sacred works, including oratorios, cantatas, Requiems, Masses, graduals, offertories, etc.; also several operas: 2 collections of 4-part songs; some 60 symphonies; serenades, marches, minuets; concertos for flute, violin, and harpsichord, and a double concerto for viola, organ, and strings; string quartets and quintets; also a sextet. A selection of his Masses and other church works was edited by A. M. Klafsky in the *Denkmäler der Tonkunst in Österreich*, vols. 45 and 62 (formerly 22 and 32.i); a selection of his instrumental works, edited and partly reorchestrated by L. H. Perger, in vol. 29 (formerly 14.ii), including a symph. in E-flat (1783), a symph. in C major (1788), a Turkish March, etc.; additional recent publications are in *Accademia Musicale* (Mainz), vols. 7, 8, 9; *Musica Rinata* (Budapest), vols. 3, 4, 7; and by the Haydn-Mozart Press in Salzburg.

BIBLIOGRAPHY: F. J. Schinn and G. Otter. *Biographische Skizze von J. M. Haydn* (Salzburg, 1808); C. Wurzbach, *Joseph Haydn und sein Bruder Michael* (Vienna, 1862); J. E. Engl, *Zum Gedenken J. M. Haydns* (Salzburg, 1906); O. Schmid, *J. M. Haydn: Sein Leben und Wirken* (Vienna, 1906); K. M. Klob, *Drei musikalische Biedermänner* (Ulm, 1911); F. Martin, *Kleine Beiträge zur Musikgeschichte Salzburgs* (Salzburg, 1913); A. M. Klafsky, "Michael Haydn als Kirchenkomponist," in Adler's *Studien zur Musikwissenschaft* (1915); G. de Saint-Foix, "Histoire de deux trios de Michael Haydn," *Revue de Musicologie* 38; H. Jancik, *Michael Haydn, ein vergessener Meister* (Zürich, 1952); H. C. Robbins Landon, "An Introduction to Michael Haydn," in *Essays on the Viennese Classical Style* (N.Y., 1970).

Haydon, Glen, eminent American musicologist; b. Inman, Kansas, Dec. 9, 1896; d. Chapel Hill, North Carolina, May 8, 1966. He studied at the Univ. of California, Berkeley (B.A., 1918; M.A., 1921); he then went to Paris where he studied clarinet playing and composition; then enrolled at the Univ. of Vienna where he obtained his Ph.D. in 1932. Returning to America, he became head of the Dept. of Music at the Univ. of North Carolina at Chapel Hill, and held this post until his death. A Festschrift in his honor, planned for his 70th birthday, was publ. posthumously in Chapel Hill (1969) under the title *Studies in Musicology. Essays in the History, Style and Bibliography of Music in Memory of Glen Haydon*, edited by J. W. Pruett. Among Haydon's theoretical publications are the valuable books, *The Evolution of the Six-Four Chord* (Berkeley, Calif., 1933), and *Introduction to Musicology* (N.Y., 1941; reprinted in 1959); he also publ. a *Graded Course of Clarinet Playing* (N.Y., 1927), and translated into English Jeppesen's *Counterpoint: The Polyphonic Vocal Style of the 16th Century* (N.Y., 1939). Haydon wrote a ballet *The Druids Weed* (1929) and several pieces of sacred choral music.

Hayes, Gerald Ravenscourt, English writer; b. London, April 18, 1889; d. there, Sept. 13, 1955. He entered the Hydrographic Dept. of the Admiralty in 1911; became chief cartographer in 1934; then transferred to Secretary's Dept. (1946–53). Apart from his writings on cartography, he became interested in musical instruments; was one of the founders of the Dolmetsch Foundation; publ. *The Treatment of Instrumental Music* (1928); *The Viols and Other Bowed Instruments* (1930); *King's Musick*, an anthology (1937); numerous articles on instruments in various publications.

Hayes, Philip, English organist and composer, son of **William Hayes**; b. Oxford, April, (baptized April 17), 1738; d. London, March 19, 1797. He studied mainly with his father; Mus. B., Oxford (May 18, 1763); became Gentleman of the Chapel Royal in 1767; organist of New College, Oxford (1776); succeeded his father as organist of Magdalen College and prof. of music in the Univ. (1777); also received his Mus. D. the same year; organist of St. John's College (1790).

WORKS: oratorio *Prophecy* (Oxford, 1781); a masque, *Telemachus*; odes, anthems, services, psalms, glees; 6 concertos for organ, harpsichord, or piano (1769); also some numbers in Dibdin's *The Two Misers* and Dr. Arnold's *Two to One*. He edited *Harmonia Wiccamica* (London, 1780).

Hayes, Roland, distinguished Negro tenor; b. Curryville, Georgia, June 3, 1887; d. Boston, Jan. 1, 1977. His parents were former slaves. He studied singing with A. Calhoun in Chattanooga, Tennessee and later at Fisk Univ. in Nashville; subsequently continued vocal studies in Boston and in Europe. He made his concert debut in Boston on Nov. 15, 1917 in a program of German lieder and arias by Mozart; he then made a successful tour in the U.S. In 1920 he went to London, where he studied the German repertory with Sir George Henschel. A grand European tour followed, with appearances in Paris, Vienna, Leipzig, Munich, Amsterdam, Madrid and Copenhagen. In 1924 he gave more than 80 concerts in the U.S., obtaining a veritable triumph for his interpretation of lyrical German and French songs, and most particularly for his poignant rendition of Negro spirituals. In 1925 he was awarded the Spingarn Medal for "most outstanding achievement among colored people" and in 1939 he received the honorary degree of Mus. D. from Wesleyan Univ., Delaware, Ohio. He publ. expert arrangements of 30 Negro spirituals, *My Songs* (N.Y., 1948).

BIBLIOGRAPHY: Mackinley Helm, *Angel Mo' and Her Son, Roland Hayes* (N.Y., 1942); F. W. Woolsey, "Conversation with Roland Hayes," and W. Marr, II, "Roland Hayes," both in *Black Perspectives in Music* (Fall 1977).

Hayes, William, English organist and composer; b. Gloucester, Dec., 1707 (baptized on Jan. 26, 1708); d. Oxford, July 27, 1777. He was a chorister at Gloucester cathedral; organist of St. Mary's, Shrewsbury (1729–31); then of Worcester cathedral (1731–34). In 1734 he became organist of Magdalen College, Oxford; Mus. Bac. (Oxford, 1735); Univ. prof. of music (1742); Mus. D. (1749). He conducted the Gloucester music festival in 1757, 1760, and 1763.

WORKS: His canons *Allelujah* and *Miserere nobis*, and his glee *Melting airs soft joys inspire* won prizes offered by the Catch Club in 1763; also, a masque, *Circe*; psalms, odes, glees, canons, ballads, and cantatas. He also wrote *Remarks on Mr. Avison's Essay on Musical Expression* (1762); *Anecdotes of the Five Music-Meetings* (1768); and was co-editor of Boyce's *Cathedral Music*.

Hayman, Richard, American composer of the extreme avant-garde; b. Sandia, New Mexico, July 29, 1951. He studied humanities and philosophy at Columbia Univ.; attended classes of Vladimir Ussachevsky in electronic music; also studied flute with Eleanor Laurence at the Manhattan School of Music and had sessions on Indian vocal music with Ravi Shankar; consulted with Philip Corner and John Cage on the problems of ultra-modern music; attended conducting seminars of Pierre Boulez at the Juilliard School of Music. He eked out a meager living by intermittent employment as construction worker, gardener, operating room assistant in a hospital and church pipe organ renovator; earned occasional few dollars as a subject in sleep laboratory experiments; as a last resort, boldly peddled earplugs in New York subways. He arranged exhibitions of his graffiti at the Univ. of Buffalo, organized assemblages of objects and sounds at the Avant-Garde Festival at Shea Stadium, N.Y., wrote provocatively titled articles. In 1975 he was appointed an editor of *Ear* magazine. Perhaps his most mind-boggling musical work is *Dali,* composed at the command of Salvador Dali, scored for large orchestra, and notated on a toothpick, with instructions "ascend chromatically in slow pulse." It was "performed" on March 23, 1974. Another work is *it is not here,* a light-and-sound piece, realized in Morse code at the Museum of Modern Art, N.Y., on June 14, 1974. Other pieces are *heartwhistle,* with the audience beating their collective pulses and whistling continuous tones (Aug. 3, 1975); *sleep whistle,* with the composer whistling while asleep in a store window during a paid sleep exhibition (Dec. 7, 1975); *roll,* with the composer rolling, lying down, in the street, covered with bells as a token of Hindu devotion (April 9, 1975); *dreamsound,* a sleep event in which the composer makes various sounds for the benefit of slumbering participants (Berkeley, California, Feb. 20, 1976); *home* for a telephone; *Boo Boo* for piano; *Buff Her Blind* for musical toys and electronic instruments; *spirits* for transduced piano.

Haynes, John C., American music publisher; b. Brighton, Mass., Sept. 9, 1829; d. Boston, May 3, 1907. He entered the employ of Oliver Ditson in 1845; was given an interest in the business in 1851, and on Jan. 1, 1857, became a co-partner, the firm name being changed to O. Ditson & Co. In 1889, after the death of O. Ditson, Haynes became president on the firm's incorporation. See the magazine *Musician* (June 1907).

Haynes, Walter Battison, English organist and composer; b. Kempsey, near Worcester, Nov. 21, 1859; d. London, Feb. 4, 1900. He studied first with his uncle, an organist, then with F. Taylor and E. Prout; also studied at the Leipzig Cons., with C. Reinecke and S. Jadassohn, where he won the Mozart scholarship. In 1884 he was appointed organist at St. Philip's Church, Sydenham; from 1890, also taught at the Royal Academy of Music.
WORKS: Symphony; Concert Overture; *Idyll* for violin and orch.; Piano Trio; organ pieces; 2 cantatas for women's voices, *Fairies' Isle* and *A Sea Dream.*

Hays, Doris, American pianist and composer of the avant-garde; b. Memphis, Tennessee, Aug. 6, 1941. She attended the Cadek Cons. of Chattanooga and studied with Richard Hervig at the Univ. of Iowa and later with Paul Badura-Skoda at the Univ. of Wisconsin; then travelled to Europe, where she took courses at the Hochschule für Musik in Munich. In 1971 she won first prize at the International Competition for Interpreters of New Music in Rotterdam. Returning to the U.S., she took lessons in advanced piano playing with Hilde Somer in N.Y.; gave numerous piano recitals in programs of ultra-modern music, taught music at Queens College, N.Y. and at the Univ. of Wisconsin; made records of piano works by contemporary American and European composers. In her own compositions she endeavors to unite auditory, visual and tactile elements; several of her works employ rhythmic patterns of lights and motorized sculptures designed by herself and programmed through computers. Typical of these multi-media works is *SensEvents* (1971-77), scored for a group of instruments instructed to play simultaneously but non-synchronously, of an indeterminate duration, with beams of colored light directed at individual musicians to indicate clues. Other works are: *Scheveningen Beach* (1973) for piccolo, several ordinary flutes and alto flute; *Duet for Pianist and Audience* (1971); *Chartres Red* (1972) for piano; *Pieces From Last Year* (1974) for 16 instruments playing non-synchronously; *Breathless* (1975) for bass flute, and numerous pieces for modernistic children.

Hays, William Shakespeare, American song composer; b. Louisville, Ky., July 19, 1837; d. there, July 22, 1907. He wrote his first song at 16 years of age; published nearly 300, having enormous sales, totaling several million. The most widely known were *Evangeline, My Southern Sunny Home, Write Me a Letter from Home, Driven from Home,* and *Mollie Darling.*

Hayton, Leonard George (Lennie), American jazz pianist, arranger and conductor; b. New York, Feb. 13, 1908; d. Palm Springs, Calif., April 24, 1971. He played piano in various jazz groups in New York; then went to California, where he was music director for Metro-Goldwyn-Mayer and for the 20th Century-Fox Film Corporation. He composed several semi-classic instrumental numbers and orchestrated scores for films. He married the black singer **Lena Horne** in 1948, and was acting as song arranger for her.

Haywood, Charles, American musicologist, b. Grodno, Russia, Jan. 2, 1905. He came to the U.S. in 1916; studied singing at the Institute of Musical Art in New York and at the Juilliard School of Music; completed his musical education at Columbia Univ. (M.A., 1940; Ph.D., 1949). His first profession was that of an opera singer; he was a member of the Chautauqua Opera Co. and Philadelphia Opera Co., and taught singing at the Juilliard School. In 1939 he joined the faculty at Queens College, N.Y. as lecturer on opera, folk music and American music. He published a valuable compendium, *A Bibliography of North American Folklore and Folksong* (N.Y., 1951; new enlarged edition, N.Y., 1961); edited *Art Songs of Soviet Russia* (N.Y., 1947); brought out *A Treasury of World Folksongs* (N.Y., 1965) and contributed numerous articles dealing with folk music of various nations.

715

Head, Michael, English singer, pianist and composer; b. Eastbourne, Jan. 28, 1900; d. Cape Town, South Africa, Aug. 24, 1976. He studied with Frederick Corder at the Royal Academy of Music in London, and in 1927 joined its faculty as piano instructor. In 1947 he made a grand tour through Asia, Canada, and Australia, performing both as singer and pianist. He published several collections of English songs; also wrote 2 children's operas, *The Bachelor Mouse* (1954) and *Key Money* (1966); Trio for Oboe, Bassoon and Piano (1966); Suite for Recorders (1968); a cantata, *Daphne and Apollo* (1964).

Headington, Christopher, English composer and pianist; b. London, April 28, 1930. He studied piano and composition at the Royal Academy of Music, London; also took private lessons with Benjamin Britten. He published the *Bodley Head History of Western Music* (London, 1974).
WORKS: Variations for Piano and Orch. (1950); Cello Sonata (1950); *Introduction and Allegro* for chamber orch. (1951); String Quartet (1953); Piano Sonata (1956); *Chanson de l'éternelle tristesse,* ballet (1957); Violin Concerto (1959); Sonatina for Oboe and Piano (1960); Sonatina for Unaccompanied Flute (1960); Toccata for Piano (1962); *Towards a Pindaric Ode* for soprano, mezzo-soprano and piano (1965).

Healey, Derek, English-born Canadian composer; b. Wargrave, May 2, 1936. He studied music theory (with Howells), flute, organ and piano at the Royal College of Music in London; then went to Italy; took courses in composition with Petrassi and conducting with Celibadache at the Accademia Chigiana in Siena (summers of 1961–63 and 1966) and composition with Porena in Rome (1962–66); then settled in Canada; taught at the Univ. of Victoria, B.C. (1969–71) and Univ. of Toronto (1971–72); in 1972 was appointed to the faculty of the Univ. of Guelph, College of Arts. His style of composition was influenced at first by Britten and Hindemith; later he began to experiment with large and discordant blocks of sonorities.
WORKS: the opera *Seabird Island* (Guelph, May 7, 1977); a children's opera, *Mr. Punch* (1969); 2 ballets: *Il Carcerato* (1965) and *The Three Thieves* (1967); *The Willow Pattern Plate* for orch. (1957); Concerto for Organ, Strings and Timpani (1960); *Ruba'i* for orch. (1968); *Butterflies* for mezzo-soprano and small orch. (Victoria, July 20, 1970); *Arctic Images* for orch. (Vancouver, Sept. 21, 1971); *Noh,* triple concerto for flute, piano, synthesizer and orch. (1974); *Primrose in Paradise,* fantasy on a shape-note hymn, for chamber orch. (1975; last movement of a projected symph.); *Tribulation* for orch. (1977; first movement of a projected symph.); String Quartet (1961); Cello Sonata (1961); *Partita bizzara* for oboe and piano (1962); *Divisions* for brass quintet (1963); *Mobile* for flute, vibraphone, celesta, harp, 2 percussionists and cello (1963); *6 Epigrams* for violin and piano (1963); *Movement* for flute, oboe, clarinet and string trio (1965); *Laudes* for flute, horn, percussion, harp, 2 violins and cello (1966); *Maschere* for violin and piano (1967); *Stinging* for alto recorder; cello, harpsichord and tape (1971). For piano: *October's Dream* (1957), *Partita Moderna* (1959), *12 Preludes* (1960), and *Lieber Robert,* with musical phrases, quoting from Schumann (1974); for organ: *Voluntaries 1–6* (1956–62), Sonata (1961), *Variants* (1964) and *The Lost Traveler's Dream* (1970); songs.

Heap, Charles Swinnerton, English pianist and choral conductor, b. Birmingham; April 10, 1847; d. there, June 11, 1900. He studied at the Leipzig Cons.; returning to England, took courses at Cambridge; obtained his degree of Mus. D. in 1872. He was then engaged in conducting choral societies in Birmingham; also led the Birmingham Philharmonic. He wrote several cantatas and orchestral overtures and a number of works of chamber music, as well as organ pieces and songs.

Heartz, Daniel, American musicologist, born Exeter, New Hampshire, Oct. 5, 1928. He studied at the Univ. of New Hampshire in Durham (A.B., 1950) and at Harvard University (A.M., 1951; Ph.D., 1957). In 1957–60 he was on the faculty of the Univ. of Chicago; in 1960 he was appointed to the music faculty of the Univ. of California, Berkeley. He published a valuable monograph, *Pierre Attaingnant, Royal Printer of Music* (Berkeley, Calif., 1969) and edited *Preludes, Chansons, and Dances for Lute, Published by P. Attaingnant, Paris* (1964); also contributed numerous articles dealing with music of the Renaissance to various music journals.

Hebenstreit, Pantaleon, German musician; b. Eisleben, 1667; d. Dresden, Nov. 15, 1750. In his early years, he was engaged variously as a violinist and a dancing master in Leipzig, but fled from his creditors to Merseburg, where the idea of improving the dulcimer was suggested to him, and he invented the instrument with which he made long and brilliant concert tours, and which Louis XIV named the "Pantaleon," after its originator's Christian name. As a precursor of the piano, it has disappeared in the process of evolution. In 1706, Hebenstreit was appointed Kapellmeister and dancing master to the court at Eisenach; in 1714, "pantaleon chamber musician" at the Dresden court.

Heckel, Emil, German music publisher and piano manufacturer; b. Mannheim, May 22, 1831; d. there, March 28, 1908. He was trained by his father Karl Ferdinand Heckel (1800–1870) in piano manufacturing. He was a great admirer of Wagner, and was one of the most important supporters of the Bayreuth Festivals, and maintained a voluminous correspondence with Wagner himself, which was published by his son Karl Heckel under the title *Briefe Richard Wagners an Emil Heckel* (Berlin, 1899; English translation by W. A. Ellis, London, 1899). Heckel had an enormous bust of Wagner sculpted by J. Hoffart installed in his palatial residence at Mannheim, but the bust was busted during the anti-Wagnerian air bombardment in World War II.

Heckel, Johann Adam, German manufacturer of musical instruments; b. Adorf, July 14, 1812; d. Biebrich, April 13, 1877. From 1824–35, he worked with the bassoonist Carl Almenräder on experiments for improving the clarinet and bassoon. His son and successor, **Wilhelm** (b. Biebrich, Jan. 25, 1856; d. there, Jan.

13, 1909), continued his experiments with success and constructed the "Heckelphone" (a baritone oboe; used by Strauss in the score of *Salome*) in 1904; also made various changes in the construction of other woodwind instruments. He wrote *Der Fagott. Kurzgefasste Abhandlung über seine historische Entwicklung, seinen Bau und seine Spielweise* (1899; new ed., 1931).

Heckel, Wolf, German lutenist at Strasbourg in the 16th century; b. Munich, c.1515. He publ. a *Lautenbuch* (Strasbourg, 1556, 1562), a valuable and interesting collection of old German, French, and Italian songs, dances, fantasias, ricercari, pavanes, and saltarelli, arranged for 2 lutes; a copy of it is in the Hamburg town library. Reprints from it have been publ. by J. Wolf and L. Nowak in *Denkmäler der Tonkunst in Österreich,* 28(14.i) and 72(37.ii), respectively, by H. D. Bruger in his *Lautenschule,* and W. Tappert in *Sang und Klang aus alter Zeit.*

Heckscher, Céleste de Longpré (*née* **Massey**), American composer; b. Philadelphia, Feb. 23, 1860; d. there, Feb. 18, 1928. Of an artistic family (her grandfather was the artist Louis de Longpré), she studied piano and participated in the musical affairs of the city; was for many years president of the Philadelphia Operatic Society. She began to compose about 1890; wrote the operas *The Flight of Time* and *Rose of Destiny* (Philadelphia, May 2, 1918); *Dances of the Pyrenees,* an orch. suite (Philadelphia, Feb. 17, 1911); a fantasy *To the Forest* for violin and piano (1902); songs and piano pieces. Her style, melodious and without pretensions, is akin to Chaminade's.
BIBLIOGRAPHY: E. E. Hipsher, *American Opera and Its Composers* (Philadelphia, 1927; pp. 256–58).

Hedley, Arthur, English musicologist; b. Shiremoor, near Newcastle-upon-Tyne, Nov. 12, 1905; d. Birmingham, Nov. 8, 1969. He studied French literature at the Federal Univ. of Durham (1923–27) and music with W. G. Whittaker at Newcastle. An ardent Chopinist, he learned the Polish language to be able to study Chopin documentation in the original; publ. a biography, *Chopin* (London, 1947); edited *Selected Correspondence of Chopin* (London, 1962); helped to dispel cumulative misconceptions and deceptions relating to Chopin's life; was instrumental in exposing the falsity of the notorious Potocka-Chopin correspondence produced by Mme. Czernicka (who killed herself in 1949 on the 100th anniversary of Chopin's death, after the fraudulence of her claims was irrefutably demonstrated by Hedley at the Chopin Institute in Warsaw). Hedley's Chopinolatry was carried to the point of fetishism; he acquired Chopin's cuff links and a lead pencil; proved the authenticity of Chopin's silk waistcoat which came to light in Paris.

Hédouin, Pierre, French lawyer and littérateur; b. Boulogne, July 28, 1789; d. Paris, Dec. 20, 1868. He studied law in Paris from 1809; became an attorney, and for 30 years practiced in Boulogne. He settled in Paris in 1842 when he was appointed head of the Ministry of Public Works. His relationship with Monsigny fostered a predilection for music and the arts, and he

occupied his leisure moments with literature, especially that of music, and in composition. He wrote novels, contributed to the *Annales archéologiques, Annales romantiques,* and to several musical periodicals; composed nocturnes, *romances,* and songs, also writing the words; furnished the libretti of several operas.
WRITINGS: *Notice historique de Monsigny* (1821); *Gossec, sa vie et ses ouvrages* (1852); *De l'abandon des anciens compositeurs; Ma première visite à Grétry; 'Richard Cœur de Lion' de Grétry; Lesueur; Meyerbeer à Boulogne-sur-Mer; Paganini; Joseph Dessauer; Trois anecdotes musicales* (on Lesueur, Mlle. Dugazon, and Gluck) in his *Mosaïque* (1856; a published collection of his miscellaneous articles); *Gluck, son arrivée en France* (1859); etc.

Hedwall, Lennart, Swedish conductor and composer; b. Göteborg, Sept. 16, 1932. He studied composition with Bäck and Blomdahl; in 1957 attended the Darmstadt composition courses. Returning to Sweden, he became active as theater conductor and pedagogue. The idiom of his music ranges from the traditional to the audaciously dissonant.
WORKS: 4 pieces for string orch., noncommittally entitled *Music* (1950–69); *Metamorphoses* for chamber ensemble (1955); Oboe Concerto (1956; Swedish Radio, Dec. 21, 1961); *Variazioni piccoli* for orch. (1958); *Lyric Music* for soprano and orch. (1959); *Canzona* for strings (1965); Concerto for Cello and String Orch. (1970); *Fantasia on Veni redemptor gentium* for string orch. (1972); 2 string trios (1952, 1960); Solo Flute Sonata (1954); Trio for Flute, Viola and Cello (1955); Duo for Clarinet and Bassoon (1955); Solo Violin Sonata (1957); 2 Suites for organ (1958–59, 1970); Piano Sonata (1960); Partita for 13 Winds (1961); Trio for Flute, Clarinet and Bassoon (1962); Wind Quintet (1965); String Quartet (1965); *6 Monologues* for solo oboe (1965); *3 Dialogues* for clarinet and cello (1969); Organ Sonata (1971); liturgical cantatas; a cappella choral pieces; songs; theater music.

Heermann, Hugo, distinguished German violinist; b. Heilbronn, Württemberg, March 3, 1844; d. Merano, Nov. 6, 1935. As a boy, he was taken to Rossini in Paris for advice; then went to Brussels where he studied with Bériot and Meerts at the Brussels Cons. graduating in 1861; subsequently took lessons with Joachim. In 1865 he became first violinist of the famous Frankfurt String Quartet; also taught at Hoch's Cons. In 1904 he founded his own violin school. He extended tours as a concert violinist in Europe, U.S.A., and Australia; from 1906–1909 he taught violin at the Chicago Musical College; returning to Europe, he taught at Stern's Cons. in Berlin, and at the Cons. of Geneva (1911–22). He had the distinction of having been the first to play the Violin Concerto of Brahms in Paris, New York and Australia. He published a book of memoirs, *Meine Lebenserinnerungen* (Leipzig, 1935).

Hegar, Friedrich, Swiss composer and conductor; b. Basel, Oct. 11, 1841; d. Zürich, June 2, 1927. He studied at the Leipzig Cons. with Hauptmann, Richter, Ferdinand David, Rietz, and Plaidy. In 1860, he played

violin in a Warsaw orch.; then taught music in Gebweiler, Alsace. In 1863, he established himself in Zürich, where he was active as violinist, conductor, and pedagogue. He conducted the Choral Society of Zürich for 37 years (1864–1901), and the concerts of the Tonhalle Orch. for 41 years (1865–1906); also led various other choral organizations. He was a founder of the Zürich Music School (later, Zürich Cons.) in 1876, and its director until 1914. He received many honors, including membership in the Berlin Academy of Arts in 1917. As a composer, he contributed a great deal to Swiss choral music, particularly in the field of romantic ballads. His most successful work is *Manasse* for soli, mixed chorus, and orch. (Zürich, Oct. 25, 1885; revised version, Jan. 10, 1888); other works are *Hymne an die Musik,* for chorus and orch. (1870); *Das Herz von Douglas,* for soli, male chorus, and orch. (1905); *Festival Overture* (1895); Cello Concerto (1919); Ballade for Violin and Orch. (1922); a string quartet, a violin sonata; 16 songs, etc.
BIBLIOGRAPHY: A. Steiner, *Friedrich Hegar, sein Leben und Wirken* (Zürich, 1928); W. Jerg, *Hegar, ein Meister des Männerchorliedes* (Lachen, 1946).

Hegedüs, Ferencz, celebrated Hungarian violinist; b. Fünfkirchen, Feb. 26, 1881; d. London, Dec. 12, 1944. His precocious talent was carefully fostered by his father, a professional cellist; his mother (of Spanish origin) was also a musician; he then studied at the Budapest Cons. with Hubay. His style of playing had the manner of the Hungarian school; but his performances of Beethoven and other classics were entirely traditional. He lived in Switzerland after 1930; then went to London.

Heger, Robert, Alsatian-born German conductor and composer; b. Strasbourg, Aug. 19, 1886; d. Munich, Jan. 14, 1978. He studied composition with Max Schillings in Munich; then engaged in opera conducting. He conducted at Nuremberg from 1913 to 1921; was subsequently engaged at the State Opera in Vienna (1925–33); at the Berlin State Opera (1933–45), and after the war at the Berlin City Opera (1945–50) and subsequently led the Bavarian State Opera in Munich
WORKS: several operas, among them *Ein Fest auf Haderslev* (Nuremberg, Nov. 12, 1919), *Der Bettler Namenlos* (Munich, April 8, 1932), *Der verlorene Sohn* (Dresden, March 11, 1936), and *Lady Hamilton* (Nuremberg, Feb. 11, 1951); 3 symphonies; a symphonic poem, *Hero und Leander;* Violin Concerto; Cello Concerto; Piano Trio; String Quartet and other pieces of chamber music; also choral works and songs.

Hegner, Anton, Danish cellist and composer; b. Copenhagen, March 2, 1861; d. New York, Dec. 4, 1915. He studied at the Copenhagen Cons.; in 1899 went to New York where he became active mainly as a cello teacher. He composed 4 string quartets; a piano trio; 2 cello concertos; a number of pieces for cello solo, and about 60 songs.

Hegner, Otto, Swiss pianist; b. Basel, Nov. 18, 1876, d. Hamburg, Feb. 22, 1907. He studied piano with Eugene d'Albert; at the age of 12 he made an American tour and was hailed as one of the most phenomenal young pianists. His early death at the age of 30 cut short his brilliant career. His sister **Anna Hegner** (b. Basel, March 1, 1881; d. there, Feb. 3, 1963) was an excellent violinist.

Hegyesi (real name **Spitzer**), **Louis,** noted Hungarian cellist; b. Arpad, Nov. 3, 1853; d. Cologne, Feb. 27, 1894. He studied with Demis in Vienna and with Franchomme in Paris. In 1888 he was appointed to the faculty of the Cons. of Cologne. He published several brilliant cello pieces and a valuable theoretical manual, *Neue rhythmische Tonleiter- und Akkordstudien.*

Heiden, Bernhard, American composer; b. Frankfurt, Germany, Aug. 24, 1910. He studied with Paul Hindemith at the Hochschule für Musik in Berlin (1929–33). In 1935 he emigrated to the U.S. and lived in Detroit where he was active as a pianist and organist. In 1946 he was appointed to the music faculty of Indiana Univ. in Bloomington. His music is neo-Classical in its formal structure, and strongly polyphonic in texture, following the general lines of Hindemith's theory and practice.
WORKS: an opera *The Darkened City* (produced at Indiana Univ., Feb. 23, 1963); 2 symphonies (1938, 1954); Concerto for Chamber Orch. (1949); *Euphorion* for orch. (1949); *Memorial* for orch. (N.Y., Oct. 4, 1956); Sinfonia for Woodwind Quintet (1949); Quintet for Horn and String Quartet (1952); Violin Sonata (1954); Horn Sonata (1939); Serenade for Bassoon and String Trio (1955); Piano Trio (1956); Cello Sonata (1958); Viola Sonata (1959); Quintet for Oboe and String Quartet (1963); *Envoy* for orch. (1963); Woodwind Quintet (1965); Cello Concerto (1967); 4 Dances for Brass Quintet (1967); *Inventions* for 2 cellos (1967); Horn Concertos (1969); Partita for Orch. (1970); *Intrada* for alto saxophone and wind quintet (1970); 3 string quartets (1947, 1951, 1964); 5 Canons for Horns (1971); choral works and piano pieces.

Heider, Werner, German composer; b. Fürth, Jan. 1, 1930. He studied in Nuremberg and Munich, and became active as pianist, conductor and composer. In 1963 he organized a modern ensemble named "Kammermusik + Jazz" and in 1968 formed an "Ars Nova Ensemble" in Nuremberg.
WORKS: *Glimpses* for soprano, piano and orch. (1958); *Choreographie* for clarinet and jazz band (1961); *Konturen* for violin and orch. (1962); *Konflikte* for percussion and orch. (1963); *Picasso-Musik* for voice and 3 instruments (1966); *Passatempo per 7 Solisti* (1967); *Kunst-Stoff* for electrified clarinet, prepared piano and tape (1971). Structurally, his music presents an empyrical surface in which thematic elements are organized in hidden serial progressions.

Heidingsfeld, Ludwig, German composer; b. Jauer, March 24, 1854; d. Danzig, Sept. 14, 1920. He studied at Stern's Cons. in Berlin, and later taught there. He subsequently settled in Danzig, and founded a conservatory there (1899). He wrote two operettas, *Der neue Dirigent* (Danzig, 1907) and *Alle Burchenherrlichkeit* (Danzig, 1911) and the symph. poems, *King Lear* and *Der Totentanz;* piano pieces and songs.

Heifetz, Jascha, celebrated violinist; b. Vilna, Feb. 2, 1901. His father, Ruben Heifetz, an able musician, taught him the rudiments of violin playing at a very early age; he then studied with Elias Malkin at the Vilna Music School, and played in public before he was 5 years old; at the age of 6, he played Mendelssohn's Concerto in Kovno. In 1910 he was taken by his father to St. Petersburg, and entered the Cons. there in the class of Nalbandian; after a few months, he was accepted as a pupil by Leopold Auer. He gave his first public concert in St. Petersburg on April 30, 1911. The following year, with a letter of recommendation from Auer, he went to Berlin; his first concert there (May 24, 1912), in the large hall of the Hochschule für Musik, attracted great attention: Artur Nikisch engaged him to play the Tchaikovsky Concerto with the Berlin Philharmonic (Oct. 28, 1912), and Heifetz obtained sensational success as a child prodigy of extraordinary gifts. He then played in Austria and Scandinavia. After the Russian Revolution of 1917, he went to America, by way of Siberia and the Orient. His debut at Carnegie Hall, N.Y. (Oct. 27, 1917) won for him the highest expression of enthusiasm from the public and in the press; veritable triumphs followed during his tour of the U.S., and soon his fame spread all over the world. He made his first London appearance on May 5, 1920; toured Australia (1921) and the Orient (1923), Palestine (1926), and South America. He revisited Russia in 1934, and was welcomed enthusiastically. He became a naturalized American citizen in 1925, and made his home at Beverly Hills, Calif.; in subsequent years he continued to travel as a concert violinist, visiting virtually every country in the world, but about 1970 ceased to appear in public as a soloist; he participated in a trio (with Piatigorsky and Pennario) and also taught classes of exceptionally talented pupils at the Univ. of Southern Calif., Los Angeles. The quality of his playing is unique in luminous transparency of texture, tonal perfection, and formal equilibrium of phrasing; he never allowed his artistic temperament to superimpose extraneous elements on the music; this inspired tranquillity led some critics to characterize his interpretations as impersonal and detached. Heifetz made numerous arrangements for violin of works by Bach, Vivaldi, and pieces by contemporary composers; his most famous transcription is *Hora Staccato* by the Rumanian composer Grigoraş Dinicu (1889-1949), made into a virtuoso piece by adroit ornamentation and rhythmic elaboration. In his desire to promote modern music Heifetz commissioned a number of composers (Walton, Gruenberg, Castelnuovo-Tedesco, and others) to write violin concertos for him, and performed several of them. Herbert R. Axelrod edited and published an "unauthorized pictorial biography" of Heifetz (1977); Heifetz filed a lawsuit for 7½ million dollars against the publisher and compiler, claiming invasion of privacy.

Heiller, Anton, significant Austrian organist and composer; b. Vienna, Sept. 15, 1923. He studied piano and organ at the Vienna Cons.; in 1952 he won first prize at the International Organ Contest in Haarlem, Holland; in 1969 he received the Austrian Grand Prize for Music; in 1971 he was appointed prof. at the Hochschule für Musik in Vienna. His own music is rooted deeply in the tradition of the Renaissance, while his contrapuntal technique adopts modern procedures. He particularly excels in sacred works, to Latin texts; in these he occasionally makes use of the 12-tone method of composition.

WORKS: a chamber oratorio *Tentatio Jesu* (1952); *Psalmenkantate* (1955); Concerto for Organ and Orch. (1963); cantata *In principio erat verbum* (1965); *Stabat mater* for chorus and orch. (1968); several Masses, including *Kleine Messe über Zwolftonmodelle*, a cappella (1962); *English Mass* (1965); *Adventsmusik* for chorus and organ (1971).

Heilman, William Clifford, American composer; b. Williamsport, Penn., Sept. 27, 1877; d. there, Dec. 20, 1946. He studied at Harvard Univ. (B.A., 1900) and in Europe with Rheinberger and Widor. He was a member of the music dept. of Harvard Univ. from 1905 till 1930. Among his works are a symph. poem, *By the Porta Catania* (1916), Piano Trio, Romance for Cello and Piano, a number of character pieces for piano, and choruses. He made arrangements of Negro spirituals.

Hein, Carl, German-American cellist and choral conductor; b. Rendsburg, Feb. 2, 1864; d. New York, Feb. 27, 1945. He studied at the Hamburg Cons.; played cello in the Hamburg Philharmonic Orch.; in 1890 he emigrated to America, and lived in New York, where he became the leader of several German choral societies, among them the Mozart-Verein and Schubert-Chor. Later he was active mainly as a vocal coach. He composed a number of male choruses.

Heinefetter. Six sisters, all well known as opera singers: **Sabina** (b. Mainz, Aug. 19, 1809; d. Illemau, Nov. 18, 1872) was an itinerant harpist as a child; at the age of 16, she went to Kassel to study with Spohr; then sang with brilliant success in Vienna, Berlin, and Milan. One of her outstanding roles was Donna Anna in *Don Giovanni*. She died insane. Her sister, **Maria (Mme. Stöckel;** b. Mainz, Feb. 16, 1816; d. Vienna, Feb. 23, 1857), achieved during her short career several notable successes; she also died insane. **Katinka** (1820-1858), **Fatima, Eva,** and **Nanette** were other sisters who appeared professionally on the opera stage.

Heinemann, Alfred, German composer; b. Bückeburg, April 10, 1908. He played piano as a child, and began to compose at the age of 10. In 1936 he left Germany and went to Johannesburg, South Africa. In 1944 he moved to Cape Town; was active mainly as a teacher. In 1949 he settled in the U.S.; in 1967 joined the staff of Broadcast Music Inc. His music follows the tenets of enlightened functionalism, without transgressing the natural capacities of the instruments.

WORKS: opera, *Torso* (1958); the ballets *Galaxy* (1941); *Roulette* (1946); *La Manie des titres et des abbréviations* (1953) and *Kobold* (1963); Piano Concerto (1941); Violin Concerto (1942); *March of the Neanderthal Men* (Cape Town, April 7, 1946); Symphony (1959-64).

Heinemeyer, Ernst Wilhelm, outstanding German flutist; b. Hannover, Feb. 25, 1827; d. Vienna, Feb. 12, 1869. He studied with his father, **Christian Heinemeyer** (1796–1872), who was the chamber flutist at Hannover. In 1847, he went to Russia, where he played the flute in the Imperial Orch. at St. Petersburg; in 1859, he returned to Hannover; in 1866, he went to Vienna. He wrote several concertos for the flute.

Heinichen, Johann David, notable German composer and theorist; b. Krössuln, near Weissenfels, April 17, 1683; d. Dresden, July 15, 1729. He was educated at the Thomasschule in Leipzig, studying with Schell and Kuhnau; at the same time, he studied law, and practiced as a lawyer in Weissenfels. His first opera, *Der angenehme Betrug,* was perf. in Leipzig in 1709; he then held a position as conductor at Zeitz. Councillor Buchta of Zeitz supplied the funds for Heinichen to accompany him to Italy (1713–18), where he produced several operas. In Venice, he joined the Elector of Saxony, Frederick Augustus, and followed him to Dresden as director of the Italian opera company there (1718). However, as a result of confusion brought about by a violent quarrel between Heinichen and the celebrated singer, Senesino, the Italian opera was dissolved. Heinichen remained in Dresden as director of church and chamber music. He was a prolific composer; a thematic catalogue of his works is found in G. A. Seibel, *Das Leben des J. D. Heinichen* (Leipzig, 1913), listing, besides his operas, 2 oratorios, 16 Masses, 63 cantatas, more than 100 other sacred works, 4 symphonies, 2 overtures, 30 concertos, 17 sonatas, 7 pieces for flute, many separate airs, etc. Most of them are preserved in the Dresden library; few of his works have been published. Heinichen's importance lies not so much in his compositions as in his basic theoretical work, *Neu erfundene und gründliche Answeisung zu vollkommener Erlernung des General-Basses* (Hamburg, 1711); new revised ed. as *Der General-Bass in der Composition* (Dresden, 1728).
BIBLIOGRAPHY: R. Tanner, *J. D. Heinichen als dramatischer Komponist* (Leipzig, 1916); G. Hausswald, *J. D. Heinichens Instrumentalwerke* (Berlin, 1937).

Heininen, Paavo, Finnish composer; b. Järvenpää, Jan. 13, 1938. He studied at the Univ. of Helsinki and at the Sibelius Academy, graduating in 1960; later studied with Bernd Alois Zimmermann at the Hochschule für Musik in Cologne; then went to America and took courses in composition with Vincent Persichetti at the Juilliard School of Music in New York. Returning to Finland, he occupied teaching posts in Turku and, since 1966, at the Sibelius Academy of Music in Helsinki.
WORKS: *The Silken Drum,* chamber opera after a Japanese Noh play (1976); 4 symphonies: No. 1 (1958; revised 1960; Helsinki, March 24, 1964); No. 2, *Petite symphonie joyeuse* (Helsinki, Dec. 7, 1962); No. 3 (1969); No. 4 (Oslo, Sept. 4, 1972); 2 piano concertos: No. 1 (Turku, Jan. 23, 1965) and No. 2 (Turku, Dec. 1, 1966); *Preambulo* for orch. (1959); *Tripartita* for orch. (1959); Concerto for Strings (1959); *Soggetto* for 14 solo strings and orch. (1963); *Adagio,* for orch., "con-

certo in the form of variations" (1963, revised 1966; London, Feb. 19, 1967); *Arioso* for strings (1967); *Cantico delle creature* for baritone, and orch. or piano or organ (1968); Quintet, for flute, saxophone, piano, vibraphone and percussion (1961); *Musique d'été* for flute, clarinet, harpsichord, violin, cello, vibraphone and percussion (1963); *Discantus I* for alto flute (1965); *Discantus II* for solo clarinet (1969); *Discantus III* for solo saxophone (1976); *Cantilena I* for solo viola (1970); *Cantilena II* for solo cello (1970); *Cantilena III* for solo violin (1976); Violin Sonata (1970); *2 Chansons* for cello and piano (1974); String Quartet (1974); Toccata for Piano (1956); Piano Sonatina (1957); *Oculus aquilae,* triptych for organ (1968); *Libretto della primavera* for piano (1971); *Poesia squillante ed incandescente,* piano sonata (1974); *Préludes-Études-Poèmes* for piano (1974); String Quartet (1975); songs.

Heiniö, Mikko, Finnish composer; b. Tampere, May 5, 1948. He studied composition with Joonas Kokkonen at the Sibelius Academy in Helsinki; then engaged in teaching.
WORKS: String Quartet No. 1 (1971); Trio for Flute, Violin and Guitar (1971); Piano Concerto No. 1 (Tampere, Nov. 17, 1972); *Luominen (The Creation)* for soprano, baritone, chorus and orch. (1972); Suite for Flute and 2 Guitars (1974); 4 *Romantische Lieder* for soprano and orchestra (1974); Piano Concerto No. 2 (Helsinki, Feb. 26, 1975).

Heinitz, Wilhelm, German musicologist; b. Altona, Dec. 9, 1883; d. Hamburg, March 31, 1963. He studied the bassoon, and played in various orchestras; then became interested in phonetics; studied primitive music and the languages of Africa and Polynesia; became a member of the Phonetic Laboratory at the Univ. of Hamburg, and led a seminar in comparative musicology until his retirement in 1949. He wrote a number of valuable papers on the structural problems of speech, which he published in special journals; also the books, *Klangprobleme im Rundfunk* (Berlin, 1926); *Strukturprobleme in primitiver Musik* (Hamburg, 1931); *Neue Wege der Volksmusikforschung* (Hamburg, 1937); *Physiologische Reaktion und Pulsationsmessung* (Hamburg, 1958).

Heinrich, Anthony Philip (Anton Philipp), American violinist and composer of Bohemian birth; b. Schönbüchel, Bohemia, March 11, 1781; d. in extreme poverty in New York, May 3, 1861. As a boy he acquired proficiency on the piano and violin, but began adult life as a wholesale merchant and banker; in 1810 he emigrated to America, settling in Philadelphia as a merchant and as an unpaid music director of the Southwark Theatre. After business reverses in 1817 he moved to the wilds of Kentucky, first to Bardstown, and then to nearby Lexington, where he managed to find enough musicians to conduct in a performance of a Beethoven symphony. Without any knowledge of harmony, he began to compose in 1818; these first songs and choral and instrumental pieces he publ. later as Op. 1, *The Dawning of Music in Kentucky, or The Pleasures of Harmony in the Solitudes of Nature* (1820), and Op. 2, *The Western Minstrel* (1820; both repr. N.Y., 1972). He became director of music at Southwark Theater, Phila.; later, in Louisville, Ky. The year 1827 found him in London, playing violin in a small orch.; there he also studied theory, and about 1830 began to write for orch.; returned to the U.S. in 1832. In 1834 he again visited England, as well as Germany and Austria (1835), and had some of his works produced at Dresden, Prague, Budapest, and Graz (his symph., *The Combat of the Condor*, was perf. at Graz in 1836; also in France); in Vienna he entered a competition with a symphony, but the prize was awarded to Franz Lachner; disappointed, he returned to America and settled in New York, where he soon gained immense popularity, generally known as "Father Heinrich." He was a commanding figure in the musical affairs of the U.S., publishing many of his piano pieces and songs, grand festivals of his works being arranged in N.Y., Philadelphia, and Boston, and the critics speaking of him as the "Beethoven of America." But a tour of Germany in 1857–58 was a dismal failure. The quality of his works is dubious at best; he wrote for an enormous orch., à la Berlioz, and his musical ideas, out of all proportion to the means employed, recall the style of Haydn's imitators; nevertheless, he is historically important, being the first to employ Indian themes in works of large dimensions and to show decided nationalist aspirations. In 1917 the Library of Congress acquired Heinrich's "Memoranda" (letters, programs, newspaper clippings, etc.), many published works and almost all the orchestral scores, enumerated in a list made by Heinrich himself in 1857. A perusal of the titles is amusing and instructive: *Grand American Chivalrous Symphony*; *The Columbiad, or Migration of American Wild Passenger Pigeons*; *The Ornithological Combat of Kings, or The Condor of the Andes and the Eagle of the Cordilleras*; *Pocahontas, the Royal Indian Maid and the Heroine of Virginia, the Pride of the Wilderness*; *The Wildwood Spirit's Chant or Scintillations of 'Yankee Doodle,' forming a Grand National Heroic Fantasia scored for a Powerful Orch. in 44 Parts*; *Manitou Mysteries, or The Voice of the Great Spirit*; *Gran Sinfonia Misteriosa-Indiana* (U.S. performance, N.Y., Dec. 2, 1975). Reprints (in addition to opp. 1 and 2): *Songs without Words*, vol. I of Piano Music in Nineteenth Century America (Chapel Hill, N.C., 1975); *Yankeedoodle* (for piano) in W. T. Marrocco and H. Gleason, *Music in America* (N.Y., 1964); *The Maiden's Dirge*, in E. Gold, *The Bicentennial Collection of American Music* (Dayton, Ohio, 1975). BIBLIOGRAPHY: F. A. Mussik, *Skizzen aus dem Leben des . . . A. Ph. Heinrich* (Leipzig, 1843); O. G. Sonneck, "Musical Landmarks in New York," *Musical Quarterly* (April 1920); *Dictionary of American Biography* (1932); Wm. T. Upton, *A. Ph. Heinrich* (N.Y., 1939); D. M. Barron, *The Early Vocal Works of Anthony Philip Heinrich* (Univ. of Illinois, 1972); L. H. Filbeck, *The Choral Works of Anthony Philip Heinrich* (Univ. of Illinois, 1973); W. R. Maust, *The Symphonies of Anthony Philip Heinrich Based on American Themes* (Indiana Univ., 1973).

Heinrich, Max, German-American baritone; b. Chemnitz, June 14, 1853; d. New York, Aug. 9, 1916. He studied at the Dresden Cons.; in 1873, came to America; taught at Marion, Alabama (1876–82), then moved to New York, where he appeared in oratorio with various orchestras. From 1888–93, he taught singing at the Royal Academy of Music in London; then lived in Chicago (1894–1903) and in Boston (1903–10). He gave numerous recitals of German lieder, the last of them shortly before his death.

Heinroth, Charles, American organist; b. New York, Jan. 2, 1874; d. Southampton, Long Island, N.Y., Jan. 8, 1963. He studied organ with John White and composition with Victor Herbert in New York; subsequently took theory lessons with Rheinberger in Munich. Returning to America he occupied various posts as church organist in New York and Brooklyn; from 1907 until 1932 he was organist at the Carnegie Institute in Pittsburgh; from 1932 to 1942 was head of the Music Dept. at the City College of New York.

Heinroth, Johann August Günther, German composer and writer; b. Nordhausen, June 19, 1780; d. Göttingen, June 2, 1846. He studied with his father, Christoph Gottlieb Heinroth, an able organist. He then attended the Univ. of Leipzig, and of Halle. In 1804, he became attached to the School of Jewish Studies organized by Israel Jacobson. This was the beginning of a lifelong study of the Jewish liturgy, which he reorganized, adding numerous original melodies that became part of the Jewish service. He also attempted the introduction of a simplified musical notation by figures. From 1818, he served as music director of the Univ. of Göttingen, in succession to Forkel.

WRITINGS: (all publ. at Göttingen): *Gesangunterrichts-Methode für höhere und niedere Schulen* (1821–23, 3 parts); *Volksnoten oder vereinfachte Tonschrift* (1828); *Kurze Anleitung, das Klavier oder Forte-Piano spielen zu lehren* (1828); *Musikalisches Hilfsbuch für Prediger, Kantoren und Organisten* (1833).

BIBLIOGRAPHY: A monograph on Heinroth is included in W. Boetticher's book, *Die Musik an der Georgia Augusta-Univ. zu Göttingen* (1958).

Heinsheimer, Hans (Walter), American publishing executive and writer on music; b. Karlsruhe, Sept. 25, 1900. He studied law in Heidelberg, Munich and Freiburg-im-Breisgau (*Juris Dr.*, 1923); then joined Universal Edition in Vienna, where he was in charge of its opera department (1924–38), and supervised the publication of such important stage works as Alban Berg's *Wozzeck*, Krenek's *Jonny spielt auf*, Weinberger's *Schwanda*, Kurt Weill's *Aufstieg und Fall der Stadt Mahagonny*, and George Antheil's *Transatlantic*. He came to the U.S. in 1938 and was associated with the New York branch of Boosey & Hawkes. In 1947 he was appointed director of the symphonic and operatic repertory of G. Schirmer, Inc.; in 1957 became director of publications and in 1972 vice-president of the firm; in these capacities he promoted the works of Samuel Barber, Gian Carlo Menotti, Leonard Bernstein and Elliott Carter. He retired in 1974 and has devoted himself mainly to writing. A brilliant stylist in both German and English, he has contributed numerous informative articles to *Melos, Musical Quarterly, Holiday, Reader's Digest,* etc. He published the entertaining books, *Menagerie in F-sharp* (N.Y., 1947) and *Fanfare for Two Pigeons* (1952) (publ. in German in a single vol. entitled *Menagerie in Fis-dur;* Zürich, 1953); *Best Regards to Aida* (publ. in German as *Schönste Grüsse an Aida;* Munich, 1968).

Heintze, Gustaf Hjalmar, Swedish pianist and composer; b. Jönköping, July 22, 1879; d. Saltsjöbaden, March 4, 1946. He was of a musical family; his father **Georg Wilhelm Heintze** (1849–95) was a well-known organist, as was his grandfather, **Gustaf Wilhelm Heintze** (1825–1909). He studied at the Stockholm Cons.; in 1910 was appointed organist at a Stockholm church, a post that he held until his death. He wrote cantatas, 2 violin concertos, chamber music, and organ pieces.

Heinze, Sir Bernard Thomas, eminent Australian conductor; b. Shepparton, near Melbourne, July 1, 1894. He studied at the Univ. of Melbourne, Royal College of Music in London, and with Vincent d'Indy at the Schola Cantorum in Paris. After service in the Royal Artillery during World War I, he returned to Australia; in 1926, was appointed prof. of music at the Univ. of Melbourne. In 1938 he made a tour of Europe as conductor. He was conductor of the Melbourne Symph. Orch. from 1933 till 1949; was knighted in 1950. In 1956, he became director of the State Cons. in Sydney.

Heinze, Gustav Adolph, German composer and conductor; b. Leipzig, Oct. 1, 1820; d. Muiderberg, near Amsterdam, Feb. 20, 1904. He received his early musical education from his father, a clarinetist in the Gewandhaus Orch. in Leipzig, and joined that orchestra as clarinetist at the age of 16. He then conducted at the Breslau Opera, and also produced 2 operas there. In 1850 he went to Amsterdam as conductor of the German Opera, and remained in Holland till the end of his life. He composed, besides his operas, several oratorios and other choral works.

Heise, Peter Arnold, Danish composer; b. Copenhagen, Feb. 11, 1830; d. Stockkerup, Sept. 12, 1879. He studied music with Niels Gade and Berggreen in Copenhagen and with Hauptmann at the Leipzig Cons. Returning to Denmark, he became a music teacher and organist at Sorö, where he remained until 1865. He then settled in Copenhagen; produced 2 successful operas, *The Pasha's Daughter* (Sept. 30, 1869) and *King and Marshal* (Sept. 25, 1878). He also wrote a symphony, chamber music, etc., which remain mostly unpublished. It was in his many lieder to Danish texts that Heise achieved enduring fame.

BIBLIOGRAPHY: G. Hetsch, *Peter Heise* (Copenhagen, 1926).

Hekking, André, French cellist; b. Bordeaux, July 30, 1866; d. Paris, Dec. 14, 1925. He was the son of the Dutch cellist, **Robert Gérard Hekking** (1820–75), who settled in France, and received his training from him. From 1909 he lived in Paris; in 1919 was appointed prof. at the Paris Cons.; also taught at the American Cons. in Fontainebleau. He publ. a practice book for cellists, *Violoncelle, exercices quotidiens* (Paris, 1927).

Hekking, Anton, notable cellist; brother of **André Hekking;** b. The Hague, Sept. 7, 1856; d. Berlin, Nov. 18, 1935. He studied at the Paris Cons. with Joseph Giese; then undertook an American tour with the pianist Mme. Essipova. Returning to Europe, he was first cellist of the Berlin Philh. (1884–88 and 1898–1902). After another American tour, he became first cellist of the Boston Symph. (1889–91) and later of the N.Y. Symph. (1895–98). He returned to Berlin in 1898; taught at Stern's Cons. there, and became a member of a trio with Schnabel and Wittenberg (1902).

Hekking, Gérard, French cellist; cousin of **André** and **Anton Hekking,** b. Nancy, Aug. 22, 1879; d. Paris, June 5, 1942. He studied at the Paris Cons., winning 1st prize (1899). He was first cellist of the Concertgebouw Orch. in Amsterdam (1903–14) and taught at the Amsterdam Cons.; also made tours in Russia, Spain, Germany, and France. He was in the French Army during World War I; from 1921–27, was again in Holland; in 1927, became prof. at the Paris Cons. He wrote several cello pieces; also revised *Principes de la technique du violoncelle* of François Gervais (Paris, 1930).

Hekster, Walter, Dutch composer; b. Amsterdam, March 29, 1937. He studied composition and clarinet at the Amsterdam Cons., graduating in 1961; then went to the U.S., where he was engaged as clarinetist with the Connecticut Symph. Orch. (1962–65); attended classes of Roger Sessions at Tanglewood in the summer of 1966; from 1965 to 1971 he taught clarinet and composition at Brandon Univ., Canada; then returned to Holland and assumed teaching posts at the Utrecht Cons. and at the Arnhem Cons.

WORKS: *Epitaphium (In Memoriam Eduard van Beinum)* for strings (1959); *Foci* for violin and chamber ensemble (1965–66); *Facets* for orch. (1967–68); *Branches* for 15 strings (1969); *Nocturnal Conversation* for orch. in 4 groups (1970–71); *Early One Morning* for 15 winds (1972); *Mobiles* for orch. in 4 groups (1973); *The Auroras of Autumn* for oboes and orch. (1975); *Pentagram* for wind quintet (1961); *Reflections* for clarinet, horn, cello, vibraphone, celesta and percussion (1964); *Dialogues* for flute and clarinet (1965); *Music for Bassoon and Piano* (1965); 2 sonatas: No. 1 for piano (1966) and No. 2 for solo cello (1967); *Interpolations* for violin and piano (1967); *Fluxus* for solo flute (1968); *Fluxions* for clarinet and piano (1968); 5 *Reliefs* scored for various instrumental combinations (1968–69); *The Snow Man* for soprano, percussion and bass clarinet (1969); *Windsong* for trumpet, flute and saxophone (1970); *Reedmusic* for oboe, clarinet and bassoon (1970); *Incenter* for flute, oboe and cello (1970); *Fresco* for clarinet and string trio (1970); *Diversities* for flute, clarinet, horn, bassoon and piano (1970); *Ambage* for string quartet (1970); *Credences of Summer* for violin, clarinet and piano (1974); *Tropos* for flute, oboe, violin, viola, cello and piano (1974–75); *Map* for solo Ondes Martenot (1975); *Epicycle I* for flute, guitar and double bass (1975); *Epicycle II* for trumpet, bass clarinet, accordion and percussion (1975); *Echoes of Summer* for oboe, clarinet and bassoon (1975); *Graffiti* for Ondes Martenot, percussion and piano (1975); *Derivations* for piano (1965); *Studies in Spatial Notation* for piano (1970).

Helder, Bartholomäus, German composer; b. Gotha, 1585; d. Remstedt, near Gotha, Oct. 28, 1635. He studied theology in Leipzig; was school teacher at a village near Gotha (1607-16); then was for 20 years a pastor at Remstedt. He died of the plague. He publ. a collection of Christmas and New Year's songs, *Cymbalum genethliacum* (1614); a book of psalm tunes, *Cymbalum Davidicum;* many of his secular songs are included in contemporary anthologies. His New Year's song *Das alte Jahr vergangen ist* became very popular.

Helfer, Walter, American composer; b. Lawrence, Mass., Sept. 30, 1896; d. New Rochelle, N.Y., April 16, 1959. He studied at Harvard Univ.; then took courses in composition with Caussade in Paris and with Respighi in Rome. Returning to the U.S., he joined the staff of Hunter College. He wrote an orchestral *Fantasy on Children's Tunes* (1935); *Symphony on Canadian Airs* (1937); Concertino for Piano and Chamber Orch. (1947); *Soliloquy* for cello and piano; String Quartet; String Trio; *Elegiac Sonata* for piano; various minor piano pieces and songs.

Helfert, Vladimír, Czech musicologist; b. Plánice, Bohemia, March 24, 1886; d. Prague, May 18, 1945. He studied with Hostinsky in Prague and with Kretzschmar and Wolf at the Berlin Univ. (1908, Mus. D., with the dissertation *G. Benda und J. J. Rousseau*); 1921 instructor, 1926 prof. of musicology at the Univ. of Brno; director of the Czech Orchestral Society there; from 1924, editor of the paper *Hudebni Rozhledy.* In 1940 he was arrested by the Nazis and held in Breslau; released in 1943; then rearrested in 1945 and taken to the Terezin concentration camp. He died a few days after his liberation.
WRITINGS: (mostly in Czech): *History of the Melodrama* (1908); *Jaroměřice and the Count J. A. Questenberg* (Prague, 1917); *The Music of the Jaroměřice Castle: A Critical Analysis of the Works of the Composer Franz Míča* (Prague, 1924); *Contribution to the Development of the History of the Marseillaise* (in Italian; Turin, 1922); *The Creative Development of Smetana* (Prague, 1924); "Zur Entwicklungsgeschichte der Sonatenform," *Archiv für Musikwissenschaft* (1925); *Histoire de la musique dans la république tchécoslovaque* (in collaboration with Erich Steinhardt; Prague, 1936); and other essays, mostly about Czech music in the 18th century; joint author of O. Pazdirek's *Dictionary of Music* (in Czech; vol. I, 1929; vol. II, 1937).

Helfman, Max, American choral conductor and composer; b. Radzin, Poland, May 25, 1901; d. Dallas, Texas, Aug. 9, 1963. He was taken to the U.S. in 1909, and studied at the David Mannes Music College, and at the Curtis Institute in Philadelphia, where his teachers were Rosario Scalero in composition and Fritz Reiner in conducting. He subsequently was ac-

tive mainly as conductor of Jewish choral groups; was in charge of Temple Emanuel in Patterson, New Jersey (1926-39); then at Temple B'nai Abraham, Newark (1940-53); and at Temple Sinai in Los Angeles (1954-57); and of Washington Hebrew Congregation (1958-62). He wrote a dramatic cantata *New Hagadah* (1949); several pieces of Jewish liturgical music, and edited a series of choral works for the Jewish Music Alliance.

Helfritz, Hans, German ethnomusicologist and composer; b. Hilbersdorf, July 25, 1902. He studied with Hindemith at the Hochschule für Musik in Berlin, and with Egon Wellesz in Vienna. In 1936 he went to South America; lived mostly in Chile where he worked on the problems of musical folklore. In 1956 he undertook a journey along the West Coast of Africa and made recordings of native songs. In 1962 he settled in Ibiza in the Balearic Islands.
WRITINGS: (books on ethnic subjects): *Amerika, Land der Inka, Maya und Azteken* (Vienna, 1965); *Die Götterburgen Mexikos* (Cologne, 1968) and *Mexiko, Land der drei Kulturen* (Berlin, 1968). He composed 2 string quartets, a violin sonata, a saxophone concerto and various short orchestral pieces; in some of them he makes use of South American and African motives.

Hellendaal, Pieter, organist and composer; b. Rotterdam, March (baptized April 1), 1721; d. Cambridge, England, April 26, 1799. In 1760, he went to England and on June 12, 1760 was appointed successor to Charles Burney as organist at St. Margaret's, King's Lynn in Norfolk.
WORKS: 12 sonatas for violin (Amsterdam, 1744); 6 concertos for violin (London, 1760); 6 solos for violin with thorough-bass (London, 1761); 8 solos for cello with thorough-bass (London, 1770); *Celebrated Rondo* for violin with instrumental accompaniment; *A Collection of Psalms for the Use of Parish Churches;* 2 glees for 4 voices.
BIBLIOGRAPHY: G. A. C. De Graaf, "Pieter Hellendaal, Musiquant *(1721-1799),*" *Mens en Melodie* (Aug. 1950).

Heller, Hans Ewald, German-American composer; b. Vienna, April 17, 1894; d. New York, Oct. 1, 1966. He studied with J. B. Foerster and Camillo Horn; was engaged in Vienna as music critic and teacher. In 1938 he settled in the U.S. Among his compositions are the light operas *Satan* (Vienna, 1927), *Messalina* (Prague, 1928), and *Der Liebling von London* (Vienna, 1930); an overture *Carnival in New Orleans* (1940); a cantata, *Ode to Our Women* (1942); 2 string quartets; Suite for Clarinet and Piano; about 150 songs.

Heller, James G., American composer; b. New Orleans, Jan. 4, 1892; d. Cincinnati, Dec. 19, 1971. He studied at Tulane Univ., New Orleans (B. A., 1912), the Univ. of Cincinnati (M. A., 1914), the Hebrew Union College (Rabbi, 1916), and the Cincinnati Cons. of Music (Mus. D., 1934); for 12 years wrote the program notes for the Cincinnati Symph. Orch.; then taught musicology at the Cincinnati Cons. of Music. Among his works are *Elegy and Pastorale* for voice and string orch. (Cincinnati, Dec. 30, 1934); String Quartet; Violin Sonata; Jewish services (New Union Hymnal, 1930–32).

Heller, Stephen, celebrated Hungarian pianist and composer; b. Budapest, May 15, 1813; d. Paris, Jan. 14, 1888. He was of a Jewish family, but was converted to Christianity as a youth. He studied piano with F. Brauer and showed such extraordinary ability that he was sent to Vienna to continue his studies; there he took lessons with Anton Halm. In 1828 he began a tour through Austria and Germany. However, the exertion of travel proved too much for him; in Augsburg, he became ill, and decided to remain there for a time; financial means were provided by a wealthy family. In 1838 he went to Paris, where he became friendly with Berlioz, Chopin, and Liszt. Soon he became very successful as a pianist; some critics even judged him as superior to Chopin. In Paris, Heller began to compose piano pieces somewhat akin to Schumann's: brilliant salon dances, studies, and character pieces that became exceedingly popular. In 1849 he visited London, where his concerts charmed a large circle of music lovers. A nervous ailment forced him to curtail his appearances; in 1862 he revisited England and played with Hallé at the Crystal Palace. He then returned to Paris, where he remained for the rest of his life. WORKS: He wrote in all several hundred piano pieces arranged in groups in 158 opus numbers; of these, the most effective are *Traumbilder; Promenades d'un solitaire; Nuits blanches; Dans les bois; Voyage autour de ma chambre; Tablettes d'un solitaire; Tarentelles;* admirable études; ballades (notably *La Chasse*); 4 sonatas, 3 sonatinas, waltzes, mazurkas, caprices, nocturnes, variations, etc. BIBLIOGRAPHY: M. Hartmann, "Stephen Heller," *Monatshefte* (1859); H. Barbedette, *Stephen Heller* (Paris, 1876; English transl., London, 1877); R. Schütz, *Stephen Heller* (Leipzig, 1911; standard biography); Isidor Philipp, "Some Recollections of Stephen Heller," *Musical Quarterly* (Oct. 1935).

Hellmesberger, Georg, Sr., renowned Austrian violinist; b. Vienna, April 24, 1800; d. Neuwaldegg, near Vienna, Aug. 16, 1873. His father, a country schoolmaster, gave him his first musical instruction; he succeeded Schubert as soprano chorister in the Imperial chapel; in 1820 became a pupil of the Vienna Cons. under Böhm (violin) and E. Förster (composition); in 1821 became assistant instructor there; in 1833, professor. In 1829 he succeeded Schuppanzigh as conductor of the Imperial Opera; 1830, member of the court chapel; pensioned in 1867. He had many distinguished pupils, including Ernst, Hauser, Auer, Joachim, and his own sons, **Georg** and **Joseph.**

Hellmesberger, Georg, Jr., Austrian violinist; son of the preceding; b. Vienna, Jan. 27, 1830; d. Hannover, Nov. 12, 1852. He studied composition with Rotter; made a successful concert tour through Germany and England. At the age of 21, he was appointed concertmaster of the Hannover Royal orch., and produced there 2 operas, *Die Bürgschaft* and *Die beiden Königinnen* (1851), when his career, so brilliantly begun,

was cut short by a lung ailment, to which he succumbed at the age of 22.

Hellmesberger, Joseph, Sr., distinguished Austrian violin virtuoso; another son of **Georg Hellmesberger, Sr.;** b. Vienna, Nov. 23, 1828; d. there, Oct. 24, 1893. In 1851, was appointed artistic conductor of the Gesellschaft der Musikfreunde (till 1859, when he was succeeded by Herbeck), and director of the Vienna Cons. till 1893, where he was violin prof. (1851–77); concertmaster at the Imperial Opera (1860); solo violinist in the court orch. (1863); court conductor (1877). From 1849–87 he led the famous string quartet bearing his name (Hellmesberger, Durst, Heissler, Schlesinger), which opened a new era for chamber music in Vienna. BIBLIOGRAPHY: A. Barthlmé, *Vom alten Hellmesberger* (Vienna, 1908); R. M. Prosl, *Die Hellmesberger; hundert Jahre aus dem Leben einer Wiener Musikerfamilie* (Vienna, 1947).

Hellmesberger, Joseph, Jr., Austrian violinist and dramatic composer; son of the preceding; b. Vienna, April 9, 1855; d. there, April 26, 1907. He was solo violinist in the Imperial orch., and prof. at the Vienna Cons. (1878); then conducted opera and ballet; in 1887 he succeeded his father as leader of the Hellmesberger quartet. WORKS: 10 operettas, produced (1880–1906) at Vienna, Munich, and Hamburg: *Kapitän Ahlström; Der Graf von Gleichen; Der schöne Kurfürst; Rikiki, oder Nelly, das Blumenmädchen; Das Orakel; Der bleiche Gast; Das Veilchenmädel; Die drei Engel; Mutzi;* and *Der Triumph des Weibes;* the ballets *Fata Morgana; Die verwandelte Katze; Das Licht; Die fünf Sinne;* etc.

Hellouin, Frédéric, French writer on music; b. Paris, April 18, 1864; d. St. Germain-en-Laye, March 26, 1924. He was a pupil of Massenet at the Paris Cons.; from 1902, lecturer at the École des Hautes Études Sociales. He publ. *Feuillets d'histoire musicale française* (1902), *Gossec et la musique française à la fin du XVIIIᵉ siècle* (1903), *Essai de critique de la critique musicale* (1906), *Le Noël musical français* (1906), *Un Musicien oublié: Catel* (1910).

Hellwig, Karl Friedrich Ludwig, German composer; b. Kunersdorf, near Wrietzen, July 23, 1773; d. Berlin, Nov. 24, 1838. He learned to play all the string instruments and piano; then studied theory with Zelter and others; at the same time, he was engaged in the manufacture of paint, which enabled him to pursue his musical studies as an avocation. In 1813 he became organist at the Berlin court. He wrote 2 operas, *Die Bergknappen* (Dresden, April 27, 1820) and *Don Sylvio di Rosalbo* (unperformed), much church music, and a number of German lieder, which show a certain poetic sensitivity and a ballad-like quality in the manner of Zelter and other early German Romanticists.

Helm, Everett, American composer and musicologist; b. Minneapolis, July 17, 1913. He studied at Harvard Univ., graduating in 1935; then went to Europe where he took courses with Malipiero in Italy and Vaughan Williams in London. Returning to the U.S., he taught at Western College, Ohio (1943–44); then toured South America (1944–46). From 1948 to 1950 he was music officer under the Military Government in Germany; then lived mostly in Germany, Austria and Italy. In 1963 he made his home in Asolo, near Venice. A linguist, he contributed articles to various music magazines in several languages; made a specialty of the music of Yugoslavia and was guest lecturer at the Univ. of Ljubljana (1966–68).

WORKS: Piano Concerto (N.Y., April 24, 1954); *Adam and Eve*, an adaptation of a medieval mystery play (Wiesbaden, Oct. 28, 1951, composer conducting); Concerto for 5 Instruments, Percussion and String Orch. (Donaueschingen, Oct. 10, 1953); *The Siege of Tottenburg*, radio opera (1956); *Le Roy fait battre tambour*, a ballet (1956); *500 Dragon-Thalers*, a singspiel (1956); Piano Concerto No. 2 (Louisville, Feb. 25, 1956); Divertimento for Flutes (1957); *Sinfonia da camera* (1961); Concerto for Double Bass and String Orch. (1968); 2 string quartets; Woodwind Quintet (1967); numerous piano pieces and songs.

WRITINGS: *Béla Bartók in Selbstzeugnissen und Bilddokumenten* (Reinbek-bei Hamburg, 1965; a reduction and translation into English was published in N.Y., 1972); *Composer, Performer, Public: A Study in Communication* (Florence, 1970; in English).

Helm, Theodor, Austrian music critic; b. Vienna, April 9, 1843; d. there, Dec. 23, 1920. He was the son of a physician; studied jurisprudence in Vienna and became a government employee; in 1867, he began writing music criticism for various Viennese publications; in 1874 became music teacher at Horák's music school; from 1875 till 1901, he was editor of Fromme's *Kalender für die Musikalische Welt;* published *Beethovens Streichquartette: Versuch einer technischen Analyse im Zusammenhang mit ihrem geistigen Gehalt* (Leipzig, 1885; 2nd ed., 1910).

Helmholtz, Hermann (Ludwig Ferdinand) von, celebrated German scientist and acoustician; b. Potsdam, Aug. 31, 1821; d. Berlin, Sept. 8, 1894. His father was a school teacher in Potsdam, and Helmholtz received his education there. His mother, Caroline Penn, was of English extraction. He studied medicine at the Military Institute of Berlin; received his M.D. and became a member of the staff of the Charité Hospital there (1842); in 1843 he was appointed military surgeon at Potsdam; then recalled to Berlin as teacher of anatomy (for artists) at the Academy of Fine Arts (1848). In 1849, he obtained a position as prof. of physiology at Univ. of Königsberg; 1855, prof. at Bonn; 1858, at Heidelberg. In 1871, abandoning the teaching of physiology and anatomy, he accepted the position of prof. of physics at the Univ. of Berlin; publ. various scientific studies. The work of most interest to musicians, and indispensable for students of acoustics, is his *Lehre von den Tonempfindungen als physiologische Grundlage für die Theorie der Musik* (Brunswick, 1863); it was translated by Alexander John Ellis and publ. in London under the title, *On the Sensations of Tone as a Physiological Basis for the Theory of Music* (London, 1875; new ed., N.Y., 1948). By a long series of experiments, Helmholtz established a sure physical foundation for the phenomena manifested by musical tones, either single or combined. He supple-

mented and amplified the theories of Rameau, Tartini, Wheatstone, Corti, and others, furnishing impregnable formulae for all classes of consonant and dissonant tone effects, and proving with scientific precision what Hauptmann and his school sought to establish by laborious dialectic processes. The laws governing the differences in quality of tone (tone color) in different instruments and voices, covering the whole field of harmonic, differential, and summational tones; the nature and limits of musical perception by the human ear are the chief results of Helmholtz's labors.

BIBLIOGRAPHY: S. Epstein, *Hermann von Helmholtz als Mensch und Gelehrter* (Stuttgart, 1896); L. Königsberger, *Hermann von Helmholtz* (3 vols., Brunswick, 1902–03; 1 vol., 1911); E. Waetzman, *Zur Helmholtzschen Resonanztheorie* (Breslau, 1907); L. S. Lloyd, "Helmholtz and the Musical Ear," *Musical Quarterly* (April 1939); H. Ebert, *Hermann von Helmholtz* (Stuttgart, 1949).

Helms, Hans G., German composer; b. Teterow, Mecklenburg, June 8, 1932. He studied literature and comparative philology; in 1957 settled in Cologne; worked on various speech problems; also supervised numerous recordings of modern music. His compositions exploit the musical possibilities of the speaking voice; of these, *Golem*, 'polemics for 9 vocal soloists' has been widely performed at modern music festivals in Germany. Other works are *Daidalos* for 4 solo singers, and a group of speaking and listening pieces, *Geschichte von Yahud* (1963).

Helps, Robert, American pianist and composer; b. Passaic, New Jersey, Sept. 23, 1928. He studied at the Juilliard School of Music in New York with Abby Whiteside (piano) and Roger Sessions (composition). He occupied teaching posts at Princeton Univ., the San Francisco Cons. of Music, Stanford Univ. and the Univ. of California at Berkeley. In 1970 he was on the staff of the New England Cons. of Music. His natural pianism helps Helps to write idiomatically for his instrument.

WORKS: Fantasy for Piano (1952); Symph. No. 1 (1955); Piano Trio (1957); *Image* for piano (1958); *Recollections* for piano (1959); *Portrait* for piano (1960); *Cortège* for orch. (1963); Serenade in 3 parts: (1) Fantasy for Violin and Piano (2) Nocturne for string quartet (3) *Postlude* for piano, violin, and horn (1964); Piano Concerto (1966); *Saccade* for piano 4 hands (1967); *Quartet* for piano solo, divided into 4 equal parts, each numbering 22 keys (1971).

Helsted, Gustaf, Danish composer; b. Copenhagen, Jan. 30, 1857; d. there, March 1, 1924. He was a pupil of Hartmann and Gade; from 1892, prof. of theory and from 1904 also of organ, at the Copenhagen Cons.; from 1915, organist of the Frauenkirche. He wrote 2 symphonies, a decimet for woodwinds and strings, a string sextet, 3 string quartets, a piano trio, 2 violin sonatas, and 2 cantatas: *Gurresånge* (Copenhagen, April 18, 1904) and *Vort Land* (Copenhagen, April 19, 1909).

Hemberg, Eskil, Swedish conductor and composer; b. Stockholm, Jan. 19, 1938. He studied at the Royal College of Music in Stockholm; took lessons in conducting from Herbert Blomstedt. He conducted the chorus of Stockholm Univ. on an extensive tour in Europe and America. Most of his works are for vocal groups; he maintains the main lines of classical polyphony in sacred music, while in his instrumental writing he ventures into modern harmony.

WORKS: an a cappella opera, *Love*, after Robert Graves (1969–70; first stage performance, Stockholm, Oct. 30, 1973); *3 Jerusalem Choruses* (1958); *2 Evangelical Motets* (1960); *Zoo*, 5 nonsense songs for chorus (1965); *Paradise*, cantata (1965); *En natt som lyste*, cantata (1966); *Eighteen Movements*, a choreographic choral suite (Stockholm, April 30, 1968); *Signposts*, to the texts of Dag Hammarskjöld, for chorus (1968); *The Gallery*, after E. A. Robinson, for bass and male chorus (1969); *Messa d'oggi* for 5 solo voices and chorus (1968–70); *Jesu lidande, död och uppståndelse*, a St. Mark Passion for soli, chorus and orch. (Stockholm, March 26, 1972); *Cantica* for soli, chorus and orch. (Bergen, Norway, Nov. 29, 1973); *En gammal saga (An Old Tale)*, cantata for soprano, harp and harpsichord (1973); *Migraine* for orch. (1973); *Zona rosa* for string quartet (1973); *Epitaffio* for organ (1974); *Pietà*, to texts by Hammarskjöld, for alto voice and piano (1974); many choruses and songs.

Hemel, Oscar van, Dutch composer; b. Antwerp, Aug. 3, 1892. He studied composition with Lodewijk Mortelmans at the Royal Flemish Cons. in Antwerp; went to Holland in 1914; was active as a violin teacher; then took lessons in composition with Pijper in Rotterdam; did not begin to compose until very late in life, but compensated for it by composing prolifically. His music reveals a type of neo-Romanticism typical of the German and Austrian symphonic style of the early 20th century; later, he adopted some dodecaphonic procedures.

WORKS: radio opera, *Viviane* (Hilversum radio, 1950); *Maria Magdalena*, sacred cantata (1941); *De bruid (The Bride)* for soprano, male chorus and orch. (1946); *Dat liet van Alianora* for soprano, male chorus and orch. (1947); *Hart van Nederland (Heart of Holland)* for male chorus, winds and percussion (1952); *Ballade van Brabant* for narrator, boys' chorus, male chorus and orch. (1952); *Le Tombeau de Kathleen Ferrier* for alto and orch. (1954); *Herdenkingshymne 1940–1945 (Memorial Hymn 1940–1945)* for mixed chorus, children's chorus, brass and percussion (1955; for full orch., 1970); *Les Mystères du Christ*, 5 psalms for alto, baritone, male chorus and orch. (1958); *Te Deum* for 4 soloists, chorus and orch. (1958); *Tuin van Holland* for soprano, baritone, chorus and orch. (1958); *Ballade van Kapitein Joos de Decker* for alto, bass, chorus and orch. (1943–59); *Trittico liturgico* for soprano and strings (1959); *Huwelijks Cantata* (1966); *Song of Freedom* for speaking chorus, mixed chorus and orch. (1968–69); 5 symphonies: No. 1 (1935); No. 2 (1948); No. 3, *Sinfonietta* for small orch. (1952); No. 4 (1962); No. 5 (1963–64, revised 1967); Suite for Chamber Orch. (1936); Suite for Flute, and Chamber Orch. or Piano (1937); Piano Concerto (1941–42); Ballade for Orch. (1942); 2 violin concertos (1943–45, 1968); *De stad (The City)*, symph. poem (1949); *Divertimento Ballet*

for orch. (1950; drawn from his opera *Viviane*); Viola Concerto (1951); *Feestelijke ouverture* (1952); *Olof Suite* for orch. (1953); *Entrada festante* (1953); *Tema con variazioni* for orch. (1953); Oboe Concerto (1955); Concerto for Wind Orch. (1960); *Concerto da camera* for flute and string orch. (1962); Violin Concertino (1963); Cello Concerto (1963); *3 Contrasts* for winds and percussion (1963); Divertimento for strings (1964); *Entrada* for orch. (1964); Serenade for 3 Solo Winds and String Orch. (1965); Polonaise for Orch. (1966); Concerto for 2 Violins and String Orch. (1970–71); Divertimento for Orch. and Piano (1974); 2 violin sonatas (1933, 1945); 6 string quartets (Nos. 3–6: 1946–47, 1953, 1956, 1961); Piano Trio (1937); Piano Quartet (1938); Viola Sonata (1942); String Trio (1951); Concertino for Trumpet and Piano (1953); *Canticum psalmorum* for contralto, chorus, 2 pianos and percussion (1954); *4 Koperkwartetten* for horn, 2 trumpets and trombone (1955); Clarinet Quintet (1958); *Divertimento II* for 12 winds and piano (1959); Trio for Flute, Oboe and Bassoon (1959); *Rondeau et Ballade* for female chorus, flute, string quartet and harp (1959); *Capriccio* for clarinet and piano (1960); Sextet for Piano and Wind Quintet (1962); *Donquichotterie* for 4 trombones (1962); Suite for 2 Violins (1966); *About Commedia dell'arte* for oboe quartet (1967); Wind Quintet (1972).

Hemke, Frederick, American saxophone virtuoso; b. Milwaukee, July 11, 1935. He studied at the Univ. of Wisconsin (1953–55, 1956–58) and Eastman School of Music (1960–62); was a student of Marcel Mule in Paris (1955–56) where he became the first American to win the Premier Prix in saxophone (1956). In 1964 he joined the Chicago Symph. Orch. as saxophonist; from 1962 was on the faculty of Northwestern Univ. In 1966 he made a tour of 11 countries in the Orient under the auspices of the State Dept. He has published a history of the saxophone.

Hemmer, Eugene, American pianist, composer and teacher; b. Cincinnati, March 23, 1929. He studied piano with Albino Gorno and composition with Felix Labunski at the College of Music of Cincinnati. After receiving his M.M. he held teaching jobs as pianist and composer: at the Univ. of Cincinnati (1950–58); Chadwick School, Palos Verdes, California (1960–68); and at El Camino College, Torrance, California (since 1969).

WORKS: Concerto for 2 Pianos and Orchestra, 10 Symphonic Dances, *The School Bus* for orch., *Sunshine Games* for orch., Divertimento, for harp, marimba, celesta and piano; 2 viola sonatas, Cello Sonata, Piano Trio, Duo for Violin and Cello.

Hempel, Frieda, brilliant German coloratura soprano; b. Leipzig, June 26, 1885; d. Berlin, Oct. 7, 1955. In 1900 she entered the Leipzig Cons. as a piano pupil; from 1902–05 she studied singing with Frau Nicklass-Kempner in Berlin; made her debut at the Berlin Opera in Nicolai's *Merry Wives of Windsor* (Aug. 28, 1905); from 1905–07, at the Court Opera in Schwerin; 1907–12, member of the Royal Opera in Berlin; 1912–19, one of the foremost members of the Metropolitan Opera, where she made her debut as the

Queen in *Les Huguenots* on Dec. 27, 1912. In 1920 she impersonated Jenny Lind in the Lind centenary celebrations in New York and throughout the U.S. (70 concerts). She was married to William B. Kahn in 1918 (divorced in 1926). From 1940 till 1955 she lived in New York. A few months before her death, knowing that she was incurably ill, she returned to Berlin. Her memoirs, *Mein Leben dem Gesang*, were published posthumously (Berlin, 1955).

Hemsi, Alberto, composer; b. (of Italian-Jewish parents) Cassaba, Turkey, Dec. 23, 1896. He studied in Smyrna, and later at the Milan Cons. with Bossi; graduated in 1919. He was wounded while serving in the Italian Army in World War I. In 1928 he went (after a brief sojourn in Rhodes) to Alexandria, where he was appointed director of the Israelite Music School; from 1932–1940 taught at the Liceo Musicale Italiano there; later became instructor in harmony at the Alexandria Cons. In 1929 he founded the Edition Orientale de Musique.
WORKS: for orch.: *Danses bibliques; Croquis Egyptiens,* orchestral suite (Alexandria, March 19, 1951); for voice and orch.: *Five Hebrew Songs, Poème biblique, Mélodie religieuse; Tre arie antiche* for string quartet; String Quintet; Violin Sonata; *Suite Séfardie* for violin and piano; *Trois danses égyptiennes* for violin and piano; *Six danses turques* for piano; *Coplas Séfardies* (six cycles of traditional Jewish chants) for voice and piano.

Henderson, Alva, American opera composer; b. San Luis Obispo, April 8, 1940. He studied voice and music theory at the San Francisco State College; devoted himself mainly to vocal works. His first opera, *Medea,* based on the play by Robinson Jeffers, was produced with a modicum of critical favor in San Diego, California, on Nov. 29, 1972; his second opera was adapted from Shakespeare's play *The Tempest.* He obtained his most decisive success with his third opera, *The Last of the Mohicans,* after the novel of James Fenimore Cooper, produced by the Wilmington Opera Society on June 12, 1976 in Wilmington, Delaware.

Henderson, Ray, American composer of popular songs; b. Buffalo, Dec. 1, 1896; d. Greenwich, Conn., Dec. 31, 1970. He studied music at the Univ. of Southern Calif.; played the organ in churches and piano in jazz groups in Buffalo; then went to New York as a song plugger in Tin Pan Alley, and soon began writing songs of his own. His first success was *Georgette* (1922); this was followed by *Sonny Boy* which he wrote for Al Jolson's early talkie *The Singing Fool;* subsequent hits were *You're the Cream in My Coffee, Button Up Your Overcoat, Alabamy Bound, Hold Everything, Three Cheers,* etc.; some of these songs were written in collaboration with B. G. DeSylva. Unlike most Broadway composers, Henderson could read and write music; he even took private lessons with Benjamin Britten. His film biography *The Best Things in Life are Free* was made in 1966.

Henderson, William James, American music critic; b. Newark, N.J., Dec. 4, 1855; d. (suicide) New York, June 5, 1937. He was a graduate (1876) of Princeton

(M.A., 1886); studied piano with Carl Langlotz (1868–73) and voice with Torriani (1876–77); chiefly self-taught in theory. He wrote many librettos of light operas, and also *Cyrano de Bergerac* for Walter Damrosch (1913). He was first a reporter (1883), then music critic of the *New York Times* (1887–1902); and for 35 years, until his death, for the *New York Sun* (1902–37); lectured on music history in N.Y. College of Music (1899–1902); from 1904, lectured on the development of vocal art at the Institute of Musical Art, N.Y. A brilliant writer, Henderson was an irreconcilable and often venomous critic of modern music; he loved Wagner, but savagely attacked Debussy and Richard Strauss. Henderson, in turn, was the butt of some of Charles Ives's caustic wit.
WRITINGS: *The Story of Music* (1889; 12th enlarged ed., 1912); *Preludes and Studies* (1891); *How Music Developed* (1898); *What Is Good Music?* (1898; 3rd ed., 1905); *The Orchestra and Orchestral Music* (1899); *Richard Wagner, His Life and His Dramas* (1901); *Modern Musical Drift* (1904); *The Art of the Singer* (1906); *Some Forerunners of Italian Opera* (1911); *Early History of Singing* (1921); "The Function of Musical Criticism," *Musical Quarterly* (Jan. 1915); "Beethoven After a Hundred Years," *Musical Quarterly* (April 1927); many other articles in various journals. In the series *Famous Composers and Their Works,* Henderson wrote the biographies of Goldmark, Tchaikovsky, and Wagner, as well as the chapter on Dutch composers.
BIBLIOGRAPHY: O. Thompson, "An American School of Criticism: The Legacy Left by W. J. Henderson, R. Aldrich and Their Colleagues of the Old Guard," *Musical Quarterly* (Oct. 1937); O. Thompson also edited excerpts from Henderson's scrapbook, published as *The Art of Singing* (N.Y., 1938); *Charles E. Ives: Memos,* ed. by J. Kirkpatrick (N.Y., 1972).

Hendl, Walter, American conductor; b. West New York, New Jersey, Jan. 12, 1917. He studied conducting with Fritz Reiner at the Curtis Institute of Music in Philadelphia. He was associate conductor of the N.Y. Philharmonic from 1945 to 1949 and musical director of the Dallas Symphony from 1949 to 1958. From 1964 to 1972 he was director of the Eastman School of Music in Rochester, N.Y. He composed some incidental music for theatrical plays.

Hendrix, Jimi (James Marshall), black American rock 'n' roll musician; b. Seattle, Nov. 27, 1942; d. London, Sept. 18, 1970, as a result of asphyxiation from vomiting while unconscious after taking an overdose of barbiturates. He rose to fame as a singer-guitarist whose erotic body movements underscored the sexual implications of his lyrics. He produced a sensation by his performance of an electronically amplified version of *The Star-Spangled Banner* at the Woodstock Festival in August, 1969. His popularity in England was enhanced by his appearance at the Isle of Wight Festival in August, 1970.
BIBLIOGRAPHY: Curtis Knight, *Jimi; An Intimate Biography of Jimi Hendrix* (New York, 1974).

Hengeveld, Gerard, Dutch pianist and composer; b. Kampen, Dec. 7, 1910. He studied piano with Carl

Friedberg; appeared as soloist with European orchestras and in recital; then was appointed to the piano faculty at The Hague Cons. He composed a Violin Sonata (1944); Concertino for Piano and Orch. (1946); Piano Concerto (1947); Cello Sonata (1965); *Musica Concertante* for oboe and chamber orch. (1968); numerous teaching pieces for piano.

Henkel, Heinrich, German pianist; son of **Michael Henkel;** b. Fulda, Feb. 17, 1822; d. Frankfurt, April 10, 1899. He was a pupil of his father; also studied with Aloys Schmitt. He settled in Frankfurt in 1849, as a teacher. He publ. a piano method, *Vorschule des Klavierspiels,* an abridged ed. of A. André's *Lehrbuch der Tonsetzkunst* (1875), *Mitteilungen aus der musikalischen Vergangenheit Fuldas* (1882); piano pieces and songs.

Henkel, Michael, German composer of church music; b. Fulda, June 18, 1780; d. there, March 4, 1851. He studied with Vierling; then served as a local music teacher. He wrote a great number of sacred works, organ pieces, and instrumental works.

Henkemans, Hans, Dutch composer and pianist; b. The Hague, Dec. 23, 1913. He took lessons in piano and composition with Bernhard van den Sigtenhorst-Meyer and Willem Pijper (1930-36); made his debut as pianist in his own piano concerto at 19. Concurrently he studied medicine at the Univ. of Utrecht, and was active as a practicing psychiatrist. As a composer, he follows the stylistic manner of the modern French school, cultivating sonorous harmonies supporting melodic lines of a modal character.
WORKS: 2 piano concertos (1932; 1936); Symphony (1934); *Voorspel (Prelude)* for orch. (1935-36); *Ballade,* for alto and chamber orch. (1936); *Driehonderd waren wij (Three Hundred Were We . . .),* cantata (1933-40); *Passacaglia and Gigue* for piano and orch. (1941-42; Amsterdam, Dec. 2, 1945); *Primavera* for 12 instruments (1944; revised 1959); Flute Concerto (1945-46); Violin Concerto (1948-50); Viola Concerto (1954); Harp Concerto (1955); Partita for Orch. (1960; Scheveningen, Dec. 8, 1960); *Barcarola fantastica* for orch. (Groningen, Nov. 13, 1962); *Dona Montana,* 3 pieces for orch. (1964); *Bericht aan de Levenden (Message to the Living)* for chorus, narration and orch. (1964; Amsterdam, May 4, 1965); *Villonnerie* for baritone and orch. after Villon's poems (1965); *Elégies* for 4 flutes and orch. (Utrecht, Oct. 18, 1967); *Tre aspetti d'amore* for chorus and orch. (1967-68; Amsterdam, July 5, 1971); *Canzoni Amorose* for soprano, baritone, piano and orch. (1972-73); 2 wind quintets (1934, 1962); 3 string quartets; Cello Sonata (1936); Violin Sonata (1944); *Epilogue* for flute and piano (1947); *4 Pieces* for harp and flute (1963); *Aere Festivo* for 3 trumpets and 2 trombones (1965); 2 Etudes for Piano (1937); 2-Piano Sonata (1943); Piano Sonata (1958); songs, including *De Tooverfluit (The Magic Flute,* 1946) and *3 Liederen)* (1964); choruses. In 1971 he orchestrated 12 of Debussy's Preludes (Amsterdam, July 5, 1971).
BIBLIOGRAPHY: M. Flothuis, "Hans Henkemans," *Sonorum Speculum* (1963).

Henneberg, Albert, Swedish composer, son of **Richard Henneberg;** b. Stockholm, March 27, 1901. He studied composition in Stockholm (1920-24) and later in Vienna and Paris (1926-30). Returning to Stockholm in 1931, he became active as a conductor.
WORKS: 5 operas: *Inka* (1935-36), *Det jäser i Småland* (1937-38), *Den lyckliga staden* (1940-41), *Bolla och Badin* (1942-44) and *I madonnans skugga* (1946); Chamber Symphony (1927); 6 symphonies: No. 1, *Pä ledungsfärd* (1925); No. 2, with baritone solo (1927); No. 3, *Värvindar* (1927); No. 4, *Pathétique* (1930-31); No. 5 (1935); No. 6, *Vinterskärgärd* (1953-54); Piano Concerto (1925); *Valborgsmässonatt,* symph. poem (1928); Serenade for String Orch. (1931; also for string quartet); *Sommar,* suite for orch. (1932); *Det ljusa landet* for soloists, chorus and orch. (1933); Trumpet Concerto (1934); Trombone Concerto (1935); *I brytningstider,* symph. suite (1943); *Gustavianska kapriser* for orch. (1943); Concertino for Flute and Strings (1944); Cello Concerto (1948); Concertino for Bassoon and Strings (1956); Concertino for Clarinet, Strings, Piano and Percussion (1960); 2 string quartets (1931); *Little Quartet* for flute, oboe, bassoon and horn; Violin Sonata.

Henneberg, Johann Baptist, Austrian conductor and composer; b. Vienna, Dec. 6, 1768; d. there, Nov. 26, 1822. He conducted at Vienna theaters (1790-1803); then became a member of the orch. of Count Esterházy; in 1818, returned to Vienna. He wrote a great number of *Singspiele,* of which the most successful were *Die Waldmänner* (Hamburg, 1787) and *Liebe macht kurzen Prozess* (Leipzig, 1799).

Henneberg, Richard, German conductor and composer; b. Berlin, Aug. 5, 1853; d. Malmö, Oct. 19, 1925. He studied piano with Liszt; then traveled as accompanist with various artists, including Wieniawski; held posts as operatic coach at the Italian Opera in London, at various theatres in Berlin and Stockholm; from 1885 until 1907 conducted at the Stockholm Opera; from 1914-20, was conductor of the Malmö Orchestra. Henneberg gave the first performance of *Tannhäuser* in Stockholm (1876) and the first complete production of the *Ring of the Nibelung* in Sweden (1907), and was an ardent propagandist of Wagner's music. He wrote a comic opera *Drottningens Vallfart* (Stockholm, 1882), incidental music to Ibsen's *Brand,* various Shakespearian pieces, a ballet *Undine,* some choral works and songs (all in a Wagnerian vein).

Hennerberg, Carl Fredrik, Swedish musicologist; b. Älgaras, Jan. 24, 1871; d. Stockholm, Sept. 17, 1932. As a young man, he was an organist at Varola; then went to Stockholm, where he studied at the Cons. (1899-1903) and remained on the faculty as harmony teacher. In 1909 he was appointed organist at the Royal Chapel; also served as librarian of the Music Academy. He specialized in the study of organ manufacture; traveled in European countries to collect information; publ. *Die schwedischen Orgeln des Mittelalters* (Vienna, 1909); *Orgelns byggnad och vard* (a treatise on organ building; Uppsala, 1912; 2nd ed.,

1928); contributed numerous bibliographical papers to musicological journals.

Hennes, Aloys, German pianist; b. Aachen, Sept. 8, 1827; d. Berlin, June 8, 1889. He studied with Hiller and Reinecke in Cologne; then taught piano in various provincial towns; in 1872 settled in Berlin. He publ. *Klavierunterrichtsbriefe,* containing ingenious teaching pieces. His daughter, **Therese,** was a child prodigy, who made an exceptionally successful tour in England in 1877.

Hennessy, Swan, American composer; b. Rockford, Ill., Nov. 24, 1866; d. Paris, Oct. 26, 1929. He was the son of an Irish-American settler; studied general subjects in Oxford, and music in Germany; then traveled in Italy, France, and Ireland, eventually settling in Paris.

WORKS: about 70 compositions, several of which are derived from Irish folk melos; his technical equipment was thorough; his idiom, impressionistic. Among his Irish-inspired works are *Petit trio celtique* for violin, viola, and cello; *Rapsodie celtique* for violin and piano; *Rapsodie gaëlique* for cello and piano, and *Sonata in Irish Style* for violin and piano; several piano albums "*à la manière de . . .*"; characteristic piano pieces in a humorous vein, such as *Epigrammes d'un solitaire, Impressions humoristiques,* etc.; 4 string quartets.

Hennig, Carl, German organist and composer; b. Berlin, April 23, 1819; d. there, April 18, 1873. A precocious musician, he brought out a psalm for soli, chorus, and orch. at the age of 14; began to conduct choral groups at an early age; then became a church organist at the Sophienkirche in Berlin; also was conductor of the Lyra Choral Society. He wrote a great number of miscellaneous pieces, sacred works, cantatas, as well as popular dances for piano.

Hennig, Carl Rafael, German music theorist and composer; son of **Carl Hennig;** b. Berlin, Jan. 4, 1845; d. Posen, Feb. 6, 1914. He studied music with his father; then with Richter in Leipzig and Kiel in Berlin; at the same time, studied law. After a brief period of teaching in Berlin, he went to Posen, where he founded the Hennig Vocal Society; also served as church organist. He composed several cantatas, choruses, songs, and instrumental pieces, but it is as a writer on theoretical subjects that he is mainly remembered.

WRITINGS: *Die Methodik des Schulgesang-Unterrichts* (Leipzig, 1885); *Die Unterscheidung der Gesangregister auf physiologischer Grundlage* (Leipzig, 1892); *Beitrag zur Wagner-Sache* (Leipzig, 1893); *Ästhetik der Tonkunst* (Leipzig, 1896); *Über die Entstehung der 'hohen Resonanz'* (Leipzig, 1902); *Musiktheoretisches Hilfsbuch* (Leipzig, 1903; 2nd ed., 1906); *Einführung in das Wesen der Musik* (Leipzig, 1906); excellent analyses of Beethoven's 9th Symph. and *Missa Solemnis.*

Henning, Ervin Arthur, American composer; b. Marion, South Dakota, Nov. 22, 1910, of German immigrant parents. He studied music in Chicago with Ros-

lyn Brogue, whom he subsequently married. In 1944 he entered New England Cons. in Boston, graduating in 1946. He writes mostly for chamber music combinations; in his later works he adopted the 12-tone method of composition.

WORKS: Quintet, for flute, horn, violin, viola and cello (1946); Partita for String Quartet (1948); Suite for Viola Concertante, 2 Violins and Cello (1950); Divertimento for Unaccompanied Bassoon (1950); Trio for Clarinet, Viola and Piano (1959); Piano Sonata (1959); pieces for recorders; arrangements of Bach for various woodwind ensembles.

Henriot, Nicole, French pianist; b. Paris, Nov. 23, 1925. She studied with Marguerite Long; entered the Paris Cons. at the age of 12, graduating with a 1st prize two years later. She toured Europe (1946–49), appearing with major orchestras; she made her American debut on Jan. 29, 1948; toured Canada and South America (1949–50).

Henriques, Fini Valdemar, Danish composer; b. Copenhagen, Dec. 20, 1867; d. there, Oct. 27, 1940. He studied violin with Valdemar Tofte in Copenhagen, and with Joachim at the Hochschule für Musik in Berlin; composition with Svendsen; returning to Copenhagen, he was violinist in the court orch. (1892–96); also appeared as soloist. He organized his own string quartet, and traveled with it in Europe; also conducted orchestras.

WORKS: As a composer, he followed the Romantic school; he possessed a facile gift of melody; his *Danish Lullaby* became a celebrated song in Denmark. He also wrote an opera *Staerstikkeren* (Copenhagen, May 20, 1922); several ballets (*The Little Mermaid,* after Hans Andersen; *Tata,* etc.); *Hans Andersen Overture;* 2 symphonies; String Quartet; Quartet for Flute, Violin, Cello, and Piano; Violin Sonata; a number of piano pieces (several cycles, *Lyrik, Erotik,* etc.).

BIBLIOGRAPHY: S. Berg, *F. V. Henriques* (Copenhagen, 1943).

Henriques, Robert, Danish cellist, conductor, and composer; b. Copenhagen, Dec. 14, 1858; d. there, Dec. 29, 1914. He studied cello with Popper, and composition with Kretschmer in Dresden. Upon his return to Copenhagen, he conducted orchestral concerts; wrote music criticism; composed an overture *Olaf Trygvason;* symph. sketch, *Aquarellen;* a number of pieces for the cello.

Henry, Harold, American pianist; b. Neodesha, Kansas, March 20, 1884; d. Orangeburg, N.Y., Oct. 15, 1956. He studied in Kansas; then went to Berlin where he took lessons with Leopold Godowsky; also studied with Moszkowski in Paris. He made his American debut in Chicago on January 30, 1906, and then launched a moderately successful concert career before settling in New York as a piano teacher. He wrote a number of character pieces for piano (*Heroic Rhapsody, Dancing Marionette, Night Sounds*) and some singable songs.

Henry, Hugh Thomas, American Roman Catholic priest, and writer on church music; b. Philadelphia,

1862; d. there, March 12, 1946. He taught church music at Overbrook Seminary from 1889 to 1917; was prof. of homiletics at Catholic Univ., Washington, from 1919–37. Besides his many religious and literary writings, he contributed the following articles to the *Musical Quarterly:* "Music Reform in the Catholic Church" (Jan. 1915), "Choir-Boys in Catholic Churches" (July 1917), and "Music in Lowell's Prose and Verse" (Oct. 1924).

Henry, Leigh Vaughan, English writer and conductor; b. Liverpool, Sept. 23, 1889; d. London, March 8, 1958. Received his earliest training from his father, John Henry, a singer and composer; then studied with Granville Bantock in London, Ricardo Viñes in France, and Buonamici in Italy; taught music at Gordon Craig's Theatrical School in Florence (1912); then was in Germany, where he was interned during World War I. Returning to England, he edited a modern music journal *Fanfare* (1921–22); also was active in various organizations promoting modern music; in 1930 he went to the U.S.; lectured at various colleges. He was music director of the Shakespeare Festival Week in London in 1938, 1945, and 1946; organized and conducted orchestral concerts of British music, and the National Welsh Festival Concerts; also at the BBC.
WRITINGS: *Music: What it Means and How to Understand It* (London, 1920); *The Growth of Music in Form and Significance* (1921); *The Story of Music* (1935); *Dr. John Bull* (largely fictional; London, 1937); *My Surging World,* autobiography (with R. Hale; 1937). Among his compositions are *The Moon Robber,* an opera; *Llyn-y-Fan,* symph. poem; various pieces on Welsh themes.

Henry, Michel, a member of the 24 "violons du roi" under Henry IV and Louis XIII; b. Paris, Feb., 1555; date of death unknown. He wrote ballets for the court. His younger brother, known as Le Jeune, also in the "violons du roi," composed some very interesting instrumental music: a *Fantaisie* for 5 violins; another *Fantaisie* for 5 *cornetti; Pavane* for 6 oboes; some of this is reproduced by P. Mersenne in his *Harmonie universelle* (vol. 3, pp. 186–277). Dolmetsch made a modern arrangement of the *Fantaisie* for 5 violins.
BIBLIOGRAPHY: F. Lesure, "Le Recueil de Ballets de Michel Henry," in *Les Fêtes de la Renaissance* (Paris, 1956).

Henry, Pierre, French composer and acoustical inventor; b. Paris, Dec. 9, 1927. He studied with Messiaen at the Paris Cons.; also took courses with Nadia Boulanger; in 1950 was a founder of Groupe de Recherche de Musique Concrète with Pierre Schaeffer, but in 1958 separated from the group to experiment on his own projects in the field of electro-acoustical music and electronic synthesis of musical sounds. In virtually all of his independent works he applied electronic effects, often with the insertion of pre-recorded patches of concrete music and sometimes "objets trouvés" borrowed partially or in their entirety from pre-existent compositions.
WORKS: In collaboration with Pierre Schaeffer he wrote *Symphonie pour un homme seul* (1950) and the experimental opera *Orphée 53* (1953); independently

he wrote *Microphone bien tempéré* (1952); *Musique sans titre* (1951); *Concerto des ambiguités* (1951); *Astrologie* (1953); *Spatiodynamisme* (1955); 4 ballets: *Haut voltage* (1956), *Coexistence* (1959), *Investigations* (1959), *Le Voyage* (1962); *Messe de Liverpool* (1967); *Ceremony* (1970); *Futuristie 1,* "electro-acoustical musical spectacle," with the reconstruction of the "bruiteurs" introduced by the Italian futurist Luigi Russolo in 1909 (Paris, Oct. 16, 1975).

Henry V, the English king; b. Monmouth, Sept. 1387; d. Bois de Vincennes, Aug. 31, 1422. During his reign (1413–22), he established a flourishing musical service at the Chapel Royal; was a musician himself; probably was the author of a Gloria and a Sanctus for 3 voices in the Old Hall MS (transcribed into modern notation, and publ. by the Plainsong and Medieval Music Society, 1933–38, vols. I and III; in that edition, these works are ascribed to Henry VI).

Henry VI, the English king; b. Windsor, Dec. 6, 1421; d. London, May 21, 1471. He reigned from 1422 till 1471. For a long time, he was regarded as the "Roy Henry" who was the author of a Gloria and a Sanctus in the Old Hall MS; however, research by M. Bukofzer tends to indicate that the works may actually be by Henry V.
BIBLIOGRAPHY: W. Barclay Squire, "Henry VI," *Sammelbände der Internationalen Musik-Gesellschaft* (1900–01, p. 342); G. R. Hayes, *King's Music,* an anthology (London, 1937).

Henry VIII, the English king; b. Greenwich, June 28, 1491; d. Windsor, Jan. 28, 1547. He reigned from 1509 to 1547. He received regular instruction in music. His compositions include 2 Masses (lost); a Latin motet for 3 voices (publ. in the *Baldwin Collection,* 1591); the anthem *O Lord, the Maker of All Kings;* a secular ballad, *Passe tyme with good cumpanye,* for 3 voices (publ. in Chappell's *Popular Music of the Olden Time*); five 4-part songs and twelve 3-part songs; also several pieces for 3 and 4 viols; 35 pieces are printed in *Music at the Court of Henry VIII,* vol. 18 of *Musica Britannica.*
BIBLIOGRAPHY: Lady Mary Trefusis, *Music Composed by Henry VIII* (Roxburghe Club, 1912; privately printed); G. R. Hayes, *King's Music* (London, 1937).

Henschel, Sir George (full name **Isador Georg Henschel**), German conductor, composer, and singer; b. Breslau, Feb. 18, 1850; d. Aviemore, Scotland, Sept. 10, 1934. Both parents were of Polish-Jewish descent but he was converted to Christianity when young. He studied with Julius Shäffer at Breslau, and with Moscheles (piano), Götze (singing), and Reinecke (theory) at the Leipzig Cons. (1867–70); then with Friedrich Kiel (composition) and Adolf Schulze (singing) in Berlin. He was a boy soprano; when his voice broke he gave concerts as a tenor; made his debut in Leipzig (1868) as Hans Sachs (baritone) in a concert performance of *Die Meistersinger;* he then toured throughout Europe; later gave recitals as a bass, and in 1914 he appeared in London singing as a basso profondo. At the age of 78 he sang a group of Schubert lieder in London (at the Schubert centennial, 1928).

An important turning point in his career came when he was selected as the first conductor of the Boston Symphony, which he led for three seasons (1881–84); he also gave concerts in Boston and New York as a singer. Settling in England, he founded the London Symphony Concerts (inaugural concert, Nov. 17, 1886), and conducted them until the series was concluded in 1897. He was a vocal teacher at the Royal College of Music (1886–88) and conductor of the Scottish Symphony Orchestra (1893–95). From 1905–08 he was professor of singing at the Institute of Musical Art, New York. In 1931, at the age of 81, he was engaged to conduct a commemorative concert on the 50th anniversary of the Boston Symphony Orchestra, identical (except for one number) with his inaugural Boston concert of 1881. In 1881 Henschel married the American singer **Lillian Bailey,** with whom he gave concerts; she died in 1901. In 1907 he was married, for a second time, to Amy Louis. He was knighted in 1914.

WORKS: His musical compositions (mostly vocal) are in the German Romantic tradition. They include the opera *Nubia* (Dresden, Dec. 9, 1899); *Stabat Mater* (Birmingham, Oct. 4, 1894); *Requiem,* in memory of his first wife (Boston, Dec. 2, 1902); Mass for 8 voices (London, June 1, 1916); String Quartet; about 200 songs (almost all published). He was the author of *Personal Recollections of Johannes Brahms* (Boston, 1907) and the autobiographical *Musings and Memories of a Musician* (1918).

BIBLIOGRAPHY: Mark Antony de Wolfe Howe, *The Boston Symphony Orchestra, 1881–1931* (Boston, 1931); H. Earle Johnson, *Symphony Hall* (Boston, 1950).

Henschel, Lillian June (*née* **Bailey**), American soprano; b. Columbus, Ohio, Jan. 17, 1860; d. London, Nov. 4, 1901. She made her professional debut in Boston at 16; then went to Paris to study with Mme. Viardot-García. On April 30, 1879 she appeared in London, at a Philh. concert, when she sang, besides her solo number, a duet with George Henschel. She then studied with him and on March 9, 1881, married him. When Henschel was appointed first conductor of the Boston Symph. Orch., she appeared as a soloist with him accompanying her at the piano, also in duets at Boston Symph. concerts. Until her untimely death, the Henschels were constantly associated in American artistic life. Her well-trained voice and fine musical feeling won her many admirers.

BIBLIOGRAPHY: Helen Henschel, *When Soft Voices Die. A Musical Biography* (London, 1944).

Hensel, Fanny Cäcilia, pianist and composer; sister of **Felix Mendelssohn;** b. Hamburg, Nov. 14, 1805; d. Berlin, May 14, 1847. Brought up in the cultured atmosphere of the Mendelssohn family, she received an excellent musical education at home. She married the painter W. Hensel on Oct. 3, 1829, but remained very close to her brother, who constantly asked her advice in musical matters; her death, which occurred suddenly, was a great shock to Mendelssohn, who died a few months afterwards. She had a talent for composing; publ. 4 books of songs; a collection of part-songs,

Gartenlieder (reprinted, London, 1878); also *Lieder ohne Worte* for piano.

BIBLIOGRAPHY: Jack Werner, "Felix and Fanny Mendelssohn," *Music & Letters* (1947); S. Hensel, *Die Familie Mendelssohn* (Berlin, 1879). See also bibliography for Felix Mendelssohn.

Hensel, Heinrich, German dramatic tenor; b. Neustadt, Oct. 29, 1874; d. Hamburg, Feb. 23, 1935. He studied in Vienna and Milan; was a member of the Frankfurt Opera (1900–06), then at Wiesbaden (1906–10), where Siegfried Wagner heard him and engaged him to create the chief tenor part in his opera *Banadietrich* (Karlsruhe, 1910) and also to sing Parsifal at the Bayreuth Festival. He obtained excellent success; subsequently sang at Covent Garden, London (1911). He made his American debut at the Metropolitan Opera House as Lohengrin (Dec. 22, 1911) and was hailed by the press as one of the finest Wagnerian tenors; he also appeared with the Chicago Opera.

Hensel, Octavia (real name **Mary Alice Ives Seymour**), American writer on music; b. 1837; d. near Louisville, May 12, 1897. She publ. *Life and Letters of Louis Moreau Gottschalk,* a regrettably unreliable volume (Boston, 1870); also *The Rheingold Trilogy* (Boston, 1884).

Hensel, Walther (real name **Julius Janiczek**), music educator; b. Moravska Trebova, Bohemia, Sept. 8, 1887; d. Munich, Sept. 5, 1956. He studied in Vienna, in Prague, and in Freiburg, Switzerland, where he obtained his *Dr. phil.* (1911); taught languages in Prague (1912–18). He traveled in Europe (1918–25) as organizer of folksong activities, with the aim of raising the standards of choral music for the young. From 1925–29, he was the head of the Jugendmusik School at the Dortmund Cons. In 1930, he went to Stuttgart, where he organized an educational program for the promotion of folk music. In 1938, he returned to Prague; taught at the German Univ. there. After 1945, he went to Munich. He edited a number of folksong collections (*Der singende Quell,* etc.); edited the periodicals *Finkensteiner Blätter, Lied und Volk,* etc.; publ. *Lied und Volk, eine Streitschrift wider das falsche deutsche Lied* (1921); "Über die gesamte Musikpflege in Schule und Haus," in H. J. Moser's *Grundfragen der Schulmusik* (1931); *Im Zeichen des Volksliedes* (1922; 2nd ed., 1936); *Musikalische Grundlehre* (Kassel, 1937); *Auf den Spuren des Volksliedes* (Kassel, 1944; reprint, 1964).

Henselt, Adolph von, distinguished German pianist and composer; b. Schwabach, May 9, 1814; d. Warmbrunn, Silesia, Oct. 10, 1889. The family moved to Munich when he was still an infant, and he studied piano there with Mme. von Fladt. In 1831, an allowance from King Ludwig I enabled him to continue piano study with Hummel at Weimar; then he took a course of theory under Sechter in Vienna. After a highly successful tour in Germany (1837), he went to St. Petersburg (1838), where he established himself as a piano teacher; was appointed chamber pianist to the Empress, and inspector of music at the Imperial Institutes for Girls in principal Russian cities. He remained in Russia for 40 years; a generation of Russian pianists studied under him. He was a virtuoso of the first rank; like Liszt (whose intimate friend he became), he developed an individual manner of playing, designed to express a personal feeling for the music. His technical specialty was the artful execution, in legato, of widely extended chords and arpeggios, for the achievement of which he composed extremely difficult extension studies. As a composer of piano pieces, he was praised by Schumann and Liszt. His principal works are a piano concerto, 2 sets of études, and a number of effective piano pieces (*Frühlingslied, La gondola*, etc.); all together, 54 works. He published a long-winded but historically and didactically interesting paper entitled *Instructions for Teaching of Playing the Fortepiano, Based on Experience of Many Years, a Manual for the Teachers and Pupils of the Educational Institutions Entrusted to Him by the Government* (in Russian, St. Petersburg, 1868).

BIBLIOGRAPHY: W. von Lenz, *Die grossen Pianoforte Virtuosen unserer Zeit* (Berlin, 1872; English ed., N. Y., 1899, revised 1971; includes a sympathetic character sketch of Henselt); La Mara, *Adolph Henselt,* in *Musikalische Studienköpfe* (vol. III, 1909; reprinted separately, 1911); H. C. Schonberg, *The Great Pianists* (N. Y., 1963).

Hentschel, Ernst Julius, German music educator; b. Zudel, near Görlitz, July 26, 1804; d. Weissenfels, Aug. 14, 1875. He was taken to Langenwaldau as a child, where he taught violin and piano; later he learned to play all the wind instruments also. He devoted himself mainly to musical education, and won the highest regard in this field. He compiled several collections of school songs; was co-founder and editor of the musical journal *Euterpe*.

Hentschel, Franz, German conductor and composer; b. Berlin, Nov. 6, 1814; d. there, May 11, 1889. He studied with A. W. Bach; after conducting theater orchestras in provincial towns, he settled in Berlin as music teacher. He wrote an opera, *Die Hexenreise,* and numerous marches for military bands.

Hentschel, Theodor, German conductor and composer; b. Schirgiswalde, March 28, 1830; d. Hamburg, Dec. 19, 1892. He studied with Reissiger and Ciccarelli in Dresden; was active as theater conductor in Bremen (1860–90), and then at Hamburg. He wrote the operas *Matrose und Sänger* (Leipzig, 1857); *Der Königspage* (Bremen, 1874); *Die Braut von Lusignan, oder die schöne Melusine* (Bremen, 1875); *Lancelot* (Bremen, 1878); *Des Königs Schwerdt* (Hamburg, 1891); overtures and symphonic marches for orch.; piano music; songs; Mass for double chorus; etc.

Henze, Hans Werner, outstanding German composer of the modern school; b. Gütersloh, Westphalia, July 1, 1926. His early studies at the Braunschweig School of Music were interrupted by military service, and for a year he was in the German Army on the Russian front. After the war he took music courses at the Kirchenmusikalisches Institut in Heidelberg; at the same time he studied privately with Wolfgang Fortner. Early in his career as a composer he became fascinated with the disciplinary aspects of Schoenberg's method of composition with 12 tones, and attended the seminars on the subject given by René Leibowitz at Darmstadt. A musician of restless temperament, he joined a radical political group and proclaimed the necessity of writing music without stylistic restrictions in order to serve the masses. In search of natural musical resources he moved to Italy; lived in Ischia from 1953 to 1956; then stayed in Naples and finally settled in Marino. He successfully attempted to integrate musical idioms and mannerisms of seemingly incompatible techniques; in his vocal works he freely adopted such humanoid effects as screaming, bellowing and snorting; he even specified that long sustained tones were to be sung by inhaling as well as exhaling. Nonetheless, Henze manages to compose music that is feasible for human performance. But political considerations continued to play a decisive role in his career. In 1967 he, in company with the German radical composer Paul Dessau, withdrew from the membership of the Academy of the Arts of West Berlin in a gesture of protest against its artistic policies. He defiantly placed the red flag on the stage at the first performance of his oratorio *Das Floss der Medusa* in Hamburg on Dec. 9, 1968; when the chorus refused to sing under such circumstances, Henze canceled the performance, and declared that revolutionary action was more important than any world première. During his stay in Italy he became a member of the Italian Communist Party.

WORKS: FOR THE STAGE: *Das Wundertheater,* operatic melodrama (Heidelberg, May 7, 1949); *Jack Pudding,* a ballet (Wiesbaden, Jan. 1, 1951); *Anrufung Apolls* (Wiesbaden, Oct. 28, 1951); opera, *Boulevard Solitude* (Hanover, Feb. 17, 1952); choreographic fantasy, *Labyrinth* (Hamburg, April, 1952); *Der Idiot,* ballet pantomime, after Dostoyevsky (Berlin, Sept. 1, 1952); *Tancred und Canthylene* (Munich, 1952); *Pas d'action* (1952); *Die schlafende Prinzessin* (Essen, 1954); *Maratona di danza* (Berlin, Sept. 24, 1957); *Undine,* ballet (London, Oct. 27, 1958); *L'Usignolo dell'Imperatore,* pantomime after Andersen (Venice, Sept. 16, 1959); *Der Prinz von Homburg,* opera (Hamburg, May 22, 1960); *Elegie für junge Liebende,* chamber opera (Schwetzingen, May 20, 1961; in English, as *Elegy for Young Lovers,* which is the original title of the text by W. H. Auden from which the German libretto was made, Glyndebourne, July 13, 1961); *Der junge Lord,* comic opera (Berlin, April 7, 1965); *Ein Landarzt,* monodrama for baritone and orch. (Berlin, Oct. 13, 1965); *Tancredi,* ballet (Vienna, May 14, 1966); *Die Bassariden,* "opera seria" with an Intermezzo, after Euripides, to the libretto of W. H. Auden and Chester Kallman (Salzburg, Aug. 6, 1966); *Moralities,* scenic cantatas after Aesop, to texts by W. H. Auden (Cincinnati May Festival, May 18, 1968); opera, *Il difficile percorso verso la casa di Natascha Ungeheuer* (Rome, May 17, 1971). ORCHESTRAL WORKS: Symph. No. 1 (Bad Pyrmont, Aug. 25, 1948; revised version, Berlin, April 9, 1964); Symph. No. 2 (Stuttgart, Dec. 1, 1949); Symph. No. 3 (Donaueschingen Festival, Oct. 7, 1951; the first movement incorporates materials taken from his ballet, *Anrufung Apolls*); *Kranichsteiner Kammerkonzert* (Darmstadt, Sept. 27, 1946); *Ballet Variations* (Cologne, Oct. 3,

1949); Violin Concerto (Baden-Baden, Dec. 12, 1948); Piano Concerto No. 1 (Düsseldorf, Sept. 11, 1952); *Ode an den Westwind,* for cello and orch. (Bielefeld, April 30, 1954); *Quattro Poemi,* symph. suite (Darmstadt, May 31, 1955); *Symphonische Etuden* (1955); Symph. No. 4 (West Berlin, Oct. 9, 1963); Symph. No. 5 (N.Y., May 16, 1963); *Los Caprichos,* fantasia for orch. (1963; Duisburg, April 6, 1967); *Doppio Concerto* for oboe, harp and strings (Zürich, Dec. 2, 1966); Fantasia for String Orch. (1966; Berlin, April 1, 1967); *Telemanniana* for orch. on themes of Telemann (Berlin, April 4, 1967); Concerto for Double Bass and Orch. (Chicago, Nov. 2, 1967); Piano Concerto No. 2 (Bielefeld, Sept. 29, 1968); *Versuch über Schweine* for baritone and chamber orch. (London, Feb. 14, 1969; the title refers to the insulting term applied by reactionaries to the rebellious Berlin students); Symph. No. 6 (Havana, Nov. 19, 1969); *Compases para Preguntas ensimismadas* for viola and 22 players (Basel, Feb. 11, 1971); *Heliogabalus Imperator* "Allegoria per musica" for orch. (Chicago Symph., commissioned work, Chicago, Nov. 16, 1972); *Tristan,* preludes for piano, electronic tapes and orch. (1973). CHAMBER MUSIC: Sonatina for Flute and Piano (1947); Violin Sonata (1947); String Quartet No. 1 (1947); String Quartet No. 2 (1952); Serenade for Cello Solo (1953); Wind Quintet (1953); *Concerto per il Marigny* for piano and instruments (Paris, March 9, 1956); *Royal Winter Musick,* "Sonata on Shakespearean characters" for guitar solo (1976); String Quartet No. 3 (1976); string quartets Nos. 4 and 5 (Schwetzingen, May 25, 1977). VOCAL MUSIC: 5 *Madrigals* for chorus and chamber orch. (Frankfurt, April 25, 1950); *Ein Landarzt,* radio cantata, after Kafka (Hamburg, Nov. 29, 1951); *Das Ende einer Welt,* radio cantata (Hamburg, Dec. 4, 1953); *Novae de infinito laudes,* cantata (Venice, April 24, 1963); *Cantata della Fiaba estrema* (Zürich, Feb. 26, 1965); *El Cimarrón* for baritone, flute, guitar and percussion, to texts from *The Autobiography of a Runaway Slave* by Esteban Montejo (Aldeburgh Festival, June 22, 1970).

BIBLIOGRAPHY: Klaus Geitel, *H. W. Henze* (Berlin, 1968); H. H. Stuckenschmidt, "Hans Werner Henze und die Musik unserer Zeit," *Universitas* XXVII/2 (1972).

Heppener, Robert, Dutch composer; b. Amsterdam, Aug. 9, 1925. He took piano lessons with Jan Öde and Johan van den Boogert at the Amsterdam Cons.; later studied composition with Bertus van Lier. He then engaged in teaching; joined the staff of the Cons. of the Music Lyceum Society in Amsterdam. In his own compositions he observes the rational boundaries of modern harmony.

WORKS: *Cantico delle creature di S. Francesco d'Assisi* for soprano, harp and strings (1952, revised 1954); Nocturne for Piano (1953); Symphony (1957); Septet (1958); *Derivazioni* for string orch. (1958); *Arcadian Sonatina* for 2 recorders and violin (1959); *A fond de fleurettes* for string quartet (1961); Sinfonietta for Small Orch. (1961); *Het derde land (The Third Country),* 3 songs for chorus and chamber orch. (1962); *Cavalcade,* overture and rondo for orch. (1963); *Eglogues* for orch. (1963); *Scherzi* for strings (1965); *Canti Carnascialeschi (Carnival Songs),* 5-movement cycle for a cappella chorus (1966); *Fanfare trionfale* for chorus, winds, timpani and piano (1967); Quartet, for alto flute, violin, viola and cello (1967); *Air et sonneries* for orch. (1969); *Canzona* for saxophone quartet (1969); *Hymns and Conversations* for 28 harps (1969; Amsterdam, July 8, 1969); 4 *Songs,* after Pound, for middle voice and piano (1968–70); *Muziek voor straten en pleinen (Music for Streets and Squares)* for orch. (Amsterdam, Oct. 31, 1970); *Del iubilo del core che esce in voce* for a cappella chorus (1974); *Pas de quatre-mains,* for piano, 4 hands (1975).

BIBLIOGRAPHY: W. Paap, "Robert Heppener," *Sonorum Speculum* 39 (1969).

Herbart, Johann Friedrich, eminent German philosopher and musician; b. Oldenburg, May 4, 1776; d. Göttingen, Aug. 14, 1841. He studied at Jena with Fichte. In 1805, appointed prof. of philosophy at Göttingen; 1809–35, at Königsberg; 1835 (to his death) again at Göttingen. Of importance to music theory are his *Psychologische Bemerkungen zur Tonlehre* (1811), treating of intervals, and the chapter "Von den schönen Künsten," in his *Kurze Enzyklopädie der Philosophie* (1931). He composed a piano sonata, which was published (Leipzig, 1808), and several other works.

BIBLIOGRAPHY: W. Kahl, *Herbart als Musiker* (Langensalza, 1926).

Herbeck, Johann (Franz) von, Austrian conductor and composer; b. Vienna, Dec. 25, 1831; d. there, Oct. 28, 1877. He was a boy chorister at the Heiligenkreuz monastery, where he had instruction in organ; then studied composition with Ludwig Rotter in Vienna; also studied philosophy at Vienna Univ.; from 1859–66, and from 1875 to his death, he was conductor of the Gesellschaft der Musikfreunde; from 1866–71, court conductor; from 1871–75, director of the court opera. He was particularly successful as conductor and organizer of several choral societies in Vienna. Herbeck publ. numerous choral works of considerable worth, if not of any originality. His son, Ludwig Herbeck, publ. a biography, *Johann Herbeck, ein Lebensbild* (Vienna, 1885), which contains a complete catalogue of his works. See also the sketch on Herbeck in Hanslick's *Suite* (Vienna, 1885).

Herberigs, Robert, Belgian composer; b. Ghent, June 19, 1886; d. Oudenaarde, Sept. 20, 1974. He studied singing at the Ghent Cons. and made a debut as a baritone at the Flemish Opera in Antwerp (1908), but soon abandoned his operatic aspirations and began an assiduous study of composition. He succeeded swiftly, and won the Belgian Grand Prix in 1909 with his cantata, *La Legénde de St. Hubert.* But he also pursued interest in literature, and published several novels. His music reflects the manner of French romanticism.

WORKS: 2 comic operas: *Le Mariage de Rosine,* after Beaumarchais (1919; Ghent, Feb. 13, 1925) and *L'Amour Médecin,* after Molière (1920); a radio play *Antoine et Cleopatra,* after Shakespeare, for 6 speakers, chorus and orch. (1949); an open-air play, *Lam Godsspel* or *Jeu de l'Agneau Mystique (Pageant of the Mystic Lamb,* 1948; Ghent, 1949); a play of "light and

sound in stereorama" *Le Château des comtes de Gand*
(1960); 2 piano concertos (1932, 1952); 2 Suites for
brass ensemble (1946); *Sinfonia Breve* (1947; 2 earlier
symphonies were withdrawn); Organ Concerto
(1957); numerous symph. poems and orchestral
suites: *Cyrano de Bergerac*, with solo horn, in the
form of a concerto (Brussels, April 12, 1912); *Le
Chant d'Hiawatha*, after Longfellow (1921); *Vlaanderen, O Welig Huis* (*Flanders, the Well-Beloved*,
1949); *De Vrolijke Vrouwtjes van Windsor* (*The Merry Wives of Windsor*, 1950); *Rapsodia alla Zingara*
(1952); *A la Fontaine Bellerie* (1954; originally for piano, 1923); *Échos et mirages* (1954); *Esquisses et impromptus* (1954); *La Chanson d'Ève*, 2 suites (1955,
1959; originally a cycle of 40 songs, 1922–24); 4 Ballades (1955); *La Petite Sirène*, after Hans Christian
Andersen (1955); *Odes aux Muses* (1955); 4 *Saisons*,
after Breughel (1956); 4 *Odes à Botticelli* (1958); *Commedia dell'arte* (1958); *De Nachtelijke Wapenschouw*
(*Nocturnal Parade*, 1961); *Hamlet* (1962); *Roméo et
Juliette* (1963); *Reinaut et Armida* (1967); *Cantata to
the memory of Jan Willems* (1946); *Te Deum Laudamus* for chorus and organ (1912); *Missa pro Defunctis*
for chorus a cappella (1926); 7 other Masses for chorus and organ, including *Messe in nativitate* (1926)
and *Messe pour la Paix* (1938); String Quartet (1921);
Poème for piano trio (1923); Violin Sonata (1932);
Concert champêtre for wind quintet (1938); Clarinet
Sonatina (1939); Piano Quartet (1939); *Suite Miniature* and sonatine for flute and string trio (both 1954);
21 piano sonatas and sonatinas (1941–45); piano
pieces; songs.

Herbert, Victor, famous composer of light music; b.
Dublin, Ireland, Feb. 1, 1859; d. New York, May 26,
1924. He was a grandson of Samuel Lover, the Irish
novelist; his father died when he was an infant; soon
his mother married a German physician and settled in
Stuttgart (1867), taking the boy with her. He entered
the Stuttgart high school, but did not graduate; his
musical ability was definitely pronounced by then,
and he selected the cello as his instrument, taking lessons from the celebrated cellist Bernhard Cossmann
in Baden-Baden. He soon acquired a degree of technical proficiency that enabled him to take a position as
cellist in various orchestras in Germany, France, Italy,
and Switzerland; in 1880, he became a cellist of the
Eduard Strauss waltz band in Vienna; in 1881, returned to Stuttgart, where he joined the court orch.,
and studied composition with Max Seifritz at the
Cons. His earliest works were for the cello with orch.;
he performed his suite with the Stuttgart orch. on Oct.
23, 1883, and the First Cello Concerto on Dec. 8, 1885.
On Aug. 14, 1886, he married the Viennese opera
singer **Therese Förster** (1861–1927); in the same year
she received an offer to join the Metropolitan Opera in
New York, and Herbert was engaged as an orchestra
cellist there, appearing in N.Y. also as soloist (played
his own Cello Concerto with the N.Y. Philh., Dec. 10,
1887). In his early years in New York, Herbert was
overshadowed by the celebrity of his wife, but soon
he developed energetic activities on his own, forming
an entertainment orchestra which he conducted in a
repertory of light music; he also participated in chamber music concerts; was soloist with the Theodore

Thomas and Seidl orchestras. He was the conductor
of the Boston Festival Orch. in 1891; Tchaikovsky
conducted this orchestra in Philadelphia in a miscellaneous program and Herbert played a solo. He was associate conductor of the Worcester Festival
(1889–91), for which he wrote a dramatic cantata, *The
Captive* (Sept. 24, 1891). In 1893 he became bandmaster of the famous 22nd Regiment Band, succeeding
P. S. Gilmore. On March 10, 1894, he was soloist with
the N.Y. Philh. in his 2nd Cello Concerto. In the same
year, at the suggestion of William MacDonald, the
manager of the Boston Ideal Opera Company, Herbert
wrote a light opera, *Prince Ananias*, which was produced with encouraging success in New York (Nov.
20, 1894). From 1898 to 1904, Herbert was conductor
of the Pittsburgh Symph. Orch., presenting some of
his own compositions: *Episodes amoureuses* (Feb. 2,
1900); *Hero and Leander* (Jan. 18, 1901); *Woodland
Fancies* (Dec. 6, 1901); *Columbus* (Jan. 2, 1903). In
1900 he directed at Madison Square Garden, New
York, an orch. of 420 performers for the benefit of the
sufferers in the Galveston flood. On April 29, 1906 he
led a similar monster concert at the Hippodrome for
the victims of the San Francisco earthquake. In 1904
he organized the Victor Herbert N.Y. Orch., and gave
concerts in New York and neighboring communities.
But it is as a composer of light operas that Herbert
became chiefly known. In the best of these he unites
spontaneous melody, sparkling rhythm, and simple
but tasteful harmony; his experience as a symphonic
composer and conductor imparted a solidity of texture to his writing that placed him far above the many
gifted amateurs in this field. Furthermore, he possessed a natural communicative power in his music,
which made his operettas spectacularly successful
with the public. In the domain of grand opera, he was
not so fortunate. When the production of his first
grand opera, *Natoma*, took place at Philadelphia on
Feb. 25, 1911, it aroused great expectations; but the
opera failed to sustain lasting interest. Still less effective was his second opera, *Madeleine*, staged by the
Metropolitan Opera Co. in New York on Jan. 24, 1914.
Herbert was one of the founders of the American Society of Composers, Authors and Publishers (ASCAP)
in 1914, and was vice-president from that date until
his death. In 1916 he wrote a special score for the
motion picture, *The Fall of a Nation*, in synchronization with the screen play.

WORKS: operettas: *Prince Ananias* (N.Y., Nov. 20,
1894); *The Wizard of the Nile* (Chicago, Sept. 26,
1895); *The Gold Bug* (N.Y., Sept. 21, 1896); *The Ser-
enade* (Cleveland, Feb. 17, 1897); *The Idol's Eye* (Troy,
N.Y., Sept. 20, 1897); *The Fortune Teller* (Toronto,
Sept. 14, 1898); *Cyrano de Bergerac* (Montreal, Sept.
11, 1899); *The Singing Girl* (Montreal, Oct. 2, 1899);
The Ameer (Scranton, Oct. 9, 1899); *The Viceroy* (San
Francisco, Feb. 12, 1900); *Babes in Toyland* (Chicago,
June 17, 1903); *Babette* (Washington, Nov. 9, 1903); *It
Happened in Nordland* (Harrisburg, Nov. 21, 1904);
Miss Dolly Dollars (Rochester, Aug. 31, 1905); *Won-
derland* (Buffalo, Sept. 14, 1905); *Mlle. Modiste* (Tren-
ton, Oct. 7, 1905; Herbert's most popular work); *The
Red Mill* (Buffalo, Sept. 3, 1906); *Dream City* (N.Y.,
Dec. 25, 1906); *The Tattooed Man* (Baltimore, Feb. 11,
1907); *The Rose of Algeria* (Wilkes-Barre, Sept. 11,

1909); *Little Nemo* (Philadelphia, Sept. 28, 1908); *The Prima Donna* (Chicago, Oct. 5, 1908); *Old Dutch* (Wilkes-Barre, Nov. 6, 1909); *Naughty Marietta* (Syracuse, Oct. 24, 1910; highly successful); *When Sweet Sixteen* (Springfield, Mass., Dec. 5, 1910); *Mlle. Rosita* (later called *The Duchess*, Boston, March 27, 1911); *The Enchantress* (Washington, Oct. 9, 1911); *The Lady of the Slipper* (Philadelphia, Oct. 8, 1912); *The Madcap Duchess* (Rochester, N.Y., Oct. 13, 1913); *Sweethearts* (Baltimore, March 24, 1913); *The Débutante* (Atlantic City, Sept. 21, 1914); *The Only Girl* (Atlantic City, Oct. 1, 1914); *Princess Pat* (Atlantic City, Aug. 23, 1915); *Eileen* (Cleveland, Jan. 1, 1917, as *Hearts of Erin*); *Her Regiment* (Springfield, Mass., Oct. 22, 1917); *The Velvet Lady* (Philadelphia, Dec. 23, 1918); *My Golden Girl* (Stamford, Conn., Dec. 19, 1919); *The Girl in the Spotlight* (Stamford, Conn., July 7, 1920); *Oui, Madame* (Philadelphia, March 22, 1920); *Orange Blossoms* (Philadelphia, Sept. 4, 1922); *The Dream Girl* (New Haven, April 22, 1924). Other stage productions: *Cinderella Man* (1915), *The Century Girl* (1916), *Ziegfeld Follies* (1917, 1920–23), *The Willow Plate* (marionette play by Tony Sarg, 1924). Nonstage works: Serenade, op. 12; 1st Cello Concerto (Dec. 8, 1885); 2nd Concerto for Cello, op. 30 (N.Y. March 10, 1894); *Pan-Americana*; *Suite of Serenades* (composed for Paul Whiteman's orch.; perf. 1924); *Golden Days*; *Dramatic Overture*; orchestral arrangements; men's choruses; songs; many pieces for piano, violin and piano, and cello and piano.

BIBLIOGRAPHY: J. Kaye, *Victor Herbert* (N.Y., 1931); Edward N. Waters, *Victor Herbert* (exhaustive biography, with a full list of works; N.Y., 1955).

Herbst, Johannes, American Moravian minister and composer; b. Kempten, Swabia, July 23, 1735; d. Salem, North Carolina, Jan. 15, 1812. Herbst came to the United States in 1786 to serve as minister at Lancaster, Pa. and later at Lititz. In 1811 Herbst was elevated to the episcopate and transferred to the Southern Province of the Moravian Church at Salem, where he died the following year. When he emigrated to the U.S. he brought with him a large number of musical manuscripts, this being the practice of those traveling to the American Moravian settlements. During the following years, in which he was a performing musician, composer, and teacher, he added to his collection, copying manuscripts brought from Europe by other Moravians, and music composed by American Moravians; altogether there are almost 12,000 pages in his hand, constituting the most extensive individual collection of 18th- and 19th-century Moravian (and non-Moravian) music in the U.S. The Herbst Collection is in the Archives of the Moravian Music Foundation in Winston-Salem, N.C., and is available complete on either microfiches or roll microfilm: A. 493 manuscript scores of about 1000 vocal-instrumental pieces (Congregation Music); B. 45 manuscript scores or parts of larger vocal works by C.P.E. Bach, Mozart and Haydn, and others, including Herbst and other Moravians; C. 6 miscellaneous vols. of keyboard works, texts, etc.; the entire collection totals 11,676 pages. An itemized *Catalog of the Johannes Herbst Collection* prepared by Marilyn Gombosi was publ. in Chapel Hill, N.C., in 1970 and includes a biographical

sketch of Herbst, and a short history of the Collection. Herbst was the most prolific of all the American Moravian composers, having to his credit some 127 choral anthems and songs (all included in the above collection; a few pieces publ. by H. W. Gray, Peters, and Boosey & Hawkes). Many of his works show him to have been a highly skilled musical craftsman. His music collection is particularly important as the principal source of music by American and European Moravian composers.

BIBLIOGRAPHY: A. G. Rau and Hans T. David, *A Catalogue of Music by American Moravians* (Bethlehem, 1938); H. T. David, "Background for Bethlehem: Moravian Music in Pennsylvania," *Magazine of Art* (April 1939), Hans T. David, "Musical Life in the Pennsylvania Settlements of the Unitas Fratrum," *Transactions of the Moravian Historical Society* (1942); repr. as Moravian Music Foundation Publication No. 6 (1959); Donald M. McCorkle, *Moravian Music in Salem: A German-American Heritage* (Indiana Univ., 1958); Joan O. Falconer, *Bishop Johannes Herbst (1735–1812), An American Moravian Musician, Collector and Composer* (Columbia Univ., 1969; 2 vols.).

Hercigonja, Nikola, Croatian composer; b. Vinkovcim, Feb. 19, 1911. He studied in Zagreb; in 1950 became a prof. of the Music Academy in Belgrade. In his music he follows a general trend of realistic composition, inspired by national folk songs.

WORKS: *Vječni Žid u Zagrebu* (*The Wandering Jew in Zagreb*), musical burlesque (1942); *Gorski Vijenac* (*Mountain Wreath*), opera-oratorio (Belgrade, Oct. 19, 1957); *Planetarium*, scenic action for voices, speaking chorus and orch. (1960); numerous choruses.

Hering, Karl (Friedrich August), German violinist; b. Berlin, Sept. 2, 1819; d. Burg, near Magdeburg, Feb. 2, 1889. He studied with Rungenhagen in Berlin and Tomaschek in Prague; established a music school in Berlin (1851); publ. *Methodischer Leitfaden für Violinlehrer* (1857) and an elementary violin method; also wrote a monograph on Kreutzer's studies (1858).

Hering, Karl Gottlieb, German music pedagogue; b. Bad Schandau, Oct. 25, 1765; d. Zittau, Jan. 4, 1853. He studied academic subjects at the Leipzig Univ.; music with J. G. Schicht. In 1811 he was appointed music teacher at the Zittau seminary, and remained there until 1836, when he retired. He publ. a number of manuals on practical music study: *Praktisches Handbuch zur leichten Erlernung des Klavier-Spielens* (Halberstadt, 1796); *Praktische Violin-Schule* (Leipzig, 1810), etc.; also compiled *Zittauer Choralbuch* (Leipzig, 1822), and other collections, including original compositions. Some of his pieces for children became celebrated in Germany and elsewhere, particularly *Steckenpferd* ("Hopp, hopp, hopp, Pferdchen lauf Galopp"); *Weihnachtsfreude* ("Morgen, Kinder, wird's was geben"), and (most famous of them all) *Grossvaterlied*, which was used by Schumann in his *Carnaval*.

BIBLIOGRAPHY: Lucy Gelber, "Karl Gottlieb Hering," in *Die Liederkomponisten* (Berlin, 1936).

Héritte-Viardot, Louise-Pauline-Marie, vocal teacher; daughter of **Pauline Viardot-García;** b. Paris, Dec. 14, 1841; d. Heidelberg, Jan. 17, 1918. She was for many years a singing teacher at the St. Petersburg Cons.; then taught in Frankfurt, Berlin, and Heidelberg. She was married to a French consular official, Héritte. She was also a composer; her opera *Lindoro* was performed in Weimar (1879); she further wrote the cantatas *Das Bacchusfest* (Stockholm, 1880) and *Le Feu de ciel;* some chamber music, and vocal exercises. Her memoirs (translated from the original German) were publ. in English as *Memories and Adventures* (London, 1913), in French as *Mémoires de Louise Héritte-Viardot* (Paris, 1923).

Herman, Jerry, American composer of popular music; b. New York, July 10, 1933. He played piano by ear but never learned to read music. He studied drama at the Univ. of Miami; then became a script writer for television in N.Y. Later he devoted himself entirely to musical comedies, for which he wrote both lyrics and music. His shows *Parade* (1960) and *Milk and Honey* (1961) were fairly successful; but he made his greatest hit with the production of *Hello, Dolly!* (N.Y., Jan. 16, 1964), which had the longest run in the history of Broadway shows, closing on Dec. 26, 1970. A comparable success was achieved by his next musical *Mame,* which opened in New York on May 24, 1966.

Herman, Reinhold (Ludwig), conductor and composer; b. Prenzlau, Germany, Sept. 21, 1849; d. probably in New York, c.1920. He studied at the Stern Cons. in Berlin; came to the U.S. in 1871 as singing teacher; from 1884, conducted the choral society "Liederkranz"; from 1898–1900, conducted the Handel and Haydn Society in Boston; then lived in Italy; returned to New York in 1917. He publ. *An Open Door for Singers* (N.Y., 1912); wrote 3 operas, of which *Wulfrin* was perf. in Kassel (Oct. 11, 1898); also several choral works.

Herman, Vasile, Rumanian composer; b. Satu-Mare, June 10, 1929. He studied piano in his home town and composition with Demian, Toduță and Comes at the Cluj Cons. (1949–57); subsequently was appointed to its staff. His music is cautiously modernistic, with occasional overflow into aleatory indeterminacy.
WORKS: an oratorio, *Balada lui Pintea Viteazul* (1957); 2 piano sonatas (*Sonata da ricercar,* 1958; 1967); *8 Small Pieces* for piano (1959); Partita for Piano (1961); *Sonata-Baladă* for oboe and piano (1961); *Variante* for 2 clarinets, piano and percussion (1963–64); *4 Ritornele* for orch. (1964; Cluj, Dec. 18, 1966); *3 Pieces* for solo violin (1964); *Microforme* for piano (1965); *Cantilaţii (Cantillations)* for orch. (Cluj, March 23, 1968); Flute Sonata (1967); *Episodes* for flute, marimba, vibraphone and percussion (1968); *Melopee* for solo flute (1968); *Polifonie* for 7 instrumental groups (1968); *Strofe* for chorus, brass and percussion (1968); *Graphie musicale* for 1 or 2 pianos (1969; of variable duration); 2 cantatas (1969, 1970); *Postlude* for orch. (1970); String Quartet (1971); choruses; songs.

Herman, Woody (real given names **Woodrow Charles**), American clarinetist and band leader; b. Milwaukee, May 16, 1913. He studied there and at Marquette Univ. In 1931, joined a jazz band as a clarinet player, and in 1937 formed his first band, and has had several since then, most being called "Herds"; i.e., the First Herd, Second Herd, etc. In the mid-1940s Herman's was the first prominent big band to make the transition from swing to a more advanced, bebop-influenced idiom characterized by "progressive" harmonies; became known as "progressive jazz." On March 25, 1946, he presented in Carnegie Hall the first performance of Stravinsky's *Ebony Concerto,* written specially for him. He is also the composer of numerous popular songs.

Hermann, Hans, German composer; b. Leipzig, Aug. 17, 1870; d. Berlin, May 18, 1931. He studied with W. Rust in Leipzig, E. Kretschmer in Dresden, and H. von Herzogenberg in Berlin; from the age of 18, played the double bass in various European orchestras; then taught at the Klindworth-Scharwenka Cons. in Berlin (1901–07). From 1907 till 1927, he lived in Dresden; then returned to Berlin. He publ. some 100 songs, of which several became fairly well known *(Drei Wanderer, Alte Landsknechte,* etc.); he had a flair for imitating the simple style of the folk ballad; he further wrote a symphony subtitled *Lebensepisoden,* a stage work *Der rote Pimpernell;* pieces for clarinet with piano, etc.

Hermann, Robert, Swiss composer; b. Bern, April 29, 1869; d. Ambach, Bavaria, Oct. 22, 1912. He studied in Frankfurt; as a youth, developed an original approach to composition; he met Grieg, who encouraged him; studied briefly with Humperdinck; his symph. was perf. by the Berlin Philh. Orch. (Nov. 7, 1895), and other works followed.
BIBLIOGRAPHY: W. Niemann, "Robert Hermann," in *Monographien moderner Musiker* III (Leipzig, 1909).

Hermannus (surnamed **Contractus** on account of his paralyzed limbs), theoretician and composer; b. Saulgau, July 18, 1013; d. Altshausen, near Biberach, Sept. 24, 1054. He was the son of Hermann, Count of Vehringen. He was a student in Reichenau monastery; under the guidance of his tutor, Abbot Berno, he acquired wide learning. In 1043 he entered the Benedictine Order. His best known work (containing valuable historical notices on music) is a chronology from the time of Christ to 1054. It has been republished several times, and is to be found in Peres' (Pertz's) *Monumenta* (vol. V). He was the author of *Opuscula Musica,* in which he gives a thorough discussion of the modes and criticizes the Daseian notation used in the 10th-century tract, *Musica enchiriadis.* He proposed his own notation by Greek and Latin letters. In the indication of a change in pitch, it had an advantage over neume notation. Hermannus' notation is written above the neume notation in some manuscripts of the 11th and 12th centuries in the Munich Library. Hermannus was the composer of the Gregorian Marian antiphons, *Salve Regina* and *Alma Redemptoris Mater.* A transcription (into modern notation) of his *Versus ad discernendum cantum* is to be found in A. Schering's *Geschichte der Musik in Beispielen* (no. 7).

BIBLIOGRAPHY: W. Brambach, *Hermanni Contracti Musica* (Leipzig, 1884); Leonard Ellinwood, *Musica Hermanni Contracti* (Rochester, N.Y., 1936), which gives the Latin text, edited after both the Vienna manuscript and an 11th-century MS now at the Eastman School, Rochester, N.Y., an English translation, and commentary; R. Crocker, "Hermann's Major Sixth," *Journal of the American Musicological Society* (Spring 1972).

Hermanson, Åke, Swedish composer; b. Mollösund, June 16, 1923. He studied piano and organ in Göteborg and Stockholm; took courses in composition with Hilding Rosenberg (1950–52). In his music he follows a type of concentrated brevity marked by an alternation of short contrasting motives; Hermanson defines this usage as "pendulum dynamics."

WORKS: *Lyrical Metamorphoses* for string quartet (1957–58); *A due voci* for flute and viola (1957–58); *Invoco* for strings (Norrköping, May 24, 1961); *Stadier* for soprano, flute, bass clarinet, viola and percussion (1960–61); *Suoni d'un flauto* for solo alto flute (1961); *In Nuce (In a Nutshell)* for orch. (1962–63; the title is justified, for the piece takes barely 3 minutes to play; first performance, Stockholm, Oct. 9, 1964); *Nenia bahusiensis* for children's chorus a cappella (1963); Symphony No. 1 (1964–67; Stockholm, Oct. 29, 1967); *Appel I–IV* for orch. (1968–69; first complete performance, Swedish Radio, Dec. 12, 1970); *Alarme* for solo horn (1969); *In sono* for flute, oboe, or English horn, viola and cello (1970); *Ultima* for orch. (Swedish Radio, Nov. 18, 1972); *Flauto d'Inverno* for bass flute solo (1976); Symphony No. 2 (Stockholm, Sept. 26, 1976).

Hermesdorff, Michael, German musicologist; b. Trier (Trèves), March 4, 1833; d. there, Jan. 1885. He entered the priesthood, and was appointed organist of Trier cathedral. He founded the Choral Society, chiefly for the exposition of Gregorian plainchant, on which he was an authority by virtue of his study of original sources. He edited the *Graduale ad usum Romanum cantus S. Gregorii* (Leipzig, 1876–82, 10 numbers) in the monthly supplements of the *Cäcilia* journal, but died before its completion. He revised the 2nd ed. of Lück's collection of sacred compositions (4 volumes); publ. German translation of the *Micrologus* and *Epistola* of Guido d'Arezzo; a *Kyriale,* and *Harmonica cantus choralis a* 4; a *Graduale,* several anthems, and *Praefatio* (prayers used in the Trier diocese); and 3 Masses of his own composition.

Hermstedt, Johann Simon, famous German clarinetist; b. Langensalza, Dec. 29, 1778; d. Sondershausen, Aug. 10, 1846. He was educated at the Annaberg school for soldiers' children; studied with Knoblauch and Baer; became clarinetist in the Langensalza regiment; then conducted a military band in Langensalza. He made improvements in his instrument; composed concertos, variations, and other pieces for clarinet. Spohr wrote a clarinet concerto for him.

Hernández, Hermilio, Mexican composer; b. Autlán, Jalisco, Feb. 2, 1931. He studied music with José Valadez and Domingo Lobato at the Escuela Superior Diocesana de Música Sagrada in Guadalajara, graduating in 1956; then studied in Italy and in Paris.

WORKS: *Cantata Adviento* (1953); *5 Pieces* for orch. (1955); Violin Concerto (1960); *Sonata* for chamber orch. (1964); *Suite* for violin and piano (1952); String Quartet (1954); Piano Trio (1955); Cello Sonata (1962); Wind Quintet (1965); *Poliédros* for oboe, bassoon and piano (1969); *Music for 4 Instruments* for flute, violin, cello and piano (1970); 2 piano sonatinas (1955, 1971); *Tema transfigurado* for piano (1962); *6 Inventions* for piano (1968); Piano Sonata (1970); *Diálogos* for 2 pianos (1970); *Fantasia* for organ (1970); songs.

Hernández-López, Rhazés, Venezuelan composer and musicologist; b. Petare, June 30, 1918. He studied in Caracas with Vicente Emilio Sojo and Juan Bautista Plaza. Apart from composition, he engaged in teaching and radio work.

WORKS: In his series of piano pieces under the title *Casualismo* he applies the 12-tone method of composition. Other works include *Las Torres desprevenidas,* symph. poem (1951); *Sonorritmo* for orch. (1953); *Mérida, geografía celeste,* symph. suite (1958); *Expansión tres* for orch. (1965); *Tres dimensiones* for strings (1967); *Cuadros* for flute, violin, viola, cello and harp (1950); viola sonata (1952); *Tres espacios* for violin, cello and piano (1965); *Horizontal* for flute and strings (1966); piano pieces; songs.

Hernández Moncada, Eduardo, Mexican composer; b. Jalapa, Sept. 24, 1899. He studied with Rafael Tello at the National Cons. in Mexico City. He conducted theater orchestras; in 1936 became assistant cond. of the Orquesta Sinfónica in Mexico. As a composer he made an impression with his Symphony, first performed in Mexico City (July 31, 1942). His ballet *Ixtepec* (1945) employs Mexican rhythms.

Hernández, Pablo, Spanish composer; b. Saragossa, Jan. 25, 1834; d. Madrid, Dec. 10, 1910. He was first a church chorister; at 14 played organ at the San Gil church in Saragossa. At 22 he went to Madrid to study with Eslava at the Madrid Cons.; graduated with a gold medal (1861) and joined the faculty in 1863 as a singing teacher. He wrote 2 zarzuelas: *Gimnasio higienico* and *Un Sevillano en la Habana;* also many sacred works.

Hernándo, Rafael José María, Spanish composer; b. Madrid, May 31, 1822; d. there, July 10, 1888. He studied with Carnicer and Saldoni at the Madrid Cons. (1837–43); then went to Paris, where he took lessons with Auber. His *Stabat Mater* was performed there, and a grand opera, *Romilda,* was accepted for performance at the Théâtre des Italiens, but the revolutionary upheaval of 1848 prevented its production. Hernándo returned to Madrid, where he produced a number of zarzuelas, of which the most successful was *El duende* (June 6, 1849); others were *Palo de ciego* (1849), *Colegialas y soldados* (1849), *Bertoldo y Comparsa, Cosas de Juan, El tambor, Aurora,* etc.;

also collaborated with Barbieri, Oudrid, and Gaztambide in *Escenas de Chamberi* and *Don Simplicio Bobadilla*. In 1852 he became secretary of the Madrid Cons.; later taught harmony there.

Hernried, Robert, writer on music and composer; b. Vienna, Sept. 22, 1883; d. Detroit, Sept. 3, 1951. He studied at the Univ. of Vienna; for some years conducted opera at provincial theaters (1908–14); taught theory at the Mannheim Academy of Music (1919–22), at the Cons. of Heidelberg (1923), in Erfurt, and in Berlin. In 1933 he left Germany and taught in New York, Davenport, Iowa, Dickinson, N.D., and at Fort Wayne, Ind. In 1946 he became prof. of music at the Detroit Institute of Musical Art. He wrote an opera, *Francesca da Rimini;* about 75 choral works; a Mass; some characteristic pieces for orch., etc.; publ. a monograph on Jaques-Dalcroze (Geneva, 1929), a biography of Brahms (Leipzig, 1934), and 2 theoretical works, *Allgemeine Musiklehre* (Berlin, 1932) and *Systematische Modulation* (Berlin, 1935; 2nd ed., 1948).

Herold, Louis-Joseph-Ferdinand, celebrated French composer; b. Paris, Jan. 28, 1791; d. Thernes, near Paris, Jan. 19, 1833. His father, **François-Joseph Hérold** (pupil of C. P. E. Bach), a piano teacher and composer, did not desire his son to become a musician, and sent him to the Hix school, where his aptitude for music was noticed by Fétis, then assistant teacher there. After his father's death (1802), Herold began to study music seriously; in 1806 he entered the Paris Cons., taking piano lessons with Louis Adam, and winning first prize for piano playing in 1810. He studied harmony under Catel, and (from 1811) composition under Méhul; in 1812 his cantata *Mlle. de la Vallière* won the Prix de Rome (the MS score is in the Cons. Library with works composed during his three years' study in Rome). From Rome he went to Naples, where he became pianist to Queen Caroline; here he produced his first opera, *La gioventù di Enrico Quinto* (Jan. 5, 1815), which was well received. From Naples he went to Vienna, after a few months' stay returned to Paris, where he finished the score of Boieldieu's *Charles de France,* an "opéra d'occasion" (Opéra-Comique, June 18, 1816), and where all the rest of his operas were produced. The flattering reception of *Charles de France* led to the successful production of *Les Rosières* (Jan. 27, 1817), *La Clochette* (Oct. 18, 1817), *Le Premier Venu* (Sept. 28, 1818), *Les Troqueurs* (Feb. 18, 1819), and *L'Auteur mort et vivant* (Dec. 18, 1820); the failure of the last-named opera caused him to distrust his natural talent, and to imitate, in several succeeding stage works, the style then in vogue—that of Rossini. With the comic opera *Marie* (Aug. 12, 1826) Herold returned, however, to his true element, and won instant and brilliant success. Meantime he had obtained the post of chorusmaster at the Italian Opera (1824); during this period he brought out *Le Muletier* (May 12, 1823), *Lasthénie* (Sept. 8, 1823), *Vendôme en Espagne* (Dec. 5, 1823), *Le Roi René* (Aug. 24, 1824), and *Le Lapin blanc* (May 21, 1825). In 1827 he was appointed to the staff of the Grand Opéra, for which he wrote several melodious and elegant ballets: *Astolphe et Jaconde* (Jan. 29,

1827); *La Somnambule* (Sept. 19, 1827); *Lydie* (July 2, 1828); *La Fille mal gardée* (Nov. 17, 1828); *La Belle au bois dormant* (April 27, 1829); *La Noce de village* (Feb. 11, 1830). *La Somnambule* furnished Bellini with the subject of his popular opera. On July 18, 1829 Herold produced *L'Illusion,* a one-act opera full of charming numbers. *Emmeline,* a grand opera (Nov. 28, 1829), was a failure, but his next opera *Zampa* (May 3, 1831) was sensationally successful and placed Herold in the first rank of French composers. He then wrote *L'Auberge d'Aurey* (May 11, 1830) jointly with Carafa; *La Marquise de Brinvilliers* (Oct. 31, 1831) in collaboration with Auber, Batton, Berton, Blangini, Boieldieu, Carafa, Cherubini, and Paër; also produced *La Médecine sans médecin* (Oct. 15, 1832). His last work published in his lifetime, *Le Pré aux clercs* (Dec. 15, 1832), had a remarkable vogue. He died of consumption shortly before his 42nd birthday. His unfinished opera *Ludovic* was completed by Halévy and produced posthumously at the Opéra-Comique on May 16, 1833. Herold's piano music, comprising 55 opus numbers, consists of sonatas, caprices, rondos, divertissements, fantasies, variations, and potpourris.

BIBLIOGRAPHY: B. Jouvin, *Herold, sa vie et ses œuvres* (Paris, 1868); Hector Berlioz, *Les Musiciens et la musique* (Paris, 1903); A. Pougin, *Herold* (Paris, 1906).

Heron-Allen, Edward, English writer on the violin; b. London, Dec. 17, 1861; d. Selsey, Sussex, March 28, 1943. He was the author of a standard manual on the history of violin manufacture: *Violin-Making, As It Was and Is* (London, 1884).

Herrera de la Fuente, Luis, Mexican conductor and composer; b. Mexico City, April 26, 1916. He studied piano and violin; took composition lessons with Rodolfo Halffter. From 1954 to 1972 he served as principal conductor of the National Symph. Orch. in Mexico City; in the interim he led the National Symph. Orch. of Peru (1965–71); was guest conductor of orchestras in the U.S., Canada, Europe, and New Zealand.

WORKS: an opera, *Cuauhtemoc;* the ballets *La Estrella y la Sirena* and *Fronteras;* he also composed chamber music.

Herriot, Édouard, French statesman and writer on music; b. Troyes, July 5, 1872; d. Lyons, March 26, 1957. He entered politics as a member of the Radical Party; was premier of France 3 times between 1924 and 1932; then became president of the Chamber of Deputies. He was arrested in 1942 for refusing to cooperate with the Vichy Government, deported to Germany, and held in a castle near Potsdam until the end of the war. Returning to France, he resumed his activities; in 1946, he was elected to the French Academy. He was the author of a popular biography, *La Vie de Beethoven* (Paris, 1929; many editions), publ. in English as *The Life and Times of Beethoven* (N.Y., 1935).

Herrmann, Bernard, American conductor and outstanding composer for films; b. New York, June 29, 1911; d. Los Angeles, Dec. 24, 1975. He won a composition prize at the age of 13; then enrolled at New

York Univ. where he studied with Philip James and Percy Grainger; later took courses with Wagenaar in composition and Albert Stoessel in conducting at the Juilliard Graduate School of Music. In 1934 he was appointed to the staff of the Columbia Broadcasting System as a composer of background music for radio programs and conductor of the CBS Symph. Orch. summer radio series; from 1940 till 1955 he was chief conductor of the CBS Symph. Orch. in boldly progressive programs of modern works, including those by Charles Ives. He became associated with Orson Welles and wrote several film scores for the radio broadcasts of the Mercury Theater. His music for *Citizen Kane* (1940), the first of his 61 film scores, is still regarded as a classic of the genre. His use of an electric violin and electric bass in the score for *The Day the Earth Stood Still* (1951) is an example of early application of electronic music in films. He subsequently wrote film scores for the thrillers of Alfred Hitchcock, succeeding in capturing the eerie spirit of Hitchcock's peculiar art by the use of atonal devices; of these, the score for *Psycho* (1960), for strings only, was particularly apt. Among Herrmann's other film scores were *The Devil and Daniel Webster* (1941; also known as *All That Money Can Buy*; received an Academy Award); *Jane Eyre* (1942); *Anna and the King of Siam* (1946); *The Ghost and Mrs. Muir* (1948); *Snows of Kilimanjaro* (1952); *Garden of Evil* (1954); *The Trouble with Harry* (1955); *The Man Who Knew Too Much* (1956); *The Wrong Man* (1957); *Vertigo* (1958); *North by Northwest* (1959); *The Man in the Gray Flannel Suit* (1956); *The Seventh Voyage of Sinbad* (1958); *Journey to the Center of the Earth* (1959); *The Birds* (1963); *Fahrenheit 451* (1966); *La Mariée était en noir* (*The Bride Wore Black*, 1967); *Sisters* (1973) and *Obsession* (1975). Herrmann spent the last ten years of his life in England, but was in Los Angeles in Dec. 1975, to conduct the score for his last film *Taxi Driver*; he died in his sleep shortly after completing the final recording session. His concert works include the 4-act opera *Wuthering Heights* (1948–50; recorded in England in 1966 but not publicly performed); 2 Christmas operas for TV: *A Christmas Carol* (CBS television, N.Y., Dec. 23, 1954) and *A Child Is Born*; 2 cantatas: *Moby Dick* (N.Y., April 11, 1940) and *Johnny Appleseed* (1940). For orch.: *The City of Brass*, symph. poem (1934); *Sinfonietta* for strings (1935); *Currier and Ives*, suite (1935); *Nocturne and Scherzo* (1936); *Fiddle Concerto* (1940); Symph. No. 1 (1940; N.Y. Philh., Nov. 12, 1942); *For the Fallen* (N.Y. Phil., Dec. 16, 1943; composer conducting); *The Fantasticks* for vocal quartet and orch. (1944). He also wrote a String Quartet (1932); *Aubade* for 14 instruments (1933); *Echoes* for string quartet (1966); clarinet quintet, *Souvenirs de Voyage* (1967).

Herrmann, Eduard, conductor and composer; b. Oberrotweil, Germany, Dec. 18, 1850; d. Miami, Fla., April 24, 1937. He studied violin with Joachim in Berlin; played in various German orchestras; from 1878–81 he was concertmaster of the Imperial Orch. in St. Petersburg. In 1881 he settled in New York; formed a quartet with Schenck, Lilienthal, and Hauser, which enjoyed an excellent reputation; one of their features was the annual performance of all of Beethoven's quartets. He wrote a Violin Concerto, a String Quintet, a String Quartet, a Sextet for oboe, clarinet, and strings, etc.

Herrmann, Hugo, German composer; b. Ravensburg, April 19, 1896; d. Stuttgart, Sept. 7, 1967. He acquired primary knowledge of music without systematic study; was drafted into the German Army during World War I and severely wounded in 1918. After the Armistice he took courses in composition with Schreker in Berlin. In 1923 he went to the U.S. and was employed as a church organist; in 1925 he returned to Germany; from 1935 to 1962 he was director of a music school in Trossingen. A believer in practical art he promoted community music; took especial interest in the accordion and wrote several works for this instrument; he also composed pieces for the mouth organ. He also wrote several operas: *Gazellenhorn, Picknick, Vasantasena, Das Wunder, Paracelsus, Der Rekord, Der Überfall, Die Heinzelmännchen;* 5 symphonies; 5 string quartets, etc. He published a manual, *Einführung in die Satztechnik für Mundharmonika-Instrumente* (Trossingen, 1958), containing instructions for performance on the mouth organ.
BIBLIOGRAPHY: A Festschrift, *Hugo Herrmann, Leben und Werk* was published for his 60th birthday (Trossingen, 1956; edited by Armin Fett).

Herschel, Friedrich Wilhelm, eminent astronomer; b. Hannover, Nov. 15, 1738; d. Slough, near Windsor, Aug. 25, 1822. Son of a military musician, he was brought up as a musician like his three brothers. At 14 years of age he entered the band of the Hannoverian guards as oboist, and was stationed at Durham when that regiment went to England (1755). He later played organ at the Halifax parish church. In 1766 he was employed at the Octagon Chapel in Bath. He devoted his leisure to astronomy, constructed the great "Herschel" telescope, discovered the planet Uranus, was appointed "Astronomer Royal" (1781), and abandoned the musical profession. He received the honor of knighthood (1816) and an Oxford degree. He composed a symphony and 2 concertos for wind instruments.

Hertog, Johannes den, Dutch conductor and composer; b. Amsterdam, Jan. 20, 1904. He studied with his father, Herman Johannes den Hertog; then with Cornelis Dopper. He occupied various posts as operatic coach; was director and conductor of the Wagner Society in Amsterdam; from 1938–41 was assistant conductor of the Concertgebouw; also conducted at The Hague; in 1948 he was appointed conductor of the Flemish Opera in Antwerp, and in 1960 he became artistic director of the Netherlands Opera in Amsterdam. He wrote an opera, *Pygmalion* (1957); a musical play, *Pandora* (1968); a number of songs and some orchestral pieces.

Hertz, Alfred, eminent German-American conductor; b. Frankfurt, July 15, 1872; d. San Francisco, April 17, 1942. After completing his academic studies he entered the Raff Cons., where he studied with Anton Urspruch; then held positions as opera conductor in Altenburg (1892–95), Barmen-Elberfeld (1895–99), and Breslau (1899–1902). In 1902 he was engaged as conductor of the German repertory at the Metropolitan Opera; he conducted the first American performance of *Parsifal* (Dec. 24, 1903), which took place against the wishes of the Wagner family; consequently, Hertz could no longer obtain permission to conduct Wagner in Germany. In 1915 he was engaged to lead the San Francisco Symph. Orch.; he retained that post until 1930. He also organized the summer series of concerts at the Hollywood Bowl (1922), and conducted more than 100 concerts there; he was affectionately known as the "Father of the Hollywood Bowl."

Hertzka, Emil, Austrian music publisher; b. Budapest, Aug. 3, 1869; d. Vienna, May 9, 1932. He studied chemistry at the Univ. of Vienna; also took courses in music. He was engaged on the staff of the music publisher Weinberger in Vienna (1893); then joined the Universal Edition organized in 1901. In 1907 he became its director, and remained in that capacity until his death. He purchased the catalogues of several other music publishing firms: the Wiener Philharmonischer Verlag, Albert J. Gutmann Co. (which published Bruckner and Mahler), and acquired the rights of publication to works by many celebrated modern composers (Bartók, Schoenberg, Alban Berg, Kurt Weill, Krenek); also represented Soviet composers. An impassioned believer in the eventual worth of experimental music, he encouraged young composers, took active part in the organization of concerts of modern music, etc. An Emil Hertzka Foundation was established by his family after his death, for the purpose of helping unknown composers secure performances and publication of their works.

Hertzmann, Erich, German-American musicologist; b. Krefeld, Germany, Dec. 14, 1902; d. Berkeley, California, March 3, 1963. He studied music at the Hoch Cons. in Frankfurt; then took courses with several eminent teachers (J. Wolf, Abert, Schering, Sachs, Hornbostel, and Friedrich Blume) at the Univ. of Berlin, where he obtained his doctorate with a dissertation on Willaert (1931). In 1938 he emigrated to the U.S., and joined the faculty of Columbia Univ.; also lectured at Princeton Univ. (1946–49). In 1949 he held a Guggenheim Fellowship; in 1955 received a stipend from Columbia Univ. to study the creative processes of Beethoven. Apart from his dissertation on Willaert, he published numerous articles in German and American music journals, mostly dealing with structural analysis of classical scores.

Hervé (properly **Florimond Ronger**), a French dramatic composer, the creator of French operetta; b. Houdain, near Arras, June 30, 1825; d. Paris, Nov. 3, 1892. He was a chorister and scholar of St.-Roch; he became organist at various churches in Paris. With his friend Kelm, in 1848, he sang in *Don Quichotte et Sancho Pansa,* an interlude of his own composition, at the Opéra National. In 1851 he conducted the orch. at the Palais Royal; in 1855 he opened the 'Folies-Concertantes,' a small theater for the production of pantomimes, *saynètes* (musical comediettas for two persons), etc., and, with phenomenal activity, developed the light French operetta from these diminutive and frivolous pieces, writing both librettos and music, conducting the orchestra, and often appearing as an actor on the stage. From 1856 to 1869 he led this feverish life in Paris, producing his works at various theaters, responding to failures by doubling his efforts. In 1870–71, when the Franco-Prussian War and the Commune stopped theatrical activities in Paris, he went to London, where he produced several of his light operas; he revisited London many times afterwards. In all, he wrote about 50 operettas, of which only one became a universal success, *Mam'zelle Nitouche* (Paris, Jan. 16, 1883, followed by numerous productions in European cities); other fairly successful works were *L'Oeil crevé* (Paris, Oct. 12, 1867) and *Le Petit Faust* (Paris, April 29, 1869). He also wrote a grand opera, *Les Chevaliers de la table ronde* (Paris, Nov. 17, 1866); the ballets, *Sport, La Rose d'Amour, Les Bagatelles,* etc.
BIBLIOGRAPHY: L. Schneider, *Les Maîtres de l'opérette française, Hervé et Charles Lecocq* (Paris, 1924).

Hervey, Arthur, composer and writer; b. (of Irish parentage) Paris, Jan. 26, 1855; d. London, March 10, 1922. At first intended for the diplomatic service, he embraced a musical career in 1880; was critic for *Vanity Fair* (1889–92); 1892–1908, on the staff of the London *Morning Post.*
WRITINGS: *Masters of French Music* (London, 1894); *French Music in the XIXth Century* (1904); *Alfred Bruneau* (1907); *Franz Liszt and His Music* (1911); *Meyerbeer* (1913); *Rubinstein* (1913); *Saint-Saëns* (1921); etc.

Hervig, Richard, American composer and teacher; b. Story City, Iowa, Nov. 24, 1917. He studied with Philip Greeley Clapp at the Univ. of Iowa; in 1955 was appointed to its faculty. He wrote 2 symphonies, 2 clarinet sonatas, choral music and piano pieces.

Herz, Henri, brilliant Austrian pianist; b. Vienna, Jan. 6, 1803; d. Paris, Jan. 5, 1888. He was taught by his father, and by Hünten at Coblenz; later (1816) by Pradher, Reicha, and Dourlen at the Paris Cons., and won 1st piano prize; improved himself in Moscheles's style after that virtuoso's visit in 1821; was in high repute as a fashionable teacher and composer, his compositions realizing 3 and 4 times the price of those of his superior contemporaries. In 1831 he made a tour of Germany with the violinist Lafont; visited London in 1834, and at his first concert Moscheles and Cramer played duets with him. In 1842, was appointed piano prof. at the Paris Cons. He suffered financial losses through partnership with a piano manufacturer, Klepfer, and thereupon undertook a concert tour through the United States, Mexico, and the West Indies (1845–51). Returning, he established a successful piano factory, his instruments receiving 1st prize at the Paris Exhibition of 1855. He resigned his professorship at the Cons. in 1874. Herz acknowledged that he courted the popular taste; his numerous works (over 200) include piano concertos, variations, sonatas, rondos, violin sonatas, nocturnes, dances, marches, fantasias, etc. He publ. an interesting and

vivid book, *Mes voyages en Amérique* (1866), a reprint of his letters to the *Moniteur Universel.*
BIBLIOGRAPHY: A. Loesser, *Men, Women, and Pianos* (N.Y., 1954); H. C. Schonberg, *The Great Pianists* (N.Y., 1963).

Herzog, Emilie, Swiss soprano; b. Ermatingen, Switzerland, Dec. 17, 1859; d. Aarburg, Switzerland, Sept. 16, 1923. She studied voice in Zürich and Munich; made a debut in a minor role at the Munich Opera in 1880, and afterwards sang in other German opera houses, including Bayreuth. In 1889 she was engaged at the Berlin Opera, where she became one of the best interpreters of soubrette roles; she also gave recitals in Germany as a lieder singer. She made guest appearances in the opera houses of London, Paris, Vienna, and Brussels, and in 1896 sang at the Bolshoi Theater in Moscow; she also sang for a season at the Metropolitan Opera in New York (1899–1900). Returning to Europe she continued to sing at the Berlin Opera (until 1910); then taught at the Zürich Cons. (1910–22).

Herzog, George, American ethnomusicologist; b. Budapest, Dec. 11, 1901. He studied musicology and anthropology in Budapest and Berlin; in 1925 he went to America and pursued his studies at Columbia Univ., where he received his Ph.D; in 1930 he joined the expedition to Liberia, organized by the Univ. of Chicago, where he made a thorough study of West African music; from 1932 to 1946 he was prof. of anthropology at Columbia Univ., and also lectured at Yale Univ. In 1948 he was appointed prof. of anthropology and folk music at the Univ. of Indiana in Bloomington, where he remained until 1961. He published numerous informative papers on folk music of American Indians and African tribes. Among his most important ethnomusicological publications are: *Musik der Karolinen-Inseln* (Hamburg, 1936); *Research in Primitive and Folk Music in the United States* (Washington, 1936).
BIBLIOGRAPHY: B. Krader, "Bibliography of George Herzog," *Ethnomusicology* (Jan. 1956).

Herzog, Johann Georg, German organist and composer; b. Hummendorf, near Kronach, Aug. 5, 1822; d. Munich, Feb. 3, 1909. He studied at the music school in Schmölz, in Bavaria, and at the age of 11 began to earn a living playing the organ. In 1843 he went to Munich, where he was church organist, and later (1850) prof. at the Munich Cons.; among his pupils was Rheinberger. In 1854, he went to Erlangen; established a series of historical organ concerts there (1861–65); he then returned to Munich. He wrote a great number of organ works; also practical manuals.

Herzog, Sigmund, pianist; b. Budapest, June 13, 1868; d. New York, Aug. 28, 1932. He studied with Julius Epstein at the Vienna Cons., graduating in 1885; later with Rafael Joseffy in New York, where he then taught at the Institute of Musical Art. He publ. *The Art of Octave-Playing* and various piano pieces.

Herzogenberg, Heinrich von, Austrian pianist and composer; b. Graz, June 10, 1843; d. Wiesbaden, Oct. 9, 1900. He studied with Dessoff at the Vienna Cons.; then lived in Graz; went to Leipzig in 1872; with Spit-

ta, Holstein, and Volkland, he founded the Bach-Verein there (1874); was its conductor from 1875–85; then was prof. of composition at the Hochschule für Musik in Berlin (1885–88); director of the 'Meisterschule' (1889–92 and 1897–1900). He was a very prolific composer; his chief influences were Brahms and Bruch.
WORKS: the oratorios *Die Geburt Christi, Die Passion, Erntefeier;* choral works with orch., *Der Stern des Liedes, Die Weihe der Nacht, Nannas Klage, Totenfeier,* and several psalms and motets; a cantata *Columbus;* a symph. poem *Odysseus;* 2 symphonies; Piano Quintet; String Quintet; 5 string quartets; Quartet for Piano, Horn, Clarinet, and Bassoon; 2 piano quartets; 2 piano trios; 2 string trios; Trio for Piano, Oboe, and Horn; 3 violin sonatas; 3 cello sonatas; several works for piano four hands; fantasies for organ. Herzogenberg's wife, **Elisabet,** *née* **von Stockhausen** (b. Paris, April 13, 1847; d. San Remo, Jan. 7, 1892), was an excellent pianist. They were great friends of Brahms, with whom they maintained a long correspondence (see M. Kalbeck, *Johannes Brahms im Briefwechsel mit Heinrich und Elisabet von Herzogenberg,* 1907).
BIBLIOGRAPHY: J. H. Spengel, *Heinrich von Herzogenberg in seinen Vokalwerken* (Leipzig, 1893); W. Altmann, *Heinrich von Herzogenberg, Sein Leben und Schaffen* (Leipzig, 1903). J. Rieter-Biedermann publ. a complete catalogue of Herzogenberg's works (1900).

Heseltine, Philip (pen name **Peter Warlock**), brilliant English composer and writer; b. London, Oct. 30, 1894; d. there, Dec. 17, 1930. He studied at Eton with Colin Taylor (1908–10); a meeting with Delius in France in 1910 influenced him profoundly in the direction of composition; he adopted a style that was intimately connected with English traditions of the Elizabethan period and yet revealed impressionistic undertones in harmonic writing. Another influence was that of Bernard van Dieren, from whom he absorbed an austerely contrapuntal technique. He publ. all his musical works under the name Peter Warlock. He was a conscientious objector during World War I; in 1917 was in Ireland; after the Armistice returned to London; in 1920 he founded the progressive journal of musical opinion, *The Sackbut;* wrote criticism; made transcriptions of old English music; participated in organizing the Delius Festival in 1929. Suffering from depression, he committed suicide by gas in his London flat.
WRITINGS: (under the name Philip Heseltine): *Frederick Delius* (London, 1923; revised ed. by Hubert Foss, London, 1952); *Carlo Gesualdo, Prince of Venosa, Musician and Murderer* (in collaboration with Cecil Gray; London, 1926); a pamphlet of 8 pages, *Thomas Whythorne: An Unknown Elizabethan Composer* (Oxford, 1927); as Peter Warlock, publ. a monograph, *The English Ayre* (London, 1926); ed. (with Ph. Wilson) 300 old songs (*English Ayres, Elizabethan and Jacobean; French Ayres*); co-editor, *Oxford Choral Songs* and the *Oxford Orchestral Series,* a collection of old English and Italian dances; transcribed for piano some lute music of John Dowland, *Forlorne Hope;* many other transcriptions. Musical compositions: song cycle *The Curlew* (with flute, English horn, and string quartet); *Saudades* (3 songs); *Lilligay* (5

songs); *Peterisms* (2 sets of 3 songs each); *Candlelight* (12 nursery songs), and many separate songs; *Capriol Suite* (on tunes from Arbeau's *Orchésographie*, in 2 versions: for string orch. and full orch.); *Corpus Christi* (2 versions, for chorus a cappella and for soprano and tenor soli with string quartet); numerous other vocal works.

BIBLIOGRAPHY: Cecil Gray, *Peter Warlock: A Memoir of Philip Heseltine* (London, 1934); G. Cockshott, "A Note on Warlock's Capriol Suite," *Monthly Musical Record* (1940); G. Cockshott, "Some Notes on the Songs of Peter Warlock," *Music & Letters* (July 1940); K. Avery, "The Chronology of Warlock's Songs," *Music & Letters* (Oct. 1948).

Hess, Dame Myra, distinguished English pianist; b. London, Feb. 25, 1890; d. there, Nov. 25, 1965. She studied at the Royal Academy of Music with Tobias Matthay; made her concert debut in London on Nov. 15, 1907, at the age of 17, playing Beethoven's G Major Concerto with Thomas Beecham, producing a highly favorable impression. She then embarked on a successful and steady career; made several tours in Germany and France; played recitals in America in 1922, repeating her American tours at regular intervals. In 1941 she was created Dame of the British Empire. Her playing was marked by classical precision and poetic imagination; although she was never attracted by the modern repertory of her time, she occasionally performed piano music by contemporary British composers.

BIBLIOGRAPHY: D. Lassimonne, ed. *Myra Hess by Her Friends* (London, 1966).

Hess, Ludwig, German tenor; b. Marburg, March 23, 1877; d. Berlin, Feb. 5, 1944. He studied singing with Vidal in Milan; gave concerts of German lieder throughout Europe, specializing in the modern repertory; made a successful tour of the U.S. and Canada in 1911; conducted a choral society in Königsberg (1917–20); then settled in Berlin. He was also a composer; wrote the operas *Abu und Nu* (Danzig, 1919) and *Vor Edens Pforte* (after Byron); *Kranion* (Erfurt, 1933); Symphony; a symph. poem *Himmelskönig mit musizierenden Engeln* (after Hans Memling); *Ariadne*, a cantata; many choral works, and numerous songs. He publ. a book *Die Behandlung der Stimme vor, während und nach der Mutation* (Marburg, 1927).

Hess, Willy, German violinist; b. Mannheim, July 14, 1859; d. Berlin, Feb. 17, 1939. His first teacher was his father, who was a pupil of Spohr. As a child, he was taken to the U.S.; at the age of 9, he played with the Thomas Orch. He then studied with Joachim in Berlin; later occupied posts as concertmaster in Frankfurt (1878–86), Rotterdam, where he taught at the Cons. (1886–88), and in Manchester, England, with the Hallé Orch. (1888–95). From 1895 to 1903, he was prof. of violin at the Cons. of Cologne; then taught at the Royal Academy of Music in London (1903–04); in 1904, he was engaged as concertmaster of the Boston Symph. Orch., and remained in that position until 1910; also organized the Hess Quartet in Boston.

From 1910–28 he taught at the Hochschule für Musik in Berlin; there he remained until his death.

BIBLIOGRAPHY: F. Bonavia, "Willy Hess," *Monthly Musical Record* (1931).

Hess, Willy, Swiss musicologist and composer; b. Winterthur, Oct. 12, 1906. He studied piano at the Zürich Cons., and also took bassoon lessons; after 1940 played the bassoon in the orchestra at Winterthur. His main vocation was musicology; he devoted himself to the elucidation of obscure points of Beethoven's biography and the rational collation of different editions of his works.

WRITINGS: *Beethovens Oper Fidelio und ihre drei Fassungen* (Zürich, 1953); a biography, *Beethoven* (Zürich, 1956). Esthetics: *Die Harmonie der Künste* (Vienna, 1960); *Die Dynamik der musikalischen Formbildung* (2 Vols., Vienna, 1960, 1964); *Vom Doppelantlitz des Bösen in der Kunst, dargestellt am Beispiel der Musik* (Munich, 1963); *Vom Metaphysischen im Künstlerischen* (Winterthur, 1963); *Parteilose Kunst, parteilose Wissenschaft* (Tutzing, 1967). He composed prolifically; wrote several fairy-tale operas; Symphony; Sonata for Bassoon and Small Orch.; Horn Concerto; numerous pieces of chamber music, including a curious work for double bassoon and string quartet; also a number of piano pieces, and choruses.

Hesse, Adolph (Friedrich), German organist and composer; b. Breslau, Aug. 30, 1808; d. there, Aug. 5, 1863. His father was an organ builder, and Hesse received his first instruction from him; he further profited by the advice of Hummel and Spohr. He was church organist at Breslau; visited Paris in 1844 for the inauguration of the new organ at St.-Eustache; his virtuoso handling of the pedal evoked praise. In 1851 he gave demonstrations of organ playing in London; then returned to Breslau; there he enjoyed a great reputation, not only as an organist, but also as conductor of the Breslau Symph. He publ. a collection, *Practical Organist*; his organ works were brought out by Steggall in a complete edition.

Hesse, Ernst Christian, German composer; b. Grossgottern, April 14, 1676; d. Darmstadt, May 16, 1762. He studied the viola da gamba, first at Darmstadt, then in Paris; gave successful demonstrations of his virtuosity in various European towns. In 1713 he married the opera singer, **Johanna Döbricht.** He wrote 2 operas and many works for viola da gamba.

Hesse, Julius, German pianist; b. Hamburg, March 2, 1823; d. Berlin, April 5, 1881. He originated and successfully introduced a new measurement for piano keys; publ. *System des Klavierspiels*.

Hesse, Max, German music publisher; b. Sondershausen, Feb. 18, 1858; d. Leipzig, Nov. 24, 1907. In 1880 he founded under his name a publishing house, with headquarters in Leipzig; in 1915 the firm moved to Berlin. Among its most important publications were 3rd–11th editions of Riemann's *Musik Lexikon* (1887–1929) and H. J. Moser's *Musik-Lexikon*. Great devastation was wreaked on the physical materials of the firm by air bombardment during World War II. After the war the firm was re-established in Berlin. See *80 Jahre Max Hesses Verlag* (Berlin, 1960).

Hesselberg, Edouard Gregory, pianist and teacher; b. Riga, May 3, 1870; d. Los Angeles, June 12, 1935. He studied at the Cons. of the Moscow Philh. Society (1888–92); later was a private pupil of Anton Rubinstein. In 1892 he came to the U.S.; taught at the Ithaca Cons. (1895–96), Music Academy in Denver (1896–1900), Cons. of Music at Wesleyan College (1900–05), Belmont College, Nashville (1905–12), and at the Toronto Cons. (1912–18). He wrote *Russian Suite* and *Russian Rhapsody,* for orch.; also piano pieces; made arrangements for 2 pianos of works by Bach, Chopin, and Schubert.

Hessen, Alexander Friedrich, Landgraf von, German musician; b. Copenhagen, Jan. 25, 1863; d. Fronhausen, March 26, 1945. In 1888 he became Landgrave of the House of Hessen. Although blind from childhood, he studied music with admirable diligence; took violin lessons in Berlin with Joachim and Bruch; studied composition with Draeseke in Dresden and with Fauré in Paris. By an extraordinary effort he managed to compose a number of works, mostly chamber music and Lieder.
BIBLIOGRAPHY: P. Hiller, *Der Liederzyklus von Alexander Friedrich von Hessen* (1910).

Hessenberg, Kurt, German composer; b. Frankfurt, Aug. 17, 1908. He studied in Leipzig with Raphael (composition) and Reichmüller (piano). In 1933 he was appointed to the faculty of the Hoch Cons. in Frankfurt. Possessing great facility in composition, Hessenberg evolved an effective idiom, fundamentally classical, but containing Wagnerian elements in dramatic passages, with occasional infusion of prudential modernistic devices.
WORKS: His most successful work was *Struwwelpeter,* a suite for small orchestra based on a well-known German children's tale. He further wrote 3 symphonies (1936, 1943, 1954); Concerto for Orch. (1958); Piano Concerto (1940); Concerto for 2 Pianos and Orch. (1950); 2 flute sonatas (1932); Cello Sonata (1941); Violin Sonata (1942); String Trio (1949); Piano Trio (1950); 5 string quartets (1934–67); numerous piano pieces; a number of cantatas and a multitude of lieder.
BIBLIOGRAPHY: Karl Laux, *Kurt Hessenberg* (Essen, 1949).

Hetsch, (Karl Friedrich) Ludwig, German conductor; b. Stuttgart, April 26, 1806; d. Mannheim, June 28, 1872. He studied with Abeille; was attached to the court of the King of Württemberg; then conducted in Heidelberg (1835–46) and in Munich (from 1846). He wrote an opera, *Ryno* (Stuttgart, 1833), orchestral works, and chamber music.

Hétu, Jacques, Canadian composer; b. Trois Rivières, Quebec, Aug. 8, 1938. He studied composition with Clermont Pépin at the Montreal Cons. (1956–61). A Canadian Council scholarship enabled him to go to Paris, where he took lessons with Dutilleux and Mes-

siaen; upon his return to Canada in 1963 he was appointed to the staff of the Laval Univ. in Quebec. In his music he makes use of permissible modern devices, while hewing to classical formal conventions.
WORKS: 3 symphonies: No. 1 for string orch. (1959), No. 2 (1961) and No. 3 for chamber orch. (1971); *Adagio and Rondo* for string quartet (1960); Trio for Flute, Oboe and Harpsichord (1960); 2-Piano Sonata (1961); *Petite Suite* for piano (1962); Variations for Piano (1964); Rondo for Cello and String Orch. (1965); *4 Pieces* for flute and piano (1965); Variations for Solo Violin, or Viola, or Cello (1967); Double Concerto for Violin, Piano and Chamber Orch. (1967); *L'Apocalypse,* symph. poem (1967); Piano Concerto (1969); *Cycle* for piano and wind instruments (1969); Passacaille for Orch. (1970); String Quartet (1972); *Fantaisie* for piano and orch. (1973).

Heuberger, Richard (Franz Joseph), Austrian conductor and composer; b. Graz, June 18, 1850; d. Vienna, Oct. 27, 1914. By profession a civil engineer, in 1876 he turned his full attention to music; became choral master of the Vienna Gesangverein and conductor of the Singakademie (1878); from 1902–09, conductor of the Männergesangverein; appointed prof. at the Vienna Cons. (1902). In 1881 he became music critic of the *Wiener Tageblatt,* then of *Neue Freie Presse* (1896–1901), after 1904, of *Neue Musikalische Presse,* and editor of *Musikbuch aus Österreich* (1904–06).
WORKS: operas: *Abenteuer einer Neujahrsnacht* (Leipzig, 1886), *Manuel Venegas* (Leipzig, March 27, 1889), remodeled as the 3-act grand opera *Mirjam, oder Das Maifest* (Vienna, Jan. 20, 1894), *Barfüssele* (Dresden, 1905); the operettas (all first performed at Vienna) *Der Opernball* (Jan. 5, 1898; exceptionally successful; in N.Y., May 24, 1909), *Ihre Excellenz* (1899; new version as *Eine entzückende Frau*), *Der Sechsuhrzug* (1900), *Das Baby* (1902), *Der Fürst von Düsterstein* (1909), *Don Quixote* (1910); the ballet *Struwwelpeter* (Dresden, 1897); cantata, *Geht es dir wohl, so denk' an mich,* from *Des Knaben Wunderhorn;* overture to Byron's *Cain;* and songs. He publ. a selection of his critiques as *Musikalische Skizzen* (Leipzig, 1901); a biography, *Franz Schubert* (Berlin, 1902; 2nd ed., 1908); *Anleitung zum Modulieren* (Vienna, 1910).

Heubner, Konrad, German composer; b. Dresden, April 8, 1860; d. Coblenz, June 6, 1905. He studied with Riemann in Leipzig, with Nottebohm in Vienna, and with Nicodé in Dresden. In 1890 he was appointed director of the Coblenz Cons. He wrote a symphony, a cantata *Das Geheimnis der Sehnsucht,* several overtures, and a violin concerto.

Heugel, Henry, Swiss-French music theorist; b. Neuchâtel, Switzerland, Sept. 26, 1789; d. Nantes, France, May 2, 1841. He studied in Paris with Galin and Reicha; developed a 'méthode de méloplaste' along the lines of Galin's system; publ. *Nouvelle méthode pour l'enseignement de la musique inventée par H. Heugel et developpée par lui de manière à permettre d'apprendre sans maître* (1832).

Heugel, Jacques-Léopold, French music publisher; son of **Henry Heugel;** b. La Rochelle, March 1, 1811; d. Paris, Nov. 12, 1883. In 1839 he joined a music publishing establishment founded in Paris by J. A. Meissonnier (1812), and became its director; the name was changed to 'Heugel et Cie.' After his death, his nephew, **Paul Chevalier Heugel** (1861–1931) became its owner. The firm is now managed by **Philippe** and **François Heugel,** successors to their father, **Jacques-Paul Heugel,** who was the grandson of Jacques-Léopold Heugel. The list of publications includes the famous Paris Cons. methods, in all branches of music, and the works of celebrated composers (Bizet, Bruneau, Charpentier, Delibes, Fauré, Franck, Honegger, Ibert, d'Indy, Lalo, Massenet, Milhaud, Offenbach, Poulenc, Ravel, Roussel, Florent Schmitt, Widor, etc.). The firm also published the important weekly, *Le Ménestrel* (founded in 1833; suspended publication during the Franco-Prussian War, 1870–71, and during World War I; ceased publishing in 1940).

Heuss, Alfred Valentin, Swiss musicologist; b. Chur, Jan. 27, 1877; d. Gaschwitz, Germany, July 8, 1934. He studied at the Stuttgart Cons. (1896–98), then at the Akademie der Tonkunst in Munich, attending the Univ. of Munich simultaneously (1898–99); from 1900–03, he studied musicology with Kretzschmar at the Univ. of Leipzig (*Dr. phil.,* 1903, with his dissertation *Die Instrumentalstücke des 'Orfeo' und die venezianischen Opernsinfonien*). He was music critic of the *Signale* (1902–05); of the *Leipziger Volkszeitung* (1905–12); of the *Leipziger Zeitung* (1912–18); editor of the *Zeitschrift der Internationalen Musik-Gesellschaft* (1904–14), to which he contributed valuable articles; editor-in-chief of the *Zeitschrift für Musik* (1921–29); wrote analyses of works by Bach, Beethoven, Liszt, Bruckner, etc., for Breitkopf & Härtel's *Kleiner Konzertführer*. Of special value are his program books of the Bach Festivals at Leipzig (1904–27); he also publ. *Bachs Matthäuspassion* (1909). Other writings include "Über die Dynamik der Mannheimer Schule," in the *Riemann-Festschrift* (1909); *Kammermusikabende* (1919); *Beethoven: Eine Charakteristik* (1921); *Beethovens Orch.-Crescendo* (Basel, 1924); etc.

Heward, Leslie, English conductor and composer; b. Littletown, Liversedge, Yorkshire, Dec. 8, 1897; d. Birmingham, May 3, 1943. He was a pupil of his father, an organist; at the age of 17 he played organ in a church; later studied at the Royal College of Music in London. He then taught at various schools and conducted opera. From 1924–27 he was conductor of the Cape Town orch. in South Africa. Returning to England, he conducted the orch. of the city of Birmingham. Heward was also a composer; he wrote several orchestral suites, choruses, and songs. A memorial volume was published after his death under the editorship of Eric Blom (London, 1944).

Hewitt, Helen, American musicologist; b. Granville, N.Y., May 2, 1900; d. Denton, Texas, March 19, 1977. She studied at the Eastman School of Music in Rochester, N.Y.; then traveled to Paris, took a course in theory with Nadia Boulanger and organ lessons with Widor. Returning to America, she enrolled in the musicology class of Paul Henry Lang at Columbia Univ. (M.A., 1933); further supplemented her studies at Heidelberg Univ., where she was a student of Besseler. She obtained her Ph.D. from Radcliffe College in 1938; received a Guggenheim Fellowship grant in 1947. From 1942 until 1968 she was on the music faculty of North Texas State College in Denton. She edited Petrucci's anthology of secular choral music of the 15th century, *Harmonice Musices Odhecaton A* (Cambridge, Mass., 1942); contributed valuable articles on the music of the Renaissance to various periodicals.

Hewitt, James, American composer, publisher, organist, and violinist; b. Dartmoor, England, June 4, 1770; d. Boston, Aug. 1, 1827. He played in the court orch. in London as a youth. In 1792 he went to America and settled in New York, where he was described as one of the 'professors of music from the Opera House, Hanover Square, and Professional Concerts under the direction of Haydn, Pleyel, etc., London.' On Sept. 21, 1792 he gave a benefit concert with the violinists J. Gehot and B. Bergmann, the flutist W. Young, and a cellist named Phillips, which included Hewitt's *Overture in 9 Movements, expressive of a battle.* Subsequently, Young and Gehot went to Philadelphia, and in 1793 Hewitt, Bergmann, and Phillips gave a series of 6 subscription concerts; at their 5th concert (March 25, 1793) they presented for the first time in America, Haydn's *Passion of Our Saviour* (i.e., *The Seven Last Words*); in 1794 Henri Capron joined Hewitt in promoting his 'City Concerts;' meanwhile, Hewitt became the leader of the Old American Co. Orch., and in 1795 gave up his activities in connection with the subscription concerts. In 1798 he bought out the N.Y. branch of Carr's 'Musical Repository' and established a publishing business of his own. In 1812 he went to Boston, where he played organ at the Trinity Church and was in charge of the music presented at the Federal Street Theatre. In 1818 he returned to N.Y.; also traveled in the South. In N.Y. he was director of the Park Theatre.

WORKS: ballad operas *Tammany* (produced in N.Y., 1794, under the auspices of the Tammany Society; only one song, "The Death Song of the Cherokee Indians," survives; repr. in W. T. Marrocco and H. Gleason, *Music in America*), *The Patriot or Liberty Asserted* (1794), *The Mysterious Marriage* (1799), *Columbus* (1799), *Pizarro, or the Spaniards in Peru* (1800), *Robin Hood* (1800), *The Spanish Castle* (N.Y., Dec. 5, 1800), *The Wild Goose Chase* (1800); an overture *Demophon*; a set of 3 piano sonatas; *Battle of Trenton,* for piano (reprinted in the collection *Music from the Days of George Washington,* ed. by Carl Engel and Oliver Strunk); *The 4th of July—A Grand Military Sonata for the Pianoforte*; some other music, much of it extant in the Library of Congress, Washington; N.Y. Public Library; and the Boston Public Library. In 1816 Hewitt published a new setting of the *Star-Spangled Banner* to Key's poem, but it never took root. His *Nahant Waltz* is reprinted in J. T. Howard's *A Program of Early American Piano Music* (N.Y., 1931). **John Hill Hewitt** (b. New York, July 11, 1801; d. Baltimore, Oct. 7, 1890), eldest son of James

Hewitt, studied at West Point Academy; was a theatrical manager, a newspaper man, and drillmaster of Confederate recruits in the Civil War; wrote poems and plays; about 300 songs (*The Minstrel's Return from the War, All Quiet Along the Potomac, Our Native Land, The Mountain Bugle*, etc.); cantatas (*Flora's Festival, The Fairy Bridal, The Revelers*, and *The Musical Enthusiast*); ballad operas (*Rip Van Winkle, The Vivandiere, The Prisoner of Monterey, The Artist's Wife*). His admirers dubbed him the 'father of the American ballad' but the form of a ballad existed in America long before him. He wrote a book of memoirs, *Shadows on the wall* (1877; repr. 1971). **James Lang Hewitt** (1807–53), another son of James, was associated with the publishing firm of J. A. Dickson in Boston (1825); after his father's death he returned to N.Y. and continued his father's publishing business.

BIBLIOGRAPHY: *Sammelbände der Internationalen Musik-Gesellschaft* (p. 459); J. T. Howard, "The Hewitt Family in American Music," *Musical Quarterly* (Jan. 1931); J. T. Howard, *Our American Music* (N.Y., 1939, and subsequent eds.); C. E. Huggins, *John Hill Hewitt: Bard of the Confederacy* (Florida State Univ., 1964); J. W. Wagner, *James Hewitt: His Life and Works* (Indiana Univ., 1969); W. C. Winden, *The Life and Music Theater Works of John Hill Hewitt* (Univ. of Illinois, 1972).

Hewitt, Maurice, French violinist; b. Asnières (Seine), Oct. 6, 1884; d. Paris, Nov. 7, 1971. He studied at the Paris Cons.; was violinist in the Capet Quartet (1908–28); taught at the Cleveland Institute of Music (1930–34); from 1934, teacher at the American Cons. of Fontainebleau; at the Paris Cons. from 1938 (chamber music class); in 1928, organized in Paris the Quatuor Hewitt; in 1939, founded the Orchestre de Chambre Hewitt.

Hey, Julius, German singing teacher; b. Irmelshausen, April 29, 1832; d. Munich, April 23, 1909. He first studied painting, but turned to music. He became an ardent Wagnerian after his introduction to the master by King Ludwig II, and worked under the direction of Hans von Bülow at the Munich School of Music (established by the King in accordance with Wagner's plans). After Bülow's departure (1869), Hey vainly tried to effect a reform from a German national standpoint in the cultivation of singing, but met with so many obstacles that he resigned when Wagner died (1883) and devoted himself to finishing his method of singing, *Deutscher Gesangsunterricht* (4 parts; 1886). It contains a complete and logical exposition of Wagner's views on vocal training. His book *Richard Wagner als Vortragsmeister* was publ. posthumously by his son Hans.

Heyden, Hans, German organist; son of **Sebald Heyden;** b. Nuremberg, Jan. 19, 1536; d. there, Oct. (buried Oct. 22), 1613. He was his father's successor as organist at St. Sebald Church, and was the inventor of the unique 'Geigen-Clavicymbel' ('Nürnbergisch Geigenwerk'), which he described in *Musicale instrumentum reformatum* (1605).

BIBLIOGRAPHY: G. Kinsky, "Hans Heyden," *Zeitschrift für Musikwissenschaft* (1924).

Heyden (Heiden, Haiden), Sebald, German composer; b. Nuremberg, Dec. 8, 1499; d. there, July 9, 1561. In 1519, he was appointed cantor of the Hospital School in Nuremberg; in 1537, became rector at the Church of St. Sebald. He was the author of the important theoretical work *Musicae, id est, artis canendi libri duo* (1537; 2nd ed., as *De arte canendi*, etc., 1540); composed the famous Passion song, O Mensch, bewein dein Sünde gross.

BIBLIOGRAPHY: A. Kosel, *Sebald Heyden* (Würzburg, 1940).

Heyer, Wilhelm, German patron of music; b. Cologne, March 30, 1849; d. there, March 20, 1913. A wealthy co-owner of the wholesale paper manufacturing firm Poensgen & Heyer, he was an enthusiastic amateur and was active in the musical affairs of Cologne in advisory capacities. In 1906 he established a historical musical museum in Cologne, in which he assembled more than 2600 instruments with accessories, about 20,000 autographs of musicians, 3500 portraits, and a library of books about music, containing many rare editions. Georg Kinsky, curator of the museum from 1909, publ. an illustrated catalogue of the Heyer collections. The museum was dissolved in 1927, and the instruments were acquired by the Musicological Institute of Leipzig Univ.; the books were dispersed by auction sales.

Heyman, Katherine Ruth Willoughby, American pianist; b. Sacramento, Calif., 1877; d. Sharon, Conn., Sept. 28, 1944. She made her debut as soloist with the Boston Symph. Orch. in 1899; from 1905 till 1915 toured the U.S. and Europe with Schumann-Heink, Marcella Sembrich, and others. She became greatly interested in the works of Scriabin, and played recitals of his works in Europe and America; also publ. many articles on Scriabin's theosophic ideas. In 1928 she founded in Paris the "Groupe Estival pour la musique moderne." She publ. *The Relation of Ultra-Modern to Archaic Music* (Boston, 1921); composed *Studies in Modern Idiom* for the piano, and songs.

Heymann, Werner Richard, German-American composer; b. Königsberg, Feb. 14, 1896; d. Munich, May 30, 1961. He studied violin and composition; wrote a number of scores of incidental music for theatrical plays; spent several years in Hollywood where he wrote the music score for the highly successful film *Ninotchka*.

Hickmann, Hans Robert Hermann, German musicologist; b. Rosslau, May 19, 1908; d. Blandford Forum, Dorset, England, Sept. 4, 1968. He studied in Halle and Berlin, where he took courses in musicology with Sachs, Schering, Schünemann, and Wolf. In 1933 he went to Egypt, where he collected materials dealing with ancient Egyptian music. In 1957 he joined the faculty of the Univ. of Hamburg; then lived in England. His principal works include the books *Das Portativ* (Kassel, 1936); *La Trompette dans l'Egypte ancienne* (Cairo, 1946); *Terminologie arabe des instruments de musique* (Cairo, 1947); *Musikgeschichte in Bildern*, vol. 2, on Egypt (Leipzig, 1962).

For other details see his autobiographical notice in *Die Musik in Geschichte und Gegenwart.*

Hidalgo, Juan, one of the earliest and most notable Spanish opera composers; b. c.1600; d. Madrid, March 30, 1685. In 1631 he became a member of the Royal Chapel in Madrid as harpist and also as player of the "clavi-harpa," an instrument he is said to have invented. A document of 1677 attests that he was 'of superior skill, and had merited the highest honors from Their Majesties at all times.' So great was his reputation that the Duke of Infantado called him "unique in the faculty of music." He composed the opera *Celos aun del aire matan,* text by Calderón de la Barca (perf. Madrid, Dec. 5, 1660); the music of Act I (voices and basso continuo) was discovered by J. Subirá and publ. by him in 1933 (this is the longest extant specimen of Spanish operatic music from the 17th century). Hidalgo also wrote music for Calderón's comedies, *Ni amor se libra de amor* (1662) and *Hado y divisa de Leónido y de Marfisa* (1680), and for *Los celos hacen estrellas* by Juan Vélez (c.1662). It is very probable that he also composed the opera *La púrpura de la rosa* (1660), text by Calderón. He was likewise known as a composer of sacred and secular songs (some preserved in the National Library, Madrid). Music by Hidalgo is reprinted in Pedrell's *Cancionero* (IV) and *Teatro lírico* (vols. III, IV, and V).
BIBLIOGRAPHY: J. Subirá, *Celos aun del aire matan, Opera del siglo XVII* (Barcelona, 1933); J. Subirá, "El operista español Don Juan Hidalgo," *Las Ciencias* I/3 (Madrid, 1934); O. Ursprung, "Die älteste erhaltene spanische Oper," in the *Schering-Festschrift* (Berlin, 1937); G. Chase, "Origins of the Lyric Theater in Spain," *Musical Quarterly* (July 1939); J. Moll, "Nuevos datos para la biografía de Juan Hidalgo" in the Festschrift for H. Anglés (Barcelona, 1958–61).

Hidas, Frigyes, Hungarian composer; b. Budapest, May 25, 1928. He studied composition with János Viski at the Academy of Music in Budapest; received the Erkel Prize in 1959. From 1955 to 1966 he served as musical director of the National Theater of Budapest.
WORKS: an opera, *Asszony és az igazság* (*Woman and the Truth,* 1965); Oboe Concerto (1951); 2 string quartets (1954, 1963); Oboe Sonata (1954); Clarinet Concerto (1954); Organ Sonata (1956); Violin Concertino (1957); Viola Concerto (1959); *De minoribus,* cantata (1959); Symphony (1960); *Színek* (*Colors*), ballet (1960); 2 wind quintets (1961, 1969); Fantasy for Clarinet and Piano (1965); Concertino for Strings (1966); Flute Concerto (1967); Horn Concerto (1968); Concertino for Winds and Strings (1969); Organ Fantasy (1969); Piano Concerto (1972); *Gyászzene* (*Funeral Music,* 1973), a requiem for the 2nd Hungarian army that perished in the battle of the River Don.

Hier, Ethel Glenn, American pianist and composer; b. Cincinnati, June 25, 1889; d. New York, Jan. 14, 1971. She studied at the Cincinnati Cons. of Music and at the Institute of Musical Art, N.Y., where she was a pupil of Goetschius; also took lessons with Ernest Bloch. She lived mostly in New York. Among her compositions are *Asolo Bells* for orch. (Rochester, Oct. 25, 1939); a cantata, *Mountain Preacher* (N.Y.,

Dec. 5, 1941); and numerous pieces of chamber music, as well as piano works.

Higgins, Richard C. (Dick), American avant-garde composer; b. Cambridge, England, March 15, 1938. He was taken to America as a child; studied piano in Worcester, Mass.; composition and mycology with John Cage in N.Y. Eventually he moved to California; became active in the mushrooming avant-garde groups; participated in staging "happenings" across the country; joined the ultra-modern group Fluxus in 1961; organized Something Else Press (1964) with the aim of publishing something else. Not averse to academic activities, he joined the faculty of the California Institute of the Arts in Los Angeles. In his productions he pursues the objective of total involvement, in which music is verbalized in conceptual designs without reification, or expressed in physical action; the ultimate in this direction is achieved by his work *The Thousand Symphonies* (1968) in which the composer shoots machine-gun bullets through manuscript paper; his Symph. No. 585, shot by a sergeant of the army at the composer's behest, was distributed in holographs in No. 6 of the avant-garde magazine *Source* (1969) under the subtitle 'the Creative Use of Police Resources.' Other major compositions include: *Graphis,* 146 works for varying groups (1958); *A Loud Symphony* (1958); Symph. No. 3½ (duration 50 seconds, 1959); *In the Context of Shoes,* a happening for tape, vacuum cleaners, drills, gardener's shears, piano and anti-dancers (1960); *In Memoriam,* 164-part canon (1960); *Musical Processes,* a cycle of 5 pieces for indeterminate ensembles (1960); *Constellations and Contributions* for multimedia (1959–60); *Symphoniae Sacrae,* conceptual works without a definite realization (1961); *The Peaceable Kingdom,* spoken opera with bells (1961); *Danger Musics,* a cycle of 43 conceptual pieces (1961–63); *Litany* for 5 pianos and tape recorder (1962–68); *Requiem for Wagner the Criminal Mayor* for tape recorder (1962); *Lavender Blue,* opera (1963); *Egg* for magnetic tape (1967); *Sophocles I and II,* fatal pieces for piano (1970). He publ. *foew&ombwhnw,* "a grammar of the mind and a phenomenology of love and a science of the arts as seen by a stalker of the wild mushroom" (N.Y., 1969). His Zodiac parameter is Aries with the Sun in Pisces.

Higginson, Henry Lee, founder of the Boston Symph. Orch.; b. New York, Nov. 18, 1834; d. Boston, Nov. 15, 1919. He studied singing and piano in Vienna (1856–60); in 1868 he established himself as a banker in Boston (Lee, Higginson & Co.). In 1881, in order to found the Boston Symph. Orch., he assumed the responsibility of providing for about $50,000 yearly of the annual budget of some $115,000, thus clearing the estimated deficit and assuring the organization's successful continuance; the orch., comprising 67 performers, gave its first concert at the old Music Hall on Oct. 22, 1881; in the summer of 1885, the series of concerts of lighter music, famous as the 'Pops,' were instituted; on Oct. 15, 1900, the Boston Symph. Orch. inaugurated its own permanent home, Symphony Hall; in 1903 the Pension Fund was established, for the benefit of which a special concert is given annually. A firm believer in the superiority of German mu-

sicians, Higginson engaged George Henschel as the first conductor of the orch. (1881–84); there followed a line of German conductors: Wilhelm Gericke (1884–89), Artur Nikisch (1889–93), Emil Paur (1893–98), Gericke again (1898–1906), Karl Muck (1906–08), Max Fiedler (1908–12), and again Karl Muck, from 1912 till 1918, when he was arrested as an enemy alien when the U.S. entered World War I. Higginson, distraught over Muck's arrest, resigned his position shortly after and selected a Board of Directors to control the orchestra. He died the following year.
BIBLIOGRAPHY: M. A. de Wolfe Howe, *The Boston Symphony Orchestra* (Boston, 1914; new augmented ed., 1931); H. Earle Johnson, *Symphony Hall* (Boston, 1950).

Hignard, (Jean-Louis) Aristide, French composer; b. Nantes, May 20, 1822; d. Vernon, March 20, 1898; studied with Halévy at the Paris Cons., taking the 2nd Grand Prix de Rome. He was an earnest composer of lofty aims, but brought out operas and other works of secondary importance; his best opera, *Hamlet,* composed in 1868, was to be performed in Paris; unluckily for him, *Hamlet* by Ambroise Thomas was produced that same year, with such spectacular success that Hignard could not compete with it; accordingly, he had to be content with a provincial production in his native city (Nantes, April 21, 1888). His other operas that reached the stage include *Le Visionnaire* (Nantes, 1851), *Le Colin-Maillard* (Paris, 1853); *Les Compagnons de la Marjolaine* (Paris, 1855); *M. de Chimpanzé* (Paris, 1858); *Le Nouveau Pourceaugnac* (Paris, 1860); *L'Auberge des Ardennes* (Paris, 1860); *Les Musiciens de l'orchestre* (Paris, 1861)

Hijman, Julius, Dutch composer and pianist; b. Almelo, Jan. 25, 1901; d. New York, Jan. 6, 1969. He studied piano privately with Dirk Schaefer, then with Paul Weingartner in Vienna; theory and composition with Sem Dresden in Holland. He went to the U.S. in 1940; was instructor at the Houston Cons., Texas (1940–42) and at the Kansas City Cons. (1945–49); then taught composition at the Philadelphia Music Academy and the New York College of Music. He composed mostly chamber music; sonatas for violin, cello, saxophone, oboe, and flute, with piano; 4 string quartets; a sonata for 2 violins and piano; published a study, *New Austrian Music* (in Dutch; Amsterdam, 1937).

Hildach, Eugen, German baritone; b. Wittenberge-on-the-Elbe, Nov. 20, 1849; d. Zehlendorf, near Berlin, July 29, 1924. He began to study voice at the age of 24; married **Anna Schubert,** a singer, and went to Dresden, where they both taught at the Cons.; also toured together in Germany. In 1904, they established their own singing school in Frankfurt. He publ. a number of songs, several of which became well known; particularly popular was *Der Lenz.*

Hiles, Henry, English composer and pedagogue; b. Shrewsbury, Dec. 31, 1826; d. Worthing, near London, Oct. 20, 1904. He filled various positions as organist and harmony teacher for nearly 60 years (1846–1904); was editor of the *Quarterly Musical Review*

(1885–88). He composed several oratorios, glees, and part-songs; publ. the manuals *Harmony of Sounds* (1871); *Grammar of Music* (2 vols., 1879); *First Lessons in Singing* (1881); *Part-Writing or Modern Counterpoint* (1884); *Harmony or Counterpoint?* (1889); *Harmony, Choral or Contrapuntal* (1894).

Hill, Alfred, Australian composer; b. Melbourne, Dec. 16, 1870; d. Sydney, Oct. 30, 1960. He went to study music in Germany; took violin lessons at the Leipzig Cons., and played violin in the Gewandhaus Orch. for 2 years, conducted among others by Brahms, Grieg and Tchaikovsky. He then went to New Zealand where he became interested in the study of aboriginal music of the Maori. From 1916 to 1934 he was professor at the Sydney Cons.
WORKS: operas: *The Weird Flute, Tapu, The Rajah of Shivapore, Giovanni the Sculptor, The Ship of Heaven, Lady Dolly* and *The Whipping Boy;* the cantatas *Hinemoa* and *Tawhaki;* 12 symphonies; 17 string quartets, other pieces of chamber music and many songs. Several of his works are based on Maori themes. He published a manual, *Harmony and Melody* (Sydney, 1927).
BIBLIOGRAPHY: A. D. McCredie, "Alfred Hill (1870–1960): Some Background and Perspectives for an Historical Edition," *Miscellanea Musicologica* (1968).

Hill, Edward Burlingame, eminent American composer; b. Cambridge, Mass., Sept. 9, 1872; d. Francestown, N.H., July 9, 1960. A member of a distinguished family of educators (his father was a professor of chemistry at Harvard, and his grandfather, president of Harvard), he pursued regular courses at Harvard Univ.; studied music with J. K. Paine; graduated in 1894 *summa cum laude;* took lessons in piano with B. J. Lang and A. Whiting, in composition with Chadwick and Bullard; also (for one summer) studied with Widor in Paris. He became greatly interested in the new tonal resources of the Impressionist school of composers; wrote articles in the *Boston Evening Transcript* and other publications dealing with French music; publ. a book *Modern French Music* (Boston, 1924). In 1908 he joined the faculty of Harvard Univ. as instructor in music; became associate prof. in 1918; prof. from 1928–37; then James E. Ditson prof. (1937–40); retired in 1940, and lived mostly in New Hampshire; member of the National Institute of Arts and Letters, American Academy of Arts and Sciences; Chevalier of the Légion d'honneur; lectured at the universities of Strasbourg and Lyons (1921). In his music, Hill reveals himself as a follower of the French school; clarity of design and elegance of expression are his chief characteristics. His best works are for orchestra; but he also composed some fine chamber and choral music.
WORKS: FOR ORCHESTRA: symph. poem, *The Parting of Lancelot and Guinevere* (St. Louis, Dec. 31, 1915); *Stevensoniana Suite No. 1* (N.Y., Jan. 27, 1918); symph. poem, *The Fall of the House of Usher,* after Poe (Boston, Oct. 29, 1920); *Stevensoniana Suite No. 2* (N.Y., March 25, 1923). The following were perf. for the first time by the Boston Symph. Orch: *Waltzes* (Feb. 24, 1922); *Scherzo* for 2 pianos and orch. (Dec.

19, 1924); symph. poem, *Lilacs* (his best work in the Impressionist manner; Cambridge, March 31, 1927; many subsequent performances); Symphony No. 1 (March 30, 1928); *An Ode* (for the 50th anniversary of the Boston Symph. Orch.; Oct. 17, 1930); Symphony No. 2 (Feb. 27, 1931); Concertino for Piano and Orch. (Boston, April 25, 1932); Sinfonietta for String Orch. (Brooklyn, April 3, 1936; also in Boston); Symphony No. 3 (Dec. 3, 1937); Violin Concerto (Nov. 11, 1938); Concertino for String Orch. (April 19, 1940); *Music for English Horn and Orch.* (March 2, 1945); *Prelude* for orchestra (N.Y., March 29, 1953). *Diversion* for small ensemble was perf. at the Saratoga Festival (Sept. 6, 1947). CHAMBER MUSIC: Flute Sonata (1926); Clarinet Sonata (1927); Sextet, for flute, oboe, clarinet, bassoon, horn, and piano (1934); String Quartet (1935); Piano Quartet (1937); Sonata for 2 Clarinets (1938); Quintet for Clarinet and String Quartet (1945); Sonata for Bassoon and Piano (1948); Sonatina for Cello and Piano (1949); Sonatina for Violin and Piano (1951). VOCAL WORKS: *Nuns of the Perpetual Adoration,* cantata for women's voices with orch. or piano (1908); *Autumn Twilight,* for soprano and orch.; *The Wilderness Shall Rejoice,* anthem for mixed chorus (1915); 2 pantomimes (with orchestral accompaniment): *Jack Frost in Midsummer* (1908); and *Pan and the Star* (1914). FOR PIANO: *Poetical Sketches* (1902); *Country Idyls,* a set of 6 pieces; *Jazz Study* for 2 pianos (1924).

Hill, Granville, English organist and music critic; b. Manchester, March 9, 1878; d. there, Dec. 26, 1953. As a youth he was church organist in Manchester; later began to study piano, achieving a commendable degree of proficiency; in 1936 he was appointed piano prof. at the Leeds College of Music; also became music critic of the *Manchester Guardian,* leaving that position shortly before his death.

Hill, Junius Welch, American organist and music editor; b. Hingham, Mass., Nov. 18, 1840; d. Hollywood, Sept. 7, 1916. After studying in Boston with J. C. D. Parker, he went to Germany, where he took courses in piano and composition with Moscheles, Plaidy, Richter, and Reinecke. Returning to Boston in 1863, he was organist at various churches; taught at Wellesley College (1884–97); then settled in California. He publ. a number of choral works for women's voices, among them *Treasures of Lyric Art, Arabesques, Mozaïques, Characteristic Piano Pieces,* etc.

Hill, Ralph, English writer on music; b. Wattingford, Oct. 8, 1900; d. London, Oct. 20, 1950. He was first active in music publishing (1920–29); was music editor of the *Radio Times* (1933–45); also wrote for the *Daily Mail* (1933–39 and 1945–50); publ. *An Outline of Musical History* (1929); *Brahms: A Study in Musical Biography* (1933); *Liszt* (1936); *Challenges: A Series of Controversial Essays* (1943); *Music Without Fears* (1945).

Hill, Richard S., American music librarian; b. Chicago, Sept. 25, 1901; d. Naples, Florida, Feb. 7, 1961. He was educated at Phillips Exeter Academy; then studied at Cornell Univ. (B.A., 1924) and did post-

graduate work at Oxford Univ., England (1924–26); held research fellowship in psychology with Kurt Koffka at Smith College (1927–29); returned to Cornell Univ. for further study in psychology and musicology, the latter under Otto Kinkeldey. He joined the staff of Music Division, Library of Congress, Washington, D.C. in 1939; served as editor of *Notes,* the quarterly journal of the Music Library Association, from 1943 to the time of his death; concurrently was president of the International Association of Music Libraries (1951–55). In 1946 he was sent by the Library of Congress to Germany and Austria to investigate the conditions of music libraries there and estimate the losses inflicted by the war; published an important account, *The Former Prussian State Library,* listing manuscripts of Mozart, Beethoven, and Haydn which were missing in the aftermath of the war (*Notes,* Sept. 1946). He contributed several important articles to music magazines, one of the most notable being "Schoenberg's Tone Rows and the Tonal System of the Future" (*Musical Quarterly,* Jan. 1936). In collaboration with Kurtz Myers, he edited a new type of discography, publ. under the title *Record Ratings* (N.Y., 1956).

Hill, Ureli Corelli, American violinist and conductor; b. New York, c.1802; d. Paterson, N.J., Sept. 2, 1875. His father, Uriah K. Hill, was a teacher of music in Boston and N.Y., and author of a manual, *Solfeggio Americano, a System of Singing* (N.Y., 1820). An admirer of Corelli, he named his son after him; the first name (Ureli) is a combination of the father's name Uriah and a friend's name, Eli. Ureli Corelli Hill played violin in various theaters in N.Y. as a boy; was violinist in the orch. of Garcia's opera company in 1825; then joined the N.Y. Sacred Musical Society, and conducted it in the first American performance, with orchestral accompaniment, of Handel's *Messiah* (1831). In 1836 he went to Germany, where he studied a year with Spohr. Returning to N.Y. he became a founder and first president of the N.Y. Philharmonic (1842–48); then went West in quest of fortune, which, however, failed to materialize. In N.Y. he exhibited a pianoforte of his own invention, in which he used small bell tuning forks in place of strings, so as to secure perfect intonation; the attempt to promote this instrument met with failure. He played the violin in the N.Y. Philharmonic until 1873, when he retired because of age; continued to play engagements in various theater orchestras throughout his life; then moved to Paterson, N.J., where he engaged (unsuccessfully) in real estate schemes. Depressed on account of constant setbacks in his ventures of promotion in music and in business, he committed suicide by swallowing morphine.

Hill, W. E. & Sons, a firm of violin makers and music dealers in London. It is claimed that 'Mr. Hill, the instrument maker,' mentioned in Pepys' Diary (1660) was an ancestor of the present owners. The founder of the firm was **Joseph Hill** (1715–84); he was an apprentice to Peter Wamsley; established his business in 1750. He had 5 sons, who were good violinists. **William Ebsworth Hill,** a great-grandson of the founder (b. London, Oct. 20, 1817; d. Hanley, April 2, 1895), adopted the present name of the firm; his instruments took first prize at the expositions in London (1851) and Paris (1867). His sons, **William Henry Hill** (b. London, June 3, 1857; d. there, Jan. 20, 1927, **Arthur Frederick Hill** (b. London, Jan. 24, 1860; d. there, Feb. 5, 1939), and **Alfred Ebsworth Hill** (b. London, Feb. 11, 1862; d. there, April 21, 1940), collaborated in the writing of *Antonio Stradivari, His Life and Work* (London, 1902), a standard work. From material also gathered by them, Lady M. L. Huggins previously wrote *Giovanni Paolo Maggini: His Life and Work* (London, 1892). William Henry, Arthur F., and Alfred Ebsworth Hill are the joint authors of *The Violin-Makers of the Guarneri Family* (with introductory note by E. J. Dent; London, 1931). The Ashmolean Museum at Oxford contains a valuable collection of stringed instruments, including a 1716 Stradivari violin with a bow dated 1694, presented by Arthur F. Hill. The firm continues to exist in the second half of the 20th century, under the direction of the descendants of the founder, **Andrew Hill** (b. London, July 3, 1942) and **David Hill** (b. London, Feb. 28, 1952).

Hill, Wilhelm, German pianist and composer; b. Fulda, March 28, 1838; d. Homburg, June 6, 1902. He studied in Frankfurt, and received a prize for his opera *Alona* in the competition for the opening of a new opera house. He was a prolific composer; publ. violin sonatas; piano quartet; piano pieces. His song *Es liegt eine Krone im tiefen Rhein* achieved immense popularity.
BIBLIOGRAPHY: K. Schmidt, *Wilhelm Hill, Leben und Werke* (Leipzig, 1910).

Hille, Eduard, German composer and conductor; b. Wahlhausen, May 16, 1822; d. Göttingen, Dec. 18, 1891. He studied music with Heinroth. In 1855 he founded a 'Singakademie' in Göttingen, and gave many concerts of choral music. He wrote an opera, *Der neue Oberst* (Hanover, 1849), and a number of part-songs.

Hillemacher, two brothers, French composers; **Paul** (b. Paris, Nov. 29, 1852; d. Versailles, Aug. 13, 1933) and **Lucien** (b. Paris, June 10, 1860; d. there, June 2, 1909). They both studied at the Paris Cons.; Paul Hillemacher won the 2nd Prix de Rome in 1875, and the 1st in 1876, with the cantata *Judith;* Lucien Hillemacher obtained 2nd Prix de Rome in 1879, and the 1st in 1880. After graduation, they decided to write music in collaboration, and adopted a common signature.—P. L. Hillemacher.
WORKS: Together they produced the following stage works: *Saint-Mégrin,* opera (Brussels, March 2, 1886); *Une Aventure d'Arlequin,* opéra-comique (Brussels, March 22, 1888); *Le Régiment qui passe* (Royan, Sept. 11, 1894); *Le Drac,* lyric drama (perf. at Karlsruhe in German as *Der Flutgeist,* Nov. 14, 1896); *Orsola,* lyric drama (Paris, May 21, 1902); *Circé,* lyric drama (Paris, April 17, 1907). Paul Hillemacher, who survived his brother by 24 years, wrote a short 'tableau musical' *Fra Angelico,* which was produced at the Paris Opéra-Comique on June 10, 1924. In addition to their operas, the brothers wrote a symph. legend *Loreley,* which won the prize of the City of Paris

(1882); 2 orchestral suites, *La Cinquantaine* and *Les Solitudes;* an oratorio, *La Légende de Sainte Geneviève* (1886); songs. They also brought out a biography of Gounod (Paris, 1905).

Hiller, Ferdinand, distinguished German conductor and composer; b. Frankfurt, Oct. 24, 1811; d. Cologne, May 10, 1885. He was a member of a wealthy Jewish family; received a fine education; studied piano with Aloys Schmitt, and appeared in public at the age of 10. In 1825 he went to Weimar to study with Hummel, whom he accompanied to Vienna in 1827, and visited Beethoven. He lived in Paris from 1828–35 and became a friend of Chopin, Liszt, Berlioz, and many other celebrated musicians. When his father died in 1836, he went back to Frankfurt, where he conducted the concerts of the Cäcilien-Verein. He went then to Italy, where he produced an opera, *Romilda* (Milan, 1839). It was unsuccessful, but an oratorio, *Die Zerstörung Jerusalems,* which he wrote in the following year, aroused the interest of Mendelssohn, who invited Hiller to Leipzig, where it was performed by the Gewandhaus Orch. (April 2, 1840). In 1841 he went to Italy, where he studied church music. His subsequent activities consisted mainly of conducting in Germany; he led the Gewandhaus concerts in Leipzig during the 1843–44 season; then conducted in Dresden, where he staged his operas *Traum in der Christnacht* (1845) and *Konradin* (Oct. 13, 1847); was municipal conductor at Düsseldorf (1847–50), then at Cologne. He established the Cologne Cons., and was its 1st director until his death; also conducted the Lower Rhine Festival, which further enhanced his reputation. His other engagements were at the Italian Opera in Paris (1851–52) and in St. Petersburg, Russia, where he led a group of symph. concerts (1870); he also visited London several times between 1852 and 1872. He never ceased to compose works in large forms, despite their indifferent success; wrote 3 more operas, *Der Advokat* (Cologne, 1854), *Die Katakomben* (Wiesbaden, Feb. 15, 1862), and *Der Deserteur* (Cologne, Feb. 17, 1865); oratorio, *Saul;* cantatas, *Lorelei, Nal und Damajanti, Israels Siegesgesang, Prometheus, Rebecca, Prinz Papagei;* a ballad, *Richard Löwenherz,* for soli, chorus, and orch.; 3 symphonies, 3 overtures, 3 piano concertos, 5 string quartets, 5 piano quartets, 5 piano trios; many choral works; more than 100 songs; piano music. In his musical leanings, he was a conservative, and violently attacked Wagner. His classical training and friendly association with Spohr, and especially Mendelssohn, naturally influenced his style. Gifted in many fields of artistic endeavor, he was also a brilliant critic; his writings were publ. in collected form as *Die Musik und das Publikum* (1864); *Beethoven* (1871); *Aus dem Tonleben unserer Zeit* (2 vols.; 1868; 1871); *Musikalisches und Persönliches* (1876); *Briefe von M. Hauptmann an Spohr und andere Komponisten* (1876); *Felix Mendelssohn-Bartholdy, Briefe und Erinnerungen* (1874); *Briefe an eine Ungenannte* (1877); *Künstlerleben* (1880); *Wie hören wir Musik?* (1881); *Goethes musikalisches Leben* (1883); and *Erinnerungsblätter* (1884).
BIBLIOGRAPHY: W. Neumann, *W. Taubert und Ferdinand Hiller* (Kassel, 1857); H. Hering, *Die Klavier Kompositionen F. Hillers* (Cologne, 1927); R.

Seitz, ed.; *Aus Ferdinand Hillers Briefwechsel*, in 7 vols. (Cologne, 1958, 1961, 1964, 1965, 1967, 1968, 1970—the final vol. with M. Sietz). R. Sietz; "Felix Mendelssohn und Ferdinard Hiller. I: Ihre persönlichen Beziehungen," *Jahr-Buch des Kölnischen Geschichtsvereins* 16 (1967); idem, ". . . II: Ihre künstlerischen Beziehungen," ibid. 43 (1971).

Hiller, Friedrich Adam, German composer; son of Johann Adam Hiller; b. Leipzig, 1768; d. Königsberg, Nov. 23, 1812. He studied music with his father; was a conductor at various provincial theaters in Germany, and wrote a number of light operas: *Biondetta* (Schwerin, 1790); *Das Schmuckkästchen* (Königsberg, 1804); *Die drei Sultaninen* (Königsberg, 1809); etc.; also chamber music.

Hiller (Hüller), Johann Adam, significant German composer; b. Wendisch-Ossig, near Görlitz, Dec. 25, 1728; d. Leipzig, June 16, 1804. After completing his primary education in his native town, he went to Dresden, where he studied music with Homilius. In 1751 he entered the Univ. of Leipzig, where he studied law; at the same time he was forced to earn his living by performing at popular concerts as a singer and flute player. In 1754 he became tutor to a nephew of Count Brühl at Dresden, whom he accompanied in 1758 to Leipzig; there he finally settled, and devoted himself to a revival of the Subscription Concerts in 1763; these developed into the famous 'Gewandhaus' concerts, of which he was appointed conductor. In 1771 he founded a singing school, and from 1789–1801 was Cantor and music director of the Thomasschule as successor of Doles. Hiller was one of the originators of the Singspiel; in order to stress the disparity of characters in his operas, he assigned arias in a grand manner to the gentry, while persons of low degree were given simple songs. WORKS: Singspiels *Lisuart und Dariolette, oder Die Frage und die Antwort* (Leipzig, Nov. 25, 1766), *Lottchen am Hofe* (Leipzig, April 24, 1767), *Die Liebe auf dem Lande* (Leipzig, May 18, 1768), *Die Jagd* (Weimar, Jan. 29, 1770; his best known work), *Der Krieg* (Berlin, Aug. 17, 1772), *Die Jubelhochzeit* (Berlin, April 5, 1773), *Das Grab des Mufti, oder Die zwey Geizigen* (Leipzig, Jan. 17, 1779). Several remained unperformed (*Das Orakel, Poltis, Die Friedensfeyer,* etc.). He further wrote many instrumental works, church music, and lieder, in which he excelled; particularly fine are his *Lieder für Kinder*, to words by C. F. Weisse (1769; new ed., 1865); also *Lieder mit Melodien an meinen Canarienvogel* (1759); *Letztes Opfer, in einigen Lieder-Melodien* (1790); setting of Horace's *Carmen ad Aelium Lamian;* 3 string quartets (1796); a symphony; keyboard compositions. He edited many Classical works, and also brought out numerous collections of contemporary pieces by German and Italian composers. He publ. *Allgemeines Choral-Melodienbuch für Kirchen und Schulen* (1793). He brought out a weekly publication on music *Wöchentliche Nachrichten und Anmerkungen, die Musik betreffend* (1766–70; repr. in 4 vols., Hildesheim, 1970), the first music periodical in Germany to report news regularly. His writings include *Lebensbeschreibungen berühmter Musikgelehrten und Tonkünstler* (1784); *Über*

Metastasio und seine Werke (1786); *Anweisung zum musikalisch-richtigen Gesang* (1774); *Anweisung zum musikalisch-zierlichen Gesang* (1780); *Anweisung zum Violinspiel* (1792). His autobiography, *Lebensläufe deutscher Musiker* was repr. in an edition by A. Einstein (Leipzig, 1914).

BIBLIOGRAPHY: K. Peiser, *Johann Adam Hiller* (Leipzig, 1894); M. Friedländer, *Das deutsche Lied im 18. Jahrhundert* (1902); G. Calmus, *Die ersten deutschen Singspiele von Standfuss und Hiller* (Berlin, 1908); H. von Hase, "Johann Adam Hiller und Breitkopf," *Zeitschrift für Musikwissenschaft* (Oct. 1919); A. Schering, *Das Zeitalter J. S. Bachs und Johann Adam Hillers* (Leipzig, 1940); V. Duckles, "Johann Adam Hiller's *Critical Prospectus for a Music Library,*" in H. C. R. Landon and R. Chapman, eds. *Studies in Eighteenth-Century Music* [Geiringer Festschrift] (London, 1970).

Hiller, Lejaren A., American composer and theorist of computer music; b. New York, Feb. 23, 1924. He studied chemistry at Princeton Univ. (Ph.D., 1947) and music at the Univ. of Illinois (M. Mus., 1958); began his career as a chemist; was assistant prof. of chemistry at the Univ. of Illinois (1953–58), and subsequently taught music there. WORKS: 2 symphonies (1953, 1960), Piano Concerto (1949), 4 string quartets (1949, 1951, 1953, and 1962), 5 piano sonatas, etc.; achieved notoriety with his computer composition *Illiac Suite* for string quartet (in collaboration with Leonard M. Isaacson; 1957), the name being an abbreviation of *Illinois Accumulator;* the result is a programmed, i.e. dictated, production which includes vast stretches of cadential C major chords. Encouraged by publicity, Hiller wrote a *Computer Cantata* for soprano, magnetic tape and chamber ensemble (1963); other works are *Man with the Oboe* (1962), *Machine Music* for piano, percussion and tape (1964); *An Avalanche for Pitchmen, Prima Donna, Player Piano, Percussion and Pre-recorded Playback* (1968). He published (with Isaacson) a manual, *Experimental Music* (N.Y., 1959) and numerous articles on the application of computers to musical composition; also some really valuable writings on chemistry.

Hillis, Margaret, American choral conductor; b. Kokomo, Indiana, Oct. 1, 1921. She studied piano as a child; also played the tuba and double bass in school bands. An energetic person, she became a junior golf champion and, fantastically, was a civilian flying instructor for the U.S. Navy during World War II. She then enrolled as a music student at Indiana Univ. (B.A., 1947) and later took a course in choral conducting with Robert Shaw at the Juilliard School of Music in New York (1947–49); Shaw engaged her as his assistant with the Collegiate Chorale (1952–53). In the interim, she led the Youth Chorale of Brooklyn (1948–51); was for a season choral director of the New York City Opera (1955–56). In 1957 she organized the Chicago Symph. Orchestra Chorus with the task of preparing and rehearsing choruses for Chicago Symphony concerts. From 1952 to 1968 she was also choral conductor of the American Opera Society in New York; was choral director of the Cleveland Orchestra

Chorus (1969–71); concurrently she was resident conductor of the Chicago Civic Orch. (from 1967); in 1971 she took charge of the Elgin, Illinois, Symph. Orch. She received numerous awards of merit, from musical, social and educational organizations, including the Golden Plate Award for American Academic Achievement (1967); was also the recipient of honorary degrees of Mus. D. from Temple Univ. (1967) and Indiana Univ. (1972). On Oct. 31, 1977 she successfully conducted in Carnegie Hall a performance of Mahler's Choral Symph. No. 8 with the Chicago Symph. Orch., substituting on short notice for the temporarily incapacitated Sir George Solti.

Hilsberg (real name **Hillersberg**), **Alexander,** violinist and conductor; b. Warsaw, April 24, 1897; d. Camden, Maine, Aug. 10, 1961. He studied violin with Auer at the St. Petersburg Cons. In 1918 he went on a concert tour in Siberia, eventually reaching Harbin in Manchuria; in 1923 he went to the U.S. via Japan. In 1926 he joined the violin section of the Philadelphia Orch.; became its concertmaster in 1931, and associate conductor in 1945. He was also on the staff of the Curtis Institute of Music in the ensemble department (1927–51). The great success that Hilsberg achieved conducting the Philadelphia Orch. at a Carnegie Hall concert in 1950 led to his engagement as permanent conductor of the New Orleans Symph. Orch. (1952); in the spring of 1956 he took this orchestra on a tour of Latin America.
BIBLIOGRAPHY: Hope Stoddard, *Symphony Conductors of the U.S.A.* (N.Y., 1957; pp. 89–95).

Hilsberg, Ignace, Russian-American pianist; b. Warsaw, July 20, 1894; d. San Diego, California, July 6, 1973. He studied at St. Petersburg Cons. with Isabelle Vengerova, Essipova, and Dubassov, graduating in 1917. After the Revolution he went to China, where he gave a series of concerts, including a command performance for Sun Yat-sen in Peking. In 1922 he taught at the Cons. of Athens, Greece. In 1923 he went to America; in 1936 he settled in Hollywood; played piano for sound films. In 1969 he moved to San Diego. As a pianist, Hilsberg represented the time-honored Russian tradition, combining romantic expressiveness with technical virtuosity.

Hilton, John (the Elder), English organist and composer; d. Cambridge, March, 1608. He was appointed organist at Trinity College, Cambridge on Jan. 26, 1594. He was probably the composer of the anthem *Lord, for Thy tender mercies' sake;* another anthem, *Call to Remembrance* (modern reprint by the Oxford Univ. Press), is also his. To distinguish him from a younger John Hilton, he is referred to as John Hilton, the Elder.

Hilton, John (the Younger), English composer; b. Oxford, 1599; d. London, March (buried March 21), 1657. He may have been the son of **John Hilton, the Elder;** obtained his degree of Mus. B. from Trinity College at Cambridge (1626); in 1628 he was appointed organist at St. Margaret's, Westminster.
WORKS: *Ayres, or Fa-las for 3 voyces* (1627; reprinted by the Musical Antiquarian Society); *Catch*

that catch can, or, a Choice collection of catches, rounds, and canons for 3 or 4 voyces (1625); 2 services; *Elegy;* anthems. The British Museum has further MSS. Other compositions are to be found in F. Keel's collection *Elizabethan Love-Songs* (N.Y., 1913), C. K. Scott's *Euterpe* (vol. 12, London, 1910), and E. H. Meyer's *Spielmusik des Barock* (vol. 1, Kassel, 1934). Six pieces for string trio have been arranged by Peter Warlock (London, 1930).
BIBLIOGRAPHY: W. H. G. Flood, "New Light on Late Tudor Composers: John Hilton," *Musical Times,* 1927.

Himmel, Friedrich Heinrich, German opera composer; b. Treuenbrietzen, Brandenburg, Nov. 20, 1765; d. Berlin, June 8, 1814. He studied theology at the Univ. of Halle; at the same time, he cultivated music. He received a stipend from Friedrich Wilhelm II to study with Naumann in Dresden; subsequently he went to Italy, where he acquired skill in stage music. His cantata *Il primo navigatore* was performed in Venice (March 1, 1794), and his opera *La Morte di Semiramide* in Naples (Jan. 12, 1795). He then returned to Berlin and was appointed court conductor. In 1798 he went to St. Petersburg, where he produced his opera *Alessandro.* In 1800 he returned from Russia by way of Sweden and Denmark; in Berlin he produced his Italian opera *Vasco di Gama* (Jan. 12, 1801). His subsequent operas, staged in Berlin, were in the nature of Singspiele, to German words: *Frohsinn und Schwärmerei* (March 9, 1801), *Fanchon das Leiermädchen* (May 15, 1804; his most successful work; many revivals), *Die Sylphen* (April 14, 1806), etc. His last opera, *Der Kobold,* was produced in Vienna (May 22, 1813). Many of his songs had great vogue (*An Alexis, Es kann ja nicht immer so bleiben,* etc.). He also composed an oratorio, *Isacco figura del Redentore* (Berlin, 1792); several works of sacred music; a piano concerto; piano sextet; piano quartet; pieces for piano solo.
BIBLIOGRAPHY: L. O. Odendahl, *Fr. H. Himmel; Bemerkungen zur Geschichte der Berliner Oper um die Wende des 18. und 19. Jahrhunderts* (Bonn, 1917).

Hinckley, Allen (Carter), American bass; b. Gloucester, Mass., Oct. 11, 1877; d. Yonkers, N.Y., Jan. 28, 1954. He studied for the ministry at Amherst College and the Univ. of Pennsylvania; then took up singing and studied with Oscar Saenger in New York. He then proceeded to Germany where he made a successful debut at the Hamburg State Opera as the King in *Lohengrin* (1903) and remained on the staff until 1908. Returning to America he made his debut at the Metropolitan Opera in the part of Hunding in *Die Walküre* (Nov. 18, 1908), and was on the staff until 1914; then devoted himself to vocal teaching in New York.

Hindemith, Paul, eminent German composer, one of the leading masters of 20th-century music; b. Hanau, near Frankfurt, Nov. 16, 1895; d. Frankfurt, Dec. 28, 1963. He began studying violin music at the age of 9; at 14 he entered the Hoch Cons. in Frankfurt, where he studied violin with A. Rebner, and composition with Arnold Mendelssohn and Sekles. His father was killed in World War I, and Hindemith was compelled to rely on his own resources to make a living. He became concertmaster of the orchestra of the Frankfurt Opera House (1915–23), and later played the viola in the string quartet of his teacher Rebner; from 1922 to 1929 he was the viola player in the Amar String Quartet; also appeared as soloist on the viola and viola d'amore; later also was engaged as conductor, mainly in his own works. As a composer he joined the modern movement and was an active participant in the contemporary music concerts at Donaueschingen, and later in Baden-Baden. In 1927 he was appointed instructor in composition at the Berlin Hochschule für Musik. With the advent of the Hitler regime in 1933, Hindemith began to experience increasing difficulties, both artistically and politically. Although his own ethnic purity was never questioned, he was married to a woman whose father was Jewish, and he stubbornly refused to cease ensemble playing with undeniable Jews. Hitler's propaganda minister Dr. Goebbels accused Hindemith of cultural Bolshevism, and his music fell into an official desuetude. Unwilling to compromise with the barbarous regime, Hindemith accepted engagements abroad. Beginning in 1934 he made 3 visits to Ankara at the invitation of the Turkish government and helped to organize the music curriculum at the Ankara Cons. He made his first American appearance at the Coolidge Festival at the Library of Congress, Washington, D.C., in a performance of his Unaccompanied Viola Sonata (April 10, 1937); after a brief sojourn in Switzerland he emigrated to the U.S.; was instructor at the Berkshire Music Center in Tanglewood in the summer of 1940; from 1940–1953 he was prof. at Yale Univ.; he was elected member of the National Institute of Arts and Letters; and during the academic year 1950–51 he was Charles Eliot Norton Lecturer at Harvard Univ. He became an American citizen in 1946. He conducted concerts in Holland, Italy and England during the summer of 1947; in 1949, revisited Germany for the first time since the war, and conducted the Berlin Philharmonic in a program of his own works (Feb. 14, 1949). In 1953 he went to Switzerland; gave courses at the Univ. of Zürich; also conducted orchestras in Germany and Austria. In 1954 he received the prestigious Sibelius Award of thirty-five thousand dollars, offered annually to distinguished composers and scientists by a Finnish ship owner. In 1959–61, he conducted guest appearances in the U.S.; in 1963 he visited America for the last time; then went to Italy, Vienna, and finally to Frankfurt, where he died.

Hindemith's early music reflects rebellious opposition to all tradition; this is noted in such works as the opera *Mörder, Hoffnung der Frauen* (op. 12, 1921) and *Suite 1922,* for piano (op. 26); at the same time he cultivated the techniques of constructivism, evident in such a work as his theatrical sketch, *Hin und Zurück* (op. 45a, 1927), in which *Krebsgang* (retrograde movement) is applied to the action on the stage, so that events are reversed; in a work of a much later period, *Ludus Tonalis* (1943), the postlude is the upside-down version of the prelude. Along constructive lines is Hindemith's cultivation of so-called *Gebrauchsmusik,* that is, music for use; he was also an ardent champion of *Hausmusik,* to be played or sung by amateurs at home; the score of his *Frau Musica* (as revised in 1944) has an obbligato part for the audience to sing. A neo-Classical trend is shown in a series of works, entitled *Kammermusik,* for various instrumental combinations, polyphonically conceived, and Baroque in style. Although Hindemith made free use of atonal melodies, he was never tempted to adopt an integral 12-tone method, which he opposed on esthetic grounds. Having made a thorough study of old music, he artfully assimilated its polyphony in his works; his masterpiece of this genre was the opera, *Mathis der Maler.* An exceptionally prolific composer, Hindemith wrote music of all types for all instrumental combinations, including a series of sonatas for each orchestral instrument with piano. Hindemith's style may be described as a synthesis of modern, Romantic, Classical, Baroque, and other styles, a combination saved from the stigma of eclecticism only by Hindemith's superlative mastery of technical means. As a theorist and pedagogue, Hindemith developed a self-consistent method of presentation derived from the acoustical nature of harmonies.

WORKS: OPERAS: *Mörder, Hoffnung der Frauen,* one act, op. 12 (Stuttgart, June 4, 1921); *Das Nusch-Nuschi,* marionette opera, op. 20 (Stuttgart, June 4, 1921; revised version, Königsberg, Jan. 22, 1931); *Sancta Susanna,* one act, op. 21 (Frankfurt, March 26, 1922); *Cardillac* (Dresden, Nov. 9, 1926; revised version, Zürich, June 20, 1952); *Hin und Zurück,* op. 45a (Baden-Baden, July 17, 1927); *Neues vom Tage* (Berlin, June 8, 1929; revised version Naples, April 7, 1954, composer conducting); *Wir bauen eine Stadt,* children's opera (Berlin, June 21, 1930); *Mathis der Maler* (Zürich, May 28, 1938); *Die Harmonie der Welt* (Munich, Aug. 11, 1957; composer conducting); *Das lange Weihnachtsmahl* (Mannheim, Dec. 17, 1961); *Tuttifäntchen,* incidental music for a Christmas fairy-tale (1922). BALLETS: *Der Dämon,* a pantomime (1922); *Triadisches Ballet* (1926–27); *Nobilissima Visione* (performed under the title *St. Francis* by the Ballet Russe de Monte Carlo, in London, July 21, 1938); *Der Ploner Musiktag,* a pantomime (1932).

ORCHESTRAL WORKS: Cello Concerto, op. 3; *Lustige Sinfonietta,* op. 4; Piano Concerto, op. 29 (1924); Concerto for Orch. with Oboe, Bassoon, and Violin Soli, op. 38 (Duisburg, July 25, 1925); *Konzertmusik* for viola and orch. (Hamburg, March 28, 1930); *Konzertmusik* for piano, brass and 2 harps (Chicago, Oct. 12, 1930); *Konzertmusik* for brass and strings (for 50th anniversary of the Boston Symph. Orch.; perf. there, April 3, 1931); *Philharmonisches Konzert* (Berlin Philh., April 15, 1932); *Mathis der Maler,* symphony from the opera (Berlin, March 12, 1934); *Der Schwanendreher,* for viola solo and orch. (Amsterdam, Nov. 14, 1935, Hindemith soloist); *Trauermusik,* for solo viola and string orch. (written for a memorial service for King George V; London, Jan. 22, 1936, Hindemith soloist); *Symphonic Dances* (London, Dec. 5, 1937); Violin Concerto (Amsterdam, March 14, 1940); Cello Concerto (Boston, Feb. 7, 1941, Piatigorsky soloist); Symphony in E-flat (Minneapolis, Nov. 21, 1941); *Cupid and Psyche,* overture for a ballet (Philadelphia, Oct. 29, 1943); *Symphonic Metamorphosis on Themes by Weber* (N.Y., Jan. 20, 1944); *The Four Temperaments,* theme with 4 variations for piano and strings (Boston, Sept. 3, 1944); *Hérodiade,* for chamber orch. (1944); *Symphonia Serena* (Dallas, Feb. 1, 1947); Piano Concerto (Cleveland, Feb. 27, 1947), Clarinet Concerto (Philadelphia, Dec. 11, 1950; Benny Goodman, Soloist); Concerto for Trumpet, Bassoon, and String Orch. (1948; 2nd version, 1953); Concerto for 4 winds, harp and orch. (N.Y., May 15, 1949); *Sinfonietta* (Louisville, March 1, 1950, composer conducting); Concerto for Horn and Orch. (Baden-Baden, June 8, 1950); Symphony in B flat for concert band (Washington, April 5, 1951); *Harmonie der Welt*, symphony from the opera (Basel, Jan. 24, 1952); *Pittsburgh Symphony* (Pittsburgh, Jan. 30, 1959, composer conducting); Concerto for Organ and Orch. (N.Y., April 26, 1963, composer conducting).

CHAMBER MUSIC: Trio for Clarinet, Horn, and Piano, op. 1; String Quartet, in C, op. 2; Piano Quintet, op. 7; *3 Stücke*, for cello and piano, op. 8 (1917); 1st String Quartet, in F minor, op. 10 (1919); a set of 6 sonatas, op. 11, of which 2 are for violin and piano (1920), 1 for cello and piano (1922), 1 for viola and piano (1922), 1 for viola unaccompanied (1923), and 1 for violin unaccompanied (1923); 2nd String Quartet, in C, op. 16 (1922); 3rd String Quartet, op. 22 (1922); *Kammermusik No. 1*, op. 24/1 (Donaueschingen Festival, July 31, 1922); *Kleine Kammermusik*, op. 24/2, for flute, oboe, clarinet, horn, and bassoon (1922); a set of 4 sonatas, op. 25: for viola alone (1923), for viola d'amore and piano (1929), for cello alone (1923), for viola and piano (1924); Quintet for Clarinet and String Quartet, op. 30 (Salzburg Festival, Aug. 7, 1923); 2 sonatas for violin alone, op. 31/1 and 31/2 (1924); *Canonic Sonatina* for 2 flutes, op. 31/3 (1924); 4th String Quartet, op. 32 (1924); 1st Trio for Violin, Viola, and Cello, op. 34 (1924); *3 Stücke*, for 5 instruments (1925); *Kammermusik No. 2*, op. 36/1, for piano and 12 instruments (Venice Festival, Sept. 3, 1925); *Kammermusik No. 3*, op. 36/2, for cello and 10 instruments (1925); *Kammermusik No. 4*, op. 36/3 for violin and small ensemble (1925); *Kammermusik No. 5*, op. 36/4, for solo viola and small ensemble (1927); *Konzertmusik* for wind instruments, op. 41 (1926); *Spielmusik*, for strings, flutes, and oboes, op. 43/1 (1927); *Kammermusik No. 6*, op. 46/1, for viola d'amore and chamber ensemble (1928); *Kammermusik No. 7*, op. 46/2, for organ and chamber ensemble (1928); Trio for Viola, Heckelphone, and Piano, op. 47 (1929), *14 Easy Duets for 2 Violins* (1932); 2 Canonic Duets for 2 Violins (1932); 2nd Trio for Violin, Viola, and Cello (1934); *Meditation* for violin (or viola, or cello) and piano (1938); 3 violin sonatas (1935, 1938, 1939); Flute Sonata (1936); Oboe Sonata (1938); Bassoon Sonata (1938); Viola Sonata (1939); Clarinet Sonata (1939); Horn Sonata (1939); Trumpet Sonata (1939); Harp Sonata (1939); English Horn Sonata (1941); Trombone Sonata (1941); *Echo* for flute and piano (1942); 5th String Quartet (1944); 6th String Quartet (1945); *A Frog He Went A-Courting*, variations for cello and piano (1946); Cello Sonata (1948).

VOCAL WORKS: *Melancholie*, for contralto and string quartet, op. 14 (1921); *Des Todes Tod*, op. 23/1, for soprano, 2 violas, and cello (1922); *Die junge Magd*, 6 poems, op. 23/2, for contralto, flute, clarinet, and string quartet (1922); *Die Serenaden*, little cantatas on romantic poems, op. 35, for soprano, oboe, viola, and cello (1925); *Frau Musica*, op. 45/1, for voices

and instruments (1928; revised, 1944, under the title *In Praise of Music*); *8 Canons* for 2 voices and instruments, op. 45/2 (1928); *Martinslied*, op. 45/3, for voice and instruments (1931); *Das Unaufhörliche*, oratorio (Berlin, Nov. 21, 1931); *When Lilacs Last in the Dooryard Bloom'd*, an American requiem after Walt Whitman, for chorus and orch. (N.Y., May 14, 1946); *Apparebit Repentina Dies*, for chorus and brass (Harvard Symposium, Cambridge, Mass., May 2, 1947); *The Demon of the Gibbet*, for chorus a cappella (1949); *Cantique de l'Espérance*, for mezzo-soprano, chorus, and 2 orchestras (1952); *6 Chansons* for mixed voices (1939); *5 Songs on Old Texts* for mixed voices (1943); Mass for mixed choir a cappella (Vienna, Nov. 12, 1963). FOR VOICE AND PIANO: *3 Hymnen*, after Walt Whitman, op. 13; *8 Songs* for soprano, op. 18 (1922); *Das Marienleben*, a cycle of songs after Rilke, op. 27 (Donaueschingen, June 17, 1923; revised radically, and perf., Hanover, Nov. 3, 1948); *9 English songs* (1944); *Bal des pendus* (1946).

FOR PIANO: *7 Waltzes*, op. 5, four hands; *In einer Nacht*, op. 15, a set of 15 piano pieces (1922); Piano Sonata, op. 17 (1917); *Tanzstücke*, op. 19 (1922); *1922 Suite*, op. 26 (1922); *Klaviermusik*, op. 37 (1927); *Übung in drei Stücken*, op. 37/1 (1925); *Reihe kleiner Stücke*, op. 37/2 (1927); 3 sonatas (1936); Sonata for 2 Pianos (1942); *Ludus Tonalis*, for piano solo (Chicago, Feb. 15, 1943). The Auftrag der Hindemith-Stiftung is issuing a Collected Works edition (begun in 1975). Thematic indexes have been compiled by Kurt Stone (for the Associated Music Publishers, N.Y., 1954; verified by the composer); and H. Rösner, *Paul Hindemith—Katalog seiner Werke, Diskographie, Bibliographie, Einführung in das Schaffen* (Frankfurt am Main, 1970).

WRITINGS: *Unterweisung im Tonsatz* (2 vols., 1937, 1939; in English as *The Craft of Musical Composition*, N.Y., 1941; revised, 1945); *A Concentrated Course in Traditional Harmony* (2 vols., N.Y., 1943, 1953); *Elementary Training for Musicians* (N.Y., 1946); *J. S. Bach: Heritage and Obligation* (New Haven, 1952; German ed., *J. S. Bach: ein verpflichtendes Erbe*, Wiesbaden, 1953); *A Composer's World: Horizons and Limitations* (Cambridge, Mass., 1952).

BIBLIOGRAPHY: Franz Willms, "Paul Hindemith," in *Von neuer Musik* (Cologne, 1925); W. Altmann, "Paul Hindemith," ibid.; Hans Kleemann, "Das Kompositionsprinzip Paul Hindemiths," in *Gedenkschrift für Hermann Abert* (Halle, 1928); Heinrich Strobel, *Paul Hindemith* (the basic biography; Mainz, 1928; 2nd enlarged ed., 1931; 3rd amplified ed., 1948); Edwin Evans, "Hindemith," in *Cobbett's Cyclopedic Survey of Chamber Music* (1929); A. Machabey, "Paul Hindemith, musicien allemand," *Revue Musicale* (1930); Willi Reich, "Paul Hindemith," *Musical Quarterly* (Oct. 1931); Paul Rosenfeld, "Neo-Classicism and Hindemith," in *Discoveries of a Music Critic* (N.Y., 1936); H. H. Stuckenschmidt, "Hindemith Today," *Modern Music* (1937); Frani B. Muser, "The Recent Works of Paul Hindemith," *Musical Quarterly* (Jan. 1944); N. Cazden, "Hindemith and Nature," *Music Review* (Nov. 1954); R. Stephan, "Hindemith's Marienleben, an Assessment of its Two Versions," *Music Review* (Nov. 1954); *Paul Hindemith, Zeugnis in Bildern*, brought out by Schott (Mainz, 1955; updated edition, *Paul Hindemith: die letzten Jahre; ein Zeugnis in Bildern*, Mainz, 1965); H. L. Schilling, *Paul Hindemith's Cardillac* (Würzburg, 1962); H. Boatwright, "Paul Hindemith as a Teacher," *Musical Quarterly* (July 1964); H. Tischler, "Remarks on Hindemith's Contrapuntal Technique," in *Essays in Musicology* (Apel Festschrift; Bloomington, Ind., 1968); A. Briner, *Paul Hindemith* (Zürich, 1970); I. Kemp, *Hindemith* (London, 1970); A. Lanza, "Libertà e determinazione formale nel giovane Hindemith," *Rivista Italiana di Musicologia* V/1 (1970); G. Skelton, *Paul Hindemith: The Man Behind the Music* (London, 1975). The Hindemith-Stiftung began publication of the *Hindemith-Jahrbuch* in 1971.

Hindle, John, English composer; b. London, 1761; d. there, 1796. He was mainly known as a composer of glees, one of which, *Queen of the Silver Bow*, became extremely popular.

Hine, William, English composer and organist; b. Brightwell, 1687; d. Gloucester, Aug. 28, 1730. He studied with Jeremiah Clarke; then served as organist at Gloucester Cathedral. A collection of his anthems under the title *Harmonia sacra Glocestriensis* was published posthumously by his widow.

Hines, Earl (Kenneth) "Fatha", black jazz pianist; b. Duquesne, Pennsylvania, Dec. 28, 1905. He played in Louis Armstrong's band, and under his influence evolved a special type of "trumpet piano style" with sharp accents, octave tremolos in the treble and insistent repeated melodic notes. In 1929 he organized his own group in Chicago; its theme song *Deep Forest* became extremely popular; a radio announcer used to introduce him as "Fatha Hines coming through deep forest with his children," and the nickname "Fatha" stuck. After a hiatus of several years Hines reappeared on the jazz horizon as a solo pianist and made a hit, first in N.Y. in 1964, in Berlin in 1965 and in Russia in 1966; was described by jazz critics as "the last of the great masters."
BIBLIOGRAPHY: Stanley Dance, *The World of Earl Hines* (N.Y., 1977).

Hines (real name **Heinz**), **Jerome,** American bass; b. Los Angeles, Nov. 8, 1921. After studying chemistry at the Univ. of California, Los Angeles, he turned to singing; took voice lessons with Gennaro Curci; sang minor operatic roles in Los Angeles and San Francisco. He was employed as a chemist during World War II. On Nov. 21, 1946 he made his debut at the Metropolitan Opera House in N.Y. in a minor part, but created a very fine impression, and was assigned the title role in *Boris Godunov* (Feb. 11, 1954). He scored a great personal triumph when he sang the role in the Russian language in the Bolshoi Theater in Moscow (Oct. 23, 1962).

Hingston, John, English composer and organist; date of birth unknown; d. London, Dec. (buried Dec. 16), 1683. He studied with Orlando Gibbons; was in the service of Oliver Cromwell and taught music to his daughter. After the Restoration, he was engaged as Keeper of the Organs at the Court. Six vols. of his works are preserved in Oxford.

Hinrichs, Gustav, German-American conductor; b. Ludwigslust, Germany, Dec. 10, 1850; d. Mountain Lake, N.J., March 26, 1942. He studied violin and piano with his father; composition with E. Marxsen in Hamburg. In 1870 he settled in America; was in San Francisco until 1885; then went to Philadelphia, where he organized his own opera company; gave the American premières of *Cavalleria Rusticana* (Philadelphia, Sept. 9, 1891) and *Pagliacci* (N.Y., June 15, 1893). From 1903–08, he conducted at the Metropolitan Opera House; then retired. He was the composer of an opera, *Onti-Ora* (Indian name of Catskill Mountains; Philadelphia, July 28, 1890).

Hinrichsen, Max, German music publisher; b. Leipzig, July 6, 1901; d. London, Dec. 17, 1965. He worked with his father, **Heinrich Hinrichsen** (1868-1942), in Peters Edition, Leipzig, until 1937, when he went to London, becoming a British subject in 1947. There he established the Hinrichsen Edition, Ltd.; in 1944 began publishing *Hinrichsen's Musical Year Book*, which appeared irregularly until 1961.

Hinrichsen, Walter, music publisher; brother of **Max Hinrichsen;** b. Leipzig, Sept. 23, 1907; d. New York, July 21, 1969. He studied at the Univ. of Leipzig; then was connected with the Peters Edition there, headed by his father **Heinrich Hinrichsen** (1868-1942; see **Peters, Carl Friedrich**). In 1936 Walter Hinrichsen came to America; was in the U.S. Army (1942–45); after the war became a government employee in the U.S. Zone in Germany (1945–47). He then returned to America and in 1948 opened new offices of the C. F. Peters Corporation in New York. After his death the firm has continued with his widow, Evelyn Hinrichsen, as president.

Hinshaw, William Wade, American baritone; b. Union, Iowa, Nov. 3, 1867; d. Washington, D.C., Nov. 27, 1947. He studied voice with L. G. Gottschalk in Chicago; was choir director at various churches; made his operatic debut as Méphistophélès in Gounod's *Faust* with the H. W. Savage Co. (St. Louis, Nov. 6, 1899); in 1903, opened the Hinshaw School of Opera in Chicago, which was later incorporated into the Chicago Cons.; Hinshaw became president of the combined institutions (1903–07). In 1909 he organized the International Grand Opera Co. of Chicago. He made his debut at the Metropolitan Opera House, N.Y., on Nov. 16, 1910; in 1912 he sang in the Wagner festival at Graz, and in 1914, in the special *Ring* festival at Berlin; then returned to America. In 1916 he offered a prize of one thousand dollars for the best 1-act opera by an American composer (awarded to Hadley for his opera *Bianca*). From 1920–26 he produced Mozart's operas in English with his own company in the U.S., Canada, and Cuba (about 800 performances in all). He then settled in Washington.

Hinton, Arthur, English composer; b. Beckenham, Nov. 20, 1869; d. Rottingdean, Aug. 11, 1941. He studied at the Royal Academy of Music in London; then taught violin there; subsequently went to Munich for further study with Rheinberger. There he composed a symphony, which he conducted at one of the concerts of the Munich Cons.; traveled in Italy; returned to London in 1896. He continued to compose; his Second Symphony was performed in London in 1903. He married the pianist **Katharine Goodson**, who gave many performances of his piano works, including a concerto. He wrote the children's operettas, *The Disagreeable Princess* and *St. Elizabeth's Rose*; also a number of songs.

Hinze-Reinhold, Bruno, German pianist; b. Danzig, Oct. 20, 1877; d. Weimar, Dec. 26, 1964. He studied at the Leipzig Cons.; taught piano at the Stern Cons. in Berlin (1901-13). In 1913 he moved to Weimar; was director of the State Music School (1916-49); then retired, but continued his activity as private piano teacher. He publ. a pedagogical manual *Technische Grundbegriffe eines natürlichen neuzeitlichen Klavierspiels.*

Hipkins, Alfred James, English authority on musical instruments; b. London, June 17, 1826; d. there, June 3, 1903. He was connected with the Broadwood piano manufacturers; acquired an excellent knowledge of the piano and was Chopin's favorite tuner on his last visit to England. He himself learned to play the piano well enough to give recitals. He publ. standard works on instruments, among them, *Musical Instruments, Historic, Rare, and Unique* (Edinburgh, 1888; contains numerous colored plates; reprinted, London, 1921) and *A Description and History of the Pianoforte, and of the Older Keyboard Stringed Instruments* (London, 1896).

Hirao, Kishio, Japanese composer; b. Tokyo, July 8, 1907; d. there, Dec. 15, 1953. He studied in Tokyo; then went to Paris where he took courses at the Schola Cantorum. Returning to Japan he devoted himself to teaching. He wrote several works for orchestra, making use of themes of old Japanese music.

Hirayoshi, Takekuni, Japanese composer; b. Kobe, July 10, 1936. He studied with Yoshio Hasegawa at the Tokyo Univ. of Arts (1955-61), later attended the graduate school there (1963-67). In 1970 he was appointed instructor at the Toho Girls High School.
    WORKS: String Quartet (1960); *Composition for orch.* (Tokyo, Nov. 5, 1962); Ballade for Orch. (1966); *Dialog* for marimba, flute, clarinet and cello (1968); Symphonic Variations (Tokyo, Oct. 23, 1969; winner of 1969 Odaka Prize); Prelude and Fantasia for solo guitar (1970); *Monodrama* for piano (1970); *Impromptu* for flute, violin and piano (1970); *Epitaph* for solo cello (1971); Octet, for 4 Japanese instruments and string quartet (1972); *Epitaph* for 2 flutes (1973); *Song of the Wind* for 2 marimbas (1973); Ballade for Organ and Orch. (1974); *Requiem* for violin and orch. (1975).

Hirsch, Paul Adolf, German bibliographer and collector; b. Frankfurt, Feb. 24, 1881; d. Cambridge, England, Nov. 25, 1951. He began collecting rare musical editions as a young man, and published successive

catalogues of his rapidly growing library. In 1936 he left Germany and was able to transport his entire collection to England; it was purchased by the British Museum in 1946; the total of items was about 20,000. In 1922 he began the publication of new editions (several in facsimile, and with commentaries) of rare works; these are Francesco Caza, *Tractato vulgare de canto figurato* (Milan, 1492; ed. J. Wolf, 1922); Giovanni Luca Conforto, *Breve et facile maniera d'essercitarsi a far passaggi* (Rome, 1593; ed. J. Wolf, 1922); *Neujahrsgrüsse Seelen; eine Sammlung von Liedern mit Melodien und Bilderschmuck aus den Jahren 1770-1800* (ed. M. Friedlaender, 1922); Georg Philipp Telemann, *Fantaisies pour le clavessin: 3 douzaines* (ed. Max Seiffert, 1923); Hercole Bottrigari, *Il desiderio, overo de' concerti di varii strumenti musicali* (Venice, 1594; ed. Kathi Meyer, 1924); Karl Friedrich Zelter, *Fünfzehn ausgewählte Lieder* (ed. Moritz Bauer, 1924); Giovanni Spataro, *Dilucide et probatissime demonstratione* (Bologna, 1521; ed. J. Wolf, 1925); Nicolaus Listenius, *Musica, ab authore denuo recognita* (Nuremberg, 1549; ed. Georg Schünemann, 1927); Carl Philipp Emanuel Bach, *Zwölf zwei- und dreistimmige kleine Stücke für die Flöte oder Violine und das Klavier* (1770; ed. Richard Hohenemser, 1928); Christoph Schultze, *Lukas-Passion* (Leipzig, 1653; ed. Peter Epstein, 1930); Martin Luther, *Deutsche Messe* (1526; ed. J. Wolf, 1934); Wolfgang Amadeus Mozart, *The Ten Celebrated String Quartets*, first authentic edition in score (ed. Alfred Einstein, 1945).
    BIBLIOGRAPHY: P. H. Muir, "The Hirsch Catalogue," *Music Review* (1948); a list of editions is found in the Jan. 1951 issue of *Music Review*.

Hirschfeld, Robert, writer on music; b. Brünn, Moravia, Sept. 17, 1857; d. there, April 2, 1914. He studied at the Universities of Breslau and Vienna; in 1884, took his degree of *Dr. phil.* at the Vienna Univ. with a dissertation on Johannes de Muris; made arrangements of several stage works by Haydn, Mozart, etc., for modern performances.

Hirt, Franz Josef, Swiss pianist; b. Lucerne, Feb. 7, 1899. He studied with Hans Huber and Ernst Lévy at the Cons. of Basel; later took lessons with Egon Petri and Alfred Cortot. In 1919 he became a teacher at the Cons. of Bern; also gave numerous piano recitals in Europe. He published *Meisterwerke des Klavierbaues* (1955; issued in English under the title *Stringed Keyboard Instruments, 1440-1880*; Boston, 1968).

Hirt, Fritz, Swiss violinist; b. Lucerne, Aug. 9, 1888; d. Chigny-sur-Morges, Switzerland, Jan. 5, 1970. He studied in Zürich and had an extended career as a concert violinist in Europe; was also a member of the Basel String Quartet.

Hitchcock, H. (Hugh) Wiley, American musicologist; b. Detroit, Sept. 28, 1923. He attended classes at Dartmouth College (A.B., 1943) and at the Univ. of Michigan (M. Mus., 1948; Ph.D., 1954); taught music at Univ. of Michigan (1948-61), Hunter College (1961-71), and since 1971 has been prof. at Brooklyn College, where he is also Director of the Institute for

Studies in American Music. He has been the recipient of numerous grants, including Fulbright Senior Research Fellowships in 1954–55 (Italy) and 1968–69 (France), and a Guggenheim Fellowship in 1968–69. He has been an officer, board member, or consultant for many learned and music organizations, including Music Library Assoc. (Vice-Pres., 1965–66; President, 1966–67; member of Bd. of Directors, 1970–72); American Musicological Society (member of Bd. of Directors, 1966–67, 1975– ; Editorial Bd., 1969–71; Publications Committee, 1969–75); President of The Charles Ives Society (1973–); Consultant to National Endowment for the Humanities (1969–), American Music Recording Project of the Rockefeller Foundation (1973–75), Martha Baird Rockefeller Fund for Music (1974–76), etc. Also active as an editor: series editor for *The Prentice-Hall Music History Series* (1965–), *Earlier American Music* (reprints of music; Da Capo Press, N.Y., 1972–), and *Recent Researches in American Music* (A-R Editions, Madison, Wisc., 1976–); Executive Committee & Area Editor of *Grove's Dictionary of Music and Musicians,* 6th ed. His research interests are widely divergent and he has done valuable work in 3 specialties: French Baroque (primarily Marc-Antoine Charpentier), Italian Baroque (primarily Giulio Caccini), and American music. Aside from journal and magazine articles, he has edited music of Caccini, Leonardo Leo, and Charpentier, and published several books: *Music in the United States: A Historical Introduction* (Englewood Cliffs, N.J., 1969; 2nd ed., 1974); *Charles Ives Centennial Festival-Conference 1974* (program book; N.Y., 1974); *Ives* (London, 1977); co-editor, with V. Perlis, of *An Ives Celebration: Papers and Panels of the Charles Ives Centennial Festival-Conference* (Urbana, Ill., 1977).

Hjort Albertsen, Per, Norwegian composer; b. Trondheim, July 27, 1919. He studied architecture, then studied organ at the Oslo Cons. and took lessons in composition with Sven Erik Tarp in Copenhagen, Ralph Dawnes in London and Hanns Jelinek in Vienna.

WORKS: a school opera, *Russicola* (1956); Flute Concertino (1948); *Villemann og Magnill,* ballad for soprano, baritone, male chorus and orch. (1951); *Symphonic Prelude* (1951); *Gunnerus Suite* for string orch. (1952); *Little Suite* for string orch. (1955); *Presentation,* overture (1958); *Notturno e Danza* for orch. (1960); *Concerto Piccolo* for violin and amateur string orch. (1961); Concerto for Piano and School Orch. (1969); *Tordenskioldiana* for orch. (1972); *Bendik og Årolilja,* ballad for tenor, chorus and piano (1943); Piano Sonata (1946); Clarinet Sonatina (1950); *4 Religious Folksongs* for violin, cello, and organ (1974); numerous choral works.

Hlobil, Emil, Czech composer; b. Veselí nad Lužnici, Oct. 11, 1901. He studied with Křička at the Prague Cons. (1921–23) and Suk at the Master School there (1924–30); taught at the Cons. (1941–58) and afterward at the Academy of Music and Dramatic Arts in Prague. He followed the national tradition of the modern Czech school, and also cautiously experimented with serial methods of composition.

WORKS: 2 operas: *Anna Karenina,* after Tolstoy (1962; České Budějovice, April 16, 1972) and *Le Bourgeois gentilhomme,* after Molière (1965); *Weekend,* symph. suite (1933); Divertimento for Small Orch. (1935); *The Song of Youth,* symph. poem (1942); *Commemoration of the Martyrs,* symph. fresco (1944–45); 7 symphonies: No. 1 (1949); No. 2, *The Day of Victory* (1951); No. 3 (1957); No. 4 (1959); No. 5 (1969); No. 6, for strings (1972); No. 7 (1973); the symph. suites *Summer in the Giant Mountains* (1950), *Folk Merry-Making* (1950); *Spring in the Gardens of Prague* (1951–53) and *In the Valachian Village* (1952); a cantata, *On the Gift of Coal* (1952); Serenade for Small Orch. (1955); Violin Concerto (1955); Rhapsody for Clarinet and Orch. (1955); Accordion Concerto (1956); *Labor Holiday* for orch. (1960); Concerto for String Orch. (1963); Organ Concerto (1963); *Concerto filharmonico* for orch. (1965); Sonata for Chamber String Orch. (1965); *Invocazioni* for orch. (1967); Double-Bass Concerto (1968); *Contemplation* for viola and string orch. (1968); *The Path of the Living* for orch. (1974); String Quintet (1925); 4 string quartets (1931, 1936, 1955, 1969); Violin Sonatina (1935); Piano Trio (1938); Wind Quintet (1940); Horn Sonata (1942, revised 1948); Quartet for Harpsichord, Violin, Viola and Cello (1943); Nonet (1946); Serenade for String Quartet (1956); Wind Octet (1956); Violin Sonata (1959); Quartet for Flute, Oboe, Clarinet and Bassoon (1964); *Chamber Music* for 2 clarinets, basset horn and bass clarinet (1965); Flute Sonata (1966); Trio for Clarinet, Horn and Double Bass (1967); Trumpet Sonata (1967); Bass-Clarinet Sonata (1970); *Dialogue* for 2 bassoons (1971); Trombone Sonata (1973); Sonata for 2 Cellos (1973); 2-Piano Sonata (1958); 2 piano sonatas (both in 1968); *Aria and Toccata* for organ (1963); songs; choruses.

Hoboken, Anthony van, eminent Dutch music bibliographer; b. Rotterdam, March 23, 1887. He studied with Iwan Knorr at the Hoch Cons. in Frankfurt and with Schenker in Vienna. In 1927 he founded the Archive for Photographs of Musical Manuscripts in the National Library at Vienna; he then began to collect first editions of classical works; his Haydn collection is particularly rich. He published the complete thematic catalogue of Haydn's work in 2 volumes (1957, 1971). He also contributed a number of articles on Haydn to music journals. A Festschrift in his honor was published on his 75th birthday, ed. by J. Schmidt-Görg (Mainz, 1962). His archive of early music publications was purchased by the Austrian government in 1974, and officially opened at the Austrian National Library in Vienna on Hoboken's 90th birthday, March 23, 1977, as a tribute to his signal accomplishments in musical bibliography; although frail, Hoboken was present on this occasion.

Hochberg, Count Bolko von (pseudonym, J. H. Franz), German composer; b. Fürstenstein Castle, Silesia, Jan. 23, 1843; d. near Salzbrunn, Dec. 1, 1926. He established and for several years maintained the Hochberg Quartet; also founded the Silesian music festivals (1876); was general intendant of the Berlin Royal Theaters (1886–1903). His works include the operas *Claudine von Villabella* (Schwerin, 1864) and *Die*

Falkensteiner (Hannover, 1876; rewritten and produced as *Der Wärwolf,* Dresden, 1881); 3 symphonies, 3 string quartets, 2 piano trios; a concerto for piano; songs and choruses.

Hochreiter, Emil, Austrian composer; b. Debreczin, Hungary, Dec. 27, 1871; d. Vienna, Aug. 3, 1938. He studied jurisprudence and music; composed mainly sacred choruses; also some symphonic overtures in a traditional romantic manner. During his sojourn of many years in Novo Mesto he collected Slovenian eucharistic songs, some of which he publ. in anthologies.

Hoddinott, Alun, Welsh composer; b. Bargoed, Aug. 11, 1929. He studied music at the University College of South Wales in Cardiff; also took private instruction with Arthur Benjamin. In 1951 he was appointed lecturer in music at Cardiff College of Music and Drama; in 1959 joined the music faculty of the Univ. College of South Wales. He also serves as organizer of the annual Cardiff Music Festival. His music follows the judicious line of humanitarian modernism, without blundering into musical chaos.

WORKS: 2 OPERAS: *The Beach of Falesá* (Cardiff, March 26, 1974); *Murder, the Magician* (Welsh Television, Feb. 11, 1976). FOR ORCH.: Symph. No. 1 (National Eisteddfod of Wales; Pwllheli, Aug. 5, 1955, composer conducting); Symph. No. 2 (Cheltenham Festival, July 11, 1962); Symph. No. 3 (Manchester, Dec. 5, 1968); Symph. No. 4 (Manchester, Dec. 4, 1969); Symph. No. 5 (London, March 6, 1973); Concerto No. 1 for piano, wind and percussion (London, Feb. 22, 1960); Concerto No. 2 for piano and orch. (National Eisteddfod of Wales, Cardiff, Aug. 5, 1969, composer conducting); Concertino for viola and chamber orch. (Llandaff Festival, June 25, 1958); Harp Concerto (Cheltenham Festival, July 16, 1958); Concerto for clarinet and string orch. (Cheltenham Festival, July 16, 1954); Concerto for organ and orch. (Llandaff Festival, June 19, 1967); Horn Concerto (Llandaff Festival, June 3, 1969); Concertino for viola and small orch. (Llandaff Festival, June 25, 1958); Violin Concerto (Birmingham, March 30, 1961); Concertino for trumpet, horn and orch. (Llangefni, April 8, 1971); Concerto Grosso No. 1 (Caerphilly Festival, June 11, 1965); Concerto Grosso No. 2 (1966); *Variants* for orch. (London, Nov. 2, 1966); *Fioriture* (London, Nov. 24, 1968); Divertimento for orch. (Llandaff, Nov. 14, 1969); *4 Welsh Dances* (London, June 28, 1958); *Investiture Dances* (commissioned to celebrate the investiture of the Prince of Wales; London, June 22, 1969); *Night Music* (Aberystwyth, Jan. 30, 1967); *Sinfonia* for string orch. (Bromsgrove Festival, April 19, 1964); *Sinfonietta No. 1* (Cardiff Festival, 1968); *Sinfonietta No. 2* (Cheltenham Festival, July 4, 1969); *Sinfonietta No. 3* (Swansea, March 10, 1970); *Sinfonietta No. 4* (Wales, July 30, 1971); *The Sun, the Great Luminary of the Universe* (Swansea, Oct. 8, 1970); CHAMBER MUSIC: 4 violin sonatas (1969, 1970, 1971, 1976); Cello Sonata (1970); Clarinet Sonata (1967); Sonata for Harp (1964); Horn Sonata (1971); Divertimenti for 8 instruments (1968); Divertimento for oboe, clarinet, horn and bassoon (1963); Piano Quintet (1972); Septet for wind, strings and piano (1956); Sextet for flute, clarinet, bassoon, violin, viola and cello

(1960); String Quartet (1966); Variations for flute, clarinet, harp, and string quartet (1962); 6 piano sonatas (1959–72); *Ritornelli* for trombone, winds and percussion (1974); *A Contemplation Upon Flowers* for soprano and orch. (1976); organ music; choruses; songs.

Hodeir, André, French music critic and jazz enthusiast; b. Paris, Jan. 22, 1921. He studied at the Paris Cons. with Messiaen and others; in 1954 founded The Jazz Group of Paris. He edited the periodical *Jazz Hot* (1947–50); published *Hommes et problèmes du jazz* (Paris, 1954; in English as *Jazz, Its Evolution and Essence* (N.Y., 1956); *Les Formes de la Musique* (Paris, 1951; in English, N.Y., 1966); *La Musique depuis Debussy* (Paris, 1961; in English, N.Y., 1961); *Toward Jazz* (N.Y. 1962); *The Worlds of Jazz* (N.Y., 1972).

Hodges, Edward, English organist and composer; b. Bristol, July 20, 1796; d. Clifton, England, Sept. 1, 1867. He was an organist at Bristol; received his Mus. Doc. at Cambridge (1825); in 1838, went to America, where he became an organist in Toronto and then in New York (1839). He returned to England in 1863. He published *An Essay on the Cultivation of Church Music* (N.Y., 1841). The Library of Congress acquired the bulk of his music library (743 vols.) including his own works in MS, in 1919. His daughter, **Faustina Hasse Hodges** (d. Philadelphia, Feb. 4, 1895), was also an organist in the U.S. She composed songs and instrumental pieces and publ. a biography of her father (N.Y., 1896). His son, **Rev. John Sebastian Bach Hodges** (1830–1915), an accomplished organist, composed many anthems and services.

BIBLIOGRAPHY: A. H. Messiter, *History of the Choir and Music of Trinity Church* (N.Y., 1906).

Hodges, Johnny (John Cornelius), American jazz alto saxophonist; b. Cambridge, Mass., July 25, 1906; d. New York, May 11, 1970. He took saxophone lessons from Sidney Bechet; joined the Duke Ellington Band in 1928, remaining with it for the rest of his career, except for a period of 5 years when he had his own band (1950–55). He became famous for his lyrical melodious mode which remained the principal characteristic of his playing.

Hodkinson, Sydney P., Canadian composer; b. Winnipeg, Jan. 17, 1934. He played the clarinet in bands; studied composition at the Eastman School of Music in Rochester, N.Y., with Louis Mennini and Bernard Rogers (1953–58); then had sessions with Sessions, Carter and Babbitt at Princeton Univ. (1960); in 1967 enrolled at the Univ. of Michigan as a student of Leslie Bassett and Ross Lee Finney (Mus. D. 1968). He was on the faculty of the Univ. of Virginia (1958–63), of Ohio Univ. (1963–68) and of the Univ. of Michigan (1968–73); in 1973 appointed to the staff of the Eastman School of Music. He held a Guggenheim Fellowship in 1978–79; received numerous awards for specific compositions. In his music he explores with pragmatic coherence all resources of modern techniques.

WORKS: *Lyric Impressions* for orch. (1956); *Threnody* for orch. (1957); *Diversions on a Chorale* for orch.

(1958); *Two Studies* for string quartet (1958); *Structure* for percussion ensemble (1958); *Stanzas* for piano trio (1959); *Litigo* for winds and percussion (1959); *Dynamics,* 5 miniatures for orch. (1960); *Lament for Guitar and Two Lovers,* a theatrical action for actors, dancers and musicians (1962); *Dialogue,* concertino for piano and wind band (1963); *Five Absurdities from Lewis Carroll* for 5 trombones (1964); *Mosaic* for brass quintet (1964); *Taiwa,* a myth for actors, dancers and musicians (Athens, Ohio, April 28, 1965); *Caricatures* for orch. (1966; Dallas, April 5, 1969); *Armistice,* a truce for dancers and musicians (1966); *Interplay,* a histrionic controversy for 4 musicians; (on flute and piccolo, clarinet and saxophone, percussion, and double bass, Montreal, July 17, 1967); *Scissors,* electronic film score (1967); *Dissolution of the Serial* for piano and one instrument (1967; Ann Arbor, Michigan, Dec. 10, 1967); *Funks,* improvisations for 7 jazz musicians (1967); *Imagin'd Quarter* "an incentive" for 4 percussionists (1967); *Shifting Trek* for 11 instruments (1967); *Fresco,* a mural for orch. (1968); *Organasm,* a scenario for organ soloist and assistants (1968); *Flux* for chamber orch. (1968); *Arc,* aria with interludes, for soprano, flute, piccolo, piano and 2 percussionists (1969); *Valence* for chamber orch. (1970); *Stabile* for youth orch. (1970); *One Man's Meat* for live and recorded double bass solo (1970); *Another Man's Poison* for brass quintet (1970); *Epigrams* for orch. (1971); *Trinity* for solo treble instrument (1972); *Incentus* for orch. (1972); *Blocks* for symph. band (1972); *Contemporary Primer* for symph. band (1972); *Vox Populous,* chamber oratorio (1972); *The Edge of the Olde One* for electrified English horn, strings and percussion (N.Y., May 13, 1977); 8 pieces for various ensembles under the generic title *Megaliths;* 8 ensembles under the title *Drawings.*

Höeberg, Georg, Danish composer, conductor, and violinist; b. Copenhagen, Dec. 27, 1872; d. Vedboek, Aug. 3, 1950. He studied at the Cons. of Copenhagen, and later in Berlin; taught at the Copenhagen Cons. from 1900 till 1914; from 1914 till 1930, was conductor at the Royal Opera; from 1915 until 1949 he appeared as guest conductor in Scandinavia and Germany. He wrote the opera *Bryllup i Katakomberne (The Wedding in the Catacombs;* Copenhagen, March 6, 1909); the ballet *The Paris Cathedral* (Copenhagen, Oct. 25, 1912); several pieces for violin and orch.; a symphony; choral works and songs.

Hoérée, Arthur, Belgian music critic and composer; b. Saint Gilles, near Brussels, April 16, 1897. He studied organ and music theory at the Brussels Cons. In 1919 he went to Paris where he studied composition with Paul Vidal and orchestration with Vincent d'Indy. He then devoted himself mainly to music criticism, without abandoning composition. He gave several courses in composition at the École Normale Supérieure de Musique in Paris and at the French Radio Center. In 1972 he was appointed instructor in musicology at the Sorbonne. His compositions include several ballets and scores of incidental music for theatrical plays; *Pastorale et danse* for string quartet (1923); *Septet* (1923); *Pour le premier jour du printemps* for piano (1949); *Crève-Coeur, le Magicien* for

soli, chorus and orch. (1961). He published a monograph *Albert Roussel* (Paris, 1938).

Hoesick, Ferdinand, Polish musicologist; b. Warsaw, Oct. 16, 1867; d. there, April 13, 1941. He received an excellent European education; studied at the Universities of Heidelberg, Cracow, and Paris, returning to Warsaw in 1891; was editor and writer on literature; his writings on music deal exclusively with Chopin; publ. (in Polish) the basic biography, *Chopin's Life and Works* (3 vols.; Warsaw, 1910–11; 2nd ed., in 2 vols., 1926); a brief preliminary biography, *Chopin* (Warsaw, 1898); *Selection from J. Elsner's Memoirs* (Warsaw, 1901); *Chopiniana* (letters, etc.; Warsaw, 1912); *Slowacki and Chopin, Historic-Literary Parallels and Sketches* (Warsaw, 1928).

Hoesslin, Franz von, German conductor; b. Munich, Dec. 31, 1885; d. (in a plane crash in southern France) Sept. 28, 1946. He studied general subjects at the Univ. of Munich; conducting with Felix Mottl, composition with Max Reger. He held the post of conductor at the Municipal Theater of St. Gall, Switzerland (1908–11); then conducted in Riga (1912–14); was in the German army during World War I; then in Lübeck (1919–20), Mannheim (1920–22), and at the Berlin Volksoper (1922–23); general music director in Dessau (1923–26); opera conductor in Barmen-Elberfeld (1926–27); later was engaged as conductor for the Bayreuth festival; conducted opera in France and Spain. He was also a composer; wrote some orchestral works, a clarinet quintet, and choruses.

Høffding, Finn, Danish composer; b. Copenhagen, March 10, 1899. He studied violin with K. Sandby (1911–21), organ with R. S. Rung-Keller (1919–21), composition and harmony with Knud Jeppesen (1918–21), and music history with Thomas Laub (1920–23); then went to Vienna where he took lessons with Joseph Marx (1921–22). He subsequently was for 38 years on the faculty of the Royal Academy of Music in Copenhagen (1931–69). His style of composition is influenced by the linear counterpoint as practiced by Carl Nielsen.
  WORKS: 3 operas: *Kejserens nye Klaeder (The Emperor's New Clothes),* after Hans Christian Andersen (1926; Copenhagen, Dec. 29, 1928); *Kilderejsen (The Healing Spring),* after Holberg (1931; Copenhagen, Jan. 13, 1942); a school opera, *Pasteur* (1935; Copenhagen, March 9, 1938); 4 symphonies: No. 1, *Sinfonia impetuosa* (1923; Copenhagen, Aug. 22, 1925); No. 2, *Il Canto de Liberato,* to a phonic text devised by the composer, for coloratura soprano, chorus and orch. (1924); No. 3, for 2 pianos and orch. (1928); No. 4, *Sinfonia Concertante,* for chamber orch. (1934); 4 symphonic fantasies: No. 1, *Evolution* (1939; Copenhagen, Sept. 4, 1940); No. 2, *Det er ganske vist (It Is Perfectly True),* after Hans Christian Andersen (1940; Copenhagen, March 6, 1944; as a pantomime, Tivoli Gardens, July 1, 1948); No. 3, *Vdr-Höst (Spring-Autumn)* for baritone and orch. (1944; Copenhagen Radio, Jan. 24, 1946); No. 4, *The Arsenal at Springfield,* after Longfellow's poem, for 3 soloists, chorus and orch. (1953; Copenhagen Radio, Sept. 22, 1955); *Overture* for small orch. (1930); Concerto for Oboe and

String Orch. (1933); *Fanfare,* concert piece for orch. (1939); *Fire Minespil,* suite for small orch. (1944); *Majfest,* fantasy on a Danish folk dance, for orch. (1945); *Fantasia Concertante* for orch. (Copenhagen Radio, April 1, 1965); *Karlsvognen* for soloists, chorus and orch. (1924); *Fem Svaner (The Five Swans)* for soloists, chorus and orch. (1937; Copenhagen, Sept. 9, 1938); *Christofer Columbus,* chaconne for male chorus, baritone solo, and orch. (1937; Copenhagen, March 5, 1941); *Giordano Bruno* for baritone solo, male chorus, winds and percussion (Univ. of Copenhagen, Dec. 8, 1968); several works for school performance, including *Da solen blev forkølet (When the Sun Caught a Cold)* for children's chorus and school orch. (1977); *Kammermusik* for soprano, oboe and piano (1927); *Das Eisenbahngleichnis* for chorus, piano and 3 saxophones (1934); *Fire Satser* for chorus and instruments (1965); *Vintersolhverv* for chorus and instruments (1965); *Årets kredsgang,* cycle for chorus and instruments (1965); *Davids 18 og 23,* 2 psalms for voice and organ (1966); several a cappella choruses, including *Agent* (1969); *2 Songs* (1977) and *4 Songs* (1977). CHAMBER MUSIC: 2 string quartets (1920, 1925); *Dialogues* for oboe and clarinet (1927); 2 wind quintets (1940; *Familien Vind,* 1954); Oboe Sonata (1943). For piano: Sonatina (1951); Canon (1959); several sets of pieces. He published the teaching manuals *Harmonilaere* (Copenhagen, 1933; enlarged edition, 1970; harmonic analysis); *Den Elementaere Horelaere (Elementary Ear-Training,* Copenhagen, 1935; 2nd edition, 1964); *Indforelse i Palestrinastil (Introduction to the Style of Palestrina,* Copenhagen, 1969; a textbook on counterpoint); *Textbook on Harmony* (Copenhagen, 1976).

Höffer, Paul, German composer; b. Barmen, Dec. 21, 1895; d. Berlin, Aug. 31, 1949. He studied piano with Walter Georgii in Cologne; then took courses in composition with Franz Schreker in Berlin. In 1923 he became piano teacher at the Hochschule für Musik in Berlin. In his compositions he adopted a fairly radical idiom, making free use of the modern techniques of polytonality and atonality. However, most of his works preserve the formal unity of the Romantic school; the influence of his teacher Schreker is discernible. WORKS: the operas *Borgia* (1931), and *Der Falsche Waldmar* (1934); the oratorios *Der reiche Tag* (1938), *Von edlen Leben* (1941), and *Mysterium der Liebe* (1942); *Sinfonie der grossen Stadt* (1937); Piano Concerto (1939); Oboe Concerto (1946); 3 string quartets; Clarinet Quintet; Wind Sextet. BIBLIOGRAPHY: Karl Laux, *Musik und Musiker der Gegenwart* (pp. 127–35; Essen, 1949).

Hoffman, Richard, pianist and composer; b. Manchester, England, May 24, 1831; d. New York, Aug. 17, 1909. He received his first instruction from his father and then studied with Leopold de Meyer, Pleyel, Moscheles, Rubinstein, Döhler, and Liszt. He spent most of his life in the U.S. and was a major figure in American musical life, but chose to retain his British citizenship. (Perhaps this was due to his having the same birthdate as Queen Victoria; on their joint birthday he would place a British flag on the mantel and play *God Save the Queen* on the piano.) He came to New York in 1847; traveled with Jenny Lind on her American tour (1850–52) as joint artist; appeared often with Louis Moreau Gottschalk for 2-piano recitals. He was a prolific composer, mainly of salon music for piano; wrote about 100 opus numbers; also songs, anthems, etc. He published *Some Musical Recollections of Fifty Years* (with biographical sketch by his wife; posthumous, 1910).

Hoffmann, Ernst Theodor Amadeus (his third Christian name was Wilhelm, but he replaced it by Amadeus from love of Mozart), famous German writer, who was also a composer; b. Königsberg, Jan. 24, 1776; d. Berlin, June 25, 1822. He was a student of law, and served as assessor at Poznan; also studied music with the organist Podbielski. He acquired considerable proficiency in music; served as music director at the theater in Bamberg; then conducted opera performances in Leipzig and Dresden (1813–14). In 1814 he settled in Berlin, where he remained. He used the pen name of **Kapellmeister Johannes Kreisler** (subsequently made famous in Schumann's *Kreisleriana*); his series of articles in the *Allgemeine Musikalische Zeitung* under that name were reprinted as *Phantasiestücke in Callot's Manier* (1814). As a writer of fantastic tales, he made a profound impression on his period, and influenced the entire Romantic school of literature; indirectly, he was also a formative factor in the evolution of the German school of composition. His own compositions are passable from the technical viewpoint, but strangely enough, for a man of his imaginative power, they lack the inventiveness that characterizes his literary productions. If his music is occasionally performed, it is only as a curiosity. WORKS: operas: *Die Maske* (1799), *Scherz, List und Rache* (Poznan, 1808), *Der Renegat* (Plozk, 1803), *Faustine* (Plozk, 1804), *Die ungeladenen Gäste, oder der Canonicus von Mailand* (Warsaw, 1805), *Lustige Musikanten* (Warsaw, 1805), *Liebe aus Eifersucht* (Warsaw, 1807), *Der Trank der Unsterblichkeit* (Bamberg, 1808), *Das Gespenst* (Warsaw, 1809), *Aurora* (performance planned in Bamberg, 1811, when Hoffmann conducted the theater there, but production failed to materialize; the opera was revised by L. Böttcher, and produced in a new version in Bamberg, Nov. 5, 1933), *Undine* (Berlin, Aug. 3, 1816; his best work; vocal score edited by Hans Pfitzner, 1907), *Julius Sabinus* (unfinished); also a ballet, *Harlekin;* some sacred works; a symphony; a piano trio; 4 piano sonatas. Two vols. of Hoffmann's collected musical works were publ. in 1922–23, edited by Gustav Becking. His writings on music were publ. separately by Hans von Ende (Cologne, 1896). BIBLIOGRAPHY: There is a large literature on Hoffmann as a writer; books and articles on Hoffmann as a musician include E. Istel, "E. T. A. Hoffmann als Musikschriftsteller," *Neue Zeitschrift für Musik* (1903); Hans von Müller, *Das Kreislerbuch* (Leipzig, 1903); Hans von Wolzogen, *E. T. A. Hoffmann und R. Wagner* (Berlin, 1906); E. Kroll, *E. T. A. Hoffmanns musikalische Anschauungen* (Königsberg, 1909); Hans Ehinger, *E. T. A. Hoffmann als Musiker und Musik-Schriftsteller* (Cologne, 1954); H. Dechant, *E. T. A.*

Hoffmanns Oper Aurora (1975); R. Murray Schafer, *E. T. A. Hoffmann and Music* (Toronto, 1975).

Hoffmann, Hans, German music scholar; b. Neustadt, Silesia, Jan. 26, 1902; d. Bielefeld, Aug. 8, 1949. He studied musicology at the Univ. of Breslau, and later in Leipzig, Berlin and Kiel. Concurrently he took instruction in singing and for several years sang in numerous oratorio performances in German. In 1933 he became choral conductor in Hamburg, and also taught music theory at Hamburg Univ. He was also active as symphony and opera conductor, and in 1940 was appointed music director of the Bielefeld Opera. Among his publications the most important are *H. Schütz und J. S. Bach* (Kassel, 1940) and *Vom Wesen der zeitgenössischen Kirchenmusik* (Kassel, 1949).

Hoffmann, Heinrich August (called **Hoffmann von Fallersleben**), German writer; b. Fallersleben, Hannover, April 2, 1798; d. at Castle Korvei, Jan. 29, 1874. He received his education at the Univ. of Göttingen; in 1835 he was appointed prof. at Breslau Univ. For some years (1842–48) he was not allowed to teach or reside in Prussia, on account of his dissenting political views; after 1848 he was librarian to Prince Lippe at Korvei. He wrote several important books dealing with music, *Geschichte des deutschen Kirchenlieds* (1832; 2nd ed., 1854); *Schlesische Volkslieder mit Melodien* (1842); etc., but his chief claim to fame is the text of *Deutschland, Deutschland, über alles,* which he wrote to Haydn's *Emperor's Hymn.*

Hoffmann, Richard, Austrian-American composer; b. Vienna, April 20, 1925. He studied violin and harmony in Vienna as a child; was in New Zealand from 1935 until 1947; graduated from the Auckland Univ. College in 1945. He settled in the U.S. in 1947; studied composition with Arnold Schoenberg, and subsequently became his amanuensis and secretary. In 1954 he joined the faculty of the Oberlin Cons. of Music. He developed a sui generis serial technique, in which intervals, meters, rhythms, timbres and dynamics are systematically organized, while the tone row is not necessarily dodecaphonic.
WORKS: String Quartet (1947); Trio for Piano, Violin and Bass Clarinet (1948); Piano Quartet (1950); *Fantasy and Fugue, in Memoriam Arnold Schoenberg,* for orch., in which the subject is a single reiterated note in five different dynamics (1951); Piano Concerto (1954); Cello Concerto (1956–59); String trio (1961–63); *Memento mori* for double male chorus, tape and orch. (1966–69); choruses; songs.

Hoffmeister, Franz Anton, German composer and publisher; b. Rottenburg, May 12, 1754; d. Vienna, Feb. 9, 1812. He went to Vienna as a law student, but became greatly interested in music, and in 1783, established his publishing firm, of historic significance owing to its publications of Mozart and Beethoven. In 1800 he went to Leipzig, where he organized (with Kühnel) a "Bureau de Musique," which eventually became incorporated into the celebrated firm of C. F. Peters. In 1805 he returned to Vienna, where he devoted himself mostly to composition. Amazingly prolific, he composed 9 operas, 66 symphonies and over-

tures, 42 string quartets, 5 piano quartets, 11 piano trios, 18 string trios, 12 piano sonatas; in addition to these he wrote a very great number of compositions for flute with various instruments. Hoffmeister's craftsmanship was of sufficient excellence to lead to confusion of his music with Haydn's. Regarding this, see E. F. Schmid, "F. A. Hoffmeister und die *Göttweiger Sonaten,*" *Zeitschrift für Musik* (1937).

Hofhaimer (Hofheimer), Paul, celebrated organist and composer; b. Radstadt, Jan. 25, 1459; d. Salzburg, 1537. Cuspinianus and Luscinius both wrote of him as an unrivalled organist and lutenist. He was greatly appreciated at the various courts where he served. He was court organist to the Archduke Sigismund of Tyrol from 1480, residing at Innsbruck, and from 1490, at the court of the Emperor Maximilian I there. He was ennobled by the Emperor in 1515, when he played in St. Stephen's Cathedral in Vienna; he was also made Knight of the Golden Spur by King Ladislas of Hungary. Little of his organ music survives; some is preserved in the Berlin State Library. Extant works comprise *Harmoniae poeticae* (odes of Horace set for 4 voices; 35 by Hofhaimer and 9 by Senfl, Nuremberg, 1539; repub. by Achtleitner, 1868); 4-part German songs in contemporary collections (5 in Oeglin's *Liederbuch,* 1512; others in Forster's *Liederbuch,* 1539); etc.
BIBLIOGRAPHY: H. J. Moser, *Paul Hofhaimer* (Stuttgart, 1929), containing transcriptions of Hofhaimer's surviving works.

Hofman, Shlomo, Polish-Israeli composer and musicologist; b. Warsaw, April 24, 1909. He studied at the Warsaw Cons., graduating in 1934; then went to Paris where he studied composition with Roger-Ducasse, Charles Koechlin and Darius Milhaud (1937–38). He subsequently settled in Palestine; in 1954 became lecturer in musicology at the Israel Academy of Music in Tel-Aviv. Among his works are Oboe Concerto (1950); Hebrew cantata *Tawashih* (1960); Quintet for Clarinet and Strings (1945); several song titles. He publ. a valuable thesis, *L'Œuvre de Clavecin de François Couperin Le Grand* (Paris, 1961); a polyglot *Dictionary of Musical Terms* (Jerusalem, 1955); *The Music of Israel* (1959); *La Musique Arabe en Israel* (1963), etc.

Hofmann, Casimir, Polish pianist; father of **Josef Hofmann**; b. Cracow, 1842; d. Berlin, July 6, 1911. He studied at the Vienna Cons.; then conducted opera in Cracow. In 1878 he moved to Warsaw, where he taught and conducted. After the spectacular success of his young son, he followed him on his extended tours throughout Europe and America. From 1886, he lived mainly in Berlin. He wrote numerous works in various genres.

Hofmann, Heinrich (Karl Johann), German pianist and composer; b. Berlin, Jan. 13, 1842; d. Gross-Tabarz, Thuringia, July 16, 1902. He studied in Berlin with Grell, Dehn, and Wüerst. He became a concert pianist, then turned to composition. Exceptionally productive, he wrote a great deal of operatic, symphonic, and chamber music, choral works and solo piano pieces, all of which were published and frequently performed. His popularity declined precipitously towards the end of his life; his music vanished from concert programs after his death. His style reflected Wagnerian procedures, particularly in heroic moods; he possessed complete mastery of technique, but his music lacked originality or distinction.

WORKS: stage works: comic opera *Cartouche* (Berlin, 1869); heroic drama *Armin* (Dresden, Oct. 14, 1877); pastoral opera *Aennchen von Tharau* (Hamburg, Nov. 6, 1878); historic opera *Wilhelm von Oranien* (1882), and the comic opera *Donna Diana* (Berlin, Nov. 15, 1886). His *Frithjof Symphony* (1874) was enormously popular, having had 43 performances during the 1874–75 season in German cities alone; it was also performed in England and America. Similarly successful was his orchestral *Hungarian Suite* (1873). He also wrote a great number of choral works and songs; characteristic piano pieces; chamber music.

Hofmann, Josef, celebrated pianist; b. Podgorze, near Cracow, Jan. 20, 1876; d. Los Angeles, Feb. 16, 1957. He was the son of the pianist **Casimir Hofmann;** his mother was a professional opera singer. At the age of 4 he began to play the piano, tutored by an older sister and an aunt; at 5, his father began giving him regular lessons. He was barely 6 when he first appeared in public in Ciechocinek; at the age of 10 he played Beethoven's Concerto No. 1 with the Berlin Philharmonic, under Hans von Bülow. He also made a tour of Scandinavia; played in France and England; his concerts as a child prodigy became a European sensation; soon an American offer of a concert tour came from the impresarios Abbey, Schoeffel & Grau. On Nov. 29, 1887, Hofmann appeared at the Metropolitan Opera House, as a soloist in Beethoven's Concerto No. 1, with an orchestra conducted by Adolf Neuendorff, and played works by Chopin and some of his own little pieces. He electrified the audience, and hardheaded critics hailed his performance as a marvel. He appeared throughout the United States, giving 42 concerts in all; then agitation was started by the Society for the Prevention of Cruelty to Children against the exploitation of his talent. Alfred Corning Clark of N.Y. offered fifty thousand dollars to the family for his continued education. The offer was accepted, and young Hofmann began serious study with Moszkowski (piano) and Urban (composition) in Berlin. Then Anton Rubinstein accepted him as a pupil in Dresden, where Hofmann traveled twice a week for piano lessons. At the age of 18 he resumed his career, giving recitals in Dresden and elsewhere in Germany with enormous success; made his first tour of Russia in 1896, attaining huge popularity there; he reappeared in Russia frequently. In 1898 he again played in the U.S.; from then on, he appeared in American cities almost every year. At the peak of his career, he came to be regarded as one of the greatest pianists of the century. He possessed the secret of the singing tone, which enabled him to interpret Chopin with extraordinary delicacy and intimacy. He was also capable of summoning tremendous power playing Liszt and other works of the virtuoso school. His technique knew no difficulties; but in his interpretations, he subordinated technical effects to the larger design of the work. When the Curtis Institute of Music was founded in Philadelphia (1924), Hofmann was engaged to head the piano department; from 1926–38 he was director of the Curtis Institute. On Nov. 28, 1937, his golden jubilee in the U.S. was celebrated with a concert at the Metropolitan Opera House, where he had first played as a child 50 years before. He performed the D minor Concerto of Anton Rubinstein, and his own *Chromaticon*, for piano and orch. From 1938 to his death he lived mostly in California. He became an American citizen in 1926. Hofmann was also a composer, under the pen name **Michel Dvorsky** (literal translation into Polish of his German name, meaning 'courtyard man'). Among his works are several piano concertos; some symph. works; *Chromaticon*, for piano and orch. (first played by him with the Cincinnati Symph. Orch., Nov. 24, 1916); numerous piano pieces. He publ. a practical manual, *Piano-Playing with Piano-Questions Answered* (1915).

Hofmann, Leopold, Austrian composer; b. Vienna, Aug. 14, 1738; d. there, March 17, 1793. He studied piano and violin; held posts as choirmaster in Vienna churches; also served as court organist. He wrote much church music; a number of instrumental concertos and chamber works, highly competent technically but lacking in invention and polyphonic strength. The article by Hermine Prohaszka in *Die Musik in Geschichte und Gegenwart* gives a detailed list of his published and unpublished works.

Hofmann, Richard, German violinist; b. Delitzsch, April 30, 1844; d. Leipzig, Nov. 13, 1918. He studied with Dreyschock and Jadassohn in Leipzig; later settled there as music teacher. He publ. instructive pieces for various instruments, and a valuable manual *Praktische Instrumentationsschule* (Leipzig, 1893; 3rd ed., 1907; in English, 1898); *Katechismus der Musikinstrumente* (many editions); *Neuer Führer durch die Violin- und Viola-Litteratur* (1909); "Die F-Trompete im 2. Brandenburgischen Konzert von J. S. Bach," *Bach-Jahrbuch* (1916).

Hofmeister, Friedrich, German music publisher; b. Strehlen, Jan. 24, 1782; d. Reudnitz, near Leipzig, Sept. 30, 1864. In 1807 he established in Leipzig the music firm that bears his name; beginning in 1829, he publ. a valuable monthly catalogue, the *Musikalisch-litterarischer Monatsbericht.* His son and successor, **Adolf Hofmeister** (b. c.1802; d. Leipzig, May 26, 1870), publ. a 3rd and enlarged ed. of Whistling's *Handbuch der musikalischen Litteratur* (1845), with supplementary vols. filled from issues of Hofmeister's *Monatsbericht.* After 1852, the 12 *Monatsberichte* for each complete year were arranged in alphabetical order and issued as a *Jahresbericht.* All these valuable editions were continued by the firm under the proprietorship of Albert Röthing (b. Leipzig, Jan. 4, 1845; d. there, Aug. 11, 1907). In 1905 Karl Günther became the head of the firm; he was succeeded by Karl Ganzenmüller. In 1935 the firm acquired the catalogue of Merseburger (Leipzig); after World War II the firm had offices both in Frankfurt and Leipzig.

Hofstetter, Romanus, German cleric and composer; b. Laudenbach (Württemberg), April 24, 1742; d. Miltenberg, May 21, 1815. He published 12 string quartets under his own name and, more importantly, is the true author of six string quartets commonly attributed to Haydn as his op. 3.
BIBLIOGRAPHY: Alan Tyson and H. C. Robbins Landon, "Who Composed Haydn's Op. 3?" *Musical Times* (July 1964).

Hogarth, George, Scottish writer on music; b. Carfrae Mill, near Oxton, Berwickshire, 1783; d. London, Feb. 12, 1870. He was a practicing lawyer in Edinburgh, and an amateur musician. He settled in London in 1830; contributed articles to the *Harmonicon;* also wrote reviews for the *Morning Chronicle.* His daughter married Charles Dickens in 1836; when Dickens became editor of the *Daily News* (1846), Hogarth began writing music criticisms for it; also wrote for other papers. From 1850–64 he was secretary to the Philharmonic Society of London.
WRITINGS: *Musical History, Biography, and Criticism* (1835); *Memoirs of the Musical Drama* (1838; 2nd ed., 1851, as *Memoirs of the Opera*); *The Birmingham Festival* (1855); *The Philharmonic Society of London* (1862), and *The Life of Beethoven.*

Hoiby, Lee, American composer; b. Madison, Wisconsin, Feb. 17, 1926. After a preliminary music study in his home town he took piano lessons with Egon Petri at Mills College, where he received his M.A. in 1952; intermittently he studied with Menotti at the Curtis Institute in Philadelphia, and then attended various courses in Rome and Salzburg. In 1957 he received an award of one thousand dollars from the National Institute of Arts and Letters. He is at his best in composing operas on contemporary subjects in the manner reminiscent of Menotti, concise, dramatic and aurally pleasing and sometimes stimulating.
WORKS: operas *The Witch* (1956); *The Scarf* after Chekhov (Spoleto, June 20, 1958); *Beatrice* after Maeterlinck (Louisville, Oct. 23, 1959); *Natalia Petrovna* after Turgenev (N.Y., Oct. 8, 1964); *Summer and Smoke* after a play by Tennessee Williams (St. Paul, Minn., June 19, 1971); also incidental music to the play *The Duchess of Malfi* (N.Y., March 19, 1957). Other works are *Noctambulation* for orch. (N.Y., Oct. 4, 1952); *Hearts, Meadows & Flags* for orch. (Rochester, Nov. 6, 1952); *Pastoral Dances* for flute and orch. (New Orleans, Nov. 6, 1956); Violin Sonata; 5 Preludes for Piano; *Design for Strings; Diversions* for woodwind quintet; *Songs of the Fool* for mixed chorus; etc.

Hol, Richard, Dutch composer, conductor, pianist, and organist; b. Amsterdam, July 23, 1825; d. Utrecht, May 14, 1904. He studied organ with Martens and theory with Bertelmann. After traveling in Germany, he taught music in Amsterdam; in 1862, became city music director at Utrecht, succeeding Kufferath; then cathedral organist (1869) and director of the School of Music (1875); conducted concerts in The Hague and Amsterdam.
WORKS: A prolific composer, he wrote the operas *Floris V* (Amsterdam, April 9, 1892), *Uit de branding* (Amsterdam, 1894), and *De schoone schaapster;* the oratorio *David* (1880), 4 symphonies, choral and orchestral works, chamber music, and songs. From 1886–1900 he was editor of *Het Orgel,* wrote a monograph on Sweelinck (1860).
BIBLIOGRAPHY: H. Nolthenius, *Richard Hol, Levensschets* (Haarlem, 1904).

Holbrooke, Josef, English composer; b. Croydon, July 5, 1878; d. London, Aug. 5, 1958. He received his primary education from his father; then studied at the Royal Academy of Music in London with F. Corder. After graduation he conducted ballet and various summer orchestras. Although he composed prolifically, and had many ardent admirers of his music, he never succeeded in establishing himself as a representative British composer. Perhaps this was owing to the fact that he stood aloof from modernistic developments of European music, and preferred to write for a hypothetical mass audience, which, however, failed to materialize at the infrequent performances of his music.
WORKS: OPERAS: *Pierrot and Pierrette* (London, Nov. 11, 1909); a trilogy (his main dramatic work): *The Cauldron of Anwyn:* I. *The Children of Don* (London, June 15, 1912), II. *Dylan, Son of the Wave* (London, July 4, 1913), III. *Bronwen, Daughter of Llyr* (Huddersfield, Feb. 1, 1929); *The Enchanter* (Chicago, 1915); *The Snob,* 1-act comic opera. BALLETS: *The Red Masque, The Moth, The Enchanted Garden.* ORCHESTRAL WORKS: symph. poems, *The Raven* (London, 1900); *The Viking; Ulalume* (1904); *Byron,* with chorus; *Queen Mab,* with chorus (Leeds Festival, 1904); *Homage to E. A. Poe,* with chorus; *The Bells,* with chorus (Birmingham, 1906); *The Skeleton in Armor; The Masque of the Red Death;* 5 symphonies; variations on *Three Blind Mice, The Girl I Left Behind Me,* and *Auld Lang Syne; Dreamland Suite; Les Hommages,* suite; *The Haunted Palace,* fantasy; *The New Renaissance,* overture. CHAMBER MUSIC: 5 string quartets; 4 string sextets; 3 violin sonatas; 2 piano quartets; 2 clarinet quintets; Piano Quintet; Trio for Violin, Horn, and Piano. He wrote many piano pieces, songs, and clarinet pieces; also, a book, *Contemporary British Composers* (1925).
BIBLIOGRAPHY: George Lowe, *Josef Holbrooke and His Work* (1920); also a symposium, *Josef Holbrooke: Various Appreciations by Many Authors* (London, 1937).

Holde, Artur, German music critic; b. Rendsburg, Oct. 16, 1885; d. New York, June 23, 1962. He studied musicology at the Univ. of Berlin; from 1910 to 1936 he was music director of the Frankfurt Synagogue; also was active as music critic. In 1937 he emigrated to the U.S.; was choirmaster at the Hebrew Tabernacle in New York (1937–43) and music critic of the German periodical *Aufbau* in New York. He published the books *Jews in Music* (N.Y., 1959); *A Treasury of Great Operas* (N.Y., 1965); contributed articles to the *Musical Quarterly* and other American publications.

Holden, Oliver, American musician, carpenter, and minister; b. Shirley, Mass., Sept. 18, 1765; d. Charlestown, Mass., Sept. 4, 1844. After serving as a marine in the navy, he settled in Charlestown in 1787 and was active there as a justice of the peace and carpenter; then abandoned carpentry and established a music store (about 1790); also offered music lessons; officiated as preacher of the Puritan Church; served as Charlestown Representative in the State House of Representatives (1818–33). He composed psalm tunes and odes; at least 21 hymns are known to be of his authorship, his best being *Coronation* (set to the words *All Hail the Power of Jesus' Name*), first published in vol. I of his *Union Harmony* (1793); it has retained its popularity until modern times. His *From Vernon's mount behold the hero rise*, one of the many works written in commemoration of George Washington's death, was sung at the Old South Meeting House, Boston, in Jan. 1800. Other publications are *The American Harmony* (1792), *The Massachusetts Compiler* (1795; with H. Gram and S. Holyoke), *The Worcester Collection* (1797; ed. and revised by Holden), *Sacred Dirges, Hymns and Anthems* (1800), *Modern Collection of Sacred Music* (1800), *Plain Psalmody* (1800), *Charlestown Collection of Sacred Songs* (1803), *Vocal Companion* (1807), and *Occasional Pieces*.

BIBLIOGRAPHY: F. J. Metcalf, *American Psalmody* (1917); F. J. Metcalf, *American Writers and Compilers of Sacred Music* (1925); *Dictionary of American Biography* IX (1932); D. W. McCormick, *Oliver Holden, Composer and Anthologist* (Union Theological Seminary, 1963); R. Patterson, *Three American "Primitives": A Study of the Musical Styles of Samuel Holyoke, Oliver Holden, and Hans Gram* (Washington Univ., 1963); G. Chase, *America's Music* (2nd ed., N.Y., 1966).

Holewa, Hans, Austrian-born Swedish composer; b. Vienna, May 26, 1905. He studied music in Vienna; in 1938 went to Stockholm, where he established himself as a pianist and pedagogue. He was the first composer living in Sweden to adopt Schoenberg's method of composing with 12 tones related only to one another. From 1949 to 1970 he served on the staff of the Swedish Broadcasting Corporation.

WORKS: opera, *Apollos förvandling* (1967–71); 2 string quartets (1939, 1965); Piano Sonata (1940); 12 *Pieces* for piano (1945); 13 *Pieces* for string quartet (1948); Symphony (1948); *Music* for 2 pianos (1949); Sonata for Cello Solo (1952); *Och vilar inom oss*, cantata (1953); String Trio (1959); Solo Violin Sonata (1960); *Concertino I* for clarinet, horn, viola, piano, harp and percussion (1960); *Miniatures* for string quartet (1961); Quintet, for clarinet, cello, trombone, percussion and piano (1962); Violin Concerto (Swedish Radio, Feb. 7, 1965); *Concertino II* for octet and percussion (1964); *Kammermusik I* and *II* for cello and piano (1964, 1973); *Composition* for orch. (Swedish Radio, Oct. 8, 1966); *Chamber Concerto* for viola and 11 strings (1966); *4 Cadenze* for cello and orch. (Swedish Radio, April 12, 1970); *Movimento espressivo* for orch. (1971); Piano Concerto (1972); Concerto for 2 pianos and string orch. (1975).

Holguín, Guillermo. See **Uribe-Holguín, Guillermo.**

Holiday, Billie (called **Lady Day**), black American jazz singer; b. Baltimore, April 7, 1915; d. New York, July 17, 1959. She began singing professionally in Harlem night clubs at age 15; was discovered by impresario John Hammond and bandleader Benny Goodman in 1933 and appeared with his band; also with Count Basie, Artie Shaw and others; toured Europe (1954, 1958). Her otherwise brilliant career was marred by personal tragedies and, above all, addiction to narcotics and alcohol. Despite the oft-quoted phrase "Lady Day sings the blues," Billie Holiday rarely sang classic blues; with her unique vocal endowments she managed to make everything she performed—mostly popular tunes of the day—sound "bluesy." She publ. (with some professional journalistic help) an autobiography, *Lady Sings the Blues* (N.Y., 1956).

Hollaender, Alexis, German pianist; b. Ratibor, Silesia, Feb. 25, 1840; d. Berlin, Feb. 5, 1924. He studied at the Berlin Royal Academy with Grell and others; became instructor at Kullak's Academy (1861); conducted choral groups (1864) and the 'Cäcilienverein' (1870). He composed piano works, choruses, songs, etc.; publ. an instructive edition of Schumann's piano music and *Methodische Übungen fürs Halten einer tieferen Stimme*.

Hollaender, Gustav, German violinist; b. Leobschütz, Silesia, Feb. 15, 1855; d. Berlin, Dec. 4, 1915. He was taught the violin by his father, appeared in public at an early age; then studied at the Leipzig Cons. with Ferdinand David, and in Berlin with Joachim. At the age of 20 he embarked on a concert career; gave concerts of chamber music with Scharwenka and Grünfeld in Berlin (1878–81); in 1881 he was appointed teacher at the Cologne Cons.; in 1894 became director of the Stern Cons. in Berlin, which post he filled until his death. He wrote numerous pieces for violin, in an effective virtuoso style.

Hollaender, Viktor (pen name, **Arricha del Tolveno**), German composer; brother of **Gustav Hollaender;** b. Leobschütz, April 20, 1866; d. Hollywood, Oct. 24, 1940. He studied with Kullak; was theater conductor in Berlin for a number of years; also theater conductor in London. He lived mostly in Berlin until 1933, when he went to America and settled in Los Angeles. His works include the light operas *San Lin, Trilby, The Bey of Morocco, Schwan von Siam, Die dumme Liebe, Der rote Kosak, Der Regimentspapa*, etc.; songs and piano pieces.

Holland, Theodore, English composer; b. London, April 25, 1878; d. there, Oct. 29, 1947. He studied with Frederick Corder at the Royal Academy of Music and with Joachim at the Hochschule für Musik in Berlin. In 1927 he became prof. of composition at the Royal Academy of Music. Although his career was mainly that of a teacher, he was an estimable composer, particularly proficient in writing for the theater. Among his works is a children's operetta, *King Goldemar;* a musical play, *Santa Claus; Evening on a Lake*, for chamber orch. (1924); *Cortège* for an ensemble of cellos (1939); *Spring Sinfonietta* (1943); 2 string quartets; 2 piano trios; Suite for Viola and Piano; and several song cycles.

Hollander, Lorin, American pianist; b. New York, July 19, 1944. He received his early musical training from his father, the violinist **Max Hollander,** and studied violin before tackling the piano. He earned the reputation of an aggressive pianist to whom technical difficulties, whether in Bach or Prokofiev, did not exist. His principal piano teacher was Steuermann at the Juilliard School of Music in New York.

Holle, Hugo, German writer on music; b. Mehlis, Thuringia, Jan. 25, 1890; d. Stuttgart, Dec. 12, 1942. He was a pupil of Max Reger; 1919–21, director of the Heilbronn Cons.; 1921–25, editor of the *Neue Musikzeitung* in Stuttgart; from 1925 teacher of music theory at the Hochschule für Musik, Stuttgart; conductor of the famous "Holle's Madrigal Choir," with which he toured Central Europe; member of the Board of the Max Reger Society; co-editor of the Musikalische Volksbücher.

WRITINGS: *Goethes Lyrik in Weisen deutscher Tonsetzer bis zur Gegenwart* (1914); *Die Chorwerke Max Regers* (Munich, 1922); and numerous articles in music periodicals. He revised Storck's *Mozartbiographie* in 1923, and has edited old choral music for the Schott publ. firm (*Die hohen Feste, Motetten alter Meister,* etc.).

Höller, Karl, German composer; b. Bamberg, July 25, 1907. He received a good musical training as a chorister at the Cathedral of Bamberg; pursued his formal studies at the Cons. of Würzburg; later took courses at the Academy of Music in Munich, where he studied composition with Joseph Haas. He subsequently was engaged as an instructor there (1933–37); then taught at the Hochschule für Musik in Frankfurt; in 1949 he succeeded Haas as composition teacher at the Hochschule für Musik in Munich.

WORKS: Symphony (1953); Chamber Concerto for Violin and Orch. (1931); *Hymnen* for orch. (1933); *Symphonic Fantasy on a Theme of Frescobaldi* for orch. (1934); Chamber Concerto for Harpsichord and Small Orch. (1934); 2 violin concertos (1938, 1948); 2 cello concertos (1941, 1949); *Sveelnick Variations* for orch. (1951); 6 string quartets; Clarinet Quintet; Piano Quartet; Piano Trio; 8 violin sonatas; Cello Sonata; 2 flute sonatas; Viola Sonata ("in memoriam Hindemith," 1967); a multitude of piano pieces and some vocal works.

Holliger, Heinz, Swiss oboe player and composer; b. Langenthal, May 21, 1939. He studied composition with Veress at the Cons. of Bern, and then with Boulez in Paris, where he also took lessons in oboe playing and piano. In 1959 he obtained the first international prize for oboe playing, and won first prize again in Munich in 1961. He embarked on a career as a concert oboist with his wife, the harpist **Ursula Hänggi,** touring in Europe and in the U.S. Several modern composers wrote special works for him, among them Penderecki, Henze, Stockhausen, Krenek, Berio and Jolivet. He composes mostly chamber music works, several of them scored, understandably, for oboe and harp.

WORKS: Sonata for Unaccompanied Oboe (1956); 3 *Liebeslieder* for voice and orch. (1960); *Erde und Himmel* for tenor and 5 instruments (1961); *Studie* for soprano, oboe, cello and harpsichord (1962); *Improvisationen* for oboe, harp and 12 instruments (1963); Trio for Oboe, Viola and Harp (1968); *Der magische Tänzer,* chamber opera for 2 men and 2 marionettes (Basel, April 26, 1970); *Pneuma* for winds, percussion, and organ (Donaueschingen, Oct. 18, 1970); *Cardiophonic* for a wind instrument and 3 magnetophones (1971); String Quartet (1973); *Atenbogen* for orch. (1975).

Hollingsworth, John, English conductor; b. Enfield, Middlesex, March 20, 1916; d. London, Dec. 29, 1963. He studied music at the Guildhall School in London; during World War II conducted a band of the Royal Air Force; after the end of the war, he was active primarily as conductor in the film studios in London.

Hollingsworth, Stanley, American composer; b. Berkeley, Calif., Aug. 27, 1924. He studied at the State College in San José, Cal.; then with Darius Milhaud at Mills College and with Gian Carlo Menotti at the Curtis Institute of Music in Philadelphia. He was then in Rome, at the American Academy (1955–56). As a composer, he follows the principles of practical modernism; in this respect he emulates Menotti.

WORKS: *Dumbarton Oaks Mass* for chorus and string orch.; Sonata for Oboe and Piano; opera *The Mother,* after Andersen (Curtis Institute, Philadelphia, March 29, 1954); Quintet for Harp and Woodwind Instruments; a television opera *La Grande Bretèche,* after Balzac (NBC production, Feb. 10, 1957); and *Stabat Mater* for chorus and orch. (San José, May 1, 1957). In some works, he used the pseudonym **Stanley Hollier.**

Hollins, Alfred, blind English pianist; b. Hull, Sept. 11, 1865; d. Edinburgh, May 17, 1942. He studied piano at several schools for the blind; then studied with Hans von Bülow in Berlin. In 1886 he made a tour of the U.S. playing in an ensemble with other blind musicians; in 1888, appeared in America once more, as soloist with several orchestras. Returning to England, he became a church organist in Edinburgh (1897–1904). Then followed tours in Australia (1904), South Africa (1907, 1909, and 1916), and the U.S. (1925). He also composed some music. He publ. an autobiography, *A Blind Musician Looks Back* (London, 1936).

Hollmann, Joseph, Dutch cellist; b. Maastricht, Oct. 16, 1852; d. Paris, Jan. 1, 1927. He studied with Servais at the Brussels Cons., winning first prize (1870); then at the Paris Cons. with Jacquard; played many concerts in Europe and America; lived mostly in Paris. Saint-Saëns wrote his 2nd cello concerto for Hollmann.

Holloway, Robin, English composer; b. London, Oct. 19, 1943. He was a boy chorister at St. Paul's Cathedral; then studied composition with Alexander Goehr. In 1974 he was appointed music lecturer at Cambridge University. His music is deeply rooted in Englishry; he resists the procrustean deformation of fashionable dodecaphony, preferring the relatively liberal discipline of neo-medieval counterpoint, clinging resolutely to basic tonality and modality. Yet he audaciously piles tonal Pelion on modal Ossa in his effort to achieve mountainous polyharmony; he also makes use of occasional "objets trouvés" from the music of Brahms, Debussy and Schoenberg treating such objects as legitimate flotsam and jetsam. His dramatizations, intensifications and amplifications of Schumann's lieder are notable.

WORKS: *Garden Music* for 6 players (1962); Concerto for Organ and Wind Instruments (1966); Concerto for Orch. (1966–72); *Souvenirs de Schumann* for orch. (1970); *Evening with Angels* for 16 players (1972); *The Death of God*, melodramatic cantata (1973); *Clarissa*, opera after the novel of Richardson (1971–77).

Holm, Mogens Winkel, Danish composer; b. Copenhagen, Oct. 1, 1936. He studied composition and oboe at the Cons. of Copenhagen (1955–61); then became music critic on the foremost Danish daily newspaper *Politiken.*

WORKS: chamber opera *Aslak* (1962; Copenhagen, Jan. 27, 1963); textless chamber opera, *Sonata for Four Opera Singers,* with jazz instruments and electronics (Copenhagen, April 19, 1968); 5 ballets: *Tropismer II* (Copenhagen, May 24, 1964), *Kontradans* (Danish Radio, July 16, 1965); *Chronicle* (Swedish Radio, May 5, 1969), *Galgarien* (Malmö, Sweden, Nov. 27, 1970) and *Rapport* (Danish Radio, March 19, 1972); *Chamber Concertante* for bassoon, string quartet and string orch. (1959); *Concerto Piccolo* for orch. (1961); *A Ghost Story,* for soloists, chorus and orch. (1964); *Cumulus* for orch. (Danish Radio, Aug. 17, 1965); *Alios,* symph. for 4 instrumental groups (Danish Radio, March 24, 1972; symph. version of the ballet *Rapport*); Trio for oboe, clarinet and bassoon (1956); Wind Quintet (1957); *Little Chamber Concerto* for 5 wind instruments, violin and cello (1958); String Quartet (1959); *ABRACADABRA* for flute, trumpet, cello and 4 timpani (1960); *Tropismer I* for oboe, bassoon, horn and piano (1961); *Annonce* for soprano and chamber group (1965; to a text from a marriage advertisement in *Politiken*); *Ricercare* for oboe and 4 continuo groups (1967); *Sonata* for wind quintet (1968); *Overtoninger I* for soprano, cymbalom and cello (1971); *Overtoninger II* for flute, piano and cello (1972); choruses.

Holmboe, Vagn, eminent Danish composer; b. Horsens, Jutland, Dec. 20, 1909. He studied composition with Knud Jeppesen and Høffding at the Royal Cons. in Copenhagen (1927–29); then took intermittent courses in Berlin with Ernst Toch and others (1930–33); traveled in Transylvania (1933–34), where he gained first-hand knowledge of Balkan folk music. Upon return to Copenhagen, he taught at the Royal Danish Institute for the Blind (1940–49), wrote music criticism for the newspaper *Politiken* (1947–55) and taught at the Copenhagen Cons. (1950–65). A recipient of a government lifetime grant, and remarkably productive, he wrote 21 symphonies (of which he withdrew 3 early ones), 13 chamber concertos for different solo instruments, and 14 extant string quartets

(after he withdrew 10 previous ones). His music evolved from the legacy of Sibelius and Carl Nielsen; he then developed a method of composition with "germ themes," that grow metamorphically; his symphonic works give an impression of grandeur, with long, dynamic crescendos in expanded tonality.

WORKS: 3-act opera, *Lave og Jon* (*Lave and Jon,* 1946–48); one-act chamber opera, *Kniven* (*The Knife,* 1959–60); symphonic fairy play, *Fanden og borgemestern* (*The Devil and the Mayor,* 1940); radio play, *Fløjten* (1946); ballet, *Den galsindede tyrk* (1942–44). FOR ORCH.: 10 numbered symphonies: No. 1 for chamber orch. (1935); No. 2 (1938–39); No. 3, *Sinfonia rustica* (1941); No. 4, *Sinfonia sacra,* with chorus (1941, revised 1945); No. 5 (1944); No. 6 (1947); No. 7 (1950); No. 8, *Sinfonia boreale* (1951–52); No. 9 (1967–68); and No. 10 (1970–71); a *Sinfonia in memoriam* (1954–55); 4 sinfonias for string orch., known collectively as *Kairos* (1957, 1957, 1958–59, 1962); 3 chamber symphonies: No. 1, *Collegium musicum concerto No. 1* (1951); No. 2 (1968); and No. 3, *Frise* (1969–70); 3 works representing symphonic metamorphoses: *Epitaph* (1956), *Monolith* (1960) and *Epilogue* (1961–62); *Tempo variable* (1971–72); Concerto for Orch. (1929); Concerto for Chamber Orch. (1931); Concerto for String Orch. (1933); *Rapsodi* for flute and chamber orch. (1935); Violin Concerto (1938); Cello Concerto (1974); Concerto for recorder, celeste, vibraphone and strings (1974); Flute Concerto (1976); Tuba Concerto (1976); 13 chamber concertos: No. 1 for piano, strings and percussion (1939); No. 2 for flute, violin, celeste, percussion and string orch. (1940); No. 3 for clarinet, 2 trumpets, 2 horns and strings (1940); No. 4, *Triple Concerto,* for violin, cello, piano and chamber orch. (1942); No. 5 for viola and chamber orch. (1943); No. 6 for violin and chamber orch. (1943); No. 7 for oboe and chamber orch. (1944–45); No. 8, *Sinfonia Concertante,* for chamber orch. (1945); No. 9 for violin, viola and chamber orch. (1945–46); No. 10, *trae-messing-tarm,* for chamber orch. (1945–46); No. 11 for trumpet, 2 horns and string orch. (1948); No. 12 for trombone and chamber orch. (1950); and No. 13, *Collegium musicum concerto No. 2,* for oboe, viola and chamber orch. (1955–56); concertino No. 1 for violin, viola and string orch. (1940) and No. 2 for violin and string orch. (1940); *Symphonic Overture* for percussion, piano and strings (1941). CHAMBER MUSIC: 14 string quartets: No. 1 (1948–49), No. 2 (1949), No. 3 (1949–50), No. 4 (1953–54, revised 1956), No. 5 (1955), No. 6 (1961); No. 7 (1964–65), No. 8 (1965), No. 9 (1965–66, revised 1969), No. 10 (1969), No. 11, *Quartetto rustico* (1972), No. 12 (1973), No. 13 (1975) and No. 14 (1975); *Musik for fugle og frøer* for 2 flutes and 16 bassoons (1971); Sextet for flute, clarinet, bassoon, violin, viola and cello (1972–73); Wind Quintet (1933); Quintet for flute, oboe, clarinet, violin and viola (1936); *Notturno* for wind quintet (1940); *Aspekter* for wind quintet (1957); *Tropos* for string quintet (1960); Brass Quintet (1961–62); *Musik til Morten* for oboe and string quartet (1970); Serenade for flute, piano, violin and cello (1940); *Primavera* for flute, piano, violin and cello (1951); *Quartetto medico* for flute, oboe, clarinet and piano (1956); Quartet for flute, violin, viola and cello (1966); *Fanden løs i Voldmosen* for clarinet, 2 violins

and double bass (1971); *Ondata* for percussion (1972); *Firefir,* quartet for 4 flutes (1977); *Rhapsody Intermezzo* for violin, clarinet and piano (1938); *Isomeric* for 2 violins and piano (1950); piano trio (1954); Trio for flute, piano and cello (1968); *Nuigen,* a piano trio (1976); an unnumbered violin sonata (1929); 3 numbered violin sonatas (1935, 1939, 1965); *Sonatina capricciosa* for flute and piano (1942); sonata for violin and viola (1963); Oboe Sonatina (1966); *Triade* for trumpet and organ (1975). FOR SOLO INSTRUMENTS: Violin Sonata (1953); Flute Sonata (1957); Double Bass Sonata (1962); Cello Sonata (1968–69). For piano: *Choral Fantasy* (1929), 2 sonatas (1929, 1930), *Allegro affettuoso* (1931), 4 suites (1930–33); *Julen 1931* (1931), *6 Sketches* (1934), *Rumaensk Suite* (1937–38), *6 Pieces* (1939), *Sonatina briosa* (1941), *Suono da bardo* (1949–50), *Moto austero* (1965) and *I venti* (1972). For organ: *Fabula I* (1972); *Fabula II* (1973); *Contrasti* (1972). FOR VOICE: *Requiem for Nietzsche* for tenor, baritone, mixed chorus and orch. (1963–64); *Skoven (The Forest)* for mixed chorus, children's chorus, and instruments (1960); *3 Inuit sange (3 Eskimo Songs)* for baritone, male chorus and percussion (1956); *Beatus parvo* for chorus and chamber orch. (1973); *Edward* for baritone and orch. (1971); *The wee-wee man* for tenor and orch. (1971); *Zeit* for alto and string quartet (1966–67); a cappella choruses, including *Solhymne* (1960) and the Latin motets, *Liber Canticorum I* (1951–52), *II* (1952–53), *III* (1953), *IV* (1953) and *V, Beatus vir* (1967); numerous cantatas for ceremonial events; songs. He wrote a book on contemporary music, *Mellemspil (Interlude,* Copenhagen, 1966).
BIBLIOGRAPHY: "Tre symfonier" in *Modern nordisk musik* (Stockholm, 1957; pp. 152–166), *Vagn Holmboe* (London, 1974); P. Rapoport, *Vagn Holmboe's Symphonic Metamorphoses* (Univ. of Ill., Urbana, 1975).

Holmes, Alfred, English violinist; b. London, Nov. 9, 1837; d. Paris, March 4, 1876. His only teacher was his father, an amateur violinist; he sang at the Oratory in London as a soprano chorister; appeared as a violinist at the age of 9, playing a duet with his brother, Henry. The 2 brothers then went on a European tour, playing in Belgium, Germany, Sweden, Denmark, and Holland (1855–61). Alfred Holmes then lived in Paris (1861–64); visited Russia in 1867; then returned to Paris, making occasional visits to London. He composed several programmatic symphonies, entitled *Robinhood, The Siege of Paris, Charles XII,* and *Romeo and Juliet;* also overtures, *The Cid* and *The Muses.* His brother, **Henry Holmes** (b. London, Nov. 7, 1839; d. San Francisco, Dec. 9, 1905), was also a precocious violinist; after 1865 he settled in London, where he taught at the Royal College of Music. In 1894, he went to San Francisco, where he remained until his death. He wrote 4 symphonies, 2 cantatas, Violin Concerto (London, Dec. 11, 1875); also some chamber music.

Holmès, Augusta (Mary Anne), French composer; b. Paris (of Irish parents), Dec. 16, 1847; d. there, Jan. 28, 1903. She progressed very rapidly as a child pianist, and gave public concerts; also composed songs under the pen name **Hermann Zenta.** She studied harmony with H. Lambert, an organist; later became a pupil of César Franck. She then began to compose works in large forms, arousing considerable attention, mixed with curiosity, for she was undoubtedly one of the very few professional women composers of the time. Her music, impartially considered, lacks individuality or strength; at best, it represents a conventional by-product of French Romanticism, with an admixture of fashionable exotic elements.
WORKS: operas: *La Montagne noire* (Paris Opéra, Feb. 8, 1895); *Héro et Léandre, Astarte, Lancelot du lac;* for orch.: *Andante pastoral* (Paris, Jan. 14, 1877); *Lutèce* (Angers, Nov. 30, 1884); *Les Argonautes* (Paris, April 24, 1881); *Irlande* (Paris, March 2, 1882); *Ode triomphale* (Paris, March 4, 1888); *Pologne, Andromède, Hymne à Apollon,* etc.; cantatas, *La Vision de la Reine; La Chanson de la Caravane; La Fleur de Neflier;* some piano pieces; 117 songs, some of which have remained in the active repertory of French singers.
BIBLIOGRAPHY: P. Barillon-Bauché, *Augusta Holmès et la femme compositeur* (Paris, 1912); R. Pichard du Page, *Augusta Holmès; une musicienne versaillaise* (Paris, 1921); R. Myers, "Augusta Holmès: A Meteoric Career," *Musical Quarterly* (July 1967).

Holmes, Edward, English pianist and author; b. London, 1797; d. there, Aug. 28, 1859. He received a fine education; was a friend of Keats at Enfield. He studied music with Vincent Novello. In 1826 he became a contributor to a literary journal, *Atlas.* He publ. *A Ramble among the Musicians of Germany* (1828; reprint, with a new introduction and indices by Charles Cudworth, N.Y., 1969); *The Life of Mozart* (his most important work; 1845; 2nd ed., 1878); *Life of Purcell; Analytical and Thematic Index of Mozart's Piano Works;* also articles in the *Musical Times* and other journals.

Holoubek, Ladislav, Slovak conductor and composer; b. Prague, Aug. 13, 1913. He studied music theory with Alexander Moyzes at the Bratislava Academy of Music (1926–33) and with Vítĕslav Novák at the Prague Cons. (1934–36). He was on the staff of the Slovak National Theater in Bratislava (1933–52 and 1959–66), and at the State Theater in Košice (1955–58).
WORKS: 5 operas, all brought out in Bratislava: *Stella* (March 18, 1939); *Svitanie (Dawn,* March 14, 1941); *Túžba (Yearning,* Feb. 12, 1944), *Rodina (Fatherland,* 1956–60); and *Professor Mamlock* (May 21, 1966); Symphony (1946); Sinfonietta (1950); *10 Variations on an Original Theme* for orch. (1950); *Defiances and Hopes,* symph. poem (1973); 2 cantatas: *Mesačná noc (Moonlight Night,* 1951) and *The Promise* (1952); Violin Sonata (1933); 3 String Quartets (1936, 1948, 1962); Wind Quintet (1938); Trio for flute, violin, and harp (1939); 2 Piano Sonatas (1931, 1947); songs.

Holst, Edvard, composer of light music; b. Copenhagen, 1843; d. New York, Feb. 4, 1899. He emigrated to America in 1874, and was active in New York as actor, dancing master, etc.; also wrote numerous pieces for military band (*Marine Band March, Battle of Ma-*

nila, etc.); a number of songs, and a comic opera, *Our Flats* (N.Y., 1897); in all, more than 2,000 numbers.

Holst, Gustav Theodore (real name, **Gustavus Theodore von Holst;** he removed the Germanic particle "von" after 1914; before World War I, his works were published under the name **Gustav von Holst**), famous English composer; b. Cheltenham, Sept. 21, 1874; d. London, May 25, 1934. He was the son of a Swedish father, an able organist, and a grand English mother, an amateur pianist. Reared in a musical family, Holst performed on the organ and led a chorus in Wyck Rissington, Gloucestershire, at the age of 19. He then entered the Royal College of Music in London, where he studied composition with Stanford; also took up the trombone, and acquired such proficiency that he was able to earn his living as trombonist with the Carl Rosa Opera Co. and in various symphony orchestras. In 1905 he became music master at St. Paul's Girls' School; from 1907, he was music director at Morley College in London, retaining both positions until his death. From 1919 he also taught composition at the Royal College of Music. In 1923 he undertook a journey to the U.S.; lectured and performed his works at Harvard Univ. and at the Univ. of Michigan. His last years were devoted entirely to composition. In his music, he was inspired equally by exotic subjects and by English folklore; oriental themes particularly fascinated him; he studied Hindu literature, and wrote several works reflecting Hindu legends. His most enduring work is the orchestral suite, *The Planets* (1914–16), depicted as astrological or mystical symbols. Also popular is his unassuming but effective work for string orch., *St. Paul's Suite* (1913). His daughter, **Imogen Holst,** (b. Richmond, Surrey, April 12, 1907), compiled a detailed biography.

WORKS: OPERAS AND OTHER STAGE WORKS: *Lansdown Castle,* operetta (Cheltenham, Feb. 7, 1893); *The Revoke* (one act; 1895); *The Youth's Choice* (1902); *Sita* (1899–1906); *Sāvitri,* chamber opera (after the Hindu epic *Mahabharata;* 1908; London, Dec. 5, 1916); *The Perfect Fool* (London, Covent Garden, May 14, 1923); *At the Boar's Head* (Manchester, April 3, 1925); *The Wandering Scholar* (1929; Liverpool, Jan. 31, 1934); choral ballet, *The Morning of the Year* (1927); choral ballet, *The Golden Goose* (Liverpool, Jan. 11, 1929). ORCHESTRAL WORKS: *Walt Whitman* (1899); *Cotswolds* (1900); symph. poem, *Indra* (1903); *Song of the Night,* for violin and orch. (1905); *Marching Song* and *Country Song,* for small orch. (1906); *Songs of the West* (1906), and *Somerset Rhapsody* (London, Queen's Hall, April 6, 1910); incidental music to *A Vision of Dame Christian* and music for the Stepney Pageant (1909); Suite No. 1 for military band (1909); Oriental Suite, *Beni Mora* (1910; London, May 1, 1912); *Invocation,* for cello and orch. (1911); Suite No. 2 for military band (1911); *Phantastic Suite* (1911); *St. Paul's Suite* for string orch. (1913); *The Planets,* suite for large orch. and voices (1914–16; London, Queen's Hall, Sept. 29, 1918); *Japanese Suite* (1915); *Fugal Overture* (London, Queen's Hall, Oct. 11, 1923); *Fugal Concerto,* for flute, oboe, and strings (London, 1923); *First Choral Symphony,* for soprano and mixed voices (Leeds Festival, Oct. 7, 1925); *Egdon Heath,* symph. poem (after Thomas Hardy; N.Y.,

Feb. 12, 1928); *Double Concerto,* for 2 violins (London, Queen's Hall, April 3, 1930); *Hammersmith,* prelude and scherzo (London, Queen's Hall, Nov. 25, 1931). CHAMBER MUSIC: *Fantasy Pieces* for oboe and strings; Piano Quintet (1896); Suite (1900; London, April 6, 1904); Woodwind Quintet (1903). CHORAL AND VOCAL WORKS: *Clear and Cool,* for chorus and orch. (1897); *Ornulf's Drapa,* scena for baritone and orch. (1898); *Ave Maria,* for 8-part women's chorus (1900); *King Estmere,* ballade for chorus and orch. (1903); *The Mystic Trumpeter,* for soprano and orch. (1904); *The Cloud Messenger,* ode for chorus and orch. (1910); *Christmas Day* (1910); 4-part Songs for children, women's chorus (1905); 4 Carols for mixed chorus; *Two Eastern Pictures,* for women's chorus and harp (1911); *Hecuba's Lament,* for contralto (1911); Choral Songs; *Choral Hymns from the Rig-Veda* (1910); 2 Psalms, for chorus, strings, and organ (1912); *Hymn to Dionysus* (1913); *Dirge for Two Veterans,* for men's chorus and brass band (1914); Part-songs for Mixed Chorus (1916); 3 Hymns for Chorus and Orch. (1916); 6 Folksongs for Chorus (1916); *Hymn of Jesus,* for 2 choruses, orch., piano, and organ (1917); Part-songs for Children; *Ode to Death,* with orch. (after Walt Whitman, 1919; Leeds Festival, 1922); Choruses to *Alcestis,* for women's chorus, harp, and flutes (1920); motet, *The Evening Watch* (1924); *Choral Fantasia,* for soprano, chorus, organ, and orch. (1930); 12 Welsh Folksongs, for mixed chorus (1930–31). Songs: *The Heart Worships; Hymns from the Rig-Veda* (1908). FOR PIANO: Toccata on the Northumbrian pipe tune *Newburn Lads* (1924); *Chrissemas Day in the Morning* (1926); *Nocturne* (1930); *Jig* (1932).

BIBLIOGRAPHY: Louise B. M. Dyer, *Music by British Composers. No. 1: Gustav Holst* (London, 1931); E. Rubbra, *Gustav Holst* (Monaco, 1947); Imogen Holst, *Gustav Holst* (London, 1938); Imogen Holst, *The Music of Gustav Holst* (London, 1951); A. E. F. Dickinson, "Gustav Holst," *The Music Masters,* vol. 4, ed. by A. L. Bacharach (London, 1954); Imogen Holst, *A Thematic Catalogue of Gustav Holst's Music* (1974); E. Rubbra, *Gustav Holst: Collected Essays* (1974); Michael Short, *Gustav Holst: A Centenary Documentation* (1974).

Holst, Henry, Danish violinist of English parentage; b. Copenhagen, July 25, 1899. He studied at the Copenhagen Cons.; then went to Berlin where he took violin lessons with Willy Hess; subsequently was engaged as concertmaster of the Berlin Philharmonic (1923–31); then taught at the Royal College of Music in Manchester, England (1931–45); from 1945 to 1954 he was prof. of violin at the Royal College of Music in London; from 1961 to 1963 taught violin classes at the Univ. of Arts in Tokyo, Japan; in 1963 returned to Denmark and was appointed violin prof. at the Cons. of Copenhagen.

Holstein, Franz (Friedrich) von, German composer; b. Braunschweig, Feb. 16, 1826; d. Leipzig, May 22, 1878. His father was an army officer; at his behest, Holstein entered the Cadet School; there he had an opportunity to study musical theory. While a lieutenant, he privately produced his operetta, *Zwei Nächte in Venedig* (1845). He fought in the Schleswig-Holstein campaign; returning to Braunschweig, he wrote a grand opera, *Waverley,* after Walter Scott. He sent the score to Hauptmann at the Leipzig Cons.; the latter expressed his willingness to accept Holstein as a student. Accordingly, he resigned from the army (1853) and studied with Hauptmann until 1856. He then undertook some travels in Italy, finally returning to Leipzig, where he settled. He was also a poet, and wrote his own librettos. The musical style of his operas was close to the French type, popularized by Auber. He was a man of means, and left a valuable legacy for the benefit of indigent music students.

WORKS: operas: *Der Haideschacht* (Dresden, Oct. 22, 1868), *Der Erbe von Morley* (Leipzig, Jan. 23, 1872), *Die Hochländer* (Mannheim, Jan. 16, 1876); another opera, *Marino Faliero,* remained unfinished; overture, *Frau Aventiure* (left in sketches only; orchestrated by Albert Dietrich; perf. posthumously, Leipzig, Nov. 13, 1879); *Beatrice,* scene for soprano solo with orch.; a piano trio; other chamber music; part-songs for mixed and men's voices, etc.

BIBLIOGRAPHY: G. Glaser, *Franz von Holstein: ein Dichterkomponist des 19. Jahrhunderts* (Leipzig, 1930).

Holt, Simeon ten, Dutch composer; b. Bergen, North Holland, Jan. 24, 1923. He studied piano with Jacob van Domselaer; later took composition lessons with Honegger in Paris. From 1960 to 1970 he was connected with the Institute for Sonologie in Utrecht; in 1970 opened his own electronic music studio.

WORKS: Suite for String Quartet (1954); *Diagonal Music* for string orch. (1956); Divertimento for 3 Flutes (1957); *Epigenese* for orch. (1964); *Triptichon* for 6 percussionists (1965); *Sandpipers* for percussion (1965); String Quartet (1965); *Atalon* for mezzo-soprano and 36 playing and talking instrumentalists (1967-68); *Differenties* for 3 clarinets, piano and vibraphone (1969); *Scenario X* for brass quintet (1970); for piano: *Compositions I-IV* (1942-45); Suite (1953); 2 sonatas (1953, 1959); *20 Bagatelles* (1954); *Allegro ex Machina* (1955); *Diagonal Suite* (1957); *Journal* (1957); *Music for Peter,* 7 little pieces (1958); *20 Epigrams* (1959); *5 Etudes* (1961); electronic compositions: *Sevenplay* (1970); *Inferno I* and *II* (1970, 1971), *Modules I-IV* (1971); *I am Sylvia* (1973); *Recital I* and *II* (1972-74).

Holter, Iver (Paul Fredrik), Norwegian composer; b. Gausdal, Dec. 13, 1850; d. Oslo, Jan. 25, 1941. He entered the Univ. of Christiania (Oslo) as a student of medicine, but devoted much more time to music, which he studied under Svendsen; then was a pupil of Jadassohn, Richter, and Reinecke at the Leipzig Cons. (1876-78); lived in Berlin (1879-81); became Grieg's successor as conductor of the "Harmonie" in Bergen (1882); from 1886 to 1911 he was conductor of "Musikföreningen" in Oslo, and from 1890-1905, also of "Handvaerkersångföreningen"; in 1907, founded (and conducted until 1921) "Holters Korförening," a society devoted to the production of large choral works (sacred and secular); was conductor of several of the great Scandinavian festivals; in 1900 he conducted with Svendsen the "Northern Concerts" in Paris. In 1919 the Norwegian Government granted him an art-

ist's stipend. He was editor of *Nordisk Musik Revue* (1900-06). His compositions include a symphony (1885), a violin concerto, and several cantatas: for the 300-year jubilee of Christiania (1924); for the 900-year Olavs-jubilee (1930); choruses, chamber music, songs.

Holtzner, Anton, German organist and composer of the early 17th century; d. 1635. He was educated in Italy. His keyboard canzonas make use of free rhythmic transformation of themes in the manner of Frescobaldi's 'variation canzonas'; one of them is reprinted in A. G. Ritter's *Geschichte des Orgelspiels im 14.-18. Jahrhundert* (1884).

Holy, Alfred, harpist; b. Oporto, Portugal, Aug. 5, 1866; d. Vienna, May 8, 1948. He studied violin and piano; then took harp lessons with Stanek at the Prague Cons. (1882-85). He subsequently was engaged as first harpist at the German Opera in Prague (1885-96); at the Berlin State Opera (1896-1903); at the Vienna Court Opera (1903-13). In 1913 he became first harpist of the Boston Symph. Orch.; retired in 1928 and returned to Vienna. He publ. studies for harp, arranged from the symphonic works of Richard Strauss, and various other harp transcriptions.

Holyoke, Samuel, American composer; b. Boxford, Mass., Oct. 15, 1762; d. East Concord, N.H., Feb. 7, 1820. His father was a clergyman, and Holyoke was naturally drawn to composing hymns. Although he received no formal training in music, he began to compose early, following his innate musical instinct. He wrote his most popular hymn tune, *Arnheim,* when he was only 16. He attended Harvard College, graduating in 1789; in 1793 he organized a school of higher education, known as the Groton Academy (later Lawrence Academy). In 1800 he went to Salem, where he was active as a teacher; was also a member of the Essex Musical Association in Salem. Holyoke was among those who did not favor the application of 'fuging' tunes in sacred music, as advocated by Billings, and generally omitted that style of composition from his collections; in the preface to his *Harmonia Americana* he states his reason for this as being because of "the trifling effect produced by that sort of music; for the parts ... confound the sense and render the performance a mere jargon of words." His first collection was the *Harmonia Americana* (Boston, 1791); then followed *The Massachusetts Compiler* (co-ed. with Hans Gram and Oliver Holden; Boston, 1795); *The Columbian Repository of Sacred Harmony* (publ. Exeter, N.H., and dedicated to Essex Musical Association; copyright entry dated April 7, 1802; contains 734 tunes, many of his own composition); *The Christian Harmonist* (Salem, 1804); and *The Instrumental Assistant* (Exeter; 2 vols., 1800-07; includes instructions for violin, German flute, clarinet, bass viol, and hautboy). He also publ. the song *Washington* (1790), *Hark from the Tombs* (music for the funeral of Washington; 1800), etc.

BIBLIOGRAPHY: F. J. Metcalf, *American Psalmody* (N.Y., 1917); F. J. Metcalf, *American Writers and Compilers of Sacred Music* (Cincinnati, 1925); J. L. Willhide, *Samuel Holyoke, American Music-Educator* (Univ. of Southern California, 1954); R. Patterson,

Three American 'Primitives': A Study of the Musical Styles of Samuel Holyoke, Oliver Holden, and Hans Gram (Washington Univ., 1963).

Holzbauer, Ignaz, Austrian composer; b. Vienna, Sept. 17, 1711; d. Mannheim, April 7, 1783. While studying law, he taught himself music with the aid of *Gradus ad Parnassum* by Fux, whom he met later, and was encouraged towards further study. For a brief time, he was musical director to Count Rottach in Moravia; in 1741 he returned to Vienna, where he produced his first opera, *Ipermestra.* He traveled to Italy; on his journey in 1747, he was accompanied by his wife, an excellent singer. In 1750, he became court conductor at Stuttgart; in 1753 he was engaged as music director at Mannheim and remained there for most of his life. In 1756 he visited Rome; in 1757, Turin; in 1759, Milan; produced some of his operas there. He was greatly respected as a musician by his contemporaries; his church music was warmly praised by Mozart, who heard it in Mannheim in 1777.

WORKS: Historically, his most significant opera is *Günther von Schwarzburg,* in which Holzbauer presented a purely German story without concession to the prevalent Italian taste. It was produced in Mannheim in 1776, and the full score publ. at the time (reprint, in vols. 8/9 of *Denkmäler deutscher Tonkunst*). He also wrote 12 Italian operas: *Il figlio delle selve* (Schwetzingen, 1753), *L'isola disabitata* (Schwetzingen, 1754), *Issipile* (Mannheim, 1754), *Don Chisciotte* (Schwetzingen, 1755), *Le nozze d'Arianna* (Mannheim, 1756), *I cinesi* (Mannheim, 1756), *La clemenza di Tito* (Mannheim, 1757), *Nitteti* (Turin, 1757), *Ippolito ed Aricia* (Mannheim, 1759), *Alessandro nell' Indie* (Milan, 1759), *Adriano in Siria* (Mannheim, 1768), *Tancredi* (Munich, 1783). In addition, he wrote 4 oratorios (of which only one is extant), 21 Masses, 37 motets, and other church music. Most importantly, he was the composer of 65 symphonies, 17 divertimentos, string quartets, instrumental concertos, etc., in the innovating style of the Mannheim school; a thematic catalogue is in vols. 4 and 13 (3 and 7) of *Denkmäler der Tonkunst in Bayern* (vol. 13 also has his Symphony in E-flat) and in vol. 16 of the *Denkmäler deutscher Tonkunst* (which also has his String Quintet in E-flat).

BIBLIOGRAPHY: K. M. Klob, *Drei musikalische Biedermänner* (Ulm, 1911).

Homer, Louise (*née* **Louise Dilworth Beatty**), American contralto; b. Shadyside, near Pittsburgh, April 28, 1871; d. Winter Park, Florida, May 6, 1947. She studied in Philadelphia, and later in Boston, where her teacher in harmony was **Sidney Homer,** whom she married in 1895. With him she went to Paris, and there continued her study of voice with Fidèle Koenig; she also took lessons with Paul Lhérie in dramatic action. She made her debut in opera as Leonora in *La Favorita* (Vichy, 1898). In 1899 she was engaged at the Théâtre de la Monnaie in Brussels, singing various parts of the French and Italian repertories. She subsequently sang Wagnerian contralto roles in German at Covent Garden, London. She made her American debut in opera as Amneris with the Metropolitan Opera Co. (then on tour) at San Francisco (Nov. 14, 1900);

sang the same part in N.Y. (Dec. 22, 1900); continued on the staff of the Metropolitan from 1900 to 1919; was then with the Chicago Opera Co. (1920–25); with the San Francisco and Los Angeles Opera companies (1926), and again with the Metropolitan, reappearing there on Dec. 13, 1927. Her classic interpretation of Orfeo at the Paris revival of Gluck's opera (1909) and subsequently in N.Y. (1910, under Toscanini) produced a great impression. One of her greatest operatic triumphs was her performance of Dalila, with Caruso singing Samson. After retiring from the opera stage, she gave recitals with her daughter, **Louise Homer Stires,** soprano. Her husband wrote a book of memoirs, *My Wife and I* (N.Y., 1939).

Homer, Sidney, American composer; b. Boston, Dec. 9, 1864; d. Winter Park, Fla., July 10, 1953. He studied in Boston, with Chadwick; then in Leipzig and in Munich. Returning to Boston, he taught theory of music. In 1895 he married **Louise Dilworth Beatty,** his pupil, and went with her to Paris. He retired in 1940 and settled in Winter Park. He publ. about 100 songs, many of which won great favor, particularly *A Banjo Song;* also *Dearest, Requiem, Prospice, Bandanna* ballads, *It was the time of roses, General William Booth enters into Heaven, The song of the shirt, Sheep and Lambs, Sing me a song of a lad that is gone, The pauper's drive;* also 17 lyrics from Christina Rossetti's *Sing-song.* Other works include Sonata for Organ (1922), Quintet for Piano and Strings (1932), Violin Sonata (1936), String Quartet (1937), Piano Trio (1937). He publ. a book of memoirs, *My Wife and I* (N.Y., 1939).

BIBLIOGRAPHY: H. C. Thorpe, "The Songs of Sidney Homer," *Musical Quarterly* (Jan. 1931).

Homilius, Gottfried August, eminent German organist and composer; b. Rosenthal, Feb. 2, 1714; d. Dresden, June 5, 1785. He was a pupil of J. S. Bach; completed his education at the Univ. of Leipzig in 1735; became organist of the Frauenkirche in Dresden; then was appointed music director of 3 main churches there (1755). Published works are: Passion (1775); a Christmas oratorio, *Die Freude der Hirten über die Geburt Jesu* (1777); *6 deutsche Arien* (1786); in MS in the Berlin State Library and in the Dresden Kreuzchor archives: Passion according to St. Mark; church music for each Sunday and Feast day in the year; motets, cantatas, fugued chorales, a thorough-bass method, 2 chorus books, etc.

BIBLIOGRAPHY: R. Steglich, "Ph. Em. Bach und G. A. Homilius im Musikleben ihrer Zeit" (*Bach-Jahrbuch,* 1915). For a complete list of works, see Georg Feder's detailed article in *Die Musik in Geschichte und Gegenwart.*

Homs, Joaquín, Catalan composer; b. Barcelona, Aug. 22, 1906. He studied cello; began to compose late in life. He took lessons in music theory with Roberto Gerhard (1931–37); formed a constructivist style with thematic contents derived from Catalan melos.

WORKS: 7 string quartets (1938–68); Duo for Flute and Clarinet (1936); Wind Quintet (1940); Concertino for Piano and Strings (1946); Sextet (1959); String trio (1968); *Impromtu for Ten* (1970).

Honegger, Arthur (Oscar), remarkable French composer; b. Le Havre (of Swiss parents), March 10, 1892; d. Paris, Nov. 27, 1955. He studied violin with Lucien Capet in Paris; then took courses at the Zürich Cons. with L. Kempter and F. Hegar. Returning to France in 1912, he entered the Paris Cons. in the classes of Gédalge and Widor; further studied with Vincent d'Indy. His name first attracted attention when he took part in a concert of 'Nouveaux Jeunes' (Paris, Jan. 15, 1918). In 1920, the Paris critic Henri Collet published an article in *Comoedia* in which he drew a parallel between the Russian Five and a group of young French composers whom he designated "Les Six," which comprised Honegger, Milhaud, Poulenc, Auric, Durey, and Germaine Tailleferre. The label persisted, even though the six composers went their separate ways and rarely gave concerts together. Honegger became famous with his "symphonic movement" *Pacific 231,* a realistic tonal portrayal of a powerful American locomotive, depicting, in a series of rhythmic pulses, a gradual progress towards full speed, the slackening of pace, and the final stop. The piece, widely performed in 1924, became, in the mind of music critics and listeners, a perfect symbol of the "machine age." However, Honegger soon turned away from literal representation towards symphonic and choral music in quasi-Classical structures. Among his cantatas, *Le Roi David* and *Jeanne d'Arc au bûcher* are fine examples of modern vocal music; of his 5 symphonies, the 3rd (*Liturgique*) and the 5th (*Di tre re,* so designated by the composer to draw attention to the endings of each movement on a thrice repeated note D) are particularly impressive. Honegger makes free use of the devices of atonality in melodic writing, and polytonality in harmonic constructions, but only to enhance the basic sense of tonal unity. He lived most of his life in Paris; married the pianist **Andrée Vaurabourg** (who often played his works) in 1926. In 1929 he visited the U.S.; in 1947 was engaged to teach summer classes at the Berkshire Music Center in Tanglewood.

WORKS: FOR THE STAGE: *Le Roi David,* dramatic Psalm (Mézières, June 11, 1921); *Antigone,* opera (Brussels, Dec. 28, 1927); *Judith,* biblical opera (Monte Carlo, Feb. 13, 1926); *Amphion,* melodrama (Paris, June 23, 1931); *Les Aventures du Roi Pausole,* operetta (Paris, Dec. 12, 1930); *Cris du monde,* stage oratorio (Paris, June 2, 1931); *La Belle de Moudon,* vaudeville (Mézières, 1933); *Jeanne d'Arc au bûcher,* stage oratorio (Basel, May 12, 1938); *L'Aiglon,* opera (Monte Carlo, March 11, 1937); *Les Mille et une Nuits,* spectacle (Paris Exhibition, 1937); *Les Petites Cardinal,* operetta (with J. Ibert; Paris, Feb. 20, 1938); *Nicolas de Flue,* dramatic legend (Neuchâtel, 1941); *Charles le Téméraire,* opera (Mézières, May, 1944). Ballets: *Vérité-Mensonge* (Paris, 1920); *Skating Rink* (Paris, Jan. 20, 1922); *Sous-marine* (Paris, June 27, 1925); *Sémiramis,* ballet-pantomime (Paris, May 11, 1934); *Le Cantique des cantiques* (Paris, Feb. 2, 1938); *L'appel de la montagne* (Paris, July 9, 1945); *Chota Roustaveli* (with Harsányi and Tcherepnin; Monte Carlo, May 5, 1946). INCIDENTAL MUSIC: *Le Dit des jeux du monde* (Paris, Dec. 2, 1918); *La Mort de Sainte Alméenne* (1918); *La Danse macabre* (1919); *Saül* (Paris, June 16, 1922); *Fantasio* (1922); *L'Impera-*

trice aux rochers (1925); *Phaedra* (1926). FILM MUSIC: *Mlle. Doctor* (1937); *Pygmalion,* after Bernard Shaw's play (1938). FOR ORCH.: *Prélude d'Aglavaine et Sélysette* (Paris Cons., April 3, 1917, composer conducting); *Le Chant de Nigamon* (Paris, Jan. 3, 1920); *Pastorale d'Été* (Paris, Feb. 12, 1921); *Les Mariés de la tour Eiffel* (with Milhaud, Auric, Poulenc, and Tailleferre; Paris, June 19, 1921); *Horace Victorieux,* 'mimed symphony' (Lausanne, Oct. 30, 1921); *Prelude pour la Tempête* (Paris, May 1, 1923); *Chant de Joie* (Paris, May 3, 1923); *Pacific 231* (designated as *Mouvement symphonique No. 1;* Koussevitzky's concert, Paris, May 8, 1924); Concertino for Piano and Orch. (Paris, May 23, 1925, Andrée Vaurabourg soloist); *Rugby* (*Mouvement symphonique No. 2;* Stade Colombe, Paris, Dec. 31, 1928, during the intermission of the International Rugby Match between France and England); Cello Concerto (Boston, Feb. 17, 1930); Symphony No. 1 (Boston, Feb. 13, 1931); *Mouvement symphonique No. 3* (Berlin, March 27, 1933); Symphony No. 2, for string orch. (Basel, May 18, 1942); suite, *Jour de fête suisse* (1943); Symphony No. 3, *Liturgique* (Zürich, Aug. 17, 1946); *Sérénade à Angélique,* for small orch. (Paris, Dec. 11, 1946); Symphony No. 4, *Deliciae Basilienses* (Basel, Jan. 21, 1947); *Concerto da camera,* for flute, English horn, and strings (1949); *Suite archaïque,* for orch. (Louisville, Feb. 28, 1951); Symphony No. 5, *Di tre re* (Boston, March 9, 1951); *Monopartita,* for orch. (Zürich, June 12, 1951). RADIO MUSIC: *Radio Panoramique,* symphonic sketch (Radio-Geneva, March 1935; in concert form, Paris, Oct. 19, 1935); *Christophe Colomb* (Radio, Lausanne, April 17, 1940); etc. CHORAL AND VOCAL WORKS: *Cantique de Pâques,* for soli, women's chorus, and orch. (1918); *Pâques à New York,* for voice and string quartet (1920); *La Danse des morts,* oratorio for soli, chorus, and orch. (Basel, March 2, 1940); *Chant de Libération,* for baritone, chorus, and orch. (Paris, Oct. 22, 1944); *Cantate de Noël* (Basel, Dec. 18, 1953). CHAMBER MUSIC: 1st String Quartet (1916–17); Rhapsody for 2 Flutes, Clarinet (or 2 violins, viola), and Piano (1917); 2 violin sonatas (1918; 1919); Viola Sonata (1920); Sonatina for 2 Violins (1920); Cello Sonata (1920); *Hymn,* for 10 strings (1920); Sonatina for Clarinet and Piano (1922); *Trois Contrepoints,* for flute, English horn, violin, and cello (1922); Sonatina for Violin and Cello (1932); 2nd String Quartet (1934); 3rd String Quartet (1936). FOR PIANO: *Trois pièces* (1910); *Hommage à Ravel* (1915); *Toccata et Variations* (1916); *Prélude et danse* (1919); *Le Cahier romand* (1923); *Hommage à Roussel* (1928); *Prélude, arioso et fughetta sur le nom de Bach* (1932); also a Partita for 2 Pianos (arranged from *Trois Contrepoints;* 1928). SONGS: 4 *Poèmes* (1914–16); 6 *Poésies de Jean Cocteau* (1920–23); 5 *Mélodies-minute* (1941); publ. a book *Je suis compositeur* (Paris, 1951; in English as *I Am a Composer,* London, 1966).

BIBLIOGRAPHY: R. Chalupt, "Arthur Honegger," *Revue Musicale* (1922); E. B. Hill, *Modern French Composers* (N.Y., 1924); Roland-Manuel, *Arthur Honegger* (Paris, 1925); A. George, *Arthur Honegger* (Paris, 1926); Willy Tappolet, *Arthur Honegger* (Zürich, 1933, in German; French ed., Neuchâtel, 1938); Claude Gérard, *Arthur Honegger: catalogue succinct des œuvres* (Brussels, 1945); José Bruyr, *Honegger et son œuvre* (Paris, 1947); M. F. G. Delannoy, *Honegger* (Paris, 1953); Jean Matter, *Honegger* (Lausanne, 1956); Willi Reich, ed. *Arthur Honegger, Nachklang: Schriften, Photos, Dokumente* (Zürich, 1957); Jacques Feschotte, *Arthur Honegger: L'Homme et son œuvre* (Paris, 1966); P. Meylan, *Arthur Honegger, humanitare Botschaft der Musik* (Frauenfeld, 1970).

Honegger, Henri, Swiss cellist; b. Geneva, June 10, 1904. He studied with Ami Briquet in Geneva; then went to Germany where he took lessons with Julius Klengel at the Leipzig Cons.; from there he traveled to Paris where he took lessons with Casals; returning to Switzerland he became first cellist in the Orchestre de la Suisse Romande, but also continued his tours as a soloist; in 1950 he presented a series of concerts in New York performing all of Bach's cello suites. In 1964 he resigned from the Orchestre de la Suisse Romande in order to devote himself exclusively to concert activities.

Honegger, Marc, French musicologist; b. Paris, June 17, 1926. He studied music history and theory at the Sorbonne with Chailley and P.-M. Masson; in 1954 was appointed to the faculty of the musicological dept. of the Univ. of Paris. In 1958 he joined the staff of the Univ. of Strasbourg; in 1970 received the degree of *Docteur-ès-lettres.* He published several valuable papers on French music of the late Renaissance; also a historical survey, *La Musique française de 1830 à 1914* (1962). He is the editor of the valuable 4-volume encyclopedia, *Dictionnaire de la Musique* (Strasbourg, 1970–77).

Hood, Helen, American song composer; b. Chelsea, Mass., June 28, 1863; d. Brookline, Mass., Jan. 22, 1949. She studied piano with B. J. Lang and composition with Chadwick; also took a piano course with Moszkowski in Berlin; lived most of her life in Boston. Among her published pieces are *The Robin* (part-song); 5 Pieces for Violin and Piano; *Song Etchings* (a set of 6 songs); she also wrote some chamber music.

Hood, Mantle, American musicologist; b. Springfield, Illinois, June 24, 1918. He studied at the Univ. of Calif., Los Angeles (A.B., 1951; M.A., 1952); then at the Univ. of Amsterdam (Ph.D., 1954). In 1954 he joined the staff of U.C.L.A. In 1956–57 he traveled to Indonesia on a Ford Foundation Fellowship. In 1961 he was appointed Director of the Institute of Ethnomusicology at U.C.L.A. He contributed numerous valuable articles on oriental music to various learned journals and musical encyclopedias; made arrangements of Indonesian melodies. He is also a composer; his works include a symph. poem, *Vernal Equinox* (1955); Woodwind Trio (1950); 6 Duets for Soprano and Alto Recorder (1954); piano pieces; etc.

Hoof, Jef van, Belgian composer; b. Antwerp, May 8, 1886; d. there, April 24, 1959. He studied composition at the Antwerp Cons. with Gilson, Mortelmas and Huybrechts; composed three operas: *Tycho-Brahe* (1911), *Meivuur* (1916) and *Jonker Lichthart* (1928); 5 symphonies (1938, 1941, 1945, 1951, 1956); choruses;

lieder; piano pieces. His style of composition is neo-Romantic, with a penchant for expansive sonorities.

Hoogstraten, Willem van, Dutch conductor; b. Utrecht, March 18, 1884; d. Tutzing, Germany, Sept. 11, 1965. He studied violin with Alexander Schmuller; then with Bram Eldering at the Cons. of Cologne and with Ševčik in Prague; played concerts with the pianist **Elly Ney,** whom he married in 1911 (divorced in 1927). From 1914–18 he conducted the municipal orch. in Krefeld; in 1922 he was engaged as conductor of the summer concerts of the N.Y. Philharmonic (until 1938); associate conductor of the N.Y. Philharmonic (1923–25). He was regular conductor of the Portland, Oregon, Symph. Orch. from 1925–37. During World War II he was in charge of the Mozarteum Orch. in Salzburg (1939–45). In 1949 he settled in Stuttgart; conducted the Stuttgart Philharmonic.

Hook, James, English organist and composer; b. Norwich, June 3, 1746; d. Boulogne, 1827. He exhibited a precocious talent as a boy; took lessons with Garland, organist of the Norwich Cathedral. In 1764 he went to London, where he played organ at various entertainment places. In 1765 he won a prize for his *Parting Catch.* He was subsequently organist and music director at Marylebone Gardens, London (1769–73) and at Vauxhall Gardens (1774–1820); his last position was at St. John's, Horsleydown.
WORKS: He was a highly industrious composer of songs; he may have written as many as 2,000 numbers; of these, only a few escaped oblivion (*Within a mile of Edinboro' Town; Sweet Lass of Richmond Hill,* etc.); many oratorios and odes; concertos for harpsichord; 117 sonatas, sonatinas, and divertimentos for piano; about 30 theater scores, all produced in London: *Cupid's Revenge* (June 12, 1772), *The Lady of the Manor* (Nov. 23, 1778), *The Fair Peruvian* (March 8, 1786), *Jack of Newbury* (May 6, 1795), *Wilmore Castle* (Oct. 21, 1800), *The Soldier's Return* (April 23, 1805), *The Invisible Girl* (April 28, 1806), *The Fortress* (July 16, 1807), *Safe and Sound* (August 28, 1809), etc. He publ. a manual, *Guida di musica,* in 2 parts (1785; 1794); some of the musical examples from it were reprinted by H. Wall in *Leaves from an Old Harpsichord Book.*

Hope-Jones, Robert, English organ manufacturer; b. Hooton Grange, Cheshire, Feb. 9, 1859; d. (by suicide) Rochester, N.Y., Sept. 13, 1914. As a boy, he entered the employ of Laird Bros., engineers at Birkenhead; then became chief electrician of the National Telephone Co.; at the same time, was engaged as church organist. In 1889 he set up his own business as organ builder. In 1903 he settled in America; was connected with the E. M. Skinner Co. of Boston; in 1907, founded the Hope-Jones Organ Co. at Tonawanda, N.Y., but sold the plant and his patents in 1910 to the Rudolph Wurlitzer Co. of N.Y. He introduced many innovations into the building of electrical organs; the development of the modern organ in the U.S. owes much to his inventive genius. One of the finest of his organs is in the Auditorium at Ocean Grove, N.J.
BIBLIOGRAPHY: G. L. Miller, *The Recent Revolution in Organ Building* (N.Y., 1913).

Hopekirk, Helen, Scottish pianist; b. Edinburgh, May 20, 1856; d. Cambridge, Mass., Nov. 19, 1945. She studied with A. C. Mackenzie; then went to Germany; made her debut with the Gewandhaus Orch., Leipzig (Nov. 28, 1878); also took lessons with Leschetizky in Vienna. She married William Wilson, a businessman, in 1882; lived in Vienna; in 1897, settled in Boston; taught at the New England Cons. In her recitals she featured many works of the modern French school (Debussy, Fauré, etc.). She was also a composer; played her own piano concerto with the Boston Symph. Orch. (Dec. 27, 1900); publ. a collection of Scottish folksongs.
BIBLIOGRAPHY: Constance Hall, *Helen Hopekirk* (Cambridge, Mass., 1954).

Hopkins, Charles Jerome (first name is sometimes erroneously given as **Edward**), American composer and musical journalist; b. Burlington, Vermont, April 4, 1836; d. Athenia, N.J., Nov. 4, 1898. Self-taught in music (he took only 6 lessons in harmony), he learned to play piano sufficiently well to attain professional status. He studied chemistry at the N.Y. Medical College; played organ in N.Y. churches, and was active in various educational enterprises; in 1856 he founded the American Music Association, which promoted concerts of music by Gottschalk, Bristow, and other American composers. In 1868 he founded the *N.Y. Philharmonic Journal,* and was its editor until 1885. In 1886 he organized several "Free Singing and Opera Schools," for which he claimed nearly 1,000 pupils. In 1889 he went to England on a lecture tour announcing himself as "the first American Operatic Oratorio composer and Pianist who has ever ventured to invade England with New World Musical theories and practices." Throughout his versatile career, he was a strong advocate of American music; his sensational methods and eccentric professional conduct brought him repeatedly into public controversy; in England he was sued for libel. Hopkins claimed a priority in writing the first "musicianly and scientific Kinder-Oper" (*Taffy and Old Munch,* a children's fairy tale, 1880). He further wrote an operatic oratorio, *Samuel,* and a great number of choruses and songs, few of which are published. He compiled two collections of church music and an *Orpheon Class-Book.*
BIBLIOGRAPHY: N. Slonimsky, "The Flamboyant Pioneer," in *A Thing or Two About Music* (N.Y., 1947, pp. 250–261).

Hopkins, Edward John, English organist and composer; b. London, June 30, 1818; d. there, Feb. 4, 1901. He was a chorister at the Chapel Royal (1826–33); then studied theory with T. F. Walmisley. In 1834 he became organist at Mitcham Church; from 1838, was at St. Peter's Islington; from 1841, at St. Luke's, and from 1843 at the Temple Church, London. There he remained for 55 years, retiring in 1898; Walford Davies was his successor. Several of his many anthems have become established in the church repertory (*Out of the Deep, God is Gone Up, Thou Shalt Cause the Trumpet of the Jubilee to Sound,* etc.). His book, *The Organ: Its History and Construction* (in collaboration with Rimbault, London, 1855; 5th ed., 1887), is a standard work. He contributed articles to *Grove's Dictio-* *nary of Music and Musicians* and to various musical publications.
BIBLIOGRAPHY: Charles W. Pearce, *The Life and Works of Edward John Hopkins* (London, 1910).

Hopkins, John Henry, American clergyman and writer of hymn tunes; b. Pittsburgh, Oct. 28, 1820; d. Hudson, New York, Aug. 13, 1891. He studied at schools of divinity and served as a deacon in several churches. His Christmas carol, *We Three Kings of Orient Are,* is a perennial favorite. He published a collection *Carols, Hymns and Songs* (1862).
BIBLIOGRAPHY: R. G. McCutchan, *Our Hymnody* (N.Y., 1937).

Hopkinson, Francis, American statesman, writer, and composer; signer of the Declaration of Independence; b. Philadelphia, Sept. 21, 1737; d. there, May 9, 1791. By profession a lawyer, he was deeply interested in music; learned to play the harpsichord; studied music theory with James Bremner; was a member of an amateur group in Philadelphia who met regularly in their homes to play music, and also gave public concerts by subscription. He was the composer of the first piece of music written by a native American, *Ode to Music,* which he wrote in 1754, and of the first original American song, *My days have been so wondrous free* (1759). At least, this is the claim he makes in the preface to his *7 Songs* (actually 8, the last having been added after the title page was engraved) *for the harpsichord or forte piano,* dated Philadelphia, Nov. 20, 1788, and dedicated to George Washington: "I cannot, I believe, be refused the Credit of being the first Native of the United States who has produced a Musical Composition." Other works: *Ode in Memory of James Bremner* (1780); a dramatic cantata, *The Temple of Minerva* (1781); there are also some songs. Hopkinson's music was couched in the conventional English style, modeled after pieces by T. A. Arne, but he undoubtedly possessed a genuine melodic gift. He also provided Benjamin Franklin's glass harmonica with a keyboard and introduced improvements in the quilling of the harpsichord, and invented the Bellarmonic, an instrument consisting of a set of steel bells. He was probably, but not certainly, the compiler of *A Collection of Psalm Tunes with a Few Anthems,* etc. A MS book of songs in Hopkinson's handwriting is in the possession of the Library of Congress. Hopkinson's son, **Joseph Hopkinson,** wrote the words to *Hail Columbia.*
BIBLIOGRAPHY: O. G. Sonneck, *Francis Hopkinson, the First American Poet Composer . . .* (Washington, 1905; repr. N.Y., 1969); H. V. Milligan, *The First American Composer: 6 Songs by Francis Hopkinson* (Boston, 1918); G. E. Hastings, *The Life and Works of Francis Hopkinson* (Chicago, 1926); O. E. Albrecht, *Francis Hopkinson, Musician, Poet and Patriot* (Philadelphia, 1938); J. T. Howard, *Our American Music* (N.Y., 1939, and subsequent eds.).

Hoppin, Richard Hallowell, American musicologist; b. Northfield, Minn., Feb. 22, 1913. He studied piano at the École Normale de Musique in Paris (1933–35); musicology at Harvard Univ. (M.A., 1938; Ph.D., 1952). He was on the music faculty of the Univ. of

Texas, Austin (1949–61); in 1961, appointed prof. of music at Ohio State Univ. In 1959–60 he was the recipient of a Guggenheim Fellowship. He edited the important collection, *The Cypriot-French Repertory of the Manuscript Torino* (4 vols., Rome, 1960–63); contributed numerous articles to scholarly musical publications.

Horák, Adolph, pianist and teacher; b. Jankovic, Bohemia, Feb. 15, 1850; d. Vienna, Jan. 14, 1921. With his brother **Eduard** he established the Horák Pianoforte School in Vienna; in collaboration, they publ. a valuable *Klavierschule;* Adolph alone wrote *Die technische Grundlage des Klavierspiels.*

Horák, Antonin, Czech composer; b. Prague, July 2, 1875; d. Belgrade, March 12, 1910. He was engaged as opera conductor in Prague and Belgrade; his own opera, *Babička (Grandmother),* was fairly successful at its first production, in Prague (March 3, 1900); he also wrote cantatas and other choral works.

Horák, Eduard, pianist and teacher; b. Holitz, Bohemia, April 22, 1838; d. Riva, Lake of Garda, Dec. 16, 1892. With his brother **Adolph** he founded in Vienna the Horák Pianoforte School, which soon acquired a European reputation. In collaboration with Fr. Spigl, who succeeded him as director of the Horák School, he published *Der Klavierunterricht in neue, natürliche Bahnen gelenkt* (Vienna, 1892; in 2 vols.), and with his brother, a practical manual, *Klavierschule.*

Horák, Josef, Czech bass clarinetist; b. Znojmo, March 24, 1931. He attended the State High School for Musical and Dramatic Arts in Prague; was a clarinetist in the Brno State Philh. and Czech Radio Orch. On Oct. 20, 1955 he made his debut as a performer on the bass clarinet, and began a unique career as a virtuoso on that instrument; along with Dutch bass clarinetist, Harry Sparnaay, Horák is responsible for the revival of interest in the bass clarinet. Hindemith transcribed for Horák his bassoon sonata. In 1963 Horák and the pianist Emma Kovárnová formed the chamber duo, "Due Boemi di Praga," and performed nearly 300 specially commissioned works by Alois Hába, André Jolivet, Frank Martin, Messiaen, Stockhausen, and many, many others.

Horák, Wenzel Emanuel, Bohemian composer and organist; b. Mscheno-Lobes, Bohemia, Jan. 1, 1800; d. Prague, Sept. 3, 1871. He studied theory by himself, with the aid of the standard manuals of Vogler, Cherubini, etc.; also played organ, and was organist at various churches in Prague; wrote 10 Masses, motets, and a theoretical work, *Die Mehrdeutigkeit der Harmonien* (1846).

Horenstein, Jascha, Russian conductor; b. Kiev, May 6, 1898; d. London, April 2, 1973. His family moved to Germany when he was a child, and he studied with Max Brode in Königsberg and with Adolf Busch in Vienna; also took advanced courses in composition with Franz Schreker in Berlin. After some concerts which he conducted in Vienna and in Berlin, he was appointed conductor of the Düsseldorf Opera; then

appeared in France (1929) and in Russia (1931); made a tour in Australia (1936–37); conducted the Ballets Russes de Monte Carlo in Scandinavia (1937) and gave a series of concerts in Palestine (1938). After 1945 he conducted in the U.S. and South America as well as in Europe. He was highly regarded for his interpretations of Mahler.

Horký, Karel, Czech composer; b. Štěmechy, near Třebíč, Sept. 4, 1909. He played in a military band as a boy; studied bassoon; took private lessons in composition with V. Polívka and Pavel Haas; then entered the Prague Cons. as a student of Křička, graduating in 1944. He taught harmony at the Brno Cons. (1945–52) and in 1964 was appointed its director.
WORKS: 4 operas: *Jan Hus* (Brno, May 27, 1950); *Hejtman Šarovec* (Brno, 1953); *Jed z Elsinoru (The Poison from Elsinor),* freely after Shakespeare's *Hamlet* (Brno, Nov. 11, 1969); *Dawn* (Brno, July 4, 1975); 2 ballets: *Lastura (The Shell,* Brno, Oct. 23, 1945) and *Král Ječmínek (King Ječmínek,* Brno, Sept. 21, 1951); a cantata, *Český sen (The Czech Dream,* 1961–62); *Klythia,* symph. poem (1941); *Romantic Sinfonietta* (1944); Cello Concerto (1953); Violin Concerto (1955); 5 symphonies (1959, 1964, 1971, 1974, 1977); Serenade for String Orch. (1963); Bassoon Concerto (1966); Horn Concerto (1971); *Fateful Preludes* for piano and orch. (1972); *Dimitrov,* symph. poem with narrator and chorus, honoring the memory of the chairman of the Bulgarian Communist Party (1972); 4 string quartets (1938, 1954, 1955, 1963); String Trio (1940); Violin Sonata (1943); Suite for Wind Quintet (1943); Oboe Sonatina (1958); Nonet (1958); Clarinet Quintet (1960); Double-Bass Sonatina (1961); Clarinet Sonatina (1965); *3 Compositions* for piano (1971); *3 Compositions* for cello and piano (1972); choruses; songs; film music.

Horn, August, German composer and arranger; b. Freiberg, Sept. 1, 1825; d. Leipzig, March 25, 1893. He was a pupil of Mendelssohn at the Leipzig Cons.; wrote overtures and light music; but became principally known as arranger of symphonies, operas, etc. for piano, 2 and 4 hands. His comic opera *Die Nachbarn* was produced in Leipzig in 1875.

Horn, Camillo, composer; b. Reichenberg, Bohemia, Dec. 29, 1860; d. Vienna, Sept. 3, 1941. He was a pupil of Bruckner at the Vienna Cons.; conducted choruses there, and was also active as music critic. Many of his works have been published; he wrote a symphony; a cantata, *Bundeslied der Deutschen in Böhmen; Deutsches Lied* for chorus and orch.; many choruses a cappella; a number of piano pieces.

Horn, Charles Edward, composer and conductor; son of **Karl Friedrich Horn;** b. London, June 21, 1786; d. Boston, Oct. 21, 1849. He studied with his father, and practiced voice under the guidance of Rauzzini. Made his debut as a singer in a light opera (June 26, 1809); sang Kaspar in the English production of *Der Freischütz.* In 1833 he emigrated to America; there he wrote several oratorios: *The Remission of Sin* (later named *Satan*), etc. In 1848 he became conductor of the Handel and Haydn Society in Boston. In the U.S., he was notable primarily as a singer and composer of ballads.

Horn, Karl Friedrich, German composer; b. Nordhausen, April 13, 1762; d. Windsor, England, Aug. 5, 1830. He settled in England at the age of 20 and with the patronage of Count Brühl, Saxon Ambassador in London, became a fashionable teacher. In 1823 he became organist of St. George's Chapel at Windsor. With Wesley he prepared an English edition of Bach's *Wohltemperierte Clavier;* also wrote a treatise on thorough-bass; composed 12 sets of piano variations with flute obbligato; 6 piano sonatas; *Military Divertimentos.*

Hornbostel, Erich Moritz von, eminent musicologist; b. Vienna, Feb. 25, 1877; d. Cambridge, Nov. 28, 1935. He studied philosophy in Vienna and Heidelberg; 1900, *Dr. Phil.;* 1905–06 assistant of Stumpf in Berlin; 1906, came to the U.S. to record and study Indian music (Pawnee); 1906–33, director of the Phonogramm-Archiv in Berlin. In 1933 he left Germany and went to England. He was a specialist in Asian, African and other non-European music; also investigated the problems of tone psychology; contributed hundreds of articles to scholarly publications on these subjects. He edited a collection of records, *Musik des Orients* (Lindström, 1932); from 1922 until death was co-editor, with C. Stumpf, of the *Sammelbände für vergleichende Musikwissenschaft.* Hornbostel's writings are being prepared for reissue, edited by K. P. Wechsmann *et al.* (1975 ff).

Horne, Lena, black American singer; b. Brooklyn, June 30, 1917. She sang in supper clubs in New York and in Las Vegas; became popular in cafe society, and invited praise by her earthy and husky voice capable of considerable depth of expression. She publ. an autobiography *In Person, Lena Horne* (N.Y., 1950).

Horne, Marilyn, American soprano; b. Bradford, Penna., Jan. 16, 1934. She studied voice with William Vennard at the Univ. of Southern Calif.; also attended master classes of Lotte Lehmann. She made her opera debut in Gelsenkirchen, Germany in 1957. Returning to the U.S., she sang the demanding part of Marie in Berg's *Wozzeck* with the San Francisco Opera Co. (Oct. 4, 1960). In 1969 she toured Italy; sang in Stravinsky's *Oedipus Rex* at La Scala in Milan (March 13, 1969). She made her Metropolitan Opera debut in N.Y. on March 3, 1970.

Horneman, Christian Emil, Danish composer; son of **Johan Ole Horneman;** b. Copenhagen, Dec. 17, 1840; d. there, June 8, 1906. He studied at the Leipzig Cons. (1858–60), where he became a friend of Grieg. He composed light music under various pseudonyms; returning to Copenhagen, he organized a concert society there; produced an opera, *Aladdin* (Nov. 18, 1888); also was active as choral conductor and teacher. He wrote, in addition, 2 string quartets and numerous songs.

Horneman, Johan Ole, Danish composer; b. Copenhagen, May 13, 1809; d. there, May 29, 1870. He composed music in a popular vein; in 1844 established a publishing firm with Emil Erslev. His collection of piano pieces, *Nordiske sange uden tekst (Nordic Songs Without Text),* enjoyed some popularity; he further published a piano manual, *Ny praktisk Pianoforteskole* (new ed. by L. Schytte).

Horner, Ralph Joseph, English conductor and composer; b. Newport, Monmouthshire, April 28, 1848; d. Winnipeg, Canada, April 7, 1926. He studied at the Leipzig Cons. (1864–67) with Moscheles, Reinecke, and Plaidy. On his return to England, he was active as choral conductor; also conducted light opera. From 1906–09 he was in New York; then settled in Winnipeg, where he became director of the Imperial Academy of Music and Arts and conductor of the Oratorio Society (1909–12). He wrote the operas *Confucius, Amy Rosbart,* and *The Belles of Barcelona;* the oratorios *St. Peter* and *David's First Victory;* a *Torch Dance* for orch.; many sacred cantatas, anthems, piano pieces, songs.

Hornstein, Robert von, German composer; b. Donaueschingen, Dec. 6, 1833; d. Munich, July 19, 1890. He studied at the Leipzig Cons.; then went to Munich where he became a teacher at the municipal school of music. He was a close friend of Wagner; composed operas in a Romantic vein; one of these, *Adam und Eva,* was produced in Munich in 1870; other works are a ballet, *Der Blumen Rache;* incidental music to Shakespeare's *As You Like It;* many songs.

Horowitz, Vladimir, fabulous Russian pianist; b. Berdichev, Oct. 1, 1904. He received his early training in piano with Sergei Tarnowsky (1914–19); then studied with Felix Blumenfeld. He made his concert debut at Kharkov at the age of 17, marking the beginning of a remarkable career; played numerous concerts in Russia before leaving for a European tour in 1924. He made his American debut on Jan. 12, 1928 as soloist with the New York Philharmonic in Tchaikovsky's First Piano Concerto with Thomas Beecham conducting, producing an indelible impression; then played annual recitals in the U.S.; appeared as soloist with major orchestras, rapidly earning the reputation of a piano virtuoso of the highest caliber, so that his very name became synonymous with pianistic greatness. In 1933 he married Wanda Toscanini, daughter of Arturo Toscanini. In 1938–39 he lived mostly in Switzerland; in 1940 returned to America and settled in New York; he became an American citizen in 1944. He is especially admired for his inspired interpretations of romantic music; his performances of Liszt's and Rachmaninoff's piano concertos are incomparable; among modern composers he prefers works of a lyrical nature; particularly remarkable are his performances of Scriabin's sonatas. On Dec. 9, 1949, he played in Havana, Cuba, the first performance anywhere of Samuel Barber's Piano Sonata. He composed a sparkling piano paraphrase on themes from *Carmen* and made a vertiginous transcription for piano of Sousa's march *Stars and Stripes Forever,* a veritable tour de force of pianistic pyrotechnics, which he occasionally performed as an encore to the delight of his audiences. Owing to a nervous ailment, he interrupted his public appearances for 12 years between 1953 and 1965, but staged a triumphant comeback at Carnegie Hall, N.Y., on May 9, 1965. Subsequently he resumed his career in concert recitals, but not as soloist with orchestras until he appeared after an interval of 25 years in Carnegie Hall, N.Y., playing Rachmaninoff's Third Piano Concerto with the N.Y. Philharmonic, Eugene Ormandy conducting, on Jan. 8, 1978, to mark the 50th anniversary of his American debut.

BIBLIOGRAPHY: Abram Chasins, *Speaking of Pianists* (N.Y., 1958; pp. 136–44); Harold Schonberg, *The Great Pianists* (N.Y., 1963).

Horsley, Charles Edward, English organist and composer; b. London, Dec. 16, 1822; d. New York, Feb. 28, 1876. He was a pupil of his father, **William Horsley;** then studied with Moscheles. In Leipzig he became friendly with Mendelssohn, who instructed him in composition. Upon his return to London, he obtained a post as organist of St. John's; wrote the oratorios *David, Joseph,* and *Gideon;* incidental music to Milton's *Comus.* In 1862 he went to Australia, and served as organist in Melbourne. There he wrote an ode, *Euterpe,* for the opening of the Town Hall (1870). He eventually settled in New York. His *Text Book of Harmony* was publ. posthumously (1876).

Horsley, William, English organist and composer; father of **Charles Edward Horsley;** b. London, Nov. 15, 1774; d. there, June 12, 1858. He had little formal study, but his friendly association with John Callcott, the composer of glees, led him to try his hand at the composition of light vocal pieces. He married Callcott's daughter in 1813. He was instrumental in the establishment of the choral society "Concentores Sodales" (1798–1847), for which he wrote many anthems, catches, and glees; was also a founder of the Philharmonic Society of London (1813); occupied various posts as church organist. Many of his songs (*See the Chariot at Hand, O Nightingale,* etc.) were frequently sung. He further publ. 5 albums of glees (1801–07), hymn tunes (1820), canons, piano pieces, etc.; also *An Explanation of Musical Intervals and of the Major and Minor Scales* (1825); *Introduction to Harmony and Modulation* (1847); edited Callcott's glees, with a biography and analysis; brought out the 1st book of Byrd's *Cantiones Sacrae.*

Horst, Anthon van der, Dutch composer, conductor and organist; b. Amsterdam, June 20, 1899; d. Hilversum, March 7, 1965. He studied composition with Bernard Zweers, and piano and organ with de Pauw at the Amsterdam Cons.; won the Prix d'Excellence for organ in 1917. He then served as an organist of the English Reformed Church in Amsterdam (1918–41) and of the Netherlands Protestant League in Hilversum; in 1936 he was appointed prof. of organ and conducting at the Amsterdam Cons. In some of his organ and piano works he adopted the scale of alternating tones and semitones known in Holland as "Pijper's scales" which he called "modus conjunctus."

WORKS: 3 symphonies: No. 1 (1935–37); No. 2, *Divertimento pittorale* (1954); No. 3, with chorus (1959); *Choros I-VIII,* 8 separate works for soloists, chorus and orch., based on various texts (1931–58); *Rembrandt Cantata* (1956); *Nocturne funèbre* for orch. (1950–51); *Concerto per Organo Romantico* for organ and orch. (1952); *Concerto spagnuolo* for violin and orch. (1953; performed posthumously in Groningen, May 26, 1965); *3 Etudes symphoniques* (1954); *Concerto in Baroque Style* for organ and strings (1960); *Reflexions sonores* for orch. (1962); *Ricercar svelato* for brass, organ and strings (1963); *Salutation joyeuse* for orch. (1964); *Hymn* for solo soprano (1935); Suite for Solo Cello (1941); *Suite in modo conjuncto* for organ (1943); *Partita diverse sopra Psalm 8* for organ (1947); *Tema con variazioni in modo conjuncto* for piano (1950); *Sonata in modo conjuncto* for 2 pianos (1951); Suite for 31-tone organ (1953); *Theme, Variations and Fugue* for flute, violin and viola (1957); Sextet for Flute and Strings; songs; choruses.

Horszowski, Mieczyslaw, Polish pianist; b. Lwów, June 23, 1892. He studied with Melcer before going to Vienna, where he became a pupil of Leschetizky; made his first public appearance at the age of 10, playing the First Piano Concerto of Beethoven with the Warsaw Philharmonic; then began extensive concert tours in Europe; played joint recitals with Casals. At several concerts he played all of Bach's preludes and fugues of the *Well-Tempered Clavier;* in 1954 he gave a series of recitals in New York in programs including all piano works of Beethoven.

Horton, Austin Asadata Dafora, Nigerian composer; b. Freetown, Sierra Leone, West Africa, Aug. 4, 1890; d. New York, March 4, 1965. As a youth, he became deeply interested in African folk dance festivals and studied the culture of many African tribes. He then went to Europe and organized a dance group in Germany. He settled in the U.S. in 1921, devoting himself to the propagation of African art, coaching singers, dancers and drummers for performance of African dances. He utilized authentic African melorhythms in several of his stage spectacles for which he also arranged the musical score. Of these, *Kykunkor, the Witch,* produced at the Unity Theatre Studio in N.Y. on May 7, 1934, attracted considerable attention. He also produced a dance drama *Tunguru.*

Horvat, Stanko, Croatian composer; b. Zagreb, March 12, 1930. He studied composition with Šulek at the Zagreb Academy of Music, graduating in 1956; then took a course with Tony Aubin at the Paris Cons. and private composition lessons with René Leibowitz (1958–59); returning to Yugoslavia, he was appointed to the music faculty of the Zagreb Academy. In his style of composition he traversed successively a period of neo-Classical mannerisms, serialism in its dodecaphonic aspect, aleatory expressionism, and sonorism; eventually he returned to a median technique of pragmatic modernism.

WORKS: a television opera *Three Legends* (Salzburg, 1971); a ballet *Izabranik (The Chosen One,* 1961); Sinfonietta (1954); Symphony (1956); *Concerto rustico* for strings (1958); Piano Concerto (1966; Zagreb, April 3, 1967); *Choral* for strings (1967); *Taches* for piano and chamber orch. (1968; Graz, Sept. 26, 1968); *Hymnus* for orch. (1969); *Perpetuum mobile* for string orch. (1971; Zagreb, May 9, 1971); *Krik (The Cry)*, after García Lorca, for mezzo-soprano and orch. (1968; Zagreb, March 19, 1969); a cantata, *Jama (The Pit,* 1971; Zagreb, Dec. 18, 1971); *Choral Variations* for string quartet (1953); *Contrasts* for string quartet (1963); *Rondo* for string quartet (1967); *Variants* for piano (1965); *Sonnant* for piano (1970).

Horvath, Josef Maria, Austrian composer of Hungarian descent; b. Pécs, Dec. 20, 1931. He studied piano and composition at the Liszt Academy in Budapest; in 1956 he went to Salzburg, where he studied composition and took instruction in electronic music. Subsequently he became a composition teacher at the Salzburg Mozarteum.
WORKS: *Entropia,* a symphony in 5 movements (1961); Trio for Violin, Horn and Piano (1963); a group of works under the generic title *Redundance,* for wind octet, string quartet, or both played together (1970); *Origines* for chamber group (1975).

Horwitz, Karl, Austrian composer; b. Vienna, Jan. 1, 1884; d. Salzburg, Aug. 18, 1925. He studied with Arnold Schoenberg, and adopted an atonal idiom. He was active in organizing the Donaueschingen Festivals (from 1921) and in other societies devoted to modern music; among his works are a symphonic poem, *Vom Tode;* 2 string quartets, and several song cycles. In 1924 he suffered a loss of hearing, as a result of disease, and died shortly afterwards.

Hosmer, Elmer Samuel, American organist and composer; b. Clinton, Mass., March 21, 1862; d. Pawtucket, R.I., April 25, 1945. He studied music in Boston with George Whiting, Percy Goetschius, and others; occupied various positions as organist; composed cantatas (*Pilgrims of 1620, The Man Without a Country,* etc.) and many anthems.

Hosmer, Lucius, American composer; b. South Acton, Mass., Aug. 14, 1870; d. Jefferson, N.H., May 9, 1935. He studied with Chadwick at the New England Cons.; lived mostly in Boston; wrote a 'romantic comic opera' *The Rose of the Alhambra* (Rochester, 1905; N.Y., Feb. 4, 1907); a comic opera, *The Walking Delegate* (revised and produced under the title *The Koreans*); various light pieces for orch.: *On Tiptoe, Chinese Wedding Procession; Southern Rhapsody, Northern Rhapsody, Ethiopian Rhapsody,* etc.; also songs.

Hostinský, Otakar, Czech writer on music; b. Martinoves, Jan. 2, 1847; d. Prague, Jan. 19, 1910. He studied at the Univ. of Prague and later in Munich; became instructor of esthetics and history of music at Charles Univ. in Prague (1877); prof. in 1892.
WRITINGS: *Das Musikalisch-Schöne und das Gesammtkunstwerk vom Standpunkt der formalen Ästhetik* (1877), as a philosophical reply to Hanslick's famous book (in Czech as *Hostinského esthetika,* Prague, 1921); *Die Lehre von den musikalischen Klängen* (1879); *Über die Entwicklung und den jetzigen Stand der tschechischen Oper* (1880); *Über die Bedeutung der praktischen Ideen Herbarts für die allgemeine Ästhetik* (1883); his articles on Smetana were

collected and publ. in 1901 (new ed., 1941); he wrote numerous articles on Czech folksongs, etc. A jubilee pamphlet was publ. in Prague on the occasion of his 60th birthday (1907).

Hothby, John, English music theorist; b. about 1415; d. probably in England, Nov. 6, 1487. He was a student at Oxford; was a member of the Carmelite order; lived in Florence, Italy, about 1440, and was known there under the Italianized name **Ottobi;** was then in Lucca (1468-86), where he taught in canonic schools. In 1486 he was recalled to England by Henry VII.
WRITINGS: about 12 treatises: *Ars musica; Regulae super proportionem; De cantu figurato; Regulae super contrapunctum; Regulae de monochordo manuali; Quid est proportio; Tractatus quarundam regularum artis musices;* etc. His *La Calliopea legale* was publ. by Coussemaker in *Histoire de l'harmonie au moyen-âge; Regulae super proportionem, De cantu figurato* and *Regulae super contrapunctum* in Coussemaker's *Scriptores de musica* (vol. 3).
BIBLIOGRAPHY: U. Kornmüller, "Johann Hothby . . . ," *Kirchenmusikalisches Jahrbuch* (1893); H. Schmidt, *Die 'Calliopea legale' des J. Hothby* (Leipzig, 1897).

Hotter, Hans, German operatic baritone; b. Offenbach, Jan. 19, 1909. He studied voice in Munich; subsequently was engaged at the German Theater in Prague (1932-34) and at the Hamburg State Opera (1934-37); he then sang at most major opera theaters in Europe and America, including La Scala of Milan, Covent Garden of London, the Teatro Colón of Buenos Aires, the Paris Opéra, and the Chicago Opera; he also gave concerts as a soloist. From 1950 to 1954 he was a member of the Metropolitan Opera in New York. He was particularly acclaimed for his Wagnerian roles; he sang the role of Wotan at the Bayreuth Festival.
BIBLIOGRAPHY: B. W. Wessling, *Hans Hotter* (Bremen, 1966).

Hotteterre, a family of French musicians: **Nicolas Hotteterre** (b. 1637; d. Paris, May 10, 1694), a hurdy-gurdy player; his brother **Martin** (d. 1712), also a hurdy-gurdy player and a performer at the court ballets; **Louis Hotteterre** (d. 1719), son of Nicolas, who played the flute at the French court for 50 years (1664-1714); his brother **Nicolas Hotteterre** (d. Paris, Dec. 4, 1727), who (like his brother) played flute and oboe in Lully's orchestra at the court of Louis XIV; **Jacques Hotteterre** (b. c.1684; d. Paris, July 16, 1762), surnamed 'le Romain' evidently owing to his long sojourns in Rome, popularized the transverse (German) flute at the French court and published several manuals on that instrument and others: *Principes de la flûte traversière ou flûte d'Allemagne, de la flûte à bec ou flûte douce et du hautbois* (Paris, 1707; sometimes attributed to his cousin **Louis;** the 1728 ed. was reprinted in facsimile, Kassel, 1941); *Méthode pour la musette* (1738); *L'Art de préluder sur la flûte traversière, sur la flûte à bec, etc.* (Paris, 1712; 2nd ed. under the title, *Méthode pour apprendre . . . ,* c.1765); also wrote sonatas, duos, trios, suites, *rondes (chansons à danser),* and minuets for flute.

BIBLIOGRAPHY: J. A. Carlez, *Les Hotteterre* (Caen, 1877); E. Thoinan, *Les Hotteterre et les Chédeville* (Paris, 1894); N. Mauger, *Les Hotteterre, nouvelles recherches* (Paris, 1912); H. M. Fitzgibbon, "Of Flutes and Soft Recorders," *Musical Quarterly* (April 1934).

Houdard, Georges, French authority on Gregorian chant; b. Neuilly-sur-Seine, March 30, 1860; d. Paris, Feb. 28, 1913. He studied with L. Hillemacher and with Massenet at the Paris Cons.; then devoted himself exclusively to old church music; publ. valuable treatises.
WRITINGS: *L'Art dit grégorien d'après la notation neumatique* (1897); *L'Evolution de l'art musical et l'art grégorien* (1902); *Aristoxène de Tarente* (1905); *La Rythmique intuitive* (1906); *Textes théoriques; Vademecum de la rythmique grégorienne des Xᵉ et XIᵉ siècles* (1912); also wrote some sacred music (a Requiem, offertories, elevations, etc.).

Houdoy (Hudoy), Jules François Aristide, French writer on music; b. Lille, Dec. 12, 1818; d. there, Jan. 28, 1883. He was President of the "Société des Sciences et des Arts" at Lille; author of *Histoire artistique de la cathédrale de Cambrai* (Lille, 1880), a very valuable work as regards the music of the 15th century.

Houseley, Henry, organist and composer; b. Sutton-in-Ashfield, England, Sept. 20, 1852; d. Denver, Colo., March 13, 1925. He studied at the Royal College of Organists in London; then filled various posts as church organist. In 1888 he emigrated to the U.S., settling in Denver, where he was active in many musical and cultural fields; produced there several light operas: *The Juggler* (May 23, 1895); *Pygmalion* (Jan. 30, 1912); *Narcissus and Echo* (Jan. 30, 1912); also wrote a cantata, *Omar Khayyám,* which was performed in Denver on June 1, 1916.
BIBLIOGRAPHY: E. E. Hipsher, *American Opera and Its Composers* (Philadelphia, 1934; pp. 268–69).

Housman, Rosalie, American composer; b. San Francisco, June 25, 1888; d. New York, Oct. 28, 1949. She studied with Arthur Foote in Boston; also took lessons in N.Y. with Ernest Bloch; composed *Color Sequence* for soprano and small orch.; women's choruses; children's pieces; songs.

Hovhaness (former spelling **Hovaness**), **Alan,** American composer of Armenian descent (father, Armenian; mother, Scottish); b. Somerville, Mass., March 8, 1911. He studied piano with Heinrich Gebhard; composition with Frederick Converse; also took lessons with Bohuslav Martinu. He traveled to Japan in 1960; to France and Germany in 1961; and to Russia in 1965. While mastering the traditional technique of composition, he became fascinated by Indian and other Oriental musical systems; from his earliest works, he made use of Armenian melorythmic patterns. As a result, he gradually evolved an individual type of art in which quasi-Oriental cantillation and a curiously monodic texture became the mainstay. By dint of ceaseless repetition of themes and relentless dynamic tension a definite impression is created of originality; the atmo-

spheric effects often suggest Impressionistic exoticism.
WORKS: 33 symphonies: No. 1, *Exile Symphony* (1937); No. 2, *Mysterious Mountain* (1955); No. 3 (1956); No. 4 for band (1958); No. 5 (1953; revised 1963); No. 6, *Celestial Gate,* for small orch. (1959); No. 7, *Nanga Parvat* for band (1959); Nos. 1–7 were destroyed in his symphonic *auto-da-fé* of 1940; No. 8, *Arjuna* (1947; Madras, Feb. 1, 1960); No. 9, *St. Vartan* (1950); No. 10 (1959); No. 11, *All Men Are Brothers* (1960); No. 12, *Chorale* (1960); No. 13; No. 14, *Ararat,* for band (1962); No. 15, *Silver Pilgrimage* (1962); No. 16 for strings and Korean percussion instruments (Seoul, Korea, Jan. 26, 1963); No. 17, *Symphony for Metal Orchestra* (commissioned by the American Metallurgical Congress; Cleveland, Oct. 23, 1963); No. 18, *Circe* (1964); No. 19, *Vishnu* (N.Y., June 2, 1967); No. 20, *Three Journeys to a Holy Mountain,* for concert band; No. 21, *Etchmiadzin* (1970); No. 22, *City of Light* (1971); No. 23, *Ani,* for concert band (1972); No. 24, *Majnun,* for chorus and orch. (1973); No. 25, *Odysseus,* for chamber orch. (1973); No. 26, *Consolation* (1975); No. 27 (1975); No. 28 (1976); No. 29, for solo baritone horn and orch. (1976); No. 30 (1976); No. 31, for strings (1976); No. 32, for small orch. (1977); No. 33, for small orch. (1977–78); 2 operas, 2 quasi-operas and one pseudo-opera, respectively: *The Blue Flame* (San Antonio, Texas, Dec. 15, 1959); *Spirit of the Avalanche* (Tokyo, Feb. 15, 1963); *Wind Drum* (Union College, Gatlinburg, Tenn., Aug. 23, 1964); *Pilate* (Pepperdine College, Los Angeles, June 26, 1966); and *The Travelers* (Foothill College, Calif., April 22, 1967); other works are: 2 *Armenian Rhapsodies* for strings (1944–45); *Elibris,* for flute and strings (San Francisco, Jan. 26, 1950); *Lousadzak (Coming of Light),* for piano and strings (Boston, Feb. 4, 1945); Concerto for Trumpet and Strings (N.Y., June 17, 1945); *Sosi* for violin, piano, percussion and strings (N.Y., March 6, 1949); *Arevakal* for orch. (N.Y., Feb. 18, 1952); *Janabar,* 5 hymns for violin, trumpet, piano and strings (N.Y., March 11, 1951); Concerto for Orch. (Louisville, Feb. 20, 1954); *Ad Lyram,* for orch. (Houston, March 12, 1957); *Meditation on Zeami,* symph. poem (N.Y., Oct. 5, 1964); *Ukiyo-Floating World,* symph. poem (Salt Lake City, Jan. 30, 1965); *The Holy City* for orch. (Portland, Maine, April 11, 1967); *And God Created Great Whales* for humpback whale solo (on tape) and orch. (N.Y., June 11, 1970); *The Way of Jesus,* a folk oratorio (St. Patrick's Cathedral, N.Y., Feb. 23, 1975); Violin Concerto (National Symph. Orch. in Wolf Trap Farm Park near Washington, Yehudi Menuhin, soloist, July 3, 1976); *Rubaiyat* for narrator, accordion and orch. (N.Y., May 20, 1977); much chamber music; piano pieces.

Hovland, Egil, Norwegian composer; b. Mysen, Oct. 18, 1924. He studied organ and composition at the Oslo Cons. (1946–49), later studying privately with Bjarne Brustad (1951–52, in Oslo), Vagn Holmboe (1954, in Copenhagen), Aaron Copland (1957, at Tanglewood) and Dallapiccola (1959, in Florence). In Norway he was active as a music critic and as an organist at a church in Fredrikstad. He cultivates a peculiarly Scandinavian type of neo-Classical polyphony, but is apt to use serial techniques.

WORKS: a church opera, *Brunnen* (*The Well*, 1971–72); Passacaglia and Fugue for string orch. (1949); *Festival Overture* (1951); 3 symphonies: No. 1, *Symphonia Veris* (*Symphony of Spring*, 1952–53); No. 2 (1954–55); No. 3, for narrator, chorus and orch. (1969–70); Suite for Orch. (1954); Concertino for 3 Trumpets and Strings (1954–55); *Music for 10 Instruments* (1957); Suite for Flute and Strings (1959); *Festival Overture* for wind orch. (1962); *Lamenti* for orch. (Oslo, April 24, 1964); *Rorate* for 5 sopranos, organ, chamber orch. and tape (1966–67); *Missa vigilate* for soprano, baritone, chorus, 2 female dancers, organ and tape (1967); *Mass to the Risen Christ* for chorus and instruments (1968); *Rapsodi 69* for orch. (1969); *All Saints' Mass* for soprano, chorus, organ and instruments (1970); *Den vakreste rosen* (*The Most Beautiful Rose*), after Hans Christian Andersen, for narrator, 4 sopranos, organ and orch. (1970); Trombone Concerto (1972); *Missa Verbi* for chorus, organ and instruments (1972–73); Violin Concerto (1974); *Noël-Variations* for orch. (1975); Suite for flute and Piano (1950); *Motus* for solo flute (1961); *Song of Songs* for soprano, violin, percussion and piano (1962–63); *Magnificat* for alto, flute and harp (1964); *Varianti* for 2 pianos (1964); Piano Trio (1965); Wind Quintet (1965); *Elemento* for organist and 2 assistants (1965, revised 1966); Variations for Oboe and Piano (1968–69); *I DAG* for chorus and instruments (1974); numerous sacred works and organ pieces.

Howard, John Tasker, eminent American writer on music; b. Brooklyn, Nov. 30, 1890; d. West Orange, N.Y., Nov. 20, 1964. He attended Williams College in Williamstown, Mass.; then studied composition with Howard Brockway and Mortimer Wilson. He then devoted himself primarily to musical journalism; was managing editor of the *Musician* (1919–22); served as educational director of the Ampico Corporation (1922–28); then edited the music section of *McCall's Magazine* (1928–30) and *Cue* (1936–38). From 1940 to 1956 he was the curator of the Americana Music Collection at the N.Y. Public Library, which he enriched to a great extent. His major achievement was the publication of several books and monographs on American music and musicians.

WRITINGS: *Our American Music* (N.Y., 1931; 4 editions, the last one posthumous, 1965); *Stephen Foster, America's Troubadour* (N.Y., 1934; revised, 1953); *Ethelbert Nevin* (N.Y., 1935); *Our Contemporary Composers, American Music in the 20th Century* (1941); *This Modern Music* (N.Y., 1942; new edition by James Lyons, 1957, under the title *Modern Music*); *The World's Great Operas* (N.Y., 1948); *A Short History of Music in America* (N.Y., 1957; with G. K. Bellows). He was also a composer of modest, but respectable attainments. He wrote a piece for piano and orch., entitled *Fantasy on a Choral Theme* (New Jersey Orch., Orange, N.Y., Feb. 20, 1929); also *Foster Sonatina* for violin and piano; piano pieces and some songs.

BIBLIOGRAPHY: G. K. Bellows, "John Tasker Howard," *Notes* (Sept. 1957; with a complete list of his published writings).

Howard, Kathleen, contralto; b. Clifton, Canada, July 17, 1884; d. Hollywood, Aug. 15, 1956. She studied in New York with Bouhy and in Paris with Jean de Reszke; sang at the Metz Opera (1907–09); then at Darmstadt (1909–12); at Covent Garden in London (1913); with the Century Opera in N.Y. (1914–15). She made her first appearance with the Metropolitan Opera in *The Magic Flute* (Nov. 20, 1916); remained on the staff until 1928. After her retirement from the stage, she was engaged in magazine work; was fashion editor of *Harper's Bazaar* (1928–33); publ. an autobiography, *Confessions of an Opera Singer* (N.Y., 1918). She married Edward Kelley Baird on June 27, 1916.

Howe, Mary, American composer; b. Richmond, Va., April 4, 1882; d. Washington, Sept. 14, 1964. She studied at the Peabody Cons. in Baltimore; was a pupil of Gustav Strube (composition) and Ernest Hutcheson (piano); in 1915, settled in Washington, where she played a prominent part in musical organizations. She was a vice-president of the Friends of Music of the Library of Congress; was a member of the Board of Directors of the National Symphony Orch.

WORKS: Violin Sonata (1922); Suite for String Quartet and Piano (1923); *Sand,* for orch. (1928); *Dirge,* for orch. (1931); *Castellana,* for 2 pianos and orch. (1935); *Spring Pastoral,* for solo violin and 13 instruments (1936); *Stars and Whimsy,* for 15 instruments (1937); *Potomac,* orchestral suite (1940); *Agreeable Overture* (1949); *Rock,* symphonic poem (Vienna, Feb. 15, 1955). Choral works: *Chain Gang Song* (1925); *Prophecy, 1792* (1943).

BIBLIOGRAPHY: M. Goss, "Mary Howe," in *Modern Music Makers* (N.Y., 1952).

Howell, Dorothy, English pianist and composer; b. Handsworth, Feb. 25, 1898. She studied at the Royal Academy of Music with Matthay (piano) and J. B. McEwen (composition); from 1924 to 1970 taught music theory there. Among her works are a piano concerto, songs and choruses.

Howells, Herbert, prominent English composer; b. Lydney, Gloucestershire, Oct. 17, 1892. He studied at the Royal College of Music in London with Stanford, Parry and others (1912–17); and in 1920 was appointed instructor there. He traveled to South Africa, Canada and the U.S. (1922–23); in 1936 succeeded Holst as music director at St. Paul's Girls' School, remaining there until 1962; was a prof. of music at the Univ. of London (1954–64). In 1953 he was awarded the Order of Commander of the British Empire.

WORKS: Piano Concerto (London, July 10, 1914); orchestral suite, *The B's* (1915); *Sine nomine* for voices and orch. (1922); Second Piano Concerto (1924); *A Kent Yeoman's Wooing Song* for voices and orch. (1933); Cello Concerto (1937); *Hymnus Paradisi,* for voices and orch. (1951); *Missa Sabrinensis* (Worcester Festival, Sept. 7, 1954); *An English Mass* (1960); many motets, organ pieces, etc.

BIBLIOGRAPHY: H. J. Foss, "Herbert Howells," *Musical Times* (Feb. 1930); W. Sutton, "The Organ Music of Herbert Howells," *Musical Times* (1971).

Howes, Frank Stewart, English writer on music; b. Oxford, April 2, 1891; d. Witney, near Oxford, Sept. 28, 1974. He studied at St. John College and at the Royal College of Music in London. From 1943 to 1960 he was chief music critic for the *Times* (London); from 1927 to 1945 he edited the *Journal of the English Folk Dance and Song Society.* He also explored problems of musical psychology. In 1954 he was awarded the Order of Commander of the British Empire.

WRITINGS: *The Borderland of Music and Psychology* (1926); *William Byrd* (1928); *Appreciation of Music* (1928); *A Key to the Art of Music* (1935); *A Key to Opera* (in collaboration with Ph. Hope-Wallace; 1939); *The Music of William Walton* (2 vols.; 1942); *Full Orchestra* (1942); *Man, Mind and Music* (1948); *Music: 1945-50* (1951); *The Music of Ralph Vaughan Williams* (1954); *Music and Its Meanings* (1958); *The English Musical Renaissance* (1966); *Folk Music of Britain and Beyond* (London, 1969).

Howland, William Legrand, American composer; b. Asbury Park, N.J., 1873; d. at his cottage, Douglas Manor, Long Island, N.Y., July 26, 1915. He studied with Philip Scharwenka in Berlin, and lived most of his life in Europe. His one-act opera, *Sarrona,* to his own libretto, was produced in Italian in Bruges, Belgium (Aug. 3, 1903) and subsequently had a number of performances in Italy; it was staged in N.Y. (in English) on Feb. 8, 1910; in Philadelphia (in German) on March 23, 1911. He wrote another opera, *Nita;* 2 oratorios (*The Resurrection* and *Ecce Homo*), and some choral works.

Hoyer, Karl, German organist and composer; b. Weissenfels, Saale, Jan. 9, 1891; d. Leipzig, June 12, 1936. He studied at the Leipzig Cons. with Reger, Straube, and Krehl; was organist in Reval (1911), Chemnitz (1912–26), and at the St. Nicholas Church in Leipzig (from 1926); also taught organ and theory at the Leipzig Cons. He wrote about 50 valuable organ works, also selections for organ and string orch.; chamber music; choral works; and songs.

Hřimalý, Adalbert (Vojtech), Czech violinist and composer; b. Pilsen, July 30, 1842; d. Vienna, June 15, 1908. A member of an exceptionally musical family, whose father was an organist, and whose 3 brothers were violinists, he received an early training at home; then studied with Mildner at the Prague Cons. (1855–61); was subsequently active as conductor, composer, and teacher in various towns in Holland, Sweden, and Rumania. He wrote a great number of works, including an opera, *Zaklety princ* (*The Enchanted Prince*; Prague, May 13, 1872).

Hřimalý, Johann (Jan), celebrated violinist and teacher; b. Pilsen, April 13, 1844; d. Moscow, Jan. 24, 1915. Like his older brother **Adalbert,** he studied at the Prague Cons. At the age of 24 he went to Moscow, where he became prof. of violin at the Cons. (1874). He remained in Moscow for 40 years until his death, and was regarded there as a great teacher; 2 generations of Russian violinists studied under him. He also organized a string quartet in Moscow; publ. *Tonleiter-*

studien und Übungen in Doppelgriffen für die Violine (Prague, 1895).

Hřimalý, Otakar, Czech violinist; son of **Adalbert Hřimalý;** b. Cernauti, Rumania, Dec. 20, 1883; d. Prague, July 10, 1945. He studied at the Vienna Cons. In 1909 he went to Moscow upon recommendation of his uncle, **Johann Hřimalý;** prof. at the Moscow Cons., and remained there until 1922; then lived in Rumania; in 1939, went to Prague. He was known not only as a violin teacher, but also as a composer; wrote an opera, 2 symphonies, the symphonic poems *Ganymed* and *Der goldene Topf;* also chamber music and violin pieces.

Hrisanidis (Hrisanide), Alexandre, Rumanian-born composer and pianist of Greek citizenship, living in Holland; b. Petrila, June 15, 1936. He studied at the Bucharest Cons. with Paul Constantinescu, Tudor Ciortea, Zeno Vancea, Mihail Jora and Alfred Mendelsohn (1953–64); continued his studies at the American Cons. in Fontainebleau, France with Nadia Boulanger (1965); attended Darmstadt summer courses in new music (1966–67); then taught at the Bucharest Academy (1959–62) and at the Bucharest Cons. (1962–72); in 1972, he left Rumania; was visiting prof. of music at the Univ. of Oregon (1972–73); in 1974 settled in Holland. To reassert his Greek ancestry, he changed the Rumanian spelling of his last name to Hrisanidis. His music follows constructivist tendencies, with the application of modified serial techniques. In 1965 he won the annual award of the Lili Boulanger Memorial Fund, Boston, for his *Volumes—Inventions* and his clarinet sonata.

WORKS: 2 cantatas, *C'était issu stellaire* for male chorus, organ, 3 trumpets, 4 trombones and percussion (1965; Zagreb, May 16, 1967) and *Les Lumières de la patrie* (1965); *Poem* for orch. (1958; Bucharest, Feb. 8, 1963); *Passacaglia* for Orch. (1959; Cluj, Nov. 25, 1962); *"Vers-Antiqua" (Hommage à Euripide)* for chamber orch. (1960; Hannover, Jan. 28, 1966); Concerto for Orch. (1964); *Ad perpetuam rei memoriam,* 3 pieces for orch. (1966; Bucharest, Dec. 22, 1967); *RO* for orch. (1968); *I-RO-LA-HAI* for voice and orch. (Nuremberg, June 8, 1971); *Sonnets,* concerto for harpsichord and orch. (Hilversum, March 26, 1973); 3 flute sonatas (1956, 1960-62, 1956); Violin Sonata (1957; its 3 movements can be played as separate pieces: *Hommages à Bartók, Enesco* and *Schoenberg*); Trio for Violin, Viola and Bassoon (1958); String Quartet (1958); Clarinet Sonata (1960-62); *Mers-Tefs* for solo violin (1960-68); *Volumes—Inventions* for cello and piano (1963); *Music* for viola and piano (1965); *À la recherche de la verticale* for solo oboe (1965); *M. P.5 (Musique pour 5)* for violin, viola, cello, saxophone (or clarinet) and piano (1966); *Directions* for wind quintet (1967-69); *Première musique pour RA* for piano and tape (1968-69); *Seconde musique pour RA* for piano and tape (1969); *Troisième musique pour RA* for piano, varying percussion instruments and tape, divided into 3 separate pieces: *Das Finale der Unendlichkeit, Vergangenheit schauende Stunde* and *glorreich ist alles* (all composed in 1970); *Quatrième musique pour RA* for piano and tape, in 2 separate pieces: *Maister Manole* and *Blaga* (both written in 1970); *Cinquième musique pour RA* for piano, celesta, harpsichord and tape (1973); *Sixième musique pour RA* for piano, varying instruments and tape, in 3 separate pieces: *Là où ça passe,* "*ZED-UE,*" and *Mnemosyne* (all 1970); *Soliloquium × 11* for string quartet (1970); *Music for 1 to 4 Violins,* quartet for violins (1970); *Chanson sous les étoiles,* duet for flute and oboe (1973); *Du soir venant* for solo bass clarinet (1974–75); *Suite Classique* for piano (1954); *Piano Pieces 1–13* (1955–56); 3 piano sonatas: No. 1 (1955–56; movements can be played independently: *Flames, Duality* and *Study No. 4*); No. 2, *Sonata piccola* (1959); No. 3, *Picasso Sonata* (1956–64); *Desseins espagnols* for prepared piano (1971); *Unda* for organ (1965); songs.

Hristić, Stevan, Serbian composer; b. Belgrade, June 19, 1885; d. there, Aug. 21, 1958. He studied in Leipzig, Rome, Paris and Moscow. Returning to Belgrade, he became conductor of the National Opera Theater; also taught at the Music Academy there. He composed a music drama *Suton* (*Sunset,* 1925), a ballet, *Legend of Okhrid* (1947), and many choral works, of which *Jesen (Autumn)* became fairly popular.

Hrušovský, Ivan, Slovak composer; b. Bratislava, Feb. 23, 1927. In 1947 he began studies of composition with A. Moyzes at the Bratislava Cons.; continued composition studies with Moyzes at the Academy of Musical Arts, graduating in 1957; then joined its faculty. His music represents the common denominator of Central European trends.

WORKS: *Suite Pastorale* for orch. (1955); Piano Concerto (1957); Sinfonietta for 2 string orch. (1959); *The Tatra Poem,* symph. poem (1960); *Hirošima,* cantata (1961–62); *Concertante Overture* for string orch. (1963); *Combinazioni sonorische* for 9 instruments (1963); *Sen o člevĕku (A Dream About a Man),* cantata (1964); *Passacaglia eroica* for orch. (1964); *Musica Nocturna* for string orch. (1971); 2 piano sonatas (1965, 1970); Sonata for Solo Violin (1969); *Sonata in Modo Classico* for solo cymbalom (1976); the electronic tape pieces, *Invocation* (1974) and *Idée Fixe* (1975); choruses.

Hubay, Jenö, celebrated Hungarian violinist; b. Budapest, Sept. 15, 1858; d. Vienna, March 12, 1937. He received his initial training from his father, Karl Hubay, prof. of violin at the Budapest Cons.; gave his first public concert at the age of 11; then studied with Joachim in Berlin (1873–76). His appearance in Paris, at a Pasdeloup concert, attracted the attention of Vieuxtemps, of whom he became a favorite pupil; in 1882 he succeeded Vieuxtemps as prof. at the Brussels Cons. In 1886 he became prof. at the Budapest Cons. (succeeding his father; from 1919 to 1934 he was its director. In Budapest he formed the celebrated Hubay String Quartet. In 1894 he married the Countess Rosa Cebrain. Among his pupils were Vecsey, Szigeti, Telmányi, Eddy Brown, and other renowned violinists. Hubay was a prolific composer.

WORKS: operas (all produced in Budapest): *Alienor* (Dec. 5, 1891); *Le Luthier de Crémone* (Nov. 10, 1894), *A Falu Rossza (The Village Vagabond;* March 20, 1896), *Moosröschen* (Feb. 21, 1903); *Anna Karenina* (Nov. 10, 1923), *Az Álarc (The Mask;* Feb. 26,

1931); 4 symphonies: No. 1 (1885); No. 2, *1914–15* (1915); No. 3, *Vita Nuova,* for soli, chorus, and organ; No. 4, *Petöfi-Sinfonie,* for soli, chorus, and orch.; also *Biedermeyer Suite,* for orch. (1913); 4 violin concertos; 14 pieces for violin and orch., in the Hungarian manner, *Scènes de la Csárda; Sonate romantique,* for violin and piano; also edited the violin études of Kreutzer (1908), Rode, Mayseder, and Saint Lubin (1910).

Hubbell, Frank Allen, American conductor, arranger and composer; b. Denver, Colorado, May 9, 1907. He was taken to California as a child and studied music at the Univ. of Southern Calif., Los Angeles; did some conducting there and conducting with Albert Coates and Vladimir Bakaleinikov. His orchestral compositions are mostly arrangements of Western country ballads.

Hubeau, Jean, French composer and pianist; b. Paris, June 22, 1917. He entered the Paris Cons. at the age of 9; studied piano with Lazare Lévy; composition with Jean and Noël Gallon and Paul Dukas. He won first prize for piano at 13, and for composition at 16; in 1934, at the age of 17, he received the 2nd Grand Prix de Rome with his cantata *La Légende de Roukmani.* He made several European tours as pianist; from 1942 to 1957 he was director of the Cons. of Versailles; afterwards joined the staff of the Paris Cons., teaching a class of chamber music.

WORKS: ballets: *Trois Fables de La Fontaine* (Paris, March 2, 1945), *La Fiancée du diable* (Paris, Dec. 8, 1945), *Un Cœur de diamant ou l'Infante* (Monte Carlo, April 7, 1949); for orch.: *Tableaux hindous* (Paris, Oct. 18, 1936), Violin Concerto (Paris, March 30, 1941), Cello Concerto (Paris, Nov. 28, 1942), *Concerto héroïque,* for piano and orch. (Paris, Dec. 22, 1946); chamber music: Violin Sonata (1941), *Sonatine-Humoresque,* for horn, flute, clarinet, and piano (1942), Sonata for Trumpet and Piano (1943), *Sonate-Caprice* for 2 violins (1944), *Air varié* for clarinet and piano (1961), *Idylle* for flute and piano (1966); a piano sonata, other piano pieces; songs and choral works.

BIBLIOGRAPHY: A. Machabey, *Portraits de trente musiciens français* (Paris, 1949; pp. 97–100).

Huber, Hans, Swiss composer; b. Eppenberg, near Olten, June 28, 1852; d. Locarno, Dec. 25, 1921. He studied at the Leipzig Cons. with Richter, Reinecke, and Wenzel (1870–74); then taught music at Wesserling, at Thann (Alsace), and at Basel; received an honorary degree of *Dr. phil.* from Basel Univ. (1892). In 1896 he became director of the Basel Cons., a post that he held until his death. Huber composed prolifically in all genres; his style combined the rhapsodic form typical of Lisztian technique with simple ballad-like writing. He often used Swiss songs for thematic material. In Switzerland his reputation is very great and his works are frequently performed, but they are virtually unknown elsewhere.

WORKS: the operas, *Weltfrühling* (Basel, March 28, 1894), *Kudrun* (Basel, Jan. 29, 1896), *Der Simplicius* (Basel, 22, 1912), *Die Schöne Bellinda* (Bern, April 2, 1916), and *Frutta di Mare* (Basel, Nov. 24, 1918); 8 symphonies (all except No. 2 performed first in Basel): No. 1, *William Tell* (April 26, 1881), No. 2, *Böcklinsinfonie* (Zürich, July 2, 1900), No. 3, *Heroische* (Nov. 9, 1917), No. 4, *Akademische* (May 23, 1909), No. 5, *Romantische* (Feb. 11, 1906), No. 6 (Nov. 19, 1911), No. 7, *Swiss* (June 9, 1917), No. 8 (Oct. 29, 1921); 4 piano concertos (Basel, 1878, 1891, 1899, 1910); Violin Concerto (1878); Sextet for Piano and Wind Instruments (1900); Quintet for Piano and Wind Instruments (1914); 2 string quintets (1890, 1907); String Quartet; 2 piano quartets; 5 piano trios; 10 violin sonatas; 5 cello sonatas, and a number of piano works, among them 48 preludes and fuges for piano 4 hands.

BIBLIOGRAPHY: E. Refardt, *Hans Huber* (Leipzig, 1906); E. Refardt, *Hans Huber, Beiträge zu einer Biographie* (1922); E. Refardt, *Hans Huber* (Zürich, 1944; supersedes his previous monographs; contains a complete list of works and full bibliography); Gian Bundi, *Hans Huber, Die Persönlichkeit nach Briefen und Erinnerungen* (1925).

Huber, Klaus, Swiss composer; b. Bern, Nov. 30, 1924. He studied with Willy Burkhard at the Zürich Cons. and with Boris Blacher in Berlin.

WORKS: *Oratio Mechtildis* for contralto and chamber orch. (Strasbourg Festival, June 9, 1958) and a cantata for voice and 4 instruments, *Des Engels Anredung an die Seele* (Rome, June 13, 1959); *Alveare vernat* for flute and 12 solo strings (1965); Tenebrae for orch. (1966-67); *James Joyce Music* for harp, horn and chamber orch. (1966-67); *Tempora,* violin concerto (1969-70); *Im Paradies oder Der Alte vom Berge* (1974-75).

Huber, Kurt, eminent Swiss musicologist; b. Chur, Switzerland, Oct. 24, 1893; executed by the Gestapo in Munich, July 13, 1943, for participation in the student protests against the Nazi government. He studied with Sandberger and Kroyer in Munich (*Dr. phil.,* 1917); from 1920, taught at the Munich Univ.; publ. *Ivo de Vento* (Munich, 1918); *Die Doppelmeister des 16. Jahrhunderts* (Munich, 1920); *Der Ausdruck musikalischer Elementarmotive* (1923). From 1925 he devoted himself to collecting and recording old Bavarian folksongs, and publ. them (with Paul Klem).

BIBLIOGRAPHY: W. H. Rubsamen, "Kurt Huber of Munich," *Musical Quarterly* (April 1944); Clara Huber, *Kurt Huber zum Gedächtnis* (Regensburg, 1947). Huber's lectures on musical esthetics were reconstructed, ed. by Otto Ursprung, and publ. as *Musikästhetik* (1954).

Huberman, Bronislaw, famous Polish violinist; b. Czenstochowa, Dec. 19, 1882; d. Corsier-sur-Vevey, Switzerland, June 15, 1947. At a very early age he began to study the violin with Michalowicz, a teacher at the Warsaw Cons.; he then studied with Isidor Lotto; in 1892 he was taken to Berlin, where he studied with Joachim. He made public appearances at the age of 11 in Amsterdam, Brussels, and Paris. Adelina Patti heard him in London and engaged him to appear with her at her farewell concert in Vienna (Jan. 12, 1895); on Jan. 29, 1896 he played Brahms's Violin Concerto in Vienna; Brahms, who was present, commended him warmly. Huberman toured the U.S. in 1896-97;

many world tours followed; he gave a series of 14 concerts in Paris (1920), 10 in Vienna (1924), 8 in Berlin (1926); toured America again in 1937. At a concert arranged on May 16, 1909 by the city of Genoa for the sufferers of the Messina earthquake, Huberman was honored by an invitation to play upon Paganini's Guarneri violin (preserved in the Museum of Genoa). He was teacher of a master class at the Vienna State Academy (1934-36); in 1936 he organized a new Palestine Symph. Orch., consisting chiefly of Jewish musicians who had lost their positions in Europe. He came to the U.S. in 1940; returned to Europe after the war. He publ. *Aus der Werkstatt des Virtuosen* (Vienna, 1912); *Mein Weg zu Paneuropa* (1925).

BIBLIOGRAPHY: *An Orchestra Is Born. The Founding of the Palestine Orchestra as Reflected in Bronislaw Huberman's Letters, Speeches, and Articles* (Tel Aviv, 1969); H. Goetz, *Bronislaw Huberman and the Unity of Europe* (Rome, 1967).

Hubert, Nicolai, Russian conductor and pedagogue; b. St. Petersburg, March 19, 1840; d. Moscow, Oct. 8, 1888. He studied with his father; then at the St. Petersburg Cons. (1863) with Zaremba and Rubinstein. In 1869 he was in Odessa as opera conductor; in 1870 engaged as prof. of music theory at the Moscow Cons.; he succeeded Nicholas Rubinstein as its director in 1881, resigning in 1883. Hubert also wrote music criticism in Moscow newspapers.

Huberti, Gustave-Léon, Belgian composer; b. Brussels, April 14, 1843; d. Schaerbeek, June 28, 1910. He studied at the Brussels Cons., where he won the Prix de Rome in 1865 for his cantata *La Fille de Jephté.* He was director of Mons Cons. (1874-78); then conductor in Antwerp and Brussels; in 1899, appointed prof. at the Brussels Cons.; director of the Music School of St.-Josse-ten-Noodle-Schaerbeek. In 1891 he was elected a member of the Belgian Academy.

WORKS: 3 oratorios, *Een Laatste Zonnestraal* (1874), *Bloemardinne,* and *Willem van Oranjes dood;* the dramatic poem *Verlichting (Fiat lux),* for soli, chorus, organ, and orch.; the symph. poem *Kinderlust en Leed,* for chorus and orch.; *Symphonie funèbre; Suite romantique; In den Garade; Triomffeest,* with organ; also various festival marches, etc.; vocal soli with orchestral accompaniment; numerous French, Flemish, and German songs with piano; an *Andante et intermezzo,* for 4 flutes and orch.; a piano concerto; compositions for the piano *(Étude, Conte d'enfant, Tarentelle, Impromptu, Historiette, Étude rythmique,* and *Valse lente);* a men's chorus, *Van Maerlantszang;* publ. a book, *Histoire de la musique religieuse des Italiens et des Néerlandais* (Brussels, 1873).

Huberty, Albert, Belgian operatic bass; b. Seraing-sur-Meuse, Feb. 2, 1879; d. Nieuport-les-Bains, March 10, 1955. He studied in Brussels; sang in Belgium, Holland, and England; then in Montreal (1909-13). He made his Paris debut at the Opéra-Comique on May 20, 1915, as Roméo; thereafter, sang 62 different roles there.

Hucbald (Hugbaldus, Ubaldus, Uchubaldus), Flemish monk and musical theorist; b. at or near Tournai, c.840; d. Saint-Amand, near Tournai, June 20, 930. He was a pupil of his uncle Milo, director of the singing school at Saint-Amand; then director of a similar school at Nevers (860); subsequently returned to Saint-Amand and succeeded his uncle. The following works are printed under his name in Gerbert's *Scriptores* (vol. I): *De Harmonica institutione; Musica enchiriadis* (gives the earliest detailed account of the beginnings of polyphonic music and of the Daseian notation, in which the Greek aspirate sign is used in various combinations and positions to produce 18 symbols indicating that many pitches); *Scholia enchiriadis;* fragments entitled *Alia musica;* and *Commemoratio brevis de tonis et psalmis modulandis.* However, it has been established (by W. Mühlmann, in *Die 'Alia Musica';* Leipzig, 1914) that Hucbald was not the author of *Musica enchiriadis.*

BIBLIOGRAPHY: C. E. H. de Coussemaker, *Memoire sur Hucbald et sur ses traités de musique* (1814); J. F. Rowbotham, *History of Music* (vol. III, p. 366 ff.); Ph. Spitta, "Die Musica enchiriadis und ihr Zeitalter," *Vierteljahrsschrift für Musikwissenschaft* (vol. 5, pp. 443–82 and vol. 6, pp. 293–309); R. Schlecht, German transl. of the *Musica enchiriadis,* in *Monatshefte für Musikgeschichte* (1874–76); H. Riemann, *Geschichte der Musiktheorie* (Leipzig, 1898); E. J. Grutchfield, "Hucbald, A Millenary Commemoration," *Musical Times* (1930; 2 installments); A. H. Fox-Strangways, "A Tenth Century Manual," *Music & Letters* (1932); J. Handschin, "Etwas Greifbares über Hucbald." *Acta Musicologica* 7; R. Weakland, "Hucbald as Musician and Theorist," *Musical Quarterly* (Jan. 1956).

Hudson, Frederick, English musicologist; b. Gateshead, Durham, Jan. 16, 1913. He studied with Edward Bairstow at the University of Durham and with Gordon Slater at Lincoln Cathedral; specialized as an organist; received the degree of Bachelor of Music at the University of Durham in 1941, and Mus. Dr. in 1950. He served as organist and choirmaster at Alnwick (1941–48); was lecturer in music at King's College, Univ. of Durham; at the Univ. of Newcastle upon Tyne (1949–70); was subsequently reader in music there. He edited works by Bach, Handel, Giovanni Gabrieli, William Byrd and others for the new editions of their works; contributed important papers dealing with watermarks of undated manuscripts and prints, making use of beta-radiography with Carbon-14 sources; also compiled a catalogue of the works of Charles Villiers Stanford (*Music Review,* May, 1976); contributed to the 6th edition of *Grove's Dictionary of Music and Musicians.*

Hüe, Georges-Adolphe, French composer; b. Versailles, May 6, 1858; d. Paris, June 7, 1948. He was a pupil in the Paris Cons. of Reber and Paladilhe; took first Grand Prix de Rome in 1879, and the Prix Crescent in 1881; lived in Paris as teacher and composer; member (succeeding Saint-Saëns) of the Académie des Beaux-Arts (1922).

WORKS: the operas *Les Pantins* (Opéra-Comique, Dec. 28, 1881), *Le Roi de Paris* (Opéra, April 26, 1901), *Titania,* after Shakespeare (Opéra-Comique, Jan. 20, 1903), *Le Miracle* (Opéra, Dec. 30, 1910), *Dans l'ombre de la cathédrale,* after Blasco Ibañez (Opéra-

Comique, Dec. 7, 1921), *Riquet à la houppe,* after Perrault (Opéra-Comique, Dec. 21, 1928); the ballet *Cœur brisé* (Paris, 1890); pantomime, *Siang Sin* (Opéra, March 19, 1924); *Rübezahl,* symphonic legend in 3 parts (Concerts Colonne, 1886); "féerie dramatique," *La Belle au bois dormant* (Paris, 1894); *Résurrection,* "épisode sacré" (1892); *Le Berger,* ballade and fantaisie for violin and orch. (1893); Symphony; *Rêverie* and *Sérénade* for small orch.; *Romance* for violin and orch.; choral works, and songs of more than average merit (6 songs from Heine's *Lyrisches Intermezzo; Croquis d'Orient; Chansons printanières; Berceuse pour les gueux; Deux chansons,* etc.).

Hueffer, Francis, English author and music critic; b. Münster, May 22, 1843; d. London, Jan. 19, 1889. He studied philology and music in London, Paris, Berlin, and Leipzig; received a Dr. phil. degree from Göttingen Univ. for his first publication (1869), a critical edition of the works of Guillem de Cabestant, troubadour of the 12th century. In 1869 he settled in London as a writer on music, and from 1878 was music critic of the *Times.* He publ. *Richard Wagner and the Music of the Future* (1874), *The Troubadours: a History of Provençal Life and Literature in the Middle Ages* (1878), *Musical Studies* (1880; reprints of his articles from the *Times* and *Fortnightly Review,* Italian transl., Milan, 1883), *Italian and Other Studies* (1883), *Half a Century of Music in England* (1889; 2nd ed., 1898); he also transl. the correspondence of Wagner and Liszt into English, and was editor of Novello's series of biographies The Great Musicians, for which he wrote *Wagner* (1881).

Huehn, Julius, American baritone; b. Revere, Mass., Jan. 12, 1904; d. Rochester, N.Y., June 8, 1971. He studied engineering at the Carnegie Institute of Technology; later took voice lessons with Anna Schoen-René at the Juilliard School in New York. He made his operatic debut with the Metropolitan Opera as the herald in *Lohengrin* on Dec. 21, 1935; then served in the U.S. Air Force and carried out missions in Europe as a bombardier. He sang again at the Metropolitan Opera after the end of the war. He was particularly noted for his performances of heroic baritone parts in Wagner's operas.

Hughes, Dom Anselm, eminent English musicologist; b. London, April 15, 1889; d. Nashdom Abbey, Burnham Bucks, Oct. 8, 1974. He studied at Oxford (B.A., 1911; M.A., 1915); lectured on medieval church music in universities and colleges in the U.S. and Canada (1932, 1934, 1939, and 1940); contributed articles to *Grove's Dictionary of Music and Musicians;* edited (with others) the *Old Hall Manuscript* (1933–38).

WRITINGS: *Early English Harmony* (vol. II; London, 1912); *Latin Hymnody* (London, 1923); *Worcester Mediaeval Harmony* (Burnham, 1928); *The House of My Pilgrimage* (London, 1929); *Anglo-French Sequelae* (London, 1934); *Index to the Facsimile Edition of MS Wolfenbüttel 677* (Oxford, 1939); *Liturgical Terms for Music Students* (Boston, 1940); *Medieval Polyphony in the Bodleian Library* (Oxford, 1951); *Catalogue of the Musical Manuscripts at Peterhouse, Cambridge* (Cambridge, 1953). He also composed

Missa Sancti Benedicti (London, 1918); and various small pieces of church music.

Hughes, Edwin, American pianist; b. Washington, D.C., Aug. 15, 1884; d. New York, July 17, 1965. He studied with S. M. Fabian in Washington, with Rafael Joseffy in New York (1906–07), and with T. Leschetizky in Vienna (1907–10); taught at the Ganapol School of Musical Art, Detroit (1910–12), Volpe Institute of Music, N.Y. (1916–17), and the Institute of Musical Art, N.Y. (1918–23); lectured at various schools. From 1920 to 1926 he was special editor of piano music for G. Schirmer, Inc.; edited Bach's *Well-Tempered Clavier* for Schirmer's Library of Musical Classics (with a preface in English and Spanish); publ. piano transcriptions of Strauss's Waltzes; wrote songs; etc.

Hughes, Herbert, Irish critic and composer; b. Belfast, March 16, 1882; d. Brighton, May 1, 1937. He studied at the Royal College of Music in London. He was one of the founders of the Irish Folksong Society and co-editor of its early journals; was music critic of the *Daily Telegraph.* He collected and edited many folksongs, including the collections Boosey's *Modern Festival Series; Irish Country Songs* (in 4 vols.); *Old Irish Melodies* (3 vols.); *Historical Songs and Ballads of Ireland; Songs from Connacht; Songs of Uladh.* He composed incidental music to the comedy *And So to Bed,* the film *Irish Hearts; Nursery Rhymes,* studies in imitation (2 vols.); *Parodies,* for voice and orch. (2 vols.); *Brian Boru's March,* for piano; *3 Satirical Songs,* for violin, flute, clarinet, and bassoon; *Shockheaded Peter,* cycle for soprano, baritone, and piano; etc.

Hughes, Robert, Scottish-born Australian composer; b. Leven, Fyfeshire, March 27, 1912. He emigrated to Australia in 1930; worked as a music librarian at the Australian Broadcasting Commission in Melbourne. He withdrew most of his early compositions; his extant works include a *Festival Overture* (1948); *Farrago,* suite for orch. (1949); *Serenade* for small orch. (1952); *Symph. No. 1* (1952); *Essay* for orch. (1953); a ballet, *Xanadu* (1954); *Masquerade Overture* (1956); Sinfonietta (1957; Manchester, England, Nov. 10, 1957); television ballet, *The Forbidden Rite* (1962); *Synthesis* for orch. (1969); *Five Indian Poems* for chorus, woodwind instruments and percussion (1971); *Sea Spell* for orch. (1973).
BIBLIOGRAPHY: James Murdoch, *Australia's Contemporary Composers* (Melbourne, 1972).

Hughes, Rupert, American writer on music; b. Lancaster, Mo., Jan. 31, 1872; d. Los Angeles, Sept. 9, 1956. He studied with W. G. Smith in Cleveland (1890–92), E. S. Kelley in New York (1899), and Ch. Pearce in London (1900–01). His publications include: *American Composers* (Boston, 1900; revised, 1914); *The Musical Guide* (2 vols., N.Y., 1903; republished as *Music Lovers' Encyclopedia,* in 1 vol., 1912; revised and newly edited by Deems Taylor and Russell Kerr as *Music Lover's Encyclopedia,* 1939; revised, 1954); edited *Thirty Songs by American Composers* (1904). He composed a dramatic monologue for baritone and

piano, *Cain* (1919); piano pieces, and songs. He was principally known, however, as a successful novelist.

Hugo, John Adam, American pianist and composer; b. Bridgeport, Conn., Jan. 5, 1873; d. there, Dec. 29, 1945. From 1888–97 he studied at the Stuttgart Cons. with Speidel, Faiszt, Doppler, and Zumpe; appeared as concert pianist in Germany, England, and Italy; returned to the U.S. in 1899. His one-act opera, *The Temple Dancer,* is one of the few operas by American composers presented by the Metropolitan Opera, N.Y. (March 12, 1919); it was also produced in Honolulu (Feb. 19, 1925). His other works are the operas, *The Hero of Byzanz* (written while studying at the Stuttgart Cons.) and *The Sun God;* Symphony; 2 piano concertos; Piano Trio; pieces for the violin; pieces for the cello; piano pieces, and songs.
BIBLIOGRAPHY: E. E. Hipsher, *American Opera and Its Composers* (Philadelphia, 1927; pp. 270–74).

Hugon, Georges, French composer; b. Paris, July 23, 1904. He studied at the Paris Cons.; received the Prix Bizet (1926). He was director of the Cons. of Boulogne-sur-Mer (1934–41); in 1941, became prof. at the Cons. of Paris.
WORKS: oratorio, *Chants de deuil et d'espérance* (1947); 2 symphonies (1941, 1949); symph. poems, *Au nord* (1930) and *La Reine de Saba* (1933); Piano Concerto (1962); Flute Sonata (1965); Piano Trio; String Quartet; various pieces for piano; songs.
BIBLIOGRAPHY: A. Machabey, *Portraits de trente musiciens français* (Paris, 1949; pp. 101–4).

Huhn, Bruno, song composer; b. London, Aug. 1, 1871; d. New York, May 13, 1950. He studied piano in London and New York; toured in Egypt, India, and Australia (1889–91). In 1891 he settled in New York, where he made a successful debut as a pianist (April 17, 1896). Subsequently he held various positions as conductor of suburban choral groups and also as accompanist to singers. He wrote many sacred choruses and solo songs, of which his setting of Henley's *Invictus* (1910) attained great popularity.

Huízar, Candelario, Mexican composer; b. Jerez, Feb. 2, 1883; d. Mexico City, May 3, 1970. He studied violin and composition; in 1917 settled in Mexico City, where he continued his studies with Gustavo Campa. He was copyist in various music schools (1920–25), and in 1931 became librarian of the Conservatorio Nacional. His compositions reflect Mexican folklore, and often contain authentic Mexican themes.
WORKS: for orch. (all first performed in Mexico City): *Imágenes,* symph. poem (Dec. 13, 1929); Symphony No. 1 (Nov. 14, 1930); *Pueblerinas,* symph. poem (Nov. 6, 1931); *Surco,* symph. poem (Oct. 25, 1935); Symphony No. 2 (Sept. 4, 1936); Symphony No. 3 (July 29, 1938); Symphony No. 4 (Aug. 7, 1942); Sonata for Clarinet and Bassoon (1931); String Quartet (1938); choral works and songs.
BIBLIOGRAPHY: J. C. Romero, "Candelario Huízar," *Nuestra Música* (Jan. 1952).

Hull, Anne, American pianist and composer; b. Brookland, Pennsylvania, Jan. 25, 1888. She studied at the Peabody Cons. in Baltimore, and upon graduation became active as piano teacher; made numerous appearances with Mary Howe in duo piano recitals. Her work for two pianos, *Ancient Ballad*, attained considerable popularity.

Hull, Arthur Eaglefield, English writer on music; b. Market Harborough, March 10, 1876; d. London, Nov. 4, 1928. He studied privately with Matthay and Charles Pearce in London; served as organist at Huddersfield Parish Church; was (from 1912) editor of the *Monthly Musical Record.* In 1918 he founded the British Music Society; was its honorary director until 1921; Mus. Doc. (Queen's College, Oxford). In 1906 he married Constance Barratt, an accomplished violinist. A man of broad culture, he was an enthusiast for new music; was an early champion of Scriabin in England. In 1924 he brought out a *Dictionary of Modern Music and Musicians.* This was a pioneer volume and, despite an overabundance of egregious errors and misconceptions, is of service as a guide; a German transl. was made by Alfred Einstein, with numerous errors corrected (1926); another volume which still retains its value is *Modern Harmony: Its Explanation and Application* (London, 1914; 3rd ed., 1923; reprint, 1934). In 1927 he publ. a book, *Music. Classical, Romantic and Modern,* which proved to be a pasticcio of borrowings from various English and American writers; this was pointed out by many reviewers, and the book was withdrawn by the publishers in 1928; this episode led directly to Hull's suicide; he threw himself under a moving train at the Huddersfield Railway Station, suffered grave injuries and loss of memory, and died a few weeks later. The list of his publications includes also *Organ Playing, Its Technique and Expression* (1911); *The Sonata in Music* (1916); *Scriabin* (1916); *Modern Musical Styles* (1916); *Design or Construction in Music* (1917); *Cyril Scott* (1918); he made English translations of Romain Rolland's *Handel* (1916) and *Vie de Beethoven;* edited the complete organ works of Bach and Mendelssohn (with annotations for students); was also editor of the series Music Lovers' Library and Library of Music and Musicians (in which his book on Scriabin appeared); other books by him in the same series were *Bach* and *Three English Composers.*

Hullah, John Pyke, English composer and organist; b. Worcester, June 27, 1812; d. London, Feb. 21, 1884. He was a pupil of William Horsley; in 1833 he studied singing with Crivelli at the Royal Academy of Music; as a composer he was entirely self-taught. At the age of 24 he produced an opera to a story by Charles Dickens, *The Village Coquette* (London, Dec. 6, 1836); 2 other operas followed: *The Barber of Bassora* (London, Nov. 11, 1837) and *The Outpost* (May 17, 1838). In the meantime, he obtained a post of church organist at Croydon. He made several trips to Paris, where he became interested in the new system of vocal teaching established by Wilhem; he modified it to suit English requirements, and, with the sanction of the National Education Committee, he opened his Singing School for Schoolmasters at Exeter Hall (1841). The school became the target of bitter criticism; nonetheless, it prospered; thousands of students enrolled; his

wealthy supporters helped him build St. Martin's Hall for performances of vocal music by his students; the hall was inaugurated in 1850; it was destroyed by fire in 1860. From 1844–74 Hullah taught singing at King's College, and later at Queen's College and Bedford College in London. He conducted the student concerts of the Royal Academy of Music (1870–73); in 1872 he became Inspector of Training Schools. He held the honorary degree of LL.D. from Edinburgh Univ. (1876); was also a member of the Cecilia Society in Rome and of the Academy of Music in Florence. He edited Wilhem's *Method of Teaching Singing Adapted to English Use* (1841); publ. *A Grammar of Vocal Music* (1843); *A Grammar of Harmony* (1852); *A Grammar of Counterpoint* (1864); *The History of Modern Music* (1862); *The Third or Transition Period of Musical History* (1865); *The Cultivation of the Speaking Voice* (1870); *Music in the House* (1877); also brought out useful collections of vocal music: *The Psalter, The Book of Praise Hymnal,* the *Whole Book of Psalms with Chants.* He was the composer of the celebrated song *O that we two were Maying;* other popular songs are *The Storm* and *Three Fishers.* A *Life of John Hullah* was publ. by his wife (London, 1886).

Hüller, Johann Adam. See **Hiller, Johann Adam.**

Hüllmandel, Nicolas-Joseph, Alsatian musician; b. Strasbourg, May 23, 1756; d. London, Dec. 19, 1823. He was an illegitimate son of **Michel Hüllmandel,** organist at the Strasbourg Cathedral and nephew of the French horn player Jean-Joseph Rodolphe. He studied with Carl Philip Emmanuel Bach in Hamburg; in 1776 he went to Paris where he taught piano and the glass harmonica; among his pupils in composition were Onslow and Aubert. After the French Revolution he went to London, where he remained until his death. There he published a manual, *Principles of Music, Chiefly Calculated for the Pianoforte* (1795).

WORKS: 17 sonatas for piano; 34 sonatas for piano with violin obbligato; 54 Airs for piano; 12 Suites for piano; 2 books of Divertissements for piano. He composed in a typical manner of his time; Mozart, in one of his letters to his father, expressed appreciation of Hüllmandel's sonatas.

BIBLIOGRAPHY: Rita Benton, "N.-J. Hüllmandel," *Revue de Musicologie* (Dec. 1961).

Humbert, Georges, Swiss organist and writer on music; b. St. Croix, Aug. 10, 1870; d. Neuchâtel, Jan. 1, 1936. He studied with Huberti at the Brussels Cons. and with Bargiel in Berlin. In 1892 he became prof. of music history at the Geneva Cons., retaining this post until 1912; from 1898 till 1918 he was organist at Morges. In 1918 he established the Neuchâtel Cons., and was its director until his death; also conducted various performing societies in Switzerland. He was editor of *Gazette Musical de la Suisse Romande* (1894–96) and *La Vie Musicale* (1918–24); publ. *Notes pour servir a l'étude de l'histoire de la musique* (1904). He was the translator into French of Riemann's *Musiklexikon* (1899; 3rd ed., 1931).

Humble, Keith, Australian composer; b. Geelong, Sept. 6, 1927. He studied at the Cons. of Melbourne (1945–51); then went to Paris where he took lessons with René Leibowitz. He returned to Australia in 1956 to teach piano and music theory at the Melbourne Cons.; the following year he went again to Paris where he organized a modernistic workshop, Le Centre de Musique. Once more in Australia, in 1966 he resumed his post at the Melbourne Cons. where he formed a studio for electronic music. In the interim, he made several visits to the U.S., where he lectured at the Univ. of California at La Jolla, and also spent some time at Princeton Univ., working with Milton Babbitt. His own compositions reflect the avant-garde tendencies of British, French and American modern music.

WORKS: *L'Armée des saluts* for singers, instrumentalists, and actors (1965); *Music for Monuments,* for instruments and voices (1967); 5 pieces for various ensembles under the generic category, *Arcade* (1968–69); *Après la légende* for piano and orch. (1969); 6 pieces titled *Nunique* (1968–71; *Nunique V* is an opera entitled *La Rountala,* which was commissioned by the Australian Opera Company, 1971).

BIBLIOGRAPHY: James Murdoch, *Australia's Contemporary Composers* (Melbourne, 1975; pp. 120–132).

Hume, Paul, American music critic; b. Chicago, Dec. 13, 1915; studied at the Univ. of Chicago; took private lessons in piano, organ, and voice; was organist, choirmaster, and a baritone soloist at various churches in Chicago and Washington; gave song recitals in Boston and in the Middle West; taught voice at Catholic Univ., Washington; in 1946, became music editor and critic of the *Washington Post;* instructor in music history at Georgetown Univ. from 1949; contributor to *Saturday Review* (N.Y.); active as lecturer and radio commentator on music; publ. *Catholic Church Music* (N.Y., 1956) and *Our Music, Our Schools, and Our Culture* (National Catholic Education Association, 1957). Paul Hume leaped to national fame in 1950 when President Truman, outraged by Hume's unenthusiastic review of Margaret Truman's song recital, wrote him a personal letter threatening him with bodily injury. Hume sold the letter to a Connecticut industrialist for an undisclosed sum of money.

Humfrey, Pelham, English composer; b. 1647; d. Windsor, July 14, 1674. He was among the first children appointed to the restored Chapel Royal in 1660, and (together with fellow-choristers John Blow and William Turner) he wrote the famous *Club Anthem.* In 1664 King Charles II sent him to study in France and Italy under the Secret Service Funds; that he worked under Lully remains unverified, nor can it be proved that he got to Italy. He returned to England in 1667 and was appointed Gentleman of the Chapel Royal on Oct. 26, 1667. An entry in Pepys' diary for Nov. 15, 1667 described him as being "full of form, and confidence, and vanity" and disparaging "everything, and everybody's skill but his own." Humfrey's justification of his self-confidence lay in his undoubted mastery of the Italian declamatory style, greater

than anyone had yet achieved in England. On July 15, 1672, he was appointed Master of the Children of the Chapel Royal. Two years later he died at the early age of 27. One of his wards was the young Henry Purcell, whose style clearly shows Humfrey's influence.

WORKS: 24 secular songs; 4 sacred songs; a dialogue, composed with John Blow; songs and vocal ensembles for Shadwell's version of Shakespeare's The *Tempest;* 3 odes, all to Charles II; 26 anthems, of which 19 are extant (one composed with John Blow and William Turner); *Have Mercy Upon Me, O God* in MS in the British Museum; *O Praise God in His Holyness* in MS at the Durham Cathedral Library; and *Hear My Prayer, O God* (in the Egerton MSS of the British Museum); etc.; one complete Service for the Anglican Church (Morning Prayer, Communion, and Evening Prayer); *The Grand Chant,* a widely used Anglican chant. Seven anthems by Humfrey are included in Boyce's *Cathedral Music;* 3 sacred songs in *Harmonia Sacra* (1714); a number of secular songs in the following collections: Playford's *Choice Songs* (1673), *Choice Ayres, Songs and Dialogues* (1676–84); J. S. Smith's *Musica Antiqua* (1812); Humfrey's *Complete Church Music* is publ. in *Musica Britannica 34–35.*

BIBLIOGRAPHY: W. Barclay Squire, "The Music of Shadwell's Tempest," *Musical Quarterly* (Oct. 1921), P. Dennison, "The Will of Pelham Humfrey." *R.M.A. Research Chronicle 7* (1970); idem, "The Church Music of Pelham Humfrey," *Proceedings of the Royal Music Assoc. 98* (1971–72).

Humiston, William Henry, American organist; b. Marietta, Ohio, April 27, 1869; d. New York, Dec. 5, 1923. He studied the organ with C. Eddy in Chicago (1885–94); held various positions in and around Chicago as church organist. In 1896 he moved to New York, where he became a pupil of MacDowell (1896–99); served as organist at suburban churches until 1909; conducted traveling opera companies (1909–12). He wrote a *Southern Fantasy,* for orch. (1906); some overtures, and songs.

Hummel, Ferdinand, German composer and harpist; b. Berlin, Sept. 6, 1855; d. there, April 24, 1928. He gave concerts as a child harpist (1864–67); then studied music at Kullak's Academy in Berlin and later at the Hochschule für Musik there. He established himself as a teacher in Berlin, and also became a prolific composer. Much impressed by the realistic school of Italian opera (Mascagni), he wrote several short operas in the same genre: *Mara* (Berlin, 1893), *Angla* (Berlin, 1894), *Assarpai* (Gotha, 1898), *Sophie von Brabant* (Darmstadt, 1899), *Die Beichte* (Berlin, 1900), *Ein treuer Schelm,* and *Die Gefilde der Seligen* (Altenburg, 1917). He also wrote a symphony, a piano concerto, chamber music, choral works, aggregating to about 120 opus numbers.

Hummel, Johann Nepomuk, celebrated German pianist and composer; b. Pressburg, Nov. 14, 1778; d. Weimar, Oct. 17, 1837. He studied with his father, **Johannes Hummel,** who was music master of the Imperial School for Military Music. In 1786 the father was appointed conductor at Schikaneder's Theater in Vienna, and there Mozart interested himself in young

Hummel and took him into his house and for 2 years instructed him. He made his debut in 1787 at a concert given by Mozart in Dresden; 1788–93 he accompanied his father on professional concert tours as pianist, visiting Germany, Denmark, Scotland, England, and Holland. In London he studied briefly with Clementi; in Oxford he presented his string quartet. In 1793 he returned to Vienna and began a course of studies with Albrechtsberger, and also profited by the counsel of Haydn and Salieri in composition. From 1804–11 he acted as deputy Kapellmeister for Haydn, in Prince Esterházy's service. In the meantime, he had his opera *Mathilde von Guise* produced in Vienna (March 26, 1810). He settled in Vienna in 1811 as a teacher; in 1816 was appointed court Kapellmeister at Stuttgart, and in 1819, at Weimar, a post he held until his death. His duties were not too rigorous, and he was allowed to make frequent professional tours. He traveled to St. Petersburg in 1822; in 1825 he was in Paris, where he was made Chevalier of the Legion of Honor; in 1826, visited Belgium and Holland; in 1827, was in Vienna, in 1828, in Warsaw, and in 1829, again in France. He conducted a season of German opera at the King's Theatre in London in 1833. The last years of his life were marred by ill health and much suffering. During the peak of his career as a pianist, he was regarded as one of the greatest virtuosos of his time; both as pianist and composer he was often declared to be the equal of Beethoven. His compositions were marked by excellent craftsmanship; his writing for instruments, particularly for piano, was impeccable; his melodic invention was rich, and his harmonic and contrapuntal skill was of the highest caliber. Yet, with his death, his music went into an immediate eclipse; performances of his works became increasingly rare, until the name of Hummel all but vanished from active musical programs. However, some of his compositions were revived by various musical societies in Europe and America, and as a result, at least his chamber music was saved from oblivion. He wrote 124 opus numbers; these include 9 operas, several ballets, cantatas; 3 Masses for 4 voices and organ; a Graduale and Offertorium, still in use in Austrian churches; 7 concertos and concertinos for piano and orch.; many works for piano solo; 6 piano trios; a piano quintet; quintet for violin, viola, cello, double bass, and piano; and septet in D minor (his most outstanding work), for flute, oboe, viola, horn, cello, double bass, and piano. He also publ. *Anweisung zum Pianofortespiel* (1828), an elaborate instruction book and one of the first to give a sensible method of fingering. His wife, **Elisabeth Hummel-Röckl** (1793–1883), was an opera singer.

BIBLIOGRAPHY: G. Sporck, *L'Interprétation des sonates de J. N. Hummel* (Paris, 1933); K. Benyovszky, *J. N. Hummel, der Mensch und Künstler* (Bratislava, 1934); Dieter Zimmerschied, *Thematisches Verzeichnis der Werke von Johann Nepomuk Hummel* (1971); J. Sachs, "Authentic English and French Editions of J. N. Hummel," *Journal of the American Musicological Society* (Summer 1972); idem, "Hummel and the Pirates: The Struggle for Musical Copyright," *Musical Quarterly* (Jan. 1973); idem, "A Checklist of the Works of Johann Nepomuk Hummel," *Notes* (June 1974; corrects and complements Zimmerschied's *Thematisches Verzeichnis*).

Humperdinck, Engelbert, celebrated German composer; b. Siegburg, near Bonn, Sept. 1, 1854; d. Neustrelitz, Sept. 27, 1921. He first studied architecture in Cologne; there he met Ferdinand Hiller, who discovered his musical talent and took him as a student at the Cologne Cons.; his other teachers there were Gernsheim and Jensen (composition), Seiss and Mertke (piano), Rensberg and Ehlert (cello). In 1876 he won a Mozart scholarship at Frankfurt; studied in Munich with Franz Lachner and Rheinberger; there he published his first works, *Humoreske*, for orch. (1880) and *Die Wallfahrt nach Kevelaar*, for chorus, which won the Mendelssohn Prize (1879); he also won the Meyerbeer prize of 7,600 marks (1881), which enabled him to visit Italy and France. In Italy he met Wagner, who invited him to be his guest at Bayreuth. Here Humperdinck assisted in preparing the score of *Parsifal* for publication; from then on the relations between Humperdinck and the Wagner family were most cordial; Siegfried Wagner became Humperdinck's pupil and received his entire musical education from him. From 1885–87 Humperdinck was prof. in the Cons. in Barcelona; after his return to Germany he taught for a short time in Cologne, and then went to Mainz in the employ of the Schott publishing firm; in 1890 he became prof. at Hoch's Cons. in Frankfurt, and music critic for the *Frankfurter Zeitung*. On Dec. 23, 1893, in Weimar, he produced the fairy-opera *Hänsel und Gretel* (text by his sister, Adelheid Wette). The work, aside from its intrinsic merit, appeared at the right psychological moment. The German public, weary of the bombast of the Wagner-imitators, were almost willing to accept the blunt realism of the Italian "verismo" as a relief from the labored dullness of pseudo-Wagnerian music dramas. And now a new composer, drawing inspiration from folk music, found musical expression for a thoroughly German subject, and the public was delighted. Before a year had passed, the work was in the repertory of every German opera house; also abroad its success was extraordinary and lasting (London, Dec. 26, 1894; N.Y., Oct. 8, 1895). A host of imitators ransacked German fairy-lore, but with ill success. Since Humperdinck's health had never been robust, he determined after this success to give up teaching, and in 1896 he retired to Boppard on the Rhine to devote himself entirely to composition. His next work was *Die sieben Geislein* (Berlin, Dec. 19, 1895), a fairy play for children, written for voice and piano. In 1898 he wrote incidental music to Rosmer's *Königskinder* (Munich, Jan. 23, 1897); in this music Humperdinck made a bold attempt to prescribe definite rhythmic and pitch inflections ("sprechnoten") to the actors in the drama; he later recast the score into an opera, which was produced at the Metropolitan Opera House, N.Y. (Dec. 28, 1910). In 1900 he became director (with practically nominal duties) of the Akademische Meisterschule in Berlin. His other operas are *Dornröschen* (Frankfurt, Nov. 12, 1902); *Die Heirat wider Willen* (Berlin, April 14, 1905); *Die Marketenderin* (Cologne, May 10, 1914), and *Gaudeamus* (Darmstadt, March 18, 1919); he wrote incidental music for Berlin productions of 5 plays of Shakespeare, *The Merchant of Venice* (Nov. 9, 1905), *The Winter's Tale* (Sept. 15, 1906), *Romeo and Juliet* (Jan. 29, 1907), *Twelfth Night* (Oct. 17, 1907), *The Tempest* (Oct. 8, 1915); to *Lysistrata,* by Aristophanes (Berlin, Feb. 27, 1908), and *The Blue Bird,* by Maeterlinck (Berlin, Dec. 23, 1912). He contributed music to Max Reinhardt's production of *The Miracle* (London, Dec. 23, 1911). He further wrote a choral ballade, *Das Glück von Edenhall* (1884), *Maurische Rhapsodie,* for orch. (1898), and a symphony. Among his songs, the cycle *Kinderlieder* is particularly fine. Humperdinck's lasting fame still rests, however, upon his one opera *Hänsel und Gretel,* which succeeded thanks to Humperdinck's ability to write melodies of ingenuous felicity, despite the almost incompatible Wagnerian instrumental and dramatic design.

BIBLIOGRAPHY: G. Münzer, *E. Humperdinck* (Leipzig, 1906); E. Istel, "German Opera since Richard Wagner," *Musical Quarterly* (April 1915); O. Besch, *E. Humperdinck* (Leipzig, 1915); H. Kühlmann, *Stil und Form in Humperdincks 'Hänsel und Gretel'* (Marburg, 1930); K. G. Fellerer, "Englebert Humperdinck und seine Stellung im deutschen Musikleben," *Heimatbuch der Stadt Siegburg* 2 (1967).

Humperdinck, Engelbert (real name **Arnold George Dorsey**), Indian-born rock singer; b. Madras, May 3, 1936; his family moved to England. As a youth, he showed innate aptitude for raucous sentimentality and unmitigated schmaltz; these propensities attracted the attention of a hustler in search of potential rock singers; dissatisfied with the lackluster name of his chosen candidate for lucre and glory, he brazenly picked up the name Engelbert Humperdinck from a music dictionary, and conferred it on Dorsey. As luck would have it, the rechristened rock singer (and his manager) prospered, making a quantum leap from his early beginnings as a hapless entertainer in British pubs to a successful crowd pleaser in England and America. His voice is bland and colorless, but his stance is sincere, and his records sell prodigiously among the low classes of British-American music fans. *Chacun à son goût.*

Humpert, Hans, German composer; b. Paderborn, April 19, 1901; killed in battle at Salerno, Sept. 15, 1943. He studied at the Frankfurt Cons. and in Berlin; then taught at Paderborn until he was called into the army. His music is marked by a neo-Romantic quality, with a strong contrapuntal structure.

WORKS: 2 symphonies (1937, 1942); 3 string quartets; String Trio; Violin Sonata; Viola Sonata; Sonata for Flute Solo; 5 cantatas; 4 Masses; 3 motets; 7 psalms; many choral and organ works.

BIBLIOGRAPHY: G. Hoffmann, "Hans Humpert," *Musica* (Sept. 1953).

Huneker, James Gibbons, brilliant American journalist and writer on music; b. Philadelphia, Jan. 31, 1857; d. Brooklyn, Feb. 9, 1921. He studied piano with Michael Cross in Philadelphia, and in 1878 in Paris with Th. Ritter; later with Joseffy at the National Cons. in N.Y.; then taught piano there (1888–98). He was music and drama critic of the *N.Y. Recorder* (1891–95), the *Morning Advertiser* (1895–97); music, drama, and art critic for the N.Y. *Sun* (1900–12). In 1917 he was music critic of the *Philadelphia Press;* after one season (1918–19) with the *N.Y. Times* he became music critic for the *N.Y. World,* a position he held until his death; also wrote for various journals in N.Y., London, Paris, Berlin, and Vienna. He published a novel dealing with artistic life in N.Y., *Painted Veils* (1921), but he devoted most of his uncommon gifts to musical journalism. He was capable of rising to true poetic style when writing about Chopin and other composers whom he loved; but he also possessed a talent for caustic invective; his attacks on Debussy were particularly sharp. He had a fine sense of humor, and candidly described himself as an "old fogy." In addition to his literary publications, he furnished introductory essays for Joseffy's edition of Chopin's works.

WRITINGS: *Mezzotints in Modern Music* (1899); *Chopin: The Man and His Music* (1900; in German, 1914); *Melomaniacs* (1902); *Overtones, a Book of Temperaments* (1904); *Iconoclasts: A Book for Dramatists* (1905); *Visionaries: Fantasies and Fiction* (1905); *Egoists: A Book of Supermen* (1909); *Promenades of an Impressionist: Studies in Art* (1910); *Franz Liszt: A Study* (1911; in German, 1922); *The Pathos of Distance* (1913); *Old Fogy, His Musical Opinions and Grotesques* (1913); *New Cosmopolis* (1915); *Ivory Apes and Peacocks* (1915); *Unicorns* (1917); *The Philharmonic Society of New York and Its 75th Anniversary* (1917); *Bedouins* (1920); *Steeplejack* (his memoirs; 1920); *Variations* (1921). A selection of his letters was publ. posthumously by Josephine Huneker (1922); a collection of essays, with an introduction by Mencken, in 1929.

BIBLIOGRAPHY: B. De Casseres, *James Gibbons Huneker* (N.Y., 1925); A. T. Schwab, *James Gibbons Huneker: Critic of the Seven Arts* (Stanford, Calif., 1963).

Hungerford, Bruce, Australian pianist; b. Korumburra, Victoria, Nov. 24, 1922; d. in an automobile accident in The Bronx, N.Y., Jan. 26, 1977. He received his education in Melbourne; studied piano with Ignaz Friedman in Sydney (1944), and later with Ernest Hutcheson at the Juilliard School of Music in New York (1945–47); took private lessons with Myra Hess in New York between 1948 and 1958, and also with Carl Friedberg from 1948 to 1955. He gave his first piano recital in New York in 1951; from then on until 1965 he appeared under the name **Leonard Hungerford.** Apart from his virtuoso technique, he possessed an extraordinary mastery of dynamic gradations and self-consistent musical phraseology. He also gained recognition as a color photographer and archeologist, specializing in Egyptology; he recorded a 17-part audio-visual lecture entitled "The Heritage of Ancient Egypt" (1971).

Hunt, Jerry, American composer; b. Waco, Texas, Nov. 30, 1943. He studied piano at North Texas State Univ.; developed a successful career as a performer of modern music; was on the faculty of Southern Methodist Univ. in Texas (1967–73) and concurrently was artist-in-residence at the Video Research Center in Dallas.

WORKS: The titles of his works indicate a preoccupation with mathematical and abstract concepts, as exemplified by his 8 pieces for varying instrumental groups bearing the generic title *Helix* (1961-71); other works are *Sur Dr. John Dee,* scored for "zero to 11 performers" (1963); *Tabulatura Soyga,* also for 0-11 instruments (1965); *Preparallel* for orchestral groups (1965); *Unit,* a "solo situation" (1967); *Infrasolo* for 10 cymbals "or something else" (1970); *Autotransform glissando* (1970); *Symphony* for electronics (1971); *Haramand Playing: Recursive/Regenerative* for electronic audio and video generating systems (1972); *Quaquaversal Transmission,* a theater work (1973); and *21 Segments* for varying numbers of instruments (1973-77).

Hünten, Franz, German pianist and composer; b. Coblenz, Dec. 26, 1793; d. there, Feb. 22, 1878. He studied with his father, an organist; at the age of 26 he went to Paris and took courses at the Cons. with Pradher (piano) and Cherubini (composition); composed salon music for piano (fantasies, variations on opera themes, waltzes, etc.), some 250 opus numbers in all, most of which he succeeded in publishing; also brought out a *Méthode nouvelle pour le piano,* and other didactic compilations which became popular among teachers and students; Hünten was very much in demand as a piano teacher in Paris. Having accumulated considerable capital from his enterprises, he returned to Coblenz in 1848, and remained there until his death.
BIBLIOGRAPHY: Gerd Zöllner, *Franz Hünten: Sein Leben und sein Werk* (Cologne, 1959).

Huré, Jean, French composer and writer on music; b. Gien, Loiret, Sept. 17, 1877; d. Paris, Jan. 27, 1930. He received his musical education at a monastery in Angers; went to Paris in 1895; there he founded the École Normale Pour Pianistes (1912) and the monthly magazine *L'Orgue et les Organistes* (1923); in 1925 he became church organist at St. Augustin; in 1926 he won the Prix Chartier for composition.
WORKS: His ballet, *Le Bois sacré,* was produced at the Opéra-Comique in Paris on June 28, 1921; he further wrote incidental music to Musset's *Fantasio,* 3 symphonies, Violin Concerto, *Andante* for saxophone and orch., 2 string quartets, Piano Quintet, Violin Sonata, 3 cello sonatas, etc.; publ. the manuals *La Technique du piano* (1908), *La Technique de l'orgue* (1918); also *L'Esthétique de l'orgue* (1923) and *Saint Augustin, musicien* (1924).
BIBLIOGRAPHY: G. Migot, *Jean Huré* (1926).

Hurley, Laurel, American coloratura soprano; b. Allentown, Pa., Feb. 14, 1927. Of a musical family, she studied with her mother, a church organist; at 16, appeared on Broadway (Aug. 21, 1943) as Kathie in Romberg's operetta *The Student Prince;* then toured with the company that produced it. She was the winner of the Walter W. Naumburg Foundation Award, which enabled her to give a song recital in N.Y. (Nov. 6, 1952). She made her debut at the Metropolitan Opera on Feb. 8, 1955, in a minor role; on Jan. 11, 1957, she appeared in the title role of *La Périchole.* On May 6, 1949, she married John Peter Butz.

Hurlstone, William Yeates, English composer and pianist; b. London, Jan. 7, 1876; d. there, May 30, 1906. A precocious musician, he composed waltzes as a young child; studied at the Royal College of Music with Stanford (composition) and Edward Dannreuther (piano); performed his Piano Concerto in 1896. In 1905 he was appointed prof. at the Royal College of Music but died in the following year; his early death was much regretted.
WORKS: the fairy suite *The Magic Mirror,* for orch.; *Variations on a Hungarian Air* and *Variations on a Swedish Air,* for orch.; Quartet, for flute, oboe, horn, and bassoon; Quintet, for flute, oboe, horn, bassoon, and piano; Piano Trio; Trio for Clarinet, Bassoon, and Piano; Clarinet Sonata; Bassoon Sonata; several song cycles.
BIBLIOGRAPHY: H. G. Newell, *W. Y. Hurlstone: Musician and Man* (London, 1936); Katharine Hurlstone, *William Hurlstone, Musician: Memories and Records by His Friends* (London, 1949).

Hurník, Ilja, Czech composer; b. Poruba, near Svinov, Nov. 25, 1922. He moved to Prague in 1938; studied composition with Řidký and was the last pupil of Novák (1941-44); studied piano at the Prague Academy of Music (1945-51); then made several concert tours in Czechoslovakia. His own works are marked with impressionistic flavor, while retaining a classical format.
WORKS: 3 operas: *Dáma a lupiči (The Lady and the Gangster),* after the film *The Ladykillers* (1966), *Mudrci a bloudi (The Wise and the Foolish,* 1968), and *Diogenes* (1974); a ballet *Ondráš* (1950); an oratorio *Noe (Noah,* 1959); 2 cantatas: *Maryka* (1948, revised 1955) and *Ezop (Aesop,* 1964); *Sulamit,* cycle of songs after the Old Testament, for female voice and orch. (1963); Flute Concerto (1953); Serenade for Strings (1954); Concerto for Winds and Percussion (1956); Concerto for Oboe, String Orch., and Piano (1959); *Musikanti (The Musicians)* for 20 instruments (1962); *Chamber Music* for strings (1962); *Kyklopes (Cyclops)* for orch. (Prague, June 4, 1965); Concerto for Piano and Small Orch. (1972); Wind Quintet (1944); 2 string quartets (1949; 2nd with a baritone solo, to Old Testament texts, 1961); Viola Sonata (1952); *Die Vier Jahreszeiten (The 4 Seasons of the Year)* for 12 solo instruments (1952); *Sonata da camera* for flute, oboe, cello and harpsichord (1953); Piano Quintet (1953); *Ballet* for 9 instruments (1954); *Esercizi* for flute, oboe, clarinet and bassoon (1958); *Moments Musicaux* for 11 winds (1962); *Gloria di flauti* for 2 flutes (1973); Preludes for Piano (1943); Piano Sonatina (1952); 3 organ sonatas (1956); Etude for Piano (1972).

Hurok, Sol, Russian-American impresario; b. Pogar, April 9, 1888; d. New York, March 5, 1974. Fleeing the political iniquities of the Czarist regime in regard to Jews, he emigrated to the U.S. in 1905, and became a naturalized citizen in 1914. In 1913 he inaugurated a series of weekly concerts announced as "Music for the Masses" at the Hippodrome in New York; then became an exclusive manager for famous Russian artists, among them Anna Pavlova, Feodor Chaliapin, Artur Rubinstein, Mischa Elman and Gregor Piatigorsky, as well as numerous celebrities in the field of the ballet and opera. He negotiated the difficult arrangements with the Soviet government for American appearances of the Bolshoi Ballet, the Ukrainian dance company and the Leningrad Kirov ballet; made frequent trips to Russia, helped by his fluency in the language. Ironically, his New York office became the target of a bomb attack by a militant Jewish organization which objected to Hurok's importation of Soviet artists, even though most of the artists were themselves Jewish.

Hurum, Alf, Norwegian-born composer and painter; b. Oslo, Sept. 21, 1882; d. Honolulu, Aug. 15, 1972. He studied with Max Bruch at the Hochschule für Musik in Berlin (1905–09); later took additional courses in Paris and in Russia. He was a co-founder of the Society of Norwegian Composers in 1917. After touring as a concert pianist he settled in Hawaii, where he established the Honolulu Symph. Orch. and was its conductor briefly (1924–26). His second career was that of a silk painter in the Japanese manner, which preoccupied him during his later years. In his music he cultivates coloristic harmonies, somewhat in an impressionist mode.
WORKS: 2 violin sonatas (1911, 1916); *3 Aquarelles* for piano (1912); String Quartet (1913); *Exotic Suite* for violin and piano (1916); *Pastels,* 4 pieces for piano (1916); *Eventyrland (Fairy Land),* suite for orch. or piano (1920); *Gotiske bilder,* 6 pieces for piano (1920); *Norse Suite* for orch. (1920); *Bendik and Aarolilja,* symph. poem (1923); Symphony (Bergen, 1927); piano pieces, songs, motets.

Husa, Karel, significant Czech-American composer; b. Prague, Aug. 7, 1921. He studied music theory and conducting at the Prague Cons. (1941–45); attended there the classes in composition of Řidký (1946); then went to Paris where he took courses at the École Normale de Musique with Honegger and Nadia Boulanger (1946–52); also received instruction in conducting with André Cluytens. In 1954 he emigrated to the U.S.; in 1959 became an American citizen. He joined the music faculty of Cornell Univ., where he taught composition; also appeared frequently as conductor in programs of his own works. In his early music he followed the modern Czech school of composition, making thematic use of folk tunes, but in the U.S. he changed his style radically and adopted the serial method of composition, with judicious deflections from doctrinaire prescriptions. In 1969 he received the Pulitzer Prize for his third string quartet.
WORKS: *3 Fresques* for orch. (1947; revised, 1967); Sinfonietta (1947); Divertimento for String Orch. (1948); Concertino for Piano and Orch. (1949); *Portrait* for string orch. (1953); Symphony (1953); *Mosaïques* for orch. (1961); Concerto for Brass Quintet and String Orch. (1965); Concerto for Alto Saxophone and Band (1967); *Music for Prague* for band (1968); Concerto for Percussion and Wind Instruments (1971); *Apotheosis of this Earth* for wind instruments (1971); Trumpet Concerto (1973); *The Steadfast Tin Soldier* for narrator and orch. (Boulder, Colorado, May 10, 1975); a ballet, *Monodrama* (Indianapolis, March 26, 1976); 3 string quartets (1948, 1953, 1968); *Evocations of Slovakia* for clarinet, viola and cello (1951); *2 Pre-*

ludes for flute, clarinet and bassoon (1966); Divertimento for Woodwind Quintet (1968); *Studies* for percussion instruments (1968); Violin Sonata (1973); *12 Moravian Songs* for voice and piano (1956); *Festive Ode* for chorus and orch. (1965); 2 piano sonatas.
BIBLIOGRAPHY: Lawrence Hartzell, "Karel Husa, The Man and His Music," *Musical Quarterly* (May 1976).

Hus-Desforges, Pierre Louis, French cellist and composer; b. Toulon, March 14, 1773; d. Pont-le-Voy, near Blois, Jan. 20, 1838. He studied at the Paris Cons.; played the cello in various orchestras; held numerous posts as theatrical conductor and teacher. He was conductor at the Théâtre-Français in St. Petersburg early in the 19th century; returning to France, was cellist at the Théâtre Saint-Martin in Paris; from 1819 until 1822 taught at Metz; in 1823 was in Bordeaux; from 1824 again in Paris. His name as composer appears for the first time as **Citoyen Desforges,** on a song entitled *L'Autel de sa patrie* (Paris, 1798); he was the author of a *Méthode de violoncelle à l'usage des commençants* (Paris, 1828); a string quartet, and a 'Sinfonia concertante' with violin and cello obbligato; he also published a historical novel, *Sapho à Leucade* (Paris, 1818).

Huss, Henry Holden, American composer and pianist; b. Newark, N.J., June 21, 1862; d. New York, Sept. 17, 1953. He was a descendant of Leonhard Huss, brother of the Bohemian martyr, John Huss. His mother, Sophia Ruckle Holden Huss, was a granddaughter of Levi Holden, a member of Washington's staff. Huss studied piano and theory with his father and with Otis B. Boise. In 1882 he went to Germany, and studied organ and composition with Rheinberger at the Munich Cons.; graduated with a *Rhapsody* for piano and orch. (1885), which he subsequently performed with several American orchestras; also played his Piano Concerto in B with the N.Y. Philharmonic, Boston Symph., etc. In 1904 he married **Hildegard Hoffmann,** a concert singer; they appeared frequently in joint recitals. He continued to compose music almost to the very end of his long life.
WORKS: the symph. poems *Life's Conflicts* (1921) and *La Nuit* (originally for piano solo, 1902; orchestrated, 1939; first perf., Washington, March 12, 1942); 4 string quartets; Violin Sonata; Cello Sonata; Viola Sonata; choral works: *The 23rd Psalm, Mankind's Own Song, Winged Messengers of Peace, The Flag, The Fool's Prayer, Captain, Oh My Captain, Lord, Make My Heart a Place Where Angels Sing,* etc.

Huston, Scott, American composer; b. Tacoma, Oct. 10, 1916. He studied with Burrill Phillips, Bernard Rogers and Howard Hanson at the Eastman School of Music (1938–42); in 1952 he was appointed to the faculty of the College-Cons. of Music in Cincinnati. Huston leans towards a modern concept of romanticism, not without an admixture of decidedly advanced techniques.
WORKS: Toccata for Piano and Orch. (Rochester, May 30, 1951); *Abstract* for orch. (Cincinnati, Nov. 20, 1955); *The Eighth Word of Christ,* cantata (1959); Organ Sonata (1960); *Intensity I* for wind ensemble

(1962); Concerto for Trumpet, String Orch., Harp and Timpani (1963); Symphony No. 3, *Phantasms* (Cincinnati, Feb. 2, 1968); *Pro Vita* for piano and brass quintet (1965); *The Wisdom of Patriotism* for chorus, band and orch. (1966); *Penta-Tholoi* for piano (1966); *Phenomena* for flute, oboe, double bass and harpsichord (1967); *Idioms* for violin, clarinet and horn (1968); *Love and Marriage*, chamber cantata (1969); *The Oratorio of Understanding* (1969); *The Song of Deborah*, cantata (1969); *Orthographics* for 4 trombones (1970); *Divinely Superfluous Beauty and Natural Music*, song cycle for soprano and chamber ensemble (1971); *A Game of Circles* for clarinet, celeste and piano (1971); *Sounds at Night* for brass choir (1971); *Life-Styles I* and *II* for piano trio or clarinet, cello and piano (1972); Symphony No. 4 for string orch. (Cincinnati, Aug. 10, 1972); *Suite: For Our Times* for brass sextet (1973); *Tamar*, monodrama for soprano and piano (1974); *Eleatron* for viola and piano (1975); many liturgical settings for chorus; songs; chamber pieces.

Hutchens, Frank, pianist and composer; b. Christchurch, New Zealand, Jan. 15, 1892; d. Sydney, Oct. 18, 1965. He studied at the Royal Academy of Music in London with Matthay (piano) and Corder (composition); taught there from 1908–14; in 1914, was appointed prof. at the State Cons. at Sydney, Australia. His compositions include *Ballade* for orch. (1938); Concerto for 2 Pianos and Orch. (1940); *Air Mail Palestine*, for voice and orch. (1942); also piano pieces.

Hutcheson, Ernest, Australian pianist and teacher; b. Melbourne, July 20, 1871; d. New York, Feb. 9, 1951. He studied piano in Australia with Max Vogrich; played concerts as a very young child; then was sent to the Leipzig Cons. to study with Reinecke, graduating in 1890. In 1898 he performed his own Piano Concerto with the Berlin Philharmonic. In 1900 he arrived in the U.S.; was head of the piano dept. at the Peabody Cons. in Baltimore (1900–12). In 1915 he created a sensation in New York by playing 3 concertos (Tchaikovsky, Liszt, and MacDowell) in a single evening; in 1919 he repeated his feat, playing 3 Beethoven concertos in one evening; during 1924–37 he was dean of the Juilliard School; in 1937, appointed its president. Among his compositions are several symphonic works and numerous piano pieces. He publ. *Elements of Piano Technique* (N.Y., 1907); *Elektra by Richard Strauss: A Guide to the Opera* (N.Y., 1910); *A Musical Guide to the Richard Wagner Ring of the Nibelung* (N.Y., 1940); *The Literature of the Piano* (N.Y., 1948).

Hutschenruyter, Wouter, Dutch composer; b. Rotterdam, Dec. 28, 1796; d. there, Nov. 18, 1878. He was a pupil of Hummel; also studied trumpet, and became a famous trumpet player. An energetic promoter of band music, he organized a music corps of the Civic Guard (1821); established a choral society called "Eruditio Musica"; also led various other music societies. He wrote an opera, *Le Roi de Bohème;* 4 symphonies; more than 150 works for military band; *Konzertstück* for 8 kettledrums with orch.; cantatas, songs.

Hutschenruyter, Wouter, Dutch conductor and musicologist, grandson of the identically named Dutch composer; b. Rotterdam, Aug. 15, 1859; d. The Hague, Nov. 24, 1943. After diligent study he became a choral conductor; in 1890, was appointed assistant conductor of the Concertgebouw in Amsterdam; from 1894 to 1917 he conducted the municipal band in Utrecht, which he brought to a high degree of excellence; performed many works by Dutch composers. From 1917–25 he taught at Rotterdam; then lived in The Hague. He wrote a number of symphonic and chamber works; publ. many books and manuals: *Orkest en orkestspel na 1600* (1903); *Mozart* (1905; new ed., 1927); *De geschiedenis der toonkunst* (1919); *Geschiedenis van het orkest en van den instrumenten* (1926); *De symphonieën van Beethoven geanalyseerd en toegelicht* (1928); *Chopin* (1926); *Mahler* (1927); *Wagner* (1928); *Brahms* (1929); *Richard Strauss* (1929); *De sonates van Beethoven toegelicht* (1930); *De Antwikkeling der Symphonie door Haydn, Mozart en Beethoven* (1931); *De Programma-Muziek* (1933); also a volume of personal memoirs (1930).

Hüttenbrenner, Anselm, Austrian composer; b. Graz, Oct. 13, 1794; d. Ober-Andritz, near Graz, June 5, 1868. At the age of 7 he studied with the organist Gell; in 1815 he went to Vienna to study law; also took lessons with Salieri there. Schubert was his fellow student, and they became close friends. Hüttenbrenner also knew Beethoven intimately, and was present at his death. He was an excellent pianist and a prolific composer; Schubert praised his works. He wrote 4 operas, 6 symphonies, 10 overtures, 9 Masses, 3 Requiems, 3 funeral marches, 2 string quartets, a string quintet, piano sonatas, 24 fugues, and other piano pieces; some 300 male quartets and 200 songs. One of his songs, *Erlkönig*, was included in the collection *12 Lieder der deutschen Romantik*, ed. by H. H. Rosenwald (1929). His reminiscences of Schubert were publ. by Otto Deutsch in 1906. It was Hüttenbrenner who came into the possession of many Schubert manuscripts after Schubert's death, among them that of the "Unfinished Symphony," which he held until 1865. It has been suggested that Hüttenbrenner had lost the 3rd and 4th movements of Schubert's work, and for that reason was reluctant to part with the incomplete manuscript, but the extant sketches for the Scherzo make that unlikely.

BIBLIOGRAPHY: K. Kurth, *Anselm Hüttenbrenner als Liederkomponist* (Cologne, 1932); T. C. L. Pritchard, "The Unfinished Symphony," *Music Review* (Jan. 1942).

Huybrechts, Albert, Belgian composer; b. Dinant, Feb. 12, 1899; d. Woluwe-St.-Pierre, near Brussels, Feb. 21, 1938. He studied at the Brussels Cons. with Martin Lunssens, Paulin Marchand, Léon Dubois and Joseph Jongen. In 1926 he gained international recognition by winning two U.S. prizes, the Elizabeth Sprague Coolidge Prize of the Library of Congress for his violin sonata, and the Ojai Valley Prize in California for his string quartet. In 1937 he was appointed prof. at the Brussels Cons., but a severe attack of uremia led to his premature death. He wrote in a judiciously modern idiom, seasoned with prudential dissonance.

WORKS: 2 symph. poems: *David* (1923) and *Poème Feerique* (1923); *Chant funèbre* for cello and orch. (1926); *Sérénade* for orch. (1929); *Chant d'Angoisse* for orch. (1930; his most distinctive work); Nocturne for Orch. (1931); *Divertissement* for brass and percussion (1931); Cello Concertino (1932); 2 string quartets (1924, 1927); Violin Sonata (1925); Trio for Flute, Viola and Piano (1926); Sextet for Wind Quintet with Second Flute (1927); Suite, for flute, oboe, clarinet, bassoon and piano (1929); *Choral* for organ (1930); *Sicilienne* for piano (1934); *Pastourelle* for cello and piano (1934); Sonatine for Flute and Viola (1934); String Trio (1935); Wind Quintet (1936); songs, of which the best known is *Horoscopes* (1926). A catalogue of his works was publ. by the Centre Belge de Documentation Musicale (1954).

Hyde, Walter, English tenor; b. Birmingham, Feb. 6, 1875; d. London, Nov. 11, 1951. He studied with Gustave Garcia; sang in light opera before he undertook Wagnerian roles, which became his specialty. He sang Siegmund at Covent Garden in 1908; his other roles included Walter in *Die Meistersinger* and also Parsifal. He was a frequent participant at many musical festivals in England.

Hyllested, August, Swedish pianist and composer; b. Stockholm, June 17, 1856; d. Blairmore, Scotland, April 5, 1946. He played in public as a child; then studied at the Copenhagen Cons. with Niels Gade, and subsequently with Th. Kullak (piano) and Fr. Kiel (composition) in Berlin; then had some lessons from Liszt. He gave concerts as pianist in England (1883) and in America (1885). From 1886–91 he was prof. and assistant director of the Chicago Musical College; from 1891–94, taught piano at the Gottschalk Lyric School, Chicago. After a concert tour in Europe, he returned to Chicago in 1897; he was in Glasgow from 1903–14; then again in the U.S. (1916–19); in Denmark and Sweden (1919–21); in 1923, retired to Blairmore, where he died shortly before his 90th birthday. He published numerous piano pieces in a Romantic style (*Album Leaf, Valse sentimentale, Suite romantique,* etc.), a suite of Scandinavian dances; also a fantasia on Scotch tunes; choral pieces; a symph. poem, *Elizabeth,* with double chorus (London, 1897, composer conducting).

I

Ibach, Johannes Adolf, German piano maker; b. Barmen, Oct. 17, 1766; d. there, Sept. 14, 1848. In 1794, he founded a piano factory at Barmen; also manufactured organs from 1834, with his son **C. Rudolf Ibach;** then traded under the name of Adolf Ibach & Sohn; from 1839, as Rudolf & Söhne, when his son **Richard** joined. From 1862 the firm was known as C. Rudolf & Richard Ibach, to distinguish it from another business founded by a third son, **Gustav J.** The same year C. Rudolf died, and in 1869 his son **Rudolf** (d. Herrenalb, Black Forest, July 31, 1892) continued the piano factory alone as Rudolf Ibach Sohn, established a branch at Cologne, gained medals for the excellence of his pianos, and became purveyor to the Prussian court. **Richard Ibach** continued the organ factory.

BIBLIOGRAPHY: *Das Haus Ibach 1794–1894* (1895).

Ibert, Jacques, French composer; b. Paris, Aug. 15, 1890; d. there, Feb. 5, 1962. He studied at the Paris Cons. with Gédalge and Fauré (1911–14); during World War I served in the French Navy; returned to the Paris Cons. after the Armistice and studied with Paul Vidal; recieved the Prix de Rome in 1919 for his cantata *Le Poète et la fée;* while in Rome, he wrote his most successful work, the symph. suite *Escales (Ports of Call),* inspired by a Mediterranean cruise while serving in the Navy. In 1937 he was appointed director of the Academy of Rome, and held this post until 1955, when he became director of the united management of the Paris Opéra and Opéra-Comique (until 1957). In his music, Ibert combines the most felicitous moods and techniques of Impressionism and neo-Classicism; his harmonies are opulent; his instrumentation is coloristic; there is an element of humor in lighter works, such as his popular orchestral *Divertissement* and an even more popular piece, *Le Petit Âne blanc* from the piano suite *Histoires.* His craftsmanship is excellent; an experimenter in tested values, he never fails to produce the intended effect.

WORKS: OPERAS: *Angélique* (Paris, Jan. 28, 1927); *Persée et Andromède* (Paris, May 15, 1929); *Le Roi d'Yvetot* (Paris, Jan. 15, 1930); *Gonzague* (Monte Carlo, 1935); *L'Aiglon,* after Edmond Rostand, in collaboration with Honegger (Monte Carlo, March 11, 1937); *Les Petites Cardinal,* with Honegger (Paris, 1938); *Barbebleue,* radio opera (Lausanne Radio, Oct. 10, 1943). BALLETS (all first performed in Paris): *Les Rencontres* (Nov. 21, 1925); *Diane de Poitiers* (April 30, 1934, produced by Ida Rubinstein); *Les Amours de Jupiter* (March 9, 1946); *Le Chevalier errant* (May 5, 1950); a ballet, *Tropismes pour des Amours Imaginaires* (1957). FOR ORCH.: symph. poem, *Noël en Picardie* (1914); *Ballade de la geôle de Reading,* after Oscar Wilde (Paris, Oct. 22, 1922); 3 symph. pictures (Paris, Jan. 6, 1924); *Féerique,* a symph. scherzo (Paris, Dec. 12, 1925); Concerto for Cello and Wind Instruments (Paris, Feb. 28, 1926); *Divertissement,* suite (Paris, Nov. 30, 1930; from incidental music to *Le Chapeau de paille d'Italie); Paris,* suite for chamber orch. (Venice, Sept. 15, 1932; from incidental music to *Donogoo,* play by Jules Romains); Flute Concerto (Paris, Feb. 25, 1934); *Concertino da Camera* for saxophone and chamber orch. (Paris, May 2, 1935); *Capriccio* (1938); *Ouverture de fête* (Paris, Jan. 18, 1942); *Suite élisabéthaine* (1944); *Symphonie Concertante,* for oboe and string orch. (Basel, Feb. 11, 1949); *Louisville Concerto* (Louisville, Feb. 17, 1954); *Hommage à Mozart* for orch. (1957); *Bacchanale* for orch. (1958); *Bostoniana* for orch. (1956–61). VOCAL WORKS: *Le Poète et la fée,* cantata (1919); *Chant de folie* for solo voices, chorus, and orch. (Boston, April 23, 1926); *Trois chansons* for voice and orch. or piano; *La Verdure dorée,* for voice and piano; *Chanson du rien,* for voice and piano; *Quintette de la peur* for chorus and piano (1946). CHAMBER MUSIC: *2 mouvements,* for 2 flutes, clarinet, and bassoon (1923); *Jeux,* sonatina for flute and piano (1924); *3 pièces brèves,* for flute, oboe, clarinet, horn, and bassoon (1930); *Pastoral,* for 4 fifes (in *Pipeaux,* by various composers, 1934); *Entr'acte,* for flute and guitar (1935); String Quartet (1944); Trio for Violin, Cello, and Harp (1944); *2 Interludes* for violin and harpsichord (1949); also 6 pieces for harp (1917); a piece for unaccompanied flute (1936). FOR PIANO: *Histoires* (10 pieces); *Les Rencontres,* arranged from the ballet (5 pieces); *Petite suite en 15 images* (1943).

BIBLIOGRAPHY: A. Hoerée, "J. Ibert," *Revue Musicale* (July 1929); G. Samazeuilh, *Musiciens de mon temps* (Paris, 1947); J. Feschotte, *Jacques Ibert* (Paris, 1959); G. Michel, *Jacques Ibert, l'homme et son œuvre* (Paris, 1968).

Idelsohn, Abraham Zevi, eminent Jewish musicologist: b. Pfilsburg, near Libau (Latvia), July 13, 1882; d. Johannesburg, South Africa, Aug. 14, 1938. He studied in Königsberg, in Berlin, and with Jadassohn and Kretzschmar at the Leipzig Cons. He possessed a powerful baritone voice and for a time was cantor of the Synagogue at Regensburg (1903); then went to Johannesburg and later (1905–21) to Jerusalem, where he founded an Institute for Jewish Music (1910) and a Jewish Music School (1919). In 1921, he returned to Germany; then went to the U.S.; lectured at the Hebrew Union College in Cincinnati (1924–34). In 1934 he suffered a paralytic stroke; was taken to Miami, and in 1937 to Johannesburg, where he finally succumbed. Idelsohn was one of the greatest authorities on Jewish Music and contributed much towards its establishment on a scientific basis.

WRITINGS: He publ. a quantity of studies in English, German and Hebrew on Oriental and Hebrew music, of which the most important are: *History of Jewish Music* (in Hebrew, 1924; 2nd ed., 1928, also publ. in English); *The Ceremonies of Judaism* (1923–30); *Diwan of Hebrew and Arabic Poetry of the Yemenite Jews* (in Hebrew; 1930); *Jewish Liturgy and Its Development* (1932; reprint issued by the Hebrew Union College, N.Y., 1956); "Musical Characteristics of East European Jewish Folk-Songs," in the *Musical Quarterly* (Oct. 1932). His most important contribution to the study of Jewish music is the monumental *Thesaurus of Hebrew-Oriental Melodies* (10 vols.; 1914–32), in which are collected, with the aid of phonograph recordings, Jewish melodies of Northern Africa, Asia Minor, Palestine, and other parts of the world. He also composed and publ. 6 Synagogue Services, Hebrew songs (1929), a music drama *Jephtah* (1922), and a *Jewish Song Book for Synagogue, Home and School* (1929).

Ifukube, Akira, Japanese composer; b. Kushiro (Hokkaido), March 7, 1914. As a young man, he was trained in forestry; then turned to music, and took lessons from Alexander Tcherepnin, who was in Japan at the time.

WORKS: Ifukube wrote several ballets based on Japanese melodies and employing Impressionistic harmonies: *Enchanted Citadel* (Tokyo, Dec. 20, 1949), *Drums of Japan* (Tokyo, Dec. 29, 1951), etc.; for orch.: *Japanese Rhapsody* (Boston, April 5, 1936); *Aboriginal Triptych* (1938); *Symphonie Concertante* for piano and orch. (Tokyo, March 3, 1942; music destroyed in an air raid); *Ballade Symphonique* (Tokyo, Nov. 20, 1943); *Arctic Forest* (Changchun, Manchuria, April 26, 1944); also Violin Concerto (Tokyo, June 22, 1948).

Igumnov, Konstantin, Russian pianist and pedagogue; b. Lebedyan, near Tambov, May 1, 1873; d. Moscow, March 24, 1948. He studied piano with Zverev and Siloti, and theory with Taneyev, Arensky and Ippolitov-Ivanov at the Moscow Cons., graduating as pianist in the class of Pabst (1894). He gave numerous concerts, specializing in Romantic music, and was regarded as an artist of impeccable taste who worked out every detail of the music to utmost perfection. But great as his artistic reputation was in Russia (he rarely, if ever, played abroad), his main accomplishment was that of a piano pedagogue. He was appointed prof. of the Moscow Cons. in 1899, and remained on its staff for nearly half a century until his death. Among his students were Nicolai Orlov, Dobrowen and Oborin.

BIBLIOGRAPHY: Yakov Milstein, *K. N. Igumnov* (Moscow, 1975).

Ikebe, Shin-ichirō, Japanese composer; b. Mito, Sept. 15, 1943. He attended the Tokyo Univ. of Arts, as a student of Ikenouchi and Miyoshi; after graduation in 1971 he joined the faculty of the Univ. and the Tokyo College of Music.

WORKS: an opera, *The Death Goddess* (produced on Tokyo television, July 25, 1971; winner of Salzburg Opera Prize, 1971); a ballet, *Creature* (1974); Piano Sonatina (1963); Solo Violin Sonata (1965); *"Crepa" in 7 capitoli,* concerto da camera for solo violin, 3 violas, cello and double bass (1966); Piano Concerto (1967); Symphony (Tokyo, March 30, 1968); *Petite Symphonie* for youth orch. (1969); *Lion* for brass ensemble (1969); *Un-en* for 3 Japanese instruments, violin, viola, cello and double bass (1970); *Energeia* for 60 performers (1970); *Clipper by 9* for 9 instruments (1971); *Trivalence I* for flute, violin and piano (1971); *Trivalence II* for clarinet, cello and harpsichord (1973); *Flash!* for flute ensemble (1972); *Monovalence I* for marimba (1972), *II* for harp (1973), *III* for voice (1973), *IV* for marimba (1975) and *V* for double bass (1975); *Ascension* for piano (1974); *Dimorphism* for organ and orch. (1974); *Quadrants* for a group of Japanese instruments and orch. (1974); several works

for solo or grouped Japanese instruments; choral works; film music.

Ikenouchi, Tomojirō, Japanese composer, b. Tokyo, Oct. 21, 1906. He received his musical education at the Paris Cons.; upon his return to Japan, was appointed professor of composition at State High School of Music in Tokyo.

WORKS: *Yuya,* music for a *Nō* drama (Tokyo, Feb. 1, 1943); 2 symph. movements (Tokyo, Nov. 4, 1951); 3 string quartets, etc.

Ikonen, Lauri, Finnish musicologist and composer; b. Mikkeli, Aug. 10, 1888; d. Helsinki, March 21, 1966. He studied at Helsinki Univ. and with Paul Juon in Berlin (1910–13); was editor of the Finnish music magazine *Suomen Musikkilehti* (1923–29). His music follows the Romantic tradition of Sibelius.

WORKS: 6 symphonies; No 1, *Sinfonia inornata* (1922); No. 2 (1937); No. 3, *Lemmin poika (Son of Lemmi,* 1941, revised 1959); No. 4, *Sinfonia concentrata* (1942); No. 5, *Sinfonia aperta* (1943); No. 6 (1956); *Koulemaantuomitun mielialoja (Thoughts of a Condemned Man),* for baritone and orch. (1936); Violin Concerto (1939); Piano Trio (1941); *Concerto Meditativo,* for cello and orch. (1942); *Concerto Intimo* for piano (1956); *Elaman lahja (The Gift of Life)* for soloists, chorus and orch. (1956); 2 violin sonatas; Piano Sonata; choral works; songs.

Ikonomov, Boyan, Bulgarian composer; b. Nikopol, Dec. 14, 1900; d. Sofia, March 27, 1973. He studied music in Sofia (1920–26); then went to Paris where he attended classes of Vincent d'Indy and Guy de Lioncourt at the Schola Cantorum in Paris (1928–32); also took a course in conducting with Weingartner in Basel (1934). Returning to Bulgaria, he was music director of the Sofia Radio (1937–48) and of the Bulgarian film center (1948–56). His music is rooted in Bulgarian folksongs, with an emphasis on modal melodic progressions and asymmetric rhythms.

WORKS: *Indje Voivoda* (1960); a children's operetta, *The Young Artful Boys* (1960); 3 ballets: *The 7 Mortal Sins* (1933). *The Tragedy of Othello* (1946) and *The Light Floods Everything* (1967); 2 oratorios: *The Legend of Shipka* (1968) and *Vassil Levsky* (1972); 2 cantatas: *George Dimitrov* (1954) and *Poem About Lenin* (1969); *Haidouk Rhapsody* for orch. (1932); Sinfonietta (1934); *Kaliakra,* symph. poem (1935); *Pastorale* for chamber orch. (1937); 4 symphonies (1937, 1947, 1955, 1971); *Pastorale and Dance* for orch. (1939); *Shar Planina,* symph. poem (1942); Violin Concerto (1951); Divertimento for String Quartet and Orch. (1956); Piano Concertino (1958); 6 string quartets (1933, 1937, 1941, 1944, 1945, 1949); 2 trios for oboe, clarinet and bassoon (1935, 1968); Cello Sonata; choral and solo songs; incidental music.

Ilerici, Kemal, Turkish composer, b. Kastamonu, Oct. 15, 1910. He studied composition with Ferit Alnar. Among his works are a symphonic suite, *In My Village* (1945), *Pastoral Fantasy* for orch. (1951), String Quartet, Suite for Oboe and Piano, and choral works. He wrote a book on Turkish music, *Türk Musikisi Tonal Sistemi ve Armonisi* (1948).

Iliev, Konstantin, Bulgarian composer and conductor; b. Sofia, March 9, 1924. He studied composition with Khadzhiev and Vladigerov and conducting with Goleminov at the Sofia Music Academy (1942–46); later took courses in composition with Řídký and Alois Hába and in conducting with Talich at the Prague Cons. (1946–48). Returning to Bulgaria, he devoted himself mainly to conducting; was a conductor at the State Opera in Sofia (1947–56); then conducted the Sofia Philharmonic Orchestra (1956–72). In 1964 he was appointed to the faculty of the State Cons. in Sofia. As a composer, he has evolved a rather stimulating idiom, adroitly exploring the asymmetric Balkan rhythms and oriental melismas to create an aura of folkloric authenticity; in non-ethnic pieces he often applies serial principles of melodic formations.
WORKS: the opera *The Master of Boyana* (Sofia, Oct. 3, 1962); an oratorio, *Eulogy to Constantin the Philosopher* (1971); 5 symphonies (1947, 1951, 1954, 1958, 1959); *Concerto Grosso* for string orch., piano and percussion (1949); *Symphonic Variations* (1951); *Tempi concertanti I* for string orch. (1967); *Tempi concertanti II* for flute, harpsichord and 12 instruments (1969); Violin Concerto (1971); 4 string quartets (1949, 1952, 1953, 1956); Piano Trio (1976); choruses.

Iliffe, Frederick, English composer; b. Smeet-on-Westerby, Leicester, Feb. 21, 1847; d. Oxford, Feb. 2, 1928. He was organist at St. John's College in Oxford; wrote an oratorio, *The Visions of St. John the Divine* (1880); a cantata, *Lara* (1885); organ music; publ. *Critical Analysis of Bach's Well-tempered Clavichord* (London, 1869).

Ilitsch, Daniza, Serbian soprano; b. Belgrade, Feb. 21, 1914; d. Vienna, Jan. 15, 1965. She studied at the Stankovic Cons. there; made her debut as Nedda in *Pagliacci* with the Berlin State Opera (Nov. 6, 1936); was on its staff for 2 seasons; then became a member of the Vienna State Opera (1938–41); the German army of occupation put her in a concentration camp in 1944, and she spent 4 months there until the liberation of Vienna. In 1947 she came to America; made her debut with the Metropolitan Opera as Desdemona (March 12, 1947).

Illica, Luigi, Italian librettist; b. Castell' Arquato, Piacenza, May 9, 1857; d. Colombarone, Piacenza, Dec. 16, 1919. He was engaged as a journalist in Milan; after 1892 devoted himself to writing librettos. He was the author (in collaboration with Giacosa) of librettos for Puccini's operas *La Bohème, Tosca,* and *Madama Butterfly;* and the sole writer of the text for Giordano's *Andrea Chenier* and Mascagni's *Le Maschere.*

Ilyinsky, Alexander, Russian composer; b. Tsarskoye Selo, Jan. 24, 1859; d. Moscow, Feb. 23, 1920. He studied in Berlin with Kullak (piano) and Bargiel (composition); upon returning to Moscow in 1885, was teacher at the Philharmonica Institute there. He wrote an opera, *The Fountain of Bakhtchissaray;* publ. *Trois valses brillantes* for piano, etc.

Imbert, Hugues, French music critic and essayist; b. Moulins-Engilbert, Nièvre, Jan. 11, 1842; d. Paris, Jan. 15, 1905. He studied violin; was on the editorial staff of *Le Guide Musical.* He publ. *Profils des Musiciens* (in 3 series: 1888, 1892, 1897); *Symphonie* (1891); *Portraits et Études* (1894); *Rembrandt et Wagner* (1897); *Charles Gounod, l'Autobiographie et les Mémoires* (1897); *Bizet* (1899); *La Symphonie après Beethoven* (1900); *Médaillons contemporains* (1902); *J. Brahms: Sa vie et son œuvre* (publ. posthumously, 1906).

Imbrie, Andrew (Welsh), notable American composer; b. New York, April 6, 1921. He studied piano with Leo Ornstein (1930–42); then served in the Signal Corps of the U.S. Army during World War II; spent a summer studying composition with Nadia Boulanger at Fontainebleau; intermittently had fruitful sessions with Sessions, first privately, then at Princeton Univ. and at the Univ. of California at Berkeley (M.A., 1947). In 1947 he was awarded the American Prix de Rome; after a sojourn in Italy he was appointed prof. of music at Berkeley. He held 2 Guggenheim grants (1953–54, 1960–61). His style of composition is marked by a sharp and expressive melodic line, while the polyphony is vigorously motile; harmonic confluence is dissonant but euphoniously tonal. Imbrie's natural propensity is towards instrumental writing; even his choral pieces possess the texture of chamber music.
WORKS: FOR ORCH.: *Ballad in D* (1947; Florence, June 20, 1949); Violin Concerto (1954; San Francisco, April 22, 1958); *Little Concerto* for piano 4-hands and orch. (1956); *Legend,* symph. poem (San Francisco, Dec. 9, 1959); Symph. No. 1 (San Francisco, May 11, 1966); Symph. No. 2 (1969); Symph. No. 3 (1970); Cello Concerto (1972); Piano Concerto No. 1 (1973); Piano Concerto No. 2 (1974); Flute Concerto (N.Y., Oct. 13, 1977); CHAMBER MUSIC: 4 string quartets (1942, 1953, 1957, 1969); Piano Trio (1946); *Divertimento* for 6 instruments (1948); *Serenade* for flute, viola and piano (1952); *Impromptu* for violin and piano (1960); Cello Sonata (1966); Chamber Symphony (1968); Piano Sonata (1947); VOCAL WORKS: *On the Beach at Night,* to words by Walt Whitman (1948); *Drum Taps,* cantata to words by Walt Whitman (1961); 2 operas: *Christmas in Peeples Town* (Berkeley, Calif., Dec. 3, 1964); *Angle of Repose,* after the novel of Wallace Stegner (San Francisco, Nov. 6, 1976).

Inch, Herbert Reynolds, American composer; b. Missoula, Montana, Nov. 25, 1904. He studied at the State Univ. of Montana and then at the Eastman School of Music in Rochester, with Howard Hanson (Mus. Bac., 1925; M.M., 1928); he was a fellow of the American Academy in Rome in 1931. After teaching for several years at the Eastman School, he became a member of the faculty at Hunter College, N.Y. (1937–65); in 1965 moved to La Jolla, Calif.
WORKS: *Variations on a Modal Theme* (Rochester, April 29, 1927); *Three Pieces,* for small orch. (Rochester, Oct. 24, 1930); Symphony No. 1 (Rochester, May 5, 1932); *Serenade,* for small orch. (Rochester, Oct. 24, 1939); Piano Concerto (1940); *Answers to a Questionnaire,* for orch. (1942); *Northwest Overture* (1943); Violin Concerto (Rochester, May 1, 1947); *Re-*

turn to Zion, for women's chorus (1945); Piano Quintet (1930); *Mediterranean Sketches,* for string quartet (1933); Divertimento, for brass (1934); String Quartet (1936); Cello Sonata (1941); *Three Conversations,* for string quartet (1944); 3 symphoniettas (1948, 1950, 1955); Piano Trio (1963); 3 piano sonatas (1935, 1946, 1966).

d'India, Sigismondo, Italian madrigal composer; b. c.1580, probably in Palermo; d. in 1629, possibly in Modena. He was director of music at the Savoy court in Turin from 1601 until 1623; then was in the service of the Cardinal of Savoy in Rome. He publ. 8 books of madrigals in 5 parts, 5 books of arias and cantatas in the monodic style, which was then coming into fashion, entitled simply *Musiche* (possibly by association with Caccini's *Le nuove musiche);* and, in the polyphonic style, two books of *Sacri Concentus* (1610) and a book of motets (1627). D'India is reputed for the comparative boldness of his harmonic progressions in the otherwise static monody affected by his Florentine contemporaries. His opera (in recitative), *Zalizura,* is extant.

d'Indy, (Paul-Marie-Théodore-) Vincent, eminent French composer; b. Paris, March 27, 1851; d. there, Dec. 2, 1931. Owing to the death of his mother at his birth, his education was directed entirely by his grandmother, a woman of culture and refinement who had known Grétry and Monsigny, and who had shown a remarkable appreciation of the works of Beethoven when that master was still living. From 1862-65 he studied piano with Diémer, and later harmony and theory with Marmontel and Lavignac. In 1869 he made the acquaintance of Henri Duparc, and with him spent much time studying the masterpieces of Bach, Beethoven, Berlioz, and Wagner; at that time, he wrote his op. 1 and 2, and contemplated an opera on Victor Hugo's *Les Burgraves* (1869-72; unfinished). During the Franco-Prussian War he served in the Garde Mobile, and wrote his experiences in *Histoire du 105ᵉ bataillon de la Garde nationale de Paris en l'année 1870-71* (1872). He then began to study composition with César Franck, continuing until 1880; when the latter was appointed prof. of organ at the Cons. (1873), he joined the class, winning a second *accessit* in 1874 and the first the following year. On his first visit to Germany in 1873 he met Liszt and Wagner, and was introduced to Brahms; in 1876, heard the first performances of the *Ring* dramas at Bayreuth, and for several years thereafter made regular trips to Munich to hear all the works of Wagner; also attended the première of *Parsifal* in 1882. From 1872-76, organist at St.-Leu; 1873-78, chorusmaster and timpanist with the Colonne Orch.; for the Paris première of *Lohengrin* in 1887 he drilled the chorus and was Lamoureux's assistant. In 1871 he joined the Société Nationale de Musique as a junior member, and was its secretary from 1876 till 1890, when, after Franck's death, he became president. In 1894 he founded with Bordes and Guilmant the famous Schola Cantorum (opened 1896), primarily as a school for plainchant and the Palestrina style. Gradually the scope of instruction was enlarged so as to include all musical disciplines, and the institution became one of the world's foremost music schools. His fame as a composer began with the performance of *Le Chant de la cloche* at a Lamoureux concert in 1886; the work itself had won the City of Paris Prize in the competition of the preceding year. As early as 1874 Pasdeloup had played the overture *Les Piccolomini* (later embodied as the second part in the *Wallenstein* trilogy), and in 1882 the 1-act opera *Attendez-moi sous l'orme* had been produced at the Opéra-Comique; but the prize work attracted general attention, and d'Indy was recognized as one of the most important of modern French masters. Although he never held an official position as conductor, he frequently, and with marked success, appeared in that capacity (chiefly upon invitation to direct his own works); thus he visited Spain in 1897, Russia in 1903 and 1907, and the U.S. in 1905, when he conducted the regular subscription concerts of Dec. 1 and 2 of the Boston Symph. Orch. In 1892 he was a member of the commission appointed to revise the curriculum of the Conservatoire, and refused a proffered professorship of composition; but in 1912 accepted an appointment as prof. of the ensemble class. Besides other duties, he discharged, from 1899, those of inspector of musical instruction in Paris; last U.S. visit in 1921. He was made Chevalier of the Legion of Honor in 1892, Officer in 1912; was also member of many academies and artistic associations (in Belgium, Holland, Spain, Italy, Sweden, etc.). Both as teacher and creative artist d'Indy continued the traditions of César Franck. Although he cultivated almost every form of composition, his special talent seemed to be in the field of the larger instrumental forms. Some French critics assign to him a position in French music analogous to that of Brahms in German music. His style rests on Bach and Beethoven; however, his deep study of Gregorian Chant and the early contrapuntal style added an element of severity, and not rarely of complexity, that renders approach somewhat difficult, and has prompted the charge that his music is lacking in emotional force.

WRITINGS: In addition to composition, d'Indy did some important editing and wrote several books. For the edition of Rameau's complete works (ed. by Saint-Saëns and Malherbe) he revised *Dardanus, Hippolyte et Aricie,* and *Zais;* also ed. Monteverdi's *Orfeo* and *Incoronazione di Poppea;* he also made piano arrangements of orchestral works by Chausson, Duparc, and other composers. His numerous articles in various journals are remarkable for critical acumen and literary finish. He publ. an important manual, *Cours de Composition musicale* (Book I, 1903; Book II: Part 1, 1909, Part 2, 1933); *César Franck* (1906; in English, 1910, reprinted, N.Y., 1965); *Beethoven: Biographie critique* (1911; English transl. by Th. Baker, Boston, 1913; reprint, N.Y., 1970); *La Schola Cantorum en 1925* (1927); *Wagner et son influence sur l'art musical français* (1930); *Introduction à l'étude de Parsifal* (1937; posthumous).

WORKS: FOR THE STAGE: op. 14, *Attendez-moi sous l'orme,* 1-act comic opera (Opéra-Comique, Feb. 11, 1882); op. 18, *Le Chant de la cloche,* dramatic legend (Brussels, Théâtre de la Monnaie, Nov. 21, 1912); op. 40, *Fervaal,* lyric drama (Brussels, March 12, 1897); op. 53, *L'Étranger,* lyric drama (Brussels, Jan. 7, 1903); op. 67, *La Légende de Saint-Christophe,* lyric drama (Paris Opéra, June 9, 1920); op. 80, *Le Rêve de Cynias,* lyric comedy (Paris, June 10, 1927). FOR ORCH.: op. 5, *Jean Hunyade,* symph. (Paris, May 15, 1875); op. 6, *Antoine et Cléopâtre,* overture (Paris, Feb. 4, 1877); op. 8, *La Forêt enchantée,* symph. legend (Paris, March 24, 1878); op. 12, *Wallenstein,* symphonic trilogy: a) *Le Camp de Wallenstein* (April 12, 1880), b) *Max et Thécla* (Jan. 25, 1874; originally *Les Piccolomini),* c) *La Mort de Wallenstein* (April 11, 1884); op. 19, *Lied* for cello and orch. (Paris, April 18, 1885); op. 21, *Saugefleurie,* legend (Paris, Jan. 25, 1885); op. 25, *Symphonie Cévenole (sur un chant montagnard français)* for orch. and piano (Paris, March 20, 1887); op. 28, *Sérénade et Valse* (from op. 16 and 17), for small orch. (1887); op. 31, *Fantaisie* for oboe and orch. (Paris, Dec. 23, 1888); op. 34, incidental music to Alexandre's *Karadec* (Paris, May 2, 1891); op. 36, *Tableaux de Voyage* (Le Havre, Jan. 17, 1892); op. 42, *Istar,* symph. variations (Brussels, Jan. 10, 1897); op. 47, incidental music to Mendès's *Medée* (1898); op. 55, *Choral varié* for saxophone and orch. (Paris, May 17, 1904); op. 57, 2nd Symphony in B-flat (Paris, Feb. 28, 1904); op. 61, *Jour d'été à la montagne* (Paris, Feb. 18, 1906); op. 62, *Souvenirs,* tone poem (Paris, April 20, 1907); op. 67, *La Queste de Dieu,* descriptive symph. (from *La Légende de Saint-Christophe;* 1917); op. 70, 3rd Symphony: *Sinfonia Brevis de Bello Gallico* (1916–18; Paris, Dec. 14, 1919); op. 77, *Le Poème des rivages* (N.Y., Dec. 1, 1921); op. 87, *Diptyque méditerranéen* (Paris, Dec. 5, 1926); op. 89, Concerto for Piano, Flute, Cello, and String Orch. (Paris, April 2, 1927). CHAMBER MUSIC: op. 7, Piano Quartet in A minor (1878); op. 24, Suite in D, for trumpet, 2 flutes, and string orch. (Paris, March 5, 1887); op. 29, Trio for Piano, Clarinet, and Cello (1888); op. 35, String Quartet No. 1 (1891); op. 45, String Quartet No. 2 (1898); op. 50, *Chansons et Danses, divertissement* for 7 wind instruments (Paris, March 7, 1899); op. 59, Violin Sonata (1905); op. 81, Piano Quintet in G minor (1925); op. 84, Cello Sonata (1926); op. 91, *Suite en 4 parties* for flute, strings, and harp (Paris, May 17, 1930); op. 92, String Sextet (1928); op. 96, String Quartet No. 3 (1929); op. 98, Trio No. 2, for piano, violin, cello (1929). VOCAL WORKS: op. 2, *Chanson des aventuriers de la mer,* for baritone solo and men's chorus (1870); op. 11, *La Chevauchée du Cid,* for baritone, chorus, and orch. (1879); op. 22, *Cantate Domino* (1885); op. 23, *Ste. Marie-Magdeleine,* cantata (1885); op. 32, *Sur la mer,* for women's voices and piano (1888); op. 37, *Pour l'inauguration d'une statue,* cantata (1893); op. 39, *L'Art et le peuple,* for men's chorus (1894); op. 41, *Deus Israël,* motet (1896); op. 44, *Ode à Valence* for soprano and chorus (1897); op. 46, *Les Noces d'or du sacerdoce* (1898); op. 49, *Sancta Maria,* motet (1898); opp. 90 and 100, 6 *Chants populaires français,* for a cappella chorus (1928 and 1931); op. 93, *Le Bouquet de printemps,* for women's chorus (1929); songs (opp. 3, 4, 10, 13, 20, 43, 48, 52, 56, 58, 64). FOR PIANO: op. 1, *Trois Romances sans paroles* (1870); op. 9, *Petite sonate* (1880); op. 15, *Poème des montagnes: Le Chant des bruyères, Danses rythmiques, Plein-air* (1881); op. 16, *Quatre Pièces* (1882); op. 17, *Helvetia,* 3 waltzes (1882); op. 21, *Saugefleurie* (1884; also arranged for orch.); op. 26, *Nocturne* (1886); op. 27, *Promenade* (1887); op. 30, *Schuman-*

niana, 3 pieces (1887); op. 33, *Tableaux de Voyage,* 13 pieces (1889); op. 60, *Petite chanson grégorienne,* for piano 4 hands (1904); op. 63, Sonata (1907); op. 65, *Menuet sur le nom de Haydn* (1909); op. 68, *13 Short Pieces;* op. 69, *12 petites pièces faciles,* in old style; op. 73, *7 Chants de terroir* for piano 4 hands; op. 74, *Pour les enfants de tous les âges,* 24 pieces; op. 85, *Thème varié, fugue et chanson;* op. 86, *Conte de fées,* suite (1926); op. 95, 6 paraphrases on French children's songs; op. 99, *Fantaisie sur un vieil air de ronde française* (1931). FOR ORGAN: op. 38, *Prélude et Petit Canon* (1893); op. 51, *Vépres du Commun d'un Martyr* (1889); op. 66, *Prélude* (1913). WITHOUT OPUS NUMBER: *O gai Soleil,* canon a 2 (1909); incidental music to *Veronica* (1920); *3 Chansons anciennes du Vivarais* (1926); *La Vengeance du mari,* for 3 soli, chorus, and orch. (1931).

BIBLIOGRAPHY: E. Deniau, *Vincent d'Indy* (Toulouse, 1903); A. Hervey, *French Music in the 19th Century* (London, 1903); F. Starczewski, *La Schola Cantorum de Paris, ou Vincent d'Indy considéré comme professeur* (Warsaw, 1905); O. Séré, *Musiciens français d'aujourd'hui* (2nd ed., Paris, 1911); L. Borgex, *Vincent d'Indy: Sa vie et son œuvre* (Paris, 1913); A. Sérieyx, *Vincent d'Indy* (Paris, 1913); Romain Rolland, *Musiciens d'aujourd'hui* (Paris, 1914); E. B. Hill, "Vincent d'Indy, an Estimate," *Musical Quarterly* (April 1915); Paul Landormy, "Vincent d'Indy," *Musical Quarterly* (July 1932); M. M. de Fraguier, *Vincent d'Indy* (Paris, 1933); L. Vallas, "The Discovery of Musical Germany by Vincent d'Indy in 1873," *Musical Quarterly* (April 1939); Léon Vallas, *Vincent d'Indy: I. La Jeunesse. II. La Maturité, La Vieillesse* (Paris, I., 1946; II., 1950; the basic biography); J. Canteloube, *Vincent d'Indy* (Paris, 1949); Norman Demuth, *Vincent d'Indy* (London, 1951); J. Guy-Ropartz, ed., *Le Centenaire de Vincent d'Indy, 1851–1951* (Paris, 1952); L. Davies, *Cesar Franck and His Circle* (Boston, 1970); C. B. Paul, "Rameau, d'Indy, and French Nationalism," *Musical Quarterly* (Jan. 1972).

Infantas, Fernando de las, Spanish musician and theologian; b. Córdoba, 1534; d. after 1609. He belonged to a noble family and enjoyed the protection of the Emperor Charles V and later of Philip II, who employed him on diplomatic missions in Italy. He went to Venice, and then to Rome, where he lived for 25 years (1572–97). He exerted a decisive influence upon the course of Catholic church music by opposing the plan for the reform of the Roman Gradual undertaken by Palestrina in 1578 at the request of Pope Gregory XIII. Backed by the authority of Philip II of Spain, he succeeded in having the project abandoned. He publ. *Sacrarum varii styli cantionum tituli Spiritus Sancti,* a collection of motets in 3 books: I for 4 voices, II for 5 voices (both publ. in Venice, 1578), III for 6–8 voices (Venice, 1579), and *Plura modulationum genera quae vulgo contrapuncta appellantur super excelso gregoriano cantu* (Venice, 1579; contains 100 contrapuntal exercises for 2–8 voices based on 1 plainsong theme; pointed the way to a new freedom and elasticity in polyphonic writing); separate compositions were also publ. in various collections of the time. A Sequence for 6 voices, *Victimae paschali,* was publ. by W. Dehn in *Sammlung älterer Musik aus dem 16. und 17. Jahrhundert*, vol. V, pp. 6–11 (Berlin, 1837–40).

BIBLIOGRAPHY: R. F. Molitor, *Die nachtridentinische Choralreform* (vol. I); R. Mitjana, *Don Fernando de las Infantas, teólogo y músico* (Madrid, 1918); R. Stevenson, *Spanish Cathedral Music in the Golden Age* (Berkeley, Calif., 1961).

Infante, Manuel, Spanish composer; b. Osuna, near Seville, July 29, 1883; d. Paris, April 21, 1958. He studied piano and composition with Enrique Morera; in 1909 he settled in Paris; gave concerts of Spanish music; wrote numerous pieces for piano, mostly on Spanish themes: *Gitanerias; Pochades Andalouses; Sevillana,* fantasy (1922); *El Vito* (variations on a popular theme); also an opera, *Almanza.*

Ingegneri, Marco Antonio, Italian composer; b. Verona, c.1545; d. Cremona, July 1, 1592. He was a pupil of Vincenzo Ruffo, organist of Verona Cathedral. He went to Cremona about 1568 and became maestro di cappella at the cathedral there (1576). Monteverdi was his pupil.

WORKS: a book of Masses *a* 5–8 (1573); a second, *a* 5 (1587); 4 of madrigals *a* 4–5 (1578, 1579, 1580, 1584); *Sacrae cantiones a* 5 (1576); *Sacrae cantiones a* 7–16 (1589). The 27 celebrated Responses, formerly attributed to Palestrina, are by Ingegneri. They had been printed in Breikopf & Härtel's edition of Palestrina's works (vol. 32) as of doubtful authenticity, but were eliminated when Haberl, in 1897, discovered a copy (printed in Venice, 1588) with the full name of Ingegneri. Many other motets and madrigals appeared in collections of the time. A reprint of one of his motets is in Johannes Wolf's *Sing- und Spielmusik aus älterer Zeit.*

BIBLIOGRAPHY: F. Haberl, "M. A. Ingegneri," *Kirchenmusikalisches Jahrbuch* (1898); R. Casimiri, in *Note d'Archivio* (1926); Ellinor Dohrn, *Marc Antonio Ingegneri als Madrigalkomponist* (Hannover, 1936); G. Cesari, "La musica in Cremona," in *Istituzioni e monumenti dell'arte musicale italiana* (vol. 6).

Ingenhoven, Jan, Dutch composer; b. Breda, May 29, 1876; d. Hoenderlo, May 20, 1951. He studied with L. Brandts-Buys in Rotterdam and Mottl in Munich; lived in Germany and Switzerland; conducted a madrigal choir in Munich (1909–12); then devoted himself mainly to composition. His works are influenced by Debussy, but he preserves an element of peculiarly native melos. Among his works are a symph. fantasy, *Brabant and Holland;* 3 symphonic poems *(Lyric; Dramatic; Romantic);* 4 string quartets; Woodwind Quintet; Trio for Violin, Cello, and Harp; Trio for Flute, Clarinet, and Harp; Trio for Piano, Violin, and Cello; several choral works in the classical tradition; songs.

BIBLIOGRAPHY: D. Ruyneman, *De komponist Jan Ingenhoven* (Amsterdam, 1938).

Inghelbrecht, Désiré Émile, French conductor and composer; b. Paris, Sept. 17, 1880; d. Paris, Feb. 14, 1965. He studied at the Paris Cons.; after graduation, conducted at various theaters in Paris; toured as conductor of the Ballets Suédois (1919–22); was director of the Opéra-Comique (1924 and 1932–33). In 1945 he

became conductor of the Paris Opéra; also conducted abroad. He publ. several books and pamphlets on conducting: *Comment on ne doit pas interpréter Carmen, Faust et Pelléas* (1932); *Diabolus in musica* (1933); *Mouvement contraire: souvenirs d'un musicien* (1947); and *Le Chef d'orchestre et son équipe* (1948; English transl. as *The Conductor's World,* 1953).

WORKS: *La Nuit vénitienne,* opera in 3 acts after Musset (1908); BALLETS: *La Bonne Aventure* (1912), *El Greco* (Ballets Suédois, Paris, Nov. 18, 1920), *Le Diable dans le beffroi* (after Edgar Allan Poe; Paris Opéra, June 1, 1927), *Jeux de Couleurs* (Opéra-Comique, Feb. 21, 1933); *Le chêne et le tilleul,* opera-ballet (Paris, 1961); FOR ORCH.: *Automne* (1905); *Pour le jour de la première neige au vieux Japon* (1908); *Rapsodie de printemps* (1925); *La Métamorphose d'Éve* (1925); *La Légende du grand St. Nicolas* (1925); *Iberiana* for violin and orch. (1948); *Vézelay, évocation symphonique* (1952); CHAMBER MUSIC: *Deux esquisses antiques,* for flute and harp (1902); *Poème sylvestre,* for woodwinds (1905); Quintet for Strings and Harp (1918); pieces for cello and piano, and viola and piano; CHORAL WORKS: *Le Cantique des créatures de Saint François d'Assise,* for chorus and orch. (1919); Requiem (1940); *Quatre chansons populaires françaises,* for mixed chorus; PIANO WORKS: *La Nursery,* four-hand pieces for children, 3 vols. (1905 and 1911); *Suite petite-russienne* (1908); *Paysages* (1918), etc.; also songs (*Mélodies sur des poésies russes,* 1905; *Au jardin de l'infante,* 1910; etc.).

Insanguine, Giacomo (Antonio Francesco Paolo Michele), called **Monopoli,** Italian composer; b. Monopoli, March 22, 1728; d. Naples, Feb. 1, 1795. He studied with Cotumacci at the Cons. of San Onofrio in Naples; then became his master's assistant (1767) and second teacher (1774); after Cotumacci's death (1785), first teacher. He concurrently was second organist at the Cappella del Tesoro di San Gennaro (1774), first organist (1776); and maestro di cappella there (1781).

WORKS: some 15 operas, among them: *Lo Fumaco revotato* (1756); *Didone abbandonata* (1772); *Arianna e Teseo* (1773); *Adriano in Siria* (1773); *Le astuzie per amore* (1777); *Medonte* (1779); *Calipso* (1782). His best work is the 71st Psalm for 3-part chorus and orch.; he also composed other psalms, hymns, Masses, etc.

Inten, Ferdinand, German-American pianist and teacher, b. Leipzig, Feb. 23, 1848; d. New York, Jan. 16, 1918. He studied at the Leipzig Cons. (1862–66) with Moscheles, Plaidy, Hauptmann, and Reinecke; in 1868, came to the U.S. and settled in New York; made his American debut as piano soloist in N.Y., on Dec. 12, 1868. He organized concerts of chamber music, which became famous. As a teacher, he also achieved success; among his pupils were Frank and Walter Damrosch.

Inzenga, José, Spanish writer on music; b. Madrid, June 3, 1828; d. there, June 28, 1891. He first studied with his father, then at the Madrid Cons. and the Paris Cons.; prof. at the Madrid Cons. (1860). He was commissioned by the Minister of Public Instruction to make a collection of Spanish folksongs, which he publ. as *Cantos y bailes populares de España* (4 vols., 1888); also wrote a treatise on accompaniment, and *Impresiones de un artista en Italia.* He was very successful as a composer of zarzuelas: *Para seguir una mujer* (1851); *Don Simplicio Bobadilla* (1853); *Un día de reino* (1854); *El campamento* (1861); *Si yo fuera rey* (1862); etc.

Ioannidis, Yannis, Greek composer; b. Athens, June 8, 1930. He studied piano in Athens (1946–55) and then music theory at the Cons. there and organ, composition, and conducting at the Vienna Musical Academy (1955–63); taught at Pierce College in Athens (1963–68); in 1968 went to live in Caracas (his family was from Venezuela), where he served as artistic director of the chamber orch. of the National Institute of Culture and Fine Arts. As a composer, he follows the precepts of the Second Vienna School, with a firm foundation of classical forms.
WORKS: 2 string quartets (1961, 1971); *Triptych* for orch. (1962); Duo for Violin and Piano (1962); *Peristrophe* for string octet (1964); *Versi* for solo clarinet (1967); *Arioso* for string nonet (1960); *Tropic* for orch. (1968); *Schemata (Figures)* for string ensemble (1968); *Projections* for strings, winds and piano (1968); *Fragments I* for cello and piano (1969) and *Fragments II* for solo flute (1970); *Metaplassis A* and *B* for orch. (1969, 1970); *Actinia* for wind quintet (1969); *Transiciones* for orch. (1971); *Estudio I, II* and *III* for piano (1971–73); *Fancy for 6* for 4 winds, cello and percussion (1972); *Nocturno* for piano quartet (1972); transcriptions of Greek folksongs for chorus.

Iparraguirre y Balerdí, José María de, Spanish-Basque composer and poet; b. Villarreal de Urrechu, Aug. 12, 1820; d. Zozobastro de Isacho, April 6, 1881. He led a wandering life; improvised songs, accompanying himself on the guitar; one of his songs, *Guernikako Arbola,* a hymn to the sacred tree of Guernica, became the national anthem of the Basques. As a result of the unrest in the Basque country, and his own participation in it, he was compelled to leave Spain; spent many years in South America; was enabled to return to Spain in 1877, and even obtained an official pension.

Ipavec, Benjamin, Slovenian composer; b. St. Jurij, Dec. 24, 1829; d. Graz, Dec. 20, 1909. He studied medicine in Vienna and became a professional physician, with music as an avocation, but he was the first to cultivate national Slovenian motives systematically and therefore became historically important. He wrote a national Slovenian opera *Teharski plemiči* (*The Nobles of Teharje;* Ljubljana, 1892); numerous songs in a romantic vein; also brought out collections of Slovenian folksongs.

Ippolitov-Ivanov, Mikhail (real name **Ivanov,** but assumed his mother's name to distinguish himself from Michael Ivanov, the music critic; the name is pronounced Ippolitov-Ivánov); important Russian composer and pedagogue; b. Gatchina, Nov. 19, 1859; d. Moscow, Jan. 28, 1935. He entered the St. Petersburg

Cons. in 1875; studied composition with Rimsky-Korsakov, graduating in 1882. He then received the post of teacher and director of the Music School in Tiflis, in the Caucasus, where he remained until 1893; he became deeply interested in Caucasian folk music; many of his works were colored by the semi-Oriental melodic and rhythmic inflections of that region. Upon Tchaikovsky's recommendation he was appointed in 1893 prof. of composition at the Moscow Cons.; in 1906 became its director, retiring in 1922. Among his pupils were the composers Glière and Vasilenko. From 1899 on, he was conductor of the Mamontov Opera in Moscow; in 1925, became conductor of the Bolshoi Theater in Moscow. Outside Russia, he is known mainly by his effective symph. suite *Caucasian Sketches* (1895).
WORKS: OPERAS: *Ruth* (Tiflis, Feb. 8, 1887); *Azra* (Tiflis, Nov. 28, 1890); *Asya* (Moscow, Sept. 28, 1900); *Treason* (1909); *Ole from Nordland* (Moscow, Nov. 21, 1916); *The Last Barricade* (1934); also completed Mussorgsky's unfinished opera *Marriage* (1931). FOR ORCH.: *Symphonic Scherzo* (St. Petersburg, May 20, 1882); *Yar-Khmel,* spring overture (St. Petersburg, Jan. 23, 1883, composer conducting); *Caucasian Sketches;* (Moscow, Feb. 5, 1895; composer conducting); *Iveria* (2nd series of *Caucasian Sketches;* Moscow, 1906); Symphony No. 1 (Moscow, 1908); *Armenian Rhapsody* (Moscow, 1909); *On the Volga* (Moscow, 1910); *Mtzyri,* symph. poem (Moscow, 1922); *Turkish March* (Baku, 1929); *From the Songs of Ossian,* 3 musical pictures (Moscow, 1927); *Episodes of the Life of Schubert* (1929); *In the Steppes of Turkmenistan; Voroshilov March; Musical Scenes of Uzbekistan;* symph. poem, *Year 1917; Catalan Suite* (1934); a suite on Finnish themes, *Karelia* (1935, last work; only the Finale was orchestrated). CHAMBER MUSIC: Violin Sonata; 2 string quartets; *An Evening in Georgia,* for harp, flute, oboe, clarinet, and bassoon. VOCAL WORKS: *Alsatian Ballad* for a cappella mixed chorus; *Five Characteristic Pieces* for chorus and orch. or piano; *The Legend of a White Swan,* for a cappella mixed chorus; *Cantata in Memory of Pushkin,* for children's chorus and piano; *Cantata in Memory of Zhukovsky,* for mixed chorus and piano; *Pythagorean Hymn to the Rising Sun,* for mixed chorus, 10 flutes, 2 harps, and tuba; *Cantata in Memory of Gogol,* for children's chorus and piano; *Hymn to Labor,* for mixed chorus and orch.; 116 songs. He publ. *The Science of the Formation and Resolution of Chords* (1897, in Russian) and *50 Years of Russian Music in My Memories* (Moscow, 1934; in English in *Musical Mercury,* N.Y., 1937).
BIBLIOGRAPHY: Sergei Boguslavsky, *Ippolitov-Ivanov* (Moscow, 1936); L. Podzemskaya, *M. M. Ippolitov-Ivanov and Georgian Musical Culture* (Tbilisi, 1963).

Ipuche-Riva, Pedro, Uruguayan composer; b. Montevideo, Oct. 26, 1924. He studied at the Cons. of Montevideo, and later in Paris with Jean Rivier and Nöel Gallon. Returning to Uruguay, he unfolded energetic activities as a music critic, lecturer, teacher and radio commentator.
WORKS: symph. poem, *El Arbol solo* (1961); 3 symphonies (1962, 1965, 1968); Cello Concerto (1962);

Fantasía concertante for trumpet and string orch. (1963); String Quartet (1962); Quartet for Flute, Violin, Cello and Piano (1963); *Espejo roto* for violin, horn and piano (1966); Concerto for small orch. (1966); *Sinfonietta-Concertino* for piano and orch. (1967); *Animales ilustres*, suite for wind quintet (1967); *Pieza* for oboe and piano (1969); *Variaciones antipianísticas* for piano (1969); other piano pieces; choruses; songs.

Ireland, John, eminent English composer; b. Inglewood, Bowdon, Cheshire, Aug. 13, 1879; d. Washington, England, June 12, 1962. A member of a literary family (both his parents were writers), he received a fine general education. As his musical inclinations became evident, he entered the Royal College of Music in 1893, studying piano with Frederick Cliffe, and composition with Stanford. His parents died while he was still a student; he obtained positions as organist in various churches; the longest of these was at St. Luke's, Chelsea (1904–26). In 1905 he received the degree of Bac. Mus. at the Univ. of Durham; honorary Mus. Doc. there in 1932. He taught at the Royal College of Music for a number of years; Benjamin Britten, Alan Bush, E. J. Moeran, and other British composers were his pupils. He began to compose early in life; during his student years, he wrote a number of works for orch., chamber groups, and voices, but destroyed most of them. His creative catalogue, therefore, begins in 1903 (with the song cycle *Songs of a Wayfarer*). His early compositions were influenced by the German Romantic school; soon he felt the impact of modern musical ideas; he adopted many devices of the French Impressionist school; his rhythmic concepts were enlivened by the new Russian music presented by the Diaghilev Ballet. At the same time, he never wavered in his dedication to the English spirit of simple melody; his writing is often modal or pentatonic, evocative of insular folk music. WORKS: FOR ORCH.: *The Forgotten Rite*, symph. prelude (1913); *Mai-Dun*, symph. rhapsody (1921); *A London Overture* (1936); *Concertino pastorale*, for strings (1939); *Epic March* (1942); *Satyricon* (1946); Piano Concerto (London, Oct. 2, 1930). CHORAL WORKS: *Morning Service*, for voices with organ (1907–20); motet, *Greater love hath no man* (1912); *Communion Service* (1913); *Evening Service* (1915); *These things shall be*, for baritone solo, chorus, and orch. (1937); a number of four-part songs a cappella; two-part songs with piano accompaniment, unison choral songs with piano accompaniment. CHAMBER MUSIC: *Fantasy Trio* for piano, violin, and cello (1906); Trio for violin, clarinet, and piano (1913; rewritten for violin, cello, and piano, 1915, and revised again in 1938); Trio No. 2, for violin, cello, and piano (1917); Violin Sonata No. 1 (1909; revised twice, 1917, 1944); Violin Sonata No. 2 (1917); Cello Sonata (1923); *Fantasy Sonata*, for clarinet and piano (1943). FOR PIANO: *The Daydream*, and *Meridian* (1895; revised 1941); *Decorations* (1913); *The Almond Trees* (1913); *Rhapsody* (1915); *London Pieces* (1917–20); *Leaves from a Child's Sketchbook* (1918); *Summer Evening* (1919); *Sonata* (1920); *On a Birthday Morning* (1922); *Soliloquy* (1922); Sonatina (1927); Ballade (1929); *Indian Summer* (1932); *Green Ways* (1937); *Sarnia*, "An Island Sequence" (1941); *Three Pastels* (1941); organ

works; about 100 songs, to words by D. G. Rossetti, Christina Rossetti, Thomas Hardy, A. E. Housman, Ernest Dowson, etc.

BIBLIOGRAPHY: A miniature essay on Ireland was publ. by J. & W. Chester, Ltd., in 1923; see also Edwin Evans's article on Ireland in Cobbett's *Cyclopedic Survey of Chamber Music;* Josef Holbrooke, *Contemporary British Composers* (London, 1925); Nigel Townshend, "The Achievement of John Ireland," *Music & Letters* (April 1943); John Longmire, *John Ireland: Portrait of a Friend* (London, 1969).

Irgens Jensen, Ludwig, Norwegian composer; b. Oslo, April 13, 1894; d. Enna, Sicily, April 11, 1969. He studied philosophy, music theory and piano in Oslo, but was mainly self-taught in composition; from 1946 was recipient of the Norwegian State Salary of Art, which is a government life pension. His output was relatively small; his compositions are influenced mainly by German Romanticism. WORKS: *Japanischer Frühling* for voice and piano (1918–19); *Der Gott und die Bajadere*, cantata (1921–32); Violin Sonata (1924); *Tema con variazioni* for orch. (1925); Passacaglia for Orch. (1926); Piano Quintet (1927); *Heimferd (The Return)*, dramatic symphony for soloists, chorus and orch., commemorating the 900th anniversary of the death of St. Olav (1929; Oslo, 1930; recast as an opera and produced in Oslo, Aug. 27, 1947); *Partita sinfonica* (1937); Symphony (1942); *Canto d'omaggio*, festival overture (Oslo, 1950); choruses; songs.

Irino, Yoshirō, Japanese composer; b. Vladivostok, Siberia, Nov. 13, 1921. He went to Japan in 1927; studied economics at the Tokyo Univ. (1941–43) and worked for the Bank of Tokyo (1943–46); meanwhile took private composition lessons from Saburo Moroi (1942–43). In 1946 he organized a composer/performer group "Shinseikai." From 1954 he has taught at the Tokyo Music School. His music is cast in an astutely modern manner, while preserving the classical format. In some of his works he applied the method of composition with 12 tones, the first Japanese composer to do so consistently. WORKS: an operetta, *The Man in Fear of God* (Tokyo, May 25, 1954); a television opera *Drum of Silk* (1962); a ballet *Woman-Mask* (1959); *Adagietto and Allegro vivace* for orch. (1949); Sinfonietta for Chamber Orch. (1953); Ricercari for Chamber Orch. (1954); Double Concerto for Violin, Piano and Orch. (1955); *Concerto Grosso* (1957); Sinfonia (1959); Concerto for String Orch. (1960); Suite for Jazz Ensemble (1960); *Music* for harpsichord, percussion and 19 string instruments (1963); Symph. No. 2 (1964); *2 Fantasies* for 17 and 20 kotos (1969); *Sai-un (Colorful Clouds)* for 15 string instruments (1972); *Wandlungen* for 2 shakuhachi and orch. (1973); 2 string quartets (1945, 1957); Flute Sonatina (1946); Piano Trio (1948); String Sextet (1950); *Chamber Concerto* for 7 instruments (1951); *Music* for violin and piano (1957); Quintet for clarinet, saxophone, trumpet, cello and piano (1958); Divertimento for 7 Winds (1958); *Music* for violin and cello (1959); *Music* for vibraphone and piano (1961); Partita for Wind Quintet (1962); String Trio (1965); *3 Movements* for 2 kotos and jushichi-gen (1966); *7 In-*

ventions for guitar and 6 players (1967); Violin Sonata (1967); *3 Movements* for solo cello (1969); Sonata for piano, violin, clarinet and percussion (1970); Trio for Flute, Violin and Piano (1970); *A Demon's Bride* for chorus, oboe, horn, piano and percussion (1970); *Globus I* for horn and percussion (1970); *Globus II* for marimba, double bass and percussion (1971); *Globus III* for violin, cello, piano, harp, shō, and 2 dancers (1975); Suite for Solo Viola (1971); *Cloudscape* for string ensemble (1972); *3 Improvisations* for solo flute (1972); *5 Days* for violin and viola (1972); *3 Scenes* for 3 kotos (1972); *Strömung* for flute, harp and percussion (1973); *Shō-yō* for Japanese instruments (1973); *Gafu* for flute, shō and double bass (1976); *Klänge* for piano and percussion (1976); *Movements* for solo marimba (1977).

Irrgang, Heinrich Bernhard, German organist; b. Zduny, July 23, 1869; d. Berlin, April 8, 1916. He was a church organist and teacher in Berlin; composed organ music and songs.

Isaac, Heinrich (or **Isaak, Izak, Yzac, Ysack;** in Italy, **Arrigo Tedesco** [Henry the German]; Low Latin **Arrighus**), Netherlandish polyphonist (the Italian term "Tedesco" was used at the time for Netherlanders as well as Germans); b. Brabant, c.1450; d. Florence, March 26, 1517. From 1480–92 he was in the service of Lorenzo de' Medici, in the capacities of organist, maestro di cappella, and teacher to Lorenzo's children. He afterwards spent several years in Rome, and finally was called to the court of Maximilian I, at Vienna, as 'Symphonista regis'; from 1514 until his death he lived in Florence. He was greatly influenced by the music of the countries in which he lived, writing with equal facility in the Netherlandish, Italian, and German styles as they flourished in his day.

WORKS: 23 Masses *a* 4–6 (of which 10 were publ. between 1506–39); those in MS are in the libraries at Vienna (8), Munich (4), and Brussels (1). Motets and psalms by Isaac were printed in some 40 collections from 1501–64 (see Eitner, *Bibliographie der Musiksammelwerke;* Berlin, 1877). One of the most beautiful of German chorales, *Nun ruhen alle Wälder,* is sung to the melody by Isaac, *Inspruk, ich muss dich lassen.* A voluminous collection of motets, *Choralis Constantinus,* was ed. by his pupil Ludwig Senfl, in 1550 (3 parts). Parts I and II were republished in the *Denkmäler der Tonkunst in Österreich* 10 and 32 (5.i and 16.i); Part III, by the Univ. of Michigan Press (1950; ed. by Louise Cuyler). Isaac's secular works were ed. by Joh. Wolf and also republished in *Denkmäler der Tonkunst in Österreich* 28 and 32 (14.i and 16.i). The *Missa carminum* and other works are publ. in F. Blume's *Das Chorwerk* 7, 81, and 100. Other reprints are in Eitner's *Publikation älterer Musikwerke* I (5 4-voiced vocal works) and A. Schering's *Geschichte der Musik in Beispielen* (a Kyrie and a canzona). 5 polyphonic Masses from Isaac's *Choralis Constantinus* were transcribed and ed. by Louise Cuyler (Univ. of Michigan, 1956).

BIBLIOGRAPHY: H. Rietsch, "Heinrich Isaac und das Innsbrucklied," *Jahrbuch der Musikbibliothek Peters* (1917); Peter Wagner, *Geschichte der Messe* (pp. 281–317); P. Blaschke, "Heinrich Isaaks Choralis Constantinus," *Kirchenmusikalisches Jahrbuch* (1931); Frank A. d'Accone, "Heinrich Isaac in Florence: New and Unpublished Documents," *Musical Quarterly* (Oct. 1963); F. Ghisi, "Arrigo il Tedesco, musicista fiorentino," *Chigiana* 24 (1967); S. Novack, "Fusion of Design and Tonal Order in Mass and Motet: Josquin Desprez and Heinrich Isaac," *Music Forum* 2 (1970).

Isamitt, Carlos, Chilean composer; b. Rengo, Colchagua, March 13, 1887; d. Santiago, July 2, 1974. He studied both music and painting in Chile; then in Italy, Spain, France and Holland. As a composer he became interested in the folk music of the Araucanian Indians, and made use of these authentic materials in several of his works. Among them are *4 movimientos sinfónicos* (1960), *Te kuduam mapuche* for voice, bassoon and the Araucanian drum kultrún (1958), Harp Concerto (1957), and Sonata for Flute Solo (1954). A catalogue of his works is found in *Compositores de América,* vol. XIII (Washington, 1967).

Ishii, Kan, Japanese composer, brother of **Maki Ishii;** b. Tokyo, March 30, 1921. He is one of two sons of Baku Ishii, a renowned scholar of modern dance. He studied in Tokyo at the Musashino Music School with Goh, Ikenouchi and Odaka (1939–43); in 1952 went to Germany and took lessons in composition with Carl Orff at the Hochschule für Musik in Munich. Returning to Japan he taught at the Toho Music Univ., and at the Aichi-Prefectural Arts Univ.; in 1970 was elected president of the All-Japan Chorus League.

WORKS: 4 operas: *Mermaid and Red Candle* (1961), *Kaguyahime (Prince Kaguya,* 1963), *En-no-Gyojia* (Tokyo, 1964), and *Lady Kesa and Morito* (Tokyo, Nov. 24, 1968); 9 ballets: *God and the Bayadere* (Tokyo, Nov. 6, 1950), *Birth of a Human* (Tokyo, Nov. 27, 1954), *Frökln Julie* (1955), *Shakuntara* (1961), *Marimo* (Tokyo, 1963), *Biruma no tategoto (Harp of Burma,* 1963), *Haniwa* (1963), *Hakai* (1965) and *Ichiyo Higuchi* (1966); a symph. poem *Yama (Mountain,* Tokyo, Oct. 7, 1954); *Kappa's Penny* for youth orch. (1956); *Sinfonia Ainu* for soprano, chorus and orch. (1958–59); *The Reef,* cantata for baritone, chorus, 4 pianos and percussion (1967); *Akita the Great* for chorus and brass (1968); *Music for Percussion* for 8 players (1970); Viola Sonata (1960); Music for Solo Flute (1972); *Footsteps to Tomorrow,* cantata for solo soprano (1972); folksongs; choruses, etc. He compiled a valuable collection of Japanese folksongs, publ. in 6 volumes.

Ishii, Maki, Japanese composer, brother of **Kan Ishii;** b. Tokyo, May 28, 1936. He received an early training in music from his father, a renowned promoter of modern dance; he studied composition with Akira Ifukube and Tomojiro Ikenouchi, and conducting with Akeo Watanabe in Tokyo (1952–58); then went to Germany where he took courses at the Berlin Hochschule für Musik with Boris Blacher and Josef Rufer (1958–61); after a brief return to Japan he went back to Germany, where he decided to remain. In his works he attempts to combine the coloristic effects of Japanese instruments with European techniques of serial music and electronic sounds.

WORKS: Prelude and Variations for 9 players (1959–60); *7 Stücke* for small orch. (1960–61); *4 Bagatelles* for violin and piano (1961); *Transition* for small orch. (1962); *Aphorismen I* for string trio, percussion and piano (1963); *Galgenlieder* for baritone, male chorus and 13 players (1964); *Characters* for flute, oboe, piano, guitar and percussion (1965); *Hamon* for violin, chamber ensemble and tape (1965); *Expressions* for string orch. (Tokyo, Jan. 11, 1968); *5 Elements* for guitar and 6 players (1967); *Piano Piece* for pianist and percussionist (1968); *Kyō-ō* for piano, orch. and tape (Tokyo, Feb. 22, 1969); *Kyō-sō* for percussion and orch. (Tokyo, Feb. 7, 1969); *La-sen I* for 7 players and tape (1969); *La-sen II* for solo cello (1970); *Sō-gū I* for shakuhachi and piano (1970); *Music for Gagaku* (1970); *Dipol* for orch. (1971); *Sō-gū II* for gagaku and symph. orchestras (Tokyo, June 23, 1971; work resulting from simultaneous performance of *Music for Gagaku* and *Dipol*); *Sen-ten* for percussion player and tape (1971); *Aphorismen II* for a pianist (1972); *Chō-etsu* for chamber group and tape (1973); *Polaritäten* for soloists and orch. (1973; work exists in 3 versions, each having different soloists: *I* for biwa and harp; *II* for biwa, shakuhachi and flute; *III* for shakuhachi and flute); *Synkretismen* for marimba, 7 soloists, strings and 3 percussionists (1973); *Anime Amare* for harp and tape (1974); *Jo* for orch. (1975).

Isidore of Seville, Spanish cleric; b. Cartagena, c.560; d. Seville, April 4, 636. He was brought to Seville as a child; in 599, became archbishop there. Between 622 and 633, compiled a treatise on the arts, *Etymologiarum sive originum libri XX;* he expressed the conviction that music can only be preserved through memory, for musical sounds could never be notated (*scribi non possunt*). The text was published in Oxford (1911); an English transl. of the pertinent parts is included in Strunk's *Source Readings in Music History* (N.Y.,1950).

BIBLIOGRAPHY: Karl Schmidt, *Quaestiones de musicis scriptoribus romanis imprimis Cassiodoro et Isidoro* (Leipzig, 1898).

Isler, Ernst, Swiss organist and music critic; b. Zürich, Sept 30, 1879; d. there, Sept 26, 1944. He studied in Zürich and Berlin; served as organist in Zürich, and taught organ there. He became music critic of the influential daily paper *Neue Zürcher Zeitung* in 1902, and held this position until his death; from 1910 to 1927 he was editor of the *Schweizerische Musikzeitung*. He publ. the monographs on Hans Huber, Max Reger, etc., also a valuable compendium, *Das Züricherische Konzertleben 1895–1914* (Zürich, 1935), and its sequel covering the years 1914–31 (Zürich, 1936).

Ísólfsson, Páll, Icelandic organist and composer; b. Stokkseyri, Oct. 12, 1893; d. Reykjavik, Nov. 23, 1974. He studied organ at the Leipzig Cons. with Straube, and later in Paris with Bonnet. Returning to Iceland he served as organist in the Reykjavik Cathedral (1939–68) and director of the Reykjavik Cons. and of the Icelandic Radio. He wrote a number of attractive piano pieces, in the manner of Grieg (humoresques, intermezzi, capriccios, etc.), choruses and a cantata on the millennial anniversary of the Icelandic Parliament (1930); also compiled (with S. Einarsson) a collection of choral pieces by various composers. In 1963–64 he published his autobiography in 2 vols. (in Icelandic).

BIBLIOGRAPHY: J. Thorarinsson, *Páll Isolfsson* (Reykjavik, 1963).

Isouard, Nicolo, important French opera composer; b. Malta, Dec. 6, 1775; d. Paris, March 23, 1818. A son of a prosperous merchant, he was sent to Paris to study engineering; afterwards, he served as a clerk in Malta, Palermo, and in Naples, where he took lessons with Sala and Guglielmi. In the spring of 1794 he produced his first opera, *L'avviso ai maritati*, in Florence; from that time on he abandoned business pursuits, dedicating himself to operatic composition. In order not to embarrass his family, and particularly his father, who was against his career as a musician, he adopted the name **Nicolo de Malte,** or simply **Nicolo.** He served as organist of St. John of Jerusalem at Malta (1795–98); in 1799, went to Paris, where he became increasingly successful as an opera composer; he was also popular as a pianist. In Paris he had to undergo strong competition with Boieldieu; but the lengthy list of productions of his operas up to 1816 shows that he had never relaxed his industry. The music of his operas demonstrates a facile melodic gift in the French manner, as well as sound craftsmanship. Besides operas, he wrote church music. The best known of his operas are *Cendrillon, Joconde,* and *Jeannot et Colin.* A list of his operas, produced in Paris, includes: *Le Petit Page* (with R. Kreutzer; Feb. 14, 1800); *La Statue* (April 26, 1802); *L'Intrigue au Sérail* (April 25, 1809); *Cendrillon* (Feb. 22, 1810); *La Victime des arts* (Feb. 27, 1811); *La Fête du village* (March 31, 1811); *Le Billet de loterie* (Sept. 14, 1811); *Le Magicien sans magie* (Nov. 4, 1811); *Lully et Quinault* (Feb. 27, 1812); *Le Prince de Catane* (March 4, 1813); *Les Français à Venise* (June 14, 1813); *Joconde* (Feb. 28, 1814); *Michel-Ange* (Dec. 11, 1802); *Les Confidences* (March 31, 1803); *Le Baiser et la quittance* (June 18, 1803); *Le Médecin turc* (Nov. 19, 1903), *L'Intrigue aux fenêtres* (Feb. 26, 1805); *Le Déjeuner de garçons* (April 24, 1805); *La Ruse inutile* (May 30, 1805); *Léonce* (Nov. 18, 1805); *La Prise de Passaw* (Feb. 8, 1806); *Idala* (July 30, 1806); *Les Rendezvous bourgeois* (May 9, 1807); *Les Créanciers* (Dec. 10, 1807); *Un Jour à Paris* (May 24, 1808); *Cimarosa* (June 28, 1808); *Jeannot et Colin* (Oct. 17, 1814); *Les Deux Maris* (March 18, 1816); *L'Une pour l'autre* (May 11, 1816); *Aladin* (Feb. 6, 1822; posthumous work, completed by Benincori and Habeneck).

BIBLIOGRAPHY: E. Wahl, *Nicolo Isouard* (Munich, 1906).

Isserlis, Julius, Russian pianist; b. Kishinev, Nov. 7, 1888; d. London, July 23, 1968. He studied with Puchalski at the Kiev Cons.; then with Safonov and Taneyev at the Moscow Cons. He taught at the Moscow Philharmonic Institute of Music (1913–23); then in Vienna (1923–28); in 1928, he settled in London. He wrote a number of character pieces for piano.

Istel, Edgar, eminent German musicologist; b. Mainz, Feb. 23, 1880; d. Miami, Florida, Dec. 17, 1948. He studied in Munich with Thuille and Sandberger; received his Dr. phil. with the dissertation *J. J. Rousseau als Komponist* (1900); then settled in Munich as a teacher; in 1919, taught in Berlin; in 1920 he moved to Madrid, where he remained until the outbreak of the civil war in 1936; then went to England, and eventually to the U.S. (1938).

WRITINGS: *Das deutsche Weihnachtsspiel und seine Wiedergeburt aus dem Geiste der Musik* (Langensalza, 1901); *Richard Wagner im Lichte eines zeitgenössischen Briefwechsels* (1902); *Peter Cornelius* (1906); *Die Entstehung des deutschen Melodramas* (1906); *Die komische Oper* (1906); *Die Blütezeit der musikalischen Romantik in Deutschland* (1909); *Das Kunstwerk Richard Wagners* (1910); *Das Libretto* (1914; English ed. as *The Art of Writing Opera Librettos*, N.Y., 1922); *Die moderne Oper vom Tode Wagners bis zum Weltkrieg* (Leipzig, 1915); *Niccolo Paganini* (Leipzig, 1919); *Revolution und Oper* (1919); *Das Buch der Oper; die deutschen Meister von Gluck bis Wagner* (Berlin, 1919); *Bizet und Carmen* (Stuttgart, 1927). Between 1915 and 1934, he contributed a number of articles on various composers to the *Musical Quarterly;* edited the musical writings of E. T. A. Hoffmann, the collected essays of Cornelius, and Dittersdorf's autobiography; published analytical brochures on works of Mahler, Humperdinck, and others. Istel was also a composer; he wrote several operas, oratorios and smaller pieces.

Istomin, Eugene, American pianist; b. New York, Nov. 26, 1925, of Russian parents. He studied with Rudolf Serkin at the Curtis Institute in Philadelphia; in 1943 he won the Leventritt Award for an appearance as soloist with the N.Y. Philharmonic Orch. (Nov. 21, 1943), playing the 2nd Concerto of Brahms. After that he developed a highly successful concert career; appeared with a number of American orchestras and also gave recitals in America and in Europe. On Feb. 15, 1975, he married Martita Casals, widow of Pablo Casals.

Istrate, Mircea, Rumanian pianist and composer; b. Cluj, Sept. 27, 1929. He studied piano and composition at the Cons. of Cluj (1945–53) and Bucharest (1954–57); subsequently taught piano in Bucharest. He composed a Flute Sonata (1954); *Burlesca,* chamber concerto for violin, oboe, clarinet, bassoon and double bass (1955); *Muzică stereofonică* for 2 string orchestras (1955–57); *Evocare* for mezzo-soprano, female chorus and orch. (1960); *Pe o plajă japoneză (On a Japanese Beach),* sequences for female chorus, orch. and tape (1961); Oboe Sonata (1962); *Algoritm* for orch. (1964); *Interferente (Interferences)* for orch. and electronics (1965); *Evenimente I-II-III,* etc., for prepared piano, percussion within a piano, electric guitar, double bass, vibraphone, horn, marimba and tape (1966; of variable duration); *Pulsations* for orch. (1973); songs.

Ištvan, Miloslav, Czech composer; b. Olomouc, Sept. 2, 1928. He studied music at the Janáček Academy in Brno with Jaroslav Kvapil (1948–52); subsequently was active mainly as a music teacher. Like many of his compatriots he cultivated a national style of composition, thematically derived from folk music, but later adopted the *modus operandi* of the cosmopolitan avant-garde. In 1963 he joined the "Creative Group A" of Brno, dedicated to free musical experimentation "uninhibited by puritanically limited didactical regulations." He also worked in the electronic music studio of the Brno Radio.

WORKS: Concerto for Horn, String Orch. and Piano (1949); Symphony (1952); *Winter Suite* for strings, piano and percussion (1956); *Concerto-Symphony* for piano and orch. (1957); *Balada o Jihu (Ballad of the South),* 3 symph. frescoes after Lewis Allan's satirical view of the American south (Brno, Dec. 8, 1960); Concertino for Violin and Chamber Orch. (1961); *6 Studies* for chamber ensemble (1964; revised for chamber orch. and performed at the International Society for Contemporary Music Fest., Prague, Oct. 9, 1967); *Zaklínání času (Conjuration of Time)* for orch. and 2 narrators (1967; Ostrava, Jan. 23, 1969); *Ja, Jakob (I, Jacob),* chamber oratorio, with tape (1968); Sonata for Violin and Chamber Orch. (1970); *In memoriam Josef Berg* for orch. (1971); *Hymn to the Sun,* small cantata (1971); *The Beauty and the Animal,* chamber oratorio (1974); *Shakespearean Variations* for orch. (1975); *Rondos* for Viola and Piano (1950); Trio for Clarinet, Cello and Piano (1950); Clarinet Sonata (1954); Suite for Horn and Piano (1955); Piano Trio (1958); *Rhapsody* for cello and piano (1961); String Quartet (1963); *Dodekameron* for 12 players (1962–64); *Refrains* for string trio (1965); *Ritmi ed antiritmi* for 2 pianos and 2 percussionists (1966); *Lamentations,* 5 songs for alto, piano and tape (1970); Cello Sonata (1970); *5 framenti* for solo salterio (1971); *Omaggio a J. S. Bach* for wind quintet (1971); *Psalmus niger* for 6 percussionists (1971); *Blacked-Out Landscape,* in memory of those fallen in World War II, for string quartet (1975); *Ad fontes intimas* for double bass or trumpet, and percussion (1975); 2 piano sonatas (1954, 1959); *Impromptus* for piano (1956); *Odyssey of a Child from Lidice* for piano (1963); *Musica aspera* for organ (1964); Variations for 2 Pianos (1972); 2 scores of "musique concrète," *Island of Toys* (1968) and *Avete morituri* (1970); many choruses and songs.

Ito, Ryuto, Japanese composer; b. Hiroshima, March 4, 1922. He was a medical student; subsequently turned to music and took lessons with Ikenouchi, Moroi, and Takata. Several of his works were awarded prizes established by the Tokyo newspaper *Mainichi.*

Iturbi, José, celebrated Spanish pianist; b. Valencia, Nov. 28, 1895. He took piano lessons with Joaquín Malats in Barcelona; as a very young boy he played in street cafés to earn a living. A local group of music lovers collected a sum of money to send him to Paris for further study; he was accepted at the Paris Cons., and graduated in 1912. He then went to Switzerland; in 1919 he became a piano teacher at the Geneva Cons. Beginning in 1923 he devoted himself to concert tours and rapidly acquired the reputation of a brilliant virtuoso; his performances of Spanish music were especially apt in their rhythmic verve. After playing a series of concerts in Europe, he made a tour of South America; in 1928 he made his U.S. debut; so successful was he that during his 2nd U.S. tour in 1930 he gave 77 concerts. In 1936 he began a career as orchestral conductor and led the Rochester Philharmonic Orch. for several seasons; also performed in the dual role of pianist and conductor playing concertos and accompanying himself as best he could. He wrote a number of pleasing pieces in the Spanish vein, of which *Pequeña danza española* is singularly attractive. His sister, **Amparo Iturbi** (b. Valencia, March 12, 1898; d. Beverly Hills, Calif., April 21, 1969), was also a talented pianist; she played piano duos with José Iturbi on numerous occasions in Europe and America.

Iturriberry, Juan José, Uruguayan composer; b. Pando, Oct. 24, 1936. He studied in Montevideo with Carlos Estrada and Héctor Tosar, and also took a course in electro-acoustical techniques. His works are quaquaversal; some require electronic applications. His *Meditation in F* (1975) is concentrated on the single note F, which is repeated *ad nauseam.*

Ivanov, Georgi, Bulgarian composer; b. Sofia, Aug. 23, 1924. He studied with Lubomir Pipkov and Veselin Stoyanov in Sofia; then went to Moscow where he studied with Shaporin (1946–50). Returning to Bulgaria, he became conductor of the National Youth Theater in Sofia.

WORKS: 2 symph. poems: *Legend of the Lopian Forest* (Sofia, Feb. 15, 1951) and *The Mutiny on the S.S. Nadezhda* (1955); Symph. (Sofia, June 22, 1960); Divertimento for clarinet, violin, harpsichord and chamber orch. (1962); *Metamorphosis* for strings (1967); *Timbres in Rhythm* for orch. (1968); Variations for orch. (1969); *Musica concertante* for orch. (1970).

Ivanov, Mikhail, Russian music critic and composer; b. Moscow, Sept. 23, 1849; d. Rome, Oct. 20, 1927. He studied mechanical sciences at the Technological Institute in St. Petersburg, graduating in 1869; then went to Moscow, where he took private harmony lessons with Tchaikovsky; from 1870 to 1875 he lived in Italy where he took music lessons with Sgambati. In 1875 he returned to St. Petersburg, where he obtained the position of music critic in the influential daily newspaper *Novoye Vremya,* which he held from 1880 to 1917. After the revolution he emigrated to Italy, where he remained until his death. A critic of reactionary tendencies, he assailed the composers of the Russian National School; endowed with a lively literary style, he made use of irony against any new musical developments; this in turn earned him the enmity of liberal musicians. He was also a composer of sorts; he wrote a ballet *Vestal Virgin* (St. Petersburg, Feb. 29, 1888); the operas, *Zabava Putiatishna* (Moscow, Jan. 15, 1899), and *Potemkin Holiday* (St. Petersburg, Dec. 16, 1902), and a number of songs; publ. *Pushkin in Music* (St. Petersburg, 1899); *The Historical Development of Music in Russia* (2 vols., St. Petersburg, 1910–12); translated into Russian Hanslick's *Von Musikalisch-Schönen.*

Ivanov-Boretzky, Mikhail, Russian musicologist; b. Moscow, June 16, 1874; d. there, April 1, 1936. He studied jurisprudence at the Univ. of Moscow, graduating in 1896; at the same time he took music lessons; in 1898 he went to St. Petersburg and became a student of composition of Rimsky-Korsakov; his own music was mainly imitative of Rimsky-Korsakov's works. He wrote the operas *Adolfina* (Moscow, Dec. 10, 1908); *The Witch* (Moscow, Aug. 14, 1918); a Symphony, piano music, choruses, songs. His importance to Russian music, however, lies in his writings. He published the monographs on Palestrina, Handel, Schumann, Mendelssohn and Beethoven; also a useful anthology of music history, with a synoptic table of 18th-century music (Moscow, 1934) and numerous articles on Russian music. From 1921 to 1936 he taught various academic subjects at the Moscow Cons. A collection of his articles was published in Moscow in 1972.

Ivanovici, Ion, Rumanian bandleader and composer of light music; b. Banat, 1845; d. Bucharest, Sept. 29, 1902. He played the flute and clarinet in a military band in Galatz, and in 1880 conducted his own band there. In the same year he wrote the waltz *Valurile Dunării (The Waves of the Danube),* which became a perennial favorite all over the world. He took part in the Paris Exposition of 1889, and conducted there a band of 116 musicians. In 1900 he was appointed Inspector of Military Music in Rumania. He published about 150 pieces for piano and dances for band.

BIBLIOGRAPHY: Viorel Cosma, *Ivanovici* (Bucharest, 1958).

Ivanov-Radkevitch, Nicolai, Russian composer; b. Krasnoyarsk, Siberia, Feb. 10, 1904; d. Moscow, Feb. 4, 1962. He studied composition with Glière and orchestration with Vasilenko at the Moscow Cons., graduating in 1928; subsequently joined its staff (1929–48). In 1952 he was appointed instructor in orchestration at the Institute of Military Bandleaders of the Soviet Army. He was particularly successful in writing popular marches for band, of which *Our Own Moscow* and *Victory March* received the State Prize. He also composed 4 symphonies (1928, 1932, 1937, 1945); 12 symphonic suites on folk motives; violin sonata; various pieces for other instruments; film music.

Ives, Burl, American folk singer; b. Hunt Township, Jasper County, Illinois, June 14, 1909. He studied briefly at N.Y. Univ.; traveled through the U.S. and Canada as an itinerant handyman, supplementing his earnings by singing and playing the banjo. He then became a dramatic actor and appeared on the stage and in films, and gave concerts of folk ballads accompanying himself on the guitar. He publ. an autobiography, *Wayfaring Stranger* (N.Y., 1948) and the anthologies, *The Burl Ives Songbook* (1953) and *Burl Ives Book of Irish Songs* (1958).

Ives, Charles Edward, one of the most remarkable American composers, whose individual genius created music so original, so universal, and yet so deeply national in its sources of inspiration that it profoundly changed the direction of American music; b. Danbury, Conn., Oct. 20, 1874; d. New York, May 19, 1954. His father, **George Ives,** was a bandleader of the First

Connecticut Heavy Artillery during the Civil War, and the early development of Charles Ives was, according to his own testimony, deeply influenced by his father. At the age of 12, he played the drums in the band and also received from his father rudimentary musical training in piano and cornet playing. At the age of 13 he played organ at the Danbury Church; soon he began to improvise freely at the piano, without any dependence on school rules; as a result of his experimentation in melody and harmony, encouraged by his father, Charles Ives began to combine several keys, partly as a spoof, but eventually as a legitimate alternative to traditional music; at 17 he composed his *Variations on America* for organ in a polytonal setting; still earlier he wrote a band piece *Holiday Quick Step* which was performed by the Danbury Band in 1888. He attended the Danbury High School; in 1894 he entered Yale Univ., where he took regular academic courses and studied organ with Dudley Buck and composition with Horatio Parker; from Horatio Parker he received a fine classical training; still in college he composed 2 full-fledged symphonies, written in an entirely traditional manner demonstrating great skill in formal structure, fluent melodic development and smooth harmonic modulations. After his graduation from Yale Univ., in 1898, Ives entered an insurance company; also played organ at the Central Presbyterian Church in New York (1899–1902). In 1907 he formed an insurance partnership with Julian Myrick of New York; he proved himself to be an exceptionally able businessman; the firm of Ives & Myrick prospered, and Ives continued to compose music as an avocation. In 1908 he married Harmony Twichell. In 1918 he suffered a massive heart attack, complicated by a diabetic condition, and was compelled to curtail his work both in business and in music to a minimum because his illness made it difficult to handle a pen. He retired from business in 1930, and by that time he had virtually stopped composing. In 1919 Ives published at his own expense his great masterpiece, *Concord Sonata*, for piano, inspired by the writings of Emerson, Hawthorne, the Alcotts and Thoreau. Although written early in the century, its idiom is so extraordinary and its technical difficulties so formidable that the work did not receive a performance in its entirety until John Kirkpatrick played it in New York in 1939. In 1922, Ives brought out, also at his expense, a volume of *114 Songs*, written between 1888 and 1921 and marked by great diversity of style, ranging from lyrical romanticism to powerful and dissonant modern invocations. Both the *Concord Sonata* and the *114 Songs* were distributed *gratis* by Ives himself to anyone wishing to receive copies. His orchestral masterpiece, *Three Places in New England,* also had to wait nearly two decades before its first performance; of the monumental *Fourth Symphony,* only the second movement was performed in 1927, and its complete performance was given posthumously in 1965. In 1947 Ives received the Pulitzer Prize for his *Third Symphony,* written in 1911. The slow realization of the greatness of Ives and the belated triumphant recognition of his music were phenomena without precedent in music history. Because of his chronic ailment, and also on account of his personal disposition, Ives lived as a recluse away from the mainstream of American musical life; he never went to concerts and did not own a record player or a radio; while he was well versed in the musical classics, and studied the scores of Beethoven, Schumann and Brahms, he took little interest in sanctioned works of modern composers; yet he anticipated many technical innovations, such as polytonality, atonality, and even 12-tone formations, as well as polymetric and polyrhythmic configurations, which were prophetic for his time. In the second movement of the *Concord Sonata* he specified the application of a strip of wood on the white and the black keys of the piano to produce an echo-like sonority; in his unfinished *Universe Symphony* he planned an antiphonal representation of the heavens in chordal counterpoint and the earth in contrasting orchestral groups. He also composed pieces of quarter-tone piano music. A unique quality of his music was the combination of simple motives, often derived from American church hymns and popular ballads, with an extremely complex dissonant counterpoint which formed the supporting network for the melodic lines. A curious idiosyncrasy is the frequent quotation of the "fate motive" of Beethoven's Fifth Symphony in many of his works. Materials of his instrumental and vocal works often overlap, and the titles are often changed during the process of composition. In his orchestrations he often indicated interchangeable and optional parts, as in the last movement of the *Concord Sonata,* which has a part for flute obbligato; thus he reworked the original score for large orchestra of his *Three Places in New England* for a smaller ensemble to fit the requirements of Slonimsky's Chamber Orchestra of Boston which gave its first performance, and it was in this version that the work was first published and widely performed until the restoration of the large score was made in 1974. Ives possessed an uncommon gift for literary expression; his annotations to his works are both trenchant and humorous; he published in 1920 *Essays Before a Sonata* as a literary companion volume to the *Concord Sonata;* his *Memos* in the form of a diary, published after his death, reveal an extraordinary power of aphoristic utterance. He was acutely conscious of his civic duties as an American, and once circulated a proposal to have federal laws enacted by popular referendum. His centennial in 1974 was celebrated by a series of conferences at his alma mater at Yale Univ., in New York, in Miami and many other American cities, and in Europe, including Russia. While during his lifetime he and a small group of devoted friends and admirers had great difficulties in having his works performed, recorded or published, a veritable Ives cult emerged after his death; eminent conductors gave repeated performances of his orchestral works and modern pianists were willing to cope with the forbidding difficulties of his works. In the number of orchestral performances, in 1976 Ives stood highest among modern composers on American programs, and the influence of his music on the new generation of composers reached a high mark, so that the adjective "Ivesian" became common in music criticism to describe certain acoustical and coloristic effects characteristic of his music. America's youth expressed especial enthusiasm for Ives, which received its most unusual tribute in the commercial marketing of a T-shirt with

Ives's portrait. All of the Ives manuscripts and his correspondence were deposited by Mrs. Ives at Yale Univ., forming a basic Ives Archive.

WORKS: FOR ORCH.: 4 symphonies: No. 1 (1896–98); No. 2 (1897–1902; N.Y., Feb. 22, 1951); No. 3 (1901–04; N.Y., April 5, 1946); No. 4 (1910–16; 2nd movement only perf. N.Y., Jan. 29, 1927; first perf. in its entirety was given in N.Y. on April 26, 1965, Leopold Stokowski conducting the American Symph. Orch.); also incomplete fragments of a *Universe Symphony* (1911–16); *Three Places in New England (Orchestral Set No. 1: The "St. Gaudens" in Boston Common; Putnam's Camp, Redding, Connecticut; The Housatonic at Stockbridge;* 1903–14; N.Y., Jan. 10, 1931, Chamber Orch. of Boston, Nicolas Slonimsky conducting); *Calcium Light Night,* for chamber orch. (1898–1907); *Central Park in the Dark* (1898–1907); *The Unanswered Question* (1908); *Theater Orchestra Set: In the Cage, In the Inn, In the Night* (1904–11); *The Pond* (1906); *Browning Overture* (1911); *The Gong on the Hook and Ladder, or Firemen's Parade on Main Street,* for chamber orch. (1911); *Lincoln, the Great Commoner,* for chorus and orch. (1912); *A Symphony: Holidays,* in 4 parts, also performed separately: *Washington's Birthday* (1913), *Decoration Day* (1912), *Fourth of July* (1913), *Thanksgiving and/or Forefathers' Day* (1904); *Over the Pavements,* for chamber orch. (1913); *Orchestral Set No. 2* (1915); *Tone Roads,* for chamber orch. (1911–15); *Orchestral Set No. 3* (1919–27). CHAMBER MUSIC: String Quartet No. 1, subtitled *A Revival Service* (1896); *Prelude,* from "Pre-First Sonata," for violin and piano (1900); Trio for Violin, Clarinet, and Piano (1902); "Pre-Second String Quartet" (1905); *Space and Duration,* for string quartet and a very mechanical piano (1907); *All the Way Around and Back,* for piano, violin, flute, bugle, bells (1907); *The Innate,* for string quartet and piano (1908); *Adagio Sostenuto,* for English horn, flute, strings, and piano (1910); Violin Sonata No. 1 (1908); Violin Sonata No. 2 (1910); Trio, for Violin, Cello, and Piano (1911); String Quartet No. 2 (1913); Violin Sonata No. 3 (1914); *Set,* for string quartet and piano (1914); Violin Sonata No. 4, subtitled *Children's Day at the Camp Meeting* (1915). VOCAL WORKS: *Psalm 67* (1898); *The Celestial Country,* cantata (1899); *Three Harvest Home Chorales,* for mixed chorus, brass, double bass and organ (1898–1912); *General William Booth Enters into Heaven,* for chorus with brass band (1914); *114 Songs* (1884–1921). PIANO PIECES: *Three-Page Sonata* (1905); *Some Southpaw Pitching* (1908); *The Anti-Abolitionist Riots* (1908); Sonata No. 1 (1909); *Twenty-Two* (1912); *Three Protests for Piano* (1914); Sonata No. 2, for piano, subtitled *Concord, Mass., 1840–1860,* in 4 movements: *Emerson, Hawthorne, The Alcotts, Thoreau* (1909–15; publ. 1919; 1st perf. in its entirety by John Kirkpatrick, N.Y., Jan. 20, 1939; the 2nd movement requires the application of a strip of wood on the keys to produce tone-clusters); *Three Quartertone Piano Pieces* (1903–24).

WRITINGS: As a companion piece to his "Concord Sonata" (Piano Sonata No. 2), Ives wrote *Essays before a Sonata* (publ. N.Y., 1920), commentaries on the Concord writers who inspired his work, and on various musical and philosophical matters; this has been reprinted as *Essays before a Sonata and Other Writings,* ed. by Howard Boatwright (N.Y., 1961). Most of his other expository writings are publ. as *Memos,* ed. by John Kirkpatrick (N.Y., 1972), composed of autobiography, explanation, and criticism.

BIBLIOGRAPHY: Henry Bellamann, "Charles Ives, The Man and His Music," *Musical Quarterly* (Jan. 1933); Henry Cowell, "Charles Ives," in *American Composers on American Music* (Stanford Univ., 1933); Paul Rosenfeld, *Discoveries of a Music Critic* (N.Y., 1936); Paul Rosenfeld, "Ives' Concord Sonata," *Modern Music* (Jan.–Feb. 1939); Madeleine Goss, *Modern Music Makers* (N.Y., 1952); N. Slonimsky, "Charles Ives, America's Musical Prophet," *Musical America* (Feb. 15, 1954); Henry and Sidney Cowell, *Charles Ives and His Music* (the basic biography; N.Y., 1955; repr. with additional material, 1969); Gilbert Chase, *America's Music* (N.Y., 1955); J. Kirkpatrick, *A Temporary Mimeographed Catalogue of the Music Manuscripts and Related Materials of Charles Edward Ives* (New Haven, 1960); S. R. Charles, "The Use of Borrowed Materials in Ives' Second Symphony," *Music Review* (May 1967); D. Marshall, "Charles Ives' Quotations: Manner or Substance?" *Perspectives of New Music,* (Spring–Summer 1968); J. Bernlef and R. de Leeuw, *Charles Ives* (Amsterdam, 1969); Dominique-René de Lerma, *Charles Edward Ives, 1874–1954: A Bibliography of His Music* (Kent, Ohio, 1970); Richard Warren Jr., compiler, *Charles E. Ives: Discography* (Yale Univ. Library, New Haven, 1972); H. Wiley Hitchcock, *Music in the United States: A Historical Introduction* (Englewood Cliffs, 1969; 2nd edition, 1974); V. Perlis, *Charles Ives Remembered: An Oral History* (New Haven, Conn., 1974; won the 1974 Kinkeldey Award); David Wooldridge, *From the Steeples and Mountains: A Study of Charles Ives* (N.Y., 1974); Frank R. Rossiter, *Charles Ives and His America* (N.Y., 1975); H. Wiley Hitchcock, *Charles Ives* (London, 1977); H. Wiley Hitchcock and Vivian Perlis, *An Ives Celebration: Papers and Panels of the Charles Ives Centennial Festival-Conference* (Urbana, Illinois, 1977). The Charles Ives Society, in New York, promotes research and publications. Letters from Charles Ives to Nicolas Slonimsky are reproduced in the latter's book *Music Since 1900* (4th edition, N.Y., 1971). A movie for television, "A Good Dissonance Like a Man," produced and directed by Theodor W. Timreck in 1977, with the supervision of Vivian Perlis, depicts the life of Ives with fine dramatic impact. See also *Modern Music . . . Analytical Index,* compiled by Wayne Shirley and ed. by William and Carolyn Lichtenwanger (N.Y., 1976; pp. 107–8).

Ives (Ive), Simon, English composer; b. Ware, July (baptized July 20), 1600; d. London, July 1, 1662. He was organist in Newgate and a choral master at St. Paul's Cathedral in London; wrote music for masques at the court. His songs, catches, and rounds were published in several 17th-century collections: Playford's *Select Ayres and Dialogues* (1669) and *Musical Companion* (1672), Hilton's *Catch that Catch can* (1652), etc. He also wrote instrumental music, some of which was included in *Musick's Recreation* (1652 and 1661).

Ivogün, Maria (real name **Inge von Gunther**), Hungarian coloratura soprano; b. Budapest, Nov. 18, 1891. She studied with Irene Schlemmer-Ambros in Vienna; was a member of the Munich Opera (1913–25); Berlin State Opera (1925–45); taught at the Music Academy in Vienna (1948–50) and at the Musik Hochschule in Berlin. She was married to the Bavarian tenor, **Karl Erb,** in 1921 (divorced, 1932); then to her accompanist, **Michael Raucheisen** (1933).

Ivry, Richard d', French opera composer; b. Beaune, Feb. 4, 1829; d. Hyères, Dec. 18, 1903. He studied music as an avocation; wrote mostly for the stage; also songs and hymns; composed several grand operas: *Les Amants de Vérone,* after *Romeo and Juliet* (Paris, Oct. 12, 1878); *Fatma, Omphale et Pénélope,* etc. He used the anagram **Yrvid** as a *nom de plume.*

Iwamoto, Marito, Japanese violinist; b. Tokyo, Jan. 19, 1926. She studied at the Music Academy in Tokyo; played at 14 with the Tokyo Symph. Orch. She made her American debut in N.Y. on June 14, 1950, with considerable success, and remained in the U.S.

J

Jacchia, Agide, Italian conductor; b. Lugo, Jan. 5, 1875; d. Siena, Nov. 29, 1932. He studied at the Cons. of Parma and at the Liceo Musicale in Pesaro; won prizes as a flute player (1896), as apprentice conductor (1897) and as composer (1898). He made his conducting debut in Brescia on Dec. 26, 1898, then filled in numerous engagements as a theater conductor in Italy. In 1902 he accompanied Mascagni on his American tour; also conducted the Milan Opera Company on its American tour in 1907–09. He was conductor of the Montreal Opera Co. (1910–13) and of the Boston National Opera (1915–16). From 1918 to 1926 he conducted the Boston Pops concerts; then returned to Italy.

Jachet of Mantua (Jaquet Collebaud de Vitré), composer; b. Vitré, France, c.1495; d. Mantua, 1559. He served at the Cathedral of Mantua as maestro di cappella (1539–58). His published works include 4-part motets (Venice, 1539); 5-part motets (Venice, 1540); Mass in 4 parts (Paris, 1554); Masses in 5 parts (Venice, 1555); *Messe del Fiore* in 5 parts (Venice, 1561); Passions in 5 parts, and other church works (Venice, 1567). Many of his motets were included in contemporary anthologies. His Mass, *La Fede non debbe esser corrotta*, was reprinted by A. Reinbrecht in 1892.
BIBLIOGRAPHY: G. Reese, *Music in the Renaissance* (N.Y., 1954; pp. 366–67).

Jachimecki, Zdzislaw, eminent Polish musicologist; b. Lwow, July 7, 1882; d. Cracow, Oct. 27, 1953. He studied in Lwow with S. Niewiadomski and H. Jarecki, and in Vienna with Adler (musicology) and Schoenberg (composition); Dr. phil. with a dissertation *150 Psalms by Mikolaj Gomolka* (1906). He then became a member of the faculty at the Univ. of Cracow. Jachimecki was one of the most renowned Polish musicologists; he was also a composer of choral works; was conductor of symphonic concerts in Cracow from 1908–24. Most of his writings are published in Polish, in Cracow. They include: *The Influence of Italian Music on Polish Music* (1911); *Organ Tablature of the Holy Ghost Cloister in Cracow, 1548* (1913); *Music of the Royal Court of King Wladyslaw Jagiello* (1915); *Outlines of Polish History of Music* (Warsaw, 1919); *Moniuszko* (Warsaw, 1921); *Chopin* (1926; in French as *F. Chopin et son œuvre,* Paris, 1930); monographs on Mozart, Haydn, Wagner, Szymanowski, etc.; contributed an article on Moniuszko to the *Musical Quarterly* (Jan. 1928); publ. *Muzyka Polska* (2 vols., 1948, 1951).

Jachino, Carlo, Italian composer; b. San Remo, Feb. 3, 1887; d. Rome, Dec. 23, 1971. He studied with Luporini in Lucca and with Riemann in Leipzig; then taught at the Parma Cons. (until 1936), at Naples (1936–38), and at the Santa Cecilia in Rome (1938–50). He then went to South America; was director of the National Cons. in Bogotá, Colombia (1953–57); returning to Italy he served as artistic director of the Teatro San Carlo in Naples (1961–69). His opera *Giocondo e il suo rè* was produced in Milan (June 24, 1924). He also wrote several works of chamber music; a treatise on the 12-tone method of composition, *Tecnica dodecafonica* (Milan, 1948); and *Gli strumenti d'orchestra* (Milan, 1950). In his early compositions he followed the Romantic Italian style; later he adopted a modified 12-tone method.

Jackson, George K., English-American organist and theorist; b. Oxford, 1745; d. Boston, Mass., Nov. 18, 1822. He was a pupil of Dr. James Narer; became a surplice boy at the Chapel Royal, London; was among the tenor singers at the Handel Commemoration in 1784; 1791, Mus. Doc., St. Andrew's College. In 1796 he came to Norfolk, Va., then to Elizabeth, N.J., and N.Y. City (1804, music director at St. George's Chapel). By 1812 he was in Boston, where he remained as organist at various churches; also gave a series of oratorios with Graupner and Mallet. A collection of his music is in the library of the Harvard Music Association, Boston. He publ. *First Principles, or a Treatise on Practical Thorough Bass* (London, 1795); *David's Psalms* (1804); *A Choice Collection of Chants* (1816); *The Choral Companion* (1817); *Watt's Divine Hymns set to music.*
BIBLIOGRAPHY: F. J. Metcalf, *American Writers and Compilers of Sacred Music* (1925); H. E. Johnson, "George K. Jackson, Doctor of Music (1745–1822)," *Musical Quarterly* (Jan. 1943).

Jackson, George Pullen, American folklorist and writer; b. Monson, Maine, Aug. 20, 1874; d. Nashville, Jan. 19, 1953. He studied philology in Dresden and at the Univ. of Chicago (Ph.B., 1904; Ph.D., 1911); was teacher of German at Vanderbilt Univ. (1918–43); founder of the Tennessee State Sacred Harp Singing Association; elected president of the Tennessee Folklore Society (1942).
WRITINGS: *The Rhythmic Form of the German Folk Songs* (1917); *White Spirituals in the Southern Uplands* (1933); *Spiritual Folksongs of Early America* (1937; 2nd ed., 1953); *White and Negro Spirituals* (1943); *Story of the Sacred Harp* (1944); *Another Sheaf of White Spirituals* (1952).

Jackson, Mahalia, black American singer; b. New Orleans, Oct. 26, 1911; d. Evergreen Park, Illinois, Jan. 27, 1972. She went to Chicago and was employed as a hotel maid; sang in Baptist churches; operated a beauty salon; owned a flower shop. She revealed an innate talent for expressive hymn singing, and soon was in demand for conventions and political meetings. She steadfastly refused to appear in night clubs. In 1952 she made a triumphant European tour; other successful appearances followed. She publ. her autobiography as a "soul singer" under the title *Movin' On Up* (N.Y., 1966).

Jackson, Samuel P., American organist; b. Manchester, England, Feb. 5, 1818; d. Brooklyn, N.Y., July 27, 1885. Son of the organ builder James Jackson, he was taken to America in 1825, and learned his father's trade. He filled in positions at various churches as an organist; for many years was music proofreader for G.

Schirmer, Inc., in New York. He publ. a variety of vocal sacred works, also a collection *Gems for the Organ* and 4 books of *Organ-Voluntaries*.

Jackson, William (I), English organist and composer; b. Exeter, May 29, 1730; d. there, July 5, 1803. He was a pupil of Sylvester, organist of Exeter Cathedral, and of J. Travers in London. After teaching for years at Exeter, he became (1777) organist and choirmaster at the cathedral. Besides the operas *The Lord of the Manor* (London, Dec. 27, 1780) and *Metamorphoses* (London, Dec. 5, 1783), he composed odes (Warton's *Ode to Fancy;* Pope's *The Dying Christian to his Soul;* etc.) and a large number of songs, canzonets, madrigals, pastorals, hymns, anthems, church services, etc.; also sonatas for harpsichord.
WRITINGS: *30 Letters on Various Subjects* (London, 1782); *Observations on the Present State of Music in London* (1791); and *The Four Ages, together with Essays on Various Subjects* (1798).

Jackson, William (II), English organist and composer; b. Masham, Yorkshire, Jan. 9, 1815; d. Bradford, April 15, 1866. A self-taught musician, he became organist at Masham in 1832; won first prize, offered by the Huddersfield Glee Club, in 1840; 1852, established a music business and became organist of St. John's Church at Bradford; later was conductor of Bradford Choral Union.

Jacob, Benjamin, English organist; b. London, May 15, 1778; d. there, Aug. 24, 1829. He was a pupil of Willoughby, Shrubsole, and Arnold (1796); served as organist at various churches, finally at Surrey Chapel (1794–1825). With Wesley and Crotch, he gave organ recitals (1808–14), which were attended by large crowds; conducted a series of oratorios in 1800, and the Lenten Oratorios at Covent Garden in 1818. Jacob was very active in spreading the Bach cult in London (see O. A. Mansfield, "J. S. Bach's First English Apostles," *Musical Quarterly,* April 1935). He publ. *National Psalmody* (London, 1819) and other collections; also glees and catches.

Jacob, Gordon, English composer and pedagogue; b. London, July 5, 1895. He studied music theory with Stanford at the Royal College of Music, and from 1926 to 1966 was on its faculty; also served as examiner of other music schools. In 1968 he was named Commander of the British Empire.
WORKS: 2 symphonies (1929, 1944); 3 sinfoniettas (1942, 1951, 1953); *Variations on an Air by Purcell* for strings (1930); Viola Concerto (1925); Concerto for Piano and String Orch. (1927); Concerto for Oboe and Strings (1933); Concerto for Bassoon, Strings, and Percussion (1947); *Rhapsody* for English horn and strings (1948); Concerto for Horn and Orch. (1951); Concerto for Violin and String Orch. (1953); Violin Concerto (1954); Cello Concerto (1955); Trombone Concerto (1952); Divertimento for Harmonica and Strings (1954); Second Piano Concerto (1956); Second Oboe Concerto (1956); *A York Symphony* for woodwind instruments (1971); also a considerable amount of chamber music: Quartet for Oboe and Strings (1938); Quintet for clarinet and strings (1942); Suite

for 4 Trombones (1968); Piano Trio (1955); Cello Sonata (1957); piano works; arrangements of Schumann's *Carnaval* and suites from works by William Byrd, Orlando Gibbons, Liszt, Chopin, etc. suitable for ballet performances; choral pieces, both secular and sacred; the books, *Orchestral Technique: A Manual for Students* (Oxford, 1931), *How to Read a Score* (Oxford, 1944), *The Composer and His Art* (London, 1955) and *The Elements of Orchestration* (London, 1962).

Jacob, Maxime, French composer; b. Bordeaux, Jan. 13, 1906; d. at the Benedictine Abbey, at En-Calcat (Tarn), Feb. 26, 1977. He studied music in Paris with Gédalge, Koechlin and Darius Milhaud. Pursuing a whimsical mode, he became associated with the so-called École d'Arcueil, named after a modest Paris suburb, where Erik Satie presided over his group of disciples; then made an 180° turn towards established religion, and in 1930 entered the Benedictine Order, where he served mainly as an organist. He continued to compose prolifically; between 1929 and 1949 he wrote 15 piano sonatas, 3 violin sonatas, 2 cello sonatas, etc.; then produced 8 string quartets (1961–69), a curious *Messe syncopée* (1968); 500 or more songs.
BIBLIOGRAPHY: Jean Roy, "Maxime Jacob," *Revue Musicale* (July 1939).

Jacobi, Erwin, Swiss musicologist; b. Strasbourg, Sept. 21, 1909. He studied economic science at Munich and Berlin; then went to Palestine, remaining there from 1934 to 1952; he studied harpsichord with Pelleg and music theory with Ben-Haim in Tel Aviv; in 1952 went to the U.S. where he took harpsichord lessons with Wanda Landowska; from 1953 to 1956 he studied musicology with Cherbuliez at the Univ. of Zürich and music theory with Hindemith; in 1957 obtained his Ph.D. for a dissertation on the evolution of music theory in England (publ. in Strasbourg in 1957–60; new edition, Baden-Baden, 1971). He was visiting Professor at the Univ. of Iowa (1970–71) and at Indiana Univ. (1971–72); in 1961 was appointed lecturer in musicology at Zürich University.

Jacobi, Frederick, American composer; b. San Francisco, May 4, 1891; d. New York, Oct. 24, 1952. He studied piano with Paolo Gallico and Rafael Joseffy, and composition with Rubin Goldmark; then took private lessons with Ernest Bloch. Subsequently he was on the faculty of the Juilliard School of Music, N.Y. (1936–50) and served as a member of the executive board of the League of Composers. In his own music he often made use of authentic American Indian themes.
WORKS: opera, *The Prodigal Son* (1944); for orch.: *The Pied Piper,* symph. poem (1915); *A California Suite* (San Francisco, Dec. 6, 1917); 2 symphonies: No. 1, *Assyrian* (San Francisco, Nov. 14, 1924); No. 2 (San Francisco, April 1, 1948); *Ode for Orchestra* (San Francisco, Feb. 12, 1943); Concertino for Piano and String Orch. (Saratoga Springs, Sept. 3, 1946); 2 *Assyrian Prayers,* for voice and orch. (1923); *The Poet in the Desert,* for baritone solo, chorus and orch. (1925); *Sabbath Evening Service,* for baritone solo and mixed chorus (1931); 3 string quartets (1924, 1933, 1945); *Im-*

pressions from the Odyssey, for violin and piano (1947); *Meditation,* for trombone and piano (1947); miscellaneous piano pieces and songs.

BIBLIOGRAPHY: David Diamond, "Frederick Jacobi," *Modern Music* (March-April 1937).

Jacobi, George, violinist and composer; b. Berlin, Feb. 13, 1840; d. London, Sept. 13, 1906. He studied in Brussels with Bériot and in Paris with Massart and Gevaert; won first prize (violin) at the Paris Cons. in 1861; became first violinist at the Paris Opéra and also conducted concerts in Paris. In 1871 he became conductor at the Alhambra Theatre in London; from 1896, taught at the Royal College of Music. He wrote about 100 ballets and a comic opera, *The Black Crook,* which attained temporary popularity.

Jacobs, Arthur, English music critic, lexicographer, opera librettist and translator; b. Manchester, June 14, 1922. He studied at Oxford Univ. From 1947 to 1952 he was music critic for the *Daily Express* and has since then written articles for a number of publications. From 1960 to 1971 he was an associate editor of the London monthly *Opera.* In 1952 he publ. a book on Gilbert and Sullivan. He then became deeply involved in musical lexicography; compiled an uncommonly intelligent, compact reference work, *A New Dictionary of Music* (London, 1958; 2nd ed., 1967; reprints with revisions, 1968, 1970; completely revised in 1977). In 1964 Jacobs was appointed lecturer in music history at the Royal Academy of Music, London; was visiting prof. at the Univ. of Illinois (1967); at the Univ. of Calif., Santa Barbara (1969) and at Temple Univ. in Philadelphia (1970, 1971); toured Australia and Russia. An accomplished linguist, he mastered Russian, as well as German, French, Italian and Spanish; translated with admirable fidelity to the syllabic and musical values of the originals, some 20 operas, among them Tchaikovsky's *The Queen of Spades,* Schoenberg's *Erwartung* and Alban Berg's *Lulu;* wrote the libretto of Nicholas Maw's opera *One Man Show* (London, 1964). Several of these translations have been adopted by the Covent Garden Opera (from 1974 the English National Opera) and Sadler's Wells Opera in London. In 1971 he was appointed editor of *Music Yearbook* publ. in London.

Jacobs-Bond, Carrie. See **Bond, Carrie Jacobs.**

Jacobson, Maurice, English publisher and composer; b. London, Jan. 1, 1896; d. Brighton, Feb. 1, 1976. He studied at the Royal College of Music in London with Stanford and Holst; wrote stage music for Shakespeare productions for the Old Vic Theatre. In 1923 he joined the music publishing house J. Curwen & Sons, Ltd., and in 1950 was elected its president. Among his compositions are the ballet *David* (1935); the cantatas *The Lady of Shalott* (1940) and *The Hound of Heaven* (1953); many short instrumental pieces and songs.

Jacobsthal, Gustav, German music theorist; b. Pyritz, Pomerania, March 14, 1845; d. Berlin, Nov. 9, 1912. He studied at the Univ. of Strasbourg (1863–70); from 1872, taught music there; publ. the valuable treatises, *Die Mensuralnotenschrift des 12. und 13. Jahr-*

hunderts (1871) and *Die chromatische Alteration im liturgischen Gesange der abendländischen Kirche* (1897). F. Ludwig and E. Schmidt published a tribute, *Trauerfeier für Gustav Jacobsthal* (Berlin, 1912).

BIBLIOGRAPHY: Friedrich Gennrich, *Die Strassburger Schule für Musikwissenschaft* (1940).

Jacoby, Hanoch, Israeli composer and violist; b. Königsberg, March 2, 1909. He studied composition with Hindemith at the Hochschule für Musik in Berlin (1927–30); was a member of the radio orch. in Frankfurt (1930–33); in 1934 emigrated to Jerusalem; taught at the Jerusalem Music Academy until 1958, when he joined the Israel Philharmonic Orch. as violist.

WORKS: 3 symphonies (1940, 1951, 1960); Viola Concerto (1939); Violin Concerto (1942); *King David's Lyre* for small orch. (1948); 7 *Miniatures* for small orch. (1945); *Capriccio Israélien* for orch. (1951); Sinfonietta (1960); *Serio Giocoso* for orch. (1964); *Partita concertata* for orch. (1970–71); *Mutatio* for orch. (1975); *Variations* for orch. (1976); *Jewish Oriental Folklore,* suite for string orch. (1977); Concertino for String Trio (1932); 2 string quartets (1937, 1938); *Theme, Variations and Finale* for piano trio (1940); Wind Quintet (1946); *Canzona* for solo harp (1960); 2 *Suites of Jewish Oriental Folklore* for brass quintet (1975); *Mutatio II* for oboe, bassoon, 2 trumpets, 2 trombones, 2 violas and double bass (1976).

Jacopo da Bologna (Jacobus de Bononia), 14th-century composer; one of the earliest representatives of the Florentine "Ars nova"; he wrote madrigals, *ballate,* etc.; his MSS are in the libraries of Florence and Paris and at the British Museum in London. His complete works are publ. in W. T. Marrocco, *The Music of Jacopo da Bologna* (Berkeley and Los Angeles, 1954). Johannes Wolf publ. 3 madrigals in his *Geschichte der Mensuralnotation* (nos. 40–42); one madrigal is in G. Reese's *Music in the Middle Ages* (N.Y., 1940; p. 363), and another in A. T. Davison and W. Apel, *Historical Anthology of Music* (Cambridge, Mass., 1947).

BIBLIOGRAPHY: J. Wolf, "L'arte del biscanto misurato secondo el maestro Jacopo da Bologna," *Kroyer-Festschrift* (1933); K. von Fischer, "'Portraits' von Piero, Giovanni da Firenze, und Jacopo da Bologna in einer Bologneser Handschrift des 14. Jahrhunderts?" *Musica Disciplina* 27 (1973).

Jacotin (real name **Jacques Godebrie**), Flemish composer; b. Antwerp, c.1445; d. there, March 23, 1529. He was for nearly half a century "chapelain" in the choir of Notre Dame in Antwerp (1479–1528). His vocal works were publ. in collections by Attaignant (1529, 1530–35) and Rhaw (1545), in Le Roy's & Ballard's *Chansons nouvellement composées* (1556), etc. He excelled especially in French chansons; of these *Trop dure m'est ta longue demeure* is reproduced in H. Expert's reprint of Attaignant's collection of 1529; and *Mon triste cœur,* in Eitner's *Selection of 60 Chansons* (1899). Several motets attributed to Jacotin and publ. by Petrucci are of doubtful authenticity. His *Sancta Divinitas unus Deus* for 8 voices appeared in Uhlhardt's collection of 1546.

Jacques de Liège (Jacobus Leoniensis), Belgian music theorist; b. Liège, c.1260; d. there, after 1330. He studied in Paris; then was a cleric in Liège. About 1330, already at an advanced age, he wrote the important compendium *Speculum musicae* in 7 parts, in 293 folios (586 pages; approximating some 2,000 pages in modern typography); it was formerly attributed to Johannes de Muris, but the authorship of Jacques de Liège is proved by the specific indication in the manuscript (Paris, Bibliothèque Nationale) that the initial letters of the 7 chapters form the name of the author; these letters are I-A-C-O-B-U-S. W. Grossmann in his book, *Die einleitenden Kapitel des Speculum Musicae von J. Muris* (Leipzig, 1924), overlooks this indication.

BIBLIOGRAPHY: For detailed discussion of the problem, see R. Bragard, "Le Speculum Musicae du Compilateur Jacques de Liège," *Musica Disciplina* (1953–54; also printed separately); H. Besseler, "Studien zur Musik des Mittelalters," *Archiv für Musikwissenschaft* (1925–27). Selections from the *Speculum musicae* are given in English transl. in O. Strunk's *Source Readings in Music History* (N.Y., 1950); the complete Latin text, ed. by R. Bragard, was publ. in the *Corpus Scriptorum de Musica* of the American Institute of Musicology (1956).

Jadassohn, Salomon, noted German pedagogue; b. Breslau, Aug. 13, 1831; d. Leipzig, Feb. 1, 1902. He studied piano and violin in Breslau; in 1848 he took courses at the Leipzig Cons.; in 1849 he was in Weimar, where Liszt accepted him as a student; then he returned to Leipzig, and studied privately with Hauptmann. He remained in Leipzig during his entire life; organized a choral society, Psalterion (1866); conducted the concerts of the Euterpe Society. In 1871 he was appointed instructor at the Leipzig Cons.; in 1887 he was made Dr. phil. (honoris causa); in 1893 he became Royal Professor. A scholar of the highest integrity and great industry, he codified the traditional views of harmony, counterpoint, and form in his celebrated manuals, which have been translated into many languages. He was a firm believer in the immutability of harmonic laws, and became the rock of Gibraltar of conservatism in musical teaching; through his many students, who in turn became influential teachers in Germany and other European countries, the cause of orthodox music theory was propagated far and wide. He was also a composer; wrote 4 symphonies; a piano concerto; 3 piano quintets; a piano quartet; 4 piano trios; 2 string quartets; a serenade for flute and string orch.; a cavatina for cello with orch.; choral works; many piano pieces and songs. He was a master of contrapuntal forms, and wrote a number of vocal duets in canon; other contrapuntal devices are illustrated in many of his works. His music is totally forgotten; but his importance as a theorist cannot be doubted.

WRITINGS: His manuals, covering a wide range of musical subjects, are: *Harmonielehre* (Leipzig, 1883; 7th ed., 1903; English ed., N.Y., 1893, under the title, *A Manual of Harmony*, transl. by Th. Baker); *Kontrapunkt* (1884; 5th ed., 1909); *Kanon und Fuge* (1884; 3rd ed., 1909); *Die Formen in den Werken der Tonkunst* (1889; 4th ed., 1910); *Lehrbuch der Instrumentation* (1889; 2d ed., 1907); *Die Kunst zu Modulieren und Präludieren* (1890); *Allgemeine Musiklehre* (1892); *Elementar-Harmonielehre* (1895); *Methodik des musiktheoretischen Unterrichts* (1898); *Das Wesen der Melodie in der Tonkunst* (1899); *Das Tonbewusstsein; die Lehre vom musikalischen Hören* (1899); *Erläuterung der in Bachs "Kunst der Fuge" enthaltenen Fugen und Kanons* (1899); *Der Generalbass* (1901).

Jadin, Louis Emmanuel, French composer and conductor; b. Versailles, Sept. 21, 1768; d. Paris, April 11, 1853. He was at first a page in the household of Louis XVI; after the Revolution, he was on the staff of the Théâtre de Monsieur; there he produced his comic opera, *Joconde* (Sept. 14, 1790). He then wrote all kinds of festive compositions to be performed on special occasions during the revolutionary years. In 1802 he became prof. of piano at the newly established Paris Cons., succeeding his brother, **Hyacinthe Jadin** (1769–1800). During the Napoleonic wars he continued to write patriotic pieces; his orchestral overture, *La Bataille d'Austerlitz,* enjoyed great popularity for a while. He also wrote pieces for piano, and piano duets.

BIBLIOGRAPHY: G. de Saint-Foix, "Les Frères Jadin," *Revue Musicale* (1925).

Jadlowker, Hermann, tenor; b. Riga, July 17, 1877; d. Tel Aviv, May 13, 1953. He left home as a boy to escape a commercial career and entered the Vienna Cons. He made his debut as operatic tenor in Cologne (1889); then sang at the Berlin State Opera and at the Vienna Opera. He made his American debut at the Metropolitan Opera House in *Faust* (Jan. 22, 1910); in 1913, went again to Berlin; from 1929 until 1938 he was cantor at the synagogue of his native town, Riga; then went to Palestine, where he settled as a teacher.

Jaëll, Alfred, noted French pianist; b. Trieste, March 5, 1832; d. Paris, Feb. 27, 1882. He studied with his father, Eduard Jaëll; appeared as a child prodigy in Venice in 1843; continual concert tours earned him the nickname of "le pianiste voyageur." He traveled in America in 1852–54; after this, he lived in Paris, Brussels, and Leipzig. In 1866 he married **Marie Trautmann;** made piano transcriptions from works of Wagner, Schumann, and Mendelssohn.

Jaëll-Trautmann, Marie, French pianist, wife of **Alfred Jaëll;** b. Steinseltz, Alsace, Aug. 17, 1846; d. Paris, Feb. 4, 1925. She studied with Henri Herz at the Paris Cons., where she won first prize. After her marriage, she accompanied her husband on his travels. She wrote many characteristic pieces for piano, and published pedagogical works: *La Musique et la psycho-physiologie* (1895); *Le Mécanisme du toucher* (1896); *Le Toucher* (1899); *L'Intelligence et le rythme dans les mouvements artistiques* (1905); *Le Rythme du regard et la dissociation des doigts* (1906); *La Coloration des sensations tactiles* (1910); *La Résonance du toucher et la topographie des pulpes* (1912); *La Main et la pensée musicale* (posthumous, 1925).

BIBLIOGRAPHY: H. Kiener, *Marie Jaëll* (1952).

Jagel, Frederick, American tenor; b. Brooklyn, June 10, 1897. His mother and father were pianists. He was a clerk for the Mutual Life Insurance Co.; studied in Milan (1923–27) and with William Brady in N.Y. (1932–42). He made his operatic debut in 1924 in Leghorn as Rodolfo; then sang in Italy and Spain; debut with the Metropolitan Opera Co. as Radames (Nov. 8, 1927). He was a member of the San Francisco Opera Co. (1931, 1939, 1942–44); at the Teatro Colón, Buenos Aires (1928, 1939–41). On June 12, 1928, he married **Nancy Weir,** an opera singer. From 1949 to 1970 he taught voice at the New England Cons. in Boston.

Jahn, Otto, learned German philologist and musicographer; b. Kiel, June 16, 1813; d. Göttingen, Sept. 9, 1869. He studied languages and antiquities at Kiel, Leipzig, and Berlin; then traveled in France and Italy; in 1839 he settled in Kiel as a lecturer on philology; in 1842 became prof. of archeology at Greifswald; was director of the Archeological Museum in Leipzig (1847); he lost this position in the wake of the political upheaval of 1848. In 1855 he was appointed prof. of archeology at Bonn Univ. He went to Göttingen shortly before his death. In the field of music, his magnum opus was the biography of Mozart (Leipzig, 1856–59, in 4 vols.; 2nd ed., 1867, in 2 vols.; 3rd ed., 1889–91, revised by H. Deiters; 4th ed., also revised by Deiters, 1905–07; 7th ed., revised by Hermann Abert, 2 vols., 1956). The English translation (by P. Townsend) appeared in 3 vols. in London (1882). Jahn's biography was the first musical life written according to the comparative critical method; it reviews the state of music during the period immediately preceding Mozart; this comprehensive exposition has become a model for subsequent musical biographies. Jahn intended to write a biography of Beethoven, according to a similar plan, but could not complete the task; Thayer utilized the data accumulated by Jahn in his own work on Beethoven; Pohl used Jahn's notes in his biography of Haydn. Numerous essays by Jahn were publ. in his *Gesammelte Aufsätze über Musik* (1866). He composed songs, of which 32 were publ. in 4 books; he also brought out a volume of songs for mixed voices; edited the vocal score of Beethoven's *Fidelio.*
BIBLIOGRAPHY: J. Vahlen, *Otto Jahn* (1870); E. Petersen, *Otto Jahn in seinen Briefen* (Leipzig, 1912); J. Pulver, "Otto Jahn," *Musical Times* (April 1913).

Jahn, Wilhelm, Austrian conductor; b. Hof, Moravia, Nov. 24, 1834; d. Vienna, April 21, 1900. At the age of 20 he became a theater conductor in Budapest; then occupied similar posts in Agram, Amsterdam, and Prague. He spent a number of years in Wiesbaden (1864–81); finally settled in Vienna, where he became musical director of the Vienna Opera. He retired in 1897, and was succeeded by Mahler.

Jähns, Friedrich Wilhelm, German vocal pedagogue and writer on music; b. Berlin, Jan. 2, 1809; d. there, Aug. 8, 1888. He studied singing with Grell; sang at the Berlin Opera as a boy soprano in the chorus. In 1845 he founded a singing society, which he conducted until 1870; in 1881 he became instructor of rhetoric at Scharwenka's Cons. He was very success-

ful as a vocal teacher in Berlin; had some 1,000 pupils. His admiration for Weber impelled him to collect all materials pertaining to Weber's life and works; his unique library, containing 300 autograph letters and many other documents, pamphlets, essays, and first editions, was acquired in 1883 by the Berlin Royal Library. He publ. a treatise on Weber, with a thematic catalogue, *Carl Maria von Weber in seinen Werken* (Berlin, 1871). Apart from exhaustive biographical data, this book is historically interesting, because in the preface the author introduced, for the first time in print, the Wagnerian term "Leitmotiv"; this was later popularized by Wolzogen and others. He was also a composer; his works include a *Grand Sonata* for violin and piano; a piano trio; a book of *Schottische Lieder,* and many other vocal pieces.

Jalas (real name, **Blomstedt**), **Jussi,** Finnish conductor; b. Jyväskylä, June 23, 1908. He studied with Krohn in Helsinki, and later in Paris with Rhené-Baton and Monteux. Since 1945 he has conducted at the Helsinki Opera. He has appeared as guest conductor in Scandinavia, Germany, France, and England; also in the U.S. (1950 and 1955). Jalas is regarded as one of the most authentic interpreters of the music of Sibelius, whose son-in-law he was.

James, Dorothy, American composer; b. Chicago, Dec. 1, 1901. She studied with Louis Gruenberg and Adolf Weidig at the Chicago Musical College, and at the American Cons. of Music, Chicago (M.M., 1927); also took courses in composition with Howard Hanson at the Eastman School of Music, Rochester, N.Y.; with Healey Willan in Toronto and Ernst Krenek at the Univ. of Michigan. For 40 years (1927–68) she valiantly taught music theory at Eastern Michigan Univ. at Ypsilanti, Michigan; continued to live in Ypsilanti after retirement.
WORKS: an opera, *Paolo and Francesca* (1930; partial performance in concert form, Rochester, April 2, 1931, on the same program with her *3 Symphonic Fragments*); *Elegy for the Lately Dead* for orch. (1938); Suite for Small Orch. (1940); chamber music: *Ballade* for violin and piano (1925); *Rhapsody* for violin, cello and piano (1929); *Pastorales,* 3 pieces for clarinet, strings and celesta (1933); *Recitative and Aria* for string quintet (1944); *Morning Music* for flute and piano (1967); *Patterns* for harp (1977); *Tears,* after Walt Whitman, for chorus and orch. (1930); *The Jumblies,* children's cantata, to the text by Edward Lear (1935); *Paul Bunyan,* children's cantata (1938); *The Golden Year* for chorus and orch. (1953); many pieces for a cappella chorus and vocal solos with piano accompaniment; *2 Satirical Dances* for piano (1934); *Tone-Row,* suite for piano (1962). She published a valuable brochure, *Music of Living Michigan Women Composers* (1976).

James, Philip, notable American composer; b. Jersey City, N.J., May 17, 1890; d. Southhampton, Long Island, N.Y., Nov. 1, 1975. He studied with Rubin Goldmark, Scalero, Norris, and Schenck. He was in the army during World War I; and after the Armistice was appointed bandmaster of the American Expeditionary Force General Headquarters Band. At various times, he conducted the Winthrop Ames Theatrical Productions (1915–16), Victor Herbert Opera Co. (1919–22), New Jersey Symph. Orch. (1922–29), Brooklyn Orchestral Society (1927–30), Bamberger Little Symphony (Station WOR; 1929–36); also was guest conductor with the Philadelphia Orch. and the N.Y. Philharmonic. In 1933 he was elected a member of the National Institute of Arts and Letters; won numerous prizes, among them one for his orchestral suite *Station WGZBX* awarded by the National Broadcasting Co. Philip James had a distinguished career as teacher. In 1923 he joined the faculty of N.Y. Univ.; became chairman of the music dept. in 1933; retired in 1955.

WORKS: FOR THE STAGE: *Judith,* dramatic reading with ballet and small orch. (1927). FOR ORCH.: Suite for Strings (N.Y. Univ., April 28, 1934); *Sea Symph.* for bass-baritone and orch. (1928); *Song of the Night,* symph. poem (1931; N.Y., March 15, 1938); *Station WGZBX,* satirical suite (NBC Symph. Orch., May 1, 1932); *Bret Harte,* overture (N.Y., Dec. 20, 1936); *Gwalia,* a Welsh rhapsody for orch. (N.Y., Feb. 18, 1940, composer conducting); Symph. No. 1 (1943); Sinfonietta (1946); 2nd Suite for strings (1943; Saratoga Springs, Sept. 5, 1946); *Miniver Cheevy,* for orch. and *Richard Cory,* for narrator and orch. (Saratoga, N.Y., Sept. 9, 1947); *Brennan on the Moor* (N.Y., Nov. 28, 1939); symph. poem *Chaumont,* for small orch. (1948); Symph. No. 2 (1949). CHAMBER MUSIC: String Quartet (1924); Suite for Flute, Oboe, Clarinet, Bassoon, and Horn (1936); Piano Quartet (1938). CHORAL WORKS: *The Nightingale of Bethlehem,* for soloists, chorus, and orch. (1919); *Song of the Future,* for mixed chorus a cappella (1922); *Missa Imaginum,* for mixed chorus and orch. (1929); *General William Booth Enters Into Heaven,* for tenor, male voices, and small orch. (1932); *World of Tomorrow,* for mixed chorus and orch. (1938); *Shirat Ha-Yam,* for mixed chorus and orch. (1944); *Mass of the Pictures* for chorus and orch. (1965); *To Cecilia,* cantata for chorus and small orch. (1966).

Jan, Karl von, German writer on music; b. Schweinfurt, May 22, 1836; d. Adelboden, Switzerland, Sept. 4, 1899. He took the degree of Dr. phil. at Berlin (1859) with the thesis *De fidibus Graecorum;* publ. several essays on ancient Greek music. An important work is his critical edition of the Greek writers on music: *Musici scriptores graeci; Aristoteles, Euclides, Bacchius, Cleonides, Nichomachus, Gaudentius, Alypius* (1895), with an appendix, *Melodiarum reliquiae,* containing all the vocal music known in his day to be extant (this also in a separate edition, augmented and revised, 1899).

Janáček, Leoš, greatly renowned Czech composer; b. Hukvaldy, Moravia, July 3, 1854; d. Ostrava, Aug. 12, 1928. At the age of ten he was placed at the Augustine monastery in Brno as a chorister; then studied at the Brno Teachers' Training College (1872–74) and at the Organ School (College of Music) in Prague, where he studied organ with Skuherský (1874–75); later took lessons in composition with L. Grill at the Leipzig Cons. and with Franz Krenn at the Vienna Cons. (1879–80). Returning to Brno, he was active as

teacher; from 1881 to 1888 he conducted the Czech Philharmonic there; from 1919 to 1925 he taught at the Cons. of Brno; many Czech composers of the younger generation were his students. Although he began to compose early in life, it was not until 1904, with the production of his opera *Její pastorkyňa* (commonly known under its German title, *Jenufa*), that his importance as a national composer was realized in the music world; the work was widely performed in Austria, Germany and Russia, and was eventually produced in America. In the field of religious music, he created a unique score, *Glagolitic Mass* (also known as *Slavonic Mass* or *Festival Mass*), to a text in old Slavonic, with an instrumental accompaniment. Janáček took great interest in Russian literature and music; he visited Russia three times; his operas *Káťa Kabanová* and *From the House of the Dead* and several other works are based on Russian literary works. There is an affinity between Janáček's method of dramatic prosody and Mussorgsky's ideas of realistic musical speech, but Janáček never consciously imitated the Russian models. He was a firm believer in the artistic importance of folksongs and collected a number of them in his native Moravia; contributed a paper on the musical structure of national songs to the Prague Academy (1901). During the last two decades of his life, Janáček was strongly influenced by the French school; the idiom of his instrumental works of that period clearly reflects Impressionist usages.

WORKS: FOR THE STAGE: 9 operas: *Šárka* (1887, revised in 1918; instrumentation of the third act and final revision of the first and second acts accomplished by Janáček's student Oswald Chlubna in 1918–19 and 1924; Brno, Nov. 11, 1925); *Počátek románu (Beginning of a Romance,* 1891; Brno, Feb. 10, 1894); *Její pastorkyňa (Her Foster Daughter;* German title, *Jenufa;* 1894–1903; Brno, Jan. 21, 1904; revised 1906, 1911 and 1916); *Osud (Fate,* 1903–04; Brno Radio, Sept. 18, 1934; first stage perf., Brno, Oct. 25, 1958); the satiric opera *Výlety páně Broučkovy (The Excursions of Mr. Broucek),* made up of 2 separately performable scenes, *Výlet pana Broučka do Měsíce (Mr. Broucek's Flight to the Moon,* 1908–17) and *Výlet pana Broučka do XV století (Mr. Broucek's Trip to the 15th Century,* 1917; both in Prague, April 23, 1920); *Káťa Kabanová* (after Ostrovsky's play, *The Storm,* 1919–21; Brno, Nov. 23, 1921); *Příhody lišky Bystroušky (The Cunning Little Vixen,* 1921–23; Brno, Nov. 6, 1924); *Věc Makropulos,* after Čapek *(The Makropulos Affair,* 1923–25; Brno, Dec. 18, 1926); *Z mrtvého domu,* after Dostoyevsky *(From the House of the Dead,* 1927–28; produced posthumously, Brno, April 12, 1930) and a ballet, *Rákocz Rákoczy* (1891; Prague, July 24, 1891). CHORAL WORKS: 6 cantatas: *Hospodine pomiluj ny (Lord, Have Mercy Upon Us)* for solo quartet, double chorus, with organ, harp, 3 trumpets, 3 trombones and 2 tubas (1896); *Amarus* for solo trio, chorus, harp and orch. (1897, revised 1901 and 1906); *Otčenáš (The Lord's Prayer)* for tenor, chorus, harp and organ (1901, revised 1906); *Na Soláni Čarták (At the Inn of Solan)* for male chorus and orch. (1911); *Věčné evangelium (The Eternal Gospel),* cantata-legend for soprano, tenor, chorus and orch. (1914) and *Glagolská mše (Glagolitic Mass* or *Slavonic Mass* or

Festival Mass) for soli, chorus and orch. (1926; Brno, Dec. 5, 1927); a cappella choruses. CHAMBER VOCAL WORKS: *Zápisník zmizelého* (*The Diary of One Who Vanished*) for tenor, alto, 3 female voices and piano (1917–19, revised 1924) and *Říkadla* (*Nursery Rhyme*) for 9 singers and chamber ensemble (1925–27); numerous folksong arrangements. FOR ORCH.: Suite for String Orch. (1877); *Idyll* for string orch. (1878); *Moravian Dances* (1888–91); *6 Lašske tance* (*6 Lachian Dances*, 1889–90); Suite (1891); *Žárlivost* (*Jealousy*), symph. poem (1894); *Šumařovo dítě* (*The Fiddler's Child*), ballad (1912; Prague, Nov. 14, 1917), *Taras Bulba*, rhapsody after Gogol (1915–18; Brno, Oct. 9, 1921); *Balada blanická* (*The Ballad of Blaník*), symph. poem (1920; Brno, March 21, 1920); Sinfonietta (1926; Prague, June 29, 1926; his most popular instrumental work); *Dunaj* (*The Danube*), symph. poem (1923–28; completed by Chlubna, 1948); Violin Concerto (1927–28; only a fragment was completed). CHAMBER MUSIC: 2 string quartets: No. 1 (inspired by Tolstoy's *Kreutzer Sonata*, 1923) and No. 2, *Intimate Letters* (1928); *Dumka* for violin and piano (1880); *Pohádka* (*Fairytale*) for cello and piano (1910); Violin Sonata (1913); *Mládí* (*Youth*) for wind sextet (1924); Concertino for Piano and Ensemble of clarinet, bassoon, horn, 2 violins and viola (1925; Brno, Feb. 16, 1926); *Capriccio* for piano left-hand and flute, piccolo, 2 trumpets, 3 trombones and tuba (1926; Prague, March 2, 1928). FOR PIANO: *Tema con variazioni* (known as the *Zdeňka Variations*, 1880); *3 Moravian Dances* (1892, 1904); *Po zarostlém chodníčku* (*On an Overgrown Path*), cycle in 2 series (1901–08); sonata, *1. X. 1905* (also known as *From the Street*, 1905); *V mlhách* (*In the Mist*, 4 pieces, 1912); *Memory* (1928). A complete list of works with exact dates of composition and performance is found in Gr. Černušák and Vlad. Helfert, *Pazdírkuv Hudební Slovník Naučny*, vol. 2 (Prague, 1937), and in Kenneth Thompson, *St. Martin's Dictionary of Twentieth-Century Composers 1911–1971* (N.Y., 1973).

BIBLIOGRAPHY: Max Brod, *Leoš Janáček* (Prague, 1924; in German, Vienna 1925); H. Hollander, "Leoš Janáček and His Operas," *Musical Quarterly* (Jan. 1929); Daniel Muller, *Leoš Janáček* (Paris, 1930); J. Procházka, *Lašske Kořeny života i díla Loeše Janáčka* (Prague, 1948); B. Štědroň, *Leoš Janáček: Letters and Reminiscences* (Prague, 1946; in English, 1955); H. Hollander, "The Music of Leoš Janáček—Its Origin in Folklore," *Musical Quarterly* (April 1955); J. Seda, *Leoš Janáček* (Prague, 1956, in Czech and English); H. Richter, *Leoš Janáček* (Leipzig, 1958); J. Vogel, *Leoš Janáček: Leben und Werk* (Prague, 1958; in English, London, 1962); B. Štědroň, *The Works of Leoš Janáček* (Prague, 1959); J. Rocek, *Leoš Janáček* (Leipzig, 1962); Hans Hollander, Leoš Janáček: *His Life and Work* (N.Y., 1963); Erik Chisholm, *The Operas of Leoš Janáček* (N.Y., 1971); T. Kneif, *Die Bühnenwerke von Leoš Janáček* (1974); Michael Evans, *Janáček's Tragic Operas* (London, 1977). A collection of documents and studies pertaining to Janáček's work was publ. in Prague under the title *O lidové písne a lidové hudbě* (1955).

Janeček, Karel, Czech composer and theorist; b. Czestochowa, Poland, Feb. 20, 1903; d. Prague, Jan. 4, 1974. He spent his boyhood in Kiev. After completing secondary education at an industrial school, he went to Prague where he took courses in composition with Křička and Novák (1924–27). From 1929 to 1941 he taught at the Pilsen Music School; then was prof. of composition at the Prague Cons. (1941–46) and later at the Prague Academy. In his early works Janeček adopted a traditional national style; later he occasionally employed a personalized dodecaphonic scheme. WORKS: *Overture* (1926–27); 2 symphonies (1935–40, 1954–55); *Lenin*, symph. triptych (1953); *Legend of Prague*, overture for string orch. (1956); Fantasy for Orch. (1962–63); Sinfonietta (1967); *Large Symposium* for 15 soloists (1967); 3 string quartets (1924, 1927, 1934); Divertimento for 8 instruments (1925–26); String Trio (1930); Trio for flute, clarinet and bassoon (1931); Duo for Violin and Viola (1938); Violin Sonata (1939); Divertimento for oboe, clarinet and bassoon (1949); Cello Sonata (1958); *Little Symposium*, chamber suite for flute, clarinet, bassoon and piano (1959); Duo for Violin and Cello (1960); *Chamber Overture* for nonet (1960); Quartet for flute, oboe, clarinet and bassoon (1966); *Trifles and Abbreviations* for piano (1926); *Tema con variazioni*, for piano, inspired by the tragedy of the village of Lidice, destroyed by the Nazis (1942); several choral works, including *To the Fallen* (1950–51), *To the Living* (1951) and *My Dream* (1972); songs. WRITINGS: *Základy moderní harmonie* (*The Basis of Modern Harmony*, written 1942–49; publ. in Prague, 1965), *Hudební formy* (*Musical Forms*, Prague, 1955), *Melodika* (Prague, 1956), *Harmonie rozborem* (*Harmony Through Analysis*; Prague, 1963; originally known as *Analytical Introduction to Harmony*), *Tektonics* (*Tectonics, the Science of Construction of Compositions*; Prague, 1968) and *Tvorba a tvůrci* (*Creativity and Creations*; Prague, 1968).

Janequin, Clément, creator and chief representative of the new 16th century French polyphonic chanson; b. Châtellerault, about 1485; d. c.1560. He was a pupil of Josquin. In his youth he may have been in the service of Louis Ronsard, father of the poet Pierre Ronsard, and may have accompanied his master during the Italian campaigns, from 1507 to the battle of Marignano, 1515. About 1520 he was in Paris and later perhaps in Spain. There is evidence that in 1529 he was in Bordeaux, subsequently in the service of the Cardinal of Lorraine (d. 1550), then chaplain of the Duke de Guise, whose victories he celebrated by extended chansons. From 1545 to 1558 he was curate at Unverre. In a dedication in verse, of 1559, he bemoans his old age and poverty.

WORKS: Besides many detached pieces in collections of the time (Attaignant's, Gardane's, etc.), and chansons in special editions, there were publ. 2 Masses (1532, 1554), *Sacræ cantiones seu motectœ 4 voc.* (1533), *Proverbs de Salomon mis en cantiques et ryme françoise* (1554); *Octante deux psaumes de David* (1559); etc. Among the most interesting "Inventions" (chansons) in 4–5 parts are *La Bataille* (portraying the battle of Marignano; Verdelot added a fifth part to the original four), *La Prise de Boulogne*, *Le Chant des oiseaux*, etc. Some of Janequin's works are ambitious examples of program music. Reprints have been made by Henri Expert in his *Maîtres Musiciens de la Renaissance Française* (chansons; vol. 7) and by Maurice Cauchie in *Les Concerts de la Renaissance*, Part 2 (a collection of 30 3- and 4-voiced chansons by Janequin; 1928). Cauchie also ed. 2 5-voiced chansons (*Le Caquet des femmes* and *La Jalouzie*). His complete chansons are publ. in 6 vols. as *Chansons polyphoniques*, ed. by T. Merritt and F. Lesure (Monaco, 1965–71).

BIBLIOGRAPHY: M. Cauchie, "Clément Janequin: Recherches sur sa famille et sur lui-même," *Revue de Musicologie* (Feb. 1923); M. Cauchie, "Clément Janequin, chapelain du duc de Guise," *Le Ménestrel* (Jan. 21, 1927); M. Cauchie, *Les Psaumes de Janequin* (Liège, 1930); J. Levron, *Clément Janequin, musicien de la Renaissance* (Paris, 1948); F. Lesure, "Clément Janequin, Recherches sur sa vie et son œuvre," *Musica Disciplina* (1951); G. Reese, *Music in the Renaissance* (N.Y., 1954; pp. 295–99 and 340).

Janigro, Antonio, Italian cellist and conductor; b. Milan, Jan. 21, 1918. He studied at the Cons. of Milan and in Paris; pursued a successful career as a solo cellist but later turned mostly to conducting. In 1950 he founded the group I Solisti di Zagreb and toured with this small ensemble extensively. In 1968 he was appointed conductor of the Radio Chamber Orch. in Saarland, and toured with it in Europe and America (1969 and 1971). In 1965 he was appointed prof. of cello playing at the Schumann Cons. in Düsseldorf.

Janis (real name **Yanks**), **Byron,** American pianist; b. McKeesport, Pennsylvania, March 24, 1928. He first studied piano with Adelle Marcus, and then was one of the few private students of Vladimir Horowitz. He made his concert debut at the age of 15, playing Rachmaninoff's 2nd Piano Concerto with the Pittsburgh Symph. Orch. (Feb. 20, 1944); then toured widely in America; also made several tours of Russia with remarkable success.

Janitsch, Johann Gottlieb, Silesian composer; b. Schweidnitz, June 19, 1708; d. Berlin, c.1763. He studied jurisprudence and was in the service of the Minister of War von Happe; in 1736 he followed crown prince Friedrich (later Frederick the Great) to Rheinsberg as his court musician; later was director of military music in Berlin. His name is known mainly through his quartet for flute, oboe, viola and piano entitled *Echo*, composed in 1757, which was reissued as part of the series *Kammermusik-Bibliothek* in Leipzig in 1938; two more quartets were published in 1963 and 1970. 30 quartets of Janitsch are extant (he assigns the name "Suonata a quatro" to them); he also wrote several harpsichord pieces. A collection of Janitsch's works has been assembled from available manuscripts by Josef Marx of the McGinnis & Marx, firm of music publishers in New York.

Jankélévitch, Vladimir, French music critic; b. Bourges, Aug. 31, 1903. He has publ. a number of biographical studies: *Gabriel Fauré et ses mélodies* (1938; new augmented ed., 1951); *Maurice Ravel* (1939); *Debussy et le mystère* (1949); also *La Rapsodie: verve et improvisation musicale* (1955); *Le Nocturne: Fauré,* *Chopin et la Nuit; Satie et le Matin* (Paris, 1957); contributed a number of articles to music magazines.

Jankó, Paul von, Hungarian pianist and inventor; b. Totis, June 2, 1856; d. Istanbul, March 17, 1919. He studied at the Polytechnic, Vienna, and also at the Cons. (under Hans Schmitt, Krenn, and Bruckner); then (1881–82) at Berlin Univ. (mathematics), and with Ehrlich (piano); from 1892 lived in Istanbul (Constantinople). His keyboard, invented in 1882, is a new departure in piano mechanics, though standing in distant relationship to the older "chromatic" keyboard advocated by the society "Chroma." It has six rows of keys; each pair of rows consists of 2 mutually exclusive whole-tone scales; the fingering of all diatonic scales is alike; chromatic scales are played by striking alternative keys in any two adjoining rows. A full description of the keyboard was published in pamphlet form by its inventor (1886). The "Jankó keyboard" was espoused by quite a few enthusiastic souls, but like many similar "inventions" it soon lapsed into innocuous desuetude.

BIBLIOGRAPHY: F. B. Boyes, *Das Jankó-Klavier* (Vienna, 1904); H. F. Münnich, *Materialen für die Jankó-Klaviatur* (1905).

Jannaconi, Giuseppe, one of the last composers in "Palestrina-style"; b. Rome, 1741; d. there, March 16, 1816. A pupil of S. Rinaldini and G. Carpani, he succeeded Zingarelli in 1811 as maestro at St. Peter's. He is noted for his scoring of many of Palestrina's works, aided by his friend Pisari. His works remain in MS in the Santini College now at Münster; they include a Mass, a *Te Deum*, a *Magnificat*, a *Dixit Dominus*, and a *Tu es Petrus*, all *a* 16; 16 Masses in 4–8 parts, with organ; 14 other Masses; 32 psalms in 4–8 parts; 10 Masses with orch.; 16 motets in 2–6 parts; 57 offertories and anthems *a* 3–8; a canon *a* 64; 2 canons *a* 16; an *Ecce terrae motus* for 6 basses; an oratorio for 2 tenors and 1 bass, *L'Agonia di Gesù Christo;* etc.

Janowka, Thomas Balthasar, Bohemian organist; b. Kuttenberg, 1660; date of death unknown. He was the compiler of *Clavis ad thesaurum magnae artis musicae* (Prague, 1701), which was the second (after Tinctoris) music dictionary in print. Only a few copies are extant.

Jansa, Leopold, Bohemian violinist and composer; b. Wildenschwert, March 23, 1795; d. Vienna, Jan. 24, 1875. He studied in Vienna; then taught violin there; was dismissed in 1849 after he took part in a concert in London for the benefit of the Hungarian revolutionists. He remained in England as a teacher for several years until the amnesty of 1868, when he returned to Vienna and received a pension. He was greatly esteemed as a violinist; he composed much violin music, including 4 concertos and 36 violin duets; other works are 8 string quartets, 3 string trios, and some church music.

Janson, Alfred, Norwegian composer; b. Oslo, March 10, 1937. His mother gave him piano lessons, but he soon turned to the accordion as his favorite musical instrument, and as a youth earned a living by playing in cafés and restaurants, mostly in jazz groups. He then took some composition lessons with Finn Mortensen. His own music is a cross-section of a variety of modern techniques.

WORKS: an opera, *Fjeldeventyret* (*A Mountain Adventure*, 1970–73; Oslo, April 9, 1973); *Vuggesang (Cradle Song)* for 48 strings and piano (1963); *Konstruksjon og hymne (Construction and Hymn)* for orch. (1963); *Canon* for saxophone, percussion, piano, Hammond organ, double bass, voice and tape (1964); *Tema* for chorus, organ, percussion and piano (1966); *Nocturne*, after Nietzsche, for 2 choruses, 2 cellos, 2 percussion groups and harp (1967); *Mot Solen (Towards the Sun)*, ballet with 2 solo saxophones, chorus and orch. ensemble (1968); *I dag død, imorgen rosenrød (Candy and Balloons)*, ballet (1969); *Röster i mänskligt landskap (Voices in Human Landscape)*, Mass for 3 actors, chorus and 10 instruments (1969); *Valse Triste* for jazz quintet and tape (1970); *Aberte*, music for a television play (1972).

Janssen, Herbert, German baritone; b. Cologne, Sept. 22, 1895; d. New York, June 3, 1965. He studied in Cologne and Berlin; gave recitals; then became a member of the Berlin State Opera. He made his American debut with the Metropolitan Opera Co. (Philadelphia, Jan. 24, 1939) as Wotan in *Siegfried;* then sang in other Wagnerian roles.

Janssen, Werner, American composer and conductor; b. New York, June 1, 1899. He studied music theory with Frederick Converse in Boston and conducting with Felix Weingartner in Basel and Hermann Scherchen in Strasbourg (1921–25); won the Prix de Rome of the American Academy (1930) and made his debut as conductor in Rome; he gave a concert of music by Sibelius in Helsinki in 1934 and was praised by Sibelius himself; received the Finnish Order of the White Rose. He made his American debut with the N.Y. Philharmonic on Nov. 8, 1934; served as regular conductor of the Baltimore Symph. (1937–39); then went to Hollywood where he organized the Janssen Symph. (1940–52) and commissioned American composers to write special works. He was subsequently conductor of the Utah Symph. Orch., Salt Lake City (1946–47), of the Portland, Oregon, Orch. (1947–49) and of the San Diego Philharmonic (1952–54). In 1937 he married the famous motion picture actress Ann Harding; they were divorced in 1963. As a composer, Janssen cultivates the art of literal pictorialism; his most successful work of this nature was *New Year's Eve in New York* (Rochester, May 9, 1929), a symph. poem for large orch. and jazz instruments; the orchestra players were instructed to shout at the end "Happy New Year!" Other works are: *Obsequies of a Saxophone,* for 6 wind instruments and a snare drum (Washington, D.C., Oct. 17, 1929); *Louisiana Suite,* for orch. (1930); *Dixie Fugue* (extracted from the *Louisiana Suite;* Rome, Nov. 27, 1932); *Foster Suite,* for orch., on Stephen Foster's tunes (1937); 2 string quartets.

Janssens, Jean-François-Joseph, Belgian composer; b. Antwerp, Jan. 29, 1801; d. there, Feb. 3, 1835. He studied with his father and later with Lesueur in Paris.

Returning to Antwerp, he became a lawyer; was a notary public until the siege of Antwerp (1832); composed in his leisure hours. Going to Cologne, he lost his manuscripts and other possessions in a fire on the night of his arrival; this misfortune so affected him that he became insane. He wrote 4 operas, 2 cantatas, 2 symphonies, 5 Masses; a number of motets, anthems, and hymns; also songs.

BIBLIOGRAPHY: Hendricks, *Simple histoire. Boutades biographiques à l'occasion du 25me anniversaire de la mort de J.-F.-J. Janssens* (Antwerp, 1860); E. van der Straeten, *J.-F.-J. Janssens, compositeur de musique* (Brussels, 1866; contains a list of his works).

Jaques-Dalcroze, Émile, composer and creator of "Eurhythmics"; b. (of French parents) Vienna, July 6, 1865; d. Geneva, July 1, 1950. In 1873 his parents moved to Geneva; having completed his course at the Univ. and also at the Cons. there, he went to Vienna for further study under R. Fuchs and A. Bruckner, and then to Paris, where he studied orchestration at the Cons. with Delibes; in 1892 he returned to Geneva as instructor of theory at the Cons. Since he laid special stress on rhythm, he insisted that all his pupils beat time with their hands, and this led him, step by step, to devise a series of movements affecting the entire body. Together with the French psychologist Édouard Claparide, he worked out a special terminology and reduced his practice to a regular system, which he called "Eurhythmics." When his application to have his method introduced as a regular course at the Cons. was refused, he resigned, and in 1910 established his own school at Hellerau, near Dresden. Even before that time the new system had attracted wide attention, and the school flourished from the beginning; within three years branches were opened in France, Russia, Germany, England, and the U.S. (Bryn Mawr College, New York, and Chicago). Conditions resulting from the war brought about the closing of the school at Hellerau in 1915. After that he founded another school at Geneva, the headquarters of which was later moved to Paris. In 1925 the Hellerau School was established in Laxenburg, near Vienna. Jaques-Dalcroze himself also taught in London; in his later years he lived in Geneva. Without question, the results obtained by Jaques-Dalcroze have contributed toward the recent development of the ballet. Aside from his rhythmical innovations, he also commanded respect as a composer of marked originality and fecundity of invention; many of his works show how thoroughly he was imbued with the spirit of Swiss folk music.

WORKS: the operas *Le Violon maudit* (Geneva, 1893), *Janie* (Geneva, March 13, 1894), *Sancho Panza* (Geneva, 1897), *Onkel Dazumal* (Cologne, 1905; as *Le Bonhomme Jadis*, Paris, 1906), *Les Jumeaux de Bergame* (Brussels, 1908), *Fête de la jeunesse et de la joie* (Geneva, 1932); an operetta, *Respect pour nous* (Geneva, 1898); a pantomime, *Écho et Narcisse* (Hellerau, 1912); *Festival vaudois,* for soli, chorus, and orch.; *La Veillée,* for soli, chorus, and orch.; *Dance Suite in A* for orch.; *Suite de ballet;* 2 violin concertos; String Quartet; Suite for Cello and Piano; *Fantasia appassionata,* for violin and piano; *Images* (1928); *Dialogues* (1931); *Ariettes* (1931); *Rondeaux* for piano (1933);

several collections of songs (*Chansons romandes et enfantines, Chansons populaires et enfantines, Idylles et chansons, Volkskinderlieder, Tanzlieder für Kinder, Chansons religieuses, Chansons de la gosse,* etc.) He publ. *Le Cœur chante; impressions d'un musicien* (Geneva, 1900); *L'Éducation par le rhythme,* a series of lectures (1907); a comprehensive *Méthode Jaques-Dalcroze* (5 parts, 1907–14); *Rhythm, Music and Education* (Basel, 1922; in German, French, and English); *Souvenirs* (Neuchâtel and Paris, 1942); *La Musique et nous* (Geneva, 1945); also "The Child and the Pianoforte," *Musical Quarterly* (April 1928); "Eurhythmics and its Implications," in the *Musical Quarterly* (July 1930); "L'Improvisation au piano," *Rhythm* (1932).

BIBLIOGRAPHY: A. Seidl, *Die Hellerauer Schulfeste und die Bildungsanstalt Jaques-Dalcroze* (Regensburg, 1912); K. Storck, *Émile Jaques-Dalcroze: seine Stellung und Aufgabe in unserer Zeit* (Stuttgart, 1912); M. E. Sadler, *Eurhythmics* (London, 1912); *Dalcroze Kongress-Bericht* (Geneva, 1926); H. Brunet-Lecomte, *Jaques-Dalcroze, sa vie, son œuvre* (Geneva, 1950).

Járdányi, Pál, Hungarian composer; b. Budapest, Jan. 30, 1920; d. there, July 27, 1966. He studied piano and violin as a child; in 1938 became a composition student of Kodály at the Academy of Music in Budapest, where he later joined the faculty. He was awarded the Erkel Prize in 1952 and the Kossuth Prize in 1954. His works follow the style of modern Hungarian music, based on national folksongs.

WORKS: Sinfonietta (1940); *Divertimento concertante* for orch. (1942–49); *Dance Music* for orch. (1950); *Tisza mentén (Along the Tisza),* symph. poem (1951); *Vörösmarty Symphony* (1953); *Rhapsody from Borsod* for orch. (1953); *Symphonic March* (1953); Harp Concerto (1959); *Vivente e moriente* for orch. (1963); Concertino for Violin and String Orch. (1964); *Székely rapszódia* for orch. (1965); violin duets (1934–37); Rondo for Piano (1939); Piano Sonata (1940); 2-Piano Sonata (1942); 2 string quartets (1947, 1953–54); Flute Sonata (1952); *Fantasy and Variations on a Hungarian Folksong* for wind quintet (1955); *Bulgarian Rhythm* for piano duet (1956); Quartet for 3 violins and cello (1958); String Trio (1959).

Jarecki, Henryk, Polish conductor and composer; b. Warsaw, Dec. 6, 1846; d. Lwow, Dec. 18, 1918. He studied with Moniuszko; from 1877 to 1900 he was conductor at the Lwow Opera; wrote 7 operas on subjects from Polish literature; also a *Polish Mass* and a number of songs.

Jarecki, Tadeusz, Polish conductor and composer; b. Lwow, Dec. 31, 1888; d. New York, April 29, 1955. He studied with his father **Henryk Jarecki;** then went to Moscow where he studied with Taneyev at the Moscow Cons., graduating in 1913. During World War I he lived in New York; then went back to Poland and conducted opera in Stanislawow (1932–37); after a brief sojourn in Paris and in London he returned to New York, where he remained until his death. He composed a symph. suite *Chimère* (1926); *Sinfonia breve* (which he conducted in Lwow, Jan. 15, 1932); 3 string quartets; songs. On Feb 23, 1921, he married the American lyric soprano **Louise Llewellyn Jarecka** (b. New York, Dec. 10, 1889; d. there, March 6, 1954).

Jarnach, Philipp, composer; b. Noisy, France, July 26, 1892. He was a son of the Catalonian sculptor E. Jarnach and a German mother. He studied at the Paris Cons. with Risler (piano) and Lavignac (theory). At the outbreak of World War I he went to Zürich, where he met Busoni; this meeting was a decisive influence on his musical development; he became an ardent disciple of Busoni; after Busoni's death, he completed Busoni's last opera, *Doktor Faust,* which was produced in Jarnach's version in Dresden on May 21, 1925. During the years 1922–27 Jarnach wrote music criticism in Berlin. In 1927 he was appointed prof. of composition at the Cologne Cons., and remained at that post until 1949; from 1949 to 1970 he taught at the Hamburg Cons. Jarnach's own music is determined by his devotion to Busoni's ideals; it is distinguished by impeccable craftsmanship, but it lacks individuality. He participated in the modern movement in Germany between the two world wars, and many of his works were performed at music festivals during that period. Among his works are a *Sinfonie Brevis* (1923); String Quintet (1920); String Quartet (1924); *Musik zum Gedächtnis des Einsamen,* for string quartet (1952); Sonatina for Flute and Piano; Cello Sonatina, etc.

BIBLIOGRAPHY: Hans Mersmann and E. G. Klussmann, *Philipp Jarnach zum 60. Geburtstag* (Hamburg, 1952); also references in E. J. Dent's *Ferruccio Busoni* (Oxford, 1933).

Järnefelt, Armas, Finnish conductor and composer; b. Viborg, Aug. 14, 1869; d. Stockholm, June 23, 1958. He studied with Wegelius at the Helsinki Cons. and also with Busoni, who taught there at the time; he then went to Berlin (1890) and to Paris (1892), where he studied with Massenet. He began his career as an opera coach in Magdeburg (1896); then was at Düsseldorf (1897). Returning to Finland in 1898, he was conductor in his native town; in 1903 he received a government stipend for travel; was for 25 years conductor of the Stockholm Opera (1907–32); conductor of the Helsinki Opera (1932–36), and of the Helsinki Municipal Orch. (1942–43). He was married to the Finnish singer, **Maikki Pakarinen** (1893; divorced in 1908), then to another singer, **Liva Edström.** He wrote several works for orch., in a national Finnish style: *Korsholm, Suomen synty, Laulu Vuokselle, Abo slott,* etc.; his *Berceuse* and *Praeludium* for small orch. became extremely popular.

BIBLIOGRAPHY: Väinö Pesola, "Armas Järnefelt," *Suomen Säveltäjiä,* edited by Sulho Ranta (Helsinki, 1945; pp. 300–06).

Järnefelt, Maikki (*née* **Pakarinen**), Finnish soprano, wife of **Armas Järnefelt;** b. Joensuu, Aug. 26, 1871; d. Turku, July 4, 1929. She studied with Mme. Marchesi in Paris; became a well-known opera singer in Europe; also lived in America for several years. She was married to Järnefelt in 1893 and divorced in 1908; then was married to Palmgren (1910).

Jarno, Georg, composer; b. Budapest, June 3, 1868; d. Breslau, May 20, 1920. He conducted opera in Breslau; produced his own operas there: *Die schwarze Kaschka* (Breslau, May 12, 1895; his most successful opera), *Der Richter von Zalamea* (1899), and *Der Goldfisch* (1907); in Vienna he produced *Die Förster-Christel* (1907), *Das Musikantenmädel* (1910), and *Die Marine-Gustel* (1912). Another opera, *Das Farmermädchen,* was produced in Berlin (1913).

Jarnowick, Giovanni. See **Giornovichi, Giovanni Mare.**

Jarnowick, Pierre Louis Hus-Desforges. See **Hus-Desforges, Pierre Louis.**

Jaroch, Jiří, Czech composer; b. Smilkov, Sept. 23, 1920. He studied composition with Řidký at the Prague Cons.; played violin in theater orchestras; then was engaged as program editor of musical broadcasts. As a composer, he takes a median line in Central European music, within the pragmatic limits of modernistic permissiveness.
WORKS: *Scherzo* for orch. (1947); *Burlesque* for orch. (1951); *Symphonic Dance* (1953); *Smuteční Fantasie (Mourning Fantasy)* for orch. (1954); 4 symphonies: No. 1 (1954–56), No. 2 (1958–60), No. 3, *Concertante,* for violin and orch. (1968–69) and No. 4 (1975); *Shakuntala,* suite for orch. (1957); *Stařec a Moře (The Old Man and the Sea),* symph. poem based on the Hemingway novel (1961); *Summer Festival,* tarantella for orch. (1964); *Fantasy* for viola and orch. (1966); 2 string quartets (1949–50; 1970); *Children's Suite* for nonet (1952); *Nonet No. 2* (1963); *Metamorphosis* for 12 winds (1967–68); *Sonata* for solo violin (1973).

Jarov, Sergei, Russian choral conductor; b. Moscow, March 20, 1896. He studied at the Academy for Church Singing at the Imperial Synod; then became an officer of the Cossacks. After the Revolution, and the defeat of the White Army, he left Russia and established a Don Cossack Chorus, with which he made successful tours in Europe; eventually settled in America. The repertory of his chorus includes popular Russian songs in artful arrangements, emphasizing dynamic contrasts, and also sacred works by Russian composers.

Jarre, Maurice, French composer for films; b. Lyon, Sept. 13, 1924. He studied electrical engineering at Lyon; in 1944 went to Paris and began to study music.
WORKS: *Mouvements en relief* for orch.; *Polyphonies concertantes* for piano, trumpet, percussion and orch.; *Passacaille,* in memory of Honegger (Strasbourg Festival, June 15, 1956); *Mobiles* for violin and orch. (Strasbourg Festival, June 20, 1961). He became a successful film composer; won the Academy Award for his emotional score to *Dr. Zhivago* (1966).

Jaubert, Maurice, French composer; b. Nice, Jan. 3, 1900; killed in action in France, June 19, 1940. He studied law and took lessons in piano and composition at the Cons. of Nice. He abandoned the legal profession in 1923, when he went to Paris. He obtained considerable success with the score for the French film *Carnet de bal* (1938). His works include: *Suite française,* for orch. (St. Louis, Nov. 10, 1933); *Sonata a due,* for violin, cello, and string orch. (Boston, Dec. 27, 1946); *Jeanne d'Arc,* symph. poem (1937), etc.

Jausions, Dom Paul, French writer on church music; b. Rennes, Nov. 15, 1834; d. Vincennes, Indiana, Sept. 9, 1870. He entered the order of St. Benedict at Solesmes in 1856, and under the direction of Dom Guéranger began to study Gregorian chant; continued his investigations in company with Dom Pothier, whose *Mélodies Grégoriennes* are the result of their joint labors. In 1869 he was sent to the U.S. to collect data for a biography of Bruté de Rémut, bishop of Vincennes (an uncle of Dom Guéranger), and died as he was about to return. His interpretation of the Gregorian melodies according to the tonic accent has become one of the guiding principles in the publications of the Benedictines of Solesmes. A complete list of his writings is found in the *Bibliographie des Bénédictins de la congrégation de France* (1907).

Jean-Aubry, Georges, French writer on music; b. Paris, Aug. 13, 1882; d. there, Nov. 14, 1949. He was a journalist; became interested in music; traveled in Europe and South America (1908–15); then lived in London, where he edited *The Chesterian,* house organ of the publishing firm J. & W. Chester. He publ. *La Musique française d'aujourd'hui* (1915; in English, London, 1919) and *La Musique et les nations* (1922; in English, London, 1923).

Jeanneret, Albert, Swiss violinist, composer and educator; b. La Chaux-de-Fonds, Feb. 7, 1886. He studied violin with Andreas Moser at the Hochschule für Musik in Berlin and with Henri Marteau at the Geneva Cons., graduating with the Premier Prix de Virtuosité in 1909; subsequently joined the staff of the Jaques-Dalcroze Institute of Eurhythmics in Hellerau. In 1919 he went to Paris where he founded a school of rhythmic gymnastics and organized a children's orchestra. In 1939 he returned to Switzerland and settled in Vevey, where he led a children's orchestra similar to the one he had in Paris. About the same time he became a follower of the Moral Rearmament Movement. On July 21, 1968 he received (and subsequently published) a telepathic message from his brother, the architect Le Corbusier (Charles Édouard Jeanneret), who had died three years before, urging him to continue his pursuits of functional art. In accordance with these ideas, which he shared with his brother, Jeanneret wrote some 25 'symphonies enfantines' for children's orchestra, employing 'bruits humanisés' produced by graduated bottles partially filled with water at different levels, metal pipes, wooden boxes, etc.; a *Suite pittoresque* for 3 violins, and choruses for Moral Rearmament meetings.
BIBLIOGRAPHY: Pierre Meylan, "Albert Jeanneret et les 'bruits humanisés'," *Revue Musicale de Suisse Romande* (March 1971).

Jeannin, Dom Jules Cécilien, French musicologist, specialist on Gregorian chant; b. Marseilles, Feb. 6, 1866; d. Hautecombe, Feb. 15, 1933. He studied in Marseilles; later traveled extensively in Syria and

Mesopotamia, gathering material for his collection, *Mélodies liturgiques syriennes et chaldéennes* (in 3 vols.: I, 1925; II, 1928; III, not publ.). Other works: *Études sur le rythme grégorien* (Lyons, 1926); *Nuove osservazioni sulla ritmica gregoriana* (Turin, 1930); "La Question rythmique grégorienne," *Revue Musicale* (1930). As a scholar he was an opponent of Dom Mocquereau, and wrote a book, *Rythme grégorien: réponse à Dom Mocquereau* (Lyons, 1928), disputing his theories. He spent the last years of his life as organist in the Hautecombe monastery.

BIBLIOGRAPHY: L. Bonvin, "Jules Cécilien Jeannin," *Kirchenmusikalisches Jahrbuch* (1930).

Jeanson, Bo Gunnar, Swedish musicologist; b. Göteborg, Oct. 10, 1898; d. Stockholm, Jan. 20, 1939. He studied at the Stockholm Cons. with L. Lundberg (piano) and T. Norlind (musicology); then took courses in Vienna with Wellesz, and in Freiburg, Switzerland, with Peter Wagner. In 1926 he received the degree of Dr. phil. for a dissertation on August Söderman; in 1927 became editor of the musicological publication *Svensk Tidskrift för Musikforskning*. He publ. a music history, *Musiken genom tiderna* (2 vols.; Stockholm, 1927 and 1931; revised by J. Rabe, 1945).

Jedliczka, Ernst, Russian pianist; b. Poltava, June 5, 1855; d. Berlin, Aug. 3, 1904. He studied at the Moscow Cons. with Tchaikovsky and Nicholas Rubinstein; then taught there (1881–88). In 1888 he settled in Berlin; was first prof. of the Klindworth Institute (1888–97); then at the Stern Cons. (from 1897).

Jeep, Johannes, German composer; b. Dransfeld, 1581; d. Hanau, Nov. 19, 1644. He studied in Göttingen and Celle; traveled in Italy; was Kapellmeister in Weickersheim (1610–33); cathedral organist in Frankfurt (1633–40); from 1640, in Hanau. He publ. a book of songs for 3, 4, 5, and 6 voices, *Studentengärtlein* (2 vols., 1607 and 1609; many subsequent reprints; included in H. J. Moser, *Studentenlust*, 1930); sacred songs (1607); secular songs, *Tricinia* (1610);

Jeffries, George, English composer; date and place of birth unknown; d. 1685. He was a member of the Chapel Royal and organist to King Charles I; went to Oxford in 1643 as organist and composer. Many of his sacred works are extant in MS, preserved in the British Library and at the Royal College of Music, among them about 190 motets and anthems and several services (in Latin); madrigals in the Italian manner; also masques, cantatas, dramatic dialogues, and other stage pieces.

Jehin, François, celebrated Belgian violinist; b. Spa, Belgium, April 18, 1839; d. Montreal, Canada, May 29, 1899. As a child he studied with Servais and with his uncle **François Prume,** whose name he added to his own, often performing as **Jehin-Prume;** then took lessons with Bériot at the Brussels Cons.; studied harmony with Fétis; won 1st prize in violin and in theory; at the age of 16, after completing advanced studies with Vieuxtemps and Wieniawski, he undertook a European tour; appeared with Anton and Nicholas Rubinstein, Jenny Lind, and other celebrities; formed a famous trio with Kontski and Monsigny. In 1863 he traveled through Mexico, Cuba, New York, to Montreal; met and married the singer **Rosita del Vecchio.** Thenceforth, his time was divided between Europe and America; he eventually settled in Montreal. Among his pupils was Eugène Ysaÿe. He wrote 2 violin concertos and many brilliant solo pieces for his instrument. He publ. in Montreal a book of memoirs, *Une vie d'artiste* (gives a list of his works from op. 1 to op. 88).

Jelich, Vincenz, Austrian composer; b. St. Veit, 1596; d. c.1636. He was a choirboy in Graz (1605–16); in 1617, went to Zabern, Alsace, as court musician. He wrote *Parnassia militia* (1622); *Arion* (2 books of sacred songs, 1628); motets, etc.

BIBLIOGRAPHY: H. Federhofer, "Vincenz Jelich," *Archiv für Musikwissenschaft* (1955).

Jelinek, Hanns, Austrian composer; b. Vienna, Dec. 5, 1901; d. there, Jan. 27, 1969. He studied with Schoenberg, and in the 1930's adopted the 12-tone method. He wrote for orch. *Sinfonia ritmica* (1932); *Divertimento No. 8,* for E-flat clarinet, clarinet, basset horn, and bass clarinet (1952); String Quartet; Suite for Strings; a series of piano pieces under the title of *Zwölftonwerk.* He is the author of the manual *Anleitung zur Zwölftonkomposition* (Vienna, 1952).

Jelmoli, Hans, Swiss pianist and composer; b. Zürich, Jan. 17, 1877; d. there, May 6, 1936. He studied with Humperdinck and Iwan Knorr at Frankfurt; then conducted operatic productions in Mainz and Würzburg. Upon his return to Zürich, he was mainly active as teacher and writer; wrote music criticism for the *Schweizerische Musikzeitung.* He composed the operas *Die Schweizer, Sein Vermächtnis,* and *Die Badener Fahrt;* incidental music to various plays; also 26 Swiss songs in the Zürich dialect. He publ. *Ferruccio Busonis Zürcher Jahre* (1928) and other pamphlets concerning musical life in Zürich.

Jemnitz, Sándor (Alexander), Hungarian composer; b. Budapest, Aug. 9, 1890; d. Balatonföldvár, Aug. 8, 1963. He studied with Koessler at the Budapest Academy (1912–16); then briefly with Max Reger in Leipzig. From 1917 to 1921 he occupied various posts as assistant conductor at German opera theaters; from 1921 to 1924 attended Schoenberg's classes at the Prussian Academy of Music in Berlin. In 1924 he returned to Budapest; was engaged as a music critic. As a composer, he followed the median line of middle European modernism of the period between the two world wars, representing a curious compromise between the intricate contrapuntal idiom of Max Reger and the radical language of atonality modeled after Schoenberg's early works. He wrote mostly instrumental music.

WORKS: Concerto for Chamber Orch. (1931); *Prelude and Fugue* for orch. (1933); *7 Miniatures* for orch. (1948); *Overture for a Peace Festival* (1951); Concerto for String Orch. (1954); Fantasy for Orch. (1956); 3 violin sonatas (1921, 1923, 1925); Cello Sonata (1922); 3 solo violin sonatas (1922, 1932, 1938); Flute Trio (1924); 2 wind trios (1925); Trumpet Quartet (1925); 2 string trios (1925, 1929); Flute Sonata (1931); Partita for 2 Violins (1932); Guitar Trio (1932); Solo Cello Sonata (1933); Solo Harp Sonata (1933); *Duet Sonata* for saxophone and banjo (1934); Solo Double Bass Sonata (1935); Solo Trumpet Sonata (1938); Solo Flute Sonata (1941); Solo Viola Sonata (1941); String Quartet (1950); 2 suites for violin and piano (1952, 1953); Trio for flute, oboe and clarinet (1958); *3 Pieces* for piano (1915); 2 piano sonatinas (1919); *17 Bagatelles* for piano (1919); 5 piano sonatas (1914, 1927, 1929, 1933, 1954); *Recueil* for piano (1938–45); Sonata for Pedal Organ (1941); *8 Pieces for Piano* (1951); 2 organ sonatas (1959); songs. His ballet, *Divertimento,* written in 1921, was not produced until 26 years later (Budapest, April 23, 1947). He also published brief monographs on Mozart, Beethoven, Mendelssohn, Schumann and Chopin.

Jeney, Zoltán, Hungarian composer; b. Szolnok, March 4, 1943. He studied piano as a child; then took courses in music theory with Zoltán Pongrácz at the Kodály Vocational Music School in Debrecen; then became a student of Farkas at the Academy of Music in Budapest (1961–66); subsequently went to Rome and attended a seminar in composition with Goffredo Petrassi at the Santa Cecilia Academy (1967–69). His music is constructivist, derived from the acoustical agglutination of kindred sounds.
WORKS: *5 Songs* for soprano, clarinet, cello and harp (1963); *Statue of Streaming* for vocal quintet (1965); *Omaggio* for soprano and orch. (1966); *Aritmie—Ritmiche* for flute and cello (1967); *Soliloquium* No. 1 for flute (1967); *Wei wu wei* for flute, clarinet, viola, cello, double bass, harp, piano, celesta and percussion (1968); *Alef (Hommage à Schönberg)* for orch. (1971–72; Budapest, June 19, 1972); *Mandala* for 3 Hammond organs (1972); *Yanta* for any number of electric organs (1972); *Round* for piano, harp and harpsichord (1972); *4 Sounds* for 3 to 11 instruments (1972); *Movements of the Eye I* for piano, *II* for 2 prepared pianos, and *III* for 3 pianos (all 1973); *For Quartet (Wei wu wei No. 2)* for string quartet (1973).

Jenkins, David, Welsh composer; b. Trecastle, Dec. 30, 1848; d. Aberystwyth, Dec. 10, 1915. He studied at the Univ. of Wales; then taught there; became widely known as choral conductor; wrote oratorios and other choral works for the Welsh festivals; his cantata, *The Ark of the Covenant,* was performed at the Caernarvon Festival in 1876. He was editor of the Welsh music periodical, *Y Cerddor.*

Jenkins, John, English composer; b. Maidstone, 1592; d. Kimberley, Norfolk, Oct. 26, 1678. His father was a carpenter by trade but was apparently musical, for upon his death, in 1617, an inventory of his possessions included "Seven Vialls and Violyns, One Bandora and a Cytherne." In John's early years he was a domestic tutor and lute player to various aristocrats; also played at the courts of Charles I and Charles II. He wrote many *Fancies* for viols or organ, and light pieces which he called *Rants;* of these, *Mitter Rant* was included in Playford's *Musick's Handmaid* (1678); *The Fleece Tavern Rant* and *The Peterborough Rant,* both in Playford's *Apollo's Banquet* (1690); his

popular air, *The Lady Katherine Audley's Bells* or *The Five Bell Consort,* appeared in Platford's *Courtly Masquing Ayres* (1662). He wrote some music for violin; an edition entitled *12 Sonatas for 2 Violins and a Base, with a Thorough Base for the Organ or Theorbo* attributed to Jenkins, and supposedly published in London in 1660, is not extant; the claim made by some historians that Jenkins was the first English composer of violin sonatas cannot be sustained inasmuch as William Young had anticipated him by publishing 11 violin sonatas in 1653. Reprints: *John Jenkins, Fancies and Ayres* ed. by Helen Joy Sleeper (Wellesley, 1950); *J. J. 3 Part Fancy and Ayre Divisions (Wellesley Ed.* 10, 1966); *J. J. Consort Music of 4 Parts,* ed. by Andrew Ashbee *(Musica Britannica 26,* 1969).
BIBLIOGRAPHY: J. T. Johnson, "How to 'Humor' John Jenkins' 3-Part Dances," *Journal of the American Musicological Society* (Summer 1967); A. Ashbee, "John Jenkins's Fantasia-Suites for Treble, 2 Basses and Organ," *Chelys* 1, 2 (1969, 1970); G. Dodd, "Provisional Index of the Works of J. J.," *Chelys* 1 (1969); A. Ashbee, "The 4-Part Consort Music of J.J.," *Proceedings of the Royal Music Association* (1969–70); A. C. Coxon, "A Handlist of the Sources of John Jenkins' Vocal and Instrumental Music," *R.M.A. Research Chronicle* 9 (1971).

Jenko, Davorin, Slovenian composer; b. Dvorje, Nov. 9, 1835; d. Ljubljana, Nov. 25, 1914. He studied jurisprudence and music in Trieste and Vienna; was a choral conductor in Belgrade (1871-1902); then settled in Ljubljana. He was the composer of the first Serbian operetta *Vračara (The Fortune Teller;* Belgrade, May 3, 1882), a musical comedy *Dido* (Belgrade, June 19, 1892) and many choral works. The melody of the royal Serbian national anthem was taken from one of Jenko's choruses.

Jenks, Alden Ferriss, American composer; b. Harbor Beach, Michigan, Aug. 10, 1940. He studied at Yale Univ. (B.A., 1962) and at the Univ. of California in Berkeley (M.A., 1968); also attended seminars with Karlheinz Stockhausen at the Univ. of California, Davis (1966–67). In 1968 he organized in Berkeley a group called "Deus ex Machina" which gave performances of acoustical and electronic music with human and mechanical participants. His productions fall into three categories: (1) written scores that can be performed by untutored players, (2) electronic music on magnetic tape and (3) conceptual composition that exists only in verbalized instructions. Inventory: *Expedition* for orch. (1964); *The Exterminator* for double chorus and individual speaking, shouting, laughing and occasionally singing voices (1965); *Quasar* for brass and percussion (1966); *Chez Elle* for magnetic tape (1968); *Q.E.D.* for amplified autoharp, amplified metal wastebasket, modulated spoken material and slide projector (1969); *Emissions,* a duet for 3 World War II short-wave receivers and a gesticulating lecturer whose discourse is inaudible (1969); *The Magic Pillow Show* for mixed media (1970); music for experimental films.

Jenner, Gustav, German composer and writer; b. Keitum, Dec. 3, 1865; d. Marburg, Aug. 29, 1920. He studied with Mandyczewski, and also took some lessons with Brahms; in 1895, became music director at Marburg. He composed fine lieder, choral works, several violin sonatas, a trio for piano, clarinet, and horn; transcribed old German songs, etc.; publ. *Johannes Brahms als Mensch, Lehrer und Künstler* (1905; 2nd ed., 1930).

BIBLIOGRAPHY: W. Kohleick, *Gustav Jenner* (1943).

Jensen, Adolf, German composer; b. Königsberg, Jan. 12, 1837; d. Baden-Baden, Jan. 23, 1879. He stemmed from a family of musicians in Königsberg; studied with Ehlert and Köhler; began to compose as a boy; at 19, went to Russia as a music tutor; then was theater conductor in Posen (1857); was in Copenhagen (1858–60), where he studied with Gade; then returned to Königsberg. He subsequently taught at Tausig's school in Berlin (1866–68); then lived in Dresden, Graz, and finally at Baden-Baden, where he died of consumption. A great admirer of Schumann, he closely imitated him in his songs, of which about 160 were published. He also wrote an opera, *Die Erbin von Montfort* (1864–65); it was revised by Keinzl, to a new libretto by Jensen's daughter, under the title *Turandot*. Other works are the canatas, *Jephthas Tochter, Der Gang der Jünger nach Emmäus, Adonisfeier,* etc., and many characteristic piano pieces.

BIBLIOGRAPHY: A. Niggli, *Adolph Jensen* (Zürich, 1895); another biography, also by Niggli, publ. in Heinrich Reimann's *Berühmte Musiker* (Berlin, 1900); G. Schweizer, *Das Liedschaffen A. Jensens* (Frankfurt, 1933). Jensen's letters were publ. by P. Kuczynski (1879).

Jensen, Gustav, German violinist and composer; brother of **Adolf Jensen**; b. Königsberg, Dec. 25, 1843; d. Cologne, Nov. 26, 1895. He studied with his brother; then with Dehn in Berlin (theory) and with Joachim (violin). In 1872 he became prof. of composition at the Cologne Cons., and held that position until his death. He wrote a symphony; a string quartet; violin sonata; cello sonata; *Ländliche Serenade,* for string orch.; various violin pieces; publ. the series *Klassische Violinmusik;* translated into German Cherubini's *Manual of Counterpoint.*

Jensen, Ludvig Irgens. See Irgens Jensen, Ludwig.

Jensen, Niels Peter, Danish organist and composer; b. Copenhagen, July 23, 1802; d. there, Oct. 19, 1846. He was blind from childhood, but learned to play the flute and organ; was organist at St. Peter's Church in Copenhagen from 1828. He wrote 2 sonatas and other pieces for the flute.

Jeppesen, Knud, eminent Danish musicologist and composer; b. Copenhagen, Aug. 15, 1892; d. Aarhus, Denmark, June 14, 1974. He studied at the Univ. there with Laub and Nielsen, and at the Univ. of Vienna with G. Adler and R. Lach (1922, Dr. phil. with the dissertation *Die Dissonanzbehandlung in den Werken Palestrinas;* English transl. by Margaret W. Hamerik, as *The Style of Palestrina and the Dissonance,* with introduction by E. J. Dent, Copenhagen, 1927; 2nd ed.,

1946; very valuable); from 1920 to 1946, taught at the Cons. in Copenhagen; 1946–1957, prof. of musicology at Univ. of Aarhus; from 1931 to 1954, editor of *Acta musicologica.* He ed. *Der Kopenhagener Chansonnier* (1927). Other writings: *Kontrapunkt* (1930; English transl., with introduction by Glen Haydon, N.Y., 1939; 2nd German ed., Leipzig, 1956); *Die mehrstimmige italienische Laude um 1500* (1935); *Die italienische Orgelmusik am Anfang des Cinquecento* (Copenhagen, 1943); etc. In his compositions Jeppesen lives up to his reputation as a profound student of polyphonic masterpieces of the Renaissance; his music is the product of his erudition, precise in its counterpoint, unfailingly lucid in its harmonic structure, and set in impeccable classical forms.

WORKS: opera, *Rosaura* (1946; Copenhagen, Sept. 20, 1950); Symphony (1939); Horn Concerto (1941); *Little Summer Trio,* for flute, cello and piano (1941); *Te Deum Danicum* (1942; Copenhagen, 1945; London, Oct. 27, 1948; *Tvesang (Twin Song),* for tenor, bass, double chorus, orch., piano, and organ (1965; Danish Radio, Copenhagen, Jan. 12, 1967).

BIBLIOGRAPHY: A Festschrift, *Natalicia musicologica: Knud Jeppesen, septuagenario collegis oblata,* co-edited by Søren Sørensen and Bjørn Hjelmborg (Copenhagen, 1962).

Jepson, Harry Benjamin, American organist; b. New Haven, Conn., Aug. 16, 1870; d. Noank, Conn., Aug. 23, 1952. He studied organ with Stoeckel, and composition with Horatio Parker; in 1895, was appointed instructor of organ at Yale Univ., and served in that capacity until 1950. He edited *Yale University Hymns* and publ. a number of works for organ.

Jepson, Helen, American soprano; b. Titusville, Penna., Nov. 28, 1905. Of a musical family, she sang in church choirs at 13 in Akron, Ohio, where she went to school; worked as a corset fitter and salesgirl; then was enabled to go to Philadelphia to study at the Curtis Institute (1923–28); in 1936, went to Paris to study with Mary Garden; also took lessons with Queena Mario; then became a member of the Philadelphia Grand Opera Co. She made her debut with the Metropolitan Opera Co. on Jan. 24, 1935, and remained on the staff until 1947; also sang with the Chicago Civic Opera Co. She was married to George Rosco Possell (1931); divorced, and married Walter Dellera (1942).

Jeremiáš, Jaroslav, Czech composer; son of the organist and composer **Bohuslav Jeremiáš** (1859–1918); b. Pisek, Aug. 14, 1889; d. Budějovice, Jan. 16, 1919. He studied at the Prague Cons.; also took lessons with Novák. He was engaged as opera conductor at Ljubljana, Yugoslavia; then returned to Prague. Although he died at the age of 29, he left several significant works: the opera *Starý král (The Old King;* produced posthumously, Prague, April 13, 1919); oratorio *Jan Hus* (also posthumous; Prague, June 13, 1919); a viola sonata; songs.

BIBLIOGRAPHY: B. Bělohlávek, *Jaroslav Jeremiáš* (Prague, 1935).

Jeremiáš, Otakar, Czech conductor and composer, brother of **Jaroslav Jeremiáš**; b. Písek, Oct. 17, 1892;

d. Prague, March 5, 1962. He studied composition, as did his brother, with Vítězslav Novák at the Prague Cons.; also took lessons in cello playing; was a cellist in the Czech Philharmonic. He subsequently directed a music school at Budějovice (1918–28); conducted the orch. of the Prague Radio (1929–45); was director of the Prague Opera (1945–51) and the first chairman of the Czech Composers Guild. His music continues the traditions of the Czech National School, with a pronounced affinity to the style of Smetana, Foerster and Ostrčil.

WORKS: 2 operas: *Bratři Karamazovi (The Brothers Karamazov,* after Dostoyevsky, 1922–27; Prague, Oct. 8, 1928) and *Enšpígl (Til Eulenspiegel,* 1940–44; Prague, May 13, 1949); 2 cantatas: *Mohamedův zpěv* (1932) and *Píseň o rodné zemi (Song of the Native Land,* 1940–41); *Písně jara (Spring Song)* for orch. (1907–08); *Podzimní suita (Autumn Suite)* for orch. (1907–08); 2 symphonies (1910–11, 1914–15); *Jarní předehra (Spring Overture,* 1912); *Fantasie* for orch. and 2 mixed choruses (1915; Prague Radio, Oct. 27, 1942); *Romance o Karlu IV,* melodrama with orch. (1917); *Láska,* 5 songs with orch. (1921); Piano Trio (1909–10); String Quartet (1910); Piano Quartet (1911); String Quintet (1911); *Fantasie na staročeské chorály (Fantasy on Old Czech Chorales)* for nonet (1938); 2 piano sonatas (1909, 1913); songs; film music.

BIBLIOGRAPHY: J. Plavec, *Otakar Jeremiáš* (Prague, 1943; gives a list of works with dates of performance).

Jeritza (real name **Jedlitzka**), **Maria,** dramatic soprano; b. Brünn, Oct. 6, 1887. She studied voice and several instruments in Brünn; appeared first as a chorus singer at the Brünn Opera; made her debut as a soloist as Elsa in *Lohengrin* at Olmütz (1910), followed by an engagement at the Vienna Volksoper (debut as Elizabeth in *Tannhäuser);* guest appearances in Stuttgart (where she created the title role of Strauss' *Ariadne),* Zürich, Berlin, Munich, Basel, Bern, etc.; member of the Vienna State Opera (1912–35); member of the Metropolitan Opera Co. (1921–32; debut as Marietta in Korngold's *Die tote Stadt,* Nov. 19, 1921), where she became especially celebrated for her interpretation of Tosca; appeared in Boston in Rudolf Friml's *Annina* (later changed to *Music Hath Charms),* with which she toured; has toured the U.S. many times in recital and as soloist with various orchestras. In 1935, she married the motion picture executive Winfield Sheehan, and settled in Hollywood; after his death, she married Irving F. Seery on April 10, 1948. Her 90th birthday was celebrated by her many friends in October 1977. She published *Sunlight and Song,* an autobiography (N.Y., 1924).

BIBLIOGRAPHY: Ernst Decsey, *Maria Jeritza* (Vienna, 1931).

Jersild, Jørgen, Danish composer and music pedagogue; b. Copenhagen, Sept. 17, 1913. He studied musicology at the Univ. of Copenhagen, obtaining his Magister Artis degree in 1940; then went to Paris where he studied with Albert Roussel; returning to Denmark he taught music history and theory at the Copenhagen Cons. His works are written in an effec-

tive neo-Classical manner with an impressionistic flavor. He composes mostly in small forms; among his works are: *Pastorale* for strings (1945); Serenade for Wind Instruments (1947); a group of *Quartetti piccoli* for string quartet (1950) and a ballet, *Lunefulde Lucinda* (1954). He published a number of informative articles dealing with Danish music history; also several useful singing manuals, among them a book on solfeggio (Copenhagen, 1948; also in English, N.Y., 1966); Harp Concerto (Aldeburg, June 9, 1972).

Jervis-Read, Harold Vincent, English composer; b. Powyke, Worcestershire, March 14, 1883; d. Salisbury, Dec. 15, 1945. He studied at the Royal Academy of Music, and later taught there. He wrote for chorus *The Hound of Heaven, Dream Tryst, That Land, To the Daughter of Earth, High Tide,* etc.; String Sextet; 2 piano sonatas; *5 Caprices,* for piano; songs; etc.

Jesinghaus, Walter, Swiss violinist and composer; b. Genoa, July 13, 1902; d. Ticino, Sept. 17, 1966. He studied violin in Milan and Lugano; gave concerts as a child virtuoso. In 1918 he went to Zürich to study academic music subjects with Andreae and Jarnach; later enrolled at the Basel Cons.; in 1921–25 was active as theater conductor in Germany; in 1925 he settled in Lugano. He wrote several operas *(Tartuffe, Sœur Béatrice, Belinda e il mostro, La luna e la città);* also a *Symphonia choralis* and much chamber music including a number of pieces for viola d'amore.

BIBLIOGRAPHY: D. Poli, *Walter Jesinghaus* (Bologna, 1929).

Jessel, Léon, German operetta composer; b. Stettin, Jan. 22, 1871; d. Berlin, Jan. 4, 1942. He began his career as a theater conductor in Germany, then produced numerous operettas, some of which enjoyed considerable popular success, among them *Die beiden Husaren* (Berlin, 1913), *Schwarzwaldmädel* (1917), *Verliebte Frauen* (1920), *Die Postmeisterin* (1921), *Schwalbenhochzeit* (1921), *Des Königs Nachbarin* (1924), *Die Luxuskabine* (1929), *Junger Wein* (1933), *Die goldene Mühle* (1940). His piano piece, *Die Parade der Zinnsoldaten (The Parade of Tin Soldiers),* composed in 1905, achieved perennial popularity.

Ježek, Jaroslav, Czech composer; b. Prague, Sept. 25, 1906; d. New York, Jan. 1, 1942. He studied composition with Jirák and Josef Suk; also experimented with quarter-tone techniques under the direction of Alois Hába. In 1928 he became resident composer for the "Liberated Theatre," a Prague satirical revue; produced the scenic music for 20 of its plays. In 1939, shortly before the occupation of Czechoslovakia by the Nazis, he emigrated to America.

WORKS: For orch.: Piano Concerto (Prague, June 23, 1927); *Nerves,* ballet (1928); Fantasy for Piano and Orch. (Prague, June 24, 1930); Concerto for Violin and Wind Orch. (Prague, Sept. 26, 1930); *Symphonic Poem* (Prague, March 25, 1936). Chamber music: Wind Quartet (1929); Wind Quintet (1931); String Quartet No. 1 (1932); Violin Sonata (1933); Duo for 2 Violins (1934); String Quartet No. 2 (1941). For piano: Suite for Quarter-tone Piano (1927); *Capriccio* (1932);

Bagatelles (1933); *Rhapsody* (1938); *Toccata* (1939); Sonata (1941).

Jiménez-Mabarak, Carlos, Mexican composer; b. Tacuba, Jan. 31, 1916. He studied piano with Jesús Castillo in Guatemala; attended classes in humanities in Santiago, Chile (1930–33); then studied musicology with Charles Van den Borren in Brussels (1933–36); returned to Mexico in 1937 and studied conducting with Revueltas. After more travel in Europe, he taught music theory at the National Cons. in Mexico (1942–65) and at the School of Arts in Villahermosa (1965–68). He draws his thematic materials from folk-songs of Mexico; his predilection is for the theater; he was one of the first to use electronic music and "musique concrète" in Mexico.

WORKS: opera, *Misa de seis* (Mexico City, June 21, 1962); incidental music to *Calígula,* after Camus (1947); the ballets: *Perifonema* (Mexico City, March 9, 1940); *El amor del agua* (Mexico City, 1950); *El Ratón Pérez* (1955); *El Paraíso de los Ahogados,* "música magnetofónica" (1960); *Pitágoras dijo...* for small ensemble (1966); several cantatas; Piano Concerto (1944); 2 symphonies (1945, 1962); *Sinfonia Concertante* for piano and orch. (1966; Mexico City, March 11, 1977); *Concierto del abuelo* for piano and string quartet (1938); Concerto for Timpani, Bells, Xylophone and Percussion (1961); *La ronda junto a la fuente* for flute, oboe, violin, viola and cello (1965); piano pieces and songs.

Jirák, Karel Boleslav, eminent Czech composer and conductor; b. Prague, Jan. 28, 1891; d. Chicago, Jan. 30, 1972. He studied privately with Vítězslav Novák and with J. B. Foerster. In 1915 he was appointed conductor of the Hamburg City Opera; in 1918 went to Brno, where he was conductor at the National Theater for a season (1918–19). He then was choral conductor and prof. of composition at the Prague Cons. (1920–30); from 1930 to 1945, music director of the Czechoslovak Radio. In 1947 he went to the U.S.; in 1948 became chairman of the theory dept. at Roosevelt College (later Univ.) in Chicago; held the same position also at Chicago Cons. College, from 1967 to 1971. His music represents the finest traditions of middle-European 20th-century romanticism.

WORKS: opera, *A Woman and God* (1911–14; Brno, March 10, 1928); 6 symphonies: No. 1 (1915–16); No. 2 (1924); No. 3 (1929–38; Prague, March 8, 1939); No. 4, *Episode from an Artist's Life* (1945; Prague, April 16, 1947); No. 5 (1949; Edinburgh Festival, Aug. 26, 1951; winner of the Edinburgh International Festival prize); No. 6 (1957–70; Prague, Feb. 17, 1972); *Overture to a Shakespearean Comedy* (1917–21; Prague, Feb. 24, 1927); Serenade for Strings (1939); *Symphonic Variations* (Prague, March 26, 1941); Overture "The Youth" (1940–41); Rhapsody for Violin and Orch. (1942); *Symphonietta* for small orch. (1943–44); Piano Concerto (1946; Prague, Dec. 12, 1968); *Symphonic Scherzo* for band or orch. (1950; orch. version, Chicago, April 25, 1953); Serenade for Small Orch. (1952; first complete performance, Santa Barbara, Calif., March 24, 1965); *Legend* for small orch. (1954; Chicago, March 20, 1962); Concertino for Violin and Chamber Orch. (1957; Chicago, May 18,

1963). CHAMBER MUSIC: 7 string quartets (1915, 1927, 1937–40, 1949, 1951, 1957–58, 1960); String Sextet, with alto voice (1916–17); Cello Sonata (1918); *Night Music* for violin and piano (1918; orchestrated, 1928); Violin Sonata (1919); Viola Sonata (1925); Divertimento for String Trio (1925); Flute Sonata (1927); Wind Quintet (1928); *3 Pieces* for violin and piano (1929); *Variations, Scherzo and Finale,* nonet (1943); Serenade for Winds (1944); Piano Quintet (1945); Violin Sonatina (1946); *Mourning Music* for viola and organ (1946; also orchestrated); Clarinet Sonata (1947); *Introduction and Rondo* for horn and piano (1951); *3 Pieces* for cello and piano (1952); Horn Sonata (1952); Oboe Sonata (1953); Trio for oboe, clarinet and bassoon (1956); *4 Essays* for violin and piano (1959–62); Suite for Solo Violin (1964); Piano Trio (1966–67); Bass Clarinet Sonatina (1968–69). VOCAL WORKS: *Psalm 23* for chorus and orch. (1919); Requiem for solo quartet, chorus, organ and orch. (1952; Prague, Nov. 17, 1971); several a cappella works for male chorus; song cycles (many also with orch.): *Lyric Intermezzo* (1913); *Tragicomedy,* 5 songs (1913); *Fugitive Happiness,* 7 songs (1915–16); *13 Simple Songs* (1917); *3 Songs of the Homeland* (1919); *Evening and Soul* (1921); *Awakening* (1925); *The Rainbow* (1925–26); *The Year* (1941); *7 Songs of Loneliness* (1945–46); *Pilgrim's Songs* (1962–63); *The Spring* (1965). FOR PIANO: *Summer Nights,* 4 pieces (1914); *Suite in Olden Style* (1920); *The Turning Point* (1923); 2 sonatas (1926, 1950); *Epigrams and Epitaphs* (1928–29); *4 Caprices in Polka Form* (1945); *5 Miniatures* (1954); *4 Pieces for the Right Hand* (1968–69). FOR ORGAN: *5 Little Preludes and Fugues* (1957); Suite (1958–64); Passacaglia and Fugue (1971); also incidental music for plays. He is the author of a textbook on musical form (in Czech, 5 editions, 1924–45).

BIBLIOGRAPHY: M. Očadlík, *Karel Boleslav Jirák* (Prague, 1941).

Jiránek, Josef, Bohemian violinist and pedagogue; b. Ledeč, March 24, 1855; d. Prague, Jan. 5, 1940. He studied music with Smetana, who legally adopted him; then took violin lessons with A. Hřímalý and harp lessons with Stanek; also became proficient as a pianist. From 1877 to 1891 he was in Russia where he held teaching posts; brought out a teaching guide, *Musical Grammar,* published in the Russian language. Upon his return to Prague he taught piano at the Prague Cons. (1891–1923). He published a number of useful piano manuals (all in German): *Schule des Akkordspiels und der Akkordzerlegungen; Theoretisch-praktische Schule der wesentlichen Verzierungen im Pianofortespiel; Anschlagübungen zur Erreichung gleichzeitig verschiedener Tongebung im mehrstimmigen Spiel; Tonleitern in Doppelgriffen; Technische Übungen in Verbindung mit praktischen Fingersatzstudien; Neue Schule der Technik und des musikalischen Vortags;* composed *Scherzo fantastique,* for orch.; piano quintet; 2 piano sonatas, and other pieces.

Jirásek, Ivo, Czech composer and conductor; b. Prague, July 16, 1920. He studied conducting with Dědeček and composition with Alois Hába, Řidký, M. Krejčí and Šín at the Prague Cons. (1938–45); conducted opera in Opava (1946-55); then was engaged as music editor with the Copyright Union in Prague.

WORKS: 5 operas: *Pan Johanes (Mr. Johanes,* 1951-52; Opava, 1956), *Svítání nad vodami (Daybreak over the Waters,* 1960; Pilsen, 1963), *Medvěd (The Bear,* after Chekhov, 1964; Prague, 1965), *The Key* (1968) and *And it was Evening and it was Morning* (on the theme of Bergman's film *The Seventh Seal,* 1971-72); *Ciaconna* for orch. (1944); *Concertant Symphony* for violin and orch. (1958); *Little Suite* for orch. (1964); Variations for Orch. (Prague, April 15, 1965); *Festive Prelude* for orch. (1971); Partita for wind orch. (Prague, June 2, 1973); symph. for baritone and orch. (1973-74; Prague, March 16, 1974); an oratorio, *Stabat Mater,* for 4 soloists, children's and mixed choruses, organ, winds and percussion (1968; Prague, March 3, 1969); 3 cantatas: *Ballad from Hospital* (1944), *Love* (1960) and *Zpěv o planetě Jménem země (Song of the Planet Called Earth,* 1976; Prague, April 2, 1977); *Riddles* for children's choir, wind quintet and percussion (1962); violin sonata (1946); *4 Studies* for string quartet (1963-66); *Sonata da camera* for 13 strings (1966); *Music* for soprano, flute and harp (1967); *Serenades* for flute, bass clarinet and percussion (1967); *3 Pieces* for flute, violin, viola and cello (1971); *Hudba k odpolední kávě (Music for Afternoon Coffee)* for 4 clarinets (1972); Piano Sonata (1940); Suite for Piano (1943); choruses; songs.

Jirko, Ivan, Czech composer; b. Prague, Oct. 7, 1926. After a period of musical study with K. Janeček and Bořkovec at the Prague Cons. he pursued the career of psychiatry; but double activity in such different fields of endeavor did not seem to hamper his development as either a practicing psychiatrist or a composer.

WORKS: 5 operas: *The Twelfth Night* (after Shakespeare, 1963-64; Liberec, Feb. 25, 1967), *The Strange Story of Arthur Rowe* (after Graham Greene's novel *Ministry of Fear,* 1967-68; Liberec, Oct. 25, 1969), *The Millionairess,* operatic divertimento (1969-71), *The Strumpet* (1970; Olomouc, June 23, 1974) and *The Way Back* (1974); 4 piano concertos (1949, 1951, 1958, 1966); *Serenade* for small orch. (1951); Clarinet Concerto (1955); 3 symphonies (1957; *The Year 1945,* 1962; 1977); *Macbeth,* symph. fantasy (1962); *Elegy on the Death of a Friend* for orch. (1965); *Divertimento* for horn and orch. (1965); *Symphonic Variations* (1966); *Serenata Giocosa* for chamber string orch. (1967; alternate version for violin and guitar); Sonata for 14 winds and kettledrums (1967); *Capriccio all'antico* for orch. (1971); *Prague Seconds,* symph. sketches (1972); Trumpet Concerto (1972); Flute Concerto (1973); *Prague Annals,* symph. triptych (1973); *At the Turning Point,* symph. fantasy (1975); *Double Concerto* for violin, piano and orch. (1976; Charleroi, Belgium, Nov. 18, 1976); *The Most Beautiful Land,* cantata (1950-51); *The Day,* cycle for baritone and orch. (1960-62); *Requiem* (1971); *Song of These Days,* 4 episodes for baritone, chorus and orch. (1973-74); *Štěstí (Happiness),* musical panorama for narrator, soprano, baritone and orch. (1975-76); Wind Quintet (1947); 6 string quartets (1954, 1962, 1966, 1969, 1972, 1974); Cello Sonata (1954-55); Suite for wind quintet (1956); Violin Sonata (1959); *Kaleidoscope* for violin

and piano (1965); *Serenata in due tempi* for nonet or oboe quartet (1970); *Guiocchi per tre* for string trio (1972); Partita for solo violin (1974); 2 piano sonatas (1956; *Élégie disharmonique,* 1970).

Joachim, Amalie (*née* **Weiss**), German concert singer; wife of **Joseph Joachim;** b. Marburg, May 10, 1839; d. Berlin, Feb. 3, 1899. Her real maiden name was **Schneeweiss,** but she abridged it to Weiss in 1854 when she appeared as a singer in Vienna. She began her career as a soprano; after her marriage to Joachim (1863) she abandoned the stage, but continued to give recitals as a lieder singer; her interpretations of Schumann's songs were particularly fine.

BIBLIOGRAPHY: Olga Plaschke, *Amalie Joachim* (Berlin, 1899).

Joachim, Joseph, one of the greatest masters of the violin; b. Kittsee, near Pressburg, June 28, 1831; d. Berlin, Aug. 15, 1907. He began to study the violin at the age of 5; his first teacher was Szervaczinski, with whom he appeared in public at the age of 7, playing a violin duet. At the age of 10 he was sent to the Vienna Cons., where he studied with Böhm; in 1843 he played in Leipzig at a concert presented by Pauline Viardot; Mendelssohn did him the honor of accompanying him on the piano. He appeared with the Gewandhaus Orch. (Nov. 16, 1843); then made his first tour in England (1844), arousing admiration for his mature musicianship and remarkable technique. Returning to Leipzig, he studied with Ferdinand David; also played as concertmaster of the Gewandhaus Orch. in David's absence. From 1849 till 1854 Joachim served as concertmaster of the court orch. in Weimar. Liszt, who reigned supreme in Weimar, did not favor young Joachim, and in 1854 Joachim went to Hannover as solo violinist at the court; in 1863 he married the singer **Amalie Weiss.** In 1868 he was appointed director of the Hochschule für ausübende Tonkunst in Berlin. His fame as a teacher spread far and wide, and aspiring violinists from all over Europe flocked there to study with him. He did not, however, abandon his career as a virtuoso; he was particularly popular in England, which he visited annually after 1862; he received an honorary degree of Doc. Mus. from Cambridge Univ. (1877), and also from Oxford and Glasgow. His style of playing, nurtured on the best classical models, was remarkable for masterful repose, dignity, and flawless technique. It was his unswerving determination to interpret the music in accordance with the intentions of the composer; this noble objectivity made him an authentic exponent of the best of violin literature. As a player of chamber music he was unexcelled in his day. The famous Joachim Quartet, organized in 1869, attained great and merited celebrity in Europe; the Joachim tradition of excellence and faithful interpretation of classical works influenced the subsequent generations of German violinists.

WORKS: His compositions for the violin are virtuoso pieces that have never ceased to attract performers; of these, the most famous is the Concerto, op. 11, in D minor, known as the *Hungarian Concerto* (marked "in ungarischer Weise"), which he wrote in Hannover in the summer of 1857, and first performed there on March 24, 1860; another Concerto in G major

(Hannover, Nov. 5, 1864, composer soloist), was revised in 1889. Other works are: Variations, for violin and orch. (Berlin, Feb. 15, 1881, composer soloist); *Andantino* and *Allegro scherzoso*, for violin and orch.; *3 Stücke (Romanze, Fantasiestück, Frühlingsfantasie)* for violin and piano; *3 Stücke (Lindenrauschen, Abendglocken, Ballade)* for violin and piano; *Hebrew Melodies*, for viola and piano; *Variations on an Original Theme* for viola and piano; *Notturno*, for violin and orch.; several overtures; cadenzas for violin concertos by Beethoven and Brahms; songs.

BIBLIOGRAPHY: A. Moser, *J. Joachim, Ein Lebensbild* (Berlin, 1898; 2nd enlarged ed., 2 vols., 1908, 1910; English transl. from 2nd German ed., London, 1900); K. Storck, *J. Joachim, Eine Studie* (Leipzig, 1902); J. A. Fuller-Maitland, *J. Joachim* (London, 1905); L. Brieger-Wasservogel, *Joachim-Gedenkbüchlein* (Dresden, 1907); H. J. Moser, *J. Joachim* (Zürich, 1908); G. Schünemann, "Aus Joachims Nachlass," in *Bericht der Hochschule* (vol. 53); S. Joachim-Chaigneau, "Trois épisodes de la vie de Joachim," *Revue Musicale* (Jan. 1940). Joachim's letters were publ. by A. Moser, *Johannes Brahms im Briefwechsel mit J. Joachim* (Berlin, 1908; vols. V. and VI); Johannes Joachim and A. Moser, *Briefe an und von J. Joachim* (3 vols., Berlin, 1911–13).

Joachim, Otto, German-born Canadian composer and violinist; b. Düsseldorf, Oct. 13, 1910. He took violin lessons with his father; later studied violin in Cologne (1928–31). He fled Germany in 1934 and spent the next 15 years in the Far East, mainly in Singapore and in Shanghai. In 1949 he emigrated to Canada; played the viola in the Montreal Symph. Orch.; in 1956 he joined the staff of the Cons. of Montreal. His music is quaquaversal, but its favorite direction is asymptotic.

WORKS: *Asia*, symph. poem (1928–39); *3 Bagatelles* for piano (1939); *Music for Violin and Viola* (1954); *L'Eclosion* for piano (1954); *Cello Sonata* (1954); *Concertante No. 1* for violin, string orch. and percussion (1955, revised 1958; Paris, Sept. 9, 1958) and *No. 2* for string quartet and string orch. (1961; Montreal, March 12, 1962); *String Quartet* (1956); *Psalm* for chorus (1960); *Interlude* for 4 saxophones (1960); *Nonet*, for strings, winds and piano (1960); *Twelve 12-Tone Pieces for the Young*, for piano (1961); *Expansion* for flute and piano (1962); *Divertimento* for Wind Quintet (1962); *Music for 4 Viols* (1962); *Dialogue* for viola and piano (1964); *Illuminations I* and *II*—aleatory works of indeterminate duration, wherein performers are cued in by a light-triggering system operated by a "conductor": *I* for live narrator and 4 instrumentalists (1965) and *II* for 10 performers and 4-track taped reading of a scientific text (1969; Grand Prix Paul Gilson, 1969); *Contrastes* for orch. (Montreal, May 6, 1967); *Katimavik* for tape (1966–67); *Kinderspiel*, aleatory music for children, for narrator, violin, cello and piano (1969; variable duration); *Twelve 12-Tone Pieces for the Young* for violin and piano (1970); *Mankind*, multi-media work for 4 synthesizers, pianist, timpanist, slides, burning incense and 4 readers who are to be ordained clerics of 4 major world religions (1972).

João IV, King of Portugal; b. Villa-Vicosa, March 19, 1604; d. Lisbon, Nov. 6, 1656. As a prince he received a fine musical training at the court chapel. He began collecting church music, gradually accumulating a magnificent library, which was totally destroyed in the earthquake of 1755. However, its contents are known, for a catalogue of it was issued in Lisbon in 1649, and reprinted by Vasconcellos in 1873. João IV was a true music scholar, well acquainted with the flow of conflicting opinions regarding musical theory. He publ. (anonymously) the pamphlets *Defensa de la musica moderna contra la errada opinion del obispo Cyrillo Franco* (in Spanish; 1649); *Respuesta a las dudas que se pusieron a la missa "Panis quem ego dabo" de Palestrina* (1654); Italian translations were made of both. He composed a considerable quantity of church music; his motets *Crux fidelis* and *Adjuva nos* are reprinted in S. Lück's *Sammlung ausgezeichneter Kompositionen für die Kirche* (1884–85).

BIBLIOGRAPHY: J. Freitas Branco, *D. João IV, Músico* (Lisbon, 1956).

Jobert, Jean, French music publisher; b. Lyons, Oct. 11, 1883; d. Paris, Nov. 27, 1957. He was an employee of the publishing firm of Fromont in Paris; he purchased the business in 1922, including the valuable catalogue of Debussy's early works (*L'Après-midi d'un faune, Clair de lune,* etc.). In 1945 he was elected president of the Syndicated Society of Music Publishers in France.

Jochum, Eugen, German conductor; brother of **Georg Ludwig** and **Otto Jochum;** b. Babenhausen, Bavaria, Nov. 1, 1902. He studied organ and piano at the Augsburg Cons. (1914–22); composition with Waltershausen at the Munich Academy of Music (1922–24), and conducting with Sigmund von Hausegger. He subsequently occupied various posts as opera coach and assistant conductor in Munich, Kiel, Mannheim and Duisburg. From 1934 to 1945 he was musical director of the Hamburg State Opera; then conducted the Radio Orchestra in Munich (1949–60); in 1961 he became conductor of the Concertgebouw Orchestra in Amsterdam; later was conductor and artistic director of the Bamberg Symph. He is reputed as one of the best conductors of the symphonic works of Bruckner and Mahler.

Jochum, Georg Ludwig, German conductor; brother of **Eugen** and **Otto Jochum;** b. Babenhausen, Dec. 10, 1909; d. Mülheim-an-der-Ruhr, Nov. 1, 1970. He studied in Munich with Hausegger and Pembaur; occupied numerous posts as conductor, at the Frankfurt Opera (1937–40); in Linz (1940–45), etc. From 1946 to 1958 he was director of the Duisburg Cons.; also filled in numerous appearances as guest conductor in Europe, Japan and South America.

Jochum, Otto, prolific German composer; brother of **Eugen** and **Georg Ludwig Jochum;** b. Babenhausen, March 18, 1898; d. Bad Reichenhall, Nov. 24, 1969. He studied at the Augsburg Cons. and at the Munich Academy of Music with Heinrich Kasper Schmid, Gustav Geierhaas, and Joseph Haas (1922–31). In 1933 he was appointed director of the Municipal Singing School in Augsburg; 1949, director of the Augsburg Cons.; retired in 1952. He composed about 150 opus numbers, among them 2 oratorios (*Der jüngste Tag* and *Ein Weihnachtssingen); 12 Masses; a great number of works for chorus, accompanied and a cappella; arrangements of folk songs; a *Goethe-Sinfonie* (1941); *Florianer-Sinfonie* (1946); songs.

Jodál, Gábor, Rumanian composer of Hungarian parentage; b. Odorhei, April 25, 1913. He studied law and music in Cluj (1930–37); then enrolled as a composition student at the Liszt Academy in Budapest with Kodály, Kósa and J. Adám (1939–42). After graduation, he devoted himself to choral coaching and teaching; in 1950 he was appointed to the faculty of the Cons. in Cluj; was its director from 1965 to 1973. As a composer, he continues an amiable but rhythmically incisive tradition of the ethnically variegated music of Transylvania.

WORKS: 2 cantatas: *Revoluţia* (1964) and *Slăvite zile* for chorus, winds, percussion and 2 pianos (1967); 2 violin sonatas (1946, 1953); *3 Pieces* for viola and piano (1946); Suite for Flute and Piano (1955); String Quartet (1955); *3 Pieces* for wind quintet (1959); *Introduction and Scherzo* for bassoon and piano (1964); Suite for Wind Quintet (1966); *3 Nocturnes* for flute, clarinet, viola, cello and piano (1967); Viola Sonata (1974); Piano Sonatina (1954); *3 Pieces* for 2 pianos (1970); choruses; songs.

Jöde, Fritz, German music educator; b. Hamburg, Aug. 2, 1887; d. Hamburg, Oct. 19, 1970. He began his career as a provincial school teacher; was in the German army during World War I; then undertook a serious study of music at the Univ. of Leipzig. He organized societies for the propagation of folk music, and was very active in various youth movements in Germany. In 1939 he became instructor at the Hochschule für Musik in Salzburg and leader of the seminar at the Mozarteum (1939–45); then instructor on school music in Hamburg (1947–52). He published a number of books on music education and collected German folksongs. Among his anthologies are *Ringel-Rangel-Rosen* (children's songs; 1913; enlarged ed., 1927); *Der Rosengarten* (1917); *Der Musikant* (1923; new ed., 1942); *Der Kanon* (in 3 parts; 1925); *Chorbuch* (6 vols., 1927–31); *Die Singstunde* (1929); *Lasst uns singen* (1930); *Frau Musika* (songs for home; 1929); *Die Weihnachtsnachtigall* (1939); *Unser Mutterlied* (1940).

WRITINGS: *Musikalische Jugendkultur* (1918); *Musik und Erziehung* (1920); *Die Lebensfrage der neuen Schule* (1921); *Unser Musikleben Absage und Beginn* (1923); *Musikschulen für Jugend und Volk* (1924); *Die Kunst Bachs* (1926); *Elementarlehre der Musik* (1927); *Musikdienst am Volk* (1927); *Das schaffende Kind in der Musik* (1928); *Musik in der Volksschule* (1929); *Kind und Musik* (1930); *Deutsche Jugendmusik* (1934); *Vom Wesen und Werden der Jugendmusik* (1954). From 1940 to 1952 he was editor of the *Zeitschrift für Spielmusik*.

BIBLIOGRAPHY: R. Stapelberg, ed., *Fritz Jöde: Leben und Werk* (Wolfenbüttel, 1957).

Johannes Chrysorrhoas (John of Damascus), Christian Saint; b. Damascus, c.700; d. at the monastery of St. Sabas, near Jerusalem, 754. He was canonized by both Greek and Roman churches; was the earliest dogmatist of the Greek church; wrote many examples of the kanon, a special type of Byzantine hymn that usually used a pre-existent melody. John is credited, by what may be a legend, with having arranged the Byzantine Oktoechos and having improved Byzantine notation.

BIBLIOGRAPHY: H. J. W. Tillyard, *Byzantine Music and Hymnography* (1923; p. 20ff.); E. Wellesz, *Byzantinische Musik* (1927; p. 33ff.); K. Wachsmann, *Untersuchungen zum vorgregorianischen Gesang* (1935; p. 78ff.).

Johannesen, Grant, brilliant American pianist; b. Salt Lake City, July 30, 1921. He studied piano with Robert Casadesus at Princeton Univ. (1941–46) and with Egon Petri at Cornell Univ.; also studied music theory and composition with Roger Sessions and Nadia Boulanger. In 1963 he married the cellist **Zara Nelsova.** He made his first debut in New York in 1944; made his first European tour in 1949, and appeared as a soloist at regular intervals in major European cities; toured South America in 1952 and 1969; played in Australia in 1960, and gave concerts in Russia in 1963, 1965 and 1971. He acquired a reputation as a pianist of a fine musicianly stature, subordinating his virtuoso technique to the higher considerations of intellectual fidelity to the composer's intents. He also composed some piano works.

Jóhannsson, Magnús Blöndal, Icelandic composer; b. Skálar, Sept. 8, 1925. He was taken to Reykjavík as an infant, and showed a precocious musical talent; at the age of 10, was admitted to the Reykjavík School of Music where he studied under F. Mixa and V. Urbantschitsch (1935–37 and 1939–45); then was sent to America and took courses in composition at the Juilliard School of Music in New York (1947–53). He returned to Iceland in 1954 and became a staff member of the Iceland State Broadcasting Service (1956–76); was also conductor for the National Theater in Reykjavík (1965–72). As a composer, he was attracted to the novel resources of electronic music; his *Study* for magnetic tape and wind quintet (1957) was the first Icelandic work employing electronic sound. His other works include *4 Abstractions* for piano (1955); *Ionization* for organ (1956); *Samstirni* for tape (1960); *Punktar (Points)* for tape and small orch. (1961); *15 Minigrams* for flute, oboe, clarinet and double bass (1961); *Dimensions* for solo violin (1961); *Sonorities I–III* for piano (1961–68); *Birth of an Island,* tape music for the film depicting the volcanic creation of an island near Iceland (1964); *Sequence,* ballet for dancers, instruments and lights (1968); *The Other Iceland,* music from the film (1973).

Johanos, Donald, American conductor; b. Cedar Rapids, Iowa, Feb. 10, 1928. He studied violin with André de Ribaupierre and Cecil Burleigh at the Eastman School of Music, Rochester, N.Y.; conducting with Eugene Ormandy, George Szell, Eduard van Beinum and Otto Klemperer (1955–57). From 1962 to 1970 he was principal conductor and music director of the Dallas Symph. Orch., achieving estimable results. Subsequently he was guest conductor with numerous American and European orchestras.

Johansen, David Monrad, Norwegian composer; b. Vefsn, Nov. 8, 1888; d. Sandvika, Feb. 20, 1974. He studied piano with Karl Nissen and music theory with Iver Holter; in 1915 he went to Berlin where he took lessons with Humperdinck; already in his middle age he continued his studies in composition in Paris (1927) and in Leipzig (1933–35), where he took a special course in counterpoint with Grabner. In the meantime he pursued an active career as a concert pianist and composer; gave a recital of his own works in Oslo in 1915. He also wrote music criticism in *Aftenposten* (1925–45). His music continued the national Norwegian tradition, in the lyric manner of Grieg; as time went by, Johansen experienced a mild influence of Russian and French music, gradually forming an innocuous modern style with sporadic audacious incursions into the domain of sharp dissonance. WORKS: *Symphonic Fantasy* (1936); symph. poem *Pan* (1939); Piano Concerto (1955); Violin Sonata (1912); Piano Quartet (1947); Quintet for flute and string quartet (1967); String Quartet (1969); oratorio *Voluspa* (1926); *Sigvat Skald* for baritone and orch. (1928); several choruses and a group of songs; piano pieces. He publ. a monograph on Grieg (Oslo, 1934; in English, Princeton, 1938). BIBLIOGRAPHY: O. M. Sandvik and O. Gaukstad, *David Monrad Johansen* (Oslo, 1968).

Johansen, Gunnar, Danish-American pianist; b. Copenhagen, Jan. 21, 1906. He studied piano with Victor Schiøler; later in Berlin with Frederic Lamond, Edwin Fischer and Egon Petri. From 1924 to 1929 he toured Europe as a concert pianist; then lived in California. In 1939 he joined the faculty of the Univ. of Wisconsin in Madison as Artist-in-Residence, a title that was specially created for him. An early admirer of Busoni, he devoted himself to the propaganda of his music. In March 1966 he presented a Busoni Centennial Commemorative program at the Univ. of Wisconsin including Busoni's formidable *Fantasia Contrappuntistica.* He recorded for Artist Direct Records the complete piano works of Busoni and his Bach transcriptions; the complete piano works of Liszt and complete clavier works of Bach. Johansen produced a sensation of seismic proportions on Jan. 14, 1969, when he played with the Philadelphia Orch. in New York the piano version of Beethoven's Violin Concerto at 30½ hours' notice. Johansen is also a composer of truly fantastic fecundity. He wrote 2 piano concertos (1930, 1970); *East-West,* cantata for wordless women's voices, piano, 3 woodwinds and percussion (1944); 31 piano sonatas (1941–51); and 246 piano sonatas improvised directly on the keyboard and recorded on tape (1952–70). A scholar as well as a musician, Johansen translated from Danish into English George Brandes's biography of Kierkegaard.

Johanson, Sven-Eric, Swedish organist and composer; b. Västervik, Dec. 10, 1919. He studied composition with H. M. Melchers and Hilding Rosenberg in

Stockholm; was a church organist in Uppsala (1944–50) and Göteborg (1950–54). In 1954 he became teacher of organ playing and harmony at the Göteborg Cons. His early works show a marked influence of Max Reger and Hindemith; later he adopted some atonal usages. WORKS: a saga-opera, *Bortbytingarna (The Changelings,* 1953); a chamber opera, *Kunskapens vin (The Wine of Knowledge,* in 2 acts; 1959–68); a microdrama, *Rivalerna (The Rivals,* 1967); an opera-buffa, *Tjuvens pekfinger (The Forefinger Thieves,* 1966–68); Concerto for Organ and Strings (1946); *Aff Sancto Christofforo,* chamber oratorio (1948); *Sinfonietta Concertante* for violin and chamber orch. (1951); 4 symphonies: No. 1, *Sinfonia Ostinata* (1949); No. 2, *Duinoelegi,* for solo voices, chorus and orch. (1954; transcribed for string orch. under the title *Sinfonia Elegiaca,* 1955; Göteborg, Feb. 8, 1956); No. 3 (1956; Göteborg, Sept. 23, 1959); No. 4, *Sånger i Förvandlingens Natt (Songs in the Night of Transformation)* for a cappella chorus (Stockholm, April 3, 1959); *Concerto da Camera* for cello and orch. (1958); *Maskarad-Divertissement* for orch. (1958); *Variations on a Värmland Folk Tune* for small orch. (1963); *Vagues* for orch. (1965); *Fotia* for orch. (1966); *Vienti* for orch. (1967); *Terra* for large orch. and tape (Göteborg, Sept. 12, 1968); *Fantyr* for orch. (1969); *Concerto Göteborg* for piano and orch. (1970); Concerto for Nyckel Harp and Strings (1971; a nyckel harp is a keyed fiddle); *Sinfonietta pastorella* for orch. (1972); 5 string quartets (1947; 1948; 1950; *Séquences variables,* 1961; 1964); *The Haze Trees,* song cycle for soprano, clarinet, violin, viola, piano and tape (1961); Wind Quintet (1964); *Ave Crax, Ave Crux* for soprano, baritone, chorus, organ and tape (1967); *Don Quixote* for flute, clarinet, cello and double bass (1971); *Purpurgreven* for flute, trumpet, violin, cello and piano (1971); 3 piano sonatas (1949, 1956, 1959); motets; organ and piano pieces; songs.

Johansson, Bengt, Finnish composer; b. Helsinki, Oct. 2, 1914. He studied composition with Sulho Ranta and Selim Palmgren; also cello at the Sibelius Academy in Helsinki, graduating in 1946; made study trips to Europe, Italy and America; upon return to Finland in 1965, he became a lecturer in music history at the Sibelius Academy. His music makes use of a wide variety of resources, including electronic sound. WORKS: FOR ORCH.: Serenade for Strings (1945); *Petite suite de ballet* (1948); *Aquarelles* (1948); Piano Concerto (1951); Suite for violin, strings, piano and timpani (1952); *Festivo,* overture (1952); *Expressions* for strings (1954); *Tema con sette variazioni in modo antico* for cello and orch. (1954). VOCAL WORKS: *Stabat Mater* for chorus a cappella (1951); *It's Perfectly True,* a "musical fairy tale" for narrator, solo voices, female chorus and orch. (1957); *Missa Sacra* for tenor, chorus and orch. (1960); *12 Passages from the Bible* for male chorus and organ (1960); *The Tomb at Akr Çaar,* to a text by Ezra Pound, for baritone and chamber chorus (1964); *Triptych* for soprano, baritone and chorus (1965); *Requiem* for baritone, 2 choruses, 2 string orchestras and timpani (1966); *3 Classic Madrigals* for chorus (1967); *Cantata Humana,* on words of Dag Hammarskjöld, for baritone, 4 narrators on tape, chorus and orch. (Helsinki, April 9, 1970); *The Song of the Bride* for soprano and orch. (1972). CHAMBER MU-SIC: *Sonata Piccola* for cello and piano (1945); *Dialogues* for cello and string quintet (1970); pieces for violin; also *3 Electronic Etudes* (1960).

John, Elton, eccentric English rock pop singer and piano player; b. Pinner, Middlesex, March 25, 1947. His real name was **Reginald Kenneth Dwight;** he attended classes at the Royal Academy in London, and actually managed to learn how to read music; he earned his living as a jazz pianist in various London clubs and pubs; then joined a rock group bearing the pretentious appellation Bluesology; it was from the sax player Elton Dean, of whom he was inordinately fond, that he annexed his first name, while his last name he took from the first name of the leader of the band, John Baldry. For all his low aspirations, Elton John was capable of forming lines of communication with kindred souls on a comparable level of intelligence among his audiences. He affects bizarre behavior, wearing multicolored attires and psychedelic eyeglasses of which he collected several hundred. In 1971 he flew across the ocean and captivated the American acid rock groups with his strangulated voice and uninhibited conduct. His songs, bearing titles such as *Honky Château* and *Madman Across the Water,* give a clue to his schizophrenic nature.

Johner, Dominicus (Franz), prior of the Beuron monastery; authority on ecclesiastical music; b. Waldsee, Dec. 1, 1874; d. Beuron, Jan. 4, 1955. He studied theology and music in Prague and also in Portugal; entered the Benedictine Order in Beuron in 1894; was ordained a priest in Lisbon in 1898; in 1900 he went back to Beuron; taught Gregorian Chant there, and at the Hochschule für Musik in Cologne (from 1925). He composed a cycle *Neue Marienlieder,* for chorus in unison with organ (2 books; 1916 and 1918) and *Neue Kommunionslieder* (1916).

WRITINGS: His writings, of great importance to students of Gregorian Chant, include *Neue Schule des gregorianischen Choralgesanges* (Regensburg, 1906; 6th ed., 1929); *Cantus ecclesiastici* (1909; 7th ed., 1925); *Die Psalmodie nach der Vaticana* (1911); *Litaniae Lauretanae octo modis accomodatae* (1921; 2nd ed., 1927); *Der gregorianische Choral* (1924; in Danish, Copenhagen, 1931); *Die Sonn- und Festtagslieder des vatikanischen Graduale* (1928); *Wie gelangen wir zu einem würdigen des gregorianischen Chorals?* (1928); *Erklärung des Kyriale* (1933); *Wort und Ton im gregorianischen Choral* (Leipzig, 1940). A collection of articles, *Der kultische Gesang der abendländischen Kirche,* ed. by F. Tack, was publ. in his honor on his 75th birthday (Cologne, 1950).

Johns, Clayton, American pianist and composer; b. New Castle, Del., Nov. 24, 1857; d. Boston, March 5, 1932. He studied architecture in Philadelphia (1875–79); then turned to music, studying at Boston with J. K. Paine (theory) and W. H. Sherwood (piano), and in Berlin (1882–83) with Kiel (composition) and Rummel (piano); settled in Boston. His works include a *Berceuse* and *Scherzino* for string orch.; several piano pieces; music for violin and piano; about 100 songs; also publ. *The Essentials of Pianoforte Playing* (1909); *From Bach to Chopin* (1911); and *Reminiscences of a Musician* (1929).

Johns, Emile, American pianist and publisher; b. in Austria about 1800; d. Paris, Aug. 10, 1860. He settled in New Orleans in 1822 and opened a music store; published *Album Louisiannais: Hommage aux dames de la Nouvelle Orléans,* containing 8 piano pieces. He eventually went to Paris, where he became friendly with Chopin and other musicians; Chopin dedicated to him his 5 mazurkas, op. 7.

BIBLIOGRAPHY: J. S. Kendall, "The Friend of Chopin and Some Other New Orleans Musical Celebrities," *Louisiana Historical Quarterly* (Oct. 1948).

Johnsen, Hallvard, Norwegian composer; b. Hamburg, Germany, June 27, 1916, to Norwegian parents. He went to Norway as a youth; studied music theory with Bjarne Brustad (1937–41) and Karl Andersen (1943–45) in Oslo and with Vagn Holmboe in Denmark. He also learned to play the flute and was employed as a flutist in Norwegian military bands.

WORKS: an opera, *The Legend of Svein and Maria* (1971; Oslo, Sept. 9, 1973); 11 symphonies: No. 1 (1949); No. 2, *Pastorale* (1954); No. 3 (1957); No. 4 (1959); No. 5 (1960); No. 6 (1961); No. 7 (1962); No. 8 (1964); No. 9 (1968); No. 10 (1973); No. 11 (1975); a cantata, *Norwegian Nature* (1952); 2 *Overtures* (1954, 1968); 2 flute concertos with string orch. (1939, 1955); 2 violin concertos, with chamber orch. (1955, 1967); Trumpet Concerto (1966); *Canzona* for wind orch. (1968); Trio for flute, violin and viola (1938); Quartet for flute and string trio (1945); *Tema con variazioni* for piano (1957); 3 string quartets (1962, 1966, 1972); Serenade for wind quintet (1962); Suite for flute and horn (1964); Quintet for winds, with vibraphone (1965); Sextet (1974); *Trio Serenade* for flute, viola and cello (1974); Quartet for 4 Saxophones (1974); Quintet for 2 cornets, horn, baritone horn and tuba (1974); Duet for 2 Flutes (1975); choral pieces.

Johnson, Bengt-Emil, Swedish composer and poet; b. Ludvika, Dec. 12, 1936. He studied composition with Knut Wiggen; at the same time pursued his abiding interest in modernistic poetry; published 4 collections of poems (1963–66) in a "concrete" idiom polyphonically elaborated in the technique of recited "text-sound compositions," a process electronically combining semantic and abstract sounds. Most of his works are of this nature; in emulation of computer-type identification (also used by Xenakis), he includes the year of composition in the title: *Semikolon; Äventyr på vägen (Semicolon; Adventure on the Way;* 1965); *1/1966: Släpkoppel (Drag-leash . . .); 1/1967: Nya släpkoppel med vida världen (New drag-leashes with the wide world); 2/1967: (Meden) (While); "from any point to any other point,"* a ballet in collaboration with Lars-Gunnar Bodin and Margaretha Åsberg (1968); *1/1969: Genom törstspegeln (första passeringen) (Through the mirror of thirst—first passage); 2/1969: För Abraham Jakobsson, på vägen (For Abraham Jakobsson, on the way),* after C. J. L. Almquist; *3/1969: Through the mirror of thirst (second passage); 1/1970: (bland) (among); 2/1970: (among) II;*

3/1970: (among) III; 4/1970: Jakter (Hunts), after C. F. Hills; *6/1970: Hyllning till Mr. Miller (Homage to Mr. Miller),* based on Henry Miller; *1/1971: under publikens jubel (Under the cheers of the people); 1/1972: (among) IV; 2/1972: (while) II; 3/1972: Släpkoppel (uppsläpp); 4/1972: Släpkoppel (Weltanschauung) (Drag-leash—World Outlook)* for a cappella chorus; *5/1972: Mimicry (Erik Rosenberg in memoriam)* for voice, cello, trombone, piano and percussion; *1/1973: Pierrot på rygg* for soprano, cello, piano and percussion; *2/1973: Subsong II; 3/1973: Ej blir det natt* for chorus; *Disappearances* for piano and tape (1974).

Johnson, "Bunk" (real Christian names **William Geary**), black American jazz trumpeter; b. New Orleans, Dec. 27, 1879; d. New Iberia, La., July 7, 1949. As a youth he played trumpet with Dixieland bands; toured with minstrel shows, circus troupes and numerous jazz aggregations. He lost all his teeth due to the ravages of pyorrhea and had to stop playing. After many years of musical inactivity he was "rediscovered" in 1937, working in sugar cane fields, by "hot jazz" aficionados; fitted with dentures, he resumed his career and enjoyed belated fame in a revival of Dixieland music.

Johnson, Edward, Canadian tenor and operatic impresario; b. Guelph, Ontario, Aug. 22, 1878; d. Guelph, Ontario, April 20, 1959. He studied at the Univ. of Toronto; in 1900, went to New York, where he sang in light opera; then went to Italy for further study; appeared there in opera under the name of **Eduardo di Giovanni.** In 1920 he returned to the U.S.; was a member of the Chicago Opera Co.; then joined the Metropolitan Opera Co. (debut, Nov. 16, 1922); in 1935 he was appointed general manager of the Metropolitan Opera, succeeding Herbert Witherspoon. He resigned in 1950.

Johnson, Hall, black American choral leader, composer and arranger; b. Athens, Georgia, June 2, 1887; d. New York, April 30, 1970. He studied at the Univ. of Atlanta and at the Univ. of Southern California in Los Angeles; also took courses with Percy Goetschius in New York. In 1925 he formed the Hall Johnson Choir, with which he gave numerous concerts; in 1936 he organized the Negro Chorus of Los Angeles. In 1951 he toured Germany and Austria with his chorus under the auspices of the U.S. State Department. He composed choral music and made arrangements for the films and television.

Johnson, Horace, American composer and journalist; b. Waltham, Mass., Oct. 5, 1893; d. Tucson, Arizona, May 30, 1964. He studied with Bainbridge Crist. He wrote several popular pieces for orch., among them *Astarte* (Richmond, Jan. 2, 1936), and *Streets of Florence* (Mexico, July 9, 1937); also songs (*The Pirate, When Pierrot Sings, The Three Cherry Trees,* and *Thy Dark Hair*).

Johnson, Hunter, American composer; b. Benson, North Carolina, April 14, 1906. He studied at the Univ. of North Carolina and at the Eastman School of Music; upon graduating he occupied various teaching posts; at the Univ. of Manitoba (1944–47), at Cornell Univ. (1948–53), at the Univ. of Illinois (1959–62), and since 1962 at the Univ. of Texas. He wrote a Symphony (1931); Piano Concerto (1935); Trio, for flute, oboe and piano (1954) and *Past the Evening Sun* for orch. (1964).

Johnson, James Weldon, black American lyricist, librettist, anthologist, and writer on music (also a poet, novelist, newspaper editor, lawyer, and international diplomat); b. Jacksonville, Florida, June 17, 1871; d. in an automobile accident at Wiscassette, Maine, June 26, 1938. He studied literature at Atlanta University; then returned to Jacksonville, becoming a teacher and school principal; after self-study, became a lawyer (1898; the first black to pass the Florida bar examinations). A poem written for school use in 1900 to commemorate Abraham Lincoln's birthday, *Lift Every Voice and Sing,* was set to music by his brother, composer **J. Rosamond Johnson,** and performed in Jacksonville the same year; though its beginnings were inauspicious, the song gradually acquired popularity, and in 15 years became known as "The Negro National Anthem." In the summer of 1899 the brothers visited N.Y. in an attempt to find a producer for their collaborative Gilbert and Sullivan-styled operetta, *Tolosa, or The Royal Document;* while their effort failed, they became acquainted with Oscar Hammerstein and many figures in the Negro musical life of N.Y. They returned to N.Y. in subsequent summers, selling some 30 songs to various musical reviews, and moved there permanently in 1902, forming, with Bob Cole, an enormously successful song-writing team called "Cole and Johnson Bros."; among their hit songs, mostly in Negro dialect, were *Under the Bamboo Tree* (1902), which was parodied by T. S. Eliot in "Fragment of the Agon," *Congo Love Song* (1903), and, under the pseudonym **Will Handy,** *Oh, Didn't He Ramble* (1902), which was to become a jazz standard; the team's success was such that they became known as "Those Ebony Offenbachs." In 1906 James Weldon Johnson was consul to Venezuela, and later, to Nicaragua. During this period he wrote his only novel, *The Autobiography of an Ex-Colored Man* (published anonymously, as if it were a true confession; Boston, 1912), in which he gives vivid descriptions of the "ragtime" musical life in N.Y. during the first decade of the century; soon afterwards, his transl. of Granados's *Goyescas* was used for the Metropolitan Opera's first performance of this work. In 1926 he compiled (with a lengthy and valuable introduction) *The Book of American Negro Spirituals* (N.Y.), with arrangements by his brother, and, in 1927, *The Second Book of American Negro Spirituals;* his book *Black Manhattan* (N.Y., 1930), a historical study of Negroes in N.Y., also draws together considerable information on black musical life. He also wrote an autobiography *Along This Way* (1931). His papers are on deposit at Yale University.

BIBLIOGRAPHY: E. Levy, *James Weldon Johnson* (Chicago, 1973).

Johnson, J. (John) Rosamond, black American composer and bass; brother of **James Weldon Johnson;** b. Jacksonville, Florida, Aug. 11, 1873; d. N.Y., Nov. 11,

1954. He studied at the Univ. of Atlanta and at the New England Conservatory of Music; took voice lessons with David Bispham. He set his brother's poem *Lift Every Voice and Sing* (1900) to music, this later becoming known as "The Negro National Anthem"; the brothers collaborated in many other songs at this time, selling them for various musical reviews in N.Y.; in 1902 they formed, with Bob Cole, the song-writing team of "Cole and Johnson Bros.," meeting with tremendous success; in addition to popular, black dialect songs, Johnson wrote some songs that were accepted on the concert stage, such as *Li'l Gal* and *Since You Went Away*. In 1912-13 he was music director of Hammerstein's Opera House in London; also sang in opera; subsequently toured America and Europe in programs of Negro spirituals; with his brother he compiled two volumes of Negro spirituals (1926, 1927), adding piano accompaniments; wrote a ballet, *African Drum Dance*, and many vocal works; also *Rolling Along in Song* (a history of Negro music with 85 song arrangements). He sang the role of Lawyer Frazier in the early performances of Gershwin's *Porgy and Bess*.

Johnson, Lockrem, American composer; b. Davenport, Iowa, March 15, 1924; d. Seattle, March 5, 1977. He studied at the Cornish School of Music in Seattle (1931-38) and at the Univ. of Washington (1939-42); subsequently was a member of its faculty (1947-49); concurrently served as pianist in the Seattle Symph. (1948-51). In 1952 he held a Guggenheim Fellowship; lived in New York, where he served as head of the Orchestra Dept. of C. F. Peters Corporation for several years. Returning to Seattle, he became head of the Music Dept. at the Cornish School (1962-69). In 1970 he founded Puget Music Publications, devoted to publishing works by composers of the Northwest. Among his own works, the most popular was the chamber opera, *A Letter to Emily* (N.Y., Jan. 25, 1955), which was performed nearly 100 times in various cities. He further wrote a ballet entitled *She;* Symphony (Seattle, Dec. 2, 1966); 6 piano sonatas; 3 violin sonatas; 2 cello sonatas, and *Suite of Noëls* for mixed voices and organ.

Johnson, Robert Sherlaw, English composer; b. Sunderland, May 21, 1932. He was educated at King's College in The Univ. of Durham; after graduation he enrolled in the Royal Academy of Music in London; in 1957 went to Paris where he studied piano with Jacques Février and composition with Nadia Boulanger; also attended classes of Olivier Messiaen at the Paris Cons.; returning to England, he gave piano recitals in programs of 20th-century music. In 1961 he became a member of the faculty of Leeds Univ., and later was Lecturer in Music at the Univ. of York. In 1970 he was appointed to the staff of Oxford Univ. In his music he recreates the Renaissance forms and mannerisms in a modern modal idiom. He composes mainly for chamber ensembles and vocal groups.
WORKS: 2 string quartets (1966, 1969); *Triptych* for flute, clarinet, violin, cello, piano and percussion (1973); Quintet for clarinet, violin, viola, cello and piano (1974); *The Praises of Heaven and Earth* for soprano, electronic tape and piano (1969); *Green Whis-*

pers of Gold for voice, electronic tape and piano (1971); *Carmina vernalia* for soprano and instruments (1972); 2 piano sonatas (1963, 1967); *Asterogenesis* for the 8-octave piano (manufactured by Bösendorfer of Vienna) extending the range to the C below the lowest C on an ordinary piano (1973).

Johnson, Thor, American conductor; b. Wisconsin Rapids, Wis., June 10, 1913 (of Norwegian parentage); d. Nashville, Tennessee, Jan. 16, 1975. He studied at the Univ. of North Carolina and later at the Univ. of Michigan (M.A., 1935); he organized a Univ. of Michigan Little Symphony with which he toured in the U.S. in 1935-36 and in 1937-41. In 1936 he won the Huntington Beebe Fellowship. This enabled him to study conducting in Europe during 1936-37. His principal teachers were Malko, Abendroth, Weingartner and Bruno Walter. Returning to America he attended Koussevitzky's conducting courses at the Berkshire Music Center; conducted the Grand Rapids (Mich.) Symph. Orch. (1940-42) and was guest conductor of the Philadelphia Orch. at Ann Arbor. He enlisted in the U.S. Army in 1942; from 1947 to 1958 he was principal conductor of the Cincinnati Symph. Orch., one of the few Americans to hold the conductorship of a major American orchestra for such a length of time. From 1958 to 1964 he was director of conducting activities at Northwestern Univ., Chicago, and from 1967, till his death, directed the Nashville (Tenn.) Orch. Association; also filled in guest engagements in Europe; in 1971 he conducted in Italy and Rumania. He also traveled as a guest conductor in the Orient.
BIBLIOGRAPHY: Hope Stoddard, *Symphony Conductors of the U.S.A.,* chap. XII (N.Y., 1957).

Johnson, Tom, American composer and music critic; b. Greeley, Colorado, Nov. 18, 1939. He studied at Yale University (B.A., 1961; M.Mus., 1967). Subsequently he was employed as instructor of the 52nd Army Band Training Unit at Fort Ord, Calif. (1963-65) and in 1967 was dance accompanist at New York Univ. In 1971 he became music critic of the radical Greenwich Village paper, *The Village Voice,* and pugnaciously proceeded to preach the gospel of asymptotic modernity. In his own compositions, he aims to displease, but much to his chagrin, often fails in his design to shock. The most beguiling of his productions is *The Four-Note Opera,* for soloists, chorus, piano and tape, to his own libretto, produced at The Cubiculo in New York on May 11, 1972; the score actually makes use of only 4 notes, A, B, D, and E, but employs them with quaquaversal expertise. Among his other works are *Pendulum* for orch. (1965); *Fission* for orch. (1966); *Four Violins* for 4 violins and percussion (1966); Trio for flute, cello and piano (1967); *Five Americans* for orch. (1969); *411 Lines,* a theater piece (1970) and several pieces of "Action Music" for dancers and piano. Apart from his activities as a composer and writer, Tom Johnson has also appeared as a singer, even though he grievously lacks the *bel canto* quality in his throaty voice; on June 11, 1976, in the summer gardens of the Museum of Modern Art in New York, he gave a rendition of a group of 18 "Secret Songs" of his composition, set to nonsense syllables; after singing each of the songs he burned the manuscript in a specially provided white bowl in which an eternal flame burns—sustained by alcohol.

Johnston, Benjamin, American avant-garde composer; b. Macon, Georgia, March 15, 1926. He was educated at the College of William and Mary (A.B., 1949), at the Cincinnati Cons. of Music (M.Mus., 1950), and at Mills College (M.A., 1952). In 1951 he joined the faculty of the Univ. of Illinois, Urbana. In 1959 he received a Guggenheim Fellowship. His works include *Celebration* for solo piano; Duo for Flute and String Bass; *9 Variations for string quartet; Knocking Piece* for percussion; *Night,* cantata (1955); *Gambit* for dancers and orch. (1959); *Sonata for Microtonal Piano* (1965); *Quintet for Groups* (1966) and a "tombstone" piece, *Ci gît Satie,* for the Swingle singers (1966); opera, *Carmilla* (1970).

Johnstone, Arthur Edward, composer and teacher; b. London, May 13, 1860; d. Wilkes-Barre, Penna., Jan. 23, 1944. He was brought to New York as a child and studied there with Leopold Damrosch (composition), William Scharfenberg and William Mason (piano), and S. P. Warren (organ). He was lecturer at Washington Univ. (summer sessions), St. Louis, for many years; composed an overture; piano works; songs; etc.; publ. a useful book, *Instruments of the Modern Symphony Orchestra and Band* (N.Y., 1917; revised ed., 1948).

Johnstone, John Alfred, Shakespearian scholar and writer on music; b. Cork, Ireland, July 6, 1861; d. Sidmouth, England, March 21, 1941. After studying literature and music in Dublin, he went to Australia in 1882; spent many years in Melbourne, where he was director of the music school of the Atheneum; returning to England, he continued to publish books and articles on the English theater and on music. In addition to his writings, he taught piano; publ. numerous manuals (*The Art of Expression in Piano Playing; The Royal Method for Scales and Arpeggios; The Simplicity Piano Tutor; Muscular Relaxation, Weight, Touch and Rotary Movement,* etc.).

Jokinen, Erikki, Finnish composer; b. Janakkala, Oct. 16, 1941. He studied with Kokkonen and Bergman at the Sibelius Academy in Helsinki; subsequently held various teaching posts. Among his works are: Cello Concerto (Helsinki, Oct. 21, 1971) and String Quartet (1972).

Jokl, Georg, composer; brother of **Otto Jokl;** b. Vienna, July 31, 1896; d. New York, July 29, 1954. He studied with Schreker; was active as accompanist and teacher in Vienna; in 1938, settled in New York. Among his works are a symph.; a symph. poem, *Heldensang* (Königsberg, 1923); *Burletta piccola,* for wind instruments (1952); music works.

Jokl, Otto, composer; brother of **Georg Jokl;** b. Vienna, Jan. 18, 1891; d. New York, Nov. 13, 1963. He studied with Hermann Grädener and Alban Berg (1926–30). His Suite for Orch. (1934) won the Hertzka Prize in Vienna; other works are *Sinfonietta seria*

(1935); 2 string quartets; etc. In 1940 he emigrated to America and settled in New York.

Jolas, Betsy, French composer of American parentage; b. Paris, Aug. 5, 1926. She went to America in 1939; studied at Bennington College (B.A., 1946); returned to Paris in 1946 and took courses with Olivier Messiaen at the Paris Cons. In her music she applies constructive methods in neo-Baroque forms and quasi-serial techniques.

WORKS: *Figures* for 9 instruments (1956); *Mots* for 5 voices and 8 instruments (1963); *Quatuor* for coloratura soprano, violin, viola and cello (1964); *J.D.E.* for 14 instruments (1966); *D'un Opéra de Voyage* for 22 instruments (1967); *Quatre Plages* for string orch. (1968); *États* for violin and percussion (1969); *Winter Music* for organ and chamber orch. (1970); *Le Pavillon au bord de la Rivière,* musical spectacle after a medieval Chinese play (Avignon, July 25, 1975); *O Wall,* a "mini-opera" as an instrumental counterpart to a line from Shakespeare's *A Midsummer Night's Dream,* for woodwind quintet (N.Y., Nov. 5, 1976).

Jolivet, André, prominent French composer; b. Paris, Aug. 8, 1905; d. there, Dec. 20, 1974. A son of artistically inclined parents, he took interest in the fine arts, wrote poetry and improvised at the piano; studied cello with Louis Feuillard and music theory with Aimé Théodas at Notre Dame de Clignancourt. At the age of 15 he wrote a ballet and designed a set for it; in 1928 he undertook a prolonged study of musical techniques with Paul Le Flem. Of decisive importance to the maturation of his creative consciousness was his meeting in 1930 with Varèse, then living in Paris, who gave him a sense of direction in composition. In 1935 Jolivet organized in Paris a progressive group "La Spirale." In 1936, in association with Yves Baudrier, Olivier Messiaen and Daniel Lesur he founded "La Jeune France" dedicated to the promotion of new music in a national French style. Jolivet was also active as conductor of his own works, and traveled all around the world, including America and Russia, Egypt and Japan, in this capacity. He served as conductor and music director of the Comédie Française (1943–59); was technical adviser of the Direction Générale et des Lettres (1959–62), and president of the Concerts Lamoureux (1963–68); he also was prof. of composition at the Paris Cons. (1965–70). Jolivet injected an empiric spirit into his music, making free use of modernistic technical resources, including the electronic sounds of Ondes Martenot. Despite these esoteric preoccupations, and even a peripheral deployment of serialism, Jolivet's music is designed mainly to provide aural stimulation and esthetic satisfaction.

WORKS: an opera buffa *Dolorès,* subtitled *Le Miracle de la femme laide* (1942; Paris Radio, May 4, 1947); 3 ballets: *Guignol et Pandore* for piano or orch. (1943; Paris, April 29, 1944); *L'Inconnue* (1950; Paris Opera, April 19, 1950) and *Ariadne* (1964; Paris, March 12, 1965); an oratorio *La Vérité de Jeanne* (1956; Domrémy Fest., May 20, 1956; 3 orch. interludes drawn from it are often played separately); 2 cantatas: *La Tentation dernière* (1941; Paris, May 16, 1941) and *Le Cœur de la matière* (1965; Paris, April 9,

1965); scenic music for radio legends and other productions such as *La Queste de Lancelot* (1943; Paris, Jan. 21, 1944); *Le Livre de Christophe Colomb* (1946; Paris, Feb. 21, 1947); *Hélène et Faust*, after Goethe (1949); 2 productions of *Antigone* (1951, 1960), *Empereur Jones* (1953), *L'Amour Médecin* (1955) and *L'Eunuque* (1959). He also wrote *Andante* for string orch. (1935); *Danse incantatoire* for orch. with 2 Ondes Martenot (1936); *Trois chants des hommes* for baritone and orch. (1937); *Poèmes pour l'enfant* for voice and 11 instruments (1937; Paris, May 12, 1938); *Cosmogonie*, prelude for orch. (1938; Paris, Nov. 17, 1947; also for piano); *5 danses rituelles* (1939; Paris, June 15, 1942); *3 complaintes du soldat* for voice, and orch. or piano (1940); *Symphonie de danses* (1940; Paris, Nov. 24, 1943); *Suite delphique* for wind instruments, harp, Ondes Martenot and percussion (1943; Vienna, Oct. 22, 1948); *Psyché* for orch. (1946; Paris, March 5, 1947); *Fanfares pour Britannicus* for brass and percussion (1946); *Concerto for Ondes Martenot and Orch.* (1947; Vienna, April 23, 1948); 2 trumpet concertos: Concertino (Concerto No. 1) for Trumpet, String Orch. and Piano (1948) and No. 2 (1954); 2 flute concertos: No. 1, with string orch. (1949) and No. 2, *Suite en concert*, for flute and percussionists (1965); Piano Concerto (1949–50; Strasbourg Music Festival, June 19, 1951); Concerto for Harp and Chamber Orch. (1952); 3 numbered symphonies: No. 1 (1953; International Society for Contemporary Music Fest., Haifa, May 30, 1954), No. 2 (1959; Berlin Fest., Oct. 3, 1959) and No. 3 (1964; Mexico City, Aug. 7, 1964, composer conducting); Concerto for Bassoon, String Orch., Harp and Piano (1954; Paris Radio, Nov. 30, 1954); *Suite transocéane* (1955; Louisville, Kentucky, Sept. 24, 1955); *Suite française* for orch. (1957); Percussion Concerto (1958; Paris, Feb. 17, 1959); *Adagio* for strings (1960); *Les Amants magnifiques* for orch. (1961; Lyon, April 24, 1961); Symphony for Strings (1961; Paris, Jan. 9, 1962); 2 cello concertos: No. 1 (1962; Paris, Nov. 20, 1962) and No. 2, with string orch. (1966; Moscow, Jan. 6, 1967); *12 Inventions* for 12 instruments (1966; Paris, Jan. 23, 1967); *Songe à nouveau rêvé* for soprano and orch. (1970); Violin Concerto (1972; Paris, Feb. 28, 1973); *La Flèche du Temps* for 12 solo strings (1973); *Yin-Yang* for 11 solo strings (1974). His chamber and solo instrumental works include *3 Temps* for piano (1930); Suite for String Trio (1930); String Quartet (1934); *Mana* for piano (1935); *2 Poèmes* for Ondes Martenot and piano (1935); *5 Incantations* for solo flute (1936); *Messe pour le jour de la paix* for voice, organ and tambourine (1940); *Ballet des étoiles* for 9 instruments (1941); *Suite liturgique* for voice, oboe, cello and harp (1942); Nocturne for Cello and Piano (1943); *Pastorales de Noël* for flute or violin, bassoon or viola, and harp (1943); *Chant des Linos* for flute and piano, or flute, violin, viola, cello and harp (1944); *Sérénade* for oboe and piano, or wind quintet (1945); 2 piano sonatas (1945, 1957); *Hopi Snake Dance* for 2 pianos (1948); *Épithalame* for 12-part vocal "orchestra" (1953; Venice, Sept. 16, 1956); *Sérénade* for 2 guitars (1956); *Rhapsodie à sept* for clarinet, bassoon, trumpet, trombone, percussion, violin and double bass (1957); Flute Sonata (1958); Sonatina for Flute and Clarinet (1961); *Hymne à l'Univers* for organ (1961); *Messe 'Uxor tua'*

for 5 voices, and 5 instruments or organ (1962); Sonatina for Oboe and Bassoon (1963); *Madrigal* for 4 voices and 4 instruments (1963); *Alla rustica* for flute and harp (1963); *Suite rhapsodique* for solo violin (1965); *Suite en concert* for solo cello (1965); *5 églogues* for solo viola (1967); *Ascèses*, 5 pieces for solo flute or clarinet (1967); *Cérémonial en hommage à Varèse* for 6 percussionists (1968); *Controversia* for oboe and harp (1968); *Mandala* for organ (1969); *Arioso Barocco* for trumpet and organ (1969); *Patchinko* for 2 pianos (1970); *Heptade* for trumpet and percussion (1971–72).

BIBLIOGRAPHY: V. Fédorov and P. Guinard, compilers, *André Jolivet: Catalogue des œuvres* (Paris, 1969).

Jommelli, Niccolò, eminent opera composer of the Neapolitan school, called "the Italian Gluck"; b. Aversa, near Naples, Sept. 10, 1714; d. Naples, Aug. 25, 1774. He received elementary musical education from Mazillo, a Neapolitan ecclesiastic. It cannot be established whether he studied at any conservatory in Naples, but undoubtedly he had acquired sufficient knowledge of composition, for at the age of 23 he produced in Naples an opera, *L'errore amoroso* (1737); this was quite successful, and he brought out another opera, *Odoardo* (Naples, 1738). He went to Rome in 1740; there he staged his operas *Ricimero* (1740) and *Astianatte* (1741). Invited to Bologna, he became acquainted with Padre Martini, who gave him valuable advice on composition. In Bologna he produced the opera *Ezio* (1741). He then went to Venice, where he produced *Merope* (1741), with such success that he was appointed director of the important Conservatorio degli Incurabili (1743); in Venice he wrote several notable sacred works. He produced new operas almost every year in various towns in Italy: *Tito Manilio* (Turin, 1743); *Demofoonte* (Padua, 1743); *Alessandro nell'Indie* (Ferrara, 1744); *Sofonisba* (Venice, 1746); *Didone abbandonata* (Rome, 1747); *L'amore in maschera* (Naples, 1748); *Demetrio* (Parma, 1749). In 1749 he went to Vienna, where he formed a warm friendship with Metastasio. In Vienna he produced *Achille in Sciro* (1749) and contributed some numbers to *Andromeda* (1750) and *Euridice* (1750). Then he returned to Rome, where he produced *Ifigenia in Aulide* (1751), *Attilio Regolo* (1753), and some intermezzi. By the good offices of Cardinal Albani, he was appointed maestro at St. Peter's, as Bencini's assistant. He remained in that position until 1753, when he received the important appointment of Kapellmeister to the Duke of Württemberg in Stuttgart. His sojourn there was most productive; his operas staged in Stuttgart included *Fetonte* (1753); *Pelope* (1755); *L'asilo d'amore* (1758); *Nitteti* (1759); *Olimpiade* (1761); *La pastorella illustre* (1763), and several serenades and other occasional pieces; also sacred works. After 15 years in Stuttgart, he returned to Italy (1769), but his operas produced in Naples, *Armida abbandonata* (1770), *Ifigenia in Tauride* (1771), and *Cerere placata* (1772), did not succeed. However, he did not suffer privation, since he enjoyed a pension from the King of Portugal; 3 of his operas were produced in Lisbon: *Le avventure di Cleomede* (1772), *Il trionfo di Clelia* (1774), and *L'Accademia di musica* (1775). Shortly before his death he wrote a *Miserere* for 2 voices, which became one of his best-known works. The position of Jommelli in Italian music is largely determined by his partial adoption of the German style during his long stay in Stuttgart; the emphasis on instrumental accompaniment, and a more solid harmonic substance, characteristic of German opera of the time, did not suit the Italian taste. On the other hand, he played a progressive role in the development of Neapolitan music, by rejecting the conventional type of the *da capo* aria; he pursued a more dramatic and realistic form of expression than that of Alessandro Scarlatti, which explains the sobriquet "the Italian Gluck." That he possessed melodic invention and contrapuntal skill of a high order is proved by his handling of solo passages in his operas and sacred works. In addition to his famous *Miserere*, he wrote a number of other church works: *Laudate* for 4 soprani soli and double choir; *Dixit* for 8 voices; *In convertendo* for 6 solo voices and double choir; *Magnificat; Hymn to St. Peter* for double choir, etc. The opera *Fetonte* was published in vols. 22/23 of the *Denkmäler deutscher Tonkunst; Salmo (Miserere),* for 2 and 4 voices with orch., by Breitkopf & Härtel; other works available in modern editions are: *Victimae paschali* for 5 voices; *Lux aeterna* for 4 voices; *Hosanna filio;* etc.

BIBLIOGRAPHY: P. Alfieri, *Notizie biografiche di Niccolò Jommelli* (Rome, 1845); H. Abert, *Niccolò Jommelli als Opernkomponist* (Halle, 1908; includes a biography); A. della Corte, *L'opera comica italiana nel 1700* (1923).

Jonák, Zdeněk, Czech composer; b. Prague, Feb. 25, 1917. He studied composition with Řídký at the Prague Cons.; devoted himself mainly to pragmatic musical tasks, such as making arrangements of folksongs and writing music for the theater.

WORKS: String Quartet No. 1 (1941); *Prelude* for orch. (1944); *Passacaglia* for orch. (1947); String Quartet No. 2 (1951); cello sonata (1951); wind quintet (1953); *Serenade* for chamber orch. (1955); Concerto for wind orch. (1963); *Chamber Symphony* (1964); *Mim* for flute and harp (1965); *Epigrams,* song cycle for chorus a cappella (1970); Trumpet Concerto (1974).

Jonás, Alberto, Spanish-American pianist; b. Madrid, June 8, 1868; d. Philadelphia, Nov. 9, 1943. He received primary music training in Madrid; then studied piano and theory of composition at the Brussels Cons. In 1890 he went to St. Petersburg, Russia, where he had some lessons with Anton Rubinstein. After a brief concert career in Europe, he went to the U.S., where he taught piano at the Univ. of Michigan (1894–98) and at the Cons. of Detroit (1898–1904). From 1904 to 1914 he lived in Berlin; after the outbreak of World War I he came back to America, settling in New York, where he established a fine reputation as a piano pedagogue. In collaboration with 16 pianists, he publ. *Master School of Modern Piano Playing and Virtuosity* (N.Y., 1922) which went through 5 editions, and also brought out several books of piano exercises for beginners. He wrote a number of attractive piano pieces in a salon manner, among them *Northern Dances, Humoresque, Nocturne and Evening Song.*

Jonas, Emile, French composer; b. Paris, March 5, 1827; d. St.-Germain-en-Laye, May 21, 1905. He studied at the Paris Cons.; received the 2nd Grand Prix de Rome for his cantata *Antonio* (1849). After graduation he became instructor at the Paris Cons. (until 1865); also was music director at the Portuguese Synagogue, and a bandmaster.

WORKS: light operas (all produced in Paris): *Le Duel de Benjamin* (1855); *La Parade* (Aug. 2, 1856); *Le Roi boit* (April 1857); *Les Petits Prodiges* (Nov. 19, 1857); *Job et son chien* (Feb. 6, 1863); *Le Manoir de La Renardière* (Sept. 29, 1864); *Avant la noce* (March 24, 1865); *Les Deux Arlequins* (Dec. 29, 1865); *Le Canard à trois becs* (Feb. 6, 1869); *Désiré, sire de Champigny* (April 11, 1869); an operetta to an English libretto, *Cinderella the Younger* (London, Sept. 25, 1871; in French as *Javotte,* Paris, Dec. 22, 1871). He publ. a valuable *Receuil de chants hébraïques* (1854) for the Portuguese Synagogue.

Jonas, Maryla, Polish pianist; b. Warsaw, May 31, 1911; d. New York, July 3, 1959. She was a precocious child pianist, and appeared in public at the age of 9; took lessons with Turczynski and was commended by Paderewski. She began her professional career as a concert pianist at the age of 15; after the invasion of Poland in 1939 she made her way to Rio de Janeiro, and gave a series of concerts in South America; then went to New York where she made an exceptionally successful debut in Carnegie Hall (Feb. 25, 1946); her auspicious career was thwarted by an irremediable illness and early death.

Jonas, Oswald, Austrian musicologist; b. Vienna, Jan. 10, 1897; d. Riverside, Calif., March 19, 1978. He studied law at the Univ. of Vienna; was a student of Schenker in musicology; subsequently taught at the Schenker Institute in Vienna (1935–38). After the annexation of Austria by the Nazis he went to America; was on the faculty of the Roosevelt University in Chicago (1940–65). In 1966 he was appointed prof. of music at the Univ. of California, Riverside. He published *Das Wesen des musikalischen Kunstwerks* (Vienna, 1934) and numerous articles dealing with Schenker's theories; also prepared for publication Schenker's posthumous work, *Kunst des Vortrags.*

Joncières, Victorin de (real name **Felix Ludger Rossignol**), French composer; b. Paris, April 12, 1839; d. there, Oct. 26, 1903. He was first a student of painting; music was his avocation. At the age of 20 he produced a light opera for a student performance; encouraged by its success with the critics, he began to study music seriously, first with Elwart, then with Leborne at the Paris Cons. He was a great admirer of Wagner, and when Leborne expressed his opposition to Wagner, Joncières impulsively left his class.

WORKS: the operas (all produced in Paris): *Sardanapale* (Feb. 8, 1867); *Le dernier jour de Pompei* (Sept. 21, 1869); *Dimitri* (May 5, 1876; his most successful work); *La Reine Berthe* (Dec. 27, 1878); *Le Chevalier Jean* (March 11, 1885; successful in Germany under the title *Johann von Lothringen*); *Lancelot du lac* (Feb. 7, 1900); he further wrote music to *Hamlet* (Nantes, Sept. 21, 1867); *Symphonie roman-*

tique (Paris, March 9, 1873); Violin Concerto (Paris, Dec. 12, 1869); a symph. ode, *La Mer;* etc.

Jones, Alton, American pianist; b. Fairfield, Nebraska, Aug. 3, 1899; d. New York, Jan. 2, 1971. He studied at Drake Univ. (B.M., 1919) and at the Institute of Musical Art in New York, where his teachers were Edwin Hughes and Richard Buhlig; he graduated in 1921; made his concert debut in N.Y. in 1924; was a soloist with the N.Y. Philharmonic in 1949; gave his last N.Y. recital in 1955. He taught at the Juilliard School of Music from 1921 until his death; his reputation as a pedagogue was high; many American pianists were his pupils.

Jones, Charles, American composer; b. Tamworth, Canada, June 21, 1910. He studied at the Juilliard School of Music in N.Y., where he later became a faculty member.

WORKS: Suite for Strings (1937); Symph. No. 1 (1939); *Galop* for orch. (1940); *Cassation* for orch. (1949); Symph. No. 2 (1957); *Suite after a Notebook of 1762* for orch. (1957); Symph. No. 3 (1962); Concerto for 4 Violins and Orch. (1963); Symph. in 5 short movements (1965); 6 string quartets (1936–70); Sonatina for Violin Alone (1938); Sonatina for Violin and Piano (1942); *Threnody* for viola unaccompanied (1947); *Sonata a tre* (1952); *Epiphany* for speaker and 4 instruments (1952); Violin Sonata (1958); *The Seasons,* a cantata (1959); *Sonata piccola* for piccolo and harpsichord (1961); 2 piano sonatas; Sonata for 2 Pianos (1957); *Keyboard Book* for harpsichord (1953); Toccata for Piano; Ballade for Piano.

Jones, Daniel, remarkable Welsh composer; b. Pembroke, Dec. 7, 1912. Both his parents were musicians, and he absorbed the natural rudiments of music instinctively at home. He then attended the Swansea Univ. College; then entered the Royal Academy of Music in London, where he studied a variety of theoretical and practical aspects of music: composition with Farjeon, conducting with Sir Henry Wood, viola with Lockyear and French horn with Aubrey Brain; in 1935 he was awarded the Mendelssohn Scholarship; received his M.A. for a thesis on Elizabethan lyric poetry and its relations with music; obtained his D.Mus. at the Univ. of Wales in 1951; honorary D.Litt. in 1970. During World War II he served in the British Intelligence Corps; continued his interests in literature and was editor of collected poems of Dylan Thomas (1971). An exceptionally prolific composer, he wrote 9 symphonies within 30 years, between 1945 and 1974, several oratorios, 2 operas, much chamber music. In 1936 he promulgated a system of "complex metres" in which the numerator in the time signature indicates the succession of changing meters in a clear numerical progression, e.g. 32-322-3222-322-32 followed by 332-3332, 332 etc.; his other innovation is a category of "continuous modes" with the final note of the mode (non-octaval) serving as the initial note of a transposed mode.

WORKS: symphonies: No. 1 (1944), No. 2 (1950), No. 3 (1951), No. 4 (1954), No. 5 (1958), No. 6 (1964), No. 7 (1971), No. 8 (1972), No. 9 (1974); operas, *The Knife* (London, Dec. 2, 1963); *Orestes* (1967); oratorios and cantatas: *The Country Beyond the Stars* (1958), *St. Peter* (1962), *The Three Hermits* (1969), *The Ballad of the Standard-Bearer* (1969), *The Witnesses* (1971); *Capriccio* for flute, harp and strings (1965); Violin Concerto (1966); Sinfonietta (1972); several concert overtures and symph. suites; a "miscellany" for small orch. (1947), etc.; 8 string quartets, 5 string trios, String Quintet, Sonata for Unaccompanied Cello (1946); Sonata for Cello and Piano (1972); Kettledrum Sonata (1947); 8 Pieces for Violin and Viola (1948); Wind Septet (1949); Wind Nonet (1950); Sonata for 4 Trombones (1955); 24 Bagatelles for Piano Solo (1943–55); 6 piano sonatas, 3 piano sonatinas. He is the author of numerous articles expounding his philosophy of music, some of them incorporated in a book, *Music and Esthetic* (1954).

Jones, Edward, Welsh musician and writer ("Barddy Brenin"); b. Llanderfel, Merionethshire, March 29, 1752; d. London, April 18, 1824. He was taught by his father, and the family organized a Welsh ensemble, consisting of harps and string instruments. In 1775 he went to London; in 1783, was appointed Welsh bard to the Prince of Wales. He publ. several anthologies of Welsh music: *Musical and Poetical Relicks of the Welsh Bards* (1784; 2nd ed., 1794; an additional vol. appeared under the title *The Bardic Museum,* 1802; 3rd vol., 1824; a supplementary vol. posthumously; the entire work contains 225 Welsh melodies); in addition to these, he publ. collections of melodies by other nations; also *Musical Trifles calculated for Beginners on the Harp.*

BIBLIOGRAPHY: T. Ellis, *Edward Jones, Barddy Brenin* (1957).

Jones, Kelsey, American-born Canadian composer; b. South Norwalk, Conn., June 17, 1922. He went to Canada in 1939; studied with Sir Ernest MacMillan, Healey Willan and Leo Smith at the Univ. of Toronto (Mus. D., 1951) and with Nadia Boulanger in Paris. Returning to Canada, he was appointed to the faculty of the Univ. of Montreal in 1954. In his compositions he follows traditional Baroque forms.

WORKS: a chamber opera, *Sam Slick* (Halifax, Sept. 5, 1967); *Miramichi Ballad,* suite for orch. (1954); Suite for flute and strings (1954); *4 Pieces* for recorder quartet (1955); *Songs of Time* for chorus and piano 4-hands (1955); *Sonata da Camera* for flute, oboe and harpsichord (1957); *Introduction and Fugue* for violin and piano (1959); *Songs of Innocence,* after Blake, for soprano and chamber orch. (1961); *Prelude, Fughetta and Finale* for violin, cello and harpsichord (1963); *Rondo* for solo flute (1963); *Prophecy of Micah* for chorus and orch. (Montreal, Feb. 5, 1964); *Sonata da Chiesa* for flute, oboe and harpsichord (1967); Wind Quintet (1968); *Hymn to Bacchus* for chorus and piano 4-hands (1972); *Adagio, Presto and Fugue* for string quartet and string orch. (1973); *Songs of Winter* for soprano, contralto and piano (1973); *Passacaglia and Fugue* for brass quintet (1975).

Jones, Parry, Welsh operatic tenor; b. Blaina, Monmouthshire, Feb. 14, 1891; d. London, Dec. 26, 1963. He studied in London, in Italy and in Germany; made his debut as tenor in 1914; toured widely in Europe and America. He was principal tenor at the Covent Garden Opera House until 1955; sang tenor parts in many modern operas, including Alban Berg's *Wozzeck.*

Jones, Quincy Delight, Jr., American pianist, trumpeter, bandleader and composer; b. Chicago, March 14, 1933. He studied hot trumpet in Seattle and in Boston; joined Lionel Hampton's band; toured with Dizzy Gillespie in the Near East; traveled in Europe (1957-60). His songs and arrangements (*Kingfish, Stockholm Sweetnin', Evening in Paris,* etc.) are sophisticated realizations of swing patterns.

Jones, Robert (I), English composer; b. c.1485; d. London, c.1536. He served as a chorister in the Chapel Royal; traveled with Henry VIII in France (1513); held a royal patent in England (1514-19); in 1520 was in France again; then returned to England, remaining in London until his death. Some of his sacred works are preserved in MS.
BIBLIOGRAPHY: W. H. Grattan Flood, *Early Tudor Composers* (London, 1925).

Jones, Robert (II), English lutenist and composer; flourished in the late 16th century and early 17th. He obtained a Mus. Bac. degree from Oxford in 1597; held grants to establish a school for children in London in 1610 and in 1615. He publ. *The First Book of Ayres* (1600), followed by 4 other books (1601, 1605, 1607, 1611); a book of madrigals, entitled *First Set of Madrigals of 3, 4, 5, 6, 7 and 8 Parts, for viols and voices or for voices alone; or as you please;* also a madrigal in 6 parts, *Oriana, seeming to wink at Folly,* in *The Triumphes of Oriana* (1601), and 3 pieces in Leighton's *Teares or Lamentacions* (1614). The 5 books of Ayres were republished, with the original accompaniment of each song transcribed into modern notation, by E. H. Fellowes (London, 1925-27).
BIBLIOGRAPHY: E. H. Fellowes, *The English Madrigal Composers* (Oxford, 1921; 2nd ed., 1948); Ph. Heseltine, "Robert Jones and His Prefaces," *Musical Times* (1923; pp. 99-101 and 168-71); E. H. Fellowes, *The English Madrigal* (London, 1925); E. H. Fellowes, *The English Madrigal School* (London, 1926); Ph. Heseltine, *The English Ayre* (London, 1926); E. H. Fellowes, "The Text of the Songbooks of Robert Jones," *Music & Letters* (1927).

Jones, Sidney, English composer of light music; b. London, June 17, 1861; d. there, Jan. 29, 1946. At an early age he became conductor of a military band; then toured the English provinces and Australia as conductor of various light opera companies; in 1905 he was appointed conductor at the London Empire Theatre. He owes his fame mainly to his enormously successful operetta, *Geisha* (London, April 25, 1896), which was for decades performed all over the world. His other operettas are: *The Gayety Girl* (London, 1893); *An Artist's Model* (London, 1895); *A Greek's Slave* (Vienna, 1899); *San Toy* (Vienna, 1899); *My Lady Molly* (London, 1903); *The Medal and the Maid* (London, 1903); *See See* (London, 1906); *The King of Cadonia* (London, 1908); *The Persian Princess* (London, 1909); *Spring Maid* (London, 1911); *The Girl*

from Utah (London, 1913); *The Happy Day* (London, 1916).

Jones, Sissieretta (real name **Matilda S. Joyner**), black American soprano, known as "the Black Patti" (with reference to Adelina Patti); b. Portsmouth, Virginia, Jan. 5, 1868; d. Providence, R.I., June 24, 1933. She studied voice at the New England Conservatory of Music; began singing professionally in 1888. Her first success was in 1892 at a Cakewalk Jubilee held in Madison Square Garden in N.Y.; afterwards gave recitals at the Academy of Music; the Metropolitan Opera considered her for African roles in *Aida* and *L'Africaine,* but racial attitudes and conservative management policies would not permit such parts to be taken by Afro-Americans. She subsequently toured the U.S., including a command performance before President Harrison at the White House. From 1893 to 1910 she led "Black Patti's Troubadours," with which she toured and sang operatic arias.
BIBLIOGRAPHY: William Lichtenwanger, in *Notable American Women* (Cambridge, Mass., 1971).

Jones, "Spike" (Lindley Armstrong), American bandleader; b. Long Beach, Calif., Dec. 14, 1911; d. Los Angeles, May 1, 1965. He played drums as a boy; then led a school band. On July 30, 1942 he made a recording of a satirical song *Der Führer's Face,* featuring a Bronx-cheer razzer; toured the U.S. with his band, The City Slickers, which included a washboard, a Smith and Wesson pistol, anti-bug Flit guns in E-flat, doorbells, anvils, hammers to break glass, and a live goat trained to bleat rhythmically. Climactically, he introduced the Latrinophone (a toilet seat strung with catgut). With this ensemble he launched a Musical Depreciation Revue. He retired in 1963 when the wave of extravaganza that had carried him to the crest of commercial success had subsided.

Jones, Tom (real name **Thomas Jones Woodward**), English singer and drummer; b. Pontypridd, South Wales, June 7, 1940. He sang, as most Welshmen do, with a natural feeling for melody; dropped out of school at 16 and got to play drums and sing in British pubs; his big chance at success came when he was heard by the famed manager Gordon Mills, a Welshman himself, who decided to propel him into fame; but first he had to abbreviate his name to plain Tom Jones. His greatest asset was lung power; he could outscream anyone in the rock field; he wore extremely tight "sexy" pants whose protuberances excited middle-aged women; with these assets he successfully invaded America.

Jones, William, known as **Jones of Nayland,** English minister and musician; b. Lowick, Northamptonshire, July 30, 1726; d. Nayland, Jan. 6, 1800. He studied at Oxford; was a vicar at Bethersden, Kent; then was a curate of Nayland. He published *A Treatise on the Art of Music* (1784; 2nd ed., 1827).

Jones, Sir William, English Orientalist; b. London, Sept. 28, 1746; d. Calcutta, April 27, 1794. He was a magistrate in India, where he lived from 1783; published *On the Musical Modes of the Hindus* (1784), which was included in vol. 6 of his collected works (1799).

BIBLIOGRAPHY: *Dictionary of National Biography* (vol. 10).

Jong, Marinus de, Dutch-born Belgian pianist and composer; b. Osterhout, Aug. 14, 1891. He studied composition with Mortelmans and piano with Bosquet at the Antwerp Cons. After several tours as pianist in Europe and America (he played a recital in New York on Feb. 7, 1921), he settled in Belgium in 1926 and in 1931 became a prof. of piano at the Antwerp Cons. He developed a neo-Impressionistic style, with polytonal counterpoint as its mainstay.

WORKS: 3 operas: *Mitsanoboe* (1962), *Die häslichen Mädchen von Bagdad (The Hateful Maidens of Baghdad;* Antwerp, Jan. 7, 1967) and *Esmoreit* (Antwerp, Sept. 11, 1970); 5 ballets: *De vrouwen van Zalongo* (1951), *De kleine haven* (1952), *De kringloop* (1955), *Carrefour* (1956) and *De Reiskameraad* (1959); 4 oratorios: *Hiawatha's Lied* (1947), *Imitatio Christi* (1956), *Kerkhofblommen* (1957) and *Proverbia Bruegeliana* (1961); the cantata *Summum Bonum* (1955); *Ode aan Peter Benoit* for baritone, chorus and orch. (1946); *Hymnus "Civitas Dei"* for soloists, chorus, children's chorus and orch. (1957); *Hymne aan de Schoonheid* for soprano, baritone, chorus and orch. (1961); 3 piano concertos (1924, 1952, 1956–57); concertos for trumpet (1937), cello (1946; revised 1969), violin (1954), viola (1958), oboe (1966–67), horn (1966–67), bassoon (1967), flute (1967), clarinet (1967) and organ (1974); 3 symphonies (1932, 1965–66, 1976); 3 *Flemish Rhapsodies:* No. 1 for orch. (1955), No. 2 for orch. (1971) and No. 3 for piano and orch. (1971); *Rhapsodie No. 4* for wind orch. (1974); *Heidestemmingen (Impressions de Bruyère)* for orch. (1937); *Hiawatha,* symph. poem (1945); *Aphoristische Tryptiek* for orch. or wind quintet (1952); *Boublitschky Suite* for orch. (1956); *Ruimteraket, Atlas (Fusée interplanétaire),* symph. poem (1964); 6 string quartets (1923, 1926, 1947, 1956, 1956, 1962); *Pacis, Doloris et Amoris,* violin sonata (1927); *Quartet for 4 Cellos* (1936); Nonet (1939); 3 wind quintets (1952, 1965, 1971); Suite for 4 Trombones (1958); Trio for oboe, clarinet and bassoon (1961); Wind Quartet (1968); Fantasia for Saxophone and Piano (1968); Piano Quartet (1971); Sextet for piano and wind quintet (1972); 3 piano sonatas (1926, 1933, 1934); *Fantaisie-Walsen* for piano (1960); *12 Preludes* for piano (1975); Concerto for Solo Organ (1964); numerous organ pieces, choruses and songs.

Jongen, Joseph, eminent Belgian composer; brother of Léon Jongen; b. Liège, Dec. 14, 1873; d. Sart-lez-Spa, July 12, 1953. He studied at the Liège Cons.; won two prizes in composition (1897); then traveled in Germany, France and Italy; returned to Belgium in 1902 and was appointed professor at the Liège Cons. During World War I he lived in England; there he formed a piano quartet with Defauw, Tertis and Doehaerd, with which he gave numerous concerts; also played organ recitals. In 1920 he became a prof. at the Brussels Cons.; from 1925 to 1939 he was its director; was succeeded by his brother, Léon. A prolific composer, he continued to write music to the end of his

life; the total of his works aggregates 137 op. numbers. While not pursuing extreme modern effects, Jongen succeeded in imparting an original touch to his harmonic style.

WORKS: His finest work was the *Symphonie concertante* for organ and orch. (1926); it was popularized by the organist Virgil Fox in guest appearances with major American orchestras. His other works with orchestra include: Symphony (1899); Violin Concerto (1899); Cello Concerto (1900); *Fantaisie sur deux Noëls populaires Wallons* (1902); *Lalla-Roukh,* symph. poem after Thomas Moore (1904); *Prélude et Danse* (1907); *2 Rondes wallonnes* (1912; also for piano); Trumpet Concertino (1913); *Impressions d'Ardennes* (1913); Suite for violin and orch. (1915); *Epithalame et Scherzo* for 3 violins, and orch. or piano (1917); *Tableaux pittoresques* (1917); *Poème héroïque* for violin and orch. (1919); *Prélude élégiaque et Scherzo* (1920); *Fantaisie rhapsodique* for cello and orch. (1924); *Hymne* for organ and strings (1924); *Pièce symphonique* for organ and orch. (1928); *Passacaille et Gigue* (1929); *Suite No. 3, dans le style ancien* (1930); *10 Pieces* (1932); *Triptyque* (1935); *Ouverture Fanfare* (1939); *Alleluia* for organ and orch. (1940); *Ouverture de fête* (1941); Piano Concerto (1943); *Bourrée* (1944); Harp Concerto (1944); Mass for organ, chorus and orch. (1946); *In memoriam* (1947); *Ballade, Hommage à Chopin* (1949); *3 Mouvements symphoniques* (1951). Chamber music: 3 string quartets (1893, 1916, 1921); Piano Trio (1897); Piano Quartet (1901); 2 violin sonatas (1903, 1909); Trio for piano, violin and viola (1907); Cello Sonata (1912); *2 Serenades* for string quartet (1918); *2 Pièces* for flute, cello and harp (1924); *2 Pièces* for 4 cellos (1929); *Sonata eroica* for organ (1930); Wind Quintet (1933); Quintet for harp, flute, violin, viola and cello (1940); Concerto for Wind Quintet (1942); Quartet for 4 Saxophones (1942); String Trio (1948); a number of piano pieces, including 24 preludes in all keys (1941); solo pieces for various instruments with piano; many songs with instrumental accompaniment; choral works. A catalogue of his works is publ. by the Centre Belge de Documentation Musicale (Brussels, 1954).

Jongen, Léon, important Belgian composer, brother of **Joseph Jongen;** b. Liège, March 2, 1884; d. Brussels, Nov. 18, 1969. He studied organ and served as a church organist in Liège; received the Belgian Grand Prix de Rome for his cantata *Les Fiancés de Noël* (1913); was in the Belgian Army during World War I; after the war traveled to the Far East and became the first conductor of the Opéra Français in Hanoi. Returning to Belgium in 1934, he became an instructor of the Brussels Cons.; from 1939 to 1949 he was successor to his brother as its director.

WORKS: For the stage: opera, *L'Ardennaise* (1909); a musical fairy tale, *Le Rêve d'une Nuit de Noël* (1917; Paris, March 18, 1918); opera, *Thomas l'Agnelet* (1922–23; Brussels, Feb. 14, 1924); the ballet, *Le Masque de la Mort rouge,* after Poe (1956). Also, he wrote 2 lyric scenes for chorus and orch.: *Geneviève de Brabant* (1907) and *La Légende de St. Hubert* (1909; first public performance, St. Hubert, July 21, 1968); *Campéador* for orch. (1932); *Malaisie,* suite for orch. (1935); *In Memoriam Regis* for orch. (1935); *Pré-*

lude, Divertissement et Final for piano and orch. (1937); *Trilogie de Psaumes* for chorus and orch. (1937–39); *Rhapsodia Belgica* for violin and orch. (1948); *Musique for a Ballet* (1954); *Divertissement en forme de variations sur un thème de Haydn* for orch. (1956); Violin Concerto (1962; compulsory work for the 12 finalists of the 1963 Queen Elisabeth violin contest held in Brussels). He further wrote String Quartet (1919); Fantasia for Piano (1930); *Divertissement* for 4 saxophones (1937); Trio for oboe, clarinet and bassoon (1937); Trio for flute, violin and viola (1937); Piano Quartet (1955); Quintet for piano, flute, clarinet, horn and bassoon (1958); songs.

Jonsson, Josef Petrus, Swedish composer; b. Enköping, June 21, 1887; d. Norrköping, May 9, 1969. He studied piano, but soon turned to musical journalism. He wrote 3 symphonies (*Nordland,* 1919–22; 1931; 1947); *Chamber Symphony* (1949); several orch. overtures and suites; Violin Concerto (Norrköping, April 10, 1960); *Festival Prelude* for orch. (1961); *Korallrevet,* symph. poem for baritone, chorus and orch. (1916); *Missa Solemnis* for chorus, orchestra and organ (1934); Cantata, for speaking chorus, female chorus, soli, 2 flutes and piano (Norrköping, May 5, 1962); chamber music; piano pieces; songs.

Joplin, Janis, American rock and blues singer; b. Port Arthur, Texas, Jan. 19, 1943; d. Hollywood, Oct. 4, 1970, of an overdose of heroin. After several attempts at formal education she held sporadic jobs as barroom singer in Austin and Los Angeles. In 1966 she joined the band of Travis Rivers in San Francisco; made a profound impression by her passionate wailing in a raspy voice; her appearances in such esoteric emporia as Psychedelic Supermarket in Boston, Kinetic Playground in Chicago, Whisky A-Go-Go in Los Angeles and Fillmore East in New York established her reputation as an uninhibited representative of the young generation. She was arrested in Tampa, Florida, in 1969 for having hurled porcine epithets at a policeman, which further endeared her to her public. On the more positive side, the Southern Comfort Distillery Co. presented her with a fur coat in recognition for the publicity she gave the firm by her habitual consumption of a quart of Southern Comfort at each of her appearances, brandishing the bottle conspicuously so as to display the brand name on its label. Her extraordinary ability to inject religious passion even into a commercial theme is illustrated by a song she composed, *Oh Lord, Won't You Buy Me a Mercedes-Benz?*

Joplin, Scott, black American pianist and composer; b. Texarkana, Nov. 24, 1868; d. New York, April 1, 1917. He learned to play the piano at home and later studied music seriously with a local German musician. He left home at 17 and went to St. Louis earning his living by playing piano in local emporia. In 1893 he moved to Chicago (drawn by the prospect of musicmaking and other gaiety of the World's Fair), and in the following year went to Sedalia, Missouri, where he took music courses at George Smith College, a segregated school for Negroes. His first music publications were in 1895, of genteel, maudlin songs and

marches, typical of the period. His success as a ragtime composer came with the *Maple Leaf Rag* (1899; the most famous of all piano rags), which he named after a local dance hall, the Maple Leaf Club. The sheet music edition sold so well that Joplin was able to settle in St. Louis and devote himself exclusively to composition; he even tried to write a ragtime ballet (*The Ragtime Dance,* 1902) and a ragtime opera, *A Guest of Honor* (copyright 1903, but the music is lost; newspaper notices indicate it was probably performed by the Scott Joplin Opera Co. in 1903). In 1907 he went to New York where he continued his career as a composer and teacher. Still intent on ambitious plans, he wrote an opera *Treemonisha* to his own libretto (the title deals with a Negro baby girl found under a tree by a woman named Monisha); he completed the score in 1911 and produced it in concert form in 1915 without any success. Interest in the opera was revived almost 60 years later; T. J. Anderson orchestrated it from the piano score, and it received its first complete performance at the Atlanta Symphony Hall on Jan. 28, 1972. Despite Joplin's ambitious attempts to make ragtime "respectable" by applying its principles to European forms, it was with the small, indigenous dance form of the piano rag that he achieved his greatest artistic success. As one noted historian phrased it, these pieces "are the precise American equivalent, in terms of a native dance music, of minuets by Mozart, mazurkas by Chopin, or waltzes by Brahms." Altogether, he wrote about 50 piano rags, in addition to the 2 operas, and a few songs, waltzes, and marches. The titles of some of these rags reflect his desire to transcend the trivial and create music on a more serious plane: *Sycamore,* "A Concert Rag" (1904); *Chrysanthemum,* "An Afro-American Intermezzo" (1904); *Sugar Cane,* "A Ragtime Classic Two Step" (1908); *Fig Leaf Rag,* "A High Class Rag" (1908); *Reflection Rag,* "Syncopated Musings" (1917). In his last years he lamented at failing to achieve the recognition he felt his music merited. Suffering from syphilis, he became insane and died shortly afterward in a state hospital. More than 50 years later, in the early 1970s, an extraordinary sequence of events—new recordings of his music and its use in an award-winning film, *The Sting* (1974)—brought Joplin unprecedented popularity and acclaim: among pop recordings, *The Entertainer* (1902) was one of the best selling discs for 1974; among classical recordings, Joplin albums represented 74 per cent of the "best sellers" of the year. In 1976 he was awarded exceptional posthumous recognition by the Pulitzer Prize Committee. Among the numerous collections of his music, the best is the 2-vol. set, facsimiles of the original editions, issued by the New York Public Library, *The Collected Works of Scott Joplin,* ed. by Vera Brodsky Lawrence (N.Y., 1971; lacks 3 rags, for which reprint permission was denied, and 2 song collaborations, discovered subsequent to publication).

BIBLIOGRAPHY: R. Blesh and H. Janis, *They All Played Ragtime* (N.Y., 1950; 4th ed., 1971; the basic biographical study); A. Reed, "Scott Joplin, Pioneer," *Black Perspective In Music* (Spring 1975; Fall 1975; corrects some biographical details); T. Waldo, *This Is Ragtime* (N.Y., 1976; treats the Joplin revival).

Jora, Mihail, Rumanian composer; b. Roman, Aug. 14, 1891; d. Bucharest, May 10, 1971. He studied piano privately in Iaşi (1901–12) and theory at the Cons. there (1909–11); then went to Germany where he became a student of Max Reger at the Leipzig Cons. (1912–14); after World War I he went to Paris where he studied with Florent Schmitt (1919–20). Returning to Rumania, he held the professorship in composition at the Bucharest Cons. (1929–62). He was a founding member of the Society of Rumanian Composers in 1920, and was consultant to the Bucharest Opera (1931–45). He was also a music critic.

WORKS: 6 ballets: *La piaţă* (*At the Market Place,* 1928; Bucharest, 1931), *Demoazela mǎriuţa* (*Damoiselle Mariutza,* 1940; Bucharest, 1942), *Curtea veche* (*The Old Court,* 1948), *Cînd strugurii se coc* (*When the Grapes Ripen;* Bucharest, 1954), *Întoarcerea din adîncuri* (*Return to the Abyss,* 1959; Bucharest, 1965) and *Hanul Dulcinea* (*The Inn Dulcinea;* Bucharest, 1967); Suite for Orch. (1915); *Poveste indicǎ* (*Hindu Tale),* symph. poem with vocalizing tenor (1920); *Privelişti moldoveneşti* (*Moldavian Landscapes),* suite for orch. (1924); *Şase cîntece şi-o rumbǎ* (*6 Songs and a Rumba)* for orch. (1932); Symphony (1937); *Burlesca* for orch. (1949); *Baladǎ* for baritone, chorus and orch. (1955); *Small Suite* for violin and piano (1917); 2 string quartets (1926, 1966); Viola Sonata (1951); Violin Sonata (1962); choruses; several song cycles. For piano he wrote *Joujoux pour ma dame* (1925); *Cortegiu* (*Marche juive,* 1925); Sonata (1942); *Variations on a Theme of Schumann* (1943); *Poze şi pozne* (*Portraits and Jokes),* miniatures in 3 sets (1948, 1959, 1963); *13 Preludes* (1960); Sonatina (1961). He published the book *Momente muzicale* (Bucharest, 1968). Jora is regarded in Rumania as one of the finest composers of the romantic national school, with a strongly pronounced lyric inspiration. Many composers of the younger generations were his students.

Jordá, Enrique, Spanish conductor; b. San Sebastian, March 24, 1911. He was a chorister in the parochial school and played organ at his parish church in Madrid; in 1929 he went to Paris as a medical student, but then turned decidedly to music, studying organ with Marcel Dupré, composition with Paul Le Flem and conducting with Frans Rühlmann. He made his debut as an orchestral conductor in Paris in 1938; then became the regular conductor of the Madrid Symph. Orch.; subsequently was principal conductor of the Cape Town Symph. Orch., South Africa (1947–51). From 1954 to 1963 he was conductor of the San Francisco Symph. Orch.; in 1970 he became conductor of the Philharmonic Orch. at Antwerp, Belgium. He publ. a popular book, *El Director de Orquesta ante la Partitura* (Madrid, 1969).

Jordan, Irene, American soprano; b. Birmingham, Alabama, April 25, 1919. Both her parents were professional music teachers and she began playing piano at the age of 5; then studied voice at Judson College in Marion, Alabama (A.B. 1939); in 1940 she went to New York where she continued her vocal studies; in 1946 she took up operatic coaching with Boris Goldovsky. She then filled in engagements in Broadway shows and on the radio; made her operatic debut in a minor role at the Metropolitan Opera in 1946; in 1954 was engaged at the Chicago Lyric Opera; in 1956 sang the Queen of the Night in Mozart's opera, *The Magic Flute,* at Covent Garden, London; subsequently sang as a soprano soloist with the Boston Symphony and other American orchestras, and appeared at the St. Louis Municipal Opera. Possessing a diversified vocal technique, she was able to sing both dramatic and lyric soprano parts. In 1962 she was engaged as prof. of voice at Northwestern University.

Jordan, Jules, American singer and composer; b. Willimantic, Conn., Nov. 10, 1850; d. Providence, March 5, 1927. He moved to Providence in 1870 and established himself as a singer, choral conductor, and teacher; for 40 years (1880–1920), conducted the Arion Club (250 voices). He was a successful composer of school operettas (*The Alphabet, Cloud and Sunshine,* etc.); wrote 6 light operas: *Star of the Sea, An Eventful Holiday, The Buccaneers, Princess of the Blood, Her Crown of Glory,* and *A Leap Year Furlough;* vaudeville sketches, *Cobbler or King, Managerial Tactics,* etc. His romantic comedy opera *Rip Van Winkle* was produced at the Providence Opera House (May 25, 1897); another opera, *Nisiea,* remained unperformed. He wrote his own librettos for his stage works as well as for his cantatas *The Night Service, Barbara Fritchie,* etc.

BIBLIOGRAPHY: E. E. Hipsher, *American Opera and Its Composers* (Philadelphia, 1934, pp. 280–81).

Jordan, Mary, American contralto; b. Cardiff, Wales, Nov. 27, 1879; d. San Antonio, Texas, May 15, 1961. She entered St. Cecilia's Convent, in Scranton, Pa.; then studied with various teachers in Seattle, San Francisco, and New York. She made her operatic debut as Amneris with the Boston Opera Co. (March 28, 1911); also sang in churches in Brooklyn and New York; toured in the Orient, and was for some years prof. at the Manila Cons.; then settled in San Antonio, Texas, as vocal teacher.

Jordan, Sverre, Norwegian composer; b. Bergen, May 25, 1889; d. there, Jan. 10, 1972. He studied piano; then traveled to Germany where he took courses in piano and composition in Berlin with Ansorge and Klatte (1907–14). In 1914 he returned to Bergen; was active as music director of the National Theater (1932–57). In his works he made liberal use of national folksongs, which met the tastes of the general public. Typical of these nationally oriented works are *Suite in Old Style* for small orch. (1911); *Norvegiani* for orch. (1921); *Smeden* (*The Smith)* for baritone, chorus and orch. (1924); *Norge i vare hjerter,* cantata for the opening of the Bergen Exhibition (1928); *Suite on Norwegian Folk Tunes and Dances* for orch. (1936); *Holberg-silhuetter* for orch. (1938); *Norwegian Rhapsody* for orch. (1950); *Suite in Old Style on Holberg Themes* for orch. (1954); *Concerto Romantico* for horn and orch. (1956) and *Kongen* (*The King),* orch. melodrama with narration and choral finale (1957). Other works are Piano Concerto (1945); Cello Concerto (1947); *Concerto Piccolo* for piano and orch. (1963); Violin Concerto (1966); 2 violin sonatas (1917, 1943); Flute Sonatina (1955); 2 piano trios (1958,

1963); Piano Sonata (1963); incidental music for many plays; over 200 songs, often with orch. accompaniment.

Jørgensen, Erik, Danish composer; b. Copenhagen, May 10, 1912. He studied theory of music with Knud Jeppesen in Copenhagen (1928–31); then took private lessons with Finn Høffding; in 1936 took conducting courses with Scherchen in Geneva. He evolved an individual idiom of composition, marked by an abundance of asymmetrical rhythmic configurations in the neo-Baroque manner; later experimented with dodecaphony; eventually adopted a technique of "controlled coincidences."

WORKS: Concerto Grosso for flute, clarinet, bassoon and string orch. (1933–34); *3 Antiphonies* for soprano, tenor and chamber orch. (1934–35); Concerto for Solo Violin, String Orch. and Piano (1937); Concertino for Flute, Clarinet, Violin and Piano (1938); *Rhapsodies* for violin and piano (1939–40); Sonatina for clarinet and bassoon (1942); *Modello per archi* for string orch. or string quartet (1957); *Figure in Tempo* for cello and piano (1960–61); Quintet for 2 pianos, 2 percussionists and double bass (1962); *Modello 2* for 4 vocal soloists and 12 instruments (1963); *Astrolabium,* chamber concerto for 11 instruments (1964); string quartet (1964–65); *Notturno* for 24 solo instruments (1965); Variations for Piano (1966); *Confrontations* for orch. (1967–68); a chamber opera, *The Shadow of a Dream* (1969); *Improvisations* for wind quintet (1971); *Moods and States,* quartet for flute, horn, violin and cello (1973); a madrigal comedy for children and grownups, *The Fairytale* (1973–77).

Jörn, Karl, tenor; b. Riga, Latvia, Jan. 5, 1876; d. Denver, Dec. 19, 1947. He studied in Riga and Berlin; then sang in provincial German towns; was on the staff of the Hamburg City Theater (1899–1902); then at the Berlin Opera; sang in London (1908); and in New York (1908–11); was particularly successful in Wagnerian roles; toured the U.S. with the German Grand Opera Co. (1931); then taught in Denver, where he remained until his death.

Joseffy, Rafael, eminent Hungarian-American pianist and teacher; b. Hunfalu, July 3, 1852; d. New York, June 25, 1915. At the age of 8 he began to study piano with a local teacher at Miskolcz, and later at Budapest. In 1866 he entered the Leipzig Cons., where his principal teacher was E. F. Wenzel, though he had some lessons with Moscheles. From 1868 to 1870 he studied with Karl Tausig in Berlin, and the summers of 1870 and 1871 he spent with Liszt in Weimar. He made his debut at Berlin in 1870; his excellent technique and tonal variety elicited much praise; his career was then securely launched. He made his American debut in 1879 playing at a symph. concert of Leopold Damrosch in New York, where he settled permanently; taught at the National Cons. from 1888 till 1906. In America he gained appreciation both as a virtuoso and as a musician of fine interpretative qualities; his programs featured many works of Brahms at a time when Brahms was not yet recognized in America as a great master. As a pedagogue, Joseffy was eminently successful; many American concert pia-

nists were his pupils. He brought out an authoritative edition of Chopin's works in 15 vols. (with critico-historical annotations by Huneker); also edited studies by Czerny, Henselt, Moscheles, Schumann, and others. His *School of Advanced Piano Playing* (1902; in German as *Meisterschule des Klavierspiels*) is a valuable practical method. Joseffy was also a composer; publ. a number of characteristic piano pieces (*Die Mühle, Romance sans paroles, Souvenir d'Amérique, Mazurka-Fantasie, Spinnlied,* etc.) and arrangements of works by Schumann, Bach, Boccherini, Gluck, Delibes.

BIBLIOGRAPHY: E. Hughes, "Rafael Joseffy's Contribution to Piano Technique," *Musical Quarterly* (July 1916).

Josephson, Jacob Axel, Swedish composer and conductor; b. Stockholm, March 27, 1818; d. Uppsala, March 29, 1880. He studied music in Uppsala; then taught at the Cathedral School there (1841–43); in 1844 he went to Germany; studied with Hauptmann and Niels Gade in Leipzig. After further study in Rome (1845–46), he returned to Uppsala, where he became conductor of the Philharmonic Society; became music director at Uppsala Univ. in 1849; in 1864, was appointed organist at the cathedral there. He wrote mostly choral works (psalms, cantatas); edited a series of articles on sacred songs, "Zion" (1867–70).

BIBLIOGRAPHY: K. Nyblom, *J. A. Josephson* (Stockholm, 1926).

Josif, Enriko, Serbian composer; b. Belgrade, May 1, 1924. He studied music theory with Milenko Živković at the Belgrade Music Academy (1947–50); then went to Italy and took a course in composition with Petrassi at the Santa Cecilia Academy in Rome (1961–62); returning to Belgrade he was appointed to the faculty of the Serbian Music Academy.

WORKS: a ballet, *Ptico, ne sklapaj svoja krila* (*Bird, Don't Break Your Wings,* 1970; Belgrade, Oct. 7, 1970); Sinfonietta (1954); *Sonata antica* for orch. (1955); *Lyrical Symphony* for 4 flutes, harp and string orch. (1956); Piano Concerto (1959); *Symphony in One Movement* (1964; Belgrade, Jan. 24, 1966); *Sinfonietta di tre re* (1968); *Oratorio profano da camera* for narrator, soprano, celesta, piano and percussion (1956); *Smrt Stefana Dečanskog* (*The Death of Stefan of Decane*), chamber motets for narrator, soloists, chorus and 16 instruments (1956; enlarged and orchestrated as a dramatic epic in 1970 under the title *Stefan Dečanski;* Belgrade, Oct. 7, 1970); *Rustikon,* cantata (1962); *Improvisations on a Folk Theme* for 14 winds (1949); String Quartet (1953); *Snovidenja* (*Dream Visions*) for flute, harp and piano (1964); *Divertimento* for wind quintet (1964); *Epigram I* for chamber ensemble and *Epigram II* for piano trio (1967); *Zapisi* (*Chronicles*) for wind quintet (1971); *Vatrenja* for piano trio (1972); *Sonata brevis* for piano (1949); *4 Priče* (*Stories*) for piano (1957); *4 Skice* (*Sketches*) for piano (1957); *3 Psalms* for piano (1963).

Josten, Werner, American composer; b. Elberfeld, Germany, June 12, 1885; d. New York, Feb. 6, 1963. He studied music theory in Munich; then took courses with Jaques-Dalcroze in Geneva; he lived in Paris from 1912 to 1914; at the outbreak of World War I, he returned to Germany; in 1918 was appointed assistant conductor at the Munich Opera. In 1920 he went to the U.S. and appeared as composer-accompanist with several singers; in 1933 he became an American citizen. He taught at Smith College in Northampton, Mass. from 1923 to 1949; also conducted the Smith College Orch., with which he presented performances of works by Monteverdi and Handel. His own compositions are couched in a lyrical manner of German romantic music, with a strong undercurrent of euphonius counterpoint within the network of luscious harmonies. During his American period, he became interested in exotic art, and introduced impressionistic devices in his works.

WORKS: *Jungle,* a symph. movement, inspired by Henri Rousseau's painting "Forêt Exotique" (Boston Symph., Oct. 25, 1929); *Batouala,* choreographic poem, also arranged as an African ballet (1931; a symphonic suite drawn from it was first performed at Smith College, Nov. 10, 1963, under the title *Suite nègre*); *Concerto sacro I-II* for piano and string orch. (1925; N.Y., March 27, 1929); *Joseph and His Brethren,* ballet (1932; N.Y., March 9, 1936; as a symph. suite, Philadelphia, May 15, 1939); *Endymion,* ballet (1933; as a symph. suite, N.Y., Oct. 28, 1936); Serenade for Small Orch. (1934); Symphony in F (Boston Symph., Nov. 13, 1936, composer conducting); *Symphony for Strings* (Saratoga Springs, N.Y., Sept. 3, 1946). CHAMBER MUSIC: String Quartet (1934); Violin Sonata (1936); Cello Sonata (1938); Sonatina for Violin and Piano (1939); Trio for flute, clarinet, and bassoon (1941); Trio for violin, viola, cello (1942); Trio for flute, cello and piano (1943); Sonata for Horn and Piano (1944); *Canzona seria,* for flute, oboe, clarinet, bassoon and piano (N.Y., Nov. 23, 1957). VOCAL WORKS: *Crucifixion* for bass solo and mixed chorus a cappella (1915); *Hymnus to the Quene of Paradys,* for women's voices, strings, and organ (1921); *Indian Serenade,* for tenor with orch. (1922); *Ode for St. Cecilia's Day,* for voices and orch. (1925); *À une Madone,* for solo tenor and orch., after Baudelaire (1929); about 50 songs.

BIBLIOGRAPHY: *Werner Josten, 1885-1963. A Summary of His Compositions With Press Reviews* (N.Y., 1964).

Joteyko, Tadeusz, Polish composer; b. Poczuiki, April 1, 1872; d. Teschen, Aug. 19, 1932. He studied in Brussels with Gevaert and in Warsaw with Noskowski; held positions as head of musical societies in Kalisz and Lodz; conducted the Warsaw Philharmonic from 1914 to 1918; taught at the Warsaw Cons. He wrote the operas *Grajek (The Player;* Warsaw, Nov. 23, 1919); *Zygmunt August* (his most successful work; Warsaw, Aug. 29, 1925); *Królowa Jadwiga (Queen Jadwiga;* Warsaw, Sept. 7, 1928); chamber music; numerous songs and piano pieces.

Joubert, John, significant South African composer; b. Cape Town, March 20, 1927. After preliminary studies in South Africa, he travelled to Great Britain with a Performing Right Scholarship in 1946 and took music courses with Howard Ferguson at the Royal Academy of Music in London (1946-50). In his music he cultivates the pragmatic goal of pleasurability, wherein harmony and counterpoint serve the functional role of support for a flowing melody; in several works he makes use of primitive elements derived from Hottentot rites, transmuting the primitive vocalizations into its modern polytonal and polyrhythmic formations. His carols, *Torches* and *There is No Rose,* enjoy wide popularity.

WORKS: *Antigone,* radio opera (BBC, London, July 21, 1954); *In the Drought,* chamber opera (Johannesburg, Oct. 20, 1956); *Silas Marner,* after the novel by George Eliot (Cape Town, May 20, 1961); *The Quarry,* opera for young people (Wembley, March 26, 1965); *Under Western Eyes,* after the novel by Joseph Conrad (Camden, England, May 29, 1969); *The Prisoner,* an opera for schools (Barnet, March 14, 1973). Other works are the cantatas *The Burghers of Calais* (1954); *Leaves of Life* (1963); *Urbs beata* (first performed at St. George's Cathedral, Cape Town, Nov. 26, 1963); *The Choir Invisible* (Halifax, May 18, 1968); *The Martyrdom of St. Alban* (London, June 7, 1969); *The Raising of Lazarus* (Birmingham, Sept. 30, 1971). VARIOUS CHORAL WORKS: *Pro Pace,* a cycle of 3 motets for unaccompanied chorus (1960); *The Holy Mountain,* a canticle for chorus and two pianos (1963); numerous sacred works, anthems and carols, including *Torches, There is No Rose, Great Lord of Lords, Welcome Yule, Christ is Risen, The Beatitudes, Te Deum;* secular part songs, among them *The God Pan* and *Sweet Content;* also *African Sketchbook (Hottentot Animal Songs)* for vocal quartet and wind instruments (1970). ORCHESTRAL WORKS: *Legend of Princess Vlei,* ballet (Cape Town, Feb. 21, 1952); Overture (Cheltenham Festival, June 12, 1953); *Symphonic Prelude* (Durban Centenary Festival, May 15, 1954); Violin Concerto (York, June 17, 1954); Symph. No. 1 (Hull, April 12, 1956); *North Country Overture* (1958); Piano Concerto (Manchester, Jan. 11, 1959); Sinfonietta for Chamber Orch. (1962); *In Memoriam, 1820* (1962); Symph. No. 2 (London, March 24, 1971). CHAMBER MUSIC: *Miniature String Quartet* (1950); Viola Sonata (1952); String Trio (1958); Octet for clarinet, bassoon, horn, string quartet and double bass (1960); *Sonata a cinque* for recorder, 2 violins, cello and harpsichord (1963); 2 Piano Sonatas (1956, 1971); organ pieces, songs.

Jouret, Léon, Belgian composer; b. Ath, Oct. 17, 1828; d. Brussels, June 6, 1905. He studied at the Brussels Cons.; in 1874, was appointed prof. of singing there. His 2 operas, *Quentin Metsys* and *Le Tricorne enchanté,* were produced semi-privately in Brussels (1865 and 1868); of more importance is his collection of folk melodies of his native region, *Chants populaires de pays d'Ath.*

Journet, Marcel, French bass singer; b. Grasse, Alpes Maritimes, July 25, 1867; d. Vittel, Sept. 5, 1933. He made his operatic debut at Bezières (1891); performed at summer seasons at Covent Garden, London (1893-1900); sang at the Théâtre de la Monnaie in Brussels (1894-1900); made his American debut at the Metropolitan Opera, N.Y., in 1908 and remained on the staff for 7 seasons; from 1908-14, was in Europe; at the outbreak of World War I in 1914, he joined the

Chicago Opera Co., leaving it in 1916; later, returned to France. His repertory included 8 Wagner operas, 27 Italian and 65 French operas.

Jousse, Jean, French music pedagogue; b. Orleans, 1760; d. London, Jan. 19, 1837. A scion of an aristocratic family, he was compelled to flee France during the Revolution, and settled in London, where he became a successful teacher of singing and piano. He publ. several textbooks, among them *Lectures on Thoroughbass* (1819; a new revised and augmented ed., N.Y., 1894, under the title, *A Catechism of Music*).

Joy, Geneviève, French pianist; b. Bernaville, Oct. 4, 1919. She studied at the Paris Cons. with Yves Nat (piano), Jean and Noël Gallon (theory); received Premier Prix in piano in 1941. In 1945 she married the composer **Henri Dutilleux.** She specialized in modern music; gave numerous first performances of piano works by French composers, some of them written especially for her.

Juch, Emma (Antonia Joanna), American operatic soprano; b. Vienna, July 4, 1863 (of American parents); d. New York, March 6, 1939. She was brought to the U.S. at the age of 4, and studied in N.Y. with Murio Celli; made her debut in the old Chickering Hall in 1881; stage debut in London (1883); sang 3 seasons under Mapleson's management in England and in the U.S.; from 1886-88 she was principal soprano of the American Opera Co.; upon its failure in 1889, she organized the Emma Juch Grand Opera Co., which presented opera in the U.S. and Mexico (until 1891); after that, she confined herself chiefly to concert appearances. On June 26, 1894, she married District Attorney Francis L. Wellman, but was divorced in 1911.
BIBLIOGRAPHY: N. S. Putnam, in *Notable American Women* (Cambridge, Mass., 1971).

Juchelka, Miroslav, Czech composer; b. Velká Polom, March 29, 1922. He studied composition with Řidký and Hlobil at the Prague Cons. (1939-43) and then with Albín Šíma at the Master School there (1943-47); in 1952 was appointed music director of the Czech Radio in Prague.
WORKS: *Symphonic Fantasy* for orch. (1952); Accordion Concerto (1954); *Burlesque* for piano and orch. (1958); Suite for String Orch. (1961); *Burlesque* for clarinet and promenade orch. (1970); *From the Beskyds,* suite for orch. (1972); Clarinet Concerto (1974); *Miniatures* for cello and piano (1951); Suite for nonet (1962); Clarinet Sonatina (1964); *Five Compositions for Due Boemi* for bass clarinet and piano (1972; Due Boemi is a Czech chamber duo, led by Josef Horák).

Judge, Jack, English composer of popular songs; b. 1878; d. West Bromwich, July 28, 1938. His song, *It's a long, long way to Tipperary,* written in 1912, attained enormous popularity in England and elsewhere as a wartime song during World War I.

Judson, Arthur, American concert manager; b. Dayton, Ohio, Feb. 17, 1881; d. Rye, New York, Jan. 28,

1975. He took violin lessons with Max Bendix; played in orchestras, and himself conducted summer resort orchestras. In 1900 he was appointed dean of the Cons. of Music of Denison Univ., Granville, Ohio. In 1907 he was in N.Y.; was connected with the editorial and advertising departments of *Musical America.* From 1915 to 1935 he was manager of the Philadelphia Orch.; in 1922 he was appointed manager of the N.Y. Philharmonic Orch., and held this position for 34 years, resigning in 1956. In 1928 his concert management took over the Wolfsohn Musical Bureau; in 1930, these organizations merged into Columbia Concerts Corporation, with Judson as president.

Juhan, Alexander, American violinist, conductor, and composer; probably son of **James Juhan;** b. Halifax, 1765; d. 1845. He was brought to Boston in 1768; was violinist and a manager in Philadelphia in 1783; later went to Charleston, S.C., where he was active from 1790 to 1792; returned to Philadelphia in 1792. He composed 6 piano sonatas, of which 3 are accompanied by a flute (or a violin); also a book of 12 songs, with instrumental accompaniment.

Juhan, James, French musician, who was active in Boston (1768-70) and in Charleston, S.C. (1771), and later in Philadelphia, where he exhibited the "great North American Forte Piano" (1786).
BIBLIOGRAPHY: O. G. Sonneck, *Early Concert Life in America* (1907).

Juilliard, Augustus D., American music patron; b. at sea, during his parents' voyage in a sailing vessel from Burgundy to America, April 19, 1836; d. New York, April 25, 1919. He was a prominent industrialist; left the residue of his estate for the creation of a Juilliard Musical Foundation (established in 1920). The objects of his Foundation are to aid worthy students of music in securing a complete musical education, and to arrange and give concerts for the education of the general public in the musical arts. The Juilliard School of Music was founded and has been maintained by the Foundation.
BIBLIOGRAPHY: *Dictionary of American Biography,* vol. X (N.Y., 1933).

Jullien, Gilles, French organist; b. c.1650; d. Chartres, Sept. 14, 1703. He became organist at the Chartres Cathedral in 1667, and held this post until his death. His *Premier Livre d'Orgue* was publ. by Lesclop in Chartres (1680); a modern reprint, with annotations and an introduction by Norbert Dufourcq, was issued in Paris (1952).

Jullien, Jean-Lucien-Adolphe, French writer on music; son of **Marcel-Bernard Jullien;** b. Paris, June 1, 1845; d. Chaintreauville, Seine-et-Marne, Aug. 30, 1932. He studied law in Paris and took private lessons with Bienaimé, a former prof. of the Paris Cons. He became a musical journalist; contributed to various magazines, and took a strong position in favor of the new music of Berlioz and Wagner.
WRITINGS: *L'Opéra en 1788* (1873); *La Musique et les philosophes au XVIIIᵉ siècle* (1873); *La Comédie à la cour de Louis XVI, le théâtre de la reine à Trianon*

(1873); *Histoire de théâtre de Mme. Pompadour, dit Théâtre des petits cabinets* (1874); *Les Spectateurs sur le théâtre* (1875); *Le Théâtre des demoiselles Verrières* (1875); *Les Grandes Nuits de Sceaux, le théâtre de la duchesse du Maine* (1876); *Un Potentat musical* (1876); *Weber à Paris* (1877); *Airs variés; histoire, critique, biographie musicales et dramatiques* (1877); *La Cour et l'opéra sous Louis XVI; Marie-Antoinette et Sacchini; Salieri; Favart et Gluck* (1878); *Goethe et la musique* (1880); *L'Opéra secret au XVIIIᵉ siècle* (1880); *Richard Wagner, sa vie et ses œuvres* (1886; also in English translation, Boston, 1892) and *Hector Berlioz* (1888); *Musiciens d'aujourd'hui* (1st series, 1891; 2nd series, 1894); *Musique* (1895); *Le Romantisme et l'éditeur Renduel* (1897); *Amours d'opéra au XVIIIᵉ siècle* (1908); *Ernest Reyer* (1909).
BIBLIOGRAPHY: F. Delhasse, *A. Jullien* (Paris, 1884).

Jullien, Louis Antoine, French conductor; b. Sisteron, April 23, 1812; d. Paris, March 14, 1860. The son of a bandmaster, he went to Paris in 1833 and studied composition with Le Carpentier and Halévy, but could not maintain the discipline of learning music, and began to compose light dances instead; of these, the waltz *Rosita* attained enormous, though transitory, popularity in Paris. He left the conservatory in 1836 without taking a degree, and became engaged as conductor of dance music at the Jardin Turc. He also attempted to launch a musical journal, but an accumulation of carelessly contracted debts compelled him to leave France (1838). He went to London, where he conducted summer concerts at Drury Lane Theatre (1840) and winter concerts with an enlarged ensemble of instrumentalists and singers (1841). He then opened a series of "society concerts" at which he presented large choral works, such as Rossini's *Stabat Mater,* as well as movements from Beethoven's symphonies. In 1847 he engaged Berlioz to conduct at the Drury Lane Theatre, which he had leased. He became insolvent in 1848, but attempted to recoup his fortune by organizing a "concert monstre" with 400 players, 3 choruses, and 3 military bands. He succeeded in giving 3 such concerts in London in 1849. He then essayed the composition of an opera, *Pietro il Grande,* which he produced at his own expense at Covent Garden on Aug. 17, 1852. He used the pseudonym **Roch Albert** for his spectacular pieces, such as *Destruction of Pompeii.* He publ. some dance music under his own name (*Royal Irish Quadrille,* etc.). In 1853 he was engaged by Barnum for a series of concerts in the U.S. For his exhibition at the Crystal Palace in N.Y. (June 15, 1854), attended by a great crowd, he staged a simulated conflagration for his *Fireman's Quadrille.* Despite his eccentricities, however, Jullien possessed true interest in musical progress. At his American concerts he made a point of including several works by American composers: *Santa Claus Symphony* by William Henry Fry and some chamber music by George Frederick Bristow. In 1854 he returned to London; his managerial ventures resulted in another failure. In 1859 he went to Paris, but was promptly arrested for debt, and spent several weeks in prison. He died a few months later in an insane asylum to which he was confined.

BIBLIOGRAPHY: J. W. Davison, *Memoirs* (London, 1912); J. T. Howard, *Our American Music* (4th ed., 1965); N. Slonimsky, *A Thing or Two About Music* (N.Y., 1948; pp. 226–35); A. Carse, *The Life of Jullien: Adventurer, Showman-Conductor and Establisher of the Promenade Concerts in England* (Cambridge, 1951).

Jullien, Marcel-Bernard, French music scholar; b. Paris, Feb. 2, 1798; d. there, Oct. 15, 1881. He was secretary general to the "Société des Méthodes d'enseignement" and a learned grammarian.
WRITINGS: *De l'étude de la musique instrumentale dans les pensions des demoiselles* (1848); *De quelques points des sciences dans l'antiquité (Physique, métrique, musique)* (1854); and *Thèses supplémentaires de métrique et de musique ancienne* (1861).

Jumilhac, Dom Pierre-Bénoit de, Benedictine monk; specialist in Gregorian chant; b. Château St. Jean-de-Ligourre, near Limoges, 1611; d. St. Germain-des-Prés, March 21, 1682. He wrote *La Science et la Pratique du plain-chant* (Paris, 1673; ed. by Nisard and Leclerq and republished in 1847), an erudite work containing many musical examples.

Junck, Benedetto, Italian composer; b. Turin, Aug. 21, 1852; d. San Vigilio, near Bergamo, Oct. 3, 1903. He was of Alsatian-Italian extraction; was trained for a commercial career, but practiced the piano in his free time; then entered the Milan Cons. for serious study, and developed a fine lyric talent for song writing; his youthful ballad *La Simona* became very popular; *Dolce sera,* from his album, *8 Romanze,* also was well known. In addition to songs, he wrote a string quartet and 2 violin sonatas.

Jüngst, Hugo, German conductor; b. Dresden, Feb. 26, 1853; d. there, March 3, 1923. He studied at the Dresden Cons.; was conductor of the Dresden Male Choral Society, which he founded in 1876, and of numerous festivals; composed many men's choruses, including the well-known *Scissors Grinder.*

Juon, Paul, Russian composer; b. Moscow, March 6, 1872; d. Vevey, Switzerland, Aug. 21, 1940. He was a pupil of Hřimaly (violin) and Taneyev and Arensky (composition) in Moscow; in Berlin, of Bargiel (1894–96); lived in Berlin; appointed professor of composition at the Hochschule für Musik in 1906.
WORKS: for orch.: Symphony in A; *Vaegtevise,* fantasy on Danish folksongs; *Aus einem Tagebuch,* suite; Serenade; 3 violin concertos; *Episodes Concertantes,* triple concerto for violin, cello, and piano with orch.; chamber music: 4 string quartets; Sextet, for 2 violins, viola, 2 cellos, and piano; Octet, for piano, violin, viola, cello, oboe, clarinet, horn, and bassoon; 2 quintets for piano and strings; Divertimento for piano and woodwinds; *Rhapsodie* for piano quartet; other piano quartets; 3 piano trios; *Caprice, Legende* and *Litaniae* for trio; 6 *Silhouettes* for 2 violins and piano; sonatas for violin, viola, cello, flute, and clarinet (with piano); pieces for violin, cello, and piano (*Satyre und Nymphen, Intime Harmonien,* etc.); compositions for piano 4 hands; songs. He published *Praktische Har-*

monielehre (1901); *Handbuch für Harmonielehre* (1920); *Anleitung zum Modulieren* (1929); *Der Kontrapunkt* (1932).

Jupin, Charles-François, French violinist and composer; b. Chambéry, Nov. 30, 1805; d. Paris, June 12, 1839. He studied with Baillot at the Paris Cons., taking 1st prize in 1823; wrote an opera, *La Vengeance italienne* (1834); numerous pieces for violin.

Jürgens, Fritz, German composer; b. Düsseldorf, April 22, 1888; killed in action in Champagne, Sept. 25, 1915. He studied music largely by himself; wrote some fine lieder; set to music 45 poems by Gustav Falke, and 35 by Martin Greif.

Jurgenson, Pyotr, Russian music publisher; b. Reval, July 17, 1836; d. Moscow, Jan. 2, 1904. The youngest son of indigent parents, he learned the music trade with M. Bernard, owner of a music store in St. Petersburg; Jurgenson served in 3 other music-selling houses there, before opening a business of his own in 1861, in Moscow. With a small investment, he gradually expanded his firm until it became one of the largest in Russia. Through Nicholas Rubinstein he met the leading musicians of Russia, and had enough shrewdness of judgment to undertake the publication of works of Tchaikovsky, beginning with his op. 1. He became Tchaikovsky's close friend, and, while making handsome profit out of Tchaikovsky's music, he demonstrated a generous regard for Tchaikovsky's welfare; he publ. full scores of Tchaikovsky's symphonies and operas, as well as his songs and piano works. His voluminous correspondence with Tchaikovsky, from 1877 to Tchaikovsky's death, was publ. in 2 vols. in Moscow (1938 and 1952). Jurgenson publ. also many works by other Russian composers; issued vocal scores of Glinka's operas; also publ. the first Russian editions of the collected works of Chopin, Schumann, Mendelssohn, and Wagner's operas. His catalogue contained some 20,000 numbers. After his death, his son **Boris Jurgenson** succeeded to the business; it was nationalized after the Russian Revolution.

Jurinac, Sena, operatic soprano; b. Travnik, Yugoslavia, Oct. 24, 1921. Her father was a Croatian physician; her mother was a Viennese. Sena Jurinac studied in Zagreb; made her debut at the Zagreb Opera as Mimi in *La Bohème* in 1942; after the end of the war she moved to Vienna and Europeanized her original Slavic first name Srebrenka (literally, the silver one) to a more vowel-rich Sena. She was very successful in Vienna, and repeated her successes with unfailing constancy at her appearances in Salzburg, Florence and Edinburgh; she also sang at La Scala in Milan and at the Teatro Colón in Buenos Aires. She made her American debut with the San Francisco Opera in 1959; this was followed by guest appearances with the Metropolitan Opera. She has earned the reputation as one of the finest interpreters of the soprano roles in Mozart's operas.

Jurjans, Andrejs, Latvian composer; b. Erlaa, Sept. 18, 1856; d. Riga, Sept. 28, 1922. He studied with Rim-sky-Korsakov (1875–82) in St. Petersburg. In 1882, he was appointed prof. at the Cons. of Kharkov, where he taught for 34 years until 1916. In 1917 he went to Riga. He wrote a symph. poem, a cello concerto, some chamber music, and a number of orchestral arrangements of Latvian folk melodies, which he employed also in his original works.

BIBLIOGRAPHY: Jahnis Straumes, *Our Musicians* (in Latvian; Riga, 1922).

Jurovský, Šimon, Slovak composer; b. Ulmanka, Feb. 8, 1912; d. Prague, Nov. 8, 1963. He attended the Bratislava Academy of Music (1931–36); then took courses in composition with Josef Marx at the Vienna Academy of Music (1943–44). He held various posts in Slovakia; was manager of the Bratislava Opera, director of the Slovak Folk Art Ensemble, etc. In his music he followed the broad tenets of national romanticism, with frequent references to folk themes.

WORKS: an opera, *Dcery Abelovy (The Daughters of Abel,* 1961); a ballet *Rytierska balada (The Song of Chivalry;* Bratislava, 1960); 2 orch. suites (1939; 1943); Serenade for String Orch. (1940); *Začatá cesta (The Journey Begun),* symph. poem (1948); *Radostné súženie (A Joyous Competition),* symph. scherzo (1949); 2 symphonies: No. 1, *Mírová (Peace),* for piano and strings (1950) and No. 2, *Heroická (Heroic),* for organ and orch. (1960); Cello Concerto (1953); Concertino for Piano and String Orch. (1962); *3 Uspávanky (Lullabies)* for soprano, piano, harp and strings (1947); Quartet for Winds (1936); *Melodies and Dialogues,* a string quartet (1944); String Trio (1948); *Concert Dance* for piano (1960); much film music; choral pieces; songs (including arrangements of folksongs).

BIBLIOGRAPHY: Zdenka Bokesová, *Šimon Jurovský* (Bratislava, 1955).

Juzeliunas, Julius, Lithuanian composer; b. Zeimelis, Feb. 20, 1916. He studied at the Kaunas Cons., graduating in 1948; subsequently taught there. He wrote the opera *Sukiléliai (The Rebels;* Vilna, 1960) and *Avarie* (Vilna, 1968); a ballet, *On the Seashore* (Vilna, May 10, 1953); 3 symphonies (1948, 1951, 1965); Concerto for Tenor and Orch. (1954); *African Sketches* for orch. (1961); *Poem-Concerto* for strings (1961); Concerto Grosso (1966); 2 String Quartets (1962, 1966); choruses.

Jyrkiäinen, Reijo, Finnish composer; b. Suistamo, April 6, 1934. He studied composition with Nils-Eric Fougstedt and Joonas Kokkonen at the Sibelius Academy in Helsinki (1956–63), and theory at the Univ. of Helsinki (1958–63); later attended modern music courses at Darmstadt (1962–63) and the electronic sessions at the Bilthoven Radio Studio in Holland (1963). From 1957 to 1966 he was librarian of music recordings at the Finnish Broadcasting Company; taught at the Sibelius Academy (1966–67). In 1972 he became managing director of the Helsinki Philharmonic Orchestra. In his own works, he has pursued advanced experimentation, ranging from classical Schoenbergian dodecaphony to electronics.

WORKS: *5 Dodecaphonic Etudes* for piano (1961); *Frammenti per il septetto d'archi,* for 3 violins, 2 violas, cello and double bass (1962); *Sounds I, II* and *III,* concrete music on tape (1963–66); *Mesto,* for flute, clarinet, guitar and percussion (1963); *For Four,* for violin, clarinet, guitar and percussion (1963); *Contra-*dictions for flute, clarinet, piano, guitar and string quartet (1965); *5 Piano Pieces for Children* (1966); *Idiopostic I* and *II,* electronic music (1963, 1966); *Varianti* for viola and piano (1967).

K

Kàan-Albest, Heinrich, Polish pianist and composer; b. Tarnopol, May 29, 1852; d. Roudná, Bohemia, March 7, 1926. He studied in Prague with Blodek and Skuherský; went with Dvořák to London in 1884; from 1889, taught piano at the Prague Cons.; was its director from 1907-18. He wrote two operas, *Escape* (1895) and *Germinal*, after Zola (1908); two ballets, *Bajaja* and *Olim;* symph. poem *Sakuntala; Frühlings-Eklogen* for orch.; many piano pieces and arrangements.

Kabalevsky, Dmitri, noted Russian composer; b. St. Petersburg, Dec. 30, 1904. When he was 14 years old, his family moved to Moscow; there he received his primary musical education at the Scriabin Music School (1919-25); also studied music theory privately with Gregory Catoire; in 1925 he entered the Moscow Cons. as a student of Miaskovsky in composition and Goldenweiser in piano; in 1932 he was appointed instructor in composition there; in 1939 became full professor. As a pedagogue, he developed effective methods of musical education; in 1962 he was elected head of the Commission of Musical Esthetic Education of Children; in 1969 became president of the Scientific Council of Educational Esthetics in the Academy of Pedagogical Sciences of the U.S.S.R.; in 1972 he received the honorary degree of President of the International Society of Musical Education. As a pianist, composer and conductor he made guest appearances in Europe and America. Kabalevsky's music represents a paradigm of the Russian school of composition in its Soviet period; his melodic writing is marked by broad diatonic lines invigorated by an energetic rhythmic pulse; while adhering to basic tonality, his harmony is apt to be rich in euphonious dissonances. A prolific composer, he writes in all musical genres; in his operas he successfully reflects both the lyrical and the dramatic aspects of the libretto, several of which are based on Soviet subjects faithful to the tenets of Socialist Realism. His instrumental writing is functional, taking into consideration the idiomatic capacities of the instruments.
WORKS: OPERAS: *Colas Breugnon,* after Romain Rolland (Leningrad, Feb. 22, 1938); *At Moscow* (Moscow, Nov. 28, 1943; revised and produced under the title *In the Fire* in Moscow, Nov. 7, 1947); *The Family of Taras* (Leningrad, Nov. 7, 1950); *Nikita Vershinin* (Moscow, Nov. 26, 1955); *The Sisters* (1969); FOR ORCH.: Symph. No. 1 (Moscow, Nov. 9, 1932); Symph. No. 2 (Moscow, Dec. 25, 1934); Symph. No. 3, subtitled *Requiem for Lenin*, with a choral ending (Moscow, Jan. 21, 1934); Symph. No. 4 (Moscow, Oct. 17, 1956); *The Comedians*, orchestral suite from incidental music to a play (1940); *Spring*, symph. poem (1960); *Pathetic Overture* (1960); 3 piano concertos: No. 1 (Moscow, Dec. 11, 1931, composer soloist); No. 2 (Moscow, May 12, 1936); No. 3 (Moscow, Feb. 1, 1953, composer conducting, Vladimir Ashkenazy soloist); Violin Concerto (Leningrad, Oct. 29, 1948); 2 cello concertos: No. 1 (Moscow, March 15, 1949); No. 2 (1964); CHAMBER MUSIC: 2 string quartets (1928, 1945); *20 Simple Pieces* for violin and piano (1965); for piano: 3 piano sonatas (1928, 1945, 1946); 24 Preludes

(1943); many other piano pieces, including 30 children's pieces (1938); *24 Simple Pieces* for children (1944); VOCAL WORKS: *7 Merry Songs* for voice and piano (1945); numerous school songs and choruses; Requiem (Moscow, Feb. 9, 1963); oratorio, *A Letter to the 30th Century* (1970); incidental music for plays; film scores.
BIBLIOGRAPHY: L. Danilevich, *Dmitri Kabalevsky* (Moscow, 1954); G. Abramovsky, *Dmitri Kabalevsky* (Moscow, 1960); L. Danilevich, *Creative Work of D. B. Kabalevsky* (Moscow, 1963); R. V. Glezer, *Kabalevsky* (Moscow, 1969); Y. Korev, *Kabalevsky* (Moscow, 1970).

Kabasta, Oswald, Austrian conductor; b. Mistelbach, Dec. 29, 1896; d. (suicide), Kufstein, Austria, Feb. 6, 1946. He studied at the Vienna Academy of Music and in Klosterneuburg, was choir-director in Florisdorf, and teacher of singing in Viennese high schools. In 1924 he was appointed music director to the Municipal Theater of Baden near Vienna; in 1926, conductor of opera and concert in Graz and guest conductor of the Gesellschaft der Musikfreunde in Vienna; 1931-1937, music director of the Austrian Radio. In 1935 he was appointed director of the Gesellschaft der Musikfreunde. As conductor of the Vienna Radio Orchestra, he toured with it in London (1936), Berlin, Warsaw, Budapest, Amsterdam, etc. He was conductor of the Bruckner Festivals in Linz in 1936 and 1937; in 1938 he succeeded Von Hausegger as conductor of the Munich Philharmonic. Having compromised himself by a close association with the Austrian Nazis, he committed suicide a few months after the conclusion of World War II.

Kabeláč, Miloslav, Czech composer; b. Prague, Aug. 1, 1908. He studied piano, conducting and composition at the Prague Cons. (1928-31); served as music director at the Czech Radio in Prague (1932-54, with the exception of the war years); from 1958 to 1962 he taught composition at the Prague Cons. In 1966 he was elected chairman of the Committee for Non-European Music of the Oriental Society. In his music he followed a moderately advanced idiom, including some devices of 12-tone composition.
WORKS: Sinfonietta (1931); Fantasy for Piano and Orch. (1934); *Little Christmas Cantata* (1937); a cantata to words urging Czechoslovakia to resist Nazi encroachments, *Neustupujte (Do Not Yield!)* for men's chorus, winds and percussion (1939; Prague, Oct. 28, 1945); 2 overtures (1939, 1947); 8 symphonies: No. 1, for strings and percussion (1941-42); No. 2 (1942-46); No. 3, for organ, brass and timpani (1948-57); No. 4, for chamber orch. (1954-58); No. 5, *Dramatica,* for soprano and orch. (1959-60); No. 6, *Concertante,* for clarinet and orch. (1961-62); No. 7, on Old Testament texts, for narrator and orch. (1967-68); No. 8, *Antiphonies,* for soprano, chorus, percussion and organ (1970); *Moravian Lullabies* for soprano and chamber orch. (1951); *Détem (For Children),* suite for orch. (1955); *6 Lullabies* for alto, women's chorus and instrumental ensemble (1955); *Mysterium času (Mystery of Time),* passacaglia for orch. (Prague, Oct. 23, 1957); *3 Melodramas* for narrators and orch. (1957);

Hamletovská improvizace (Hamlet Improvisations) for orch. (1962–63; Prague, May 26, 1964; commemorating the 400th anniversary of Shakespeare's birth); *Zrcadlení (Reflections),* 9 miniatures for orch. (Prague, Feb. 2, 1965); *Tajemství ticha (Euphemias Mysterion)* for soprano and chamber orch. (Warsaw Autumn Festival, Sept. 30, 1965); Wind Sextet (1940); *3 Pieces* for cello and piano (1941); Oboe Sonatina (1955); Ballade for Violin and Piano (1956); Suite for Saxophone and Piano (1959); *8 Inventions* for percussion group (1963; in the form of a ballet, Strasbourg, April 22, 1965); *8 Ricercari* for percussion group (1966–67); *Laments and Smiles,* 8 bagatelles for flute and harp (1969); *Fated Dramas of Man,* for narrator, trumpet, percussion and piano (1975–76); *8 Preludes* for piano (1955–56); *Motifs,* piano cycle (1959); *E Fontibus Bohemicis (From Bohemian Annals),* concrete music (1970–73); choruses; songs.

Kačinkas, Jeronimas, Lithuanian composer and conductor; b. Viduklé, April 17, 1907. He studied with his father, a church organist; then at the State Music School in Klaipeda and at the Cons. of Prague with Jaroslav Křička and Alois Hába. Returning to Lithuania, he became conductor of the Klaipeda Symph. Orch. (1932–38); in 1938 was appointed music director for the Lithuanian Radio in Kaunas; during World War II conducted the Vilna Philharmonic; left Lithuania in 1944; from 1945 to 1949 lived in a Displaced Persons Camp in Augsburg, Germany. In 1949 he settled in the U.S.; he lives mostly in Boston. His music reflects the influences of Scriabin and French Impressionists. Among his works are a trumpet concerto; 2 string quartets; sacred choruses; piano pieces.

Kade, Otto, German musicologist; b. Dresden, May 6, 1819; d. Doberan, near Rostock, July 19, 1900. He studied composition with J. Otto Schneider; also took courses in choral conducting. In 1848 he established in Dresden the singing society "Cäcilia" for the promotion of old church music. In 1860 he became conductor of the court choir in Schwerin. He publ. a number of useful papers dealing with German choral music, among them an *Offizielles Melodienbuch,* and a *Choralbuch* for the Mecklenburg Landeskirche; edited the musical supplements to vol. 1 of Ambros's *Geschichte der Musik* (1881, publ. as vol. 5) and the revised edition of its vol. 3 (1893). His major accomplishment in musical bibliography was the compilation of *Die Musikalien-Sammlung des grossherzoglich Mecklenburg-Schweriner Fürstenhauses aus den letzten zwei Jahrhunderten* (Schwerin, 1893; in 2 vols.; a supplement, *Der Musikalische Nachlass der Frau Erbgrossherzogin Auguste von Mecklenburg-Schwerin,* appeared in 1899). Some of his own compositions are collected in the *Cantional* which he published for the Mecklenburg Landeskirche.

Kadosa, Pál, prominent Hungarian composer and pianist; b. Léva (now Levice, Czechoslovakia), Sept. 6, 1903. He studied composition with Kodály and piano with Arnold Székely at the Academy of Music in Budapest (1921–27); gave piano recitals in Hungary; taught piano at the Fodor Music School in Budapest (1927–43). In 1945 he was appointed prof. of piano at the Academy of Music. He won the Kossuth Prize in 1950 and the Erkel Prize in 1955 and 1962; was made an honorary member of the Royal Academy of Music in London (1967). In his music he combines the elements of the cosmopolitan modern idiom with a strong feeling for Hungarian rhythms and folk-like melodies; in his treatment of these materials, he is closer to the style of Bartók than to that of his teacher Kodály. The lyrical element is as distinctive in his works as the energetic rhythmic factor.

WORKS: an opera, *A huszti kaland (The Adventure of Huszt,* 1949–50; Budapest, Dec. 22, 1951); 5 cantatas: *De amore fatale* (1939–40), *Terjed a fény (Light Is Spreading,* 1949), *Sztálin esküje (Stalin's Oath,* 1949), *A béke katonai (The Soldiers of Peace,* 1950) and *Március fia (Son of March,* 1950); Chamber Symphony (1926); 2 divertimentos for orch. (1933; 1933–34, revised 1960); 8 symphonies: No. 1 (1941–42; Budapest, 1965); No. 2, *Capriccio* (Budapest, 1948); No. 3 (1953–55; Budapest, 1957); No. 4, for string orch. (1958–59; Budapest, 1961); No. 5 (1960–61; Hungarian Radio, 1962); No. 6 (1966; Hungarian Radio, Aug. 19, 1966); No. 7 (1967; Budapest, 1968); No. 8 (1968; Hungarian Radio, 1969); *Partita* for orch. (1943–44); *Morning Ode* for orch. (1945); March, overture (1945); *Honor and Glory,* suite (1951); Suite for Orch. (1954); *Pian e forte,* sonata for orch. (1962); Suite for Small Orch. (1962); Sinfonietta (1974); 4 piano concertos: No. 1 (1931; Amsterdam ISCM Festival, June 9, 1933, composer soloist); No. 2, concertino (1938); No. 3 (1953); No. 4 (1966); 2 violin concertos (1932, revised 1969–70; 1940–41, revised 1956); Concerto for String Quartet and Chamber Orch. (1936); Viola Concertino (1937); 3 string quartets (1934–35, 1936, 1957); Serenade for 10 instruments (1967); solo sonatinas for violin (1923) and cello (1924); Sonatina for Violin and Cello (1923); 2 violin sonatas (1925, revised 1969–70; 1963); Suite for Violin and Piano (1926, revised 1970); 2 string trios (1929–30, 1955); *Partita* for violin and piano (1931); Suite for Solo Violin (1931); Wind Quintet (1954); Piano Trio (1956); *Improvisation* for cello and piano (1957); Flute Sonatina (1961); Violin Sonatina (1962); 3 suites for piano (1921; 1921–23, revised 1970); several piano cycles: *7 Bagatelles* (1923), *8 Epigrams* (1923–24), *5 Sketches* (1931), *6 Hungarian Folksongs* (1934–35), *6 Little Preludes* (1944), *10 Bagatelles* (1956–57), *4 Caprichos* (1961), *Kaleidoscope* (8 pieces, 1966) and *Snapshots* (1971); 4 piano sonatas (1926, revised 1970; 1926–27; 1930; 1959–60); Piano Sonatina (1927); 2-Piano Sonata (1947); Suite for Piano Duet (1955); *3 Radnóti Songs* (1961); *7 Attila József Songs* (1964); folksong arrangements; piano albums for children.

Kaempfert, Max, German violinist and composer; b. Berlin, Jan. 3, 1871; d. Solothurn, June 2, 1941. He studied violin in Paris and Munich; was concertmaster of the Kaim Orch. in Munich (1893–98); in 1899 went to Frankfurt, where he remained most of his life. He wrote an opera, *Der Schatz des Sultans,* in a folk style; a grand opera, *Der tote Gast;* 3 rhapsodies for orch.; chamber music and songs.

Kaffka, Johann Christoph (real name **J. C. Engelmann**), German composer and singer; b. Regensburg,

1754; d. Riga, Jan. 29, 1815. He studied with Riepel; appeared on the stage as a singer and actor in Berlin (1778), Breslau, and Dessau (1800); in 1803, settled in Riga as a bookseller. He wrote a dozen operas, several ballets, 2 oratorios, Masses, vespers, etc.

Kafka, Johann Nepomuk, Bohemian composer; b. Neustadt, May 17, 1819; d. Vienna, Oct. 23, 1886. He composed numerous popular salon pieces (many based on Austrian themes) for the piano.

Kagel, Mauricio, leading composer of the cosmopolitan avant-garde; b. Buenos Aires, Dec. 24, 1931. He studied in Buenos Aires with Juan Carlos Paz and Alfredo Schiuma; also attended courses in philosophy and literature at the Univ. of Buenos Aires. In 1949 he became associated with the Agrupación Nueva Música. From 1949 to 1956 he was choral director at the Teatro Colón. In 1957 he obtained a stipend of the Academic Cultural Exchange with West Germany, and went to Cologne which he made his permanent home. From 1960 to 1966 he was guest lecturer at the International Festival Courses for New Music in Darmstadt; in 1961 and 1963 he gave lectures and demonstrations of modern music in the U.S., and in 1965 was prof. for composition at the State University of New York in Buffalo; in 1967 he was guest lecturer at Academy for Film and Television in Berlin; in 1968 he presented a course in new music in Göteborg, Sweden; in 1969 returned to Cologne as director of the Institute for New Music at the Musikschule in Cologne; was named professor there in 1974. As a composer, Kagel evolved an extremely complex system in which a fantastically intricate and yet wholly rational serial organization of notes, intervals and durations is supplemented by aleatory techniques; some of the latter are derived from linguistic permutations, random patterns of lights and shadows on exposed photographic film, and other seemingly arcane processes. In his hyper-serial constructions, Kagel endeavors to unite all elements of human expression, ultimately aiming at the creation of a universe of theatrical arts in their visual, aural and societal aspects. WORKS: *Palimpsestos* for chorus a cappella (1950); String Sextet (1953); *Traummusik* for instruments and musique concrète (1954); *Anagrama* for speaking chorus, 4 vocalists and chamber ensemble (1958); *Transición I* for electronic sounds (1958); *Transición II* for piano, percussion and two magnetic tapes (1959); *Pandora's Box* for magnetic tape (1961); *Sonant* for electric guitar, harp, double bass and 20 instruments (1961); *Sur scène* for 6 participants in mixed media, with musicians instructed to interfere with actors and singers (concert performance; Radio Bremen, May 6, 1962); *Phonophonie,* 4 melodramas for 2 voices and sound sources (1963); *Composition & Decomposition,* a reading piece (1963); *Diaphonie* for chorus and orch. and slide projections (1964); *Music for Renaissance Instruments* for 23 performers (1966); String Quartet (1967); *Montage* for different sound sources (1967); *Ornithologica Multiplicata* for exotic birds (1968); *Ludwig van,* a surrealistic film score bestrewed with thematic fragments from Beethoven's works (1970; a bicentennial homage to Beethoven); *Staatstheater,* "scenic composition" involv-

ing a ballet for "non-dancers" and orchestrated for a number of household objects, including a chamber pot and medical appurtenances such as a large clyster filled with water held in readiness to administer a rectal enema (Hamburg Staatsoper, April 25, 1971); *Variations ohne Fuge* for orch. (1972); *Con voce* for 3 mute actors (1972); *Mare nostrum,* scenic play (1975); *Kantrimiusik* (phonetic rendition into German of "country music"; 1975). BIBLIOGRAPHY: Dieter Schnebel, *Mauricio Kagel: Musik, Theater, Film* (Cologne, 1970).

Kagen, Sergius, Russian-American pianist and composer; b. St. Petersburg, Aug. 22, 1909; d. New York, March 1, 1964. He went to Berlin in 1921; emigrated to the U.S. in 1925; studied at the Juilliard School of Music, N.Y., graduating in 1930; later joined its faculty. He wrote an opera *Hamlet* (Baltimore, Nov. 9, 1962); piano pieces and vocal works; edited *40 French Songs* (2 vols.; N.Y., 1952).

Kahl, Willi, German musicologist; b. Zabern, Alsace, July 18, 1893; d. Cologne, Oct. 3, 1962. He studied in Freiburg, Munich, and Bonn (Dr. phil., 1919); in 1923, became instructor and librarian at the Univ. of Cologne. WRITINGS: *Das lyrische Klavierstück zu Beginn des 19. Jahrhunderts* (Bonn, 1919); *Musik und Musikleben im Rheinland* (Cologne, 1923); *Herbart als Musiker* (Langensalza, 1936); *Verzeichnis des Schrifttums über Franz Schubert* (Regensburg, 1938); edited a collection, *Lyrische Klavierstücke der Romantik,* Norbert Burgmüller's *Ausgewählte Lieder,* J. A. P. Schulz's *Stücke für Klavier,* G. Benda's sonatinas; compiled the important documentary volume, *Selbstbiographien deutscher Musiker des 18. Jahrhunderts* (Cologne, 1948).

Kähler, Willibald, German conductor and composer; b. Berlin, Jan. 2, 1866; d. Klein-Machnow, Oct. 17, 1938. He was a pupil of Kiel and Herzogenberg at the Hochschule für Musik in Berlin; then occupied various posts as conductor; from 1891 in Mannheim, and from 1906, court conductor at Schwerin; after 1931 lived in retirement at Gauting near Munich. He wrote music for Goethe's *Faust;* symphonic prologue to Kleist's *Der Prinz von Homberg;* choral works; piano pieces, etc.; publ. a guide to Bruckner's 8th Symphony and *Te Deum;* revised the unfinished orchestral scores of some *Lieder* by Hugo Wolf and Weber's *Silvana* (1928).

Kahlert, August Karl Timotheus, German writer on music and composer; b. Breslau, March 5, 1807; d. there, March 29, 1864. He taught at Breslau Univ.; wrote *Blätter aus der Brieftasche eines Musikers* (1832); *Tonleben* (1838); contributed articles to the *Allgemeine musikalische Zeitung* and Dehn's *Caecilia;* also composed songs.

Kahn, Erich Itor, German-American pianist and composer; b. Rimbach, Germany, July 23, 1905; d. New York, March 5, 1956. He studied at the Hoch Cons. in Frankfurt; went to France in 1933; in 1938–39 toured as accompanist of Casals in France and North Africa;

in 1941 emigrated to America; organized the Albeneri Trio (the name being derived from assorted syllables of the first names of the participants, Alexander Schneider, violin, Benar Heifetz, cello, and Erich Kahn, piano). In 1948 he was awarded the Coolidge Medal for eminent service to chamber music. He was held in high esteem as a composer of inventive intellect.

WORKS: Suite for Violin and Piano (1937); *Ciaccona dei tempi di guerra* for piano (40 variations on a 12-tone theme in the bass; 1943); String Quartet (1953); 4 Nocturnes for Voice and Piano (1954); *Symphonies bretonnes* for orch. (1955); *Actus Tragicus* for 10 instruments (Baden-Baden Festival, June 18, 1955).

BIBLIOGRAPHY: Dika Newlin, "In Memoriam: Erich Itor Kahn, Retrospect and Prospect," *American Composers Alliance Bulletin* 3 (1957); R. Leibowitz and K. Wolff, *Erich Itor Kahn, un grand représentant de la musique contemporaine* (Paris, 1958).

Kahn, Otto Hermann, American patron of music; b. Mannheim, Feb. 21, 1867; d. New York, March 29, 1934. He was engaged in the banking profession in London (1888–93); settled in N.Y. in 1893; member of the firm Kahn, Loeb & Co.; became interested in the musical affairs of N.Y. City; from 1907 to his death was on the board of the Metropolitan Opera Co.; was vice president of the N.Y. Philharmonic. He was a brother of **Robert Kahn,** the composer.

BIBLIOGRAPHY: M. J. Matz, *The Many Lives of Otto Kahn* (N.Y., 1963).

Kahn, Robert, German pianist and composer; b. Mannheim, July 21, 1865; d. Biddenden, Kent, May 29, 1951. He studied music with Lachner in Mannheim and with Rheinberger in Munich. In 1885 he went to Berlin, and in 1890 moved to Leipzig where he organized a Ladies' Choral Union which he conducted; in 1893 he was appointed instructor of piano at the Berlin Hochschule für Musik, retiring in 1931. After the advent of the Nazi government in Germany he went to England where he remained until his death. He composed a considerable amount of respectable chamber music and a lot of singable choruses. He was a brother of the banker **Otto Kahn.**

BIBLIOGRAPHY: E. Radecke, *Robert Kahn* (Leipzig, 1894).

Kahnt, Christian Friedrich, German music publisher; b. May 10, 1823; d. Leipzig, June 5, 1897. He was the founder and, till 1886, head of the music publishing firm of C. F. Kahnt at Leipzig and Zwickau; from 1857 publisher, and after 1868, titular editor, of Schumann's *Neue Zeitschrift für Musik.* The firm and the magazine were acquired by Oscar Schwalm ("C. F. Kahnt Nachfolger") in 1886, by Dr. Paul Simon in 1888, and by Alfred Hoffmann in 1903. After Hoffmann's death in 1926, his wife, Maria, directed the business; when she died in 1959, the firm was taken over by her son.

Kahowez, Günter, Austrian composer; b. Vöcklabruck, Dec. 4, 1940. He studied at the Bruckner Cons. in Linz and later at the Vienna Music Academy with Karl Schiske. With neo-classical precepts as

points of departure, he rapidly progressed in the direction of modern serialism.

WORKS: Wind Quintet (1959); String Quartet (1960); *Klangrhythmen* for piano (1962); *Flächengitter* for flute solo (1962); *Megalyse* for electronic instruments (1962); *Duale* for clarinet and guitar (1963); *Schichtungen* for orch. (1963); *Ouverture & Pantomime* for orch. (1964); *Elementalichemie* for cello and percussion (1975).

Kaim, Franz, German impresario; b. Kirchheim unter Tech, near Stuttgart, May 13, 1856; d. Munich, Nov. 17, 1935. Having built a concert hall and organized an orch. in Munich, he established there (1893) the celebrated series of concerts bearing his name, the "Kaimkonzerte," which presented classical works and also new compositions by German composers; the successive conductors were Hans Winderstein (1893), Zumpe (1895), Löwe (1897), Hausegger and Weingartner (1898), Raabe (1903), and Schneevoigt (1904, until the dissolution of the orch. in 1908). Besides the regular symph. concerts, a series of Volkssinfoniekonzerte was given. Immediately after the dissolution of the orch., its members formed the Konzertverein under the direction of Löwe (later under Pfitzner and Hausegger).

Kaiser, Alfred, Belgian-born British composer; b. Brussels, Feb. 29, 1872; d. Bournemouth, Oct. 1, 1917. He studied composition with Bruckner in Vienna and with Foerster in Prague; went to London to live. During World War I he changed his name to **De Keyser** to escape the odium attached to the Kaiser of Germany. Among his works are the operas *Le Billet de Joséphine* (Paris, 1902), *Die schwarze Nina* (Elberfeld, 1905), and *Stella Maris* (Düsseldorf, 1910). He also wrote a symphony, a piano concerto and some chamber music.

Kajanus, Robert, outstanding Finnish conductor; b. Helsingfors, Dec. 2, 1856; d. there, July 6, 1933. He studied at the Helsingfors Cons., and later at the Leipzig Cons., with Reinecke, Richter, and Jadassohn (1877–79); he then went to Paris, where he studied with Svendsen (1879–80); then lived for some time in Dresden. In 1882 he returned to Helsingfors, where he devoted himself to composition and conducting. Kajanus was the earliest champion of the music of Sibelius. In 1900 he was engaged by the French Government to present a concert of Finnish music with the Helsingfors Philharmonic at the World Exposition in Paris. He was also the composer of some orchestral and choral pieces on Finnish themes (symph. poems *Kullervo* and *Aino;* orch. suite *Sommarminnen;* 2 Finnish rhapsodies; piano pieces and songs).

BIBLIOGRAPHY: K. Flodin, *Finska musiker* (in Swedish; Helsingfors, 1900); Yrjö Suomalainen, *Robert Kajanus* (Helsingfors, 1952).

Kalabis, Viktor, Czech composer; b. Červený Kostelec, Feb. 27, 1923. He studied music theory with J. Řídký at the Academy of Arts in Prague; after the end of the war in 1945 attended classes of E. Hlobil at the Prague Cons.; from 1953 to 1972 he served as music programmer on the Radio Prague. In his early works

he adhered to traditional methods of composition, but later adopted modified serial procedures.
WORKS: Cello Concerto (1951); Piano Concerto (1954); Symph. No. 1 (1957); Violin Concerto (1958); Symph. No. 2 (*Sinfonia Pacis;* 1960); *Symphonic Variations* (1964); Concerto for Orch. (1966); Symph. No. 3 (1971); Symph. No. 4 (1972); Trumpet Concerto (1973); Concerto for Harpsichord and String Orch. (1975); Divertimento, for flute, oboe, clarinet, horn and bassoon (1952); *Classical Nonet* (1956); 2 string quartets (1949, 1962); Wind Quintet (1952); Cello Sonata (1968); Sonata for Clarinet and Piano (1969); Variations for Horn and Piano (1969); Sonata for Trombone and Piano (1970); Nonet No. 2 (1977).

Kalafati, Vassili, Russian composer and pedagogue of Greek extraction; b. Eupatoria, Crimea, Feb. 10, 1869; d. Leningrad, during the siege, Jan. 30, 1942. He studied at the St. Petersburg Cons. with Rimsky-Korsakov, graduating in 1899; subsequently was appointed to the teaching staff. A musician of thorough knowledge of every aspect of music theory, he was held in great esteem by his colleagues and students; Rimsky-Korsakov sent Stravinsky to Kalafati for additional training in harmony. As a composer, Kalafati faithfully continued the traditions of the Russian National School; many of his works were published by Belaieff; he wrote a symphony, a piano quintet, 2 piano sonatas and a number of songs, all set in impeccably euphonious harmonies.

Kalbeck, Max, German music historian; biographer of Brahms; b. Breslau, Jan. 4, 1850; d. Vienna, May 4, 1921. He studied at Munich Univ.; in 1875 went to Breslau, where he wrote music criticism; his collected articles were publ. as *Wiener Opernabende* (1881), *Gereimtes und Ungereimtes* (1885), and *Opernabende* (2 vols., 1898); also *Humoresken und Phantasien* (1896). His most important publication was the monumental biography *Johannes Brahms* (8 vols., 1904-14). He also edited Brahms' correspondence with Hanslick and E. von Herzogenberg (2 vols., 1906), with P. J. and Fritz Simrock, and with Jos. Widmann; and the correspondence of Keller-Heyse (1918).

Kalhauge, Sophus Viggo Harald, Danish composer and teacher; b. Copenhagen, Aug. 12, 1840; d. there, Feb. 19, 1905. He studied with P. Heise, C. Rongsted, and J. C. Gebauer; also studied in Germany, Switzerland, and Italy; returned to Copenhagen as teacher of piano and singing.
WORKS: the operas *Zouavens Hjemkomst* (1868), *Paa Krigsfod* (1880), and *Mantillen* (1889); *An den Frühling,* for soli, chorus, and orch.; piano pieces and songs.

Kálik, Václav, Czech composer; b. Opava, Oct. 18, 1891; d. Prague, Nov. 18, 1951. He studied with J. Novotný and V. Novák at the Charles Univ. in Prague; later with J. Suk at the Master School there; was active as a choral conductor and concert pianist. Among his works are 3 operas: *A Spring Morning* (1933; Olomouc, 1943), *Lásky div* (*Love's Miracle,* 1942-43; Liberec, Nov. 20, 1950) and *Consecration of Youth*

(1946-48); *Fantazie* for orch. (1915); *Moře* (*The Sea*), symph. poem (1924); 2 symphonies: No. 1, *Mírová (Peace),* for soprano and orch. (1927) and No. 2 (1941-43); Prelude for Orch. (1931); *Venezia* for string orch. (1932); *Intermezzo* for tenor, violin and piano (1913); *Evil Love* for soprano, violin and piano (1919); Violin Sonata (1919); *Pražské obrazy* (*Prague Pictures*) for male chorus (1949-50) and several piano pieces.

Kalinnikov, Vassili, Russian composer; b. Voin, near Mtzensk, Jan. 13, 1866; d. Yalta, Crimea, Jan. 11, 1901. He studied in Orel; in 1884 he enrolled in the Moscow Cons., but had to leave it a year later because of inability to pay; he then studied the bassoon at the Music School of the Moscow Philharmonic Society, which provided free tuition. He earned his living by playing bassoon in theater orchestras; also studied composition with A. Ilyinsky and Blaramberg. Still as a student, he composed his first work, a symph. poem, *The Nymphs* (Moscow, Dec. 28, 1889); later wrote another symph. poem, *The Cedar and the Palm;* the overture and entr'actes for *Tsar Boris,* and a prelude to the opera *In the Year 1812.* In 1895 he completed his most successful work, Symphony in G minor (Kiev, Feb. 20, 1897); a second symphony, in A (Kiev, Mar. 12, 1898), was not as successful; he also wrote a cantata, *John of Damascus;* a *Ballade* for women's chorus and orch.; songs, and piano pieces. Owing to his irregular habits and undernourishment, he contracted tuberculosis, and was sent to Yalta for treatment; there he died a few months later. Kalinnikov possessed a fine lyric talent; there is a definite trend in Russia towards greater recognition of his music. Several of his manuscript works (Serenade for Strings; the overture *Bylina,* etc.) were published on the 50th anniversary of his death (1951).
BIBLIOGRAPHY: V. Paskhalov, *V. S. Kalinnikov, Life and Works* (Moscow, 1938; greatly enlarged ed., 1951); a collection of his letters and other materials was publ. in Moscow, in 2 vols., in 1959.

Kalisch, Paul, German tenor; b. Berlin, Nov. 6, 1855; d. St. Lorenz am Mondsee, Salzkammergut, Austria, Jan. 27, 1946. He studied architecture; then went to Milan where he took voice lessons with Leoni and Lamperti; he sang with considerable success in Italy (Milan, Rome, Florence); then at the Munich Opera and in Berlin; in 1887 he sang the Wagner roles at the Metropolitan Opera House with **Lilli Lehmann,** whom he married in New York the following year. At the first Paris performance of *Tristan und Isolde* (1904) he and his wife sang the title roles; they were later separated (though not legally divorced); after Lilli Lehmann's death in 1929, he lived on her estate in Salzkammergut, remaining there until his death at the age of 90.

Kalischer, Alfred, German writer on music; b. Thorn, March 4, 1842; d. Berlin, Oct. 8, 1909. After taking the degree of Dr. phil. at Leipzig, he studied music with Burgel and Bohmer at Berlin, where he edited the *Neue Berliner Musikzeitung* (from 1873). Of special value are his writings about Beethoven; he also published philosophical works, poems, and dramas.

WRITINGS: *Lessing als Musikästhetiker* (1889); *Die "Unsterbliche Geliebte" Beethovens* (1891); *Die Macht Beethovens* (1903); *Beethoven und seine Zeitgenossen* (4 vols., 1908: I, *Beethoven und Berlin;* II and III, *Beethovens Frauenkreis;* IV, *Beethoven und Wien*). He also edited *Neue Beethovenbriefe* (1902); *Beethovens sämtliche Briefe* (5 vols., 1906–08; in English, 1909).

Kalkbrenner, Christian, German composer and writer; father of **Friedrich W. M. Kalkbrenner;** b. Minden, Hannover, Sept. 22, 1755; d. Paris, Aug. 10, 1806. He studied piano with Becker and violin with Rodewald in Kassel; was choirmaster at the court of the Queen in Berlin (1788), then in the court of Prince Heinrich at Rheinsberg (1790–96); in 1797, went to Naples; in 1798 he became choirmaster at the Paris Opéra. At the Opéra he produced his opera *Olimpie* (Dec. 18, 1798); also some pasticcios from music by Mozart and Haydn; he further wrote 2 symphonies, a piano concerto, several piano sonatas, *Theorie der Tonkunst* (1789), and *Kurzer Abriss der Geschichte der Tonkunst* (1792).

Kalkbrenner, Friedrich Wilhelm Michael, celebrated German pianist; b. near Kassel, between Nov. 2 and Nov. 8, 1785; d. Deuil, Seine-et-Oise, June 10, 1849. He was taught by his father, **Christian Kalkbrenner.** In 1798 he was enrolled at the Paris Cons., where he studied with Adam (piano) and Catel (harmony), taking first prizes in 1801. From 1803 he studied counterpoint with Albrechtsberger in Vienna; appeared as a concert pianist in Berlin, Munich (1805), and Stuttgart; also in Paris, with great success, in 1806. As a teacher, too, he was in great vogue. The years 1814–23 he spent in London; in 1818 he took up Logier's newly invented Chiroplast, simplified it, and applied it practically. After a German tour in 1823 with the harpist Dizi, Kalkbrenner settled (1824) in Paris as a partner in the Pleyel piano factory (the future Mme. Camilla Pleyel was one of his pupils). He revisited Germany in 1833 and Belgium in 1836. Kalkbrenner was inordinately vain of the success of his method of teaching, which aimed at the independent development of the fingers and wrist; his practical method of octave playing became a standard of modern piano teaching. He likewise developed left-hand technique, and a proper management of the pedals. As a player, his technique was smooth and well-rounded, his fingers supple and of equal strength, and his tone full and rich; his style, while fluent and graceful, lacked emotional power. His numerous études (among them several for left hand alone) are interesting and valuable. Chopin took some advice from him in Paris, but did not become his pupil despite Kalkbrenner's urging to do so.
WORKS: 4 piano concertos (the last, op. 125, for 2 pianos); Piano Septet, with strings and two horns; Quintet, for piano, clarinet, horn, bassoon, and double bass; 2 piano sextets; piano quintets; 3 piano quartets; 7 piano trios; 15 sonatas; also rondos, fantasies, variations, caprices, etc., of a light character; *Méthode pour apprendre le pianoforte à l'aide du guide-mains* (1830); *Traité d'harmonie du pianiste* (1849).
BIBLIOGRAPHY: "Memoir of Mr. Frederick Kalk-

brenner," *Quarterly Mus. Magazine and Review* (1824); L. Boivin, *Kalkbrenner* (Paris, 1840).

Kallenberg, Siegfried Garibaldi, German composer; b. Schachen, near Lindau, Nov. 3, 1867; d. Munich, Feb. 9, 1944. He studied at the Cons. of Stuttgart with Faisst; from 1892, taught at Stettin, Königsberg, and Hannover. In 1910 he settled in Munich; a Kallenberg Society was established there in 1921 to promote his creative output. As a composer, Kallenberg was inspired by neo-Romanticism; in some of his works there are touches of Impressionism; his absorption in symbolic subjects brought him into a kinship with the Expressionist school in Germany. Apart from works on exotic subjects, he wrote music in a traditional style; he was particularly strong in choral polyphony.
WORKS: operas: *Sun Liao, Das goldene Tor,* and *Die lustigen Musikanten;* choral works: *90th Psalm, Germania an ihre Kinder,* Requiem, *Den Gefallenen, Eine kleine Passionmusik, Eine Pfingstmusik;* 3 symphonies; *Impressionen,* for orch.; *Konzertante Fantasie,* for piano and orch.; about 10 chamber works; 3 piano sonatas, a set of *Miniaturen* for piano; and some 300 songs. He wrote monographs on Richard Strauss (Leipzig, 1926) and Max Reger (Leipzig, 1930).

Kalliwoda, Johann Wenzel, famous Bohemian violinist and composer; b. Prague, Feb. 21, 1801; d. Karlsruhe, Dec. 3, 1866. He studied at the Prague Cons. with Pixis (1811–17); played in the Prague Orch. (1817–23). In 1823 he became conductor of Prince Fürstenberg's orch. in Donaueschingen; there he spent 30 years, eventually retiring to Karlsruhe. He enjoyed an enviable reputation; some of his music was highly praised by Schumann.
WORKS: 2 operas, *Blanda* (Prague, Nov. 29, 1827) and *Prinzessin Christine* (1827); 10 Masses; 7 symphonies; 14 overtures and 13 fantasias for orch.; Violin Concerto; Concerto for 2 Violins; 7 concertinos; 3 string quartets; 3 string trios, and a variety of solos for violin; also choruses, duets, and songs.
BIBLIOGRAPHY: K. Strunz, *J. W. Kalliwoda* (Vienna, 1910).

Kalliwoda, Wilhelm, German pianist and composer; son of **Johann Wenzel Kalliwoda;** b. Donaueschingen, July 19, 1827; d. Karlsruhe, Sept. 8, 1893. He studied with Hauptmann in Leipzig; also took some lessons from Mendelssohn; wrote piano pieces and songs; was also a reputable conductor.

Kallmann, Helmut, Canadian librarian and musicologist; b. Berlin, Aug. 7, 1922. He studied music with his father; left Germany in 1939 for London. In 1940 he was sent to Canada; was interned in refugee camps; upon release took music courses at the Univ. of Toronto, graduating in 1949. In 1951 he became music librarian for the Canadian Broadcasting Corporation. In 1970 he was appointed Chief of Music Division of the National Library of Canada in Ottawa. He publ. a valuable *Catalogue of Canadian Composers* (Toronto, 1952) and *A History of Music in Canada 1534–1914* (Toronto, 1960); collaborated in various publications dealing with Canadian composers.

Kallstenius, Edvin, Swedish composer; b. Filipstad, Aug. 29, 1881; d. Stockholm, Nov. 22, 1967. He first studied science at Lund Univ. (1898–1903); then took courses in music at the Leipzig Cons. (1903–07); returning to Stockholm he became music critic of the *Svenska Dagbladet;* was a music librarian at Radio Sweden (1928–46), a board member of the Society of Swedish Composers (1932–61). In his early works he followed the romantic traditions of Scandinavian music; but later turned to advanced modern techniques, including explicit application of dodecaphonic configurations.

WORKS: FOR ORCH.: *Scherzo fugato* for small orch. (1907, revised 1923); *Sista Striden,* dramatic overture (1908); *En serenad i sommarnatten (A Serenade in the Summer Night,* 1918); *Sinfonia concertata* for piano and orch. (1922); 4 sinfoniettas (1923; 1946; *Dodicitonica,* 1956; *Semi-seriale,* 1958); 5 symphonies (1926, revised 1941; 1935; 1948; 1954; *Sinfonia su temi 12-tonici,* 1960); *Dalarapsodi* (1931); *Dalslandsrapsodi* (1936); *Romantico,* overture (1938); *Högtid och fest,* trilogy (1940); *Musica gioconda* for strings (1942); *Cavatina* for viola and orch. (1943); *Passacaglia enarmonica* (1943); *Kraus-variationer* (1947); *Sonata concertate* for cello and orch. (1951); *Musica Sinfonica* for strings (1953; full orchestral version, 1959); *Nytt vin i gamla läglar (New Wine in Old Bottles)* for small orch. (1954); *Choreographic Suite* (1957); *Prologo seriale* (1966). Vocal works: *När vi dö (When Mankind Perishes),* requiem for chorus and orch. (1919); *Sångoffer (Song Offering),* cantata for baritone and orch. (1944); *Stjärntändningen* for chorus and orch. (1949); *Hymen, o, Hymenaios* for soli, chorus and orch. (1955). CHAMBER MUSIC: 8 string quartets (1904; 1905; 1913; *Divertimento alla serenata,* 1925; 1945; 1953; *Dodecatonica,* 1957; 1961); Cello Sonata (1908); Violin Sonata (1909); Clarinet Quintet (1930); Suite for winds and percussion (1938); Wind Quintet (1943); *Trio Divertente* for flute, violin and viola (1950); *Piccolo trio seriale* for flute, English horn and clarinet (1956); *Trio svagante* for clarinet, horn and cello (1959); solo sonatas for cello (1961), flute (1962), and violin (1965); *Lyric Suite* for flute, saxophone and cello (1962); String Trio (1965).

Kálmán, Emmerich (Imre), Hungarian composer of light opera; b. Siófok, Oct. 24, 1882; d. Paris, Oct. 30, 1953. He studied with Kössler in Budapest; won the Imperial Composition Prize (1907). Settling in Vienna, he produced a great number of tuneful and successful operettas; in 1938 he left Vienna; was in Paris until 1940; then came to America; lived in New York and Hollywood; in 1949 went again to Europe.

WORKS: He made his debut as composer with a symph. scherzo *Saturnalia,* performed by the Budapest Philharmonic Orch. (Feb. 29, 1904); later dedicated himself exclusively to the composition of operettas in the Viennese style. His first success was with *Ein Herbstmanöver* (first performed in Hungarian, Budapest, Feb. 22, 1908; performed in N.Y. in the same year as *The Gay Hussars*); his other popular operettas were *Gold gab ich für Eisen* (Vienna, Oct. 16, 1914; N.Y., Dec. 6, 1916 as *Her Soldier Boy*), *Fräulein Susi* (Budapest, Feb. 23, 1915; English and American productions as *Miss Springtime*), *Die Csardasfürstin*

(Vienna, Nov. 17, 1915; in England as *Gypsy Princess;* in America as *The Riviera Girl*), *Gräfin Mariza* (Vienna, Feb. 28, 1924), and *Die Zirkusprinzessin (Circus Princess;* Vienna, March 26, 1926). The following were moderately successful: *Der gute Kamerad* (first version of *Gold gab ich für Eisen;* Vienna, Oct. 10, 1911); *Der kleine König* (Vienna, Nov. 27, 1912); *Die Faschingsfee* (Vienna, Jan. 31, 1917); *Die Bajadere* (Vienna, Dec. 23, 1921); *Golden Dawn* (N.Y., Nov. 30, 1927); *Die Herzogin von Chicago* (Vienna, April 6, 1928); *Ronny* (Berlin, Dec. 22, 1931); *Kaiserin Josephine* (Zürich, Jan. 18, 1936); *Marinka* (N.Y., July 18, 1945). His last work, *Arizona Lady,* was performed posthumously in Bern in 1954.

BIBLIOGRAPHY: J. Bistron, *Emmerich Kálmán* (Vienna, 1932); R. Oesterreicher, *Emmerich Kálmán* (Vienna, 1954); V. Kálmán, *Mein Leben mit Emmerich Kálmán* (Bayreuth, 1966).

Kalmár, László, Hungarian composer and music editor; b. Budapest, Oct. 19, 1931. He studied composition with Ervin Major and Farkas; in 1957 was appointed Editor of the Editio Musica Budapest.

WORKS: a cantata *Soldiers Weep at Night,* after Quasimodo (1962); *4 Canons* for piano (1966); *Symmetriae* for string orch. (1966); Trio for flute, marimba and guitar (1968); *3 Monologos:* No. 1 for solo guitar (1968), No. 2 for solo violin (1973) and No. 3 for solo flute (1973); *Toccata concertante* for piano and string orch. (1968–70); Flute Sonata (1970–71); *Triangoli* for clarinet, horn, harp, violin and cello (1970–71); *Distichon* for piano, harp and percussion (1970–71); *Memoriale* for chorus, percussion and string orch. (1969–71); *Cicli* for 18 strings (1971); *Cantus* for 2 contraltos, clarinet, cello and harp (1969–72); *2 Duets* for 2 Trumpets (1972); Quartet for English horn, viola, vibraphone and harpsichord (1972); String Trio (1972); *Combo* for guitar, conga and double bass (1971–73); *Sotto voce* for harmonium, vibraphone and harp (1973); *Sereno* for cello and harp (1974–75).

Kalniņš, Alfreds, Latvian composer; b. Zehsis, Aug. 23, 1879; d. Riga, Dec. 23, 1951; studied at the St. Petersburg Cons. with Homilius (organ) and Liadov (composition); was organist at various Lutheran churches in Dorpat, Libau, and Riga; also played organ recitals in Russia. While in Riga, he was active as teacher and composer. From 1927 till 1933 he lived in New York; then returned to Latvia and settled in Riga.

WORKS: the operas *Banuta* (first national Latvian opera; Riga, May 29, 1920); *Salinieki (The Islanders;* Riga, 1925); *Dzimtenes Atmoda (The Nation's Awakening;* Riga, Sept. 9, 1933); symph. poem, *Latvia;* piano pieces; some 100 choruses; about 200 songs; arrangements of Latvian folksongs (publ. in Riga).

BIBLIOGRAPHY: J. Vitolins, *Alfreds Kalniņš* (in Latvian; Riga, 1968).

Kalniņš, Janis, Latvian composer and conductor; son of **Alfreds Kalniņš;** b. Riga, Nov. 2, 1904. He studied in Riga with Vitols and in Leipzig with H. Abendroth; was conductor at the Latvian National Theater in Riga (1924–33), and at the Riga Opera House (1933–44). In 1948 he settled in Canada. From 1962 to 1968 he conducted the New Brunswick Symphony.

WORKS: *Hamlet*, opera (Riga, Feb. 17, 1936); 3 symphonies: No. 1 (1939-44); No. 2, *Symphony of the Beatitudes*, with chorus (1953); No. 3 (1972-73); Violin Concerto (1945-46); *Theme and Variations* for clarinet, horn and orch. (1963); String Quartet (1948); choruses; songs.

Kalomiris, Manolis, distinguished Greek composer; b. Smyrna, Turkey, Dec. 26, 1883; d. Athens, April 3, 1962. He studied piano with A. Sturm and composition with Herman Grädener at the Vienna Cons. (1901-06); then went to Russia, where he taught piano at a private school in Kharkov. In 1910 he settled in Greece; was instructor of the Athens School of Music (1911-19) and founder of the Hellenic Cons. of Athens (1919-26). In 1926 he founded the Cons. of Athens; was its director until 1948. As a music educator, he was greatly esteemed in Greece; two generations of Greek composers were his pupils. Kalomiris was the protagonist of Greek nationalism in music; almost all of his works are based on Greek folksong patterns, and many are inspired by Hellenic subjects. In his harmonies and instrumentation he followed the Russian school of composition, with a considerable influx of lush Wagnerian sonorities. His catalogue of works, published in Athens in 1964 lists 222 opus numbers; he also brought out several text books on harmony, counterpoint, and orchestration.
WORKS: OPERAS: *O Protomastoras* (*Master-Builder*), to a libretto by Nikos Kazantzakis, the first opera by a Greek composer on a native subject (Athens, March 24, 1916); *Mother's Ring*, music drama (1917); *Anatoli* (*The Orient*), musical fairy tale, to a libretto by Kalomiris, after Cambyssis (1945-48); *The Shadowy Waters*, opera to a libretto after Yeats (1950-52); *Constantin Palaeologus*, music legend after a story by Kazantzakis (Athens, Aug. 12, 1962); FOR ORCH: *Greek Suite* (1907); *The Olive Tree* for women's chorus and orch. (1909); *Iambs and Anapests*, suite (1914); *Valor Symphony* for chorus and orch. (1920); *Greek Rhapsody* for piano and orch. (orchestrated by Gabriel Pierné and conducted by him for the first time in Paris, April 3, 1926); *Island Pictures* for violin and orch. (1928); *Symphony of the Kind People* for mezzo-soprano, chorus and orch. (1931); *3 Greek Dances* (1934); Piano Concerto (1935); *At the Ossios Loukàs Monastery* for narrator and orch. (1937); *Triptych* (1940); *Minas the Rebel*, tone poem (1940); *The Death of the Courageous Woman*, tone poem (1945); Concertino for violin and orch. (1955); *Palamas Symphony* for chorus and orch. to texts by the Greek poet Palamas (Athens, Jan. 22, 1956); CHAMBER MUSIC: Piano Quintet, with soprano (1912); String Trio (1921); *Quartet quasi fantasia* for harp, flute, English horn and viola (1921); Violin Sonata (1948); FOR PIANO: *Sunrise* (1902); *3 Ballads* (1906); *For Greek Children* (1910); *2 Rhapsodies* (1921); *5 Preludes* (1939); choruses; songs.

Kamburov, Ivan, Bulgarian writer on music; b. Leskovec, Oct. 8, 1883; d. Sofia, Jan. 23, 1955. He studied music with Max Reger and Krehl at the Leipzig Cons.; 1910-14, high school teacher at Plovdiv, Bulgaria; 1922-24 and 1929-30, traveled for scientific research purposes.

WRITINGS: (in Bulgarian): *Bulgarian Music* (1926); *Operatic Art* (1926); *Music and Nation* (1932); *Illustrated Music Dictionary*; *Music for All* (Sofia, 1934); *Polish Music* (Sofia, 1939); *Yugoslav Music* (Sofia, 1940); *Bulgarian Folksongs* (Sofia, 1941); *Dvořák* (Sofia, 1941).

Kamensky, Alexander, Russian pianist; b. Geneva, Switzerland (of Russian parentage), Dec. 12, 1900; d. Leningrad, Nov. 7, 1952. The family returned to Russia early in the century, and Kamensky studied piano at the Petrograd Cons., graduating in 1923. He developed an energetic career as a concert pianist; did not interrupt his activities even during the siege of Leningrad in 1941-42, when he played almost 500 recitals under the most dangerous conditions. In his programs he featured many works by Soviet composers and also by modern Western music masters, including Schoenberg and Stravinsky. In 1934 he was appointed prof. of piano of the Leningrad Cons. He made a number of transcriptions for piano of selections from Russian operas.
BIBLIOGRAPHY: A. Bushen, "A Pianist's Heroism," in his book, *Music on the Fronts of the Great Patriotic Wars* (Moscow, 1970, pp. 217-32).

Kamieński, Lucian, Polish composer; b. Gniezno, Jan. 7, 1885; d. Thorn, July 27, 1964. He studied composition with Max Bruch in Berlin; musicology with Kretzschmar and Johannes Wolf; Dr. phil. for his dissertation, *Die Oratorien von J. A. Hasse* (1910). He then was music critic at Königsberg (until 1919); in 1920 appointed instructor at the Music Academy in Poznan; taught musicology at the Univ. of Poznan. In 1939 he was forced to leave his post; returning to Poznan after 1945, he established himself as a private teacher.
WORKS: 2 comic operas, *Tabu* (Königsberg, April 9, 1917) and *Dami i huzary* (Poznan, Oct. 2, 1938); *Sinfonia paschalis* (1928); *Silesia sings*, a symph. sketch (1929); Violin Sonata; several piano suites on Polish themes; an album of 60 workers' songs to his own words (Berlin, 1905-10), which he issued under the name **Dolega-Kamieński.**

Kamieński, Mathias, earliest composer of Polish opera; b. Ödenburg, Hungary, Oct. 13, 1734; d. Warsaw, Jan. 25, 1821. He studied composition in Vienna, and settled in Warsaw as a teacher. On May 11, 1778, his first opera, *Nędza uszczęśliwiona* (*Poverty Made Happy*), was produced in Warsaw and enthusiastically received; he produced 4 more Polish operas, and also wrote a ballad opera, *Zośka* (Warsaw, Jan. 21, 1781); a cantata for the unveiling of the Sobieski monument (1788), Masses, offertories, and polonaises.

Kaminski, Heinrich, eminent German composer; b. Tiengen, Baden, July 4, 1886; d. Ried, Bavaria, June 21, 1946. He studied at Heidelberg Univ. with Wolfrum and in Berlin with Kaun, Klatte, and Juon; taught a master class at the Berlin Academy of Music (1930-32). In 1933 he settled in Ried, where he remained to the end of his life. His writing is strictly polyphonic and almost rigid in form; the religious and mystic character of his sacred music stems from his family origins (he was the son of a clergyman of Polish extraction); the chief influences in his work were Bach and Bruckner. Interest in his music was enhanced after his death by posthumous editions of his unpublished works.

WORKS: an opera, *Jürg Jenatsch* (Dresden, April 27, 1929); a music drama for narrator and orch., *Das Spiel vom König Aphelius* (his last work, completed in 1946; produced posthumously, Göttingen, Jan. 29, 1950); a Passion, after an old French mystery play (1920); many choral works: *69th Psalm* (1914), *Introitus und Hymnus* (1919), *Magnificat* (1925), *Der Mensch*, motet (1926), *Die Erde*, motet (1928), etc.; for orch.: Concerto Grosso for Double Orch. (1922), *Dorische Musik* (1933), Piano Concerto (Berlin, 1937), *In Memoriam Gabrielae*, for orch., contralto, and solo violin (1940), *Tanzdrama* (1942); chamber music: Quartet for clarinet, viola, cello, and piano (1912), 2 string quartets (1913 and 1916), Quintet for clarinet, horn, violin, viola, and cello (1924), *Music for 2 Violins and Harpsichord* (1931), *Hauskonzert* (1941), *Ballade* for horn and piano (1943); organ works: Toccata (1923), *Chorale-Sonata* (1926), 3 Chorale Preludes (1928), Toccata and Fugue (1939); piano works: *Klavierbuch* (1934), *10 kleine Übungen für das polyphone Klavierspiel* (1935); songs: *Brautlied* for soprano and organ (1911), *Cantiques bretons* (1923), *3 geistliche Lieder* for soprano, violin, and clarinet (1924), *Triptychon* for alto and organ (1930), *Lied eines Gefangenen* (1936), *Weihnachtsspruch* (1938), *Hochzeitsspruch* for 2 altos and organ (1940), *Dem Gedächtnis eines verwundeten Soldaten* for 2 sopranos and piano (1941); folksong arrangements.

BIBLIOGRAPHY: S. Günther, "Heinrich Kaminski," *Die Musik* XXII/7; E. Krieger, "Heinrich Kaminski," *Zeitschrift für Musik* (1933); K. Schleifer, *Heinrich Kaminski* (Kassel, 1945); K. Schleifer and R. Schwarz-Stilling, *Heinrich Kaminski: Werkverzeichnis* (Kassel, 1947); I. Samson, *Das Vokalschaffen von Heinrich Kaminski, mit Ausnahme der Opern* (Frankfurt, 1956).

Kaminski, Joseph, Israeli violinist and composer; b. Odessa, Russia, Nov. 17, 1903; d. Gedera, Israel, Oct. 14, 1972. He studied in Warsaw, Berlin, and Vienna; in 1935, went to Palestine and settled in Tel Aviv; was concertmaster of the Israel Symph. Orch. there; traveled with this orch. on its tour in the U.S. in 1951.

WORKS: *Concertino* for trumpet and orch.: (Tel Aviv, May 5, 1941); *Ballad*, for harp and chamber orch. (Tel Aviv, Feb. 2, 1946); Violin Concerto (1949); Symphonic Overture (1960).

Kämpf, Karl, German organist and composer; b. Berlin, Aug. 31, 1874; d. Mönchengladbach, Nov. 4, 1950. He was a pupil of F. E. Koch; became a professional performer on the harmonium; in 1925, was appointed conductor of the choral society "Liedertafel" in Mönchengladbach. He wrote several symph. marches on literary subjects: *Hiawatha, Aus baltischen Landen, Andersens Märchen,* etc.; also a choral symph. in 6 movements, *Die Macht des Liedes;* piano works; various pieces for the harmonium, etc.

BIBLIOGRAPHY: J. Hagemann-Bonn, *Karl Kämpf* (Leipzig, 1907).

Kamu, Okko, Finnish violinist and conductor; b. Helsinki, March 7, 1946. He studied violin at the Sibelius Academy in Helsinki under Onni Suhonen; at the age of 23 he won the international competition for conductors arranged by the Herbert von Karajan Foundation; in 1971 was appointed conductor with the Finnish Radio Symphony Orchestra.

Kandler, Franz Sales, Austrian writer on music; b. Klosterneuburg, Aug. 23, 1792; d. Baden, near Vienna, Sept. 26, 1831. As a boy he sang in the court choir in Vienna; studied with Albrechtsberger, Salieri, and Gyrowetz. He was an Imperial military draughtsman; when ordered to Italy (1815–26), he pursued the study of Italian music and its history as an avocation. He publ. *Cenni storico-critici intorno alla vita ed alle opere del celebre compositore Giovanni Adolfo Hasse, detto il Sassone* (1820); *Über das Leben und die Werke des G. Pierluigi da Palestrina, genannt der Fürst der Musik* (1834); and *Cenni storico-critici sulle vicende e lo stato attuale della musica in Italia* (1836).

BIBLIOGRAPHY: L. Schiedermair, "Venezianer Briefe F. S. Kandlers," in *Riemann-Festschrift* (Leipzig, 1909).

Kanitz, Ernst, Austrian-American composer; b. Vienna, April 9, 1894; d. Menlo Park, California, April 7, 1978. He changed his first name to Ernest in order to distinguish himself from a homonymous concert manager in Vienna. He studied with Richard Heuberger (1912–14) and with Franz Schreker (1914–20). In 1922 he joined the staff of the Neues Konservatorium in Vienna; after the *Anschluss* of Austria in 1938 he emigrated to the U.S.; he taught music theory in various American colleges, among them at the Univ. of Southern California (1945–59) and at Marymount College in Palos Verdes, Calif. (1960–64).

WORKS: *Heitere Ouvertüre* (1918); an oratorio *Das Hohelied* (1921); a radio cantata *Zeitmusik* (1931); *Dance Sonata* for flute, clarinet, trumpet, bassoon and piano (1932); Concertino for Theremin and Orch. (1938); *Quintettino* for piano and wind instruments (1945); sonata for violin and cello (1947); *Intermezzo Concertante* for saxophone and orch. (1948); *Divertimento* for Viola and Cello (1949); Concerto Grosso (1949); *Notturno* for flute, violin and viola (1950); String Trio (1951); *Sonata breve* for violin, cello and piano (1952); *Sonata Californiana* for alto saxophone and piano (1952); 1-act opera *Kumana* (1953); Sonata for Cello Unaccompanied (1956); *Room No. 12* and *Royal Auction,* a pair of 1-act operas (Los Angeles, Feb. 26, 1958); Sonatina for Viola and Piano (1958); *The Lucky Dollar,* an opera (1959); Suite for Brass Quintet (1960); *Perpetual,* an opera (Los Angeles, April 26, 1961); *Cantata 1961* for mixed chorus and 2 pianos (1961); *Visions at Midnight,* opera-cantata (Los Angeles, Feb. 26, 1964); Bassoon Concerto (San Francisco, April 8, 1964); *Sinfonia Seria* (St. Louis, Oct. 17, 1964); Symph. No. 2 (1965; San Francisco, Dec. 11, 1968); *Little Concerto* for unaccompanied saxophone (Chicago, Dec. 15, 1970). He also publ. *A Counterpoint Manual: Fundamental Techniques of Polyphonic Music Writing* (Boston, 1948).

Kann, Hans, Austrian pianist and composer; b. Vienna, Feb. 14, 1927. He studied piano with A. Göllner; composition with Pollnaur. After the end of World War II, he gave a series of piano recitals in Europe; won prizes at piano competitions in Geneva, Munich, and Vienna. He taught at the Academy of Music in Vienna (1950–52); then taught piano at the Univ. of Arts in Tokyo, Japan (1955–58). Returning to Europe, he gave courses in advanced piano techniques at the Institute of New Music in Darmstadt (1963–69); published several collections of piano exercises.

Kanner, Jerome Herbert, American violinist, composer, and arranger; b. New York, Nov. 17, 1903. He made his debut as a violinist in N.Y. at the age of 8; studied violin with Kneisel, Stoeving, and Auer; conducting with Walter Damrosch and Albert Stoessel; composition with Edward Kilenyi; also took some lessons with Ravel in Paris. After 1925 he gave up the violin and devoted himself mainly to composing and conducting for radio and motion pictures. He composed 2 symphonies, a symph. poem, *The Rubayat,* and songs in the light vein.

Kanner-Rosenthal, Hedwig, piano pedagogue; b. Budapest, June 3, 1882; d. Asheville, North Carolina, Sept. 5, 1959. She studied with Leschetizky and Moriz Rosenthal, whom she married; appeared with him in duo recitals; taught in Vienna; in 1939 settled in New York as a teacher.

Kapell, William, brilliant American pianist; b. New York, Sept. 20, 1922, of Russian and Polish parents; d. in an airplane crash at King's Mountain, near San Francisco, Oct. 29, 1953. He studied with Olga Samaroff at the Philadelphia Cons. of Music; made his N.Y. debut on Oct. 28, 1941; subsequently appeared as soloist with all major American orchestras and also in Europe, specializing in modern music. He met his death returning from an Australian concert tour.

Kapp, Arthur, Estonian composer; b. Suure-Iani, Feb. 28, 1875; d. Tallinn (Reval), Jan. 14, 1952. He studied at the St. Petersburg Cons. with Rimsky-Korsakov. From 1904 to 1920 he was director of the Cons. of Astrakhan, on the Volga. From 1920 to 1943, director of the Reval (Tallinn) Cons. in Estonia. In that capacity he was the teacher of a generation of Estonian musicians.
WORKS: 4 symphonies, concertos (for piano, violin, cello, clarinet, and French horn), and a string sextet. His Symphony No. 4, subtitled *Youth Symphony* (1949), was awarded the State Prize in 1949, and the First Stalin Prize in 1950; he also wrote a cantata *For Peace* (1951).

Kapp, Eugen, notable Estonian composer, son of **Arthur Kapp;** b. Astrakhan, May 26, 1908. He studied with his father, who was director of the Astrakhan Cons.; followed him to Estonia in 1920, and was graduated from the Tallinn Cons. there in 1931.
WORKS: His operas, *Flames of Vengeance* (Tallinn, July 21, 1945) and *Freedom's Singer* (Tallinn, July 20, 1950), were awarded Stalin prizes. Other works: a ballet, *Kalelvipoeg* (1949), a *Patriotic Sym-*

phony, a cantata, *Power of the People,* 2 violin sonatas, piano pieces, and choral works. Kapp succeeded his father as prof. of composition at the Tallinn Cons. and served as its director until 1965. See G. A. Polyanovsky, *Eugen Kapp* (Moscow, 1951); H. Kyrvits, *Eugen Kapp* (Moscow, 1959).

Kapp, Julius, German writer on music; b. Seelbach in Baden, Oct. 1, 1883; d. Sonthofen, March 18, 1962. He studied in Marburg, Berlin, and Munich; Dr. Phil. in 1906; from 1904–07, editor of *Literarischer Anzeiger,* which he founded in 1904; from 1923–45, was stage director of the Berlin State Opera and edited its bulletin, *Blätter der Staatsoper,* from 1948–54 he held a similar post at the Berlin Municipal Opera.
WRITINGS: *Wagner und Liszt* (1908); *Franz Liszt* (1909; went through 20 printings before 1924); *Register zu Liszts Gesammelten Schriften* (1909); *Liszt-Brevier* (1910); *Liszt und die Frauen* (1911); *Wagner und die Frauen* (1912; 16th printing, 1929; completely rewritten and publ. in English transl. as *The Loves of Richard Wagner,* London, 1951); *Paganini* (1913; many editions; 15th ed., 1969); *Berlioz* (1914); *Das Dreigestirn: Berlioz—Liszt—Wagner* (1920); *Meyerbeer* (1920; 8th printing, 1932); *Franz Schreker* (1921); *Das Opernbuch* (1922; 16th printing, 1928); *Die Oper der Gegenwart* (1922); *Weber* (1922; 5th rev. ed., 1931); *Die Staatsoper 1919 bis 1925* (1925); *Wagner und seine erste Elisabeth* (with H. Jachmann, 1926); *185 Jahre Staatsoper* (1928); *Wagner und die Berliner Staatsoper* (1933); *Wagner in Bildern* (1933); *Geschichte der Staatsoper Berlin* (1937); *200 Jahre Staatsoper in Bild* (1942). He edited Liszt's *Gesammelte Schriften* (4 vols., 1910) and Wagner's *Gesammelte Schriften und Briefe* (24 vols., 1914).

Kapp, Villem, Estonian composer; nephew of **Arthur Kapp,** first cousin of **Eugen Kapp;** b. Suure-Jöani, Sept. 7, 1913; d. Tallinn, March 24, 1964. He studied music at the Tallinn Cons.; from 1944 was prof. of composition there. He wrote in an expansive romantic style rooted in folksong; his opera *Lembitu* (Tallinn, Aug. 23, 1961) glorifies Estes Lembitu, the leader of the Estonian struggle against the invading Teutonic crusaders in 1217. He also wrote 2 symphonies, chamber music and choral pieces.
BIBLIOGRAPHY: Helga Tönson, *Villem Kapp* (Tallinn, 1967).

Kappel, Gertrude, German soprano; b. Halle, Sept. 1, 1884; d. Munich, April 3, 1971; studied with Nikisch and Noe at the Leipzig Cons.; made her debut in 1903 at the Hannover Opera, after which she was engaged in Munich, Berlin, and Vienna for the leading Wagner roles; appeared also in Amsterdam, Brussels, Madrid, London, and Paris; made her first American appearance as Isolde with the Metropolitan Opera on Jan. 16, 1928, and remained a member until 1936; 1932, sang the title part in *Elektra* at its first Metropolitan performance; in 1933 she joined the roster of the San Francisco Opera Co.; retired in 1937 and returned to Germany.

Kapr, Jan, Czech composer; b. Prague, March 12, 1914. He studied first with his father, who was a professional musician; then took courses at the Prague Cons. with Řídký and later with J. Křička (1933–40). He was music producer with the Czech Radio (1939–46), a music critic (1946–49) and an editor in music publishing (1950–54); from 1961 to 1970 he taught at the Janáček Academy of Musical Arts in Brno. His style of composition is derived from the Czech National School; in his later works he audaciously introduced modernistic serial procedures.

WORKS: an opera, *Muzikantská pohádka (Musicians' Fairytale*, 1962); 2 piano concertos (1938, 1953); *Marathon*, symph. scherzo (1939); Sinfonietta for small orch. (1940); 8 symphonies: No. 1 (1943); No. 2 (1946); No. 3, for small orch. (1946); No. 4 (1957); No. 5, *Olympijská (Olympic*, 1959); No. 6 (1960, revised 1964); No. 7, *Krajina dětstvi (Country of Childhood)* for children's chorus and orch. (1968); No. 8, *Campanae Pragenses (The Bells of Prague)*, for chorus, orch. and bell sounds on tape (1970); 2 cantatas: *A Song to the Native Land* (1950) and *In the Soviet Land* (1950); *Harvested*, symph. rhapsody (1950); *Zitra (Tomorrow)*, symph. picture (1953); *Léto (Summer)* for chamber orch. (1954); *Allegretto* for violin and orch. (1955); Violin Concerto (1955); Variations for flute and string orch. (1958); Concertino for Viola and Wind Orch. (1965); *Omaggio alla tromba* for 2 solo trumpets, wind orch., piano and timpani (1967–68; Prague, March 6, 1970); *Anachron* for chamber orch. (1974); Concertino for Clarinet and Chamber Ensemble (1975); 7 string quartets (1937; 1941; 1954; 1957; 1961; with solo baritone, 1963; 1965); Nonet (1943); Fantasy for Violin and Piano (1958); *4 Moods* for nonet (1959); *Contrario Romana* for baritone and piano (1965); *Dialogues* for flute and harp (1965); *Šifry (Ciphers)* for piano, percussion and tape (1966); *Oscilace (Oscillation)* for violin, clarinet, trumpet, piano, cello and percussion (1965); *Rotation 9* for piano quartet (1967); *Shadow Play and Dreambook* for soprano, flute and harp (1968); Sonata for Solo Cimbalom (1968); *Testimonies* for cello, bass clarinet, piano and light source (1969); *Woodcuts* for 8 brass (1973); *Colors of Silence* for 8 instruments (1973); *Circuli* for violin and accordion (1974); *Vendanges* for soprano, baritone and piano (1974); *Molto Vivo* for solo flute (1974); *Signals* for trumpet and piano (1976); Sonata for Flute, Horn and Piano (1976); 3 piano sonatas (1945, 1947, 1958); *Home*, cycle for piano (1953–55); *Bagatelles* for piano (1957); *Momente* for piano (1957); Variations for Piano (1961); *Chess Sonata* for 2 pianos (1972; one piano live and one on tape); *Příležitosti (Opportunities)* for piano (1976); choruses; film music. He publ. a volume on new music: *Konstanty (The Constants)* (Prague, 1967).

Kaprál, Václav, Czech composer (father of **Vítězslava Kaprálová**); b. Určice, near Prostějova, Moravia, March 26, 1889; d. Brno, April 6, 1947. He studied composition with Janáček in Brno (1907–10) and with Novák in Prague (1919–20); then took piano lessons with Alfred Cortot in Paris (1923–24). He established his own music school in Brno in 1911; lectured at the Univ. of Brno (1927–36); then taught at the Brno Cons. from 1936 until his 3-year internment in a concentration camp in Svatobořice during World War II; in

1946, became a prof. at the Music Academy in Brno. In his works he shows a fine eclectic talent.

WORKS: He wrote mostly for piano: 4 sonatas (1912, 1921, 1924, 1939); Nocturne (1915); *Spring Lullabies* (1916–17); *Suita romantica* (1918); the highly modern *Miniatures* (1924); *Con duolo* for left hand alone (1926); 3 sonatinas (1930; *Sonatina bucolica*, 1936; 1943); Fantasy (1934); also *Wedding March* for orch. (1923); 2 string quartets (1925, 1927); *Pizeň podzimu (Song of Autumn)* for voice and string quartet (1929); *5 Uspávanky (5 Lullabies)* for voice, and small orch. (1932–33; performed at the International Society for Contemporary Music Festival, Barcelona, April 20, 1936); *Ballad* for cello and piano (1946).

Kaprálová, Vítězslava, Czech composer; daughter of **Václav Kaprál** (family names in Slavic languages assume adjectival gender endings); b. Brno, Jan. 24, 1915; d. Montpellier, France, June 16, 1940. She received her early education from her father; then studied conducting and composition at the Brno Cons. under Vilém Petrželka (1930–35); later at the Prague Cons. with Novák (composition) and Talich (conducting). In 1937 she received a scholarship to Paris, where she took lessons in conducting with Munch and composition with Martinů. Her early death, of tuberculosis, cut short a remarkable career.

WORKS: *Suite en miniature* for orch. (1932–35); Piano Concerto (Brno, June 17, 1935); *Military Sinfonietta* (Prague, Nov. 26, 1937); *Suita Rustica* (Brno, April 16, 1939); *Partita* for string orch. and piano (performed posthumously; Brno, Nov. 12, 1941); *Christmas Prelude* for chamber orch. (1939); Concertino for Violin, Clarinet and Orch. (1940; unfinished); *Legenda a Burleska* for violin and piano (1932); *Sonata appassionata* for piano (1933); String Quartet (1936); *6 Variations on the Bells of the Church of Saint Étienne in Paris* for piano (1938); *2 Ritournelles* for cello and piano (1940).

Kapsberger, Johann Hieronymus von, 17th-century composer of a noble German family (known in Italy as **Giovanni Geronimo Tedesco della Tiorba,** because of his ability as a player); b. 1575; d. Rome, 1661. He was a noted virtuoso on the theorbo, chitarrone, lute, and trumpet. He lived in Venice about 1604, and then in Rome, enjoying the favor of Pope Urban VIII. His compositions are in the then "modern" Florentine style; those for lute are written in a much simplified lute tablature.

WORKS: *Intavolatura di chitarrone* (3 books: 1604, 1616, 1626); *Villanelle a 1, 2 e 3 voci* (4 books: 1610, 1619, 1619, 1623); *Arie passeggiate* (2 books: 1612, 1623); *Intavolatura di lauto* (2 books; 1611, 1623); *Motetti passeggiati* (1612); *Balli, gagliarde e correnti* (1615); *Sinfonie a 4 con il basso continuo* (1615); *Capricci a due stromenti, tiorba e tiorbino* (1617); *Missae Urbanae*, 4–8 voices (1631); *Apotheosis of St. Ignatius de Loyola;* a musical drama, *Fetonte* (1630); wedding cantatas, etc.

BIBLIOGRAPHY: J. Wolf, *Handbuch der Notationskunde* (vol. 2, pp. 194ff.).

Karajan, Herbert von, celebrated Austrian conductor; b. Salzburg, April 5, 1908. He was a scion of a

cultured musical family; his great-grandfather **Theodor von Karajan,** was an eminent music theorist. Karajan learned to play the piano as a child and gave a public concert at the age of 11. He studied music at the Mozarteum in Salzburg. In 1926 he entered the Vienna Music Academy where he studied conducting with Franz Schalk. He made his conducting debut with the orch. of the Vienna Music Academy on Dec. 17, 1928; then conducted opera at the Stadttheater in Ulm (1929–34), and concurrently was in charge of the summer courses in conducting in Salzburg; then was engaged as conductor of the Aachen Opera (1934–41); in 1938 he was appointed conductor of the Berlin State Opera; inaugurated his season there with *Fidelio* on Sept. 30, 1938, while continuing his tenure at Aachen. His second marriage to a woman with an undeniably Jewish grandparent created difficulties for him with the Hitler regime, even though he was a member in good standing of the Austrian National Socialist Party from 1935, that is, even before the *Anschluss;* however, he continued to conduct at the Berlin State Opera until its destruction in an air raid in 1944. After the war he was subjected by the Allied military authorities to a lengthy process of de-Nazification, but eventually was cleansed of Nazi taint and was able to conduct at the Salzburg Festival in 1948; in the same year he was appointed conductor of the Vienna Symph. Orch.; he subsequently conducted opera at La Scala in Milan and at the Bayreuth Festival. In 1954 he succeeded Furtwängler as musical director of the Berlin Philharmonic; concurrently was artistic director of the Vienna State Opera (1956–64) and at the Salzburg Festival (1956–60). He was for a season artistic adviser of the Orchestre de Paris (1969–70). In 1969 he established the Karajan Foundation for the purpose of promoting biennial international competitions for young conductors. As his fame spread he appeared as guest conductor all over the world, including the U.S.; also gave performances in Russia with the Vienna Philharmonic Orch. (1962), with La Scala Opera (1964) and the Berlin Philharmonic (1969). His world reputation is based on his extraordinary capacity for systematic work, his emotional strength and his self-assurance; both in opera and in symphony he is capable of achieving superlative performances; his cycles of Beethoven's symphonies and Wagner's music dramas are recognized as exemplary in fidelity to style and excellence of execution.
BIBLIOGRAPHY: Ernst Haeussermann, *Herbert von Karajan* (Gütersloh, 1968); Christian Spiel, editor, *Anekdoten um Herbert von Karajan* (Munich, 1968).

Karajan, Theodor Georg von, Austrian writer on music; b. Vienna, Jan. 22, 1810; d. there, April 28, 1873. He studied history, philology, and law; after holding various minor posts, he became president of the Austrian Academy of Science (1866–1869). His important monograph *J. Haydn in London, 1791 und 1792* (Vienna, 1861) contains Haydn's correspondence with Maria Anna von Genzinger; he also publ. *Aus Metastasios Hofleben* (Vienna, 1861). He was the great-grandfather of **Herbert von Karajan.**

Karasowski, Moritz, Polish writer on music; b. Warsaw, Sept. 22, 1823; d. Dresden, April 20, 1892. He

was a cellist in the opera orch. in Warsaw from 1851, and later court cellist at Dresden. He publ. (in Polish) *History of Polish Opera* (Warsaw, 1859) and *Life of Mozart* (1868), but his most important contribution was his book *Chopin's Youth* (1862), and particularly the first comprehensive biography of Chopin, publ. in German as *F. Chopin, sein Leben, seine Werke und Briefe* (Dresden, 1877; in English, N.Y., 1878).

Karastoyanov, Assen, Bulgarian composer; b. Samokov, June 3, 1893; d. Sofia, Sept. 8, 1976. He studied flute at the Sofia State Music School (1914–18); then went to Germany where he took lessons in music theory with Paul Juon at the Berlin Hochschule für Musik (1921–22); later took a course in composition with Paul Dukas at the École Normale de Musique in Paris (1930–31); went again to Germany and enrolled at the Leipzig State Cons. as a composition student of Günther Raphael. Returning to Bulgaria, he taught for 25 years at the State Cons. in Sofia (1933–58).
WORKS: 7 operettas, including *Michel Strogoff,* after Jules Verne (1937–40); 7 patriotic cantatas; *A Balkan Suite* for orch. (1928); 4 symphonies: No. 1, *Miner's Symphony* (1940); No. 2 *Danubian,* for brass orch. (1960); No. 3 *Rhodopean* (1973) and No. 4, *Proto-Bulgarian* (1975); Flute Concerto (1959); *A Bogomil Legend* for string orch. (1973); 2 string quartets (1937, 1970); 2 suites for flute and piano (1955, 1968); *Capriccio* for violin and piano (1970); *Scherzino* for piano (1933); Piano Sonata (1938); songs.

Karatygin, Vyacheslav, Russian writer on music; b. Pavlovsk, Sept. 17, 1875; d. Leningrad, Dec. 23, 1925. He learned to play the piano from his mother who was a professional pianist, but entered the Univ. of St. Petersburg as a student of chemistry; from 1898 to 1907 he worked in a chemical factory in St. Petersburg, but at the same time took lessons in composition with Sokolov; from 1907 until 1917 he served as a music critic on various publications and gave courses in several conservatories and music schools. A broad-minded musician, he welcomed the music of Scriabin, Stravinsky and Prokofiev at the time when most Russian critics regarded them as unacceptable, and he enunciated the idea of a "musical revolution." He published the monographs on Mussorgsky, Chaliapin and Scriabin, and he himself composed some piano pieces and songs. A memorial collection of articles, *V. G. Karatygin, His Life and Work,* was publ. by the Russian Institute for the History of Art (Leningrad, 1927).

Kardoš, Dezider, Slovak composer; b. Nadlice, Dec. 23, 1914. He studied composition with Alexander Moyzes at the Bratislava Academy of Music and Drama (1932–37); composition with Vítězslav Novák at the Prague Cons. (1937–39). He worked at the Czech Radio in Prešov (1939–45) and Košice (1945–51) in eastern Slovakia. In 1961 he was appointed prof. of composition at the Academy of Music in Bratislava. The thematic sources of his musical inspiration are found in eastern Slovak folklore.
WORKS: *Peace Cantata* (1951); 6 symphonies: No. 1 (1942); No. 2, *Of Native Land* (1955); No. 3 (1961); No. 4, *Piccola* (1962); No. 5 (1965); No. 6 (1974–5); 2 overtures, *My Home* (1946) and *East Slovak Overture*

(1950); Concerto for Orchestra (1957); *Heroic Ballad* for string orchestra (1959); Concerto for String Orch. (1963); Piano Concerto (1969); *Res philharmonica,* overture (1970); *Partita* for 12 strings (1972); *Songs About Life,* cycle of 4 microdramas for soprano, tenor and orch. (1973-74); *Slovakophonia,* variations on a folk theme for orch. (1975-76); 2 string quartets (1935, 1966); 2 Suites for piano (1937); Wind Quintet (1938); *Preludium quasi una fantasia* for organ (1940); *Bagatelles* for piano (1948); *3 Compositions for Violin and Piano* (1966); *Elevazioni* for organ (1967); choruses and songs.

Kardos, István, Hungarian composer; b. Debrecen, June 6, 1891; d. Budapest, Dec. 22, 1975. He studied composition at the Academy of Music in Budapest. From 1917 to 1946 he conducted musical plays in Hungary, Germany and Switzerland; taught at the Budapest Academy of Music (1948-59).
WORKS: *Dance* for orch. (1918); 4 symphonies (1919, 1958, 1967, 1968); *Hungarian Scherzo* for orch. (1936); Violin Concertino (1947); *Áprilisi hajnal (Dawn in April),* cantata (1950); *Janus* for orch. (1950); 2 piano concertos (1956, 1963); Concertino for Double Bass and Orch. (1959); Double Concerto for Viola, Double Bass and Orch. (1964); *Alliage* for violin and chamber orch. (1966); *Intrada* for orch. (1968); *Visitation* for orch. (1969); 6 string quartets (1917, 1925, 1951, 1960, 1967, 1971); Viola Sonata (1942); Double-Bass Sonata (1949); Flute Sonata (1957); Wind Quintet (1959); String Trio (1960); *Bipartitum* for bassoon and piano (1963); Sonata for Solo Clarinet (1965); *Poem and Burlesque* for double bass and piano (1969); 2 sextets for clarinet, string quartet and piano (1971); *Grotesque* for octave flute, cello and double bass (1971); *Notturno* for horn, flute, violin and harp (1971); Piano Sonata (1916); the piano pieces, *Dickens Suite* (1957), *Toccata* (1960), *Variations and Fugue* (1969); songs.

Karel, Rudolf, Czech composer; b. Pilsen, Nov. 9, 1880; d. at the Terezín concentration camp, March 6, 1945. He was the last student of Dvořák, with whom he studied in Prague for one year during Karel's term at the Prague Cons. (1901-04). In 1914 he went to Russia as a teacher and remained there during World War I. After the Revolution he made his way to Irkutsk, Siberia; during the Russian civil war he became a member of the Czechoslovak Legion and conducted an orchestra organized by the legionnaires. He returned to Prague in 1920; from 1923 to 1941 taught at the Prague Cons. As a member of the Czech resistance in World War II, he was arrested by the Nazis in March, 1943; was transferred to Terezin in Feb., 1945, and died there of dysentery shortly before liberation. His music reflects the Romantic concepts; he had a predilection for programmatic writing; the national element is manifested by his treatment of old modal progressions; his instrumental writing is rich in sonority; the polyphonic structure is equally strong.
WORKS: a lyric comedy, *Ilseino srdce (Ilsea's Heart,* 1906-09; Prague, Oct. 11, 1924); 2 musical fairytales: *Smrt Kmotřička (Godmother Death,* 1928-33; Brno, Feb. 3, 1933) and *Tři vlasy děda Vševěda (3 Hairs of the Wise Old Man,* 1944-45; his last

work, written in camp, left as a draft only, arranged by his student Zbyněk Vostřák, and performed posthumously in Prague, Oct. 28, 1948); Suite for Orch. (1903-04); *Comedy Overture* (1904-05); Fantasy for Orch. (1905); *Ideály (The Ideals),* symph. epic from an artist's life (1906-09); 2 symphonies (*Renaissance,* 1910-11, and *Spring,* 1935-38; two other symphonies of 1904 and 1917 are lost); a symphony, *Vzkříšení (Resurrection),* for soli, chorus and orch. (1923-27; Prague, April 9, 1928); *Capriccio* for violin and orch. (1924); *4 Slavonic Dance Moods* for orch. (1912); *The Demon,* symph. poem (1918-20); *Revolutionary Overture* (1938-41); *Sladká balada dětská (Sweet Ballad for a Child)* for soprano, chorus and orch. (1928-30); *Černoch (A Negro),* exotic ballad for baritone, and orch. or piano (1934); 3 string quartets (1902-03, 1907-13, 1935-36); Piano Trio (1903-04); Violin Sonata (1912); Nonet for wind quintet and string quartet (1945; left in draft form and completed by F. Hertl); Piano Sonata (1910) and the piano pieces *5 Pieces* (1902); *Notturno* (1906-07); *Thema con variazioni* (1910); *3 Waltzes* (1913) and *Burlesques* (1913-14); choruses; songs; incidental music.
BIBLIOGRAPHY: O. Šourek, *Rudolf Karel* (Prague, 1947).

Karg-Elert, Sigfrid, distinguished German organist and composer; b. Oberndorf, Württemberg, Nov. 21, 1877; d. Leipzig, April 9, 1933. He studied at the Leipzig Cons. with Reinecke and Jadassohn; in 1919 was appointed to its staff. Concurrently with his teaching activities, he began to give organ recitals, and soon became known as one of the greatest virtuosos on the instrument; he also played on the "Kunstharmonium," for which he wrote many original compositions. His real name, Karg, sounded unattractive to his audiences (it means "avaricious"), and he changed it to Karg-Elert. As a composer he developed a brilliant style, inspired by the music of the Baroque, but he embellished this austere and ornamental idiom with Impressionistic devices; the result was an ingratiating type of music with an aura of originality. In 1932 he undertook a concert tour in the U.S.
WORKS: for the Kunstharmonium: sets of pieces: *Skizzen* (1903), *Aquarellen* (1906), *Miniaturen* (1908), *Intarsien* (1911), *Impressions* (1914), *Idyllen* (1915), *Innere Stimmen* (1918); fundamental technical works: *Die Kunst des Registrierens; Die ersten grundlegenden Studien; Hohe Schule des Legatospiels; Die Harmoniumtechnik (Gradus ad Parnassum); Theoretische-praktische Elementarschule;* for organ: 66 chorale improvisations (1908-10); 20 Chorale Preludes and Postludes (1912); 10 *Poetic Tone Pictures;* 3 *Pastels,* Cathedral Windows (on Gregorian themes); Wind Quintet; two clarinet sonatas; Sonata for Flute unaccompanied; *Trio bucolico* for violin, flute, and piano; a number of lieder. He published *Akustische Ton-, Klang-, und Funktionsbestimmung* (1930) and *Polaristische Klang- und Tonalitätslehre* (1931). Hans Avril publ. a catalogue of Karg-Elert's works: *Kompositions-verzeichnis mit einer monographischen Skizze* (Berlin, 1928).
BIBLIOGRAPHY: A. Eaglefield Hull, "Karg-Elert," *Musical Times* (Feb. and March 1913); H. B. Gaul, "Bonnet, Bossi, Karg-Elert," *Musical Quarterly* (July

1918); Paul Schenk, *Sigfrid Karg-Elert* (Berlin, 1927); Godfrey Sceats, *The Organ Works of Karg-Elert* (Orpington, 1940; revised ed., London, 1950); Walter Kwasnik, *S. Karg-Elert: Sein Leben und Werk in Heutiger Sicht* (1971).

Karjalainen, Ahti, Finnish composer; b. Oulu (Uleaborg), March 20, 1907. He studied composition at the Helsinki Cons., Viipuri (Vyborg) Institute and Sibelius Academy; played violin and trombone in various orchestras; later conducted the Jyväskylä City Orch.
WORKS: *Polonaise* for trombone and orch. (1935); *Scherzo* for trumpet, trombone and orch. (1940); Trombone Concerto (1942); *Summer Scenes* for oboe and orch. (1944); *Winter Scenes* for orch. (1948); symph. No. 1 (1948); *Concert Suite* for bassoon and orch. (1949); Duo for 2 Trumpets and Orch. (1950); Violin Concerto (1952); *Ostinato* for cello and orch. (1954); 2 cello concertos (1956, 1966); *The Eagle's Way* for chorus and orch. (1965); *Setting Out* for narrator, baritone, mixed chorus, male chorus and orch. (1968); *The Song of Wood,* cantata (1971); 6 partitas for various instrumental combinations (1936, 1940, 1945, 1961, 1964, 1965); Wind Sextet (1945); other chamber music; songs; solo pieces.

Karkoff, Maurice Ingvar, prominent Swedish composer; b. Stockholm, March 17, 1927. He studied piano and conducting at the Royal Academy of Music in Stockholm (1948-53); composition with Blomdahl, Lars-Erik Larsson, Erland von Koch in Stockholm, with Holmboe in Copenhagen, and later with Nadia Boulanger and André Jolivet in Paris (1957), Wladimir Vogel in Switzerland (1959-61) and Alexander Boscovich in Tel Aviv (1963). Returning to Sweden in 1965, he devoted himself principally to teaching. In his music he absorbed many cultures, which are reflected in his style of composition, which may be described as romantic modernism; thematically he is sensitive to exotic resources and coloristic instrumental timbres.
WORKS: FOR ORCH.: *Serenade* for strings (1953); *Short Variations* for string quartet (1953; revised in 1956); Sinfonietta (1954); *Saxophone Concertino* (1955); 6 symphonies: No. 1 (1955-56; Bergen, Norway, Oct. 22, 1956); No. 2 (1957; Swedish Radio, Jan. 5, 1959); No. 3, *Sinfonia Breve* (1958-59; Gävle, Jan. 10, 1960); No. 4 (1963; Stockholm, April 4, 1964); No. 5, *Sinfonia da Camera* (1964-65; Gävle, Nov. 11, 1965); No. 6 (1972-73; Stockholm, Oct. 12, 1974); Violin Concerto (1956); Piano Concerto (1957); Cello Concerto (1957-58); *Lyric Suites I and II* for chamber orch. (1958); Trombone Concerto (1958); Horn Concerto (1959); *9 Aphoristic Variations* (1959); Clarinet Concerto (1959); *Variations* (1961); *Serenata* for chamber orch. (1961); *7 Pezzi* (1963); *Oriental Pictures* (1965-66; also for piano); Suite for Harpsichord and Strings (1962); *Concerto da Camera* for balalaika and orch. (1962-63); Concerto for Orchestra (1963); *Transfigurate mutate* (1966); *Tripartita* (1966-67); *Textum* for strings (1967); *Metamorphoses* (1967); *Sinfonietta Grave* (1968-69); *Epitaphium* for small chamber orch. (1968; also for nonet); *5 Summer Scenes* (1969); *Triptyk* (1970); *Partes caracteris* (1971); *Symphonic Relexions* (1971); *Passacaglia* for strings (1971). VOCAL MUSIC: *6 Allvarliga Songs* for

high voice and orch. (1955); *Det Svenska Landet,* festival cantata (1956); *Livet,* songs and recitation for low voice and orch. (1959); *Gesang des Abgeschiedenen,* 5 songs for baritone and orch. or piano (1959-60); *10 Japanese Songs* for high voice and orch. or piano (1959); *Himmel och Jord,* cantata (1960); *Sieben Rosen später,* cantata (1964); *Das ist sein Erlauten,* cantata (1965); *Landscape of Screams,* after Nelly Sachs, for soprano, narrator and instruments (1967); *6 Chinese Impressions* for high voice and instrumental ensemble (1973). CHAMBER MUSIC: Flute Sonata (1953); Cello Sonata (1954-55); Violin Sonata (1956); Wind Quintet (1956-57); String Quartet (1957); Quartet for 2 trumpets, horn and trombone (1958); String Trio (1960); *Chamber Concerto* for 14 winds, timpani, percussion and string basses (1961); *Metamorphoses* for 4 horns (1966); *Terzetto* for flute, cello and piano (1967); *3 Episodes* for clarinet, cello and piano (1968); *Quattro parte* for 13 brasses and percussion (1968); *4 Momenti* for violin and piano (1970); *Epitaphium* for accordion, electric guitar and percussion (1970); *6 Pezzi breve* for oboe solo (1972). PIANO MUSIC: Piano Sonata (1956); *Partita Piccola* (1958); *Capriccio on Football* (1961; musical report on a football game); *Monopartita* (1969); *3 Expressions* for 2 pianos (1971). Songs; minor chamber and piano pieces. Under the impression of his travels to Israel, he wrote a chamber opera, *The Boundary Kibbutz* (1972-73).

Karkoschka, Erhard, German composer; b. Ostrava, Bohemia, March 6, 1923. He studied music in Stuttgart and in Tübingen; in 1958 was appointed to the staff of the Musikhochschule in Stuttgart. He adopted the serial method of composition, following the example of Anton Webern; often incorporated electronics in his works; also resorted to graphic notation in order to achieve greater freedom of resulting sonorities. He wrote *Symphonische Evolutionen* (1953); *Kleines Konzert* for violin and chamber orch. (1955); *Undarum continuum* for orch. (1960); *Antinomie* for wind quintet (1968); *Quattrologe* for string quartet (1966); *Tempora Mutantur* for string quartet (1971); electronic works; much choral music and stage melodramas. He publ. *Zur rhythmischen Struktur in der Musik von heute* (Kassel, 1962); *Das Schriftbild der neuen Musik* (Celle, 1966; in English as *Notation in New Music,* London, 1972), and many magazine articles, dealing with problems of new music.

Karl, Tom, Irish tenor; b. Dublin, Jan. 19, 1846; d. Rochester, N.Y., March 19, 1916. He studied in England with Henry Phillips, and in Italy with Sangiovanni. He sang in Italy for many years, then settled in N.Y. His remarkable success as Ralph in *Pinafore* (1879) determined him to abandon grand opera; some years later he organized (with H. C. Barnabee and W. H. MacDonald) the famous light opera company, The Bostonians. He had a repertory of about 150 operas and operettas. He retired in 1896; had an operatic school in N.Y.; then went to Rochester, where he taught singing.

Karlins, M. William, American composer; b. New York, Feb. 25, 1932. He studied composition in New York with Frederick Piket (1954-57); then at the Manhattan School of Music (1958-61) with Vittorio Gianinni, and later at the Univ. of Iowa (1963-65). He taught at Western Ill. Univ. (1965-67) and since 1967 at Northwestern Univ.

WORKS: *Concert Music I* for orch. (1959); 3 piano sonatas (1959, 1962, 1965); *Concerto Grosso I* for 9 instruments (1959-60); *Concerto Grosso II* for 7 solo instruments (1961); String Quartet, with Soprano (1960); *Concert Music II* for chorus and orch. (1960; Milwaukee, Feb. 14, 1971); *Outgrowths-Variations* for piano (1961); *Birthday Music I* for flute, bass clarinet and double bass (1962), *II* for flute and double bass (1962); String Trio (1962-63); *Concert Music III* for winds, brass, piano and percussion (Urbana, Ill., April 17, 1964); *Concert Music IV* for orch. (Evanston, Ill., May 14, 1965); *Solo Piece with Passacaglia* for clarinet (1964); *Variations on "Obiter Dictum"* for cello, piano and percussion (1965); *Music for Solo Cello* (1966); *Music for Oboe, Bass Clarinet and Piano* (1966); Quartet for Saxophones (1966-67); *Lamentations—In Memoriam* for narrator and chamber group (1968); *Music for Saxophone and Piano* (1969); *Graphic Mobile* for any 3 or multiple of 3 instruments (1969); Wind Quintet (1970); *Reflux*, a concerto for double bass and wind ensemble (Chicago, April 8, 1972); *Concert Music V* for orch. (Chicago, Dec. 20, 1973); Quintet for saxophone and string quartet (1973-74); *4 Etudes* for double bass and tape or 3 double basses (1974).

Karlowicz, Jan, Polish music scholar; father of **Mieczyslaw Karlowicz;** b. Subortowicze, near Troki, May 28, 1836; d. Warsaw, June 14, 1903. He studied music in Wilno, Moscow, Paris, Brussels, and Berlin. Settling in Warsaw, he publ. translations of several German textbooks on harmony; also publ. (in English, German, and French) a pamphlet, *Project of a New Way of Writing Musical Notes* (Warsaw, 1876); composed some songs.

BIBLIOGRAPHY: F. Starczewski, *The Musical Activities of Jan Karlowicz* (Warsaw, 1904).

Karlowicz, Mieczyslaw, Polish composer; b. Wiszniewo, Dec. 11, 1876; d. Zakopane, Galicia, Feb. 8, 1909. He was the son of the theorist **Jan Karlowicz;** was sent to Germany to study violin as a child. In 1887 he began composition studies in Warsaw with Noskowski, Roguski, and Maszynski; violin with Barcewicz; later he continued his studies in Berlin with H. Urban (1895-1900). Returning to Warsaw, he devoted himself to composition and teaching; was director of the Warsaw Music Society (1904-06); after a sojourn in Germany (where he studied conducting with Nikisch in Leipzig), he settled in Zakopane; also traveled to France, Austria, and Germany. An enthusiastic mountain climber, he was killed in an accident, under an avalanche. Essentially a Romantic composer, he succeeded in blending the national elements of Polish folk music with the general European genre of mild modernism; there is an influence of Richard Strauss in his expansive tone painting. The appreciation of his music in Poland rose rather than declined after his death; some of his piano pieces and songs have been established in the concert repertory.

WORKS: Serenade for String Orch. (1898); Symphony in E minor, subtitled *Renaissance* (1900); symph. poem, *Returning Waves* (1904); symph. trilogy, *Eternal Songs* (1907); *Lithuanian Rhapsody* for orch. (1908); *Stanislaw and Anna of Oswiecim,* symph. poem (1908); *Sad Story,* symph. poem (1908); *Episode at the Masquerade,* symph. poem (1908-09; unifinished; completed by G. Fitelberg). He publ. for the first time some theretofore unknown letters of Chopin (Warsaw, 1904; in French as *Souvenirs inédits de F. Chopin,* Paris, 1904).

BIBLIOGRAPHY: F. Kecki, *Karlowicz* (Warsaw, 1934); A. Chybinski, *Karlowicz* (Cracow, 1947); Igor Boelza, *Karlowicz* (Moscow, 1951).

Karow, Karl, German composer; b. Alt-Stettin, Nov. 15, 1790; d. Bunzlau, Dec. 20, 1863. He taught music at Bunzlau; publ. a *Choralbuch,* a *Leitfaden für den Schulgesang-Unterricht,* motets, piano pieces, etc.

Karpath, Ludwig, Austrian singer and music critic; b. Budapest, April 27, 1866; d. Vienna, Sept. 8, 1936. He was a pupil at the Cons. in Budapest; studied singing in Vienna; was a member of the National Opera Co. in the U.S. (singing minor bass roles) for 3 seasons (1886-88); returning to Vienna, he became an influential music critic; for many years (1894-1921) wrote for the *Neues Wiener Tageblatt.* He publ. *Siegfried Wagner als Mensch und Künstler* (1902), *Zu den Briefen Wagners an eine Putzmacherin* (1906), *R. Wagner, der Schuldenmacher* (1914), *Wagners Briefe an Hans Richter* (1924).

Karpeles, Maud, English ethnomusicologist; b. London, Nov. 12, 1885, d. there, Oct. 1, 1976. She was educated at private schools in England and Germany, and soon after 1900 became associated with Cecil Sharp in his collecting and promoting of English folk songs and dances. During the summers of 1915 through 1918 she assisted him in teaching and on field trips in the U.S.; materials collected on the field trips appear in two distinct, if often confused, 2-vol. collections: (1) *English Folk Songs from the Southern Appalachians* (London, 1917, in collaboration with Olive Dame Campbell); and (2) *English Folk Songs from the Southern Appalachians* (London, 1932, ed. by Karpeles, representing songs collected entirely by Sharp and Karpeles; reprinted 1966). In 1929-30 she collected 191 songs in Newfoundland from which *Folk Songs from Newfoundland* (London, 1934; 2nd ed. 1970) was issued with piano arrangements by Ralph Vaughan Williams and others. In 1935 she helped organize at London the English Folk Dance Conference and Festival in conjunction with the English Folk Dance and Song Society. Following World War II Karpeles was largely responsible for the gathering at London of a delegation of specialists from 28 countries that founded the International Folk Music Council, with Karpeles as Hon. Secretary and Ralph Vaughan Williams as President. From 1949 through 1963 she edited the annual *Journal of the International Folk Music Council,* compiled manuals for collectors, and wrote articles for other related journals. After 1963 she was Hon. President of the International Folk Music Council, and continued her writing and counseling projects. She was honored with the

Order of the British Empire in 1960 and with degrees from the University of Quebec and Memorial University of Newfoundland (1970). Among her many publications were: *Cecil Sharp* (London, 1933, reprinted, 1955, in collaboration with A. H. Fox Strangways; 1967 ed., *Cecil Sharp; His Life and Work,* Chicago, enlarged and rewritten by Maud Karpeles alone); *Folk Songs of Europe* (London, 1956; N.Y., 1964); *An Introduction to English Folk Song* (London, 1973); and at least 5 editions (1920, 1932, 1952, 1966, 1974) of *English Folk Songs,* published in London, the last retitled *Cecil Sharp's Collection of English Folk Songs.*
BIBLIOGRAPHY: Willard Rhodes, "Memorial Obituary: Maud Karpeles 1885–1976," *Ethnomusicology* (May 1977).

Karr, Gary, American virtuoso double-bass player; b. Los Angeles, Nov. 20, 1941. He was a scion of a family of musicians which numbered 7 bass players (his father, grandfather, 2 uncles and 3 cousins). He absorbed the technique of manipulating this mastodon of string instruments by natural selection: studied with a cellist, a pianist, and a singer (Jennie Tourel) before taking lessons with Herman Reinshagen, former first double-bass player of the N.Y. Philharmonic. He then took an additional course with the cellist Gabor Rejto at the Univ. of Southern California; subsequently studied at the Aspen Music School and finally at the Juilliard School of Music in New York. He launched his spectacular career as a soloist with major American orchestras, and then played with the London Philharmonic and the Oslo Philharmonic. His solo recitals attracted a great deal of curiosity and elicited astounded praise from even the most skeptical of music critics. To expand the meager repertory for the instrument, he commissioned Hans Werner Henze, Gunther Schuller, Alec Wilder, Sir Malcolm Arnold and other modern composers to write special works for him. He also introduced some works in the jazz manner. As an instructor, he gave courses at several music schools in the U.S. and Canada.

Kartzev, Alexander, Russian composer; b. Moscow, July 19, 1883; d. there, July 3, 1953. He was a pupil of Juon in Berlin, and Taneyev and Glière in Moscow. He wrote an opera, *Undine;* a symphony; violin concerto; string quartet; piano quintet; violin sonata, etc.

Karyotakis, Theodore, Greek composer; b. Argos, July 21, 1903. He studied composition with Dimitri Mitropoulos and Varvoglis; concurrently enrolled as a law student at the Univ. of Athens.
WORKS: an opera, *Moon Flower* (1953–55); oratorio, *Song of Songs* (1956); *Symphonic Study* (1938); *Ballade* for piano, strings and percussion (1939); *Rhapsody* for violin and orch. (1940); *Sinfonietta* for strings (1942); *Epic Song* for orch. (1944); *Short Suite* for small orch. (1946); Divertimento for Orch. (1948); *Serenade* for small orch. (1955); *Serenities,* 10 songs for voice, clarinet, celesta, string orch. and percussion (1962); *3 Pieces for Orch.* (1965); Concerto for Orch. (1967); *Adagio* for voice and strings (1968); *Essay* for orch. (1969); Symphony in One Movement (1974); 2 violin sonatas (1945, 1955); *6 Erotic Songs* for voice, flute and harp (1948); String Trio (1949); *Rhapsody* for

cello and piano (1963); Viola Sonatina (1963); Solo Cello Sonatina (1963); String Quartet with Voice (1963); *11 Sketches* for flute and viola (1963); *9 Inventions* for violin and piano (1966); Trio for clarinet, viola and piano (1969); Duo for Flute and Clarinet (1969); *Music for Flute, Clarinet, Horn and Bassoon* (1973). For piano: Sonatina (1935); *Variations of a Folksong* (1944); *Improvisations* (1968). He also wrote a dramatic scene on XXII of *The Iliad* for 2 narrators, tenor, soprano, mezzo-soprano and chorus (1964) and many songs, including *Orion,* 7 inventions for voice and violin (1968), and *Nocturnal Heptastichs,* 7 songs for voice and various instruments (1969).

Kasemets, Udo, Estonian-born Canadian composer; b. Tallinn, Nov. 16, 1919. He studied at the Tallinn Cons., at the Stuttgart State Academy of Music, and attended a Darmstadt summer course in new music under Krenek (1950). He emigrated to Canada in 1951 and became an organist, accompanist, and teacher; later became music critic for the Toronto *Daily Star;* was also lecturer on mixed-media music at the Ontario College of Arts in Toronto. In 1966 he became editor of *Canavangard,* an annotated catalogue of avant-garde Canadian composers. His early music is set in peaceful romantic modalities with Estonian undertones, but soon he espoused serialism and pantheatricalism of the most uninhibited avant-garde.
WORKS: *Estonian Suite* for chamber orch. (1950); *Sonata da Camera* for solo cello (1955); Violin Concerto (1956); String Quartet (1957); *Logos* for flute and piano (1960); *Haiku* for voice, flute, cello and piano (1961); *Squares* for piano, 4 hands (1962); $\sqrt{5}$ for 2 performers on 2 pianos and percussion (1962–63); *Trigon* for 1 or 3 or 9 or 27 performers, a multi-dimensional score in which thematic information is provided by a deoxyribonucleic matrix (1963; 11 subsequent versions, 1964–66); *Communications,* a non-composition to words by e. e. cummings, a cybernetic manifestation for singular or plural singers, speakers, instrumentalists or dancers of an indeterminate duration (1963); *Cumulus* for any solo instrument or ensemble, and 2 tape recorders, the score consisting of 9 segments to be played in any order (1963–64; 2 later versions, 1966, 1968); *Calceolaria,* time/space variations on a floral theme, for any number of performers (1966; version for 4-channel tape, 1967); *Contactics,* a choreography for musicians and audience (1966); *Variations on Variations on Variations* for singers, instrumentalists and 4 loudspeakers (1966); *Quartets of Quartets,* 4 separate works for varying ensembles of readers, tape, calibrators, windbells, windgenerators, opaque projectors and any sound-producing media: *Music for Nothing, Music for Anything (Wordmusic), Music for Something (Windmusic),* and *Music for Everything* (all 1971–72); *Music(s) for John Cage,* incorporating *Guitarmusic for John Cage* for any number of guitars, projections and dimmers, *Voicemusic for John Cage* for any number of voices, *Saladmusic for John Cage* for any number of saladmakers, and *Walking/Talking* for any number of walkers/talkers (all 1972); *Time-Space Interface* for any number of participants and any media, in both indoor and outdoor versions (1971–73); *Quadraphony (Music of the Quarter of the Moon of*

the Lunar Year), an acoustical/architectural time/-space exploration project (1972–73); *La Crasse du Tympan* for record/tape mix (1973); *WATEAR-THUNDAIR: Music of the Tenth Moon of the Year of the Dragon*, a nature-sound-mix with verbal and visual commentary (1976); *KANADANAK*, a "celebration of our land and its people . . . ," for readers, drummers, and audience participation (1976–77).

Kashin, Daniil, Russian composer; b. Moscow, 1769; d. there, Dec. 22, 1841. He was a serf, property of an aristocratic landowner, Gavril Bibikov. His master engaged Sarti, who was in Russia at the time, to teach Kashin; when Sarti accompanied Potemkin to southern Russia, Kashin went along. Returning to Moscow, he demonstrated his ability by presenting a piano concerto and an overture of his own composition (March 17, 1790). Bibikov sent him to Italy for further study; there Kashin spent 7 years; upon his return in 1798, he was given his liberty. On April 10, 1799, he gave in Moscow a monster concert with the participation of 200 executants, including an ensemble of Russian horns; at this concert he presented several of his Russian songs, which later became popular. He wrote 3 operas: *Natalia, the Boyard's Daughter* (Moscow, Oct. 21, 1801), *Fair Olga* (Moscow, Jan. 14, 1809), *The One-Day Reign of Nourmahal*, after Thomas Moore's *Lalla Rookh* (1817, not produced); also collections of "patriotic songs" and an album of Russian folksongs. In 1806 he publ. 6 issues of a periodical, *Musical Journal of Russia.*
BIBLIOGRAPHY: R. A. Mooser, *Annales de la Musique et des Musiciens en Russie au XVIIIᵉ Siècle* (vol. 2, Geneva, 1950, pp. 491–493).

Kashkin, Nikolai, Russian music critic; b. Voronezh, Dec. 9, 1839; d. Kazan, March 15, 1920. After receiving rudimentary instruction in music from his father, an amateur, Kashkin became a private tutor in elementary music in his native town. In 1860 he settled in Moscow, where he studied piano; in 1866 he joined the staff of the Moscow Cons., where he taught for 30 years. He became music critic of 2 Moscow papers, and his opinions exercised considerable influence in the musical life of Moscow in the last quarter of the 19th century. He was an intimate friend of Tchaikovsky; his little pamphlet *Reminiscences of Tchaikovsky* (Moscow, 1896) is valuable for authentic biographical and psychological data. A selection of his articles was publ. in Moscow (1953).

Kashperov, Vladimir, Russian composer; b. in Tchufarovo, Simbirsk region, Sept. 6, 1826; d. Romantsevo, near Mozhaisk, July 8, 1894. He studied with Voigt and Henselt in St. Petersburg and with Dehn in Berlin (1856); went to Italy to study singing (1858), and remained there until 1864; he wrote several operas in the Italian style which were produced in Italy: *Maria Tudor* (Milan, 1859), *Rienzi* (Florence, 1863), and *Consuelo* (Venice, 1865). In 1865 he returned to Russia and taught voice at the Moscow Cons. (1866–72); in 1872 opened his own school of singing. In Moscow he produced 2 operas with Russian librettos: *The Storm*, after Ostrovsky (1867) and *Taras Bulba*, after Gogol (1893). Even in his Russian works, Kashperov

remained faithful to the Italian style of composition, taking Donizetti as a model.

Kaskel, Karl von, German composer; b. Dresden, Oct. 10, 1866; d. Berlin, Nov. 22, 1943. While a law student at Leipzig, he studied music in the Cons. under Reinecke and Jadassohn (1886–87) and later at Cologne under Wüllner and Jensen. He lived many years in Dresden; later in Munich. He was a fairly successful composer.
WORKS: operas, *Hochzeitsmorgen* (Hamburg, 1893), *Sjula* (Cologne, 1895), *Die Bettlerin vom Pont des Arts* (Kassel, 1899), *Der Dusle und das Babeli* (Munich, 1903), *Der Gefangene der Zarin* (Dresden, 1910), *Die Nachtigall* (Stuttgart, 1910), *Die Schmiedin von Kent* (Dresden, 1916); for orch., *Lust-spielouvertüre; Humoresque; Ballade;* piano pieces; songs.
BIBLIOGRAPHY: E. Schmitz, "Karl von Kaskel," *Monographien moderner Musiker* (Leipzig, 1909).

Kassern, Tadeusz Zygfrid, Polish composer; b. Lwow, March 19, 1904; d. New York, May 2, 1957. He studied with M. Soltys at the Lwow Cons. and with Opienski in Poznan. He also took a course in law; in 1931, went to Paris. In 1945 he was appointed cultural attaché at the Polish Consulate in N.Y. However, he broke with the Communist government in Poland, and remained in N.Y.; became an American citizen in 1956. Among Polish composers, he pursued a cosmopolitan trend; although many of his works are inspired by Polish folk music, the idiom and the method are of a general European modern character.
WORKS: 2 operas, *The Anointed* (1951) and *Sun-Up* (1952; N.Y., Nov. 10, 1954); *Dies irae*, symph. poem in memory of Marshal Pilsudski (1935); Concerto for Soprano (1928); Concerto for Double Bass and Orch. (1937); Concerto for String Orch. (1944); Concertino for Oboe and String Orch. (1946); Concertino for Flute, String Orch., Xylophone, and Celesta (1948); *Teen-Age Concerto*, for piano and orch. (N.Y., May 1956); choruses; chamber music; piano pieces; songs.

Kässmayer, Moritz, Austrian violinist and composer; b. Vienna, March 20, 1831; d. there, Nov. 9, 1884. He studied with Sechter at the Vienna Cons.; then played violin in the orch. of the Vienna Opera; later became ballet conductor there. He wrote a comic opera, *Das Landhaus zu Meudon* (1869); symphonies; Masses and other church music; 5 string quartets; songs. His *Mesalliansen* for string quartet with piano 4 hands, and *Volksweisen und Lieder* for string quartet 'humoristisch und kontrapunktisch bearbeitet,' are amusing specimens of old-fashioned humor.

Kastalsky, Alexander, Russian choral conductor and composer; b. Moscow, Nov. 28, 1856; d. there, Dec. 17, 1926. He was a pupil of Tchaikovsky, Taneyev, and Hubert at the Moscow Cons. (1875–82). In 1887 he became instructor of piano at the Synodal School in Moscow; in 1891, assistant conductor of the Synodal Chorus; in 1910, appointed director of the school and principal conductor of the choir. In 1911 he took it on an extended European tour. In 1918 the Synodal School became a choral academy; in 1923 it merged with the Moscow Cons. Kastalsky was also teacher of conducting at the Moscow Philharmonic Institute (1912–22); in 1923, appointed prof. of choral singing at the Moscow Cons. He was a notable composer of Russian sacred music, into which he introduced modern elements, combining them with the ancient church modes.

WORKS: the opera *Clara Militch,* after Turgenev (Moscow, 1916); oratorio *The Furnace of Nabucho* (1909); Requiem (1916; in memory of Allied soldiers fallen in World War I; in 12 sections, based on the modes of Greek Orthodox, Roman Catholic, and Anglican Churches); *Rustic Symphony* (Moscow, Dec. 13, 1925); incidental music to *Stenka Rasin* (Moscow, 1918), to Shakespeare's *King Lear* (Moscow, 1919), and to Hauptmann's *Hannele* (Moscow, 1920); a cantata, *1812;* symph. suite *Pictures of Russian Festivities* (1912); *A Market Place in Ancient Russia* (completed 1924); 5 choruses on patriotic texts; about 80 sacred choruses a cappella; *In Georgia,* suite for piano; *Ancient Times* (4 vols. of restorations of ancient music, for piano: I. China, India, Egypt; II. Greece, Judea, Islam; III. Early Christianity; IV. Ancient Russia). He publ. a valuable paper, *Peculiarities of the National Russian Musical System* (Moscow, 1923), greatly expanded by him during the last 3 years of his life, and publ. posthumously as *Foundations of National Polyphony,* ed. by Victor Belaiev (Moscow, 1948).

BIBLIOGRAPHY: His autobiographical sketch, *My Musical Career and My Thoughts on Church Music,* was publ. in the *Musical Quarterly* (April 1925). See also W. S. Pring, "Kastalsky and Russian Folk Polyphony," *Music & Letters* (1929).

Kastendieck, Miles Merwin, American music critic; b. Brooklyn, April 16, 1905. He studied at Yale Univ. with D. S. Smith. He became critic of the *New Haven Journal-Courier* (1929–38), of the *Brooklyn Eagle* (1938–46), the *N.Y. Journal-American* since 1946, and N.Y. correspondent for the *Christian Science Monitor* (1945–72). He wrote *England's Musical Poet, Thomas Campion* (N.Y., 1938).

Kastle, Leonard, American composer; b. New York, Feb. 11, 1929. He studied composition with George Szell and piano with Frank Sheridan and Paul Wittgenstein. In 1945 he entered the Curtis Institute and studied with Isabelle Vengerova (piano) and Rosario Scalero (composition); continued his studies with Gian-Carlo Menotti and Carl Bamberger (conducting); graduated in 1950. Among his works are a Piano Sonata (1950); a one-act opera for television, *The Swing* (NBC television network, June 11, 1956); a choral work, *Whispers of Heavenly Death* (1956); *Deseret* (NBC Opera Co., N.Y., Jan. 1, 1961).

Kastner, Alfred, Austrian harpist; b. Vienna, March 10, 1870; d. Hollywood, May 24, 1948. He studied with Zamara at the Vienna Cons.; then played first harp in the orchestras of the Dresden Opera and Warsaw Opera; later taught harp in Budapest (1892–98); was in the U.S. (1898–1900); then in Switzerland. From 1904–19 he was harpist in the Queen's Hall Orch. in London; also taught at the Royal Academy of Music there. In 1919 he was engaged as first harpist of the Los Angeles Philharmonic. He publ. several concert pieces for the harp and various arrangements.

Kastner, Emmerich, Austrian writer on music; b. Vienna, March 29, 1847; d. there, Dec. 5, 1916. He published several valuable works dealing with Wagner: *Richard Wagner-Katalog* (1878); *Wagneriana* (1885); *Briefe R. Wagners an seine Zeitgenossen 1830–38* (1885); *Die dramatischen Werke R. Wagners* (1899). Other writings are *Bayreuth* (1884) and *Neuestes und vollständigstes Tonkünstler- und Opern-Lexikon* (1889; only A-Azzoni printed); edited *Beethovens sämmtliche Briefe* (Leipzig, 1911). He was editor of the *Wiener musikalische Zeitung.*

Kastner, Georg Friedrich, Alsatian acoustician; son of **Johann Georg Kastner;** b. Strasbourg, Aug. 10, 1852; d. Bonn, April 6, 1882. He followed his father's ideas of music as a science; at the age of 20, read a paper before the Académie des Sciences in Paris, *Pyrophone: Flammes chantantes,* subsequently published; constructed the Pyrophone, an organ of 3 octaves on which the sound was produced by burning gas jets. Description and picture of the Pyrophone are in vol. 3 of H. Ludwig von Jan's biography of Kastner's father.

Kastner, Jean Georges, Alsatian composer and theorist; b. Strasbourg, March 9, 1810; d. Paris, Dec. 19, 1867. He studied organ as a child; later entered the Strasbourg Lutheran Seminary. He then gave up his theological studies and went to Paris. There he resumed his musical education, taking lessons with Berton and Reicha. An industrious scholar, Kastner acquired enormous erudition in various arts and sciences. He pursued the study of acoustics and formulated a theory of the cosmic unity of the arts. At the same time he took great interest in practical applications of music; he was active in organizing the contest of bands of 9 nations held at the Paris Exposition of 1867. He was a founder and vice-president of the Association des Artistes-Musiciens. He was elected a member of the "Institut" and an Officer of the Legion of Honor. Among the grandiose projects that he carried out were several volumes of "Livres-Partitions," that is, symphony-cantatas illustrating musico-historical subjects, preceded by essays upon them. Of these the following were published: *Les Danses des morts; dissertations et recherches historiques, philosophiques, littéraires et musicales sur les divers monuments de ce genre qui existent tant en France qu'à l'étranger;* and *Danse macabre, grande ronde vocale et instrumentale* (Paris, 1852; 310 pages); *La Harpe d'Éole, et la musique cosmique;* and *Stéphen, ou la Harpe d'Éole, grand monologue avec chœurs* (1856); *Les Sirènes,* and *Le Rêve d'Oswald ou les Sirènes, grande symphonie dramatique vocale et instrumentale* (1858); *Parémiologie musicale de la langue française* and *La Saint-Julien des ménétriers, symphonie-cantate à grand orchestre, avec solos et chœurs* (1862; 659 pages); *Les Voix de Paris* and *Les Cris de Paris, grande symphonie humoristique vocale et instrumentale,* making use of vendors' cries with orchestral accompaniment (1875). Kastner wrote several operas; 4 were produced in Strasbourg: *Gustav*

Wasa (1832), *Oskars Tod* (1833), comic opera *Der Sarazene* (1834), and *Die Königin der Sarmaten* (1835). In Paris he produced 2 operas: *La Maschera* (June 17, 1841) and *Le Dernier Roi de Juda* (1844). He also wrote 5 overtures, a sextet for saxophones, and 2 collections of men's choruses (*Les Chants de la vie,* 1854; *Chants de l'armée française,* 1855); publ. a useful and highly practical *Manuel général de musique militaire à l'usage des armées françaises* (Paris, 1848). His great project, *Encyclopédie de la musique,* was left uncompleted at his death.

BIBLIOGRAPHY: H. Ludwig (real name, H. Ludwig von Jan), *J. G. Kastner, ein elsässischer Tondichter, Theoretiker und Musikforscher* (Leipzig, 1886; 3 parts in 2 vols.).

Kastner, Santiago, musicologist; b. London, Oct. 15, 1908. He studied at Amsterdam, Leipzig, Berlin, Barcelona; settled in Lisbon in 1933; lectured throughout Europe, made many appearances as concert pianist and harpsichordist. His writings include *Música hispanica* (Madrid, 1936); *Contribución al estudio de la música española y portuguesa* (Lisbon, 1941); *Federico Mompou* (Madrid, 1947); *Carlos de Seixas* (Coimbra, 1947); *Francisco Correa de Arauxo* (Barcelona, 1948). He edited 80 keyboard sonatas by Seixas (1965) and several other works by Portuguese and Spanish composers.

Katchen, Julius, American pianist; b. Long Branch, N.J., Aug. 15, 1926; d. Paris, April 29, 1969. He studied in New York with David Saperton; made his debut with the Philadelphia Orch. on Oct. 21, 1937. He studied academic subjects at Haverford College, graduating in 1945. In 1948 he toured Palestine; then settled in Paris; gave a series of successful concerts in Europe.

Kate, André ten, Dutch composer and cellist; b. Amsterdam, May 22, 1796; d. Haarlem, July 27, 1858. He studied cello with Bertelmann. He wrote the operas *Seid e Palmira* (1831) and *Constantia* (1835); also other operas; chamber music; part-songs; etc.

Kates, Stephen, American cellist; b. New York, May 7, 1943. He studied at the Juilliard School of Music; in 1963 won a honorable mention and a medal of merit at the International Cello Competition in Budapest; appeared at the Young People's Concerts with the N.Y. Philharmonic under Leonard Bernstein; in 1964 toured Europe with the Pittsburgh Symph. Orch.; then went to study with Gregor Piatigorsky in Los Angeles. In 1965 he won a debut grant of the Young Musicians Foundation in California. In 1966 he won the 2nd prize in the Tchaikovsky competition in Moscow.

Katims, Milton, American conductor and violist; b. New York, June 24, 1909. He attended Columbia Univ.; studied viola and conducting with L. Barzin. From 1935–43 he was viola player and assistant conductor at WOR; in 1943, joined the NBC Symph. Orch. as 1st violist and subsequently assistant conductor under Toscanini. From 1954 to 1974 he was conductor and musical director of the Seattle Symph. Orch. In 1976 was appointed artistic director of the School of Music at the University of Houston, Texas.

Katwijk, Paul van, pianist and composer; b. Rotterdam, Dec. 7, 1885; d. Dallas, Texas, Dec. 11, 1974. He studied at the Cons. of The Hague; then in Berlin with Klatte and in Vienna with Godowsky; then devoted himself chiefly to conducting and teaching. In 1912 he settled in the U.S.; taught at Drake Univ., Des Moines, Iowa (1914–18) and also conducted the Des Moines Symph. Orch.; in 1919, appointed dean of music at Southern Methodist Univ., Dallas, Texas; resigned in 1949, but continued to teach piano there until 1955. He was conductor of the Dallas Municipal Opera (1922–25) and from 1925 till 1936 conductor of the Dallas Symph. Orch. He composed several symph. works; his orch. suite *Hollandia* was perf. by the Dallas Symph. Orch. on March 15, 1931.

Katz, Israel J., American musicologist; b. New York, July 21, 1930. He studied at the Univ. of Calif., Los Angeles, with Klaus P. Wachsmann and Boris Kremenliev, earning his B.A. in 1956 and Ph.D. in 1967. He specialized in Jewish and Spanish music; publ. a monograph, *Judeo-Spanish Traditional Ballads from Jerusalem* (2 vols., Brooklyn, 1971); contributed scholarly articles to the *Encyclopedia Judaica, Ethnomusicology* and other publications.

Kauder, Hugo, Austrian composer; b. Tobitschau, Moravia, June 9, 1888; d. Bussum, Holland, July 22, 1972. He studied violin; was a member of the Konzertverein Orch. in Vienna. In 1938 he came to America and settled in New York. His music is contrapuntal, with canonic devices much used in free and often asymmetric rhythm, while the harmonies are conservative. He wrote 4 symphs., a cello concerto, and a great number of works for chamber music combinations. He publ. *Entwurf einer neuen Melodie- und Harmonielehre* (Vienna, 1932) and *Counterpoint* (N.Y., 1960).

Kauer, Ferdinand, Austrian composer; baptized at Klein-Tajax (Znaim), Moravia, Jan. 18, 1751; d. Vienna, April 13, 1831. As a boy he played organ in a Jesuit church at Znaim; in 1784 he played violin in a Vienna theater, and also supplied music for a number of plays performed there. He wrote some 100 operettas and other stage works; of these, *Das Donauweibchen* (Vienna, Jan. 11, 1798) was sensationally successful and was performed all over Europe for many years; other works (an oratorio *Die Sündflut,* a quantity of church music, symphonies, concertos, etc.) also enjoyed favor. Most of his manuscripts were lost in the flood of 1830; a list of extant works is given by Eitner in his *Quellen-Lexikon.* Kauer publ. a *Singschule nach dem neuesten System der Tonkunst* (1790), and a *Kurzgefasste Generalbass-Schule für Anfänger* (1800).

BIBLIOGRAPHY: Th. Haas, "Ferdinand Kauer," *Neue Musik Zeitung* (1925); K. Manschinger, *Ferdinand Kauer* (Vienna, 1929).

Kauffmann, Emil, German composer and writer on music; son of **Ernst Friedrich Kauffmann;** b. Ludwigsburg, Nov. 23, 1836; d. Tübingen, June 17, 1909. He studied at the Stuttgart Cons. with Keller, Faiszt, Jung, and Singer; joined the court orch. in 1863 as violinist; teacher in the music school at Basel (1868–77); musical director at Tübingen Univ. (Dr. phil., 1885). He wrote *Die Nacht;* over 60 lieder; male choruses; sonatas and other piano pieces; also the essays *Entwickelung der Tonkunst von der Mitte des 18. Jahrhunderts bis zur Gegenwart* (1884) and *Justinus Heinrich Knecht: ein schwäbischer Tonsetzer* (1892); contributed articles to the Leipzig *Musikalisches Wochenblatt.*

Kauffmann, Ernst Friedrich, German composer; father of **Emil Kauffmann;** b. Ludwigsburg, Nov. 27, 1803; d. Stuttgart, Feb. 11, 1856. He studied at Tübingen Univ. (1825–27); became principal of the Realschule at Ludwigsburg, but because of his connection with revolutionists he lost his position in 1835; was imprisoned in Asperg (1838–42), where he wrote 6 sets of songs, which became popular.

Kauffmann, Fritz, German composer; b. Berlin, June 17, 1855; d. Magdeburg, Sept. 29, 1934. He was an apothecary; began to study music seriously at 23, with Kiel in Berlin; 3 years later, won the Mendelssohn Prize for composition. After a sojourn in Vienna, he lived mostly in Berlin; in 1889 became choral conductor in Magdeburg; from 1897 till 1920 he conducted the Kirchengesangverein there. He wrote a comic opera, *Die Herzkrankheit;* a symphony; 2 violin concertos; piano concerto; cello concerto; 2 piano sonatas; *Tanz-Improvisationen* for piano; choruses; songs.

Kauffmann, Leo Justinus, Alsatian composer; b. Dammerkirch, Sept. 20, 1901; killed in an air raid, Strasbourg, Sept. 25, 1944. He studied with Marie Joseph Erb in Strasbourg and with Jarnach and Abendroth in Cologne; 1932–40, was active in radio work in Cologne; then taught at the Strasbourg Cons.; served as its director until he was killed. He wrote the opera *Die Geschichte vom schönen Annerl* (Strasbourg, June 20, 1942); a Mass; a symph.; and Concertino for Double Bass with Chamber Orch.

Kaufman, Harry, American pianist; b. New York, Sept. 6, 1894; d. Beverly Hills, Calif., Aug. 22, 1961. He studied at the Institute of Musical Art with Stojowski; later was a pupil of Josef Hofmann; in 1924 he was appointed teacher of the art of accompanying at the Curtis Institute, Philadelphia. Though principally known as an excellent accompanist, he also appeared as soloist with the N.Y. Philharmonic, the Philadelphia Orch., etc., and as a member of several chamber music groups.

Kaufman, Louis, distinguished American violinist; b. Portland, Oregon, May 10, 1905. He studied with Kneisel; won the Loeb Prize in 1927 and the Naumburg Award in 1928. In 1950 he regularly gave concerts in Europe. On Oct. 21, 1950 he presented in Paris, as violinist and conductor, the 12 concertos by Vivaldi, op. 8; in 1954 he played 12 concertos by Torelli, op. 8, in London; also performed Vivaldi's concertos in Rio de Janeiro and Buenos Aires (1952). He gave numerous first performances of works by contemporary composers, among them a violin concerto by Dag Wiren (Stockholm, Oct. 25, 1953), and first American performances of violin works by Darius Milhaud, Lev Knipper, Bohuslav Martinu, and others; also played American works in Europe; gave the first performance in England of Walter Piston's Violin Concerto (London, April 6, 1956). He edited 6 Sonatas for Violin by G. Ph. Telemann, *Sonata Concertante* by L. Spohr; published *Warming Up Scales and Arpeggios* for violinists (1957).

Kaufmann, Armin, Rumanian composer; b. Itzkany, Bukovina, Oct. 30, 1902. In 1914 his family settled in Austria; he studied with Joseph Marx at the Vienna Academy of Music; from 1938 to 1966 he played the viola in the Vienna Symph. Orch. As a composer, he wrote mostly instrumental music.

WORKS: 4 symphonies (1929, 1962, 1966, 1968); Piano Concerto (1970); Quintet for piano, violin, viola, cello, double bass (1965); 7 string quartets; Trio for violin, zither and guitar (1962); Trio for flute, viola and harp (1967); Rhapsody for solo guitar (1970); a curious Concerto for Tárogató and Orch. (1967).

Kaufmann, Friedrich, German inventor; b. Dresden, Feb. 5, 1785; d. there, Dec. 1, 1866. He invented a trumpet automaton (1808), the "Belloneon," the "Klaviatur-Harmonichord," the "Chordaulodion," and the "Symphonion." In 1851 his son, **Friedrich Theodor Kaufmann** (b. Dresden, April 9, 1823; d. there, Feb. 5, 1872), made an "Orchestrion" from the "Symphonion."

Kaufmann, Helen, American writer on music; b. New York, Feb. 2, 1887. She studied at Barnard College; was active in various educational organizations.

WRITINGS: *From Jehovah to Jazz* (1937); *Home Book of Music Appreciation* (1942); *Story of One Hundred Great Composers* (1943); *Little Book of Music Anecdotes* (1948); *Little Guide to Music Appreciation* (1948); *The Story of Music Through the Ages* (1949); *The Story of Mozart* (1955); *The Story of Sergei Prokofiev* (Philadelphia, 1971); etc.

Kaufmann, Walter, conductor and composer; b. Karlsbad, April 1, 1907. He studied composition with Schreker in Berlin; also took courses in musicology in Prague. In 1935 he traveled to India, where he remained for 10 years; studied the Hindu systems of composition; served as music director of the Bombay Radio. In 1947 he moved to Nova Scotia and taught piano at the Halifax Cons. there; from 1948 to 1957 he was conductor of the Winnipeg Symph. Orch.; in 1957 he settled in America, and joined the staff of Indiana Univ. in Bloomington; he became an American citizen in 1964. A prolific composer, he devotes his chief interest to stage works; he wrote the following operas: *Der Himmel bringt es an den Tag* (1934); *Anasuya,* a radio opera (Bombay, Oct. 1, 1938); *A Parfait for Irene* (Bloomington, Feb. 21, 1952); *Bashmashkin* (after Gogol's *The Coat;* 1952); *The Scarlet Letter,* after Hawthorne (Bloomington, May 6, 1961); *Sganarelle* (1962); *A Hoosier Tale* (Bloomington; July 30, 1966). He further wrote 6 symphonies (1930, 1933, 1936, 1939, 1940, 1956); *Madras Express,* a fantasy for orch. (Boston Pops, June 23, 1948); Piano Concerto (1950); *Rubayyat,* for voice and orch. (1951–52); 4 12-tone pieces for small orch. (1956); 7 string quartets; 2 piano trios; 2 string trios; piano pieces; songs. He also contributed several informative articles on Eastern music to various American magazines; published *Musical References in the Chinese Classics* (Detroit, 1976).

Kaul, Oskar, German musicologist; b. Heufeld, Oct. 11, 1885; d. Unterwössen, July 17, 1968. He studied music at the Cologne Cons.; then took courses in musicology with Sandberger in Munich; obtained his degree of Dr. phil. at the Univ. of Munich in 1911. He was in the army during World War I; in 1922, became privat docent in Würzburg; in 1930, prof.; also director of the State Cons. there. He retired in 1945; lived in Unterwössen, Bavaria. He edited 5 symphonies and chamber music by Rosetti for the *Denkmäler der Tonkunst in Bayern* (vols. 12 and 25) and publ. a dissertation, *Die Vokalwerke Anton Rosettis* (Cologne, 1911); other writings include *Geschichte der Würzburger Hofmusik im 18. Jahrhundert* (Würzburg, 1924), *Athanasius Kircher als Musikgelehrter* (Würzburg, 1932), and many valuable papers on the music history of Bavaria.

Kaun, Hugo, German composer; b. Berlin, March 21, 1863; d. there, April 2, 1932. He studied piano with Oskar Raif and composition with Friedrich Kiel in Berlin; composed industriously as a very young man. In 1887 he went to live in America, settling in Milwaukee, where he remained for 14 years (1887–1901); was a successful teacher, and continued to compose. In 1902 he returned to Berlin to teach privately; in 1922, became prof. at the Klindworth-Scharwenka Cons.; publ. an autobiography, *Aus meinem Leben* (Berlin, 1932); also a manual for students, *Harmonielehre und Aufgabenbuch.* A cultured composer, thoroughly versed in the craft, he wrote a great number of works, and enjoyed recognition among large groups of friends; his musical style contained elements of both Brahmsian and Wagnerian idioms.

WORKS: operas: *Sappho* (Leipzig, Oct. 27, 1917), *Der Fremde* (Dresden, Feb. 23, 1920), and *Menandra* (staged in Kiel and several other German opera houses simultaneously, Oct. 29, 1925); for orch.: 3 symphonies; 2 piano concertos; *Der Sternenbanner,* a festival march on the *Star-Spangled Banner;* overture, *Der Maler von Antwerpen* (Chicago, Feb. 3, 1899); *Im Urwald,* 2 symph. poems, after Longfellow's *Minnehaha* and *Hiawatha* (Chicago, Feb. 7, 1903); etc.; *Auf dem Meere,* for baritone, chorus, and orch.; several settings of psalms; a Requiem, and other church music; chamber music: Octet for wind and string instruments; String Quintet; 4 string quartets; piano trio; Violin Sonata; numerous piano pieces.

BIBLIOGRAPHY: W. Altmann, *Hugo Kaun* (Leipzig, 1906); G. R. Kruse, "Hugo Kaun," *Die Musik* (1909–10); R. Schaal, *Hugo Kaun, Leben und Werk* (Regensburg, 1946).

Kay, Hershy, American composer and arranger; b. Philadelphia, Nov. 17, 1919. He studied at the Curtis Institute of Music in Philadelphia; then went to N.Y.; orchestrated Leonard Bernstein's musical comedies *On the Town* (1944) and *Candide* (1956). He made numerous arrangements for Balanchine's ballet company, among them *Concert* (1956) from Chopin's music. His original ballet, *Western Symphony,* was produced by Balanchine with the N.Y. City Ballet Co. on Sept. 7, 1954, and was included in its Russian tour in 1962.

Kay, Ulysses Simpson, eminent black American composer; b. Tucson, Arizona, Jan. 7, 1917. He received his early music training at home; on the advice of his mother's uncle **"King" Oliver,** a leading jazz cornetist, he studied piano. In 1934 he enrolled at the Univ. of Arizona at Tucson (Mus. B., 1938); he then went to study at the Eastman School in Rochester where he was a student of Bernard Rogers and Howard Hanson (M.M., 1940); later attended the classes of Paul Hindemith at the Berskshire Music Center in Tanglewood (1941–42). He served in the U.S. Navy (1942–45); went to Rome, Italy, as winner of the American Rome Prize, and was attached there to the American Academy in Rome (1949–52). From 1953 to 1968 he was employed as consultant by Broadcast Music Inc., N.Y.; was on the faculty of the Boston University (1965) and at the Univ. of California, Los Angeles (1966–67); in 1968 was appointed prof. of music at the Herbert H. Lehman College, N.Y. In 1964 he held a Guggenheim Fellowship; in 1969 he was awarded an honorary doctorate in music by the Univ. of Arizona. Kay's music follows a distinctly American idiom, particularly in its rhythmic intensity, while avoiding ostentatious ethnic elements; in harmony and counterpoint, he pursues a moderately advanced idiom, marked by prudentially euphonious dissonances; his instrumentation is masterly.

WORKS: operas: *The Boor,* after Chekhov (1955; Louisville, April 3, 1968), *The Juggler of Our Lady* (1956; New Orleans, Feb. 3, 1962), *The Capitoline Venus* (Quincy, Illinois, March 12, 1971), *Jubilee* (Jackson, Mississippi, Nov. 20, 1976); Oboe Concerto (Rochester, April 16, 1940); *5 Mosaics* for chamber orch. (Cleveland, Dec. 28, 1940); ballet, *Dance Calinda* (Rochester, April 23, 1941); *Of New Horizons,* overture (N.Y., July 29, 1944); *A Short Overture* (N.Y.; March 31, 1947); Suite for Strings (Baltimore, April 8, 1949); *Sinfonia in E* (Rochester, May 2, 1951); *6 Dances* for strings (1954); Concerto for Orch. (N.Y., 1954); *Song of Jeremiah,* cantata (Nashville, April 23, 1954); Serenade for Orch. (Louisville, Sept. 18, 1954); *3 Pieces After Blake,* for soprano and orch. (1952; N.Y., March 27, 1955); *Fantasy Variations* for orch. (1963); *Umbrian Scene* for orch. (New Orleans, March 31, 1964); *Markings,* symphonic essay, dedicated to the memory of Dag Hammarskjöld (Rochester, Michigan, Aug. 8, 1966; television performance, with scenes from Hammarskjöld's life, on "The Black Composer," shown on Education TV on June 19, 1972); *Theater Set* for orch. (1968); *Scherzi musicali* for chamber orch. (1971); *Aulos* for flute and chamber orch. (Bloomington, Ind., Feb. 21, 1971); *Quintet Concerto* for 5 brass soli and orch. (N.Y., March 14, 1975); *Southern Harmony* for orch. (North Carolina Symphony, Feb. 10, 1976); 2 string quartets (1953; 1956); Quintet for flute and strings (1947); Piano Quintet (1949); Piano Sonata (1940); film score for *The Quiet One* (1948); many choral pieces and songs.

BIBLIOGRAPHY: N. Slonimsky, "Ulysses Kay," *American Composers Alliance Bulletin* (Fall 1957);

L. M. Hayes, *The Music of Ulysses Kay, 1939–1963* (Univ. of Wisconsin, 1971); R. T. Hadley, *The Published Choral Music of Ulysses Simpson Kay, 1943–1968* (Univ. of Iowa, 1972); C. Dower, "Ulysses Kay: Distinguished American Composer," *Musart* (Jan.–Feb. 1972); L. R. Wyatt, "Ulysses Kay's *Fantasy Variations:* An Analysis," *Black Perspective in Music* (Spring 1977).

Kayser, Heinrich Ernst, German violinist; b. Altona, April 16, 1815; d. Hamburg, Jan. 17, 1888. He was a theater violinist in Hamburg (1840–57); then became a violin teacher there; wrote numerous violin studies that became standard exercises, and a violin method.

Kayser, Leif, Danish composer; b. Copenhagen, June 13, 1919. He studied at the Copenhagen Cons., and later took courses with Rosenberg in Stockholm; then went to Rome where he studied theology (1942–49), and was ordained a priest of the Catholic church. Returning to Copenhagen he served as chaplain of the Catholic Cathedral. He wrote 4 symphonies (1939, 1940, 1956, 1963), *Christmas Oratorio* (1943); Sinfonietta for an amateur orch. (1967); Divertimento for 4 recorders (1968); Organ Sonata; several sacred choruses; 4 psalms for women's chorus, etc.

Kayser, Philipp Christoph, German composer and pianist; b. Frankfurt, March 10, 1755; d. Zürich, Dec. 23, 1823. In 1775 he settled in Zürich as a teacher. From Goethe's correspondence with him it appears that he wrote music to several of Goethe's singspiele, but only one, *Scherz, Liszt und Rache,* is preserved, in manuscript. He publ. a *Weihnachtskantate; Deux Sonates en symphonie,* for piano and 2 horns; and songs.
BIBLIOGRAPHY: C. A. Burkhardt, *Goethe und der Komponist Philipp Christoph Kayser* (Leipzig, 1879); E. Refardt, *Hist-biogr. Mus.-Lexikon der Schweiz* (1928).

Kazachenko, Grigori, Russian composer; b. St. Petersburg, May 3, 1858; d. there (Leningrad), May 18, 1938. He studied piano and composition at the St. Petersburg Cons.; then was chorusmaster at the Imperial Opera and appeared as conductor. In 1924 he became prof. of choral singing at the Leningrad Cons. He wrote 2 operas, *Prince Serebryanny* (St. Petersburg, 1892) and *Pan Sotnik* (St. Petersburg, Sept. 17, 1902); Symphony; *An Armenian Overture; Fantasia on Russian Themes* for viola and orch.; several choral works, songs and piano pieces.

Kazandjiev, Vasil, Bulgarian composer and conductor; b. Ruse, Sept. 10, 1934. He studied composition with Vladigerov and conducting with Simeonov at the Bulgarian State Cons., graduating in 1957; in 1964 was appointed to its faculty. He is one of the few composers in Bulgaria to employ elements of serial techniques; he endeavors to amalgamate non-tonal ingredients of modern music with the national melorhythms of Bulgarian folk motives.
WORKS: Concerto for String Orch. (1951); *Variations* for string orch. (1952); Sinfonietta (1954); Trumpet Concerto (1955); *Divertimento* for orch. (1957); Concerto for Piano, Saxophone and Orch.

(1957–60); Violin Concerto (1961); *Complexi Sonori* for strings (1965); *Symphony of Timbres* (1968); *The Living Icons* for chamber orch. (1970; Sofia, Jan. 26, 1972); *Pictures from Bulgaria* for string orch. and percussion (1971); *Festive Music* for orch. (1972); *Capriccio* for orch. (1974); Wind Quintet (1951); *Variations* for oboe, clarinet, violin, viola, cello and piano (1954); Horn Sonata (1955); Clarinet Sonata (1956); Sonata for Solo Violin (1957); 2 string quartets (1965; 1970); *Concert Improvisations* for flute, viola, harp and harpsichord (1974); Piano Sonata (1957); *The Triumph of the Bells* for piano (1974); choruses; songs; incidental music.

Kazanly, Nikolai, Russian composer; b. Tiraspol, Dec. 17, 1869; d. St. Petersburg, Aug. 5, 1916. He received his primary education in music in Odessa (1879–83); then went to St. Petersburg where he entered the class in composition of Rimsky-Korsakov at the St. Petersburg Cons., graduating in 1894. In 1897 he traveled to Germany where he conducted symphony concerts in Munich; returning to Russia he supervised music education in military schools. He wrote an opera, *Miranda* (1910); a symphony and several symphonic poems, among them *La Nuit du Carnaval;* cantatas and songs, all in the traditional Russian style. Under the general title of "Philharmonica" he published over 100 classical pieces in arrangement for small orchestra.

Kazuro, Stanislaw, Polish composer; b. Teklinapol, near Wilno, Aug. 1, 1881; d. Warsaw, Nov. 30, 1961. He studied in Warsaw, Paris, and Rome; after his return to Warsaw he was active mainly as a pedagogue and chorus conductor; he also published several school manuals. His compositions, in an academic style, were chiefly designed for pedagogic purposes; among them are 2 folk operas, several choral works, albums of pieces for piano, etc.

Każyński, Wiktor, Polish composer; b. Wilno, Dec. 30, 1812; d. St. Petersburg, March 18, 1867. He studied jurisprudence in Wilno; was mostly self-taught in music. From 1836 to 1840 he was a church organist; then went to Warsaw where he took lessons with Chopin's teacher Elsner. In 1843 he went to St. Petersburg; in 1845 he conducted the orchestra of the Alexandrinsky Theater in St. Petersburg. He was one of the first pianists to play Chopin's works in Russia. His own compositions are of little importance, but they are of historical interest as early examples of Polish romanticism. He wrote an opera to a Polish libretto, *Zyd wieczny tulacz (The Wandering Jew),* which was produced in Wilno in 1840, and an opera to a French libretto, *Mari et femme* (St. Petersburg, 1848); he also published a *History of Italian Opera* (St. Petersburg, 1851; in Polish and in a Russian translation).

Keats, Donald, American composer; b. New York, May 27, 1929. He studied piano at the Manhattan School of Music; composition at Yale Univ. with Quincy Porter and Paul Hindemith (Mus. B., 1949) and at Columbia Univ. with Otto Luening, Douglas Moore and Henry Cowell (M.A., 1953); musicology with Alfred Einstein and Leo Schrade at Yale and with Paul Henry Lang at Columbia. Subsequently he obtained a Ph.D. in composition from the Univ. of Minnesota. In 1954 he received a Fulbright Grant for study in Germany, and took lessons with Philipp Jarnach in Hamburg. In 1957 he joined the staff of Antioch College. In 1964–65 he held a Guggenheim Fellowship.

WORKS: Clarinet Sonata (1948); String Trio (1949); Divertimento for winds and strings (1949); *The Hollow Men* for chorus and instruments (1955); String Quartet No. 1 (1956); Variations for Piano (1956); Symph. No. 1 (1957); Piano Sonata (1960); *The Naming of Cats* for chorus (1961); Symph. No. 2 (*Elegiac Symphony*; Kansas City, April 28, 1964); String Quartet No. 2 (1965).

Kee, Cor, Dutch organist and composer, father of **Piet Kee**; b. Zaandam, Nov. 24, 1900. He studied the organ in Holland; was especially praised for his talent in improvisation; in 1951 began a class in organ improvising in connection with the annual International Organ Improvisation Competition in Haarlem. He published 3 collections of *Psalms* for organ, which treat old psalm tunes contrapuntally. In some of his own compositions (almost exclusively for organ) he applies polyphonic devices of the classical Flemish School in a modern way, including serial procedures.

WORKS: *Reeksveranderingen* (*Serial Permutations;* 1966); *Phases* for organ (1966); *Phases* for organ (1969); *Blijde Incomste (Joyful Entry),* variations on a traditional song, for brass, percussion and piano (1969); *Sweelinck Variations* for horn, 2 trumpets, 2 trombones and organ (1973); numerous teaching pieces for organ.

Kee, Piet, Dutch organist and composer, son of **Cor Kee;** b. Zaandam, Aug. 30, 1927. He studied organ with his father and with Horst at the Amsterdam Cons., graduating in 1948; won the International Organ Improvisation Contest for 3 consecutive years (1953–55); in 1956 became organist of the St. Bavo Church in Haarlem where the annual contest is held; from 1954 was prof. of organ at the Muzieklyceum in Amsterdam. Like his father, he has written music almost exclusively for organ: *Triptych on Psalm 86* (1960); *Variations on a Carol* (1952–60); *Music and Space,* a rondo for 2 organs, 3 trumpets and 2 trombones (1969); made arrangements of hymns and folksongs; traveled as a concert organist in Europe and the U.S.

Keene, Christopher, American conductor; b. Berkeley, Calif., Dec. 21, 1946. He studied piano and cello; took courses at the Univ. of California, in Berkeley, majoring in history in 1963. While still a student he organized an opera company, with which he staged several modern works including the West Coast première of Henze's *Elegy for Young Lovers;* was guest conductor of the Spoleto Festivals in the summers of 1968, 1969 and 1971. Concurrently, he was musical director of the American Ballet Company, for which he wrote a ballet of his own, *The Consort* (1970). In 1970 he joined the conducting staff of the New York City Opera as the winner of the Julius Rudel Award; made a brilliant debut in Ginastera's opera *Don Rod-*

rigo; on March 12, 1971, conducted the world première of Menotti's opera *The Most Important Man;* on Aug. 12, 1971 he conducted the posthumous world première of the opera *Yerma* by Villa-Lobos, with the Santa Fe Opera Co. At his New York appearances he was enthusiastically acclaimed by the critics as one of the brightest precocious talents in the profession. In April 1971 he distinguished himself with the N.Y. City Opera by a highly competent performance of *La Traviata,* and later conducted also at the Metropolitan Opera. These accomplishments are all the more remarkable since he never took a regular course in conducting, but learned to lead orchestras by instinctual instrumental navigation. In 1975 he was appointed music director of the Syracuse, N.Y., Symph. Orchestra.

Kéfer, Paul, French cellist; b. Rouen, Dec. 30, 1875; d. Rochester, N.Y., May 22, 1941. He studied cello at the Paris Cons. with Delsart; won first prize in 1900. After coming to the U.S. in 1913, he formed, in N.Y., the Trio de Lutèce with Barrère (flute) and Salzedo (harp); was also founder and a member of the Franco-American Quartet. In 1923 he became prof. of cello at the Eastman School of Music in Rochester, N.Y.

Keil, Alfredo, Portuguese composer; b. Lisbon, July 3, 1850; d. Hamburg, Oct. 4, 1907. He was of German extraction and received his education in Germany. Returning to Portugal, he devoted his energies to the furtherance of national music, and was the first to produce an opera on a Portuguese subject in the Portuguese language. His song *Herois do mar* (1890) was adopted as the national anthem of the Republic of Portugal in 1910.

WORKS: the operas, *Donna Bianca* (Lisbon, March 10, 1888), *Irene* (Turin, March 22, 1893), *Serrana* (the first grand opera in Portuguese; Lisbon, March 13, 1899); 2 symph. sketches, *India* and *Simao;* songs.

BIBLIOGRAPHY: Lavignac's *Encyclopédie de la Musique* (vol. 4, p. 2453).

Keilberth, Joseph, German conductor; b. Karlsruhe, April 19, 1908; d. Munich, July 20, 1968. A member of a musical family, he was a conductor at the Karlsruhe State Opera (1935–40), of the Berlin Philharmonic Orch. (1940–45), at the Dresden Opera (1945–51); also guest conductor at the Berlin State Opera and in Hamburg. He founded the Philharmonic Orch. in Bamberg, and in 1951 toured with it in Switzerland, Holland, France, Spain, and Portugal. In 1953 he conducted the Wagner Festival in Bayreuth; in 1954, toured with the Bamberg Philharmonic Orch. in Cuba and Mexico; U.S. debut at Carnegie Hall, April 4, 1954.

Keiser, Reinhard, notable German composer of opera; b. Teuchern, near Weissenfels, Jan. 9, 1674; d. Hamburg, Sept. 12, 1739. He studied with his father Gottfried Keiser, an organist; he was then sent to Leipzig, where he studied at the Thomasschule with Johann Schelle. In 1692 he was in Brunswick, where the success of his pastoral *Ismene* encouraged him to try his hand at a serious opera, *Basilius* (1693). In

1695 he went to Hamburg, which then possessed the best operatic stage in Germany, and remained there. During his long years of unremitting labors in Hamburg he wrote no fewer than 77 operas, 39 singspiele and intermezzos; his first opera was *Mahmuth II* (Hamburg, 1696), and *Circe* (Hamburg, March 1, 1734) was the last. He was the first German to employ popular subjects in opera; he also made use of his native language (instead of Italian) for his librettos; his productions frankly aimed to please, but at least they were original works, not mere copies of Italian models. Among his more popular operas in German were *Störtebecker unde Goedje Michel* (Hamburg, 1701), *Die Leipziger Messe* (1710), *Der Hamburger Jahrmarkt* (Hamburg, 1725), and *Die Hamburger Schlachtzeit* (1725). In his grasp of dramatic expression, in the facility of his melodic invention, and in the mastery of his orchestration, he was easily the foremost composer of German opera of the day. Furthermore, he was proficient in administrative affairs; in 1703 he became director and manager of the Hamburg Opera, and brought it to a high degree of excellence. In 1709 he married into a wealthy family, which contributed further to the security of his social status in Hamburg. In 1717 he was in Copenhagen, which he revisited in 1722–24; produced several of his operas there; was given an honorary appointment as conductor to the King. Returning to Hamburg in 1724, he continued to write for the Hamburg Opera; in 1728 he was appointed canon and cantor at the Hamburg Katharinenkirche. He also wrote many sacred works (oratorios, cantatas, motets, psalms, Passions, etc.) of which a number were publ.: *R. Keisers Gemüths-Ergötzung, bestehend in einigen Sing-Gedichten, mit einer Stimme und unterschiedlichen Instrumenten* (1698); *Divertimenti serenissimi* (duets and airs with harpsichord; 1713); *Musikalische Landlust* (cantatas with continuo for harpsichord; 1714); *Kaiserliche Friedenspost* (songs and duets with harpsichord; 1715); a *Weihnachts-Cantate*, etc. The opera *Jodelet* was ed. by F. Zelle in *Publikationen der Gesellschaft für Musikforschung* (vols. 20–22); *Octavia* was ed. by F. Chrysander as a supplement to the Handel *Gesamtausgabe* (1902); the opera *Crösus* and selected numbers from *L'Inganno fedele* were publ. by Schneider in *Denkmäler deutscher Tonkunst* 37/38.

BIBLIOGRAPHY: E. O. Lindner, *Die erste stehende deutsche Oper* (Leipzig, 1855); F. A. Voigt, "Reinhard Keiser," *Vierteljahrsschrift für Musikwissenschaft* (1890); Hugo Leichtentritt, *Reinhard Keiser in seinen Opern* (Berlin, 1901); R. Petzoldt, *Die Kirchenkompositionen und weltlichen Kantaten Reinhard Keisers* (Berlin, 1934); A. Loewenberg's *Annals of Opera* (1943; new ed., 1955; contains details on the production of the operas); J. Rudolph, "Reinhard Keiser und Masaniello," *Musik und Gesellschaft* (Oct. 1967); M. A. Peckham, "First Performance of Reinhard Keiser's *Croesus*," *Current Musicology* 6 (1968); W. Paap, "De *Markus Passion* von Reinhard Keiser," *Mens en Melodie* (March 1970); J. Rudolph, "Probleme der Hamburger deutschen Frühoper," *Händel-Jahrbuch* (1969–70); R. D. Brenner, "Emotional Expression in Keiser's Operas," *Music Review* (Aug. 1972).

Kelbe, Theodore, German conductor; b. Brunswick, Oct. 6, 1862; d. Milwaukee, Oct. 12, 1922. He studied violin in his native town; from 1879–82, was a member of the court orch. there; in 1882, joined the opera orch. in Cologne. In 1901 he came to America as concertmaster of the Milwaukee Symph. Orch.; in 1904, became conductor of the Sängerbund des Nordwestens there; was in charge of its festivals in Milwaukee (1904), St. Paul (1906), Omaha (1910), St. Paul (1912), and Kansas City (1917).

Kelberine, Alexander, pianist; b. Kiev, Feb. 22, 1903; d. (suicide) New York, Jan. 30, 1940. He studied at the Kiev Cons.; then at the Univ. of Vienna; took lessons from Busoni in Berlin; in 1923, came to America and studied at the Juilliard Graduate School, N.Y., with Siloti (piano) and Rubin Goldmark (composition); later also studied with Ernst Toch. A victim of acute depression, he programmed his last recital for pieces in minor keys and of funeral connotations, concluding with Liszt's *Todtentanz;* he then went home and took an overdose of sleeping pills. His body was discovered on Jan. 30, 1940. He was married to the pianist **Jeanne Behrend,** but was estranged from her.

Keldorfer, Robert, Austrian composer and conductor; son of **Viktor Keldorfer;** b. Vienna, Aug. 10, 1901. He studied with his father; then at the Musical Academy in Vienna with Carl Prohaska and Max Springer. He occupied various posts as organist and choral conductor while studying; upon graduation in 1930 he went to Linz, where he became director of the Bruckner Cons.; was director of the District Cons. in Klagenfurt (1941–1966).

WORKS: an opera, *Verena* (Klagenfurt, 1951); Concerto for Oboe and Strings (1965); *Sonata ritmica* for alto recorder and piano (1964), Viola Sonata (1964); Sonata for Recorder and Guitar (1967); a great number of choral works, church music, lieder, etc. His music is influenced by Richard Strauss.

Keldorfer, Viktor, Austrian conductor and composer; father of **Robert Keldorfer;** b. Salzburg, April 14, 1873; d. Vienna, Jan. 28, 1959. He was a student at the Mozarteum in Salzburg; then conducted choruses in Vienna; in 1922, became director of the Vienna Schubertbund and conductor of the Ostdeutscher Sängerbund, which became a model for many Austrian male choruses. He publ. 150 opus numbers; a *Missa solemnis,* 2 vols. of *Lieder für grosse und kleine Kinder,* many men's choruses, and arrangements of Strauss waltzes for men's chorus and orch. He also edited a complete collection of Schubert's men's choruses.

Kelemen, Milko, significant Croatian composer; b. Podrawska Slatina, March 30, 1924. He was taught to play piano by his grandmother; in 1945 entered the Zagreb Academy of Music where he studied theory with Šulek; then went to Paris where he took courses with Messiaen and Aubin at the Paris Cons. (1954–55); supplemented his studies at Freiburg with Fortner (1958–60); then worked on electronic music at the Siemens studio in Munich (1966–68); in the interim he taught composition at the Zagreb Cons. (1955–58; 1960–65). He was co-founder of the Zagreb

Biennial Festival of New Music, and became its president in 1961. In 1969 he was appointed to the faculty of the Schumann Cons. in Düsseldorf; in 1973 he became prof. of composition at the Hochschule für Musik in Stuttgart. As a composer, Kelemen began his career following the trend of European modernism well within academically acceptable lines, but changed his style radically about 1956 in the direction of the cosmopolitan avant-garde, adopting successively or concurrently the techniques of serialism, abstract expressionism, constructivism and sonorism, making use of electronic sound; he further writes alternatively valid versions for a single piece.

WORKS: A "theater-of-the-absurd" musical scene, *Novi Stanar (The New Tenant,* after Ionesco, 1964; Münster, Germany, Sept. 20, 1964); 2 operas: *König Ubu* (1965; Hamburg, 1965) and *Der Belagerungszustand (State of Siege),* after Camus' novel *The Plague* (1968–69; Hamburg, Jan. 10, 1970); a "scenic action," *Opera bestial* (1973–74); 2 ballets: *Le Héros et son miroir (The Hero and His Mirror;* 1959; Paris, May 10, 1961) and *Napuštene (Abandoned;* 1964; Lübeck, Nov. 4, 1964); FOR ORCH.: *Prelude, Aria and Finale* for string orch. (1948); sinfonietta (1950); symph. (1951; Zagreb, Feb. 18, 1952); piano concerto (1952; Zagreb, Dec. 22, 1953); violin concerto (1953; Zagreb, April 19, 1957); *Koncertantne improvizacije* for strings (1955); *Adagio and Allegro* for strings (1955); *Concerto Giocosa* for chamber orch. (1956; Zagreb, Jan. 4, 1957); concerto for bassoon and strings (1956; Zagreb, April 11, 1957); *Simfonijska muzika 1957* (Zagreb, June 4, 1958); *3 Dances* for viola and strings (1957); *Konstelacije* for chamber orch. (1958; Zagreb, April 27, 1960); Concertino for double bass and strings (1958); *Skolion* (1958); *5 Essays* for strings (1959); *Ekvilibri* for 2 orch. (1961); *Transfiguracije* for piano and orch. (1961; Hamburg, April 6, 1962); *Sub Rosa* (1964; Zagreb, May 23, 1965); *Surprise* for chamber string orch. (1967; Zagreb, May 13, 1967); *Composé* for 2 pianos and orch. groups (1967; Donaueschingen, Oct. 22, 1967); *Changeant* for cello and orch. (1967–68); *Floreal,* in 3 versions (1969–70; Coolidge Festival, Washington, Oct. 30, 1970); *Oliphant* for 5 winds and chamber ensemble (1971); *Sonabile* for piano with ring modulator, and orch. (1972); *Abecedarium* for chamber string orch. (1973; Graz, Oct. 13, 1974); *Mirabilia II* for piano with ring modulator and 2 orch. groups (Graz, Oct. 12, 1977); FOR VOICE: *Igre (Games),* song cycle for baritone and strings (1955; Zagreb, Sept. 29, 1956); *Epitaph* for mezzo-soprano and chamber orch. (1961); *O Primavera,* cantata for tenor and strings (1964); *Hommage à Heinrich Schütz* for chorus a cappella (1964); *Le Mot* for mezzo-soprano and 2 orch. (1964–65); *Musik für Heinssenbüttel* for voice and chamber ensemble (1967); *Passionato* for flute and choral group (1971); *Yebell* for narrator, pantomime and chamber ensemble (1972; Munich, Sept. 1, 1972); *For You* for voice and ring modulator (1972); *Gassho* for 4 choruses (1974); CHAMBER MUSIC: *Musika* for solo violin (1957); *Études contrapunctiques* for wind quintet (1959); Oboe Sonata (1960); *Studija* for solo flute (1961); *Radiant* for flute, viola, piano or celeste, harpsichord and percussion (1961); *Entrances* for wind quintet (1966); *Motion* for string quartet (1968); *Varia melodia* for string quartet (1972); *Fabliau* for

solo flute (1972); *Tantana,* 5 movements of instrumental "happening," with voices in one movement (1972); FOR PIANO: *Theme and Variations* (1949), Sonata (1954), *5 Studies* (1958) and *Dessins commentées* (1963).

Kéler-Béla (real name **Albert von Keler**), Hungarian violinist, band conductor, and composer of light music; b. Bartfeld, Feb. 13, 1820; d. Wiesbaden, Nov. 20, 1882. He was a law student; then became a farmer; finally took up music in 1845, studying under Sechter and Schlesinger in Vienna, and playing the violin at the Theater-an-der-Wien, where he developed his specialty, the composition of dance music. In 1854 he went to Berlin for a time to conduct the Gungl Orch.; the following year he succeeded Lanner as the conductor of his band in Vienna. From 1856–63 he conducted an army band; then the Spa Orch. at Wiesbaden, resigning in 1873 owing to ill health. He wrote a great number of dances and other light pieces, some of which attained enormous popularity, such as the waltz *Hoffnungssterne,* the galop *Hurrah-Sturm,* and particularly his *Lustspiel Ouverture.*

BIBLIOGRAPHY: Z. Sztehlo, *Kéler-Béla* (Budapest, 1930).

Kell, Reginald, English clarinet virtuoso; b. York, June 8, 1906. He studied with Haydn Draper at the Royal Academy of Music in London; in 1932, was engaged as 1st clarinetist in the London Philharmonic Orch.; also 1st clarinetist with the London Symph. Orch. (from 1937); from 1935–48 taught clarinet at the Royal Academy of Music, as successor to his teacher Draper. In 1948 he went to America; settled in New York.

BIBLIOGRAPHY: R. Gelatt, *Music Makers* (N.Y., 1953; pp. 189–94).

Keller, Gottfried (called **Godfrey**), German harpsichord teacher who was active in England late in the 17th century; d. London, 1704. He publ. *A Complete Method for Attaining to Play a Thorough-bass upon either Organ, Harpsichord, or Theorbo-lute* (1707; posthumous; reprinted in W. Holder's *Treatise on Harmony,* London, 1731); 6 suites for 2 violins, trumpet or oboe, viola, and continuo and 6 suites for 2 flutes with continuo.

Keller, Hans, Austrian-British musicologist; b. Vienna, March 11, 1919. He emigrated to England in 1938; studied violin and viola, and played in orchestras and string quartets; mastered the English language to an extraordinary degree, and soon began pointing out solecisms and other infractions on the purity of the tongue to native journalists; wrote articles on film music, and boldly invaded the sports columns in British newspapers flaunting his mastery of the lingo. In 1945 he founded (with Donald Mitchell) the periodical *Music Survey;* launched a system of "functional analysis," applying symbolic logic and pseudo-Babbagean taxonomy to render esthetic judgment on the value of a given musical work. He published several articles expounding the virtues of his ratiocination; among them, the fundamental essay,

"Functional Analysis: Its Pure Application," *The Music Review*, 1957.

BIBLIOGRAPHY: H. Raynor, "Hans Keller and Pontius Pilate," *The Music Review*, 1957.

Keller, Harrison, American music educator; b. Delphos, Kansas, Oct. 8, 1888. He studied violin at Bethany College, Lindsborg, Kansas (B.M., 1907; honorary D.M., 1954); then in Germany, at Stern's Cons., Berlin (1907–11); in Prague, with Anton Witek (1912), and in St. Petersburg, Russia, with Leopold Auer (1913–14). He served in the U.S. Army in World War I; received the French Legion of Honor. Returning to the U.S., he organized a string quartet in Boston; was head of the string dept. at the New England Cons. (1922–46); then became its director (1947–52) and president (1952–58). In 1978 he was living in Maine.

Keller, Hermann, German organist and musicologist; b. Stuttgart, Nov. 20, 1885; d. in Freiburg im Breisgau, Aug. 17, 1967, in an automobile accident; studied with Max Reger (composition), Straube (organ), and Teichmüller (piano). He filled various posts as organist in Weimar, Stuttgart, etc.; from 1920 till 1950 taught at the Württemberg Hochschule für Musik.

WRITINGS: *Reger und die Orgel* (1923); *Schule des Generalbassspiels* (1931); *Schule der Choralimprovisation* (1939); *Die Kunst des Orgelspiels* (1941); *Bachs Orgelwerke* (1948); *Bachs Klavierwerke* (1950); *Phrasierung und Artikulation* (Kassel, 1955; in English, N.Y., 1965); *Domenico Scarlatti* (Leipzig, 1957); *Das wohltemperierte Klavier von J. S. Bach* (Kassel, 1965).

Keller, Karl, German composer and flutist; b. Dessau, Oct. 16, 1784; d. Schaffhausen, July 19, 1855. His father was a court organist and chamber musician. Keller was a flute virtuoso; he was court musician at Berlin (until 1806), Kassel (until 1814), Stuttgart (until 1816), and Donaueschingen (1817), where he later became chorusmaster. He married the opera singer Wilhelmine Meierhofer. In 1849 he received a pension and retired to Switzerland. He wrote 3 flute concertos; 4 polonaises with orch.; 2 divertissements with orch.; 6 part-songs for male chorus; duos and solos for flute; and songs.

Keller, Matthias, German violinist and composer; b. Ulm, Germany, March 20, 1813; d. Boston, Oct. 12, 1875. He studied music in Stuttgart and Vienna; at 16 became first violinist of the Royal Chapel in Vienna (for 5 years); then bandmaster in the army (for 7 years); in 1846, went to America and played in theater orchestras in Philadelphia; became interested in violin making and founded "Keller's Patent Steam Violin Manufactory" (1857). He then went to New York and won a five hundred dollar prize for his *American Hymn* (Speed our Republic, O Father on high), for which he wrote both words and music; composed over 100 songs, including some patriotic songs for the Civil War; also a *Ravel Polka* (1846); publ. *A Collection of Poems* (1874).

BIBLIOGRAPHY: F. J. Metcalf, *American Writers and Compilers of Sacred Music* (1925); *Dictionary of American Biography* (1933).

Keller, Max, Bavarian composer and organist; b. Trostberg, Oct. 7, 1770; d. Altötting, Sept. 16, 1855. He was organist at Altötting; publ. 6 Latin Masses; 6 German Masses; other sacred works and organ music.

Keller, Otto, Austrian writer on music; b. Vienna, June 5, 1861; d. Salzburg, Oct. 25, 1928. He studied music history with Hanslick and theory with Bruckner; publ. biographies of Beethoven (1885), Goldmark (1900), von Suppé (1905), Tchaikovsky (1914), and Mozart (2 vols., 1926–27); also an illustrated history of music (5th ed., 1926) and *Die Operette* (1926); compiled a valuable collection of source material relating to music and the theater.

Keller, Walter, American organist; b. Chicago, Feb. 23, 1873; d. there, July 7, 1940. He studied at the American Cons. of Music in Chicago (1891–94) and at the Leipzig Cons. (1894–96). Returning to America, he occupied various teaching posts; also was church organist in Chicago from 1903. He wrote a comic opera, *The Crumpled Isle;* a melodrama, *Alaric's Death;* and a *Synchronous Prelude and Fugue* for orch. (Chicago, 1924); also a number of works for organ; sacred choruses; songs.

Kellermann, Christian, Danish cellist; b. Randers, Jutland, Jan. 27, 1815; d. Copenhagen, Dec. 3, 1866. He studied with Merk in Vienna; made many concert tours; in 1847, was appointed soloist in the royal orch. at Copenhagen. He publ. solos for cello.

Kelley, Edgar Stillman, important American composer and writer; b. Sparta, Wis., April 14, 1857; d. New York, Nov. 12, 1944. He studied first with F. W. Merriam (1870–74), then with Clarence Eddy and N. Ledochowsky in Chicago (1874–76). In 1876 he went to Germany, where he took courses at the Stuttgart Cons. (until 1880) with Seifritz (composition), Krüger and Speidel (piano), and Friedrich Finck (organ). Returning to the U.S., he served as organist in Oakland and San Francisco; conducted performances of light opera companies in New York; taught piano and theory in various schools and in the N.Y. College of Music (1891–92); was music critic for the *San Francisco Examiner* (1893–95); lecturer on music for the University Extension of New York Univ. (1896–97); then acting prof. at Yale Univ. (1901–02). In 1902 he went to Berlin, where he taught piano and theory (until 1910). In 1910 he was appointed dean of the dept. of composition at the Cincinnati Cons., retaining this post until his death, at the same time holding a fellowship in composition at Western College, Oxford, Ohio; honorary Litt. D., Miami Univ. (1916); honorary LL.D., Univ. of Cincinnati (1917). He contributed articles to various music journals; also publ. correspondence from Germany during his stay there. With his wife, **Jessie Stillman Kelley,** he organized the Kelley Stillman Publishing Co., which publ. several of his scores. Although his stage works and his symphonic pieces were quite successful when first performed (some critics described him as a natural successor to MacDowell in American creative work), little of his music survived the test of time.

WORKS: Theme and Variations for string quartet

(c.1880); *Wedding Ode,* for tenor solo, men's chorus, and orch. (c.1882); incidental music to *Macbeth,* for orch. and chorus (San Francisco, Feb. 12, 1885); comic opera *Puritania* (Boston, June 9, 1892; 100 consecutive performances; publ. in vocal score); *Aladdin,* Chinese suite for orch. (San Francisco, April, 1894); incidental music to *Ben Hur,* for soli, chorus, and orch. (N.Y., Oct. 1, 1900; highly successful, used for performances of that popular play some 6000 times up to 1918); music to Fernald's play, *The Cat and the Cherub* (N.Y., June 15, 1901); *Alice in Wonderland,* suite for orch. (Norfolk, Conn., Festival, June 5, 1919; composer conducting; *Gulliver* (Cincinnati, April 9, 1937); 2nd Symph., *New England* (Norfolk, Conn., Festival, June 3, 1913; composer conducting); *The Pilgrim's Progress,* a musical miracle play for soli, chorus, children's chorus, organ, and orch. (Cincinnati May Festival, May 10, 1918); *A California Idyll,* for orch. (N.Y., Nov. 14, 1918); *The Pit and the Pendulum,* symph. suite, after Poe (1925); *Israfel* and *Eldorado,* for voice and orch.; Piano Quintet; 2 piano quartets; many choral works, of which the best known are *My Captain,* after Whitman, and *The Sleeper,* after Poe; 3 pieces for piano: *The Flower Seekers, Confluentia* (also arranged for string orch., 1913), *The Headless Horseman;* a song, *The Lady Picking Mulberries* (1888); song cycle *Phases of Love* (1890). He also publ. *Chopin the Composer* (N.Y., 1913); *Musical Instruments* (Boston, 1925).

Kelley, Jessie Stillman (Mrs. Edgar S. Kelley), American piano pedagogue; b. Chippewa Falls, Wis., 1866; d. Dallas, April 3, 1949. She studied piano with William Mason and theory with Edgar Stillman Kelley (whom she later married); L.H.D., Western College, Oxford, Ohio; Litt. D., Miami Univ.; for many years, taught piano in San Francisco, New York, and Berlin; 1910-34, director of music, Western College; was active in music clubs.

Kellie, Lawrence, English tenor and song composer; b. London, April 3, 1862; d. there, Aug. 20, 1932. He was apprenticed to a solicitor; began to study music in 1884 at the Royal Academy of Music; appeared in a minor operatic role at Covent Garden in 1886; made his American debut in a vocal recital in New York (May 23, 1887). His songs have had a great vogue; among them, the most popular were *Is it too late? Sleeping Tide, All for thee, This heart of mine,* and *Douglas Gordon.*

Kellner, Ernst August, English pianist and singer; b. Windsor, Jan. 26, 1792; d. London, July 18, 1839. He began to study piano at the age of 2; at 5 he played a Handel concerto before the court; also studied voice in England with W. Parsons, and in Italy with Nozzari, Casella, and Crescentini in Naples in 1815. Returning to England in 1820, he won acclaim as pianist and baritone; sang in Venice (1824); sang and played in St. Petersburg (1828); and Paris (1833); in 1834, became organist at the Bavarian Chapel in London.
BIBLIOGRAPHY: a biographical sketch by Richard Cull, *Case of Precocious Musical Talent,* publ. in London (1839).

Kellogg, Clara Louise, famous American soprano; b. Sumterville, S.C., July 9, 1842; d. New Hartford, Conn., May 13, 1916. She received her vocal training in New York, from Manzocchi, Errani, and Muzio; made her professional debut at the Academy of Music, N.Y. (Feb. 27, 1861); then sang in Boston. She sang Marguerite in the N.Y. première of *Faust* (Nov. 25, 1863); made her London debut as Marguerite on Nov. 2, 1867. In 1872 she organized an opera company with Pauline Lucca, but the rivalry between them precluded its success. In 1873 she launched an opera enterprise of her own, known as the English Opera Co.; she extended her supervision to the translations of the librettos, the stage settings, and the training of the soloists and chorus. She herself sang 125 performances in the winter of 1874-75. After that, she divided her time between Europe and America. In 1887 she married her manager, Karl Strakosch, nephew of Maurice and Max Strakosch, and retired from the stage. She wrote *Memoirs of an American Prima Donna* (N.Y., 1913).

Kelly, Michael, Irish singer and composer; b. Dublin, Dec. 25, 1762; d. Margate, Oct. 9, 1826. He studied singing under Rauzzini, and in Naples (1779) under Fenaroli and Aprile. He then sang in Palermo, Leghorn, Florence, Bologna, and Venice. Visiting Vienna, he was engaged at the court opera for 4 years, becoming the friend of Mozart, and taking the role of Basilio in the production of *Figaro.* In 1787 he appeared for the first time at Drury Lane, and sang leading tenor roles there until his retirement. In 1789 his debut as composer was made with *False Appearances* and *Fashionable Friends;* up to 1820 he wrote the music for 62 stage pieces, also many songs. He had a music shop from 1802-11; when it failed, he went into the wine trade; it was Sheridan who said, considering the quality of his music and wines, that he was "a composer of wines and an importer of music." His *Reminiscences,* publ. in the year of his death (1826), were written by Theodore Hook from material supplied by him (reprinted with new introduction by A. H. King, N.Y., 1968); the volume is replete with amusing musical anecdotes.

Kelly, Robert, American composer; b. Clarksburg, West Virginia, Sept. 26, 1916. He studied composition with Scalero at the Curtis Institute in Philadelphia and violin with Samuel Gardner. After service in the U.S. Army, he joined the faculty of the Univ. of Illinois at Urbana, retiring in 1970.
WORKS: *Adirondack Suite,* for orch. (1941); *A Miniature Symphony* (Austin, Texas, Oct. 15, 1950); *The White Gods,* opera in 3 acts on the Aztec impression of the conquistadores (Urbana, Illinois, July 3, 1966); Symph. No. 2 (1958); Concerto for Violin, Cello and Orch. (Urbana, Illinois, March 8, 1961); Symph. No. 3, *Emancipation Symphony* (Washington, D.C., Feb. 5, 1963); *An American Diptych* for orch. (Austin, Texas, April 26, 1963); *Colloquy* for chamber orch. (Chicago, April 17, 1965); Violin Concerto (1968); chamber music: 2 string quartets (1944, 1952); Viola Sonata (1950); Violin Sonata (1952); Sonata for Trombone and Piano (1952); Sonata for Oboe and Harp (1955); Quintet for clarinet and strings (1956); Cello

Sonata (1958); *Toccata* for marimba and percussion (1959); *Triptych* for cello and piano (1962); *Tod's Gal*, opera (Norfolk, Virginia, Jan. 8, 1971); *Mosaic* for string quartet (1975); choruses; songs; band music.

Kelterborn, Rudolf, Swiss composer; b. Basel, Sept. 3, 1931. He studied piano and rudimentary music theory in high school; then entered the Univ. of Basel and studied musicology with Jacques Handschin; later took a course in composition with Willy Burkhard in Zürich and Boris Blacher in Salzburg; for one semester he studied in Detmold with Wolfgang Fortner (1955). In 1960 he was engaged as teacher of composition at the Music Academy in Detmold; in 1968 he became prof. at the Musikhochschule in Zürich. In 1975 he was appointed music director of the Basel Radio. He was also active as conductor, mostly of his own music. In his music, Kelterborn applies a precisely coordinated serial organization wherein quantitative values of duration form a recurrent series; the changes of tempi are also subjected to serialization. Both melody and harmony are derived from a tone row in which the dissonant intervals of major seventh and minor second are the mainstays.
WORKS: OPERAS: *Die Errettung Thebens* (Zürich, June 23, 1963); *Kaiser Jovian* (Karlsruhe, March 4, 1967). FOR ORCH.: Suite for Woodwinds, Percussion and Strings (1954); Concertino for Violin and Chamber Orch. (1954); Sonata for 16 Solo Strings (1955); *Canto appasionato* (1959); Concertino for Piano, Percussion and Strings (1959); *Metamorphosen* (1960); Cello Concerto (1962); *Phantasmen* (1966); Symph. No. 1 (Vienna, April 26, 1968); Symph. No. 2 (1969); *Musik* for piano and 8 wind instruments (1970); *Traummusik* for small orch. (1971); *Kommunikationen* for 6 instrumental groups (1972); *Changements* (1973); *Tableaux encadrés* (1974). CHAMBER MUSIC: 4 string quartets (1954, 1956, 1962, 1970); *5 Fantasien* for wind quintet (1958); *Esquisses* for harpsichord and percussion (1962); *Meditationen* for 6 wind instruments (1962); *Kammersonate* for flute, oboe, string trio and harpsichord (1963); *Fantasia a tre* for piano, violin and cello (1967); *4 Stücke* for clarinet and piano (1970); *9 Momente* for viola and piano (1973); *Reaktionen* for violin and piano (1974). VOCAL WORKS: *Cantata profana* (1960); *Ewige Wiederkehr*, chamber cantata (1960); *Musica spei* for soprano, chorus and orch. (1968); *Dies unus* for voices and orch. (1971); *3 Fragmente* for chorus and orch. (1968); *Dies unus* for voices and orch. (1971); *3 Fragmente* for chorus a cappella (1973).
BIBLIOGRAPHY: D. Larese and F. Goebels, *Rudolf Kelterborn* (Amriswil, 1970).

Kemp, Barbara, German dramatic soprano; b. Cochem, Dec. 12, 1881; d. Berlin, April 17, 1959. She sang in opera in Rostock and Breslau before being engaged as a member of the Berlin State Opera in 1914. She married the composer **Max von Schillings** in 1923; in the same year (March 1) she sang the title role in his opera *Mona Lisa* at the Metropolitan Opera, N.Y. She returned to Germany; sang Wagnerian roles at Bayreuth; continued on the roster of the Berlin State Opera until 1932, when she retired.

BIBLIOGRAPHY: Oscar Bie, *Barbara Kemp* (Berlin, 1921).

Kemp, Joseph, English composer and pedagogue; b. Exeter, 1778; d. London, May 22, 1824. He studied organ with W. Jackson; organist of Bristol cathedral (1802); Mus. Bac. from Cambridge (1808), Mus. Doc. (1809); then taught in London. As one of the earliest promoters of music instruction by classes, he publ. a pamphlet on a *New System of Musical Education* (1819). He composed *The Jubilee*, an "occasional piece" (1809); *The Siege of Isca*, a melodrama (1810); *Musical Illustrations of the Beauties of Shakespeare; Musical Illustrations of The Lady of the Lake;* psalms; anthems, songs, etc.

Kemp, Robert, known as "Father Kemp"; b. Wellfleet, Mass., June 6, 1820; d. Boston, May 14, 1897. He was a shoe dealer but loved music; in 1854 organized "Old Folks Concerts" in Boston. His book, *Father Kemp and His Old Folks* (Boston, 1868) contains his autobiography.

Kempe, Rudolf, German conductor; b. Niederpoyritz, near Dresden, June 14, 1910; d. Zürich, May 11, 1976. He studied oboe, and became first oboist in the Gewandhaus Orch. at Leipzig in 1929. In 1936 he began to conduct various German orchestras; was musical director of the Dresden State Orch. (1949–52) and later of the Munich State Opera (1952–54). He then conducted opera in Berlin, Vienna, Salzburg, London, Barcelona, and at the Metropolitan Opera, N.Y.; made a tour in Australia and South America.
BIBLIOGRAPHY: H. Jäckel and G. Schmiedel, *Bildnis des schaffenden Künstlers: ein Dirigent bei der Arbeit* (Leipzig, 1955).

Kempff, Wilhelm, German pianist and composer; b. Jüterbog, Nov. 25, 1895. He studied piano with his father, also named Wilhelm Kempff; composition with Robert Kahn in Berlin. He made several tours in Germany and Scandinavia as a pianist, featuring improvisation as part of his programs. He taught classes in Stuttgart; after 1957 gave annual courses in Positano, Italy. He was especially appreciated as an interpreter of Beethoven's sonatas.
WORKS: several symphonies; Piano Concerto; Violin Concerto; *Arkadische Suite* for orch. (1939); *Deutsches Schicksal*, dramatic cantata (1937); the short operas *König Midas, Die Familie Gozzi, Die Fasnacht von Rottweil;* ballets; several string quartets; many pieces for piano and for organ. He publ. his autobiography, *Unter dem Zimbelstern* (1951).
BIBLIOGRAPHY: B. Gavoty and Roger Hauert, *Wilhelm Kempff*, in the series "Les grands interprètes" (Geneva, 1954).

Kempter, Karl, German organist and composer; b. Limbach, Jan. 17, 1819; d. Augsburg, March 11, 1871. He was choirmaster at Augsburg cathedral. He wrote 4 oratorios, numerous Masses and graduals; also publ. *Der Landchorregent*, a collection for use in small churches.

Keneman, Feodor, Russian pianist and composer of German descent; b. Moscow, April 20, 1873; d. there, March 29, 1937. He was a piano student of Safonov at the Moscow Cons. (graduated in 1895) and a student of composition of Ippolitov-Ivanov there (graduated in 1897); also attended classes of counterpoint of Taneyev. From 1899 to 1932 he taught music theory at the Moscow Cons. He gave piano recitals and was the favorite accompanist of Chaliapin, for whom he composed the popular Russian ballad "As the King Went to War" and arranged the folk song "Ei ukhnem!" which became one of the greatest successes at Chaliapin's concerts. Keneman made an American tour with Chaliapin in 1923–24. He also composed a number of military marches and band pieces.

Kenessey, Jenö, Hungarian composer; b. Budapest, Sept. 23, 1906; d. there, Aug. 19, 1976. He studied with Lajtha and Siklós in Budapest and attended Franz Shalk's conducting course in Salzburg; in 1932 he was appointed a member of the conducting staff at the Budapest Opera House; conducted his opera *Gold and the Woman* (1942) there on May 8, 1943, and his ballet *May Festival* (1948) on Nov. 29, 1948. His other works include 5 more ballets: *Montmartre* (1930), *Johnny in Boots* (1935), *Mine Is the Bridegroom* (1938); *The Kerchief* (1951) and *Bihari's Song* (1954); *Dance Impressions* for orch. (1933); Divertimento for Orch. (1945); *Dances from Sárköz* for orch. (1953); *Beams of Light,* cantata (1960); *Canzonetta* for flute and chamber orch. (1970); *Dawn at Balaton,* symph. poem with narrator and female voices (1972); Piano Quartet (1928–29); Sonata for Harp and Flute (1940); Sonata for Harp, Flute and Viola (1940); Divertimento for Viola and Harp (1963); Trio for violin, viola and harp (1972); *Elegy and Scherzo* for piano (1973); songs and choruses.

Kenins, Talivaldis, Latvian-born Canadian composer; b. Liepaja, April 23, 1919. He studied composition with Wihtol at the State Cons. in Riga (1940–44); during the final years of the Nazi-Soviet War he was conscripted as a laborer in Germany. After the war he traveled to France and studied with Aubin, Plé-Caussade and Messiaen at the Paris Cons. (1945–50) winning a first prize in composition. In 1951 he emigrated to Canada; settled in Toronto; served as music director of the Latvian Lutheran Church of Toronto; in 1952 joined the music faculty of the Univ. of Toronto; in 1956 received Canadian citizenship. In his music he maintains a rigorous formality of classical design; his thematic material draws on folksong resources of his native Latvia and the pentatonic Indian melos of his adoptive country; he also applies cosmopolitan modern techniques.
WORKS: Piano Concerto (1946); Duo for piano and orch. (1951); *Scherzo Concertante* for orch. (1953); 5 symphonies: No. 1 for chamber orch. (1959); No. 2, *Sinfonia Concertante,* for flute, oboe, clarinet and orch. (1967); No. 3 for orch. (1970); No. 4 for chamber orch. (1972); No. 5 for full orch. (1975); *Nocturne and Dance* for string orch. (1963); *Folk Dance, Variations and Fugue* for school orch. (1964); Concerto for Violin, Cello and String Orch. (1964); *Fantaisies Concertantes* for piano and orch. (1971; Toronto, June 20,

1973); Violin Concerto (1974); *Naačnaača (Trance),* symph. poem (1975); Sinfonietta (1976); *Beatae Voces Tenebrae* for orch. (1977); *To a Soldier,* cantata for 2 soloists, chorus and organ (1953); *Daniel,* Biblical scene after the Second Book of Daniel, for 2 soloists, chorus and organ (1956); *Lyrical Suite* for 2 soloists, chorus and organ (1962); *Gloria (Chants of Glory and Mercy)* for 4 soloists, chorus and orch. (Guelph, May 3, 1970); *Lagalai: Legend of the Stone,* chamber drama for chorus, flute, horn and percussion (1970); *Sawan-Oong (The Spirit of the Winds)* for narrator, solo bass, chorus and small orch. (1973); *Baltica,* cantata for solo bass or alto, chorus, 2 trumpets, timpani and organ (1974); a cappella choruses; String Quartet (1948); *Prelude and Scherzo* for flute, clarinet and bassoon (1947); Septet (1949); Cello Sonata (1950); Piano Trio (1952); Violin Sonata (1955); *Suite Concertante* for cello and piano (1955); *Diversions on a Gypsy Song* for cello and piano (1958); Piano Quartet (1958); Divertimento for clarinet and piano (1960); *Little Suite* for string quartet (1966); *Concertante* for flute and piano (1966); *Fantasy-Variations* for flute and viola (1967); *Concertino à Cinque* for flute, oboe, viola, cello and piano (1968); *2 Dialogues* for cello and piano (1968); *Partita brève* for viola and piano (1971); Serenade for oboe and cello (1973); *Concerto-Fantasy* for organ and percussion (1976); Concertino for 2 Pianos (1956); Piano Sonata (1961); other piano pieces; songs.

Kennan, Kent Wheeler, American composer and teacher; b. Milwaukee, Wisconsin, April 18, 1913. He studied composition with Hunter Johnson at the Univ. of Michigan (1930–32); then took courses with Howard Hanson and Bernard Rogers at the Eastman School of Music in Rochester, N.Y. (M.B., 1934; M.M., 1936; spent 3 years in Europe after winning the American Prix de Rome, and took some lessons with Pizzetti in Rome. Returning to the U.S., he taught at Kent State Univ., Ohio (1939–40) and at the Univ. of Texas, Austin (1940–42); during World War II served as bandleader in the U.S. Army (1942–45); then taught again at the Univ. of Texas (1945–46) and at Ohio State Univ. (1947–49). In 1949 he joined the staff of the Univ. of Texas on a permanent basis, and in 1964 was appointed chairman of the Music Dept. there.
WORKS: His music is so conducive to listening pleasure that Toscanini himself chose one of his innocent little symphonic pieces, *Night Soliloquy,* for flute and orch. to conduct with the NBC Symph. Orch. (Feb. 26, 1943), a rare distinction for an American composer. Kennan's other works are *Il campo dei fiori* for trumpet and orch. (1937); Nocturne for Viola and Orch. (1937); *Promenade* for orch. (1938); Symphony (1938); *Blessed Are They That Mourn* for chorus and orch. (1939); *Andante* for oboe and orch. (Philadelphia, March 7, 1947; Trumpet Sonata (1956). A protracted hiatus in composition that followed was filled by the publication of useful teaching manuals: *The Technique of Orchestration* (N.Y., 1952; revised edition, 1970); *Counterpoint Based on 18th-Century Practice* (N.Y., 1959); 2 workbooks on orchestration (1952, 1969) and a counterpoint workbook (1959).

Kennedy-Fraser, Marjory, Scottish singer, pianist, and folksong collector; b. Perth, Oct. 1, 1857; d. Edinburgh, Nov. 21, 1930. She was the daughter of the famous Scottish singer **David Kennedy** (1825–1886) and traveled with him as his accompanist from the age of 12. She then studied with Mathilde Marchesi in Paris; also took courses in piano with Matthay and in music history with Niecks. Inspired by the example of her father, she became a dedicated collector of folksongs. In 1905 she went to the Outer Hebridean Isles, after which she made a specialty of research in Celtic music, including the adaptation and arranging of Gaelic folk material into art forms; publ. the famous collection *Songs of the Hebrides* with texts in Gaelic and English, in 3 vols. (1909, 1917, 1921); also wrote a *Hebridean Suite* for cello and piano; several collections of folk music for schools, piano pieces based on Hebridean folksongs, etc. She also publ. the important handbook *Hebridean Song and the Laws of Interpretation* (Glasgow, 1922); a similar volume for Lowland Scots songs; also an autobiography, *A Life of Song* (London, 1928); wrote the libretto for Bantock's opera *The Seal Woman.* She was married to A. J. Fraser, a school teacher in Glasgow.

Kent, James, English organist and composer; b. Winchester, March 13, 1700; d. there, May 6, 1776. He was chorister in Winchester cathedral and in the Chapel Royal; organist of Trinity College, Cambridge (1731–37), then of Winchester cathedral (1737–74). He wrote 2 services; also *Kent's Anthems* (2nd ed., 2 vols.; London, 1844).

Kentner, Louis, Hungarian pianist; b. Karwin, Silesia, July 19, 1905. He studied piano in Budapest with Arnold Szekely and composition with Kodály. As a youth he gave a series of concerts in Budapest, performing all of Beethoven's sonatas. In 1935 he settled in England; toured India with Yehudi Menuhin in 1954; made his American debut in N.Y., Nov. 28, 1956. He publ. some valuable articles on Liszt.

Kenton (real name **Kornstein**), **Egon F.,** Hungarian-American musicologist; b. Nagyszalonta, Hungary, May 22, 1891. He studied violin with Hubay at the Budapest Academy of Music, graduating in 1911; was violist in the Hungarian String Quartet (1911–23); then emigrated to the U.S.; in 1947 received his M.A. in musicology from N.Y. Univ.; subsequently taught musicology at the Univ. of Connecticut in Storrs (1950–61); from 1961 to 1971 served as librarian of the Mannes College of Music in N.Y.; in 1975 went to Paris to live. He publ. a valuable biography of Giovanni Gabrieli (Rome, 1967; published in English by the American Institute of Musicology in Rome).

Kenton, Stan (Stanley Newcomb), American jazz band leader, composer and pianist; b. Wichita, Kansas, Feb. 19, 1912. He spent his youth in California; began arranging and composing at the age of 16; in 1941 he organized his own band; in 1950 toured with an orch., including strings, and instituted a type of "progressive jazz" by discovering such obsolescently modernistic things as whole-tone scales and consecutive major 9th-chords; however, his style of playing varied, according to arrangers he used at each particular time. He dabbled in theoretical speculation, and took a course in the Schillinger System of Composition.

Kepler, Johannes, the illustrious German astronomer; b. Weil, Württemberg, Dec. 27, 1571; d. Regensburg, Nov. 15, 1630; he explored Pythagorean concepts on harmony and relationships between music, mathematics, and physics, in Books 3 and 5 of his *Harmonices mundi.*
BIBLIOGRAPHY: D. P. Walker, "Kepler's Celestial Music," *Journal of the Warburg and Courtland Institutes* 20 (1967); R. Haase, "Keplers harmonikale Denkweise," *Musikerziehung* (Dec. 1969); idem, "Johannes Keplers wahre Bedeutung," in *Kunstjahrbuch der Studt Linz 1970* (1971); R. Hannas, "Johann Kepler's Excursion into Political Proportions," *Diapason* (April 1972); R. Haase, "Fortsetzungen der Keplerschen Weltharmonik," in *Johannes Kepler, Werk und Leistung* (1971).

Kerle, Jacobus de, Flemish organist and composer; b. Ypres, 1531/32; d. Prague, Jan. 7, 1591. He served as church organist at the Cathedral of Orvieto (1555–61); then was ordained a priest and in 1561 went to Venice where he supervised the publication of his *Liber Psalmorum;* then was at the court of Cardinal Otto Truchsess in Augsburg; in 1563 he traveled to Barcelona, and later was in Dillingen, Bavaria (1564). He returned to Ypres in 1565; went to Rome once more; was in Augsburg in 1568 and in Cambrai in 1579. His further ascertainable movements find him in the service of the Elector Gebhard Truchsess of Waldburg in Cologne, and from September, 1582, chaplain at the Imperial Court in Prague under Rudolph II. He exerted a considerable influence on the musical culture of his time.
WORKS: *Preces speciales pro salubri generalis concilii successu,* for the Council of Trent (Venice, 1562); Masses (Venice, 1562; Munich, 1572, with the *Cantio de sacro foedere contra Turcas*); also hymns, psalms, madrigals, and various works in manuscript. The *Preces* were transcribed by O. Ursprung in the *Denkmäler der Tonkunst in Bayern* 34 (26; 1926), together with a list of Kerle's published works, extant manuscripts, reprints, etc.
BIBLIOGRAPHY: O. Ursprung, *Jacobus de Kerle* (Munich, 1913); Glen Haydon, "The Hymns of Jacobus de Kerle," in the Festschrift for Gustave Reese (N.Y., 1966).

Kerll (or **Kerl, Kherl, Cherl**), **Johann Kaspar,** German organist and composer; b. Adorf, Saxony, April 9, 1627; d. Munich, Feb. 13, 1693. He received his musical apprenticeship from his father, an organist and organ manufacturer, Kaspar Kerll; then went to Rome where he converted to Catholicism, and where he received instruction from Carissimi and Frescobaldi. On Feb. 27, 1656 he was appointed Court Kapellmeister in Munich, and held this post until 1674. He was ennobled in 1664.
WORKS: preludes, interludes and postludes for organ; toccatas and suites for harpsichord; a number of Masses; sacred concertos, etc. In Munich he produced

several operas to Italian librettos, among them *Applausi festivi* (Aug. 28, 1658); *Antiopa giustificata* (Sept. 26, 1662); *Atalanta* (Jan. 30, 1667); *Le pretensioni del sole* (Nov. 6, 1667; *Amor tiranno* (Oct. 31, 1672). Of importance is his organ work, *Modulatio organica super Magnificat octo tonis* (1689). Modern editions of his works are found in the *Denkmäler der Tonkunst in Österreich* 49 and 59, and *Denkmäler der Tonkunst in Bayern* 3 (2.ii).

BIBLIOGRAPHY: K. Weitzmann-Seiffert, *Geschichte der Klaviermusik* (vol. 1, pp. 185ff.); Fr. W. Riedel, "Eine unbekannte Quelle zu Johann Kaspar Kerlls Musik für Tasteninstrumente," *Die Musikforschung* (1960).

Kerman, Joseph, American musicologist; b. London, England (of American parents), April 3, 1924. He studied musicology at Princeton Univ. with Oliver Strunk (Ph.D., 1950). In 1951 he was appointed to the staff of the Univ. of California at Berkeley. His Ph.D. thesis, *The Elizabethan Madrigal: A Comparative Study* was publ. in the series American Musicological Society Studies and Documents (N.Y., 1962); he also publ. *Opera as Drama* (N.Y., 1956), *The Beethoven Quartets* (N.Y., 1967) and *A History of Art and Music* (N.Y., 1968); 1971-74 prof. of music, Oxford Univ.

Kern, Jerome (David), famous American composer; b. New York, Jan. 27, 1885; d. there, Nov. 11, 1945. He was educated in N.Y. public schools; studied music with his mother; then with Paolo Gallico and Alexander Lambert (piano); with Austin Pearce and Albert von Doenhoff (theory). After a sojourn in London (1903), where he was connected with a theatrical production, he went to Germany, where he continued to study composition; returned to New York in 1904; became a pianist and salesman for a publishing firm; publ. his first song, *How'd You Like to Spoon With Me,* in 1905; and it became famous. In 1911 he obtained his first success as a composer for the stage with his musical comedy, *The Red Petticoat.* After that he continued to produce musical comedies in rapid succession; in 1917 alone he produced 7 shows on Broadway; altogether, he composed more than 60 works for the stage, including several motion picture scores. His most important productions include *Very Good, Eddie* (N.Y., Dec. 23, 1915), *Have a Heart* (N.Y., Jan. 11, 1917), *Head Over Heels* (N.Y., Aug. 29, 1918), *Sally* (N.Y., Dec. 21, 1920; extremely successful), *Stepping Stones* (N.Y., Nov. 6, 1923), *Sunny* (N.Y., Sept. 22, 1925), *Show Boat* (Washington, Nov. 15, 1927; N.Y., Dec. 27, 1927; his most remarkable score, one of the finest American works of its genre; includes the famous bass aria *Ol' Man River*), *The Cat and the Fiddle* (N.Y., Oct. 15, 1931), *Music in the Air* (N.Y., Nov. 8, 1932), *Roberta* (N.Y., Nov. 18, 1933), *The Three Sisters* (London, 1934), *Gentlemen Unafraid* (1938), *Very Warm for May* (N.Y., Nov. 17, 1939). He also composed an orchestral work, *Portrait of Mark Twain* (Cincinnati, May 14, 1942). A motion picture on his life, *As the Clouds Roll By,* was produced posthumously (1946). A selection of his songs are in *The Jerome Kern Song Book,* introduction by Oscar Hammerstein II (N.Y., 1955).

BIBLIOGRAPHY: Robert Simon, "Jerome Kern,"

Modern Music (Jan. 1929); David Ewen, *The Story of Jerome Kern* (N.Y., 1953); A. Wilder, *American Popular Song* (N.Y., 1972).

Kerr, Harrison, American composer; b. Cleveland, Oct. 13, 1897. After completing his general studies in Cleveland, he went to France where he took courses with Nadia Boulanger at the American Cons. Upon returning to America he became active mainly as pedagogue; also organized musical exchange agencies in Europe and the Far East. From 1949 to 1968 he was Dean of the College of Fine Arts at the Univ. of Oklahoma. He composed 4 symphonies, a violin concerto, some chamber music and piano pieces.

Kersters, Willem, Belgian composer; b. Antwerp, Feb. 9, 1929. He studied at the Antwerp and Brussels Cons. with Jean Louel, Jean Absil, Marcel Quinet and Marcel Poot; then taught music at various schools; in 1968 was appointed prof. at the Cons. in Maastricht, Holland. His music reveals traits of the classical Flemish school of composition, with lucidly sonorous contrapuntal lines in which tonality is ingeniously intertwined with atonal melodic progressions. Most of his works are written for instruments.

WORKS: Sinfonietta (1955); *Sinfonia Concertante* for flute, clarinet, bassoon and string orch. (1957); *Sinfonia Piccola* (1958); Divertimento for String Orch. (1958); 4 symphonies (1962; 1963; 1967; *De Apocalypsis,* 1968); *Suite in the Form of a French Overture* for 4 clarinets and string orch. (1964); Sinfonietta for wind orch. (1967); *Contrasts* for percussion, and orch. or piano (1969); *Anaglyphos* for 10 percussion players (1969); *Capriccio* for orch. (1972); *Laudes* for brass and percussion (1973); Wind Quintet (1954); Viola Sonata (1954); *Berceuse and Humoresque* for oboe, clarinet and bassoon (1956); *Partita* for violin and piano (1956); 2 string quartets (1962, 1964); Solo Violin Sonata (1965); *De drie tamboers,* septet for 4 clarinets, percussion, timpani and piano (1966); *Variations on a Theme of Giles Farnaby* for 4 clarinets (1967); *Notturno* for solo guitar (1968); 3 Rondos for brass quintet (1969); Variations for flute, oboe, clarinet and bassoon (1969); *Ballade* for violin and piano (1970); Piano Quartet (1970); Quartet for clarinet, violin, viola and cello (1971); Oboe Sonatina (1974); organ pieces; oratorio *Marianna Alcoforado* (1961); the ballets, *Parwati* (1956), *Le Triomphe de l'Esprit* (1961) and *Halewijn* (1973).

Kertész, István, Hungarian conductor; b. Budapest, Aug. 28, 1929; d. Kfar Saba, Israel, April 16, 1973 (drowned while swimming in the Mediterranean). He studied at the Academy of Music in Budapest and at Santa Cecilia, Rome (1958); was conductor at Györ (1953-55), at the Budapest Opera (1955-57) and of the London Symph. Orch. (1965-68).

Kes, Willem, violinist, composer, and conductor; b. Dordrecht, Holland, Feb. 16, 1856; d. Munich, Feb. 21, 1934. He studied with various teachers in Holland; in 1871 went to Germany, where he took lessons with Ferdinand David at the Leipzig Cons., and with Wieniawski in Brussels and Joachim in Berlin. However, he did not pursue the career of a virtuoso, but turned to conducting. In 1876 he became conductor of the Park Orch. in Amsterdam, and in 1888 assumed the conductorship of the Concertgebouw. In 1895 he succeeded Henschel as conductor of the Scottish Orch. in Glasgow. In 1898 he went to Russia, where he conducted the Moscow Philharmonic Society. In 1905 he became director of the Cons. of Coblenz; retired in 1926, and settled in Munich. Among his works are a symph., several overtures, a violin concerto, a cello concerto, a choral work with orch. *Der Taucher;* a violin sonata; piano pieces; songs.

Kessler, Ferdinand, German composer, violinist, and teacher; b. Frankfurt, Jan., 1793; d. there, Oct. 28, 1856. He studied with his father and Vollweiler. One of his pupils was Franz Wüllner. He publ. sonatas, rondos, etc., for piano.

Kessler (real name **Kötzler**), **Joseph Christoph,** German pianist and pedagogue; b. Augsburg, Aug. 26, 1800; d. Vienna, Jan. 14, 1872. He studied with the organist Bilek in Feldsberg; then was tutor with the family of Count Potocki in Lemberg; there he spent 20 years; from 1855 lived in Vienna. He publ. a series of practical studies for piano; Moscheles used them in his teaching, and Liszt recommended them. Pyllemann publ. his reminiscences of Kessler in the *Allgemeine musikalische Zeitung* (1872).

Kessler, Thomas, Swiss composer; b. Zürich, Sept. 25, 1937. He studied literature in Zürich and Paris; in 1962 moved to Berlin where he enrolled at the State Hochschule für Musik, graduating in 1968. His works include the ballets *Countdown for Orpheus* (1967) and *Revolutionsmusik* (1968); Trombone Concerto (1968); String Trio (1969) and several other pieces of chamber music.

Kestenberg, Leo, eminent Hungarian music educator and writer; b. Rosenberg, Nov. 27, 1882; d. Tel Aviv, Jan. 14, 1962. He studied in Berlin, piano with Franz Kullak and Busoni, and composition with Draeseke; then taught at the Klindworth-Scharwenka Cons. and played piano recitals, distinguishing himself as a fine interpreter of Liszt's works. In 1918 he was appointed chairman of the music dept. of the Prussian Ministry of Art; in 1929, councilor in the ministry. In that capacity, he reorganized the system of musical education in Prussia, along the lines set forth in 3 pamphlets which he prepared in collaboration with W. Günther: *Prüfung, Ausbildung und Anstellung der Musiklehrer an den höheren Lehranstalten in Preussen* (1925); *Schulmusikunterricht in Preussen* (1925); *Privatunterricht in der Musik* (1929). In 1933 he was compelled to leave Germany; he settled temporarily in Prague, where he was active in music education. After the occupation of Czechoslovakia by the Nazis in 1939, Kestenberg went to Palestine; from 1939 to 1945 he was musical director of the Palestine Symph. Orch.; then lived in Tel Aviv as a teacher. In 1957 Kestenberg received from the West German government a large sum compensating him for his unlawful removal from his position in the Prussian Ministry of Art by the Nazi government.
WRITINGS: *Musikerziehung und Musikpflege*

(Berlin, 1921); editor of *Jahrbuch der deutschen Musikorganisation* (with Beidler; 1929; 2nd ed., 1931) and of the magazines *Die Musikpflege* (with E. Preussner) and *Musik und Technik* (1930); general editor of a series of books, *Musikpädagogische Bibliothek.* He also wrote a book of memoirs, *Bewegte Zeiten; Musisch-musikantische Lebenserinnerungen* (Zürich, 1961).
BIBLIOGRAPHY: P. Bekker, *Briefe an zeitgenössische Musiker* (Berlin, 1932; pp. 44ff.).

Ketèlbey, Albert William, English composer of light music; b. Aston, Aug. 9, 1875; d. Cowes, Isle of Wight, Nov. 26, 1959. He was of remote Danish origin. Precociously gifted in music, he wrote a piano sonata at the age of 11, and played it at the Worcester Town Hall; Elgar heard it and praised it. At the age of 13, he competed for a Trinity College scholarship, and was installed as Queen Victoria Scholar; at 16 he obtained the post of organist at St. John's Church at Wimbledon; at 20 began tours as conductor of a musical comedy troupe. For some years he was music director of Columbia Gramophone Co. and music editor at Chappell's Music Publishing Company. Among his works are: Quintet for Woodwinds and Piano, String Quartet, *Caprice* for piano and orch., a comic opera *The Wonder Worker,* etc. He achieved fame with a series of remarkably popular instrumental pieces on exotic subjects (*In a Persian Market, In a Monastery Garden, Sanctuary of the Heart, In a Chinese Temple Garden,* etc.). He also published many small pieces under various pseudonyms.

Ketten, Henri, Hungarian pianist, b. Baja, March 25, 1848; d. Paris, April 1, 1883. He studied at the Paris Cons. with Halévy and Marmontel; wrote a number of ingratiating and successful piano pieces in the salon genre, also suitable as teaching material (*Chasse au papillon, Romance sans paroles, Tranquillité, Mélancolie,* etc.).

Kettenus, Aloys, Belgian violinist and composer; b. Verviers, Feb. 22, 1823; d. London, Oct. 3, 1896. He studied at the Liège Cons. and in Germany; 1845, leader of the Mannheim orch.; in 1855, became a member of the Hallé Orch. in London, and of the Royal Italian Orch. He wrote an opera, *Stella Monti* (1862); a violin concerto; a concertino for 4 violins and orch.; a duet for violin and piano; etc.

Ketterer, Eugene, French pianist and composer; b. Rouen, 1831; d. Paris, Dec. 18, 1870. He studied at the Paris Cons. He publ. 290 piano pieces in drawing-room style, many of which became popular (*Grand caprice hongrois, L'Argentine, La Châtelaine, Gaëtana, Rondo oriental,* etc.).

Ketting, Otto, Dutch composer, son of **Piet Ketting;** b. Amsterdam, Sept. 3, 1935. He studied composition at The Hague Cons. (1952–58); played trumpet in various orchestras (1955–61); taught composition at the Rotterdam Cons. (1967–71) and The Hague Cons. (1971–74). His music represents a valiant effort to adapt classical modalities to the esthetics of the 20th century.

WORKS: opera *Dummies* (The Hague, Nov. 14, 1974); 6 ballets: *Het laatste bericht* (*The Last Message*, 1962), *Intérieur* (1963), *Barrière* (1963), *The Golden Key* (1964), *Choreostruction* (1963) and *Theater Piece* (1973); *Kerstliederen* (*Christmas Songs*) for chorus and small orch. (1953); Sinfonietta (1954); *Due canzoni* for orch. (1957); Passacaglia for Orch. (1957); Concertino for 2 Solo Trumpets, String Orch., 3 Horns and Piano (1958); Symphony (1957–59); Concertino for Jazz Quintet and Orch. (1960); Variations for wind orch., harp and percussion (1960); *Pas de deux*, choreographic commentary for orch. (1961); a series of "collages," among which the most uninhibited is *Collage No. 9* for 22 musicians (conductor, 16 brass and 5 percussionists, 1963; Amsterdam, Jan. 26, 1966; audience reaction, hopefully that of outrage, is part of the performance: the conductor is instructed to treat his environment with disdain and contempt, to arrive late, leave early and refuse to acknowledge social amenities); *In Memoriam Igor Stravinsky* for orch. (1971); *Time Machine* for winds and percussion (Rotterdam, May 5, 1972); *For Moonlight Nights* for flutist (alternating on piccolo and alto flute) and 26 players (1973; Hilversum, April 17, 1975); Concerto for Solo Organ (1953); Sonata for Brass Quartet (1955); Piano Sonatina (1956); Serenade for Cello and Piano (1957); *A Set of Pieces* for flute and piano (1967); *A Set of Pieces* for wind quintet (1968); *Minimal Music* for 28 toy instruments (1970).

Ketting, Piet, Dutch composer, conductor and pianist, father of **Otto Ketting;** b. Haarlem, Nov. 29, 1904. He studied singing and choral conducting at the Utrecht Cons.; then took lessons in composition with Willem Pijper. As a pianist, he formed a duo with the flutist Johan Feltkamp (1927) and a unique trio with Feltkamp and oboist Jaap Stotijn (1935) that toured the Dutch East Indies in 1939; from 1949 to 1960 he conducted the Rotterdam Chamber Orch.; was also founder and conductor of the Rotterdam Chamber Choir (1937–60). From 1960 till 1974 he immersed himself in the numerical symbolism of J. S. Bach's works, with some startling, though unpublished results. In his own music he pursues a modern Baroque system of composition, with a discreet application of euphonious dissonance. He allowed himself a 20-year hiatus in composition between 1942 and 1962, partly on account of the war, but then resumed production with renewed vigor.
WORKS: 2 symphonies (1929, 1975); Sinfonia for Cello and Orch. (1963; radio performance, Dec. 1, 1965); *De Minnedeuntjes* (*The Love Songs*) for chorus and orch. (1966–67; Dutch Radio, May 9, 1968); Bassoon Concertino (1968); Clarinet Concertino (1973); String Trio (1925); 3 string quartets (1927–28); Cello Sonata (1928); Trio for flute, clarinet and bassoon (1929); Flute Sonata (1930); Sonata for Flute, Oboe and Piano (1936); *Partita* for 2 flutes (1936); *Fantasia No. 1* for harpsichord, descant and treble recorders and flute (1969); *Fantasia No. 2* for harpsichord (1972); *Preludium e Fughetta* for alto flute and piano (1969); 4 piano sonatinas (1926, 1926, 1927, 1929); *Prelude, Interlude and Postlude* for 2 pianos (1971); *Jazon and Medea*, dramatic scene for chorus, piano, flute and clarinet (1975).

Keuris, Tristan, Dutch composer; b. Amersfoort, Oct. 3, 1946. He studied music theory and composition first with Jan van Vlijmen; then with Ton de Leeuw; also took piano lessons at the Utrecht Cons. He subsequently became an instructor in 20th-century music at the Amsterdam Cons. His music is austerely structural.
WORKS: *Quartet* for orch. in 4 groups (1966–67); *Play* for clarinet and piano (1967); *Choral Music I* for orch. (1969); Quartet for 4 saxophones (1970); Piano Sonata (1970); *Soundings* for orch. (1970); Saxophone Concerto (1971); *Concertante Music* for clarinet, oboe, bassoon, piano and 5 strings (1972–73); *Music for violin, clarinet and piano* (1973); Sinfonia (1972–74; Amsterdam Radio, Jan. 31, 1976); *Fantasia* for solo flute (1976); Serenade for Oboe and Orch. (1974–76); Concertino for bass clarinet and string quartet (1977).

Keurvels, Edward H. J., Belgian conductor and composer; b. Antwerp, March 8, 1853; d. Eckeren (Hogblom), Jan. 29, 1916. He studied with Peter Benoit; was choirmaster and later conductor at the National Flemish Theater in Antwerp. In 1896 he established a series of symph. concerts at the Antwerp Zoological Gardens, which assumed considerable importance in Antwerp's musical life. He wrote an opera, *Parisina* (Antwerp, 1890); also numerous songs.

Keussler, Gerhard von, German composer and conductor; b. Schwanenburg, Latvia, July 5, 1874; d. Niederwartha, near Dresden, Aug. 21, 1949. He studied biology in St. Petersburg; then went to Leipzig, where he took courses in music theory with Riemann and Kretzschmar at the Leipzig Univ. and with Reinecke and Jadassohn at the Cons. From 1906 to 1918 he conducted a German chorus in Prague; then went to Hamburg where he conducted the "Singakademie." In 1931 he toured in Australia as conductor; returning to Germany in 1934 he lived in Berlin; in 1941 he settled in Niederwartha, near Dresden, where he remained until his death. He wrote operas in a Wagnerian vein, of which several were performed: *Wandlungen* (1904); *Gefängnisse* (Prague, April 22, 1914), and *Die Gesselfahrt* (Hamburg, 1923); he further composed 2 symphonies and a symph. poem *Australia* (1936).

Kewitsch, Theodor, German composer and writer on music; b. Posilge, Feb. 3, 1834; d. Berlin, July 18, 1903. He studied organ with his father; was teacher and organist in various towns; received a pension in 1887 and went to Berlin; edited the *Musikkorps* (1891–92), the *Hannoverische Musikzeitung* (1893–97), and the *Deutsche Militärmusiker-Zeitung*; also wrote articles for other music journals. He publ. a *Vade-mecum* for organists; much church music; 4-part songs for mixed and male chorus; piano pieces, etc.; also wrote *Vermächtnis an die deutschen Militärmusikmeister* (1901).

Key, Francis Scott, a Baltimore lawyer, author of the words of the American national anthem; b. Carroll County, Maryland, Aug. 1, 1779; d. Baltimore, Jan. 11, 1843. He wrote the text of the anthem aboard a British ship (where he was taken as a civilian emissary to intercede for release of a Maryland physician) on the morning of Sept. 14, 1814, setting it to the tune of a British drinking song *To Anacreon in Heaven*, popular at the time, written by John Stafford Smith. The text and the tune did not become an official national anthem until March 3, 1931, when the bill establishing it as such was passed by Congress and signed by President Hoover.

BIBLIOGRAPHY: O. G. Sonneck, *Report on the Star Spangled Banner, Hail Columbia, Yankee Doodle* (1909); O. G. Sonneck, *The Star Spangled Banner* (1914); J. Muller, *The Star Spangled Banner* (N.Y., 1935); J. A. Kouwenhoven and L. M. Patten, "New Light on *The Star Spangled Banner,*" *Musical Quarterly* (April 1937); W. Lichtenwanger, "The Music of *The Star-Spangled Banner,*" *Quarterly Journal of the Library of Congress* (Washington, D.C., July 1977).

Key, Pierre van Rensselaer, American music lexicographer; b. Grand Haven, Mich., Aug. 28, 1872; d. New York, Nov. 28, 1945. He was educated at the Chicago Musical College; then held positions as music critic of the *Chicago Times-Herald, Chicago American, Chicago Examiner,* and the *New York World* (1907–19). He was the editor of valuable compilations: *Pierre Key's Musical Who's Who* (1931); *Pierre Key's Music Year Book; Pierre Key's Radio Annual;* and the periodical *Music Digest;* publ. *John McCormack: His Own Life Story* (1919); *Enrico Caruso,* with Bruno Zirato (1922); *This Business of Singing* (1936).

Khachaturian, Aram, brilliant Russian composer of Armenian extraction; b. Tiflis, June 6, 1903; d. Moscow, May 1, 1978. His father was a bookbinder. The family stayed in Tiflis until 1920; Khachaturian played the tuba in the school band, and also studied mathematics. He then went to Moscow and entered the Gnessin School to study cello, and later, composition with Gnessin himself. In 1929 he became a student at the Moscow Cons., graduating in 1934 in the class of Miaskovsky. Although he started to compose rather late, he developed rapidly, and soon progressed to the first rank of Soviet composers. His music is in the tradition of Russian Orientalism; he applies the characteristic scale progressions of Caucasian melos, without quoting actual folksongs. His *Sabre Dance* from his ballet, *Gayane*, became popular all over the world. In 1948 Khachaturian was severely criticized by the Central Committee of the Communist Party, along with Prokofiev, Shostakovich, and others, for modernistic tendencies; although he admitted his deviations in this respect, he continued to compose essentially in his typical manner, not shunning highly advanced harmonic combinations and impressionistic devices.

He traveled in Europe as conductor of his own works; he visited the U.S. as a member of the Soviet delegation; he made his American debut as conductor and composer in Washington on Jan. 23, 1968, with the National Symph. Orch., and then conducted it in N.Y., on Jan. 28, 1968, with a rousing popular reception. He was married to Nina Makarova (1908–76).

WORKS: *Gayane,* ballet (Molotov, Dec. 9, 1942); received the Stalin Prize); *Spartak,* ballet (1953); Symph. No. 1 (1932); Symph. No. 2 (Moscow, Dec. 30,

1943); *Symphonie-Poème* (1947; criticized for its modernism); *Poem About Stalin,* for orch. (1938); Violin Concerto (Moscow, Nov. 16, 1940); Cello Concerto (Moscow, Oct. 30, 1946); *Masquerade,* symph. suite from incidental music to Lermontov's play (1944); *Concerto-Rhapsody* for violin and orch. (Moscow, Nov. 3, 1962); String Quartet (1932); Trio for clarinet, violin, and piano (1932); Violin Sonata (1932); several piano pieces (*Poem, Toccata, Scherzo, Dance,* etc.). He conducted a concert of his works in London on Dec. 5, 1954, and also visited several other European capitals.

BIBLIOGRAPHY: I. Martynov, *Aram Khachaturian* (Moscow, 1956); G. Schneerson, *Aram Khachaturian* (Moscow, 1958); G. Khubov, *Aram Khachaturian* (Moscow, 1962).

Khachaturian, Karen, Soviet composer; nephew of **Aram Khachaturian;** b. Moscow, Sept. 19, 1920. He studied at the Moscow Cons. with Litinsky; during World War II served in the entertainment division of the Red Army. He resumed his studies in 1945 at the Moscow Cons. with Shebalin, Shostakovitch and Miaskovsky. His music is distinguished by formal elegance and rhythmic power. Among his works are: Symph. (Moscow, March 12, 1955); several overtures; a number of symph. suites; Violin Sonata; Cello Sonata; songs.

Khadjiev, Parashkev, Bulgarian composer; b. Sofia, April 14, 1912. He studied composition with Vladigerov and piano with Stoyanov at the Bulgarian State Cons. in Sofia, graduating in 1936; then went to Vienna where he studied composition with Joseph Marx (1937) and to Berlin where he took a course in composition with Thiessen at the Hochschule für Musik in Berlin (1938–40). Returning to Bulgaria, he occupied various teaching positions.

WORKS: 9 operas: *Imalo edno vreme* (*Once Upon a Time,* 1957; Sofia, April 11, 1957), *Lud gidiya* (*Madcap,* 1959; Sofia, Nov. 15, 1959), *Albena* (1962; Varna, Nov. 2, 1962), *Jukka nosht* (*July Night,* 1964; Plovdiv, Feb. 16, 1965), *The Millionaire* (1964; Sofia, March 14, 1965), *Master Woodcarvers* (1966; Sofia, Oct. 9, 1966), *The Knight* (1969; Varna, 1969), *The Three Brothers and the Golden Apple* (1970; Sofia, Jan. 28, 1971) and *The Year 893* (1972; Ruse, March 26, 1973); 4 operettas: *Delyana* (1952), *Aika* (1955), *Madame Sans-Gêne* (1958) and *King Midas Has Ass's Ears* (1976); a musical, *Job Hunters* (1972); a ballet, *Srebarnite pantofki* (*The Silver Slippers,* 1961; Varna, March 20, 1962); *Skici* (*Sketches*) for orch. (1940); Violin Concertino (1941); Flute Concertino (1945); *Capriccio* for orch. (1951); *Small Dance Suite* for orch. (1952); *Rondino* for orch. (1969); 2 violin sonatas (1940, 1946); *3 Pieces* for wind quintet (1942); 2 string quartets (1948, 1953); piano pieces; choruses; arrangements of Bulgarian folksongs. He has publ. 4 theoretical texts: *Harmonia* (Sofia, 1959; second ed., 1973), *Textbook on Harmony* (Sofia, 1962; second ed., 1964), *Short Practical Course in Harmony* (Sofia, 1974) and *Elementary Theory of Music* (Sofia, 1974).

Khandoshkin, Ivan, Russian violinist and composer; b. 1747; d. St. Petersburg, March 28, 1804. He was the first Russian violin virtuoso, and the first to write instrumental music on Russian folk themes. He studied in St. Petersburg with an Italian musician, Tito Porta; then was sent to Italy, where he was a student at the Tartini school in Padua; it is probable that he took lessons from Tartini himself. Returning to Russia in 1765, he became a violinist in the Imperial Chapel; was concertmaster of the Court Orch. in 1773; also taught violin at the Academy of Arts in St. Petersburg, and later in Moscow and in Ekaterinoslav. These appointments were highly unusual honors to one of Khandoshkin's origin (he was a liberated serf). The following pieces were publ. during his lifetime: *6 Sonates pour deux violons* (Amsterdam, 1781); *Chansons russes variées pour violon et basse* (Amsterdam, 1781); *Nouvelles variations sur des chansons russes,* for violin (St. Petersburg, 1784). A set of Russian songs for unaccompanied violin was publ. in 1820; a number of works by Khandoshkin came to light in Russian archives in recent times; his concerto for viola and string orch. was publ. in 1947; a *Sentimental Aria* for unaccompanied violin was publ. in 1949.

BIBLIOGRAPHY: G. Fesetchko, "Ivan Khandoshkin," *Sovietskaya Musica* (Dec. 1950); R. Aloys Mooser, *Annales de la Musique et des Musiciens en Russie au XVIIIe siècle* (Geneva, 1950; vol. II, pp. 386–92); I. Yampolsky, *Russian Violin Art* (Moscow, 1951; vol. I, pp. 76–121; contains musical examples from Khandoshkin's works).

Khodzha-Einatov, Leon, Russian composer; b. Tiflis, March 23, 1904; d. Leningrad, Nov. 1, 1954. He studied with Spendiarov; in 1927, went to Leningrad, where he wrote music for the stage. He wrote the opera *Rebellion* (Leningrad, May 16, 1938); 3 Armenian operas, *Arshak* (1945), *David Bek* (1951), and *Namus* (1952); also *Symphonic Dances* (16 numbers) and a symphony (1953).

Khrennikov, Tikhon, Russian composer; b. Elets, June 10, 1913. He studied composition with Litinsky and Shebalin at the Moscow Cons.; also became a proficient pianist. During the Nazi-Soviet War he was musical advisor to the Red Army; in 1948 he was elected Secretary General of the Union of Soviet Composers. In this capacity he was a spokesman for Soviet musical policy along the lines of Socialist Realism. His own works express very forcefully the desirable qualities of Soviet music, a flowing melody suggesting the broad modalities of Russian folksongs, a vibrant rhythm and a touch of lyricism.

WORKS: the operas *Brothers* (later renamed *In the Storm;* Moscow, May 31, 1939), *Frol Skobeyev* (Moscow, Feb. 24, 1950), *Mother* (Moscow, Oct. 26, 1957) and 2 light operas, *100 Devils* (Moscow, May 16, 1963) and *White Nights* (Moscow, Nov. 3, 1967); 2 symphonies: No. 1 (Moscow, Oct. 10, 1935) and No. 2 expressing "the irresistible will to defeat the fascist foe" (Moscow, Jan. 10, 1943); 2 piano concertos (1933, 1970); Violin Concerto (Moscow, Oct. 21, 1959); Cello Concerto (Moscow, May 13, 1964); chamber music; piano pieces, and songs.

BIBLIOGRAPHY: V. Kukharsky, *Tikhon Khrennikov* (Moscow, 1957).

Kidson, Frank, English musical folklorist and bibliographer; b. Leeds, Nov. 15, 1855; d. there, Nov. 7, 1926. Originally a landscape painter, he became interested in historical studies and began to collect English, Scottish, and Irish folksongs and dance melodies; subsequently became one of the founders of the Folksong Society in England. He publ. *Old English Country Dances* (1890); *Traditional Tunes* (1891); *British Music Publishers, Printers and Engravers* . . . (1900); *English Folksong and Dance* (1915); *The Beggar's Opera, its Predecessors and Successors* (1922); contributed valuable articles to the *Musical Antiquary* and the *Musical Quarterly;* with A. Moffat, he ed. *The Minstrelsy of England; Songs of the Georgian Period; British Nursery Rhymes; Children's Songs of Long Ago; 80 Singing Games for Children;* etc.

Kiel, Friedrich, German music pedagogue and composer; b. Puderbach, near Siegen, Oct. 7, 1821; d. Berlin, Sept. 13, 1885. He studied the rudiments of music with his father, a schoolmaster. One of his youthful works, a set of variations (1832–34), attracted the attention of Prince Karl von Wittgenstein, who gave him violin lessons in 1835, and took him into his orchestra. Kiel further studied with Kaspar Kummer at Coburg, becoming leader of the ducal orchestra there (1840); then moved to Berlin, and studied with Dehn (1842–44). He received a stipend from King Friedrich Wilhelm IV; in 1865 he was elected to the Prussian Academy of Fine Arts. From 1866 to 1870 he taught composition at Stern's Cons., Berlin. He wrote the oratorios *Christus* and *Der Stern von Bethlehem; Stabat Mater;* a *Requiem; Te Deum;* 4 piano sonatas. He was a prolific composer, but it was as a pedagogue that he gained distinction. W. Altmann publ. a complete list of his works in *Die Musik* 1 (1901).

Kielland, Olav, Norwegian conductor and composer; b. Trondheim, Aug. 16, 1901. He studied music theory at the Leipzig Cons. (1921–23) and took Weingartner's conducting class in Basel (1929). He conducted in Göteborg (1925–31), Oslo (1931–45), Trondheim (1946–48), Bergen (1948–55) and filled some conducting engagements in London and New York. In 1952 he organized, in Reykjavik, Iceland's first symph. orchestra.

WORKS: 3 sinfonias: *I* (1935), *II* (1961) and *III* (1966); Violin Concerto (1939–40); *Overtura tragica* (1941); *Mot Blåsnøhøgdom (The Whitecapped Mountains),* symph. suite for high voice and orch. (1945–46); *Concerto Grosso Norvegese* for 2 horns and string orch. (1952); *Tvileikar* for 4 instruments (1954); String Quartet (1964); *Marcia del Coraggio* for orch. (1968); *Ouverture Solenne* (1974).

BIBLIOGRAPHY: Bjarne Kortsen, *Contemporary Norwegian Orchestral Music* (Bergen, 1969; pp. 244–82).

Kienle, Ambrosius, an authority on Gregorian chant; b. Sigmaringen, May 8, 1852; d. in the monastery at Beuron, June 18, 1905. He entered the monastery in 1873, and devoted himself to the study of Gregorian chant. He publ. *Choralschule* (1884; 3d ed., 1899); *Kleines kirchenmusikalisches Handbuch* (1892); *Mass* *und Milde in kirchenmusikalischen Dingen* (1901), and essays in periodicals.

Kienzl, Wilhelm, Austrian composer; b. Waizenkirchen, Jan. 17, 1857; d. Vienna, Oct. 3, 1941. He studied music at Graz Gymnasium with Ignaz Uhl, and with W. A. Remy (composition); later with Josef Krejči at Prague, with Rheinberger in Munich, and with Liszt at Weimar, at length receiving his Ph.D. in Vienna in 1879 for the dissertation *Die musikalische Deklamation* (Leipzig, 1880). A second work, *Miscellen* (Leipzig, 1885), concerning impressions received in Bayreuth (1879), created a stir by its bold criticism. During 1880 he lectured on music in Munich; in 1881–82, made a pianistic tour in Hungary, Rumania, and Germany; in 1883, was appointed conductor of the German opera in Amsterdam. Shortly thereafter, he went to Krefeld to take up a similar position; in 1886 he married the concert singer Lili Hoke. From 1886–90 he was artistic director of the Styrian Musikverein at Graz, directed the symph. concerts and the programs of the provincial vocal and instrumental schools. From 1890–92 he held the position of 1st conductor at the Hamburg Opera; and from 1892–94, court conductor at Munich, before returning to Graz. In 1917, he received the honorary degree of Doc. Mus. from the Univ. of Graz; and, later, in Vienna, was music critic for various papers. His early operas include *Urvasi* (Dresden, Feb. 20, 1886; rewritten, 1909), *Heilmar, der Narr* (Munich, March 8, 1892; very successful), and *Der Evangelimann* (Berlin, May 4, 1895; his most famous work). Then followed *Don Quichote,* a "musical tragi-comedy" (Berlin, Nov. 18, 1898); *In Knecht Rupprechts Werkstatt,* a 'Märchenspiel' (Graz, 1906); *Der Kuhreigen (Ranz des Vaches;* Vienna, Nov. 23, 1911); *Das Testament* (Vienna, Dec. 6, 1916); *Hassan der Schwarmer* (Chemnitz, 1925); *Sanctissimum* (Vienna, 1925); *Hans Kipfel,* a Singspiel (Vienna, 1928). Kienzl finished Adolf Jensen's opera *Turandot,* and edited Mozart's *Titus.* His own published compositions comprise about 120 songs; much light piano music; incidental music to *Die Brautfahrt; Septuaginta* (1937); 3 *Phantasiestücke* for piano and violin; Piano Trio; 2 string quartets; choral music. He also composed the new Austrian national anthem, with a text by the future president of Austria, Karl Renner, to replace that written by Haydn in 1797; its adoption was announced by the Republican government on June 6, 1920, but on Dec. 13, 1929, the Haydn melody was once more adopted as a national anthem (with a different set of words). Kienzl edited Brendel's *Grundzüge der Geschichte der Musik* (Leipzig, 1886); Brendel's *Geschichte der Musik in Italien, Deutschland und Frankreich* (7th ed., Leipzig, 1889). In addition he wrote *Richard Wagner* (1904; 2nd ed., 1908); *Aus Kunst und Leben* (1904); *Im Konzert* (1908); *Betrachtungen und Erinnerungen* (1909); *Meine Lebenswanderung,* an autobiography (1926); *Hans Richter* (1930).

BIBLIOGRAPHY: M. Morold, *Wilhelm Kienzl* (Leipzig, 1909); *Festschrift zum 60. Geburtstag von Wilhelm Kienzl* (1917); *Festschrift zum 80. Geburtstag* (Vienna, 1937); Hans Sittner, ed., *Wilhelm Kienzl's Lebenswanderung* (Vienna, 1953; includes his correspondence with Peter Rosegger).

Kiepura, Jan, Polish tenor; b. Sosnowiec, May 16, 1902; d. Rye, New York, Aug. 15, 1966. He studied in Warsaw, where he made his first public appearance in 1923; was then engaged as opera singer by a number of European opera houses (Vienna, Berlin, Milan, etc.). He made his American debut in Chicago in 1931; appeared at the Metropolitan Opera in N.Y. as Rodolfo in *La Bohème* (Feb. 10, 1938). He then settled in the U.S., making frequent tours in Europe as well. He was married to the Austrian singer **Martha Eggerth.**

Kiesewetter, Raphael Georg, Edler von Wiesenbrunn, Austrian scholar and writer on musical subjects; b. Holleschau, Moravia, Aug. 29, 1773; d. Baden, near Vienna, Jan. 1, 1850. He was educated for an official career as an Austrian functionary; was connected with the War Ministry; traveled in various European countries; in 1801 settled in Vienna. His musical interests impelled him to undertake serious study with Albrechtsberger, who instructed him in counterpoint. He was an indefatigable collector of old musical manuscripts, and archeological research became his specialty. He received the rank of nobility in 1845. **A. W. Ambros** was his nephew.

WRITINGS: *Die Verdienste der Niederländer um die Tonkunst* (received the prize of the Netherlands Academy in 1826; Dutch transl., 1829); *Geschichte der europäisch-abendländischen, das ist unserer heutigen Musik* (Leipzig, 1834; English transl., 1846); *Über die Musik der neuern Griechen, nebst freien Gedanken über altägyptische und altgriechische Musik* (1838); *Guido von Arezzo, sein Leben und Wirken* (1840); *Schicksale und Beschaffenheit des weltlichen Gesangs vom frühen Mittelalter bis zur Erfindung des dramatischen Styles und den Anfangen der Oper* (1841); *Die Musik der Araber nach Originalquellen* (1842); *Der neuen Aristoxener; zerstreute Aufsätze* (1846); *Über die Oktave des Pythagoras* (1848); *Galerie der alten Kontrapunktisten* (1847; a catalogue of his old scores, bequeathed to the Vienna Library); also essays on old music and on Gregorian notation in German periodicals.

Kiesewetter, Tomasz, Polish composer and conductor; b. Sosnowka, Sept. 8, 1911. He studied composition with Rytel and conducting with Berdiayev at the Warsaw Cons.; during the German occupation of World War II, was active in resistance groups; after the war taught at the State College of Music in Lodz.

WORKS: operetta, *The Lonely Ones* (1963); a ballet, *King's Jester* (1954); *Polish Dances* for orch. (1947, 1950); 3 symphonies (1949, 1952, 1958); Viola Concerto (1950).

Kijima, Kiyohiko, Japanese composer; b. Tokyo, Feb. 19, 1917. He studied composition with Ikenouchi at Nihon Univ.; later joined its faculty. He received 2 prizes given by the Tokyo newspaper *Mainichi* (1938, 1948). His works include *Satsukino,* poem for soprano and small orch. (1940); *Symphonic Overture* (1942); *Prelude and Fugue* for orch. (1948); String Quartet (1950); Violin Sonata (1951); *5 Meditations* for orch. (1956); *Trio* for Flute, Violin and Piano (1958, revised 1970); *Divertimento* for orch. (1963); *Mi-Chi-No-Ku* for chorus, flute, piano, and percussion (1963); Piano Quintet (1965); *2 Legends* for piano (1969); songs.

Kiladze, Grigory, Soviet Georgian composer; b. Batum, Oct. 25, 1902; d. Tbilisi, April 3, 1962. He studied at the Tbilisi Cons. with Ippolitov-Ivanov (1924–27); then at the Leningrad Cons. with Vladimir Shcherbachev (1927–29). Kiladze was one of the most active proponents of ethnic Georgian music in a modern idiom derived thematically from folk melorhythms. He wrote operas on subjects from Caucasian revolutionary history: *Bakhtrioni* (1936); *Lado Ketzkhoveli* (1941); ballet, *Sinatle* (1947); also *Poem about Stalin* for chorus and orch. (1935); *Heroic Symphony* (1944); an oratorio, *Childhood and Adolescence of the Leader* (1951); overture, *Triumph* (1957).

Kilar, Wojciech, Polish composer; b. Lwów, July 17, 1932. He studied piano and composition with Woytowicz at the State College of Music in Katowice (1950–55); later took courses at the Cracow Academy (1955–58); then went to Paris where he took private lessons with Nadia Boulanger (1959–60). Returning to Poland, he became a teacher at the College of Music in Katowice. Of an experimental turn of mind, he makes use of a variety of modern techniques, while retaining essential classical forms.
WORKS: *The Mask of the Red Death,* ballet after Poe (1962); *Little Overture* (1955); 2 symphonies; No. 1 for strings (1955) and No. 2, *Sinfonia concertante,* for piano and orch. (1956); *Béla Bartók in Memoriam* for solo violin, winds and 2 percussion groups (1957); Concerto for 2 Pianos and Percussion (1958); *Herbsttag,* after Rilke, for soprano and string quartet (1960); *Riff 62* for orch. (1962); *Générique* for orch. (1963); *Diphthongs* for chorus, 6 percussionists, 2 pianos and strings (1964); *Springfield Sonnet* for orch. (1965); *Solenne* for soprano, strings and brasses (1967); *Training 68* for clarinet, trombone, cello and piano (1968); *Upstairs-Downstairs* for 2 children's choruses without words and orch. (Warsaw, Sept. 25, 1971); *Prelude and a Carol* for 4 oboes and string orch. (1972); *Bogurodzica (Mother of God)* for chorus and orch. (1975); incidental music for theatrical plays; film scores.

Kilburn, Nicholas, English choral conductor and composer; b. Bishop Auckland, Durham, Feb. 7, 1843; d. there, Dec. 4, 1923. He studied in Cambridge, then conducted a musical society in his native town and the Philharmonic Society of Sunderland (from 1885); these posts he filled until his death. He publ. *Notes and Notions on Music; How to Manage a Choral Society; Wagner, a Sketch; Parsifal and Bayreuth; The Story of Chamber Music,* etc.; also wrote some choral works.

Kilenyi, Edward, Jr., American pianist; son of **Edward Kilenyi, Sr.**; b. Philadelphia, May 7, 1911. In 1927 he went to Budapest to study with Dohnányi at the Cons. there; after graduating (1930), he traveled in Europe, giving concerts; returning to America, he continued his career as concert pianist; American debut, N.Y., Oct. 21, 1940, in recital.

Kilenyi, Edward, Sr., Hungarian composer and pedagogue; b. Bekes, Jan. 25, 1884; d. Tallahassee, Florida, Aug. 15, 1968. He studied in Budapest, at the Cons. of Cologne, and in Italy (with Mascagni). In 1908 he settled in the U.S.; took courses at Columbia Univ. with Rybner and Daniel Gregory Mason (M.A., 1915). In 1930 he went to Hollywood, where he remained as pedagogue and composer for the films. He was for 5 years the teacher of George Gershwin.

Killmayer, Wilhelm, German composer; b. Munich, Aug. 21, 1927. He studied in Munich with H. W. von Waltershausen (1945–50); then at the Univ. of Munich (1950–52), and later with Carl Orff; was engaged as conductor of the Marionette Theater of Munich. He has written mostly for choral groups, in a modern madrigal manner, with rapidly altering rhythmic patterns and massive harmonies; the influence of Carl Orff is decidedly apparent. Among his works are a *Missa Brevis; Chansons* for tenor, flute, strings, and percussion; *Canti amorosi* for 6 voices a cappella; *Lauda* for chorus (1968); *Sinfonie "Folgi"* (Hannover, Feb. 9, 1971); music for marionettes.

Kilpinen, Yrjö, Finnish song composer; b. Helsingfors, Feb. 4, 1892; d. Helsinki, Mar. 2, 1959. He had very little academic education in music; took a few courses at the Helsingfors Cons., in Berlin, and in Vienna. His chosen form was that of lyric song; possessing an exceptional talent for expressing poetic lines in finely balanced melodies, he attained great renown in Finland, and has been called the Finnish Hugo Wolf. He composed about 800 lieder to words in German, Finnish, and Swedish, by classical and modern poets. In 1948 he was appointed member of the Academy of Finland. About 300 of his songs are publ.; other works are *Pastoral Suite* for orch. (1944); *Totentanz* for orch. (1945); 6 piano sonatas; Cello Sonata; Suite for viola da gamba with piano; etc.
BIBLIOGRAPHY: M. Pulkkinen, *Yrjö Kilpinen: Gedruckte Kompositionen* (Helsinki, 1960).

Kim, Earl, American composer; b. Dinuba, Calif., Jan. 6, 1920. He studied at the Univ. of Calif., Berkeley (M.A. 1952); was associate prof. at Princeton Univ. (1952–67) and subsequently on the staff of Harvard Univ. His works include *Dialogues* for piano and orch. (1959); *They are Far Out,* for soprano, violin, cello and percussion (1966); *Gooseberries, She Said,* for soprano, 5 instruments and percussion (1968); *Letter Found Near a Suicide,* a song cycle; and *Exercises en Route,* a multimedia composition. He received in 1971 the Brandeis Univ. Creative Arts Award.

Kimball, Jacob, Jr., American composer; b. Topsfield, Mass., Feb. 22, 1761; d. in the almshouse there, Feb. 6, 1826. In 1775 he was a drummer in the Massachusetts militia; then entered Harvard University (graduated 1780); subsequently studied law and was admitted to the bar, but soon gave up that profession for music, teaching in various New England towns. He wrote hymns, psalm tunes, and "fuguing pieces," in the style of Billings; compiled *The Rural Harmony* (71 original compositions for 3 and 4 voices; Boston, 1793). Another collection, *The Essex Harmony* (44 tunes and 2 anthems) is also attributed to him; it was publ. in Exeter, N.H., 1800, and dedicated to the Essex, Mass., Music Association; the Boston Public Library possesses an imperfect copy.

BIBLIOGRAPHY: F. J. Metcalf, *American Psalmody* (1917); F. J. Metcalf, *American Writers and Compilers of Sacred Music* (1925); G. Wilcox, *Jacob Kimball, Jr.: His Life and Works* (Los Angeles, 1957).

Kinder, Ralph, American organist; b. Stalybridge, near Manchester, England, Jan. 27, 1876; d. Bala, suburb of Philadelphia, Nov. 14, 1952. He was taken to the U.S. at the age of 5; was a chorister in Bristol, R.I.; studied in America, and then in London with E. H. Lemare. He held various posts as church organist in Bristol (1890–98), Providence (1898), and in Philadelphia (from 1899). He wrote numerous organ pieces of considerable charm; of these the following are published: *Arietta, Berceuse, Caprice, Festival March, Jour de Printemps, Moonlight, Souvenir, In Springtime.*

Kindermann, Johann Erasmus, German organist and composer; b. Nuremberg, March 29, 1616; d. there, April 14, 1655. He was a student of J. Staden; in 1634, went to Venice, where he took lessons with Cavalli; returning to Nuremberg in 1636, he became a church organist. His works include *Cantiones pathetikai* (1639); *Friedensklag* (1640); *Opitianischer Orpheus* (1642); *Concentus Salomonis* (1642); *Musica catechetica* (1643); *Deliciae studiosorum* (1640–48, many reprints); *Intermedium musico-politicum* (a collection of quodlibets, 1643); *Harmonia organica* (in tablature; 1645; 2nd ed., 1665); *Göttliche Liebesflamme* (1640–75; 20 sacred songs), also various instrumental works.

BIBLIOGRAPHY: H. J. Moser, *Corydon* (1933; vol. 1, pp. 31–42; vol. 2, pp. 77–88).

Kindler, Hans, Dutch-American cellist and conductor; b. Rotterdam, Jan. 8, 1892; d. Watch Hill, R.I., Aug. 30, 1949. He studied at the Rotterdam Cons., receiving first prize for piano and cello in 1906. In 1911 he was appointed prof. at the Scharwenka Cons. in Berlin, and first cellist at the Berlin Opera. In 1912–13 he made a successful tour of Europe; in 1914, came to the U.S. to become first cellist of the Philadelphia Orch., a post he held until 1920. In 1927 he made his debut as a conductor in Philadelphia; in 1928 he conducted the world première of Stravinsky's ballet *Apollon Musagète* at the Library of Congress Festival in Washington, D.C.; in 1929 appeared as cellist in 110 concerts throughout the U.S. and Europe, also touring as far as Java and India. In 1931 he organized the National Symphony Orch. in Washington, D.C., of which he was permanent conductor until his resignation on Nov. 30, 1948.

King, Harold Charles, Swiss-born Dutch composer; b. Winterthur, Dec. 30, 1895. He came to Holland to study engineering at the Delft Technical Univ.; served as a management consultant with a municipal corporation in Amsterdam; while thus occupied, he took composition lessons with **Cornelis Dopper** and **Henk Badings.**

WORKS: Serenade for String Orchestra (1934); *Per Ardua,* symph. suite (1946–49); *Concerto da camera* for flute and strings (1962); *Triptyque symphonique* (1964); Sinfonietta (1965); Organ Concerto (1966); Cello Sonata (1940); *Trio patetico* for violin, viola and cello (1942); *3 Impressions* for solo cello (1948); Wind Quintet (1949); 2 string quartets (1953, 1962); *A fleur d'eau* for flute, violin, spinet and viola da gamba (1964); Sonata for Solo Cello (1966); Duo for 2 cellos (1966); *Piccolo Quartetto* for string quartet (1976); *Little Laddie,* piano sonatina (1966); *King David's Dance* for 4-octave carillon (1975).

King, Karl L. (Lawrence), American Midwestern bandmaster and composer of band music; b. Painterville, Ohio, Feb. 21, 1891; d. Fort Dodge, Iowa, March 31, 1971. After 8 grades of public schools in Cleveland and Canton, Ohio, during which he began to play brass instruments (primarily the baritone horn) under the tutelage of local musicians, he quit school to learn the printing trade but soon began to play in and compose for local bands. In 1910 he initiated his short career as a circus bandsman, bandmaster, and composer, ending it in 1917–1918 as bandmaster of the Barnum & Bailey Circus Band (for which he had already written what was to remain his most famous march, *Barnum & Bailey's Favorite*). On Sept. 13, 1920, he conducted his first concert with the Fort Dodge, Iowa, Military Band, with which he was to be associated for half a century. It was a time when the small-town band in the United States was passing its heyday; but King took a group of only 18 bandsmen, added to them, and in a very few years had created a notable institution not only in Iowa but in the whole Midwestern rural culture (and this over a period when most town bands were disappearing under the competition of radio, recordings, the school band movement, and faster transportation and communications). In 1922 the Band began to receive municipal tax support under the Iowa Band Law (for which one of King's marches is named) and its name was changed to "the Fort Dodge Municipal Band" although it was known commonly as Karl L. King's Band. For 40 years it toured widely over its region, especially to play at county fairs, and King himself traveled even more widely to conduct or judge at band contests, conventions, massed band celebrations, and all manner of band events. He was one of the founders, in 1930, of the American Bandmasters Association; he served as president of that group in 1939, and in 1967 was named Honorary Life President. Among his 260-odd works for band (most published by the firm of C. L. Barnhouse in Oskaloosa, Iowa) are concert works, novelties, waltzes and all manner of dance forms; but marches predominate, from the circus marches of his early days to sophisticated marches for university bands (such as *Pride of the Illini* for Illinois and *Purple Pageant* for Northwestern) and especially to easy but tuneful and well-written marches for the less accomplished school bands. The musical *The Music Man* (1957) was inspired in part by King's music, according to its composer and fellow-Iowan, **Meredith Willson.**

BIBLIOGRAPHY: T. J. Hatton, *Karl L. King, An American Bandmaster* (Evanston, Ill., 1975).

King, Matthew Peter, English composer; b. London, 1773; d. there, Jan., 1823. He composed 10 or 12 operas for the Lyceum Theatre; an oratorio, *The Intercession;* a quintet for piano, flute, and strings; piano sonatas; etc.; also publ. *A General Treatise on Music* (London, 1800) and an *Introduction* to sight singing (1806).

King, Oliver A., English pianist; b. London, July 6, 1855; d. there, Aug. 23, 1923. He was a pupil of J. Barnby; later studied piano with Reinecke at the Leipzig Cons. (1874–77). From 1880–83 he toured Canada, giving recitals, and visited New York. In 1893 he was appointed prof. of piano at the Royal Academy of Music in London.

WORKS: 3 cantatas, *The Romance of the Roses, Prosperina,* and *The Naiades; 137th Psalm* (Chester Festival, 1888); a symph. poem, *Night;* 2 overtures; Piano Concerto; Violin Concerto; pieces for piano solo and for organ.

Kinkel, Johanna (*née* **Mockel**), German composer; b. Bonn, July 8, 1810; d. London, Nov. 15, 1858. She studied music in Berlin with Karl Böhmer, and married Gottfried Kinkel, the poet, in 1843. She wrote *Die Vogel-Cantate;* the operetta *Otto der Schutz,* and the well-known song, *The Soldier's Farewell;* also publ. *Acht Briefe an eine Freundin über Klavierunterricht* (1852).

Kinkeldey, Otto, eminent American musicologist; b. New York, Nov. 27, 1878; d. Orange, New Jersey, Sept. 19, 1966. He graduated from the College of the City of N.Y. in 1898 (B.A.); then from N.Y. Univ. in 1900 (M.A.); then took lessons with MacDowell at Columbia Univ. (until 1902). After that he went to Germany, where he undertook a course of study with Radecke, Egidi, and Thiel at the Akademisches Institut für Kirchenmusik in Berlin; studied musicology at the Univ. of Berlin with Fleischer, Friedlaender, Kretzschmar, and J. Wolf (1902–06). He received his Ph.D. from the Univ. of Berlin in 1909; Kinkeldey had been organist and choirmaster at the Chapel of the Incarnation, N.Y. (1898–1902); was organist and music director of the American Church in Berlin (1903–05); from 1909 to 1914 was instructor in organ and theory, lecturer on musicology, and music director at the Univ. of Breslau; named Royal Prussian Professor in 1910. Returning to the U.S. at the outbreak of World War I, he became organist and choirmaster at All-Souls Church, N.Y. (1915–17); was captain of infantry in the U.S. Army (1917–19); in 1915–23, and again in 1927–30, he was chief of the Music Division of the New York Public Library; 1923–27, prof. of music at Cornell Univ.; 1930–46, prof. of musicology and librarian there; Professor Emeritus, 1946. He was guest prof. at Harvard Univ. (1946–48); Univ. of Texas (1948–50); Princeton Univ. (1950–51); North Texas State College (1952–53); Univ. of Illinois (1953–54); Univ. of California, Berkeley (1954–55); Boston Univ. (1957); Univ. of Washington, Seattle (1958). He was elected president of the American Musicological Society for 1934–36, and re-elected for 1940–42; was also nominated an honorary member of the Musical Association, London. In 1947 he received a Litt.D. (*honoris*

causa) from Princeton Univ. He published the valuable book (in German), *Orgel und Klavier in der Musik des 16. Jahrhunderts* (Leipzig, 1910); many articles in the *Musical Quarterly,* the *Proceedings* of the Music Teachers' National Association, etc., and edited Erlebach's *Harmonische Freude musikalischer Freunde* for vols. 46 and 47 of the *Denkmäler deutscher Tonkunst* (1914). Later publications include *A Jewish Dancing Master of the Renaissance, Guglielmo Ebreo* (reprinted in 1929 from A. S. Freidus Memorial Volume) and *Music and Music Printing in Incunabula* (reprinted in 1932 from the *Papers of the Bibliographical Society of America,* vol. 26).

BIBLIOGRAPHY: articles by E. J. Dent and G. S. Dickinson in the *Musical Quarterly* (Oct. 1938); Carleton Sprague Smith, "Otto Kinkeldey," *Notes* (Dec. 1948); Ch. Seeger, ed., *A Musicological Offering to Otto Kinkeldey Upon the Occasion of his 80th Birthday* (Philadelphia, 1960).

Kinsky, Georg, German musicologist; b. Marienwerder, Sept. 29, 1882; d. Berlin, April 7, 1951. He was self-taught in music; after working under Kopfermann at the Royal Library in Berlin, he was appointed curator of the private museum of W. Heyer in Cologne (1909). The Heyer Library was dissolved in 1927. In 1921 Kinsky was appointed teacher at the Univ. of Cologne; in 1925, received his Ph.D. there. He publ. a very valuable illustrated catalogue of the Heyer collections: Vol. I, Keyed Instruments (1910); vol. II, Stringed Instruments (1912); vol. III, Wind and Percussion Instruments (remains in manuscript); vol. IV (in manuscript, 1916). He also publ. a condensed *Handkatalog,* containing valuable historical notes (1913); *Briefe Glucks an Kruthoffer* (Vienna, 1927); *Geschichte der Musik in Bildern* (Leipzig and Paris, 1929; London, New York, and Milan, 1930; new ed. with introduction by Eric Blom, London, 1937); *Die Originalausgaben der Werke J. S. Bachs* (Vienna, 1937); *Manuscripte-Briefe-Dokumente von Scarlatti bis Stravinsky,* catalogue of autographs in the Louis Koch Collection (Stuttgart, 1953, posthumous); a thematic catalogue of Beethoven's works (completed by H. Halm and publ. 1955).

Kipnis, Alexander, eminent Russian bass singer; b. Zhitomir, Feb. 13, 1891; d. Westport, Conn., May 14, 1978. He studied voice in Berlin with Grenzbach at the Klindworth-Scharwenka Cons.; made his professional debut as a singer in Hamburg in 1916. In 1923 he emigrated to the U.S.; sang with the German Opera Co. in N.Y., appearing first as Pogner in *Die Meistersinger* (Feb. 12, 1923); then was with the Chicago Civic Opera (1924); subsequently traveled widely giving recitals in the U.S., South America, Australia and Europe; sang opera in Berlin, Munich, Vienna, Bayreuth and Salzburg. On Jan. 6, 1940 he made his first appearance at the Metropolitan Opera House, N.Y., as Gurnemanz in *Parsifal,* and later sang the part of Boris Godunov, in which he excelled. Through the years, he appeared as a soloist with Toscanini, Richard Strauss, Nikisch, Siegfried Wagner, and other celebrated conductors.

Kipnis, Igor, American harpsichordist; son of the singer **Alexander Kipnis;** b. Berlin, Sept. 27, 1930. He studied at Westport, Conn., School of Music and at Harvard Univ. (A.B., 1952); after holding various jobs as music director for radio programs, he devoted himself to the study of the harpsichord, achieving a fine reputation both as scholar and performer; gave concerts on the harpsichord; toured in America and in Europe; taught at the Berkshire Music Center (1964–67); lectured widely on the subject of proper interpretation of Baroque music; made numerous recordings; edited collections of music for the harpsichord.

Kipper, Hermann, German composer; b. Koblenz, Aug. 27, 1826; d. Cologne, Oct. 25, 1910. He studied with Anschütz and H. Dorn. He was a music teacher and critic in Cologne. He wrote the comic operettas *Der Quacksalber, oder Doktor Sägebein und sein Famulus; Incognito, oder Der Fürst wider Willen; Kellner und Lord; Der Haifisch;* etc.

Kircher, Athanasius, highly significant Jesuit scholar; b. Geisa, near Fulda, Germany, May 2, 1601; d. Rome, Nov. 27, 1680. He attended the Jesuit Seminary in Fulda (1612–18), and was ordained in Paderborn in 1618. He subsequently studied philosophy and theology in Cologne (1622), Koblenz (1623) and Mainz (1624–28); from 1629 to 1632 he taught theology and philosophy at the Univ. of Würzburg; in 1632 he went to Avignon, and in 1635 to Rome where he remained until the end of his life. His *Oedipus aegiptiacus* contains a curious chapter on hieroglyphic music; in his treatise *De arte magnetica* he gives examples of musical airs which were popularly regarded as a cure for tarantism (a nervous condition supposedly induced by the bite of a tarantula). Indeed, his writings present a curious mixture of scientific speculation and puerile credulity. His principal work is the Latin compendium *Musurgia universalis sive ars magna consoni et dissoni* (Rome, 1650; in German, 1662; a facsimile edition was issued in 1969).
BIBLIOGRAPHY: U. Scharlau, *Athanasius Kircher (1601–1680) als Musikschriftsteller* (Kassel, 1969).

Kirchner, Fritz, German pianist and composer; b. Potsdam, Nov. 3, 1840; d. there, May 14, 1907. He studied piano with Theodor Kullak, and with Wüerst and Seyffert (theory) at Kullak's Academy; taught there (1864–89); then at the "Mädchenheim" school in Berlin. He wrote educational pieces and other piano works (*Ball-Scenes; 24 Preludes*), and songs.

Kirchner, Leon, significant American composer; b. Brooklyn, Jan. 24, 1919 of Russian-Jewish parents. In 1928 the family moved to Los Angeles; there he studied piano with Richard Buhlig; in 1938 he entered the Univ. of California, Berkeley, where he took courses in music theory with Albert Elkus and Edward Strickland (B.A. 1940); he also took lessons with Ernest Bloch in San Francisco. In 1942 he went to New York where he had some fruitful private sessions with Sessions; in 1943 he entered military service in the U.S. Army; after demobilization in 1946 he was appointed to the faculty of the San Francisco Conservatory, concurrently teaching at the Univ. of California, Berkeley; in 1948 he received a Guggenheim Fellowship; in 1950 he became associate prof. at the Univ. of Southern California, Los Angeles; from 1954 to 1961 he taught at Mills College in Oakland, California, and in 1961 was named prof. of music at Harvard Univ.; during the academic year 1970–71 he was guest prof. at the Univ. of California at Los Angeles. He received the New York Music Critics Award in 1950 and 1960, and in 1967 he was awarded the Pulitzer Prize. In his music Kirchner takes the prudential median course, cultivating a distinct modern idiom, without espousing any particular modernistic technique, but making ample and effective use of euphonious dissonance; the contrapuntal fabric in his works is tense but invariably coherent. Through his natural inclinations towards classical order, he prefers formal types of composition, often following the established Baroque style.
WORKS: the opera, *Lily,* after Saul Bellow's novel, *Henderson, The Rain King* (N.Y., April 14, 1977); Sinfonia (New York, Jan. 31, 1952); *Toccata* for strings, wind instruments, and percussion (San Francisco, Feb. 16, 1956); Piano Concerto No. 1 (N.Y., Feb. 23, 1956; composer soloist); Piano Concerto No. 2 (Seattle, Oct. 28, 1963); *Music for Orchestra* (1969); chamber music: Duo for violin and piano (1947); String Quartet No. 1 (1949); *Sonata Concertante* for violin and piano (1952); Piano Trio (1954); String Quartet No. 2 (1958); Concerto for violin, cello, 10 instruments and percussion (1960); String Quartet No. 3, with electronic sound (1966; awarded the Pulitzer Prize for 1967); *Lily,* for violin, viola, cello, woodwind quintet, piano, percussion and voice (1973; material from this work was used in his opera, *Lily*); vocal works: *Letter* (1943) and *The Times are Nightfall* for soprano and piano (1943); *Dawn,* for chorus and organ (1946); *Of Obedience and The Runner,* after Walt Whitman, for soprano and piano (1950); *Words from Wordsworth* for chorus (1966); for piano: Sonata (1948); *Little Suite* (1949).
BIBLIOGRAPHY: A. L. Ringer, "Leon Kirchner," *Musical Quarterly* (Jan. 1957).

Kirchner, Theodor, distinguished German composer; b. Neukirchen, near Chemnitz, Dec. 10, 1823; d. Hamburg, Sept. 18, 1903. On Mendelssohn's advice, he studied in Leipzig with K. F. Becker (theory) and J. Knorr (piano), and, in the summer of 1842, with Johann Schneider in Dresden. He was engaged as organist at Winterthur (1843–62) and then taught at the Zürich Music School (1862–72); later held the post of director of the Würzburg Cons. (1873–75). He then returned to Leipzig; finally went to Hamburg in 1890. As a youth, he enjoyed the friendship of Mendelssohn and Schumann, who encouraged and aided him with their advice. He wrote about 90 piano works, in the style of Schumann; some of his miniatures are of very high quality; also made numerous transcriptions for piano solo and piano duet (*Alte Bekannte in neuem Gewande*); *Kinder-Trios* for piano, violin, and cello; a piano quartet; a string quartet; 8 pieces for piano and cello; etc.
BIBLIOGRAPHY: A. Niggli, *Theodor Kirchner*

(Leipzig, 1880); Otto Klauwell, *Theodor Kirchner* (Langensalza, 1909); *Theodor Kirchner, Briefe aus den Jahren 1860-1868,* ed by P. O. Schneider (Zürich, 1949).

Kiriac-Georgescu, Dumitru, Rumanian musician; b. Bucharest, March 18, 1866; d. there, Jan. 8, 1928. As a young man he went to Paris and studied with Vincent d'Indy at the Schola Cantorum; returning to Rumania in 1900, he was appointed prof. at the Bucharest Cons. In 1901 founded the Choral Society Carmen in Bucharest. His chief work is a collection of sacred choruses in 5 vols. He was a noted folklorist, and also contributed to a resurgence of interest in the church music of the Orthodox faith.

Kirigin, Ivo, Croatian composer and music critic; b. Zadar, Feb. 2, 1914; d. Zagreb, Oct. 21, 1964. He studied in Italy with Pizzetti; was active as theater conductor in Zagreb; among his works are Concertino for Piano and Orch.; Symph. work (1950); cantata *Pjesma o Zemlji* (*Song of the Land;* 1952); *Kameni Horizonti* (*Stone Horizons;* Zagreb, March 16, 1955); 5 Movements for Strings (1958); numerous songs.

Kirk, Roland, black American jazz musician; b. Columbus, Ohio, Aug. 7, 1936; d. Bloomington, Indiana, Dec. 5, 1977. He lost his sight in infancy and was brought up at the Ohio State School for the Blind; learned to play trumpet, tenor saxophone, flute, clarinet, trumpet, manzello (a saxophone hybrid), strichophone (an abortion of a French horn), and a nose flute. He had an uncanny ability to play two or three wind instruments simultaneously. In 1963 he organized his own band, with which he toured Europe, Australia and New Zealand. He composed a lot of songs of the pop variety; typical titles are "Here Comes the Whistleman," "I Talk with the Spirits," "Rip, Rig and Panic," "Funk Underneath." A converted Muslim, he changed his first name to **Rahsaan.**

Kirkby-Lunn, Louise, English dramatic contralto; b. Manchester, Nov. 8, 1873; d. London, Feb. 17, 1930. She studied at the Royal College of Music in London; appeared as an opera singer at various London theaters; then toured with Sir Augustus Harris' company, and with the Carl Rosa Opera Co., until 1899, when she married W. J. Pearson, and retired from the stage for two years. In 1901 she reappeared as a member of the Royal Opera at Covent Garden, where she soon became one of the popular favorites. In 1902 she sang for the first time at the Metropolitan Opera, N.Y., where her interpretations of Wagnerian roles (Ortrud and Brangäne) made a deep impression; in 1904 she sang Kundry in Savage's production of *Parsifal* in English. In 1906-08 and 1912-14 she was again with the Metropolitan Opera; later toured in Australia.

Kirkman (real name **Kirchmann**), **Jakob,** founder of the firm of Kirkman and Sons, the harpsichord makers in London; b. Bischweiler, near Strasbourg, March 4, 1710; d. Greenwich, June (buried June 9), 1792. He settled in London about 1730; there he was associated with a Flemish harpsichord maker, Hermann Tabel. After Tabel's death, Kirkman married his widow, and

acquired Tabel's tools. In 1755 he was naturalized as a British subject. In 1773 Kirkman, who was childless, formed a partnership with his nephew, **Abraham Kirkman** (1737-94). The descendants of Abraham Kirkman continued the business until 1896, when the firm was merged with Collard; it was eventually absorbed by Chappell. For details and a list of surviving instruments, see the exhaustive article on Kirkman in Donald Boalch, *Makers of the Harpsichord and Clavichord* (London, 1956).

Kirkpatrick, John, eminent American pianist and pedagogue; b. New York, March 18, 1905. He studied at Princeton Univ.; then took courses in Paris with I. Philipp, C. Decreus, and Nadia Boulanger; returning to America in 1931, he became an energetic promoter of the cause of American music. His most signal achievement was the first performance of the *Concord Sonata* by Charles Ives, which he gave in New York on Jan. 20, 1939, playing it from memory, an extraordinary feat for the time; this performance, which earned enthusiastic reviews for both Ives and Kirkpatrick, played an important role in the public recognition of Ives. As a pedagogue, he taught at Mount Holyoke College and at Cornell Univ. (1946-68); later joined the faculty of Yale Univ. (1968-75), where he is also curator of the Charles Ives Collection. His compendia, *A Temporary Mimeographed Catalogue of the Music Manuscripts of Ives* (1960; reprinted, 1973); and *Charles E. Ives: Memos* (1972) are primary sources of the Ives studies.

Kirkpatrick, Ralph, American harpsichord player and musicologist; b. Leominster, Mass., June 10, 1911. He studied piano at home; theory at Harvard Univ. (A.B., 1931) and with Nadia Boulanger in Paris; there he also took lessons in harpsichord playing with Wanda Landowska. He then worked with Arnold Dolmetsch at Haslemere in order to acquaint himself with old instruments; also with Heinz Tiessen in Berlin. He received a Guggenheim Fellowship in 1937 and undertook a journey throughout Europe, studying early studies of old chamber music; visited Spain, where he uncovered unknown materials on Domenico Scarlatti. In 1940 he was appointed to the staff of Yale Univ.; presented numerous harpsichord concerts and participated in festivals. He publ. valuable new eds. of Bach's *Goldberg Variations,* 60 keyboard sonatas of Domenico Scarlatti, etc. In 1953 he publ. *Domenico Scarlatti,* an exhaustive biography coupled with scholarly analysis of the music, and containing a numbered list of the works that quickly became standard.

Kirnberger, Johann Philipp, noted German theorist; b. Saalfeld, April 24, 1721; d. Berlin, July 27, 1783. He first studied with P. Kellner at Gräfenroda, and with H. N. Gerber at Sondershausen. In 1739 he became a pupil of Bach in Leipzig, and spent 2 years with him. He then traveled in Poland (1741-50) as tutor in various noble Polish families; in 1751 he became violinist to Frederick the Great, and in 1758, Kapellmeister to Princess Amalie. He was greatly renowned as a teacher; among his pupils were Schulz, Fasch, and Zelter. As a theoretical writer, he was regarded as one of the greatest authorities of his time. In his own compositions he displayed an amazing contrapuntal technique, and seriously strove to establish a scientific method of writing music according to basic rules of combination and permutation; his *Der allzeit fertige Menuetten- und Polonaisen-Komponist* (1757) expounded the automatic method of composition. Other works are: *Die Kunst des reinen Satzes in der Musik aus sicheren Grundsätzen hergeleitet und mit deutlichen Beispielen versehen* (2 vols., 1771, 1779, his *magnum opus*); *Grundsätze des Generalbasses, als erste Linien zur Komposition* (1781; often republ.); *Gedanken über die verschiedenen Lehrarten in der Komposition, als Vorbereitung zur Fugenkenntniss* (1782); *Die Konstruction der gleichschwebenden Temperatur* (1760). *Die wahren Grundsätze zum Gebrauch der Harmonie* (1773) was claimed by a pupil of Kirnberger's, J. A. P. Schulz, as his work.

BIBLIOGRAPHY: H. Riemann, *Geschichte der Musiktheorie* (Leipzig, 1898; pp. 478 ff.); A. Schering, "Kirnberger als Herausgeber Bachscher Choräle," *Bach Jahrbuch* (1918); S. Borris, *Kirnbergers Leben und Werk* (Berlin, 1933).

Kirsten, Dorothy, American soprano; b. Montclair, N.J., July 6, 1917. She studied singing at the Juilliard School of Music in N.Y.; Grace Moore took an interest in her and enabled her to go to Italy for further voice training. She studied in Rome with Astolfo Pescia; the outbreak of war in 1939 forced her to return to the U.S. She became a member of the Chicago Opera Co. (debut, Nov. 9, 1940); made her first appearance in N.Y. as Mimi with the San Carlo Opera Co. (May 10, 1942); appeared with the Metropolitan Opera in the same role on Dec. 1, 1945. In 1947 she went to Paris, where she sang Louise in Charpentier's opera, coached by Charpentier himself. On New Year's Eve, 1975 she made her farewell appearance at the Metropolitan Opera, in the role of Tosca, after a 30-year career with the company.

Kisielewski, Stefan, Polish composer; b. Warsaw, March 7, 1911. He studied piano and composition at the Warsaw Cons. (1927–37); was also active as a music journalist and teacher.

WORKS: a musical, *Terrible Manor House* (1963); 3 ballets: *Polish Devils* (1957), *System of Doctor Tar, after Poe* (1962) and *Amusement Grounds* (1966); Concerto for Chamber Orch. (1948); *Rustic Rhapsody* for orch. (1950); Symph. No. 2 (1951); *Little Overture* (1953); *Perpetuum mobile* for orch. (1955); Chamber Symph. (1956); Symph. for 15 Performers (1961); Divertimento for flute and chamber orch. (1964); *Journey in Time* for string orch. (1965); *Sport Signals,* overture (1966); *Rencontres dans un désert* for 10 performers (1969); *Intermezzo* for clarinet and piano (1942); Suite for Oboe and Piano (1957); *Capriccio energico* for violin and piano (1960); Clarinet Sonata (1972); *Toccata* for piano (1945); 2 piano sonatas; songs.

Kist, Florentius Cornelis, Dutch writer on music and teacher; b. Arnhem, Jan. 28, 1796; d. Utrecht, March 23, 1863. He was a physician, practicing in The Hague (1818–25); as a youth, he played the flute and horn. In 1821 he gave up medicine and founded the "Diligen-

tia" music society; in 1841, settled in Utrecht, where he edited the *Nederlandsch muzikaal. Tijdschrift* (1841–44). In Utrecht he also established amateur concerts and the singing society "Duce Apolline." He publ. *De toestand van het protestantsche kerkgezang in Nederland* (1840); *Levensgeschiedenis van Orlando de Lassus* (1841); translated Brendel's *Grundzüge der Geschichte der Musik* (1851); contributed articles to German musical journals; also wrote vocal music and pieces for the flute.

Kistler, Cyrill, German composer; b. Gross-Aitingen, near Augsburg, March 12, 1848; d. Kissingen, Jan. 1, 1907. He was a schoolteacher (1867–76); then studied music at Munich under Wüllner, Rheinberger, and Franz Lachner (1876–80). In 1883 he was called to the Sondershausen Cons.; from 1885 he lived in Bad Kissingen as principal of a music school and music publisher; he also edited the *Musikalische Tagesfragen.* An enthusiastic admirer of Wagner, he unsuccessfully attempted to employ the master's forms and principles in his 10 operas, among them, *Kanhild* and *Eulenspiegel.* Besides these, he wrote 104 works (festive marches, funeral marches for orch., choruses, songs, pieces for organ and harmonium), a *Harmonielehre* (1879); based on Wagner's innovations; 2nd augmented ed., 1903); *Musikalische Elementarlehre* (1880); *Der Gesang- und Musikunterricht an den Volksschulen* (1881); *Volksschullehrer-Tonkünstlerlexikon* (3rd ed., 1887); *Jenseits des Musikdramas* (1888); *Franz Witt* (1888); *Über Originalität in der Tonkunst* (1894; 2nd ed., 1907); *Der einfache Kontrapunkt und die einfache Fuge* (1904); *Der drei- und mehrfache Kontrapunkt* (1908).

BIBLIOGRAPHY: A. Eccarius-Sieber, *Cyrill Kistler* (Leipzig, 1906).

Kistner, Karl Friedrich, German music publisher; b. Leipzig, March 3, 1797; d. there, Dec. 21, 1844. In 1831 he took over Probst's music publishing business, which he carried on from 1836 under the firm name of 'Friedrich Kistner.' He acquired many works by Mendelssohn, Schumann, and Chopin for his catalogue. His son, **Julius Kistner,** succeeded him; in 1866 he sold his business to Karl Friedrich Ludwig Gurckhaus (1821–1884). In 1919 it was bought by Linnemann, and in 1923 merged with C. F. W. Siegel, and operated under the name Fr. Kistner & C. F. W. Siegel.

Kitson, Charles Herbert, notable English theorist and music pedagogue; b. Leyburn, Yorks, Nov. 13, 1874; d. London, May 13, 1944. He studied for an ecclesiastical career, but also took a D.Mus. degree at Oxford (1902). He was organist of Christ Church Cathedral in Dublin (1913–20); also taught at the Royal Irish Academy of Music. In 1920 he was appointed prof. of music at the Univ. of Dublin, resigning in 1935. Returning to London, he was prof. of harmony and counterpoint at the Royal College of Music. He publ. a number of valuable manuals, distinguished by their clarity of presentation and didactic logic. The most important of these are: *The Art of Counterpoint* (1907); *Studies in Fugue* (1909); *Evolution of Harmony* (1914); *Applied Strict Counterpoint* (1916); *Elementary Harmony* (1920); *Invertible Counterpoint and Canon*

(1927); *Rudiments of Music* (1927); *Elements of Fugal Construction* (1929); *Contrapuntal Harmony for Beginners* (1931); *The Elements of Musical Composition* (1936). He also wrote some church music.

Kitt, Eartha, black American singer of popular songs; b. in the town named North, South Carolina, Jan. 26, 1928. She moved to Brooklyn and sang in various emporia around town. In 1948 she went to Paris where she attracted attention as an exotic chanteuse. She excelled particularly in earthy, passion-laden songs delivered in low-key monotone. She published an autobiography *Thursday's Child* (N.Y., 1956; her date of birth indeed fell on a Thursday).

Kittel, Bruno, German violinist and conductor; b. Entenbruch, near Posen, May 26, 1870; d. Wassenberg, near Cologne, March 10, 1948. He studied in Berlin; played in theater orchestras there. From 1901 till 1907 he was conductor of the Royal Theater Orch. in Brandenburg; also was director of the Brandenburg Cons. (until 1914). In 1902 he established the Kittelsche Chor, which soon developed into one of the finest choral societies of Europe, and with which he made many tours. In 1935 he was appointed director of the Stern Cons. in Berlin.

Kittel, Johann Christian, German organist and composer; b. Erfurt, Feb. 18, 1732; d. there, May 18, 1809. He studied at the Thomasschule in Leipzig, and was one of Bach's last students there. After Bach's death, he became organist at Langensalza (1751); then at the Predigerkirche in Erfurt (from 1756). Despite the meager remuneration, he remained in Erfurt almost all his life; in search of betterment, he undertook several tours in nearby towns; even as an old man, in his late sixties, he traveled as organist giving concerts in Göttingen, Hannover, Hamburg, and Altona. He stayed in Altona for a few years; publ. a book of church melodies, *Neues Choralbuch,* there in 1803. In his last years he obtained a small stipend from Prince Primas of Dalberg. Among his other works are *Der angehende praktische Organist* (3 books; Erfurt, 1801–8; 3rd ed., 1831); 6 sonatas and a fantasia for clavichord; *Grosse Präludien, Hymne an das Jahrhundert* (1801); smaller organ pieces. The famous organist C. H. Rinck was one of his pupils.
BIBLIOGRAPHY: A. Dreetz, *J. C. Kittel, der letzte Bach-Schüler* (Leipzig, 1932).

Kittl, Johann Friedrich, Bohemian composer; b. Castle Worlik, May 8, 1806; d. Lissa, in German Poland, July 20, 1868. He studied at a music school in Prague with Tomaschek; at the age of 19 brought out his opera *Daphnis Grab* (1825). In 1837 he wrote a *Jagdsinfonie,* which was performed by the Gewandhaus Orch. in Leipzig on Jan. 9, 1840, at Mendelssohn's behest, and subsequently enjoyed considerable vogue in Germany. In 1843 Kittl was appointed director of the Prague Cons., resigning in 1864. He was a friend of Wagner, who wrote for him a libretto, *Bianca und Giuseppe,* which Kittl set to music and produced as *Die Franzosen vor Nizza* (Prague, Feb. 19, 1848). He further wrote the operas *Waldblume* (1852) and *Die*

Bilderstürmer (1853); some symphonic and chamber music.
BIBLIOGRAPHY: W. Neumann, *J. F. Kittl* (Kassel, 1857); E. Rychnovsky, *J. F. Kittl* (2 vols.; Prague, 1904–05); Jan Branberger, *Das Konservatorium für Musik in Prag* (Prague, 1911); M. Tarantová, *J. F. Kittl* (Prague, 1948).

Kitzinger, Fritz, German conductor; b. Munich, Jan. 27, 1904; d. New York, May 23, 1947. He studied at the Munich Cons. and the Univ. of Munich, graduating in 1924; conductor of the Dortmund Opera (1925–27), Berlin State Opera (1927–30), and Chemnitz Opera (1930); toured China and Japan as a symphonic conductor. In 1934 he came to the U.S. and subsequently settled in N.Y.

Kitzler, Otto, German conductor and cellist; b. Dresden, March 16, 1834; d. Graz, Sept. 6, 1915. He studied with Johann Schneider, J. Otto, and Kummer (cello); then at the Brussels Cons. with Servais and Fétis; was cellist in the opera orchestras at Strasbourg and Lyons; chorusmaster at theaters in Troyes, Linz, Königsberg, Temesvar, Hermannstadt, and Brünn. In 1868 he became director of the Brünn Music Society and of the Brünn Music School; also conductor of the Männergesangverein; retired in 1898. His reputation was very high. Bruckner, 10 years his senior, took orchestration lessons from him in 1861–63. He wrote orchestral music, piano pieces, songs, etc.; also *Musikalische Erinnerungen* (1904; containing letters from Wagner, Brahms, and Bruckner).

Kiurkchiysky, Krasimir, Bulgarian composer; b. Troyan, June 22, 1936. He studied composition with Vladigerov at the Bulgarian State Cons. in Sofia, graduating in 1962; went to Moscow and took some lessons with Shostakovich. His own music reflects Shostakovich's influence in its rhapsodic compactness.
WORKS: an opera, *Yula* (1969; Zagora, 1969); Piano Concerto (1958); Trio for violin, clarinet and piano (1959); String Quartet (1959); *Adagio* for string orch. (1959); Cello Sonata (1960); *Symphony Concertante* for cello and orch. (1960); Violin Sonata (1961); *Symphony-Requiem* (1966); *Diaphonous Study* for orch. (1967); Concerto for Orch. (1975); choruses; incidental music.

Kiyose, Yasuji, Japanese composer; b. Oita, Jan. 13, 1900. He studied with Yamada, Pringsheim, and Alexander Tcherepnin.
WORKS: Piano Concerto (Tokyo, March 10, 1955); *Sketch of Japan* for orch. (1963); 2 piano trios (1938, 1955); 3 violin sonatas (1941, 1948, 1950); String Trio (1949); String Quartet (1952); Quintet for harp and Woodwinds (1957); Buddhist cantata, *Mt. Itajiki* (1955).

Kjellsby, Erling, Norwegian composer and conductor; b. Oslo, July 7, 1901; d. there, Feb. 18, 1976. He studied composition with Brustad and Valen; became a lecturer at Oslo Teacher's College in 1923. He wrote *Norwegian Rhapsody* for small orch. (1937); *Melody* for orch. (1938); 4 string quartets (1940–57); piano pieces, choruses.

Kjellström, Sven, Swedish violinist; b. Lulea, March 30, 1875; d. Stockholm, Dec. 5, 1950. He studied in Stockholm and later in Paris. Returning to Sweden in 1909, he was active in chamber music societies; was director of the Stockholm Cons. (1929–40). He also formed a string quartet, with which he traveled to remote communities in Scandinavia, including Lapland; he was an ardent collector of Swedish folksongs.
BIBLIOGRAPHY: O. Ottelin, *Sven Kjellström och folkets musikliv* (1945).

Kjerulf, Halfdan, Norwegian song composer; b. Christiania, Sept. 15, 1815; d. Grefsen, near Christiania, Aug. 11, 1868. He was a member of a family of artists and scholars; took lessons with a resident German musician, Carl Arnold; already in his prime, he went to Leipzig to study counterpoint; returned to Norway in 1851. He limited himself to composition in small forms; although he followed the German model, he injected melodic and rhythmic elements of a national Norwegian character into his songs. Grieg was deeply influenced by his example and frequently expressed admiration for his music; many celebrated singers (Jenny Lind, Christine Nilsson, Henriette Sontag among them) included his songs in their programs, and thus made them known. He wrote 108 songs in all, among which the most popular are *Last Night, Tell Me, The Nightingale,* and *Synnöve's Song;* he also composed some 30 works for men's chorus and 10 albums of piano pieces marked by a strong Scandinavian cast (*Elfin Dance, Shepherd's Song, Cradle Song, Spring Song, Album-leaf, Capriccio, Scherzo, Scherzino,* etc.); also publ. an album, *25 Selected Norwegian Folk Dances* for piano (1861) and *Norwegian Folk Songs* for piano (1867); these are arrangements of Norwegian melodies from collections by Lindeman and others. In 1874 a monument was erected to him in Christiania.
BIBLIOGRAPHY: A. Grønvold, "Halfdan Kjerulf," in *Norske Musikere* I (Christiania, 1883); K. Nyblom, *Halfdan Kjerulf* (1926); Dag Schjelderup-Erbe, "Modality in Halfdan Kjerulf's Music," *Music & Letters* (July 1957).

Klafsky, Anton Maria, Austrian musicologist and composer; nephew of Katharina Klafsky; b. Winden, Burgenland, July 8, 1877; d. Baden, near Vienna, Jan. 1, 1965. He studied at the Univ. of Vienna; took lessons in composition with Hermann Grädener. He composed much church music, 3 symphonies, piano pieces, and songs; edited sacred choral works of Michael Haydn for the *Denkmäler der Tonkunst in Österreich* vols. 44 and 62 (22 and 32.i).

Klafsky, Katharina, Hungarian soprano; b. St. Johann, Sept. 19, 1855; d. Hamburg, Sept. 22, 1896. She studied with Mme. Marchesi in Vienna; began her career as a chorus singer in various opera houses; in 1881 she attracted attention as a Wagnerian singer; appeared in Hamburg (1885), in London (1892, 1894) and in the U.S. (1895–96). She was one of the most spectacular prima donnas of her day, and her early

death was mourned by opera lovers as a great loss.
BIBLIOGRAPHY: L. Ordemann, *Aus dem Leben und Wirken von Katharina Klafsky* (Hameln, 1903).

Klami, Uuno, Finnish composer; b. Virolahti, Sept. 20, 1900; d. Helsinki, May 29, 1961. He studied the rudiments of music in Helsinki schools; then traveled to Paris and Vienna for further advancement as a composer. In 1938 he received from the Finnish government a life pension. In 1959 he was elected to the Academy of Finland. His music was influenced by the folk modalities of the Karelian region which was his birthplace; the impact of the profundities of the idiom of Sibelius was considerable, but Klami ornamented it with impressionistic detail.
WORKS: for orch.: *Sérénades espagnoles* (1924; revised 1944); *Karelian Rhapsody* (1927); *Rhapsody* (1927); *Merikuvia* (*Sea Pictures;* 1928–30); 3 symphonies (*Symphonie enfantine,* 1928; No. 1, 1937; No. 2, 1944); *Opernredoute* (1929); *Kuvia maalaiselämästä* (*Rustic Scenes;* 1930); *Helsinki March* (1930); *Kalevala Suite* (1932; revised 1943); *Sérénades joyeuses* (1933); *Lemminkäinen* (1934); *Karelian Dances* (1935); *Suomenlinna* (*Fortress of Finland;* 1940); *Revontulet* (*Aurora Borealis;* 1946); *Pyöräilijä* (*The Cyclist,* orch. rondo; 1946); *Karjalainen tori* (*Karelian Market Place;* 1947); 2 piano concertos (No. 1, *Night in Montmartre,* 1924; No. 2, 1950); *4 Folk Songs* for piano and strings (1930); *Cheremissian Fantasy* for cello and orch. (1930); Violin Concerto (1942); *Theme and Variations* for cello and orch. (1950). Vocal and choral works: *Psalmus* for soloists, chorus and orch. (1935–36); *Vipusessa käynti* (*In the Belly of Vipunen*) for baritone, male chorus and orch. (1938); *Laulu Kuujärvestä* (*The Song of Kuujarvi*) for baritone and orch. (1956); *Kultasauvalliset* (*The People with the Golden Staffs*), festive cantata (1961). Chamber music: string quartet, *Nain tragédie* (1920); Piano Quartet (1921); Piano Quintet (1923). At the time of his death, Klami left over a thousand pages of an unfinished ballet score.

Klatte, Wilhelm, German music critic and writer; b. Bremen, Feb. 13, 1870; d. Berlin, Sept. 12, 1930. He studied music in Leipzig, and took lessons with Richard Strauss in Weimar. For some time he held various positions as conductor and music critic; from 1904 he taught at Stern's Cons. in Berlin; in 1925 he was appointed prof. at the Academy for Church and School Music in Berlin. He publ. (in collaboration with A. Seidl) *Richard Strauss, eine Charakterskizze* (1895); "Zur Geschichte der Programm-Musik," in the collection of monographs founded by Richard Strauss, *Die Musik* (1905); *Franz Schubert* (1907); *Grundlagen des mehrstimmigen Satzes* (1922; 3rd ed., 1930).

Klauser, Julius, American writer on music; b. New York, July 5, 1854; d. Milwaukee, April 23, 1907. He studied with his father, Karl Klauser; also took courses at Leipzig Cons. (1871–74); returning to America he settled in Milwaukee as a music teacher. He wrote a book on harmony according to his own system, *The Septonate and the Centralization of the Tonal System* (1890); also *The Nature of Music* (1909).

Klauser, Karl, music editor and arranger; b. St. Petersburg, Russia, Aug. 24, 1823 (of Swiss parents); d. Farmington, Conn., Jan. 5, 1905. He studied music in Germany; went to New York in 1850 and settled in Farmington as a music teacher in 1856. He edited *Half-hours with the Best Composers* and also (with Theodore Thomas and J.K. Paine) *Famous Composers.*

Klauwell, Adolf, German music pedagogue; b. Langensalza, Dec. 31, 1818; d. Leipzig, Nov. 21, 1879. He publ. elementary class books, and instructive piano pieces *(Goldnes Melodien-Album).*

Klauwell, Otto, German writer on music, b. Langensalza, April 7, 1851; d. Cologne, May 11, 1917. He served in the Franco-Prussian War; then entered Leipzig Univ., where he studied mathematics and music; obtained his degree of Dr. phil. with the dissertation *Die historische Entwickelung des musikalischen Canons* (1874). In 1875 he was appointed prof. at Cologne Cons.
WRITINGS: *Musikalische Gesichtspunkte* (1881; 2nd ed., 1892, as *Musikalische Bekenntnisse); Der Vortrag in der Musik* (1883; in English, N.Y., 1890); *Die Formen der Instrumentalmusik* (1894; 2nd ed., 1918); *Geschichte der Sonate* (1899); *Beethoven und die Variationenform* (1901); *Studien und Erinnerungen* (1904); *Geschichte der Programm-Musik* (1910). He was also a composer; wrote 2 romantic operas, *Das Mädchen vom See* (Cologne, 1899) and *Die heimlichen Richter* (Elberfeld, 1902); overtures; chamber music; piano pieces; songs.

Klebe, Giselher, German composer; b. Mannheim, June 28, 1925. He studied at the Berlin Cons. with Kurt von Wolfurt (1942–43), with Josef Rufer and with Boris Blacher (1946–51). He worked in the program division of the Berlin Radio (1946–49); in 1957 was appointed to the faculty of the Nordwestdeutsche Musik Akademie in Detmold; was elected member of the Academy of Arts in Berlin. An experimenter by nature, he has written music in widely ranging forms, from classically conceived instrumental pieces to highly modernistic inventions; his technique is basically dodecaphonic, the chief influences being Schoenberg and Anton von Webern; coloristic and sonoristic schemes play an important role.
WORKS: 10 OPERAS: *Die Räuber,* after Schiller (1951–56; Düsseldorf, June 3, 1957; revised 1962); *Die tödlichen Wünsche,* after Balzac (1957–59; Düsseldorf, June 14, 1959); *Die Ermordung Cäsars,* after Shakespeare (1958–59; Essen, Sept. 20, 1959); *Alkmene,* after Kleist (1961; Berlin, Sept. 25, 1961); *Figaro lässt sich scheiden,* opera buffa after von Horváth (1962–63; Hamburg, June 28, 1963); *Jakobowsky und der Oberst,* comic opera after Werfel (1965; Hamburg, Nov. 2, 1965); *Das Märchen von der schönen Lilie,* fairytale opera after Goethe (1967–68; Schwetzingen, May 15, 1969); *Ein wahrer Held,* after Synge's *Playboy of the Western World,* adapted by Boll (1972–73; Zürich Festival, Jan. 18, 1975); and *Das Mädchen aus Domremy,* after Schiller (1975–76; Stuttgart, June 19, 1976); *Das Rendez-vous* (Hannover, Oct. 7, 1977); 5 BALLETS: *Pas de trois* (1951; Wiesbaden, 1951); *Signa-*

le (1955, Berlin, 1955); *Fleurenville* (1956; Berlin, 1956); *Menagerie* (1958); and *Das Testament* (symph. No. 4, 1970). FOR ORCH: *Con moto* (1948; Bremen, Feb. 23, 1953); *Divertissement joyeux* for chamber orch. (1949; Darmstadt, July 8, 1949); *Die Zwitschermaschine (The Twittering Machine),* metamorphosis on Klee's famous painting (1950; Donaueschingen, Sept. 10, 1950); *2 Nocturnes* (1951; Darmstadt, July 20, 1952); 4 symphonies: No. 1 for 42 strings (1951; Hamburg, Jan. 7, 1953), No. 2 (1953), No. 3 (1967) and No. 4, *Das Testament,* ballet-symph. for orch. and 2 pianos tuned a quarter-tone apart (1970–71; Wiesbaden, April 30, 1971); *Rhapsody* (1953); *Double Concerto* for violin, cello and orch. (1954; Frankfurt, June 19, 1954); *Moments musicaux* (1955); Cello Concerto (1957); *Omaggio* (1960); *Adagio and Fugue* (on a motif from Wagner's *Die Walküre,* 1962); *Herzschläge,* 3 symphonic scenes for beat band and orch. (1969); Concerto for electronically altered harpsichord and small orch. (1971–72); *Orpheus,* dramatic scenes (1976); FOR VOICE: *Geschichte vom lustigen Musikanten* for tenor, chorus and 5 instruments (1946–47); *5 Römische Elegien,* after Goethe, for narrator, piano, harpsichord and double bass (1952; Donaueschingen, Oct. 10, 1953); *Raskolnikows Traum,* dramatic scene after Dostoyevsky, for soprano, clarinet and orch. (1956); *5 Lieder* for alto and orch. (1962); *Stabat Mater* for soprano, mezzo-soprano, alto, chorus and orch. (1964); *Gebet einer armen Seele (The Prayer of a Poor Soul),* dodecaphonic mass for chorus and organ (1966); choruses; songs; CHAMBER MUSIC: wind quintet (1948); 2 string quartets (1949, 1963); viola sonata (1949); 2 solo violin sonatas (1952, 1955); 2 violin sonatas (1953, 1972); *Elegia Appasionata,* piano trio (1955); *Dithyrambe* for string quartet (1957); *7 Bagatelles* for bassett horn, trombone, harp and tubular bells (1961); *9 Duettini* for flute and piano (1962); *Missa "Miserere nobis"* for 18 winds (1965); *Concerto a cinque* for piano, harpsichord, harp, percussion and double bass (1965); *Quasi una fantasia,* piano quintet (1967); *Scene and Aria* for 3 trumpets, 3 trombones, 2 pianos and 8 cellos (1967–68); *Variations on a Theme of Berlioz* for organ and 3 drummers (1970); double bass sonata (1971); *Nenia* for solo violin (1975). He has pieces for piano: *Nocturnes* (1949), 2-piano sonata (1949); and *4 Inventions* (1956).

Kleber, Leonhard, German organist and composer; b. Göppingen, Württemberg, c.1490; d. Pforzheim, March 4, 1556. He studied in Heidelberg; from 1521 was organist at Pforzheim. In 1524 he compiled a book of 112 pieces by Hofhaimer, Josquin, Obrecht, and others, arranged in keyboard tablature. Modern transcriptions are to be found in the following: A. G. Ritter, *Zur Geschichte des Orgelspiels* (1884); R. Eitner, *Monatshefte für Musikgeschichte* (1888); H. J. Moser, *Frühmeister der deutschen Orgelkunst* (1930); W. Apel, *Musik aus früher Zeit* (1934); W. Apel & A.T. Davison, *Historical Anthology of Music* (1946); W. Apel, "Early German Keyboard Music," *Musical Quarterly* (April 1937); *Denkmäler der Tonkunst in Österreich* 28 and 72 (14.i and 37.ii). H. Löwenfeld, *Leonhard Kleber und sein Orgeltabulaturbuch* (Berlin, 1897; repr. Hilversum, 1968).

Klecki, Paul. See **Kletzki, Paul.**

Klee, Eugen, German choral conductor; b. Kaiserslautern, Dec. 15, 1869; d. Philadelphia, Dec. 18, 1929. He studied with his father, Jacob Klee, and later with Thuille in Munich. In 1894 he emigrated to America and settled in Philadelphia, where he was active as leader of German choral societies; also trained similar societies in Brooklyn.

Klee, Ludwig, German pianist and pedagogue; b. Schwerin, April 13, 1846; d. Berlin, April 14, 1920. He was a pupil at the Kullak Academy in Berlin, and then taught there until he established a music school of his own. He publ. *Die Ornamentik der klassichen Klaviermusik*, treating ornamentation from Bach to Beethoven; also edited 2 vols. of *Klassische Vortragsstücke*.

Kleefeld, Wilhelm, German writer on music; b. Mainz, April 2, 1868; d. Berlin, April 2, 1933, on his 65th birthday. He was a pupil of Spitta in Berlin; took his degree of Dr. phil. at Berlin Univ. with the dissertation *Das Orchester der ersten deutschen Oper, Hamburg, 1678–1738* (publ., 1898); in 1898 he became teacher at the Klindworth-Scharwenka Cons.; from 1904 taught at Berlin Univ. He wrote numerous valuable articles on opera; under the title *Opernrenaissance* he ed. a number of early operas; publ. a monograph on Clara Schumann (1910). He wrote many songs and piano pieces (for 2 and 4 hands).

Kleffel, Arno, German composer and conductor; b. Pössneck, Sept. 4, 1840; d. Nikolassee, near Berlin, July 15, 1913. He studied with Hauptmann in Leipzig; then conducted theater orchestras and opera in Riga, Cologne, Amsterdam, Berlin, Augsburg, Magdeburg, etc. In 1904 he became conductor of Stern's Gesangverein in Berlin; in 1910, head of the operatic dept. at the Musikhochschule. He wrote an opera, *Des Meermanns Harfe* (Riga, 1865); music to Goethe's *Faust*; many characteristic piano pieces (*Ritornelles, Jungbrunnen,* etc.); teaching pieces; *Fête d'enfants*; *Nuits italiennes,* for 4 hands; also songs.

Klega, Miroslav, Slovak composer; b. Ostrava, March 6, 1929. He studied composition with Křička in Prague and with Suchoň and Cikker at the Bratislava Cons. (1946–50); taught at the Cons. of Ostrava (1955–73; director 1967–73).
WORKS: *Suite Bagatelle* for piano (1948); *Černá země (Black Soil),* Symph. Variations (1951); Symph. (1959); Concertino for 4 String Instruments (1961); *Pantomima,* suite for orch. (1963); *Concerto-Partita* for violin and orch. (1965); *Confessions of the Lonely Infantryman* for narrator and orch. (1968).

Kleiber, Carlos, German conductor; son of **Erich Kleiber;** b. Berlin, July 3, 1930. He accompanied his parents to South America after the advent of Hitler to power in Germany, and received his musical education in Buenos Aires. Inheriting his father's flair for command of an orchestra, he made his debut in Munich as theater conductor in 1953, and subsequently conducted opera in Potsdam (1954) and in Düsseldorf

(1956). In 1964 he appeared as opera conductor in Zürich and in 1966 in Stuttgart. Subsequently he was engaged as guest conductor in Vienna (1967), Prague (1968) and Munich (1968). Following his father's precepts of the optimum balance between instrumental and vocal masses, he obtains excellent results.

Kleiber, Erich, eminent Austrian conductor; b. Vienna, Aug. 5, 1890; d. Zürich, Jan. 27, 1956. He studied at the Cons. and Univ. of Prague; in 1911, conductor at the Prague National Theater; then conducted opera in Darmstadt (1912–18), Barmen-Elberfeld (1919–21), and in Düsseldorf and Mannheim (1922–23). In 1923 he was appointed general music director of the Berlin State Opera; conducted the world première of Berg's opera *Wozzeck* (Dec. 14, 1925). In 1935, in protest against the German National Socialist government, he emigrated to South America, where he toured as guest conductor; also appeared in Mexico, Cuba, and the U.S.; in 1936–49, conducted German opera at the Teatro Colón in Buenos Aires. He conducted the Havana Philharmonic Orch. (1944–47); appeared as guest conductor of the NBC Symph. Orch. (1945–46); was engaged as chief conductor of the Berlin Opera in 1954, but resigned in March, 1955, before the opening of the season, because of difficulties with the officials of the German Democratic Republic. He wrote a violin concerto, a piano concerto, orchestral variations, a *Capriccio* for orch., an overture, numerous chamber music works, piano pieces, and songs.
BIBLIOGRAPHY: J. Russell, *Erich Kleiber: A Memoir* (London, 1957).

Klein, Bernhard, German composer; b. Cologne, March 6, 1793; d. Berlin, Sept. 9, 1832. He went to Paris in 1812 to study with Cherubini at the Paris Cons.; returning to Cologne, he was appointed music director of the Cathedral. In 1818 he settled in Berlin; from 1820 taught at the Royal Institute for Church Music. During his lifetime he was greatly praised for his contrapuntal craftsmanship in sacred works, and was even described by some as "the Berlin Palestrina."
WORKS: 2 operas: *Dido* (Berlin, Oct. 15, 1823) and *Ariadne* (1825; unperformed); another opera, *Irene,* remained unfinished; 3 oratorios: *Job* (Leipzig, 1820), *Jephtha* (Cologne, 1828), and *David* (Halle, 1830); the cantata *Worte des Glaubens* (1817); an 8-part *Pater noster,* a 6-part Magnificat, 6-part responses, 8 books of psalms, hymns, motets for men's voices, etc.; sonatas and variations for piano; songs. His younger brother, **Joseph Klein** (1801–1862), was also a composer; he lived mostly in Berlin.
BIBLIOGRAPHY: C. Koch, *Bernhard Klein* (Rostock, 1902).

Klein, Bruno Oscar, composer, pianist, and pedagogue; b. Osnabrück, Germany, June 6, 1858; d. New York, June 22, 1911. He studied with his father, Karl Klein, organist of the Osnabrück Cathedral, and later at the Munich Cons. In 1878 he settled in America. From 1884 till his death in 1911 he was head of the piano dept. at the Convent School of the Sacred Heart, N.Y.; also served as organist in various churches. His opera *Kenilworth* was performed in

Hamburg (Feb. 13, 1895); he also wrote a piano concerto; a violin concerto; *American Dances* for orch.; choral music; chamber music; piano pieces.

Klein, Fritz Heinrich, Austrian composer and theorist of an original bent; b. Budapest, Feb. 2, 1892; d. Linz, July 11, 1977. He took piano lessons with his father; then went to Vienna where he studied composition with Schoenberg and Alban Berg, and became their devoted disciple. From 1932 to 1957 he taught music theory at the Bruckner Cons. in Linz. His most ingenious composition is *Die Maschine* (1921; first performed in N.Y., Nov. 24, 1924), subtitled "eine extonale Selbstsatire" and publ. under the pseudonym "Heautontimorumenos" (i.e., self-tormentor); this work features instances of all kinds of tonal combinations, including a "Mutterakkord," which consists of all 12 different chromatic tones and all 11 different intervals, the first time such an arrangement was proposed. He also published an important essay bearing on serial techniques then still in the process of formulation, "Die Grenze der Halbtonwelt," in *Die Musik* (Jan. 1925). He made the vocal score of Alban Berg's opera *Wozzeck*. Among his own works are *Partita* for 6 instruments (1953); *Divertimento* for String Orch. (1954); *Ein musikalisches Fliessband* for orch. (1960); *Musikalisches Tagebuch* for orch. (1970); he further wrote several stage works, among them a mystery opera *Nostradamus,*

Klein, Herman, English music journalist; b. Norwich, July 23, 1856; d. London, March 10, 1934. He studied voice with Manuel Garcia; then taught singing; at the same time wrote music criticism; was critic of the *Sunday Times* from 1881 to 1901; from 1902 till 1909 he was in America as critic of the *N.Y. Herald.* He then returned to London as critic of the *Saturday Review* (1917–21).
WRITINGS: *30 Years of Musical Life in London* (N.Y., 1903); *Unmusical New York* (London, 1910); *The Reign of Patti* (N.Y., 1920); *The Art of the Bel Canto* (London, 1923); *Musicians and Mummers* (London, 1925); *Great Women Singers of My Time* (London, 1931); *The Golden Age of Opera* (London, 1933). He was co-editor of Manuel Garcia's *Hints on Singing* (London, 1894); edited *Musical Notes 1886–89; Lieder in English* (a collection of about 60 translations of songs of Schubert, Schumann, Brahms, etc.). He also made a translation of *Carmen.*

Klein, Ivy Frances (born **Salaman**), English song composer; b. London, Dec. 23, 1895. She has written a number of songs to texts by English poets and has appeared in concerts singing and accompanying herself. In 1924 she married Daryl Klein. Among her songs are: *Ode on Solitude* (after Pope); *Music When Soft Voices Die* (Shelley). Her choral work *She Walked in Beauty* (Byron) was performed at Queen Elizabeth's coronation (1952).

Klein, John, American organist, conductor, and composer; b. Rahns, Penna., Feb. 21, 1915. He studied with Ornstein in Philadelphia; later, studied conducting with Bruno Walter and Felix Weingartner in Salzburg; composition with Nadia Boulanger in Paris and

Hindemith at the Berkshire Music Center. After several years as church organist, he wrote music for films. His works include a Violin Concerto (1944), *Horace, the Bear,* for narrator and orch. (1946), and chamber music.

Klein, Kenneth, talented American conductor; b. Los Angeles, Sept. 5, 1939. He studied violin at the Univ. of Southern California School of Music with Eudice Shapiro, Vera Barstow, and Peter Meremblum; also took piano lessons with Gerhard Albersheim. Subsequently he was trained as a conductor; his instructors were Fritz Zweig in Los Angeles, Izler Solomon at the Aspen School of Music, and Richard Lert in Asilomar, California. Klein played violin under the direction of Lert in the Pasadena Symph. Orch., and in the All State Symph. of California. In 1963 he organized the Westside Symph. Orch. in Los Angeles, and conducted it until 1967, when he was engaged as music director of the Symph. Orch. of Guadalajara, Mexico; conducted with it a series of ambitious programs, including works by contemporary composers. Concurrently, he started on an international career as guest conductor; in 1968 he appeared in Buenos Aires; in 1973 he gave concerts in Puerto Rico; in 1974 he was guest conductor in Paris; also conducted in Austria, Germany, Switzerland, and Scandinavia. He made two tours in Russia, in 1974 and 1977, conducting symphonic concerts in major Soviet cities, including Siberia. Music critics globally praised him for both his romantically inspired interpretations of classical and modern music and incisive sense of dynamics and rhythm.

Klein, Lothar, German-born Canadian composer; b. Hannover, Jan. 27, 1932. He moved to England in 1939 and to the U.S. in 1941; studied composition with Paul Fetler at the Univ. of Minnesota, graduating in 1954, and orchestration with Dorati (1956–58); took courses in composition with Josef Rufer at the Free Univ. of Berlin and with Blacher at the Hochschule für Musik there (1958–60). Returning to the U.S., he taught at the Univ. of Minnesota (1962–64) and Univ. of Texas, Austin (1964–68); in 1968 was appointed to the faculty of the Univ. of Toronto, where he became chairman of the graduate music department (1971–76). His early music is essentially tonal, esthetically derived from neo-Romantic procedures; he then experimented with various branches of serialism; also wrote collage pieces embodying elements of all historical periods through linkage of stylistic similarities.
WORKS: 2 *Cantatas: I* for soli, chorus, harp and wind ensemble (1957) and *II (On Epigrams of Sappho)* for actress and 6 solo instruments (1958); 3 ballets: *Charades, Lost Love* and *La Ronde* (all 1950–56); a dance drama, *The Prodigal Son* (1966); Divertimento for Band (1953); Piano Concerto (1954); *Eclogues* for horn and strings (1954); 3 symphonies (1955, 1965, 1972); Concerto for wind quartet, brass, timpani and strings (1956); *Symmetries* for orch. (1958); *Appasionato* for orch. (1958); *Trio Concertante* for string trio and orch. (1961; New Orleans, April 4, 1965); *Epitaphs,* dedicated to the memory of Hemingway, Camus and President Kennedy, for orch. (1963; New Orleans, April 4, 1965); *Janizary Music* for winds,

percussion and celli (1970); *Prelude, Madrigal and Fantastic Sprites,* suite for orch. (1971); *Passacaglia of the Zodiac* for 14 solo strings (1971); *Music for Violin and Orch.* (1972); *Le Trésor des Dieux,* suite for guitar or harpsichord, and orch. (1972); *Slices of Time* for trumpet, and string orch. (1973); *The Philosopher in the Kitchen,* "gastronomic meditation," for contralto and orch. (1974; Toronto, July 8, 1975); *Invention, Blues and Chase* for free bass accordion and strings (1975); *Musica Antiqua,* allegory for consort and orch. (1975; performers also sing); *Orpheus: A Lyrical Essay* for narrator, chorus, winds and piano (1976); *Wind Quintet* (1952); *Piano Quintet* (1953); *Music for Violin and Piano* (1963); *Hommage à Satie* for piano (1966); *Piano Sonata* (1968); *Trio Sonata,* "third-stream music" for clarinet, cello, piano and jazz drums (1969); *4 for 1,* suite for solo double bass (1970); *6 Exchanges* for solo saxophone (1972); songs; choral works; incidental music for 10 plays.

Klein, Manuel, English-American conductor and composer; b. London, Dec. 6, 1876; d. New York, June 1, 1919. He studied in London; settled in N.Y. in 1904, where he was music director of the N.Y. Hippodrome and composer of the music for a great many of the productions there.

Kleinheinz, Franz Xaver, German composer and conductor; b. Mindelheim, June, 1765 (baptized June 26); d. Budapest, Jan. 26, 1832. He played in the Munich Orch.; in 1803 he went to Vienna to study with Albrechtsberger; then was active in Brünn; subsequently in Budapest (1814–23). He made transcriptions for string quartet of Beethoven's early piano sonatas; wrote the operas *Harald* (Budapest, March 22, 1814) and *Der Käfig* (Budapest, 1816); much chamber music; sacred choral works; a piano concerto; etc.
   BIBLIOGRAPHY: Emil Haraszti, "Les Compositions inconnues de F. X. Kleinheinz," *Revue Musicale* (March 1930).

Kleinknecht, Jakob Friedrich, German flutist, violinist, and composer; b. Ulm, April (baptized, April 8), 1722; d. Ansbach, Aug. 14, 1794. In 1743 he was engaged as flutist in the Margrave's orch. in Bayreuth, and in 1756 was appointed its Kapellmeister. He wrote a number of pieces of chamber music, almost all of them including solo parts for the flute.

Kleinmichel, Richard, German pianist and composer; b. Posen, Dec. 31, 1846; d. Charlottenburg, Aug. 18, 1901. He studied with his father, Friedrich Kleinmichel (1827–1894), a bandmaster; subsequently took courses at the Leipzig Cons.; taught music in Hamburg for some years; returned to Leipzig in 1876, and in 1882 became music director of the Municipal Theater there; then was active in similar positions in Danzig and Magdeburg. He married **Clara Monhaupt,** a soprano. He wrote 2 operas, *Der Pfeiffer von Dusenbach* (Hamburg, 1881) and *Manon* (Hamburg, 1883); 2 symphs.; many characteristic pieces for piano; 4 books of piano études "für kleine und grosse Leute" and other pedagogical studies. He arranged for piano several of Wagner's scores, including the entire *Ring.*

Kleinsinger, George, American composer; b. San Bernardino, Calif., Feb. 13, 1914. He was taken to New York as a child; first studied dentistry; then entered N.Y. Univ. as a music student of Philip James; later studied at the Juilliard Graduate School with Jacobi and Wagenaar. He acquired a taste for simple American songs and rhythms; sophisticated pieces on native subjects, often with a satiric purpose, and with colorful instrumental effects, became his specialty; in this vein he wrote *Tubby the Tuba* for narrator and orch. (1942); *Pan the Piper* (1946), *Pee-Wee the Piccolo* (1946), *Street Corner Concerto* for harmonica and orch. (1947), *Brooklyn Baseball Cantata* (1948), and the chamber opera *Archy and Mehitabel* (N.Y., Dec. 6, 1954), which enjoyed an excellent success.

Klemetti, Heikki, Finish composer and choral conductor; b. Kuortane, Feb. 14, 1876; d. Helsinki, Aug. 26, 1953. He studied philosophy, and then music at the Stern Cons. in Berlin. In 1900 he founded the famous men's choir, Suomen Laulu (became a mixed choir in 1907), with which he toured Scandinavia and Europe (1901–25); also the U.S. (1939). He publ. a history of music (in Finnish; several vols. since 1916), a textbook of choral singing (1917), and a textbook of voice production (1920); composed numerous choruses, Masses, and antiphons (collected and officially approved as the hymnal of the State Church of Finland in 1924); also arranged songs for school and home (3 vols., 1927–28) and some early church music.

Klemm, Johann Gottlob. See **Clemm, Johann Gottlob.**

Klemperer, Otto, distinguished German conductor; b. Breslau, May 14, 1885; d. Zürich, July 6, 1973. His family moved to Hamburg when he was a child; he received rudimentary musical training from his mother; in 1901 he entered the Hoch Cons. in Frankfurt; then went to Berlin where he took courses with Ph. Scharwenka, James Kwast, and Pfitzner. He met Mahler, who was impressed with his musical talent and recommended him to the management of the German National Theater in Prague as conductor in 1907; with Mahler's support, Klemperer received engagements to conduct opera in Hamburg (1910), Barmen (1913), Strasbourg (1914), Cologne (1917) and Wiesbaden (1924). He conducted the N.Y. Symph. Orch. during the 1925–26 season with excellent success; also was guest conductor in England, South America and Australia, and 3 times in Russia. In 1927 he was appointed music director of the Kroll Opera in Berlin. The seizure of Germany by the Nazis in 1933 compelled him to flee the country; he went to the U.S.; from 1933 to 1939 he was conductor of the Los Angeles Philharmonic. His career suffered a serious setback in 1939 when he had an operation for the removal of a brain tumor, but he recovered remarkably well and was able to resume his artistic activities. From 1947 to 1950 he conducted at the Budapest Opera; in 1959 he was appointed principal conductor of The Philharmonia Orch. in London; in 1971 was given an honorary membership in the Royal Academy of Music. In 1970 he conducted in Jerusalem and accepted Israeli citizenship; then lived in Switzerland. Klemperer was also a composer; he wrote 6 symphonies; 9 string quartets; 17 pieces for voice and orch.; and about 100 Lieder. He publ. *Meine Erinnerungen an Gustav Mahler* (Zürich, 1960; in English as *Minor Recollections*, London, 1964).

BIBLIOGRAPHY: *Conversations with Klemperer* (London, 1973).

Klenau, Paul (August) von, Danish conductor and composer; b. Copenhagen, Feb. 11, 1883; d. there, Aug. 31, 1946. He studied with Hilmer (violin) and Malling (composition) in Copenhagen; then in Berlin with Halir (violin) and Max Bruch (composition); in Munich with Thuille, and in Stuttgart with Max von Schillings. He began his conducting career in 1907 in Freiburg; from 1922 till 1930 he conducted the Philharmonic in Copenhagen.

WORKS: operas, *Kjartan und Gudrun* (Mannheim, April 4, 1918; revised version as *Gudrun auf Island*, Hagen, Nov. 27, 1924); *Die Lästerschule*, after Sheridan's *School for Scandal* (Frankfurt, 1926); *Michael Kohlhaas* (Stuttgart, 1933); *Rembrandt van Rijn* (Berlin, Jan. 23, 1937); *Elisabeth von England* (Kassel, March 29, 1939; title changed to *Die Königin* after the outbreak of World War II); 7 symphonies; *Inferno* (3 fantasies for orch., after Dante); chamber music; piano pieces; songs. His most successful work was a ballet after Hans Christian Andersen, *Klein Idas Blumen*.

Klengel, August Alexander, German pianist and composer; b. Dresden, Jan. 27, 1783; d. there, Nov. 22, 1852. He studied with Milchmayer, and from 1803, with Clementi, with whom he traveled through Germany, and in 1805, to St. Petersburg, where he remained as private tutor to aristocratic families until 1811. He then lived in Paris; visited London in 1815; returned to Dresden in 1816, and was appointed organist at the Roman Catholic Court Church. He was a fine organist and pianist, particularly distinguished by his *legato* piano style; as a composer, he was a master of contrapuntal forms; his canons were so ingenious that he was known under the sobriquet "Kanon-Klengel."

WORKS: His piano canons were publ. under the title *Les Avantcoureurs* (Dresden, 1841); he also wrote 48 canons and 48 fugues, taking Bach's *Well-Tempered Clavier* as the model (publ. posthumously, 1854). His other published piano works include 2 concertos; a 4-hand fantasia; a rondo; *Promenade sur mer, interrompue par une tempête,* and other salon music.

BIBLIOGRAPHY: R. Jäger, *A. A. Klengel, und seine Kanons und Fugen* (Leipzig, 1928).

Klengel, Julius, German cellist; brother of **Paul Klengel;** b. Leipzig, Sept. 24, 1859; d. there, Oct. 27, 1933. Brought up in a musical atmosphere (virtually all members of his family were professional or amateur musicians), he developed rapidly; studied cello with Emil Hegar and theory with Jadassohn. He joined the Gewandhaus Orch. in Leipzig when he was 15; in 1881 he became 1st cellist, and remained in that post until his resignation in 1924. He also taught at the Leipzig Cons. He traveled widely in Europe as a soloist; composed a number of works for his instrument, among

them 4 concertos; a *Konzertstück* for cello with piano; *Hymnus* for 12 cellos; Double Concerto for Violin and Cello; 2 string quartets; Piano Trio; edited a number of cello works; publ. cello exercises.

Klengel, Paul, German conductor and composer; brother of **Julius Klengel;** b. Leipzig, May 13, 1854; d. there, April 24, 1935. He studied at the Leipzig Cons. and at Leipzig Univ.; took the degree of Dr. phil. with the dissertation *Zur Ästhetik der Tonkunst.* From 1881–86 he conducted the Leipzig Euterpe Concerts; 1888–93, 2nd court conductor at Stuttgart; then again in Leipzig; from 1898 to 1902 he conducted German choral societies in New York; then went back to Germany. He was a versatile musician and was proficient as a violinist as well as a pianist, although he did not engage in a concert career. He wrote numerous works for violin, and also publ. many skilful arrangements for various combinations.

BIBLIOGRAPHY: Eva Klengel, *Stammtafel der Familie Klengel* (Leipzig, 1929).

Klenovsky, Nikolai, Russian composer; b. Odessa, 1853; d. St. Petersburg, July 6, 1915. He studied violin with Hřimalý and harmony with Tchaikovsky at the Moscow Cons. In 1893 he was appointed director of the Cons. of Tiflis in the Caucasus, and in 1902 was engaged as conductor of the Court Chapel in St. Petersburg. He composed 3 ballets, *Hashish* (Moscow, 1885), *Svetlana* (Moscow, 1886) and *Salanga* (St. Petersburg, 1900); an orchestral suite *Fata Morgana* and a number of choruses; some of his songs had merit.

Klenovsky, Paul. Pseudonym of **Wood, Sir Henry.**

Klerk, Albert de, Dutch organist and composer; b. Haarlem, Oct. 4, 1917. He served as assistant organist in a Haarlem church as a boy; then studied at the Amsterdam Cons. In 1964 he became a prof. of organ and improvisation at the Amsterdam Cons.; has also been active as a choral conductor. He has written much music for the church and made arrangements of old Flemish songs.

WORKS: Concerto for Organ and Orch. (1941); *Jam lucis orto sidere* for high voice and orch. (1942–43); *Cantabile* for orch. (1952); *Stabat Mater* for alto, tenor, chorus and chamber orch. (1952); a sacred cantata, *Super Omnia,* for alto, chorus and organ (1960); *Adagium-Suite* for school chorus and orch. (1960); *5 Noëls français* for alto and 10 wind instruments (1963); Concerto for organ-positive and string orch. (1964); Concerto for solo organ, 2 horns, 2 trumpets and 2 trombones (1967); *Laudate Dominum (Psalm 150)* for chorus and orch. (1968); *Suite Concertante* for organ and string orch. (1976); a number of sacred works, including *Mater Sanctus Laelitiae (Mother of Blessed Happiness)* for female chorus, flute, English horn and bassoon (1957) and *Ad Modum Tubae* for chorus, wind quartet and organ; sonatina for violin and cello (1937); *Aria met variaties* for piano, 4 hands (1944); *Fantasy* for violin and piano (1949–50); numerous organ pieces, including Prelude and Fugue (1940); Sonata (1942); *6 Inventions* (1945); *Ricercare (Hommage à Sweelinck)* (1950), *8 Fantasies on a Gregorian Theme* (1954) and *Images.*

Kletzki (originally spelled **Klecki**), **Paul,** Polish conductor; b. Lodz, March 21, 1900; d. Liverpool, March 5, 1973. He studied violin with Emil Mlynarski; during World War I was a member of the Lodz Philharmonic; then lived in Berlin (1921–33) and in Italy. After World War II he occupied various conducting posts, including a season with the Liverpool Philharmonic (1954–55). From 1958 to 1964 he conducted the Dallas Symph.; then went to Switzerland where he conducted the Bern Orch. (1964–66) and the Orchestre de la Suisse Romande (1967–70); also was guest conductor in South America and Australia. He wrote about 50 compositions for various combinations, including 2 symphonies.

Kleven, Arvid, Norwegian composer and flutist; b. Drontheim, Nov. 29, 1899; d. Oslo, Nov. 23, 1929. He studied in Oslo, Paris, and Berlin; from 1919, played flute in the National Theater Orch. in Oslo, and in the Philharmonic Orch. there. He wrote a tone poem, *Lotusland* (Oslo, 1922); 2 *Aquarelles,* for orch. (1923); *Sinfonia libera* (1927); several works for violin; piano pieces; songs.

Klička, Josef, Bohemian organist and composer; b. Klattau, Dec. 15, 1855; d. there, March 28, 1937. He studied with Skuhersky in Prague; then conducted various choral societies there; from 1906–20 he was inspector of music in Bohemia. He was appointed prof. of organ at the Prague Cons. in 1885 and taught until his retirement in 1924. He wrote an opera, *The Miller's Beautiful Wife* (Prague, 1886); 9 Masses; 2 oratorios; many organ works, including a fantasia on the chorale melody *St. Wenzeslaus,* and *Legend* (both published in *Les Maîtres contemporains d'orgue,* Paris); chamber music; also pieces for harp.
BIBLIOGRAPHY: K. Hoffmeister, *Josef Klička* (Prague, 1944).

Klimov, Mikhail, Russian choral conductor and pedagogue; b. Moscow, Oct. 21, 1881; d. Zavidovo, near Tver, Feb. 20, 1937. He studied composition with Rimsky-Korsakov and conducting with Nicolas Tcherepnin at the St. Petersburg Cons., graduating in 1908. In 1919 he was called upon to reorganize the former Imperial Church Choir as a secular group, and toured with it in Europe in 1928. He also taught choral singing at the St. Petersburg Cons. He publ. a textbook of solfeggio (1929).
BIBLIOGRAPHY: V. Muzalevsky, *M. G. Klimov* (Leningrad, 1960).

Klindworth, Karl, eminent German pianist, pedagogue, and editor; b. Hannover, Sept. 25, 1830; d. Stolpe, near Potsdam, July 27, 1916. He learned to play violin and piano as a child; obtained work as conductor of a traveling opera company when he was only 17; also traveled in Germany as concert pianist; then went to Weimar to study with Liszt. In 1854 he went to London, where he remained until 1868, establishing himself as a popular piano teacher. When Wagner was in London in 1855, they became friends; as a result of his admiration for Wagner, Klindworth undertook the most important work of his life, the arrangement in vocal scores of Wagner's tetralogy, *The*
Ring of the Nibelung. In 1868, he was engaged as prof. at the newly-founded Moscow Cons. at the invitation of its director, Nicholas Rubinstein; after Rubinstein's death in 1881 Klindworth returned to Germany; was for a time conductor of the Berlin Philharmonic. In 1884 he established in Berlin his own "Klavierschule"; in 1893 it was merged with the Scharwenka Cons. of Music in Berlin, as Konservatorium der Musik Klindworth-Scharwenka, which became one of the most famous music schools in Germany. Klindworth was an exceptionally competent arranger and music editor; apart from his masterly transcriptions of Wagner's operas, he made an arrangement for 2 pianos of Schubert's C Major Symphony. He also wrote a number of virtuoso pieces for piano, of which the brilliant *Polonaise-Fantaisie* and 24 grand études in all keys enjoyed some vogue among pianists.
BIBLIOGRAPHY: Hugo Leichtentritt, *Das Konservatorium der Musik Klindworth-Scharwenka, 1881–1931* (Berlin, 1931).

Klingenberg, Friedrich Wilhelm, German pedagogue; b. Sulau, June 6, 1809; d. Görlitz, April 2, 1888. He was director of the Music Academy at Breslau (1830–37); from 1840–85, cantor at the Peterskirche in Görlitz. He wrote a symphony, overtures, piano pieces, vocal church music, and songs.

Klitzsch, Karl Emanuel, German conductor and composer; b. Schönhaide, Oct. 30, 1812; d. Zwickau, March 5, 1889. He lived most of his life in Zwickau; co-founder and conductor of the Music Society there. Under the pen name of **Emanuel Kronach** he composed the opera *Juana, oder ein Tag auf St. Domingo;* the 96th Psalm, for soli, chorus, and orch.; also songs.

Klose, Friedrich, Swiss composer; b. Karlsruhe (of Swiss parents), Nov. 29, 1862; d. Ruvigliana, Lugano, Dec. 24, 1942. He studied in Karlsruhe and Geneva; in 1886 he went to Vienna, where he took a course with Bruckner. He traveled in Germany, Austria, and Switzerland, occupying teaching posts for a year or two in various places, until 1907, when he was appointed prof. of composition at the Akademie der Tonkunst in Munich. In 1920 he went to Switzerland. He wrote several large works that reveal the influence of Bruckner and Wagner; of these, the most important is *Ilsebill,* described as "dramatic symphony" (Munich, Oct. 29, 1905); another important work is an oratorio, *Der Sonne-Geist* (Basel, 1918); he further wrote a symph. poem, *Das Leben ein Traum;* organ works; a string quartet; songs. He publ. the books *Meine Lehrjahre bei Bruckner* (Regensburg, 1927), and *Bayreuth* (1929).
BIBLIOGRAPHY: R. Louis, *Friedrich Klose* (Munich, 1905); H. Knappe, *Friedrich Klose* (1921). A symposium of articles, *Friedrich Klose, zum 80. Geburtstag,* was publ. at Lugano (1942).

Klosé, Hyacinthe-Éléonore, noted clarinetist and pedagogue; b. Isle of Corfu, Oct. 11, 1808; d. Paris, Aug. 29, 1880. He studied at the Paris Cons.; then taught there for nearly 30 years (1839–68). In 1843 he introduced an important innovation into Böhm's system of ring-keys, which was widely adopted; publ.

Grande méthode pour la clarinette à anneaux mobiles (1844) based on that system; also studies and exercises. He did much to promote the then-novel saxophone, and wrote some music for it.

Klose, Margarete, German contralto; b. Berlin, Aug. 6, 1902; d. there, Dec. 14, 1968. She studied music at the Klindworth-Scharwenka Cons. in Berlin; made her debut in Ulm in 1927; then sang in Mannheim (1928–31) and finally at the Berlin State Opera, where she obtained a decisive popular and musical success; she continued her active career until her 60th year; sang in Italy, England and the U.S. She was particularly praised for her Wagnerian contralto roles.

Kloss, Erich, German writer on music; b. Görlitz, Feb. 19, 1863; d. (in an automobile accident) Berlin, Nov. 1, 1910. He began his career as a teacher, but because of deafness he was obliged to give it up; directed his attention to writing.

WRITINGS: *20 Jahre Bayreuth* (1896); *Wagner, wie er war und ward* (1901); *Ein Wagner-Lesebuch* (1904); *Wagner-Anekdoten* (1908); *R. Wagner in seinen Briefen* (1908); *R. Wagner an siene Künstler* (1909); *R. Wagner im Liede* (1910); *R. Wagner über die Meistersinger* (1910); *R. Wagner über den Ring des Nibelungen* (1913; publ. posthumously); also edited *Richard Wagner an Freunde und Zeitgenossen* (1909), and the 3rd augmented ed. of the Wagner-Liszt correspondence (1910).

Klotz, a family of Bavarian violin makers at Mittenwald. Their instruments were brought into repute by **Matthias Klotz** (b. Mittenwald, June 11, 1653; d. there, Aug. 16, 1743), the son of Ägidius Klotz; he is believed to have learned the art of violin making from Nicola Amati, during his travels in Italy; he manufactured his best instruments between 1670 and 1696. His son **Sebastian Klotz** (b. Mittenwald, Jan. 18, 1696; d. there, Jan. 20, 1775) is regarded as even superior in making violins after Italian models. There followed, in the 18th century, several other violin makers named Klotz, but their relationship to the family cannot be established.

Klughardt, August (Friedrich Martin), German composer; b. Cöthen, Nov. 30, 1847; d. Dessau, Aug. 3, 1902. He was a pupil of Blassmann and Reichel at Dresden. In 1867 he was appointed theater conductor at Posen; had similar posts in Lübeck (1868) and Weimar (1869–73); he then was active in Neustrelitz (1873–82) and Dessau (from 1883).

WORKS: 4 operas: *Miriam* (Weimar, 1871), *Iwein* (Neustrelitz, 1879), *Gudrun* (Neustrelitz, 1882), and *Die Hochzeit Mönchs* (Dessau, Nov. 10, 1886; given in Prague as *Astorre,* 1888); 5 symphonies, chamber music, songs, and piano pieces.

BIBLIOGRAPHY: L. Gerlach, *August Klughardt, Sein Leben und seine Werke* (Leipzig, 1902).

Klusák, Jan, Czech composer; b. Prague, April 18, 1934. He studied composition with Řídký and Bořkovec at the Prague Academy of Music (1953–57). In his music he draws upon multiple resources of modern

techniques, especially the 12-tone method of composition.

WORKS: an opera after Kafka, *Proces (The Trial,* 1966); *Music to the Fountain* for wind quintet (1954); concertino for flute and strings (1955); *Partita* for strings (1955); 2 string quartets (1955–56, 1961–62); 3 symphonies (1956, 1959, 1960); *Concerto Grosso* for wind quintet and strings (1957); *4 Small Vocal Exercises,* on texts by Kafka, for narrator and 11 winds (1960); *Obrazy (Images)* for 12 winds (1960); Concertino for 8 instruments (1960); 6 *Inventions:* No. 1 for chamber orch. (1961), No. 2 for chamber orch. (1962), No. 3 for strings (1962), No. 4 for orch. (1964), No. 5, *Hra v šachy (Game of Chess),* for wind quintet (1965) and No. 6 for wind quintet, violin, viola, cello and double bass (1969); *Variations on a Theme of Mahler* for orch. (1960–62; based on a theme from Mahler's 5th symph.); *Monoinvention* for solo cello (1962); *Risposte* for solo violin (1963); *2 Czech Dances* for wind orch. (1964); *3 Pieces* for organ (1964); Sonata for violin and wind instruments (1964–65); *Lyric Fantasy (Homage to Grieg)* for orch. (1965); *Contrapunto fiorito* for 8 instruments (1966); *Le Forgeron Harmonieux,* variations on a theme of Handel, for orch. (1966); *Rondo* for piano (1967); *Ein Friesischer Freitag* for orch. (1970).

Knab, Armin, German composer; b. Neu-Schleichach, Feb. 19, 1881; d. Bad Wörishofen, June 23, 1951. He studied piano in Würzburg; from 1934–43, taught at the Hochschule für Musick-Erziehung, in Berlin.

WORKS: the sacred cantatas *Mariae Geburt* (1928), *Vanitas mundi* (1946), *Engelsgruss* (1950), etc.; the musical fairy tales, *Sneewittchen* and *Rumpelstilzchen;* folksong cantatas *Singt und klingt* (1934), *Grüss Gott, du schöner Maien* (1935), and *Glück auf, ihr Bergleute* (1946); a great number of choral works; many instrumental pieces for school use. Knab was particularly esteemed in Germany as a composer of lieder. He followed the Romantic tradition, but tended towards a more severe modal style in his larger works.

BIBLIOGRAPHY: O. Lang, *Armin Knab, ein Meister deutscher Liedkunst* (Munich, 1937).

Knabe, William (Valentine Wilhelm Ludwig), founder of the celebrated piano manufacturing firm of Baltimore; b. Kreuzberg, near Oppeln, Prussia, June 3, 1803; d. Baltimore, May 21, 1864. He opened his business in 1839 with Henry Gaehle; in 1854 the partnership was dissolved. His successors were his sons **William Knabe** (1841–89) and **Ernest Knabe** (1827–94), joined later by Charles Keidel, and his grandsons **Ernest J. Knabe** and **William Knabe** (1872–1939). The firm was later amalgamated with the American Piano Corp.

Knap, Rolf, Dutch composer; b. Amsterdam, Oct. 17, 1937. He studied oboe at the Amsterdam Cons.; took private composition lessons with Karel Mengelberg; then studied electronic music at the Institute of Sonology of the Univ. of Utrecht. He was an orchestral oboist (1960–67); taught oboe at several schools of music in Holland (1967–74).

WORKS: *(Sym)phonic Piece* for orch. (1971); *Le Couple(t)* for voice, piano and electronics (1971); *Dilemmaniana for Marrie* for narrator, cello and live electronics (1972); *Zelomanniana* for oboe and piano (1974); 2 song cycles *Liederen van Doofstommen (Songs of Deaf-Mutes;* 1974, 1976).

Knape, Walter, German composer; b. Bernburg, Jan. 14, 1906. He studied at the Univ. of Leipzig, receiving his Ph.D. in 1934 for a dissertation on the symphonies of Carl Abel. In 1961 he began editing the complete works of Abel. He was subsequently connected with various music schools in Berlin, in Hannover, and lectured at the Univ. of Hamburg. He composed several symphonic and choral works as well as chamber music and a considerable number of piano pieces. He further published *Instrumentenkunde* (Berlin, 1957). In 1961 he made his home in Cuxhaven.

Knapp, Phoebe Palmer, American hymn-tune writer; b. New York, 1839; d. Poland Springs, Maine, July 10, 1908. She and her husband, the founder of the Metropolitan Life Insurance Company, supported much philanthropic work as members of the Methodist Episcopal Church. She wrote both verse and music for church hymns; her most popular hymn is *Assurance* (1873).
BIBLIOGRAPHY: R. G. McCutchan, *Our Hymnody* (N.Y., 1937).

Knappertsbusch, Hans, eminent German conductor; b. Elberfeld, March 12, 1888; d. Munich, Oct. 25, 1965. He studied with Steinbach and Lohse at the Cons. of Cologne (1908–12); then occupied various positions as opera conductor, in Elberfeld (1913–18), Leipzig (1918–19) and Dessau (1919–22). From 1922 to 1935 he was principal conductor of the Bavarian State Opera in Munich; then went to Vienna, where he conducted the Vienna Philh. and the Vienna Opera (1937–45). In 1951 he was a regular conductor at the Bayreuth Festivals; also was guest conductor in Russia (1926 and 1929). He was regarded as the keeper of German romantic traditions in his interpretations of the classics, and was particularly praised for his performances of the operas of Wagner and Richard Strauss.
BIBLIOGRAPHY: R. Betz and W. Panofsky, *Knappertsbusch* (Ingolstadt, 1958).

Knecht, Justin Heinrich, German composer and organist; b. Biberach, Sept. 30, 1752; d. there, Dec. 1, 1817. He was organist and music director in Biberach from 1771 to the end of his life, traveling only briefly to Stuttgart, where he was court conductor from 1807 till 1809. Despite his provincial field of activity he attained considerable repute in Germany through his compositions and theoretical writings. He was a follower of the Vogler system of harmony; taught chord building by thirds up to chords of the eleventh on all degrees of the scale. His publications include: *Erklärung einiger missverstandenen Grundsätze aus der Vogler' schen Theorie* (Ulm, 1785); *Gemeinnützliches Elementarwerk der Harmonie und des Generalbasses* (4 parts, 1792–8); *Kleines alphabetisches Wörterbuch der vornehmsten und interessantesten Artikel aus der musikalischen Theorie* (1795); *Vollständige Orgelschule für Anfänger und Geübtere* (3 parts, 1795–98); *Theoretisch-praktische Generalbass-Schule; Kleine Klavierschule für die ersten Anfänger* (republ. as *Bewährtes Methodenbuch beim ersten Klavierunterricht*); *Allgemeiner musikalischer Katechismus* (Biberach, 1803); *Luthers Verdienst um Musik und Poesie* (1817). He wrote about 15 operas, several sacred works, and a piece for 15 instruments, *Tongemälde der Natur,* to which he supplied a programmatic description, seemingly anticipating Beethoven's "Pastoral" Symphony. However, the resemblance is superficial and there is no reason to believe that Beethoven was influenced by Knecht in this "tone painting" of nature.
BIBLIOGRAPHY: E. Kauffmann, *J. H. Knecht* (Tübingen, 1892); A. Bopp, *J. H. Knecht* (Kassel, 1930).

Kneisel, Franz, violin virtuoso; b. Bucharest (of German parentage), Jan. 26, 1865; d. New York, March 26, 1926. He studied at the Cons. of Bucharest, graduating at the age of 14; in 1879 went to Vienna, where he became a pupil of Grün and Hellmesberger at the Vienna Cons.; made his debut on Dec. 31, 1882 in Vienna; in 1884 he went to Berlin, where he was concertmaster of the Bilse Orch. (1884–85). In 1885 he was engaged as concertmaster of the Boston Symph. Orch.; made his debut as soloist in Boston on Oct. 31, 1885, playing the Beethoven Concerto. In 1886 he organized the celebrated Kneisel Quartet (Emmanuel Fiedler as 2nd violin; Louis Svecenski, viola; Fritz Giese, cello), which gave performances of high quality in Boston, New York, and other American cities, and also in Europe, obtaining world fame. The Kneisel Quartet was dissolved in 1917. Kneisel was admirable in ensemble playing; his service to the cause of chamber music in America was very great. He was made honorary Mus. Doc. by Yale Univ. (1911) and by Princeton Univ. (1915). In 1903 he resigned his post as concertmaster of the Boston Symph.; from 1905 he taught violin at the Institute of Musical Art in N.Y. He composed *Grand Concert Etude* for violin; publ. *Advanced Exercises* for violin (1900); edited a collection of violin pieces (3 vols., 1900).

Kniese, Julius, German conductor; b. Roda, near Jena, Dec. 21, 1848; d. Dresden, April 22, 1905. He was a pianist and organist; studied with W. Stade in Altenburg; then in Leipzig with Brendel and C. Riedel (1868–70). From 1871–76 he was director of the Singing Academy at Glogau; then conducted the singing society at Rühl and the Wagnerverein at Frankfurt; music director at Aix (1884–89); from 1882 he was also chorusmaster for the festival operas at Bayreuth, where he settled in 1889; became director of the Preparatory School for Stage Singers (1890). He wrote an opera, *Jery und Bätely* (Bayreuth, 1890); publ. 4 albums of songs.

Knight, Joseph Philip, English song composer and clergyman; b. Bradford-on-Avon, July 26, 1812; d. Great Yarmouth, June 2, 1887. He studied organ with Corfe at Bristol. He began to compose songs at the age of 20, and from the very first revealed an exceptional knack of contriving a melody with suitable harmony that was memorable and conveyed a sincere sentiment. While in the U.S. in 1839–41 he brought out his most celebrated song, *Rocked in the Cradle of the Deep;* another successful song was *Why Chime the Bells so Merrily?* After 2 years as vicar and organist at St. Agnes, Scilly Islands, he married, lived abroad for a time, and then returned to England. Among his songs written in England are: *Venice, Say What Shall My Song Be Tonight?, The Dream, All on the Summer Sea, She Wore a Wreath of Roses, Of What is the Old Man Thinking?*

Knipper, Lev, important Russian composer; b. Tiflis, Dec. 3, 1898; d. Moscow, July 30, 1974. He studied piano, and took lessons in composition with Glière in Moscow; traveled to Germany and took private lessons with Jarnach in Berlin and Julius Weissmann in Freiburg. Under the influence of western European trends he wrote music in a fairly advanced style of composition, but soon abandoned these experiments and devoted himself to the study of folk music of different nationalities of the Soviet Union; notated folk songs of Turkestan, Kirghiziya, etc.
WORKS: An extraordinarily prolific composer, he wrote 20 symphonies; the choral finale of his 4th symphony was arranged as a song, which became extremely popular not only in Russia, but in the U.S. (as *Meadowland*); several ballets and orchestral suites on ethnic motives; overtures; 3 violin concertos (1944, 1965, 1967); 2 cello concertos (1962, 1972); Clarinet Concerto (1966); Oboe Concerto (1967); Bassoon Concerto (1969); 3 string quartets and other chamber music; piano pieces; songs, and the operas *The North Wind* (Moscow, March 30, 1930) and *On the Baikal Lake* (1948), making use of Mongol themes.

Knittl, Karl, Bohemian conductor and composer; b. Polna, Oct. 4, 1853; d. Prague, March 17, 1907. He was a pupil of Skuherský at the Prague School for Organists; later studied singing with Pivoda and conducting with Smetana. From 1877–90, and again from 1897–1901, he conducted the choral society "Hlahol" in Prague; in 1890 he was appointed prof. at the Prague Cons.; in 1902 became its administrative director. He composed cantatas; choruses; songs; piano pieces; also *Beispiele zur allgemeinen Musiklehre* and *Lehre vom homophonen Satze.*

Knoch, Ernst, German conductor; b. Karlsruhe, Aug. 1, 1875; d. New York, Mar. 20, 1959. He studied at the Karlsruhe Cons., and later took a course in conducting with Felix Mottl, whose assistant he became at the Karlsruhe Opera (1898–1901). He made his professional debut as conductor in Strasbourg (1901), where he remained till 1907; conducted at Bayreuth (1904–07), Essen (1907–09), and Cologne (1909–12). He then made a world tour in the Thomas Quinlan Co. as conductor of Wagner's operas; gave the first Australian performance of *Tristan und Isolde* (Melbourne, July 14, 1912). In 1913–14 he conducted 20 performances of *Parsifal* in Elberfeld. In 1914 he went to America; conducted opera in New York, Chicago, and Cleveland; settled in N.Y. as opera coach and teacher in 1938.

Knorr, Ernst Lothar von, German composer; b. Eitorf, near Cologne, Jan. 2, 1896; d. Heidelberg, Oct. 30, 1973. He studied at the Cologne Cons. with Bram Eldering (violin), Franz Bölsche (composition) and Fritz Steinbach (conducting). After graduation he played violin in various provincial orchestras; in 1925 he moved to Berlin and taught violin at the Hochschule für Musik. During the air raid on Frankfurt in 1944 almost all of his manuscript works were destroyed; among extant scores are several cantatas; Concerto for 2 Orchestras; Chamber Concerto for piano, saxophone, chorus, and small orch.; some choral works; after the end of the war he composed a Wind Quintet (1958); *Diaphonia* for 2 pianos (1971); some chamber music. He served as director of the Academy of Music in Hannover (1952–61); then was in charge of the Hochschule für Musik in Heidelberg (until 1969). He was principally known for his educational work; his school cantatas are well adapted to performance.

Knorr, Iwan, eminent German music pedagogue and composer; b. Mewe, Jan. 3, 1853; d. Frankfurt, Jan. 22, 1916. His family went to Russia when he was 3 years old, returning to Germany in 1868; he then entered Leipzig Cons., where he studied piano with Moscheles and theory with Richter and Reinecke. In 1874 he went back to Russia, where he taught at the Kharkov Cons., and also at the Imperial Institute for Noble Ladies in St. Petersburg. He finally settled in Frankfurt in 1883 as teacher at the Hoch Cons.; in 1908, became its director. He had many distinguished pupils, among them Cyril Scott, Pfitzner, Braunfels, and Ernst Toch. He wrote music in a Romantic vein; several of his works are inspired by Ukrainian folksongs which he had heard in Russia.
WORKS: operas *Dunja* (Coblenz, March 23, 1904) and *Durchs Fenster* (Karlsruhe, Oct. 4, 1908); *Ukrainische Liebeslieder,* for vocal quartet and piano, op. 6 (1890); *Variationen* (on a Ukrainian folksong), op. 7 (1891); Variations for piano, violin, and cello, op. 1; Piano Quartet, op. 3; Variations for piano and cello, op. 4; etc. He wrote a biography of Tchaikovsky for the series *Berühmte Musiker* (1900) and several pedagogic works: *Aufgaben für den Unterricht in der Harmonielehre* (1903), *Lehrbuch der Fugenkomposition* (1911), *Fugen des Wohltemperirten Klaviers in bildlicher Darstellung* (1912; 2nd ed., 1926); also a number of analyses for Schlesinger's *Musikführer.*
BIBLIOGRAPHY: Moritz Bauer, *Iwan Knorr* (Frankfurt, 1916; contains a complete list of works).

Knorr, Julius, eminent German pianist and pedagogue; b. Leipzig, Sept. 22, 1807; d. there, June 17, 1861. He made his debut as pianist at the Gewandhaus, Leipzig, in 1831; was an intimate friend of Schumann and an editor of the *Neue Zeitschrift für Musik* during its first year. Knorr introduced the preparatory technical exercises that have become the groundwork of technical study on the piano.
WRITINGS: *Neue Pianoforteschule in 184 Übungen* (1835; 2nd ed., 1841, as *Die Pianoforteschule der neuesten Zeit; ein Supplement zu den Werken von Cramer, Czerny, Herz, Hummel, Hünten, Kalkbrenner, Moscheles*); *Das Klavierspiel in 280 Übungen; Materialien für das mechanische Klavierspiel* (1844);

Methodischer Leitfaden für Klavierlehrer (1849); *Ausführliche Klaviermethode*, in 2 parts: *Methode* (1859) and *Schule der Mechanik* (1860); *Erklärendes Verzeichniss der hauptsächlichsten Musikkunstwörter* (1854).

Knote, Heinrich, German tenor; b. Munich, Nov. 26, 1870; d. Garmisch, Jan. 12, 1953. He studied with Kirchner; was appointed to the staff of the Munich Opera in 1892; from 1904 to 1908 he sang at the Metropolitan Opera in New York; in 1908 he joined the roster of the Hamburg Opera; also sang in Wiesbaden, Berlin, and Würzburg. In 1923-24 he made a North American tour; then returned to Munich. He was particularly noted for his interpretations of Wagnerian roles.
BIBLIOGRAPHY: J. H. Wagenmann, *Der 60-jährige deutsche Meistersänger Heinrich Knote* (Munich, 1930).

Knussen, Oliver, English composer; b. Glasgow, June 12, 1952. Remarkably precocious, he began playing piano as a very small boy and showed unusual diligence also in his studies of music theory, mostly with John Lambert. On April 7, 1968 he made musical headlines when, at the age of 15, he conducted the London Symph. Orch. in the first performance of his own First Symph., written in an eclectic, but astoundingly effective modern style. He was awarded fellowships for 3 years in Tanglewood (1970, 1971, 1973), where he studied advanced composition with Gunther Schuller.
WORKS: 3 symphonies: No. 1 (1966-67; London, April 7, 1968); No. 2, for soprano and orch. (1970-71; Tanglewood, Aug. 18, 1971); No. 3 (1973-76); *Pantomime* for chamber ensemble (1968, revised 1971); Concerto for Orchestra (1968-69; London, Feb. 1, 1970; revised 1974); *Masks* for solo flute (1969); *Fire-Capriccio* for flute and string trio (1969); *Tributum,* overture (1969); *Vocalise with Songs of Winnie-the-Pooh* for soprano and 6 instruments (1970; revised without text, 1974-75); *Choral* for wind orch. (1970-72; Boston, Nov. 8, 1973); *Rosary Songs* for soprano, clarinet, viola and piano (1972); *Océan de Terre* for soprano and chamber ensemble (1972-73, revised 1975); *Puzzle Music,* 4 pieces after puzzle canons by John Lloyd, for flute, clarinet, 2 percussionists, harp, guitar or mandolin, and celesta (1972-73); *Chiara* for soprano, female chorus and small orch. (1971-75).

Knyvett, Charles, Jr., English vocalist and organist; son of **Charles Knyvett, Sr.;** b. London, 1773; d. there, Nov. 2, 1859. He studied organ with Samuel Webbe; in 1801 he participated in the Vocal Concerts in London; in 1802 he became organist at St. George's; also was active as a teacher. He publ. a *Selection of Psalm Tunes* (1823).

Knyvett, Charles, Sr., English organist and tenor; father of Charles and William Knyvett; b. Norfolk, Feb. 22, 1752; d. London, Jan. 19, 1822. He was a chorister in London; in 1786, was appointed a Gentleman of the Chapel Royal, and in 1796, an organist there. In 1791-94 he led the Vocal Concerts (with S. Harrison).

Knyvett, William, English singer, conductor, and composer; son of **Charles Knyvett, Sr.,** brother of **Charles Kynvett, Jr.;** b. London, April 21, 1779; d. Ryde, Ise of Wight, Nov. 17, 1856. He sang alto at the Concerts of Ancient Music; in 1797, became a Gentleman of the Chapel Royal, and in 1802, a composer there. He participated in concerts in London as a singer for many years; also composed a number of glees, of which one, *When the Fair Rose,* won a prize of the Harmonic Society in 1800.

Kobald, Karl, Austrian writer on music; b. Brno, Aug. 28, 1876; d. Vienna, Oct. 12, 1957. He studied at Vienna Univ. with Guido Adler, Hellmesberger, and Hans Richter; also took lessons with Bruckner. In 1918 he became music adviser in the Austrian Ministry of Education; in 1932-38, and again in 1945-46, was president of the State Academy; then retired.
WRITINGS: *Alt-Wiener Musikstätten* (1919; 2nd ed., 1923); *Schubert und Schwind* (1920); *Franz Schubert* (1922); *In Memoriam Anton Bruckner* (1924); *Johann Strauss* (1925); *Beethoven* (1927; new eds. 1936, 1946, and 1952); *Franz Schubert und seine Zeit* (1927); *Klassische Musikstätten* (1929); *Joseph Haydn* (1929); *Wo unsterbliche Musik entstand* (1950).

Kobbé, Gustav, American writer on music; b. New York, March 4, 1857; killed in his sailboat by a Navy seaplane maneuvering in the bay near Babylon, Long Island, July 27, 1918. He studied piano and composition with Adolf Hagen in Wiesbaden (1867-72), and with Joseph Mosenthal in New York. He attended Columbia College (School of Arts, 1877; School of Law, 1879). He was a frequent contributor, on musical and other subjects, to the daily press and to magazines.
WRITINGS: *Wagner's Life and Works* (N.Y., 1890; 2 vols., containing analyses, with the *Leitmotive* of the music dramas); *The Ring of the Nibelung* (1899; part of preceding, printed separately); *Opera Singers* (1901); the novel *Signora, A Child of the Opera House* (1902); *Loves of the Great Composers* (1905); *How to Appreciate Music* (1906); *Wagner and His Isolde* (1906); *Famous American Songs* (1906). Shortly before his accidental death, he finished his *Complete Opera Book,* which was publ. posthumously (N.Y., 1919) and proved so successful that 20 printings were issued before 1950; a revised and enlarged edition, *Kobbé's Complete Opera Book,* compiled by the Earl of Harewood (1246 pages; includes stories of many operas by modern composers), was publ. in 1954.

Koch, Caspar Petrus, German-American organist and pedagogue; b. Carnap, Nov. 25, 1872; d. Pittsburgh, April 3, 1970. He was taken to the U.S. as a child and was employed as a church organist in Pittsburgh and elsewhere. From 1914 to 1941 he taught organ playing at the Carnegie Institute of Technology in Pittsburgh. He edited several collections of Bach's organ pieces and composed some organ music.

Koch, Eduard Emil, German scholar and authority on Lutheran church music; b. Schloss Solitude, near Stuttgart, Jan. 20, 1809; d. Stuttgart, April 27, 1871. He was pastor at Gross-Anspach (1837), at Heilbronn (1847); then superintendent there (1853-64). He wrote the valuable work *Geschichte des Kirchenliedes und Kirchengesanges, insbesondere der deutschen evangelischen Kirche* (1847; 3rd ed. in 8 vols., 1866–77).

Koch, Erland von (full Christian name **Sigurd Christian Erland**), Swedish composer; son of **Sigurd von Koch;** b. Stockholm, April 26, 1910. He studied music with his father, then at the Stockholm Cons. (1931–35); went to Germany, where he studied composition with Paul Höffer and conducting with Clemens Krauss (1936–38). He returned to Stockholm in 1939. He conducted the Swedish Radio Orch. (1943–45); in 1953 was appointed to the staff of the Royal College of Music. In some of his later works he endeavors to create a curious amalgam of folk motives with 12-tone rows ("12-tone and folk-tone").
WORKS: FOR THE STAGE: a children's opera, *Pelle Svanslös* (*Tailless Peter,* 1948; revised 1966); 2 ballets, *Askungen* (*Cinderella,* 1942; also an orch. suite) and *Samson and Delila* (1963; orch. suite, 1964; revised 1972), music for the radio play *Bjälbojarlen,* after Strindberg (Swedish Radio, Jan. 25, 1968). FOR ORCH.: *Little Suite* for chamber or string orch. (1933); 3 piano concertos: No. 1 (1936); No. 2 (1962); No. 3, with wind orch. (1970; version with full orch., 1972); Violin Concerto (1937); Concertino for Strings (1938); 4 symphonies: No. 1 (1938); No. 2, *Sinfonia Dalecarlia* (1944); No. 3 (1948); No. 4, *Sinfonia seria* (1952–53, revised 1962); *Nordic Capriccio* (1943); *Rural Suite* for strings (1945); Viola Concerto (1945, revised 1966); *Concertino Pastorale* for flute and strings (1947, revised 1963); Sinfonietta (1949); *Triptychon* for violin and orch. (1949); *Arkipelag* (1950); *Musica Intima* for strings (1950, revised 1965); Cello Concerto (1951); *Musica malinconica* for strings (1952); *Concert Music* (1955); Concerto for Small Orch. (1955); the Oxberg trilogy: *Oxberg Variations* (1956), *Lapland Metamorphoses* (1957) and *Dance-Rhapsody* (1957); *Dalecarlia Suite* (1957); Concerto for Saxophone and String Orch. (1958); *12 Scandinavian Dances* (1958–60); *Concerto lirico* for strings (1959; revised version of Fourth String Quartet); *Concerto piccolo* for 2 saxophones (soprano and alto) and strings (1962); *Fantasia Concertante* for violin and orch. (1964); the Impulsi trilogy: *Impulsi* (1964), *Echi* (1965) and *Ritmi* (1966); *Arioso e Furioso* for strings (1967); *Polska svedese* (1968); *Musica Concertante* for 8 winds, strings and percussion (1969); Double Concerto for Flute, Clarinet and Strings (1971); *A Swede in New York* (1973). CHAMBER MUSIC: 6 string quartets: No. 1 (1934); No. 2 (1944); No. 3, *Musica intima* (1950); No. 4 (1956, revised 1959); No. 5 (1961); No. 6, *Serenata espressiva* (1963); *Larghetto* for cello, or viola, and piano (1937, revised 1965); *Berceuse* for violin and piano (1953); *Sonatina semplice* for violin and piano (1960); *Varianti virtuosi II* for violin and piano (1968); *Quattro tempi* for wind quintet (1968); *Miniatures* for saxophone quartet (1970). VOCAL MUSIC: *Midsommardalen* (*Midsummer Valley*) for baritone, chorus and orch. (1960–61); *Sångarkväll* (*Evening Song*) for baritone, male chorus and wind orch. (1972); FOR PIANO: *Rhythmic Bagatelles* (1957); *Intermezzi concertanti* (1963); *Varianti virtuosi* (1965); songs.

Koch, Friedrich E., German composer and teacher; b. Berlin, July 3, 1862; d. there, Jan. 30, 1927. He studied cello with Hausmann and theory with Bargiel; played cello in the Court Orch. in Berlin (1883–91); then taught privately; in 1901 was elected a member of the Academy. As a composer, he cultivated almost exclusively the large forms; his style was somewhat severe in its elevation.
WORKS: the opera *Die Halliger* (Cologne, 1897); the oratorios *Von den Tageszeiten* and *Die Sündflut;* 2 symphonies; *Deutsche Rhapsodie,* for violin and orch.; String Trio; Piano Trio; many choral works.
BIBLIOGRAPHY: K. Kämpf, *F. E. Koch* (Leipzig, 1907).

Koch, Heinrich Christoph, German music theorist; b. Rudolstadt, Oct. 10, 1749; d. there, March 19, 1816. He studied with Göpfert at Weimar; he was violinist in the orchestra at Rudolstadt (1768); then leader of chamber music there (1777). He publ. *Musikalisches Lexikon* (1802); *Versuch einer Anleitung zur Composition* (3 vols., 1782–93); *Handbuch bei dem Studium der Harmonie* (1811); a manual of enharmonic modulation (1812); contributed articles to periodicals. He also wrote a *Choralbuch* for wind band, and cantatas. He started the *Journal der Tonkunst* in 1795, but it was unsuccessful.

Koch, Helmut, German conductor; b. Wuppertal-Barmen, April 5, 1908; d. East Berlin, Jan. 26, 1975. He studied conducting with Scherchen; was for many years leader of workers' choruses; after 1945 was chorus director of the East Berlin Radio; in 1963 became director of the East Berlin Singakademie. He made numerous arrangements of German folksongs for various groups.

Koch, Karl, Austrian organist and composer of sacred music; b. Biberwier, Tyrol, Jan. 29, 1887; d. Innsbruck, Sept. 20, 1971. He studied religion and music at a theological seminary in Brixen; took courses in conducting with Max Springer at the Musical Academy in Vienna. In 1926 he settled in Innsbruck as choral conductor. He wrote a number of sacred choruses and much organ music; a symphony *Aus den Bergen* (1942); String Quartet; 2 piano sonatas; publ. a manual, *Harmonielehre* (Vienna, 1948).
BIBLIOGRAPHY: Wilhelm Isser, *Karl Koch: Das Bild eines zeitgenössischen Komponisten* (Innsbruck, 1969).

Koch, Sigurd von (full Christian name **Richert Sigurd Valdemar**), Swedish composer; b. Ägnö, near Stockholm, June 28, 1879; d. Stockholm, March 16, 1919. He studied piano in Germany; composed several symphonic works, instrumental concertos, and much chamber music; his violin sonata has been published.

Kochan, Günter, German composer; b. Luckau, Oct. 2, 1930. He studied with Blacher in West Berlin and with Eisler in East Berlin; in 1950 he became an instructor in music theory at the Hochschule für Musik; in 1967 promoted to prof. of composition there. His music is marked by a sober feeling for classical form, but is not devoid of functional modernistic devices.

WORKS: Several of his choral works are politically oriented, among them the cantata *Ernst Thälmann* (1959; in memory of the head of the German Communist Party who died in a concentration camp); *Aurora* for women's voices, chorus and orch. (1966; a tribute to the sailors of the Russian ship that bombarded the Winter Palace on the day of the Soviet revolution in 1917); *Das Testament von Ho Chi-Minh* for speaker, chamber orchestra and 9 solo instruments (1971); *Wir, unaufhaltsam* for baritone, speaker, chorus and orch., a "symphonic demonstration" (1971); in other forms, Piano Concerto (1958); Violin Concerto (1962); 3 symphonies (1963, 1968, 1972); Concertino for Flute (1964); Cello Concerto (1967); Viola Concerto (1974); Cello Sonata (1961); Violin Sonata (1962); String Quartet (1965); piano pieces; songs.

Kochanski, Paul, Polish violinist; b. Odessa, Sept. 14, 1887; d. New York, Jan. 12, 1934. He studied with Mlynarski in Warsaw; in 1901 became concertmaster of the Warsaw Philharmonic; in 1903 went to Brussels to study with César Thomson; in 1907 was appointed prof. at the Warsaw Cons. From 1916 to 1918 he taught violin at the Petrograd Cons.; then joined the staff of the Cons. of Kiev (1919–20); in 1920 he left Russia, reaching America in 1921; made his American debut with the N.Y. Symph. Orch., Feb. 14, 1921. From 1924 he taught at the Juilliard Schoool. He excelled in the performance of modern works; did a great service in promoting the violin music of Szymanowski; publ. several transcriptions for violin and piano, among them a *Spanish Popular Suite* (after 7 *Spanish Popular Songs* of Manual de Falla).

Köchel, Ludwig von, Austrian musicographer, compiler of the famous Mozart catalogue; b. Stein, near Krems, Jan. 14, 1800; d. Vienna, June 3, 1877. He studied natural sciences, and attained distinction in botany and mineralogy; music was his hobby; his love for Mozart's art moved him to compile a Mozart catalogue as methodically as he would a descriptive index of minerals; the result of this task of devotion was the monumental *Chronologisch-thematisches Verzeichnis sämmtlicher Tonwerke W. A. Mozarts* (Leipzig, 1862). The 'K numbers' used to identify Mozart's works have been supplemented by secondary numbers in Alfred Einstein's revision of the catalogue (1937; reprinted, with further alterations and corrections, in 1947). Köchel himself publ. some supplementary matter in the *Allgemeine musikalische Zeitung* (1864); the 2nd ed. of the catalogue was prepared by Waldersee (1905). Köchel's writings on music include further *Über den Umfang der musikalischen Produktivität W. A. Mozarts* (1862), which preceded the publication of the catalogue; *Die kaiserliche Hofmusikkapelle in Wien von 1543 bis 1867* (1869); and *Johann Josef Fux* (1872); he also edited *83 neuaufgefundene Originalbriefe L. van Beethovens an den Erzherzog Rudolph* (1865).

Kocher, Conrad, German composer; b. Ditzingen, near Stuttgart, Dec. 16, 1786; d. Stuttgart, March 12, 1872. In 1803 he went to St. Petersburg, where he studied piano with Klengel and Berger, and composition with J. H. Müller; traveled in Italy (1819). Returning to Germany in 1820, he settled in Stuttgart and devoted himself to composition; received the honorary degree of Dr. phil. from Tübingen Univ. in 1827. He wrote 2 operas, an oratorio, etc.; also publ. a piano method; a manual of composition, *Die Tonkunst in der Kirche* (1823); and *Zionsharfe* (ancient and modern chorales).

Kocián, Jaroslav, Czech violinist; b. Ústí nad Orlicí, Feb. 22, 1883; d. Prague, March 9, 1950. He studied violin with Ševčik at the Prague Cons., and also took lessons in composition with Dvořák. After his graduation in 1901 he traveled widely as a concert violinist, almost rivaling the success of his famous compatriot Jan Kubelik. He made 4 American tours; also appeared in Asia and Africa. After 1920 he confined himself mainly to teaching; became prof. at the Master School of the Prague Cons. in 1929; retired in 1943. He composed several effective violin pieces (2 *Humoresques*, *Sérénade, Intermezzo pittoresque, Hymne au printemps, Dumka, Berceuse,* etc.).

BIBLIOGRAPHY: A memorial vol., *Jaroslav Kocian: sborník statí a vzpomínek,* was published at Prague in 1953.

Kocsár, Miklós, Hungarian composer; b. Debrecen, Dec. 21, 1933. He studied with Farkas at the Budapest Academy of Music; upon graduation he devoted himself to theater conducting and teaching. In 1973 he won the National Erkel Prize.

WORKS: a cantata *Hegyi legények* (*Mountain Lads,* 1957); Horn Concerto (1957); *Serenata* for string quartet (1959, revised for string orch., 1971); *Capriccio* for orch. (1961); *Magányos ének* (*Lonely Song*), a song cycle for soprano and chamber ensemble (1969); 2 wind quintets (1956, 1959); Piano Sonatina (1956); Violin Sonata (1957); Trio for 2 Trombones and Trumpet (1958); *Movimento* for violin (1961–62); *Dialoghi* for bassoon and piano (1964–65); Variations for Wind Quintet (1968); *Repliche* for flute, and cimbalom or harpsichord (1971); *Improvisazioni* for piano (1972); Brass Septet (1972); choruses; many songs.

Koczalski, Raoul (Armand Georg), Polish pianist; b. Warsaw, Jan. 3, 1884; d. Posnań, Nov. 24, 1948. He was trained by his mother; at the age of 4 he played at a charity concert in Warsaw and was at once proclaimed an "infant phenomenon"; his progress was watched by psychologists, and a detailed biography of him was publ. by B. Vogel when he was only 12. He gave concerts in Vienna (1892), Russia, Paris, and London (1893); made nearly 1000 public appearances before 1896. His sensational success diminished as he grew out of the prodigy age, but he was appreciated as a mature pianist for his sensitive playing of Chopin. He lived mostly in France, Germany, and Sweden; after World War II he returned to Poland and taught in Posnań; shortly before his death he was appointed to a state teaching post in Warsaw. He was precocious not only as a pianist but also as a composer; wrote some 50 opus numbers before he was 10. His opera *Rymond,* written at the age of 17, was produced at Elberfeld, Oct. 14, 1902; he wrote another opera, *Die Sühne* (Mühlhausen, 1909); many piano pieces.

Koczirz, Adolf, Austrian music scholar; b. Wierowan, Moravia, April 2, 1870; d. Vienna, Feb. 22, 1941. He was a government functionary; studied musicology with Guido Adler in Vienna (Dr. phil., 1903); ed. vols. 37 and 50 (18.ii and 25.ii) of the *Denkmäler der Tonkunst in Österreich* (lute music of the 16th and 17th centuries); contributed many essays on old instrumental music to various publications.

Kodalli, Nevit, Turkish composer; b. Mersin, Jan. 12, 1924. He studied with Necil Kazim Akses at the Ankara Cons. graduating in 1948; then went to Paris where he took lessons with Honegger. His music preserves the traits of Turkish folk melos, but the harmonic and contrapuntal treatment is in the manner of the French modern school. Among his works are a symphony (Ankara, May 20, 1950); an oratorio *Ataturk* (Ankara, Nov. 9, 1953); an opera, *Gilgamesch* (Ankara, 1962); 2 string quartets (1947, 1966).

Kodály, Zoltán, illustrious Hungarian composer; b. Kecskemét, Dec. 16, 1882; d. Budapest, March 6, 1967. He was brought up in a musical family; received general education at a high school in Nagyszombat; at the same time, he took lessons in piano and violin; soon began to compose; wrote a Mass at the age of 16. He then enrolled at the Univ. of Budapest, and also studied composition with Hans Koessler at the Budapest Academy of Music. His early works were mostly sacred choral compositions and chamber music; his doctor's thesis, *Strophic Structure in the Hungarian Folksong* (1906), indicates his growing interest in folk music. He became associated with Béla Bartók in collecting, organizing, and editing the vast wealth of national folksongs; he also made use of these melodies in his own works. He published his findings in the bulletins of the Hungarian Ethnographic Society. In 1906 he went to Paris, where he took some lessons with Widor; in 1907 he was appointed instructor at the Budapest Academy of Music; wrote music criticism for several newspapers in Budapest; also contributed correspondence to the *Revue Musicale,* the *Musical Courier,* and other journals. In 1913 he issued, with Bartók, a detailed paper dealing with the subject of collecting national songs. During World War I he continued to teach and compose, but his activity in collecting and publishing Hungarian folksongs was inevitably curtailed. In 1919 Kodály was appointed assistant director of the Academy of Music in Budapest; for political reasons he was relieved of this post; however, he resumed his teaching in 1922. In 1923 he was commissioned to write a commemorative work in celebration of the half-century of the union of Buda and Pest; for this occasion he wrote a *Psalmus Hungaricus,* which proved to be one of his most significant works. The initial performance in Budapest was followed by numerous productions all over Europe, and also in America. Another signal success was the presentation of Kodály's national opera, in a comic style, *Háry János* (1926); an orchestral suite from this work is widely played. Two suites of folk dances, arranged in a modern manner, *Marosszék Dances* and *Galanta Dances,* won for Kodály a world-wide popularity. His reputation as one of the most significant national composers was firmly established with the repeated performances of these works. During the turbulent events of 1939-45, Kodály remained in Budapest, working on his compilations of folksongs. In 1946-47 he visited the U.S. and conducted concerts of his works. On Dec. 18, 1959, he married Sarolta Péczely, a student (b. 1940). In 1965 he visited the U.S. as a lecturer. Kodály's musical style is not as radical as that of Bartók; he never departs from basic tonality, and his experiments in rhythm do not reach the primitivistic power of Bartók's percussive idiom. Kodály prefers a Romantic treatment of his melodic and harmonic materials; there is also a decided tinge of Impressionism in his orchestration. But there is no mistaking his ability to present nationally colored melorhythms in a pleasing and stimulating manner.

WORKS: OPERAS: *Háry János* (Budapest, Oct. 16, 1926); *Székelyfonó* (*The Spinning Room,* lyric scenes based on Hungarian folksongs and dances; Budapest, April 24, 1932); *Czinka Panna* (Budapest, March 15, 1948). FOR ORCH.: *Summer Evening,* tone poem (1906; revised 1930; N.Y. Philharmonic, April 3, 1930; Toscanini conducting); orch. suite from *Háry János* (N.Y., Dec. 15, 1927); *Ballet Music* (1925); *Theater Overture* (1927); *Marosszék Dances* (Dresden, Nov. 28, 1930); *Dances of Galanta* (for the 80th anniversary of the Budapest Philharmonic Society, 1934; Philadelphia, Dec. 11, 1936); *Variations on a Hungarian Folksong* (*Peacock Variations;* Amsterdam, Nov. 23, 1939); Concerto for Orch. (Chicago, Feb. 6, 1941); Symphony in C (Lucerne, Aug. 16, 1961). FOR CHORUS: *Psalmus Hungaricus,* for tenor solo, chorus, and orch. (based on the 55th Psalm; his most important work; Budapest, Nov. 19, 1923; U.S. première, N.Y. Philharmonic, Dec. 19, 1927; Mengelberg conducting); *Te Deum,* hymn for soli, chorus, and orch. (for 250th anniversary of delivery of Budapest from the Turks; performed in the Budapest Cathedral, Sept. 11, 1936); *Missa Brevis,* for chorus and orch. (1945); *Kallo,* folk dances for mixed choir and small orch. (1951); numerous choruses (*Transylvanian Lament, Jesus and the Traders, Ode to Franz Liszt,* etc.). CHAMBER MUSIC: 1st String Quartet (1908); Cello Sonata (1909-10); Duo for violin and cello (1914); Sonata for Cello Unaccompanied (1915); 2nd String Quartet (1916-17); Serenade for 2 violins and viola (1919-20); an arrangement for cello and piano of 3 Chorale Preludes by Bach (1924). FOR PIANO: *Meditation* (1907); *9 Pièces pour piano* (1910); *Marosszék Dances* (1927); *24 Little Canons on the Black Keys* (1945); *Children's Dances* (1946). FOR VOICE AND PIANO: *20 Hungarian Folksongs* (with Béla Bartók; 1906); *Magyar nepzene* (*Hungarian Folk Music;* 57 arrangements of folksongs; 1917-32; publ. in English, N.Y., 1960); numerous songs and choruses for children and music students: *Bicinia Hungarica* (1937-42); *333 Reading Exercises* (1943); *441 Melodies,* collected in 4 books, subtitled *Pentatonic Music* (1945-48); etc.; also song collections for general use; numerous articles in ethnographic and musical publications. He edited the periodical *Studia Musicologica Academiae Scientiarum Hungaricae;* wrote the book *Die ungarische Volkmusik* (Budapest, 1962). His collected writings are publ. as *Kodály Zoltán: Visszatekintés,* ed. by F. Bónis (Budapest, 1964).

BIBLIOGRAPHY: M. D. Calvocoressi, "Zoltán Kodály," *Monthly Musical Record* (April 1922); A. Toth, "Zoltán Kodály," *Revue Musicale* (Sept.–Oct. 1929); Imre Waldbauer, "Kodály," in Cobbett's *Cyclopedic Survey of Chamber Music* (London, 1930); H. Mersmann, *Kodály*, in *Kammermusik* (vol. IV, pp. 186ff); E. Haraszti, "Zoltán Kodály et la musique hongroise," *Revue Musicale* (Feb. 1947); *Emlékkönyv Kodály Zoltán* (on the occasion of his 70th birthday; 1953); L. Eösze, *Zoltán Kodály: His Life and Work* (in English; Budapest, 1962); Percy M. Young, *Zoltán Kodály* (London, 1964); C. Jolly, "Kodály—A Personal View," *Tempo* 83 (Winter 1967); H. Stevens, "The Choral Music of Zoltán Kodály," *Musical Quarterly* (April 1968); C. Kokas, "Kodály's Concept of Music Education," *Council for Research in Music Education Bulletin* (Fall 1970); L. Eösze, *Zoltán Kodály: His Life in Pictures* (N.Y., 1971); L. Wheeler and L. Raebeck, *Orff and Kodály Adapted for the Elementary School* (Dubuque, Iowa, 1972). The Kodály Musical Training Institute in Wellesley, Mass., issues a newsletter.

Koeberg, Frits Ehrhardt Adriaan, Dutch composer; b. The Hague, July 15, 1876; d. there, Nov. 9, 1961. He studied with H. Viotta in Holland and with Xaver Scharwenka in Berlin; returned to The Hague in 1902; taught at the Cons. and conducted the orch. "Musica" there.

WORKS: opera *Bloemenkind* (1917); 3 symphonies; symph. poems, *Zeelandia* (1920); *Chimères* (1941); *Suite de Lage Landen,* for orch. (1946); *Dances in the Village,* for orch. (1948); *Hollandia,* for band (1933); chamber music; songs.

Koechlin, Charles, notable French composer; b. Paris, Nov. 27, 1867; d. Canadel, Var, Dec. 31, 1950. He studied at the Paris Cons. with Gedalge, Massenet, and Fauré, graduating in 1897. He lived mostly in Paris, where he was active as composer, teacher, and lecturer; made 3 visits to the U.S. (1918, 1928, 1937), lecturing on French music (in English); contributed to various journals (*Gazette des Beaux Arts, Chronique des Arts,* etc.) and to Lavignac's *Encyclopédie* (valuable and comprehensive essays on modern music). He also participated in modern-music societies, and worked in various social organizations for the promotion of world-wide music culture. In his own compositions he created a style that is unmistakably French in its clarity and subtlety of nuance and dynamics; although highly sympathetic to all innovation, he stopped short of crossing the borders of perceptible tonality and coherent rhythmic patterns; he was a master of orchestration. As a pedagogue he possessed a clear insight into the problems of musical technique; publ. several manuals of fundamental value: *Traité d'harmonie* (3 vols., 1927–30); *Étude sur les notes de passage* (1922); *Étude sur l'écriture de la fugue d'école* (1933); *Précis des règles du contrepoint* (1927; also in English as *A Summary of the Rules of Counterpoint*); *Traité d'orchestration* (4 vols.); *Théorie de la musique* (1935); also an advanced paper, *Essai sur la musique polytonale et atonale. A Traité de polyphonie modale* is in MS. He also publ. monographs on Gabriel Fauré (1927) and Debussy (1927).

WORKS: *Jacob chez Laban,* biblical pastoral (1896–1908; Paris, May 19, 1925); the ballets *La Forêt païenne* (Paris, June 17, 1925) and *L'Âme heureuse* (1947); for orch.: *La Forêt,* symph. poem (1896–1907); *En mer, la nuit,* symph. poem (1899–1904); *L'Automne,* symph. suite (1896–1909); *Nuit de Walpurgis classique,* symph. poem (1901–07); *Études antiques,* symph. suite (1908–14); symph. poems, *Le Printemps, L'Hiver, Nuit de juin, Midi en août* (1910–12); *Suite légendaire* (1915–20); *Rapsodie sur des chansons françaises* (1916); *La Course de printemps,* symph. poem after Kipling's *Jungle Book* (1925–27); *The 7 Stars Symphony,* symph. suite (1933); *Symphonie d'hymnes* (1936); *La Loi de la jungle,* after Kipling (1939); Partita for chamber orch. (1945); also 2 symphonies, arranged mostly from earlier works; *Ballade* for piano and orch. (1919); *20 Chansons Bretonnes* for cello and chamber orch. (1934); *Offrande musicale sur le nom de B.A.C.H.* (15 pieces), for organ and orch. (1942); *Silhouettes comiques* (12 pieces), for bassoon and orch. (1943); 3 string quartets; several fugues for string quartet; *Suite en quatuor,* for flute, violin, viola, and piano; Sonata for 2 Flutes; Piano Quintet; *Divertissement,* for 2 flutes and bass flute; Trio for flute, clarinet, and bassoon; Modal Sonatina for Flute and Clarinet; *Primavera,* for flute, violin, viola, cello, and harp; Septet for flute, oboe, English horn, clarinet, bassoon, horn, and saxophone; Flute Sonata; Viola Sonata; Oboe Sonata; Violin Sonata; Cello Sonata; Horn Sonata; Bassoon Sonata; and 2 clarinet sonatas; several suites of pieces for unaccompanied flute; several sets of piano pieces (*Paysages et marines, Les Heures persanes, Douze Pastorales, L'Ancienne Maison de campagne, Douze Petites Pièces très facile,* etc.); organ music; vocal duets, trios, and quartets; several cycles of songs.

BIBLIOGRAPHY: M. D. Calvocoressi, "Charles Koechlin's Instrumental Works," *Music & Letters* (1924); W. H. Mellers, "A Plea for Koechlin," *Music Review* (1942); Pierre Renaudin, *Charles Koechlin* (Paris, 1952); Henri Sauguet, *L'Œuvre de Charles Koechlin* (Paris, 1975).

Koellreutter, Hans Joachim, German composer; b. Freiburg im Breisgau, Sept. 2, 1915. He studied flute, piano and composition in Berlin and in Geneva. In 1937 he went to Brazil and unfolded an energetic program of performances of modern music. In 1939 he formed in São Paulo the group "Música Viva Brasil" and also publ. a magazine of the same name. He was prof. at the Instituto Musical in São Paulo (1942–44) and directed an international course on new music in Teresópolis. In 1952 he founded an orchestra in Bahia, which he conducted until 1962; then was in charge of the music programs of the Goethe Institute in Munich (1963–65); the years 1965–69 he spent in New Delhi, India, where he founded a music school. From 1969 to 1975 he was music instructor and director of performances at the Goethe Institute in Tokyo, Japan; then returned to Brazil. His music follows classical forms, while the thematic materials are modeled after the 12-tone method of composition; in several of his works he makes use of exotic motives of South America, India and Japan.

WORKS: *American Psalm,* for chorus and orch. (1945); *Proletarian Psalm* (1946); *Konzertmusik,* for piano and chamber orch. (1946); *Systatica* for flute, percussion and dancing (1955); *Concretion* for orch. (1960); *Constructio ad synesin* for orch. (1962); *8 Haikai* for voice, flute, guitar, piano and percussion (1963); *Indian Report* for voices, chamber orch. and a group of Indian instruments (1969); *Sunyata* for flute and instrumental ensemble, including Indian percussion instruments (1969); Concerto for Sitar and Orch. (1969); *Tanka* for Koto (1971). He published *Three Lectures on Music* (Mysore, 1968) and *Attitudes of Consciousness in Indian and Western Music* (New Delhi, 1966).

Koemmenich, Louis, German-American conductor; b. Elberfeld, Germany, Oct. 4, 1866; d. New York, Aug. 14, 1922. He studied at Kullak's Academy in Berlin; in 1890 emigrated to the U.S., settling in N.Y., where he became active as a choral conductor and a singing teacher; founded the Oratorio Society of Brooklyn for the production of new works (1898) and the New Choral Society of N.Y., which gave its 1st concert on April 4, 1918 (Verdi's *Requiem*). He wrote many choruses for men's voices, including *Lockung* and *Wer weiss wo,* which received prizes in 1894 and 1900.

Koenemann, Theodore. See **Keneman, Feodor.**

Koenen, Friedrich, German composer; b. Rheinbach, near Bonn, April 30, 1829; d. Cologne, July 6, 1887. He studied piano and organ with his father, and cello with Biermann; in 1854, was ordained priest; from 1862–63, studied church music at Regensburg with Haberl, Schrems, and Witt. Went to Cologne, where he was appointed choirmaster of the cathedral; also taught music at the Seminary for Priests; in 1869, founded the Cäcilienverein. Among his 58 compositions are 7 Masses, 2 church cantatas, a *Te Deum,* motets, psalms, organ preludes, and songs.

Koenen, Tilly (Mathilde Caroline), Dutch mezzo-soprano; b. Salatiga, Java, Dec. 25, 1873; d. The Hague, Jan. 4, 1941. She studied piano, on which she became a proficient performer; then took up voice with Cornelia van Zanten. She toured Germany and Austria from 1900 with excellent success; visited America in 1909–10 and in 1915–16. She was particularly impressive in her interpretations of German Romantic songs; also performed some songs by her compatriots.

Koenig, Gottfried Michael, German composer; b. Magdeburg, Oct. 5, 1926. He studied in Braunschweig, in Detmold, Cologne and Bonn. In 1954 he became a member of the studio for electronic music at the Cologne Radio; in 1964 appointed artistic director of the studios of electronic music at the University of Utrecht. His philosophical attitude towards music is that it should represent the past, present and the future; accordingly he is apt to give abstract and scientific titles to his works, particularly for electronic music, such as *Terminus I* (1963), *Terminus II* (1967); *Funktion Grün* (1968); *Funktion Gelb* (1968); *Funktion Orange* (1968); *Funktion Rot* (1968). He also wrote two quintets for wind instruments (1959, 1965); String Quartet (1962) and piano pieces; published a

number of papers dealing with the application of serial and aleatory procedures to electronic music.

Koering, René, French composer; b. Andlau, Alsace, May 27, 1940. He studied piano; in 1960 went to Darmstadt where he absorbed some modernistic notions at a festival for new music. He then began to compose experimentally in every conceivable classical and popular genre. The denouement was his decision to write understandable music with a minimum of feasible modernities.

WORKS: *Triple et Trajectoires* for piano and 2 orchestras (1963); *Combat T 3 N* for piano and orch. (1970); Symph. No. 1 (Royan, March 23, 1974).

Koessler, Hans, German organist and composer; b. Waldeck, Jan. 1, 1853; d. Ansbach, May 23, 1926. He studied with Rheinberger in Munich; then taught at the Dresden Cons.; in 1882, went to Budapest to teach organ and, later, composition at the Academy of Music, remaining on the staff until 1908. In 1918 he retired to Ansbach. In his music he follows the tradition of Brahms; although his technical achievements inspire respect, his works lack any durable quality that would distinguish them from the mass of other competent compositions by German composers of his generation.

WORKS: an opera, *Der Münzenfranz* (Strasbourg, 1903); oratorio *Triumph der Liebe; Silvesterglocken,* for voices and orch.; *Hymne an die Schönheit,* for men's chorus and orch.; 2 symphonies; Violin Concerto; Cello Concerto; 2 string quartets; String Quintet; String Sextet; Violin Sonata; Cello Sonata; songs.

Koetsier, Jan, Dutch conductor and composer; b. Amsterdam, Aug. 14, 1911. He studied in Berlin at the Stern Cons. (1924–26) and at the Hochschule für Musik there (1927–34); was a conductor in Lübeck and Berlin; returned to Holland and conducted in The Hague (1941–42), and was 2nd conductor of the Concertgebouw in Amsterdam (1942–49), then again in The Hague (1949–50). In 1950 he moved to Germany and became principal conductor of the Bavarian Radio Orch. in Munich. In his music he explores the modern applications of the Baroque techniques.

WORKS: an opera, *Frans Hals* (1951); *Symphony "Demeter"* (1943); *Variations on a Children's Song* for orch. (1932, revised 1967); 3 Baroque suites: for orch., for violin and string orch., and for cello and 12 woodwinds (all 1935); *Adagietto e Scherzino* for orch. (1933); *Serenata Serena* for string orch. (1935); Oboe Concertino (1936); Piano Concertino (1936); *Duo Concertante* for flute, violin and orch. (1936); *Vision Pastorale* for English horn and string orch. (1937); Cello Concerto (1938); *Symphonische Musik* (1939); Viola Concerto (1940); *Valerius Overture* (1942, revised in 1966); *Siciliano e Rondino* for 2 oboes and orch. (1942); *Music for 2 String Orch.,* 3 trumpets, 3 trombones and timpani (1943); *Symphonietta* (1943); Divertimento for Orch. (1944); *Music for 4 Orch.* (1944); 3 symphonies: No. 1 (1945); No. 2, for chorus and orch. (1946); No. 3 (1954); *Music for Chamber Orch.* (1948); *Trauermusik* for flute, clarinet and strings (1954); *Musical Sketch,* fantasia for piano and orch. (1956); *De Mann Lot* for narrator, baritone, male chorus and orch. (1940–62); Concerto for Trumpet, Trombone and Orch. (1965); *Kreisleriana,* concertino for 2 pianos and orch. (1965); *Valerius Suite* for orch. (1966); *Valerius Rhapsody* for orch. (1967); *Symphonia Concertante* for oboe, clarinet, bassoon, horn and strings (1967); *Concertino lirico* for violin, cello and string orch. (1968); *Homage to Gershwin* for orch. (1966–69); *Intrada Classica* for wind orch., timpani and harp (1971); *March of Twins,* scherzo for 2 solo percussionists and orch. (1971); *Hymnus Monaciensis* for orch. (1971); *Müldorfer Serenade* for orch. (1971); *Concerto capriccioso* for piano and orch. (1975); much chamber music, including Quintet for flute, oboe, violin, viola and cello (1932, revised 1964); Septet (1932, revised 1957); Violin Sonatina (1933); 2 divertimentos for wind quintet (1937, 1947); *Gesang der Geister über Wassern* for chorus and 7 instruments (1939, revised 1973); *Von Gottes und des Menschen Wesen,* 7 madrigals for chorus and 7 instruments (1940, revised 1968); *Amsterdam,* chamber cantata for soprano or tenor, and 7 instruments; *Choral-fantasy* for organ with ad lib. 3 trumpets and 3 trombones (1955, revised 1974); *Introduction and 8 Etudes* for string quartet (1956); Octet for 2 oboes, 2 clarinets, 2 horns and 2 bassoons (1968); *Bamberger Promenade* for 2 trumpets and 3 trombones (1970); *5 Impromptus* for 4 trombones (1970); sonatinas for trumpet, for trombone, and for tuba (all 1970); Trio for alto flute, viola da gamba and harpsichord (1971); *5 Miniatures* for 4 horns (1971); Sonatina for Trumpet and Organ (1971, revised 1974); Sonata for Cello and Harp (1972); *Colloquy* for 12 horns (1972); Horn Sonatina (1972); Brass Quintet (1974); piano and organ pieces.

Koffler, Jósef, Polish composer; b. Stryj, Nov. 28, 1896; killed with his wife and child in Wieliczka, near Cracow, during a street roundup of Jews in 1943. He was a pupil of Schoenberg and Guido Adler; graduated from the Univ. of Vienna in 1923; then went to Lwow where he taught at the Cons., edited the Polish monthly review *Orchestra,* and contributed to other music magazines. He was the first Polish composer to use the method of composition with 12 tones according to Schoenberg's principles; his *15 Variations* for string orch. (Amsterdam Festival, June 9, 1933) are derived from a 12-tone row. He composed 3 symphonies; his 3rd Symphony was performed at the London Festival on June 17, 1938; other works are String Trio (Oxford Festival, July 23, 1931); Divertimento for oboe, clarinet and bassoon; String Quartet; *40 Polish Folksongs* for piano; *Quasi una sonata;* a cycle of piano pieces; *Love Cantata; 4 Poems* for voice and piano.

Kofler, Leo, Austrian organist and singing teacher; b. Brixen, March 13, 1837; d. New Orleans, Nov. 29, 1908. He studied at Stern's Cons. in Berlin; in 1866, came to America, and held various positions as organist in St. Louis, Cincinnati, Brooklyn, and N.Y. He publ. *The Act of Breathing as the Basis of Tone Production* (7th ed., N.Y., 1897) and *Take Care of Your Voice, or, The Golden Rule of Health;* also ed. *Selected Hymn-tunes and Hymn-anthems.*

Kogan, Leonid, outstanding Russian violinist; b. Dniepropetrovsk, Nov. 14, 1924; studied violin with his father, a photographer and amateur musician. At the age of 10 he was taken to Moscow; studied with Abram Yampolsky at the Moscow Cons., graduating in 1948; then appointed teacher there. In Moscow he organized a concert trio with the pianist Emil Gilels and the cellist Mstislav Rostropovitch; married a sister of Gilels, a violinist; appeared often with her in works for 2 violins. In 1951 he received the 1st prize at the International Competition in Brussels; then traveled widely; gave concerts in England, Italy, France, China, South America, etc. In 1958 he undertook his 1st American tour, playing with the Boston Symph., N.Y. Philharmonic, Philadelphia Orch., Los Angeles Philharmonic, etc. His son **Pavel** (b. Moscow, June 6, 1952) inherited his talent as a violinist; in 1970 he won first prize at the International Competition in Helsinki, Finland.

Kogel, Gustav Friedrich, German conductor; b. Leipzig, Jan. 16, 1849; d. Frankfurt, Nov. 13, 1921. He studied at the Leipzig Cons.; was editor for C. F. Peters (1870–74); then was active as conductor in various provincial theaters; conducted the Berlin Philharmonic in 1888; was conductor of the Museum Concerts in Frankfurt from 1891 till 1903; also filled engagements as guest conductor in Russia, Spain, etc.; was guest conductor at the N.Y. Philharmonic in 1906. He edited full scores and piano scores of several operas; wrote piano pieces.

Köhler, Ernesto, Italian flutist; b. Modena, Dec. 4, 1849; d. St. Petersburg, May 17, 1907. He studied flute with his father; became 1st flutist of the court orch. at Modena; then at the Karltheater in Vienna; in 1871, became 1st flutist of the Imperial Orch. in St. Petersburg. He wrote numerous compositions for the flute; also an opera, *Ben Achmed,* and several ballets.

Köhler, Ernst, German organist and pianist; b. Langenbielau, May 28, 1799; d. Breslau, May 26, 1847. He was 1st organist of the Elisabethkirche in Breslau from 1827 until his death. He wrote 2 symphonies, 9 overtures, 12 church cantatas, 12 large vocal works with orch., organ works, and piano pieces.

Kohler, Franz, American violinist and conductor; b. Clinton, Iowa, Feb. 20, 1877; d. Erie, Pa., Dec. 22, 1918. He studied with Karl Halir (violin) in Weimar and Berlin; returning to America in 1898, he joined the Pittsburgh Symph. Orch. as a violinist; was concertmaster briefly in 1910; in 1911–13 taught violin at Oberlin College; from 1913 till his death, conducted the Erie Symph. Orch.

Köhler, Louis, German composer of celebrated piano studies; b. Brunswick, Sept. 5, 1820; d. Königsberg, Feb. 16, 1886. He studied piano in Brunswick with Sonnemann; then took courses in composition in Vienna (1839–43) with Sechter and Seyfried; also studied piano there with Bocklet. After a season of theater conducting, he settled in Königsberg (1847) and established there a successful school for piano playing. He wrote 3 operas, a ballet, a symphony, overtures, cantatas, and other works, but he is remembered exclusively for his albums of piano studies, which have been adopted in music schools all over the world; next to Czerny, he is the most popular purveyor of didactic piano literature; it must be observed that while his studies are of great instructive value, they are also worthwhile from the purely musical standpoint. His chief work, in which he laid the foundation of methodical piano pedagogy, is *Systematische Lehrmethode für Klavierspiel und Musik*, in 2 vols.: I, *Die Mechanik als Grundlage der Technik* (1856; 3rd ed., revised by Riemann, 1888); II. *Tonschriftwesen, Harmonik, Metrik* (1858); other publications are *Führer durch den Klavierunterricht* (6th ed., 1879); *Der Klavierfingersatz* (1862); *Der Klavieruntericht, oder Studien, Erfahrungen und Ratschläge* (4th ed., 1877); *Die neue Richtung in der Musik* (1864); *Leichtfassliche Harmonie- und Generalbasslehre* (a valuable manual of harmony; 3rd ed., 1880); *Brahms und seine Stellung in der neueren Klavierliteratur* (1880); *Der Klavierpedalung* (1882); *Allgemeine Musiklehre* (1883).

Kohn, Karl, American pianist and composer; b. Vienna, Aug. 1, 1926. After the Nazi absorption of Austria in 1938, his family emigrated to the U.S.; he studied piano with Carl V. Werschinger and conducting with Prüwer at N.Y. College of Music (1940–44); then took courses in music theory and composition at Harvard Univ. with Walter Piston, Irving Fine and Randall Thompson (B.A., 1950; M.A., 1955). In 1956 he traveled to Finland on a Fulbright grant; upon return to the U.S. he taught piano and music theory at Pomona College in Claremont, Calif. and at the Claremont Graduate School of Music. He also taught several summers at the Berkshire Music Center at Tanglewood, Mass.; held a Guggenheim Fellowship in 1961–62; in 1975 was awarded a grant by the National Endowment for the Arts. As a pianist, he specializes in modern music, deploying a virtuoso technique in tackling the most formidable piano works; also gave 2-piano concerts with his wife **Margaret Kohn.** In his compositions he tends towards prudential serialism, but also explores diatonic modalities, applying the power of pervicacious iteration of pandiatonic chordal complexes; he successfully adopts medieval polyphonic devices to contemporary usages, such as the integration of the pre-composed thematic fragments, a technique anciently known as "centone" (literally "patchwork quilt"). He makes use of topological rearrangements of classical pieces, as in *Son of Prophet Bird*, dislocated and paraphrased from Schumann's *Bird as a Prophet*. WORKS: *Sinfonia Concertante* for piano and orch. (1951); *Overture* for string orch. (Helsinki, April 17, 1956); *Castles and Kings*, symph. suite for children (1958); *3 Scenes* for orch. (1958–60); *Concerto mutabile* for piano and orch. (1962); *Interlude* for orch. (1964); *Episodes* for piano and orch. (1966); *Interlude I* for flute and string orch. (1969); *Interlude II* for piano and string orch. (1969); *Esdras* for flute, piano, chorus and orch. (1969–70); *Centone per Orchestra* (1973; Claremont Music Festival, June 27, 1973, composer conducting); *Innocent Psaltery*, "colonial music" for orch. (1976); *The Prophet Bird* (a metamorphosis of Schumann's *Bird as a Prophet*, 1976); CHAMBER MUSIC:

Fanfare for brass and percussion (1952); *Motets* for 8 horns (1953); *Song* for violin (or clarinet) and piano (1956); *Concert Music* for 12 wind instruments (1956); *Quartet* for horns (1957); *3 Pieces* for flute and piano (1958); Divertimento, for flute, oboe, clarinet and bassoon (1959); *Capriccio* for flute, clarinet, cello, harp and piano (1962); Serenade for wind quintet and piano (1962); *Little Suite* for wind quintet (1963); *Kaleidoscope* for string quartet (1964); *Sonata da camera* for alto flute, clarinet and piano (1964); *Encounters I* for flute, piccolo and piano (1965); *Encounters II* for horn and piano (1967); *Introduction and Parodies* for clarinet, horn, bassoon, string quartet and piano (1967); *4 Musical Pictures* for violin and piano (1967); *Rhapsodies* for marimba, vibraphone and percussion (1968); *Impromptu* for 8 wind instruments (1969); *Reflections* for clarinet and piano (1970); Variations for horn and piano (1971); *Souvenirs* for violin and piano (1971); *Encounters III* for violin and piano (1971); Trio for violin, horn and piano (1972); *Encounters IV* for oboe and piano (1972); *Romanza* for flute and piano (1972); *Encounters V* for bassoon and piano (1973); *3 Duets* for 2 violins (1973); *Paronyms* for flutes and piano (1974); Concerto for Horn and Piano (1974); *Son of Prophet Bird* for harp solo (1977). For piano solo: *3 Rhapsodies* (1960, 1971, 1977); *5 Bagatelles* (1961); *Partita* (1963); *Recreations* for piano 4-hands (1968); *Bits and Pieces* (1973); sacred choruses; songs.

Kohoutek, Ctirad, Czech composer; b. Zábřeh, March 18, 1929. He studied composition with Petřelka at the Brno Cons.; then with Kvapil at the Janáček Academy of Music there (1949–53); joined its faculty after graduation. His music follows the traditions of Central European modernism, well contained within classical forms, but diversified by serial procedures and glamorized by electronic sound. WORKS: Oboe Sonatina (1950); *Ukolébavka černošské mámy (The Lullaby of the Negro Mother)*, cantata (1952); *Munich,* symph. poem (1953); *Festival Overture* (1954); Suite for Viola and Piano (1957); Violin Concerto (1958); Suite for Wind Quintet (1959); String Quartet (1959); *Velký přelom (The Great Revolution),* symph. (1960); *Ballads from the Rebellion,* 2 cantatas (1960); *Symphonic Dances* (1961); *Pátý živel (The Fifth Element),* melodrama for narrator and orch. (1962); Symphonietta (1963); *Rapsodia eroica* for organ (1963); Concertino for Cello and Chamber Orch. (1964); *Preludes* for chamber orch. (1965); *Inventions* for piano (1965); *Miniatures* for 4 horns (1965; version for string orch., 1966); *Memento 1967,* concerto for percussion and winds (1966); *Panychida letní noci (Panychide of the Summer Night),* music for 2 sound layers of 2 violas, 2 pianos, percussion and tape (1968); *Teatro del mondo,* symphonic rotation in 4 movements (1968–69); *Loutkové scény (Puppet Scenes),* piano pieces for children (1969); *Pantheon,* sound picture for orch. (1970); *Sluneční zaře (Sunshine),* symph. poem (1975); several children's choruses. He publ. 2 books: *Novodobé skladebné teorie západoevropské hudby (Modern Composing Theories of West European Music,* Prague, 1962; second ed., revised and retitled *Novodobé skladebné směry v hudbě [Modern Composing Trends in Music],* Prague,

1965) and *Projektová hudební kompozice (Project Musical Composition,* Brno, 1968).

Kohs, Ellis B., notable American composer; b. Chicago, May 12, 1916. He studied at the Univ. of Chicago with Carl Bricken, at the Juilliard School of Music, N.Y. with Bernard Wagenaar, and at Harvard Univ. with Walter Piston. He served in the U.S. Army (1941–46); then occupied various teaching positions; taught at Wesleyan Univ. (1946–48), Cons. of Kansas City (1948–50); in 1950 he was appointed to the faculty of the Univ. of Southern California, Los Angeles. In his music he pursues the aim of classical clarity; he is particularly adept in variation structures; the rhythmic patterns in his works are often asymmetrical, and the contrapuntal fabric highly dissonant; in some of his works he makes use of a unifying 12-tone row, subjecting it to ingenious metamorphoses, as particularly revealed in his opera *Amerika;* a humorous streak is shown in his choral piece *The Automatic Pistol,* to words from the U.S. Army weapons manual which he composed during his military service. As a pedagogue, he published the useful manuals, *Music Theory, a Syllabus for Teacher and Student* (2 vols., N.Y., 1961); and *Musical Form: Studies in Analysis and Synthesis* (Boston, 1976).
WORKS: Concerto for Orch. (San Francisco, Aug. 9, 1942); *Legend* for oboe and string orch. (Columbus, Ohio, Feb. 27, 1947); Cello Concerto (1947); Chamber Concerto for viola and string nonet (1949); Symph. No. 1 (1950); Symph. No. 2, with chorus (Univ. of Illinois, Urbana, April 13, 1957); String Quartet (1942); *Night Watch* for flute, horn, and kettledrums (1943); Sonatina for Bassoon and Piano (1944); Sonatina for Violin and Piano (1948); *Short Concert* for string quartet (1948); Clarinet Sonata (1951); Variations for Recorder (1956); *The Automatic Pistol,* for male voices a cappella (Washington, Army Music Chorus, Sept. 5, 1943); *25th Psalm* (1947); *Lord of the Ascendant,* for chorus, soloists, dancers, and orch. (1956); incidental music to Shakespeare's *Macbeth* (1947); *Passacaglia* for organ and string orch. (1946); *Capriccio* for organ (1948); *Etude in Memory of Bartók* for piano (1946); Piano Toccata (1948); *Fantasy on La, Sol, Fa, Re, Mi* (1949); *10 Inventions* for piano (1950); *Studies in Variation,* in 4 parts: for woodwind quintet, for piano quartet, for piano solo, for unaccompanied violin (1962); Sonata for Snare-Drum and Piano (1966); opera, *Amerika* (1969; abridged concert version produced in Los Angeles, May 19, 1970). See his autobiographical sketch *Thoughts from the Workbench,* in *American Composers Alliance Bulletin* (Autumn 1956).

Kohut, Adolf, German writer on music; b. Mindszent, Hungary, Nov. 10, 1847; d. Berlin, Sept. 21, 1917. He published *Moses Mendelssohn und seine Familie* (1886); *Weber-Gedenkbuch* (1887); *Friedrich Wieck* (1888); *Das Dresdener Hoftheater in der Gegenwart* (1888); *Die grössten deutschen Soubretten im 19. Jahrhundert* (1890); *Joseph Joachim* (1891); *Bilder aus der Musikwelt* (1891); *Aus dem Zauberlande Polyhymnias* (1892); *Dur- und Mollakkorde* (1894); *Schiller in seinen Beziehungen zur Musik* (1905); *Die Gesangsköniginnen in den letzten drei Jahrhunderten*

(1906); also wrote biographies of Auber, Meyerbeer, and Rossini for Reclam's *Universalbibliothek.*

Kókai, Rezsö, Hungarian composer; b. Budapest, Jan. 15, 1906; d. there, March 6, 1962. He studied composition with János Koessler and piano with Emanuel Hegyi at the Budapest Academy (1919–26); he received his doctorate from the Univ. of Freiburg (1933) with a dissertation on Liszt's early piano music. In 1929 he joined the faculty of the National Academy of Music in Budapest.
WORKS: an oratorio, *István király (King Stephen,* 1942); a ballet, *A rossz feleség (The Bad Wife,* 1946); *2 Rondos* for small orch. (1947); *Recruiting Suite* for orch. (1950); Violin Concerto (1952); *Dances from Szék* for orch. (1952); *Concerto all'Ungherese* for orch. (1957); *Hungarian Dance* for youth orch. (1960); *Toccata* for piano (1927); Serenade for String Trio (1949–50); 2-Piano Sonata (1949); *4 Improvisations* for piano (1949–50); Quartet for clarinet and string trio (1952); *Capriccio* for violin and piano (1952); music for radio plays and films; songs. He wrote 2 books, *Methodical Aesthetics of Music* (Budapest, 1938) and *The Music of Our Century* (Budapest, 1961).

Kokkonen, Joonas, prominent Finnish composer; b. Iisalmi, Nov. 13, 1921. He studied composition with Selim Palmgren at the Sibelius Academy in Helsinki, and later taught there. In 1963 he was elected to the membership of the Finnish Academy; in 1965 he became chairman of the Union of Finnish Composers. In 1973 he was awarded the Sibelius Prize. Like all composers of his generation in Finland, he experienced the inevitable influence of Sibelius, but soon abandoned the characteristic diatonic modalities of Finnish folk music and formed an individual style of composition marked by a curiously anfractuous chromaticism and involuted counterpoint, freely dissonant but hewing to clearly identifiable tonal centers. For a period he dabbled in dodecaphonic writing, but found its doctrinaire discipline uncongenial. He derives his techniques from the contrapuntal procedures of Bach and, among the moderns, from Bartók. Thematically, he adopts an objective method of formal structure, in which a free succession of formative motives determines the content.
WORKS: opera, *Viimeiset Kiusaukset (The Last Temptations),* on the subject of the life of a 19th-century Finnish evangelist (Helsinki, Sept. 2, 1975); 4 symphonies: No. 1 (1960); No. 2 (1961); No. 3 (Helsinki, Sept. 12, 1967); No. 4 (1970; Helsinki, Nov. 7, 1971); *Lintujen Tuonela (The Hades of the Birds)* for mezzo-soprano and orch. (1959); *Sinfonia da camera* for string orch. (1962); *Opus Sonorum* for orch. (1964); Cello Concerto (1969); *Inauguratio,* suite for orch. (1971); Piano Trio (1948); Piano Quintet (1953); Duo for violin and piano (1955); 2 string quartets (1959, 1966); Wind Quintet (1973); several sacred choruses; also piano pieces and songs.

Kolar, Victor, American conductor; b. (of Bohemian parentage) Budapest, Feb. 12, 1888; d. Detroit, June 16, 1957. He studied violin with Ševčik and composition with Dvořák at the Prague Cons. In 1900 he emigrated to America; played violin in the Pittsburgh

Orch. (1905–08) and in the N.Y. Symph. Orch. (1908–20). In 1920 he became associate conductor at the Detroit Symph. Orch., and later was appointed principal conductor there, until 1941. As assistant conductor of the N.Y. Symph. Orch. he brought out several of his own works, among them a symphony (Jan. 28, 1916); his other works were *Hiawatha*, a symph. poem (Pittsburgh, Jan. 31, 1908); *3 Humoresques* for violin and piano; numerous songs and 7 marches.

Kolbe, Oskar, German music theorist; b. Berlin, Aug. 10, 1836; d. there, Jan. 2, 1878. He studied with Grell and Löschhorn in Berlin; taught theory at Stern's Cons. (1859–75). He publ. a *Kurzgefasstes Handbuch der Generalbasslehre* (1862) and a *Handbuch der Harmonielehre* (1873); also wrote an oratorio, *Johannes der Täufer;* an overture to *Wallensteins Tod;* piano music; songs.

Kolberg, Oskar, Polish composer and song collector; b. Przysucha, near Radom, Feb. 22, 1814; d. Cracow, June 3, 1890. He studied at the Warsaw Cons. with Chopin's teacher Elsner; then in Berlin; returned to Warsaw in 1840. He devoted a major part of his life to traveling in the country in order to collect folksongs, while earning his living as an employee of the Warsaw-Vienna Railroad. He started a series of publications on Polish folklore, including folk music, in 1860; 23 vols. were issued before his death, and publication of the materials assembled by him was continued later by the Polish Academy. He also wrote a number of Polish dances for piano, and composed an opera, *Krol Pasterzy* (*The Shepherd's Inn;* Warsaw, March 2, 1859).

Kolchinskaya, Camilla, Russian conductor; b. Moscow, 1940. She studied violin, and was accepted at the age of 6 at a Moscow School for musically gifted children, where she conducted choral rehearsals. She played the violin in the orchestra of Moscow Film studios; then ventured to compete for the post of conductor of the orchestra of the city of Yaroslavl; she won the contest and conducted a season of classical and modern programs there. She also was guest conductor of orchestras in Siberia; in 1975, after 8 years of conducting in provincial cities, she returned to Moscow where she became guest conductor of the USSR National Symph. Orch. In 1976 she applied for an exit visa to Israel; conducted her first concert there with the Israel Philharmonic in Tel Aviv on Jan. 12, 1977.

Kolessa, Filaret, Ukrainian ethnomusicologist; b. Chodowitschi, near Lwów, July 17, 1871; d. Lwów, March 3, 1947. He studied in Vienna with **Bruckner** (composition) and with **Guido Adler** (musicology); in 1898 was appointed to the faculty of the State High School in Lwów; in 1939 he became prof. at Lwów Univ. and director of the Ethnographic Museum there. He published a number of important papers dealing with Ukrainian folk songs: *Rhythmics of Ukrainian Folk Songs* (1906–07); *Melodies of Ukrainian Historical Dumas* (1910–13; reprint, Kiev, 1969); *Genesis of Ukrainian Historical Dumas* (1921); *Folk Songs of the South Carpathians* (1923); *Recitative Forms in Ukrai-*

nian Folk Poetry (1927); *Folk Songs of Galician Lemko Region* (1929).

Kolff, J. van Santen, Dutch-born German writer on music; b. Rotterdam, April 19, 1848; d. Berlin, Nov. 29, 1896. A polyglot, he contributed hundreds of articles and essays on music to publications in German, French, and Dutch; of value is his historical analysis of the Leitmotiv, published in vols. VIII and IX of *Bayreuther Blätter,* under the title "Geschichtliches und Ästhetisches über das Erinnerungsmotiv." He was the first to use the term "reminiscence motive" in reference to Wagner's works.

Kolisch, Rudolf, Austrian violinist; b. Klamm, July 20, 1896; d. Watertown, Mass., Aug. 1, 1978. He studied violin with Ševčik at the Univ. of Vienna; also took private lessons in composition with Schoenberg. In 1922 he organized the Kolisch Quartet, which systematically presented works by modern composers. His was the first string quartet that performed its programs from memory. In 1935 he went to the U.S.; in 1942 he became the leader of the Pro Arte Quartet; taught at the Univ. of Wisconsin until 1967, and then was "artist in residence" at the New England Cons. of Music in Boston. He was one of the few professional left-handed violinists.

Kollmann, August Friedrich Christoph, German composer; b. Engelbostel, March 21, 1756; d. London, March 21, 1829. He was organist in the German Chapel, St. James', London. Among his works are a symphony, *The Shipwreck;* 100 Psalms harmonized in 100 ways; Rondo for piano on the chord of the diminished 7th, etc.; also publ. *Essays on Practical Harmony* (1796), *First Beginning on the Pianoforte,* etc.

Kollo, Walter, German operetta composer; b. Neidenburg, March 28, 1878; d. Berlin, Sept. 30, 1940. He studied in Sondershausen and Königsberg. In 1901 he settled in Berlin and was active as theater conductor; wrote songs that became popular favorites. Among his most successful operettas are *Drei alte Schachteln* (Berlin, Oct. 6, 1917) and *Die Frau ohne Kuss* (Berlin, July 6, 1924).

Kolman, Petr, Slovak composer; b. Bratislava, May 29, 1937. He studied theory with Očenáš and Cikker at the Bratislava Cons. (1951–56) and advanced composition with Alexander Moyzes at the High School for Musical Arts in Bratislava (1956–60); was editor of symph. music at the Bratislava Radio (1961–65) and later worked in an electronic music studio. He adopted the serial method of composition, according to Schoenberg's practice.
WORKS: *Romeo and Juliet,* symph. poem (1956); String Trio (1957); Violin Concerto (1959–60); *3 Piano Pieces in Memory of Schoenberg* (1960); *Participazioni* for 12 instruments (1962); *Sonata Canonica* for clarinet and bass clarinet (1963); *Panegyrikos* for 16 instruments (1964); *Homage to Kandinsky* for string quartet (1964); *Monumento per 6,000,000* for orch. (1964); *Mollisation mobile* for flute and vibraphone (1965).

Kolneder, Walter, Austrian violinist and musicologist; b. Wels, July 1, 1910. He studied composition with Johann Nepomuk David, conducting with Bernhard Paumgartner, and violin playing with Max Strub. He was employed as a violinist in the orch. of the Mozarteum in Salzburg (1929–35) and subsequently occupied various positions as an orchestral player in Austria. From 1953 to 1959 he was director of the Cons. of the city of Luxembourg; from 1959 to 1965 he taught in Darmstadt; in 1966 was appointed director of the Hochschule für Musik in Karlsruhe. He publ. several valuable monographs on old and new music, among them *Die vokale Mehrstimmigkeit in der Volksmusik der österreichischen Alpenländer* (Innsbruck, 1949); *Aufführungspraxis bei Vivaldi* (Leipzig, 1955); *Anton Webern: Einführung in Werk und Stil* (Rodenkirchen, 1961; in English, as *Anton Webern: An Introduction to His Works,* Los Angeles, 1968); *Antonio Vivaldi* (Wiesbaden, 1965; in English, Berkeley, California, 1970); edited violin music of Corelli, Stradella, Vivaldi, etc.

Kolodin, Irving, American music critic; b. New York, Feb. 22, 1908. He studied at the Institute of Musical Art, N.Y.; was music critic on the *N.Y. Sun* (1932–50); in 1947 he became editor of the music section of *The Saturday Review.* He published a number of valuable reference works and monographs: *The Metropolitan Opera 1883–1935* (N.Y., 1936; new revised edition as *The Story of the Metropolitan Opera, 1883–1950,* N.Y., 1953; 4th edition, N.Y., 1966); *The Kingdom of Swing* (with Benny Goodman; N.Y., 1939); *A Guide to Recorded Music* (N.Y., 1941; new edition, as *New Guide to Recorded Music,* Garden City, N.Y., 1946; 3rd revised edition, 1950); *Mozart on Records* (N.Y., 1942); *Orchestral Music,* in the series "The Guide to Long-Playing Records" (N.Y., 1955); editor, *The Saturday Review Home Book of Recorded Music and Sound Reproduction* (N.Y., 1956); *Musical Life* (N.Y., 1958); *The Continuity of Music: A History of Influence* (N.Y., 1969); *The Interior Beethoven: A Biography of the Music* (N.Y., 1975); *The Opera Omnibus: Four Centuries of Critical Give and Take* (N.Y., 1976).

Komorous, Rudolf, Czech composer of avant-garde tendencies; b. Prague, Dec. 8, 1931. He studied bassoon at the Prague Cons. (1946–52) and composition with Pavel Bořkovec at the Prague Academy of Musical Arts (1952–59); concurrently served as first bassoonist at the Prague Opera. From 1959 to 1961 he was in China as a teacher of bassoon at the Cons. of Peking. Returning to Prague, he took active part in the modern music movement; in 1961 he was one of the organizers of the progressive group "Musica Viva Pragensis." After the Soviet occupation of Czechoslovakia in 1968, Komorous left Prague and went with his family to Canada. In 1971 he was appointed prof. of composition at the Univ. of Victoria in British Columbia. In his works he explores the ultra-modern potentialities of composition, often resorting to graphic music notation. WORKS: chamber opera for voices a cappella, *Lady Whiterose* (1964–66); *Chamber Music* for bassoon and small orch. (1959); *The Green Twig* for basset horn, triangle, harmonium, piano, viola and cello (1960); *Still Life with Florets* for 2 clarinets, bassoon, cymbal and 3 violas (1961); *The Sweet Queen* for mouth harmonica, bass drum and piano (1962–63); *Venus* for strings and percussion (1963); *Olympia* for flexatone, harmonica, nightingale, acolyte bells, sleigh bells and rattle (1964); *Piccolomini* for 4 piccolos (1964); *The Devil's Trills* for piano (1964); *Mignon* for 4 four-string instruments (1965); *Chanson* for guitar, spirale and viola (1965); *York* for flute, oboe or trumpet, bassoon, triangle, piano, mandolin and double bass (1967); *The Gloomy Grace* for 11 instruments and nightingale (1968); *Bare and Dainty* for orch. (1970); *Lethe* for orch. and tape (1971); *Dingy Yellow* for soprano saxophone, piano and tape (1972); *Untitled 1* for tape (1973), *2* for solo trumpet (1973), *3* for 10 instruments (1974), *4* for 4 oboes, 2 trumpets and violin (1974) and *5* for flute, horn, viola and double bass (1974); *Preludes* for 13 early instruments (1974); *The Grand Chopper* for tape (1974); *Anatomy of Melancholy* for tape (1974); *Rossi* for small orch. (1975); *At Your Memory the Transparent Tears Are Like Molten Lead* for viola da gamba and harpsichord (1976); *The Gentle Touch (In Answer to Assistant Magistrate Chang)* for 5 flutes, 4 violas, 3 cellos and piano (1977).

Komorzynski, Egon, Austrian musicologist; b. Vienna, May 7, 1878; d. there, March 16, 1963; studied musicology with Guido Adler at the Univ. of Vienna and with Riemann at the Univ. of Leipzig. He devoted himself to the study of Mozart; publ. a fundamental work on Mozart's librettist Schikaneder (Vienna, 1901; revised ed., 1951); a monograph on Mozart (Berlin, 1941; 2nd ed., 1955); a novel about Schubert, *Genius zwischen 2 Welten* (Berlin, 1944).

Kondorossy, Leslie, Hungarian-American composer; b. Pressburg, June 25, 1915. He studied at the Academy of Music in Budapest; after World War II he emigrated to America and settled in Cleveland; there he evolved fruitful activity as a teacher, conductor and composer. He is especially proficient in producing short operas; among them are *Night in the Puszta* (Cleveland, June 28, 1953); *The Voice* (Cleveland, May 15, 1954); *The Pumpkin* (Cleveland, May 15, 1954); *Unexpected Visitor* and *The Two Imposters* (Cleveland, Oct. 21, 1956); *The Fox* (Cleveland, Jan. 28, 1961); *The Baksis* (1964); *Nathan the Wise* (1964); the radio operas *The Midnight Duel* (Cleveland Radio, March 20, 1955); *The String Quartet* (Cleveland Radio, May 8, 1955); children's operas *The Poorest Suitor* (Cleveland, May 24, 1967); *Shizuka's Dance* (Cleveland, April 22, 1969; also performed on Tokyo Television, Japan, July 31, 1974); *Kalamona and the Four Winds* (Cleveland Radio, Sept. 12, 1971); church opera, *Ruth and Naomi* (Cleveland, April 28, 1974); *Kossuth Cantata* (Cleveland, March 16, 1952); *David, A Son of Jesse,* oratorio (Cleveland, June 4, 1967); Trombone Concerto (1958); Trumpet Concerto (1959); Harp Concerto (1961); *Jazz Mass* for voices and jazz band (1968); Harpsichord Concerto (1972); numerous organ pieces.

Kondracki, Michal, Russian-born composer; b. Poltava, Oct. 5, 1902; studied with Statkowski and Melcer at the Warsaw State Cons., graduating in 1926 with honors; then went to Paris, where he was a pupil of Paul Dukas; later also studied with Szymanowski; from 1928–33 lived in Paris; in 1933 returned to Warsaw as music critic; left Poland after the outbreak of war in 1939 and reached Brazil; stayed in Rio de Janeiro from 1940 till 1943; then settled in N.Y.

WORKS: opera, *Popieliny* (Warsaw, May 3, 1934); a ballet, *Metropolis* (1929); *Cantata ecclesiastica* (1937); *Partita* for chamber orch. (1928); Symph. (1942); a set of Brazilian dances for orch. (1944).

Königslöw, Johann Wilhelm Cornelius, German organist and composer; b. Hamburg, March 16, 1745; d. Lübeck, May 14, 1833. He was organist at the Marienkirche in Lübeck from 1773 until his death. He composed many "Abendmusiken," following Buxtehude's example.

Königslöw, Otto Friedrich von, German violinist and conductor; b. Hamburg, Nov. 13, 1824; d. Bonn, Oct. 6, 1898. He studied at the Leipzig Cons. with David (violin) and Hauptmann (theory); following 12 years of concert tours, he became conductor of the Gürzenich Orch. at Cologne (1858–81); also was a member of the staff of the Cologne Cons. In 1884 he settled in Bonn.

Koning, David, Dutch pianist and composer; b. Rotterdam, March 19, 1820; d. Amsterdam, Oct. 6, 1876. He studied with Aloys Schmitt in Frankfurt; from 1840, was conductor of the choral society "Felix Meritis" in Amsterdam; was a member of various music organizations in Europe; was active mainly as a piano teacher. He wrote a comic opera, *The Fishermaiden;* an *Elegy on the Death of an Artist,* for soli, chorus, and orch.; much vocal music; many piano pieces and studies.

Konius, Georgy. See **Conus, Georgy.**

Konjović, Petar, eminent Serbian composer; b. Sombor, May 6, 1882; died Belgrade, Oct. 1, 1970. He studied at the Prague Cons. with Novák; was choral director and teacher in Zemun and Belgrade (1906–14). In 1920 he toured Europe as pianist; from 1921–26 was music director of the Zagreb Opera. From 1927–33 he was director of national theaters in Osijek, Split, and Novi Sad; from 1933–39, intendant of the national theater in Zagreb. In 1939 he settled in Belgrade as rector and prof. of the Academy of Music.

WORKS: the operas *Vilin Veo* or *Ženidba Miloševa* (*The Wedding of Milos;* Zagreb, April 25, 1917), *Koštana* (Zagreb, April 16, 1931), *Knez od Zete* (*The Duke of Zeta;* Belgrade, May 25, 1929) and *Sel jaci* (*The Peasants;* Belgrade, March 3, 1952); Symphony in C (1908); *Capriccio Adriatico,* for violin and orch. (1920); *Makar Chudra,* symph. poem after Maxim Gorky (1944); 2 string quartets; solo pieces for violin, cello, and piano; 24 songs; 100 Yugoslav folksongs *Moja Zemlja* (of which 25 are arranged for voice and small orch.). He publ. a book of essays, *Ličnosti* (*Personalities;* Zagreb, 1920), and a monograph on Miloje Milojević (Belgrade, 1954).

Kono, Kristo, Albanian composer; b. Tirana, July 17, 1907. He studied at the Milan Cons.; wrote the first national Albanian operetta *The Dawn* (1954); also an opera, *Flowers of Memories* (1959) and many choruses.

Konoye, Hidemarō, Japanese composer and conductor; b. Tokyo, Nov. 18, 1898; d. there, June 2, 1973. A member of an aristocratic Japanese family, he received his education in Japan and in Europe; attended classes in composition of Vincent d'Indy at the Schola Cantorum in Paris; then took courses with Franz Schreker and Georg Schumann at the Berlin Cons. He made his European debut as conductor with the Berlin Philharmonic on Jan. 18, 1924. Returning to Japan he was principal conductor of the New Symph. Orch. in Tokyo (1926–34), specializing in new works of Japanese, European, and American composers. He conducted in the U.S. in 1937 and 1957. He is the composer of several orchestral pieces based on Japanese subjects; also orchestrated old Japanese court music for the modern Western orch.; arranged the music of *Madama Butterfly* for the films (inserting many Japanese folk melodies).

Kont, Paul, Austrian composer; b. Vienna, Aug. 19, 1920. He studied violin and piano in his early youth; then took courses in conducting with Krips and Swarowsky at the Musikakademie in Vienna. In 1948 he went to Paris, where he studied composition with Milhaud, Honegger and Messiaen. Returning to Vienna, he adopted a serial method applying the statistical principles of valid recurrences of all musical parameters, including pitch, rhythm and dynamics. Typical of this idiom are his *Celestina* for "total theater" (1966) and *Inzwischen,* a "mystery play for our time" (Vienna Television, Jan. 5, 1967). His other works are: *Indische Legende,* a radio cantata (1951); *Peter und Susanne* (Vienna Television, June 26, 1959); chamber ballets *Annoncen* (1956); *Die traurigen Jäger* (1958); *Italia passata* (1967); a choreographic symphony (1970); 2 wind quartets; Trio for flute, cello and harp; piano pieces; film music. He published *Antianorganikum,* essays on new music (Vienna, 1967).

Kontarsky, Alfons, German pianist; brother of **Aloys** and **Bernhard Kontarsky;** b. Iserlohn, Westphalia, Oct. 9, 1932. He studied piano with Else Schmitz-Gohr at the Hochschule für Musik in Cologne (1953–55) and with Erdmann in Hamburg (1955–57); in 1955 received, along with his older brother Aloys, the first prize for duo piano playing at the International Competition of the Bavarian Radio in Munich; made with Aloys a concert tour of duo recitals through the U.S., South America, South Africa and Japan; in 1967 appointed prof. of piano at the Hochschule für Musik, Cologne.

Kontarsky, Aloys, German pianist; brother of **Alfons** and **Bernhard Kontarsky;** b. Iserlohn, Westphalia, May 14, 1931. He studied piano at the Hochschule für Musik in Cologne with Else Schmitz-Gohr and with Erdmann in Hamburg; in 1955 he received, along with his younger brother Alfons, the first prize for duo piano playing at the International Competition of the Bavarian Radio in Munich; then embarked with him on a worldwide tour of duo piano recitals in the U.S., South America, South Africa and Japan. He specialized in ultra-modern music; gave première performances of works by Stockhausen, Berio, Earle Brown, Pousseur, Bussotti and B. A. Zimmermann. In 1960 he joined the faculty of the International Festival Series of New Music in Darmstadt.

Kontarsky, Bernhard, German pianist and conductor; brother of **Alfons** and **Aloys Kontarsky;** b. Iserlohn, Westphalia, April 26, 1937. He studied at the Hochschule für Musik in Cologne and at the Univ. of Cologne. In 1964 he received the Mendelssohn Prize in Chamber Music. He is the principal conductor of the Stuttgart State Opera; is also active as a concert pianist, both as a soloist and ensemble with his brothers.

Kontski, Antoine de, Polish pianist; brother of **Apollinaire** and **Charles de Kontski;** b. Cracow, Oct. 27, 1817; d. Ivanichi, near Okulova, Novgorod District, Russia, Dec. 7, 1889. He was the most famous member of the Kontski family of precocious musicians. He studied with John Field in Moscow (1830); went to Paris in 1851; then was in Berlin (1853); from 1854–67 he was in St. Petersburg; then he lived in London as piano teacher. He toured the U.S. in 1883 and again in 1885; lived for a time in Buffalo. At the age of nearly 80, he undertook a world tour (1896–98), giving concerts in Australia, Japan, and Siberia. He died at the estate of friends near St. Petersburg.

WORKS: He was a composer of effective salon music and virtuoso pieces for piano; his picturesque *Réveil du lion* was enormously successful for many years; it was an epitome of Romantic exuberance to the point of being ludicrous; he also wrote 2 piano concertos, the waltzes *La Victorieuse* and *Souvenir de Biarritz; Grande Polonaise;* a characteristic piece, *La Nuit sur la mer,* and several orchestral overtures; also 2 light operas, *Les Deux Distraits* (London, 1872), and *Le Sultan de Zanzibar* (N.Y., May 8, 1886).

Kontski, Apollinaire de, Polish violinist; brother of **Antoine** and **Charles de Kontski;** b. Cracow, Oct. 23, 1825; d. Warsaw, June 29, 1879. He studied with his elder brother Charles; he appeared with his brothers as a small child in Russia and later in Germany, frankly exploited by his family for sensational publicity and gain. In 1837 he played for Paganini in Paris; in 1861 he became director of the Warsaw Cons., of which he was a founder, and remained in that post until his death. He publ. some violin music.

Kontski, Charles de, Polish pianist; brother of **Antoine** and **Apollinaire de Konstki;** b. Cracow, Sept. 6, 1815; d. Paris, Aug. 27, 1867. Like his brothers, he was a child prodigy, and made appearances with them at various public exhibitions and concerts. He studied in Warsaw and in Paris, eventually settling in Paris as a private piano teacher, enjoying considerable success in society.

Koole, Arend, Dutch musicologist; b. Amsterdam, April 22, 1908. He studied at the Amsterdam Cons. (1925–30) and later at Utrecht; his doctoral dissertation is a valuable monograph on Locatelli (Amsterdam, 1949). He also took lessons in conducting with Pierre Monteux; made appearances as guest conductor in Holland and Belgium. In 1949 he went to South Africa where he served as Senior Lecturer in Musi-

cology at the Univ. of Bloemfontein; from 1964 to 1973 he was prof. in music history at the Univ. of Southern California in Los Angeles; in 1974 he returned to South Africa. Besides his book on Locatelli, he published a monograph on Mendelssohn (1953); contributed numerous articles to music periodicals and encyclopedias.

Kopelent, Marek, Czech composer; b. Prague, April 28, 1932. He studied composition with Řídký at the Academy of Musical Arts in Prague (1951–55); was editor for contemporary music at Supraphon, the state publishing house of music (1956–71). In his music he experiments with a wide variety of musical resources of the multi-media avant-garde.

WORKS: 4 string quartets (1954, 1955, 1963, 1967); *3 Movements* for string orch. (1958); *Nénie s flétnou (Nenie with Flute)* for flute, 9 female voices and chamber ensemble (1961); *Small Pantomime* for wind quintet (1961); Trio for flute, clarinet and bassoon (1962); Trio for flute, bass clarinet and piano (1962); *Reflexe* for flute, violin, viola and cello (1962); an oratorio, *Chléb a ptáci (Bread and Birds,* 1957–62); *Canto Intimo* for flute and vibraphone (1963); *Matka (The Mother),* fresco for chorus and flute (1964); *Hudba pro pět (Music for Five)* for oboe, clarinet, bassoon, viola and piano (1964); *Modlitba kamene (Prayer of Stones)* for narrator, 2 small choruses, 3 gongs and tam-tam (1965); *Rozjímání (Contemplation)* for chamber orch. (1966); *Game,* a happening for string quartet (1965–66); *Snehah* (Sanskrit for "love") for soprano and chamber ensemble (1967); *Bijoux de Bohème* for harpsichord (1967); *Sváry (Quarrels)* for 12 solo instruments and orch. (1967–68; Prague, March 7, 1969); *Zátiší (Seclusion)* for viola and chamber orch. (1968); *Žaloby (Complaints)* for 2 choruses, trumpet, percussion and ad lib tape (1969); *Bludný hlas (The Wandering Voice)* for actress, chamber ensemble, tape and ad lib film and light projection (1969–70); *Appassionato* for piano and orch. (1970–71); *Secret Signals from Outer Space,* piece for young pianist (1971); *Intimissimo* for chamber ensemble (1971); *Musique piquante* for violin and cimbalom (1971); *A Few Minutes with an Oboist* for oboe and chamber orch. (1972); Wind Quintet (1972); *Black and White Tears* for solo voices (1972); *Syllabes mouvementées* for vocal soloists (1972); *Veroničina rouška (Veronika's Veil),* sonata for 11 strings (1972–73); *Rondo* for 5 percussionists (1973); *T'ukáta (Taps)* for harp, harpsichord, cimbalom and guitar (1974); *Hrátky (A Cozy Chat)* for saxophone and orch. (1974–75).

Koppel, Herman David, Danish composer; b. Copenhagen, Oct. 1, 1908. He studied piano and composition at the Royal Academy of Music in Copenhagen (1926–29); made his debut in 1930 as a concert pianist; toured widely in Europe and the Soviet Union; upon return to Denmark, was appointed to the staff of the Copenhagen Cons. (1949). In his piano recitals he emphasized modern Danish music, especially that of Carl Nielsen; his own compositions are, in turn, influenced by Nielsen's works.

WORKS: Koppel is a prolific composer; he wrote 7 symphonies: No. 1 (1930); No. 2 (1943); No. 3 (1944–45); No. 4 (1946); No. 5 (1955); No. 6, *Sinfonia breve* (1957); No. 7 (1960–61; Copenhagen, May 16,

1961); Violin Concerto (1929); *Music for Strings* (1930); 4 piano concertos (1931–32, 1936–37, 1948, 1960–63); *Music for Jazz Orch.* (1932); *Capriccio* for violin and orch. (1934); Variations for small orch. (1935); 2 Concertinos for Strings (1937–38, 1957); Clarinet Concerto (1941); Sinfonietta (1945); Concerto for Violin, Viola and Orch. (1947); *3 Psalms of David* for tenor, chorus and orch. (1949); Cello Concerto (1952); *Immortalis Mortalium* for baritone, boys' chorus and orch. (1954); *2 Biblical Songs* for soprano and orch. or piano (1955); *The Song of the Sun* for children's chorus, strings and piano (1958); *Moses,* oratorio (1963–64; Copenhagen, Oct. 21, 1965); *Requiem* (1965–66); Oboe Concerto (1970); Chamber Concerto for Violin and Strings (1970); Flute Concerto (1971); *Hymns of Thanksgiving* for soli, chorus and orch. (1974); 5 string quartets (1928–29, 1939, 1944–45, 1964, 1975); Duo for violin and piano (1930); Trio for clarinet, violin and piano (1931); Duo for clarinet and bassoon (1932); Sextet for winds and piano (1942); *Fantasy* for solo clarinet (1947); Piano Sonata (1950); *Ternio I* for cello or violin and piano (1951); Piano Quintet (1953); Cello Sonata (1956); Variations for clarinet and piano (1961); *Capriccio* for flute and piano (1961); *Macbeth,* opera after Shakespeare (1968; Copenhagen, 1970); *9 Variations* for piano trio (1969); Suite for Solo Cello (1971); Piano Trio (1971); *8 Variations and Epilogue* for piano and 13 players (1972); Divertimento for string trio (1972); *Ternio II* for solo saxophone (1973); *Pastorale Variations* for flute, violin, viola and cello (1975); incidental music for plays; music to 29 films; songs.

Koppel, Thomas Herman, Danish composer, son of **Herman David Koppel;** b. Orebro, Sweden, April 27, 1944. He studied piano and theory with his father at the Royal Danish Cons. in Copenhagen (1963–67). In 1968 he organized in Copenhagen a pop-group, "Savage Rose," and joined the Danish avant-garde in other venturesome activities.

WORKS: operas, *Historien om en moder (The Story of a Mother),* after H. C. Andersen (Copenhagen, Oct. 17, 1965) and *Bérénice* (1968); 3 string quartets (1963, 1964, 1966); *Cloches* for voice, clarinet, horn, celesta, piano, cello and percussion (1964); a cantata, *Phrases,* for 2 sopranos, 12 mezzo-sopranos, 4 solo instruments and orch. (Danish Radio, April 6, 1967); *Visions Fugitives* for piano and orch. (1965); *Concert héroïque* for 3 pianos, orch., chorus and wind machine (Copenhagen, Jan. 9, 1967); *Petit Air* for soprano and 4 instruments (1966); *Ouverture solennelle* (1967); *Impressions Lyriques* for percussion (1968); music for the ballet, *Dødens triumf* (Triumph of Death; Danish Radio, May 23, 1971).

Kopylov, Alexander, Russian composer; b. St. Petersburg, July 14, 1854; d. Strelna, near St. Petersburg, Feb. 20, 1911. He studied violin and piano at the Court Chapel (1862–72); upon graduation took lessons in composition with Rimsky-Korsakov and Liadov. From 1872 till 1896 he taught at the Court Chapel. He wrote a symphony; a concert overture; 5 string quartets; *Souvenir de Peterhof* for violin and piano; 2 albums of *Tableaux musicaux de la vie enfantine,* for piano; and other piano pieces, most of them publ. by Belaieff. He was an epigone of the Romantic school of minor Russian composers, emulating Tchaikovsky. A complete list of his publ. works is found in the *Verzeichnis russischer Komponisten* publ. by Fr. Hofmeister (Leipzig, 1949).

Korbay, Francis Alexander, Hungarian tenor and composer; b. Budapest, May 8, 1846; d. London, March 9, 1913. He was a pupil of Gustave Roger; sang at the Hungarian Opera in Budapest (1865–68); at the same time he pursued piano study, profiting by advice from Liszt, who was his godfather; made a rather successful tour as pianist in Europe (1869–71), and then went to the U.S., settling in N.Y. in 1871 as teacher of voice and piano. In 1894 he went to London; was prof. of singing at the Royal Academy of Music (1894–1903); remained in London until his death. He wrote an orchestral work, *Nuptiale; Hungarian Overture; Le Matin,* for solo voice and piano, which was arranged by Liszt for orch.; also numerous lieder and piano pieces.

Korchmarev, Klimenty, Russian composer; b. Verkhnedneprovsk, July 3, 1899; d. Moscow, April 7, 1958. He studied at the Odessa Cons. with Maliszewski; then went to Moscow. He was one of the first Soviet composers who began to write on revolutionary themes; in 1923 he wrote *March on the Left* to words by Mayakovsky. In 1927 he produced an operatic fairy tale *Ivan the Soldier* and a ballet *The Serf Ballerina* (Leningrad, Dec. 11, 1927). His other works of social significance and revolutionary content were the choral symphonies *October* (1931) and *The Peoples of the Soviet Land* (1935). In 1939 he went to Turkmenistan where he collected native songs; also composed the first Turkmenian ballet, *The Merry Deceiver.* In 1950 he wrote a cantata, *Free China,* for which he received a Stalin prize.

Koreshchenko, Arseny, Russian composer; b. Moscow, Dec. 18, 1870; d. Kharkov, Jan. 3, 1921. He studied piano with Taneyev and composition with Arensky at the Moscow Cons.; later was instructor in music theory there; from 1906 to 1919 he taught composition at the Moscow Philh. Institute; then went to Kharkov where he taught piano and composition at the local Music Academy, until his death. He wrote music imitative of Tchaikovsky and Arensky; his songs have a certain obsolete charm. He composed 3 operas, *Belshazzar's Feast* (Moscow, 1892), *The Angel of Death* (1893), and *The House of Ice* (Moscow, Nov. 19, 1900); a ballet, *The Magic Mirror* (Moscow, 1902); several orchestral pieces: an *Armenian Suite* for orch.; *Concerto Fantasy* for piano and orch.; a string quartet; choruses; piano pieces; songs.

Korganov, Genari, Armenian pianist and composer; b. Kvarely, May 12, 1858; d. Rostov-on-the-Don, March 7, 1890. He studied with Reinecke at the Leipzig Cons. and with L. Brassin in St. Petersburg. In 1879 he settled in Tiflis. In his works he often used authentic Caucasian motives while his harmonic treatment was modeled after Rimsky-Korsakov's Oriental pieces. His fantasia for piano on Caucasian themes, *Bayati,* presents a certain interest.

Kořínek, Miroslav, Slovak composer; b. Brno, Jan. 29, 1925. He studied composition with Alexander Moyzes at the Bratislava Cons.; in 1950 joined its staff as a lecturer in music.

WORKS: Concertino for Viola and Orch. (1951); Accordion Concerto (1956); *Divertimento Concertato* for string orch. (1962); Flute Concerto (1964); *Chamber Concerto* for clarinet and orch. (1966); Horn Concerto (1968); *Atlantide,* cantata (1972); 2 String Quartets (1951, 1963); Trio for 2 oboes and English horn (1961); Piano Quintet (1967); Wind Quintet (1970); *2 Capriccios* for trombone and piano (1973); *Concertante Fantasy* for flute and guitar (1974); *Apocryphas* for piano (1968); numerous instructive pieces for schools.

Korn, Clara Anna, German composer and teacher; b. Berlin, Jan. 30, 1866; d. New York, July 14, 1940. She was brought to America at an early age; studied with Horatio Parker and Bruno Oscar Klein; taught at the National Cons. in N.Y. (1893–98); afterwards, settled in Brooklyn as a private teacher. She wrote an opera, *Their Last War;* a symphony; a symph. poem *Morpheus;* an orchestral suite, *Rural Snapshots;* a piano concerto; violin concerto; piano pieces; songs.

Korn, Peter Jona, German-American composer; b. Berlin, March 30, 1922; left Germany as a child in 1933; studied in England (1934–36); lived in Jerusalem (1936–39); in 1941 emigrated to the U.S., settling in Los Angeles. His teachers in composition were Edmund Rubbra in London, Stefan Wolpe in Jerusalem, Hanns Eisler and Ernst Toch in Los Angeles; he also attended Schoenberg's classes at the Univ. of Calif., Los Angeles (1942) and studied the technique of composition for films with Ingolf Dahl and Miklós Rózsa. The resulting style ultimately adopted by Korn is that of pragmatic romanticism marked by polycentric tonality in the framework of strong rhythmic counterpoint. In 1965 he returned to Germany; in 1967 he was appointed director of the Richard Strauss Konservatorium in Munich.

WORKS: an opera *Heidi* (1961–63); 3 symphonies (1946, 1952, 1956); Variations on a tune from *Beggar's Opera,* for orch. (Louisville, Oct. 1, 1955); *Tom Paine Overture* (1950; Malmö, Sweden, Dec. 8, 1959, composer conducting; *In Medias Res,* symph. overture (1953); *Rhapsody* for oboe and strings (1952); Concertino for Horn and Double String Orch. (1952); Saxophone Concerto (1956); Cello Sonata (1949); Oboe Sonata (1949); Horn Sonata (1953); String Quartet No. 1 (1950); Serenade for 4 horns (1957); Passacaglia and Fugue for 8 horns (1952); String Quartet No. 2 (1963); *Quintettino* for flute, clarinet, bassoon, cello and piano (1964); Violin Concerto (1965); *Semi-Symphony* (1966), Wind Quintet (1966). He wrote a polemical book of essays *Musikalische Umwelt Verschmutzung* (Wiesbaden, 1975).

Kornauth, Egon, Austrian composer; b. Olmütz (Olomouc), May 14, 1891; d. Vienna, Oct. 28, 1959. He studied in Vienna with Fuchs, Schreker, and Schmidt; took a course in musicology with Guido Adler at the Univ. (Ph.D., 1915). In 1926 he was engaged to organize an orchestra in Medan, Sumatra; despite the difficulties of such an undertaking he maintained this orchestra for 2 seasons; later he toured through Java, Celebes, and Ceylon with the Vienna Trio, which he had founded. Kornauth's music is marked by considerable contrapuntal skill; his instrumental pieces and songs are mostly in a Romantic vein.

WORKS: 4 symph. suites (1913–39); Symph. Overture (1914; revised 1925); *Ballade* for orch., with cello obbligato (Vienna, Feb. 20, 1919); Nonet, for various instruments; String Sextet; String Quintet; Piano Quintet; Clarinet Quintet; String Quartet; Piano Quartet; Piano Trio; Violin Sonata, Viola Sonata, Cello Sonata, Clarinet Sonata; various choral works and several song cycles.

BIBLIOGRAPHY: E. H. Müller von Asow, *Egon Kornauth* (Vienna, 1941; includes a complete list of works).

Körner, Christian Gottfried, German music theorist; b. Leipzig, July 2, 1756; d. Berlin, May 13, 1831. He was the father of Theodor Körner, the poet. He publ. an essay "Über den Charakter der Töne oder über Charakterdarstellung in der Musik," in the *Horen* (1775); also composed songs, etc.

BIBLIOGRAPHY: W. Seifert, *C. G. Körner: ein Musikästhetiker der deutschen Klassik* (Regensburg, 1960).

Körner, Gotthilf Wilhelm, German music publisher; b. Teicha, near Halle, June 3, 1809; d. Erfurt, Jan. 3, 1865. He founded his music-publishing firm in 1838 and publ. many organ works; in 1886 the company merged with C. F. Peters.

Kornerup, Thorwald Otto, Danish writer on musical subjects; b. Copenhagen, March 11, 1864; d. there, Dec. 20, 1938. His publications, which deal mostly with the problems of acoustics and various special tone systems, include *The 19-Tone and 31-Tone Precursors of the Well-Tempered Systems; The Acoustical Theory of Atonality; From the Original Prototype of the 5-Tone Scales to the Golden Tones of Electrical Musical Instruments; The Indian Tone System with its 22 Srutis* (all in Danish).

Korngold, Erich Wolfgang, Austrian composer of remarkable and precocious gifts; b. Brno, May 29, 1897; d. Hollywood, California, Nov. 29, 1957. He received his earliest musical education from his father, **Julius Korngold;** he then studied with Fuchs, Zemlinsky, and Grädener in Vienna. His progress was astounding; at the age of 12 he composed a piano trio, which was soon published, revealing a competent technique and an ability to write in a modern style (strongly influenced by Richard Strauss). About the same time he wrote (in piano score) a pantomime, *Der Schneemann;* it was orchestrated by his teacher, Zemlinsky, and performed at the Vienna Court Opera (Oct. 4, 1910), creating a sensation. In 1911 Nikisch played his *Schauspiel-Ouvertüre* in a Gewandhaus concert at Leipzig; in the same year the youthful composer gave a concert of his works in Berlin, appearing also as a pianist; his Sinfonietta was given by Felix Weingartner and the Vienna Philharmonic in 1913. Korngold was not quite 19 when his two short operas, *Der Ring des Polykrates* and *Violanta,* were produced in Munich. His first lasting success came with the opera, *Die tote Stadt,* produced first in Hamburg (1920), and then on many opera stages all over the world. In 1929 he entered a fruitful collaboration with the famous director, Max Reinhardt; in 1934 he went to Hollywood to arrange Mendelssohn's music for the Reinhardt film production of *A Midsummer Night's Dream.* He was intermittently in Europe, taught at the music academy in Vienna (1930–34) before settling in Hollywood; composed a number of film scores; conducted light opera with the N.Y. Opera Co. in 1942 and 1944. He became an American citizen in 1943; after 1945 he divided his time between the U.S. and Europe; lived for some time in Vienna.

Korngold's music represents the last breath of the romantic spirit of Vienna; it is marvelously consistent with the melodic, rhythmic, and harmonic style of the judicious modernity of the nascent 20th century. When Mahler heard him play some of his music as a young boy he kept repeating: "Ein Genie! Ein Genie!" Korngold never altered his established idiom of composition, and was never tempted to borrow modernistic devices, except for some transitory passages in major seconds or an occasional whole-tone scale. After the early outbursts of incautious enthusiasms on the part of some otherwise circumspect critics nominating Korngold as a new Mozart, his star, his erupting nova, began to sink rapidly, until it became a melancholy consensus to dismiss his operas at their tardy revivals as derivative products of an era that had itself little to exhibit that was worthwhile. Ironically, his film scores, in the form of orchestrated suites, experienced long after his death a spontaneous renascence, particularly on records, and especially among the unprejudiced and unopinionated American musical youth who found in Korngold's music the stuff of their own new dreams.

WORKS: OPERAS: *Der Ring des Polykrates* and *Violanta* (Munich, March 28, 1916); *Die tote Stadt* (Hamburg, Dec. 4, 1920); Metropolitan Opera, N.Y., Nov. 19, 1921); *Das Wunder der Heliane* (Hamburg, Oct. 7, 1927); *Kathrin* (Stockholm, Oct. 7, 1939); *Die stumme Serenade* (Dortmund, Dec. 5, 1954); pantomime, *Der Schneemann* (Vienna, Oct. 4, 1910); FOR ORCH: *Schauspiel-Ouvertüre* (Leipzig, 1911); Sinfonietta (Vienna, Nov. 28, 1913); Suite from the music to Shakespeare's *Much Ado About Nothing,* for chamber orch. (Vienna, 1919); *Sursum Corda,* symph. overture (1919); Piano Concerto for the Left Hand Alone (1923; written for Paul Wittgenstein); Cello Concerto (1946); Violin Concerto (Jascha Heifetz with the St. Louis Symph. Orch., Feb. 15, 1947); *Symphonic Serenade* for string orch. (1949); Symph. in F-sharp (1950; first public performance, Munich, Nov. 27, 1972); *Theme and Variations* for orch. (1953); CHAMBER MUSIC: Piano Trio (1910); Violin Sonata; String Sextet; Piano Quintet; 3 string quartets (1922, 1935, 1945); 3 piano sonatas (1908, 1910, 1932).

BIBLIOGRAPHY: R. S. Hoffmann, *Erich Wolfgang Korngold* (Vienna, 1923); L. Korngold, *Erich Wolfgang Korngold. Ein Lebensbild* (Vienna, 1967).

Korngold, Julius, noted Austrian music critic; b. Brno, Dec. 24, 1860; d. Hollywood, Sept. 25, 1945. He was a law student; at the same time he studied music with Franz Krenn at the Vienna Cons. In 1902 he became music critic of the influential *Neue Freie Presse.* He was much in the limelight when his son **Erich** began his spectacular career at the age of 13 as child composer, and an unfounded suspicion was voiced that Korngold was using his position to further his son's career. He published a book on a contemporary German opera, *Deutsches Opernschaffen der Gegenwart* (1922). In 1938 he joined his son in the U.S., settling in Hollywood, where he remained until his death.

Kornmüller, Utto, German writer on church music; b. Straubing, Jan. 5, 1824; d. Metten, Feb. 13, 1907. He was ordained to the priesthood in 1847; became choirmaster of the Benedictine monastery at Metten (1858); also president of the Regensburg branch of the Cäcilienverein until 1903. He publ. a *Lexikon der kirchlichen Tonkunst* (1870); *Der katholische Kirchenchor* (1868); *Die Musik beim liturgischen Hochamt* (1871); contributed articles to the *Kirchenmusikalisches Jahrbuch* and *Monatshefte für Musikgeschichte;* also wrote a number of Masses and motets.

Korte, Oldřich František, Czech composer; b. Šala-on-Váh, April 26, 1926. He studied with Picha at the Prague Cons. (1943–49); then toured as a pianist and an actor with the modernistic group "Laterna Magica" and also worked as a photographer. His music is similarly quaquaversal and quite uninhibited in its methods and resources.

WORKS: *Iniuria* for piano (1942–44); *The Drinker's Transformations,* variations for piano (1945); Sinfonietta (1945–47); *In Praise of Death* for piccolo and glockenspiel (1948); *Příběh fléten (The Story of the Flutes)* for orch. (1949–51; Prague Radio, Oct. 23, 1953); Concerto Grosso for strings, trumpets and piano (1954–62; revised 1968); *Philosophical Dialogues* for violin and piano (1964–68); a 2-act musical, *The Pirates of the Fortune* (Vienna, April 15, 1974).

Korte, Werner, German musicologist; b. Münster, May 29, 1906; studied there, in Freiburg and Berlin (with Johannes Wolf); received his Dr. phil. degree with the dissertation, *Die Harmonik des frühen 15. Jahrhunderts in ihrem Zusammenhang mit der Formtechnik* (publ. 1929); was assistant in musicology at the Univ. of Heidelberg (1928–31); from 1932 at the Univ. of Münster. He publ. *Studie zur Geschichte der Musik in Italien im ersten Viertel des 15. Jahrhunderts* (1933); *J. S. Bach* (1934); *Beethoven* (1936); *Schumann* (1937); *Musik und Weltbild* (1940); *Händel und der deutsche Geist* (1942); *Bruckner und Brahms* (Tutzing, 1963).

Kortschak, Hugo, Austrian violinist and conductor; b. Graz, Feb. 24, 1884; d. Honolulu, Hawaii, Sept. 20, 1957. He studied violin with Ševčik at the Prague Cons.; went to America and organized the Kortschak Quartet in Chicago (1913), later renamed Berkshire String Quartet. He helped in organizing the Coolidge Chamber Music Festival at Pittsfield, Mass. in 1918, and in 1938 received the Coolidge Medal for "distinguished services to chamber music."

Kortsen, Bjarne, Norwegian musicologist; b. Hauge-sund, July 4, 1930. He studied music and electrical engineering; was employed by the Norwegian rail-ways for 3 years while studying musicology at the Univ. of Oslo (M.A., 1962); later studied at the Univ. of Glasgow (Ph.D., 1964), at the Univ. of Cologne, and at the Musik-Hochschule in Berlin. He publ. a number of valuable books in Norwegian, German and English: *Fartein Valen, Life and Music* (3 vols.; Oslo, 1965); *Modern Norwegian Chamber Music* (Haugesund, 1965); *Contemporary Norwegian Orchestral Music* (West Berlin, 1969); *Chamber Music Works by Johan Svendsen* (Bergen, 1971).

Kósa, György, Hungarian composer and pianist; b. Budapest, April 24, 1897. He exhibited a precocious talent for music, and when he was 7 years old Béla Bartók accepted him as a piano student. At 13 he en-tered the Budapest Academy of Music where he stud-ied with Kodály, Siklós and Victor Herzfeld; he con-tinued his piano studies in the class of Dohnányi and received his diploma in 1917. He then traveled as an accompanist with violinists and other artists in Ger-many, Austria and Italy; returned to Budapest in 1921 and in 1927 became prof. of piano at the Budapest Academy of Music. He remained in Budapest during World War II and was compelled to serve as a manual laborer in a war camp; after 1945 he resumed his teaching at the Academy where he stayed until retire-ment in 1962. The primary influence in his music is that of Bartók, but he also experienced the attraction of Impressionist techniques.
WORKS: 7 operas: *The King's Robe* (1926–27); *The Two Knights,* opera buffa (1934; Budapest, 1936); *Ce-nodoxus,* mystery opera (1941–42); *The Scholar An-selmus* (1944–45); *Tartuffe* (1950); *Knight Pázmány* (1962–63); *The Wedding of Mihály Kocsonya,* opera buffa (1971); 7 biblical oratorios; 6 secular oratorios, including *Villon* (1960–61) and *Manole* (1965); 3 bibli-cal cantatas; 6 secular cantatas, including *Orpheus, Eurydike, Hermes* (1967), *Cantata humana* (1967) and *Susanna* (1971); 3 Masses (1946, 1949, 1951); 2 Requi-ems (1944, 1966); ballets and pantomimes, including *White Pierrot* (Budapest, 1920), *Laterna Magica* (with voices, 1922; Budapest, Feb. 23, 1927), *The Three Mir-acles of Joe the Orphan* (1932; Budapest, Feb. 26, 1933), *King David,* biblical ballet, (1936), *Burlesque* (1947) and *Song About the Eternal Sorrow* (1955). For orch.: *6 Pieces* (1919); 9 symphonies (1921; 1927; for chamber orch., 1933; 1934; for chamber orch., 1937; 1946; *Mohács,* 1957; 1959; 1969); *Fairy Tale Suite* (1931); *Fantasy on 3 Hungarian Folksongs* (1948); *Ballad and Rondo* for violin and wind orch. (1961). Chamber music: 8 string quartets (1920, 1929, 1933, 1937, 1956, 1959–60, 1963, 1965); Duet for violin and double bass (1928); *Music for 17 instruments* (1928); Quintet for Harp and Winds (1938); Trio for flute, vio-lin and cello (1941); Trio for 2 violins and viola (1946); Trio for wordless soprano, violin and clarinet (1947); 2 wind quintets (1955, 1960); *Cello Cantata* for cello, organ, piano and percussion (1963); Duet for violin and cello (1964). He also wrote 3 piano sonatas (1941, 1947, 1956); Solo Cello Sonata (1928); Variations for piano (1933); Violin Sonata (1937); *Gaby Sonata* for violin and piano (1958); *Concerto Patetico* for violin

and piano (1960); *Elegy* for solo violin (1964); Cello Sonata (1965); many songs, often with string quartet and other ensemble accompaniment; choruses.

Kosakoff, Reuven, American pianist and composer; b. New Haven, Conn., Jan. 8, 1898. He studied at Yale Univ. and at Juilliard School of Music in N.Y.; then went to Berlin as a private piano student of Artur Schnabel. He has written several biblical cantatas; 2 Sabbath services; a piano concerto on Hebrew themes (Pittsburgh, March 24, 1941); *Jack and the Beanstalk* for narrator and orch. (New Haven, April 22, 1944).

Koschat, Thomas, Austrian bass singer and com-poser; b. Viktring, near Klagenfurt, Aug. 8, 1845; d. Vienna, May 19, 1914. He sang in chorus at various churches; then turned to composition; publ. his first vocal quartets in the Carinthian dialect in 1871; they became so successful that he publ. some 100 more. In 1875 he organized the famous Kärnthner Quintett with 4 other singers; their performances were exceed-ingly popular. His "Liederspiel" *Am Wörthersee* (Vi-enna, March 22, 1880), containing many of his favor-ite vocal numbers, had great vogue; he also produced a 4-act "Volksstück mit Gesang," *Die Rosenthaler Nachtigall,* and the "Singspiel" *Der Bürgermeister von St. Anna* (Vienna, May 1, 1884; given in Italian as *Un Colpo di fuoco).*
BIBLIOGRAPHY: Karl Krobath, *Thomas Koschat, der Sänger Kärnthners* (Leipzig, 1912).

Köselitz, Heinrich (pen name **Peter Gast**), German writer and composer; b. Annaberg, Jan. 10, 1854; d. there, Aug. 15, 1918. He studied with Richter at the Leipzig Cons. While in Basel, he formed an intimate friendship with Nietzsche, from whom he also took lessons in composition; after Nietzsche's death, he be-came his literary executor; edited Nietzsche's letters. As composer he elaborated the Wagnerian system of *Leitmotive;* he used the pen name of Peter Gast for his musical productions, among them the operas *Wil-bram und Siegeheer* (1879), *Scherz, List und Rache* (1881), *Die heimliche Ehe* (Danzig, 1891; publ. in 1901 as *Der Löwe von Venedig);* *König Wenzel* (not pro-duced), and *Orpheus und Dionysos* (not produced); a festival play, *Walpurgisnacht* (1903); a symph. poem, *Helle Nächte;* choruses; songs.
BIBLIOGRAPHY: L. Brieger-Wasservogel, *Peter Gast* (Leipzig, 1906); F. Götz, *Peter Gast* (Annaberg, 1934); F. Tutenberg, "Peters Gasts Löwe von Vene-dig," *Zeitschrift für Musik* (Feb. 1940).

Koshetz, Nina, Russian soprano; b. Kiev, Dec. 30, 1894; d. Santa Ana, Calif., May 14, 1965. She studied piano as a child; then began to study singing. She toured Russia with Rachmaninoff, of whose songs she was a congenial interpreter. After the revolution she went to the U.S.; appeared as soloist with major American orchestras and also sang recitals of Russian songs. In 1941 she went to California and devoted her-self to teaching.

Kosleck, Julius, German trumpet and cornet virtu-oso; b. Neugard, Dec. 3, 1825; d. Berlin, Nov. 5, 1904. He was a trumpeter in the court orch. in Berlin; in 1871 he founded the Kaiser Cornett Quartett; also a wind band, Patriotischer Bläserbund; from 1873 taught at the Hochschule für Musik in Berlin. He was influential in reviving the historic art of the fanfare; publ. a method for the trumpet and cornet à pistons. In 1884 he introduced a trumpet with a broad, funnel-shaped mouthpiece, which was regarded as a "Bach trumpet," capable of playing high florid parts.

Kosma, Joseph, Hungarian-French composer; b. Budapest, Oct. 22, 1905; d. La Roche-Guyon, near Paris, Aug. 7, 1969. He studied at the Music Academy there. In 1933 he went to Paris and settled there as a composer of ballet and film music.

WORKS: ballets, *Le Rendez-vous* (Paris, June 15, 1945), *Baptiste* (1946), *L'Ecuyère* (1948); *Le Pierrot de Montmartre* (1952); film scores to *La Grande Illusion, Les Enfants du paradis;* etc.; comic operas, *Les Chansons de Bilitis* (1954); *Un amour électronique* (Paris, 1962); *La Révolte des canuts* (Lyons, 1964); *Les Hussards* (Lyons, Oct. 21, 1969). He also wrote an oratorio, *Les Ponts de Paris* (1947), a number of characteristic piano pieces (*Danse des automates,* etc.), and songs.

Kössler, Hans. See **Koessler, Hans.**

Kossmaly, Carl, German writer on music and conductor; b. Breslau, July 27, 1812; d. Stettin, Dec. 1, 1893. He studied in Berlin with Berger, Zelter, and Klein; then was chorusmaster at theaters in Wiesbaden, Mainz, Amsterdam, Bremen, Detmold, and Stettin, where he settled as teacher and concert conductor. He publ. *Schlesisches Tonkünstler-Lexikon* (1846–47); *Mozarts Opern* (1848); *Über die Anwendung des Programmes zur Erklärung musikalischer Compositionen* (1858); *Über Richard Wagner* (1873, anti-Wagnerian); contributed articles to music periodicals; also wrote symphonies, overtures, instrumental and vocal works, songs, etc.

Kostelanetz, André, Russian-American conductor; b. St. Petersburg, Dec. 22, 1901. He studied at the St. Petersburg Cons. In 1922 he left Russia and went to America. He was employed as a rehearsal accompanist at the Metropolitan Opera, N.Y.; in 1930 was engaged to conduct the CBS Symph. Orch. On June 2, 1938, he married the famous soprano **Lily Pons;** they were divorced some years later. During World War II he organized concerts for the U.S. Armed Forces; subsequently conducted numerous popular concerts in America and in Europe, particularly summer concerts. He also made successful arrangements of light music; his technique of massive concentration of instrumental sonorities and of harmonic saturation by means of filling in harmonies with inner thirds and sixths influenced film music. An intelligent musician, he commissioned special works from American composers, of which the most successful was Copland's *Lincoln Portrait.*

Kostić, Dušan, Croatian composer; b. Zagreb, Jan. 23, 1925. He studied at the Music Academy in Belgrade; later took a course in conducting with Scherchen. He incorporated neo-classical, impressionistic and serial techniques in his music; also wrote occasional pieces on national folk themes.

WORKS: 2 symphonies (1957, 1961); symph. poem *Contrasts* (1954); *Crnogorska suita* for orch. (1957); *Sonata amorosa* for violin and piano (1957); opera buffa, *Majstori su prvi ljudi* (Belgrade, April 23, 1962); *Kragujevac,* symph. poem for voices and orch., commemorating the execution of the schoolboys at Kragujevac in 1941 by the Nazi occupation forces (Belgrade, Feb. 5, 1962); choruses; songs; piano pieces.

Kostić, Vojislav, Serbian composer; b. Belgrade, Sept. 21, 1931. He studied in his native city; adopted a sophisticated style of utilitarian music. His *Karakteri* for clarinet, piano and 18 percussion instruments (1958) had numerous performances in Yugoslavia. He also wrote a Divertimento for Wind Quintet; Suite for Bassoon and Piano; and *Ciganska priča (Gypsy Tale)* for male chorus and chamber orch., to Gypsy texts (1964).

Köstlin, Heinrich Adolf, theologian and organizer of church festivals; b. Tübingen, Oct. 4, 1846; d. Cannstadt, June 4, 1907. He was the son of **Josephine Lang-Köstlin,** the song composer (1815–1880). In 1875 he united the choirs of 3 towns (Sulz, Kalw, Nagold) for church music performances, which became the nucleus of the Württemberg Evangelical "Kirchengesangverein," organized by him in 1877, the festivals of which he also conducted. In 1883, he organized, with L. Hallwachs, a similar society for all Germany, with annual meetings in different cities; this led to the establishment of more choral branches for sacred music (more than 2,000 choirs in 1916). Köstlin publ. *Geschichte der Musik im Umriss* (1873; 6th ed., revised by W. Nagel, 1910); *Die Tonkunst: Einführung in die Ästhetik der Musik* (1878); *Luther als Vater des evangelischen Kirchenliedes* (1882); *Geschichte des christlichen Gottesdienstes* (1886); also a biographical sketch of his mother (Leipzig, 1881).

Köstlin, Karl Reinhold, German music theorist; b. Urach, Sept. 28, 1819; d. Tübingen, April 12, 1894. He taught esthetics and art history at Tübingen Univ. He publ. *Ästhetik* (2 vols., 1863–69); an essay on musical esthetics in Vischer's *Ästhetik* (vol. 3); and a pamphlet on Wagner.

Kostov, Georgi, Bulgarian composer; b. Sofia, Jan. 21, 1941. He studied composition with Pantcho Vladigerov and Peter Stoyanov at the Bulgarian State Cons., graduating in 1966; pursued his studies at the Moscow Cons. (1972); returning to Bulgaria he became an instructor at his alma mater.

WORKS: a ballet *The Broadside of "Avrora"* (1967); 2 oratorios: *Glorious Days* (1969) and *Alive He Is* (1976); 2 cantatas: *The Communist Man* (1964) and *We Are Proud of You, Our Party* (1975); Clarinet Concerto (1958); Viola Concertino (1965); Concerto for Horn, String Orch. and Timpani (1966); *Youth Overture* (1967); *3 Diaphonous Dances* for orch. (1972); *Poem* for trumpet, percussion and string orch. (1973); *Prelude, Chorale and Fugue* for orch. (1974); *Rhythmic Movements* for orch. (1974); *Antiphonous Dialogues* for orch. (1974); *September Ballad* for orch. (1974); chamber music; choral songs; popular music.

Kotek, Joseph, Russian violinist; b. Kamenetz-Podolsk, Oct. 25, 1855; d. Davos, Switzerland, Jan. 4, 1885. He studied violin with Ferdinand Laub and composition with Tchaikovsky at the Moscow Cons.; later took violin lessons with Joachim in Berlin. He was an intimate friend of Tchaikovsky, and often served as mediator in financial matters between him and Nadezhda von Meck; also worked over the solo part of Tchaikovsky's violin concerto, and played it with the composer at the piano, privately, at Clarens, Switzerland (April 3, 1878); however, he was reluctant to try it out in public performance despite Tchaikovsky's urgings. From 1878–82 he taught violin at the Hochschule für Musik in Berlin. He died of tuberculosis at the age of 29; Tchaikovsky made a special trip to Davos to see him before his death.

Kothe, Aloys, German music teacher; brother of **Bernhard** and **Wilhelm Kothe;** b. Gröbnig, Oct. 3, 1828; d. Breslau, Nov. 13, 1868. He studied with Grell in Berlin; taught at the Teachers' Seminary in Breslau. He publ. a Mass for men's voices; piano pieces, songs, etc.

Kothe, Bernhard, German writer on music; brother of **Aloys** and **Wilhelm Kothe;** b. Gröbnig, May 12, 1821; d. Breslau, July 25, 1897. He studied in Berlin with A. B. Marx; in 1851, became church music director and teacher at Oppeln; then succeeded his brother Aloys Kothe as music teacher at the Teachers' Seminary in Breslau, where he founded the Cäcilien-Verein for Catholic church music. He publ. *Musica Sacra;* 2 pamphlets, *Die Musik in der katholischen Kirche* (1862) and *Abriss der Musikgeschichte für Lehrerseminare und Dilettanten* (1874); also edited the 4th ed. of Seidel's *Die Orgel und ihr Bau* (1887); and, with Forchhammer, a *Führer durch die Orgellitteratur* (1890). He also publ. a book of organ preludes; other organ pieces; motets.

Kothe, Robert, German singer and folksong arranger; b. Straubing, Feb. 6, 1869; d. Gräfelfing, near Munich, May 24, 1944. He appeared as a singer, accompanying himself on the lute; established a school for lutenists in Gelsenkirchen; publ. 12 albums of folksong arrangements; also a method of lute playing (1929).
BIBLIOGRAPHY: Fritz Jöde, *Robert Kothe* (1916).

Kothe, Wilhelm, German music teacher; brother of **Aloys** and **Bernhard Kothe;** b. Gröbnig, Jan. 8, 1831; d. Habelschwerdt, Dec. 31, 1897. He studied organ in Berlin; from 1871 until his death he was music teacher at the Teachers' Seminary in Habelschwerdt. He publ. a pamphlet on *Friedrich der Grosse als Musiker;* also methods for violin and voice, songs, and piano music.

Kothen, Karl Axel, Finnish singer and composer; b. Frederikshamm, Aug. 15, 1871; d. Helsinki, July 7, 1927. He studied in Helsinki, Rome, St. Petersburg, Vienna, Paris, and Munich; returning to Helsinki in 1908, became prof. of singing at the Helsinki Cons. He wrote several choral works, among them *Vagorna sjunga* and *Finlands namm* (both for the Finland Jubilee of 1920); also a cantata for the festival of the tercentenary of Vasa; incidental music to *Kristina Vasa;* piano pieces and songs.

Kotík, Petr, Czech flutist and composer; b. Prague, Jan. 27, 1942. He studied in Prague and later at the Vienna Music Academy with Schiske and Jelinek; in 1966 formed there an experimental music ensemble Quax. His works tend to embrace all manners of contemporary techniques; among them are *Spontano* for piano and 10 wind instruments (1964); *Contrabandt* for several players and electronic music (1967); *6 Švestek (6 Plums)* for 24 instruments (1968).

Kotilainen, Otto, Finnish composer; b. Heinävesi, Feb. 5, 1868; d. Helsinki, Aug. 9, 1936. He studied with Wegelius and Sibelius at the Helsingfors Cons., and in Berlin. He wrote a cantata, *Cygneus; Festsang* for chorus and horns; Orchestral Suite; *Legend* for string orch.; incidental music for plays; pieces for violin and piano; choruses; songs.

Kotoński, Włodzimierz, Polish composer of the avant-garde; b. Warsaw, Aug. 23, 1925. He studied theory with Piotr Rytel at the Warsaw Cons. (1945–51) and also took private lessons with Tadeusz Szeligowski in Poznań. He became a research worker in Polish folk music at the State Institute of Art, and simultaneously began experimenting with alteration of sound by electronic means; at an early date produced an *Étude concrète* in which a single stroke of cymbals was electronically metamorphosed and expanded into a work of considerable length (1949). In 1959–60 he attended the summer sessions of new music at Darmstadt; then went to Paris, where he researched the problems of musique concrète with Pierre Schaeffer; in 1966–67 he worked at the Electronic Music Studio of the West German Radio in Cologne.
WORKS: *Poème* for orch. (1949); *Quartettino* for 4 horns (1950); *Danses montagnardes* for orch. (1950); *Prelude and Passacaglia* for orch. (1953); *6 Miniatures* for clarinet and piano (1957); *Chamber Music* for 21 instruments and percussion (1958; Warsaw Fest., Oct. 2, 1958); *Musique en rélief,* cycle of 5 miniatures for 6 orch. groups (1959; Darmstadt, Sept. 5, 1959); *Étude concrète* for a single stroke of cymbals electronically metamorphosed (1960; Darmstadt, July 9, 1960); Trio for flute, guitar and percussion (1960); *Concerto per quattro* for harp, harpsichord, guitar, piano and chamber orch. (1960); *Canto* for 18 instruments (1961); *Selection I* for 4 jazz players (1962); *Pezzo* for flute and piano (1962); *Musica per fiati e timpani* (1964); 2 wind quintets (1964, 1967); *Monochromie* for solo oboe (1964); *a battere* for guitar, viola, cello, harpsichord and percussion (1966); *Pour quatre* for clarinet, trombone, cello and piano (1968); *Action* for electronic sound (Cracow, June 5, 1969); *Music for 16 cymbals and strings* (1969; Warsaw, Sept. 20, 1969); *Multiplay,* an instrumental theater for brass quintet (1971); *Musical Games,* an instrumental theater for 5 players (1972); Oboe Concerto (1972); *Aeolian Harp* for soprano and 4 instruments (1972–73); *Promenade* for clarinet, trombone, cello (all electronically amplified) and 2 synthesizers (1973); *Wind Rose* for orch. (1976). He publ. a book, *Instrumenty perkusyjne we współczesnej orkiestrze* (*Percussion Instruments in the Modern Orchestra,* Cracow, 1963).

Kotter, Hans, Alsatian organist and composer; b. Strasbourg, c.1480; d. Bern, 1541. He was a disciple of Paul Hofhaimer; served as organist at Freiburg, Switzerland (1504–22) until he was banished for espousing the doctrines of the reformer Zwingli. In 1532 Kotter was able to return to Switzerland, and he took up residence in Bern as a schoolmaster. He compiled a collection of keyboard pieces in tablature (1513), including preambles, fantasies, dances, transcriptions of vocal music, and settings of plainchant. There is also in existence a setting of a *Nobis post hoc* by Kotter interpolated in a *Salve Regina* by Hofhaimer.
BIBLIOGRAPHY: W. Merian, *Die Tabulaturen des Organisten Hans Kotter* (Leipzig, 1916); W. Apel, "Early German Keyboard Music," *Musical Quarterly* (April 1937); G. Reese, *Music in the Renaissance* (N.Y., 1954).

Kottlitz, Adolf, German violinist; b. Trier, Sept. 27, 1820; killed while hunting in Uralsk, Russia, Oct. 26, 1860. He began his career as a child prodigy; gave public concerts at the age of 10; spent 3 years in Paris, where he was a protégé of Liszt; then played violin in the orch. of the Königsberg Opera (1848–56). In 1856 he undertook a long tour in Russia, and finally settled in Uralsk as violin teacher. He publ. 2 string quartets. His wife **Clothilde,** *née* **Ellendt** (1822–67), was a singing teacher in Königsberg.

Kotzeluch, Leopold Anton. See **Koželuch, Leopold Anton.**

Kotzolt, Heinrich, German vocal teacher; b. Schnellewalde, Aug. 26, 1814; d. Berlin, July 2, 1881. He first studied philology in Breslau, but turned to music, studying in Berlin with Dehn and Rungenhagen (1836–38); then sang at the Danzig Opera (1838–42). Returning to Berlin, he founded a singing society there in 1849. He publ. a method for a cappella singing; also the 54th Psalm, for double chorus a cappella; *Lobet den Herrn, alle Heiden,* for 8-part chorus; etc.

Kotzschmar, Hermann, organist; b. Finsterwalde, Germany, July 4, 1829; d. Portland, Maine, April 12, 1909. As a child, he learned to play the organ and virtually all the orchestral instruments; then studied seriously in Dresden. In 1848 he came to America with the Saxonia Band and settled in Portland, Maine, as teacher; was for 47 years organist at the First Unitarian Church there. He publ. many vocal quartets, songs, and piano pieces. His *Te Deum* in F was often sung in American churches. He was also esteemed as a teacher; **J. K. Paine** was his pupil.
BIBLIOGRAPHY: G. T. Edwards, *Music and Musicians of Maine* (Portland, 1928; pp. 167–69).

Kotzwara (*recte* **Kočvara**), **Franz,** Bohemian composer; b. Prague, 1730; d. London (by hanging himself), Sept. 2, 1791. He traveled in Europe; then settled in London towards the end of the 18th century. In 1790 he went to Dublin as a viola player in the orchestra at the King's Theatre; returning to London the same year, he played in the orchestra at the Handel Commemoration in May. He is remembered solely for his piano piece, *The Battle of Prague,* which attained tremendous popularity in the 19th century.

Kouguell, Arkadie, Russian-American pianist and composer; b. Simferopol, Dec. 25, 1898. He studied at the St. Petersburg Cons. From 1928 to 1948 he lived in Beirut; then in Paris. In 1952 he settled in New York as piano teacher.
WORKS: *Impressions of Damascus* for orch. (1930); *Rapsodi tartare* for orch. (1947); Piano Concerto (1930); Piano Concerto for Left Hand (1934); Cello Concerto (1950); Concertino for Trombone and Piano (1956); *Bédouin Dance* for an ensemble of 60 cellos (1932); 2 string quartets; 3 piano sonatas; Violin Sonata; 2 cello sonatas; suites for various chamber groups.

Kounadis, Arghyris, Greek composer; b. Constantinople, Feb. 14, 1924; moved to Athens in his infancy; studied piano at home and jurisprudence at the Univ. of Athens; at the same time began to compose. In 1958 he went to Freiburg, Germany, where he studied composition with Wolfgang Fortner; became interested in the theater; wrote incidental music for Greek plays produced at Epidaurus (1958, 1960, 1961). In his instrumental works he follows the dodecaphonic technique. Of these, his *Chorikon* for orchestra was performed by the Berlin Philharmonic on May 15, 1962. This was followed by other symph. works in the same manner, *Triptychon* (1964) and *Heterophonika Idiomela* (1967).

Kountz, Richard, American composer; b. Pittsburgh, July 8, 1896; d. New York, Oct. 14, 1950. From 1927–39 he was manager of the Standard and Educational Publications dept. of M. Witmark & Sons in N.Y. He wrote *The Sleigh* and other songs; a *Pastorale* for organ, etc.; also made arrangements for various choral combinations.

Koussevitzky, Serge, celebrated Russian conductor; b. Vishny-Volochok, July 26, 1874; d. Boston, June 4, 1951. His father and his three brothers were all amateur musicians. Koussevitzky learned to play the trumpet and took part, with his brothers, in a small wind ensemble, numbering eight members in all; they earned their living by playing at balls and weddings and occasionally at village fairs. At the age of 14 he went to Moscow; since Jews were not allowed to live there, he became baptized. He then received a fellowship with free tuition at the Musico-Dramatic Institute of the Moscow Philharmonic, in the class of the double bass; his teacher was the famous double-bass player Rambousek; he also studied music theory with Blaramberg and Kruglikov. In 1894 he joined the orchestra of the Bolshoi Opera Theater, where his teacher Rambousek held the first chair in the double-bass section. Upon Rambousek's death in 1901, Koussevitzky succeeded him at his post. However, in 1905 he decided to leave the Bolshoi Theater, and in an open letter to the Russian publication *Musical Gazette,* explained the reason for his resignation as the economic and artistic difficulties in the orchestra. In the meantime Koussevitzky had already become known as a soloist on the double bass of the first magnitude who was able to achieve high artistic performance on this supposedly unwieldy instrument. On March 25, 1901 he gave his first public concert in

Moscow in a program which included an adaptation of Handel's Cello Concerto; on subsequent occasions he performed his own arrangement for double bass of Mozart's Bassoon Concerto and of Bruch's *Kol Nidrei.* On March 27, 1903 he gave a double-bass recital in Berlin, attracting great attention. To supplement the meager repertory, he wrote several pieces for the double bass and performed them at his concerts; with some aid from Glière, he composed a double-bass concerto, which he performed for the first time in Moscow on Feb. 25, 1905. On Sept. 8, 1905, he married Natalie Ushkov, of a wealthy tea-merchant family. He soon resigned from the orchestra of the Bolshoi Opera Theater and went to Germany, where he continued to give double-bass recitals; played the 1st Cello Concerto by Saint-Saëns on the double bass. In 1907 he conducted a student orchestra at the Berlin Hochschule für Musik; his first public appearance as conductor took place on Jan. 23, 1908 with the Berlin Philharmonic. In 1909 he established a publishing house, Editions Russes de Musique; in 1915 he purchased the catalogue of the Gutheil Co.; among composers with whom he signed contracts were Scriabin, Stravinsky, Prokofiev, Medtner, and Rachmaninoff; the association with Scriabin was particularly fruitful, and in subsequent years Koussevitzky became the greatest champion of Scriabin's music. In 1909 he organized his own symph. orch. in Moscow, featuring works by Russian composers, but also including classical masterpieces; played many Russian works for the first time, among them Scriabin's *Prometheus.* In the summer of 1910 he took his orch. to the towns along the Volga River in a specially chartered steamboat. He repeated the Volga tour in 1912 and 1914. The outbreak of World War I made it necessary to curtail his activities; however, he continued to give his concerts in Moscow; in 1915 he presented a memorial Scriabin program. After the Revolution of 1917, Koussevitzky was offered the directorship of the State Symph. Orch. (former Court Orch.); in Petrograd he conducted it until 1920; also presented concerts in Moscow despite the hardships of the revolutionary times. In 1920 he left Russia; went first to Berlin, then to Rome, and finally to Paris, where he settled for several years. There he organized the Concerts Koussevitzky with a specially assembled orchestra; presented many new scores by French and Russian composers, among them Ravel's orchestration of Mussorgsky's *Pictures at an Exhibition,* Honegger's *Pacific 231,* and several works by Prokofiev and Stravinsky. In 1924 Koussevitzky was engaged as permanent conductor of the Boston Symph. Orch., a post that he was to hold for 25 years, the longest tenure of any conductor of that organization; until 1928 he continued his Paris series (during the summer months). Just as in Russia he championed Russian composers, in France the French, so in the U.S. he encouraged American composers to write works for the Boston Symph. Orch. Symphonic compositions by Aaron Copland, Roy Harris, Walter Piston, Samuel Barber, Howard Hanson, Edward Burlingame Hill, William Schuman, and others were performed by Koussevitzky for the first time. For the 50th anniversary of the Boston Symph. Orch. (1931) Koussevitzky commissioned works from Stravinsky *(Symphony of Psalms),*

Hindemith, Honegger, Prokofiev, Albert Roussel, Ravel (piano concerto), Copland, Gershwin, etc. In 1950 he conducted in Rio de Janeiro, Israel, and in Europe; also was guest conductor at several concerts of the Boston Symph. after his successor, Charles Munch, became principal conductor. A highly important development in Koussevitzky's American career was the establishment of the Berkshire Music Center at Tanglewood, Mass. This was an outgrowth of the Berkshire Symph. Festival, organized in 1934 by Henry Hadley; Koussevitzky and the Boston Symph. Orch. presented summer concerts at the Berkshire Festival in 1935 for the first time; since then, the concerts have become an annual institution. The Berkshire Music Center was opened on July 8, 1940, with Koussevitzky as director, and Copland as assistant director; among the distinguished guest instructors were Hindemith, Honegger, and Messiaen; Koussevitzky himself taught conducting; he was succeeded after his death by his former student, Leonard Bernstein. Koussevitzky held many honorary degrees; Mus. Doc. from Brown Univ. (1926), Rutgers Univ. (1937), Yale Univ. (1938), Rochester Univ. (1940), Williams College (1943), and Boston Univ. (1945); an LL.D. degree from Harvard Univ. (1929) and from Princeton Univ. (1947); he was a member of the French Legion of Honor; held the Cross of Commander of the Finnish Order of the White Rose (1936). Besides his double-bass concerto, he wrote *Humoresque, Valse miniature, Chanson triste,* and other small pieces for his instrument; and an orchestral work, *Passacaglia on a Russian Theme* (Boston Symph., Oct. 12, 1934). Koussevitzky became an American citizen on April 16, 1941. In 1942 his wife died; he established the Koussevitzky Foundation as a memorial to her, the funds to be used for commissioning works by composers of all nationalities. He married Olga Naoumoff (1901–78), a niece of Natalie Koussevitzky, on Aug. 15, 1947. As a conductor, Koussevitzky possessed an extraordinary emotional power; in Russian music, and particularly in Tchaikovsky's symphonies, he was unexcelled; he was capable of achieving the subtlest nuances in the works of the French school; his interpretations of Debussy were notable. As a champion of modern music, he introduced a great number of compositions for the first time anywhere; his ardor in projecting unfamiliar music before new audiences in different countries served to carry conviction among the listeners and the professional music critics. He was often criticized for the liberties he allowed himself in the treatment of classical masterpieces; undoubtedly his performances of Bach, Beethoven, Brahms, and Schubert were untraditional; but they were none the less musicianly in the sincere artistry that animated his interpretations.

BIBLIOGRAPHY: A. Lourié, *S. A. Koussevitzky and His Epoch* (N.Y., 1931); Hugo Leichtentritt, *Serge Koussevitzky, The Boston Symph. Orch. and the New American Music* (Cambridge, Mass., 1946); M. A. DeWolfe Howe, *The Boston Symph. Orch. 1881–1931* (Boston, 1931); M. A. DeWolfe Howe, *The Tale of Tanglewood* (Boston, 1946); Moses Smith, *Koussevitzky* (N.Y., 1947, a controversial biography; Koussevitzky instituted suit against the author and publisher for invasion of his right of privacy, but lost his case in court).

Koutzen, Boris, Russian-American violinist and composer; b. Uman, near Kiev, April 1, 1901; d. Mount Kisco, N.Y., Dec. 10, 1966. He studied violin with Leo Zetlin and composition with Glière at the Moscow Cons. (1918–22). In 1922 he went to the U.S. and joined the violin section of the Philadelphia Orch.; also taught violin at the Philadelphia Cons. His music possesses an attractive romantic flavor in an old Russian manner. He composed a number of orchestral pieces, among them *Solitude* (Philadelphia, April 1, 1927, composer conducting); *Valley Forge,* symph. poem (N.Y., Feb. 19, 1940); Concerto for 5 Solo Instruments (Boston, Feb. 23, 1940); Violin Concerto (Philadelphia, Feb. 22, 1952, **Nadia Koutzen,** daughter, soloist); Piano Concertino (1959); an opera, *You Never Know* (1962); *Concertante* for 2 flutes and orch. (1965).

Koval, Marian, Russian composer; b. Pristan Voznesenya, Olonetz district, Aug. 17, 1907; d. Moscow, Feb. 15, 1971. He studied composition with Gnessin and Miaskovsky at the Moscow Cons. (1925–30). Inspired by the revolutionary ideas of a new collective society, he organized with others a group named "Procoll" ("Productive Collective") dedicated to the propaganda of music in its sociological aspects; in 1929–31 he was also a member of the Russian Association of Proletarian Musicians until it was disbanded by the Soviet government as being counterproductive. He became known mainly through his choruses and solo songs on socialist subjects; all of his music is derived from modalities of Russian folksongs and those of the ethnic group of the Urals, to which he belonged. He wrote the operas *Emelian Pugatchev* (Moscow, Nov. 25, 1939) and *Sevastopoltzy* (Perm, Nov. 28, 1946); the cantatas *The People's Sacred War* (1941), *Valery Tchkalov* (1942), *The Kremlin Stars* (1947); a children's opera, *The Wolf and Seven Little Goats* (1939); 2 cycles of songs about Lenin, etc.
BIBLIOGRAPHY: G. Polyanovsky, *Marian Koval* (Moscow, 1968).

Kovalev, Pavel, Russian composer; b. Nikolayev, Jan. 6, 1890; d. Paris, Nov. 16, 1951. He studied at the Cons. of Odessa; then took courses at the Leipzig Cons. with Teichmüller and Max Reger. Returning to Russia he taught at the Odessa Cons. (1919–22). In 1927 he left Russia via China and Japan and settled in Paris, where he remained until his death. He wrote an opera *Ariane et Barbe-bleue;* some ballet scores and a number of chamber music pieces and songs.

Kovaříček, František, Czech composer; b. Litětiny near Pardubice, May 17, 1924. He studied with Řidký at the Prague Academy of Music, graduating in 1952; was musical director of the Czech Radio (1953–57); in 1966 joined the staff of the Prague Cons.
WORKS: a comic opera, *The Stolen Moon* (1966); Cello Sonata (1958); *Serenade* for 9 instruments (1958); *Divertimento* for strings (1960); *Larghetto* for clarinet and piano (1963); Clarinet Concerto (1964); *Capriccio* for chamber orch. (1970–71); 2 piano sonatas; songs.

Kovařovic, Karel, noted Czech conductor and composer; b. Prague, Dec. 9, 1862; d. there, Dec. 6, 1920. He studied clarinet, harp, and piano at the Prague Cons., and composition with Fibich. In 1900 he was appointed opera conductor of the National Theater in Prague, and held this post until his death; he also led symph. concerts in Prague. As conductor, he demonstrated great craftsmanship and established a high standard of excellence in his operatic productions; his interpretations of Dvořák and Smetana were particularly notable; an ardent believer in the cause of Czech music, he promoted national compositions. In his own music, he also made use of national materials, but his treatment was mostly imitative of the French models; the influences of Gounod and Massenet are particularly noticeable. He publ. some of his lighter works under a series of humorously misspelled names of French opera composers (C. Biset, J. Héral, etc.).
WORKS: the operas (all produced in Prague): *Ženichové* (The Bridegrooms; May 13, 1884), *Cesta Oknem* (Through the Window; Feb. 11, 1886), *Noc Šimona a Judy* (The Night of Simon and Jude; original title, *Frasquita;* Nov. 5, 1892), *Psohlavci* (The Dog-Heads; his most famous opera; April 24, 1898), *Na starém bělidle* (At the Old Bleaching-House; Nov. 22, 1901); ballets, *Hashish* (June 19, 1884), *Pohádka o nalezeném štěstí* (A Tale of Found Happiness; Dec. 21, 1886), *Na zaletech* (Flirtation; Oct. 24, 1909); symph. works, a piano concerto; 2 string quartets; etc.

Koven, Reginald de. See **De Koven, Reginald.**

Kowalski, Henri, French pianist and composer; b. Paris, 1841; d. Bordeaux, July 8, 1916. He studied piano with Marmontel and composition with Reber; wrote characteristic piano pieces (*Marche hongroise, 12 Caprices en forme d'études, Barcarolle chinoise, Sérénade japonaise,* etc.). He described his American tour in a book, *A travers l'Amérique; impressions d'un musicien* (Paris, 1872; contains a list of his compositions).

Kowalski, Július, Slovak composer; b. Ostrava, Feb. 24, 1912. He studied composition with Rudolf Karel and Alois Hába at the Prague Cons. (1929–33); subsequently took courses in composition with Suk and conducting with Talich at the Master School there (1933–34); then went to Vienna where he studied conducting with Clemens Krauss (1939). After the end of the war he occupied administrative and managerial positions in Bratislava. In 1971 he became concert manager of the Music and Arts Center. As a student of Alois Hába he wrote some microtonal pieces, e.g., Suite for violin and viola in the sixth-tone system (1936) and Duo for violin and cello in the quarter-tone system (1937), but later composed in a more or less traditional style.
WORKS: chamber opera, *Lampionová slávnost* (The Chinese Lantern Celebration, 1961; Ostrava, 1963); *Russian Rhapsody* for orch. (1933–34); *Serbian Fantasy* for orch. (1934); 5 symphonies (1954, 1957, 1959, 1970, 1974); Concertino for Violin and Chamber Orch. (1955); *Impressions* for orch. (1965); Concerto for Cello and String Orch. (1970); Concerto for String Quartet and Orch. (1973–74; Bratislava, Nov. 14,

1974); *Concertante Symphonietta* for wind quintet and orch. (1976; Bratislava, Feb. 7, 1977); 2 piano trios (1931, 1975); 4 string quartets (1932, 1954, 1965, 1975); *Divertimento* for flute, oboe and bassoon (1966); violin sonatina (1966); *Little Fantasy* for flute and piano (1969); *Grimaces* for flute, clarinet, trombone and tuba (1970).

Kowalski, Max, German composer and pedagogue; b. Kowal, Poland, Aug. 10, 1882; d. London, June 4, 1956. He was taken to Frankfurt as an infant, and received his primary education there; studied law, obtaining his Dr. juris at Marburg Univ.; returning to Frankfurt, he studied music with Bernhard Sekles; in 1912 wrote a cycle of songs to Guiraud's *Pierrot Lunaire* (independently from Schoenberg's work of the same year) and during the following 20 years composed a number of lieder, which were widely performed in Germany. After 1933 he was put in the Buchenwald concentration camp, but was released in 1939, and went to England; settled in London as teacher and a synagogal cantor; eked out his existence by also tuning pianos.

Kox, Hans, Dutch composer; b. Arnhem, May 19, 1930. He studied at the Utrecht Cons., then became a private student of Henk Badings; subsequently taught at the Doetinchem Music School (1956–70). He became fascinated with mathematical properties of music, both in formal structure and in the intervallic divisions; in some of his works he applies a scale of 31 equal intervals invented by the Dutch physicist Adriaan Fokker. In his series of *Cyclophonies (Sound Cycles)* he experimented with "open-end" forms.
WORKS: He wrote an opera, *Dorian Gray,* after Wilde (1972–73; Scheveningen, March 30, 1974); *Little Lethe Symphony* (1956); *Concertante Music* for horn, trumpet, trombone and orch. (1956); Flute Concerto (1957); *Macbeth,* overture (1958); Concerto for Orch. (1959); 2 symphonies: No. 1, for string orch. (1959) and No. 2 (1960–66; incorporates the orch. pieces *Ballade* and *Paraklesis*); *Ballet "Spleen"* for orch. (1960); Piano Concerto (1961); *De Kantate van St. Juttemis* for baritone, tenor, chorus and piano (1962); Violin Concerto (1963); 2-Violin Concerto (1964); 9 *Cyclophonies:* No. 1, for cello and small orch. (1964); No. 2, for 3 orch. groups (1964); No. 3, for piano and tape (1964); No. 4, for treble recorder and 9 strings (1965); No. 5, for oboe, clarinet, bassoon and 19 strings (1966); No. 6, for violin, trumpet, piano, vibraphone and 16 strings (1967); No. 7, for violin, piano and 6 percussionists (1971); No. 8, for wind quintet, violin, viola, cello and double bass (1971); No. 9, for solo percussion and small orch. (1974); *Zoo,* cantata (1964); *Litania* for female chorus, percussion and strings (1965); *Music for Status Seekers* for orch. (1966); *L'Allegria* for soprano and orch. (1967); Cello Concerto (1969); *In Those Days* for chorus and orch. (1969; Prix Italia, 1970); *Phobos* for orch. (1970); *Puer natus est,* European carols for chorus and orch. (1971); *Requiem for Europe* for 4 choruses and orch. (1971); *6 One-Act Plays* for 29 musicians (1971); *Gedächtnislieder* for voice and orch. (1972); *Concerto Bandistico* for orch. (1973); *Gothic Concerto* for harp and chamber orch. (1975); 4 violin sonatas (1952,

1955, 1961, 1966); 2 trios for 2 violins and viola (1952, 1954); 4 sextets of varying instrumental combinations (1957, 1957, 1959, 1961); String Quartet (1955); Trio No. 3A for violin, viola and cello (1955); String Quintet (1957); *Amphion* for 2 narrators, brass and percussion (1958); *3 Pieces* for solo violin, in the 31-tone system (1958); 2 piano quartets (1959, 1968); Sonata for Solo Cello (1959); *4 Pieces* for string quartet, in the 31-tone system (1961); the 31-tone *4 Pieces* for 2 trumpets and trombone (1964); Serenade for 3 violins (1968); *Préludes* for violin (1971); *De Vierde Kraai oftewel De Kraaiende Vier* for male chorus, brass quartet and percussion (1972); *Capriccio* for 2 violins and piano (1974); *The Jealous Guy Plays His Tune* for violin and piano (1975); 2 piano sonatas (1954, 1955); *3 Etudes* for piano (1961); Prelude and Fugue for organ (1954); the 31-tone Passacaglia and Chorale for organ (1960).

Koyama, Kiyoshige, Japanese composer; b. Nagano, Jan. 15, 1914. He studied composition with Komei Abe; wrote a number of works in a Japanese national style, among them *Shina no Bayashi* for orch. (Tokyo, June 3, 1946); *Kobiki-Uta* for orch. (Tokyo, Oct. 3, 1957); symph. suite *Nomen,* for a Noh play (Tokyo, Dec. 5, 1959); *Ubusuna* for koto and other Japanese instruments (1962); *Ainu no Uta* for string orch. (Tokyo, May 23, 1964); an opera, *Sansho Dayū* (Tokyo, March 29, 1972); several pieces for Japanese instruments.

Koželuch, Johann Anton, Bohemian composer, cousin of **Leopold Koželuch;** b. Welwarn, Dec. 14, 1738; d. Prague, Feb. 3, 1814. He studied in Prague and Vienna; served as choirmaster at the Prague Cathedral from 1784. He wrote 2 operas: *Alessandro nell'Indie* (Prague, 1769) and *Demofoonte* (Prague, 1772); 2 oratorios; a *Missa solennissima* and 44 other Masses; 4 Requiems; many other church works; also 5 symphonies, Piano Concerto, Bassoon Concerto, Oboe Concerto, and a great number of other instrumental works; the bulk of these remain in manuscript.
BIBLIOGRAPHY: R. Fikrle, *J. A. Koželuch* (Prague, 1944).

Koželuch (Kotzeluch), Leopold Anton, Bohemian composer; b. Welwarn, June 26, 1747; d. Vienna, May 7, 1818. He was a law student at Prague; studied music with his cousin **Johann Anton Koželuch.** The success of a ballet of his own at the National Theater, Prague, in 1771 caused him to adopt the profession of music. Within six years he wrote 24 more ballets, 3 pantomimes, and incidental music; became music master to the Archduchess Elisabeth at Vienna in 1778, and followed Mozart as court composer in 1792. He was a brilliant pianist, and in high favor as a teacher among the aristocracy. His compositions include the operas *Le Mazet, Giudita, Deborah,* and *Didone abbandonata;* cantatas, symphonies, numerous piano compositions (about 50 concertos), chamber works, etc., but they are of scant interest. Beethoven referred to him contemptuously in a letter of 1812 as "miserabilis."

Kozina, Marjan, Slovenian composer; b. Novo Mesto, June 4, 1907; d. there, June 19, 1966. He studied at the

Cons. of Ljubljana; later took courses with Josef Marx at the Vienna Academy of Music and with Josef Suk at the Prague Cons. During the occupation of Yugoslavia by the Nazi armies, Kozina took part in the armed resistance movement; after the liberation he taught at the Musical Academy of Ljubljana. He wrote music in a fine unaffected manner, making circumspect use of modern harmonies, while deriving his melorhythmic essence from native Slovenian folksong patterns. His most important work is the music drama *Equinox* (Ljubljana, May 2, 1946) which had numerous revivals in Yugoslavia, and was also performed in Prague and Moscow. Other works are the ballet *Diptihon* (1952) and a cantata *Lepa Vida* (*Beautiful Vida;* 1939).

Kozma, Matei, Rumanian composer and organist; b. Tîrgu-Mureş, July 23, 1929. He acquired the rudiments of music from his father, **Géza Kozma,** a Rumanian composer and cellist; then studied at the Cluj Cons. (1947-54), where his teachers were Jodál and Demian. He served as organ soloist (1955-57) and director (1959-66) of the Tîrgu-Mureş Philh.; then became an instructor at the Music Institute there.
WORKS: *Rondo* for piano (1954); 2 ballets: *Baladă lacului Sf. Ana* (1957) and *Baladă celui care cînta in cătuşe* (1963); Organ Concerto (1961, revised 1965); *Trandafirii roşii,* poem for chorus and orch. (1962); *Theme and Variations* for organ (1963); Trio for Solo Clarinet (1965); *Omagiu eroilor,* overture (1967); *Toccata, Trio and Ricercari* for organ (1968); choruses; songs.

Kraft, Anton, Austrian cello virtuoso; b. Rokitzán, near Pilsen, Dec. 30, 1749; d. Vienna, Aug. 28, 1820. He began to study at an early age with his father, an amateur cellist; then went to Prague, and later to Vienna; there he enjoyed the friendship of Haydn, who recommended him for a post as cellist in the chapel of Prince Esterházy (1778); he was subsequently in the employ of Prince Grassalkowicz; in 1795 entered the service of Prince Lobkowitz in Vienna. Among Kraft's works are 3 sonatas, 3 grand duos for violin and cello, and several grand duos for 2 cellos; Divertissement for Cello and Double Bass; etc. For a time it was thought that Haydn's famous Cello Concerto in D was actually written by Kraft, but it is now generally agreed by specialists that it is an authentic work by Haydn. Since it was written for Kraft, he may have made technical suggestions that were adopted by Haydn.

Kraft, Leo, American composer and pedagogue; b. New York, July 24, 1922. He studied composition with Karol Rathaus at Queens College, N.Y. (B.A., 1945), with Randall Thompson at Princeton Univ. (M.A., 1947), and with Nadia Boulanger in Paris (1954-55). In 1947 he was appointed prof. at Queens College. Kraft's craftsmanship preserves formal ties with the revered past along with a salute to the turbulent present and a wink at an ominous future.
WORKS: *Let Me Laugh,* for chorus and piano (1954); *Two's Company* for 2 clarinets (1957); 3 partitas: No. 1 for piano, No. 2 for violin and viola, No. 3 for wind quintet (1969); *5 Pieces* for clarinet and piano

(1969); *Toccata* for band (1970); *Fantasy* for flute and piano (1971); *Dualities* for 2 trumpets (1971); *Line Drawings* for flute and percussion (1974); *10 Short Pieces* for piano (1976); *Trios and Interludes* for flute, viola, and piano (1977); *Statements and Commentaries* for piano (1978); *Diaphonies* for oboe and piano (1978); He published the textbooks: *A New Approach to Sight Singing* (with S. Berkowitz and G. Fontrier; N.Y., 1960); *A New Approach to Ear Training* (N.Y., 1967); *Gradus: An Integrated Approach to Harmony, Counterpoint, and Analysis* (N.Y., 1976).

Kraft, Nicolaus, Hungarian cellist and composer; son of **Anton Kraft;** b. Esterház, Hungary, Dec. 14, 1778; d. Eger, May 18, 1853. He studied cello with his father, and went with him on concert tours while quite young; he and his father played chamber music with Mozart at the Dresden court (1789); when the Krafts went to Vienna in 1790, Nicolaus became a member of the famous 'Schuppanzigh Quartet.' He was subsequently chamber musician to Prince Lobkowitz, who sent him to Berlin in 1791 to study for a year with Duport. After concerts in Germany, he returned to Vienna, and joined the court orch. (1809); then entered the court orch. at Stuttgart in 1814. He retired after an accident to his hand, in 1834. He wrote 5 cello concertos; 6 duos and 3 'divertissements' for 2 cellos; Cello Fantasia with String Quartet; *Polonaise* and *Bolero* for cello with orch.; and other cello music. His son, **Friedrich Kraft** (b. Vienna, Feb. 13, 1807; d. Stuttgart, Dec. 4, 1874), was also a cellist, and played in the Stuttgart court orch. for many years.

Kraft, William, American composer and percussion virtuoso; b. Chicago, Sept. 6, 1923. He went to New York as a child; studied musical analysis with Miriam Gideon; then entered Columbia Univ., and studied composition with Jack Beeson, Henry Cowell, Seth Bingham, Otto Luening and Vladimir Ussachevsky; and musicology with Paul Henry Lang (B.S., 1951; M.A., 1954); he also attended the summer classes in composition with Irving Fine and conducting with Leonard Bernstein at the Berkshire Music Center; then went to England where he had composition lessons with Boris Orr at Cambridge Univ. He took private lessons in timpani playing with Saul Goodman and general percussion with Morris Goldenberg; selected percussion as his main specialty, achieving a high degree of virtuosity on all manners of drums and other rhythm instruments, both according to the classical tradition and in jazz. In 1955 he joined the percussion section of the Los Angeles Philharmonic Orchestra. In 1977 he gave lectures on contemporary techniques and modern notation at the Univ. of Southern California, Los Angeles. As a composer he explores without prejudice all genres of techniques, including serial precedures; he develops the rhythmic element to the full. He held numerous awards, including 2 Guggenheim Fellowships (1967, 1972).
WORKS: *Three Miniatures* for percussion and orch. (Los Angeles, Feb. 14, 1959); *Variations on a Folksong* for orch. (Los Angeles, March 26, 1960); *Symphony* for Strings and Percussion (New York, Aug. 21, 1961); *Concerto Grosso* (San Diego, Calif. March 22, 1963); *Concerto for Four Percussion Solo-*

ists and Orchestra (Los Angeles, March 10, 1966); *Contextures: Riots—Decade '60* (Los Angeles, April 4, 1968); *Configurations* for four percussion soloists and jazz orch. (Los Angeles, Nov. 13, 1966); *Games: Collage No. 1* for brass and percussion (Pasadena, Calif. Nov. 21, 1969); Piano Concerto (Los Angeles, Nov. 21, 1973); Nonet for brass and percussion (Los Angeles, Oct. 13, 1958); *Six Pieces* for string trio (1963); *Double Trio* for piano, prepared piano, amplified guitar, tuba and percussion (Los Angeles, Oct. 31, 1966); *Triangles*, a concerto for percussion and 10 instruments (Los Angeles, Dec. 8, 1969); *Mobiles* for 10 instruments (Berkeley, Calif., Oct. 18, 1970); *Cadenze* for 7 instruments (1972); Tuba Concerto (Los Angeles, Jan. 26, 1978).

Kramer, A. Walter, American music critic and composer; b. New York, Sept. 23, 1890; d. there, April 8, 1969. He studied music with his father, Maximilian Kramer and took violin lessons with Carl Hauser and Richard Arnold. After graduating from the College of the City of N.Y. in 1910, he joined the staff of *Musical America* (1910–22) and served as its editor-in-chief from 1929 till 1936. His music criticism was journalistically voluble and knowledgeable. He wrote many pleasant and entirely singable songs and also essayed an ambitious *Symphonic Rhapsody* for violin and orch. (1912).
    BIBLIOGRAPHY: J. T. Howard, *A. Walter Kramer* (N.Y., 1926); W. T. Upton, *Art-Song in America* (N.Y., 1930; pp. 225–35).

Kranich & Bach, well-known firm of piano makers founded in New York, 1864, by **Helmuth Kranich** (b. Grossbreitenbach, Germany, Aug. 22, 1833; d. N.Y., Jan. 29, 1902) and **Jacques Bach** (b. Lorentzen, Alsace, June 22, 1833; d. N.Y., Oct. 29, 1894). The business, incorporated in 1890, has been continued by the founders' descendants: **Frederick Kranich** served as president from 1902–20, and was succeeded by **Louis P. Bach** from 1920–30; in 1930 **Jacques Bach Schlosser** (grandson of Jacques Bach) was elected president; **Helmuth Kranich,** son of Helmuth, Sr., was appointed a member of the Board of Directors in 1894; secretary of the firm in 1902, and president in 1946; retired in 1950. He died in N.Y. on Oct. 24, 1956. Other members of the Board of Directors included **Philip Schlosser** (grandson of Jacques Bach), **Victor Kranich** (son of Helmuth Kranich, Sr.), **Lucy Bach** (daughter of Jacques Bach), and **John J. Kuhn** (grandnephew of Jacques Bach). Frederick Kranich invented the "Isotonic" pedal, doing away with the shifting keyboard in grand pianos, and the "Violyn" plate for upright pianos, and perfected various improvements in piano construction.
    BIBLIOGRAPHY: A. Dolge, *Pianos and Their Makers,* vol. II (Covina, California, 1913).

Krantz, Eugen, German pianist; b. Dresden, Sept. 13, 1844; d. Gohrisch, near Königstein, May 26, 1898. He studied at the Dresden Cons.; was chorusmaster at the court opera there (1869–84); taught at the Dresden Cons., becoming director in 1890, when he bought the institution. He publ. some songs and a *Lehrgang im*

Klavierunterricht (1882); was also critic for the Dresden *Presse* and for the *Nachrichten.*

Krapf, Gerhard, German-American organist and composer; b. Meissenheim-bei-Lahr, Dec. 12, 1924. He studied piano and organ in Karlsruhe; was church organist in Offenburg, Germany (1939–42); was drafted into the German army and taken prisoner of war in Russia; upon his release he returned to Karlsruhe where he continued to study organ, choral conducting and composition (1950). In 1951 he went to America where he studied organ at the Univ. of Redlands, California, and took a course in composition with Paul A. Pisk. He then taught music at Albion, Michigan (1953–54), at the Northwest Missouri State College, Maryville, (1954–58) and at the Univ. of Wyoming, Laramie (1958–61). In 1961 he joined the faculty of the Univ. of Iowa, where he was appointed head of the organ dept. He composed a great number of organ pieces and sacred choral works; publ. a manual *Liturgical Organ Playing* (Minneapolis, 1964) and *Organ Improvisation: A Practical Approach to Chorale Elaborations for the Service* (Minneapolis, 1967).

Krása, Hans, Czech composer; b. Prague, Nov. 30, 1899; d. Auschwitz, Oct. 16, 1944. He was of Czech-German (Jewish) extraction; studied in a German high school in Prague; took lessons in music with Zemlinsky and Keussler in Prague. He made rapid progress, and had his first orchestral piece *Grotesques* performed in Prague on May 20, 1921; also successful were his beginnings as conductor; he was engaged as chorusmaster at the German Theater in Prague; then went to Berlin where he conducted at the Kroll Opera. He returned to Prague in 1928, and in 1942 was interned at the Theresienstadt concentration camp; nevertheless he continued to compose and produced an opera *Brundibár,* which had several performances arranged by an opera group of the Jewish inmates. On Oct. 16, 1944 he was transported to Auschwitz and put to death. He was a composer of some interesting works in a "hedonistic" manner, aiming at sophisticated entertainment; his idiom was mildly atonal. So promising was his career as a composer that his *Pastorale* and *March* (originally first and second movements from a symphony) were performed in Paris (April 24, 1923) and also by the Boston Symph. Orch. (Nov. 19, 1926). His string trio was performed posthumously at the Aspen, Colorado, Festival (Oct. 22, 1951). He also wrote incidental music to *Lysistrata,* and the cantata *Die Erde ist des Herrn.* Other works were *Theme With Variations* for string quartet (1942); a group of songs to words by Rimbaud, and some piano pieces.

Krasner, Louis, American violinist; b. Cherkassy, Russia, June 21, 1903; was taken to the U.S. as a small child; studied at the New England Cons., Boston, graduating in 1923; then went abroad, where he studied violin with Carl Flesch, Lucien Capet, and Ševčik. From 1944 to 1949 he was concertmaster of the Minneapolis Symph. Orch.; then became prof. of violin and chamber music at Syracuse Univ. In 1974 he joined the staff of the New England Cons. He commissioned Alban Berg in 1934 to write a violin concerto for him; gave its world première at the Barcelona Festival of the International Society for Contemporary Music (April 19, 1936); also gave the world première of Schoenberg's Violin Concerto (Philadelphia, Dec. 6, 1940, Stokowski conducting).

Krásová, Marta, Czech contralto; b. Protovin, March 16, 1901; d. Vráz, near Beroun, Feb. 20, 1970. She studied voice in Prague and Vienna; made her debut in Bratislava in 1924; subsequently joined the National Theater in Prague; made highly successful guest appearances in Hamburg, Dresden, Madrid, Paris, Moscow and Warsaw; toured the United States in 1938–39. In 1935 she married the Czech composer **Karel Boleslav Jirák;** divorced, 1946. She achieved distinction in the principal parts in national Czech operas; was also notable as a Wagnerian singer.

Kraus, Alessandro, German collector of musical instruments; b. Frankfurt, Aug. 6, 1820; d. Florence, Sept. 22, 1904. He was noted for his extensive and valuable collection of musical instruments; co-founder of the "Tonkünstlerhilfsverein" in Frankfurt and of the Florentine "Società del Quartetto."

Kraus, Ernst, German tenor; b. Erlangen, June 8, 1863; d. Wörthsee, Sept. 6, 1941. He studied in Milan with Cesare Galliera and in Munich with Frau Schimon-Regan; made his debut as a concert singer at a Kaim Concert in Munich (Jan. 18, 1893); opera debut in Mannheim on March 26, 1893, as Tamino in *Die Zauberflöte;* then remained there as a member of the opera (1893–96); from 1896–1923, engaged at the Court Opera in Berlin; in 1924, returned to Munich as singing teacher.

Kraus, Felix von, Austrian bass singer; b. Vienna, Oct. 3, 1870; d. Munich, Oct. 30, 1937. He first studied musicology at the Univ. of Vienna (Dr. phil., 1894); then singing with Stockhausen. In 1899, after a European tour as a concert singer, he appeared at the Wagner Festival in Bayreuth as Hagen, and subsequently participated in the festivals every summer for many years; established himself as one of the finest interpreters of Wagnerian bass roles. He also taught dramatic singing in Munich. In 1899 he married the American singer, **Adrienne Osborne.**

Kraus, Joseph Martin, important German-Swedish composer; b. Miltenberg, near Mainz, June 20, 1756; d. Stockholm, Dec. 15, 1792. He studied at the Jesuit School in Mannheim; later in Mainz (1773), Erfurt, and Göttingen (1776). In 1778 he went to Sweden and worked as a theater conductor in Stockholm; he became greatly interested in Swedish culture; wrote operas to Swedish texts; traveled with Gustaf III on the continent and in England (1782–87); was appointed court conductor in 1789. During his short life (he was almost an exact contemporary of Mozart) he wrote an enormous amount of operatic and instrumental music of high quality; he preserved the style of Gluck; his mastery of the craft established a high standard for Swedish music; Swedish historians gave an increasingly appreciative account of his importance; editions of his unpublished manuscripts are beginning to be issued. His first Swedish opera was *Proserpine* (1781); there followed *Aeneas in Carthage* (1782; produced posthumously, Stockholm, Nov. 18, 1799) and *Soliman II* (his most successful opera; Stockholm, Sept. 22, 1789). When Gustaf III was assassinated in 1792, Kraus wrote a memorial cantata for his funeral. His symphonies, overtures, and other instrumental works are preserved at the Uppsala Library. He wrote an autobiography and publ. (anonymously) a pamphlet *Etwas von und über Musik* (1777); also some poetical works in German.

BIBLIOGRAPHY: K. F. Schreiber, *Biographie über den Odenwälder Komponisten J. M. Kraus* (Baden, 1928); R. Engländer, *J. M. Kraus und die Gustavianische Oper* (Uppsala and Leipzig, 1943).

Kraus, Lili, Hungarian pianist; b. Budapest, April 3, 1905. She studied at the Budapest Academy of Music, graduating at 17; took courses with Bartók and Kodály (theory) and with Schnabel (piano). After teaching at the Vienna Cons. for several years, she embarked upon a tour of the world; in 1942 she was detained by the Japanese in the Dutch East Indies; after the end of the war she played in Australia (1946–47), in England, and in South Africa (1948); became a British subject in 1948. She also made several appearances in the U.S., playing with major symph. orchestras and in recital.

Krause, Anton, German pianist and conductor; b. Geithain, Nov. 9, 1834; d. Dresden, Jan. 31, 1907. He began to study piano at an early age; then studied at Dresden; from 1850 to 1853 studied at the Leipzig Cons. with Wenzel, Moscheles, Hauptmann, Richter, Rietz, and David; taught music and also conducted in Leipzig. In 1859 he succeeded Reinecke at Barmen as director of the Singverein and the Konzertgesellschaft, retiring in 1897. He wrote *Prinzessin Ilse,* for soli, female chorus, piano, and declamation; choral works; songs; also instructive piano pieces. He publ. a collection of classical sonatinas and a *Library for Two Pianofortes* (18 vols.).

Krause, Eduard, German pianist and teacher; b. Swinemünde, March 15, 1837; d. Berlin, March 28, 1892. He studied with Kroll in Berlin and Hauptmann in Leipzig; then went to Stettin as pianist and teacher. He publ. characteristic pieces for the piano (*Berceuse, Impromptu, Grosse Sonate, Ungarische Rhapsodie, Konzertfantasie über schwedische Volkslieder,* etc.).

Krause, Emil, German piano pedagogue and music critic; b. Hamburg, July 30, 1840; d. there, Sept. 5, 1916. He was a pupil of Hauptmann, Richter, Rietz, Moscheles, and Plaidy at the Leipzig Cons. In 1860 he went to Hamburg, where he taught piano and wrote music criticism for the *Fremdenblatt* from 1864 until 1907. He publ. *Beiträge zur Technik des Klavierspiels,* with supplementary matter in *Ergänzungen; Aufgabenbuch für die Harmonielehre* (1869; 8th ed., 1908); *Praktische Klavierschule* (1892); *Neuer "Gradus ad Parnassum"* (100 études); and *Anleitung zum Studium der Musikgeschichte* (1906); *Johannes Brahms in seinen Werken* (Hamburg, 1892; contains a catalogue of works); *Kurzgefasste Darstellung der Passion, des*

Oratoriums und modernen Konzertwerkes für chor, soli und orchester (Langensalza, 1902). His compositions include an oratorio, *Den Heimgegangenen, Trio non difficile* for piano, violin, and cello (1863); songs; piano pieces.

Krause, Karl Christian Friedrich, German writer on music; b. Eisenberg, May 6, 1781; d. Munich, Sept. 27, 1832. He publ. many philosophical works; also *Darstellungen aus der Geschichte der Musik* (1827), *Vollständige Anweisung* (1808), and *Anfangsgründe der allgemeinen Theorie der Musik* (1838).

Krause, Martin, German pianist and pedagogue; b. Lobstadt, near Leipzig, June 17, 1853; d. Plattling, Bavaria, Aug. 2, 1918. He was a pupil of his father, a cantor, and of Wenzel and Reinecke at the Leipzig Cons. After successful tours in Holland and Germany (1878–1880), he was prostrated by nervous exhaustion for 2 years. He played before Liszt in 1883, and for 3 years, until Liszt's death, was in constant communication with the master and his pupils. In 1885 Krause, Siloti, Frau Moran-Olden, and others gave two grand concerts in Leipzig, which marked the establishment of the "Lisztverein," of which Krause was the chief promoter, chairman, and manager till 1900, when it was discontinued. After 1900 he taught in Leipzig, Dresden, and at Stern's Cons, in Berlin.

Krause, Theodor, German choir conductor and teacher; b. Halle, May 1, 1833; d. Berlin, Dec. 12, 1910. He was a theological student; studied music with Hentschel, Hauptmann, and Grell. He organized church choirs in Berlin; was conductor of the Seiffert a cappella society; taught singing at sight by using the "Wandernote" (movable Do). He wrote church music, part-songs, and songs; was music critic for several Berlin papers; publ. *Die Wandernote* (1888) and *Deutsche Singschule* (1888).

Kraushaar, Otto, German writer on music; b. Kassel, May 31, 1812; d. there, Nov. 23, 1866. He studied with Hauptmann, whose idea of the opposition of the major and minor modes he developed in a treatise on *Der accordliche Gegensatz und die Bergründung der Scala* (1852), prior to Hauptmann's *Natur der Harmonik.* He also publ. *Die Construktion der gleichschwebenden Temperatur ohne Scheiblerische Stimmgabeln* (1838); contributed essays to periodicals; wrote songs.

Krauss, Clemens, eminent Austrian conductor; b. Vienna, March 31, 1893; d. Mexico City, May 16, 1954. He was a chorister at the Imperial Chapel; then studied at the Vienna Cons. with Reinhold (piano), Grädener, and Heuberger (theory), graduating in 1912. He was then choral director at the State Theater in Brno; subsequently acted as second conductor of opera in Riga (1913–14), in Nuremberg (1915–16), 1st conductor in Stettin (1916–21), opera and symph. conductor in Graz (1921–22), conductor at the Vienna State Opera and teacher of conducting at the Vienna Academy of Music (1922), and of the Tonkünstlerkonzerte (1923–27), conductor of the Frankfurt Opera and of the Museum Concerts in Frankfurt (1924–29), director of the Vienna State Opera and conductor of the Vi-

enna Philharmonic (1929–34), 1st conductor at the Berlin State Opera (1934–36), musical director of the Munich Opera (1937–40), of the Mozarteum in Salzburg (1939–45). In 1929 he made guest appearances in the U.S. with the N.Y. Philharmonic and Philadelphia Orch. In 1945 he was appointed conductor of the Vienna Opera and the Vienna Philharmonic. He was married to the singer **Viorica Ursuleac,** whom he often accompanied at the piano at her recitals. Krauss was a close collaborator and friend of Richard Strauss; he wrote the libretto of Strauss's opera *Capriccio.* He was regarded as one of the finest operatic and symph. conductors in Austria and Germany. He died suddenly on a tour in Mexico.

BIBLIOGRAPHY: A. Berger, *Clemens Krauss* (Graz, 1924; 3rd ed., 1929); J. Gregor, *Clemens Krauss, seine musikalische Sendung* (Vienna, 1953); Oscar von Pander, *Krauss in München* (Munich, 1955).

Krauss, Gabrielle, Austrian soprano; b. Vienna, March 24, 1842; d. Paris, Jan. 6, 1906. She studied general music subjects at the Vienna Cons.; voice with Mathilde Marchesi. She made her first important appearance at the Vienna Opera on July 20, 1860, in Rossini's *Wilhelm Tell;* remained on the roster until 1867; then went to Paris; sang Leonora in *Il Trovatore* at the Théâtre-Italien (Apr. 6, 1867) and became a favorite. The Franco-Prussian War of 1870 compelled her to leave Paris; she sang in Italy and in Russia. When the new building of the Paris Grand Opéra was opened in 1875, she sang *La Juive* (Jan. 5, 1875); remained with the opera until 1888, when she retired.

Krauze, Zygmunt, Polish composer and pianist; b. Warsaw, Sept. 19, 1938. He studied composition with Sikorski and piano with Maria Wilkomirska at the Warsaw Cons., graduating in 1962 (M.A., 1964); completed studies with Nadia Boulanger in Paris (1966–67). He is an inventive composer, cultivating with equal devotion primitive rustic instruments and electronic sounds. As a pianist, he specializes in new music; he taught piano at Cleveland State Univ. (1970–71).

WORKS: *3 Malay Pantuns,* to Indonesian texts, for 3 flutes and contralto (1961); *5 Unitary Piano Pieces* (1963); *Triptych* for piano (1964); *Voices* for 5–15 optional instruments (1968); *Polychrony* for clarinet, trombone, cello and piano (1968); 2 string quartets (1960, 1969); *Piece for Orch. No. 1* (1969); *Piece for Orch. No. 2* (1970); *Folk Music* for orch. (1971–72); *Aus aller Welt stammende* for 10 strings (1973); *Vibrations* for piano, 8 hands (1973); *Song* for flute, clarinet, bassoon, violin, cello, double bass and 3 automatophones (1974); *Automatophone* for 15 musical boxes and 15 plucked instruments (1974); *Fête galante et pastorale,* space music for a castle, for 13 tapes and 6 instruments groups (1974; Graz, Austria, Oct. 12, 1974); *Idyll* for tape, 4 hurdy-gurdies, 4 bagpipes, 4 zlobcoki, 8 fifes, 16 bells and 4 whistles (1974).

Krebs, Carl, German music scholar and critic; b. Hanseberg, Feb. 5, 1857; d. Berlin, Feb. 9, 1937. He studied musicology at the Univ. of Berlin with Ph. Spitta. From 1896 to 1923 he lectured on music history at the

Berlin Hochschule für Musik; in 1911 was elected secretary of the Academy. He wrote music criticism for several Berlin newspapers; publ. various historical essays in the scholarly musical journals; in 1898 he edited Beethoven's sonatas in their original form. He also publ. a valuable monograph on Dittersdorf, entitled *Dittersdorfiana* (Berlin, 1900); other publications were *Schaffen und Nachschaffen in der Musik* (Berlin, 1902); *Haydn, Mozart, Beethoven* (Leipzig, 1906; 3rd ed., 1920); *Meister des Taktstocks* (Berlin, 1919) and an interesting treatise *Die Frauen in der Musik,* published in 1895 under the auspices of the feminist group, "Der Existenzkampf der Frau."

Krebs (real name **Miedcke**), **Carl August,** German composer; b. Nuremberg, Jan. 16, 1804; d. Dresden, May 16, 1880. He studied music with the opera singer Johann Baptist Krebs, who legally adopted him. A precocious child, he is said to have composed an opera *Feodore* at the age of 7. He became a conductor at the Vienna Opera in 1826; in 1850 he was appointed principal conductor of the Dresden Opera succeeding Wagner who had been involved in revolutionary activities in Saxony; Krebs continued at his Dresden post until 1872. He produced 2 operas, *Silva* (Hamburg, 1830) and *Agnes* (Hamburg, Oct. 8, 1833; revised under the title *Agnes Bernauer* and produced in Dresden in 1858), but he was successful mainly as a song composer; his religious hymn *Vater unser* was popular for many years; he also wrote several Masses and some brilliant piano pieces. He was married to the opera singer **Aloysia Michalesi** (1826–1904). Their daughter **Mary Krebs** (1851–1900) was a talented pianist.

Krebs, Johann Ludwig, German organist and composer; b. Buttelstädt, Oct. 10, 1713; d. Altenburg, Jan. 2, 1780. He received methodical training in musical subjects from his father, an organist, and was sent to study at the Thomasschule in Leipzig, where he became a pupil of Bach for 9 years (1726–35); was Bach's assistant at the harpsichord in Bach's Collegium Musicum there. Later he was organist at Zeitz, Zwickau, and Altenburg. He publ.: *Klavierübungen* in 4 parts (Nuremberg, 1743–49); sonatas for clavier and flute; suites and preludes for clavier; string trios; organ pieces (including an organ fugue on the name B-A-C-H); these were reprinted in the series *Masterpieces of Organ Music* (N.Y., 1944–45); Partita No. 2 is found in Pauer's *Alte Meister,* a trio with continuo in Riemann's *Collegium Musicum.*
BIBLIOGRAPHY: Hans Löffler, "J. L. Krebs," *Bach-Jahrbuch* (1930).

Kreger, James, American violoncellist; b. Nashville, Tennessee, March 30, 1947. He received his early musical training taking piano lessons with local teachers. In 1965 the family moved to Beverly Hills, Calif., where he studied cello with Gabor Rejto; in 1966 he went to New York and enrolled at the Juilliard School of Music as a student of Leonard Rose and Harvey Shapiro. He also took courses at the Michigan State Univ., and played the cello in a student orchestra in Tanglewood. On March 16, 1971 he gave an auspicious recital in New York, eliciting high praise from hardened music critics.

Krehbiel, Henry Edward, noted American music critic; b. Ann Arbor, Mich., March 10, 1854; d. New York, March 20, 1923. He was music critic of the *Cincinnati Gazette* (1874–80); then editor of the *N.Y. Musical Review* and critic for the *N.Y. Tribune;* the latter post he held for some 40 years until his death; in 1909, received the honorary degree of M.A. from Yale Univ. He publ. *Notes on the Cultivation of Choral Music, and the Oratorio Society of New York* (1884); *Review of the N.Y. Musical Seasons 1885–90* (5 vols.); *Studies in the Wagnerian Drama* (1891); *The Philharmonic Society of New York: A Memorial* (1892); *How to Listen to Music* (1896); *Annotated Biography of Fine Art* (with R. Sturgis; 1897); *Music and Manners in the Classical Period* (1898); *Chapters of Opera* (1908; 2nd ed., 1911); *A Book of Operas* (1909); *The Pianoforte, and Its Music* (1911); *Afro-American Folksongs* (1914); *A Second Book of Operas* (1917); *More Chapters of Opera* (1919); transl. of Courvoisier's *Technic of Violin Playing* (N.Y., 1880; 2nd ed., 1896), Kerst's *Beethoven* (1905), and Kerst's *Mozart* (1905); also publ. and edited the English version of Thayer's *Beethoven* (3 vols., 1921); he was consulting editor of *The Music of the Modern World* (1895–97) and American editor of the 2nd ed. of *Grove's Dictionary of Music and Musicians* (1904–10); was also author, for many years, of the program notes of the N.Y. Philharmonic Society. He was a brilliant writer of music criticism, and was able to project his opinions (and his prejudices) in vivid prose in his newspaper reviews. He was an ardent champion of Wagner, and he also wrote with warm admiration for the late Romantic composers; but he deprecated the modern school of composition, hurling invectives on Stravinsky, Prokofiev and Schoenberg (whose music he described as excrement).

Krehl, Stephan, German theorist and composer; b. Leipzig, July 5, 1864; d. there, April 7, 1924. He studied at the Cons. of Leipzig and Dresden. In 1889 he was appointed teacher of piano and theory at the Karlsruhe Cons.; from 1902, at the Leipzig Cons.; in 1911, director there. He publ. the manuals, *Praktische Formenlehre* (1902); *Allgemeine Musiklehre* (1904; 2nd ed., 1912; in Spanish, 1930); *Fuge: Erläuterung und Anleitung zur Komposition derselben* (1908); *Kompositionsunterricht und moderne Musik* (1909); *Musikerelend* (1912); *M. Hauptmann; ein Dank- und Gedenkwort* (1918); *Theorie der Tonkunst und Kompositionslehre* (vol. I: *Elementarmusiklehre,* 1921; vol. II: *Harmonielehre,* 1923; 2nd ed., 1928). He also composed a quintet for clarinet, 2 violins, viola, and cello; a cello sonata; *Slovenische Tänze* for piano 4-hands; a cantata, *Trostung,* and a prelude to Hauptmann's play *Hannele.*
BIBLIOGRAPHY: F. Reuter, *Stephan Krehl* (1921).

Krein, Alexander, Russian composer; b. Nizhni-Novgorod, Oct. 20, 1883; d. Staraya Ruza, near Moscow, April 21, 1951. At the age of 13 he entered the Moscow Cons. and studied cello; also studied composition privately with Nikolayev and Yavorsky. Later he became instructor at the People's Cons. of Moscow (1912–17); after the revolution he worked in the Music Division of the Commissariat of Education and in the Ethnographic Department. From 1923 he was associated with the productions of the Jewish Drama Theater in Moscow, and wrote music for many Jewish plays. Together with Gnessin, he was a leader of the National Jewish movement in Russia. In general, his style was influenced by Scriabin and Debussy, but he made considerable use of authentic Hebrew material.

WORKS: operas, *Zagmuk*, on a revolutionary subject based on an ancient Babylonian tale (Moscow, May 29, 1930) and *Daughter of the People* (1946); a ballet after Lope de Vega, *Laurencie* (1938); incidental music to the Jewish plays *The Eternal One* (1923), *Sabbati Zewi* (1924), *Ghetto* (1924), *The People* (1925), *The Doctor* (1925); for orch.: *Salome* (1923); *Elegy* for string orch. (1914); *La Rose and la Croix*, symph. fragments (1917–21); *Kaddisch*, symphonic cantata for tenor solo, mixed choir, and orch. (1921); Symphony (1922–25); *U.S.S.R., Shock Brigade of the World Proletariat*, symph. dithyramb for narrator, chorus, and orch. (1925); *Threnody in Memory of Lenin*, for chorus and orch. (1925); various symph. suites on Hebrew themes; chamber music: a string quartet, *Jewish Sketches* for clarinet and string quartet, *Elegiac Trio*, for violin, cello, and piano; *Jewish Capriccio* for violin and piano; Piano Sonata; *3 Poems* for piano; *Jewish Songs* (to Russian words); vocalises.

BIBLIOGRAPHY: L. Sabaneyev, *Alexander Krein* (Moscow, 1928; in Russian and German).

Krein, Grigory, Russian composer, brother of **Alexander Krein**; b. Nizhni-Novgorod, March 18, 1879; d. Komarovo, near Leningrad, Jan. 6, 1955. He studied with Juon and Glière. His music underwent the influence of Jewish culture, and he wrote many works on Jewish themes; however, he also cultivated strict classical forms, adapting them to his needs. He wrote a descriptive symph. cycle on Lenin's life (1937); other works are a violin concerto, a string quartet, a *Hebrew Rhapsody* for clarinet and orch., and piano pieces.

Krein, Julian, Russian composer, son of **Grigory Krein**; b. Moscow, March 5, 1913. He studied with his father; wrote his first compositions at the age of 13. In 1927 he went to Paris; took some lessons with Paul Dukas. In 1933 he went back to Moscow and remained there. Besides composing, he also wrote music criticism. His music is marked by a lyric quality; in his harmonic procedures he adopts advanced methods bordering on polytonality. Among his works are *Five Preludes* for orch. (1927); a symph. prelude *Destruction* (1929); Cello Concerto (Barcelona, Oct. 18, 1931, Eisenberg soloist); *Spring Symphony* (1938); piano pieces; songs.

Kreisler, Fritz, celebrated violinist; b. Vienna, Feb. 2, 1875; d. New York, Jan. 29, 1962. His talent manifested itself at an early age and was carefully fostered by his father, under whose instruction the boy made such progress that at the age of 6 he was sent to study with Jacob Dont; then was admitted to the Vienna Cons., where he studied with Jacques Auber and Hellmesberger (1882–85); in 1885, carried off the gold

medal. He then entered the Paris Cons., where he was a pupil of Massart (violin) and Delibes (composition); graduated in 1887 as winner of the Grand Prix (gold medal) over 40 competitors. He made his American debut at Steinway Hall, N.Y., on Nov. 10, 1888. In the following year, he made a very successful tour of the U.S. with Moriz Rosenthal. On his return to Europe, he abandoned music for some years; studied medicine in Vienna, and art in Rome and Paris; then entered the Austrian army, serving as an officer in an Uhlan regiment. At his reappearance in Berlin (March 1899) his playing created a sensation. Not only had he regained his outstanding virtuosity, but he had also developed into a great interpreter. On his second visit to the U.S. in 1900–01, when he appeared as soloist and in ensemble with Hofmann and Gerardy, he carried his audiences by storm; on his tour of England in the spring of 1901, he scored similar triumphs. In 1904 the London Philharmonic Society honored him by awarding him the Beethoven gold medal. At the outbreak of World War I in 1914, he joined his former regiment, was wounded at Lemberg (Sept. 6, 1914), and excused from further service. Fortunately his wound was slight (his hip and shoulder were injured in a Russian cavalry attack) so that at the end of 1914 he resumed his artistic career in the U.S. He remained in the U.S. throughout the rest of World War I despite the embarrassment of his status as an enemy alien; after the Armistice, went back to Europe, but continued to make frequent visits to America. He was made Commander of the Legion of Honor by the French government, and received many other honors from foreign governments. In 1938 he became a French citizen; in 1940 he returned to N.Y.; in 1943, became an American citizen. Kreisler's repertory contained almost everything of value written for the violin since the 17th century. He was the owner of a Guarneri violin and of instruments by other masters; gathered a rich collection of invaluable manuscripts; in 1949 donated to the Library of Congress the original scores of Brahms' Violin Concerto and Chausson's *Poème* for violin and orch. He wrote some of the most popular violin pieces in the world, among them *Caprice Viennois, Tambourin Chinois, Schön Rosmarin, Liebesfreud*, etc. He also publ. a number of pieces in the classical vein, which he ascribed to various old composers (Vivaldi, Pugnani, Couperin, Padre Martini, Dittersdorf, Francoeur, Stamitz, and others). In 1935 he reluctantly admitted that these pieces were his own, with the exception of the first 8 bars from the "Couperin" *Chanson Louis XIII*, taken from a traditional melody; he explained his motive in doing so by the necessity of building up well-rounded programs for his concerts that would contain virtuoso pieces by old composers, rather than a series of compositions under his own, as yet unknown, name. He also wrote the operettas *Apple Blossoms* (N.Y., Oct. 7, 1919) and *Sissy* (Vienna, Dec. 23, 1932); publ. numerous arrangements of early and modern music (Corelli's *La Folia*, Tartini's *The Devil's Trill*, Dvořák's *Slavonic Dances, Spanish Dance* by Granados, *Tango* by Albéniz, etc.). He publ. a book of reminiscences of World War I, *Four Weeks in the Trenches: The War Story of a Violinist* (Boston, 1915).

BIBLIOGRAPHY: L. P. Lochner, *Fritz Kreisler*

(N.Y., 1950; not fully reliable as to factual details); Olin Downes, "Kreisler's Delectable Musical Hoax," *N.Y. Times* (March 3, 1935), reprinted in *Olin Downes on Music*, ed. by Irene Downes (N.Y., 1957).

Kreissle von Hellborn, Heinrich, Austrian writer; b. Vienna, Jan. 19, 1822; d. there, April 6, 1869. He studied law; was Dr. juris, and secretary in the Ministry of Finance, Vienna. A passionate admirer of Schubert, he publ. *Franz Schubert, eine biographische Skizze* (1861), followed in 1865 by the exhaustive biography *Franz Schubert* (condensed English transl. by Wilberforce, 1866; full transl. by A. D. Coleridge, 1869, in 2 vols., with an appendix by Sir George Grove).

Krejčí, Iša, important Czech composer and conductor; b. Prague, July 10, 1904; d. there, March 6, 1968. He studied composition with Jirák and Novák and conducting with Talich at the Prague Cons., graduating in 1929; was active in Bratislava as a conductor (1928–32), then at the Prague National Theater (1933–34) and at the Prague Radio (1934–45). From 1945 till 1958 he headed the opera in Olomouc; from 1958 to his death, he was music director of the National Theater in Prague. His music, in a neo-Classical idiom, is distinguished by vivacious rhythms and freely flowing melody; the national Czech element is not ostentatious, but its presence is well marked.
WORKS: 2 operas: *Antigone*, after Sophocles (1934); *Pozdviženi v Efesu (The Revolt at Ephesus)*, after Shakespeare's *Comedy of Errors* (1939–43; Prague, Sept. 8, 1946); Sinfonietta (1929); *Malý Balet (Small Ballet)* for chamber orch. (1927–30); Concertino for Piano and Wind Instruments (1935); Concertino for Violin and Wind Instruments (1936); *Antické motivy (Antique Motifs)* for low male voice, and orch. or piano (1936); Suite for Orch. (1939); *Sinfonietta-Divertimento* for orch. (1939); Cello Concertino (1939–40); *20 Variations on an Original Theme* for orch. (1946–47); Serenade for Orch. (1947–50); *14 Variations* on the folksong *Goodnight, My Beloved*, for orch. (1951–52); 4 symphonies (1954–55, 1956–57, 1961–63, 1961–66); *Vivat Rossini*, overture (1967); *Divertimento-Cassation* for flute, clarinet, bassoon and trumpet (1925); 5 string quartets (1928, revised 1935; 1953; 1960; 1962; 1965); Viola Sonatina (1928–29); Clarinet Sonatina (1929–30); Trio for oboe, clarinet and bassoon (1935); Trio for clarinet, double bass and piano (1936); Nonet (1937); *Sonatina concertante* for cello and piano (1939); Wind Quintet (1964); *4 Pieces* for violin and piano (1967); *A Little Mourning Music* for alto, violin, cello, double bass and piano (1936); *Ohlasy (Night Sounds)* for voice and wind quintet (1936); Piano Trio, with female voice to words of a psalm (1967); Piano Sonatina (1934); *3 Scherzinos* for piano (1945); songs.

Krejčí, Josef, Bohemian organist and composer; b. Milostin, Dec. 17, 1821; d. Prague, Oct. 19, 1881. He studied with Josef Proksch in Prague; was active as church organist; in 1858 he became director of the Organ School in Prague, and in 1865 was appointed director of the Prague Cons. He wrote mainly for the organ and also composed many sacred choruses.

Krejčí, Miroslav, Czech composer; b. Rychnov nad Kněžnou, Nov. 4, 1891; d. Prague, Dec. 29, 1964. He studied science at Charles Univ. in Prague (1910–14); then became a schoolmaster there, remaining in that employment for nearly 30 years (1914–43). He was a prof. at the Prague Univ. until his retirement (1943–53). His own music education was desultory; he studied 2 years with Vítězslav Novák as a youth (1911–13) and acquired a mastery of technique through actual composition.
WORKS: 2 operas: *Léto (Summer*, 1937; Prague, Dec. 4, 1940) and *Poslední Hejtman (The Last Captain*, 1944; Prague, March 18, 1948); the cantatas *The Wedding Song* (1926), *Smrt Kristova (The Death of Christ*, 1937–40), *Better Love* (1954), *Rodné Zemi (Homeland*, 1958) and *Mír (Peace*, 1959); Vocal Symphony (1930); 3 numbered symphonies (1944–46, 1952–54, 1955); *King Lávra*, symph. poem (1917); *Life and Time* for string orch. and horn (1927); Viola Concerto (1947); Clarinet Concerto (1949); *Capriccio* for viola, winds and percussion (1950); *Dance Suite* for orch. (1950); Violin Concerto (1953); *Funeral Music* for wind orch. (1960); 7 string quartets (1913; 1918; 1926; 1941; 1943; 1953; 1955); Clarinet Quintet (1920); 3 string quintets (1926, 1952, 1957); Divertimento, for flute, clarinet, horn and bassoon (1926); 2 violin sonatas (1926, 1952); Viola Sonata (1942); Cello Sonata (1943); Sonatina, for bassoon, or oboe, or horn, and piano (1950); Septet (1950); Nonet (1953); Quartet, for oboe, clarinet, bassoon and piano (1955); Wind Octet (1956); Suite for Solo Horn (1956); *3 Pieces* for 3 violas and piano (1957); Flute Sonata (1958); Divertimento for 10 winds (1958); Horn Sonata (1959); Organ Sonata (1954); choruses; songs.

Krek, Uroš, Slovenian composer; b. Ljubljana, May 21, 1922. He studied composition with Škerjanc at the Music Academy in Ljubljana, graduating in 1947; in 1967 joined its staff as a lecturer in music. His style of composition is classical in form, but contains some elements of folk modalities.
WORKS: Violin Concerto (1949); Bassoon Concerto (1954); *Mouvements concertants* for string orch. (1956); Horn Concerto (1960); *Inventiones ferales* for violin and orch. (1962); Concerto for Piccolo and Orch. (1966); *Capriccio* for Viola and 10 instruments (1971); Sinfonia for strings (1973); *Old Egyptian Stanzas* for tenor and orch. (1967); Violin Sonata (1946); Sonata for 2 violins (1971).

Kremenliev, Boris, Bulgarian-American composer and musicologist; b. Razlog, May 23, 1911. In 1929 he came to the U.S., and studied composition with La Violette in Chicago and with Howard Hanson in Rochester. He was a member of the Psychological Warfare Branch of the U.S. Army in Europe during World War II. In 1947 he was appointed to the staff of the Univ. of California in Los Angeles. Several of his works are imbued with Bulgarian melorhythms; of these the most interesting are *Pravo Horo* for orch. (Rochester, April 18, 1940) and *Bulgarian Rhapsody* for orch. (1952); he also composed several pieces of chamber music and publ. a valuable treatise, *Bulgarian-Macedonian Folk Music* (Los Angeles, 1952).

Kremer, Isa, Jewish folk singer; b. Beltzi, Bessarabia, 1885; d. Cordoba, Argentina, July 7, 1956. She acquired early fame as a singer of Russian, Yiddish, Polish, and German ballads; made many tours in Russia and Eastern Europe before coming to the U.S. in 1923; in New York, she appeared in vaudeville; gave her final concert in America at Carnegie Hall on Dec. 3, 1950. She married Dr. Gregorio Bermann, an Argentinian psychiatrist, in 1940.

Kremlev, Yuly, Russian musicologist and composer; b. Essentuki, June 19, 1908; d. in Leningrad, Feb. 15, 1971. He studied at the Leningrad Cons.; devoted himself mainly to musical biography; publ. monographs on Chopin (Moscow, 1949; revised ed. 1960), Grieg (Moscow, 1958) and Debussy (Moscow, 1964) and essays on esthetics. He also wrote a symphony, several piano sonatas and songs.

Krempelsetzer, Georg, Bavarian composer; b. Vilsburg, April 20, 1827; d. there, June 9, 1871. He was by trade a cloth weaver; studied music in Munich with Franz Lachner; became chorusmaster at theaters in Munich (1865), Görlitz (1868), and Königsberg (1870). He wrote the opera *Der Onkel aus der Lombardei* (1861), and the operettas *Die Franzosen in Gotha, Der Vetter auf Besuch* (1863), *Die Kreuzfahrer* (1865), *Das Orakel in Delphi* (1867), *Die Geister des Weins* (1867), *Aschenbrödel, Rotmantel* (1868).

Kremser, Eduard, Austrian composer; b. Vienna, April 10, 1838; d. there, Nov. 27, 1914. He studied in Vienna; in 1869, became chorusmaster of the "Männergesangverein" there; also conducted various other choral societies. He wrote the light operas *Der Botschafter* (Vienna, Feb. 25, 1886), *Der kritische Tag* (Vienna, Dec. 6, 1891), etc.; several symph. sketches with voices: *Balkanbilder, Prinz Eugen, Das Leben ein Tanz,* etc.; many part-songs (his settings of *6 altniederländische Volkslieder* are especially fine; of these the most celebrated is the Dutch *Prayer of Thanksgiving*); *Das Herzklopfen, Erinnerungen,* and *Fröhliche Armuth,* for men's chorus and orch.; songs (*Jagdlied,* with accompaniment of 4 horns; 2 songs from *Der Trompeter von Säkkingen,* with solo cornet); piano music; also edited *Wiener Lieder und Tänze* (2 vols., 1912, 1913).
BIBLIOGRAPHY: H. von Paumgarten, *Eduard Kremser* (Vienna, 1915).

Krenek, Ernst, noted modern composer; b. Vienna, Aug. 23, 1900. (Being of Czech origin, he used to spell his name Křenek (pronounced Krshenek) with a diacritical sign on r, but dropped it after coming to America). He studied in Vienna, and in Berlin with Franz Schreker; lived in Zürich (1923–25); then was an opera coach in Kassel, under Paul Bekker (1925–27); in 1928 he returned to Vienna and became a correspondent of the *Frankfurter Zeitung;* also traveled widely in Europe as lecturer and accompanist in programs of his own songs. In 1937 he came to the U.S.; was prof. of music at Vassar College (1939–42); then head of the music dept. at Hamline Univ., St. Paul, Minn. (1942–47); lived in Hollywood (1947–50). In the summer of 1950 and in following years he made successful tours of Germany as lecturer and conductor of his own works. He became an American citizen on Jan. 24, 1945. He was married to Anna Mahler (daughter of Gustav Mahler) in 1923; divorced in 1925, and married Berta Hermann, an actress. His evolution as a composer mirrors the development of modern music in general. The tradition of Mahler, strengthened by the domestic ties of his first marriage, was the dominant influence of his early life in music; he then became associated with the modern groups in Vienna, particularly Schoenberg, Berg, and Anton von Webern. In Germany he was associated with Hindemith as a creator of modern opera in a satiric manner. He achieved a masterly technique of composition in his earliest works, and developed his melodic and harmonic idiom in the direction of atonality and polytonality. His first international success came to him at the age of 26, with the production of his opera *Jonny spielt auf,* generally described as a "jazz opera" (although no such title appears in the score). It deals with a jazz fiddler whose fame sweeps the world; in the apotheosis, Jonny sits atop a gigantic globe. The opera was first performed in Leipzig (Feb. 10, 1927), producing a sensation; it was subsequently translated into 18 languages and performed all over the world; a brand of Austrian cigarettes was named after it; it was staged at the Metropolitan Opera House, New York (Jan. 19, 1929) with the hero as a black-faced musician rather than a Negro as in the original. However, the opera fell into desuetude a few years later. Krenek produced several short operas, to which he wrote his own librettos, with transitory success. He also composed symphonic, choral, and chamber music; wrote books and articles on music history and modern methods of composition. In 1933 he adopted the 12-tone method of composition; his opera *Karl V* was written in this idiom; subsequent works use various ingenious applications of Schoenberg's basic method. In 1950 he completed a voluminous autobiography, the manuscript of which he deposited at the Library of Congress, not to be opened until 15 years after his death. Excerpts were publ. under the title *Self-Analysis.* He made his home in Palm Springs, California, but traveled widely as conductor and pianist in his own works in Europe. In 1963 he was awarded the Grand State Prize of Austria.
WORKS: OPERAS AND DRAMAS WITH MUSIC: *Zwingburg* (Berlin, Oct. 16, 1924), *Der Sprung über den Schatten* (Frankfurt, June 9, 1924), *Orpheus und Eurydike* (Kassel, Nov. 27, 1926), *Jonny spielt auf* (Leipzig, Feb. 10, 1927), *Leben des Orest* (Leipzig, Jan. 19, 1930), *Karl V* (Prague, June 15, 1938), *Tarquin* (Vassar College, May 13, 1941), *What Price Confidence?* (1946), *Dark Waters* (1951), *Pallas Athene weint* (Hamburg, Oct. 17, 1955), *The Bell Tower* (Urbana, March 17, 1957), 3 short operas: *Der Diktator; Das geheime Königreich; Schwergewicht oder Die Ehre der Nation* (Wiesbaden, May 6, 1928); *Ausgerechnet und verspielt,* comic opera (Vienna, June 27, 1962), *Der goldene Bock,* fantastic chamber opera (Hamburg, June 16, 1964, composer conducting), *Das kommt davon, oder Wenn Sardakai auf Reisen geht (That's What Happened or, If Sardakai Goes Traveling),* to his own libretto (Hamburg State Opera, June 27, 1970). FOR ORCH.: 5 symphonies (No. 1, 1921; No.

2, 1922; No. 3, 1922; No. 4, N.Y., Nov. 27, 1947; No. 5, Albuquerque, March 16, 1950), *2 Concerti grossi* (1921); *Symphonische Musik* for 9 solo instruments (Donaueschingen, July 30, 1922); Piano Concerto No. 1 (1923); Concertino for Flute, Violin, Harpsichord, and String Orch. (1924); Violin Concerto (Dessau, Jan. 5, 1925); *Symphonie* for brass and percussion (1924-25); *3 Military Marches* (Donaueschingen, 1926); *Potpourri* (Cologne, Nov. 15, 1927); *Kleine Symphonie* (Berlin, Nov. 1, 1928); *Theme and Variations* (1931); *Music for Wind Orch.* (1931); Piano Concerto No. 2 (Amsterdam, March 17, 1938); *Symphonic Piece* for string orch. (Ann Arbor, Mich., Aug. 1, 1939); *Little Concerto,* for piano and organ, with chamber orch. (1940); *I Wonder as I Wander,* variations on a North Carolina folksong (1942); *Tricks and Trifles,* orchestral version of the *Hurricane Variations* (1945); *Symphonic Elegy* for strings, on the death of Anton von Webern (1946); Piano Concerto No. 3 (Minneapolis, Nov. 22, 1946, Mitropoulos pianist-conductor; the 12-tone system consistently used by Krenek after 1936 is not applied in this concerto); Piano Concerto No. 4 (1950); Double Concerto for Violin, Piano, and Chamber Orch. (Donaueschingen Festival, Oct. 6, 1951); Concerto for Harp and Chamber Orch. (Philadelphia, Dec. 12, 1952); Concerto for 2 Pianos and Orch. (N.Y., Oct. 24, 1953); *Medea,* for contralto and orch. (Philadelphia, March 13, 1953); *Eleven Transparencies* (Louisville, Feb. 12, 1955); *Spass mit Karten,* ballet (1957); *Kette, Kreis und Spiegel,* symph. poem (1957); *Spiritus Intelligentiae, Sanctus* for voices and electronic sounds (1957); *Hexaeder,* 6 pieces for chamber ensemble (1958); *Missa duodecim tonorum* for mixed chorus and organ (1958); *Sestina* for soprano and small ensemble (1958); *Quaestio Temporis* for chamber orch. (Hamburg, Sept. 30, 1960); *La Corona,* cantata (1959); *From Three Make Seven,* for chamber orch. (1961); *5 + 1* (*Alpbach Quintet;* 1962). CHAMBER MUSIC: Violin Sonata (1919); Serenade for quartet (1919); 8 string quartets (No. 1, 1921; No. 2, 1921; No. 3, 1923; No. 4, 1923-24; No. 5, 1930; No. 6, 1937; No. 7, 1943; No. 8, 1952); Suite for clarinet and piano (1924); Solo Violin Sonata (1924-25); Suite for cello solo (1939); Sonatina for Flute and Viola (1942); Sonata for Violin Solo (1942); Sonata for Viola and Piano (1948); String Trio (1948); *Parvula Corona Musicalis ad honorem J. S. Bach,* for string trio (1950). PIANO WORKS: *Double Fugue* for piano, 2 hands (1918); *Dance Studies,* in *Grotesken-Album* (ed. by K. Seeling, 1922); Piano Sonata No. 1 (1919); 5 sonatinas (1920); *Toccata and Chaconne* on the chorale, *Ja, ich glaub' an Jesum Christum* (1922, also a suite of pieces on the chorale); 2 suites (1924); 5 pieces (1925); Piano Sonata No. 2 (1928); *12 Short Piano Pieces* (1938); Piano Sonata No. 3 (1943); *Hurricane Variations* (1944); *8 Piano Pieces* (1946); Piano Sonata No. 4 (1948); *George Washington Variations* (1950); Piano Sonata No. 5 (1950); Piano Sonata No. 6 (1951). FOR CHORUS: *Concert Aria,* text from Goethe's *Stella* (1928); *Von der Vergänglichkeit des Irdischen,* cantata (1932); *Reisebuch aus den Österreichischen Alpen* (1935); 2 a cappella choruses for women's voices on Elizabethan poems (1939); *Proprium Missae in Festo SS. Innocentium,* for women's voices (1940); *Lamentatio*

Jeremiae Prophetae, Secundum Brevarium Sacrosanctae Ecclesiae Romanae (1941); *Cantata for Wartime* (1943); *5 Prayers,* for women's voices, from the *Litanie* by John Donne (1944); *The Santa Fe Time Table,* for chorus a cappella, to the text of names of railroad stops between Albuquerque and Los Angeles (1945); *In Paradisum,* motet for women's voices a cappella (1946). Krenek also composed an Organ Sonata (1941) and revised and orchestrated Monteverdi's *L'Incoronazione di Poppea* (1937); he is the author of the books *Über neue Musik* (collected lectures; Vienna, 1937; in English as *Music Here and Now,* N.Y., 1939); *Studies in Counterpoint* (N.Y., 1940; in German as *Zwölfton-Kontrapunkt Studien,* Mainz, 1952); *Selbstdarstellung,* autobiography (Zürich, 1948; in English as *Self-Analysis,* Albuquerque, 1953); *Musik im goldenen Westen; das Tonschaffen des U.S.A.* (Vienna, 1949); *Johannes Ockeghem* (N.Y., 1953); *De rebus prius factis* (Frankfurt, 1956); *Gedanken Unterwegs* (Munich, 1959).

BIBLIOGRAPHY: A. Weissmann, "Ernst Krenek," *Modern Music* (Dec. 1928); E. Evans, "Ernst Krenek," *Cobbett's Cyclopedic Survey of Chamber Music* (London, 1930; vol. 2, pp. 76-79); J. M. Schneider, "Ernst Krenek," *Revue Musicale* (Aug. 1930); F. Saathen, *Ernst Krenek, Ein Essay* (Munich, 1959); Lothar Knessl, *Ernst Krenek* (Vienna, 1967); W. Rogge, *Ernst Kreneks Opern—Spiegel der zwangiger Jahre* (Wolfenbüttel, 1970).

Krenn, Franz, Austrian composer and pedagogue; b. Dross, Feb. 26, 1816; d. St. Andrä, June 18, 1897. He studied music with his father; occupied posts as church organist in Vienna; from 1869-93 was prof. of harmony and counterpoint at the Vienna Cons. Gustav Mahler was his pupil. Krenn left a large number of works, among them 29 Masses, a symphony, chamber music, and a manual, *Musik- und Harmonielehre* (1890).

Krentzlin, Richard, German piano pedagogue and composer; b. Magdeburg, Nov. 27, 1864; d. Oldendorf (Hesse), Nov. 27, 1956, on the morning of his 92nd birthday. He studied at the Kullak Academy; became a successful piano teacher; publ. numerous character pieces (*Bunte Bilder, Aus meiner Jugendzeit,* etc.) and 8 books of piano studies, *Der gute Pädagoge.*

Krenz, Jan, Polish conductor and composer; b. Wloclawek, July 14, 1926. He studied composition with Sikorski and conducting with Wilkomirski; then was conductor of the Lódź Philharmonic (1945), of the Poznań Philharmonic (1948-49), and the Polish Radio Symph. in Katowice (1952-67), with which he toured in Germany, England, Japan and Australia. Returning to Poland, he became a principal conductor of Warsaw Opera (1967-73).

WORKS: *Toccata* for piano and orch. (1943); Symph. No. 1 (1947-49); *Nocturnes* for orch. (1950); *Classical Serenade* for orch. (1950); cantata, *Rozmowa dwóch miast (Conversation of Two Towns)* (1950); *Rustic Serenade* for small orch. (1951); Piano Concertino (1952); *Rhapsody* for xylophone, tam-tam, timpani, celesta, and string orch. (1952); *Capriccio* for

24 instruments (1962); 2 string quartets and other chamber music.

Kresánek, Jozef, Slovak musicologist; b. Čičmany, Dec. 20, 1913. He studied composition with Karel and Novák in Prague; in 1939 he joined the staff of Bratislava Univ. As a composer and music scholar he dedicated himself mainly to the codification of Slovak folksongs, and publ. numerous treatises on the subject. He composed 2 orchestral suites; some chamber music and songs.

Kretschmer, Edmund, German composer; b. Ostritz, Aug. 31, 1830; d. Dresden, Sept 13, 1908. He studied with Julius Otto (composition) and Johann Schneider (organ) in Dresden. In 1863 he became organist of the court, retiring in 1901. He was a successful composer; his choral work, *Geisterschlacht,* won a prize at the Dresden singing festival (1865); a 3-part Mass for men's chorus won the Brussels Academy's prize in 1868. He wrote several operas to his own librettos in a Wagnerian manner; at least 2 of them were successful: *Die Folkunger* (Dresden, March 21, 1874) and *Heinrich der Löwe* (Leipzig, Dec. 8, 1877); he also produced 2 light operas: *Der Flüchtling* (Ulm, 1881) and *Schön Rotraut* (Dresden, 1887); several choral works for festive occasions; church music; etc.
BIBLIOGRAPHY: O. Schmid, *Edmund Kretschmer* (Dresden, 1890).

Kretzschmar, August Ferdinand Hermann, eminent German music scholar; b. Olbernhau, Jan. 19, 1848; d. Nikolassee, near Berlin, May 10, 1924. He was a chorister and a pupil of Julius Otto in Dresden; then studied with Richter, Reinecke, Oskar Paul, and Papperitz at the Leipzig Cons.; took his degree of Dr. phil. at Leipzig with a thesis on ancient notation prior to Guido d'Arezzo, *De signis musicis* (1871). He then became teacher of organ and harmony at the Leipzig Cons.; also conducted choral societies there. In 1876 he was a theater conductor at Metz; 1877, music director at Rostock Univ.; 1880, municipal music director there. In 1887 he joined the faculty of the Leipzig Univ.; from 1888–97, Riedel's successor as conductor of the "Riedelverein"; conducted the "Akademische Orchesterkonzerte" initiated by himself (1890–95). In 1904 he went to Berlin as prof. at the Univ. there; from 1909–20, was also the director of the Hochschule für Musik. He was a thoroughly educated musician, a good organist as well as choral conductor, and composer of some secular and sacred vocal music. But his importance in musicology lies in his establishment of certain musical and esthetic concepts that elucidate the historical process. He introduced a convenient term (taken from theology) "Hermeneutik," applying it to the explanation of musical melodies and intervallic progressions as expressive of human emotions.
WRITINGS: *Peter Cornelius* (1880); *Führer durch den Konzertsaal,* in 3 vols.; I (1887; 6th ed., 1921), II (1888; 2nd ed., 1932, supplemented by Noack and Botstiber), III (1890; 4th ed., 1920; enlarged by Schnoor, 1932); *Geschichte des neuen deutschen Liedes* (1912; vol. 1 only, up to the songs of Zelter); *Geschichte der Oper* (1919); *Einführung in die Musikgeschichte* (1920); *Bach-Kolleg* (1922). His articles in various periodicals were publ. as *Gesammelte Aufsätze* (2 vols., 1911). He edited vols. 8, 9, and 42 of the *Denkmäler deutscher Tonkunst,* of which he was general editor from 1911–19; brought out a new edition of Lobe's *Lehrbuch der musikalischen Komposition* (4 vols., 1884–87).
BIBLIOGRAPHY: *Festschrift zu Kretzschmars 70. Geburtstag* (Leipzig, 1918); H. Abert, "Kretzschmar," *Jahrbuch der Musikbibliothek Peters* (1924).

Kreubé, Charles Frédéric, French conductor and composer; b. Luneville, Nov. 5, 1777; d. near Saint-Denis, 1846. He studied violin in Paris with R. Kreutzer (1800); joined the orch. of the Paris Opéra-Comique as violinist; from 1816–28, first conductor. He wrote 16 operas; also violin pieces.

Kreutz, Arthur, American composer; b. La Crosse, Wisconsin, July 25, 1906. He studied music at the Univ. of Wisconsin and at Columbia Univ. in New York; then was lecturer there (1946–52); in 1952 he was appointed to the staff of the music department of the Univ. of Mississippi. His works include a "ballad opera," *Acres of Sky* (Fayetteville, Ark., Nov. 16, 1951); symph. poem, *Winter of the Blue Snow* (1942); 2 symphonies (1945, 1946); opera, *The University Greys* (Clinton, Miss., March 15, 1954); folk opera, *Sourwood Mountain* (ibid., Jan. 8, 1959); also *Dance Concerto* for clarinet and orch. (1958); Violin Concerto (1965); 2 "jazz sonatas" for violin and piano, and other pieces in a jazz vein; also *New England Folksing* for chorus and orch. (Brooklyn, Feb. 17, 1948) and *Mosquito Serenade* for orch. (N.Y. Philharmonic, Feb. 21, 1948).

Kreutzer, Auguste, French violinist; brother of **Rodolphe Kreutzer;** b. Versailles, Sept. 3, 1778; d. Paris, Aug. 31, 1832. He studied with his brother at the Paris Cons.; played in the orch. of the Paris Opéra-Comique and Opéra; also in the court orchestras; taught at the Paris Cons. He wrote 2 violin concertos, 3 sonatas, etc.

Kreutzer, Konradin, important German composer; b. Messkirch, Baden, Nov. 22, 1780; d. Riga, Dec. 14, 1849. He was pupil of J. B. Rieger at Zwiefalten Abbey and of Ernst Weihrauch (1792–96). He then studied law at Freiburg for one year (1799–1800) before devoting himself to music. In 1800 he brought out his first operetta, *Die lächerliche Werbung,* in Freiburg. He lived for 5 years in Constance, and then in Vienna until 1811, studying counterpoint under Albrechtsberger. He produced, with considerable success, *Jerry und Bätely,* after Goethe (May 19, 1810); not being able to bring out 2 operas, *Konradin von Schwaben* and *Der Taucher,* in Vienna, he went, after a pianistic tour of a year, to Stuttgart, where, after the production of *Konradin von Schwaben* (March 30, 1812), he was appointed court conductor. In Stuttgart he produced 8 dramatic works, and then went to Donaueschingen in 1817 as conductor to Prince von Fürstenberg. There he produced *Adele von Budoy* in 1819, which was later successful in a revision entitled *Cordelia.* Returning to Vienna, he brought out *Libussa* (Dec. 4, 1822); was conductor at the Kärnthnerthor

Theater (1825, 1829–32, and 1837–40) and at the Josephstadt Theater (1833–37); his most successful work, *Das Nachtlager von Granada* (Jan. 14, 1834), appeared, and was followed a month later by *Der Verschwender* (Feb. 20, 1834), incidental music for Ferdinand Raimund's play of that name. Together with *Jerry und Bätely*, these 2 works held the stage until the end of the century. From 1840–42 he was conductor at the Municipal Theater in Cologne; after 2 years in Vienna (1847–49), he accompanied his daughter Cäcilie, a singer, to Riga, where he died. Besides his many operas, he wrote an oratorio, *Die Sendung Mosis*, and a cantata, *Die Friedensfeier;* also church music, chamber music, and piano pieces; songs, and some noteworthy men's choruses (*Die Capelle, Sonntagsmorgen, Der Tag des Herrn,* etc.).

BIBLIOGRAPHY: W. H. Riehl, *Musikalische Charakterköpfe* (vol. I, Stuttgart, 1879); R. Rossmayer, "Kreutzers Klaviermusik," *Zeitschrift für Musikwissenschaft* (vol. XIII, pp. 80 ff.); H. Burkard, *Konradin Kreutzers Ausgang* (Tübingen, 1920); A. Landau, *Das einstimmige Kunstlied Konradin Kreutzers* (Leipzig, 1930).

Kreutzer, Léon, French composer and music critic; son of **Auguste Kreutzer;** b. Paris, Sept. 23, 1817; d. Vichy, Oct. 6, 1868. He studied piano with Fleche and composition with Benoist. He wrote for the *Revue et Gazette Musicale, Revue Contemporaine, La Quotidienne, L'Union,* etc.; publ. an *Essai sur l'art lyrique au théâtre* (1845); also wrote an orchestral prelude to Shakespeare's *The Tempest;* string quartets, piano sonatas, etc.; and a treatise on modulation.

Kreutzer, Leonid, Russian pianist and pedagogue; b. St. Petersburg, March 13, 1884; d. Tokyo, Oct. 30, 1953. He studied piano with Anna Essipova and composition with Glazunov at the St. Petersburg Cons. In 1906 he went to Germany; from 1921 to 1932 taught at the Hochschule für Musik in Berlin. After the advent of the Nazi regime in 1933 he went to the U.S., and in 1938 traveled to Japan where he became prof. of piano at the Cons. of Tokyo; earned a fine reputation as a teacher there; many Japanese concert pianists were his pupils. He published *Das Wesen der Klaviertechnik* (Berlin, 1923).

Kreutzer, Rodolphe, famous violinist; b. Versailles, Nov. 16, 1766; d. Geneva, Jan. 6, 1831. His father, a German violinist in the Chapelle du Roi, and Anton Stamitz were his teachers. At the age of 13 he played a violin concerto of his own composition at a Concert Spirituel; in 1782 he was appointed 1st violin in the Chapelle du Roi, and in 1790 solo violin in the Théâtre-Italien, bringing out his first opera, *Jeanne d'Arc à Orleans* (May 10, 1790). It was followed by over 40 others, given at the Opéra, the Opéra-Comique, or the Théâtre-Italien; *Lodoiska* (Aug. 1, 1791) was perhaps his best. A year after his appointment as a teacher of violin at the Cons., he made a triumphant concert tour through Italy, Germany, and Holland. In 1801 he succeeded Rode as solo violin at the Opéra, of which he became second conductor in 1816, and first conductor in 1817. From 1802 he was also chamber musician to Napoleon; from 1815, to Louis XVIII; retired in 1826,

and so far lost influence that his last opera, *Mathilde,* was contemptuously rejected by the direction of the Opéra. Although his own music could not withstand the test of time, his name became immortal because it was to him that Beethoven dedicated the celebrated *Kreutzer Sonata.*

WORKS: 43 operas; 19 violin concertos; 2 double concertos; *Symphonie concertante* for violin and cello, with orch.; 15 string quartets; 15 string trios; also duets, sonatas, variations, etc., for violin; but his masterwork, wherein his worthiness to rank with the great masters of the classic Parisian school of violin playing is convincingly proved, is the *40 Etudes ou Caprices* for violin solo, republished in countless editions, revised by Vieuxtemps and others. Kreutzer was joint author, with Rode and Baillot, of the great violin method used in the Paris Cons.

BIBLIOGRAPHY: H. Kling, *R. Kreutzer* (Brussels, 1898); B. Cutter, *How to Study Kreutzer* (1907); J. Hardy, *R. Kreutzer; sa jeunesse à Versailles* (Paris, 1910); A. Moser, *Geschichte des Violinspiels* (p. 394 ff.).

Křička, Jaroslav, eminent Czech composer and pedagogue; b. Kelč, Moravia, Aug. 27, 1882; d. Prague, Jan. 23, 1969. He first studied law in Prague (1900–02); then studied music at the Cons. there (1902–05) and in Berlin (1905–06); 1906, taught music in Ekaterinoslav, Russia; 1909, returned to Prague and conducted (1911–20) the famous choral society 'Hlahol'; 1919, became prof. at the Cons., remaining on its staff until 1945; then devoted his time to composition.

WORKS: the operas *Hypolita* (1910–16; Prague, Oct. 10, 1917); *Bílý pán* (The White Gentleman), after Oscar Wilde's *The Canterville Ghost* (1927–29; Brno, 1929; revised in 1930 as *Today Ghosts Have a Difficult Time;* Breslau, Nov. 14, 1931); *Kral Lavra* (King Lawrence, 1936–37 and revised 1938–39; Prague, June 7, 1940); *České jesličky* (The Czech Christmas Manger, 1936–37 and revised 1948; Prague, Jan. 15, 1949); *Jáchym a Juliána* (Joachim and Julia, 1945–48; Opava, 1951); *Serenáda* (Pilsen, 1950; opera buffa); *Kolébka* (The Cradle, 1950; Opava, 1951; musical comedy); *Zahořanský hon* (The Zahořany Hunt, Opava, 1955) and the children's operas: *Ogaři* (Country Lads, 1918; Nové Město in Moravia, Sept. 7, 1919); *Dobře to dopadlo* or *Tlustý pradědeček* (It Turned Out Well or The Fat Great-Grandfather, 1932) and *Lupici a Detekotyvove* (Robbers & Detectives, 1932; both operas, Prague, Dec. 29, 1932); several small operas for children's theater; a television opera *Kalhoty* (A Pair of Trousers; Czech television 1962); a symphony, *Jarní* (Spring, 1905–06; revised 1942); *Nostalgie* for string orch. and harp (1905); *Faith,* symph. poem (1907); *A Children's Suite* for orch. (1907); *Scherzo Idyllic* for orch. (1908; Prague, Nov. 13, 1910; 3rd movement of an uncompleted Symph. No. 2); *Modrý pták* (A Blue Bird), overture after a Maeterlinck fairy tale (1911; Prague, March 3, 1912, composer conducting); *Adventus,* symph. poem (1920–21; Prague, Nov. 6, 1921); *Matěj Kopecký,* overture (1928); *Horácká suita (Suite montagnarde)* for orch. (1935; Prague, Sept. 8, 1935); Sinfonietta for string orch. and timpani (1940–41); *Majales,* overture (1942); Violin Concerto (1944); Concertino for Horn, and String Quartet (or string orch.;

1951); *Variations on a Theme of Boccherini* for bassoon, and string quartet or string orch. (1952); *Sinfonietta semplice* (1962); the cantatas: *Pokušeni na pousti* (*Temptation in the Desert*, 1921–22); *Jenny, the Thief* (1927–28); *Tyrolese Elegies* (1930–31); *A Eulogy to a Woman* (1933); *Recollections of Student Years* (1934); *Moravian Cantata* (1935–36); *The Golden Spinning Wheel* (1943); *To Prague* (1960); *Small Suite in Old Style* for 2 violins and piano (1907); 3 string quartets (1907; 1938–39; *Wallachian*, 1949); *Doma* (*At Home*), piano trio (1924–25); Violin Sonata (1925); Sonatina for 2 Violins (1926–27; revised for violin and viola); Concertino (septet) for Violin, Wind Quintet and Piano (1940); *Partita* for solo violin (1941); Divertimento for wind quintet (1950); Flute Sonatina (1951); Variations for solo violin (1956); Violin Sonatina (1962); several albums of piano pieces; a number of songs; also arrangements of folksongs.

Krieger, Adam, German composer; b. Driesen, Neumark, Jan. 7, 1634; d. Dresden, June 30, 1666. He studied with Samuel Scheidt in Halle; from 1655–57 he was organist at the Nikolaikirche in Leipzig; then went to Dresden as court organist. He was one of the most important of the early composers of German lieder; he called his "Arien" and for most of them wrote the words as well as the music; they contain instrumental ritornels, for two violins and continuo in the early songs, for five strings and continuo in the later ones. Many of these "Arien" have been preserved, although his original collection (1657) is lost; it was reconstructed by H. Osthoff (1929); the 2nd collection (1667) is reproduced in vol. 19 of the *Denkmäler deutscher Tonkunst*. H. Osthoff, *Adam Krieger* (Leipzig, 1929).

Krieger, Armando, Argentine composer; b. Buenos Aires, May 7, 1940. He studied composition with Alberto Ginastera; gave piano concerts in programs of advanced modern music. In his compositions he adopts a serial technique in which rhythmic, melodic and harmonic elements follow a predetermined formula of contrasts. Among his works the most significant is *Métamorfosis d'après une lecture de Kafka* for piano and 15 instruments (1968); he also wrote 2 chamber cantatas (1959, 1963); 2 string quartets (1960, 1963) and other chamber music.

Krieger, Edino, Brazilian composer; b. Brusque (Santa Catarina), March 17, 1928. He studied music with his father Aldo Krieger, director of the local Cons., and H. J. Koellreutter. In 1948 he studied with Aaron Copland at the Berkshire Music Center in Tanglewood; then at the Juilliard School of Music, N.Y., with Peter Mennin; also with Ernst Krenek in Brazil in 1952 and with Lennox Berkeley in London. He adopted the dodecaphonic method of composition, but in 1953 turned toward neo–Classicism with national allusions. To the first period belong his *Epigramas* for piano; Sonatina for flute and piano; *Música de Câmara* for flute, trumpet, violin and timpani and *Melopeia* for voice, viola, oboe, saxophone and trombone; to the second, *Abertura sinfonica*; String Quartet; 2 piano sonatas; *Concertante* for piano and orch.; *Fantasia* for orch.; *Divertimento* for string

orch.; *Brasiliana* for viola and orch.; and 4-hand piano sonata. However, he applies dodecaphonic techniques in his Brazilian work *Chôro* for flute and string orch. and in *Variações elementares* for chamber orch. (1965).

Krieger (or **Krüger**), **Johann,** famous German contrapuntist and organist, brother of **Johann Philipp Krieger;** b. Nuremberg, Dec. 28, 1651; d. Zittau, July 18, 1735. He studied with his brother, and became his successor as chamber organist at Bayreuth in 1672. He was subsequently a court musician at Greiz (1678–81); then went to Zittau, where he was active as municipal organist; he remained there for 54 years, until his death. His music was appreciated by Handel; some of his organ compositions are regarded as presaging the grand style of Bach.

WORKS: *Neue musikalische Ergetzligkeit*, arias for 5–9 voices (Frankfurt, 1684); *6 musikalische Partien*, dance music for clavichord (Nuremberg, 1697); *Anmuthige Clavier-Übung*, containing preludes, fugues, etc. (Nuremberg, 1699); also sacred music. Max Seiffert ed. (in the *Denkmäler deutscher Tonkunst*) 2 sacred choral works by Krieger (vol. 6, part 1) and complete keyboard works, with critical notes, lists of sacred and secular vocal music, dates of performance, notes on extant MSS, biographical details, etc. (vol. 18); an aria from the *Neue musikalische Ergetzligkeit* is reprinted in Schering's *Geschichte der Musik in Beispielen*, no. 235.

Krieger, Johann Philipp, German composer; b. Nuremberg, Feb. 25, 1649; d. Weissenfels, Feb. 7, 1725. He was a pupil of Johann Drechsel and Gabriel Schütz in Nuremberg; went to Copenhagen, where he became a pupil and later assistant of court organist Johann Schröder (1663–69). In 1670 he was appointed court organist and chamber composer at Bayreuth, with an interval of study in Italy (1673). He was subsequently court musician at Kassel, and at Halle (from 1677); on Dec. 23, 1680 he was appointed court conductor at Weissenfels and Halle, remaining in this capacity until his death. He received the rank of nobility from Emperor Leopold I during a visit to Vienna (1677). He produced some 20 stage works in Halle, Weissenfels, Hamburg, and other German towns; publ. 12 trio sonatas for 2 violins with continuo (op. 1, 1688); 12 sonatas for violin with viola da gamba (op. 2, 1693); *Musikalischer Seelenfriede*, 20 sacred arias for violin with bass (1697); *Lustige Feldmusik*, 6 overtures for wind or other instruments (1704), etc. Modern reprints, ed. by Seiffert, are in vols. 53/54 of the *Denkmäler deutscher Tonkunst* (contains a selection of 21 sacred compositions by Krieger with critical commentary, as well as a complete list of his sacred works perf. at Weissenfels, notes of extant MSS, biographical details, etc.), vol. 6 (2 sacred choral works with a practical transcription of one of them), and the appendix to vol. 18 (3 keyboard pieces). Other reprints are: instrumental suite from *Lustige Feldmusik*, in *Perlen alter Kammermusik* (ed. by Schering, for strings; 1912); in *Organum*, ed. by Seiffert (vol. 3, containing no. 3 of the *Feldmusik*, for chamber orch.); selected organ pieces are in vol. 4 of *Organum*, etc.; 24 arias, in *Haus- und Kammermusik aus dem XVI.–XVIII. Jahrhundert*, ed. by H. J. Moser (1930); 2

arias in Schering's *Geschichte der Musik in Beispielen;* Eitner ed. 2 partitas, 2 sonatas, and various vocal works in *Monatshefte für Musikgeschichte* (supplement to vol. 30).

Kriens, Christian, Dutch-American pianist, violinist, and composer; b. Brussels, April 29, 1881; d. Hartford, Conn., Dec. 17, 1934. He was taken to Holland as a child; studied with his father, a clarinetist, and later at the Royal Cons. at The Hague. At 14 he made his debut at Amsterdam, playing the *Emperor Concerto* and conducting his own 2nd Symphony. From 1896–99 he toured Europe as a violinist; then taught at The Hague Cons. He came to America as conductor of the French Opera Co. (1906); settled in New York in 1907; was violinist in the N.Y. Symph., N.Y. Philh., and at the Metropolitan Opera. He then became director of the Traveller's Broadcasting Co., Station WTIC, Hartford, Conn. Despondent over his inability to find further work, he committed suicide.

Krigar, Hermann, German pianist; b. Berlin, April 3, 1819; d. there, Sept. 5, 1880. He studied at Leipzig with Schumann, Mendelssohn, and Hauptmann (1843–45); organized a singing society in Berlin; taught there. He wrote incidental music, motets, psalms, piano pieces, and songs.

Krips, Josef, noted Austrian conductor; b. Vienna, April 8, 1902; d. Geneva, Oct. 13, 1974. He studied with Mandyczewski and Weingartner in Vienna; was violinist at the Volksoper there (1918–21); then became operatic coach and choirmaster of the Volksoper (1921). In 1924 he conducted opera in Aussig; in 1925, at the Municipal Theater in Dortmund; from 1926–33, general music director at Karlsruhe. In 1933 he was appointed conductor at the Vienna State Opera; in 1935, became prof. at the Vienna Academy of Music. In 1938 he lost these positions, after the annexation of Austria to Germany; conducted a season of opera in Belgrade (1938–39). In 1945 he rejoined the staff of the Vienna State Opera; conducted in England, France, and Russia in 1947, producing an excellent impression. In 1950 he was appointed conductor of the London Symph. Orch.; from 1953 to 1963 he was conductor of the Buffalo Symph. Orch.; then conductor of the San Francisco Symph. Orch. (1963–69); also guest conductor of the N.Y. Philharmonic and other American and European orchestras.

Kriukov, Nikolai, Russian composer; brother of **Vladimir Kriukov;** b. Moscow, Feb. 14, 1908; d. there (suicide), April 5, 1961. He studied with Vassilenko; devoted himself chiefly to folksong arrangements and film music. He has written orchestral suites on folk themes gathered in various republics of the Soviet Union, sometimes including native instruments. He received 2 Stalin prizes for his film scores.

Kriukov, Vladimir, Russian composer; b. Moscow, July 22, 1902; d. Staraya Rusa, near Moscow, June 14, 1960. He studied with Gretchaninov, Miaskovsky, and Catoire. He wrote the operas *Miserly Night* (composed at the age of 15), *The King at the Marketplace* (after Alexander Blok), and *The Station Master* (after

Pushkin); (1951, 1955); Violin Concerto (1950); 2 concerto grossos (1950, 1963); String Quartet (1954); songs.

Křivinka, Gustav, Czech composer; b. Doubravice, April 24, 1928. He studied violin and composition in Brno, graduating in 1954 from the Brno Cons. He wrote 2 symphonies; 2 violin concertos; 2 piano concertos; several song cycles; chamber music.

Křížkovský, Karel (Pavel), Bohemian choral composer; b. Holasovice, Jan. 9, 1820; d. Brno, May 8, 1885. He was a chorister at Opava; then attended the Gymnasium there; became a school teacher; in 1845, joined the order of the Austin Friars, and assumed the name Pavel; was ordained priest in 1848. He was greatly interested in Moravian folksongs and collected many of them in the field. At the same time, he began to compose choruses in the national manner; one of his earliest works, *Utonulá (The Girl That Drowned),* became popular; other favorites are *Žaloba (The Plaint)* and particularly *Odvedeného prosba (The Recruit's Prayer).* He also wrote much sacred music (Roman Catholic) for the Olomouc Cathedral, where he was music director from 1873. Among his pupils was Janáček. Publication of his collected works was begun at Prague in 1949.

BIBLIOGRAPHY: J. Geissler, *Křížkovský* (Prague, 1885); K. Eichler *Křížkovský* (Brno, 1904); J. Racek, *Křížkovský* (Olomouc, 1946).

Kroeger, Ernest Richard, American organist and composer; b. St. Louis, Aug. 10, 1862; d. there, April 7, 1934. He studied piano in St. Louis; then was organist at various churches there; taught and lectured at a number of schools in the U.S. He composed orchestral works, including the overtures *Thanatopsis, Endymion, Sardanapalus, Hiawatha, Atala* and the symph. suites *Lalla Rookh* and *The Mississippi; A Masque of Dead Florentines,* for declamation or action with music; Piano Trio; Piano Quartet; Piano Quintet; 4 string quartets; Violin Sonata; pieces for organ; songs.

Kroeger, Karl, American composer; b. Louisville, Kentucky, April 4, 1932. He studied music at the Univ. of Louisville and Univ. of Illinois; then moved to New York, where he became head of the Americana Collection of the New York Public Library's Music Division. In 1964 he was appointed composer-in-residence at the Univ. of Oregon; in 1972 became director of the Moravian Music Foundation in Salem, North Carolina; has written numerous articles on Moravian music and has edited manuscripts from the Foundation archives. He has written symphonic and chamber music in a neo-Classical manner.

Krohn, Ernst C., American musicologist; b. New York, Dec. 23, 1888; d. Santa Fe, March 21, 1975. He settled in St. Louis in 1898; studied piano with his father and with Ottmar Moll, attaining a modicum of virtuosity; gave recitals and taught piano in various schools in St. Louis from 1909 to 1963; also composed songs and piano pieces. He was co-founder of the Bach Society of St. Louis in 1942.

WRITINGS: *A Century of Missouri Music* (St.

Louis, 1924); *The History of Music: An Index to the Literature Available in a Selected Group of Musicological Publications* (St. Louis, 1952).

Krohn, Felix (Julius Theofil), Finnish conductor and composer; b. Tampere, May 20, 1898; d. Lahti, Nov. 11, 1963. He studied with his father; later at the Helsinki School of Music and the Hochschule für Musik in Berlin. Returning to Finland in 1922, he was active as conductor and teacher.
WORKS: *Sotarukous (War Prayer)* for orch. (1918); *Sinfonia Brevis, Vuodenajat (The Seasons,* 1921); *Kyllikki,* cantata (1923); *Odalisque* for orch. (1924); 4 suites for orch.: *Sysmäläinen (The Man from Sysma,* 1938), *Vihreä kulta (Green Gold,* 1939), *Anu and Mikko* (1940), and *Linnaisten kartanon vihreä kamari (The Green Room at Linnainen Manor,* 1944); *Uskollinen sisar (The Faithful Sister),* opera for children (1945); chamber music.

Krohn, Ilmari (Henrik Reinhold), eminent Finnish music scholar; b. Helsingfors, Nov. 8, 1867; d. there, April 25, 1960. After studying with Richard Faltin in Helsingfors, he went to Germany, where he took courses at the Leipzig Cons. with Papperitz and Reinecke (1886–90); obtained his Dr. phil. with the thesis *Über die Art und Enstehung der geistlichen Volksmelodien in Finnland* (Helsingfors, 1899). Returning to Finland, he joined the staff of the Univ. of Helsingfors (1900); also taught at the Cons. there; lectured at musical congresses in London, Paris, Basel, Vienna, and Rome (1891–1914). In 1906 he founded the musical journal *Säveletär,* was a member of the Songbook Commission (1918–23); proposed the construction of an "Acoustic Harmonium" of his own invention, and publ. a paper on it, *System Krohn* (Vienna, 1906).
WRITINGS: *Guide for Acoustic Intonation* (Helsingfors, 1911; in Swedish, 1912); a course of music theory, in 5 parts: I. *Rhythm* (1911–14); II. *Melody* (1917); III. *Harmony* (1923); IV. *Polyphony* (1929); V. *Form* (1937); *Der Formenbau in den Symphonien von Jean Sibelius* (Helsinki, 1942); *Der Stimmungsgehalt in den Symphonien von Jean Sibelius* (Helsinki, 1945–46; 2 vols.); *Sävelmuistoja elämäni varrelta* (memoirs; Helsinki, 1951). His most significant accomplishment is the compilation of some 7000 Finnish folksongs, *Suomen Kansan Sävelmiä,* which he began in 1886, and methodically arranged in 4 categories: I. sacred melodies; II. secular melodies; III. dance melodies; IV. runic melodies. The publication of these important materials stretched from 1898 till 1933. He also edited psalms (1903), introits (1908), antiphons (1915), Easter matins, New Year vigils, vespers, and the Order of the Mass for the church year (1925); *Iltakellot, Completorium I–IV* (1928); began a complete edition of the Finnish Psalter in 1952. He contributed valuable articles on Finnish music to various journals. Krohn was also a composer; wrote an opera, *Tuhotulva (Deluge,* Helsinki, Oct. 25, 1928); 2 oratorios, *Ikiaartehet (Eternal Treasures,* 1914) and *Viottajat (Victors,* 1937); many sacred choral works; a number of songs. On the occasion of his 60th birthday, his students publ. a collection of musical essays in his honor (Helsinki, 1927).

BIBLIOGRAPHY: Sulho Ranta, *Ilmari Krohn* in *Suomen Säveltäjiä* (Helsinki, 1945; pp. 273–284).

Kroll, Erwin, German music critic and author; b. Deutsch-Eylau, Feb. 3, 1886. He studied at Königsberg and at the Munich Academy of Music and Munich Univ., with Pfitzner and Sandberger; was music critic in Königsberg until 1930, when he moved to Berlin; from 1945–53 he was musical director of the Northwest Radio. He publ. biographies of E. T. A. Hoffmann (1923); Pfitzner (1924), and Weber (1933); also wrote a number of songs and some chamber music.

Kroll, Franz, German pianist and music editor; b. Bromberg, June 22, 1820; d. Berlin, May 28, 1877. He was first a student of medicine; then took lessons from Liszt; settled in Berlin as a music teacher. He was the editor of Bach's *Well-Tempered Clavier* for the Bach Gesellschaft, to which he contributed an introduction, summarizing bibliographical data; also edited Mozart's piano works.

Kroll, William, American violinist; b. New York, Jan. 30, 1901. He studied in Berlin and at the Institute of Musical Art, N.Y. (graduated in 1922); then became 1st violinist of the Coolidge String Quartet, and appeared with it at numerous chamber music festivals in the U.S. and in Europe; subsequently organized a string quartet of his own, The Kroll Quartet.

Krombholc, Karlo, Hungarian-Serbian composer; b. Budapest, Dec. 20, 1905. He studied at the Vienna Academy of Music; was active as a concert pianist from 1927 to 1939; in 1945 he went to Yugoslavia and settled in Novi Sad as piano teacher. His works are influenced mainly by Béla Bartók, with ethnic modalities gadrooned by atonal extrapolations. Typical of these is his extensive piano work *Sazvezda (Constellation;* 1969). He also wrote orchestral works based on Hungarian and Balkan folk tunes.

Krommer, Franz, violinist and composer; b. Kamenitz, Moravia, Nov. 27, 1759; d. Vienna, Jan. 8, 1831. He first studied with his uncle, an organist; went to Vienna; joined the orch. of Count Styrum-Limburg at Simontornya as violinist, then conductor; became choirmaster at Fünfkirchen, Pecs; then bandmaster of the Karólyi regiment; went to Gödöllö as Kapellmeister of Count Grassalkovic's orch. He returned to Vienna, and in 1818 became Imperial Kapellmeister. He wrote a Mass; 5 symphonies; 5 violin concertos; a quantity of chamber music; quintets and quartets for wind instruments; etc.
BIBLIOGRAPHY: W. H. Riehl, *Musikalische Charakterköpfe* (vol. 3, Stuttgart, 1879).

Kromolicki, Joseph, eminent musicologist; b. Posen, Jan. 16, 1882; d. Berlin, Oct. 11, 1961. He received a thorough education in music, studying with Haberl and Haller in Regensburg; and with Pfitzner, Kretzschmar, and Johannes Wolf in Berlin; received his Dr. phil. in 1909 with a thesis, *Die Practica artis musicae des Amerus.* He was active as choral conductor in Berlin churches; edited *Musica sacra* from 1908 and vols. 45, 48, and 57 of the *Denkmäler deutscher Tonkunst;* composed 5 Masses, a *Te Deum,* organ preludes, sacred songs, etc.

Kronke, Emil, German pianist and composer; b. Danzig, Nov. 29, 1865; d. Dresden, Dec. 16, 1938. He was a pupil of Reinecke in Leipzig and of Nicodé and Kirchner in Dresden; won 1st prize for piano playing at the Dresden Cons. (1886). He was an ardent admirer of Liszt, and wrote several virtuoso pieces for piano; also publ. several manuals: *Das virtuose Arpeggiospiel; Chopin-Etüden; Die moderne Technik; Die hohe Schule des 4. und 5. Fingers;* edited over 200 of Chopin's works.

Kronold, Hans, cellist; brother of **Selma Kronold;** b. Cracow, July 3, 1872; d. New York, Jan. 10, 1922. He studied in Leipzig and Berlin; came to America at the age of 14; joined the orch. of the Metropolitan Opera; then played in the N.Y. Symph. Orch.; taught at the N.Y. College of Music. He publ. cello pieces and songs.

Kronold, Selma, soprano; sister of **Hans Kronold;** b. Cracow, Aug. 18, 1861; d. New York, Oct. 9, 1920. She made her debut as Agatha in *Der Freischütz,* at Leipzig, when she was 16; then was engaged to sing Wagnerian roles in various European cities. In 1888 she came to America; sang the leading roles in the American premières of *Cavalleria Rusticana* (Philadelphia, Sept. 9, 1891) and *I Pagliacci* (N.Y., June 15, 1893); in 1896, joined the Metropolitan Opera; retired in 1904 and founded the Catholic Oratorio Society. Her repertory included some 45 parts.

Krow, Josef Theodor, Czech singer and composer; b. Nove Straseci, Dec. 19, 1797; d. Draguignan, near Nice, March 1, 1859. He studied cello, theory and voice; appeared as an opera singer in minor roles in Hungary, Poland and Holland. From 1835 to 1840 he lived in London as a singing teacher; in 1858 he went to Nice, where he died a year later. His claim to a small niche in music history is that in 1825 he published a song to the Czech words "Těšme se blahou nadeji," claiming it to be an authentic melody of the time of the Bohemian religious reformer, martyr and saint, Ján Hus. This claim was widely believed; Liszt wrote a piano paraphrase on Krow's song under the title *Hussittenlied aus dem 15. Jahrhundert* ("a Hussite song from the 15th century"). Under the same misapprehension Balfe made use of it in his opera *The Bohemian Girl,* and an Italian composer Angelo Tessaro in the opera *Giovanni Huss.* Even more spectacular was Krow's success in setting the same tune to his own German words "Polen wird für ewig Polen," published under the pseudo-Polish pseudonym Workinski (*Work* is the crab form of *Krow*) in 1831; the song was caught in the wave of universal sympathy for Poland after the unsuccessful Polish rebellion, achieving tremendous popularity all over Europe.

Kroyer, Theodor, eminent German musicologist; b. Munich, Sept. 9, 1873; d. Wiesbaden, Jan. 12, 1945. He studied piano with Lang, counterpoint with Rheinberger, and musicology with Sandberger; took the degree of Dr. phil. in 1897; then became music critic of the *Münchener Allgemeine Zeitung;* was on the staff of the Univs. of Munich (1902–20), Heidelberg (1920–23), and Leipzig (1923–33). In 1925 he purchased for the Univ. of Leipzig the rich collection of instruments, manuscripts, and portraits from the famous Heyer Museum in Cologne; also in 1925 he began issuing the valuable series *Publikationen älterer Musik* (Deutsche Gesellschaft für Musikwissenschaft). In 1932 be became prof. at the Univ. of Cologne; retired in 1938. He edited a volume (motets and Magnificat) of the complete works of Senfl in the *Denkmäler der Tonkunst in Bayern* 5 (1903); also edited a selection from the works of G. Aichinger for the same series (vol. 8).

BIBLIOGRAPHY: *Kroyer-Festschrift* (1933); O. Ursprung, "Theodor Kroyer," *Zeitschrift für Musikwissenschaft* (Nov. 1933).

Krstič, Petar, Serbian composer; b. Belgrade, March 2, 1877; d. Belgrade, Jan. 21, 1957; studied at the Vienna Cons. with R. Fuchs. Returning to Belgrade, he conducted opera at the National Theater; in 1930, became inspector of several music schools. His works, based on Serbian national tunes, included the opera *Zulumćar* (Belgrade, Nov. 23, 1927); cantata *Jutro Slobode* (1919); several orchestral suites of national dances; choruses and songs. He edited a Serbian music dictionary.

Krückl, Franz, Moravian baritone; b. Edlspitz, Nov. 10, 1841; d. Strasbourg, Jan. 13, 1899. He studied with Dessoff; made his debut in 1868 in Brünn; then sang in Kassel, Augsburg, Hamburg, and Cologne (1874–86); taught at the Hoch Cons. in Frankfurt; in 1892, became director of the Municipal Theater in Strasbourg. He publ. *Der Vertrag zwischen Direktor und Mitglied der deutschen Bühne* (1899).

Krueger, Felix Emil, German music psychologist; b. Posen, Aug. 10, 1874; d. Basel, Feb. 24, 1948. He studied at the Univs. of Strasbourg, Berlin, and Munich (Dr. phil., 1897), also at the Leipzig Psychological Institute and the Kiel Psychological and Physiological Institute. After lecturing at the Univ. of Leipzig (1903–06), he went to Argentina and was prof. at the Univ. of Buenos Aires (1906–08); was prof. at Halle Univ. (1910–12); exchange prof. at Columbia Univ., N.Y. (1912–13); in 1918, was appointed prof. and director of the Psychological Institute of Leipzig Univ., succeeding Wilhelm Wundt; held an honorary LL.D. degree from Columbia Univ.; also honorary degrees from European institutions of learning. He retired in 1938; lived in Potsdam; then went to Switzerland, where he remained until his death.

WRITINGS: *Beziehungen der experimentellen Phonetik zur Psychologie* (1907); *Mitbewegungen beim Singen, Sprechen und Hören* (Leipzig, 1910); *Über Entwicklungspsychologie* (1915); *Über psychische Ganzheit* (1926). In 1934 his students and admirers publ. a Festschrift on his 60th birthday.

Krueger, Karl, American conductor; b. Atchison, Kansas, Jan. 19, 1894. He first studied philosophy and law, then music, at the Univs. of Vienna and Heidelberg; recieved his M.A. from the Univ. of Kansas (1916); took courses with Chadwick and Goodrich in Boston, Widor in Paris, and R. Fuchs (composition) in Vienna; also conducting with Schalk, Nikisch, and Weingartner. From 1919-24 he was assistant conductor at the Vienna State Opera; he was conductor of the Seattle Orch. (1926-32), the Kanas City Philharmonic Orch. (1933-43), the Detroit Symph. Orch. (1943-49). In 1950 he organized a radio orch., but the broadcasts were discontinued after a season. He publ. a book, *Way of the Conductor* (N.Y., 1958).

Krug, Dietrich, German music teacher; b. Hamburg, May 25, 1821; d. there, April 7, 1880. He studied with Melchert and J. Schmitt. He wrote studies for the piano; also publ. a method.

Krug, Freidrich, German composer; b. Kassel, July 5, 1812; d. Karlsruhe, Nov. 3, 1892. He was a baritone singer; court musical director at Karlsruhe. He wrote the operas *Die Marquise* (Kassel, 1843), *Meister Martin der Kufer und seine Gesellen* (Karlsruhe, 1845), *Der Nachtwächter* (Mannheim, 1846).

Krug, (Wenzel) Joseph (called **Krug-Waldsee**), German composer and conductor; b. Waldsee, Nov. 8, 1858; d. Magdeburg, Oct. 8, 1915. He developed precociously; entered the Stuttgart Cons. at 14, studying violin, piano, singing, and theory; graduated in 1880, and went to Switzerland, where he was active as a teacher in Hofwyl; then conducted a choral society in Stuttgart (1882-89); was subsequently chorusmaster in Hamburg (1889-92), in Nuremberg and Augsburg (from 1894); then lived in Magdeburg. He wrote several cantatas in a grand manner; 4 operas; chamber music; songs.

Krüger, Eduard, German writer on music; b. Lüneburg, Dec. 9, 1807; d. Göttingen, Nov. 9, 1885. He studied philology in Berlin and Göttingen; also studied music; in 1861, became prof. of music at Göttingen Univ. He publ. *De musicis Graecorum organis circa Pindari tempora* (1830); *Grundriss der Metrik* (1838); *Beiträge für Leben und Wissenschaft der Tonkunst* (1847); *System der Tonkunst* (1866); also contributed articles to various periodicals.

Krüger, Wilhelm, German pianist and composer; b. Stuttgart, Aug. 5, 1820; d. there, June 16, 1883. He studied piano with Ziegele and composition with Lindpaintner. In 1845 he settled in Paris, where he enjoyed an excellent reputation as pianist and teacher; in 1870, the outbreak of the Franco-Prussian War compelled him to return to Germany; he was then active as a pedagogue. He publ. a number of brilliant salon pieces for piano (168 opus numbers in all), which included caprices, nocturnes, genre pieces (*Harpe éolienne, Guitare*), a *Polonaise-Boléro*, études (*Les Six Jours de la semaine*, etc.), and transcriptions, fantasias, etc., of and on operatic airs. He edited a 2-vol. edition of Handel's clavier works.

Kruis, M. H. van't, Dutch organist and composer; b. Oudewater, March 8, 1861; d. Lausanne, Feb. 14, 1919. He studied in The Hague; then filled various posts as organist and teacher; in 1886, founded a musical monthly *Het Orgel*. He publ. *Beknopt overzicht der muziekgeschiedenis* (1892); also wrote an opera, *De bloem van Island*, 3 symphonies, 8 overtures, organ music, piano pieces, etc.

Krul, Eli, Polish-American composer; b. Pabianice, Jan. 1, 1926; studied at the Hochschule für Musik in Munich (1945-49). In 1950 he settled in New York. His works include a string quartet (1958); *O Come, Let Us Sing* for chorus and organ (1960); *Alleluia* for chorus a cappella (1962), etc.

Krumpholtz, Johann Baptist, Bohemian harpist and composer; b. Budenice, near Zlonice, May 8, 1742; d. Paris, Feb. 19, 1790. He received his first instruction from his father, a bandmaster in a Paris regiment; gave concerts in Vienna in 1772; studied composition with Haydn; from 1773-76, was a member of Prince Esterházy's orch. Following a long concert tour in Germany, he returned to France, and in Metz he married a **Fräulein Meyer,** a 16-year-old harpist, with whom he subsequently gave concerts in Paris and London. Krumpholtz added to his fame as harpist by inventing a harp with 2 pedals, loud and soft; he also stimulated Erard to make experiments that led to the invention of the modern pedal machinism. His life ended tragically; he drowned himself in the Seine when his young wife eloped to England with another man. He wrote 6 concertos for harp and orch., a duo for 2 harps, 52 sonatas and other works entitled *Sonates pathétiques*, a symph. for harp with a small orch.; many short pieces.

Krumpholtz, Wenzel, Austrian violinist; brother of **Johann Baptist Krumpholtz;** b. Budenice, near Zlonice, 1750; d. Vienna, May 2, 1817. He was a member of the orch. at the Vienna Opera in 1796, and was friendly with Beethoven; when Krumpholtz died, Beethoven was moved to write a *Gesang der Mönche*, dedicated to his memory. Wenzel Krumpholtz wrote several pieces for unaccompanied violin, among them *Abendunterhaltung* and *Eine Viertelstunde für eine Violine.*

Krupa, Gene, American jazz drummer; b. Chicago, Jan. 15, 1909; d. Yonkers, N.Y., Oct. 16, 1973. He joined a jazz band when still in his adolescence; made his first recording at 18. In 1935 he became Benny Goodman's drummer and scaled the heights of the swing world; having a phenomenal technique and being a natural showman, he "popularized" the drums with extended, virtuosic solos. He left Goodman in 1938, forming his own band; he toured Europe and the Orient and became internationally famous. A largely fictional film, *The Gene Krupa Story*, was produced in 1959.

Kruse, Georg Richard, German conductor and writer on music; b. Greiffenberg, Jan. 17, 1856; d. Berlin, Feb. 23, 1944. He studied at the Univ. of Bern and also in Leipzig; then was opera director and conductor in Germany. In 1894-96 he toured the U.S. as conductor of a troupe presenting Humperdinck's *Hansel und Gretel;* returned to Europe and was municipal theater director in Bern, St. Gall, and Ulm (1896–1900); from 1900 to 1909 he edited the *Deutsche Bühnengenossenschaft*. In 1906 he founded and was director of the Lessing Museum in Berlin; in 1908, founded the Lessing Society and the *Musik-Volksbibliothek des Tonkünstlerverein;* also was editor of dramatic and musical works for *Reclams Universalbibliothek* and contributed articles to various journals. He publ. a comprehensive biography of A. Lortzing (1899); *Lortzings Briefe* (1901; enlarged 2nd ed., Regensburg, 1913); biographies of Otto Nicolai and Hermann Götz; essays; etc.

Kruseman, Jacob Philip, Dutch music publisher; b. Amsterdam, Nov. 17, 1887; d. The Hague, Jan. 31, 1955. He studied singing, and appeared in recitals and light opera in Holland until 1909, when he founded a publishing firm in The Hague, specializing in books on music and art; issued about 25 vols. of biographies of famous composers, and himself wrote a booklet, *Beethoven's Eigen Woorden* (The Hague, 1947). His most important publication is *Geïllustreerd Muzieklexicon,* ed. by himself with G. Keller (The Hague, 1932; supplemented, ed. by Kruseman and Zagwijn, 1949); it is modelled after Riemann's *Musiklexikon,* but contains a great deal of information on Dutch musicians not available in other reference books. After his death, the management of his publishing firm was assumed by his widow.

Kruyf, Ton de, Dutch composer; b. Leerdam, Oct. 3, 1937. He studied violin; attended seminars in new music in Darmstadt led by Maderna, Boulez, Stockhausen and Ligeti; then took a course in composition with Wolfgang Fortner in Heidelberg. In his music he pursues the goal of maximum effect with a minimum of means; he makes use of serialism when it is structurally justified.
WORKS: the opera *Spinoza* (Amsterdam, June 15, 1971); a short radio opera *Quauhquauhtinchan in den vreemde* (*Quauhquauhtinchan in Foreign Parts*; Hilversum, June 3, 1972); a ballet, *Chronologie II* (The Hague, 1968); *Mouvements symphoniques* for orch. (1955, revised 1966); *Sinfonietta,* 3 dances for strings (1956, revised 1965); *5 Impromptus* for small orch. (1958); *Einst dem Grau der Nacht enttäuscht,* after poems by the modern painter Paul Klee, for mezzo-soprano and chamber ensemble (Hilversum, Sept. 15, 1964); *Pour faire le portrait d'un oiseau,* after Jacques Prévert, for mezzo-soprano and chamber ensemble (Hilversum, Sept. 17, 1965); *De blinde zwemmers,* 3 fragments for youth chorus and 2 instrumental groups (1966); *Töne aus der Ferne,* after a poem by Paul Klee, for alto and chamber orch. (Amsterdam, Sept. 11, 1968); *Sinfonia II* (Hilversum, May 14, .1969; developed from an orchestral interlude in opera *Spinoza*); *Quatre pas de deux* for flute and orch. (1972); *Echoi* for oboe and string orch. (1973); *Twee uur (Two Hours)* for speaker and orch. (1973); Quartet for flute, violin, trumpet and bassoon (1959); Flute Sonatina (1960); *Music* for string quartet (1962); *Partita* for string quartet (1962); Solo Cello Sonata (1964); *Aubade* for horn, 2 trumpets, trombone and tuba (1965); *Fragments IV from Shakespeare Sonnets* for mezzo-soprano, flute and cello (1965); *Pas de deux* for flute and piano (1968); *Serenata per complesso da camera* for flute, clarinet, harp and string quintet (1968); *Mosaico* for oboe and string trio (1969); *Séance* for percussion, piano and harp (1969); *Echoi* for solo oboe (1973); *Sgrafitti* for piano (1960); *Arioso* for piano, 4 hands (1975).
BIBLIOGRAPHY: E. Vermeulen, "Ton de Kruyf: Spinoza," *Sonorum Speculum* 47 (1971).

Krygell, Johan Adam, Danish organist; b. Naestved, Sept. 18, 1835; d. Copenhagen, July 27, 1915. He began his career as a painter, but turned his attention to music; entered the Copenhagen Cons. in 1867, studying organ under G. Matthison-Hansen; won the Ancker stipend, and spent 1874–75 studying in Germany; returning to Copenhagen in 1880, he became organist at St. Matthew's Church; also taught. He wrote an opera, *Saul* (not produced); an oratorio; a Mass; 24 string quartets; a septet; symphonies; overtures; organ works.

Krylov, Pavel, Russian composer; b. Tver, March 3, 1885; d. Moscow, April 21, 1935. He studied at the Philharmonic Institute in Moscow; graduated in 1910 with honors. In 1920 he joined the staff of the Moscow Cons. Among his works are an opera, *The Fountain of Bakhtchissaray;* a symphony; a symph. poem, *The Spring;* a symph. suite, *Volga;* concerto for clarinet and orch.; 3 piano sonatas; songs.

Kryzhanovsky, Ivan, Russian theorist and composer; b. Kiev, March 8, 1867; d. Leningrad, Dec. 9, 1924. He studied medicine and music; took lessons with Rimsky-Korsakov at the St. Petersburg Cons.; worked in Pavlov's laboratory of conditioned reflexes; served in the medical corps in the Russian Army during World War I, and was taken prisoner. After his release, he lectured on the physiology of piano technique. He wrote several symphonic works, chamber music and a piano concerto. His paper, *Biological Bases of the Evolution of Music,* was published in an English translation (London, 1928).

Kubelík, Jan, famous Czech violinist; b. Michle, near Prague, July 5, 1880; d. Prague, Dec. 5, 1940. He was taught by his father, who was a gardener; since he showed extraordinary talent, he was accepted by Ševčik as a student at the Prague Cons.; later he studied in Vienna, where he made his professional debut on Nov. 26, 1898. In 1900 he began a series of triumphant concerts in Europe and America. He was regarded as a counterpart to Paderewski in virtuosity, dramatic appeal, and ability to communicate his art to audiences everywhere. In 1903 he married a Hungarian countess and became a naturalized Hungarian citizen. His career as a great virtuoso was stopped short with World War I; he appeared much less frequently than before; lived mostly in Prague. He composed 6 violin concertos in a brilliant style; also a symphony and some chamber music.
BIBLIOGRAPHY: J. Čeleda, *Jan Kubelík* (Prague, 1930); K. Hoffmeister, *Jan Kubelík* (Prague, 1941); a symposium in his memory, ed. by J. Dostál, was publ. at Prague in 1942.

Kubelík, Rafael, eminent Czech conductor; son of **Jan Kubelík;** b. Býchory, near Kolín, June 29, 1914. He studied at the Prague Cons.; made his conducting debut with the Czech Philharmonic in Prague on Jan. 24, 1934; he was subsequently conductor at the National Theater in Brno (1939–41); from 1942 to 1948 he was musical director of the Czech Philharmonic; between 1948 and 1950 he conducted in England and elsewhere in Europe. In 1950 he was appointed principal conductor of the Chicago Symph. Orch.; he made it a rule to feature modern works (about 60 pieces in all) in his programs; this and his insistence on painstaking work on details in rehearsals antagonized some critics in the Chicago press, so that he was compelled to resign (1953). From 1955 to 1958 he was director of the Covent Garden Opera in London; during his tenure there he presented the complete performance of *Boris Godunov* in Mussorgsky's original version. In 1961 he became chief conductor of the orchestra of the Bavarian Radio, and toured with it in Japan (1965) and the U.S. (1968); for a brief time he was music director of the Metropolitan Opera in New York (1972–74), where he also became the epicenter of controversy; these contretemps, however, did not undermine his artistic integrity. In 1978 he was engaged to conduct 6 weeks of guest appearances with the N.Y. Philharmonic. In 1967 he became a Swiss citizen. Kubelík is also a composer; he wrote 2 operas, *Veronika* (Brno, April 19, 1947) and *Cornelia Faroli* (1966); 3 symphonies; Violin Concerto; Cello Concerto; a Requiem, and other choral works; *4 Forms* for string orch. (1965).

Kubik, Gail, American composer; b. South Coffeyville, Oklahoma, Sept. 5, 1914; he was partly of Czech, partly of Irish extraction. He had primary training in music from his mother, an accomplished singer. He then enrolled at the Eastman School of Music in Rochester, N.Y., where he studied composition with Bernard Rogers (Mus.B., 1934) and also took lessons in piano and violin; subsequently went to Chicago where he studied composition at the American Cons. of Music with Leo Sowerby (M.M., 1935); in 1938 he took courses with Walter Piston and Nadia Boulanger at Harvard Univ. During World War II he served in the U.S. Air Force in the rank of a sergeant. In 1943 he received a Guggenheim Fellowship; also served as music director of the Bureau of Motion Pictures on the Office of War Information. After the war he traveled in Europe as conductor and lecturer; in 1952 was guest lecturer at the Accademia di Santa Cecilia in Rome; in 1966 lectured at Oxford Univ. He occupied various teaching positions in the U.S., and in 1970 was appointed composer-in-residence at Scripps College, Claremont, California. From his association with the musical theater and the motion pictures, he developed a great skill in writing scores for documentary films. His gift of musical humor is expressed in his score for the animated film cartoon *Gerald McBoing-Boing* (1950), which received the Motion Picture Academy Award, and also the British Film Institute Award, and incidentally launched a vogue of twangy rhinogenic tunes in popular music. In his symphonic and chamber music he cultivates a manner that is modern without being aggressively destructive of tonality; his rhythmic patterns are apt to be asymmetric.

WORKS: *Mirror for the Sky,* folk opera on the life of Audubon (Eugene, Oregon, May 23, 1939); *Boston Baked Beans,* "opera piccola" (N.Y., March 9, 1952); *Frankie and Johnnie,* ballet for dance band and folk singer (1946); *American Caprice,* for piano and orch. (1936); Symph. No. 1 (1949); Symph. No. 2 (1955); Symphony No. 3 (N.Y., Feb. 28, 1957); *Symphonie-Concertante* (N.Y., Jan. 7, 1952; received the Pulitzer Prize); *Thunderbolt Overture* (1953); *Scenario for Orchestra* (1957); *2 Divertimenti* for orch. (1959, 1960); Violin Concerto, winner of 1st prize of the Jascha Heifetz competition (1941); *Trivialities,* for flute, horn, and string quartet (1934); *Puck,* for speaker, strings and wind instruments (1940); Suite for 3 recorders (1941); Sonatina for Violin and Piano (1944); Toccata for organ and strings (1946); *Little Suite* for flute and 2 clarinets (1947); Divertimento for piano, violin and cello (1971); *A Record of Our Time,* "a protest piece" for chorus, narrator, soloist and orch. (1970); film scores: *The World at War* (1942); *Memphis Belle* (1943); *Gerald McBoing-Boing* (1950); *Two Gals and a Guy* (1951); *Translantic* (1952); *The Desperate Hours* (1955); *Down to Earth* (1959).

Kubín, Rudolf, Czech composer; b. Moravská Ostrava, Jan. 10, 1909; d. there, Jan. 11, 1973.He studied cello and music theory at the Prague Cons.; took a course in quarter-tone and sixth-tone composition from Alois Hába (1925–27). After World War II, he was a co-founder of the Ostrava Cons. and was its first director. He wrote music in disparate styles, some extremely modern, others designed for utilitarian purposes (Mass songs, military marches, patriotic cantatas, etc.).

WORKS: 3 operas: *Letní noc* (*A Summer Night,* 1930–31; Czech Radio, 1931; first Czech radio opera), *Naši furianti* (*Our Wild Ones,* 1942–45; Ostrava, Sept. 18, 1949) and *Koleje mládí* (*The Rails of Youth,* 1948–49; radio opera); numerous operettas, including *Heva* (1955–57); *Prolog* for orch. (1929); *Czech Overture* (1932); *Sinfonietta* for orch. and organ (1935–36); Overture to the unfinished opera, *Zpěv uhlí* (*Song of Coal,* 1936); Trombone Concerto (1936); *Symphony Concertante* for 4 horns and string orch. (1937); Clarinet Concerto (1939); 2 violin concertos (1940, 1960); *Moravian Rhapsody* for orch. (1942); the overture *Květen* (*May,* 1945); Accordian Concerto (1950); symphonic cycle, *Ostrava* (1950–51), consisting of 5 separate works: *Vítězství* (*Victory*), *Maryčka Magdónova, Ostrava, V Beskydách* (*In The Beskid Mountains*) and *Ocelové srdce* (*Heart of Steel*); symph. poem *Geroj, In Memoriam K. Gottwalda* (1953); dramatic overture, *Julius Fučík* (1954); Cello Concerto (1960); *Salutation to Frenštát,* melodrama for orch. (Ostrava, Jan. 9, 1969); *Reminiscence,* a symphony (Ostrava, Jan. 9, 1969); String Quartet (1925–26); *Scherzo* for 2 clarinets and piano (1933); *Jazzety* for piano (1940); *Scherzo* for violin and piano (1942); Ballade for 4 Cellos (1942); Nonet (1946); Suite for Solo Cello (1970); songs; choruses; numerous quarter-tone pieces written during his studies with Alois Hába: 2 suites for piano (1926, 1927); 2 fantasies for piano (1926, 1927); Fantasy for Clarinet and Piano (1926); *5 Pieces* for cello and piano (1926); *Piano Piece* (1927).

Kučera, Václav, Czech composer; b. Prague, April 29, 1929. He studied music at the Charles Univ. in Prague (1948–51); then went to Russia where he took a course in composition with Shebalin at the Moscow Cons. (1951–56). Upon return to Prague he was appointed head of foreign music at the Czech Radio (1956–59); then occupied various administrative posts; in 1972 was appointed to the music department of the Academy of Arts of Czechoslovakia. In his music he tends to observe abstract concepts of formal composition, along with multi-media works on historic and patriotic subjects.
WORKS: a musical-dramatic fresco for radio, *Lidice,* for 2 narrators, 2 reporters, speaking chorus, mixed chorus, instruments, and electronic and concrete sound (1972); *Drama* for 9 instruments (1961); symph. (1962); *Protests,* chamber-cycle for violin, piano and kettledrums (1963); *Krysař (The Pied Piper),* concertino stereophonico for flute and 2 chamber orchestras (1964); *Genesis,* duet for flute and harp (1965); *Hic sunt homines,* chamber-cycle for piano quartet (1965); *Spectra* for dulcimer (1966); *Diptychon* for flute, bass clarinet, piano and percussion (1966); *Obraz (A Picture)* for piano and orch. (1966); *Duodrama* for bass clarinet and piano (1967); *Invariant* for bass clarinet, piano and tape (1968); *Argot,* 3 movements for brass quintet (1970); *Scenario* for flute, violin, viola and cello (1970); *Diario (Homage to Che Guevara),* concert-cycle for solo guitar (1971); *Spring Manifesto (In Memory of Prague, May 1945)* for flute, bass clarinet, piano and percussion (1974); *Amoroso,* cycle for mezzo-soprano, flute and harp (1975).

Kucharz, Johann Baptist, Bohemian organist; b. Chotecz, March 5, 1751; d. Prague, Feb. 18, 1829. He studied at the Jesuit College in Königsgratz, at the Jesuit Seminary in Gitschin, then with Seegert in Prague; organist at the Heinrichskirche, then at Strahow Monastery; conductor of the Prague Opera (1791–1800). He made the first piano scores of Mozart's operas.

Kücken, Friedrich Wilhelm, German conductor and composer; b. Bleckede, Nov. 16, 1810; d. Schwerin, April 3, 1882. He studied with his brother-in-law Lührss, an organist, and Aron at Schwerin; in 1832, went to Berlin, where he studied counterpoint with Birnbach; in 1841, studied with Sechter in Vienna; conducted festivals of male choruses in Switzerland; was Kapellmeister in Stuttgart (1851–61). He wrote the operas *Die Flucht nach der Schweiz* (Berlin, Feb. 26, 1839) and *Der Prätendent* (Stuttgart, April 21, 1847); also sonatas for violin and for cello, etc. He most noted for his songs (*Ach wie wär's möglich dann; Das Sternelein; O weine nicht; Trab, trab; The Maid of Judah; The Swallows,* etc.).

Kuczinski, Paul, composer; b. Berlin, Nov. 10, 1846; d. there, Oct. 21, 1897. He was a banker by profession; also an excellent musician (studied with Bülow and Kiel). He was a friend of Adolf Jensen, whose letters he publ. in part as *Aus Briefen Adolf Jensens* (1879); also publ. *Erlebnisse und Gedanken, Dichtungen zu Musikwerken* 1898), showing his admiration for Wag-

ner. He wrote the poems for his own numerous vocal scores.
WORKS: *Die Bergpredigt,* for baritone solo, chorus, and orch.; *Gesang des Turmwächters,* for tenor solo. and orch.; *Geschenke der Genien,* for female chorus and orch.; *Neujahrgesang,* for tenor solo, chorus, and orch.; also piano pieces (*Humoreske, Intermezzo, Karnevalswalzer, Phantasiestücke*).

Kudelski, Karl Matthias, German violinist; b. Berlin, Nov. 17, 1805; d. Baden-Baden, Oct. 3, 1877. He studied with Lafont; played 1st violin in the orch. of the City Theater in Berlin; in a quartet in Dorpat (1830); Kapellmeister to a Russian Prince (1839); from 1841–51, leader and director in the Imperial Theater, Moscow. He publ. a *Kurzgetfasste Harmonielehre* (1865); also violin concertos; cellos concertos; violin sonatas; piano trios; fantasies for violin and piano; etc.

Kufferath, Hubert Ferdinand, German pianist and organist; brother of **Johann Hermann** and **Louis Kufferath;** b. Mülheim-on-Ruhr, June 11, 1818; d. Brussels, June 23, 1896. He studied first with his brothers; then with Hartmann (violin) in Cologne; with Ferdinand David and Mendelssohn in Leipzig. From 1841–44 he was conductor of the Männergesangverein of Cologne; then settled in Brussels, where he taught members of the royal family; in 1872, became prof. at the Brussels Cons. He wrote symphonies, piano concertos, piano pieces (*Capriccio, Etudes de concert, Charakterstücke,* etc.); also wrote a *Praktische Chorschule für 4 Vocal- oder Instrumentalstimmen zum Studium der Harmonie, des Kontrapunktes und der Orgel* (1896).

Kufferath, Johann Hermann, German violinist and composer; brother of **Hubert Ferdinand** and **Louis Kufferath;** b. Mülheim-on-Ruhr, May 12, 1797; d. Wiesbaden, July 28, 1864. He studied violin with Spohr and composition with Hauptmann; in 1823, became musical director at Bielefeld; in 1830, at Utrecht, where he also taught singing at the School of Music and conducted various societies; retired to Wiesbaden in 1862. He wrote cantatas (*Jubelkantate,* etc), overtures, and motets; also a *Manuel de chant.*

Kufferath, Louis, pianist and teacher; brother of **Hubert Ferdinand** and **Johann Hermann Kufferath;** b. Mülheim-on-Ruhr, Nov. 10, 1811; d. near Brussels, March 2, 1882. He studied with his brother, Johann Hermann, and with Schneider at Dessau. From 1836–50 he was director of the Cons. at Leeuwarden, Holland; then in Ghent and Brussels. He publ. a Mass, 250 canons, a cantata, *Artevelde;* songs; etc.

Kufferath, Maurice, Belgian cellist and writer on music; son of **Hubert Ferdinand Kufferath;** b. Brussels, Jan 8, 1852; d. there, Dec. 8, 1919. He studied cello with the Servais (*père* and *fils*); then at Brussels Univ.; from 1873–1900, wrote for *L'Indépendence Belge,* editor of the *Guide musical,* then proprietor; in 1900, became director of the Théâtre de la Monnaie, together with Guillaume Guidé; co-founder of the Ysaÿe concerts, with Ysaÿe and Guidé. He publ. essays on Wagner's operas, and a comprehensive work, *Le Théâtre de Wagner de Tannhäuser à Parsifal* (Brussels, 1891–98; 6 vols.; of these, *Parsifal* was publ. in English transl., (N.Y., 1904); also a brochure, *L'Art de diriger l'orchestre* (Brussels, 1891; an account of Hans Richter's conducting in Brussels); a sketch of Henri Vieuxtemps (Brussels, 1883). He wrote the report on the musical instruments at the Brussels Exposition of 1880. Under the pen name **Maurice Reymont** he translated Wagner's librettos and texts of songs by Brahms into French. He was an ardent propagandist for Wagner's ideas in Belgium.

BIBLIOGRAPHY: L. Solvay, *Notice sur Maurice Kufferath* (Brussels, 1923).

Küffner, Joseph, German composer; b. Würzburg, March 31, 1776; d. there, Sept. 8, 1856. He wrote 2 operas, *Sporn und Schärpe* and *Der Cornett;* 7 symphonies; 10 overtures; music for military band and wind instruments; Fantasy for Violin with Orch.; Quintet for flute and strings; string quartets; trios and duets for flutes; duets for clarinet; guitar music; violin sonatas; etc.

Kuhač, Franz Xaver, Croatian music theorist; b. Escheck, Croatia, Nov. 20, 1834; d. Agram, June 18, 1911. He studied at the Budapest Cons. and at the Leipzig Cons.; also with Hanslick in Vienna and Liszt in Weimar. He publ. several valuable studies on the music system, instruments, and notation of the South Slavic nations, and 4 vols. of Slavic folksongs. He claimed Haydn and Tartini as Croatian composers; publ. *Josip Haydn i hrvatske narodne popievke* (*Joseph Haydn and Croatian folk melodies;* Agram, (1880); *Das türkische Element in der Musik der Kroaten, Serben und Bulgaren* (1900); numerous minor essays.

Kuhe, Wilhelm, Bohemian pianist; b. Prague, Dec. 10, 1823; d. London, Oct. 9, 1912. He studied with Proksch, Tomaschek, and Thalberg. He went to London with the singer Pischek in 1845 and settled there; from 1886–1904, prof. at the Royal Academy of Music. He wrote salon music (*Feu follet, Gondola, Rosée du soir, Étude de concert,* etc.); operatic fantasias for piano; also publ. *My Musical Recollections* (London, 1897).

Kuhlau, Friedrich, prolific German composer; b. Ülzen, Germany, Sept. 11, 1786; d. Copenhagen, March 12, 1832. He lost an eye in a childhood accident; during his recovery studied piano; became a private tutor in Hamburg and studied composition there with E. F. G. Schwenke. He went to Copenhagen in 1810 in order to avoid conscription into Napoleon's army; there he prospered, and in 1813 was appointed court musician.

WORKS: He produced several stage works in Copenhagen: *Røverborgen* (*The Robber's Castle;* May 26, 1814); *Trylleharpen* (*The Magic Harp;* Jan. 30, 1817); *Elisa* (April 17, 1820); *Lulu* (Oct. 29, 1824); *William Shakespeare* (March 28, 1826); *Elverhøj* (*The Fairies' Mound;* Nov. 6, 1828; his most celebrated dramatic work); wrote 3 flute quartets; trios concertants, duets, etc., for flute; 8 violin sonatas; 2 piano concertos; in-

structive piano sonatas, and perennially popular sonatinas, much used for teaching purposes; also various pieces for 4 hands; songs and male quartets, once in great vogue.

BIBLIOGRAPHY: C. Thrane, *Danske Komponister* (Copenhagen, 1875; with a list of works); C. Thrane, *Friedrich Kuhlau. Zur 100-jährigen Wiederkehr seines Geburtstages* (Leipzig, 1886).

Kühmstedt, Friedrich, notable German theorist; b. Oldisleben, Dec. 20, 1809; d. Eisenach, Jan. 10, 1858. He studied with Rinck at Darmstadt; then taught music there (1831–36); settled in Eisenach, where he taught at the seminary. He publ. a *Gradus ad Parnassum; Kunst des Vorspiels für Orgel; Theoretisch-praktische Harmonie- und Ausweichungslehre* (1838); composed organ music (a double fugue, a *Fantasia eroica,* fugues, preludes, and postludes); also oratorios, a Mass, motets, piano concertos, etc.

Kuhnau, Johann, erudite German musician, organist, and theorist; b. Geising, Apr. 6, 1660; d. Leipzig, June 5, 1722. He studied at the Kreuzschule in Dresden with Hering and Albrici; then with Edelmann at Zittau, where he became cantor. He attended the Univ. of Leipzig from 1682–84; then succeeded Kühnel as organist at the Thomaskirche; in 1688 he organized a Collegium Musicum and also studied law. He became musical director of the Univ. of Leipzig in 1700; the following year he was appointed cantor at the Thomaskirche; was Bach's predecessor in the post. He publ. *Jura circa musicos ecclesiasticos* (Leipzig, 1688); *Der Musikalische Quacksalber . . . in einer kurtzweiligen und angenehmen Historie . . . beschrieben* (Dresden, 1700; a satire on Italian music); 3 treatises are in MS. Kuhnau was the first to publish a harpsichord sonata imitated from the instrumental sonata (properly a suite) in several movements. It is found in Part II of his *Neue Clavier-Übung* (1692) and contains 3 movements, Allegro, Adagio, and Allegro (Rondo); there followed 7 sonatas in his *Frische Clavier-Früchte* (1696), which show a marked advance in treatment and melodic invention; 6 more harpsichord sonatas appeared under the title *Biblische Historien nebst Auslegung in sechs Sonaten,* in the highly original form of illustrations to biblical stories, thus presaging the development of program music; they set forth the fight between David and Goliath, David's cure of Saul, Jacob's Wedding, etc. (1700; new ed. of the first 2 by J. S. Shedlock, 1895; new ed. of the 1st by H. Bauer, 1927). Kuhnau's complete clavier works were publ. by Päsler in vol. 2 of the *Denkmäler deutscher Tonkunst;* Schering publ. 4 church cantatas and a list of Kuhnau's sacred works in vols. 58/59.

BIBLIOGRAPHY: H. Bischoff, *Uber J. Kuhnaus Vorstellung einiger biblischen Historien* (1877); J. S. Shedlock, *The Pianoforte Sonata* (London, 1895; p. 38 ff.); R. Münnich, "Kuhnaus Leben," *Sammelbände der Internationalen Musik-Gesellschaft* (1902; p. 473ff.); J. C. Martin, *Die Kirchenkantaten J. Kuhnaus* (Leipzig, 1928); H. F. Menck, "J. Kuhnaus 'Musikalische Quacksalber,'" in *Der Musiker im Roman* (Heidelberg, 1931; p. 61ff.)

Kühner, Basil, German composer; b. Stuttgart, April 1, 1840; d. Vilna, Aug. 1911. He studied at the Stuttgart Cons. with Faiszt and Lebert; then studied violin with Massart in Paris, and piano with Henselt in St. Petersburg; then was director of the Tiflis Cons. (1870-76). In 1878 he settled in St. Petersburg, where he established his own music school (1892). He wrote the opera *Tarass Bulba* (after Gogal; St. Petersburg, Dec. 24, 1880; had only 3 performances); a symph. subtitled *Liberation of the Serfs in Russia* (St. Petersburg, 1866); a string quintet; 2 string quartets; a suite for cello and piano; *Snowflakes,* suite for piano; other piano pieces.

Kühner, Konrad, German pianist and teacher; b. Markt-Streufdorf, Meiningen, March 2, 1851; d. Schmalkalden. Feb. 5, 1909. He studied at the Stuttgart Cons.; from 1889-99 he lived in Dresden as a piano teacher, then in Brunswick. He wrote the symph. poem *Maria Stuart;* piano music; a *Technik des Klavierspiels; Schule des 4-händigen Spiels* (12 vols.); a *Vortragsalbum* (5 vols); *Etüdenschule des Klavierspielers* (12 vols.); also edited many works for the *Edition Litolff.*

Kulenkampff, Gustav, German composer; b. Bremen, Aug. 11, 1849; d. Berlin, Feb. 10, 1921. He studied music with Barth (piano) and Bargiel (composition). He organized in Berlin his own women's choir; taught musical subjects at various music schools; appeared as pianist. He wrote the operas *Der Page* (Bremen, 1890), *Der Mohrenfürst* (Magdeburg, 1892), *Die Braut von Cypern* (Schwerin, 1897), *König Drosselbart* (Berlin, 1899), *Ammarei* (1903), *Anneliese* (Kassel, 1904); women's choruses; a piano sonata; songs; etc.

Kullak, Adolf, German music theorist and critic, brother of **Theodor Kullak;** b. Meseritz, Feb. 23, 1823; d. Berlin, Dec. 25, 1862. He studied general subjects at the Univ. of Berlin, and also music with Bernhard Marx; then taught at his brother's Academy; contributed music criticism to various periodicals; publ. some piano pieces and songs. He wrote *Das Musikalisch-Schöne* (Leipzig, 1858) and *Ästhetik des Klavierspiels* (Berlin, 1861; 4th ed. by W. Niemann, 1906; 5th ed., 1916; in English, N.Y., 1892), a valuable and instructive summary of piano methods.

Kullak, Franz, German pianist and composer; son of **Theodor Kullak;** b. Berlin, April 12, 1844; d. there, Dec. 9, 1913. He studied with his father; also with Liszt for a brief while. In 1867 he became piano teacher in his father's Academy; assumed its directorship at his father's death in 1822, dissolving the institution in 1890. He wrote an opera, *Ines de Castro* (Berlin, 1877); piano pieces; songs; also an essay, *Der Vortrag in der Musik am Ende des 19. Jahrhunderts* (Leipzig, 1898).

Kullak, Theodor, famous German pianist and pedagogue; b. Krotoschin, Sept. 12, 1818; d. Berlin, March 1, 1882. He studied piano with local teachers; in 1837 he went to Berlin at his father's behest to study medicine; also studied music there with Dehn (theory); then in 1842 went to Vienna, where he took lessons

with Czerny. Returning to Berlin in 1846, he became court pianist to the King of Prussia. In 1850 he founded a conservatory in Berlin in partnership with Julius Stern and Bernhard Marx; however, dissension soon arose among them and, in 1855, Kullak established his own school, the Neue Akademie der Tonkunst, which greatly prospered and became famous as "Kullak's Academy." He publ. valuable pedagogic works: *Materialien für den Elementar-Unterricht* (3 vols.); *Schule des Oktavenspiel;* various characteristic pieces for piano in a salon manner (*Ondine, Les Etincellese, Les Danaides, La Gazelle,* etc.); also *Kinderleben* (2 albums of piano pieces).
    BIBLIOGRAPHY: O. Reinsdorf, *Theodor Kullak und seine Neue Akademie der Tonkunst in Berlin* (1870); H. Bischoff, *Zur Erinnerung an Theodor Kullak* (1883).

Kullman, Charles, American tenor; b. New Haven, Jan. 13, 1903. He studied at Yale Univ. (graduated in 1924) and at the Juilliard Graduate School (graduated in 1927); made a successful debut at the Kroll Opera in Berlin as Pinkerton in *Madama Butterfly* (Feb. 24, 1931); then appeared at various European opera houses: at the Berlin State Opera (1932-36), Vienna State Opera, and Covent Garden in London (1934-36). On Dec. 19, 1935 he made his debut with the Metropolitan Opera as Faust: remained on its roster until 1956, when he was engaged as resident tenor at the Indiana Univ. School of Music.

Kummer, Friedrich August, German cellist, oboist, and composer; b. Meiningen, Aug. 5, 1797; d. Dresden, Aug. 22, 1879. His family moved to Dresden, where Kummer studied cello with Dotzauer; then he studied oboe in order to enter the court orch., which he did in Nov. 1814; in 1817 he again studied the cello and became a virtuoso of the first rank. He also taught at the Dresden Cons. He was a prolific composer; 163 of his compositions were printed; he wrote concertos, a concertino divertissements, etc., for the cello; also concert pieces for oboe, clarinet, horn, trumpet; and a method for cello.

Kummer, Kaspar, German flutist and composer; b. Erlau, Dec. 10, 1795; d. Koburg, May 21, 1870. He was a member of the court orch. at Koburg; then musical director there. He wrote quintets and quartets for flute and strings; flute concertos, trios, duos, etc.; and a method for flute.

Kümmerle, Salomon, German collector of vocal music; b. Malmsheim, near Stuttgart, Feb. 8, 1838; d. Samaden, Aug. 28, 1896. He taught at a school in Samaden (1875-90); publ. several collections of vocal music, among them *Musica sacra; Grabgesänge; Zionsharfe; Choralbuch für evangelische Kirchenchöre; Encyklopädie der evangelischen Kirchenmusik* (3 vols., 1888-96).

Kunad, Rainer, German composer; b. Chemnitz, Oct. 24, 1936. He studied in Leipzig with Finke, Gerster and Schenk; became active as a teacher. He excels particularly in light opera and ballet.
    WORKS: a pantomime with singing *Das Schloss*

(1962), one-act opera *Bill Brook* (1965), *Ich: Orpheus* for actors, dancers and singers (1965); also orchestral works, among them *Aphorismen* (1956), *Sinfonia variatione*, (1959); *Sinfonie* (1964), *Sinfonietta* (1969), *Concerto per archi* (1967); Piano Concerto (1969); chamber music: Wind Quintet (1965), *Die Ehe* for oboe, bassoon and piano (1970); Piano Sonata; Overture for two pianos; organ pieces and several cantatas and various choral works.

Kunc, Božidar, Croatian-American pianist and composer; b. Zagreb, July 18, 1903; d. Detroit, April 1, 1964. He received his academic training at the Music Academy in Zagreb, graduating in 1927; taught there from 1929 to 1950, when he emigrated to the U.S. He was a brother of the singer **Zinka Milanov.** His music is impressionistic in its harmonic palette.

WORKS: 2 violin concertos (1928, 1955); *Dramatic Prologue* for orch. (1929); *Symphonic Intermezzo* (1934); 2 piano concertos: No. 1 (Zagreb, April 27, 1934; composer soloist) and No. 2 (1962); *Marcia Funebre* for orch. (1936); *Triptihon* for cello and orch. (1940); *3 Episodes* for piano and string orch. (1955); symphonies; several chamber works, including Cello Sonata (1927), *Cycle* for piano and percussion (1956), *Pieces* for solo double bass (1959); 4 piano sonatas (1930–43) and several cycles and pieces; songs.

BIBLIOGRAPHY: K. Kovačević, *Hrvatski Kompozitori i njihova djela* (Zagreb, 1960).

Kunc, Jan, Czech composer; b. Doubravice, Moravia, March 27, 1883; d. Brno, Sept. 11, 1976. He studied with Janácek in Brno and with Novák in Prague; was music critic in Brno (1909–18); in 1918–19 he toured as accompanist with his wife, a concert singer. In 1919 he became instructor at the Brno Cons.; from 1923 till 1945 was its director; lectured at the Masaryk Univ. in Brno (1947–52).

WORKS: an unfinished opera *The Lady from the Seashore* (begun 1919); *Song of Youth,* symph. poem (1915–16); *Stála Kačenka u Dunaja (Catherine Stood by the Danube)*, ballad for alto and orch. (1918–19); Piano Sonata (1903); Piano Trio (1905); String Quartet (1909); *4 Compositions* for piano (1917); *Chronicle,* 20 variations on a Slovak folksong for piano (1926); Violin Sonata (1931); *Serenade* for violin and piano (1952); *Miniatures* for piano (1954–57; also for wind quintet, 1958); *Sedmdesát tisíc (Seventy Thousand)* for chorus (1907); *Ostrava* for male chorus (1912); *35 Folksongs of Moravian Slovakia* for female chorus (1960); many folksong arrangements.

Kunits, Luigi von, Austrian violinist and conductor; b. Vienna, July 20, 1870; d. Toronto, Canada, Oct. 8, 1931. He studied composition with Anton Bruckner, history of music with Hanslick, and violin with Ševčik. In 1893 he came to America; from 1897–1910 was concertmaster of the Pittsburgh Symph.; taught at the Pittsburgh Cons.; later founded his own music school. After 2 years in Europe (1910–12), he went to Canada and settled in Toronto; taught at the Canadian Academy of Music; founded the *Canadian Journal of Music* (1915–19); from 1923 till 1931 was conductor of the New Symph. Orch. of Toronto (renamed Toronto Symph. Orch. in 1927). He publ. a book *The Hero as Musician: Beethoven* (1913); also contributed articles to various periodicals. His compositions include 2 violin concertos, a string quartet, a viola sonata, *Three Etudes* for violin and piano; *Romanza,* for violin and piano; songs.

Kunkel, Charles, German-American pianist and publisher; b. Sipperfeld, Rheinpfalz. July 22, 1840; d. St. Louis, Dec. 3, 1923. He was taken to America in 1848 by his father who gave him elementary musical training. In 1868 he and his brother **Jacob,** also a musician, went to St. Louis, where he established a music publishing business and started a music periodical, *Kunkel's Musical Review,* which included sheet music and articles; with his brother he also opened a music store selling pianos and other instruments; in 1872 he founded the St. Louis Cons. of Music which continued in business for several years; furthermore he presented an annual series of concerts in St. Louis known as "Kunkel's Popular Concerts" (1884–1900). He taught piano almost to the last years of his life; also publ. a method of piano playing, which was commended favorably by Liszt; Anton Rubinstein praised him as a pianist during his visit to St. Louis in 1873. Kunkel was reputed to be quite formidable as a sight reader. Altogether, he was certainly a shining light in the German musical colony in middle America in the second half of the 19th century. With his brother he gave, to tumultuous applause, a series of concerts playing piano duets. His publishing business put out a cornucopia of his own piano solos with such titles as *Nonpareil, Galop Brilliant, Philomel Polka, Snow-drops Waltz,* and *Southern Jollification,* most of these highly perishable; however, one piece, *Alpine Storm* deserves retrieval, if for no other reason than its dedication: "To my son, Ludwig van Beethoven Kunkel." (This piece also contains "tone clusters" played with the palm of the hand in the bass to imitate thunder.)

Kunkel, Franz Joseph, German theorist and composer; b. Dieburg, Aug. 20, 1808; d. Frankfurt, Dec. 31, 1880. From 1828–54 he was rector and music teacher in the Bensheim Teachers' Seminary. He wrote a *Kleine Musiklehre; Die Verurteilung der Konservatorien zu Pflanzschulen des musikalischen Proletariats* (1855); *Kritische Beleuchtung des C. F. Weitzmannischen Harmonie-Systems; Die neue Harmonielehre im Streit mit der alten* (1863); etc.; also a cantata, psalms, motets, etc.

Kunkel, Jacob, German-American pianist; b. Kleiniedesheim, Oct. 22, 1846; d. St. Louis, Oct. 16, 1882. He studied with his elder brother, **Charles Kunkel,** and was also a nominal pupil of Tausig who, according to the Kunkel family report, refused to teach him because he thought that the younger man was equal to the master. He was taken to America, with his brother, and participated in most of the latter's enterprises, in the music publishing business and in a general music store. The two brothers also gave a series of concerts playing piano duets. Jacob Kunkel composed piano pieces in a salon manner.

Künneke, Eduard, German operetta composer, b. Emmerich, Jan. 27, 1885; d. Berlin, Oct. 27, 1953. He studied with Max Bruch in Berlin; was subsequently engaged as a choirmaster in various theaters in Germany; produced two operas, *Robins Ende* (Mannheim, 1909) and *Coeur As* (Dresden, 1913, with little success; he then turned to light opera, and his first work in this genre, a Singspiel, *Das Dorf ohne Glocke* (Berlin, April 5, 1919) was received with great acclaim. His next light opera, *Der Vetter aus Dingsda* (Berlin, April 15, 1921), was no less successful; there followed *Lady Hamilton* (1926); *Glückliche Reise* (Berlin, Nov. 23, 1932); *Lockende Flamme* (1933); *Herz über Bord* (1935); *Der grosse Name* (1938); etc. His last operetta was *Hochzeit mit Erika* (1949). Besides his stage works, he wrote many film scores, an overture, a piano concerto, and other instrumental compositions.

Kunsemüller, Ernst, German conductor; b. Rehme, June 24, 1885; d. (as a result of war wounds) Düsseldorf, April 25, 1918. He studied at the Univs. of Berlin and Bonn (Dr. phil., 1909); then at the Cologne Cons. with Friedberg, Wölsche, and Steinbach; from 1910–12, conducted an a cappella chorus at Neuss; in 1912, became conductor of the Verein der Musikfreunde and Gesangverein in Kiel; in 1914, appointed musical director at the Univ. of Kiel. He wrote a serenade for small orch., 2 piano sonatas, choruses, songs, etc.

Kunst, Jos, Dutch composer; b. Roermond, Jan. 3, 1936. He studied composition with Ton de Leeuw at the Amsterdam Cons. (1965–70); upon graduation joined its staff. In his music he utilizes a great variety of modernistic techniques, especially metamorphoses of given thematic material.
WORKS: *Stenen eten (The Stone Eaters)* for 2 pianos (1965); *Ijzer (Iron)* for violin and piano (1965); *Insecten* for 13 strings (1966); *Glass Music* for piano (1966); *Extérieur* for 2-track tape (1967); *Arboreal* for orch. (Rotterdam, Sept. 11, 1969); *Expulsion* for 2-track tape (1969); *Trajectoire* for 16 voices and 11 instruments (1970); *XVII One Way* for small orch. (Amsterdam, March 13, 1971); *XVIII Outward Bound* for solo harp (1971); *Solo Identity I* for solo bass clarinet (1972); *Solo Identity II* for piano (1973); *Elements of Logic* for wind orch. (in collaboration with Jan Vriend, 1972; Scheveningen, Feb. 25, 1973); *No Time at All* for bass clarinet and piano (1973; a fusion of the 2 *Solo Identities); No Time* for 3 clarinets, bass clarinet, piano and 3 percussionists (1974; an amplified version of *No Time at All*); *XXII: Any Two* for woodwinds (1975).

Kuntze, Karl, German composer; b. Trier, May 17, 1817; d. Delitzsch, Sept. 7, 1883. He studied in Berlin with A. W. Bach, Marx, and Rungenhagen; cantor and organist at Pritzwalk; then organist at Aschersleben (1858); in 1873, settled in Delitzsch, where he taught at the seminary. He is best known for his humorous male choruses (*Adam und Eva, Der Hecht im Karpfenteich, Weingalopp, Der neue Bürgermeister, Die Schweigermutter*); also wrote an operetta, *Im Gebirge* (Dessau, 1875); motets and songs for mixed chorus; organ pieces; etc. He edited the 3rd ed. of Seidel's *Die Orgel und ihr Bau* (1875).

Kunwald, Ernst, Austrian conductor; b. Vienna, April 14, 1868; d. there, Dec. 12, 1939. He studied law at Vienna Univ. (Dr. juris, 1891); at the same time studied piano with Leschetizky and J. Epstein, and composition with H. Grädener; then at the Leipzig Cons. with Jadassohn. His first engagement as opera conductor was in Rostock (1895–97); then conducted opera in Sondershausen (1897–98), Essen (1898–1900), Halle (1900–01), Madrid (1901–02), Frankfurt (1902–05), and at Kroll's Theater in Berlin (1905–07); appointed conductor of the Berlin Philharmonic Orch. (1907–12). In 1906 he was guest conductor of the N.Y. Philharmonic Society; in 1912, became regular conductor of the Cincinnati Symph. Orch., and from 1914, also of the May Festival. He was arrested as an enemy alien on Dec. 8. 1917, but was released on bail and allowed to continue to conduct until his internment. In 1919 he went to Germany and conducted symph. concerts in Königsberg (1920–27); 1928–31, conducted the Berlin Symph. Orch.; then returned to Vienna, where he remained until his death.

Kunz, Alfred, Canadian composer; b. Neudorf, Saskatchewan, May 26, 1929. He studied with Delamont and Weinzweig in Toronto (1949–55); then went to Europe; attended Stockhausen's classes of new music in Darmstadt and Cologne; returning to Canada, he held various teaching posts in Ontario.
WORKS: an operetta for high school, *The Watchful Gods* (1962); 7 ballets, including *Moses* (1965); 2 sinfoniettas (1957, 1961); *Violin Sonata* (1959); *The Song of the Clarinet* for narrator, flute, oboe, clarinet, bassoon and string quintet (1961); *Behold the Beauty of the Sky* for high school chorus and orch. (1961); *Excursion* for orch. (1964); *Emanation No. 1* for violin, horn and piano (1962); *Emanation No. 2* for flute, clarinet, horn and bassoon (1964); *Fun for Two* for 2 bassoons or 2 bass clarinets (1964); *Love, Death and Full Moonnights* for baritone and instrumental ensemble (1964); *Wind Quintet* (1964); *The Big Land,* oratorio (1967); *In the Park of October Colour,* a "song of love" for solo piano, chorus and orch. (1969); *5 Night Scenes* for orch. (1971); *The Creation* for narrator, 3 sopranos, alto, chorus and orch. (1972); Concerto for 8 Percussion Players and Orch. (1973); Piano Concerto (1975).

Kunz, Ernst, Swiss composer and conductor; b. Bern, June 2, 1891. He studied in Munich; from 1916 to 1918 he conducted the Munich Opera; returning to Switzerland he was active mainly as a theater conductor. His music is neo-Romantic in essence; the influences of Richard Strauss and Pfitzner are especially pronounced. He wrote the operas *Der Fächer* (1924; Zürich, 1929), *Vreneli ab em Guggisberg* (in Swiss dialect; 1935), *Die Bremer Stadtmusikanten* (1937); *Der Traum ein Leben* (1968); a Singspiel, *Die Hochzeitsreise* (1960); the oratorios, *Vom irdischen Leben* (1931–49), *Christmas Oratorio* (1936); *Weisheit des Herzens* (1946), *Einkehr* (1951), *Psalter und Harfe* (1956); 5 symphonies (1917, 1921, 1942, 1966, 1966); a symphonic triptych, *Drei Lebensalter* (1964); *Serenata strana* for orch. (1971); Viola Concerto (1952); Chamber Concerto for strings, solo flute and piano

(1971); 3 string quartets; piano quartet; piano pieces; about 500 choruses; several song cycles.

Kunz, Konrad Max, German composer; b. Schwandorf, Dec. 30, 1812; d. Munich, Aug. 3, 1875. He studied in Munich with Hartmann Stuntz; co-founder and conductor of the Munich Liedertafel. He wrote many popular male quartets (*Elstein; Odin, der Schlachtengott;* etc.); also *200 Canons for Piano;* publ. the satirical pamphlet, *Die Gründung der Moosgau-Brüderschaft Moosgrillia* (1866).

Kunzen, Adolf Carl, German pianist and organist; b. Wittenberg, Sept. 22, 1720; d. Lübeck, July, 1781. At the age of 8 he toured in Holland and England. Finally settled in Wittenberg as organist at the Marienkirche. He wrote an oratorio, a Passion, symphonies, 21 violin concertos, piano sonatas, etc. (many MSS are in the library of the Brussels Cons.)

Kunzen, Friedrich Ludwig Aemilius, composer; son of **Adolf Carl Kunzen;** b. Lubeck, Sept. 24, 1761; d. Copenhagen, Jan. 28, 1817. He studied music with his father, and jurisprudence at Kiel Univ. (1784–87); then settled in Copenhagen, where he taught music. He spent a few years in Berlin, and was Kapellmeister at Frankfurt and Prague; then became court conductor in Copenhagen (1795).
WORKS: the operas *Holger Danske* (Copenhagen, March 31, 1789); *Die Weinlese* (Frankfurt, May 3, 1793); *Hemmeligheden* (*The Secret*; Copenhagen, Nov. 22, 1796); *Dragedukken* (*The Good Fairy*; Copenhagen, March 14, 1797); *Erik Ejegod* (Copenhagen, Jan. 30, 1798); *Min Bedstemoder* (*My Grandmother*; Copenhagen, May 15, 1800); *Kœrlighed paa Landet* (*Love in the Country*; Copenhagen, March 23, 1810); also wrote oratorios; overtures; sonatas; his musical style paralleled the models of Mozart and Haydn.

Kuosmanen, Kari, Finnish composer; b. Helsinki, March 11, 1946. He studied piano with Flodin; composition with Allis Sallinen at the Sibelius Academy in Helsinki. After graduation, he obtained a teaching post at the Oulu (Uleaborg) School of Music.
WORKS: *Abacus* for violin, viola, cello and orch. (1968); *Sinfonia da Chiesa* for 4 string quartets (Helsinki, Feb. 28, 1973).

Kupfermann, Meyer, American composer; b. New York, July 3, 1926. He attended Queens College; in 1951 joined the staff of Sarah Lawrence College. His works include 7 symphonies, 5 string quartets, *Cycle of Infinities* (a number of pieces for various ensembles); Concertino for 11 Brass Instruments; *Sonata on Jazz Elements* for piano; *Tunnel of Love* for jazz combo (N.Y., May 22, 1971); several short operas: *In a Garden* (N.Y. Dec. 29, 1949); *The Curious Fern,* and *Voices for a Mirror* (both produced in N.Y. on June 5, 1957) and *Draagenfut Girl* (Bronx, N.Y., May 8, 1958); *Abracadabra Quartet* for piano and string trio (1976); *The Red King's Throne* for clarinet, piano, cello, and percussion (1978).

Kupkovič, Ladislav, Slovak composer of the avant-garde; b. Bratislava, March 17, 1936. He studied violin in Bratislava at the High School of Music (1950–55)

and at the Cons. (1955–61); played violin in the Slovak Philharmonic. In 1963 he organized the chamber ensemble "Hudba Dneška" ("Music of Today"). He left Czechoslovakia after the Soviet incursion in 1968 and went to Germany; lived in Berlin and Cologne until 1973, when he was appointed instructor at the Hochschule für Musik in Hannover. His music utilizes the cosmopolitan resources of ultra-modern music.
WORKS: *Dialogues* for flute and bassoon (1961); *Maso kríza* (*Flesh of the Cross*), an impression of a surrealist painting of the crucifix for trombone and 10 percussion players (1961–62); *Psalm* for 4 horns (1962); *Skica* (*Sketch*) for 6 players (1962); *Otázky a odpovedi* (*Questions and Answers*) for 3 flutes and tam-tam (1962); *Decolleté* for 4 oboes, 4 trumpets and 12 percussion players (1964); *Výkřiky* (*Exclamations*) for flute, bass clarinet, piano and percussion (1964); *Rozhovor času s hmotou* (*A Conversation between Time and Matter*) for bassoon and 3 percussion players (1965); *Ozveny* (*Echoes*) for 31 players (1966); *Písmená* (*Letters*) for 4 female and 4 male voices (1967); *Menej i viac* (*More and Less*) for bass clarinet and piano (1967); *Pred s za* (*Before and After*) for chamber ensemble (1967); *Cluster—Dynamika—Glissando* for string quartet (1967); *Dioe* for orch. with conductor (1968); *Oktoedr* (*Octohedron*) for chamber ensemble (1968); *Präparierte Texte* Nos. 1–7 for various combinations of instruments (1968); *Les Adieux* for piano (1968); *Etude* for ensemble (1968); *Ad libitum,* a "happening" for a random group of performers (1969); *Klanginvasion auf Bonn,* a spectacle of indeterminate duration representing the invasion of noise on the population of Bonn (1970); *Treffpunkt* for 4 groups of wind instruments (1970); *Notausgang* for orch. and microphones (1970); *Musikalische Ausstellung* for chamber ensemble (1970); *Erinnerungen* for orch. and tape (1970); *Souvenir* for violin and piano or string orch. (1971); *Monolith* for 48 strings (1971); *Ein Gespräch mit Gott* (*A Conversation with God*) for orch. (1972); *Das Gebet* (*The Prayer*) for string orch. and percussion (1972–73); *Concours* for the "orchestra of the future" (1973). Kupkovič also initiated "walking concerts" in which a group of musicians walk in the streets playing segments of familiar pieces ad nauseam.
BIBLIOGRAPHY: Monica Lichtenfeld, "Porträt des Komponisten und Dirigenten Ladislav Kupkovič," *Musica* (March-April 1975).

Kuri-Aldana, Mario, Mexican composer; b. Tampico, Aug. 15, 1931. He studied piano with Carlos del Castillo at the Academia Juan Sebastián Bach in Mexico City (1948–51) and theory with Juan Tercero at the National School of Music of the Autonomous Univ. of Mexico (1952–60); took conducting courses from Igor Markevitch and Jean Giardino at the National Institute of Fine Arts in Mexico City (1957–58); privately studied advanced techniques of composition with Rodolfo Halffter and Luis Herrera de la Fuente (1961–62); took lessons in Buenos Aires with Ginastera. Returning to Mexico he gave himself to teaching.
WORKS: 3 symphonies; No. 1, *Sacrificio* (1959); No. 2 for string orch. (1966); No. 3, *Ce Actal-1521* (1976); *Los Cuatro Bacabs,* suite for double wind

orch. and optional narrator (1960); *Máscaras,* concerto for marimba and wind orch. (1962); *Pasos* for piano and orch. (1963); *Bacab de las Plegarias* for 2 flutes, 2 clarinets, trumpet, harp and strings (1966); *Formas de otros tiempos* for string orch. and harp (1971); *Concierto de Santiago* for flute, string orch. and 2 percussion players (1973); *Concertino Mexicano* for violin and string orch. (1974); numerous songs accompanied by various instrumental combinations, among them *Cantares para una niña muerta* for mezzo-soprano, flute and guitar (1961); *Este, ese y aquel (This, That and the Other)* for mezzo-soprano, flute, violin, viola, cello and vibraphone (1964); *Amarillo era el color de la Esperanza (Yellow Was the Color of Hope),* secular cantata for narrator, mezzo-soprano and jazz band (1966); *Noche de Verano* for narrator, soprano and small orch (1975); *A mi hermano* for baritone, chorus and orch. (1977); chamber music: *Canto de 5-Flor* for cello and piano (1957); *Sonatina Mexicana* for violin and piano (1959); *Xilofonías* for piccolo, oboe, bass clarinet, double bassoon and percussion (1963); *Puentes* for string quartet (1965, revised 1977); *Candelaria,* suite for wind quintet (1965); *3-Silvestre,* concerto for 9 instruments (1966); *Fuga para metales* (1968). For piano: *Suite Ingenua* (1953), *Villancico, Canción y Jarabe* (1965), Sonata (1972).

Kurka, Robert, American composer of Czech descent; b. Cicero, Illinois, Dec. 22, 1921; d. New York City, Dec. 12, 1957. He studied violin with Kathleen Parlow and Hans Letz; composition with Otto Luening and Darius Milhaud; received a Guggenheim Fellowship in 1951 and 1952. His opera *The Good Soldier Schweik,* completed shortly before his untimely death of leukemia, was produced with extraordinary success at the New York City Center on April 23, 1958, and has since been widely performed in America and in Europe. His other works include 2 symphonies; Serenade for chamber orch.; Violin Concerto; Concerto for 2 Pianos, String Orch. and Trumpet; Concerto for Marimba and Orch.; *Ballad* for French horn and strings; 5 string quartets; Piano Trio; 4 violin sonatas; piano pieces; choruses.

Kurpiński, Karol, Polish composer; b. Wloszakowice (Luschwitz), March 6, 1785; d. Warsaw, Sept. 18, 1857. He studied with his father, Marcian Kurpiński, an organist; in 1810 became a violinist at a Warsaw theater; then second conductor at the Warsaw Opera; also taught at the Warsaw Cons. He wrote the operas *Jadwiga* (Warsaw, Dec. 23, 1814), *The New Cracovians, The Castle of Czorsztyn* (Warsaw, May 11, 1819), and others; also many Polish dances. Wagner used one of his themes in his symph. overture *Polonia.* Kurpiński publ. a collection, *Historical Songs* (Warsaw, 1816).

Kürsteiner, Jean Paul, American pianist and pedagogue; b. (of French-Swiss father and American mother) Catskill, N.Y., July 8, 1864; d. Los Angeles, March 19, 1943. He studied in Leipzig with Jadassohn and R. Hofmann; piano with Weidenbach and Teichmüller. Returning to America in 1893, he was appointed instructor of piano and theory at the Ogontz

School in Philadelphia, holding this position until 1930. In 1938 he moved to Los Angeles. He wrote a number of piano pieces, of which *Invocation to Eros* became fairly well known. His works comprise 33 opus numbers. He publ. *Essays on Expert Aid to Artistic Piano Playing.*

Kurt, Melanie, Austrian soprano; b. Vienna, Jan. 8, 1880; d. New York, March 11, 1941. She studied piano at the Vienna Cons. (1887–94), winning the gold medal and Liszt prize; then took singing lessons from Fannie Mütter in Vienna, and made a successful operatic debut as Elisabeth in *Tannhäuser* (Lübeck, 1902). From 1905 to 1908 she sang in Braunschweig; then (1908–12), at the Berlin Opera. She became an outstanding Wagner interpreter and appeared in London, Brussels, Milan, Budapest, etc. When the Deutsches Opernhaus in Charlottenburg was opened in 1912, she was engaged as chief soprano for heroic roles. On Feb. 1, 1915, she made her debut at the Metropolitan Opera House as Isolde. In 1917 she returned to Europe, living in Berlin and Vienna as singing teacher. In 1939 she settled in N.Y., where she remained until her death.

Kurtág, György, Hungarian composer; b. Lugoj, Feb. 19, 1926. He learned to play piano as a child; then studied composition with Kadosa, Leo Weiner, Veress and Farkas at the Budapest Academy of Music (1946–53); went to Paris and took lessons with Milhaud and Messiaen (1957–58); upon return to Budapest he taught at the Academy of Music. In his music he sometimes applies serial principles to classical melodic configurations and forms.

WORKS: *Suite* for piano duet (1950); Piano Suite (1951); *Cantata* (1953); Viola Concerto (1954); String Quartet (1959); Wind Quintet (1959); *8 Piano Pieces* (1960); *8 Duets* for violin and cimbalom (1960–61); *Jelek (Signs)* for solo viola (1961); *5 Merrycate* for guitar (1962); *Bornemissza Péter mondásai (The Sayings of Péter Bornemissza),* concerto for soprano and piano (1963–68); *In Memory of a Winter Sunset,* 4 fragments for soprano, violin and cimbalom (1969); *4 Capriccios* for soprano and chamber ensemble (1971–72); *Game* for piano (1974–75); *4 Songs* (1975); *Szálkák (Splinters)* for solo cimbalom (1975).

Kurth, Ernst, eminent Austrian musicologist; b. Vienna, June 1, 1886; d. Bern, Aug. 2, 1946. He studied at the Vienna Cons. with Guido Adler; received his Dr. phil. with the thesis *Der Stil der Opera seria von Chr. W. Gluck bis zum Orfeo* (1908), which was publ. in Adler's *Studien zur Musikwissenschaft* (vol. 1); held various posts as teacher and conductor in Germany; then went to Bern in 1912, where he founded a Collegium Musicum; became prof. in 1927. His principal work, *Grundlagen des linearen Kontrapunkts: Bachs melodische Polyphonie* (Bern, 1917), exercised a profound influence on musicology, and on practical composition as well; the term "linear counterpoint" which he introduced in it became part of scientific nomenclature in music; a companion volume, *Romantische Harmonik und ihre Krise in Wagners Tristan* (Bern, 1920), is a psychological analysis of Romantic music. His volume *Musikpsychologie* (Berlin, 1931) repre-

sents a synthesis of his theoretical ideas on musical perception. He also publ. a comprehensive biography of Bruckner (Berlin, 1925; 2 vols.) and several valuable studies: "Zur Ars cantus mensurabilis des Franko von Köln," in *Kirchenmusikalisches Jahrbuch* (1908); *Die Voraussetzungen der theoretischen Harmonik und der tonalen Darstellungssysteme* (Bern, 1913); "Zur Motivbildung Bachs," *Bach Jahrbuch* (1917).
BIBLIOGRAPHY: E. Bücken, "Kurth als Musiktheoretiker," *Melos* IV/7–8; K. von Fischer, "In memoriam Ernst Kurth," in *Musikalmanach* (Munich, 1948).

Kurtz, Edward Frampton, American violinist and composer; b. New Castle, Pa., July 31, 1881; d. Cedar Falls, Iowa, June 8, 1965. He studied at the Univ. of Iowa, the Detroit Cons., and the Cincinnati Cons.; took violin lessons with Eugène Ysaÿe, during which time the latter was conductor of the Cincinnati Symph. Orch.; studied composition with Clapp, Goetschius, and E. S. Kelley. After teaching at various midwestern colleges, he became head of the music dept. of Iowa State Teachers College, in 1940, and lived mostly in Iowa. He wrote 3 symphonies (1932, 1939, 1940), several symphonic poems, a suite for string quartet, subtitled *From the West;* violin pieces.

Kurtz, Efrem, Russian-American conductor; b. St. Petersburg, Nov. 7, 1900. He studied academic subjects in Riga; then went to Germany and took music courses at the Stern Cons. in Berlin, graduating in 1922. Subsequently he devoted himself to ballet conducting. He came to the U.S. in 1943; was conductor of the Kansas City Philharmonic (1943–48) and of the Houston Symph. Orch. (1948–54). In 1966 he conducted some concerts in Moscow and Leningrad; then was active as guest conductor in Europe and America; in 1977 he conducted in Tokyo; also filled in engagements with the Kansas City Philharmonic and with the Zürich Tonhall Orch. He makes his permanent home in Switzerland.

Kurz, Selma, coloratura soprano; b. Bielitz, Silesia, Nov. 15, 1874; d. Vienna, May 10, 1933. She studied with Pless; made her first appearances in Hamburg, 1895. In 1899 she was engaged by Mahler at the Vienna Court Opera, and remained on the roster until 1926. She made her London debut at Covent Garden as Gilda (June 7, 1904), creating a profound impression; subsequently appeared in America, also with success. She was married to the famous Viennese gynecologist, Josef Halban.

Kurz, Siegfried, German composer and conductor; b. Dresden, July 18, 1930. He studied composition with Fidelio Finke, trumpet and conducting at the Dresden State Academy (1945–50); was conductor at the Dresden State Theater (1949–60) and a conductor at the Dresden State Opera since 1960 and music director there since 1971. His own music combines the principles of classical lucidity with the dissonant counterpoint of the mid-modern era.
WORKS: Concerto for the Trumpet and String Orch. (1953); *Sinfonia Piccola* (Dresden, June 26, 1954); *Dance Suite* for orch. (1955); 2 symphonies

(1958, 1959); *Music for Orchestra* (1960); *Chamber Concerto* for wind quintet and string orch. (1962); Piano Concerto (Dresden, Oct. 2, 1964); Variations for Orch. (1968); Sonatine for Orch. (1969); *Music for winds, percussion and strings* (1969); Horn Concerto (Dresden, Dec. 20, 1973); Wind Quintet (1950); Sonatina for 7 wind instruments (1952).

Kusevitsky, Moshe, Jewish cantor; b. Smorgon, Poland, June 9, 1899; d. Kings Point, Long Island, N.Y., Aug. 23, 1966. He studied in Wilna; became cantor at Warsaw in 1926, and also pursued a concert career; made his Paris debut as a concert singer in 1930; then appeared several times in England; in 1934, gave concerts in Palestine; in 1938, sang in the U.S. He returned to Warsaw before the outbreak of World War II; escaped to Russia, where he remained from 1939 until 1946, and gave concerts in Leningrad, Moscow, Odessa, etc.; in 1946–47, toured in England; then settled in New York. Although his name is identical (in Russian characters) with that of Serge Koussevitzky, the two are not related.

Kusser (or **Cousser**), **Johann Sigismund,** composer; b. Pressburg, Feb. 13, 1660; d. Dublin, Nov. 1727. He received his early musical training from his father, Johann Kusser (1626–75), a minister and organist. He lived in Stuttgart as a boy; then spent 8 years in Paris (1674–82), where he became a pupil of Lully. He subsequently was in Ansbach (1682–83); then in Brunswick (1690). In 1694 he became co-director of the Hamburg Opera, but left 2 years later, and was active in Nuremberg and Augsburg as opera composer. He was again in Stuttgart from 1700–04. In 1705 he appeared in London, and after a year proceeded to Dublin, where he held the posts of chapelmaster and instructor. He revisited Stuttgart briefly, but returned to Dublin, and remained there until his death. He was greatly esteemed as operatic conductor; Mattheson, in his *Volkommener Capellmeister*, holds him up as a model of efficiency. Kusser's historical significance lies in that he was the mediator between the French and the German styles of composition, and the first to use Lully's methods and forms in German instrumental music. Lully's influence is shown in Kusser's set of 6 suites for strings, *Composition de musique suivant la méthode française* (Stuttgart, 1682).
WORKS: operas: for Brunswick, *Julia* (1690, *Kleopatra* (1691), *Ariadne* (Feb. 15, 1692), *Andromeda* (Feb. 20, 1692), *Jason* (Sept. 1, 1692), *Narcissus* (Oct. 14, 1692), *Porus* (1693); for Hamburg, *Erindo* (1694) and *Der grossmüthige Scipio Africanus* (1694); for Stuttgart, *Der verliebte Wald* (1698) and *Erminia* (Oct. 11, 1698). 18 suites from the lost operas *Le Festin des Muses, La Cicala delle cetra d'Eunomio,* and *Apollon enjoué,* 6 operatic overtures, and several arias are extant. An aria from *Erindo* is publ. in Schering's *Geschichte der Musik in Beispielen* (No. 250). An overture was edited by H. Osthoff (1933).
BIBLIOGRAPHY: F. Chrysander, "Die Hamburger Oper unter der Direktion von J. S. Kusser," *Allgemeine musikalische Zeitung* (1879); Hans Scholz, *J. S. Kusser* (Munich, 1911).

Kussevitsky, Serge. See **Koussevitzky, Serge.**

Küster, Hermann, German writer on music; b. Templin, July 14, 1817; d. Herford, March 17, 1878. He studied in Berlin with A. W. Bach, Ludwig Berger, Marx, and Rungenhagen; from 1845–52, musical director at Saarbrücken; then settled in Berlin as music teacher; in 1857, became court and cathedral organist. He publ. *Über Händels Israel in Ägypten* (1854); *Populäre Vorträge über Bildung und Bergründung eines musikalischen Urteils* (4 vols., 1870–77); *Methode für den Unterricht im Gesang auf höheren Schulanstalten* (1872); *Über die Formen in der Musik* (1872), etc.; also wrote 7 oratorios; orchestral music; church music, songs; etc.

Kutev, Filip, Bulgarian choral leader and composer; b. Aytos, June 13, 1903. After completing his education in Sofia he became a military band leader; in 1951 he organized an ensemble of largely untutored folk singers, musicians and dancers; he brought it to a high point of virtuosity and toured in Europe (1958) and in the U.S. (1963), eliciting great praise. Virtually all of his compositions are derived from Bulgarian melorhythms; among these are *Bulgarian Rhapsody* for orch. (1937); cantata, *September the Ninth*, in honor of the entry of the Soviet Army into Bulgaria in 1944; *Stalin Cantata* (1949); Symphony (1950).
BIBLIOGRAPHY: S. Stoyanov, *Filip Kutev* (Sofia, 1962).

Kutschera, Elsa, Austrian operatic soprano; b. Vienna, June 1, 1867; d. there Dec. 29, 1945. She studied with Pauline Viardot-Garcia and Padilla; sang in Berlin in 1892; made U.S. tours in 1895 and 1915.

Kutzschbach, Hermann Ludwig, German conductor; b. Meissen, Aug. 30, 1875; d. Dresden, Feb. 9, 1938. He studied at the Dresden Cons. with Draeseke and others; was opera coach at various German theaters; from 1906–09, conductor of the court opera at Mannheim; then returned to Dresden, where he became conductor of the court opera (1914).

Kuula, Toivo, Finnish composer; b. Vasa, July 7, 1883; d. Viipuri (Vyborg), May 18, 1918. He studied at the Helsinki Cons. with Wegelius, Järnefelt and Sibelius (1900–08); then went to Italy, where he took courses with Bossi in Bologna; also in Paris with Marcel Labey; in 1910 he was appointed conductor of the orchestra at Oulu; from 1911 to 1916 was assistant conductor of the Helsinki Philharmonic; then conductor of the orch. in Viipuri. He was shot to death during a street fight in the aftermath of the Finnish Civil War. His music, rooted in Finnish folksong, is occasionally touched with Impressionism. To commemorate his achievement, two societies were formed in Helsinki and Stockholm in 1948 and 1949.
WORKS: At his death he left unfinished a *Jupiter Symphony;* his *Stabat Mater* (for chorus, organ, and orch; 1914–18) was completed by Madetoja and first performed in 1919 in Helsinki. Completed works: 2 *South Ostrobothnian Suites,* for orch. (1906 and 1912); *Prelude and Fugue,* for orch. (1909); *Prelude and Intermezzo,* for strings and organ (1909); *Orjanpoika (The Son of a Slave),* symph. legend (1910); *Kuolemattomuuden toivo (Hope of Immortality)* for

baritone, chorus and orch. (1910); *Merenkylpijäneidot (Maids on the Seashore)* for soprano and orch. (1910); *Impi ja pajarinpoika (The Maid and the Boyar's Son)* for soprano and orch. (1911). Violin Sonata; music for plays; piano pieces; songs.
BIBLIOGRAPHY: T. Elmgreen-Heinonen and E. Roiha, *Toivo Kuula* (Helsinki, 1952).

Kuusisto, Ilkka Taneli, Finnish composer, son of **Taneli Kuusisto;** b. Helsinki, April 26, 1933. He studied organ at the Sibelius Academy in Helsinki; also composition with Arre Merikanto and Nils-Eric Fougstedt. In 1958 he went to New York to study organ with Seth Bingham; later continued his studies in Germany and in Vienna.
WORKS: 3 *Introductions* for brass, percussion and organ (1956); 3 *Chinese Songs* for soprano, flute and piano (1956); Duo for flute and cello (1957); *Valkeneva päivä (Daybreak)* cantata for solo voices, youth chorus and organ (1957); *Coelestis aulae nuntius* for trombone and organ (1959); *Crucifixus* for baritone and string quartet (1959); *Cassazione* for 2 clarinets and 2 horns (1961); *Jazzationes,* suite for jazz quartet and string quartet (1965); *Ritornells* for viola and marimba (1970); *The Pain* and *Alfhid,* 2 songs for baritone, 2 clarinets and strings (1972); music for Brecht's play *Saint Joan of the Stockyards* (1972); music for films; anthems; songs.

Kuusisto, Taneli, Finnish composer, b. Helsinki, June 19, 1905. He studied at the Univ. of Helsinki, in Paris, and in Leipzig with J. N. David; 1936–42, assistant conductor at the Helsinki Radio; 1942–46, chorus director at the Opera there. In 1948 he began teaching at the Sibelius Academy; was Director there 1959–71; vice-chairman of the board of directors of the Finnish National Opera, 1960–70; a member of the Swedish Royal Academy of Music.
WORKS: Sonatina, for string quartet (1927); *Pastorale,* for orch. (1934); Nocturne, for cello and orch. (1936); *Sonatina di Natale,* for flute, cello and piano (1936); *Psalm 40,* for baritone, chorus, organ and strings (1939); *Jouluyö (Christmas Night)* for chorus, organ and orch. (1941); *Laatokka (Lake Ladoga),* symph. legend (1944); *Kangastuksia (Mirages)* for mezzo-soprano and orch. (1945); Trio for flute, viola and piano (1945); *Saimoon helmi (The Pearl of Saimaa),* cantata (1949); *Toccata,* for orch. (1953); piano pieces, organ pieces; sacred music.
BIBLIOGRAPHY: Sulho Ranta, "Taneli Kuusisto," in *Suomen Saveltajia* (Helsinki, 1945; pp. 655–64).

Kuyper, Elisabeth, Dutch conductor and composer; b. Amsterdam, Sept. 13, 1877; d. Lugano, Feb. 26, 1953. She studied with Max Bruch in Berlin. From 1908–20 she taught theory at the Hochschule there; founder (1908) and conductor of the Berlin Tonkünstlerinnen Orch.; in 1922 she led a few concerts of the London Women's Symph. Orch., and 1923 conducted the New York Women's Symph. Orch.; later returned to Europe and lived at Lago Maggiore in Brissago. She composed a symphony, a violin concerto, several violin sonatas, a ballade for cello and piano, a piano trio, songs.

Küzdö, Victor, Hungarian violinist and teacher; b. Budapest, Sept. 18, 1859; d. Glendale, Calif., Feb. 24, 1966, at the age of 106. He studied at the Budapest Cons. with Karl Huber; made his debut there in 1882; toured in Europe, and visited the U.S. in 1884 and 1887. In 1894 he settled in New York; from 1918-31, taught at the summer school of Chicago Musical College; in 1932, settled in Glendale, Calif. He became totally blind in 1950. He published several violin pieces, among them a Serenade and *Witches' Dance.*

Kuznetzov, Konstantin, Russian musicologist; b. Novocherkassk, Sept. 21, 1883; d. Moscow, May 25, 1953. He studied at the Univ. of Heidelberg (Dr. phil., 1906); was instructor at the Univ. of Moscow (1912-14); prof. at the Univ. of Odessa (1914-20); in 1921, returned to Moscow, where he remained until his death. An erudite musician, he wrote on music history from a broad sociological standpoint; publ. *Introduction to the History of Music* (Moscow, 1923); *Glinka and His Epoch* (Moscow, 1927); edited several publications for the Musicological Institute of Moscow.

Kvandal, Johan, Norwegian composer; b. Oslo, Sept. 8, 1919. He studied piano and composition at the Oslo Cons.; later with Joseph Marx in Vienna and Nadia Boulanger in Paris. He was a church organist in Oslo (1959-74) and a member of the governing board of the Society of Norwegian Composers (1960-75); wrote music criticism in the Oslo newspapers *Morgenposten* (1959-74) and *Aftenposten* (after 1974).

WORKS: Piano Sonatina (1942); Divertimento for strings (1945); String Trio (1951); *Song of Stella* for soprano and string orch. (1952); 3 solo cantatas: No. 1 for soprano or tenor, and orch. (1953); No. 2, *O Domine Deus,* for soprano and organ (1966); No. 3 for baritone and organ (1970); 2 string quartets (1954, 1966); *Variations and Fugue* for orch. (1954); *Norwegian Overture* (1959); Symphony No. 1 (1959); Duo for violin and cello (1959); *Symphonic Epos* for orch. (1961-62); Concerto for flute and strings (1963); *Aria, Cadenza and Finale* for violin and piano (1964); orch. suite from incidental music to the play *Skipper Worse* (1967); *Sinfonia Concertante* (1968); *Introduction and Allegro* for horn and piano (1969); *3 Fantasy Country Dances* for piano (1969); *Da lontano* for flute and piano (1970); Wind Quintet (1971); *Nature,* chamber cantata for baritone, violin and piano (1972); *Antagonia,* concerto for 2 string orchestras and percussion (1972); *Duo Concertante* for 2 pianos (1974); Quartet for flute, violin, viola and cello (1975); songs.

Kvapil, Jaroslav, significant Czech composer; b. Fryšták, April 21, 1892; d. Brno, Feb. 18, 1958. He studied with Janáček in Brno (1906-09) and at the Leipzig Cons. (1911-13) with Leichtmüller (piano) and Max Reger (composition). He was in the Austrian army during World War I; then was music director of the Philharmonic Society in Brno (1919-47); taught at the Janáček Academy of Music in Brno (1947-57). His works show the double influence of Janáček's national and rhapsodic style and Max Reger's strong polyphonic idiom.

WORKS: an opera, *Pohádka máje (A Romance in May,* 1940-43; Prague, May 12, 1950; revised 1955; Brno, 1955); an oratorio, *Lví srdce (The Lion's Heart,* 1928-31; Brno, Dec. 7, 1931); 2 cantatas: *A Song on Time That Is Passing* (1924) and *Small Italian Cantata* (1950); 4 symphonies: No. 1 (1913-14); No. 2 (1921); No. 3 (1936-37); No. 4, *Vítězná (Victory,* 1943); *Thema con variazioni e fuga* for orch. (1912); 2 violin concertos (1927-28, 1952); *Z těžkých dob (From Anxious Times),* symph. variations (1939); *Slavonic (Jubilee) Overture* (1944); *Burlesque* for flute and orch. (1945); *Svítání (Daybreak),* symph. poem (1948-49); Oboe Concerto (1951); Piano Concerto (1954); 3 violin sonatas with piano (1910; 1914; 1931); Sonata for Violin and Organ (1931); Piano Trio (1912); Cello Sonata (1913); 6 string quartets (1914; 1926, 1931, 1935, 1949, 1951); Piano Quintet (1914-15); Brass Quintet (1925); Variations for Trumpet and Piano (1929); Suite for Trombone and Piano (1930); *Intimate Pictures* for violin and piano (1934); Wind Quintet (1935); Violin Sonatina (1941); *Fantasy* for cello and piano (1942); Nonet (1944); Quartet for flute, violin, viola and cello (1948); Duo for violin and viola (1949); Suite for Viola and Piano (1955). He also wrote 3 piano sonatas (1912, 1925, 1946); Variations for Piano (1914); *Fantasy in the Form of Variations* for piano (1952); Piano Sonatina (1956); *10 Pieces* for piano (1957); Fantasy for Organ (1935); several song cycles; many transcriptions of folksongs; a piano album of 100 folksongs from Moravian Slovakia (1914).

BIBLIOGRAPHY: L. Kundera, *Jaroslav Kvapil* (Prague, 1944).

Kvernadze, Alexander, Georgian composer; b. Signahi, Georgia, June 29, 1928. He studied with Andrey Balanchivadze at the Cons. of Tbilisi, graduating in 1953. Among his works are 2 Piano Concertos (1950, 1965); Violin Concerto (1956); *Dance-Fantasy* for orch. (1959); Symphony (1961); violin pieces; film music.

Kwalwasser, Helen, American violinist; daughter of Jacob Kwalwasser; b. Syracuse, Oct. 11, 1927. She showed a gift for violin playing at an early age; studied with Louis Persinger (1936-39), with Zimbalist at the Curtis Institute of Music in Philadelphia (1939-41), then with Galamian (1941-48); made her debut in N.Y. on March 25, 1947; then toured Europe (1949); returning to N.Y., was active as violinist and teacher.

Kwalwasser, Jacob, music psychologist and educator; b. New York, Feb. 27, 1894; d. Pittsburgh, Aug. 7, 1977. He received his education at the Univ. of Pittsburgh and the Univ. of Iowa, obtaining his Ph.D. in 1926; taught in the public schools in Pittsburgh (1918-23); head of public school music at the Univ. of Iowa (1923-26); in 1926, was appointed prof. and head of the dept. of music education at Syracuse Univ. He is the co-author of the Kwalwasser-Dykema Music Tests; publ. a manual on the subject in 1913; also collaborated in establishing the Kwalwasser-Ruch Musical Accomplishment Test, and various other melodic, harmonic, and instrumental tests; publ. numerous magazine articles on music education.

WRITINGS: *Tests and Measurements in Music* (1927; an influential code of rules, adopted in many educational institutions); *Problems in Public School Music* (1932; rev. ed., 1941; treats objectives of music education); *Exploring the Musical Mind* (N.Y., 1955).

Kwast, James, famous German pianist and teacher; b. Nijkerk, Holland, Nov. 23, 1852; d. Berlin, Oct. 31, 1927. He studied with his father and Ferdinand Böhme; later with Reinecke and Richter at the Leipzig Cons.; also with Th. Kullak and Wüerst at Berlin, and with Brassin and Gevaert at Brussels. In 1874 he became instructor at the Cons. of Cologne; from 1883 till 1903 he taught at the Hoch Cons. in Frankfurt; from 1903 to 1906, was prof. of piano at the Klindworth-Scharwenka Cons. in Berlin; then at Stern's Cons. there. He was greatly esteemed by his colleagues and students as a piano pedagogue; many well-known pianists were his pupils at Frankfurt and Berlin. His first wife, Antonia (d. Stuttgart, Feb. 10, 1931), was a daughter of Ferdinand Hiller; his second wife, **Frieda Hodapp-Kwast** (b. Bargen, Aug. 13, 1880; d. Bad Wiessee, Sept. 14, 1949), was a concert pianist. He wrote a piano concerto and other piano music; edited works of Handel and Clementi for the *Tonmeister* edition.

Kyung-Wha Chung, brilliant Korean violinist; b. Seoul, March 26, 1948. She comes from a musical family; her sister is a cellist, her brother a pianist. She began playing violin as a small child; in 1961 she went to the U.S., and became a pupil of Ivan Galamian in N.Y. In 1967 she shared first prize with Pinchas Zukerman in the Leventritt Competition. As a soloist, she developed an active career, in America, Asia and Europe, giving an average of 110 concerts annually. She also gives frequent performances in a trio with her brother and sister.

L

La Barbara, Joan, American composer and experimental vocalist; b. Philadelphia, June 8, 1947. Her grandfather taught her to play nursery songs on piano; then she sang in church and school choirs; joined a folk music group in Philadelphia; then went to New York where she sang radio commercials and at the same time made contacts with the most uninhibited representatives of the American avant-garde. In her compositions she usually makes use of graphic notation. Among her works are *Ides of March* for strings and voices (1974); *An Exaltation of Larks* for voice and electronics (1975); *Cyclone,* a sound sculpture for white noise and voices (1975; first performed in Bonn, Germany, May 14, 1977); *Thunder* for voice electronics and timpani (1976); *Circular Song* for voice employing circular breathing (1975); introduced many other vocal improvements, vocalizing while breathing in and out.

Labarre, Théodore, eminent French harpist; b. Paris, March 5, 1805; d. there, March 9, 1870. He studied privately with Cousineau, Boscha, and Naderman; then at the Paris Cons. with Dourlen, Eler, Fétis, and Boieldieu. From 1824–47 he lived alternately in London and Paris; became conductor of the Opéra-Comique; in 1851, was appointed conductor of Louis Napoleon's private orchestra; in 1867, prof. of harp at the Paris Cons. He wrote 4 operas, 5 ballets, numerous pieces for the harp, songs, etc.; also a *Méthode complète* for harp.

La Bassée, Adam de, medieval poet; b. La Bassée; d. Lille, Feb. 25, 1286. He was an ecclesiastic at Lille; created religious songs by adapting his own words to sacred and secular melodies; published by Abbé D. Charnel in the *Messager des sciences historiques* (Ghent, 1858).

Labatt, Leonard, Swedish tenor; b. Stockholm, Dec. 4, 1838; d. there, March 7, 1897. He studied with J. Günther; then with Masset in Paris; made his debut in Stockholm as Tamino in *Die Zauberflöte* (1866); in 1868–69 was at the Dresden Opera; from 1869 till 1883 at the Vienna Opera; sang in London in 1881; made an American tour in 1888–89. He was especially fine in Wagnerian roles.
BIBLIOGRAPHY: F. Hedberg, *Svenska opera-sängare* (Stockholm, 1885).

L'Abbé, Joseph Barnabé Saint-Sevin (real name **Saint-Sevin**), French violinist and composer; b. Agen, June 11, 1727; d. Paris, July 20, 1803. A precocious musician, he began his study with his father and became a member of the orchestra of the Comédie-Française at the age of 12; then studied with Leclair; was violinist at the Opéra (1742–62); also played at the Concert Spirituel (1741–55); devoted his later years to teaching and composition. He had an excellent violin technique, and was an innovator in that he wrote out cadenzas in full.
WORKS: 2 books of violin sonatas with continuo (1748–64); symphonies for 3 violins and continuo (c.1754); 5 collections of airs arranged for 1 and 2 violins; a manual, *Les Principes du violon* (1761).
BIBLIOGRAPHY: L. de la Laurencie, *L'École française de violon de Lully à Viotti* (vol. 2, Paris, 1923).

Labey, Marcel, French conductor and composer; b. Le Vésinet, Seine-et-Oise, Aug. 6, 1875; d. Nancy, Nov. 25, 1968. He studied law in Paris, receiving his degree in 1898; then turned his attention to music, studying piano with Delaborde, harmony with Lenormand, and composition with Vincent d'Indy at the Schola Cantorum; taught piano there, and at d'Indy's death in 1931, became vice-principal of the school.
WORKS: an opera, *Bérengère* (1912; Le Havre, April 12, 1929); 3 symphonies (1903; 1908; 1934); *Suite champêtre* for orch. (1923); *Ouverture pour un drame* (Paris, Jan. 22, 1921); Piano Sonata; Viola Sonata; 2 violin sonatas; String Quartet; Piano Trio; Piano Quartet; Piano Quintet; songs; etc. He publ. piano arrangements of several orchestral works of d'Indy (Symph. in B-flat, *Jour d'été à la montagne,* etc.).

Labia, Fausta, Italian opera singer; sister of **Maria Labia;** b. Verona, April 3, 1870; d. Rome, Oct. 6, 1935. She became a great favorite in Sweden, but retired in 1908 after her marriage. She then lived many years in Rome and taught at the Santa Cecilia. Her method, *L'Arte del respiro nello recitazione e nel canto,* was publ. posthumously in 1936.

Labia, Maria, Italian soprano; sister of **Fausta Labia;** b. Verona, Feb. 14, 1880; d. Malcesine del Garda, Feb. 10, 1953. She received her musical education from her mother, an excellent amateur singer; made her operatic debut in Stockholm on May 19, 1905 as Mimi. From 1906 to 1908 she was on the roster of the Komische Oper in Berlin. She was then engaged by the Manhattan Opera, where she first appeared on Nov. 9, 1908, as Tosca. After the demise of that company she joined the Vienna Opera; then taught voice at the Music Academy of Siena. She was an actress of great emotional power, and was particularly successful in such dramatic roles as Carmen, Santuzza, Nedda, and Violetta.

Labitzky, August, German violinist and conductor; son of Joseph Labitzky; b. Bečov (Petschau), Oct. 22, 1832; d. Reichenhall, Aug. 28, 1903. He studied at the Prague Cons., and with Ferdinand David and Hauptmann in Leipzig. He became conductor of the Karlsbad resort orch. in 1853; composed piano pieces, etc.

Labitzky, Joseph, German dance composer and violinist; father of **August Labitzky;** b. Schönfeld, Eger, July 5, 1802; d. Karlsbad, Aug. 19, 1881. He studied with Veit in Bečov (Petschau); in 1820, joined the orchestra in Marienbad as 1st violinist; then occupied a similar post in Karlsbad; organized his own orchestra and toured southern Germany. He studied with Winter in Munich, where he publ. his first dances (1827); returning to Karlsbad in 1835, he organized an orchestra and toured Europe. Many of his waltzes, galops, quadrilles, etc. (about 300 opus numbers) enjoyed a great vogue.

Lablache, Luigi, famous Italian bass of French and Irish descent; b. Naples, Dec. 6, 1794; d. there, Jan. 23, 1858. He studied voice with Valesi at the Naples Cons. della Pietà dei Turchini; at 18 he commenced his career there as a *basso buffo.* In 1812 he married Teresa Pinotti, the daughter of an actor. In 1813 he went to Palermo as *primo basso cantante;* then appeared at La Scala in Milan; made his debut in London as Geronimo in *Il Matrimonio Segreto* (March 30, 1830) with instantaneous success; in Paris, in the same role on Nov. 4, 1830. From 1836–37 Lablache lived in England as singing master to Queen Victoria. He also sang in Naples, Vienna, and St. Petersburg, always winning acclaim. He was greatly esteemed by his contemporaries; Schubert dedicated to him his 3 Italian songs (1827).
BIBLIOGRAPHY: F. H. J. Castil-Blaze, *Biographie de Lablache* (Paris, 1850); G. Widén, *Luigi Lablache* (Göteborg, 1897).

Labor, Josef, Austrian pianist, organist, and composer; b. Horowitz, June 29, 1842; d. Vienna, April 26, 1924. He lost his sight as a youth; studied with Sechter at the Vienna Cons.; in 1863 was tutor to the princesses of Hannover, who were living then in exile with their family in Vienna. He played in London (1865), Paris, and in Russia; in 1868 returned to Vienna, where he settled as a teacher; among his students were Julius Bittner and Arnold Schoenberg. He wrote several sonatas; a piano quartet; pieces for organ and for piano; church music; songs; etc.; also edited Biber's violin sonatas for the *Denkmäler der Tonkunst in Österreich.*
BIBLIOGRAPHY: P. Kundi, *Josef Labor, Sein Leben und Wirken* (Vienna, 1963; contains a thematic catalogue).

Laborde, Jean Benjamin de, French violinist and composer; b. Paris, Sept. 5, 1734; d. there (on the guillotine), July 22, 1794. He studied violin with Dauvergne and composition with Rameau; was chamberlain to Louis XV, and a member of the Compagnie des Fermiers-Généraux; then withdrew from the court and devoted himself to composition. He wrote 32 operas, and songs; also an *Essai sur la musique ancienne et moderne,* containing an early study of folksongs (1780); *Recueils de chansons avec un accompagnement de violon et la basse continue; Choix de chansons mises en musique* (4 vols., 1773); *Mémoires historiques sur Raoul de Coucy* (1781).
BIBLIOGRAPHY: Jacques Devisme, *J. B. de La Borde, un favori des dieux* (Paris, 1936).

Labroca, Mario, Italian composer; b. Rome, Nov. 22, 1896; d. there, July 1, 1973. He was a composition pupil of Malipiero and Respighi and graduated from the Parma Cons. in 1921. He held numerous administrative and teaching posts; was music director of the Teatro La Fenice in Venice (from 1959); lectured at the Univ. of Perugia (from 1960). He was closely connected with the theater and the cinema in Italy and composed many scores for plays and films.

WORKS: 2 operas, *La Principessa di Perepepè* (Rome, Dec. 11, 1927) and *Le tre figliuole di Pinco Pallino* (Rome, Jan. 27, 1928); Stabat Mater for soprano, mixed chorus, and orch. (Rome, Dec. 15, 1935); Symphony (1934); *Sinfonia* for string orch. (1927); 2 string quartets (1925 and 1934); Piano Trio (1925); Suite for viola and piano (1926); *Tre cantate dalla Passione secondo San Giovanni* (1950).

Labunski, Felix, Polish-American composer and teacher, brother of **Wiktor Labunski** (1895–1974); b. Ksawerynów, Dec. 27, 1892. Brought up in a musical environment (his father, a civil engineer, was an amateur singer; his mother played the piano), he began studying piano as a child; then entered the Warsaw Cons., where he was a student of Marczewski and Maliszewski. He met Paderewski, who arranged for him a stipend at the École Normale de Musique in Paris, where he studied with Nadia Boulanger and Paul Dukas. In 1927 he formed, with Czapski, Perkowski and Wiechowicz, the "Association of Young Polish Musicians in Paris." Returning to Poland, Labunski held the post of Director of the Dept. of Classical Music of the Polish Radio in Warsaw (1934–36). In 1936 he emigrated to America; became a naturalized citizen in 1941. He lived in New York until 1945, when he joined the staff of the Cincinnati College of Music, continuing in this position when it merged with the Cincinnati Cons. of Music in 1955; he retired in 1964 as Prof. Emeritus in composition. In his music, Felix Labunski remains faithful to the legacy of romanticism as cultivated in Poland and Russia.

WORKS: Between 1923 and 1931, Labunski wrote mainly for piano; his first orchestral work of importance was *Triptyque champêtre* (1931). Other works were *Polish Cantata* (1932), *Ptaki (The Birds)* for soprano and orch. (1934); String Quartet No. 1 (1935); *Divertimento* for flute and piano (1936); *In Memoriam,* symph. poem in memory of Paderewski (1941); *Suite* for string orch. (1941; performed at the Festival of the International Society for Contemporary Music, Berkeley, Calif., Aug. 2, 1942); *Song Without Words* for soprano and strings (1946); *There Is No Death,* cantata (1950); Variations for Orchestra (1951); Symphony in D (1954); *Elegy* for orch. (Cincinnati, Dec. 11, 1955); *Images of Youth,* cantata (Cincinnati May Festival, May 11, 1956); *Xaveriana,* fantasy for two pianos and orch., commissioned for the 125th anniversary of Xavier Univ. (1956); *Divertimento* for flute, oboe, clarinet and bassoon (1956); *Diptych* for oboe and piano (1958); *Symphonic Dialogues* (Cincinnati, Feb. 9, 1961); String Quartet No. 2 (1962); *Canto di Aspirazione* for orch. (a revision of the slow movement of the Second Symphony, 1963); *Polish Renaissance Suite* for orch. (1967); *Intrada Festiva* for brass choir (1968); *Salut à Paris,* ballet suite for orch. (1968); *Music* for piano and orch. (1968); *Primavera* for orch. (Cincinnati, April 19, 1974).

Labunski, Wiktor, pianist and composer; brother of **Felix Labunski;** b. St. Petersburg, April 14, 1895; d. Kansas City, Jan. 26, 1974. He studied at the St. Petersburg Cons. with Nikolayev (piano), Kalafati and Vitols (composition); later, piano with Felix Blumenfeld and Safonov, and conducting with Emil Mlynarski. From 1919 till 1928 he was head of the piano dept. at the Cons. of Cracow; then came to the U.S.; made his debut in 1928 as a pianist at Carnegie Hall, N.Y.; was instructor at the Nashville Cons. (1928-31); prof. and director of the Memphis, Tenn., College of Music (1931-37); in 1937, appointed prof. and director of the Cons. of Music of Kansas City. In 1920 he married Wanda Mlynarska, daughter of his teacher Emil Mlynarski.

WORKS: Symph. in G minor (1936); Piano Concerto (Kansas City, Feb. 16, 1939, composer soloist); Concerto for 2 Pianos and Orch. (Kansas City, May 31, 1957); many piano pieces (*Impromptu, Minuet, 4 Variations on a Theme by Paganini, Reminiscence,* etc.).

Laccetti, Guido, Italian singer and composer; b. Naples, Oct. 1, 1879; d. Cava dei Tirreni, Oct. 8, 1943. He studied at the Cons. of Naples; from 1925 taught at the Palermo Cons. His works include the operas *La contessa di San Remo* (1904), *Hoffmann* (Naples, 1912), *Il miracolo* (Naples, 1915), *Carnasciali* (Rome, 1925), and *La favola dei gobbi* (1935).

Lacerda, Francisco de, Portuguese conductor and musicologist; b. Ribeira Seca, S. Jorge, Azores, May 11, 1869; d. Lisbon, July 18, 1934. He studied at the Lisbon Cons.; received a government stipend for study in Paris, where he took a course with Vincent d'Indy at the Schola Cantorum. In Paris he associated himself with Bourgault-Ducoudray and worked with him in the International Folklore Association; also conducted concerts. At the outbreak of World War I he returned to Portugal; in 1913 he organized the Orquestra Filarmonica in Lisbon. He compiled the important *Cancioneiro musical portugues,* containing some 500 folksongs; wrote a number of original compositions, among them the symph. works, *Adamastor, Almorol, Rapsodia insular,* etc.

BIBLIOGRAPHY: A. Pinot, *Musica moderna portuguesa* (Lisbon, 1930; pp. 70-73); F. de Sousa, *Exposição commemorativa do primeiro centenario do nascimento, Francisco de Lacerda,* a centennial memoir (Lisbon, 1969).

Lach, Robert, Austrian musicologist and composer; b. Vienna, Jan. 29, 1874; d. Salzburg, Sept. 11, 1958. He was a pupil of R. Fuchs at the Vienna Cons. (1893-99); also studied philosophy and musicology with Wallaschek, Rietsch, and Adler; Dr. phil., Prague, 1902. After some years of research and study, he publ. *Studien zur Entwicklungsgeschichte der ornamentalen Melopöie* (Leipzig, 1913), viewing the entire field of musical history in the light of new discoveries of ethnographic investigation. From 1911 to 1920 he was chief of the music division of the Vienna State Library; in 1915, joined the faculty of the Vienna Univ. He recorded for the Phonogram Archives of Vienna the songs of Russian prisoners of World War I (with particular emphasis on Asian and Caucasian nationalities) and publ. numerous papers on these melodies. He was pensioned in 1939, and lived in Vienna in retirement, devoting his time to the compilation of oriental glossaries (Babylonian, Sumerian, Egyptian, etc.). The dedicatory brochure, *Robert Lach, Persön-*

lichkeit und Werk, zum 80. Geburtstag (Vienna, 1954), contains a complete list of his works and scientific writings. His list of musical works attains 150 opus numbers, among them 10 symphonies; 25 string quartets; 14 string quintets; 7 string sextets; septet, octet, nonet, and decet; trios; sonatas; cantatas; 8 Masses; etc. He also wrote philosophical poems and mystical plays; contributed dozens of articles on various subjects to music periodicals.

Lachenmann, Helmut, German composer; b. Stuttgart, Nov. 27, 1935. He studied piano with Jürgen Uhde and composition with Johann Nepomuk David at Stuttgart and later took lessons with Nono in Venice. He subsequently worked in electronic music at the Univ. of Ghent, Belgium. In 1966 he was appointed to instructor in music theory at Music High School in Stuttgart; also conducted a master class in composition at the Basel Music Academy. Among his works are *Souvenir* for 41 instruments (1959); *Introversion I and II* for 6 instrumentalists (1964, 1966); String Trio (1966); *Trio fluido* for clarinet, marimba and viola (1968); *Pression* for cello solo (1969); *Kontrakadenz* for orch. (1970); *Gran Torso* for string quartet (1971); *Fassade* for orch. (1973).

Lachmann, Robert, noted German musicologist; b. Berlin, Nov. 28, 1892; d. Jerusalem, May 8, 1939. He studied languages in Berlin and London; served in the German army during World War I, when he began to collect folk melodies from the African and Indian war prisoners; later studied musicology with Stumpf and Johannes Wolf, and Arabic with Mittwoch at Berlin Univ.; received his Ph.D. (1922) with the thesis *Die Musik in den tunisischen Städten,* publ. in the *Archiv für Musikwissenschaft* (1923). He was librarian of the music division of the Prussian State Library from 1927 until 1933, when he was ousted by the Nazi authorities as a Jew. In 1935 he went to Jerusalem, where he worked at the Hebrew Univ.

WRITINGS: *Musik des Orients* (Breslau, 1929); *Die Musik der aussereuropäischen Natur- und Kulturvölker,* in Bücken's *Handbuch* series (1929); *Jewish Cantillation and Song in the Isle of Djerba* (Jerusalem, 1940; contains a list of Lachmann's publications).

Lachmund, Carl Valentine, American pianist and teacher; b. Booneville, Mo., March 27, 1857; d. Yonkers, N.Y., Feb. 20, 1928. He studied at the Cologne Cons. with Hiller, and later with Liszt, of whom he was one of the last pupils (1881-84); taught at the Scharwenka Cons. in Berlin, and appeared as pianist, touring America with August Wilhelmj in 1880. Settling in New York in 1891, he established his own conservatory. He also founded the Women's String Orch., which he directed for 12 seasons.

Lachner, Franz, German composer and conductor; brother of **Ignaz** and **Vincenz Lachner;** b. Rain-on-Lech, April 2, 1803; d. Munich, Jan. 20, 1890. He studied with Sechter and Stadler in Vienna; became an intimate friend of Schubert; from 1827-34, conductor of the Kärnthnertor Theater in Vienna; in 1834, became conductor of the Mannheim Opera; in 1836, court conductor in Munich, then general music director (1852–65).

WORKS: 2 oratorios, *Moses* and *Die vier Menschenalter;* 4 operas, *Die Bürgschaft* (Pest, 1828), *Alidia* (Munich, 1839), *Catarina Cornaro* (Munich, Dec. 3, 1841), *Benvenuto Cellini* (Munich, 1849); 8 symphonies; a Requiem; Masses; choral works; much chamber music; piano pieces; songs.

BIBLIOGRAPHY: O. Kronseder, "Franz Lachner," *Altbayrische Monatsschrift* 4 (contains a complete catalogue of works); M. von Schwind, *Die Lachner-Rolle* (Munich, 1904); A. Würz, *Franz Lachner als dramatischer Komponist* (Munich, 1927); G. Wagner, *Franz Lachner als Liederkomponist* (Giebing, 1970).

Lachner, Ignaz, German organist, conductor, and composer; brother of **Franz** and **Vincenz Lachner;** b. Rain-on-Lech, Sept. 11, 1807; d. Hannover, Feb. 24, 1895. He studied music with his father; in 1824, joined Franz in Vienna, where he became an assistant conductor at the Kärnthnertor Theater (1825). In 1831 he went to Stuttgart as court music director; in 1842, occupied a similar post in Munich; conductor at the theater in Hamburg (1853); in 1858, became court conductor in Stockholm; in 1861, settled in Frankfurt, as musical director.

WORKS: 3 operas: *Der Geisterturm* (Stuttgart, 1837), *Die Regenbrüder* (Stuttgart, May 20, 1839), *Loreley* (Munich, 1846); several Singspiele, among them the popular *Letzte Fensterle*; ballets; melodramas; symphonies; chamber music; Masses; piano compositions; violin pieces; etc.

Lachner, Vincenz, German organist, conductor, and composer; brother of **Franz** and **Ignaz Lachner;** b. Rain-on-Lech, July 19, 1811; d. Karlsruhe, Jan. 22, 1893. He first studied with his father, and later in Vienna with his brothers, succeeding Ignaz as organist there in 1834, and Franz as court Kapellmeister at Mannheim in 1836. He conducted the German opera in London in 1842, and the municipal opera in Frankfurt in 1848. In 1873 he received a pension and settled in Karlsruhe, joining the faculty of the Cons. there in 1884. His 4-part male choruses are celebrated, particularly his settings of nearly all of Scheffel's songs, among the best being *Alt Heidelberg, du feine; Im schwarzen Wallfisch; Nun grüss' dich Gott;* also wrote symphonies, overtures, string quartets, a piano quartet, and numerous songs.

Lachnith, Ludwig Wenzel, Bohemian composer; b. Prague, July 7, 1746; d. Paris, Oct. 3, 1820. He was a member of the court orch. in Pfalz-Zweibrücken; in 1773 went to Paris and studied with Rudolph (horn) and Philidor (composition). He is known chiefly for his pasticcios, works in which he combined the music of several different composers; an instance is his oratorio *Saul,* with music taken from scores by Mozart, Haydn, Cimarosa, Paisiello, Gossec and Philidor. He also arranged the music of Mozart's *Zauberflöte,* to a libretto reworked by Etienne Morel de Chefdeville, and produced it under the title *Les Mystères d'Isis,* justly parodied as *Les Misères d'ici.* In several of his ventures he had the older Kalkbrenner as his collaborator. Original compositions by Lachnith include the

operas *L'Heureuse Réconciliation* (1785), *L'Antiquaire* (1789), and *Eugénie et Linval* (1798); 3 piano concertos; chamber music.

Lack, Théodore, French pianist and composer; b. Quimper, Finisterre, Sept. 3, 1846; d. Paris, Nov. 25, 1921. A precocious musician, Lack was appointed organist of his village church when he was only 10 years old. He entered the Paris Cons. at 14, where he studied piano with Marmontel, harmony with Bazin, and theory with Lefébure-Wély. Graduating from the Conservatory at 18, he became piano instructor there, and held this position for 57 years (1864–1921) until his death, without ever leaving Paris. He wrote a great many salon pieces for piano (*Tarentelle, Boléro, Études élégantes, Valse espagnole, Scènes enfantines, Souvenir d'Alsace, Polonaise de concert,* etc.).

Lacombe, Louis (Trouillon), French pianist and composer; b. Bourges, Nov. 26, 1818; d. Saint-Vaast-la-Hougue, Sept. 30, 1884. He studied at the Paris Cons. with Zimmermann, winning the 1st piano prize at the age of 13. After touring through France, Belgium, and Germany, he took courses with Czerny, Sechter, and Seyfried in Vienna. Following another concert tour, he settled in Paris (1839), concentrating on composition.

WORKS: a melodrama, *L'Amour* (Paris, Dec. 2, 1859); a one-act opera, *La Madone* (Paris, Jan. 16, 1861); a 2-act comic opera, *Le Tonnelier* (produced as *Meister Martin und seine Gesellen* at Coblenz, March 7, 1897); a 4-act grand opera, *Winkelried* (Geneva, Feb. 17, 1892); the cantata *Sapho* (1878; won a prize at the Paris Exhibition); a grand *Épopée lyrique* for orch.; 2 dramatic symphonies with soli and chorus: *Manfred* (1847) and *Arva ou les Hongrois* (1850); *Lassan et Friss,* Hungarian fantasy for orch.; *Au tombeau d'un Héros,* elegy for violin and orch.; Quintet for piano, violin, cello, oboe, and bassoon; 2 piano trios; numerous piano pieces (*Études en octaves; Six romances sans paroles;* etc.); also choruses. His essay on *Philosophie et musique* was publ. posthumously (Paris, 1895).

BIBLIOGRAPHY: E. Bourdin, *Louis Lacombe* (Paris, 1882); H. Boyer, *Louis Lacombe et son œuvre* (Paris, 1888); L. Gallet, *Conférence sur Louis Lacombe et son œuvre* (Paris, 1891); E. Jongleux, *Un Grand Musicien méconnu: Louis Lacombe* (Bourges, 1935).

Lacombe, Paul, French composer; b. Carcassonne, Aude, July 11, 1837; d. there, June 5, 1927. He studied in Carcassonne with François Teysserre, an organist. He was a prolific composer; his works total more than 150, including an *Ouverture symphonique* (1876); 3 symphonies (Symph. No. 3 won the prize of the Société des Compositeurs de Musique, 1886); *Suite pastorale* for orch.; *Marche dernière,* for orch.; *Scène au camp* for orch.; *Dialogue sentimental,* for flute, bassoon, and piano (1917); 3 violin sonatas; Cello Sonata; 3 trios; String Quartet; a Mass; a Requiem; songs; characteristic piano pieces (*Aubade aux mariés, Arabesques,* etc.).

BIBLIOGRAPHY: Léon Moulin, *Paul Lacombe et son œuvre* (Paris, 1924).

Lacome, Paul (Paul-Jean-Jacques Lacome de l'Estalenx), French composer; b. Houga, Gers, March 4, 1838; d. there, Dec. 12, 1920. In 1860 he went to Paris; became known as a composer of operettas, including *Jeanne, Jeannette et Jeannot* (1876); *Le Beau Nicolas* (1880); *Madame Boniface* (1883); *Myrtille* (1885); *Ma mie Rosette* (1890); *Le Cadeau de noces* (1893); *La Bain de Monsieur* (1895); *Le Maréchal Chaudron* (1898); and *Les Quatre Filles Aymon* (1898); also the orchestral suites *Clair de lune, Suite ancienne, La Verbena;* quartets; trios; psalms; piano pieces (*Les Succès de famille,* etc.); over 200 songs (*L'Estudiantina,* etc.). He publ. *Introduction à la vie musicale* (1911).

Laderman, Ezra, American composer; b. New York, June 29, 1924. He studied at Brooklyn College and at Columbia Univ. with Otto Luening and Douglas Moore (composition) and Paul Henry Lang (musicology); received 3 Guggenheim grants.

WORKS: the operas *Jacob and the Indians* (Woodstock, N.Y., July 26, 1957); *Sarah,* television opera (N.Y., Nov. 30, 1958); *Goodbye to the Clown* (N.Y., May 22, 1960); *The Hunting of the Snark,* children's opera after Lewis Carroll (N.Y., March 25, 1961); *Galileo Galilei,* opera oratorio for television (N.Y., May 14, 1967); *Magic Prison* for two narrators and orch. (N.Y., June 12, 1967); Symphony; Concerto for Orchestra; Violin Concerto; *Celestial Bodies* for flute and strings; *Double Helix* for flute, oboe, and strings; Nonet, for wind instruments; Octet, for wind instruments; 2 piano sonatas. He also wrote the score for the film *The Eleanor Roosevelt Story,* which won an Oscar. His cantata *And David Wept* was produced by CBS Television in N.Y. on April 10, 1971.

Ladmirault, Paul-Émile, French composer; b. Nantes, Dec. 8, 1877; d. Kerbili, near Penestin (Morbihan), Oct. 30, 1944. As a child, he studied piano, organ, and violin; entered the Nantes Cons. in 1892, winning 1st prize in 1893; he was only 15 when his 3-act opera *Gilles de Retz* was staged in Nantes (May 18, 1893); he entered the Paris Cons. in 1895, studying with Gédalge and Fauré; subsequently returned to Nantes, where he taught at the Cons. His *Suite bretonne* (1902–03) and symph. prelude *Brocéliande au matin* (Colonne concert, Nov. 28, 1909) were extracts from a second opera, *Myrdhin* (1902–09), which was never performed; the ballet *La Prêtresse de Koridwen* was produced at the Paris Opéra (Dec. 17, 1926). Other works include the operetta *Glycère* (Paris, 1928); Symphony (1910); *La Brière,* for orch. (Paris, Nov. 20, 1926); *En forêt,* symph. poem (1932); incidental music to *Tristan et Iseult* (1929); *Valse triste,* for piano and orch.; *Airs anciens,* for tenor, string quartet, and piano (1897); *Ballet bohémien,* for flute, oboe, double string quartet and piano (1898); *Fantaisie* for violin and piano (1899); *Chanson grecque* for flute and piano (1900); Violin Sonata (1901); *De l'ombre à la clarté,* for violin and piano (1936); piano pieces; songs; many arrangements of Breton folksongs. He contributed articles on music to various periodicals.

BIBLIOGRAPHY: Claude Debussy, "Paul-Emile Ladmirault," in *Gil Blas* (March 9, 1903); Octave Séré, *Musiciens français d'aujourd'hui* (Paris, 1922).

Ladunka, Naum, Russian composer; b. Dec. 13, 1730; d. St. Petersburg, Aug. 2, 1782. One of the few secular Russian composers of the 18th century, he is chiefly known for his arrangements of many Russian folksongs.

Ladurner, Ignaz Anton Franz Xaver, Austrian composer; b. Aldein, Tyrol, Aug. 1, 1766; d. Massy, Seine-et-Oise, March 4, 1839. He studied at the monastery of Benediktbeuren, succeeding his father as organist there (1782–84); studied in Munich under the patronage of Countess Heimhausen. In 1788 he settled in Paris, teaching at the Cons. there; Auber was one of his students. He wrote 2 operas, *Wenzel, ou Le Magistrat du peuple* (Paris, 1794) and *Les Vieux Fous* (Paris, 1796); 12 piano sonatas; 6 violin sonatas; a sonata for piano 4 hands; variations; divertissements; etc.

La Fage, Juste-Adrien-Lenoir de, eminent French writer on music; b. Paris, March 28, 1801; d. Charenton, March 8, 1862. He studied in Paris with Perne and Choron, and in Rome with Baini. Returning to Paris, he devoted himself to scholarly analysis of music theory. He ended his life at the Charenton Insane Asylum.

WRITINGS: *Manuel complet de musique vocale et instrumentale* (6 vols.; 1836–38; elaborated from Choron's sketches and notes); *Séméiologie musicale,* elements of music after Choron's principles (1837; an epitome was also publ. in 1837, as *Principes élémentaires de musique*); *De la chanson considérée sous le rapport musical* (1840); *Histoire générale de la musique et de la danse* (2 vols.; 1844; incomplete); *De l'unité tonique et de la fixation d'un diapason universel* (1859); *Essais de diphthérographie musicale* (1864; a valuable collection of source material); many works on plainsong: *De la réproduction des livres de plain-chant romain* (1853); *Cours complet de plain-chant* (2 vols.; 1855–56; an important manual); *Nouveau traité de plain-chant;* (1859; a supplement to the former); *Routine pour accompagner le plain-chant;* etc.

BIBLIOGRAPHY: R. D. Denne-Baron, *La Fage* (Paris, 1863).

L'Affilard, Michel, French 17th- and 18th-century composer. He was a singer at the Sainte-Chapelle in 1679, and at the royal chapel (1696–1709). His major work is a book on sight singing, *Principes très faciles, pour bien apprendre la musique* (Paris, 1691; Amsterdam, 1717), which is notable because the tempo of the airs is indicated according to a pendulum, thus anticipating the use of a metronome. Some of L'Affilard's manuscripts are in the Versailles Library.

BIBLIOGRAPHY: M. Brenet, *Les Musiciens de la Sainte-Chapelle du Palais* (Paris, 1910).

Lafont, Charles-Philippe, French violinist and composer; b. Paris, Dec. 1, 1781; d. Tarbes, Aug. 14, 1839. He received his first violin instruction from his mother; then studied in Paris with Kreutzer and Rode. From 1801–08 he toured Europe; then became Rode's successor at the Russian court in St. Petersburg (1808); returned to Paris in 1815 as solo violinist to

Louis XVIII. He engaged in a violin-playing debate with Paganini in Milan (1816). During an extended tour with the pianist Henri Herz, beginning in 1831, Lafont was killed in a carriage accident in southern France. He wrote 7 violin concertos; fantasias, variations, etc., for violin with various instrumental groups; about 200 *romances* for voice; and 2 comic operas.

La Forge, Frank, American pianist, vocal teacher, and composer; b. Rockford, Ill., Oct. 22, 1879; d. New York, May 5, 1953. He studied piano with Leschetizky in Vienna; toured Germany, France, Russia, and the U.S. as accompanist to Marcella Sembrich (1908–18), and to Schumann-Heink (1919). In 1920 he settled in New York as voice teacher; among his students were Lawrence Tibbett, Marian Anderson, Lucrezia Bori, and Richard Crooks. He died while playing the piano at a dinner given by the Musicians Club in N.Y. He wrote many effective songs (*To a violet, Retreat, Come unto these yellow sands, My love and I, To a messenger, I came with a song, Before the crucifix,* etc.) and piano pieces (*Gavotte and Musette, Valse de Concert, Improvisations,* etc.).

Lagoanère, Oscar de, French composer; b. Bordeaux, Aug. 25, 1853; d. Paris, May 23, 1918. He studied at the Paris Cons. with Marmontel, Duprato, and Savard. From 1876–1908 he conducted operettas at various theaters in Paris; from 1908–14, administrator and director of music at the Théâtre de la Gaité. He was a prolific composer of operettas, the most successful of which were *Le Cadeau d'Alain* (Paris, Sept. 14, 1902), *L'Habit de César* (Paris, May 14, 1906), *Amour et sport* (Paris, July 28, 1907), *Un Ménage au violon;* also piano pieces and songs.

La Guerre, Elisabeth Jacquet de, French composer, organist, and clavecinist; b. Paris, 1659; d. there, June 27, 1729. A member of a family of professional musicians, she evinced talent at an exceptionally early age; was favored by the court of Louis XIV, completing her education under the patronage of Mme. de Montespan. She married Marin de La Guerre, organist of several Paris churches. Her works include an opera, *Céphale et Procris* (Paris, March 15, 1694); a ballet (1691); keyboard suites; violin sonata; cantatas, mostly sacred; etc.

La Guerre, Michel, French organist and composer; b. Paris, c.1605; d. there, Nov. 13, 1679. He was organist at Sainte-Chapelle from 1633 until his death. His historical importance rests upon his being the author of the first French opera, a "comédie de chansons," *Le Triomphe de l'amour sur bergers et bergères* (Paris, Louvre, Jan. 22, 1655), to a libretto by Charles de Beys, court poet. At least, this is the claim made for La Guerre by H. Quittard, in his article "La Première comédie française en musique " (*Bulletin Français de la Société Internationale de Musique,* April and May, 1908). The claim is disputed by Romain Rolland and others.

Lahee, Henry, English pianist and composer; father of **Henry Charles Lahee;** b. Chelsea, April 11, 1826; d.

London, April 29, 1912. He studied with Sterndale Bennett, C. Potter (piano), and J. Goss (composition). He was organist at Holy Trinity Church, Brompton (1847–74); also a concert pianist; member of the Philharmonic Society. He wrote madrigals and glees: *Hark, how the birds* (1869), *Hence, loathed melancholy* (1878), *Away to the hunt* (1879), *Love in my Bosom* (1880), etc.

Lahee, Henry Charles, American writer on music; son of **Henry Lahee;** b. England, July 2, 1856; d. Hingham, Mass., April 11, 1953, as a result of injuries sustained in an automobile accident. He served in British mercantile marine (1871–79); in 1880, settled in Boston; was secretary of the New England Cons. (1891–99); then established a musical agency (1899); retired in 1951.

WRITINGS: (all publ. in Boston): *Famous Singers of Today and Yesterday* (1898; new ed., 1936); *Famous Violinists of Today and Yesterday* (1899; 2nd ed., 1912); *Famous Pianists of Today and Yesterday* (1901); *Grand Opera in America* (1902); *The Organ and Its Masters* (1903; new revised ed., 1927); *The Grand Opera Singers of Today* (1922); *Annals of Music in America* (1922; very valuable; contains a chronology of performances of major works); *The Orchestra: A Brief Outline of its Development in Europe and America* (1925).

La Hèle, George de, composer; b. Antwerp, 1547; d. Madrid, 1587. After early training as a chorister, he was sent to Madrid to join the royal chapel of Philip II in 1560, remaining in Spain for 10 years; in 1571, entered the Univ. of Louvain; 1572, choirmaster at the church of Saint-Rombaud in Malines, remaining there until 1574, when he accepted a similar post at the Tournai Cathedral; returned to Madrid in 1582 to take charge of music in the royal chapel. In 1576 he won prizes in the competition at Evreux for his motet *Nonne Deo subjecta* and his chanson *Mais voyez mon cher esmoy.* His 8 Masses (1577; printed by Plantin, Antwerp, 1578), dedicated to Philip II, are all parody Masses and are modeled on works by Josquin, Lassus, Rore, and Crecquillon; also wrote other sacred works.

BIBLIOGRAPHY: G. van Doorslaer, *George de la Hèle, maître de chapelle-compositeur* (Antwerp, 1924).

Lahire, Philippe de, French writer; b. Paris, 1640; d. there, April 21, 1719. He was prof. of mathematics at Paris Univ.; wrote *Explications des différences des sons de la corde tendue sur la trompette marine,* and *Expériences sur le son.*

Lahoussaye, Pierre, French violinist and composer; b. Paris, April 12, 1735; d. there, 1818. He studied with Pagin; later in Padua with Tartini. He played in the court orch. of Parma; in 1768 went to London with Guglielmi, becoming leader at the King's Theatre; returning to Paris, was appointed *chef d'orchestre* of the Concert Spirituel (1777–82); conductor of the Comédie-Italienne (1782–90); then conductor at the Théâtre de Monsieur (1790–1801); also taught at the Paris Cons. He wrote a comic opera, *Les Amours de Courcy*

(Paris, Aug. 22, 1790); of his compositions, 6 violin sonatas were published.

Laidlaw, Anna Robena, English pianist; b. Bretton, Yorkshire, April 30, 1819; d. London, May 29, 1901. She studied in Edinburgh with Robert Müller, in Königsberg, and in London with Henry Herz. In 1837 she played with the Gewandhaus Orch. in Leipzig; continued her successful career as concert pianist until her marriage in 1855. She was an acquaintance of Schumann, whose *Fantasiestücke* are inscribed to her.

Laistner, Max, German musician; b. Stuttgart, Feb. 16, 1853; d. London, July 3, 1917. He settled in London where he founded the first German Glee Club; wrote a number of choral works. His arrangement of Chopin's "Minute Waltz" is included in the anthology *13 Transcriptions of Chopin's Waltz in D-flat, Op. 64,* edited by D. M. Garvelmann (N.Y., 1969).

Lajarte, Théodore-Edouard Dufaure de, French writer on music and composer; b. Bordeaux, July 10, 1826; d. Paris, June 20, 1890. He studied at the Paris Cons. with Leborne; was archivist of the Grand Opéra (1873–90). He is best known for his writings on music: *Bibliothèque musicale du Théâtre l'Opéra* (2 vols., 1876–78; reprint, Geneva, 1969); *Instruments Sax et fanfares civiles* (1867); *Traité de composition musicale* (with Bisson; 1880); *Grammaire de la musique* (1880); *Petite Encyclopédie musicale* (1881–84); *Curiosités de l'Opéra* (1883); also publ. a collection of *Airs à danser de Lulli à Méhul;* and the series, *Chefs-d'œuvre classiques de l'opéra français.* Early in his career Lajarte wrote the operettas *Monsieur de Floridor* (Paris, Oct. 11, 1880), *Mamzelle Pénélope, Duel du Commandeur, Portrait, Roi de Carreau;* the ballet *Les Deux Jumeaux de Bergame* (Paris, Jan. 26, 1886); also marches and dances for military band.

Lajeunesse, Marie Louise Cecilia Emma. See Albani, Emma.

Lajtha, László, significant Hungarian composer; b. Budapest, June 30, 1892; d. there, Feb. 16, 1963. He studied piano with Arpád Szendy and theory with Victor von Herzfeld at the Budapest Academy of Music; traveled to Leipzig, Geneva and Paris; returned to Budapest in 1913 to become an associate of the Ethnographical Dept. of the Hungarian National Museum. From 1919 to 1949 he was a professor at the National Cons. and after 1952 was prof. of musical folklore at the Academy of Music in Budapest. In 1951 he was awarded the Kossuth Prize for his work on Hungarian folk music. He was a brilliant symphonist; his instrumental music is distinguished by consummate mastery of contrapuntal writing. WORKS: 3 ballets: *Lysistrata* (1933; Budapest, Feb. 25, 1937), *Le Bosquet des quatre dieux* (1943), and *Capriccio* (1944); 9 symphonies: No. 1 (1936); No. 2 (1938); *Les Soli,* symphony for string orch., harp and percussion (1941); No. 3 (1947–48); No. 4, *Le Printemps* (*The Spring*, 1951); No. 5 (1952; Paris, Oct. 23, 1954); No. 6 (1955; Brussels, Dec. 12, 1960); No. 7 (1957; Paris, April 26, 1958); No. 8 (1959; Budapest,

May 21, 1960); No. 9 (1961; posthumous, Paris, May 2, 1963); *Hortobágy Suite* for orch. (1935); 2 divertissements for orch. (1936, 1939); *3 Nocturnes* for chorus and orch. (1941); *In Memoriam* for orch. (1941); 2 sinfoniettas for string orch. (1946, 1956); *11 Variations* for orch. (1947); *Missa in tono phrygio* for chorus and orch. (1949–50); *Dramma per musica,* piano quintet (1922); 10 string quartets (1923; 1926; 1929; 1930; *Cinque Études,* 1934; *Quatre Études,* 1942; 1950; 1951; 1953; *Suite Transylvaine,* 1953); Piano Quartet (1925); 3 string trios (1927, 1932, 1945); Piano Trio (1928); Violin Sonatina (1930); Cello Sonata (1932); 2 trios for harp, flute and cello (1935, 1949); 2 quintets for flute, violin, viola, cello and harp (*Marionettes,* 1937; 1948); *Sonata en concert* for cello and piano (1940); *Sonata en concert* for flute and piano (1958); *Sonata en concert* for violin and piano (1962); *Des esquisses d'un musicien* for piano (1913); *Contes I* for piano (1913); Piano Sonata (1914); *Scherzo and Toccata* for piano (1930); Mass for chorus and organ (1951–52).

Lake, George Ernest, English organist and composer; b. London, May 29, 1854; d. there, March 15, 1893. He served as church organist in London and Edinburgh; wrote anthems and hymns; also a musical comedy, *Sweepstakes* (London, May 21, 1891).

Lakner, Yehoshua, Czech-born Israeli composer; b. Bratislava, April 24, 1924. He went to Palestine in 1941; studied there with Partos, Boscovich and Pelleg in Haifa, Jerusalem and Tel Aviv; in 1952 attended Copland's classes in composition at the Berkshire Music Center in Tanglewood; in 1959–60 went to West Germany where he worked with Stockhausen and Kagel in the electronic studio of the West German Radio and with Bernd-Aloys Zimmermann in Cologne. He then moved to Zürich, Switzerland, where he wrote music for the municipal theater; in 1974 joined the faculty of the Zürich Cons. His music follows the tenets of the modern Central European School of abstract expressionism and its concomitant atonality, with an application of serial techniques. WORKS: Flute Sonata (1948); Sextet for piano and woodwinds (1951); *Toccata* for orch. (1953); *Improvisations* for solo viola (1958); *Hexachords* for orch. (1960); *Kaninchen* for speaker, percussion and tape (1973); *Umläufe* for flute, bass clarinet, piano and 2 tapes (1976).

Laks, Simon, Polish composer; b. Warsaw, Nov. 1, 1901. He studied at the Warsaw Cons. with Melcer (conducting) and Statkowski (composition); went to Paris in 1925, continuing his musical studies under Rabaud and Vidal at the Paris Cons. In 1941 he was interned by the Nazis at the Auschwitz concentration camp, but survived and returned to Paris in May, 1945. WORKS: symph. poem *Farys* (1924); *Symphonic Blues,* jazz fantasy (1928); *Suite polonaise* (1936); Sinfonietta for strings (1936); *Suite on Silesian Tunes,* for small orch. (1945); *Songs of the Polish Earth,* for orch. (1946); *3 Warsaw Polonaises,* for chamber orch. (1947); 5 string quartets; Quintet for flute, oboe, clarinet, bassoon, and horn; Piano Trio, etc. He published his reminiscences, *La Musique d'unautre monde* (Paris, 1948).

Lalande, Michel-Richard de. See **Delalande.**

La Laurencie, Lionel de, important French musicologist; b. Nantes, July 24, 1861; d. Paris, Nov. 21, 1933. After studying law and science, he became a pupil of Léon Reynier (violin) and Alphonse Weingartner (harmony), and Bourgault-Ducoudray at the Paris Cons. In 1898 he became lecturer at the École des Hautes Études Sociales; contributed regularly to several musical journals.

WRITINGS: *La Légende de Parsifal et le drame musical de R. Wagner* (1888–94); *España* (1890); *Le Goût musical en France* (1905); *L'Académie de musique et le concert de Nantes* (1906); *Rameau,* in *Musiciens célèbres* (1908); *Lully,* in *Les Maîtres de la Musique* (1911); "Contribution à l'histoire de la symphonie française vers 1750," *L'Année Musicale* (with G. de Saint-Foix; 1911); *Les Créateurs de l'opéra français* (1920; 2nd ed., 1930); *L'École française de violon, de Lully à Viotti* (3 vols.; 1922–24); *Les Luthistes,* in *Musiciens célèbres* (1928); *La Chanson royale en France* (1928); *Inventaire critique du fonds Blancheton à la Bibliothèque du Conservatoire* (2 vols.; 1930–31); *Chansons au luth et airs du XVIe siècle* (with Thibault and Mairy; 1931); *Orfée de Gluck* (1934). In 1916 La Laurencie became editor of Lavignac's *Encyclopédie de la musique et dictionnaire du Conservatoire,* to which he contributed on French music of the 17th and 18th centuries. *Catalogue des livres de musiciens de la bibliothèque de l'Arsénal à Paris,* edited by La Laurencie and A. Gastoué, was publ. in 1936.

BIBLIOGRAPHY: *Mélanges de musicologie offerts à M. Lionel de la Laurencie* (Paris, 1933); B. Brook, "Lionel de la Laurencie's *L'École francaise de violon,*" *Notes* (Sept. 1969).

Lalewicz, Georg, Russian pianist; b. Suwalki, Poland, Aug. 21, 1875; d. Buenos Aires, Dec. 1, 1951. He studied piano with Annette Essipov and composition with Liadov and Rimsky-Korsakov at the St. Petersburg Cons. Upon graduation, he taught piano at the Odessa Cons. (1902–05), Cracow Cons. (1905–12), and the Vienna Imperial Academy (1912–19). In 1921 he went to Argentina, settling in Buenos Aires as prof. at the Conservatorio Nacional; changed his name to Jorge Lalewicz. An international prize for piano performance was established in his memory in 1952.

Laliberté, Alfred (full Christian name **Joseph François Alfred**), Canadian pianist and composer; b. St. Jean, Quebec, Feb. 10, 1882; d. Montreal, May 7, 1952. He studied in Berlin (1900–05) with Lutzenko (piano) and Klatte (theory); later took lessons with Teresa Carreño. In 1906 he formed a friendship with Scriabin and became an ardent propagandist of his music. Laliberté wrote an opera, *Sœur Béatrice* (after Maeterlinck), 2 string quartets, several piano pieces (some on Canadian themes); also made arrangements of some 800 Canadian songs. Most of his music remains in manuscript; a few original songs have been published.

Lalo, Charles, French writer on musical matters; b. Périgueux, Feb. 24, 1877; d. Paris, April 1, 1953. He studied philosophy in Bayonne and Paris.

WRITINGS: *L'Esthétique expérimentale contemporaine* (1908); *Esquisse d'une esthétique musicale scientifique* (1908; 2nd ed., 1939, as *Éléments d'une esthétique*); *Les Sentiments esthétiques* (1909); *Introduction à l'esthétique* (1912); *L'Art et la vie sociale* (1921).

Lalo, Édouard (Victor-Antoine-Édouard), distinguished French composer (of Spanish descent); b. Lille, Jan. 27, 1823; d. Paris, April 22, 1892. He studied with Baumann at the branch of the Paris Cons. in Lille; then at the Paris Cons. with Habeneck (violin) and Schulhoff and Crèvecœur (composition); played with equal skill on the violin and viola, and was violist of the Armingaud-Jacquard Quartet, a group organized in Paris for the purpose of spreading the works of the German masters. In 1848–49 he publ. his first songs (*L'Adieu au désert, L'Ombre de Dieu, Le Novice, 6 Romances populaires de Béranger*) and subsequently some chamber music. All of this music met with indifference and Lalo was discouraged to the point of abandoning composition for several years; his ambition, however, was stimulated again by his marriage (in 1865) to **Mlle. Bernier de Maligny,** a fine contralto singer who performed many of his songs. He wrote a 3-act opera, *Fiesque,* and sent the score to the competition established in 1867 by the Théâtre-Lyrique; it was ranked 3rd, and failed to reach production; the ballet music from it was performed under the title *Divertissement* at the Concert Populaire (Dec. 8, 1872) with excellent success. His next signal success was the performance of his Violin Concerto, played by Sarasate (Jan. 18, 1874) at a Châtelet concert; then came his most famous work, *Symphonie espagnole,* also performed by Sarasate (Feb. 7, 1875). This work, a true virtuoso piece with vibrant Spanish rhythms, became one of the greatest favorites in the violin repertory, and secured for Lalo international fame. His *Fantaisie norvégienne* for violin and orch. followed; it was subsequently re-arranged for orch. alone, and performed as *Rapsodie norvégienne* (Colonne Concerts, Oct. 26, 1879). He had not abandoned, however, his efforts at writing for the stage. As early as 1875 he began work on the opera *Le Roi d'Ys;* after several revisions, the work was produced at the Opéra-Comique (May 7, 1888), obtaining enormous success; repeated performances followed, in France and elsewhere in Europe; the American première took place at New Orleans, Jan. 23, 1890. In 1888 he was made officer of the Legion of Honor; also was awarded the Prix Monbinne by the Académie des Beaux-Arts. Besides the works already mentioned, there were the following: 1 act from an unfinished opera, *La Jacquerie* (completed by Artur Coquard; posthumously produced in Monte Carlo, March 9, 1895); the ballets *Namouna* (Paris, March 6, 1882) and *Néron* (Paris, March 28, 1891); 3 symphonies, 2 of them unpublished; Cello Concerto (Paris, Dec. 9, 1877); Piano Concerto (1889); 3 piano trios; String Quartet; Violin Sonata; 4 impromptus for violin and piano; *Soirées parisiennes,* for violin and piano; *Guitare,* for violin and piano; Cello Sonata; songs.

BIBLIOGRAPHY: M. Dufour, *Édouard Lalo* (Lille, 1908); centennial issue of the *Revue Musicale,* with articles by Paul Dukas, Adolphe Jullien, and Pierre Lalo (May, 1923); J. Tiersot, "Édouard Lalo," *Musical Quarterly* (Jan. 1925); G. Servières, *Lalo* (Paris, 1925).

Lalo, Pierre, French critic; son of **Édouard Lalo;** b. Puteaux, Seine, Sept. 6, 1866; d. Paris, June 9, 1943. He became music critic of *Le Temps* in Oct. 1898; publ. *La Musique,* a selection of his articles (Paris, 1898–99); *De Rameau à Ravel: portraits et souvenirs* (Paris, 1947; posthumous).

Laloy, Louis, French musicologist and critic; b. Grey, Haute-Saône, Feb. 18, 1874; d. Dôle, March 3, 1944. He studied philosophy in Paris, receiving the degree of Dr. ès Lettres in 1904; from 1899–1905, was also a pupil of Bréville and d'Indy at the Schola Cantorum. He was co-founder (1901) of the *Revue d'Histoire et de Critique Musicale;* in 1905 he founded, with J. Marnold, the *Mercure Musical;* contributed articles to *Revue de Paris, Grande Revue, Mercure de France,* and *Gazette des Beaux-Arts.* He publ. *Aristoxène de Tarente et la musique de l'antiquité* (1904); *Rameau* (1908); *Debussy* (1909; new ed., 1944); *Notes sur la musique cambodgienne* (in the *Bericht über den zweiten Kongress* of the Internationale Musik-Gesellschaft at Basel, 1906; publ. Leipzig, 1907); *La Musique chinoise* (1910); *The Future of Music* (London, 1910); "L'Opéra," in *Cinquante ans de musique française, 1874–1923* (1924); *La Musique retrouvée, 1902–27* (1928); *Une Heure de musique avec Beethoven* (1930). He also provided the poem for Roussel's opera-ballet *Padmâvati* and for Debussy's *Ode à la France;* publ. a volume of transcriptions of Chinese compositions; and supplied the French versions of a number of Russian opera librettos.

La Mara. See **Lipsius, Marie.**

LaMarchina, Robert, American cellist and conductor; b. New York, Sept. 3, 1928. He studied cello with his father; appeared as a *wunderkind* in public; continued his studies with Gregor Piatigorsky and Emanuel Feuermann; in 1944 played in the NBC Symphony under Toscanini; later joined the Los Angeles Philharmonic; sporadically conducted orchestras near and around Los Angeles; ultimately became primarily a conductor. In 1967 he was engaged as conductor of the Honolulu Symphony Orchestra.

La Marre (Lamare), Jacques-Michel-Hurel de, French cellist; b. Paris, May 1, 1772; d. Caen, March 27, 1823. He toured Europe, including Russia, with great success; Clementi called him "the Rode of the violoncello." Four cello concertos and an *air varié* publ. under La Marre's name are actually by Auber.

Lambardi, Camillo, Italian tenor and composer; b. Naples, c.1560; d. there, 1634. He sang at the Santa Casa dell'Annunziata at Naples; studied there with Gian Domenico da Nola, whom he succeeded as a maestro di cappella in 1592. He publ. music for Holy Week for 2 choirs (1592), 2 books of madrigals, etc.

Lambardi (Lombarodo), Francesco, Italian tenor, organist, and composer; son of **Camillo Lambardi;** b. Naples, 1587; d. there, July 25, 1642. As a youth he was a "sopranello" in the Santa Casa dell'Annunziata at Naples; later tenor there; then organist of the royal chapel; first organist there (1615–36). He publ. 3 sets of *villanelle* for 3–5 voices (Naples, 1607; 1614; 1616).

Lambelet, George, Greek composer and musicologist; b. Corfu, Dec. 24, 1875; d. Athens, Oct. 30, 1945. Both his father and older brother were musicians. He studied in Naples; returned to Greece in 1901; co-edited *Critique* with Axiotis, and *Musical Chronicles* with J. Papadopoulos; publ. a number of studies on Greek folk music, including *Nationalism in Art and Greek Folk Music* (Athens, 1928). He is noted for *La Musique populaire grecque* (Athens, 1934), a collection of 60 Greek folksongs and dances, together with harmonizations and a critical study. Lambelet's musical compositions have a strong national flavor. He wrote choral works: *The Hymn to Peace; Balkan Hymn; Hymn to Greece;* etc.; *The Feast,* symph. poem; *Elegy,* for orch.; *Dirge,* for orch.; songs.

Lambert, Alexander, Polish-American pianist, composer, and teacher; b. Warsaw, Nov. 1, 1862; d. New York, Dec. 31, 1929. He studied piano with his father and with Julius Epstein at the Vienna Cons.; also worked with Liszt at Weimar for a brief period. He went to New York in 1880; director of the N.Y. College of Music (1887–1905); taught piano privately. He publ. a number of effective piano pieces (*Etude and Bourrée, Tarantella, Mazurka, Valse-Impromptu, Canzonetta,* etc.), and a valuable piano method, *A Systematic Course of Studies* (3 vols., 1907); also a brief *Piano Method for Beginners.*

Lambert, Constant, English composer, conductor, and writer on music; b. London, Aug. 23, 1905; d. there, Aug. 21, 1951. He was a member of an artistic family; studied at the Royal College of Music with R. O. Morris and Vaughan Williams. While he was still a student, Diaghilev commissioned a ballet from him (*Romeo and Juliet;* Monte Carlo, May 4, 1926). This early association with the dance proved decisive, for Lambert spent most of his life as a composer and conductor of ballets. His compositions are notable for the assimilation of a jazz idiom, in his *Elegiac Blues* (1927), in his very successful *Rio Grande* (on a poem of Sacheverell Sitwell), for solo piano, chorus, and orch. (Manchester, Dec. 12, 1929), and in his Piano Sonata (1928–29) and Piano Concerto with small orch. (1931). He wrote the ballets *Pomona* (Buenos Aires, Sept. 9, 1927) and *Horoscope* (London, Jan. 27, 1938); *The Bird Actors,* overture for orch. (1925); *Summer's Last Will and Testament,* masque for chorus and orch. (after Thomas Nashe; London, Jan. 29, 1936); *King Pest,* for orch. (London, 1937); *Aubade héroïque,* for orch. (1942); *Prizefight,* for band (1923); *8 Chinese Songs* (on poems by Li-Po); transcribed and edited works by Boyce, Handel, Roseingrave, etc.; rescored Vaughan Williams's *Job* for theater orch. (1931). Lambert was music critic of the *Sunday Referee,* and published a provocative book, *Music Ho!: A Study of Music in Decline* (London, 1934).

BIBLIOGRAPHY: R. J. McGrady, "The Music of Constant Lambert," *Music & Letters* (July 1970); C. Palmer, "Constant Lambert—A Postscript," *Music & Letters* (April 1971).

Lambert, Herbert, English clavichord and harpsichord maker; b. Bath, Dec. 22, 1881; d. there, March 7, 1936. Originally a professional photographer, he turned his craftsmanship and research activity to the building of old keyboard instruments, especially clavichords. His name is perpetuated in *Lambert's Clavichord* (1928), a small book of compositions for this instrument by Herbert Howells.

Lambert, Johann Heinrich, German music theorist; b. Mühlhausen, Aug. 29, 1728; d. Berlin, Sept. 25, 1777. A member of the Berlin Academy, he wrote *Sur quelques instruments acoustiques* (1763; German ed., 1796); *Sur la vitesse du son* (1768); *Remarques sur le tempérament en musique* (1774; German transl. in Marpurg's *Historisch-kritische Beiträge*, vol. 5); and *Observations sur les sons des flûtes* (1775); all of the above are printed in the reports of the Berlin Academy.

Lambert, Juan Bautista, Catalan composer; b. Barcelona, 1884; d. there, May 4, 1945. He studied with Morera; was active in Barcelona as organist and conductor. He composed a successful light opera, *La Alborada;* a symph. poem, *Vallencis;* also wrote numerous choral works, marches, and songs.

Lambert, Lucien, French composer and pianist; b. Paris, Jan. 5, 1858; d. Oporto, Portugal, Jan. 21, 1945. He studied first with his father; after a tour of America and Europe, returned to Paris to study at the Cons. there with Dubois and Massenet, taking the Prix Rossini in 1885 with his cantata *Prométhée enchaîné.* He settled in Portugal in 1914; was prof. of composition at the Oporto Cons. (1922–37).
WORKS: the operas *Brocéliande* (Rouen, Feb. 25, 1893), *Le Spahi* (Paris, Oct. 18, 1897), *La Marseillaise* (Paris, July 14, 1900), *La Flamenca* (Paris, Oct. 31, 1903); *Harald* (1937), *Penticosa,* and *La Sorcière;* the ballets *La Roussalka* (Paris, Dec. 8, 1911) and *Les Cloches de Porto* (1937); *Florette,* lyric comedy (1921); *Légende roumaine,* symph. poem; *Fantaisie monothématique,* for orch., on an oriental theme (Paris, March 19, 1933); *Tanger le soir,* Moorish rhapsody for orch.; *Esquisses créoles,* orchestral suite, on themes by Gottschalk; *Andante et fantaisie tzigane,* for piano and orch.; String Quartet; String Sextet; Mass; piano pieces; songs.

Lambert, Michel, French lutenist and singer; b. Champigny-sur-Veude, near Chinon (Indre-et-Loire), 1610; d. Paris, June 29, 1696. He was master of chamber music in the court of Louis XIV; also a celebrated singing teacher. His daughter married Lully. He publ. *Airs et brunettes* (1666; 2nd ed., 1689) and *Airs et dialogues* (1698; posthumous).

Lambeth, Henry Albert, British organist, conductor, and composer; b. Hardway, near Gosport, Jan. 16, 1822; d. Glasgow, June 27, 1895. He studied with Thomas Adams; went to Glasgow about 1853 as city organist; was conductor of the Glasgow Choral Union (1859–80); harmonized Scottish melodies; wrote several songs and piano pieces; with D. Baptie, edited the *Scottish Book of Praise* (1876).

Lambillotte, Louis, French writer and church composer; b. Charleroi, Hainault, March 27, 1796; d. Vaugirard, Feb. 27, 1855. He was organist at Charleroi, then at Dinant; in 1822, became *maître de chapelle* at the Jesuit Seminary at St.-Acheul, joining the order in 1825; subsequently settled in Vaugirard.
WORKS: 4 Masses, one in the Lydian mode; other sacred music; organ pieces; fugues, etc.; he publ. an *Antiphonaire de Saint-Grégoire, facsimile du manuscrit de Saint-Gall* (1851); *Clef des Mélodies grégoriennes* (1851); *Quelques mots sur la restauration du chant liturgique* (1855); *Esthétique, Théorie et Pratique du chant grégorien* (1855); other essays.
BIBLIOGRAPHY: J. Dufour, *Mémoire sur les chants liturgiques restaurés par Lambillotte* (Paris, 1857); T. Nisard, *Le Père Lambillotte et Dom A. Schubiger* (Paris, 1857); M. de Monter, *Lambillotte et ses frères* (Paris, 1871).

Lambord, Benjamin, American organist and composer; b. Portland, Maine, June 10, 1879; d. Lake Hopatcong, N.J., June 6, 1915. He studied in Boston with A. Whiting, at Columbia Univ. with MacDowell, and in Paris with Vidal. He was organist and choirmaster in various churches in New York; organized the Lambord Choral Society and the Modern Music Society. He wrote *Introduction and Variations on an English Dance Theme,* for orch.; *Clytie,* for soprano and orch.; *Verses from Omar Khayyam,* for mixed chorus and orch.; *Ten Lyric Studies for Piano;* piano pieces; partsongs; songs.

Lamm, Pavel, Russian musicologist; b. Moscow, July 27, 1882; d. Nicolina Gora, near Moscow, May 5, 1951. He studied piano at the Moscow Cons.; toured Europe as accompanist of the singer Olenine d'Alheim; then was on the editorial board of the Russian State Publishing Dept. He edited the vocal score of Mussorgsky's original version of *Boris Godunov* (Moscow, 1928); was editor-in-chief for Mussorgsky's complete works in the aborted edition begun in 1928.

Lammers, Julius, German composer; b. Leipzig, April 20, 1829; d. there, Sept. 20, 1888. He taught at the Leipzig Cons.; composed numerous songs and some piano pieces.

Lamond, Frederic Archibald, Scottish pianist; b. Glasgow, Jan. 28, 1868; d. Stirling, Feb. 21, 1948. He played organ as a boy in a local church; also studied oboe and violin; in 1882, entered the Raff Cons. in Frankfurt, studying with Heermann (violin), Max Schwarz (piano), and Urspruch (composition); then piano with Hans von Bülow, Clara Schumann, and Liszt. A brilliant concert pianist, Lamond appeared in Berlin, Vienna, London, Russia, and New York. He became renowned for his skillful interpretation of Beethoven; publ. an edition of Beethoven's sonatas (1923). He married Irene Triesch, a German actress, in

1904 and settled in Berlin, until the outbreak of World War II, when he moved to London. He was also a composer; wrote a symphony (Glasgow, Dec. 23, 1889), some chamber music, and numerous piano pieces. He published an interesting volume of reminiscences about Liszt and others, *Memoirs* (Glasgow, 1949).

La Montaine, John, American composer; b. Oak Park, Illinois, March 17, 1920. He studied piano with Rudolph Ganz in Chicago and in Rochester, at the Eastman School of Music, with Howard Hanson and Bernard Rogers; at the Juilliard School, New York, with Bernard Wagenaar, and with Nadia Boulanger. He received 2 Guggenheim Fellowships in composition (1959 and 1960); in 1962 served as Composer in Residence at the American Academy in Rome; was visiting prof. at the Eastman School of Music in 1964–65. He received the Pulitzer Prize for his Piano Concerto in 1959. In 1977 he became holder of the Nixon Chair as a Nixon distinguished Scholar at Nixon's alma mater, Whittier College, California.
    WORKS: Piano Concerto (Washington, Nov. 25, 1958); *Jubilant Overture; Colloquy* for string orch.; Symph. No. 1; *From Sea to Shining Sea* for orch.; *Novellis, Novellis,* a Christmas pageant opera (Washington Cathedral, Dec. 24, 1961); *The Shepherdes Playe,* opera television production (Washington, Dec. 24, 1967); *Erode the Great,* cantata (Washington, Dec. 30, 1969); *Be Glad, Then, America,* a Bicentennial opera (University Park, Pennsylvania, Feb. 6, 1976); *Birds of Paradise* for piano and orch.; *Te Deum; Songs of the Rose of Sharon* for soprano and orch.; Cello Sonata; String Quartet; organ pieces; songs.

Lamote de Grignon, Juan, Catalan conductor and composer; b. Barcelona, July 7, 1872; d. there, March 11, 1949. He studied at the Cons. of Barcelona, and upon graduation, taught piano there; made his debut as conductor in Barcelona (April 26, 1902). In 1910 he founded the Orquesta Sinfónica of Barcelona, which carried on its activity until 1924; also led the municipal band (from 1914).
    WORKS: a 1-act opera, *Hesperia* (Barcelona, Jan. 25, 1907); works for orch. (*Andalucía, Hispanicas, Scherzo, Cantos populares españoles, Poema romántico*); the oratorio *La Nit de Nadal;* numerous songs (*12 Chansons catalanes, Violetas, Tres motetes, Tres cantos espirituales, Passioneras,* etc.). He publ. *Musique et musiciens français à Barcelona, catalans à Paris* (Barcelona, 1935).

Lamote de Grignon, Ricard, Catalan cellist, conductor, and composer; son of **Juan Lamote de Grignon;** b. Barcelona, Sept. 23, 1899; d. there, Feb. 5, 1962. Studied cello and composition at the Barcelona Cons.; played cello in the Orquesta Sinfónica, conducted by his father; then conducted provincial orchestras; became assistant conductor of the municipal band of Barcelona.
    WORKS: an opera, *La Caperucita verde,* and a children's opera, *La Flor;* a symph. poem, *Boires; Tríptico de Rabindranath Tagore,* for soprano and orch.; Piano Trio; songs. On April 19, 1936, he conducted, at the Barcelona Festival of the International Society for

Contemporary Music, his symph. legend *Joan de Os;* his *Enigmas* for orch. received the municipal prize of Barcelona in 1951. He publ. a manual, *Síntesis de técnica musical* (Barcelona, 1948).

Lamothe, Georges, French composer; b. 1837; d. Courbevoie, Oct. 15, 1894. He was a very prolific composer of dance music; wrote more than 1,000 opus numbers.

Lamoureux, Charles, noted French conductor and violinist; b. Bordeaux, Sept. 28, 1834; d. Paris, Dec. 21, 1899. He studied at the Paris Cons. with Girard (violin), taking 1st prize in 1854; also studied with Tolbecque (harmony), Leborne (counterpoint), and Alexis Chauvet (theory). In 1850 he became solo violinist in the Théâtre du Gymnase orch.; then became a member of the Paris Opéra orch. In 1860 he and Colonne, Adam, and A. Pilet founded a society for chamber music; in 1873, organized the Société de l'Harmonie Sacrée; became known as conductor of the Conservatoire Concerts (1872–77); conductor of the Paris Opéra (1877–79). He founded the celebrated Concerts Lamoureux (Nouveaux Concerts) on Oct. 23, 1881. More than any other French musician, Lamoureux educated Parisians to appreciate Wagner; he was responsible not only for highly competent performances of classical masterpieces, but also for presentation of compositions of his contemporaries.
    BIBLIOGRAPHY: Romain Rolland, *Musiciens d'aujourd'hui* (Paris, 1914; p. 234 ff.).

Lampe, Walther, German pianist, composer and pedagogue; b. Leipzig, April 28, 1872; d. Munich, Jan. 23, 1964. He studied piano with Clara Schumann; composition with Knorr in Frankfurt and with Humperdinck in Berlin; was prof. of piano at the Munich Academy of Music from 1920 to 1937. His edition of Mozart piano sonatas (2 vols., Munich, 1954), according to the original manuscripts, is valuable. Among his works are piano pieces and songs.

Lamperti, Francesco, Italian singing teacher; b. Savona, March 11, 1811; d. Cernobbio, May 1, 1892. He studied at the Milan Cons.; director at the Teatro Filodrammatico in Lodi; tutored many distinguished singers, including Albani, Mme. Artôt, both Cruvelis, Campanini, Collini, and Mme. Lagrange; taught at the Milan Cons. (1850–75). He publ. *Guida teorico-pratico-elementare per lo studio del canto; Studî di bravura per soprano; Esercizi giornalieri per soprano o mezzo-soprano; L'Arte del canto; Osservazioni e consigli sul trillo; Solfeggî;* etc. His methods and studies in voice production have also appeared in English transl.: *Studies in bravura singing for the soprano voice* (N.Y., 1875); *A Treatise on the Art of Singing* (London, 1877; revised ed., N.Y., 1890).

Lamperti, Giovanni Battista, Italian singing teacher; son of **Francesco Lamperti;** b. Milan, June 24, 1839; d. Berlin, March 18, 1910. At the age of 9 he was a choirboy at the Milan Cathedral; studied piano and voice at the Milan Cons.; served as accompanist in his father's class there. He taught first in Milan; in Dresden for 20 years; then in Berlin. Among his pupils were Sembrich, Schumann-Heink, Bulss, Stagno, etc. He publ. *Die Technik des Bel Canto* (1905; English transl. by Th. Baker; N.Y., 1905); *Scuola di Canto* (8 vols. of solfeggi and vocalises); other technical exercises. His pupil W. E. Brown publ. *Vocal Wisdom; Maxims of G. B. Lamperti* (N.Y., 1931; new ed., 1957).

Lampugnani, Giovanni Battista, Italian teacher and composer; b. Milan, 1706; d. after 1784. In 1743 he became conductor of the Italian Opera in London; later, *maestro al cembalo* at La Scala, Milan. Over the period of 1732–69, he wrote 32 operas in the style of Hasse, presented in London, Venice, and Milan; publ. some trio sonatas; also wrote symphonies and concertos.

Lancen, Serge Jean Mathieu, French composer and pianist; b. Paris, Nov. 5, 1922. He studied at the Paris Cons. with Aubin, Büsser and Noël Gallon. During World War II he went to Switzerland; returning to Paris he continued his studies; obtained Premier Prix de Rome for composition in 1949.
WORKS: *La mauvaise conscience,* chamber opera (Paris, Jan. 4, 1964); *Les Prix,* ballet (Bordeaux, March 13, 1954); Piano Concerto (1947); Concerto for Mouth Harmonica, written for Larry Adler (1955); Concerto for Double Bass and Orch. (1960); *Manhattan Symphony* (1962); *Concert à six* for 6 clarinets (1962); light pieces for radio: *Cadence, Promenade, Bahamas, Brazilia, En route for Monte-Carlo, Suite Gastronomique, Futilités;* also *Marche triomphale* commissioned by the convention of the League against Rheumatism (Amsterdam, June 15, 1955).

Land, Jan Pieter Nicholaas, Dutch orientalist and musicologist; b. Delft, April 23, 1834; d. Arnhem, April 30, 1897. In 1864 he was prof. of classical and oriental languages and of philosophy at the Amsterdam Academy; then was prof. of philosophy at Leyden Univ. (1872–94). He was an accomplished linguist, specializing in Semitic philology; was deeply interested in musico-historical research, to which he made most valuable contributions.
WRITINGS: *Noord Nederlands muziekgeschiedenis* (1874–81); *Over de toonladders der arabische muziek* (1880); *Musique et musiciens au XVIIᵉ siècle. Correspondance et œuvres musicales de Constantijn Huygens* (with Jonckbloet; Leyden, 1882); *Recherches sur l'histoire de la gamme arabe* (Leyden, 1884); *Essai de notation musicale chez les arabes et les persans* (1885); *Over onze kennis der javaansche muziek* (Amsterdam, 1891).

Landau, Siegfried, German-American conductor and composer; b. Berlin, Sept. 4, 1921. He studied at the Stern Cons. in Berlin and also at the Klindworth-Scharwenka Cons. He went to England early in 1939, where he continued his studies at Trinity College; in November 1940 he arrived in the U.S., where he studied conducting with Pierre Monteux. In 1955 he organized the Brooklyn Philharmonia, which he conducted until 1971; concurrently conducted performances of the Chattanooga Opera Co. (1960–73).
WORKS: *Chassidic Suite* for viola and piano (1941); *Longing for Jerusalem,* for soprano and orchestra (1941); ballet, *The Golem* (1946); *The Sons of Aaron,* opera (Scarsdale, N.Y., Feb. 28, 1959); etc.

Landi, Stefano, Italian singer and composer; b. Rome, c.1590; d. there, Oct. 28, 1639. He was maestro di cappella to Bishop Cornaro of Padua; returned to Rome in 1620, and was appointed to a similar post at Santa Maria dei Monti (1624); in 1629, became contralto singer at the Cappella Giulia, St. Peter's. He was one of the most eminent contrapuntists of the Roman school; pupil of the 2 Naninis; one of the creators of the cantata, and one of the earliest operatic composers in Rome.
WORKS: *La morte d'Orfeo,* pastoral opera (Venice, 1619); *Il Sant' Alessio,* sacred opera (Rome, Feb. 23, 1632); also a *Missa in benedictione nuptiarum,* for 6 voices (1628); a book of Masses a cappella for 4–5 voices; madrigals for 4–5 voices (1619 and 1624); arias for 1–2 voices (5 vols., 1620–38); etc.

Landini, Benedetto, Italian organist and composer; b. Calenzano, Jan. 31, 1858; d. Florence, July 11, 1938. He studied at the Florence Cons., graduating in 1886; became a teacher of organ there in 1888; also for many years, organist of the Church of Santissima Annunziata in Florence, and choirmaster at San Lorenzo and Santa Trinità; from 1891, active in church music reforms in Tuscany. He wrote a Mass, a Requiem, *De Profundis, Hymnus,* psalms and other sacred works; also a children's opera, *L'Arancia di Codino* (1913); edited works of Frescobaldi, Marco da Gagliano, and Corteccia, and numerous old Tuscan folksongs.

Landini (Landino), Francesco, Italian instrumentalist and composer; b. Fiesole, 1325; d. Florence, Sept. 2, 1397. Blinded as a youth, he turned early to music, becoming proficient in the art of playing the lute, guitar, flute, and organ. He was one of the most celebrated organ virtuosos of his time; was known as "Francesco degli organi." He studied with Giovanni da Cascia and Jacopo da Bologna; for many years (1369–96) was organist at the Church of Lorenzo in Florence. Although not the first, he was probably the most famous master of the Florentine "Ars nova" of the 14th century; his works, of which more than 150 are preserved in the libraries of Europe, represent over a third of extant Italian 14th-century music; he wrote madrigals, *cacce, ballate,* etc. Modern reprints: *The Works of Francesco Landini,* ed. by L. Ellinwood (Medieval Academy of America Publication 36; Cambridge, Mass., 1939); *The Works of Francesco Landini,* ed. by L. Schrade (Polyphonic Music of the 14th Century, vol. 4; Monaco, 1958).
BIBLIOGRAPHY: F. Villani, *Liber de civitatis Florentiae famosis civibus* (written c.1400); edited by C. Galletti; 1874); F. Ludwig, "Die mehrstimmige Musik des 14. Jahrhunderts," *Sammelbände der Internationalen Musik-Gesellschaft* (1902); J. Wolf, *Geschichte der Mensuralnotation* (3 vols., 1904); J. Wolf, *Florenz in der Musikgeschichte des 14. Jahrhunderts, Sammelbände der Internationalen Musik-Gesellschaft* 3; F. Ludwig in Adler's *Handbuch* (vol. 1); F. Ludwig in *Zeitschrift für Musikwissenschaft* 5; G. Carducci in *Opere* 8; H. Riemann in *Handbuch der Musikgeschichte* (vol. 2); H. Riemann, "Das Kunstlied im 14.–15.

Jahrhundert," *Sammelbände der Internationalen Musik-Gesellschaft* 7; A. Schering, "Das Kolorierte Orgelmadrigal des Trecento," *Sammelbände der Internationalen Musik-Gesellschaft* 13; A. Schering, *Studien zur Musikgeschichte der Frührenaissance* (1914); M. Schneider, *Die Ars nova des 14. Jahrhunderts in Frankreich und Italien* (Wolfenbüttel, 1930); H. Besseler, *Die Musik des Mittelalters und der Renaissance* (1931); E. Li Gotti and N. Pirrotta, *Il Sacchetti e la tecnica del trecento italiano* (Florence, 1935); L. Ellinwood, "Francesco Landini and His Music," *Musical Quarterly* (April 1936); Hélène Noltenius, *Renaissance in Mei; Florentijns leven rond Francesco Landino* (Utrecht, 1956); C. Schachter, "Landini's Treatment of Consonance and Dissonance," *Music Forum* 2 (1970).

Landon, H. C. Robbins, eminent American musicologist; b. Boston, March 6, 1926. He studied music history with Alfred J. Swan at Swarthmore College and composition with Harl McDonald there; then musicology with Karl Geiringer at Boston Univ. (B. Mus., 1947). In 1948 he went to Vienna, where he was active in the field of Haydn research. In 1960 went to live in Italy. In his major work, *The Symphonies of Joseph Haydn* (London, 1955; Supplement 1961), he analyzes and discusses every symphony, suggests solutions for numerous problems of authenticity, origin, and chronology, and presents a new perspective of Haydn as a musician of his time; complementing this monumental achievement, he issued, between 1963–68, new editions of all of the Haydn symphonies. In 1957 he discovered the Hadyn Mass in G (No. 13), regarded as lost; and also the MS of the score of the so-called *Jena Symphony*, which he established as being by Friedrich Witt, not by Beethoven. Further publications are: *The Collected Correspondence and London Notebooks of J. Haydn* (London, 1959); *Beethoven, A Documentary Study* (London & N.Y., 1970); edited (with Donald Mitchell) *The Mozart Companion* (London, 1956; revised ed., 1965); *Haydn: Chronicle and Works,* announced in 5 vols.; Vol. III, *Haydn in England,* publ. 1976; Vol IV, *Haydn: The Years of "The Creation"* 1796-1800, publ. 1977.

Landormy, Paul (Charles-René), French musicologist and critic; b. Issy, Jan. 3, 1869; d. Paris, Nov. 17, 1943. For a number of years he taught philosophy in the provinces; going to Paris in 1892, he studied singing with Sbriglia and Pol Plançon. With Romain Rolland he organized a series of lectures on music history at the École des Hautes Études Sociales; established an acoustic laboratory there; music critic of *La Victoire* (1918); also contributed articles to *Le Temps* and various other journals. He publ. *Histoire de la musique* (Paris, 1910; augmented ed., 1923; English transl., N.Y., 1923); *Brahms* (1920) and *Bizet* (1924), in the series Les Maîtres de la musique; *La Vie de Schubert* (Paris, 1928); *Gluck* (Paris, 1941); *Gounod* (Paris, 1942); *La Musique française de Franck à Debussy* (Paris, 1943).

Landowska, Wanda, celebrated harpsichordist and authority on old music; b. Warsaw, July 5, 1877; d. Lakeville, Conn., Aug. 16, 1959. She studied piano at the Warsaw Cons. with Michalowski and in Berlin with Moszkowski. In 1900 she went to Paris, where she married Henry Lew, a writer. She traveled widely in Europe as pianist; in 1909 made a tour of Russia, and played for Tolstoy, who showed great interest in her ideas on classical music. Subsequently, she devoted her efforts principally to reviving the art of playing upon the harpsichord. In 1912 she commissioned the Pleyel firm of Paris to construct a harpsichord for her; this was the first of the many keyboard instruments built for her in subsequent years. In 1913 she was invited by Kretzschmar to give a special course in harpsichord playing at the Berlin Hochschule für Musik. The outbreak of World War I found her in Germany, and she was interned there until the Armistice; in 1918 her husband was killed in an automobile accident in Berlin. In 1919 she gave master classes of harpsichord playing at the Basel Cons.; then returned to Paris. In 1925 she bought a villa in St.-Leu-la-Forêt, near Paris, and established there a school for the study of early music. A concert hall was built there in 1927; she presented regular concerts of early music, and gave lessons on the subject; also assembled a large collection of harpsichords. Her school attracted students from all over the world; she also taught at the Cons. of Fontainebleau, and frequently appeared at concerts in Paris, both as pianist and harpsichordist. She commissioned Manuel de Falla to compose a chamber concerto for harpsichord, and played the solo part in its first performance in Barcelona (Nov. 5, 1926); another commission was Poulenc's *Concert champêtre* for harpsichord and small orch. (Paris, May 3, 1929). She appeared for the first time in America on Nov. 20, 1923, as soloist with the Philadelphia Orch., under Stokowski; then returned to France. When the Germans invaded France in 1940, Landowska fled to Switzerland, abandoning her villa, her library, and her instruments. In 1941 she reached New York; presented a concert of harpsichord music in N.Y. on Feb. 21, 1942; then devoted herself mainly to teaching; also made recordings; settled in her new home at Lakeville, Conn. She is acknowledged as one of the greatest performers on the modern harpsichord; her interpretations of Baroque music are notable in their balance between classical precision and freedom from rigidity, particularly in the treatment of ornamentation. She wrote *Bach et ses interprètes* (Paris, 1906); *Musique ancienne* (Paris, 1909; 7th ed., 1921; English transl. N.Y., 1924); many articles in various French and German magazines (on Bach, Chopin, harpsichord playing, etc.). A collection of her articles was publ. posthumously under the title *Landowska on Music,* edited and translated by Denise Restout and Robert Hawkins (N.Y., 1964). She also wrote cadenzas for Mozart's concertos, etc.

BIBLIOGRAPHY: A. Schaeffner, "Wanda Landowska et le retour aux 'humanités' de la musique," *Revue Musicale* (June 1927); R. Gellat, *Music Makers* (N.Y., 1953; pp. 254–86); B. Gavoty, *Wanda Landowska* (Geneva, 1957).

Landowski, Mme. W.-L. (Alice-Wanda), French writer on music; b. Paris, Nov. 28, 1899; d. there, April 18, 1959. She studied piano in Paris at the Marguerite Long School; theory with Gustave Bret. She taught music history at the Cons. of Clermont; in 1945, became prof. at the Rouen Cons., a branch of the Paris Cons.; also was engaged as music critic of *Le Parisien.* She adopted the initials W.-L. (L. for Ladislas, her father's name) to avoid confusion with Wanda Landowska, no relation.

WRITINGS: *L'Année musicale* (Paris, 1936–39; annual reports of musical events); *La Musique à travers les âges* (1937); *Maurice Ravel* (1938); *Les Grands Musiciens* (1938); *Histoire universelle de la musique moderne* (1941); *Histoire générale de la musique* (1945); *L'Œuvre de Claude Delvincourt* (1947); *Chopin et Fauré* (1946); *Le Travail en musique* (1949); *La Musique américaine* (1952); *Paul Paray* (1956).

Landowski, Marcel, French composer; b. Prêt L'Abbé (Finistère), Feb. 18, 1915. He studied with Büsser, Gaubert, and Munch; has been active as conductor. His works include the opera *Le Rire de Nils Halerius* (Mulhouse, Jan. 19, 1951); oratorio *Rythmes du monde* (1941); *Clairs-Obscurs,* suite for orch. (Paris, 1938); *Edina,* symph. poem (1946); *Le Petit Poucet,* symph. suite (Paris, 1947); Symphony (Paris, 1949); Piano Concerto (Paris, March 1, 1942); Cello Concerto (Paris, 1946); *Le Ventriloque,* lyric comedy (Paris, Feb. 8, 1957); *Les Adieux,* one-act lyric drama (Paris, Oct. 8, 1960); *L'Orage,* symph. poem (1961); *L'Opéra de poussière,* opera in two acts (Avignon, Oct. 25, 1962); *Les Notes de nuit* for narrator and orch. (Boulogne, Dec. 16, 1962); Piano Concerto No. 2 (Paris, Feb. 28, 1964); Symph. No. 2 (Strasbourg, June 24, 1965); Symph. No. 3 (1965); Concerto for Flute and String Orch. (1968); also music for films.

BIBLIOGRAPHY: A. Goléa, *Marcel Landowski: L'Homme et son œuvre* (Paris, 1969).

Landré, Guillaume (Louis Frédéric), important Dutch composer, son of **Willem Landré;** b. The Hague, Feb. 24, 1905; d. Amsterdam, Nov. 6, 1968. He took music lessons from Zagwijn and Pijper (1924–29); studied jurisprudence at the Utrecht Univ., receiving a master's degree in 1929; then was teacher of economics in Amsterdam (1930–47). He was general secretary of the Netherlands Arts Council (1947–58) and president of the Society of Netherlands Composers (1950–62). As a composer, he endeavored to revive the spirit and the polyphonic technique of the national Flemish School of the Renaissance in a 20th-century guise, with euphonious dissonances and impressionistic dynamics creating the modern aura. In his later works he experimented with serial devices.

WORKS: 3 operas: *De Snoek (The Pike),* comic opera (1934; Amsterdam, March 24, 1938); *Jean Lévecq,* after Maupassant (1962–63; Holland Festival, Amsterdam, June 16, 1965); *La Symphonie pastorale,* after André Gide (1965–67; Rouen, March 31, 1968); 4 symphonies: No. 1 (1932; Amsterdam ISCM Festival, June 9, 1933); No. 2 (1942; The Hague, March 6, 1946); No. 3 (Amsterdam, June 16, 1951); No. 4, *Symphonie concertante* (1954–55; Stockholm ISCM Festival, June 5, 1956); Suite for string orch. and piano (1936); *4 Pieces* for orch. (1937); *Concert Piece* for orch. (1938); Cello Concerto (1940); *Sinfonietta* for violin and orch. (1941); *Piae memoriae pro patria mortuorum* for chorus and orch. (1942); *Groet der Martelaren (Salute to the Martyrs)* for baritone and orch. (1943–44); *Symphonic Music* for flute and orch. (1947–48); *Sinfonia Sacra in Memoriam Patris* (1948; Rotterdam, Nov. 7, 1948; uses motifs from his father's *Requiem*); *4 Mouvements Symphoniques* (1948–49; The Hague, Jan. 17, 1950); *Berceuse voor moede mensen* for soloists, chorus and orch. (1952); Chamber Symphony for 13 instruments (1952; Amsterdam, Feb. 24, 1953); *Sonata festiva* for chamber orch. (1953); *Kaleidoscope,* symph. variations (1956); *Symphonic Permutations* (1957); Clarinet Concerto (Amsterdam, June 25, 1959); *Concertante* for contrabass clarinet and orch. (1959); *Anagrams* for orch. (1960); *Variazioni senza tema* for orch. (Amsterdam, Dec. 11, 1968); Violin Sonata (1927); 4 string quartets (1927, 1942–43, 1949, 1965); Piano Trio (1929); 2 wind quintets (1930, 1960); *4 Miniatures* for clarinet, and string quartet or string orch. (1950); Sextet for flute, clarinet and string quartet (1959); *Quartetto piccolo* for 2 trumpets, horn and trombone (1961); incidental music to the play *Cortez.*

Landré, Willem, Dutch writer on music and composer; father of **Guillaume Landré;** b. Amsterdam, June 12, 1874; d. Eindhoven, Jan. 1, 1948. He was a pupil of Bernard Zweers. In 1901 he became music critic of the *Oprechte Haarlemsche Courant* in Haarlem; music editor of the *Nieuwe Courant* in The Hague (1901–05), then of the *Nieuwe Rotterdamsche Courant* in Rotterdam (1905–37); taught theory, composition, and the history of music at the Rotterdam Cons.; editor of *Caecilia, Het Muziekcollege.*

WORKS: the operas *De Roos van Dekama* (Haarlem, 1897) and *Beatrix* (The Hague, 1925); the orchestral works *In memoriam Matris; 3 Mood Pictures; Le Jardin de Marguerite;* a *Requiem in memoriam uxoris; Fragments from the Book of Baruch,* for chorus; Piano Concerto; Piano Trio; numerous part-songs and songs.

Landshoff, Ludwig, German musicologist and conductor; b. Stettin, June 3, 1874; d. New York, Sept. 20, 1941. He studied music with Thuille, Urban, and Max Reger in Munich and Berlin; musicology with Sandberger, Max Friedlaender, and O. Fleischer; Dr. phil. (1901) from the Univ. of Munich with his treatise *Johann Rudolph Zumsteeg: ein Beitrag zur Geschichte des Liedes und der Ballade.* He established concerts at which old music was played on instruments of its time; was director of the Munich Bach Society (1919–28). He went to Paris in 1933, and to New York in 1939. He edited *Alte Meister des Belcanto* (5 vols., 1912–27; contains numerous 17th and 18th century unpubl. arias); Bach's *15 zweistimmige Inventionen und 15 dreistimmige Sinfonien, Trio-Sonaten; Musikalisches Opfer; 6 suites avec leurs préludes.*

BIBLIOGRAPHY: A. Einstein, "In Memoriam, Ludwig Landshoff," *Musical Quarterly* (April 1942).

Lane, Eastwood, American composer; b. Brewerton, N.Y., May 22, 1879; d. Central Square, Oswego County, N.Y., Jan. 22, 1951. He attended Syracuse Univ.; then devoted himself to composition. His works are mostly in a light, descriptive vein, for piano; two of his piano sketches, *Sea Burial* and *Persimmon Pucker,* were orchestrated by Ferde Grofé for performance by Paul Whiteman; other works are piano suites, *Sleepy Hollow, Adirondack Sketches,* and *5 American Dances;* he also wrote 2 ballets, *Abelard and Heloise* and *A Caravan From China Comes.*

BIBLIOGRAPHY: J. T. Howard, *Eastwood Lane* (N.Y., 1925); N. P. Gentieu, "Eastwood Lane," *Journal of Jazz Studies* (Spring 1976).

Lane, Louis, American conductor; b. Eagle Pass, Texas, Dec. 25, 1923. He studied at the Univ. of Texas, the Eastman School of Music and at the Berkshire Music Center in Tanglewood. In 1947 he won a competition to become apprentice conductor to George Szell, the musical director of the Cleveland Orch.; in 1956 he was appointed assistant conductor to Szell. In 1959 he was appointed regular conductor of the Akron, Ohio, Symph. Orch. In addition, he appeared as guest conductor with the Chicago Symph. Orch. and with the Detroit Symph. Orch. He conducted several Cleveland orchestra concerts during its 1965 European (and Russian) tour.

Lang, Benjamin Johnson, American pianist and conductor; b. Salem, Mass., Dec. 28, 1837; d. Boston, April 3, 1909. He studied with his father and with Alfred Jaëll. In 1855 he went to Berlin for advanced studies; for a time took piano lessons with Liszt. Returning to America, he was engaged as church organist; was also organist of the Handel and Haydn Society in Boston for many years (1859–95); then was its conductor (1895–97); directed the Apollo Club and the Cecilia Society, from their foundation (1868 and 1874, respectively); gave numerous concerts of orchestral, choral, and chamber music on his own account. As a pianist, teacher, conductor, and organizer, he was in the first rank of Boston musicians for a third of a century, and brought out a long list of important works by European and American composers. Among his pupils were Arthur Foote and Ethelbert Nevin. He was also a composer; wrote an oratorio, *David,* and a great many sacred works; songs and piano pieces.

Lang, Hans, Austrian operetta composer; b. Vienna, July 15, 1908; studied at the Vienna Cons.; wrote popular songs; composed the operettas *Lisa, benimm dich!* (Vienna, March 21, 1939; his most successful work); *Der Hofrat Geiger; Der alte Sünder; Mädel im Frack; X für ein U; Höchste Eisenbahn;* etc.

Lang, Henry Albert, American pianist, teacher, and composer; b. (of German parents) New Orleans, Oct. 9, 1854; d. Philadelphia, May 27, 1930. He studied at the Stuttgart Cons. Following a concert tour of Germany, he taught piano at the Karlsruhe Cons.; then at Riga and Königsberg. He came to the U.S. in 1890; settled in Philadelphia, where he was instructor at several music schools. He wrote 2 symphonies; *Fantastic Dances* for orch.; violin concerto; cello sonata; piano quintet; 2 piano trios; 2 string quartets; songs.

Láng, István, Hungarian composer; b. Budapest, March 1, 1933. He studied with Viski (1951–56) and Ferenc Szabó (1956–58) at the Budapest Academy of Music; in 1966 he was appointed director of the Hungarian Marionette Theatre. His music is rooted in euphonious dissonance, without venturing into fashionable ugliness.

WORKS: 2 operas: *Pathelin mester (Master Pathelin;* Budapest, 1958) and *A gyáva (The Coward;* Budapest, 1968); 4 ballets: *Mario és a varázsló (Mario and the Magician,* after Thomas Mann's novel, 1962), *Hiperbola* (1963; suite, 1968), *Lebukott (Nabbed,* 1968) and the ballet-cantata *Csillagra-török (Star Fighters,* 1971); Viola Concerto (1957); Concerto for String Orch. (1960); Concertino for Xylophone and Orch. (1961, revised 1967); *Variazioni ed Allegro* for orch. (1965; revision of a discarded symphony); *Gyászzene (Funeral Music)* for orch. (1969); *Impulsioni* for oboe and instrumental groups (1969); *3 Sentences from Romeo and Juliette* for strings (1969–70); *Concerto bucolico* for horn and orch. (1970–71); *Tüzoszlop (Firepillar)* for orch. (1972); Symphony No. 2 (1972–74); Chamber Cantata for soprano, clarinet, cello, piano and percussion (1962); Solo Cello Sonata (1960); 2 string quartets (1961, 1966); Duo for 2 flutes (1963); 3 wind quintets (1964; *Transfigurazioni,* 1965; 1975); *Pezzi* for soprano, flute, clarinet, viola and 2 percussionists (1964); *Monodia* for solo clarinet (1965); *Dramma breve* for solo flute (1970); *Cassazione* for brass septet (1971); *Töredékek (Fragments)* for female voice, oboe, bassoon and harp (1971–72); *Rhymes* for flute, clarinet, viola, cello and piano (1972); *Villanások (Flashes)* for solo violin (1973); *Improvisazioni* for solo cimbalom (1973); *Constellations* for oboe, violin, viola and clarinet (1974–75); *Surface Metamorphosis* for tape (1975); *Solo* for bass flute (1975); *Monologue* for horn (1975); *Waves* for soprano and vibraphone (1975); *Constellations* for oboe and string trio (1975–76).

Lang, Josephine, German composer of art songs; daughter of the German singer **Sabina Hitzelberger;** b. in Munich, March 14, 1815; d. Tübingen, Dec. 2, 1880. She studied music with her mother and also took lessons with Mendelssohn; composed and published a considerable number of surprisingly competent lieder in an amiably songful Germanically romantic vein, in addition to some very playable piano pieces. She was married to a poet who wrote under the *nom de plume* Christian Reinhold.

Lang, Margaret Ruthven, American composer; daughter of **Benjamin J. Lang;** b. Boston, Nov. 27, 1867; d. Boston, May 29, 1972, at the age of 104(!). She studied in Boston with her father and later in Munich; also with Chadwick and MacDowell. Her works include the overture *Witichis* (1893), *Dramatic Overture* (1893), the overture *Totila; Ballade* for orch. (1901); *Sappho's Prayer to Aphrodite,* aria for contralto with orch. (1895); *Phoebus,* aria for baritone and orch.; *In the Manger,* for mixed choir; *The Heavenly Noël,* for solo, women's chorus, piano, and string orch.; *Christmas Cycle* for vocal quartet; piano pieces; some 200 songs. She stopped composing about 1930. She attended Boston Symph. concerts since its foundation; she was present at a concert 3 days before her 100th birthday, at which Erich Leinsdorf included in the program the psalm tune *Old Hundredth* in her honor.

Lang, Paul Henry, eminent American musicologist and teacher; b. Budapest, Aug. 28, 1901. He studied bassoon and piano; took courses in composition at the Budapest Music Academy with Kodály and Leo Weiner; played bassoon in various orchestral groups in Budapest; also appeared as pianist in chamber music recitals; was chorus répétiteur at the Royal Opera in Budapest (1923–24); then attended the Univ. of Heidelberg, and the Sorbonne in Paris, where he studied musicology with André Pirro (1924–28); in 1928 he went to the U.S. where he enrolled in Cornell Univ. in the class of Otto Kinkeldey; obtained his Ph.D. in 1934 with the dissertation *A Literary History of French Opera.* He was assistant prof. at Vassar College (1930–31); associate prof., Wells College (1931–33); visiting lecturer, Wellesley College (1934–35); associate prof. of musicology, Columbia Univ. (1933–39); full prof. 1939; emeritus, 1970. He was vice-president of the American Musicological Society (1947–49) and President of the International Musicological Society (1955–58). From 1945 to 1972 he was editor of the *Musical Quarterly;* from 1954 to 1963, music editor of the *N.Y. Herald Tribune.* He published a valuable and very popular volume, *Music in Western Civilization* (N.Y., 1941; many subsequent reprints); an important biography, *George Frideric Handel* (N.Y., 1965); *Critic at the Opera* (N.Y., 1971); further brought out *A Pictorial History of Music* (with O. Bettman, N.Y., 1963); edited *One Hundred Years of Music,* a collection of articles marking the centennial of G. Schirmer, Inc., music publishing house (N.Y., 1961); *Problems of Modern Music* (N.Y., 1962; separate publication of articles from the *Musical Quarterly,* 1960); *Stravinsky. A New Appraisal of His Work* (N.Y., 1963); *The Creative World of Mozart* (N.Y., 1963); *Contemporary Music in Europe. A Comprehensive Survey* (with Nathan Broder; N.Y., 1965; a reprint of the semicentennial issue of the *Musical Quarterly*).

Lang, Walter, Swiss pianist and composer; b. Basel, Aug. 19, 1896; d. Baden, Switzerland, March 17, 1966. He was a pupil of Jaques-Dalcroze; taught at the Dalcroze School in Geneva; then studied in Munich with Klose, and in Zürich with Andreae and W. Frey; appeared as a concert pianist and as an accompanist; taught theory in Basel (1920–22); prof. of piano at Zürich Cons. (1922–41); music director of Monte Ceneri Radio (1942–48); in 1948, became instructor at the Basel Cons. He is married to the coloratura soprano **Mimi Lang-Seiber.**
    WORKS: Symphony (1946); overture *Jour de Fête* (1947); *Scherzo fugato* for string orch. (1939); Piano Concerto (1940); Cello Concerto (1951); String Quartet (1919); 2 violin sonatas (1920, 1939); Piano Trio (1925); Flute Sonata (1956); numerous piano pieces.

Langbecker, Emanuel Christian Gottlieb, German authority on Protestant chorales; b. Berlin, Aug. 31, 1792; d. there, Oct. 24, 1843. He was secretary to Prince Waldemar of Prussia; his researches on the origin of the Protestant chorale are embodied in *Das deutsch-evangelische Kirchenlied* (1830); *Johann Crügers Choral-Melodien* (1835); *Gesangblätter aus dem 16. Jahrhundert* (1838); and *Paul Gerhardts Leben und Lieder* (1841).

Langdon, Richard, English composer and organist; b. Exeter, c.1729; d. there, Sept. 8, 1803. He studied at Oxford (Mus. Bac., 1761); was organist of Exeter Cathedral (1753–77), Bristol Cathedral (1778–82), Armagh Cathedral (1782–94); publ. *Divine Harmony,* a collection of psalms and anthems (1774); also *12 Glees* for 3–4 voices (1770); 2 cantatas; 12 songs.

Lange, Daniel de, Dutch cellist and composer; brother of **Samuel de Lange;** b. Rotterdam, July 11, 1841; d. Point Loma, Calif., Jan. 31, 1918. He studied cello with Servais and composition with Verhulst. As a young man he taught at the Lwow Cons. (1860–63); returning to Amsterdam, he occupied various teaching posts; in 1895 became director of the Amsterdam Cons., remaining in that post until 1913; gave numerous choral concerts of old Dutch music; also wrote music criticism. In 1913 he went to California, where he lived at the headquarters of the Universal Brotherhood and Theosophical Society at Point Loma. He wrote an opera, *De val van Kuilenburg;* 2 symphonies; a cello concerto; chamber music; sacred works; also publ. an *Exposé d'une théorie de la musique.*
    BIBLIOGRAPHY: Henry Viotta, *Onze hedendaagsche toonkunstenaars* (Amsterdam, 1894); A. Averkamp, *Levensbericht van Daniel de Lange* (Leyden, 1918). See also the *Theosophical Field* (March 1918).

Lange, Francisco Curt, German musicologist; b. Eilenburg, Dec. 12, 1903. He studied music with Abert, Bekker, Bücken, and Sandberger. In 1930 he went to Uruguay; established the Instituto Interamericano de Música, and Editorial Cooperativo Interamericano de Compositores, which published a long series of works by Latin American composers. Beginning in 1935, he edited the *Boletín Latino-Americano de Música,* a series of bulky volumes containing documentary data on Latin American music and composers; separate volumes appeared in Montevideo, Lima, Bogota, Caracas, Rio de Janeiro, etc. He also publ. numerous essays and pamphlets dealing with literature, philosophy, pedagogy, and sociology (all in Spanish); brought out an anthology *Latin-American Art Music for the Piano* (G. Schirmer, Inc., N.Y., 1942) with biographical sketches of 12 composers; also published a collection of Brazilian church music of the 18th century.

Lange, Gustav, German pianist and composer; b. Schwerstedt, near Erfurt, Aug. 13, 1830; d. Wernigerode, July 19, 1889. He studied with A. W. Bach, Grell, and Löschhorn. For many years, he lived in Berlin; wrote more than 400 piano pieces, generally facile, elegant, and effective, and many of which gained great vogue.

Lange, Hans, German-American violinist and conductor; b. Istanbul, Feb. 17, 1884 (of German parents); d. Albuquerque, New Mexico, Aug. 13, 1960. He studied the violin as a child, then at the Prague Cons. with Ševčik, graduating in 1902 with highest honors. In 1903 he made his debut as solo violinist with the Berlin master of the Frankfurt Opera; settled in the U.S. in 1923; was assistant conductor of the N.Y. Philharmonic (1923–33) and later an associate conductor (1933–36); then associate conductor of the Chicago Symph. Orch. (1936–46). He was conductor of the Albuquerque Symphony Orch. from 1951 to 1958.

Lange, Konrad von, German esthetician; b. Göttingen, March 15, 1855; d. Tübingen, July 28, 1921. In his theories he introduced the basic concept of "illusion" in the creation and appreciation of art and music. He publ. *Die Bewusste Selbsttäuschung* (1895); *Das Wesen der Kunst* (2 vols., 1907); *Das Wesen der künstlerischen Erziehung* (1902); *Der Zweck der Kunst* (1912).

Lange-Müller, Peter Erasmus, Danish composer; b. Frederiksborg, near Copenhagen, Dec. 1, 1850; d. Copenhagen, Feb. 26, 1926. He studied at the Copenhagen Cons. His early compositions show the influence of J. P. E. Hartmann; those of his later period exhibit distinct individuality.
WORKS: operas (all produced in Copenhagen), *Tove* (Jan. 19, 1878), *Spanske Studenter* (Oct. 21, 1883), *Fru Jeanna* (Feb. 4, 1891), *Vikingeblod* (April 29, 1900); incidental music for *Fulvia* and *Det var en gang; Niels Ebbeson,* for baritone, men's chorus, and orch.; 2 symphonies; the orchestral suites *Alhambra* and *Weyerburg;* trio for violin, cello, and piano; piano pieces, etc.; some 200 songs, many of which gained great popularity.

Lange, Samuel de, Dutch organist and composer; brother of **Daniel de Lange;** b. Rotterdam, Feb. 22, 1840; d. Stuttgart, July 7, 1911. He studied with Verhulst in Holland and with Winterberger in Vienna. He was with his brother in Lwow (1859–63); then taught successively at the Rotterdam Music School (1863–74), the Basel Music School (1874–76), and the Cologne Cons. (1876–85); then was conductor of the Oratorio Society at The Hague (1885–93); finally was prof. of organ and composition at the Stuttgart Cons. (1894); became its director in 1900. He wrote a piano concerto; 3 symphonies; 4 string quartets; 2 piano trios; 4 violin sonatas; 2 cello sonatas; 8 sonatas for organ; an oratorio, *Moses;* 3 cantatas, *De Opstanding, Die Totenklage,* and *Eines Königs Tränen;* male choruses; songs.

Langendorff, Frieda, German contralto; b. Breslau, March 24, 1868; d. New York, June 11, 1947. She studied with Mme. Leffler-Burckard; made her debut in Strasbourg (1901); sang at the Metropolitan Opera, N.Y. in 1907–08 and 1910–11. She then made an extensive concert tour throughout the U.S. (1912–13). In 1914 she was engaged by the Dresden Royal Opera; also sang at Bayreuth, Berlin, Helsinki, Brussels, and Amsterdam. She returned to New York after World War II. Among 76 operatic roles (which included mezzo-soprano parts) in her repertory were Ortrud, Fricka, Amneris, Azucena, and Dalila.

Langenus, Gustave, Belgian clarinetist; b. Malines, Aug. 6, 1883; New York, Jan. 30, 1957. He studied at Brussels Cons. As a youth of 18, he traveled with Sousa's band in Europe; then lived in England; in 1910, came to the U.S.; was clarinetist with the N.Y. Symphony (1910–20); was one of the founders of the Chamber Music Society in N.Y. (1914); member of the N.Y. Philharmonic from 1920–23; taught at the Juilliard School of Music, and the Dalcroze School of Music. He publ. *Fingered Scale Studies for the Boehm Clarinet* (N.Y., 1911); *Modern Clarinet Playing* (N.Y., 1913); *Virtuoso Studies and Duos for Clarinet* (N.Y., 1915); *Complete Method for the Boehm Clarinet* (8 vols., N.Y., 1916).

Langer, Eduard, Russian pianist and composer; b. Moscow, May 3, 1835; d. there, June 5, 1905. He was a pupil at the Leipzig Cons. of Moscheles, Richter, and Hauptmann; upon returning to Moscow, he taught at the Cons. there; publ. numerous arrangements for 2 pianos (4 and 8 hands) of operas and orchestral works by Russian composers; his own compositions include a string quartet, a string trio, 2 violin sonatas, and many piano pieces.

Langer, Ferdinand, German composer and cellist; b. Leimen, near Heidelberg, Jan. 21, 1839; d. Kirneck (Black Forest), Aug. 5, 1905. An excellent cellist, he joined the orchestra of the Mannheim court theater; later became 2nd Kapellmeister there. With Emil Heckel, he founded the first "Wagnerverein" in Germany (1883). He produced several locally successful operas in Mannheim: *Die gefährliche Nachbarschaft* (1868), *Dornröschen* (1873), *Aschenbrödel* (1878), *Murillo* (1887), and the "romantische Volksoper" *Der Pfeiffer von Haardt* (1894). He revised Weber's *Silvana* for its revival in 1885.

Langer, Hermann, German organist and theorist; b. Höckendorf, near Tharandt, July 6, 1819; d. Dresden, Sept. 8, 1889. He studied in Leipzig with K. F. Becker; in 1843, became organist of the Univ. of Leipzig church; 1845, teacher of liturgical song at Leipzig Univ.; 1857, musical director there; went to Dresden in 1887 as Inspector of Organ Building. He publ. a *Repertorium für Männergesang; Der erste Unterricht im Gesang* (3 courses; 1876–77); also edited the *Musikalische Gartenlaube.*

Langer, Victor, Hungarian composer; b. Budapest, Oct. 14, 1842; d. there, March 19, 1902. He studied in Budapest with R. Volkmann, and later at the Leipzig Cons. Returning to Budapest, he was active as a teacher, theater conductor, and editor of a Hungarian music journal. His songs *Ögyek dalai,* Hungarian dances, arrangements, etc., publ. under the pen name of **Aladar Tisza,** are in the genuine national vein; they enjoyed great popularity.

Langert, Johann August Adolf, German composer; b. Coburg, Nov. 26, 1836; d. there, Dec. 27, 1920. He was theater conductor in Coburg, Mannheim, and Basel; in 1873, became court conductor at Gotha, retiring in 1897 to his native town. He composed several operas: *Die Jungfrau von Orleans* (Coburg, 1861), *Des Sängers Fluch* (Coburg, 1863), *Dona Maria* (Darmstadt, 1866), *Die Fabier* (Coburg, 1866), *Dornröschen* (Leipzig, 1871), and *Jean Cavallier* (Coburg, 1880; rewritten and produced as *Die Camisarden,* 1887).

Langey, Otto, German-American cellist and composer; b. Leichholz, near Frankfurt on the Oder, Oct. 20, 1851; d. New York, March 16, 1922. He studied cello with Specht in Sorau, Ullrich in Halle, and Cabisius in Bremen; theory and composition with W. Fritze in Liegnitz. In 1877 he went to London, playing in the Hallé and Richter concerts; came to the U.S. in 1889, and made a tour as soloist with the Boston Symph. Club; settled in N.Y. as teacher; in 1909, became arranger of orchestral music for G. Schirmer, Inc. He publ. the *Langey Tutors* (methods for 28 different instruments) and numerous compositions for orch. (*Arabian Serenade, Liberty Overture, 3 Oriental Sketches,* etc.).

Langgaard, Rued, Danish composer and organist; b. Copenhagen, July 28, 1893; d. Ribe, July 10, 1952. His father, **Siegfried Langgaard** (1852–1914), was a pupil of Liszt and an accomplished pianist. Rued Langgaard studied organ with Gustav Helsted; from his early youth he was occupied mainly as a church organist. As a composer, he followed neo-Romantic trends, in the manner of Bruckner and Mahler, scaling heights and plumbing depths of grandiose designs.
  WORKS: Biblical opera, *Antichrist* (1921–30); and 16 symphonies: No. 1, *Klippepastoraler* (1908–11; Berlin, 1913); No. 2, *Vaarbrud (Spring Song),* with solo soprano (1912–13; Copenhagen, 1914; revised and performed on the Danish Radio, 1948); No. 3, *Ungdomsbrus (The Sound of Youth),* with piano, and chorus and ad lib. (1915; Copenhagen, 1918; revised, 1926); No. 4, *Løvfald (The Fall of the Leaf,* 1916; Copenhagen, 1917); No. 5, *Steppenatur* (1918; Copenhagen, 1926; revised, Danish Radio, 1938); No. 6, *Det Himmelrivende (The Heaven Rending,* 1919); No. 7, *Ved Tordenskjold i Holmens Kirke* (1925–26; Copenhagen, 1926; revised and given on the Danish Radio, 1935); No. 8, *Minder om Amalienborg* (1928); No. 9, *Dronning Dagmar* (1942; Danish Radio, 1943); No. 10, *Hin Tordenbolig* (1944); No. 11 *Ixion* (1945; Danish Radio, July 29, 1968); No. 12, *Helsingeborg* (1946); No. 13, *Undertro (Belief in Miracles,* 1947); No. 14, *Morgenen (Morning),* suite for chorus and orch. (1948); No. 15, *Søstormen (The Storm at Sea,* 1948); No. 16, *Syndflod af Sol (Flood of Sun,* 1951; Copenhagen, March 17, 1966); for voices with orch.: *Musae triumphantes* (1906); *Angelus (The Gold Legend,* 1915–37); *Sfaerernes Musik (Music of the Spheres,* 1916–18; his most interesting work; performed in Karlsruhe, Germany, 1921); *Endens Tid (The End of Time,* 1921–39); 2 church cantatas, *Krematio* (1928–36) and *Jephta* (1948); *Højsangen (Song of Solomon,* 1949; Danish Radio, Feb. 24, 1969). Other works include *Heltedød (Death of a Hero)* for orch. (1907); *Drapa* for orch. (1907); *Sfinx,* overture (1909); *Saga blot* for orch. (1917); Violin Concerto (1943–44; Danish Radio, July 29, 1968); a dedicatory overture, *Carl Nielsen vor store Komponist (Carl Nielsen Our Great Composer)* for orch. (1948); 6 string quartets (1914–31); 5 violin sonatas (1915–49); *Dies Irae* for tuba and piano (1948); many minor organ pieces, motets and songs.

Langhans, Friedrich Wilhelm, German composer, and violinist; b. Hamburg, Sept. 21, 1832; d. Berlin, June 9, 1892. He studied at the Leipzig Cons. with David (violin) and Richter (composition); then in Paris with Alard (violin). In 1852–56 he played violin in the Gewandhaus Orch. at Leipzig; 1857–60, concertmaster at Düsseldorf; then teacher and violinist in Hamburg, Paris, and Heidelberg; Dr. phil. from Heidelberg (1871). He taught music history at Kullak's Neue Akademie der Tonkunst in Berlin (1874–81); in 1881, joined the faculty of the Scharwenka Cons. In 1858 he married the concert pianist **Louise Japha** (divorced in 1874). He publ. *Das musikalische Urteil* (1872; 2nd ed., 1886); *Die königliche Hochschule für Musik in Berlin* (1873); *Musikgeschichte in 12 Vorträgen* (1878); *Die Geschichte der Musik des 17., 18. und 19. Jahrhunderts* (2 vols.; 1882–86; a well-written continuation of Ambros' great work). He composed a symphony, a string quartet, a violin sonata, and studies for violin.

Lang-Köstlin, Josephine, German song composer; mother of **Heinrich Adolf Köstlin;** b. Munich, March 14, 1815; d. Tübingen, Dec. 2, 1880. She studied with Frau Berlinghof-Wagner and Mendelssohn; publ. many lieder. See a biographical sketch of her life by her son (Leipzig, 1881).

Langlais, Jean, French organist and composer; b. La Fontenelle, Feb. 15, 1907. He was blind from infancy; studied organ with Dupré at the Paris Cons., winning 1st prize in 1930; studied composition with Paul Dukas. He became organist at Montrouge; from 1945, organist at Ste.-Clotilde in Paris; also taught organ at the School for the Blind. His works are mainly for organ (*Deux offertoires pour tous les temps, Trois paraphrases grégoriennes,* etc.); also wrote a symph. poem, *Cloches;* Suite for Cello and Orch.; numerous choral works; Trio for Flute, Violin, and Viola.
  BIBLIOGRAPHY: A. Machabey, *Portraits de trente musiciens français* (Paris, 1949; pp. 109–13).

Langlé, Honoré François Marie, French music theorist and composer; b. Monaco, 1741; d. Villiers-le-Bel, near Paris, Sept. 20, 1807. He studied in Naples at the Conservatorio della Pietà dei Turchini, with Cafaro. In 1768 he went to Paris, becoming a singing teacher at the École Royale de Chant in 1784; then was prof. of harmony and librarian at the Paris Cons. He wrote an important *Traité d'harmonie et de modulation* (1793; 2nd ed., 1797; chord building by thirds); *Traité de la basse sous le chant* (1798); *Nouvelle méthode pour chiffrer les accords* (1801); *Traité de la fugue* (1805); also collaborated with Cherubini on the latter's *Méthode de chant;* edited Mengozzi's *Méthode de chant du Conservatoire* after Mengozzi's death. Langlé composed a number of operas, only one of which was presented: *Corisandre, ou Les Fous par enchantement* (Paris, March 8, 1791).

Langley, Allan Lincoln, American violinist; b. Newport, R.I., June 11, 1892; d. (of a heart attack) in a Hudson tube train between Jersey City and New York City, Nov. 12, 1949. He studied at Brown Univ., Providence (B.A., 1914), and at the New England Cons. with Shepherd, Chadwick, Winternitz, and Mason; played violin and viola in the Boston Symph. (1918),

National Symph. (1920–21), N.Y. Philharmonic (1921–27), and Richmond Symph. Orch. (1932–33).

Langlotz, Karl A., German-American composer; b. Saxe-Meiningen, Germany, June 20, 1834; d. Trenton, N.J., Nov. 25, 1915. He was a member of the Liszt circle in Weimar; in 1853, came to America; lived in Philadelphia as music teacher; 1857–68, instructor of German at Princeton; 1868, entered the Theological Seminary, graduating in 1871; 1874, moved to Trenton, where he taught music. He is known for composing the famous Princeton song *Old Nassau* (1859), at the suggestion of the Princeton students and teachers who gathered regularly to sing college songs; the song was first publ. in the earliest Princeton song book, *Songs of Old Nassau* (N.Y., 1859).
BIBLIOGRAPHY: W. S. Conrow, "Old Nassau" (N.Y., 1905).

Langstroth, Ivan Shed, American pianist, teacher, and composer; b. Alameda, Calif., Oct. 16, 1887; d. New York, April 18, 1971. He studied in San Francisco with T. Vogt, then in Berlin with Juon, Humperdinck, and Lhevinne. In 1915 he was coach at the Kiel Opera; 1916, organist at the American Church in Berlin; 1917–20, toured Scandinavia as concert pianist; 1921–28, teacher at the New Cons. in Vienna; then returned to America; from 1943–45 he was lecturer on music at Brooklyn College; then taught privately in New York. He wrote orchestral and choral works, chamber music, piano pieces, songs.

Lanier (Laniere), Nicholas, English composer, lutenist, and painter; b. Greenwich (baptized Sept. 10), 1588; d. London, Feb. 24, 1666. He is important as having been probably the first to introduce the Italian recitative style into England, in his music to masques, of which the first was Ben Jonson's *Lovers made Men* (London, Feb. 22, 1617). He was Master of the King's Musick under Charles I and Charles II. He wrote a pastoral on the birth of Prince Charles, a funeral hymn for Charles I, a cantata *Hero and Leander,* and some New Year's songs; his songs are found in MS in the British Museum, Bodleian Music School, Christ Church, and Fitzwilliam Museum; also in the published collections *Select Musicall Ayres and Dialogues* (1653, 1659), *The Musical Companion* (1667), *The Treasury of Musick* (1669), *Choice Ayres and Songs* (1685), and J. S. Smith's *Musica Antiqua* (1812).
BIBLIOGRAPHY: J. Pulver, *A Biographical Dictionary of Old English Music* (1927); *Dictionary of National Biography* (vol. II; reprinted Oxford, 1921–22); V. Duckles, "English Song and the Challenge of Italian Monody," in *Words to Music* (includes a complete transcription of *Hero and Leander;* Los Angeles, 1967).

Lanier, Sidney, American poet and musician; b. Macon, Ga., Feb. 3, 1842; d. Lynn, N.C., Sept. 7, 1881. Best known for his poetry, Lanier learned as a child to play the piano, flute, guitar, violin, and organ. After serving in the Civil War, he was organist and choirmaster for a short period at a church in Montgomery, Ala. In 1873 he became first flutist of the Peabody

Symph. Orch. in Baltimore. He wrote a number of articles on music (collected in *Music and Poetry: Essays upon Some Aspects and Interpretations of the Two Arts,* 1898; repr. N.Y., 1969) and composed songs and flute pieces.
BIBLIOGRAPHY: H. C. Thorpe, "Sidney Lanier: A Poet for Musicians," *Musical Quarterly* (July 1925); A. H. Starke, "Sidney Lanier as a Musician," *Musical Quarterly* (Oct. 1934).

Lankow, Anna, noted German singing teacher; b. Bonn, Jan. 13, 1850; d. there, March 19, 1908. She studied singing in Cologne, Leipzig, and Dresden; began her career as a concert singer; then was engaged as contralto in the Weimar Opera; however, because she had been lame since childhood, she was forced to abandon the stage. In 1883 she married the sculptor Paul Pietsch of Berlin; after his death in 1885, she came to America, settling in New York as a singing teacher; subsequently returned to Germany. She published a valuable treatise, *Die Wissenschaft des Kunstgesangs* (1899, in German and English).

Lanner, August (Joseph), Austrian violinist and composer; son of **Joseph (Franz Karl) Lanner;** b. Vienna, Jan. 23, 1834; d. there, Sept. 27, 1855. A talented violinist, dance composer, and conductor, he died in his 22nd year.

Lanner, Joseph (Franz Karl), historically significant Austrian violinist and dance composer; b. Vienna, April 12, 1801; d. Oberdöbling, near Vienna, April 14, 1843. A self-taught violinist and composer, he joined Pamer's dance orch. when he was 12. In 1818 he formed a trio which Johann Strauss, Sr., joined, making it a quartet. The group grew in size, and by 1824 it was a full sized classical orchestra which became famous and performed in coffee houses, taverns, at balls, etc. The orchestra was subsequently divided into two ensembles, with Lanner leading one, and Strauss the other. Lanner and Strauss are credited with the creation of the mid-19th century Viennese waltz. Lanner's output totals 207 popular pieces, including 112 waltzes, 25 Ländler, 10 quadrilles, 3 polkas, 28 galops, and 6 marches; an overture to *Der Preis einer Lebensstunde; Banquet-Polonaise; Tarantella;* and *Bolero.* His complete works in 8 vols., ed. by E. Kremser, were publ. by Breitkopf & Härtel in 1889 (repr. N.Y., 1971); selections were brought out by Oscar Bie (Munich, 1920) and Alfred Orel, in the *Denkmäler der Tonkunst in Österreich* 65 (33.ii).
BIBLIOGRAPHY: H. Sachs, *J. Lanner* (Vienna, 1889); F. Rebay and O. Keller, *J. Lanner* (Vienna, 1901); F. Lange, *J. Lanner und Johann Strauss, Ihre Zeit, ihr Leben und ihre Werke* (Vienna, 1904; 2nd ed., 1919).

Lannoy, Eduard, Austrian composer; b. Brussels, Dec. 4, 1787; d. Vienna, March 28, 1853. His family moved to Graz when he was a child; he studied there and in Paris. In 1813 he went to Vienna, where he became an active promoter of the Gesellschaft der Musikfreunde; from 1830–35 he was a member of the executive board of the Vienna Cons. He wrote several operas and Singspiele, a symphony, overtures, chamber music, piano pieces, songs.

Lans, Michael J. A., Dutch composer and authority on Gregorian chant; b. Haarlem, July 18, 1845; d. Amsterdam, Feb. 3, 1908. A Roman Catholic priest, he started publication of an ecclesiastical periodical *Gregoriusblad* (1876); composed several Masses; publ. *Palestrina* (1882), and a manual of strict counterpoint (1889).

Lantins, Arnold de, Netherlands composer; b. probably at Lantin, near Liège, c.1400; date of death unknown. He traveled to Italy about 1427; was a singer in the Papal Chapel in Rome between Nov., 1431 and July, 1432. His employment of carefully connected chords suggesting purely harmonic procedures is of historical interest. Two motets, *Tota pulchra es* and *O pulcherrima mulierum* (from the *Song of Solomon*), are reproduced in Charles Van den Borren's *Polyphonia Sacra: A Continental Miscellany of the 15th Century* (1932). Other works are found in J. Stainer, *Dufay and His Contemporaries* (London, 1898), in J. Wolf, *Geschichte der Mensural-Notation,* and in vol. 61 (31) of *Denkmäler der Tonkunst in Österreich.*
BIBLIOGRAPHY: Charles Van den Borren, *Hugo et Arnold de Lantins* (Liège, 1935); G. Reese, *Music in the Renaissance* (N.Y., 1954).

Lantins, Hugo de, Netherlands singer and composer; possibly related to **Arnold de Lantins;** b. probably at Lantin, near Liège, shortly before 1400; death date unknown. As a young man, he was in Italy, where he wrote an ode *Tra quante regione* for the marriage of Theodore Palaiologos (1421); several motets and other ecclesiastical pieces are extant.
BIBLIOGRAPHY: Charles Van den Borren, *Arnold et Hugo de Lantins* (Liège, 1935); G. Reese, *Music in the Renaissance* (N.Y., 1954).

Lanza, Mario (real name **Alfredo Arnold Cocozza**), American singer of Italian descent; b. Philadelphia, Jan. 31, 1921; d. Rome, Oct. 7, 1959. He studied singing with Enrico Rosati; appeared in recitals and opera. In 1951 he starred in the title role of a highly successful film, *The Great Caruso.*

Lanzetti, Salvatore, Italian cellist; b. Naples, c.1710; d. Turin, c.1780. He was one of the earliest virtuosos on the cello; during his residence in London (about 1739–56) he succeeded in establishing the cello there as a favorite solo instrument; returned to Italy as a member of the royal chapel at Turin. He publ. 2 books of cello sonatas (1736), 6 solos, and 6 sonatas for 2 cellos with continuo; also a method, *Principes de doigter pour le violoncelle dans tous les tons.*

Laparra, Raoul, French composer; b. Bordeaux, May 13, 1876; killed during an air raid near Paris, April 4, 1943. He studied at the Paris Cons. with Gédalge, Massenet, and Fauré; won the Grand Prix de Rome with his cantata *Ulysse* (June 27, 1903). He was music critic of *Le Matin,* resigning in 1937 to dedicate himself entirely to composition. He was at his best in music inspired by Spanish subjects.

WORKS: the operas *Peau d'âne* (Bordeaux, 1899), *La Habanera* (Paris, Feb. 26, 1908; his best known work), *La Jota* (Paris, April 26, 1911), *Le Joueur de viole* (Paris, Dec. 24, 1925), *Las Toreras* (Lille, Feb., 1929), *L'Illustre Fregona* (Paris, Feb. 16, 1931); incidental music to *El Conquistador; Un Dimanche basque,* suite for orch. and piano, etc.

Laporte, André, Belgian composer; b. Oplinter, July 12, 1931. He studied musicology and philosophy at the Catholic Univ. of Louvain, graduating in 1956; studied organ with Flor Peeters and counterpoint with Marinus De Jong (1956–58). In 1963 he was engaged as a producer for the Belgian Radio; in 1968 he was appointed to the faculty of the Brussels Cons.
WORKS: Piano Sonata (1954); *Psalm* for 6 voices and brass (1956); *Introduction and Fughetta* for guitar (1956); *Sequenza I* for solo clarinet (1964); *Sequenza II* for bass clarinet and 3 clarinets (1965); *Jubilius* for 12 brasses and 3 percussionists (1966); *Ludus fragilis* for solo oboe (1967); *Story* for 3 violas de gamba and harpsichord (1967); *Ascension* for piano (1967); *Inclinations* for flute (1968); *Alliances* for cello and piano (1968); *De profundis* for mixed choir (1968); *Le Morte Chitarre,* for tenor, flute and 14 string soloists (1969); *Reflection* for clarinet (1970); *Night Music* for orch. (1970; Brussels, March 15, 1971); *La vita non è Sogno,* for narrator, tenor, baritone, chorus and orch. (Ghent, Sept. 13, 1972); *Péripétie* for brass sextet (1973); *Arboreal,* film music for piano and tape (1974); *Chamber Music* for soprano, flute, clarinet, violin and piano (1975).

Laporte, Joseph de, French writer on theater and music; b. Belfort, 1713; d. Paris, Dec. 19, 1779. He was a Jesuit abbé; wrote *Anecdotes dramatiques* (3 vols., 1775; contains all varieties of theatrical works); *Dictionnaire dramatique* (3 vols., 1776); *Almanach des spectacles de Paris, ou Calendrier historique des théâtres de l'Opéra, des Comédies française et italienne et des foires* (48 vols. in all; those from 1750–79 by Laporte; the rest by Duchesne and others).

La Pouplinière, Alexandre-Jean-Joseph Le Riche de, French musical amateur; b. Chinon, July 26, 1693; d. there, Dec. 5, 1762. A wealthy member of the nobility and a statesman, he was a patron of music; pupil of Rameau. The musical soirées he gave in his private theater were famous; he engaged Gossec as music director (1751); introduced Johann Stamitz to the Parisian public; upon Stamitz's advice, he added horns, clarinets, and a harp to his orchestra, instruments seldom heard in a concert orchestra before that time. La Pouplinière wrote a number of arias, some of which Rameau incorporated into his own works.
BIBLIOGRAPHY: Ancelet, *Observations sur la musique et les instruments* (Amsterdam, 1757); P. Hédouin, *Gossec* (Paris, 1852); P. Hédouin, *Mosaïque* (Paris, 1856); G. Cucuel, *La Pouplinière et la musique de chambre au XVIIIe siècle* (Paris, 1913).

La Prade, Ernest, American composer; b. Memphis, Tenn., Dec. 20, 1889; d. Sherman, Conn. April 20, 1969. He studied violin at the Cincinnati College of Music; at the Royal Cons. in Brussels with César

Thomson, and in London with J. Jongen (composition). He subsequently taught at the Cincinnati College of Music; member of the Cincinnati Symph. Orch. (1909-12), of the Belgian and Holbrook Quartets in London (1914-17), of the N.Y. Symph. Orch. (1919-28); in 1929, joined the staff of NBC; in 1950, supervisor of music research there. He wrote a comic opera, *Xantha* (London, 1917), and songs; publ. *Alice in Orchestralia* (1925); *Marching Notes* (1929); *Broadcasting Music* (1947).

La Presle, Jacques de, French composer; b. Versailles, July 5, 1888; d. Paris, May 6, 1969. He studied at the Paris Cons.; received the Grand Prix de Rome in 1921; in 1937, appointed prof. of harmony at the Paris Cons. His works include *Apocalypse de St.-Jean* (1928); *Album d'images,* a suite for orch. (1935); Piano Concerto (1949); chamber music; songs.

Laquai, Reinhold, Swiss composer; b. Zürich, May 1, 1894; d. Oberrieden, Oct. 3, 1957. He studied at the Zürich Cons.; later with Busoni in Berlin. In 1920 he became a teacher at the Zürich Cons.
WORKS: the operas *Der Schleier der Tanit* and *Die Revisionsreise;* many orchestral works (3 symphonies, 5 overtures, 2 serenades, a concert piece for piano and orch., etc.): chamber music (trios, sonatas for violin, flute, cello, bassoon and horn, clarinet, etc., piano quintet); piano pieces and more than 200 songs.

Lara, Agustín, Mexican composer of popular songs; b. Tlacotalpán, Oct. 14, 1900; d. Mexico City, Nov. 5, 1970. He learned to play piano by ear; earned his living as an entertainer in a Mexican house of tolerance, where he wrote his first successful song *Rosa;* an encounter with a woman who impulsively slashed his face during an altercation inspired him to write a paean to womanhood, *Morucha,* which acquired great popularity. His other songs that became famous are *Tus Pupilas, Gotas de Amor,* and the most famous, *Mujer.*

Lara-Bareiro, Carlos, Paraguayan composer; b. Capiatá, March 6, 1914. He played in the boy scout band conducted by his father; then studied violin in Asunción and in Rio de Janeiro; during his stay in Brazil he also took lessons in composition and conducting. Returning to Paraguay in 1951 he organized in Asunción the Symph. Orch. of the Association of Musicians of Paraguay. Eventually he moved to Buenos Aires. His works reflect the modes and moods of Paraguayan folk music. He wrote several symphonic suites on Paraguayan themes and a piano concerto.

Lara, Isidore de. See **De Lara, Isidore.**

Laredo, Jaime, Bolivian violinist; b. Cochabamba, June 7, 1941. He was sent to the U.S. as a child; studied with Ivan Galamian at the Curtis Institute in Philadelphia. In 1959, a week before his 18th birthday, he won the Queen Elisabeth of Belgium Competition in Brussels, and subsequently made a brilliant career, both in America and in Europe. The Bolivian government issued a series of airmail stamps with his picture, bearing the notes A, D, C in the treble clef, spelling out his name in Latin notation (La-Re-Do). In 1960 he married the pianist **Ruth Meckler** (divorced 1974).

La Rocca, Nick (Dominick James), American jazz cornetist; b. New Orleans, April 11, 1889; d. New Orleans, Feb. 22, 1961. After graduating from high school he became a cornetist and local bandleader. He formed the Original Dixieland Jazz Band, which gained wide popularity and brought attention to the New Orleans style of jazz; it played at Reisenweber's in New York during World War I and toured throughout the United States and Europe; the group is most noted for having made, in 1917, the first jazz recordings, these becoming a major influence on the next generation (the "Chicago School") of white jazz musicians.
BIBLIOGRAPHY: H. O. Brunn, *The Story of the Original Dixieland Jazz Band* (Baton Rouge, La., 1960). La Rocca's memorabilia are on deposit at Tulane University.

Laroche, Hermann, Russian music critic; b. St. Petersburg, May 25, 1845; d. there, Oct. 18, 1904. He studied with Rubinstein and Zaremba at the St. Petersburg Cons., and with Tchaikovsky in Moscow. He became prof. at the Moscow Cons. (1867-70); then at the St. Petersburg Cons. (1872-79); contributed numerous articles to Russian journals; collected his essays and criticisms and published them in 1894. His most important work is *M. I. Glinka and His Place in Russian Music* (1868; new ed., 1953); with N. Kashkin he wrote *Reminiscences of Tchaikovsky* (1894).

La Rotella, Pasquale, Italian composer and conductor; b. Bitonto, Feb. 26, 1880; d. Bari, March 20, 1963. He studied in Naples; was choral conductor at the Bari Cathedral (1902-13); from 1934-49, taught at the Liceo Musicale there; toured Italy as opera conductor. His works include the operas *Ivan* (Bari, Jan. 20, 1900); *Dea* (Bari, April 11, 1903); *Fasma* (Milan, Nov. 28, 1908); *Corsaresca* (Rome, Nov. 13, 1933); *Manuela* (Nice, March 4, 1948); much sacred music.

Larrocha, Alicia de, brilliant Spanish pianist; b. Barcelona, May 23, 1923. She studied piano with Frank Marshall and theory with Ricardo Lamote de Grignon. She made her first public appearance at the age of 5; was soloist with the Orquesta Sinfónica of Madrid at the age of 11. In 1940 she launched her career in earnest; from 1947 made extensive concert tours in Europe and America. Her interpretations of Spanish music have evoked universal admiration for their authentic quality, but she has also been exuberantly praised by sober-minded critics for her impeccable taste and exquisitely polished technique in classical works.

L'Arronge, Adolf, composer and conductor; b. Hamburg, March 8, 1838; d. Berlin, May 25, 1908. He studied at the Leipzig Cons. with R. Genée; theater conductor in Cologne, Danzig, Königsberg, Würzburg, Stuttgart, Budapest, etc.; in 1866, became director of the Kroll Opera, Berlin; then of the Lobetheater in Breslau (1874-78). Returning to Berlin, he bought the Friedrich-Wilhelmstädtisches Theater in 1881, and managed it until 1894 as the Deutsches Theater. He brought out many musical farces, Singspiele, etc. at the Wallnertheater, including his comic operas *Das Gespenst* and *Der zweite Jakob*, the "Volksstücke" *Das grosse Los* (1868) and *Mein Leopold*, etc.; also wrote many songs.

Larsen, Jens Peter, Danish musicologist; b. Frederiksberg, June 14, 1902. He studied at the Univ. of Copenhagen with Th. Laub, taking an M.A. in 1928 and a Ph.D. in 1939; church organist (1930–45). From 1949 to 1965 he was the head of the Musicological Institute at the Univ. of Copenhagen; in 1961 was guest lecturer at the Univ. of California, Berkeley. On his 70th birthday he was honored with a Festschrift, containing a bibliography of his publications (Copenhagen, 1972). His chief work was a thorough investigation of all aspects of the life and music of Haydn. He published *Die Haydn-Überlieferung* (Copenhagen, 1939); *Drei Haydn Kataloge in Faksimile* (Copenhagen, 1941); also *Handel's Messiah* (N.Y., 1957); was general editor of a collected edition of Haydn's works (Boston and Vienna, 1949–51; Cologne, 1955–60).

Larsen, Nils, Norwegian pianist; b. Oslo, June 7, 1888; d. there, Nov. 7, 1937. He studied in Oslo with M. Knutzen and in Berlin with Ganz and da Motta. He wrote a number of piano pieces; edited the works of Christoph Graupner.

Larsén-Todsen, Nanny, Swedish soprano; b. Hagby, Kalmar län, Aug. 2, 1884. She studied at the Stockholm Cons. and in Germany and Italy. In 1906 she made her debut at the Royal Theater in Stockholm as Agatha in *Der Freischütz;* was a member of the Royal Theater (1907–22), specializing in Wagnerian roles; sang at La Scala in Milan (1923–24), the Metropolitan Opera House in N.Y. (1925–27; debut Jan. 31, 1925 as Brünnhilde in *Götterdämmerung*), at Bayreuth (1927–31), and made guest appearances at most of the European opera houses. Her principal roles were the 3 Brünnhildes, Isolde, Fricka, and Leonore. She married H. Todsen in 1916; following her retirement from the stage she became a teacher in Stockholm.

Larsson, Lars-Erik, important Swedish composer; b. Åkarp, near Lund, May 15, 1908. He studied composition (with Ellberg) and conducting (with Olallo Morales) at the Royal Academy of Music in Stockholm (1925-29); then went to Vienna where he took lessons with Alban Berg (1929-30); upon return to Sweden, he was choirmaster of the Royal Opera in Stockholm (1930-31) and conducted the Swedish Radio orchestra (1937-54); taught at the Royal Academy (1947-59) and was musical director of Uppsala Univ. (1961-65). His early compositions were in a classical spirit, but with time his idiom became increasingly complex; there are also some instances of the application of dodecaphonic procedures in his later compositions.
WORKS: STAGE WORKS: opera, *Prinsessan av Cypern* (*The Princess of Cyprus*, 1930-36; Stockholm, April 29, 1937); an opera-buffa, *Arresten pd Bohus* (*The Arrest at Bohus*, 1938-39); a ballet, *Linden* (1958). FOR ORCH.: 3 symphonies (1927-28, 1936-37, 1945; all 3 later withdrawn from his catalogue); 3 con-

cert overtures (1929, 1934, 1945); *Symphonic Sketch* (1930); *Sinfonietta* for strings (1932); *Little Serenade* for strings (1934); Saxophone Concerto (1934); *Divertimento* for chamber orch. (1935); *Little March* (1936); *Ostinato* (Stockholm, Nov. 24, 1937); *En vintersaga* (*A Winter Tale*), suite (1937); *Pastoral Suite* (1938); *The Earth Sings*, symph. poem (1940); *The Land of Sweden*, suite (1941); *Gustavian Suite* for flute, harpsichord and strings (1943); Cello Concerto (1947); *Music for Orchestra* (1948-49); Violin Concerto (1952); 12 concertinos, with string orch., for solo instruments: flute, oboe, clarinet, bassoon, horn, trumpet, trombone, violin, viola, cello, double bass and piano (1953-57); *Adagio* for strings (1960); *3 Pieces* (1960); *Orchestral Variations* (1962); *Lyric Fantasy* for small orch. (1967); *Due Auguri* (1971); *Barococo*, suite (1973). VOCAL MUSIC: *Förklädd gud* (*The Disguised God*), a lyric suite for narrator, soprano, baritone, chorus and orch. (1940); *Väktarsånger* (*Watchman's Songs*) for narrator, baritone, male chorus and orch. (1940); *Missa Brevis* for a cappella chorus (1954); *Intrada Solemnis* for 2 choruses, boys' chorus, winds and organ (1964); *Soluret och urnan* (*The Sundial and the Urn*), cantata (1965-66). CHAMBER MUSIC: Violin Sonatina (1928); *Duo* for violin and viola (1931); *Intimate Miniatures* for string quartet (1938); 3 string quartets (1944, 1955, 1975); *Quattro Tempi*, a divertimento for wind quintet (1968); Cello Sonatina (1969); *3 Pieces* for clarinet and piano (1970); *Aubade* for oboe, violin, and cello (1972). PIANO MUSIC: 3 sonatinas (1936, 1947, 1950); *Croquiser* (1947); *7 Little Preludes and Fugues* (1969).

La Rue, Jan (full Christian name **Adrian Jan Pieters**), eminent American musicologist; b. in Kisaran, Sumatra, July 31, 1918, of native American parentage (his ancestor was a French Huguenot who fled first to the Palatinate and then came to America, landing in Massachusetts in 1670; LaRue's parents spent three years in Indonesia, where his father served as a botanist and developed a basic budding process used on rubber trees). He studied at Harvard Univ. (Ph.D., 1952) and at Princeton Univ.; taught at Wellesley College; in 1957 became prof. at N.Y. Univ. His dual specialties are 18th-century music and style analysis. He prepared a thematic catalogue of about 10,000 entries on symphonies and instrumental concertos of the classic period; contributed to various publications a number of original articles bringing informing light on obscure subjects. His most important papers include: "Native Music in Okinawa," *Musical Quarterly* (April 1946); "The Okinawan Notation System," *Journal of the American Musicological Society* (1951); "Die Datierung von Wasserzeichen im 18. Jahrhundert," *Kongress-Bericht*, Mozart-Jahr, 1956 (also in English, "Watermarks and Musicology," *Acta Musicologica*, 1961). He publ. *Guidelines for Style Analysis* (N.Y., 1970); was editor of the *Report of the Eighth Congress of the International Musicological Society, New York 1961* (Kassel, 1961); co-editor of the Festschrift for Otto Erich Deutsch (Kassel, 1963) and of the Festschrift for Gustave Reese (N.Y., 1965). In 1966-68 he was president of the American Musicological Society.

La Rue, Pierre de (Petrus Platensis, Pierchon, Pierson, Pierzon, Perisone, Pierazon de la Ruellien), eminent

Netherlands contrapuntist and composer; b. in all probability between 1455 and 1460, in Tournai, where his family is known to have resided; d. Courtrai, Nov. 20, 1518. He was at the court of Burgundy (1477); a singer at the Cathedral of Siena from 1482-85; attached to the chapel of Archduke Maximilian of Austria (April 1485), and the chapel of Notre-Dame in Bois-le-Duc (1490-91); chapel singer at the court of Burgundy (1492-1510); at the court of Margaret of Austria; canon at the court of Philippe le Beau in Malines (1501); prebend at Courtrai, Namur, and Termonde (from 1501); *cantor principis* at Courtrai (1502). He wrote about 33 Masses, of which many were publ.; others are in MS in libraries in Brussels, Malines, Rome, Vienna, Berlin, etc. One of Petrucci's early publications using movable type was 7 "Misse Petri de La Rue" issued at Venice in 1503. Motets and chansons were printed in collections of the time. A motet was scored by Dreher in his *Cantiones sacrae* (1872); Mass *Ave Maria* was publ. by H. Expert in *Les Maîtres-Musiciens de la renaissance française* (1890); a Kyrie in A. Schering, *Geschichte der Musik in Beispielen* (no. 65); some motets in R. J. van Maldeghem, *Trésor musical* (1865-93); motets and a Requiem in F. Blume, *Das Chorwerk* (vols. 11 and 91); 3 Masses in *Monumenta musicae belgicae* 8.
BIBLIOGRAPHY: A. W. Ambros, *Geschichte der Musik* (vol. 3, p. 234 ff.); P. Wagner, *Geschichte der Messe* (p. 166ff.); K. E. Roediger, *Die geistlichen Musikhandschriften der Universitäts-Bibliothek Jena* (1935); H. Riemann, *Handbuch der Musikgeschichte* (vol. 2, p. 286ff.); Josef Robyns, *Pierre de la Rue* (Brussels, 1954; in Flemish); G. Reese, *Music in the Renaissance* (N.Y., 1954); M. Staehelin, "Pierre de la Rue in Italien," *Archiv für Musikwissenschaft* (April-June 1970).

La Salette, Joubert de, French theorist; b. Grenoble, Sept. 4, 1743; d. there, Feb. 4, 1833. He wrote *Sténographie musicale* (1805; an unsuccessful invention on the lines of German tablature); *Considérations sur les divers systèmes de la musique ancienne et moderne* (1810; his best work); *De la notation musicale en général, et en particulier de celle du système grec* (1817); *De la fixité et de l'invariabilité des sons musicaux* (1824); and other essays.

Lasalle, Jean-Louis. See **Lassalle, Jean Louis.**

Laserna, Blas, Spanish composer; b. Corella, Navarre, Feb. 4, 1751; d. Madrid, Aug. 8, 1816. He was official musician for several theaters; composed the music for Ramón de la Cruz's comedy *El café de Barcelona* (Barcelona, Nov. 4, 1788); also the operas *La gitanilla por amor* (Madrid, 1791; successful) and *Idomeneo* (Madrid, Dec. 9, 1792); incidental music to plays of Calderón, Lope de Vega, Moreto, etc.; composed many *tonadillas, sainetes,* etc.

Las Infantas, Fernando de. See **Infantas, Fernando de las.**

Láska, Gustav, Bohemian composer and double-bass player; b. Prague, Aug. 23, 1847; d. Schwerin, Oct. 16, 1928. He studied at the Prague Cons. with Hrabe,

Kittl, and Krejči. Following a year of giving double-bass concerts, he joined the court orch. in Kassel (1868-72); then in Sondershausen (1872-75); was theater conductor in Göttingen, Eisleben, and Halberstadt; played double bass in Berlin; in 1878, became double-bass player in the court orch. in Schwerin.
WORKS: an opera, *Der Kaisersoldat;* a cantata, *Deutsches Aufgebot;* 2 symphonies; 2 overtures; Double-Bass Concerto; 3 Masses; several works for double bass and piano (3 *Romanzen, Rhapsodie, Erotik, Ballade und Polonaise, Schlummerlied, Karneval von Venedig,* etc.); piano pieces; songs.

Lasner, Ignaz, cellist; b. Drosau, Bohemia, Aug. 8, 1815; d. Vienna, Aug. 18, 1883. He studied with Goltermann in Prague, and Merk and Servais in Vienna. He was an orchestra player in Vienna; composed cello pieces.

Lassalle, Jean-Louis, French baritone; b. Lyons, Dec. 14, 1847; d. Paris, Sept. 7, 1909. After training in industrial designing and painting, he entered the Paris Cons. to study voice; also studied privately with Novelli. In 1869 he sang in Liège, Lille, Toulouse, and Brussels; debut at the Paris Opéra, June 7, 1872; remained there for more then 20 years, with extended leaves of absence during which he toured throughout Europe, Russia, and the U.S. (debut, Metropolitan Opera House, N.Y., Jan. 15, 1892, as Nelusco in *L'Africaine);* remained at the Metropolitan until 1897. He returned to Paris in 1901 and settled there as a singing teacher; in 1903, became prof. at the Paris Cons. His repertory comprised about 60 operas, ranging from Donizetti to Wagner.

Lassen, Eduard, eminent Danish conductor and composer; b. Copenhagen, April 13, 1830; d. Weimar, Jan. 15, 1904. His family moved to Brussels when he was a child; he entered the Brussels Cons., taking the Belgian Prix de Rome (1851). Following a tour through Germany and Italy, he went to Weimar, where Liszt fostered the presentation of his 5-act opera *Landgraf Ludwigs Brautfahrt* (1857). He became court music director in Weimar (1858); then conductor of the Weimar Opera (1860-95); led the world première of Saint-Saëns' opera *Samson et Dalila* (Weimar, Dec. 2, 1877). He also wrote the operas *Frauenlob* (Weimar, 1860) and *Le Captif* (Brussels, April 24, 1865); a ballet, *Diana;* 2 symphonies; *Fest-Cantate;* 2 overtures; *Te Deum;* a set of *Biblische Bilder,* for chorus and orch.; songs, etc.; also incidental music to *Oedipus* (1874), Hebbel's *Nibelungen,* Goethe's *Faust* (parts 1 and 2; 1876), Scheffel's *Die Linde am Ettersberg* (1878), *Circe* (1881), Goethe's *Pandora* (1886).

Lassus, Ferdinand de, eldest son of **Roland de Lassus;** d. Aug. 27, 1609; musician at Munich court (1583-85); court conductor at Sigmaringen; tenor singer in Munich (1590); went with the court to Landshut (1595) and later became court conductor there. He brought out a book of *Cantiones sacrae suavissimae* (1587; motets); edited, with his brother **Rudolph,** his father's *Magnum opus musicum.*
BIBLIOGRAPHY: H. Delmotte, *Notice biographique*

sur *Roland Delattre* (Valenciennes, 1836; includes biography and list of works of Ferdinand de Lassus).

Lassus, Ferdinand de, son of **Ferdinand** and grandson of **Roland de Lassus;** d. c.1635; studied in Rome (1609); court conductor (1616) and official (1629) under the Duke of Bavaria. Of his works, written for 8 to 16-voiced double choruses in the style made popular by the Venetian school, few remain. He publ. *Apparatus musicus* (motets, Mass, Magnificat, Litany, etc.; 8 voices; 1622).

Lassus, Roland de (Latin, **Orlandus Lassus**; Italian, **Orlando di Lasso**; French, **Roland Delattre),** one of the greatest of the Netherlands composers and one of the foremost contrapuntists of the Renaissance; b. Mons, 1532; d. Munich, June 14, 1594. He was a chorister in the church of St. Nicolas, Mons; his voice was exceptionally beautiful, so that he was kidnapped three times to secure him for other choruses. His parents finally allowed him to enter the service of Ferdinando Gonzaga, viceroy of Sicily (1544); he followed Gonzaga to Palermo and to Milan; at the age of 18, he was placed in the service of Marchese della Terza (1550). From April, 1553 to Dec., 1554 he was chorusmaster at San Giovanni in Laterano. His parents died in 1554; Lassus subsequently joined Cesare Brancaccio, a music lover from Naples; with him he supposedly visited England and France; this visit was of brief duration, if it took place at all. In 1555 he settled in Antwerp. Both socially and artistically, he enjoyed a fine reputation in Antwerp, despite his youth; he had his first works printed in Venice (1555), containing 22 madrigals to poems of Petrarch; in the same year, he publ. in Antwerp a collection of madrigals and motets to words in Italian, French, and Latin. In 1556 he was offered a highly desirable post at the court of Albert V of Bavaria, and settled in Munich; in 1558 he married an aristocratic lady, Regina Wechinger. He remained in Munich for 38 years, until his death, with the exception of a trip to Italy (1567-68), which he undertook to engage musicians and singers for the Bavarian court, and a further visit to Paris in 1571. He brought Giovanni Gabrieli to Munich in 1575. On Dec. 7, 1570 he received from the Emperor Maximilian a hereditary rank of nobility. His last journey was to Regensburg a year before his death. Lassus represents the culmination of the great era of Franco-Flemish polyphony; his superlative mastery in sacred as well as secular music renders him one of the most versatile composers of his time; he was equally capable of writing in the most elevated style and in the popular idiom; his art was supranational; he wrote Italian madrigals, German lieder, French chansons, and Latin motets. Musicians of his time described him variously as the "Belgian Orpheus" and the "Prince of Music." The sheer scope of his production is amazing; he left more than 2000 works in various genres. The *Patrocinium musices* (1573-98), a 12-volume series published in Munich by Adam Berg, under ducal patronage, contains 7 vols. of Lassus' works: vols. I, 21 motets; vol. II, 5 Masses; vol. III, Offices; vol. IV, a Passion, vigils, etc.; vol. V, 10 Magnificats; vol. VII, 13 Magnificats; vol. VIII, 6 Masses. Lassus' sons publ. 516 of his motets under the title *Magnum opus musicum* (1604). Eitner publ.

Chronologisches Verzeichnis der Druckwerke des Orlando di Lassus (Berlin, 1874). The publication of his collected works was issued by Breitkopf & Härtel of Leipzig (21 vols., 1894-1926), under the editorship of Haberl and Sandberger; a new series was begun in 1956 (12 vols. completed as of 1977) by the Bärenreiter Verlag under the editorship of W. Boetticher, who also publ. a complete catalogue of works (Berlin, 1956). Various works are contained in vols. 13, 34, 37, 41, and 48 of *Das Chorwerk,* and there are a considerable number in the catalogues of leading publishers.

BIBLIOGRAPHY: H. Delmotte, *Notice biographique sur Roland Delattre connu sous le nom d'Orland de Lassus* (Valenciennes, 1836); A. Mathieu, *Biographie de Roland de Lattre* (Mons, 1851); *Register für die Geschichte der Musik in Bayern,* ed. by D. Mettenleiter (Brixen, 1868); W. Bäumker, *Orlandus de Lassus, der letzte grosse Meister der niederländischen Tonschule* (Freiburg, 1878); J. Declève, *Roland de Lassus: sa vie et ses œuvres* (Mons, 1894); F. X. Haberl, "Synchronistische Tabelle über den Lebensgang von Giovanni Pierluigi da Palestrina und Orlando di Lasso," *Kirchenmusikalisches Jahrbuch* 9 (1894); A. Sandberger, *Beiträge zur Geschichte der bayrischen Hofkapelle* (vols. I and III; Leipzig, 1894); E. Destouches, *Orlando di Lasso: ein Lebensbild* (Munich, 1894); E. Schmitz, *Orlando di Lasso* (Leipzig, 1915); E. Closson, *Roland de Lassus* (1919); R. Casimiri, *Orlando di Lasso, maestro di cappella al Laterano nel 1553* (Rome, 1920); Charles Van den Borren, *Orlande de Lassus* (Paris, 1920); A. Sandberger, *Ausgewählte Aufsätze* (Munich, 1921); A. Sandberger, *Orlando di Lasso und die geistigen Strömungen seiner Zeit* (Munich, 1926); Charles Van den Borren, *En quelle année Roland de Lassus est-il né?* (The Hague, 1926); E. Lowinsky, *Der Motettenstil Orlando di Lassos* (Heidelberg, 1933); L. Behr, *Die deutschen Gesänge Orlando di Lassos* (Erlangen, 1935); E. Lowinsky, *Das Antwerpener Motettenbuch Orlando di Lassos und seine Beziehungen zum Motettenschaffen der niederländischen Zeitgenossen* (The Hague, 1937); Lucie Balmer, *Orlando di Lassos Motetten* (Berne, 1938); J. Huschke, *Orlando di Lassos Messen* (Leipzig, 1941); F. Blume, "Lasso und Palestrina," *Deutsche Musikkultur* 9 (1944); C. Van den Borren, *Roland de Lassus* (1944); A. Einstein, *The Italian Madrigal* (Princeton, 1949); G. Reese, *Music in the Renaissance* (N.Y., 1954); W. Boetticher, *Orlando di Lasso* (2 vols., Berlin, 1956; contains complete list of works); Horst Leuchtmann, *Die musikalischen Wortausdeutungen in den Motetten des Magnum Opus Musicum von Orlando di Lasso* (Strasbourg, 1959); Horst Leuchtmann, *Orlando di Lasso, Sein Leben; Briefe* (2 vols., Wiesbaden, 1977).

Lassus, Rudolph de, organist and composer; son of **Roland de Lassus;** d. Munich, 1625. He was a musician in the court orch. at Munich from 1585 until his death; was an organist and composer of merit and repute; various works were publ.; 3 Masses and 3 Magnificats are in MS in Munich. Two motets are included in Proske's *Musica divina* (vol. I). With his brother Ferdinand he edited his father's *Magnum opus musicum.*

BIBLIOGRAPHY: H. Delmotte, *Notice biographique sur Roland Delattre connu sous le nom d'Orland de*

Lassus (Valenciennes, 1836; includes biography and list of works).

László, Alexander, Hungarian composer; b. Budapest, Nov. 22, 1895; studied at the Budapest Academy with A. Szendy (piano) and Herzfeld (composition); in 1915 he went to Berlin; was active as a pianist; also worked on the radio and in film enterprises. In 1938 he emigrated to the U.S.; in 1945, settled in Hollywood. He cultivated the idea of music expressed through colors; introduced a specially constructed "color pianoforte" *(Farblichtklavier)* at the Kiel music festival (June 14, 1925); for the projection of the colors corresponding to music in proportional wave lengths he invented the Sonchromatoscope and a new system of notation called Sonchromography. His book *Die Farblichtmusik* (1925) discusses this new technique. His works include, besides special compositions for color lights, the pantomimes *Marionetten* (Budapest, 1916), *Die schöne O-sang* (Hamburg, 1919), *Panoptikum,* etc.; *News of the Day, Hungarian Dance Suite,* and *Fantasy of Colors,* for piano; *Mechanized Forces,* for orch.; *Hollywood Concerto* and *The Ghost Train of Marshall Pass,* for piano and orch.; arrangements for piano of various works by classical composers; film music. His sophisticated ideas about music and color found a fertile ground in Hollywood, where he supplied many musical scores to television; also wrote a musical, *Wanted: Sexperts and Serpents for Our Garden of Maidens* (1968); *Pacific Triptych* for orch. (1962) and a symph. fantasy *Roulette hématologique* (1969).

Latham, William Peters, American composer; b. Shreveport, Louisiana, Jan. 4, 1917. He attended the Cons. of Music in Cincinnati, where he studied trumpet; then took courses in composition at the Eastman School of Music, Rochester, with Herbert Elwell and Howard Hanson. He served in the U.S. Army as a Cavalry Bandsman and later as Infantry Platoon Leader, and was in active combat in Germany in 1945. Returning to America, he was on the faculty of Iowa State Teacher's College (1946-65); in 1965 was appointed prof. of music at North Texas State Univ., Denton. As a composer he excels in sacred choruses; in his concert band music he boldly experiments with modern techniques, as exemplified by his *Dodecaphonic Set,* and most spectacularly in *Fusion,* in which he endeavors to translate the process of atomic fusion into musical terms through an ingenious application of asymmetrical rhythms.

WORKS: *The Lady of Shalott,* symph. poem (Cincinnati, March 7, 1941); *Fantasy* for violin and orch. (1946); Symph. No. 1 (Rochester, N.Y., April 25, 1950); Symph. No. 2 (1953). For concert band: *Proud Heritage,* concert march (his most popular work, 1955); *Plymouth Variations* (1962); *Escapades* (1965); *Dionysian Festival* (1966); *Dodecaphonic Set* (1966); *Prayers in Space* (1971); *The Music Makers,* with chorus and rock group (1972); *Dilemmae* (1973); *Prolegomena* (1974); *Revolution!* (1975); *Fusion* (1975; New Orleans, April 12, 1976). Chamber music: 3 string quartets (1938-40); 3 string trios (1938-39); *Fantasy Concerto* for flute and strings (1941); *5 Pieces* for solo clarinet (1941; later renamed "5 Atonal Studies");

Sonata for oboe and piano (1947); Violin Sonata (1949); Suite for trumpet and strings (1951); *Sisyphus* for alto saxophone and piano (1971); *Preludes Before Silence,* 9 pieces for solo flute and piccolo (1974). Vocal works: *Peace* for chorus and orch. (1943); *Prayer after World War* for chorus a cappella (1945); *Prophecy of Peace* for chorus and orch. (1952); several settings of psalms and other religious texts; also overtures and concert marches; songs; piano pieces.

Latilla, Gaetano, Italian composer; b. Bari, Jan. 21, 1711; d. Naples, Jan. 15, 1788. As a child, he sang in the choir of the cathedral in Bari; then studied at the Conservatorio di Sant' Onofrio in Naples. He was 2nd maestro di cappella at Santa Maria Maggiore in Rome from 1738-41, when illness forced him to return to Naples; in 1756 he became chorusmaster at the Conservatorio della Pietà in Venice; 1762, 2nd maestro di cappella at St. Mark's in Venice. In 1772 Latilla again returned to Naples, where he remained until his death. He wrote about 50 operas, including *Li mariti a forza* (Naples, 1732); *Angelica ed Orlando* (Naples, 1735); *Gismòndo* (Naples, 1737; also known as *La finta giardiniera;* perf. as *Don Colascione* in London, 1749); *Madama Ciana* (Rome, 1738; perf. as *Gli artigiani arrichiti* in London, 1750, and in Paris, 1753); *I sposi incogniti* (Naples, 1779); also the oratorio *L'onnipotenza e la misericordia divina;* 6 string quartets; church music; etc.

La Tombelle, Fernand de, French organist and composer; b. Paris, Aug. 3, 1854; d. Château de Fayrac, Dordogne, Aug. 13, 1928. He first studied with his mother; then at the Paris Cons. with Guilmant (organ) and Dubois (composition); also with Saint-Saëns. From 1885-98 he was assistant organist at the Madeleine; 1896-1904, prof. of theory at the Schola Cantorum.

WORKS: the oratorios *Crux, L'Abbaye,* and *Jeanne d'Arc;* operettas *Un bon numéro* and *Un Rêve au pays du bleu* (1892); ballets *La Muse fleurie* and *La Roche aux Fées;* orchestral suites *Impressions matinales, Livres d'images, Tableaux musicaux, Suite féodale;* symph. poem *Antar;* cantatas *Ste.-Cécile* and *Ste.-Anne;* incidental music to *La Magdaléenne, Yannic, Conte bleu;* chamber music (quartets, trios, sonatas for violin and piano); a Mass; numerous sacred choruses; works for organ; songs. He also wrote a method for the harmonium.

Lattuada, Felice, Italian composer; b. Caselle di Morimondo, Milan, Feb. 5, 1882; d. Milan, Nov. 2, 1962. He studied at the Milan Cons. with Ferroni, graduating in 1911.

WORKS: the operas *La tempestà* (Milan, Nov. 23, 1922), *Sandha* (Genoa, Feb. 21, 1924), *Le preziose ridicole* (Milan, Feb. 9, 1929), *Don Giovanni* (Naples, May 18, 1929), *La caverna di Salamanca* (Genoa, March 1, 1938), *Caino* (Milan, Jan. 10, 1957); *Canto augurale per la Nazione Eletta,* for tenor, chorus, and orch.; orchestral works: *Sinfonia romantica* (1911); *Cimitero di guerra; Il mistero della Passione di Cristo; Incanti della notte; Divertimento rustico; Prelude and Fugue;* other choral, orchestral, and chamber works; also music for films.

Laub, Ferdinand, Austrian violinist and composer; b. Prague, Jan. 19, 1832; d. Gries, near Bozen, Tyrol, March 18, 1875. A precocious violinist, he entered the Prague Cons. as a child; under the patronage of the Grand Duke Stephen, he went to Vienna for further study (1847); then made a German tour, visited Paris, and played in London; 1853, concertmaster at Weimar; in 1855, leader of the court orch. in Berlin; 1855-57, taught at the Stern Cons. After spending some time in Vienna (1862-65), he went on a Russian tour, following which he became prof. of violin at the Moscow Cons. (1866). He spent his last years in Karlsbad and Tyrol. He wrote an opera, *Die Griesbäcker;* brought out 2 collections of Czech melodies; publ. violin pieces.

BIBLIOGRAPHY: B. Šich, *Ferdinand Laub* (Prague, 1951).

Lauber, Joseph, Swiss composer; b. Ruswil, Canton Lucerne, Dec. 27, 1864; d. Geneva, May 28, 1952. He studied in Zürich with Hegar, in Munich with Rheinberger, and in Paris with Massenet and Diémer. Returning to Switzerland, he taught at the Zürich Cons.; then conducted a theater orch. in Geneva (1905-07). He wrote more than 200 compositions, including the opera *Die Hexe;* oratorio *Ad gloriam Dei;* 6 symphonies, and other orchestral works; 5 concertos (including one for double bass with orch.); chamber works; choral music; piano pieces; songs; etc.

Launis, Armas Emanuel (real name **Lindberg**), Finnish musicologist and composer; b. Hämeenlinna (Tavastehus), April 22, 1884; d. Nice, Aug. 7, 1959. He studied composition with Sibelius in Helsinki; took courses at the Univ. of Helsinki with Ilmari Krohn; earned his doctorate with the valuable thesis *Über Art, Entstehung und Verbreitung der Estnisch-Finnischen Runenmelodien* (Helsinki, 1913). In 1930 he settled in Nice.

WORKS: operas *Seitsemän veljestä* (The 7 Brothers; Helsinki, April 11, 1913), *Kullervo* (Helsinki, Feb. 28, 1917), *Aslak Hetta* (Helsinki, 1922), *Noidan laulu* (The Sorcerer's Song; 1932), *Lumottu silkkihuivi (The Magic Silk Kerchief;* 1937), *Jehudith* (1940); 2 cantatas (1906 and 1910); *Andante Religioso,* for violin and orch. (1932); *Northern Suite,* for violin and orch. (1950); *Karelian Suite,* for orch. (1952); piano quintet and other chamber music; piano pieces; songs.

Laurence, Frederick, English composer; b. London, May 25, 1884. After beginning his career in business, he studied music privately with Josef Holbrooke; also in Germany, France, and Austria. Returning to London, he was for a while active in both music publishing and organization.

WORKS: for orch.: *The Spirit's Wayfaring* (London, Oct. 2, 1918), *The Dance of the Witch Girl* (London, Oct. 12, 1920), *A Miracle, Enchantment, Fire Earth, Milandor, Night, The Dream of Harlequin, The Passionate Quest, The Gate of Vision;* chamber music; piano pieces.

Laurencie, Lionel de la. See **La Laurencie, Lionel de.**

Laurencin, Ferdinand Peter, Bohemian writer on music; b. Kremsier, Moravia, Oct. 15, 1819; d. Vienna, Feb. 5, 1890. He studied in Prague with Tomaschek and Pitsch; subsequently settled in Vienna as a writer; publ. the essays *Zur Geschichte der Kirchenmusik bei den Italienern und Deutschen* (1856), *Das Paradies und die Peri von R. Schumann* (1859), *Dr. Hanslicks Lehre vom Musikalisch-Schönen: Eine Abwehr* (1859), and *Die Harmonik der Neuzeit* (1861); also contributed articles to the *Neue Zeitschrift für Musik,* which printed a biographical sketch of him by J. Schucht after his death (1890).

Laurens, Edmond, French composer and pedagogue; b. Bergerac, Nov. 10, 1852; d. Paris, Nov. 27, 1925. He studied with Guiraud at the Paris Cons.; later became teacher of harmony and composition there.

WORKS: *La Harpe et le glaive,* grand opera; *Les Amours d'un soldat de plomb,* pantomime; *La Neuvaine,* lyric play; other works for the stage: (*Irlande, Conte d'amour, Roses d'automne); Suite Japonaise* for orch.; *Silhouettes* for piano and orch.; piano pieces; numerous songs. He also was the author of the manuals, *Cours d'enseignement musical pianistique* and *L'Art du Correcteur.*

Laurenti, Bartolomeo Girolamo, Italian violinist and composer; b. Bologna, c.1644; d. there, Jan. 18, 1726. He played violin at the Basilica San Petronio; was one of the earliest members of the Accademia Filarmonica in Bologna. He wrote *Sonate per camera a violino e violoncello* (1691); *Sei concerti a 3, cioè violino, violoncello ed organo* (1720); a sonata for violin and continuo; etc.

Laurischkus, Max, German composer; b. Insterburg, Feb. 18, 1876; d. Berlin, Nov. 17, 1929. He studied with Bargiel and Herzogenberg at the Hochschule für Musik in Berlin. He wrote *Zug des Todes,* for chorus and orch.; Cello Concerto; *Konzertstück* for violin and orch.; *Pastorale* for "Mustel" harmonium and celesta; choruses for women's voices; etc.

Lauri-Volpi, Giacomo, Italian tenor; b. Lanuvio, near Rome, Dec. 11, 1892. He studied law; then went to Rome where he took singing lessons with Enrico Rosati. He made his debut in Viterbo in 1919; then sang in the opera houses in Florence and at La Scala in Milan. He made his first American appearance at the Metropolitan Opera House in New York, on Jan. 26, 1923 as the Duke in *Rigoletto;* remained a member of the Metropolitan until 1934, while filling guest engagements at Covent Garden in London, the Paris Opera and at the Teatro Colón in Buenos Aires. In 1934 he returned to Europe, and lived mostly in Burjasot, near Valencia. During World War II he continued to sing in Spain in concert and in opera, and in a remarkable demonstration of his professional mettle, he sang an aria of Calaf from Puccini's opera *Turandot* at the Teatro Liceo in Barcelona in 1972, at the age of 80. He publ. several books of reminiscences, among them *L'equivovo* (Milan, 1930); *Cristalli viventi* (Rome, 1948); *A visa aperto* (Milan, 1953); 2 books on voices of the present and past, *Voci paralele* (Milan, 1955) and *Misteri della voce umana* (Milan, 1957).

BIBLIOGRAPHY: A. Gustarelli, *Chi è Giacomo Lauri-Volpi?* (Milan, 1932).

Lauro, Antonio, Venezuelan guitarist and composer; b. Ciudad Bolívar, Aug. 3, 1917. He studied in Caracas; became a proficient guitar player; was soloist in the first performance of his Guitar Concerto (Caracas, July 25, 1956). He wrote many pieces for guitar, a choral symph. poem *Cantacharo,* several symph. suites, choruses and songs.

Lauska, Franz (Seraphinus Ignatius), Bohemian pianist and composer; b. Brünn, Jan. 13, 1764; d. Berlin, April 18, 1825. He studied in Vienna with Albrechtsberger; was chamber musician in Munich; 1794-98, taught in Copenhagen; settled in Berlin in 1798; became a teacher at the court; among his pupils was Meyerbeer. He wrote 24 sonatas *(Grande sonate, Sonate pathétique,* etc.); Cello Sonata; 4-hand pieces *(6 Easy and Agreeable Pieces, Polonaise,* etc.); rondos, variations for 2 hands, etc.

Lauterbach, Johann Christoph, German violinist and composer; b. Culmbach, July 24, 1832; d. Dresden, March 28, 1918. He studied in Würzburg with Bratsch and Fröhlich; then at the Brussels Cons. with Bériot and Fétis, receiving a gold medal in 1851; taught violin there; 1853, prof. of violin and concertmaster at the Munich Cons.; 1861, at the court orch. in Dresden; also head of the violin dept. of the Dresden Cons. (1861-77). He wrote a *Cavatine* for violin and orch.; *Capriccio* for violin and orch.; works for violin and piano *(Zwei Konzertetüden, Legende, Allegro scherzoso, Polonaise, Tarentelle,* etc.).

Lavagne, André, French composer; b. Paris, July 12, 1913. He studied at the Paris Cons.; won first prize in piano (1933), Premier Second Grand Prix de Rome (1938); in 1941, appointed inspector of music in Paris schools.
WORKS: the operas, *Comme ils s'aiment* (Paris, 1941) and *Corinne* (Enghiens-les-Bains, 1956); *Concert dans un parc,* for piano and orch., inspired by Watteau's painting (1941); *Concerto romantique,* for cello and orch. (1941); *Nox,* symph. poem for voice and orch.; *Spectacle rassurant,* for voice and orch.; several ballets *(Le Pauvre Jongleur, Kermesse,* etc.).
BIBLIOGRAPHY: A. Machabey, *Portraits de trente musiciens français* (Paris, 1949; pp. 115-19).

Lavagnino, Angelo Francesco, Italian composer; b. Genoa, Feb. 22, 1909. He studied with Renzo Rossi and Vito Frazzi at the Milan Cons., graduating in 1933; from 1948 to 1962 he was prof. of film music at the Accademia Musicale in Siena.
WORKS: opera *Malafonte* (Antwerp, 1952); for orch.: *Volo d'api* (1932); *Tempo alto* (1938); Violin Concerto (1941); Piano Quintet (1942); Violin Sonata (1943); *Pocket Symphony* (title in English; 1949).

Lavallée, Calixa, Canadian pianist and composer; b. Verchères, Quebec, Dec. 28, 1842; d. Boston, Jan. 21, 1891. He first studied with his father; then at the Paris Cons. with Marmontel (piano), and Bazin and Boieldieu *fils* (composition). Returning to Canada, he made

tours of his native country and the U.S.; took part in the Civil War; in 1881, soloist in the company of Mme. Gerster, the German singer. He wrote the music to the Canadian national song *O Canada* (first perf. in Montreal, June 24, 1880; poem by Judge Routhier). He subsequently settled in Boston, where he became instructor at the Petersilea Academy; wrote a comic opera, *The Widow* (Springfield, Ill., March 25, 1882).
BIBLIOGRAPHY: S. Salter, "Early Encouragement to American Composers," *Musical Quarterly* (Jan. 1932); E. Lapierre, *C. Lavallée, Musicien National du Canada* (Montreal, 1937).

Lavalle-García, Armando, Mexican composer; b. Ocotlán, Jalisco, Nov. 23, 1924. He studied violin at the National Cons. of Music in Mexico City and took courses in composition with Bernal Jiménez, Revueltas, and Rodolfo Halffter; subsequently played the viola with the National Symph. Orch. of Mexico City and conducted the Xalapa Symph. Orch. His music is permeated with the essence of Mexican folklore, even in pieces of ostensibly abstract connotations.
WORKS: 3 ballets: *La Canción de los Buenos Principios* (1957), *3 Tiempos de Amor* (1958) and *Corrido* (1959); *Mi Viaje,* symph. poem (1950); *Estructuras geométricas* for string orch. and percussion (1960); Concerto for Viola and String Orch. (1965); Concerto for Violin, String Orch. and Percussion (1966); *Divertimento* for wind quintet (1953); Violin Sonata (1966); Oboe Sonata (1967); *Potencial* for Spanish guitar, psaltery, harp and percussion (1967); *Trígonos* for flute, clarinet and bassoon (1968); Trio for oboe, bassoon, and cello, with percussion accompaniment (1969).

Lavigna, Vincenzo, Italian composer and eminent music teacher; b. Altamura, Feb. 21, 1776; d. Milan, Sept. 14, 1836. He studied at the Cons. di Santa Maria di Loreto in Naples; subsequently went to Milan, where he was "maestro al cembalo" at La Scala until 1832; also prof. of solfeggio at the Milan Cons.; he was a teacher of Verdi. He wrote 10 operas, of which his first, *La muta per amore, ossia Il medico per forza* (Milan, 1803), was his best; also 2 ballets.
BIBLIOGRAPHY: G. De Napoli, *La Triade Melodrammatica Altamurana: G. Tritto, V. Lavigna, S. Mercadante* (Milan, 1931; pp. 47-66).

Lavignac, (Alexandre Jean) Albert, eminent French musicologist and pedagogue; b. Paris, Jan. 21, 1846; d. there, May 28, 1916. He studied at the Paris Cons. with Marmontel (piano), Bazin and Benoist (harmony), and A. Thomas (composition), winning first prize for *solfège* in 1857, 1st for piano in 1861, 1st for harmony and accompaniment in 1863, 1st for counterpoint and fugue in 1864, 2nd for organ in 1865; appointed assistant prof. of *solfège* there (1871); prof. of *solfège* (1875); prof. of harmony (1891).
WRITINGS: His *Cours complet théorique de dictée musicale* (6 vols., 1882) attracted considerable attention and led to the introduction of musical dictation as a regular subject in all important European conservatories; followed (1900) by *Dictées musicales* (additional exercises). His *magnum opus* was the famous *Encyclopédie de la musique et Dictionnaire du Con-*

servatoire, which he edited from 1913 until his death. Other works: *Solfèges manuscrits* (6 vols.); *50 Leçons d'harmonie; École de la Pédale du piano* (1889); *La Musique et les musiciens* (1895; 8th edition, 1910; entirely revised, 1950; English transl. with additions on American music by H. E. Krehbiel, 1899); *Le Voyage artistique à Bayreuth* (1897; English transl. as *The Music Dramas of Richard Wagner*, 1898); *Les Gaîtés du Conservatoire* (1900); *L'Éducation musicale* (1902; English transl., 1903); *Notions scolaires de musique* (1905; Spanish transl., 1906); *Théorie complète des principes fondamentaux de la musique moderne* (1909). Lavignac's compositions (chiefly for the piano) are of little importance; together with T. Lack, he publ. arrangements for 2 pianos of Beethoven's Symphonies No. 1 and 2.

Lavigne, Antoine-Joseph, French oboist; b. Besançon, France, March 23, 1816; d. Manchester, Aug. 1, 1886. He studied at the Paris Cons.; settled in England in 1841; played in the Drury Lane Promenade Concerts; then in Hallé's Manchester orch. He applied Böhm's ring-key system to the oboe. In his later years he became destitute and died in the poorhouse at Manchester.

La Violette, Wesley, American composer; b. St. James, Minn., Jan. 4, 1894. He studied at Northwestern Univ. and at Chicago Musical College (M.M.; Mus. Doc., 1925); taught at Chicago Musical College (1923-33); in 1940 he went to California and lived in La Jolla.
WORKS: the opera *Shylock* (1927; awarded the David Bispham Memorial Medal, 1930; excerpts performed, Chicago, Feb. 9, 1930); an opera on the life of Buddha, *The Enlightened One* (1955); Symph. No. 1 (Rochester, Oct. 19, 1938); Symph. No. 2, subtitled *Miniature,* or *Tom Thumb Symphony* (Chicago, May 25, 1942); *The Song of the Angels,* choral symph. (1952); cantata, *The Road to Calvary* (1952); 2 violin concertos (1929; 1938); *Penetrella,* for divided strings, 18 parts (Chicago, Nov. 30, 1928); *Osiris,* an Egyptian tone poem (1929); *Chorale* for large orch. (Chicago, July 31, 1936); *Music from the High Sierras* (San Francisco, March 4, 1941); Concertino for flute and orch. (1943); 3 string quartets; Piano Quintet (1927); Octet (1937); Sextet for piano, flute, oboe, clarinet, bassoon, and horn (1940); Flute Quintet (1943); Flute Sontata, 2 violin sonatas, viola sonata, piano sonata, etc. He is the author of several publications on philosophy and religion: *The Creative Light* (N.Y., 1947), *The Wayfarer* (Los Angeles, 1956), etc. His book *The Crown of Wisdom* (Bombay, 1960) was nominated for the Nobel Prize in literature.

Lavista, Mario, Mexican composer of the extreme avant-garde; b. Mexico City, April 3, 1943. He studied harmony with Rodolfo Halffter and composition with Héctor Quintanar; then attended classes and seminars of Stockhausen, Pousseur, Xenakis and Ligeti in Darmstadt and Cologne. Returning to Mexico in 1970, he founded "Quanta," an improvisational music group. In his music he explores all resources of sound, and all idiomatic textures, from deliberate homophony to horrendous explosions of ear-splitting dissonance.

WORKS: *Monologue,* after Gogol's *Diary of a Madman,* for baritone, flute, vibraphone and double bass (1966); *5 Pieces* for string quartet (1967); *Divertimento* for wind quintet, 5 woodblocks and 3 short-wave radios (1968); *Homage to Samuel Beckett* for 3 amplified choruses (1968); *Diacronia* for string quartet (1969); *Kronos* for a minimum of 15 alarm clocks, and loudspeakers and tapes, with an indeterminate chronometric duration of 5 to 1,440 minutes (1969); *Piece for One Pianist and One Piano* (1970; also a version called *Piece for Two Pianists and Two Pianos,* in which a second pianist maintains an absolute silence that must be "communicated" to the listeners); *Game* for solo flute (1970); *Continuo* for brass, percussion, 2 prepared pianos and strings (1970); Trio, for 2 string instruments and ring modulator (1972); *Diafonia* for one performer on 2 pianos and percussion (1973); *Cluster* for piano (1973); *Antinomia* for tape (1973); *Antifonia* for flute, 2 bassoons and percussion (1974); *Dialogos* for violin and piano (1974); *Espejos (Mirrors)* for piano, 4 hands (1975); *Quotations* for cello and piano (1975); *Lyhannh* for orch. (1976; the title is Swift's word for the "swallow" in Part 4 of *Gulliver's Travels);* Piano Trio (1976); *Jaula* for any number of prepared pianos and pianists (1976).

Lavoix, Henri-Marie-François, French writer on music; b. Paris, April 26, 1846; d. there, Dec. 27, 1897. He was graduated from the Sorbonne; then studied harmony and counterpoint with H. Cohen; in 1865, became librarian of the Bibliothèque Nationale; contributed articles to the *Revue et Gazette musicale.*
WRITINGS: *Les Traducteurs de Shakespeare en musique* (1869); *La Musique dans l'ymagerie du moyen-âge* (1875); *La Musique dans la nature* (1873); *Histoire de l'instrumentation* (1878; his chief work); *Le Chant, ses principes et son histoire,* in collaboration with T. Lemaire (1881); *La Musique du siècle de Saint-Louis* (1884); *La Musique française* (1891). His chief work was *Histoire de la musique* (Paris, 1884; reprinted 1891; translated into Spanish and publ. in Buenos Aires in 1943).

Lavrangas, Denis, Greek conductor and composer; b. Argostoli, Cephalonia, Oct. 17, 1864; d. Razata, Cephalonia, July 30, 1941. He studied first in Argostoli with N. Serao (violin) and N. Tzanis (theory); then at the Cons. of San Pietro a Maiella in Naples; and at the Paris Cons. with Delibes, Massenet, and Dubois; conducted an opera company touring through France; went to Italy and conducted theater orchestras in Turin, Venice, etc. Returning to Greece in 1894, he became artistic director of the Philharmonic Society of Athens.
WORKS: the operas *Elda di Vorn* (Naples, 1890), *The Two Brothers* (Athens, July 22, 1900), *The Sorceress* (Athens, 1901), *Dido* (Athens, April 19, 1909; his best work), *Black Butterfly* (Athens, 1928), *Redeemer* (Corfu, 1935), *Facanapas* (1935; performed posthumously, Athens, Dec. 2, 1950); the operettas *White Hair* (Athens, 1915), *Sporting Club* (Athens, 1919); *Ouverture grecque, Suites grecque,* and other works for orch.; 2 Masses; choruses; piano pieces; songs. He also publ. teaching manuals.

Lavry, Marc, significant Israeli composer; b. Riga, Dec. 22, 1903; d. Haifa, March 20, 1967. He studied with Teichmüller at the Leipzig Con.; then was active as conductor in Germany and in Sweden. In 1935 he went to Palestine; in 1951 he was appointed head of the music section of the Jerusalem Broadcasting Service. In 1952 he visited the U.S. His music is imbued with intense feeling for Jewish folk motives. Among his works prior to his going to Palestine, the most notable was *Fantastische Suite* for orch. (1932). He was the composer of the first Palestinian opera in Hebrew that received a stage performance, *Dan Hashomer (Dan the Guard)* which he conducted in Tel Aviv on Feb. 17, 1945; another opera, *Tamar and Judah,* in the form of a series of cantillations with homophonic instrumental accompaniment, composed in 1958, was first performed in concert form, at the Jewish Arts Festival of Congregation Rodeph Sholom in New York, posthumously, March 22, 1970; he further composed *Israeliana I* for orch. (1966); the symph. poems *Stalingrad* and *Emek (The Valley);* 2 piano concertos; many songs and smaller works, *The Song of Emek* having appeared in numerous editions.

Law, Andrew, American singing teacher and composer; b. Milford, Conn., March, 1749; d. Cheshire, Conn., July 13, 1821. He graduated from Rhode Island College, M. A., 1778, then studied theology and was ordained in Hartford (1787); subsequently he was active as a preacher in Philadelphia and Baltimore; later as pioneer singing teacher in New England. He invented a new system of notation, patented in 1802, which employed 4 (later increased to 7) different shapes of notes without the staff; it was not successful and was used in only a few of his own books. A second innovation (at least as far as American usages were concerned) was his setting of the melody in the soprano instead of in the tenor. In 1786 he received an honorary M. A. degree, Yale; 1821, LL. D. from Allegheny College, Meadville, Penna. He compiled *A Select Number of Plain Tunes Adapted to Congregational Worship* (1775); *Select Harmony* (Cheshire, Conn., 1778); *A Collection of Hymns for Social Worship* (Cheshire, 1782); *The Rudiments of Music* (Cheshire, 1783); *The Art of Singing,* in 3 parts, each separately paged: I. *The Musical Primer;* II. *The Christian Harmony;* III. *The Musical Magazine* (Cheshire, 1792-93; 4th ed., Windsor, Vt., 1803; part III contains 6 books of tunes); *Harmonic Companion, and Guide to Social Worship: Being a Choice Selection of Tunes Adapted to the Various Psalms and Hymns* (Philadelphia, 1807); *The Art of Playing the Organ and Pianoforte* (Philadelphia, 1809); *Essays on Music* (Philadelphia, 1814). Only one of his hymn tunes, *Archdale,* acquired some popularity; but his teaching books, quaintly but clearly written, contributed considerably to early music education in America.
BIBLIOGRAPHY: F. J. Metcalf, *American Psalmody* (N.Y., 1917); F. J. Metcalf, *American Writers and Compilers of Sacred Music* (N.Y., 1925); *Dictionary of American Biography* (vol. 11); Richard Crawford, *Andrew Law, American Psalmodist* (Evanston, Ill., 1968).

Lawes, Henry, English composer; brother of **William Lawes;** b. Dinton, Wilts, Jan. 5, 1596; d. London, Oct. 21, 1662. He studied in London with Coperario; in 1626, became Epistler and Gentleman of the Chapel Royal, then clerk; member of the King's private band; also music master to the Earl of Bridgewater; lost appointments during the Protectorate, but was reinstated in 1660. He is interred in the cloisters of Westminster Abbey. He is historically important because his infinite care in setting texts with proper note and accent marked a step in the development of vocal composition which culminated in Purcell.
WORKS: *Coelum Britannicum,* masque (London, Feb. 17, 1634); *Comus,* masque (Sept. 29, 1634); *The Triumphs of Peace,* masque; *A Paraphrase upon the Psalmes of David* (1637); *Choice Psalmes put into Musick for 3 Voices* (1648; includes many compositions by his brother **William Lawes);** *Ayres and Dialogues for 1, 2, and 3 Voices* (3 vols., 1653, 1655, 1658); music to poems by Milton, Herrick, W. Cartwright, Davenant, etc.; songs and anthems in contemporary collections: *The Treasury of Musick* (1669); Clifford's *Divine Services and Anthems* (1664); manuscripts are in the libraries of the British Museum and Christ Church, Oxford.
BIBLIOGRAPHY: *Dictionary of National Biography,* vol. 11 (Oxford, 1921-22); Willa McClung Evans, *Henry Lawes, Musician and Friend of Poets* (N.Y., 1941); E. F. Hart, "Introduction to Henry Lawes," *Music & Letters* (1951); J. G. Demaray, *Milton and the Masque Tradition* (Cambridge, Mass., 1968); A. Davidson, "Milton on the Music of Henry Lawes," *Milton Newsletter* (May 1968); R. J. McGrady, "Henry Lawes and the Concept of just note and accent," *Music & Letters* (Jan. 1969); Pamela J. Willett, *The Henry Lawes Manuscript* (London, 1969); N. C. Carpenter, "Milton and Music: Henry Lawes, Dante, and Casella," *English Literary Renaissance* (1972).

Lawes, William, English composer; brother of **Henry Lawes;** b. Salisbury (baptized May 1), 1602; d. Chester, 1645. He studied with Coperario, London; Musician in Ordinary to Charles I. He was killed in the service of the Royalist Army during the Civil War. He is best known for his part-song *Gather ye rosebuds while ye may;* other works include music to Shirley's *The Triumph of Peace* (with Simon Ives; 1633); *The Triumph of Prince d'Amour* (1635); one of his anthems appears in Boyce's *Cathedral Music;* songs and vocal works in *Select Musicall Ayres and Dialogues* (1653 and 1659); *Catch that catch can* (1652), *The Treasury of Musick* (1669), *Choice Psalms* (1648); instrumental music in *Courtly Masquing Ayres* (1662); *The Royal Consort* (66 short pieces for viols, lutes, etc.), and some *Airs* for violin and bass can be found in the British Museum; his *Great Consort* (6 suites for 2 treble viols, 2 theorbos, and 2 bass viols) is in the library of Christ Church, Oxford; other MSS of his anthems and canons are in the British Museum and the library of Christ Church, Oxford; *Select Consort Music of William Lawes* is publ. in *Musica Britannica* 21.
BIBLIOGRAPHY: *Dictionary of National Biography,* vol. 11; J. Pulver, *A Biographical Dictionary of Old English Music* (1927); R. Erlebach, "William

Lawes," *Proceedings of the Musical Association* (London, 1933).

Lawrence, Marjorie, Australian soprano; b. Dean's March, near Melbourne, Feb. 17, 1909. She studied in Melbourne with Ivor Boustead; then in Paris with Cécile Gilly. In 1932 she made her debut at the Monte Carlo Opera as Elisabeth in *Tannhäuser;* 1932-36, member of the Paris Opéra. She came to the U.S. and made her debut at the Metropolitan Opera House on Dec. 18, 1935 as Brünnhilde in *Die Walküre;* then joined the company; made guest appearances with the Chicago, San Francisco, St. Louis, and Cincinnati Operas, and in Buenos Aires. An attack of infantile paralysis while she was in Mexico (1941) interrupted her career. However, she staged a remarkable return at a concert in N. Y. on Nov. 9, 1942, when she sang reclining upon a couch. She appeared as Venus in *Tannhäuser,* Jan. 22, 1943, sitting in a chair. She subsequently devoted herself to teaching; was prof. of voice at Tulane Univ., Louisiana (1956-60); in 1960 directed an opera class at the Univ. of Southern Illinois. She was awarded a doctor's degree, honoris causa, by Ohio Univ. in 1969. She publ. an autobiography, *Interrupted Melody, The Story of My Life* (N.Y., 1949), which was made into a motion picture in 1955.

Lawrence, William John, writer on music; b. Belfast, Ireland, Oct. 29, 1862; d. Dulwich, Aug. 8, 1940. He was first in the wholesale wine business; then became interested in drama; lectured at Harvard Univ. on the Elizabethan theater (1925-26). He publ. *The Physical Conditions of the Elizabethan Public Playhouse* (Cambridge, Mass., 1927), *Pre-Restoration Stage Studies* (1927), *Those Nut-Cracking Elizabethans* (London, 1935); also a valuable study on the stage jig of the Elizabethan era, an early form of the ballad opera.

Lawton, Dorothy, English music librarian; b. Sheffield, England, July 31, 1874; d. Bournemouth, England, Feb. 19, 1960. She came to the U.S. as a child; studied in N.Y. with Stojowski (piano), lectured on and taught piano, theory, and history of music until 1920, when she organized and became director of the Music Branch (Circulation Dept.) of the N.Y. Public Library; established a similar department in the American Library in Paris in 1930. She returned to England in 1946, and settled in London.

Layton, Billy Jim, American composer and musicologist; b. Corsicana, Texas, Nov. 14, 1924. He studied at the New England Cons. with Carl McKinley, graduating in 1948; then at Yale Univ. with Quincy Porter and at Harvard Univ. with Walter Piston (composition) and Gombosi and Pirrotta (musicology); obtained his Ph.D. with the dissertation, *Italian Music for the Ordinary of the Mass* (1960); was on the faculty of Harvard Univ. (1960-66); in 1966 was appointed prof. of music at the State Univ. of N.Y. at Stony Brook.
WORKS: *An American Portrait,* symph. overture (1957); *Dante Fantasy* for orch. (1964); *3 Dylan Thomas Poems* for chorus and brass sextet (1955); chamber music of various descriptions.

Lazar, Filip, Rumanian composer; b. Craiova, May 18, 1894; d. Paris, Nov. 3, 1936. He studied with Kiriac and Castaldi at the Bucharest Cons. (1907-12) and with Teichmüller and Krehl at the Leipzig Cons. (1913-14). In 1915 he went to Paris; was a founding member of the modern musical society "Triton" (1928). His music is brilliantly hedonistic, with the ethnic Rumanian element furnishing an exotic element à la moderne.
WORKS: *Prelude* for orch. (1919); *Suita română* for orch. (1921); *Divertissement* for orch. (1924); *Suite valaque* for small orch. (1925); *Tziganes,* scherzo for orch. (Boston, Oct. 29, 1926); *Music for an Orchestra* (Boston, March 23, 1928); *Le Ring: Un round de 4 minutes* (Paris, Jan. 10, 1930); 4 Concertos: No. 1, *Concerto Grosso in the Old Style* (Boston, Feb. 21, 1930); No. 2, Concerto for Piano and Small Orch. (1931); No. 3, Concerto for Piano and Orch. (Paris, Nov. 4, 1934); No. 4, *Concerto da camera* for percussion and 12 instruments (Paris, Dec. 11, 1935); *Musică pentru radio (Music for Radio),* overture for small orch. (Paris, "Triton" concerts, Feb. 26, 1931); 2 piano sonatas (1913, 1929); Violin Sonata (1919); 2 suites for piano (1924, 1925); *Bagatelles* for cello and piano (1925); *3 Dances* for violin and piano (1927); *Bagatelles* for piano (1927); Trio for oboe, clarinet and bassoon (1934); String Trio (1935); *Petite Suite* for oboe, clarinet and bassoon (1936); choruses; songs.

Lazare, Martin, Belgian pianist and composer; b. Brussels, Oct. 27, 1829; d. there, Aug. 6, 1897. He studied in The Hague with van der Does, and at the Paris Cons. with Zimmerman; traveled to London, Germany, the U.S., and Canada.
WORKS: opera *Le Roi de Bohème* (The Hague, 1852); operetta *Les Deux Mandarins* (Brussels, 1878); chamber music; piano works (*Sicilienne, Valses de salon, 6 études de concert, 6 études de genre).*

Lazarof, Henri, brilliant Bulgarian-American composer; b. Sofia, April 12, 1932. He left Bulgaria in 1948 for Palestine, and studied composition with Paul Ben-Haim in Jerusalem; then took courses with Goffredo Petrassi at Santa Cecilia in Rome (1955-57). He received a study fellowship from Brandeis Univ., where he studied with Harold Shapero (1957-59); in 1962 he joined the music faculty at the Univ. of Calif., Los Angeles. His music is marked by inventive originality in its thematic structure and subtle "sonorism" in instrumentation, without imperiling the pragmatic quality of the basic design; instances of serial procedures are unobtrusive.
WORKS: Piano Concerto (1957); *Piccola Serenata* for orch. (Boston, June 14, 1959); Viola Concerto (Monaco, Feb. 20, 1962; 1st prize at the International Competition of Monaco); Concerto for Piano and 20 Instruments (Milan Radio, May 28, 1963); *Odes* for orch. (1963); *Concertino da camera* for woodwind quintet (1959); *Tempi Concertati,* a double concerto for violin, viola, and chamber orch. (1964); 2 string quartets (1956, 1962); String Trio (1957); Sonata for violin solo (1958); *Inventions* for viola and piano (1962); *Asymptotes* for flute and vibraphone (1963); *Quantetti* (a telescoped title for "Quattro Canti per Quartetto di pianoforte") scored for 4 pianos (1964);

Structures Sonores for orch. (1966; received first International Prize of the City of Milan, La Scala Award); *Rhapsody* for violin and piano (1966); *Espaces* for 10 instruments (1966); Octet for wind instruments (1967); *Mutazione* for orch. (1967); Concerto for Cello and Orch. (1968; Oslo, Norway, Sept. 12, 1969); *Omaggio* chamber concerto for 19 players (1968); *Divertimenti* for 5 players (1969); *Textures* for piano and 5 ensembles (1970); *Continuum* for strings (1970).

Lazarus, Daniel, French composer; b. Paris, Dec. 13, 1898; d. there, June 27, 1964. He studied at the Paris Cons., taking 1st prize in composition (1915). His works include the ballet *Le Roseau* (Paris, Nov. 15, 1924); *Symphonie avec Hymne,* a large work in 5 parts for chorus and orch. portraying the destiny of the Jewish people; an "épopée lyrique," *Trumpeldor* (Paris, April 30, 1946; perf. in concert form); *Fantaisie* for cello and orch.; violin sonata; piano pieces; etc.

Lazarus, Gustav, German pianist and composer; b. Cologne, July 19, 1861; d. Berlin, May 24, 1920. He studied with I. Seiss, G. Jensen, and F. Wüllner; prof. of piano at the Scharwenka Cons. in Berlin (1887-99); 1899, became director of Breslaur's Cons. and Seminary in Berlin; appeared with success as a pianist in Germany, France, and England. He wrote 170 opus numbers, including the operas *Mandanika* (Elberfeld, 1899) and *Das Nest der Zaunkönige;* choral works with orch.; orchestral suite; chamber music; choruses; piano works; songs.

Lazzari, Sylvio, French composer; b. Bozen, Dec. 30, 1857; d. Paris, June 18, 1944. He entered the Paris Cons. in 1883, studying with César Franck and Guiraud; became a naturalized French citizen, settling in Paris. Up to 1894 he was an active propagandist for the works of Wagner, contributing essays to various journals; then he devoted himself entirely to composition, adopting the principles of Impressionism. He visited the U.S. to conduct the world première of his opera *Le Sautériot* (Chicago, Jan. 19, 1918). He also wrote the operas *Armor* (Prague, Nov. 7, 1898), *La Lépreuse* (Paris, Feb. 7, 1912), *Melaenis* (Mulhouse, 1927), *La Tour de feu* (Paris, Jan. 16, 1928); a pantomime, *Lulu* (1887); orchestral works: a symphony; *Rapsodie espagnole; Ophélie,* symph. poem; *Impressions d'Adriatique; Effet de nuit,* symph. poem (1904); *Marche pour une fête joyeuse; Tableau symphonique d'après Verlaine; Chanson de Moulin; Au bois de Misène; Cortège nocturne; Fête bretonne; Et la jeune fille parla; Perdu en mer; Rapsodie* for violin and orch.; *Le Nouveau Christ,* for baritone and orch.; *Des choses des choses,* for soprano and orch.; *Apparitions* for soprano and orch.; incidental music to *Faust;* Piano Trio; String Quartet; Octet for wind instruments; Violin Sonata; piano works; songs; etc.

Lear, Evelyn, American soprano; b. New York, Jan. 18, 1927. She studied piano and horn; appeared as a pianist in concerts; then began taking singing lessons at the Juilliard School of Music. In 1957 she went to Berlin on a Fullbright grant and studied there at the Hochschule für Musik. In 1958 she was engaged by the Deutsche Staatsoper in Berlin; in 1962 she sang the title role of Lulu in Alban Berg's unfinished opera in Vienna. Returning to America she sang Marie in Berg's *Wozzeck* at the Chicago Lyric Opera in 1966. She made her Metropolitan Opera debut in the first performance of Marvin David Levy's opera *Mourning Becomes Electra* on March 16, 1967. She continued her appearances in Europe, both in classical and in modern repertory, earning for herself a fine reputation as a dramatic singer and interpretive artist. She is married to the American baritone **Thomas Stewart.**

Le Bé, Guillaume, early French type-founder; b. Troyes, 1525; d. Paris, 1598. He was trained in Rome and Venice; in 1552 he settled in Paris. He followed the method of Petrucci, printing notes and staff lines separately, and thus necessitating 2 impressions. He also made tablature type. His punches and other equipment were acquired by Ballard, and were in use for another couple of centuries.

Lebègue, Nicolas-Antoine, French organist; b. Laon, 1631; d. Paris, July 6, 1702, as court organist. He publ. 3 books of organ music (I, 1676; II and III, after 1678), a vol. of *Pièces de clavessin* (1677), and *Airs* for 2–3 voices with continuo. His complete organ works are to be found in Guilmant's *Archives des maîtres de l'orgue* 9 (1909); a new edition of his complete keyboard works is N. Dufourcq's *Œuvres de clavecin* (Monaco, 1956); selections from his clavecin music in Farrenc's *Trésor Musical.*
BIBLIOGRAPHY: N. Dufourcq, *Nicolas-Antoine Lebègue* (Paris, 1954).

Lebert, Siegmund (real name **Sigmund Levi**), German pianist and pedagogue; b. Ludwigsburg, near Stuttgart, Dec. 12, 1821; d. Stuttgart, Dec. 8, 1884. He was a pupil of Tomaschek in Prague. In 1856 he founded, with Faiszt, Stark, Brachmann, and Speidel, the Stuttgart Cons. His *Grosse Klavierschule* (which included numerous studies of his own composition), publ. in cooperation with Stark, ran through many editions (revised by Max Pauer, 1904), and appeared also in English, French, Italian, and Russian translations. He also publ. an *Instructive Edition* of classical piano works and edited Clementi's *Gradus ad Parnassum.*

Lebeuf, Abbé Jean, French music scholar; b. Auxerre, March 6, 1687; d. Paris, April 10, 1760. In 1740 he succeeded to Lancelot's chair in the Académie. He wrote about 180 essays on all manner of subjects, including a series publ. in the *Mercure de France* (1725–28) dealing with plainchant, in strong opposition to Motz's newly invented style of notation; other musical essays by him are: *Lettre sur les orgues,* in the *Mercure de France* (1737); *Traité historique et pratique sur le chant ecclésiastique précédé d'une nouvelle méthode pour l'enseigner et l'apprendre facilement* (1741).

Leborne, Aimé-Ambroise-Simon, French composer; b. Brussels, Dec. 29, 1797; d. Paris, April 2, 1866. He went to France as a child; studied at the Paris Cons. with Berton and Cherubini; 2nd Prix de Rome (1818); 1st Prix de Rome (1820); joined the faculty of the

Paris Cons., first as prof. of counterpoint, then of fugue, and finally of composition; retained this post until his death; was also librarian of the Paris Opéra and of the Royal Chapel. He wrote the operas *Le Camp du drap d'or* (Paris, Feb. 28, 1828), *Cinq Ans d'entr'acte,* and *Lequel* (Paris, March 21, 1838); adapted Carafa's *Les Deux Figaros;* also edited a new edition of Catel's *Traité d'harmonie,* making numerous additions to the practical part (1848).

Leborne, Fernand, French music critic and composer; b. Charleroi, March 10, 1862; d. Paris, Jan. 15, 1929. He was a pupil at the Paris Cons. of Massenet, Saint-Saëns, and César Franck. He lived mostly in Paris; was music critic for *Le Monde artiste,* later for the *Petit Parisien;* as a composer, he won the Prix Chartier in 1901.
WORKS: operas *Daphnis et Chloé* (Brussels, May 10, 1885), *Hedda* (Milan, 1898), *Mudarra* (Berlin, April 19, 1899), *Les Girondins* (Lyons, March 25, 1905), *La Catalane* (Paris, May 24, 1907), *Cléopâtre* (Rouen, 1914), *Néréa* (Marseilles, Jan. 12, 1926); the orchestral works *Suite intime, Symphonie dramatique, Aquarelles, Temps de guerre, Fête bretonne, Marche solennelle, Ouverture guerrière, Ouverture symphonique, Symphonie-Concerto* for violin and piano with orch.; incidental music to *L'Absent* (Paris, 1903); String Quartet; Piano Trio; Violin Sonata; a Mass, motets; piano pieces; songs.

Lebouc, Charles-Joseph, French cellist and composer; b. Besançon, Dec. 22, 1822; d. Hyères, March 6, 1893; studied at the Paris Cons. with Franchomme, Halévy, and Colet (composition), winning 1st prize for cello (1842) and 1st prize for harmony (1844). He played in the Paris Opéra orch. (1844–48); was a member of the Société des Concerts from 1842; founder of the "Soirées de musique classique." He wrote a *Trio de concert,* for piano, violin, and cello; *Ave verum,* for voice with piano and cello; duos for cello with piano; cello pieces; also a method for cello.

Lebrun, Franziska (neé **Danzi**), renowned German soprano; wife of **Ludwig August Lebrun;** b. Mannheim, March 24, 1756; d. Berlin, May 14, 1791. She made her debut in Schwetzingen on Aug. 9, 1772 as Sandrina in Sacchini's *La contadina in corte;* London debut on Nov. 8, 1777 as Ariene in Sacchini's *Creso;* sang in Paris at the Concert Spirituel, and in Milan during the first season of the Teatro alla Scala; also appeared in Naples and Berlin. She was also a composer; publ. 36 sonatas for violin and piano.

Lebrun, Jean, French horn player; b. Lyons, April 6, 1759; d. Paris, c.1809. He studied in Paris with Punto. His playing was remarkable for its purity of tone and for the ease with which he took the high notes. He played 1st horn in the Paris Opéra orch. (1786–92); after a visit to England, he entered the court orch. at Berlin; following extended tours, returned to Paris in 1806, but found no employment, and in despair, committed suicide. The mute for the horn is his innovation.

Lebrun, Louis-Sébastien, French tenor and composer; b. Paris, Dec. 10, 1764; d. there, June 27, 1829. Unsuccessful as a singer in the Paris Opéra and Opéra-Comique, he became one of the 4 "maîtres de chant" at the Opéra; in 1807, tenor in Napoleon's chapelle, and in 1810, "chef du chant" there. He wrote 16 operas, the most successful being *Marcelin* (Paris, March 22, 1800) and *Le Rossignol* (Paris, April 23, 1816); also a *Te Deum* (1809); a Solemn Mass (1815); and a collection of *romances.*

Lebrun, Ludwig August, German oboe player, one of the greatest of his time; b. Mannheim (baptized May 2), 1752; d. Berlin, Dec. 16, 1790. He studied with his father; was a member of the court orch. at Mannheim (1764–78); then toured with his wife, the singer **Franziska Lebrun,** in Germany, Italy, Austria, France and England; his concerts in London (1781) and Paris (1784), both solo and with his wife, created a sensational success. He composed the ballets *Armida* and *Agus;* also 7 oboe concertos; 12 trios for oboe, violin, and cello; duos for flutes.

Lebrun, Paul Henri Joseph, Belgian conductor and composer; b. Ghent, April 21, 1863; d. Louvain, Nov. 4, 1920. He was a pupil at the Cons. in Ghent; won the Belgian Prix de Rome in 1891 with his cantata *Andromeda,* and 1st prize of the Belgian Académie for a symph.; 1890, prof. of theory at the Ghent Cons. and conductor of the "Orpheon" at Cambrai; 1895, also conductor of the "Cercle artistique" at Ghent; from 1913 until his death, director of the music school in Louvain. He wrote an opera, *La Fiancée d'Abydos* (Ghent, 1897); orchestral and choral works; chamber music; etc.

Leça, Armando, Portuguese composer and folksong specialist; b. Leça da Palmeira, Aug. 9, 1893. He studied with Oscar da Silva; was active as choral conductor and collector of native folksongs; publ. an authoritative edition of popular Portuguese music (1922; expanded ed. in 2 vols., 1947). He wrote several dance suites for orch., of which the *Dansa de Don Pedro* attained considerable popularity; 2 operettas, *Maio florido* (1918) and *Bruxa* (1919); many piano pieces of pictorial character, and songs.

Le Caine, Hugh, Canadian acoustician; b. Port Arthur, Ontario, May 27, 1914. He held a B.Sc. degree at Queen's Univ., Kingston, Ontario in 1938 and M.Sc. in 1939; obtained his Ph.D. in nuclear physics from the Univ. of Birmingham, England, in 1952; cooperated with the first Canadian Electronic Music Studio at the Univ. of Toronto in 1959, and at McGill Univ. in Montreal in 1964; exhibited electronic music instruments at Expo '67 in Montreal. He has contributed papers on electronic music to various scholarly journals; realized a number of electronic compositions for the radio and television studios in Toronto and Montreal, among them *Dripsody* (1959), *Alchemy* (1964) and *Perpetual Motion* for data systems computer (1970).

Le Carpentier, Adolphe-Clair, French pianist and composer; b. Paris, Feb. 17, 1809; d. there, July 14, 1869. He was a pupil of Lesueur and Fétis at the Cons.

(1818), winning several prizes. He publ. an excellent *Méthode de piano pour les enfants*, also 25 *Études élémentaires* (op. 59), and a collection of 24 études, *Le Progrès;* also nearly 300 fantasias on operatic and national airs, well arranged and of moderate difficulty.

Lechner, Leonhard (Leonardus Lechner Athesinus), composer; b. in the valley of Adige (Athesinus; hence his surname) in the Austrian Tyrol, c.1550; d. Stuttgart, Sept. 9, 1606. He was a boy-chorister under Roland de Lassus in Munich and Ivo de Vento in Landshut; then teacher in Nuremberg (1570); Kapellmeister in Hechingen (1584); from 1585, in Tübingen; finally, Kapellmeister in Stuttgart (from 1587). His later works, as illustrated by his *Johannispassion, Hohelied Salomonis* and *Deutsche Sprüche vom Leben und Tod,* show him to be one of the most gifted of the German composers in the period immediately preceding Heinrich Schütz. He publ. *Motectaesacrae* (in 4-6 voices; 2 vols., 1575 and 1581; the latter vol. bearing the title *Sacrae Cantiones,* partly reprinted by Commer); *Newe teutsche Lieder* (3-voiced villanellas; 2 vols., 1576 and 1577; collected ed., 1586 and 1590); *Newe teutsche Lieder* (in 4-5 voices; 1577); *Newe teutsche Lieder* (in 4-5 voices; 1582; reprinted by E. Fritz Schmid, 1926); 8 Magnificats (in 4 voices; 1578); 3 Masses (in 5-6 voices; 1584); 10 introits (in 5-6 voices; 1584); *Newe lustige teutsche Lieder, nach Art der welschen Canzonen* (in 4 voices; 1586 and 1588); 7 *Psalmi Poenitentiales* (in 6 voices; 1587); *Harmoniae miscellae,* collection (1583); *Johannispassion* (1594; reprinted by Ameln, 1926); *Hohelied Salomonis* (in 4 voices; 1606; ed. by Ameln and Lipphardt, 1927); *Deutsche Sprüche vom Leben und Tod* (in 4 voices; 1606; ed. by Ameln and Lipphardt, 1927); other psalms and motets for 4-18 voices (1575-1604). He also made arrangements for 5 voices of 3-part villanellas by Regnart (1579; partly reprinted in *Monatschefte für Musikgeschichte,* vol. 19, ed. by Eitner); publ. works of Lassus. A complete edition of Lechner's works was begun in 1954 under the general editorship of Konrad Ameln; by 1977, vols. 1-5, 7-9, and 12-13 were issued.

BIBLIOGRAPHY: O. Kade, "Leonhard Lechner und sein Streit mit dem Grafen Eitel Friedrich von Hohenzollern im Jahre 1585," *Monatshefte für Musikgeschichte* (vol. 1, 1869, with musical supplement); J. Sittard, in *Zur Geschichte der Musik und des Theaters am Württembergischen Hofe* (1890; p. 27 et seq.); O. Koller, "Leonhard Lechner," *Musikbuch aus Österreich* (1904); M. Schreiber, *Leonhard Lechner* (Munich, 1932); M. Schreiber, *Die Kirchenmusik des Kapellmeisters Leonhard Lechner Athesinus* (Regensburg, 1935); K. Ameln, *Gedenkrede auf Leonhard Lechner* (Lüdenscheid, 1961); K. Ameln, "Leonhard Lechner in His Time," in J. Riedel, ed. *Cantors at the Crossroads* (Buszin Festschrift; St. Louis, 1967).

Lechthaler, Josef, Austrian church composer and musicologist; b. Rattenberg, Dec. 31, 1891; d. Vienna, Aug. 21, 1948. He studied philology in Innsbruck, and musicology with Guido Adler in Vienna; obtained his degree of Dr. phil. in 1919; from 1925, taught theory at the Vienna Academy of Music, and was director of the church music school there from 1933 until 1938,

and again from 1945 to his death. He wrote "Der katholische Organist als Baumeister des Gesamtkunstwerks," in *Kongress-Bericht für Kirchenmusik* (Berlin, 1927); composed the cantatas *Der lichte Tag* and *Lieder der Wanderschaft;* a cappella choruses; 2 string quartets; Trio for Violin, Viola da Gamba, and Harpsichord; a song cycle *Conjunx conjugi;* a sonata for piano, choruses, much guitar music, various songs and pieces for children.

BIBLIOGRAPHY: E. Tittel, *Josef Lechthaler* (Vienna, 1966).

Leclair, Jean Marie (l'aîné), celebrated French violinist; b. Lyons, May 10, 1697; d. Paris, Oct. 22, 1764. At first he was a dancer; was ballet master at Turin, where the violinist Somis was attracted by dance music he wrote, and gave him further instruction. From 1729-31, he played the violin in the orch. of the Paris Opéra; was a frequent performer at the Concert Spirituel (1728-34). Thenceforth he lived in Paris as composer and teacher; made brief visits to Holland and Spain in 1743-44. He was assassinated in his own house; the circumstances that no robbery was attempted and that he was stabbed 3 times, in the front part of his body, suggest that the murderer was known to him; it may have been his estranged wife, who was also his publisher and engraver of his music. (See "The Murder of Leclair" in N. Slonimsky's *A Thing or Two About Music;* N.Y., 1948; pp. 86-90.) Leclair was one of the best composers for the violin in the 18th century; although he followed the Italian school in his early works, he developed a distinct style in his later music; he used technical devices in the virtuoso category.

WORKS: opera *Glaucus et Scylla* (Paris, Oct. 4, 1746); opera ballet *Apollon et Climène* (1750); *Concerti grossi* for 3 violins, viola, cello, and organ; 6 trios, and 2 easy trios, for 2 violins with bass; duos for violins; and (his finest compositions) 48 sonatas for violin with continuo. New editions have been publ. by F. David (in his *Hohe Schule des Violinspiels* and *Vorschule*), Eitner (in *Publikationen der Gesellschaft für Musikforschung,* vol. 31), D. Alard, M. Herwegh, Bouillard, Moffat, L. Lichtenberg, etc. The violin sonatas opp. 5, 9, and 15 are issued in the series *Recent Researches in the Music of the Baroque Era* (Madison, Wisconsin, 1968-69). A complete edition of his works in 16 vols. was begun in Paris in 1953, under the direction of M. Pincherle.

BIBLIOGRAPHY: L. de la Laurencie, "Le Rôle de Leclair dans la musique instrumentale," *Revue Musicale* (April 1923); A. Moser, *Geschichte des Violinspiels* (1923; p. 372 et seq.); H. Engel, *Das Instrumentalkonzert* (Part I, vol. 3, of Kretzschmar's *Führer*, p. 172 et seq.); M. Pincherle, *Jean-Marie Leclair l'aîné* (Paris, 1952); G. Nutting, "J.-M. Leclair," *Musical Quarterly* (Oct. 1964); N. Zaslaw, "Handel and Leclair," *Current Musicology* 9 (1969).

Leclair, Jean Marie (le cadet), younger brother of the preceding; b. Lyons, Sept. 23, 1703; d. there, Nov. 30, 1777. Like his brother, he was a violinist; he spent most of his life in his native town; publ. a book of violin sonatas; wrote several divertissements.

BIBLIOGRAPHY: Léon Vallas, "Une Famille de violinistes lyonnais, les Leclair," *Bulletin de la Société Française de Musicologie* (July 1921).

Lecocq, Charles, French composer of light opera; b. Paris, June 3, 1832; d. there, Oct. 24, 1918. He studied at the Paris Cons. under Bazin (harmony), Halévy (composition), and Benoist (organ); obtained 1st prize for harmony (1850) and 2nd prize for fugue (1852). In 1857 he shared with Bizet a prize offered by Offenbach for the best opera buffa, with his *Le Docteur Miracle* (Paris, April 8, 1857). From that time on, he composed industriously for the stage; after several transient successes he produced an operetta, *Fleur de thé* (1868), which had a run of a hundred nights in Paris, and was also well received in England and Germany. He produced 9 more operettas before *La Fille de Mme. Angot* (Brussels, Dec. 4, 1872; Paris, Feb. 21, 1873), which brought him fame. In Paris alone it enjoyed an uninterrupted series of performances for over a year. It was closely followed by its rival in popularity, *Giroflé-Girofla* (Brussels, March 21, 1874). Altogether, he produced some 40 operettas and comic operas, distinguished by melodic grace, instrumental finish, and dramatic acumen, not inferior to the productions of Offenbach and Hervé. His serious opera *Plutus* (Opéra-Comique, March 31, 1886) was unsuccessful. He publ., for piano, a ballet pantomime, *Les Fantoccini;* 24 "morceaux de genre," *Les Miettes;* and a gavotte; also an *Aubade; mélodies* and *chansons* for voice with piano; sacred songs for women's voices (*La Chapelle au couvent*); etc.

BIBLIOGRAPHY: L. Schneider, *Les Maîtres de l'operette, Hervé et Charles Lecocq* (Paris, 1924).

Le Couppey, Félix, French pianist; b. Paris, April 14, 1811; d. there, July 5, 1887. He was a pupil at the Paris Cons.; from 1843, taught piano and harmony there. He publ. several successful piano methods: *École du mécanisme du piano, 24 études primaires; Cours de piano élémentaire et progressif; L'Art du piano* (50 études with annotations); and a pamphlet, *De l'enseignement du piano: conseils aux femmes professeurs* (1865); also piano character pieces and songs.

Lecuna, Juan, Venezuelan composer; b. Valencia, Carabobo, Nov. 20, 1894; d. Rome, April 15, 1954. He studied in Caracas; later went to the U.S.; took lessons with Gustave Strube in Baltimore. He also engaged in diplomatic service, and during the last years of his life was a member of the Venezuelan legation at the Vatican. He wrote a *Suite Venezolana* for 4 guitars; a string quartet; a piano concerto and a suite of 4 Venezuelan dances for piano.

Lecuona, Ernesto, Cuban composer of popular music; b. Havana, Aug. 7, 1896; d. Santa Cruz de Tenerife, Canary Islands, Nov. 29, 1963. He played piano as a child, and wrote his first song when he was 11 years old. He graduated from the National Cons. of Havana (1911); toured South America and Europe as leader of a Cuban dance band. Among his melodies, the most successful are *Malagueña, Andalucía,* and *Siboney.*

Ledbetter, Huddie (Leadbelly), black American folk singer and guitarist; b. Mooringsport, Louisiana, 1885; d. N.Y., Dec. 6, 1949. He never had an education but possessed a genuine talent for folksong singing. He was jailed for murder in 1918; released in 1925; served another term for attempted homicide (1930–34) and for assault (1939–40). It was during this last incarceration that he was discovered by folk researchers John and Alan Lomax, and they were instrumental in obtaining his early release and starting him on a career as a professional and renowned performer. The recordings of prison songs he made for the Lomaxes are now on deposit at the Library of Congress. After release, he played and sang in night clubs. The authenticity of his performance gives him a historic niche in folksong history. A cult arose around his name after his death; the "hootenanny" movement was much influenced by his style. He is the composer of the song *Good Night, Irene,* but it did not become popular until after his death.

Ledebur, Carl, German writer on music; b. Schildesche, near Bielefeld, April 20, 1806; d. Stolp, Oct. 25, 1872. He was a Prussian cavalry officer; publ. a *Tonkünstlerlexikon Berlins von den ältesten Zeiten bis auf die Gegenwart* (1861; reprint, Tutzing, 1965) and essays on Berlin court music.

Ledent, Félix-Étienne, Belgian pianist and composer; b. Liège, Nov. 20, 1816; d. there, Aug. 23, 1886. He studied at the Liège Cons. with J. Jalheau, and in Paris with Daussoigne-Méhul, taking the 2nd Prix de Rome (1843); in 1844, became prof. of piano at the Liège Cons. He publ. an *Adagio et Rondo* for piano and orch.; piano pieces and songs.

Lederer, Felix, Bohemian conductor; b. Prague, Feb. 25, 1877; d. Berlin, March 26, 1957. He studied at the Prague Cons.; then at the Vienna Cons.; was conductor at the Municipal Theater in Nuremberg (1899–1903), at Augsburg (1903–05), Barmen (1905–08), Bremen (1908–10), and Mannheim (1910–22); in 1922, appointed opera conductor at Saarbrücken; from 1945 until his death, in Berlin as prof. at the Hochschule für Musik.

Leduc, Alphonse, French music publisher; b. Nantes, March 9, 1804; d. Paris, June 17, 1868. He studied with Reicha at the Paris Cons.; played piano and bassoon. In 1841 he founded a music business in Paris; after his death, his son **Alphonse II** (1844–1892) inherited the business; at the death of the latter, his widow directed the firm until 1904, when their son **Émile Alphonse III** (b. Nov. 14, 1878; d. Paris, May 24, 1951) became the next owner; his sons **Claude** and **Gilbert Leduc** (partners of their father from 1938) continued the business. From 1860–95 the firm publ. *L'Art Musical,* which was then assimilated with the *Guide Musical.*

BIBLIOGRAPHY: Cecil Hopkinson, *Parisian Music Publishers, 1700–1950* (London, 1954).

Leduc, Jacques, Belgian composer; b. Jette, near Brussels, March 1, 1932. He studied music at the Royal Cons. in Brussels and privately with Jean Absil. In 1962 he was appointed to the faculty of the Music Academy in Uccle.

WORKS: a lyric comedy *Nous attendons Sémira-*

mis (Belgian television, Feb. 6, 1973); a cantata *L'Aventure* (1961); *Antigone*, symph. poem (1960); Concertino for Oboe and String orch. (1962); *Divertissement* for flute and string orch. (1962); *Fantaisie sur le thème de 'La Folia'* for clarinet, and chamber orch. or piano (1964); *4 Etudes* for chamber orch. (1966); *Le Printemps*, symph. sketch (1967); *Ouverture d'été* (1968); Symphony (1969); Piano Concerto (1970); *5 croquis* for orch. (1971); *Dialogue* for clarinet, and chamber orch. or piano (1972); *Instantanés*, 5 pieces for string ensemble (1972); Wind Quintet (1960); *3 Petites Pièces en Quatuor* for 4 flutes or clarinets (1963); String Trio (1963); *Suite en Quatuor* for 4 saxophones (1964); *3 Impromptus* for harp (1964); *Sortilèges Africains*, sequence for voice, saxophone, percussion and piano (1966); Flute Sonata (1966); *Ballade* for clarinet and piano (1967); Violin Sonata (1967); *Capriccio* for wind quartet (1969); *3 Pièces* for solo cello (1973); *4 pièces brèves* for piano (1965); *Prelude, Variations and Fugato* for piano (1965); *Contrastes* for piano (1967); *Apostrophes* for piano (1971); choruses; songs.

Le Duc, Simon, French composer; b. about 1745; d. Paris, Jan. 20, 1777. He studied violin with Gaviniès; made his debut as a soloist on Sept. 8, 1763 at the Concert Spirituel in Paris. He subsequently became active as a composer of instrumental music and a publisher. His works comprise 3 symphonies, a *Symphonie Concertante* and concertante string trios with orchestra.
BIBLIOGRAPHY: Barry S. Brook, "Simon Le Duc l'aîné, a French Symphonist at the Time of Mozart," *Musical Quarterly* (Oct. 1962).

Lee, Dai-Keong, Hawaiian composer of Chinese parentage; b. Honolulu, Sept. 2, 1915. He studied in the U.S. with Roger Sessions, Frederick Jacobi, and Aaron Copland.
WORKS: the operas, *The Poet's Dilemma* (N.Y., April 12, 1940); *Speakeasy* (N.Y., Feb. 8, 1957); *Hawaiian Festival Overture* (1942); Symph. No. 1 (1942); Violin Concerto (1946); 2nd Symph. (San Francisco, March 14, 1952); *Polynesian Suite* for orch. (1958); *Canticle of the Pacific* for chorus and orch. (1968).

Lee, Ernest Markham, English organist and writer on music; b. Cambridge, June 8, 1874; d. Eastbourne, Nov. 13, 1956. While a student at Emanuel Coll., he acted as organist at All Saints', Woodford Green; in 1917 he was appointed prof. of organ at the Guildhall School of Music and examiner at the Univs. of London, Oxford, and Cambridge; visited Canada and New Zealand (1929–30), Jamaica and Canada (1933), and India (1934); then lived in London.
WORKS: services, anthems, sacred and secular songs, piano pieces *(Hesperis, Serapis, Modern Suite); Edvard Grieg* (1908); *The Story of Opera* (1909); *Brahms: The Man and His Music* (1915); *The Story of Symphony* (1916); *On Listening to Music* (1918); *Musical Theory and Knowledge* (1923); *Brahms' Orchestral Works* (1931).

Lee, Louis, German cellist and composer; brother of **Maurice** and **Sebastian Lee;** b. Hamburg, Oct. 19, 1819; d. Lübeck, Aug. 26, 1896. He studied cello with J. N. Prell; gave concerts at the age of 12 in German cities and in Copenhagen. He organized chamber music soirées (with Hafner, then with Boie) in Hamburg; taught at the Hamburg Cons. until 1884; also was 1st cellist of the Philharmonic Society. He publ. a piano quartet; a piano trio; a cello sonata; a cello sonatina; pieces for piano and cello; piano pieces; music to Schiller's *Jungfrau von Orleans* and *Wilhelm Tell;* etc.

Lee, Maurice, German piano teacher; brother of **Louis** and **Sebastian Lee;** b. Hamburg, Feb., 1821; d. London, June 23, 1895, where he had long resided as a piano teacher and composer of popular salon music.

Lee, Sebastian, German cellist and composer; brother of **Louis** and **Maurice Lee;** b. Hamburg, Dec. 24, 1805; d. there, Jan. 4, 1887. He studied with J. N. Prell; from 1837–68, was solo cellist at the Opéra in Paris; returned to Hamburg in 1868, remaining there until his death. He publ. an excellent method for cello; also variations, divertissements, and fantasies for cello with orch.; variations for cello with string quartet; cello duos.

Leedy, Douglas, American composer; b. Portland, Oregon, March 3, 1938. He studied at Pomona College (B.A., 1959) and at the Univ. of California, Berkeley (M.A., 1962). He played the French horn in the Oakland, Calif., Symph. Orch. and at the San Francisco Opera (1961–65); 1965–66 held a U.S. grant for study in Poland; was on the faculty of the Univ. of California, Los Angeles (1967–70). He cultivates avant-garde methods of electronic application to mixed media.
WORKS: *Exhibition Music* (1965; continued indefinitely); *Decay*, theater piece for piano, Wagner tuba and tape (1965); *Antifonia* for brass quartet (1965); *Usable Music I for Very Small Instruments with Holes* (1966); *Usable Music II* for brass (1966); *Teddy Bears Picnic*, audio-tactile electronic theater piece (1968); *Ave Maris Stella* for soprano, instrumental trio, organ and electronic sound (1968); *88 is Great*, theater piece for many-handed piano (1968); *The Electric Zodiac*, electronic music (1969); *Entropical Paradise: Six Sonic Environments* for electronic recordings (1970); *Gloria* for soprano, chorus and instruments (1970).

Lees, Benjamin, outstanding American composer; b. Harbin, Manchuria, Jan. 8, 1924, of Russian parents; (his family name was **Lysniatsky**). He was brought to the U.S. in infancy; studied piano in San Francisco and Los Angeles; served in the U.S. Army (1942–45); then enrolled at the Univ. of Southern California, Los Angeles, as a student in theory of composition with Halsey Stevens, Ingolf Dahl and Ernst Kanitz; also took private lessons with George Antheil. He held a Guggenheim Fellowship in 1955. In 1956 he went to Finland on a Fulbright Fellowship, returning to America in 1962, after several years in Europe; in 1967 he visited Russia under the auspices of the State Dept. He taught composition at the Peabody Cons. in Baltimore, and at Queens College and Manhattan School of Music in N.Y. Eventually he made his home in Great Neck, Long Island, N.Y., and devoted himself mainly to composition. He writes mostly for instruments; his music possesses an ingratiating quality, modern but not arrogantly so; his harmonies are lucid and are couched in euphonious dissonances; he favors rhythmic asymmetry, the formal design of his works is classical in its clarity. An interesting idiosyncracy is the use of introductory instrumental solos in most of his symphonies and concertos. The accessibility of his musical expression makes his music attractive to conductors and soloists.

WORKS: 4 piano sonatas (1949, 1950, 1951, 1963); Sonata for 2 pianos (1951); *Profile* for orch. (1952; NBC Symph., N.Y., Milton Katims conducting, April 18, 1954); String Quartet No. 1 (1952); Sonata for horn and piano (1952); *Declamations* for string orch. and piano (1953; Oklahoma, Feb. 15, 1956); Toccata for Piano (1953); Symph. No. 1 (1953); *Fantasia* for piano (1954); Violin Sonata No. 1 (1954); *10 Kaleidoscopes* for piano (1954); *Three Variables* for wind quartet and piano (1955); *The Oracle*, music drama, libretto by the composer (1955); String Quartet No. 2 (1955); Piano Concerto No. 1 (Vienna, April 26, 1956); *Divertimento Burlesca* for orch. (1957); Symph. No. 2 (Louisville, Dec. 3, 1958); Violin Concerto (1958; Boston, Feb. 8, 1963); *Concertante breve* for oboe, two horns, piano and strings (1959); *Prologue, Capriccio, and Epilogue* (Portland, April 9, 1959); *Concerto for Orchestra* No. 1 (1959; Rochester, N.Y., Feb. 22, 1962); *Epigrams* for piano (1960); *Visions of Poets*, dramatic cantata to texts of Walt Whitman's words (Seattle, May 15, 1962); Concerto for Oboe and Orch. (1963); *Spectrum* for orch. (1964); *The Gilded Cage*, opera (N.Y., 1964); Concerto for String Quartet and Orch. (Kansas City, Jan. 19, 1965); *Invenzione* for solo violin (1965); Concerto for Chamber Orch. (1966); Piano Concerto No. 2 (Boston, March 15, 1968); *Silhouettes* for wind instruments and percussion (1967); *Medea of Corinth*, for vocal soloists, wind quintet and timpani (London, Jan. 10, 1971); *Odyssey* for piano (1970); *Study No. 1* for cello solo (1970); *The Trumpet of the Swan* for narrator and orch. (Philadelphia, May 13, 1972); *Collage* for string quartet, woodwind quintet and percussion (Milwaukee, May 8, 1973); Violin Sonata No. 2 (1972); *Etudes* for piano and orch. (Houston, Texas, Oct. 28, 1974); *Labyrinths* for wind ensemble (Bloomington, Indiana, Nov. 18, 1975); Variations for Piano and Orch. (Dallas, March 31, 1976); *Passacaglia* for orch. (Washington, April 13, 1976); Concerto for Woodwind Quintet and Orch. (Detroit, Oct. 7, 1976); *Dialogue* for cello and piano (N.Y., March 2, 1977).

BIBLIOGRAPHY: Deryck Cooke, "The Music of Benjamin Lees," *Tempo* (Summer 1959); Deryck Cooke, "The Recent Music of Benjamin Lees," *Tempo* (Spring 1963); N. Slonimsky, "Benjamin Lees in Excelsis," *Tempo* (June 1975).

Leeuw, Reinbert de, Dutch composer and pianist; b. Amsterdam, Sept. 8, 1938. He studied at the Amsterdam Cons.; in 1963 was appointed to the faculty of the Cons. of The Hague. Apart from his professional occupations, he became a political activist; collaborated with Louis Andriessen, Mischa Mengelberg, Peter Schat and Jan van Viljmen on the anti-American multimedia spectacle *Reconstructie*, produced during the Holland Festival in Amsterdam, on June 29, 1969.

He further wrote an opera *Axel* (with Vlijmen, 1975-76); *Solo I* for solo cello (1961); *3 Positions* for solo violin (1963); String Quartet (1963); *Interplay* for orch. (1965); *Hymns and Chorals* for 15 winds, 2 electric guitars and electric organ (Amsterdam, July 5, 1970); *Duets* for solo recorder (1971); *Abschied (Farewell)*, symph. poem, a stylistically historical recapitulation of the late Romantic period of German music between 1890 and 1910, culminating with the emergence of Schoenberg (1971-73; Rotterdam, May 11, 1974). Leeuw published a book about Ives (in collaboration with J. Bemlef; Amsterdam, 1969) and a collection of 17 articles, *Muzikale Anarchie* (Amsterdam, 1973).

BIBLIOGRAPHY: E. Schonberger, "Reinbert de Leeuw" *Key Notes* 1 (Amsterdam, 1975; pp. 3-18).

Leeuw, Ton de, Dutch composer; b. Rotterdam, Nov. 16, 1926. He studied piano and theory with Louis Toebosch in Breda (1947-49), composition with Badings in Amsterdam (1947-49) and with Messiaen and Thomas de Hartmann in Paris (1949-50); also took courses in ethnomusicology with Jaap Kunst in Amsterdam (1950-54). He was director of sound for the Netherlands Radio Union in Hilversum (1954-59); then was engaged as teacher of music in Utrecht and Amsterdam. In his works he explores all thinkable, and some unthinkable but conceptually plausible, ways, pathways and byways of musical techniques. A government grant enabled him to make a tour of Iran and India in 1961, to study non-European systems of composition.

WORKS: a television opera, *Alceste* (Dutch Television, March 13, 1963); an opera, *De droom (The Dream)* based on 14 Haiku (Holland Festival, June 16, 1965); a radio oratorio, *Hiob (Job)* for soloists, chorus, orch. and tape (1956); a television play, *Litany of Our Time* for soprano, chorus, instruments, and electronic sound (1969; Dutch Television, Jan. 1, 1971); 2 ballets: *De bijen (The Bees;* Arnhem, Sept. 15, 1965) and *Krishna and Radha* for flute, harp and percussion (1964); Concerto Grosso for string orch. (1946); *Treurmuziek in memoriam Willem Pijper* for chamber orch. (1948); Symphony for strings and percussion (1950); Symphony for string orch. (1951); *Plutos-Suite* for chamber orch. (1952); 2 violin concertos (1953, 1961); *Suite* for youth orch. (1954); *10 Mouvements rétrogrades* for orch. (1957); *Brabant*, symph. song for middle voice and orch. (1959); *Nritta*, orch. dance (1961); *Ombres* for orch. (1961); *Symphonies for Winds*, an homage to Stravinsky, for 29 winds (1962-63); *Haiku I* for voice and piano (1963); *Haiku II* for soprano and orch. (Rotterdam, July 5, 1968); *Spatial Music I* for 32 to 48 players (1965-66); *Spatial Music II* for percussion (1971); *Spatial Music III* for orch. in 4 groups (1967) and *IV (Homage to Stravinsky)* for 12 players (1968); *Syntaxis I* for tape (1966) and *II* for orch. (1966; Utrecht, May 16, 1966); *Lamento pacis* for chorus and 16 instruments (1969); *Music for 12 strings* (1970); *Music* for organ and 12 players (Zwolle, June 29, 1972); *Gending* for Javanese gamelan orch. (Hilversum, Oct. 11, 1975); String Trio (1948); Flute Sonata (1949); Violin Sonata (1951); Trio for flute, clarinet and piano (1952); *5 Sketches* for oboe, clarinet, bassoon, violin, viola and cello (1952);

2 string quartets (1958; with tape, 1964); *Antiphony* for wind quintet and 4 electronic tracks (1960); *Schelp* for flute, viola and guitar (1964); *The 4 Seasons* for harp (1964); *Night Music* for 1 performer on 3 different flutes (1966); *Music* for 1 or 2 violins (1967); *Music for solo oboe* (1969); *Reversed Night* for solo flute (1971); *Midare* for solo marimba (1972); *Music for solo trombone* (1973–74); *Canzone* for 4 horns, 3 trumpets and 3 trombones (1973–74); *Rime* for flute and harp (1974); *Mo-Do* for amplified harpsichord (1974); Piano Sonatina (1949); *Introduzione e Passacaglia* for organ (1949); 2-piano sonata (1950); *5 Etudes* for piano (1951); *4 Rhythmic Etudes* for piano (1952); *Lydische Suite* for piano (1954); *3 African Studies* for piano (1954); *Men Go Their Ways* for piano (1964); *Sweelinck Variations* for organ (1972–73); *De Toverfluit*, 4 songs for soprano, flute, cello and piano (1954); *Electronic Suite* for tape (1958); solo songs; choruses. He publ. a book *Muziek van de Twintigate Eeuw* (*Music of the Twentieth Century*, Utrecht, 1964). See *Key Notes* 3 (1976; pp. 67–74).

LeFanu, Nicola, British composer; daughter of **Elizabeth Maconchy;** b. Wickham Bishops, Essex, April 28, 1947. She studied music at St. Hilda's College, Oxford (B.A., 1968); also took private lessons with Goffredo Petrassi in Italy and with Thea Musgrave and Peter Maxwell Davies in England. Although she scrutinized her mother's works with great interest, she never had formal instruction from her. Brought up in an extremely cultured and sophisticated environment (her father William LeFanu is well known in the literary world), she absorbed the seemingly conflicting and quaquaversal musical influences with elegance and ease; her own style of composition is that of median vigesimosecular modernism, without prejudice even in regard to overt triadic harmonies. In 1970 she won first prize at the BBC National Competition for her Variations for oboe quartet (1968). Her other works include *Soliloquy* for oboe solo (1965); *Preludio* for chamber orch. (1967); *Chiaroscuro* for piano (1969); *Quartettsatz* for string quartet (1970); Quintet for clarinet and strings (1970).

Lefébure, Louis-François Henri, French musician; b. Paris, Feb. 18, 1754; d. there, Nov. 1840. He was a government official until 1814; publ. several instructive books on singing: *Nouveau Solfège,* a 23-page pamphlet (1780), containing ideas put into practice by Gossec in the *École royale de chant;* a polemical brochure, *Bévues, erreurs et méprises de différents auteurs célèbres en matières musicales* (1789); etc. He also composed 2 oratorios and other choral works.

Lefébure-Wély, Louis James Alfred, French organist and composer; b. Paris, Nov. 13, 1817; d. there, Dec. 31, 1869. A pupil of his father, he took, at the age of 8, the latter's place as organist of the church of Saint-Roch, becoming regular organist at 14. Entering the Paris Cons. in 1832, he was taught by Benoist (organ) and Laurent and Zimmerman (piano); studied composition with Berton and Halévy. From 1847–58 he was organist at the Madeleine; then at St. Sulpice. WORKS: opera, *Les Recruteurs* (1861); a cantata, *Après la victoire* (1863); 3 Masses; 3 symphonies; a string quintet and a string quartet; much elegant salon music for piano (his most celebrated piece is *The Monastery Bells*); 50 piano études; harmonium music.

Lefebvre, Charles Édouard, French composer; b. Paris, June 19, 1843; d. Aix-les-Bains, Sept. 8, 1917. He studied at the Paris Cons.; won the Premier Grand Prix de Rome in 1870 for his cantata *Le Jugement de Dieu;* following his study in Rome, joined the faculty of the Paris Cons. in 1895. WORKS: the operas *Lucrèce, Le Trésor* (Angers, 1883), *Zaïre* (Lille, 1887), *Djelma* (Paris, May 25, 1894), *Singoalla; Judith,* biblical drama (Paris, 1879); *Ouverture dramatique; Dalila,* symph. poem; *Éloa,* a "poème lyrique"; the legend *Melka; Sainte Cécile,* for solo voice, chorus, and orch. (Paris, 1896); Serenade for Orch.; *Toggenburg,* overture (Paris, 1904); *La Messe du fantôme,* for voice and orch.; chamber music (sonatas, trios, quartets, suites for both strings and woodwinds, etc.).

Lefèvre, Jean Xavier, French clarinetist; b. Lausannne, March 6, 1763; d. Paris, Nov. 9, 1829. He studied with Michel Yost in Paris; from 1787, played in concerts; from 1791–1817, was at the Paris Opéra; from 1795–1825, prof. at the Cons. He wrote a clarinet method (1802); also 6 concertos for clarinet, trios, duos, sonatas, etc., for his instrument. He popularized the sixth key of the clarinet, but did not invent it, as often stated.
BIBLIOGRAPHY: F. G. Rendall, *The Clarinet* (London, 1954; p. 74).

Leffler-Burckard, Martha, German soprano; b. Berlin, June 16, 1865; d. Wiesbaden, May 14, 1954. She made her debut as coloratura soprano in Strasbourg (1890); then sang at Breslau, Cologne, and Bremen; from 1898–1900, was at the court theater in Weimar; 1900–02, at Wiesbaden; after that, at the principal German opera houses; in 1906, at Bayreuth; in 1908, at the Metropolitan Opera House in Wagner roles; from 1912–19, member of the Berlin Opera. Her best roles were Fidelio, Isolde, and the 3 Brünnhildes.

Le Flem, Paul, French composer; b. Lézardieux, Côtes-du-Nord, March 18, 1881. He was a pupil of Lavignac at the Paris Cons., and of Vincent d'Indy and Albert Roussel at the Schola Cantorum; also studied philosophy and literature; then taught at the Schola Cantorum. He became music critic for *Comoedia,* taking a strong stand in favor of modern music; was instrumental in organizing a modern music society called La Spirale (1935). His own music is influenced by Debussy and Roussel; in several of his stage works, he employs the melodic idioms of his native Brittany. WORKS: *Aucassin et Nicolette,* fairy tale with voices (Paris, July 20, 1923); operas, *Le Rossignol de Saint Malo* (Opéra-Comique, May 5, 1942), *La Clairière des fées* (1943), and *La Magicienne de la mer* (Paris, Oct. 29, 1954); 3 symphonies (1908, 1958, 1967); *Konzertstück* for violin and orch. (1965); *La Maudite,* dramatic legend for voices and orch. (1967; new version, 1971); chamber music.

Le Fleming, Christopher (Kaye), English composer; b. Wimborne, Feb. 26, 1908. He studied piano, and has been active in teaching at primary schools. He has written *The Singing Friar,* for tenor solo, chorus, and orch.; 5 Psalms; *Peter Rabbit Music Books* for piano; an orch. suite, *London River* (1956); incidental music for plays.

Le Gallienne, Dorian, Australian composer; b. Melbourne, April 19, 1915; d. there, July 27, 1963. He graduated from Melbourne Univ. in 1938; then went to England, and studied with Arthur Benjamin and Howells at the Royal College of Music in London; during World War II he worked with the Department of Information and the Australian Broadcasting Commission. On another trip to England he took private lessons in composition with Gordon Jacobs; in 1953 returned to Melbourne. His music is marked by clear linear procedures, often in dissonant counterpoint.

WORKS: 2 ballets: *Contes Heraldiques* (1947) and *Voyageur* (1954); *3 Psalms* for chorus and orch. (1948); *Overture* (1952); Symphony in E (1952-53); Sinfonietta (1951-56); *Symphonic Study* for orch. (1962-63; a posthumous work derived from material intended as a Second Symphony); Flute Sonata (1943); Violin Sonata (1945); Duo for violin and viola (1956); Trio for oboe, violin and viola (1957); 2 *Pieces:* No. 1 for violin, cello, clarinet, percussion and harp; No. 2 for 2 clarinets and string quartet (both 1959); piano pieces, numerous songs, including *3 Sonnets of Shakespeare* (1946) and *4 Divine Poems of John Donne* (1947-50); incidental and film music.

Leginska, Ethel (real name **Liggins**), English pianist, teacher, and composer; b. Hull, England, April 13, 1886; d. Los Angeles, Feb. 26, 1970. She showed a natural talent for music at an early age; the pseudonym Leginska was given to her by Lady Maud Warrender, under the illusion that a Polish-looking name might help her artistic career. She studied piano at the Hoch Cons. in Frankfurt, and later in Vienna with Leschetizky. She made her debut as a pianist in London; also toured Europe; on Jan. 20, 1913, she appeared for the first time in America, at a recital in New York. Her playing was described as having masculine vigor, dashing brilliance, and great variety of tonal color; however, criticism was also voiced against an individualistic treatment of classical works. In the midst of her career as a pianist, she developed a great interest in conducting; she organized the Boston Philharmonic Orch. (100 players), later the Women's Symph. Orch. of Boston; appeared as guest conductor with various orchestras in America and in Europe. In this field of activity she also elicited interest, leading to a discussion in the press of a woman's capability of conducting an orchestra. While in the U.S., she took courses in composition with Rubin Goldmark and Ernest Bloch; wrote music in various genres, distinguished by rhythmic display and a certain measure of modernism. She married the composer **Emerson Whithorne** in 1907 (divorced in 1916). In 1939 she settled in Los Angeles as a piano teacher.

WORKS: operas: *Gale* (Chicago Civic Opera Co., Nov. 23, 1935, composer conducting), *The Rose and the Ring* (1932; perf. for the first time, Los Angeles,

Feb. 23, 1957, composer conducting); *From a Life,* for 13 instruments (N.Y., Jan. 9, 1922); *Beyond the Fields We Know,* symph. poem (N.Y., Feb. 12, 1922); *2 Short Pieces* for orch. (Boston Symph., Feb. 29, 1924, Monteux conducting); *Quatre Sujets Barbares,* inspired by Gauguin, suite for orch. (Munich, Dec. 13, 1924, composer conducting); *Fantasy* for orch. and piano (N.Y., Jan. 3, 1926); *Triptych,* for 11 instruments (Chicago, April 29, 1928); String Quartet, after 4 poems of Tagore (Boston, April 25, 1921); *6 Nursery Rhymes* for soprano and chamber orch.; piano pieces; songs.

Legley, Victor, outstanding Belgian composer; b. Hazebrouck, French Flanders, June 18, 1915. He studied viola and music theory at the Brussels Cons. (1933-35); also took private lessons in composition with Jean Absil (1941), who was mainly influential in shaping Legley's style; in 1947 he became a programmer for the Flemish Broadcasts of the Belgian Radio; from 1949 taught at the Brussels Cons. In his works he adheres to the pragmatic tenets of modern music, structurally diversified and unconstricted by inhibitions against dissonance.

WORKS: an opera, *La Farce des deux nus* (Antwerp, Dec. 10, 1966); a ballet, *Le Bal des halles* (1954); *Symphonic Variations on an Old Flemish Folksong* (1941); 5 symphonies (1942, 1947, 1953, 1964, 1965); *Concert à treize,* chamber symphony (1944); *Suite* for orch. (1944); *Music for a Greek Tragedy* for orch. (1946); *Symphonic Miniature* for chamber orch. (1946); 2 violin concertos: No. 1 (1947), No. 2 (1966; Brussels, May 22, 1967; mandatory work of the 1967 Queen Elisabeth violin competition finals); *The Golden River,* symph. sketch (1948); Piano Concerto (1952); *Divertimento* for orch. (1952); *Little Carnaval Overture* (1954); Concertino for Timpani and orch. (1956); *Serenade* for string orch. (1957); *La Cathédrale d'Acier* (The Steel Cathedral), symph. sketch after a painting by Fernand Steven (1958); *Overture to a Comedy by Goldoni* (1958); *3 Pieces* for chamber orch. (1960); *Dyptiek* for orch. (1964); *Harp Concerto* (1966); *Paradise Regained* for orch. (1967); *Prélude for a Ballet* (1969); *3 Movements* for brass and percussion (1969); *Espaces* for string orch. (1970); Viola Concerto (1971); 5 string quartets (1941; 1947; 1956; 1963; *Esquisses,* 1970); Trio for oboe, clarinet, and bassoon (1942); Quartet for 4 flutes (1943); Violin Sonata (1943); Viola Sonata (1943); Sextet for piano and wind quintet (1945); Cello Sonata (1945); *Musique de Midi,* nonet (1948); Clarinet Sonata (1952); Trumpet Sonata (1953); *Serenade* for 2 violins and piano (1954); *Burlesque* for violin and piano (1956); *Poème d'Eté* for violin and piano (1957); *Serenade* for flute, violin and cello (1957); *5 Miniatures* for 4 saxophones (1958); Trio for flute, viola and guitar (1959); Wind Quintet (1961); *4 Pieces* for guitar (1964); *Rhapsodie* for trumpet and piano (1967); Piano Quartet (1973); Piano Trio (1973); String Trio (1973); *4 Ballades,* for either violin, viola, cello or double bass, each with piano (1975); 2 piano sonatas (1946, 1974); *4 Portraits* for piano (1954-55); *Music for 2 pianos* (1966); *3 Marches* for piano (1968); *Brindilles* for piano (1974); *Brieven uit Portugal* for voice and piano (1955); *Zeng* for soprano, and string quartet or string orchestra (1965); other works for voice.

Legrand, Michel, French composer of popular music; b. Paris, Feb. 24, 1932. He entered the Paris Cons. at the age of 11; still a student, began making professional jazz arrangements; wrote for radio, television and the cinema. His inventive score for the motion picture *Les Parapluies de Cherbourg* (1965), written throughout in sing-song fashion, received merited praise.

Legrenzi, Giovanni, celebrated Italian composer; b. Clusone, near Bergamo, Aug. 12, 1626; d. Venice, May 26, 1690. He was a pupil of Pallavicino; organist at Bergamo; maestro di cappella to the Duke of Ferrara; produced his first opera, *Achille in Sciro,* at Ferrara in 1663; from 1664 in Venice, becoming director of the Cons. de' Mendicanti in 1672, and in 1685 succeeding Natale Monferrato as maestro at San Marco, where he enlarged the orch. to 34 pieces (8 violins, 11 violette, 2 tenor viols, 3 viole da gamba and bass viols, 4 theorbos, 2 cornetti, 1 bassoon, and 3 trombones). His 18 operas show a noteworthy advance over those of his predecessors in the orchestral support of the vocal parts, and he treats the recitative and the melodic phrase with greater freedom. He was one of the most important composers of chamber music before Corelli. He was a noted teacher; among his pupils were Gasparini, Lotti, and Caldara.
WORKS: *Concerto di messe e salmi a 3-4 con violini* (1654); *Motetti a 2-4 voci* (1655); *Motetti a 5 voci* (1660); *Sacri e festivi concerti, messe e salmi a due cori* (1657); *Sentimenti devoti a 2 e 3 voci* (1660; 2 vols.); *Compiete con litanie ed antifona della Beata Vergine* (a 5; 1662); *Cantata e canzonette a voce sola* (1674); *Idee armoniche* (a 2 and 3; 1678); *Echi di riverenza* (14 cantatas for solo voice; 1679); *Motetti sacri con voce sola con 3 strumenti* (1692); *Suonate per chiesa* (1655); *Suonate da chiesa e da camera a tre* (1656); *Una muta di suonate* (1664); *Suonate a 2 violini e violone* (with organ continuo; 1667); *La Cetra* (sonatas for 2-4 instruments; 1673); *Suonate a 2 violini e violoncello* (1677); *Suonate da chiesa e da camera* (1693).
BIBLIOGRAPHY: G. Tebaldini, "Giovanni Legrenzi," *Musica d'oggi* (April 1937); P. Fogaccia, *Giovanni Legrenzi* (Bergamo, 1954).

Lehár, Franz, celebrated Austrian operetta composer; b. Komorn, Hungary, April 30, 1870; d. Bad Ischl, Oct. 24, 1948. He was first instructed in music by his father, Franz Lehár (1840–1898), a military bandmaster; entered the Prague Cons. at 12 and studied violin with A. Bennewitz and theory with J. Foerster. In 1885 he was brought to the attention of Fibich, who gave him lessons in composition independently from his studies at the Cons. In 1887 Lehár submitted 2 piano sonatas to Dvořák, who encouraged him in his musical career. In 1888 he became a violinist in a theater orchestra in Elberfeld; in 1889, entered his father's band (50th Infantry) in Vienna, and assisted him as conductor; after 1890 he led various military bands in Pola, Trieste, Budapest, and Vienna. His first success as stage composer came with the production of his operetta *Kukuschka* (Leipzig, Nov. 28, 1896); most of his subsequent productions took place in Vienna. His most celebrated operetta is *Die lustige*

Witwe (The Merry Widow), produced at Vienna in 1905; this was followed by innumerable performances throughout the world; in Buenos Aires it was played simultaneously in 5 languages (1907); other operettas that achieved tremendous success were *Der Graf von Luxemburg* (1909) and *Zigeunerliebe* (1910). Lehár's music exemplifies the spirit of gaiety and frivolity that was the mark of Vienna early in the century; his superlative gift of facile melody and infectious rhythms is combined with genuine wit and irony; a blend of nostalgia and sophisticated humor made a lasting appeal to audiences, undiminished by the upheavals of wars and revolutions.
WORKS: the opera *Kukuschka* (Leipzig, Nov. 28, 1896; rewritten as *Tatjana,* Brünn, Feb. 24, 1905); the operettas *Wiener Frauen* (Vienna, Nov. 25, 1902; in Berlin as *Der Klavierstimmer;* rewritten as *Der Schlüssel zum Paradiese,* Leipzig, 1906); *Der Rastelbinder* (Vienna, Dec. 20, 1902); *Der Göttergatte* (Vienna, Jan. 20, 1904); *Die Juxheirat* (Vienna, Dec. 22, 1904); *Die lustige Witwe* (Vienna, Dec. 28, 1905); *Mitislaw der Moderne* (Vienna, Jan. 5, 1907); *Der Mann mit den drei Frauen* (Vienna, Jan. 21, 1908); *Das Fürstenkind* (Vienna, Oct. 7, 1909); *Der Graf von Luxemburg* (Vienna, Nov. 12, 1909); *Zigeunerliebe* (*Gypsy Love;* Vienna, Jan. 8, 1910); *Eva* (Vienna, Nov. 24, 1911); *Endlich allein* (Vienna, Feb. 10, 1914; revised and produced as *Schön ist die Welt,* Vienna, Dec. 21, 1934); *Der Sterngucker* (Vienna, Jan. 14, 1916; revised and produced in Milan as *La Danza delle libellule,* Sept. 27, 1922); *Wo die Lerche singt* (Budapest, Feb. 1, 1918); *Die blaue Mazur* (Vienna, May 28, 1920); *Die Tangokönigin* (Vienna, Sept. 9, 1921); *Frasquita* (Vienna, May 12, 1922); *Die gelbe Jacke* (Vienna, Feb. 9, 1923; revised and produced as *Das Land des Lächelns,* Berlin, Oct. 10, 1929); *Clo-Clo* (Vienna, March 8, 1924); *Paganini* (Vienna, Oct. 30, 1925); *Der Zarewitsch* (Vienna, Feb. 21, 1927); *Friederike* (Berlin, Oct. 4, 1928); *Giuditta* (Vienna, Jan. 20, 1934). Besides his operettas, Lehár wrote an *Ungarische Fantasie* for violin and small orch.; *Huldigungsouvertüre; Ein Märchen aus 1001 Nacht; Il Guado,* symph. poem for orch. and piano; *Eine Vision,* overture; a symph. poem *Fieber;* a song cycle, *Musikalischer Roman* (1936); numerous marches and dances for orch.
BIBLIOGRAPHY: E. Decsey, *Franz Lehár* (Vienna, 1924; 2nd ed., Munich, 1930); A. von Lehár, *Unsere Mutter* (1930); A. Rivoire, *Une Heure de musique avec Franz Lehár* (Paris, 1930); S. Czech, *Franz Lehár, Weg und Werk* (Berlin, 1942); M. von Pereani, *Franz Lehár* (Vienna, 1949); W. Macqueen-Pope and D. L. Murray, *Fortune's Favorite: The Life and Times of Franz Lehár* (London, 1953); W. Zentner and A. Würz, eds. *Reclams Opern- und Operettaführer* (contains the plots of Lehár's most famous operettas; Stuttgart, 1955); *Katalog der Bühnenwerke von Franz Lehár* (Vienna, 1955); B. Grun, *Gold and Silver: The Life and Times of Franz Lehár* (London, 1970); M. Schönherr, *Franz Lehár, Bibliographie zu Leben und Werk* (Baden at Vienna, 1970).

Lehmann, Friedrich J., American music pedagogue; b. Cleveland, Sept. 17, 1866; d. Oberlin, Ohio, April 23, 1950. He studied piano and voice at the Oberlin Cons., Ohio; then went to Germany, and took lessons with

Fritz von Bose and Gustav Schreck in Leipzig. He taught at the Oberlin Cons. for 30 years (1902–32). He publ. *A Treatise on Simple Counterpoint in 40 Lessons* (N.Y., 1907); *Harmonic Analysis* (Oberlin, 1910); *The Analysis of Form in Music* (Oberlin, 1919).

Lehmann, George, American violinist; b. New York, July 31, 1865; d. Yonkers, N.Y., Oct. 14, 1941. He was a pupil at the Leipzig Cons., studying with Schradieck (violin), Lammers (harmony), and Jadassohn (counterpoint and fugue); then took some violin lessons with Joachim in Berlin. In 1886 he returned to the U.S.; was concertmaster of the Cleveland Symph. Orch. (1886–89); then was in Europe (1889–92). In 1893 he settled in N.Y.; 1907–14, lived in Berlin; after 1914, again in N.Y. He publ. *True Principles of the Art of Violin Playing* (N.Y., 1899) and *The Violinist's Lexicon* (N.Y., 1918), also *Four Melodious Sketches* for violin and piano; etc.

Lehmann, Hans Ulrich, Swiss composer; b. Biel, May 4, 1937. He studied cello in Biel and music theory in Zürich; took courses in advanced composition at seminars of Pierre Boulez and Karlheinz Stockhausen in Basel (1960–63). In 1964 he was appointed to the faculty of the Musik-Akademie in Basel; from 1969, teaching music theory at the Univ. of Zürich. As a composer, he adheres to progressive neo-Classicism with serial connotations.

WORKS: *Structures transparentes* for piano, viola and clarinet (1961); *Quanti I* for flute and chamber ensemble (1962); *Régions pour un flûtiste* (1963); *Episoden* for wind quintet (1964); *Mosaik* for clarinet (1964); *Komposition für 19,* for a chamber group (1965); *Spiele* for oboe and harp (1965); *Rondo* for voice and orch. (1967); *Instants* for piano (1968); *Konzert* for 2 wind instruments and strings (1969); *Régions III* for clarinet, trombone and cello (1970); *Monodie* for a wind instrument (1970).

Lehmann, Lilli, celebrated German soprano; b. Würzburg, Nov. 24, 1848; d. Berlin, May 16, 1929. Her mother, **Marie Loew** (1807–83), who had sung leading soprano roles and had also appeared as a harpist at the Kassel Opera under Spohr, became harpist at the National Theater in Prague in 1853, and there Lilli Lehmann spent her girlhood. At the age of 6 she began to study piano with Cölestin Müller, and at 12 progressed so far that she was able to act as accompanist to her mother, who was the only singing teacher she ever had. She made her professional debut in Prague on Oct. 20, 1865, as the First Page in *Die Zauberflöte;* then sang in Danzig (1868) and Leipzig (1869–70). In 1870 she became a member of the Berlin Opera, and soon established a reputation as a brilliant coloratura singer. During the summer of 1875 she was in Bayreuth, and was coached by Wagner himself in the parts of Wöglinde (*Rheingold* and *Götterdämmerung*), Helmwige, and the Forest Bird; these roles she created at the Bayreuth Festival the following summer. She then returned to Berlin under a life contract with the Berlin Opera; she was given limited leaves of absence, which enabled her to appear in the principal German cities, in Stockholm (1878), and in London (debut as Violetta, June 3, 1880; as Isolde, July 2,

1884; as Fidelio in 1887). She made her American debut at the Metropolitan Opera, N.Y., on Nov. 25, 1885, as Carmen; 5 days later she sang Brünnhilde in *Die Walküre;* then sang virtually all Wagner roles through subsequent seasons until 1889; also appeared as Norma, Aida, Donna Anna, Fidelio, etc. She sang Isolde at the American première of *Tristan* (Dec. 1, 1886), and appeared in Italian opera with the De Reszkes and Lassalle during the season of 1891–92. In the meantime her contract with the Berlin Opera was cancelled (1889) owing to her protracted absence, and it required the intervention of Wilhelm II to reinstate her (1891). In 1896 she sang the three Brünnhildes at the Bayreuth Festival. Her great admiration for Mozart caused her to take an active part in the annual Mozart Festivals held at Salzburg, and from 1905 she was practically the chief organizer of these festivals. In 1909 she still sang Isolde (in Vienna). Her operatic repertory comprised 170 roles in 114 operas (German, Italian, and French). She possessed in the highest degree all the requisite qualities of a great interpreter; she had a boundless capacity for work, a glorious voice, and impeccable technique; she knew how to subordinate her fiery temperament to artistic taste; on the stage she had plasticity of pose, grace of movement and regal presence; her ability to project her interpretation with conviction to audiences in different countries was not the least factor of her universal success. Although she was celebrated chiefly as an opera singer, she was equally fine as interpreter of German lieder; she gave recitals concurrently with her operatic appearances, and continued them long after she had abandoned the stage; her repertory of songs exceeded 600. She was also a successful teacher; among her pupils were Geraldine Farrar and Olive Fremstad. On Feb. 24, 1888, she married the tenor **Paul Kalisch** in New York; they appeared together as Tristan and Isolde; some years later, they were legally separated (but not actually divorced). After Lilli Lehmann's death, Paul Kalisch inherited her manor at Salzkammergut, and remained there until his death in 1946, at the age of 90.

Lilli Lehmann was the author of the books *Meine Gesangskunst* (1902; English translation by Richard Aldrich, under the title *How to Sing,* N.Y., 1902; 3rd revised and supplemented ed., transl. by Clara Willenbücher, N.Y., 1924; reprint, 1949); *Studie zu Fidelio* (1904); *Mein Weg,* an autobiography (1913; 2nd ed., 1920; in English as *My Path Through Life,* 1914). She also edited arias of Mozart and many classical songs for the Peters Edition.

BIBLIOGRAPHY: J. H. Wagenmann, *Lilli Lehmanns Geheimniss der Stimmbänder* (Berlin, 1905; 2nd ed., 1926); L. Andro, *Lilli Lehmann* (Berlin, 1907).

Lehmann, Liza (Elizabetha Nina Mary Frederica), English soprano and composer; b. London, July 11, 1862; d. Pinner, Middlesex, Sept. 19, 1918. She was of German-Scotch parentage; she grew up in an intellectual and artistic atmosphere; her grandfather was a publisher, her father a painter, her mother a singer. From her childhood she lived in Germany, France, and Italy; among guests at her house in Rome was Liszt. She studied voice with Alberto Randegger in London, and composition with Wilhelm Freudenberg in Wiesbaden. She made her professional debut as a singer at a Monday Popular Concert in London (Nov. 23, 1885), and subsequently appeared at various festivals in England. On Oct. 10, 1894, she married the English painter and composer **Herbert Bedford,** and retired from the stage; she then applied herself with great earnestness to composition, with remarkable results, for she was able to produce a number of works (mostly vocal) of undeniable merit, and was the first English woman composer to enjoy success with a large public, in England and in America. Her best known work, which has become a perennial favorite, is *In a Persian Garden,* to words from Omar Khayyám's *Rubaiyát,* in Fitzgerald's version; it is a song cycle, with recitatives, scored for 4 voices with piano accompaniment; while the music itself is entirely conventional, the vocal parts are eminently effective, both in dramatic and in lyrical passages. In 1910 Liza Lehmann made a tour in the U.S., presenting concerts of her songs, with herself at the piano.

WORKS: *Sergeant Brue,* a musical farce (London, June 14, 1904); *The Vicar of Wakefield,* a "Romantic light opera" (Manchester, Nov. 12, 1906); *Everyman,* one-act opera (London, Dec. 28, 1915); *Once upon a Time,* a "fairy cantata" (London, Feb. 22, 1903); *Young Lochinvar,* for baritone solo, chorus, and orch.; *Endymion,* for soprano and orch.; *Romantic Suite,* for violin and piano; *In a Persian Garden,* for vocal quartet and piano (London, Jan. 10, 1897, 1st American performance, Boston, Jan. 5, 1910); song cycles (several of a humorous nature): *The Daisy Chain* (12 songs of childhood), *More Daisies, Prairie Pictures, In Memoriam* (after Tennyson), *Nonsense Songs* (from *Alice in Wonderland*), *The Cautionary Tales and a Moral* (after Hilaire Belloc); piano pieces (*Cobweb Castles,* etc.). Her memoirs, *The Life of Liza Lehmann, by Herself,* were publ. shortly after her death (London, 1919).

Lehmann, Lotte, celebrated German soprano; b. Perleberg, Feb. 27, 1888; d. Santa Barbara, California, Aug. 26, 1976. She studied in Berlin with Erna Tiedke, Eva Reinhold, and Mathilde Mallinger. She made her debut in a minor role at the Hamburg Opera, but soon was given important parts in Wagner's operas, establishing herself as one of the finest Wagnerian singers. In 1914 she was engaged at the Vienna Opera. Richard Strauss selected her to sing the Young Composer in *Ariadne auf Naxos* when it was first performed in Vienna; then she appeared as Octavian in *Der Rosenkavalier,* and later as the Marschallin, which became one of her most famous roles. In 1922 she sang in South America; in 1930, made her U.S. debut as Sieglinde with the Chicago Civic Opera; she sang the same part with the Metropolitan Opera, N.Y., on Jan. 11, 1934; became a member of the company, appearing chiefly in Wagnerian roles. In 1937 she toured Australia; in 1938 she settled in the U.S.; lived mostly in California. She publ. a novel, *Orplid Mein Land* (1937; in English as *Eternal Flight,* 1938), and an autobiography, *Anfang und Aufstieg* (Vienna, 1937; London, as *Wings of Song,* and N.Y., as *Midway in My Song,* 1938); *More than Singing* (N.Y., 1945); *My Many Lives* (N.Y., 1948; a sequel to the previous volume); also

publ. a book of reminiscences, *Five Operas and Richard Strauss* (N.Y., 1964).

BIBLIOGRAPHY: B. W. Wessling, *Lotte Lehmann, mehr als eine Sängerin* (Salzburg, 1969).

Lehmann, Marie, dramatic soprano; sister of **Lilli Lehmann;** b. Hamburg, May 15, 1851; d. Berlin, Dec. 9, 1931. She was a pupil of her mother, and later of her sister; made her debut in Leipzig (May 1, 1867); in 1876 she created the parts of Wellgunde (*Rheingold* and *Götterdämmerung*) and Ortlinde (*Walküre*) at Bayreuth; from 1881 until her retirement in 1902 she was a member of the Vienna court opera; then lived in Berlin as a teacher.

Lehmann, Robert, German cellist; b. Schweidnitz, Silesia, Nov. 26, 1841; d. Stettin, June 12, 1912. He studied organ and cello; settled in Stettin in 1875 as church organist and conductor. He publ. a series of waltzes for orch. under the title *Briefe aus Wien,* melodious pieces for cello, and some church music; also wrote an autobiography, *Erinnerungen eines Künstlers* (1895).

Leibowitz, René, Polish-French composer and theorist; b. Warsaw, Feb. 17, 1913; d. Paris, Aug. 28, 1972. His family settled in Paris in 1926; from 1930 till 1933 he studied in Berlin with Schoenberg and in Vienna with Anton von Webern; under their influence he adopted the 12-tone method of composition; upon his return to France he became the foremost exponent of the 12-tone method in France; he had numerous private students, among them Boulez. He published *Schoenberg et son école* (Paris, 1947; in English, N.Y., 1949); *Introduction à la musique de douze sons* (Paris, 1949); a manual of orchestration, *Thinking for Orchestra* (with Jan Maguire; N.Y., 1958); *Histoire de l'Opéra* (Paris, 1957); *Erich Itor Kahn, un grand représentant de la musique contemporaine* (with Konrad Wolff; Paris 1958; in English, N.Y. 1958).

WORKS: operas, *La Nuit close* (1949); *La Rumeur de l'espace* (1950); *Ricardo Gonfolano* (1953); *Les Espagnols à Venise,* opera buffa (1963; Grenoble, Jan. 27, 1970); *Labyrinthe,* after Bandelaire (1969); *Todos caerán,* to Leibowitz's own libretto (1970–72); for orch.: *Fantaisie symphonique* (1956); Violin Concerto (1959); *3 Bagatelles* for string orch. (1959); Concertino for Trombone (1960); Cello Concerto (1962); *Rapsodie Symphonique* (1964–65); chamber music: *Marijuana* for violin, trombone, vibraphone and piano (1960); *Sinfonietta da camera* (1961); *Capriccio* for flute and strings (1967); *Suite* for 9 instruments (1967); Saxophone Quartet (1969); *Petite Suite* for clarinet sextet (1970); 8 string quartets (1940, 1950, 1952, 1958, 1963, 1965, 1966, 1968); vocal works: *Tourist Death* for soprano and chamber orch. (1943); *L'Explication des Métaphores* for speaker, 2 pianos, harp and percussion (1947); *Chanson Dada* for children's chorus and instruments (1968); *Laboratoire central* for speaker and chorus (1970); numerous solo songs.

Leibrock, Joseph Adolf, German cellist and harpist; b. Brunswick, Jan. 8, 1808; d. Berlin, Aug. 8, 1886. He studied in Berlin; Dr. phil.; cellist and harpist in the court orch. at Brunswick. He wrote music to Schiller's

Räuber; part-songs; arrangements for piano and cello; *Musikalische Akkordenlehre;* etc.

Leichtentritt, Hugo, eminent German-American music scholar; b. Pleschen, Posen, Jan. 1, 1874; d. Cambridge, Mass., Nov. 13, 1951. He was educated at Harvard Univ. (1891–94) and took a music course with Prof. Paine; went to Berlin in 1895 to complete his musical studies; obtained the degree of Dr. phil. at Berlin Univ. with the dissertation *Reinhard Keiser in seinen Opern* (1901); he subsequently taught at the Klindworth–Scharwenka Cons. and wrote music criticism for German and American publications. In 1934 he left Germany and became lecturer on music at Harvard Univ. Although known chiefly as a scholar, Leichtentritt was also a composer; he wrote a symphony, a violin concerto, a cello concerto, a piano concerto, much chamber music, several song cycles and numerous piano pieces. He also wrote a comic opera, *Der Sizilianer,* which was produced in Freiburg on May 28, 1920. All his music manuscripts were donated after his death to the Library of Congress in Washington, D.C.
WRITINGS: *Chopin* (1905); *Geschichte der Motette* (Leipzig, 1908; a fundamental source on the subject); *Musikalische Formenlehre* (Leipzig, 1911; 5th ed., 1952; in English as *Musical Form,* Cambridge, Mass., 1951); *Erwin Lendvai* (Berlin, 1912); *Ferruccio Busoni* (Leipzig, 1916); *Analyse der Chopinschen Klavierwerke* (2 vols.; Berlin, 1920, 1922); *Händel* (Berlin, 1924; very valuable); *The Complete Piano Sonatas of Beethoven* (analytical notes; N.Y., 1936); *Everybody's Little History of Music* (N.Y., 1938); *Music, History, and Ideas* (Cambridge, Mass. 1938; very successful; 14 printings); *Boston Symph. Orch. and the New American Music* (Cambridge, Mass., 1946); *Music of the Western Nations* (posthumous; edited and amplified by N. Slonimsky; Cambridge, Mass., 1956).

Leider, Frida, German opera soprano; b. Berlin, April 18, 1888; d. Berlin, June 3, 1975. After several years of study in Milan, she became a member of the Berlin Opera; made her American debut with the Chicago Opera as Brünnhilde in *Die Walküre* in 1928; appeared with the Metropolitan Opera for the first time on Jan. 16, 1933 as Isolde; then returned to Germany. She published an autobiography, *Das war mein Teil, Erinnrungen einer Opernsängerin* (Berlin, 1959); in English, *Playing My Part* (N.Y., 1966).

Leifs, Jón, foremost Icelandic composer and writer; b. Sólheimar, May 1, 1899; d. Reykjavik, Iceland, July 30, 1968. After completing his primary education at Reykjavik, he went to Germany, where he studied at the Leipzig Cons. with Teichmüller, Szendrei, Scherchen, Lohse, and Graener; then conducted concerts in various German towns; in 1926 led the Hamburg Philharmonic when it visited Iceland; from 1934–37, musical director of the Icelandic Radio; also president of the Council of Northern Composers (1951) and other musical societies in Iceland and Scandinavia. His music is technically derived from the German Romantic tradition; but in several of his works he makes use of Icelandic melodies and rhythms; often he abandons

opulent harmonic accoutrements to portray Arctic nature in bleak, organum-like diaphony.
WORKS: wordless music dramas, *Loftr* (Copenhagen, Sept. 3, 1938) and *Baldr* (1950); *Hljomkvida,* symph. trilogy (Karlsbad, 1925); *Icelandic Overture* (Oslo, 1926; his most successful work); *Kyrie on Icelandic Themes* for a cappella chorus; *Island-Kantate* (Greifswald, 1930); *Saga–symfoni* (Helsinki, Sept. 18, 1950); 2 string quartets; several piano cycles based on Icelandic dance tunes; songs. He publ. (in Icelandic) a manual on musical forms; in German, *Islands künstlerische Anregung* (Reykjavik, 1951); contributed articles on Icelandic music to *Die Musik* (Oct. 1923), *Volk und Rasse* (Munich, 1932), and other publications.

Leigh, Walter, English composer; b. London, June 22, 1905; killed in action near Tobruk, Libya, June 12, 1942. He was a student of Edward Dent at Cambridge; also took lessons with Harold Darke and later with Paul Hindemith at the Hochschule für Musik in Berlin (1927–29). He was particularly adept in his writing for the theater.
WORKS: 2 light operas, *The Pride of the Regiment or Cashiered for His Country* (Midhurst, England, Sept. 19, 1931) and *The Jolly Roger, or The Admiral's Daughter* (Manchester, England, Feb. 13, 1933); a musical revue, *Nine Sharp* (London, 1938); several pieces designated for amateur orchestra; Sontina for viola and piano (performed at the Festival of the International Society for Contemporary Music, Vienna, June 17, 1932); Trio for 3 pianos (1934); Trio for flute, oboe, and piano (1935); several scores of incidental music for the theater; piano pieces and songs.

Leighton, Kenneth, English composer; b. Wakefield, Yorkshire, Oct. 2, 1929. He enrolled at the Queen's College, Oxford, to study classics and music (B. Mus., 1951); later took courses with Goffredo Petrassi in Rome. In 1956–68 he was lecturer in composition at the Univ. of Edinburgh; then Lecturer in Music at Worcester College, Oxford (1968–70), and from 1970 again at the Univ. of Edinburgh.
WORKS: Symph. for strings (1948); *Primavera romana,* overture (1951); Piano Concerto (1951); Concerto for Viola, Harp, Timpani and Strings (1952); Violin Concerto (1952); Concerto for Oboe and Strings (1953); Concerto for 2 Pianos, Timpani and Strings (1953); Cello Concerto (1956); Piano Quintet (1962); 2 violin sonatas (1951, 1956); 2 string quartets (1956, 1957); *Fantasia contrapuntistica* for piano (1956); *Sinfonia sacra, The Light Invisible* for tenor, chorus and orch. to texts from the Bible and poems by T.S. Eliot (1958); other choral music.

Leighton, Sir William, English musician, "gentleman pensioner"; b. c.1560; d. before 1617. He publ. *The Teares or Lamentacions of a Sorrowfull Soule Composed with Musicall Ayres and Songs both for Voyces and Divers Instruments* (1614), containing 54 metrical psalms and hymns, 17 being for 4 voices with accompaniments in tablature for the lute, bandora, and cittern, and 13 for 4 voices and 24 for 5 voices without accompaniment. The first 8 are by Leighton himself;

the others are by Bull, Byrd, Dowland, Gibbons, Coperario, Weelkes, Wilbye, etc. Excerpts have been transcribed into modern notation and scored by S. Beck (New York Public Library, 1934).

BIBLIOGRAPHY: M. Seiffert, in the *Bulletin de la Société Musicologique* (1922); J. Pulver, *A Biographical Dictionary of Old English Music* (1927).

Leimer, Kurt, German pianist and composer; b. Wiesbaden, Sept. 7, 1920; d. Vaduz, Liechtenstein, Nov. 20, 1974. He studied piano with his great-uncle Karl Leimer (1858–1944), who was the teacher of Gieseking. After a brief concert career, he took lessons in composition with Kurt von Wolfurt; made rapid progress as a composer, and produced 4 piano concertos (one for left hand), all very effective in their highflown Romantic style; he was soloist in his 4th Piano Concerto in N.Y., on Oct. 14, 1956, with Stokowski conducting; Karajan also conducted some of his works. Leimer became an Austrian citizen in 1956, but lived in Vaduz.

Leinsdorf, Erich, eminent Austrian conductor; b. Vienna, Feb. 4, 1912. He studied with Paul Emerich and Hedwig Kammer-Rosenthal at the Vienna Staatsakademie; in 1934 he became assistant to Bruno Walter and Toscanini at the Salzburg Festival; subsequently he appeared as symphony conductor in Italy and in France. In 1938 he was engaged as a conductor of the Metropolitan Opera House, N.Y., and made his American debut in *Die Walküre* (Jan. 21, 1938) with excellent success; he then conducted other Wagner operas and soon established a reputation as a first ranking interpreter of Wagner's music drama. He conducted the Cleveland Orch. in 1943; then was in the U.S. Army; conducted in Europe after the end of the war. From 1947 to 1956 he was conductor and music director of the Rochester Philharmonic Orch. From 1955 to 1962 he conducted at the N.Y. City Opera and also fulfilled guest engagements in Europe and in the U.S. His most important position was that of conductor and music director at the Boston Symph. Orch., a post which he held from 1962 till 1969; afterwards he conducted opera and symphony concerts mainly in Europe. He publ. a semi-autobiographical book and rather candid book of comments, *Cadenza, a Musical Career* (New York, 1976).

Leisinger, Elisabeth, German coloratura soprano; b. Stuttgart, May 17, 1864; d. there, Dec. 15, 1933. She was a daughter of the singer **Bertha Leisinger** (1825–1913), and received her training from her; subsequently studied with Pauline Viardot–Garcia in Paris. In 1884 she was engaged at the Berlin Opera; sang there for ten seasons; she married in 1894, and retired from the stage.

Leite, Antonio da Silva, Portuguese composer; b. Oporto, May 23, 1759; d. there, Jan 10, 1833. He was conductor at the Oporto Cathedral from 1787 to 1826. He wrote 2 operas; publ. *Rezumo de todas as regras e preceitos de cantoria assim da musica metrica como da cantochão* (Oporto, 1787) and a guitar method, *Estudo de guitarra* (Oporto, 1796).

Leitert, Johann Georg, German pianist and composer; b. Dresden, Sept. 29, 1852; d. Hubertusburg, near Dresden, Sept. 6, 1901. He studied with Kragen and Reichel (piano) and Rischbieter (harmony). In 1865 he made his concert debut in Dresden; then played in Leipzig, Berlin, Prague, etc.; toured successfully in England in 1867; also gave concerts in Austria and Russia. From 1879–81 he taught at the Horák Music School in Vienna; wrote many characteristic pieces for piano: *Esquisses, Chants du crépuscule, Herbstblätter, Strahlen und Schatten, Aus schönern Stunden, Feuilles d'amour, Lose Blätter, Valse Caprice,* etc.; also transcriptions for piano (chiefly from Wagner's works).

Leitzmann, Albert, German theorist and musicologist; b. Magdeburg, Aug. 3, 1867; d. Jena, April 16, 1950. He studied chiefly literature and esthetics; established himself as Privatdozent for German language and literature at the Univ. of Jena. Besides numerous books dealing with literature and philology, he publ. *Beethovens Briefe* (1909; 3d ed. 1933); *Mozarts Briefe* (1910); *Mozarts Persönlichkeit* (1914); *Beethovens Persönlichkeit* (2 vols., 1914); *Beethovens persönliche Aufzeichnungen* (1918); *Ludwig van Beethoven. Berichte der Zeitgenossen* (2 vols., 1921); *W.A. Mozart. Berichte der Zeitgenossen* (1926).

Leiviskä, Helvi, Finnish composer; b. Helsinki, May 25, 1902. She studied under Erkki Melartin at the Helsinki School of Music, and with Arthur Willner in Vienna; subsequently served as a librarian of the Sibelius Academy in Helsinki. She is one of the very few women composers of symphonic music in Finland.

WORKS: *Folk Dance Suite* for orch. (1929, revised 1971); Piano Concerto (1935); 2 orch. suites (1934, 1938); *Triple Fugue* for orch. (1935); *Pimeän peikko (Goblin of Darkness)* for chorus and orch. (1942); 3 symphonies (1947, 1954, 1971); *Mennyt manner (The Lost Continent)* for solo voices, chorus, and orch. (1957); *Sinfonia Brevis* (1962, revised 1972); Piano Quartet (1926); String Quartet (1926); Violin Sonata (1945).

Le Jeune, Claude (or **Claudin**), French composer; b. Valenciennes, 1528; d. Paris, Sept. 25, 1600. He was active chiefly in Paris, where he appears to have been for some time associated with the poet Antoine de Baïf in the Académie de Musique, founded to encourage the growth of a new style of musical composition known as "musique mesurée," in which the music is made to follow the metrical rhythm of the text in conformity with the rules of classical prosody. The type of poetry set to music in this manner was called "vers mesurez," and 33 examples of such settings by Le Jeune are to be found in the work entitled *Le Printemps,* publ. posthumously at Paris in 1603 by his sister Cécile Le Jeune. The metrical scanning is given at the head of each song. In the preface to this work Le Jeune is given credit for having been the first to achieve the "mating of ancient rhythm and modern harmony"; if not the first, he was at least, together with his contemporary and friend, Jacques Mauduit, one of the earliest and most notable cultivators of this new and significant style. Le Jeune also cultivated every other variety of vocal music known in his time, such as French chansons in "vers rimez," Italian madrigals, Latin motets, etc. Special mention must be made of his settings of the Psalms, of which several collections appeared from 1564-1606. So great was his renown even during his lifetime that a wood engraving dated 1598 bore the legend: "Le Phénix des Musiciens." His best-known work is his setting of the Genevan Psalter *a* 4 and 5, publ. by Cécile Le Jeune in 1613. This simple contrapuntal setting of the Psalms was widely used in the Reformed churches of France and Holland, and it was also publ. in a German transl. Some of these harmonizations even found their way into early New England psalm books, such as *The Ainsworth Psalter* (cf. *Early Psalmody in America,* ed. by C. S. Smith for the New York Public Library, 1939). A more elaborate setting of some psalms, *Douze Psaumes de David,* in motet style for 2 to 7 voices, was contained in the work entitled *Dodecacorde,* publ. at La Rochelle in 1598. On the title page of this work, Le Jeune is described as "compositeur de la musique de la chambre du roy," showing that he was then attached to the court of Henri IV. It is known that he had espoused the Huguenot cause during the wars of the Catholic League, and it is said that his manuscripts narrowly escaped destruction during the siege of Paris in 1588, having been saved only by the intervention of his Catholic colleague Mauduit. In 1612 a nephew of Le Jeune publ. a *Second livre de meslanges à 4-10,* containing miscellaneous vocal pieces and two instumental fantasias. The most important works of Le Jeune have been reprinted by H. Expert in his *Maîtres musiciens de la renaissance française,* as follows: *Dodecacorde* (vol. 11), *Le Printemps* (vols. 12-14), one part of the *Livre de meslanges* (vol. 16), *Psaumes en vers mesurez* (vols. 20-22); also, in *Monuments de la musique française* (vols. 1 and 8) are *Octonaires de la vanité et inconstance du monde* and other works; *Missa ad placitum* is in *Le Pupitre* 2; chansons in *Florilège du concert vocal de la renaissance* 6; the *Airs* (1608) are publ. in 4 vols. by D.P. Walker in the *Miscellenea* series of the American Institute of Musicology.

BIBLIOGRAPHY: E. Bouton, *Esquisse biographique et bibliographique sur Claude Le Jeune* (Valenciennes, 1845); M. Cauchie, "La Mort de Claude Le Jeune," *Revue de Musicologie* (Aug. 1927); D. P. Walker and F. Lesure, "Claude Le Jeune and *Musique mesurée*," *Musica Disciplina* (1949).

Lekeu, Guillaume, talented Belgian composer; b. Heusy, near Verviers, Jan. 20, 1870; d. Angers, Jan. 21, 1894. He went to school in Poitiers; after graduation followed his family to Paris, where he studied with Gaston Vallin; he also received some advice from César Franck and took a course with Vincent d'Indy. He subsequently went to Brussels to compete for the Belgian Prix de Rome; won second prize with his cantata *Andromède* (1891). Returning to Paris he wrote several works of excellent quality, but death (of typhoid fever) intervened when he was barely 24 years old. His style of composition was influenced mainly by César Franck; his most durable work, a violin sonata with modal inflections and chromatic progres-

sions, closely follows the procedures of Franck's Violin Sonata.

WORKS: The list of his works is necessarily small; Cello Sonata (1888); *Adagio* for strings (1888); *Chant de triomphale délivrance* for orch. (1889); *Hamlet* for orch. (1890); *Fantaisie sur un cramignon liégois* for orch. (1890); *Chant lyrique* for chorus and orch. (1891); *Introduction et Adagio* for tuba and wind orch. (1891); Piano Trio (1891); Violin Sonata (1891; his most frequently performed work); Piano Sonata (1891); *Fantaisie sur deux airs angevins* for orch. (1892); *Suite* for voice and orch. (1892); *Barberine* (fragments for an opera); *Chanson de mai,* for chorus and orch.; *Adagio* for string quartet; *Épithalame* for strings, trombones and organ; String Quartet; *Meditation* and *Minuet* for string quartet; *Noël* for soprano, string quartet and piano; Piano Quartet (unfinished; completed by Vincent d'Indy); Piano Sonata; *Tempo di mazurka* for piano; a group of songs.

BIBLIOGRAPHY: A. Tissier, *Guillaume Lekeu* (Verviers, 1906); R. Vandelle, "Guillaume Lekeu," *Revue Musicale* (1921); M. Lorrain, *Guillaume Lekeu, Sa correspondance, sa vie et son œuvre* (Liège, 1923); R. Stengel, *Lekeu* (Brussels, 1944); P. Prist, *Guillaume Lekeu* (Brussels, 1946).

Lemacher, Heinrich, German composer; b. Solingen, June 26, 1891; d. Cologne, March 16, 1966. He studied at the Cons. of Cologne; 1928, he became a teacher at the Cologne Hochschule für Musik. A disciple of the German Romantic school, he elaborated its principles in a number of choral and instrumental works; the chief influences are Bruckner and Reger; he wrote several symph. suites; chamber music; piano pieces. More important than these are his compositions for the Catholic service: several Masses, offertories, motets, cantatas with organ accompaniment, etc., in which he succeeded in establishing a practical style of modern polyphony. Written shortly before his death, his last work, Sextet for 3 trumpets, 2 trombones and tuba, bears the op. number 208. He published several books on music theory: *Lehrbuch des Kontrapunktes* (Mainz, 1950; 4th ed., 1962); *Harmomielehre* (Cologne, 1958; 5th ed., 1967) and *Formenlehre der Musik* (with H. Schroeder, Cologne, 1962; in English as *Musical Form* 1967).

BIBLIOGRAPHY: Karl Laux "Heinrich Lemacher," in *Musik und Musiker der Gegenwart* (Essen, 1949; pp. 153-62).

Lemaire (or **Le Maire**), **Jean,** French musician; b. Chaumont en Bassigny, 1581; d. about 1650. He is said to have proposed the adoption of a 7th solmisation syllable *si* (so asserted by Rousseau in his *Dictionnaire de Musique; za,* according to Mersenne's *Harmonie universalle*). However, the designation *si* seems to have been proposed even earlier, so the question of priority remains moot. Lemaire constructed a lute which he called "almérie" (anagram of Lemaire).

BIBLIOGRAPHY: J. R. Knowlson, "Jean Le Maire, the Almérie, and the 'Musique Almerique': A set of Unpublished Documents," *Acta Musicologica* (1968).

Lemaire, Jean Eugène Gaston, French composer; b. Château d'Amblainvilliers, Seine-et-Oise, Sept. 9,

1854; d. (suicide; body found in the Seine) Paris, Jan. 9, 1928. He studied at the École Niedermeyer; was a prolific composer of light music (operettas, piano pieces, and characteristic pieces for orch.).

WORKS: *Perrette et le pot au lait*, pantomime (Paris, Feb. 11, 1891); *Conte de printemps*, pantomime (Paris, May 18, 1892); *La Belle Tunisienne*, opera in 1 act (Paris, Aug. 26, 1892); the operettas *Les Maris de Juanita*, *Le Supplice de Jeannot*, *Le Rêve de Manette*; *Rose*, lyric fairy tale (Paris, March 14, 1895); the ballets *Feminissima* (1902) and *Pierrot venge son Rival* (1917). He also wrote a number of fox-trots, one of which, *La Grenouille*, became popular, and songs, of which *Vous dansez, marquise*, was a great favorite.

Le Maistre (or **Le Maître**), **Mattheus,** Flemish composer; b. near Liège, c.1505; d. Dresden, 1577. In 1554 he succeeded J. Walter as Kapellmeister at the court in Dresden; retired on a pension Feb. 12, 1568. Fétis and Otto Kade wrongly identified him with Hermann Matthias Werrekoren, choirmaster in Milan.

WORKS: *Magnificat octo tonorum* (1577); *Catechesis numeris musicis inclusa* (1563; for the choirboys of the Dresden Chapel); *Geistliche und weltliche teutsche Gesänge*, for 4-5 voices (1566); motets for 5 voices (1570); *Officia de nativitate et Ascensione Christi*, for 5 voices (1574); *Schöne und auserlesene teutsche und lateinische geistliche Lieder* (1577). A motet, *Estote prudentes* (4 voices) is in Commer's *Collectio* (vol. 8); 2 lieder for 4 voices are in Ambros' *Geschichte der Musik* (vol. 5, *Beispielband*, ed. by O. Kade, 1882).

BIBLIOGRAPHY: O. Kade, monograph on Le Maistre (Mainz, 1862); René Vannes, *Dictionnaire des Musiciens* (Brussels, 1947; pp. 242–44).

Lemare, Edwin Henry, British-American organist; b. Ventnor, Isle of Wight, Sept. 9, 1865; d. Los Angeles, Sept. 24, 1934. He received his early training from his father, an organist; then studied at The Royal Academy of Music in London; at the age of 19 he played at the Inventions Exhibition in London; in 1892 he began a series of weekly organ recitals at Holy Trinity Church, London; from 1897 to 1902 he was organist at St. Margaret's Westminister. In 1901 he made a concert tour through the U.S. and Canada; from 1902 to 1905 he was organist of the Carnegie Institute of Pittsburgh; then held the post of municipal organist in San Francisco (1917–21), Portland, Maine (1921–23) and Chattanooga, Tennessee (1924–29). He publ. about 200 organ works and made many arrangements. His *Andantino in D-flat* acquired wide popularity when it was used for the American ballad *Moonlight and Roses.* His booklet of reminiscences, *Organs I Have Met,* was publ. posthumously in 1957.

Lemit, William, French ethnomusicologist; b. Paris, Dec. 15, 1908; d. there (by suicide), Aug. 21, 1966. He was entirely autodidact in music; traveled through the French countryside collecting popular songs. He publ. several song anthologies of French children's rhymes, among them *La Vie du garçon* (1950); *Les Jeux chantés enfantins du folklore français* (1957).

Lemmens, Nicolas Jacques, Belgian organist; b. Zoerle-Parwys, Jan. 3, 1823; d. Castle Linterport, near Malines, Jan. 30, 1881. He was trained in music by his father; then attended the Brussels Cons., where he was appointed prof. of organ in 1849. He composed principally for organ and publ. the useful *École d'orgue.* His book *Du chant grégorien, sa mélodie, son rhythme, son harmonisation,* was publ. posthumously in 1886; 4 vols. of his sacred choral works and organ pieces were publ. by Breitkopf & Härtel.

Lemoine, Antoine-Marcel, French music publisher, violinist, and guitar player; father of **Henry Lemoine;** b. Paris, Nov. 3, 1753; d. there, April 10, 1816. A self-taught musician, he played viola at the Théâtre de Monsieur, conducted at minor Parisian theaters, and finally founded a music publishing firm.

Lemoine, Henry, French music publisher, son of **Antoine-Marcel Lemoine;** b. Paris, Oct. 21, 1786; d. there, May 18, 1854. He studied at the Paris Cons. (1798–1809); in 1821 he also had harmony lessons from Reicha; taught the piano; at his father's death, in 1817, succeeded to the latter's music publishing business. He publ. methods for harmony, piano, and solfeggio; *Tablettes du pianiste: memento du professeur de piano*; sonatas, variations, dances, etc., for piano.

Lemont, Cedric Wilmont, organist; b. Fredericton, New Brunswick, Canada, Dec. 15, 1879; d. New York, April 27, 1954. He studied with Carl Faelten (piano) and Dunham (organ) in Boston; filled various positions as organist and choirmaster in Canada; in 1907, settled in the U.S.; taught in Chicago and Brooklyn. He publ. over 600 compositions, including piano pieces, anthems, etc.; brought out 3 vols. of *American History and Encyclopedia of Music.*

Lemoyne, Jean Baptiste, French conductor and composer; b. Eymet, Périgord, April 3, 1751; d. Paris, Dec. 30, 1796. He studied with Graun and Kirnberger at Berlin, where he became 2nd Kapellmeister to Frederick the Great. Returning to Paris, he brought out an opera, *Électre* (1782), pretending to be a pupil of Gluck, an imposture that Gluck did not see fit to expose until the failure of Lemoyne's piece. In his next operas, Lemoyne abandoned Gluck's ideas, copied the style of Piccinni and Sacchini, and produced several successful works, including *Phèdre* (Fountainebleau, Oct. 26, 1786) and *Nephté* (Paris, Dec. 15, 1789).

Lenaerts, Constant, Belgian conductor and composer; b. Antwerp, March 9, 1852; d. there, March 20, 1931. He studied with Peter Benoît; began to conduct at the Flemish National Theater at the age of 18; in 1914, was appointed teacher at the Antwerp Cons. He wrote a cantata, *De triomf van't licht* (1890), songs, and some instrumental music.

Lendvai, Erwin, Hungarian conductor and composer; b. Budapest, June 4, 1882; d. Epsom, Surrey, March 31, 1949. He studied with Koessler; later went to Milan, where he had some lessons with Puccini; taught at Jaques-Dalcroze's School of Eurhythmics for a season (1913–14); then was instructor of dramatic composition at Hoch's Cons. in Frankfurt; later at the Klindworth-Scharwenka Cons. in Berlin (1919–22); teacher at the Hamburg Volksmusikschule (1923–25); choral conductor in Coblenz (1926–27); then in Munich and in Erfurt; in 1938 he went to Switzerland, and later to London, where he remained until his death. He composed a symphony (1909); *Archaische Tänze* for small orch.; *Masken*, an orchestral scherzo; *Nippon*, choral suite for women's voices; string quartet; several piano trios and other chamber music; also an opera *Elga* (Mannheim, Dec. 6, 1916); publ. a valuable method, *Chorschule*.

BIBLIOGRAPHY: Hugo Leichtentritt, *Erwin Lendvai* (Berlin, 1912).

Lendvay, Kamilló, Hungarian composer; b. Budapest, Dec. 28, 1928. He studied composition with Viski at the Budapest Academy of Music; devoted himself mainly to the musical theater, as composer and conductor; in 1973 was appointed conductor of the Capitol Operetta Theater; also taught at the Budapest Academy.

WORKS: A television opera buffa *Abűvös szék (The Magic Chair*, 1972); 4 musicals: *The 3 Muskateers* (1962), *10 Days That Shook the World* (1967), *Ex* (1968) and *Knock Out* (1968); 2 ballets: *Eszmélés (Awakening*, 1964) and *Musica leggiera*, jazz ballet (1965); an oratorio *Orogenesis* (1969); *Tragic Overture* (1958); *Mauthausen* for orch. (1958); Concertino for piano, wind instruments, percussion and harp (1959); *The Indomitable Tin Soldier*, orch. suite with narrator (1961); Violin Concerto (1961–62); *4 Invocations* for orch. (1966); Chamber Concerto for 13 instruments (1969); *Kifejezések (Expressions)* for 11 strings or string orch. (1974); *Pezzo concertato* for cello and orch. (Trieste, Oct. 18, 1975); *Fantasy* for violin and piano (1951); *Rhapsody* for violin and piano (1955); String Quartet (1962); *4 Duos* for flute and piano (1965); *Disposizioni* for solo cimbalom (1975); choruses; songs.

Lenepveu, Charles (Ferdinand), French composer and pedogogue; b. Rouen, Oct. 4, 1840; d. Paris, Aug. 16, 1910. As a law student he took music lessons from Servais; won 1st prize at Caen in 1861 for a cantata; entered Ambroise Thomas' class at the Paris Cons. in 1863, and in 1865 took the Grand Prix de Rome with the cantata *Renaud dans les jardins d'Armide* (Paris, Jan. 3, 1866). His comic opera *Le Florentin* also won a prize, offered by the ministry of Fine Arts (1867), and was performed at the Opéra-Comique (Feb. 26, 1874). The grand opera *Velléda* was produced at Coven Garden, London (July 4, 1882), with Adelina Patti in the title role. In 1891 Lenepveu succeeded Guiraud as harmony prof. at the Cons., and in 1893 again succeeded him as prof. of composition, taking an advanced class in 1894. In 1896 he was elected to Ambroise Thomas' chair in the Académie des Beaux–Arts; was Chevalier of the Legion of Honor, and Officer of Public Instruction.

BIBLIOGRAPHY: R. de Saint–Arroman, *Charles Lenepveu* (Paris, 1898).

Léner, Jenö, Hungarian violinist; b. Szabadka, April 7, 1894; d. New York, Nov. 4, 1948. He studied at the Hungarian Music Academy in Budapest; worked as a violinist in theater orchestras; in 1918 organized the Léner String Quartet (with Joseph Smilovits, Sándor Roth amd Imre Hartmann), which became one of the most renowned string quartets of modern times; it was particularly noted for its interpretation of Beethoven's quartets. In 1925 Léner took his quartet to London, and in 1929 to the U.S.; it was disbanded in 1942, but reorganized, with a partly new membership, in 1945. The fame enjoyed by the Léner quartet can be judged by Aldous Huxley's discussion of its performance of Beethoven's last quartets in his novel *Point Counterpoint* (1928).

BIBLIOGRAPHY: Antal Molnár, *The Léner Quartet* (Budapest, 1968; also in English, in the series Great Hungarian Performers, 1969).

Leng, Alfonso, Chilean composer; b. Santiago, Feb. 11, 1884; d. there, Nov. 7, 1974. He was of mixed German and English descent; studied dentistry, and became a professional dentist in Santiago; also took music lessons with Enrique Soro. In his leisure time, he composed short symphonic sketches in a Romantic vein, songs, and evocative piano pieces.

WORKS: *5 Dolores* for orch. (1920); *La Muerte de Alsino*, symph. poem (1920; Santiago, May 30, 1931); *Canto de Invierno* for orch. (1932); *Fantasia* for piano and orch. (Santiago, August. 28, 1936); *Psalm 77* for soloists, chorus and orch. (1941); *Fantasia quasi Sonata* for piano (1909); *10 Preludes* for piano (1919–32); *Andante* for piano and string quartet (1922); *2 Otoñales* for piano (1932); 2 piano sonatas (1927, 1950); many songs. A special issue of the *Revista Musical Chilena* (Aug.–Sept., 1957) was publ. in his honor with articles by Domingo Santa Cruz, Alfonso Letelier, and others.

Lennon, John (Winston), English rock 'n' roll singer, guitarist, poet and instinctive composer, member of the celebrated rock group The Beatles; b. Liverpool, Oct. 9, 1940, during a German air raid on the city. He was educated by an aunt after his parents separated; played the mouth organ as a child; later learned the guitar; was encouraged to become a musician by the conductor of a Liverpool-Edinburgh bus. Emotionally rocked over by Elvis Presley's animal magnetism, he became infatuated with American popular music. With three other rock-crazed Liverpudlians, Paul McCartney, George Harrison and Stuart Sutcliffe, he formed a pop combo. Inspired by the success of a local group, The Crickets, Lennon hit upon the name The Beatles which possessed the acoustical ring of the coleopterous insect, beetle, and the rock-associated beat. The Beatles opened at the pseudo-exotic Casbah Club in Liverpool in 1959; soon moved to the more prestigious Cavern Club, where they co-opted Pete Best as a drummer. In 1960 they played in Hamburg, scoring a gratifyingly vulgar success with the beer-sodden customers by their loud, electrically amplified sound. Back in England, The Beatles crept on to fame. In 1961 they were taken up by the perspicacious promoter Brian Epstein who launched an extensive publicity campaign to put them over the footlights. Sutcliffe died of a brain hemorrhage in 1962. Pete Best left the group and was replaced by Richard Starkey, whose "nom-de-beatle" became Ringo Starr. The quartet opened at the London Palladium in 1963 and drove the youthful audience to a frenzy, a scene that was to be repeated in America, in Europe, in Japan and in Australia. After a period of shocked recoil, the British establishment acknowledged the beneficent contribution of The Beatles to British art and the Exchequer. In 1965 Queen Elizabeth II bestowed upon them the Order of the British Empire. Although American in origin, the type of popular music plied by John Lennon and The Beatles as a group has an indefinably British lilt. The meter is square; the main beat is accentuated; syncopation is at a minimum; the harmony is modal, with a lowered submediant in major keys as a constantly present feature; a propensity for plagal cadences and a proclivity for consecutive triadic progressions create at times a curiously hymnal mood. But professional arrangers employed by The Beatles invested their bland melodies in raucous dissonance; electronic amplification made the music of The Beatles the loudest in the world for their time. The lyrics, most of them written by John Lennon and Paul McCartney, are distinguished by suggestive allusions, sensuous but not flagrantly erotic, anarchistic but not destructive, cynical but also humane. There are covert references to psychedelic drugs. The Beatles produced the highly original films: *A Hard Day's Night, Help!, Yellow Submarine* and *Let It Be.* The most successful individual songs in the Beatles' repertory are: *Love Me Do, I Want To Hold Your Hand, Can't Buy Me Love, Ticket to Ride, Day Tripper, All My Loving, I Wanna Be Your Man, And I Love Her, Eight Days a Week, Yesterday, Michelle, Eleanor Rigby, With a Little Help from My Friends, Sergeant Pepper's Lonely Hearts Club Band, Magical Mystery Tour, Lady Madonna, Your Gonna Lose That Girl, Norwegian Wood, Good Day Sunshine, Hey Jude;* also title songs of the films.

BIBLIOGRAPHY: Hunter Davies, *The Beatles,* "the authorized biography" (N.Y., 1968); Ned Rorem, "The Beatles," *N.Y. Review of Books* (Jan. 18, 1968); G. Geppert, *Songs der Beatles. Texte und Interpretationen* (2nd ed. Munich, 1968); E. Davies, "The Psychological Characteristics of Beatle Mania," *Journal of the History of Ideas* (April-June 1969); P. McCabe and R. D. Schonfeld, *Apple to the Core: The Unmaking of the Beatles* (N.Y., 1972); F. Seloron, *Les Beatles* (Paris, 1972); W. Mellers, *Twilight of the Gods: The Music of the Beatles* (N.Y., 1973).

Lenormand, René, French composer; b. Elbeuf, Aug. 5, 1846; d. Paris, Dec. 3, 1932. He recieved his musical training from his mother, who was an excellent pianist; in 1868, went to Paris, where he studied with Damcke. Lenormand's main interest was in the creation of an international type of the German lied, and for that purpose he organized in Paris a society which he called "Le Lied en tous pays." Besides his songs, Lenormand wrote an opera, *Le Cachet rouge* (Le Havre, 1925); a piano concerto; *Le Lahn de Mabed* (on an old Arabian theme), for violin and orch.; *Le Voyage imaginaire,* symph. tableaux after Loti; *Deux Esquisses sur des thèmes malais,* for orch.; piano pieces *(Une Journée à la campagne, Le Nuage vivant, Valses sérieuses, Pièces exotiques,* etc.; for 4 hands: *Diver-*

tissement américain, La Nouba Medjenneba, etc.); also publ. a valuable manual on harmony, *Étude sur l'harmonie moderne* (Paris, 1912; English transl. as *A Study of Modern Harmony,* London, 1915).

BIBLIOGRAPHY: H. Woollett, *Un mélodiste français: René Lenormand* (Paris, 1930).

Lent, Ernest, German cellist and composer; b. Brandenburg, Sept. 18, 1856; d. Washington, D.C., Dec. 22, 1922. He studied at the Leipzig Cons. (1878-81); toured in Europe as a concert cellist; in 1884, settled in Washington as a teacher. He publ. numerous pieces for cello and piano, and some songs; also a manual, *Elementary Technics for the Violin* (4 books).

Lentz, Daniel, American composer of the avant-garde; b. Latrobe, Pennsylvania, March 10, 1942. He began his career as as follower of the medieval troubadours and goliards; like they, he traveled far and wide; like they, he was the recipient of bounties from foundations and individuals in power. He received two grants from the National Endowment for the Arts, a Fulbright Grant, and a Tanglewood Composition Fellowship. He traveled in Holland in 1970 and in Germany in 1973 and presented concerts and multimedia exhibitions in California and other receptive regions of the U.S. The titles of some of his works are inscrutable, as in *Fermentation Notebooks, North American Eclipse,* or alliterative, as in *The Iridescence of Eurydice.* Perhaps his most startling composition is *Love and Conception,* in sonata form, in which two naked young people of the opposite gender are told to crawl under the lid of a grand piano and simulate sexual intercourse; the piece was actually performed at the Univ. of California, Santa Barbara, on Feb. 26, 1969, but as a result, the composer was fired from his teaching job there.

Lenz, Wilhelm von, Russian writer on music; b. Riga, June 1, 1809; d. St. Petersburg, Jan. 31, 1883. He traveled in Europe; was a piano pupil, in Paris, of Liszt and also of Chopin (1842); returning to Russia, he became a government councillor in St. Petersburg. His writings are historically valuable because of the intimate personal experience that they reflect. His most notable book is *Beethoven et ses trois styles* (2 vols.; St. Petersburg, 1852; new ed., by Calvocoressi, Paris, 1909), in which he proposed for the first time the division of Beethoven's works into 3 chronological periods, the first (opp. 1-21) being entirely Classical, the second (opp. 22-95) and to Lenz the best, truly Beethovenian in its nobility and individuality, and the third (from op. 96) as marking partly a decline, partly an attempt to scale unattainable heights. He further publ. *Beethoven: eine Kunststudie* (6 vols., 1855-60); vols. 4-6 separately publ. as *Kritischer Katalog der sämmtlichen Werke nebst Analysen derselben* (Hamburg, 1860), and vol. 1 as *Beethoven: eine Biographie* (2nd ed., 1879; reprinted, with additions by A. Kalischer, 1908); and *Die grossen Pianoforte-Virtuosen unserer Zeit* (brief character sketches of Liszt, Chopin, Tausig, and Henselt; 1872; English transl., N.Y., 1899).

Leo, Leonardo (Lionardo Oronzo Salvatore de Leo), one of the founders of the Neapolitan School of composition; b. San Vito degli Schiavi, near Brindisi, Aug. 5, 1694; d. Naples, Oct. 31, 1744. He studied with N. Fago at the Cons. della Pietà de' Turchini in Naples (1703–15); in 1716, 2nd maestro there, and maestro at the cathedral; 1717, maestro at Santa Maria della Solitaria and organist of the Royal Chapel, of which he was appointed 3rd maestro di cappella in 1731; vice maestro (1738); 1st maestro (1741); in 1725, succeeded A. Scarlatti as instructor in the Cons. di Sant' Onofrio, where he remained until his death, training many illustrious pupils, including Pergolesi, Jommelli, Piccinni, Sacchini, Traetta; simultaneously taught at the Cons. della Pietà.

WORKS: In 1713 he brought out a dramatic oratorio, *Il trionfo della castità di Sant' Alessio,* at the Cons. His first opera was *Pisistrato* (Naples, May 13, 1714); it was followed by nearly 60 others, *La Contesa dell' Amore colla Virtù* being the last; a list of the most important operas includes: *Sofonisba* (Naples, 1718); *Lucio Papirio* (Naples, 1720); *Caio Gracco* (Naples, 1720); *Arianna e Teseo* (Naples, 1721); *Timocrate* (Venice, 1723); *L'amore fedele* (Naples, 1724); *Lo pazzo apposto* (Naples, 1724); *Zenobia in Palmira* (Naples, 1725); *Il trionfo di Camilla* (Rome, 1726); *La semmeglianza di chi l'ha fatta* (Naples, 1726); *Dalli sdegni d'amore, ovvero L'Orismene* (Naples, 1726); *Il Cid* (Rome, 1727); *Lo matrimonio annacuso* (Naples, 1727); *Argeno* (Venice, 1728); *La pastorella commattuta* (Naples, 1728); *Catone in Utica* (Venice, 1729); *La schiava per amore* (Naples, 1729); *Rosmene* (Naples, 1730); *Evergete* (Rome, 1731); *Componimento drammatico pastorale* (Rome, Nov. 19, 1733); *Il castello d'Atlante* (Naples, 1734); *La clemenza di Tito* (Venice, 1735); *Demetrio* (Torre Maggiore, 1735); *Demofoonte* (Naples, 1735); *Emira* (Naples, 1735); *Onore vince amore* (Naples, 1736); *Farnace* (Naples, 1736); *Siface* (Bologna, 1737); *Ciro riconosciuto* (Naples, 1737); *L'amico traditore* (Naples, 1737); *La simpatia del sangue* (Naples, 1737); *L'Olimpiade* (Naples, 1737); *Il conte* (Naples, 1738); *Le nozze di Amore e di Psiche* (Naples, 1738); *Temistocle* (Florence, 1739); *Amor vuol sofferenze* (Naples, 1739); *Achille in Sciro* (Turin, 1739); *Ezio* (Modena, Dec. 26, 1739); *Carlo in Alemagnia* (Milan, 1740); *Viriati* (Pistoia, 1740); *Il verbo eterno e la religione* (Florence, 1741); *L'Andromaca* (Naples, 1742); *L'ambizione delusa* (Naples, 1742); *Il fantastico od Il nuovo Don Chisciotte* (Naples, 1743); *La fedeltà odiata* (Naples, 1744); *Vologeso* (Turin, 1744); Besides operas, he wrote 5 more oratorios, 5 Masses, *Magnificats, Misereres, Credos, Dixits,* motets, hymns, responses, etc.; most celebrated of all is his grand *Miserere* for double (8-part) chorus, ranking with Pergolesi's famous *Stabat Mater;* also 6 cello concertos with string quartet; 2 books of organ fugues; several harpsichord toccatas; etc. Most are in MS at Naples, Rome, Berlin, and Paris. A few have been publ. in modern editions: a duet from *Demofoonte* and an aria from *La clemenza di Tito* in Gevaert's *Gloires d'Italie;* the above mentioned *Miserere* in Commer's *Musica sacra* (vol.8), also separately by Choron (Paris) and Schlesinger (Berlin) and in a Concordia edition by H. Wiley Hitchcock, St. Louis, 1961; one *Dixit dominus a 8* by Stanford (London) and another *a 5* by Kummel in his *Sammlung,* etc.; a *Credidi propter,* a *Tu es sacerdos,* a *Miserere a 4* in Braune's *Cäcilia;* a *Di quanta pena* and an *Et incarnatus est,* in Rochlitz's *Sammlung vorzüglicher Gesangstücke;* many solfeggi with bass, in Levesque's and Bêche's *Solfèges d'Italie.*

BIBLIOGRAPHY: C. V. Leo, *Leonardo Leo e sua epoca musicale* (Brindisi, 1894); G. Leo, *Leonardo Leo, musicista del secolo XVIII e le sue opere musicali* (Naples, 1905); F. Schlitzer, T. Traetta, L. Leo, V. Bellini (Siena, 1952); F. Piovano, "À propos d'une récente biographie de Leonardo Leo," *Sammelbände der Internationalen Musik-Gesellschaft* (1906–07; pp. 70–95); E. J. Dent, "Leonardo Leo," *Sammelbände der Internationalen Musik-Gesellschaft* 8, (pp. 550–66); Karl Geiringer, "Eine Geburtstagskantate von P. Metastasio und Leonardo Leo," *Zeitschrift für Musikwissenschaft* (1927); F. Walker, "Cav. Giacomo Leo and His Famous 'Ancestor,' " *Music Review* (Nov. 1948); G. A. Pastore, *Leonardo Leo* (Galatina, 1957).

Léonard, Hubert, Belgian violinist and pedagogue; b. Bellaire, near Liège, April 7, 1819; d. Paris, May 6, 1890. His first violin teacher was Rouma; at Liège; he then became a pupil of Habeneck at the Paris Cons.; in 1844 he embarked on an extended European tour; then succeeded Bériot as violin prof. at the Brussels Cons. In 1867 he went to Paris, where he remained until his death. He publ. *Petite gymnastique du jeune violiniste; 24 Études classiques; Études harmoniques;* a method for violin, *École Léonard; L'ancienne école italienne,* a collection of special studies in double stopping, including examples from Corelli, Tartini, Geminiani, and Nardini; *Le Violon au point de vue de l'orchestration;* also 5 violin concertos; 6 concert pieces with piano; a serenade for 3 violins; a concert duo for 2 violins; fantasias and character pieces.

Leoncavallo, Ruggero, Italian dramatic composer; b. Naples, April 23, 1857; d. Montecatini, Aug. 9, 1919. He attended Naples Cons. where his teachers were B. Cesi (piano), and M. Ruta and L. Rossi (composition), and at 16 made a pianistic tour. His first opera, *Tommaso Chatterton,* was about to be produced in Bologna (1878), but the manager disappeared, and the production was called off. Leoncavallo earned his living as a young man by playing piano in cafés; this life he continued for many years, traveling through Egypt, Greece, Turkey, Germany, Belgium, and Holland before settling in Paris. There he found congenial company; composed chansonettes and other popular songs; wrote an opera *Songe d'une nuit d'été* (Midsummer Night's Dream, after Shakespeare), which was privately sung in a salon. He began to study Wagner's scores, and became an ardent Wagnerian; he resolved to emulate the master by producing a trilogy *Crepusculum,* depicting in epical traits the Italian Renaissance; the separate parts were to be *I Medici, Girolamo Savonarola,* and *Cesare Borgia.* He spent 6 years on the basic historical research; having completed the first part, and with the scenario of the entire trilogy sketched, he returned to Italy in 1887. There, the publisher Ricordi became interested in the project, but kept delaying the publication and production of the work. Annoyed, Leoncavallo turned to

Sonzogno, the publisher of Mascagni, whose opera *Cavalleria Rusticana* had just obtained tremendous vogue. Leoncavallo submitted a short opera in a similarly realistic vein; he wrote his own libretto based on a factual story of passion and murder in a Calabrian village, and named it *Pagliacci.* The opera was given with sensational success at the Teatro dal Verme in Milan under the direction of Toscanini (May 21, 1892), and rapidly took possession of the operatic stages throughout the world; it is often played on the same evening with Mascagni's opera, both works being of brief duration. Historically, these 2 operas signalized the important development of Italian operatic "verismo," which influenced composers of other countries also. The holograph score of *Pagliacci* is in the Library of Congress.

The enormous success of *Pagliacci* did not deter Leoncavallo from carrying on his more ambitious projects. The first part of his unfinished trilogy, *I Medici,* was finally brought out at La Scala, Milan, on Nov. 9, 1893, but the reception was so indifferent that Leoncavallo turned to other subjects; the same fate befell his youthful *Tommaso Chatterton* at its production in Rome (March 10, 1896). His next opera, *La Bohème* (Venice, May 6, 1897), won considerable success, but had the ill fortune of coming a year after Puccini's masterpiece on the same story, and was dwarfed by comparison. There followed a light opera, *Zazà* (Milan, Nov. 10, 1900), which was fairly successful, and was produced repeatedly on world stages. In 1904 Leoncavallo was commissioned by the German Emperor Wilhelm II to write an opera for Berlin; this was *Der Roland von Berlin,* on a German historic theme; it was produced in Berlin on Dec. 13, 1904, but despite the high patronage it proved a fiasco. In 1906 Leoncavallo made a tour of the U.S. and Canada, conducting his *Pagliacci* and a new opera, *La Jeunesse de Figaro,* specially written for his American tour; it was so unsuccessful that Leoncavallo never attempted to stage it in Europe. Back in Italy he resumed his industrious production; 2 new operas, *Maia* (Rome, Jan. 15, 1910) and *Malbruk* (Rome, Jan. 19, 1910), were produced within the same week; another opera, *La Reginetta delle Rose,* was staged simultaneously in Rome and in Naples (June 24, 1912). In the autumn of that year, Leoncavallo visited London, where he presented the première of his *Gli Zingari* (Sept. 16, 1912); a year later, he revisited the U.S., conducting in San Francisco. He wrote several more operas, but they made no impression; 3 of them were produced during his lifetime: *La Candidata* (Rome, Feb. 6, 1915), *Goffredo Mameli* (Genoa, April 27, 1916), and *Prestami tua moglie* (Montecatini, Sept. 2, 1916); the following were produced posthumously: *A chi la giarettiera?* (Rome, Oct. 16, 1919). *Edipo re* (Chicago, Dec. 13, 1920), and *Il primo bacio* (Montecatini, April 29, 1923). Still another opera, *Tormenta,* remained unfinished. Salvatore Allegra collected various sketches by Leoncavallo and arranged from them a 3-act operetta, *La maschera nuda,* which was produced in Naples on June 26, 1925.

Leonhard, Julius Emil, German composer; b. Lauban, June 13, 1810; d. Dresden, June 23, 1883. He became prof. of piano at the Munich Cons. in 1852; at the Dresden Cons. in 1859. He wrote an oratorio, *Johannes der Täufer;* 3 cantatas for soli, chorus, and orch.; a symphony; overture to Oehlenschläger's *Axel und Walpurg;* a piano sonata; 2 violin sonatas; 3 string trios; a piano quartet; etc.

Leonhardt, Gustav, eminent Dutch organist and harpsichord player; b. 'sGraveland, May 30, 1928; studied in Holland and Switzerland; toured widely in Europe; made 6 tours in America as performer and lecturer. He edited collections of keyboard music; published *The Art of Fugue, Bach's Last Harpsichord Work* (The Hague, 1952).

Leoni, Franco, Italian composer; b. Milan, Oct. 24, 1864; d. London, Feb. 8, 1949. He studied at the Milan Cons. with Dominiceti and Ponchielli; in 1892, went to London, where he remained for 25 years, until 1917; then lived in France and Italy, eventually returning to England.

WORKS: operas: *Raggio di Luna* (Milan, June 5, 1890); *Rip van Winkle* (London, Sept. 4, 1897); *Ib and Little Christina,* subtitled "a picture in 3 panels" (London, Nov. 14, 1901); *The Oracle* (London, June 28, 1905; Metropolitan Opera, N.Y., Feb. 4, 1915; his most successful opera); *Tzigana* (Genoa, Feb. 3, 1910); *Le Baruffe chiozzotte* (Milan, Jan. 2, 1920); *La Terra del sogno* (Milan, Jan. 10, 1920); the cantatas *Sardanapalus* (1896), *Golgotha* (1911); oratorio, *The Gate of Life* (London, March 16, 1898); songs.

Leoni, Leone, Italian composer; b. c.1560; d. c.1627. He was maestro di cappella in Vicenza (1588). He was a disciple of the Venetian school; his works are characteristic for their application of chromatic devices in harmony, and antiphonal choral usages. He publ. 5 books of madrigals for 5 voices (Venice, 1588–1602); 4 books of motets with organ, under the title *Sacri fiori* (1606–22); *Aurea corona* for 4 voices accompanied by 6 instruments (1618). His motets are particularly fine.

Leonin (Leoninus), great master of the Notre Dame School and of the Ars Antiqua; probably flourished before the cornerstone of Notre Dame de Paris was laid in 1163; was theretofore active at the earlier church, Beatae Mariae Virginis; according to the treatise of Anonymus IV (Coussemaker, *Scriptores,* I, 342), he complied the *Magnus Liber organi de graduali et antiphonario pro servitio divino multiplicando,* a cycle of 2-part liturgical settings for the whole church year, a work later revised by Leonin's successor, Perotin. The original of this collection has not been preserved, but there are 4 extant MSS containing music from it; of these, MS Wolfenbüttel 677 (formerly Helmstedt 628), dating from the 14th century (facsimile reprint in J. H. Baxter, *An Old St. Andrews Music Book,* 1931), though not the oldest, appears to preserve music from the *Magnus Liber* in purest form; the other 3 MSS are Pluteus 29.1 in the Biblioteca Medicea–Laurenziana of Florence, Wolfenbüttel 1206, and Madrid Biblioteca Nacional 20486. Leonin was the chief figure of his period, standing midway between the St. Martial school and Perotin; his technique is characterized by the juxtaposition in individual pieces of the note-against-note style, and the style in which, over a lower part characterized by long sustained notes, an upper part moves in freely flowing rhythm. (Both styles had already been used at St. Martial.)

BIBLIOGRAPHY: Fr. Ludwig, "Die liturgische Organa Leonins und Perotins," *Reimann–Festschrift* (1909); Fr. Ludwig, *Repertotium organorum recentioris et motetorum vetustissimi stili:* vol. I, *Catalogue raisonné der Quellen* (1910); J. Handschin "Zur Notre Dame Rhythmik," *Zeitschrift für Musikwissenschraft* (1925); H. Schmidt, "Zur Melodiebildung Leonins und Perotins," *Zeitschrift für Musikwissenschaft* (1931); M. Schneider, "Zur Satztechnik der Notre Dame-Schule," *Zeitschrift für Musikwissenschraft* (1932); G. Reese, *Music in the Middle Ages,* chap. 11 (N.Y., 1940); W. G. Waite, *The Rhythm of Twelfth Century Polyphony* (New Haven, 1954); F. Salzer, "Tonality in Early Medieval Polyphony," *Music Forum* I (1967).

Leonova, Darya, Russian contralto; b. Vyshny-Volochok, March 9, 1829; d. St. Petersburg, Feb. 6, 1896. She studied singing in St. Petersburg; in 1852 sang the part of Vania in Glinka's *A Life for the Tsar,* and was greatly praised by Glinka himself. In 1875 she went on a concert tour around the world, through Siberia, China, Japan, and America. In 1879 she traveled in Southern Russia and the Crimea with Mussorgsky as accompanist; sang arias from Mussorgsky's operas and his songs; in 1880 opened a singing school in St. Petersburg, with Mussorgsky acting as coach.

BIBLIOGRAPHY: V. Yakovlev, *D. Leonova* (Moscow, 1950).

Leopold I, Austrian Emperor who reigned from 1658 till 1705; b. Vienna, June 9, 1640; d. there, May 5, 1705. During his reign Vienna became the center of the world's operatic activity, no fewer than 400 new operas having been produced at that time; he was not only an enthusiastic patron but also a practically trained musician and diligent composer. His complete works are in MS in the State Library at Vienna: 15 oratorios, 7 operas, 17 ballet suites, 155 arias, 79 sacred compositions (2 Masses, 5 Offices for the Dead, 4-part *Miserere* with instruments, etc.).

Leplin, Emanuel, American composer; b. San Francisco, Oct. 3, 1917; d. Martinez, California, Dec. 1, 1972. He studied violin with Georges Enesco; conducting with Pierre Monteux; composition with Roger Sessions.

WORKS: *Galaxy* for 2 cellos and orch. (1942); *Cosmos* for violin and orch. (1949); 2 symph. poems, *Landscapes* and *Skyscrapers* (San Francisco, May 5, 1960); Symph. (San Francisco, Jan. 3, 1962); 3 string quartets; chamber music for various instrumental combinations; piano pieces.

Leppard, Raymond, English conductor and harpsichordist; b. London, Aug. 2, 1927. He studied at Trinity College, Cambridge; was lecturer in music at Cambridge Univ. (1958–68). In 1963 he organized the English Chamber Orch. and traveled with it to Japan in 1970. In 1973 he became principal conductor of the Northern Symph. Orch., England. In 1978 he was guest conductor of the N.Y. Philharmonic. He takes particular interest in early Baroque music; gives harpsichord recitals.

Leps, Wassili, Russian conductor and composer; b. St. Petersburg, May 12, 1870; d. Toronto, Dec. 22, 1943. He went to Germany, where he studied at the Dresden Cons. with Draeseke, Wüllner, and Theodor Kirchner. In 1894 he settled in America; taught at the Philadelphia Music Academy; then became conductor of the Philadelphia Operatic Society, which he led until 1923, producing 47 operas. In 1932 he organized the Providence Symph. Orch.; was its conductor until 1941, when he retired and went to Toronto to reside with a daughter. He wrote an opera on a Japanese subject, *Hoshi–San,* which he conducted with the Philadelphia Operatic Society on May 21, 1909; a cantata, *Yo–Nennen,* and some symphonic music.

BIBLIOGRAPHY: E. E. Hipsher, *American Opera and Its Composers* (Philadelphia, 1934; pp. 290–94).

Le Roux, Maurice, French composer and conductor; b. Paris, Feb. 6, 1923. He studied with Messiaen at the Paris Cons.; then worked at the electronic studios of the Radiodiffusion Française. In his music he adopts serial procedures. In 1952 he embarked on a conductor's career.

WORKS: *Le Petit Prince,* ballet (1950); *Sables,* ballet (1956); *Le Cercle des métamorphoses* for orch. (1953); *Trois visages* for trumpet and piano; *Pièces dodécaphoniques* for piano; songs. He publ. *Introduction à la musique contemporaine* (Paris, 1947); *Claudio Monteverdi* (Paris, 1951).

Leroux, Xavier, French composer; b. Velletri, Papal States, Oct. 11, 1863; d. Paris, Feb. 2, 1919. He was a pupil of Dubois and Massenet at the Paris Cons.; 1st Grand Prix de Rome, 1885; appointed prof. at the Cons. in 1896.

WORKS: the operas *Cléopâtre* (Paris, Oct. 23, 1890), *Évangeline* (Brusseke, 1895), *Astarté* (Paris, Feb. 15, 1901), *La Reine Fiammette* (Paris, Dec. 23, 1903; Metropolitan Opera, N.Y., Jan. 24, 1919), *Vénus et Adonis* (Nîmes, 1905), *William Ratcliff* (Nice, Jan. 26, 1906), *Théodora* (Monte Carlo, March 19, 1907), *Le Chemineau* (Paris, Nov. 6, 1907; Metropolitan Opera, N.Y., Jan. 31, 1919); *Le Carillonneur* (Paris, March 20, 1913); *La Fille de Figaro* (Paris, March 11, 1914); *Les Cadeaux de Noël* (Paris, Dec. 25, 1915), *1814* (Monte Carlo, April 6, 1918), *Nausithoé* (posthumous; Nice, April 9, 1920), *La Plus Forte* (posthumous; Paris, Jan. 11 1924), *L'Ingénu* (Bordeaux, Feb. 13, 1931); songs; piano pieces.

Le Roy, René, French flutist; b. Maisons-Laffitte, near Paris, March 4, 1898. He studied at the Paris Cons. with Hennebains, Lafleurance, and Gaubert. In 1918 he won first prize for flute playing; in 1919 succeeded his teacher Gaubert as director of the Société des Instruments à Vent; in 1922 he founded the Quintette Instrumental de Paris, with which he gave numerous concerts in Europe and America. He subsequently occupied various teaching positions; was prof. of chamber music for wind instruments at the Paris Cons. (1955–64). He compiled (with Cl. Dorgeuille) a manual *Traité de la flûte, historique, technique et pédagogique* (Paris, 1966).

Lert, Ernst Josef Maria, Austrian opera intendant and writer; b. Vienna, May 12, 1883; d. Baltimore, Jan. 30, 1955. He studied at the Univ. of Vienna with G. Adler; 1908, Dr. phil.; was dramatic coach at the Municipal Theater in Breslau and in Leipzig; 1920-23, opera director of the Municipal Theater and teacher at the Hoch Cons., Frankfurt; 1923-29, stage director at La Scala, Milan (with Toscanini); 1929-31, stage director at the Metropolitan Opera House, N.Y.; 1936-38, head of the opera department of Curtis Inst. of Music; after 1938, head of the opera department of the Peabody Cons., Baltimore. He publ. *Mozart auf dem Theater* (Berlin, 1918; 4th ed., 1922); *Otto Lohse,* a biography (Leipzig, 1918).

Lert, Richard Johannes, Austrian conductor; brother of **Ernst Lert;** b. Vienna, Sept 19, 1885. He studied at the Vienna Academy of Music; held posts as conductor in Düsseldorf, Darmstadt, Frankfurt, and Hannover; conducted in Paris. He emigrated to the U.S. in 1934; settled in Pasadena, Calif., as conductor and teacher. He married the novelist Vicki Baum (July 17, 1916). He celebrated his 90th birthday in 1975; continued to conduct summer concerts of Baroque music at Orkney Springs, Virginia for the Eastern Institute of Orchestral Studies; also gave courses in conducting.

Leschetizky, Theodor, great Austrain pianist and famous pedagogue; b. Lancut, Austrian Poland, June 22, 1830; d. Dresden, Nov. 14, 1915. He first studied with his father, who took him to Vienna, where he became a pupil of Czerny. He acquired a mastery of the piano in an amazingly short time, and he was only 15 when he himself began to teach. He also attended Vienna Univ. as a student of philosophy, until its closure in the wake of the 1848 revolution. In 1852 he went to Russia; his initial concerts in St. Petersburg were extremely successful, and gradually he attracted many pupils. He was also active as music director to the Grand Duchess Helen. In 1862 Anton Rubinstein, director of the newly opened St. Petersburg Cons., engaged him as teacher. After 16 years in Russia, Leschetizky returned to Vienna; there he married his former pupil Anna Essipova (she was his second wife); they were divorced in 1892; Leschetizky contracted 2 more marriages after that. He continued to make occasional concert tours, but he concentrated mainly on teaching; his fame grew, and pupils flocked from all over the world to his studio in Vienna. His most celebrated pupil was Paderewski; other pupils were Gabrilowitsch, Schnabel, Isabelle Vengerova, etc., as well as his third and fourth wives, Dominirska Benislavska and Marie Rozborska. His method of playing with the "Kugelhand" (arched hand) was to secure fullness of tone and finger dexterity, with the flexible wrist reserved for octave playing and chord passages. A Leschetizky Society, composed of his pupils, was organized after his death; a branch was established in the U.S.

Leschetizky was also a composer; he wrote an opera, *Die erste Falte* (Prague, Oct. 9, 1867), and some

chamber music; but it is his piano pieces that still remain of interest and value; of these, the following are the most effective: *Les Deux Alouettes; Grand Polka de Caprice; La Cascade; Perpetuum mobile; Valse chromatique; Souvenirs d'Italie; À la Campagne,* and *Trois Études caractéristiques.*

BIBLIOGRAPHY: Malwine Brée, *Die Grundlage der Methode Leschetizky* (Vienna, 1902; also in English and French transls.); Countess Angèle Potocka, *Theodor Leschetizky* (London, 1903); Annette Hullah, *Theodor Leschetizky* (London, 1906); Ethel Newcomb, *Leschetizky as I Knew Him* (London, 1921).

Leslie, Henry David, English conductor and composer; b. London, June 18, 1822; d. Llansaintfraid, near Oswestry, Feb. 4, 1896. He was a pupil of Charles Lucas; cellist in the Sacred Harmonic Society, and its conductor from 1853-61. In 1855 he organized (with Heming) an a cappella singing society, which won 1st prize at Paris in 1878. He composed the operas *Romance, or Bold Dick Turpin* (1857); *Ida* (1864); the oratorios *Immanuel* (1853) and *Judith* (1858); the cantatas *Holyrood* (1860), *Daughter of the Isles* (1861), and a "biblical pastoral," *The First Christian Morn* (1880); a symphony; an overture, *The Templar.*

Lessel, Franz, Polish pianist and composer; b. Pulawy, c.1780; d. Petrikow, Dec. 26, 1838. He went to Vienna in 1797 to study medicine, but became a pupil of Haydn and one of his few intimate friends. He returned to Poland upon Haydn's death, continuing to compose; he left in MS a great number of instrumental works; his published compositions show a fine talent; he wrote a piano concerto, 2 fantasias for piano, 3 piano sonatas, a piano trio, and several symphonies; his songs (to Polish words) were often performed.

Lessmann, Otto, German pianist and critic; b. Rüdersdorf, near Berlin, Jan. 30, 1844; d. Jena, April 27, 1918. He studied with Hans von Bülow (piano), Kiel (theory), and Teschner (voice); taught piano at Stern's Cons.; was owner and editor of the *Allgemeine Musik-Zeitung* (1882-1907).

Lester, Thomas William, English organist and composer; b. Leicester, England, Sept. 17, 1889; d. Berrien Springs, Mich., Dec. 4, 1956. He came to the U.S. in 1902; studied with Wilhelm Middelschulte in Chicago; wrote music criticism for the *Chicago Record-Herald;* also served as organist in various Chicago churches. He wrote 8 cantatas (sacred and secular); several suites for piano; organ pieces; numerous choruses; songs.

Le Sueur (or **Lesueur**), **Jean François,** French composer; b. Drucat-Plessiel, near Abbeville, Feb. 15, 1760; d. Paris, Oct. 6, 1837. At 7 he was a choirboy at Abbeville; at 14, in Amiens, where he took a course of studies; interrupting his academic education, he became maître de musique at the cathedral of Séez; then an assistant at the Church of the Innocents in Paris. Abbé Roze gave him some instruction in harmony; this comprised practically all of his musical training; he developed his musical talent without teachers. His subsequent positions were as maître de musique in the cathedral of Dijon (1781), at Le Mans (1783), and at Tours (1784). He then returned to Paris, now serving (upon the recommendation of Grétry) as maître de chapelle at the Innocents. When the competition for the post of maître de chapelle at Notre Dame was announced in 1786, Le Sueur entered it, and won. He organized an orch. for the chief festive days, and brought out Masses, motets, services, etc., using a full orch., thus completely transforming the character of the services; he was greatly successful with the congregation, but the conservative clergy strongly objected to his innovations; other critics called his type of musical productions "opéra des gueux" (beggars' opera). He expounded his ideas of effective and descriptive music in a pamphlet, *Essai de musique sacrée ou musique motivée et méthodique, pour la fête de Noël, à la messe de jour* (1787); this evoked an anonymous attack, to which he replied with another publication, *Exposé d'une musique unie, imitative, et particulière à chaque solennité* (1787), reasserting his aim of making church music dramatic and descriptive. He retired temporarily in 1788, and spent 4 years in the country. Upon his return to Paris, he brought out at the Théâtre Feydeau 3 operas: *La Caverne* (Feb. 16, 1793), which had a popular success, *Paul et Virginie* (Jan. 13, 1794), and *Télémaque* (May 11, 1796). When the Paris Conservatoire was organized in 1795, Le Sueur was appointed inspector, and a member of the Committee on Instruction; with Méhul, Langlé, Gossec, and Catel, he wrote the *Principes élémentaires de la musique* and the *Solfèges du Conservatoire*. Le Sueur was dismissed in 1802 on account of an altercation ensuing after the rejection, by the Opéra, of 2 of his operas in favor of *Sémiramis*, written by Catel. For 2 years he lived in poverty and suffering, until Napoleon, in 1804, raised him to the highest position attainable by a musician in Paris, by appointing him as maître de chapelle, succeeding Paisiello. His rejected opera, *Les Bardes*, was then produced (Paris, July 10, 1804) with great applause, and *La Mort d'Adam*, the other rejected work, was also staged (Paris, March 21, 1809). After the restoration of the monarchy, and despite Le Sueur's avowed veneration for Napoleon, the government of Louis XVIII appointed him superintendent and composer to the Chapelle du Roi; from 1818 he was also prof. of composition at the Paris Cons.; he had several celebrated pupils, among them Berlioz, Gounod, and Ambroise Thomas. He taught at the Cons. until his death; was a member of the Institut (1813), and held several other honorary positions. His last 3 operas were accepted for performance, but were not produced; these were *Tyrtée* (1794), *Artaxerse* (1797), and *Alexandre à Babylone;* other works were 2 secular cantatas, *L'Inauguration du temple de la Victoire* (Paris, Jan. 2, 1807) and *Le Triomphe de Trajan* (Paris, Oct. 23, 1807); several sacred oratorios (*Debora, Rachel, Ruth et Noémi, Ruth et Booz);* a Solemn Mass for 4 voices, chorus, and orch.; a cantata, *L'Ombre de Sacchini;* 3 *Te Deums;* 2 *Passions;* a *Stabat Mater;* these, and some other works, were publ.; he left many more (over 30 Masses, etc.) in MS. He publ. a *Notice sur la mélopée, la rythmopée, et les grands caractères de la musique ancienne* (Paris, 1793); a sketch of Paisiello (1816); and some pamphlets.

BIBLIOGRAPHY: C. P. Ducanel, *Mémoire pour J. F. Lesueur* (Paris, 1802); Raoul-Rochette, *Notice historique sur la vie et les œuvres de Jean-François Le Sueur* (Paris, 1837); Stéphen de la Madeleine, *Biographie de Jean-François Le Sueur* (Paris, 1841); P. O. Fouque, "Le Sueur comme prédecesseur de Berlioz," in *Les Révolutionnaires de la musique* (Paris, 1882); H. Berlioz, *Les Musiciens et la musique* (Paris, 1903; on Le Sueur's oratorios); C. Pierre, *Hymnes et chants de la Révolution* (Paris, 1904); W. Buschkötter, *Jean François Le Sueur* (Halle, 1912); F. Lamy, *Jean François Le Sueur* (Paris, 1912); G. Servières, "Les Oratoires de Jean-François Le Sueur," in *Episodes d'histoire musicale* (Paris, 1912); J. Mongrédien, "La Musique du sacre de Napoléon Ier," *Revue de Musicologie* (1967); W. Dean, "Opera under the French Revolution," *Proceedings of the Royal Music Association* (1967–68); M. M. Herman, "The Turbulent Career of Jean-François Le Sueur," *Recherches sur la Musique Français Classique* (1969).

Lesur, Daniel, French composer, pianist, and organist; b. Paris, Nov. 19, 1908. He studied at the Paris Cons. with Tournemire, Caussade, and Ferté; assistant organist at Ste.-Clothilde (1927–37; prof. of counterpoint at the Schola Cantorum (1935–39). In 1936 he and Yves Baudrier, O. Messiaen, and Jolivet organized "La Jeune France." His works include the ballet *L'Infante et le monstre* (with A. Jolivet, 1938); *Ave Maria sur un Noël,* for soprano, contralto, women's chorus, and organ (1938); *Andrea del Sarto,* symph. poem (Paris, June 21, 1949); *Andrea del Sarto,* opera (Marseille, Jan. 24, 1969); *Suite française,* for orch. (1935); *Pastorale* for chamber orch. (1938); *Ricercare,* for orch. (1939); *Passacaille* for piano and orch. (1937); *L'Étoile de Séville,* suite for chamber orch. (1941); *Chansons cambodgiennes,* for voice and chamber orch. (1947); Suite for piano and string trio (1943); *Suite médióvale,* for flute, violin, viola, cello, and harp (1946); *Le Village imaginaire,* for 2 pianos (1947); piano pieces (*Soirs, Les Carillons, Bagatelle, Pavane, Deux Noëls, Pastorale variée, Ballade,* etc.); organ music; songs (*Les Harmonies intimes, La Mort des voiles, 3 Poèmes de Cécile Sauvage, L'Enfance de l'art, Clair comme le jour,* etc.).

Lesure, François, French music librarian, musicologist and writer; b. Paris, May 23, 1923. He studied at the École des Chartres, then at the École Pratique des Hautes Études and the Sorbonne, and musicology at the Paris Conservatory. A member of the Music Department at the Bibliotheque Nationale since 1950, he was made its Chief Curator in 1970. From 1953 to 1967 he headed the Paris office (responsible for Series B) of the Répertoire International des Sources Musicales (RISM), for which he himself edited 3 volumes: *Recueils imprimés XVIe-XVIIe siècles* (Munich, 1960), *Recueils imprimés XVIIIe siècle* (Munich, 1964; supplement in *Notes,* March 1972, vol. XXVIII, pp. 397–418, and the 2 vols. of *Écrits imprimés concernant la musique* (Munich, 1971). His other posts have included a professorship at the Free University of Brussels and editorship, since 1967, of the series reprinting early music known as *Le Pupitre* (Paris, 56 volumes by 1977). He has also edited such non-serial works as the report of the 1954 Arras Conference, *La Renaissance dans les provinces du Nord* (Paris, 1956), the *Anthologie de la chanson parisienne au XVIe siècle* (Monaco, 1953), 6 vols. of *Chansons polyphoniques* (Monaco, 1967–1972; with A. T. Merritt, the first 5 volumes constituting the collected works of C. Janequin), P. Trichet's *Traité des instruments de musique (vers 1640)* (Neuilly, 1957), and a collected edition of Debussy's writings on music, *Monsieur Croche et autres écrits* (Paris, 1971; in English, N.Y. 1977). In 1971 he became President of the Société française de musicologie, and in 1973 director of the published *Archives* of the École Pratique des Hautes Études. His own publications include a *Bibliographie des éditions d'Adrian Le Roy et Robert Ballard, 1551–1598* (with G. Thibault, Paris, 1955; supplement in *Revue de Musicologie*, 1957); *Musicians and Poets of the French Renaissance* (N.Y., 1955); *Mozart en France* (Paris, 1956); *Collection musicale A. Meyer* (with N. Bridgman, Abbeville, 1961); *Musica e società* (Milan, 1966; German version as *Musik und Gesellschaft im Bild: Zeugnisse der Malerei aus sechs Jahrhunderten*, Kassel, 1966; in English as *Music and Art in Society*, Univ. Park, Pennsylvania, 1968); *Bibliographie des éditions musicales publiées par Estienne Roger et Michel-Charles Le Cene, Amsterdam, 1696–1743* (Paris, 1969); and *Musique et musiciens français du XVIe siècle* (Geneva, 1976, a reprinting in book form of 24 of Lesure's many articles originally published 1950–1969). He contributed *L'Opéra classique français 17e et 18e siècles* (Geneva, 1972) and *Claude Debussy* (Geneva, 1975) to the series *Iconographie Musicale*. For the Bibliothèque Nationale he prepared a series of exhibition catalogs, most notably one on Berlioz (Paris, 1969). The culmination of his Debussy studies is a *Catalogue de l'œuvre de Claude Debussy* (Geneva, 1977).

Letelier, Alfonso, Chilean composer and teacher; b. Santiago, Oct. 4, 1912. He studied with Allende at the Cons. Nacional in Santiago, where he became prof. of harmony (1947); aided in establishing the Escuela Moderna de Música. His compositions include a symph. poem, *La vida del campo*, for piano and orch.; *Aculeo*, suite for orch. (Louisville, Jan. 30, 1957); *Los sonetos de la muerte*, for female voice and orch.; a string quartet; Variations for piano; a Mass for chorus, string orch., and organ; songs. From 1952 to 1962 he was dean of the Faculty of Fine Arts of the Univ. of Chile.

Letorey, Omer, French composer; b. Châlon-sur-Saône, May 4, 1873; d. Paris, March 21, 1938. He studied at the École Niedermeyer, and with Pessard at the Paris Cons.; in 1895, won the Prix de Rome with his scena *Clarisse Harlowe*. Other works include the operas *Cléopâtre* (1918); *L'Oeillet blanc* (1930), and *Le Sicilien ou l'Amour Peintre* (Paris, Opéra-Comique, March 19, 1930).

Letz, Hans, German violinist; b. Ittenheim, Alsace, March 18, 1887; d. Hackensack, N.J., Nov. 14, 1969. He studied violin with H. Schuster at the Strasbourg Cons., and later with Joachim at the Hochschule für Musik in Berlin. In 1908 he emigrated to the U.S.; made his debut in New York (Nov. 3, 1908); subse-

quently was concertmaster of the Chicago Symph. Orch. (1909–12), and 2nd violinist of the Kneisel Quartet (1912–17). In 1917 he settled in N.Y. as a teacher at the Institute of Musical Art; also formed his own string quartet. He publ. a guide, *Music for the Violin and Viola* (N.Y., 1949).

Leuckart, F. Ernst Christoph, German music publisher; b. Halberstadt, March 21, 1748; d. Breslau, Feb. 2, 1817. He established a music business at Breslau in 1782; it was acquired by Constantin Sander in 1856, who removed it to Leipzig in 1870, and added to it by buying out the firms of Weinhold & Förster (Breslau), Damköhler (Berlin), and Witzendorf (Vienna). The new firm, "Constantin Sander, vormals F. E. C. Leuckart," publ. many learned works (e.g., by Ambros, Lussy, Westphal, Niecks, Molitor, etc.) and compositions of R. Franz, Rheinberger, Draeseke, Bossi, Hausegger, Huber, Klose, Duparc, Richard Strauss, Max Reger, Atterberg, Bantock, Ernest Bloch, Johan Wagenaar, Schjelderup, and others. Constatin Sander's son, Martin (b. Breslau, Nov. 11, 1859; d. Leipzig, March 14, 1930) was head of the firm until his death.

Lev, Ray, Russian pianist; b. Rostov, May 8, 1912; d. New York, May 20, 1968. Her father was a synogogue cantor, and her mother a singer. The family came to the U.S. in 1913; she sang in her father's synagogue choirs in New York; studied piano with Walter Ruel Cowles in New Haven and with Gaston Déthier. She also took lessons with Tobias Matthay in London (1930–33); then returned to New York and appeared in recitals.

Leva, Enrico de, Italian composer of popular music; b. Naples, Jan. 19, 1867; d. there, July 28, 1955. He studied with d'Arienzo; early in life, began writing popular ballads that proved of wide appeal *(Non mi guarda, E spingole frangese, Triste aprile, Ultima serenata,* etc.) and earned him great financial returns. He also wrote an opera, *La Camargo* (Turin, March 2, 1898).

Levadé, Charles (Gaston), French composer; b. Paris, Jan. 3, 1869; d. there, Oct. 27, 1948. He was a pupil of Massenet at the Paris Cons.; won the Grand Prix de Rome in 1899.

WORKS: the opera *Les Hérétiques* (Béziers, Aug. 27, 1905); the lyric comedies *La Rôtisserie de la reine Pédauque* (after Anatole France; Paris, Jan. 12, 1920) and *La Peau de chagrin* (after Balzac; Paris, April 24, 1929); orchestral suites; chamber music; piano pieces; songs.

Levant, Oscar, American pianist and composer; b. Pittsburgh, Dec. 27, 1906; d. Beverly Hills, Calif., Aug. 14, 1972. He studied piano with Stojowski; also took a few composition lessons with Schoenberg and Schillinger. As a pianist, he established himself by his authentic performances of Gershwin's music *(Rhapsody in Blue, Concerto in F);* also emerged as a professional wit on the radio; publ. a brilliant book, *A Smattering of Ignorance* (N.Y., 1940). He wrote music of considerable complexity, in the modern vein; was soloist in his Piano Concerto (NBC Symph. Orch., Feb. 17,

1942); other works are *Nocturne* for orch. (Los Angeles, April 14, 1937); String Quartet (1937); piano pieces; film scores.

Levarie, Siegmund, Austrian-American musicologist and conductor; b. Lemberg (outside Vienna), July 24, 1914. He was raised and trained in Vienna; studied conducting with Joseph Mertin at Vienna Conservatory, musicology with Robert Haas at University of Vienna (Ph.D., 1938); concurrently, took private lessons in composition with Hugo Kauder. He emigrated to the U.S. in 1938; became a U.S. citizen in 1943. He was Director of Concerts at Univ. of Chicago (1938–52); conducted the Collegium Musicum there, mostly in programs of medieval and Renaissance music; in 1954 was appointed prof. of music at Brooklyn College.
WRITINGS: *Fugue and Form* (Chicago, 1941); *Mozart's "Le Nozze di Figaro"* (Chicago, 1952; reprint, N.Y., 1977); *Fundamentals of Harmony* (N.Y., 1954; reprint, N.Y., 1962); *Guillaume de Machaut* (N.Y., 1954; reprint, N.Y., 1970); *Musical Italy Revisited* (N.Y., 1963; reprinted 1973); *Tone: A Study in Musical Acoustics* (with Ernst Lévy; Kent, Ohio, 1968); edited music of Salomone Rossi: *Sinfonie* a 3 (Vienna, 1937), and *Canzoni* a 4 (N.Y., 1942); contributed articles on early music, opera, and acoustics to various journals.

Levasseur, Jean-Henri, French cellist and composer; b. Paris, c.1765; d. there, 1823. He studied with Cupis and Duport; a member of the Paris Opéra orch. (1789–1823); professor of cello at the Paris Cons., and belonged to the Imperial Chapel. He publ. sonatas, études, and duets for cello; was co-editor of the cello method used at the Paris Cons.

Levasseur, Nicolas-Prosper, French bass; b. Bresles, March 9, 1791; d. Paris, Dec 7, 1871. He was admitted to the Paris Cons. in 1807, and he entered Garat's singing class in 1811; made his debut at the Paris Opéra (Oct. 14, 1813); sang subordinate roles until 1820, when his success at Milan in Meyerbeer's *Marguerite d'Anjou* (Nov. 14, 1820) attracted attention, and he was engaged for 5 years at the Théâtre Italien, Paris; later took leading bass roles at the Opéra. He was also prof. at the Paris Cons. (1841–69).

Levasseur, Rosalie (real Christian names **Marie Claude Josèphe**), French soprano; b. Valenciennes, Oct. 8, 1749; d. Neuwied-on-Rhine, May 6, 1826. She was the daughter of Jean-Baptiste Levasseur and Marie-Catherine Tournay, born out of wedlock; but the parents were married when she was 11. She was described by contemporaries as being not at all attractive; still she must have possessed a fine voice and musical ability, for she was a formidable rival of Sophie Arnould. She first appeared on the stage under the name of **Mlle. Rosalie;** in 1775 she assumed the name Levasseur. The Austrian ambassador in Paris used his influence to promote her career; they lived as husband and wife.
BIBLIOGRAPHY: J.-G. Prod'homme, "Rosalie Levasseur: Ambassadress of Opera," *Musical Quarterly* (April 1916).

Levens, Charles, French music theorist and organist; b. Marseilles, 1689; d. Bordeaux, March 11, 1764. He received his musical training at the St.-Sauveur Cathedral in Aix-en-Provence; subsequently was maître de chapelle at the Cathredral St.-Pierre in Vannes; then went to Bordeaux where he was maître de musique at St.-André Church. He publ. in 1743 an eleborate book on harmony, *Abrégé des règles de l'Harmonie, pour apprendre la composition, avec un nouveau projet sur un système de musique sans tempérament ni cordes mobiles,* in which he attempted to correlate the ascending harmonic progression, in natural overtones, with the descending arithmetical progression in undertones, thereby obtaining a dual harmonic basis; his elucubrations proved futile in practice.

Levenson, Boris, Russian composer and conductor; b. Ackerman, Bessarabia, March 10, 1884; d. New York, March 11, 1947. He studied at the St. Petersburg Cons. with Glazunov and Rimsky-Korsakov, graduating in 1907; in 1920, emigrated to America; lived mostly in New York. He wrote a symphony, an orch. suite *Palestine* (N.Y., 1927); *Night in Bagdad,* Oriental tone poem (N.Y. Philharmonic, Aug. 17, 1938); *Volga,* tone poem; *Hebrew Suite,* for 8 instruments; 2 string quartets; songs.

Leveridge, Richard, English singer and composer; b. London, c.1670; d. there, March 22, 1758. According to contemporary reports, he possessed a powerful bass voice, and was a successful singer in Italian operas; sang at Covent Garden and Drury Lane. He publ. a collection of songs (1727) in a popular style; of these, *The Roast Beef of Old England* became a favorite. He wrote incidental music for *Macbeth,* a number of masques, etc. He was also the owner of a coffee house in London.

Levey, Richard Michael, Irish composer and conductor; b. Dublin, Oct. 25, 1811; d. there, June 28, 1899. He received a practical musical education playing in various orchestras in Dublin and writing incidental music for production of plays. About 1835 he became a theater conductor; wrote some 50 overtures and a number of ballad scores. He publ. a collection of old Irish airs.

Levey, William Charles, Irish conductor and composer; son of **Richard Michael Levey;** b. Dublin, April 25, 1837; d. London, Aug. 18, 1894. He studied with Auber, Thalberg, and Prudent in Paris; then became conductor at Drury Lane, London (1868–74), at Covent Garden, and other theaters. He wrote the operettas *Fanchette* (London, Jan. 4, 1864), *Punchinello* (London, Dec. 28, 1864), and *The Girls of the Period* (London, Feb. 25, 1869); incidental music to *Anthony and Cleopatra, King o' Scots, Amy Robsart, Lady of the Lake, Rebecca, Esmeralda;* various pantomimes; 3 cantatas; many songs; piano pieces; etc.

Levi, Hermann, eminent German conductor; b. Giessen, Nov. 7, 1839; d. Munich, May 13, 1900. He was a pupil of Vincenz Lachner in Mannheim (1852–55) and at the Leipzig Cons. (1855–58). He conducted at Saar-

brücken (1859-61) and at the German Opera in Rotterdam (1861-64). He became court conductor at Karlsruhe in 1864, and in 1872 he recieved his most important appointment, at the court theater in Munich, retaining this position until 1896. He enjoyed great respect among German musicians, and was influential in spreading the Wagnerian gospel. He conducted the first performance of *Parsifal* at Bayreuth (July 28, 1882), and his interpretation received complete approval from Wagner himself, who, for the nonce, repressed his opposition to Jews. Levi conducted the musical program at Wagner's funeral. He was also a friend of Brahms; his correspondence with Brahms was publ. in vol. 7 of *Brahms Briefwechsel* (Berlin, 1912). He wrote *Gedanken aus Goethes Werken* (1901; 3rd ed., 1911).
BIBLIOGRAPHY: E. Possart, *Erinnerungen an Hermann Levi* (Munich, 1901); A. Ettlinger, "Hermann Levi," necrology in Bettelheim's *Biographisches Jahrbuch* (1903).

Levidis, Dimitri, Greek composer; b. Athens, April 8, 1886; d. there, May 30, 1951. He studied at the Athens Cons., then with A. Denéréaz in Switzerland; in 1910, settled in Paris; from 1939 till his death, was again in Greece. He was the first to write works for the Martenot "Ondes Musicales," including *Poème Symphonique pour solo d'Ondes Musicales et Orchestre* (Paris, Dec. 23, 1928) and *De Profundis* for voice and 2 soli of Ondes Musicales (Paris, Jan. 5, 1930). Other works include a ballet, *Le Pâtre et la Nymphe* (Paris, April 24, 1924); *Divertissement* for English horn, harps, strings, celesta, and persussion (Paris, April 9, 1927); an oratorio, *The Ilaid;* poem for violin and orch. (1927); *Chant payen* for oboe and strings; compositons for the "Dixtuor æolien d'orchestre"; pieces for chamber ensembles; song cycles; piano pieces.

Levina, Zara, Soviet composer; b. Simferopol, Crimea, Feb. 5, 1906; d. Moscow, June 27, 1976. She studied piano at the Cons. of Odessa, graduating in 1923; then entered the Moscow Cons., where she was a student of Felix Blumenfeld in piano and of Maiskovsky in composition, graduating in 1931. She subsequently gave piano recitals. She distinguished herself primarily as composer of children's songs which achieved great popularity; also set music to some 100 texts by Russian poets. She wrote 2 piano concertos (1945, 1975), 2 violin sonatas (1928, 1948), and piano pieces.
BIBLIOGRAPHY: N. Mikhailovskaya, *Zara Levina* (Moscow, 1960).

Levine, James, brilliant American pianist and conductor; b. Cincinnati, June 23, 1943. Of a musical family, he absorbed music by osmosis and began playing the piano as a small child. At the age of 10 he was soloist in Mendelssohn's 2nd Piano Concerto with the Cincinnati Symph. Orch.; in 1956 he took piano lessons with Rudolf Serkin at the Marlboro Music Festival in Vermont. In 1961 he enrolled in the Juilliard School of Music in N.Y., where he studied conducting with Jean Morel and piano with Rosina Lhévinne. In 1962 he conducted Bizet's opera *The Pearl Fishers* at Aspen, Colorado; also became assistant conductor of the Cleveland Orch., the youngest to occupy a compa-

rable position (1965-70). On June 5, 1971, Levine made his debut as an opera conductor at the Metropolitan Opera in N.Y., conducting *Tosca;* in 1973 he became the principal conductor of the Metropolitan Opera and in 1976 became its music director. Concurrently he was music director at the summer concerts of the Ravinia Festival with the Chicago Symph.; also conducted guest appearances in America and in Europe.

Levitzki, Mischa, Russian pianist; b. Kremenchug, Russia, May 25, 1898; d. Avon-by-the-Sea, New Jersey, Jan. 2, 1941. When he was 8 years old, his parents, who were naturalized American citizens, returned to the U.S. He studied at the Institute of Musical Art, N.Y. , with Stojowski (1906-11). In 1911 he went to Germany, where he studied with Dohnányi at the Hochschule für Musik in Berlin; won the Mendelssohn Prize. In 1915 he returned to America; appeared in a N.Y. recital on Oct. 17, 1916; subsequently made numerous tours in the U.S. and in the Orient. He publ. a number of attractive piano pieces *(Valse in A, Arabesque valsante, Valse tzigane, Gavotte, The Enchanted Nymph, etc.).*

Lévy, Alexandre, Brazilian composer; b. São Paulo, Nov. 10, 1864; d. there, Jan. 17, 1892. He studied with Emile Durand in Paris. His compositions include a symph. which recieved a Columbus Celebration prize in 1892; *Comala,* symph. poem; *Suite Brasileira* for orch.; chamber music and piano works *(Schumanniana,* suite; *Allegro appassionato,* etc.). Although his music is steeped in the European Romantic tradition, and his technique is limited, he appears an important figure in Brazilian music because of his contribution to the nationalist musical movement; he was one of the earliest Brazilian composers to use native folk material in instrumental works.
BIBLIOGRAPHY: Renato Almeida, *Compendio de Historia da musica brasileira* (Rio de Janeiro, 1947).

Levy, Burt, American composer; b. Brooklyn, Aug. 5, 1936. He studied composition with George Rochberg, Salvatore Martirano and others; received degrees from the Univ. of Oregon and Temple Univ. in Philadelphia. He joined the faculty at the Univ. of Illinois in Urbana. His works are of an experimental variety. In *Orbs with Flute* he applies such effects as slapping keys, pitchless clacks, tongue blocking the embouchure hole, etc.

Lévy, Ernst, distinguished Swiss pianist and composer; b. Basel, Nov. 18, 1895. He studied in Basel with Huber and Petri, and in Paris with Pugno. In 1941 he came to the U.S.; taught at the New England Cons. in Boston (1941-45), at Bennington College, Vermont (1946-51), at Chicago Univ. (1951-54), at the Massachusetts Institute of Technology in Boston (1954-59) and at the Brooklyn College of the City Univ. of New York (1959-66). In 1966 he went to Switzerland and lived in Morges. A man of profound culture, he is also a virtuoso pianist; his interpretations particularly in the works of Beethoven, are praised for their deep perception; similarly his own music is much admired if rarely performed; besides his musical accomplishments, he is an alpinist and a master carpenter; unpublished remain his writings on philosophical subjects. He composed 15 symphonies between 1920 and 1967; much chamber music and choral works; pieces for solo cello, solo viola, solo violin; *Soliloquy* clarinet solo; 55 pieces for clavichord; a study on whole-tone scales for piano; organ pieces, etc. He also published a theoretical study (with S. Levarie), *Tone. A Study in Musical Acoustics* (Kent, Ohio, 1968).

Levy, Frank, American cellist and composer, son of **Ernst Lévy;** b. Paris, Oct. 15, 1930. He went to America with his father; studied at the Juilliard School of Music in New York (B.S., 1951) and at the Univ. of Chicago (M.A., 1954); studied cello with Leonard Rose and Janos Starker in New York; was cellist in various orchestras.
    WORKS: *Ricercar* for 4 celli (1958); Sonata for unaccompanied cello (1959); Quintet for flute and strings (1959); Bassoon Concerto (1961); Trio for clarinet, horn and bassoon (1961); Sonata for bassoon and piano (1963); *Fantasy* for tuba, harp, timpani and strings (1965); choruses and solo songs.

Lévy, Heniot, Polish-American pianist and composer; b. Warsaw, July 19, 1879; d. Chicago, June 16, 1946. He was a pupil at the Hochschule für Musik in Berlin, and of Max Bruch (composition); made his debut as pianist with the Berlin Philharmonic Orch. (1899); in 1900 he emigrated to America, and became piano teacher at the American Cons. in Chicago. Among his works are *24 Variations on an Original Theme* for orch. (Chicago, April 9, 1942); piano concerto; string sextet; string quintet; 2 piano quintets; 4 string quartets; 2 piano trios; cello sonata; numerous piano pieces; songs.

Levy, Jules, Bulgarian composer; b. Salonika, June 19, 1930. He studied in Sofia with Stoyanov at the Bulgarian State Cons., graduating in 1957; was subsequently engaged as conductor of the Stefan Makedonsky Theater of Music in Sofia.
    WORKS: 3 musicals, *The Girl I Was in Love With* (1963), *The World Is Small* (1970) and *The Phone Which...* (1975); a ballet *Fair in Sofia* (1968); a choreographic oratorio *Onward to the Rising World* (1973); *Youth Concerto* for violin and orch. (1953); 3 symphonies: No. 1, *Life and Death* (1958); No. 2 (1970); No. 3 (1976); *Divertimento-Concertante No. 1* for trumpet and pop orch. (1961) and *No. 2* for flute and orch. (1971); *Overture-Poem* (1962); *The Blacksmith,* symph. fantasy (1964); *Pirin Mountain Rhapsody* for jazz and symph. orchestras (1972); string quartet *Masks* (1974); chamber pieces; choral songs; popular music.

Lévy, Lazare, distinguished French pianist and pedagogue; b. (of French parents) Brussels, Jan. 18, 1882; d. Paris, Sept 20, 1964. He studied with Diémer at the Paris Cons. (1894–98), where he was awarded 1st prize for piano; also studied harmony with Lavignac and composition with Gédalge; gave concerts with the principal orchs. of Europe; in 1920 succeeded Alfred

Cortot as prof. at the Paris Cons. He publ. numerous piano pieces.

Levy, Marvin David, American composer; b. Passaic, N.J., Aug. 2, 1932. He studied composition with Philip James at N.Y. Univ., and with Otto Luening at the Columbia Univ.; was awarded an American Prix de Rome and a Guggenheim fellowship. He showed a particular disposition towards the musical theater. In his vocal and instrumental writing Levy adopts an expressionistic mode along atonal lines, in an ambience of cautiously dissonant harmonies vivified by a nervously asymmetric rhythmic pulse.
    WORKS: the one-act operas *Sotoba Komachi* (N.Y., April 7, 1957); *The Tower* (Sante Fe, Aug. 2, 1957); and *Escorial* (N.Y., May 4, 1958). In 1961 he was commissioned to write an opera for the Metropolitan Opera at Lincoln Center, N.Y., to a libretto from O'Neill's play *Mourning Becomes Electra*. It was produced at the Metropolitan on March 17, 1967; although critical reception was indecisive, the opera was retained in the repertory for several seasons, a signal honor to an American composer. His other works include String Quartet (1955); *Rhapsody* for violin, clarinet and harp (1956); *Chassidic Suite* for French horn and piano (1956); a Christmas oratorio, *For the Time Being* (1959); *Caramoor Festival Overture* (1959); Symphony (1960); *Sacred Service* for the Park Avenue Synagogue in N.Y. (1964); Piano Concerto (Chicago, Dec. 3, 1970).

Lévy, Michel-Maurice, French composer; b. Ville-d'Avray, June 28, 1883; d. Paris, Jan. 24, 1965. He studied at the Paris Cons. with Lavignac and Leroux. From 1920–32 he was popular as a musical parodist in vaudeville under the name of **Bétove** (i.e., Beethoven); wrote operettas under that name: *Pom-Pom* (1928), *Les Exploits galants du Baron de Crac* (1932), *D'Artagnan* (1945). Under his own name he wrote the operas *Le Cloître* (Lyons, 1932), *Dolorés* (Paris, 1952); operettas *Lydia* (Brussels, 1936), *La Demoiselle de Carentan* (Paris, 1951); *Les Trois Pantins de bois,* ballet suite for orch.; *Le Chant de la terre,* symph. poem (1945); *Moïse,* a "fresque lyrique" (Mulhouse, 1955); film music; choral works; songs.

Lewandowski, Louis, eminent Jewish scholar; b. Wreschen, near Posen, April 3, 1821; d. Berlin, Feb. 3, 1894. He studied at the Academy of Music in Berlin; became music director of the Berlin Synagogue from 1840; established himself as a voice teacher. His greatest accomplishment is the compilation of the Jewish service music for use by Berlin's Jewish community; in his arrangements of the traditional tunes, Lewandowski applied the technique of German Romantic music, and often reduced the exotic and asymmetrical pattern of the Jewish cantilena to simple song meters; his compositions for organ also employed ordinary 19th-century harmonies. This treatment contributed to the popularity of Lewandowski's service music, but at the same time traduced the true spirit of Jewish cantillation, so that the more nationalistic Jewish scholars refused to accept it.

Lewenthal, Raymond, American pianist; b. San Antonio, Texas, Aug. 29, 1926. He was taken to Hollywood as a child; studied piano with local teachers. He then enrolled at the Juilliard School of Music in N.Y., as a student of Olga Samaroff; continued his studies in Europe with Alfred Cortot; spent a year in Rio de Janeiro as a piano teacher. Returning to the U.S., he devoted himself to promoting the piano music by neglected romantic composers, among them Thalberg, Hummel and Henselt, whose works he performed at his recitals. Particularly meritorious is his redemption from undeserved oblivion of the voluminous output of Charles-Valentin Alkan. He edited a collection of Alkan's piano works for G. Schirmer, Inc.

Lewinger, Max, Polish violinist and composer; b. Sulkow, near Cracow, March 17, 1870; d. Dresden, Aug. 31, 1908; He studied at the Conservatories of Cracow, Lwow, and Vienna; in 1893 became teacher of violin at the Bucharest Cons.; then played in the Gewandhaus orch. in Leipzig (1897) and in Dresden (from 1898). He publ. *Legende* for violin and orch., and a number of pieces for violin and piano *(Tarantella, Polonaise, Capriccio, Dumka, Serenade,* etc.).

Lewis, Henry, black American conductor; b. Los Angeles, Oct. 16, 1932. He learned to play piano and string instruments as a child; at the age of 16 was engaged as double-bass player in the Los Angeles Philharmonic; from 1955–59 played double-bass in the 7th Army Symph. Orch. overseas, and also conducted it in Germany and in Holland. Returning to the U.S., he founded the Los Angeles Chamber Orch.; in 1963 traveled with it in Europe under the auspices of the State Department. From 1968 to 1975 he was conductor and musical director of the New Jersey Symph. Orch. in Newark; subsequently conducted opera and orchestral guest engagements.

Lewis, John Aaron, American jazz pianist and composer; b. La Grange, Illinois, May 3, 1920. He served in the U.S. Army during World War II; enrolled in the Manhattan School of Music, N.Y. (M.A., 1953); became an arranger. From 1952 to 1977 he led the Modern Jazz Quartet (piano, vibraphone, drums, double bass), a group that for 25 years was one of the focal points of both "cool" jazz and "classical" jazz, a merger known as Third Stream. To this end Lewis composed and arranged works that, while leaving room for jazz improvisation, also includes such formal devices as fugal counterpoint; he has also composed extended compositions requiring the additional forces of string quartet or orchestra, and has written several movie scores *(Odds Against Tomorrow, No Sun in Venice, A Milanese Story)* and a ballet, *Original Sin* (San Francisco Ballet, March 1961). Significantly, the Modern Jazz Quartet (known as MJQ) abandoned the usual night-club habitat of jazz in favor of formal, tuxedoed performances in concert halls. Lewis has taught at several colleges, and in 1966 became a member of the Board of Trustees of the Manhattan School of Music.

Lewis, Leo Rich, American music educator; b. South Woodstock, Vt., Feb. 11, 1865; d. Cambridge, Mass.

Sept. 8, 1945. He graduated from Tufts College (A.B., 1887); attended Harvard Univ. (M.A., 1889); then studied composition with Rheinberger at the Akademie der Tonkunst in Munich. From 1895 until his death he headed the music department and taught theory and music history at Tufts College. He originated a card system of thematic cataloguing of music.
BIBLIOGRAPHY: H. A. Hersey, *A History of Music in Tufts College* (Manchester, N.H., 1947; pp. 302–16).

Lewis, Richard, English tenor; b. Manchester, May 10, 1914. He studied in London; made his operatic debut at Glyndebourne in 1947, and remained with the Festivals there for several years. He joined the staff of the San Francisco Opera Co. in 1955.

Lewisohn, Adolph, German-American musical philanthropist; b. Hamburg, May 27, 1849; d. Saranac Lake, N.Y., Aug. 17, 1938. A prominent industrialist, his principal service to music and education was the erection of the Lewisohn Stadium in 1914, which he donated to the College of the City of N.Y., and the inauguration of summer concerts by the N.Y. Philharmonic there. He also founded the Lewisohn chamber music education courses at Hunter College, N.Y.

Lewkowitch, Bernhard, Danish organist and composer; b. Copenhagen, May 28, 1927 (of Russian parents). He studied organ and composition at the Cons. of Copenhagen (1946–50) with Schierbeck and Jersild. From 1947 to 1963 he served as organist and choirmaster at the Catholic Church of St. Ansgar, in Copenhagen. In 1953 he founded in Copenhagen a choral society Schola Cantorum, with which he performed medieval and Renaissance music. In 1963 he was awarded the prestigious Carl Nielsen Prize; in 1966 he was given a lifetime Danish government pension. His own music is primarily choral, to Latin texts, and is derived essentially from the Renaissance paradigms of modal counterpoint; it has an affinity with sacred works of Stravinsky, but is otherwise *sui generis* in its stylized archaisms; several of these works have become repertory pieces in Denmark, and were also performed at the international festivals of contemporary music in Haifa (1954), Cologne (1960), Amsterdam (1963), and Copenhagen (1964).
WORKS: *Mariavise* for chorus (1947); *Tres orationes* for tenor, oboe and bassoon (1958); *Il cantico delle creature* for 8 voices, after Francis of Assisi (1963); *Laudi a nostra Signora* for chorus, to medieval texts (1969); 4 piano sonatas; madrigals; lieder.

Ley, Henry George, English organist and composer; b. Chagford, Dec. 30, 1887; d. Ottery-Saint-Mary, Devonshire, Aug. 24, 1962. He studied with Parratt at the Royal College of Music in London; was active mainly as church organist in Oxford and London; was musical director at Eton College (1926–45); also taught organ at the Royal College of Music in London. He wrote *Variations on a Theme by Handel* for orch.; some chamber music, and many organ pieces.

Ley, Salvador, Guatemalan pianist and composer; b. Guatemala City, Jan. 2, 1907. At the age of 15 he went to Berlin, where he studied piano with Georg Bertram and theory with Hugo Leichtentritt. He appeared as a pianist in Berlin in 1927; returned to Guatemala in 1934; in 1938 he gave a recital in New York; then became teacher of piano at the Cons. of Guatemala.

WORKS: *Lera,* opera in 2 acts (1959); *Danza exotica* for piano (1959); Suite for flute and piano (1962); *Concertante* for viola and string orch. (1962); *Toccatina* for piano (1965); *Introduction and Movement* for unaccompanied cello (1965); piano pieces; songs.

Leybach, Ignace, Alsatian pianist and composer; b. Gambsheim, July 17, 1817; d. Toulouse, May 23, 1891. He studied in Paris with Pixis, Kalkbrenner, and Chopin; in 1844, became organist at the cathedral of Toulouse. He publ. some 225 piano pieces, in a facile and pleasing manner; his 5th Nocturne, op. 52, became famous and its popularity continued among succeeding generations of piano students, reprinted in countless anthologies of piano music; other piano compositions are: *Boléro brillant; Ballade; Valse poétique; Les Batelières de Naples,* etc.; he also publ. an extensive organ method (3 vols.; 350 pieces).

Leygraf, Hans, Swedish pianist; b. Stockholm, Sept. 7, 1920. He appeared as soloist with the Stockholm orch. at the age of 10; then studied at the Stockholm Cons., in Munich and in Vienna; acquired a fine reputation as a concert pianist; was particularly noted as a Mozart interpreter. In 1944 he married the Viennese pianist **Margarete Stehle** (b. Vienna, April 26, 1921). In 1956 he joined the faculty of the Salzburg Mozarteum.

Lhévinne, Josef, celebrated Russian pianist; b. Orel, Russia, Dec. 13, 1874; d. New York, Dec. 3, 1944. After some preliminary study in his native town, he was taken to Moscow, and entered Safonov's piano class at the Moscow Cons.; at the age of 15 he played the *Emperor Concerto* with Anton Rubinstein conducting; he graduated in 1891; won the Rubinstein Prize in 1895. In 1900 he traveled to the Caucasus; taught piano at the Cons. of Tiflis; 1902–06, at the Moscow Cons. In 1906 he went to the U.S.; made his American debut in N.Y. with the Russian Symph. Orch., conducted by Safonov (Jan. 27, 1906); afterwards he made numerous concert tours in America. He lived mostly in Berlin from 1907 till 1919; was interned during World War I, but was able to continue his professional activities. In 1919 he returned to the U.S.; appeared in recitals, and with major American orchestras; also in duo recitals with his wife. They established a music studio where they taught numerous pupils; also taught at the Juilliard Graduate School. Lhévinne's playing was distinguished not only by its virtuoso quality, but by an intimate understanding of the music, impeccable phrasing, and fine gradations of singing tone. He was at his best in the works of the Romantic school; his performances of the concertos of Chopin and Tchaikovsky were particularly notable.

Lhévinne, Rosina, Russian pianist and teacher, wife of **Josef Lhévinne;** b. Kiev, March 28, 1880; d. (at the age of 96) Glendale, Calif. Nov. 9, 1976. She graduated from the Kiev Cons. in 1898, winning the gold medal; in 1899 she married Josef Lhévinne in Moscow; appeared as soloist in Vienna (1910), St. Petersburg (1911), Berlin (1912); remained in Berlin with her husband through World War I; in 1919, came to the U.S.; taught at the Juilliard Graduate School; also privately in N.Y., establishing a reputation as a fine pedagogue. Among her many pupils was Van Cliburn.

Lhotka, Fran, Czech-Yugoslav composer and teacher; b. Wožice, Dec. 25, 1883; d. Zagreb, Jan. 26, 1962. He took lessons with Dvořák in Prague, and with Janáček and Klička (1899–1905). After a season of teaching in Ekaterinslav, Russia (1908–09), he settled in Zagreb; in 1919, was appointed instructor at the Cons. of Zagreb, and conductor of the 'Lisinski Chorus,' with which he toured Central Europe; from 1923 to 1940 and again from 1948 to 1952 he was rector of the State Music Academy in Zagreb.

WORKS: the operas *Minka* (Zagreb, 1918) and *The Sea* (Zagreb, 1920); the ballets *The Devil of the Village* (Zürich, 1935; also performed in Vienna, Prague, etc.), *Ballad of Medieval Love* (Zürich, 1937; also at the Edinburgh Festival, 1951), *Luk* (Munich, 1938); a symphony; *Yugoslav Capriccio* for orch.; Violin Concerto; Suite for 4 flutes; choral works; songs; a manual of harmony (Zagreb, 1948).

Lhotka-Kalinski, Ivo, Croatian composer, son of **Fran Lhotka;** b. Zagreb, July 30, 1913. He studied with Pizzetti in Rome; after the end of World War II taught singing at the Music Academy of Zagreb; in 1967 became its regional director. He has a natural flair for stage composition in the folk style; he wrote several brilliant musical burlesques, among them *Analfabeta (The Illiterate;* Belgrade, Oct. 19, 1954); *Putovanje (The Journey),* first television opera in Yugoslavia (Zagreb, June 10, 1957); *Dugme (The Button;* Zagreb, April 21, 1958); *Vlast (Authority;* Zagreb Television, Oct. 18, 1959); *Svjetleći Grad (The Town of Light;* Zagreb, Dec. 26, 1967); also a children's opera *Velika coprarija (The Great Sorcerer;* 1952); *Misli (Thoughts)* for clarinet and strings (1965); a number of choral works, songs and piano pieces.

Liadov, Anatoly, significant Russian composer, son of **Konstantin Liadov;** b. St. Petersburg, May 10, 1855; d. on his estate of Polynovka, in the district of Novgorod, Aug. 28, 1914. He was a member of an exceptionally gifted musical family. His father was an outstanding opera conductor; his grandfather was conductor of the St. Petersburg Philharmonic Society; Liadov's uncles were also professional musicians. After his primary education at home, Liadov entered the St. Petersburg Cons. (1870); studied piano with G. G. Kross, theory with J. Johannsen, composiition with Rimsky-Korsakov; he was expelled from the school for failing to attend classes (1876), but was allowed to compete for a diploma in 1878, and passed the final examination brilliantly. He was immediatly engaged as instructor of theory and harmony at the Cons., and held this post until his death. Among his students were Prokofiev, Miaskovsky, Asafiev, and other notable Russian composers. From his first attempts at composition, Liadov was fascinated by Russian folklore, and most of his works possess the imaginative quality of Russian fairy tales. He was not a prolific composer; he was at his best in miniatures, which he worked out with a fine artistic sense; of these, the piano cycle *Birulki* (1876) and *Tabatière à musique (Music Box,* 1893) are particularly popular; for orchestra he wrote the symph. tableaux, *Baba Yaga, Enchanted Lake,* and *Kikimora,* which are still in the permanent repertory of Russian orchestras; his arrangements of Russian songs are valuable for their authentic harmonization.

WORKS: for orch.: *Scherzo* (1887); *Mazurka* (1888); *Polonaise* (1900); *Baba Yaga* (St. Petersburg, March 18, 1904); *8 Russian Folksongs* (1906); *Enchanted Lake* (St. Petersburg, Feb. 21, 1909); *Kikimora* (St. Petersburg, Dec. 12, 1909); *Fragments from Apocalypse* (St. Petersburg, Dec. 8, 1912); *Nenie,* threnody (1914); for piano: *Birulki* (1876); *4 Arabesques* (1879); *4 Intermezzos* (1882-83); *2 Mazurkas* (1887); *Novellette* (1889); *Ballade* (1890); *Marionnettes* (1892); *Bagatelle* (1892); *Tabatière à musique* (1893; also for small orch.); *Variations on a Polish Theme* (1901); *4 pieces: Grimaces, Twilight, Temptation, Recollection* (1910); several sets of preludes and études, etc.; vocal works: 120 Russian folksongs for voice and piano (1903); other Russian song arrangements and harmonizations. Liadov contributed a movement to the string quartet on the theme B-La-F, in honor of the publisher Belaiev (1895), and a polka to the collection *Fridays* (1899), for string orch.

BIBLIOGRAPHY: M. D. Calvocoressi and Gerald Abraham, *Masters of Russian Music* (London, 1936; pp. 424-30); N. Zaporozhetz, *A. K. Liadov, Life and Work* (Moscow, 1954).

Liadov, Konstantin, Russian conductor; b. St. Petersburg, May 10, 1820; d. there, Dec. 19, 1868. He studied at the Theatrical School; in 1850 became conductor of the Imperial Opera; resigned shortly before his death, and was succeeded by Napravnik. He was an efficient drillmaster, and did much to raise the standard of performance; produced several Russian operas for the first time, and was instrumental in encouraging Russian music; he was greatly appreciated by his coworkers; Glinka often sought his advice on details of production of his operas.

Liapunov, Sergei, important Russian pianist and composer; b. Yaroslavl, Nov. 30, 1859; d. Paris, Nov. 8, 1924. He studied piano at the Moscow Cons. with Pabst and Klindworth and composition with Hubert and Taneyev. From 1894 to 1902 he was subdirector of the Imperial Choir at St. Petersburg; from 1902 to 1910, inspector of music at St. Helen's Institute; in 1910 became prof. at the St. Petersburg Cons.; following the Russian Revolution, he lived in Paris. He was a member of the Imperial Geographic Society, which commissioned him to collect the folksongs of the regions of Vologda, Viatka, and Kostroma (publ. with piano accompaniments in 1897). As a composer he followed the tradition of the Russian National School, but was also willing to experiment with harmonic innovations; his writing for piano possesses excellent expertise; his First Piano Concerto is still in the repertory of Russian pianists.

WORKS: Symph. No. 1 (1887; St. Petersburg, April 23, 1888; also performed in Berlin, Jan. 15, 1907);

Ouverture solennelle, on Russian themes (St. Petersburg, May 6, 1896); *Zelazova Vola,* named after Chopin's birthplace and composed for Chopin's centennial (1910); *Hashish,* oriental symph. poem (1914); Symph. No. 2 (1910-17; Leningrad, Dec. 28, 1950); Violin Concerto; 2 piano concertos (1890, 1909); *Ukrainian Rhapsody* for piano and orch. (Berlin, March 23, 1908, with Busoni as soloist); numerous piano compositions, of which *12 études d'exécution transcendante,* all in sharp keys, were written in emulation of Liszt's similarly titled piano studies in flat keys.

BIBLIOGRAPHY: M. Shifman, *S. Liapunov* (Moscow, 1960).

Liatoshinsky, Boris, Ukrainian composer; b. Zhitomir, Jan. 3, 1895; d. Kiev, April 15, 1968. He studied jurisprudence at the Univ. of Kiev, simultaneously taking lessons in composition at the Kiev Cons. with Glière, graduating in 1919. In 1920 he was appointed prof. at the Kiev Cons.; also taught at the Moscow Cons. (1935-38 and 1941-43). His style of composition follows the broad outlines of national music, with numerous thematic allusions to folksongs.

WORKS: the operas *The Golden Hoop* (Odessa, March 26, 1930); *Shchors* (Kiev, Sept. 1, 1938; glorifying the exploits of the Soviet partisan leader Nicolai Shchors); *Grazina,* symph. ballad (Kiev, Nov. 26, 1955); 5 symphonies (1918-67); *Reunion,* symph. poem (1949); *Slavonic Concerto* for piano and orch. (1953); 4 string quartets (1915-43); 2 piano trios (1925, 1942); a Ukrainian quintet for piano (1946); numerous arrangements for chorus of Ukrainian folksongs; piano pieces, etc.

BIBLIOGRAPHY: Igor Boelza, *Boris Liatoshinsky* (Moscow, 1947).

Liberace, Walter (Wladziu Valentino), popular American pianist of Italian-Polish parentage; b. West Allis, Wisconsin, May 16, 1919. He received rudimentary musical training from his father, a French horn player. Encouraged by Paderewski, he began to study piano; played at night clubs, billed as **Walter Busterkeys.** In 1940 he moved to New York; evolved a facile repertoire of semi-classical arrangements; made a synthesis of the first movement of Beethoven's *Sonata quasi una fantasia* and Rachmaninoff's Prelude in C-sharp minor, taking advantage of the fact that both works are in the same key. He prospered; made lucrative inroads on television; built a home in California with a piano-shaped swimming pool. Inspired by a movie on Chopin, he placed a candelabra on the piano at his concerts; this decorative object identified him as a Romantic pianist, an impression enhanced by the dress suit of white silk mohair he habitually wears. In 1959 he won a suit for defamation of character against the London *Daily Mirror* and its columnist W. Connor (Cassandra) who suggested in print that Liberace was a deviate.

Libert, Henri, French organist; b. Paris, Dec. 15, 1869; d. there, Jan. 14, 1937. He studied at the Paris Cons. with Marmontel and Diémer (piano), César Franck and Widor (organ), and Massenet and Godard (composition); took 1st organ prize (1894); was titular organist at the Basilica of St. Denis in Paris, and prof. of organ at the American Cons. in Fontainebleau. He wrote many organ works, including *Variations symphoniques, Chorals, Préludes et fugues;* piano pieces; motets; songs; also publ. didactic works.

Libon, Philippe, French violinist and composer; b. (of French parents) Cadiz, Aug. 17, 1775; d. Paris, Feb. 5, 1838. He studied in London with Viotti; in 1796, became chamber violinist in Lisbon; in 1798, was a member of the court orch. in Madrid. In 1800 he settled in Paris as a member of the court orch. He publ. 6 violin concertos; 6 string trios; duets; 2 vols. of *Airs variés; Trente caprices* for violin solo.

Lichard, Milan, Slovak authority on folksongs; b. Uhorská Skalica, Feb. 24, 1853; d. Užhorod, April 21, 1935. He studied music in Budapest; also worked for the railway administration. He devoted his entire life to collecting and editing Slovak songs; contributed numerous articles on the subject to various scholarly magazines. From 1921 he lived in Užhorod, where he was also active as choral conductor.

Lichey, Reinhold, German organist and composer; b. Pohlsdorf, near Liegnitz, March 26, 1879; d. Plaue, Dec. 5, 1957. He studied music in Breslau; then went to Berlin where he took lessons with Max Bruch. He subsequently held numerous positions as church organist and chorus leader in Aachen, Königsberg, Naumburg, Pforta and finally at Plaue, near Arnstadt, where he remained until his death. He was a voluminous composer; wrote mostly for organ and chorus; also composed the *Goethe-Symphonie* (1948) and *Deutsches Friedens-Quartett.*

Lichnowsky, Prince Carl, a nobleman of Polish origin; a friend of Mozart and Beethoven; b. Vienna, June 21, 1761; d. there April 15, 1814. He received the title of nobility from the Russian government in 1773, but spent most of his life in Vienna. He was a pupil of Mozart, who accompanied him on a visit to the Prussian court in 1789. Beethoven's op. 1, 13, 26, and 36 are dedicated to Lichnowsky. In his home, Lichnowsky presented regular chamber music concerts with a quartet composed of Schuppanzigh, Sina, Weiss, and Kraft. Lichnowsky's younger brother, Count Moritz (1771–1837), was also a friend of Beethoven, who dedicated his op. 35, 51, and 90 to the Count and his wife.

Lichtenberg, Leopold, American violinist; b. San Francisco, Nov. 22, 1861; d. Brooklyn, N.Y., May 16, 1935. As a child, he began to study with Wieniawski; traveled as a concert violinist in Belgium and Holland; then returned to America; was a member of Theodore Thomas's Orch. in N.Y., and also of the Boston Symph.; in 1899, was appointed head of the violin dept. of the National Cons. in N.Y.; gave chamber music concerts.

Lichtenberger, Henri, French writer on music; b. Mulhouse, March 12, 1864; d. Biarritz, Nov. 4, 1941. In 1887 he became prof. of literature at the Univ. of Nancy; from 1905, prof. of German language and literature at the Univ. of Paris. He made a special study of Wagner's art and ideas, and publ. *Richard Wagner poète et penseur* (1890) and *Wagner,* a biography (1909; revised ed., 1925).

Lichtenstein, Karl August von, German theater manager and composer; b. Lahm, Franconia, Sept. 8, 1767; d. Berlin, Sept. 10, 1845. He studied music in Göttingen with Forkel; then was intendant of court theaters at Dessau (1798), Vienna (1800), Bamberg (1811), and Berlin (1823); in 1825, became director of the Berlin Opera; composed 11 operas and vaudevilles.

Lichtenthal, Peter, Austrian composer and writer on music; b. Pressburg, May 10, 1780; d. Milan, Aug. 18, 1853. He was a doctor by profession, and composed music as an avocation; settled in Milan in 1810; produced 3 operas and 5 ballets at La Scala; publ. a string quartet, 2 piano trios, and piano pieces. His chief writings are: *Cenni biografici intorno al celebre maestro Wolfgang Amadeus Mozart* (1814); *Dizionario e bibliografia della musica* (1826; 4 vols.); *Estetica, ossia dottrina del bello e delle belle arti* (1831); *Mozart e le sue creazioni* (1842).

Lichtenwanger, William, learned American librarian; b. Asheville, North Carolina, Feb. 28, 1915. He studied at the Univ. of Michigan at Ann Arbor (B. Mus., 1937; M. Mus., 1940); played oboe and other instruments in the band and orch.; wrote pieces with whimsical titles, e.g., *Phrygidair* (in Phrygian mode, naturally). He served as Assistant Reference Librarian of the Music Division at the Library of Congress, Washington, D.C. (1940–53, except for service in the Army of the U.S., 1941–45); Assistant Head (1953–60) and Head of the Music Reference Section there (1960–74); Associate Editor of *Notes* of the Music Library Association (1946–60) and its Editor (1960–63); in 1975 he was made a Member Emeritus of the Music Library Association. Furthermore, he was music editor of Collier's Encyclopedia (1947–50) and consultant for a biographical dictionary, *Notable American Women* (1971); also contributor to supplements II and III of the *Dictionary of American Biography;* chairman and compiler of *A Survey of Musical Instrument Collections in the U.S. and Canada* published by the Music Library Association (1974). A polyglot and a polymath, he is fluent in German, French and Turkish; nearly fluent in Japanese and fairly fluent in personalized Russian. With his excellent wife Carolyn he edited an analytic index to *Modern Music* (N.Y., 1976). Among his scholarly achievements perhaps the highest is his incandescent essay, "The Music of *The Star-Spangled Banner*—From Ludgate Hill to Capitol Hill," in the *Quarterly Journal of the Library of Congress* (July 1977), in which he furnishes documentary proof that the tune of the American national anthem was indeed composed by John Stafford Smith, all demurrings by various estimable historians to the contrary notwithstanding. To the present edition of *Baker's Biographical Dictionary of Musicians,* he contributed incalculably precious verifications, clarifications, rectifications and refutations of previous inadvertent and/or ignorant fabrications and unintentional prevarications.

Lichtveld, Lou (Lodewijk Alphonsus Maria), Dutch composer; b. Paramaribo, Surinam, Nov. 7, 1903. He went to Amsterdam in 1922 and was active as an organist and music critic. In 1936 he joined the International Brigade on the Loyalist side in the Spanish Civil War. During the Nazi occupation of Holland he served in the resistance movement, and became its representative in the emergency parliament of 1945. Lichtveld returned to Surinam in 1949, and served as Minister of Education and Public Health and later President of the Exchequer; organized the facilities for musical education. From 1961 to 1969 he was in the diplomatic service of The Netherlands, stationed in Washington and the United Nations; then retired and lived mostly on the island of Tobago in the West Indies. He wrote about 2 dozen novels and essays under the pen name of **Albert Helman.** His musical works include an oratorio *Canciones* (1934, manuscript lost in the Spanish Civil war); Piano Concertino (1932); Flute Sonata (1930); Violin Sonata (1931); *Triptych* for piano (1925); Piano Sonata (1927); also experimental pieces employing oriental scales. He used a 24-tone scale for the Dutch documentary films produced by Joris Ivens, *Regen* (1929; the musical score added in 1932) and *Philips-Radio* (1930; also known as *Industrial Symphony*). He also composed several choruses a cappella.

Lickl, Johann Georg, Austrian composer and conductor; b. Korneuburg, April 11, 1769; d. Pécs, May 12, 1843. He was associated with Schikaneder in Vienna, where he wrote the music for various light operas. His large opera *Slawina von Pommern* was produced in Vienna in 1812. He settled in Pécs as a church choir leader. Among his published works are several string quartets. He also publ. a periodic edition, *Wiener Salon-Musik* (arrangements for piano and harmonium from popular classics).

Lidholm, Ingvar, Swedish composer; b. Jönköping, Feb. 24, 1921. He studied violin and music theory at the Royal College of Music in Stockholm (1940–45) with Charles Barkel, Hilding Rosenberg and Tor Mann; was a stipendiary of the Jenny Lind Foundation for studies in France, Switzerland and Italy; then had private lessons with Mátyás Seiber in England. He played viola; then was engaged as conductor of the municipal orch. in Örebro (1947–56) and director of chamber music at the Swedish Broadcasting Corp. (1956–65); from 1965 to 1971 he taught at the Royal College of Music in Stockholm, and in 1974 became head of planning at the music dept. of the Swedish Radio. He became associated with the cosmopolitan avant-garde active in Sweden; contributed greatly to the formulation of methods and aims of modern music; with Ligeti and Lutoslawski he compiled a brochure *Three Aspects of New Music. From the Composition Seminar in Stockholm,* publ. in English (Stockholm, 1968). In his own works he applies constructivist methods with various serial algorithms. WORKS: *Toccata e canto* for chamber orch. (1944); Concerto for String Orch. (1945); Solo Flute Sonata (1945); *Laudi* for a cappella chorus (1947); Piano Sonata (1947); *Music* for string orch. (1952); Concertino for Flute, Oboe, English Horn and Cello

(1954); *Ritornell* for orch. (Stockholm, Feb. 17, 1956); *4 Pieces* for cello and piano (1955); *Canto LXXXI,* for a cappella chorus, after Ezra Pound (1956); *Skaldens Natt (The Night of the Poet)* for soprano, chorus and orch. (Hamburg, April 6, 1959); *Mutanza* for orch. (Örebro, Nov. 15, 1959); a ballet, *Riter (Rites;* Stockholm, March 26, 1960); *Motus Colores* for orch. (Cologne Festival, June 13, 1960); *Poesis* for orch. (Stockholm, Jan. 14, 1964); *Nausikaa ensam (Nausikaa Alone),* lyrical scene, based on a section of Eyvind Johnson's novel *Return to Ithaca,* for soprano, chorus and orch. (Ingesund, June 2, 1963); *Holländarn (The Dutchman),* opera, after Strindberg (Swedish Television, Dec. 10, 1967); *Stamp Music,* an improvisatory piece in graphic notation for variable performers (1970; composed for a Swedish postage stamp; version for soprano and tam-tam, 1971).

Lídl, Václav, Czech composer; b. Brno, Nov. 5, 1922. He studied at the Brno Cons., graduating in 1948; devoted himself principally to composing for the films. However, he took time off to write a *Romantic Sonata* for violin and piano; 2 string quartets; a Divertimento for flute, clarinet and bassoon; children's choruses.

Lidón, José, Spanish organist and composer; b. Béjar, June 2, 1748; d. Madrid, Feb. 11, 1827. He first served as organist in Málaga; in 1787 obtained the post of organist at the Chapel Royal in Madrid. He wrote an opera, *Glauca y Coriolano,* which was performed in Madrid (1792); music for organ and keyboard pieces. A keyboard sonata is printed in S. Kastner's collection, *Silva iberica* (Mainz, 1954). Lidón also publ. *Reglas muy útiles para los organistas y aficionados al piano.*

Lie (Lie-Nissen), Erika, Norwegian pianist; b. Kongsvinger, Jan. 17, 1845; d. Christiania, Oct. 27, 1903. She studied with Kjerulf in Christiania and with Th. Kullak in Berlin; later taught at Kullak's Academy there. She made concert tours throughout Europe; was particularly noted for her interpretation of Chopin. In 1870 she joined the faculty of the Copenhagen Cons. Returning to Norway, she married Dr. Oscar Nissen in 1874 and settled in Christiania.

Lie, Harald, Norwegian composer; b. Oslo, Nov. 21, 1902; d. there, May 23, 1942. At the age of 21 he went to America, where he earned his living as a piano tuner; then studied piano manufacturing in Leipzig. Returning to Norway in 1929, he took lessons in composition with Fartein Valen. During 12 years of composing he produced 2 symphonies (1934; 1937); *Symphonic Dance* (1942); some choral works; only 12 op. numbers in all. He died of tuberculosis.

Lie, Sigurd, Norwegian composer; b. Drammen, May 23, 1871; d. there, Sept. 29, 1904. He was a pupil of Lindeman and Holter; then studied at the Leipzig Cons. (1891–93); spent several years in Berlin; then returned to Norway, where he was appointed conductor of the "Handelsstand Sangforening" in Christiania (1902).
WORKS: Symphony in A minor (Christiania, Feb.

28, 1903); *Oriental Suite* for orch. (Christiania, Oct. 28, 1899); Violin Concerto (Bergen, Feb. 13, 1896); *Erling Skjalgson* for baritone solo, men's chorus, and orch. (Christiania, Oct. 28, 1899); *Norske Dans* for violin and piano; men's choruses; a song cycle *Wartburg,* and many separate songs, of which *Schnee* became famous.

Liebe, Eduard Ludwig, German composer; b. Magdeburg, Nov. 19, 1819; d. Chur, Feb. 4, 1900. He studied in Kassel with Spohr and Baldewein; then was music director at Coblenz, Mainz, and Worms; went to Strasbourg as teacher; later in London. He wrote an opera, *Die Braut von Azola* (Karlsruhe, 1868); also publ. popular songs and piano pieces.

Liebermann, Rolf, Swiss composer and opera director; b. Zürich, Sept. 14, 1910. He studied composition with Wladimir Vogel, then resident in Switzerland; most of his works were in an experimental idiom, sharing the influence of hedonistic eclecticism, French neo-Classicism and Viennese dodecaphony; he became particularly attracted to theatrical applications of modernistic procedures. He soon veered away from composition and made an extremely successful career as an opera administrator. In 1959 he became intendant of the Hamburg State Opera, and in 1962 its artistic director; in this post he instituted an audacious program of commissioned works from avant-garde composers (among them Krenek, Schuller, and Penderecki). Concurrently he was program director of the North German Radio and the West Berlin Radio. In 1973 he was named director of the Paris Opéra.
WORKS: the operas *Leonore 40/45* (Basel, March 25, 1952), *Penelope* (Salzburg, Aug. 17, 1954), *The School for Wives* (Louisville, Dec. 3, 1955; revised as a 3-act opera, *Die Schule der Frauen* and produced in Salzburg in 1957); *Furioso* for orch. (1947; Dallas, Dec. 9, 1950); *Concerto for Jazzband and Orchestra* (Donaueschingen Festival, Oct. 17, 1954); cantatas *Streitlied zwischen Leben und Tod* and *Une des fins du monde; Les Échanges* for 52 industrial machines recorded on tape, and composed for an exhibition in Lausanne, where it was performed on April 24, 1964; several piano pieces and songs. A Festschrift in his honor was presented to him on his 60th birthday (Hamburg, 1970).

Lieberson, Goddard, American composer and music executive; b. Hanley, Staffordshire, England, April 5, 1911; d. New York, May 29, 1977. He was brought to the U.S. as a child; studied at the Eastman School of Music, Rochester, N.Y.; settled in N.Y. in 1936. In 1939 he became a member of the staff of Columbia Records, Inc., and rapidly progressed in business; was President of Columbia Records (1955–66, 1973–75); in 1964 he was named president of the Record Industry Association of America while continuing as head of Columbia Records, Inc. In this latter position he was the chief catalyst in promoting longplaying records since their introduction in 1948, and was also responsible for a liberal policy in recording modern works by Columbia Records. He composed the orchestral suites *Five Modern Painters* (1929); *Piano Pieces for Ad-*

vanced Children or Retarded Adults; edited *Columbia Book of Musical Masterpieces* (N.Y., 1950).

Liebeskind, Joseph, German music editor; b. Leipzig, April 22, 1866; d. there, Aug. 10, 1916. He studied at the Leipzig Cons. with Sitt, Reinecke, and Jadassohn; lived most of his life in Leipzig; edited and arranged a number of works by Gluck, Mozart, Dittersdorf. He was a notable music collector; owned a large library rich in Gluck items, including some manuscripts.

Liebich, Ernst (Johann Gottlob), eminent German violin maker; b. Breslau, April 13, 1830; d. there, Sept. 23, 1884. His father and grandfather were violin makers, and he was trained in their workshop; also worked with Vuillaume in Paris, Hart in London, and Bausch in Leipzig. His instruments were awarded several prizes at international exhibitions.

Liebig, Karl, German conductor; b. Schwedt, July 25, 1808; d. Berlin, Oct. 6, 1872. He was engaged as an oboist in the Alexander Grenadier Regiment in Berlin; in 1843 he organized the Berlin Symphoniekapelle, which under his leadership attained a very high standard of performance; in 1867 the orchestra elected another conductor; Liebig's attempts to form a rival organization proved futile.

Liebling, Emil, German-American pianist; brother of **Georg Liebling;** b. Pless, Silesia, April 12, 1851; d. Chicago, Jan. 20, 1914. He studied piano with Th. Kullak in Berlin, Dachs in Vienna, and Liszt in Weimar; composition with Dorn in Berlin. In 1867 he came to America and lived in Chicago from 1872, actively engaged as a concert pianist and teacher. He wrote a number of effective piano pieces in a light vein (*Florence Valse, Feu follet, Albumblatt, Two Romances, Cradle Song, Canzonetta, Menuetto scherzoso, Mazurka de concert, Spring Song*). He edited *The American History and Encyclopedia of Music* and co-edited a *Dictionary of Musical Terms.*

Liebling, Estelle, American singer and vocal pedagogue; sister of **Leonard Liebling;** niece of **Emil** and **Georg Liebling;** b. New York, April 21, 1880; d. New York, Sept. 25, 1970. She studied with Mathilde Marchesi in Paris and S. Nicklass-Kempner in Berlin; made her debut as Lucia at the Dresden Royal Opera; also appeared at the Stuttgart Opera, the Opéra-Comique, Paris, and the Metropolitan Opera House, N.Y. (1903–4); was soloist with leading symph. orchestras in the U.S., France, Germany; also with Sousa; in 1936–38 was prof. at the Curtis Institute of Music; then settled in N.Y. as vocal teacher. She publ. *The Estelle Liebling Coloratura Digest* (N.Y., 1943).

Liebling, Georg, German-American pianist and composer; brother of **Emil Liebling;** b. Berlin, Jan. 22, 1865; d. New York, Feb. 7, 1946. He studied piano with Theodor and Franz Kullak, and Liszt; composition with Urban and Dorn; toured through Europe (1885–89); was court pianist to the Duke of Coburg (1890). In 1894–97 he directed his own music school in Berlin; 1898–1908, in London as prof. at the Guildhall School of Music. He came to the U.S. in 1924; made his N.Y. concert debut, Nov. 19, 1924. He used the pseudonym **André Myrot.**

WORKS: *Great Mass,* for soli, chorus, orch., and organ (Los Angeles, 1931); 2 violin concertos; *Concerto Eroico,* for piano and orch. (1925); 2 violin sonatas; 3 Preludes for violin and piano; *Aria e Tarantella* for cello and piano; *Légende* for violin and piano, etc.; piano pieces; songs.

BIBLIOGRAPHY: G. Braun, *Hofpianist Georg Liebling* (Berlin, 1896).

Liebling, Leonard, American music critic and editor; nephew of **Georg** and **Emil Liebling;** brother of **Estelle Liebling;** b. New York, Feb. 7, 1874; d. there, Oct. 28, 1945. He studied at the College of the City of New York, and privately with Leopold Godowsky (piano); then in Berlin with Kullak and Barth (piano) and Urban (composition); toured Europe and America as pianist. In 1902 he joined the staff of the *Musical Courier,* N.Y., and in 1911 became its editor-in-chief; his weekly columns on topical subjects were both entertaining and instructive. He also served as music critic of the *N.Y. American* (1923-34; 1936-37). He wrote some chamber music, piano pieces, and songs, as well as librettos of several light operas, including Sousa's *The American Maid.*

Lienau, Robert, German music publisher; b. Neustadt, Holstein, Dec. 28, 1838; d. there, July 22, 1920. In 1864 he purchased Schlesinger's business in Berlin, and in 1875, Haslinger's in Vienna; with the latter, he acquired the most important works of Weber, Meyerbeer, Liszt, Spohr, and others. In 1910 the management of the business was taken over by his sons **Robert** and **Wilhelm Lienau.**

Liepe, Emil, German singer and composer; b. Potsdam, Jan. 16, 1860; d. Berlin, Feb. 18, 1940. He studied in Leipzig and Vienna; from 1884-90, sang in various German opera theaters; in 1891-92 he appeared at the Bayreuth Festival; then retired from the stage, and taught voice at the Cons. of Sondershausen (1903-7) and, after 1907, in Berlin. He wrote an opera, *Colomba* (Danzig, 1894); symph. poems *Fatum* and *Rückblick;* Symphony; also a number of songs.

Lier, Bertus van. See **Van Lier, Bertus.**

Lier, Jacques van. See **Van Lier, Jacques.**

Lierhammer, Theodor, Austrian baritone and teacher; b. Lwow, Nov. 18, 1866; d. Vienna, Jan. 6, 1937. He was a practicing physician when he began to study singing with Ress in Vienna, Carafa in Milan, and Stockhausen in Frankfurt; made his debut at Vienna in 1894 in a concert with Fritz Kreisler; toured Austria and Hungary (1896), Germany (1898), Russia (1899), France and England (1900), and the U.S. (1904). From 1904-14 he was prof. of singing at the Royal Academy of Music in London; served as army physician during World War I; 1922-24, in London as singer and teacher; 1924, named prof. of singing at the State Academy of Music in Vienna; 1932-35, taught at the Austro-American Summer Cons., Mondsee (Salzburg). One of his American pupils was Roland Hayes.

Lieurance, Thurlow, American composer; b. Oskaloosa, Iowa, March 21, 1878; d. Boulder, Colorado, Oct. 9, 1963. He studied at the Cincinnati College of Music; served as army bandmaster during the Spanish-American War. He became interested in American Indian music, and lived on various reservations, studying the culture of Indian tribes; this research resulted in the composition of music showing the influence of Indian melodies; one of the songs, *By the Waters of Minnetonka,* achieved tremendous popularity; he publ. futher *9 Indian Songs* (1919), *Songs of the North American Indian* (1921), *8 Songs From the Green Timber* (1922), *Forgotten Trails* (1923); wrote several symph. pieces: *Medicine Dance, Colonial Exposition Sketches, Scenes Southwest, Prairie Sketches, Water Moon Maiden,* etc. In 1940 he was appointed dean of the music dept., Municipal Univ. of Wichita, Kansas; 1957, Dean Emeritus.

Ligeti, György, innovative Hungarian composer of the avant-garde; b. Dicsöszentmartin, Transylvania, May 28, 1923. He studied composition with Sándor Veress and Ferenc Farkas at the Budapest Music Academy (1945-49) and became instructor there (1950-56). In 1956 he left Budapest; worked in the Studio for Electronic Music in Cologne (1957-59); then lived mostly in Vienna (1959-69) and in Berlin (1969-73); in summers he lectured at the International Courses for New Music in Darmstadt; from 1961 was guest prof. of composition at the Musical High School in Stockholm; besides, he gave lectures in Spain, in Holland, in Germany, in Finland and in Tanglewood, U.S.; in 1972 was composer-in-residence at Stanford Univ.; in 1973 was appointed prof. of composition at the Hochschule für Musik in Hamburg. In his bold and imaginative experimentation with musical materials and parameters, Ligeti endeavors to bring together all aural and visual elements in a synthetic entity, making use of all conceivable effects, employing homely kitchen utensils and plebeian noise makers or grandiose electronic blasts; alternating tremendous sonorous upheavals with static chordal masses and shifting dynamic colors.

WORKS: *Rumanian Concerto* for orch. (1951); *Glissandi* for electronic sound (1957); *Articulation* for electronics (1958); *Apparitions* for orch. (1959); *Atmospheres* for orch. (1961); *Volumina* for organ (1962); *Aventures* for 3 singers and 7 instruments (1962); *Nouvelles Aventures* for soprano and 7 instruments (1962-65); *Requiem* for soprano, mezzo-soprano, 2 choruses and orch. (1963-65; Stockholm, March 14, 1965; *Kyrie* from it was used in the film score for *2001: A Space Odyssey);* Cello Concerto (Berlin, April 19, 1967); *Lontano* for orch. (Donaueschingen, Oct. 22, 1967); *10 Pieces* for wind quintet (Malmö, Jan. 19, 1969); *Ramifications* for string orch. (1969); *Chamber Concerto* for 13 instruments (Ottawa, April 2, 1970); Double Concerto for Flute, Oboe and Orch. (1972); *Clocks and Clouds* for female chorus and orch. (1973); *San Francisco Polyphony* for orch. (1974); also 2 string quartets (1954, 1968). Ligeti's *Poème symphonique* for 100 metronomes, all running at different speeds, was performed at the Buffalo Festival of The Arts Today (March 4, 1965) causing a sensation.

BIBLIOGRAPHY: Erkki Salmenhaara, *György Ligeti* (Helsinki, 1969).

Lilburn, Douglas, New Zealand composer; b. Wanganui, Nov. 2, 1915. He studied with Vaughan Williams at the Royal College of Music in London; then returned to New Zealand where he became prof. of music at the Victoria Univ. in Wellington. Among his works are *Forest,* symph. poem (1937); *Aoteroa,* overture (London, April 16, 1940); *Song of the Antipodes,* for orch. (Wellington, Aug. 20, 1947); *Diversions,* for string orch. (London, June 28, 1947); Symph. No. 1 (first full-fledged symphony by a New Zealand composer; Wellington, May 12, 1951); Symph. No. 2 (1955); Symph. No. 3 (1961); 2 string quartets; 3 violin sonatas; String Trio; Clarinet Sonata; Piano Sonata; other piano pieces; songs.

Liliencron, Rochus von, eminent German music scholar; b. Plön, Dec. 8, 1820; d. Coblenz, March 5, 1912. He studied law and theology in Kiel and Berlin; took a course of Nordic philology in Copenhagen, in 1850, became prof. of Norse literature at Kiel Univ.; in 1852, prof. of German literature at Jena Univ.; then privy-councillor at Saxe-Meiningen (1855–68); in 1869, went to Munich; there he edited the *Allgemeine deutsche Biographie* (1875–1900); collected and annotated German folksongs of the Middle Ages, publ. as *Historische Volkslieder der Deutschen vom 13.-16. Jahrhundert* (4 vols. and an appendix; Leipzig, 1865–69); from 1876 he lived in Schleswig as provost of St. John's Monastery; in 1894, appointed editor of the *Denkmäler deutscher Tonkunst.*
WRITINGS: *Lieder und Sprüche aus der letzten Zeit des Minnesangs* (1854; contains 20 melodies with texts from the Jena Minnesänger Codex, c.1320); *Über den Chorgesang in der evangelischen Kirche* (1881); *Deutsches Leben im Volkslied um 1530,* containing 147 polyphonic German folksongs of the 16th century (1885; 2nd ed., 1925); *Chorordnung für die Sonn- und Festtage des evangelischen Kirchenjahres* (1900; 2nd ed., by H. J. Moser, 1929). He wrote an autobiography, *Frohe Jugendtage* (1902). In 1910, in honor of his 90th birthday, a Festschrift was publ., to which many of the foremost German musicologists contributed (Riemann, Adler, Friedlaender, Kretzschmar, Sandberger, Seiffert, and others).
BIBLIOGRAPHY: A. Bettelheim, *Leben und Wirken des Freiherrn Rochus von Liliencron* (1917).

Lilienthal, Abraham W., American composer and teacher; b. New York, Feb. 13, 1859; d. there, March 15, 1928. He received his entire musical training in New York; for many years, played the viola in the N.Y. String Quartet; then lived in N.Y. as teacher and composer. He wrote a string quartet; a string quintet; a string sextet; a piano trio; a cello sonata; and a series of orchestral dances.

Liljeblad, Ingeborg, Finnish soprano; b. Helsinki, Oct. 17, 1887; d. there, Feb. 28, 1942. She studied in Berlin with Etelka Gerster, and in Paris with Félia Litvinne; was engaged at the Mannheim Opera (1911–13) and in Hamburg for the season of 1913–14. Returning to Helsinki in 1927, she taught at the Sibelius Academy. She was married to the conductor **Leo Funtek.**

Liljefors, Ingemar, Swedish composer, son of **Ruben Liljefors;** b. Göteborg, Dec. 13, 1906. He studied at the Royal Academy of Music in Stockholm (1923–27 and 1929–31); in 1938 was appointed to its staff. From 1947 to 1963 he was chairman of the Association of Swedish composers. He published a manual on harmony from the functional point of view (1937) and one on harmonic analysis along similar lines (1951). His compositions frequently employ elements of Swedish folk music.
WORKS: the opera *Hyrkusken (The Coachman,* 1951); *Rhapsody* for piano and orch. (1936); *3 Studies* for piano (1939); Piano Concerto (1940); 2 piano trios (1940, 1961); Symphony (1943); Piano Concertino (1949); Violin Sonatina (1954); 3 piano sonatinas (1954, 1964, 1965), Violin Concerto (1956); Cello Sonatina (1958); *En Tijdh-Spegel (A Mirror of the Times)* for soli, chorus and orch. (1959; Swedish Radio, April 16, 1961); Sinfonietta (1961); String Quartet (1963); *2 Intermezzi* for strings (1966); Sonatina for solo violin (1968); *Divertimento* for strings (1968).

Liljefors, Ruben, Swedish composer and conductor; b. Uppsala, Sept. 30, 1871; d. there, March 4, 1936. He studied in Uppsala; then with Jadassohn at the Leipzig Cons.; later in Dresden with Draeseke; and with Max Reger in Leipzig. Returning to Sweden, he was active as choral conductor in Uppsala (1902) and in Göteborg (1903–11); in 1912 he went to Gävle as conductor of the Orchestral Society.
WORKS: the cantata *Blomsterfursten (The Flower-Prince);* Symphony (1906); *Sommer-Suite* (1920); *3 Bagatelles* for string orch.; *Romance* for violin and orch.; Piano Concerto (1899; rewritten, 1922); incidental music to *Fritjof och Ingeborg;* Violin Sonata; men's choruses; piano pieces; songs; etc.

Lillo, Giuseppe, Italian composer; b. Galatina, Lecce, Feb. 26, 1814; d. Naples, Feb. 4, 1863. He studied at the Naples Cons. with Furno, Lanza, and Zingarelli; in 1846, became teacher of harmony at the Naples Cons.; later (1859), teacher of counterpoint and composition there. He had to retire from active life in 1861 because of mental illness.
WORKS: the operas *Una moglie per 24 ore* (Naples, 1834), *L'osteria d'Andujar* (Naples, 1840; his most successful work), etc.; symphonies; a piano quartet; much good piano music; also church music.

Limantour, José Yves, Mexican conductor; b. Paris (of Mexican parents), Aug. 9, 1919. He was educated at Trinity College, Cambridge; settled in Mexico in 1939; studied there at the Conservatorio Nacional; in 1940–41 he was in the U.S., where he took courses with Hindemith; from 1942–43 he was conductor of the orch. of the Ballet Russe de Monte Carlo in Mexico; 1944–51, conductor of the Jalapa Symph. Orch.

Limbert, Frank, conductor and composer; b. New York (of German parents), Nov. 15, 1866; d. Hanau, Nov. 19, 1938. He was taken to Germany at the age of 8, and remained there; studied at the Hoch Cons. in

Frankfurt; Dr. phil. at the Univ. of Strasbourg (1894), with the dissertation *Beitrag zur Kenntnis der volkstümlichen Musik, insbesondere der Balladen-Komposition in England*; from 1895 lived mostly in Hanau, where he conducted an oratorio society. He publ. a *Konzertstück* for piano and orch.; Violin Sonata; Viola Sonata; *Ein Zyklus von Sonetten* for chorus a cappella; other choruses, songs; piano pieces.

Limnander de Nieuwenhove, Armand Marie Ghislain, Belgian composer; b. Ghent, May 22, 1814; d. Moignanville, near Paris, Aug. 15, 1892. He studied in Freiburg with Lambillotte and in Brussels with Fétis; in 1835, became choral director in Malines; in 1845, settled in Paris.
WORKS: the grand opera *Le Maître-chanteur* (Paris 1853); the comic operas *Les Monténégrins* (Paris, 1849), *Le Château de la Barbe-Bleue* (1851), and *Yvonne* (1859); the symphony *La Fin des Moisson*; *Scènes druidiques*, for orch.; a string quartet; a cello sonata; church music; songs; etc.

Lincke, Joseph, Austrian cellist; b. Trachenberg, Silesia, June 8, 1783; d. Vienna, March 26, 1837. He was cellist in Schuppanzigh's famous quartet (1808–16) in Vienna; was 1st cellist at the Theater an der Wien (1818); finally at the Vienna Court Opera (1831). He composed some cello pieces.

Lincke, Paul, German composer of light music; b. Berlin, Nov. 7, 1866; d. Klausthal-Zellerfeld, near Göttingen, Sept. 3, 1946. He was active in many fields; played violin and bassoon; conducted theater orchestras; engaged in music publishing; after World War I he conducted revues at the Folies-Bergère in Paris (1918–20). His chief fame comes from his operettas; he is generally credited as being the progenitor of a special type of "Berlin operetta" as distinguished from the Vienna genre. The best-known of these are *Venus auf Erden* (1897), *Im Reiche des Indra* (Berlin, Dec. 17, 1899); *Frau Luna* (Berlin, Dec. 31, 1899); *Fräulein Loreley* (Berlin, 1900); *Lysistrata* (Berlin, 1902), which contains the famous tune *Glühwürmchen-Idyll (Glow-worm)*; *Prinzessin Rosine* (1905); *Grigri* (1911) and *Casanova* (1913). His last operetta was *Ein Liebestraum*, which was produced in Hamburg in 1940; a postage stamp in Lincke's honor, with a musical example showing the melody *Berliner Luft* from *Frau Luna*, was issued by the West German Government in 1957.
BIBLIOGRAPHY: Edmund Nick, *Paul Lincke* (Hamburg, 1953).

Lincoln, Robert Dix, American pianist and composer; b. Woodstock, Ohio, Dec. 3, 1924. He studied with Nadia Boulanger in Paris. Upon return to the U.S. he taught at various colleges. He wrote numerous teaching pieces for piano of a descriptive nature, among them *Lions and Tigers, Bouncing Clowns, Marching Musicians*, etc.

Lind, Jenny, famous soprano, called "the Swedish Nightingale"; b. Stockholm, Oct. 6, 1820; d. at her villa, Wynd's Point, Malvern Wells, England, Nov. 2, 1887. She studied singing at a school connected with the court theater; her early teachers there were C. M. Craelius and I. Berg; she later studied with A. F. Lindblad and J. A. Josephson. She made her professional debut as Agathe in *Der Freischütz* at the Stockholm Opera on March 7, 1838; she then sang Euryanthe in Weber's opera, and several parts in French operas. In 1840 she was appointed a regular member of the Royal Swedish Academy of Music, and was also given the rank of court singer. However, she felt the necessity of improving her voice, and went to Paris, where she studied for about a year with Manuel Garcia, who gave her a thorough training according to his well-known "scientific" method. In Paris Meyerbeer heard her, and was so impressed that he wrote for her the part of Vielka in his opera *Ein Feldlager in Schlesien*. Jenny Lind returned to Stockholm in 1842; in 1844 she went to Berlin; sang there, and also in Hannover, Hamburg, Cologne, and Coblenz; then appeared in Frankfurt, Darmstadt, Copenhagen, and again in Berlin; her other important engagements were at the Gewandhaus, Leipzig (Dec. 6, 1845), and at the Vienna Opera (April 18, 1846). By this time, her fame became legendary in Europe; she was engaged to sing in London, and her appearance there was preceded by an extraordinary publicity campaign. She made her London debut as Alice in *Robert le Diable* on May 4, 1847, with sensational success; as Chorley reported, the town "went mad about the Swedish Nightingale." If her success in England was great, her American tour exceeded all expectations in public agitation and monetary reward. She arrived in America in 1850, under the sponsorship of P. T. Barnum, the circus manager, who presented Jenny Lind as a natural phenomenon rather than an artist; nonetheless, she produced a fine impression on the musical public as well; she sang recitals in New York, Boston, St. Louis, and other cities; a 4-page broadside in folio format with golden type was issued in anticipation of her Boston appearance by the F. Gleason Publishing Co. (1850); poems were written in her honor, and accounts of her concerts were published in hundreds of newspapers. She earned fantastic fees, and made generous donations to various charitable institutions in Sweden. On Feb. 5, 1852, she married, in Boston, her accompanist **Otto Goldschmidt;** with him she returned to Europe; remained for some time in Dresden; in 1856 she went to London, and remained in England for the rest of her life, with the exception of a few appearances in Europe. She had left the operatic stage in 1849, before her American tour; in England she sang with her husband's Bach Choir; her final public appearance was at the Rhenish Music Festival, in 1870, when she sang the principal part in her husband's oratorio *Ruth*. Unlike many other celebrated singers of her era, Jenny Lind was a paragon of domestic virtue, and was distinguished by her lack of vanity; even her most ardent worshippers did not claim that she was beautiful, but there was no disagreement as to the quality of her voice and her musicianship. She possessed a fine coloratura, with a compass reaching high G; never striving for dramatic effect, she was able to maintain a perfect phrase. Among her best operatic parts were La Sonnambula and Lucia. A bust of Jenny Lind was unveiled in Westminster Abbey on April 20, 1894. A Jenny Lind Association was formed in N.Y. in 1922, and a Jenny Lind society was organized in Stockholm in 1943.

BIBLIOGRAPHY: J. B. Lyser, *G. Meyerbeer und Jenny Lind* (Vienna, 1847); C. G. Rosenberg, *Jenny Lind in America* (N.Y., 1851); H. S. Holland and W. S. Rockstro, *Memoir of Mme. Jenny Lind-Goldschmidt* (2 vols., London, 1891; condensed edition, 1 vol., 1893); W. S. Rockstro and O. Goldschmidt, *Jenny Lind-Goldschmidt: A Record and Analysis of the Method of the Late Jenny Lind-Goldschmidt* (London, 1894); C. A. Wilkens, *Jenny Lind: Ein Cäcilienbild aus der evangelischen Kirche* (Gütersloh, 1854; 5th ed., 1926); "Jenny Lind's Singing Method" (a letter written by her), *Musical Quarterly* (July 1917); T. Norlind, *Jenny Lind* (Stockholm, 1919); M. R. Werner, *Barnum* (N.Y., 1923); Mrs. Raymond Maude, *The Life of Jenny Lind* (London, 1926); Grace Humphrey, *Jenny Lind* (Philadelphia, 1928); E. C. Wagenknecht, *Jenny Lind-Goldschmidt* (Boston, 1931); Laura Benet, *Enchanting Jenny Lind* (N.Y., 1939); H. Headland, *The Swedish Nightingale: A Biography of Jenny Lind* (Rock Island, Ill., 1940); M. Pergament, *Jenny Lind* (Stockholm, 1945); K. Rotzen and T. Meyer, *Jenny Lind* (Stockholm, 1945); Joan Bulman, *Jenny Lind* (London, 1956); G. D. Schultz, *Jenny Lind, the Swedish Nightingale* (Philadelphia, 1962); W. P. Ware and T. C. Lockard, Jr., translators and editors, *The Lost Letters of Jenny Lind* (London, 1966); A. M. Dunlop, *The Swedish Nightingale* (N.Y., 1965); E. P. Myers, *Jenny Lind, Songbird from Sweden* (Champaign, Illinois, 1968).

Lindberg, Oskar Fredrik, Swedish composer and organist; b. Gagnef, Feb. 23, 1887; d. Stockholm, April 10, 1955. He studied at the Stockholm Cons. with Andreas Hallén and Ernst Ellberg; was organist at Trinity Church, Stockholm (1906–14); in 1919, appointed teacher of harmony at the Stockholm Cons.
WORKS: the opera *Fredlös* (after Selma Lagerlöf's story *The Outlaw*; Stockholm, Nov. 25, 1943); *Det ljusa Landet*, for chorus and orch. (1935); *Skansen Cantata; Bergslags Cantata* (1947); Symphony (1912); *Dalmålningar (Pictures from Dalarna*; 1908); the symph. poems *Florez och Blanzeflor, Från de stora skogarna, Hemifrån, Vildmark, Gesunda*; overtures; orchestral suites; Piano Quartet; Piano Quintet; a Requiem; piano pieces; songs.

Lindblad, Adolf Fredrik, Swedish composer; b. Skänninge, near Stockholm, Feb. 1, 1801; d. Linköping, Aug. 23, 1878. He studied in Berlin with Zelter. His numerous songs, tinged with national color, won deserved popularity, especially after Jenny Lind, his pupil, sang them in public; he was called the "Schubert of the North."
WORKS: an opera, *Frondörerna (The Frondists*; Stockholm, May 11, 1835); 2 symphonies; 7 string quartets; Piano Trio; Duo for piano and violin; songs (*The Song of the Dalecarlian Maiden, Lament, The Wood by the Åren Lake, A Day in Spring, A Summer's Day, Autumn Evening*, etc.).
BIBLIOGRAPHY: M. Grandinson, *Brev till A. F. Lindblad från Mendelssohn* (Stockholm, 1913).

Lindblad, Otto (Jonas), Swedish composer; b. Karlstorp, March 31, 1809; d. Mellby, Jan. 26, 1864. He is chiefly known for his vocal ensemble music; formed a vocal and instrumental trio; also was opera and choral conductor. He wrote 66 vocal quartets; 5 choruses with solos; 14 vocal trios; 3 duets; 36 solo songs.
BIBLIOGRAPHY: Ture Nerman, *Otto Lindblad* (Uppsala, 1930).

Linde, Bo, Swedish composer; b. Gävle, Jan. 1, 1933; d. there, Oct. 2, 1970. He studied composition with Lars-Erik Larsson at the Royal Academy of Music in Stockholm; then took courses in conducting in Vienna (1953–54). In 1960 he returned to Gävle. In his music he follows a healthy Scandinavian style of composition, liberally diversified with cosmopolitan neo-Classical techniques, bordering on polytonality.
WORKS: *Sinfonia fantasia* (1951); *6 Character Studies* for piano (1952); *Ballet blanc* (1953; Gävle, May 11, 1969); 2 piano trios (1953, 1969); String Quartet (1953); Violin Sonata (1953); 2 piano concertos (1954, 1956); *Suite in an Old Style* for orch. (1954); 2 piano sonatinas (1955, 1962); *Preludium and Final* for strings (1955); Violin Concerto (1957); Suite for orch. (1959); *Slotts-skoj (Fun in the Castle)*, a children's opera for radio (1959); *Sinfonia* (1960); Concerto for Orchestra (1961–62); *6 Pieces* for piano (1962); *Concert Music* for small orch. (1963); *Vårbilder (Spring Scenes)* for soli, chorus and orch. (1963); Cello Concerto (1964); *Serenata nostalgica* for 11 strings (1965); *Quartet in Miniature* for clarinets (1965); *Suite Boulogne* for orch. (1966); *Little Concerto* for wind quintet and strings (1966); *Pensieri sopra un Cantico Vecchio* for orch. (Gävle, Jan. 1, 1968); String Trio (1968); *Pezzo concertante*, a concertino for bass clarinet and strings (Gävle, Sept. 9, 1970); *6 Italian Songs* for baritone, violin, cello and piano (1970).

Lindegren, Johan, Swedish teacher and authority on church music; b. Ullared, Jan. 7, 1842; d. Stockholm, June 8, 1908. He studied at the Stockholm Cons., where he became teacher of counterpoint in 1881; 1884, organist and cantor of St. Nicholas' Church. Among his pupils were Alfvén, Melchers, Bäck, Håkanson, and Wiklund. An authority on church music, he edited *Tidning för kyrkomusik* (1881–82); also publ. a *Koralbok* (1905). Of his numerous compositions, only a few were published: *Hösttankar (Autumn Thoughts)*, an elegy; *Till Vegas jhältar (For Vega's Heroes)*, festival march; a string quartet; a piano sonata and fugue.

Lindeman, Ludvig Mathias, Norwegian organist and folksong collector; b. Trondhjem, Nov. 28, 1812; d. Christiania, May 23, 1887. He turned from theology to the study of music; in 1839, became organist at Our Saviour's Church in Christiania; in 1849, teacher of church singing at the Theological Seminary of Christiania Univ.; in 1883 he and his son Peter Lindeman (1858–1930) founded a music school which later developed into the Christiania Cons. He was one of the earliest and most active collectors of Norwegian folksongs; publ. nearly 600 folk melodies in the collection *Older and Newer Norwegian Mountain Melodies* (3 vols., 1853–67); also *68 Norwegian Mountain Melodies* (1841); *50 Norwegian Melodies* (1862); and *30 Norwegian Ballads* (1863). His *Chorale Book for the*

Norwegian Church (1877) remains a standard work; it contains some melodies by Lindeman, including *Kirken den er et gammelt hus,* one of the best-known Norwegian hymn tunes; also composed *Draumkvoedet (Dream chant)* for chorus; organ fugues; etc.

BIBLIOGRAPHY: O. M. Sandvik, *Ludvig Mathias Lindeman og folkemelodien* (Oslo, 1950).

Lindeman, Osmo, Finnish composer; b. Helsinki, May 16, 1929. He studied with Eino Linnala and Nils-Eric Fougstedt at the Sibelius Academy in Helsinki. In 1959 he was awarded a UNESCO grant to the Munich Music Academy, where he studied for a year with Carl Orff; upon returning to Finland he taught at the Sibelius Academy. In his works he at first adopted a traditional romantic manner, but after 1968 devoted himself to electronic music.

WORKS: Symph. No. 1, surnamed *Sinfonia Inornata* (1959); Piano Concerto No. 1 (1963); Symph. No. 2 (1964); Piano Concerto No. 2 (1965); *Music* for chamber orch. (1966); Concerto for Chamber Orch. (1966); *Huutokauppa (Auction),* ballet with 6 reciters, chorus, 2 pianos and orch. (1967); *Variabile* for orch. (1967); String Trio (1958); *Partita* for percussion (1962); *2 Expressions* for vibraphone and marimba (1965); String Quartet (1966). For tape: *Kinetic Forms* (1969); *Mechanical Music* (1969); *Tropicana* (1970); *Midas* (1970); *Ritual* (1972; won first prize in the electronic and computer music category of the VI International Composition Contest, in Italy).

Lindley, Robert, English cellist; b. Rotherham, Yorkshire, March 4, 1776; d. London, June 13, 1855. He studied cello with Cervetto; from 1794–1851 was 1st cellist at the Royal Opera in London; in 1882 became prof. of cello at the Royal Academy of Music. He wrote pieces for the cello.

Lindner, August, German cellist; b. Dessau, Oct. 29, 1820; d. Hannover, June 15, 1878. He studied with Drechsler; in 1837 he became 1st cellist in the court orch. at Hannover. He composed a cello concerto and numerous vocal pieces.

Lindner, Ernst Otto Timotheus, German music scholar; b. Breslau, Nov. 28, 1820; d. Berlin, Aug. 7, 1867. He was editor of the *Vossische Zeitung;* also conducted the Berlin Bach-Verein. He wrote *Meyerbeers "Prophet" als Kuntswerk beurteilt* (1850); *Die erste stehende deutsche Oper* (1855); *Geschichte des deutschen Liedes im 18. Jahrhundert* (1871; edited by Erk).

Lindpaintner, Peter Joseph von, German conductor and composer; b. Coblenz, Dec. 9, 1791; d. Nonnenhorn, Lake Constance, Aug. 21, 1856. He studied violin and piano in Augsburg; theory in Munich with Winter and Joseph Grätz; in 1812, became musical director of the Isarthor Theatre in Munich; from 1819 until his death, conductor of the court orch. at Stuttgart, where his ability made the orchestra famous.

WORKS: 28 operas, including *Der Bergkönig* (Stuttgart, Jan. 30, 1825), *Der Vampyr* (Stuttgart, Nov. 21, 1828), *Die Genueserin* (Vienna, Feb. 8, 1839), *Lichtenstein* (Stuttgart, Aug. 26, 1846); 3 ballets *(Joko,* etc.); 5 melodramas; 5 oratorios; symphonies; overture to *Faust;* incidental music to *Lied von der Glocke;* 6 Masses; *Stabat Mater;* songs *(Die Fahnenwacht, Roland,* etc.).

BIBLIOGRAPHY: R. Hänsler, *Lindpaintner als Opernkomponist* (Munich, 1928).

Lineva, Evgenia (*née* **Papritz**), Russian folksong collector; b. Brest-Litovsk, Jan. 9, 1854; d. Moscow, Jan. 24, 1919. She studied voice with her mother, who was a pupil of Glinka; then took lessons with Mathilde Marchesi in Vienna; later sang opera in Paris, London, and Moscow. In 1889 she married the engineer A. L. Linev (1840–1916); because of his revolutionary activities, he served a prison term, and was then forced to emigrate. Lineva was with him in London (1890–92) and in America; she gave concerts with a Russian choir (which she organized) at Carnegie Hall, New York (Dec. 10, 1892) and at the Chicago Exposition (1893). In America they experimented with phonograph recording. Upon their return to Russia (1894), Lineva undertook a series of trips in the Volga region, using a phonograph constructed by her husband to record folksongs. She published her findings in 2 vols. (with photographs and musical examples) in Russian and in English under the title *The Peasant Songs of Great Russia* (St. Petersburg, 1904); she further publ. *Songs of the Novgorod Region* (1909).

BIBLIOGRAPHY: E. Kann-Novikova, *Evgenia Lineva* (Moscow, 1952).

Linjama, Jouko, Finnish composer; b. Kirvu, Feb. 4, 1934. He studied with Aarre Merikanto and Joonas Kokkonen at the Sibelius Academy in Helsinki; then at the Staatliche Hochschule für Musik in Cologne with Bernd Alois Zimmermann and G. M. Koenig (1962–64); later taught at the Sibelius Academy (1964–68). His production is marked with serial canonic techniques following the paradigm of Anton von Webern.

WORKS: *5 Metamorphoses on 5 Canons from Op. 16 of Anton Webern* for piano, harpsichord, guitar, celesta and vibraphone (1963); *Orationes St. Thomae Aqvinatis* for chorus, flute, oboe, clarinet, bassoon, trumpet and trombone (1964, revised 1973); *Millaista on (How It Is),* chamber oratorio, to fragments of S. Beckett's text, for baritone, 6 male voices, 3 tapes and orch. (1964–68); *Kiittäkäät Herraa (Thank the Lord),* cantata for soprano, chorus and organ (1967); organ sonata, *Veni Creator Spiritus* (1968); *Missa de angelis* for chorus, English horn, clarinet, bassoon, horn and trombone (1969); Concerto for Organ (1971); *Triptychon* for 2 organs (1971); *Partita* for organ (1973); incidental music; numerous choral pieces a cappella; songs.

Linko, Ernst, Finnish composer and pianist; b. Helsinki, July 14, 1889; d. there, Jan. 28, 1960. He studied piano at the Helsinki School of Music (1909–11); then in Berlin, St. Petersburg and Paris. He was director of the Sibelius Academy (1939–59); for many years was active as a concert pianist. He wrote 4 piano concertos (1916, 1920, 1931, 1957), *Symphonie chevaleresque* (1949), *Ariette* for wind ensemble, *Rigaudon* for strings, Piano Trio, String Quartet, numerous piano pieces.

Linley, George, English composer and author; b. Leeds, 1798; d. London, Sept. 10, 1865. He settled in London, where he wrote words and music of songs, many of which acquired great vogue (*Ever of thee; I cannot mind my wheel, mother; Thou art gone from my gaze,* etc.); he also wrote the cantata *The Jolly Beggars;* the operas *Francesca Doria* (1849), *La Poupée de Nuremberg* (London, 1861), *The Toy-Makers* (1861), *Law versus Love* (1862); part-songs, trios, duets, hymns; edited the collections *Scottish Melodies, Songs of the Camp, Original Hymn Tunes,* etc.; publ. *The Musical Cynics of London* (1862), a satirical poem aimed at the critic Chorley, and *Modern Hudibras* (1864).

Linley, Thomas, Sr., English composer; b. Badminton, Jan. 17, 1733; d. London, Nov. 19, 1795. He first studied with a church organist in Bath; then with Paradisi. He organized performances of oratorios in Bath; in 1774 he went to London, where he produced several oratorios, and various stage works, to which he contributed an occasional song; also arranged and orchestrated ballets, comic operas, etc., by other composers. He publ. *6 Elegies* for 3 voices (his finest work) and *12 Ballads;* 2 vols. of miscellaneous vocal pieces by him were publ. posthumously. The writer Sheridan was his son-in-law; Linley wrote 7 numbers for the production of *The Duenna* of Sheridan, and arranged the rest of the work from music by others; it was produced at Covent Garden, London, on Nov. 21, 1775, and became one of the most successful comic operas in England in the 18th century (about 75 performances during the season). Linley's 3 sons and 3 daughters were also professional musicians.
BIBLIOGRAPHY: C. Black, *The Linleys of Bath* (London, 1926).

Linley, Thomas, Jr., English violinist and composer; eldest son of the preceding; b. Bath, May 7, 1756; d. Grimsthorpe, Aug. 5, 1778. He was extremely gifted as a child, and played a violin concerto in public at the age of 8. He studied music in London with his father and with Boyce; was then sent to Florence, where he studied violin with Nardini, and while there, met Mozart, with whom he subsequently formed a close friendship. Returning to England, he played at his father's concerts at Bath and in London. He wrote incidental music for various plays in London. He lost his life by drowning at the early age of 22. Some of his vocal pieces were included in the posthumous collection of his father's music.
BIBLIOGRAPHY: G. Beechey, "Thomas Linley, Junior," *Musical Quarterly* (Jan. 1968; includes a list of surviving works).

Linnala, Eino, Finnish composer; b. Helsinki, Aug. 19, 1896; d. Helsinki, June 8, 1973. He studied composition with Melartin at the Univ. of Helsinki and with Arthur Willner in Vienna. Upon return to Finland he acted as chairman of the Finnish Composer's Copyright Bureau, TEOSTO (1960–68); published music textbooks. He composed 2 symphonies (1927 and

1935), *Finnish Rhapsody* (1932), *Overture* (1934), 3 cantatas, numerous choral works and songs.

Linstead, George Frederick, Scottish pianist and composer; b. Melrose, Jan. 24, 1908. He wrote an oratorio at the age of 13, and an opera, *Agamemnon,* at 16; was church organist at Sheffield; in 1947, was appointed prof. at Sheffield Univ. Besides his youthful compositions, he has written an opera, *Eastward of Eden* (1937); *Moto perpetuo* for orch. (1947); Violin Sonata (1934); String Quartet (1941); piano pieces.

Lintermans, François-Joseph, Belgian composer and conductor; b. Brussels, Aug. 18, 1808; d. Ixelles, May 14, 1895. He was director of the Brussels choral society Les Artisans Réunis; composed choruses (*Cri de guerre, Réveil, Chœur des buveurs,* etc.)

Lioncourt, Guy de, French composer; b. Caen, Dec. 1, 1885; d. Paris, Dec. 24, 1961. He studied at the Schola Cantorum with Vincent d'Indy, who was his uncle by marriage; 1918, he won the Grand Prix Lasserre with his fairy-tale opera *La Belle au bois dormant* (1912). In 1935 he was co-founder, with L. de Serres, of the École César Franck in Paris.
WORKS: dramatic: *Le Petit Faune aux yeux bleus* (1911), *Les Dix Lépreux* (1920), *Jean de la lune* (1921), *Mystère de l'Emmanuel* (Liège, 1924), *Le Mystère de l'Alléluia* (1927), *Le Réniement de St.-Pierre* (1928), *Le Dict de Mme. Sante-Barbe* (1937), *Le Navrement de Notre Dame* (1944), *Le Mystère de l'Esprit* (1946); String Quartet; Piano Quartet; 3 *Mélodies grégoriennes,* for organ; *Élevations liturgiques* for organ; 3 Masses; motets. He publ. *Un Témoignage sur la musique et sur la vie au XXᵉ siècle* (Reims, 1956).

Lipatti, Dinu, outstanding Rumanian pianist and composer; b. Bucharest, April 1, 1917; d. Chêne-Bourg, near Geneva, Dec. 2, 1950. His father was a violinist who had studied with Sarasate, and his mother a pianist. He received his early training from his parents; then studied with Florica Musicescu at the Bucharest Cons. (1928–32). He received a 2nd prize at the International Competition at Vienna in 1934; then studied piano with Cortot, conducting with Munch, and composition with Paul Dukas and Nadia Boulanger in Paris (1934–39). He gave concerts in Germany and Italy, returning to Rumania at the outbreak of World War II. In 1943 he made his way to Stockholm, and then to Geneva, where he taught piano at the Geneva Cons. He visited England 4 times between 1946 and 1950; projected tours in America and Australia had to be canceled owing to his illness (lymphogranulomatosis), which led to his early death. He was generally regared as one of the most sensitive interpreters of Chopin, and was also praised for his deep understanding of the Baroque masters. Lipatti was married to **Madeleine Cantacuzene,** herself a concert pianist. He was also a fine composer.
WORKS: Piano Sonata (1932); Violin Sonatina (1933); *Şātrarii,* symph. poem (1933); *Concertino in the Classic Style* for piano and string orch. (1936; Bucharest, Oct. 5, 1939); *Fantasy* for piano trio (1936); *Nocturne* for piano (1937); *Suite* for 2 pianos (1938); *Symphonie concertante* for 2 pianos and orch. (1938);

Improvisation for piano trio (1939); *3 Nocturnes* for piano (1939); *Fantasy* for piano (1940); Piano Sonatina for the left hand (1941); *3 Rumanian Dances* for 2 pianos (1943), or piano and orch. (1945; Geneva, Oct. 11, 1945); *Aubade* for wind quartet (1949); songs.

BIBLIOGRAPHY: *Hommage à Dinu Lipatti* (Geneva, 1952); A. Lipatti, *La Vie du pianiste Dinu Lipatti, écrite par sa mère* (1954).

Lipawsky, Josef, Austrian composer; b. Hohenmauth, Bohemia, Feb. 22, 1769; d. Vienna, Jan. 7, 1810. He studied philosophy in Prague; then settled in Vienna, where he enjoyed the friendship of Mozart, who gave him some instruction; was house musician for Count Adam Teleky; also gave public piano concerts. He wrote a symphony; *Grande sonate pathétique* for piano; songs. His music was highly regarded by his contemporaries.

Lipinsky, Carl, Polish violinist and composer; b. Radzyn, Oct. 30, 1790; d. near Lwow, Dec. 16, 1861. His father was a professional musician and gave him his primary education. He met Paganini, who agreed to teach him the violin; in 1835 he visited Leipzig; Schumann was greatly impressed by his playing and dedicated *Carnaval* to him. Lipinsky appeared in London on April 25, 1836, as soloist in his *Military Concerto* for violin and orch.; in 1839 he settled in Dresden as concertmaster of the Dresden Orch.; Liszt once played at the same concert with him. Lipinsky wrote a comic opera, *Klótnia przez zaklad* (Lwow, May 27, 1814), and other stage pieces; polonaises and *Rondos alla polacca* for violin and piano, and numerous technical violin studies.

Lipkin, Malcolm Leyland, English composer; b. Liverpool, May 2, 1932. He studied at Liverpool College (1944–48) and at the Royal College of Music in London (1949–53); also took private lessons with Mátyás Seiber in London. In 1967 he was appointed Tutor in the Department of External Studies at Oxford Univ. He wrote *Sinfonia di Roma* (1965); *Mosaics* for chamber orch. (1966); 2 violin concertos (1952, 1962); Piano Concerto (1957); Violin Sonata (1957); *Pastorale* for horn and strings (1963); *Suite* for flute and cello (1961); String Trio (1964); *Capriccio* for piano and string quartet (1966); 4 piano sonatas, some choruses and lieder.

Lipkovska, Lydia, Russian soprano; b. Babino, Khotin District, Bessarabia, May 10, 1884; d. Beirut, Lebanon, Jan. 22, 1955. She studied voice with Madame Iretzkaya in St. Petersburg, and made her professional debut there in the spring of 1909. She sang in Paris with great success, and received a contract for an American tour. Her American debut took place with the Boston Opera on Nov. 12, 1909, when she sang *Lakmé;* on Nov. 18, 1909, she appeared at the Metropolitan Opera House in *La Traviata* with Caruso. She was reengaged for the following season in the U.S.; also appeared in London (July 11, 1911). During World War I she was in Russia; after the Revolution she went to France; in 1919 she married Pierre Bodin, lieutenant in the French Army; toured the U.S. again in 1920. She then lived in France and

her native Bessarabia; during the Rumanian occupation of Odessa (1941–44) she appeared at the Odessa Opera in her favorite role of Violetta; also acted in drama. In 1944 she went to Paris; then accepted a teaching position in Beirut (Lebanon); during her last years of life she was supported by the Tolstoy Foundation of America.

Lipowsky, Felix Joseph, German music lexicographer and composer, son of **Thad Ferdinand Lipowsky;** b. Wiesensteig, Jan. 25, 1764; d. Munich, March 21, 1842. He was engaged in many scholarly pursuits, as a legal scientist, politician, art historian, etc. He was active as a church organist and choir leader; in 1787 he obtained his Dr. jur. degree; then served as municipal officer in Bavaria. He publ. *Bairische Musiklexikon* (Munich, 1811), which contains valuable material despite many faults of commission and omission. He wrote several sacred choral works and some instrumental music.

Lipowsky, Thad Ferdinand, German composer; b. St. Martin, Bavaria, Dec. 28, 1738; d. Wiesensteig, March 18, 1767. He studied with Leopold Mozart in Salzburg; obtained a law degree in Wiesensteig (1763); composed many violin pieces. A lengthy account of his career is found in the *Baierisches Musik-Lexikon* compiled by his son, **Felix Joseph Lipowsky.**

Lipps, Theodor, German writer on music; b. Wallhalben, July 28, 1851; d. Munich, Oct. 17, 1914. He occupied the chair of philosophy at the universities of Bonn (1889), Breslau (1890–94), and Munich (from 1894). Besides the musical sections of his *Ästhetik* (2 vols., 1903–6), his writings on music comprise *Zur Theorie der Melodie* (1901); *Psychologische Studien* (vol. 2: *Das Wesen der musikalischen Harmonie und Disharmonie;* 1885; 2nd ed., 1905); "Tonverwandtschaft und Tonverschmelzung," *Zeitschrift für Psychologie und Physiologie* (1899).

BIBLIOGRAPHY: P. Moos, *Theodor Lipps als Musikästhetiker* (1907); F. Liuzzi, *Essenza dell' arte e valore estetico nel pensiero di Theodor Lipps* (Bologna, 1924).

Lipsius, Marie (pen name **La Mara**), German writer on music; b. Leipzig, Dec. 30, 1837; d. Schmölen, near Wurzen, March 2, 1927. She received her entire education from her father, Dr. Adalbert Lipsius, rector of the Thomasschule in Leipzig; through R. Pohl, she was introduced to Liszt; in Liszt's circle at Weimar she had the happy fortune of meeting the foremost musicians of the time. Her writings on Liszt and Wagner, and on other German composers of the Romantic school, possess a stamp of authority and intimate understanding.

WRITINGS: *Beethoven* (1870; 2nd ed. 1873); *Musikalische Studienköpfe* (1868–82; 5 vols., often republished); *Musikalische Gedanken-Polyphonie: eine Sammlung von Aussprüchen berühmter Musiker über ihre Kunst* (1873); *Das Bühnenfestspiel in Bayreuth* (1877); *Musikerbriefe aus fünf Jahrhunderten* (1886; 2 vols.); *Klassisches und Romantisches aus der Tonwelt* (1892); *Briefe an August Roeckel, von Richard Wagner* (Leipzig, 1895); *Briefe von H. Berlioz an die Für-*

stin Carolyne zu Sayn-Wittgenstein (1903); *Aus der Glanzzeit der Weimarer Altenburg, Bilder und Briefe aus dem Leben der Fürstin C. Sayn-Wittgenstein* (1906); *Marie von Muchanov-Kalergis in Briefen an ihre Tochter* (1907; 2nd ed., 1911); *Beethovens "Unsterbliche Geliebte." Das Geheimnis der Gräfin Brunswik und ihre Memoiren* (1909); *Liszt und die Frauen* (1911); *Durch Musik und Leben im Dienste des Ideals* (autobiography; 2 vols., 1917; 2nd ed., 1926); *Beethoven und die Brunsviks* (1920); *An der Schwelle des Jenseits: Letzte Erinnerungen an die Fürstin Carolyne Sayn-Wittgenstein* (1925). She also publ. popular biographies of many composers (Wagner, Berlioz, Rubinstein, Schumann, etc.).

Lirou, Jean François Espic, Chevalier de, French composer and theorist; b. Paris, 1740; d. there, 1806. He was an officer in the 'Mousquetaires du roi,' for whom he wrote a *Marche des Mousquetaires,* which was performed until the Revolution. He publ. an *Explication du système de l'harmonie* (1785); this was the first French theory of harmony that opposed Rameau's system and sought to establish the laws of chord progressions from the inherent affinities of tonality.

Lishin, Grigory, Russian composer; b. St. Petersburg, May 5, 1854; d. there, June 27, 1888. He studied piano with his mother; became a proficient accompanist; also wrote music criticism. He composed 2 operas, *Don Caesar* (Kiev, 1888) and *Count Nulin* (after Pushkin), to his own librettos. His sentimental ballad, *She laughed,* was extremely popular with Russian singers.

Lisinski, Vatroslav, important Croatian composer; b. Zagreb, July 8, 1819; d. there, May 31, 1854. He was a student of Sojka and Wiesner von Morgenstern in Zagreb; as late as 1847, he went to Prague to study with Pitsch and Kittl. Although he never acquired a solid technique of composition, he was notable in that he tried to establish a national style in dramatic writing. He was the composer of the first Croatian opera, *Ljubav i zloba* (*Love and Malice*), for which he wrote only the vocal score; it was orchestrated by his teacher Wiesner von Morgenstern, and performed in Zagreb on March 28, 1846. His second opera, *Porin,* also in Croatian, was given many years after his death, in Zagreb, on Oct. 2, 1897. He further wrote 7 overtures and a number of choruses and songs.
BIBLIOGRAPHY: F. Kuhač, *Vatroslav Lisinski* (Zagreb, 1887); L. Zupanović, *Vatroslav Lisinski* (Zagreb, 1969).

Liška, Zdeněk, Czech composer; b. Smečno, March 16, 1922. He studied at the Prague Cons.; since 1945 active as composer for the State Studios of Documentary Films. For the Czechoslovak spectacle, *Laterna Magica,* he wrote a violin concerto in a modern virtuoso manner. This concerto, first performed in Leningrad on Dec. 5, 1960, was a featured work in the presentation of *Laterna Magica* in New York in the summer of 1964.

Lissa, Zofia, outstanding Polish musicologist; b. Lwow, Oct 19, 1908. She studied with Chybinski. The outbreak of the war interrupted her further studies; in 1947–54 she was vice-president of the Union of Polish Composers; in 1957 was appointed prof. of musicology at the Warsaw Univ.; she also served as a member correspondent with the Berlin Academy of Fine Arts (since 1957) and of the Academy of Sciences & Literature of Mainz (1972). She wrote voluminously on a variety of subjects connected with music history, education, broadcasting, film music, psychology of music and social implications of music; publ. *The Outlines of Musical Science* (Lwow, 1934; new ed., 1948); *Some Problems of Musical Esthetics* (Cracow, 1952; also publ. in Japanese, 1956, and in Chinese, 1962); *Essays on Musical Esthetics* (Cracow, 1964; in German, Berlin, 1969; in Hungarian, Budapest, 1973; in Serbian, Belgrade, 1973); of peculiar interest is her publication *The Marxist Method in Musicology* (Cracow, 1951) in which she propounds the interpretation of socialist realism and other doctrines of Marxist science as applied to both musical composition and musical evaluation. She contributed numerous articles on Polish music to *Die Musik in Geschichte und Gegenwart.*

Lissenko, Nikolai, significant Ukrainian composer; b. Grinki, near Kremenchug, March 22, 1842; d. Kiev, Nov. 6, 1912. He was the son of a landowner; grew up in a musical atmosphere; the singing of Ukrainian songs by local peasants produced a lasting impression on him, and determined his future as a national composer. He studied natural sciences at the Univ. of Kiev, graduating in 1864; was a justice of the peace in the Kiev district (1864–66); then abandoned his nonmusical pursuits and went to Leipzig, where he entered the Cons., and took courses with Richter (theory), Reinecke (piano), and Papperitz (organ). Returning to Russia in 1868, he taught piano at the Kiev Institute of the Daughters of Nobility; from 1874–76 studied orchestration with Rimsky-Korsakov in St. Petersburg. As early as 1868 he published his first collection of Ukrainian songs (printed in Leipzig); subsequent issues comprised 240 songs in 5 books, arranged according to their categories (Spring Songs, Midsummer Night Songs, Christmas Songs, etc.); he set to music a great number of poems from *Kobzar* by the Ukrainian poet Shevchenko (5 albums for 2, 3, and 4 voices; publ. in Kiev, 1870–97). In 1903, on the occasion of the 35th anniversary of the publication of his first collection of Ukrainian songs, Lissenko received a gift of 5,000 rubles from his admirers.

In his pamphlet *The Characteristics of the Ukrainian Dumki* (1874), Lissenko presents a theory that Ukrainian modes are derived from Greek music, and that antiphonal construction is one of the main features of Ukrainian songs, while the persistence of symmetrical rhythms distinguishes them from Russian songs. In his original compositions, Lissenko asserted himself as an ardent Ukrainian nationalist; he wrote several operas to Ukrainian librettos: *Chernomortsy* (1870); *Rizdviana Nitch,* after Gogol's *Christmas Eve Night* (1870); *Winter and Spring* (1880); *Utoplena,* after Gogol's *May Night* (1885); *Taras Bulba,* after Gogol's novel of the same name (1890; Kiev, Dec. 20, 1903; revised by Liatoshinsky and produced in Kiev in 1937); and his most popular stage work, after Kotlarevsky's play, *Natalka-Poltavka* (*Natalie from Pol-tava*), originally in the form of incidental music, then expanded into a 3-act opera (1890). He further wrote an opera, *Sappho*, with a Ukrainian text, which was unsuccessful; and 2 children's operas, *Pan Kotsky* (*Puss-in-Boots*, 1891) and *Koza-Dereza* (Kiev, April 20, 1901). Other works include 2 cantatas: *The Tor-rents Roar* (1877) and *Rejoice, Field Unplowed* (1883); also a *Cossack Scherzo*, for orch. (1872); *Capriccio elegiaco*, for violin and orch. (1894); 2 rhapsodies on Ukrainian themes, for piano; vocal pieces.

List, Emanuel, Austrian bass; b. Vienna, March 22, 1891; d. there, June 21, 1967. He was a chorister at the Theater-an-der-Wien; studied voice in Vienna, and made his debut at the Volksoper there in 1922 as Méphistophélès in *Faust*; in 1923, was engaged at the Berlin State Opera, remaining there until 1933; spe-cialized in Wagnerian roles. On Dec. 27, 1933 he made his first American appearance at the Metropolitan Op-era, N.Y., as the Landgraf in *Tannhäuser*; in subse-quent seasons, sang almost all Wagnerian bass roles; also appeared as singer of German lieder.

List, Eugene, American pianist; b. Philadelphia, July 6, 1918; was taken to Los Angeles when a year old; studied there at the Sutro-Seyler Studios and made his debut with the Los Angeles Philharmonic at the age of 12; later studied in Philadelphia with Olga Samaroff, and at the Juilliard Graduate School in N.Y.; made his New York debut playing the solo part in the American première of Shostakovich's Piano Concerto with the N.Y. Philharmonic (Dec. 19, 1935). As a sergeant in the U.S. Army, he was called upon to play the piano at the Potsdam Conference in July 1945, in the presence of Truman, Churchill, and Sta-lin. He married the violinist **Carroll Glenn** (Aug. 16, 1943). In 1964 he was appointed prof. of piano at the Eastman School of Music, Rochester, N.Y.; then joined the faculty of N.Y. University.

List, Kurt, Austrian-American musician; b. Vienna, June 21, 1913; d. Milan, Nov. 16, 1970. He studied mu-sic at the Vienna Academy of Music (M.A., 1936) and at the Univ. of Vienna (Ph.D., 1938); also took private lessons with Alban Berg (1932–35) and Anton von Webern (1935–38). He went to the U.S. in 1938; be-came active in the field of recording; wrote music criticism. After World War II he returned to Europe and lived mostly in Italy. His string quartet and a wind quintet were performed in New York; he also wrote two unperformed operas, *Der Triumph des Todes* and *Mayerling*, stylistically influenced by Rich-ard Strauss.

Listemann, Bernhard, German-American violinist and conductor; b. Schlotheim, Aug. 28, 1841; d. Chi-cago, Feb. 11, 1917. He studied with Ferdinand David in Leipzig, with Vieuxtemps in Brussels, and with Jo-achim in Hannover; became concertmaster of the court orch. in Rudolstadt (1859–67); then went with his brother **Fritz Listemann** to America; from 1871–74, was concertmaster in the Thomas Orch., N.Y.; in 1874 he went to Boston, where he founded the "Philharmonic Club," and later the "Philharmonic

Orch.," which he conducted until 1881, when he be-came concertmaster of the newly established Boston Symph. Orch.; meanwhile, he started the "Listemann Quartet;" also was director of the "Listemann Con-cert Co." (1885–93). In 1893 he went to Chicago, where he taught violin at the Chicago College of Mu-sic.

Listemann, Franz, American cellist; son of **Bernhard Listemann**; b. New York, Dec. 17, 1873; d. Chicago, March 11, 1930. He studied with Fries in Boston, with Julius Klengel in Leipzig, and with Haussmann in Ber-lin. After a year as 1st cellist in the Pittsburgh Orch., he settled in N.Y.; he was soloist at the American pre-mière of Dvořák's Cello Concerto (1896).

Listemann, Fritz, German violinist; brother of **Bern-hard Listemann**; b. Schlotheim, March 25, 1839; d. Boston, Dec. 28, 1909. Like his brother, he studied with Ferdinand David at the Leipzig Cons.; was a member of the court orch. at Rudolstadt (1858–67); together with his brother he went to America; played violin in the Thomas Orch. in N.Y. (1871–74); then was in Boston, where he played in various chamber music organizations, and (from 1878) in his brother's "Philharmonic Orch."; from 1881–85, was a violinist in the Boston Symph. Orch.; then played in the "Liste-mann Concert Co." directed by his brother. He wrote 2 violin concertos; violin pieces.

Listemann, Paul, American violinist; son of **Bernhard Listemann**; b. Boston, Oct. 24, 1871; d. Chicago, Sept. 20, 1950. He was taught by his uncle **Fritz Listemann**, and also by his father; as a boy participated in the various organizations directed by his father; then went to Germany, where he studied in Leipzig with Brodsky and in Berlin with Joachim; he was subse-quently engaged as orchestral violinist in Pittsburgh, New York, etc.; was a member of the Metropolitan Opera Orch. from 1903 to 1920. In 1930 he moved to Chicago.

Listov, Konstantin, Russian composer; b. Odessa, Aug. 19, 1900. He learned music by ear; then studied piano in Tsaritsin (Stalingrad) and in Saratov. In 1923 he went to Moscow and began to write music for the theater. His Red Army song *Tachanka* became im-mensely popular. He also wrote a symphony in com-memoration of the centennial of Lenin (1970).
    BIBLIOGRAPHY: A. Tishchenko, *Konstantin Listov* (Moscow, 1962).

Liszt, Franz (Ferencz), greatly celebrated Hungarian pianist and composer; creator of the symphonic poem and a reformer of modern piano technique; b. Raiding, near Ödenburg, Oct. 22, 1811; d. Bayreuth, July 31, 1886. His father was an excellent amateur musician and trained him in music from earliest childhood; at the age of 9 young Liszt played the difficult Piano Concerto by Ries. A group of Hungarian aristocrats provided sufficient funds (600 florins annually) to fi-nance his musical education for 6 years. In 1821 the family moved to Vienna where Liszt became a pupil of Czerny in piano and studied music theory with Sa-lieri. Liszt's ambitious father was eager to introduce him to Beethoven, and as a legend (supported by Liszt himself in his later years) had it, Beethoven kissed him on the brow after Liszt played an arrangement of Beethoven's Trio, op. 97, for him, entirely from memory. Beethoven's factotum Schindler made an earnest effort to persuade Beethoven to come to Liszt's concert in Vienna on April 13, 1823, but Beethoven did not acquiesce. After concerts in Munich and Stuttgart, young Liszt proceeded to Paris where he applied for admission to the Cons.; but Cherubini, then director of the Paris Cons., who was opposed to infant prodigies, refused to accept him as a student using as an excuse a rule forbidding the entrance of foreigners. As a consequence, Liszt took no more piano lessons; he studied composition for a short time with Paër and then with Reicha. At the age of 13 Liszt composed an operetta *Don Sanche, ou le Château d'Amour*, which was performed 5 times at the Académie Royale de Musique in 1825. Liszt's father died in 1827, and he settled in Paris. He was already well-known as a virtuoso pianist, and in Paris he moved in the highest circles of letters and arts; he was fascinated by the new romantic spirit of the age; the socialistic ideas of St. Simon, the revolutionary rumblings of 1830, greatly affected him. Paganini's spectacular performances on the violin inspired Liszt to emulate him in creating a new pianistic technique that exploited all possible sonorities of the instrument; the corresponding ideas of Berlioz in enlarging orchestral sonorities found in Liszt an enthusiastic supporter. At the same time Liszt never abandoned the basic romantic feeling for music as an expressive art, the voice of the human soul translated into musical tones; in this he was an ardent companion of Chopin, his close contemporary. He formed a liaison with the Countess d'Agoult, who wrote literary works under the *nom de plume* of Daniel Stern, and went to live with her in Geneva (1835–39). Three children were born to them: Cosima, the younger of two daughters, eventually became the wife of Richard Wagner. After his Geneva sojourn he set out on a concert tour through Europe, which proved to be a series of triumphs. To underline the narrative romantic quality of his playing and his compositions, Liszt accepted the suggestion of his London manager who used the word "recital" for this purpose, and the term became universally accepted. Since Liszt himself acknowledged that in his piano works he set Paganini as a model, it was only natural that he was often described as the "Paganini of the piano." But he maintained that his virtuosity was but a means of recreating great music, and held that the interpreter's duty was to reveal the composer's innermost intentions. His spiritual affinity with Beethoven moved him to superlative renditions of the master's piano sonatas; but he was also able to give intimate interpretations of Chopin. Withal, Liszt was a man of the world, a practical musician who was willing to give to his public what was expected of him. On stage he was often an actor; he wore white gloves, as was the custom of the day, and took them off ceremoniously in front of the audience; at some concerts he had two pianos on the stage, and played a group of pieces on each in alternation so that his hands could be seen from every side of the audience. He included in some of his programs free improvisations on themes proffered to him by musical amateurs. His private life underwent another upheaval when he formed a new liaison with the Russian Princess Carolyne Sayn-Wittgenstein, who left her husband and took up her residence with Liszt; she was very influential in turning him towards established religion. Liszt became a Freemason in 1841, a tertiary of St. Francis in 1858. In 1865 the Pope Pius IX conferred on him the dignity of Abbé. In 1879 he received the tonsure and the four minor orders: ostuary, lector, exorcist and acolite, and an honorary canonry; however, he was never ordained a priest, and could not say Mass, or hear Confession. But he could discard his cassock and even marry if he so wished. He practically abandoned his concert career in 1848, when he accepted the position of court Kapellmeister at Weimar. When Wagner was exiled from Saxony, Liszt arranged the production of his opera *Lohengrin* in Weimar on Aug. 28, 1850; he also was instrumental in supervising performances of Wagner's *Der fliegende Holländer* and *Tannhäuser* and the music of Berlioz. In 1861 he left Weimar and lived for the most part in Rome. In 1870 he returned to Weimar to conduct a centennial Beethoven festival there. In 1875 he was made president of the New Hungarian Academy of Music in Budapest; the last years of his life were spent in Weimar, Budapest and Rome. In Weimar he formed a faithful retinue of loyal and admiring students, and he displayed great interest in new movements in musical composition. He was an eager correspondent; his letters, many of them still unpublished, number in the thousands, written in French and German, in longhand; he did not employ a secretary. According to a will he made in 1860, Liszt's manuscripts passed into the possession of the Princess Carolyne Sayn-Wittgenstein; after the latter's death in 1887, they were inherited by her daughter Marie Hohenlohe-Schillingsfürst. She in turn left these materials to the Weimar Court; eventually they became part of the "Liszt Museum." Liszt's achievement as a composer is of revolutionary significance. He created the transcendental style of piano playing and introduced a new concept of the spiritual relationship between music and literature; he was allied with Wagner in the movement that was called, both in derision and admiration, *Zukunftsmusik*, the music of the future. The term applied to a mystical synthesis of the arts, which for Liszt implied the adoption of a programmatic design in a musical composition and a liberation from the classical rules of musical form. Such a synthesis was accomplished by Liszt in the creation of a symphonic poem, explicitly descriptive and connected with a literary work or a philosophical idea. "Music of the future" also embraced the field of harmony, modulation and melody. Both Liszt and Wagner greatly enhanced the type of chromatic harmony resulting from instant modulation into unrelated keys. In the last years of his life, Liszt experimented with melodic patterns, such as those derived from the whole-tone scale, which tend to obscure tonality, and with harmonic combinations rich in dissonance produced by long delayed resolutions. Liszt defied tradition when he boldly outlined the main subject of his *Faust Symphony*, formed of 4 arpeggiated, chromatically descending, augmented triads, the whole aggregating into 12 different notes. In his orchestration he summoned large sonorities following the precedent of Berlioz. It was this unremitting flow of sound that outraged the music critics of Liszt's day and moved them to denounce Liszt as a purveyor of noise in guise of music. But Liszt was also capable of writing music of intimate lyric quality; his songs to German or French words possess the deepest lyrical expressiveness; his piano pieces distil the poetry and the drama of the literary program to the finest gradation of sentiment. His B-minor Piano Sonata introduces a new dimension into this classical form; in place of an orderly succession and development of basic themes, Liszt cultivates here an association of motives, thus transforming the work into a musical narrative. His 3 albums of *Années de Pèlerinage* for piano are tone paintings evoking the scene with pictorial vividness. His two piano concertos, his brilliant *Hungarian Rhapsodies*, his *Mephisto-Waltz*, and particularly his *Études d'exécution transcendante*, are unsurpassed in their sonorous grandeur and authentic virtuosity. In his transcriptions of Schubert's and Schumann's songs, he transmutes their vocal lines and accompanying harmonies into new tonal creations. Finally his flamboyant arrangements of operatic arias by Auber, Donizetti, Gounod, Meyerbeer, Mozart, Rossini, Verdi and Wagner, are exhibitions of the highest art of transmutation from one medium into another. Liszt never wrote a full-fledged opera, but he composed oratorios that are operatic in substance and presentation. His many sacred works enhance the originality of his secular harmonies without losing their devotional character. Liszt was deeply conscious of his Hungarian heritage, but he spent most of his life in France, Germany and Italy; he could barely converse in Hungarian; he never went into the countryside in quest of the folk origins of Hungarian music as the two modern Hungarians, Kodály and Bartók, did; rather he gathered the ethnic materials that he so brilliantly used in his *Hungarian Rhapsodies* and other works of Hungarian inspiration from Gypsy bands he frequently heard in public places in Budapest; in one extraordinary instance, he borrowed the theme for the most famous of these, No. 2, from an unpublished work by an obscure Austrian musician named Heinrich Ehrlich who had sent him his manuscript on approval; Ehrlich recounted this episode in his *30 Jahre Künstlerleben* (1893).

WORKS: FOR STAGE: *Don Sanche, ou le Chateau d'Amour*, one-act operetta, a juvenile work (1825; the score, believed to have been lost, was discovered in 1903; the overture and an aria from it were publ. in the May 1904 issue of *Die Musik*).

FOR ORCH.: the symphonic poems (all conducted for the first time by Liszt himself, except when otherwise noted): *Ce qu'on entend sur la montagne*, after Victor Hugo (Weimar, Jan. 7, 1857); *Tasso, Lamento e Trionfo* (Weimar, Aug. 28, 1849; revised version, Weimar, April 19, 1854); *Les Préludes*, after Lamartine's "Méditations poétiques" (Weimar, Feb. 23, 1854); *Orpheus* (Weimar, Feb. 16, 1854); *Prometheus* (Weimar, Aug. 24, 1850), *Mazeppa*, after Victor Hugo (Weimar, April 16, 1854); *Festklänge* (Weimar, Nov. 9, 1854); *Héroïde funèbre* (sketched in 1830 as *Symphonie révolutionnaire*; revised and orchestrated in 1850; Breslau, Nov. 10, 1857, Moritz Schön conducting);

Hungaria (sketched in 1848; revised in 1856; first performance, Budapest, Sept. 8, 1856), *Hamlet* (1858; Sondershausen, July 2, 1876, Max Erdmannsdörfer conducting; *Hunnenschlacht*, after Kaulbach's painting (Weimar, Dec. 29, 1857); *Die Ideale*, after Schiller (Weimar, Sept. 5, 1857); *Eine Faust-Symphonie*, in 3 characteristic pictures, after Goethe, with a choral finale (Weimar, Sept. 5, 1857); a *Symphony* to Dante's *Divina Commedia*, with a female chorus (Dresden, Nov. 7, 1867); *2 Episodes* from Lenau's "Faust" (1860–61); *2 Mephisto Waltzes* (1860; 1880); *Trois odes funèbres*, with male chorus (1860–66); *Salve Polonia* (1863); *Festival March* for Goethe's jubilee (1849); for piano and orch.: Concerto No. 1, in E-flat (the "Triangle Concerto", so nicknamed because of the prominent use of a triangle solo; 1849; revised 1853; Weimar, Feb. 16, 1855; Berlioz conducting, Liszt at the piano), Concerto No. 2, in A major (1848; revised 1856–61; Weimar, Jan. 7, 1857, Hans von Bronsart soloist, Liszt conducting); *Fantasie* on motifs from Beethoven's *Ruins of Athens* (Budapest, June 1, 1853); *Totentanz*, paraphrase on *Dies irae* (1849; revised 1853–59; The Hague, April 15, 1865, Hans von Bülow soloist).

FOR PIANO SOLO: *Album d'un voyageur* (3 books); *3 apparitions*; *Rondo sur un thème espagnol (El Contrabandista)*; *Napolitana*; *Rhapsodie espagnole* (arranged for piano and orch. by Busoni); *3 Études de concert*; *2 Études de concert (Waldesrauschen, Gnomenreigen)*; *Harmonies poétiques et religeuses* (10 pieces); *Liebesträume* (3 nocturnes; originally they were songs); *3 Sonetti del Petrarca; Valse Impromptu; Mazurka brillante; 2 Polonaises; Scherzo and March; Grand Solo de concert* (also for 2 pianos); *Grand Galop chromatique; 12 Grandes Études* (originally publ. as *Études en forme de douze exercices pour piano*); *Ab irato, étude de perfectionnement*; Sonata in B minor (1854); *Berceuse; 2 Ballades; 3 Valses-Caprices; 6 Consolations; 20 Hungarian Rhapsodies* (No. 3 is the *Héroïde funèbre*; No. 9, the *Carnaval de Pest*; No. 15 the *Rákoczy March*; No. 20 is unpublished; the manuscript in the Liszt Museum at Weimar); *3 Airs Suisses; Années de pèlerinage* (3 series; contains such famous pieces as *Au bord d'une source, Venezia e Napoli*, and *Les Jeux d' eau à la Villa d'Este*; Book I is a revised version of Book I of the *Album d'un voyageur*); *Ave Maria; 3 Élégies; 12 Études d'exécution transcendante; 6 Consolations; Mephisto-Waltz* (originally for orch.; *3 versions for piano solo*; No. 4 [unpublished], subtitled "Bagatelle sans tonalité"); *Via Crucis; Epithalamium; Bülow March; 3 Valses oubliées; Valse élégiaque; Weihnachtsbaum* (12 pieces); *Mosonyi's Grabgeleit; Mephisto-Polka; Impromptu* in F-sharp; *2 Légendes: St. François d'Assise prédicant aux oiseaux, St. François de Paule marchant sur les flots; La lugubre gondole; Heroischer Marsch im ungarischen Stil; 2 Arabesques; Czardas obstiné; Czardas macabre; Hymne du Pape; 7 Ungarische Bildnisse; Rhapsody, nach Siebenbürgischen und Walachischen Motiven; Phantasy and Fugue on B-A-C-H; Variations on a theme from Bach's B minor Mass; Variations on Bach's prelude, Weinen, Klagen; Technische Studien* (12 books); transcriptions of Beethoven's symphonies, of Berlioz's *Symphonie fantastique, Harold en Italie*, and overtures to *Les Francs-juges* and *King Lear*, of

Wagner's overture to *Tannhäuser*, of 6 of Chopin's *Chants polonais*, of 10 songs by Robert Franz, 7 songs by Mendelssohn, songs from several cycles by Schubert (*Schwanengesang, Winterreise, Geistliche Lieder, Müllerlieder*, also *Die Forelle*, etc.), Schumann's *Liebeslied*, and other songs, etc.

VOCAL WORKS: *Missa solemnis* (the *Gran* festival Mass); *Hungarian Coronation Mass*; Mass in C minor with organ; *Missa choralis* in A minor with organ; Requiem; 3 oratorios: *Die Legende von der Heiligen Elisabeth, Christus*, and *Stanislaus* (unfinished); 9 choruses with organ; *Die Seligkeiten*, for baritone solo, chorus and organ; *Pater noster*, for mixed chorus, and organ; *Pater noster* and *Ave Maria*, for men's voices and organ; *Psalm 13*, for tenor solo, chorus, orch.; *Psalm 18*, for men's chorus, orch., and organ; *Psalm 23*, for tenor (or soprano) solo, with harp (or piano) and organ (or harmonium); *Psalm 116*, for soli, men's (or mixed) chorus, organ, and orch.; *Psalm 137*, for solo, women's chorus, violin, harp, piano, and organ; *Christus ist geboren*, for chorus with organ; *An den heiligen Franziskus*, for men's voices, organ, trombones, and drums; *Les Morts*, for men's chorus and orch.; numerous minor sacred compositions; the cantatas *Die Glocken des Strassburger Münsters, Die heilige Cäcile, An die Künstler* (for soli, men's chorus, and orch.), *Hungaria* (for soli, mixed chorus, and orch.; the last has nothing in common with the symph. poem bearing the same title; score lost for many years, discovered by P. Raabe in 1912; *Zur Säcular-Feier Beethovens; Festalbum* (for Goethe's 100th birthday); *Festchor* (for the unveiling of the Herder monument, Weimar, 1850); numerous 4-part men's choruses (*Das Lied der Begeisterung; Weimars Volkslied; Was ist das Deutsche Vaterland?* with piano; *Festgesang*, with organ); about 60 songs with piano, many strikingly beautiful (*Du bist wie eine Blume, Es muss ein wunderbares sein, Die Macht der Musik, Jeanne d'Arc au búcher*). Vol. 2 of Peter Raabe's biography (1931) includes a complete catalogue of works. Thematic catalogues of Liszt's works were publ. by Breitkopf & Härtel in 1855 and 1876; a complete catalogue of the publ. works by A. Göllerich appeared in the *Neue Zeitschrift für Musik* (1887–88); a *Chronologisch-systematisches Verzeichnis* by L. Friwitzer was publ. in the *Wiener musikalische Chronik* (Nov. 1887–March 1888).

In 1905 plans were made to publish Liszt's complete works, to be issued periodically by Breitkopf & Härtel. Volume I appeared in 1907; by 1936 Breitkopf & Härtel of Leipzig had issued 34 volumes, but world conditions put an end to the project. In 1950 the Liszt Society of London, with E. J. Dent as President, began to issue a new series, but by 1968 only 56 volumes had appeared, 5 of them devoted to Liszt's lesser-known piano works, one to selected songs. A *Neue Liszt-Ausgabe* was begun in 1970 under the editorial direction of Zoltán Gárdonyi and István Szelényi, and by 1977, 8 volumes had been issued jointly by the Bärenreiter Verlag of Kassel and Editio Musica of Budapest.

WRITINGS: *De la fondation Goethe* (Goethestiftung) *à Weimar* (1851); *Lohengrin et Tannhäuser de Richard Wagner* (1851; also in German); *Frédéric Chopin* (1852; 2nd ed., in French, Leipzig, 1879; in English, 1901); *Über Fields Notturnos* (1859); *Des Bohémiens et de leur musique en Hongrie* (French, 1859; also Hungarian, German; in English as *The Gypsy in Music*); *Robert Franz* (1872); *Keine Zwischenaktmusik mehr* (1879). His *Gesammelte Schriften* were ed. by Lina Ramann and publ. in 6 vols. (Leipzig, 1800–83); also a selection as *Volksausgabe* (4 vols., Leipzig, 1910); J. Kapp publ. an *Allgemeine Inhaltsübersicht* with full indices (1910).

BIBLIOGRAPHY: BIOGRAPHY: J.W. Christern, *Franz Liszt* (Hamburg, 1841); Lina Ramann, *Franz Liszt als Künstler und Mensch* (3 vols., Leipzig, 1880–94; English transl. of vol. 1, London, 1882); R. Pohl, *Franz Liszt: Studien und Erinnerungen* (Leipzig, 1883); L. Nohl, *Liszt* (Leipzig, 1884; Part 2 by A.Göllerich, 1887; English transl., Chicago, 1887); T. C. Martin, *Franz Liszt* (London, 1886); E. Reuss, *Franz Liszt* (Dresden, 1898); R. Louis, *Franz Liszt* (Berlin, 1900); A. O. von Pozsony, *Liszt und Hans von Bülow* (Munich, 1900); M.-D. Calvocoressi, *Franz Liszt* (Paris, 1905; English transl., in the *Musical Observer*, N.Y., 1910–11); A. Göllerich, *Franz Liszt* (Berlin, 1908); J. Kapp, *Richard Wagner und Franz Liszt: Eine Freundschaft* (Berlin, 1908); J. Kapp, *Franz Liszt. Eine Biographie* (Berlin, 1909; 20th ed., 1924; a standard biography); A. W. Gottschalg, *Franz Liszt in Weimar und seine letzten Lebensjahre* (publ. posthumously, 1910); J. Chantavoine, *Liszt* (Paris, 1910; 5th ed., 1928); R. Ledos de Beaufort, *Franz Liszt: The Story of His Life* (Boston, 1910; with a list of works and pupils); A. Hervey, *Franz Liszt and His Music* (London, 1911); J. Kapp, *Franz Liszt und die Frauen* (Berlin, 1911); La Mara, *Liszt und die Frauen* (Leipzig, 1911); Cosima Wagner, *Franz Liszt: Ein Gedenkblatt von seiner Tochter* (Munich, 1911); J. G. Huneker, *Franz Liszt* (N.Y., 1911; in German, Munich, 1922); F. Barberio, *Liszt e la principessa de Sayn-Wittgenstein* (Rome, 1912); A. von Schorn, *Zwei Menschenalter, Erinnerungen und Briefe aus Weimar und Rom* (Stuttgart, 1913); Sir A. Mackenzie, *Liszt* (London, 1913); B. Schrader, *Franz Liszt* (Leipzig, 1914); K. Grunsky, *Franz Liszt* (Leipzig, 1924); R. Wetz, *Franz Liszt* (Leipzig, 1925); F. Corder, *Liszt* (London, 1925; new ed., 1933); Guy de Pourtalès, *La Vie de Franz Liszt* (Paris, 1926; also in English, N.Y., 1926); C. van Wessem, *Franz Liszt* (The Hague, 1927); Marie d'Agoult, *Erinnerungen an Franz Liszt* (ed. by Siegfried Wagner; 2 vols., 1928); A. Stradal, *Erinnerungen an Franz Liszt* (Bern, 1929); M. Herwegh, *Au banquet des dieux: Franz Liszt, Richard Wagner et leurs amis* (Paris, 1931); P. Raabe, *Franz Liszt* (2 vols., Stuttgart and Berlin, 1931); B. Kellermann, *Erinnerungen an Franz Liszt* (1932); Sacheverell Sitwell (London, 1934; revised, 1955); R. Bory, *Liszt et ses enfants: Blandine, Cosima et Daniel* (Paris, 1936); R. Bory, *La Vie de Franz Liszt par l'image* (Geneva, 1936); A. de Hevésy, *Liszt, ou de roi Lear de la musique* (Paris, 1936); R. Hill, *Liszt* (London, 1936); H. Engel, *Liszt* (Potsdam, 1936); Blandine Ollivier, *Liszt, le musicien passionné* (Paris, 1936); Z. Harsányi, *Magyar Rapszódia: Franz Liszt* (Budapest, 1936; in English, publ. in London, 1936, as *Hungarian Melody*, and in N.Y., 1937, as *Immortal Franz*); E. von Liszt, *Franz Liszt* (Vienna, 1937; family documents, etc.); M. Tibaldi Chiesa, *Vita romantica di Liszt* (Milan, 1937); C. Aragonnès, *Marie d'Agoult: une destinée romantique*

(Paris, 1938); P. Raabe, *Wege zu Liszt* (Regensburg, 1943); Y. Milstein, *Liszt* (Moscow, 1956); J. Rousselot, *Franz Liszt* (London, 1960); C. Rostand, *Liszt* (Paris, 1960); W. G. Armando, *Franz Liszt: eine Biographie* (Hamburg, 1961); J. Hankiss, *Wenn Liszt ein Tagebuch geführt hätte* (Budapest, 1961); M. Bagby, *Liszt's Weimar* (N. Y., 1961); A. Leroy, *Franz Liszt* (Lausanne, 1967); C. V. Lachmund, *Mein Leben mit Franz Liszt* (Eschwege, 1970); E. Perényi, *Liszt: The Artist as Romantic Hero* (Boston, 1974). Pictorial biographies: W. Füssmann and Béla Mátéka, *Franz Liszt. Ein Künstlerleben in Wort und Bild* (Berlin, 1936); Z. László and B. Mátéka, *Franz Liszt: sein Leben in Bildern* (Budapest, 1967).

APPRECIATION, CRITICISM: W. Lenz, *Die grossen Pianoforte Virtuosen unserer Zeit* (Berlin, 1872; English transl., N.Y., 1899); L. Nohl, *Beethoven, Liszt, Wagner* (Vienna, 1874); R. Wagner, *Über Franz Liszts Symphonische Dichtungen*, in *Gesammelte Schriften und Dichtungen* (vol. 5; Leipzig, 1883); Otto Lessmann, *Franz Liszt: eine Huldigung* (in German and English; N.Y., 1883); B. Vogel, *Franz Liszt als Lyriker* (Leipzig, 1887); A. Habets, *A. Borodin et Franz Liszt* (Paris, 1893; English transl., London, 1895); O. Bie, *Das Klavier und seine Meister* (Munich, 1898); E. Segnitz, *Franz Liszt und Rom* (Leipzig, 1901); H. Gerstenberg, *Aus Weimars nachklassischer Zeit* (Hamburg, 1901); E. O. Nodnagel, *Jenseits von Wagner und Liszt* (Königsberg, 1902); La Mara, *Aus der Glanzzeit der Weimarer Altenburg* (Leipzig, 1906); F. H. Clark, *Liszts Offenbarung: Schlüssel zur Freiheit des Individuums* (Berlin, 1907); A. de Angelis, *Franz Liszt a Roma* (Turin, 1911); A. Kohut, *Franz Liszt in seinen Wirken als Mensch und als Tonkünstler* (Leipzig, 1911); A. von Schorn, *Das nachklassische Weimar unter der Regierungszeit Karl Friedrichs und Maria Paulownas* (Weimar, 1911; also *Zweiter Teil: unter der Regierungszeit von Karl Alexander und Sophia*, Weimar, 1912); E. Segnitz, *Liszts Kirchenmusik* (Langensalza, 1911); E. Hughes, "Liszt as a Lieder Composer," *Musical Quarterly* (April 1917); O. G. Sonneck, "Liszt's Huldigungsmarsch and Weimar's Volkslied," *Musical Quarterly* (Jan. 1918); C. Boissier, *Liszt pédagogue* (Paris, 1928); J. Heinrichs, *Über den Sinn der Lisztschen Programmmusik* (Kempen, 1929); H. Arminski, *Die ungarischen Fantasien von Franz Liszt* (Vienna, 1929); T. Weber, *Die symphonischen Dichtungen Liszts* (Vienna, 1929); E. Major, *Liszt's Hungarian Rhapsodies* (in Hungarian; Budapest, 1929); J. Bergfeld, *Die formale Struktur der symphonischen Dichtungen Franz Liszts* (Eisenach, 1931); Z. Gárdonyi, *Die ungarischen Stileigentümlichkeiten in den musikalischen Werken Franz Liszts* (Berlin, 1931); K. Isóz, *Liszt and Budapest* (in Hungarian; Budapest, 1931); H. Dobiey, *Die Klaviertechnik des jungen Liszt* (Berlin, 1931); I. Philipp, *La Technique de Liszt* (2 vols.; Paris, 1932); R. Kokai, *Franz Liszt in seinen frühen Klavierwerken* (Leipzig, 1933); E. Newman, *The Man Liszt: A Study of the Tragi-Comedy of a Soul Divided against Itself* (London, 1934); H. Westerby, *Liszt the Composer and His Piano Works* (London, 1936); Liszt issue of the *Musical Quarterly* (July 1936); G. Falk, *Liszt Breviarium* (in Hungarian; Budapest, 1936); E. Haraszti, "Franz Liszt—Author Despite Himself," *Musical Quarterly* (Oct. 1947); H. Searle, *The Music*

of Liszt (London, 1954); E. N. Waters, "Liszt and Longfellow," *Musical Quarterly* (Jan. 1955); P. Rehberg, *Franz Liszt: die Geschichte seines Leben, Scheffens und Wirkens* (Zürich, 1961); Alan Walker, ed., *Franz Liszt: The Man and His Music* (N.Y., 1970). Separate analyses of all the larger works, including the oratorios, Masses, and psalms, are found in H. Kretzschmar's *Führer durch den Konzertsaal* (3 vols.; Leipzig, 1887; 4th ed., 1913); in Breitkopf & Härtel's *Kleiner Konzertführer* (Leipzig), Schlesinger's *Der Musikführer* and *Meisterführer* (Berlin).

CORRESPONDENCE: *Briefwechsel zwischen Wagner und Liszt* (2 vols.; Leipzig, 1887, 2nd ed., 1900; English transl., London, 1888; 2nd ed., 1897, with index; these 2 eds. contain only the letters from 1841-61, and many passages referring to persons still living at the time of publication were omitted; in the 3rd ed., prepared by Erich Kloss in 1910, all letters up to Wagner's death are included, and the omitted portions restored); La Mara, *Franz Liszts Briefe* (8 vols.; Leipzig, 1893-1905; about 2,500 letters in the original French or German; those to Carolyne Sayn-Wittgenstein, in vols. 4-7, all in French); C. Bache, *Letters of Franz Liszt* (2 vols.; London, 1894; in English transl.); La Mara, *Briefwechsel zwischen Franz Liszt und Hans von Bülow* (Leipzig, 1898); R. von Seydlitz, *Ungedruckte Originalbriefe des Meisters an G. Freiherrn von Seydlitz* (Dresden, 1902); A. Stern, *Franz Liszts Briefe an Karl Gille* (Leipzig, 1903); La Mara, *Franz Liszt et Charles-Alexandre, grand-duc de Saxe: Correspondance* (Leipzig, 1909); C. A. René, 48 letters to A. W. Gottschalg, in *Franz Liszt in Weimar und seine letzten Lebensjahre* (1910); E. Reuss, *Franz Liszt in seinen Briefen* (Stuttgart, 1911); W. von Csapó, *Franz Liszts Briefe an Baron Anton Augusz, 1846-1878* (Budapest, 1911); N. de Gutmannsthal, *Souvenirs de Franz Liszt: Lettres inédites* (Leipzig, 1913); K. von Schlözer, *Römische Briefe, 1864-69* (Stuttgart, 1913); P. Raabe, *Briefwechsel zwischen Franz Liszt und dem Grossherzog Karl Alexander von Sachsen* (1918); A. Orel, *Briefe Liszts* (Vienna, 1930); correspondence with Mme. d'Agoult (in French), publ. by Daniel Ollivier, 1st series, 1833-40 (1933), 2nd series, 1840-64 (1934); correspondence with Liszt's daughter, Blandine, publ. by Ollivier, in *Revue des Deux Mondes* (Dec. 15, 1935; Jan. 1, 1936); *The Letters of Franz Liszt to Marie Sayn-Wittgenstein*, ed. by H. E. Hugo (N.Y., 1953). Liszt's letters to Olga von Meyendorff (1871–86), translated by William B. Tyler, were published, with an introduction and notes by Edward N. Waters (Washington, D.C., 1978). See also La Mara, *Briefe hervorragender Zeitgenossen an Franz Liszt* (3 vols.; Leipzig, 1895-1904).

Litaize, Gaston, French composer and organist; b. Ménil-sur-Belvitte, Aug. 11, 1909. He was blind from infancy; studied at the National Institute of the Blind; also at the Paris Cons.; won 2nd Prix de Rome (unprecedented for a blind person); was appointed organist at the church of St.-François Xavier, Paris; also on the staff of the National Institute of the Blind. In the autumn of 1957 he made his 1st American tour as concert organist. He holds the post of organ teacher at the Institution Nationale des Jeunes Aveugles in Paris. He composed a number of organ pieces and several sacred choruses, among them *Messe solennelle en français* (1966).

Literes Carrión, Antonio, Spanish composer; b. Arta, Majorca, c.1670; d. Madrid, Jan. 18, 1747. He was a composer and cello player under Charles II, Philip V, and Ferdinand VI. In 1693 he was appointed to the royal chapel as violinist. After the fire at the old Alcazar in Madrid on Christmas Eve, 1734, Literes and Nebra were charged with the reconstruction of musical MSS that were damaged or completely burned. They also wrote new music for church services to replace the material destroyed. Literes composed excellent church music (14 Psalms, 8 *Magnificats*, etc.); some of his sacred works are reprinted in Eslava's *Lira Sacro-Hispana*; also wrote an opera, *Los Elementos,* and a zarzuela, *Accis y Galatea* (1709). His son **Antonio Literes Montalbo** (d. Madrid, Dec. 2, 1768), was a composer and organist under Ferdinand VI.

BIBLIOGRAPHY: N. A. Solar Quintes, "Antonio Literes Carrión y sus hijos," *Anuario Musical* vol. 5 (Barcelona, 1950); F. Pedrell, *Teatro Lírico Español* (vols. 2 and 4); J. Nin, *Classiques espagnols du chant* (Paris, 1926).

Litinsky, Genrik (Heinrich), distinguished Russian composer; b. Lipovetz, March 17, 1901. He studied composition with Glière at the Moscow Cons., graduating in 1928; subsequently taught there (1928–43); among his students were Khrennikov, Zhiganov, Arutunian and other Soviet composers. In 1945 he went to Yakutsk as an ethnomusicologist; in collaboration with native Siberian composers he produced the first national Yakut operas, based on authentic folk melorhythms and arranged in contemporary harmonies according to the precepts of Socialist Realism: *Nurgun Botur* (Yakutsk, June 29, 1947), *Sygy Kyrynastyr* (Yakutsk, July 4, 1947), and *Red Shaman* (Yakutsk, Dec. 9, 1967). He wrote three Yakut ballets: *Altan's Joy* (Yakutsk, June 19, 1963); *Field Flower* (Yakutsk, July 2, 1947); *Crimson Kerchief* (Yakutsk, Jan. 9, 1968). Other works include: Symphony (1928); *Dagestan Suite* for orch. (1931); Trumpet Concerto (1934); *Festive Rhapsody* for orch. (1966); 12 string quartets (1923–61); String Octet (1944); 12 concert studies for cello (1967); 12 concert studies for trumpet and piano (1968); 15 concert studies for oboe and piano (1969). He published the valuable manuals, *Problems of Polyphony* (3 vols., 1965, 1966, 1967), ranging from pentatonic to dodecaphonic patterns and from elementary harmonization to polytonality; also *Formation of Imitation in the Strict Style* (1970). In 1964 he was named People's Artist of the Yakut Soviet Socialist Republic and of the Tatar Soviet Socialist Republic.

Litolff, Henry Charles, pianist, composer, and publisher; b. London (of an Alsatian father and English mother), Feb. 6, 1818; d. Colombes, near Paris, Aug. 6, 1891. A precocious pianist, he studied with Moscheles; made his professional debut in London on July 24, 1832, at the age of 14. An early marriage (at 17) forced him to seek a livelihood in Paris, where he attracted attention by his brilliant concerts; then he became an itinerant musician, traveling in Poland, Germany, and Holland; was in Vienna during the Revolution of 1848, and became involved, so that he was compelled to flee. He then settled in Brunswick; after the termination of his first marriage, he married the widow of the music publisher Meyer, acquiring the business. Litolff was one of the pioneers in the publication of cheap editions of classical music (Collections Litolff). In 1860 he turned over the firm to his adopted son **Theodor Litolff** (1839-1912). Then he went to Paris, marrying for a third time (Comtesse de Larochefoucauld); after her death (1870) he married a 15-year-old girl.

WORKS: Besides his business pursuits, he was a prolific composer; 115 of his works were publ.; of these, the most famous is the overture *Robespierre* (Paris, Feb. 2, 1870), which carries the idea of programmatic music to its utmost limit, with a vivid description of Robespierre's execution (drum beats, etc.); the operas *Die Braut von Kynast* (Brunswick, 1847), *Les Templiers* (Brussels, Jan. 25, 1886); *Héloïse et Abélard* (Paris, Oct. 17, 1872); oratorio *Ruth et Booz* (1869); *Szenen aus Goethes Faust,* for soli, chorus, and orch.; 5 *Concertos-Symphonies* for piano and orch., of which the 4th contains a brilliant scherzo which became a perennial favorite; the *Eroica* violin concerto; a funeral march for Meyerbeer; 3 piano trios; 6 *Études de concert* for piano; many character pieces for piano, of which *Chant de la Fileuse* became popular.

BIBLIOGRAPHY: H. Berlioz, *Les Musiciens et la Musique* (Paris, 1878); P. Magnette, *Litolff* (Paris, 1914).

Litta, Giulio, Italian composer; b. Milan, 1822; d. Vedano, near Monza, May 29, 1891. A composer of precocious talent and excellent training, he produced an opera at 20, *Bianca di Santafiora* (Milan, Jan. 2, 1843), followed by 6 more operas: *Sardanapalo* (Milan, Sept. 2, 1844); *Maria Giovanna* ((Turin, Oct. 28, 1851); *Edita di Lorno* (Genoa, June 1, 1853); *Il Viandante* (Milan, April 17, 1873); *Raggio d'amore* (Milan, April 6, 1879), and *Il Violino di Cremona* (Milan, April 18, 1882). He also wrote an oratorio, *La Passione;* church music; songs.

Litvinne, Félia (real name **Françoise-Jeanne Schütz**), Russian soprano; b. St. Petersburg, 1861; d. Paris, Oct. 12, 1936. She studied in Paris with Mme. Barth-Banderoli and Victor Maurel; made her debut there in 1885 at the Théâtre des Italiens; then sang at the Academy of Music, N.Y., with Mapleson's company; made successful appearances in St. Petersburg, Moscow, and in Italy; returned to Paris, where she sang at the Opéra-Comique and the Théâtre Lyrique de la Gaîté, at Monte Carlo, at La Scala, Covent Garden, the Metropolitan Opera House; made a tour of South America. In 1927 she was appointed prof. of singing at the American Cons. of Fontainebleau. She publ. her memoirs, *Ma vie et mon art* (Paris, 1933).

Litzau, Johannes Barend, Dutch organist and composer; b. Rotterdam, Sept. 9, 1822; d. there, July 18, 1893. He studied with J. B. Bremer and B. Tours; in 1855, succeeded Bremer as organist of the Lutheran church in Rotterdam. He founded an organ school and wrote a number of organ works in the Classical style: 3 organ sonatas; *Konzertsatz im strengen Stil mit 4 Subjekten,* etc.; also a cantata, *Sneeuw-vermaak.*

Litzmann, Berthold, German writer on music; b. Kiel, April 18, 1857; d. Munich, Oct. 13, 1926. He wrote an exhaustive biography, *Clara Schumann, ein Künstlerleben, nach Tagebüchern und Briefen* (3 vols., Leipzig, 1902–10; English transl., 1913); also prepared for publication the correspondence between Brahms and Clara Schumann (2 vols., Leipzig, 1927; English transl., N.Y., 1927).

Liuzzi, Fernando, Italian composer and musicologist; b. Senigallia, Dec. 19, 1884; d. Florence, Oct. 6, 1940. He studied in Bologna with Fano, and at the Liceo di S. Cecilia in Rome; then went to Munich, where he studied with Mottl and Reger. He taught at the Cons. of Parma (1910–17), the Cons. "Luigi Cherubini," Florence (1917–23), Univ. of Florence, Royal Italian Univ. of Perugia, Royal Univ. in Rome (1926–38).
WORKS: the operetta *L'Augellin bel verde* (Rome, 1917); *Le Vergini Savie e le Vergini Folli (The Wise and the Foolish Virgins),* a liturgical drama transcribed and rearranged for soli, chorus, and orch. from a French MS of the 12th century (Florence, 1930); *La Passione,* for soli, chorus, and orch., based on religious melodies of the 13th century (1930); *Hyla,* symph. poem; *Gaiola e Marechiaro,* Neapolitan rhapsody for orch.; Violin Sonata; *Sonata-fantasia* for violin and organ; songs; etc.
WRITINGS: *Estetica della musica* (Florence, 1924); *Essenza dell'arte e valore estetico nel pensiero di T. Lipps* (Bologna, 1924); *La Lauda e i primordi della melodia Italiana* (2 vols. of facsimiles and transcriptions of medieval Italian music; Rome, 1935).
BIBLIOGRAPHY: E. T. Ferand, "In Memoriam: Fernando Liuzzi," *Musical Quarterly* (Oct. 1942).

Liverati, Giovanni, Italian composer; b. Bologna, March 27, 1772; d. Florence, Feb. 18, 1846. He studied voice, and was engaged as a tenor in Spain; in 1796 he traveled with an Italian opera company in Germany; then turned to composition, and wrote various operas for traveling troupes. He was in Stockholm in 1803, in Paris in 1808, in Vienna in 1811, in London in 1815; remained in London until about 1840; then went back to Italy.
WORKS: operas: *La prova mancata* (1801), *Enea in Cartagine* (1809), *I selvaggi* (London, June 27, 1815), *Gastone e Bajardo* (London, Feb. 26, 1820); an oratorio, *David* (1811); he contributed a setting of *In questa tomba oscura* to Mollo's collection (1808), which includes also the famous Beethoven setting of these words.

Liviabella, Lino, Italian composer; b. Macerata, April 7, 1902; d. Bologna, Oct. 21, 1964. He studied with Respighi at the Santa Cecilia Academy in Rome; was director of the Cons. of Pesaro from 1953 to 1959; then taught at Parma.
WORKS: *L'Usignola e la Rosa,* for chamber orch. (1926); *I canti dell' amore,* triptych for string orch. (1929); *Suite per una fiaba,* for orch. (1933); *Il Vincitore,* written for the Berlin Olympiad (1936); *Il poeta e sua moglia,* for orch. (1938); *La mia terra,* for orch. (1942); the oratorios, *Sorella Chiara* (1947), *Caterina da Siena* (1949), *O Crux Ave* (1953); *Conchiglia,* dramatic musical play (1955); 3 violin sonatas; a string quartet; songs.

Ljungberg, Göta (Albertina), Swedish soprano; b. Sundsval, Oct. 4, 1893; d. Lidingö, near Stockholm, June 28, 1955. She studied at the Royal Academy of Music and the Royal Opera School in Stockholm; also privately in Berlin; in 1918, made her debut (as Elsa) at the Royal Stockholm Opera; appeared in London, in the title role of *Judith* by Goossens (1929); then sang at the Strauss Festival in Mannheim, etc.; American debut at the Metropolitan Opera, N.Y., on Jan. 20, 1932; remained on the roster until 1935; created the role of Lady Marigold Sandys in Hanson's *Merry Mount.* After World War II, she lived in N.Y. as voice teacher; then returned to Sweden.

Llobet, Miguel, Catalan guitar virtuoso; b. Barcelona, Oct. 18, 1875; d. there, Feb. 22, 1938. He began his career as a painter; then turned to music and studied with Tarrega; lived in Paris (1904–14); toured in Argentina (1910), Chile (1912), the U.S. (1915–17), and throughout Europe. Manuel de Falla composed his *Homenaje* (for the *Tombeau de Debussy)* for him, and Llobet himself made many arrangements for the guitar.

Llongueras y Badía, Juan, Catalan composer; b. Barcelona, June 6, 1880; d. there, Oct. 13, 1953. He studied in Barcelona with Morera, Millet, and Granados, and with Jaques-Dalcroze in Dresden and Geneva; founded the Institut Catala de Rítmica i Plástica in Barcelona for the exposition in Spain of the Dalcroze methods; was also music critic, writer, and prof. of music education in Barcelona. His compositions include piano pieces (*La vida sencilla, L'estiu efimer,* etc.), a quantity of *Canciones y juegos infantiles* and other songs; also wrote *Les cançons de Nadal* (Catalan Christmas songs); publ. the essays, *Couperin o la gracia; Bach o el fervor; Beethoven o la Passió;* etc., also a book of reminiscences, *Evocaciones y recuerdos de mi primera vida musical en Barcelona* (Barcelona, 1944).

Lloyd, Charles Harford, English organist and composer; b. Thornbury, Gloucestershire, Oct. 16, 1849; d. Slough, Oct. 16, 1919. He attended Magdalen Hall, Oxford (Mus. Bac., 1871; B.A., 1872; M.A., 1875; Mus. Doc., 1892); 1887–92, teacher of organ and composition at the Royal College of Music; 1892, instructor at Eton College; from 1914 until his death, organist at the Chapel Royal, St. James'.
WORKS: cantatas *Hero and Leander* (Worcester, 1884), *The Song of Balder* (Hereford, 1885), *Andromeda* (Gloucester, 1886), *A Song of Judgment* (Hereford, 1891), *Sir Ogie and Lady Elsie* (Hereford, 1894); church music, including the anthems *Art thou weary?, Blessed is he, Fear not, O land, Give the Lord the honor,* and *A Hymn of Thanksgiving;* organ works.

Lloyd, George, English composer; b. St. Ives, June 28, 1913. He learned to play piano and violin at home;

then studied composition with Harry Farjeon. He was in the Royal Marines during World War II; served in the Arctic on convoys to Russia and nearly lost his life when his ship was sunk. He composed mainly for the theater; among his works are the operas *Iernin* (Penzance, Nov. 6, 1934), *The Serf* (London, Oct. 20, 1938), *John Socman* (Bristol, May 15, 1951); also wrote 6 symphonies; 4 piano concertos; a violin concerto, and pieces of chamber music.

Lobe, Johann Christian, German flutist, writer on music, and composer; b. Weimar, May 30, 1797; d. Leipzig, July 27, 1881. He studied with A. E. Müller; played a flute solo with the Gewandhaus Orch. in Leipzig (1811); then flutist, later viola player, in the Weimar court orch. until 1842; founded a music school; 1846–48, in Leipzig as editor of the *Allgemeine Musikzeitung;* 1853, published the periodical *Fliegende Blätter für Musik;* music editor of *Illustrierte Zeitung;* also contributed articles to various journals. WORKS: the operas (all produced in Weimar) *Wittekind, Die Flibustier, Die Fürstin von Granada* (Sept. 28, 1833), *Der rote Domino, König und Pächter;* 2 symphonies; overtures; concertos; piano quartets; variations and solos for flute. WRITINGS: *Die Lehre von der thematischen Arbeit* (1846); *Lehrbuch der musikalischen Komposition* (vol. I, *Harmony,* 1850; revised by Kretzschmar, 5th ed., 1884; vol. II, *Instrumentation,* 3rd ed., 1879; vol. III, *Canon, Fugue, etc.,* 1860; vol. IV, *Opera,* 1867; revised by Kretzschmar, 1884–87); *Katechismus der Musik* (1851; 28th ed., 1904; revised by Leichtentritt, 1926; English transl., N.Y., 1896); *Musikalische Briefe eines Wohlbekannten* (1852; 2nd ed., 1860); *Fliegende Blätter für Musik* (1853–57, 3 vols.); *Aus dem Leben eines Musikers* (1859); *Vereinfachte Harmonielehre* (1861); *Katechismus der Kompositionslehre* (1872; 7th ed., 1902; English transl., N.Y., 1891); *Consonanzen und Dissonanzen* (1869). BIBLIOGRAPHY: W. Bode, ed., *Goethes Schauspieler und Musiker, Erinnerungen von Eberwein und Lobe* (1912); O. Coon, ed., *A New Catechism of Music on the Plan of Johann Christian Lobe* (N.Y., 1905).

Lobkowitz, Prince Franz Joseph (Maximilian Ferdinand) von, Austrian art patron; b. Vienna, Dec. 7, 1772; d. Raudnitz an der Elbe, Dec. 16, 1816. Beethoven dedicated to him the quartet op. 18; the 3rd, 5th, and 6th symphonies; the Triple Concerto; the quartet op. 74; and the song cycle *An die ferne Geliebte.*

Lobo, Duarte (also Latinized as **Eduardus Lupus),** Portuguese composer; b. Alcáçovas, c.1565 (he was not identical with the person of the same name baptized on Sept. 19, 1565; his date of birth must therefore remain uncertain); d. Lisbon, Sept. 24, 1646. He was a pupil of Manuel Mendes at Evora; served as choirmaster there before moving to Lisbon; in 1594, became master of the chapel at the Cathedral. As a composer of church music, he enjoyed considerable renown; his mastery of polyphony inspired respect, but comparisons with Victoria Benevoli, and other great composers of his time, are exaggerations. The following works were printed in his lifetime: *Natalitiae noctis responsoria, a* 4–8; *Antiphonae, a* 8; *Salve,*

a 3–11 (Antwerp, 1602); *Officium defunctorum* (Lisbon, 1603); *Magnificat, a* 4 (Antwerp, 1605); 2 books of Masses, *a* 4–8 (Antwerp, 1621 and 1639); MSS in the British Museum, the Fitzwilliam Collection in Cambridge, at the Cathedrals of Granada and Toledo. An antiphon and 2 Masses are reprinted in J. E. dos Santos, *A polifonia clássica portuguêsa* (Lisbon, 1937); 16 Magnificats for 4 voices, transcribed by M. Joaquim (Lisbon, 1945). BIBLIOGRAPHY: Manuel Joaquim, *20 libros de música polifónica* (Lisbon, 1953; pp. 58–59).

Locatelli, Pietro, Italian violinist and composer; b. Bergamo, Sept. 3, 1695; d. Amsterdam, March 30, 1764. He studied in Rome with Corelli; after long professional tours, he settled in Amsterdam, establishing regular public concerts, and enjoying great fame there. His technical feats, particularly in double stops, were considered marvelous at the time; by changing the tuning of his violin, he produced apparently impossible effects; Paganini is said to have profited by Locatelli's innovations. WORKS: 12 *Concerti grossi* (Amsterdam, 1721); Flute Sonatas with bass (Amsterdam, 1732); *L'arte del violino,* containing 12 concertos and 24 caprices for 2 violins, viola, cello, and continuo (1733); 6 *Introduzioni teatrali* and 6 concertos (1735); 6 *Sonates en trio* (1737); 6 Sonatas for Solo Violin (1737); 6 *Concerti a quattro* (1741); Trios for 2 violins and bass (1741); *L'arte di nuova modulazione: caprices énigmatiques; Contrasto armonico: concerto a quattro.* Some of Locatelli's works appear in modern editions: 6 Sonatas for Solo Violin; a few pieces in Alard's and David's methods; a theme with variations in Schering's *Alt-Meister des Violinspiels;* "Tragic Symphony" publ. by Schering; 2 trio sonatas, publ. by Moffat, etc. BIBLIOGRAPHY: J. W. von Wasielewski, *Die Violine und ihre Meister* (1920); C. Vanbianchi, "Un celebre violinista bergamasco percursore di Nicolo Paganini," *Bolletino della Civica Biblioteca di Bergamo* (May 1920); A. Schering, *Geschichte des Instrumental-Konzerts* (1927); A. Moser, *Geschichte des Violinspiels* (1923; pp. 224ff.); M. Pincherle, *Les Violinistes* (Paris, 1924); A. Koole, *Leven en Werken van Pietro Locatelli* (Amsterdam, 1949); A. Koole, *Pietro Antonio Locatelli. Conferenza* (Bergamo, 1970).

Locke, Matthew, English composer; b. Exeter, c.1630; d. London, Aug., 1677. He was a chorister in Exeter Cathedral, studying under Edward Gibbons and William Wake; then was composer to Charles II (1661); became a Roman Catholic, and was appointed organist to Queen Catherine. Prominent among English composers of his era, he wrote music to *The Tempest* and *Macbeth,* and to Shadwell's *Psyche* (London, March 9, 1675: the music for *The Tempest* and *Psyche* were publ. in 1675 as *The English Opera*); to Shirley's masque *Cupid and Death* and Stapleton's comedy *The Stepmother;* also 6 suites, anthems, etc.; the first English work on thoroughbass, *Melothesia, or Certain General Rules for Playing Upon A Continued Bass* (1673); and pamphlets versus Salmon's attempt at reducing music notation to one universal character. P. Warlock and A. Mangeot published 6 *Consorts a* 4

(London, 1932). Chamber music is repr. in vols. 31–32 of *Musica Brittanica,* anthems and motets in vol. 38. R. E. M. Harding compiled *A Thematic Catalogue of the Works of Matthew Locke* (1971).

BIBLIOGRAPHY: J. Pulver, *A Biographical Dictionary of Old English Music* (1927); R. Covell, "17th-Century Music for *The Tempest,*" *Studies in Music* 2 (1968); C. D. S. Field, "Matthew Locke and the Consort Suite," *Music & Letters* (Jan. 1970); M. Tilmouth, "Revisions in the Chamber Music of Matthew Locke," *Proceedings of the Royal Music Association* 98 (1971–72).

Lockspeiser, Edward, English writer on music; b. London, May 21, 1905; d. there, Feb. 3, 1973. He studied in Paris with Alexandre Tansman and Nadia Boulanger; then attended the classes of C. H. Kitson and Malcolm Sargent at the Royal College of Music in London. He dedicated himself to musical journalism, particularly to the cause of French music; publ. the valuable monographs on Debussy (London, 1936; revised edition, 1951); Berlioz (1940) and Bizet (1947), and an exhaustive biography, *Debussy: His Life and Mind* (2 vols.; London, 1962, 1965). He also edited *Claude Debussy: Lettres inédites à André Caplet, 1908–1914* (Monaco, 1957).

Lockwood, Anna, composeress of the militant avant-garde; b. Christchurch, New Zealand, July 29, 1939. She studied at Canterbury Univ. in New Zealand; then went to London, where she took courses with Peter Racine Fricker at the Royal College of Music; subsequently attended classes at the Musikhochschule in Cologne and at the Electronic Music Center in Bilthoven, Holland. In 1968 she gave non-lectures at the Anti-University of London. With her husband, Harvey Matusow, she undertook a series of experiments in total art, including aural, oral, visual, tactile, gustatory and olfactory demonstrations and sporadic transcendental manifestations; of these, the most remarkable was the summoning (in German) of Beethoven's ghost at a séance held in London on Oct. 3, 1968, with sound recorded on magnetic tape, which in playback revealed some surprisingly dissonant music of apparently metapsychic origin, tending to indicate that Beethoven was a posthumous avant-garde composer (the tape was not released in order to avoid unanswerable controversy); the séance was preceded by the burning of a combustible piano and of an inflammable microphone. Not content with setting the piano afire, she also demonstrated the drowning of an upright piano in a lake in Amarillo, Texas (Dec. 27, 1972). Anna Lockwood also experimented with surgical piano transplants. Her other works, some of them consisting of controlled glossolalia and notated optically on graphic paper, are *À Abélard, Héloïse* for mezzo-soprano and 10 instruments (1962); *Aspects of a Parable* for baritone and 12 instruments (1963); *Love Field,* for tape, a lament for John F. Kennedy (1964); *Glass Concert I* (1967); *Glass Concert II,* scored for sheets of armor plate glass, spotlight bulbs, wine glasses, milk bottles, glass curtains, fluorescent tubes, glass mobiles and other vitreous objects (1969; blueprint and directions publ. in *Source* 5); *Dark Touch* for tactile-aural equip-

ment (1970); *Gentle Grass,* a ritual for 6 players (1970); *Humm,* for 70 or more hummers (1971); *Bus Trip,* a moving event with food, free love and realistic sound effects (1971); *River Archives,* an anthology of sounds from world rivers (1971); *World Rhythms,* incorporating ambient recorded sounds, inspired by long sessions of transcendental meditation (1975).

Lockwood, Normand, American composer; b. New York, March 19, 1906. He studied at the Univ. of Michigan; in 1925 went to Europe where he took lessons with Respighi in Rome and Nadia Boulanger in Paris; he was Fellow at the American Academy in Rome (1929–31); upon his return to America he was instructor in music at the Oberlin (Ohio) Cons. (1932–43); from 1945 to 1953, lecturer at Columbia Univ.; then at Trinity Univ., San Antonio, Texas (1953–55); also taught at the Univ. of Hawaii and at the Univ. of Oregon. In 1961 he was appointed member of the faculty of Denver, Colorado, Univ.; prof. emeritus, 1974.

WORKS: the operas *Scarecrow* (Columbia Univ., N.Y., May 19, 1945), *Early Dawn* (Denver, Aug. 7, 1961), *The Wizards of Balizar* (Denver, Aug. 1, 1962), *The Hanging Judge* (Denver, March, 1964), *Requiem for a Rich Young Man* (Denver, Nov. 24, 1964); *Moby Dick* for chamber orch. (1946); oboe concerto (1966); *Symphonic Sequences* (1966); *From an Opening to a Close* for wind instruments and percussion (1967); 2 concertos for organ and brass (1950, 1970); Clarinet Quintet (1960); Mass for children and orch.; 8 duets for 2 trumpets; Flute Sonata; *Sonata-Fantasia* for accordion; *Valley Suite* for violin and piano; 4 *Excursions* for 4 string basses; 4 *Songs from James Joyce's "Chamber Music"* for medium voice and string quartet (N.Y., March 28, 1948); oratorios, *Light out of Darkness* (1956), *Children of God* (Cincinnati, Feb. 1, 1957); numerous other sacred works.

Loeb, John Jacob, American composer of popular songs; b. Chicago, Feb. 18, 1910; d. Valley Stream, Long Island, N.Y., March 2, 1970. He began writing songs for Broadway shows and jazz bands at the age of 18. Among his best-known songs are *Sweetie Pie, Masquerade* and *Reflections in the Water.* In collaboration with Carmen Lombardo, he wrote the tune of *Boo Hoo.*

Loeffler, Charles Martin (Tornow), outstanding American composer; b. Mulhouse, Alsace, Jan. 30, 1861; d. Medfield, Mass., May 19, 1935. His father was a writer, who sometimes used the *nom de plume* Tornow, which Loeffler later added to his name. When he was a child, the family moved to Russia, where his father was engaged in government work in the Kiev district; later they lived in Debrecen in Hungary, and in Switzerland. In 1875 Loeffler began taking violin lessons in Berlin with Rappoldi, who prepared him for study with Joachim; he studied harmony with Kiel; also took lessons with Bargiel. He then went to Paris, where he continued his musical education with Massart (violin) and Guiraud (composition). He was engaged briefly as violinist in the Pasdeloup Orch.; then was a member of the private orch. of the Russian Baron Paul von Derwies, at his sumptuous residences near Lugano and in Nice (1879–81). When Derwies died in 1881, Loeffler went to America, with letters of recommendation from Joachim. He played in the orch. of Leopold Damrosch in N.Y. In 1882 he became 2nd concertmaster of the newly organized Boston Symph. Orch., but was able to accept other engagements during late spring and summer months; in the spring of 1883, he traveled with the Thomas Orch. on a transcontinental tour; the summers of 1883 and 1884 he spent in Paris, where he took violin lessons with Hubert Léonard. He resigned from the Boston Symph. in 1903, and devoted himself to teaching and composition, living in Boston and suburban Medfield. He was married to Elise Burnett Fay (1910). After his death, she donated to the Library of Congress all of his MSS, correspondence, etc.; by his will, he left the material assets of his not inconsiderable estate to the French Academy and the Paris Cons. He was officer of the French Academy (1906); Chevalier in the French Legion of Honor (1919); member of the American Academy of Arts and Letters; Mus. Doc. (*honoris causa*), Yale Univ. (1926).

Loeffler's position in American music is unique: he was brought up under many different national influences, Alsatian, French, German, Russian, and Ukrainian. One of his most vivid scores, *Memories of My Childhood*, written as late as 1924, reflects the modal feeling of Russian and Ukrainian folksongs. But his esthetic code was entirely French, with definite leanings toward Impressionism; the archaic constructions that he sometimes affected, and the stylized evocations of "ars antiqua," are also in keeping with the French manner. His most enduring work, *A Pagan Poem*, is cast in such a neo-archaic vein. He was a master of colorful orchestration; his harmonies are opulent without saturation; his rhapsodic forms are peculiarly suited to the evocative moods of his music. His only excursion into the American idiom was the employment of jazz rhythms in a few of his lesser pieces.

WORKS: *The Nights in the Ukraine* (after Gogol, suite for violin and orch., Boston, Nov. 20, 1891); *Fantastic Concerto* for cello and orch. (Boston, Feb. 2, 1894); *Divertimento*, for violin and orch. (Boston, Jan. 4, 1895); *La Mort de Tintagiles* (after Maeterlinck), dramatic poem for 2 viole d'amore and orch. (revised for orch. and viola d'amore, 1900; 1st perf., Boston, Feb. 16, 1901); *Divertissement espagnol* for orch. and saxophone (1901); *La Villanelle du Diable*, symph. fantasy for orch. and organ (Boston, April 11, 1902); *Poem* for orch., inspired by Verlaine's *La Bonne Chanson* (Boston, April 11, 1902; reorchestrated, and perf. by the Boston Symph., Nov. 1, 1918); *A Pagan Poem* (after Virgil), for orch. with piano, English horn, and 3 trumpets obbligati (originally as chamber music, 1901; revised for orch. and piano, 1906; 1st perf., Boston Symph., Nov. 22, 1907, Karl Muck conducting); *Hora Mystica* for orch. and men's chorus (Boston Symph., March 2, 1917, Karl Muck conducting); *5 Irish Fantasies*, for voice and orch. (3 numbers perf., Boston, March 10, 1922); *Memories of My Childhood* (*Life in a Russian Village*), for orch. (awarded the Chicago North Shore Festival Association prize, 1924; Chicago Symph., Evanston, Illinois, May 30, 1924); *Canticum Fratris Solis (The Canticle of the Sun)*, for

solo voice and chamber orch. (commissioned by the E. S. Coolidge Foundation; 1st perf. at the Library of Congress Festival of Chamber Music, Oct. 28, 1925); *Evocation* for women's voices and orch. (on lines from the *Select Epigrams of Greek Anthology* by J. W. Machail; commissioned for the opening of Severance Hall, Cleveland; perf. there, Feb. 5, 1931); Psalm 137, *By the Rivers of Babylon*, for 4-part women's chorus with organ, harp, 2 flutes, and cello obbligato (1907); *For one who fell in battle*, for 8-part mixed chorus a cappella (1911); *Beat! Beat! Drums!* (after Whitman), for men's chorus in unison, 6 piccolos, 3 saxophones, brass, drums, and 2 pianos (1917; Cleveland, Nov. 17, 1932); 2 rhapsodies for oboe, viola, and piano (*L'Étang* and *La Cornemuse;* after poems by Maurice Rollinat; 1905); Octet for 2 clarinets, 2 violins, viola, cello, double bass, and harp; String Sextet; *Music for Four Stringed Instruments* (in memory of the American aviator Victor Chapman; 1917); Quintet for 3 violins, viola, and cello; *4 Melodies* for voice and piano (poems by G. Kahn; 1903); *4 Poems* for voice, viola, and piano (1904); *4 Poems* for voice and piano (1906); *The wind among the reeds*, for voice and piano (poems by W. B. Yeats; 1908); *The Reveller*, for solo voice, violin, and piano (1925); *Partita* for violin and piano (1930); in MS, a 4-act Chinese opera, *Life is but a Dream*, and an opera based on a short play by Cecil Sharp. Also wrote *Violin Studies for the Development of the Left Hand* (publ. 1936).

BIBLIOGRAPHY: Carl Engel contributed an extensive essay on Loeffler to the *International Cyclopedia of Music and Musicians*, ed. by Oscar Thompson (N.Y., 1938); Engel also wrote articles on Loeffler in the *Chesterian* (March 1920), in *Musical Quarterly* (July 1925), and in *Cobbett's Cyclopedic Survey of Chamber Music* (1929); L. Gilman, *Nature in Music and Studies in Tone Poetry of Today* (1914); Paul Rosenfeld, *Musical Portraits* (1923) and *An Hour with American Music* (N.Y., 1929; pp. 52–59).

Loeillet, Jacques, oboe player, brother of **Jean-Baptiste Loeillet;** b. Ghent, July 7, 1685; d. Versailles, Nov. 28, 1746. He played in court orchestras in Brussels and Munich. In 1727 he went to France; demonstrated his virtuosity, performing on several wind instruments and on the violin, at the Versailles court, and was appointed chamber musician to Louis XV. He publ. 6 sonatas for 2 flutes and 6 sonatas for solo flute with continuo.

Loeillet, Jean-Baptiste (known in England as **John Loeillet**), notable harpsichordist and flutist; brother of **Jacques Loeillet;** b. Ghent, Nov. 18, 1680; d. London, July 19, 1730. The family name has been variously spelled **L'Oeillet, Luly, Lulli, Lullie,** and even **Lully,** which latter form led to a great deal of confusion, so that Loeillet's Minuet in A has been misattributed in some editions to the great Lully. Loeillet studied in Ghent and in Paris. In 1705 he went to London, where he played the oboe and the flute at the Queen's Theatre (until 1710). He became extremely successful as teacher, player on the harpsichord, and collector of musical instruments. He popularized the German transverse flute in England. In his music he followed the Italian tradition; his writing for the flute shows a thorough understanding of the virtuoso possibilities of the instrument.

WORKS: He publ. in London, under the name of John Loeillet, the following works: 6 suites of lessons for the harpsichord; 6 sonatas for various instruments; 12 sonatas for violins, German flutes, and common flutes; 12 solos for a German flute, common flute, and violin; the following were publ. under the name of **Jean-Baptiste Loeillet de Gand:** 4 books of solos for a flute and a bass; 6 sonatas for 2 flutes; and 6 sonatas for 2 German flutes. There are 2 different sets of opus numbers, which suggests that there was another Loeillet, possibly identifiable with John Loeillet's cousin, also named Jean-Baptiste, and active in Lyons. Reprints of authentic and putative works by John Loeillet include a set of sonatas, ed. by Béon (Paris, 1911); a sonata ed. by Moffat; harpsichord pieces ed. by J. Watelet (Antwerp, 1932); 2 sonatas for flute and piano, ed. by J. van Etsen (Antwerp, 1938); etc.

BIBLIOGRAPHY: Paul Bergmans, *Une Famille de musiciens belges du XVIIIᵉ siécle: Les Loeillet* (Brussels, 1927); prime source book, providing documentary information on members of the family; but see B. Priestman, "Catalogue thématique des œuvres de Jean-Baptiste, John et Jacques Loeillet," *Revue Belge de Musicologie* (Oct.–Dec. 1952; pp. 219–74), separating John Loeillet's works from those purported to be by his cousin; see also Priestman's article, "The Keyboard Works of John Loeillet," *Music Review* (May 1955).

Loeillet, John. See **Jean-Baptiste Loeillet.**

Loeschhorn, Albert. See **Löschhorn, Albert.**

Loesser, Arthur, brilliant American pianist and imaginative writer on music; b. New York, Aug. 26, 1894; d. Cleveland, Jan. 4, 1969. He studied with Stojowski and Goetschius at the Institute of Musical Art, N.Y.; began an auspicious concert career in 1913; toured Australia and the Orient in 1920–21. In 1926 he was appointed prof. of piano at the Cleveland Institute of Music. In 1943 he was commissioned in the U.S. Army as an officer in the Japanese intelligence dept.; mastered the language and, after the end of the war, gave lectures in Japanese in Tokyo; was the first American musician in uniform to play for a Japanese audience (1946). He publ. *Humor in American Song* (N.Y., 1943) and an entertaining volume, *Men, Women and Pianos: A Social History* (N.Y., 1954). He was a brother of **Frank Loesser.**

Loesser, Frank, American composer of popular music; brother of **Arthur Loesser;** b. New York, June 29, 1910; d. there, July 28, 1969. He was educated at the College of the City of N.Y., where he began writing songs for college activities; he subsequently was active as a reporter, singer, and vaudeville performer. In 1931 he settled in Hollywood and devoted himself mainly to writing musical comedies. During World War II he was in the U.S. Army, and wrote several Army songs (*What Do You Do in the Infantry?; Salute to the Army Service Forces; Praise the Lord and Pass the Ammunition; They're Either Too Young or Too Old;* etc.); continued to produce popular songs after the war (*On A Slow Boat to China; Small Fry; The Moon of Manakoora; Dolores; How Sweet You Are; Now That I Need You; Roger Young; Just Another Polka; Two Sleepy People; Spring Will Be a Little Late This Year; A Touch of Texas; Jingle Jangle Jingle; I Wish I Didn't Love You So; My Darling, My Darling; Baby, It's Cold Outside,* etc.); also wrote music for several highly successful Broadway plays: *Where's Charley?, Guys and Dolls, The Most Happy Fella,* etc.

BIBLIOGRAPHY: Arthur Loesser, "My Brother Frank," *Notes* (March 1950).

Loevendie, Theo, Dutch composer and saxophone player; b. Amsterdam, Sept. 17, 1930. He studied composition and clarinet at the Amsterdam Cons. (1956–61); taught clarinet at the Toonkunst Music School in Haarlem and at the Amsterdam Cons. (1960–65); in 1968 was appointed instructor in improvisation at the Rotterdam Cons. In 1973 he organized STAMP concerts with the purpose of presenting contemporary music of various styles (jazz, folk music, avant-garde, etc.).

WORKS: an opera for young people, *Esperanza* (Holland Festival, Amsterdam, July, 1971); *Confluxus* for jazz and symphony orchestras (1966); *3 Pieces* for 3 different clarinets (1968); *Scaramuccia* for clarinet and orch. (Utrecht, April 14, 1971); *Music for Bass Clarinet and Piano* (1971); *Music for Double Bass and Piano* (1971); *Aulos* for winds and/or strings (1972); *2 Trios* for 3 percussionists (1973); *Timbo* for 6 percussionists (1974); *Prelude* for 6 percussionists (1974); *De nachtegaal,* musical theater piece (1974); *Incantations* for bass clarinet and orch. (The Hague, Oct. 25, 1975); *Orbits* for solo horn, 4 obbligato horns and orch. (Rotterdam, Feb. 28, 1976); *Strides* for piano (1976); *6 Turkish Folk Poems* for female voice and 7 instruments (Holland Festival, The Hague, June 21, 1977).

Loevensohn, Marix, Belgian cellist; b. Courtrai, Belgium, March 31, 1880; d. Montauban, France, April 24, 1943. He studied at the Brussels Cons.; made his public debut in London at the age of 14; then toured England as a joint artist with celebrated musicians, among them Paderewski and Adelina Patti; was, successively, member of the string quartets of Wilhelmj, Ysaÿe, and Thomson. In the interim, he taught in Berlin, Amsterdam and Brussels.

Loewe, Carl (Gottfried), outstanding German composer of lieder; b. Löbejün, near Halle, Nov. 30, 1796; d. Kiel, April 20, 1869. His father, a schoolmaster and cantor, taught him the rudiments of music; when he was 12 he was sent to the Francke Institute in Halle, where his attractive manner, excellent high voice, and early ability to improvise, brought him to the attention of Jerome Bonaparte, who granted him a stipend of 300 Thaler annually until 1813. His teacher was Türk, the head of the Francke Institute; after Türk's death in 1813, Loewe joined the Singakademie founded by Naue. He also studied theology at the Univ. of Halle, but soon devoted himself entirely to music. He began to compose as a boy; under the influence of Zelter, he wrote German ballades, and developed an individual style of great dramatic force and lyrical inspiration; he perfected the genre, and was regarded by many musicians as the greatest song composer after Schubert and before Brahms. His setting of Goethe's poem *Erlkönig* (1818), which came before the publication of Schubert's great song to the same poem, is one of Loewe's finest creations; other songs that rank among his best are *Edward, Der Wirthin Töchterlein, Der Nöck, Archibald Douglas, Tom der Reimer, Heinrich der Vogler, Oluf, Die verfallene Mühle,* etc. Loewe was personally acquainted with Goethe, and also met Weber. In 1820 he became schoolmaster at Stettin, and organist at St. Jacobus there. He lived in Stettin, except for frequent travels, until 1866, when he settled in Kiel. He visited Vienna (1844), London (1847), Sweden and Norway (1851), and Paris (1857), among other places. Loewe was an excellent vocalist, and was able to perform his ballades in public.

WORKS: 5 operas, only one of which, *Die drei Wünsche,* was performed (Berlin, Feb. 18, 1834); 17 oratorios; cantata, *Die Hochzeit der Thetis;* a ballade for soli, chorus, and orch., *Die erste Walpurgisnacht* (after Goethe); 368 ballades for voice and piano, publ. in his collected edition and in numerous anthologies (Peters and Schlesinger publ. "Loewe-Albums" containing 20 and 16 numbers respectively). Loewe's instrumental works (symphonies, overtures, 3 string quartets, a piano trio, several piano sonatas, etc.) are mostly in MS. He publ. several pedagogic works: *Gesanglehre für Gymnasien, Seminarien und Bürgerschulen* (Stettin, 1826; 5th ed., 1854); *Musikalischer Gottesdienst; methodische Anweisung zum Kirchengesang und Orgelspiel* (1851, and subsequent eds.); *Klavier- und Generalbass-Schule* (2nd ed., 1851). A *Gesamtausgabe der Balladen, Legenden, Lieder und Gesänge,* in 17 vols., ed. by Max Runze, was publ. by Breitkopf & Härtel (1899–1905). A Loewe-Verein was founded in Berlin in 1882.

BIBLIOGRAPHY: *Selbstbiographie,* ed. by K. H. Bitter (Berlin, 1870); A. Wellmer, *Carl Loewe: Ein deutscher Tonmeister* (Leipzig, 1886); M. Runze, *Loewe redivivus* (Berlin, 1888); A. B. Bach, *The Art-Ballad: Loewe and Schubert* (London, 1890; 3rd ed., 1891); M. Runze, *Ludwig Giesebrecht und Carl Loewe* (Berlin, 1894); W. Wossidlo, *Carl Loewe als Balladenkomponist* (Berlin, 1894); A. Niggli, *Carl Loewe* (Zürich, 1897); H. Bulthaupt, *Carl Loewe, Deutschlands Balladenkomponist* (Berlin, 1898); M. Runze, *Goethe und Loewe* (as introduction to vols. 11 and 12 of the *Gesamtausgabe* of Loewe's works; Leipzig, 1901); M. Runze, *Die musikalische Legende* (introduction to vols. 13 and 14 of the same; Leipzig, 1902); H. Draheim, *Goethes Balladen in Loewes Komposition* (Langensalza, 1905); K. Anton, *Beiträge zur Biographie Carl Loewes* (Halle, 1912); K. Anton, "Carl Loewe als Lehrer Walter von Goethes," *Goethe Jahrbuch* 23 (1913); H. Kleemann, *Beiträge zur Ästhetik und Geschichte der Loeweschen Ballade* (Halle, 1913); L. Hirschberg, *Loewe als Instrumentalkomponist* (Langensalza, 1919); O. Altenburg, *Carl Loewe* (Stettin, 1924); Hans Engel, *Carl Loewe: Überblick und Würdigung* (Greiswald, 1934); W. Serauky, "Zu Carl Loewes Biographie und musikalischen Schaffen," in

Festschrift A. Schering (Berlin, 1937); R. Sietz, *Carl Loewe: ein Gedenkbuch zum 150. Geburtstag* (Cologne, 1948).

Loewe, Ferdinand. See **Löwe, Ferdinand.**

Loewe, Frederick, Austrian-American composer of popular music; b. Vienna, June 10, 1904. He studied piano in Berlin with Busoni and Eugène d'Albert; composition with Rezniček. In 1924 he emigrated to the U.S.; was active as concert pianist; then devoted himself chiefly to production of popular music. Adapting himself adroitly to the American idiom, he became one of the most successful writers of musical comedies; among them are *Salute to Spring; Great Lady; The Life of the Party; What's Up?; The Day Before Spring; Brigadoon; Paint Your Wagon;* and (the most spectacularly successful of them all) *My Fair Lady,* after Shaw's *Pygmalion* (1956; 2717 performances); this was followed by another hit, *Camelot* (1960); in all these his lyricist was Alan Jay Lerner.

BIBLIOGRAPHY: David Ewen, *Great Men of American Popular Song* (Englewood Cliffs, N.J., 1970).

Loewenberg, Alfred, German musicologist; b. Berlin, May 14, 1902; d. London, Jan. 3, 1950. He studied at Jena Univ. (Ph.D., 1925); settled in London in 1934. His unique achievement is the compilation of *Annals of Opera: 1597–1940* (Cambridge, 1943; new ed., Geneva, 1955; rev. and corrected 1970), tabulating in chronological order the exact dates of first performances and important revivals of some 4,000 operas, with illuminating comments of a bibliographical nature. Also publ. *Early Dutch Librettos and Plays with Music in the British Museum* (London, 1947), and a number of articles.

Loewengard, Max Julius, German writer on music and pedagogue; b. Frankfurt, Oct. 2, 1860; d. Hamburg, Nov. 19, 1915. He was a pupil of Raff in Frankfurt; from 1891 to 1904 he was on the faculty of the Scharwenka Cons. in Berlin, and wrote music criticism for the *Börsen-Zeitung;* from 1904–8, taught at the Hamburg Cons.; founded the Institut für Musikwissenschaft there. His compositions include an opera, *Die vierzehn Nothelfer* (Berlin, 1896), a serenade for orch., and many songs.

WRITINGS: several highly successful manuals: *Lehrbuch der Harmonie* (1892; 6th ed., 1906; English transl. by H. M. Peacock, 1905; F. Liebing, 1907; Th. Baker, 1910); *Lehrbuch des Kontrapunkts* (1902; English transl. by F. Liebing, 1907); *Aufgabenbuch zur Harmonielehre* (1903); *Lehrbuch des Kanons und der Fuge* (1903); *Lehrbuch der musikalischen Formen* (1904); *Praktische Anleitung zum Generalbassspiel, Harmonisieren, Transponieren und Modulieren* (1913).

Logan, Frederick Knight, American composer of popular songs; b. Oskaloosa, Iowa, Oct. 15, 1871; d. June 11, 1928. He wrote a number of sentimental ballads in collaboration with his mother **Virginia Logan.** He was the composer of the celebrated *Missouri Waltz* which he published as a piano solo in 1914, with his name on the cover of the sheet music as an "arranger," for he was reluctant to admit the authorship of the tune that seemed beneath his own estimate as a composer. But when the words were added in 1916, the thing became a sensational hit. The State of Missouri accepted it as its official song. Harry Truman loved to play it on the piano and, for better or for worse, the *Missouri Waltz* became associated with his (Truman's) political deeds and misdeeds.

Logar, Mihovil, Croatian composer; b. Fiume, Oct. 6, 1902. He studied in Prague with K. B. Jirák and J. Suk. In 1927 he returned to Belgrade and became prof. of composition at the Belgrade Musical Academy. A highly prolific composer, he writes in all genres, employing a restrained modern idiom.
WORKS: the operas *Pokondirena Tikva (Middle-Class Noblewoman;* Belgrade, Oct. 20, 1956); *Četrdesetprva (The Year of 1941;* Sarajevo, Feb. 10, 1961); ballet *Zlatna ribica (Goldfish,* after Pushkin's tale; Belgrade, Nov. 11, 1953); *4 Scenes from Shakespeare,* incidental music for orch. (1954); *Rondo rustico* for orch. (1945); *Violin Concerto* (1954); *Clarinet Concerto* (1956); *Vatra (Fire),* cantata (Belgrade, Sept. 27, 1960); *Kosmonauti,* concert overture in honor of the Soviet cosmonauts (Belgrade, June 8, 1962); *Sinfonia italiana* (Belgrade, Nov. 24, 1964); *Doppio Concerto* for clarinet and French horn (Belgrade, April 5, 1968).

Logier, Johann Bernhard, German pianist, teacher and composer; b. Kassel, Feb. 9, 1777; d. Dublin, July 27, 1846. He received his early musical training at home; as a youth he went to England and played the flute in a regimental band; he was employed as an organist in Westport, Ireland, where he perfected his invention of the "chiroplast," for holding the hands in the most convenient positions during piano practice; he patented it in 1814 and promoted it with fanatic persistence. Amazingly enough, it obtained great vogue in England, and was equally successful in Germany; he spent 3 years (1823–26) in Berlin to promote it, then returned to Ireland, and settled in Dublin. In reply to numerous polemical attacks on his invention Logier publ. equally bitter assaults on his detractors, among them the pamphlets *An Explanation and Description of the Royal Patent Chiroplast, or Hand-Director for Pianoforte* (London, 1816) and *An Authentic Account of the Examination of Pupils Instructed on the New System of Musical Education, by J. B. Logier* (London, 1818). He further publ. *The First Companion to the Royal Patent Chiroplast* (London, 1818; it went through numerous editions) and *Logier's Practical Thorough-Bass,* and in German, *System der Musikwissenschaft und der musikalischen Komposition* (Berlin, 1827). He also introduced a method of simultaneous practice on different pianos, which for a time was adopted even in such a bastion of traditional music instruction as the Paris Conservatoire. In the end, Logier's "chiroplast" joined a number of other equally futile pseudo-scientific inventions in the repository of musical curiosities.

Logothetis, Anestis, Bulgarian-born avant-garde composer of Greek extraction; b. Burgas, Oct. 27, 1921. He was trained in mechanical engineering in Vi-

enna (1942–45); then took lessons in composition there with Ratz and Uhl (1945–51); exhibited in Vienna galleries a series of polymorphic graphs capable of being performed as music by optional instrumental groups. He employs a highly personalized "integrating" musical notation, making use of symbols, signs and suggestive images playing on a performer's psychological associations.
WORKS: *Integration* for violin, cello and piano (1953); *Peritonon* for horn and piano (1954); *Polynom* for orch. in 5 groups (1958); *2 Textures* for 2 piano groups (1959); *Kompression* for any instrument (1959); *Textur—Struktur—Spiegel—Spiel* (1959); *Fantasmata and Meditation,* tape ballet music (1959); *Agglomeration* for solo violin (1960); *5 Portraits of Love,* ballet (1960); *Koordination* for 5 orch. groups (1960); *Himmelsmechanik,* ballet (1960); *Katalysator* for horns (1960). The following "polymorphic" pieces are for variable chamber instrumental groups: *Kulmination I + II + III* (1961); *Meditation* for any instruments or voices (1961); *Impulse* (1961); *Vibration* (1962); *Mäandros* (1963); *Odyssee* (1963); *Dynapolis* (1963); *Dispersion* (1963); *Kentra* (1964); *Seismographie I* and *II* (1964); *Osculations* (1964); *Ichnologia* (1964); *Labyrinthos* (1965); *Reversible Bijunktion* (1965); *1.65AL* (1965); *Orbitals* (1965); *Enósis* (1965); *Diffusion* (1965); *Integration* (1966); *Enclaves* (1966); *Diptychon* for piano (1966); *Desmotropie* for orch. (1967); *Karmadharmadrama,* musical theater (1967; Graz, Oct. 12, 1972); *Polychron* (1967); *Syrroi* (1967); *Konvektionsströme* for orch. (1968); *Styx* for orch. of plucked strings (1968); *Evektion* (1968); *Anastasis,* stage piece for voices, tape film, television and instruments (1969); *Kollisionen* (1970); *Komplementäres* (1970); *Pyrifleghethon—Acheron—Kokkytos* for 3 choirs and optional instruments (Athens, Sept. 26, 1971; refers to the 3 rivers of the Greek nether world); *Klangraum I* and *II* for orch. (1972); *Musik-Fontane für Robert Moran* (1972); *Emanationen* for clarinet and tape (1973).

Logroscino, Nicola, Italian composer; b. Bitonto (baptized Oct. 22), 1698; d. Palermo, after 1765. He was a pupil of Veneziano and Perugino (1714–27) at the Cons. di Santa Maria di Loreto in Naples; 1728–31, was organist at Conza (Avellino); in 1731, again in Naples. In 1747 he became first prof. of counterpoint at the Cons. dei Figliuoli Dispersi in Palermo; then went to Naples where he produced his most successful operas; he is regarded as the creator of Neapolitan *opera buffa* in the local dialect, among them *Il Governatore, Il vecchio marito* and *Tanto bene che male.* Of his serious operas *Giunio Bruto* (1748) and *Olimpiade* (1753) were the most notable.
BIBLIOGRAPHY: H. Kretzchmar, "Zwei Opern Nicola Logroscinos," *Jahrbuch Peters* (1908); U. Prota-Giurleo, *Nicola Logroscino, il dio dell'opera buffa* (Naples, 1927); E. P. Morello, *A Scarlatti e Nicolò Logroscino* (1927); A. della Corte, *L'opera comica italiana nel 1700* (Bari, 1923; vol. 1; p. 172 *et seq*).

Löhlein, Georg Simon, German composer; b. Neustadt, near Coburg, July (baptized July 16), 1725; d. Danzig, Dec. 16, 1781. On account of his tall stature (6 ft. 2 inches), he was seized on a journey and forced

into the Prussian Guard; he was stationed at Potsdam and served at the palace of Frederick the Great. He was severely wounded at the battle of Collin during the Seven Years' War, but recovered and went to Jena, where he completed his interrupted musical education; at the age of 38 he enrolled at the Univ. of Leipzig; there he was active as both violinist and pianist. In 1781 he received a post as organist at the St. Mary Church in Danzig, but suffered from the rigors of the climate, and died a few months after arrival there. Löhlein wrote a singspiel, *Zemire und Azor* (Leipzig, 1775), several instrumental concertos, chamber music, etc., but he became known mainly through his pedagogical work, *Clavier-Schule* in 2 vols. (1765 and 1781), which passed through many editions and was revised by Czerny; he also publ. a *Violinschule* (1774).
BIBLIOGRAPHY: F. von Glasenapp, *G. S. Löhlein* (Halle, 1937).

Lohmann, Peter, German poet and writer on music; b. Schwelm, April 24, 1833; d. Leipzig, Jan. 10, 1907. From 1856 he lived in Leipzig, and wrote (1858–61) for the *Neue Zeitschrift für Musik.* He publ. *Über R. Schumanns Faustmusik* (1860) and *Über die dramatische Dichtung mit Musik* (1861; 2nd ed., 1864; 3rd ed. as *Das Ideal der Oper,* 1886).

Lohse, Otto, German conductor and composer; b. Dresden, Sept. 21, 1858; d. Baden-Baden, May 5, 1925. He was a pupil at the Dresden Cons. of Richter (piano), Grützmacher (cello), Draeseke and Wüllner (composition). In 1880 he went to Russia and conducted theater music in Riga; in 1893 he was in Hamburg; there he married the famous singer **Katharina Klafsky,** and in the spring of 1896 both artists were members of the Damrosch Opera Co. in N.Y., with Lohse as conductor. From 1897 to 1904, Lohse conducted opera in Strasbourg; 1904–11, in Cologne; 1911–12, at the Théâtre de la Monnaie, Brussels; 1912–23, at the Leipzig Stadttheater. He composed an opera, *Der Prinz wider Willen* (Riga, 1890), and songs.
BIBLIOGRAPHY: Ernst Lert, *Otto Lohse* (Leipzig, 1918).

Lolli, Antonio, Italian violinist and composer; b. Bergamo, c.1730; d. Palermo, Aug. 10, 1802. Little is known of his early life; he was in Stuttgart at the court of the Duke of Württemberg from 1762 till 1772; asked for a leave of absence, but did not return to Stuttgart; however, he drew his salary until 1774. He gave violin concerts in Hamburg, Lübeck, and Stettin in 1773–74; then proceeded to St. Petersburg, where he became a special favorite of Catherine II, and also ingratiated himself with Potemkin. He received 4,000 rubles annually as violinist to the Empress and chapel master of the court. In Dec. 1777 he visited Stockholm, and then went to Germany. An incorrigible gambler, he dissipated the fortune of 10,000 florins he had accumulated from the Russian emoluments, and in 1780, after protracted journeys through Europe, went back to St. Petersburg; there he was able to regain his social and artistic position; gave concerts at Potemkin's palace in St. Petersburg, and also played in Moscow. Despite his frequent derelictions of duty,

he was retained at the court until 1783, when his contract was cancelled and he was succeeded as chapel master by Paisiello. However, he continued to give some public concerts, and also lessons, before leaving Russia in 1784. In 1785 he appeared in London, then was in Paris and in Naples, finally settling in Palermo. Contemporary accounts indicate that Lolli was a violinist of great ability, but also addicted to eccentricities in playing technical passages. He composed and publ. several sets of violin works, among them *5 Sonates et Divertissement* for violin with continuo (1776; dedicated to Potemkin); other violin pieces (concertos, sonatas, etc.); also an *École du violon en Quatuor* (Berlin, 1776; many reprints by various German and French publishers).
BIBLIOGRAPHY: A. Moser, "Arcangelo Corelli und Antonio Lolli; zwei künstlerische Ehrenrettungen," *Zeitschrift für Musikwissenschaft* (April 1921); R.-Aloys Mooser, *Annales de la Musique et des Musiciens en Russie* (Geneva, 1950; vol. II, pp. 161–68).

Lomakin, Gavriil, Russian singer and composer; b. St. Petersburg, April 6, 1812; d. Gatchina, May 21, 1885. He studied theory with Sapienza; in 1830, became choirmaster, and singing master at several institutions in St. Petersburg, and later conductor of the court chapel (1848–59). Together with Balakirev, he established in 1862 the Free School for Music, and had charge of the singing classes until 1870. He wrote 10 *Cherubim Songs;* 14 *Penitential Songs;* a Liturgy, etc.; publ. a *Treatise on Choral Singing;* arrangements for chorus of old Russian hymns.

Lomax, Alan, American ethnomusicologist; b. Austin, Texas, Jan. 31, 1915. He acquired his métier from his father, **John Avery Lomax;** studied at the Univ. of Texas in Austin (B.A., 1936) and at Columbia Univ. During the years 1933–42 he undertook the task of collecting folksongs of South-Western and Mid-Western regions of the U.S.; in 1963 he was appointed head of the Bureau of Applied Social Research. With his father he brought out several collections of unknown American folksongs: among them, *The Folk Songs of North America in the English Language* (N.Y., 1960); *Hard-Hitting Songs for Hard-Hit People* (N.Y., 1967); *Folk Song Style and Culture* (Washington, D.C., 1968). They also supervised field recordings of rural and prison work songs, and it was on one such occasion that they discovered Leadbelly. Another "discovery" was "Jelly Roll" Morton, and their recorded interviews, made at the Library of Congress in 1938, resulted in the book *Mr. Jelly Roll* (N.Y., 1950; 2nd ed., Berkeley, 1973).

Lomax, John Avery, American ethnomusicologist; b. Goodman, Mississippi, Sept. 23, 1867; d. Greenville, Miss., Jan. 26, 1948. He began collecting and notating American folksongs since his early youth; studied music at the Univ. of Texas in Austin; founded the Texas Folklore Society. In 1933 his son **Alan Lomax** joined him in his research. Publications: *American Ballads and Folk Songs* (N.Y., 1934); *Cowboy Songs and Other Frontier Ballads* (with Alan Lomax, N.Y., 1938; enlarged edition, 1945); *Our Singing Country* (with Alan Lomax, N.Y., 1941); *Best Songs from the Lomax Col-*

lections for Pickers and Singers (posthumous, edited by Alan Lomax, N.Y., 1966). He publ. an autobiography, *Adventures of a Ballad Hunter* (N.Y., 1947).

Lombardo, Carmen, Canadian-born American song writer and saxophone player; b. London, Ontario, July 16, 1903; d. North Miami, Florida, April 17, 1971. He was a brother of **Guy Lombardo** and played the saxophone in his band from 1929 until the year of his death. His lush saxophone tone contributed greatly to the emotional euphony of the Lombardo sound and his vibrato was most ingratiating. He was also a composer; among his popular hits are such tunes as *Sailboat in the Moonlight, Powder Your Face with Sunshine* and the lachrymose classic *Boo Hoo,* which he composed in collaboration with John Jacob Loeb.

Lombardo, Guy, Canadian-born American bandleader; b. London, Ontario, June 19, 1902, of Italian parents; d. Houston, Texas, Nov. 5, 1977. With his brother **Carmen Lombardo,** he organized a dance band, "The Royal Canadians" and took it to the U.S. in 1924; two other brothers, **Lebert** and **Victor,** were also members of the band. The band rapidly rose to success on the commercial wave of pervasive sentimentality; in 1928 it was publicized as the purveyor of "the sweetest music this side of Heaven." The rendition of *Auld Lang Syne* by the Guy Lombardo Band at the Waldorf-Astoria Hotel in N.Y. at New Year's Eve celebrations every winter from 1929 to 1977 (with the exception of 1959) became a nostalgic feature. In his arrangements, Guy Lombardo cultivated unabashed emotionalism; in his orchestrations all intervallic interstices are well filled, and saxophones are tremulous with vibrato. The result is a velvety, creamy, but not necessarily oleaginous harmoniousness, which possesses an irresistible appeal to the obsolescent members of the superannuated generation of the 1920's. His preferred dynamics was *mezzo-forte,* and his favorite tempo, *Andante moderato;* he never allowed the sound of his band to rise to a disturbing *forte* or to descend to a squeaking *pianissimo.* He was a wizard of the golden mean, and his public loved it.

London, George, American bass-baritone; b. Montreal, Can., May 30, 1919, of Russian-Jewish parents. His real name was **Burnstein.** The family moved to Los Angeles in 1935; there he took lessons in operatic interpretation with Richard Lert; made his public debut in the opera *Gainsborough's Duchess* by Albert Coates (L.A., April 20, 1941). After further study he toured the U.S. as a member of the Bel Canto Trio, with Frances Yeend, soprano, and Mario Lanza, tenor; made his debut with the Metropolitan Opera Co. as Amonasro on Nov. 13, 1959; produced a very fine impression singing Boris Godunov there on March 6, 1953; he also sang this role, in Russian, in Moscow in 1960; he remained on the staff of the Metropolitan Opera until 1965. From 1971 to 1976 he was executive director of the National Opera Institute in Washington. In 1975 he became General director of the Washington Opera.
BIBLIOGRAPHY: J. Wechsberg, "The Vocal Mis-

sion," a "profile" of George London, in the *New Yorker* (Oct. 26 and Nov. 2, 1957).

Long, Marguerite, notable French pianist and pedagogue; b. Nimes, Nov. 13, 1874; d. Paris, Feb. 13, 1966. She studied piano with Marmontel at the Paris Cons.; appointed instructor there in 1906; in 1920 she founded her own music school; in 1940 Jacques Thibaud, the violinist, joined her; with him she gave numerous recitals and established the Long-Thibaud Competitions. She played an important role in promoting French music; in 1931 gave the first performance of the Piano Concerto by Ravel, dedicated to her. She was married to Joseph de Marliave. She publ. *Au Piano avec Claude Debussy* (Paris, 1960); *Au Piano avec Gabriel Fauré* (Paris, 1963).
BIBLIOGRAPHY: Janine Weill, *Marguerite Long: une vie fascinante* (Paris, 1969).

Longas, Federico, Spanish pianist and composer; b. Barcelona, July 18, 1893; d. Santiago, Chile, June 17, 1968. He was a pupil of Granados and Malats; toured widely in the U.S., South America, and Europe as accompanist of Tito Schipa and as soloist. He founded a piano school, the Acad. Longas, in Barcelona; later he went to Paris; then to the U.S., settling in N.Y. His works include effective piano pieces (*Jota, Aragon,* etc.); over 100 songs (*Castilian Moonlight, La Guinda, Muñequita,* etc.).

Longhurst, William Henry, English organist and composer; b. London, Oct. 6, 1819; d. Canterbury, June 17, 1904. He was a chorister in Canterbury Cathedral (1828–36); then assistant organist (1836–73); in 1873, became first organist, retiring in 1898 after 70 years of uninterrupted service in the Cathedral. He received the degree of Mus. Doc. in 1875; was music lecturer at St. Augustine's College, Canterbury. He wrote an oratorio, *David and Absalom* (1872); a cathedral service; other church music; etc.

Longo, Achille, Italian composer, son of **Alessandro Longo;** b. Naples, March 28, 1900; d. there, May 28, 1954. He studied at the Naples Cons.; taught harmony there (1926–30); then at the Cons. of Parma (1930–34); in 1934 returned to Naples and taught composition at the Cons. until his death.
WORKS: Suite for flute, oboe, clarinet, bassoon, and piano (1926; won the Bellini Prize); Piano Concerto (Venice, 1932); Piano Quintet (1934); Violin Concerto (1937); *Notturno* and *Corteo* for orch. (1942); Requiem (1947); *Serenata in do,* for orch. (1950).

Longo, Alessandro, Italian pianist and music editor; b. Amantea, Dec. 30, 1864; d. Naples, Nov. 3, 1945. He studied with Cesi (piano) and Serrao (composition); in 1887, was appointed prof. of piano at the Naples Cons. In 1892 he founded the Circolo Scarlatti to promote the works of Domenico Scarlatti; from 1914, edited the periodical *L'arte pianistica.* His most important achievement is the complete edition of Domenico Scarlatti's harpsichord works (10 vols. and a supplement; the order of sonatas was partly superseded by Kirkpatrick's catalogue). He was also a prolific composer; publ. numerous pieces for piano solo and piano 4-hands; Piano Quintet; *Tema con variazioni* for harp; Suite for clarinet and piano; songs.

Longy, Georges, French oboe virtuoso; b. Abbeville, Aug. 29, 1868; d. Mareuil (Dordogne), March 29, 1930. He studied at the Paris Cons. (1st prize, 1886); was a member of the Lamoureux Orch. (1886–88) and of the Colonne Orch. (1888–98). In 1898 he was engaged as first oboe player of the Boston Symph. Orch., and remained there until 1925. From 1899 to 1913 he conducted the Boston Orchestral Club. In 1900 he founded the Longy Club for chamber music; in 1916 he established his own music school in Boston (later Longy School of Music, Cambridge, Mass.).

Lonque, Georges, Belgian composer; b. Ghent, Nov. 8, 1900; d. Brussels, March 3, 1967. He studied with Moeremans, Mathieu and Lunssens at the Ghent Cons.; was awarded Second Prix de Rome for his cantatas *Le Rossignol* in 1927 and *Antigone* in 1929. He was a prof. in harmony at his alma mater after 1932 and was director of the music academy in Renaix (1938–64). His music was influenced mainly by Debussy, Fauré and Ravel.

WORKS: *Impressions d'Hemelrijk* for orch. (1925); *Vieux quai* for violin or cello, and orch. (1928); *Aura,* symph. poem and ballet (1930); *Wiener Walzer* for small orch. (1933); *Poème de la Mer* for cello and orch. (1935); *Images d'Orient* for saxophone or viola, and orch. (1935); *Porcelaines de Saxe* for small orch. (1939); *Prélude et Aria* for cello and orch. (1943); *Estrelle* for violin and orch. (1944); Violin Concerto (1948); *Afgoden (Idoles)* for clarinet and orch. (1950); Violin Sonata (1925); *Caprice* for violin and piano (1930); String Quartet (1937); piano pieces, including *Nuit d'automne* (1929), 2 sonatinas (1939, 1944), *Voilier* (1952), *Tableaux d'une chambre bleue* (1952) and *Nocturne* (1955); *Missa pro Pace* for male chorus and organ (1941); numerous songs, including *Faune* (1933), *Why Don't You Come?* (1944), *La Question* (1957) and *Portrait* (1957).

Loomis, Clarence, American pianist and composer; b. Sioux Falls, S.D., Dec. 13, 1889; d. Aptos, Calif., July 3, 1965. He studied at the American Cons. of Chicago with Heniot Levy (piano) and Adolph Weidig (composition); subsequently took lessons with Leopold Godowsky in Vienna. Returning to the U.S., he held various positions as music teacher; taught piano and organ at Highland Univ., New Mexico (1945–55); in 1960 he settled in Aptos, California.

WORKS: As a composer he was mainly successful in writing light operas in a romantic vein; among them are *Yolanda of Cyprus* (London, Ont., Sept. 25, 1929; also given in Chicago, Washington and N.Y.), *A Night in Avignon* (Indianapolis, July 1932), *The White Cloud* (1935), *The Fall of the House of Usher* (Indianapolis, Jan. 11, 1941), *Revival* (1943), *The Captive Woman* (1953); he further wrote a comic ballet *The Flapper and the Quarterback,* which was first performed in Kyoto, Japan at the coronation of Emperor Hirohito, Nov. 10, 1928; for orch.: *Gargoyles,* symph. prelude (1936); *Gaelic Suite* for strings (1953); *Fantasy* for piano and orch. (1954); *Macbeth* (1954); The

Passion Play for chorus and orch.; 2 string quartets (1953, 1963); cantata, *Song of the White Earth* (1956); numerous sacred choruses; *Susanna Don't You Cry,* a stage extravaganza (1939); piano suites; songs; organ pieces.

BIBLIOGRAPHY: E. E. Hipsher, *American Opera and Its Composers* (Philadelphia, 1934; pp. 298–301).

Loomis, Harvey Worthington, American composer; b. Brooklyn, Feb. 5, 1865; d. Boston, Dec. 25, 1930. He was a pupil in composition of Dvořák at the National Cons., N.Y. (1891–93), when Dvořák was director there; later lived mostly in Boston; became interested in Indian music, and published many arrangements of Indian melodies; also original works in that style (*Lyrics of the Red Man,* etc.).

WORKS: a grand opera, *The Traitor Mandolin;* 2 melodramas, *The Song of the Pear* and *The Story of a Faithful Soul;* 4 comic operas, *The Maid of Athens, The Burglar's Bride, Going Up?, The Bey of Baba;* the musical pantomimes *Put to the Test, Her Revenge, In Old New Amsterdam, The Enchanted Fountain, Love and Witchcraft, Blanc et Noir;* incidental music to *The Tragedy of Death* and *The Coming of the Prince; Fairy Hill; Song Flowers for Children to Gather* (2 books), *Toy Tunes,* etc. Many of his manuscripts are in the Music Division of the Library of Congress.

BIBLIOGRAPHY: Rupert Hughes, *Contemporary American Composers* (Boston, 1900; pp. 77–92).

Looser, Rolf, Swiss cellist and composer; b. Niederscherli, near Bern, May 3, 1920. He studied cello with Richard Sturzenegger at the Cons. of Bern and theory with Moeschinger; he received his concert diploma in 1944 and subsequently took additional cello lessons with Pierre Fournier in Paris; he also continued his composition study with Willy Burkhardt in Zürich and with Frank Martin in Geneva. In 1953 he joined the staff of the Bern Cons. as cello instructor; in 1963 he took up residence in Biel. Among his works are a *Fantasie* for cello and orch. (1958); *Rhapsodie* for cello and chamber orch. (1961); *Fantasia a quattro* (1966); and *Alyssos,* 5 pieces for string orch. and percussion (1968).

Lopatnikoff, Nikolai, outstanding Russian-American composer; b. Reval, Estonia, March 16, 1903; d. Pittsburgh, Oct. 7, 1976. He studied at the St. Petersburg Cons.; after the Revolution continued his musical training in Helsinki; then went to Karlsruhe and Berlin where he studied with Ernst Toch and Grabner. In 1934 he proceeded to London; in 1939 went to the U.S.; became naturalized as an American citizen in 1944. In 1945 he was appointed prof. of composition at the Carnegie Institute of Technology, Pittsburgh, retiring in 1968. His music is cast in a neo-Classical manner, distinguished by a vigorous rhythmic pulse, a clear melodic flow and a wholesome harmonic investment. A prolific composer, he composed music in all genres; being a professional pianist he often performed his own works with orchestras.

WORKS: opera *Danton* (1931–33; excerpts from it were performed by the Pittsburgh Symph. Orch., March 25, 1967); *Introduction and Scherzo* for orch. (Boston, April 27, 1928); Symph. No. 1 (Karlsruhe,

Jan. 9, 1929); Symph. No. 2 (Boston, Dec. 22, 1939); Symph. No. 3 (Pittsburgh, Dec. 10, 1954); Symph. No. 4 (Pittsburgh, Jan. 21, 1972); Sinfonietta (Festival of International Society for Contemporary Music, Berkeley, Calif., Aug. 2, 1942); *Opus Sinfonicum* (1933-41; 1st prize of the Cleveland Orch.; perf. Cleveland, Dec. 9, 1943); Concertino for Orch. (Boston, March 2, 1945); Piano Concerto No. 1 (Cologne, Nov. 3, 1925); Piano Concerto No. 2 (Düsseldorf, Oct. 16, 1930); Violin Concerto (Boston, April 17, 1942); Concerto for 2 Pianos and Orch. (Pittsburgh, Dec. 7, 1951); *2 Russian Nocturnes* for orch. (1945); *Music for Orchestra* (Louisville, Kentucky, Jan. 14, 1959); *Variazioni concertanti* (Pittsburgh, Nov. 7, 1958); *Festival Overture* (Detroit, Oct. 12, 1960); Concerto for Orch. (Pittsburgh, April 3, 1964); 3 string quartets (1925, 1929, 1956); Duo for violin and cello (1926); Sonata for piano, violin and snare drum (1926); Cello Sonata (1928); Piano Trio (1938); *Variations and Epilogue* for cello and piano (1946); a number of solo piano pieces; also pieces for mechanical piano (1928).

Lopes-Graça, Fernando, eminent Portuguese pianist, composer and musicologist; b. Tomar, Dec. 17, 1906. He took piano lessons at home; studied composition with Tomás Borba and musicology with Luís de Freitas Branco at the Lisbon Cons. (1923-31); subsequently was instructor at the Instituto de Música in Coimbra (1932-36); was compelled to leave Portugal in 1937 for political reasons, and went to Paris where he studied composition with Charles Koechlin. After the outbreak of World War II he returned to Lisbon and became active in the modern musical movement; taught at the Academia de Amadores de Música there (1940-54); in 1958 went to Brazil as a pianist; in 1959 made a concert tour in Angola, a Portuguese colony at the time, and in 1977 toured the Soviet Union with the Portuguese tenor Fernando Serafim. His music is inspired by nationalistic themes, and is inherently lyrical. WORKS: FOR THE STAGE: cantata-melodrama in 2 parts, *D. Duardos e Flérida,* for narrator, 3 soloists, chorus and orch. (1964-69; Lisbon, Nov. 28, 1970); revue-ballet, *La Fièvre du temps,* for 2 pianos (1938). FOR ORCH.: *Poemeto* for strings (1928); *Prelúdio, Pastoral e Dança* (1929); 2 piano concertos (1940; 1942); 3 Portuguese Dances (1941); Sinfonia (1944); 5 *Estelas Funerárias* (1948); *Scherzo Heróico* (1949); *Suite Rústica No. 1* (1950-51); *Marcha Festiva* (1954); Concertino for piano, strings, brass and percussion (1954); 5 Old Portuguese Romances (1951-55); *Divertimento* for winds, kettledrums, percussion, cellos and double basses (1957); *Poema de Dezembro* (1961); Viola Concertino (1962); *4 Bosquejos (4 Sketches)* for strings (1965); *Concerto da camera,* with cello obbligato (Moscow, Oct. 6, 1967; Rostropovich soloist); *Viagens na minha Terra (Travels in My Country,* 1969-70); *Fantasia* for piano and orch., on a religious song from Beira-Baixa (1974). FOR VOICE: *Pequeno Cancioneiro do Menino Jesus (Little Songbook of the Child Jesus)* for women's chorus, 2 flutes, string quartet, celeste and harp (1936-59); *História Trágico-Marítima* for baritone, contralto, chorus and orch. (1942-59); *9 Portuguese Folk Songs* for voice and orch. (1948-49); 4 Songs of

Federico García Lorca for baritone, 2 clarinets, violin, viola, cello, harp and percussion (1953-54); *Cantos do Natal (Christmas Carols)* for female voices and instrumental ensemble (1958); *9 cantigas de amigo* for voice and chamber ensemble (1964); *6 cantos Sefardins (Sephardite Songs)* for voice and orch. (1971); choruses; songs.

CHAMBER MUSIC: *Estudo-Humoresca* for flute, oboe, clarinet, 2 violins, viola and cello (1930); 2 violin sonatinas (1931, revised 1951; 1931, revised 1970); Piano Quartet (1939, revised 1963); *Prelúdio, Capricho e Galope* for violin and piano (1941, revised 1951); *Página esquecida (Forgotten Leaf)* for cello and piano (1955); *Pequeno Tríptico* for violin and piano (1960); *Prelúdio e Fuga* for solo violin (1961); *Canto de Amor e de Morte* for piano quintet (1961); *4 Invençoēs* for solo cello (1961); String Quartet (1964); *Suite Rústica No. 2* for string quartet (1965); *14 Anotaçoēs (14 Annotations)* for string quartet (1966); *7 Souvenirs for Vieira da Silva* for wind quintet (1966); *The Tomb of Villa-Lobos* for wind quintet (1970); *3 Inflorescências* for solo cello (1973); *3 Capriccetti* for flute and guitar (1975); *2 Airs* for solo flute (1976); *2 Movements* for solo flute (1977). FOR PIANO: 5 sonatas (1934; 1939, revised 1956; 1952; 1961; 1977); *8 Bagatelles* (1939-48; No. 4, 1950); *Glosas (Glosses,* 1950); *24 Preludes* (1950-55); *Album do jovem pianista (Album for a Young Pianist,* 1953-63); *Duas sonatinas recuperadas (2 Restored Sonatinas,* 194?; rewritten, 1960); *In Memoriam Béla Bartók,* 8 progressive suites (1960-75); *4 Impromptus* (1961); *Piano Music for Children* (1968-76); *4 Pieces* for harpsichord (1970-71). FOR GUITAR: *Prelúdio e baileto* (1968), *Partita* (1970-71), and Sonatina (1974). He published about 25 books, including *Música e músicos modernos* (Oporto, 1943); *Dicionário de Música* (with Borba, Lisbon: Vol. 1, 1956; Vol. 2, 1958) and *Escritos Musicológicos* (Lisbon, 1977); biographies of Mozart, Chopin, Bartók; essay on Portuguese music. In 1960 he edited, with Michel Giacometti, the first vol. of the *Antologia da Música Regional Portuguesa,* the first attempt to collect, in a systematic way, the regional songs of Portugal.

BIBLIOGRAPHY: M. V. Henriques, *Fernando Lopes Graça na música portuguesa contemporanea* (Sacavém, 1956).

Lopez, Vincent, American jazz pianist, composer and bandleader; b. Brooklyn, Dec. 30, 1894; d. North Miami Beach, Florida, Sept. 20, 1975. His father, of Portuguese ancestry, a bandmaster in the U.S. Navy, taught Lopez the rudiments of music. However, he sent him to St. Mary's Passionist Monastery in the hope that he would become a Roman Catholic priest. But Lopez turned to music, and as a teenager played in the beer halls of Brooklyn. Later he led restaurant orchestras in New York. On Nov. 27, 1921 he inaugurated a regular broadcasting hour of dance band music over the radio station WJX in Newark, on which he popularized the song *Nola,* using it as a signature, opening with a greeting, "Hello, everybody . . . Lopez speaking." He had the first sustaining television show, *Dinner Date with Lopez,* which featured show business personalities. Among his song hits were *Rockin' Chair Swing, Knock, Knock, Who's There?,* and *The*

World Stands Still. He also gave lectures on numerology and related pseudo-sciences.

López-Buchardo, Carlos, Argentine composer; b. Buenos Aires, Oct. 12, 1881; d. there, April 21, 1948. He studied piano and harmony in Buenos Aires; composition with Albert Roussel in Paris; became director of the National Cons. in Buenos Aires. His music is set in a vivid style, rooted in national folksong; particularly successful in this respect is his symph. suite, *Escenas Argentinas* (Buenos Aires, Aug. 12, 1922, under Felix Weingartner). Other works are: the opera *El Sueño de Alma* (Buenos Aires, Aug. 4, 1914; won the Municipal Prize); lyric comedies, *Madame Lynch* (1932), *La Perichona* (1933), *Amalia* (1935); several piano pieces in Argentine folk manner; songs.

Lo Presti, Ronald, American composer; b. Williamstown, Mass., Oct. 28, 1933. He studied composition with Louis Mennini and Bernard Rogers at the Eastman School of Music in Rochester, N.Y. (M.M., 1956); subsequently was engaged as a clarinet teacher in public schools; in 1964 was appointed instructor in music theory at Arizona State Univ. at Tempe. He obtained popular success with his score *The Masks* which was commissioned for the space exhibit at the aerospace building at the Smithsonian Institute.
WORKS: a 1-act opera *The Birthday* (1962; Winfield, May 1962); a children's opera *Playback* (Tucson, Arizona, Dec. 18, 1970); *The Masks* for orch. (Rochester, N.Y., May 8, 1955); *Nocturne* for small orch. (1955–56); *Nocturne* for viola and string orch. (1959); *Kansas Overture* (1960); *Kanza Suite* for orch. (1961); *Llano Estacado (The Staked Plain)* for orch. (1961); *Port Triumphant* for orch. (1962); 2 symphonies (1966, 1968); *From the Southwest* for orch. (1967); *Rhapsody* for marimba, vibraphone and orch. (1975). For voice: *Alleluia* for chorus, brass and timpani (1960); *Kanza* for 4 narrators, chorus and orch. (1961); *Tribute* for chorus, and orch. and/or band (1962); *Scarecrow* for children's ballet company, mixed voices and cello orch. (1973); *Ode to Independence* for baritone, chorus and band (1974); *Requiem* for chorus and orch. (1975); *Memorials* for chorus and orch. (1975); choruses; songs. For symph. band: *Pageant* (1956); *Prelude* (1959); *Introduction, Chorale and Jubilee* (1961); *Tundra* (1967); *A Festive Music* (1968). Chamber music: *Suite* for 8 horns (1952); *Sketch* for percussion (1956); *Suite* for 4 horns (1958); *5 Pieces* for violin and piano (1960); *Scherzo* for violin quartet (1960); *Chorale* for 3 tubas (1960); *Fanfare* for 38 brasses (1960); *Requiescat* for brass ensemble (1961); *Suite* for 5 trumpets (1961); *Miniature* for brass quartet (1962); *Rondo* for timpani and piano (1969); Trio for 3 percussionists (1971); String Quartet (1970); *Suite* for 6 bassoons (1971); Fantasy for 5 horns (1972); *Cantalena* for cello orch. (1972); Wind Quintet (1975).

Lorentz, Alfred, German composer and conductor; b. Strasbourg, March 7, 1872; d. Karlsruhe, April 23, 1931. He studied with Rheinberger in Munich (composition), and with Mottl at Karlsruhe (conducting). He was chorusmaster, and later conductor, at the Municipal Theater in Strasbourg; from 1899 to 1925, was court conductor in Karlsruhe. He wrote the operas *Der Mönch von Sendomir* (Karlsruhe, 1907), *Die beiden Automaten* (Karlsruhe, 1913), *Liebesmacht* (Karlsruhe, 1922), *Schneider Fips* (Coburg, 1928), and an operetta, *Die Mondscheindame* (Karlsruhe, 1919); also some orchestral works.

Lorenz, Alfred Ottokar, Austrian musicologist, composer, and conductor; b. Vienna, July 11, 1868; d. Munich, Nov. 20, 1939. He studied at the Univ. of Vienna with Spitta; conducted opera at Königsberg and Elberfeld (1894–97), and at Coburg-Gotha (1898–1916); from 1920, lived in Munich; lectured at Munich Univ. from 1923. He made a specialty of Wagnerian research; publ. the comprehensive work *Das Geheimnis der Form bei Richard Wagner,* in 4 vols.: *Die musikalische Formgebung in Richard Wagners Ring des Nibelungen* (1924), *Der musikalische Aufbau von Tristan und Isolde* (1926), *Die Meistersinger* (1930), *Parsifal* (1933); the musical architecture and form of the operas are here analyzed in minute detail. He further publ. *Alessandro Scarlattis Jugendoper* (1927); *Abendländische Musikgeschichte im Rhythmus der Generationen* (1928), and numerous smaller essays in various music magazines, on Bach, Mozart, Beethoven, Weber, Wagner, Richard Strauss, etc. He composed an opera, *Helges Erwachen* (Schwerin, 1896); incidental music to various plays; the symph. poems *Bergfahrt* and *Columbus;* some chamber music; and songs.

Lorenz, Franz, Austrian writer on music; b. Stein, April 4, 1805; d. Vienna, April 8, 1883. He was a physician by profession; took great interest in music, and publ. valuable pamphlets on Mozart: *In Sachen Mozarts* (Vienna, 1851), *Mozart als Klavier-Komponist* (Breslau, 1866); numerous articles in Vienna newspapers and magazines.

Lorenz, Julius, German composer; b. Hannover, Oct. 1, 1862; d. Glogau, Oct. 1, 1924. He was a pupil of Reinecke and Jadassohn at the Leipzig Cons.; from 1884–95, he conducted the singing academy at Glogau; in 1895 he settled in New York as choral conductor; led the singing society "Arion"; in 1911, returned to Glogau. He wrote an opera, *Die Rekruten;* many choral works, both sacred and secular; and some chamber music.

Lorenz, Karl Adolf, German composer; b. Köslin, Aug. 13, 1837; d. Stettin, March 3, 1923. He studied music in Berlin with Dehn, Kiel, and Gehrig; also at Berlin Univ. (Dr. phil., 1861). He settled in Stettin, becoming conductor of the symph. concerts of the Lehrer-Gesangverein; succeeded Loewe as municipal director of music; founded the Stettiner Musikverein (for oratorio).
WORKS: the secular oratorios *Otto der Grosse, Winfried, Krösus, Die Jungfrau von Orleans, Das Licht;* a passion cantata, *Golgotha;* 2 operas, *Die Komödie der Irrungen* and *Harald und Theano;* a symphony; a piano trio; etc.
BIBLIOGRAPHY: K. König, *Karl Adolph Lorenz* (Stettin, 1937).

Lorenz, Max, German tenor; b. Düsseldorf, May 17, 1901; d. Salzburg, Jan. 11, 1975. He studied with Grenzebach; sang with the Dresden Opera; made his American debut with the Metropolitan Opera Co., N.Y., as Walther in *Die Meistersinger* (N.Y., Nov. 12, 1931). From 1934 to 1939 he sang in Berlin and in Vienna; joined the Chicago Opera for one season; also made appearances in London, at La Scala, Milan, and at the Paris Opéra. He sang the roles of Tristan and Siegfried at the Bayreuth Festival (1933, 1942, 1952).

Lorenzani, Paolo, Italian composer; b. Rome, 1640; d. there, Oct. 28, 1713. He was a pupil of Orazio Benevoli at the Vatican; having failed to obtain Benevoli's position after the latter's death in 1672, he was given the post of maestro di cappella at the Jesuit College in Rome; then held a similar position at the Cathedral of Messina; when Sicily was captured by the French, the Duc de Vivonne, who was the French viceroy, induced Lorenzani to go to Paris (1678); he found favor with Louis XIV, and became court musician; in 1679 he was sent to Italy to recruit singers for the French court; he produced his Italian pastoral, *Nicandro e Fileno,* at Fontainebleau (1681); from 1679–83 he was sur-intendant of music to the Queen; when the Queen died (1683) he became choirmaster at the Italian religious order of Théatins in Paris. For several years Lorenzani was supported by the Paris faction opposed to Lully; after Lully's death, Lorenzani produced an opera with a French libretto, *Orontée* (Paris, Aug. 23, 1687). This having failed, Lorenzani turned to the composition of motets, which proved his best works; the famous Paris publisher Ballard brought them out in an impressively printed edition; Ballard also publ. a book of Italian airs by Lorenzani. In 1694 he returned to Italy, and was appointed maestro of the Cappella Giulia at St. Peter's, the post that he had tried unsuccessfully to secure in 1672; there he remained until his death. His printed works include 25 motets for 1–5 voices (Paris, 1693); 6 Italian airs (Paris, 1690), and several separate vocal numbers; Henry Prunières reproduced a scene from Lorenzani's opera *Nicandro e Fileno* in the *Revue Musicale* (Aug. 1922).
BIBLIOGRAPHY: M. Brenet, *Les Concerts en France sous l'ancien régime* (Paris, 1900); Henry Prunières, *L'Opéra italien en France avant Lulli* (Paris, 1913); Henry Prunières, "Paolo Lorenzani à la cour de France," *Revue Musicale* (Aug. 1922).

Lorenzi-Fabris, Ausonio de, Italian composer; b. Montebelluna, Jan. 18, 1861; d. Venice, July 30, 1935. He studied at the Liceo Benedetto Marcello in Venice. He composed the operas *Gli Adorati del fuoco* (Venice, Jan. 27, 1891), *Maometto II* (Venice, July 9, 1892; revised, Florence, May 9, 1903), *Il re si annoia* (Trieste, Dec. 19, 1904); and a religious play *Refugium Peccatorum* (Venice, March 24, 1897).

Lorenzo, Leonardo de, Italian flutist; b. Viggiano, Aug. 29, 1875; d. Santa Barbara, Calif., July 27, 1962. He studied at the Naples Cons.; from 1897 to 1907, was flutist in various traveling orchestras. In 1910 he emigrated to the U.S.; was 1st flutist of the N.Y. Philharmonic (1910–12); later with the Minneapolis Symph. Orch., the Los Angeles Philharmonic, and the Rochester Philharmonic; taught flute at the Eastman School of Music in Rochester; in 1935, settled in California. He publ. several books of flute studies and some solo pieces, and an informative book on flute playing and flute players, *My Complete Story of the Flute* (N.Y., 1951).

Loriod, Yvonne, French pianist; b. Houilles, Jan. 20, 1924. She studied at the Paris Cons. with Lazar Lévy and composition with Messiaen and Milhaud. She toured as a concert pianist in Germany and Austria; made her American debut in 1949 as piano soloist in Messiaen's work *Turangalila.* She subsequently joined the faculty of the Paris Cons.

Lortzing, (Gustav) Albert, celebrated German opera composer; b. Berlin, Oct. 23, 1801; d. there, Jan. 21, 1851. His parents were actors, and the wandering life led by the family did not allow him to pursue a methodical course of study. He learned acting from his father, and music from his mother at an early age. After some lessons with Rungenhagen in Berlin, he continued his own study, and soon began to compose songs. At the age of 21 he married the actress Rosina Regina Ahles in Cologne; they had 11 children. In 1824 he wrote his first opera (to his own libretto), *Ali Pascha von Janina,* which, however, was not produced until 4 years later (Münster, Feb. 1, 1828). In 1832 he brought out 2 vaudevilles, *Der Pole und sein Kind* and *Scenen aus Mozarts Leben,* which were well received on several German stages. From 1833 to 1844 he was engaged at the Municipal Theater of Leipzig as a tenor; there he launched a light opera, *Die beiden Schützen* (Feb. 20, 1837), which became instantly popular; on the same stage he produced on Dec. 22, 1837, his undoubted masterpiece, *Czaar und Zimmermann* (later spelling, *Zar und Zimmermann*), to his own libretto derived from various French plays, and based on the true history of Peter the Great of Russia, who worked as a carpenter in Holland. The opera was produced in Berlin in 1839, and from then on its success was assured; after a few years it became a favorite on most European stages. Lortzing's next opera, *Caramo, oder Das Fischerstechen* (Leipzig, Sept. 20, 1839), was a failure; there followed *Hans Sachs* (Leipzig, June 23, 1840) and *Casanova* (Leipzig, Dec. 31, 1841), which passed without much notice; subsequent comparisons showed some similarities between *Hans Sachs* and *Die Meistersinger,* not only in subject matter, which was derived from the same source, but also in some melodic patterns; however, no one seriously suggested that Wagner was influenced by Lortzing's inferior work. There followed a romantic opera, *Der Wildschütz* (Leipzig, Dec. 31, 1842), which was in many respects the best that Lortzing wrote, but its success, although impressive, never equalled that of *Zar und Zimmermann.* At about the same time, Lortzing attempted still another career, that of opera impresario, but it was short-lived; his brief conductorship at the Leipzig Opera was similarly ephemeral. Composing remained his chief occupation; he produced *Undine* in Magdeburg (April 21, 1845) and *Der Waffenschmied* in Vienna (May 31, 1846). In Vienna he also acted as conductor; after a season or two at the Theater an der Wien, he returned to Leipzig, where he produced the light opera *Zum Grossadmiral* (Dec. 13, 1847), which was only moderately successful. The revolutionary events of 1848 seriously affected his positions both in Leipzig and Vienna; after the political situation became settled, he produced in Leipzig an opera of a romantic nature, *Rolands Knappen* (May 25, 1849). Although at least 4 of his operas were played at various German theaters, Lortzing received no honorarium, owing to a flaw in the regulations protecting the rights of composers. He was compelled to travel again as an actor, but could not earn enough money to support his large family left behind in Vienna. In the spring of 1850 he was engaged as musical director at a small theater in Berlin; on Jan. 20, 1851 his last opera, *Die Opernprobe*, was produced in Frankfurt, while he was on his deathbed in Berlin; he died the next day. His opera *Regina, oder die Marodeure*, written in 1848, was edited by Richard Kleinmichel, with the composer's libretto revised by Adolf L'Arronge, and performed in Berlin on March 21, 1899; another opera, *Der Weihnachtsabend*, was not produced. Lortzing also wrote an oratorio, *Die Himmelfahrt Christi;* some incidental music to various plays, and songs. But it is as composer of characteristically Germanic Romantic operas that Lortzing holds a distinguished, if minor, place in the history of dramatic music. He was a follower of Weber, without Weber's imaginative projection; in his lighter works, he approached the type of French operetta; in his best creations he exhibited a fine sense of facile melody, and infectious rhythm; his harmonies, though unassuming, were always proper and pleasing; his orchestration, competent and effective.

BIBLIOGRAPHY: P. J. Düringer, *Albert Lortzing, sein Leben und Wirken* (Leipzig, 1851); G. R. Kruse, *Albert Lortzing* (Berlin, 1899; standard biography); R. Bürner, *Albert Lortzing in Detmold* (Detmold, 1900); G. R. Kruse, *Lortzings Briefe* (Leipzig, 1902; augmented ed., 1913; 3rd ed., 1947); H. Wittmann, *Lortzing* (Leipzig, 1902); H. Laue, *Die Operndichtung Lortzings* (Bonn, 1932; a valuable analysis); H. Killer, *Albert Lortzing* (Potsdam, 1938); O. Schumann, *Albert Lortzing, sein Leben in Bildern* (Berlin, 1941); E. W. Böhme, *Albert Lortzing in Lüneburg* (1951); J. Knodt, *Albert Lortzing* (1955).

Löschhorn, Albert, German pianist, composer and pedagogue; b. Berlin, June 27, 1819; d. there, June 4, 1905. He studied at the Royal Institute for Church Music with L. Berger, Killitschgy, Grell, and A. W. Bach; became piano teacher there in 1851. He publ. a series of excellent piano studies, including *Melodious Studies, La Vélocité, Universal Studies, Le Trille, School of Octaves*, which became standard pedagogical works; also wrote attractive piano solos, *La Belle Amazone, 4 Pièces élégantes, Tarentelle, Deux Valses*, the barcarolle *À Venise*, and *Trois Mazurkas;* suites, sonatas, sonatinas, etc. With J. Weiss he publ. a *Wegweiser in die Pianoforte-Literatur* (1862; 2nd ed., 1885 as *Führer durch die Klavierliteratur*).

Lotti, Antonio, Italian organist and composer; b. Venice, c.1667; d. there, Jan. 5, 1740. He was a pupil of Legrenzi in Venice; produced an opera, *Giustino*, at the age of 16; in 1687 he became chorister at San Mar-

co; in 1690, assistant organist there, and in 1692, 2nd organist. On Aug. 17, 1704 he was appointed 1st organist; in 1736 he was elected maestro di cappella. While at San Marco, he industriously composed church music, Masses, anthems, etc.; he also wrote dramatic music. As a teacher, he was highly renowned; among his pupils were Alberti, Gasparini, Galuppi, and Marcello. He absented himself from Venice but once (1717–19), when he went to Dresden at the Crown Prince's invitation.

WORKS: 21 operas, including *Alessandro Severo* (Venice, Dec. 26, 1716), *Giove in Argo* (Dresden, Oct. 25, 1717), *Teofane* (Dresden, Nov. 13, 1719), *Costantino* (Vienna, Nov. 19, 1716; in collaboration with Fux and Caldara); 4 oratorios: *Il voto crudele, L'umiltà coronata, Gioa re di Giuda*, and *Giuditta;* many Masses, motets, etc., none of which were publ. by him. Lück's *Sammlung ausgezeichneter Compositionen* contains 4 Masses and other numbers; Rochlitz, Proske, Trautwein, Commer, Schlesinger, and others have printed Misereres and other sacred music by Lotti; 8 Masses were edited by H. Müller in the *Denkmäler deutscher Tonkunst* 60. During Lotti's lifetime his only work published was *Duetti, terzetti e madrigali a più voci* (Venice, 1705, dedicated to Joseph I; includes the madrigal, *In una siepe ombrosa*, the appropriation of which caused Bononcini's downfall).

BIBLIOGRAPHY: Charlotte Spitz, *Antonio Lotti in seiner Bedeutung als Opernkomponist* (Leipzig, 1918); Charlotte Spitz, "Ottone von Händel und *Teofane* von Lotti," in *Sandberger-Festschrift;* A. Moser, "Arcangelo Corelli und Antonio Lotti: Zwei künstlerische Ehrenrettungen," *Zeitschrift für Musik* (April 1921); A. Schering, *Geschichte des Oratoriums* (p. 202ff.). The correspondence regarding the controversy with Bononcini was reproduced in *Letters from the Academy of Ancient Music at London to Signor Antonio Lotti of Venice with his Answers and Testimonials* (London, 1732); the case was described in the article "The Fall of Bononcini," *Musical Times* (Jan. 1892).

Lotze, Rudolf Hermann, German writer on music; b. Bautzen, May 21, 1817; d. Berlin, July 1, 1881. He became prof. of philosophy at Leipzig Univ. in 1842; in 1844, prof. in ordinary, and court councillor, at Göttingen; settled in Berlin shortly before his death. He publ. *Geschichte der Ästhetik in Deutschland* (1868), which contains criticism of Helmholtz, Hauptmann, and others; also interesting ideas on musical esthetics.

Loudová, Ivana, Czech composer; b. Chlumec nad Cidlinou, March 8, 1941. She studied composition with Kabeláč at the Prague Cons. (1958–61) and with Hlobil at the Prague Academy of Arts (1961–66); in 1971 she went to Paris where she took lessons with Messiaen and André Jolivet. Her music is richly dissonant and impressionistically colorful.

WORKS: *Fantasy* for orch. (1961); Concerto for Chamber Orch. (1962); Symph. No. 1 (1964); Symph. No. 2 for contralto, chorus and orch. (1965); *Spleen (Hommage à Charles Baudelaire)* for orch. (1971); *Chorale* for wind orch., percussion and organ (1971); *Hymnos* for wind orch. and percussion (1972); Concerto for Orch. (1974); Violin Sonata (1960–61); Clarinet Sonata (1963); String Quartet (1964); *Per tromba,*

5 studies for solo trumpet (1969); *Agamemnon* for solo percussionist (1973); *Romeo and Juliet,* suite for flute, 2 violins, cello and harp (1973); a children's cantata, *Le Petit Prince,* after Saint-Exupéry (1967); *Gnomai* for soprano, flute and harp (1970).

Louel, Jean, Belgian composer and conductor; b. Ostend, Jan. 3, 1914. He studied at the Ghent Cons. with Joseph Ryelandt (composition) and at the Brussels Cons. with Joseph Jongen (theory) and Désiré Defauw (conducting); then went to Paris to study conducting with Eugene Bigot and Paul Paray. He was director of music academies in Alost (1945–49) and Anderlecht (1949–56); in 1956 became inspector of music schools in Flemish Belgium. He obtained the Belgian Prix de Rome in 1943 for his cantata *La Navigation d'Ulysse.*
WORKS: *Fantaisie sur 2 Chanson de Trouvères* for orch. (1942); *Suite* for chamber orch. or piano (1942); *Burlesque* for bassoon and orch. (1943); *March funèbre* and *Triomfmarch* for orch. (both in 1945); 2 piano concertos (1945, 1949); *Concerto da camera* for flute and orch. (1946–47); 2 violin concertos (1950, 1971); Symphony No. 2 for string orch. (1968; his youthful Symph. No. 1 had been withdrawn); *Toccata and Fugue* for winds (1974); Clarinet Sonata (1935); Brass Trio (1951); *Theme and Variations* for violin and piano (1953); *Sonatina* for 2 violins and piano (1955); Wind Quintet (1958); Violin Sonata (1960); *Suite* for flute, cello, vibraphone and harp (1967); *Invention* for solo horn (1973).

Louis Ferdinand, Prince of Prussia, nephew of **Frederick the Great;** b. Friedrichsfelde, near Berlin, Nov. 18, 1772; fell at Saalfeld, Oct. 10, 1806. He was an excellent amateur musician. While traveling in 1804, he met Beethoven, and showed great interest in the master's music. Beethoven's 3rd Piano Concerto in C minor is dedicated to Louis Ferdinand, which testifies to their mutual esteem. However, the statement sometimes made that Louis Ferdinand imitated Beethoven in his own works is untenable inasmuch as the Prince fell in battle two years after his first acquaintance with Beethoven's music. The following compositions by Louis Ferdinand are published: 2 piano quintets; 2 piano quartets; 4 piano trios; Octet for clarinet, 2 horns, 2 violins, 2 cellos, and piano; *Notturno* for flute, violin, cello, and piano; *Andante and Variations* for viola, cello, and piano; *Rondo* for piano and orch., and a *Rondo* for piano solo. H. Kretzschmar edited his Collected Works (Leipzig, 1915–17).
BIBLIOGRAPHY: Elisabeth Wintzer, *Louis Ferdinand, als Mensch und Musiker* (1916); H. Wahl, *Prinz Louis Ferdinand von Preussen* (1917); F. Lewald, *Prinz Louis Ferdinand* (1929); A. Semrau, *Prinz Louis Ferdinand* (1930); R. Hahn, *Louis Ferdinand* (Breslau, 1934); E. Poseck, *Prinz Louis Ferdinand* (Berlin, 1938; 2nd ed., 1943).

Louis XIII, King of France from 1610 to 1643. He was an amateur musician, and wrote madrigals. The well known *Amaryllis,* arranged by Henri Ghis, and widely published as "Air of Louis XIII," is a misattribution; the melody first appears in print as "La Clochette" in the *Ballet-Comique de la Reine* by Balthazar de Beau-

joyeux, produced in 1582, long before Louis XIII was born. A gavotte, also entitled *Amaryllis,* with a melody totally different from the apocryphal "Air of Louis XIII" and dated 1620, may be an authentic composition of Louis XIII.

Louis, Rudolf, German writer on music; b. Schwetzingen, Jan. 30, 1870; d. Munich, Nov. 15, 1914. He studied philosophy at the Universities of Geneva and Vienna (Dr. phil., 1894); music with Klose and Mottl; was conductor at the State Theater in Landshut (1895–96), and in Lübeck (1896–97); in 1897, settled in Munich, where he became critic for the influential periodical, *Neueste Nachrichten* (from 1900).
WRITINGS: *Der Widerspruch in der Musik* (1893); *Richard Wagner als Musikästhetiker* (1897); *Die Weltanschauung Richard Wagners* (1898); *Franz Liszt* (1900); *Hector Berlioz* (1904); *Anton Bruckner* (1905); *Die deutsche Musik der Gegenwart* (1909; 3rd ed., 1912); *Aufgaben für den Unterricht in der Harmonielehre* (1911); with L. Thuille he wrote *Harmonielehre* (1907; 8th ed., 1924; abridged as *Grundriss der Harmonielehre,* 1908). He was also a composer; publ. a symph. fantasy, *Proteus* (1903); *Zum Hochzeitstage* and *Albumblatt* for piano, 4-hands; songs.

Loulié, Étienne, 17th-century French writer on music; inventor of the "chronomètre," the precursor of the metronome; place and date of birth unknown: d. Paris, 1702. He studied with Gehenault and Ouvrard under the patronage of Mlle. de Guise; was at the Saint-Chapelle in Paris from 1663–73. He publ. *Éléments ou principes de musique dans un nouvel ordre . . . avec l'estampe et l'usage du chronomètre* (Paris, 1696), which describes and illustrates his invention, an unwieldy device 6 feet tall; and a *Nouveau système de musique* (1698), describing the "sonomètre" (a monochord to aid in tuning), which he also invented.

Lourié, Arthur (Vincent), Russian composer; b. St. Petersburg, May 14, 1892; d. Princeton, N.J., Oct. 13, 1966. He studied at the St. Petersburg Cons.; participated in various modernistic groups, and wrote piano music, influenced by Scriabin (*Préludes fragiles, Synthèses,* etc.); experimented in futuristic composition (e.g., *Formes en l'air,* dedicated to Picasso, and graphically imitating a cubist design by omitting the staves instead of using rests); also composed religious music (*Lamentations de la Vierge,* etc.). After the Soviet Revolution, he was appointed chief of the music dept. of the Commissariat for Public Instruction; in 1921 he left Russia, and lived in Paris; in 1941, emigrated to the U.S., and became an American citizen. In his music written after 1920 he followed mainly Stravinsky's practice of stylizing old forms, secular and sacred.
WORKS: *Nash Marsh (Our March,* poem by Mayakovsky), for declamation with piano (1918); *La Naissance de la beauté,* cantata for a chorus of 6 sopranos, soprano solo, and piano (1922); *Dithyrambes* for flute solo (1923); *Liturgical Sonata,* for orch., piano, and chorus (1928); *Concerto Spirituale,* for piano, chorus, and double basses (N.Y., March 26, 1930); *Sinfonia Dialectica* (Symph. No. 1; Philadelphia, April 17, 1931); *Kormtschaya* (Symph. No. 2; Boston, Nov. 7,

1941); *The Feast During the Plague,* opera-ballet after Pushkin (1935; arranged for soprano solo, mixed chorus, and orch.; Boston, Jan. 5, 1945); *De ordinatione angelorum,* for chorus (1948); *Piano Gosse* (1917; republished in N.Y., 1944 under the title *8 Scenes of Russian Childhood*); 2 pieces for piano: *Berceuse de la chevrette* (1936) and *A Phoenix Park Nocturne* (1938); *The Mime* for solo clarinet (1956); *Concerto da Camera* for violin solo and string orch. (1957); *The Blackamoor of Peter the Great,* opera (1961). He published a biography of Koussevitzky (N.Y., 1931).

BIBLIOGRAPHY: "The Music of Arthur Lourié," *Ramparts* (Menlo Park, Calif., Jan. 1965); D. Gojowy, "Zwölftontechnik in Russland," *Melos* (May–June 1972).

Løveberg, Aase (*née* **Nordmo**), Norwegian soprano; b. Målselv, June 10, 1923, in a peasant family; spent her childhood on a farm near the Arctic Circle. When she was 19 she went to Oslo, where she studied voice with Haldis Ingebjart; made her opera debut in Oslo on Dec. 3, 1948; then sang in Stockholm, Vienna, Paris, and London. She made her 1st American appearance as soloist with the Philadelphia Orch. (Dec. 6, 1957).

Løvenskjold, Herman Severin, Norwegian organist and composer; b. Holdensjärnbruk, July 30, 1815; d. Copenhagen, Dec. 5, 1870. At the age of 13 his parents took him to Copenhagen, where he studied music; in 1836 brought out his ballet *Sylphiden* there with much success. After the production of his second ballet, *Sara,* in 1839, he went to Vienna, where he took some lessons with Seyfried; returned to Denmark in 1851; was appointed organist at the Slottskyrka in Christiansborg. He wrote an opera, *Turandot* (Copenhagen, Dec. 3, 1854); *Festouvertüre* (for the coronation of Christian VIII); *Ouverture de concert idyllique;* the overture *Fra Skoven ved Fureso;* Piano Trio; Piano Quartet; piano pieces for 2 and 4 hands.

Lover, Samuel, Irish novelist, poet, painter, and composer; b. Dublin, Feb. 24, 1797; d. St. Heliers, Jersey, July 6, 1868. He wrote music to several Irish plays, and to many songs; publ. *Songs and Ballads* (London, 1859). Among his most popular songs (some of which are set to old Irish tunes) are *The Angel's Whisper, Molly Bawn,* and *The Low-Backed Car.* He wrote an opera, *Grana Uile, or the Island Queen* (Dublin, Feb. 9, 1832). He devised a very successful musical entertainment, *Irish Evenings* (1844), with which he toured the British Isles, also the U.S. (1846). He was **Victor Herbert's** grandfather.

Löw, Joseph, Bohemian pianist and composer; b. Prague, Jan. 23, 1834; d. there, Oct. 5, 1886. In 1854 he toured through Moravia, Silesia, Galicia, and the Bukovina; returning to Prague in 1856, he was active as a concert pianist and composer. He publ. over 450 numbers of light piano music, including *Jugend-Album; Deux Impromptus romantiques; Allegro brillant* for 2 pianos; *Soir de printemps; Maiengruss,* etc.

Löwe, Ferdinand, Austrian conductor; b. Vienna, Feb. 19, 1865; d. there, Jan. 6, 1925. He studied with Dachs, Krenn, and Bruckner at the Vienna Cons.; then taught piano and choral singing there (1883–96). In 1897 he became conductor of the Kaim Orch. in Munich; then of the court opera in Vienna (1898–1900); of the Gesellschaftskonzerte (1900–04); in 1904 he became conductor of the newly organized Vienna Konzertverein Orch., which he made one of the finest instrumental bodies in Europe; returned to Munich as conductor of the Konzertverein (1908–14), which comprised members of the former Kaim Orch.; also conducted in Budapest and Berlin; from 1919–22, was head of the Vienna Staatsakademie für Musik. He was a friend and trusted disciple of Bruckner; edited (somewhat liberally) several of Bruckner's works even during the master's lifetime; conducted the 3 finished movements of Bruckner's posthumous 9th Symphony (Vienna, Feb. 11, 1903), with considerable cuts and alterations, adding Bruckner's *Te Deum* in lieu of the unfinished finale.

Löwe, Karl. See **Loewe, Carl.**

Lowens, Irving, eminent American musicologist, librarian and music critic; b. New York, Aug. 19, 1916. He studied at Teachers College, Columbia Univ. (B.S. in Music, 1939); Univ. of Maryland (Ph.D. in American Civilization, 1965). In 1953 he joined the music staff of the *Washington Star;* in 1961 became its chief music critic. From 1959 to 1966 he served as librarian in the Music Division of the Library of Congress in Washington; was president of the American Music Critics Association (1971–75); member of numerous musicological societies; in 1962 was recipient of a travel grant to Germany given by the American Council of Learned Societies; was sole American representative at the Enesco Festival in Bucharest (1970). In 1977 he joined the staff of Peabody Cons. in Baltimore.

WRITINGS: *The Hartford Harmony: a Selection of American Hymns from the Late 18th and Early 19th Centuries* (Hartford, 1953); *Music and Musicians of Early America* (N.Y., 1964); *Source Readings in American Music History* (N.Y., 1966); *Lectures on the History and Art of Music at the Library of Congress, 1946-63* (N.Y., 1968); *A Bibliography of American Songsters Published before 1821* (Worcester, Mass., 1976); *Haydn in America* (Smithsonian Institution, Washington, 1977). He edited *An Introduction to the Singing of Psalm-Tunes, 1726* (Philadelphia, 1954); *Benjamin Carr's Federal Overture, 1794* (Philadelphia, 1957); *Sonneck-Upton, Bibliography of Early Secular American Music, 1945* (Philadelphia, 1964); *MacDowell's Critical and Historical Essays, 1912* (Philadelphia, 1969); *Kentucky Harmony, 1816* (Philadelphia, 1976); *A Bibliography of Songsters Printed in America Before 1821* (Philadelphia, 1976).

Lowinsky, Edward, eminent German-American musicologist; b. Stuttgart, Jan. 12, 1908. He studied at the Hochschule für Musik in Stuttgart and at the Univ. of Heidelberg (Dr. phil., 1933); emigrated to the U.S. and in 1947 became an American citizen. He occupied several important positions in American universities and colleges; was on the staff of Black Mountain College (1942–47); at Queens College (1949–52 and 1954–56), at the Institute for Advanced Study at Princeton Univ.

(1952–54); at the Univ. of California, Berkeley (1956–61), and at the Univ. of Chicago (1961–78). He is the editor-in-chief of *Monuments of Renaissance Music.*

WRITINGS: *Orlando di Lassos Antwerpener Motettenbuch* (The Hague, 1937); *Secret Chromatic Art in the Netherlands Motet* (N.Y., 1946); *Tonality and Atonality in Sixteenth-Century Music* (Berkeley, Calif., 1961).

Lowry, Robert, American hymn writer; b. Philadelphia, March 12, 1826; d. Plainfield, N.J., Nov. 25, 1899. He was a Baptist preacher and studied music in his middle age. His most popular hymn tune is *Something for Jesus.*

BIBLIOGRAPHY: R. G. McCutchan, *Our Hymnody* (N.Y., 1937).

Lowtzky, Hermann, Russian composer; b. Kamenetz-Podolsk, June 20, 1871; d. Zürich, Dec. 8, 1957. He studied law, philosophy and music; went to St. Petersburg in 1899 and enrolled in Rimsky-Korsakov's class at the Conservatory there. He moved to Switzerland in 1910. His music preserves the Russian elements of style and idiom. Among his published works are the opera *Lucretia* to his own libretto (Kiev, Dec. 18, 1912); Piano Trio (1905); and a cantata *Paradies und Peri.* In manuscript are an opera *Mozart* and *Kol Nidre* for cello and orch.

Loy, Max, German conductor and composer; b. Nuremberg, June 18, 1913. He studied piano and composition at the Nuremberg Cons. and at the Univ. of Erlangen (Dr. phil., 1938). Since 1938 he was conductor of the Nuremberg Opera; in 1971 became its general musical director; also traveled as pianist-accompanist to celebrated singers (Erna Sack, Sigrid Onegin, Patzak, etc.). In 1965 he was guest conductor in Los Angeles and elsewhere in the U.S.; also conducted in Japan. He composed a piano concerto, 5 string quartets, a piano quintet and songs.

Lualdi, Adriano, Italian composer, conductor and critic; b. Larino, Campobasso, March 22, 1885; d. Milan, Jan. 8, 1971. He studied composition with Falchi in Rome and Wolf-Ferrari in Venice; began his musical career as an opera conductor; in 1918 went to Milan, where he was active as a music critic and government administrator on musical affairs; from 1936 to 1943 he was director of the Cons. of San Pietro a Maiella in Naples; then was appointed director of the Florence Cons. (1947–56). He was a voluminous composer, excelling particularly in opera. His opera *Le nozze di Haura,* written in 1908, had a concert performance by the Radio Italiano on Oct. 15, 1939 and its first stage production in Rome on April 17, 1943. His subsequent operas were *La figlia del re,* after the *Antigone* of Sophocles (Turin, March 18, 1922); *Le furie d'Arlecchino* (Milan, May 10, 1915); *Il diavolo nel campanile* (La Scala, Milan, April 22, 1925), *La Granceola* (Venice, Sept. 10, 1932), *La Luna dei Caraibi,* one-act opera after O'Neill (Rome, Jan. 29, 1953); a mimodrama *Lumawig e la Saetta* (Rome, Jan. 23, 1937); *Il testamento di Euridice,* lyric tragedy (1939–52); a satiric radio comedy, *Tre alla radarstra-*totropojonosferaphonotheca del Luna Park (1953–58); the cantatas, *La Rosa di Saron* (1915; also titled as *Il cantico;* Milan, May 10, 1915); the symph. poems, *La Leggenda del vecchio marinaio* (1910) and *L'interludio del sogno* (1917); *Suite Adriatica* for orch. (1932); *Africa,* rhapsody for orch. (1936); *Divertimento* for orch. (1941); numerous choruses and minor pieces for various instruments. Lualdi was also an industrious writer on musical subjects. He publ. several volumes of reminiscences of his "musical voyages:" *Viaggio musicale italiano* (1931); *Viaggio musicale in Europa* (1928); *Viaggio musicale nel Sud-America* (Milan, 1934); *Viaggio musicale nel l'U.R.S.S.* (1941); also *L'Arte di dirigere l'orchestra* (1940); *Tutti vivi,* a collection of miscellaneous articles (Milan, 1955).

Lübeck, Ernst, Dutch pianist and composer; son of **Johann Heinrich Lübeck;** b. The Hague, Aug. 24, 1829; d. Paris, Sept. 17, 1876. He was trained as a pianist by his father; as a youth made a voyage to America, played concerts in the U.S., Mexico and Peru (1849–54); then returned to Europe and settled in Paris where he acquired the reputation of a virtuoso; Berlioz wrote enthusiastically about his playing. He became mentally unbalanced following the events of the Paris Commune of 1871; there his career ended. He wrote some pleasing salon pieces for piano, among them *Berceuse; Tarentelle; Polonaise; Trilby the Sprite: Rêverie caractéristique.*

Lübeck, Johann Heinrich, Dutch violinist and composer; b. Alphen, Feb. 11, 1799; d. The Hague, Feb. 7, 1865. He was a Prussian regimental musician (1813–15); studied music in Potsdam; then was a player in theater orchestras in Riga and Stettin; in 1823, settled in Holland, giving violin concerts. From 1827 until his death he was director of the Cons. of The Hague; was also conductor of the "Diligentia" concerts there, and in 1829, became court conductor.

Lübeck, Louis, Dutch cellist; son of **Johann Heinrich Lübeck;** b. The Hague, Feb. 14, 1838; d. Berlin, March 8, 1904. He studied with Jacquard in Paris; from 1863–68, taught cello at the Leipzig Cons.; toured Germany, Holland, England, and the U.S. (1875–81); in 1881 he settled in Berlin as cellist in the court orch. He wrote 2 concertos for cello, and solo pieces.

Lübeck, Vincentius (Vincenz), German organist and composer; b. Padingbüttel, Sept., 1654; d. Hamburg, Feb. 9, 1740. He was organist at Stade for almost 30 years; in 1702, became organist at the Nicolaikirche in Hamburg, remaining in that post until his death. Lübeck's works, including 3 cantatas, chorale preludes for organ, etc., were publ. by Gottlieb Harms (Klecken, 1921).

Luboshutz (real name **Luboshits**), **Léa,** Russian violinist; b. Odessa, Feb. 22, 1885; d. Philadelphia, March 18, 1965. She studied violin with her father; played in public at the age of 7; after study at the Odessa Music School, she went to the Moscow Cons., graduating with a gold medal (1903); gave concerts in Germany and France, and also took additional lessons from Eugène Ysaÿe in Belgium; returned to Russia, and organized a trio with her brother **Pierre** (piano) and sister **Anna** (cello); left Russia after the Revolution and lived in Berlin and Paris (1921–25). In 1925 she settled in New York; played the American première of Prokofiev's 1st Violin Concerto (Nov. 14, 1925); made several appearances in joint recitals with her son, **Boris Goldovsky**, pianist. From 1927, she was on the faculty of the Curtis Institute of Music.

Luboshutz, Pierre, Russian pianist; brother of **Léa Luboshutz;** b. Odessa, June 17, 1891; d. Rockport, Maine, April 17, 1971. He studied violin with his father; then turned to the piano, and entered the Moscow Cons. as a pupil of Igumnov, graduating in 1912; also studied in Paris with Edouard Risler; returning to Russia, he played in a trio with his two sisters, **Léa** (violin) and **Anna** (cello); in 1926 went to America as accompanist to Zimbalist, Piatigorsky, and others. In 1931 he married **Genia Nemenoff** (b. Paris, Oct. 23, 1905); with her he formed a piano duo (N.Y. debut, Jan. 18, 1937); as Luboshutz-Nemenoff, they gave annual concerts with considerable success. From 1962 to 1968, they headed the Piano Dept. at Michigan State Univ.; then returned to New York.

Lubrich, Fritz, Jr., German organist; son of **Fritz Lubrich, Sr.;** b. Neustädtel, Jan. 26, 1888; d. Hamburg, April 15, 1971. He received his early training from his father; then was a student of Straube in organ playing in Leipzig and of Max Reger in composition. From 1948 to 1952 he was the choir leader of the Hamburg Singakademie. He publ. several valuable articles on the history of choral organizations in Germany.

Lubrich, Fritz, Sr., German organist and writer on music; b. Bärsdorf, July 29, 1862; d. Eberswalde, March 29, 1952. He studied music in Breslau; was active as a church organist in various cities in Silesia. He edited several periodicals of Protestant Church music and publ. a number of valuable articles on Lutheran liturgy.

Lucantoni, Giovanni, Italian composer and singing teacher; b. Rieti, Jan. 18, 1825; d. Paris, May 30, 1902. He studied with his parents, who were both good amateur musicians; then with Giovanni Pacini in Lucca and Nicola Vaccaj in Milan. In 1857 he settled in Paris as a singing teacher; also lived in London. His vocal compositions were very popular for a time; particularly well known was the vocal duet *Una notte a Venezia;* he also wrote an opera, *Elisa* (Milan, June 20, 1850); a 4-part Mass; a cantata; a symphony; and various "ballabili" for piano.

Lucas, Leighton, English conductor and composer; b. London, Jan. 5, 1903. He was trained to be a dancer and for several years (1918–21) was a member of the Diaghilev Russian Ballet in Paris and in London. Then he learned conducting and traveled with various ballet companies. He also made arrangements of classical pieces for ballet and composed his own ballet scores, among them *The Wolf's Ride* (1935) and *The Horses* (1946). He also wrote some chamber music, including *Divertissement* for harp and 8 instruments

(1955), Clarinet Concerto (1956), *Disquisition* for 2 cellos and piano 4-hands (1967), String Trio (1969), etc. He publ. a pamphlet *Mini-Music* (London, 1967).

Lucas, Mary Anderson, English composer; b. London, May 24, 1882; d. there, Jan. 14, 1952. She studied piano at the Dresden Cons.; later took lessons in composition with R. O. Morris and Herbert Howells. She adopted an advanced harmonic style of composition; her works include a ballet, *Sawdust* (1941), which had considerable success; 6 string quartets; Trio for clarinet, viola, and piano; *Rhapsody* for flute, cello, and piano; and many songs.

Lucca, Pauline, Austrian soprano; b. Vienna, April 25, 1841; d. there, Feb. 28, 1908. She was a daughter of an Italian father and a German mother; she studied singing in Vienna and sang in the chorus of the Vienna Opera. Her professional debut took place in Olmütz as Elvira in *Ernani* on Sept. 4, 1859. Her appearance in Prague as Norma attracted the attention of Meyerbeer, who arranged her engagements in Berlin. In 1863 she sang in London with excellent success; in 1872 she made her first appearance in the U.S. Returning to Europe, she joined the staff of the Vienna Opera (1874–89); then retired from the stage. In her prime she was regarded as "prima donna assoluta," and her private life and recurring marriages and divorces were favorite subjects of sensational press stories; a curious promotional pamphlet, entitled *Bellicose Adventures of a Peaceable Prima Donna,* was publ. in New York, in 1872, presumably to whip up interest in her public appearances, but it concerned itself mainly with a melodramatic account of her supposed experiences during the Franco-Prussian War.
BIBLIOGRAPHY: Anna Mara-Jansen and D. Weisse-Zehrer, *Die Wiener Nachtigall; der Lebensweg der Pauline Lucca* (Berlin, 1935).

Luciani, Sebastiano Arturo, Italian musicologist; b. Acquaviva delle Fonti, June 9, 1884; d. there, Dec. 7, 1950. He studied in Naples and Rome; devoted his energies mainly to documentation of biographies of Italian composers. He published a monograph on Domenico Scarlatti (Turin, 1942); edited *Antonio Vivaldi: note e documenti sulla vita e sulla opere* (1939) and *La Scuola veneziana* (1940).

Lucier, Alvin, American composer; b. Nashua, N.H., May 14, 1931. He studied theory with Quincy Porter at Yale Univ. and with Arthur Berger, Irving Fine and Harold Shapero at Brandeis Univ.; also took a course with Lukas Foss at Tanglewood. He spent two years in Rome on a Fulbright Scholarship. Returning to America in 1962, he was appointed to the faculty at Brandeis Univ.
WORKS: In his works he exploits serial and electronic techniques. Among them are *Music for solo performer* (1965), derived from amplified electroencephalographic waves, which activate percussion instruments; *Whistlers,* depicting magnetic disturbances in the ionosphere; *Shelter 999,* amplifications of mini-sounds in the immediate environment with parietal filters; *Music for High Structures; Chambers,* derived from the noises of displaced objects; *Vespers,*

produced by acoustic orientation by means of echolocation; *The Only Talking Machine of Its Kind in the World,* for mixed media, featuring electronic ventriloquy (1969). He wrote a computer controlled environmental work for the Pepsi Cola Pavilion of Expo '70 in Osaka, Japan, a sound mosaic, with hundreds of tape recorders; also a biographical composition for oboe, accompanied by the Atlantic Ocean, a chest of drawers and the Federal Bureau of Investigation (1970); also produced an experimental composition, *Still and Moving Lines of Silence in Families of Hyperbolas* (N.Y., Feb. 21, 1975); and 4 pieces for multimedia (1975–77), involving electronic sound and a modified bird call. In 1970 he resigned from Brandeis Univ. and joined the staff of Wesleyan University. In 1977 he was teaching at Wesleyan Univ.; was music director of the Viola Farber Dance Co. and a member of the Sonic Arts Union.

Luciuk, Juliusz, Polish composer; b. Brzeźnica, Jan. 1, 1927. He studied musicology with Jachimecki at the Jagiellonian Univ. in Cracow (1947–52), concurrently taking courses in composition with Wiechowicz at the State College of Music in Cracow (1947–56); then had lessons with Nadia Boulanger and Max Deutsch in Paris (1948–49). He evolved a *sui generis* technique according to the pragmatic purposes of each specific composition.
WORKS: ballets *Niobe* (1962), *Battleship Potemkin* (1967), *Orpheus* (1973), *Medea* (1975), *So Pass Five Years,* for prepared piano and chamber ensemble (Amsterdam, Oct. 9, 1972); oratorio, *Francis of Assisi* (Cracow, Oct. 3, 1976); cantata, *Dzikie Wino* (*Virginia Creeper,* 1955); *Pour un Ensemble* for narrator and 24 strings (1961); *Melorythmes* for orch. (1962); *Lirica di Timbri,* 5 pieces for prepared piano (1963); *Metamorphoses* for orch. (1963); *Pacem in Terris* for vocalizing soprano and prepared piano (1964); *Variété* for trumpet and orch. (1965); *Poème de Loire,* 5 songs for soprano and orch. (1968); *Speranza sinfonica* (1969); *Lamentazioni in memoriam Grazyna Bacewicz* for orch. (1970); *Mini-Opus* for piano, 4 hands (1971); Concertino for Piano and Chamber Orch. (1973); *Portraits lyriques* for mezzo-soprano, 2 violins, cello and piano (1974).

Lucký, Štěpán, Czech composer; b. Žilina, Jan. 20, 1919. He studied quarter-tone composition with Alois Hába at the Prague Cons. (1936–39). During the occupation of Czechoslovakia he was interned in concentration camps at Bucharest, Auschwitz and Buchenwald, but survived; after the war he enrolled in the Prague Cons. where he studied with Řídký, graduating in 1947. His music is couched in a pragmatic modernistic manner without circumscription by any particular doctrine or technique.
WORKS: opera *Půlnoční překvapení* (*Midnight Surprise,* 1958; Prague, 1959); *Divertimento* for 3 trombones and string ensemble (1946); Cello Concerto (1946); Piano Concerto (1947); Violin Concerto (1963–65); Octet for strings (1970); *Double Concerto* for violin, piano and orch. (1971); Wind Quintet (1946); *Sonata brevis* for violin and piano (1947); *Elegy* for cello and piano (1948); Brass Quartet (1949); *Elegy* for horn and piano (1965); Sonata for solo violin

(1967–69); *3 Pieces for Due Boemi* for bass clarinet and piano (1969–70; "Due Boemi" is a Czech duo); *Sonata doppia* for 2 violins (1971); Flute Sonata (1973); *Divertimento* for wind quintet (1974); Piano Sonata (1940); Piano Sonatina (1945); *3 Etudes* for quarter-tone piano (1946); *Little Suite* for piano (1971); songs.

Ludford, Nicholas, English composer; b. c.1485; d. c.1557. He was one of the musicians at St. Stephen's Westminster; in 1521 he was admitted to the Fraternity of St. Nicholas, a guild of musicians. His surviving works (all in manuscript) include Masses, motets, and a Magnificat. His *Collected Works,* ed. by J. D. Bergsagel, are being issued by the American Institute of Musicology (1965–).
BIBLIOGRAPHY: H. Baillie, "Nicholas Ludford," *Musical Quarterly* (April 1958).

Ludikar, Pavel, Austrian bass; b. Prague, March 3, 1882; d. Vienna, Feb. 19, 1970. He studied law in Prague; then took piano lessons acquiring sufficient proficiency to be able to play accompaniments to singers; then finally devoted himself to his real profession, that of opera singing. He appeared in Vienna, Dresden, Milan and Buenos Aires; was a member of the Boston Civic Opera (1913–14); from 1926 to 1935 he was on the staff of the Metropolitan Opera Co.; his most successful role was that of Figaro in *Il Barbiere di Siviglia,* which he sang more than 100 times in the U.S.; he was also renowned for bass parts in Russian operas, and sang the title role of Krenek's opera *Karl V* in Prague on June 22, 1938. His repertory included about 18 operatic roles in 4 languages.

Ludkewycz, Stanislaus, Polish composer; b. Jaroslav, Austrian Galicia, Dec. 24, 1879. He studied music in Lwow, and later in Vienna with Grädener and Zemlinsky; received his Dr. phil. in 1908. From 1910–14 he was in Lwow as director of the Lissenko Society and Institute of Music; was recruited in the Austrian Army, and was taken prisoner by the Russians (1915). After the Revolution he was evacuated to Tashkent; liberated in 1918, he returned to Lwow. He was prof. of composition of the Cons. of Lwow until the age of 93 (1939–72). In 1949 he received the Order of the Red Banner from the Soviet government.
WORKS: the operas *Bar Kochba* and *Dovbush* (1952); the symph. poems *Valse mélancolique* (1916), *Stone Carvers* (1926), *Dnieper* (1947), etc.; 2 piano concertos (1919; 1950); *Carpathian Symphony* (1951); *Caucasus,* a symph. ode for chorus and orch. (1911); *Salute to Lwow,* for chorus (1944); *Song About Stalin,* for chorus (1949); chamber music; a collection of Ukrainian songs for chorus (1906–14). He publ. a handbook of choral singing; 1500 Ukrainian melodies of Austria, in the ethnographic studies of the Musicological Society of Lwow (1900–02); a manual of music history and other pedagogical works.
BIBLIOGRAPHY: S. Pavlishin, *S. Ludkewicz* (Kiev, 1974).

Ludwig, August, German composer and musical journalist; b. Waldheim, Jan. 15, 1865; d. Dresden, April 9, 1946. He studied at the Cons. of Cologne, and later in Munich; brought out a number of orchestral compositions, notably the overtures *Ad Astra* and *Luther-Ouvertüre;* also a comic opera, *Kunst und Schein* (1906). From 1894 till 1903 he was editor of the *Neue Berliner Musikzeitung.* He publ. *Geharnischte Aufsätze über Musik* (a collection of essays); *Der Konzertagent* (1894); *Stachel und Lorbeer* (1897); *Zur Wertschätzung der Musik* (1898); *Tannhäuser redivivus* (1908). He attracted unfavorable attention by his abortive attempt to "complete" Schubert's "Unfinished" Symphony, adding 2 movements, a *Philosophen-Scherzo* and a *Schicksalsmarsch.*

Ludwig, Christa, excellent German soprano; b. Berlin, March 16, 1928. Both her parents were professional singers, and she took her first music lessons with her mother. She began her career as a contralto; appeared in opera in Darmstadt (1952–54), in Hannover (1954–55), in Vienna (1955), in Berlin, Hamburg, Rome and Milan. She made her American debut at the Metropolitan Opera, N.Y., on Dec. 10, 1959 as Cherubino in the *Marriage of Figaro;* remained on the staff, off and on, until 1971; among her roles were Amneris in *Aida,* Kundry in *Parsifal* and Leonore in *Fidelio.*

Ludwig, Franz, Bohemian composer and musicologist; b. Graslitz, July 7, 1889; d. Münster, June 15, 1955. He studied first with his father, director of the Graslitz Music School; then with Pembaur, Reger, and Krehl at the Leipzig Cons., and with Riemann (musicology) at Leipzig Univ. He publ. a *Kurzgefasste Musikgeschichte des Erzgebirges* (1924); biographies of Franz Wüllner, etc. He composed an opera, *Schlag zwölf* (Münster, 1928); a scenic oratorio, *Das Lambertusspiel* (Bremerhaven, 1933); *Lustspielouvertüre* for orch.; Piano Concerto; Horn Concerto; *Serenade* for 8 wind instruments; sonatas and other pieces for piano; men's choruses; songs.

Ludwig, Friedrich, German musicologist; b. Potsdam, May 8, 1872; d. Göttingen, Oct. 3, 1930. He studied music history at the Univ. of Marburg, and later at Strasbourg; in 1911 became a member of the faculty at the Univ. of Strasbourg; then went over to the Univ. of Göttingen. He was an authority on medieval music and publ. numerous valuable articles on the subject, covering all aspects of the period. He also edited the musical works of Guillaume de Machaut (1926–34).
BIBLIOGRAPHY: J. Müller-Blattau, *Dem Andenken Friedrich Ludwigs* (Kassel, 1931).

Ludwig, Leopold, Austrian conductor; b. Witkowitz (Ostrava), Jan. 12, 1908. He studied piano in Vienna; then conducted provincial theater orchestras in Austria and Germany; from 1936 to 1939 was conductor in Oldenburg, and from 1939 conducted at the State Opera in Vienna (1939–43), and conducted opera after the end of the war, in Berlin, until 1951. He then became musical director of the Hamburg State Opera (1951–70), with which he made special appearances in Paris, Edinburgh, London and New York. In 1968 he returned to Hamburg, and was mainly active as prof. of music at Hamburg Univ.

BIBLIOGRAPHY: B. W. Wessling, *Leopold Ludwig* (Bremen, 1968).

Ludwig II, Bavarian King, royal patron of Wagner; b. in the Nymphenburg castle in Munich, Aug. 25, 1845; d. insane, by suicide, in the Starnberg Lake, June 13, 1883. Already as a crown prince he conceived an extreme adulation for Wagner, and when he became King, at 19, he declared his intention to sponsor all of Wagner's productions, an event that came at the most difficult time of Wagner's life, beset as he was by personal and financial problems. In sincere gratitude, Wagner spoke of his future plans of composition as "a program for the King." In his total devotion to Wagner, Ludwig converted his castle Neuschwanstein into a "worthy temple for my divine friend," installing in it architectural representations of scenes from Wagner's operas. His bizarre behavior caused the government of Bavaria to order a psychiatric examination of Ludwig, and he was eventually committed to an asylum near the Starnberg Lake. During a walk, he overpowered the psychiatrist who escorted him, and apparently dragged him to his death in the lake, and drowned himself, too. Much material on Ludwig II is found in Wagner's bibliography; for a detailed account of his life see Wilfrid Blunt, *The Dream King, Ludwig II of Bavaria* (London, 1970).

Luening, Otto, outstanding American composer; b. Milwaukee, June 15, 1900. His family moved to München before World War I and Luening attended classes at the Akademie der Tonkunst there, studying flute and theory; then went to Switzerland where he took courses with Jarnach and Andreae at the Cons. of Zürich; subsequently had some private lessons in composition with Busoni. Returning to the U.S. in 1920 he participated in organizing the American Grand Opera Co. in Chicago; was executive director of the Opera Department at the Eastman School of Music, Rochester, N.Y. (1925–28). In 1930 he was awarded a Guggenheim Fellowship, which he held again in 1974; was on the faculty at the Univ. of Arizona (1933–34), at Bennington College (1934–44) and at Barnard College (1944–47); subsequently was a member of the faculty of philosophy at Columbia Univ. (1949–68) and music chairman of the School of the Arts at Columbia (1966–70); taught composition at the Juilliard School of Music in N.Y. (1951–53). In 1959 he participated in the formation of the Columbia-Princeton Electronic Music Center; with Ussachevsky and others he was instrumental in writing music combining live instruments with electronic sound; the earliest experiments were made by them in 1952. Luening holds numerous honorary degrees and consulting positions with industrial and educational organizations; he is life member of the National Institute of Arts and Letters.
WORKS: the opera *Evangeline* (1932; produced at the Columbia Univ. Festival, May 5, 1948, composer conducting); numerous orchestral scores: Concertino, for flute, harp, celesta and strings (1923; Philadelphia, Jan. 30, 1935); *2 Symphonic Interludes* (1935; N.Y., April 11, 1936); *Prelude to a Hymn Tune* (after William Billings) for piano and small orch. (N.Y., Feb. 1, 1937); *Fuguing Tune* for flute, oboe, clarinet, bassoon

and horn (1941); *Kentucky Concerto* (1951); *Legend for oboe and strings* (1951); *Sonority Canon* for 37 flutes; and literally hundreds of pieces for various, and sometimes very unusual, instrumental combinations; also sonatas for double bass solo, cello solo, viola solo, violin solo, accordion solo and flute solo; many of these pieces exist in alternative settings; thus the *Sonority Canon* for 37 flutes exists also in a version for 4 solo flutes accompanied by 33 flutes on tape. His early electronic works include *Low Speed* in 2 sections: *Invention* and *Fantasy in Space* (first perf. at the Museum of Modern Art, N.Y., Oct. 28, 1952); with Vladimir Ussachevsky, he prepared the score of the first work expressly written for live instruments combined with electronic sound, *Rhapsodic Variations,* which was first performed by the Louisville Orch. in New York on March 20, 1954. Another work with Ussachevsky, *Poem in Cycles and Bells* for tape and orch. was written for the same combination; it was first performed in Los Angeles, Nov. 18, 1954. As a commissioned work he wrote *A Wisconsin Symphony* (Milwaukee, Jan. 4, 1976).

BIBLIOGRAPHY: J. Beeson, "Otto Luening," *American Composers Alliance Bulletin* (Autumn 1953).

Lugert, Josef, Bohemian music educator and composer; b. Frohnau, Oct. 30, 1841; d. Prague, July 24, 1936. He studied organ in Prague; in 1868 was appointed to the faculty of the Prague Cons.; later organized schools for instrumentalists in the provinces. He wrote a symphony, several pieces of chamber music and publ. a manual *Musikalische Formenlehre* and various school manuals.

Luigini, Alexandre (-Clément-Léon-Joseph), French composer; b. Lyons, March 9, 1850; d. Paris, July 29, 1906. He was the son of the Italian musician Giuseppe Luigini (1820–1898), who conducted at the Théâtre-Italien in Paris; studied at the Paris Cons. with Massart (violin) and Massenet (composition); then entered his father's orch. at Lyons (1869) as violinist, and began his very successful career as ballet composer with the production of his first stage work *Le Rêve de Nicette* (Lyons, 1870); in 1877 he became conductor at the Grand Théâtre at Lyons and prof. of harmony at the Lyons Cons.; after 20 years there, went to Paris as conductor at the Opéra-Comique, where he remained till his death, except during 1903, when he conducted the orch. at the Théâtre-Lyrique. His greatest success as composer came with the production of *Ballet égyptien* (Lyons, Jan. 13, 1875), still one of the most popular ballet scores; it was inserted, with Verdi's permission, in the 2nd act of *Aida* at its performance in Lyons in 1886. Other works: comic operas: *Les Caprices de Margot* (Lyons, 1877), *La Reine des fleurs* (Lyons, 1878), *Faublas* (Paris, 1881); ballets: *Ballet égyptien* (Lyons, 1875), *Anges et démons* (1876), *Les Noces d'Ivanovna* (1883), *Le Bivouac* (1889), *Les Écharpes* (1891), *Rayon d'or* (1891), *Rose et Papillon* (1891), *Le Meunier* (1892), *Arlequin écolier* (1894), *Dauritha* (1894); also *Romance symphonique* for orch.; 3 string quartets (all won prizes); marches for orch.; numerous piano pieces.

Lukačić, Ivan, Croatian organist and composer; b. Šibenik (baptized April 17), 1587; d. Split, Sept. 20, 1648. He studied music in Italy and in 1597 entered the Franciscan order. In 1615 he became the music master at the Cathedral of Split. His book of *Sacrae Cantiones* (1620) includes 27 motets; they reflect the influence of the early Baroque style and employ instrumental accompaniment.

Lukáš, Zdeněk, Czech composer; b. Prague, Aug, 21, 1928. He studied music theory with Kabeláč in Prague; then lived mostly in Pilsen as choral conductor (1955–65). In his music he avails himself of several advanced techniques of composition, including serialism.

WORKS: a radio opera, *At žije mrtvý* (*Long Live the Dead Man,* 1967; Prague, Dec. 11, 1968); a one-act opera, *Domácí karneval* (*Home Carnival,* 1968; Prague, March 29, 1969); Piano Concerto (1955); Violin Concerto (1956); Cello Concerto (1957); 4 symphonies (1960; 1961; 1965; 1966); Concerto for Soprano Saxophone and Orch. (1962); *Concerto Grosso* for string quartet and string orch. (1964); *Symphonietta Solemnis* (1965); *Sonata concertata* for piano, winds and percussion (1966); *Musica ritmica* for percussion and winds (1966); Concerto for Violin, Viola and Orch. (Prague, March 7, 1969); Variations for Piano and Orch. (1970); 3 string quartets (1960, 1965, 1973); Trio for violin, piano and side drum (1962); *Partita semplice* for 4 violins and piano (1964); Wind Quintet (1969); *Amoroso* for clarinet, bagpipes and double bass (1970); *Thou Shalt Not Kill,* electronic oratorio for chorus, instruments and tape (1971); *Verba Laudata,* 4 songs for soprano, string quartet and piano (1967); *Modlitba (Prayer)* for chorus, organ and percussion (1968).

Lully (or Lulli), Jean-Baptiste, celebrated Italian-born French composer; b. Florence, Nov. 28, 1632; d. Paris, March 22, 1687. Son of a poor Florentine miller, he was taught the elements of music by a Franciscan monk, and also learned to play the guitar, and later the violin. Attracted by his vivacious temperament and a talent for singing, the Chevalier de Guise took him to Paris in 1646 as a page to Mademoiselle d'Orléans, a young cousin of Louis XIV. He soon adapted himself to the ways and manners of the French court, and quickly mastered the language, although he could never rid himself of a pronounced Italian accent. The story that he was ever a scullery boy is apocryphal, but he kept company with the domestic servants, and his talent as a violin player was first revealed by his improvisations in the royal kitchen; Count de Nogent heard him, and secured for him a position in the private band of Mademoiselle d'Orléans. When he set to music a satirical poem reflecting on his patroness, he lost favor with her, but entered the service of young Louis XIV (1652), winning his first success as a ballet dancer. He contrived to obtain instruction on the harpsichord and in composition from Nicolas Métru, organist of St. Nicolas-des-Champs, and François Roberday, organist at the Église des Petits-Pères. He attended opera and concerts at the court, led by his compatriot Luigi Rossi, and conceived a passion for the theater, which became the determining factor in his entire career. After a brief association with the King's private orchestra, "les 24 violons du roi," he organized his own band of 17 instruments (later 21), "les petits violons," which he developed into a fine ensemble. He rose fast in royal favor; became a favorite composer of court ballets for various occasions; in several of these productions Louis XIV himself took part next to Lully, who danced and acted as "M. Baptiste." In 1661 he received the lucrative post of composer to the king, and in 1662, a further appointment as maître de musique of the royal family. In 1662 he married Madeleine Lambert, daughter of the court musician Michel Lambert. From 1663 to 1671 he wrote music for several comic ballets by Molière, including *Le Mariage forcé, L'Amour Médecin,* and *Le Bourgeois Gentilhomme,* which foreshadowed the development of opéra-comique. In 1672 he obtained letters patent for the establishment of the Académie Royale de Musique (which eventually became the Grand Opéra), taking the privilege from Perrin and Cambert, who originally launched the enterprise in 1668. With the formation of a national opera house, Lully found his true calling, that of creating French operatic art, setting French texts to music with sensitivity to the genius of the language, and abandoning the conventional Italian type of opera, with its repetitive extensions of arias, endless fiorituras, etc. In the theater, Lully did not confine himself to the composer's functions, but also acted as director, stage manager, conductor, and even, upon occasion, machinist. From 1672 he worked in close cooperation with a congenial librettist, Quinault, who followed Lully's ideas with rare understanding. Lully developed a type of overture which became known as the "Lully Overture" or "French Overture" and of which the earliest example occurs in his ballet *Alcidiane* (1658); this type of overture opens with a slow, solemn, homophonic section with sharply dotted rhythms, followed by a fast section with some elements of imitation; frequently the overture ends with a return to tempo and rhythm of the opening. In vocal writing, Lully demonstrated his mastery of both dramatic recitative and songful arias; he imparted dramatic interest to his choral ensembles; the instrumental parts were also given more prominence than in early Italian opera. That an Italian-born musician should have become the founder of French opera is one of the many paradoxes of music history. As a man, Lully was haughty, arrogant, and irascible, tolerating no opposition; his ambition was his prime counsellor; considerations of morality played a small part in his actions. With those in power, he knew how to be submissive; a shrewd courtier, he often gained his aims by flattery and obsequiousness; the manner in which he secured for himself the directorship of the Académie Royale de Musique, through the royal favorite Mme. de Montespan, moved some of his critics to berate him savagely. Yet, thanks to his volcanic energy and his disregard of all obstacles, he was able to accomplish an epoch-making task. His death resulted from a symbolic accident: while conducting, he vehemently struck his foot with a sharp-pointed cane used to pound out the beat; gangrene set in and he died of blood poisoning.

WORKS: BALLETS (produced at court in Paris, Versailles, Saint-Germain, and Fontainebleau): *La Nuit*

(Feb. 23, 1653); *Alcidiane* (Feb. 14, 1658; *La Raillerie* (Feb. 19, 1659); *L'Impatience* (Feb. 19, 1661); *Les Saisons* (July 30, 1661); *Hercule amoureux* (ballet music for Cavalli's opera *Ercole amante;* Feb. 7, 1662); *Les Arts* (Jan. 8, 1663); *Les Noces de village* (Oct. 3, 1663); *Le Mariage forcé* (Jan. 29, 1664); *Les Amours déguisés* (Feb. 15, 1664); *Les Plaisirs de l'isle enchantée* (May 8, 1664); *La Naissance de Vénus* (Jan. 26, 1665); *L'Amour Médecin* (Sept. 15, 1665); *Les Muses* (Dec. 2, 1666); *Le Sicilien, ou l'Amour peintre* (Feb. 10, 1667); *Le Carnaval* (Jan. 18, 1668); *Georges Dandin* (July 18, 1668); *Flore* (Feb. 13, 1669); *Monsieur de Pourceaugnac* (Oct. 6, 1669); *Les Amants magnifiques* (Feb. 4, 1670); *Le Bourgeois Gentilhomme* (Oct. 14, 1670); *Psyché* (Jan. 17, 1671).

OPERAS: *Cadmus et Hermione* (April 27, 1673); *Alceste, ou Le Triomphe d'Alcide* (Jan. 19, 1674); *Thésée* (Jan. 12, 1675); *Atys* (Jan. 10, 1676); *Isis* (Jan. 5, 1677); *Psyché* (a different work from the similarly named ballet; April 19, 1678); *Bellérophon* (Jan. 31, 1679); *Proserpine* (Feb. 3, 1680); *Le Triomphe de l'Amour* (Jan. 21, 1681); *Persée* (April 18, 1682); *Phaéton* (Jan. 9, 1683); *Amadis de Gaule* (Jan. 18, 1684); *Roland* (Jan. 8, 1685); *Idylle sur la paix* (July 16, 1685); *Le Temple de la paix* (Oct. 20, 1685); *Armide et Renaud* (Feb. 15, 1686); *Acis et Galatée* (Sept. 17, 1686); *Achille et Polyxène* (Nov. 7, 1687). For further details about productions and revivals of Lully's operas, see A. Loewenberg, *Annals of Opera* (1943; new ed., 1955). Ten stage works produced at the French court between 1653 and 1657 had several numbers contributed by Lully. Most of Lully's operas have been publ. by Breitkopf & Härtel, in *Chefs-d'œuvre classiques de l'opéra français; Armide et Renaud* in Eitner's *Publikationen älterer Musikwerke* (vol. 14; full score, and a piano score). Besides his stage works, Lully wrote a *Te Deum,* a *Miserere,* a 4-part Mass a cappella, many motets; instrumental works (string trios, airs for violin, etc.). Henry Prunières undertook a complete ed. of Lully's works (9 vols. publ. from 1930–39).

BIBLIOGRAPHY: Le Prevost d'Exmes, *Lully Musicien* (Paris, 1779); Th. Lajarte, *Lully* (Paris, 1878); E. Radet, *Lully, Homme d'affaires, propriétaire et musicien* (Paris, 1891); R. Gandolfi, *Accademia dedicata a G. B. Lulli e Luigi Cherubini* (Florence, 1902); Romain Rolland, *Musiciens d'autrefois* (Paris, 1908; in English, 1915); Henry Prunières, *Lully* (Paris, 1909); L. de La Laurencie, *Lully* (Paris, 1911); Henry Prunières, *L'Opéra italien en France avant Lully* (Paris, 1913); Henry Prunières, *Le Ballet de cour en France avant Lully* (Paris, 1914); special issue of the *Revue Musicale* (Jan. 1925); Henry Prunières, "Lully and the Académie de Musique et de Danse," *Musical Quarterly* (Oct. 1925); Henry Prunières, *La Vie illustre et libertine de J. B. Lully* (Paris, 1929; a somewhat romanticized biography, based on factual data); F. Böttger, *Die Comédie-Ballets von Molière und Lully* (Berlin, 1931); E. Borrel, *J.-B. Lully: le cadre, la vie, la personnalité, le rayonnement, les œuvres* (Paris, 1949); Th. Valensi, *Louis XIV et Lully* (Nice, 1951); N. Slonimsky's article in the *Guide du Concert* (Feb. 1, 1952), which reproduces the text of Lully's birth certificate, establishing the date as Nov. 28, 1632; J. Eppelsheim, *Das Orchester in den Werken J. B. Lullys* (Tutzing, 1961); M. Ellis, "Inventory of the Dances of Jean-Baptiste Lully," *Recherches sur la Musique Française Classique* 9 (1969); A. Ducrot, "Les Représentations de l'Académie royale de musique à Paris au temps de Louis XIV (1671-1715)," *Recherches sur la Musique Française classique* 10 (1970).

Lumbye, Hans Christian, Danish composer of light music; b. Copenhagen, May 2, 1810; d. there, March 20, 1874. He played in military bands as a youth; in 1839 formed his own orch., soon achieving fame as a conductor and composer of dance music, especially with his concerts in the Tivoli amusement park in Copenhagen. He composed about 400 pieces of dance music (waltzes, galops, polkas, marches, etc.), which earned him the sobriquet of 'the Johann Strauss of the North.' His two sons were also musicians; the elder, **Carl Lumbye** (b. Copenhagen, July 9, 1841; d. there, Aug. 10, 1911), was a violinist, conductor, and composer of dance music. The younger son, **Georg Lumbye** (b. Copenhagen, Aug. 26, 1843; d. there, Oct. 30, 1922), studied at the Paris Cons., and conducted dance music in Copenhagen; wrote the operetta *Heksefløjten* (*The Witch's Flute;* 1869) and numerous vaudevilles.
BIBLIOGRAPHY: G. Skjerne, *H. C. Lumbye og hans Samtid* (Copenhagen, 1912; 2nd ed., 1946).

Lumsdaine, David, Australian composer; b. Sydney, Oct. 21, 1931. He studied piano, viola and composition at the Sydney Cons. and at the Univ. of Sydney (B.A., 1953). After graduation in 1954 he moved to England where he took private lessons in composition with Mátyás Seiber in London. A precocious composer, he wrote his first pieces at the age of 12. In his mature works he developed a highly complex idiom of composition. In 1961 he was engaged by the Royal Academy of Music in London to organize a series of seminars on contemporary composition; in 1970 he obtained a lectureship in music at Durham Univ., where he established an electronic music studio.
WORKS: *Variations for Orchestra* (1957); *Short Symphony* (1959); *Annotations from Auschwitz,* chamber cantata (1964; his most powerful work); *Cantata No. 2* (1964); *Missa brevis* (1964); *Bach Music* for large orchestra, based on material from Bach's *The Art of the Fugue,* transformed into a complex continuum of metric elements; *Cantata No. 3, Story from a Time of Disturbance,* for baritone and chamber ensemble (1965); *Easter Frescoes* for soprano and chamber orchestra, after the *New Testament* (1966); *Flights* for two pianos (1967); *Mandala I* for wind quintet (1968); *Bourbon* for computer and tape (1968); *Babel* for magnetic tape (1968); *Episodes* for orchestra (1969); *Mandala II* for flute, clarinet, viola, cello and percussion (1969); *Looking Glass Music* for brass quintet and magnetic tape (1971); *Kangaroo Hunt* for piano and percussion (1971); *Caliban Impromptu* for piano trio and electronic instruments, after Shakespeare's play *The Tempest* (1972); *Salvation Creek with Eagle* for chamber orch. (1974); *Sunflower* for chamber orch. (1975); *Evensong* for brass ensemble (1975); *Hagoromo* for orch. (1975).
BIBLIOGRAPHY: James Murdoch, *Australia's Contemporary Composers* (Melbourne, 1972); R. Cooke,

"David Lumsdaine," *Music and Musicians* 21 (1972-73).

Lund, Signe, Norwegian composer; b. Oslo, April 15, 1868; d. there, April 6, 1950. She studied in Berlin, Copenhagen and Paris; spent several years in America. As a composer she was completely under the lyrical domination of Grieg's music, and her works are eminently perishable. She wrote a ceremonial overture, *The Road to France* on the occasion of America's entry into World War I in 1917; also various instrumental pieces and songs. She publ. an autobiography, *Sol gjennem skyer* (Oslo, 1944).

Lundquist, Torbjörn, Swedish composer; b. Stockholm, Sept. 30, 1920. He studied composition with Dag Wirén; acquired proficiency on the accordion, and wrote many works for this popular instrument. In his music he followed the Romantic "Scandinavian" tradition; during his travels in the North he collected songs of Lapland, which he used in heterophonic counterpoint in some of his works. He also experimented with ultra-modern techniques of "organized spontaneity."
WORKS: *Divertimento* for chamber orch. (1951); 3 symphonies: No. 1, *Kammarsymfoni* (1952-56, revised 1971); No. 2, *For Freedom* (1956-70); No. 3, *Sinfonia dolorosa* (1971-75); *Elegies from Bergen* for tenor, male chorus and orch. (1958); *Via Tomheten (Via the Emptiness),* "visions" for soli, chorus and chamber orch. (1959); *Anrop (Call)* for soprano and orch. (1963-64); works for solo concert accordion: *Partita Piccola* (1964), *Metamorphoses* (1965), *9 Two-Part Inventions* (1966), *Plasticity* (1966), *Sonatina piccola* (1967), *Botany Play* (1968) and *Microscope* (1971); *Concerto da Camera* for accordion and orch. (1965; Gävle, Feb. 20, 1966); *Movements* for accordion and string quartet (1966); *Duell* for accordion and percussion (1966); *Combinazione* for violin and percussion (1966); 2 string quartets (1966, 1969); *Férvor* for violino grande and orch. (1967); *Hangarmusik,* a "concerto sinfonico" for piano and orch. (1967); *Teamwork* for wind quintet (1967); *Confrontation* for orch. (Stockholm, Oct. 5, 1968); *Evoluzione* for strings (1968); *Intarzia* for accordion and strings (1968); *Sogno* for oboe and strings (1968); *Sound on Sound* for audience, speaker, composer and stereo orch. (Stockholm, Jan. 25, 1969); *Stereogram III* for xylorimba, electric guitar and accordion (1969); *Quatre Rondeaux* for wind quartet and piano (1969); *Tempera* for 6 brass instruments (1969); *Galax* for orch. (1971); marimba concerto (1972); an opera, *Sekund av evighet* (Stockholm, May 27, 1974); *Concerto Grosso* for violin, cello and string orch. (1974); *Marimba Concerto* (1972-75); *Trio fiorente* for piano trio (1975).

Lundsten, Ralph, Swedish composer and film director; b. Neder-Luleå, Oct. 6, 1936. He is a pioneer in Swedish electronic composition.
WORKS: His electronic works include many ballets (often in collaboration with choreographer Ivo Cramér): *Ristningar (Carvings,* 1969), *Erik XIV* (1969), *Nattmara (Nightmare,* 1970), *Gustav III* (1971), *Fader Vår (Our Father,* 1971), *Ringbunden* (1971), *Midnattstimmen* (1972), *Stretch* (1972), *Nor-*

disk natursymfoni Nr 1, Strömkarlen (The Water Sprite, 1972), *Gunnar på Lidarände* (1973), *Isländska dansbilder* (1974), *Johannes og anima* (ballet version of the *Nordic Nature Symphony No. 2,* 1975); other electronic scores include *Främmande planet (Unknown Planet,* 1959–60), *Composition in 3 Movements* (1964), *Atomskymning (Atom Nightfall,* 1964), *EMS Nr 1* (1966), *Vintermusik* (1968), *Suite for Electronic Accordion* (1968), *Burmusik (Cage Music,* 1968), *Cosmic Love* (1970), *Through a Landscape of Mirrors* (1970), *Cosmic Love—Trial and Discussion* (1970); *Landskapsmusik* (1972), *På vingliga tår* (1973), *Shangri-La* (1973), *Terje möter Monstret och Mobben* (1973), *Heaven by Night* (1975), *Nordisk natursymfoni Nr 2, Johannes och huldran* (1975), *Spöken dansar* (1975) and *Vattensymfoni (Water Symphony,* 1975). Electronic works in collaboration with Leo Nilson: *Kalejdoskop* (1965), *Aloha Arita* (1965–66), *3 Electronic Pop Pieces* (1966), *Visioner av flygande tefat (Visions of Flying Saucers,* 1966), *Music for the Ether Hypothesis* (1967), *Lyckomusik (Bliss Music,* 1968), *Feel* (1968), *It* (1968), *Sveagris* (1968), *Tellus* (1968), *Mizar* (1968), *Holmia* (1969) and *Fågel blå (Bluebird,* 1969).

Lunetta, Stanley G., American avant-garde composer; b. Sacramento, Calif., June 5, 1937. He received his B.A. at Sacramento State College and completed graduate work at the Univ. of California, Davis, where he studied composition with Larry Austin, Jerome Rosen and Richard Swift; also took a course with Karlheinz Stockhausen when he lectured at Davis. In 1963 he formed the New Music Ensemble devoted to contemporary music. His works explore the potentialities of electronic media; a major project is to build a computer capable of independent creative composition, both in ultra-modern and infraclassical fields.

WORKS: His pieces, most of them for mixed media characterized by disestablishmentarian latitudinarianism, include *A Piece for Bandoneon and Strings* (1966); *Funkart* for mixers, lights and audio-visual input material (1967); *TA-TA* for chorus with mailing tubes (Santa Barbara, Calif., May 15, 1969); *I Am Definitely Not Running for Vice President* for photocells, modulators and 4 governors (1967); *TWOMANSHOW,* an evening of environmental theater (1968); *Spider-Song,* a comic-book and a situation (in collaboration with Larry Austin, first demonstrated in N.Y., Dec. 17, 1968); *Mr. Machine* for flute and electronics (1969); an epithalamium for a married percussionist couple (1970). He was one of the editors of the fantastically screwed-up hyper-modern music magazine *Source,* published (where else?) in California.

Lunn, Charles, English tenor; b. Birmingham, Jan. 5, 1838; d. London, Feb. 28, 1906. He studied in Italy with Sangiovanni, Cattaneo, and Vizione; then sang in concert and oratorio (1864–67); settled as a teacher in Birmingham, where his pupils' concerts, given in the Town Hall, became important local events; in 1895 he moved to London. He wrote *The Philosophy of Voice,* a valuable work (1874; 10th ed., 1906), followed by a sequel, *Vox Populi* (1880); also *Vocal Expression, Empirical or Scientific* (1878).

Lunssens, Martin, Belgian conductor and composer; b. Molenbeek-Saint-Jean, April 16, 1871; d. Etterbeek, Feb. 1, 1944. He studied with Gevaert, Jehin, and Kufferath at the Brussels Cons., gaining the 1st Belgian Prix de Rome in 1895 with the cantata *Callirhoé;* then became prof. at the Cons. of Brussels; subsequently was director of the Music Academy at Courtrai (1905–16); at Charleroi (1916–21); at the Cons. of Louvain (1921–24); and finally at Ghent (from 1924). He was also known as an excellent conductor; was in charge of the Flemish Opera in Antwerp, where he conducted many Wagner operas.

WORKS: 4 symphonies, the first 3 with the programmatic titles *Symphonie romaine, Symphonie florentine,* and *Symphonie française;* several symph. poems *(Roméo et Juliette; Phèdre; Le Cid; Timon d'Athènes);* 3 violin concertos; Viola Concerto; Cello Concerto; much chamber music; songs.

Lupi, Roberto, Italian composer and music scholar; b. Milan, Nov. 28, 1908; d. Dornach, Switzerland, April 17, 1971. He studied at the Cons. of Milan; then became prof. of harmony and counterpoint at the Cherubini Cons. in Florence. Among his works are the cantata, *Orfeo, Sacra Sinfonia;* Cello Sonata; songs. He publ. a treatise, *Armonia di gravitazione* (Rome, 1946), emphasizing the importance of the focal tone in composition rather than key. He edited several works by Galuppi, Caldara, Stradella, and other Italian composers.

Luporini, Gaetano, Italian opera composer; b. Lucca, Dec. 12, 1865; d. there, May 12, 1948. He was a pupil of Primo Quilici, and a protégé of Ricordi, the publisher. After graduating from the Pacini Music Institute in Lucca, he studied at the Milan Cons. with Carlo Angeloni and Catalani; returning to Lucca in 1902, he became director of the Pacini Music Institute; also choirmaster of the Lucca cathedral.

WORKS: OPERAS: *I dispetti amorosi* (Turin, Feb. 27, 1894); *La Collana di Pasqua* (Naples, Nov. 1, 1896; renamed *Nora,* and performed under that title in Lucca, Sept. 7, 1908); *L'aquila e le colombe* (Rome, Feb. 17, 1914); *Chiaro di luna* (Bologna, Nov. 20, 1925); also orchestral pieces and songs.

Lupus, Eduardus. See **Lobo, Duarte.**

Lupus (Latinized name of **De Wolf), Michael,** Flemish composer; b. c.1500; d. Lierre, July 15, 1567. Biographical data are scant, and identity uncertain. He had a prebend at Soignies in 1535; in the same year was named chaplain to the court of Charles V at Naples. Upon his return to the Netherlands, he received a new prebend at Lierre. He traveled with Charles V in Germany (1547–48); when the Emperor abdicated in 1555, Lupus lost his positions. 4 motets by Lupus are found in Fuenllana's collection of 1554, and in Petrucci's *Motetti de la Corona* (1526).

BIBLIOGRAPHY: René Vannes, *Dictionnaire des Musiciens* (Brussels, 1947).

Lussan, Zélie de, American soprano; b. Brooklyn, Dec. 21, 1862; d. London, Dec. 18, 1949. She was trained in singing by her mother, and made her public appearance at the age of 16 at the Academy of Music in Brooklyn; in 1885 joined the Boston Ideal Opera Co., and in 1889 went to London where she sang with the Carl Rosa Co.; in 1894 she made an appearance with the Metropolitan Opera, N.Y., and sang with it again in 1900. On Sept. 11, 1907 she married the pianist **Angelo Fronani** in London; after his death in 1918 she remained in London until her own death.

Lussy, Mathis, Swiss writer on music and piano teacher; b. Stans, April 8, 1828; d. Montreux, Jan. 21, 1910. He studied with Businger and Nägeli; went to Paris in 1847 as a piano teacher. He wrote *Exercices de mécanisme* (1863); *Traité de l'expression musicale* (1873; partial reprint as *Le Rythme musical*, 1883); *Histoire de la notation musicale* (1882; written with E. David); *L'Anacrouse dans la musique moderne* (1903); "De la diction musicale et grammaticale," in *Riemann-Festschrift* (1909); *La "Sonate pathétique" de Beethoven* (publ. posthumously, 1912; edited by A. Dechevrens).
BIBLIOGRAPHY: E. Monod, *Mathis Lussy et le Rythme Musical* (Neuchâtel, 1912).

Lütgendorff, Willibald Leo, German art historian; b. Augsburg, July 8, 1856; d. Weimar, Dec. 31, 1937. He studied at the Kunstakademie in Munich; in 1889, became director of the Kunstschule and curator of the Art Gallery in Lübeck. Besides writings on the plastic arts, he publ. *Die Geigen- und Lautenmacher vom Mittelalter bis zur Gegenwart* (1904; enlarged ed., 1913; in 2 vols., 1922), which is regarded as a standard authority.

Luther, Martin, the great religious reformer; b. Eisleben, Nov. 10, 1483; d. there, Feb. 18, 1546. His reform of the church extended to the musical services, in which he took the deepest interest. After leaving the Wartburg, near Eisenach (March 22, 1522), he gave his ideas practical shape; his *Formula missae* (1523) and *Deutsche Messe* (German Mass; 1526; facsimile ed. by J. Wolf, Kassel, 1934) established the new service. He changed the order of the Mass; a German psalm took the place of the introit; the German Creed was substituted for the Latin Credo. The German Mass was sung for the first time in the Parish Church at Wittenberg on Christmas Day, 1524. Kapellmeister Conrad Rupsch and cantor Johann Walter aided Luther in organizing the musical part of the Mass. Walter states that Luther invented chorale melodies on the flute (he was an excellent flutist), and that these were noted down by Walter and Rupsch. It is impossible to establish with certainty which hymn tunes ascribed to Luther are really his; *Jesaia dem Propheten das geschah* is definitely Luther's; and the celebrated hymn tune, *Ein' feste Burg ist unser Gott,* is most probably authentic. Most importantly, the words of many chorales were written, arranged, or translated from Latin by Luther. Koch in *Geschichte des Kirchenlieds* gives a list of 36.
BIBLIOGRAPHY: A. J. Rambach, *Über Luthers Verdienst um den Kirchengesang* (Hamburg, 1813); K. von Winterfeld, *Luthers deutsche geistliche Lieder* (Leipzig, 1840); Karl Loewe, *Lutherstudien* (1846; publ. Wittenberg, 1918); H. von Stephen, *Luther als*

Musiker (Bielefeld, 1899); M. Rade, *Martin Luthers Leben, Taten und Meinungen* (3 vols.; Tübingen, 1883; 2nd ed., 1901); F. Zelle, *Das älteste lutherische Haus-Gesangbuch* (Göttingen, 1903; with commentary); J. W. Lyra, *Luthers Deutsche Messe* (1904); F. Spitta, *Die Lieder Luthers in ihrer Bedeutung für das evangelische Kirchenlied* (Göttingen, 1905); F. Spitta, *Studien zu Luthers Liedern* (Göttingen, 1907); H. Lehmann, *Luther im deutschen Lied* (Halle, 1910); H. Kretzschmar, "Luther und die Musik," in *Jahrbuch Peters* (1917); K. Anton, *Luther und die Musik* (1918); H. Preuss, *Luther der Künstler* (1931); H. J. Moser, *Die Melodien der Lutherlieder* (Leipzig, 1935); G. Wolfram, "Ein' feste Burg ist unser Gott" (Berlin, 1936); C. Mahrenholz, *Luther und die Kirchenmusik* (Kassel, 1937); Charles Schneider, *Luther poète et musicien et les Enchiridiens de 1524* (Geneva, 1942); Walter E. Buszin, "Luther on Music," *Musical Quarterly* (Jan. 1946); F. Smend, *Luther und Bach* (Berlin, 1947); Paul Nettl, *Luther and Music* (Philadelphia, 1948); W. Stapel, *Luthers Lieder und Gedichte* (Stuttgart, 1950).

Lutkin, Peter Christian, American organist and hymnologist; b. Thompsonville, Wis., March 27, 1858; d. Evanston, Ill., Dec. 27, 1931. He studied music in Chicago; then went to Europe, and took lessons with A. Haupt (organ) and W. Bargiel (composition) in Berlin; and had further instruction in piano from Moszkowski in Paris and Leschetizky in Vienna. Returning to America, he filled various posts as organist in Chicago; taught theory at the American Cons. of Music in Chicago. In 1883 he became instructor in piano and organ at Northwestern Univ., Evanston, Illinois; from 1895 to 1928 was Dean of the School of Music there; also taught church music at the Garrett Biblical Institute at Evanston (1915–28); for 20 seasons conducted the Chicago North Shore Festival Association (1909–30); publ. church music and pedagogical works for piano; edited the *Methodist Sunday School Hymnal;* was co-editor of the *Episcopal Church Hymnal.*

Lutoslawski, Witold, outstanding Polish composer; b. Warsaw, Jan. 25, 1913. He played piano and violin as a child; then took formal piano lessons with Lefeld (1932–36) and composition with Maliszewski (1932–37) at the Warsaw Cons. At the beginning of World War II he was in the Polish Army; became a German prisoner of war, but got back to Warsaw; earned a living by playing piano in cafés and cabarets. After the war he dedicated himself to composition and teaching. His renommée soon reached the outside world; he received invitations to give seminars and to lecture in England, West Germany, Denmark and Sweden; he gave a seminar at the Berkshire Music Center in Tanglewood in 1962; was composer-in-residence at Dartmouth College, Hanover, N.H. in 1966. He received numerous awards: 3 first mentions in the International Rostrum of Composers, UNESCO (1958, 1964, 1968); Grand Prix du Disque, Paris (1965); Ravel Prize, Paris (1971), Sibelius Prize, Helsinki (1973); was made an honorary member of the Free Academy of Arts in Hamburg (1966); extraordinary member of the Academy of Arts in West Berlin (1968); honorary member of the International Society for Contemporary Music (1969); associate member of the German Academy of Arts in East Germany (1970); a corresponding member of the American Academy of Arts and Letters (1975) and Royal Academy of Music in London (1976). He received honorary D. Mus. degrees from the Cleveland Institute of Music (1971), University of Warsaw (1973) and an honorary degree of Doctor of Fine Arts from Northwestern Univ. (1974). His early works are marked by a neo-Classical tendency, with an influx of national Polish motives; gradually he turned to a more structural type of composition in which the melodic and rhythmic elements are organized into a strong unifying network, with occasional incursions of dodecaphonic and aleatory practices; the influence of Béla Bartók is felt in the constantly changing colors, angular intervallic progressions and asymmetrical rhythms. In this respect, Lutoslawski's *Musique funèbre* for string orch., dedicated to the memory of Béla Bartók, thematically built on a concatenation of upward tritones and downward semitones, is stylistically significant.

WORKS: *Symphonic Variations* (1936–38; Cracow, June 17, 1939); 2 symphonies: No. 1 (1941–47; Katowice, April 6, 1948); No. 2 (1966–67; Katowice, June 9, 1967); *Overture* for strings (1949; Prague, Nov. 9, 1949); *Little Suite* for chamber orch. (1950; Warsaw, April 20, 1951); Concerto for Orchestra (1950–54; Warsaw, Nov. 26, 1954); *5 Dance Preludes* for clarinet, harp, piano, percussion and strings (1955; a version for nonet, 1959); *Musique funèbre* for string orch., in memory of Béla Bartók (1958; Katowice, March 26, 1958); *3 Postludes*: No. 1 for the centennial of the International Red Cross (1958); No. 2 (1960); No. 3 (1960); *Jeux vénitiens* (1961; Venice, April 24, 1961); *Livre* (The Hague, Nov. 18, 1968; individual movements are called Chapters); Cello Concerto (1970; London, Oct. 14, 1970; Rostropovich soloist); *Mi-parti* (Rotterdam, Oct. 22, 1976). Chamber music: Trio for oboe, clarinet and bassoon (1945); *Recitativo e Arioso* for violin and piano (1951); *5 Folk Melodies* for strings (1952); *Bucoliche,* 5 pieces for viola and piano (1952); *Preludia taneczne* for clarinet and piano (1954); string quartet (1964); *Preludes and Fugues* for 13 solo strings (1971; Festival of the International Society for Contemporary Music, Graz, Oct. 22, 1972). Vocal music: *Belated Nightingale* and Mr. *Tralala,* 2 songs for voice and orch. (1947); *A Straw Chain* for soprano, mezzo-soprano, flute, oboe, 2 clarinets and bassoon (1951); *Silesian Triptych* for soprano and orch. (Warsaw, Dec. 2, 1951); *5 Songs* for female voice and 30 solo instruments (1958); *3 Poèmes d'Henri Michaux* for choir, wind instruments, percussion, 2 pianos and harp (Zagreb, May 9, 1963; performance requires 2 conductors reading from separate scores); *Paroles tissées* for tenor, string ensemble, harp, piano and percussion (Aldeburgh, England, Festival, June 20, 1965); *Les Espaces du Sommeil* for baritone and orch. (1975; Berlin, March 12, 1978); piano pieces.

BIBLIOGRAPHY: S. Jarociński, "Witold Lutoslawski," in *Polish Music* (Warsaw, 1965; in English; pp. 191–99); Ove Nordwall, *Lutoslawski* (Stockholm, 1968).

Lütschg, Karl, renowned piano pedagogue; b. St. Petersburg, Oct. 15, 1839; d. Blankenburg, Germany,

June 6, 1899. He studied piano with Henselt in Russia, and with Moscheles in Germany; composition with Richter and Kiel. Returning to St. Petersburg, he became prof. at the Cons. there; publ. a number of valuable piano studies and instructive editions of classical works: *École d'études* (12 books), *Bibliothèque des œuvres classiques et modernes* (420 numbers); etc. His son, **Waldemar Lütschg** (b. St. Petersburg, May 16, 1877; d. Berlin, Aug. 29, 1948), was also a pianist; after his father's death in 1899 he settled in Berlin; taught piano at the Chicago Musical College in 1905–06.

Lutyens, Elisabeth, English composer; b. London, July 9, 1906. She is the daughter of the noted architect Sir Edwin Lutyens. She studied composition with Harold Darke and viola with Ernest Tomlinson at the Royal College of Music in London (1926–30) and later in Paris (1930–31). In her autobiography, *A Goldfish Bowl* (London, 1972), she recounts a life of artistic frustration: as a composer she progressed from an early Romantic style to an austere, intense Expressionist idiom, with the application of a *sui generis* dodecaphonic technique. In 1969 she received the honorary title of Commander of the British Empire.

WORKS: FOR THE STAGE: a dramatic scene, *The Pit,* for tenor, bass, women's chorus and orch. (Palermo, April 24, 1949); a radio opera, *Penelope* (1950); a chamber opera, *Infidelio* (1956; London April 17, 1973); an opera, *The Numbered* (1965–67); a "charade in 4 acts and 3 interruptions," *Time Off? Not a Ghost of a Chance!,* for actor, baritone, vocal quartet, chorus and 11 instruments (1967–68; Sadler's Wells, London, March 1, 1972); a lyric drama, *Isis and Osiris,* for 8 voices and small orch. (1969); a ballet, *The Birthday of the Infanta* (London, 1932); *Ballet* for 9 wind instruments and percussion (1949). FOR ORCH.: *5 Pieces* (1939); 6 Chamber Concertos, some with solo instruments (1939–48); *3 Symphonic Preludes* (1942); Viola Concerto (1947); *Music I-III* for orch. (1954, 1962, 1964); *Choral* for orch. (1956); *Quincunx* for orch. with optional mezzo-soprano and baritone (1960); *En Voyage,* suite (London, July 2, 1960); *Symphonies* for solo piano, wind, harps and percussion (London, July 28, 1961); *Music* for piano and orch. (1964); *Novenaria* for orch. (1967); *Plenum II* for oboe and chamber orch. (London, June 14, 1974); *The Winter of the World* for cello and chamber ensemble (London, May 5, 1974). FOR VOICE: *ô saisons, ô châteaux!* cantata for soprano, mandolin, guitar, harp and strings (1946); *Requiem for the Living* for soloists, chorus and orch. (1948); *Bienfaits de la lune* for soprano, tenor, chorus, strings and percussion (1952); *De Amore,* cantata (1957; London, Sept. 7, 1973); *Catena* for soprano, tenor and 21 instruments (1961-62); *Encomion* for chorus, brass and percussion (1963); *The Valley of Hatsu-Se* for soprano and instrumental ensemble (1965); *Akapotik Rose* for soprano and instrumental ensemble (1966); *And Suddenly It's Evening* for tenor and 11 instruments (1967); *Essence of Our Happiness,* cantata (1968; London, Sept. 8, 1970); *Phoenix* for soprano, violin, clarinet and piano (1968); *Anerca* for women's speaking chorus, 10 guitars and percussion (1970); *Vision of Youth* for soprano, 3 clarinets, piano and percussion (1970); *Islands* for soprano, tenor, narrator and instrumental ensemble (London, June 7, 1971); *The Tears of Night* for countertenor, 6 sopranos and 3 instrumental ensembles (1971); *Voice of Quiet Waters* for chorus and orch. (1972; Huddersfield, April 14, 1973); *Counting Your Steps* for chorus, 4 flutes and 4 percussionists (1972); choruses; songs. CHAMBER MUSIC: solo Viola Sonata (1938); 6 String Quartets (1938-52); 9 Bagatelles for cello and piano (1942); *Aptote* for solo violin (1948); *Valediction* for clarinet and piano (1954); *Nocturnes* for violin, cello and guitar (1956); *Capriccii* for 2 harps and percussion (1956); *6 Tempi* for 10 instruments (1957); Wind Quintet (1960); String Quintet (1963); Trio for flute, clarinet and bassoon (1963); String Trio (1964); *Scena* for violin, cello and percussion (1964) *Music for Wind* for double wind quintet (1964); *Music for Three* for flute, oboe and piano (1964); *The Fall of the Leaf* for oboe and string quartet (1967); *Horai* for violin, horn and piano (1968); *The Tides of Time* for double bass and piano (1969); *The Rape of the Moon* for chamber ensemble (1973); *Plenum III* for string quartet (1974); *Eos* for ensemble (1975). FOR PIANO: *5 Intermezzi* (1942); *Piano e Forte* (1958); 5 Bagatelles (1962); *Plenum I* (1973). FOR ORGAN: Suite (1948), *Sinfonia* (1956) and *Plenum IV* (1975). She has also composed scores for nearly 200 film, radio and theater productions.

Lutz, Wilhelm Meyer, operetta composer and conductor; b. Männerstadt, near Kissingen, 1822; d. London, Jan. 31, 1903. He studied music with his father, an organist, and later at Würzburg. In 1848 he settled in England; played organ in various churches in Birmingham, Leeds, and London; conducted theater music in London from 1851; in 1869 was appointed musical director at the Gaiety Theatre, for which he wrote numerous light operas; the following were successful: *Faust and Marguerite* (1855); *Blonde and Brunette* (1862), *Zaida* (1868), *Miller of Milburg* (1872), and *Legend of the Lys* (1873). He also wrote the popular dance *Pas de quatre*.

Lux, Friedrich, German composer; b. Ruhla, Nov. 24, 1820; d. Mainz, July 9, 1895. He studied with his father, a cantor at Ruhla; at 12 he gave an organ concert at Gotha; then studied with F. Schneider at Dessau, where he remained for 10 years as music director at the court theater. From 1851 to 1877 he was conductor at the City Theater in Mainz; from 1867 also conducted the Oratorio Society there. WORKS: the operas *Das Käthchen von Heilbronn* (Dessau, March 23, 1846), *Der Schmied von Ruhla* (Mainz, March 28, 1882), and *Die Fürstin von Athen* (Frankfurt, 1890); 4 symphonies (No. 3 subtitled *Die vier Menschenalter*; No. 4, *Durch Nacht zum Licht*, with chorus); 3 string quartets; Piano Trio; many choral works and songs. He publ. transcriptions of Beethoven's symphonies (except the Ninth) for piano, 4-hands. BIBLIOGRAPHY: A. Reissmann, *F. Lux: Sein Leben und seine Werke* (Leipzig, 1888).

Luython, Charles, Flemish composer; b. Antwerp, c.1556; d. Prague, 1620. After receiving elementary training as a chorister in his native land, he was sent, at the age of 10, to the Imperial Chapel in Vienna, where he remained until he was 15. He wrote 2 Masses for Emperior Maximilian II; in 1582 was appointed court organist by Rudolph II, for whom wrote a book of madrigals (publ. by Gardano in Venice). He remained with Rudolph II at his residence in Prague; in 1603 became successor to Philippe de Monte as court composer, while continuing to hold his post as court organist. He retired from the service in 1611. Apart from his book of madrigals (Venice, 1582), he publ. *Sacrae Cantiones* for 6 voices (Prague, 1603); *Lamentationes* for 6 voices (Prague, 1604); 9 Masses for 3-7 voices (Prague, 1609). Among his extant works for instruments, there is a *Fuga suavissima* (publ. in Woltz's *Tabulatur-Buch,* 1617). Luython was a composer of considerable ingenuity; Michael Praetorius recounts in his *Syntagma musicum* that Luython owned a keyboard instrument with 3 manuals, representing the diatonic, chromatic, and enharmonic intervals (18 notes to the octave), thus securing theoretically correct modulations through sharps or flats.
BIBLIOGRAPHY: L. de Burbure, *Charles Luython* (Brussels, 1880); A. A. Smijers, *Luython als Motettenkomponist* (Vienna, 1917); A. G. Ritter, *Zur Geschichte des Orgelspiels* (1884; pp. 51-52).

Luzzaschi, Luzzasco, Italian composer; b. Ferrara, 1545; d. there, Sept. 11, 1607. He studied with Cypriano de Rore as a child (until 1558); became organist at the ducal court, and attained great renown as a teacher; Frescobaldi was one of his many pupils.
WORKS: 7 books of madrigals for 5 voices, of which 5 are extant (1575-1604); *Sacrae cantiones,* also for 5 voices (1598); madrigals for 1-3 sopranos, with keyboard accompaniment (1601). Diruta's collection *Il Transilvano* contains an organ toccata and 2 ricercari by Luzzaschi; the toccata is reprinted in Ritter's *Zur Geschichte des Orgelspiels;* a 4-part *Canzon da sonar* is given in Rauerij's collection (1608); the accompanied madrigal *Ch'io non t'ami,* in Otto Kinkeldey's *Orgel und Klavier in der Musik des 16. Jahrhunderts* (Leipzig, 1910; p. 291). Other reprints are found in L. Torchi's *L'Arte Musicale in Italia* (vol. 4), in Riemann's *Musikgeschichte in Beispielen* (no. 73), and in Schering's *Geschichte der Musik in Beispielen* (no. 166).
BIBLIOGRAPHY: Otto Kinkeldey, "Luzzasco Luzzaschis Solo Madrigale mit Klavierbegleitung," *Sammelbände der Internationalen Musik-Gesellschaft* (1908); A. Einstein, *The Italian Madrigal* (Princeton, 1949); G. Reese, *Music in the Renaissance* (N.Y., 1954, pp. 411-13).

Luzzi, Luigi, Italian composer; b. Olevano di Lomellina, March 28, 1828; d. Stradella, Feb. 23, 1876. He studied medicine at Turin, but later entered the musical profession; wrote successful songs (*Mia madre,* etc.); an opera, *Tripilla* (Novara, Feb. 7, 1874); Symphony; hymns for chorus and orch.; piano pieces.

Lvov, Alexei, Russian violinist and composer; author of the Russian national anthem under the Tsars; b. Reval, June 5, 1798; d. Romano, near Kovno, Dec. 28, 1870. He was the son of the director of the Imperial

Court Chapel in St. Petersburg; received his primary education at home; attended the Institute of Road Engineering (graduated in 1818); at the same time studied violin. In 1827 he was sent to the Turkish front in Bulgaria; then was attached to the Court. He wrote the national anthem "God save the Tsar" in 1833, and it was first performed in Moscow on the name day of Tsar Nicholas I, on Dec. 6 (18), 1833; it remained the official anthem until the Revolution of 1917. In 1837 he succeeded his father as director of the Imperial Chapel (until 1861); in 1839 he organized instrumental classes there; edited a collection of services for the entire ecclesiastical year of the Greek Orthodox Church. In 1840 he traveled in Europe; played his Violin Concerto with the Gewandhaus Orchestra in Leipzig (Nov. 8, 1840); Schumann greatly praised his playing. Returning to Russia, he established a series of orchestral concerts in St. Petersburg, presenting classical programs. Growing deafness forced him to abandon his activities in 1867. As a composer, he followed slavishly the Italian school.
WORKS: 3 operas: *Bianca* (Dresden, Oct. 13, 1844), *Ondine* (in Russian; St. Petersburg, Sept. 20, 1847), and *Starosta Boris, or Russian Muzhik and the French Marauders* (on the subject of the 1812 war; St. Petersburg, May 1, 1854); several violin works, including a concerto; publ. an essay, *On Free or Non-Symmetrical Rhythm* (St. Petersburg, 1858).
BIBLIOGRAPHY: I. Yampolsky, *Russian Violin Art* (Moscow, 1951; vol. 1, pp. 205-27).

Lybbert, Donald, American composer; b. Cresco, Iowa, Feb. 19, 1923. He studied at the Univ. of Iowa (B.M., 1946); at Columbia Univ. with Elliott Carter and Otto Luening (M.A., 1950); and with Nadia Boulanger at Fontainebleau, France (1961). He is prof. of music at Hunter College, N.Y. His style of composition is evolved from firm classical foundations, but he applies dodecaphonic and other serial techniques; without abandoning central tonality, he refrains from using key signatures; his rhythmic patterns are asymmetrical but his polymetry maintains a strong common denominator.
WORKS: operas *Monica* (Amsterdam, Nov. 2, 1952) and *Scarlet Letter* (1965); *Introduction and Toccata* for brass and piano (1955); Trio for clarinet, horn and bassoon (1957); Chamber Sonata for horn, viola and piano (1958); *Leopardi Canti*, song cycle for soprano, flute, viola and bass clarinet (1959); *Sonorities* for 11 instruments (1960); *Sonata brevis* for piano (1962); *Praeludium* for brass and percussion (1962); *Variants for 5 Winds* (1973); *Octagon*, for soprano and 7 chamber players, on Molly Bloom's monologue from James Joyce's *Ulysses* (1975); *Zap* (for the centennial of Hunter College); *Lines for the Fallen*, for soprano and 2 pianos tuned a quarter-tone apart; 2 piano sonatas; choral pieces; song cycles.

Lyford, Ralph, American composer; b. Worcester, Mass., Feb. 22, 1882; d. Cincinnati, Sept. 3, 1927. He began to study piano and violin as a child; entered the New England Cons. in Boston at 12, studying piano with Helen Hopekirk, organ with Goodrich, and composition with Chadwick; then went to Leipzig to study conducting with Artur Nikisch (1906). Returning to America, he became assistant conductor of the San Carlo Opera Co. (1907-8); then was with the Boston Opera Co. (1908-14). In 1916 he settled in Cincinnati, where he taught at the Cons., and also conducted the summer seasons of opera at the Zoölogical Gardens there; in 1925 he became associate conductor of the Cincinnati Symph. Orch.
WORKS: opera *Castle Agrazant* (Cincinnati, April 29, 1926; won the David Bispham Medal); Piano Concerto (1917); chamber music; songs.
BIBLIOGRAPHY: E. E. Hipsher, *American Opera and Its Composers* (Philadelphia, 1934; pp. 304-8).

Lyman, Howard Wilder, American voice teacher; b. Lancaster, Mass. Feb. 2, 1879. He studied at the New England Cons. (graduated, 1909); was for many years on the music faculty at the Univ. of Syracuse (1912-45); also director of music at the Methodist Church there (1926-53); then taught privately. He was still living at the age of 99, in 1978, at Folts Home in Herkimer, New York.

Lyne, Felice, American soprano; b. Slater, Mo., March 28, 1887; d. Allentown, Pa., Sept. 1, 1935. Her family moved to Allentown when she was a child; studied there with F. S. Hardman; then in Paris with Mme. Marchesi, J. de Reszke, and L. d'Aubigne. She made a successful debut as Gilda in *Rigoletto* at Hammerstein's London Opera (Nov. 25, 1911), and appeared there 36 times that season, creating the principal soprano parts in the English premières of Massenet's *Don Quichotte* and *Jongleur de Notre-Dame,* and Holbrooke's *Children of Don;* toured with the Quinlan Opera Co. Returning to the U.S., she became a member of the Boston Opera Co.; also appeared in concerts.

Lynes, Frank, American composer and organist; b. Cambridge, Mass., May 16, 1858; d. Bristol, N.H., June 24, 1913. He was a student at the New England Cons.; later studied piano and organ with B. J. Lang and harmony with J. K. Paine. He then went to Germany and enrolled in the Leipzig Cons. (1883-85), where his teachers were Reinecke (piano) and Jadassohn (theory). Returning to America, he settled in Boston. He held various positions as church organist; for some years conducted the Cantabrigia Ladies' Chorus. He wrote mainly for piano.
WORKS: *Analytical Sonatinas* (a set of 4, so named to emphasize the formal element), *10 Bagatelles, 12 Recreations, 8 Fairy Tales for Musical Children, Woodland Notes* (6 pieces), *Scenes from Alice in Wonderland* (10 pieces), *Independence* (16 studies); also pedagogical works: *Key Circle Exercises; 10 Special Studies;* pieces for piano 4-hands and 6-hands; pieces for 2 pianos, 8-hands; many songs; anthems.
BIBLIOGRAPHY: Olin Downes, *Frank Lynes* (Boston, 1914; contains a complete list of works).

Lynn, George, American choral conductor and composer; b. Edwardsville, Penna., Oct. 5, 1915. He studied composition with Roy Harris at Westminster Choir College, organ with Carl Weinrich and conducting with John Finley Williamson. In 1964 he succeeded Williamson as director of Westminster Choir College and conductor of Westminster Choir.

WORKS: Symph.; Piano Concerto; *Gettysburg Address* for baritone solo, chorus and orch.; *Greek Folksong Rhapsody* for contralto, chorus and orch.; 3 Sacred Symphonies for chorus; 3 string quartets; 30 organ pieces; 40 songs; about 130 choruses. He is editor of Westminster Choir Series, publ. by G. Schirmer, Inc.

Lyon, David, English composer; b. Walsall, Staffordshire, Dec. 29, 1938. He was educated in London. His compositions include a String Quartet (1962); *Divertimento* for small orch. (1963); Piano Concerto (1964); *Partita* for solo horn (1964); *Dance Prelude* for small orch. (1964).

Lyon & Healy, American manufacturers of musical instruments. The firm was founded in Chicago in 1864 by **George Washburn Lyon** (b. 1820) and **Patrick Joseph Healy** (b. March 17, 1840; d. Chicago, April 3, 1905). They began originally as dealers in sheet music, books, and the smaller musical instruments; in 1871 they took over the piano business of Smith & Dixon and gradually began also to manufacture other instruments. After the retirement of Lyon in 1889, Healy became the sole head and general manager; he expanded the manufacturing dept. and erected larger factories. Among the firm's instruments, the Lyon & Healy harp, put on the market in 1899, has become universally known; its collection of old violins once rivaled those of the world's most famous dealers. Besides the parent store in Chicago, there are several branches in other cities.

Lyon, James, an early American composer; b. Newark, N.J., July 1, 1735; d. Machias, Maine, Oct. 12, 1794. He graduated from Princeton in 1759; in 1765, accepted a pastorate in Nova Scotia; then in Machias, Maine (1771 until his death). The *N.Y. Mercury* of Oct. 1, 1759 speaks of an ode composed by Lyon, a member of the graduating class of Princeton, and mentions its performance at the graduation exercises on Sept. 26; but the music of this work, written in the same year that Hopkinson wrote his first songs, is lost. The first known compositions of Lyon are 6 psalm tunes publ. by him in a collection, *Urania* (Philadelphia,

1761; facsimile reproduction, with introduction by R. Crawford, N.Y., 1973); also wrote settings of 2 poems by Watts, *A Marriage Hymn* and *Friendship,* and of Psalms 8, 17, 19, 23, 95, 104, and 150.

BIBLIOGRAPHY: O. G. Sonneck, *Francis Hopkinson and James Lyon: Two Studies in Early American Music* (Washington, 1905; repr., with new introduction by R. Crawford, N.Y., 1969); G. T. Edwards, *Music and Musicians of Maine* (Portland, 1928); *Dictionary of American Biography* vol. 11 (N.Y., 1933).

Lyons, James, American music critic and editor; b. Peabody, Mass., Nov. 24, 1925; d. New York, Nov. 13, 1973. He studied musicology with Karl Geiringer at Boston Univ. and music history with Warren Storey Smith at the New England Cons. of Music. He subsequently dedicated himself to musical journalism; settled in New York in 1952; was a music critic for the *N.Y. Herald Tribune* (1953–62); in 1957 became editor and publisher of the *American Record Guide.* He was co-author (with John Tasker Howard) of *Modern Music* (N.Y. 1957); contributed articles to various music journals on a variety of subjects, ranging from Oriental music to musical psychology.

Lyra, Justus Wilhelm, German cleric and song composer; b. Osnabrück, March 23, 1822; d. Gehrden, Dec. 30, 1882. He studied philosophy and theology in Berlin; filled various church offices in Germany; eventually became "pastor primarious" at Gehrden and Hannover. As a student, he wrote many scholastic songs, which became very popular in German universities (e.g., *Der Mai ist gekommen, Durch Feld und Buchenhallen, Zwischen Frankreich und dem Böhmerwald, Meine Mus' ist gegangen*); he also wrote church music (Christmas cantata, 1872); publ. 5 books of songs, ranging from one voice to mixed chorus; *Die liturgischen Altarweisen des lutherischen Hauptgottesdienstes* (1873); *Andreas Ornithoparchus und dessen Lehre von den Kirchenakzenten* (Gütersloh, 1877); *Luthers Deutsche Messe* (posthumously publ., 1904).

BIBLIOGRAPHY: Bär and Ziller, *J. W. Lyra* (Leipzig, 1901).

Lysberg, Charles-Samuel. See **Bovy-Lysberg, Charles-Samuel.**

M

Maag, Peter, Swiss conductor; b. St. Gallen, May 10, 1919. He received his early musical training from his father, Otto Maag, a Lutheran minister and music scholar; studied piano with Cortot in Paris and conducting with Ansermet in Geneva; was assistant conductor of the Canton theaters at Biel-Solothurn (1942–46) and became its music director for the years 1949–51. Expanding his activities, he conducted opera at Düsseldorf (1952–54); from 1955 to 1959 was general music director at the Bonn Opera; from 1964 to 1968 he was conductor at the Vienna Volksoper; in 1972 he was appointed artistic director at the Teatro Regio in Parma; also conducted opera at La Scala in Milan, at the State Opera in Vienna, at Covent Garden in London, and at the Teatro Colón in Buenos Aires; was guest conductor of the Orchestre de la Suisse Romande in Geneva and of the Berlin Philharmonic; made tours of both South America and Japan. He made his American debut as conductor in Cincinnati in 1959; gave concerts in N.Y. in 1968. On Sept. 23, 1972 he conducted *Don Giovanni* at the Metropolitan Opera, and in 1974 conducted *Falstaff* at the Lyric Opera in Chicago.

Maas, Louis (Philipp Otto), composer and pianist; b. Wiesbaden, Germany, June 21, 1852; d. Boston, Sept. 17, 1889. He studied with Reinecke and Papperitz at Leipzig Cons. (1867–71), and for 3 summers with Liszt. From 1875–80 he taught at the Leipzig Cons.; in 1880 he emigrated to the U.S., settling in Boston; conducted the Boston Philharmonic Concerts (1881–82). As a token of gratitude to his adoptive country, he wrote an "American Symphony," *On the Prairies,* dedicated to President Chester A. Arthur, which he conducted in Boston, Dec. 14, 1882. This symphony, Germanic in form and harmonic language, contained some Indian themes. Maas further wrote overtures, suites, marches, fantasias, etc., for orch.; a string quartet; a piano concerto; 3 sonatas, 3 impromptus and 12 *Phantasiestücke* for piano; violin sonatas; and songs.

Maasalo, Armas, Finnish composer; b. Rautavaara, Aug. 28, 1885; d. Helsinki, Sept. 9, 1960. He studied at the Helsinki School of Music; for 34 years directed the National Chorus (1915–49) and later headed the music department of the Sibelius Academy in Helsinki (1951–55). As a composer he excelled particularly in Finnish church music.

WORKS: *Ricordanza* for cello, piano and orch. (1919); Piano Concerto (1919); *Karelian Scenes* for orch. (1920); *The Path of Man,* cantata (1926); *Two Stars* for alto, chorus and orch. (1929); *Partita seria* for strings (1934); *Christmas Oratorio* (1945); organ pieces; religious songs for chorus and solo voice.

Ma'ayani, Ami, Israeli composer; b. Ramat-Gan, Jan. 13, 1936. He studied composition privately with Ben-Haim (1956–60); concurrently attended courses in architecture at the Technion School in Haifa (diploma, 1960); then worked on electronic music with Ussachevsky at Columbia Univ. in N.Y. (1964–65). In 1971 he was appointed conductor of the Israeli National Youth Orch.

WORKS: opera-oratorio, *The War of the Sons of Light,* for 4 soloists, chorus, ballet and orch. (1970–72); *Divertimento Concertante* for chamber orch. (1957); 2 harp concertos (1960, 1966); *Mizorim (Psalms)* for soprano, flute, bass clarinet, harp, percussion and strings (1965); Concerto for 8 wind instruments and percussion (1966); *Regalim (Festivals)* for soprano or tenor, and orch. (1966); Violin Concerto (1967); Cello Concerto (1967); 2-Piano Concerto (1969); *Symphony Concertante* for wind quintet and orch. (1972); *Poème* for flute and string trio (1965); *Improvisation variée* for flute, viola or violin, and harp (1966); *4 Preludes* for 4 percussionists and piano (1968); *2 Madrigals* for harp and wind quintet (1969); 2 pieces for harp solo, *Maqamat* (1960) and *Toccata* (1962); piano pieces.

Maazel, Lorin, brilliant American conductor; b. Neuilly, France, March 6, 1930, of American parents. He was brought to the U.S. as a child; at a very early age showed innate musical ability; he had perfect pitch and could assimilate music osmotically. He took lessons in conducting with Vladimir Bakaleinikoff in Pittsburgh; in August 1939, at the age of 9, he appeared as conductor at the New York World's Fair producing a sensation and eliciting the inevitable jocular comments (he was compared to a trained seal). Still as a very young boy he conducted concerts at the Hollywood Bowl, and led the NBC Symph. Orch. and the N.Y. Philharmonic in several summer concerts at the Lewisohn Stadium. He survived these traumatic exhibitions; in 1952 received a Fulbright Scholarship for travel in Italy, where he undertook a serious study of Baroque music. He made several tours in Europe and South America, conducting from memory. A polyglot, he is fluent in French, German, Italian, Spanish, Portuguese and Russian, which facilitates his international travels. In 1972 he was appointed music director and conductor of the Cleveland Orchestra, and after some hesitant comments by captious critics, asserted himself as an intellectual artist of the highest caliber.

Mabellini, Teodulo, Italian composer; b. Pistoia, April 2, 1817; d. Florence, March 10, 1897. He studied with Pilotti in his native town, and then in the Istituto Reale Musicale at Florence; at the age of 19, he produced there an opera, *Matilda a Toledo* (Aug. 27, 1836), which made so favorable an impression that Grand Duke Leopold II gave him a stipend to study with Mercadante at Novara. His second opera, *Rolla* (Turin, Nov. 12, 1840), was no less successful; thereupon he wrote many more operas, among them *Ginevra degli Almieri* (Turin, Nov. 13, 1841), *Il conte di Lavagna* (Florence, June 4, 1843), *I Veneziani a Costantinopoli* (Rome, 1844), *Maria di Francia* (Florence, March 14, 1846), and *Fiammetta* (Florence, Feb. 12, 1857). He also wrote several effective oratorios and cantatas: *Eudossia e Paolo* (Florence, 1845), *Etruria* (Florence, August 5, 1849), *Lo spirito di Dante* (Florence, May 15, 1865), and a patriotic hymn *Italia* *risorta* (Florence, Sept. 12, 1847); *Grande Fantasia* for flute, clarinet, horn, trumpet, and trombone; sacred works for chorus and orch. He lived in Florence from 1843 until his death; conducted the concerts of the Società Filarmonica (1843–59); taught composition at the Istituto Reale Musicale (1859–87).

BIBLIOGRAPHY: M. Giannini, *Mabellini e la musica* (Pistoia, 1899); A. Simonatti, *Teodulo Mabellini* (Pistoia, 1923).

MacArdle, Donald Wales, American musicologist; b. Quincy, Massachusetts, July 3, 1897; d. Littleton, Colorado, Dec. 23, 1964. He studied science at the Mass. Institute of Technology, obtaining an M.S. in chemical engineering; then turned to music; took courses at the Juilliard School in N.Y. He devoted his scholarly research mainly to the minutiae of Beethoven's biography; contributed a number of valuable articles on the subject to the *Musical Quarterly* and other journals. He earned his living as an engineer.

Macbeth, Allan, Scottish organist and composer; b. Greenock, March 13, 1856; d. Glasgow, Aug. 25, 1910. He studied at the Leipzig Cons. with Richter, Reinecke, and Jadassohn (1875–76). His subsequent musical activities were largely confined to playing the organ in Glasgow churches and directing choral groups; from 1890 he was principal of the School of Music at the Glasgow Athenaeum. He wrote an operetta, *The Duke's Doctor*; 2 cantatas, *The Land of Glory* (1890) and *Silver Bells; Jubilee Chorus* (1896); *Intermezzo* for strings; *Danze pizzicate,* for orch.; also chamber music and songs.

Macbeth, Florence, American coloratura soprano; b. Mankato, Minnesota, Jan. 12, 1891; d. Hyattsville, Maryland, May 5, 1966. She studied in Europe; in 1913 made her operatic debut as Rosina in *Il Barbiere di Siviglia* in Braunschweig, Germany. On Jan. 14, 1914, she made her American debut with the Chicago Opera Co. and remained on its staff as prima coloratura soprano until 1930; for a season she undertook an American tour with the Commonwealth Opera Co., singing in Gilbert and Sullivan operettas. So melodious and mellifluous were her fiorituras that she was dubbed the "Minnesota Nightingale." In 1947 she married the novelist James M. Cain and settled in Maryland.

MacCunn, Hamish, Spanish composer and conductor; b. Greenock, March 22, 1868; d. London, Aug. 2, 1916. He studied at the Royal College of Music (1883–86) with Parry; then taught at the Royal Academy of Music (1888–94); in 1898, became conductor of the Carl Rosa Opera Co.; from 1900 to 1905 conducted at the Savoy Theatre; later he toured with various troupes, conducting light opera.

WORKS: operas: *Jeanie Deans,* after Scott's *The Heart of Midlothian* (Edinburgh, Nov. 15, 1894), *Diarmid* (London, Oct. 23, 1897), *The Masque of War and Peace* (London, Feb. 13, 1900); *The Golden Girl,* musical comedy (Birmingham, Aug. 5, 1905); the cantatas, *Lord Ullin's Daughter,* after Walter Scott (London, Feb. 18, 1888), *Bonny Kilmeny* (Edinburgh, Dec. 15, 1888), *The Lay of the Last Minstrel* (Glasgow, Dec. 18, 1888), *The Cameronian's Dream* (Edinburgh, Jan. 27, 1890), *Queen Hynde of Caledon* (Glasgow, Jan. 28, 1892), *The Wreck of the Hesperus,* after Longfellow (London, Aug. 28, 1905); the overtures *Cior Mhor* (London, Oct. 27, 1885), *The Land of the Mountain and the Flood,* after Scott (London, Nov. 5, 1887), *The Ship o' the Fiend* (London, Feb. 21, 1888), *The Dowie Dens o' Yarrow* (London, Oct. 13, 1888); *Highland Memories,* orchestral sketch (London, March 13, 1897); *Scotch Dances* for piano; songs; etc.

MacDermid, James G., American pianist, vocalist, and composer; b. Utica, Ontario, June 10, 1875; d. Brooklyn, Aug. 16, 1960. He studied in London, Ontario; in 1893 went to Chicago for further studies, and remained in the U.S.; became an American citizen in 1906; for several seasons toured as accompanist to his wife, **Sibyl Sammis MacDermid,** soprano (b. Foreston, Ill., May 15, 1876; d. New York, Nov. 2, 1940). He published about 75 sacred and secular songs.

MacDowell, Edward Alexander, greatly significant national American composer, b. New York, Dec. 18, 1860; d. there, Jan. 23, 1908. His early teachers were Teresa Carreño in piano and Desvernine in music theory. In 1876 he went to France and enrolled as an auditor in Savard's class at the Paris Cons.; was admitted as a regular student on Feb. 8, 1877, and withdrew on Sept. 30, 1878. From 1877 to 1879 he studied piano with Antoine-François Marmontel and solfège with Marmontel's son. He then went to Germany where he took a brief course with Louis Ehlert in Wiesbaden; then enrolled in the Frankfurt Cons. in 1879 as a piano student of Karl Heymann and, in composition, of Joachim Raff. Both Heymann and Raff recognized MacDowell's unusual talent, and when Heymann resigned his post in 1881, he recommended MacDowell as his successor; his suggestion, however, was not followed, and MacDowell accepted a teaching position at the Darmstadt Cons. In 1882 Raff introduced him to Liszt, who arranged for him to play his own piano work, *Modern Suite,* at the annual concert of the Allgemeiner Musikverein (Weimar, July 11, 1882). In 1884 MacDowell returned to America; on July 9, 1884 he married his former pupil Marian Nevins, who during her long life (1857–1956) was his devoted helper and after his death a faithful keeper of his musical legacy. In 1888 the MacDowells settled in Boston. The Boston Symph. Orch., under its successive conductors, Gericke, Nikisch and Paur, regularly performed MacDowell's compositions. He was the soloist in his own Piano Concerto with the Boston Symph. on April 12, 1889. When Columbia Univ. established a music department in 1896, the trustees invited MacDowell as the first incumbent, citing him as the "the greatest musical genius America has produced." Unfortunately, mutual disenchantment soon developed between MacDowell and the university authorities; MacDowell was outspoken in his dissatisfaction with the organization of the Division of Fine Arts; the trustees in turn accused MacDowell of a lack of propriety. In 1904 he resigned his post. The shock of these events probably affected MacDowell's mental state, which was already unstable; the physicians found a disintegrating process in the brain tissues, which eventually resulted in total insanity. MacDowell spent the last years of his life in a childlike state, unaware of his surroundings and incapable of performing vital functions. In 1906 a public appeal was launched to raise funds for MacDowell; the signers included Horatio Parker, Victor Herbert, Arthur Foote, George Chadwick, Frederick Converse, Andrew Carnegie, J. Pierpont Morgan, and former President Grover Cleveland. After MacDowell's death, which came when he was only 47 years old, the sum of fifty thousand dollars was raised for the organization of the MacDowell Memorial Association; Mrs. MacDowell deeded to the Association her husband's summer residence at Peterborough, New Hampshire. This property became a pastoral retreat for American composers and writers who could spend summers and work undisturbed in separate cottages, paying a minimum rate for lodgings and food. During the summer of 1910 Mrs. MacDowell arranged an elaborate pageant with music from MacDowell's works; the success of this project led to the establishment of a series of MacDowell festivals in Peterborough.

Among American composers MacDowell occupies an exalted position. He was a musical poet whose talent found its most felicitous expression in small forms of lyrico-dramatic inspiration. He possessed the gift of fertile invention; his musical themes are admirably defined and logically developed. His sense of proportion, symmetry and artistic unity was impeccable; with unerring instinct he maintained the given mood of a work, avoiding irrelevant or incompatible elements. His harmonic scheme is bold within the limits of the romantically beautiful, his rhythm varied and incisive, his melody noble, his dramatic climaxes emotionally stirring. Directness, freshness, and vitality constitute the perennial charm of MacDowell's music. Stylistically, he belonged to the romantic age; he was a kindred spirit of Schumann and Grieg. MacDowell was the first American composer of stature who incorporated American rhythms and melodic patterns into his music and depicted in romantic colors the landscape of America.

WORKS: (opp. 1–7 were publ. under the pseudonym of **Edgar Thorn**):

FOR ORCH.: *Hamlet and Ophelia*, symph. poem, op. 22 (1885; Boston Symph., Jan. 27, 1893); *Lancelot and Elaine*, symph. poem, op. 25 (1888; Boston Symph., Jan. 10, 1890); *Lamia*, symph. poem, op. 29 (1889; Boston Symph., Oct. 23, 1908); *The Saracens* and *The Lovely Alda*, 2 symph. poems, op. 30 (Boston Philharmonic, Nov. 5, 1891); Suite No. 1 for orch., op. 42 (Worcester Festival, Sept. 24, 1891); Suite No. 2 (*Indian Suite*; N.Y., Jan. 23, 1895; Boston Symph. Orch., Jan. 31, 1895); Piano Concerto No. 1, in A minor, op. 15 (1882; Zürich, July 11, 1882, composer soloist); Piano Concerto No. 2, in D minor, op. 23 (N.Y., March 5, 1889, composer soloist); *Romance* for cello and orch., op. 35 (1888).

FOR CHORUS: 2 choruses for men's voices, op. 3, *Love and Time* and *The Rose and the Gardener* (1897); *The Witch*, for men's chorus, op. 5 (1898); *War Song*, for men's chorus, op. 6 (1898); 3 songs for men's chorus, op. 27 (1887); 2 songs for men's chorus, op. 41 (1890); *Two Northern Songs*, for mixed voices, op. 43 (1891); 3 choruses for men's voices, op. 52 (1897); *Two*

Songs from the 13th Century, for men's chorus (1897); 2 choruses for men's voices, op. 53 (1898); 2 choruses for men's voices, op. 54 (1898); *College Songs*, for men's voices (1901); *Summer Wind*, for women's chorus (1902).

FOR VOICE AND PIANO: *Two Old Songs*, op. 9 (1894); 3 Songs, op. 11 (1883); 2 Songs, op. 12 (1883); *From an Old Garden* (6 songs), op. 26 (1887); 3 Songs, op. 33 (1888; revised 1894); 2 Songs, op. 34 (1888); *6 Love Songs*, op. 40 (1890); 8 Songs, op. 47 (1893); 4 Songs, op. 56 (1898); 3 Songs, op. 58 (1899); 3 Songs, op. 60 (1902).

FOR PIANO: *Amourette*, op. 1 (1896); *In Lilting Rhythm*, op. 2 (1897); *Forgotten Fairy Tales* (*Sung Outside the Prince's Door, Of a Tailor and a Bear, Beauty in the Rose Garden, From Dwarfland*), op. 4 (1898); *6 Fancies* (*A Tin Soldier's Love, To a Humming Bird, Summer Song, Across Fields, Bluette, An Elfin Round*), op. 7 (1898); *Waltz*, op. 8 (1895); *First Modern Suite*, op. 10 (1880); *Prelude and Fugue*, op. 13 (1883); *Second Modern Suite*, op. 14 (1881); *Serenata*, op. 16 (1883); *2 Fantastic Pieces* (*Legend, Witches' Dance*), op. 17 (1884); *2 Pieces* (*Barcarolle, Humoresque*), op. 18 (1884); *Forest Idyls* (*Forest Stillness, Play of the Nymphs, Revery, Dance of the Dryads*), op. 19 (1884); *4 Pieces* (*Humoresque, March, Cradle Song, Czardas*), op. 24 (1887); *6 Idyls* after Goethe (*In the Woods, Siesta, To the Moonlight, Silver Clouds, Flute Idyl, The Bluebell*), op. 28 (1887); *6 Poems* after Heine (*From a Fisherman's Hut, Scotch Poem, From Long Ago, The Post Wagon, The Shepherd Boy, Monologue*), op. 31 (1887); *4 Little Poems* (*The Eagle, The Brook, Moonshine, Winter*), op. 32 (1888); *Etude de Concert* in F-sharp, op. 36 (1889); *Les Orientales*, after Victor Hugo (*Clair de Lune, Danse le Hamac, Danse Andalouse*), op. 37 (1889); *Marionettes*, 8 Little Pieces (*Prologue, Soubrette, Lover, Witch, Clown, Villain, Sweetheart, Epilogue*), op. 38 (1888; originally only six pieces; *Prologue* and *Epilogue* were added in 1901); 12 Studies, Book I (*Hunting Song, Alla Tarantella, Romance, Arabesque, In the Forest, Dance of the Gnomes*); Book II (*Idyl, Shadow Dance, Intermezzo, Melody, Scherzino, Hungarian*), op. 39 (1890); Sonata No. 1, *Tragica*, op. 45 (1893); 12 Virtuoso Studies (*Novelette, Moto Perpetuo, Wild Chase, Improvisation, Elfin Dance, Valse Triste, Burleske, Bluette, Träumerei, March Wind, Impromptu, Polonaise*), op. 46 (1894); *Air and Rigaudon*, op. 49 (1894); Sonata No. 2, *Eroica*, op. 50 (1895); *Woodland Sketches*, 10 pieces (*To a Wild Rose, Will o' the Wisp, At an Old Trysting Place, In Autumn, From an Indian Lodge, To a Water Lily, From Uncle Remus, A Deserted Farm, By a Meadow Brook, Told at Sunset*), op. 51 (1896); *Sea Pieces* (*To the Sea, From a Wandering Iceberg, A.D. 1620, Star-light, Song, From the Depths, Nautilus, In Mid-Ocean*), op. 55 (1898); Sonata No. 3, *Norse*, op. 57 (1900); Sonata No. 4, *Keltic*, op. 59 (1901); *Fireside Tales* (*An Old Love Story, Of Br'er Rabbit, From a German Forest, Of Salamanders, A Haunted House, By Smouldering Embers*), op. 61 (1902); *New England Idyls*, 10 pieces (*An Old Garden, Midsummer, Midwinter, With Sweet Lavender, In Deep Woods, Indian Idyl, To an Old White Pine, From Puritan Days, From a Log Cabin, The Joy of Autumn*), op. 62 (1902); 6 Little Pieces on

Sketches by J. S. Bach (1890); Technical Exercises, 2 Books (1893; 1895). MacDowell's writings were collected by W. J. Baltzell and publ. as *Critical and Historical Essays* (1912); repr., with new intro. by I. Lowens (N.Y., 1969).

BIBLIOGRAPHY: L. Gilman, *Edward MacDowell: A Study* (N.Y., 1908; corrected reprint, N.Y., 1969); E. F. Page, *Edward MacDowell: His Works and Ideals* (N.Y., 1910); J. Adams, *What the Piano Writings of MacDowell Mean to the Piano Student* (Chicago, 1913); T. P. Currier, "MacDowell as I Knew Him," *Musical Quarterly* (Jan. 1915); O. G. Sonneck, *Suum cuique: Essays in Music* (N.Y., 1916); O. G. Sonneck, *Catalogue of First Editions of Edward MacDowell* (Washington, D.C., 1917; reprint, N.Y., 1973); W. H. Humiston, *MacDowell* (N.Y., 1921); J. F. Porte, *A Great American Tone Poet: Edward MacDowell* (London, 1922); J. B. Matthews, *Commemorative Tributes to MacDowell* (N.Y., 1922); Abbie F. Brown, *The Boyhood of Edward MacDowell* (N.Y., 1924); Upton Sinclair, "MacDowell," *American Mercury* (1926); J. F. Cooke, *Edward MacDowell, A Short Biography* (Philadelphia, 1928); R. W. Brown, "A Listener to the Winds, Edward MacDowell," in *Lonely Americans* (N.Y., 1929); Paul Rosenfeld, *An Hour with American Music* (Philadelphia, 1929, pp. 31–51); Anita Brown, *A Mosaic of Muses of the MacDowell Club of New York* (N.Y., 1930); *Catalogue of an Exhibition Illustrating the Life and Work of Edward MacDowell* (N.Y., 1938); J. T. Howard, *Our American Music* (N.Y., 1939; 4th ed., 1965); Marian MacDowell, "MacDowell's Peterborough Idea" *Musical Quarterly* (Jan. 1932); Marian MacDowell, *Random Notes on Edward MacDowell and his Music* (Boston, 1950); Arnold T. Schwab, "Edward MacDowell's Birthdate: A Correction," *Musical Quarterly* (April 1975).

Macfarlane, William Charles, English-born American organist and composer; b. London, Oct. 2, 1870; d. North Conway, N.H., May 12, 1945. In 1874 he was taken to N.Y.; was taught by his father, Duncan Macfarlane (1836–1916), and by S. P. Warren. He made his debut as organist in N.Y. on March 22, 1886; from 1898 to 1919 held various positions as organist and choral conductor; in 1941, retired to North Conway. He wrote *America First, a Boy Scout Operetta* (1917); the light operas, *Little Almond Eyes* (Portland, 1916) and *Sword and Scissors* (1918); cantata *The Message from the Cross* (1907); *The Church Service Book* (N.Y., 1912); numerous anthems and other sacred music; organ pieces (*Lullaby, Serenade, Scherzo, Romanza,* etc.).

Macfarren, Sir George Alexander, eminent English composer and pedagogue; b. London, March 2, 1813; d. there, Oct. 31, 1887. He studied with his father, George Macfarren, the dramatist, and with Charles Lucas and C. Porter (1829) at the Royal Academy of Music, where he became a professor in 1834. After many years of teaching there, he was appointed in 1875 successor to Sterndale Bennett as prof. of music at Cambridge Univ.; in 1876 he became principal of the Royal Academy of Music. He was knighted in 1883. In the last years of his life he became blind. WORKS: the operas (all performed in London) *Don Quixote* (Feb. 3, 1846), *Charles II* (Oct. 27, 1849), *Robin Hood* (Oct. 11, 1860), *Helvellyn* (Nov. 3, 1864); the oratorios *St. John the Baptist* (Bristol, Oct. 23, 1873), *The Resurrection* (Birmingham, 1876), *Joseph* (Leeds, 1877), *King David* (Leeds, 1883); cantata, *The Lady of the Lake* (Glasgow, Nov. 15, 1877); many sacred works; songs, including the well-known *Pack, clouds, away;* chamber music. He publ. *Rudiments of Harmony* (1860; 14 eds.) and *Six lectures on Harmony* (1867; 3rd ed., 1880); also *Addresses and Lectures* (London, 1888). He edited *Old English Ditties* (2 vols.), *Old Scottish Ditties, Moore's Irish Melodies, Songs of England, British Vocal Album;* also Purcell's *Dido and Aeneas,* Handel's *Belshazzar, Judas Maccabaeus, Jephtha,* and *Messiah,* etc. His wife, **Natalie Macfarren** (*née* Clarina Thalia Andrae; b. Lübeck, Dec. 14, 1826; d. Bakewell, April 9, 1916), received her early education in New York; later studied singing in London; also took a course in composition with Macfarren, whom she married in 1844. She appeared as an opera singer (contralto) in New York, and in her husband's operas in England. She was a successful singing teacher; publ. a *Vocal Method* and an *Elementary Course of Vocalising and Pronouncing the English Language.*

BIBLIOGRAPHY: H. C. Banister, *George Alexander Macfarren: His Life, Works, and Influence* (London, 1892).

Macfarren, Walter Cecil, English pianist and composer; brother of **George Alexander Macfarren;** b. London, Aug. 28, 1826; d. there, Sept. 2, 1905. He was a chorister at Westminster Abbey; then studied at the Royal Academy of Music, with Holmes (piano) and with his brother (composition). From 1846 until 1903 he was professor of piano at the Royal Academy of Music; conducted its concerts from 1873 till 1880. He composed a number of overtures on Shakespearian subjects; a piano concerto; many piano pieces; edited Beethoven's sonatas, and several albums of piano pieces under the title *Popular Classics.* He publ. *Memories; an Autobiography* (London, 1905).

Mach, Ernst, eminent German acoustician; b. Turas, Moravia, Feb. 18, 1838; d. Vaterstetten, near Munich, Feb. 19, 1916. He was a professor of physics in Prague (1864) and in Vienna (1895). Besides his scientific works of far-reaching importance, he published a number of books and studies dealing with musical acoustics: *Zwei populäre Vorträge über musikalische Akustik* (1865); *Einleitung in die Helmholtz'sche Musiktheorie* (1866); *Zur Theorie des Gehörorgans* (1872); *Beitrag zur Geschichte der Musik* (1892); *Die Analyse der Empfindungen und das Verhältnis des Physischen zum Psychischen* (5th ed., 1906); "Zur Geschichte der Theorie der Konsonanz," in *Populärwissenschaftliche Vorträge* (3rd ed., 1903). The unit of velocity of sound "Mach" is named after him.

Mácha, Otmar, Czech composer; b. Ostrava, Oct. 2, 1922. He studied with Jaroslav Řídký at the Prague Cons. (1942–46); was chief dramaturgist for musical programs at the Czech Radio in Prague (1945–62); from 1969 worked at the Czech Radio. WORKS: 3 operas: *Polapená nevěra (Entrapped*

Faithlessness, 1956-57; Prague, Nov. 21, 1958), *Jezero Ukereve* (*Lake Ukereve*, 1960-63; Prague, May 27, 1966) and the opera buffa *Svatba na oko* (*Feigned Wedding*, 1974-76); a musical comedy, *Cradle for Sinful Maidens* (1975-76); an oratorio *The Heritage of Jan Amos Comenius* (1952-55); *Symphonic Intermezzo* (1958); *Noc a Naděje* (*Night and Hope*), symph. poem (Prague Spring Fest., May 26, 1960); *Azur Tarantella* for orch. (1962); *Variations on a Theme by and the Death of Jan Rychlík* for orch. (Prague, March 15, 1966); *4 Monologues* for soprano, baritone and orch. (1966); *Variants*, short studies for orch. (Czech Radio, April 21, 1969); *Janinka zpívá* (*Janinka Sings*), suite for soprano and orch. (1969); Sinfonietta (1970-71); *Double Concerto* for violin, piano and orch. (1975-76); String Quartet (1943); Violin Sonata (1948); Cello Sonata (1949); Bassoon Sonata (1963); *Funeral Toccata* for organ (1964); *The Weeping of the Saxophone* for saxophone and piano (1968); *Folklore* for piano (1969); *Psalm No. 2* for baritone and organ (1969); *Small Triptych*, 3 songs for soprano, flute and tam-tam (1971); *Wedding Toccata* for organ (1974); *Eyes and Hands*, chamber cantata for mezzo-soprano, clarinet, viola and piano (1975-76); choruses; songs.

Machabey, Armand, French musicologist; b. Pont-de-Roide, Doubs, May 7, 1886; d. Paris, Aug. 31, 1966. He studied at the Univ. of Paris; *docteur ès lettres*, 1928; subsequently active as a music historian and essayist.
WRITINGS: *Histoire et évolution des formules musicales* (dissertation, 1928; revised, and publ. in 1955 as *Genèse de la tonalité musicale classique, des origines au XVe siècle*); *Précis-manuel d'histoire de la musique* (1942); *Anton Bruckner* (1946); *Maurice Ravel* (1947); *Traité de la critique musicale* (1947); *Le Bel Canto* (1948); *Portraits de trente musiciens français* (1949); *La Notation musicale* (1952); *Frescobaldi* (1952); *Guillaume de Machaut: la vie et l'œuvre musicale* (2 vols., 1955). He contributed numerous valuable articles to various magazines; also wrote several orchestral suites and songs.

Machado, Augusto, Portuguese composer; b. Lisbon, Dec. 27, 1845; d. there, March 26, 1924. He was a pupil of Junior, Lami, and D'Almeide in Lisbon, and of Lavignac and Danhauser in Paris; 1892-1908, director of the San Carlos Theater in Lisbon; 1894-1910, director of the Cons. there. Besides numerous operettas, he wrote the operas *A Cruz de oiro* (Lisbon, 1873), *A Maria da Fonte* (Lisbon, 1879), *Lauriane* (Marseilles, Jan. 9, 1883; his most successful work), *Os Dorias* (Lisbon, 1887), *Mario Wetter* (Lisbon, 1898), *Venere* (Lisbon, 1905), and *La Borghesina* (Lisbon, 1909). For the third centenary of the death of Camoens he wrote the symph. ode *Camões es os Luziadas* (1880); also organ and piano pieces.

Machaut (or **Machault, Machaud**), **Guillaume de (Guillelmus de Mascaudio),** important French composer and poet; probably a native of Machaut in the Champagne; b. c.1300; d. Rheims, 1377. He studied theology; took holy orders; in 1323-40 was in the service of King John of Bohemia (Duke of Luxembourg) as almoner (1330), notary (1332), and secretary (1335), traveling widely with that prince (their visits extended to Russia). Later he was at the court of Charles V of France. He held various ecclesiastical benefices (Houdain, Arras, Verdun), and from 1337 was canon of Rheims, where he resided from 1340 until his death (he visited Paris in 1363). His works include ballades, rondeaux, virelais, and motets. He wrote the earliest polyphonic (4 voices) setting of the complete Mass by a single composer. A complete ed. of Machaut's musical works was prepared by Friedrich Ludwig for the *Publikationen älterer Musik* (vols. I, 1; III, 1; IV, 2; 1926-34, containing about two-thirds of his *opera omnia* and a commentary); the Mass, lais and hocket, not included in Ludwig's collection, were brought out for the *Publikationen* by H. Besseler in 1943, but the printed copies were destroyed in an air raid. After the war, several editions of the Mass were publ. (by Chailley, Paris, 1948; by Machabey, Liège, 1948; by de Van, Rome, 1949; by Hübsch, Heidelberg, 1953; and Besseler's again, Leipzig, 1954). The complete works are publ. in L. Schrade, ed., *Polyphonic Music of the 14th Century* (vols. 2 and 3; Monaco, 1956). 14 works (including parts of the Mass) are found in J. Wolf's *Geschichte der Mensuralnotation von 1250-1450* (Leipzig, 1904); 2 pieces in Schering's *Geschichte der Musik in Beispielen*; other pieces in Davison and Apel, *Historical Anthology of Music* (Cambridge, Mass., 1946). *La louange des dames*, lyric poems, was ed. by N. Wilkins (Edinburgh, 1972).
BIBLIOGRAPHY: Machaut's poems were publ. by V. Chichmaref, as *Poésies lyriques de Guillaume Machaut* (2 vols., Paris, 1909). H. Quittard, "Notes sur Guillaume de Machaut et son œuvre," *Bulletin de la Société Française de Musicologie* (1918); H. Besseler, in the *Freiburger-Orgelbericht* (1926; pp. 146 ff.); A. Machabey, "Guillaume de Machaut, la vie et l'homme," *Revue Musicale* (May 1930; April and May 1931); G. Reese, *Music in the Middle Ages*, chapter 12 (N.Y., 1940); A. Douce, *Guillaume de Machaut, Musicien et poète rémois* (Rheims, 1948); George Perle, "Integrative Devices in the Music of Machaut," *Musical Quarterly* (April 1948); Otto Gombosi, "Machaut's Messe Notre-Dame," *Musical Quarterly* (April 1950); S. Levarie, *Guillaume de Machaut* (N.Y., 1954); A. Machabey, *Guillaume de Machaut: la vie et l'œuvre musicale* (2 vols.; Paris, 1955); G. Reaney, "Notes on the Harmonic Technique of Guillaume de Machaut," in H. Tischler, *Essays in Musicology* (Apel Festschrift; Bloominton, Ind., 1968); H. H. Eggebrecht, "Machauts Motette Nr. 9," *Archiv für Musikwissenschaft* (Aug. 1968); S. J. Williams, "Vocal Scoring in the Chansons of Machaut," *Journal of the American Musicologist Society* (Fall 1968); W. Dömling, *Die mehrstimmigen Balladen, Rondeaux und Virelais von Guillaume de Machaut* (Tutzing, 1970); M. Hasselman and T. Walker, "More Hidden Polyphony in a Machaut Manuscript," *Musica Disciplina* (1970); G. Reaney, *Guillaume de Machaut* (London, 1971).

Machavariani, Alexei, Georgian composer; b. Gory, Sept. 23, 1913. He studied at the Cons. of Tiflis, graduating in 1936; in 1940 became instructor in music theory there. His music is profoundly infused with Caucasian melorhythms. He wrote the operas *Deda da shvili* (*Mother and Son;* Tiflis, May 1, 1945) on a patriotic subject connected with the struggle for independence in the Caucasus, and *Hamlet* (1964); a ballet, *Knight in a Tiger's Skin* (1965); symph. poems, *Mumly Muhasa* (1939), *Satchidao* (1940), *On the Death of a Hero* (1948); overture, *The People's Choice* (1950); cantata, *For Peace, for Fatherland* (1951); Piano Concerto (1944); Violin Concerto (1950); an oratorio, *The Day of My Fatherland* (1954); many songs, of which *Blue Light* (1949) achieved great popularity in Russia; *Khorumy*, a Georgian military dance, for piano (1941; very popular); 2 symphonies (1947, 1973).

Machl, Tadeusz, Polish organist, composer and pedagogue; b. Lwów, Oct. 22, 1922. He studied composition with Malawski and organ with Rutkowski at the State College of Music in Cracow (1949–52); subsequently occupied various teaching and administrative positions in Cracow.
WORKS: *3 miniatury symfoniczne* (1946); 5 symphonies: No. 1, with chorus (1947); No. 2 (1948); No. 3, *Tatry* (1949); No. 4 (1954); No. 5 for soprano, female chorus and orch. (1963); many concertos, including 4 for organ (1950; 1952; 1953; 1958) and one each for soprano (1958), violin (1960), harpsichord (1962), piano (1965) and harp (1967); *Double Concerto* for piano, harpsichord and orch. (1967); 2 triple concertos: No. 1 for 3 organs (1969) and No. 2 for 2 pianos, organ and orch. (1971); *Lyrical Suite* for orch. (1956); *Jubilee Overture* (1971); *Dzień pracy* (*Labor Day*) for chorus and small orch. (1948); 3 string quartets (1952, 1957, 1962); Piano Sonata (1940); pieces for organ solo and for piano; choruses; songs.

Machlis, Joseph, American music historian and pedagogue; b. Riga, Latvia, Aug. 11, 1906; was brought to the U.S. as an infant. He studied at the College of the City of N.Y. (B.A., 1927), and at the Institute of Musical Art of the Juilliard School (Teachers Diploma, 1927); also took an M.A. in English literature from Columbia Univ. (1938). In 1938 he was appointed to the music faculty at Queens College of the City Univ. of N.Y. He publ. several well-written texts: the immensely popular *The Enjoyment of Music* (N.Y., 1955; 3rd ed., 1970); *Introduction to Contemporary Music* (N.Y., 1961); *American Composers of Our Time* for young people (N.Y., 1963); *Getting to Know Music* for high school students (N.Y., 1966). He translated a number of operatic librettos for the NBC Opera Company (*Rigoletto, La Traviata, Fidelio, La Bohème, Cavalleria Rusticana,* Prokofiev's *War and Peace,* etc.); *Boris Godunov, Tosca* and Manuel de Falla's *Atlántida* for other opera companies. He is the author of a novel *57th Street* about the "concert industry" (N.Y., 1970), published under the phonetically palindromic pseudonym **George Selcamm.**

Mackenzie, Sir Alexander Campbell, distinguished British composer and educator; b. Edinburgh, Aug. 22, 1847; d. London, April 28, 1935. A scion of a musical family (there were 4 generations of musicians in his paternal line), he showed musical aptitude as a child; was sent to Germany, where he studied violin with K. W. Uhlrich and theory with Eduard Stein, at the Sondershausen Cons. (1857–62); returning to England, he studied violin with Sainton and music theory with Charles Lucas; subsequently was active in Edin-

burgh as violinist and teacher (1865–79). Between 1879 and 1888 he spent part of each year in Florence. In 1888 he was elected principal of the Royal Academy of Music in London, holding this post until 1924. From 1892 to 1899 he conducted the concerts of the Philharmonic Society of London. His reputation as an educator and composer was very high among musicians. He was knighted in 1895. As a composer, he was a staunch believer in programmatic music; he introduced national Scottish elements in many of his works; his *Pibroch Suite* for violin and orch., first introduced by Sarasate at the Leeds Festival (1889), acquired considerable popularity; Paderewski gave the first performance of his *Scottish Concerto* with the London Philharmonic (1897).
WORKS: OPERAS: (all first performed in London); *Colomba* (April 9, 1883), *The Troubadour* (June 8, 1886), *His Majesty* (Feb. 20, 1897), *The Cricket on the Hearth* (composed 1900; perf. June 6, 1914), *The Knight of the Road* (Feb. 27, 1905); CANTATAS: *Jason* (1882), *The Rose of Sharon* (Norwich Festival, Oct. 16, 1884), *The Story of Sayid* (1886), *The Witches' Daughter* (1904), *The Sun-God's Return* (1910); FOR ORCH: *Cervantes,* overture (1877), *Scottish Rhapsody* No. 1 (1880), *Burns* (*Scottish Rhapsody* No. 2, 1881), *La Belle Dame sans merci,* after Keats (1883), *Twelfth Night,* after Shakespeare (1888), *Coriolanus,* suite (1901), *London Day by Day,* suite (1902), *Canadian Rhapsody* (1905), *Tam o'Shanter* (*Scottish Rhapsody* No. 3, 1911), *Youth, Sport and Loyalty,* overture (1922), Violin Concerto (1885), *Pibroch Suite* for violin and orch. (Leeds, Oct. 10, 1889), Suite No. 2 for violin and orch. (London, Feb. 18, 1897), *Scottish Concerto* for piano and orch. (London, March 24, 1897); CHAMBER MUSIC: Piano Trio (1874), String Quartet (1875), Piano Quartet (1875), *From the North,* 9 pieces for violin and piano (1895), *4 Dance Measures,* for violin and piano (1915); several characteristic piano suites (*Rustic Suite, In the Scottish Highlands, Odds and Ends, Jottings, In Varying Moods);* a number of songs; arrangements of Scottish songs, etc. He publ. an autobiography, *A Musician's Narrative* (London, 1927).

Mackerras, Charles, American conductor; b. Schenectady, N.Y., Nov. 17, 1925, of Australian parentage. He was taken to Sydney at the age of 2; studied oboe playing at the Sydney Cons. and served as first oboist at the Sydney Symph. Orch. In 1946 he went to England; in 1947–48 he studied conducting with Vaclav Talich in Prague; returned to England and held several positions as conductor, first at Sadler's Wells Opera in London (1948–54), then with the BBC Concert Orchestra (1954–56); subsequently he conducted guest appearances with orchestras in Europe, Canada, Australia and South Africa; from 1966 to 1969 he was principal conductor of the Hamburg State Opera. In 1969 he was appointed musical director at the Sadler's Wells Opera.

Mackinlay, Malcolm Sterling, English bass and singing teacher; son of the famous contralto, **Antoinette Sterling;** b. London, Aug. 7, 1876; d. there, Jan 10, 1952. He studied at Trinity College, Oxford (M.A., 1901); studied singing with Manuel Garcia; then traveled as joint artist with his mother; in 1904 he gave up his concert career and established himself in London as a singing teacher; organized the Sterling Mackinlay Operatic Society. He publ. the following books: *Antoinette Sterling and Other Celebrities* (1906); *Garcia, the Centenarian, and His Times* (1908); *The Singing Voice and Its Training* (1910); *Light Opera* (technique and theatercraft; 1926); *Origin and Development of Light Opera* (1927); also 2 novels.

Maclean, Alexander Morvaren (Alick), English composer and conductor; son of **Charles Donald Maclean;** b. Eton, near Windsor, July 20, 1872; d. London, May 18, 1936. He studied with Sir Joseph Barnby; later conducted the Spa Orchestra at Scarborough (from 1911) and the New Queen's Hall Light Orchestra (1915–23). He wrote several operas; of these, 2 were produced in German, in Mainz: *Die Liebesgeige* (April 15, 1906) and *Waldidyll* (March 23, 1913); and 3 in London: *Petruccio* (June 29, 1895), *The King's Price* (April 29, 1904), and *Maître Seiler* (Aug. 20, 1909). His most successful opera, *Quentin Durward* (after Walter Scott), written in 1892, was not produced until many years later, at Newcastle-on-Tyne (Jan. 13, 1920). He also wrote an oratorio, *The Annunciation* (London, 1910); *Rapsodie monégasque* for orch. (1935); choral works.

Maclean, Charles Donald, English organist; b. Cambridge, March 27, 1843; d. London, June 23, 1916. He studied theory with Ferdinand Hiller in Cologne; later at Oxford Univ. (D. Mus., 1865). He was musical director at Eton College (1871–75); then entered the Indian Civil Service, returning to London in 1898. He was the English editor of the International Musical Society.

Maclean, Quentin Stuart Morvaren, English-Canadian organist and composer; b. London, May 14, 1896; d. Toronto, July 9, 1962. He studied organ with Karl Straube and composition with Max Reger in Leipzig (1912–14); was interned as an enemy alien in Germany during World War I. Upon his return to London, he was active as an organist; in 1939 he emigrated to Canada.
WORKS: *Concert Piece* for organ and orch. (1932); *Rhapsody on Two English Folk Tunes* for harp and small orch. (1938); *Stabat Mater* for tenor, chorus, organ and strings (1941); *Concerto Grosso in Popular Style* for 4 electric instruments (solovox, electric organ, electric guitar, theremin) and small orch. (1942); *Concerto For Electric Organ* and dance orch. (1945); *The Well-Tempered Orchestra.* prelude and fugue on a tuning formula, for orch. (1950); *Concerto Romantico* for piano and orch. (1953); *Rustic Rhapsody* for orch. (1954); *Theme and Variatons* for harpsichord and orch. (1954); *Concerto Rococo* for violin and orch. (1957); String Quartet (1937); Piano Trio (1937); Trio for flute, viola and guitar (1937); organ pieces; choruses; songs.

Maclennan, Francis, American tenor; b. Bay City, Mich., Jan. 7, 1879; d. Port Westminster, Long Island, July 17, 1935. He studied voice in N.Y., and later with Henschel in London and Franz Emerich in Berlin;

made his debut as Faust at Covent Garden (1902); in 1904 he sang Parsifal in Savage's Opera Co. on a tour of the U.S.; from 1907 till 1913 he sang at the Berlin Opera, where he had the distinction of being the first foreigner to sing Tristan in Germany; also performed Wagnerian roles in England; from 1915–17 he was a member of the Chicago Opera Co., appearing chiefly as a Wagnerian singer. In 1904 he married **Florence Easton,** with whom he appeared in duo recitals.

MacMillan, Sir Ernest Campbell, eminent Canadian conductor and composer; b. Mimico, Ontario, Aug. 18, 1893; d. Toronto, May 6, 1973. He studied organ in Toronto and then at Edinburgh Univ. with Alfred Hollins and Frederick Niecks; in the summer of 1914 he went to Bayreuth to attend the Wagner Festival and was interned as an enemy alien at the outbreak of World War I; after the Armistice he returned to Canada and settled in Toronto; was director of the Toronto Cons. (1926–42) and dean of the faculty of music, Univ. of Toronto (1927–52); was also conductor of the Toronto Symph. Orch. (1931–56) and the Mendelssohn Choir in Toronto (1942–57); filled in engagements as guest conductor in the U.S., England, Australia and South America. He held several important administrative posts, including presidency of the Canadian Music Council (1947–66), and of the Canadian Music Centre (1959–70). He was knighted by King George V in 1935 and received 9 honorary doctorates from Canadian and U.S. universities.
WORKS: *England,* an ode, after Swinburne, for soprano, baritone, chorus and orch. (composed in the prisoner-of-war camp in Germany, 1914–18; first performed Sheffield, England, March 17, 1921); *Overture* (1924); *Two Sketches* on French-Canadian airs, for string orch. (1927); *A Song of Deliverance* for chorus and orch. (1944); *Fantasy on Scottish Melodies* for orch. (1946); *6 Bergerettes du Bas Canada* for soprano, alto, tenor, oboe, viola, cello and harp; *3 Indian Songs of the West Coast* for voice and piano and many other songs and choruses; etc. He published several educational works: *On the Preparation of Ear Tests; Graded Piano Sight Reading Exercises* (with Healey Willan); *The Modern Piano Student* (with Boris Berlin); edited *Music in Canada* (Toronto, 1955).

Macmillen, Francis, American violinist; b. Marietta, Ohio, Oct. 14, 1885; d. Lausanne, Switzerland, July 14, 1973. A precocious child, he was sent to Germany at the age of 10 and was accepted by Joachim as a pupil; later he studied with César Thomson at the Brussels Cons., winning the first prize in 1901; continued his studies with Carl Flesch in Berlin and Leopold Auer in St. Petersburg. He made his professional debut as a concert violinist at the age of 17 in Brussels (March 30, 1903); appeared with the N.Y. Symph. Orch. on Dec. 7, 1906; then embarked on a concert tour of Europe; after the outbreak of World War I in 1914 he returned to the U.S. and taught violin at Ithaca, N.Y.; resumed his European tours in 1929; then lived in New York, Florence, Italy, and lastly, in Switzerland.

MacNeil, Cornell, American opera baritone; b. Minneapolis, Sept. 24, 1922. He began to earn his living as a machinist, and simultaneously made appearances as a radio actor and operetta singer. His professional debut was in the baritone role in Menotti's opera *The Consul* in New York on March 15, 1950. He joined the New York City Opera in 1953; also made guest appearances in San Francisco, Chicago and Mexico City. On March 5, 1959 he sang the role of Charles V in Verdi's opera *Ernani* at La Scala in Milan. On March 21, 1959 he sang Rigoletto at the Metropolitan Opera in N.Y. and became a regular member of the company in 1960; also sang in Europe. He attracted unexpected notoriety when he walked off the stage during the third act of Verdi's opera *Un Ballo in Maschera* on Dec. 27, 1964 in Parma, Italy, in protest against the offensive attitude of the audience, and engaged in a fist fight with the opera manager. Pacified, he resumed his career in America, but also became active in labor union affairs; in 1969 he was elected president of the American Guild of Musical Artists.

Maconchy, Elizabeth, significant English composer of Irish extraction; b. Broxbourne, Herts., March 19, 1907. She studied with Vaughan Williams at the Royal College of Music in London (1923–29); went to Prague in 1930 where she absorbed the styles and techniques of expressionism; upon return to England she composed prolifically in all genres; developed a style peculiarly her own, tonally tense, contrapuntally dissonant and coloristically sharp in instrumentation.
WORKS: 3 one-act operas: *The Sofa*, to a libretto by Ursula Vaughan Williams (London, Dec. 13, 1959); *The Departure* (London, Dec. 16, 1962); *The Three Strangers* after Thomas Hardy (London, June 5, 1968); an operatic extravaganza, *The Birds*, after Aristophanes (London, June 5, 1968, on the same day with *The Three Strangers*); a church masque, *The Jesse Tree* (Dorchester Abbey, Oct. 7, 1970); the ballets, *Great Agrippa* (1933), *The Little Red Shoes* (1935), *Puck Fair* (1940); numerous works for orch.: *The Land*, symph. suite (1929), Piano Concerto (1930), Viola Concerto (1938), *Theme and Variations* for strings (1942), Symphony (1945–48), Viola Concerto (1937), *Dialogue*, for piano and orch. (1940), Concertino, for clarinet and strings (Copenhagen Festival of the International Society for Contemporary Music, June 2, 1947, *Proud Thames*, overture (1953), *Serenata Concertante* for violin and orch. (1962), *An Essex Overture* (1966), *3 Cloudscapes* for orch. (1968); chamber music: 11 string quartets (1933–77), Quintet for oboe and strings (1932), *Prelude, Interlude, and Fugue* for 2 violins (Prague Festival of the International Society for Contemporary Music, Sept. 4, 1935), Viola Sonata (1938), Violin Sonata (1944), Concertino for Piano and Strings (1951), Concertino for Bassoon and Strings (1954), String Trio (1957), Double Concerto for Oboe, Bassoon and Strings (1957), *Reflections* for oboe, clarinet, viola and harp (1960), Clarinet Quintet (1963), *Music* for double bass and piano (1970), *3 Bagatelles* for oboe and harp (1972); vocal works: *Samson at the Gates of Gaza* for chorus and orch. (1963), *The Starlight Night and Peace*, for soprano and chamber orch. (1964), *Witnesses* for 2 sopranos, flute, oboe, clarinet, horn, cello, percussion and ukulele (1966); several song cycles; piano pieces.
BIBLIOGRAPHY: F. Howes, "Elizabeth Maconchy," *Monthly Musical Record* (July–Aug. 1938); Elizabeth Maconchy, "A Composer Speaks," *Composer* (1971–72).

Macpherson, Charles, Scottish organist and composer; b. Edinburgh, May 10, 1870; d. London, May 28, 1927. He was a chorister at St. Paul's Cathedral; studied organ with George Martin; then took courses at the Royal Academy of Music; held various positions as organist; succeeded his teacher George Martin as organist of St. Paul's in 1916; conducted the London Church Choirs Association from 1914 until his death. He wrote several overtures on Scottish themes; a number of choral works; edited 144 Scottish songs in 8 vols.; publ. *A Short History of Harmony* (London, 1917).

Macpherson, Stewart, English organist and educator; b. Liverpool, March 29, 1865; d. London, March 27, 1941. He studied with W. C. Macfarren at the Royal Academy of Music (piano) and with G. A. Macfarren (composition); then taught harmony there; conducted the Westminster Orchestral Society (1885–1902); in 1898 was appointed examiner to the Associated Board, in which capacity he visited Canada, Australia, and New Zealand (1900). He wrote a symphony, several overtures, and a Mass; edited the *Music Student's Library* and the Joseph Williams *Handbooks on Music* series; publ. *Practical Harmony* (1894); *Practical Counterpoint* (1900); *Rudiments of Music* (1907); *350 Exercises in Harmony* (1907); *Evolution of Musical Design; Form in Music* (1908); *Music and Its Appreciation* (1910); *Aural Culture Based upon Musical Appreciation* (with Ernest Read; in 3 parts: 1912, 1914, and 1918); *Studies in Phrasing and Form* (1911); *Musical Education of the Child* (1915); *Studies in the Art of Counterpoint* (1928); *A Simple Introduction to the Principles of Tonality* (1929); *Cameos of Musical History* (1937).

Macque, Giovanni (Jean) de, Flemish composer; b. Valenciennes, c.1550; d. Naples, Sept. 1614. In his marriage certificate (1592) he is named "Fiammingo della città di Valencena"; a book of motets (Rome, 1596) describes him as a Belgian from Valenciennes. He studied with Philippe de Monte; then went to Rome (about 1570), where he became a member of the Compagnia dei Musici di Roma (organized in 1584; among its members were Palestrina and Marenzio. In 1586 Macque went to Naples and entered the service of Don Fabrizio Gesualdo da Venosa, father of the composer Carlo Gesualdo. On May 20, 1590, Macque was appointed 2nd organist of the Church of the Annunciation in Naples. In 1594 he was appointed organist of the viceregal chapel, and in Dec. 1599 became its choir director. Among his pupils in Naples were Ascanio Mayone, Giovanni Maria Trabaci, Luigi Rossi, and Falconieri. Several of Macque's madrigals are found in Younge's *Musica Transalpina* (1588) and in Morley's collection of Italian works (1598); extant keyboard pieces are reproduced in the *Monumenta Musicae Belgicae* (Antwerp, 1938; with a list of sources and a biographical sketch). Macque was one of the first to employ rhythmic transformations of a single theme (in canzonas), which were later used extensively by Frescobaldi; Macque also applied the keyboard technique of Cabezón's "diferencias" (variations).

BIBLIOGRAPHY: U. Prota-Giurleo, "Notizie storico-biografiche sul musicista belga Jean Macque," *Report of the First Congress of the International Society for Musical Research* (1930); A. Davison and W. Apel, *Historical Anthology of Music* (Cambridge, Mass., 1946); G. Reese, *Music in the Renaissance* (N.Y., 1954).

Madatov, Grigori, Russian flutist and composer; b. Baku, April 2, 1898; d. Moscow, March 14, 1968. He studied at the Moscow Cons. Upon graduation, he taught flute playing in Baku (1920–37) and at the Cons. of Tbilisi (1938–44). In 1947 he joined the staff of the Musical Pedagogical Institute in Moscow. He wrote many pieces for flute suitable as teaching material.

Maddy, Joseph Edgar, American educator and conductor; b. Wellington, Kansas, Oct. 14, 1891; d. Traverse City, Mich., April 18, 1966. He studied at Bethany College, Wichita College, and at the Columbia School of Music, Chicago; played the viola and clarinet; was a member of the Minneapolis Symph. Orch. (1909–14) and St. Paul Symph. (1914–18); supervisor of instrumental music in the public schools of Rochester, N.Y. (1918–20) and Richmond, Ind. (1920–24); instructor of public school methods at Earlham College (1922–24); in 1924, appointed to the faculty of the Univ. of Michigan as prof. of music education; founder and conductor of the National High School Orch., for which he established, with T. P. Giddings, the National Music Camp at Interlochen, Michigan.

Madeira, Francis, American conductor; b. Jenkintown, Pennsylvania, Feb. 21, 1917. He studied piano and conducting at the Juilliard School of Music, N.Y. (1937–43). He was appointed to the faculty of Brown Univ. in 1943. In 1945 he organized the Rhode Island Philharmonic Orch. in Providence; announced his resignation for 1980. He was also active as a concert pianist in the U.S. and in Europe; composed a number of symphonic and other works.

Madeira, Jean (*née* **Browning**), American contralto; b. Centralia, Illinois, Nov. 14, 1918; d. Providence, July 10, 1972. She studied piano with her mother, and was regarded as a child prodigy; at the age of 12, she was piano soloist with the St. Louis Symph. Orch.; took vocal lessons in St. Louis; then studied both piano and voice at the Juilliard School, N.Y. Subsequently she became a member of the Chautauqua Opera Co., and the San Carlo Opera Co. In 1948 she sang minor roles at the Metropolitan Opera; went to Europe; sang Carmen with the Vienna State Opera on Sept. 18, 1955, obtaining extraordinary success; on March 19, 1956 she appeared as Carmen with the Metropolitan Opera, N.Y., and this role became one of her best. Her European tours included appearances at Covent Garden, La Scala, Paris Opéra and Bayreuth. She was married to **Francis Madeira** on June 17, 1947.

Maderna, Bruno, eminent Italian conductor and composer of modern tendencies; b. Venice, April 21, 1920; d. Darmstadt, Nov. 13, 1973. He studied conducting with Scherchen and composition with Malipiero. As a conductor he promoted the most advanced compositions; from 1958 to 1967 he led the International Chamber Ensemble in Darmstadt; then taught at the Cons. of Rotterdam; also gave summer courses at the Berkshire Music Center in Tanglewood (1971, 1972). He lived mostly in West Germany, was naturalized as a German citizen in 1963. He was held in great respect by composers of the international avant-garde who wrote special works for him. He was also a composer in his own right; among his works are *Introduzione e passacaglia* for orch. (1947); Piano Concerto (1948); *Serenata* for 11 instruments (1946); *Studi per "Il Processo" di Kafka,* for recitation, soprano, and small orch. (1950); *Musica per due dimensioni* (1952); *Sintaxis* for 4 different but unspecified timbres produced electronically (1956); a radio opera, *Don Perlimplin,* after Lorca (1962); 3 oboe concertos (1962, 1967, 1973); Violin Concerto (1969); *Serenata per un satellite* for 7 instruments (1969); *Œdipe-Roi,* electronic ballet (Monte Carlo, Dec. 31, 1970); *Von A bis Z,* opera (1970); *Aura* for orch. (1971); *Ausstrahlung* for soprano, chorus and orch. (1971); *Juilliard Serenade* for chamber orch. and taped sounds (N.Y., Jan. 31, 1971, Maderna conducting); opera, *Satyrikon,* after Petronius (The Hague, 1973).

Madetoja, Leevi, outstanding Finnish composer; b. Oulu (Uleaborg), Feb. 17, 1887; d. Helsinki, Oct. 6, 1947. He studied in Helsinki with Järnefelt and Sibelius (1906–10); took lessons in Paris with Vincent d'Indy (1910–11) and in Vienna with Robert Fuchs (1911–12). Returning to Finland, he conducted the Helsinki Philharmonic (1912–14) and the Viipuri (Vyborg) Orch. (1914–16); taught at the Helsinki Cons. (1916–39); was also active as music critic. Madetoja's music is inspired by Finnish melos; he is held in great esteem in Finland as a worthy continuator of the national Finnish school of composition, according to precepts established by Sibelius.

WORKS: 2 operas, *Pohjalaisia* (*The Ostrobothnians,* Helsinki, Oct. 25, 1924) and *Juha* (Helsinki, Feb. 17, 1935); *Symphonic Suite* (1910); *Concert Overture* (1911); *Tanssinäky* for orch. (*Dance Vision,* 1911–12); *Kullervo,* symph. poem (1913); 3 symphonies (1916, 1918, 1926); *Comedy Overture* (1923), ballet-pantomime, *Okon Fuoko* (Helsinki, Dec. 2, 1930); Piano Trio (1909); Violin Sonatina (1914); *Lyric Suite* for cello and piano (1922); many cantatas and solo songs; 40 a cappella works for male chorus; incidental music for plays; film music.

BIBLIOGRAPHY: K. Tuukkanen, *Leevi Madetoja* (Helsinki, 1947).

Madey, Boguslaw, Polish conductor and composer; b. Sosnowiec, May 31, 1932. He received diplomas in composition, piano and conducting from the Academy of Music in Poznań; then went to England where he took a course in conducting with Norman del Mar at the Guildhall School of Music in London (1959–60). Returning to Poland, he became conductor at the Warsaw Opera (1960–72); later was music director at the Grand Theater of Opera and Ballet in Lodz. He composed a Piano Concerto (1957); Flute Concerto

(1960); concerto for voice and instruments entitled *Transfiguration* (1965); and some short piano pieces.

Madriguera, Enrique, Catalan-born composer of light music; b. Barcelona, Feb. 17, 1904; d. Danbury, Connecticut, Sept. 7, 1973. His rumba *Adiós* attained considerable popularity. He studied violin in Europe; then settled in the United States where he led a Latin American orchestral group.

Maegaard, Jan, Danish composer; b. Copenhagen, April 14, 1926. He studied music theory with Poul Schierbeck and B. Hjelmborg; counterpoint with Knud Jeppesen and orchestration with J. Jersild at the Royal Cons. in Copenhagen (1945–50), and at the Univ. of Copenhagen, where he took a course in musicology with Jens Peter Larsen (*magister artis,* 1957). He then went to the U.S., where he studied musicography with Robert Nelson at the Univ. of California, Los Angeles (1958–59). Returning to Denmark, he taught at the Copenhagen Cons.; appointed to the faculty of the Musicological Institute of the Univ. of Copenhagen; received his Dr. phil. for a 3-vol. dissertation, *Studies of the Evolution of Schoenberg's Dodecaphonic Method* (Copenhagen, 1970). Once more in America, he was guest lecturer at the State Univ. of N.Y. at Stony Brook (1974) and at the Univ. of California, Los Angeles (1978). He served on the board of the Society for Publishing Danish Music (1958–78).
WORKS: *Chamber Concerto No. 1* (1949); *Chamber Concerto No. 2* (1961–62); *Gaa udenom sletterne (Avoid the Plains)* for chorus and orch (1953; Copenhagen, March 21, 1957); *Due tempi* for orch. (Copenhagen, Aug. 31, 1961); music for a television production of *Antigone* for chorus, orch. and tape (1966); *Suite* for violin and piano (1949); Trio for oboe, clarinet and bassoon (1950); Wind Quintet (1951); *Suite* for 2 violins (1951); *Den gyldne harpe (The Golden Harp)* for mezzo-soprano, oboe, cello and piano (1951); *Quasi una sonata* for viola and piano (1952); Bassoon Sonata (1952); *Variations impromptus* for violin, viola, cello and piano (1953); *Jaevndøgnselegi (Equinox Elegy)* for soprano, cello and organ (1955); *Alter Duft aus Märchenzeit* for piano trio (1960); *Movimento* for clarinet, horn, Hammond organ, string quartet and percussion (1967); *Musica riservata No. 1* for string quartet (1970); *Musica riservata No. 2* for oboe, clarinet, saxophone and bassoon (1976); *Pastorale* for 2 clarinets (1976); piano sonata (1955); choruses; songs; cadenzas and transcriptions of Bach, Mozart and Schoenberg. He publ. a textbook on new music, *Musikalsk Modernisme 1945–62* (Copenhagen, 1964; 2nd ed., 1971).

Maelzel, Johannes Nepomuk, German inventor of the metronome; b. Regensburg, Aug. 15, 1772; d. on board the brig *Otis* in the harbor of La Guiara, Venezuela, en route to Philadelphia, July 21, 1838. He studied music with his father, an organ manufacturer. He went to Vienna in 1792, where he began constructing mechanical instruments, which attracted great attention in Vienna and subsequently in other European cities; of these the Panharmonicon was particularly effective; in 1812 he inaugurated an Art Cabinet, where he exhibited his inventions, including an automatic trumpeter. In 1816 he constructed the Metronome, the idea for which he obtained from Winkel, of Amsterdam (who had exhibited similar instruments, but without the scale divisions indicating the number of beats per minute). Maelzel put the Metronome on the market, despite a lawsuit brought by Winkel, and the initial of his last name was thenceforth added to the indication of tempo in musical compositions (M.M., Maelzel's Metronome), Beethoven wrote a piece for Maelzel's Panharmonicon, which he subsequently orchestrated and published as *Wellington's Victory.* Maelzel also exhibited an "automatic chess player." He claimed it as his invention but it was really designed and built by Wolfgang von Kempelen. He was able to impress the public by his "scientific" miracle but it was soon exposed by skeptical observers, among them Edgar Allan Poe, as an ingenious mechanical contrivance concealing a diminutive chessmaster behind its gears. (In this connection, see C. M. Carroll, *The Great Chess Automaton,* N.Y., 1975).

Maes, Jef, Belgian composer and violist; b. Antwerp, April 5, 1905. He enrolled at the Royal Flemish Cons. in Antwerp in 1922 and studied viola and chamber music; took private lessons in composition with Karel Candael. He played viola in several orchestras in Antwerp; from 1932 he taught violin at the music academy in Boom (near Antwerp), becoming its director in 1943; from 1942 to 1970 was on the faculty of the Flemish Cons. in Antwerp. In his compositions he continues the traditions of the Belgian national school.
WORKS: an opera buffa *Marise* (1946); a television opera *De antikwaar (The Antique Dealer,* 1959; Antwerp Television, March 1963); a ballet *Tu auras nom . . . Tristan* (1960; Geneva, June 1963; orch. suite, 1963–64); *3 rythmen in Dansvorm* for orch. (1931); *Légende* for violin and orch. (1933); Viola Concerto (1937); *Concertstück* for orch. (1938); *Ouvertura buffa* (1939); *Concertstück* for trombone and orch. (1944); Piano Concerto (1948); Violin Concerto (1951); 3 symphonies (1953, 1965, 1975); Concerto for Harpsichord and String Orch. (1955); *Burlesque* for bassoon and orch. (1957); *Rosa Mystica* for soprano, and orch. or piano (1959); *Kempische Suite* for orch. or wind orch. (1960); *Concertante Ouverture* (1961); *Arabesque en Scherzo* for flute and orch. (1963); *Praeludium, Pantomime, Scherzo,* suite for orch. (1966); *Partita* for string orch. (1966); *Ouverture op een Belcanto Thema van Verdi* for orch. or wind orch. (1967); *De verloofden* for orch. (1969); *Mei 1871* for narrator and orch. (1971); *Music pour le podium* for wind orch. (1971); *Dialogue* for violin and orch. (1972); Sonatina for flute and viola (1934); Violin Sonata (1934); *Concertstück* for trumpet and and piano (1957); *Prelude and Allegro* for 2 trumpets, horn, trombone and tuba (1959); *Fantasia* for 2 pianos (1960); Duo for Violin and Piano (1962); Trio for violin, viola and percussion (1964); *4 Contrastes* for 4 clarinets (1965); *Suite* for percussion and piano (1968); Piano Quartet (1970); songs.

Magaloff, Nikita, Russian-Swiss pianist; b. St. Petersburg, Feb 21, 1912. His family left Russia after the Revolution; he enrolled in the Paris Cons. as a student of Isidor Philipp; graduated with Premier Prix at the age of 17. In 1939 he settled in Switzerland; in 1947 made his first American tour; also toured South America, South Africa, etc. From 1949 to 1960 he conducted a school of piano virtuosity at the Geneva Cons.; then gave summer courses at Taormina, Sicily, and at the Accademia musicale Chigiana in Siena. In 1956 he became a Swiss citizen, living mostly in Coppet (Vaud). He is renowned for his lyrico-dramatic interpretations of Chopin, with lapidary attention to detail. He is also a composer; he wrote a Piano Toccata; Sonatina for violin and piano; songs; cadenzas for Mozart's piano concertos.

Maganini, Quinto, American flutist, conductor, arranger, and composer; b. Fairfield, Calif., Nov. 30, 1897; d. Greenwich, Connecticut, March 10, 1974. He played the flute in the San Francisco Symph. Orch. (1917) and in the N.Y. Symph. (1919–28); studied flute playing with Barrère in N.Y., composition with Nadia Boulanger in France, at the American Cons. in Fontainebleau; 1927, won a Pulitzer scholarship; 1928–29, awarded a Guggenheim Fellowship; 1930, conductor of the N.Y. Sinfonietta; in 1932 he organized his own orch., the Maganini Chamber Symph., with which he toured widely. From 1939 till 1970 he was conductor of the Norwalk, Conn., Symph.
WORKS: *Toulumne,* a Californian Rhapsody, for orch., with trumpet obbligato (N.Y., Aug. 9, 1924); *South Wind,* orchestral fantasy (N.Y., April 7, 1931); *Sylvan Symphony* (N.Y., Nov. 30, 1932); *Napoleon,* an orchestral portrait (N.Y., Nov. 10, 1935); *The Royal Ladies,* orchestral suite on airs ascribed to Marie Antoinette, (Greenwich, Conn., Feb. 3, 1940); an opera, *Tennessee's Partner* (American Opera Festival, Radio Station WOR, N.Y., May 28, 1942); numerous arrangements for small orch. of classical and modern works.

Mager, Jörg, German music theorist and pioneer in electronic music; b. Eichstätt, Nov. 6, 1880; d. Aschaffenburg, April 5, 1939. After completing his university studies, he became interested in electronic reproduction of sounds; constructed several instruments capable of producing microtonal intervals by electronic means, which he named Sphärophon, Elektrophon and Partiturophon; he was also active in visual music for film. He publ. *Vierteltonmusik* (Aschaffenburg, 1916) and *Eine neue Epoche der Musik durch Radio* (Berlin, 1924).

Maggini, Giovanni Paolo, Italian violin maker; b. Brescia, Nov. 1579 (baptized Nov. 29, 1579); d. there, c.1630. He worked in the shop of Gasparo da Salò; after his marriage in 1615, he set up his own workshop and became prosperous thanks to the excellence of his manufacture; about 50 violins and 20 violas and cellos are extant; his instruments are prized particularly because of the softness of their tone in deep registers. His label reads: Gio. Paolo Maggini, Brescia.
BIBLIOGRAPHY: M. L. Huggins, *Giovanni Paolo Maggini, His Life and Work* (London, 1892); A. Berenzi, *Gli artefici liutai bresciani* (Brescia, 1890); A. Berenzi, *Di Giovanni Paolo Maggini* (Cremona, 1907).

Maggioni, Aurelio Antonio, Italian composer; b. Milan, April 8, 1908. He studied at the Milan Cons.; graduated as a pianist (1926) and composer (1933). He subsequently taught music theory in Parma (1938, in Florence (1939–51), in Milan, (1952–54, in Lima, Peru (1954–59) and again in Milan from 1959. He wrote the opera *Il Gioco di Soleima* (Bergamo, 1955); during his stay in Peru he composed a *Suite incaici* for orch., making use of indigenous themes; also a mandatory amount of chamber music and minor pieces, all set in a competent Italianate style.

Magnard, (Lucien-Denis-Gabriel-) Albéric, French composer; b. Paris, June 9, 1865; d. Baron, Oise, Sept. 3, 1914 (killed by German soldiers in his house). He was brought up in an intellectual family; his father was editor of *Le Figaro.* He studied at the Paris Cons. with Dubois and Massenet, and later with Vincent d'Indy. He fell under the influence of Wagner, but succeeded in generating an element of national French music in his works; his mastery of instrumentation is incontestable, and the rhapsodic sweep of his symphonies is impressive. Despite these qualities, Magnard's symphonic music never gained a stable place in the orchestral repertory; his operas were even less successful.
WORKS: operas: *Yolande* (Brussels, 1892), *Guercœur* (1904; revised by Guy-Ropartz, and produced at the Paris Opéra, April 24, 1931), and *Bérénice* (Paris, Opéra-Comique, Dec. 15, 1911); 4 symphonies (1894; 1899; 1902; 1913); *Suite dans le style ancien,* for orch. (1892); *Hymne à la Justice* (1903); *Hymne à Vénus* (1906); Quintet for wind instruments and piano (1904); String Quartet (1904); Piano Trio (1906); Violin Sonata; Cello Sonata; songs.
BIBLIOGRAPHY: M. Boucher, *Albéric Magnard* (Lyons, 1919); G. Carraud, *La Vie, l'œuvre et la mort d'Albéric Magnard* (Paris, 1921); C. Laforêt, "L'Esthétique d'Albéric Magnard," *Revue Musicale* (1920).

Magne, Michel, French composer; b. Lisieux, March 20, 1930. He began to compose as a very young man, adopting at once an ultramodern method; his film score *Le Pain Vivant* (1955) received critical acclaim; he has also experimented with electronic music; on May 26, 1955, he conducted in Paris his *Symphonie Humaine* for 150 performers, making use of inaudible "infrasounds" to produce a physiological reaction by powerful low frequencies. He wrote the musical score for Françoise Sagan's ballet, *Le Rendez-vous manqué* (1957).

Magomayev, Muslim, Azerbaijani composer; b. Shusha, Sept. 18, 1885; d. Baku, July 28, 1937. He began his musical career as an improviser, and his first opera, *Shah Ismail* (1916), was a series of songs and interludes on native themes. His second opera *Nergiz* (Baku, Jan. 1, 1936), is based on the events of the Russian Revolution.
BIBLIOGRAPHY: G. Ismailova, *Muslim Magomayev* (Baku, 1975).

Mahaim, Ivan, Swiss physician, amateur violinist, and writer on music; b. Liège, June 25, 1897; d. Lausanne, Dec. 3, 1965. He studied violin with Alfred Pochon in Lausanne; held the post of associate prof. in cardiology at the Univ. of Lausanne. He publ. a highly valuable 2-vol. edition, *Beethoven, Naissance et Renaissance des Derniers Quatuors* (Paris, 1964); contributed many articles on Beethoven to various publications.

Mahillon, Victor, Belgian manufacturer of musical instruments, and a writer on acoustics; b. Brussels, March 10, 1841; d. Saint-Jean, Cap-Ferrat, June 17, 1924. He was the son of **Charles Mahillon** (1813-87), founder of the manufacturing firm of that name; he worked in his father's shop as a youth; applied himself to a study of acoustics; in 1869 he began publishing a periodical, *L'Écho musical,* which he abandoned shortly before his father's death; then assumed the management of the factory; made excellent reproductions of rare instruments, among them a complete collection of all the wind instruments in use during the 16th and 17th centuries. In 1876 he became custodian of the instrumental museum of the Cons. of Brussels (founded by Fétis) and greatly enlarged the collection (more than 3500 specimens).

WRITINGS: *Tableau synoptique des voix et de tous les instruments de musique; Tableau synoptique de la science de l'harmonie; Éléments d'acoustique musicale et instrumentale* (1874); *Catalogue descriptif et analytique du Musée instrumental du Conservatoire Royal de Musique de Bruxelles* (1880; 2nd ed., 5 vols., 1893-1922); *Le Matériel sonore des orchestres de symphonie, d'harmonie, et de fanfares* (1897); *Les Instruments à vent: I. Le Trombone, son histoire, sa théorie, sa construction; II. Le Cor; III. La Trompette* (1907).

Mahler, Fritz, Austrian-American conductor; nephew of **Gustav Mahler;** b. Vienna, July 16, 1901; d. Winston-Salem, North Carolina, June 18, 1973. He studied composition in Vienna with Schoenberg, Anton von Webern, and Alban Berg; musicology with Guido Adler at the Univ. of Vienna (1920-24); conducting with Leopold Reichwein. He conducted summer orchestras in Bad Hall (1924-26); light opera at the Volksoper in Vienna; from 1930-35, conductor of the radio orch. in Copenhagen; in 1936 emigrated to America, where he taught at the Juilliard Summer School; conductor of the Erie, Penn., Philharmonic Orch. (1947-53); in 1953 appointed conductor of the Hartford, Conn., Symph. Orch.

Mahler, Gustav, great Austrian composer and conductor; b. Kalischt, Bohemia, July 7, 1860; d. Vienna, May 18, 1911. He attended the Iglau Gymnasium; then entered the Vienna Cons., where he studied with Julius Epstein (piano), Robert Fuchs (harmony), and Franz Krenn (composition). He also took courses in history and philosophy at the Univ. of Vienna (1877-79). In the summer of 1880 he received his first appointment as conductor, in the town of Hall; from then on, he held posts as theater conductor at Ljubljana (1881), Olmütz (1882), Vienna (1883), and Kassel (1883-85). In 1885 he succeeded Anton Seidl at the Prague Opera, where he directed performances of Wagner's music dramas. From 1886-88 he was assistant to Arthur Nikisch in Leipzig; in 1888 he received the important engagement of music director of the

Royal Opera in Budapest; he thoroughly reorganized the management and repertory there; after three seasons, he was summoned to Hamburg, where he reasserted his growing competence as opera conductor (1891-97). In 1897 he was offered the directorship of the Vienna Court Opera; he held this position for ten years; under his guidance, the Vienna Opera reached a very high standard of artistic excellence; Mahler displayed an extraordinary talent as an organizer and an inspired conductor. His performances were admired for the perfection of ensemble, fidelity to the composer's intentions, and superlative theatrical effectiveness. He was also known as a relentless taskmaster who refused to sacrifice his artistic ideals to managerial expediency, or defer to the fame of the prima donnas. In 1907, he accepted the post of principal conductor of the Metropolitan Opera, where he made his debut on Jan 1, 1908, with a superb performance of *Tristan und Isolde;* also noteworthy were his revivals of *Fidelio* and *Don Giovanni.* In 1909, he was elected conductor of the N.Y. Philharmonic Soc., and endowed with autocratic powers, so that he could carry out his plans for the improvement of performing standards and the enlargement of the repertory. His uncompromising zeal aroused opposition among the conservative elements in the administration of the New York Philharmonic, and he was constantly engaged in a struggle with the board of trustees; when he left New York at the conclusion of the season of 1910-11, he was spiritually a broken man. He was imprudent enough to conduct his last New York concert (Feb. 21, 1911) while he was in a high fever. He returned to Vienna in May 1911, and died shortly afterwards of pneumonia, at the age of 50. Mahler was the last great composer of the Romantic School of Vienna. His symphonies and other works were drawn on the grandest scale, and the technical means employed for the realization of his ideas was correspondingly elaborate. The sources of his inspiration were twofold: the lofty concepts of universal art, akin to those of Bruckner, and ultimately stemming from Wagner; and the simple folk melos of the Austrian countryside, in pastoral moods recalling the intimate episodes in Beethoven's symphonies. Mahler himself attached programmatic titles to several of his symphonies, but later repudiated them, insisting that his music should be perceived and judged by its absolute value without any literary, pictorial or emotional associations. The description of the 8th Symphony as a "symphony of a thousand" was the inspiration of Mahler's enthusiastic manager; indeed, by some counts, 1003 performers were employed at its premiere (Munich, Sept. 12, 1910). Mahler was not an innovator in his harmonic writing; he never departed entirely from the traditions of 19th-century music, but he brought the Romantic era to a culmination by virtue of the expansiveness of his emotional expression and the grandiose design of his musical structures. Morbid by nature, Mahler brooded upon the idea of death; one of his most poignant compositions is the cycle for voice and orch., *Kindertotenlieder;* the marginal remarks in the manuscript of his unfinished 10th Symphony, invoking death and annihilation, point to serious mental trouble. There was conflict in Mahler's religious persuasion: born in the Jewish faith, he became a Catholic in

1897; but his true philosophy was pantheistic. On March 10, 1902, he married Alma Maria Schindler; of their two daughters, one died in infancy; the other, Anna Justina (b. 1904), was briefly married to Ernst Krenek. Mahler's importance in the development of modern music in Austria was very great; the early works of Arnold Schoenberg and Alban Berg show the influence of his concepts. Festivals of Mahler's music were given in various countries; a society was formed in the U.S. in 1931 "to develop in the public an appreciation of the music of Bruckner, Mahler, and other moderns." An International Gustav Mahler Society was formed in Vienna in 1955, with Bruno Walter as honorary president.

WORKS: SYMPHONIES: No. 1, in D, *Titan* (1883–88; Budapest, Nov. 20, 1889, Mahler conducting); No. 2, in C minor, *Resurrection,* with soprano, contralto, and chorus (1887–94; Berlin, Dec. 13, 1895, Mahler conducting); No. 3, in D minor, *Ein Sommermorgen-traum* (1893–96; Krefeld, June 9, 1902, Mahler conducting); No. 4, in G (1889–1901; Munich, Nov. 25, 1901, Mahler conducting); No. 5, in C-sharp minor, *The Giant* (1901–02; Cologne, Oct. 18, 1904, Mahler conducting); No. 6, in A minor (1903–05; Essen, May 27, 1906, Mahler conducting); No. 7, in E minor (1904–06; Prague, Sept. 19, 1908, Mahler conducting); No. 8, in E-flat, Symphony of a Thousand, with 8 solo voices and choruses (1906–07; Munich, Sept. 12, 1910, Mahler conducting); No. 9, in D (1908–10; posthumous, Vienna, June 26, 1912, Bruno Walter conducting); No. 10 (unfinished, 1909; 2 movements *Adagio* and *Purgatorio,* performed in Vienna, Oct. 12, 1924, Franz Schalk conducting; publ. in facsimile by Alma Mahler, 1924; a "realization" of the 10th Symph. was made by Deryck Cooke, who used fragments from Mahler's other works in order to complete the score; it was broadcast by the BBC from London for the first time, on Dec. 9, 1960; Alma Mahler expressed her approval of Deryck Cooke's work, and it had several more performances).

VOCAL WORKS: *Lieder und Gesänge aus der Jugendzeit,* 14 songs for voice and piano (1880–92); *Das klagende Lied,* for soprano, contralto, tenor, chorus, and orch. (1880–99); *Lieder eines fahrenden Gesellen,* 4 songs with orch. (1883–85); *Des Knaben Wunderhorn,* 10 songs, with piano or orch. (1888); 5 songs, to poems by Rückert (1902); *Kindertotenlieder,* 5 songs with piano or orch. (1901–04); *Das Lied von der Erde,* for contralto, tenor, and orch. (1907–10; posthumous; Munich, Nov. 20, 1911, Bruno Walter conducting). Mahler destroyed the manuscripts of several of his early works, among them a piano quintet, performed in Vienna on July 11, 1878, with Mahler at the piano, and three unfinished operas: *Herzog Ernst von Schwaben,* to a drama by Uhland; *Die Argonauten,* from a trilogy by Grillparzer, and *Rübezahl,* after Grimm's fairy tales. He further made an arrangement of Weber's *Die drei Pintos* and *Oberon.* The collected works are being issued by the International Gustav Mahler Gesellschaft founded in Vienna in 1960.

BIBLIOGRAPHY: L. Schiedermair, *Gustav Mahler* (Leipzig, 1901); Paul Stefan, *Gustav Mahlers Erbe* (Munich, 1908; a polemic against Felix Weingartner, Mahler's successor in Vienna); *Gustav Mahler. Ein Bild seiner Persönlichkeit in Widmungen* (Munich, 1910); Paul Stefan, *Gustav Mahler. Eine Studie über Persönlichkeit und Werk* (Munich, 1910; 4th augm. ed., 1921; English transl., N.Y., 1913); R. Specht, *Gustav Mahler* (Berlin, 1913); Guido Adler, *Gustav Mahler* (Vienna, 1916); A. Neisser, "Gustav Mahler," *Reclams Universal-Bibliothek* (Berlin, 1918); H. F. Redlich, *Gustav Mahler: eine Erkenntnis* (Nuremberg, 1919); Paul Bekker, *Mahlers Sinfonien* (Berlin, 1921); A. Roller, *Die Bildnisse Gustav Mahlers* (Leipzig, 1922); R. Mengelberg, *Gustav Mahler* (1923); Natalie Bauer-Lechner, *Erinnerungen an Gustav Mahler* (Vienna, 1923); Alma Maria Mahler, *Briefe Gustav Mahlers* (Berlin, 1924); W. Hutschenruyter, *Gustav Mahler* (The Hague, 1927); H. Holländer. "Gustav Mahler," *Musical Quarterly* (Oct. 1931); G. Engel, *Gustav Mahler: Song-Symphonist* (N.Y., 1932); Bruno Walter, *Gustav Mahler* (Vienna, 1936; also in English transl., N.Y., 1957); Alma Maria Mahler, *Gustav Mahler: Erinnerungen und Briefe* (Amsterdam, 1940; in English as *Memories and Letters,* London, 1946); Egon Wellesz, "The Symphonies of Gustav Mahler," *Music Review* (Jan.-April 1940); Bruno Walter (with Ernst Krenek), *Gustav Mahler* (N.Y., 1941); Dika Newlin, *Bruckner-Mahler-Schoenberg* (N.Y., 1947); Arnold Schoenberg, "Gustav Mahler," *Style and Idea* (N.Y., 1950); N. Loeser, *Gustav Mahler* (Haarlem, 1950); Hans Tischler, "Mahler's Impact on the Crisis of Tonality," *Music Review* (April 1951); Theodore Reik, *The Haunting Melody* (N.Y., 1953); Erwin Stein, *Orpheus in New Guises* (London, 1953); H. F. Redlich, *Bruckner and Mahler,* The Master Musicians Series (London, 1955). Detailed analyses of Mahler's symphonies, by Istel, Schiedermair, Teibler, Weigl, and Gräner, are found in vol. 10 of *Meisterführer;* 3rd Symph., by L. Schiedermair, in the series *Der Musikführer* (Leipzig, 1902); another analysis of the 3rd symph., by E. O. Nodnagel (Darmstadt, 1904), attacking Schiedermair's interpretation; see also Donald Mitchell, "Some Notes on Mahler's Tenth Symphony," *Musical Times* (Dec. 1955). Vol. I of Donald Mitchell's monumental biography was publ. in London, 1958, under the title, *Gustav Mahler: The Early Years;* Willi Reich, ed., *Gustav Mahler: Im eigenen Wort, im Wort der Freunde* (Zürich, 1958); T. Adorno, *Mahler: eine musikalische Physiognomik* (Frankfurt, 1960); S. Vestdijk, *Gustav Mahler* (The Hague, 1960); N. Cardus, *Gustav Mahler: His Mind and His Music* (vol. I; London, 1965); Heinrich Kralik, *Gustav Mahler* (Vienna, 1968); Jack Diether, "Notes on Some Mahler Juvenilia," *Chord and Discord* III/1 (1969); Kurt Blaukopf, *Gustav Mahler, oder Zeitgenosse der Zukunft* (Vienna, 1969); Henry-Louis de La Grange, *Mahler,* vol. I (N.Y. 1973); Donald Mitchell, *Gustav Mahler: The Wunderhorn Years* (Boulder, Colorado, 1976); Anne Shelley, ed., *Gustav Mahler in Vienna* (N.Y., 1976); Kurt Blaukopf, ed., *Mahler. A Documentary Study* (N.Y., 1976); P. Ruzicka, *Mahler: Eine Herausforderung* (Wiesbaden, 1977); C. Floros, *Gustav Mahler* (2 vols.; Wiesbaden, 1977); Egon Gartenberg, *Mahler: The Man and His Music* (N.Y., 1978).

Mahrenholz, Christhard, German musicologist and writer on ecclesiastical subjects; b. Adelebsen, near Göttingen, Aug. 11, 1900. He studied organ as a youth; took courses at the Leipzig Cons. with Schering; upon graduation devoted himself mainly to the cause of Lutheran music. In 1933 he was elected president of the Association of Evangelical German Church Choirs; was co-editor of the magazine *Musik und Kirche*. In 1960 he was designated Abbott of Amelungsborn Cloister; in 1967 he retired from active work. Among his publications are *Luther und die Kirchenmusik* (Kassel, 1937); *Samuel Scheidt, sein Leben und sein Werk* (1924; reprint 1968); *Die Orgelregister* (1944; reprint 1968); *Die Berechnung der Orgelpfeifenmensuren vom Mittelalter bis zur Mitte des 19.Jh.* (1938). He edited works by Scheidt and other German composers; was co-editor of *Handbuch der deutschen evangelischen Kirchenmusik* (Göttingen, several vols., beginning 1932). A collection of his articles *Musicologica et liturgica: Gesammelte Aufsätze von Christhard Mahrenholz*, edited by K. F. Müller, was publ. in Kassel in 1960, as an homage on his 60th birthday; a Festschrift, *Kerygma und Melos*, was publ. for his 70th birthday in 1970 in Kassel and Berlin, containing a bibliography of his writings from 1960 to 1970.

Maichelbeck, Franz Anton, German composer of keyboard music; b. Reichenau, July 6, 1702; d. Freiburg-im-Breisgau, June 14, 1750. He publ. *Die auf dem Clavier spielende Caecilia* (1736; contains 8 sonatas) and *Die auf dem Clavier lehrende Caecilia* (1738; a book of studies).

Maier, Guy, American pianist; b. Buffalo, Aug. 15, 1892; d. Santa Monica, Calif., Sept. 24, 1956. He studied at the New England Cons. in Boston, and privately with Schnabel. After a series of solo appearances in the U.S., he formed a partnership with Lee Pattison as duo pianist, and gave numerous concerts with him (until 1931). From 1933 till 1946 he taught at the Juilliard School of Music, N.Y.; in 1946 he went to California. He made numerous transcriptions of various classical works for piano.

Maier, Julius Joseph, German music scholar; b. Freiburg, Baden, Dec. 29, 1821; d. Munich, Nov. 21, 1889. He studied for a government career, but in 1849 took up music under Haussmann in Leipzig; taught for a time at the Munich School of Music; in 1857 was appointed custodian of the music dept. of the Munich Library. He publ.: *Klassische Kirchenwerke alter Meister* (1845; arranged for men's chorus); *Auswahl englischer Madrigale* (1863); the valuable catalogue, *Die musikalischen Handschriften der Königlichen Hof- und Staatsbibliothek in München* (1879; only Part I, *Die Handschriften bis zum Ende des 17. Jahrhunderts*).

Maillart, Louis (called **Aimé**), French composer; b. Montpellier, March 24, 1817; d. Moulins, May 26, 1871. He studied at the Paris Cons. with Halévy and Leborne (composition) and with Guérin (violin); won the Grand Prix de Rome in 1841.

WORKS: 6 operas, all first performed at Paris: *Gastibelza* (Nov. 15, 1847); *Le Moulin des tilleuls* (1849), *La Croix de Marie* (1852), *Les Dragons de Villars* (Sept. 19, 1856; his most successful opera, performed also in Germany under the title *Das Glöckchen des*

Eremiten), *Les Pêcheurs de Catane* (Dec. 19, 1860), and *Lara* (March 21, 1864); also several canatas and other sacred works.

Maillart, Pierre, Belgian theorist; b. Valenciennes, 1551; d. Tournai, July 16, 1622. He was chorister at the Flemish chapel in Madrid; returning to his native land, he entered the Univ. of Louvain; was later in Antwerp (1574) and Tournai, where he was cantor (1606). He publ. *Les Tons, ou Discours sur les modes de musique* (Tournai, 1610).

Mailly, Alphonse-Jean-Ernest, Belgian organist and composer; b. Brussels, Nov. 27, 1833; d. there, Jan. 10, 1918. He studied at the Cons. of Brussels; taught piano and organ there; gave numerous and successful organ concerts in France and England; wrote various pieces for piano and organ.

Mailman, Martin, American composer; b. New York, June 30, 1932. He studied composition with Louis Mennini, Wayne Barlow, Bernard Rogers and Howard Hanson at the Eastman School of Music, Rochester, N.Y., graduating in 1954 (M.M., 1955; Ph.D., 1960); taught at the U.S. Navy School of Music (1955–57), Eastman School (1958–59), East Carolina College (1961–66); in 1966 was appointed to the faculty of North Texas State Univ., Denton.

WORKS: opera, *The Hunted* (Rochester, N.Y., April 27, 1959); for symphonic band: *4 Miniatures* (1960); *Geometrics 1* (1961), *2* (*Geometrics in Sound*, 1962), *3* (1965) and *4* (1968); *Alarums* (1962); Concertino for Trumpet and Band (1963); *Liturgical Music* (1964); *4 Variations in Search of a Theme*, with narrator (1965); *Associations 1* (1968–69); *Shouts, Hymns and Praises* (1972); *Partita* for string orch. (1960); *Genesis Resurrected* for orch., narrator and chorus (1961); *Sinfonietta* (1964); Symph. No. 1 (1969); *Generations* for 3 string orchestras and percussion (1969); *Promenade* for brass and percussion (1953); *Petite Partita* for piano (1961); String Quartet (1962); *4 Divisions* for percussion ensemble (1966).

Mainardi, Enrico, Italian cellist and composer; b. Milan, May 19, 1897; d. Munich, April 11, 1976. He studied in Milan; then went to Berlin where he was a student of Hugo Becker. He played chamber music; appeared in concerts with Dohnányi; formed a trio with the flutist Gazzelloni and the pianist Agosti; taught cello at the Academy of Santa Cecilia in Rome; then went to live in Germany. He wrote a Cello Concerto (Rome, May 13, 1947, composer soloist); Concerto for 2 Cellos and Orch. (1969); String Quintet (1970); Piano Quartet (1969); Trio for clarinet, cello and piano (1969); *Burattini*, a suite of 12 pieces for cello and piano (1968); *21 Etudes* for cello solo; various other pieces.

Maine, Basil Stephen, English writer on music; b. Norwich, March 4, 1894; d. Sheringham, Norfolk, Oct. 13, 1972. He studied with Stanford Rootham and Dent at Queen's College in Cambridge; was active after graduation as a school teacher and occasionally an actor; in 1921 he became a music director in London. He was ordained a priest in 1939. He publ. a number of monographs about music, among them biographies of *Elgar* (London, 1933; 2 vols.); *Chopin* (London 1933); also collections of essays, *The Glory of English Music* (1937); *The Best of Me; A Study in Autobiography* (London, 1937); *Basil Maine on Music* (1945); *Twang With Our Music, Being a Set of Variants to Mark the Completion of Thirty Years' Practice in the Uncertain Science of Music Criticism* (London, 1957). He also composed some choral works and organ pieces.

Mainwaring, John, English writer; b. 1735; d. Cambridge, April, 1807. In 1760 he publ. *Memoirs of the Life of the late G. F. Handel,* which was the first biography in book form of any composer; it was translated into German by J. Mattheson (1761).

Mainzer, Joseph, German singing teacher and musical journalist; b. Trier, Oct. 21, 1801; d. Salford, Lancashire, Nov. 10, 1851. He was a chorister at the Trier Cathedral; then studied music in Darmstadt, Munich, and Vienna; returning to his native town, he was ordained priest; taught at the seminary there, and publ. a sight-singing method, *Singschule* (1831). He then abandonded priesthood; moved to Brussels (1833), and then to Paris (1834), where he started the short-lived *Chronique Musicale de Paris* (1838). In 1841 he went to England; lived for a time in London, and finally established himself in Manchester as a singing teacher. In 1844 he began publication of the monthly *Mainzer's Musical Times and Singing Circular* which in 1846 became *The Musical Times* (publ. without interruption through more than a century). Mainzer mastered the English language to such an extent that he was able to engage in aggressive musical journalism. His methods of self-advertising were quite uninhibited; he arranged singing courses in open-air gatherings, and had pamphlets printed with flamboyant accounts of receptions tendered him.
WRITINGS: *Singschule* (Trier, 1831); *Méthode de chant pour les enfants* (Paris, 1835); *Méthode de chant pour voix d'hommes* (Paris, 1836); *Bibliothèque élémentaire de chant* (Paris, 1836); *Méthode pratique de piano pour enfants* (Paris, 1837); *Abécédaire de chant* (Paris, 1837); *École chorale* (Paris, 1838); *Esquisses musicales, ou souvenirs de voyage* (Paris, 1838–39); *Cent mélodies enfantines* (Paris, 1840); *Singing for the Million* (London, 1841).
BIBLIOGRAPHY: Percy A. Scholes, "The Mainzer Movement," in *The Mirror of Music* (London, 1947; vol. 1, pp. 3–10).

Mair, Franz, Austrian composer; b. Weikersdorf, in the Marchfeld, March 15, 1821; d. Vienna, Nov. 14, 1893. He was founder (1883) and conductor of the Vienna Schubertbund; composed music to *Die Jungfrau von Orleans* and other theatrical productions; wrote a number of male choruses and a cycle of 15 folksongs of various nations, arranged for men's chorus and orch., as *Die Völker und ihre Lieder.* His reminiscences were publ. by the Schubertbund under the title *Aus meinem Leben* (Vienna, 1897).

Maison, René, Belgian tenor; b. Frameries, Nov. 24, 1895; d. Mont-Dore, France, July 15, 1962. He studied at the Cons. of Brussels, and later went to the Paris Cons.; was on the roster of the Monte Carlo Opera (1922), then at the Opéra-Comique in Paris, and at Covent Garden, London. He was a member of the Chicago Civic Opera Co. (1927–32), at the Teatro Colón, Buenos Aires (1934–37); then joined the Metropolitan Opera, N.Y. (debut as Walther in *Die Meistersinger,* Feb. 3, 1936).

Maitland, John Alexander Fuller. See **Fuller-Maitland, John Alexander.**

Maitland, Rollo F., American organist; b. Williamsport, Pa., Dec. 10, 1884; d. Philadelphia, April 7, 1953. He was taught the rudiments of music by his father; then studied violin, piano and organ with various teachers in Philadelphia; was active as a church organist there; taught theory and other subjects at the Zeckwer-Hahn Music Academy in Philadelphia. He publ. a number of compositions for organ; also contributed articles to the *Diapason* and other publications.

Majeske, Daniel, American violinist; b. Detroit, Sept. 17, 1932. He began studying violin at the age of 4 and at 16 appeared as soloist with the Detroit Symphony Orchestra; continued his studies at the Curtis Institute in Philadelphia with Ivan Galamian. In 1955 he joined the violin section of the Cleveland Orchestra; in 1969 he was named its concertmaster. He appeared as a soloist with major American orchestras; in 1965 he was appointed to the faculty of the Cleveland Music School Settlement. He owns the "Marquis de Riviera" Stradivarius violin of 1718.

Majo, Gian Francesco (called **Ciccio di Majo**), Italian composer; son of **Giuseppe Majo**; b. Naples, March 27, 1732; d. there, Nov., 1770. He received his primary education from his father; was church organist; then began to compose for the stage; wrote some 20 operas, of which the first was *Ricimero, re dei Goti* (Rome, Feb. 7, 1759); also wrote separate arias for various pasticcios.

Majo, Giuseppe, Italian composer; father of the preceding; b. Naples, Dec. 5, 1697; d. there, Nov. 18, 1771. He studied with Nicola Fago at the Conservatorio della Pietà dei Turchini in Naples; in 1744 became master of the royal chapel in Naples, retaining this post until his death. He wrote a considerable amount of church music; also several comic operas and 2 serious operas.

Majone (Mayone), Ascanio, Neapolitan organist and composer; lived in the late 16th to early 17th centuries. He was a pupil of Giovanni Macque, and his assistant at the viceregal chapel at Naples, c.1600. Existing musical publications by Majone are: *Primo libro di diversi capricci per sonare* (Naples, 1603); *Il primo libro di madrigali a 5 voci* (Naples, 1604); *Secondo libro di diversi capricci per sonare* (Naples, 1609; repr. in *Orgue et Liturgie* 63 and 65; Paris, 1964). Two of his madrigals are included in the collection *Teatro di Madrigali a 5 v. de div. excell. musici Napolitani, posti in luce da Scipione Ricci, Libraro* (Naples, 1609). Majone is mentioned in Scipione

Cerreto's *Della Prattica Musica vocale e strumentale* (Naples, 1601) as an outstanding performer on the organ and harp. Majone's keyboard toccatas are among the earliest examples of the affective Baroque style found later in Frescobaldi.

BIBLIOGRAPHY: W. Apel, "Neapolitan Links between Cabezón and Frescobaldi," *Musical Quarterly* (Oct. 1938); M. Bukofzer, *Music in the Baroque Era* (N.Y., 1947).

Major, Ervin, Hungarian music scholar and composer; b. Budapest, Jan. 26, 1901; d. there, Oct. 10, 1967. He studied with his father, **Jakab Gyula Major**; then took lessons with Kodály (1917–21). He made a profound study of Hungarian folk music as it relates to the works of classical composers, and published numerous essays on the subject. He composed mostly in small forms; among his works are a bassoon sonata (1938), a sonata for double bass and piano (1943), piano pieces and choruses.

Major (real name **Mayer**), **Jakab Gyula,** Hungarian pianist, conductor, and composer; b. Kosice, Dec. 13, 1858; b. Budapest, Jan. 30, 1925. He studied with Robert Volkmann; graduating from the Budapest Cons. in 1882, he became a teacher in Hungarian schools. He toured in Europe as a pianist; then returned to Budapest. His music follows the Romantic tradition of the German school. He wrote the operas, *Erzsike* (Budapest, Sept. 24, 1901), *Széchy Mária* (1906), and *Mila* (1913), 5 symphonies, Piano Concerto, Violin Concerto, Cello Concerto, 4 string quartets, Piano Quintet, 2 violin sonatas, and much piano music.

Makarova, Nina, Russian composer; b. Yurino, Aug. 12, 1908; d. Moscow, Jan. 15, 1976. She studied with Miaskovsky at the Moscow Cons., graduating in 1936. Her early works show a romantic flair, not without some coloristic touches of French impressionism. She wrote an opera, *Zoya* (1955); a symphony (1938) which she conducted herself in Moscow on June 12, 1947; a number of violin pieces, a sonatina and 6 etudes for piano, several song cycles and a cantata, *The Saga of Lenin* (1970). She was married to **Aram Khachaturian.**

BIBLIOGRAPHY: Ivan Martinov, *Nina Makarova* (Moscow, 1973).

Makeba, Miriam, black South African singer; b. Prospect, near Johannesburg, March 4, 1932. She sang in a mission choir in Pretoria; then joined an itinerant minstrel show. She first attracted attention when she sang the leading part in the African opera *King Kong* (Johannesburg, Feb. 2, 1959). In 1959 she went to the U.S.; appeared in New York night clubs and on television; testified at the United Nations on racist policies of South Africa; made a successful tour of Europe; also traveled to Ethiopia and Kenya as a representative of Negro art.

BIBLIOGRAPHY: *Current Biography* (June 1965).

Makedonski, Kiril, Macedonian composer; b. Bitol, Jan. 19, 1925. After completing his academic schooling in Skoplje, he studied with Krso Odak at the Music Academy in Zagreb; later continued his composition studies with Brkanović in Sarajevo, and in Ljubljana with Škerjanc. He is the composer of the first national Macedonian opera *Goce* (Skoplje, May 24, 1954); his second opera was *Tsar Samuil* (Skoplje, Nov. 5, 1968). He also wrote 4 symphonies: chamber music and a number of choruses. His idiom follows the fundamental vocal and harmonic usages of the Russian National School.

BIBLIOGRAPHY: Branko Karakaš, *Muzicki Stvaraoci u Makedoniji* (Belgrade, 1970; pp. 68–70).

Maklakiewicz, Jan Adam, Polish composer; b. Chojnaty, near Warsaw, Nov. 24, 1899; d. Warsaw, Feb. 7, 1954. He studied with Statkowski at the Warsaw Cons. and with Paul Dukas in Paris. Returning to Poland, he became instructor in harmony at the Warsaw Cons.; from 1932 he was organist at the Church of the Holy Cross; in 1934, he established the musical periodical *Chor* and was also active as music critic.

WORKS: Under the influence of French modernism, Maklakiewicz wrote a number of works in an advanced style; his *4 Japanese Songs* were performed at the Oxford Festival of the International Society for Contemporary Music (July 23, 1931). Other works include a ballet, *Cagliostro in Warsaw* (Poznan, Oct. 1, 1946); a symph. poem *Grünewald* (Cracow, Sept. 1, 1945); *Uwertura praska* (*The Prague Overture*; Prague, May 8, 1947); Cello Concerto (1932); Violin Concerto (1933); some chamber music; many arrangements of Polish folksongs. From 1947 to his death Maklakiewicz was director of the Cons. of Cracow.

Maksimović, Rajko, Serbian composer; b. Belgrade, July 27, 1935. He studied at the Academy of Music in Belgrade; later joined its faculty; also took a postgraduate course at Princeton Univ. His style of composition combines formal neo-Classicism with serial procedures and ethnic Balkan thematics.

WORKS: *Muzika posta-janja* based on an atonally treated motive B-A-C-H (Belgrade, July 20, 1965); *Partita concertante* for violin and strings (1965); *Kad su živi zavideli mrtvima* (*When the Living Envied the Dead*), cantata to texts from medieval Serbian chronicles (Belgrade, April 21, 1964); *Three Haiku* for female choir and chamber orch., with the application of aleatory devices (Zagreb, May 16, 1967).

BIBLIOGRAPHY: Vlastimir Peričić, *Muzički Stvaraoci u Srbiji* (Belgrade, 1969; pp. 238–43).

Malashkin, Leonid, Russian composer; b. 1842; d. Moscow, Feb. 11, 1902. He was an ardent song collector; his anthology *50 Ukrainian Folksongs* is valuable. His original compositions were not successful; he wrote an opera, *Ilya Murometz* (Kiev, 1879), a *Russian Symphony on Folk Themes* (Moscow, March 27, 1873), and a great deal of church music.

Malawski, Artur, Polish violinist and composer; b. Przemyśl, July 4, 1904; d. Cracow, Dec. 26, 1957. He graduated as a violinist from the Cracow Cons. in 1928; then studied composition with Kazimierz Sikorski, and conducting at the Warsaw Cons. (1936–39). In his music he utilized Polish folksongs as thematic material; the treatment is in a general modern idiom.

WORKS: *Allegro capriccioso* for small orch.

(1929); *Sinfonietta* (1936); *Symphonic Variations* (1937); cantata, *Wyspa Gorgon* (*Gorgons' Island*, 1939); 2 symphonies (1938–43, 1955); a ballet-pantomime, *Wierchy* (*The Peaks;* 1944, revised 1950); *6 Symphonic Etudes* for piano and orch. (Sopot, April 30, 1948); *Tryptyk góralski* (*Highland Triptych*) for small orch. or piano (1949); *Toccata and Fugue* for piano and orch. (1949); cantata, *Stara baśń* (*The Old Tale*, 1950); *Suite popularna* for orch. (1952); *Hungaria 1956* for orch. (1957; Warsaw, Feb. 14, 1958; descriptive of the Hungarian insurrection of 1956); 2 string quartets (1926, 1943); String Sextet (1935); *Ziabia Ballad* (*Ballad of the Frogs*), 2 recitations for voice and wind ensemble (1934); *Burlesque* for violin and piano (1940); *Miniatures* for piano (1947); Violin Sonata (1951); Piano Trio (1953).
    BIBLIOGRAPHY: B. Schäffer, editor, *Artur Malawski: zycie i twórczość* (Cracow, 1969).

Malcuzynski, Witold, outstanding Polish pianist; b. Warsaw, Aug. 10, 1914; d. Palma, Majorca, July 17, 1977. He studied with Turczynski at the Warsaw Cons.; graduated in 1936; then took lessons with Paderewski in Switzerland. After his marriage to the French pianist **Colette Gaveau,** he went to Paris (1939); then toured in South America (1940–42); made his American debut in 1942; gave concerts in Australia in 1950. He made in all 14 U.S. tours, 9 South American tours, and 2 world tours (1949; 1956). He was particularly distinguished as an interpreter of Chopin.
    BIBLIOGRAPHY: B. Gavoty, *Witold Malcuzynski* (London, 1957).

Maldeghem, Robert Julien van, Belgian music editor; b. Denterghem, Oct. 9, 1806; d. Brussels, Nov. 13, 1893. He studied with Fétis at the Brussels Cons., winning the Belgian Prix de Rome; obtained a post as church organist; undertook a thorough research of old Flemish music, and eventually publ. an anthology of choral works in 29 vols., *Trésor musical,* an edition of great documentary and historic importance, despite many errors of transcription; comments and rectifications were made by Charles Van den Borren, in *Acta Musicologica* 5/6 and by G. Reese, "Maldeghem and His Buried Treasure: a Bibliographical Study," in *Notes* (Dec. 1948).

Maldere (Malderre), Pierre van, Belgian violinist and composer; b. Brussels, Oct. 16, 1729; d. there, Nov. 1, 1768. In 1746 he became a member of the ensemble of the Royal Chapel of Brussels. From 1751 to 1753 he was in Dublin as violinist, conductor, and composer. He then traveled to Paris (1754) and Austria (1757–58); returning to Brussels, he became conductor of the Opera, and also wrote stage works for production there.
    WORKS: operas *Les Amours champêtres* (1758); *Les Précautions inutiles* (1760); *La Bagarre* (1762); *Les Sœurs rivales* (1762); *Le Médecin de l'amour* (1766); *Le Soldat par amour* (1766); a number of instrumental works, of which many were published during his lifetime: 6 symphonies (Brussels, 1759), *6 sinfonie a più stromenti* (Paris, 1760), and a similar set,

publ. in Paris (1768); also violin sonatas. Three of his brothers were also violinists.
    BIBLIOGRAPHY: S. Clercx, *Pierre van Maldere* (Brussels, 1948).

Maleingreau (or **Malengreau**), **Paul de,** Belgian composer and organist; b. Trélon-en-Thiérache, Nov. 23, 1887; d. Brussels. Jan. 9, 1956. He studied with Edgar Tinel at the Brussels Cons.; in 1913, became prof. of harmony there; in 1919, appointed instructor of organ; in 1946 he was elected president of the Froissart Academy. His performances of Bach organ works were highly regarded in Belgium. Among his compositions are 2 symphonies: *Légende de St. Augustin,* for solo voices, chorus, and orch. (1934); an Easter Mass (1925); 2 Dipthychs, for orch. (1947); organ works; piano pieces.

Maler, Wilhelm, German composer and music educator; b. Heidelberg, June 21, 1902; d. Hamburg, April 29, 1976. He studied music history with Kroyer and composition with Grabner in Heidelberg; then took courses with Haas in Munich and Jarnach in Berlin. He subsequently occupied several teaching positions in Cologne, Bonn, Detmold and Hamburg; also was active in theatrical organizations. His music is marked by a strong polyphonic strain; in his works as well as in his theoretical writings he developed structural ideas promulgated by Hindemith.
    WORKS: Concerto for Cembalo and Chamber Orch. (1927); *Orchesterspiel* (1930); Violin Concerto (1932); *Flämisches Rondo* for orch. (1937); 2 string quartets; String Trio; 6 piano sonatas and various minor pieces. He published a manual of harmony, *Beitrag zur Harmonielehre* (Leipzig, 1931; revised as *Beitrag zur durmolltonalen Harmonielehre,* 1950; 3rd revised ed., 1957).

Malherbe, Charles-Théodore, French writer on music and conductor; b. Paris, April 21, 1853; d. Cormeilles, Eure, Oct. 5, 1911. First he studied law, and was admitted to the bar; but then took up music under A. Danhauser, A. Wormser, and J. Massenet. After a tour (as Danhauser's secretary) through Belgium, Holland, and Switzerland in 1880–81, to inspect the music in the public schools, he settled in Paris; in 1896, was appointed assistant archivist to the Grand Opéra, succeeding Nuitter as archivist in 1899. He edited *Le Ménestrel,* and contributed to many leading reviews and musical journals. His collection of musical autographs, which he left to the Paris Cons., was probably one of the finest private collections in the world.
    WRITINGS: *L'Œuvre dramatique de Richard Wagner* (1886); *Précis d'histoire de l'Opéra-Comique* (1887); *Notice sur Ascanio* (1890); *Mélanges sur R. Wagner* (1891); *Histoire de la seconde Salle Favart* [Opéra-Comique] (2 vols., 1893–93, 'couronnée par l'Institut'); *Catalogue des œuvres de Donizetti* (1897); *Programmes et concerts* (1898); *Auber* (1911). Malherbe was secretary of the edition of Rameau's complete works publ. by Durand, editing the historical and biographical notices therein; also ed., with Weingartner, of the complete edition of Berlioz's works (Breitkopf & Härtel).

Malherbe, Edmond Paul Henri, French composer; b. Paris, Aug. 21, 1870; d. Corbeil-Essonnes (Seine-et-Oise), March 7, 1963. He studied at the Paris Cons. with Massenet and Fauré; 1898, won the Premier Second Prix de Rome, and in 1899, the Deuxième Premier Grand Prix; 3 times winner of the Prix Trémont of the Académie des Beaux-Arts (1907, 1913, 1921); in 1950 received the Grand Prix Musical of the City of Paris for the total of his works. A productive composer, he continued to write music in his 80's, but very few of his larger compositions were performed, and virtually none published.
    WORKS: operas: *Madame Pierre* (1903; Paris, 1912); *L'Avare,* after Molière (1907); *L'Émeute* (1911; Paris, 1912); *Cléanthis* (1912); *Anna Karénine* (1914); *Le Mariage forcé,* after Molière (1924); *Néron* (1945); *L'Amour et Psyché,* lyric tragedy with ballet (1948; State Prize, 1950); *Monsieur de Pourceaugnac,* pantomime with chorus, after Molière (1930); a series of "tableaux symphoniques" after great paintings; 3 symphonies (1948; 1956; 1957); Violin Concerto; Nonet; Sextet; many choruses, songs piano pieces. He publ. *L'Harmonie du système musical actuel à demi-tons* (1920) and *Le Tiers-de-ton: Deux Systèmes: Tempéré et non-tempéré* (1900; 1950).

Malibran, María Felicità (*née* **García**), famous contralto; daughter of **Manuel García;** b. Paris, March 24, 1808; d. Manchester, Sept. 23, 1836. Taken to Naples, she played a child's part in Paër's opera *Agnese;* later she studied solfeggio with Panseron; from the age of 15, however, she was her father's pupil in singing. Her debut in London (June 7, 1825), as Rosina in the *Barbiere,* procured her engagement for the season. The family then voyaged to New York, where for two years she was the popular favorite, singing in *Otello, Romeo, Don Giovanni, Tancredi, Cenerentola,* and the 2 operas which her father wrote for her, *L'Amante astuto* and *La Figlia dell'aria.* In N.Y. she married the French merchant Malibran; he soon became bankrupt, and they separated. Returning to Paris, her immense success led to an engagement at a salary of 50,000 francs; after 1829 she sang every season at London; also appeared at Rome, Naples, Bologna, and Milan. She married the violinist **Bériot** in 1836, only a few months before her death, which was caused by over-exertion after a severe fall from her horse. As a singer and actress she exercised the fascination of a highly endowed personality over her audiences. Her voice was of extraordinary compass, but the medium register had several "dead" tones. She was also a good pianist, and composed numerous nocturnes, romances, and chansonnettes, publ. in album form as *Dernières pensées.*
    BIBLIOGRAPHY: *Cenni biografici* (Venice, 1835); G. Barbieri, *Notizie biografiche di Maria Malibran* (Milan, 1836); I. Nathan, *The Life of Mme. Maria Malibran de Bériot* (London, 1836); A. von Treskow, *Mme. Malibran* (Leipzig, 1837); Comtesse Merlin, *Loisirs d'une femme de monde* (Paris, 1838; German transl. by G. Lotz as *Maria Malibran als Weib und Künstlerin,* Leipzig, 1839; English transl., London, 1844; more romantic than trustworthy); E. Legouvé, "Maria Malibran," in *Études et souvenirs de théâtre* (Paris, 1880); E. Heron-Allen, "A Contribution Towards an Accurate Biogr. of Ch. de Bériot and Maria Malibran," *De fidiculis opuscula* 6 (1894); A. Pougin, *Maria Malibran: Histoire d'une cantatrice* (Paris, 1911; English transl., London, 1911); Clément Lanquine, *La Malibran* (Paris, 1911); J.-G. Prod'homme, "La Fayette et Maria Malibran," *Chesterian* (Sept. 1919); Louise Héritte-Viardot, *Une Famille de grands musiciens* (1923); Carl Engel, "Again La Fayette and Maria Malibran," *Chesterian* (Jan.–Feb. 1925); *6 Unpubl. Letters from La Fayette to Maria Malibran, Chesterian* (March–April 1925); A. Flament, *Une Étoile en 1830: La Malibran* (Paris, 1928); Phyllis Crump, *Musset and Malibran* (Cambridge, England, 1932); P. Larionoff, *Maria Malibran e i suoi tempi* (Florence, 1935); D. Bielli, *Maria Malibran* (1936); M. Lorenzi de Bradi, *La brève et merveilleuse vie de la Malibran* (Paris, 1936); G. G. Bernardi, "La Malibran a Venezia," *Musica d'oggi* (Aug.–Sept. 1936); H. Malherbe, *La Passion de la Malibran* (Paris, 1937); A. Flament, *L'Enchanteresse errante, la Malibran* (Paris, 1937); S. Desternes and H. Chandet, *La Malibran et Pauline Viardot* (Paris, 1969); Carmen de Reparaz *María Malibran* (Madrid, 1976).

Malipiero, Francesco, Italian composer; grandfather of **Gian Francesco Malipiero;** b. Rovigio, Jan. 9, 1824; d. Venice, May 12, 1887. He studied with Melchiore Balbi at the Liceo Musicale in Venice. At the age of 18 he wrote an opera, *Giovanna di Napoli,* which was produced with signal success; Rossini praised it. Other operas by Malipiero were *Attila* (Venice, Nov. 15, 1845; renamed later *Ildegonda di Borgogna*), *Alberigo da Romano* (his best; Venice, Dec. 26, 1846), *Fernando Cortez* (Venice, Feb. 18, 1851).

Malipiero, Gian Francesco, greatly distinguished Italian composer; b. Venice, March 18, 1882; d. Treviso (near Venice), Aug. 1, 1973. He was reared in a musical environment; his grandfather, **Francesco Malipiero,** wrote operas; his father **Luigi Malipiero** was also a musician. In 1898 Malipiero enrolled at the Vienna Cons. as a violin student; in 1899 he returned to Venice where he studied at the Liceo Musicale Benedetto Marcello with Enrico Bossi, whom he followed to Bologna in 1902; he took a diploma in composition at the Liceo Musicale G. B. Martini in Bologna in 1904. In 1913 he went to Paris, where he absorbed the techniques of musical impressionism, cultivating parallel chord formations and amplified tonal harmonies with characteristic added sixths, ninths and elevenths. However, his own style of composition was determined by the polyphonic practices of the Italian Baroque. In 1921 Malipiero returned to Italy; taught composition at the Univ. of Parma (1921–23); afterwards lived mostly in Asolo, near Venice. He became director of the Liceo Musicale Benedetto Marcello in Venice in 1939; was named a member of the National Institute of Arts and Letters in N.Y. in 1949, of the Royal Flemish Academy in Brussels in 1952, of the Institut de France in 1954, and of the Akademie der Künste in West Berlin in 1967. Apart from his activities as composer and educator, Malipiero was the erudite and devoted editor of collected works of Monteverdi and Vivaldi.
    WORKS: OPERAS: *Canossa* (Rome, Jan. 24, 1914);

Sogno d'un tramonto d'autunno (1914; not performed until nearly half a century later, when it was brought out in concert production on the Milan Radio, Oct. 4, 1963); *L'Orfeide* (Düsseldorf, Nov. 5, 1925), in 3 parts (*La Morte delle maschere; Sette Canzoni; Orfeo*); the 2nd part, *Sette Canzoni* (Paris, July 10, 1920), is often performed separately; *Tre commedie goldoniane* (*La Bottega da caffè; Sior Todaro Brontolon; Le Baruffe chiozzotte;* 1st performance in its entirety, Darmstadt, March 24, 1926); *Filomela e l'Infatuato* (Prague March 31, 1928); *Merlino maestro d'organi* (Rome Radio, Aug. 4, 1934); *Il mistero di Venezia*, in 3 parts (*Le Aquile di aquileia; Il finto Arlecchino; I Corvi di San Marco;* 1st performance in its entirety, Coburg, Dec. 15, 1932); *Torneo notturno* (Munich, May 15, 1931); *Il festino* (Turin Radio, Nov. 6, 1937); *La favola del figlio cambiato* (Brunswick, Jan. 13, 1934); *Giulio Cesare* (Genoa, Feb. 8, 1936); *Antonio e Cleopatra* (Florence, May 4, 1938); *Ecuba* (Rome, Jan. 11, 1941); *La vita è sogno* (Breslau, June 30, 1943); *I Capricci di Callot* (Rome, Oct. 24, 1942); *L'allegra brigata* (Milan, May 4, 1950); *Mondi celesti e infernali* (Turin Radio, Jan. 12, 1950); *Il figliuol prodigo* (Florence May Festival, May 14, 1957); *Venere prigioniera* (Florence May Festival, May 14, 1957); *Il marescalco* (1960); *Il Capitan Spavento* (Naples, March 16, 1963); *Don Giovanni*, opera after Pushkin (Naples, Sept. 22, 1963); *Il Marescalco* (1964); *Le Metamorfosi di Bonaventura*, (Venice, Sept. 5, 1966); *Don Tartuto bacchetone* (1966; Venice, Jan. 20, 1970); *L'iscariota* (1971); *Uno dei dieci* (1971).

BALLETS: *Pantea* (Venice, Sept. 6, 1932); *La mascherata delle principesse prigioniere* (Brussels, Oct. 19, 1924); *Stradivario* (Florence, June 20, 1949); *Il mondo novo* (Rome, Dec. 16, 1951).

FOR ORCH.: *Sinfonia degli eroi* (1905); *Sinfonia del mare* (1906); *Sinfonie del silenzio e della morte* (1908); *Impressioni dal vero* in 3 parts (1st part, Milan, May 15, 1913; 2nd part, Rome, March 11, 1917; 3rd part, Amsterdam, Oct. 25, 1923); *Armenia*, on Armenian folksongs (1917); *Ditirambo tragico* (London, Oct. 11, 1919); *Pause del silenzio* in 2 parts (1st part, his most famous orchestral work, Rome, Jan. 27, 1918; 2nd part, Philadelphia, April 1, 1927); *Per una favola cavalleresca* (Rome, Feb. 13, 1921); *Oriente immaginario*, for chamber orch. (Paris, Dec. 23, 1920); *Variazioni senza tema*, for piano and orch. (Prague, May 19, 1925); *L'Esilio dell'Eroe*, symph. suite (1930); *Concerti per orchestra* (Philadelphia, Jan. 29, 1932); *Inni* (Rome, April 6, 1933); *Sette invenzioni* (Rome, Dec. 24, 1933); *Quattro invenzioni* (Dresden, Nov. 11, 1936); *Fantasie di ogni giorni*, for orch. (Louisville, Nov. 17, 1954); *Serenata mattutina* for 10 instruments (1959); *Concerto di concerti* for baritone, violin and orch. (1960); *Serenata* for bassoon and chamber orch. (1961); *Serenissima* for saxophone and orch. (1961); *Sinfonia per Antigenida* (1962); *Abracadabra* for baritone and orch. (1962); 11 symphonies: No. 1 (Florence, April 2, 1934); No. 2, *Elegiaca* (Seattle, Jan. 25, 1937); No. 3, *Delle campane* (Florence, Nov. 4, 1945); No. 4, *In Memoriam* (Boston, Feb. 27, 1948; dedicated to the memory of Natalie Koussevitzky); No. 5, *Concertante, in eco* (London, Nov. 3, 1947); No. 6, *Degli archi* (Basel, Feb. 11, 1949); No. 7, *Delle canzoni* (Milan, Nov. 3, 1949); No. 8, *Di un tempo* (Rome, March 21, 1951); No. 9, *Dello Zodiaco* (Lausanne, Jan. 23, 1952); No. 10 (1967); No. 11, *Delle Cornamuse* (1970); Violin Concerto No. 1 (Amsterdam, March 5, 1933); Violin Concerto No. 2 (1963); Cello Concerto (Belgrade, Jan. 31, 1939); 1st Piano Concerto (Rome, April 3, 1935); 2nd Piano Concerto (Duisburg, March 6, 1939); *Concerto a tre*, for violin, cello, piano and orch. (Florence, April 9, 1939); 3rd Piano Concerto (Louisville, March 8, 1949); 4th Piano Concerto (Turin Radio, Jan. 28, 1951); 5th Piano Concerto (1958); 6th Piano Concerto, *Delle machine* (Rome, Feb. 5, 1966); Concerto for 2 Pianos and Orch. (Besancon Festival, Sept. 11, 1957); Flute Concerto (1968).

VOCAL WORKS: *San Francesco d'Assisi*, mystery for soli, chorus, and orch. (N.Y., March 29, 1922); *La Principessa Ulalia*, cantata (N.Y., Feb. 19, 1927); *La Cena*, for soli, chorus, and orch. (Rochester, N.Y., April 25, 1929); *La Passione*, for soli, chorus, and orch. (Rome, Dec. 15, 1935); *De Profundis*, for solo voice, viola, bass drum, and piano (1937); *Missa pro mortuis*, for baritone solo, chorus, and orch. (Rome, Dec. 18, 1938); *Quattro vecchie canzoni*, for solo voice and 7 instruments (Washington, April 12, 1941); *Santa Eufrosina* for soli, chorus, and orch. (Rome, Dec. 6, 1942); *Le sette allegrezze d'amore*, for solo voice and 14 instruments (Milan, Dec. 4, 1945); *Vergilii Aeneis*, for 11 soli, chorus, and orch. (Turin, June 21, 1946); *La Terra*, for chorus and orch. (Cambridge, Mass., May 2, 1947, with organ); *Mondi celesti*, for solo voice and 12 instruments (Capri, Feb. 3, 1949); *Le sette peccati mortali*, for chorus and orch. (Monteceneri, Nov. 20, 1949); *La festa de la Sensa*, for baritone solo, chorus, and orch. (1950); *Cinque Favole*, for solo voice and small orch. (Washington, Oct. 30, 1950); *Passer mortuus est*, for a cappella chorus (Pittsburgh, Nov. 24, 1952); *L'asino d'oro* for baritone and orch., after Apuleius (1959); *Ave Phoebe, dum queror* for chorus and 20 instruments (1964).

CHAMBER MUSIC: *Ricercari*, for 11 instruments (Washington, Oct. 7, 1926); *Ritrovari*, for 11 instruments (Gardone, Italy, Oct. 26, 1929); 8 string quartets: No. 1, *Rispetti e Strambotti* (1920); No. 2, *Stornelli e Ballate* (1923); No. 3, *Cantari alla madrigalesca* (1931); No. 4 (1934); No. 5, *Dei capricci* (1940); No. 6, *L'arca di Noè* (1947); No. 7 (1950); No. 8, *Quartetto per Elisabetta*, E. S. Coolidge Foundation Commission (1964); *Epodi e giambi*, for violin, viola, oboe, and bassoon (1932); *Sonata a cinque* for flute, violin, viola, cello, and harp (1934); *Sonata a tre*, for violin, cello, and piano (1927); Cello Sonatina (1942). For piano: *Six Morceaux* (1905); *Bizzarrie luminose dell'alba, del meriggio e della notte* (1908); *Poemetti lunari* (1910); *Preludi autunnali* (1914); *Poemi asolani* (1916); *Barlumi* (1917); *Risonanze* (1918); *Maschere che passano* (1918); *Tre omaggi* (1920); *Omaggio a Claude Debussy* (1920); *Cavalcate* (1921); *La siesta* (1921); *Il tarlo* (1922); *Pasqua di Risurrezione* (1924); *Preludi a una fuga* (1926); *Epitaffio* (1931); *Omaggio a Bach* (1932); *Preludi, ritmi e canti gregoriani* (1937); *Preludio e fuga* (1941); *Hortus conclusus* (1946). Editions of works by Bassani, Cavalieri, Galuppi, Jommelli, Marcello, Tartini, Leo, Monteverdi (several individual works, and a collected edition, 16 vols., 1926–42), Vivaldi.

WRITINGS: *L'Orchestra* (Bologna, 1920; English transl. by Eric Blom, London, 1921); *Claudio Monteverdi* (Milan, 1930); *Stravinsky* (Venice, 1945); *Antonfrancesco Doni musico, ovvero L'armonioso labirinto* (Venice, 1946); *Così va lo mondo: 1922-45* (autobiography; Milan, 1946); *La Pietra del bando* (1947); and many articles in various European and American magazines. A collection of Malipiero's writings was published under the title *Il Filo d'Arianna* (Turin, 1966).

BIBLIOGRAPHY: biography, Massimo Bontempelli, *Gian Francesco Malipiero* (Milan, 1942); Guido M. Gatti, ed., *L'opera di Gian Francesco Malipiero* (Bologna, 1952; a collection of articles on Malipiero, reprinted from numerous sources, and a comprehensive list of works, up to 1950, annotated by the composer, with a chronology of performances, etc.); magazine articles: H. Prunières, "G. F. Malipiero," *Musical Quarterly* (July 1920); G. M. Gatti, "G. F. Malipiero," *Il Pianoforte* (May 1925); G. M. Gatti, "G. F. Malipiero," in *Musicisti moderni d'Italia e di fuori* (Bologna, 2nd ed., 1925; pp. 75-86); M. Labroca, "G. F. Malipiero," *Musikblätter des Anbruch* (special Italian issue, Aug.-Sept. 1925); H. F. Redlich, "G. F. Malipiero und die neue Oper," *Anbruch* (Nov.-Dec. 1929); G. Rossi-Doria, "Le Théâtre et l'oratorio de G. F. Malipiero," *Musique* (Dec. 1929-Jan. 1930); S. Goddard, "Malipiero's L'Orfeide," *Chesterian* (Nov. 1930); G. F. Malipiero, "The Sette Canzoni, An Explanation; *Chesterian* (Dec. 1930); H. F. Redlich, "Francesco Malipiero, Dramaturge lyrique," *Revue Musicale* (Nov. 1931); M. Saint Cyr, "G. F. Malipiero," *Rassegna dorica* (Feb. 1932); H. O. Boehm, "G. F. Malipiero," *Der Aufsteig* (Sept. 1932); H. H. Stuckenschmidt, "Zu Malipieros Bühnenwerken," *Melos* (Feb. 1934); special issue of the *Rassegna Musicale* for his 60th birthday (March 1942), containing articles by Pizzetti, Casella, Labroca, and others; Everett Helm, "Gian Francesco Malipiero: An Introduction," *Soundings 1* (Cardiff; Autumn 1970). See also *"Modern Music"*... *Analytic Index*, compiled by Wayne Shirley, ed. by Wm. and C. Lichtenwanger (N.Y., 1976; p. 131).

Malipiero, Riccardo, Italian composer; nephew of **Gian Francesco Malipiero**; b. Milan, July 24, 1914. He studied piano and composition at the Milan and Turin Cons. (1930-37); completed studies with his uncle at the Benedetto Marcello Cons. in Venice (1937-39); traveled as lecturer and pianist in Europe, South America and U.S. As a composer, he followed Italian neo-Baroque, but about 1950 adopted a fairly consistent method of 12-tone composition.

WORKS: 3 operas: *Minnie la Candida* (Parma, Nov. 19, 1942); *La Donna è mobile*, opera buffa (1954; Milan, Feb. 22, 1957); television opera, *Battono alla Porta* (Italian television, Feb. 12, 1962; stage version, Genoa, May 24, 1963); Piano Concerto (1937); *3 Dances* for orch. (1937); 2 cello concertos (1938, 1957); *Balleto* for orch. (1939); *Piccolo concerto* for piano and orch. (1945); *Antico sole* for soprano and orch. (1947); *Cantata sacra* for soprano, chorus and orch. (1947); 3 symphonies: No. 1 (1949), No. 2, *Sinfonia Cantata*, for baritone and orch. (1956; N.Y., March 19, 1957) and No. 3 (1959; Univ. of Florida, Miami, April 10, 1960); Violin Concerto (1952; Milan,

Jan. 31, 1953); *Studi* for orch. (1953; Venice Festival, Sept. 11, 1953); *Ouverture-Divertimento "del Ritorno"* (1953); Concerto for Piano and Chamber Orch. (1955); *Concerto breve* for ballerina and chamber orch. (1956; Venice Festival, Sept. 11, 1956); *Cantata di natale* for soprano, chorus and orch. (1959; Milan, Dec. 21, 1959); Sonata for oboe, and strings (1960); *Concerto per Dimitri* for piano and orch. (1961; Venice Festival, April 27, 1961); *Nykteghersia* for orch. (1962); *Cadencias* for orch. (1964; Geneva Radio, Jan. 13, 1965); *Muttermusik* for orch. (1965-66; Milan, Feb. 28, 1966); *Mirages* for orch. (1966; Milan, Feb. 6, 1970); *Carnet de notes* for chamber orch. (1967); *Rapsodia* for violin and orch. (1967); *Serenata per Alice Tully* for chamber orch. (1969; N.Y., March 10, 1970); *Monologo* for female voice and strings (1969); Concerto for Piano Trio and Orch. (1971; Milan, Jan. 16, 1976); *Requiem 1975* for orch. (Florence, Nov. 6, 1976); *Go Placidly* for baritone and chamber orch. (1976; N.Y., Nov. 10, 1976); chamber music: *Musik I* for cello and 9 instruments (1938); 3 string quartets 1941, 1954, 1960); Violin Sonata (1956); Piano Quintet (1957); *Musica da camera* for wind quintet (1959); Oboe Sonata (1959); *6 Poesie di Dylan Thomas* for soprano and 10 instruments (1959); *Mosaico* for wind and string quintets (1961); *Preludio Adagio e Finale* for soprano, 5 percussionists and piano (1963); *In Time of Daffodils*, to poems by E. E. Cummings, for soprano, baritone and 7 instrumentalists (Washington, Oct. 30, 1964); *Nuclei* for 2 pianos and percussion (1966); *Cassazione* for string sextet (1967); Piano Trio (1968); *Ciaccona di Davide* for viola and piano (1970); *Memoria* for flute and piano (1973); *Giber Folia* for clarinet and piano (1973); for piano: *14 Inventions* (1938); *Musik* for 2 pianos (1939); *Piccolo musica* (1941); *Invenzioni* (1949); *Costellazioni* (1965) and *Le Rondini de Alessandro* (1971). He published several monographs: *J. S. Bach* (Brescia, 1948); *Debussy* (Brescia, 1948); *Guida alla dodecafonia* (Milan, 1961); *Musica ieri e oggi* (with E. Radius and G. Severi; 6 vols., Rome, 1970).

BIBLIOGRAPHY: Claudio Sartori, *Riccardo Malipiero* (in English; Milan, 1957).

Maliszewski, Witold, Polish composer; b. Mohylev-Podolsk, July 20, 1873; d. Zalesie, July 18, 1939. He studied piano in Warsaw and violin in Tiflis; then enrolled in the St. Petersburg Cons., in the class of Rimsky-Korsakov. He became director of the Odessa Cons. in 1908; went to Poland in 1921, and was active there mainly as a teacher; in 1932 he joined the staff of the Warsaw Cons. As a composer, he followed the Russian Romantic tradition; some of his symph. works had a modicum of success. He wrote the operas *The Mermaid* (Warsaw, 1928) and *Boruta* (1930); 4 symphonies; a piano concerto (1932); 4 string quartets; violin sonata; cello sonata; many piano pieces, and songs.

BIBLIOGRAPHY: See E. Wrocki, *Witold Maliszewski* (Warsaw, 1932).

Malkin, Jacques, Russian-American violinist; b. Slobodka, near Odessa, Dec. 16, 1875; d. New York, Dec. 8, 1964. He studied in Odessa, and later enrolled at the Paris Cons.; in 1893 he played the viola d'amore in the

Société des Instruments Anciens in Paris. In 1918 he went to America and settled in New York as a violin teacher; with his brothers **Joseph** and **Manfred**, he formed a trio.

Malkin, Joseph, Russian-American cellist; b. Propoisk, near Odessa, Sept. 24, 1879; d. New York, Sept. 1, 1969. After studying in Odessa he went to Paris and studied cello at the Paris Cons., graduating in 1902; then went to Germany and became the first cellist at the Berlin Philharmonic (1902-08); toured America as a member of the Brussels Quartet. He remained in the U.S.; was first cellist of the Boston Symph. Orch. (1914-19) and of the Chicago Symph. (1919-22); with his brothers **Jacques** and **Manfred** he organized the Malkin Trio, which presented concerts in New York and Boston. In 1933 he organized the Malkin Cons. in Boston, and was instrumental in inviting Arnold Schoenberg to teach at the Malkin Cons. during Schoenberg's first American season (1934-35); the Malkin Cons. closed in 1943; from 1944 to 1949, Malkin played cello in the New York Philharmonic, before retiring. He died in a nursing home. He publ. a number of arrangements and studies for the cello.

Malkin, Manfred, Russian-American pianist; b. Odessa, Aug. 11, 1884; d. New York, Jan. 8, 1966. He studied at the Paris Cons.; in 1905 went to the U.S.; established his own music school in New York (1914-31); with his brothers **Jacques** and **Joseph**, formed a piano trio.

Malko, Nikolai, eminent Russian conductor; b. Brailov, May 4, 1883; d. Sydney, Australia, June 23, 1961. He studied philology at the Univ. of St. Petersburg; composition and orchestration with Rimsky-Korsakov, Liadov and Glazunov; conducting with Tcherepnin. After graduation he went to Munich where he took a conducting course with Mottl. Returning to Russia, he conducted opera in St. Petersburg; was conductor of the Leningrad Philharmonic (1926-29), with which he performed many new works by Soviet composers, including the première of Shostakovich's 1st Symph. In 1928 he left Russia; conducted orchestras in Vienna, Buenos Aires, Prague, etc.; was particularly successful in Denmark, where he made frequent appearances, and established a conducting class; many Danish musicians became his pupils, including the King of Denmark, who was a talented amateur. In 1938 he visited the U.S. as a lecturer; also appeared as guest conductor with several American orchestras; became an American citizen on May 7, 1946. He subsequently conducted the Yorkshire Symph. Orch., England (1954-56). In 1956 his was appointed resident conductor of the Sydney Symph. Orch., Australia, where he established a fine tradition of orchestral performance, striving above all for clarity and balance of sonorities. He publ. a manual *The Conductor and His Baton* (Copenhagen, 1950); also composed various works, among them a clarinet concerto (Copenhagen, Sept. 27, 1952). The Danish Radio inaugurated in his honor a triennial Malko International contest for conductors.

Malling, Jørgen, Danish composer; b. Copenhagen, Oct. 31, 1836; d. there, July 12, 1905. He studied with Gade; was first winner of the Ancher stipend in 1861; went to Paris and there became enthusiastic over Chevé's system of vocal notation, which he tried (unsuccessfully) to introduce in various cities in Scandinavia and Russia; was organist in Svendborg (1869-72); lived in Vienna from 1879 to 1882, and in Munich from 1882 to 1895; returned to Copenhagen in 1901; was active there as a teacher and composer. He wrote the operas *Lisenka* and *Frithjof;* a cantata, *Küvala;* a string quartet; a piano trio; numerous piano pieces and songs.

Malling, Otto (Valdemar), , Danish composer; b. Copenhagen, June 1, 1848; d. there, Oct. 5, 1915. He studied with Gade and J. P. E. Hartmann at the Copenhagen Cons.; conducted the Student's Choral Society (1872-84); was organist at various churches in Copenhagen (1878-1910); became conductor of the Concert Society there (1874-93); in 1885 was appointed instructor of music theory at the Copenhagen Cons.; in 1899 became its director.
WORKS: His published works, comprising about 100 op. numbers, include a symph.; Fantasia for violin and orch.; *Oriental Suite, Musique de ballet;* Piano Concerto; several cantatas. works for organ; numerous songs; characteristic pieces for piano; a ballet, *Askepot (Cinderella;* Copenhagen, Sept. 25, 1910); and a treatise on instrumentation.

Mallinger, Mathilde (*née* **Lichtenegger**), soprano; b. Agram, Croatia, Feb. 17, 1847; d. Berlin, April 19, 1920. She studied in Prague and Vienna; made her debut in Munich as Norma (Oct. 4, 1866), and created the role of Eva in *Die Meistersinger* (Munich, June 21, 1868). In 1873 she appeared in the U.S.; also sang in Russia. Subsequently she was active mainly as a singing teacher, in Prague (1890-95) and, after 1895 in Berlin. She was married to Baron von Schimmelpfennig of Berlin.

Mallinson, Albert, English composer and organist; b. Leeds, Nov. 13, 1870; d. Elsinore, Denmark, April 5, 1946. He was a pupil of W. Creser; then church organist in Leeds; in 1903 married the Danish singer **Anna Steinhauer,** and with her made successful tours of Denmark and Germany, introducing his own songs; from 1904 until 1914 he was organist of the English Church in Dresden; at the outbreak of World War I he went to Denmark, where he remained most of his life. He wrote about 300 songs to German, English, and Danish texts.

Malotte, Albert Hay, American organist and song composer; b. Philadelphia, May 19, 1895; d. Los Angeles, Nov. 16, 1964. He was a chorister at St. James Episcopal Church; studied with W. S. Stansfield, and later in Paris with Georges Jacob; then moved to Hollywood, where he became a member of the music staff of the Walt Disney Studios; composed the scores for some of Disney's "Silly Symphonies" and "Ferdinand, the Bull." He was the composer of the enormously popular setting, *The Lord's Prayer* (1935); he also set to music the 23rd Psalm and other religious texts.

Malovec, Jozef, Slovak composer; b. Hurbanovo, March 24, 1933. He studied with A. Moyzes at the High School of Musical Arts in Bratislava (1951-53) and with Sommer and Řidký at the Prague Academy (1953-57); subsequently was active in program making on the Bratislava Radio.
WORKS: *Scherzo* for orch. (1956); *3 Studies* for string quartet (1962); *Little Chamber Music* for flute, clarinet, trumpet, vibraphone, viola, cello and percussion (1964); *Kryptogram* for piano, bass clarinet and percussion (1965); *Suite* for strings and harpsichord (1974); *5 National Songs* for alto and orch. (1975); *Prelude and Burlesque* for wind quintet (1976); electronic pieces, *Orthogenesis* (1967), *Punctum Alpha* (1968) and *Theorem* (1971).

Malten (real name **Müller**), **Therese,** German soprano; b. Insterburg, June 21, 1855; d. Neuzchieren, near Dresden, Jan. 2, 1930. She studied with Gustav Engel in Berlin; made her operatic debut in Dresden in 1873, and remained for some 30 years the principal singer on the roster of the Dresden Opera; also sang in Berlin, Vienna, and London. Wagner heard her and suggested her engagement as Kundry at the première of *Parsifal* at Bayeuth in 1882. She was particularly renowned as a Wagnerian singer; was also a fine dramatic actress.

Mamangakis, Nikos, Greek composer; b. Rethymnon, Crete, March 3, 1929. He studied music at the Hellikon Cons. in Athens (1947-53); then composition with Carl Orff and Harald Genzmer at the Hochschule für Musik in Munich (1957-61) and electronic music at the "Siemens" Studio in Munich (1961-62); subsequently divided his time between Athens and Berlin. His works reflect modern quasi-mathematical procedures, with numerical transformations determining pitch, rhythm and form.
WORKS: *Music for 4 Protagonists* for 4 voices and 10 instrumentalists, on a text by Kazantzakis (1959-60); *Constructions* for flute and percussion (1959-60); *Combinations* for solo percussionist and orch. (1961); *Speech Symbols* for soprano, bass and orch. (1961-62); "Cycle of Numbers": No. 1, *Monologue* for solo cello (1962); No. 2, *Antagonisms* for cello and one percussionist moving in an arc along the stage (1963); No. 3, *Trittys (Triad)* for guitar, 2 double-basses, santouri and percussion (1966); and No. 4, *Tetraktys* for string quartet (1963-66); *Kassandra* for soprano and 6 performers (1963); *Erotokritos,* ballad for 3 voices and 5 instruments in an old style (1964); *Ploutos,* popular opera after Aristophanes *Theama-Akroama,* visual-auditive event (happening) for actor, dancer, painter, singer and 8 instruments (Athens, April 3, 1967); *Scenario for 2 Improvised Art Critics* for voice, instruments and tape (1968); *Antinomies* for solo voice, flute, electric double bass, 2 harps, 4 cellos, 2 percussionists, Hammond organ, 4 basses and 4 sopranos (Athens, Dec. 18, 1968); *Bolivar,* folk cantata in pop-art style (1968); *The Bacchants,* electronic ballet (1969); *Parastasis* for various flutes, voice and tape (1969); *Askesis* for solo cello (1969-70); *Perilepsis* for

solo flute (1970); *Erophili,* popular opera (1970); *Anarchia* for solo percussion and orch. (Donaueschingen, Oct. 16, 1971); *Penthima,* in memory of Jani Christou, for solo guitar (1970-71); *Monologue II* for violin and tape (1971); *Kykeon* for several solo instruments (1972); *Olophyrmos* for magnetic tape (1973).

Mamiya, Michio, brilliant Japanese composer; b. Asahikawa, Hokkaido, June 29, 1929. He studied with Ikenouchi at the State Music School in Tokyo; upon graduation he devoted himself mainly to the cultivation of national Japanese music in modern forms, with inventive uses of dissonant counterpoint and coloristic instrumentation.
WORKS: an opera *Mukashi banashi hitokai Tarobê (A Fable from Olden Times about Tarobê, the Slavedealer,* 1959); oratorio, *15 June 1960,* an homage to an activist Japanese student killed during the demonstration against the renewal of the Japanese-American defense treaty (1961); a musical, *Elmer's Adventure* (Tokyo Radio, Aug. 28, 1967); 2 piano concertos (1954, 1970); Sonata for Violin, Piano, Percussion and Double Bass (1966); Violin Concerto (Tokyo, June 24, 1959); Quartet for Japanese Instruments (1962); Sonata for Violin Solo (1971); Nonet (1972); a number of choral works.

Mana-Zucca, (real name **Augusta Zuckermann**), American pianist and composer; b. New York, Dec. 25, 1887. She studied piano with Alexander Lambert in N.Y., then took lessons with Leopold Godowsky and Busoni in Berlin; also studied singing in London and Paris, and composition with Herman Spielter in London. Returning to the U.S. she was exhibited as a piano prodigy, playing a Beethoven concerto at the age of 11 with the N.Y. Symph. under the direction of Walter Damrosch. In 1916 she changed her name by transposing the syllables of her patronymic, and rearranging its vowels, and dropping her first name altogether (Zuckermann→Mana-Zucca). She was soloist in her own Piano Concerto in N.Y. on Aug. 20, 1919; also wrote 2 operas, *Hypatia* and *The Queue of Ki-Lu*; a ballet, *The Wedding of the Butterflies*; several short orchestral works (*Cuban Dance, Frolic for Strings, Fugato Humoresque, Bickerings, Havana Nights,* etc.); Violin Sonata, Cello Sonata, Piano Trio, and a number of solo violin pieces; a great amount of teaching material for piano, and a collection of 366 piano pieces under the general title *My Musical Calendar,* consisting of 12 books, one for each month. Her Violin Concerto, op. 224, was performed in N.Y., Dec. 9, 1955. Mana-Zucca became known mainly for her lyrical songs, of which *I Love Life* was quite popular; other successful songs were *There's Joy in My Heart, Big Brown Bear, Honey Lamb, Time and Time Again.* In 1940 she settled in Miami, Florida.

Mancinelli, Luigi, Italian conductor; b. Orvieto, Feb. 5, 1848; d. Rome, Feb. 2, 1921. He studied piano and cello; also took composition lessons with Mabellini. In 1874 he began to conduct opera in Italy; subsequently conducted at Drury Lane in London (1886-88) and at Covent Garden (1888-1906); concurrently he conducted opera at Madrid (1888-95); from 1894 to 1902 he was on the staff of the Metropolitan Opera House,

N.Y. In 1906 he inaugurated the Teatro Colón in Buenos Aires, and was its principal conductor until 1912 when he returned to Italy. He was particularly renowned as a conductor of Wagner's operas, and was known in Italy as "il Wagnerista."

WORKS: operas: *Isora de Provenza* (Bologna, Oct. 2, 1884), *Tizianello* (Rome, June 20, 1895), *Ero e Leandro* (Madrid, Nov. 30, 1897; his most famous opera, produced all over Europe, and also at the Metropolitan Opera House, N.Y.), *Paolo e Francesca* (Bologna, Nov. 11, 1907); a posthumous opera, *Sogno di una notte d'estate* (after Shakespeare's *Midsummer Night's Dream),* was not produced. He also wrote the oratorios *Isaia* (Norwich, England, Oct. 13, 1887) and *Santa Agnese* (Norwich, Oct. 27, 1905); a cinematic cantata *Giuliano l'Apostata* (Rome, 1920); and *Intermezzi sinfonici* for *Cleopatra* by Cossa, a symph. suite that became very popular.

BIBLIOGRAPHY: L. Arnedo, *Luigi Mancinelli y su opera Hero y Leandro* (Madrid, 1898); G. Orefice, *Luigi Mancinelli* (Rome, 1921).

Mancini, Francesco, Italian composer; b. Naples, Jan. 16, 1672; d. there, Sept. 22, 1737. He studied at the Conservatorio di S. Maria della pietà dei Turchini in Naples; in 1704 held the post of first organist in the chapel, and in 1720 was a maestro di cappella at the Conservatorio S. Maria di Loreto in Naples. He wrote some 20 operas for Naples, which established his reputation as a notable composer. His opera *Idaspe fedele* was sung in Italian at the Haymarket Theater in London on March 23, 1710, with considerable success.

Mancini, Henry, American composer of film and television music; b. Cleveland, April 16, 1924, of Italian parents. He took piccolo lessons from his father, a member of the Sons of Italy band in Aliquippa, Pennsylvania. After playing in dance bands, he studied at Carnegie Institute in Pittsburgh and at the Juilliard School of Music, N.Y. He further studied composition in Los Angeles with Castelnuovo-Tedesco, Ernst Krenek and Alfred Sendrey. In 1952 he became a composer for Universal-International film studios and in 1958 began writing background music for television. His jazzy theme for the Peter Gunn series placed him at once as one of the most adroit composers of melodramatic music; he won 5 television awards and several Academy Awards for film scores.

Mandić, Josip, Croatian composer; b. Trieste, April 4, 1883; d. Prague, Oct. 5, 1959. He studied music in Trieste, Zagreb and Vienna; composed 4 symphonies (1929, 1930, 1953, 1954); a Croatian Mass; several cantatas and other vocal music; a nonet and string quartet; also the operas *Mirjana* (Olomouc, Feb. 20, 1937) and *Kapetan Niko* (1944).

Mandl, Richard, Austrian composer; b. Prossnitz, May 9, 1859; d. Vienna, April 1, 1918. He studied at the Vienna Cons.; then went to Paris, where he attended the classes of Delibes at the Cons.; returned to Vienna in 1900. He wrote a one-act comic opera, *Nächtliche Werbung* (Prague, 1888); a cantata, *Griselidis;* a symph. poem, *Stimme des Orients;* a symph. rhapsody, *Algier;* a dance suite, *Viennensia;* several

violin pieces; a string quintet; songs. He was married to **Camilla Barda** (1872–1922), who publ. a valuable pedagogical work, *Kompendium der gesamten Klaviertechnik* (3 vols).

Mandyczewski, Eusebius, eminent Austrian musicologist; b. Czernowitz, Aug. 17, 1857; d. Vienna, July 13, 1929. He studied with Robert Fuchs and Nottebohm in Vienna; in 1880 he became choirmaster of the Vienna Singakademie, and archivist to the Gesellschaft der Musikfreunde; in 1896 he joined the faculty of the Vienna Cons., where he taught music history and composition. He was subsequently engaged as one of the editors of the great edition of Haydn's works, undertaken by Breitkopf & Härtel; collaborated in many other scholarly editions, including the complete works of Brahms, who was a personal friend of his; his correspondence with Brahms was publ. by Karl Geiringer in the *Zeitschrift für Musikwissenschaft* (May 1933).

Manelli, Francesco, Italian composer; b. Tivoli, 1595; d. Parma, Sept. 1667. He served as a chorister at the Cathedral of Tivoli in 1605, and continued his service there as chapel singer (1609–24); he then was maestro di cappella there (1627–28). He produced an opera, *Gelia,* in Bologna (1630); in 1636 he went to Venice, where he was chapel singer at San Marco; from 1645 to his death he was in the service of the Duke of Parma. In 1637, the Teatro San Cassiano in Venice, the first public opera house in Europe, was opened with Manelli's opera *Andromeda;* he wrote several other operas, which enjoyed considerable popularity. All the musical scores of Manelli are lost, but some librettos are preserved. His op. 4, *Musiche varie* (Venice, 1636), a collection of canatatas, arias, *canzonette* and *ciacone,* shows that he had adopted the "parlando" recitative.

BIBLIOGRAPHY: G. Radicotti, *L'Arte musicale in Tivoli nei secoli XVI, XVII e XVIII* (1907; 2nd ed., 1921).

Manén, Joan, Catalan composer; b. Barcelona, March 14, 1883. He studied both piano and violin, and was first exhibited as a piano prodigy; later appeared as a violinist; gave numerous concerts, and was particularly successful in Germany, where he spent many years (from 1908). He wrote the operas *Giovanna di Napoli* (Barcelona, 1902), *Der Fackeltanz* (Frankfurt, 1909), *Nero und Akté* (Karlsruhe, Jan. 28, 1928; a revision of an earlier opera, *Acté,* originally produced in Barcelona, 1903), and *Soledad* (Barcelona, 1952); also a "theater symphony," *Camino del Sol* (Braunschweig, May 2, 1926); a ballet, *Triana* (1952); *Petite suite espagnole,* for violin and piano; *Nova Catalonia,* for orch.; *Fantasia-Sonata* for guitar; *Sinfonia Iberica* (1966); *Rapsodia catalana* for piano and orch. (1968); also *Romanza mistica* and *Romanza amorosa* for violin, strings and harp. He wrote an autobiography *Mis experiencias,* of which 2 vols. were published under the titles *El niño prodigioso* and *El jóven artista* (1944, 1964).

Manfredini, Francesco, Italian violinist and composer; b. Pistoia, c.1680; d. there, 1748. He was engaged as violinist in Ferrara and Bologna (1704-11); at the Munich Court in 1711; maestro di cappella at the Cathedral of Pistoia from 1734. He publ. *Concertini per camera* (1704); *12 Sinfonie da chiesa* (1709); *12 concerti grossi* (1718). His *Concerto grosso per il santissimo natale* (which includes a fine *Pastorale*) was publ. for 2 violins, string quartet, and piano (Leipzig, 1906); his 6 sonatas for 2 violins and cello appeared in London (c.1750); Sinfonia No. 10, in Vienna (1935); Concerto Grosso No. 9 was ed. for string orch. by E. Bonelli (Padua, 1948); Sinfonia No. 12, ed. by R. Nielsen (Rome, 1949).

Manfredini, Vincenzo, Italian composer; son of **Francesco Manfredini;** b. Pistoia, Oct. 22, 1737; d. St. Petersburg, Aug. 16, 1799. He was a pupil of his father; later studied with Perti in Bologna and with Fioroni in Milan. In 1758 he went to Russia, where he was attached to the court (until 1769); then returned to Italy; lived in Bologna and Venice; in 1798 was engaged by Paul I (who was his former pupil) to come to Russia again; he died there the following year. During his first visit to Russia he produced the following works: *Amour et Psyché,* ballet (Moscow, Oct. 20, 1762); *L'Olimpiade,* opera (Moscow, Nov. 24, 1762); *Pygmalion,* ballet (St. Petersburg, Sept. 26, 1763); *Carlo Magno,* opera (St. Petersburg, Nov. 24, 1763); wrote 6 clavecin sonatas for Catherine the Great (1765).
BIBLIOGRAPHY: "Les Dernières Œuvres de Vincenzo Manfredini," in R.-Aloys Mooser, *Annales de la musique et des musiciens en Russie au XVIIIᵉ siècle* (Geneva, 1950; vol. II, pp. 28-43).

Mangold, Karl (Ludwig Amand), German composer; brother of **Wilhelm Mangold;** b. Darmstadt, Oct. 8, 1813; d. Oberstdorf, Aug. 5, 1889. He studied at the Paris Cons. with Berton and Bordogni; returning to Darmstadt, became a violinist in the court orch.; from 1848-69, was court music director; also conducted various choral societies there. He wrote an opera, *Tannhäuser,* which was produced in Darmstadt on May 17, 1846, only a few months after the première of Wagner's great work; in order to escape disastrous comparisons, the title was changed to *Der getreue Eckart,* and the libretto revised; the new version was produced posthumously in Darmstadt on Jan. 17, 1892. Mangold wrote two more operas, *Gudrun* and *Dornröschen;* several "Concert dramas" (*Frithjof, Hermanns Tod, Ein Morgen am Rhein, Barbarossas Erwachen);* also oratorios (*Abraham, Wittekind, Israel in der Wüste);* chamber music; and a number of male quartets, which attained great popularity in Germany.

Mangold, (Johann) Wilhelm, German composer and violinist; brother of **Karl Mangold;** b. Darmstadt, Nov. 19, 1796; d. there, May 23, 1875. He studied with Rinck and Abbé Vogler; then went to Paris for lessons with Cherubini at the Paris Cons.; in 1825, became court conductor at Darmstadt; was pensioned in 1858. He wrote 3 operas, chamber music, and melodies for clarinet with piano, which were popular for a time.

Mankell, Henning, Swedish composer; b. Härnösand, June 3, 1868; d. Stockholm, May 8, 1930. He studied

piano and composition in Stockholm; composed a number of works, mostly for piano; in his style he followed some models of French Impressionist music. Among his works are a Piano Concerto (1917); 3 piano sonatas; 8 ballads for piano; 3 string quartets; Piano Quintet; Piano Trio; songs.

Mann, Alfred, American musicologist; b. Hamburg, Germany, April 28, 1917. He emigrated to the U.S. at an early age; studied at the Curtis Institute of Music in Philadelphia, graduating in 1942; later took courses in musicology at Columbia Univ. (Ph.D., 1955). In 1947 he was appointed prof. of music at Rutgers Univ. in Newark, N.J.
WRITINGS: *Die Lehre vom Kontrapunkt* (Celle, 1938); *Steps to Parnassus* (English edition of J. J. Fux's *Gradus ad Parnassum;* N.Y., 1943; new edition, under the title *The Study of Counterpoint,* N.Y., 1965); *The Study of Fugue* (New Brunswick, 1958); articles in the *Musical Quarterly* and other scholarly journals.

Mann, Arthur Henry, English organist and editor; b. Norwich, May 16, 1850; d. Cambridge, Nov. 19, 1929. He studied at Oxford (B. Mus., 1882); from 1876 to his death was organist at King's College, Cambridge. He was a noted student of Handel's music; with Ebenezer Prout, he discovered at the Foundling Hospital the original wind-instrument parts of Handel's *Messiah,* and reconstructed the score in accordance with these parts; the work was performed in London in this version on June 13, 1894. Mann was co-editor (with Fuller-Maitland) of the Fitzwilliam Catalogue (publ. 1893); edited Tallis's motet for 40 voices, *Spem in alium* (1888), was music editor of *The Church of England Hymnal* (1895). He composed an oratorio, *Ecce Homo* (1882), and several sacred works.

Mann, Leslie, Canadian composer and clarinetist; b. Edmonton, Alberta, Aug. 13, 1923. He studied music in Toronto; in 1957 went to Winnipeg and became first clarinetist of the CBC Winnipeg Orch. there. His music follows tradition, and contributes to listening pleasure without straining.
WORKS: a chamber opera, *The Donkey's Tale* (1971); *Concertino in the Old Style* for string orch. (1955); Flute Concerto (1964); Clarinet Concerto (1970); *Sinfonia Concertante* for bassoon and chamber orch. (1971); *Concerto Grosso No. 1* for chamber orch. (1972); 2 symphonies (1973, 1974); *Weep You No More Sad Fountains,* 7 songs to Elizabethan poems, for voice and chamber orch. (1974); *5 Bagatelles* for clarinet or viola, and piano (1951); Trio for flute, clarinet and cello (1952); Cello Sonata (1953); *5 Improvisations* for flute and piano (1954); *Toccata alla Barocco* for flute, clarinet and cello (1956); Wind Quintet (1961); Clarinet Sonata (1962); *Suite* for clarinet solo (1963); *Suite* for flute solo (1963); Trio for clarinet, cello and piano (1967); *4 Studies in the Blues Idiom* for wind quintet (1969); *Music* for clarinet, viola and piano (1971); *Partita* for violin and bassoon (1972); Sonata for solo violin (1974); *Vocalise* for oboe or clarinet, and piano (1974); songs.

Mann, Robert, American violinist, composer and conductor; b. Portland, Oregon, July 19, 1920. He studied violin with Édouard Déthier at the Juilliard Graduate School in N.Y., and had instruction in chamber music with Adolfo Betti, Felix Salmond and Hans Letz; also took courses with Edgar Schenkman in conducting, and Bernard Wagenaar and Stefan Wolpe in composition. In 1941 he won the Naumburg Competition, and made his New York debut as violinist. From 1943 to 1946 he was in the U.S. Army; then joined the faculty of the Juilliard School and in 1948 founded the Juilliard String Quartet, in which he plays first violin, and which was to become one of the most highly regarded chamber music groups; in 1962 it was established as the quartet in residence under the Whittall Foundation at the Library of Congress, without suspending its concert tours in America and abroad. As a conductor, Robert Mann specializes in contemporary music; was associated as performer and lecturer with the Music Festival and Institute at Aspen, Colorado, and also served with the National Endowment for the Arts; in 1971 he was appointed President of the Walter W. Naumburg Foundation, with his wife Lucy Rowan as Secretary and Executive Administrator. He has composed a String Quartet (1952); *Suite* for string orch. (1965); several "lyric trios" for violin, piano and narrator.

Manneke, Daan, Dutch composer; b. Kruiningen, Nov. 7, 1939. He studied organ at the Brabant Cons. (1960-66) and compostion with Ton de Leeuw in Amsterdam (1967-73); in 1973 was appointed lecturer on modern music at the Amsterdam Cons.
WORKS: an opera, *De passie van Johannes Lanckohr* (1977); *Walking in Fog Patches* for wind quintet (1971); *Jeu* for solo flute (1971); *Plein Jeu* for brass quintet (1972); *4 Sonatas* for youth orch. (1972); *Stages* for variable ensemble (1972); *Music About Poor and Bad People* for a cappella chorus (1972); *Three Times* for chorus and small orch. (1974; winner of the 1976 Fontein Tuynhout Prize for best performance by amateurs); *Ordre* for 4 recorders (1975); *Sinfonia* for 13 string instruments (1975); *Job* for male chorus, 4 brasses and 3 percussionists (1976); *En passant (Touching in Passing)* for small orch. (1977).

Manners, Charles (real name **Southcote Mansergh**), English bass singer and impresario; b. London, Dec. 27, 1857; d. Dublin, May 3, 1935. He studied at the Dublin Royal Academy of Music; then in London and in Florence. In 1882 he made his stage debut with the D'Oyly Carte company, creating the role of Private Willis in Sullivan's *Iolanthe*. In 1890 he married the soprano **Fanny Moody** and organized the Moody-Manners Opera Co. with her as a partner, for the production of grand opera in the English language; in 1902, after several successful seasons in the provincial theaters, he took his enterprise to London.

Mannes, Clara Damrosch, pianist; daughter of **Leopold Damrosch**; b. Breslau, Dec. 12, 1869; d. New York, March 16, 1948. At the age of 6 she began to study piano in N.Y.: then went to Dresden, where she took lessons with H. Scholtz; later also was a pupil of Busoni in Berlin (1897). On June 4, 1898, she married the violinist **David Mannes,** with whom she toured the U.S. and England for 20 years in joint recitals; was co-director of the Mannes School in N.Y. See *Notable American Women* (N.Y., 1971, Vol. II).

Mannes, David, American violinist and conductor; b. New York, Feb. 16, 1866; d. there, April 25, 1959. He studied violin in Berlin, and was briefly a student of Ysaÿe in Brussels (1903). He was a member of the N.Y. Symph. Orch. conducted by Walter Damrosch, beginning with 1891, and was its concertmaster from 1898 to 1912; married **Clara Damrosch,** June 4, 1898. In 1912 he founded in N.Y. the Music School Settlement for Colored People; conducted a series of free symphonic concerts at the Metropolitan Museum in N.Y. (1919-47). In 1916 he opened his own music school in New York, known as the David Mannes School of Music; continued to be active until a very advanced age; on his 90th birthday in 1956 a special concert was organized in his honor at the Metropolitan Museum. He publ. an autobiography *Music is My Faith* (N.Y., 1938).

Mannes, Leopold Damrosch, American pianist; son of **David Mannes** and **Clara Damrosch Mannes**; b. New York, Dec. 26, 1899; d. Martha's Vineyard, Cape Cod, Mass., Aug. 11, 1964. He graduated from Harvard Univ. (B.A., 1920); studied at the David Mannes School and at the Institute of Musical Art, N.Y.; pupil of Elizabeth Quaile, Guy Maier, and Alfred Cortot (piano) and Schreyer, Scalero, and Goetschius (theory); won a Pulitzer Scholarship (1925) and a Guggenheim Fellowship (1926); subsequently taught composition and piano at the Institute of Musical Art and at the Mannes School; succeeded his father as its director. He temporarily abandoned music as a profession to enter the research laboratory of the Eastman Kodak Co. at Rochester N.Y., and was a co-inventor, with Leopold Godowsky (son of the pianist), of the Kodachrome process of color photography. Among his works are: Suite for 2 pianos (1924); String Quartet (1928; performed many times by Kneisel Quartet); *3 Short Pieces,* for orch. (1926); incidental music to Shakespeare's *Tempest* (1930).

Manney, Charles Fonteyn, American music editor and composer; b. Brooklyn, N.Y., Feb. 8, 1872; d. New York, Oct. 31, 1951. He was first a church singer; then studied theory with W. A. Fisher in N. Y., and with Goodrich and Goetschius in Boston. In 1898 he was engaged as music editor for the Oliver Ditson Co., and held this position until 1930; also conducted the Footlight Orch. and various choral groups; after retirement, he moved to N. Y. He wrote an opera, 3 cantatas, songs, and piano pieces.

Manning, Kathleen Lockhart, American composer; b. Hollywood, Calif., Oct. 24, 1890; d. Los Angeles, March 20, 1951. She played as a child pianist in public concerts; took lessons with Moszkowski in Paris; also appeared as an opera singer with the Hammerstein Opera Co. in London (1911-12). She wrote 2 operas *(Mr. Wu* and *For the Soul of Rafael)* and several song cycles: *Sketches of Paris* (which includes *In the Luxemburg Gardens), Sketches of London, Songs of*

Egypt, Sketches of New York, etc.; also piano pieces
(3 Dance Impressions, In the Summer, etc.).

Mannino, Franco, Italian pianist, composer and conductor; b. Palermo, April 25, 1924. He studied piano
with R. Silvestri and composition with V. Mortari at
the St. Cecilia Academy in Rome, graduating in 1940;
toured as a pianist in Europe, America and Africa. He
wrote the operas Vivi (Naples, March 28, 1957); Il
Diavolo in giardino (Palermo, Feb. 28, 1963); Il Quar-
dro delle meraviglie (Rome, April 24, 1963); Le Notti
della paura (radio opera, broadcast from Rome, May
24, 1963); La Speranza (Trieste, Feb. 14, 1970); ballet,
Mario e il mago (Milan, La Scala, Feb. 25, 1956); and a
Sinfonia Americana for orch. (Florence, Nov. 11,
1956). After 1952, he was active mainly as opera conductor; in 1969 was appointed music director of the
Teatro San Carlo in Naples. His operas and other
works are written in a traditional melodramatic Italian style, diversified by occasional modernistic procedures.

Manns, Sir August, German-English conductor; b.
Stolzenberg, near Stettin, March 12, 1825; d. London,
March 1, 1907. He learned to play the violin, clarinet
and flute; was a member of various bands in Danzig
and Berlin; then conducted bands in Königsberg and
Cologne. In 1854 he went to London where he became
a conductor at the Crystal Palace; in 1856 he inaugurated the famous Saturday Concerts at the Crystal
Palace, which he conducted for 45 seasons, until 1901,
presenting about 14,000 concerts in all, in programs of
a regular symphonic repertory. He became a celebrated musical and social figure in London, and was
knighted in 1903. Besides the Saturday Concerts, he
conducted 6 Triennial Handel Festivals (1883–1900)
and the orchestral concerts of the Glasgow Choral
Union (1879–92).
  BIBLIOGRAPHY: H. S. Wyndham, August Manns
and the Saturday Concerts (London, 1909); Dictionary of National Biography (Supplement; Oxford,
1920).

Mannstädt, Franz, German conductor; b. Hagen, July
8, 1852; d. Weisbaden, Jan. 18, 1932. He studied at the
Stern Cons., in Berlin; was Hans von Bülow's assistant conductor at Meiningen, and also conducted some
concerts of the Berlin Philharmonic; then went to
Wiesbaden as court conductor, retiring in 1924.

Manojlović, Kosta, Serbian composer; b. Krnjevo,
Dec. 3, 1890; d. Belgrade, Oct. 2, 1949; studied in Munich and at Oxford Univ., receiving a bachelor's degree in 1919. He wrote a Serbian liturgy, and a cantata, By the Waters of Babylon; characteristic piano
pieces (Danse Fantastique, etc.) and songs. He publ.
several studies on Serbian folk music; his collection of
337 songs of East Serbia was publ. posthumously
(Belgrade, 1953).

Manrique de Lara, Manuel, Spanish composer and
student of folklore; b. Cartagena, Oct. 24, 1863; d. St.
Blasien, Germany, Feb. 27, 1929. He entered the Spanish Army and rose to the rank of brigadier general;
studied music with Chapí; became a leading authority

on old Spanish ballads, including those sung by Jewish communities in the Near East. He wrote La Ores-
tiada, symph. trilogy (1900); chamber music; etc.

Manschinger, Kurt, Austrian composer; b. Zeil-Wie-
selburg, in a castle of which his father was an administrator, July 25, 1902; d. New York, Feb. 23, 1968. He
studied musicology at the Univ. of Vienna, and at the
same time took private lessons with Anton von Webern (1919–26). After graduation he was mainly active as theatrical conductor in Austria and Germany.
His practical acquaintance with operatic production
led to his decision to write operas, for which his wife,
the singer **Greta Hartwig,** wrote librettos. Of these,
his first opera Madame Dorette was to be performed
by the Vienna State Opera, but the invasion of Austria
by the Nazi troops in 1938 made it impossible. Manschinger and his wife fled to London, where they organized an émigré theater, "The Lantern." In 1940 they
emigrated to America; Manschinger changed his
name to **Ashley Vernon** and continued to compose;
earned his living as a musical autographer by producing calligraphic copies of music scores for publishers.
  WORKS: the operas: The Barber of New York
(N.Y., May 26, 1953); Grand Slam (Stamford, Conn.,
June 25, 1955); Cupid and Psyche (Woodstock, N.Y.,
July 27, 1956); The Triumph of Punch (Brooklyn, Jan.
25, 1969); Der Talisman for voices, violin, viola, cello
and piano (London, Feb. 24, 1940); Sinfonietta (1964);
Symphony (1967); chamber music.

Mansfield, Orlando Augustine, English organist and
composer; b. Warminster, Nov. 28, 1863; d. Cheltenham, July 6, 1936. He studied with E. H. Turpin in
London and later at Trinity Univ. in Toronto; held various positions as organist in England; from 1892 to
1912 was examiner for London College of Music. He
published about 600 works for piano and for organ;
and some 100 arrangements of choral and other
works; publ. his original compositions under the pen
names of **Oscar Liemann** and **Sofie N. Adlam.** He contributed numerous articles to English and American
journals; publ. Student's Harmony (1896), which
passed through several editions.

Mansfield, Purcell James, English organist; son of **Orlando Augustine Mansfield;** b. Torquay, May 24, 1889;
d. London, Sept. 22, 1968. He received his entire education from his father. In 1905 he won the gold and
silver medals at the Bristol Eisteddfod (Welsh Festival); then was organist at various churches in London
and Glasgow. He arranged 24 Scottish airs for mixed
chorus; publ. 50 Miscellaneous Pieces for organ and 6
Scottish Song Books.

Manski, Dorothée, American soprano; b. New York,
March 11, 1895; d. Atlanta, Georgia, Feb. 24, 1967.
She went to Germany as a child; appeared at Berlin in
Max Reinhardt's productions; made her first Ameri-
can appearance with the Metropolitan Opera, N.Y., on
Nov. 6, 1927, as the Witch in Hänsel und Gretel; re-
mained with the Metropolitan Opera until 1941; then
joined the faculty of the School of Music, Indiana
Univ., as a vocal teacher.

Manskopf, (Jakob Friedrich) Nicholas, German collector of musical materials; b. Frankfurt, April 25, 1869; d. there, July 2, 1928. After extensive travels in France and England, he founded in his native city the Musikhistorisches Museum containing MSS, books, documents, rare scores, theater programs, medals, caricatures, autographs, etc., of musicians from the 14th to the 20th centuries; about 30,000 items in all.

Mantovani, Annunzio Paolo, Italian conductor of popular music; b. Venice, Nov. 15, 1905. He went to London as a youth; studied at the Trinity College of Music there; became a British subject in 1933. He formed an orchestra of his own in Birmingham at the age of 18; then led bands in hotels and in theaters. His ingratiatingly harmonious orchestral arrangements made his name famous; the "Mantovani sound" became a byword with sedentary music lovers seeking relaxation and listening pleasure an as antidote to the dramatic enervation of hazardous modern living and raucous popular music.

Mantovani, Tancredi, Italian writer on music; b. Ferrara, Sept. 27, 1863; d. Rome, Feb. 24, 1932. He was a pupil of A. Busi in Bologna; in 1894 he became prof. of music history and librarian at the Liceo Rossini in Pesaro; editor of the *Cronaca Musicale* (1896-1904); in 1919 appointed prof. of literature at the Academy of Santa Cecilia in Rome.
WRITINGS: *Estetica musicale* (1892); *Orlando di Lasso* (1895); *Rossini a Lugo* (1902); *Cristoforo Gluck* (1914); *Angelo Mariani* (1921); a guide to Berlioz' *Damnation de Faust* (1923); etc.

Mantuani, Josef, Austrian music scholar; b. Laibach (Ljubljana), March 28, 1860; d. there, March 18, 1933. He studied composition with Bruckner and others in Vienna; musicology at the Univ. of Vienna, obtaining the degree of Dr. phil.; became librarian in the Vienna Library in 1893, and later chief of the music division; from 1909 taught in his native town of Laibach. He edited several volumes of the *Denkmäler der Tonkunst in Österreich*; publ. *Tabulae codicum manuscriptorum . . . asservatorum* (2 vols., 1897 and 1899; a complete catalogue of the MSS in the Vienna Library); *Katalog der Ausstellung anlässlich der Centenafeier D. Cimarosas* (1901); *Über den Beginn des Notendrucks* (1901); *Ein unbekanntes Druckwerk* (1902); *Geschichte der Musik in Wien. I. Teil: Von den Römerzeiten bis zum Tode des Kaisers Max I.* (1904); "Die Musikpflege Laibachs zur Zeit Schuberts," in the *Adler Festschrift* (1930).

Manuel, Roland. See **Roland-Manuel, Alexis.**

Manzoni, Giacomo, Italian composer; b. Milan, Sept. 26, 1932. He studied music in Messina and Milan; taught composition at the Milan Cons. (1962-64) and at the Bologna Cons. (1965-75). His opera *Atomtod* (*Atom Death*), descriptive in apocalyptic sounds of the ultimate atomic war, attracted a great deal of attention at its production (Milan, March 17, 1965). Other works: opera *La sentenza* (Bergamo, Oct. 13, 1960); *5 Vicariote* for chorus and orch. (Radio Turin, Nov. 29, 1968); *Don Chisciotte* for soprano, small chorus and chamber orch. (1961; Venice Festival, Sept. 14, 1964); *4 poesie spagnole* for baritone, clarinet, viola, and guitar (1961); *Studio per 24* for chamber orch. (1962); *Studio No. 2* for orch. (Milan, April 20, 1963); *Studio No. 3* for tape (1964); *Musica notturna* for 5 wind instruments, piano and percussion (1966); *Insiemi* for orch. (Milan, Oct. 30, 1969); *Spiel* for 11 strings (1969); *Parafrasi con finale* for 10 instruments (1969); *Variabili* for orch. (1973); *Percorso C* for bassoon and string orch. (1976).

Mapleson, Col. James Henry, English impresario; b. London, May 4, 1830; d. there, Nov. 14, 1901. He studied at the Royal Academy of Music in London; subsequently was engaged as a singer and a viola player; sang in Italy under the name of **Enrico Mariani.** In 1861 he became the manager of the Italian Opera at the Lyceum Theatre in London; then of Her Majesty's Theatre (1862-67); at Drury Lane (1868-69); in partnership with Gye at Covent Garden (1869-71); again at Drury Lane (1871-77); at the reconstructed (after the fire of 1868) Her Majesty's Theatre (from 1877). He gave several seasons of opera in the U.S. (during intervals of his London enterprises); his American ventures fluctuated between success and disaster; his last season was 1896-97 at the N.Y. Academy of Music. On March 17, 1890, he married the American singer **Laura Schirmer.** An exuberant personality, he dominated the operatic news both in England and America by his recurrent professional troubles and his conflicts with, and attachments to, prima donnas. He was known as "Colonel" Mapleson by his intimates, but held no such rank. He publ. *The Mapleson Memoirs* (2 vols., London 1888). His nephew, **Lionel S. Mapleson** (b. London, Oct. 23, 1865; d. N.Y., Dec. 21, 1937), came to the U.S. as a violinist; in 1889 joined the orchestra of the Metropolitan Opera in N.Y.; then, for a half century, was librarian there; left his own valuable library to the Metropolitan Opera, including the first recordings, made by himself, ever taken of actual performances, with the voices of de Reszke, Calvé, and others.

Mara, Gertrud Elisabeth (*née* **Schmeling**), German soprano; b. Kassel, Feb. 23, 1749; d. Reval, Russia, Jan. 20, 1833. She learned to play the violin as a child; gave concerts in Vienna and London; returning to Germany, she studied voice and developed an extraordinary range reaching high E; she sang with the Dresden Opera (1766-71) and then was engaged by the Berlin Opera. She married the cello player Mara, and appeared under her married name. From 1784 to 1802 she lived mostly in London; in 1799 she separated from her husband; then went to Russia where she supported herself as a singing teacher; she lived in Moscow until 1812, when Napoleon's invasion forced her to seek refuge elsewhere; from 1813 she was a singing teacher in Reval, where she remained until the end of her life. She was a famous prima donna in her time, and there was much literature written about her.
BIBLIOGRAPHY: G. C. Grosheim, *Das Leben der Künstlerin Mara* (Kassel, 1823; reprint, 1972); G. Bürkli, *Gertrud Elisabeth Mara* (Zürich, 1835); "Autobiographie" (ed. by Riesemann), *Allgemeine musikali-*

sche Zeitung (1875); A. Niggli, "Gertrud Elisabeth Mara," in Waldersee's *Sammlung musikalischer Vorträge* (Leipzig, 1881; after the autobiography); E. Wolff, *Mignon* (Munich, 1909); Rosa Kaulitz-Niedeck, *Die Mara: das Leben einer berühmten Sängerin* (Heilbronn, 1929); O. Anwand, *Die Prima Donna Friedrichs des Grossen* (Berlin, 1930); also V. Huber, *Flirt und Flitter; Lebensbilder aus der Bühnenwelt* (Düsseldorf, 1970).

Maragno, Virtú, Argentinian composer; b. Santa Fé, March 18, 1928. He studied in Buenos Aires and later in Rome with Goffredo Petrassi. Returning to Argentina, he became active as a choral conductor and teacher. He writes in a distinctly modernistic vein, leaning toward serial techniques.

WORKS: *Triste y Danza* for small orch. (1947); *Divertimento* for wind quintet (1952); *Scherzo Sinfónico* (Buenos Aires, June 16, 1953); Concertino for Piano and 14 Instruments (1954); 2 string quartets (1958, 1961); *Expresión* for double orch. and percussion (Rome, June 23, 1961); *Intensidad y Espacio* for orch. (1962); *Composición I* for voices, instruments and magnetic tape (Buenos Aires, Oct. 5, 1962); music for the theater; film scores; choruses; songs.

Marais, Josef, American folk singer and composer; b. Sir Lowry Pass, South Africa, Nov. 17, 1905; d. Los Angeles, April 27, 1978. He studied at the South African College of Music and at the Royal Academy of Music in London; then took violin lessons with Otakar Sevčik in Prague. He emigrated to the U.S. in 1939; worked at the Office of War Information in N.Y. and broadcast songs from the South African *veld;* in 1947 married Roosje Baruch de la Bardo, a Dutch immigrant *chanteuse,* who took on the professional name Miranda. Together they published a number of song collections; Marais wrote the music for several stage productions, including Alan Paton's *Too Late the Phalarope,* he composed an orchestral work, *Paul Gauguin Suite,* and other descriptive pieces.

Marais, Marin, great French player of the viola da gamba and composer; b. Paris, May 31, 1656; d. there, Aug. 15, 1728. He was apprenticed as a choirboy at the Sainte-Chapelle; studied viola da gamba with Hottemann and composition with Lully (whom he addresses as teacher in a letter published in his first book of pieces for his instrument). He then became "joueur de viole du roi" (Aug. 1, 1679). In 1636 he presented at Versailles an *Idylle dramatique;* in 1701 he was called upon to write a *Te Deum* for the convalescence of the Dauphin. Marais possessed matchless skill as a virtuoso on the viola da gamba, and set a new standard of excellence by enhancing the sonority of the instrument. He also established a new method of fingering which had a decisive influence on the technique of performance. As a composer, he followed Lully's French manner; his recitatives comport with the rhythm of French verse and the inflection of the rhyme. The purely instrumental parts in his operas were quite extensive; in *Alcione* (Paris, Feb. 18, 1706) he introduced a "tempeste," which is one of the earliest attempts at stage realism in operatic music. His other operas are *Alcide* (1693), *Ariane et Bacchus*

(1696), and *Sémélé* (1709). He published 5 books of pieces for gamba (1686–1717); trios (or "symphonies") for violin, flute, and viola da gamba (1692); a book of trios for violin, viola da gamba, and harpsichord under the title *La Gamme* (1723). He was married on Sept. 21, 1676 and had 19 children; in 1709 he played a concert with three of them for Louis XIV. His son **Roland** was also a talented gambist; he publ. 2 books of pieces for the instrument with a *basso continuo* and a *Nouvelle méthode de musique pour servir d'introduction aux acteurs modernes* (1711).

BIBLIOGRAPHY: L. de La Laurencie, *L'École Française de violon* (Paris, 1924); F. Lesure, "Marin Marais" and M. Barthélemy, "Les Opéras de Marin Marais" (both *Revue Belge de Musicologie,* 1953).

Marazzoli, Marco, Italian composer; b. Parma, between 1602 and 1608; d. Rome, Jan. 26, 1662. From 1637 to 1640 he was a singer in the Papal Chapel; subsequently served as maestro di cappella for Queen Christina of Sweden who had her court in Rome at the time; then lived in Ferrara and Venice; in 1643 he was engaged by the Cardinal Mazarin in Paris; in 1645 he returned to Rome where he entered the service of Pope Urban VIII. Marazzoli's importance in music history lies in the fact that he was the composer of the first comic opera, which he wrote in collaboration with Virgilio Mazzocchi, *Chi soffre, speri,* produced in Rome on Feb. 27, 1639. He was also the author of the serious opera *La Vita Umana* (Rome, Jan. 31, 1656). For further details see A. Loewenberg, *Annals of Opera* (Cambridge, 1943; rev. 1955).

Marbé, Myriam, Rumanian composer; b. Bucharest, April 9, 1931. She began her musical studies at home with her mother, a professional pianist; then entered the Bucharest Cons., where she studied with Negrea (1944–54). In 1954 she joined the staff of the Bucharest Cons. Her compositions are permeated with Rumanian melorhythms, but her harmonic investiture is quite modern. In later works she experiments with "sonorism," serialism and "spatial" music.

WORKS: *The World of Children* for piano (1952); Viola Sonata (1955); Piano Sonata (1956); a cantata *Noapte țărănească* (*Night of the Land,* 1958); *Lyrical Piece* for oboe, string orch., 2 horns, piano, celesta and percussion (1959); Clarinet Sonata (1961); *Musica Festiva,* divertissement for strings, brass and percussion (1961); *Incantation,* sonata for solo clarinet (1964); Sonata for 2 violas (1965); *Clime* for mezzo-soprano and chamber orch. (1966); *Ritual pentru setea pămîntului* (*Ritual for the Thirst of the Earth*) for 7 singers scattered and staggered through the hall, and optional percussion (1968); *Le Temps inévitable* for piano (1968); ditto for piano and orch. (1971); *Jocus secundus* for small vocal group, tape, violin, viola, cello, clarinet, piano and percussion (1969); *Cluster Studies* for piano (1970); *Accents* for piano (1971); *Temps et espace* for orch. (1972); *Cycle* for flute, guitar and percussion (1974); *Petite musique du Soleil* for orch. (1974); *Vocabulaire I—Chanson* for soprano, clarinet, piano and bells (1974); choruses; songs.

Marbeck (Merbecke), John, English composer and theologian; b. Windsor, c.1510; d. there, c.1585. He was a chorister in St. George's Chapel, Windsor (1531); narrowly escaped burning as a heretic in 1544; was imprisoned, but pardoned by Henry VIII; Mus. Bac., Oxford, 1550; lay clerk, and organist of St. George's Chapel. His chief work is *The Booke of Common Praier noted* (1550), an adaptation of the plainchant of earlier rituals to the first ritual of Edward VI; reprinted in facsimile, 1939: republished in Jebb's *Choral Responses and Litanies* (1857; vol. II). One of his hymns appears in Hawkins' *General History of the Science and Practice of Music*. Marbeck was also the compiler of a concordance of the English Bible (1550).

BIBLIOGRAPHY: J. Pulver, *A Biographical Dictionary of Old English Music* (London, 1927); J. Eric Hunt, *Cranmer's First Litany, 1544, and Merbecke's Book of Common Prayer noted, 1550* (London, 1939); R. Stevenson, "John Marbeck's *Noted Booke* of 1550," *Musical Quarterly* (April 1951).

Marcel (real name **Wasself**), **Lucille,** American soprano; b. New York, 1885; d. Vienna, June 22, 1921. She studied in Paris with Jean de Reszke, who recommended her for the role of Elektra at the Vienna première of Strauss' opera; she made her debut in this very difficult part on March 24, 1908, under the direction of **Felix Weingartner,** whom she married in 1907; she was the principal soprano when Weingartner became conductor of the Hamburg Opera (1912–14). She sang with the Boston Opera Company, making her American debut as Tosca on Feb. 14, 1912; later she returned to Vienna where she remained until her death.

Marcelli, Nino, Chilean composer and conductor; b. Santiago, Jan. 21, 1890; d. San Diego, California, Aug. 16, 1967. He studied at the National Cons. of Santiago. In 1920 he went to the U.S.; played cello in the San Francisco Symph.; in 1927 organized the San Diego Symph. Orch., which he conducted until 1937. He composed several orchestral marches and overtures, and also a *Suite Araucana* based on motives of Chilean Indians.

Marcello, Alessandro, Italian scholar and composer; brother of **Benedetto Marcello;** b. Venice, Aug. 24, 1669; d. Padua, June 19, 1747. He publ. his works under the name of **Eterico Stinfalico;** extant are *Concerti a cinque con violino solo e violoncello obbligato* (op. 1); various pieces for flutes and oboes with strings, etc. Alessandro Marcello seems to have been the composer of the oboe concerto transcribed by Bach, which is usually attributed to Benedetto Marcello.

BIBLIOGRAPHY: F. C. Walker, "A Little Bach Discovery," *Music & Letters* (April 1950).

Marcello, Benedetto, famous composer and poet; b. Venice, Aug. 9, 1686; d. Brescia, July 24, 1739. He received an excellent education; studied jurisprudence as well as music, was a pupil of Gasparini and Lotti; had a political career: was a member of the Council of Forty for 14 years, then "Provveditore" at Pola for 8 years, and finally papal chamberlain at Brescia, a position he retained until his death. His masterwork is the settings of Giustiniani's paraphrases of the first 50 Psalms (*Estro poetico-armonico; Parafrasi sopra i*

cinquanta primi Salmi; Venice, publ. by D. Lovisa, 1724–26, in 8 vols. folio); they are for 1, 2, 3, and 4 voices, with basso continuo for organ or clavicembalo; a few with cello obbligato, or 2 violas; they have been often republished (by Carli in Paris, etc.). He also publ. *Concerti grossi* for 5 parts (1701); *Sonate per cembalo, Sonate a cinque, e flauto solo con basso continuo* (1712), *Canzoni madrigaleschi ed Arie per camera a 2–4* (1717); a satire on operatic manners, *Il teatro alla moda, o sia Metodo sicuro e facile per ben comporre ed eseguire opere italiane in musica* (1720; 2nd ed. 1722; modern ed. by E. Fondi, Lanciano, 1913; English transl. by R. G. Pauly in the *Musical Quarterly,* July 1948, and January 1949; German transl. by A. Einstein in *Perlen älterer romanischer Prosa,* 24; the pamphlet *Lettera famigliare* (1705), a rather captious critique of Lotti, was printed incomplete, with a statement that it no longer corresponded to the views of the author. Both *Il teatro alla moda* and *Lettera famigliare* were publ. anonymously, but Marcello's authorship was never in dispute. Besides the works named above, Marcello composed several cantatas, preserved in MS in the libraries of Dresden and Vienna, and sacred works.

BIBLIOGRAPHY: G. Sacchi, *Vita di Benedetto Marcello* (Venice, 1788; transl., with supplementary material, of F. L. Fontana's Latin biography of Marcello in vol. 9 of *Vitae Italorum Doctrinae Excellentium,* Pisa, 1787); O. Chilesotti, *I nostri maestri del passato* (Milan, 1882; pp. 83–91); Leonida Busi, *Benedetto Marcello* (Bologna, 1884); O. Chilesotti, *Sulla Lettera Critica di Benedetto Marcello contro A. Lotti* (Bassano, 1885; contains polemics with Busi; appends a list of Marcello's publications and bibliography); E. Fondi, *La vita e l'opera letteraria del musicista Benedetto Marcello* (Rome, 1909); A. Della Corte, "La Morale d'una satira," *Il Pianoforte* (1921); U. Rolandi, "I 50 salmi," *Musica d'Oggi* (XI/1); A. d'Angeli, *Benedetto Marcello* (Milan, 1940); R. G. Pauly, "Benedetto Marcello's Satire on Early 18th-Century Opera," *Musical Quarterly* (April 1948); W. S. Newman, "The Keyboard Sonatas of Benedetto Marcello," *Acta Musicologica* (1957).

Marchand, Louis, French organist; b. Lyons, Feb. 2, 1669; d. Paris, Feb. 17, 1732. He was the organist of the Chapel Royal in Paris (1708–14); publ. 3 books of music for the clavecin, and one for the organ. A vol. of his organ compositions was publ. by Guilmant in *Archives des maîtres de l'orgue*. His *Plein Jeu* (in 6 parts) appears in J. Bonnet's *Historical Organ Recitals* (vol. 1). Marchand's name is connected with Bach's because the two organists were scheduled to meet in open competition at Dresden in 1717 and Marchand failed to appear.

BIBLIOGRAPHY: A. Pirro, "Louis Marchand" *Sammelbände der Internationalen Musik-Gesellschaft* 6.

Marchant, Sir Stanley (Robert), English organist and composer; b. London, May 15, 1883; d. there, Feb. 28, 1949. He studied organ at the Royal Academy of Music in London; occupied various posts as organist in London churches; was on the staff of the Royal Academy of Music from 1913, in executive as well as teaching capacities. He was knighted in 1943. As a composer, he confined himself to organ music, vocal works for church services, and school manuals.

Marchesi, Blanche (Baroness André Caccamisi), famous dramatic soprano; daughter of **Salvatore** and **Mathilde Marchesi;** b. Paris, April 4, 1863; d. London, Dec. 15, 1940. She was first trained as a violinist; took lessons with Nikisch in Germany and with Colonne in Paris. In 1881 she began to study singing with her mother, and, until her marriage to Baron Caccamisi, acted as her mother's assistant. She made her debut in Berlin (1895); when she sang in London (1896), the reception was so enthusiastic that she made England her home; sang the Wagner roles at Covent Garden; made tours of Russia and Central Europe; also made 2 concert tours of the U.S. (1899; 1909); gave her farewell concert in 1938. In her last years, she established herself as a highly esteemed teacher in London. She publ. her memoirs under the title *Singer's Pilgrimage* (London, 1923).

Marchesi, Luigi, celebrated male soprano, known as "Marchesini," b. Milan, Aug. 8, 1754; d. Inzago, Dec. 14, 1829. He was a chorister in Milan; made his debut at Rome, scoring an immediate success. His fame as a sopranist grew rapidly after his visits to other Italian cities. In 1785 he was engaged as a singer at the court of Catherine the Great; on his way to St. Petersburg, he stopped over in Vienna, where he sang at the Imperial court of Joseph II. He made his Russian debut in St. Petersburg, early in 1786, as Rinaldo in Sarti's opera *Armida e Rinaldo;* the Italian female soprano Luiza-Rosa Todi intrigued against him, and despite his successes, he left Russia before the expiration of his contract. On March 9, 1787, he sang in Berlin, winning great acclaim; then toured through Switzerland and Italy. He sang for the last time at the age of 66 in Naples; then returned to Milan.

BIBLIOGRAPHY: R.-Aloys Mooser, *Annales de la Musique et des Musiciens en Russie au XVIIIᵉ siècle* (Geneva, 1950; vol. II, pp. 497–98).

Marchesi de Castrone, Mathilde, famous German vocal teacher; b. Frankfurt, March 24, 1821; d. London, Nov. 17, 1913. She studied singing in Vienna with Nicolai and in Paris with Manuel García. In 1849 she went to London; in 1852 she married the Italian baritone **Salvatore Marchesi de Castrone.** Later in life she devoted herself mainly to teaching; had classes at the Vienna Cons. (1854–61 and 1869–78); also taught privately in Paris. Among her famous pupils were Murska, Gerster, Melba, Eames, Calvé, and Sanderson. She wrote an autobiography *Erinnerungen aus meinem Leben* (Vienna, 1877) which was publ. in a revised and amplified edition under the title *Marchesi and Music: Passages from the Life of a Famous Singing Teacher* (N.Y., 1897). She further publ. a vocal manual, *10 Singing Lessons* (N.Y., 1910) which was reprinted under a new title *Theoretical and Practical Vocal Method* (N.Y., 1970, with an introduction by Philip L. Miller).

Marchesi de Castrone, Salvatore (complete name and title **Cavaliere Salvatore de Castrone, Marchese della Rajata**), baritone and famous teacher; b. Palermo,

Jan. 15, 1822; d. Paris, Feb. 20, 1908. Of a noble family, he was destined for a government career and studied law in Palermo; however, he turned to music, and took lessons in singing and theory with Raimondi in Palermo, and with Lamperti in Milan. He was involved in the revolutionary events of 1848, and was compelled to leave Italy; went to New York, where he made his operatic debut in Verdi's *Ernani.* He then studied with García in London; married **Mathilde Graumann** in 1852, and sang with her in opera on the Continent. From 1854 till 1861, they both taught at the Vienna Cons.; later at the Cologne Cons. (1865–68), and again in Vienna (1869–78); after that they resided in Paris.

Marchetti, Filippo, Italian opera composer; b. Bolognola, near Camerino, Feb. 26, 1831; d. Rome, Jan. 18, 1902. He was a pupil of Lillo and Conti at the Royal Cons., Naples. His first opera, *Gentile da Varano* (Turin, 1856), was extremely well received, and he repeated his success with another opera, *La Demente,* for Turin (Nov. 27, 1856); however, his next opera, *Il Paria,* never reached the stage. He was not discouraged by this and wrote his *Romeo e Giulietta* (Trieste, Oct. 25, 1865), which had a pronounced success in performances at La Scala, Milan, and other Italian theaters. He achieved his greatest success with *Ruy-Blas* (La Scala, April 3, 1869), which was produced also in Germany and England; the remaining operas were *Gustavo Wasa* (La Scala, Feb. 7, 1875) and *Don Giovanni d'Austria* (Turin, March 11, 1880). In 1881 he was appointed president of the Academy of Santa Cecilia in Rome.

Marchetto da Padua, an early proponent of *Ars Nova* who flourished in the 14th century and worked in Florence; author of the important treatises *Lucidarium in arte musicae planae* (on plainsong, early 14th century) and *Pomerium artis musicae mensurabilis* (on mensural music, 1318); the latter is included (in part) in Strunk's *Source Readings in Music History* (N.Y., 1950).

BIBLIOGRAPHY: O. Strunk, "Intorno a Marchetto da Padua," *Rassegna Musicale* (Oct. 1950).

Marco, Tomás, Spanish composer; b. Madrid, Sept. 12, 1942. He studied violin and composition at the Univ. of Madrid (1959–64). An ardent modernist, he founded in 1967 the magazine *Sonda,* dedicated to new music. His own compositions are of an experimental, almost exhibitionistic, theatrical nature.

WORKS: *Los Caprichos* for orch. (1959–67); *Trivium* for piano, tuba and percussion (1963); *Roulis-Tangage* for trumpet, cello, guitar, piano, vibraphone and 2 percussionists (1962–63); *Glasperlenspiel* for chamber orch. (1963–64); *Car en effet* for 3 clarinets and 3 saxophones (1965); *Piraña* for piano (1965); *Jabberwocky* for actors, tenor, saxophone, piano, 4 percussionists, tape, 6 radios, lights and slides (1966); *Schwan* for trumpet, trombone, viola, cello and 2 percussionists (1966); *Cantos del pozo artesiano* for actress, 3 chamber ensembles and lights (1967); *Vitral (Música Celestial No. 1)* for organ and string orch. (1968); *Maya* for cello and piano (1968–69); *Anábasis* for orch. (1968–70); *Rosa-Rosae,* quartet for flute, clarinet, violin and cello (1969); *Tea Party* for 4 vocal soloists, clarinet, trombone, cello and vibraphone (1969); *Floreal* for a percussionist (1969); *Kukulcan* for wind quintet (1969–72); *Mysteria* for chamber orch. (1970–71); *Albor* for flute, clarinet, violin, cello and piano (1970); *Evos* for piano (1970); *Necronomicon*, choreography for 6 percussionists (1971); *L'Invitation au voyage* for soprano, optional narrator, 3 clarinets, piano and percussion (1971); *Angelus novus (Hommage à Mahler)* for orch. (1971); *Jetztzeit* for clarinet and piano (1971); *Violin Concerto,* subtitled *Les Mécanismes de la mémoire* (1971–72; Royan Festival, April 19, 1973); *Nuba* for flute, oboe, clarinet, violin, cello and percussion (1973); *Ultramarina* for soprano, clarinet, piano and percussion (1975).

Marcoux, Vanni (full name **Jean Émile Diogène Marcoux**), dramatic baritone; b. (of French parents), Turin, June 12, 1877; d. Paris, Oct. 21, 1962. He was a law student at the Univ. of Turin; then went to France where he enrolled at the Paris Cons. He made his debut in a minor role as Frère Laurent in Gounod's *Roméo et Juliette* in Bayonne on Jan. 28, 1900; subsequently obtained considerable success at his debut at the Paris Opéra as Colonna in the première of Février's *Monna Vanna* (Jan. 13, 1909). Massenet entrusted to him the part of Don Quichotte in the première of his opera of that name (Monte Carlo, Feb. 19, 1910). In 1912 he sang with the Boston Opera Company, and later with the Chicago Opera Company. His repertory included more than 200 roles in several languages. He eventually returned to Paris and was instructor in lyric declamation at the Paris Cons. In his professional appearances, he used the hyphenated name **Vanni-Marcoux.**

Maréchal, Henri-Charles, French composer; b. Paris, Jan. 22, 1842; d. there, May 12, 1924. He studied piano and theory at the Paris Cons.; composition with Victor Massé; won the Grand Prix de Rome (1870) with the cantata *Le Jugement de Dieu.* After his return from Rome he produced an oratorio, *La Nativité* (1875), and several operas: *Les Amoureux de Catherine* (Paris, May 8, 1876), *La Taverne des Trabans* (1881), *Calendal* (Rouen, Dec. 21, 1894), *Ping-Sin* (Paris, Jan. 25, 1918), etc.; also wrote several orchestral suites; choral works; etc.. He published 2 vols. of reminiscences: *Rome: Souvenirs d'un musicien* (Paris, 1904; 2nd ed., 1913) and *Paris: Souvenirs* (Paris, 1907); also *Monographie universelle de l'Orphéon* (Paris, 1910; on singing societies); and *Lettres et Souvenirs, 1871–1874* (Paris, 1920).

Maréchal, Maurice, French cellist; b. Dijon, Oct. 3, 1892; d. Paris, April 19, 1964. He won first prize at the Paris Cons. in 1911; then gave concerts as cello soloist in Paris, London, Boston, Chicago, New York and other European cities; also toured in Russia, China and Japan. Returning to Paris he taught cello at the Paris Cons. (1942–63).

Marek, Czeslaw, Polish composer and pianist; b. Przemysl, Sept. 16, 1891. He studied piano with Leschetizky in Vienna and composition with Pfitzner in Strasbourg. In 1915 he went to Zürich, and in 1932 became a Swiss citizen. In his later years he devoted himself mainly to pedagogy; publ. a manual *Lehre des Klavierspiels* (Zürich, 1972). He composed a symphony (1927); *Échos de la jeunesse* for piano (1914); and several minor piano pieces as well as songs.

Marenco, Romualdo, Italian composer; b. Novi Ligure, March 1, 1841; d. Milan, Oct. 10, 1907. He played the violin, then the bassoon in the Doria Theater, Genoa, for which he wrote his first ballet, *Lo sbarco di Garibaldi a Marsala.* He studied counterpoint under Fenaroli and Mattei; traveled; and became in 1873 director of ballet at La Scala, Milan. He composed over 20 ballets (*Sieba, Excelsior, Sport,* etc.), also the operas, *Lorenzio de' Medici* (Lodi, 1874), *I Moncada* (Milan, 1880), *Le Diable au corps* (Paris, 1884), and the "idilio giocoso" *Strategia d'amore* (Milan, 1896). A posthumous opera, *Federico Struensea,* was produced in Milan in 1908.

Marenzio, Luca, important Italian composer; b. Coccaglio, near Brescia, 1553; d. Rome, Aug. 22, 1599. He was a chorister at the Cathedral of Brescia and pupil of Giovanni Contini there. From 1572–78 he was maestro di cappella to Cardinal Madruzzo at Rome and subsequently entered the service of Cardinal Luigi d'Este, often visiting the court of the latter's brother (Alfonso d'Este) at Ferrara and other courts. He also visited Paris, and in 1588–89 was at Florence. From 1591–95 he was in the service of Cardinal Aldobrandini at Rome, and in 1596–98 at the Polish court of Sigismund III. Upon his return to Rome he was in the service of Roman noblemen. He was called "il più dolce cigno d'Italia" and "divino compositore" by his contemporaries. WORKS: His madrigals, which are unsurpassed, were publ. as follows: 9 books *a* 5 (1580–99); 6 books *a* 6 (1584–95); 1 book *a* 4–6 (1588); 1 book of 5-part *Madrigali spirituali* (1584); 2 books of *Mottett a* 4 (1585, 1592); 1 book of *Mottitti a* 12 (1614); a book of *Sacri concernti a* 5-7 (1616); 5 books of *Villanelle ed Arie alla napoletana a* 3 (1584–91); 1 book of motets *a* 5-7 (1616, youthful work, ed. Giovanni Maria Piccioni); also antiphons and other church music. Some pieces in modern notation are in Proske's *Musica divina,* Choron's *Principes de composition,* Padre Martini's *Counterpoints,* etc. Some of his motets have been publ. by the Universal Edition; one madrigal is to be found in A. Einstein's *The Golden Age of the Madrigal;* another in Einstein's *Beispielsammlung zur älterer Musikgeschichte,* 2 pieces in A. Schering's *Geschichte der Musik in Beispielen* (nos. 140, 165), other selections in F. Jöde's *Alte Madrigale,* F. Blume's *Das Chorwerk* (vol. 8), and Davison and Apel, *Historical Anthology of Music* (Cambridge, Mass., 1947). Six books of his 5-part madrigals have been publ. in *Publikationen älterer Musik* (IV/1, 1929; VI, 1931; ed. by Alfred Einstein). A new edition *The Secular Works,* in 20 vols., ed. by S. Ledbetter and P. Myers is in preparation.

BIBLIOGRAPHY: P. Guerrini, in *Santa Cecilia* 9 and 10 (1908); A. Einstein, "Eine Caccia im Cinquecento," in the *Liliencron-Festschrift* (1910); A. Einstein, "Dante im Madrigal," *Archiv für Musikwissenschaft* 3 (1921); J. A. F. Orbaan, "Notizie inedite su Luca Marenzio," *Bolletino bibliografico musicale* III/3 (1928); A. Einstein, *The Italian Madrigal* (Princeton, 1949; pp. 614-18, 628-37); G. Reese, *Music in the Renaissance* (N.Y., 1954; pp. 420-24). H. Engel, *Luca Marenzio* (Florence, 1956; contains a bibliography and a list of works; supersedes Engel's earlier publications on Marenzio); D. Arnold, *Marenzio* (London, 1965); J. Steele, "The Later Madrigals of Luca Marenzio," *Studies in Music* (1969); Roland Jackson, "Two Newly-Found Motets by Marenzio (?)," *Journal of the American Musicological Society* (Spring 1971); W. Kirkendale, "Franceschina, Girometta, and Their Companions in a Madrigal *a diversi linguaggi* by Luca Marenzio and Orazio Vecchi," *Acta Musicologica* (1972).

Maresch, Johann Anton, inventor of the Russian "hunting-horn music," in which each player has a horn producing a single tone; b. Chotěboř, Bohemia, 1719; d. St. Petersburg, June 10, 1794. He studied horn with Hampel in Dresden, and cello in Berlin. In 1748 he was engaged by the Russian Chancellor Bestuzhev as horn player in his private orch. in St. Petersburg, and later became chamber musician to the Russian court. In 1751 he was commissioned to organize an ensemble of hunting horns for the court; he formed a group comprising 2 complete octaves tuned chromatically, adding large drums with church bells suspended within them; also constructed wooden horns for soft accompaniment to operas. The vogue of horn orchestras in Russia continued for about 50 years after Maresch's death; the players were recruited usually from serfs. After the emancipation of serfs in Russia in 1861, the horn orchestras gradually disappeared.
BIBLIOGRAPHY: J. C. Hinrichs, *Entstehung, Fortgang und jetzige Beschaffenheit der russischen Jagdmusik* (St. Petersburg, 1796); K. Vertkov, *Russian Horn Music* (Moscow, 1948); "Les Orchestres de cors russes," in R.-Aloys Mooser, *Annales de la Musique et des Musiciens en Russie au XVIIIe siècle* (Geneva, 1951, vol. III, pp. 859-76).

Mareschall, Samuel, Flemish composer; b. Tournai, May 22, 1554; d. Basel, 1640. As a young man, he was organist at the Basel Cathedral; in 1576 was appointed prof. at the Univ. there. His collection of 4-part vocal settings of the Psalms (1606) became a traditional Lutheran hymn book; another book of Psalms (including hymns by Luther) appeared in 1616. He also compiled *Melodiae suaves* (1622); much earlier he publ. a disquisition, *Porta Musica, mit einem kurtzen Bericht und Anleitung zu den Violen* (Basel, 1589).
BIBLIOGRAPHY: R. Kendall, "The Life and Works of Samuel Mareschall," *Musical Quarterly* (Jan. 1944).

Marescotti, André-François, Swiss composer; b. Carouge, near Geneva, April 30, 1902. He studied at the Geneva Cons., and in Paris with Roger-Ducasse; from 1924 he was chorusmaster at the St. Joseph church in Geneva, and, from 1931, prof. at the Geneva Cons.
WORKS: *Aubade,* for orch. (Geneva, Jan. 27, 1938); *Concert Carougeois,* for orch. (1942); *Les Anges du Greco,* ballet (Zürich, June 1, 1947); *Giboulées,* for

bassoon and orch. (1949); *La Lampe d'argile,* dramatic legend (Strasbourg, April, 1951); overture, *Festa* (1961); *Concert carougeois* for orch. (1966); numerous piano pieces. He publ. a valuable volume (in folio), *Les Instruments d'orchestre, leurs caractères, leurs possibilités et leur utilisation dans l'orchestre moderne,* with 900 musical examples (Paris, 1950).

Maretzek, Max, operatic impresario; b. Brünn, Moravia, June 28, 1821; d. Staten Island, N.Y., May 14, 1897. He studied medicine and law at the Univ. of Vienna; music with Ignaz von Seyfried (a pupil of Mozart and Haydn). He progressed rapidly, and at the age of 22 conducted his first opera, *Hamlet* (Brünn, 1843). He then traveled as theater conductor and composer of ballet music, in France and England. In 1848 he arrived in N.Y. as conductor and manager of the Italian Opera Co. He presented Adelina Patti for the first time in opera (as Lucia, 1859); in 1876 he staged his own play with music, *Baba;* conducted his pastoral opera *Sleepy Hollow; or, The Headless Horseman,* after Washington Irving (N.Y., Sept. 25, 1879). As a worldly impresario, he was extremely successful; traveled to Mexico and Cuba, but lived mostly in N.Y., and became an American citizen. He publ. a book of reminiscences, *Crotchets and Quavers, or Revelations of an Opera Manager in America* (N.Y., 1855); and a sequel, *Sharps and Flats* (N.Y., 1870).
BIBLIOGRAPHY: E. Hipsher, *American Opera and Its Composers* (Philadelphia, 1934; pp. 310-12).

Marez Oyens, Tera de, Dutch composer; b. Velzen, Aug. 5, 1932. She studied piano, violin, composition and conducting at the Amsterdam Cons., graduating in 1953; attended a course in electronic music given by Koenig; was subsequently associated with the Institute of Sonology in Utrecht.
WORKS: 2-Piano Sonatina (1961); *Der Chinesche Spiegel,* 3 songs for tenor and orch. (1962); *2 Sketches* for wind quintet (1963); *Deducties* for oboe and harpsichord (1964); *Photophonie I* for tape (1969); *Introduzione* for orch. (1969); *Communication* for chorus and dancers (1970); *Ryoanji Temple* for contralto, oboe, violin, viola and cello (1972); *Transformation* for orch. (1972); Wind Octet (1972); *Canzone per Sonar* for variable instrumentation (1972); *Delta Ballet* for tape (1973); *Mixed Feelings* for 4-track tape and percussion (1973); *3 Modi* for 3 violins, cello and recorder quartet (1973); *From Death to Birth* for chorus (1974); *Starmobile* for variable instrumentation (1974); Trio for cello, percussion and tape (1974); *Human* for orch. and tape (1975); *Ode to Kelesh* for chorus and instruments (1975); *Shoshadre,* in 2 parts, for strings (1976); *Episodes* for orch. and variable ensemble (1976); *Inter-Times* for oboe, bassoon, piano and harpsichord (1977); music for radio broadcasts of poetry, plays and various "verbosonic" compositions.

Margaritis, Loris, Greek pianist; b. Aigion, Aug. 15, 1895; d. Athens, Sept. 27, 1953. He began his career as an infant prodigy; studied in Berlin and Munich. When his early promise failed to materialize, he returned to Greece in 1915, and became an instructor at the Cons. of Salonika.

Margola, Franco, Italian composer; b. Orzinuovi, near Brescia, Oct. 30, 1908. He studied violin and composition at the Cons. of Parma; then took a course in advanced music theory with Casella at the Conservatorio di Santa Cecilia in Rome. He then taught at the Cons. of Cagliari and at the Cons. of Parma. He wrote an opera *Il Mito di Caino* (Bergamo, 1940); 2 symphonies; a children's Concerto for Piano with Small Orch., and a similar Concerto for Violin; also a Piano Concerto (Florence, Feb. 12, 1944); Cello Concerto (1955); Horn Concerto (1960); Double Concerto for Violin, Piano and String Orch. (1960); Oboe Concerto with String Orch. (1962); *4 Episodi* for flute and guitar (1970); 10 string quartets; 4 violin sonatas; 3 cello sonatas, etc. He publ. a manual *Guida pratica per lo studio della composizione* (Milan, 1954).

Maria Antonia Walpurgis, Electress of Saxony; daughter of the Elector of Bavaria (Emperor Charles VII); b. Munich, July 18, 1724; d. Dresden, April 23, 1780. She was not only a generous patroness of the fine arts, but a trained musician, pupil of Hasse and Porpora (1747–52); under the pseudonym **E.T.P.A. (Ermelinda Talea Pastorella Arcada,** her name as member of the Academy of Arcadians) she produced and publ. 2 Italian operas to her own librettos, *Il Trionfo della Fedeltà* (Dresden, 1754) and *Talestri* (Nymphenburg, near Munich, Feb. 6, 1760; Dresden, Aug. 24, 1763; the former was one of the earliest publications of Breitkopf & Härtel printed from their new types (1765); she also wrote texts of oratorios and cantatas for Hasse and Ristori.
BIBLIOGRAPHY: K. von Weber, *Maria Antonia Walpurgis* (2 vols., Dresden, 1857); H. Drewes, *Maria Antonia Walpurgis als Komponistin* (Leipzig, 1934); A. Yorke-Long, *Music at Court: 4 Eighteenth-Century Studies* (London, 1954).

Mariani, Angelo, Italian conductor and composer; b. Ravenna, Oct. 11, 1821; d. Genoa, June 13, 1873. He studied violin and composition; had some lessons with Rossini in Bologna; made his principal career as opera conductor, first in Italy (1844–47), then in Denmark (1847–48). He took part in the Italian war of independence of 1848; then was compelled to leave Italy, and spent 4 years in Istanbul. In 1852 he returned to Italy as opera conductor; introduced Wagner's *Lohengrin* in Bologna; was also favorably known as a composer; wrote several attractive songs (*Liete e tristi rimembranze, Il Trovatore nella Liguria, Rimembranze del Bosforo*, etc.); also some orchestral music. He arranged 3 operas by Verdi (in their entirety) for string quartet: *Macbeth, I Vespri Siciliani,* and *Un Ballo in Maschera.*
BIBLIOGRAPHY: T. Mantovani, *Angelo Mariani* (Rome, 1921); U. Zoppi, *Mariani, Verdi e la Stolz* (Milan, 1947).

Marić, Ljubica, remarkable Serbian composer; b. Kragujevac, March 18, 1909. She studied with Josip Slavenski in Belgrade; then went to Prague where she took composition courses with J. Suk and Alois Hába; also studied conducting with Malko in Prague (1929–32) and with Scherchen in Strasbourg (1933); she returned to Prague for more study with Hába in his special quarter-tone classes (1936–37). She subsequently taught at a music school in Belgrade. During the period of Nazi occupation of Serbia she was an active participant in the resistance. After the war she was a member of the teaching staff of the Belgrade Music Academy (1945–67). In her music she adopted a global type of modern technique, utilizing variable tonal configurations, atonal melodic progressions and microtonal structures, while adhering to traditional forms of composition.
WORKS: String Quartet (1931); Wind Quintet (1932); Trio for clarinet, trombone and double bass in quarter-tones (1937); Violin Sonata (1948); *Passacaglia* for orch. (Belgrade, April 21, 1958); the cantatas, *Pesme prostora (Songs of Space)*, based on inscriptions on the graves of Bogomils, a heretical religious sect of the Middle Ages (Belgrade, Dec. 8, 1956; her most acclaimed work); *Slovo svetlosti (Sound of Light)*, oratorio to texts from medieval Serbian poetry (1966); *Prag sna (Threshold of Dream)*, chamber cantata for narrator, soprano, alto and instrumental ensemble (1961; Opatija, Oct. 30, 1965); numerous piano pieces and songs. Apart from her experimental works, Ljubica Marić became deeply immersed in the study of ancient Byzantine chants, and wrote several modern realizations of the Serbian Octoichos; to this category belong her *Muzika Oktoiha No. 1* for orch. (Belgrade, Feb. 28, 1959); *Vizantijski koncert (Byzantine Concert)* for piano and orch. (Belgrade, June 4, 1963); *Ostinato super thema octoicha* for string quintet, harp and piano (Warsaw, Sept. 27, 1963) and *Simfonija oktoiha*, begun in 1964.
BIBLIOGRAPHY: V. Peričić, *Muzički Stvaraoci u Srbiji* (Belgrade, 1969; pp. 251–62).

Marie, Gabriel, French composer of light music; b. Paris, Jan. 8, 1852; d. Puigcerda, Catalonia, Aug. 29, 1928. He studied at the Paris Cons.; was chorusmaster of the Lamoureux Concerts (1881–87); conductor of the orch. concerts of the Société Nationale de Musique (1887–94); of Ste.-Cécile in Bordeaux; at Marseilles and (during the summer months) at the Casino in Vichy. He wrote a number of melodious pieces for orch., of which *La Cinquantaine* (in arrangements for violin or cello with piano) became immensely popular. He also wrote music criticism, collected in *Pour la musique* (Paris, 1930).

Marini, Biagio, Italian violinist and composer; b. Brescia, 1597; d. Venice, March 20, 1665. He was a pupil of Monteverdi in Mantua; then was a violinist at San Marco, Venice (1615–18); in Brescia (1620); in Parma (1622); then in the service of the courts in Neuberg and Düsseldorf (1623–45); in Milan (1649); in Ferrara (1652). He publ. some 25 op. numbers of vocal and instrumental chamber music, noteworthy for technical devices presupposing a high standard of performance. His op. 1, *Affetti musicali* (1617), contains the earliest specimen of the Italian solo violin sonata, entitled *La Gardana* (reprinted in Schering's *Geschichte der Musik in Beispielen,* no. 182); other reprints are in J. von Wasielewski, *Die Violine im 17. Jahrhundert,* L. Torchi, *L'Arte Musicale in Italia* (vol. 8), etc.
BIBLIOGRAPHY: A. Einstein, *Italienische Musiker am Hofe der Neuberger-Wittelsbacher, Sammelbände*

der Internationalen Musik-Gesellschaft IX/3; A. Schering, in *Riemann-Festschrift* (1909); A. Moser, *Geschichte des Violinspiels* (p. 55ff., 93ff); Dora J. Iselin, *Biagio Marini, sein Leben und seine Instrumentalwerke* (dissertation; Basel, 1930).

Marinov, Ivan, Bulgarian composer and conductor; b. Sofia, Oct. 17, 1928. He studied conducting with Goleminov and composition with V. Stoyanov and Khadjiev at the Bulgarian State Cons. in Sofia, graduating in 1955. In 1956 he became a conductor of the People's Opera in Plovdiv; then was appointed conductor of the Sofia State Opera House. He wrote *Dvuboj* (*Deul*), poem for tenor and orch. (1953); *Suite on 4 Folk Songs* for orch. (1955); *Ilinden,* symph. poem (1956); *Paraphrases* for orch. (1957); *Fantastic Scenes* for orch. (1959); *Divertimento* for orch. (1961); *Pentagram* for bass, string orch., piano and timpani (1965–66); *Symphony No. 1* for bass and orch. (1967); *Festive Suite* for orch. (1968); *Ode on Liberty* for orch. (1969); chamber music; songs.

Marinuzzi, Gino, Italian conductor and composer, son of **Giuseppe Marinuzzi;** b. New York, April 7, 1920. He studied at the Milan Cons. with Renzo Bossi, graduating as pianist and composer in 1941. He began his career as conductor at the Rome Opera in 1946. He was one of the first Italian composers to explore the potentialities of electronic music; in collaboration with Ketoff he developed an electronic synthesizer, the "Fonosynth," and was a founder of an electronic studio in Rome. His compositions include a Violin Concerto, Piano Concerto, and several other works for various instrumental combinations; also a radio opera *La Signora Paulatim* (Naples, 1966) as well as a number of pieces specially adapted for electronic tape.

Marinuzzi, Giuseppe (Gino), Italian conductor and composer; b. Palermo, March 24, 1882; d. Milan, Aug. 17, 1945. He studied with Zuelli at the Palermo Cons.; began his career as conductor in Catania; conducted in Italy and Spain; went to South America on tour with the Teatral Opera Co.; then was director of the Liceo Musicale in Bologna (1915–18); in 1919 conducted in Rome; in 1920 came to the U.S. as artistic director of the Chicago Opera Association; returned to Italy in 1921; was chief conductor of the Rome Opera in 1928–34, and of La Scala from 1934 to his death. False dispatches about his assassination at the hands of the Italian anti-fascists found their way into periodicals and eventually into reputable reference works, but upon verification, it appears that he died peacefully in a hospital, a victim not of a bullet but of hepatic anemia. He wrote 3 operas: *Barberina* (Palermo, 1903), *Jacquerie* (Buenos Aires, Aug. 11, 1918), *Palla de' Mozzi* (La Scala, Milan, April 5, 1932), and several works for orch., on Italian themes.

Mario, Giovanni, celebrated tenor; b. Cagliari, Sardinia, Oct. 17, 1810; d. Rome, Dec. 11, 1883. He was of noble birth (his real name was **Mario Cavaliere di Candia**), and was destined for a military career; after a period of training at the Turin Military Academy, he joined the regiment of which his father was the colonel, but eloped to Paris with a ballerina in 1836; there he studied with Bordogni and Boncharde at the Cons., and made his debut at the Opéra in *Robert le Diable* (Nov. 30, 1838); in 1840 he joined the roster of the Italian Opera in Paris, and won triumphs by the freshness and power of his voice and his exquisite vocal style; this was combined with a handsome figure, which made him the idol of the pleasure-loving women of Paris. In order not to embarrass his aristocratic relatives, he appeared under his Christian name, Mario, without a surname, achieving fame not only in opera, but also in concerts; he was as successful in London and St. Petersburg as in France. For some years, he, Tamburini, Lablache, and Giulia Grisi formed a celebrated vocal quartet; he married Grisi; retired in 1867, and lived in Paris and Rome.

BIBLIOGRAPHY: L. Engel, *From Mozart to Mario* (London, 1886); Mrs. Godfrey Pearce (Cecilia Maria de Candia, Mario's daughter) and F. Hird, *The Romance of a Great Singer* (London, 1910).

Mario, Queena (real name **Tillotson**), American soprano; b. Akron, Ohio, Aug. 21, 1896; d. N.Y., May 28, 1951. She was a practicing journalist in N.Y. before she began to study music; took voice lessons with Oscar Saenger and Marcella Sembrich; made her debut with the San Carlo Opera in N.Y. (Sept. 4, 1918); then joined the staff of the Metropolitan Opera; her first appearance there was as Micaela in *Carmen* (Nov. 30, 1922); retired from the opera stage in 1938, but continued to give concerts; taught at the Curtis Institute of Music from 1931 as successor to Marcella Sembrich. She married the conductor **Wilfred Pelletier** in 1925; divorced in 1936. She was the author of several mystery novels (*Murder in the Opera House,* etc.).

Mariotte, Antoine, French opera composer; b. Avignon, Dec. 22, 1875; d. Izieux (Loire), Nov. 30, 1944. He was trained at the Naval Academy; in 1897 he became a pupil of Vincent d'Indy at the Schola Cantorum; in 1899 was appointed conductor of the symph. concerts at St.-Etienne, Loire; from 1902 until 1919 he taught at the Cons. of Orléans; in 1920 was appointed its director; from 1936 to 1938 he was director of the Paris Opéra-Comique.

WORKS: operas: *Salomé* (Lyons, Oct. 30, 1908); *Le Vieux Roi* (Lyons, 1911); *Léontine Sœurs* (Paris, May 21, 1924); *Esther, Princesse d'Israël* (Paris, May 5, 1925); *Gargantua* (Paris, Feb. 13, 1935); also a symph. suite, *Impressions urbaines,* numerous teaching pieces for piano, and songs.

Mariz, Vasco, Brazilian singer and musicologist; b. Rio de Janeiro, Jan. 22, 1921. He studied composition with Oscar Lorenzo Fernandez and voice with Vera Janacopoulos. Concurrently he took courses in jurisprudence at the Univ. of Rio de Janeiro, obtaining his doctorate in 1943. In the same year he appeared as an opera singer in Porto Alegre, in the role of Bartolo in *Le Nozze di Figaro.* He then entered diplomatic service; was Brazilian consul at Oporto, Portugal (1948); secretary of the Brazilian Embassy in Belgrade (1949–51); then served in Rosario, Argentina, in Washington and in Brazilia. In 1977 he was appointed Brazilian ambassador to Israel. He wrote the books

Figuras da musica brasileira contemporánea (Oporto, 1948); *Dicionário bio-bibliográfico musical* (Rio de Janeiro, 1948); *Heitor Villa-Lobos, Compositor brasileiro* (Rio de Janeiro, 1949; 5th edition, revised and augmented, 1977); *Vida musical 1946-50* (Oporto, 1950).

Markevitch, Igor, brillant Russian-born composer and conductor; b. Kiev, July 27, 1912. He was taken to Switzerland as a small child; at the age of 14 he went to Paris where he took composition lessons with Nadia Boulanger and Vittorio Rieti. He attracted the attention of Diaghilev, who commissioned from him the ballet *Rebus* for his troupe. Diaghilev died before the work could be produced, but when Markevitch conducted a symphonic suite from it in Paris on Dec. 15, 1931, at the age of 19, he was acclaimed as a major new talent, and hailed, only half-facetiously, as "Igor II" (the first Igor being, of course, Stravinsky). After producing several other symphonic and choral works, Markevitch turned to conducting; took lessons from Scherchen and made several auspicious appearances with European orchestras. During World War II he was in Italy; after the war he conducted in Stockholm (1952-55); then led the Philharmonic Orch. in Havana (1957-58) and concurrently conducted the Orchestre Symphonique de Montreal (1956-60), the Orch. Lamoureux in Paris (1957-61); subsequently conducted the Spanish Radio Orch. in Madrid (1965-69) and the opera in Monte Carlo (1968-73). In 1973 he was appointed conductor of the chorus and orch. of Accademia Nazionale di Santa Cecilia in Rome. In the interim he conducted in the U.S., making his American debut with the Boston Symph. Orch. on March 18, 1955; he also conducted in Russia during several successive seasons. In 1963 the Moscow Cons. established a special chair for orchestral conducting for him. From 1968 to 1972 he monitored the International Conducting Competition in Monte Carlo. He makes his home in southern France. He composed relatively little after his initial successes. His works include his second ballet, *L'Envoi d'Icare* (Paris, June 25, 1933); Concerto Grosso (Paris, Dec. 8, 1930); *Le Nouvel Âge,* for orch. (London Festival of the International Society for Contemporary Music, June 17, 1938) and *Lorenzo the Magnificent,* historic oratorio (Rome, April 20, 1941).
BIBLIOGRAPHY: B. Gavoty, *Igor Markevitch* (Monaco, 1954).

Marks, Alan, talented American pianist; b. Chicago, May 14, 1949. His family moved to St. Louis when he was a child; he studied piano with Shirley Parnas Adams. In 1965 he won a prize in Interlocken; gave his first piano recital in St. Louis in 1966. In 1967 he went to New York where he studied at the Juilliard School of Music with Irwin Freundlich until 1971; then with Leon Fleisher at the Peabody Cons. in Baltimore (1971-72). Subsequently he gave successful recitals in Boston, Washington, Philadelphia, Los Angeles, San Francisco and other cities. In 1976 played the first performance of *Caprichos* for piano by Carlos Chávez; also particpated in numerous concerts of chamber music. He possesses an innate virtuoso technique, and seems to be able to interpret with perfect stylistic fidelity piano works by classical as well as modern composers.

Markull, Friedrich Wilhelm, German composer; b. Reichenbach, near Elbing, Prussia, Feb. 17, 1816; d. Danzig, April 30, 1887. He studied organ playing and in 1836 was appointed organist at a Danzig church. He also gave concerts as a pianist. His 3 operas were performed in Danzig: *Maja und Alpino* (Dec. 23, 1843), *Der König von Zion* (March 22, 1850), and *Das Walpurgisfest* (Jan. 14, 1855). He also wrote 2 oratorios, symphonies, and organ pieces.
BIBLIOGRAPHY: W. Neumann, *F. W. Markull* (Kassel, 1857).

Markwort, Johann Christian, German writer; b. Reisling, near Brunswick, Dec. 13, 1778; d. Bessungen, near Darmstadt, Jan 13, 1886. A theological student, he adopted the career of a tenor; appeared on the stage at Feldsberg, Trieste, Munich; was chorus director at Darmstadt (1810-30), then pensioned. He publ. *Umriss einer Gesammt- Tonwissenschaft überhaupt wie auch einer Sprach- und Tonsatzlehre und einer Gesang-, Ton-, und Rede-Vortraglehre* (1826); *Über Klangveredelung der Stimme* (1847); and an elementary piano method.

Marley, Bob, Jamaican reggae singer; b. in the village of Rhoden Hall, Feb. 6, 1945, of a white father, a British Army captain, and a native black mother. He was taken to Kingston at the age of 9, went to school and worked as an electric welder. He picked up popular music of the streets, the radio and jukeboxes, opened a small record shop and then began recording some of his own tunes, a mixture of the current calypso and American "soul" music. He was also active as a member of the Rastafarian religious group, followers of Haile Selassie of Ethiopia (whose original name was Ras Tafari). In 1976, he became embroiled in politics, supporting the People's National Party; as he was preparing to sing at a band concert on Dec. 3, 1976, he was shot and wounded. After that episode, he went to Europe, scoring an unexpected popular acclaim in England, Sweden, Holland and West Germany. In 1977 he made a tour of the U.S., where his fame was already preceded him via his recording albums. His songs, in black Jamaican dialect, preach revolution; typical of these are *Rebel Music, Everywhere Be War* and *Death to the Downpressors.*

Marliani, Marco Aurelio, Italian composer; b. Milan, Aug. 1805; d. Bologna, May 8, 1849. He studied philosophy; took some lessons with Rossini in Paris, where he went in 1830; under Rossini's influence, he wrote several operas, which reached the stage in Paris: *Il Bravo* (Feb. 1, 1834), *Ildegonda* (March 7, 1837), *Xacarilla* (Oct. 28, 1839); a ballet, *La Gypsy* (with A. Thomas; Jan. 28, 1839). He returned to Italy in 1847; produced another opera in Bologna, *Gusmano il Buono* (Nov. 7, 1847). He was involved in the revolutionary struggle of 1848; was wounded in a skirmish near Bologna, and died as a result of his injuries.

Marliave, Joseph de, French writer on music; b. Toulouse, Nov. 16, 1873; killed in battle at Verdun, Aug.

24, 1914. He wrote a valuable monograph, *Les Quatuors de Beethoven*, which was publ. posthumously in Paris in 1917 and reprinted, with preface by Gabriel Fauré, in 1925. He was the husband of the pianist **Marguerite Long.**

Marmier, Jules, German composer; b. Freiburg, March 15, 1874; d. Estavayer, July 28, 1975, at the age of 101. He composed several operatic works and organized religious spectacles for amateurs.

Marmontel, Antoine-François, celebrated French pedagogue and pianist; b. Clermont-Ferrand, July 16, 1816; d. Paris, Jan. 17, 1898. He studied at the Paris Cons. with Zimmerman (piano), Dourlen (harmony), Halévy (fugue), and Lesueur (composition); won 1st prize for piano playing in 1832. In 1837 he became instructor in solfeggio at the Cons.; in 1848 he succeeded Zimmerman as head of a piano class, and won enduring fame as an imaginative and efficient teacher; among his pupils were Bizet, Vincent d'Indy, Th. Dubois, E. Guiraud, Paladilhe, Diémer, Planté, and Debussy. He continued to teach until 1887. He publ. numerous didactic works: *L'Art de déchiffrer* (100 easy studies); *École élémentaire de mécanisme et de style* (24 studies); *École de mécanisme; 5 Études de salon; L'Art de déchiffrer à 4 mains;* also sonatas, serenades, characteristic pieces, salon music, dances, etc.

WRITINGS: *Les Pianistes célèbres* (1878); *Symphonistes et virtuoses* (1880); *Virtuoses contemporains* (1882); *Éléments d'esthétique musicale, et considérations sur le beau dans les arts* (1884); *Histoire du piano et de ses origines* (1885).

Marmontel, Antonin Emile Louis, French pianist, son of **Antoine-François Marmontel;** b. Paris, Nov. 22, 1850; d. there, July 23, 1907. He studied at the Paris Cons., and in 1901 was appointed to its faculty as instructor and piano player.

Maros, Miklós, Hungarian-born Swedish composer, son of **Rudolf Maros;** b. Pécs, Nov. 14, 1943. He studied with Rezso Sugár and Ferenc Szabó in Budapest; settled in Stockholm in 1968, where he took composition lessons with Lidholm. In 1971 he became a member of the Electronic Music Studio Foundation in Stockholm.

WORKS: a one-act opera *Jag önskar jag vore...* (*If Only...*, 1971); *Inversioni* for soprano and chamber ensemble (1968); *Turba* for chorus (1968); *Coalottino* for baritone saxophone, 3 pianos, harpsicord, Hammond organ, 2 violins, viola and 2 cellos (1969); *Spel* for clarinet, trombone, percussion and cello (1969); *Dénique* for soprano and orch. (Norrköping, Jan. 14, 1972); *Anenaika* for soprano, clarinet, trombone, viola and cello (1970); *Cartello* for piano, flute, harp and strings (1970); *Pantomim* for piano, celeste, harpsichord, Hammond organ and tape (1970); *Viola Sonata* for tape (1970); *Izé,* musical theater for flute and percussion (1970); *In H* for tape (1970); *Mutazioni* for winds (1971); Concertino, for double bass or tuba, and 6-24 winds (1971); *Descort* for soprano, flute and double bass (1971); *Diversion* for soprano, alto, alto flute, guitar, viola and 3 percussionists (1971); *HCAB-BACH* for piano (1971); *Sorg,* musical theater for clarinet,

trombone, piano and ad lib instruments (1971); *Örömhir* for trumpet, violin and viola (1971); *Aspectus* for 10 instruments (1972); *Laus Pannoniae* (*Praise for Hungary*) for soprano, chorus, recorder, oboe, harp, harpsicord, and organ (1972); *Causerie* for flute and piano (1972); *Confluentia* for small string orch. (1972); *Sirens* for 4 harps (1972); *Oratio* for male chorus and tape (1973); *Proportio* for wind orch. (1973); *Etyder* for tuba (1973); *Air* for bassoon (1973); Symph. No. 1 (1974); *Oolit* for 11 instruments (1974); *3 Epigrams* for horn, cello and piano (1975).

Maros, Rudolf, Hungarian composer; b. Stachy, Jan. 19, 1917. He studied composition with Kodály and Siklós and viola at the Budapest Academy of Music (1938–42); played viola in the Budapest Concert Orch. while teaching at the Pécs Cons. (1942–49); in 1949 joined the faculty of the Budapest Academy of Music. The early period of his creative work is marked by nationalistic tendencies; by 1959 he adopted serial techniques; then began to explore the field of "sonorism," or sound for sound's sake, making use of all available resources, such as tone clusters and microtones. To his first period belong his ballet *The Wedding at Ecser* (1950); *Puppet Show Overture* (1944); 2 sinfoniettas (1944; 1948); String Quartet (1948); *Sérénade* for oboe, clarinet and bassoon (1952); Bassoon Concertino (1954); Symphony for string orch. (1956); *Musica leggiera* for wind quintet (1956); String Trio (1957). To the second period belong 7 ballets: *Bányászballada* (*Miner's Ballad,* 1961), *5 Studii* (1967); *Quadros Soltos* (1968; adaptation of his suite *Musica da ballo*), *Reflexionen* (1970); *Dance Pictures* (1971), *Metropolis* (1972) and *The Poltroon* (1972); *Ricercare* for orch. (1959); *5 Studii* for orch. (1960); *Musica da ballo,* suite for orch. (1961); *3 Eufonias: I* for strings, 2 harps and percussion (1963); *II* for 24 winds, 2 harps and percussion (1964); and *III* for orch. (1965); *Musica da camera per 11* (Dartmouth College, Hanover, N.H., July 12, 1967); *Gemma* for orch. (1968); *Monumentum* for orch. (1969); *Notices* for strings (1972); *6 Bagatelles* for organ (1961); *2 Laments* for soprano, alto flute, harp, piano and percussion (1962); *Suite* for harp (1965); Trio for harp, violin and viola (1967); *Lament* for soprano and chamber ensemble (1967); *Consort* for wind quintet (1970); Trio for violin, viola and cimbalon (1973); *Landscapes* for chamber ensemble (1974); *Joke* for winds (1974); *Pages* for double bass (1974).

Marpurg, Friedrich, German opera composer; great-grandson of **Friedrich Wilhelm Marpurg;** b. Paderborn, April 4, 1825; d. Wiesbaden, Dec. 2, 1884. He played the violin and piano as a child; studied composition later with Mendelssohn and Hauptmann at Leipzig. He became conductor at the Königsberg Theater; at Sondershausen (1864); succeeded Mangold as court music director at Darmstadt (1868); at Freiburg (1873); and Laibach (1875); then went to Wiesbaden, where he became conductor of the Cäcilienverein.

WORKS: Operas: *Musa, der letzte Maurenkönig* (Königsberg, 1855), *Agnes von Hohenstaufen* (Freiburg, 1874), and *Die Lichtensteiner* (not performed).

Marpurg, Friedrich Wilhelm, German theorist; b. Seehausen, Brandenburg, Nov. 21, 1718; d. Berlin, May 22, 1795. While secretary to General von Rothenburg at Paris (1746–49), he became acquainted with Rameau and his theories; after a short stay in Berlin, and a prolonged sojourn in Hamburg, he was appointed director of the Prussian lottery at Berlin (1763).

WRITINGS: *Die Kunst das Clavier zu spielen* (2 vols.; Vol. I, 1750; Vol. II, 1761); *Anleitung zum Clavier-spielen, der schönern Ausübung der heutigen Zeit gemäss entworfen* (1755; 2nd ed., 1765; also in French and Dutch); *Abhandlung von der Fuge* (his *magnum opus;* 1753–54, in 2 parts; French ed. by Marpurg himself, 1756; revised by Sechter, Vienna, 1843, and Dehn, Leipzig, 1858); *Historisch-kritische Beyträge zur Aufnahme der Musik* (5 vols., 1754–78); *Handbuch bey dem General basse und der Composition* (1755–58: 3 parts; supplement 1760; 2nd ed., 1762: French by Choron and Lafage, 1836–38); a German translation of d'Alembert's *Éléments de la musique* (*Systematische Einleitung in die musikalische Setzkunst* according to Rameau; 1757); *Kritische Einleitung in die Geschichte und Lehrsätze der alten und neuen Musik* (1759; only on ancient music); *Kritische Briefe über die Tonkunst* (a weekly publication appearing 1759–63); *Anleitung zur Musik überhaupt und zur Singkunst besonders* (1763); *Neue Methode, allerley Arten von Temperaturen dem Claviere aufs bequemste mitzutheilen* (1790); etc. He composed 6 keyboard pieces, and organ music, songs (sacred and secular), and an unfinished 4-part Mass.

BIBLIOGRAPHY: H. Riemann, *Geschichte der Musiktheorie* (2nd ed., 1921, p. 496 ff.); E. Bieder, *F. W. Marpurgs System* (Berlin, 1923).

Marqués y García, Pedro Miguel, Spanish composer of light opera; b. Palma de Mallorca, May 20, 1843; d. there, Feb. 25, 1918. He studied in Paris with Alard and Armingaud, then at the Paris Cons. with Massart (violin) and Bazin (composition); also studied privately with Berlioz, and in 1867 at Madrid with Monasterio. From 1870–96 he was one of the most successful of "zarzuela" composers, his most popular works being *El anillo de hierro* (1878), *El reloj de Lucerna, La monja alférez, El plato de dia,* etc. He wrote orchestral variations, and was the author of a number of books (mostly on philosophy).

Marriner, Neville, outstanding English violinist and conductor; b. Lincoln, April 15, 1924. He studied at the Royal College of Music in London and at the Paris Cons.; was a member of the Martin String Quartet (1946–53); then was assistant concertmaster with the London Symph. Orch. (1956–68); Monteux, who conducted same, encouraged Marriner himself to become a symphonic conductor. Following this advice, Marriner joined a summer class in conducting which Monteux had maintained at Hancock, Maine. In 1959 Marriner organized the Academy of St.-Martin-in-the-Fields in a London church of that name; this being an "academy" in the old German nomenclature descriptive of concert activity. In 1969 he was invited to Los Angeles to organize a local chamber orchestra; as at his London "academy," so with the Los Angeles

Chamber Orch., Marriner presented programs of Baroque music; he made a European tour with it in 1974. He founded, concurrently, a similar organization in Australia. In 1977 he was named artistic director of the Meadow Brook Music Festival in Rochester, Michigan. In 1978 he accepted the prestigious appointment as conductor and music director of the Minnesota Symph. Orch., Minneapolis, effective for the season 1979–80.

Marrocco, William Thomas, American violinist and musicologist; b. West New York, New Jersey, Dec. 5, 1909. After initial music studies in the U.S. he went to Italy and entered the Conservatorio di Musica S. Pietro a Majella in Naples, receiving his diploma di Magistero in 1930; then studied violin and musicology at the Eastman School of Music in Rochester, N.Y. (M.A., 1940); earned his Ph.D. at the Univ. of California in Los Angeles with the dissertation *Jacopo da Bologna and His Works* (publ. as *The Music of Jacopo da Bologna,* Berkeley, 1954); was on the music faculty of the Univ. of Kansas in Lawrence (1946–49); in 1950 appointed prof. of music at the Univ. of California in Los Angeles. He publ. numerous informative essays dealing with old Italian and American music; edited *14th-Century Italian Cacce* (Cambridge, Mass., 1940; revised, 1961); an anthology *Music in America* (in collaboration with Harold Gleason, N.Y., 1964).

Marschalk, Max, German music critic; b. Berlin, April 7, 1863; d. Poberow-on-the-Ostsee, Germany, Aug. 24, 1940. He was a pupil of H. Urban; from 1894 until its dissolution in 1933, music critic of the *Vossische Zeitung;* from 1934, music director of the publishing company Dreililien in Berlin. He composed a short opera, *In Flammen* (Gotha, 1896); a "Liederspiel" *Aucassin und Nicoletna* (Stuttgart, 1907); incidental music to Hauptmann's *Hanneles Himmelfahrt* (1894), *Die versunkene Glocke* (1898), *Und Pippa tanzt* (1906), to Maeterlinck's *Sœur Béatrice, etc.*

Marschner, Franz, Bohemian pianist, pedagogue and writer on music; b. Leitmeritz, March 1855; d. Weissphyra, Aug. 22, 1932. He studied with Skuhershý at the Prague Cons. and Bruckner in Vienna. He publ. some valuable essays on the techniques of piano playing, among them *Entwurf einer Neugestaltung der Theorie und Praxis des kunstgemässen Anschlags* (on piano touch; Vienna, 1888); also wrote essays on musical esthetics; composed choral pieces, some chamber music and songs.

Marschner, Heinrich (August), German opera composer; b. Zittau, Saxony, Aug. 16, 1795; d. Hannover, Dec. 14, 1861. He entered Leipzig Univ. in 1813 as a law student; but his passion for music, and the encouragement he received from influential music critic Rochlitz, decided his vocation. Becoming a pupil of cantor Schicht, he began composing minor pieces; in 1817 he was invited to Vienna by Count Thaddäus von Amadee, and met Beethoven. Obtaining, through the count's aid, a place as music teacher in Pressburg, he wrote his first (one-act) opera, *Der Kieffhäuserberg* (Pressburg, 1816). There followed *Saidor und Zulima* (Pressburg, Nov. 22, 1818) and *Heinrich IV. und d'Au-*

bigné; the latter was brought out at Dresden (July 19, 1820) by Weber, and caused him to invite Marschner there. In 1821 he went to Dresden, where, in 1823, he was made director of the German and Italian operas, jointly with Weber and Morlacchi. After Weber's death (1826), Marschner became Kapellmeister of the Leipzig theater, where he produced his operas *Der Vampyr* (March 29, 1828) and *Der Templer und die Jüdin* (Dec. 22, 1829; after Walter Scott's *Ivanhoe*), the latter carrying his fame throughout Germany. In 1831 he was appointed court Kapellmeister at Hannover, and retained this post 28 years; he retired on a pension, with the title "General Musikdirektor," in 1859. In 1834 the Univ. of Leipzig made him Dr. phil. In Hannover his greatest work, *Hans Heiling,* was written; it was first performed on May 24, 1833, at Berlin, with tumultuous applause; it is still in the repertory of most German theaters. In his operas, Marschner stands between Weber and Wagner; from Weber he retained the Romantic flavor of musical invention and his predilection for the supernatural, and he approached Wagner in the pathos of humanized emotion and the fullness of the orchestral accompaniment. His other dramatic works are: *Der Holzdieb* (Dresden, Feb. 22, 1825); *Lucretia* (Danzig, Jan. 17, 1827); *Des Falkners Braut* (Leipzig, March 10, 1832); *Das Schloss am Ätna* (Leipzig, Jan. 29, 1836); *Der Bäbu* (Hannover, Feb. 19, 1838); *Kaiser Adolf von Nassau* (Hannover, Jan. 5, 1845); and *Austin* (Hannover, Jan. 26, 1852). A posthumous opera, *Hjarne der Sängerkönig,* was produced at Frankfurt (Sept. 13, 1863). Marschner publ. about 20 sets of songs, and 10 sets of men's choruses (*Zigeunerleben,* etc.); also piano compositions and chamber music.

BIBLIOGRAPHY: M. E. Wittmann, *Heinrich Marschner* (Leipzig, 1879); G. Münzer, *Heinrich Marschner* (Berlin, 1901); G. Fisher, *Musik in Hannover* (Hannover, 1902); H. Gaartz, *Die Opern Heinrich Marschners* (Leipzig, 1912); G. Fischer, *Marschner Erinnerungen* (Hannover, 1918); A. Gnirs, *Hans Heiling* (Karlsbad, 1931); V. Köhler, *Heinrich Marschners Bühnenwerke und Verzeichnis der . . . im Druck erschienenen Werke des Komponisten* (Göttingen, 1955).

Marsh, Robert Charles, American music critic; b. Columbus, Ohio, Aug. 5, 1924. He studied journalism at Northwestern Univ. (B.S., 1945) and philosophy (A.M., 1946); earned a doctorate in education at Harvard (1951); synchronously he took courses in music theory with Robert Palmer at Cornell Univ. (1946–47) and attended lectures of Hindemith at Harvard (1949–50); studied musicology with Thurston Dart and theory of criticism with H.S. Middleton at Cambridge, England (1955–56). He held teaching positions at the Univ. of Illinois (1947–49); Chicago City Junior College (1950–51); Univ. of Kansas City (1951–52); State Univ. of New York (1953–54) and Univ. of Chicago (1956–58). He became music critic with the *Chicago Sun Times* in 1956; contributed articles on music to various literary publications and philosophical journals; edited *Logic and Knowledge of Bertrand Russell* (1956); publ. *Toscanini and the Art of Orchestral Performance* (Philadelphia, 1956; revised as *Toscanini*

and the Art of Conducting, 1962); also a book on the Cleveland Orchestra (1967).

Marshall, John Patton, American music educator; b. Rockport, Mass., Jan. 9, 1877; d. Boston, Jan. 17, 1941. He studied music with MacDowell, Chadwick, B. J. Lang, and others; was organist at various churches; lectured on music at the Harvard Summer School. In 1903 he was appointed prof. at Boston Univ., and in 1928 became dean of the College of Music there. He publ. the teaching manuals, *Syllabus of History of Music* (1906), *Syllabus of Music Appreciation* (1911), etc.

Marsick, Armand, eminent Belgian composer (nephew of **Martin-Pierre-Joseph Marsick**); b. Liège, Sept. 20, 1877; d. Haine-Saint-Paul, April 30, 1959. He studied with his father Louis Marsick; then took a course in composition with Sylvain Dupuis at the Liège Cons.; became first violinist in the Théâtre Municipal in Nancy; completed composition studies with Guy Ropartz at the Cons. there. In 1898 he became concertmaster at the Concerts Colonne in Paris. In 1908 he obtained the position of instructor at the Cons. of Athens; he remained in Greece until 1921; was appointed conductor at the Music Academy of Bilbao, Spain, in 1922. He returned to Belgium in 1927; was prof. at the Liège Cons. (1927–42) and conductor of the Société des Concerts Symphoniques (1927–39).

WORKS: 3 operas: *La Jane* (1903; first produced as *Vendetta Corsa* in Rome, 1912; then at Liège, March 29, 1921), *Lara* (1913; Antwerp, Dec. 3, 1929) and *L'Anneau Nuptial* (1920; Brussels, March 3, 1928); a radio play, *Le Visage de la Wallonie* (1937); the symph. poems *Stèle funéraire* (1902) and *La Source* (1908); *Improvisation et Final* for cello and orch. (1904); 2 suites: *Scènes de Montagnes* (1910) and *Tableaux Grecs* (1912); *Tableaux de Voyage* for small orch. (1939); *Loustics en Fête* for small orch. (1939); *3 Morceaux Symphoniques* (1950); Violin Sonata (1900); Quartet for 4 horns (1950); *4 Pièces* for piano (1912); several sets of songs; choruses. A catalogue of his works was publ. by the Centre Belge de Documentation Musicale (Brussels, 1955).

Marsick, Martin-Pierre-Joseph, distinguished violinist; b. Jupille, near Liège, Belgium, March 9, 1848; d. Paris, Oct. 21, 1924. He studied at the Liège Cons.; at the age of 12 played the organ at the cathedral; then studied violin with Léonard at the Brussels Cons. and with Massart at the Paris Cons., taking 1st prize there. In 1870 he became a pupil of Joachim in Berlin. After a brilliant debut at Paris in the Concerts Populaires (1873), he undertook long tours in Europe; also played in the U.S. (1895–96). In 1892 he was appointed prof. of violin at the Paris Cons. Among his pupils were Carl Flesch and Jacques Thibaud. He wrote 3 violin concertos and numerous solo pieces for the violin (*Adagio scherzando; 2 Reveries; Songe; Romance; Tarentelle; Agitato; Intermezzo; Berceuse;* etc.).

Marsop, Paul, German librarian and writer on music; b. Berlin, Oct. 6, 1856; d. Florence, Italy, May 31, 1925. He studied with Hans von Bülow; from 1881 lived in

Munich and (during the winter) in Italy. He founded in Munich the Musikalische Volksbibliothek, which he turned over to the city in 1907; also aided in the establishment of similar libraries in other cities.

WRITINGS: *Musikalische Essays* (1899); *Studienblätter eines Musikers* (1903); *Neue Kämpfe* (1913); *Musikalische Satiren und Grotesken* (1924); and various pamphlets dealing mostly with Wagner (*Die Aussichten der Wagnerschen Kunst in Frankreich, Der Kern der Wagnerfrage,* etc).

Marston, George W., American organist, choral conductor, and composer; b. Sandwich, Mass., May 23, 1840; d. there, Feb. 2, 1901. He studied organ; moved to Portland, Maine as a youth and established himself there as church organist and music teacher. He composed some choral music suitable for performances by amateur groups.

Marteau, Henri, famous French violinist; b. Reims, March 31, 1874; d. Lichtenberg, Bavaria, Oct. 3, 1934. He studied violin with Léonard at the Paris Cons. and began his concert career as a youth; was soloist with the Vienna Philharmonic at the age of 10, and played a concert in London at 14. In 1892, 1893, 1894, 1898 and 1906 he also toured the U.S.; gave concerts in Scandinavia, in Russia, France and Germany. In 1900 he was appointed prof. of violin at the Geneva Cons., and in 1908 succeeded Joachim as violin teacher at the Hochschule für Musik in Berlin. In 1915 he left Germany and went to Sweden, becoming a Swedish citizen in 1920; then taught at the German Music Academy in Prague (1921-24), at the Leipzig Cons. (1926-27), and (from 1928) at the Dresden Cons. He was greatly appreciated by musicians of Europe; Max Reger, who was a personal friend, wrote a violin concerto for him, as did Massenet; his teacher Léonard bequeathed to him his magnificent Maggini violin, formerly owned by the Empress Maria Theresa. Marteau was also a competent composer; he wrote an opera *Meister Schwabe* (Plauen, 1921); a symph. work *Gloria Naturae* (Stockholm, 1918); 2 violin concertos; Cello Concerto; *Sonata fantastica* for violin alone; 3 string quartets; String Quintet; Clarinet Quintet; numerous violin pieces and arrangements of classical works.

BIBLIOGRAPHY: B. Marteau, *Henri Marteau, Siegeszug einer Geige* (Tutzing, 1971).

Martelli, Henri, French composer; b. Bastia, Corsica, Feb. 25, 1895. He studied law at the Univ. of Paris; simultaneously took courses in composition with Widor and Caussade. He was secretary of the Société Nationale de Musique (1945-67) and director of programs there since 1968; from 1953 to 1973 was president of the French section of the International Society for Contemporary Music. In his compositions he attempts to recreate the spirit of old French music in modern techniques.

WORKS: an opera *La Chanson de Roland* (1921-23, revised 1962-64; Paris, April 13, 1967); an opera buffa *Le Major Cravachon* (1958; French Radio, June 14, 1959); 2 ballets: *La Bouteille de Panurge* (1930; Paris, Feb. 24, 1937) and *Les Hommes de sable* (1951); *Rondo* for orch. (1921); *Sarabande, scherzo et final* for orch. (1922); *Divertissement sarrasin* for orch. (1922); *Sur la vie de Jeanne d'Arc* for orch. (1923); *Scherzo* for violin and orch. (1925); *Mors et Juventas* for orch. (1927); *Bas-reliefs assyriens* for orch. (1928; Boston, March 14, 1930); *Passacaille sur un thème russe* for orch. (1928); Concerto for Orch. (1931; Boston, April 22, 1932); 3 suites for orch.: No. 1, *Suite sur un thème corse* (1936); No. 2 (1950); No. 3 (1971); Concerto No. 1 for Violin and Chamber Orch. (1938); *Ouverture pour un conte de Boccace* (1942); *Suite Concertante* for wind quintet and orch. (1943); *Divertimento* for wind orch. (1945); *Fantaisie* for piano and orch. (1945); Sinfonietta (1948); 3 symphonies: No. 1, for strings (1953; French Radio, March 13, 1955); No. 2, for strings (1956; Paris, July 17, 1958); No. 3 (1957; Paris, March 8, 1960); Concertino No. 2, for violin and chamber orch. (1954); Concertino for oboe, clarinet, horn, bassoon and string orch. (1955); Double Concerto for Clarinet, Bassoon and Orch. (1956); *Le Radeau de la Méduse,* symph. poem (1957); *Variations* for string orch. (1959); *Scènes à danser* for orch. (1963); *Rapsodie* for cello and orch. (1966); Oboe Concerto (1971); *Le Temps,* cantata for voice and 8 instruments (1945); *Chrestomathie* for a cappella chorus (1949); *Invention* for cello and piano (1925); Duo for oboe and English horn (1925); 2 string quartets (1932-33, 1944); Piano Trio (1935); Violin Sonata (1936); *Suite* for 4 clarinets (1936); *Introduction et final* for violin and piano (1937); Wind Octet (1941); *Scherzetto, berceuse et final* for cello and piano (1941); Bassoon Sonata (1941); Cello Sonatina (1941); Flute Sonata (1942); *3 Esquisses* for saxophone and piano (1943); *Préambule et Scherzo* for clarinet and piano (1944); *7 Duos* for violin and harp (1946); *Fantaisiestück* for flute and piano (1946); Wind Quintet (1974); Cornet Sonatina (1948); *Adagio, Cadence et Final* for oboe and piano (1949); 2 quintets for flute, harp, and string trio (1950, 1952); Trio for flute, cello and piano (1951); *Cadence, Interlude et Rondo* for saxophone and piano (1952); *15 Études* for solo bassoon (1953); Bass Trombone Sonata (1956); Viola Sonata (1959); *Suite* for solo guitar (1960); *Concertstück* for viola and piano (1962); Concertino for Cornet and Piano (1964); *Dialogue* for trombone, tuba or bass saxophone, and piano (1966); Oboe Sonata (1972); String Trio (1973-74); Trio for flute, cello and harp (1976); *Suite galante* for piano (1924); *Guitare* for piano (1931); *3 Petites Suites* for piano (1935, 1943, 1950); *Suite* for piano (1939); 2-Piano Sonata (1946); *Sonorités* for piano, left hand (1974); 17 radiophonic works; songs.

Martenot, Maurice, French inventor of the electronic instrument "Ondes musicales," a.k.a. "Ondes Martenot"; b. Paris, Oct. 14, 1898. He studied composition at the Paris Cons. with Gédalge; began to work on the construction of an electronic musical instrument with a keyboard, which he called "Ondes musicales." He gave its first demonstration in Paris on April 20, 1928; publ. a *Méthode pour l'enseignement des Ondes musicales* (Paris, 1931). The instrument became popular among French composers. Honegger included it in *Jeanne d'Arc au bûcher;* Messiaen, Milhaud, Koechlin, Jolivet and others also wrote for it. His sister **Ginette Martenot** (b. Paris, Jan. 27, 1902) became the chief exponent of the Ondes Martenot in concert performances with orchestras in Europe and America.

Martens, Frederick Herman, American writer on musical subjects; b. New York, July 6, 1874; d. Mountain Lakes, N.J., Dec. 18, 1932. He studied in N.Y. with local teachers; from 1907 was active mainly as a writer; publ. *Leo Ornstein: The Man, His Ideas, His Work* (1918); *Violin Mastery* (1919); *Art of the Prima Donna and Concert Singer* (1923); *String Mastery* (1919; revised ed., 1923); *A Thousand and One Nights of Opera* (1926); *Book of the Opera and the Ballet* (1925); contributed articles to *The Musical Quarterly* and other publications.

Martienssen, Carl Adolf, German musicologist and pedagogue; b. Güstrow, Dec. 6, 1881; d. Berlin, March 1, 1955. He studied with Klindworth and Wilhelm Berger in Berlin; musicology with Kretzschmar. In 1914 he was appointed prof. of piano at the Leipzig Cons.; in 1932 became prof. at the Musical Institute for Foreigners in Berlin. He taught at Rostock from 1948 to 1950; then returned to Berlin.
WRITINGS: *Die individuelle Klaviertechnik auf der Grundlage des schöpferischen Klangwillens* (1930); *Methodik des individuellen Klavierunterrichts* (1934); *Grundlage einer deutschen Klavierlehre* (1942); *Das Klavierkunstwerk* (1950); and shorter studies.

Martín, Edgardo, Cuban composer and writer on music; b. Cienfuegos, Oct. 6, 1915. He studied with his maternal grandmother, the pianist **Aurea Suárez;** later took piano lessons in Havana with Jascha Fischermann and composition with José Ardévol. He taught music history at the Conservatorio Municipal (1945-68) and music analysis in the Escuela Nacional de Arte (1969-73) in Havana. He also occupied numerous offical posts; was executive secretary of the National Committee of Music for UNESCO (1962-71). Among his compositions are a ballet, *El Caballo de coral* (Havana, 1960); 2 symphonies (1947, 1948); Concerto for 9 Wind Instruments (1944); 2 string quartets (1967, 1968); *Canto de héroes* for voices with orch. (1967); *La Carta del soldado* for narrator, tenor, chorus, speaking chorus and orch. (1970). He publ. *Catálogo biográfico de compositores de Cuba* (Havana, 1970) and *Panorama histórico de la música en Cuba* (Havana, 1971).

Martin, Frank, greatly renowned Swiss composer; b. Geneva, Sept. 15, 1890; d. Naarden, Holland, Nov. 21, 1974. He studied with Joseph Lauber in Geneva (1906-14); then took courses in Zürich (1918-20), Rome (1921-23) and Paris (1923-25). He returned to Geneva in 1926 as a pianist and harpsichordist; taught at the Institute Jaques-Dalcroze (1927-38); was founder and director of the "Technicum moderne de musique" (1933-39); was president of the Association of Swiss Musicians (1942-46). He moved to Holland in 1946 and while living there taught classes in composition at the Cologne Hochschule für Musik (1950-57). His early music showed the influence of César Franck and French Impressionists, but soon he succeeeded in creating a distinctive style supported by a consummate mastery of contrapuntal and harmonic writing, and a profound feeling for emotional consistency and continuity. Still later he became fascinated by the logic and self-consistency of Schoenberg's method of composition with 12 tones, and adopted it in a modified form in several of his works. He also demonstrated an ability to stylize folksong materials in modern techniques. In 1944, the director of Radio Geneva asked Martin to compose an oratorio to be broadcast immediately upon the conclusion of World War II. He responded with *In Terra Pax* for 5 soli, double chorus and orch., which was given its broadcast première from Geneva at the end of the war in Europe, May 7, 1945; a public performance followed in Geneva 24 days later.
WORKS: FOR THE STAGE : Operas: *Der Sturm* (*The Tempest*), after Shakespeare (1952-54; Vienna, June 17, 1956) and *Monsieur de Pourceaugnac,* after Molière (1960-62; Geneva, April 23, 1963). Ballets: *Das Märchen vom Aschenbrödel,* after the Cinderella legend (1941; Basel, March 12, 1942) and *Ein Totentanz zu Basel im Jahre 1943* (Basel, May 27, 1943); a play with music, *La Nique à Satan,* for baritone, male and female and children's choruses, winds, percussion, 2 pianos and double bass (1930-31; Geneva, Feb. 25, 1933); incidental music to *Oedipus Rex* (1923), *Oedipus Coloneus* (1924), *Le Divorce* (1928), *Romeo and Juliet* (1929) and *Athalic* (1946).
VOCAL WORKS: in addition to *In Terra Pax,* 3 *Poèmes païens* for baritone and orch. (1910); *Les Dithyrambes* for 4 soli, mixed chorus, children's chorus and orch. (1918); *4 Sonnets à Cassandre* for mezzo-soprano, flute, viola, and cello (1921); *Messe* for double chorus a cappella (1922); *Musique pour les Fêtes du Rhône* for chorus and winds (1929); *Cantate sur la Nativité* for soli, chorus, string orch. and piano (1929, unfinished); *Chanson en canon* for chorus a cappella (1930); *Le Vin herbé,* oratorio after the Tristan legend, for 12 solo voices, 7 strings and piano (1938-41; first complete production, Zürich, March 26, 1942); *Cantate pour le 1er août* for chorus, and organ or piano (1941); *Der Cornet* or *Die Weise von Liebe und Tod des Cornets Christoph Rilke,* after Rilke, cycle for alto and orch. (1942-43; Basel, Feb. 9, 1945); *Sechs Monologe aus "Jedermann"* (6 *Monologues from "Everyman"*), after Hofmannsthal, for baritone or alto, and piano (1943; orchestrated 1949); *Dédicace* for tenor and piano (1945); 3 *Chants de Noël* for soprano, flute and piano (1974); *Golgotha,* oratorio for 5 soli, chorus, orch. and organ (1945-48; Geneva, April 29, 1949); 5 *Chansons d'Ariel* for small chorus a cappella (1950); *Psaumes de Genève,* psalm cantata for chorus, children's chorus, orch. and organ (1958); *Le Mystère de la Nativité,* oratorio (1957-59; Geneva, Dec. 24, 1959); 3 *Minnelieder* for soprano and piano (1960); *Ode à la Musique* for chorus, trumpet, 2 horns, 3 trombones, double bass and piano (1961); *Verse à boire* for chorus a cappella (1961); *Pilate,* short oratorio (Rome, Nov. 14, 1964); *Maria Triptychon* for soprano, violin and orch. (consists of the separate works, *Ave Maria, Magnificat* and *Stabat Mater,* 1967-69; Rotterdam, Nov. 13, 1969); *Poèmes de la Mort* for 3 male voices and 3 electric guitars (1969-71); *Requiem* (1971-72; Lausanne, May 4, 1973); *Et la vie l'emporta,* chamber cantata for small

vocal and instrumental ensembles (1974; his last work; orchestration completed by Bernard Reichel in 1975).

INSTRUMENTAL WORKS: Suite for orch. (1913); 2 violin sonatas (1913, 1931–32); *Symphonie pour orchestre burlesque sur des Thèmes savoyards*, with children's instruments (1915); Piano Quintet (1919); *Esquisses* for small orch. (1920); *Pavane Couleur de Temps* for string quintet, or string orch., or small orch. (1920); *Foxtrot*, overture for 2 pianos (1924; also for orch.); Piano Trio on popular Irish themes (1924); *Rythmes*, 3 symph. movements (1926; International Society for Contemporary Music Festival, Geneva, April 6, 1929); *Guitare*, 4 small pieces for guitar (1933; versions for piano and orch.); 2 piano concertos No. 1 (1933–34; Geneva, Jan. 22, 1936) and No. 2 (1968–69; The Hague, June 27, 1970); *Rhapsodie* for string quintet (1935); *Danse de la Peur* for 2 pianos and small orch. (1936; music from an uncompleted ballet, *Die blaue Blume*); String Trio (1936); Symphony, with jazz instruments (1937; Geneva, March 10, 1938); *Ballade* for saxophone, strings, piano and percussion (1938); *Sonata da chiesa* for viola d'amore or flute, and organ or orch. or string orch. (1938); *Ballade* for flute, and orch. or string orch. (1939); *Ballade* for piano and orch. (1939); *Ballade* for trombone or saxophone, and piano or orch. (1940); *Passacaille* for organ (1944; versions for string orch., 1952, and for full orch., 1962); *Petite Symphonie concertante* for harp, harpsichord, piano and double string orch. (1944–45; Zürich, May 17, 1946; an alternate version, retitled *Symphonie concertante*, was created in 1946 for full orch., eliminating the solo instruments); *8 Preludes* for piano (1947–48); Concerto for 7 winds, strings and percussion (1949; Bern, Oct. 25, 1949); *Ballade* for cello, and piano or small orch. (1949); Violin Concerto (1950–51; Basel, Jan. 24, 1952); Concerto for Harpsichord and Small Orch. (Venice, Sept. 14, 1952); *Clair de Lune* for piano (1953); *Etudes* for string orch. or 2 pianos (1955–56); *Ouverture en hommage à Mozart* (1956); *Pièce brève* for flute, oboe and harp (1957); *Ouverture en Rondeau* (1958); *Inter arma caritas* for orch. (1963); *Les quatre Eléments* for orch. (1963–64; Geneva, Oct. 7, 1964); *Etude rythmique* and *Etude de déchiffrage* for piano (both 1965); Cello Concerto (1965–66; Basel, Jan. 26, 1967); String Quartet (1966–67); *Erasmi Monumentum* for orch. and organ (Rotterdam, Sept. 24, 1969); *3 Danses* for oboe, harp and string orch. (Zürich, Oct. 9, 1970); *Ballade* for viola, winds, harp and harpsichord (1972); *Polyptyque*, 6 images of the Passion of Christ, for violin and 2 string orchs. (1972–73; Lausanne, Sept. 9, 1973); *Fantaisie sur des rythmes flamenco* for piano (1973).

BIBLIOGRAPHY: R.-Aloys Mooser, *Regards sur la musique contemporaine, 1921–1946* (Lausanne, 1947); B. Billeter, *Frank Martin, Ein Aussenseiter der neuen Musik* (Basel, 1970). The Sept./Oct. 1976, issue of *Schweizerische Musikzeitung*, devoted to Frank Martin, includes an extensive bibliography.

Martin, Sir George (Clement), English organist and composer; b. Lambourne, Berks, Sept. 11, 1844; d. London, Feb. 23, 1916. He was a pupil of J. Pearson and Dr. Stainer; received the degree of Bachelor of Music at Oxford in 1868, and Mus. Doc. (Canterbury) in 1883. He was knighted in 1897. In 1888 he succeeded Stainer as organist of St. Paul's Cathedral, which post he held until his death. He publ. the primer *The Art of Training Choir Boys.*

Martin, Jean-Blaise, famous French baritone; b. Paris, Feb. 24, 1768; d. Ronzières, Rhône, Oct. 28, 1837. He made his debut at the Théâtre de Monsieur in 1788; sang at the Théâtre Feydeau and the Théâtre Favart until they were united as the Opéra-Comique in 1801, and there until 1823. From 1816–18 and again from 1832–37, he was a professor at the Paris Cons. His voice, while essentially a baritone in quality, had the extraordinary range of three full octaves, reaching high C.

Martin, Riccardo (real name **Hugh Whitfield Martin**), American tenor; b. Hopkinsville, Ky., Nov. 18, 1874; d. New York, Aug. 11, 1952. He studied violin in Nashville and singing in N.Y.; was a pupil in composition of MacDowell at Columbia Univ.; went to Paris in 1901, where he took singing lessons with Sbriglia; made his debut as Faust in Nantes (1904); American debut as Canio (*Pagliacci*) with the San Carlo Opera Co. in New Orleans (1906); was a member of the Metropolitan Opera Co. from 1907 to 1913; then with the Boston Grand Opera Co. (1916–17), with the Chicago Opera Co. (1920–22); subsequently settled in N.Y. as a singing teacher.

Martinček, Dušan, Slovak composer, b. Prešov, June 19, 1936. He studied piano at the Bratislava Cons. and composition with Cikker and Zimmer; upon graduation devoted himself to teaching.

WORKS: *Dialogues in the Form of Variations* for piano and orch. (1961); *Simple Overture* (1963); *Rhapsody* for piano and orch. (1965–66); 3 piano sonatas; *Elegy* for string orch (1973); Sonata for solo viola (1974).

Martinelli, Giovanni, Italian tenor; b. Montagnana, near Venice, Oct. 22, 1885; d. New York, Feb. 2, 1969. He studied singing with Mandolini; made his concert debut in Milan (Dec. 3, 1910) in Rossini's *Stabat Mater;* made a decidedly favorable impression as an opera singer at the European première of Puccini's opera *The Girl of the Golden West* (Rome, 1911). In 1912 he sang at Covent Garden in London; made his American debut as Cavaradossi in *Tosca* with the Metropolitan Opera, N.Y.; remained on its roster until 1946, then opened an opera studio in New York and taught singing.

Martinet, Jean-Louis, French composer; b. Ste.-Bazeille, Nov. 8, 1912. He studied music theory with Charles Koechlin, Roger-Ducasse and Messiaen; also took lessons in conducting with Charles Munch and Roger Desormière. He naturally absorbed the harmonic essence of French Impressionism and the contrapuntal rigor of the neo-Classical style as practiced by Stravinsky and Béla Bartók; in later works he succumbed to the fashionable temptation of dodecaphony à la française. Among his works are a symphonic poem *Orphée* (1945); 6 pieces, each entitled

Mouvement symphonique (1953–59); *Variations* for string quartet (1946, in dodecaphonic technique); cantatas, *Épisodes* (1950), *Elsa* (1959), *Les Amours* for chorus a cappella (1960), *Les Douze* for narrator, chorus and orch., after a revolutionary poem by Alexander Blok (1961); symphony, *In memoriam* (1963); *Divertissement pastoral* for piano and orch. (1966); *2 Images* for orch. (1966).

Martinez, Marianne di, Austrian vocalist and pianist; b. Vienna, May 4, 1744; d. there, Dec. 13, 1812. She was a pupil of Metastasio and of Haydn. She wrote oratorios, motets, psalms, symphonies, piano concertos, etc. (all MSS in possession of the Gesellschaft der Musikfreunde in Vienna).

Martini, Giovanni Battista, known as Padre Martini; illustrious Italian composer and teacher; b. Bologna, April 24, 1706; d. there, Aug. 3, 1784. His musical education was conducted by his father, a violinist; he then took lessons with Padre Predieri (harpsichord and voice) and Riccieri (counterpoint). He entered the Franciscan Order at Lago, and was ordained priest in 1722; in 1725 he became maestro di cappella at the church of San Francesco in Bologna. A man of unquenchable intellectual curiosity, he studied mathematics with Zanotti, and took a course in ecclesiastical music with Giacomo Perti. He accumulated a magnificent musical library, which, after his death, went to the Liceo Musicale of Bologna and the court library in Vienna. He composed Masses and oratorios of great merit; but it was as a teacher that his name became widely known. Students of all nationalities sought his instruction (among them Gluck, Mozart, Grétry, Jommelli, Mattei), and scholars submitted complex questions regarding musical science to him for settlement. He was a member of the Accademia Filarmonica of Bologna; also of the Accademia degli Arcadi, Rome, in which his "Arcadian" title was "Aristosseno Anfioneo" (Aristoxenos Amphion).
    WORKS: Of his compositions, in the style of the Roman school (of which he was a warm partisan), the following were publ.: *Litaniae atque antiphoniae finales, a 4,* with organ and instruments (1734); *12 Sonate d'intavolatura per l'organo e cembalo* (1742); *6 Sonate d'intavolatura per l'organo e cembalo* (1747); *Duetti da camera a diversi voci* (1763). In MS, 2 oratorios, Masses, a "farsetta," 3 intermezzi, etc. His principal work is *Storia della musica* (3 vols.; Bologna, 1757, 1770, 1781), dealing only with ancient music; the *Esemplare ossia saggio fondamentale pratico di contrappunto* (2 vols.; 1774, 1775) is a collection of contrapuntal models; he also wrote *Regole per gli organisti per accompagnare il canto fermo* (1756), other learned dissertations and essays, etc.
    BIBLIOGRAPHY: G. della Valle, *Elogio del Padre Giambattista Martini* (Bologna, 1784); G. della Valle, *Memorie storiche del Padre Giambattista Martini* (Naples, 1785); F. Parisini, *Della vita e delle opere del padre Martini* (Bologna, 1887); L. Busi, *Il padre Giambattista Martini* (vol. I, Bologna, 1891); G. Gandolfi, *Elogio di Giambattista Martini* (1913); W. Reich, *Padre Martini als Theoretiker* (Vienna, 1934); A. Pauchard, *Ein italienischer Musiktheoretiker. Pater G. B.*

Martini (Lugano, 1941). Martini's voluminous correspondence was publ. by F. Parisini (Bologna, 1888).

Martini (real name **Schwarzendorf**), **Jean Paul Égide** (properly **Johann Paul Ágid**), German organist and composer; b. Freystadt in the Palatinate, baptized Aug. 31, 1741; d. Paris, Feb. 10, 1816. In 1760, having studied organ, he settled in Nancy, and Italianized his name; then was attached to the retinue of King Stanislas at Lunéville (1761–66). In 1766 he went to Paris, where he won a prize for a military march for the Swiss Guard; this introduced him into army circles in France; he enlisted as an officer of a Hussar regiment, and wrote more band music; also composed an opera, *L'Amoureux de quinze ans,* which was produced with extraordinary success at the Italian Opera in Paris (April 18, 1771). Leaving the army, he became music director to the Prince of Condé, and later to the Comte d'Artois. He purchased the reversion of the office of First Intendant of the King's Music, a speculation brought to naught by the Revolution, which caused him to resign in haste his position as conductor at the Théâtre Feydeau, and flee to Lyons in 1792. He returned to Paris in 1794, and was appointed Inspector of the Paris Cons. in 1798; also taught composition there until 1802. In appreciation of his royalist record, he was given the post of Royal Intendant at the Restoration in 1814, but died 2 years later. He wrote 12 operas, a Requiem for Louis XVI, Psalms and other church music, but he is chiefly remembered as the composer of the popular air *Plaisir d'amour,* which was arranged by Berlioz for voice and orch.
    BIBLIOGRAPHY: A Pougin, *J. P. E. Martini* (Paris, 1864).

Martini, Nino, Italian tenor; b. Verona, Aug. 7, 1902; d. there, Dec. 9, 1976. He studied voice in Italy and in the U.S.; took lessons with Giovanni Zenatello in N.Y. In 1931 he made his American debut as an opera singer with the Philadelphia Opera Co.; sang at the Metropolitan Opera House in N.Y. for the first time as the Duke in *Rigoletto* on Dec. 28, 1933, and remained on its roster for several seasons.

Martino, Donald, American composer; b. Plainfield, New Jersey, May 16, 1931. He played clarinet, oboe and saxophone as a youth; then studied composition with Ernst Bacon at Syracuse Univ., N.Y. (B.Mus., 1952); subsequently went to Princeton Univ. where he was a pupil of Babbitt in electronic composition; also took in sessions with Sessions (M.F.A., 1954); then went to Italy where he had lessons with Dallapiccola in Florence (1954–56). He was subsequently instructor of music at Princeton Univ. (1957–59) and associate prof. in music theory at Yale Univ. (1965–69). In 1970 he was appointed prof. of composition at the New England Cons. of Music, Boston. In his music he adopts a quasi-mathematical method of composition based on arithmetical permutations of tonal and rhythmic ingredients.
    WORKS: *Quodlibets* for flute (1954); *Portraits* for voices and orch. (1956); *Sette canoni enigmatici* for string quartet or any other combination of string instruments (1956); *Contemplations* for orch. (1957); Trio for violin, clarinet and piano (1959); *5 Fragmenti* for oboe and double bass (1962); Concerto for Wood-

wind Quintet (1964); *Parisonatina al' dodecafonia* for cello solo (1964); Piano Concerto (1965); *Strata* for bass clarinet (1966); *Mosaic* for orch. (1967); *Pianissimo*, piano sonata (1970); *Paradiso choruses* for soloists, chorus, tape and orch. (1974); *Ritorno* for orch. (1976); Triple Concerto for clarinet, bass clarinet, contrabass clarinet, and chamber orch. (1977). He received the Pulitzer Prize for his chamber piece *Notturno* (1974).

Martinon, Jean, significant French conductor and composer; b. Lyons, Jan. 10, 1910; d. Paris, March 1, 1976. He studied violin at the Paris Cons., winning first prize (1928); then took lessons in composition with Albert Roussel and in conducting with Charles Munch. During World War II he was in the French Army, and was taken prisoner in 1940; spent 2 years in a German prison camp, where he wrote *Stalag 9 ou Musique d'exil* for orch. and a motet *Absolve Domine* in memory of French musicians killed in the war. He was released in 1944, and conducted the Concerts du Conservatoire de Paris until 1946 when he was appointed conductor of the Bordeaux Symph. Orch.; later traveled as orchestral conductor in England and South America; made his American debut with the Boston Symph. Orch., March 29, 1957; was musical director of the Düsseldorf Symph. (1960-63); in 1963 he was appointed conductor of the Chicago Symph. Orch., with which he conducted numerous works of the modern school, including his own; despite his superior qualities as a musician and conductor, he was not successful with the Chicago audiences and some Chicago critics, and returned to France in 1968; there he conducted the Orchestre National of the Paris Radio.

WORKS: *Symphonietta* (1935); *Concerto giocoso* for violin and orch. (1937-42); *Stalag 9* (1940-42); *Absolve Domine* (1940-42); *Ode au soleil*, for narrator, chorus and orch. (1945); a ballet, *Ambohimanga*, with chorus (1946); 4 symphonies: No. 1 (1934-36); No. 2, *Hymne à la vie* (1942-44); No. 3, entitled *Irish Symphony* (1948); No. 4, *Altitudes* (1965); *Symphonies de voyages* for chamber orch. (1957); Cello Concerto (1963); octet (1969); Flute Concerto (1971); Wind Quintet (1938); String Trio (1943); Piano Trio (1945); 2 string quartets (1946, 1966); 7 sonatinas for violin (interchangeable with flute) and piano, or unaccompanied; choral works; songs; also an opera, *Hécube*, after Eurypides (1949; Strasbourg, 1956); oratorio, *Le Lis de Saron* (1952).

BIBLIOGRAPHY: A. Machabey, *Portraits de trente musiciens français* (Paris, 1950; pp. 121-25).

Martinů, Bohuslav, remarkable Czech composer; b. Policka, Dec. 8, 1890; d. Liestal, near Basel, Switzerland, Aug. 28, 1959. He studied violin at home; in 1906 he enrolled at the Prague Cons.; played in the second violin section in the Czech Philh. in Prague (1913-14), returning to Policka (1914-18) to avoid service in the Austrian Army; after World War I he re-entered the Prague Cons. as a pupil of Suk, but again failed to graduate. In 1923 he went to Paris and participated in the progressive musical circles there; took private lessons with Albert Roussel. In a relatively short time his name became known in Europe through increasingly frequent performances of his chamber works, ballets and symph. pieces; several of his works were performed at the festivals of the International Society for Contemporary Music. He remained in Paris until June, 1940, when he fled the German invasion and went to Portugal and finally to America in 1941; settled in N.Y. He became prof. at the Berkshire Music Center in Tanglewood and was a visiting prof. of music at Princeton; paid a brief visit to Prague in 1946; during his last years of life he made his home mostly in Switzerland. His music is characterized by a strong feeling for Bohemian melorhythms; his stylizations of Czech dances are set in a modern idiom without losing their simplicity. In his large works he followed the neo-Classical trend, with some Impressionistic undertones; his mastery of modern counterpoint was extraordinary. In his music for the stage, his predilections were for chamber forms; his sense of operatic comedy was very strong, but he was also capable of poignant lyricism.

WORKS: FOR STAGE: 16 operas: *Voják a tanečnice* (The Soldier and the Dancer), in 3 acts (1926-27; Brno, May 5, 1928); *Les Larmes du couteau* (The Knife's Tears), in 1 act (1928); *Trois Souhaits, ou Les Vicissitudes de la vie* (The 3 Wishes or the Fickleness of Life), an "opera-film in 3 acts" (1929; performed posthumously, Brno, June 16, 1971; the normal orchestra is augmented by a jazz flute, saxophones, flexatone, banjo, and accordion); *La Semaine de bonté*, in 3 acts (1929; unfinished); *Hry o Marii* (The Miracle of Our Lady) in 4 parts (1933-34; Brno, Feb. 23, 1935); *Hlas lesa* (The Voice of the Forest), radio opera in 1 act (1935; Czech Radio, Oct. 6, 1935); *Divadlo za bránou* (The Suburban Theater), opera buffa in 3 acts (1935-36; Brno, Sept. 20, 1936); *Veselohra na mostě* (Comedy on a Bridge), radio opera in 1 act (1935, revised 1950; Czech Radio, March 18, 1937); *Julietta, or the Key to Dreams,* lyric opera in 3 acts (1936-37; Prague, March 16, 1938); *Alexandre bis,* opera buffa in 1 act (1937; Mannheim, Feb. 18, 1964); *What Men Live By* (Čím člověk žije), pastoral opera, after Tolstoy, in 1 act (1951-52; N.Y., May 20, 1955); *The Marriage* (Ženitba), television opera, after Gogol, in 2 acts (1952; NBC television, N.Y., Feb. 7, 1953); *La Plainte contre inconnu,* in 3 acts (1953; unfinished); *Mirandolina,* comic opera in 3 acts (1954; Prague, May 17, 1959); *Ariadne,* lyric opera in 1 act (1958; Gelsenkirchen, West Germany, March 2, 1961); *Greek Passion* (Řecké pašije), musical drama, after Kazantzakis, in 4 acts (1955-59; Zürich, June 9, 1961).

BALLETS: *Noc* (Night), a "meloplastic scene" in 1 act (1913-14); *Stín* (The Shadow), in 1 act (1916); *Istar,* in 3 acts (1918-22; Prague, Sept. 11, 1924); *Who Is the Most Powerful in the World?* (Kdo je na světě nejmocnější), ballet comedy, after an English fairy tale (1922; Brno, Jan. 31, 1925); *The Revolt* (Vzpoura), ballet sketch in 1 act (1922-23; Brno, Feb. 11, 1928); *The Butterfly that Stamped* (Motýl, ktery dupal), after Kipling, in 1 act (1926); *La Revue de cuisine* (The Kitchen Revue, Prague, 1927); *On tourne* (Natáčí se), for a cartoon and puppet film (1927); *Le Raid merveilleux* (Báječný let), a "ballet mechanique" for 2 clarinets, trumpet and strings (1927); *Echec au roi* (Checkmating the King), jazz ballet in 1 act (1930); *Špaliček* (The Chap Book), with vocal soloists and chorus

(1931, revised 1940; Prague, Sept. 19, 1933; revision, Prague, April 2, 1949); *Le Jugement de Paris* (1935); *The Strangler (Uškreovač)*, for 3 dancers (1948; New London, Connecticut, Aug. 15, 1948). FOR ORCH.: 6 symphonies: No. 1 (1942; Boston, Nov. 13, 1942), No. 2 (1943; Cleveland, Oct. 28, 1943), No. 3 (1944; Boston, Oct. 12, 1945), No. 4 (1945; Philadelphia, Nov. 30, 1945), No. 5 (1946; Prague, May 27, 1947) and No. 6, *Fantaisies symphoniques* (1951–53; Boston, Jan. 7, 1955). For soloist and orch.: Concertino for cello, wind instruments and piano (1924); 5 piano concertos: No. 1 (1925; Prague, Nov. 21, 1926), No. 2 (1934, rescored 1944; Prague, 1935), No. 3 (1947–48; Dallas, Nov. 20, 1949), *Incantation* (No. 4) (1955–56; N.Y., Oct. 4, 1956) and *Fantasia concertante* (No. 5) (1957; Berlin, Jan. 31, 1959); Concertino for piano left hand and chamber orch. (1926; Prague, Feb. 26, 1947; originally titled *Divertimento*); 2 cello concertos: No. 1, for cello and chamber orch. (1930; revised for full orch., 1939 and rescored in 1955) and No. 2 (1944–45); Concerto for String Quartet and Orch. (1931; also known as String Quartet with Orchestra); 2 violin concertos: No. 1 (1931–32; Chicago, Oct. 25, 1973) and No. 2 (1943; Boston, Dec. 31, 1943); *Divertimento (Serenade No. 4)* for violin, viola, oboe, piano and string orch. (1932); Concertino for Piano Trio and Orch. (1933; Basel, Oct. 16, 1936); Concerto for Harpsichord and Chamber Orch. (1935); Concerto for Flute, Violin and Chamber Orch. (1936); *Duo Concertante* for 2 violins and orch. (1937); *Suite Concertante* for violin and orch. (1937, revised 1945); Piano Concertino (1938; London, Aug. 5, 1948); *Sonata da camera* for cello and chamber orch. (1940); *Sinfonietta giocosa* for piano and chamber orch. (1940, revised 1941; N.Y., March 16, 1942); *Concerto da camera* for violin, string orch., piano and timpani (1941; Basel, Jan. 23, 1942); 2-Piano Concerto (1943; Philadelphia, Nov. 5, 1943); *Sinfonia Concertante* for oboe, bassoon, violin, cello, and small orch. (1949; Basel, Dec. 8, 1950); 2-Violin Concerto (1950; Dallas, Jan. 8, 1951); *Rhapsody-Concerto* for viola and orch. (1952; Cleveland, Feb. 19, 1953); Concerto for Violin, Piano and Orch. (1953); Oboe Concerto (1955). OTHER WORKS FOR ORCH.: *Smrt Tintagilova (The Death of Tintagile)*, music for the Maeterlinck drama (1910); *Anděl smrti (Angel of Death)*, symph. poem (1910; also for piano); *Nocturno No. 1* (1914); *Ballada* (1915); *Míjející Půlnoc (Vanishing Midnight*, 1921–22); *Half-Time*, rondo (1924; Prague, Dec. 7, 1924); *La Bagarre (The Tumult)*, rondo (1926; Boston, Nov. 18, 1927); *Jazz Suite* (1928); *La Rhapsodie* (1928; Boston, Dec. 14, 1928); *Praeludium* (in the form of a scherzo) (1930); *Serenade* for chamber orch. (1930); *Sinfonia Concertante* for 2 orchs. (1932); *Partita* (Suite No. 1) (1932); *Invence (Inventions*, 1934); Concerto Grosso for small orch. (1938; Boston, Nov. 14, 1941); *Tre Ricercari* for chamber orch. (1938; Venice, 1938); Double Concerto for 2 String Orchestras, Piano and Timpani (1938; Basel, Feb. 9, 1940); *Memorial to Lidice* (1943; N.Y., Oct. 28, 1943); *Thunderbolt P–47*, scherzo (1945; Washington, Dec. 19, 1945); *Toccata e due canzone* for small orch. (1946; Basel, Jan. 21, 1947); *Sinfonietta La Jolla* for chamber orch. and piano (1950); *Intermezzo* for orch. (1950; Louisville Orch., Carnegie Hall, N.Y., Dec. 29, 1950); *Les Fresques de Piero della*

Francesca, impressions of 3 frescoes (1955; Salzburg Fest., Aug. 28, 1956); *The Rock*, symph. prelude (1957; Cleveland, April 17, 1958); *Parables* (1957–58; Boston, Feb. 13, 1959); *Estampes*, symph. suite (1958; Louisville, Feb. 4, 1959). FOR VOICE: *Nipponari*, 7 songs for female voice and chamber ensemble (1912); a cantata, *Česká Rapsódie* (1918; Prague, Jan. 12, 1919); *Kouzelné noci (Magic Nights)*, 3 songs for soprano and orch. (1918); *Le Jazz*, movement for voice and orch. (1928); a cantata on Czech folk poetry, *Kytice (Bouquet of Flowers*, 1937; Czech Radio, May, 1938); *Polní mše (Field Mass)* for male chorus, baritone and orch. (1939; Prague, Feb. 28, 1946); *Hora tří světel (The Hill of 3 Lights)*, small oratorio for soloists, chorus and organ (1954; Bern, Oct. 3, 1955); *Hymnus k sv. Jakubu (Hymn to St. James)* for narrator, soloists, chorus, organ and orch. (1954; Polička, July 31, 1955); *Gilgameš (The Epic of Gilgamesh)* for narrator, soloists, chorus and orch. (1954–55; Basel, Jan. 24, 1958); *Otvírání studánek (The Opening of the Wells)* for narrator, soloists, female chorus, 2 violins, viola and piano (1955); *Legend from the Smoke of Potato Fires* for soloists, chorus and chamber ensemble (1957); *Mikeš z hor (Mikesh from the Mountains)* for soloists, chorus, 2 violins, viola and piano (1959); *The Prophesy of Isaiah (Proroctví Izaiášovo)* for male chorus, soloists, viola, trumpet, piano and timpani (1959; Jerusalem, April 2, 1963; his last work; posthumous performance); numerous part-songs and a cappella choruses. CHAMBER MUSIC: 7 string quartets: No. 1 (1918; reconstructed, with the addition of a newly discovered fourth movement, by Jan Hanuš in 1972), No. 2 (1925), No. 3 (1929), No. 4 (1937), No. 5 (1938), No. 6 (1946), No. 7, *Concerto da camera* (1947); 5 violin sonatas: in C major (1919), in D minor (1926), No. 1 (1929), No. 2 (1931) and No. 3 (1944); 2 string trios (1923, 1934); Quartet for clarinet, horn, cello and drum (1924); 2 unnumbered nonets: for violin, viola, cello, flute, clarinet, oboe, horn, bassoon and piano (1924–25) and for violin, viola, cello, double-bass, flute, clarinet, oboe, horn and bassoon (1959); 2 duos for violin and cello (1927, 1957); *Impromptu* for violin and piano (1927); String Quintet (1927); Sextet for winds and piano (1929); *5 Short Pieces* for violin and piano (1929); Wind Quintet (1930); *Les Rondes*, 6 pieces for 7 instruments (1930); 3 piano trios (*5 Brief Pieces*, 1930; 1950, 1951); Sonatina for 2 violins and piano (1930); *Études rythmiques* for violin and piano (1931); *Pastorales* and *Nocturnes* for cello and piano (both 1931); *Arabesques* for violin or cello, and piano (1931); String Sextet (1932); Sonata for 2 violins and piano (1932); *Serenade* No. 1 for 6 instruments; No. 2 for 2 violins and viola; No. 3 for 7 instruments (all 1932; No. 4 is the *Divertimento* for violin, viola, oboe, piano and string orch.); 2 piano quintets (1933, 1944); Sonata for flute, violin and piano (1936); *4 Madrigals* for oboe, clarinet and bassoon (1937); Violin Sonatina (1937); *Intermezzo*, 4 pieces for violin and piano (1937); Trio for flute, violin and bassoon (1937); 3 cello sonatas (1939, 1944, 1952); *Bergerettes* for piano trio (1940); *Promenades* for flute, violin and harpsichord (1940); Piano Quartet (1942); *Madrigal Sonata* for flute, violin and piano (1942); *Variations on a Theme of Rossini* for cello and piano (1942); *Madrigal Stan-*

zas, 5 pieces for violin and piano (1943); Trio for flute, cello and piano (1944); Flute Sonata (1945); *Czech Rhapsody* for violin and piano (1945); *Fantasia* for theremin, oboe, string quartet and piano (1945); 2 Duos for violin and viola (*3 Madrigals*, 1947; 1950); Quartet for oboe, violin, cello and piano (1947); *Mazurka-Nocturne* for oboe, 2 violins and cello (1949); *Serenade* for violin, viola, cello and 2 clarinets (1951); Viola Sonata (1955); Clarinet Sonatina (1956); Trumpet Sonatina (1956); *Divertimento* for 2 flutes-à-bec (1957); *Les Fêtes nocturnes* for violin, viola, cello, clarinet, harp and piano (1959); *Variations on a Slovak Theme* for cello and piano (1959).

FOR PIANO: *Puppets*, small pieces for children (in 3 sets, 1914-24); *Scherzo* (1924, discovered 1971); *Fables* (1924); *Film en Miniature* (1925); *3 Czech Dances* (1926); *Le Noël* (*Christmas*, 1927); *4 Movements* (1928); *Borová*, 7 Czech dances (1929; also for orch.); *Préludes (en forme de . . .)* (1929); *Fantaisie* for 2 pianos (1929); *À trois mains* (1930); *Esquisses de danse*, 5 pieces (1932); *Les Ritournelles* (1932); *Dumka* (1936); *Fenêtre sur le jardin* (*The Window in the Garden*), 4 pieces (1938); *Fantasia and Toccata* (1940); *Mazurka* (1941); *Etudes and Polkas* (in 3 books, 1945); *The Fifth Day of the Fifth Moon* (1948); *3 Czech Dances* for 2 pianos (1949); Sonata (1954); *Reminiscences* (1957). FOR HARPSICHORD: *2 Pieces* (1935); Sonata (1958); *Impromptus* (1959). FOR ORGAN: *Vigilie* (1959).

BIBLIOGRAPHY: M. Šafránek, "Bohuslav Martinů," *Musical Quarterly* (July 1943); M. Šafránek, *Bohuslav Martinů: The Man and His Music* (N.Y., 1944); Jan Löwenbach, *Martinů pozdravuje domov* (Prague, 1947); M. Šafránek, *Bohuslav Martinů: His Life and Works* (London, 1962); H. Halbreich, *Bohuslav Martinů* (Zürich, 1968); C. Martinů, *Můj život s Bohuslavem Martinů* (*My Life with Bohuslav Martinů*, Prague, 1971), reminiscences by his wife, Charlotte; B. Large, *Martinů* (1975). See also *"Modern Music" . . . Analytic Index*, compiled by Wayne Shirley, ed. by Wm. and C. Lichtenwanger (N.Y., 1976; pp. 132-33).

Martín y Soler, Vicente, Spanish opera composer; b. Valencia, June 18, 1754; d. St. Petersburg, Jan. 30, 1806. He was church organist at Alicante as a youth, before going to Madrid, where he produced his first opera *I due avari* (1776). He then went to Italy, where he was known as Martini lo Spagnuolo (the Spaniard); wrote operas for Naples, Turin, and Lucca. He secured the services of Da Ponte as librettist, and produced with him the operas *Il Burbero di buon cuore* (*The Grumbler with a Good Heart;* Vienna, Jan. 4, 1786; much acclaimed; revived there, Nov. 9, 1789, with 2 additional airs written expressly for it by Mozart), *Una Cosa rara* (his undoubted masterpiece; Vienna, Nov. 17, 1786; numerous productions in other European capitals; Mozart borrowed a theme from this opera for his *Don Giovanni*), and *L'Arbore di Diana* (Vienna, Oct. 1, 1787). Having achieved fame in Italy, where he was favorably compared with Cimarosa and Paisiello, Martín y Soler was engaged as court composer by Catherine the Great (1788). In St. Petersburg, he produced the operas *Gorye Bogatyr Kosometovitch* (libretto by Catherine II; Feb. 9, 1789), *La Me-*

lomania (Jan. 7, 1790), *Fedul and His Children* (Jan. 16, 1791), and *La Festa del villaggio* (Jan. 26, 1798); the ballets, *Didon abandonnée* (1792), *L'Oracle* (1793), *Amour et Psyché* (1793) and *Tancrède* (1799). In 1795 he went to London; his operas *La Scola de' maritati* (Jan. 27, 1795) and *L'Isola del piacere* (May 26, 1795), both to librettos by Da Ponte, were presented there with excellent success. In 1796 he returned to Russia, and remained there until his death.

BIBLIOGRAPHY: J. R. de Lihory, *La Música en Valencia* (Valencia, 1903); R.-Aloys Mooser, "Un Musicien espagnol en Russie," *Rivista Musicale Italiana* (1936); R.-Aloys Mooser, *Annales de la musique et musiciens en Russie au XVIIIe siècle*, vol. II (Geneva, 1951; pp. 455-61).

Martirano, Salvatore, American composer; b. Yonkers, N.Y., Jan. 12, 1927. He studied piano and composition at the Oberlin Cons. of Music (B.M., 1951); then at the Eastman School of Music, Rochester, N.Y., with Bernard Rogers (M.M., 1952); later went to Italy where he took courses with Luigi Dallapiccola at the Cherubini Cons. of Music in Florence (1952-54). He served in the U.S. Marine Corps; played clarinet and cornet with the Parris Island Marine Band; in 1956-59 he held a fellowship to the American Academy in Rome, and in 1960 received a Guggenheim Fellowship and the American Academy of Arts and Letters Award. In 1968 he joined the faculty of the Univ. of Illinois at Urbana. He writes in a progressive avant-garde idiom, applying the quaquaversal techniques of unmitigated radical modernism, free from any inhibitions.

WORKS: Sextet for wind instruments (1949); Prelude for orch. (1950); Variations for flute and piano (1950); String Quartet No. 1 (1951); *The Magic Stones*, chamber opera after the *Decameron* (Oberlin Cons., April 24, 1952); *Piece for Orchestra* (1952); Violin Sonata (1952); *Contrasto* for orch. (1954); *Chansons Innocentes* for soprano and piano (1957); *O, O, O, O, That Shakespeherian Rag* for mixed chorus and instrumental ensemble (1958); *Cocktail Music* for piano (1962); *Octet* (1963); *Underworld* for 4 actors, 4 percussion instruments, 2 double basses, tenor saxophone and tape (1965); *Ballad* for amplified nite-club singer and instrumental ensemble (1966); *L's.G.A.* for a gas-masked politico, helium bomb, 3-16mm movie projectors and tape (1968); *The Proposal* for tapes and slides (1968); *Action Analysis* for 12 people, Bunny and controller (1968); *Selections* for alto flute, bass clarinet, viola and cello (1970).

Marttinen, Tauno, Finnish composer; b. Helsinki, Sept. 27, 1912. He studied piano, composition and conducting at the Viipuri (Vyborg) Institute of Music and Sibelius Academy in Helsinki; conducted the Hameenlinna (Tavastehus) City Orchestra. A remarkably prolific composer, he began writing music in a traditional "Scandinavian" manner; about 1955 he adopted a serial technique. His adventurous style, marked by a sense of enlightened eclecticism, while drawing his inspiration from national sources, caused some enthusiastic Finnish commentators to compare him to Charles Ives.

WORKS: FOR THE STAGE: *Neiti Gamardin talo*

(The House of Lady Gamard), opera after Balzac (1960–71); *Päällysviitta (The Cloak),* TV opera after Gogol's story (1962–63); *Kihlaus (The Engagement),* opera after Aleksis Kivi (1964); *Apotti ja ikäneito (The Abbot and the Old Maid),* opera based on Balzac (1965); *Hymy tikkaiden juurella (The Smile at the Foot of the Ladder),* ballet after Henry Miller (1965); *Tulitikkuja lainaamassa (Borrowing Matches),* opera after Maiju Lassila (1965); *Lea,* opera after Aleksis Kivi (1967); *Poltettu oranssi (Burnt Orange),* TV opera after Eva-Liisa Manner (1968); *Dorian Grayn muotokuva (The Portrait of Dorian Gray),* ballet after Oscar Wilde (1969); *Lumikuningatar (The Snow Queen),* children's ballet after H. C. Andersen (1970); *Beatrice,* ballet from the play after Dante's *Divine Comedy* (1970; Helsinki, Feb. 24, 1972); *Mestari Patelin (Master Patelin),* chamber opera (1969–72).

FOR ORCH.: 5 symphonies: No. 1 (1957–58); No. 2 (1959); No. 3 (1963); No. 4 (1965; co-winner of first prize in the orch. section of the 1967 Camden Festival of Finnish music held in London); No. 5, *The Shaman* (1967, revised 1972); *Suite* (1960); *Linnunrata (The Milky Way),* variations (1960–61); *Rembrandt* for cello and orch. (1962); Violin Concerto (1958–62); *Panu, tulen jumala (Panu, God of Fire,* 1963); *Manalan linnut (Birds of the Underworld,* 1964); 2 piano concertos (1964, 1973); *Fauni,* fantasy (1965); cello concerto, *Dalai Lama* (1964–66); *Maailman luominen (The Creation of the World),* symph. poem (1966); *Intrada* for wind ensemble (1967); Bassoon Concerto (1966–68); *Mont Saint Michel* (1969); *Vanha linna (An Old Castle,* 1969); *Pentalia* (1969); *Harmonia* (1970; Hämeenlinna, Sept. 27, 1972); *Concert Piece* for trumpet and chamber orch. (1971); *Pohjola (The North)* for wind orch. (1972; Helsinki, Nov. 22, 1972); Flute Concerto (1974).

VOCAL WORKS: *Kokko, ilman lintu (Eagle, Bird of the Air)* for mezzo-soprano and orch. (1956; the first work in his new style); *Tumma maa (Dark Land)* for alto and orch. (1960); *Pidot (Feast)* for soprano, tenor and orch. (1962); *Gabbata,* cantata for reciter, tenor, baritone, 2 choruses and strings (1965); 3 cantatas based on Kalevala themes (1964–65); *Kuoleman unia (Dreams of Death)* for alto and orch. (or piano) (1967); *Ohikulkija (Passer-by)* for soprano and chamber ensemble (1969); *Raahab* for soloists, male chorus and wind orch. (1971); *Ääniä Nooan arkista (Voices in Noah's Ark)* for male chorus and instrumental ensemble (1971).

CHAMBER MUSIC: *Delta* for clarinet and piano (1962); *Hahmoja (Silhouettes)* for piano and percussion (1962); *Loitsu (Incantation)* for percussion trio (1963); *Alfa* for flute and 7 cymbals (1963); *Nonetto* (1963); *Vipusessa käynti (Visiting Vipunen)* for 7 double basses (1969); 2 string quartets (1969, 1970); *Kupoli (Cupola)* for organ and tam-tam (1971); Duo for clarinet and percussion (1971). FOR PIANO: 4 *Preludes* (1965); *Titisee* (1965); *Taara* (1967); sonatina (1970); *Easter* (1971); also *Himalaja* for solo percussionist (1969); numerous songs and a cappella choral works; music for films and plays.

Martucci, Giuseppe, eminent Italian composer and conductor; b. Capua, Jan. 6, 1845; d. Naples, June 1, 1909. A pupil of his father (a trumpet player), he made his debut as a child pianist at the age of 7; at 11 he was admitted to the Cons. di San Pietro a Maiella in Naples; there he studied piano with B. Cesi, and composition with P. Serrao, but left in 1871. Subsequently he traveled as pianist in Italy, France, Germany, and England; in 1880 he became prof. of piano at the Naples Cons.; conducted symph. concerts established by Prince d'Ardore, and was the director of the Neapolitan Società del Quartetto. From 1886 until 1902 he was director of the Bologna Cons.; in 1902 he returned to Naples, and became director of the Cons. there, a post he held until his death. His activities as a fine symph. conductor contributed much to Italian musical culture, and he was greatly esteemed by his colleagues and the public; an ardent admirer of Wagner, he conducted the Italian première of *Tristan und Isolde* (Bologna, June 2, 1888); also led performances of other operas by Wagner. In his own works, he follows the ideals of the German school; the influences of Wagner and Liszt are particularly pronounced. As a composer he was greatly admired by Toscannini who repeatedly performed his orchestral music.

WORKS: 2 symphonies (1895 and 1904); *4 piccoli pezzi* for orch.; 2 piano concertos; Piano Quintet; 2 piano trios; *Momento musicale e minuetto* for string quartet; Cello Sonata; several sets of piano pieces; numerous songs; piano arrangements of classical works.

BIBLIOGRAPHY: R. Prati, *Giuseppe Martucci* (Turin, 1914); a commemorative vol., *Capua a Giuseppe Martucci* (Capua, 1915); Perrachio, "L'opera pianistica di Martucci," *Il Pianoforte* (March 1922); M. Limoncelli, *Giuseppe Martucci* (Naples, 1939); F. Fano, *Giuseppe Martucci* (Milan, 1950; contains complete chronology of life, and exact dates of first performances of works).

Martucci, Paolo, Italian pianist, son of **Giuseppe Martucci;** b. Naples, Oct. 8, 1883. He studied with his father; made his concert debut in Bologna with Tchaikovsky's First Piano Concerto on June 27, 1902; from 1904 to 1911 he lived in England; then went to the U.S.; taught at the Cincinnati Cons. (1911–13); in 1913 moved to N.Y. and taught piano. He celebrated his 94th birthday in 1977 in seeming good health.

Marty, Georges-Eugène, French composer and conductor; b. Paris, May 16, 1860; d. there, Oct. 11, 1908. He attended the Paris Cons. (1872–82), winning the Grand Prix de Rome with the cantata *Edith;* in 1894 was appointed instructor at the Paris Cons.; in 1903 succeeded Taffanel as conductor of the famous Société des Concerts du Conservatoire. He wrote 3 operas *(Le Duc de Ferrare, Daria,* and *La Grande Mademoiselle);* a symph. poem, *Merlin enchanté; Suite romantique* for orch.; choruses, songs, much piano music.

Marvin, Frederick, American pianist; b. Los Angeles, June 11, 1923. He studied voice with his mother and appeared as a boy soprano on the radio; then took piano lessons with Rudolf Serkin at the Curtis Institute of Music in Philadelphia. During World War II he worked as a musical therapist in U.S. Army hospitals; resuming his performing career after 1945 he gave concerts in the U.S.; made his first European tour in 1954. He did research in Spain on the works of Antonio Soler; edited 6 vols. of Soler's music, including an interesting *Fandango*.

Marx, Adolf Bernhard, eminent German theorist and writer; b. Halle, May 15, 1795; d. Berlin, May 17, 1866. Intended for the law, he matriculated at the Univ. of Halle, but likewise studied music with Türk, and gave up a subsequent legal appointment at Naumburg to gratify his love for art. He continued the study of composition in Berlin with Zelter; in 1824 he founded the *Berliner Allgemeine musikalische Zeitung* (with the publisher Schlesinger); he edited this publication with ability, and proved himself a conspicuous advocate of German music; however, the publication ceased in 1830. After taking the degree of Dr. phil at Marburg (1827), Marx lectured on music at the Berlin Univ.; was appointed prof. in 1830; became music director of the scholastic choir there in 1832. He was cofounder (with Kullak and Stern) of the Berlin Cons. (1850), retiring in 1856 to devote himself to literary and university work. He was an intimate friend of the Mendelssohn family, and advised young Mendelssohn in musical matters.

WRITINGS: His writings on musical theory and esthetics include: *Die Lehre von der musikalischen Komposition* (4 vols., 1837–47; several times reprinted; new eds. by Hugo Riemann, 1887–90); *Allgemeine Musiklehre* (1839; 10th ed., 1884; transl. into English); *Über Malerei in der Tonkunst* (1828); *Über die Geltung Händelscher Sologesänge für unsere Zeit* (1829); *Die alte Musiklehre im Streit mit unserer Zeit* (1841); *Die Musik des 19. Jahrhunderts und ihre Pflege* (1855); *Ludwig van Beethoven, Leben und Schaffen* (1859; 6th ed., by G. Behnke, 1911); *Gluck und die Oper* (1863; 2 vols.); *Anleitung zum Vortrag Beethoven'scher Klavierwerke* (1863; new ed. by E. Schmitz, 1912; English transl., 1895); *Erinnerungen aus meinem Leben* (1865; 2 vols.); *Das Ideal und die Gegenwart* (1867). A collection of his essays was publ. by L. Hirschberg as *Über Tondichter und Tonkunst* (3 vols., 1912–22). While Marx was greatly esteemed as a music theorist, his own compositions were unsuccessful; he wrote a Singspiel *Jery und Bätely,* after Goethe (1824), the oratorio *Mose* (1841), etc.

BIBLIOGRAPHY: G. F. Selle, *Aus Adolf Bernhard Marx's literarischem Nachlass* (Berlin, 1898); L. Hirschberg, "Der Tondichter Adolf Bernhard Marx," *Sammelbände der Internationalen Musik-Gesellschaft* (1908).

Marx, (Walter) Burle, Brazilian conductor; b. São Paulo, July 23, 1902. He studied piano with his mother; then went to Germany where he took lessons with Barth and Kwast; also studied composition with Reznicek. In 1930 he returned to Brazil, where he became active primarily as conductor. He conducted a concert of Brazilian music at the N.Y. World's Fair in 1939; after 1953 taught at the Settlement Music School in Philadelphia. He wrote several effective orchestral pieces; contributed articles on Brazilian music to various publications.

Marx, Joseph, Austrian composer and pedagogue; b. Graz, May 11, 1882; d. there, Sept. 3, 1964. He studied with Degner; musicology at the Univ. of Graz, taking the degree of Dr. phil. with the dissertation *Über die Funktionen von Intervallen, Harmonie und Melodie beim Erfassen von Tonkomplexen.* In 1914 he went to Vienna, where he taught at the State Academy; was its director (1922–24); then rector of the Hochschule für Musik in Vienna (1924–27); for 3 years was adviser to the Turkish government on music education, and traveled to Ankara; later resumed his teaching in Vienna; from 1947 taught at the Univ. of Graz. As a composer, he styled himself a "Romantic Realist."

WORKS: *Eine Herbst-Symphonie* (1922); *Eine symphonische Nachtmusik* (1926); *Nordlands-rhapsodie* (1929); *Alt-Wiener Serenaden* (1942); *Feste im Herbst* (1946); *Castelli romani,* for piano and orch. (1931); *Verklärtes Jahr,* for voice and orch. (1932); *Quartett in Form einer Rhapsodie,* for violin, viola, cello, and piano; String Quartet "In modo antico" (1940); String Quartet "In modo classico" (1942); 2 violin sonatas; about 150 songs; etc. He published *Betrachtungen eines romantischen Realisten* (Vienna, 1947).

BIBLIOGRAPHY: J. Bistron, *Joseph Marx* (Vienna, 1923); A. Liess, *Joseph Marx: Leben und Werk* (Graz, 1943); E. Werba, *Joseph Marx: Eine Studie* (Vienna, 1964).

Marx, Karl, German composer and pedagogue; b. Munich, Nov. 12, 1897. He served in the German Army during World War I and was a prisoner of war in England; after the Armistice, studied with Carl Orff, Hausegger, Beer-Walbrunn, and Schwickerath. In 1924 he was appointed to the faculty of the Akademie der Tonkunst in Munich; in 1928 became the conductor of the Bach Society in Munich; from 1939 to 1946 was instructor at the Hochschule für Musikerziehung in Graz; subsequently taught at the Hochschule für Musik in Stuttgart (1946–66). A master of German polyphony, Marx excels in choral composition, both sacred and secular; he is greatly esteemed as a pedagogue.

WORKS: FOR ORCH: Concerto for 2 Violins and Orch. (1926); Piano Concerto (1929, revised 1959); Viola Concerto (1929); *Passacaglia* (1932); Violin Concerto (1935); Concerto for Flute and Strings (1937); *15 Variations on a German Folk Song* (1938); *Musik nach alpenländischen Volksliedern* for strings (1940); *Festival Prelude* (1956); Concerto for String Orch. (1964; a reworking of his 1932 *Passacaglia*); *Fantasia sinfonica* (1967, revised 1969); *Fantasia concertante* for violin, cello and orch. (1972).

VOCAL MUSIC: several large cantatas, including *Die heiligen drei Könige* (1936); *Rilke-Kantate* (1942); *Und endet doch alles mit Frieden* (1952), *Raube das Licht aus dem Rachen der Schlange* (1957), *Auftrag und Besinnung* (1961); chamber cantatas, including *Die unendliche Woge* (1930); also cantatas for special seasons, children's cantatas and the like; a cappella pieces; songs, many with orch., including *Rilke-Kreis* for voice and piano (1927; version for mezzo-soprano and chamber orch., 1952) and *3 Songs,* to texts by Stefan George, for baritone and chamber orch. (1934). Also, *Fantasy and Fugue* for string quartet (1927); *Variations* for organ (1933); *Divertimento* for 16 winds (1934); *Turmmusik* for 3 trumpets and 3 trombones (1938); *Divertimento* for flute, violin, viola, cello and piano (1942); 6 sonatinas for various instrumental combinations (1948–51); *Kammermusik* for 7 instruments (1955); Trio for piano, flute and cello (1962); Cello Sonata (1964); *Fantasy* for solo violin (1966); *Partita über "Ein' feste Burg"* for string quartet or string orch. (1967); Wind Quintet (1973).

BIBLIOGRAPHY: R. von Saalfeld, "Karl Marx," *Zeitschrift für Musik* (May 1931).

Marxsen, Eduard, German organist and teacher; b. Nienstädten, near Altona, July 23, 1806; d. Altona, Nov. 18, 1887. He was a pupil of his father, an organist; later studied with Seyfried and Bocklet in Vienna; then returned to Hamburg, where he became well known as a pedagogue. He was the first teacher of Brahms; composed about 70 works in various genres.

Maryon, Edward (full name **John Edward Maryon-d'Aulby**), English composer; b. London, April 3, 1867; d. there, Jan. 31, 1954. He began to compose early in life; went to Paris, where his first opera, *L'Odalisque,* won the Gold Medal at the Exposition of 1889; however, he regarded the work as immature and destroyed the score. In 1891 he studied with Max Pauer in Dresden; later took lessons with F. Wüllner in Cologne; he then lived in France; from 1914–19 he was in Montclair, N.J., where he established a conservatory with a fund for exchange of music students between England and America; in 1933 he returned to London. Besides *L'Odalisque,* Maryon wrote the following operas: *Paolo and Francesca; La Robe de Plume; The Smelting Pot; The Prodigal Son; Werewolf; Rembrandt; Greater Love;* and *Abelard and Heloise.* In his opera *Werewolf* he applied a curious system of musical symbolism, in which the human part was characterized by the diatonic scale and the lupine self by the whole-tone scale; Maryon made a claim of priority in using the whole-tone scale consistently as a leading motive in an opera. His *magnum opus* was a grandiose operatic heptalogy under the title, *The Cycle of Life,* comprising seven mystical dramas: *Lucifer, Cain, Krishna, Magdalen, Sangraal, Psyche,* and *Nirvana.* He further wrote a symph. poem, *The Feather Robe,* subtitled *A Legend of Fujiyama* (1905), which he dedicated to the Emperor of Japan; and *Armageddon Requiem* (1916), dedicated to the dead of World War I. Of his works, only the following were published: the *Beatitudes* for baritone, double chorus, and orch. (1907), *Six Melodies* for voice and piano (1907), and *The Paean of Asaph,* a festival cantata (1931). After Maryon's death, his complete manuscripts were donated by his heirs to the Boston Public Library. Maryon developed a theory of universal art, in which colors were associated with sounds; an outline of this theory was published in his pamphlet *Marcotone* (N.Y., 1919).

BIBLIOGRAPHY: E. E. Hipsher, *American Opera and Its Composers* (Philadelphia, 1934; pp. 313–16).

Marzo, Eduardo, Italian pianist, organist, and composer; b. Naples, Nov. 29, 1852; d. New York, June 7, 1929. As a boy of 15, he settled in N.Y., and appeared in concerts as a pianist; was accompanist to many celebrated artists, among them Carlotta Patti, Mario, and Sarasate on their American tours. From 1878 he played the organ in various New York churches. He held numerous honorary orders, conferred on him by the King of Italy; was co-founder of the American Guild of Organists. He wrote many Masses and other sacred choral works; cantatas; operettas; songs; piano pieces. See F. H. Martens, in *Dictionary of American Biography,* VI.

Mascagni, Pietro, famous Italian opera composer; b. Leghorn, Dec. 7, 1863; d. Rome, Aug. 2, 1945. His father was a baker who wished Mascagni to continue in that trade, but yielded to his son's determination to study music. He took lessons with Alfredo Soffredini in his native town, until he was enabled, by the aid of an interested patron, to enter the Cons. of Milan, where he studied with Ponchielli and Saladino. However, he became impatient of the school discipline, and left the Cons. in 1884. The following year he obtained a post as conductor of the municipal band in the small town of Cerignola. He composed industriously; in 1888 he sent the manuscript of his 1-act opera *Cavalleria Rusticana* to the music publisher Sonzogno for a competition, and won first prize. The opera was performed at the Costanzi Theater in Rome on May 17, 1890, with sensational success; the dramatic story of village passion and Mascagni's emotional score, laden with luscious music, combined to produce an extraordinary appeal to opera lovers. The short opera made the tour of the world stages with amazing rapidity, productions being staged all over Europe and America with never-failing success; the opera was usually presented in 2 parts, separated by an "intermezzo sinfonico" (which became a popular orchestral number performed separately). *Cavalleria Rusticana* marked the advent of the operatic style known as "verismo," in which stark realism was the chief aim, and the dramatic development condensed to enhance the impressions. When, 2 years later, another "veristic" opera, Leoncavallo's *Pagliacci,* was taken by Sonzogno, the 2 operas became twin attractions on a single bill. Ironically, Mascagni could never duplicate or even remotely approach the success of his first production, although he continued to compose industriously, and opera houses all over the world were only too eager to stage his successive operas. Thus, his opera *Le Maschere* was produced on Jan. 17, 1901, at six of the most important Italian opera houses simultaneously (Rome, Milan, Turin, Genoa, Venice, Verona); it was produced 2 days later in Naples. Mascagni himself conducted the première in Rome, but the opera failed to fire the imagination of the public; it was produced in a revised form in Turin 15 years later (June 7, 1916), but was not established in the repertory even in Italy. In 1902 Mascagni made a tour of the U.S., conducting his *Cavalleria Rusticana* and other operas, but owing to mismanagement, the visit proved a fiasco; a South American tour in 1911 was more successful. Mascagni also appeared frequently as conductor of symph. concerts. In 1890 he was made Knight of the Crown of Italy; in 1929 he was elected member of the Academy. At various times he also was engaged in teaching; from 1895 until 1902 he was director of the Rossini Cons. in Pesaro. His last years were darkened by the inglorious role that Mascagni assumed in his ardent support of the Fascist regime, so that he was rejected by many of his old friends, including Toscanini. It was only after his death that his errors of moral judgment were forgiven; his centennial was widely celebrated in Italy in 1963.

WORKS: operas: *Pinotta* (written in 1880; score recovered after 50 years, and first produced in San Remo, March 23, 1932); *Guglielmo Ratcliff* (c.1885; Milan, Feb. 16, 1895); *Cavalleria Rusticana* (Rome, May 17, 1890); *L'Amico Fritz* (Rome, Oct. 31, 1891; the only fairly successful opera by Mascagni after *Cavalleria Rusticana;* still performed in Italy); *I Rantzau* (Florence, Nov. 10, 1892); *Silvano* (Milan, March 25, 1895); *Zanetto* (Pesaro, March 2, 1896); *Iris* (Rome, Nov. 22, 1898); *Le Maschere* (première in 6 cities, Jan. 17, 1901); *Amica* (Monte Carlo, March 16, 1905); *Isabeau* (Buenos Aires, June 2, 1911); *Parisina* (Milan, Dec. 15, 1913); *Lodoletta* (Rome, April 30, 1917); *Scampolo* (1921); *Il piccolo Marat* (Rome, May 2, 1921); *Nerone* (Milan, Jan. 16, 1935); *I Brianchi ed i Neri* (1940). Other works include *Poema Leopardiano* (for the centenary of G. Leopardi, 1898); Hymn in honor of Admiral Dewey (July 1899); *Rapsodia Satanica* for orch. (music for a film, Rome, July 2, 1917); *Davanti Santa Teresa* (Rome, Aug. 1923); chamber music.

BIBLIOGRAPHY: G. Monaldi, *Pietro Mascagni: L'uomo e l'artista* (Rome, 1899); G. Marvin, *Pietro Mascagni: Biografia aneddotica* (Palermo, 1904); G. Bastianelli, *Pietro Mascagni, con nota delle opere* (Naples, 1910); E. Pompei, *Pietro Mascagni, nella vita e nell'arte* (Rome, 1912); G. Orsini, *L'arte di Pietro Mascagni* (Milan, 1912); G. Scuderi, *Iris* (1923); T. Mantovani, *Iris* (1930); A. Donno, *Modernità di Pietro Mascagni* (1931); G. Cogo, *Il nostro Mascagni* (1931); "Bibliografia delle opere di Pietro Mascagni," *Bolletino Bibliografico Musicale* (Milan, 1932); A. de Donno, *Mascagni nel 900 musicale* (Rome, 1935); A. Jeri, *Mascagni, 15 Opere, 1000 Episodi* (Milan, 1940); D. Cellamare, *Mascagni e la "Cavalleria" visti da Cerignola* (Rome, 1941); *Mascagni parla* (Rome, 1945). Numerous publications were issued on Mascagni's centennial in 1963: *Comitato nazionale delle onoranze a Pietro Mascagni nel primo centenario della nascità* (Livorno, 1963); M. Morini, ed., *Pietro Mascagni*, 2 vols. (Milan, 1964); G. Gavazzeni, *Discorso per Mascagni nel centenario della nascità* (Rome, 1964); D. Cellamare, *Pietro Mascagni* (Rome, 1965).

Maschera, Fiorenzo, Italian organist and composer of the late 16th century. He was a pupil of Merulo; on Aug. 1, 1557, he became organist at the Cathedral of Brescia, succeeding Merulo in this post. He publ. instrumental *Canzoni a 4 voci* (Brescia, 1584; reprinted in Venice, 1588 and 1593); in this collection are some of the earliest examples of the ensemble canzona, with sections organized in terms of repetition. One such work is included in Davison and Apel, *Historical Anthology of Music,* vol. I (Cambridge, Mass., 1949).

Mascheroni, Edoardo, Italian conductor and composer; b. Milan, Sept. 4, 1852; d. Ghirla, near Varese, March 4, 1941. As a boy, he showed special interest in mathematics and literature; wrote literary essays for the journal *La vita nuova* before he decided to study music seriously; took lessons with Boucheron in Mi-

lan, and composed various pieces. In 1883 he began a career as conductor, and it was in that capacity that he distinguished himself. He was first a theater conductor in Leghorn; then went to Rome, where he established his reputation as an opera conductor. Upon Verdi's explicit request, he was selected to conduct the première of *Falstaff* at La Scala (1893); he remained on the staff of La Scala until 1897; then conducted in Germany, Spain, and South America; also was successful as a symph. conductor. He wrote 2 operas: *Lorenza* (Rome, April 13, 1901) and *La Perugina* (Naples, April 24, 1909).

Mašek, Vincenz, Bohemian pianist; b. Zwikovecz, April 5, 1755; d. Prague, Nov. 15, 1831. He was a pupil of Seegert and Dussek; became an accomplished player of the piano and harmonica; after long tours, he settled in Prague as an organist and music-dealer. His brother **Paul Mašek** (1761–1826) was a good pianist and a teacher in Vienna.

Masetti, Enzo, Italian composer; b. Bologna, Aug. 19, 1893; d. Rome, Feb. 11, 1961. He studied with Franco Alfano at the Liceo Musicale in Bologna; he devoted his life mainly to film music; from 1942 until his death he was connected with the Centro Sperimentale di Cinematografia in Rome; publ. *La musica nel film* (Rome, 1950) and composed about 60 film scores. He wrote several dramatic fables, among them *La fola delle tre ochette* (Bologna, 1928), *La mosca mora* (Bologna, 1930), and *La bella non può dormire* (Bologna, 1957). His other works included *Contrasti,* for orch. (1921); *Il gioco del cucù,* for piano and orch. (1928); a number of piano pieces and songs.

Mason, Colin, English music critic; b. Northampton, Jan. 26, 1924; d. London, Feb. 6, 1971. He studied at the Trinity College of Music in London; after the war he received a Hungarian state scholarship for the purpose of writing a book on Béla Bartók and entered as a student at the Budapest Academy of Music (1947–49). Returning to England he was the music critic of the *Manchester Guardian* (1951–64) and of the *Daily Telegraph* (from 1964); also edited the music magazine *Tempo* (from 1962); was editor of the revised printing of Cobbett's *Cyclopedic Survey of Chamber Music* (London, 1963; with a supplementary 3rd vol.).

Mason, Daniel Gregory, eminent American composer and educator; b. Brookline, Mass., Nov. 20, 1873; d. Greenwich, Conn., Dec. 4, 1953. He was a scion of a famous family of American musicians; grandson of **Lowell Mason** and nephew of **William Mason;** his father, **Henry Mason,** was a co-founder of the piano manufacturing firm Mason & Hamlin. He entered Harvard Univ., where he studied with John K. Paine (B.A., 1895); after graduation he continued his studies with Arthur Whiting (piano), P. Goetschius (theory), and Chadwick (orchestration). Still feeling the necessity for improvement of his technique as composer, he went to Paris, where he took courses with Vincent d'Indy. Returning to America, he became active as teacher and composer. In 1910 he became a member of the faculty of Columbia Univ.; in 1929, appointed

MacDowell Professor of Music; he was chairman of the Music Dept. until 1940, and continued to teach there until 1942, when he retired. As a teacher, he developed a high degree of technical ability in his students; as a composer, he represented a conservative trend in American music; while an adherent to the idea of an American national style, his conception was racially and regionally narrow, accepting only the music of Anglo-Saxon New England and "the old South"; he was an outspoken opponent of the "corrupting" and "foreign" influences of 20th-century Afro-American and Jewish-American music. His ideals were the German masters of the Romantic school; but there is an admixture of Impressionistic colors in his orchestration; his harmonies are full and opulent; his melodic writing expressive and songful. The lack of strong individuality, however, has resulted in the virtual disappearance of his music from the active repertory, with the exception of the overture *Chanticleer* and the clarinet sonata.

WORKS: FOR ORCH.: Symph. No. 1, in C minor (Philadelphia, Feb. 18, 1916; revised radically, and perf. in a new version, N.Y., Dec. 1, 1922); *Chanticleer*, a festival overture (Cincinnati, Nov. 23, 1928); Symph. No. 2, in A (Cincinnati, Nov. 7, 1930); Symph. No. 3, *Lincoln* (N.Y., Nov. 17, 1937); *Prelude and Fugue*, for piano and orch. (Chicago, March 4, 1921); *Scherzo-Caprice*, for chamber orch. (N.Y., Jan. 2, 1917); *Suite after English Folksongs* (1934); *Russians*, for baritone and orch. (1918); CHAMBER MUSIC: Quartet for piano and strings (1912); *Pastorale*, for violin, clarinet, and piano (1913); Sonata for clarinet and piano (1915); *String Quartet on Negro Themes* (1919); 3 pieces for flute, harp, and string quartet (1922); *Variations on a Theme of John Powell*, for string quartet (1926); *Divertimento*, for flute, oboe, clarinet, horn, and bassoon (1927); *Fanny Blair*, folksong fantasy for string quartet (1929); *Serenade*, for string quartet (1932); *Sentimental Sketches*, 4 short pieces for violin, cello, and piano (1935); *Variations on a Quiet Theme* (1939); a choral work, *Songs of the Countryside* (1926).

WRITINGS: *From Grieg to Brahms* (1902; revised ed., 1930); *Beethoven and His Forerunners* (1904); *The Romantic Composers* (1906; reprint, Westport, Conn., 1970); *The Appreciation of Music* (1907; with T. W. Surette); *The Orchestral Instruments And What They Do* (1909; reprint, Westport, Conn., 1971); *A Guide to Music* (1909); *A Neglected Sense in Piano Playing* (1912); *Great Modern Composers* (1916); *Short Studies of Great Masterpieces* (1917); *Contemporary Composers* (1918); *Music as a Humanity: and Other Essays* (1921); *From Song to Symphony* (1924); *Artistic Ideals* (1925); *The Dilemma of American Music* (1928; reprint, Westport, Conn., 1970); *Tune In, America!* (1931; reprint, 1969); *The Chamber Music of Brahms* (1933); *Music in My Time and Other Reminiscences* (1938; reprint, Westport, Conn., 1970); *The Quartets of Beethoven* (1947); contributed articles to the *Musical Quarterly* and other periodicals; was editor-in-chief of *The Art of Music*.

BIBLIOGRAPHY: B. C. Tuthill, "Daniel Gregory Mason," *Musical Quarterly* (Jan. 1948); Sister Mary Justina Klein, *The Contribution of Daniel Gregory Mason to American Music* (Washington, 1957); H.

Earle Johnson, in *Dictionary of American Biography, Supplement V* (N.Y., 1977).

Mason, Lowell, American composer, organist, and conductor; b. Medfield, Mass., Jan. 8, 1792; d. Orange, N.J., Aug. 11, 1872. A self-taught musician, at 16 he directed the church choir at Medfield; 1812–27, bank clerk at Savannah, Ga., also teaching and conducting; 1827, went to Boston, becoming church organist; president of the Handel and Haydn Soc. (1827–32); established classes on Pestalozzi's system, teaching it privately from 1829 and in the public schools from 1838. He founded the Boston Academy of Music in 1832, with George J. Webb; 1835, made honorary Mus. Doc. by N.Y. Univ. (one of the 1st instances of the conferring of that degree in America); studied pedagogic methods in Zürich in 1837; publ. his experiences in *Musical Letters from Abroad* (N.Y., 1853); 1851, went to N.Y.; after 1854, resided in Orange, N.J. He became wealthy through the sale of his many collections of music: *Handel and Haydn Society's Collection of Church Music* (1822; 16 later eds.); *Juvenile Psalmist* (1829); *Juvenile Lyre* (1830); *Lyra Sacra* (1832); *Sabbath School Songs* (1836); *Boston Academy Collection of Church Music* (1836); *Boston Anthem Book* (1839); *The Psaltery* (1845); *Cantica Laudis* (1850); *New Carmina Sacra* (1852); *Normal Singer* (1856); *Song Garden* (3 parts; 1864–65); etc. Many of his own hymn tunes, including *Missionary Hymn (From Greenland's Icy Mountains)*, *Olivet*, *Boylston*, *Bethany*, *Hebron*, and *Olmutz*, are still found in hymnals. His valuable library, including 830 MSS and 700 vols. of hymnology, was given to Yale College after his death.

BIBLIOGRAPHY: T. F. Seward, *The Educational Work of Dr. Lowell Mason* (Boston, 1885); F. J. Metcalf, *American Writers and Compilers of Sacred Music* (1925); E. B. Birge, *History of Public School Music in the U.S.* (1928); H. L. Mason, *Hymn Tunes of Lowell Mason, a Bibliography* (Cambridge, Mass., 1944); A. L. Rich, *Lowell Mason; The Father of Singing Among the Children* (Chapel Hill, N.C., 1946); J. V. Higginson, "Notes on Lowell Mason's Hymn Tunes," *Hymn* (April 1967); E. J. O'Meara, "The Lowell Mason Library," *Notes* (Dec. 1971).

Mason, Luther Whiting, American music educator; b. Turner, Maine, April 3, 1828; d. Buckfield, Maine, July 4, 1896. He was chiefly self-taught; 1853, superintendent of music in Louisville schools, later in Cincinnati, where he invented the 'National System' of music charts and books, which had instant success, and made him famous. He settled in Boston 1865, and reformed music instruction in the primary schools; in 1879 he was invited by the Japanese government to supervise music in the schools of Japan, where he labored 3 years with notable results (school music in Japan is termed "Mason-song"). He spent some time in Germany perfecting his principal work, *The National Music-Course*.

Mason, William, American pianist and pedagogue; b. Boston, Mass., Jan. 24, 1829; d. New York, July 14, 1908. The son of **Lowell Mason,** his opportunities for study were excellent; after piano lessons from Henry Schmidt in Boston, and frequent public appearances (first in Boston, March 7, 1846, at an Academy of Music concert), he studied in Leipzig (1849) under Moscheles, Hauptmann, and Richter, in Prague under Dreyschock, and under Liszt at Weimar. He played in Weimar, Prague, and Frankfurt; 1853, in London; 1854–55, in various American towns, settling 1855 in New York. With Theodore Thomas, Bergmann, and Matzka, he founded the "Mason and Thomas Soirées of Chamber Music," a series of classic concerts continued until 1868; thereafter he won wide celebrity as a composer and teacher. In 1872 Yale College conferred on him the degree of Mus. Doc. His principal textbook for piano playing is *Touch and Technic* (op. 44); others are *A Method for the Piano*, with E. S. Hoadley (1867); *System for Beginners* (1871); and *Mason's Pianoforte-Technics* (1878). His compositions, classical in form and refined in style and treatment, include a *Serenata* for cello and piano; some 40 numbers for piano solo, including *Amitié pour moi, Silver Spring, Monody, Rêverie poétique,* etc.; publ. *Memories of a Musical Life* (1901). See F. H. Martens, in *Dictionary of American Biography*, Vol. VI.

Mason & Hamlin Co., celebrated firm of piano manufacturers. The house was founded as the M. & H. Organ Co. in Boston in 1854 by **Henry Mason,** a son of **Dr. Lowell Mason,** and **Emmons Hamlin.** The latter, a brilliant mechanic, turned his attention to improving the quality of the reeds and obtaining great variety of tonal color, with the result that in 1861 the firm introduced the American Cabinet Organ. The firm became internationally famous, when at the Paris Exposition of 1867 its organs were awarded the 1st prize over numerous European competitors; since then they have exhibited at every important expositon in Europe and America. In 1882 they began the construction of pianofortes, introducing a new system of stringing which found immediate favor; of several improvements patented by them the most important is the Tension-Resonator (1902; described in the *Scientific American*, Oct. 11, 1902), a device for preserving the tension of the sounding board. The firm subsequently became a subsidiary of the Aeolian American Corporation and eventually of the American Piano Corp. **Henry Lowell Mason,** son of the founder, was president of the firm until 1929. He died in Boston, Oct. 18, 1957, at the age of 93.

Massa, Juan Bautista, Argentinian composer; b. Buenos Aires, Oct. 29, 1885; d. Rosario, March 7, 1938. He studied violin and composition; became a choral conductor; moved to Rosario, where he was active as a teacher.
WORKS: the operas *Zoraide* (Buenos Aires, May 15, 1909), *L'Evaso* (Rosario, June 23, 1922), *La Magdalena* (Buenos Aires, Nov. 9, 1929); 3 operettas: *Esmeralda* (1903); *Triunfo del Corazón* (1910), and *La Eterna Historia* (1911); a ballet, *El Cometa* (Buenos Aires, Nov. 8, 1932); symph. poem *La Muerte del Inca* (Buenos Aires, Oct. 15, 1932); 2 Argentine Suites for orch.; other pieces on native themes.
BIBLIOGRAPHY: F. C. Lange, "Juan Bautista Massa," *Boletín Latino-Americano de Música* (Dec. 1938).

Massa, Nicolò, Italian composer; b. Calice Ligure, Oct. 26, 1854; d. Genoa, Jan. 24, 1894. He studied at the Milan Cons. with Bazzini; wrote the operas *Aldo e Clarenza* (Milan, April 11, 1878), *Il Conte di Chatillon* (Reggio Emilia, Feb. 11, 1882), *Salammbò* (Milan, April 15, 1886; his most successful opera), *Eros* (posthumous; Florence, May 21, 1895); also composed an *Inno al Lavoro* (1892).

Massarani, Renzo, Italian composer; b. Mantua, March 26, 1898; d. Rio de Janeiro, March 28, 1975. He studied in Rome with Respighi; in 1935 went to Rio de Janeiro where he was active as a music critic and teacher. He wrote mainly for the stage; among his works are the ballets *Guerin meschino* (Darmstadt, 1928), *Boè* (Bergamo, 1937); violin pieces and songs.
BIBLIOGRAPHY: "Renzo Massarani," *Il Pianoforte* (Dec. 1924).

Massart, Lambert-Joseph, eminent violinist; b. Liège, July 19, 1811; d. Paris, Feb. 13, 1892. He was a pupil of R. Kreutzer at Paris, where he was refused admission to the Cons., as a foreigner, by Cherubini, but became so celebrated as a teacher that he was appointed professor of violin there (1843–90). Wieniawski, Marsick, Sarasate, and Teresina Tua were his pupils. His wife, **Louise-Aglaë Massart** (b. Paris, June 10, 1827; d. there, July 26, 1887), was a pianist and teacher. In 1875 she succeeded Farrenc as teacher at the Paris Cons.

Massart, Nestor-Henri-Joseph, Belgian tenor; b. Ciney, Oct. 20, 1849; d. Ostend, Dec. 19, 1899. He was an officer in the Belgian Army when his remarkable voice attracted the attention of the royal family, through whose influence he was granted leave of absence for study. He sang with success in Brussels, Lyons, Cairo, New Orleans, San Francisco, and Mexico.

Massé, Victor (real name **Félix-Marie**), French opera composer; b. Lorient, Morbihan, March 7, 1822; d. Paris, July 5, 1884. He was a child prodigy; was accepted at the Paris Cons. at the age of 12, and studied with Zimmerman (piano) and Halévy (composition); in 1844 he won the Grand Prix de Rome with the cantata *La Renégat de Tanger*. While in Rome, he sent home an Italian opera, *La Favorita e la schiava*. After his return, his *romances* had great vogue, and his first French opera, *La Chambre gothique* (Paris, 1849), was fairly successful. In 1866 he succeeded Leborne as prof. of counterpoint at the Paris Cons.; and in 1872 he was elected member of the Institut de France, as successor to Auber. His most successful light opera was *Les Noces de Jeannette* (Paris, Feb. 4, 1853); the list of his other operas, performed in Paris, includes: *La Chanteuse voilée* (Nov. 26, 1850), *Galathée* (April 14, 1852), *La Reine Topaze* (Dec. 27, 1856), *La Fiancée du Diable* (June 3, 1854), *Miss Fauvette* (Feb. 13, 1855), *Les Saisons* (Dec. 22, 1855), *Fior d'Aliza* (Feb. 5, 1866), and *Le Fils du Brigadier* (Feb. 25, 1867); his last opera *Une Nuit de Cléopatre,* was performed posthumously (April 25, 1885).
BIBLIOGRAPHY: L. Delibes, *Notice sur Victor Massé* (Paris, 1885); J. G. M. Ropartz, *Victor Massé*

(Paris, 1887); C. Delaborde, *Notice sur la vie et les ouvrages de Victor Massé* (Paris, 1888).

Masselos, William, American pianist; b. Niagara Falls, N.Y., Aug. 11, 1920. He studied piano with Carl Friedberg at the Juilliard School of Music, N.Y. (1932–42) and ensemble playing with Felix Salmond and Louis Persinger; music theory with Bernard Wagenaar. He made his professional debut in N.Y. in 1939; was soloist with the N.Y. Philharmonic in 1952 under Mitropoulos; then played with Monteux in 1959 and with Bernstein in 1973. He served as pianist in residence at Indiana Univ. (1955–57); at Catholic Univ. of America in Washington (1965–71); and at the Georgia State Univ. in Atlanta (1972–75); in 1976 he was appointed to the piano faculty of the Juilliard School of Music.

Massenet, Jules (-Émile-Frédéric), illustrious French composer; b. Montaud, near St.-Etienne, Loire, May 12, 1842; d. Paris, Aug. 13, 1912. At the age of 9 he was admitted to the Paris Cons.; studied with Laurent (piano), Reber (harmony), Savard and Ambroise Thomas (composition); after taking 1st prizes for piano playing and fugue (1859), he carried off the Grand Prix de Rome with the cantata *David Rizzio* (1863). In 1878 he was appointed prof. of composition at the Paris Cons., and at the same time was elected member of the Académie des Beaux-Arts; he continued to teach at the Paris Cons. until his death; among his students were Alfred Bruneau, Gabriel Pierné, and Gustave Charpentier. As a pedagogue he exercised a profound influence on French opera, and it is only with the decisive turn towards modern music that his influence began to decline. After Gounod, Massenet was the most popluar French opera composer; he possessed a natural sense of graceful melody in a distinctive French style; his best operas, *Manon, Werther,* and *Thaïs,* enjoy tremendous popularity in France, and have become favorites on opera stages all over the world; the celebrated *Meditation* for violin and orch. from *Thaïs* is a regular repertory number among violinists.
WORKS: OPERAS: *La Grand'-Tante* (Paris, April 3, 1867); *Don César de Bazan* (Paris, Nov. 30, 1872); *Le Roi de Lahore* (Paris, April 27, 1877); *Hérodiade* (Brussels, Dec. 19, 1881); *Manon* (Paris, Jan. 19, 1884); *Le Cid* (Paris, Nov. 30, 1885); *Esclarmonde* (Paris, May 14, 1889); *Le Mage* (Paris, March 16, 1891); *Werther* (Vienna, Feb. 16, 1892); *Thaïs* (Paris, March 16, 1894); *Le Portrait de Manon* (Paris, May 8, 1894); *La Navarraise* (London, June 20, 1894); *Sapho* (Paris, Nov. 27, 1897); *Cendrillon* (Paris, May 24, 1899); *Grisélidis* (Paris, Nov. 20, 1901); *Le Jongleur de Notre Dame* (Monte Carlo, Feb. 18, 1902); *Chérubin* (Monte Carlo, Feb. 14, 1905); *Ariane* (Paris, Oct. 31, 1906); *Thérèse* (Monte Carlo, Feb. 7, 1907); *Bacchus* (Paris, May 5, 1909); *Don Quichotte* (Monte Carlo, Feb. 19, 1910); *Roma* (Monte Carlo, Feb. 7, 1912); posthumous: *Panurge* (Paris, April 25, 1913); *Cléopatre* (Monte Carlo, Feb. 23, 1914); *Amadis* (Monte Carlo, April 1, 1922). INCIDENTAL MUSIC: *Les Érynnies* (1873); *Un Drame sous Philippe II* (1875); *Nana-Sahib* (1883); *Théodora* (1884); *Le Crocodile* (1886); *Phèdre* (1900); *Le Grillon du foyer* (1904); *Le Manteau du Roi*

(1907); *Perce-Neige et les sept gnomes* (1909). BALLETS: *Le Carillon* (1892); *La Cigale* (1904); *Espada* (1908). ORATORIOS: *Marie-Magdeleine* (1873); *Ève* (1875); *La Terre Promise* (1900). OTHER CHORAL WORKS: *Narcisse; La Vierge; Biblis.* FOR ORCH.: 7 suites: No. 1 (1865); No. 2, *Scènes hongroises* (1871); No. 3, *Scènes dramatiques* (1873); No. 4, *Scènes pittoresques* (1874); No. 5, *Scènes napolitaines* (1876); No. 6, *Scènes de Féérie* (1879); No. 7, *Scènes alsaciennes* (1881); 3 overtures: *Ouverture de Concert* (1863); *Phèdre* (1873); *Brumaire* (1899); a symph. poem, *Visions* (1890); *Parade militaire* (1887); *Devant la Madone* (1897); *Marche solennelle* (1897); *Les Rosati* (1902); *Fantasie* for cello and orch. (1897); Concerto for Piano and Orch. (1903). About 200 songs, 12 vocal duets; piano pieces for 2 and 4 hands. Massenet completed and orchestrated Delibes's opera *Kassya* (1893).

BIBLIOGRAPHY: E. de Solenière, *Massenet: étude critique et documentaire* (Paris, 1897); A. Bruneau, *La Musique française* (Paris, 1901); C. Fournier, *Étude sur le style de Massenet* (Amiens, 1905); L. Aubin, *Le Drame lyrique* (Tours, 1908); L. Schneider, *Massenet: l'homme et le musicien* (Paris, 1908; the most comprehensive biography; new ed., 1926); H. T. Finck, *Massenet and His Operas* (N.Y., 1910); O. Séré, *Musiciens français d'aujourd'hui* (rev. ed. Paris, 1921); A. Soubies, *Massenet historien* (Paris, 1913); A. Pougin, *Massenet* (Paris, 1914); G. Jean-Aubry, "Un Mot sur Massenet," in *La Musique française d'aujourd'hui* (Paris, 1916); René Brancour, *Massenet* (1922; 2nd ed., 1930); J. Loisel, *Manon de Massenet* (Paris, 1922); C. Bouvet, *Massenet* (Paris, 1929); J. d'Udine, *L'Art du lied et les mélodies de Massenet* (1931); A. Bruneau, *Massenet* (Paris, 1935); A. Morin, *Jules Massenet et ses opéras* (Montreal, 1944). Massenet's autobiography (completed by X. Leroux) appeared shortly after his death as *Mes souvenirs* (Paris, 1912; English transl., as *My Recollections,* Boston, 1919); James Harding, *Massenet* (London, 1970).

Masséus, Jan, Dutch composer; b. Rotterdam, Jan. 28, 1913. He studied at the Cons. in Rotterdam; then moved to Leeuwarden, where he taught music.
WORKS: Sinfonietta for chamber orch. (1952); Concerto for Violin and Chamber Orch. (1953); Concerto for 2 Flutes and Orch. (1956); *Cassazione,* 4 dances for small orch. (1960); Piano Concerto (1966); *Schermutselingen (Skirmishes)* for chorus and orch. (Leeuwarden, Dec. 17, 1975); *Gezelle Liederen* for soprano, alto, piano (4 hands), and percussion (1955); *Camphuysen-liederen* for chorus, 3 trumpets, 3 trombones and tuba (1967); *4 Songs* for chorus, 9 brasses, double bass and percussion (1970); *The 7 Tile Tableaux,* for baritone, brass instruments, double bass and percussion (1973); 2 violin sonatas (1946, 1950); Trio for flute, violin and piano (1948); *Quintetto* for piano and string quartet (1952); *Introduction and Allegro* for oboe, clarinet and piano (1952); *Partita* for violin and piano (1956); Flute Sonata (1957); *Serenade* for oboe, bassoon, violin and viola (1958); *7 Minutes of Organized Sound* for 3 winds, guitar and percussion (1968); *Symphonic Fantasy* for 2 pianos (1947); *Helicon Suite* for piano 4 hands (1952); *Zoological Impressions* for piano 4 hands (1954), *Balletto piccola*

for 2 pianos (1955); *Confetti* for piano 4 hands (1969); *Pentatude*, 5 studies for piano (1974).

Masson, Gérard, French composer; b. Paris, Aug. 12, 1936. He took courses in advanced techniques with Stockhausen, Pousseur and Earle Brown, working along the lines of serial methods and acoustical coordination of sonorous blocs; experienced profound influence of the theory and practice of Varèse's 'organized sound.' His music is marked by strict constructivism, enlivened by lyric exoticism.

WORKS: *Piece* for 14 instruments and percussion (1964); *Dans le Deuil des Vagues I* for 14 instruments (Royan Festival, April 1, 1967); *Ouest I* for 10 instruments (Vienna, April 25, 1968); *Dans le Deuil des Vagues II* for orch. (London, Nov. 20, 1968); *Ouest II* for voice and instruments (Paris, April 26, 1971). Stravinsky, who had an opportunity to examine some of Masson's scores, commended him in one of his last published interviews.

Masson, Paul-Marie, eminent French musicologist; b. Sète, Hérault, Sept. 19, 1882; d. Paris, Jan. 27, 1954. He studied music history with Romain Rolland at the Sorbonne; received his degree with the dissertation, *La Musique mesurée à l'Antique au XVIᵉ siècle* (1907); subsequently enrolled in the Schola Cantorum as a pupil of Vincent d'Indy; also took lessons with Koechlin. In 1910 he was appointed prof. of the history of music at the Univ. of Grenoble, and entrusted with the organization of the "Institut français de Florence," with the aim of publishing complete editions of works of the early Italian masters. He taught music history at the Sorbonne (1931–52); in 1937 he was elected vice-president of the Société française de musicologie, and in 1949, its president. He publ. a valuable books: *Lullistes et Ramistes* (1912), *Musique italienne et musique française* (1912), *Berlioz* (1923, *L'Opéra de Rameau* (1930); ed. *Chants de carnaval florentins* (vol. I) and 5-part madrigals by Gesualdo; contributed numerous articles to European music magazines, etc. He was also a competent composer; his works include a cantata to his own words, *Chant des peuples unis;* a *Suite Pastorale,* for wind quintet; songs and piano pieces. A 2-vol. offering, *Mélanges d'histoire et d'esthétique musicale offertes à Paul-Marie Masson* (containing a brief biographical sketch and bibliography), was presented to him by his colleagues, friends, and pupils on his retirement from the Sorbonne in 1952; publ. posthumously (Paris, 1955).

Maszynski, Piotr, Polish choral composer; b. Warsaw, July 3, 1855; d. there, Aug. 1, 1934. He studied piano and composition at the Warsaw Cons.; taught there from 1892 till his death; also conducted a choral society. He wrote several attractive choruses, two cantatas, a violin sonata, and some 100 songs; publ. textbooks for music schools; edited instructive anthologies of vocal music.

Mata, Eduardo, noted Mexican conductor and composer; b. Mexico City, Sept. 15, 1942. He studied composition with Rodolfo Halffter at the National Cons. of Mexico (1954–60); then took lessons in composition and conducting with Carlos Chávez (1960–65) and Ju-

lian Orbón (1960–63); in 1964 went to the Berkshire Center in Tanglewood, Mass. where he attended conducting seminars led by Max Rudolf, Gunther Schuller and Erich Leinsdorf. He was conductor of the Symph. Orch. of Guadalajara (1964–66); in 1970 became principal conductor of the Phoenix, Arizona, Symph. Orch.; in 1977 was appointed conductor and music director of the Dallas Symph. Orch. He proved his excellence as an interpreter of Classical and Romantic music to the satisfaction and even delectation of audiences that expect to be pleased by beautiful music, and his success with the public made it possible for him to introduce into his programs some decidedly unpleasing pieces by such unromantic composers as Boulez and Berio and by such forbidding representatives of the uncompromising avant-garde as Stockhausen and Cage. Eduardo Mata's own music finds the golden mean between neo-Classicism and ultramodernism; however, during the most hectic period of his activities as conductor, beginning with 1970, he practically abandoned composition.

WORKS: *Trio a Vaughan Williams* for clarinet, snare drum and cello (1957); Piano Sonata (1960); incidental music for Shakespeare's *Twelfth Night* for soprano recorder, viola and guitar (1961); *Improvisaciones* for clarinet and piano (1961); 3 symphonies: No. 1, *Clásica* (Mexico City, March 24, 1962), No. 2, *Romántica* (Mexico City, Nov. 29, 1963) and No. 3 for horn obbligato and wind orch. (1966–67); *Débora,* ballet music (1963); *La Venganza del Pescador,* suite for 2 flutes, trombone, violin, guitar and percussion (1964); *Improvisaciones No. 1* for string quartet and piano, 4-hands (1964), *No. 2* for strings and 2 pianos (1965) and *No. 3* for violin and piano (1965); *Aires sobre un tema del siglo XVI* for mezzo-soprano, 2 flutes, oboe, bassoon, 2 violas, cello and double bass (1964); Cello Sonata (1966).

Matěj, Josef, Czech composer; b. Brušperk, Feb. 19, 1922. He learned to play the trombone from his father; studied composition with Emil Hlobil at the Prague Conservatory (1942–47) and Jaroslav Řidký at the Academy of Musical Arts (1947–51). His early works are characterized by folksong inflections of the Lachian region of his birth; after 1960 he introduced into his works some coloristic Oriental elements; also made discreet use of dodecaphonic techniques.

WORKS: 2 string quartets (1948–49, 1966); Quartet for trombones (1950); 2 trombone concertos (1951, 1952); Symph. No. 1, for soloists, chorus and orch. (1953–55); *Sonata da Camera* for oboe and chamber orch. (1955); Wind Quintet (1955–56); Symph. No. 2 (1959–60); *Rhapsody* for viola and orch. (1961–63); Violin Concerto (1961–63); Trumpet Concerto (1961–63; Prague, April 15, 1965); *Informatorium* for trombone and piano (1964); *Jewish Folk Poetry* for chorus (1964); Sonata for trombone, 12 strings and piano (1966); Concerto for Flute, Strings and Harpsichord (1966); ten 2-part and ten 3-part *Inventions* for 2 and 3 trombones (1967); *Initials,* vocal fantasy on the text of a letter of St. Paul to the Corinthians, for tenor, speaker, chorus and orch. (1968); Concertino for Trumpet, French Horn and Trombone (1969); Symph. No. 3, *Sinfonia Dramatica* (1969); Concerto for Clarinet, Strings and Piano (1970); Violin Sonata

(1971); Cello Concerto (Prague, March 7, 1973); *Triple Concerto* for trumpet, French horn, trombone and chamber orch. (1973); songs.

Materna, Amalie, Austrian soprano; b. St. Georgen, Styria, July 10, 1844; d. Vienna, Jan. 18, 1918. She was a church singer; married actor Karl Friedrich, and together they sang in light opera. In 1869 she made her opera debut at the Vienna State Opera, and remained on its staff until 1897. Her dramatic talent, powerful voice and beauteous features attracted the notice of Wagner, who selected her for the role of Brünnhilde in the first Bayreuth Festival of 1876; the following year she sang at the Wagner Festival in London, under the composer's own direction, and also sang in the Wagner Festivals in New York, Chicago and Cincinnati. Her American opera debut took place on Jan. 5, 1885 as Elisabeth in *Tannhäuser* during the first season of German opera at the Metropolitan Opera House; in 1894 she became a member of Walter Damrosch's German company in N.Y. In 1902 she returned to Vienna and opened a singing studio there.

Mather, Bruce, Canadian composer and pianist; b. Toronto, May 9, 1939. He studied composition with Ridout, Morawetz and Weinzweig at the Toronto Cons. (1952–59); took summer courses in piano with Alexandre Uninsky at the Aspen School of Music in Colorado (1957–58); then went to Paris and studied with Simone Plé-Caussade, Messiaen and Milhaud (1959–61); returning to America, he continued his musical education with Leland Smith at Stanford Univ. (M.A., 1964) and studied for his doctorate at the Univ. of Toronto (Ph.D., 1967). In 1966 he joined the faculty of McGill Univ. in Montreal; in 1970 became prof. at the Univ. of Montreal. Mather's own music follows the path of unprejudiced modernism, extending from neo-Classicism to expressionism and comprising elements of serialism and microtonality.

WORKS: Violin Sonata (1956); *2 Songs,* after Thomas Hardy, for bass-baritone and small orch. (1956); *Venice,* after Byron, for soprano, clarinet, cello and piano (1957); *3 Songs,* to poems of Robert Graves, for soprano and string orch. (1957–58); Concerto for Piano and Chamber Orch. of wind quintet and string quartet (Aspen, Aug. 20, 1958; composer soloist); *Elegy* for saxophone and strings (1959); *Cycle Rilke* for voice and guitar (1959–60); *Étude* for solo clarinet (1962); *Orphée* for soprano, piano and percussion (1963); *Symphonic Ode* for orch. (Toronto, March 28, 1965); *Orchestra Piece 1967* (Toronto, Jan. 11, 1967); *Ombres* for orch. (Montreal, May 1, 1968); 5 *Madrigals: I* for soprano, alto, flute, mandolin, harp, violin and cello (1967), *II* for soprano, alto, flute, harp, violin, viola and cello (1968), *III* for alto, marimba, harp and piano (1971), *IV* for soprano, flute, piano and tape (1972) and *V* for soprano, alto and 17 instrumentalists (1972–73); *Music for Vancouver* for small orch. (1969); *2-Piano Sonata* (1970); *Musique pour Rouen* for string orch. (1970–71); *Mandola* for mandolin and piano (1971); *Music for Organ, Horn and Gongs* (1973); *In memoriam Alexandre Uninsky* for piano (1974); *Eine Kleine Bläsermusik* for wind quintet (1975); *Au Château de Pompairain* for mezzo-so-

prano and orch. (Ottawa, May 4, 1977); *Clos de Vougeot* for 4 percussionists (1977).

Mathews, William Smythe Babcock, American organist and writer on music; b. London, N.H., May 8, 1837; d. Denver, Colo., April 1, 1912. He studied music in Boston; occupied various teaching posts in Georgia, North Carolina, Alabama, Chicago, and Denver; was organist in Chicago churches; edited the *Musical Independent* (1868–72); was music critic of the *Chicago Tribune* (1878–86); 1891, founded and edited the monthly magazine *Music.* He published *Outlines of Musical Form* (1867); *Emerson Organ-Method,* with L. O. Emerson (1870); *Mason's Piano Techniques,* with William Mason (1876); *How to Understand Music* (2 vols., 1880 and 1888); *100 Years of Music in America* (1889); *Popular History of Music* (1889; 2nd ed., 1906); *Pronouncing and Defining Dictionary of Music* (1896); *Music, Its Ideals and Methods* (1897); *The Masters and Their Music* (1898); *The Great in Music* (3 vols., 1900–03).

Mathias, Franz Xaver, Alsatian church musician; b. Dinsheim, July 16, 1871; d. Strasbourg, Feb. 2, 1939. He studied in Germany with Hugo Riemann; was organist at the Strasbourg Cathedral (1898–1908); then prof. of sacred music at the Univ. of Strasbourg. Among his works the best known is the oratorio *Mystère de Joseph,* containing an instrumental *Ballet égyptien.* He also wrote an oratorio of gigantic dimensions, *Urbem Virgo tuam serva* for two choruses (with the assistance of a "crowd" of many voices); 28 cantatas; several Masses; psalms; motets; many organ pieces; publ. a manual of accompaniment of Gregorian Chant.

Mathias, Georges (-Amédée-Saint-Clair), French composer; b. Paris, Oct. 14, 1826; d. there, Oct. 14, 1910. As a youth he had the privilege of taking piano lessons with Chopin; studied composition with Halévy and others at the Paris Cons.; in 1862 was appointed prof. of piano there, and taught until 1893. He composed 2 piano concertos, 6 piano trios, *5 morceaux symphoniques* for piano and strings and a number of studies, under the promising titles *Études de style et de mécanisme* and *Études de genre.* He also publ. a collection of attractive piano pieces for 2 and 4 hands; his overtures and other symphonic works are less interesting.

Mathias, William, English composer; b. Whitland, Dyfed, Nov. 1, 1934. He studied at the Univ. College of Wales, Aberystwyth (B.Mus., 1956); then at the Royal Academy of Music with Lennox Berkeley (composition) and Peter Katin (piano). In 1965 he was elected a Fellow of the Royal Academy of Music; was awarded the D.Mus. degree by the Univ. of Wales in 1966; in 1968 he received the Bax Society Prize for composition. In 1969 he became a lecturer in music at the Univ. College of North Wales; in 1970 was appointed prof. and head of the Dept. of Music at the Univ. College of North Wales, Bangor. His style of composition may be described as civilized modernism, sophisticated but free of exhibitionistic affectation, optimistically tonal but occasionally somber, brilliantly idiomatic in instrumentation, and unequivocally populist in its euphonious appeal.

WORKS: FOR ORCH.: *Divertimento* for string orch. (1958); *Dance Overture* (London, Aug. 10, 1962); *Invocation and Dance* (Cardiff Festival, March 1, 1962); *Serenade* for chamber orch. (1962); *Concerto for Orch.* (Liverpool, March 29, 1966); Symph. No. 1 (Birmingham, June 23, 1966); *Sinfonietta* (1967); *Litanies* (1968); *Festival Overture* (1970); *Holiday Overture* (BBC radio broadcast, Sept. 30, 1971); *Vistas* (Swansea Festival, Oct. 25, 1975); Piano Concerto No. 1 (1955); Piano Concerto No. 2 (1960); Piano Concerto No. 3 (Swansea, Oct. 15, 1968); Harp Concerto (Bournemouth, June 1, 1970); Concerto for Harpsichord, Strings and Percussion (1971); Clarinet Concerto (North Wales Music Festival, Sept. 22, 1975). CHAMBER MUSIC: Violin Sonata (1961); Quintet for flute, oboe, clarinet, horn and bassoon (1963); *Divertimento* for flute, oboe and piano (1963); *Concertino*, for flute, oboe, bassoon and harpsichord (1964); String Quartet (1967); several organ pieces; choruses; songs; anthems; carols and psalms with organ or a cappella; piano pieces.

Mathieu, Émile (-Louis-Victor), Belgian composer and pedagogue; b. Lille, France (of Belgian parentage), Oct. 18, 1844; d. Ghent, Aug. 20, 1932. He studied at the Brussels Cons. with Fétis and Auguste Dupont; taught at Louvain (1867–73); then was in Paris as theater conductor; returning to Louvain, he became director of the music school there (1881–98); in 1898 was appointed director of the Ghent Cons. In 1869, and again in 1871, he won the 2nd Grand Prix de Rome in Brussels.

WORKS: the cantatas, *La Dernière Nuit de Faust, Le Songe de Colomb, Debout, Peuple,* and *Les Bois;* the comic operas, *L'Échange* (Liège, 1863), *Georges Dandin* (Brussels, 1877), and *La Bernoise* (Brussels, 1880); grand operas, *Richilde* (Brussels, 1888) and *L'Enfance de Roland* (1895); a violin concerto, and other instrumental works; symph. poems, *Noces féodales, Le Lac,* etc.

Mathieu, Rodolphe, Canadian composer; b. Grondines, Portneuf, Quebec, July 10, 1890; d. Montreal, June 29, 1962. He moved to Montreal at the age of 16; had composition lessons from Alexis Contant; then went to Paris where he took courses with Vincent d'Indy and Louis Aubert at the Schola Cantorum (1920–27); in 1927 returned to Montreal. His music is cast in a modern French manner.

WORKS: *Les Yeux noirs* for tenor and piano (1911); *Chevauchée* for piano (1911); *3 Preludes* for piano (1912–15); *Un Peu d'Ombre* for tenor and chamber orch. (1913); String Quartet (1920); Piano Trio (1921); *12 Études modernes* for solo violin (1920–23); *Harmonie du soir* for high voice, violin and orch. (1924); Piano Sonata (1927); Violin Sonata (1928); *2 Poèmes* for voice and string quartet (1928); *Lève-toi, Canadien* for chorus and orch. (Montreal, Oct. 25, 1934); Piano Quintet (1942).

Mathis, Edith, Swiss soprano; b. Lucerne, Feb. 11, 1938. She studied in Zürich; made her operatic debut at the age of 18; was subsequently engaged at the Co-

logne Opera (1959); at the Salzburg Festival (1960) and in Glyndebourne (1962). In 1963 she joined the staff of the Berlin Opera; in 1964–65 was at the Hamburg State Opera.

Matičić, Janez, Slovenian composer; b. Ljubljana, June 3, 1926. He studied in Paris and worked in the electronic studios of the Radiodiffusion française; wrote numerous works using the resources of musique concrète. He also composed music in a traditional manner: a symph. (1953); songs; piano pieces.

Mátray, Gábor, Hungarian music scholar; b. Nágykáta, Nov. 23, 1797; d. Budapest, July 17, 1875. He studied law and at the same time learned to compose. In 1812, at the age of 15, he wrote the earliest Hungarian piece of stage music, *Cserni György;* also publ. a general history of music (1828–32), the first such history in the Hungarian language; wrote treatises on folk music and Gypsy music, and made arrangements of Hungarian folksongs. His own works (for piano, guitar, and chorus) are mostly salon music, but some of them are historically important because of the use of native rhythms.

BIBLIOGRAPHY: P. Varnai, "Gábor Mátray," *Zenetudományi Tanulmányok,* vol. II (Budapest, 1954).

Matsudaira, Yori-Aki, Japanese composer of the avant-garde, son of **Yoritsuné Matsudaira;** b. Tokyo, March 27, 1931. He studied biology in Tokyo (1948–57); then formed a composing collective, "Group 20.5," with which he produced *Variation on the Theme of Noh* for flute, clarinet, 3 percussionists, piano, violin, viola and cello (1960). His own works include: *Variations* for piano trio (1957); *Speed Coefficient* for flute, piano and keyboard percussion (1958); *Orbits I-III* for flute, clarinet and piano (1960); *Instruction* for piano (1961); *Configuration* for chamber orch. (1961–63; Tokyo, March 29, 1967); *Co-Action I & II* for cello and piano (1962); *Parallax* for flute, oboe, clarinet, bassoon and saxophone (1963); *Tangent '64* for tape (1964); *Rhymes for Gazelloni* for solo flute (1965–66); *Distribution* for string quartet and ring modular (1966–67); *What's Next!* for soprano and 2 noise makers (1967, revised 1971); *Alternation for Combo* for trumpet, percussion, piano, double bass and ring modulator (1967); *Assemblage* for tape (1968); *Assemblage* for female voice and ring modulator (1968); *Wand Waves* for narrator and tape (1970); *Allotropy* for piano (1970); *Why Not?* for 4-5 operators with live electronics (1970); *"The Symphony"* for 14 players (1971); *Gradation* for violin, viola and oscillator (1971); *Substitution* for soprano and piano (1972); *Messages* for wind orch. and tape (1972).

Matsudaira, Yoritsuné, Japanese composer; b. Tokyo, May 5, 1907. He studied composition with Alexander Tcherepnin when the latter was in Japan; won the Weingartner Prize in 1937 and the International Composition Competition Prize in Rome in 1962. His music amalgamates old Japanese modalities with modern harmonies.

WORKS: *Theme and Variations,* on popular Japanese songs for orch. (Tokyo, Dec. 17, 1939); *Ancient Japanese Dance* for orch. (Berlin, Oct. 9, 1953); *Nega-*

tive and Positive Figures for orch. (Tokyo, May 28, 1954); *Metamorphoses on "Saibara"* (an old Japanese melody) for soprano and 18 instruments (Haifa Festival, June 3, 1954); *Koromogae (Love Song)* for soprano and 19 instruments (1954; Venice, Dec. 11, 1968); *Figures sonores* for orch. (1956; Zürich Festival, June 1, 1957); *U-Mai, ancient dance for orch.* (Darmstadt, Sept. 11, 1958); *Samai* for chamber orch. (Rome Festival, June 15, 1959); *Dance Suite* for 3 orch. (Donaueschingen, Oct. 18, 1959); *Bugaku* for chamber orch. (Palermo, Oct. 6, 1962); *3 Movements* for piano and orch. (Stockholm, March 20, 1964); *Ritual Dance and Finale* for orch. (1963); *Serenata* for flute and 10 instruments (1963); Piano Concerto (Madrid Festival, May 20, 1965); *Concerto da camera* for harpsichord, harp and instrumental ensemble (1964); *Dialogo coreografico* for 2 pianos and chamber ensemble (1966; Royan, France, April 3, 1967); *Roei "Jisei" (Two Stars in Vega)* for voice and instrumental ensemble (1967); *Music for 17 instruments* (1967); *Mouvements circulatoires* for 2 chamber orch. (Graz Festival, Oct. 10, 1972); *Prelude, Interlude and Apréslude* for orch. (1973); Sonatina for flute and clarinet (1940); Cello Sonata (1942); Concerto for 2 Solo Pianos (1946); Piano Trio (1948); 2 string quartets (1948, 1951); 2 violin sonatas (1948, 1952); *Suite* for flute, bassoon and piano (1950); Piano Sonata (1953); *Katsura* for soprano, harp, harpsichord, guitar and percussion (1957, revised 1967); *Somaksah* for solo flute (1961); *Portrait B* for 2 pianos and 2 percussionists (1967-68); *12 pezzi facili* for piano (1968-69).

Matsumura, Teizo, Japanese composer; b. Kyoto, Jan. 15, 1929. He studied composition with Akira Ifukube, Tomojiro Ikenouchi and Yosuji Kiyose; subsequently lectured at the Tokyo Institute Geijutsu Daigaku. Among his works are *Introduction et Allegro Concertant* for orch. (1955); *Achimè* for soprano, percussion and 11 instruments (1957); *Cryptogram* for chamber orch. (1958); Symphony (1965); *Flute of Evil Passions,* a poetic drama for baritone, male chorus, 2 Japanese instruments and orch. (1965); *Prélude* for orch. (Tokyo, Feb. 28, 1969); *Poem I* for shakuhachi (Japanese vertical flute) and koto (1969); *Totem Ritual* for chorus and orch. (1970); *Poem II* for shakuhachi (1972); Piano Concerto (1973).

Matsushita, Shin-ichi, Japanese composer; b. Osaka, Oct. 1, 1922. He graduated in mathematics from the Kyushu Univ. in Fukuoka in 1947; concurrently studied music. In 1958 he went to work in an electronic-music studio in Osaka; taught both mathematics and music at the Univ. of Osaka City. In his music he follows cosmopolitan modernistic techniques, mostly of a functional, pragmatic nature.

WORKS: *Ouvrage Symphonique* for piano and orch. (1957); *Correlazioni per 3 gruppi* for 12 players (1958); *Composizione da camera per 8* (1958); *Isomorfismi* for orch. (1958); *5 Tempi per Undici* for 11 instruments (1958-59); *Le Croître noir* for chorus, electronic and musique concrète sounds, piano, harp and percussion (1959; Osaka, Nov. 14, 1959); *Faisceaux* for flute, cello and piano (1959); *Jet Pilot* for narrator, orch., string quartet and female chorus (1960); 2 radio operas: *Comparing Notes on a Rainy Night* and *Ama-*

yo (both 1960); *Sinfonia "Le Dimensioni"* (1961); *Cube for 3 Players* for flute, celeste and viola (1961); *Successioni* for chamber orch. (Radio Palermo, Oct. 1, 1962); *Meta-Musique* No. 1 for piano, horn and percussion (1962); *Uro* for chamber ensemble (1962); *Sinfonia "Vita"* (1963); *Musique* for soprano and chamber ensemble (Osaka, Sept. 14, 1964); *Fresque Sonore* for 7 instruments (1964); *Hexahedra A, B* and *C* for piano and percussion (1964-65); *Spectra 1-4* for piano (1964; 1967; for 2 players, 1971; 1971); *Kristalle* for piano quartet (1966); *Alleluja in der Einsamkeit* for guitar, piccola and 2 percussionists (1967); *Serenade* for flute and orch. (1967); *Subject 17* for piano, percussion, horn, trumpet and trombone (San Francisco, Oct. 31, 1967); *Sinfonie Pol* for orch., harp and piano (1968); *Haleines astrales* for chamber ensemble (1968); *Astrate Atem* for orch., harp and piano (1969-70); *Requiem on the Place of Execution* for 4 soloists, chorus, orch. and tape (1970); *Musik von der Liebe* for flute, vibraphone, harp, piano, electone, and tape (1970); *Musik der Steinzeit* for violin, Ondes Martenot, tape, and the sound of cracking stone (1970); *Ostinato Obbligato* for piano (1972).

Mattei, Tito, Italian pianist and composer, b. Campobasso, near Naples, May 24, 1841; d. London, March 30, 1914. He studied with Parisi, Conti, and Thalberg; made rapid progress, so that at the age of 11 he obtained a nominal appointment as 'professore' of the Accademia di Santa Cecilia in Rome; received a gold medal for playing before Pope Pius XI, and was appointed pianist to the King of Italy. About 1865 he settled in London, where he was active principally as opera conductor. He himself composed several operas, *Maria di Gand* (London, 1880), *The Grand Duke* (London, 1889), *La Prima Donna* (London, 1889); a ballet, *The Spider and the Fly* (London, 1893); also songs and piano pieces.

Matteis, Nicola, Italian violinist, who settled in London in 1672, and publ. there 4 books of violin pieces (airs, preludes, fugues, allemandes, sarabands, etc.) under varying Italian and English titles; also *The False Consonances of Musick, or, Instructions for playing a true Base upon the Guitarre, with Choice Examples and Clear Directions to enable any man in a short time to play all Musicall Ayres,* etc. He was likewise the author of *A Collection of New Songs* (2 vols., London, 1696). His son, also named **Nicola** (d. 1749), lived in Vienna, and in Shrewsbury, England. He was Burney's teacher.

BIBLIOGRAPHY: Paul Nettl, "An English Musician at the Court of Charles VI in Vienna," *Musical Quarterly* (April 1942).

Matteo da Perugia, Italian church composer; b. Perugia in the 2nd half of the 14th century; date of death unknown. He was principal maestro di cappella of the Milan Cathedral; occupied this post from 1402 to 1416. He wrote 4 Glorias in 3 parts; one Gloria in 4 parts; a number of motets and other sacred works for services at the Milan Cathedral. The 1st vol. of the new series of the *Istituzioni e monumenti dell'arte musicale italiana* (1957) is devoted to music by Matteo, ed. by F. Fano; 22 pieces are transcribed in modern notation by Willi Apel in his anthology, *French Secular Music of the Late 14th Century* (Cambridge, Mass., 1950).

BIBLIOGRAPHY: F. Fano in the *Rivista Musicale Italiana* (Jan.–March 1953); C. Sartori, "Matteo da Perugia e Bertrand Feragut," *Acta Musicologica* (1956).

Mattfeld, Julius, American librarian, and musicographer; b. New York, Aug. 8, 1893; d. there, July 31, 1968. He studied at the N.Y. German Cons. In 1910 he joined the staff of the N.Y. Public Library; resigned in 1926 to become music librarian of the National Broadcasting Co. (until 1929); then was librarian of the Columbia Broadcasting System; was also organist of the Fordham Lutheran Church, N.Y. (1915–32). He publ. *The Folk Music of the Western Hemisphere* (1925), *A Hundred Years of Grand Opera in New York, 1825–1925* (1927); *Variety Music Cavalcade, 1620–1950* (N.Y., 1952; revised ed., 1962); *A Handbook of American Operatic Premieres, 1731–1962* (Detroit, 1963).

Mattfeld, Victor Henry, American organist and music editor; b. Bunceton, Mo., Sept. 1, 1917. He studied at Concordia College, River Forest, Ill.; then at the Univ. of Chicago (B.A., 1942) and at the American Cons. of Music in Chicago (M. Mus., 1946); took a course in conducting with Malko; was organist and choirmaster at Zion Lutheran Church, Chicago (1938–47); instructor at the American Cons. of Music (1945–47); from 1947 till 1956 was organist and choirmaster at various churches in N.Y. and New Haven; instructor in music history at the Yale School of Music (1952–55).

Matthay, Tobias (Augustus), eminent English pianist and pedagogue; b. London, Feb. 19, 1858; d. High Marley, near Haslemere, Surrey, Dec. 14, 1945. He began to play the piano at the age of 6; was taught by private teachers; in 1871 he entered the Royal Academy of Music as a pupil of Dorrell (piano); won the Sterndale Bennett scholarship, and continued to study piano (with Macfarren); took courses with Sterndale Bennett, and after the latter's death (1875) completed his studies with Ebenezer Prout and Arthur Sullivan; appointed sub-professor of piano at the Royal Academy of Music in 1876; sub-professor of harmony in 1878, and full professor of piano in 1880. In that year he gave his first public recital, and for the next 15 years appeared frequently on the concert platform; but his interest in teaching gradually engrossed his attention, so that in 1895 he gave up his career as concert pianist, and established his own piano school in London. The Matthay System, as his teaching method was known, became famous not only in England, but on the Continent and in America. Students flocked to him and carried his method abroad. Matthay wrote about 100 piano pieces, a *Konzertstück* for piano and orch., a piano quartet, and some other works. His didactic publications include: *The Art of Touch* (1903); *The First Principles of Pianoforte Playing* (1905); *Relaxation Studies* (1908); *Commentaries on the Teaching of Pianoforte Technique* (1911); *The Rotation Principle* (1912); *The Child's First Steps in Piano Playing* (1912); *Musical Interpretation* (1913); *Pianist's First Music Making* (3 books); *The Nine Steps towards Finger-individualization; On Memorizing*; etc.

BIBLIOGRAPHY: Jessie Henderson Matthay; *The Life and Works of Tobias Matthay* (London, 1945).

Mattheson, Johann, famous German composer and lexicographer; b. Hamburg, Sept. 28, 1681; d. there, April 17, 1764. A student of law, and master of several languages, he studied music under Braunmüller, Praetorius, and Kellner; at the age of 9 he sang, composed, and played the organ and harpsichord; entered the chorus at the Hamburg Opera, and later sang tenor roles, also bringing out his own operas. He befriended Handel in Hamburg, and together they made a futile journey to Lübeck in 1703, to visit Buxtehude and, possibly, apply for the position as organist to succeed him. The unwritten requirement for the gaining of that position being marriage to one of Buxtehude's daughters, Mattheson declined the opportunity. In 1704 he became tutor in the English ambassador's family; 1706, secretary of legation; later ambassador *ad interim*. In 1715 he was appointed musical director and cantor at the Hamburg Cathedral; a growing deafness obliged him to resign his directorship in 1728. Of his operas, the most important is *Cleopatra*, performed at the Hamburg Opera on Oct. 20, 1704, with Mattheson acting both as singer and conductor, in alternation, Handel taking care of the direction when Mattheson was on the stage; it was during a later performance of *Cleopatra* that a quarrel arose between Mattheson and Handel when Handel refused to give up the direction even when Mattheson was back in the pit; however, they soon were reconciled and Mattheson became Handel's first German biographer. He wrote 7 other operas, which had but little success, 24 oratorios and cantatas, a Passion, a Mass, suites for harpsichord, 12 flute sonatas with violin; etc. (88 publ. works in all; some are included in Pauer's *Old German Composers*). His importance in music history lies in the many published treatises on various musical subjects; his most significant work was the unique biographical dictionary, *Grundlage einer Ehren-Pforte, woran der tüchtigsten Capellmeister, Componisten, Musikgelehrten, Tonkünstler etc., Leben, Werke, Verdienste, etc., erscheinen sollen* (1740; new ed. by Max Schneider, with addenda, Berlin, 1910; in this work Mattheson gives himself 31 pages, as against 8 for Handel). Other publications are: *Das neu-eröffnete Orchester, oder gründliche Anleitung, wie ein 'galant homme' einen vollkommenen Begriff von der Hoheit und Würde der edlen Musik erlangen möge* (1713); *Das beschützte Orchester* (1717); *Die exemplarische Organistenprobe* (1719; 2nd ed. as *Grosse Generalbass-Schule*, 1731); *Critica musica* (2 vols.; 1722); *Der brauchbare Virtuos* (1720); *Das forschende Orchester* (1721); *De eruditione musica* (1732); *Der vollkommene Capellmeister* (1739; facsimile reprint, Kassel, 1954); *Die neueste Untersuchung der Singspiele* (1744); *Mithridat, wider den Gift einer welschen Satyre des Salvator Rosa, genannt: "La Musica," übersetzt und mit Anmerkungen, etc.* (1749); *Georg Friedrich Händels Lebensbeschreibung*

(1761; based almost entirely on Mainwaring's English biography of Handel, publ. in London, 1760); etc.

BIBLIOGRAPHY: L. Meinardus, *Mattheson und seine Verdienste um die deutsche Tonkunst*, in Waldersee's *Sammlung musikalischer Vorträge* (Leipzig, 1879); H. Schmidt, *Johann Mattheson im Lichte seiner Werke* (Erlangen, 1897); B. C. Cannon, *Johann Mattheson, Spectator in Music* (New Haven, 1947).

Matthews, (Harry) Alexander, American organist and composer; b. Cheltenham, England, March 26, 1879; d. Middletown, Connecticut, April 12, 1973. He studied with his father, John A. Matthews; then went to America; taught at the Univ. of Pennsylvania. He retired in 1954, and lived in Middletown, Conn.; he died at the age of 94. He publ. *The Introits and Graduals of the Church Year* (Philadelphia, 1924) and wrote a cantata, *The Story of Christmas*. His brother, **John Sebastian Matthews** (b. Cheltenham, Dec. 11, 1870; d. Pawtucket, R.I., July 23, 1934), was also an organist, who went to America. He publ. several anthems, organ pieces and songs.

Matton, Roger, Canadian composer; b. Granby, Quebec, May 18, 1929. He studied piano at the Cons. of Montreal; later was a composition student of Claude Champagne there (1946–49). He then went to Paris and studied with Nadia Boulanger and others. In 1956 he was appointed prof. of composition at the Laval Univ. in Quebec City. His music is marked by dramatic lyricism enlivened by propulsive rhythms.

WORKS: *Danse brésilienne* for 2 pianos (1946); *Etude* for clarinet and piano (1946); *Danse lente (Gymnopédie)* for small orch. (1947); Concerto for Saxophone and Strings (1948); *3 Préludes* for piano (1947–49); *Esquisse* for string quartet (1949); *Pax*, symph. suite (1950); *Suite on Gregorian Themes* for organ (1952); Concerto for 2 Pianos and Percussion (1954–55); *L'Escaouette*, suite of folk songs for 4 soloists, chorus and orch. (1957); *L'Horoscope*, choreographic suite (Toronto, Oct. 12, 1958); *4 Mouvements symphoniques*: No. 1 (Quebec City, Nov. 14, 1960); No. 2, *Music for a Drama* (Montreal, April 17, 1962); No. 3 (Quebec City, May 7, 1974); No. 4 (1977); concerto for 2 pianos and orch. (1964; Quebec City, Nov. 30, 1964); *Te Deum* for baritone, chorus, and orch. with electronic sound (Quebec City, Nov. 27, 1967).

Matys, Jiří, Czech composer; b. Bakov, Oct. 27, 1927. He studied organ with František Michálek at the Brno Cons., graduating in 1947; then took course in composition with Kvapil at the Janáček Academy of Music in Brno; joined its faculty after graduation (1953–57); then was headmaster of the School of Music at Královo Pole in Brno (1957–60). In 1960 he moved to Ostrava, where he was active as a music administrator.

WORKS: Horn Sonata (1948); *Fantasy* for string orch. (1949); *Partita* for piano trio (1949); *To Those Fallen in May 1945*, symph. poem (1949); Piano Sonata (1950); Wind Quartet (1951); Symph. (1951); Viola Sonata (1954); *The Bells of Velice*, chamber canata (1954); *Impromptus* for violin and piano (1955); 4 string quartets (1957, 1961, 1962–63, 1973); *Lyrical Melodramas* for narrator and piano 1957); *Children's Ballets* for wind quintet (1959); *Variace na smrt (Vari-*

ations on Death), for narrator, horn and string quartet (1959); Quartet for 4 violins (1960); *Inventions* for 3 violins (1960); *Jitřní hudba (Mourning Music)* for string orch., 2 trumpets and percussion (1961–62); *Pictures of Winter* for piano (1962); Solo Viola Sonata (1963); Duet for violin and viola (1963); Violin Sonata (1964–65); *Sonata Balladica* for piano (1966); *5 Bagatelles* for accordion (1966); *Inventions* for flute and cello (1969); *3 Movements* for wind quintet (1969); *Suite* for trumpet and piano (1969); *Music* for wind quintet (1970); *Pictures*, 3 pieces for cello and piano (1970); *Allusions*, 3 compositions for 4 flutes (1971); *Music* for string quartet and orch. (1971); *Written by Grief into Silence* for medium voice and orch. (1972); *Suite* for viola and bass clarinet (1972–73); *Symphonic Overture* (1973–74); *Partita* for solo oboe (1974); *Poetic Movements*, 3 compositions for flute, violin and piano (1975).

Matz, Rudolf, Croatian cellist and composer; b. Zagreb, Sept. 19, 1901. He studied cello and composition at the Music Academy of Zagreb; in 1950 was appointed instructor in cello there; then taught chamber music at the Music Academy of Ljubljana. He publ. a manual for cello playing (Zagreb, 1951).

WORKS: *Classical Concert* for cello and orch. (1949); *Lyric Sketches* for cello solo and string orch. (1959); Flute Concerto (1963); 4 string quartets (1924, 1932, 1935, 1944); *Baroque Concerto* for 3 cellos and piano (1952); *12 Pieces* for 3 cellos and piano (1960); Violin Sonata (1941); 2 cello sonatas (1941, 1942); *11 Caprices* in 12-tone technique for cello solo (1964); *24 Songs on Croatian Folk Poems* and other pieces based on native themes.

Matzenauer, Margarete, celebrated Hungarian-born singer; b. Temesvar, June 1, 1881; d. Van Nuys, Calif., May 19, 1963. Her father was a symph. conductor, and her mother a dramatic soprano; she grew up in favorable musical surroundings, and began to study singing at an early age, first in Graz, then in Berlin. In 1909 she joined the staff of the Strasbourg Opera; then sang contralto roles at the Munich Court Opera (1904–11). She made her American debut as Amneris in *Adia* at the Metropolitan Opera House in N.Y. (Nov. 13, 1911) and remained one of its leading members until 1930; in the interim she sang in opera in Germany and South America. She began her operatic career as a contralto, but also sang soprano parts; from 1914 on she called herself a soprano singer. After a farewell concert recital in Carnegie Hall, N.Y., in 1938, she retired from the stage and lived in California.

Matzka, George, German-American violinist and composer; b. Coburg, Oct. 31, 1825; d. New York, June 15, 1883. He was a member of the N.Y. Philharmonic, and its conductor in 1876. He wrote overtures, choruses and some chamber music.

Matzke, Hermann, German musicologist; b. Breslau, March 28, 1890; d. Constance, Switzerland, May 22, 1976. He studied musical sciences in Breslau with Kretzschmar, J. Wolf and Kinkeldey; then in Berlin, where at the Univ. of Bern, he received his Ph.D. in

1920; in 1924 returned to Breslau and developed a concept of musical technology, dealing mainly with instrumental construction; edited *Zeitschrift für Instrumentenbau* (1934-43); in 1946 settled in Constance. He publ. *Musikökonomik und Musikpolitik* (Breslau, 1927); *Grundzüge einer musikalischen Technologie* (Breslau, 1931); *Musikgeschichte der Welt im Überblick* (Bonn, 1949; new amplified edition, 1961).

Mauceri, John, American conductor; b. New York, Sept. 12, 1945. He studied at Yale Univ. (B.A., 1967); served as conductor of the Yale Symph. Orch. (1968-74), with which he toured France and Austria. In 1976-77 he conducted the Israel Philharmonic on its tour of Germany and Austria, as well as in Tel Aviv and Jerusalem. He also was guest conductor of the Los Angeles Philharmonic (1974), San Francisco Symph. (1974), National Symph. Orch. in Wolf Trap Farm Park (1975), L'Orchestre National de France (1975), in Paris (1975), Scottish National Orch. (Edinburgh, 1976) and Philadelphia Orch. at Robin Hood Dell (1976).

Mauduit, Jacques, French composer; b. Paris, Sept. 16, 1557; d. there, Aug. 21, 1627. He served as registrar in a Paris court, and studied music by himself, progressing so well that at the age of 24 he won the 1st prize for a motet at a competition. When the poet Antoine Baïf established in Paris the Académie Française de Musique et de Poésie (1570), Mauduit became associated with him, and made several settings of Baïf's poems (Paris, 1586; reprinted by Henry Expert in *Les Maîtres-Musiciens de la Renaissance française*). He is reputed to have saved the musical manuscripts of Le Jeune when the latter was arrested for his Huguenot sympathies. Mauduit's 5-part Requiem, included in Mersenne's *Harmonie Universelle,* is reprinted in R. E. Chapman's English transl. of Mersenne's books on instruments (The Hague, 1957).
BIBLIOGRAPHY: G. Reese, *Music in the Renaissance* (N.Y., 1954; pp. 385-86).

Mauersberger, Rudolf, German choral conductor and composer; b. Mauersberg, Jan. 29, 1889; d. Dresden, Feb. 22, 1971. He studied piano with Teichmüller, organ with Straube and music theory with Krehl at the Leipzig Cons. He held posts as choral conductor and organist in Aachen and Eisenach (1919-30); in 1930 went to Dresden; became a foremost proponent of choral singing methods in the classical tradition. He composed a number of liturigical works, mostly for chorus a cappella; also a *Dresdner Requiem* (1948), commemorating the destruction of Dresden in the air raid of March 1945.

Mauke, Wilhelm, German composer; b. Hamburg, Feb. 25, 1867; d. Wiesbaden, Aug. 24, 1930. He first studied medicine; then turned to music; was a pupil of Huber in Basel. He then established himself as a music critic in Munich; wrote the operas *Der Taugenichts* (1905), *Fanfreluche* (1912), *Die letzte Maske* (1917), *Das Fest des Lebens* (1926); other stage works: a *Romantische Sinfonie;* an oratorio, *Die Vertreibung aus dem Paradies;* a symph. poem, *Einsamkeit,* after Nietzsche; a piano concerto; 160 songs. A list of his works was publ. by F. X. Osterrieder (Munich, 1927).
BIBLIOGRAPHY: : W. Nagel, *Wilhelm Mauke* (1919).

Maunder, John Henry, British composer of sacred oratorios and hymns; b. London, 1858; d. there, in 1920. He studied at the Royal Academy of Music in London; was organist in several London churches; also acted as piano accompanist. He began as a composer by writing an operetta, *Daisy Dingle* (1885); later devoted himself exclusively to oratorios, of which *The Martyrs* (Oxford, May 25, 1894), *Penitence, Pardon and Peace* and *From Olivet to Calvary* became perennial favorites in church performances well into the twentieth century.

Maurel, Victor, famous French baritone; b. Marseilles, June 17, 1848; d. New York, Oct. 22, 1923. He studied singing at the Paris Cons,; made his debut at the Paris Opéra in 1868; then sang in Italy, Spain, England and Russia; in 1874 he made an American tour. Returning to Paris, he was on the staff of the Opéra (1879-94); from 1895 to 1904 he was a member of the Opéra-Comique. In 1909 he emigrated to the U.S., where he remained until his death; in his last year he was active as stage designer in N.Y. He created the roles of Iago in Verdi's *Otello* (Milan, Feb. 5, 1887) and *Falstaff* (Milan, Feb. 9, 1893); also distinguished himself in Wagnerian roles. He publ. several monographs on the esthetics of singing and also autobiographical reminiscences, among them *Le Chant renové par la science* (1892); *Un problème d'art* (1893); *L'Art du chant* (1897); *Dix ans de carrière* (1898).
BIBLIOGRAPHY: F. Rogers, "Victor Maurel: His Career and His Art," *Musical Quarterly* (Oct. 1926).

Maurer, Ludwig (Wilhelm), German violinist and composer; b. Potsdam, Feb. 8, 1789; d. St. Petersburg, Oct. 25, 1878. A precocious child musician, he appeared in concerts at the age of 13; at 17 he went to Russia, remaining there for 10 years, giving concerts, and serving as house musician to Russian aristocrats. From 1817 until 1832 he traveled in Europe, and was successful as a violinist in Berlin and in Paris. He was in Russia again (1832-45), then lived in Dresden, eventually returning to St. Petersburg. He produced 2 operas in Hannover, *Der neue Paris* (Jan. 27, 1826) and *Aloise* (Jan. 16, 1828); also wrote many stage pieces in Russia; with Aliabiev and Verstovsky, he contributed the music to Chmelnitsky's comedy *A Novel Prank, or Theatrical Combat* (1822). Besides, he wrote a curious quadruple concerto, *Symphonie concertante,* for 4 violins with orch. (1838); 3 violin concertos; string quartets and other chamber music. His 2 sons **Vsevolod** (1819-92), a violinist, and **Alexis,** a cellist, remained in Russia.

Maurice, Alphons, German composer; b. Hamburg, April 14, 1862; d. Dresden, Jan. 27, 1905. He studied with Dessoff, Krenn, and Grädener at the Vienna Cons.; wrote the operas *Josepha, Schatz,* and *Der Wundersteg; Waldestraum,* for orch.; *Spanische Serenade,* for violin and orch.; choruses; piano pieces; songs.

Maurice, Pierre, Baron de, Swiss composer; b. Geneva, Nov. 13, 1868; d. there, Dec. 25, 1936. He attended the Cons. at Geneva, then for a short time studied at Stuttgart, finishing his musical education with Lavignac and Massenet at the Paris Cons. He lived many years in Munich; composed the operas *Die weisse Flagge* (Kassel, 1903), *Misé brun* (Stuttgart, 1908), *Lanval* (Weimar, 1912), and *Kalif Storch* (not performed); a biblical drama, *La Fille de Jephthé* (Geneva, 1899); a symph. suite, *Die Islandfischer* (after Loti); *Chanson des quatre saisons,* for piano, and other piano pieces; songs.

Mauricio, José, Portuguese composer and theorist; b. Coimbra, March 19, 1752; d. Figueira, Sept. 12, 1815. He studied theology; was maestro di cappella at Santa Cruz in Coimbra; then at Santa Cecilia in Lisbon. He wrote a great deal of church music; also some instrumental works, in close imitation of Haydn. He also publ. a *Metodo de musica* (Coimbra, 1806).
BIBLIOGRAPHY: J. Vasconcellos, *Os Musicos Portugueses* (Oporto, 1870; pp. 229–48).

Maurin, Jean-Pierre, French violinist; b. Avignon, Feb. 14, 1882; d. Paris, March 16, 1894. He studied violin with Abillot and Habeneck at the Paris Cons., where he succeeded Alard as teacher in 1875. He was co-founder of the Société des Derniers Quatours de Beethoven, in Paris.

Maury, Lowndes, American composer; b. Butte, Montana, July 7, 1911. He earned his B.A. degree in music at the Univ. of Montana in 1931; went to Los Angeles where he studied composition with Wesley La Violette and Schoenberg; became active in Hollywood as pianist, arranger and teacher.
WORKS: violin sonata *In Memory of the Korean War Dead* (1952); *Proud Music of the Storm,* canata to words by Walt Whitman (1953); *Night Life* for cello and piano (1956); *Passacaglia* for string orch. (1959); *Springtime Digressions* for piano, flute and string quintet (1961); *Man Is My Song,* canata (1963); *Speculations* for piano and 3 string instruments (1964); *Summer of Green,* rhapsody for alto flute and string orch. (1964); *Scène de Ballet* for piccolo and string quartet (1965); *11 Sketches* for piano trio (1968); *The Imprisoned Cellist,* suite for solo cello (1973); *Magic Lines and Spaces,* series of piano instruction books in correlated notation, a system employing a 3-line staff (1974).

Maus, Octave, Belgian journalist and musician; b. Brussels, June 12, 1856; d. Lausanne, Nov. 26, 1919. He studied music with Louis Brassin. An ardent admirer of Wagner, he went to Bayreuth to attend the first Wagner Festival in 1876; in 1881 he was co-founder of the weekly magazine *L'Art Moderne,* in Brussels, which promoted Wagnerian ideas; then participated in the musical society "XX," the title of which symbolized the future 20th century; it was active from 1884 to 1893. From 1894 to the outbreak of World War I in 1914 he led in Brussels a concert group, "Libre Esthétique." He spent the last years of his life in Switzerland.
BIBLIOGRAPHY: Madeleine Maus, *Trente années*

de lutte pour art (a memoir by his wife, describing his activities on behalf of new music); Albert Van Der Linden, *Octave Maus et la vie musicale belge* (Brussels, 1950; contains 55 letters from Vincent d'Indy to Maus).

Maw, Nicholas, English compoer; b. Grantham, Lincolnshire, Nov. 5, 1935. He played clarinet and piano; studied composition with Lennox Berkeley at the Royal Academy of Music in London (1955–58) and with Nadia Boulanger in Paris (1958–59). In his music he makes use of serial methods of composition without abandoning the principle of tonality.
WORKS: *8 Chinese Lyrics* for mezzo-soprano (1956); *Flute Sontina* (1957); *Requiem* for female choir, soprano, contralto, string trio and string orch. (1957); *Nocturne* for mezzo-soprano and orch. (1958); *6 Chinese Songs* for contralto and piano (1955–58); *5 Epigrams* for chorus a cappella (1960); *Chamber Music* for oboe, clarinet, horn, bassoon and piano (1962); *Scenes and Arias* for solo voices and orch. (1962); *One-Man Show,* opera-buffa (London, Nov. 12, 1964); *Sinfonia* (Newcastle-upon-Tyne, May 1, 1966); *The Rising of the Moon,* opera (Glyndebourne, July 19, 1970).
BIBLIOGRAPHY: Susan Bradshaw, "Nicholas Maw," *The Musical Times* (Sept. 1962).

Maxfield, Richard (Vance), American avant-garde composer; b. Seattle, Washington, Feb. 2, 1927; d. (by self-defenestration from a hotel room), Los Angeles, June 27, 1969. He studied at the Univ. of California, Berkeley, with Roger Sessions, and at Princeton Univ. with Milton Babbitt; also took courses with Ernst Krenek and Luigi Dallapiccola. He became deeply engaged in acoustical electronics; taught experimental music at the New School for Social Research in New York and at the San Francisco State College; contributed essays to avant-garde publications; two of them, in free verse, were published in *Contemporary Composers on Contemporary Music,* edited by Elliot Schwartz and Barney Childs (N.Y., 1967). He acquired an excellent technique of composition in the traditional idiom before adopting an extreme avant-garde style.
WORKS: *Classical Overture* (1942); Trio for clarinet, cello and piano (1943); Septet for 2 flutes, 3 clarinets, French horn and bassoon (1947); Sonata for unaccompanied violin (1949); Violin Sonata (1950); String Trio (1951); Sonata for unaccompanied flute (1951); *Structures* for 10 wind instruments (1951); *11 Variations* for string quartet (1952); *5 Movements* for orch. (1956); Chamber Concerto for 7 instruments (1957); *Structures* for orch. (1958); *Sine Music* (1959); *Stacked Deck,* opera for tape, actors and lighting (1959); *Perspectives* for violin and tape (1960); *Peripeteia* for violin, saxophone, piano and tape (1960); *Clarinet Music* for 5 clarinets and tape (1961); *Cough Music,* with sonic materials obtained from coughs and other bronchial sound effects recorded during a modern dance recital and electronically arranged in a piece of tussive polyphony, (performed for the first time as the opening number in an audio-visual spectacle, "Musical Essays in Time, Space and Sound" by the Division of Adult Education of the Cooper Union

for the Advancement of Science and Art in New York City on Jan. 13, 1961); *Toy Symphony* for flute, violin, wooden boxes, ceramic vase and tape (1962); *African Symphony* (1964); *Venus Impulses* for electronic sound (1967).

Maxson, Frederick, American organist and composer; b. Beverly, N.J., June 13, 1862; d. Philadelphia, Jan. 21, 1934. He studied with Guilmant in Paris; for many years played organ in Philadelphia churches; was a successful teacher; publ. organ pieces, anthems, and songs.

May, Edward Collet, English organist and singing teacher; b. Greenwich, Oct. 29, 1806; d. London, Jan. 2, 1887. He studied with C. Potter and Crivelli; was organist of Greenwich Hospital (1837–69); prof. of vocal music at Queen's College, London. A disciple of Hullah, he taught in numerous schools and private classes, doing much to popularize singing among the masses; publ. *Progressive Vocal Exercises for Daily Practice* (1853); songs.

May, Florence, English pianist and writer; daughter of **Edward Collett May;** b. London, Feb. 6, 1845; d. there, June 29, 1923. She studied music with her father and with an uncle, Oliver May; began a promising career as a pianist in London; in 1871 went to Germany; took lessons with Clara Schumann in Baden-Baden; there she made the acquaintance of Brahms, who gave her some lessons. She became his enthusiastic admirer; upon her return to England, she started a vigorous campaign for performances of the music of Brahms; she herself gave many first performances in London. The important result of her dedication to Brahms was her comprehensive work, *The Life of Johannes Brahms* (2 vols., London, 1905; revised ed., publ. posthumously, 1948); she also publ. *The Girlhood of Clara Schumann* (London, 1912).

Maybrick, Michael (pseudonym **Stephen Adams**), English baritone and composer; b. Liverpool, Jan. 31, 1844; d. Buxton, Aug. 25, 1913. He studied at the Leipzig Cons. with Plaidy, Moscheles, and Richter (1866–68), and was a vocal pupil of Nava at Milan. He sang at the principal concerts in London and the provinces, and toured the U.S. and Canada in 1884. Many of his songs (sung by himself) had great vogue (e.g., *Nancy Lee*). His sacred solo *The Holy City* is still sung in churches in England and America.

Mayer, Charles, German pianist and composer; b. Königsberg, March 21, 1799; d. Dresden, July 2, 1862. He was taken to Russia as a child; was taught by John Field, who was in Russia at the time; lived in Moscow until Napleon's invasion in 1812; then went to St. Petersburg, and in 1814 to Paris. He returned to Russia in 1819 and formed a large class of pupils in St. Petersburg; in 1845 he made a tour of Scandinavia and Germany; in 1850 he settled in Dresden. He publ. an enormous number of piano pieces, in salon style; one of his mazurkas was once misattributed to Chopin.

Mayer, Frederick Christian, American organist; b. Columbus, Ohio, March 4, 1882; d. Amarillo, Texas, Oct. 20, 1973, in consequence of an automobile accident, while driving alone, at the age of 91, across the continent from a visit in California to his retirement home in Florida. He studied at the Cincinnati Cons., graduating in 1905; then went to Europe for further study of organ playing, at the Stern Cons. in Berlin and at the Cons. of Fountainebleau. Returning to the U.S., he taught at the Cincinnati Cons.; in 1911 was appointed organist of Cadet Chapel, West Point Military Academy; although he reached the mandatory retirement age of three-score and ten in 1952, he was allowed to carry on for another couple of years. He was reputed as a fine carillon builder; inspected and supervised dozens of carillons in the U.S., Canada and Belgium.

Mayer, Joseph Anton, German composer and pedagogue; b. Pfullendorf, Baden, Dec. 5, 1855; d. Stuttgart, Dec. 3, 1936. He studied at the Stuttgart Cons., and later in Berlin with Bargiel; then taught at the Stuttgart Cons. He wrote the operas *Der Stern von Bethlehem* and *Magdelenenbrunnen;* the choral works with orch. *Der Geiger von Gmünd, Jephtha, Würde der Frauen,* etc.; also piano pieces and songs.

Mayer, Max, pianist and pedagogue; b. Hamburg, May 31, 1859; d. Manchester, England, Oct. 26, 1931. He studied with local teachers; then with Seyfriz in Stuttgart, and finally with Liszt in Weimar. In 1883 he settled in Manchester; appeared frequently in chamber music concerts, and as accompanist in his own songs, which were first introduced by Muriel Foster. From 1908 he taught at the Royal College of Music in Manchester.

Mayer, Wilhelm (pseudonym **W. A. Rémy**), Austrian pianist and pedagogue; b. Prague, June 10, 1831; d. Graz, Jan. 22 1898. He studied with C. F. Pietsch; also took a course in law; Dr. jur. (1856). In 1862 he became conductor of the Graz Musical Society, resigning in 1870 to apply himself to pedagogy; he taught both piano and composition, and achieved great renown; among his pupils were Busoni, Kienzl, Reznicek, and Weingartner.

Mayer, William, American composer; b. New York, Nov. 18, 1925. He studied at Yale Univ. and the Mannes College of Music; then had theory sessions with Sessions. His most successful compositions are for the theater and the radio.
WORKS: *The Greatest Sound Around,* short children's opera (1954); *Hello World!* ("a musical trip around the world"), children's opera for narrator, orch. and audience participation (N.Y., Nov. 10, 1956); *One Christmas Long Ago,* one-act opera (Philadelphia, Dec. 12, 1964); *Brief Candle,* "micro-opera" (1964); *The Snow Queen,* ballet (1963); *Andante for Strings* (1955); *Hebraic Portrait* for orch. (1957); *Overture for an American* (1958); *Two Pastels* for orch. (1960); *Country Fair* for brass trio (1962); *Elegy* for brass quintet (1964); *Octagon* for piano and orch. (N.Y., American Symphony, William Masselos soloist, Leopold Stokowski conducting, March 21, 1971); many choruses (*The Passionate Shepherd to His Love, The Nymph's Reply to the Passionate Shepherd, Co-*

rinna's Going A-Maying, etc.); string quartet and other chamber music; piano sonata; children's pieces for piano; songs

Mayer-Mahr, Moritz, German pianist and teacher; b. Mannheim, Jan 17, 1869; d. Göteborg, Sweden, July 30, 1947. After a course of study in Mannheim, he went to Berlin; in 1892, appointed prof. of piano at the Klindworth-Scharwenka Cons. In 1933 he left Germany and settled in Sweden, remaining there until his death. He publ. *Die Technik des Klavierspiels* (3 vols.) and *Der musikalische Klavier-Unterricht;* edited the studies of Czerny and Heller.

Mayer-Reinach, Albert, German musicologist; b. Mannheim, April 2, 1876; d. Örebro, Sweden, Feb. 25, 1954. He studied in Munich and Berlin; received his Dr. phil. with the dissertation *K. H. Graun als Opernkomponist* (Berlin, 1899); was lecturer on music at the Univ. of Kiel (1904–30); conducted various choral societies; edited 2 vols. of works by early Königsberg composers; publ. valuable papers on German operas, etc. In 1933 he went to Sweden; in 1936 he became director of a music school in Örebro.

Mayer-Serra, Otto, eminent Spanish musicologist; b. Barcelona, Spain, July 12, 1904, of German-Catalan parentage; d. Mexico City, March 19, 1968. He studied in Germany with H. Abert, Curt Sachs, J. Wolf, and E. von Hornbostel. He returned to Spain in 1933, and was music critic of the Catalan weekly, *Mirador.* In 1936, at the outbreak of the Spanish Civil War, he was appointed head of the music division of the propaganda ministry of the Catalan Government; served in the Loyalist Army in 1938–39; after its defeat, he fled to France. In 1940 he reached Mexico, where he became active as writer, editor, lecturer, and manager. WRITINGS: *El Romanticismo Musical* (Mexico, 1940); *Panorama de la Música Mexicana* (Mexico, 1941); *Panorama de la Música Hispano-americana* (Mexico, 1944); *Música y Músicios de Latino-América* (of fundamental importance; contains detailed biographies of Latin American musicians and descriptions of folksongs; 2 vols.; Mexico, 1947).

Maykapar, Samuil, Russian pianist, composer, and teacher; b. Kherson, Dec. 18, 1867; d. Leningrad, May 8, 1938. He studied at the St. Petersburg Cons. with B. Cesi (piano) and Soloviev (theory); then in Vienna with Leschetizky; gave concerts in Germany (1903–10). From 1910 to 1930 he was prof. at the St. Petersburg Cons. He composed almost exclusively for piano; was particularly successful in miniature forms. His piano works include: *Biriulki* (a suite of 26 pieces); 24 Miniatures; *The Marionette Theater* (an album of 7 pieces); 2 sonatinas; etc.; also piano studies and special exercises (for pedaling, for wrist actions, etc.). He publ. the books *The Musical Ear* (Moscow, 1900) and *The Years of Study and of Musical Activity* (partly autobiographical; Moscow, 1938).

Maylath, Heinrich, pianist and pedagogue; b. Vienna, Dec. 4, 1827; d. New York, Dec. 31, 1883. He was a pupil of his father; traveled as a concert pianist in Europe, including Russia. In 1867 he settled in America,

and became a teacher in N.Y. He pub. some excellent, instructive piano music, as well as concert pieces; made numerous transcriptions of various works for piano.

Maynor, Dorothy, American soprano; b. Norfolk, Virginia, Sept. 3, 1910. Her father was a Methodist minister; she entered Hampton Institute as a young woman and later toured Europe with the Institute's famous Negro chorus. She made her New York debut on November 19, 1939, creating an excellent impression. In 1963 she founded the Harlem School of the Arts, dedicated to the music education of underprivileged children.

Mayr, Richard, Austrian bass; b. Henndorf, near Salzburg, Nov. 18, 1877; d. Vienna, Dec. 1, 1935. He was a student of medicine in Vienna. At the age of 21, he enrolled in the Vienna Cons.; studied voice, and in 1902 made his operatic debut at Bayreuth as Hagen. He was then engaged by Gustav Mahler at the Vienna Opera, of which he remained a member until his death. He made his American debut on Nov. 2, 1927, with the Metropolitan Opera Company as Pogner. He possessed a rich and powerful voice, equally suited for tragic and comic parts; was particularly distinguished as Wotan; his performance of Baron Ochs in *Der Rosenkavalier* was also notable.
BIBLIOGRAPHY: H. J. Holz, *Richard Mayr* (Vienna, 1923); Otto Kunz, *Richard Mayr* (Vienna, 1933).

Mayr, Simon (Christian names **Johann Simon** or **Giovanni Simone**), outstanding composer of operas; b. Mendorf, Bavaria, June 14, 1763; d. Bergamo, Dec. 2, 1845. He was of Italian parentage; was educated at the Jesuit Seminary at Ingolstadt; went to Bergamo, where he studied with Lenzi; then to Venice where he took lessons with Bertoni. He began his career as a composer of oratorios; several of these (*Jacob a Labano fugiens, David, Tobiae matrimonium, Sisera*) were successfully presented in Vienna. Piccinni encouraged him to write operas, and Mayr produced his 1st stage work, *Saffo, ossia I riti d'Apollo Leucadio,* in Venice with excellent success (1794). After that he wrote one opera after another for 30 years, bringing out about 60 works in all; they held the Italian stage until the success of Rossini's operatic style put Mayr's operas in the shade. Mayr possessed a fine talent for melody of the Italian type; his harmonization and orchestration followed the German model, somewhat in the tradition of Jommelli. In 1802 Mayr was appointed maestro di cappella at Santa Maria Maggiore, Bergamo, and, on the foundation of the Musical Institute there in 1805, was made its director. His most eminent pupil was Donizetti. He also founded 2 institutions for unable musicians. After 1816 he wrote much church music; he became blind towards the end of his life.
WORKS: operas: *Lodoiska* (Venice, Jan. 26, 1796); *Che originali* (Venice, Oct. 18, 1798); *Adelaide di Guesclino* (Venice, May 1, 1799); *Il Carretto del venditore d'aceto* (Venice, June 28, 1800); *Ginevra di Scozia* (Trieste, April 21, 1801); *I Misteri eleusine* (Milan, Jan. 16, 1802); *Alonso e Cora* (Milan, Dec. 26, 1803); *Elisa* (Venice, July 5, 1804); *Adelasia e Aleramo* (Milan, Dec. 26, 1806); *La Rosa rossa e la rosa bianca*

(Genoa, Feb. 21, 1813); *Medea in Corinto* (Naples, Nov. 28, 1813); *L'amor coningale* is publ. in *Monumenta Bergomensia* 22. He also publ. a commemorative book on Haydn, *Breve notizie istoriche della vita e delle opere di Giuseppe Haydn* (1809); compiled theoretical works, which remained in MS. His *Biografie di scrittori ed artisti musicali bergamaschi nativi ed oriundi* was ed. by A. Alessandri (Bergamo, 1875).

BIBLIOGRAPHY: F. Alborghetti and M. Galli, *Gaetano Donizetti e G. Simone Mayr, notizie e documenti* (Bergamo, 1875); C. Schmidl, *Cenni biografici su G. S. Mayr* (Trieste, 1901); C. G. Scotti, *S. Mayr* (Bergamo, 1903); H. Kretzschmar, *Die musikgeschichtliche Bedeutung S. Mayrs* (Leipzig, 1904); L. Schiedermair, *Beiträge zur Geschichte der Oper um die Wende des 18. und 19. Jahrhunderts: Simon Mayr* (2 vols.; Leipzig, 1907 and 1910); J. Freeman, "Johann Simon Mayr and His *Ifigenia in Aulide*," *Musical Quarterly* (April 1971); M. Carner, "Simone Mayr and His *L'amor coningale*," *Music & Letters* (July 1971); A. Gazzaniga, "Su *L'amor coningale* di Giovanni Simone Mayr," *Nuova Rivista Musicale Italiana* (Sept.-Oct. 1971).

Mayseder, Joseph, Austrian violinist and composer; b. Vienna, Oct. 26, 1789; d. there, Nov. 21, 1863. He was a pupil of Suche and Wranitzky (violin); and of E. Förster (piano and composition). He joined the famous Schuppanzigh Quartet as 2nd violin; entered the court orch. in 1816; became solo violinist at the court opera in 1820 and chamber violinist to the Emperor in 1835. He never went on tours, and rarely gave concerts; yet he was a finished virtuoso, admired even by Paganini. In Vienna he was very successful as a teacher. His works include several violin concertos, 5 string quintets and 8 string quartets, trios, and solo violin pieces, all effectively written.

Mayuzumi, Toshirō, eminent Japanese composer; b. Yokohama, Feb. 20, 1929. He studied at the National Music Academy in Tokyo (1945-51); then took courses at the Paris Cons. with Aubin. Returning to Japan he organized the modern group Ars Nova Japonica and also worked at the electronic studio in Tokyo. He became known in Europe with the production of his *Sphenogramme,* a modernistic piece for voice and instruments (Frankfurt Festival of the International Society for Contemporary Music on June 25, 1951) and *Ectoplasme* for electronic instruments, percussion and strings (Stockholm Festival of the International Society for Contemporary Music on June 5, 1956). His style of composition embodies sonorous elements from old Japanese music, serial techniques and electronic sound, all amalgamated in a remarkably effective manner; he was quite successful in writing film scores and spent several years in Hollywood.

WORKS: Violin Sonata (1946); *Divertimento* for 10 instruments (1948); *Symphonic Mood* (1950); *Mikrokosmos* for 7 instruments (Modern Music Festival, Karuizawa, Japan, Aug. 12, 1957); *Phonologie symphonique* (Tokyo, May 28, 1957); *Nirvana Symphony* (Tokyo, April 2, 1958); *U-So-Ri,* oratorio (Tokyo, June 12, 1959); *Mandala-Symphonie* (Tokyo, March 27, 1960); *Bunraku* for cello solo (1960); *Music with Sculpture* for winds (Pittsburgh, June 29, 1961); *Pre-* lude for string quartet (1961); *Bugaku,* ballet (N.Y., March 20, 1963); *Samsara,* symph. poem (Tokyo, June 12, 1962); *Texture* for band (Pittsburgh, June 10, 1962); *Essay in Sonorities* (Osaka, Jan. 21, 1963); *Fireworks* for band (Pittsburgh, June 13, 1963); *Pratidesana,* Buddhist cantata (Kyoto, Sept. 5, 1963); *The Ritual Overture* for band (Pittsburgh, July 2, 1964); *The Birth of Music,* symph. poem (Tokyo, Oct. 10, 1964); symph. poem, *Showa Tempyo Raku* (Old and Present Music;* Tokyo, Oct. 31, 1970); the opera, *Kinkakuji* (*The Temple of the Golden Pavilion;* Berlin, June 23, 1976).

Mazas, Jacques-Féréol, French violinist; b. Lavaur (Tarn), Sept. 23, 1782; d. Bordeaux, Aug. 25, 1849. He was a pupil of Baillot at the Paris Con., winning 1st prize as violinist (1805); then played in the orch. of the Italian Opera in Paris; toured Europe (1811-29); then was a teacher in Orléans, and director of a music school in Cambrai (1837-41). He spent the last years of his life in Bordeaux. He wrote a method for violin (new ed. by J. Hřímalý) and numerous valuable studies; also a method for viola; concertos, string quartets, trios, violin duets, fantasias, variations, *romances,* etc.; also 3 operas, one of which, *Le Kiosque,* was performed at Paris in 1842. A set of 6 études was publ. in a new ed. by Hubay.

Mazzinghi, Joseph, English pianist and composer; b. London, Dec. 25, 1765; d. Downside, near Bath, Jan. 15, 1844. He was the son of Thomas Mazzinghi, of Corsican extraction, who made his home in England. Joseph Mazzinghi studied with John Christian Bach in London; he was a mere child when his father died, and he succeeded him as organist of the Portuguese Chapel. He subsequently took lessons with Anfossi and Sacchini. He wrote 2 Italian operas for the King's Theatre: *La Bella Arsena* (1795) and *Il Tesoro* (1796), and a number of light stage works to English texts; *A Day in Turkey* (1791), *The Turnpike Gate* (1799), *The Wife of Two Husbands* (1803). He also wrote a large number of arias, glees, and songs; one of them, *Tell Me Shepherds,* attained great popularity.

Mazzocchi, Domenico, Italian composer; b. Veja, near Città Castellana, (baptized Nov. 8), 1592; d. Rome, Jan. 21, 1665. A learned Roman lawyer, he studied music with Nanini; publ. a book, *Madrigali a 5 voci in partitura* (1638), in which appear, for the 1st time, the conventional symbols for *crescendo* $<$ and *decrescendo* $>$, *piano* (*p*), *forte* (*f*), and *trillo* (*tr*), which he explains in a preface. He also composed the operas *La Catena d'Adone* (Rome, 1626) and *L'Innocenza difesa,* several oratorios, and various pieces of church music.

Mazzocchi, Virgilio, Italian composer, brother of **Domenico Mazzocchi;** b. Veja, July (baptized July 22), 1597; d. there, Oct. 3, 1646. He was chorusmaster at St. Peter's from 1629 until his death. With M. Marazzoli he composed the 1st comic opera, *Chi soffre, speri* (Rome, Feb. 27, 1639). Excerpts from this opera were publ. by H. Goldschmidt (1901); an *Argomento et allegoria* relating to it was publ. at the time of the 1st performance (a copy is in the Library of Congress, Washington).

BIBLIOGRAPHY: H. Prunières, *L'Opéra italien en France avant Lulli* (Paris, 1913); A. Salza, "Mazzocchi," *Rivista Musicale Italiana* (1917); A. Cardinali, *Cenni biografici su Domenico e Virgilio Mazzocchi* (1926).

Mazzolani, Antonio, Italian composer; b. Ruina, near Ferrara, Dec. 26, 1819; d. Ferrara, Jan. 25, 1900. He studied with Zagagnoli (composition) and Lodi (piano); wrote the operas *Gismonda* (Ferrara, May 17, 1854) and *Enrico Charlis* (Ferrara, Nov. 25, 1876); his choruses, with extensive soli, were very popular in Italy during his time.

Mazzoleni, Ettore, conductor and composer, of Italian and Swiss extraction; b. Brusio, Switzerland, June 18, 1905; d. Toronto, as a result of an automobile accident, June 1, 1968. He studied music in Oxford and London; in 1929 he was appointed teacher at Upper Canada College, Toronto; later became a member of the faculty of the Toronto Cons., and conducted concerts there; also appeared as a guest conductor in other Canadian towns. He made several transcriptions of folksongs for various instrumental and vocal groups.

Mazzucato, Alberto, Italian violinist, composer, and writer on music; b. Udine, July 28, 1813; d. Milan, Dec. 31, 1877. He first studied mathematics; then turned to music, his teacher being Bresciano in Padua, where his 1st opera *La Fidanzata di Lammermoor* was given (Feb. 24, 1834); he wrote 6 more operas: *Don Chisciotte* (Milan, April 26, 1836), *Esmeralda* (Mantua, Feb. 10, 1838; his most successful stage work), *I Corsari* (Milan, Feb. 15, 1840), *I Due Sergenti* (Milan, Feb. 27, 1841), *Luigi V* (Milan, Feb, 25, 1843), and *Hernani* (Genoa, Dec. 26, 1843); Verdi's ascendance soon put him into the shade. From 1859 till 1869 he was concertmaster in the orch. of La Scala, Milan; for several years was editor of the influential *Gazzetta Musicale*; publ. *Trattato d'estetica musicale.*

McBride, Robert Guyn, American composer; b. Tucson, Arizona, Feb. 20, 1911. He learned to play the clarinet and the saxophone and played in dance bands as a youth. He studied music theory at the Univ. of Arizona (1928-35); was subsequently a member of the Tucson Symph. Orch. (1928-35). From 1935 to 1946 he taught wind instrument playing at Bennington College; was then arranger for Triumph Films, N.Y. (1946-57); from 1957 to 1978 he was on the music faculty of the Univ. of Arizona. An exceptionally prolific composer, he wrote over 1000 pieces in various genres, many of them on American or Mexican themes with an infusion of jazz elements.
WORKS: *Mexican Rhapsody* for orch. (1934); *Workout* for oboe and piano (1936); *Swing Stuff* for clarinet and piano (1938); *Jam Session,* for woodwind quintet (1941); *Side Show* for orch. (1944); Violin Concerto (1954); *Swing Foursome* for string quartet (1957); *Five Winds Blowing* for wind quintet (1957); *Hill Country Symphony* (1964); *Lament for the Parking Problem* for trumpet, horn and trombone (1968).

McCabe, John, English pianist and composer; b. Liverpool, April 21, 1939, of mixed Scottish-Irish stock on his father's side and of German-Scandinavian-Spanish ancestry on his mother's. He played piano, violin, and cello as a child and, according to family lore, composed 13 symphonies and an opera before puberty. He studied composition with Thomas Pitfield at Manchester Univ. (Mus. B., 1960); at the Royal Manchester College of Music and in Munich with Harald Genzmer; was pianist in residence at Univ. College in Cardiff (1965-68); then settled in London. In 1978 he made a tour of the U.S. as pianist-composer.
WORKS: *Movements* for clarinet, violin and cello (1964); Symph. No. 1 (1965); *Concertante* for harpsichord and chamber ensemble (1965); Piano Concerto No. 1 (1966); string trio (1966); *Nocturnal* for piano quintet (1966); *Miniconcerto* for organ, percussion and 485 penny-whistles (1966); *Dance Movements* for horn, violin and piano (1967); *Rounds* for brass quintet (1967); cantata *Aspects of Whiteness* for mixed chorus and piano (1967); *Concertante Music* for orch. (1968); Sonata for clarinet, cello and piano (1969); Quartet for Oboe and String Trio (1969); *This Town's a Corporation Full of Crooked Streets,* an entertainment for speaker, tenor, children's chorus, mixed chorus and instrumental ensemble (1969); *The Lion, the Witch and the Wardrobe,* children's opera (1969); Piano Concerto No. 2 (1970); Symph. No. 2 (1970); *Metamorphoses* for harpsichord and orch. (1972); many piano pieces, organ works and choruses.

McCartney, John Paul, English rock 'n' roll singer and composer; member of the famous Liverpudlian quartet The Beatles; b. Liverpool, June 18, 1942. He picked out chords on a family piano (his father was an amateur ragtime player), and at puberty began playing a left-handed guitar. He is the only Beatle who attended college, and studied English literature. Fascinated by Elvis Presley, he tried to emulate the spirit of American rock 'n' roll à l'anglaise. He joined John Lennon and George Harrison in the Casbah Club in Liverpool in 1959; this fruitful and fantastically lucrative association with them, and later with Ringo Starr, continued until the breakup of the group in 1970 when McCartney went to High Court to end the partnership and asked for an accounting of assets and income. Endowed with an authentic poetic gift, McCartney infused a literary quality into the lyrics used by The Beatles, fashioning them in archaic English prosody, which in combination with the modal harmony of the arrangements, imparted a somewhat distant quality to their products. Like his co-Beatles, McCartney went through a period of transcendental meditation when he sat at the feet of a hirsute Indian guru, but his British common sense soon overrode this metaphysical infatuation.
BIBLIOGRAPHY: Hunter Davies, *The Beatles* (N.Y., 1968); Ned Rorem, "The Beatles," *N.Y. Review of Books* (Jan. 18, 1968); G. Geppert, *Songs der Beatles. Texte und Interpretationen* (2nd ed.; Munich, 1968); E. Davies, "The Psychological Characteristics of Beatle Mania," *Journal of the History of Ideas* (April-June 1969); P. McCabe and R. D. Schonfeld, *Apple to the Core: The Unmaking of the Beatles* (N.Y., 1972); F.

Seloron, *Les Beatles* (Paris, 1972); W. Mellers, *Twilight of the Gods: The Music of the Beatles* (N.Y., 1973).

McCauley, William, Canadian composer; b. Tofield, Alberta, Feb. 14, 1917. He studied piano with Margaret Parsons and music theory with Healy Willan at the Royal Cons. of Toronto (1945-47); later took courses in composition with Bernard Rogers and Howard Hanson at the Eastman School of Music in Rochester, N.Y. (1957-60; Mus. D.). He was a musical director at Crawley Films (1949-60), where he composed and conducted music for over 100 television films and documentaries; then was director of music at York Univ. (1961-69); in 1970 was appointed head of the music dept of Seneca College in Toronto. His music is pleasing, lyrical and inoffensive, with some officious modernities.

WORKS: *Newfoundland Scene* for orch. (1952); *Saskatchewan Suite* for orch. (1956); *5 Miniatures* for flute and strings (1958); *Contrasts* for orch. (1958); *Horn Concerto* (1959); *5 Miniatures* for bass trombone, harp and strings (1959); *Theme and Deviations* for orch. (1960); *Wilderness,* for orch. music from the film (1963); *Canadian Folk Song Fantasy* for symph. band (1966); *Metropolis,* concert suite for symph. band (1967); *2 Nocturnes* for strings (1968); *Sunday Morning at Wahanowin* for string orch. (1968); *Concerto Grosso* for solo brass quintet and orch. (1973); *Christmas Carol Fantasies* for orch. (1975); *5 Miniatures* for 6 percussionists (1962); *5 Miniatures* for 10 winds (1968); *5 Miniatures* for 4 saxophones (1972); *Miniature Overture* for brass quintet (1973); *Kaleidoscope Québécois* for flute, clarinet, violin, cello and 2 pianos (1974); *5 Miniatures* for brass quintet (1974); *Space Trip* for piano (1968); choruses, songs, many with instrumental accompaniment.

McClellan, John Jasper, American organist and conductor; b. Payson, Utah, April 20, 1874; d. Salt Lake City, Aug. 2, 1925. He studied piano with A. Jonás, organ with A. A. Stanley, and composition with J. E. Schmaal. In 1900 he became organist at the Mormon Tabernacle at Salt Lake City; made a transcontinental tour with its choir. In 1905 he founded the Salt Lake City Symph. Orch., and conducted it until 1910; Bachelor of Didactics, Mormon Church; composed an *Ode to Irrigation;* organ pieces; numerous anthems

McCorkle, Donald Macomber, American musicologist; b. Cleveland, Feb. 20, 1929; d. Vancouver, Feb. 7, 1978. He studied clarinet, and took courses in musicology at Indiana Univ. with Willi Apel and Paul Nettl; was granted a Ph.D. degree there (1958). In 1954 he was appointed assistant prof. of musicology at Salem College, Winston-Salem, N.C.; served as music editor of the Moravian Church in America; executive director of the Moravian Music Foundation; then went to Vancouver where he was active as a teacher. He wrote a valuable dissertation, *Moravian Music in Salem: A German-American Heritage* (Indiana Univ., 1958).

McCormack, John, famous Irish tenor; b. Athlone, June 14, 1884; d. Glena, Booterstown, Sept. 16, 1945.

Without previous training he took part in the National Irish Festival at Dublin in 1903, and carried off the gold medal; in 1903 he became a member of the Dublin Cathedral Choir and began to study seriously with the organist and choirmaster, Vincent O'Brien; he made his debut as a concert singer at a concert of the Sunday League in London (Feb. 17, 1907) and his operatic debut as Turiddu in *Cavalleria Rusticana* at Covent Garden (Oct. 5, 1907), becoming instantly a prime favorite; in 1909 he sang at the San Carlo in Naples, and was engaged by Hammerstein for the Manhattan Opera House in N.Y., where he made his American debut on Nov. 10, 1909, as Alfred Germont in *La Traviata;* during the 1910-11 season he was with the Boston Opera Co.; 1912-14, with Chicago Opera Co.; after that, he appeared seldom in opera, but became tremendously successful as a concert tenor. He was naturalized as an American citizen in 1919; was given the title of Count by Pope Pius XI in 1928 and named Papal Chamberlain.

BIBLIOGRAPHY: L. A. G. Strong, *John McCormack* (London, 1941; reprint, 1949); Lily McCormack (his widow), *I Hear You Calling Me* (Milwaukee, 1949); L. F. X. McDermott Roe, *John McCormack, the Complete Discography* (London, 1956); R. Foxall, *John McCormack* (N.Y., 1964); *Dictionary of American Biography,* Supplement III (N.Y., 1973).

McCoy, William J., American composer; b. Crestline, Ohio, March 15, 1848; d. Oakland, Calif., Oct. 15, 1926. His family moved to California when he was a child; he began to compose at the age of 12; then was sent to N.Y. to study with William Mason; later studied at the Leipzig Cons. with Reinecke and Hauptmann. His Symphony in F was conducted in Leipzig by Reinecke in 1872. He returned to California and wrote some theater music for the Bohemian Club there (*Harmadryads, The Cave Man,* etc.); also wrote an opera, *Egypt* (2 acts presented at the Berkeley Music Festival, Sept. 17, 1921), for which he received the Bispham Medal of the American Opera Society of Chicago; *Yosemite,* overture; *Violin Concerto;* a suite from *A Masque of Apollo* (*Prelude, Dance,* and *The Naiad's Idyl*); numerous songs, and a textbook, *Cumulative Harmony.*

BIBLIOGRAPHY: E. E. Hipsher, *American Opera and Its Composers* (Philadelphia, 1934; pp. 317-20).

McCutchan, Robert Guy, American choral conductor and hymnologist; b. Mount Ayr, Iowa, Sept. 13, 1877; d. Claremont, Calif., May 15, 1958. He was active as music educator and choral conductor in the schools and churches of Iowa, Kansas and Indiana; made a thorough study of American hymnals and publ. a valuable compilation, *Our Hymnody* (Nashville, 1937; 2nd ed. 1942; contains detailed biographical information on American hymn composers); also *Hymn Tune Names: Their Sources and Significance* (Nashville, 1957).

McDonald, Harl, American composer and music administrator; b. near Boulder, Colorado, July 27, 1899; d. Princeton, N.J., March 30, 1955. He studied at the Univ. of Southern California; became a professional pianist; also did research in the measurement of instrumental and vocal tones; published its results in *New Methods of Measuring Sound* (Philadelphia, 1935). In 1939 he was appointed business manager of Philadelphia Orch., but continued to compose. His music gained performance almost exclusively by courtesy of the Philadelphia Orch., conducted by Stokowski and Ormandy.

WORKS: (all performed in Philadelphia): 4 symphonies: No. 1, *The Santa Fé Trail* (Nov. 16, 1934), No. 2, *The Rhumba Symph.* (Oct. 4, 1935), No. 3, *Lamentations of Fu Hsuan*, for orch., chorus and soprano solo (Jan. 3, 1936), No. 4 (April 8, 1938); *Festival of the Workers* (April 26, 1934); *3 Poems on Traditional Aramaic Themes* (Dec. 18, 1936); Concerto for 2 Pianos and Orch. (April 2, 1937); Violin Concerto (March 16, 1945); *Saga of the Mississippi* (April 9, 1948); *From Childhood*, suite for harp and orch. (Jan. 17, 1941); 2 nocturnes for orch., *San Juan Capistrano* (Boston Symph., Oct. 30, 1939); *Arkansas Traveler*, a humoresque (Detroit, March 3, 1940); *Bataan*, a tone poem (Washington, July 3, 1942); chamber music: 2 piano trios (1931; 1932); *Fantasy* for string quartet (1932); *Quartet on Negro Themes* (1933); many choral works.

BIBLIOGRAPHY: Madeleine Goss, *Modern Music-Makers* (N.Y., 1952; pp. 303-13).

McDonald, Susann, American harpist; b. Rock Island, Illinois, May 26, 1935. She studied with Lily Laskine in Paris; received Premier Prix de harpe at the Paris Cons. (1955); her principal harp teacher was Henriette Renié, whose method she adopted in her own playing and teaching; she received some advice from Marcel Grandjany. She made her American debut in Los Angeles in 1956; then gave concerts in N.Y. (1959) and toured Europe and South America; in 1967 she was appointed prof. of harp at the Univ. of Southern Calif., Los Angeles; also taught at the Univ. of Arizona, in 1975 she joined the faculty of the Juilliard School, N.Y. She is noted for her excellent interpretations of contemporary music, for which she has developed a perfect technique.

McDowell, John Herbert, American composer; b. Washington, D.C., Dec. 21, 1926. He studied at Colgate Univ. (B.A., 1948) and at Columbia Univ. with Otto Luening, Jack Beeson and Roger Goeb (M.A., 1957); held a Guggenheim Fellowship in 1962. He devoted his energies chiefly to music for the theater and dance.

WORKS: a cantata, *Good News from Heaven* (1957); *Four Sixes and a Nine* for orch. (1959); *Accumulation* for 35 flutes, strings and percussion (1964); 100-odd pieces for dance, among them *Insects and Heroes* (1961); *From Sea to Shining Sea*, a homage to Ives (1965); *Dark Psalters* (1968).

McEwen, Sir John Blackwood, Scottish composer and pedagogue; b. Harwick, April 13, 1868; d. London, June 14, 1948. He studied at Glasgow Univ. (M. A., 1888) and at the Royal Academy of Music in London, with Corder, Matthay, and Prout; taught piano in Glasgow (1895-98) and composition at the Royal Academy of Music in London (1898-1936); in 1924 he succeeded Alexander MacKenzie as principal. He was

knighted in 1931. He continued to compose until his last years.

WORKS: several symphonies, of which one subtitled *Solway* (1911) was the best known; 4 orch. suites (1893-1941); *7 Bagatelles* for strings; Viola Concerto (1901); 17 string quartets (1893-1947); 6 violin sonatas (1913-29); Viola Sonata (1930); *Scottish Rhapsody* for violin and piano (1915); piano pieces; songs. He publ. *Text Book of Harmony and Counterpoint* (1908); *The Elements of Music* (1910); *A Primer of Harmony* (1911); *The Thought in Music* (1912); *Tempo Rubato* (1928); *Introduction to the Piano Sonatas of Beethoven* (1931).

BIBLIOGRAPHY: S. Dyke's article on McEwen's string quartets in Cobbett's *Cyclopedic Survey of Chamber Music* (London, 1930; 2nd ed., 1963).

McGill, Josephine, American composer and collector of American folksongs; b. Louisville, Ky., Oct. 20, 1877; d. there, Feb. 24, 1919. She studied with Alexander Lambert at the New York College of Music; collected material for the publ. *Folk Songs of the Kentucky Mountains* (1917, 1922, 1926, and 1937).

McHugh, Jimmy, American composer of popular songs; b. Boston, July 10, 1894; d. Beverly Hills, May 22, 1969. He was a rehearsal accompanist for the Boston Opera Company before embarking on composition. He moved to New York in 1921. His first Broadway show was *Blackbirds of 1928* which included his greatest hit song *I Can't Give you Anything but Love, Baby*. In 1930 he went to Hollywood and began to write for the films; one of his most famous songs of the period was *South American Way*. During the war he wrote the inspirational song *Comin' in on a Wing and a Prayer*. He was awarded a Presidential Certificate of Merit for his work on War Bonds. He also received honorary doctor's degrees from Harvard Univ., Georgetown Univ. and Holy Cross College.

McKay, George Frederick, American composer; b. Harrington, Wash., June 11, 1899; d. Stateline, Nevada, Oct. 4, 1970. He studied at the Univ. of Washington, Seattle, and subsequently at the Eastman School of Music in Rochester, with Palmgren and Sinding; graduated in 1923. In 1941 he was appointed to the faculty of the Univ. of Washington, where he retired in 1968.

WORKS: 4 sinfoniettas (1925-42); *Fantasy on a Western Folk Song* (Rochester, May 3, 1933); *Bravura Prelude*, for brass ensemble (Rochester, April 30, 1939); *To a Liberator*, symph. poem (Indianapolis, March 15, 1940); *Introspective Poem*, for strings (Philadelphia, April 3, 1941); *A Prairie Portrait* (San Francisco, Sept. 4, 1941); *Pioneer Epic* (Oakland, Feb. 17, 1942); Wind Quintet (1930); Piano Trio (1931); a quintet subtitled *American Street Scenes*, for clarinet, trumpet, saxophone, bassoon, and piano (1935); 2 organ sonatas; Violin Concerto (1940); Cello Concerto (1942); a suite on Negro folksongs for strings, entitled *Port Royal, 1861* (1939).

McKinley, Carl, American composer and organist; b. Yarmouth, Maine, Oct. 9, 1895; d. Boston, July 24, 1966. He studied with Edward Burlingame Hill at Harvard Univ.; in 1929 was appointed instructor of organ and composition at the New England Cons. in Boston. Many of his works are inspired by American subjects. He wrote *The Blue Flower*, symph. poem (N.Y., Jan. 18, 1924); *Masquerade*, American rhapsody for orch. (his most popular work; Chicago North Shore Festival, May 29, 1926); *Caribbean Holiday* (Boston, Nov. 18, 1948); String Quartet, Cello Sonata and other pieces of chamber music, as well as organ pieces and songs.

McKinney, Mathilde, American pianist and composer; b. South Bend, Indiana, Jan. 31, 1904. She studied piano and composition at the Juilliard School of Music in New York; was a member of the faculty of Westminster State College, Princeton, New Jersey (1960-70). Among her piano pieces are *Rain Drops* and *Sad Waltz*.

McKuen, Rod, American minstrel and lyricist; b. Oakland, Calif., April 29, 1933; ran away from previously broken home at the age of 11; bummed as logger, roadman, roping calves and dogging bulls in and out of rodeo shows; became a disc jockey and a script writer in a psychological warfare unit during the Korean war. Returning to the U.S., he appeared as a folksy balladeer in San Francisco night clubs; obtained a music theory book and learned to write tunes; supported himself by playing supporting roles in otherwise unsupportable bit parts in the movies; eked out a posh living by crashing parties and gorging himself on choice comestibles. He became a roving poet, dispensing a plethora of facile country style songs with monosyllabic assonances for rhymes and a simple appeal of scenes of non-obscene free love against an artificially flavored pastoral landscape. His first anthology of verse, *An Autumn Came*, was a failure, but he stumbled into a poetic bonanza with the commercially issued volumes *Stanyan Street* and *Listen to the Warm*. He never indentured himself to an agent, and so was able to reap a lucrative harvest of success, blandly chanting, "I have no special bed, I give myself to those who offer love." He publ. a memoir, *Finding My Father* (N.Y., 1976) in which he stated, "I was born a bastard; some people spend their entire lives becoming one." His putative natural father was a lumberjack who died about 1965.

McNaught, William (Gray), English music journalist and editor; b. London, March 30, 1849; d. there, Oct. 13, 1918. He studied at the Royal Academy of Music; was active as a choral conductor; in 1892 began to edit the *School Music Review* publ. by Novello; in 1909 became editor of the *Musical Times*. His son, also named **William McNaught** (b. London, Sept. 1, 1883; d. there, June 9, 1953), was assistant editor of the *Musical Times* when his father was editor; wrote program notes and reviews for many years; in 1944 he became editor of the *Musical Times*, succeeding Harvey Grace. He publ. *A Short Account of Modern Music and Musicians* (London, 1937).

McPhee, Colin, outstanding American composer; b. Montreal, Canada, March 15, 1901; d. Los Angeles, Jan. 7, 1964. He studied at the Peabody Cons. with Gustav Strube, graduating in 1921; then took piano lessons with Arthur Friedheim in Toronto and with Isidor Philipp in Paris. Returning to America in 1926, he joined the modern movement in New York; wrote Concerto for Piano and Wind Octet (Boston, March 11, 1929) and also scores for the experimental films H_2O and *Mechanical Principles*. In 1934 he went to live on the island of Bali in Indonesia; in 1936 he was in Mexico, where he wrote his major work *Tabuh-Tabuhan*, for 2 pianos and orch.; then was again in Bali, until 1939. From 1958 until his death he was at the Institute of Ethnomusicology at the Univ. of California in Los Angeles. He wrote *Balinese Ceremonial Music* for flute and 2 pianos (1942); *Transitions* for orch. (1951); 3 symphonies (1955, 1957, 1962); *4 Iroquois Dances* for orch.; *Invention and Kinesis* for piano; published *A House in Bali* (N.Y., 1946); and *Music in Bali* (posthumous, New Haven, Conn., 1966). See "Modern Music" . . . *Analytic Index*, compiled by Wayne Shirley and ed. by Wm. and C. Lichtenwanger (N.Y., 1976; pp. 129–130).

Meader, George, American tenor; b. Minneapolis, July 6, 1888; d. Hollywood, Dec. 19, 1963. He studied law at the Univ. of Minnesota; after graduation in 1908 he went to Germany where he took voice lessons with Anna Schoen-René; remained in Germany and sang at the Stuttgart Opera (1911–19). Returning to America in 1919, he gave recitals before making his operatic debut with the Metropolitan Opera, N.Y., as Victorin in Korngold's opera *Die tote Stadt* (Nov. 19, 1921); resigned from the Metropolitan Opera in 1931 and sang in operetta; was particularly successful in Jerome Kern's *Cat and the Fiddle*.

Meck, Nadezhda von, friend and benefactress of Tchaikovsky; b. Znamenskoye, near Smolensk, Feb. 10, 1831; d. Wiesbaden, Jan. 13, 1894. She became interested in Tchaikovsky's music through Nicholas Rubinstein, director of the Moscow Cons., of which she was a patroness. At first offering Tchaikovsky commissions, she later granted him a yearly allowance of 6000 rubles in order that he might compose undisturbed by finanical considerations. He lived for long periods in close proximity to her, at Brailov (near Kiev) and in Florence, Italy, but although they carried on an extensive and intimate correspondence (publ. in 3 vols., Moscow, 1934–36), they never met face to face. Tchaikovsky's allowance was abruptly cut off in 1890, on the pretext of financial difficulties, leading to a complete break between him and Mme. von Meck in 1891. She employed youthful Debussy as pianist in her household.

BIBLIOGRAPHY: Barbara von Meck and Catherine Drinker Bowen, *Beloved Friend* (biographical romance; N.Y., 1937); Olga Bennigson, "More Tchaikovsky-von Meck Correspondence," *Musical Quarterly* (April 1938).

Medinš, Jānis, foremost Latvian composer; b. Riga, Oct. 9, 1890; d. Stockholm, March 4, 1966. He was a pupil at the music school there; 1904-13, orch. player; 1914-16, head of the piano department of the firm of A. Diederichs in St. Petersburg; 1916-20, military bandmaster there. In 1920 he returned to Riga; conducted opera at the Latvian National Theater; also was prof. at the Riga Cons. In 1944, as the Soviet armies approached Latvia, Mediņš went to Stockholm. He wrote the operas *Uguns un Nakts* (*Fire and Night;* Riga, May 26, 1921) and *Deevi un Cilveki* (Riga, May 23, 1922); symph. and chamber music; choruses.

Medtner, Nikolai, notable Russian composer; b. (of German parents) Moscow, Jan. 5, 1880; d. London, Nov. 13, 1951. He first studied with his uncle Theodore Goedicke; in 1892 entered Moscow Cons., where he took courses with Sapelnikov and Safonov (piano), and with Taneyev (composition); graduated in 1900, winning the gold medal; in the same year he won the Rubinstein prize in Vienna; for the next 2 years he appeared with much success as a pianist in the European capitals; returning to Russia, he taught at the Moscow Cons. for one academic year (1902–03); was again prof. there from 1918 till 1921, when he left Russia; lived in Berlin and Paris; eventually settled in London; made U.S. tours in 1924–25 and in 1929–30. In Russian music he was a solitary figure; he never followed the nationalist trend, but endeavored to create a new type of composition, rooted both in the Classical and the Romantic tradition; his sets of fairy tales in sonata form are unique examples of his favorite genre. He wrote his best compositions before he left Russia; although he continued to compose during his residence abroad, his late music lacks the verve and Romantic sincerity that distinguishes his earlier works. He wrote almost exclusively for the piano and for the voice. A revival of his music was begun in Russia after his death.
WORKS: 3 piano concertos (1916–18, 1927, 1943; he was soloist in the première of his 3rd concerto with the London Philharmonic, Feb. 19, 1944); String Quintet (1950). For piano: *3 Mood Pictures* (1902); *3 Improvisations* (1902); *3 Arabesques* (1905); *34 Fairy Tales* (1905–29); *3 Dithyrambs* (1906); *Sonata-Triad* (1907); *3 Novels* (1909); *4 sonatas* (1909–14); *Fairy-tale Sonata* (1912); *Sonata-Ballade* (1913); *Sonata romantica* (1930); *Sonata minacciosa* (1931); *Sonata idillica* (1935); *4 Lyric Fragments* (1912); 3 sets of *Forgotten Melodies* (1919–20); 4 sets of *Romantic Sketches* (1933); *2 Elegies* (1945). Vocal works: 104 songs; *Sonata-Vocalise*, for voice and piano, without words (1921); *Suite-Vocalise* (1923). Chamber music: 2 violin sonatas and various pieces for violin and piano. A collection of Medtner's literary essays was published in an English transl. by Alfred Swan, as *The Muse and the Fashion* (Haverford, Pa, 1951).
BIBLIOGRAPHY: E. Newman, "N. Medtner," *Musical Times* (Jan. 1915); V. Yakovlev, *N. Medtner,* in Russian and German (Moscow, 1927); A. Swan, "Medtner and the Music of Our Time," *Music & Letters* (Jan. 1927); R. Holt, *Medtner and His Music* (London, 1948); R. Holt, editor, *N. Medtner,* a symposium (London, 1956); B. Dolinskaya, *Nicolai Medtner* (Moscow, 1966). His collected works were publ. in 12 vols. in Moscow (1959–63).

Meerens, Charles, Belgian acoustician; b. Bruges, Dec. 26, 1831; d. Schaerbeek, n. Brussels, Jan. 14, 1909. He studied cello under Bessems, Dumont, and Servais; then became a tuner in his father's piano factory, and devoted himself to acoustical researches.
WRITINGS: *Le Métromètre, ou moyen simple de connaître le degré de vitesse d'un mouvement indiqué* (1859); *Instruction élémentaire de calcul musical* (1864); *Phénomènes musico-physiologiques* (1868); *Hommage à la mémoire de M. Delezenne* (1869); *Examen analytique des expériences d'acoustique musicale de M. A. Cornu et E. Mercadier* (1869); *Le Diapason et la notation musicale simplifiées* (1873); *Mémoire sur le diapason* (1877); *Petite méthode pour apprendre la musique et le piano* (1878); *La Gamme musicale majeure et mineure* (1890); *Acoustique musicale* (1892); *L'Avenir de la science musicale* (1894); *La Science musicale à la portée de tous les artistes et amateurs* (1902).

Meerts, Lambert (-Joseph), Belgian violinist and pedagogue; b. Brussels, Jan. 6, 1800; d. there, May 12, 1863. He studied with Lafont and Habeneck at Paris; from 1835, prof. at Brussels Cons. Among his important instructive works for violin are *Études pour violon avec accompagnement d'un second violon; Mécanisme du violon* (advanced studies); 12 books of studies on rhythm, on motifs by Beethoven; etc.

Mees, Arthur, American conductor; b. Columbus, Ohio, Feb. 13, 1850; d. New York, April 26, 1923. He was a pupil, at Berlin, of Kullak (piano), Weitzmann (theory), and Dorn (conducting); from 1880 to 1886, he conducted the Cincinnati May Festival Chorus; from 1888 to 1911, conductor of the Orange Mendelssohn Union; 1891–1913, conductor of the Albany Musical Association; from 1913, also conductor of the Bridgeport Oratorio Society; from 1896, assistant conductor of the Chicago Symph. Orch.; wrote analytical program notes for it, and also for the N.Y. Philharmonic Society (1887–96). He publ. *Choirs and Choral Music* (1901); also composed piano studies.

Meester, Louis De, Belgian composer; b. Roeselare, Oct. 28, 1904. He traveled widely in his youth as a popular musician; lived in Algeria (1928–30); was a teacher at the Cons. in Meknes, French Morocco (1932–37); returned to Belgium in 1938 and studied briefly with Jean Absil; served as acoustical director at the Belgian Radio (1945–61). From 1961 to 1969 he was director of the Institute for Psychoacoustics and Electronic Music at Ghent Univ.
WORKS: 3 operas: *La Grande Tentation de Saint Antoine,* opera buffa (1957; Antwerp, Nov. 11, 1961); *2 is te weinig, 3 is te veel* (*2 Is Too Little, 3 Is Too Much,* 1966; Palermo, June 13, 1969); *Paradijsgeuzen* (*Beggars in Heaven,* 1966; Ghent, March 26, 1967); *Van een trotse vogel,* musical comedy for narrator and small orch. (1948); *Magreb* for viola and orch. (1946); *Capriccio* for orch. (1948); *Sprookjesmuziek* for orch. (1949); 2 works serving as introductions for children to instruments of the orch.: *Betje Trompet* for narrator and small orch. (1949) and *Betje Trompet en de Reus* (*Betje Trumpet and the Giant*) for 2 narrators and orch. (1965); *Sinfonietta Buffa* (1950); 2 piano concertos (1952, 1956); *La Voix du silence,* cantata for baritone, narrators, female chorus and chamber orch. (1951–54); *Musica per archi* (1955); *Amalgames* for

orch. (1956); *Marine* for orch. (1957); Concertino for 2 String Orchestras (1965); *Serenade* for flute, oboe and strings (1967); Cello Sonatina (1945); *Divertimento* for wind quintet (1946); 3 string quartets (1947, 1949, 1954); String Trio (1951); *Tafelmuziek* for flute, oboe, violin, viola and cello (1953); Sonata for solo guitar (1954); Violin Sonata (1957); *Serenade* for harpsichord and 11 strings (1958–59); *Postludium* for organ and brass (1959); *Divertimento* for piano quartet (1970); Piano Sonata (1946); *3 Nocturnes* for piano (1947); *Variations* for 2 pianos (1947); *Petite Suite* for piano (1953); *Petites Variations* for piano (1954); *Mimes* for piano (1958); Piano Sonatina (1964); 9 electronic pieces; choruses; film music.

Meeuwisse, Willy, Dutch pianist and composer; b. Arnhem, Dec. 18, 1914; d. Amsterdam, Aug. 6, 1952. He was a student of Sem Dresden in Amsterdam; his *Suite of Old Dutch Dances* for piano solo enjoyed a certain popularity. He also was active as a concert pianist.

Méfano, Paul, French composer; B. Basra, Iraq, March 6, 1937. He studied at the Paris Cons. with Dandelot, Messiaen, Martenot and Milhaud; attended seminars of Boulez, Stockhausen and Pousseur in Basel. He received a grant of the Harkness Foundation for residence in the U.S. (1966–68) and in Berlin (1968–69). In his music he pursues a constructivist style, with an emphasis on rhythmic percussion and electronic sound; the influences of Stravinsky and Varèse are particularly in evidence.

WORKS: *Incidences* for orch and piano (1960); *Paraboles* for soprano and chamber ensemble (Paris. Jan. 20, 1965); *Interférences* for a chamber group (1966); *Lignes* for bass voice, brass, percussion, bassoon, and amplified double bass (1968); *Aurélia* for 3 choruses, 3 orchestras and 3 conductors (1968); *La Cérémonie* for voices, instrumental groups and speaking choruses (1970); *Intersection,* electronic piece for 2 generators and ring modulator (1971).

Mehrkens, Friedrich Adolf, German conductor and teacher; b. Neuenkirchen, near Ottendorf-on-Elbe, April 22, 1840; d. Hamburg, May 31, 1899. He studied at the Leipzig Cons. (1861–62), then settled in Hamburg as pianist, teacher, and conductor of singing societies. He was conductor of the Bach-Gesellschaft from 1871. He wrote a symphony, a *Te Deum,* and chamber music.

Mehta, Mehli, Indian violinist and conductor, father of **Zubin Mehta;** b. Bombay, Sept. 25, 1908. He studied violin in Bombay and at the Trinity College in London, obtaining his licentiate there in 1929. In 1935 he founded the Bombay Symph. Orch.; in 1942 organized the Bombay String Quartet. He was assistant concertmaster of the Hallé Orch. in Manchester from 1955 to 1959; then settled in the U.S. In 1964 he became conductor of the orchestra of the Univ. of Calif., Los Angeles, which he brought up to a high degree of excellence.

Mehta, Zubin, brilliant and glamorous Indian conductor, son of **Mehli Mehta;** b. Bombay, April 29, 1936. He received his early musical training from his father; in 1954 he went to Vienna where he studied conducting with Hans Swarowsky. In 1958 he won an international competition for young conductors in Liverpool, England. In 1959 he was engaged as guest conductor of the Vienna Philharmonic, and subsequently conducted in Canada, France, England, Switzerland, Italy, Hungary, Rumania, Czechoslovakia, Poland and Russia. Making prodigious progress in his career, he became the youngest conductor to lead a major symphony orchestra when at the age of 24 he was appointed associate conductor of the Los Angeles Philharmonic and its music director in Dec. 1961. In 1962 he became concurrently conductor of the Montreal Symphony Orchestra. His romantic approach to conducting, combined with a superlative technical ability, contributed to his spectacular success with audiences in Europe and America. He was especially appreciated in Israel, where he made frequent appearances. In 1978 he was appointed music director and conductor of the New York Philharmonic.

Méhul, Étienne-Nicolas, famous French opera composer; b. Givet, Ardennes, June 22, 1763; d. Paris, Oct. 18, 1817. By dint of hard work, and with the friendly aid of a blind old organist, he learned to play the organ, and at the age of 10 performed the functions of organist of the Couvent des Récollets at Givet. The fame of Wilhelm Hauser, organist at Lavaldieu monastery, attracted him; the Abbot admitted him as a novice, so that he might be taught by Hauser, whose assistant he became in 1777. In 1778 he went to Edelmann in Paris for lessons in piano playing and composition. When he heard a performance of Gluck's *Iphigénie en Tauride,* he was deeply moved, and succeeded in meeting Gluck himself, by whose advice he turned towards dramatic composition. For the sake of practice he wrote 3 operas (*Psyché, Anacréon,* and *Lausus et Lydie*); a fourth early opera, *Alonzo et Cora,* though accepted by the Académie de Musique, was not performed until 1791; meanwhile *Euphrosine et Coradin, ou le Tyran corrigé,* came out at the Comédie-Italienne, on Sept. 4, 1790, and was crowned with encouraging success; good fortune likewise attended the production of *Stratonice* (May 3, 1792). There followed the operas *Le Jeune Sage et le vieux fou* (March 28, 1793), *Horatius Coclès* (Feb. 18, 1794), *Le Congrès des rois* (Feb. 26, 1794), *Mélidore et Phrosine* (May 6, 1794), and *Doria, ou la Tyrannie détruite* (March 12, 1795). During the turbulent years of the French Revolution, Méhul shrewdly selected subjects for his operas allegorically suitable to the times, but he also wrote in a melodious and forceful style that pleased those who sought artistic entertainment. In 1795 he was appointed one of the four inspectors of the newly established Conservatoire, and was also elected member of the Institut. For 2 years he wrote little, but he then resumed production with renewed energy, bringing out one opera after another (given mostly at the Opéra-Comique): *Le Jeune Henri* (May 1, 1797); *Le Pont de Lodi* (Dec. 15, 1797); *Adrien* (June 4, 1799); *Ariodant* (Oct. 11, 1799); *Épicure* (March 14, 1800); *L'Irato ou L'Emporté* (Feb. 18, 1801); *Une Folie* (April 5, 1802); *Le Trésor supposé* (July 29, 1802); *Joanna* (Nov. 23, 1802); *Héléna* (March 1, 1803); *Le Baiser et* la quittance (June 18, 1803); *L'Heureux malgré lui* (Dec. 28, 1803); *Les Deux Aveugles de Tolède* (Jan. 28, 1806); *Uthal* (May 17, 1806); *Gabrielle d'Estrées, ou Les Amours d'Henri IV* (June 25, 1806); *Joseph* (Feb. 17, 1807); *Le Prince troubadour* (May 24, 1813); *La Journée aux aventures* (Nov. 16, 1816); *Les Amazones* was produced at the Opéra (Dec. 17, 1811), as was *L'Oriflamme* (Jan. 31, 1814); *Valentine de Milan* was produced posthumously (Opéra-Comique, Nov. 28, 1822). Of these, the greatest was *Joseph*; after a *succès d'estime* at its initial production in Paris, performances followed in Germany, Austria, Hungary, Russia, Holland, Belgium, Switzerland, England, Italy, and America. Some of his operas were written in collaboration: *Épicure* with Cherubini; *Le Baiser et la quittance*, with Boieldieu, Kreutzer, and Isouard: *L'Oriflamme* , with Paer, Berton, and Kreutzer. The early opera *Le Congrès des rois* was the product of collaboration with 11 other composers. He wrote only a few ballets: *Le Jugement de Paris* (Opéra, March 5, 1793; music in large part from Haydn and Pleyel), *La Dansomanie* (Opéra, June 14, 1800), *Daphnis et Pandrose* (Opéra, Jan. 14, 1803), and *Persée et Andromède* (Opéra, June 8, 1810). He composed also numerous pieces of incidental music, patriotic hymns, and the like, and some interesting symphonic works, rather bold in character for his time; piano sonatas; chamber music. Some of his choral works (*Chant du départ, Chant de victorie, Chant de retour*, etc.) attained a certain vogue. There is extant in MS an *Ouverture burlesque*, scored for violin, woodwind, and piano.

BIBLIOGRAPHY: P. Viellard, *Méhul, sa vie et ses œuvres* (Paris, 1859); A. Pougin, *Méhul: sa vie, son génie, son caractère* (Paris, 1889); René Brancour, *Méhul* (Paris, 1912); A. L. Ringer, "A French Symphonist at the Time of Beethoven: Étienne Nicolas Méhul," *Musicial Quarterly* (Oct. 1951). See also A. Loewenberg, *Annals of Opera* (Cambridge, 1943; 2nd ed., 1955).

Meibom (or **Meibomius, Meiboom, Meybom**), **Marcus,** erudite scholar; b. Tönning, Schleswig, c.1620; d. Utrecht, Feb. 15, 1710. He was for some years prof. at the Univ. of Uppsala; in 1674 visited England; lived thereafter principally in Utrecht. His chief work is *Antiquae musicae auctores septem, graece et latine, Marcus Meibomius restituit ac notis explicavit* (Amsterdam, 1652; 2 vols.); it contains treatises on music by Aristoxenos, Euclid (*Introductio harmonica*), Nicomachos, Gaudentius Philosophos, Bacchius Senior, Aristides Quintilianus, and M. Capella (Book IX of the *Satyricon*); until the publication of the new ed. of those authors by Karl Jan, Meibom's work was the only accessible source of information.

Meiland, Jakob, German composer; b. Senftenberg, Lausitz, 1542; d. Hechingen, Dec. 31, 1577; Kapellmeister in Ansbach to 1574, then in Frankfurt and Celle.

WORKS: *Sacrae cantiones, a 5, 6* (1564; 3rd ed., 1573); *Newe auserlesene teutsche Liedlein a 4, 5* (1569); *Sacrae aliquot cantiones* (1575); *Sacrae aliquot novae cantiones* (1576; 2nd ed., 1588); *Cygneae cantiones* (1577); 3 Passions; a Mass; secular songs; etc.

BIBLIOGRAPHY: R. Oppel, *Jakob Meiland* (dissertation; Munich, 1911).

Meinardus, Ludwig (Siegfried), , German composer and writer; b. Hooksiel, Oldenburg, Sept. 17, 1827; d. Bielefeld, July 10, 1896. A pupil of Leipzig Cons.; also studied in Berlin, in Weimar (with Liszt), and with Marx at Berlin. 1853-65, conductor of the Singakademie at Glogau; then teacher in Dresden Cons.; from 1874 till 1887 he lived in Hamburg as a composer and critic, then going to Bielefeld.

WRITINGS: *Kulturgeschichtliche Briefe über deutsche Tonkunst* (2 ed., 1872); *Ein Jugendleben* (1874, 2 vols.; a sort of autobiography); *Rückblick auf die Anfänge der deutschen Oper* (1878); *Mattheson und seine Verdienste um die deutsche Tonkunst* (1879); *Mozart: Ein Künstlerleben* (1882); *Die deutsche Tonkunst im 18.-19. Jahrhundert* (1887); *Klassizität und Romantik in der deutschen Tonkunst* (1893); *Eigene Wege* (1895).

Meitus, Yuli, Ukrainian composer; b. Elizavetgrad, Jan. 28, 1903. He studied in Kharkov; from 1942 to 1946 he worked in Turkestan; then lived mostly in Kiev. Meitus is one of the most prolific opera composers in the Soviet Union; virtually all of his operas deal with subjects of the Russian Revolution and Civil War. They are: *Perekop* (Kiev, Jan. 20, 1939); *Gaidmaki* (Ashkhabad, Oct. 15, 1943); *Leili and Medzhun* (Ashkhabad, Nov. 2, 1946); *The Young Guard* (Kiev, Nov. 7, 1947; revised, Leningrad, Feb. 22, 1950); *Dawn Over the Dvina* (Kiev, July 5, 1955); *Stolen Happiness* (Lwów, Sept. 10, 1960); *Makhtumkuli* (Ashkhabad, Dec. 29, 1962); *The Daughter of the Wind* (Odessa, Oct. 24, 1965); *The Brothers Ulyanov* (Ufa, Nov. 25, 1967; revised and produced in Alma-Ata, 1970); *Yaroslav the Wise* (Donetsk, March 3, 1973); He also wrote a *Turkmenian Symphony* (1946) and 5 symph. suites on Ukrainian and other ethnic motives.

BIBLIOGRAPHY: Y. Malyshev, *Yuli Meitus, Essays on His Work* (Moscow, 1962).

Melachrino, George Miltiades, English bandleader; b. London, May 1, 1909; d. there, June 18, 1965. He studied at the Trinity College of Music; formed his own band; then launched a new group, the Melachrino Strings, which he imbued with an aura of black-velvet coloration that made the "Melachrino sound" a byword among music lovers. He could play every instrument except harp and piano. His recording albums bore titles of irresistible sentimentality, e.g. *Music for Two People Alone, Music for a Nostalgic Traveler* (known in Europe under the name of *Reverie*) and *Music for Relaxation*.

Melani, Jacopo, Italian opera composer; b. Pistoia, July 6, 1623; d. there, Aug. 19, 1676. He was a member of an exceptionally gifted family of Italian musicians; his 8 brothers were singers and composers. He specialized in comic operas, of which the following performed in Florence, are the most important: *Il Podestà di Colognole* (Dec. 1656), *Ercole in Tebe* (July 8, 1661), and *Girello* (Jan. 20, 1670); regarding the last, see the discussion of its authenticity in Loewenberg's *Annals of Opera* (Cambridge, 1943; 2nd ed. 1955). See also Hugo Goldschimdt, *Studien zur Geschichte der italienischen Oper im 17. Jahrhundert*, vol. 1, (1901).

Melartin, Erkki Gustaf, Finnish composer; b. Käkisälmi (Kexholm), Feb. 7, 1875; d. Pukinmäki (near Helsinki), Feb. 14, 1937. He was a pupil of Wegelius at the Cons. in Helsinki and of Robert Fuchs in Vienna; taught theory at the Helsinki Cons. (1901-08); succeeded Wegelius as director in 1911, and remained at this post until his death. His compositions are marked by a lyrical strain, with thematic materials often drawn from Finnish folksongs.
WORKS: opera, *Aino* (1907; Helsinki, Dec. 10, 1909); 6 symphonies (1902; 1904; 1906-07; 1912; *Sinfonia Brevis*, 1916; 1924-25); Violin Concerto (Helsinki, 1913); ballet, *Sininen helmi* (*The Blue Pearl*, 1930); numerous symph. suites and poems; incidental music for 10 plays; 2 commemorative cantatas; 4 string quartets; a piano sonata, a violin sonata; piano pieces; choruses; about 300 songs.
BIBLIOGRAPHY: K. Flodin, *Finska musiker* (Stockholm, 1900); E. Marvia, "Erkki Melartin," in *Suomen Säveltäjiä,* ed. by Sulho Ranta (Helsinki, 1945; pp. 342-59).

Melba, Nellie (stage name of **Mrs. Helen Porter Armstrong,** *née* **Mitchell**), famous Australian coloratura soprano; b. Burnley, near Richmond, May 19, 1859; d. Sydney, Feb. 23, 1931. Her father, who had decided objections to anything connected with the stage, was nevertheless fond of music and proud of his daughter's talent. When she was only 6 years old he allowed her to sing at a concert in the Melbourne Town-Hall, but would not consent to her having singing lessons; instead, she was taught piano, violin, and harp, and even had instruction in harmony and composition. As she grew older she frequently played the organ in a local church and was known among her friends as an excellent pianist, while all the time her chief desire was to study singing. Not until after her marriage in 1882 to Captain Charles Armstrong was she able to gratify her ambition, when she began to study with a local teacher, Cecchi; her first public appearance as a singer was on May 17, 1884, in a performance of Handel's *Messiah* in Sydney. The next year her father received a government appointment in London, and she accompanied him, determined to begin an operatic career. Her first concert in London (June 1, 1886) convinced her of the necessity of further study, and she went to Mme. Marchesi in Paris. Her debut as Gilda at the Théâtre de La Monnaie in Brussels (Oct. 12, 1887) created a veritable sensation; the famous impresario Sir Augustus Harris immediately engaged her for the spring season at Covent Garden, where she appeared on May 24, 1888, as Lucia, arousing great enthusiasim; a similar success attended her appearance in Paris, where she sang Ophelia in Ambroise Thomas' *Hamlet* (May 8, 1889), St. Petersburg (1890), Milan (La Scala, 1893; immense triumph over a carefully planned opposition), Stockholm and Copenhagen (Oct. 1893), New York (Metropolitan Opera, as Lucia, Dec. 4, 1893), Melbourne (Sept. 27, 1902). From her first appearance at Covent Garden she sang there regularly with only the exception of the seasons of 1909, 1912, and 1913; besides being one of the most

brilliant stars of several seasons at the Metropolitan Opera, she also sang with Walter Damrosch's Opera Co. (1897-98) and at Hammerstein's Manhattan Opera (1906-07 and 1908-09), and made several transcontinental concert tours of the U.S. Bemberg wrote for her *Elaine* (1892) and Saint-Saëns *Hélène* (1904), in both of which she created the title roles. In 1926, she returned to Australia and retired from the stage; she then became president of the Melbourne Cons. Melba was by nature gifted with a voice of extraordinary beauty and bell-like purity; through her art she made this fine instrument perfectly even throughout its entire compass (b-flat–f^3) and wonderfully flexible, so that she executed the most difficult *fioriture* without the least effort. As an actress she did not rise above the conventional, and for this reason she was at her best in parts demanding brilliant coloratura (Gilda, Lucia, Violetta, Rosina, Lakmé, etc.). On a single occasion she attempted the dramatic role of Brünnhilde in *Siegfried* (Metropolitan Opera, N.Y., Dec. 30, 1896), and met with disaster. In 1918 she was created a Dame of the British Empire. She was a typical representative of the golden era of opera; a prima donna *assoluta*, she exercised her powers over the public with perfect self-assurance and a fine command of her singing voice. As a measure of Melba's universal popularity, it may be mentioned that her name was attached to a tasty dessert (Peach Melba) consisting of half a cooked peach served with vanilla ice cream and a clear raspberry sauce (Melba sauce); also a Melba toast, a crisp thinly sliced toasted bread, patented in 1929 by Bert Weil (1890-1965), president of the Devonsheer Melba Corporation. A motion picture, based on her life, was produced in 1953, with Patrice Munsel as Melba. She wrote an autobiography, *Melodies and Memories* (London, 1925).
BIBLIOGRAPHY: Agnes Murphy, *Melba, a Biography* (London, 1909; contains a chapter on singing written by Melba); P. Colson, *Melba; An Unconventional Biography* (London, 1931); J. Wechsberg, *Red Plush and Black Velvet: The Story of Melba and Her Times* (Boston, 1961); G. W. Hutton, *Melba* (Melbourne, 1962); J. Hetherington, *Melba* (London, 1967).

Melcer, Henryk, Polish pianist and composer; b. Kalisch, Sept. 21, 1869; d. Warsaw, April 18, 1928. He was a pupil of Moszkowski at the Warsaw Cons. and of Leschetizky in Vienna (1892-94). After successful concert tours of Russia, Germany, and France, he taught piano for a short time at the Cons. of Helsinki; then taught in Lwow and at the Vienna Cons. (1903-06); in 1908, became conductor of the Warsaw Philharmonic Society; from 1922 to 1927 was director of the Warsaw Cons.
WORKS: the operas *Marja* (Warsaw, Nov. 16, 1904) and *Protasilaos and Laodamia;* a choral ballad, *Pani Twardowska;* 2 piano concertos: No. 1 in E minor (won the Rubinstein prize, 1895) and No. 2 in C minor (won the Paderewski prize, 1898); a piano trio; a violin sonata; piano pieces; songs.

Melchers, Henrik Melcher, Swedish violinist and composer; b. Stockholm, May 30, 1882; d. there, April 9, 1961. He studied there at the Cons. and with J. Lindegren; later at the Paris Cons. He lived in Paris

(1905-19), then in Brussels, and in Sondershausen. In 1925 became prof. at the Stockholm Cons.

WORKS: *Swedish Rhapsody* for orch. (Stockholm, 1914), the symph. poems *Näcken* (1916), *La Kermesse* (1919), and others; *Poem* for violin and orch. (1922); songs.

Melchior, Lauritz, celebrated tenor; b. Copenhagen, March 20, 1890; d. Santa Monica, California, March 18, 1973. He studied with Paul Bang at the Royal Opera School, Copenhagen; in 1913, made his operatic debut in *Pagliacci* (as a baritone) at the Royal Opera, where he was engaged from 1914-21; studied at the same time with Wilhelm Herold, and in 1918 appeared as a tenor; 1921-23, studied with Beigel in London, then with Grenzebach in Berlin and Anna Bahr-Mildenburg in Munich; made his London debut at Covent Garden on May 14, 1924; studied the Bayreuth traditions under Kittel, at the invitation of Cosima and Siegfried Wagner, and made his first appearance at the Festspielhaus there on July 23, 1924, as Siegfried; sang at Bayreuth regularly till 1931, and acquired the reputation of being one of the finest Wagnerian tenors. He sang Tannhäuser at his first appearance with the Metropolitan Opera, N.Y. (Feb. 17, 1926); remained on its roster until 1950; then settled in California. He became an American citizen on June 13, 1947.

Melichar, Alois, Austrian music critic; b. Vienna, April 18, 1896; d. Munich, April 9, 1976. He studied theory at the Vienna Academy of Music with Joseph Marx (1917-20) and at the Hochschule für Musik in Berlin with Schreker (1920-23). In 1923-26 he was in the Caucasus where he collected materials on Caucasian folk songs; then lived in Berlin and Vienna. In his compositions he follows the safe footpath of Reger, Pfitzner and Graener; he wrote a symph. poem *Der Dom* (1934); *Rhapsodie über ein schwedisches Volkslied* (1939); *Lustspiel-Ouvertüre* (1942); lieder; film music. As a music critic, he acquired notoriety by his intemperate attacks on better composers than himself. His publications, written in his virulent, polemical manner, include *Die unteilbare Musik* (Vienna, 1952); *Musik in der Zwangsjacke* (Vienna, 1958) and (particularly vicious), *Schönberg und die Folgen* (Vienna, 1960).

Melik-Pashayev, Alexander, Soviet conductor; b. Tiflis, Georgia, Oct. 23, 1905; d. Moscow, June 18, 1964. He received his primary music education at home; learned to play the piano; served as rehearsal pianist at the opera house in Tbilisi; made his debut as conductor there in 1923. He then went to Leningrad where he took a course in conducting with Gauck at the Leningrad Cons., graduating in 1930. In 1931 he was engaged as a member of the conducting staff of the Bolshoi Theater in Moscow, and served as its principal conductor from 1953 to 1962. For the excellence of his productions of Russian operas he received 2 consecutive Stalin Prizes (1942, 1943). He also conducted performances of the Bolshoi Theater abroad (London, 1961; Budapest, 1963).

Melis, Carmen, Italian dramatic soprano; b. Cagliari, Sardinia, Aug. 14, 1885; d. Longone al Segrino, Dec. 19, 1967. She studied with Teresina Singer and Carlo Carignani in Milan, and later with Jean de Reszke in Paris; made a successful debut at Naples in 1906; then sang in Rome, Milan, Venice, Cairo, Warsaw, and Odessa. She was engaged by Hammerstein for the Manhattan Opera, and made her American debut there as Tosca (N.Y., Nov. 26, 1909); subsequently was a member of the Boston Opera Co. (1911-13). Later became a teacher; Renata Tebaldi studied with her for 3 years.

Melkikh, Dmitri, Russian composer; b. Moscow, Feb. 11, 1885; d. there, Feb. 22, 1943. He studied at the People's Cons. in Moscow with Yavorsky, under whose influence he wrote music in archaic Russian modes; his few symphonic works reveal traits of French Impressionism. Among his works are 3 symphonies (1925, 1933, 1938); 4 string quartets; a symph. poem *Alladine et Palomides* (after Maeterlinck) and several song cycles.

Mellers, Wilfrid Howard, English musicologist and composer; b. Leamington, April 26, 1914. He studied composition with Egon Wellesz at Cambridge Univ. (1933-38); upon graduation was instructor at the Univ. of Birmingham; held positions at Downing College in Cambridge (1945-48); then returned to Birmingham and taught there until 1959. His subsequent teaching appointments were at the Univ. of Pittsburgh (1960-63) and from 1964 at the Univ. of York.

WRITINGS: *Music and Society* (London, 1946); *Studies in Contemporary Music* (London, 1947); *François Couperin and the French Classical Tradition* (London, 1950); *The Sonata Principle* (London, 1957); *Romanticism and the 20th Century* (London, 1957); *Music in a New Found Land: Themes and Developments in the History of American Music* (London, 1964); *Harmonious Meetings: A Study of the Relationships between English Music, Poetry and Theater c. 1600-1900* (London, 1965); *Caliban Reborn: Renewal in Twentieth-Century Music* (N.Y., 1967); *Twilight of the Gods: The Music of the Beatles* (N.Y., 1973).

WORKS: the operas *The Ancient Wound* (Univ. of Victoria, British Columbia, July 27, 1970) and *The Tragical History of Christopher Marlowe* (1952); several cantatas, *Sinfonia ricercata* (1947); *Alba in Nine Metamorphoses* for flute and orch. (1961); *Noctambule and Sun-Dance* for wind orch. (1962); *Voices and Creatures* for speaker, flute and percussion (1962); *De vegetalibus et animalibus* for soprano, clarinet, violin, cello, and harp (1971); *Venery for Six Plus* for "dancing singers" and an instrumental ensemble (1972); *The Gates of the Dream* for soloists, chorus, and orch. (York, May 8, 1974).

Mellnäs, Arne, Swedish composer; b. Stockholm, Aug. 30, 1933. He studied with Larsson and Blomdahl at the Royal Academy of Music in Stockholm (1953-63), in Berlin with Blacher (1959), in Vienna with Ligeti (1961-62), and in Bilthoven with Koenig (1962-63) where Mellnäs specialized in electronic music. In 1964 he traveled to America and worked at the San Francisco Tape Music Center.

WORKS: Oboe Sonata (1957); Concerto for Clarinet and Strings (1957); *Music* for orch. (1959); *Chiasmos* for orch. (1961); *Växlingar* for flute, or piccolo, and clarinet (1961); *Collage* for orch. (1962); *Per caso* for saxophone, trombone, violin, double bass and 2 percussionists (1963); *Tombola* for horn, trombone, electric guitar and piano (1963); the electronic pieces: *Cem/63* (1963), *Nite Music* (1964), *Intensity 6.5* (1966; dedicated to the memory of Edgar Varèse, containing electronically modified quotations from Varèse's works, particularly from *Density 21.5*), *Conglomérat* (1968), *Eufoni* (1969), *Monotrem* (1969), *Kaleidovision,* ballet for television (1969), *Appassionato* (1970), *Far Out* (1970), *Splinters* (1970), *Aura* for orch. (Malmö, June 5, 1964); *Gestes Sonores* for any ensemble (1964); *Sic Transit* for instruments and tape (1964); *Succsim* for chorus (1964); *Siamfoni* for trumpet, horn and trombone (1964); *Minibuff,* an opera for 2 singers and tape (1966); *Drones* for jazz combo (1967); *Fixations* for organ (1967); *Quasi niente* for one to 4 string trios (1968); *Spots and Spaces,* after e. e. cummings, for male chorus, 11 strings and winds (1968); *Aglepta* for chorus (1969); *Capricorn Flakes* for piano, harpsichord and vibraphone (1970); *Cabrillo* for clarinet, trombone, cello and percussion (1970); *Schizofoni* for 1, 2 or 3 pianos (1971); *Noël,* after e. e. cummings, for 2 sopranos, children's chorus and instrumental ensemble (1971); *Transparence* for orch. (1972); *Vae* for chorus and organ (1972); *Ceremus* for flute, clarinet, trumpet, trombone, double bass and percussion (1973); *Sub luna* for soprano, flute, violin and harp (1973); *Mara Mara Minne* for chorus and tape (1973); *Fragile* for any kind and number of instruments (1973); *Blow* for wind orch. (1974); a church opera, *Erik den helige* (Erik, the Holy; Stockholm, May 18, 1976).

Melnikov, Ivan, Russian baritone; b. St. Petersburg, March 4, 1832; d. there, July 8, 1906. He was a choirboy in school; was engaged in trade, and for a time served as inspector of Volga boats; he began to study seriously late in life; took lessons with Lomakin (1862); then went to Italy, where he studied with Repetto. He made his debut in Bellini's *Puritani* (St. Petersburg, Oct. 6, 1867); created the title role in Mussorgsky's *Boris Godunov* (St. Petersburg, Feb. 8, 1874).

Melton, James, American tenor; b. Moultrie, Ga., Jan. 2, 1904; d. New York, April 21, 1961. He attended high school and college in Florida; later entered the Univ. of Georgia, where he played the saxophone in the college band. Subsequently, he went to Vanderbilt College, Nashville, Tenn., where he took lessons in singing with Gaetano de Luca. He obtained several lucrative engagements on the radio; made his concert debut in N.Y. on April 22, 1932; made his first opera appearance in Cincinnati, June 28, 1938. On Dec. 7, 1942 he appeared for the first time with the Metropolitan Opera, remaining on its roster until 1950; also toured the U.S. as a concert singer.

Meltzer, Charles Henry, English journalist and translator; b. London, 1852; d. New York, Jan. 14, 1936. He studied music in London and Paris; was foreign correspondent for the *N.Y. Herald* and the *Chicago Tribune*; settled in N.Y. in 1888. He was an ardent proponent of opera in English, and translated the librettos of *Die Walküre* and *Das Rheingold, Les Contes d'Hoffmann,* Monteverdi's *Orfeo,* etc.

Meluzzi, Salvatore, Italian composer of church music; b. Rome, July 22, 1813; d. there, April 17, 1897. He was maestro di cappella at the basilica of St. Peter's in the Vatican, and for 45 years director of the Cappella Giulia. Thoroughly versed in the art of the old Italian masters, he emulated them in writing Masses, Requiems, antiphons, motets, hymns, psalms; among his best pieces are a *Stabat Mater* and a *Miserere.*

Membrée, Edmond, French composer; b. Valenciennes, Nov. 14, 1820; d. Château Damont, near Paris, Sept. 10, 1882. He studied at the Paris Cons. with Alkan and Zimmerman (piano) and Carafa (composition).

WORKS: the operas *François Villon* (Paris, April 20, 1857), *L'Esclave* (Paris, July 17, 1874), *Les Parias* (Paris, Nov. 13, 1876), and *La Courte Échelle* (Paris, 1879); a cantata *Fingal* (Paris, May 14, 1861); ballads, songs, etc.

BIBLIOGRAPHY: L. Mention, *Un Compositeur valenciennois: Edmond Membrée* (Paris, 1908).

Menager, Laurent, Luxembourg composer; b. Luxembourg, Jan. 10, 1835; d. there, Feb. 7, 1902. He was a song composer and a respected pedagogue. A postage stamp was issued in his honor by the Government of Luxembourg in 1951.

Menasce, Jacques de, Austrian pianist and composer; b. Bad Ischl, Austria, Aug. 19, 1905, of a French-Egyptian father and a German mother; d. Gstaad, Switzerland, Jan. 28, 1960. He studied in Vienna with Sauer (piano) and with J. Marx, Paul Pisk, and Alban Berg (composition). From 1932 until 1940 he gave concerts in Europe as a pianist; in 1941 came to America, living mostly in N.Y., but continued his concert career in Europe.

WORKS: 2 piano concertos (1935; 1939); *5 Fingerprints,* for piano (1943); *Romantic Suite,* for piano (1950); *Divertimento,* for piano and string orch. (1940); *Le Chemin d'écume,* for soprano and orch. (Geneva, 1942); a ballet, *Status Quo* (1947); Violin Sonata (1940); Viola Sonata (1955); songs, choruses.

Menchaca, Angel, Paraguayan music theorist; b. Asunción, March 1, 1855; d. Buenos Aires, May 8, 1924. He was trained as a jurist; also taught history and literature at the National College in Buenos Aires. In 1914 he publ. a provocative book, *Sistema teórico-gráfico de la Música,* in which he proposed a new system of notation, employing a basic alphabet of 12 notes and dispensing with the established signatures, staff, etc. He toured Europe for the purpose of lecturing on this device; invented a special keyboard to facilitate its application. He was also a composer; his compositions include songs and school choruses.

Mendel, Arthur, eminent American music scholar; b. Boston, June 6, 1905. He studied at Harvard Univ.; also took courses in theory with Nadia Boulanger in Paris; returning to America, he was literary editor of G. Schirmer, Inc. (1930–38); also wrote music criticism in *The Nation* (1930–33); from 1936 to 1953 he conducted in N.Y. a chorus "The Cantata Singers," specializing in Baroque music; he was then prof. of music and chairman of the music department at Princeton Univ. (1952–67). He edited (with H. T. David) the valuable "documentary biography," *The Bach Reader* (N.Y., 1945; revised N.Y., 1966); edited Bach's *St. John Passion* (1951), Schütz's *Christmas Story* (1949) and *Musicalische Exequien* (1957), and other works of the Baroque period. He publ. numerous important articles on the history of pitch, reprinted in *Studies in the History of Musical Pitch* (Amsterdam, 1969) and also promoted the possibility of music analysis with the aid of a computer, publ. in *Computers and the Humanities* (1969–70). A Festschrift, *Studies in Renaissance and Baroque Music in Honor of Arthur Mendel*, was publ. in N.Y. in 1975.

Mendel, Hermann, German music lexicographer; b. Halle, Aug. 6, 1834; d. Berlin, Oct. 26, 1876. He was a pupil of Mendelssohn and Moscheles in Leipzig, and of Wieprecht in Berlin. In 1870 he founded and edited the *Deutsche Musiker-Zeitung*; also edited *Mode's Opernbibliothek* (about 90 librettos, with commentaries and biographies of composers) and a *Volksliederbuch*. He publ. 2 small books on Meyerbeer (1868 and 1869). His great work was the *Musikalisches Conversations-Lexikon*, which he began to publ. in 1870, but was able to continue only to the letter M; the rest was completed by August Reissmann; the entire edition was in 11 vols.; a supplementary vol. was publ. in 1883.

Mendelsohn, Alfred, Rumanian composer; b. Bucharest, Feb. 17, 1910; d. there, May 9, 1966. He studied in Vienna with Joseph Marx, Franz Schmidt, Egon Wellesz and others (1927–31) and at the Bucharest Cons. with Jora (1931–32). From 1946 to 1954 he was conductor of the Rumanian Opera in Bucharest; in 1949 was prof. at the Bucharest Cons. An exceptionally prolific composer, he produced a great amount of highly competent, technically accomplished music. Influenced primarily by the programmatic Romanticism of the Vienna School, he also probed the potentialities of motivic structures, suggesting the serial concepts of modern constructivists, while remaining faithful to basic tonalitarianism.
WORKS: a dramatic symph., with libretto, in 7 tableaus *Imnul iubirii (The Love Hymn*, 1946); the operas *Meşterul Manole* (1949), *Michelangelo* (1964; Timisoara, Sept. 29, 1964) and *Spinoza*, a lyrical scene (1966); operetta *Anton Pann* (Bucharest, 1963); the ballets *Harap Alb (The White Moor*, 1948) and *Călin* (1956); the oratorios and cantatas *1917* (1956; on the Russian Revolution), *Inimă vitează* (1952), *Canata Bucureştiului* (1953), *Horia* (1955), *1907* (1957; deals with the 1907 peasant uprising in Rumania), *Glasul lui Lenin (The Voice of Lenin*, 1957), *Sub cerul de vară* (1959), *Pentru Marele Octombrie* (1960) and *Cei puternici* (1965); *Suite Concertante* for flute and

string orch. (1957); *Suite* for chamber orch. (1940); *Suită comemorativă* for string orch. (1943); 9 symphonies: No. 1 (1944); No. 2, *Veritas* (1947); No. 3, *Reconstrucţia* (1949); No. 4, *Apelul păcii* (1951); No. 5 (1953); No. 6 (1955); No. 7 (1960); No. 8 (1963); No. 9, *Concertante*, for organ and orch. (1964); the symph. poems *Prăbuşirea Doftanei (Doftana's Assault*, 1949), *Eliberarea (Liberation*, 1954), *Va înflori acel Arminden (The May Tree Will Blossom*, 1959), and *Schite dobrogene (Dobrudjan Sketches*, 1961); Chamber Symph. (1961); 2 piano concertos (1946, 1949); Cello Concerto (1949); 3 violin concertos (1953, 1957, 1964); Concertino for Harp and Strings (1955); *Divertimento* for horn and strings (1957); Concerto Grosso, for string quartet and strings (1958); Concerto for Organ and Chamber Orch. (1960); Viola Concerto (1965); *Epitaph* for orch. (1965); Concerto for Orch. (1965); Concerto for String Orch. (1965); 10 string quartets (1930–64); Piano Quintet (1953); Harp Quintet (1955); String Sextet (1957); Piano Trio (1959); *Theme and Variations* for 7 cellos (1963); Octet for 8 cellos (1963); numerous sonatas for violin, viola and cello; Piano Sonata (1947) and smaller pieces; song cycles.

Mendelssohn, Arnold, German composer; son of a cousin of **Felix Mendelssohn**; b. Ratibor, Dec. 26, 1855; d. Darmstadt, Feb. 19, 1933. He studied law at the Univ. of Tübingen; then entered the Hochschule für Musik in Berlin, where he studied with Löschhorn (piano), Haupt (organ), Grell, Kiel, and Taubert (composition). He was subsequently instructor in Bielefeld (1883–85); prof. at the Cologne Cons. (1885–90); then director of church music in Darmstadt. In 1912 he was appointed prof. at Hoch's Cons. in Frankfurt; among his pupils there was Hindemith. He wrote 3 operas: *Elsi, die seltsame Magd* (Cologne, 1896), *Der Bärenhäuter* (Berlin, Feb. 9, 1900), and *Die Minneburg* (Mannheim, 1909); 2 cantatas: *Aus tiefer Not* and *Auf meinen lieben Gott*; a German Mass, for 8-part chorus a cappella; 3 symphonies; a violin concerto; 2 string quartets; a cello sonata; 2 piano sonatas; several sets of songs. He edited Schütz's oratorios and some of Monteverdi's madrigals. His book on esthetics, *Gott, Welt und Kunst*, was brought out by W. Ewald (Wiesbaden, 1949).
BIBLIOGRAPHY: E. O. Nodnagel, *Jenseits von Wagner und Liszt* (Königsberg, 1902); W. Nagel, *Arnold Mendelssohn* (Leipzig, 1906); H. Hering, *Arnold Mendelssohn: die Grundlagen seines Schaffens und seiner Werke* (Regensburg, 1930).

Mendelssohn, Fanny. See **Hensel, Fanny Cäcilia.**

Mendelssohn, Felix (full name **Jacob Ludwig Felix Mendelssohn-Bartholdy**), illustrious German composer; b. Hamburg, Feb. 3, 1809; d. Leipzig, Nov. 4, 1847. He was a grandson of the philosopher Moses Mendelssohn and the son of the banker Abraham Mendelssohn; his mother was Lea Salomon; the family was Jewish, but upon its settlement in Berlin the father decided to become a Protestant and added Bartholdy to his surname. Mendelssohn received his first piano lessons from his mother; subsequently studied piano with Ludwig Berger and violin with Henning; he also had regular lessons in foreign languages and in painting (he showed considerable talent in drawing with pastels); he also had piano lessons with Hummel and Marie Bigot in Paris, where he went with his father for a brief stay in 1816. His most important teacher in his early youth was Zelter, who understood the magnitude of Mendelssohn's talent; in 1821 Zelter took him to Weimar and introduced him to Goethe, who took considerable interest in the boy Mendelssohn after he heard him play. Zelter arranged for Mendelssohn to become a member of the Singakademie in Berlin in 1819 as an alto singer; on Sept. 18, 1819, Mendelssohn's *19th Psalm* was performed by the Akademie. In 1825 Mendelssohn's father took him again to Paris to consult Cherubini on Mendelssohn's prospects in music; however, he returned to Berlin where he had better opportunities for development. Mendelssohn was not only a precocious musician, both in performing and in composition; what is perhaps without a parallel in music history was the extraordinary perfection of his works written during adolescence. He played in public for the first time at the age of 9, on Oct. 24, 1818, in Berlin, performing the piano part of a trio by Wölffl. He wrote a remarkable octet at the age of 16; at 17 he composed the overture for the incidental music to Shakespeare's *A Midsummer Night's Dream*, an extraordinary manifestation of his artistic maturity, showing a mastery of form equal to that of the remaining numbers of the work which were composed 15 years later. Mendelssohn proved his great musicianship when he conducted Bach's *St. Matthew Passion* in the Berlin Singakademie on March 11, 1828, an event that gave an impulse to the revival of Bach's vocal music. In the spring of 1829 Mendelssohn made his first journey to England where he conducted his Symphony in C minor (seated, after the fashion of the time, at the keyboard); later he performed in London the solo part in Beethoven's "Emperor Concerto"; he then traveled through Scotland, where he found inspiration for the composition of his overture *Fingal's Cave (Hebrides)*, which he conducted for the first time during his second visit to London, on May 14, 1832; 10 days later he played in London the solo part of his G minor Concerto and his *Capriccio brillante*. He became a favorite of the English public; Queen Victoria was one of his most fervent admirers; altogether he made 10 trips to England as a pianist, conductor and composer. In 1830–32 he traveled in Germany, Austria, Italy, Switzerland and also went to Paris. In May, 1833, he led the Lower-Rhine Music Festival in Düsseldorf; then conducted at Cologne in June, 1835. He was still a very young man when, in 1836, he was offered the conductorship of the celebrated Gewandhaus Orchestra in Leipzig; the Univ. of Leipzig bestowed upon him an honorary degree of Dr. phil. Mendelssohn's leadership of the Gewandhaus Orchestra in Leipzig was of the greatest significance for the development of German musical culture; he engaged the violin virtuoso Ferdinand David as concertmaster of the orchestra, which soon became the most prestigious symphonic organization in Germany. On March 28, 1837, Mendelssohn married Cécile Charlotte Sophie Jeanrenaud of Frankfurt, the daughter of a French Protestant clergyman. Five children (Carl, Marie, Paul, Felix and Elisabeth) were born to them, and their marriage was

exceptionally happy. At the invitation of King Friedrich Wilhelm IV, Mendelssohn went in 1841 to Berlin to take charge of the music of the court and in the cathedral; Mendelssohn received the title of Royal General Music Director, but residence in Berlin was not required. Returning to Leipzig in 1842, Mendelssohn organized, with von Falkenstein, Keil, Kistner, Schleinitz, and Seeburg as directors, and Schumann, Hauptmann, David, Becker, and Pohlenz as teachers, the famous "Conservatorium" which was officially opened on April 3, 1843. Mendelssohn himself taught there when his other duties allowed the necessary time. The financial nucleus of the foundation was a bequest from Blümner of 20,000 Thaler, left at the disposal of the King of Saxony for the promotion of the fine arts, and Mendelssohn made a special journey to Dresden to petition the King on behalf of the Leipzig Cons. During Mendelssohn's frequent absences, the Gewandhaus Concerts were conducted by Hiller (1843–44) and Gade (1844–45). In the summer of 1844 Mendelssohn conducted the Philharmonic Concerts in London; this was his 8th visit to England; during his 9th visit he conducted the first performance of his oratorio *Elijah* in Birmingham, on Aug. 26, 1846. It was in England that the "Wedding March" from Mendelssohn's music to *A Midsummer Night's Dream* began to be used to accompany the bridal procession; it became particularly fashionable when it was played at the wedding of the Princess Royal in 1858. Mendelssohn made his 10th and last visit to England in the spring of 1847; this was a sad period of his life, for his favorite sister, Fanny, died on May 14, 1847. Mendelssohn's own health began to deteriorate and he died in Leipzig at the age of 38. The exact cause of his early death is not determined; he suffered from severe migraines and chills before he died, but no evidence could be produced by the resident physicians for either a stroke or heart failure. A detailed account of Mendelssohn's illness and death is found in Dieter Kerner's *Krankheiten grosser Musiker* (Stuttgart, 1969; vol. 2, pp. 23–44). The news of Mendelssohn's death produced a profound shock in the world of music; not only in Germany and in England, where he was personally known and beloved, but in distant America and Russia as well, there was genuine sorrow among musicians. Mendelssohn societies were formed all over the world; in America the Mendelssohn Quintette Club was founded in 1849. A Mendelssohn Scholarship was established in England in 1856; its first recipient was Arthur Sullivan. Mendelssohn's influence on German, English, American and Russian music was great and undiminishing through the years; his symphonies, his concertos, his chamber music, his piano pieces and his songs became perennial favorites in concerts and at home, the most popular being the overture *Fingal's Cave*, the ubiquitously played Violin Concerto, the *Songs without Words* for piano, and the "Wedding March" from incidental music to *A Midsummer Night's Dream*. Professional music historians are apt to place Mendelssohn below the ranks of his great contemporaries, Schumann, Chopin and Liszt; in this exalted company Mendelssohn is often regarded as a phenomenon of Biedermeier culture. A barbaric ruling was made by the Nazi regime to forbid performances of Mendelssohn's music as that of a

Jew; his very name was removed from music history books and encyclopedias published in Germany during that time. This shameful episode was but of a transitory nature, however; if anything, it served to create a greater appreciation of Mendelssohn's genius.

WORKS: FOR THE STAGE: *Die Hochzeit des Camacho,* an opera composed in early childhood and performed in Berlin, April 29, 1827; fragments of another childhood opera *Lorelei,* comprising an *Ave Maria,* a vintage chorus, and an attractive finale to Act I; a "Liederspiel," *Die Heimkehr aus der Fremde,* which Mendelssohn wrote for the silver wedding of his parents, and which was performed at their house in Berlin on Dec. 26, 1829; 5 other juvenile operas are extant in manuscript. ORATORIOS: *St. Paul* (Lower-Rhine Festival, Düsseldorf, May 22, 1836, Mendelssohn conducting) and *Elijah* (Birmingham, England, Aug. 26, 1846, Mendelssohn conducting). OTHER VOCAL WORKS: the ballade, *Die erste Walpurgisnacht* (op. 60) for soli, chorus and orch.; 2 "Festgesänge," *An die Künstler* (for men's chorus and brass), and *Zur Säcularfeier der Buchdruckerkunst* ("Gutenberg Cantata," for men's chorus and orch.); music to *Antigone* (op. 55), *Athalie* (op. 74), *Œdipus in Colonos* (op. 93), and *A Midsummer Night's Dream* (op. 61); *Hymn* for alto solo, chorus, and orch. (op. 96); *Lauda Sion,* for chorus and orch. (op. 73); *Tu es Petrus,* for chorus with orch. (op. 111); Psalms 115 (op. 31) and 95 (op. 46) for soli, chorus, and orch.; Psalms 114 (op. 51) and 98 (op. 91), for men's chorus and orch.; the prayer *Verleih' uns Frieden,* for chorus and orch.; the concert aria for soprano, *Infelice!* (op. 94).

VOCAL WORKS WITHOUT ORCH.: Psalm 42, for chorus and organ; Psalms 2, 22, and 43, *a* 8, a cappella; Funeral Song for mixed chorus (op. 116); *Kyrie eleison* for double chorus; 6 anthems ("Sprüche") for 8-part chorus (op. 79); 3 motets for soli, chorus, and organ (op. 23); 3 motets for women's chorus and organ (op. 39); 3 motets for solo and chorus a cappella (op. 69); 21 quartets for men's voices, and 28 quartets for mixed voices (among these vocal quartets are some of Mendelssohn's finest compositions); 13 vocal duets; 83 songs for solo voice with piano (*Es ist bestimmt in Gottes Rat, Wer hat dich, du schöner Wald, O Täler weit, o Höhen,* etc.).

ORCHESTRAL WORKS: Symph. No. 1 (op. 11), in C minor (1824); Symph. No. 2 (op. 52), *Lobgesang,* with voices (Leipzig, June 25, 1840); Symph. No. 3 (op. 56), in A minor, *Scotch* (1830–42; Leipzig, March 3, 1842); Symph. No. 4 (op. 90), in A major, *Italian* (Berlin, May 13, 1833); Symph. No. 5 (op. 107), in D major, *Reformation* (1831; Berlin, Nov. 15, 1832); 12 early string symphonies, *Sinfoniesatz* in C minor; the concert overtures *A Midsummer Night's Dream* (op. 21), *Fingal's Cave* or *Hebrides* (op. 26), *Calm Sea and Prosperous Voyage (Meeresstille und glückliche Fahrt;* op. 27), *The Lovely Melusine (Die schöne Melusine;* op. 32), *Ruy Blas* (op. 95), and the "Trumpet" overture (op. 101); also an overture for wind band (op. 24); *Andante, Scherzo, Capriccio and Fugue,* for string orch. (op. 81); Funeral March (op. 103) and March (op. 108); Piano Concerto No. 1, in G minor (op. 25), and No. 2, in D minor (op. 40); *Capriccio brillante,* for piano with orch. (op. 22); *Rondo brillante,* for piano with orch. (op. 29); *Serenade and Allegro giojoso,* for piano with orch. (op. 43); Violin Concerto in E minor (op. 64; a classic, and one of the finest for the instrument; while writing it, Mendelssohn constantly consulted and often deferred to the judgment of Ferdinand David, who performed it for the 1st time with the Gewandhaus Orch., Leipzig, on March 13, 1845); the score of a juvenile violin concerto by Mendelssohn, written at the age of 12 (1822) was rediscovered and publ. in 1952; played, from MS, for the 1st time by Yehudi Menuhin, N.Y., Feb. 4, 1952.

CHAMBER MUSIC: Octet for strings (op. 20); 2 string quintets (opp. 18, 87); Piano Sextet (op. 110); 7 string quartets (opp. 12, 13, 44, 44a, 44b, 80, 81); 3 piano quartets (opp. 1, 2, 3); 2 piano trios (opp. 49, 66); 2 trios for clarinet, basset horn, and piano (opp. 113, 114); 2 sonatas for cello and piano (opp. 45, 58); Sonata for violin and piano (op. 4); *Variations concertantes* (op. 17); *Lied ohne Worte* (op. 109), for cello with piano; an unpubl. clarinet sonata (performed in N.Y., 1939).

PIANO MUSIC: 3 sonatas (op. 6, 105, 106); *Capriccio* (op. 5); *Charakterstücke* (op. 7); *Rondo capriccioso* (op. 14); Fantasia of "The Last Rose of Summer" (op. 15); *3 Fantasias* (op. 16); the original and popular *Songs without Words (Lieder ohne Worte),* in 8 books (opp. 19b, 30, 38, 53, 62, 67, 85, 102); *Fantasia in F-sharp minor,* or *Sonate écossaise* (op. 28); *3 Caprices* (op. 33); 6 Preludes and Fugues (op. 35); *Variations sérieuses* (op. 54); 6 *Kinderstücke* (op. 72); Variations in E-flat (op. 82); Variations in B-flat (op. 83); 3 Preludes and 3 Studies (op. 104); *Albumblatt* (op. 117); *Capriccio* in E (op. 118); *Perpetuum mobile* (op. 119); etc.; 4-hand *Allegro brillant* (op. 92); *Duo concertant* (with Moscheles) for 2 pianos on the march theme of Weber's *Preciosa;* also organ music: 3 Preludes and Fugues (op. 37); 6 Organ Sonatas (op. 65); preludes etc., Mendelssohn's collected works, ed. by Julius Rietz, were publ. by Breitkopf & Härtel (1874–77); the same firm publ. a *Thematisches Verzeichnis* (1846; 2nd ed., 1853; 3rd ed., 1882, with a bibliography).

BIBLIOGRAPHY: BIOGRAPHY: A new edition of the complete works, still in progress, was begun in 1960 by the International Felix Mendelssohn Gesellschaft. W. A. Lampadius, *Felix Mendelssohn-Bartholdy. Ein Denkmal für seine Freunde* (Leipzig, 1848; in English, Philadelphia, 1865; 2nd greatly enlarged ed. as *Felix Mendelssohn-Bartholdy. Ein Gesammtbild seines Lebens und Wirkens,* 1886); J. Benedict, *A Sketch of the Life and Works of the late Felix Mendelssohn-Bartholdy* (London, 1850; 2nd ed., 1853); J. Schubring, "Erinnerungen an Felix Mendelssohn-Bartholdy," *Daheim* 26 (Leipzig, 1866; English transl. in the *Musical World,* May 12 and 19, 1866); A. Reissmann, *Felix Mendelssohn-Bartholdy. Sein Leben und seine Werke* (Berlin, 1867); K. Mendelssohn-Bartholdy, *Goethe und Mendelssohn* (Leipzig, 1871; in English, London, 1874); S. Hensel, *Die Familie Mendelssohn* (3 vols,; Berlin, 1879; 18th ed., 1924; English transl., in 2 vols., London, 1881); W. S. Rockstro, *Mendelssohn* (London, 1884; revised ed., 1911); E. David, *Les Mendelssohns-Bartholdy et Robert Schumann* (Paris, 1887); J. Eckardt, *Ferdinand David und die Familie Mendelssohn-Bartholdy* (Leipzig, 1888); B. Schrader, *Mendelssohn* (Leipzig, 1898); S. Stratton, *Mendelssohn* (London, 1901; revised ed., 1934); J. C. Hadden, *Life of*

Mendelssohn (London, 1904); B. Blackburn, *Mendelssohn* (London, 1904); E. Wolff, *Felix Mendelssohn-Bartholdy* (Berlin, 1906); C. Bellaigue, *Mendelssohn* (Paris, 1907); J. Hartog, *Felix Mendelssohn-Bartholdy en zijne werken* (Leyden, 1908); W. Dahms, *Mendelssohn* (Berlin, 1919); P. de Stoecklin, *Mendelssohn* (Paris, 1927); Cyril Winn, *Mendelssohn* (London, 1927); E. Vuillermoz, *Une Heure avec Mendelssohn* (Paris, 1930); R. B. Gotch, *Mendelssohn and His Friends in Kensington* (including letters from F. Horley; London, 1934); J. Erskine, *Song without Words. The Story of Felix Mendelssohn* (N.Y., 1941); J. Petit-pierre, *Le Mariage de Mendelssohn* (Lausanne, 1937; in English as *The Romance of the Mendelssohns;* London, 1947); B. Bartels, *Mendelssohn-Bartholdy: Mensch und Werk* (Bremen, 1947); K. H. Wörner, *Felix Mendelssohn-Bartholdy* (Wiesbaden, 1947); M. F. Schneider, *Mendelssohn im Bildnis* (Basel, 1953); P. Radcliffe, *Mendelssohn* (London, 1954); H. E. Jacob, *Felix Mendelssohn und seine Zeit* (Frankfurt, 1959); Eric Werner, *Felix Mendelssohn. A New Image of the Composer and His Age* (N.Y., 1963); Willi Reich, *Felix Mendelssohn im Spiegel eigener Aussagen und zeitgenössischer Dokumente* (Zürich, 1970); Herbert Kupferberg, *The Mendelssohns: Three Generations of Genius* (N.Y., 1972); G. Marek, *Gentle Genius: The Story of Felix Mendelssohn* (N.Y., 1972).

CRITICISM, ANALYSIS, APPRECIATION: C. Seldon, *La Musique en Allemagne: Mendelssohn* (Paris, 1867); F. G. Edwards, *The History of Mendelssohn's Oratorio Elijah* (London, 1896; 2nd ed., 1900); J. W. Hathaway, *An Analysis of Mendelssohn's Organ Works* (London, 1908); M. Clerjot and G. Marchet, *Mendelssohn et ses quatuors à cordes* (Reims, 1901); O. A. Mansfield, *Organ-parts of Mendelssohn's Oratorios, analytically considered* (London, 1907); O. A. Mansfield, "Some Characteristics and Peculiarities of Mendelssohn's Organ Sonatas," *Musical Quarterly* (July 1917); H. W. Waltershausen, *Mendelssohns Lieder ohne Worte* (Munich, 1920); G. Schünemann, "Die Bachpflege der Berliner Singakademie," *Bach-Jahrbuch* (1928); R. Werner, *Felix Mendelssohn-Bartholdy als Kirchenmusiker* (Frankfurt, 1930); C. Wilkinson, *How to Interpret Mendelssohn's "Songs without Words"* (London, 1930); T. Armstrong, *Mendelssohn's "Elijah"* (London, 1931); G. Kinsky, "Was Mendelssohn Indebted to Weber?" *Musical Quarterly* (April 1933); Schima Kaufmann, *Mendessohn: A Second Elijah* (N.Y., 1934); H. Foss, *Felix Mendelssohn-Bartholdy* (Oxford, 1934); J. Horton, *The Chamber Music of Mendelssohn* (Oxford, 1946); Luise and Hans Tischler, "Mendelssohn's Songs without Words," *Musical Quarterly* (Jan. 1948); Percy M. Young, *Introduction to the Music of Mendelssohn* (London, 1949); D. Mintz, "Melusine: A Mendelssohn Draft," *Musical Quarterly* (Oct. 1957): Hans C. Worbs, *Felix Mendelssohn-Bartholdy: Wesen und Wirken im Spiegel von Selbsterzeunissen und Berichten der Zeitgenossen* (Leipzig, 1958); G. Friedrich, *Die Fugenkomposition in Mendelssohns Instrumentalwerke* (Bonn, 1969); S. Grossmann-Vendrey, *Felix Mendelssohn-Bartholdy und die Musik der Vergangenheit* (Regensberg, 1969); P. Krause, *Autographen, Erstausgaben und Frühdrucke der Werke von Felix Mendelssohn-Bartholdy in Leipziger Bibliotheken und Archiven* (Leipzig, 1972).

CORRESPONDENCE: P. Mendelssohn-Bartholdy, *Reisebriefe . . . aus den Jahren 1830–32* (Leipzig, 1861; 5th ed., 1882; English transl., by Lady Wallace, as *Letters from Italy and Switzerland,* London, 1862); P. Mendelssohn-Bartholdy, *Briefe aus den Jahren 1833–47* (Leipzig, 1863; 8th ed., 1915; English transl. by Lady Wallace, London, 1863); L. Nohl, *Musikerbriefe* (Leipzig, 1867); E. Polko, *Erinnerungen an Felix Mendelssohn-Bartholdy* (Leipzig, 1868; English transl. by Lady Wallace, London, 1869); E. Devrient, *Meine Erinnerungen an Felix Mendelssohn-Bartholdy und seine Briefe an mich* (Leipzig, 1869; English transl. by Lady Macfarren, London, 1869; *Acht Briefe und ein Faksimile* (Leipzig, 1871; English transl. in *Macmillan's Magazine,* June, 1871); F. Hiller, *Felix Mendelssohn, Briefe und Erinnerungen* (Cologne, 1874; English transl., by M. E. von Glehn, London, 1874); S. Hensel, *The Mendelssohn Family, 1729–1847, from Letters and Journals* (2 vols; 1882; repr. N.Y., 1969); F. Moscheles, *Briefe von Felix Mendelssohn an Ignaz und Charlotte Moscheles* (Leipzig, 1888; English transl. as *Letters of Felix Mendelssohn,* London, 1888); M. Friedlaender, "Briefe an Goethe," *Goethe-Jahrbuch* (1891); E. Wolff, *Felix Mendelssohn-Bartholdy. Meisterbriefe* (Berlin, 1907; 2nd augmented ed., 1909); K. Klingemann, *Felix Mendelssohn-Bartholdys Briefwechsel mit Legationsrat Karl Klingemann* (Essen, 1909); G. Selden-Goth, *Mendelssohn's Letters* (selections from the letters transl. by Lady Wallace, with additional correspondence; N.Y., 1945); R. Sietz, ed., *Felix Mendelssohn-Bartholdy: sein Leben in Briefen* (Cologne, 1948). A new collection of letters is being published by the Veröffentlichungen der Historischen Kommission zu Berlin: vol. 1, *Briefe an deutsche Verleger,* ed. by R. Elvers (Berlin, 1968); H.-J. Rothe and R. Szeskus, eds. *Briefe aus Leipziger Archiven* (Leipzig, 1972).

Mendelssohn, Felix Robert, German cellist, great-grand-nephew of the famous composer; b. Berlin, Sept. 27, 1896; d. Baltimore, May 15, 1951. He studied at the Stern Cons.; later taught cello there. In 1936 he settled in the U.S.; taught in N.Y.; in 1941 joined the Baltimore Symph. Orch. He died in Cadoa Hall, Baltimore, while playing Dohnányi's *Konzertstück.*

Mendoza, Emilio, Venezuelan composer; b. Caracas, Aug. 8, 1953. He played guitar as a child; in his compositions he first followed conventional forms, but expanded his musical resources to include a lot of creative noise. His *Alborada* for viola and piano (1975) represents a dialogue between traditional and raucous sounds.

Mengal, Jean-Baptiste, Belgian horn virtuoso and composer; b. Ghent, Feb. 21, 1792; d. Paris, Dec. 19, 1878. He learned the rudiments of music from his father, who was an experienced horn player, and from his brother **Martin-Joseph Mengal,** whom he succeeded as first horn player at the Ghent municipal theater. In 1812 he entered the Paris Cons., graduating with 1st prize; then played in the orchestra of the Grand Opéra. He wrote a number of works for his instrument; fantasies, duets, solos; also publ. a method of horn playing.

Mengal, Martin-Joseph, Belgian horn player and conductor; brother of **Jean-Baptiste Mengal;** b. Ghent, Jan. 27, 1784; d. there, July 4, 1851. He studied with his father; played in Paris orchestras; in 1825 was appointed director of the Ghent municipal theater; then was conductor at Antwerp; in 1835 became director of the Ghent Cons. He wrote a great number of sacred works; his MSS are preserved at the Ghent Cons.

Mengelberg, Karel, Dutch composer and conductor; b. Utrecht, July 18, 1902. He studied with Pijper and later took a course at the Hochschule für Musik in Berlin. He conducted theater orchestras in provincial German towns and was a musician with the Berlin Radio (1927-30); subsequently was conductor of the municipal band in Barcelona (1932); then went to Kiev, Russia, where he was in charge of the music department in the Ukrainian film division. He returned to Amsterdam in 1938.

WORKS: 2 ballets: *Bataille* (1922) and *Parfait Amour* (1945); *3 songs from Tagore's "The Gardener"* for soprano and orch. (1925); String Quartet (1938); Sonata for solo oboe (1939); Trio for flute, oboe and bassoon (1940); a short *Requiem* for orch. (1946); *Divertimento* for small orch. (1948); Horn Concerto (1950); *Toccata* for piano (1950); *Jan Hinnerik* for a cappella chorus (1950); *Anion,* symph. sketch (1950); *Soliloquio* for solo flute (1951); *Ballade* for flute, clarinet, harp and string quartet (1952); *Serenade* for string orch. (1952); *Recitatief* for baritone, viola da gamba and harpsichord (1953); *Suite* for small orch. (1954); *Roland Holst,* cantata for chorus and small orch. (1955); *Soneria, Romanza e Mazurca* for harp (1958). In 1961 he completed the revision, with a simplified orchestration, of Willem Pijper's Second Symphony (Pijper's own revised score was destroyed during the Nazi air raid on Rotterdam in May 1940).

Mengelberg, Kurt Rudolf, German-born musicologist and composer of Dutch descent, nephew of the conductor **Willem Mengelberg;** b. Krefeld, Feb. 1, 1892; d. Beausoleil, near Monte Carlo, Oct. 13, 1959. He studied piano with Neitzel in Cologne and musicology with Hugo Riemann at the Univ. of Leipzig, receiving his doctorate in 1915. He then went to Amsterdam, where he studied music theory with his uncle; from 1925 to 1954 served as artistic director of the Concertgebouw Company in Amsterdam. Among his publications are the valuable program book *Das Mahler-Fest, Amsterdam Mai 1920* (Vienna, 1920); a biography of Mahler (Leipzig, 1923); *Nederland, Spiegeleener Beschaving (Holland, Mirror of a Culture;* Amsterdam, 1929); a commemorative publication on the semicentennial of the Concertgebouw (Amsterdam, 1938); *Muziek, Spiegel des Tijds (Music, Mirror of Time,* Amsterdam, 1948); and a biography of Willem Mengelberg. His own compositions are mainly liturgical; among them are *Missa pro Pace* (1932); *Stabat Mater* (1940) and *Victimae Paschali laudes* (1946); he also wrote *Symphonic Variations* for cello and orch. (1927); Violin Concerto (1930); *Capriccio* for piano

and orch. (1936); Concertino for Flute and Chamber Orch. (1943); solo songs and piano pieces.

Mengelberg, Misha, Dutch composer (son of **Karel Mengelberg**); b. Kiev, June 5, 1935. He was born in Kiev while his father was working in the USSR; came to Holland in 1938, where he studied with Kees van Baaren at the Royal Cons. in The Hague, graduating in 1964. He was a co-founder of the Instant Composers Pool in 1967; in 1972 became president of the Guild of Improvising Musicians, a jazz organization.

WORKS: *Musica* for 17 instruments (1959); *Medusa* for string quartet (1962); *Commentary* for orch. (1965); *Exercise* for solo flute (1966); *Omtrent een componistenactie (Concerning a Composer's Action)* for wind quintet (1966); *3 Piano Pieces + Piano Piece 4* (1966); *Amaga* for 3 different guitars and electronic equipment (1968); *Anatoloose* for orch. and tape (1968; Holland Fest., July 8, 1971); *Hello Windy Boys* for double wind quintet (1968); *Met welbeleefde groet van de kameel (With the Very Polite Greetings of the Camel)* for orch. with electronic sawing and excavating drills (1971-73); *Onderweg (On the Way)* for orch. (1973; Bergen, Norway, Jan. 13, 1974). He was a participant in the creation of an anti-imperialistic, collective opera, *Reconstructie* (1968-69; Holland Festival, June 29, 1969; in collaboration with Louis Andriessen, Reinbert de Leeuw, Peter Schat and Jan van Vlijmen).

Mengelberg, Willem, celebrated Dutch conductor; b. Utrecht, March 28, 1871; d. Chur, Switzerland, March 21, 1951. He studied at the Cons. of Utrecht, and later at the Cologne Cons. with Seiss, Jensen, and Wüllner. He was appointed municipal music director in Lucerne in 1891, and his work there attracted so much attention that in 1895 he was placed at the head of the famous Concertgebouw Orch. in Amsterdam; during his directorship, he elevated that orchestra to a lofty position in the world of music. In addition, he became conductor of the choral society "Toonkunst" in Amsterdam (1898); appeared frequently as guest conductor in all European countries; in England was an annual visitor from 1913 until World War II; appeared with the N.Y. Philharmonic in 1905; came to the U.S. again in 1921, conducting the National Symph. Orch. in N.Y., which was absorbed at his suggestion by the Philharmonic Orch.; he led the Philharmonic at various intervals from 1922 till 1930; in 1928 he received the degree of Mus. Doc., Columbia Univ. *(honoris causa);* in 1933 was appointed prof. of music at Utrecht Univ. During the occupation of Holland by the Germans, Mengelberg openly expressed his sympathies with the Nazi cause, and lost the high respect and admiration that his compatriots had felt for him; after the liberation of Holland he was barred from professional activities there, the ban to be continued until 1951, but he died in that year in exile in Switzerland. Mengelberg was one of the finest representatives of the Romantic tradition in symphonic conducting; his interpretations extracted the full emotional power from the music, and yet he never transgressed the limits imposed by the structural forms of classical music; his renditions of Beethoven's symphonies were inspiring. He was a great admirer of Mahler and conducted a festival of Mahler's music in Amsterdam in May 1920; he was also a champion of works by Richard Strauss (who dedicated the score of *Ein Heldenleben* to him), Max Reger, and Debussy.

BIBLIOGRAPHY: Hugo Nolthenius, *Willem Mengelberg* (Amsterdam, 1920); Rudolf Mengelberg, *Das Mahlerfest in Amsterdam* (Amsterdam, 1920); A. Van den Boer, *De Psychologische beteekenis van Willem Mengelberg als Dirigent* (Amsterdam, 1925); Edna R. Sollitt, *Mengelberg and the Symphonic Epoch* (N.Y., 1930); Edna R. Sollitt, *Mengelberg spreckt* (speeches of Mengelberg; The Hague, 1935).

Menges, Herbert, English conductor, brother of **Isolde Menges;** b. Hove, Aug. 27, 1902; d. London, Feb. 20, 1972. He played violin as a child; then took piano lessons with Mathilda Verne and attended courses in composition with Vaughan Williams at the Royal College of Music in London. He began his conducting career in Brighton, and conducted the Brighton Philharmonic Society (which was founded by his mother) from 1925 until his death. He was also a music director of the Old Vic Theatre (1931-50); in 1945 he became conductor of the Southern Philharmonic Orch. at Southsea.

BIBLIOGRAPHY: Donald Brook, *International Gallery of Conductors* (Bristol, 1951; pp. 113-16).

Menges, Isolde, English violinist; sister of **Herbert Menges;** b. Hove, May 16, 1893. Her parents were violinists, and she studied at home; then for 3 years with Leopold Auer in St. Petersburg and in Dresden (1909-12); made her London debut on Feb. 4, 1913; toured the U.S. in 1916-19 (debut in N.Y., Oct. 21, 1916), and again in 1921. In 1931 she became prof. at the Royal College of Music; also organized the Menges Quartet; at the Brahms Centennial in 1933, the Menges Quartet presented in London a series of concerts of chamber music by Brahms.

Mengewein, Karl, German composer and teacher; b. Zaunroda, Thuringia, Sept. 9, 1852; d. Berlin, April 7, 1908. From 1876 until 1886 he was a teacher at Freudenberg's Cons., Wiesbaden, and with the latter founded a Cons. at Berlin in 1886, of which he was co-director till 1896. He founded the Oratorienverein (1895) and the next year the "Madrigal" for the production of a cappella music. He wrote an oratorio, *Johannes der Täufer* (1892); festival cantata, *Martin Luther;* operetta, *Schulmeisters Brautfahrt* (Wiesbaden, 1884); overture, *Dornröschen;* several Singspiele, a Requiem, female choruses, etc. He also publ. *Die Ausbildung des musikalischen Gehörs* (1908).

Ménil, Félicien de, French musicologist; b. Boulogne-sur-Mer, July 16, 1860; d. Neuilly, near Paris, March 28, 1930. He studied with Henri Maréchal and Lenepveu at the Paris Cons.; undertook extensive travels in America, India, and Africa; returning to Paris, he was appointed prof. of history of music at the École Niedermeyer (1899). His publications include: *Monsigny* (1893); *Josquin des Prés* (1897); *L'École flamande du XVe siècle* (Paris, 1895; considerably augmented and publ. as *L'École contrapuntique flamande au XVe et au XVIe siècle*, 1905); *Historie de la danse à travers les*

âges (1904). He was an ardent adherent of Esperanto, and wrote the hymn of the Esperantists (1928).

Mennicke, Karl, German writer on music; b. Reichenbach, May 12, 1880; killed in action during World War I in Galicia, late June 1917. He studied music with Hugo Riemann; received his Dr. phil. in 1905 with the dissertation *Hasse und die Brüder Graun als Symphoniker* (with thematic catalogue).

Mennin, Peter, eminent American composer; b. Erie, Pennsylvania, May 17, 1923, of Italian parents (his real name was **Mennini**). He studied music at the Oberlin Cons.; served in the U.S. Army Air Force; after demobilization he resumed his music study at the Eastman School of Music, where his teachers in composition were Howard Hanson and Bernard Rogers; he received his Mus. M. in 1945 and his Ph.D. in 1947; subsequently he took a summer course in conducting with Koussevitzky at the Berkshire Music Center, Tanglewood. He subsequently taught at the Juilliard School of Music, N.Y. (1947-58); then served as director of the Peabody Cons. in Baltimore (1958-62). In 1962 was appointed President of the Juilliard School of Music, N.Y. His music is characterized by a strong sense of purposeful thematic developement and formal cohesion; he is at his best in purely instrumental works cast in a neo-classical mold.

WORKS: 8 symphonies: No. 1 (1942), No. 2 (1944), No. 3 (N.Y., Feb. 27, 1947), No. 4, *The Cycle*, for chorus and orch. (N.Y., March 18, 1949), No. 5 (1951), No. 6 (Louisville, Nov. 18, 1953), No. 7, subtitled *Variation Symphony* (Cleveland, Jan. 23, 1964); No. 8 (1973; N.Y., Nov. 21, 1974); Sinfonia for chamber orch. (Rochester, May 24, 1947); *Fantasia* for string orch. (N.Y., Jan. 11, 1948); *Folk Overture* (Washington, Dec. 19, 1945); Violin Concerto (1950); *Concertato "Moby Dick"* for orch. (1952); Cello Concerto (1955); Piano Concerto (Cleveland, Feb. 27, 1958); Concertino for Flute, Strings, and Percussion (1945); *Canto for Orchestra* (1964); *Cantata de Virtute* for narrator, soloists, chorus, and orch. (1968-69); *Pied Piper of Hamelin* for narrator and orch., after the poem of Robert Browning (Cincinnati, May 2, 1969); *Symphonic Movements* (Minneapolis, Jan. 21, 1971; later performed under the title *Sinfonia*); *Voices* for voice, percussion, piano, harp and harpsichord, after poems of Thoreau, Melville, Whitman and Dickinson (N.Y., March 28, 1976); 2 string quartets (1941, 1951); *Sonata Concertante* for violin and piano (1956); Piano Sonata (1963); other piano pieces; songs.

Mennini, Louis, American composer; brother of **Peter Mennin** (whose real name was **Mennini**); b. Erie, Pa., Nov. 18, 1920. He studied at Oberlin Cons. (1939-42); then served in the U.S. Army Air Force (1942-45); subsequently studied composition with Bernard Rogers and Howard Hanson at the Eastman School of Music, Rochester, N.Y. (B.M., 1947; M.M., 1948); was on its faculty from 1949 to 1965; then served as Dean of the School of Music, North Carolina School of the Arts at Winston-Salem (1965-71); in 1973 appointed Chairman of the Dept. of Music of Mercyhurst College in Erie, Pennsylvania. His music is pragmatic and functional, with occasional modernistic touches.

WORKS: 2 chamber operas: *The Well* (Rochester, May 8, 1951) and *The Rope*, after Eugene O'Neill (Berkshire Music Festival, Aug. 8, 1955); *Overtura Breve* (1949); 2 symphonies: No. 1, *Da Chiesa* (1960); No. 2, *Da Festa* (1963); String Quartet (1961); *Tenebrae* for orch. (1963); Concerto Grosso for orch. (1975); numerous pieces for violin and for piano.

Menotti, Gian Carlo, remarkable composer; b. Cadegliano, Italy, July 7, 1911; was the sixth of ten children. He learned the rudiments of music from his mother, and began to compose as a child, making his first attempt at an opera, entitled *The Death of Pierrot*, at the age of 10. He studied for several years (1923-27) at the Milan Cons.; then came to the U.S., and entered the Curtis Institute, Philadelphia (1927-33), where he studied with Rosario Scalero; subsequently taught composition at the Curtis Institute; traveled often to Europe; made his home at Mt. Kisco, N.Y. Although Menotti has associated himself with the cause of American music, and spends most of his time in the U.S., he has retained his Italian citizenship. As a composer, he is unique on the American scene, being the first to create American opera possessing such an appeal to audiences as to become established in permanent repertory. Inheriting the natural Italian gift for operatic drama and expressive singing line, he has adapted these qualities to the peculiar requirements of the American stage and to the changing fashions of the period; his serious operas have a strong dramatic content in the realistic style stemming from the Italian "verismo." He writes his own librettos, marked by an extraordinary flair for drama and for the communicative power of the English language; with this is combined a fine, though subdued sense of musical humor. Menotti makes no pretensions at extreme modernism, and does not fear to approximate the successful formulas developed by Verdi and Puccini; the influence of Mussorgsky's realistic prosody is also in evidence, particularly in recitative. When dramatic tension requires a greater impact, Menotti resorts to atonal and polytonal writing, leading to climaxes accompanied by massive dissonances. His first successful stage work was *Amelia Goes to the Ball*, an opera buffa in 1 act (originally to an Italian libretto by the composer, as *Amelia al Ballo*), staged at the Academy of Music, Philadelphia, on April 1, 1937. This was followed by another comic opera, *The Old Maid and the Thief*, commissioned by the National Broadcasting Co., first performed on the radio, April 22, 1939, and on the stage, by the Philadelphia Opera Co., on Feb. 11, 1941. Menotti's next operactic work was *The Island God*, produced by the Metropolitan Opera, N.Y., on Feb. 20, 1942, with indifferent success; but with the production of *The Medium* (N.Y., May 8, 1946) Menotti established himself as the foremost composer-librettist of modern opera. The imaginative libretto, dealing with a fraudulent spiritualist who falls victim to her own practices when she imagines that the ghostly voices are real, suited Menotti's musical talent to perfection; the opera had a long and successful run in N.Y., an unprecedented occurrence in the history of the American lyric theater. A short humorous opera, *The Telephone*, was first produced by the N.Y. Ballet Society, Feb. 18, 1947, on the same bill with *The Medium;* these 2 contrasting works were subsequently staged all over the U.S. and in Europe, often on the same evening. Menotti then produced *The Consul* (N.Y., March 15, 1950), his best tragic work, describing the plight of political fugitives vainly trying to escape from an unnamed country, but failing to obtain the necessary visa from the consul of an anonymous power; very ingeniously, the author does not include the title character in the cast, since the consul never appears on the stage, but remains a shadowy presence. *The Consul* exceeded Menotti's previous operas in popular success; it had a long run in N.Y., and received the Pulitzer Prize. On Christmas Eve, 1951, the National Broadcasting Co. presented Menotti's television opera *Amahl and the Night Visitors,* a Christmas story of undeniable poetry and appeal; it became an annual television production every Christmas in subsequent years. His next opera was *The Saint of Bleecker Street,* set in a New York locale (N.Y., Dec. 27, 1954); it won the Drama Critics Circle Award for the best musical play of 1954, and the Pulitzer Prize of 1955. A madrigal ballet, *The Unicorn, the Gorgon and the Manticore,* commissioned by the Elizabeth Sprague Coolidge Foundation, was first presented at the Library of Congress, Washington, Oct. 21, 1956. His opera *Maria Golovin,* written expressly for the International Exposition at Brussels, was staged there on Aug. 20, 1958. In 1958 he organized the Festival of Two Worlds in Spoleto, Italy, staging old and new works; in 1977 he inaugurated an American counterpart of the Festival in Charleston, North Carolina. In many of the Festival productions Menotti acted also as stage director. In the meantime he continued to compose; he produced in quick succession: *Labyrinth,* television opera to Menotti's own libretto (N.Y., March 3, 1963); *Death of the Bishop of Brindisi,* dramatic cantata with the text by the composer (Cincinnati, May 18, 1963); *Le Dernier Sauvage,* opera buffa, originally with an Italian libretto by Menotti, produced at the Opéra-Comique in Paris in a French translation (Oct. 21, 1963; produced in English at the Metropolitan Opera, N.Y., Jan. 23, 1964); *Martin's Lie,* chamber opera to Menotti's text (Bath, England, June 3, 1964); *Help, Help, the Globolinks!,* "an opera in one act for children and those who like children" to words by Menotti, with electronic effects (Hamburg, Dec. 19, 1968); *The Most Important Man,* opera to his own libretto (N.Y., March 12, 1971); *The Hero,* comic opera (Philadelphia, June 1, 1976); *The Egg,* a church opera to Menotti's own libretto (Washington Cathedral, June 17, 1976); *The Trial of the Gypsy* for treble voices and piano (N.Y., May 24, 1978). Among Menotti's non-operatic works are the ballets *Sebastian* (1944) and *Errand into the Maze* (N.Y., Feb. 2, 1947); Piano Concerto (Boston, Nov. 2, 1945); *Apocalypse,* symph. poem (Pittsburgh, Oct. 19, 1951); Violin Concerto (Philadelphia, Dec. 5, 1952, Zimbalist soloist); *Triplo Concerto a Tre,* triple concerto in 3 movements (N.Y., Oct. 6, 1970); *Landscapes and Remembrances,* cantata to his own autobiographical words (Milwaukee, May 14, 1976); *First Symphony,* subtitled *The Halcyon* (Philadelphia, Aug. 4, 1976). He also wrote a number of *pièces d'occasion* such as *Trio for a House-Warming Party,* for piano, cello and flute (1936); *Vari-*

ations on a Theme by Schumann; *Pastorale* for piano and string orch.; *Poemetti per Maria Rosa* (piano pieces for children); etc. Menotti is the author of the librettos for Samuel Barber's operas *Vanessa* (Metropolitan Opera, N.Y., Jan. 15, 1958) and *A Hand of Bridge* (1959), and wrote a play without music, *The Leper* (Tallahassee, Florida, April 22, 1970).

After many years in America, he bought an estate, Yester House, in Scotland, and made it his permanent abode in 1974 with his legally adopted son, Francis Phelan, who thenceforth bears his name.

BIBLIOGRAPHY: Robert Tricoire, *Gian Carlo Menotti, l'Homme et son œuvre* (Paris, 1966); John Gruen, *Menotti: A Biography* (N.Y., 1978).

Menter, Joseph, German cellist; b. Teisbach, Bavaria, Jan. 23, 1808; d. Munich, April 18, 1856. He began his career as a violinist, then studied cello with Moralt in Munich and became a member of the orchestra of the Bavarian Royal Opera (1833). His daughter **Sophie Menter** was a celebrated pianist.

Menter, Sophie, German pianist and teacher; daughter of **Joseph Menter**; b. Munich, July 29, 1846; d. there, Feb. 23, 1918. She studied piano with Niest in Munich and with Lebert in Stuttgart; made her professional debut in 1867 at the Gewandhaus Concerts in Leipzig, and later took lessons with Tausig and Liszt. In 1872 she married the cellist **David Popper** (divorced 1886). From 1883 to 1887 she taught piano at the St. Petersburg Cons.; then lived mostly in the Tyrol. She composed a number of attractive pieces. Tchaikovsky orchestrated her work *Ungarische Zigeunerweisen* for piano and orch., and she played it under his direction in Odessa, on Feb. 4, 1893.

Menuhin, Hephzibah, American pianist; sister of **Yehudi Menuhin**; b. San Francisco, May 20, 1920. Like her brother, she was a *wunderkind*, appearing in public practically since infancy. She devoted herself mainly to chamber music and played numerous sonata recitals with her brother.

Menuhin, Yehudi, celebrated American violinist; b. New York, April 22, 1916, of Russian-Jewish parents (his father's family name was **Mnuhin**). He was taken to San Francisco as a child, where he began to study violin with Sigmund Anker; later he became a pupil of Louis Persinger. He made his public debut at the age of 7 playing the Mendelssohn concerto in San Francisco, creating a sensation. He then went to Europe where he took lessons with Adolf Busch and Enesco; played in Paris at the age of 10 with the Lamoureux orch., performing 3 violin concertos on the same program. Returning to America he made his N.Y. debut in the Beethoven concerto, with the N.Y. Symph. Society, Fritz Busch conducting (Nov. 25, 1927). The following season he played concertos by Bach, Beethoven and Brahms in one evening with the Berlin Philharmonic, under the direction of Bruno Walter. He made his London debut on Nov. 4, 1929, with the Brahms concerto; on the sesquicentennial of the Gewandhaus Orch. in Leipzig he was the soloist playing the Mendelssohn concerto (Nov. 14, 1931). In 1934 he completed his first world tour playing concerts in 73 cities in 13 countries, including Australia. After World War II Menuhin became increasingly interested in organizing music festivals and establishing an educational institution; he also began to appear as a conductor; lived mostly in Switzerland and England. In 1959 he established music festivals in Gstaad, in the Bern canton; in 1969 he opened festival performances in Windsor, Berkshire, England; he was also artistic director of the Bath Festival, Somershire, and took over the Bath Festival Orch. with which he undertook numerous tours. In 1963 he founded the Yehudi Menuhin School in Stoke d'Abernon, Surrey. He became interested in Indian music and gave concerts with the proponent of classical Indian playing, Ravi Shankar. In 1972 he succeeded Barbirolli as president of the Trinity College of Music in London. In 1970 he received the honorary citizenship of the community of Saanen, Switzerland, and assumed Swiss national allegiance, while preserving his American citizenship. In 1976 he was awarded an honorary doctorate by the Sorbonne Univ. of Paris, the first musician to be so honored since the founding of the Sorbonne in 1235. He publ. a collection of essays under the title *Theme and Variations* (London, 1972) and an autobiography, *Unfinished Journey* (N.Y., 1977).

BIBLIOGRAPHY: B. Gavoty, *Yehudi Menuhin et Georges Enesco* in the series Les Grands Interprètes (Geneva, 1955); Robert Magidoff, *Yehudi Menuhin: the Story of the Man and the Musician* (Garden City, 1955); N. Wymer, *Yehudi Menuhin* (London, 1961); Eric Fenby, *Menuhin's House of Music* (London, 1969).

Mercadante, (Giuseppe) Saverio (Raffaele), important Italian composer; b. Altamura, near Bari, Sept. (baptized Sept. 17) 1795; d. Naples, Dec. 17, 1870. He was born out of wedlock; taken to Naples at the age of 13, he enrolled at the Collegio di San Sebastiano. He studied violin; after preliminary theoretical courses with Furno and Tritto, he entered the class of Zingarelli, whose favorite pupil he became. He began to compose while still in school; wrote 2 symphonies (which were praised by Rossini), several concertos, string quartets, a Mass, etc. He began his career as a dramatic composer auspiciously with the production of his first opera, *L'Apoteosi d'Ercole* (Naples, Jan. 4, 1819). He exhibited a typical Italian dramatic flair for comedy in his next opera, *Elisa e Claudio*, produced at La Scala, Milan, on Oct. 30, 1821, and subsequently staged at all important opera houses in Europe, and, within a decade, in America. Other important operas were *Caritea, Regina di Spagna* (Venice, Feb. 21,1826), *Gabriella di Vergy* (Lisbon, Aug. 8, 1828), *I Normanni a Parigi* (Turin, Feb. 7, 1832), *I Briganti* (Paris, March 22, 1836), *Il Giuramento* (Milan, March 10, 1837; his best work; performed many times, and in the repertory of Italian opera houses well into the 20th century), *Elena da Feltre* (Naples, Dec. 26, 1838), *Il Bravo* (Milan, March 9, 1839), *La Vestale* (Naples, March 10, 1840; successful in Italy), *Leonora* (Naples, Dec. 5, 1844), *Gli Orazi ed i Curiazi* (Naples, Nov. 10, 1846), and *Virginia* (Naples, April 7, 1866; his last opera, composed in 1851, but not staged, for political reasons; although not successful with the public, the score is regarded as of fine workmanship). Mercadante composed operas for different towns, residing, after the manner of Italian opera composers, in the city for which he was writing; thus he lived in Rome, Bologna, Madrid (1827-28), Lisbon (1828-29), and Vienna (where he produced 3 operas in 1824), as well as the cities already mentioned. In 1833 he became maestro di cappella at the Cathedral of Novara; here he lost the sight of one eye, and in 1862 total blindness ensued. In 1839 he was engaged as maestro di cappella at Lanliano; and in 1840 he succeeded Zingarelli as director of the Naples Cons. Besides his operas (about 60 in all) he wrote much chamber music; a *Messa solenne,* and some 20 other Masses; *Le 7 parole di Nostro Signore,* for 4 voices with string quartet; a *Salve Regina,* a *De profundis,* 2 *Tantum ergo,* litanies, vespers, psalms, cantatas, hymns (one to Garibaldi in 1861; to Rossini in 1866); funeral symphonies to Rossini, Donizetti, Bellini, Pacini; orchestral fantasies (*L'Aurora, La Rimembranza, Il Lamento dell'Arabo, Il Lamento del Bardo,* the last composed after he had become blind); pieces for various instruments; many songs; solfeggi for the Cons.; etc.

BIBLIOGRAPHY: R. Colucci, *Biografia di Saverio Mercadante* (Venice, 1867); G. Bustico, "Saverio Mercadante a Novara," *Rivista Musicale Italiana* (1921); Guido Pannain, "Saggio su la musica a Napoli nel secolo XIX," *Rivista Musicale Italiana* (1928); G. De Napoli, *La Triade Melodrammatica Altamurana: G. Tritto, V. Lavigna, S. Mercadante* (Milan, 1931); G. Solimene, *La Patria ed i genitori di Mercadante* (Naples, 1940); B. Notarnicola, *Saverio Mercadante: biografica critica* (Rome, 1945; 3rd, much revised ed., 1951, as *Saverio Mercadante nella gloria e nella luce; Verdi non ha vinto Mercadante*); a sesquicentennial publ., *Saverio Mercadante: note e documenti* (Bari, 1945; publ. by the committee "Pro Mercadante"); Frank Walker, "Mercadante and Verdi," *Music & Letters* (Oct. 1952; Jan. 1953).

Mercadier, Jean Baptiste, French music theorist; b. Belesta, Ariège, April 18, 1750; d. Foix, Jan. 14, 1815. He wrote *Nouveau système de musique théorique et pratique* (1776), a critique of Tartini's and Rameau's systems, favoring Rameau.

Mercer, Johnny, American lyricist and composer of popular songs; b. Savannah, Georgia, Nov. 18, 1909; d. Los Angeles, June 25, 1976. He went to New York as a youth, and attracted the attention of Paul Whiteman; subsequently wrote songs for him, Benny Goodman and Bob Crosby. In 1940 he went to Hollywood, where he founded Capitol Records. His first success as a lyric writer was *Lazybones,* with music by Hoagy Carmichael; another great success was *Accentuate the Positive,* which he wrote for his psychoanalyst. He wrote both words and music for *Something's Gotta Give,* and several other hits. He received 4 Academy Awards ("Oscars") for his lyrics.

Mercure, Pierre, Canadian composer; b. Montreal, Feb. 21, 1927; d. in an ambulance between Avallon and Auxerres, France, on Jan. 29, 1966, after an automobile crash while driving from Paris to Lyon. He studied composition with Claude Champagne at the

Montreal Cons. (1944-49) and in Paris with Nadia Boulanger (1949-50); also took courses with Dallapiccola at the Berkshire Music Center in Tanglewood, and at Darmstadt and Dartington with Pousseur, Nono and Berio. He played bassoon with the Montreal Symph. (1947-52); then became producer of musical broadcasts on the French radio network in Montreal. In his music he explored electronic sonorities in combinations with traditional instrumentation.

WORKS: *Kaléidoscope* for orch. (1947-48); *Pantomime* for winds and percussion (1948); 3 short choreographed pieces: *Dualité,* with trumpet and piano; *La femme archaïque,* with viola, piano and timpani; and *Lucrèce Borgia,* with trumpet, piano and percussion (all composed in 1949); *Emprise* for clarinet, bassoon, cello and piano (1950); *Cantate pour une joie* for soprano, chorus and orch. (1955); *Divertissement* for solo string quartet and string orch. (1957); *Triptyque* for orch. (1959); 6 tape pieces with optional choreography: *Improvisation, Incandescense, Structures Métalliques I* and *II* (all 1961); *Manipulations* (1963) and *Surimpressions* (1964); *Répercussions,* for Japanese wind-chimes on tape (1961); *Jeu de Hockey* on tape (1961); *Structure Métalliques III* for tape (1962); *Tétrachromie,* ballet for 3 winds, 4 percussionists and tape (1963); *Psaume pour abri,* radiophonic cantata for narrator, 2 choirs, chamber ensemble and tape (Montreal, May 15, 1963); *Lignes et Points* for orch. (1964; Montreal, Feb. 16, 1965); H_2O *per Severino* for 4-10 flutes and/or clarinets (1965); film scores.

Merian, Hans, Swiss musicologist; b. Basel, 1857; d. Leipzig, May 28, 1905. He publ. *Mozarts Meisteropern* (1900); *Geschichte der Musik im 19. Jahrhundert* (1902; 3rd ed. as *Illustrierte Geschichte der Musik,* 1914) and wrote a number of analytical notes of instrumental and operatic masterpieces.

Merian, Wilhelm, Swiss musicologist; b. Basel, Sept. 18, 1889; d. there, Nov. 15, 1952. He studied with Nef in Basel and with Rezniček in Berlin; also studied musicology at the Univ. of Berlin; Dr. phil., 1915, with the dissertation, *Die Tabulatur des Organisten H. Kotter.* From 1920, music editor of the *Basler Nachrichten;* docent (1921), then (1930) prof. of musicology, at the Univ. of Basel.

WRITINGS: *Gedenkschrift zum 50-jährigen Bestehen der Allgemeinen Musikschule in Basel* (1917); *Basels Musikleben im 19. Jahrhundert* (1920; *Die Klaviermusik der deutschen Koloristen* (1921); *Der Tanz in den deutschen Tabulaturbüchern* (1927); *Formuntersuchung zu Mozarts Klaviersonaten,* in the Nef-Festschrift (1932); *Hermann Suter: der Dirigent und der Komponist* (Basel, 1936); *Hermann Suter: ein Lebensbild als Beitrag zur schweizerischen Musikgeschichte* (Basel, 1936). He was the editor of the *Basel Kongress-Bericht* (1924), *Geistliche Werke des 16. Jahrhunderts,* and other publications.

Mériel, Paul, French composer; b. Mondonbleau, Loire-et-Cher, Jan. 4, 1818; d. Toulouse, Feb. 24, 1897. As a boy, he earned his living playing the violin in theater orchestras; later studied with Napoleão in Lisbon; produced a comic opera, *Cornelius l'argentier,* in Amiens; then settled in Toulouse, where he brought out a symph. poem, *Le Tasse* (*Tasso*), a grand opera, *L'Armorique* (1854), and the comic opera *Les Précieuses ridicules* (1877).

Merikanto, Aarre, Finnish composer, son of **Oskar Merikanto**; b. Helsinki, June 29, 1893; d. there, Sept. 29, 1958. He studied in Leipzig with Max Reger (1912-14) and with Vassilenko in Moscow (1916-17). In 1951, he succeeded Palmgren as head of the dept. of composition at the Sibelius Academy in Helsinki, and held this post until his death. Like his father, he wrote on themes of Finnish folklore, but he also produced a few pieces that had elements of French Impressionism.
WORKS: opera, *Juha* (1920-22; first performed on the Finnish Radio in Helsinki, Dec. 3, 1958, as a memorial to him; first stage performance took place in Lahti, Oct. 28, 1963); 3 piano concertos (1913, 1937, 1955); 3 symphonies (1916, 1918, 1953); 4 violin concertos (1916, 1925, 1931, 1954); symph. suite *Lemminkainen* (1916); 2 cello concertos (1919, 1941-44); *Pan*, symph. poem (1924); Concerto, for violin, clarinet, French horn and string sextet (1925); *Concert Piece*, for cello and chamber orch. (1926); *Notturno*, symph. poem (1929); *Kyllikin ryöstö* (*The Abduction of Kyllikki*), symph. poem (1935); *Scherzo* for orch. (1937); *3 Impressions* for orch. (1940); *Soitelma kesäyölle* (*Music to the Summer Night*) for orch. (1942); *Genesis* for soprano, chorus and orch. (1956); *Tuhma* (*Simpleton*) for male chorus and orch. (1956); 2 string quartets (1913, 1939); String Trio (1912); Piano Trio (1917); Nonet (1926); String Sextet (1932); *Partita* for harp and woodwinds (1936); songs.

Merikanto, Oskar, Finnish composer; b. Helsinki, Aug. 5, 1868; d. Hausjärvi-Oiti, Feb. 17, 1924. After preliminary study in his native city, he went to Leipzig and Berlin to continue his musical education (1887). Returning to Finland, he became organist of St. John's Church, and from 1911 till 1922 was conductor of the National Opera in Helsinki. He wrote a great number of songs, which became very popular in Finland; organ works and manuals for organ playing; various instrumental pieces; and 3 operas: *Pohjan Neiti* (*The Maid of Bothnia;* Viborg, June 18, 1908), *Elinan Surma* (*Elina's Death;* Helsinki, Nov. 17, 1910), and *Regina von Emmeritz* (Helsinki, Jan. 30, 1920).
BIBLIOGRAPHY: Yrjö Suomalainen, *Oskar Merikanto* (Helsinki, 1950).

Merilainen, Usko, Finnish composer; b. Tampere, Jan. 27, 1930. He studied with Aarre Merikanto and Leo Funtek at the Sibelius Academy in Helsinki (1951-55); then took private lessons with Ernst Krenek at Darmstadt and with Wladimir Vogel in Switzerland. In his music he adopted a pragmatic modern idiom, with structural foundations of tonal and/or dodecaphonic procedures, depending on the basic concept.
WORKS: 2 ballets: *Arius* (1958-60; 2 suites, 1960 and 1962, and an *Introduction and Variations*, 1964, from the ballet) and *Psyche*, for tape (1973); *Sumu* (*The Mist*), symph. fantasy (1952); 5 symphonies: No. 1 (1952-55); No. 2 (1964); No. 3 (1971); No. 4, *The An-*

vil, dance pantomime for tape (1975); No. 5 (1976); 2 piano concertos (1955, 1969); *Concerto for orch.* (1956); *Chamber Concerto* for solo violin, double string orch. and percussion (1962); *Epyllion 1* for orch. (1963); *Musique du Printemps* for orch. (1969); Cello Concerto (1975); *Partita* for brass (1954); *4 Bagatelles* for string quartet (1962); *Arabesques* for solo cello (1963); *Hommage à Jean Sibelius* for violin and piano (1965); *Impression* for wind quintet, piano, viola, cello, double bass and percussion (1965); String Quartet (1965); *Divertimento* for wind quintet, harp, viola and cello (1968); *Metamorfora for 7* for clarinet, bassoon, trumpet, trombone, percussion, violin, and double bass (1969); *Concerto for 13* for 7 violins, 3 violas, 2 cellos and double bass (1971); *Concerto for double bass and percussion* (1973); *Aspects of the ballet "Psyche"* for tape instrumental ensemble (1973); *Suite* for piano (1955); Piano Sonatina (1958); 4 piano sonatas (1960, 1966, 1972, 1974); *Riviravi*, small piano pieces for children (1962); *3 Notturni* for piano (1967); *Papillons* for 2 pianos (1969); *4 Love Songs* for soprano and piano (1961).

Merk, Joseph, Austrian cellist; b. Vienna, March 18, 1795; d. Ober-Döbling, June 16, 1852. He was trained in Vienna; in 1818 became 1st cellist at the Vienna Opera; in 1823, teacher at the Cons. He wrote 2 cello concertos, fantasias, polonaises, etc.; his cello études are of value to students.

Merkel, Gustav (Adolf), German organist and composer; b. Oberoderwitz, Nov. 12, 1827; d. Dresden, Oct. 30, 1885. He studied organ with J. Schneider and theory with J. Otto. He was organist in several churches in Dresden; wrote many organ works: 9 sonatas (for 4 hands, with double pedal); 5 fantasias; 30 pedal studies; an organ method; also motets and songs.

Merklin, Joseph, German organ builder; b. Oberhausen, Baden, Jan. 17, 1819; d. Nancy, France, June 10, 1905. He worked in his father's workshop in Freiburg; in 1843 went to Brussels; in 1853 took his brother-in-law, **F. Schütze**, into partnership, changing the name of his firm to "Merklin, Schütze & Cie." In 1855 he bought out the Ducroquet firm in Paris; in 1858 he reorganized his partnership as Société anonyme pour la fabrication des orgues, établissement Merklin-Schütze. The firm supplied organs to several cathedrals in Europe. Merklin publ. an interesting technical paper, *Notice sur l'électricité appliquée aux grandes orgues* (Paris, 1887), containing some surprising insights on possible manufacture of electric organs. His nephew **Albert Merklin** (1892-1925) went to Madrid at the outbreak of World War I in 1914 and established a Spanish branch of the firm. Merklin's Paris factory was acquired by Guttschenritter in 1899, and his branch in Lyon was bought in 1906 by the Swiss organ builder Theodor Kuhn; it was incorporated in 1926 as Société Anonyme des Anciens Établissements Michel, Merklin & Kuhn. After several further changes of ownership, the firm was taken over in 1967 by Fredrich Jakob in Zürich.

Merli, Francesco, Italian tenor; b. Milan, Jan. 27, 1887; d. there, Dec. 11, 1976. He studied with Borghi; had a successful career singing in the provincial opera house in Italy, culminating in his appearance at La Scala in Milan in 1922, in role of Walther in *Die Meistersinger*; he continued to be on its roster until 1946; he also made frequent guest appearances at the Teatro Colón in Buenos Aires; between 1926 and 1930 he sang at the Covent Garden in London. He retired from the stage in 1950 and was active mainly as a voice teacher.

Merö, Yolanda, Hungarian-American pianist; b. Budapest, Aug. 30, 1887; d. New York, Oct. 17, 1963. She studied piano with her father; made her American debut with the Russian Symph. Orch. in New York on Nov. 3, 1909; married Hermon Irion of Steinway & Sons, and remained in the U.S.

Merola, Gaetano, conductor and impresario; b. Naples, Jan. 4, 1881; d. San Francisco, Aug. 30, 1953. He studied at the Naples Cons.; came to the U.S. in 1899, and was appointed assistant conductor at the Metropolitan Opera House; also conducted with the Henry Savage English Opera, N.Y. (1903), the Manhattan Opera Co., N.Y. (1906), etc.; in 1923 became general director of the San Francisco and Los Angeles Operas. He collapsed and died while conducting a concert at the Sigmund Stern Grove in San Francisco.

Merrick, Frank, English pianist and composer; b. Clifton, Bristol, April 30, 1886. After studying at home he took lessons with Leschetizky in Vienna. Returning home to England he taught at the Royal College of Music in Manchester (1911-29); then taught piano at the Royal College of Music at the Trinity College of Music in London. He composed a symphony and 2 piano concertos; also some character pieces for small instrumental combinations, such as *Celtic Suite* and *Dream-Pageant* and a number of songs to texts in Esperanto.

Merrill, Robert, American baritone; b. Brooklyn, June 4, 1917. He studied voice with his mother and began his career as a popular singer on the radio; on Dec. 15, 1945 he made his debut as Germont in *La Traviata* at the Metropolitan Opera, N.Y. and remained on its staff until 1964. Merrill publ. a couple of autobiographical books, *Once More from the Beginning* (N.Y., 1965) and *Between Acts* (N.Y., 1977).

Merriman, Nan (Katherine-Ann), American mezzo-soprano; b. Pittsburgh, April 28, 1920. She studied with Alexia Bassian in Hollywood; made her debut as soloist with the NBC Symph. Orch. under Toscanini on July 25, 1943; appeared subsequently with numerous other orchestras in Europe and America, in Beethoven's *Missa Solemnis*, Mahler's *Lied von der Erde*, etc. She excels in songs by Mahler, Debussy, Ravel and Manuel de Falla.

Merritt, Arthur Tillman, American musicologist and pedagogue; b. Calhoun, Mo., Feb. 15, 1902. He received the A.B. degree at the Univ. of Missouri (1924) and A.M. from Harvard Univ. (1927). He then went to Europe, on the J. K. Paine traveling scholarship from Harvard, and studied in Paris with Nadia Boulanger and Paul Dukas. He taught at Trinity College, Hartford, Conn. (1930-32); in 1932 was appointed to the staff of the music dept. of Harvard; prof., 1946. From 1932 to 1972 he taught at Harvard Univ.; on his retirement he was honored by a Festschrift, *Words and Music, the Scholar's View* (Cambridge, Mass., 1972). He is the author of a valuable treatise, *16th Century Polyphony: a Basis for the Study of Counterpoint* (Cambridge, Mass., 1939).

Merseburger, Carl Wilhelm, founder of the music-publishing firm in Leipzig bearing his name; b. 1816; d. 1885. In 1849 he purchased the publishing business of Carl Fredrich Meusel; specializing in school music, he brought out a great number of useful manuals and song books; also was the publisher of *Euterpe*, a periodical on education. His successor was his brother **Otto Merseburger** (1882–1898); the latter was succeeded by his son, **Max Merseburger** (1852-1935). The entire stock was destroyed during the air raids on Leipzig in 1945; after the end of the war, the business was resumed, with headquarters in Darmstadt, and a branch in Berlin. A centennial Festschrift was publ. in Leipzig, 1949, by the grandson of the founder.

Mersenne, Marin, important French theorist; b. La Soultière (Maine), Sept. 8, 1588; d. Paris, Sept. 1, 1648. He was a member of the Franciscan Order (from 1613); between 1640 and 1645 made 3 trips to Italy; maintained a correspondence with the leading philosophers and scientists of his time. His writings provide source material of fundamental importance for the history of 17th-century music.

WRITINGS: *Traité de l'harmonie universelle* (1627), later expanded to *Harmonie universelle* (1636-37; 2 large folio vols. with illustrations and musical examples; includes a *Traité des instruments*, depicting and describing all instruments of the 17th century; his most important work); *Quaestiones celeberrimae in Genesim* (1623; chiefly on Hebrew music); *Questions harmoniques* (1634); *Les Préludes de l'harmonie universelle* (1634); *Harmonicorum libri XII* (1635; enlarged ed., 1648); etc.

BIBLIOGRAPHY: C. Adam, *Le Père Mersenne et ses correspondants en France* (Paris, 1897); A. Pirro, "Les Correspondants du Père Mersenne," *Bulletin de la Société Internationale de Musique* (1909); P. Tannery, *Correspondance du Père Marin Mersenne* (Paris, 1933); H. Ludwig, *Marin Mersenne und seine Musiklehre* (Halle, 1934); R. Lenoble, *Mersenne ou la naissance du mécanisme* (Paris, 1943). The 7 books of the *Traité des instruments* were translated into English for the first time by Roger E. Chapman and publ. under the title, *Harmonie Universelle: The Books on Instruments* (The Hague, 1957); *Marin Mersenne: Correspondance*, ed. by C. de Waard (Paris, 1959).

Mersmann, Hans, German musicologist; b. Potsdam, Oct. 6, 1891; d. Cologne, June 24, 1971. He studied in Munich with Sandberger and in Leipzig and Berlin with Kretzschmar; Dr. phil. with the dissertation *Beiträge zur Ansbacher Musikgeschichte* (1916). He subsequently occupied various teaching positions: at the Stern Cons. in Berlin, and the Technische Hochschule there, until 1933; was in charge of folksong archives of the Prussian Volksliederkommission (1917-33); also organized numerous seminars on musicology and modern music; edited the periodical *Melos*; wrote music critcism. In 1947 he was appointed director of the Hochschule für Musik in Cologne. As a historian and analyst of modern music, Mersmann occupies an important position in contemporary research.

WRITINGS: Apart from numerous papers in German periodicals, he publ. *Angewandte Musikästhetik* (collected papers on esthetics; Berlin, 1926); *Kulturgeschichte der Musik in Einzeldarstellungen* (Berlin, 1923-25; 4 vols.: *Das deutsche Volkskied; Beethoven; Musik der Gegenwart; Mozart*); *Die moderne Musik seit der Romantik*, in Bücken's *Handbuch der Musikwissenschaft* (1928); "Die Tonsprache der neuen Musik," in *Melosbücherei* (ed. by Mersmann, 1928; 2nd ed., 1930); *Das Musikseminar* (Leipzig, 1931); *Kammermusik* (Leipzig, 1930-34; in 4 vols.: *Die Kammermusik des 17. und 18. Jahrhunderts; Beethoven; Deutsche Romantik; Europäische Kammermusik des 19. und 20. Jahrhunderts*); *Eine deutsche Musikgeschichte* (Potsdam, 1934; enlarged to include music history of other Western nations, publ. as *Musikgeschichte in der abendländischen Kultur*, 1955); *Volkslied und Gegenwart* (Potsdam, 1936); *Musikhören* (Berlin, 1938; enlarged ed., 1952); *Neue Musik in den Strömungen unserer Zeit* (1949); *Die Kirchenmusik im XX. Jahrhundert* (Nuremberg, 1958); *Stilprobleme der Werkanalyse* (Mainz, 1963); *Die moderne Oper und die Neue Musik unserer Zeit* (1967).

BIBLIOGRAPHY: W. Wiora, ed., *Musikerkenntnis und Musikziehung. Dankesgaben für H. Mersmann zu seinem 65. Geburtstag* (1957).

Mertens, Joseph, Belgian composer; b. Antwerp, Feb. 17, 1834; d. Brussels, June 30, 1901. He was the 1st violinist at the Opéra in Brussels; violin teacher at the Cons.; conductor of the Flemish Opera there (1878-89); then inspector of the Belgian music schools, and finally director of the Royal Theater at The Hague. He composed a number of Flemish and French operettas and operas which had local success: *De zwaarte Kapitein* (The Hague, 1877); *De Vrijer in de strop* (1866); *La Méprise* (1869); *L'Egoïsa* (1873); *Thécla* (1874); *Liederik l'intendent* (1875); *Les Trios Étudiants; Le Vin, le jeu et le tabac; Le Capitaine Robert; Les Evincés;* etc.

Mertke, Eduard, pianist and composer; b. Riga, June 17, 1833; d. Cologne, Sept. 25, 1895. He studied with S. von Lützau (piano) and Agthe (theory); appeared in public as a child pianist; toured Russia and Germany; in 1869, was appointed to the faculty of the Cologne Cons., where he continued to teach until his death. He wrote 3 operas: *Lisa, oder die Sprache des Herzens* (Mannheim, Feb. 24, 1872), *Resi vom Hemsensteig,* and *Kyrill von Thessalonica;* many piano pieces; technical exercises for piano; publ. a collection, *Melodies of the Ukraine.*

Mertz, Joseph Kasper, Hungarian guitar virtuoso; b. Pressburg, August 17, 1806; d. Vienna, Oct. 14, 1856. He supported himself as a youth by playing in popular theater bands; made successful tours in Bohemia and Poland; in 1842 he married the pianist **Josephine Plantin,** with whom he gave concerts in Germany before settling in Vienna.

Merula, Tarquinio, Italian composer; b. Cremona, c.1600; date of death unknown. He was maestro di cappella at the Church of Santa Maria in Bergamo (1623); organist at the court of Sigismund III of Poland (1624); organist at Sant' Agata in Cremona and maestro di cappella of the Cathedral in Cremona (1628); again at Santa Maria in Bergamo (1639); maestro di cappella and organist of the Cathedral there (1640); then at Cremona as maestro di cappella of the Cathedral (1652).

WORKS: *Canzoni a 4 per stromenti, lib. 1* (Venice, 1615); *Madrigali et altre musiche concertate a 1-5* (Venice, 1623); *Madrigaletti a 3, lib. 1, op. 4* (Venice, 1624); *Madrigali a 4-8 voci, lib. 1, op. 5* (Venice, 1624); *Satiro e Corsica, dialogo* (Venice, 1626); *Concerti spirituali a 2-5 voci, lib. 2* (Venice, 1628); *Canzoni, overe Sonate concertate per chiesa, lib. 2, op. 12* (Venice, 1637); *Curtio precipiato et altri capricii lib. 2, op. 13* (Venice, 1638); *Canzoni da suonare a tre, op. 9* (Venice, 1639); *Concerto decimo quinto Messi, salmi concertati, a 2-12* (Venice, 1639); *Arpa Davidica, Pegaso, salmi, motetti, a 2-5, lib. 3, op. 11* (Venice, 1640); *Arpa Davidica, salmi et messa, op. 16* (Venice, 1640); *Canzoni da suonare a 2-3, lib. 4, op. 17* (Venice, 1651); *Salmi et messa concertati a 3-4, lib. 3, op. 18* (Venice, 1652); etc. A *Sonata cromatica* for organ was publ. by L. Torchi in *L'Arte Musicale in Italia* (vols. 4); examples of Merula's violin music are in Riemann's *Alte Kammermusik.*

BIBLIOGRAPHY: article by M. Seiffert in *Vierteljahrsschrift für Musikwissenschaft* (VII, 410).

Merulo (real name **Merlotti**), **Claudio,** Italian organist and composer; called da Correggio; b. Correggio, April 8, 1533; d. Parma, May 4, 1604. He was a pupil of Menon and G. Donati; organist at Brescia in 1556; on July 2, 1557, chosen 2nd organist at San Marco, Venice; in 1566, succeeded Padovano as 1st organist, and held this position until 1584, when he went to Mantua, and then to Parma, where he became court organist (1586). He was reputed to be one of the greatest organists of his time; as composer, he was an important representative of the Venetian School; his works opened a new era of independent composition for the organ. He also produced a drama in madrigal style, *La Tragedia* (Venice, July 21, 1574); was renowned as a teacher; Conforti was of his pupils. Most of Merulo's works were publ. posthumously; they include: *Canzoni d'intavolatura d'organo* (1592), *Toccate d'intavolatura d'organo* (1604; 2 books), and *Ricercari d'intavolatura d'organo* (1605); 4 vols. of madrigals for 3, 4, and 5 voices (1566-1604); 2 vols. of motets for 5 voices (1578), *Ricercari da cantare* for 4 voices (1607; 1608); *Canzoni alla francese* (1620). Reprints of his organ works have been publ. by C. G. Winterfeld in *Johann Gabrieli und sein Zeitalter* (1 piece), A. Catelani in *Claudio Merculo* (2 pieces), K. F. Weitzmann in *Geschichte des Klavierspiels* (1 piece), A. Reissmann in *Allgemeine Geschichte der Musik* (1 piece), A. G. Ritter in *Zur Geschichte des Orgelspiels im 14.-18. Jahr-*

hundert (1 piece), Torchi in *L'Arte Musicale in Italia* IV (4 pieces), Riemann, in *Musikgeschichte in Beispielen* (1 piece), A. Einstein in the musical supplement to his *Geschichte der Musik* (1 piece), J. Wolf in *Sing- und Spielmusik aus älterer Zeit* (La Leonora), A. Schering in *Geschichte der Musik in Beispielen* (no. 149), A. T. Davison & W. Apel in *Historical Anthology of Music* (no. 153), etc.

BIBLIOGRAPHY: A. Catelani, *Memorie della vita e delle opere di Claudio Merulo* (Milan, 1859; reprinted in the *Bollettino bibliografico Musicale*, Milan, 1930-31); Q. Bigi, *Di Claudio Merulo* (Parma, 1861); *Claudio Merulo da Correggio* (Parma, 1905; essays by 8 Italian scholars); A. Einstein, "Claudio Merulos Ausgabe der Madrigale des Verdelot," *Sammelbände der Internationalen Musik-Gesellschaft* VIII/2 (1907); O. Kinkeldey, *Orgel und Klavier in der Musik des 16. Jahrhunderts* (1910); G. Reese, *Music in the Renaissance* (N.Y., 1954).

Merz, Karl, German-American musician; b. Bensheim, near Frankfurt, Sept. 19, 1836; d. Wooster, Ohio, Jan. 30, 1890. He was a pupil of his father and F. J. Kunkel; went to the U.S. in 1854, and lived in Philadelphia as a teacher. He was a contributor to various periodicals; his collected essays, *Music and Culture*, edited by his son, Dr. Charles H. Merz, were publ. in Philadelphia (1890).

Messager, André (-Charles-Prosper), celebrated French composer and conductor; b. Montluçon, Allier, Dec. 30, 1853; d. Paris, Feb. 24, 1929. He studied at the École Niedermeyer in Paris with Gigout (composition), A. Laussel (piano), and C. Loret (organ); then took lessons with Saint-Saëns. In 1874 he became organist at St.-Sulpice; subsequently was choir director at Sainte-Marie des Batignoles (1882-84). He began his career as conductor at the Opéra-Comique (1898-1908); also directed the opera at Covent Garden, London (1901-17). From 1907 till 1915 he was the regular conductor of the Paris Opéra; was in charge of the Société des Concerts du Conservatoire from 1908 until his death; under the auspices of the French government he visited the U.S. with that orchestra, giving concerts in 50 American cities (1918). Returning to Paris, he again conducted at the Opéra-Comique; led a season of Diaghilev's Ballets Russes in 1924. As conductor, he played an important role in Paris concert life; he directed the première of *Pelléas et Mélisande* (1902, with 21 rehearsals), the score of which Debussy dedicated to him. His initial steps as a composer were auspicious; his symph. (1875) was awarded the gold medal of the Société des Compositeurs and performed at the Concerts Colonne (Jan. 20, 1878); his dramatic scene, *Don Juan et Haydée* (1876), was awarded a gold medal by the Academy of St. Quentin. He wrote several other works for orch. (*Impressions orientals, Suite funambulesque,* etc.) and some chamber music, but he was primarily a man of the theater. His style may be described as enlightened eclecticism; his music is characteristically French, and more specifically, Parisian, in its elegance and gaiety. He was honored in France; in 1926 he was elected to the Académie des Beaux Arts. He was married to **Hope Temple** (real name **Dotie Davis,** 1858-1938), who was the author of

numerous songs. His operas (first performed in Paris except where otherwise indicated) include *François les-bas-bleus* (Jan. 20, 1878; score begun by F. Bernicat and completed after his death by Messager); *La Fauvette du Temple* (Nov. 17, 1885); *La Béarnaise* (Dec. 12, 1885); *Le Bourgeois de Calais* (April 6, 1887); fairy tale, *Isoline* (Dec. 26, 1888; ballet suite from it is popular); *La Basoche* (May 30, 1890; greatly acclaimed); *Madame Chrysanthème* (after Loti; Jan. 30, 1893; to a story similar to Puccini's *Madame Butterfly* produced 11 years later; but Puccini's dramatic treatment eclipsed Messager's lyric setting); *Le Chevalier d'Harmental* (May 5, 1896); *Véronique* (Dec. 10, 1898; successful); *Les Dragons de l'Impératrice* (Feb. 13, 1905); *Fortunio* (June 5, 1907); *Béatrice* (Monte Carlo, March 21, 1914); *Monsieur Beaucaire* (Birmingham, April 7, 1919). Among his successful operettas were *Le Mari de la Reine* (1889); *Miss Dollar* (1893); *La Fiancée en Loterie* (1896); *Les P'tites Michu* (Paris, Nov. 16, 1897; many subsequent performances); *La Petite fonctionnaire,* dance-hall operetta (Paris, May 14, 1921); *Passionnément* (Paris, Jan. 15, 1926). His ballets include *Fleur d'Oranger* (1878); *Les Vins de France* (1879); *Mignons et Vilains* (1879); *Les Deux Pigeons* (1886); *Scaramouche* (1891); *Amants éternels* (1893); *Le Chevalier aux Fleurs,* in collaboration with Pugno (1897); *Le Procès des Roses* (1897); *Une Aventure de la Guimard* (1900). He also wrote incidental music to Delair's *Hélène* (1891) and Moreau's and Carré's *La Montagne enchantée,* in collaboration with Leroux (1897). An autobiographical sketch and articles on Messager are found in *Musica* (Paris, Sept. 1908); see also O. Séré, *Musiciens français d'aujourd'hui* (1911; revised ed., 1921); H. Février, *André Messager; mon maître, mon ami* (Paris, 1948); M. Augé-Laribé, *André Messager, musicien de théâtre* (Paris, 1951).

Messchaert, Johannes Martinus, Dutch baritone; b. Hoorn, Aug. 22, 1857; d. Zürich, Sept. 9, 1922. He studied violin, then changed to singing; was a pupil of Stockhausen in Frankfurt and Wüllner in Munich; began his career as choral conductor in Amsterdam; then appeared as singer of the German repertory; lived for many years in Berlin; in 1920 went to teach at the Cons. of Zürich.

BIBLIOGRAPHY: F. Martienssen, *Johannes Messchaert. Ein Beitrag zum Verständnis echter Gesangskunst* (Berlin, 1914; 2nd ed., 1920); F. Martienssen, *Johannes Messchaert, Eine Gesangsstunde;* F. Martienssen also edited 2 vols. of Schubert's songs with Messchaert's dynamic marks (Mainz, 1928). A collection of reminiscences about Messchaert was edited by M. C. Canneman in 1968.

Messiaen, Olivier, outstanding French composer; b. Avignon, Dec. 10, 1908. A scion of an intellectual family (his father was a translator of English literature; his mother, Cécile Sauvage, a poet), he absorbed the atmosphere of culture and art as a child. A mystical quality was imparted by his mother's book of verses *L'Âme en bourgeon* (Burgeoning Soul), dedicated to her as yet unborn child. He learned to play piano; at the age of 8 composed a song *La Dame de Shalott* to a poem by Tennyson. At the age of 11 he entered the

Paris Cons., where he attended the classes of Jean and Noël Gallon, Marcel Dupré, Maurice Emmanuel and Paul Dukas, specializing in organ, improvisation and composition; he carried first prizes in all these departments. After graduation in 1930 he became organist at the Trinity Church in Paris. In 1936, he organized, with André Jolivet, Ives Baudrier and Daniel-Lesur, a group "La jeune France" with the aim of promoting modern French music. He was in the French Army at the outbreak of World War II in 1939; was taken prisoner; spent 2 years in a German prison camp in Görlitz, Silesia; he composed there his *Quatuor pour la fin du temps;* was repatriated in 1942 and resumed his post as organist at the Trinity Church in Paris; was also appointed to the faculty of the Paris Cons. where he taught harmony and musical analysis. After the end of the war he gave courses at the Berkshire Music Center in Tanglewood (1948) and at Darmstadt (1950–53). Young composers seeking instruction in new music became his eager pupils; among them were Pierre Boulez, Jean-Louis Martinet, Stockhausen, Xenakis and others, who were to become important composers in their own right. He received numerous honors; was created Grand Officier de la Légion d'honneur; was elected a member of the Institut de France, of the Bavarian Academy of the Fine Arts, of the Accademia nazionale di Santa Cecilia in Rome, of the American Academy of Arts and Letters and other organizations. He is married to the pianist **Yvonne Loriod.** Messiaen is one of the most original of modern composers; in his music he makes use of a wide range of resources, from Gregorian chant to Oriental rhythms. A mystic by nature and Catholic by religion, he strives to find a relationship between progressions of musical sounds and religious concepts; in his theoretical writing he strives to postulate an interdependence of modes, rhythms and harmonic structures. In quest of new musical resources he employs in his scores the "Ondes Martenot" and exotic percussion instruments; a synthesis of these disparate tonal elements finds its culmination in his grandiose orchestral work, *Turangalîla-Symphonie.* One of the most fascinating aspects of Messiaen's innovative musical vocabulary is the phonetic emulation of birdsong in several of his works; in order to attain ornithological fidelity he made a detailed study notating the rhythms and pitches of singing birds in many regions of several countries.

WORKS: FOR ORCH.: *Le Banquet eucharistique* (1928); *Simple chant d'une âme* (1930); *Les Offrandes oubliées* Paris, Feb. 19, 1931); *Le Tombeau resplendissant* (Paris, Feb. 12, 1933); *Hymne au Saint Sacrement* (Paris, March 23, 1933); *L'Ascension* (1934); *Trois Petites Liturgies de la Présence Divine* for voices and orch. (Paris, April 21, 1945); *Hymne* (N.Y., March 13, 1947); *Trois Talas* for piano and orch. (Paris, Feb. 15, 1948); *Turangalîla-Symphonie* (Boston, Dec. 2, 1949, Leonard Bernstein conducting); *Réveil des Oiseaux,* for piano and orch. (Donaueschingen, Oct. 11, 1953); *Chronochromie* (Donaueschingen, Oct. 16, 1960); *La Transfiguration de notre Seigneur Jésus Christ,* in 13 movements for voices and orch. (Lisbon, June 7, 1969); *Des Canyons aux Etoiles* (N.Y., Nov. 20, 1974); CHAMBER MUSIC: *Mort du nombre,* for soprano, tenor, violin, and piano (Paris, March 25, 1931);

Quatuor pour la fin du temps, for violin, clarinet, cello and piano (performed in a prison camp at Görlitz, in Silesia, with composer at the piano, Jan. 15, 1941); *Le Merle noir,* for flute and piano (1952); *Oiseaux exotiques* for piano, 2 clarinets, xylophone, glokenspiel, percussion and wind ensemble (1955); *7 Haï-kaï,* for piano, xylophone, marimba and instruments (1963); *Couleurs de la cité céleste* for piano, winds, and percussion (1964); *Et expecto resurrectionem mortuorum* for woodwinds, brass, metal percussion (1964); VOCAL WORKS: Mass for 8 sopranos and 4 violins (1933); *O sacrum convivium* (1937); *Chœurs pour une Jeanne d'Arc,* for chorus a cappella (1941); *Harawi,* "chant d'amour et de mort" for dramatic soprano and piano (1945); *5 Rechants* for 12-voice chorus (1949); FOR PIANO: *La Vision de l'Amen,* for 2 pianos (1942); *20 Regards sur l'enfant Jésus* (1944); *4 Etudes de rythme* (1949); *Catalogue d'oiseaux* (1956); numerous organ pieces: *La Nativité du Seigneur* (1935); *Le Corps glorieux* (1939); *Messe de la Pentecôte* (1950); *Livre d'orgue* (1951); *Verset pour la fête de la dédicace* (1960); *Méditations sur le mystère de la Sainte Trinité* (1969); several works for Ondes Martenot and musique concrète. The theoretical works include *20 Leçons de solfèges modernes* (Paris, 1933); *20 Leçons d'harmonie* (Paris, 1939); *Technique de mon language musical* (2 vols., Paris, 1944; English translation under the title, *The Technique of My Musical Language,* in 2 vols., 1957); individual articles on musical ornithology and other subjects.

BIBLIOGRAPHY: B. Gavoty, *Musique et mystique: le "cas" Messiaen* (Paris, 1945); Virginie Zinke-Bianchini, *Olivier Messiaen. Notice biographique; catalogue détaillé de œuvres éditées* (Paris, 1946); Claude Rostand, *Olivier Messiaen* (Paris, 1958; contains a list of works and a discography); A. Goléa, *Recontres avec Olivier Messiaen* (Paris, 1961); Claude Samuel, *Entretiens avec Olivier Messiaen* (Paris, 1967); Stuart Waumsley, *The Organ Music of Olivier Messiaen* (Paris, 1969; revised ed., 1975); Robert Sherlaw Johnson, *Messiaen* (Berkeley, Calif., 1975); Roger Nicols, *Messiaen* (London, 1975).

Messiter, Arthur Henry, organist; b. Frome, Somersetshire, England, April 12, 1834; d. New York, July 2, 1916. He was for 31 years (1866–97) organist and choirmaster at Trinity Church, N.Y.; publ. *A History of the Choir and Music of Trinity Church* (1906).

Messner, Joseph, Austrian organist; b. Schwaz (Tyrol), Feb. 27, 1893; d. St. Jakob Thurn, near Salzburg, Feb. 23, 1969. He studied in Innsbruck; then went to Munich where he took courses in organ playing and composition with Fr. Klose; in 1922 he was appointed cathedral organist in Salzburg; from 1926 to 1967 he led the concerts at the Salzburg Cathedral. At the same time he gave a seminar in church music at the Mozarteum there. He wrote 4 operas: *Hadassa* (Aachen, March 27, 1925), *Das letzte Recht* (1932), *Ines* (1933), *Agnes Bernauer* (1935); 3 symphonies; Violin Concerto; Cello Concerto; String Quartet; several sacred works, including 11 Masses. He ed. a collection of old Salzburg masters (Bernardi, Caldara, M. Haydn, Leopold Mozart, W. A. Mozart); also transcribed Bruckner's Mass in C and the Choral Mass.

Mester, Jorge, American conductor; b. Mexico City, April 10, 1935, of Hungarian parents. He attended an American school in Mexico City and later a military academy in Hollywood. In 1952 he enrolled at the Juilliard School of Music as a student in conducting with Jean Morel, graduating in 1958. He also attended conducting classes with Leonard Bernstein in Tanglewood; at 22 was appointed to the Juilliard faculty. In 1959–60 he was music director of the St. Louis Philharmonic Orch.; in 1961–62 was musical director of the Greenwich Village Symph. Orch. in N.Y. In 1965 he became musical director for the parodisitic P. D. Q. Bach Series at Lincoln Center; in 1965–66 conducted orchestras in Japan, Germany, Switzerland and Italy. In 1967 he was engaged as musical director and conductor of the Louisville Symph. Orch.; in 1967–71 appeared as guest conductor with the Los Angeles Philharmonic, Pittsburgh Symph. Orch., New Orleans Philharmonic, Philadelphia Orch., Cincinnati Symph. Orch. and the Boston Symph. Orch.; also conducted opera and ballet at the Spoleto summer festivals. In 1969 he was appointed music director of the Aspen Music Festival. He is the recipient of the Naumburg award for excellence, competence and elegance in his performances (1968). Equally at home in the classical and modern repertory, in symphonic music and in opera, Mester's interpretations are marked by a rhapsodic sense of color combined with a precision of technical detail.

Mestres-Quadreny, Josep Maria, Spanish composer; b. Manresa, March 4, 1929. He studied composition with Cristòfor Taltabull at the Univ. of Barcelona (1950–56); in 1960 he collaborated in the founding of "Música abierta," an organization of avant-garde musical activity; later he joined composers Xavier Benguerel, Joaquim Homs and Josep Soler in founding the "Conjunt Català de Música Contemporània," for the propagation of Catalan music. In 1968 he went to work in an electronic music studio. In his music he consciously attempts to find a counterpart to abstract expressionism in art, as exemplified by the paintings of Miró; for this purpose he applies serial techniques and aleatory procedures.
WORKS: Piano Sonata (1957); *Epitafios,* cantata for soprano, strings, harp and celesta (1958); opera, *El Ganxo* (1959); *Triade per a Joan Miró,* composed of *Música da cámara I* for flute, piano, percussion, violin and double bass, *Música da cámara II* for 3 clarinets, English horn, trumpet, trombone, percussion and string trio, and *Tres Moviments per a orquesta de cámara* for 15 instruments, formed by superimposing the previous 2 works (all 1961); 3 *Invenció mòvils: I* for flute, clarinet and piano, *II* for voice, trumpet and electric guitar, and *III* for string quartet (all 1961); *Tramesa a Tàpies* for violin, viola and percussion (1961); 3 ballets: *Roba i ossos (Things and Bones,* 1961), *Petit diumenge (Little Sunday,* 1962) and *Vegetació submergida (Submerged Vegetation,* 1962); *Quartet de Catroc* for string quartet (1962); *Digodal* for string orch. (1963); *Concert per a representar,* musical theater for 6 voices, 6 instrumentalists and tape (1964); *3 Cànons en homenatge a Galile,* in 3 versions: for piano, for percussion, and for Ondes Martenot, each with tape (1965, 1968, 1969); *Conversa* for chamber orch. (1965); *Suite bufa,* musical theater for ballerina, mezzo-soprano, piano and electronic sound (1966); *Tríptic carnavalesc,* cantata for soprano, flute, clarinet, trumpet, trombone, 2 percussionists and piano (1966); *Música per a Anna* for soprano and string quartet (1967); String Trio (1968); *Ibemia* for 13 instrumentalists (1969); *Quadre* for chamber orch. (1969); *Micos i Papellones* for guitar and metal percussion (1970); *Double Concerto* for Ondes Martenot, percussion and orch. (1970); *Variacions essencials* for string trio and percussion (1970); *Homenatge a Joan Prats* for 6 actors, electroacoustical installation, string quartet, 4 percussionists, flute, clarinet, trumpet, 2 trombones and tuba (1972); *Frigoli-Frigola* and *Aronada* for any number or type of instruments (1969, 1972).

Metallov, Vassili, Russian musicologist; b. Saratov, March 13, 1862; d. Moscow, June 1, 1926. He studied theology and Russian church music; in 1901, appointed prof. of history of Russian church singing at the Moscow Cons. His works on Russian church music possess great authority; they include *Alphabet of the Neume Songs* (Moscow, 1899); *The Synodal Singers* (1898); *Outline of the History of the Orthodox Church Song in Russia* (1893); *The Strict Style* (1897); etc. Metallov twice received awards from the Russian Academy of Science.

Metastasio, Pietro Antonio Domenico Bonaventura, famous Italian poet and opera librettist; b. Rome, Jan. 3, 1698; d. Vienna, April 12, 1782. He was the son of a papal soldier named Trapassi, but in his professional career assumed the Greek translation of the name, both Trapassi (or Trapassamento) and Metastasio meaning transition. He was a learned classicist; began to write plays as a young boy; studied music with Porpora; he achieved great fame in Italy as a playwright; in 1730 was appointed by Emperor Charles VI court poet at Vienna. He wrote about 35 opera texts, which were set to music by Handel, Gluck, Mozart, Hasse, Porpora, Jommelli and many other celebrated composers; some of them were set to music 60 or more times. His librettos were remarkable for their melodious verse, which naturally suggested musical associations; the libretto to the opera by Niccolo Conforto, *La Nitteti* (1754; first performed in Madrid, Sept. 23, 1756), was on the same subject as *Aida,* anticipating the latter by more than a century. Metastasio's complete works were publ. in Paris (1780–82; 12 vols.), Mantua (1816–20; 20 vols.); ed. by F. Gazzani (Torino, 1968); ed. by M. Fubino (Milano, 1968); see also A. Wotquenne, *Verzeichnis der Stücke in Versen . . . von Zeno, Metastasio und Goldoni* (Leipzig, 1905).
BIBLIOGRAPHY: S. Mattei, *Memorie per servire alla vita del Metastasio* (Colle, 1785); C. Burney, *Life and Letters of Metastasio* (3 vols., 1796; repr. N.Y., 1973); M. Zito, *Studio su Pietro Metastasio* (Naples, 1904); E. M. Leonardi, *Il Melodramma del Metastasio* (Naples, 1909); L. Russo, *Metastasio* (1921); A. Gustarelli, *Metastasio* (1930); M. Apollonio, *Metastasio* (1931); A. Bonaventura, "Pietro Metastasio musicista," *Musica d'Oggi* (1932); A. Vullo, *Confronto fra i melodrammi di Zeno e Metastasio* (Agrigento, 1935);

A. Salazar, "Un Antecedente de Aida en España," *Nuestra Música* (Mexico, 1950); H. C. Wolff, "Das Märchen von der Neapolitanischen Oper und Metastasio,"*Amulecta Musicologica* 9 (1970).

Metcalf, Frank J., American hymnologist; b. Ashland, Mass., April 4, 1865; d. Washington, D.C., Feb. 25, 1945. He studied at Boston Univ. (B.A., 1886); was for 42 years a clerk in the War Department. He owned a private collection of more than 2000 hymn books, including Lyon's *Urania* (1761) and other rare editions; also a MS bibliography containing about 10,000 entries. He publ. *American Psalmondy* (N.Y, 1917); *American Writers and Compilers of Sacred Music* (N.Y., 1925); *Stories of Hymn Tunes* (N.Y., 1928); also numerous articles.

Methfessel, Albert Gottlieb, German composer; b. Stadtilm, Thuringia, Oct. 6, 1785; d. Heckenbeck, near Gandersheim, March 23, 1869. From 1832 until 1842 he was court composer at Brunswick, then retired on pension.
WORKS: the opera *Der Prinz von Basra;* oratorio, *Das befreite Jerusalem;* sonatas and sonatinas for piano; part-songs, publ. in his *Liederbuch, Liederkranz,* and other collections.
BIBLIOGRAPHY: W. H. Riehl, *Musikalische Charakterköpfe* vol. 3 (Stuttgart, 1879). His brother, **Friedrich Methfessel** (b. Stadtilm, Aug. 27, 1771; d. there, May 14, 1807), publ. songs with guitar accompaniment.

Metianu, Lucian, Rumanian composer; b. Cluj, June 3, 1937. He studid with Olah, Vancea, Paul Constantinescu and Chirescu at the Bucharest Cons. (1957–63).
WORKS: *Cantata de camera* for chorus and chamber orch. (1953); Concerto for String Orch. (1959); *2 Choreographic Tableaux* for orch. (1964); *Echo* for orch. (1966); *Ergodica* for orch. (1967); *Conexe* for speaking chorus and orch. (1969); *Elogiu* for orch. (1969); Piano Quintet (1960); 2 string quartets (1961, 1968); Piano Sonata (1962); *Pithagoreis* for tape (1970–71).

Metner, Nikolai. See **Medtner, Nikolai.**

Métra, (Jules-Louis-Olivier), French composer of light music; b. Reims, June 2, 1830; d. Paris, Oct. 22, 1889. An actor's son, he became an actor himself as a boy; was first taught music by Ed. Roche; then was a pupil at the Paris Cons. of Elwart (1849–54). He played violin, cello, and double bass at Paris theaters; then conducted at various dance halls; the masked balls at the Opéra-Comique (1871); the orch. at the Folies-Bergère (1872–77); the balls at the Théâtre de la Monnaie, Brussels (1874–76); finally the balls at the Paris Opéra. His waltzes, mazurkas, polkas, quadrilles, etc. were extremely popular; at the Folies-Bergère he produced 19 operettas and ballet divertissements; and at the Opéra the ballet *Yedda* (1879).

Métru, Nicolas, French organist and composer; b. Bar-sur-Aube, c.1600; d. Paris, c.1670. He was organist at St.-Nicholas-des-Champs in Paris; was Lully's teacher. Ballard publ. his *Fantaisies* in 2 parts for string instruments (1642), 2 books of airs (1646), and an *Air sur la paix et le mariage du roy* (1662).

Mettenleiter, Dominicus, German music historian, brother of **Johann Georg Mettenleiter;** b. Tannenhausen, Württemberg, May 20, 1822; d. Regenburg, May 2, 1868; Dr. theol. and phil. He wrote *Musikgeschichte der Stadt Regensburg* (1866), *Musikgeschichte der Oberpfalz* (1867); and contributed to his brother's *Enchiridion.* His fine music library was united with Proske's in the Bishop's Library at Regensburg.

Mettenleiter, Johann Georg, German church composer, brother of **Dominicus Mettenleiter;** b. St. Ulrich, near Ulm, April 6, 1812; d. Regensburg, Oct. 6, 1858, as choirmaster and organist at the cathedral. An erudite church composer, he publ. *Manuale breve cantionum ac precum* (1852) and an *Enchiridion chorale . . .* (1855), both with added organ accompaniments; also Psalm 95, for 6 male voices (1854); other works in MS (Masses; a *Stabat Mater; 2 Miserere; Ave Maria* for double chorus, etc.). His brother wrote his biography, *Johann Georg Mettenleiter, ein Künstlerbild* (1866).

Metzler, Valentin, music publisher and instrument dealer in London; b. Bingen, Germany; d. London, 1833. He settled in London about 1788 and opened a shop for the sale of musical instruments; after his death, his son **George Richard Metzler** (1797–1867) became the owner, and the name of the firm was G. Metzler & Co. In 1816 the firm began to publish music; in 1867 G. Metzler entered into partnership with Frank Chappell; the firm continued to carry on its business in London until 1930.

Meulemans, Arthur, Belgian composer; b. Aarschot, May 19, 1884; d. Brussels, June 29, 1966. He studied with Edgar Tinel in Mechelen; in 1916 founded the Limburg School for organ at Hasselt; then moved to Brussels; conducted the radio orch. there (1930–42); in 1954 was elected president of the Royal Flemish Academy of Fine Arts. He produced a prodigious amount of highly competent works in all genres.
WORKS: 3 operas: *Vikings* (1919), *Adriaen Brouwer* (1926) and *Egmont* (1944; Antwerp, 1960); 15 symphonies: No. 1 (1931); No. 2 (1933); No. 3, *Dennensymphonie* (1933); No. 4, for winds and percussion (1934); No. 5, *Danssymphonie,* with female chorus (1939); No. 6, *Zeesymphonie,* with contralto and mixed chorus (1940); No. 7, *Zwaneven* (1942); No. 8, *Herfstsymphonie,* with soli and chorus (1942); No. 9 (1943); No. 10, *Psalmen-Symphonie,* with 2 narrators, soli and chorus (1943); No. 11 (1946); No. 12 (1948); No. 13, *Rembrandt-Symphonie* (1950); No. 14 (1954); No. 15 (1960); 3 sinfoniettas (1952, 1959–60, 1960); 2 ballet suites: *Josaphatpark* (1933) and *De Vogels* (1947); 3 oratorios: *Sacrum mysterium* (1917), *De zeven weeën* (1920) and *De dochtor van Jairus* (1922); various symph. poems, suites and pieces that include: *Meinacht* (1912), *Plinius Fontein* (1913), *Karnaval-Suite* (1926), *Stadspark,* prelude and scherzo (1928), *Vlaamse Rapsodie* (1932), *Verworvenheden* (1939), *Adagio* for strings (1939), *4 Symphonic Sketches* (1940), *Fusillé à l'Aube* (1948), *De Witte,* with chorus

(1949), *Symphonic Triptych* (1951), *Meterologisch Instituut* (1951), *Tableaux* (1952), *Peter Breugel* (1952), *Hertog Jan van Brabant*, with baritone (1953), *Social Security*, a masquerade (1954), *Ionisatie*, choreographic movements (1956), *Relais* (1957), *Symphonic Dances* (1957), *Esquisses symphoniques* (1958), *Divertimento*, with chorus (1958), *Aforismen* (1961), *Middelheim* (1961), *Partita* (1961), *Cirkus* (1961), *Torenhof* (1963); 2 *Concertos for Orchestra* (1953, 1956); many works for soloist and orch.: 3 piano concertos (1941, 1956, 1960), 2–Piano Concerto (1959); 3 violin concertos (1942, 1946, 1950); Viola Concerto (1942); 2 cello concertos (1920, 1944); Flute Concerto (1942); Oboe Concerto (1942); *Sonata concertante* for clarinet and string orch. (1948); 4–Clarinet Concertino (1963); 4–Clarinet Suite (1964); 4–Saxophone Concerto Grosso (1958); 4–Saxophone Concertino (1962); 2 horn concertos (1940, 1961); Trumpet Concerto (1943); Trombone Concertino (1953); Timpani Concerto (1954); Harp Concerto (1953); Harpsichord Concerto (1958); 2 organ concertos (1942, 1958); Concerto Grosso, for 6 winds, strings, harp and percussion (1962). Chamber music: 5 string quartets (1915, 1932, 1933, 1944, 1952); 2 violin sonatas (1915, 1953); Viola Sonata (1953); Cello Sonata (1953); Trumpet Sonata (1959); Piano Trio (1941); String Trio (1941); 2 woodwind trios (1933, 1960); 2 brass trios (1933, 1960); Piano Quartet (1915); Woodwind Quartet (1962); Saxophone Quartet (1953); *Suite* for 4 trombones (1942); 3 wind quintets (1931, 1932, 1958); Concerto for organ, trumpet, horn and trombone (1962); many other works and solo pieces. For piano: 3 sonatas (1916, 1917, 1951); 3 sonatinas (1927, 1928, 1941); *Refleksen* (1923); *Préludes* (1951); *Atmosferiliën* (1962). For organ: Sonata (1915); 2 symphonies (1949); 7 *Pieces* (1959); *Pièce heroïque* (1959). He also wrote many pieces for carillon, a cappella choruses and songs.

Mey, Kurt Johannes, German musicologist; b. Dresden, June 24, 1864; d. there, Sept. 21, 1912. He studied with K. A. Fischer in Dresden and with Spitta at the Univ. of Berlin; after filling various positions as répétiteur in provincial opera houses, he returned to Dresden. He publ. *Der Meistergesang in Geschichte und Kunst* (1892; revised ed., 1901); *Die Musik als tönende Weltidee* (part I, *Die metaphysischen Urgesetze der Melodik*, 1901); etc.

Meybom, Marcus. See **Meibom.**

Meyer, Ernst Hermann, German musicologist and composer; b. Berlin, Dec. 8, 1905. He studied musicology at the Univ. of Berlin with Johannes Wolf, Curt Sachs, Friedrich Blume and Hornbostel; then took a course with Besseler at the Univ. of Heidelberg and took lessons in modern composition with Hanns Eisler and Hindemith. With the advent of the Nazi regime he went to England where he was associated with the Free German Cultural Society; in 1951 he returned to Germany; founded the periodical *Musik und Gesellschaft* in East Berlin. He is one of the most prominent theoreticians of Socialist Realism in music. Among his publications are *English Chamber Music* (1946; reprint, N.Y., 1971); *Beethoven's Works and Their Significance for the Contemporary Socialist Realistic Composition* (East Berlin, 1970); numerous articles on music from the orthodox Marxist standpoint.

WORKS: an opera, *Reiter der Nacht* (1969–72); Symphony (1967); *Poem* for viola and orch. (1962); Violin Concerto (1964); Concerto Grosso for 2 trumpets, trombones, timpani and percussion (1966); Harp Concerto (1969); Clarinet Quintet (1944); 3 string quartets (1956, 1959, 1967); numerous piano pieces and choral works.

Meyer, Leonard B., American musicologist and writer on esthetics; b. New York, Jan. 12, 1918. He studied philosophy and composition at Columbia Univ. (M.A. in music, 1948) and humanities at the Univ. of Chicago (Ph.D., 1954); also took private lessons in composition with Stefan Wolpe and Aaron Copland. In 1946 he was appointed to the staff of the Univ. of Chicago; in 1961, chairman of the Music Dept. He publ. an important book dealing with the problems of communication and cultural contexts in the human response to music, *Emotion and Meaning in Music* (Chicago, 1956) and *The Rhythmic Structure of Music* (with Grosvenor Cooper; Chicago, 1960); also contributed valuable articles to various scholarly journals.

Meyer, Leopold von (called **Leopold de Meyer**), celebrated piano virtuoso; b. Baden, near Vienna, Dec. 20, 1816; d. Dresden, March 5, 1883. He studied with Czerny and Fischhof; from the age of 19, embarked on a series of pianistic tours in Europe, and in America (1845–47). At his concerts, he invariably included his own compositions, written in a characteristic salon style; his agents spread sensational publicity about him in order to arouse interest. A *Biography of Leopold de Meyer* was publ. in London in 1845.

Meyer-Baer, Kathi, musicologist; b. Berlin, July 27, 1892; studied piano there with Frieda Kwast-Hodapp and G. Bertram; then musicology at the Univ. of Berlin with Kretzschmar, Riemann, and Johannes Wolf. In 1922 she became librarian of the Paul Hirsch Music Library in Frankfurt (transferred in 1936 to Cambridge, England); was music critic for the *Frankfurter Zeitung* (1923–33). In 1936 she went to Paris; in 1939 settled in N.Y., where she was active as librarian, teacher, and writer. She publ. *Der chorische Gesang der Frauen* (Leipzig, 1917), *Das Konzert* (Stuttgart, 1925), *Bedeutung und Wesen der Musik* (Strasbourg, 1932), and a great number of valuable publications, among them *Liturgical Music Incunabula. A Descriptive Catalogue* (London, 1962); *Music of the Spheres and the Dance of Death. Studies in Musical Iconology* (Princeton, 1970).

Meyer-Eppler, Werner, Dutch-German physicist and pioneer in electronic music; b. Antwerp, April 30, 1913; d. Bonn, July 8, 1960. He studied physics and mathematics in Cologne and Bonn. In 1949 he joined the faculty of the Bonn University, working on communication theory. He published a valuable treatise, *Musik, Raumgestaltung und Elektroakustik* (Mainz, 1955).

Meyer-Helmund, Erik, composer; b. St. Petersburg, April 25, 1861; d. Berlin, April 4, 1932. He studied music with his father; then in Berlin with Kiel; was first a singer, and traveled extensively in Europe, introducing his own songs; from 1911 he lived in Berlin. He is best known as a song composer; more than 200 of his light vocal numbers were published; also composed 5 operas: *Margitta* (Magdeburg, 1889), *Der Liebeskampf* (Dresden, 1892), *Taglioni* (Berlin, 1912), *Traumbilder* (Berlin, 1912), and *Die schöne Frau Marlies* (Altenburg, 1916); also the operettas *Trischka* (Riga, 1894) and *Lucullus* (Riga, 1905); the ballet *Rübezahl* (Leipzig, 1893); male choruses; and piano pieces in a Romantic vein (*Wonnetraum, Sérénade rococo,* etc.); a *Fantasie* for violin and orch.; etc.

Meyer-Olbersleben, Max, German pianist and composer; b. Olbersleben, near Weimar, April 5, 1850; d. Würzburg, Dec. 31, 1927. He first studied with his father; then with Liszt at Weimar. On Liszt's recommendation he received a liberal allowance from the Duke for further study; took lessons in Munich with Cornelius and Rheinberger. In 1876 he became teacher of piano and theory at Wüllner-Hartung's orchestra school in Weimar; in 1877, he was appointed to the staff of the Würzburg Cons., of which he became director in 1907; also conducted the famous "Liedertafel" from 1879. He was a composer of talent and ability; his chamber music is effectively and competently written; he also publ. songs and piano pieces. His "romantic opera" *Clare Dettin* was produced in Würzburg (1896); the comic opera *Der Haubenkrieg,* in Munich (1902).

Meyerbeer, Giacomo, famous dramatic composer; b. Berlin, Sept. 5, 1791; d. Paris, May 2, 1864. Of Jewish family, his real name was **Jakob Liebmann Beer;** He prefixed the name "Meyer" to his surname and "Giacomo" (Jacob Italianized) was later assumed as an artist name. He was a piano pupil of Lauska; also had a few piano lessons with Clementi, when the latter was a guest at Meyerbeer's house in Berlin. He began the study of theory under Zelter, but soon left this strict master for Anselm Weber, and from 1810–12 lived and studied with Abbé Vogler at Darmstadt, C. M. von Weber and Gänsbacher being his fellow pupils. There he wrote an oratorio, *Gott und die Natur* (Berlin, May 8, 1811), and 2 operas, *Jephthas Gelübde* (Munich, Dec. 23, 1812), and *Wirt und Gast, oder Aus Scherz Ernst* (Stuttgart, Jan. 6, 1813); the first two were failures, but *Wirt und Gast,* later known as *Alimelek,* was accepted for Vienna, and Meyerbeer followed his opera there. Already a brilliant pianist, Hummel's suave style so impressed him that he deferred his own debut at Vienna for several months, successfully working to acquire the same fluent ease and finish. His opera was rather coolly received in Vienna (and later in Prague and Dresden); still, despite pianistic triumphs, he felt dramatic composition to be his real vocation. Acting on Salieri's suggestion that Italian melody would prove a corrective for his heavy contrapuntal style, Meyerbeer went to Venice in 1815; the vogue of Rossini's operas indicated the path to popularity, and Meyerbeer entered it with a series of operas in the Italian vein—*Romilda e Costanza*

(Padua, July 19, 1817), *Semiramide riconosciuta* (Turin, Jan. 1819), *Emma di Resburgo* (Venice, June 26, 1819; in Germany as *Emma von Leicester*), *Margherita d'Angiù* (Milan, Nov. 14, 1820), *L'Esule di Granata* (Milan, March 12, 1822), and *Il Crociato in Egitto* (Venice, March 7, 1824), this last with immense success. While writing it, he had visited Berlin with the vain hope of bringing out a 3–act German opera, *Das Brandenburger Thor,* and embraced the opportunity to call on his old friend Weber, in Prague, whose strong remonstrances against Meyerbeer's Italian tranformation of himself seem to have borne fruit; for six years Meyerbeer produced no more operas. In 1826 he went to Paris to prepare the first representation of *Il Crociato.* After this, his father's death, his own marriage, and the death of two of his children, also serve to explain his silence. But at this time he was also (according to Mendel) immersed in the study of French opera, from Lully onward; the result being Meyerbeer's third style of operatic composition, in which "he united to the flowing melody of the Italians and solid harmony of the Germans the pathetic declamation and the varied, piquant rhythm of the French." Combining with these Meyerbeer's undeniable fecundity and originality of orchestral effect, and the theatrical ability and routine of his librettist, Scribe, it is no wonder that Meyerbeer's first French grand opera, *Robert le Diable* (Nov. 21, 1831), fairly electrified the Parisians, and caused the Opéra to prosper financially. *Les Huguenots* followed on Feb. 29, 1836, and was recognized by cultured critics as vastly superior to *Robert,* though the general public, enjoying the flamboyant unrealities of *Robert,* was disappointed at first. Two years later Meyerbeer began the composition of *L'Africaine,* which was destined to occupy him through life; irritated by the composer's continued demand for changes, Scribe after awhile testily withdrew the libretto, but was mollified by Meyerbeer's entering heart and soul into the composition of another of his texts, *Le Prophète,* finished in 1842–43. After the production of *Les Huguenots* at Berlin, 1842, Meyerbeer was called to that city by King Friedrich Wilhelm IV as General Musical Director. Here his opera, *Ein Feldlager in Schlesien* (Dec. 7, 1844), achieved only moderate success until Jenny Lind assumed the role of Vielka in 1847. He visited Vienna and London in 1847; on his return to Berlin, he brought out Wagner's *Rienzi.* In 1849, *Le Prophète* was at last produced at the Grand Opéra, Paris, on April 16; on Feb. 16, 1854, it was followed by *L'Étoile du Nord* at the Opéra-Comique (much of the music taken from *Ein Feldlager in Schlesien*), where *Dinorah, ou le Pardon de Ploërmel* was brought out in 1859. Last in the series was *L'Africaine* (Grand Opéra, April 28, 1865), just a year after his death; he had returned to Paris to take charge of the rehearsals in the spring of 1864. Other works: incidental music to *Struensee* (tragedy by Michael Beer, his brother; Berlin, Sept. 19, 1846), one of his finest works; choruses to Aeschylus' *Eumenides;* festival play *Das Hoffest von Ferrara;* monodrama *Thevelindens Liebe,* for soprano solo, chorus, and clarinet obbligato (Munich, Nov. 9, 1817); *Gutenberg* cantata; cantata *Maria und ihr Genius,* for the silver wedding of Prince and Princess Carl of Prussia; serenade *Brautgeleite aus der*

Heimat, for wedding of Princess Luise of Prussia; cantata *Der Genius der Musik am Grab Beethovens;* ode to Rauch (the sculptor), for soli, chorus, and orch.; 7 sacred odes by Klopstock, for 4 voice parts a cappella; *Festhymnus* for the King of Prussia's silver wedding, for 4 voices and chorus; *Freundschaft,* for 4-part men's chorus; Psalm 91, *a* 8; *Pater noster a* 4 with organ; in MS are 12 Psalms for double choir, a *Te Deum,* a *Stabat Mater,* and a *Miserere. Quarante mélodies à une et plusieurs voix* were published in Paris; other works are *Neben dir,* for tenor with cello obbligato; *Des Jägers Lied,* for bass with horns obbligato; *Des Schäfers Lied,* for tenor with clarinet obbligato; *A Venezia,* barcarolle; *Dichters Wahlspruch,* canon for 3 voices. Instrumental: 4 *Fackeltänze* for wind band (also scored for orch.); Grand March for the Schiller Centenary (1859); Overture in march form (for opening of London Exhibition, 1862); Coronation March for King Wilhelm I (1863); piano music in MS. Meyerbeer left by will 10,000 Thaler ($7,500) for the foundation of a Meyerbeer Scholarship; only Germans under 28, and pupils of the Berlin Hochschule, the Stern Cons. and the Cologne Cons., could compete.

BIBLIOGRAPHY: A. de Lasalle, *Meyerbeer, sa vie et le catalogue de ses œuvres* (Paris, 1864); A. Pougin, *Meyerbeer* (Paris, 1864); H. Blaze de Bury, *Meyerbeer, sa vie, ses œuvres et son temps* (1865); H. Mendel, *G. Meyerbeer* (Berlin, 1868); A. Kohut, *Meyerbeer* (Leipzig, 1890); J. Weber, *Meyerbeer, Notes et souvenirs d'un de ses secrétaires* (Paris, 1898); H. de Curzon, *Meyerbeer. Biographie critique* (Paris, 1910); H. Eymieu, *L'Œuvre de Meyerbeer* (Paris, 1910); L. Dauriac, *Meyerbeer* (Paris, 1913; 2nd ed., 1930); A. Hervey, *G. Meyerbeer* (London, 1913); H. Abert, "G. Meyerbeer," *Jahrbuch Peters* (1918); J. Kapp, *G. Meyerbeer* (Berlin, 1920; rev. ed., 1930); E. Istel, "Meyerbeer's Way to Mastery," *Musical Quarterly* (Jan. 1926); J. F. Cooke, *Meyerbeer* (Philadelphia, 1929); H. Becker, *Der Fall Heine-Meyerbeer. Neue Dokumente revidieren ein Geschichtsurteil* (Kassel, 1958); Heinz Becker, *Giacomo Meyerbeer Briefwechsel und Tagebücher,* in 3 vols., (Berlin, 1960, 1970, 1975).

Meyerowitz, Jan, German-American composer; b. Breslau, April 23, 1913. In 1927 he went to Berlin where he studied with Gmeindl and Zemlinsky at the Hochschule für Musik. Compelled to leave Germany in 1933, he went to Rome where he took lessons in advanced composition with Respighi, Casella and conducting with Molinari. In 1938 he moved to Belgium and later to southern France where he remained until 1946; he then emigrated to the U.S., becoming a naturalized citizen in 1951. He married the French singer **Marguerite Fricker** in 1946. He held a Guggenheim Fellowship twice (1956, 1958). In the U.S. he taught at the Berkshire Music Center in Tanglewood and at Brooklyn College; in 1962 was appointed to the faculty of the City College of N.Y. In 1977 he received a grant from the National Endowment for the Arts. His music is imbued with expansive emotionalism akin to that of Mahler; in his works for the theater there is a marked influence of the tradition of 19th-century grand opera. His technical idiom is modern, enlivened by a liberal infusion of euphonious disso-

nance, and he often applies the rigorous and vigorous devices of linear counterpoint.

WORKS: OPERAS: *The Barrier,* to a libretto by Langston Hughes (N.Y., Jan. 10, 1950); *Eastward in Eden* (title changed later to *Emily Dickinson;* Detroit, Nov. 16, 1951); *Simoon* (Tanglewood, Aug. 2, 1950); *Bad Boys in School* (Tanglewood, Aug. 17, 1953); *Esther,* libretto by Langston Hughes (Univ. of Illinois, Urbana, May 17. 1957); *Port Town,* libretto by Langston Hughes (Tanglewood, Aug. 4, 1960); *Godfather Death* (Brooklyn, June 2, 1961); *Die Doppelgängerin,* after Gerhart Hauptmann (title changed later to conform with the original title of Hauptmann's play, *Winterballade;* Hannover, Germany, Jan. 29, 1967). FOR ORCH.: *Silesian Symphony* (1957); *Symphony Midrash Esther* (N.Y. Philharmonic, Jan. 31, 1957); *Flemish Overture* (Cleveland, 1959); Flute Concerto (1962); Oboe Concerto (1963); *Sinfonia brevissima* (Corpus Christi, Texas, 1965); *6 Pieces for Orchestra* (Pittsburgh, May 27, 1967); *7 Pieces for Orchestra* (Turin, 1972). CANTATAS: *Music for Christmas* (N.Y., 1954); *The Glory Around His Head* (N.Y. Philharmonic, April 14, 1955); *Missa Rachel Plorans* (N.Y., Nov. 5, 1955); *The Rabbis* (text from the Talmud; Turin, 1965); several solo cantatas, among them *Emily Dickinson Cantata; 6 Songs* to poems by August von Platen for soprano and orch. (Cologne, Feb. 12, 1977). CHAMBER MUSIC: Woodwind Quintet (1954); String Quartet (1955); Cello Sonata (1946); Trio for flute, cello and piano (1946); Violin Sonata (1960); Flute Sonata (1961); Piano Sonata (1958); *Homage to Hieronymus Bosch* for 2 pianos 4-hands (1945); songs to German, French and English texts. Meyerowitz published a monograph on Schoenberg (Berlin, 1967); also a booklet, *Der echte jüdische Witz* (Berlin, 1971).

Meylan, Pierre, Swiss musicologist and editor; b. Lucens (Vaud), Oct. 22, 1908; d. Lausanne, May 7, 1974. He studied philology at the Universities of Lausanne, Halle and Leipzig, and piano in Lausanne. He publ. *Les Écrivains et la musique* (2 vols.; Lausanne, 1944, 1952); edited the collections *Richard Strauss: Anecdotes et Souvenirs* (Lausanne, 1951); *Les Plus Belles Lettres de Mozart* (Lausanne, 1956). He was the editor of *Revue Musicale de Suisse Romande.*

Meyrowitz, Selmar, German conductor; b. Bartenstein, East Prussia, April 18, 1875; d. Toulouse, March 24, 1941. He studied at the Cons. of Leipzig, and later with Max Bruch in Berlin; in 1897, became assistant conductor at the Karlsruhe Opera under Mottl, with whom he went to America as conductor at the Metropolitan Opera House (1903); subsequently conducted in Prague (1905–06), Berlin (1907–10), and Hamburg (1913–16), where he was also director of the Cons. In 1917 he returned to Berlin; was conductor at the State Opera (1924–27); toured with the German Grand Opera Co. in the U.S. (1929–31); after a brief sojourn in Germany, he went to France in 1933, and remained there until his death.

Mézeray, Louis-Charles-Lazare-Costard de, conductor and composer; b. Brunswick, Nov. 25, 1810; d. Asnières, near Paris, April 1887. As a young man he conducted theater orchestras in Strasbourg and elsewhere; at 17, obtained the post of conductor at the Liège Theater; at 20, became conductor at the Court Theater in The Hague, where he brought out his heroic opera *Guillaume de Nassau;* subsequently studied with Reicha in Paris; again traveled as theater conductor in France, and also appeared as baritone singer; finally, in 1843, he became chief conductor at the Grand Théâtre in Bordeaux, and brought the standard of performance there to a very high level, establishing a fine reputation for himself.

Miaskovsky, Nikolai, eminent Russian composer; b. Novogeorgievsk, near Warsaw, April 20, 1881; d. Moscow, Aug. 8, 1950. His father was an officer of the dept. of military fortification; the family lived in Orenburg (1888) and in Kazan (1889–93). In 1893 he was sent to a military school in Nizhny-Novgorod; in 1895 he went to a military school in St. Petersburg, graduating in 1899. At that time he developed an interest in music, and tried to compose; took lessons with the composer Kazanli; his first influences were Chopin and Tchaikovsky. In 1902–03 he was in Moscow, where he studied harmony with Glière. Returning to St. Petersburg in 1903, he took lessons with Kryzhanovsky, from whom he acquired a taste for modernistic composition in the Impressionist style. In 1906, at the age of 25, he entered the St. Petersburg Cons. as a pupil of Liadov and Rimsky-Korsakov, graduating in 1911. At the outbreak of World War I in 1914, Miaskovsky was called into active service in the Russian army; in 1916 he was removed to Reval to work on military fortification; he remained in the army after the Soviet Revolution of 1917; in 1918 he became a functionary in the Maritime Headquarters in Moscow; was finally demobilized in 1921. In that year he became prof. of composition at the Moscow Cons., remaining at that post to the end of his life. A composer of extraordinary ability, a master of his craft, Miaskovsky wrote 27 symphonies, much chamber music, piano pieces, and songs; his music is marked by structural strength and emotional élan; he never embraced extreme forms of modernism, but adopted workable devices of tonal expansion short of polytonality, and freely modulating melody short of atonality. His style was cosmopolitan; only in a few works did he inject folkloric elements.

WORKS: symphonies (all first performed in Moscow, unless otherwise indicated); No. 1, C minor (1908; Pavlovsk, June 2, 1914); No. 2, C-sharp minor (July 24, 1912); No. 3, A minor (Feb. 27, 1915); No. 4, E minor (Feb. 8, 1925); No. 5, D major (July 18, 1920); No. 6, E-flat minor (May 4, 1924); No. 7, B minor (Feb. 8, 1925); No. 8, A major (May 23, 1926); No. 9, E minor (April 29, 1928); No. 10, F minor (April 7, 1928); No. 11, B-flat minor (Jan. 16, 1933); No. 12, G minor (June 1, 1932); No. 13, B minor (world première, Winterthur, Switzerland, Oct. 16, 1934); No. 14, C major (Feb. 24, 1935); No. 15, D minor (Oct. 28, 1935); No. 16, F major (Oct. 24, 1936); No. 17, G-sharp minor (Dec. 17, 1937); No. 18, C major (Oct. 1, 1937); No. 19, E-flat (Feb. 15, 1939); No. 20, E major (Nov. 28, 1940); No. 21, F-sharp minor (Nov. 16, 1940; performed by the Chicago Orch. as a commissioned work, on Dec. 26, 1940, under the title *Symphonie Fantaisie*); No. 22, subtitled *Symphonie Ballade* (Tiflis, Jan. 12, 1942); No. 23, A minor,

Symphony-Suite (July 20, 1942); No. 24, F minor (Dec. 8, 1943); No. 25, D-flat (March 6, 1947); No. 26, C major (1948; on old Russian themes; Dec. 28, 1948); No. 27, C minor (performed posthumously, Dec. 9, 1950). Other orchestral works: *Silence,* symph. poem after Edgar Allan Poe (Moscow, June 13, 1911); *Alastor,* symph. poem after Shelley (Moscow, Nov. 18, 1914); Serenade for small orch. (Moscow, Oct. 7, 1929); *Lyric Concertino,* for small orch. (Moscow, Oct. 7, 1929); Sinfonietta, for string orch. (Moscow, May 1930); Violin Concerto (Leningrad, Nov. 14, 1938); *Salutatory Overture,* on Stalin's 60th birthday (Moscow, Dec. 21, 1939); Cello Concerto (Moscow, March 17, 1945). Also cantata, *Kirov is With Us* (1942); marches for military band; choruses; 13 string quartets; 2 cello sonatas; violin sonata; 9 piano sonatas; several sets of piano pieces; song cycles; etc. His collected works were issued in 12 vols. in Moscow in 1953–56.

BIBLIOGRAPHY: Miaskovsky's "Autobiographical Notes," *Sovietskaya Musica* (June 1936); L. Sabaneyev, *Modern Russian Composers* (N.Y., 1927); A. Ikonnikov, *Miaskovsky, His Life and Works* (Moscow, 1944; English transl., N.Y., 1946); T. Livanova, *Miaskovsky* (Moscow, 1953); V. Vinogradov, *Guide to the Symphonies of N. Miaskovsky* (Moscow, 1954); S. Shlifstein, ed., *Miaskovsky, Articles, Letters, Reminiscences,* 2 vols. (Moscow, 1959).

Michael, David Moritz, German wind instrument player, violinist, and composer; b. Künhausen, near Erfurt, Oct. 27, 1751; d. Neuwied, on the Rhine, 1825. He spent some years as a Hessian army musician; in 1781 joined the Moravian church; from 1795 till 1815 he lived in the Moravian settlements at Nazareth and Bethlehem, Pennsylvania, and was the leading spirit in the musical performances in both towns; he played violin and most winds, and, as a novelty, would amuse his audience by performing simultaneously on 2 French horns. A list of programs of the Collegium Musicum at Nazareth beginning with 1796 is preserved in the Moravian Historical Society at Nazareth. Michael's compositions are listed in *A Catalogue of Music by American Moravians,* compiled by A. G. Rau and H. T. David (Bethlehem, Pa., 1938). They include a dozen choral works and 16 *Partien,* or suites, for 5, 6, and 7 wind instruments, among them one, a programmatic work, written for a boat ride on the Lehigh River.

BIBLIOGRAPHY: H. T. David, "Background for Bethlehem: Moravian Music in Pennsylvania," *American Magazine of Art* (April 1939); H. T. David, "Musical Life in the Pennsylvania Settlements of the *Unitas Fratrum,*" *Transactions of the Moravian Historical Society* (1942; repr. as Moravian Music Foundation Publication No. 6, Winston-Salem, N.C., 1959); K. Kroeger, "David Moritz Michael's Psalm 103," *Moravian Music Foundation Bulletin* (Fall-Winter 1976).

Michaelides, Solon, Greek musicologist, conductor and composer; b. Nicosia, Cyprus, Nov. 25, 1905. He studied first at the Trinity College of Music in London; then took courses in composition at the École Normale de Musique in Paris with Nadia Boulanger and later in conducting with Marcel Labey at the Schola Cantorum. Upon his return to Cyprus, he founded a cons. at Limassol in 1934 and was its director until 1956; subsequently was director of the Salonika State Cons. (1957–70) and permanent conductor of the Symph. Orch. of Northern Greece (1959–70). In 1970 he was pensioned and moved to Athens. He published *Modern British Music* (Nicosia, 1939), *Cyprus Folk Music* (ibid., 1944; second ed., 1956), *Modern Greek Music* (ibid., 1945; second ed., 1952), the 2-volume *Harmony of Contemporary Music* (Limassol, 1945), *The Neo-Hellenic Folk Music* (ibid., 1948) and *A Dictionary of Ancient Greek Music* (London, 1977). Among his compositions are an opera to his own libretto, *Ulysses* (1951); a ballet, *Nausicaa* (1961); *At the Cypriot Marriage*, symph. sketch for flute and strings (1934); *2 Byzantine Sketches* for strings (1936); *2 Greek Symphonic Pictures* (1936); 2 cantatas: *The Tomb* (1936) and *Free Besieged* (1955); *Byzantine Offering* for strings (1944); *Archaic Suite* for flute, oboe, harp and strings (1962); Piano Concerto (1966); String Quartet (1934); Piano Trio (1946); *Suite* for cello and piano (1966); *Suite* for piano (1966); *Hymn and Lament for Cyprus* for a cappella chorus (1975).

Michalsky, Donal, American composer; b. Pasadena, California, July 13, 1928; d. (asphyxiated in a fire and burned to death with his wife, 2 small children, a house guest and her daughter), Newport Beach, California, Dec. 31, 1975. He studied clarinet as a youth; then attended the Univ. of Southern Calif., Los Angeles as a student in theory with Halsey Stevens and in orchestration with Ingolf Dahl, obtaining his doctorate in 1965. In 1958 he went to Germany where he took a course with Wolfgang Fortner in Freiberg. In 1960 he was appointed prof. of composition at the California State College at Fullerton, holding this position until his tragic death. In his music he adopted a powerful modern idiom in robust dissonant counterpoint, often written in dodecaphonic technique, and yet permeated with a lyric and almost romantic sentiment.

WORKS: 3 symphonies: No. 1, choral symph. *Wheel of Time* (1967), No. 2, *Sinfonia Concertante* (1969), No. 3 (1975); Concertino, for 19 wind instruments and percussion (1964); Quintet for 2 trumpets, 2 trombones and piano (1951); *Divertimento* for 2 clarinets and bass clarinet (1952); *Partita* for oboe d'amore, string trio and string orch. (1956); Cello Sonata (1958); *Sonata Concertante* for piano solo (1961); *Trio Concertino* for flute, oboe, and horn (1961); *Cantata da Requiem* (1962); *Variations* for clarinet and piano (1962); *Partita piccola* for flute and piano (1964); *3 × 4* for saxophone quartet (1972); a number of pieces for band; songs. The manuscript of his projected opera *Der Arme Heinrich* was burned in the fire that took his life.

Micheelsen, Hans Friedrich, German composer of sacred music; b. Hennstedt, Dithmarschen, June 9, 1902; d. Glüsing, Holstein, Nov. 23, 1973. He studied in Hamburg and Berlin; was active as church organist until 1938 when he was drafted into the German army; after demobilization he settled in Hamburg, where he taught at the Hochschule für Musik. He retired in 1962 and lived mostly in Schwarzwald. He

wrote mostly choral music and pieces for organ; among his works are a *Luther Mass* (1933); a German Requiem, *Tod und Leben* (1938); oratorio, *Wachstum und Reife* (1953); *Passion According to St. Mark* (1954); cantata, *Land der Väter* (1955); evangelical Mass, *Unser Wandel ist im Himmel* (1957); *St. John's Passion* chorus a cappella (1961); also a Singspiel, *Münchhausen; Organ Concerto* (1952); *Suite* for flute and piano (1970); some songs in the Hamburg dialect.

Michel, Paul-Baudouin, Belgian composer; b. Haine-St.-Pierre, Sept. 7, 1930. He studied humanities at the Cons. in Mons; then took composition with Absil at the Queen Elisabeth Music Chapel in Brussels (1959–62) and conducting at the Royal Cons. in Brussels; attended summer courses in Darmstadt with Ligeti, Boulez, Maderna and Messiaen. He was later appointed director of the Academy of Music in Woluwé-St.-Lambert. His music adheres to the doctrine of precisely planned structural formations in a highly modern idiom.

WORKS: *Rex Pacificus*, radiophonic motet for bass, chorus, orch. and tape (1968); *La Boîte de Pandore*, ballet (1961); *Equateur*, cantata (1962); *Le Feu et le Monde* for narrator, soli, chorus, organ, 12 trumpets and percussion (1970); *Variations symphoniques* (1960); *5 Inframorphoses* for string orch. (1963); *Symphonium* for orch. (1966); *Concaténation* for chamber orch. (1967); *Hors-Temps* for orch. (1970); *Confluences* for 2 chamber groups (1974); String Trio (1956); Violin Sonata (1960); *Hommage à François Rabelais,* wind quintet (1960); Clarinet Sonatina (1960); String Quartet (1961); *Sérénade concertante* for violin and piano (1962); *Motet aléatoire sur le "Veni creator"* for chorus, 19 instruments and percussion (1962); *Quadrance* for string quartet (1965); *Conduit et Danse hiératique* for solo harp (1964); *Monologue double* for flute and tape (1965); *Ultramorphoses* for flute, clarinet, saxophone, percussion, piano, violin, viola and cello (1965); *Clarbussonance* for bass clarinet and tape (1966); *Bassonance* for bassoon and tape (1966); *Oscillonance* for 2 violins and piano (1967); *Colloque* for piano, trumpet and percussion (1967); *Gravures* for 2 trumpets and horn (1972); *Intonations* for brass (1972); *Systoles—Diastoles* for soprano and instruments (1973); *Parélléloide* for clavichord and tape (1974); several piano works, including *Partita No. 1* (1955); *Transsonance* (1965), *Libration I* (1971, revised 1973); *Lithophanie* (1971, for prepared piano); *Points cardinaux* (1968); *Variations concentriques* (1971); *Musicoïde* (1971, for 2 prepared pianos) and *Orbe* (1972); *Transphonies pour plusieurs nefs* for organ (1969); *Puzzlephonie* for organ (1972); choruses.

Michelangeli, Arturo Benedetti, Italian pianist; b. Brescia, Jan. 5, 1920. He studied piano first with his father, then with Anfossi at the Milan Cons., from which he received his diploma at the age of 13; won the International Piano Contest in Geneva at 19, and was appointed prof. of piano at the Bologna Cons. At the same time he studied medicine. During World War II he served in the Italian Air Force; after the war embarked on a spectacular career as a virtuoso pianist receiving enormous acclaim from critics and audiences. His playing seemed to revive the best traditions of classical virtuosity, marked by a superbly modulated tone and overpowering technique. He founded in Bologna a private school for exceptionally gifted pianists, but after a few years abandoned teaching.

Michelet, Michel (real name **Levin**), Russo-American composer; b. Kiev, June 26, 1894. He studied cello in Kiev and at the Vienna Cons. with Julius Klengel; then went to Leipzig where he took lessons with Max Reger. Returning to Kiev in 1914, he studied composition with Reinhold Glière. He left Russia in 1921; went to Vienna and subsequently to Paris, where he became a composer of film music. In 1941 he made his way from France to the U.S. under difficult wartime conditions, and settled in Hollywood. His music has a certain lyric quality, in a Russian vein, with an infusion of characteristic devices of early French Impressionism.
WORKS: an opera, *Hannele,* after Hauptmann (1972); Violin Concerto (1943); *Lisztiana,* "romantic trio" for violin, cello and piano (1943); Cello Sonata No. 1 (1937); Cello Sonata No. 2 (1977); 3 violin sonatas; Sonata for balalaika and piano (1972); piano pieces; songs; nearly 200 film scores.

Michi, Orazio, called **della Arpa** (because of his virtuosity on the harp), Italian composer; b. Alifa Caserta, c.1595; d. Rome, Oct. 26, 1641. From 1614 till 1623 he was in Rome; after that, with Cardinal Maurice of Savoy. Until 1914 nothing was known of his works except 5 arias publ. in Bianchi's *Raccolta d'arie* (Rome, 1640) and a 6th one publ. by Torchi in vol. 5 of *L'Arte Musicale in Italia.* Then, A. Cametti publ., in the *Rivista Musicale Italiana* (April 1914), a full description and complete thematic catalogue of 43 pieces for 1–3 voices with continuo (chiefly arias) by Michi which he had discovered in various Italian libraries, and which prove that Michi was one of the earliest and most important Roman masters of the monodic style.

Middelschulte, Wilhelm, eminent German organist; b. Werne, near Dortmund, April 3, 1863; d. there, May 4, 1943. He studied at the Institut für Kirchenmusik in Berlin with Löschhorn (piano), Haupt (organ), Commer and Schröder (composition). After serving as organist at the Church of St. Luke in Berlin (1888–91), he went to America and settled in Chicago; was organist there at the Cathedral of the Holy Name (1891–95); prof. of organ at the Wisconsin Cons. of Music, Milwaukee. He was greatly distinguished as a Bach player and pedagogue; in 1935 became instructor of theory and organ at the Detroit Foundation Music School; in 1939 returned to Germany.
BIBLIOGRAPHY: J. J. Becker, "Wilhelm Middelschulte," *Musical Quarterly* (April 1928).

Middleton, Hubert Stanley, British organist and music educator; b. Windsor, May 11, 1890; d. London, Aug. 13, 1959. He studied at the Royal Academy of Music in London and at the Univ. of Cambridge (M.A., 1920). He was appointed organist and director of music at Trinity College, Cambridge, in 1931; also taught at the Royal Academy of Music in London. His specialty was cathedral music. He himself composed

a certain number of anthems and organ pieces. He was greatly esteemed as an educator, and his teaching methods exercised profound influence on his students, many of whom became educators in their own right.

Miedel, Rainer, German cellist and conductor; b. Regensburg, June 1, 1938. He studied cello with Franco Ferrara in Siena and André Navarra in Paris. He then studied conducting with István Kertesz. In 1967 he became a cellist with the Stockholm Philharmonic; also won first prize in the Swedish Broadcasting Corporation competition for young conductors; he made his conducting debut with the Stockholm Philharmonic in 1967; from 1969 to 1976 he was assistant to Antal Dorati at the Stockholm Philharmonic. In the interim he conducted guest engagements in Berlin, Leningrad, Bucharest and Hamburg. In 1969 he was engaged as assistant conductor of the Baltimore Symph. He also made a tour of Japan as guest conductor with the Nippon Orch. of Tokyo. In 1976 he was appointed principal conductor and music director of the Seattle Symphony Orchestra.

Mieg, Peter, Swiss composer; b. Lenzburg, Sept. 5, 1906. He studied piano and theory in Basel; took courses in literature and archeology in Paris; received his Ph.D. in Zürich for a dissertation on art. He subsequently studied composition with Frank Martin; simultaneously was active as a professional painter. His works comprise a String Trio (1937); 2 string quartets (1938, 1945); Concerto for 2 Pianos and Orch. (1941); ballet, *Daphne* (1945); 2 piano concertos (1947, 1961); Violin Concerto (1949); *Concerto Veneziano* for string orch. (1955); Concerto for Oboe and Orch. (1957); *Sinfonie* (1958); Concerto for flute and String Orch. (1962); several piano sonatas and other piano pieces; songs.

Mielck, Ernst, Finnish composer; b. Viipuri (Vyborg), Oct. 24, 1877; d. Locarno, Italy, Oct. 22, 1899 (two days before his 22nd birthday). He studied piano in St. Petersburg, and composition with Max Bruch in Berlin. His early death deprived Finland of a major musical talent. He left several works showing considerable technical skill and inventive power; among these are String Quartet (1895); *Macbeth Overture* (1895); String Quintet (1896–97); *Finnish Symphony* (1897); *Dramatic Overture* (1898); two piano concertos (1895, 1898); *Finnish Suite* for orch. (1899). A monograph on Mielck was published by W. Mauke (Leipzig, 1901).

Mielke, Antonia, German dramatic soprano; b. Berlin, c.1852; d. there, Nov. 15, 1907. At first she sang chiefly coloratura roles, but gradually assumed the great dramatic parts, for which she was particulary gifted. She sang the Wagner heroines at the Metropolitan Opera during the season of 1890–91 (succeeding Lilli Lehmann); also toured the U.S. in concert recitals; returning to Germany, she continued her operatic career until 1902, when she settled in Berlin as a teacher.

Miereanu, Costin, Rumanian composer; b. Bucharest, Feb. 27, 1943. He studied with Alfred Mendelsohn, Varga, and Dan Constantinescu at the Bucharest Cons. (1960–66); attended seminars with Günther Becker and Ligeti at the summer courses in new music held in Darmstadt (1967, 1968) and also had sessions with Pierre Schaeffer at the Cons. of Paris (1968–69) and with the "Groupe de recherches musicales" there. His music presents a totality of the cosmopolitan avant-grade: serialism, electronic sound, aleatory production, and musical-verbal theater. Some of his compositions have optional parts for magnetic tape and film.

WORKS: *Donum sacrum Brancusi* for voice and orch. (1963); *Espace dernier,* aleatory music for chorus, 6 instrumental groups and tape (1965; Royan, April 14, 1973); *Variante* for solo clarinet (1966); *Finis coronat opus* for pianist and 6 instrumental groups (1966); *Cadenza* for 1 or more pianists (1966); *Monostructures I* for 2 orchestras of strings and brass (1967) and *II* for strings, brass and tape (1967); *Sursum corda* for piano, violin, viola, cello and clarinet (1967–68); *Nuit* for soprano and a cappella chorus (1968); *Dans la nuit des temps,* aleatory music for variable ensemble and tape (1968–69); *Couleurs du temps (Colors of Time)* in 3 versions: for string orch. (1968), for string quartet and tape (1968) and for double string quartet and double bass (1969); *Espaces audelà du dernier,* aleatory music for chamber ensemble (1969); *Espaces II* for 20 strings, piano and tape (1967–69); *Polymorphies 5 X 7,* in concert version, for ad lib chorus, variable ensemble and tape, or in stage version, for actors, chorus, variable ensemble and tape (1968–69); *Night Music* for tape (1968–70); *Alba* for 12 voices and 4 percussionists (1972; version for 2 voices and objects, 1973); *Source de Juin* for flute, clarinet, trombone, trumpet, electric guitar and percussion (1972); *Altar* in 3 versions that mix voices, instruments, film and tape in various combinations (1973); 5 separate works (*Amnar, Rod, Amurg, Zbor,* and *Apo*) all subtitled "réécriture spatio-temporelle," for varying combinations of instrumental and vocal soloists, chamber ensembles, film and tape (1973; all 5 works, Paris, Feb. 5, 1974); *Silence Tisse* for variable vocal and instrumental ensembles (1973–74); *Domingo* for variable quintet of voices and instruments (1974); *Quintafeira* for 2 trumpets, horn, trombone and tuba (1974); *Segundafeira* for 5 different flutes (1974); *Luna Cinese* for narrator, 1 performer and 1 or more electrophones (1975); *Planetarium I* for piano, 2 flutes, trombone and vibraphone (1975); *Rêve sans (T)rêve,* a "kinéaquarium vidéophonique" (1975); *Sempre Azzuro* for variable ensemble (1975); *Rosario* for orch. and optional tenor (1973–76); *Musiques élémentaires pour la Messe,* cycle of 6 pieces for variable instruments (1976).

Miersch, Paul Friedrich Theodor, cellist and composer; b. Dresden, Jan. 18, 1868; d. New York, March 1, 1956. He studied at the Munich Academy with Werner (cello) and Rheinberger (composition); came to the U.S. in 1886, and lived in Washington; during Tchaikovsky's American tour in 1891, he played the cello part in Tchaikovsky's trio in Washington, in the composer's presence. In 1892 he moved to N.Y., was 1st cellist of the N.Y. Symph. Orch. (1893–98); then in similar post at the Metropolitan Opera (1898–1912). After retirement from concert life, he remained in N.Y. as a teacher. He wrote a number of compositions, 46 of which have been published.

Mies, Paul, German musicologist and pedagogue; b. Cologne, Oct. 22, 1889; d. there, May 15, 1976. He studied musicology, mathematics and physics in Bonn; received his Dr. phil. with the dissertation *Über die Tonmalerei* (1912); then was active as teacher in mathematics in Cologne (1919–39) while continuing his work in music; then was director of the school of music in Cologne (1946–54). He publ. a number of musicological and educational monographs, among them *Die Bedeutung der Skizzen Beethovens zur Erkenntnis seines Stiles* (Leipzig, 1925; in English, London, 1929); *Musik im Unterricht der höherer Lehranstalten* (2 vols.; Cologne, 1926); *Skizzen aus Geschichte und Ästhetik der Musik* (1926); *Das romantische Leid und Gesänge aus Wilhelm Meister; Musik und Musiker in Poesie und Prosa,* 2 vols. (Berlin, 1926); *Schubert, der Meister des Liedes* (Berlin, 1928); *Johannes Brahms* (1930); *Der Charakter der Tonarten* (Cologne, 1948). He produced *Reihenfolge,* a collection for school orchestras, in 30 vols.; also ed. works of Bach, Mozart, Beethoven and Schubert.

Miessner, Benjamin Franklin, American inventor of electronic instruments; b. about 1890 in Indiana; d. in Miami, Florida, March 25, 1976. He studied electrical engineering at Purdue University. About 1925 organized his own company, Miessner Inventions, Inc. He perfected the Wurlitzer Organ and electronic pianos before his retirement in 1959.

Mignan, Édouard-Charles-Octave, French organist and composer; b. Paris, March 17, 1884; d. there, Sept. 17, 1969. He studied at the Paris Cons. with Widor (organ) and Paul Vidal (compostion); was church organist at Orléans and later on at the Madeleine in Paris. He wrote a number of melodious orchestral suites, a symphony, sacred choruses, numerous motets and organ pieces.

Mignone, Francisco, eminent Brazilian composer; b. São Paulo, Sept. 3, 1897. He studied music with his father; in 1920 he went to Italy for further musical education; returning to Brazil he was appointed to the faculty of the Escola Nacional de Música in Rio de Janeiro (1929), and taught there until 1967. His music shows the influence of the modern Italian school of composition; his piano pieces are of virtuoso character; his orchestration shows consummate skill. In many of his works he employs indigenous Brazilian motives, investing them in sonorous modernistic harmonies not without a liberal application of euphonious dissonances.

WORKS: OPERAS: *O Contractador dos diamantes* (Rio de Janeiro, Sept. 20, 1924), *O inocente* (Rio de Janeiro, Sept. 5, 1928); operetta *Mizú* (1937); BALLETS: *Maracatú de Chico-Rei* (Rio de Janeiro, Oct. 29, 1934), *Quadros Amazónicos* (Rio de Janeiro, July 15, 1949), *O guarda chuva* (São Paulo, 1954); FOR ORCH.: *Suite campestre* (Rio de Janeiro, Dec. 16, 1918), *Con-*

gada, from the opera, *O Contractador dos diamantes* (São Paulo, Sept. 10, 1922; his most popular piece), *Scenas da Roda*, symph. dance (São Paulo, Aug. 15, 1923), *Festa dionisiaca* (Rome, Oct. 24, 1923), *Intermezzo lirico* (São Paulo, May 13, 1925), *Momus*, symph. poem (Rio de Janeiro, April 24, 1933), *Suite Brasileira* (Rio de Janeiro, Dec. 9, 1933), *Sonho de um Menino Travesso* (São Paulo, Oct. 30, 1937), *4 Fantasias Brasileiras*, for piano and orch. (1931–37), *Seresta*, for cello and orch. (Rio de Janeiro, March 31, 1939), *Miudinho*, symph. dance (São Paulo, June 28, 1941), *Festa das Igrejas* (N.Y., April 22, 1942), *Sinfonia tropical* (1958), Piano Concerto (1958), Violin Concerto (1961), Concerto for Violin, Piano and Orch. (1966), Concertino, for clarinet and small orch. (1957), Bassoon Concertino (1957). CHAMBER MUSIC: String Octet (1956), 2 wind quintets (1960, 1962), 2 string quartets (1956, 1957), Sonata for 4 bassoons (1966), 2 wind trios (1967, 1968), 3 violin sonatas (1964, 1965, 1966), Cello Sonata (1967), 2 sonatas for 2 bassoons (1960, 1965), 2 sonatas for flute and oboe (1969, 1970), Sonata for trumpet solo (1970); FOR PIANO: 4 sonatas (1941, 1962, 1964, 1967), *Rondo* (1969); several waltzes in Brazilian popular style; *Samba rítmico* (1953; for 2 pianos), *Sonata humorística* for 2 pianos (1968); VOCAL MUSIC: an oratorio, *Alegrias de Nossa Senhora* (Rio de Janeiro, July 15, 1949), oratorio, *Santa Clara* (1962); many songs.

BIBLIOGRAPHY: N. Slonimsky, *Music of Latin America* (N.Y., 1945; pp. 134–36); Luiz Heitor Correa de Azevedo, "Francisco Mignone," *Música Brasileña Contemporánea* (Rosario, Argentina, 1952; pp. 125–57). An autobiographical brochure, *A parte do anjo* was publ. for his 50th birthday, containing articles by Correa de Azevedo, Mario de Andrade and L. Chiaffarelli (São Paulo, 1947); special issue of *Inter-American Music Bulletin* (1970–71).

Migot, Georges, significant French composer; b. Paris Feb. 27, 1891; d. Levallois, near Paris, Jan. 5, 1976. He began taking piano lessons at the age of 6; entered the Paris Cons. in 1909; after preliminary courses in harmony, he studied composition with Widor, counterpoint with André Gedalge and music history with Maurice Emmanuel; orchestration with Vincent d'Indy and organ with Gigout and Guilmant. Before completing his studies at the Paris Cons., he was mobilized into the French Army, wounded at Longuyon in 1914 and was released from military service. In 1917 he presented in Paris a concert of his own works; received the Lily Boulanger Prize in 1918. He competed twice for the Prix de Rome in 1919 and 1920, but failed to win and abandoned further attempts. In the meantime he engaged in a serious study of painting; in fact, he was more successful as a painter than as a composer in the early years of his career; exhibited his paintings in Paris art galleries in 1917, 1919, 1923 and in subsequent years. He also wrote poetry; virtually all of his vocal works are written to his own words. In his musical compositions he endeavored to recapture the spirit of old French polyphony, thus emphasizing the continuity of national art in history. His melodic writing is modal, often with archaic inflections, while his harmonic idiom is diatonically translucid; he obtains subtle coloristic effects through unusual instrumental registration. Profoundly interested in the preservation and classification of old musical instruments, Migot served as curator of the Instrumental Museum of the Paris Cons. (1949–61).

WORKS: *Hagoromo*, "symphonie lyrique et chorégraphique" for baritone, chorus and orch., to the text by Migot and Laloy (Monte Carlo, May 9, 1922); *Le Rossignol en amour*, chamber opera to the text by Migot (1926–28; Geneva, March 2, 1937); *La Sulamite*, concert opera to a libretto by Migot (1969–70); *L'Arche*, "polyphonie spatiale" for soprano, female chorus and orch., to a poem by Migot (1971; Marseille, May 3, 1974); 13 symphonies (some material of them was derived from earlier pieces of chamber music, and their numeration does not follow chronological order): No. 1, *Les Agrestides* (1919–20; Paris, April 29, 1922); No. 2 (1927; Festival of Besançon, Sept. 7, 1961); No. 3 (1943–49); No. 4 (1946–47); No. 5, *Sinfonia da Chiesa* for wind instruments (1955; Roubaix, Dec. 4, 1955); No. 6, for strings (1944–51; Strasbourg, June 22, 1960); No. 7, for chamber orch. (1948–52); No. 8, for 15 wind instruments and 2 double basses (1953); No. 9 for strings (imcomplete); No. 10 (1962); No. 11, for wind instruments (1963); No. 12 (1954–64; Lille, May 29, 1972); No. 13 (1967); also *Petite Symphonie en trois mouvements enchaînés* for string orch. (1970; Béziers, July 23, 1971); OTHER ORCH. WORKS: *Le Paravent de laque aux cinq images* (1920; Paris, Jan. 21, 1923); *Trois ciné-ambiances* (1922); *La Fête de la bergère* (1921; Paris, Nov. 21, 1925); *Prélude pour un poète* (Paris, June 7, 1929); *Le Livre des danceries*, orch. suite (Paris, Dec. 12, 1931); *Le Zodiaque* (1931–39); *Phonie sous-marine* (1962); *Dialogue* for piano and orch. (1922–25; Paris, March 25, 1926); *Dialogue* for cello and orch. (1922–26; Paris, Feb. 7, 1927); *Suite* for violin and orch. (1924; Paris, Nov. 14, 1925); *Suite* for piano and orch. (Paris, March 12, 1927); *Suite en concert* for harp and orch. (Paris, Jan. 15, 1928); *La Jungle*, "polyphonie" for organ and orch. (1928; Paris, Jan. 9, 1932); Piano Concerto (1962; Paris, June 26, 1964); Concerto for Harpsichord and Chamber Orch. (Paris, Dec. 12, 1967). CHAMBER MUSIC: *Les Parques* for 2 violins, viola and piano (1909); 3 string quartets (1921, 1957, 1966); Quartet for flute, violin, cello and piano (1960); Quartet for violin, viola, cello and piano (1961); Quartet for 2 clarinets, corno di bassetto and bass clarinet (1925); Quartet for saxophones (1955); Quartet for 2 violins and 2 cellos (1955); Quintet for flute, oboe, clarinet, horn and bassoon (1954); *Introduction pour un concert de chambre* for 5 strings and 5 wind instruments (1964); Trio for oboe, violin and piano (1906); Trio for violin, viola and piano (1918); Piano Trio (1935); Trio for oboe, clarinet and bassoon (1944); String Trio (1944–45); Trio for flute, cello and harp (1965); Guitar Sonata (1960); *Sonate luthée* for harp solo (1949); 2 sonatas for violin solo (1951, 1959); Violin Sonata (1911); *Dialogue No. 1* for violin and piano (1923); *Dialogue No. 2* for violin and piano (1925); Sonata for viola solo (1958); Sonata for cello solo (1954); *Dialogue No. 1* for cello and piano (1922); *Dialogue No. 2* for cello and piano (1929); Sonata for cello and piano (1958); *Suite* for 2 cellos (1962); *Suite* for flute solo (1931); Flute Sonata (1945); *Pastorale* for 2 flutes (1950); *Suite* for English horn and piano (1963); Sonata for clarinet solo (1953); Sonata for bassoon solo (1953); VOCAL WORKS: *6 Tétraphonies* for baritone, flute, violin and cello, to words by Migot (1945); *7 petites Images du Japon* for voice and piano (1917); *Vini vinoque amor* for 2 voices, flute, cello and piano (1937); numerous unaccompanied vocal trios and quartets; sacred choruses a cappella; double and triple choruses a cappella; *Liturgie œcuménique* for 3 voices and organ (1958); oratorio, *La Mise au tombeau* to Migot's text (1948–49); "lyric mystery" *La Nativité de Notre Seigneur* for soloists, chorus and instruments, to text by Migot (1954); *La Passion*, oratorio (1939–46; Paris, July 25, 1957); *L'Annonciation*, oratorio (1943–46); *Mystère orphique* for voice and orch. (1951; Strasbourg, March 18, 1964); *Cantate d'Amour*, concert opera, to texts by Migot (1949–50); *La Résurrection*, oratorio (1953; Strasbourg, March 28, 1969); *Du ciel et de la terre*, "space symphony" for a film (1957); *Le Zodiaque*, "chorégraphie lyrique" with libretto by Migot (1958–60); *La plate, vaste savane* for soprano and instruments (1967); *3 chansons de joie et de souci* for voice and guitar (1969); *3 Dialogues* for voice and cello (1972); *5 Chants initiatiques* for voice and piano (1973); much liturgical music; a group of albums of character pieces for piano; numerous works for organ. Migot published an autobiography, *Kaléidoscope et Miroirs* (Toulouse, 1970); *Essais pour une esthétique générale* (Paris, 1920); *Jean-Philippe Rameau et le génie de la musique française* (Paris, 1930); *Lexique de quelques termes utilisés en musique* (Paris, 1947); 2 vols. of poems (Paris, 1950, 1951).

BIBLIOGRAPHY: Léon Vallas, *Georges Migot* (Paris, 1923); Pierre Wolff, *La Route d'un musicien: Georges Migot* (Paris, 1933); Maurice Henrion, "La Musique vocale de Georges Migot," *La Revue Musicale* (Nov. 1946); Marc Honegger, "Georges Migot," *Revue Musicale Suisse* (1954); Max Pinchard, *Connaissance de Georges Migot, musicien français* (Paris, 1959); Marc Honegger, ed., *Catalogue des œuvres musicales de Georges Migot* (Strasbourg, 1977). A collection of Migot's articles was published under the title *Les Écrits de Georges Migot* in 4 vols. (Paris, 1932).

Miguez, Leopoldo, Brazilian composer; b. Rio de Janeiro, Sept. 9, 1850; d. there, July 6, 1902. He was a conductor, and was associated with various theatrical enterprises; began to compose marches and walzes; won 1st prize for his *Hymn of the Republic* (1889). In 1890 he was appointed director of the Instituto Nacional de Musica in Rio de Janeiro, retaining this post until his death. In his theater works he pursued Wagnerian ideas, but his technique was insufficient for adequate orchestration.

WORKS: operas: *Pelo Amor* (Rio de Janeiro, 1897) and *Os Saldunes* (Rio de Janeiro, Sept. 20, 1901); overtures; songs; marches.

BIBLIOGRAPHY: "Leopoldo Miguez e o Instituto Nacional de Musica," *Revista Brasileira de Musica* (1940).

Mihalovich, Edmund (Ödön) von, Hungarian composer; b. Fericsancze, Sept. 13, 1842; d. Budapest, April 22, 1929. He studied with Mosonyi in Budapest, and with Hauptmann in Leipzig; also took lessons with Peter Cornelius in Munich. From 1887 to 1919 he taught at the Hungarian Academy of Music in Budapest. He was an ardent Wagnerite and opposed Hungarian musical nationalism; the melodic materials of his own works are entirely Germanic.

WORKS: operas: *Hagbart und Signe* (Dresden, March 12, 1882), *Eliane* (Budapest, Feb. 16, 1908), *Toldi szerelme* (*Toldi's Love*; Budapest, March 18, 1893); 4 symphonies (1879, 1892, 1900, 1902); *Hero and Leander*, symph. poem (1875); *Faust*, a fantasy for orch. (1880); Violin Sonata; piano pieces; songs.

Mihalovici, Marcel, significant Rumanian-French composer; b. Bucharest, Oct. 22, 1898. He studied composition privately with Cuclin in Burcharest; in 1919 went to Paris where he settled; became a French citizen in 1955. He studied violin with Nestor Lejeune, Gregorian Chant with Amédée Gastoué and composition with Vincent d'Indy at the Schola Cantorum (1919–25). With Martinu, Conrad Beck and Tibor Harsányi he formed a freely associated "École de Paris," consisting of emigrants, which later attracted several other Parisian composers, among them Alexandre Tcherepnin of Russia, Alexandre Tansman of Poland and Alexander Spitzmueller of Austria. Mihalovici was a founding member of the modern music society "Triton" (1932); was elected a member of the Institute de France in 1964. He married the noted pianist **Monique Haas.** Mihalovici's music presents a felicitous synthesis of French and eastern European elements, tinted with a roseate impressionistic patina and couched in euphoniously dissonant harmonies.

WORKS: OPERAS: *L'Intransigeant Pluton* (1928; Paris, April 3, 1939); *Phèdre* (1949; Stuttgart, June 9, 1951); *Die Heimkehr* (Frankfurt, June 17, 1954); *Krapp ou La Dernière Bande*, libretto by Samuel Beckett (1959–60; Bielefeld, Germany, Feb. 25, 1961); opera-buffa *Les Jumeaux* (1962; Braunschweig, Germany, Jan. 23, 1963); BALLETS: *Une Vie de Polichinelle* (Paris, 1923); *Le Postillon du Roy* (Paris, 1924); *Divertimento* (Paris, 1925); *Karagueuz*, ballet for marionettes (Paris, 1926; Chicago, 1926); *Thésée au labyrinthe* (1956; Braunschweig, April 4, 1957; revised version as *Scènes de Thésée*, Cologne, Oct. 15, 1958); *Alternamenti* (1957; Braunschweig, Feb. 28, 1958) and *Variations* (Bielefeld, March 28, 1960); FOR ORCH.: *Notturno* (1923); *Introduction à un mouvement symphonique* (1923; Bucharest, Oct. 17, 1926); *Fantaisie* (1927; Liège Festival, Sept. 6, 1930); *Cortège des divinites infernales* (1928; Bucharest, Dec. 7, 1930); *Chindia* for 13 wind instruments and piano (1929); *Concerto quasi una Fantasia* for violin and orch. (1930; Barcelona Festival, April 22, 1936); *Divertissement* (1934); *Capriccio roumain* (1936); *Prélude et Invention* for string orch. (1937; Warsaw Festival, April 21, 1939); *Toccata* for piano and orch. (1938, revised 1940); *Symphonies pour le temps présent* (1944); *Variations* for brass and strings (1946); *Séquences* (1947); *Ritournelles* (1951); 5 symphonies: *Sinfonia Giocosa* (Basel, Dec. 14, 1951), *Sinfonia Partita* for strings (1952), *Sinfonia Variata* (1960), *Sinfonia Cantata* for baritone, chorus and orch. (1953–63), and No. 5 for dramatic soprano and orch. (in memory of Hans Rosbaud, 1966–69; Paris Dec. 14, 1971); *Étude en deux parties* for piano concertante, 7 wind instruments, celesta and percussion (Donaueschingen, Oct. 6, 1951); *Élégie* (1955); *Ouverture tragique* (1957); *Esercizio* for strings (1959); *Musique nocturne* for clarinet, string orch., harpsichord and celesta (1963); *Aubade* for strings (1964); *Périples* for orch. with piano concertante (1967; Paris, March 22, 1970); *Prétextes* for oboe, bass clarinet, and chamber orch. (1968); *Variantes* for horn, and orch. or piano (1969); *Borne* (1970); *Rondo* (1970); *Chant Premier* for saxophone and orch. (1973–74); *Follia*, paraphrases for orch. (1976–77); VOCAL MUSIC: a cantata, *La Genèse* (1935–40); *Cantilène* for mezzo-soprano and chamber orch. (1972); *Cascando*, invention for music and voice (1962); *Mémorial*, 5 a cappella motets, each dedicated to a different deceased composer (1952); the songs, *Abendgesang* (1957), *Stances* (1967) and *Textes* (1974); CHAMBER MUSIC: 2 violin sonatas (1920, 1941); Piano Quartet (1922); 3 string quartets (1923, 1931, 1943–46); Oboe Sonatina (1924); *Serenade* for string trio (1929); Sonata for 3 clarinets (1933); Viola Sonata (1942); Sonata for violin and cello (1944); *Églogue* for flute, oboe, clarinet, bassoon and piano (1945); Sonata for violin solo (1949); Sonata for cello solo (1949); Wind Trio (1955); *Pastorale triste* for flute and piano (1958); Bassoon Sonata (1958); Clarinet Sonata (1958); *Improvisation* for percussion (1958); *Dialogues* for clarinet and piano (1965); *Serioso* for bass saxophone and piano (1971); *Récit* for solo clarinet (1973); *Melopeia* for solo oboe (1973); FOR PIANO: *3 Nocturnes* (1928); *4 Caprices* (1929); *Ricercari* (1941); *3 Pièces nocturnes* (1948); Sonata (1964), *Cantus Firmus* for 2 pianos (1970); *Passacaglia* for the left hand (1975); incidental music for productions of *Sappho* (1946), *Le Paradis perdu* (1951), *Meurtre dans la cathédrale* (1952), *Orphée* (1954), *Mélusine* (1957) and *Herakles* (1975).

BIBLIOGRAPHY: Georges Beck, *Marcel Mihalovici* (Paris, 1954); Viorel Cosma, *Muzicieni români* (contains a list of works with dates of performance; Bucharest, 1970).

Mihály, András, Hungarian composer and conductor; b. Budapest, Nov. 6, 1917. He studied cello with Adolf Schiffer and chamber music with Leo Weiner and Imre Waldbauer at the Budapest Academy of Music (1933–38); took private composition lessons from Paul Kadosa and István Strasser. He played cello in the orch. of the Budapest Opera House (1946–48); in 1950 was appointed prof. of the Budapest Academy of Music. In 1968 he organized the Budapest Chamber Ensemble and conducted it in a series of concerts with programs of new music. As a composer, he writes in a compact contrapuntal style oxygenated by a breath of lyricism. He won the Kossuth Prize in 1955 and the Erkel Prize 3 times (1952, 1954, 1964).

WORKS: an opera, *Együtt és egyedül* (*Together and Alone*, 1964–65; Budapest, Nov. 5, 1966); 3 symphonies (*Sinfonia da requiem*, 1946; 1950; 1962); the cantatas: *My Beloved Hungarian Fatherland* (1952), *The Red Cart* (1957), *Memory and Warning* (1959), *1871* (1960) and *Fly, Poem!* (1967); Cello Concerto (1953); Piano Concerto (1954); *Fantasy* for wind quintet, string orch., harp, celesta and percussion (1955); *Festive Overture* (1959); Violin Concerto, with piano obbligato (1959); *3 Movements* for chamber ensemble

(1969); *Monodia* for orch. (1971); *Musica per 15* (1975); Piano Trio (1940); 2 string quartets (1942, 1960); *Rhapsody* for viola and piano (1947); *Serenade* for wind trio (1956); *Suite* for cello and piano (1957); Piano Sonata (1958); *3 Apocrypha* for female vocal trio or chorus, clarinet and percussion (1962); *Movement* for cello and piano (1962); the song cycles *Chamber Music*, after Joyce (1958), *Attila József Songs* (1961) and *Psalms of Rapture*, after Radnóti (1969); incidental music to plays and films.

Miki, Minoru, Japanese composer; b. Tokyo, March 16, 1930. He studied composition with Akira Ifukube and Ikenouchi at the Tokyo Univ. of Arts, graduating in 1955; organized the Ensemble Nipponia with 15 other members (1964); then appointed a lecturer at the Tokyo College of Music.

WORKS: an operetta, *Husband the Hen* (1963); a musical drama for children, *Kikimimi* (Tokyo, Feb. 27, 1968); *Trinita Sinfonia* (1953); *Osabai* for 12 winds and percussion (1955); *Sinfonia Gamula* (1957); *Poema estiva* for piano (1958); *Symphony "Joya"* (1960); *Requiem* for baritone, male chorus and orch. (1963); Sextet for piano and wind quintet (1965); *Time* for solo marimba (1968); Marima Concerto (Tokyo, Oct. 11, 1969); *Jo-No-Kyoku*, prelude for shakuhachi, koto, sangen, and strings (1969); *Convexity*, concerto for 3 groups of "sankyoku" and a Japanese drum (1970); *Hakuyoh* for violin and koto (1973); *Ha-No-Kyoku*, koto concerto (1974); many pieces for Japanese instruments solo.

Mikorey, Franz, German composer and conductor; b. Munich, June 3, 1873; d. there, May 11, 1947. He studied in Munich with Thuille and H. Levi; later in Berlin with H. von Herzogenberg; conducted in Bayreuth (1894); then in Prague, Regensburg, Elberfeld, and Vienna; in 1902 was engaged as court conductor in Dessau; appointed music director there in 1912. He conducted opera at Helsinki from 1919 to 1924; then returned to Germany.

WORKS: the opera *Der König von Samarkand* (Dessau, 1910); 2 symphonies (*Tragische; An der Adria*); *Sinfonia Engadiana*, for soli, chorus, and orch.; Piano Concerto; Piano Quintet; Piano Trio; male choruses; songs; publ. *Grundlagen des Dirigierens* (1929).

BIBLIOGRAPHY: E. Hamann, *Franz Mikorey* (Leipzig, 1907).

Miksch, Johann Aloys, famous baritone and singing teacher; b. Georgental, Bohemia, July 19, 1765; d. Dresden, Sept. 24, 1845. He was a chorus boy in Dresden; then singer at the Court Church (1786), baritone in the Italian Opera of Dresden (1797), chorusmaster of the German Opera (1820); pensioned in 1831. He was greatly renowned as a teacher; among his pupils was Schröder-Devrient.

BIBLIOGRAPHY: A. Kohut, *J. Miksch* (Leipzig, 1890).

Mikuli, Karl, Polish painist and composer; b. Czernowitz, Oct. 20, 1819; d. Lwow, May 21, 1897. He first studied medicine in Vienna, but his pronounced talent for music made him decide to go to Paris for serious study; there he became a pupil of Chopin (1844); also studied composition with Reicha. After the outbreak of the revolution of 1848 he left Paris and made several tours in Russia and Austria; was appointed director of the Lwow Cons. (1958); 30 years later he established a music school of his own there. His edition of Chopin's works contains numerous emendations made by Chopin himself as marginal remarks in Mikuli's student copies. He publ. a number of piano pieces of his own, greatly influenced by Chopin's style; also *43 airs nationaux roumains* for piano.

Mila, Massimo, Italian writer on music; b. Turin, Aug. 14, 1910. He studied literature at the Univ. of Turin, upon graduation, he became a regular contributor to Italian musical publications; was music critic of *L'Espresso* (1955–67); subsequently wrote for *La Stampa.* In 1960 he was appointed prof. of music history at the Univ. of Turin.
WORKS: *Il melodramma di Verdi* (Bari, 1933); *Cent' anni di musica moderna* (Milan, 1944); *Saggi mozartiani* (Milan, 1945); *Breve storia della musica* (Milan, 1946); *L'Esperienza musicale e l'estetica* (Turin, 1950); *La musica pianistica di Mozart* (Turin, 1963); *Le sinfonie di Mozart* (Turin, 1967).

Milán, Luis, Spanish musician, courtier, and poet; b. Valencia, c.1500; d. after 1561. He was a favorite at the viceregal court of Valencia under Germaine de Foix and her third husband, Don Fernando of Aragón. In 1535–36 he brought out his most important work, *Libro de música de vihuela de mano intitulado El Maestro,* intended as an instruction book for learning to play the vihuela (large six-stringed guitar). This was the first book of its kind to be publ. in Spain, and it is valuable for its many musical examples (tientos, fantasias, pavanes, and solo songs with guitar accomp.: villancicos, romances, and sonetos), which reveal Milán's high qualities as a composer. Milán also publ. *El Cortesano* (1561), giving a description of courtly life at Valenica in his day. *El Maestro,* with the original tablature and the transcription into modern notation, was edited by Leo Schrade in the *Publikationen älterer Musik 2* (Leipzig, 1927); selections are also found in Morphy's *Les Luthistes espagnols du XVIᵉ siècle* (Leipzig, 1902); but the transcriptions are questionable.
BIBLIOGRAPHY: J. B. Trend, *L. Milán and the Vihuelistas* (London, 1925).

Milanov (*née* **Kunc**), **Zinka,** famous soprano; b. Zagreb, Yugoslavia, May 17, 1906. She studied with Milka Ternina in Zagreb, and made her professional debut with the Ljubljana Opera (1927); then sang opera in Hamburg and Vienna; in 1937 was soloist in Verdi's Requiem under the direction of Toscanini. She made her American debut at the Metropolitan Opera House, N.Y., on Dec. 17, 1937, in *Il Trovatore*; remained on its staff until 1966. In 1937 she married Predrag Milanov; divorced in 1946; married Ljubomir Ilic in 1947.

Milburn, Ellsworth, American composer; b. Greensburg, Pennsylvania, Feb. 6, 1938. He studied with Scott Huston at the College-Cons. of Music in Cincinnati (1956–58); later with Roy Travis and Henri Lazarof at the Univ. of California at Los Angeles (1959–62)

and at Mills College with Milhaud (1966–68). He was teacher at the Cincinnati Cons. (1970–75); in 1975 appointed to the faculty of Rice Univ., Houston, Texas.
WORKS: *5 Inventions* for 2 flutes (1965); *Massacre of the Innocents* for chorus (1965); Concerto for Piano and Chamber Orch. (1967); String Trio (1968); *Soli* for five players on ten instruments (1968); String Quintet (1969); *Soli II* for two players on flutes and double bass (1970); *Voussoirs* for orch. (1970); *Soli III* for clarinet, cello and piano (1971); *Soli IV* for flute, oboe, double bass and harpsichord (1972); Violin Sonata (1972); *Lament* for harp (1972).

Milde, Hans Feodor von, opera baritone; b. Petronell, near Vienna, April 13, 1821; d. Weimar, Dec. 10, 1899. He studied singing with Manuel García; was a life member of the Weimar Court Opera, and created the role of Telramund in *Lohengrin* (1850). His wife, **Rosa Agthé** (b. Weimar, June 25, 1827; d. there, Jan 26, 1906), created the role of Elsa, and sang at Weimar until 1876.
BIBLIOGRAPHY: Natalie von Milde, *P. Cornelius. Briefe . . . an Feodor und Rosa von Milde* (Weimar, 1901).

Mildenberg, Albert, American composer; b. Brooklyn, N.Y., Jan. 13, 1878; d. there, July 3, 1918. He was a member of a musical family; studied piano with his mother; then took lessons with Rafael Joseffy (piano) and Bruno Oscar Klein (composition). In 1905 he went to Rome, where he studied with Sgambati; later in Paris with Massenet; in 1907 he made a public appearance in Paris as a conductor. Returning to America, he became dean of the dept. of music of Meredith College at Raleigh, N.C. He wrote a number of songs, many of them to his own texts; also wrote his own opera librettos. His style was in the Italian tradition; Massenet commended his gift of melody. His light opera *The Wood Witch* was produced in N.Y. on May 25, 1903; another comic opera, *Love's Locksmith,* was given in N.Y. in 1912.
BIBLIOGRAPHY: E. E. Hipsher, *American Opera and its Composers* (Philadelphia, 1934, pp. 320–22).

Mildenburg, Anna von, famous dramatic soprano; b. Vienna, Nov. 29, 1872; d. there, Jan. 27, 1947. She studied at the Vienna Cons. with Rosa Papier and Pollini; made her opera debut in Hamburg, where her fine voice and acting ability attracted a great deal of attention; in 1897 she was engaged to sing in Bayreuth; in 1898 she became a member of the Vienna Opera; retired from the stage in 1917; went to Munich, where she taught singing at the State Academy; later taught in Berlin; eventually returned to Vienna. Her repertory included all the great Wagner roles. In 1909 she married the playwright Hermann Bahr, with whom she wrote *Bayreuth und das Wagner Theater* (Leipzig, 1910; English transl., London, 1912); she also publ. *Erinnerungen* (1921) and *Darstellung der Werke Richard Wagner aus dem Geiste ser Dichtung und Musik* (vol. 1, *Tristan und Isolde*; Leipzig, 1936). Bahr alone wrote *Parsifalschutz ohne Ausnahmegesetz* (Berlin, 1912).
BIBLIOGRAPHY: P. Stefan, *Anna Bahr-Mildenburg* (Vienna, 1922).

Milder-Hauptmann, Pauline Anna, soprano; b. Istanbul, Dec. 13, 1785; d. Berlin, May 29, 1838. She was the daughter of an Austrian diplomatic official; in Vienna she attracted the notice of Schikaneder, who recommended her to Tomaselli and Salieri, who taught her opera singing. She made her debut at the Vienna Opera on April 9, 1803, and soon became so well regarded as an artist and a singer that Beethoven wrote the role of Fidelio for her. Her voice was so powerful that Haydn reportedly said to her: "Dear child, you have a voice like a house." In 1810 she married a Vienna merchant, Hauptmann. In 1812 she went to Berlin, where she created a sensation, particularly as Gluck's heroines *(Iphigenia, Alcestis, Armida)*; then sang in Russia, Sweden, and Austria.

Miles, Maurice, English conductor; b. Epsom, Feb. 25, 1908. He studied piano and violin at home; then at the Royal Academy of Music, with Clifford Curzon (piano) and Sir Henry J. Wood (conducting). Later he took lessons with Clemens Krauss in Salzburg. Returning to England, he conducted the summer orch. at Buxton, and the regular season at Bath. He was in the British Army from 1940 till 1943, when he was placed in charge of overseas music broadcasts at the BBC. In 1947 he was appointed conductor of the newly formed Yorkshire Symph. Orch.
BIBLIOGRAPHY: Donald Brook, *International Gallery of Conductors* (Bristol, 1951; pp. 117–20).

Miles, Philip Napier, English composer; b. Shirehampton, Jan. 21, 1865; d. Kingsweston, Bristol, July 19, 1935. He studied in London with Parry and Dannreuther; organized the Shirehampton Choral Society on his own estate and conducted festivals in various localities in England. He wrote several operas: *Westward Ho!* (London, Dec 4, 1914); *Fire Flies* (Clifton, England, Oct. 13, 1924; on the same program with his opera *Markheim*); *Good Friday, Demeter* and *Queen Rosamond*; also some chamber music and many songs.
BIBLIOGRAPHY: H. C. Colles, "Philip Napier Miles," *Music & Letters* (1936).

Miletić, Miroslav, Croatian violinist and composer; b. Sisak, Aug. 22, 1925. He studied in Zagreb; organized there the renowned Pro Arte String Quartet, specializing in performances of modern music.
WORKS: operas, *Hasanaginica* and *Der Fall Ruženka*; radio-opera *Auvergnanski Senatori* (1957); *Vision,* television ballet (1958); Suite for string orch. (1955); Violin Concerto (1958); Viola Concerto (1959); Symph. (1959); *Rhapsodic Variations* for violin and piano (1962); 4 string quartets; violin sonata; *Proportions* for 6 instruments; *Lamentation* for viola and magnetic tape; piano pieces; Croatian songs arranged for recorder.

Milford, Robin, English composer; b. Oxford, Jan. 22, 1903; d. Lyme Regis, Dec. 29, 1959. He studied with Holst, Vaughan Williams, and R. O. Morris, at the Royal College of Music in London. Still as a student, he composed a number of works, mostly in small forms, in a clear rhythmic manner, with thematic materials suggesting English folk music.

WORKS: ballet *The Snow Queen,* after Hans Christian Andersen (1946); oratorio, *The Pilgrim's Progress,* after John Bunyan (1932); *The Forsaken Merman,* after Matthew Arnold, for tenor, women's chorus, strings, and piano (1938–50); *A Litany to the Holy Spirit,* after Robert Herrick (1947); Suite for chamber orch. (1924); *Miniature Concerto* for strings (1933); *Ariel,* for small orch. (1940); *Miniature Concerto* for harpsichord and chamber orch. (1927); Violin Concerto (1937); *Elegiac Meditation,* for viola and strings (1947); *Fantasia* for string quartet (1945); Trio for clarinet, cello, and piano (1948); Trio for 2 violins and piano (1949); Flute Sonata (1944); Violin Sonata (1945); *A Festival* for strings (1951); *Fishing by Moonlight* for piano and strings (1952); opera, *The Scarlet Letter* (1959); piano pieces; songs; other works in various forms.

Milhaud, Darius, eminent French composer; b. Aix-en-Provence, Sept. 4, 1892; d. Geneva, June 22, 1974. He was the descendant of an old Jewish family, settled in Provence for many centuries. His father was a merchant of almonds; there was a piano in the house, and Milhaud improvised melodies as a child; then began to take violin lessons. He entered the Paris Cons. in 1909, almost at the age limit for enrollment; studied with Berthelier (violin), Lefèvre (ensemble), Leroux (harmony), Gédalge (counterpoint), Widor (composition and fugue) and Vincent d'Indy (conducting); played violin in the student orch. of the Paris Cons. under the direction of Paul Dukas. He received 1st "accessit" in violin and counterpoint, and 2nd in fugue; won the Prix Lepaulle for composition. Still as a student, he wrote music in a bold modernistic manner; became associated with Erik Satie, Jean Cocteau, and Paul Claudel. When Claudel was appointed French minister to Brazil, he engaged Milhaud as his secretary; they sailed for Rio de Janeiro early in 1917; returned to Paris (via the West Indies and New York) shortly after the Armistice of Nov. 1918. Milhaud's name became known to a larger public as a result of a newspaper article by Henri Collet in *Comœdia* (Jan. 16, 1920), grouping him with 5 other French composers of modern tendencies (Auric, Durey, Honegger, Poulenc, and Germaine Tailleferre) under the sobriquet "Les Six," even though the association was stylistically fortuitous. In 1922 Milhaud visited the U.S.; lectured at Harvard Univ., Princeton, and Columbia; appeared as pianist and composer in his own works; in 1925, traveled in Italy, Germany, Austria, and Russia; returning to France, he devoted himself mainly to composition and teaching. At the outbreak of World War II, he was in Aix-en-Provence; in July 1940, came to the U.S.; taught for several years at Mills College, Oakland, Calif. In 1947 he returned to France; was appointed prof. at the Paris Cons., but continued to visit the U.S. as conductor and teacher almost annually, despite his illness (arthritis), which compelled him to conduct while seated. Exceptionally prolific since his student days, he wrote a great number of works in every genre; introduced a modernistic type of music drama, "opéra à la minute," and also the "miniature symphony." He experimented with new stage techniques, incorporating cinematic interludes; has also successfully revived the Greek type of tragedy with vocal accompaniment; has composed works for electronic instruments, and has demonstrated his contrapuntal skill in such compositions as his 2 string quartets (No. 14 and No. 15) that can be played together as a string octet. He was the first to exploit polytonality in a consistent and deliberate manner; has applied the exotic rhythms of Latin America and the West Indies in many of his lighter works; of these, his *Saudades do Brasil* are particularly popular; Brazilian movements are also found in his *Scaramouche* and *Le Bœuf sur le toit;* in some of his works he has drawn upon the resources of jazz. His ballet, *La Création du monde,* produced in 1923, portraying the Creation in terms of Negro cosmology, constitutes the earliest example of the use of the blues and jazz in a symphonic score, anticipating Gershwin in this respect. Despite this variety of means and versatility of forms, Milhaud has succeeded in establishing a style that is distinctly and identifiably his own; his melodies are nostalgically lyrical or vivaciously rhythmical, according to mood; his instrumental writing is of great complexity and difficulty, and yet entirely within the capacities of modern virtuoso technique; he has arranged many of his works in several versions each.

WORKS: OPERAS: *La Brebis égarée,* "roman musical" (1910–15; Paris, Dec. 10, 1923); *Agamemnon* (1913; Paris, April 16, 1927); *Le Pauvre Matelot,* "complainte en trois actes" (1926; Paris, Dec. 12, 1927); *Les Choéphores* (Paris, June 15, 1919, in concert form; stage performance, Brussels, March 27, 1935); *Les Euménides* (1922; Antwerp, Nov. 27, 1927); *Les Malheurs d'Orphée* (Brussels, May 7, 1926); *Esther de Carpentras,* opéra-bouffe (1925; Paris, Feb. 1, 1938); 3 "minute operas": *L'Enlèvement d'Europe* (Baden-Baden, July 17, 1927), *L'Abandon d'Ariane,* and *La Délivrance de Thésée* (Wiesbaden, April 20, 1928); *Christophe Colomb,* grand opera in 26 scenes, to a book by Paul Claudel (Berlin, May 5, 1930); *Maximilien* (Paris, Jan. 4, 1932); *Médée* (Antwerp, Oct. 7, 1939); *Bolivar* (1943; Paris, May 12, 1950); *Le Jeu de Robin et Marion,* mystery play after Adam de la Halle (Wiesbaden, Oct. 28, 1951); *David,* opera in 5 acts and 12 scenes (Jerusalem, June 1, 1954, to celebrate the establishment of Jerusalem as the capital of Judea); *La Mère coupable,* to a libretto by Madeleine Milhaud, after Beaumarchais (Geneva, June 13, 1966); *Saint Louis, Roi de France,* opera-oratorio to the poem by Paul Claudel (1970–71; Rio de Janeiro, April 14, 1972). *Jeux d'enfants* (short plays for children for voice and instruments); *À propos de bottes* (1932), *Un Petit Peu de musique* (1933), *Un Petit Peu d'exercise* (1937).

BALLETS: *L'Homme et son désir* (Paris, June 6, 1921); *Le Bœuf sur le toit* (Paris, Feb. 21, 1920); *Les Mariés de la Tour Eiffel* (Paris, June 19, 1921; with Honegger, Auric, Poulenc, and Tailleferre); *La Création du monde* (Paris, Oct. 25, 1923); *Salade,* "ballet chanté" (Paris, May 17, 1924); *Le Train bleu,* "danced operetta" (Paris, June 20, 1924); *Polka* for a ballet, *L'Éventail de Jeanne,* homage to Jeanne Dubost, patroness of music (other numbers contributed by Ravel, Ibert, Roussel and others; Paris, June 16, 1927); *'adame Miroir* (Paris, May 31, 1948); *Jeux de printemps* (Washington, D.C., Martha Graham choreographer, Oct. 30, 1944); *The Bells,* after Poe (Chicago, April 26, 1946); *Vendange* (1952; produced 20 years

later, Nice, April 17, 1972); *La Rose des vents* (Paris, 1958); *La Branche des oiseaux* (Nice, 1965).

FOR ORCH: *Suite symphonique* No. 1 (Paris, May 26, 1914); *Suite symphonique* No. 2 (from incidental music to Paul Claudel's *Protée;* Paris, Oct. 24, 1920); 5 symphonies for small orch.: No. 1, *Le Printemps* (1917), No. 2, *Pastorale* (1918), No. 3, *Sérénade* (1921), No. 4, *Dixtuor à cordes* (1921), No. 5, *Dixtuor d'instruments à vent* (1922); 12 symphonies for large orch.: No. 1 (Chicago, Oct. 17, 1940; composer conducting); No. 2 (Boston, Dec. 20, 1946, composer conducting); No. 3, *Hymnus ambrosianus* with chorus (Paris, Oct. 30, 1947); No. 4 (Paris, May 20, 1948, composer conducting); No. 5 (Turin, Oct. 16, 1953); No. 6 (Boston, Oct. 7, 1955; composer conducting); No. 7 (Chicago, March 3, 1956); No. 8, subtitled *Rhodanienne* (Univ. of California, Berkeley, Festival, April 22, 1958); No. 9, (Fort Lauderdale, Florida, March 29, 1960); No. 10 (Portland, Oregon, April 4, 1961); No. 11, *Romantique* (1960; Dallas, Texas, Dec. 12, 1960); No. 12, *Rural* (Davis, California, Feb. 16, 1962); *Cinéma-Fantaisie sur le Bœuf sur le toit,* for violin and orch. (Paris, Dec. 4, 1920); *Caramel mou,* a shimmy, for jazz band (1920); *Cinq études,* for piano and orch. (Paris, Jan. 20, 1921); *Saudades do Brasil,* suite of dances (also for piano; 12 numbers; 1920–21); *Ballade* for piano and orch. (1921); *3 Rag Caprices* (Paris, Nov. 23, 1923); *Le Carnaval d'Aix,* for piano and orch. (N.Y., Dec. 9, 1926, composer soloist); *Deux hymnes* (1927); Violin Concerto No. 1 (1927); Viola Concerto (Amsterdam, Dec. 15, 1929); Concerto for Percussion and Small Orch. (Paris, Dec. 5, 1930); Piano Concerto No. 1 (Paris, Nov. 23, 1934); *Concertino de printemps,* for violin and orch. (Paris, March 21, 1935); Cello Concerto No. 1 (Paris, June 28, 1935); *Suite provençale* (Venice Festival, Sept. 12, 1937); *L'Oiseau* (Paris, Jan. 30, 1938); *Cortège funèbre* (N.Y., Aug. 4, 1940); Piano Concerto No. 2 (Chicago, Dec. 18, 1941, composer soloist); Concerto for 2 Pianos and Orch. (Pittsburgh, Nov. 13, 1942); *Opus Americanum* (San Francisco, Dec. 6, 1943); Clarinet Concerto (1941; Washington, Jan. 30, 1946); *Suite française* (Goldman Band, N.Y., June 13, 1945; for orch., N.Y. Philharmonic, July 29, 1945); *Cain and Abel,* for narrator and orch. (Hollywood, Oct. 21, 1945); *Le Bal martiniquais* (N.Y., Dec. 6, 1945, composer conducting); *2 Marches* (CBS, N.Y., Dec. 12, 1945); *Fête de la Victoire* (1945); Cello Concerto No. 2 (N.Y., Nov. 28, 1946); *Suite* for harmonica and orch. (1942; Paris, May 28, 1947, Larry Adler, soloist; also for violin and orch., Philadelphia, Nov. 16, 1945, Zino Francescatti, soloist); Concerto No. 3 for Piano and Orch. (Prague, May 26, 1946); Violin Concerto No. 2 (Paris, Nov. 7, 1948); *L'Apothéose de Molière,* for harpsichord and strings (Capri, Sept. 15, 1948); *Kentuckiana* (Louisville, Jan. 4, 1949); Concerto, for marimba, vibraphone, and orch. (St. Louis, Feb. 12, 1949); Piano Concerto No. 4 (Boston, March 3, 1950); Piano Concerto No. 5 (N.Y., June 25, 1956); *West Point Suite* for band (West Point, May 30, 1952); *Concertino d'hiver* for trombone and string orch. (1953); *Ouverture méditerranéenne* (Louisville, May 22, 1954); Harp Concerto (Venice, Sept. 17, 1954); Oboe Concerto (1957); Concerto No. 3 for violin and orch. (*Concerto royal,* 1958); *Aubade* (Oakland; California, March 14, 1961); *Ouverture philharmonique*

(N.Y., Nov. 30, 1962); *A Frenchman in New York* (Boston, June 25, 1963); *Odes pour les morts des guerres* (1963); *Murder of a Great Chief of State,* in memory of John F. Kennedy (Oakland, California, Dec. 3, 1963); *Pacem in terris,* choral symph. (Paris, Dec. 20, 1963); *Music for Boston* for violin and orch. (1965); *Musique pour Prague* (Prague, May 20, 1966); *Musique pour l'Indiana* (Indianapolis, Oct. 29, 1966); *Musique pour Lisbonne* (1966); *Musique pour Nouvelle Orléans* (commissioned by the New Orleans Symph. Orch., but unaccountably cancelled, and performed for the first time instead in Aspen, Colorado, Aug. 11, 1968, with Milhaud conducting); *Musique pour l'Univers Claudelien* (Aix-en-Provence, July 30, 1968); *Musique pour Graz* (Graz, Nov. 24, 1970); *Musique pour San Francisco,* "with the participation of the audience"(1971); *Suite in G* (San Rafael, California, Sept. 25, 1971); *Ode pour Jerusalem* (1972).

CHAMBER MUSIC: 18 string quartets (1912–51), of which No. 14 and No. 15 are playable together forming an octet; first performed in this form at Mills College, Oakland, California, Aug. 10, 1949); 2 violin sonatas (1911, 1917); Sonata for piano and 2 violins (1914); *Le Printemps,* for piano and violin (1918); Sonata for piano, flute, clarinet, and oboe (1918); Sonatina for flute and piano (1922); *Impromptu,* for violin and piano (1926); *3 Caprices de Paganini,* for violin and piano (1927); Sonatina for clarinet and piano (1927); *Pastorale,* for oboe, clarinet, and bassoon (1935); *Suite* for oboe, clarinet, and bassoon (1937); *La Cheminée du Roi René,* suite for flute, oboe, clarinet, horn, and bassoon (1939); Sonatina for 2 violins (1940); *Sonatine à trois,* for violin, viola, and cello (1940); Sonatina for violin and viola (1941); *Quatre Visages,* for viola and piano (1943); 2 viola sonatas (1944); *Élégie,* for cello and piano (1945); *Danses de Jacarémirim* for violin and piano (1945); Sonata for violin and harpsichord (1945); Duo for 2 violins (1945); String Trio (1947); *Aspen Serenade* for 9 instruments (1957); String Sextet (1958); Chamber Concerto, for piano, wind instruments and string quintet (1961); String Septet (1964); Piano Quartet (1966); Piano Trio (1968); *Stanford Serenade* for oboe and 11 instruments (Stanford, California, May 24, 1970); *Musique pour Ars nova* for 13 instruments, with aleatory episodes (1969); Wind Quintet (1973).

VOCAL WORKS: 3 albums of songs to words of Francis Jammes (1910–12); *7 Poèmes de la Connaissance de l'Est,* to words by Paul Claudel (1913); *3 Poèmes romantiques,* for voice and piano (1914); *Le Château,* song cycle (1914); *4 Poèmes,* for baritone, to words by Paul Claudel (1915–17); *8 Poèmes juifs* (1916); *Child poems,* to Tagore's words (1916); *Trois poèmes,* to words by Christina Rossetti (1916); *Le Retour de l'enfant prodigue,* cantata for 5 voices and orch. (1917; Paris, Nov. 23, 1922, composer conducting); *Chansons bas,* to Mallarmé's words, for voice and piano (1917); *2 Poèmes de Rimbaud* for voice and piano (1917); *Psalm 136,* for baritone, chorus, and orch. (1918); *Psalm 129,* for baritone and orch. (1919); *Les Soirées de Pétrograd,* in 2 albums: *L'Ancien Régime* and *La Révolution* (1919); *Machines agricoles,* for voice and 7 instruments, to words from a commercial catalogue (1919); *3 Poèmes de Jean Cocteau,* for voice and piano (1920); *Catalogue de fleurs,* for voice with piano or 7 instruments (1920); *Feuilles de température,* for voice and piano (1920); *Cocktail,* for voice and 3 clarinets (1921); *Psalm 126,* for chorus a cappella (1921); *4 Poèmes de Catulle,* for voice and violin (1923); *6 Chants populaires hébraïques,* for voice and piano (1925); *Hymne de Sion,* for voice and piano (1925); *Pièce de circonstance,* to words by Jean Cocteau, for voice and piano (1926); *Cantate pour louer le Seigneur,* for soli, choruses, and orch. (1928); *Pan et Syrinx,* cantata (1934); *Les Amours de Ronsard,* for chorus and small orch. (1934); *Le Cygne,* for voice and piano, to words by Paul Claudel (1935); *La Sagesse,* for voices and small orch., to words by Paul Claudel (1935; Paris Radio, Nov. 8, 1945); *Cantate de la Paix,* to words by Paul Claudel (1937); *Cantate nuptiale,* after *Song of Songs* (Marseilles, Aug. 31, 1937); *Les Deux Cités,* cantata a cappella (1937); *Chanson du capitaine,* for voice and piano (1937); *Les Quatre Éléments,* for soprano, tenor, and orch. (1938); *Récréation,* children's songs (1938); *Trois élégies,* for soprano, tenor, and strings (1939); *Incantations,* for male chorus (1939); *Quatrains valaisans,* for chorus a cappella, to Rilke's words (1939); *Cantate de la guerre,* for chorus a cappella, to Paul Claudel's words (1940); *Le Voyage d'été,* suite for voice and piano (1940); *Quatre chansons de Ronsard,* for voice and orch. (1941); *Rêves,* song cycle (1942); *La Libération des Antilles,* for voice and piano (1944); *Kaddisch,* for voice, chorus, and organ (1945); *Sabbath Morning Service,* for baritone, chorus, and organ (1947); *Naissance de Vénus,* cantata for mixed chorus a cappella (Paris Radio, Nov. 30, 1949); *Ballade-Nocturne,* for voice and piano (1949); *Barba Garibo,* 10 French folksongs with orch. (for the celebration of wine harvest in Menton, 1953); *Cantate de l'initiation* for chorus and orch. (1960); *Cantate de la croix de charité* (1960); *Invocation à l'ange Raphael* for 2 women's choruses and orch. (1962); *Adam* for vocal quintet (1964); *Cantate de Psaumes* (Paris, May 2, 1968); choral comedy, *Les Momies d'Égypte* (1972).

FOR PIANO: *Le Printemps,* suite (1915–19); 2 sonatas (1916 and 1949); *Saudades do Brasil,* 12 numbers in 2 books (1921); *Trois Rag Caprices* (1922; also for small orch.); *L'Automne,* suite of 3 pieces (1932); *Quatre Romances sans paroles* (1933); 2 sets of children's pieces: *Touches noires; Touches blanches* (1941); *La Muse ménagère,* suite of 15 pieces (1944; also for orch.); *Une Journée,* suite of 5 pieces (1946); *L'Enfant aimé,* suite of 5 pieces (also for orch.; 1948); *Le Candélabre à sept branches,* piano suite (Ein Gev Festival, Israel, April 10, 1952); *Scaramouche,* a version for 2 pianos (1939); *Le Bal martiniquais,* a version for 2 pianos (1944); etc. *Paris,* suite of 6 pieces for 4 pianos (1948); *6 Danses en 3 mouvements* for 2 pianos (Paris, Dec. 17, 1970). Film music; incidental music for plays by Claudel, Romain Rolland, etc. Milhaud publ. a collection of essays, *Études* (Paris, 1926), and an autobiography, *Notes sans musique* (Paris, 1949; in English, as *Notes without Music,* London, 1952); also *Entretiens avec Claude Rostand* (Paris, 1952), *Ma vie heureuse* (Paris, 1973).

BIBLIOGRAPHY: Paul Landormy, "Darius Milhaud," *Le Ménestrel* (Aug. 14, 21, 28, 1925); Géa Augsbourg, *La Vie de Darius Milhaud en images* (Paris, 1935); Ernst Krenek, "Darius Milhaud," in *The*

Book of Modern Composers, ed. by David Ewen (N.Y., 1942); Marion Bauer, "Darius Milhaud," *Musical Quarterly* (April 1942); Paul Collaer, *Darius Milhaud* (Antwerp, 1947); Georges Beck, *Darius Milhaud: étude suivie du catalogue chronologique complet* (Paris, 1949; a detailed list of works, with dates of composition and perfomance; with a supplement, 1957); Colin Mason, "The Chamber Music of Milhaud," *Musical Quarterly* (July 1957); Antonio Braga, *Darius Milhaud* (Naples, 1969) See also *"Modern Music"* . . . *Analytic Index,* compiled by Wayne Shirley, ed. by W. and C. Lichtenwanger (N.Y., 1976; pp. 137-139).

Millard, Harrison, American composer; b. Boston, Nov. 27, 1829; d. there, Sept. 10, 1895. He sang in the chorus of the Handel and Haydn Society as a child; then went to Italy to study voice; was a concert tenor for several years, and made tours in England with the Irish soprano Catherine Hayes. Returning to America in 1854, he became a vocal instructor, first in Boston, then (from 1856) in N.Y. He publ. about 350 songs; wrote also many church works, and an opera, *Deborah,* to an Italian libretto (not performed). He also set to music *Uncle Tom's Cabin* by Harriet Beecher Stowe.

Miller, Dayton Clarence, American physicist and flutist; b. Strongsville, Ohio, March 13, 1866; d. Cleveland, Feb. 22, 1941. After graduation from Baldwin Univ. and Princeton (D. Sc., 1890), he became prof. of physics at Case School of Applied Science (from 1893). An early interest in the flute led to his experimentation with various versions of the instrument (including a double-bass flute); he accumulated an extensive collection of flutes and various materials relating to the flute, which he left to the Library of Congress, Washington. A leading authority in the field of acoustics and light, he was president of the American Physical Society (1925-26), and of the Acoustical Society of America (1931-32), and vice-president of the American Musicological Society (1939). He publ. *The Science of Musical Sounds* (1916; revised 1926; reprinted, 1934); *Catalogue of Books and Literary Material relating to the Flute and Other Musical Instruments* (1935); *Anecdotal History of the Science of Sound to the Beginning of the 20th Century* (1935); *Sound Waves, Their Shape and Speed* (1937); etc. He also transl. and annotated Böhm's *The Flute and Flute Playing* (Cleveland, 1908; revised ed., 1922).
BIBLIOGRAPHY: H. Fletcher, *Biographical Memoir of Dayton Clarence Miller* (Washington, 1944; contains an extensive list of writings); L. E. Gilliam and W. Lichtenwanger, *The Dayton C. Miller Flute Collection: A Checklist of the Instruments* (Washington, 1961). See also *Dictionary of American Biography,* Supplement III.

Miller, Glenn, American trombonist and band leader; b. Clarinda, Iowa, March 1, 1904; perished in a plane during the war on a flight from England to France, Dec. 16, 1944. He studied at the Univ. of Colorado; went to N.Y. in 1930; in 1935 joined Ray Noble's band. He then went to Joseph Schillinger to study orchestration; began experimenting with special effects, combining clarinets with saxophones in the same register; the resultant sound became the Glenn Miller hallmark. At the outbreak of World War II, he assembled a large band and flew to England where he played for the American Air Force. A motion picture, *The Glenn Miller Story,* was produced in 1953.
BIBLIOGRAPHY: John Flower, *Moonlight Serenade: A Bio-Discography of the Glenn Miller Civilian Band* (New Rochelle, N.Y., 1972). See also G. T. Simon, in *Dictionary of American Biography,* Supplement III.

Miller, Mildred, American soprano; b. Cleveland, Dec. 16, 1924. Her parents came from Germany; the original family name was Müller. She studied at the Cleveland Institute of Music (B.M., 1946), then with Sundelius at the New England Cons. in Boston (diploma, 1948). In 1949 she went to Germany; sang with the Stuttgart Opera and with the Munich Opera. In 1950 she married the American pilot Wesley W. Posvar. Returning to the U.S. she made her debut with the Metropolitan Opera Co., N.Y., as Cherubino in *Le Nozze di Figaro* (Nov. 17, 1951).

Miller, Philip Lieson, American librarian and musicologist; b. Woodland, N.Y., April 23, 1906. He studied at the Manhattan Music School and the Juilliard School of Music, N.Y.: from 1927, in the Music Division of the N.Y. Public Library; assistant chief (1946-59); chief (1959-1966). He was one of the principal founders and first president (1966-68) of the Association for Recorded Sound Collections; 1963-64, was president of the Music Library Association. He publ. many articles and reviews, dealing especially with singers and singing, and the books, *Vocal Music* (N.Y., 1955) and *The Ring of Words. An Anthology of Song Texts* (very valuable; N.Y., 1963).

Millet, Luis, Catalan composer and conductor; b. Masnou, near Barcelona, April 18, 1867; d. Barcelona, Dec. 7, 1941. He studied with Vidiella and Pedrell; then became a choral conductor. In 1891 he founded the famous choral society "Orfeó Català," which he continued to lead until the last years of his life; was also director of the municipal music school in Barcelona; composed several orchestral fantasies on Catalan folksongs and many choral works; publ. two books on folk music; *De la canción popular catalana* and *Pel nostre ideal* (1917).
BIBLIOGRAPHY: Baltasar Sampler, *Luis Millet* (Barcelona, 1926).

Milligan, Harold Vincent, American organist and composer; b. Astoria, Oregon, Oct. 31, 1888; d. New York, April 12, 1951. He studied with Carl and Noble; was church organist in Portland, Ore., before coming to N.Y., in 1907; then taught organ at various schools and colleges; was church organist in Brooklyn and N.Y.; also lectured on American music. He publ. 4 collections of early American songs: *Pioneer American Composers* (2 vols.); *Washington Garland; The First American Composer; Colonial Love Lyrics;* also a biography of Stephen Foster (N.Y., 1920); *Stories of the Famous Operas* (N.Y., 1950); and with G. Souvaine, edited *The Opera Quiz Book* (N.Y., 1948).

Millöcker, Karl, Austrian operetta composer; b. Vienna, April 29, 1842; d. Baden, near Vienna, Dec. 31, 1899. His father was a jeweler, and Millöcker was destined for that trade, but showed irrepressible musical inclinations and learned music as a child; played the flute in a theater orchestra at 16; later took courses at the Cons. of the Gesellschaft der Musikfreunde in Vienna. Upon the recommendation of Franz von Suppé, he received a post as theater conductor in Graz (1864); produced his operettas *Der tote Gast* and *Die beiden Binder* there (both in 1865). In 1866 he returned to Vienna; from 1869 to 1883 was conductor of the Theater an der Wien; there he presented a number of his operettas, among them *Drei Paar Schuhe* (Jan. 5, 1871); *Wechselbrief und Briefwechsel,* or *Ein nagender Wurm* (Aug. 10, 1872); *Ein Abenteuer in Wien* (Jan. 20, 1873); *Gräfin Dubarry* (Oct. 31, 1879); *Apajune der Wassermann* (Dec. 18, 1880); *Die Jungfrau von Belleville* (Oct. 29, 1881); *Der Bettelstudent* (Dec. 6, 1882; his most successful work; popular also in England and America as *Student Beggar;* N.Y., Oct. 29, 1883); *Gasparone* (Jan. 26, 1884); *Der Vice-Admiral* (Oct. 9, 1886); *Die sieben Schwaben* (Oct. 29, 1887); *Der arme Jonathan* (Jan. 4, 1890; new version by Hentschke and Rixner, 1939; quite successful); *Das Sonntagskind* (Jan. 16, 1892); *Der Probekuss* (Dec. 22, 1894); *Das Nordlicht* (Dec. 22, 1896). Millöcker possessed a natural gift for melodious music; although his popularity was never as great as that of Johann Strauss or Lehár, his operettas captured the spirit of Viennese life.
BIBLIOGRAPHY: C. Preiss, *Karl Millöcker* (Vienna, 1905).

Mills, Charles, American composer; b. Asheville, N.C., Jan. 8, 1914. He studied off and on with Aaron Copland and Roy Harris; also had sessions with Sessions. His style is Baroque *à l'américaine;* he is at his best in instrumental works. Among his compositions are 3 symphonies (1940, 1942, 1955); he also composed something called *Crazy Horse Symphony* (1958); Flute Concerto (1939); Piano Concerto (1948); *Theme and Variations* for orch. (N.Y., Nov. 8, 1951); 5 string quartets; 4 violin sonatas; Concertino for Oboe and Strings; *4 Stanzas* for violin solo; *Concerto Sereno* for 8 wind instruments and several choral works.

Mills, Frederick Allen "Kerry", American composer and music publisher (composed as Kerry Mills; publishing house called F. A. Mills); b. Philadelphia, Feb. 1, 1869; d. Hawthorne, California, Dec. 5, 1904. In 1892-93 he taught violin at Univ. of Michigan; in 1895 he publ. in Detroit his own cakewalk march *Rastus on Parade;* encouraged by favorable sales, he moved to N.Y. where he became one of the most important publishers of minstrel songs, cakewalks, early ragtime, and other popular music. His own compositions were particularly successful; *At a Georgia Campmeeting* (1897) became the standard against which all other cakewalks were measured and, performed in Europe by John Philip Sousa, became popular there as well; it was roundly denounced in the Leipzig *Illustrierte Zeitung* (Feb. 5, 1903), and could well have been the inspiration for Debussy's *Golliwog's Cakewalk.* Some of his other hits also reached Europe; his *Whistling*

Rufus (1899) was publ. in Berlin as *Rufus das pfeifergigerl.*

Mills-Cockell, John, Canadian composer; b. Toronto, May 19, 1943. He studied composition and electronic music at the Univ. of Toronto and at the Royal Cons. of Music there. In 1966 he developed, in collaboration with the writer Blake Parker, artist Michael Hayden and designer Dick Zander, a method of composition and performance called Intersystems; joined the rock bands "Kensington Market" in Toronto and "Hydroelectric Streetcar" in Vancouver, utilizing the Moog Synthesizer; in 1970 organized his own band "Syrinx," a trio including electric hand drums, electric saxophone and Moog Synthesizer. He also wrote electronic music for films. His works include *Canonic Variations* for prepared piano, bassoon and stereo tape; a wind quartet; *Reverberations* for solo trombone and 2 stereo tape loops; numerous pieces for mixed media, among them *Journey Tree, Father of Light, Apaloosa-Pegasus, Hollywood Dream Trip,* and *Gold Rush.*

Milner, Anthony, English composer; b. Bristol, May 13, 1925. He studied with Herbert Fryer and R. O. Morris at the Royal College of Music, London, and privately with Mátyás Seiber. He taught at Morley College in London (1947-62); appointed to the staff of Royal College of Music, London, in 1962. In 1965 he was appointed lecturer, Univ. of London, King's College.
WORKS: *Variations* for orch. (1958); *Divertimento* for string orch. (1961); *April Prologue* for orch. (1961); *Sinfonia pasquale* for string orch. (1963); Symph. (1964); cantatas: *Salutatio Angelica* (1948), *The City of Desolation* (1955), *St. Francis* (1956), *The Water and the Fire* (1961); Quartet for oboe and strings (1953); String Quartet (1964); Quintet for wind instruments (1964); sacred choruses a cappella; song cycles; He publ. *Harmony for Class Teaching* (2 vols.; 1950).

Milojević, Miloje, Serbian composer and writer on music; b. Belgrade, Oct. 27, 1884; d. there, June 16, 1946. He was taught piano by his mother; then entered the Serbian school at Novi Sad. Returning to Belgrade after graduation (1904), he became a student of literature at Belgrade Univ. and a pupil at the Serbian School of Music. In 1907 he married the singer **Ivanka Milutinović;** they settled in Munich until 1910; Milojević served at the headquarters of the Serbian Army in 1914. From 1917-19 he was in France; from 1919 again in Belgrade. He publ. a school manual, *Elements of the Art of Music* (1922). As a composer, he wrote mostly in small forms; was influenced successively by Grieg, Strauss, Debussy, and Russian modernists; his music contains an original treatment of Balkan folksongs. His piano suite, *Grimaces rythmiques* (in a modern vein), was performed at the Paris Festival on June 26, 1937. His list of works contains 89 opus numbers.
BIBLIOGRAPHY: P. Konjović, *Miloje Milojević,* in Serbian, with a summary in French (Belgrade, 1954).

Milstein, Nathan, Russian-American violinist; b. Odessa, Dec. 31, 1904. He studied violin at the Odessa

Music School; then went to St. Petersburg, where he became a pupil of Leopold Auer at the Cons. As a very young man he supported himself by giving concerts in Russia with Vladimir Horowitz. He left Russia in 1925 and went to Paris, where he established his reputation. He arrived in the U.S. in 1929; made his American debut with the Philadelphia Orch. in Oct. 1929; appeared with major orchestras in the U.S. and in Europe, eliciting much praise for his virtuoso technique and discriminating taste in the interpretation of classical violin concertos.

BIBLIOGRAPHY: B. Gavoty, *Nathan Milstein* (Geneva, 1956).

Milstein, Yakov, Russian pianist, pedagogue and writer on music; b. Voronezh, Feb. 4, 1911. He studied piano with Igumnov at the Moscow Cons., graduating in 1932. In 1935 he joined the piano faculty of the Moscow Cons. Apart from his teaching, he edited piano works of Liszt, Chopin, Brahms, Tchaikovsky and Scriabin; published a fundamental biography of Liszt in 2 vols. (Moscow, 1956; 2nd ed., 1971); monographs on Chopin and Igumnov (Moscow, 1975).

Milton, John, father of the poet; b. Stanton St. John, near Oxford, c.1563; d. London, March 1647. He was a chorister at Christ Church, Oxford (1573–77); apparently remained at Oxford for several years, and in 1585 went to London where he was admitted to the Scriveners' Company in 1600; in that year he married Sarah Jeffrey. His fine 6–part madrigal *Fayre Oriana in the Morn* was publ. in Morley's *Triumphes of Oriana* (1601); 4 anthems were publ. in Leighton's *Teares or Lamentacions* (1614); a motet and 5 anthems in Myriell's *Tristitiae remedium* (1616); and 3 psalm settings in Ravenscroft's *Whole Booke of Psalms* (1621); 3 fantasias for 5 viols, and other works, are in MS.

BIBLIOGRAPHY: E. Brennecke, Jr., *John Milton the Elder and His Music* (N.Y., 1938; with bibliography and 16 musical examples).

Milveden, (Jan) Ingmar (Georg), Swedish composer, organist and musicologist; b. Göteborg, Feb. 15, 1920. He studied cello and organ; then took a course in composition with Sven Svensson and musicology with C. A. Moberg in Uppsala; earned his doctorate in Uppsala in 1972 with the dissertation *Zu den liturgischen "Hystorie" in Schweden. Liturgie- und choralgeschichtliche Untersuchungen*. Milveden is one of the most important Swedish composers of modern church music; he is a lecturer at the Univ. of Uppsala, and organist at St. Pers Church there.

WORKS: *Serenade* for string orch. (1942); Piano Sonatina (1943); Duo for flute and piano (1953, revised 1975); Trio for flute, clarinet and viola (1955, revised 1973); *Canticula Linnaeana* for chorus a cappella (1965); *Mässa i skördetid* (*Mass of the Harvest Time*) for congregation, liturgist, 2 choruses, 2 organs, 2 orch. groups, and tape (1969); *Pezzo Concertante* for orch. (1969; Uppsala, Feb. 5, 1970); *Concerto al Fresco*, for clarinet and orch. (1970; Uppsala, Nov. 25, 1971); *Threnodia* for 3 cellos (1970); a church opera, *Vid en Korsväg* (1971; Lund, Nov. 30, 1974); *Nu . . .*, 4 Linne quotations for solo voices, chorus, and instrumental groups (1972; Ingesund, March 17, 1974); *Mag-*

nificat for 2 choral groups, organ, winds and percussion (1973); *Toccata* for organ (1973); *Tre assaggi* for solo cello (1975); choruses; songs.

Mimaroglu, Ilhan Kemaleddin, Turkish-American composer and writer on music; b. Istanbul, March 11, 1926. He studied law at the Univ. of Ankara; in 1955 traveled to the U.S. on a Rockefeller Fellowship, and settled in New York, where he studied theory with Jack Beeson and Chou Wen-chung, musicology with Paul Henry Lang, and electronic music with Vladimir Ussachevsky at Columbia Univ.; took lessons in modern composition with Stefan Wolpe, and also received inspiring advice from Edgar Varèse. He was subsequently a recipient of a Guggenheim Fellowship (1971–72). He published several books in Turkish (*Sounds of America, Jazz as an Art, 11 Contemporary Composers, A History of Music, Little Encyclopedia of Western Music*, etc.). In 1963 he began his association with the Columbia-Princeton Electronic Music Center, where he composed most of his electronic works, among them *Le Tombeau d'Edgar Poe* (1964), *Anacolutha* (1965), *Wings of the Delirious Demon* (1969), and music for Jean Dubuffet's *Coucou Bazar* (1973). He developed compositional methods viewing electronic music in a parallel to cinema, resulting in works for tape in which recorded performance dominates individual rendition. Concurrently he displayed a growing political awareness in his choice of texts, conveying messages of New Left persuasion in such works as *Sing Me a Song of Songmy*, a protest chant against the war in Vietnam (1971) and *To Kill a Sunrise* (1974). Other works include *Parodie sérieuse* for string quartet (1947); Clarinet Concerto (1950); *Metropolis* for orch. (1955); *Pièces futiles* for clarinet and cello (1958); *Epicedium* for voice and chamber ensemble (1961); *2 × e.e.* for vocal quartet, on poems of e. e. cummings (1963); *September Moon* for orch. (1967); *Music Plus One* for violin and tape (1970); *Cristal de Bohème* for percussion ensemble (1971); various piano pieces and songs.

Minchev, Georgi, Bulgarian composer; b. Sofia, Jan. 29, 1939. He studied composition with Goleminov at the Bulgarian State Cons. in Sofia, graduating in 1963; went to Moscow and studied there with Shchedrin (1968–70); in 1972 he traveled to France, Great Britain and the U.S. on a UNESCO scholarship. Returning to Bulgaria, he became chief of productions at the Committee for Television and Radio in Sofia.

WORKS: an oratorio *Starobulgarski Hroniky* (*Old Bulgarian Chronicles*) for narrator, soloists, mixed chorus, folk music chorus and orch. (Sofia, Dec. 22, 1971); *Music for 3 orch. groups* (1968); *Intermezzo and Aquarelle* for strings, 2 flutes and harpsichord (1972); *3 Poems* for mezzo-soprano and orch. (1973); *Concerto Music* for orch. (1975); Piano Concerto (1976); choral and solo songs; folksong arrangements.

Mingus, Charles, American jazz musician; b. Nogales, Arizona, April 22, 1922. He played the bass fiddle in various combos; composed jazz pieces with sophisticated titles, such as *Pithecanthropus Erectus* and many mock-sentimental ballads. See *Beneath the Un-*

derdog: *His World as Composed by Mingus* (dictated autobiography, edited by Nel King; N.Y., 1971).

Minkus, Alois (Louis), Austrian composer of ballet music; b. Vienna, March 23, 1826; d. there, Dec. 7, 1917. (The exact date of his death was established in 1976 from documentation available in the parish register and the burial records of the city of Vienna.) He was a violinist by profession; as a young man he went to Russia, where he was engaged by Prince Yusupov as leader of his serf orchestra in St. Petersburg (1853–55). From 1861 to 1872 he was concertmaster of the Bolshoi Theater in Moscow. In 1869 the Bolshoi Theater produced his ballet *Don Quixote* to the choreography of the famous Russian ballet master Petipa; its success was extraordinary, and its appeal to the Russian audiences so durable that the work retained its place in the repertory of Russian ballet companies for more than a century, showing no signs of diminishing popularity. Equally popular was his ballet *La Bayadère,* produced by Petipa in St. Petersburg in 1877; another successful ballet by Minkus was *La Fiametta or The Triumph of Love,* originally produced in Paris in 1864. From 1872 to 1885 Minkus held the post of court composer of ballet music for the Imperial Theaters in St. Petersburg; he remained in Russia until 1891; then returned to Vienna, where he lived in semi-retirement until his death at the age of 91. The ballets of Minkus never took root outside Russia, but their cursive melodies and bland rhythmic formulas suit old-fashioned Russian choreography to the airiest *entrechat.*

Minoja, Ambrosio, Italian composer and singing teacher; b. Ospedaletto, near Lodi, Oct. 22, 1752; d. Milan, Aug. 3, 1825. He taught composition at the Cons. of Milan (1814–24); publ. celebrated books of solfeggi and *Lettere sopra il canto* (Milan, 1812); wrote sacred music; a symphony; an opera, *Tito nelle Gallie* (Milan, 1787).

Mirecki, Franz, Polish composer and singing teacher; b. Cracow, April 1, 1791; d. there, May 29, 1862. He was a pupil of Hummel in Vienna (1814) and of Cherubini in Paris (1817); lived in Milan (1822–26), in Genoa (1831–38); and after that in Cracow, where he was director of a singing school.
WORKS: the operas *Cyganie* (Warsaw, May 23, 1822), *Evandro in Pergamo* (Genoa, Dec. 26, 1824), *I due forzati* (Lisbon, March 7, 1826), *Cornelio Bentivoglio* (Milan, March 18, 1844), and *Nocleg w Apeninach* (*A Night in the Apennines;* Cracow, April 11, 1845); numerous piano pieces; also publ. (in 12 vols.) 50 psalms of Benedetto Marcello with added instrumental accompaniment.

Mirouze, Marcel, French composer and conductor; b. Toulouse, Sept. 24, 1906; d. Aude (in an automobile accident), Aug. 1, 1957. He studied with Busser at the Paris Cons.; conducted the Paris Radio Orch. (1935–40) and in Monte Carlo (1940–43). He wrote an opera, *Geneviève de Paris,* for the 2,000th anniversary of the founding of the City of Paris; it was produced first as a radio play with music in 1952, and then on stage in Toulouse in the same year; also composed 2

ballets, *Paul et Virginie* (1942) and *Les Bains de Mer* (1946); 2 symph. tableaux, *Afrique* (1936) and *Asie* (1938); Piano Concerto (1948); film music; piano pieces; songs.

Mirovitch, Alfred, Russian-American pianist; b. St. Petersburg, May 4, 1884; d. Whitefield, N.M., Aug. 3, 1959. He graduated from the St. Petersburg Cons. with the first prize in piano as a student of Anna Essipova in 1909; began his court career in 1911; made 9 world tours; made his American debut in 1921. He conducted master classes in piano at the Juilliard School of Music, N.Y. (1944–52); then joined the faculty of Boston Univ. He edited, for G. Schirmer, Inc., a number of collections of classical piano music for students: *Early Classics for the Piano; Introduction to Piano Classics* (3 vols. for different grades); *Introduction to the Romantics; Introduction to the Study of Bach* (2 vols.); *Introduction to Chopin* (2 vols.); also edited piano pieces by Russian composers; wrote original piano compositions (*Spring Song, Toccata,* etc.).

Miry, Karel, Belgian composer; b. Ghent, Aug. 14, 1823; d. there, Oct. 5, 1889. He studied with Gevaert in Brussels; then taught at the Ghent Cons.; in 1859 became its director. He cultivated the national Flemish style of composition; he wrote 18 operas and operettas, in French and in Flemish; his opera *Bouchard d'Avesnes* (Ghent, Feb. 5, 1864) was particularly successful. But he owes his fame to the patriotic song, *De Vlaamse Leeuw,* which he wrote at the age of 22, and which became the Flemish anthem of Belgium.

Mirzoyan, Edvard, Armenian composer; b. Gori, Georgia, May 12, 1921. He studied at the Erevan Cons., graduating in 1941; then went to Moscow and entered the composition class of Litinsky at the Moscow Cons. In 1948 he was appointed instructor at the Erevan Cons.; in 1965 became prof. there. In his music he follows a lucid neo-Classical style, while his thematic materials are of native Armenian provenance. He wrote a string quartet (1947); the cantatas *Soviet Armenia* (1948) and *Lenin* (in collaboration with Arutyunian, 1950); a symph. for strings (1962, his strongest composition); songs.
BIBLIOGRAPHY: M. Ter-Simonyan, *Edvard Mirzoyan* (Moscow, 1969).

Misch, Ludwig, German-American musicologist; b. Berlin, June 13, 1887; d. New York, April 22, 1967. He studied music theory with Max Friedlaender at the Univ. of Berlin; simultaneouly took courses in law, obtaining his doctor's degree in Heidelberg in 1911. He was music critic for the *Allgemeine Musikzeitung* (1909-13); conducted theater orchestras in Berlin, Essen and Bremen. From 1921 to 1933 he was music critic of the *Berliner Lokalanzeiger.* Under the Nazi regime he conducted a Jewish Madrigal Choir in Berlin until he was sent to a concentration camp. In 1947 he emigrated to New York, where he became active as organist and musicologist. He publ. the valuable books *Johannes Brahms* (Berlin, 1922); *Beethovens-Studien* (Berlin, 1950; also in English, in an enlarged edition, Norman, Oklahoma, 1953); translated and annotated (with Donald W. MacArdle) *New Beethoven Letters* (Norman, Oklahoma, 1957).

Mischakoff, Mischa, Russian-American violinist; b. Proskurov, Russia, April 3, 1895. His original name was Mischa Fischberg; owing to a plethora of Russian Jewish violinists named Fischberg, he decided to change his name to Mischakoff, formed by adding the Russian ending "koff" to his first name, which in itself is a Russian diminutive for Michael. He studied with Leopold Auer at the St. Petersburg Cons., graduating in 1912, with a gold medal for excellence; then taught at the Cons. of Nizhni-Novgorod (1918–20); emigrated to the U.S. in 1921; became a naturalized citizen in 1927. He was concertmaster of the N.Y. Symph. Orch. (1924–27), of the Philadelphia Orch. (1927–29); of the Chicago Symph. Orch. (1930–36), of the NBC Symph. Orch. under Toscanini (1937–45), and of the Detroit Symph. Orch. (1951–68); from 1940 to 1952 he was a member of the faculty of the Juilliard School of Music, N.Y.

Misón, Luis, Spanish musician; b. Barcelona; d. Madrid, Feb. 13, 1776. He was a flutist in the Royal Chapel and the Royal Opera, Madrid (from 1748), and composed stage music; was the first to introduce the "tonadilla escénica," a sort of miniature comic opera that developed from the musical interludes in early Spanish plays; also wrote "sainetes" (dramatic dialogues) and zarzuelas (operettas); his sonatas for flute and bass are in MS.
BIBLIOGRAPHY: J. Subirá, *La Música en la Casa de Alba* (Madrid, 1927); J. Subirá, *Tonadillas teatrales ineditas* (Madrid, 1932; with musical examples); J. Subirá, *Los Maestros de la tonadilla esénica* (Barcelona, 1933; with musical examples).

Misra, Mahapurush, Indian virtuoso on the tabla; b. Calcutta, Jan. 1, 1933. He studied with eminent swamis and gurus; toured in Europe in 1959 and in the U.S. in 1961.

Missa, Edmond Jean Louis, French opera composer; b. Reims, June 12, 1861; d. Paris, Jan. 29, 1910. He studied with Massenet at the Paris Cons.; received an honorable mention for the Prix de Rome in 1881; then served as organist at St. Thomas d'Aquin.
WORKS: OPERAS: *Babette* (London, Oct. 22, 1900); *Muguette,* based on Ouida's *Two Little Wooden Shoes* (Paris, March 18, 1903; his most successful work; also performed in Germany and England); *Maguelone* (London, July 20, 1903); several other operas were produced in Paris and Reims.

Mitchell, Donald, eminent English music scholar and publishing executive; b. London, Feb. 6, 1925. He studied at Dulwich College in London (1939–42); after non-combatant wartime service (1942–45) he was co-editor (with Hans Keller) of *Music Survey* (1947–52); in 1953–57 he was London music critic of the *Musical Times.* In 1958 he was appointed music editor and adviser of Faber & Faber Ltd., book publishers; in 1965 became business manager, and in 1973, director of the firm. He edited *Tempo* (1958-62); was on the music staff of the *Daily Telegraph* (1959-64); in 1963-64

served as music adviser to Boosey & Hawkes Ltd.; in 1967 was a member of BBC Central Music Advisory Council; in 1971, visiting Professor of Music at the Univ. of Sussex; in 1973 was awarded by it an honorary M. A. degree. He lectured widely on musical subjects in the United Kingdom, U.S. and Australia; contributed articles to the *Encyclopædia Britannica* and other reference publications; was active in broadcasting plans for BBC dealing with musical subjects. As a music scholar, Mitchell made a profound study, in Vienna and elsewhere, of the life and works of Gustav Mahler; was awarded in 1961 the Mahler Medal of Honor by the Bruckner Society of America. His major work is a Mahler biography: vol. 1, *Gustav Mahler: The Early Years* (London, 1958); vol. 2, *The Wunderhorn Years* (London, 1976); other publications are *The Language of Modern Music* (London, 1963; 3rd ed., 1970), *The Faber Book of Nursery Songs* (London, 1968) and *The Faber Book of Children's Songs* (London, 1970). He edited and annotated Alma Mahler's *Gustav Mahler: Memories and Letters* (1968; 3rd revised ed., 1973); also publ. *W. A. Mozart: A Short Biography* (London, 1956). With Hans Keller he compiled the symposium, *Benjamin Britten: A Commentary on All His Works from a Group of Specialists* (London, 1952); with H. C. Robbins Landon, *The Mozart Companion* (N.Y., 1956).

Mitchell, Dwike, American jazz pianist; b. Jacksonville, Florida, Feb. 14, 1930. He studied at the Philadelphia Music Academy; formed a duo with the French horn player and bassist Willie Ruff, a Yale Univ. graduate, and together they played in night clubs with complete popular acceptance despite their academic education and ability to read music. In 1959 they gave impromptu sessions of jazz in Russia, arousing unrestrained enthusiasm among the young Soviet audiences.

Mitchell, Howard, American cellist and conductor; b. Lyons, Nebraska, March 11, 1911. His family moved to Sioux City, Iowa when he was a child, and he studied piano and trumpet before taking up the cello at Peabody Cons. in Baltimore; then enrolled in the Curtis Institute, Philadelphia, as a cello student of Felix Salmond, graduating in 1935. He was first cellist at the National Symph. Orch. in Washington (1933-46); then served as its associate conductor (1946-49) and principal conductor (1949-70).
BIBLIOGRAPHY: Hope Stoddard, *Symphony Conductors of the U.S.A.* (N.Y., 1957; pp. 119-25).

Mitchell, William John, American musicologist; b. New York, Nov. 21, 1906; d. Binghamton, N.Y., Aug. 17, 1971. He studied at Columbia Univ. (M. A., 1938); then went to Vienna for further studies (1930-32). Upon his return to N.Y. he was on the staff of Columbia Univ., serving as Chairman of the Music Dept. from 1962 to 1967; concurrently he taught at the Mannes College of Music in N.Y. (1957–68); subsequently joined the faculty of the State Univ. of N.Y. in Binghamton. Among his publications are *Elementary Harmony* (N.Y., 1939; revised, 1949); translated C. P. E. Bach's *Versuch über die wahre Art das Clavier zu spielen* (publ. N.Y., 1949, as *Essay on the True*

Art of Playing Keyboard Instruments); with F. Salzer, he ed. the *Music Forum* (a hardcover, unperiodical periodical emphasizing Schenkerian analysis; 1967–), contributed articles on the *Tristan Prelude* and a work of Orlando di Lasso). He also wrote valuable articles dealing with the evolution of chromaticism and chord symbolism.

Mitjana y Gordón, Rafael, eminent Spanish music historian; b. Málaga, Dec. 6, 1869; d. Stockholm, Aug. 15, 1921. He studied music with Eduardo Ocón in Málaga, Felipe Pedrell in Madrid, and Saint-Saëns in Paris; was employed in the Spanish diplomatic service in Russia, Turkey, Morocco, and Sweden.

WRITINGS: His most important work is the extensive contribution on the history of Spanish music in Lavignac's *Encylopédie de la musique* (Paris, 1920; Part I, vol. IV). He also wrote numerous valuable works of a critical or historical nature, including: *L'Orientalisme musical et la musique arabe; El Cancionero de Uppsala; Catalogue critique et descriptif des imprimés de musique des XVIᵉ et XVIIᵉ siècles conservés à la Bibliothèque de l'Université Royale d'Uppsala* (vol. 1 only; Uppsala, 1911; vols. 2 and 3 completed by A. Davidsson); *Don Fernando de Las Infantas teólogo y músico* (Madrid, 1918); *Estudios sobre algunos músicos españoles del siglo XVI* (Madrid, 1918); *Francisco Guerrero* (Madrid, 1922); *Cristóbal Morales* (Madrid, 1922); etc.

Mitrea-Celarianu, Mihai, Rumanian composer; b. Bucharest, Jan. 20, 1935. He studied with Rogalski, Alfred Mendelsohn, Vancea and Negrea at the Bucharest Cons. (1948-53); also took private lessons with Jora (1949-51); was a prof. of harmony and music history in Bucharest (1954-60, 1962-68); then attended summer courses in new music given by Aloys Kontarsky, Caskel and Karkoschka in Darmstadt (1968), and further studied with the "Groupe de recherches musicales" in Paris (1968-69) and with Pierre Schaeffer and Pousseur at the Paris Cons. (1968-69). His trademarks in composition are aleatory, electronic and variable scoring. WORKS: Violin Sonata (1957); Piano Sonata (1958); *Variations* for orch. (1958); Piano Sonatina (1960); *Le Chant des étoiles,* cantata for mezzo-soprano and 33 instruments (1964); *Glosă (Comment)* for solo viola (1965); *Petite histoire d'avant-monde* for small chamber ensemble (1967); *Convergences II (Colinda)* for electronic instruments and percussion (1967), *III (Idéophonie M),* aleatory music for narrator, children's choir and 19 instruments (1968), *IV* for one performer on optional instrument or variable ensemble (1968) and *V (Jeux dans le blanc)* for chorus, percussion and tape (1969); *Trei pentru cinci* for aleatorily structured orch. (in collaboration with Miereanu and Bosseur, 1969); *Seth* for 7 instruments (1969); *ZN* "idéogramme photographique" for 3, 4 or 5 performers (1971); *Signaux (Sur l'Océan U)* for 13 players (1971); *Inaugural 71,* "action" for a flutist, with electro-acoustical devices and a projector (1971); *Piano de matin (Écoute pour Anne Frank),* "action" for 5 instruments, 5 persons manipulating divergent sound sources, electro-acoustical devices, and projec-

tors (1972); *Prérève* for voice, harpsichord, flute and percussion (1975); songs.

Mitropoulus, Dimitri, celebrated Greek conductor and composer; b. Athens, March 1, 1896; d. while on the podium conducting a La Scala rehearsal of Mahler's Third Symphony, Milan Nov. 2, 1960. He studied composition with Armand Marsick, the Belgian musician who spent many years in Greece, at the Odeon in Athens; wrote an opera after Maeterlinck, *Soeur Béatrice* (1918), performed at the Odeon (May 20, 1919); in 1920, after graduation from the Odeon, he went to Brussels, where he studied composition with Paul Gilson, and in 1921 to Berlin, where he took piano lessons with Busoni; served as an assistant conductor at the Berlin Opera (1921-24); then returned to Greece, where he became conductor of the municipal orch. in Athens. In 1930 he was invited to conduct a concert of the Berlin Philharmonic; when the soloist Egon Petri became suddenly indisposed, Mitropoulos substituted for him as soloist in Prokofiev's Piano Concerto No. 3, conducting from the keyboard (Feb. 27, 1930). He played the same concerto in Paris in 1932, as a pianist-conductor, and later in the U.S. His Paris debut as a conductor (1932) obtained a spontaneous success; he conducted the most difficult works from memory, which was a novelty at the time; also led rehearsals without a score. He made his American debut with the Boston Symph. on Jan. 24, 1937, with immediate acclaim; that same year he was engaged as permanent conductor of the Minneapolis Symph. Orch.; there he frequently performed modern music, including works by Schoenberg, Alban Berg, and other representatives of the atonal school; the opposition that naturally arose was not sufficient to offset his hold on the public as a conductor of great emotional power. He resigned from the Minneapolis Symph. in 1949 to accept the post of conductor of the N.Y. Philharmonic; shared the podium with Stokowski for a few weeks, and in 1950 became musical director. In 1956 Leonard Bernstein was engaged as associate conductor with Mitropoulos, and in 1958 succeeded him as musical director. With the N.Y. Philharmonic, Mitropoulos continued his policy of bringing out important works by European and American modernists; he also introduced the innovation of programming modern operas (*Elektra, Wozzeck*) in concert form. A musician of astounding technical ability, Mitropoulos became very successful with the general public as well as with the musical vanguard whose cause he so boldly espoused. While his time was engaged mainly in the U.S., Mitropoulos continued to appear as guest conductor in Europe; also appeared on numerous occasions as conductor at the Metropolitan Opera House and at various European opera theaters. He became an American citizen in 1946. Mitropoulos was one of the earliest among Greek composers to write in a distinctly modern idiom. WORKS: a violin sonata entitled *Ostinata,* in a nearly precise Schoebergian idiom (1925-26) *Burial* for orch. (1925); Concerto Grosso for orch. (1928); *Concert Piece* for violin and piano (1913); Piano Sonata (1915); *Fauns* for string quartet (1915); *Piano Piece* (1925); *Passacaglia, Preludio e Fuga* for piano (c. 1925); *10 Inventions* for soprano and piano (1926);

4 Dances from Cythera for piano (1926); incidental music for *Electra* and *Hippolytus* (1936, 1937).

BIBLIOGRAPHY: Harold Schonberg, *The Great Conductors* (N.Y., 1968).

Mitsukuri, Shukichi, Japanese composer; b. Tokyo, Oct. 21, 1895; d. Chigasaki, Kanagawa Prefecture, May 10, 1971. He graduated in applied chemistry from the engineering dept. of the Imperial Univ. in Tokyo in 1921; then went to Berlin and studied composition with Georg Schumann; returned to Japan in 1925 and became an Imperial Navy engineering officer. In 1930 he founded a contemporary Japanese composers' society "Shinko Sakkyokuka;" in 1954, was appointed a prof. at the Music Academy in Tokyo.
WORKS: *Sinfonietta Classica* (Paris, March 6, 1936); *10 Haikai de Basho* for orch. (Paris, Dec. 10, 1937); *Elegy* for chorus and orch. (1949); Symphony No. 1 (Tokyo, Aug. 22, 1951); Symphony No. 2 (1963); Piano Concertino (Tokyo, Aug. 22, 1953); Piano Concerto (Tokyo, April 23, 1955); Violin Sonata (1935); Piano Quintet (1955); *Night Rhapsody* for piano (1935); other piano pieces; 3 albums of Japanese folk songs (1950, 1954, 1955).

Mittelmann, Norman, Canadian baritone; b. Winnipeg, May 25, 1932. He studied with Martial Singher at the Curtis Institute in Philadelphia, and with Lotte Lehmann in Santa Barbara, Calif. He was a member of the staff of the Toronto Opera. On Oct. 28, 1961 he made his debut in a minor role at the Metropolitan Opera.

Mitterer, Ignaz Martin, Austrian composer of church music; b. St. Justina, Feb. 2, 1850; d. Brixen, Aug. 18, 1924. He studied singing with his uncle, Anton Mitterer; piano and organ with B. Huber; was ordained priest in 1874; studied again (1876–77) at the Kirchenmusikschule in Regensburg with F. X. Haberl; Kapellmeister at the Cathedral there (1882–84); then at the Cathedral in Brixen. He won for himself a distinguished place among modern masters of the Palestrina style; wrote more than 200 opus numbers for the church; publ. *Praktischer Leitfaden für den römischen Choralgesang* (1896), *Die wichtigsten kirchlichen Vorschriften für Kirchenmusik* (4th ed., 1905), *Praktische Chor-Singschule* (4th ed., 1908), *Vademecum für Harmoniumspieler,* etc.

Mitterwurzer, Anton, famous Austrian baritone; b. Sterzing, April 12, 1818; d. Döbling, near Vienna, April 2, 1876. He was a nephew of Gänsbacher, and studied with him; after serving as chorister at St. Stephen's, Vienna, he sang in Austrian provincial theaters. In 1839 he was engaged by the Dresden Court Opera, and remained there for 30 years, until he was pensioned in 1870. He was particularly notable in Wagnerian roles.

Mittler, Franz, Austrian composer and pianist; b. Vienna, April 14, 1893; d. Munich, Dec. 28, 1970. Studied there with Heuberger and Prohaska; later in Cologne with Fritz Steinbach and Carl Friedberg. From 1921 to 1938 he lived in Vienna as pianist and accompanist; in 1939 went to America, and settled in N.Y.

WORKS: opera, *Rafaella* (Duisburg, 1930); Piano Trio; a number of piano pieces. In America he wrote numerous popular songs (*In Flaming Beauty, From Dreams of Thee, Soft Through My Heart, Over the Moutains*); also light piano suites: *Manhattan Suite, Suite in 3/4 Time, Newsreel Suite, Boogie-Woogie, Waltz in Blue, One-Finger Polka.*
BIBLIOGRAPHY: Diana Mittler Battipaglia, *Franz Mittler: Composer, Pedagogue and Practical Musician* (Univ. of Rochester, 1974).

Mittmann, Paul, German composer of choral music; b. Habelschwerdt, June 18, 1868; d. Breslau, Jan. 11, 1920. He studied with G. Kothe at the seminary in Habelschwerdt, and later with Riemenschneider; served as church organist in Breslau; also music critic for the *Breslauer Zeitung.* He wrote a number of fine male and mixed choruses (several in Silesian dialect), and some 150 opus number for the church.

Miyagi, Michio, Japanese virtuoso on the koto and composer; b. Kobe, April 7, 1894; d. near Tokyo (in a railroad accident), June 25, 1956. He lost his eyesight at the age of 7; instructed in koto playing by a blind musician named Nakajima; in 1908 went to Korea; in 1917 moved to Tokyo, where he remained most of his life. In 1918 he introduced a koto with 17 strings. He was named a member of the Academy of Fine Arts in Tokyo in 1948; was the Japanese delegate at the Folk Music and Dance Festival in Europe in 1953. He composed more than 1,000 works for the koto and for other Japanese instruments; all of these are descriptive of poetic moods, or suggest a landscape. His concerto for koto, flute, and orch., entitled *Haru no Umi (Sea at Springtime)* was presented by André Kostelanetz with the N.Y. Philharmonic on Dec. 31, 1955, with Shinichi Yuize, a member of the Kabuki Dance Group, as soloist on the koto. Other works are: *Variations on Etenkagu,* for koto and orch. (1925); *Ochiba no Odori (Dance of Falling Leaves)* for koto solo; etc. He also publ. a book, *Ame no Nembutsu (Prayers for Rain).*

Miyoshi, Akira, Japanese composer; b. Tokyo, Jan. 10, 1933. He joined Jiyû-Gakuen children's piano group at the age of 3, graduating at the age of 6. He studied French literature; in 1951 began to study music with Hirai, Ikenouchi and the French musician Raymond Gallois-Montbrun who was in Tokyo at that time. He obtained a stipend to travel to France and took lessons in composition with Henri Challan and, again, with Gallois-Montbrun (1955-57); upon return to Japan, he resumed his studies in French literature at the Univ. of Tokyo, obtaining a degree in 1961. In 1965 he was appointed instructor at the Toho Gakuen School of Music in Tokyo.
WORKS: 2 poetical dramas: *Happy Prince* (1959) and *Ondine* (1959); *Symphonie Concertante* for piano and orch. (1954); *Mutation symphonique* (1958); *3 Mouvements symphoniques* (1960); Piano Concerto (1962); *Duel* for soprano and orch. (1964); Concerto for Orch. (Tokyo, Oct. 22, 1964); Violin Concerto (1965); *Odes metamorphosées* for orch. (1969); Concerto for Marimba and String Ensemble (1969); 2 works of musical poesy: *The Red Mask of the Death I*

for narrator, orch. and electronic sound (1969); and *II* for voice, chorus, orch. and electronic sound (1970); *Ouverture de Féte* (1973); Sonata for clarinet, bassoon, and piano (1953); Violin Sonata (1954-55); Sonata for flute, cello and piano (1955), *Torse I* for chamber orch. (1959), *II* for chorus, piano, electone and percussion (1962), *III* for solo marimba (1968), *IV* for string quartet and 4 Japanese instruments (1972) and *V* for 3 marimbas (1973); 2 string quartets (1962, 1967); *Conversation*, suite for solo marimba (1962); *8 Poèmes* for flute ensemble (1969); *Transit* for electronic and concrete sounds, percussion and keyboard instruments (1969); *Hommage à musique de chambre, I, II, III* and *IV* for flute, violin and piano (1970, 1971, 1972, 1974); *Nocturne* for marimba, percussion, flute, clarinet and double bass (1973); *Protase de loin à rien* for 2 guitars (1974); Piano Sonata (1958); *In Such Time*, suite for piano (1960); *Études en forme de Sonate* for piano (1967); choruses; songs.

Mizelle, John, American avant-garde composer; b. in Stillwater, Oklahoma, June 14, 1940. He studied at the Sacramento State College (B.A., 1965) and at the Univ. of California in Davis (M.A., 1967) where he took courses with Larry Austin, Jerome Rosen, Karlheinz Stockhausen, Richard Swift, and David Tudor. He later joined the staff at Davis as associate prof. in music. He is a professional trombone player and a member of the New Music Ensemble. In his music he affects technological associations; uses graphic notation.
WORKS: *Piano Opus* (1966); *Light Sculpture* (1967); *Radial Energy I* (1967); *Mass for Voices and Electronics* (1967); *Tangential Energy II* (1968); *Wave Forms* (1968).

Mizler, Lorenz Christoph, German music scholar; b. Heidenheim, Württemberg, July 25, 1711; d. Warsaw, March, 1778. He was a pupil of J. S. Bach (clavier and composition) from 1731 to 1734; *magister* of Leipzig Univ. with his *Dissertatio, quod musica ars sit pars eruditionis philosophiae* (1734; 2nd ed., 1736); then was lecturer in philosophy at Leipzig Univ. (1736-43); established the Societät der musikalischen Wissenschaften (1738); from 1743, private tutor in Warsaw; was ennobled by the Polish Court as Mizler von Kolof. His *Neu eröffnete musikalische Bibliothek* (1739-54) was one of the earliest musical periodicals. He publ. *Die Anfangsgründe des Generalbasses, nach mathematischer Lehrart abgehandelt* (1739); a translation of Fux's *Gradus* as *Gradus ad Parnassum, oder Anführung zur regelmässigen musikalischen Composition* (1742); etc.
BIBLIOGRAPHY: F. Wöhlke, *Lorenz Christoph Mizler* (Berlin, 1940).

Mlynarski, Emil, Polish conductor and composer; b. Kibarty, July 18, 1870; d. Warsaw, April 5, 1935. He studied at the St. Petersburg Cons. (1880-89), taking up both the violin, with Leopold Auer, and piano with Anton Rubinstein; also took a course in composition with Liadov. He embarked on a career as a conductor; in 1897 he was appointed principal conductor of the Warsaw Opera, and concurrently conducted the concerts of the Warsaw Philharmonic (1901-1905); from 1904 to 1907 he was director of the Warsaw Cons. He achieved considerable success as conductor in Scotland, where he appeared with Scottish Orch. in Glasgow and Edinburgh. From 1929 to 1931 he taught conducting at the Curtis Institute of Music in Philadelphia; in 1931 returned to Warsaw. He composed some effective violin music, including 2 concertos, of which the first won the Paderewski prize (1898). He also composed a comic opera *Noc letnia* (*Summer Night*; Warsaw, March 29, 1924).

Moberg, Carl Allan, Swedish musicologist; b. Östersund, June 5, 1896. He studied with Norlind at the Univ. of Uppsala (1917-24); then took some lessons with Alban Berg in Vienna, and took a course in musicology with Peter Wagner in Freiburg, Switzerland (1924-27). Returning to Sweden, he was prof. at the Univ. of Uppsala (1927-61). Among his signal achievements was a journey to Lapland in the north to collect native songs. He was honored with a Festschrift on his 65th birthday in 1961. Most of his writings deal with Swedish music history; among them are *Über die schwedischen Sequenzen* (2 vols., Uppsala, 1927); *Tonkonstens historia i Västerlandet* (2 vol., 1935); *Buxtehude* (1945); *Die liturgische Hymnen in Schweden* (1947); *Musikens historia i Västerlander intill 1600* (Oslo, 1973).

Mocquereau, Dom André, distinguished French scholar; authority on Gregorian chant; b. La Tessoualle, near Cholet (Maine-et-Loire), June 6, 1849; d. Solesmes, Jan. 18, 1930. In 1875 he joined the Order of Benedictines at the Abbey of Solesmes, devoted himself to the study of Gregorian chant under the direction of Dom Pothier, and became teacher of choral singing in the Abbey. After the expulsion, in 1903, of the Order from France, they found a refuge of the Isle of Wight (Quarr Abbey, Ryde), where Mocquereau then became prior; later he returned to Solesmes. He was the founder and editor of the capital work *Paléographie musicale*, of which 17 volumes appeared between 1889 and 1958. Works by Mocquereau include *Le Nombre musical grégorien ou rythmique grégorienne* (very valuable; 1908-27); *L'Art grégorien, son but, ses procédés, ses caractères; Petit traité de psalmodie; La Psalmodie romaine et l'accent latin* (1895); *Notes sur l'influence de l'accent et du cursus tonique latins dans le chant ambrosien* (1897); *Méthode de chant grégorien* (1899).
BIBLIOGRAPHY: F. Kosch, in the *Zeitschrift für Musikwissenschaft* 12; J. Ward, *De greg. Zangen naar Dom Mocquereau* (Doornik, 1929); J. A. de Donostia, *À propos du nombre musical grégorien de Dom Mocquereau* (Paris, 1930); Maurice Blanc, *L'Enseignement musical de Solesmes* (Paris, 1953; chapter 3); see also special issues of the *Gregorian Review* (Jan.-Feb. 1955) and *Revue Grégorienne* (Jan.-April 1955).

Moeck, Hermann, German music publisher and instrument maker; b. Elbing, July 9, 1896. He established his publishing business in Celle in 1930; in 1960 he handed it over to his son **Hermann Moeck, Jr.** (b. Lüneburg, Sept. 16, 1922); the firm was influential in the revival of the vertical flute (recorder) and also in the manufacture of violas da gamba, quintfidels and other old stringed instruments; Moeck's firm publ. numerous arrangements and authentic pieces by old and modern composers for recorders of various sizes and for the theretofore obsolete fidels. The firm possesses one of the greatest collections of old instruments. Hermann Moeck, Jr., wrote a valuable dissertation *Ursprung und Tradition der Kernspaltflöten der europäischen Folklore und die Herkunft urgeschichtlichen Kernspaltflötentypen* (2 vols., 1951).

Moeller, Mathias, Danish organ builder; b. Bornholm, Denmark, Sept. 29, 1855; d. Hagerstown, Maryland, April 13, 1937. He came to the U.S. in 1872 and established a factory in Hagerstown, Maryland, which became the largest organ factory in the world and built the organs for West Point, the New York Hippodrome, etc. Moeller contributed a number of important improvements to the construction of the organ.

Moeran, Ernest John, English composer of Irish descent; b. Heston, Middlesex, Dec. 31, 1894; d. Kenmare, County Kerry, Ireland, Dec. 1, 1950. His father was a clergyman, and he learned music from hymnbooks; then studied at the Royal College of Music; was an officer in the Bristish Army in World War I, and was wounded. Returning to London, he took lessons in composition with John Ireland (1920-23); also became interested in folk music; collected numerous folksongs in Norfolk, some of which were publ. by the Folksong Society (1922). Most of his compositions were inspired by simple folk patterns; his folksong arrangements are aptly made and are authentic in feeling.
WORKS: 2 Rhapsodies for orch. (1st, Manchester, 1924; 2nd, Norwich Festival, 1924); Symph. in G minor (London, Jan. 13, 1938); Violin Concerto (London, July 8, 1942); *Rhapsody* for piano and orch. (London, Aug. 19, 1943); Cello Concerto (Dublin, Nov. 25, 1945; with Moeran's wife, **Peers Coetmore,** as soloist); *Serenade* in G major for orch. (London, Sept. 2, 1948); Quartet for oboe and strings (1946); Cello Sonata (1947); piano and organ works; many songs.
BIBLIOGRAPHY: S. Wild, *E. J. Moeran* (1973).

Moeschinger, Albert, Swiss composer; b. Basel, Jan. 10, 1897. He studied in Bern, Leipzig, and Munich. In his works he shows influences of German neo-Romanticism and French Impressionism. A prolific composer, he has written some 100 opus numbers; his works include 3 symphonies; 3 piano concertos; Violin Concerto; 6 string quartets; 2 piano trios; Quintet for clarinet and strings; 2 trios for flute, clarinet, and bassoon; 2 cello sonatas; Sonata for violin and organ; *Variations mystérieuses* for chamber orch. (1977); *Blocs sonores* for orch. (1977); many pieces for piano, organ, etc.; canatas and other choral works.

Moevs, Robert W., American composer; b. La Crosse, Wisconsin, Dec. 2, 1921. He studied at Harvard Univ. (A. B., 1942); after service as a pilot in the U.S. Air Force, he took courses in Paris with Nadia Boulanger (1946–51); was a Fellow at the American Academy in Rome (1952–55); returning to the U.S. he was on the music faculty at Harvard Univ. (1955–63); from 1963, prof. of music at Rutgers Univ. in New

Brunswick, New Jersey. His music is marked by sonorous exuberance and rhythmic impulsiveness; his use of percussion is plangent. He favors ornamental variation forms.
WORKS: *14 Variations for Orchestra* (Boston, April 6, 1956); *Symphony in Three Movements* (Cleveland, April 10, 1958); *Attis* for orch. with chorus and tenor solo (Boston, Feb. 24, 1960); *Et Occidentem Illustra* (Boston, Feb. 24, 1967); Piano Concerto (1960); *Cantata sacra* for baritone, male chorus, flute, 4 trombones and timpani, to a Latin text from the Easter liturgy (1952); *Musica da camera* for chamber orch. (1968); *Pan* for unaccompanied flute (1951); *Fanfara canonica* for 6 trumpets (1966); numerous choral works and solo songs.

Moffat, Alfred Edward, Scottish music editor and arranger; b. Edinburgh, Dec. 4, 1863; d. London, June 9, 1950. He studied with L. Bussler in Berlin (1882-88); then went to London where he became active as editor of violin music by old English composers; publ. the series *Old English Violin Music* (London) and *Meisterschule der alten Zeit* (Berlin); numerous arrangements: *The Minstrelsy of Scotland* (200 Scottish songs); *The Minstrelsy of Ireland; 40 Highland Reels and Strathspeys; Songs and Dances of All Nations* (with J. D. Brown); various other editions of string and vocal music; etc.

Moffo, Anna, American soprano; b. Wayne, Pennsylvania, June 27, 1932, of Italian parentage. She studied voice at the Curtis Institute of Music in Philadelphia; later went to Italy on a Fulbright fellowship studying at the Accademia de Santa Cecilia in Rome. She made her debut in Rome and, progressing rapidly in her career, was engaged at La Scala, Milan, at the Vienna State Opera and in Paris. Returning to America, she sang with the Chicago Lyric Opera; on Nov. 14, 1957, made her debut at the Metropolitan Opera in N.Y. as Violetta, obtaining a gratifying success; she continued to sing regularly at the Metropolitan Opera, earning a stellar reputation for both her singing and acting ability.

Mohaupt, Richard, German composer; b. Breslau, Sept. 14, 1904; d. Reichenau, Austria, July 3, 1957. He studied with J. Prüwer and R. Bilke; began his musical career as an opera conductor; also gave concerts as pianist. After the advent of the Nazi regime in 1933 he was compelled to leave Germany because his wife was Jewish; settled in New York in 1939, and continued to compose; was also active as a teacher. In 1955 he returned to Europe.
WORKS: OPERAS: *Die Wirtin von Pinsk* (Dresden, Feb. 10, 1938), *Die Bremer Stadtmusikanten* (Bremen, June 15, 1949), *Double Trouble* (Louisville, Dec. 4, 1954), *Der grüne Kakadu* (Hamburg, Sept. 16, 1958); BALLETS: *Die Gaunerstreiche der Courasche* (Berlin, Aug. 5, 1936), *Lysistrata* (1946), *The Legend of the Charlatan,* pantomime (1949), *Max und Moritz,* dance-burlesque, after Wilhelm Busch (Karlsruhe, Dec. 18, 1950); Symphony (N.Y. Philharmonic, March 5, 1942); *Stadtpfeifermusik* (London Festival of the International Society for Contemporary Music, July 7, 1946); *Bucolica,* for double chorus and orch. (1948);

Trilogy for contralto solo and orch. (1951); Violin Concerto (N.Y. Philharmonic, April 29, 1954); chamber music; songs; piano pieces.

Moiseiwitsch, Benno, pianist; b. Odessa, Feb. 22, 1890; d. London, April 9, 1963. Studied there, and won the Anton Rubinstein prize at the age of 9; went to Vienna, where he studied with Leschetizky. He made his debut in Reading, England, on Oct. 1, 1908, and subsequently made London his home; made his American debut in N.Y. on Nov. 29, 1919, and toured many times in Australia, India, Japan, etc. He represented the traditional school of piano playing, excelling mostly in Romantic music.
    BIBLIOGRAPHY: M. Moiseiwitsch, *Benno Moiseiwitsch* (London, 1965).

Mojsisovics, Roderich von, Austrian composer; b. Graz, May 10, 1877; d. there, March 30, 1953. He studied with Degner in Graz, with Wüllner and Klauwell at the Cologne Cons., and with Thuille in Munich. He conducted a choral group in Brno (1903-07); then taught in various Austrian towns; was director of the Graz Cons. from 1920 till 1934. In his music he was a decided follower of Wagnerian precepts. He wrote 8 operas; 5 symphonies; a symph. poem, *Stella;* 2 overtures; a violin concerto; numerous chamber works; songs; publ. the biographies, *Max Reger* (1911) and *E. W. Degner* (1919); *Bachprobleme* (1930); etc.
    BIBLIOGRAPHY: M. Morold, *Roderich Mojsisovics* (1924).

Mokranjac, Stevan, Serbian composer; b. Negotin, Jan. 9, 1856; d. Skoplje, Sept. 28, 1914. He studied in Munich with Rheinberger, and in Leipzig with Jadassohn and Reinecke; in 1887 became director of the Serbian Choral Society in Belgrade, with which he also toured. In 1899 he founded a Serbian Music School in Belgrade, and remained its director until his death. He wrote 15 choral rhapsodies on Serbian and Macedonian melodies; a Liturgy of St. John Chrysostomos (publ. in Leipzig, 1901; also with an English transl. as *Serbian Liturgy,* London, 1919); a Funeral Service ("Opelo"); compiled a large collection of church anthems according to the Serbian usage and derived from old Byzantine modes; wrote a collection of songs for mixed chorus, *Rukoveti (Bouquets).*

Mokranjac, Vasilije, Serbian composer; b. Belgrade, Sept. 11, 1923. He was brought up in a musical enviroment (his father was a cellist, a nephew of the famous Serbian composer Stevan Mokranjac). He studied piano and composition at the Belgrade Academy of Music; his early works are romantic in style, but he gradually began experimenting with serial techniques, while safeguarding the basic tonal connotations.
    WORKS: Symph. No. 1 (Belgrade, Feb. 2, 1962); Symph. No. 2 (Belgrade, April 1, 1966); Symph. No. 3 (Belgrade, Oct. 25, 1968); *Dramatic Overture* (1950); *Concertino* for piano, string orch. and two harps (Belgrade, March 15, 1960); chamber music; piano pieces; incidental music for dramatic plays.
    BIBLIOGRAPHY: Vlastimir Peričić, *Muzički Stvaraoci u Srbiji* (Belgrade, 1969).

Mokrejs, John, American pianist, composer and teacher of Czech descent; b. Cedar Rapids, Iowa, Feb. 10, 1875; d. there, Nov. 22, 1968. He studied piano with Leopold Godowsky and theory with Adolph Weidig at the American Cons. of Music in Chicago; was active as piano teacher in New York; from 1945 to 1966 lived in Los Angeles; then returned to Cedar Rapids.
    WORKS: an opera, *Sohrab and Rustum;* an operetta *The Mayflower;* an *American Cantata* (on the life of Abraham Lincoln); Piano Trio; String Quartet; songs. He is best known, however, for his teaching pieces for piano: *Valcik (Little Waltz), Boutade, Bird Rondo, Day in Summer, Indian Dance, Harvest Moon, Military Nocturne, Moravian Lullaby, Carillon* and *Rainbow Pieces.* He also publ. instruction books: *Lessons in Sight Reading* (Chicago, 1909); *Lessons in Harmony* (N.Y., 1913); *Natural Counterpoint* (Chicago, 1941).

Mokrousov, Boris, Russian composer; b. Nizhny-Novgorod, Feb. 27, 1909; d. Moscow, March 27, 1968. He studied at the Moscow Cons. with Miaskovsky, graduating in 1936. Still as a student, he wrote an orchestral suite, *The Pioneers* (1933); a quartet for 2 trumpets and 2 trombones (1934); and a trombone concerto (1935). His graduation piece was a politically inspired work, *Anti-Fascist Symphony,* for orch., chorus, and military band (Moscow, Aug. 1, 1937). He also wrote an opera, *Tchapayev,* depicting the life of a Soviet hero.

Molchanov, Kirill, Soviet composer; b. Moscow, Sept. 7, 1922. He was attached to the Red Army Ensemble of Song and Dance during World War II; after demilitarization he studied composition with Anatoly Alexandrov at the Moscow Cons., graduating in 1949. From 1973 to 1975 he served as director of the Bolshoi Theater, and accompanied it on its American tour in 1975. He is primarily an opera composer; he is apt to select for his librettos the events of the Soviet Revolution and the war of 1941–45; the musical style of his operas closely follows the precepts of Socialist Realism.
    WORKS: operas are *The Stone Flower* (Moscow, Dec. 10, 1950); *Dawn* (1956); *Romeo, Juliet and Darkness* (1963); *The Unknown Soldier* (1967); *A Women of Russia* (1969); *The Dawns are Quiet Here* (his most successful work), to the story from the Russian struggle against the Nazis; its Moscow production at the Bolshoi Theater on April 11, 1975, became a melodramatic occasion, with the audience yielding to an unabashed display of tearful emotion; however, its American performance during the visit of the Bolshoi Theater in New York in June 1975 met with a disdainful dismissal on the part of the critics as an unoriginal piece of theatrical propaganda. Among Molchanov's other works are 3 piano concertos (1945, 1947, 1953); conatata *Song of Friendship* (1955) and *Black Box,* suite for voice, recitation and piano (1968).
    BIBLIOGRAPHY: Y. Korev, *Kirill Molchanov* (Moscow, 1971).

Moldavan, Nicolas, Russian-American viola player; b. Kremenetz, Russia, Jan. 23, 1891; d. New York,

Sept. 21, 1974. He studied at the St. Petersburg Cons., graduating in 1912. In 1918 he left Russia and went on a tour of the Far East; settled in the U.S.; was a member of the Flonzaley Quartet (1925-29); then played in the Coolidge Quartet.

Moldenhauer, Hans, German-American musicologist; b. Mainz, Dec. 13, 1906. He studied music with Dressel, Zuckmayer and Rosbaud in Mainz; was active as pianist and choral conductor there. In 1938 he went to the U.S., and settled in Spokane, Wasington; as an expert alpinist, he served in the U.S. Mountain Troops during World War II. After the end of the war he organized the Spokane Cons. (founded by him in 1942), incorporated as an educational institution in 1946. With his wife, the pianist **Rosaleen Moldenhauer,** he inaugurated a series of radio broadcasts of 2-piano music; the outgrowth of this was the publication of his valuable book *Duo-Pianism* (Chicago, 1950). As a music reseacher, he became profoundly interested in the life and works of Anton von Webern; organized 6 international Webern festivals, in Seattle (1962), Salzburg (1965), Buffalo (1966), Dartmouth College, Hanover, New Hampshire (1968), Vienna (1972) and at Louisiana State Univ., Baton Rouge (1976). His major achievement in research was the formation of the Moldenhauer Archives ("Music History from Primary Sources") embodying a collection of some 10,000 musical autographs, original manuscripts, correspondence, etc., of unique importance to musical biography. Particularly rich is the manuscript collection of works of Webern, including some newly discovered works; for this accomplishment, Moldenhauer was awarded in 1970 the Austrian Cross of Honor for Science and Art. Moldenhauer's publications concerning Anton von Webern include *The Death of Anton Webern. A Drama in Documents* (N.Y., 1961; establishes for the first time the circumstances of Webern's tragic death in 1945); *Anton von Webern: Perspectives* (Seattle, 1966): *Anton von Webern, Sketches 1926–1945* (N.Y., 1968) and *Anton von Webern: Chronicle of his Life and Work* (in collaboration with Rosaleen Moldenhauer, N.Y., 1978).

Moldovan, Mihai, Rumanian composer; b. Dej, Nov. 5, 1937. He studied with Toduța and Comes at the Cluj Cons. (1956–59); then with Vancea, Vieru and Jora at the Bucharest Cons. (1959–62); was active in various branches of the Rumanian radio and television. His music fuses a Rumanian ethos with modern harmonic textures.

Works: the cantatas *Soare al păcii* (*Sun of Peace,* 1962), *Prefigurarea primăverii,* chamber cantata, (1962), *Bocet* (1963), *6 stări de nuanță* (1966) and *Cintare omului* (1967); Oboe Concerto (1964); *Texturi,* piece for orch. (1967); *Poem* for chamber orch., with Ondes Martenot (1967); *Vitralii* (*Stained Glass Windows*), 6 pieces for orch. (1968); *Scoarțe* (*Tapestry*) for orch. (1969); *Tulnice* for 4 flutes, 8 horns, harp, 4 cellos, 4 double basses and percussion (1971); *Sinfonia* for strings (1972); Violin Sonatina (1967); String Quartet (1968); *Incantations* for clarinet and piano (1968); *Cadenza I* for trombone and percussion, *II* for solo double bass, and *III* for flute and percussion (all 1971);

Cîntece străbune (*Ancient Songs*) for soprano, flute, clarinet, horn, trumpet, trombone, piano, vibraphone, xylophone and string quintet (1972).

Molina, Antonio J., Philippine composer and conductor; b. Quiapo, Manila, Dec. 26, 1894; received his primary education at the Boy's Catholic School in his native town; then studied with Bibiano Morales in Manila; founded and directed a string group, Rondalla Ideal; also was engaged as conductor of various theater and cinema orchestras in Manila; wrote popular waltzes; then began to compose more ambitious theater music; conducted at Manila the première of his lyric drama *Ritorna Vincitor* (March 10, 1918) and his zarzuelas, *Panibuglo* (*Jealousy*; April 16, 1918) and *Ang Ilaw* (Nov. 23, 1918); in 1925 became teacher of harmony at the Univ. of the Philippines; in 1934 joined the staff of the President's Committee on Filipino Folksongs and Dances; wrote a Christmas carol for mixed chorus and orch., *The Living Word* (Manila, Dec. 18, 1936); a quintet for piano and strings, based on native folksongs (Manila, Jan 21, 1950); also numerous piano pieces and songs.

Molinari, Bernardino, eminent Italian conductor; b. Rome, April 11, 1880; d. there, Dec. 25, 1952. He studied with Falchi and Renzi at the Liceo di Santa Cecilia in Rome; in 1912, became conductor of the Augusteo orch. in Rome; also conducted throughout Europe and South America. In 1928 he made his American debut with the N.Y. Philharmonic, which he conducted again during the 1931–32 season; also appeared with other American orchestras. He was a champion of the modern Italian school, and brought out many works by Respighi, Malipiero, and other outstanding Italian composers; publ. a new ed. of Monteverdi's *Sonata sopra Sonata Maria* (1919) and concert transcriptions of Carissimi's oratorio *Giona,* Vivaldi's *Le quattro stagioni,* etc.; also orchestrated Debussy's *L'Isle joyeuse.*

BIBLIOGRAPHY: E. Mucci, *Bernardino Molinari* (Lanciano, 1941).

Molinari, Pradelli Francesco, Italian conductor; b. Bologna, July 4, 1911. He studied in Bologna and in Rome. In 1946 he conducted at La Scala in Milan; in 1951 he was guest conductor in London; also conducted opera at San Carlo, Naples; from 1957 led successful opera performances in San Francisco and Los Angeles. He is particulary renowned for his interpretations of Wagner and Puccini.

Molique, Wilhelm Bernhard, German violinist and composer; b. Nuremburg, Oct. 7, 1802; d. Cannstadt, near Stuttgart, May 10, 1869. He first studied with his father; King Maximilian I, hearing of his uncommon gifts, sent him to Munich (1816) to study with Rovelli, concertmaster of the Munich Court orch.; he succeeded Rovelli in that post in 1820; in 1826 he became concertmaster of the Stuttgart orch., with the title "Musikdirektor." He won fame abroad with extended tours in Holland, Russia, England, and France. The political crisis of 1849 caused him to settle in London, where he remained until 1866; then returned to Germany. His works include 6 violin concertos; 8 string quartets; pieces for violin and piano, and for violin and flute; fantasias, rondos, etc., for solo violin; etc.

BIBLIOGRAPHY: Fritz Schröder, *Bernhard Molique und seine Instrumentalkompositionen* (Stuttgart, 1923).

Molitor, Rapheal, German musicologist; b. Sigmaringen, Feb. 2, 1873; d. Beuron, Oct. 14, 1948. He was the son of Johann Baptist Molitor, cathedral organist; studied philosophy and theology in the Benedictine Monastery of Beuron; ordained priest in 1897; lectured there on canon law (1898-1904); in 1904, was appointed a member of the advisory board of the *Editio Vaticana.* He was one of the foremost authorities on Gregorian Chant.

WORKS: *Reformchoral* (1901), *Die nach-tridentinische Choralreform zu Rom* (2 vols., 1901; 1902), *Choralweigendrucke, Der gregorianische Choral als Liturgie und Kunst, Josef Rheinberger,* etc.; contributed important articles to the *Gregoriusblatt, Kirchenmusikalisches Jahrbuch, Sammelbände der Internationalen Musik-Gesellschaft,* etc.

Möllendorff, Willi von, German pianist and composer; b. Berlin, Feb. 28, 1872; d. Stettin, April 27, 1934. He studied with Bargiel at the Berlin Hochschule für Musik (1891-93); was subsequently active as pianist and theater conductor in Giessen, Berlin, and finally Stettin. He was known especially for his experimentation with quarter-tones, for the exposition of which he invented a bichromatic harmonium with a new keyboard. For this instrument he composed an *Adagio religioso* (with cello solo); also *5 kleine Stücke.* In addition, he wrote operas, a ballet, 2 symphonies, choral works, etc.

Mollenhauer, Eduard, German violinist; b. Erfurt, April 12, 1827; d. Owatoma, Minnesota, May 7, 1914. He was a violin pupil of Ernst (1841) and Spohr (1843); after a brief concert career in Germany, he went to London, where he joined Jullien's Orch., of which an older brother, **Friedrich Mollenhauer** (1818-85), also a violinist, was a member; after a tour with Jullien's Orch. in the U.S. (1853), the brothers settled in New York as teachers; Eduard Mollenhauer also appeared as a soloist with the N.Y. Philharmonic Society. He wrote operas *The Corsican Bride* (N.Y., 1861) and *Breakers* (N.Y., 1881); 3 symphonies; a violin concerto; solo pieces for violin (*La Sylphide,* etc.); songs.

Mollenhauer, Emil, American violinist and conductor; son of **Friedrich Mollenhauer;** b. Brooklyn, Aug. 4, 1855; d. Boston, Dec. 10, 1927. He studied violin with his father; in 1872 entered Theodore Thomas' orch.; then joined the Damrosch Orch.; from 1885 to 1888 was a member of the Boston Symph. Orch.; then assumed the conductorship of the Boston Festival Orch., and toured the U.S. with it, featuring many celebrated soloists (Calvé, Nordica, Melba, Campanari, Joseffy, Ysaÿe, Marteau, etc.). In 1899 he was elected conductor of the Boston Handel and Haydn Society, which he led until 1927.

BIBLIOGRAPHY: article on Mollenhauer in the *Dictionary of American Biography* (vol. 13).

Mollenhauer, Henry, German cellist; brother of **Friedrich** and **Eduard Mollenhauer;** b. Erfurt, Sept. 10, 1825; d. Brooklyn, N.Y., Dec. 28, 1889. In 1853 he was a member of the Royal Orch. in Stockholm; toured the U.S. (1856-58) with Thalberg, Gottschalk, and Carlotta Patti; then settled in Brooklyn as teacher; founded the Henry Mollenhauer Cons., which later flourished under the direction of his sons **Louis, Henry,** and **Adolph.**

Mollenhauer, Louis, American violinist; son of **Henry Mollenhauer;** b. Brooklyn, Dec. 17, 1863; d. there, Feb. 9, 1926. He studied with his uncle, **Eduard Mollenhauer;** was a member of the Mollenhauer Quintet Club; after his father's death, was director of his Cons. (1889-91); then founded his own Cons. in Brooklyn.

Möller, Heinrich, German musicologist; b. Breslau, June 1, 1876; d. Naumburg, March 3, 1958. He studied musicology with Riemann, Kretzschmar, and Friedlaender; lived in New York from 1914 to 1921; then returned to Germany. From 1937 till 1945 he was docent at the Univ. of Jena; in 1953, appointed instructor at the Hochschule für Musik in Weimar. He was editor of the valuable collection, *Das Lied der Völker* (14 vols.); also translated the librettos of operas of Mussorgsky and Rimsky-Korsakov into German.

Moller (or **Möller**), **Joachim.** See **Burck, Joachim.**

Moller, John Christopher, German composer and organist; b. 1755; d. New York, Sept. 21, 1803. In 1790 he appeared in New York as a harpsichordist, but left immediately after his concerts for Philadephia, where he became organist and composer for Zion German Lutheran Church (appointed Oct. 11, 1790) and (in 1791-92) took part in the City Concerts (with Reinagle, and later Henri Capron) both as manager and performer. Apparently he was also proficient as pianist, violinst and a performer on the glass harmonica. In 1793 he was joint proprietor, with Capron, of a music store, which was also used as a music school. Due to the destruction of Zion Church by fire on Dec. 26, 1794, Moller's income was severely reduced and, in Nov. 1795, he returned to N.Y. In 1796 he succeeded Hewitt in the management of the New York City Concerts with the Van Hagens. His attempt to continue this subscription series by himself, when Van Hagen later left for Boston, was unsuccessful.

WORKS: *6 Quartettos* (publ. in London by J. Betz); *Progressive Lessons for the Harpsichord* (op. 6, London); *Compleat Book of Instruction for the Pianoforte* (op. 6, London); *6 Sonatas for the forte piano or harpsichord, with a violin or violoncello accompaniment* (London); *12 Variations pour le clavecin* (1798); and *Sinfonia, Rondo, Overture, Quartetto* for "harmonica" (Benjamin Franklin's *armonica,* a glass harmonica), 2 violas, and cello, and *Duetti* for clarinet and piano in the first issue of Moller & Capron's *Monthly Numbers* (1793); a cantata, *Dank und Gebet . . .* (1794).

BIBLIOGRAPHY: J. T. Howard, *Our American Music* (N.Y., 1939; 4th ed., 1965); E. C. Wolf, *Lutheran Church Music in America during the 18th and Early*

19th Centuries (Univ. of Illinios, 1960; contains a copy of Moller's only extent cantata); R. D. Stetzel, *John Christopher Moller and His Role in Early American Music* (State Univ. of Iowa, 1965); E. C. Wolf, "Music in Old Zion, Philadephia, 1750–1850," *Musical Quarterly* (Oct. 1972).

Molloy, James Lyman, Irish composer of light music; b. Cornalaur, King's County, Aug. 19, 1837; d. Wooleys, Bucks, Feb. 4, 1909. His operettas (*Students' Frolic, My Aunt's Secret, Very Catching*), numerous songs (*Love's Old Sweet Song, London Bridge, The Kerry-dance, The Postilion, Punchinello,* etc.), and Irish melodies with new accompaniments enjoyed great popularity.
BIBLIOGRAPHY: *Dictionary of National Biography* (Supplement; Oxford, 1920).

Molnár, Antal, Hungarian musicologist and composer; b. Budapest, Jan. 7, 1890. He studied violin and composition with Viktor Herzfeld at the Budapest Academy; then played viola in the Waldbauer String Quartet (1910–13) and later in the Dohnányi-Hubay Piano Quartet (1917–19); subsequently for 40 years on the faculty of the Budapest Academy of Music (1919–59).
WORKS: (in Hungarian, in Budapest): *The Spirit of Music History* (1914); *Spiritual Basis of Bach and Handel* (1920); *History of European Music before 1750* (1920); *Sociology of Music History* (1923); *The New Hungarian Music* (1925); *Jazzband* (1931); a monograph on Kodály (1936); *Music and Life* (1946); *The Spirit of New Music* (1948); *The Art of Béla Bartók* (1948); *Johannes Brahms* (1959); *Repertory to the History of Baroque Music* (1959); *Papers on Music,* collection of essays (1961); *On Music* (1963); *The Léner String Quartet* (1968; also in English, Budapest, 1969); *The World of the Composer* (1969); *Practical Aesthetics of Music* (1971). He is also a prolific composer; among his works are *Savitri,* stage music (1912); *Grotesque March* for orch. (1914); Cello Concerto (1916); *Hugarian Dances* for orch. (1917); *Operetta Music* for orch. (1920); *Oriental Tale* for orch. (1921); *Budapest,* overture (1921); *Past and Present* for violin and orch. (1923); *Suite* for orch. (1925); *Variations on a Hungarian Theme* for orch. (1928); *Hungarian Comedy Overture* (1928; *Kuruc-Music* for 4 tárogatós (Hungarian instrument) and chamber orch. (1936); *Overture to a Comedy* (1948); Harp Concerto (1952); 2 piano trios (1912, 1917); 3 string quartets (1912, 1926, 1928); Wind Quintet (1926); songs; choruses; folksong arrangements.

Momigny, Jérôme-Joseph de, French music theorist; b. Philippeville, Jan. 20, 1762; d. Paris, Jul. y 1838. At 12, he was organist at St.-Omer, later at Ste.-Colombe, and 1785 at Lyons; established a music business in Paris, 1800; lived later in Tours, but returned to Paris.
WORKS: *Cours complet d'harmonie et de composition d'après une théorie neuve* (3 vols., 1806; bases the scales on the overtone series up to 13); and other books supporting his theories. In this work he lays the foundations of the theory of phrasing. Lussy, Westphal, and Hugo Riemann elaborated the principles

laid down by Momigny. He also wrote the musical articles for vol. II (1818) of Framéry's and Ginguené's *Encyclopédie méthodique,* presenting in condensed form the theories advanced in his *Cours complet* (under *Mesure, Motif, Période, Phrase, Ponctuation, Proportion, Rythme*); wrote chamber music and an opera.
BIBLIOGRAPHY: Albert Palm, *Jérôme-Joseph de Momigny* (Paris, 1957).

Mompou, Federico, significant Spanish composer; b. Barcelona, April 16, 1893. After preliminary studies at the Cons. of Barcelona he went to Paris where he studied piano with Isidor Philipp and composition with S.S. Rousseau. He returned to Barcelona during World War I; then again was in Paris until 1941, when he once more went back to Spain. He visited N.Y. in 1970, 1973, and in 1978. His music is inspired by Spanish and Catalan melos, but its harmonic and instrumental treatment is entirely modern. He wrote mostly for piano: *6 Impressions intimes* (1911–14), *Scènes d'enfants* (1915), *Suburbis* (1916–17), *3 Pessebres* (1918), *Cants magics* (1919), *Festes Llunyanes* (1920), *6 Charmes* (1921), *3 Variations* (1921), *Dialogues* (1923), a series *Canción y danza* (1918–53), *10 Preludes* (1927–51), *3 Paisajes* (1942, 1947, 1960), *Música callada* (4 albums, 1959–67); *Suite compostelana* for guitar (1963); choral works and songs.
BIBLIOGRAPHY: Santiago Kastner, *Federico Mompou* (Madrid, 1946).

Monaco, Mario del. See **Del Monaco, Mario.**

Monasterio, Jesús de, famous Spanish violinist and pedagogue; b. Potes, near Santander, March 21, 1836; d. Casar del Periedo, Sept. 28, 1903. He made his debut in 1845 in Madrid, as an infant prodigy; studied at Brussels Cons. with Bériot (violin) and with Fétis (theory). In 1857 he returned to Madrid; was appointed prof. of violin at the Madird Cons., and taught there for many years; was its director from 1894 to 1897; conducted the Sociedad de Conciertos (1869–76), and was influential in forming a taste for classical music in Spain. He publ. a number of violin pieces, some of which (e.g., *Adíos a la Alhambra*) were very popular.
BIBLIOGRAPHY: J. M. Alonso, *Jesús de Monasterio* (Santander, 1954; contains a list of works).

Moncada, Eduardo Hernández. See **Hernández Moncada, Eduardo.**

Moncayo, José Pablo, Mexican composer; b. Guadalajara, June 29, 1912; d. Mexico City, June 16, 1958. He studied with Chávez; in company with Ayala, Contreras, and Galindo (also pupils of Chávez) he formed the so-called "Grupo de Los Cuatro" for the purpose of furthering the cause of Mexican music.
WORKS: opera, *La Mulata de Córdoba* (Mexico City, Oct. 23, 1948); *Huapango* for orch. (1941), *Homenaje a Cervantes* for 2 oboes and strings (Mexico City, Oct. 27, 1947), *Cumbres* for orch. (Louisville, June 12, 1954); piano pieces, choruses.

Mondonville, Jean-Joseph Cassanea de (de Mondonville was his wife's maiden name), French violinist and composer; b. Narbonne, Dec. (baptized Dec. 25),

1711; d. Belleville, near Paris, Oct. 8, 1772. He appeared as a violinist in the Concert Spirituel, Paris (1734); wrote numerous motets for that organization; succeeded Gervais in 1744 as intendant of the "musique de la chapelle" at Versailles; was musical director of the Concert Spirituel from 1755 till 1762. He produced several operas and pastorales: *Isbé* (Paris, April 10, 1742), *Le Carnaval du Parnasse* (Sept. 23, 1749; included ballet scenes), *Titon et l'Aurore* (Paris, Jan. 9, 1753), *Daphnis et Alcimadure* (Fontainebleau, Oct. 29, 1754); also wrote some instrumental music: *Pièces de clavecin en sonates* (with violin; 1734), *Les Sons harmoniques*, for violin and continuo (1736), and various other works.

BIBLIOGRAPHY: L. Galibert, *Jean-Joseph Cassanea de Mondonville* (Narbonne, 1856); F. Hellouin, *Feuillets d'histoire* (Paris, 1903); L. de La Laurencie, *L'École française de violon de Lulli à Viotti* (Paris, 1922-24); A. Moser, *Geschichte des Violinspiels* (1923; p. 377ff.); A. Tessier, "Madame de Mondonville," *Revue Musicale* (July 1926).

Monestel, Alejandro, Costa Rican composer; b. San José, April 26, 1865; d. there, Nov. 3, 1950. He studied music at the Brussels Cons.; returning to Costa Rica in 1884, he was organist at the San José Cathedral (1884-1902); then lived in New York (1902-37), where he was active as church organist and composer. He wrote 14 Masses, 4 Requiems, 5 cantatas on the life of Jesus; also *Rapsodia Costarricense* for orch. (San José, Aug. 28, 1935); and publ. arrangements of Costa Rican songs.

Monfred, Avenir H. de, composer of Franco-Russian ancestry; b. St. Petersburg, Sept. 17, 1903; d. Paris, April 11, 1974. He studied piano, organ and composition at the St. Petersburg Cons., graduating in 1922. In 1924 he went to Paris and studied with Vincent d'Indy at the Schola Cantorum (1925-27). He promulgated an interesting theory of composition, "Diatonic Polymodality" expounded in detail in his book, *The New Diatonic Modal Principle of Relative Music* (N.Y., 1970).

WORKS: 2 symphonies (1955, 1957); a symph. poem *Vienna, 1850* (1941); ballet, *Suite New-yorkaise* (Monte Carlo, Nov. 19, 1956); symph. suite *Manhattan Sketches* (1958); *Rapsodie Juive* for orch. (1926); String Quartet (1939); 3 violin sonatas (1922, 1926, 1947); Cello Sonata (1938); many pieces for piano and for organ; choruses; film scores.

Moniuszko, Stanislaw, famous Polish composer; b. Ubiel, province of Minsk, Russia, May 5, 1819; d. Warsaw, June 4, 1872. He studied with August Freyer in Warsaw (1827-30) and with Rungenhagen in Berlin (1837-39); served as church organist in Vilna (1840-58), where he also produced a number of his operas. In 1858 he settled in Warsaw; was prof. at the Warsaw Cons. He wrote about 20 operas and operettas; his masterpiece was *Halka*, the first genuinely national Polish opera, which attained a lasting success in Poland, Russia, and to some extent in Germany. It was first presented in 2 acts in Vilna, by an amateur group (Jan. 1, 1848); then expanded to 4 acts, and produced ten years later in Warsaw (Jan. 1, 1858). Other operas are: *Loterya* (Warsaw, Sept. 12, 1846), *Jawnuta* (Vilna, May 20, 1852), *Flis (The Raftsman;* Warsaw, Sept. 24, 1858), *Hrabina (The Countess;* Warsaw, Feb. 7, 1860), *Verbum nobile* (Warsaw, Jan. 1, 1861), *Straszny dwór* (The Haunted Castle; Warsaw, Sept. 28, 1865), *Paria* (Warsaw, Dec. 11, 1869), *Beata* (Warsaw, Feb. 2, 1872); also wrote about 270 songs (some of which are very popular in Poland); choral works; a symph. poem, *Bajka (Fairy Tale);* etc. Several biographies of Moniuszko have been publ. in Polish: by A. Walicki (1873); J. Karlowicz (1885); B. Wilczynski (1900); A. Koehler (1919); Z. Jachimecki (1921); H. Opienski (1924); S. Niewiadomski (1928); E. Wrocki (1930); T. Joteyko (1932); W. Hulewicz (1933); K. Stromenger (1946). Witold Rudzinski publ. a comprehensive biography with a complete list of works (Warsaw, 1952) and also brought out an *Almanach moniuszkowski 1872-1952,* on the 50th anniversary of Moniuszko's death (Warsaw, 1952).

BIBLIOGRAPHY: Z. Jachimecki, "Stanislaw Moniuszko," *Musical Quarterly* (Jan. 1928); Jan Prosnak, *Stanislaw Moniuszko* (Cracow, 1968).

Monk, Edwin George, English organist and music editor; b. Frome, Somerset, Dec. 13, 1819; d. Radley, near Oxford, Jan. 3, 1900. He studied with G. A. Macfarren; Mus. Bac., Oxford, 1848; Mus. Doc., 1856. From 1858 till 1883 he was organist of York Minster. He edited *The Anglican Chant Book, The Anglican Choral Service Book, The Anglican Hymn Book* (with Singleton), *The Psalter and Canticles pointed for chanting* (with Ouseley), and *Anglican Psalter Chants* (with Ouseley).

Monk, Thelonious "Sphere," black-American jazz pianist; b. Rocky Mount, N.C., Oct. 10, 1918. One of the most admired and influential jazz musicians since the advent of bebop in the early 1940s, he has been closely associated with Dizzy Gillespie, Charlie Parker, Milt Jackson, John Coltrane, and other innovative jazz figures. He is self-taught and his pianistic technique is wholly unorthodox, sometimes appearing to border on the inept; despite this apparent lack of facility, he has a musicality that gives his playing unquestionable value; his rhythms shift erratically, his harmonic changes seem outlandish, his melodic lines veer unexpectedly, yet they all come together for an effect that is convincingly "right" and never ceases to delight. He has composed several pieces that have become jazz "classics": *Round 'bout Midnight, Well You Needn't, Epistrophy, Misterioso,* and *Criss-Cross;* this last was used by composer Gunther Schuller for his *Variations on a Theme of Thelonious Monk.* Despite or perhaps because of his lack of professional expertise, he scored a great success in Japan in 1963 and in Europe in 1964.

BIBLIOGRAPHY: "Thelonious Monk," *Current Biography* (Oct. 1964).

Monk, William Henry, English music editor; b. London, March 16, 1823; d. there, March 1, 1889. He was a pupil of T. Adams, J. A. Hamilton, and G. A. Griesbach; served as organist in various London churches; taught music at King's College, London; at the School for the Indigent Blind, at the National Training

School, etc. He edited for the Church of Scotland *The Book of Psalms in Metre, Scottish Hymnal, The Psalter,* and *Book of Anthems,* was the music editor of *Hymns, Ancient and Modern,* and composed many popular hymn tunes (*Eventide,* etc.); edited *The Parish Choir.*

BIBLIOGRAPHY: *Dictionary of National Biography* (vol. 13).

Monleone, Domenico, Italian opera composer; b. Genoa, Jan. 4, 1875; d. there, Jan. 15, 1942. He studied at the Cons. of Milan; from 1895 to 1901 was active as theater conductor in Amsterdam and in Vienna. He attracted attention by producing in Amsterdam (Feb. 5, 1907) an opera, *Cavalleria Rusticana,* to a libretto by his brother **Giovanni,** on the same subject as Mascagni's celebrated work; after its first Italian performance (Turin, July 10, 1907), Mascagni's publisher Sonzogno brought a lawsuit against Monleone for infringement of copyright; Moneleone was forced to change the title; his brother rewrote the libretto, and the opera was produced as *La Giostra dei falchi* (Florence, Feb. 18, 1914). Other operas were: *Una Novella di Boccaccio* (Genoa, May 26, 1909); *Alba eroica* (Genoa, May 5, 1910); *Arabesca* (Rome, March 11, 1913; won 1st prize at the competition of the City of Rome); *Suona la ritrata* (Milan, May 23, 1916); *Il Mistero* (Venice, May 7, 1921); *Fauvette* (Genoa, March 2, 1926); *La Ronda di notte* (Genoa, March 6, 1933); also an opera in Genovese dialect, *Scheûggio Campann-a* (Genoa, March 12, 1928). For some of his works he used the pseudonym **W. di Stolzing.**

Monn, Georg Matthias, Austrian composer; b. Lower Austria, April 9, 1717; d. Vienna, Oct. 3, 1750. For many years he was organist of the Karlskirche there. He wrote instrumental works marking a transition from the Baroque to the new style perfected by Johann Stamitz. A selection of his extant works appears in the *Denkmäler der Tonkunst in Österreich* 31 (15.ii), ed. by Horwitz and Riedel: 3 symphonies, of which one, in E-flat may possibly be by a younger relative, **Johann Christoph Monn** or **Mann** (1726–1782), and a trio sonata; in vol. 39 (19.ii), ed. by W. Fischer and Arnold Schoenberg: 5 symphonies, Cello Concerto in G minor, and Harpsichord Concerto in D (together with thematic catalogue of instrumental works of Georg Matthias Monn and Johann Christoph Monn). He wrote several symphonies; one, in E-flat major, formerly ascribed to him, has been proved to be a work by F. X. Pokorný (for that, see *Notes,* Summer 1966, p. 1179). The Quartet Fugues reprinted by Albrechtsberger are by Johann Christoph Monn. G. M. Monn's Harpsichord Concerto was transcribed by Schoenberg for cello and orch. (1933).

Monnikendam, Marius, Dutch composer; b. Haarlem, May 28, 1896; d. Amsterdam, May 22, 1977. He studied composition with Sem Dresden and organ and piano with de Pauw at the Amsterdam Cons.; in 1925 went to Paris where he took courses with Louis Aubert and Vincent d'Indy at the Schola Cantorum. Returning to Holland, he taught composition at the Rotterdam Cons. and in Amsterdam; also served as music critic of the newspaper combine *De Tijd* and *De Maasbode.* He wrote a number of church works, in which he revived the most ancient form of plainchant, but injected asymmetric rhythms in a modern style; in his larger works, he employed the resources of advanced harmony, including polytonality. He publ. monographs on César Franck (Amsterdam, 1949), Igor Stravinsky (Haarlem, 1951), *50 Masterpieces of Music* (The Hague, 1953) and *Nederlandse Componisten van heden en verleden* (Amsterdam, 1968).

WORKS: FOR ORCH.: *Arbeid* (*Labour*), symph. movement (1931); *Sinfonia super "Merck toch hoe sterck"* for chamber orch. (1944); *Mouvement symphonique* (1950); Concerto for Trumpet, Horn and Orch. (1952); *Variations symphoniques super "Merck toch hoe sterck"* (1954); Concerto for organ and strings (1958); *Ouverture* for organ and orch. (1960); *Vision* for chamber orch. (1963); Concerto, for organ, wind instruments, harp, double bass and percussion (1968); Piano Concertino (1974). FOR VOICE: 2 *Te Deums* for chorus and orch. (1919, 1946); *Missa Nova* for 3 voices and organ (1928); *7 Boetpsalmen* (*7 Penitential Psalms*) for chorus and orch. (1934); *Noah,* oratorio (1937); *Samson,* oratorio (1938); *Solomon,* oratorio (1939); *Missa Antiphonale* (1939); *Sinfonia Sacra I* for male chorus and orch. (1947); *Sinfonia sacra II* (*Domine Salvum Fac*) for chorus and orch. (1952); *Passion* for speaker, chorus and orch. (1948); *Van Riebeeck-Taferelen* for 2 speakers, chorus and orch. (1952); *Noé ou la Destruction du Premier Monde,* oratorio (1955); *Magnificat* for soprano, male chorus and orch. without strings (1956; transcribed for mixed chorus and full orch., 1965); *Missa Festiva* for chorus and orch. (1956); *Hymne* for alto, male chorus and orch. (1957); *Lamentations of Jeremiah* for chorus and orch. (1956); *Missa solenissima* for chorus, organ and 7 wind instruments (1959); *Missa pro defunctis* for 3 soloists, organ and percussion (1961); *Apocalypse* for chorus and organ (1966); *Madrigalesca* for chorus, 9 winds and percussion (1966); *De Kinderkruistocht* (*The Children's Crusade*) for mixed or female chorus, 7 woodwinds and percussion (1967); *Via Sacra* (*Way of the Cross*) for speaker, chorus, organ, percussion and projection slides (1969); *3 Psaumes pour le temps présent* for soloists, chorus and chamber orch. (1971); *Missa concertana* for soloists, chorus and orch. (1971); *Elckerlyc* (*Everyman*), mystery play for chorus, organ and orch. (The Hague, May 28, 1976); *Heart Rhythm* for speaker, male chorus, organ, double bass and percussion (1975); *Gloria* for chorus, organ, orch. (1976); CHAMBER WORKS: Cello Sonata (1925); 2 *toccatas* for organ (1931, 1970); Concerto for organ, 2 trumpets and 2 trombones (1956); *10 Inventions* for organ (1959); *Suite* for flute, oboe, clarinet, bassoon and harp (1960); Piano Sonatina (1967); *Suite biblique* for piano, 4–hands (1967); *The Bells,* prelude for organ (1971); *Toccata batalla* for organ, 2 trumpets and 2 trombones (1972); numerous small organ pieces.

Mononen, Sakari, Finnish composer; b. Korpiselkä, July 27, 1928. He studied composition with Nils-Eric Fougstedt and Einar Englund at the Sibelius Academy in Helsinki, graduating in 1961. In 1967 he was appointed director of the dept. of sacred music of Kuopio Music Institute. He composed a Symphony (1961);

Concerto Grosso for winds and strings (1968); *Divertimento* for orch. (1971); *Legenda con espressione* for orch. (1971); *Perspectives* for orch. (1972); 2 suites for piano (1959, 1970); String Trio (1960); String Quartet (1961); 3 organ sonatas (1963, 1964, 1965); *Vuorela Suite* for a cappella chorus (1972); Clarinet Sonata (1973).

Monrad Johansen, David, Norwegian composer and music critic; b. Vefsn, Nov. 8, 1888; d. Oslo, Feb. 20, 1974. He studied at the Oslo Cons. (1904–09); also took private lessons with Elling and Holter (1909–15). In 1915 he went to Berlin where he took a course in composition with Humperdinck. Upon returning to Norway, he was engaged in musical journalism; was music critic of *Aftenposten* (1925–45); publ. a monograph on Grieg (1934; in English, Princeton, 1938; new printings, 1943 and 1956). In his music he followed the lyrico-dramatic tradition of Grieg, inspired by Scandinavian folk melos.

WORKS: *Suite* for orch. (1915); incidental music to the play *Jo Gjende* (1924); *Voluspaa* (*The Wise Woman's Prophesy*), after Edda poetry, for soloists, chorus and orch. (1922–26); *Sigvat Skald* for voice and orch. (1928); *Me vigjer vår sang*, cantata (1930); *Ignis Ardens*, cantata (1930–32); *Symphonic Fantasy* (1936); *Pan*, symph. poem (1939); *Symphonic Variations* (1944–46); Piano Concerto (1954); *Epigrams on Norwegian Motifs* for orch. (1960); *Lamento* for string orch. (1964); Violin Sonata (1912–13); 3 suites for piano: *Nordlandsbilleder* (*Scenes from Northern Norway*, 1918), *Fra Gudbrandsdalen* (*From the Gudbrandsdal Valley*, 1922) and *Prillar-Guri* (1924); *Nordslands trompet*, song cycle (1925); *Balladesk Suite* for cello and piano (1942); Piano quartet (1947–48); *Nordlandske Danser* for piano (1958); Flute Quintet (1967); String Quartet (1969); songs; choruses.

Monsigny, Pierre-Alexandre, French opera composer; b. Fauquembergues, near St.-Omer, Oct. 17, 1729; d. Paris, Jan. 14, 1817. He was forced at an early age, by his father's death, to support his family; abandoned his study of music, and took a position as clerk in the Bureaux des Comptes du Clergé (1749); then became "maître d'hôtel" (majordomo) to the Duke of Orléans; in 1754, a performance of Pergolesi's *Serva padrona* so fired his imagination that he decided to try his own skill at comic opera. He took a rapid course of harmony with the double-bass player Gianotti, and soon completed his first stage work, *Les Aveux indiscrets*, produced at the Théâtre de la Foire Saint-Germain (Feb. 7, 1759). In quick succession, and with increasing success, the same theater brought out 3 more of Monsigny's operas: *Le Maître en droit* (Feb. 13, 1760), *Le Cadi dupé* (Feb. 4, 1761), and *On ne s'avise jamais de tout* (Sept. 14, 1761). The members of the Comédie-Italienne, alarmed at the rising prestige of its rival enterprise, succeeded in closing it, by exercise of vested privilege, and took over its best actors. Monsigny thereafter wrote exclusively for the Comédie-Italienne; a few of his operas, however, were first presented at the private theater of the Duke of Orléans, at Bagnolet. The operas produced at the Comédie-Italienne in Paris were: *Le Roi et le fermier* (Nov.

22, 1762), *Rose et Colas* (March 8, 1764), *Aline, reine de Golconde* (April 15, 1766), *L'Île sonnante* (Jan. 4, 1768), *Le Déserteur* (March 6, 1769), *Le Faucon* (March 19, 1772), *La Belle Arsène* (Aug. 14, 1775), and *Félix, ou l'enfant trouvé* (Nov. 24, 1777). Here Monsigny stopped abruptly, perhaps (as he himself modestly explained it) for lack of ideas. After the Revolution, he lost the stewardship of the estates of the Duke of Orléans, but the Opéra-Comique allowed him a pension of 2,400 francs; in 1800 he was made Inspector of Instruction at the Cons. (resigning in 1802). In 1813 he was elected to Grétry's chair in the Institut de France. Monsigny possessed an uncommon and natural melodic invention, and sensibility in dramatic expression, but his theoretical training was deficient; still, his works attained the foremost rank among the precursors of the French comic operas.

BIBLIOGRAPHY: Quatremère de Quincy, *Notice historique sur la vie et les ouvrages de Monsigny* (Paris, 1818); M. Alexandre, *Éloge historique de Pierre Alexandre Monsigny* (Arras, 1819); M. Hédouin, *Éloge de Monsigny* (Paris, 1820); F. de Ménil, *Les Grand Musiciens du Nord: Monsigny* (Paris, 1893); A. Pougin, *Monsigny et son temps* (Paris, 1908); P. Druilhe, *Monsigny, sa vie et son œuvre* (Paris, 1955).

Montagu-Nathan, Montagu, English writer on music; b. Banbury, Sept. 17, 1877; d. London, Nov. 15, 1958. His original name was **Montagu Nathan;** he changed it legally to Montagu Montagu-Nathan on March 17, 1909. He studied in Birmingham; then took violin lessons under Ysaÿe in Brussels, with Heermann in Frankfurt, and Wilhelmj in London. He appeared as a violinist in Belfast and Leeds, but soon abandoned concerts in favor of music journalism. He learned the Russian language and wrote several books on Russian music; *A History of Russian Music* (1914), *Handbook to the Piano Works of A. Scriabin* (1916; reprinted 1922); *Contemporary Russian Composers* (1917); and monographs on Glinka, Mussorgsky, and Rimsky-Korsakov.

Montani, Nicola Aloysius, American choral conductor and composer; b. Utica, N.Y., Nov. 6, 1880; d. Philadelphia, Jan. 11, 1948. He studied with Lorenzo Perosi and others in Rome; had training in Gregorian music under Dom Mocquereau and Dom Eudine on the Isle of Wight (1905–06); was organist and choirmaster of the Church of St. John the Evangelist, Philadelphia (1906–23). In 1914 he founded the Society of St. Gregory of America (officially recognized by Pope Benedict XV) for the restoration of Gregorian Chant and the early polyphonic style recommended in the "Motu Proprio" of Pius X; edited the *Catholic Choirmaster*. Montani was also, for a time, editor-in-chief of the liturgical music department of G. Schirmer, Inc., and of the Boston Music Co. He wrote 8 Masses; a *Stabat Mater;* motets, songs, etc.; publ. *Essentials of Sight Singing* and *The Art of A Cappella Singing: St. Gregory Hymnal, Catholic Choir Book* (1920; also in Braille type, for use by the blind). The *Caecilia* devoted its Aug. 1935 issue to Montani, listing biographical data and a catalogue of works.

Monte, Philippe de (Filippo di Monte, or Philippe de Mons), great Belgian contrapuntist; b. Malines, 1521; d. Prague, July 4, 1603. From about 1541–54 he was in Naples as tutor in the Pinelli family, and while there struck up a friendship with Roland de Lassus. In 1554 was in Rome for a brief sojourn, but soon went to Antwerp, and then to England, as singer in the choir of Philip II, husband of Queen Mary Tudor. In Sept. 1555, he left England and went to Italy again. In 1567 he was in Rome, and in 1568 he was appointed maestro di cappella to the Emperor Maximilian II in Vienna, holding this position until his death, which occurred while the court was at Prague during the summer. In 1572 he was appointed treasurer of Cambrai Cathedral, and in 1577, canon (without being required to reside there). He publ. Masses and many books of motets and madrigals; numerous others are in MS. In his *General History,* Hawkins reprinted a madrigal for 4 voices by Monte; Dehn's *Sammlung* and Commer's *Collectio* each contains a motet; a Mass for 6 voices, *Benedicta es,* was reproduced by A. Smijers in the *Publications of the Vereeniging voor Nederlandsche Muziekgeschiedenis* (vol. 38); 3 madrigals for 5–7 voices are in the *Denkmäler der Tonkunst in Österreich* 77 (41). The complete works were edited by C. Van den Borren and J. Van Nuffel in 31 vols. (Bruges, 1927–39); a new complete edition, under the direction of R. B. Lenaerts, began publication in 1975.
BIBLIOGRAPHY: G. van Doorslaer, *Philippe de Monte* (Malines, 1895); G. van Doorslaer, *Philippe de Monte: la vie et les œuvres* (Brussels, 1921); P. Bergmans, *Quatorze lettres inédites du compositeur Philippe de Monte* (Brussels, 1921); A. Einstein, *Philippe de Monte als Madrigalkomponist* (in the report of the Liège Congress, 1930); J. van Nuffel, "Philippe de Monte," *Proceedings of the Music Association* 57 (1931); G. Reese, *Music in the Renaissance* (N.Y., 1954).

Monte, Toti dal. See **Dal Monte , Toti.**

Montéclair, Michel Pignolet de, French composer; b. Andelot, Dec. (baptized Dec. 4), 1667; d. near St.-Denis, Sept. 22, 1737. He was one of the early players of the modern double bass; from 1699 to his death he played in the orch. of the Académie Royale de Musique; there he produced his ballet-opera *Les Fêtes de l'été* (June (June 12, 1716) and a lyric tragedy *Jephté,* in 5 acts (Feb. 28, 1732), the first stage work on a biblical subject to be presented at the Académie. He also wrote a Requiem, 6 trio sonatas, flute duets, and "brunettes" (French love songs); publ. a *Nouvelle Méthode pour apprendre la musique* (Paris, 1700; revised eds., 1709, 1736), a *Méthode facile pour apprendre à jouer du violon* (Paris, 1712; a pioneer violin method); and *Principes de musique* (Paris, 1736).
BIBLIOGRAPHY: E. Voillard, *Essai sur Montéclair* (Chaumont, 1879); J. Carlez, *Un Opéra biblique au XVIIIᵉ siècle* (on *Jephté;* Paris, 1879); A. Moser, *Geschichte des Violinspiels* (1923; p. 176 ff.); M. Pincherle, "Elementary Musical Instruction in the 18th Century: an Unknown Treatise by Montéclair," *Musical Quarterly* (Jan. 1948).

Montella, Giovanni Domenico, Italian lutenist and composer; b. Naples, c.1570; d. there, 1607. In 1591 he was engaged as lutenist in the Royal Chapel, Naples; was also organist and harpist. He wrote psalms and other church music; publ. 2 vols. of *villanelle,* a vol. of motets, and 10 vols. of madrigals. Some of his sacred music is included in *Istituzioni e Monumenti dell'arte musicale italiano* (vol. V, 1934).

Montemezzi, Italo, eminent Italian opera composer; b. Vigasio, near Verona, Aug. 4, 1875; d. there, May 15, 1952. He was a pupil of Saladino and Ferroni at the Milan Cons., and graduated in 1900; his graduation piece, conducted by Toscanini, was *Cantico dei Cantici,* for chorus and orch. He then devoted himself almost exclusively to opera. In 1939 he went to the U.S.; lived mostly in California; in 1949 he returned to Italy. Montemezzi's chief accomplishment is the maintenance of the best traditions of Italian dramatic music, without striving for realism or overelaboration of technical means. His masterpiece in this genre is the opera *L'Amore dei tre re* (Milan, La Scala, April 10, 1913), which has become a standard work in the repertory of opera houses all over the world. Other operas are: *Giovanni Gallurese* (Turin, Jan. 28, 1905), *Hellera* (Turin, March 17, 1909), *La Nave* (libretto by Gabriele d'Annunzio; Milan, Nov. 1, 1918), *La Notte di Zoraima* (Milan, Jan. 31, 1931), *L'Incantesimo* (radio première, NBC, Oct. 9, 1943, composer conducting); he also wrote the symph. poems *Paolo e Virginia* (Rome, 1930) and *Italia mia!* (1944), etc.
BIBLIOGRAPHY: L. Tretti and L. Fiumi, eds., *Omaggio a Italo Montemezzi* (Verona, 1952).

Monteux, Pierre, celebrated French conductor; b. Paris, April 4, 1875; d. Hancock, Maine, July 1, 1964. He studied at the Paris Cons. with Berthelier (violin), Lavignac (harmony), and Lenepveu (composition); received 1st prize for viola (1896); then was viola player in the Colonne Orch., and later chorusmaster there; also played viola in the orch. of the Opéra-Comique. He then organized his own series, Concerts Berlioz, at the Casino de Paris. In 1911 he became conductor for Diaghilev's Ballets Russes; his performances of modern ballet scores established him as one of the finest technicians of the baton. He led the world premières of Stravinsky's *Petrouchka, Le Sacre du printemps,* and *Le Rossignol,* Ravel's *Daphnis et Chloé,* and Debussy's *Jeux;* conducted at the Paris Opéra (1913–14); founded the Société des Concerts Populaires in Paris (1914); appeared as guest conductor in London, Berlin, Vienna, Budapest, etc. In 1916–17 he toured the U.S. with the Russian Ballet; in 1917, conducted the Civic Orch. Society, N.Y.; in 1917–18, at the Metropolitan Opera House. In 1919 he was engaged as conductor of the Boston Symph. Orch., and held this post until 1924 (succeeded by Koussevitzky); in 1929 he founded the Orchestre Symphonique de Paris, and was its principal conductor until 1938. From 1936 until 1952 he was conductor of the reorganized San Francisco Symph. Orch.; then continued to conduct in Europe and America; was a frequent guest conductor with the Boston Symph. (conducted it on his 80th birthday, April 4, 1955); also led its concerts at Tanglewood; shared the podium with Munch during the European tour of the Boston Symph. in 1956 (which included Russia). As an interpreter, Monteux endeavored to bring out the inherent essence of the music, without imposing his own artistic personality; unemotional and restrained in his podium manner, he nonetheless succeeded in producing brilliant performances.

Monteverdi, Claudio (Giovanni Antonio), great Italian composer; founder of modern opera; renowned madrigalist; b. Cremona (baptized May 15), 1567; d. Venice, Nov. 29, 1643. He was a chorister at the Cathedral of Cremona and studied there under the choirmaster Marc' Antonio Ingegneri, learning to play the organ and the viol. His first published work (a collection of 3–part motets) dates from 1582, when he was only 15. About 1590 he entered the service of Vincenzo Gonzaga, Duke of Mantua, as viol player and madrigal singer. With him, he traveled to Hungary (1595) and Flanders (1599). In the meantime he had publ. a collection of *canzonette a 3* (1584) and the first three books of madrigals (1587, 1590, 1592). 1602, maestro di cappella to the Duke; the 4th and 5th books of madrigals appeared in 1603 and 1605; on Feb. 22, 1607, his first musical drama, *Orfeo*, was performed at Mantua with instant success. Also in 1607 he publ. the *Scherzi musicali a tre voci*. In 1608 he set to music Rinuccini's tragedy *Arianna*, for the wedding of Francesco, Prince of Mantua (May 28, 1608). The music is lost, except the *Lamento d'Arianna*, which Monteverdi publ. separately (1623) as well as in a 5-part arrangement in book 6 of his madrigals (Venice, 1614); this aria, unsurpassed in its expressive melancholy, is one of Monteverdi's finest creations. He also wrote a ballet-opera, *Il Ballo delle Ingrate* (Mantua, June 4, 1608). In 1610 he wrote a Mass and Vespers, and took them to Rome in quest of assistance from Pope Paul V; when this proved futile, he returned to Mantua; after the death of his patron Vincenzo (1612), he lost his Mantuan position, but in 1613 was elected to succeed Martinengo as maestro di cappella at San Marco, Venice, at a salary of 300 ducats (raised to 500 in 1616), and a house, besides traveling expenses. He remained in Venice until his death, composing mainly for the church, but not neglecting the stage and the secular madrigal forms. The 7th book of madrigals was publ. in 1619. In 1624 he brought out, at the palace of Senator Mocenigo, his great dramatic scene, *Il Combattimento di Tancredi e Clorinda,* in which a narrator ("testo") connects the dialogue. In 1627 he composed 5 dramatic intermezzi for the plays *Melissa e Bradamente* and *Didone e gli Argonauti,* for the court of Parma; and in 1630 the opera *Proserpina rapita,* for the wedding of Mocenigo's daughter. In 1632 he took holy orders, out of gratitude for having escaped the terrible plague of the previous year. The *Madrigali guerrieri et amorosi,* the 8th book of madrigals, was publ. in 1638. In 1637 the first opera house was opened in Venice, the Teatro di S. Cassiano (up to that time, operas were presented at the palaces of the nobility); other theaters were soon established. Monteverdi produced *Il Ritorno di Ulisse in patria* at the Teatro di S. Cassiano (1641); two operas at the Teatro SS. Giovanni e Paolo: *Le Nozze di Enea con Lavinia* (1641) and (his last) *L'Incoronazione di Poppea* (1642). The authenticity of the opera *Adone* (Venice, Dec. 21, 1639), attributed to Monteverdi, is in dispute; the music is lost, but according to the libretto, the composer is Francesco Manelli.

The role of Monteverdi in music history is of great magnitude. He established modern opera, conceived as true drama; he enlarged the orchestra, selected and skillfully combined the instruments accompanying the voices; he was among the first, if not the first, to employ the tremolo for strings, and also pizzicato; his recitative assumes dramatic power, at times expanding to arioso. Even his early works show a remarkably advanced style of composition; the harmonic progressions reveal a strong sense of modern tonality, and the dominant seventh and other dissonances are used without preparation. In all this, he ran counter to the established tradition, and became involved in a bitter polemical exchange with Giovanni Maria Artusi of Bologna, who published several pamphlets attacking Monteverdi as a representative of the "musica moderna."

WORKS: *Orfeo* (first publ., 1609): reproduced by Sandberger (1927; facsimile of the 1616 ed.); modern eds. by Eitner in *Publikationen . . . der Gesellschaft für Musikforschung* (1881), G. Orefice (1909), Vincent d'Indy (1915), G. F. Malipiero (1923), J. A. Westrup (1925), Respighi (1935), Redlich (1936), Orff (1940, very free), Benvenuti (1942), Denis Stevens (London, 1967), and Bruno Maderno (Milan, 1967). A facsimile of the MS of *L'Incoronazione di Poppea* has been published (1938); the score was republished by Goldschmidt in his *Studien zur Geschichte der italienischen Oper* 2 (1904); by d'Indy (1908), Charles van den Borren (1914), Westrup (1927), Malipiero (1937), Krenek (1937), Benvenuti (1937), Redlich (1939), and Ghedini (1953). A reprint of *Il Ballo delle Ingrate* appears in *L'Arte musicale in Italia* 6 by L. Torchi (1897); newly ed. by Carl Orff as *Tanz der Spröden* (1929), by A. Toni (Milan, 1932), and by E. J. Dent (London, 1945). *Il Combattimento di Tancredi e Clorinda* has been reproduced by L. Torchi in *L'Arte musicale in Italia* 6 (1897); modern editions by A. Toni (1921), Malipiero (1931), and Redlich (1946). *Il Ritorno d'Ulisse* was publ. by R. Haas in the *Denkmäler der Tonkunst in Österreich* 57 (29. i); new editions by Vincent d'Indy (1927), Charles Van den Borren (1927), J. A. Westrup (1927), and Luigi Dallapiccola (1942). A 9th book of madrigals was publ. posthumously in 1651. Numerous madrigals and sacred works have been reprinted in modern eds., e.g., a 4-part Mass by Tirabassi and Charles van den Borren (1914); Vespers (1610) by Redlich (Vienna, 1949), Ghedini (Milan, 1952), Schrade (N.Y., 1953); chamber duets by Landshoff (in *Alte Meister des Bel Canto,* 1927), etc. A Mass *a* 6, Masses *a* 4, psalms *a* 1–8, with litanies to the Virgin and *Selva morale e spirituale* (containing Masses, psalms, hymns, Magnificats, motets, *Salve,* and a *Piano della Madonna* on the *Lamento* from *Arianna*) have been preserved; the arioso *Cruda Amarilli* (from the 5th book of madrigals) is included in many anthologies. The collected ed., in 16 vols., was assembled and edited by G. F. Malipiero (Vienna, 1926–42). There are 2 new complete editions in progress: one, by the Claudio Monteverdi Foundation, began publication in 1970; the other, edited by B. B. de

Surcy, issues simultaneously critical and facsimile editions (1972–).

BIBLIOGRAPHY: S. Davari, *Notizie biografiche del distinto maestro di musica Claudio Monteverdi* (Mantua, 1885); E. Vogel, "Claudio Monteverdi," *Vierteljahrsschrift für Musikwissenschaft* (1887); G. Sommi Picenardi, *Claudio Monteverdi a Cremona* (Milan, 1896); A. Heuss, "Die Instrumentalstücke des *Orfeo*," *Sammelbände der Internationalen Musik-Gesellschaft* (1903); Hugo Leichtentritt," *Claudio Monteverdi als Madrigalkomponist,*" ibid. (1910); A. Heuss, *Claudio Monteverdi als Charakteristiker in seinen Madrigalen*, in the Liliencron-Festschrift (1910); R. Mitjana, *Claudio Monteverdi y los orígines de la ópera italiana* (Málaga, 1911); L. Schneider, *Claudio Monteverdi* (Paris, 1920); A. Tessier, "Les Deux Styles de Monteverdi," *Revue Musicale* (1922); H. Prunières, *La Vie et l'œuvre de Claudio Monteverdi* (Paris, 1924; English transl., 1926); Charles Van den Borren, "Il Ritorno d'Ulisse" *de Claudio Monteverdi* (Brussels, 1925); A. Striggio, *L'Orfeo di Monteverdi* (Bologna, 1928; reprint of the libretto); issue of the *Rassegna Musicale* devoted to Monteverdi (Oct. 1929); G. F. Malipiero, *Monteverdi* (Milan, 1930); K. F. Müller, *Die Technik der Ausdrucksdarstellung in Monteverdi's monodischen Frühwerken* (Berlin, 1931); H. Redlich, *Claudio Monteverdi: vol. I: Das Madrigalwerk* (Berlin, 1932); G. F. Malipiero, "Monteverdi," *Musical Quarterly* (July 1932); G. Cesari, "La Musica in Cremona," *Istituzioni e Monumenti dell'arte musicale italiano* 6 (1939); J. A. Westrup, "Monteverdi's Lamento d'Arianna," *Music Review* (April 1940); J. A. Westrup, "Monteverdi and the Orchestra," *Music & Letters* (July 1940); D. de Paoli, *Claudio Monteverdi* (Milan, 1945); M. Bukofzer, *Music in the Baroque Era—from Monteverdi to Bach* (London, 1948); H. F. Redlich, *Claudio Monteverdi, Leben und Werk* (Olten, 1949; in English, *Monteverdi, Life and Works*, London, 1952); L. Schrade, *Monteverdi, Creator of Modern Music* (N.Y., 1950); M. Le Roux, *Claudio Monteverdi* (Paris, 1951); C. Sartori, "Monteverdiana," *Musical Quarterly* (July 1952); C. Sartori, *Monteverdi* (Brescia, 1953); Anna Amalie Abert, *Claudio Monteverdi und das musikalische Drama* (Lippstadt, 1954); H. F. Redlich, "Claudio Monteverdi: Some Problems of Textual Interpretation," *Musical Quarterly* (Jan. 1955); W. Osthoff, "Monteverdi-Funde," *Archiv für Musikwissenschaft* (1957); R. Roche, *Monteverdi* (Paris, 1959); H. Redlich, "Claudio Monteverdi. Some Editorial Problems of 1967," *Consort* 24 (1967); D. Arnold and N. Fortune, *The Monteverdi Reader* (N.Y., 1968); *Congresso internazionale sul tema Claudio Monteverdi e il suo tempo* (Verona, 1969); D. Stevens, "Monteverdi's Necklace," *Musical Quarterly* (July 1973).

Monteverdi, Giulio Cesare, Italian organist and composer; brother of **Claudio Monteverdi;** b. Cremona, Jan. 31, 1573; d. c.1630. He was the author of the important "Dichiarazione" appended to Monteverdi's *Scherzi musicali a 3 voci* (1607), in which he expounded the musical ideas of his brother, and gave a vigorous reply to the attacks on Monteverdi by Artusi. Only a few madrigals by Giulio Cesare Monteverdi are extant.

BIBLIOGRAPHY: Claudio Sartori, "Giulio Cesare

Monteverdi a Salò. Nuovi Documenti Inediti," *Nuova Rivista Italiana* (Nov.-Dec. 1967).

Montgomery, Merle, American pianist and composer; b. Davidson, Oklahoma, May 15, 1904. She studied at the Univ. of Oklahoma, and at the Eastman School of Music; then went to Paris where she took piano lessons with Isidor Philipp and composition with Nadia Boulanger at the American Cons. in Fontainebleau. Returning to the U.S. she became active as music editor, compiler of educational textbooks, etc. Under the pen name of **Aline Campbell** she published a number of characteristic piano pieces, often with exotic titles, such as *A Camel Ride.*

Montsalvatge, Bassols Xavier, Catalan composer; b. Gerona, March 11, 1911. He studied with Morera and Pahissa; in 1936 received the Pedrell prize for his *Pequeña suite burlesca* for violin and woodwinds. He wrote the musical fables *El gato con botas* (Barcelona, 1947) and *Viaje a la luna* (in Catalan, Barcelona, 1966); *Sinfonia mediterránea* (1949); string quartet, *Cuarteto indiano* (1952); *Concerto breve* for piano and orch. (1956); *3 Danzas inciertas* for 2 violins (1956); *Cant espiritual* for chorus and orch. (1958); a song cycle, *5 Invocaciones al crucificado* for soprano and 12 instruments (1969).

Moodie, Alma, Australian violinist; b. Brisbane, Sept. 12, 1900; d. Frankfurt, Germany, March 7, 1943. She studied with César Thomson in Brussels (1907–10); played at a concert as a child prodigy (with Max Reger); gave concerts in Germany, where she lived most of her life; taught at the State Academy of Music at Frankfurt. Her prestige as a musician was high in Germany; she performed many new works; Pfitzner wrote his violin concerto for her.

Moody, Fanny (Manners), English dramatic soprano; b. Redruth, Cornwall, Nov. 23, 1866; d. Dundrum, County Dublin, July 21, 1945. She studied singing with Mme. Sainton-Dolby; after several appearances in the provinces, she sang Micaela at Drury Lane, London (April 30, 1887). She married **Charles Manners,** the singer and impresario, on July 5, 1890, and thereafter accompanied her husband on his tours; she was at her best in lyric roles; also appeared successfully in Wagnerian parts (Elsa, Elizabeth, etc.).

Moog (pronounced Mohg), **Robert A.,** American electric engineer, inventor of the Moog music synthesizer; b. Flushing, N.Y., May 23, 1934. He attended the Bronx High School of Science (1948–52), Queens College (1952–55), Columbia Univ. (1955–57) and Cornell Univ. (1957–65); received his B.S. in Physics from Queens College (1957); B.S. in electrical engineering from Columbia Univ. (1957); Ph.D. in Engineering Physics from Cornell Univ. (1965). He established The R. A. Moog Co. in 1954 for the purpose of perfecting electronic musical instruments; introduced components of electronic music synthesizers in 1964; the company was incorporated in 1968, with the office at Trumansburg, N.Y. His synthesizer, which has colloquially been dubbed as "The Moog," rapidly acquired popularity. Although even pre-Moog electronic generators could synthesize tone colors, the Moog has achieved a high degree of vitality, which made it an artistic musical medium. The 1969 Moog has a manual of 5½ octaves, with the keys responding to the touch of the fingers, enabling the player to secure an extended spectrum of dynamic gradations. As the technology of the Moog continued to improve, there arose a whole generation of Moog virtuosos; among these Walter Carlos earned enviable fame for his colorful renditions of Bach's keyboard music in a manner which was popularized as "switched-on Bach."

Moór, Emanuel, Hungarian pianist and inventor; b. Kecskemét, Feb. 19, 1863; d. Mont Pèlerin, near Montreux, Switzerland, Oct. 20, 1931. He studied in Budapest and Vienna; toured the U.S. from 1885 to 1887, as director of the Concerts Artistiques, for which he engaged Lilli Lehmann, Ovide Musin, and other celebrated artists, and also acted as their accompanist. He then lived in London, Lausanne, and Munich. He invented the Moór-Duplex piano, consisting of a double keyboard with a coupler between the two manuals (an octave apart). With the introduction of this piano a new technique was made possible, facilitating the playing of octaves, tenths, and even chromatic glissandos. Some piano manufacturers (Steinway, Bechstein, Bösendorfer) have put the Moór mechanism into their instruments. Moór's second wife, **Winifred Christie** (b. Stirling, Feb. 26, 1882; d. London, Feb. 8, 1965), English pianist, aided him in promoting the Moór keyboard, and gave many performances on it in Europe and America. She publ. (in collaboration with her husband) a manual of technical exercises for the Moór piano. Needless to say, Moór's invention sank into innocuous desuetude along with phonetic alphabets, Volapük and similar elucubrations of earnest but impractical innovators. Moór was also a composer; his works include 5 operas: *La Pompadour* (Cologne, Feb. 22, 1902), *Andreas Hofer* (Cologne, Nov. 9, 1902), *Hochzeitsglocken* (Kassel, Aug. 2, 1908; in London, under the title *Wedding Bells*, Jan. 26, 1911), *Der Goldschmied von Paris,* and *Hertha*; 8 symphonies and other orchestral works; 4 piano concertos; 3 violin concertos; 2 cello concertos; Triple concerto, for violin, cello, and piano; Concerto for 2 Cellos and Orch.; 2 piano quintets; 2 string quartets; 2 piano trios; *Suite* for 4 cellos; 12 violin sonatas; 7 cello sonatas; 3 piano sonatas; Hungarian Dances for piano; Harp Sonata; Sonata for 4 harps; a great number of songs.

BIBLIOGRAPHY: L. Deutsch, *Die Technik der Doppelklaviatur Moór* (Leipzig, 1932); W. Reich, "Das Moórsche Doppelklavier," *Die Musik* XXIV/4; D. Tovey, "The Pianoforte of Emanuel Moór," *Music & Letters* (Jan. 1922); Max Pirani, *Emanuel Moór* (London, 1959; with a preface by Pablo Casals).

Moor, Karel, Czech composer; b. Bělohrad, Dec. 26, 1873; d. Prague, March 30, 1945. His real name was **Mohr.** He studied at the Cons. of Prague; then went for further study to Vienna. From 1900 to 1923 he was active as a theatrical director and conductor in Bohemia and Serbia; then lived mainly in Prague. He achieved his first success as a composer with the operetta *Pan profesor v pekle* (*Professor in Hell*), produced in Brno in 1908; his other operas *Viy,* after Go-

gol's fantastic tales (Prague, July 14, 1903) and *Hjoerdis* (Prague, Oct. 22, 1905), were also successful. A facile writer, he publ. an autobiography in the form of a novel (Prague, 1906), a volume of reminiscences (Pilsen, 1917) and a semi-fictional book *V dlani osudu* (*In the Hand of Destiny;* publ. posthumously in 1947).

Moore, Carman, American composer; b. in Ohio, 1939. He studied with Hall Overton and Vincent Persichetti in N.Y.; later took lessons with Stefan Wolpe and Luciano Berio, who inculcated in him the most advanced, though diverse, methods of ultramodern composition. In 1968 he organized, with a few colleagues, a Society of Black Composers. In 1976 he received a commission from the N.Y. Philharmonic to compose a piece derived from the music of his racial background; the piece, entitled *Wild Fires and Field Songs,* was performed Jan. 24, 1973. Another piece by Moore that attracted attention was *Museum Piece,* performed in N.Y. on April 22, 1975.

Moore, Douglas Stuart, distinguished American composer and music educator; b. Cutchogue, N.Y., Aug. 10, 1893; d. Greenport, Long Island, N.Y., July 25, 1969. He studied at Yale Univ. with D. S. Smith and Horatio Parker; wrote several university songs, among them the football song *Good Night, Harvard,* which became popular among Yale students; after obtaining his B.A. (1915) and Mus. Bac. (1917), he joined the U.S. navy; following the Armistice of 1918, he attended classes of Vincent d'Indy at the Schola Cantorum in Paris and also took lessons in organ playing with Tournemire and in composition with Nadia Boulanger and Ernest Bloch. Returning to the U.S. he served as organist at the Cleveland Museum of Art (1921–23) and at Adelbert College, Western Reserve Univ. (1923–25); in 1925 he received a Pulitzer traveling scholarship in music and spent a year in Europe. In 1926 he was appointed to the faculty of Columbia Univ.; in 1940 succeeded Daniel Gregory Mason as the head of the music dept. there; many American composers were his students. He retired in 1962. A fine musical craftsman, Moore applied his technical mastery to American subjects in his operas and symphonic works. He achieved popular success with his "folk opera" *Ballad of Baby Doe,* dealing with the true story of an actual historic figure during the era of intensive silver mining; the opera was staged on July 7, 1956 at Central City, Colorado, where its action took place; the opera had numerous revivals in America, and also in Europe. His other operas were *The Headless Horseman* (1936); *The Devil and Daniel Webster* (N.Y., May 18, 1939); *White Wings,* chamber opera (Hartford, Feb. 2, 1949); *The Emperor's New Clothes* (N.Y., Feb. 19, 1949); *Giants in the Earth* (N.Y., March 28, 1951; awarded the Pulitzer Prize); *Gallantry, a "Soap Opera"* (N.Y., March 15, 1958); *The Wings of the Dove* (N.Y., Oct. 12, 1961); *The Greenfield Christmas Tree* (Baltimore, Dec. 8, 1962); and *Carrie Nation,* to the story of a notorious temperance fighter (Lawrence, Kansas, April 28, 1966); he wrote for orch. *Pageant of P. T. Barnum* (Cleveland, April 15, 1926); *Moby Dick,* symph. poem (1927); *A Symphony of Autumn* (1930); *Overture on an American Tune* (N.Y., Dec. 11, 1932); *Village Music* (N.Y.,

Dec. 18, 1941); *In Memoriam* (Rochester, N.Y., April 27, 1944); Symph. in A (Paris, May 5, 1946; received honorable mention by the N.Y. Music Critics' Circle, 1947); *Farm Journal* for chamber orch. (N.Y., Jan. 19, 1948); Violin Sonata (1929); String Quartet (1933); Wind Quintet (1942); Quintet for clarinet, 2 violins, viola and cello (1946); Piano Trio (1953). He publ. *Listening to Music* (N.Y., 1932; revised, 1963) and *From Madrigal to Modern Music: A Guide to Musical Styles* (N.Y., 1942).

Moore, Earl Vincent, American music educator; b. Lansing, Michigan, Sept. 27, 1890. He studied at the Univ. of Michigan (B.A., 1912; M.A., 1915) and later in Europe with Widor, Holst, Boult, Heger, and others. He was organist and teacher of theory at the Univ. of Michigan (1914–23); then was Director of the School of Music, while continuing to teach (1923–46, prof.); from 1946 to 1960 was Dean of the School of Music. In 1939–40 he was National Director of the WPA Music Project; 1960–70, chairman of the Music Dept., Univ. of Houston. He served at various times as consultant to the War Dept. and to universities; 1959–72, member of the E. S. Coolidge Foundation Committee in the Library of Science; was a founder-member of the National Association of Schools of Music and president, 1936–38. He composed parts of the Michigan Union Operas and other pieces, but is famous at Michigan U. as composer of the football song "Varsity."

Moore, Gerald, English pianist; b. Watford, July 30, 1899. After a brief career as a concert pianist, he devoted himself almost exclusively to the art of accompaniment, in which he attained the foremost rank; also made transcriptions for piano of many songs and other works. He publ. an entertaining book, *The Unashamed Accompanist* (London, 1943); *Singer and Accompanist: The Performance of 50 Songs* (London, 1953) and *Am I Too Loud?* (N.Y., 1962).

Moore, Grace, American soprano; b. Slabtown, Tenn., Dec. 5, 1898; d. Copenhagen, Jan. 26, 1947. She studied at the Wilson Greene School of Music in Chevy Chase, Maryland, and with Marafioti; first appeared in musical comedy in N.Y. (1921–26); then studied in France. Upon returning to America, she made her operatic debut as Mimi at the Metropolitan Opera House (Feb. 7, 1928); made successful appearances also at the Paris Opéra-Comique (1928); at Covent Garden, London (1935); and at other European centers; also sang with the Chicago City Opera (1937); appeared in several motion pictures. She was killed in an airplane accident, on a flight from Copenhagen to Stockholm. She published an autobiography, *You're Only Human Once* (1944).

Moore, John Weeks, pioneer American musicologist and lexicographer; b. Andover, N.H., April 11, 1807; d. Manchester, N.H., March 23, 1889. He was a newspaper publisher and editor at Bellows Falls, Vt., where he publ. the *Bellows Falls Gazette* (1838–55); also was for a time editor of the musical journals *World of Music* and *Musical Library.* His *magnum opus* is the *Complete Encyclopedia of Music, Elementary, Technical, Historical, Biographical, Vocal, and Instrumen-*

tal (Boston, 1854; 1004 pages; Appendix, 1875); also *Dictionary of Musical Information* (1876); publ. the collections *Sacred Minstrel* (1842), *American Collection of Instrumental Music* (1856), and *The Star Collection of Instrumental Music* (1858); also *Puritanism of Music in America* (18 numbers), *Musical Record* (5 vols.; 1867–70), *Song and Song Writers of America* (200 numbers; 1859–80), etc.

BIBLIOGRAPHY: *Dictionary of American Biography.*

Moore, Mary Carr, American composer; b. Memphis, Tenn., Aug. 6, 1873; d. Ingleside, California, Jan. 11, 1957. In 1885 the family moved to California, where she studied singing; then theory with her uncle, John Harraden Pratt, H. B. Pasmore, and others. She began to compose as a child; her first publ. work was a lullaby, written at 16. She sang the leading part in her operetta, *The Oracle* (San Francisco, 1894); other stage works are: *The Flaming Arrow,* "Indian intermezzo" (San Francisco, March 27, 1922, composer conducting); *Narcissa* (1912; San Francisco, Sept. 7, 1925; the first grand opera by an American woman, performed under her own direction); *Rizzio* (Los Angeles, May 26, 1932); *Los Rubios* (Los Angeles, Sept. 10, 1931). She also wrote songs (*My Dream,* etc.) and piano pieces (*Murmur of Pines,* etc.).

BIBLIOGRAPHY: E. E. Hipsher, *American Opera and Its Composers* (Philadelphia, 1934; pp. 328–36).

Moore, Thomas, famous Irish poet, ballad singer, and song composer; b. Dublin, May 28, 1779; d. near Devizes, Wilts, Feb. 25, 1852. He had no regular musical training, but learned to play the piano with the aid of the organist William Warren. He was in London from 1799 to 1803; then received a position as a government functionary in Bermuda; however, he stayed there only a few months; then returned to London by way of the U.S. and Canada. In London he became extremely popular as a ballad singer in the houses of aristocracy; in 1807 he publ. a volume of poetry, *Irish Melodies,* set to music by Sir John Stevenson. In 1817 he issued his celebrated poem, *Lalla Rookh.* An ardent Irish nationalist, he played an important role in the creation and revival of Irish poetry and music. Among his own melodies are *Love thee, dearest, When midst the gay, One dear smile,* and *The Canadian Boat-Song.* He freely borrowed his musical materials from popular Irish tunes and in some cases modified them sufficiently to produce apparently new songs. He also composed short concerted vocal pieces; the terzetto *O lady fair,* and the 3-part glee *The Watchman* won wide popularity. In 1895 Sir Charles Stanford publ. *The Irish Melodies of Thomas Moore: the Original Airs Restored.*

BIBLIOGRAPHY: article on Moore in the *Dictionary of National Biography.*

Moos, Paul, German writer on esthetics; b. Buchau, March 22, 1863; d. Raeren, Belgium, Feb. 27, 1952. He studied with Thuille, Rheinberger, and others in Munich; publ. *Moderne Musikästhetik in Deutschland* (1902; 2nd ed., 1922, entitled *Die Philosophie der Musik von Kant bis Eduard von Hartmann*); *Richard Wagner als Ästhetiker* (1906); *Die psychologische Äs-*

thetik in Deutschland (1919); *Die deutsche Ästhetik der Gegenwart* (vol. I, 1929; vol. II, 1931); also contributed many valuable essays to German music magazines.

Mooser, Aloys, Swiss organ manufacturer; b. Niederhelfenschwyl, June 27, 1770; d. Freiburg, Dec. 19, 1839. He studied with his father, an Alsatian organist; attained fame as one of the greatest masters in organ building; the quality of the "Vox humana" in his organs was particularly admired.

Mooser, R.-Aloys, Swiss writer on music; great-grandson of the preceding; b. Geneva, Sept. 20, 1876; d. there, Aug. 24, 1969. His mother was a Russian, and he acquired the knowledge of the Russian language in childhood. He studied with his father and Otto Barblan in Geneva. In 1896 he went to St. Petersburg, where he served as organist at the French church, wrote music criticism for the *Journal de St. Petersbourg* and made an extensive study of Russian music in the archives. He took courses with Balakirev and Rimsky-Korsakov. In 1909 he returned to Geneva and became active as music critic there. His reviews were collected in the volumes: *Regards sur la Musique Contemporaine: 1921–46* (Lausanne, 1946); *Panorama de la Musique Contemporaine: 1947–1953* (Geneva, 1953); *Aspects de la Musique Contemporaine: 1953–1957* (Geneva, 1957). Books on Russian music: *L'Opéra-comique français en Russie au XVIIIᵉ siècle* (Geneva, 1932; 2nd ed., 1954); *Violonistes-compositeurs italiens en Russie au XVIIIᵉ siècle* (Milan, 1938–50); *Opéras, intermezzos, ballets, cantates, oratorios joués en Russie durant le XVIIIᵉ siècle* (Geneva, 1945; 2nd ed., 1955); *Annales de la musique et des musiciens en Russie au XVIIIᵉ siècle* (of prime importance for new, detailed, and accurate documentation; 3 vols.; Geneva, 1948–51); *Visage de la musique contemporaine, 1957–1961* (Paris, 1962); *Deux violonistes genevois, G. Fritz et Chr. Haensel* (Geneva, 1968).

Morales, Cristóbal de, eminent Spanish composer; b. Seville, c.1500; d. Málaga, 1553 (between Sept. 4 and Oct. 7). He was a pupil of Fernández de Castilleja, who was chapel master at the Seville Cathedral. From 1526 to 1530, Morales was choirmaster of the Avila Cathedral. In 1535 he entered the papal choir in Rome (until 1540); he composed much sacred music during this period. After a brief journey to Spain, he returned to Rome and increased his productivity as composer; he also traveled in the retinue of the Pope to various towns in Italy. From 1545 to 1547 he was choirmaster at the cathedral of Toledo; in 1551 he obtained a similar post at Málaga, where he remained until his death. Morales was one of the outstanding masters of the polyphonic style; he was greatly esteemed by contemporary musicians; Bermudo described him as "the light of Spain in music." 2 books of Masses, many motets, Magnificats, ballets, and Lamentations were publ. during his lifetime. Modern reprints are found in Eslava's *Lira sacro-hispana:* Pedrell's *Hispaniae Schola musica sacra,* Martini's *Esemplare;* Rochlitz's *Sammlung;* etc. The *Opera omnia* are appearing in *Monumentos de la Música Española,* vols. 11, 13, 15, 17, 20, 21, 24, 34 (Madrid, 1952–).

BIBLIOGRAPHY: H. Collet, *Le Mysticisme musical espagnol au XVIᵉ siècle* (Paris, 1913); R. Mitjana, *Cristóbal de Morales, Estudio crítico-biográfico* (Madrid, 1920); F. R. Piqueras, *Música y músicos toledanos* (Toledo, 1922); J. B. Trend, "Cristóbal Morales," *Music & Letters* (Jan. 1925); Elústiza and Castrillo Hernández, *Antología Musical* (Barcelona, 1933); R. Stevenson, "Cristóbal Morales, A Fourth-Centenary Biography," *Journal of the American Musicological Society* (Spring 1953); R. Stevenson, "The Earliest Polyphonic Imprint in South America," *Notes* (March 1967); H. Anglès, "Problemas que presenta la nueva edición de las obras de Morales y de Victoria," in J. Robijns *et al.,* eds., *Renaissance-Muziek* (Leuven, 1969).

Morales, Melesio, Mexican composer; b. in Mexico City, Dec. 4, 1838; d. San Petro de los Pinos, May 12, 1908. He began to compose salon music for piano and soon acquired sufficient technique to write for the stage; produced two operas, *Romeo y Julieta* (Mexico City, Jan. 27, 1863) and *Ildegonda* (Mexico City, Jan. 27, 1866); then went to France and Italy for additional study. Returning to Mexico after 4 years abroad, he presented two more operas: *Gino Corsini* (Mexico City, July 14, 1877) and *Cleopatra* (Mexico City, Nov. 14, 1891). Despite his passionate advocacy of national music, he followed conventional Italian models in his own works.

Morales, Olallo Juan Magnus, writer and composer; b. (of a Spanish father and Swedish mother) Almeria, Spain, Oct. 15, 1874; d. Tällberg, April 29, 1957. Taken to Sweden as a child, he received his education there, first at Göteborg, then at the Stockholm Cons. with W. Stenhammar and others (1891–99), and in Berlin with H. Urban (composition) and Teresa Carreño (piano). In 1901 he returned to Sweden; was conductor of the Göteborg Symph. Orch. (1905–09). From 1909 he lived in Stockholm; was prof. at the Stockholm Cons. (1917–39); secretary of the Academy of Music (1918–40). With T. Norlind he compiled a history of the Royal Academy of Music on its sesquicentennial (1921); also publ. a handbook of conducting (Stockholm, 1946). His works include a symph.; several overtures; Violin Concerto (1943); String Quartet; Piano Sonata; *Balada andaluza,* for piano (1946); *Nostalgia,* and other character pieces for piano; choral works; songs.

Moralt, Joseph, the eldest brother and 1st violin in a famous Munich string quartet of brothers; b. Schwetzingen, Aug. 5, 1775; d. Munich, Nov. 13, 1855. **Johann Baptist Moralt,** the 2nd violin (b. Mannheim, March 10, 1777; d. Munich, Oct. 7, 1825), wrote symphonies and string quartets; **Philipp Moralt,** the cellist (b. Munich, Dec. 29, 1780; d. there, Jan. 10, 1830), also played in the Munich municipal band; **Georg Moralt,** the viola player (b. Munich, 1781; d. there, 1818), was a member of the quartet until his death.

Moran, Robert Leonard, American composer of the avant-garde; b. Denver, Jan. 8, 1937. He studied piano; went to Vienna in 1958, where he took lessons in 12-tone composition with Hans Erich Apostel. Returning to America, he enrolled at Mills College, where he attended seminars of Luciano Berio and Darius Milhaud (M.A., 1963). At the same time he painted in the manner of abstract expressionism. In 1959 he toured Sweden as pianist in programs of hyper-modernistic compositions. His music is written in graphic notation, and is animated by surrealistic imagination.

WORKS: *Eclectic Boogies* for 13 percussionists (N.Y., Jan. 14, 1965); *Interiors* for any instrumental ensemble (San Francisco, April 12, 1965); *Within the Momentary Illumination* for 2 harps, electric guitar, timpani and brass (Tokyo, Dec. 1, 1965); *L'Après-midi du Dracoula* for any group of instruments capable of producing any kind of sound (1966); *Elegant Journey with Stopping Points of Interest* for orch. (1967); *Smell Piece for Mills College* for frying pans and foods (Mills College, Nov. 20, 1967; originally intended to produce a conflagration sufficiently thermal to burn down the college); *Scream Kiss No. 1* for harpsichord and stereophonic tape (1968); *Let's Build a Nut House*, opera in memory of Paul Hindemith (San Jose, April 19, 1969); *Titus* for amplified automobile and players (1969); *39 Minutes for 39 Autos*, environmental work for 30 skyscrapers, 39 auto horns, Moog synthesizer and players, employing 100,000 persons, directed from atop Twin Peaks in San Francisco, and making use of autos, airplanes, searchlights and local radio and television stations (San Francisco, Aug. 20, 1969); *Silver and the Circle of Messages* for chamber orch. (San Francisco, April 24, 1970); *Hallelujah*, "a joyous phenomenon with fanfares" for marching bands, drum and bugle corps, church choirs, organs, carillons, rock 'n' roll bands, television stations, automobile horns and any other sounding implements, commissioned by Lehigh Univ. for the city of Bethlehem, Pennsylvania, with the participation of its entire population of 72,320 inhabitants (staged in Bethlehem, April 23, 1971); *Divertissement No. 3*, a "street opera" (BBC Television, London, 1971); *Evening Psalm of Dr. Dracula* for prepared piano and tape (1973).

Moran-Olden, Fanny, German soprano; b. Oldenburg, Sept. 28, 1855; d. Berlin Feb. 13, 1905. She took lessons with Götze in Dresden, where she made her debut as Fanny Olden (her real name was **Tappenhorn**) in the role of Norma (1877); she then was at the Frankfurt Opera (1878–83), at the Leipzig City Theater (1884–91), and at the Munich Opera (1892–93); sang in New York during the 1888–89 season. She was twice married: in 1879 to the tenor **Karl Moran,** and in 1897 to **Bertram,** court singer in Munich.

Moravec, Ivan, Czech pianist; b. Prague, Nov. 9, 1930. He studied at the Prague Cons.; graduated in 1948 gaining the first prize in piano playing. He subsequently toured in Europe with considerable success. He made his American debut with the Cleveland Orch., Jan. 30, 1964.

Morawetz, Oskar, significant Czech-born Canadian composer; b. Svetla, Jan. 17, 1917. He studied with Jaroslav Křička at Prague Univ. (1933–36); after the invasion of Czechoslovakia by the Nazis in 1939 he went to Paris; then proceeded to Canada by way of

Italy and the Dominican Republic; entered the Univ. of Toronto (B.M., 1944; D. Mus., 1953). He taught at the Royal Cons. of Music in Toronto (1946–51) and from 1951 at the Univ. of Toronto. His music is Classical in format, Romantic in spirit, Impressionistic in coloring, and modernistic in harmonic usage.

WORKS: *Carnival Overture* (1946; Montreal, July 1, 1947); *Divertimento* for strings (1948); 2 symphonies: No. 1 (1951–53; first complete perf., Toronto, March 5, 1956; each movement is titled for separate performance—*Fantasy, Dirge* and *Scherzo*) and No. 2 (1959; Toronto, Feb. 2, 1960); *Overture to a Fairy Tale* (1956; Halifax, Feb. 8, 1957); *Capriccio* for orch. (1960); *Piano concerto* (1962; Montreal, April 23, 1963); *Sinfonietta* for strings (1963, revised 1968); *Passacaglia on a Bach Chorale* for orch. (1964; Toronto, Nov. 24, 1964); Sinfonietta for winds and percussion (1965; Montreal, Feb. 22, 1966); Concerto for Brass Quintet and Orch. (Toronto, March 28, 1968); *Memorial to Martin Luther King,* elegy for cello and orch. (1968; the last movement employs the popular spiritual *Free at Last*); *Reflections after a Tragedy* for orch. (1969); *Symphonic Intermezzo* (1971); *Improvisation* for cello and orch. (1973); *Harp Concerto* (1976); *Keep Us Free* for chorus and orch. (1951); *From the Diary of Anne Frank* for soprano or mezzo-soprano, and orch. (1970; Toronto, May 26, 1970); *A Child's Garden of Verses,* after R. L. Stevenson, for mezzo-soprano or alto or baritone, and orch. (Toronto, Feb. 10, 1973); 3 string quartets (1944, 1952–55, 1959); Duo for violin and piano (1947); Violin Sonata (1956); Trio for flute, oboe, and harpsichord or piano (1960); *2 Fantasies* for cello and piano (1962, revised 1970); *2 Preludes* for violin and piano (1965); piano works, including a *Sonata Tragica* (1945), *Scherzo* (1947), *Fantasy in D minor* (1948), *Tarantelle* (1949), *Ballade* (1950), *Fantasy on a Hebrew Theme* (1951), *Scherzino* (1953), *Fantasy, Elegy and Toccata* (1958), *10 Preludes* (1966), *Suite* (1968) and *Fantasy* (1973); many songs, some with orch., all listed in *Contemporary Canadian Composers* (Toronto, 1975; pp. 156–160).

Moreau, Jean-Baptiste, French composer; b. Angers, 1656; d. Paris, Aug. 24, 1733. He was a chorister at the Cathedral of Angers; then was choirmaster at the Cathedral of Langres. After a year in Dijon, he went to Paris in 1686; was introduced at the French court by the Dauphine, and was commissioned by Louis XIV to write several divertissements, among them *Les Bergers de Marly* (1687). He won great success with his musical interludes (recitatives and choruses) for Racine's *Esther* (1698) and *Athalie* (1691), performed at the royal school of St.-Cyr, where Moreau was maître de chapelle; also wrote music for Racine's *Cantiques spirituels,* for performance at St.-Cyr. His success at court was marred by his dissolute habits; however, he was greatly esteemed as a teacher of singing and composition; among his pupils were Montéclair, J. F. Dandrieu, Clérambault, and the singers Louise Couperin and his own daughter Marie-Claude Moreau. The music to *Esther* and *Athalie,* and the *Cantiques spirituels,* were publ. in the music supplement to P. Mesnard's *Oeuvres de J. Racine* (Paris, 1873).

BIBLIOGRAPHY: Th. Lavallée, *Historire de la mai-*

son royale de St.-Cyr (Paris, 1856); A. Taphanel, *Le Théâtre de St.-Cyr* (Paris, 1876); J. Tiersot, "Les Chœurs d'Esther et d'Athalie de Moreau," *Revue Musicale* (Jan. 1903); Kathi Meyer, *Der chorische Gesang der Frauen* (Leipzig, 1917); N. Demuth, "A Musical Backwater," *Musical Quarterly* (Oct. 1954).

Moreau, Léon, French composer; b. Brest, July 13, 1870; d. Paris, April 11, 1946. He studied at the Paris Cons., won the Grand Prix de Rome in 1899. Among his works are the operas *Myriade* and *Pierrot décoré;* the symph. poems *Sur la mer lointaine* and *Dionysos;* a piano concerto; many songs.

Moreira, Antonio, Portuguese composer; b. Lisbon; c.1750; d. there, Nov. 21, 1819. He studied at a seminary in Lisbon, and in 1775 became an instructor there. He wrote a number of operas in Italian, and 2 in Portuguese, for production at the Teatro San Carlos, where he was conductor until 1800. His Italian opera *Il Disertore* was given at La Scala, Milan (1800).

Morel, Auguste-François, French composer; b. Marseilles, Nov. 26, 1809; d. Paris, April 22, 1881. He lived in Paris from 1836 to 1850; then returned to Marseilles, and became director of the Cons. there; produced a grand opera *Le Jugement de Dieu* (1860); wrote a great deal of chamber music of excellent quality, for which he won the "Prix Chartier" twice; also 2 symphonies and a number of overtures.

Morel, François d'Assise, Canadian composer; Montreal, March 14, 1926. He studied piano with Trudel and composition with Claude Champagne, Isabelle Delorme and Germaine Malépart at the Quebec Provincial Cons. in Montreal (1944–53); in 1958 was a founding member (along with Joachim, Garant and Geanne Landry) of "Musique de notre temps," an organization specializing in performances of new music; then joined the faculty of the Institut Nazareth in Montreal. His music parallels the esthetic fashions of the modern times, from Debussyan coloristic imagism to motoric neo-Classicism to the organized sound of Varèse to the stern serialism of the cosmopolitan avant-garde.
WORKS: *Esquisse* for orch (1946–47; Montreal, Oct. 7, 1947; *Diptyque* for 23 instruments (1948, revised 1956; originally titled *Suite pour petit orchestre); Rondo Enfantin* for piano (1949); *Quatre chants japonais* for soprano and piano (1949); 2 string quartets (1952, 1962–63); *Antiphonie* for orch. (1953; N.Y., Oct. 16, 1953; Stokowski conducting); *2 Études de sonorité* for piano (1952–54); *Cassation* for woodwind septet (1954); *Les Rivages perdus* for soprano or tenor, and piano (1954); *Litanies* for winds, brass, harp, piano, celesta and percussion (1956, revised 1970); *Spirale* for winds, brass, harp, celesta and percussion (1956); *Symphonie* for brass and percussion (1956); *Intrada* for chorus and orch. (1957); *Rythomologue* for 8 percussionists (1957, revised 1970); *Rituel de l'Espace,* symph. poem (1956–58; Montreal, April 6, 1960); *Beatnik* for jazz band (1959); *Boréal* for orch. (1959; Montreal, April 26, 1960); *Le Mythe de la Roche Percée* for double woodwinds and percussion (1960–61; Pittsburgh, June 10, 1961); Brass Quintet

(1962); *L'Étoile Noire* for orch. (Montreal, March 13, 1962); *Requiem* for winds (1963); Sinfonia for jazz band (1963); *Trajectoire* for orch. (1967; Montreal, April 20, 1967); *Neumes d'Espace et Reliefs* for orch. (1967; Edmonton, Oct. 29, 1967); *Prismes-Anamorphoses* for winds, percussion, harp, piano and celesta (1967); *Départs* for 14 solo strings, harp, guitar and 2 percussionists (Montreal, March 17, 1969); *Iikkii (Froidure)* for 18 solo instruments (Montreal, Feb. 3, 1972); *Radiance* for small orch. (1970–72); *Me duele España,* variations for solo guitar (1975).

Morel, Jean, French conductor; b. Abbeville, Jan. 10, 1903; d. New York, April 14, 1975. He studied piano with Isidor Philipp, music theory with Noel Gallon, music theory with Maurice Emmanuel, opera conducting with Reynaldo Hahn and composition with Pierné; subsequently taught at the American Cons. in Fountainebleau (1921–36). At the outbreak of war in 1939 he emigrated to the U.S.; taught at Brooklyn College (1940–43); then conducted opera in Brazil and Mexico. In 1949 he was appointed to the faculty of the Juilliard School of Music, N.Y., and conductor of the Juilliard Orch. He also conducted at the Metropolitan Opera House.

Morelli, Carlo (real name **Carlos Zanelli**), Chilean baritone; b. Valparaiso, Dec. 25, 1897; d. Mexico City, May 12, 1970. He studied voice in Bologna with Angelo Queize, and in Florence with Leopoldo Mugnone. He sang at La Scala, Milan; toured South America (1925–31); made his first U.S. appearence with the Chicago City Opera in 1932; then sang at the Metropolitan Opera (1935–40) and with the San Carlo Opera at the City Center, N.Y. (1940–49). In 1949 he settled in Mexico.

Morelli, Giacomo, Italian librarian and music scholar; b. Venice, April 14, 1745; d. there, May 5, 1819. He was librarian at San Marco; discovered fragments of the *Art of Rhythm* by Aristoxenos, and published them in 1785.

Morelli, Giuseppe, Italian conductor; b. Rome, Aug. 2, 1907. He served as a choirboy in St. Peter's in Rome and studied at the St. Ceclia Cons., obtaining his diploma in composition in 1930. He subsequently took a course in conducting with Bernardino Molinari; rapidly earned the reputation as a fine opera conductor; in Italy he has had engagements with the Rome Opera, in Naples, Palmero, Parma, Bologna, and Venice. He also appeared as an opera conductor in Paris, Madrid, Vienna, Brussels, Amsterdam, West Berlin, in Scandinavia and Japan. He made a successful American debut as conductor at the New York City Opera in 1970.

Morelot, Stéphen, French scholar; authority on sacred music; b. Dijon, Jan. 12, 1820; d. Beaumont, Oct. 7, 1899. He was dean of the faculty of jurisprudence at Dijon Univ.; was co-editor (from 1845) of the *Revue de la musique religieuse, populaire et classique;* went to Italy in 1847 to study church music. He publ. numerous essays on the subject, among them *De la musique au XVᵉ siècle . . .* (1856), *Éléments de l'harmonie* *appliqués à l'accompagnement du plain-chant, d'après les traditions des anciennes écoles* (1861). His *Manuel de Psalmodie en fauxbourdons à 4 voix . . .* (1855) is an ingenious attempt to revive the ancient style of harmonization.

Morena (real name **Meyer**), **Berta,** German soprano; b. Mannheim, Jan. 27, 1878; d. Rottach-Eggern, Oct. 7, 1952. Her buxom beauty attracted the attention of the famous painter von Lenbach; at his behest, she was engaged (after brief training under Sophie Röhr-Brajnin in Munich) to sing Agathe in *Der Freischütz* at the Munich Opera (1898), and was immediately successful. She remained at the Munich Opera for more than 20 years; made her American debut with the Metropolitan Opera, N.Y., as Sieglinde (March 4, 1908), and remained a favorite for 5 consecutive seasons. Her talent as an actress greatly helped her in her career; she was regarded in Germany as one of the most intelligent and musicianly singers; excelled particularly in the Wagnerian parts (Elisabeth, Elsa, Eva, Isolde, the three Brünnhildes, etc.).
BIBLIOGRAPHY: A. Vogl, *Berta Morena und ihre Kunst* (Munich, 1919).

Moreno, Segundo Luis, Ecuadorian composer; b. Cotacachi, Aug. 3, 1882; d. Quito, Nov. 18, 1972. He played the clarinet in a civil band in Quito. He studied at the Quito Cons.; then was active as a military band leader in various localities in Ecuador; in 1937 took over the newly established Conservatorio Nacional de Música in Cuenca; later was director of the Cons. of Guayaquil. He composed mostly for military band; many of his pieces celebrate various patriotic events in Ecuador, as the canata, *La emancipación* (1920); overture, *9 de Julio* (1925) and various pieces on native motives, among them *3 Suites ecuatorianas* for orch. (1921, 1944, 1945). He publ. the valuable ethnomusicological treatises, *Música y danzas del Ecuador* (1949, in Spanish and in English) and *La música de los Incas* (1957).

Morera, Enrique, Spanish composer; b. Barcelona, May 22, 1865; d. there, March 11, 1942. As a child, he was taken to Argentina, and studied in Buenos Aires; then took courses at the Cons. of Brussels. Returning to Barcelona, he studied piano with Albéniz and harmony with Felipe Pedrell. In 1896 he founded a choral society, "Catalunya Nova," which he conducted for several years; taught at the Escuela Municipal de Música in Barcelona (1910–28). He was an ardent propagandist of Catalan music, and wrote a number of songs to Catalan words; also collected 193 melodies of popular origin. His opera *Emporium,* originally to a Catalan text, was performed first in Italian (Barcelona, Jan. 20, 1906); he wrote more than 50 other stage works (lyric comedies, zarzuelas, operettas, intermezzos, etc.); several symph. poems (*Atlántida, Traidoría,* etc.); a cello concerto; some chamber music; a set of 5 sardanas (national dances of Catalonia) for piano, etc.
BIBLIOGRAPHY: I. Iglesias, *E. Morera* (Barcelona, 1921; in Catalan).

Moreschi, Alessandro, the last of the artificial male sopranos; b. Montecompatri, near Rome, Nov. 11, 1858; d. Rome, April 21, 1922. He studied with Capocci in Rome; from 1883 to 1913 was sopranist at the Sistine Chapel in the Vatican. His voice was of such purity and beauty that he was nicknamed "l'angelo di Roma."
BIBLIOGRAPHY: Angus Heriot, *The Castrati in Opera* (London, 1956; appendix; pp. 225–27).

Morgan, Maud, American harpist; b. New York, Nov. 22, 1860; d. there, Dec. 2, 1941. She received her musical training from her father, George Washbourne Morgan (1823–1892); then studied in London; made her public debut in 1875 in a concert with Ole Bull.

Morgan, Russ, popular American trombonist and band leader; b. Scranton, Pa., April 29, 1904; d. Las Vegas, Aug. 7, 1969. A son of a coal-mine foreman, he worked the mines from the age of 9; learned piano from his mother; then studied the trombone. In 1923 he formed his first band The Scranton Sirens. Later he went to New York and became an arranger for John Philip Sousa. Subsequently he played in night clubs and theaters; in 1936 he formed a band to assist Rudy Vallee on his radio show. He ingratiated himself with audiences by the emotional use of the waah-waah mute on the trombone, obtaining effective contrasts in the mellow style of "sweet jazz."

Mori, Frank, English musician; son of **Nicolas Mori;** b. London, March 21, 1820; d. Chaumont, France, Aug. 2, 1873. He received his education from his father; wrote light music; his operetta *The River-Sprite* (London, Feb. 9, 1865) was fairly successful.

Mori, Nicolas, English violinist and music publisher (of Italian extraction); b. London, Jan. 24, 1796; d. there, June 14, 1839. He studied violin with Barthélemon and Viotti; gave many concerts as a soloist at an early age; also was a member of the London Philharmonic. He brought out the English editions of works by Mendelssohn, and other music. An eccentric, he wrote flamboyant advertisements about his career, and shortly before his death, announced his own memorial concert, punning on his name ("Memento Mori").
BIBLIOGRAPHY: E. W. Duffin, *Particulars of the Illness and Death of the Late Mr. Mori* (London, 1839).

Morillo, Roberto García, Argentine composer and music critic; b. Buenos Aires, Jan. 22, 1911. He studied composition with Aguirre and Juan José Castro; later took courses with Gaito and Ugarte. From 1926 to 1930 he was in Paris. Returning to Argentina he taught at the National Cons. in Buenos Aires and wrote music criticism for *La Nación.* His music is marked by propulsive rhythms and a strong sense of dissonant counterpoint. Among his works are a symph. poem, *Bersaerks* (Buenos Aires, Dec. 29, 1932); Piano Concerto (Buenos Aires, Nov. 7, 1940); *Las Pinturas negras de Goya,* for 6 instruments (Montevideo, May 27, 1940); *The Fall of the House of Usher,* after Poe (Buenos Aires, May 12, 1943); 3 symphonies (1948, 1955, 1961); *Variaciones olímpicas* for orch. (1958); *3 Pinturas de Piet Mondrian* (1960); *Ciclo de Dante Alighieri* for chamber orch. (1970); Quartet for violin, cello, clarinet and piano (1937); *Concerto a 9* for 3 clarinets and strings (1943); String Quartet (1951); 5 piano sonatas (1935–62); *Canata de los Caballeros* for soprano and orch. to words by García Lorca (1965); *Canata féstiva* a cappella (1971); also film music. Morillo publ. the monographs on Mussorgsky (1943), Rimsky-Korsakov (1945) and Carlos Chávez (1960); also publ. *Julian Bautista en la música española contemporánea* (1949). His biographical sketch and a list of works are found in *Compositores de América*, Vol. VIII (Washington, 1962).

Morin, Gösta, Swedish musicographer; b. Ludvika, April 14, 1900. He studied with T. Norlind at Uppsala Univ., and later in Germany, Austria, and Italy; in 1937 visited the U.S. He held the position of librarian at Uppsala Univ.; then at the Royal Music Academy in Stockholm; editor-in-chief of the valuable new edition of *Sohlmans Musik Lexikon* (Stockholm, 1948–53; 4 vols.).

Morini, Erica (originally **Erika**), violinist; b. Vienna, Jan. 5, 1904. Her father was Italian, her mother Viennese. She studied at her father's school of music in Vienna; then with Ševčik; made her professional debut as a child prodigy, at the age of 12; played with the Gewandhaus Orch. in Leipzig, under the direction of Nikisch (1918). She made her U.S. debut in N.Y. on Jan. 26, 1921; in subsequent years, played with virtually all major American orchestras; also toured South America, Australia, and the Orient; eventually settled in New York.

Morlacchi, Francesco, Italian composer; b. Perugia, June 14, 1784; d. Innsbruck, Oct. 28, 1841. He was a pupil of Caruso in Perugia, and of Zingarelli at Loreto; received the diploma of "maestro compositore" from the Liceo Filarmonico of Bologna (1805). At the time of graduation, he wrote a cantata for the coronation of Napoleon as King of Italy (1805); even earlier he wrote church music and an opera. His first stage work to be performed was an operetta *Il Poeta spiantata, o il Poeta in campagna* (Florence, 1807); he showed his contrapuntal skill in the composition of a Miserere in 16 parts; then produced a comic opera, *Il Ritratto* (Verona, 1807), and a melodrama, *Il Corradino* (Parma, 1808). His first signal success as an opera composer was the production of *Le Danaide* in Rome (Feb. 11, 1810). He was engaged as musical director of the Italian Opera in Dresden in 1811; wrote there several operas and, in 1814, a Mass in celebration of the return of the King of Saxony to Dresden; also wrote music for the Russian governor of Dresden during the occupation, and other occasional pieces. He continued to compose operas, for Naples, Milan, Venice, and Genoa, among them *Gianni di Parigi* (Milan, May 30, 1818), *Tebaldo ed Isolina* (Venice, Feb. 4, 1822; his most famous work; produced also in London, Paris, Leipzig, Prague, etc.), and *Colombo* (Genoa, June 21, 1828). When the King of Saxony died in 1827, Morlacchi wrote a Requiem, one of his finest works. He spent the last years of his life partly in Dresden and partly in Italy; he died on his way to Italy, at Innsbruck.

BIBLIOGRAPHY: G. B. Rossi-Scotti, *Della vita e delle opere del cav. Francesco Morlacchi . . . memorie istoriche* (Perugia, 1860); E. Magni-Dufflocq, "Francesco Morlacchi," *Bolletino Bibliografico Musicale* (1934).

Morley, Thomas, famous English composer; b. 1557; d. Oct. 1602; was a pupil of Byrd; Mus. Bac., Oxford, 1588; organist at St. Paul's Cath.; Gentleman of the Chapel Royal, 1592, also Epistler and Gospeller.

WORKS: *Conzonets, or Little Short Songs to three voyces* (1593); *Madrigalls to Foure Voyces* (1594); *The First Booke of Ballets to fiue Voyces* (1595; reprinted 1842 in score by the Musical Antiquarian Society); *The First Booke of Canzonets to Two Voyces* (1595); *Canzonets, or Little Short Aires to fiue and sixe voices* (1597); *The First Booke of Aires or Little Short Songs to sing and play to the Lute with the Base-Viol* (1600; contains the song *It was a lover and his lass* from *As You Like It*, reprinted in Knight's *Shakespeare* and Chappell's *Popular Music of the Olden Time*; the entire book was republ. by E. H. Fellowes, London, 1932). The canzonets *a* 3–4 and madrigals were publ. in modern score by Holland and Cooke; 5 sets of harpsichord lessons are in *Queen Elizabeth's Virginal Book*; services and anthems are in Barnard's and Boyce's collections. The complete secular works are publ. in E. H. Fellowes's *The English Madrigal School* (4 vols., 1914 ff.; I. *Canzonets to 2 voices* [1595] and *Canzonets to 3 voices* [1593]; II. *Madrigals to 4 voices* [1594]; III. *Canzonets to 5 and 6 voices* [1597]; IV. *Ballets to 5 voices* [1600]. Morley edited *Canzonets or Little Short Songs for Four Voyces. Collected out of the best and approued Italian Authors* (1598); *Madrigals to fiue voyces* [ditto] (1598); and *The Triumphes of Oriana, to fiue and six voyces composed by divers seurall aucthors* (1601; reprinted in score by Wm. Hawes). He wrote the first regular treatise on music publ. in England: *A Plaine and Easie Introduction to Practicall Musicke* (1597; reprinted by E. H. Fellowes, London, 1937; modernized ed., by R. Alec Harman, London, 1952); ed. the collection of instrumental music, *The First Booke of Consort Lessons, made by divers exquisite Authors for six Instruments to play together, viz. the Treble Lute, the Pandora, the Citterne, the Base Violl, the Flute, and the Treble Violl* (1599; revised ed. 1611; new ed. by Sidney Beck, N.Y., 1958).

BIBLIOGRAPHY: O. Becker, *Die englischen Madrigalisten W. Bird, Th. Morley und J. Dowland* (Bonn, 1901); E. H. Fellowes, *The English Madrigal Composers* (London, 1921; 2nd ed., 1948); Margaret Glyn, *About Elizabethan Virginal Music and Its Composers* (London, 1924); E. H. Fellowes, *The English Madrigal* (London, 1925) and *The English Madrigal School, a Guide to Its Practical Use* (London, 1926); J. E. Uhler's *Morley's Canzonets for Two Voices* (Univ. of Louisiana, Baton Rouge, 1954) and *Morley's Canzonets for Three Voices* (Baton Rouge, 1957), with facsimile eds., transcriptions of texts, and commentaries.

Mornington, Garrett Colley Wellesley, Earl of, the father of the Duke of Wellington; b. Dangan, Ireland,

July 19, 1735; d. London, May 22, 1781. He was a glee composer. In 1776 and 1777 the Catch Club awarded him prizes for catches; and in 1779 for the glee *Here in a cool grot.* Sir Henry Bishop edited a complete collection of his glees and madrigals (1846). Mornington was Mus. Doc., Dublin, and prof. at Dublin Univ. from 1764 to 1774.

Moroi, Makoto, Japanese composer, son of **Saburo Moroi;** b. Tokyo, March 12, 1930. He studied composition with his father and Tomojiro Ikenouchi at the Tokyo Academy of Music (1948-52); later taught at the Osaka Univ. of Arts and Science. His music partakes of three different sources which sometimes fuse into a unified modality; ancient Japanese elements, serialism, and sonorism, i.e. organized sound with electronic instruments.
WORKS: *Composition No. 1* for orch. (1951-53), *No. 2* for orch. (1958), *No. 3* for narrator, male chorus and orch. (1958), *No. 4* for narrator, 3 speaking sopranos, chorus and orch. (1960), and *No. 5, Ode to Arnold Schoenberg,* for chamber orch. (Osaka, Aug. 26, 1961); *Suite Classique* for orch. (1953); *Suite Concertante* for violin and orch. (Kyoto, Sept. 7, 1963); Piano Concerto (1966); Symph. (Tokyo, Nov. 7, 1968); Concerto for shakuhachi (Japanese bamboo flute), string orch. and percussion (1970-71); *Pitagorasu no hoshi (Stars of Pythagoras)* for narrator, chorus, tape and chamber orch. (1959); *Cantata da camera No. 1* for Ondes Martenot, harpsichord, 3 percussionists, male chorus and narrator (1959); *Cantata da camera No. 2, Blue Cylinder,* for narrator, solo soprano, chorus and chamber orch. (1959); *The Red Cocoon* for narrator, pantomime, 2 choruses, tape and orch. (1960); *Phaeton, the Coachman* for narrator, solo voice, chorus and tape (1965); *Vision of Cain,* symph. sketch for ballet (1966); *Izumo, My Home!* for baritone, soprano, chorus, orch. and tape (1970); Symphony for voice, percussion, Japanese instruments and tape (1972); *Musica da camera No. 3* for viola and wind quintet (1951); *Musica da camera No. 4* for string quartet (1954); *Partita* for solo flute (1953); *Albumblätter* for solo oboe (1953); *Développements raréfiants* for soprano and chamber group (Karuizawa, July 12, 1957); *Ordre* for Cello and Piano (1958); *5 Épigrammes* for flute, clarinet, vibraphone, celeste, harp, violin and cello (Tokyo, Feb. 29, 1964); *Kusabira (Mushrooms)* for 2 voices and electronic sound (1964); *Toccata, Sarabande and Tarantella* for strings and piano (1964); *5 Dialogues* for 2 shakuhachi (1965); *Les Farces* for solo violin (1970); the piano pieces, *Alpha and Beta* (1953-54), Sonatina (1966) and *8 Parables* (1967); *Contradiction I* and *II* (1972) and several other works for Japanese instruments alone.

Moroi, Saburo, Japanese composer, father of **Makoto Moroi;** b. Tokyo, Aug. 7, 1903. He studied literature at Tokyo Univ. (1926-28), later took lessons in composition with Max Trapp, orchestration with Gmeindl, and piano with Robert Schmidt at the Hochschule für Musik in Berlin (1932-34). Upon returning to Japan he was active as a music teacher; among his students who achieved a reputation as composers in their own right were Dan, Irino and his son Makoto Moroi.
WORKS: Piano Concerto (1933); 5 symphonies:

No. 1 (Berlin, Oct. 2, 1934), No. 2 (Tokyo, Oct. 12, 1938), No. 3 with organ (Tokyo, May 26, 1950), No. 4 (Tokyo, March 26, 1951) and No. 5 (Tokyo, 1971); Cello Concerto (1936); Bassoon Concerto (1937); Violin Concerto (1939); *2 Symphonic Movements* (1942); Sinfonietta (1943); *Allegro* for piano and orch. (1947); *2 Songs* for soprano and orch. (1935); a fantasy-oratorio, *A Visit of the Sun* (Tokyo, June 30, 1969); Violin Sonata (1930); String Quartet (1933); Piano Quartet (1935); Viola Sonata (1935); Flute Sonata (1937); String Sextet (1939); String Trio (1940); 2 piano sonatas (1933, 1940); *Preludio ed Allegro giocoso* for piano (1971). Among his numerous publications are a text *Junsui talicho,* on strict counterpoint, and the 5-vol. edition, *Historical Research of Musical Forms* (Tokyo, 1957-67).

Moross, Jerome, American composer; b. Brooklyn, Aug. 1, 1913. He studied music at the Juilliard School, N.Y.; became associated with various ballet groups; wrote several scores for dance, among them *Paul Bunyan* (1934), *American Pattern* (1937), *Frankie and Johnny* (1938), *Guns and Castanets* (1939), *Robin Hood* (1946); and ballet-operas: *Susanna and the Elders* (1940), *Willie the Weeper* (1945), *The Eccentricities of Davy Crockett* (1946), *The Golden Apple* (1952), *Gentlemen, Be Seated!* (N.Y., Oct. 10, 1963); the ballet suite, *The Last Judgment* (1953); also Symphony (Seattle, Oct. 18, 1943); *Beguine,* for orch. (N.Y., Nov. 21, 1934); *A Tall Story,* for orch. (N.Y., Sept. 25, 1938); Sonatina for clarinet choir (1966); Sonatina for strings, bass and piano (1967); Sonatina for brass quintet (1968); Sonatina for woodwind quintet (1970).

Morphy, Guillermo, Conde de, Spanish courtier and musician; b. Madrid, Feb. 29, 1836; d. Baden, Switzerland, Aug. 28, 1899. He was taken to Germany as a child; there he studied music; took courses with Fétis in Brussels, where he wrote an orchestral *Serenata española,* which had several performances. In 1864 he was named "chamber gentleman" to the Prince of Asturias, the future Alfonso XII, and then became his secretary; received his nobiliary title in 1885. He spent much time in Vienna and Paris, and took up the study of Spanish tablature music of the 16th century. His transcriptions (marred by inaccuracies) were publ. posthumously, with an introduction by Gevaert, as *Les Luthistes espagnols du XVIe siècle* (2 vols., Leipzig, 1902; German text by Riemann). In his influential position at the Spanish court, Morphy helped many talented musicians; was instrumental in procuring a stipend for Albéniz to enable him to study in Brussels.

Morris, Harold, American composer and pianist; b. San Antonio, Texas, March 17, 1890; d. New York City, May 6, 1964. He studied at the Univ. of Texas (B.A.) and the Cincinnati Cons.; lectured at the Rice Institute of Houston, Texas (1933), at Duke Univ. (1939-40), etc.; was on the faculty of Juilliard School of Music (1922-39); Teachers College, Columbia Univ. (1939-46); received many awards (National Federation of Music Clubs, Philadelphia Music Guild Award, etc.); was one of the principal founders of the American Music Guild (N.Y., 1921). In his music, he reveals himself as a Romanticist; in the main direction of his creative development, he was influenced by Scriabin. Many of his works are of programmatic content; some of them include American thematic material.

WORKS: for orch: *Poem*, after Tagore's *Gitanjali* (Cincinnati, Nov. 29, 1918); *Dum-A-Lum*, variations on a Negro spiritual, for chamber orch. (1925); Piano Concerto (Boston, Oct. 23, 1931, composer soloist; very successful); Symph. No. 1, after Browning's *Prospice* (1934); *Passacaglia and Fugue* (1939); *Suite*, for chamber orch. (N.Y., Nov. 1, 1941); Violin Concerto (N.Y., May 25, 1939); *American Epic* (1942); Symph. No. 2, subtitled *Victory* (Chicago, Dec. 23, 1952); *Heroic Overture* (1943); Symph. No. 3, subtitled *Amaranth*, after Edwin A. Robinson (Houston, March 13, 1948); chamber music: 2 piano trios, 2 string quartets, 2 piano quintets, violin sonata, *Prologue and Scherzo*, for flute, violin, cello, and piano, *Rhapsody*, for flute, cello, and piano; 4 piano sonatas; other piano pieces.

Morris, Reginald Owen, English composer and eminent pedagogue; b. York, March 3, 1886; d. London, Dec. 15, 1948. He studied at the Royal College of Music, with Charles Wood; from 1920, taught at the Royal College of Music, with the exception of 2 years (1926–28), when he taught theory at the Curtis Institute of Music in Philadelphia.

WORKS: Symph. in D; Violin Concerto; *Concerto Piccolo* for 2 violins and string orch.; *Fantasy* for string quartet; songs. It is mainly as an excellent teacher that Morris established himself; he gave considerable freedom to his students in expressing their individuality without adhering too closely to academic dogma. He publ.: *Contrapuntal Technique in the XVIth Century* (1922); *Foundations of Practical Harmony and Counterpoint* (1925); *Preparatory Exercises in Score Reading* (with H. Ferguson; 1931); *Figured Harmony at the Keyboard* (1933); *The Structure of Music* (1935); *The Oxford Harmony* (vol. 1 only; 1946).

BIBLIOGRAPHY: E. Rubbra, "R. O. Morris: An Appreciation," *Music & Letters* (Jan. 1949).

Morse, Charles Henry, American organist; b. Bradford, Mass., Jan. 5, 1853; d. Boston, June 4, 1927. He studied at the New England Cons. and at the Boston Univ. College of Music, with J. K. Paine; then taught at various Boston schools, at Minneapolis, and in Brooklyn, before returning to Boston. He publ. a number of anthems, Christmas carols, etc.; many arrangements for organ, and several valuable compilations (*The Contemporary Organist, The Church Organist, The Junior Church Organist,* etc.).

Mortari, Virgilio, Italian composer and pianist; b. Passirana di Lainate, near Milan, Dec. 6, 1902. He studied at the Milan Cons. with Bossi and Pizzetti; after a few years of activities as a concert pianist he became instructor at the Cons. Benedetto Marcello in Venice; in 1940 was appointed prof. of music at the S. Cecilia in Rome; in 1963 he became Vice-President there. His music combines the traits of the Italian Baroque and the modern French school of composition.

He wrote the operas *Secchi e Sberlecchi* (1927), *La Scuola delle moglie* (1930), *La Figlia del diavolo* (Milan, March 24, 1954) and *Il contratto* (1962); he also completed Mozart's unfinished work *L'Oca del Cairo*, which was performed in his version in Salzburg, Aug. 22, 1936. He further wrote the ballets *L'Allegra piazetta* (1945), *Specchio a tre luci* (1973), and numerous orchestral works, among them Fantasia, for piano and orch. (1933), *Notturno incantato* (1940), Piano Concerto (1952), the overture, *Eleonora d'Arborea* (1968), *Tripartita* (1972); concertos for solo instruments with orch.: Piano Concerto (1960), Viola Concerto (1966), Double-Bass Concerto (1966), Violin Concerto (1967), Double Concerto for violin and piano (1968), Cello Concerto (1969), Harp Concerto (1972); also Concerto for String Quartet and Orch. (1937); Sonatina for harp (1938), *Piccola serenata* for cello solo (1946), *Piccola seranata* for violin solo (1947), *Duettini concertati* for violin and double bass (1966), *Capriccio* for violin solo (1967); vocal works: *2 Funeral Psalms* in memory of Alfred Casella for voice and instruments (1947); *Alfabeto a sorpresa* for 3 voices and 2 pianos (1959); songs with piano. He publ. *La tecnica dell'orchestra contemporanea* (in collaboration with Casella; Milan, 1947); also arranged fragments from operas by Galuppi, Pergolesi and Monteverdi.

Mortelmans, Ivo, Belgian composer; son of **Lodewijk Mortelmans**; b. Antwerp, May 19, 1901. He studied at the Antwerp Con.; upon graduation he taught academic subjects and theory in Berchem (1925-66), and concurrently at Deurne (1930-70) and Mortsel (1946-67). He was active as an opera conductor. He wrote an oratorio, *Eeuwig vlecht de bruid haar kroon* (1964) and numerous other choral works, both sacred and secular.

Mortelmans, Lodewijk, Belgian composer; b. Antwerp, Feb. 5, 1868; d. there, June 24, 1952. He was a chorister in the Dominican Church; then studied with Benoit in Antwerp. In 1889 he won the 2nd Belgian Prix de Rome; gained 1st prize with his cantata *Lady Macbeth* in 1893; then taught at the Antwerp Cons. In 1921 he made a tour in the U.S.; was director of the Antwerp Cons. from 1924 to 1933.

WORKS: opera, *De Kinderen der Zee* (Antwerp, 1920); symph. poems, *Helios* (1894), *Mythe du Printemps* (1895), *Avonlied* (1928), *Weemoedig Aandenken* (1950); church cantata *Jong Vlaanderen* (1907); *Symphonie homérique* (1898); 4 elegies for orch.: *In memoriam* (1917), *Elevation du Cœur* (1917), *Solitude* (1919), *Treurdicht* (1925); 3 sets of *Miniatures* for piano; *27 Old Flemish Folksongs*, for piano; a number of songs to Flemish words, which are his finest creations. Paul Gilson called him "Prince of the Flemish song."

BIBLIOGRAPHY: The Belgian Center of Musical Documentation publ. a complete catalogue of his works, with a brief biography in Flemish, French, and English (Brussels, 1954). See also: J. L. Broeckx, *Lodewijk Mortelmans* (Antwerp, 1945).

Mortensen, Finn, Norwegian composer; b. Oslo, Jan. 6, 1922. He studied harmony with Thorleif Eken (1942), vocal polyphony with Egge (1943), and in the winter of 1956, composition with Niels Viggo Bentzon in Copenhagen. In 1970 he was appointed to the faculty of the Cons. of Oslo; in 1972 succeeded Egge as chairman of the Norwegian Society of Composers. He adopted in his later works a modified 12-tone idiom supplemented by the devices of permutation and thematic rotation.

WORKS: Symphony (1953); *Pezzo Orchestrale* (1957); *Evolution* for orch. (1961); *Tone Colors* for orch. (1962); Piano Concerto (1963); *Fantasy* for piano and orch. (Oslo, May 6, 1966); *Per Orchestra* (1967); 2 piano sonatinas (1943; 1949); String Trio (1950); 2 wind quintets (1951, 1972); Solo Flute Sonata (1953); Piano Sonata (1956); Duo for soprano and violin (1956); Sonatina for solo clarinet (1957); Sonatina for balalaika and piano (1957); *5 Studies* for solo flute (1957); *Fantasy and Fugue* for piano (1958); Sonata for viola solo (1959); Sonata for viola and piano (1959); Oboe Sonatina (1959); *Fantasy* for solo bassoon (1959); Piano Quartet (1960); *3 Pieces* for violin and piano (1961-63); 12 short dodecaphonic piano pieces for children (1961-64); 12-tone music for amateur wind players (1961-64); 2-Piano Sonata (1964); *Drawing* for piano (1966); *Chamber Music* for clarinet, bassoon, trumpet, trombone, percussion, violin and double bass (1968); *Impressions* for 2 pianos (1971); *Constellations* for accordion, guitar and percussion (1971); *Serenata* for cello and piano (1972).

Mortensen, Otto, Danish composer; b. Copenhagen, Aug. 18, 1907. He studied piano, organ and composition at the Cons. of Copenhagen; in 1939 went to Paris where he studied with Darius Milhaud. In 1942 he joined the staff of the Cons. of Copenhagen. He composes mostly vocal music; among his instrumental works are: String Quartet (1937); Quartet for flute, violin, cello and piano (1938); Wind Quintet (1944); Oboe Sonata (1947); Piano Concerto (1948); Symph. (1957).

Morthenson, Jan W., Swedish composer; b. Örnsköldsvik, April 1, 1940. He studied academic musical subjects with Lidholm in Stockholm; then went to Cologne where he worked with G. M. Koenig in electronic techniques; also attended the summer courses on new music in Darmstadt; in 1970 he visited the U.S., and gave lectures at the Cons. of San Francisco. In his compositions he devised a "non-figurative" method in which "individual changes in sound are imperceptible," and publ. a treatise *Non-figurative Musik* (Copenhagen, 1966).

WORKS: 4 pieces entitled *Coloratura: I* for strings and tape (1960); *II* for orch. (1962), *III* for chamber orch. (1962–63) and *IV* for orch. (1963), 3 *Wechselspiel: I* for cello (1960), *II* for flute and 3 loudspeakers (1961) and *III* for piano and percussion (1961); *Canzona* for 6 choral groups, percussion and loudspeakers (1961); *Chains-Mirrors*, electro-acoustical work for soprano (1961); *Some of these . . .*, graphic music for organ (1961); *Courante I, II and III*, graphic music for piano (1962); *Pour Madame Bovary* for organ (1962); 3 *Antiphonia: I* for orch. (1963), *II* for chamber orch. (1963) and *III* for chamber orch. (1970); *Eternes* for organ (1964); the computer pieces, *Neutron Star* (1967), *Spoon River* (1967), *Ultra* (1971) and *Sensory*

Project I and *II* (1971); the electronic pieces, *Interferences* (1967), *Epsilon Eridani* (1967), *Ionosphères* (1969) and *Zero* (1969); *Decadenza I* for organ and tape (1968); *Decadenza II* for orch. with tape and film (1970; Uppsala, Jan. 18, 1972); *Colossus* for orch. (1970; Berlin, Nov. 26, 1972); *Farewell* for organ (1970); *Senza* for strings (1970); *Labor* for chamber orch. (1971); *Life* for tenor, orch. and instrumental group (1972); *Video I* for 8 solo strings (1972); *Alla Marcia* for female chorus, orch., tape and 8 stroboscopes (1972-73; Stockholm, March 31, 1974); *5 Pieces* for orch. (1973). He also wrote several experimental picture-sound productions for video projection, including *Supersonics* (1970), *Camera Humana* (1972) and *Sensory Project III* (1972); film score, *Interferences I* (1967).

Morton, "Jelly Roll" (real Christian names **Ferdinand Joseph La Menthe**), black-American (actually, a "Creole-of-color," having mixed African and French-American ancestry) ragtime-blues-jazz pianist and composer; b. New Orleans, Sept. 20, 1885; d. Los Angeles, July 10, 1941. Born into a French-speaking family that proudly recalled its former days of wealth and position, Morton grew up surrounded by musical instruments and frequently attended performances at the New Orleans French Opera House. He played several instruments, but settled on the piano and (against the wishes of his family) was playing professionally by the time he was 15; he worked with Bunk Johnson in 1900, and was particularly successful as a pianist in the local bordellos of "Storyville" (the red-light district of New Orleans). He left New Orleans in 1907 and traveled through much of the U.S., both spreading his concept of ragtime and jazz, and learning the various regional styles; he was in N.Y. in 1911, Tulsa in 1912, San Francisco and Chicago in 1915, etc.; also traveled in Mexico and Canada. He was a colorful and flamboyant figure, given to extravagant boasting and flashy living; in addition to his being a musician, he was a professional gambler (cards and billiards), night club owner, and producer; he made and lost several fortunes. His early compositions (*King Porter Stomp*, comp. 1902, publ. 1924; *Jelly Roll Blues*, comp. 1905, publ. 1915) are important samples of the styles of the period. Around 1922 he made his first piano rolls, and in 1923 began recording, both solo and with the New Orleans Rhythm Kings (unusual, for this was a white group); his own band, the Red Hot Peppers, recorded during the years 1926-30 and produced some of the finest samples ever made of the New Orleans Dixieland style. In 1938 he recorded for the Library of Congress, playing piano, singing, demonstrating styles, relating anecdotes and stories, and creating, in sound, his view of the history of jazz; a major outgrowth of these recordings is his biography, Alan Lomax's *Mister Jelly Roll. The Fortunes of Jelly Roll Morton, New Orleans Creole and "Inventor of Jazz"* (N.Y., 1950; 2nd ed. Berkeley, 1973).

Morton, Robert, English composer; b. c.1440; d. 1475. He was clerk of the chapel of Philip the Good and Charles the Bold of Burgundy; possibly identical with **Robertus Anglicus** (d. 1485), a singer at St. Peter's, Rome. Some of his compositions are preserved in the

Kopenhagener Chansonnier publ. by K. Jeppesen (1927); several manuscripts are in Belgian archives.

Mosca, Giuseppe, Italian composer of operas; b. Naples, 1772; d. Messina, Sept. 14, 1839. He studied with Fenaroli; was engaged as *répétiteur* at the Théâtre-Italien, Paris (1803–09); then was maestro di cappella in Palmero (1817–21); director of music at the Messina Theater (after 1823). He was a prolific composer; wrote 44 operas, which were produced on leading Italian stages; also ballets and other theatrical pieces.

Mosca, Luigi, Italian composer; brother of **Giuseppe Mosca**; b. Naples, 1775; d. there, Nov. 30, 1824. He was pupil of Fenaroli; served as maestro al cembalo at the San Carlo Theater in Naples; later taught singing. He produced 14 operas, of which *I Pretendenti delusi* (Milan, Sept. 7, 1811) was the most successful.

Moscheles, Ignaz, eminent pianist, pedagogue, and composer; b. Prague, May 23, 1794; d. Leipzig, March 10, 1870. Of a well-to-do family (his father was a Jewish merchant), he was trained in music as soon as his ability was discovered; his 1st piano teacher was Dionys Weber at the Prague Cons.; at the age of 14, Moscheles performed publicly a concerto of his own composition. On his father's death, shortly after, he went to Vienna to study under Albrechtsberger and Salieri, at the same time earning his living as a teacher. His conspicuous talents won him access to the best circles; he prepared the piano score of Beethoven's *Fidelio*. At concerts in Munich, Dresden, and Leipzig (1816), and in Paris (1820), his remarkable playing was much applauded; he was a pioneer in developing various modifications of tone by touch, afterwards exploited by Liszt. In 1821 Moscheles settled in London; made frequent trips to the Continent, and gave Mendelssohn piano lessons at Berlin in 1824. The teacher and the pupil became close friends; on July 13, 1829, they gave the first performance in London of Mendelssohn's Concerto for 2 Pianos and Orch. After the foundation of the Leipzig Cons. in 1846, Mendelssohn invited Moscheles to join its staff. There, a host of pupils from all quarters of the globe were trained by him with sympathetic consideration, and yet with unflinching discipline in musical matters. He was noted for his energetic, brilliant, and strongly rhythmical playing; his virtuosity equalled his emotional absorption in the music; his romantic pieces for piano expressed clearly his ideas of the extent and the limitations of the instrument.

WORKS: 8 piano concertos, of which Nos. 3, 5, and 6 were favorites; also wrote, for piano and orch., *Marche d'Alexandre, Souvenirs d'Irlande, Souvenirs de Danemark,* etc.; *Grand Septuor,* for piano, violin, viola, clarinet, horn, cello, and double bass; *Grand Sextuor,* for piano, violin, flute, 2 horns, and cello; Piano Trio; piano duos with violin, with horn, and with guitar; for 2 pianos, *Hommage à Haendel;* for 2 pianos, 8 hands, *Les Contrastes;* for piano, 4 hands, *Sonate mélancolique, Allegro di bravura, La Tenerezza, Les Charmes de Paris;* also excellent studies (*Characteristics Studies,* in 2 books; *54 Études de concert;* the études

L'Ambition and *L'Enjouement,* etc.). His output totals 142 opus numbers. See his thematic index, *Thematisches Verzeichnis im Druck erschienener Compositionen* (1885; repr. London, 1967). Moscheles translated Schindler's biography of Beethoven into English (with numerous additions), publ. as *The Life of Beethoven* (2 vols., London, 1841). His wife **Charlotte Moscheles,** *née* **Embden** (d. Detmold, Dec. 13, 1889), wrote *Aus Moscheles' Leben* (Leipzig, 1872; 2 vols.; English transl., London, 1873). His correspondence with Mendelssohn was publ. by his son, **F. Moscheles,** who also publ. his father's memoirs, as *Fragments of an Autobiography* (London, 1899).

BIBLIOGRAPHY: Excerpts of Moscheles's diaries and letters were published in transl. by A. O. Coleridge: *Recent Music and Musicians as Described in the Diaries and Correspondence of Ignaz Moscheles* (1873; repr. N.Y., 1970). G. Servières, "Moscheles," *Revue Pleyel* (Paris, Dec. 1926); H. Engel, *Die Entwicklung des deutschen Klavierkonzertes von Mozart bis Liszt* (1927); J. Roche, "Ignaz Moscheles," *Musical Times* (March 1970).

Moscona, Nicola, Greek operatic bass; b. Athens, Sept. 23, 1907; d. Philadelphia, Sept. 17, 1975. He studied singing at the Athens Cons. with Elena Theodorini. He sang opera in Greece and Eygpt; then went to Milan; in 1937 he was engaged to sing at the Metropolitan Opera, N.Y., and made a successful American debut there as Ramphis in *Aida* (Dec. 13, 1937); remained on its staff until 1962; then went to Philadelphia where he taught at the Academy of Vocal Arts.

Mosel, Ignaz Franz von, Austrian composer, conductor, and writer on music; b. Vienna, April 7, 1772; d. there, April 8, 1844. He began his career as an opera conductor, and was the first in Vienna to use a baton (1812). In 1816 he conducted the first concert of the Gesellschaft der Musikfreunde. In 1820 he was appointed vice-director of the court theaters in Vienna, and in 1829, custodian of the Imperial Library.

WORKS: 3 of his operas were produced at the Court Opera in Vienna: *Die Feuerprobe* (April 28, 1811), *Salem* (March 5, 1813), and *Cyrus und Astyages* (June 13, 1818); publ. 3 collections of songs. WRITINGS: *Versuch einer Ästhetik des dramatischen Tonsatzes* (1813); *Über das Leben und die Werke des Anton Salieri* (1827); *Über die Originalpartitur des Requiems von W. A. Mozart* (1829); *Geschichte der kaiserl. königl. Hofbibliothek zu Wien* (1835); and *Die Tonkunst in Wien während der letzten fünf Dezennien* (1818, in the Vienna *Allgemeine musikalische Zeitung;* separate reprint, 1840).

BIBLIOGRAPHY: R. Batka, "Moseliana," *Musikbuch aus Österreich* (1911 and 1912).

Mosenthal, Joseph, German violinist and composer; b. Kassel, Nov. 30, 1834; d. New York, Jan. 6, 1896. He was a pupil of his father and Spohr, and played in the court orch. of Kassel under Spohr's direction. He emigrated to America in 1853; was organist at the Calvary Church, N.Y. (1860–87); from 1867, was conductor of the N.Y. Mendelssohn Glee Club; also was a violinist in the N.Y. Philharmonic (for 40 years). He publ. anthems, hymns, and other sacred works for the

Episcopal Church, and part-songs for male chorus (*Thanatopsis, Blest pair of Sirens, Music of the Sea,* etc.); *Sunday Lyrics* (6 songs); psalm, *The Earth is the Lord's;* numerous songs.

Moser, Andreas, notable German violinist and music scholar; b. Semlin, Hungary, Nov. 29, 1859; d. Berlin, Oct. 7, 1925. He studied first in Zürich, with Hegar; also took courses in engineering and architecture in Stuttgart; in 1878 he became a violin pupil of Joachim in Berlin; in 1883 was concertmaster in Mannheim; in 1884 settled in Berlin. In 1888 he was appointed teacher at the Hochschule für Musik, a post he held until his death. He publ. a number of valuable studies on the history of the violin.

WRITINGS: *Joseph Joachim. Ein Lebensbild* (1899; 2nd enlarged ed., in 2 vols., 1908; 1910); *Methodik des Violinspiels* (2 parts; 1920); *Geschichte des Violinspiels* (1923; also in English); *Technik des Violinspiels* (2 vols.; 1925); collaborated with Joachim in a 3-vol. *Violinschule* (1902–05; French by Marteau; English by Moffat); ed. *Johannes Brahms im Briefwechsel mit Joseph Joachim* (1908; vols. V and VI of the Brahms correspondence) and, with Johannes Joachim, *Briefe von und an Joseph Joachim* (3 vols., 1911–13); edited (with Joachim) Beethoven's string quartets and Bach's partitas for violin; also various other violin works.

BIBLIOGRAPHY: H. J. Moser, *Andreas Moser,* in Ebel's *Berliner Musikjahrbuch* (1926, p. 106ff.).

Moser, Hans Joachim, eminent German musicologist; son of **Andreas Moser;** b. Berlin, May 25, 1889; d. there, Aug. 14, 1967. He studied violin with his father; musicology with Kretzschmar and Johannes Wolf in Berlin, with Jenner and Schiedermair in Marburg, with Riemann and Schering in Leipzig; also took courses in singing with Oskar Noë and Felix Schmidt; composition with H. van Eyken and Robert Kahn; he received his Dr. phil. at the Univ. of Rostock, with the dissertation *Die Musikergenossenschaften im deutschen Mittelalter* (1910). Returning to Berlin, he was active as a concert singer (bass baritone); was in the German army during World War I. In 1919, he became privatdozent of musicology at the Univ. of Halle; in 1922, prof. there; 1925, prof. at the Univ. of Heidelberg; 1927, honorary prof. at the Univ. of Berlin; from 1927 to 1933, director of the State Academy for Church- and School-music in Berlin; in 1931 he received the degree of Dr. theol., Königsberg. During World War II he worked in Berlin as music editor; in 1947 became prof. at Jena Univ. and the Hochschule für Musik in Weimar; in 1950, appointed director of the Berlin Cons. As a music historian and lexicographer, he was preëminent; particularly important are his writings on German church music. His unquestionable scholarship was marred by his ardent espousal of the Nazi racial philosophy; so ferocious was his anti-semitism that he excluded Mendelssohn from his books published during the Nazi years.

WRITINGS: *Technik der deutschen Gesangskunst* (after Oskar Noë; 1911; 2nd ed., 1955); *Geschichte der deutschen Musik* (3 vols.: I. 1920, 5th ed. 1930; II. 1922, 5th ed. 1930; III. 1924, 2nd ed. 1928); *Musikalischer Zeitenspiegel* (1922); *Musikalisches Wörterbuch*

(1923); *Die evangelische Kirchenmusik in volkstümlichem Überblick* (1926); *Paul Hofhaimer* (1929); *Das Studium der Musikwissenschaft in Deutschland* (1929); *Die Epochen der Musikgeschichte* (1930; 2nd ed., 1956); *Die mehrstimmige Vertonung des Evangeliums* (2 vols.; 1931, 1934); *Corydon; das ist: Geschichte des mehrstimmigen Generalbassliedes und des Quodlibets im deutschen Barock* (2 vols., 1933); *Die Melodien der Lutherlieder* (1935); *Tönende Volksaltertümer* (1935); *J. S. Bach* (1935; 2nd ed., 1954); *Heinrich Schütz* (1936; 2nd. ed., 1954); *Lehrbuch der Musikgeschichte* (1936; 12th ed., 1954); *Das deutsche Lied seit Mozart* (1937); *Kleine deutsche Musikgeschichte* (1938; 4th ed., 1955); *Kleines Heinrich-Schütz-Buch* (1940; 2nd ed., 1950); *Allgemeine Musiklehre* (1940; 2nd ed., 1954); *G. F. Händel* (1941; 2nd ed., 1952); *Chr. W. Gluck* (1940); *C. M. von Weber* (1941; 2nd ed., 1955); *Bernhard Ziehn* (1949); *Musikgeschichte in 100 Lebensbildern* (1952); *Die evangelische Kirchenmusik in Deutschland* (1954); *Dokumente der Musik geschichte* (1954); *Die Musikleistung der deutschen Stämme* (1955); *Robert Schumann* (1956); *Die Tonsprachen des Abendlandes: 10 Essais als Wesenkunde der europäischen Musik* (Berlin, 1960); *Musik in Zeit und Raum* (Berlin, 1960); *Orgelromantik* (Ludwigsburg, 1961); numerous articles in German music magazines, some publ. separately; pamphlets for various occasions. His major work is the *Musik Lexikon* (1931; 2nd ed., 1943, withdrawn; 3rd ed., 1951; 4th ed., in 2 vols., 1956; Moser was editor (from 1926) of a projected collected ed. of Weber's works; wrote an entirely new libretto for Weber's *Euryanthe* and produced the opera under the title *Die sieben Raben* (Berlin, March 5, 1915); edited *Alte Meister des deutschen Liedes* (1912; 2nd ed., 1931); *Minnesang und Volkslied* (1925; 2nd enlarged ed., 1933); *Lutherlieder* (1930); facsimile editions of German music and old treatises; a collection of Alsatian songs; etc. He also wrote a number of songs and choruses; a school opera, *Der Reisekamerad,* after Andersen; fictional works (*Die verborgene Symphonie, Ersungenes Traumland, Der klingende Grundstein,* etc.).

Moser, Rudolf, Swiss composer; b. Niederuzwyl, St. Gall, Jan. 7, 1892; d. in a fall, while mountain climbing in Silvaplana, (Graubünden), Aug. 20, 1960. He studied theology at Basel Univ. and musicology (with Nef); then at the Leipzig Cons. (1912–14), with Max Reger, Sitt, and Klengel; further with Huber in Basel and Lauber in Geneva. He became conductor of the cathedral choir in Basel; also active as a pedagogue.

WORKS: *Der Rattenfänger,* dance play (1950); Concerto grosso, for string orch. (Basel, June 26, 1927); several suites for orch.; 3 violin concertos; Organ Concerto; Concerto for Violin, Viola, and Cello; Piano Concerto; Viola Concerto; 4 string quartets; Piano Trio; String Sextet; *Das Lied von der Sonne,* for soli, chorus, orch., and organ; *Odes of Horace,* for baritone, chorus, and orch.; other vocal music; organ pieces.

BIBLIOGRAPHY: H. Buchli, *Rudolf Moser* (Zürich, 1964).

Mosewius, Johann Theodor, German conductor and musicologist; b. Königsberg, Sept. 25, 1788; d. Schaffhausen, Sept. 15, 1858. He began his career an an opera singer in Königsberg, and later in Breslau. In 1829, he became music director at the Univ. of Breslau; in 1831, director of the Institute for Church Music there. By establishing the Singakademie (1825), and giving competent performances of works of Bach to Beethoven, he exercised cultural influence on the musical life of Breslau. He also publ. articles on composers; of these, 2 were reprinted separately; *J. S. Bach in seinen Kirchencantaten und Choralgesängen* (1845) and *J. S. Bachs Matthäus Passion* (1852).

BIBLIOGRAPHY: A. Kempe, *Erinnerungen an J. T. Mosewius* (Breslau, 1859).

Moskowa, Prince de la, Joseph Napoléon, eldest son of **Marshal Ney;** French musician; b. Paris, May 8, 1803; d. St.-Germain-en-Laye, July 25, 1857. A senator, and brigadier general under Napoleon III, he was also a talented musician. In 1843 he established the "Société de musique vocale, religieuse et classique" (for the performance of works of the 16th–17th centuries), himself conducting the concerts in his palace; the society publ. 11 volumes of these works, as *Recueil des morceaux de musique ancienne,* which included works by Allegri, Arcadelt, Bach, Bononcini, Carissimi, the 2 Gabrielis, Gesualdo, Orlando Gibbons, Gluck, Handel, Haydn, Janequin, Josquin Des Prez, Lotti, Marcello, Orlando Lasso, Palestrina, Scarlatti, Stradella, Victoria, etc. He composed 2 comic operas, *Le Cent-Suisse* (Paris, June 7, 1840) and *Yvonne* (Paris, March 16, 1855); also a Mass with Orch. in 1831.

Mosonyi, Mihály (real name **Michael Brandt**), Hungarian composer; b. Frauenkirchen, Sept. 2, 1814; d. Budapest, Oct. 31, 1870. He learned to play violin, double bass, and organ as a child; then took some lessons with Karl Turányi in Pressburg; subsequently earned his living as a private tutor in aristocratic families in Hungary and Vienna; he also played double bass in various orchestras. Although he was a product of the school of composition he became enamored of Hungarian national music; began to write in the Hungarian idiom, while his harmonies remained Germanic. Liszt took great interest in his works, and proposed to bring out Mosonyi's German opera *Kaiser Max auf der Martinswand* (1857), but Mosonyi delayed the final revision of the work, and it never reached performance. His 2nd opera, *Szép Llon (Pretty Helen),* was produced at Budapest on Dec. 19, 1861; another opera, *Almos,* was not staged until Dec. 6, 1934, 64 years after Mosonyi's death. He further wrote 5 Masses and other church music; 2 symphonies; 6 string quartets; several choruses for men's voices; songs. His *Funeral Music for Széchenyi* employs the so-called Hungarian mode, and its strong national character established Mosonyi as one of the founders of the Hungarian School.

BIBLIOGRAPHY: K. Ábrányi, *Mosonyi* (Budapest, 1872); J. Káldor, *Michael Mosonyi* (Dresden, 1936); Béla Bartók, "Three Unpublished Liszt Letters to Mosonyi," *Musical Quarterly* (Oct. 1921).

Moss, Lawrence, American composer; b. Los Angeles, Nov. 18, 1927. He studied music at Pomona Col-

lege, at Univ. of Calif., Los Angeles (A. B., 1949), at Eastman School of Music in Rochester (A.M., 1951), and at Univ. of Southern Calif. (Ph.D., 1957). In 1956-59 he taught at Mills College in Oakland, Calif.; in 1959 received a Guggenheim Fellowship for travel in Italy; in 1960 appointed to the faculty of Yale Univ. His stylistic usages tend to polycentric tonality, with sporadic application of serial techniques. He wrote the operas *The Brute,* after Chekhov (Norfolk, Conn., July 15, 1961) and *The Queen and the Rebels* (N.Y., Nov. 1, 1962); *Suite* for orch. (1950); *Fantasia* for piano (1952); Trio for flute, violin and cello (1953); *Song of Myself,* to Whitman's words, for baritone and chamber ensemble (1957); 2 string quartets (1958, 1975); Violin Sonata (1959); *Music for Five* for wind quintet (1965); *Windows* for flute, clarinet and double bass (1966); *Remembrances* for chamber ensemble (1968); *Patterns* for flute, clarinet, viola and piano (1968); *Exchanges* for chamber ensemble (1968); *Ariel* for soprano and orch. (1969); *Paths* for orch. (1971); *Unseen Leaves* for soprano, oboe, tapes, slides, and lights (Washington, Oct. 20, 1975); *Symphonies* for brass quintet and chamber orch. (1977).

Moss, Piotr, Polish composer; b. Bydgoszcz, May 13, 1949. He graduated from the State Academy of Music in Warsaw; became engaged mainly in composing music for radio, television and films in a mandatory semi-classical manner. However, he writes concert pieces in an adult and civilized style.

WORKS: Violin Concerto (1971); Wind Quintet (1971); *Per esempio,* music for 13 performers, (1972); String Quartet (1973); *Charon,* a symphony (1973); Piano Concertino (1973); *Vowels* for 12 voices and instrumental ensemble (1974); Piano Trio (1974); *Giorno* for 10 performers (1975); Cello Concerto (1975).

Mossolov, Alexander, Russian composer of avant-garde tendencies; b. Kiev, Aug. 11, 1900; d. Moscow, July 12, 1973. He fought in the Civil War in Russia (1918-20); was wounded and decorated twice with the Order of the Red Banner for heroism. After the war, he studied composition with Glière in Kiev; also privately with Miaskovsky in Moscow; took piano lessons with Igumnov at the Moscow Cons., graduating in 1925. He played his First Piano Concerto in Leningrad on Feb. 12, 1928. In his earliest works he adopted modernistic devices; wrote songs to texts of newspaper advertisements. His ballet entitled *Zavod (Iron Foundry;* Moscow, Dec. 4, 1927), attracted attention because of the attempt to imitate the sound of a factory at work by shaking a large sheet of metal. However, Mossolov's attempt to produce "proletarian" music by such means elicited a sharp rebuke from official arbiters of Soviet music. On Feb. 4, 1936, he was expelled from the Union of Soviet Composers for staging drunken brawls and behaving rudely to waiters in restaurants. He was sent to Turkestan to collect folksongs as a move towards his rehabilitation.

WORKS: 4 operas: *The Hero* (Baden-Baden, July 15, 1928), *The Dam* (Leningrad, 1929), *Masquerade* (1940) and *The Signal* (1941); an anti-Facist musical comedy, *Friedrich Barbarossa;* 6 symphonies (1928; 1932; 1937; 1942; 1947; 1950); 2 piano concertos (1927; 1932); 5 suites for orch.: No. 1, *Turkmenian* (1933); No. 2, *Uzbekian Dance* (1935); No. 3, *Native Lands,* with folk instruments (1951); No. 4 (1955); No. 5, *Festive* (1955); Harp Concerto (1939; Moscow, Nov. 18, 1939); Concerto for Orch. (1943); Cello Concerto (1946); *Elegiac Poem* for orch. (1961); 4 oratorios, among them *M. I. Kalinin* (1940) and *Moscow* (1948); a patriotic cantata *Minin and Pozharsky; Kirghiz Rhapsody* for mezzo-soprano, chorus and orch. (1933); *Ukraine* for soloist, chorus and orch. (1942); 2 string quartets (1926, 1942); Trio for clarinet, cello and piano (1926); Piano Trio (1927); Cello Sonata (1927); Viola Sonata (1928); *Dance Suite* for piano trio (1928); 4 Piano Sonatas (1923, 1924, 1925, 1926); choruses; songs.

Moszkowski, Alexander, music critic; brother of **Moritz Moszkowski;** b. Pilica, Poland, Jan. 15, 1851; d. Berlin, Sept. 26, 1934. He lived most of his life in Berlin; wrote criticism for various publications there; was also editor of *Lustige Blätter* (a humorous magazine); publ. the entertaining booklets, *Anton Notenquetschers Neue Humoresken* (1893; 9th ed., 1904), *Anton Notenquetschers heitere Dichtungen* (1894); etc. A serious work is *Die Kunst in 1000 Jahren* (1910).

Moszkowski, Moritz, famous pianist, teacher, and composer; b. Breslau, Aug. 23, 1854; d. Paris, March 4, 1925. He studied at the Dresden Cons.; later at the Stern Cons. and at the Kullak Academy in Berlin; then became a teacher at the latter institution. He gave his first public concert in Berlin in 1873; then played elsewhere in Germany, and in Paris, where he established his reputation as a pianist; in 1897, he made Paris his headquarters. As a composer, he is most widely known by his pieces in the Spanish vein, particularly the two books of *Spanish Dances*, for piano solo, or piano duo; also popular were his études, concert waltzes, gavottes, *Skizzen*, a tarantella, *Humoresque*, etc. In larger forms he essayed an opera, *Boabdil der Maurenkönig* (Berlin, April 21, 1892), which contains a ballet number that became popular; also wrote a ballet, *Laurin* (1896); a symph. poem, *Jeanne d'Arc; Phantastischer Zug* for orch.; *Aus aller Herren Länder* for orch.; Violin Concerto; Piano Concerto.

Moszumańska-Nazar, Krystyna, Polish composer; b. Lwów, Sept. 5, 1924. She studied composition with Wiechowicz and piano with Jan Hoffman at the State College of Music in Cracow (1948-55); in 1964 was appointed to its faculty. Her music is classic in its formal organization, but densely dissonant in harmony.
WORKS: Piano Concertino (1954); 2 overtures (1954, 1956); *Allegro Symphonique* (1957); *4 Symphonic Essays* (1957); *5 Duets* for flute and clarinet (1959); *Hexaèdre* for orch. (1960); *Music for Strings* (1961); *Exodus* for orch. and tape (1964); *Variazioni concertanti* for flute and chamber orch. (1965-66); *Interpretations* for flute, percussion and tape (1967); *Intonations* for 2 choruses and orch. (1968); *Implications* for 2 pianos and percussion (1968); *Pour Orchestre* (1969; Poznań, March 29, 1973); *Bagatelles* for piano (1971); *Bel canto* for soprano, celesta and percussion (1972); String Quartet (1973-74); *Polish Madonnas*, poem for chorus and orch. (1974).

Motta, José Vianna da. See **Da Motta, José Vianna.**

Mottl, Felix, celebrated Austrian conductor; b. Unter-St. Veit, near Vienna, Aug. 24, 1856; d. Munich, July 2, 1911. After preliminary studies at a seminary, he entered the Vienna Cons., and studied there with Door (piano), Bruckner (theory), Dessoff (composition), and Hellmesberger (conducting), graduating with high honors. In 1876 he acted as one of the assistants at the first Wagner festival at Bayreuth. In 1880 he succeeded Dessoff as court conductor at Karlsruhe; in 1893 was appointed general musical director there. He conducted *Tristan und Isolde* at the Bayreuth festival in 1886; led a Wagner concert in London in 1894, and gave the entire *Ring* tetralogy at Covent Garden in 1898. In 1903 he was engaged to conduct the projected performances of *Parsifal* at the Metropolitan Opera in N.Y., but withdrew owing to the protests of the Wagner family. Mottl secured recognition for Peter Cornelius' *Der Barbier von Bagdad* by re-orchestrating the score, and producing it first at Karlsruhe, on Feb. 1, 1884; additional changes were made by him with Hermann Levi, and in this form the work finally became established in the opera repertory. In Dec. 1905, he conducted, also in Karlsruhe, the 1st complete performance of both parts of Berlioz's *Les Troyens* (in German); he orchestrated Wagner's *Fünf Gedichte*, and edited Wagner's early overtures. Mottl composed 3 operas: *Agnes Bernauer* (Weimar, 1880), *Rama*, and *Fürst und Sänger;* String Quartet; numerous songs. Among his arrangements, that of Chabrier's *Bourrée fantasque* enjoys continued popularity in the concert hall.

Mottu, Alexandre, Swiss pianist, organist and composer; b. Geneva, June 11, 1883; d. there, Nov. 24, 1943. He studied organ with Otto Barblan in Geneva; piano with Teresa Carreño in Berlin. He was appointed prof. of piano and organ at the Cons. of Geneva in 1907. His works include various pieces of piano, violin and organ, and much choral music.

Moulaert, Pierre, Belgian composer, son of **Raymond Moulaert;** b. Brussels, Sept. 24, 1907; d. there, Nov. 13, 1967. He studied at the Royal Cons. in Brussels with his father and Joseph Jongen, and taught there from 1937 until his death. He was not a prolific composer, and wrote mostly in small forms, but his music has a distinctive quality of fine craftsmanship.
WORKS: *Passepied en Rondo* for wind quintet (1940); Concertino for Flute, Oboe and Strings (1954); String Quartet (1956); *Sérénade* for orch. (1956); *Petite musique concertante* for orch. (1961); *Introduction et Fugue* for flute, oboe, clarinet, bassoon and strings (Uccle, March 7, 1963); *Séquences* for orch. (1964).

Moulaert, Raymond, Belgian composer, father of **Pierre Moulaert;** b. Brussels, Feb. 4, 1875; d. there, Jan. 18, 1962. He studied at the Brussels Cons. with Arthur de Greef (piano) and Edgar Tinel (theory); then was appointed to its staff and taught composition (1939); concurrently was director of his own music school in St.-Gilles for 25 years (1913-38); also lectured at the Queen Elizabeth Chapel of Music in Brussels.

WORKS: *Theme and Variations* for trumpet and orch. (1910); *Appels pour un tournoi de chevalerie (Invitation to a Tournament of Chivalry)* for wind orch. (1923); *Passacaglia* for orch. (1931); *Symphonie de valses* (1936); Trumpet Concertino (1937); Piano Concerto (1938); *Rhapsodie écossaise* for clarinet and orch. (1940); *Tango-caprice* for saxophone and orch. (1942); *Études symphoniques* (1943); *Symphonie de fugues* (1942-44); *Eroica* for horn and chamber orch. (1946); *Légende* for flute and orch. (1951); *Variations symphoniques* (1952); Sinfonietta for strings 1955; lost); *Andante* for 4 horns (1903); *Andante, Fugue et Final* for 4 saxophones (1907); Sextet for wind quintet and piano (1925); *Passacaglia* for solo double bass (1928); *Études rythmiques* for percussion (1929); *Divertimento* for string trio (1936); *Choral varié* for 4 cellos (1937); *Suite* for 3 trombones (1939); *Sonata en forme de passacaille* for cello and piano (1942); *Concert* for wind quintet and harp (1950); *Bagatelles* for 2 violins (1960); organ works, include Sonata (1907), *2 Pieces* (1910), *3 Poèmes bibliques* (1916-20), *2 Fugues* (1929) and *Prelude et choral* (1948); piano works, including Sonata (1917), *Toccata* (1938), *Ciels* (1938) and *Études-paraphrases*, after Paganini (1948); 5 sets of *Poèmes de la Vieille France* for variable vocal groups (1917-43); *L'Eau passe*, song cycle for solo voice. A catalogue of his works was publ. by the Centre Belge de Documentation Musicale (Brussels, 1954).

Mount-Edgcumbe, Richard, British nobleman (second Earl of Mount-Edgcumbe) and music amateur; b. Plymouth, Sept. 13, 1764; d. Richmond, Surrey, Sept. 26, 1839. He was the author of the book, *Musical Reminiscences, containing an Account of the Italian Opera in England from 1773*, which he publ. anonymously in 1825. He also wrote an opera, *Zenobia* (in Italian), which was produced at London in 1800.

Mouquet, Jules, French composer; b. Paris, July 10, 1867; d. there, Oct. 25, 1946. He studied at the Paris Cons. with Leroux (harmony) and Dubois (composition); won 1st Prix de Rome in 1896 with his canata *Mélusine*, the Prix Trémont in 1905, and the Prix Chartier (for chamber music) in 1907; in 1913 became prof. of harmony at the Paris Cons.

WORKS: the oratorios *Le Sacrifice d'Isaac* and *Le Jugement dernier*; the symph. poems, *Diane et Endymion* and *Persée et Andromède*; *Danse grecque* for orch.; *Divertissement grec*, for flute and harp; Sonata for flute and piano; pieces for oboe and piano, bassoon and piano, saxophone and piano, etc.; Sept'et for wind instruments; *Études antiques* for solo piano. He also publ. a *Cours complémentaire d'harmonie*.

Mouret, Jean Joseph, French composer; b. Avignon, April 11, 1682; d. Charenton, Dec. 20, 1738. He was attached to the court in Paris; produced an opera-ballet, *Les Festes de Thalie* (Paris, Aug. 19, 1714); an opera, *Ariane* (Paris, April 6, 1717); *Les Amours des dieux*, opera-ballet (Paris, Sept. 14, 1727). He was director of the Concert Spirituel (1728-34); wrote motets for performances there; also divertissements for

the Comédie-Italienne; about 50 of his chamber pieces were publ. during his lifetime.

BIBLIOGRAPHY: R. Viollier, *J. J. Mouret, le musicien des grâces* (Paris, 1950).

Moussorgsky, Modest. See **Mussorgsky, Modest.**

Mouton, Jean, important French composer; b. Haut-Wignes (Holluigue), near Boulogne, 1459; d. St.-Quentin, Oct. 30, 1522. At the age of 7 he became a "chantre écolâtre" (chorister) in the choir of Notre Dame at Nesle, near St. Quentin; in 1500, was in charge of the choirboys at the Cathdral of Amiens; in 1501, in a similar position at the Cathedral of Grenoble. In 1513 he became a chapel singer to Louis XII, and later to Francis I; then served as canon at Thérouanne, and later at St. Quentin. He was the teacher of Willaert. He wrote almost exclusively sacred music, and was one of the greatest masters of counterpoint of the period; in his works he followed the precepts of Josquin Des Prez; excelled particularly in the art of canon. His Masses and motets were publ. between 1508 and 1540 (in collections by Petrucci, Attaignant, and others); his canons are cited by Glareanus in his *Dodecachordon* (republ. by P. Bohn, 1889); other examples of his works are found in the histories of Burney, Forkel, Hawkins, and Busby; in Commer's *Collectio;* etc. A Mass, *Alma Redemptoris*, was republished by H. Expert in his *Maîtres Musiciens 9*. His *Opera omnia*, in 10 vols., ed. by A. Minor, is publ. in the *Corpus Mensurabilis Musicae* series of the American Institute of Musicology.

BIBLIOGRAPHY: F. Lesure, "Un Document sur la jeunesse de Jean Mouton," *Revue Belge de Musicologie* (1956); G. Reese, *Music in the Renaissance* (N.Y., 1954).

Moyse, Louis, French flutist, son of **Marcel Moyse**; b. Scheveningen, Holland, July 14, 1912. He was taken to Paris as an infant; learned to play the piano and flute at home; later took private piano lessons with Isidore Philipp (1925-27); in 1930 he entered the Paris Cons. where he studied flute with Philippe Gaubert and composition with Eugène Bigot; graduated in 1932, with the Premier Prix in flute; then was his father's teaching assistant at the Paris Cons., and filled in various jobs playing at movie theaters and restaurants. He served in the French Army during World War II; after the end of the war he organized the Moyse Trio, with his father as flutist, his wife **Blanche Honegger-Moyse** as violinist and himself as pianist. In 1948 he went with his wife to the U.S.; became an American citizen in 1959. He joined his father at the Marlboro College, Vermont, where he taught until 1975; then was appointed prof. of flute and chamber music at the Univ. of Toronto, Canada. He published in N.Y. several educational collections of flute pieces, among them *Solos for the Flute Players, 40 Little Pieces for the Beginner Flutists, Album of Flute Duets, 30 Easy Duets for Flutes*, etc.

WORKS: *Suite* for 2 flutes and viola (1957); *4 Dances* for flute and violin (1958); Woodwind Quintet (1961); *Divertimento* for double woodwind quintet, 2 cellos, double bass and timpani (1961); *4 Pieces* for 3 flutes and piano (1965); *3 Pieces* for flute and guitar

(1968); *Marlborian Concerto* for flute, English horn and orch. (1969); *A Ballad for Vermont* for narrator, soloists, chorus and orch. (1971-72); Flute Sonata (1975); *Serenade* for piccolo, 4 flutes, alto flute, bass flute and piano (1977); arranged for flute and various instrumental groups works by Bach, Telemann, Handel, Mozart, Beethoven and Weber.

Moyse, Marcel, celebrated French flutist; b. Saint-Amour (Jura), May 17, 1889. He studied flute with Taffanel at the Paris Cons.; upon graduation was first flutist in several Paris orchestras (Lamoureux, Cologne, Pasdeloup, etc.). In 1932 he succeeded Philippe Gaubert as prof. of flute at the Paris Cons. In 1949 he went to the U.S.; in 1952 organized, with his son **Louis Moyse**, Rudolf Serkin, Adolf Busch and Herman Busch the Marlboro School and Festival of Music in Brattleboro, Vermont; also conducted master classes in flute and chamber music in Switzerland; gave similar courses in Japan in 1973. He published a series of excellent flute studies, among them *20 Exercises et études , 24 petites études mélodiques, 25 Études mélodiques, 100 Études faciles et progressives, 25 Études de Virtuosité* (after Czerny), *12 Études de grande virtuosité* (after Chopin), etc.; also wrote 50 variations on the Allemande from Bach's Flute Sonata in A minor and compiled a manual for flute, *Tone Developement Through Interpretation.*

Moyzes, Alexander, Slovak composer, son of **Mikuláš Moyzes**; b. Kláštor pod Znievom, Sept. 4, 1906. He studied conducting with Ostrčil, composition with Karel and Šín, and organ with Wiedermann at the Prague Cons. (1925-28); continued studies at the Master School there with Vítězslav Novák (1929-30). Upon graduation from the Cons. in 1928, he taught at the Prague Academy of Music, transferring to the High School of Musical Arts in Bratislava in 1949; was chief of the music section of the Czech Radio (1937-48). His music uses the melodic resources of Slovak folksongs; his Symph. No. 1 is the first national Slovak symphony.

WORKS: an opera, *Udatný král'* (*The Brave King*, 1966; Bratislava, 1967); 9 symphonies: No. 1 (Bratislava, Feb. 11, 1929); No. 2 (1932, revised 1941), No. 3 (1942; orchestral version of the wind quintet), No. 4 (1939-47), No. 5 (1948), No. 6 (1951), No. 7 (Bratislava, Oct. 23, 1955), No. 8 (1968) and No. 9 (1971); *Symphonic Overture* (1929); Concertino for Orch. (1933); *Jánošik's Rebels* for orch. (1933); *Nikola Šuhaj*, overture (1933); *Down the River Váh*, symph. suite (1936, revised 1945); *Dances from the Hron Region* for orch. (1950); *February Overture* (1952); *Dances from Gemer*, suite for orch. (1955); Violin Concerto (1958); *Sonatina giocosa* for violin, chamber string orch. and harpsichord (1962); Flute Concerto (1966); *Keeper of the House*, overture (1972); *Bonfires on the Mountains*, symph. suite (1973); *Musica Istropolitana* for chamber string orch. (1974); *Music to Woman*, symph. study (1975; Bratislava, May 13, 1976); *The Tale about Jánošik*, rhapsodic suite for orch. (1976); the cantatas *Svätopluk* (1935), *Znejú piesne na chotari* (*Songs Resound in the Meadows*, 1948); 2 song cycles, *Jeseň* (*In Autumn*) for mezzo-soprano, and orch. or piano (1960) and *Morning Dew* for mezzo-

soprano, and orch. or piano (1963); 2 string quartets (1928, 1969); Wind Quintet (1933); *Poetic Suite* for violin and piano (1948); *Duetta* for violin and piano (1960); *Small Suite* for violin and piano (1968); Sonatina for flute and guitar (1975); *Divertimento* for piano (1929); *Jazz Sonata* for 2 pianos (1932); Piano Sonata (1942).

Moyzes, Mikuláš, Slovak composer; b. Velká Slatina, Dec. 6, 1872; d. Prešov, April 2, 1944. He studied at the Budapest Academy of Music; in 1907 became director of the Municipal School of Music in Prešov, where he remained. He wrote a *Missa Solemnis;* many choruses; a wind quintet; a wind sextet; made arrangements of Slovak songs. His popular overture *Naše Slovensko* (*Our Slovakia*) was reorchestrated by his son **Alexander Moyzes.**

Mozart, Anna (nickname **Nannerl**), daughter of **Leopold Mozart** and sister of **Wolfgang Amadeus Mozart**; b. Salzburg, July 30, 1751; d. there, Oct. 29, 1829. Taught by her father from her earliest childhood, she quickly developed into an excellent pianist, and appeared in public with her brother; after their trip to Vienna in 1768, she remained mostly at home, helping to support the family by teaching. In 1784 she married Baron von Berchthold zu Sonnenburg; after his death, she resumed her teaching until her eyesight failed in 1820,

Mozart, Leopold (Johann Georg Leopold), the father of **Wolfgang Amadeus**, and himself an important musician; b. Augsburg, Germany, Nov. 14, 1719; d. Salzburg, Austria, May 28, 1787. A poor bookbinder's son, he learned music as a chorister in Augsburg; went to Salzburg to study at the Univ. there; at the same time learned to play the violin; was in the service of Count Thurn and Taxis at Salzburg (1740-43); then entered the private orch. of the Archbishop of Salzburg (1743); appointed court composer (1757); then became Vice-Kapellmeister (1762). He married Anna Maria Pertl of Salzburg in 1747; of their 7 children only two, "Nannerl" and Wolfgang, passed the age of one year. He dedicated himself to the musical education of his children wholeheartedly; his methods of presentation of their concerts at times approached frank exploitation, and his advertisements of their appearances were often in poor taste, but there is no denying that he succeeded in fostering and developing his son's genius. Leopold Mozart was a noteworthy composer in his own right; among his works are operas, pantomimes, 12 oratorios, other sacred music; many symphonies (18 publ.), serenades, divertimentos (the *Musikalische Schlittenfahrt* was publ.), concertos, chamber music (6 trio sonatas for 2 violins with basso continuo were publ.), organ music, piano music (12 pieces, *Der Morgen und der Abend*, were publ.). The attribution of the *Kindersinfonie* (*Toy Symphony*) to Leopold Mozart is doubtful, but see E. F. Schmid, "Leopold Mozart und die Kindersinfonie," in the *Mozart Jahrbuch*, and R. Münster "Wer ist der Komponist der Kindersinfonie?" in the *Mozart Jahrbuch*, 1969. His most signal accomplishment, however, is the publication of a violin method, *Versuch einer gründlichen Violinschule* (Augsburg, 1756;

2nd revised ed., 1770; transl. into several languages; English transl. by Editha Knocker, London, 1948; a facsimile ed. was publ. in Vienna, 1922; another facsimile ed., by H. J. Moser, Leipzig, 1956). A selection from his works was publ. by M. Seiffert in *Denkmäler der Tonkunst in Bayern* 17 (9. ii). His *Nannerls Musikbuch* was republished in Munich, 1956, with an introduction by E. Valentin.

BIBLIOGRAPHY: M. Friedlaender, "Leopold Mozarts Klaviersonaten" *Die Musik* IV/1 (1901); J. E. Engl, *Aus Leopold und des Sohns Wolfgang Mozarts irdischem Lebensgange* (Salzburg, 1902); H. Abert, "Leopold Mozarts Notenbuch von 1762," *Gluck-Jahrbuch* (1917); A. Schurig, *Leopold Mozart: Reise-Aufzeichnungen 1763 bis 1771* (1920); A. Moser, *Geschichte des Violinspiels* (1923; p. 345ff.); E. L. Theiss, *Die Instrumentalwerke Leopold Mozarts* (Giessen, 1942). His letters to his wife are publ. in Schiedermair's ed. of *Mozart's Letters;* those to his daughter, ed. by O. E. Deutsch and B. Paumgartner (Salzburg, 1936); English transl. of all them in Emily Anderson, *Letters of Mozart and His Family,* 3 vols. (London, 1938). See also the literature on Mozart, in which Leopold Mozart is constantly referred to.

Mozart, Wolfgang Amadeus (baptismal names **Johannes Chrysostomus Wolfgangus Theophilus**), supreme genius of music whose works in every genre are unsurpassed in lyric beauty, rhythmic gaiety and effortless melodic invention; b. Salzburg, Jan. 27, 1756; d. Vienna, Dec. 5, 1791. In his fourth year he manifested such eager and intelligent interest in his sister's harpsichord lessons that his father began teaching him as well; he also composed little pieces. His progress was so rapid that in January 1762, the father ventured to introduce his children to the public on a concert trip to Munich, and in September to Vienna; the Emperor, Francis I, frequently invited the children to the palace, where Wolfgang was wholly at his ease amid the brilliant assemblage, caring only for the approval of connoisseurs. Some of the pieces he played were sonatas by D. Paradies and J. C. Bach, and a concerto by Lucchesi. While in Vienna, a small violin was given him, on which he learned to play without instruction; he learned the organ in the same manner, after the use of the pedals had been explained. A longer journey, to Paris, was undertaken in 1763; the brother and sister gave private and public concerts on the way, and in Frankfurt Wolfgang played concertos both on the harpsichord and the violin, accompanied symphonies on the harpsichord and ended with long improvisations. (The clavichord and harpsichord were his principal keyboard instruments while he was in Salzburg, where pianos were still scarce, but from 1774 on, when visiting places like Munich and Paris, where the new instruments were plentiful, and after he settled in Vienna, he played on, and wrote for, the piano.) In Paris they performed before the royal family, and gave two brilliant public concerts. Here Wolfgang's first publ. compositions appeared, op. 1 and 2, each comprising *Il Sonates pour le clavecin* (2 harpsichord sonatas) with violin *ad libitum*. The travelers' reception in England (1764) was so cordial that they remained there about 15 months; the King tried Mozart's faculty for sight-reading with works by J. C.

Bach, Handel, Abel, etc., and greatly admired his playing. Here Wolfgang composed several sonatas for violin and harpsichord, and his first symphonies, which were performed repeatedly. Of his marvelous progress his father wrote home: "Our high and mighty Wolfgang knows everything in this, his eighth year, that one can require of a man of forty." On the return journey they passed through Lille, The Hague, Paris, Dijon, Bern, Zürich, Donaueschingen, Ulm, Munich, etc.; and arrived in Salzburg in November 1766, having been absent three years. After an interval of rest and serious study, during which Mozart composed his first oratorio (1767), they revisited Vienna in 1768, and Mozart wrote, at the Emperor's request, his first opera, *La finta semplice (The Pretended Simpleton)*; its production was prevented by intrigues, although Hasse and Metastasio declared that thirty operas, in no way equal to the boy's, had been given there (it was brought out at Salzburg in 1769). However, the "Liederspiel" *Bastien und Bastienne* was privately performed; and Mozart made his first appearance at a large public concert as a conductor, directing his own Solemn Mass (Dec. 7, 1768). Returning to Salzburg, he was appointed Konzertmeister to the Archbishop. For the purpose of broadening his son's education, Leopold Mozart decided on an Italian tour, leaving home in Dec. 1769. The program of a concert at Mantua, Jan. 16, 1770, exhibits Mozart's versatility at the age of 14: "A Symphony of his own composition; a harpsichord concerto, which will be handed to him, and which he will immediately play *prima vista;* a Sonata handed him in like manner, which he will provide with variations, and afterwards repeat in another key; an Aria, the words for which will be handed to him and which he will immediately set to music and sing himself, accompanying himself on the harpsichord; a Sonata for harpsichord on a subject given him by the leader of the violins: a Strict Fugue on a theme to be selected, which he will improvise on the harpsichord; a Trio in which he will execute a violin part *all'improvviso;* and finally, the latest Symphony composed by himself." It was in Rome that Mozart, after twice hearing Allegri's famous *Miserere,* wrote out the entire score from memory, without a mistake. The journey was a veritable triumphal progress; his concerts were crowded, his genius recognized by the highest musical authorities; the Pope conferred on him the order of the Golden Spur, and he was elected a member of the Bologna Philharmonic Academy, after passing the required examinations. At Milan his 3-act opera seria *Mitridate, rè di Ponto* was enthusiastically received on Dec. 26, 1770, and had 20 consecutive performances under Mozart's own direction. He returned to Salzburg in March, 1771; in August again visited Milan to bring out a "theater serenade," *Ascanio in Alba,* written for the wedding festivities of Archduke Ferdinand (Oct. 17, 1771); it quite eclipsed Hasse's festival opera *Ruggiero.* Next year his friendly protector, the Archbishop of Salzburg, died; the unmusical successor, Hieronymus, Count of Colloredo, cared little for Mozart's genius, and in the end heaped indignities upon him. It was for his installation (1772) that Mozart's "dramatic serenade" *Il Sogno di Scipione* was penned. *Lucio Silla* (Milan, Dec. 26, 1772) and *La finta giardiniera (The*

Girl Disguised as Gardener; Munich, Jan. 13, 1775) were the occasion of trips to those cities of their production. On April 23, 1775, *Il Rè pastore* (*The King as Shepherd*) was brought out at Salzburg during Archduke Maximilian's visit. Mozart obtained leave of absence in 1777, and, accompanied by his mother, repaired to Munich, in hopes of obtaining an appointment commensurate with his abilities; disappointed there, and also in Augsburg and Mannheim, they journeyed to Paris, where a symphony of Mozart was performed at a Concert Spirituel. But the war between the Gluckists and Piccinnists was at its height, and little attention was paid to the young composer. He had the further misfortune to lose his mother, who died in Paris, July 3, 1778. His expectations unrealized, Mozart resumed his function of Konzertmeister at Salzburg, also succeeding Adlgasser as court organist in 1779, with a salary of 400 florins. The opera *Idomeneo* (Munich, Jan. 29, 1781) was the first dramatic work in his mature style. In the summer of that year Mozart definitively left the service of the Archbishop, whose treatment had grown unbearable, and settled in Vienna. Commissioned by the Emperor to write an opera, Mozart composed *Belmonte und Constanze, oder Die Entführung aus dem Serail* (*Belmonte and Constance, or The Abduction from the Seraglio*), which was most successfully produced, despite the machinations of the theatrical clique, on July 16, 1782; a month later he married Constanze Weber, the sister of his youthful flame Aloysia, whom he had met in Mannheim. A period of real poverty set in. Mozart was improvident by nature; the meager receipts for compositions and concerts were quickly spent and, though an indefatigable worker, he was never free from money troubles. Periodically, he would send begging letters to his merchant friend Michel Puchberg, asking for a "loan" (which he never repaid); Puchberg invariably obliged. A Singspiel *Der Schauspieldirektor* (*The Impresario*), was produced at Schönbrunn, Feb. 7, 1786; on May 1, 1786, his fine opera buffa *Le Nozze di Figaro* (*The Marriage of Figaro*) came near failing in Vienna through the intentional lapses of the jealous Italian singers (at that time the works of Paisiello, Sarti, and Cimarosa set the standard of musico-dramatic taste in Vienna). But the hearty and spontaneous welcome accorded to this masterpiece and its author in Prague partially made up for this rebuff; he was invited to lodge in the palace of Count Thun, and every attention was bestowed on him. Next year, the unexampled success of his *Don Giovanni,* at Prague (Oct. 29, 1787), coupled with the fear that Mozart might accept favorable offers to go to England, moved the Emperor to show tardy and scanty recognition of his genius by appointing him "chamber composer" at 800 florins annually (Gluck, just deceased, as court composer had 2,000 florins). In this year (1788) Mozart ceased giving public concerts at Vienna, appearing there but once more, in 1791. In 1789 he accompanied Prince Carl Lichnowsky to Berlin, on the way playing before the Dresden court, and in the Thomaskirche at Leipzig. According to an unverified story, King Friedrich Wilhelm II, after hearing him at Potsdam, offered him the post of 1st Royal Kapellmeister, with a salary of 3,000 Thaler a year; but Mozart, with a simple trust in and loyalty to the

Austrian Emperor, refused the benevolent offer—his last opportunity, as it proved, of ridding himself of money troubles. The Emperor's only response to the news of the King's offer was an order for a new opera, *Così fan tutte* (literally, *Thus do all; tutte* being the feminine plural, the meaning is *All women are like that*), produced in Vienna on Jan. 26, 1790; but it made little impression beside the fashionable Italian works. In October Mozart attended the coronation of Emperor Leopold II at Frankfurt, full of joyful anticipations which, as usual, were not realized. He came back to Vienna in time to bid farewell to his fatherly friend Haydn, then about to set out for London. For the coronation of Leopold II at Prague, as King of Bohemia, Mozart was invited to write a festival opera and *La Clemenza di Tito* (*The Clemency of Titus*), was performed on Sept. 6, 1791, the eve of the ceremony. Already suffering from illness, overwork, and the excitement and fatigue of the journey, he returned to Vienna, and still, at Schikaneder's entreaty, composed *Die Zauberflöte* (*The Magic Flute*; Vienna, Sept. 30, 1791). The writing of his last work, the Requiem, was interrupted by fainting fits. The Requiem was incomplete when he died; it was finished by a student, Franz Xaver Süssmayr. The immediate cause of Mozart's death is believed to have been acute nephritis. A detailed discussion of the clinical aspects is found in Dieter Kerner's *Krankheiten Grosser Musiker* (Stuttgart, 1973; Vol. I, pp. 9–87); see also A. I. Borowitz, "Salieri and the 'Murder' of Mozart," *Musical Quarterly* (April 1973). Several myths and fantasies have been put in circulation: that Mozart's body was taken to the cemetery of St. Mark's during a blizzard, a story refuted by the records of the weather bureau in Vienna for the day (see in this connection N. Slonimsky, "The Weather at Mozart's Funeral," *Musical Quarterly,* Jan. 1960); that Mozart was buried in a pauper's grave (it was not so, but his body was indeed removed from the original location because the family neglected to pay the mandatory dues); and, the most fantastic tale of them all, that Mozart was poisoned by Salieri because of the latter's jealousy; this particular piece of morbid invention gained circulation in some cheap journals and eventually found its way into literature; Pushkin made it into a play *Mozart and Salieri,* which Rimsky-Korsakov set to music in his opera of the same title.

WORKS: Mozart is one of the brightest stars in the musical firmament. In his melody, German depth of emotion is expressed with Italian frankness, making his great dramatic works perennially fresh. Among his symphonies the "Jupiter" in C, and those in G minor and E-flat (1788), are prominent. His productivity was astounding, and embraced all departments of musical composition. The first complete edition of Mozart's works (528 compositions), prepared by Köchel, Nottebohm, Rietz, Espagne, Reinecke, Brahms, and others, was issued by Brietkopf & Härtel from 1876 to 1886; it contains: (1) CHURCH MUSIC (Series 1–4): 15 Masses, 4 litanies, 1 *Dixit,* 1 *Magnificat,* 4 Kyries, a madrigal, a *Veni Sancte,* a *Miserere,* an antiphon, 3 *Regina coeli,* a *Te Deum,* 2 *Tantum ergo,* 2 German church songs, 9 offertories, a *De profundis,* an aria, a motet for soprano solo, a 4-part motet, a Gradual, 2 hymns, a Passion cantata, and the cantatas

Davidde penitente and (Masonic) *Maurerfreude* and *Kleine Freimaurer-cantate.* —(2) STAGE WORKS (Series 5): *Die Schuldigkeit des ersten Gebotes* (sacred play with music), *Apollo et Hyacinthus* (Latin comedy with music), *Bastien und Bastienne, La finta semplice, Mitridate, Ascanio in Alba, Il Sogno di Scipione, Lucio Silla, La finta giardiniera, Il Rè pastore, Zaïde* (German opera; unfinished), *Thamos, König in Ägypten* (heroic drama; choruses and entr'actes); *Idomeneo, rè di Creta, Die Entführung aus dem Serail, Der Schauspieldirektor, Le Nozze di Figaro, Don Giovanni, Così fan tutte, La Clemenza di Tito, Die Zauberflöte.* English transls. of the most important librettos have been made by E. J. Dent and others. —(3) VOCAL CONCERT MUSIC (Series 6): 27 arias, and 1 rondo, for soprano with orchestra; 1 alto aria; 8 tenor arias; 5 arias and an arietta for bass; a German warsong; a duet for 2 sopranos; a comic duet for soprano and bass; 6 terzets; 1 quartet —(4) SONGS, ETC. (Series 7): 34 songs for solo voice with piano; a song with chorus and organ; a 3-part chorus with organ; a comic terzet with piano; 20 canons *a* 2–12. —(5) ORCHESTRAL WORKS (Series 8–11): 49 symphonies, 2 symphonic movements, 31 divertimentos, serenades, and cassations, 9 marches, 25 dances, Masonic Funeral Music; *Ein musikalischer Spass* (satirical; employs deliberate discords, consecutive fifths, etc.) for strings and 2 horns; also (for various instruments) a sonata for bassoon and cello, an Adagio for 2 basset-horns with bassoon, an Adagio for 2 clarinets and 3 basset horns, an Adagio for harmonica, Adagio and Allegretto for harmonica, flute, oboe, viola, and cello, a fantasy and an Andante for a clockwork organ. —(6) CONCERTOS AND SOLO PIECES WITH ORCH. (Series 12 and 16): 5 violin concertos, 6 solos for violin, a *Concertone* for 2 violins, a *Concertante* for violin and viola, a bassoon concerto, a concerto for flute and harp, 2 flute concertos, an Andante for flute, 4 horn concertos, a clarinet concerto, 21 piano concertos, a Concert Rondo for piano, a double concerto for 2 pianos, a triple concerto for 3 pianos. The so-called "Adelaide Concerto" for violin and orch., widely performed after its alleged discovery in 1934 as Mozart's work, was in reality composed by the French violinist Marius Casadesus in 1931; it was supposedly dedicated to Princess Adélaide, the daughter of Louis XV, by the boy Mozart during his visit to Paris at the age of 10. —(7) CHAMBER MUSIC (Series 13–15, 17, 18): 7 string quintets (with 2 violas); a quintet for violin, 2 violas, horn (or cello), and cello; a quintet for clarinet and strings; 26 string quartets; *Eine kleine Nachtmusik* for strings (including double bass); Adagio and Fugue for string quartet; a quartet for oboe with string trio; a divertimento for string trio; 2 duos for violin and viola; 1 duo for 2 violins; a quintet for piano, horn, oboe, clarinet, and bassoon; 2 piano quartets; 7 piano trios; 1 trio for piano, clarinet, and viola; 42 violin sonatas; an Allegro for piano and violin; 2 sets of variations for piano and violin. —(8) PIANO MUSIC (Series 19–22): (a) 4 hands: 5 sonatas, and an Andante with variations; (b) for 2 pianos: a Fugue, and a Sonata; (c) solo pieces: 17 sonatas; a Fantasia and fugue; 3 Fantasias; 15 sets of variations; 35 cadenzas to piano concertos; several minuets; 3 rondos, a suite, a fugue, 2 Allegros, an Allegro and Andante, Andantino, Adagio, Gigue. —(9) FOR ORGAN

(Series 23): 17 sonatas, mostly with 2 violins and cello; SUPPLEMENT (Series 24): unfinished works, doubtful works, and arrangements.

Mozart's works are designated by the numbers in the Köchel Catalogue (K. numbers), which have been universally accepted. Since the publication of the Breitkopf & Härtel edition, Wyzewa and St.-Foix and other authorities have shown that certain works published in that ed. are not original works of Mozart but copies in his handwriting of works by other composers. These works include the Symphony No. 3 (Köchel 18), which is by K. F. Abel, and Symphony No. 37 (K. 444), by Michael Haydn (except the Introduction). Among other works listed by Köchel, the following are spurious: Symphony in B-flat (K. 17); Sonatas for piano and violin (K. 55–60); *Salve Regina* (K. 92); Symphony in F (K. 98); *Tantum ergo* (K. 142); 2 Small Fugues (K. 154a); *Tantum ergo* (K. 197); 2 canons, *O Schwestern traut dem Amor nicht* and *O wunderschön ist Gottes Erde* (K. 226–7); Kyrie (K. 340); 9 Country Dances or Quadrilles (K. 510). The following are by other composers: Minuet and Trio in C major (K. 25a), probably by Beethoven; Sonata for piano and violin (K. 61), by H. F. Raupach; *De profundis clamavi* (K. 93), by C. G. Reutter; *Offertorium sub exposito venerabili* (K. 177 and 342), by Leopold Mozart; Kyrie (K. 221), by J. E. Eberlin; Fugue in D (K. 291), by M. Haydn, finished by S. Sechter; *Justum deduxit Dominus,* hymn (K. 326), by Eberlin; *Adoramus te,* hymn (K. 327), by Q. Gasparini; *Wiegenlied, Schlafe, mein Prinzschen* (K. 350), by B. Flies; Rondo in B-flat (K. 511a), probably by Beethoven; *Momento Domine David* (K. Anh. 22), by Reutter; *Lacrimosa* (K. Anh. 21), by Eberlin. The first four piano concertos (K. 37, 39, 40, 41) are arrangements of sonata movements, by Honauer, Raupach, Schobert, Eckard, and K. P. E. Bach; the 5th piano concerto (K. 107) consists of arrangements of 3 sonatas by Joh. Chr. Bach.

A new Complete Edition of Mozart's works (*Neue Mozart-Ausgabe*), under the general editorship of Ernst Fritz Schmid, began publication in 1955. The Mozarteum at Salzburg, a municipal musical institute founded in 1842, consists of an orchestral society, pledged to perform Mozart's church music in the 14 churches of the town, and to give 12 concerts yearly; a music school, in which the musicians of the orchestra give instruction; and an interesting museum of Mozart relics, etc. From 1880 a yearly report was issued. A series of summer courses, given by outstanding teachers in all musical branches during the Salzburg Festival in July and August, was also founded by the Mozarteum. Under the collective title of "Internationale Mozartgemeinde," branches were established in 1888 in Austria and Germany, of which those in Berlin and Dresden were especially active.

BIBLIOGRAPHY: BIOGRAPHY: Fr. v. Schlichtegroll, "Mozart," in his *Nekrolog auf das Jahr 1791* (new ed. by L. Landshoff, 1924); F. Niemtschek, *W. A. Mozarts Leben, nach Originalquellen beschrieben* (Prague, 1798; 2nd augm. ed., 1808; facsimile reprint of this ed., 1905; English transl., London, 1956); J. F. Arnold, *Mozarts Geist* (Erfurt, 1803); G. N. von Nissen, *Biographie W. A. Mozarts* (Leipzig, 1828); A. D. Oulibisheff, *Nouvelle biographie de Mozart* (Moscow, 1843; German transl., 3 vols., Stuttgart, 2nd ed. augm. by L.

Gantter, 4 vols., 1859); E. Holmes, *Life and Correspondence of Mozart* (London, 1845; 2nd ed., 1878; reprint, 1912); O. Jahn, *W. A. Mozart* (4 vols., Leipzig, 1856–9; 2nd ed., 2 vols., 1867; 3rd ed., 1891–93; 4th ed., rev. and augm. by H. Deiters, 1905, 1907; Engl. transl. by P. D. Townsend, London, 1882 [3 vols.]; the most exhaustive and standard biography; entirely rewritten and revised by H. Abert in 2 vols., 1919 and 1921; this ed. further revised by A. A. Abert, 1956); L. Nohl, *Mozarts Leben* (Leipzig, 1863; 3rd ed. by P. Sakolowski, Berlin, 1906; Engl. transl. by Lady Wallace, London, 1877); L. Nohl, *Mozart nach den Schilderungen seiner Zeitgenossen* (Leipzig, 1880); V. Wilder, *Mozart, l'homme et l'artiste* (Paris, 1880; 4th ed., 1889; English transl., London, 1908, 2 vols.); L. Meinardus, *Mozart. Ein Künstlerleben* (Leipzig, 1882); F. Gehring, *Mozart* (London, 1883; new ed., 1911); L. Klasen, *W. A. Mozart. Sein Leben und seine Werke* (Vienna, 1897); O. Fleischer, *Mozart* (Berlin, 1899); E. J. Breakspeare, *Mozart* (London, 1902); E. Prout, *Mozart* (London, 1903); L. Mirow, *Mozarts letzte Lebensjahre. Eine Künstlertragödie* (Leipzig, 1904); C. Belmonte, *Die Frauen im Leben Mozarts* (Augsburg, 1905); C. Bellaigue, *Mozart* (Paris, 1906); F. Lentner, *Mozarts Leben und Schaffen* (Innsbruck, 1906); H. von der Pfordten, *Mozart* (Leipzig, 1908); K. Storck, *Mozart. Sein Leben und Schaffen* (Stuttgart, 1908); L. Schmidt, *W. A. Mozart* (Berlin, 1912); Th. de Wyzewa and G. de Saint-Foix, *W. A. Mozart. Sa vie musicale et son œuvre de l'enfance à la pleine maturité* (5 vols., Paris, 1912–1946; the most valuable work since Jahn-Abert, especially on the origin and development of Mozart's style; the last three vols. were written by St.-Foix alone); A. Schurig, *W. A. Mozart. Sein Leben und sein Werk* (2 vols., Leipzig, 1913; 2nd ed., 1923; French transl., 1925); J. Kreitmaier, *Mozart* (1919); L. Schiedermair, *Mozart* (Munich, 1922); E. K. Blümml, *Aus Mozarts Freundes und Familien Kreis* (Vienna, 1923); O. Keller, *W. A. Mozart* (Berlin, 1926); B. Paumgartner, *Mozart* (Berlin, 1927; 4th ed., 1945); D. Hussey, *Mozart* (London, 1928; 2nd ed., 1933); M. Morold, *Mozart* (1931); R. Tenschert, *Mozart* (1931); E. Buenzod, *Mozart*, in *Maîtres de la Musique* (1931); S. Sitwell, *Mozart* (N.Y., 1932); R. Haas, *Mozart* (Potsdam, 1933; 2nd ed., 1950); Marcia Davenport, *Mozart* (N.Y., 1932; reprinted, 1956); A. il Mantovano, *Mozart fra noi* (Milan and Rome, 1933); H. Ghéon, *Promenades avec Mozart* (Paris, 1933; English transl. as *In Search of Mozart*, London, 1934); J. E. Talbot, *Mozart* (London, 1934); E. F. Schmid, *Mozart* (Lübeck, 1934); A. Boschot, *Mozart* (Paris, 1935); E. Blom, *Mozart* (London, 1935; 2nd ed., 1947); Ch. Perriolat, *Mozart, révélateur de la beauté artistique* (Paris, 1935); A. Kolb, *Mozart* (Vienna, 1937); H. de Curzon, *Mozart* (Paris, 1938); W. J. Turner, *Mozart: The Man and His Works* (N.Y., 1938); P. Nettl, *Mozart in Böhmen* (1938); I. Gyomai, *Le Cœur de Mozart* (Paris, 1939); W. Goetz, *Mozart: sein Leben in Selbstzeugnissen, Briefen und Berichten* (Berlin, 1941); E. Komorzynski, *Mozart* (Berlin, 1941; Vienna, 1955); G. Schaeffner, *W. A. Mozart* (Bern, 1941); E. Valentin, *Wege zu Mozart* (Regensburg, 1942); A. Albertini, *Mozart. La vita, le opere* (Milan, 1942); *Augsburger Mozartbuch* (Augsburg, 1943); A. Einstein, *Mozart: His Character, His Work* (N.Y., 1945); L. Parrot, *Mozart* (Paris, 3rd

ed., 1945); P. Espil, *Les Voyages de Chérubin, ou l'enfance de Mozart* (Bayonne, 1946); M. Mila, *W. A. Mozart* (Turin, 1946); E. Valentin, *Mozart* (Hameln, 1947); E. F. Schmid, *Ein schwäbisches Mozartbuch* (Stuttgart, 1948); R. Tenschert, *W. A. Mozart* (Salzburg, 1951; English transl., London, 1952); M. Kenyon, *Mozart in Salzburg* (London, 1952); K. Röttger, *W. A. Mozart* (Stuttgart, 1952); L. Biancolli, ed., *The Mozart Handbook* (N.Y., 1954); E. Schenk, *Mozart* (Zürich, 1955); N. Medici and R. Hughes, *A Mozart Pilgrimage* (London, 1955); J. Dalchow, *W. A. Mozarts Krankheiten, 1756–1763* (Bergisch Gladbach, 1955); M. Brion, *Mozart* (Paris, 1955); A. Ostoja, *Mozart e l'Italia* (Bologna, 1955); C. Fusero, *Mozart* (Turin, 1956); D. Kerner, "W. A. Mozarts Krankheiten und sein Tod," *Neue Zeitschrift für Musik* (Dec. 1956); E. Blom, "Mozart's Death," *Music and Letters* (Oct. 1957); Erich Schenk, *W. A. Mozart: Eine Biographie* (Vienna, 1955; in English, N.Y., 1959); O. Schneider & A. Algatzy, *Mozart: Handbuch* (Vienna, 1962); Otto Erich Deutsch, ed., *Mozart: Dokumente seines Lebens* (Munich, 1963; also in English, Palo Alto, Calif., 1965); S. Sadie, *Mozart* (London, 1965); Jean and Brigitte Massin, *W. A. Mozart* (Paris, 1970); Arthur Hutchins, *Mozart—The Man, The Musician* (N.Y., 1976).

CRITICISM, APPRECIATION: F. Lorenz, *W. A. Mozart als Clavier-Componist* (Breslau, 1866); K. F. Pohl, *Mozart und Haydn in London* (Vienna, 1867); W. Pole, *The Story of Mozart's Requiem* (London, 1879); E. Sauzay, *Haydn, Mozart, Beethoven, Étude sur le quatuor* (Paris, 1884); K. Prieger, *Urteile bedeutender Dichter, Philosophen und Musiker über Mozart* (Wiesbaden, 1886); A. Farinelli, *Don Giovanni: Note critiche* (Turin, 1896); A. J. Weltner, *Mozarts Werke und die Wiener Hoftheater: Statistisches und Historisches* (Vienna, 1896); D. Schultz, *Mozarts Jugendsinfonien* (Leipzig, 1900); E. von Komorzynski, *Mozarts Kunst der Instrumentation* (Stuttgart, 1906); A. Cametti, *Mozart a Roma* (Rome, 1907); K. Söhle, *Mozart. Dramatisches Zeitbild* (Leipzig, 1907); G. Schünemann, *Mozart als achtjähriger Komponist. Ein Notenbuch Wolfgangs* (1908; English transl., 1909); W. Nagel, *Mozart und die Gegenwart* (Langensalza, 1912); E. J. Dent, *Mozart's Operas. A Critical Study* (London, 1913; 2nd ed., 1947); A. Leitzmann, *Mozarts Persönlichkeit* (Leipzig, 1914); H. Cohen, *Die dramatische Idee in Mozarts Operntexten* (1916); E. Lert, *Mozart auf dem Theater* (Berlin, 1918; 4th ed., 1922); R. Lach, *Mozart als Theoretiker* (1919); H. W. von Waltershausen, *Die Zauberflöte* (1921); A. Lorenz, "Das Finale in Mozarts Meisteropern," *Die Musik* XIX/9; H. Mersmann, *Mozart* (1925); F. H. Marks, *Questions on Mozart's Pianoforte-sonatas* (London, 1929); E. Schenk, ed., *Bericht über die musikwissenschaftliche Tagung der Internationalen Stiftung Mozarteum in Salzburg, 1931* (Leipzig, 1932); V. P. Heinrich, *Komik und Humor bei Mozart* (Vienna, 1931); O. Beer, *Mozart und das Wiener Singspiel* (Vienna, 1932); G. de Saint-Foix, *Les Sinfonies de Mozart* (Paris, 1932; English transl., 1947); S. Anheisser, "Die Urfassung des Figaro," *Zeitschrift für Musikwissenschaft* 15 (p. 301ff.); N. Broder, "The Wind Instruments in Mozart's Symphonies," *Musical Quarterly* (July 1933); H. G. Farmer and H. Smith, *New Mozartiana* (Glasgow, 1935); C. M. Girdlestone, *Mozart's Pi-*

ano Concertos (in French, 2 vols., Paris, 1939; in English, 1 vol., London and Norman, Okla., 1948); A. Einstein, "Two Missing Sonatas of Mozart" (with music), *Music & Letters* (Jan. 1940); P. A. Hirsch, *Some Early Mozart Editions,* reprinted from *Music Review* (1940); N. Broder, "Mozart and the 'Clavier,'" *Musical Quarterly* (Oct. 1941); P. J. Jouve, *Le Don Juan de Mozart* (Freiburg, 1942; 3rd ed., Paris, 1948; English transl., London, 1957); E. A. Ballin, *Die Klavierlieder Mozarts* (Bonn, 1943); L. Conrad, *Mozarts Dramaturgie der Oper* (Würzburg, 1943); H. Socnik, *Das Pedal bei Mozart* (Danzig, 1943); M. Mila, *Saggi Mozartiani* (Milan, 1945); F. C. Benn, *Mozart on the Stage* (N.Y., 1946); A. Hutchings, *A Companion to Mozart's Piano Concertos* (London, 1948); J. Chantavoine, *Mozart dans Mozart* (Paris, 1948); G. Hausswald, *Mozarts Serenaden* (Leipzig, 1951); H. Dennerlein, *Der unbekannte Mozart: Die Welt seiner Klavierwerke* (Leipzig, 1951); S. Levarie, *Mozart's "Le Nozze di Figaro"* (Chicago, 1952); D. Lauener, *Die Frauengestalten in Mozarts Opern* (Zürich, 1954); A. Hyatt King, *Mozart in Retrospect* (London, 1955); K. G. Fellerer, *Mozarts Kirchenmusik* (Salzburg, 1955); R. Dumesnil, *Le Don Juan de Mozart* (Paris, 1955); A. Greither, *Die sieben grossen Opern Mozarts* (Heidelberg, 1956); R. Giazotto, *Annali Mozartiani* (Milan, 1956); G. Barblan and A. Della Corte, eds., *Mozart in Italia* (Milan, 1956); A. Einstein, *Essays on Music* (N.Y., 1956); H. C. Robbins Landon and D. Mitchell, eds., *The Mozart Companion* (N.Y., 1956); P. Nettl, *Mozart and Masonry* (N.Y., 1957); A. Della Corte, *Tutto il teatro di Mozart* (Turin, 1957); H. Albrecht, ed., *Die Bedeutung der Zeichen Keil, Strich, und Punkt bei Mozart* (Kassel, 1957); Brigid Brophy, *Mozart the Dramatist* (a Freudian interpretation; N.Y., 1964); R. B. Moberly, *Three Mozart Operas* (N.Y., 1968).

CORRESPONDENCE AND ICONOGRAPHY: L. Nohl, *Mozarts Briefe nach den Originalen herausgegeben* (Salzburg, 1865; 2nd augm. ed., Leipzig, 1877; English transl. by Lady Wallace, London, 1866); G. Nottebohm, *Mozartiana* (Leipzig, 1880); H. de Curzon, *Nouvelles lettres des dernières années de la vie de Mozart* (Paris, 1898); K. Storck, *Mozarts Briefe in Auswahl* (Stuttgart, 1906); M. Weigel, *Mozarts Briefe* (Berlin, 1910); A. Leitzmann, *Mozarts Briefe ausgewählt* (Leipzig, 1910); H. Leichtentritt, *Mozarts Briefe* (Berlin, 1912); L. Schiedermair, *Die Briefe W. A. Mozarts und seiner Familie. Erste kritische Gesamtausgabe* (5 vols., of which the last is an iconography; Munich, 1914); also correspondence ed. by H. de Curzon (in French, Paris, 1928), H. Mersmann (1928, in English and German), and H. Leichtentritt (Berlin, 1936); R. Tenschert, *Mozarts Leben in Bildern* (Leipzig, 1935); Emily Anderson, *The Letters of Mozart and His Family* (3 vols., London and N.Y., 1938, the most complete collection in English); E. H. Müller von Asow, *Briefe und Aufzeichnungen der Familie Mozart,* 5 vols. (Berlin, 1942); I. Voser-Hoesli, *W. A. Mozarts Briefe* (Zürich, 1948); R. Bory, *The Life and Works of W. A. Mozart in Pictures* (Geneva, 1948; also publ. in French and German); E. H. Mueller von Asow, *W. A. Mozart Briefwechsel und Aufzeichnungen,* 2 vols. (1769–79 only; Lindau im Bodensee, 1949); W. A. Bauer and O. E. Deutsch, *Mozart Briefe und Aufzeichnungen* (vol. 1, Kassel, 1962).

CATALOGUES, YEAR-BOOKS: *W. A. Mozart. Verzeichnis alle meiner Werke,* facsimile ed. by O. E. Deutsch, (Oxford, 1938); another ed. by E. H. Müller von Asow (Vienna, 1943); see also A. André, *Thematischer Katalog wie Mozart solchen von 1784–91 eigenhändig geschrieben hat* (Offenbach, 1805; 2nd augm. ed., 1828); L. von Köchel, *Chronologisch-thematisches Verzeichniss sämmtlicher Tonwerke W. A. Mozarts* (Leipzig, 1862; supplements 1864 [by Köchel in the *Allgemeine Musik Zeitung*] and 1889; 2nd ed., rev. and augm. by P. von Waldersee, 1905. An entirely new ed., greatly enlarged and containing the latest information on Mozart's works, was published by Alfred Einstein, 1937 (reprint, Ann Arbor, Michigan, 1947); the 6th edition, prepared by Fr. Giegling, A. Weinmann and G. Sieyers was issued in Wiesbaden, 1964, and reprinted in Leipzig, 1969. K. Moyses, *Systematischer Katalog der im Mozarteum befindlichen Autographe Mozarts* (Salzburg, 1862); J. Horner, *Katalog des Mozarts-Museums zu Salzburg* (Salzburg, 1882; 2d ed., by J. Engl, 1898); H. de Curzon, *Revue critique des ouvrages relatifs à W. A. Mozart et ses œuvres. Essai de bibliographie mozartienne* (Paris, 1906); also works on Mozart bibliography by P. Hirsch (1905), R. Tenschert (1925), and O. Keller (1927).—*Jahresbericht des Mozarteums* (from 1880); *Mitteilungen für die Mozart-Gemeinde* (Berlin, from 1895); *Bericht des Dresdener Mozart-Vereins* (from 1897); *Mozarteums-Mitteilungen* of Salzburg (1918–21; quarterly); *Mozart-Jahrbuch* (1st series, ed. by H. Abert, Munich, 1923, 1924, 1929; 2nd series, ed. by E. Valentin, Regensburg, 1941–43; 3rd series, Salzburg, from 1950); *Acta Mozartiana* from 1954; a quarterly publ. by the Deutsche Mozart-Gesellschaft).

The bicentennial celebration in 1956 produced a flood of books, articles, special editions, etc. Only the most important of the books are included in the above lists. See also the special Mozart issues of the *Musical Quarterly* (April 1956), the *Schweizerische Musikzeitung* XCVI/2 (1956), the *Neue Zeitschrift für Musik* (Jan. 1956), *High Fidelity* (Jan. 1956), etc.

Mozart, Wolfgang Amadeus, son of the great composer; b. Vienna, July 25, 1791; d. Karlsbad, July 29, 1844. He studied with Hummel and Salieri in Vienna; gave a concert as pianist at the age of 13; lived many years as a private tutor in Lwow, where he founded the Cecilia Society. He wrote 2 piano concertos, a string quartet, a piano trio, a violin sonata, many pieces for piano.

BIBLIOGRAPHY: J. Fischer, *W. A. Mozart* (Karlsbad, 1888); Karl Geiringer, "W. A. Mozart the Younger," *Musical Quarterly* (Oct. 1941); W. Hummel, *W. A. Mozarts Söhne* (Kassel, 1956); A. Vander Linden, "Le Dernier Fils de W. A. Mozart," *Bulletin des Beaux-Arts de l'Academie Royale de Belgique* (1968).

Mraczek, Joseph Gustav, Czech composer; b. Brno, March 12, 1878; d. Dresden, Dec. 24, 1944. He received his first instruction from his father, the cellist **Franz Mraczek;** was a chorister in various churches in Brno before going to Vienna, where he studied with Hellmesberger, Stocker, and Löwe at the Cons.; from 1897 to 1902, was concertmaster at the Stadttheater in Vienna; then taught violin in Brno (until 1918). In

1919, he went to Dresden to teach composition at the Cons. there; conducted the Dresden Philharmonic (1919–24); remained in Dresden to the end of his life. He wrote 6 operas: *The Glass Slipper* (Brno, 1902); *Der Traum* (Brno, Feb. 26, 1909), *Aebelö* (Breslau, 1915), *Ikdar* (Dresden, 1921), *Herrn Dürers Bild,* or *Madonna am Wiesenzaun* (Hannover, Jan. 29, 1927), *Der Liebesrat* (not produced); his most successful piece was a symph. burlesque, *Max und Moritz* (Brno, 1911; also widely played through Germany, and in the U.S.); other works include: *Oriental Sketches* for small orch. (1918); symph. poem, *Eva* (1922); *Oriental Dance Rhapsody* (1931); a piano quintet; a string quartet; piano pieces; songs.

BIBLIOGRAPHY: E. H. Müller, *J. G. Mraczek* (Dresden, 1918).

Mravinsky, Evgheny, eminent Russian conductor; b. St. Petersburg, June 4, 1903. He studied biology at St. Petersburg Univ.; then joined the Imperial Ballet as a pantomimist and rehearsal pianist; in 1924 he enrolled in the Leningrad Cons., where he studied conducting with Gauk, graduating in 1931; also took additional training with Malko; had courses in composition with Vladimir Shcherbachev; then was conductor of the Leningrad Theater of Opera and Ballet (1932–38). In 1938 he was appointed principal conductor of the Leningrad Philharmonic. Mravinsky represents the best of the Soviet school of conducting in which technical precision and fidelity to the music are combined with individual and even romantic interpretations. He is especially noted for his fine performances of Tchaikovsky's operas, ballets and symphonies; gave first performances of several symphonies of Prokofiev and Shostakovich; also conducted works by Béla Bartók and Stravinsky. In 1973 he was awarded the order of the Hero of Socialist Labor.

BIBLIOGRAPHY: V. Bogdanov-Berezovsky, *The Soviet Conductor Mravinsky* (Leningrad, 1956); V. Fomin, *Mravinsky Conducts* (Leningrad, 1976).

Mshvelidze, Shalva, Georgian composer; b. Tbilisi, May 28, 1904. He studied at the Tbilisi Cons., graduating in 1930; then was associated with various theatrical groups in the Caucasus, and also worked in Leningrad. He joined the faculty of the Tbilisi Cons. in 1929. Virtually all of his works for the theater are dedicated to the exploration of the national music of Soviet Georgia. He wrote the operas *Legend of Tariel* (Tbilisi, Feb. 25, 1946); *The Grandmaster's Right Hand* (Tbilisi, June 3, 1961); the oratorios *Caucasiana* (1949); and *The Legacy of Posterity,* for the centennial of Lenin's birth (1970); 5 symphonies (1943, 1944, 1952, 1968, 1974); symph. poems: *Azar* (1933), *Zviadauri* (1940), *Mindia* (1949), *Youngling and Tiger* (19621); chamber music; songs; incidental music to about 25 plays; film scores. He publ. a manual on orchestration in the Georgian language (1965).

Muck, Karl, great German conductor; b. Darmstadt, Oct. 22, 1859; d. Stuttgart, March 3, 1940. He received his first musical instruction from his father; also studied piano with Kissner in Würzburg; later pursued academic studies (classical philology) at the Univ. of Heidelberg and at Leipzig; received his Dr. phil. in 1880. He also attended the Leipzig Cons., and shortly before graduation made a successful debut as pianist with the Gewandhaus Orch. However, he did not choose to continue a pianistic career; obtained a position as chorusmaster at the municipal opera in Zürich; his ability soon secured him the post of conductor there; in subsequent years he was theater conductor in Salzburg, Brünn, and Graz; there Angelo Neumann, impresario of a traveling opera company, heard him, and engaged him as conductor for the Landestheater in Prague (1886), and then as Seidl's successor for his traveling Wagner Co. It was during those years that Muck developed his extraordinary qualities as a masterful disciplinarian and faithful interpreter, possessing impeccable taste. In 1889 he conducted the Wagner tetralogy in St. Petersburg, and in 1891 in Moscow. In 1892 he was engaged as first conductor at the Berlin Opera, and also frequently conducted symph. concerts of the Royal Chapel there. From 1894 to 1911 he led the Silesian Music Festivals; in 1899 he conducted the Wagner repertory at Covent Garden; from 1903 to 1906, he conducted the concerts of the Vienna Philharmonic (alternating with Mottl); besides, he appeared with outstanding success in Paris, Rome, Brussels, Madrid, Copenhagen, and other European centers. In 1901 he was selected to conduct the performances of *Parsifal* at Bayreuth. In 1906 he was engaged as conductor of the Boston Symph. Orch., and led it for 2 seasons, returning to Berlin in 1908, as general music director. He returned to America in the autumn of 1912 and assumed the post of permanent conductor of the Boston Symph. His farewell appearance at the Berlin Opera, conducting *Tristan und Isolde,* was made the occasion of a tumultuous demonstration. During the 20 years of his activity in Berlin he conducted 1,071 performances of 103 operas, of which 35 were novelties. With the entry of the U.S. into the war in the spring of 1917, Muck's position in Boston became ambiguous; he was known as a friend of Wilhelm II, and did not temper his intense German nationalism. Protests were made against the retention of Muck as conductor in Boston, and despite the defense offered by Major Higginson, the founder of the Boston Symph., Muck was arrested at his home on March 25, 1918, and interned as an enemy alien until the end of the war. In 1919 he returned to Germany; conducted the Hamburg Philharmonic from 1922 until 1933; then went to Stuttgart.

BIBLIOGRAPHY: N. Stücker, *Karl Muck* (Graz, 1939); Irving Lowens, "L'Affaire-Muck," *Musicology* I/3 (1947).

Muczynski, Robert, American composer (of Polish descent); b. Chicago, March 19, 1929. He began to study piano as a child, and received his formal training at De Paul Univ. with Alexander Tcherepnin. For his graduation, he played his own *Divertimento* for piano and orch. (1950). Other works include: Piano Concerto (Louisville, Jan. 1955; composer soloist); Symphony; *Music for Brass Sextet and Timpani; Suite* for clarinet and piano; *Fantasy* for violin and piano; for piano solo: *5 Sketches* (1952); 6 Preludes (1954); Sonata No. 1 (1957); *Galena, A Town* for orch. (1958); Trumpet Trio (1959); *Dovetail Overture* (1959); *3 Designs* for 3 timpani (1960); *Statements* for percussion (1961); *3 Preludes* for unaccompanied flute (1962). His style follows the trend of French neo-Classicism, without chromatic elaboration, but containing some polytonal usages.

Mudarra, Alonso, Spanish lutenist; b. c.1508; d. Seville, April 1, 1580. He was appointed canon of the Seville Cathedral in 1566. His important work, *Tres libros de música en cifra para vihuela* (i.e., lute music in tablature), originally publ. in Seville in 1546, was printed in modern notation by Emilio Pujol (Barcelona, 1946); this edition contains 77 works by Mudarra and his contemporaries, a biographical sketch, and commentary.

Mudge, Richard, English composer; b. Bideford, 1718; d. Great Packington, near Birmingham, April 3, 1763. He publ. 6 concertos for strings, and also an adagio for string orch. with a finale for voices singing the melody of Byrd's canon *Non Nobis Domine.* He entered Pembroke College, Oxford, in 1735 (B.A., 1738; M.A., 1741); ordained curate at Great Packington.
BIBLIOGRAPHY: S. R. Flint, *Mudge Memoirs* (1883); privately printed).

Mudie, Thomas Mollison, English composer and organist; b. London, Nov. 30, 1809; d. there, July 24, 1876. He studied at the Royal Academy of Music with Crotch and Potter; then taught piano there (1832–34); was organist at Galton, Surrey (1834–44); then taught at Edinburgh (1844–63), eventually returning to London. He wrote 4 symphonies; a piano quintet; a piano trio; and some vocal works.

Muench, Gerhart, German-born Mexican pianist and composer; b. Dresden, March 23, 1907. He studied piano with his father, a prof. at the Dresden Cons.; gave a public piano recital in Dresden at the age of 9. His auspicious career was halted by the Nazi takover in Germany; Muench was drafted into German Army, but was discharged in 1944 as physically unfit; emigrated to America in 1947; settled in Mexico in 1953; taught at the Univ. Nacional in Mexico City. In his piano recitals he introduced the new music of Stockhausen, Boulez, Pousseur and others to Mexican audiences.
WORKS: He began composing at an early age; his *Concerto da camera* for piano and chamber orch. was performed at the 1926 Contempoary Music Festival in Donaueschingen. His other works include a Cello Sonata (1938); *Capriccio Variato* for piano and orch. (1941); a chamber opera, *Tumulus Veneris* (1950); *Tesauras Orphei* for oboe, clarinet, viola, double bass and harp (1951); *Vocationes* for piano and chamber orch. (1951); Bassoon Concerto (1956); *Muerte sin Fin* for orch. (1957); Concerto for Piano and Strings (1957); Violin Concerto (1959); *Evoluta*, in 3 parts, for 2 pianos (1961); *Pièce de Résistance* for piano (1962); *Tessellata Tacambarensia,* a cycle of 9 chamber pieces for various instrumental groups or soloists (1964–76); *Labyrinthus Orphei* for orch. (1965); *Itinera Duo* for piano and orch. (1965); *Oxymora* for orch. (1967); *Auditur* for orch. (1968); *Asociaciones* for coloratura, soprano and instruments (1969); *Epi-*

tomae Tacambarensiae for orch. (1974); *Out of Chaos* for cello and piano (1975); *Signa Flexanima* for piano trio (1975); *Tetrálogo* for string quartet (1977); *Mini-Dialogos* for violin and cello (1977); *Proenza* for piano trio (1977); *Yuriko* for violin and piano (1977); 5 Masses; choruses; songs.

Muffat, Georg, important organist and composer; b. Megève, Savoy, baptized June 1, 1653; d. Passau, Feb. 23, 1704. He was named organist at the Molsheim Cathedral on March 31, 1671; in 1674, went to Austria; 1678, entered the service of the Archbishop of Salzburg, In 1681 he was in Italy; studied with Corelli and Pasquini in Rome; also spent several years in Paris, when he made a careful study of Lully's music. In 1687 he was appointed organist to the Bishop of Passau; in 1690, became Kapellmeister there. He was a significant composer; developed the German type of concerto grosso; publ. organ works, sonatas for various instruments, orchestral; suites, etc.
WRITINGS: *Armonico tributo,* polyphonic sonatas (1682; partly reprinted in the *Denkmäler der Tonkunst in Österreich* 89; *Florilegium,* orchestral suites in the style of Lully (2 vols., 1695–96; reprinted by Rietsh in the *Denkmäler der Tonkunst in Österreich* 2, 4 [1.ii, 2.ii]); *Apparatus musico-organisticus,* toccatas for organ (1960; reprinted by Lange, 1888, and by Kaller-Valentin, 1933); 12 concerti grossi, publ. under the title *Auserlesener . . . Instrumentalmusik erste Versamblung* (1701; reprinted in the *Denkmäler der Tonkunst in Österreich* 23 [11.ii]); a toccata is included in J. Bonnet's *Historical Organ Recitals* (vol. 1).
BIBLIOGRAPHY: L. Stollbrock, *Die Komponisten Georg und Gottlieb Muffat* (Rostock, 1888); F. Raugel, "Georg Muffat en Alsace," *Revue de Musicologie* (Dec. 1954); W. Kolneder, *Georg Muffat: Zur Aufführungspraxis* (1970).

Muffat, Gottlieb (Theophil), Austrian organist and composer; son of **Georg Muffat;** b. Passau, April (baptized April 25), 1690; d. Vienna, Dec. 9, 1770. In 1704 he went to Vienna, where he studied with J. J. Fux; from 1714, was in charge of the accompaniment of operas, church festivals, and chamber music at the Vienna court; became 2nd court organist in 1717; 1st organist, 1741; retired on a pension in 1763.
WORKS: *72 Versetl samt 12 Toccaten,* for organ (1726; reprinted by Guido Adler, in the *Denkmäler der Tonkunst in Österreich* 58 [29.ii]); *Componimenti musicali,* for harpsichord (ibid., 7 [3.iii]; includes an essay on ornaments; Handel used this material for ornamental phrases in his oratorios).
BIBLIOGRAPHY: L. Stollbrock, *Die Komponisten Georg und Gottlieb Muffat* (Rostock, 1888); H. Knöll, *Die Klavier- und Orgelwerke von Theophil Muffat* (Vienna, 1916); F. Chrysander in *Supplement, enthaltend Quellen zu Händels Werken* (vol. 5 of the complete ed. of Handel's works).

Mugellini, Bruno, Italian composer; b. Potenza, Dec. 24, 1871; d. Bologna, Jan. 15, 1912. He studied with Busi and Martucci in Bologna; appeared as a concert pianist in Italy; then was appointed prof. of piano at the Liceo Musicale in Bologna (1898), and succeeded Martucci as its director in 1911. He wrote an opera,

Catullo; a symph. poem, *Alla Fonte del Clitumno*; Piano Quartet; Cello Sonata; several sonatas and other pieces for piano; church music.

Mugnone, Leopoldo, Italian conductor; b. Naples, Sept. 29, 1858; d. there, Dec. 22, 1941. He studied with Cesi and Serrao at the Naples Cons.; began to compose as a young student; when he was 16, he produced a comic opera, *Don Bizarro e le sue figlie* (Naples, April 20, 1875); other operas were *Il Biricchino* (Venice, Aug. 11, 1892; fairly successful) and *Vita Bretone* (Naples, March 14, 1905). He also composed an attractive Neapolitan song, *La Rosella*, and other light music. But it was as a fine opera conductor that Mugnone achieved fame; his performances of Italian stage works possessed the highest degree of authority and an intense musicianly ardor. He also brought out Wagner's music dramas in Italy; conducted the first performance of Mascagni's *Cavalleria Rusticana* (Rome, in May 17, 1890).

Mühlfeld, Richard, famous German clarinetist; b. Salzungen, Feb. 28, 1856; d. Meiningen, June 1, 1907. He first studied the violin and played in the Meiningen court orch.; then practiced on the clarinet without a teacher, and in 1876, at the age of 20, became 1st clarinetist at Meiningen. From 1884 to 1896 he was 1st clarinetist at the Bayreuth Festivals. Brahms wrote for him the trio, op. 114 (clarinet, cello, and piano), the quintet, op. 115 (clarinet, 2 violins, viola, and cello), and the 2 clarinet sonatas, op. 120.

Mühling, August, German organist and composer; b. Raguhne, Sept. 26, 1786; d. Magdeburg, Feb. 3, 1847. He was for many years organist at the Magdeburg Cathedral; wrote the oratorios *Abbadona, Bonifazius, David, Die Leidensfeier Jesu*; 2 symphonies; Concerto for Bassoon and Orch.; 3 string quartets; Quintet for flute, 2 violins, viola, and cello; sacred duets and songs.

Mul, Jan, Dutch composer; b. Haarlem, Sept. 20, 1911; d. there, Dec. 30, 1971. He studied with H. Andriessen and with Sem Dresden at the Amsterdam Cons.; was an organist and choral conductor in Overveen (1931–60); served as music editor of the Amsterdam daily *De Volkskrant* and chairman of the Guild of Dutch Composers. He orchestrated Sem Dresden's opera *François Villon* from the vocal score for the production at the 1958 Holland Festival (Amsterdam, June 12, 1958) and Sweelinck's keyboard *Variations on an Old Song* (Amsterdam, June 12, 1963). He wrote some fine sacred choral music; his secular works show the influence of the French modern school.
WORKS: 2 short operas, *De Varkenshoeder (The Swineherd)*, after H. C. Andersen (1953) and *Bill Clifford* (1964); several Masses; *Stabat Mater* for chorus and small orch. (1934); *Te Deum Laudamus* for chorus and orch. (1955); *4 Coplas* for voice and orch. (1936); *Egmont onthalsd (Egmont Beheaded)* for chorus and orch. (1938); Piano Concerto (1938); Sonata for mezzo-soprano, baritone and small orch. (1940–53); *Galant Quartet* for soprano, and small orch. or flute, cello and piano (1952); *Felicitatie* for

orch. (1952); Concerto for Orch. (1956); Sinfonietta (1957; an orchestration of his piano sonata); *Mein junges Leben* for orch. (1961); *Lettre de M. l'Abbé d'Olivet à M. le President Bouhier* for baritone and orch. (1962); Concerto for piano 4-hands and small orch. (1962); *Confetti musicali* for orch. (1965); *Ik, Jan Mul (I, Jan Mul)* for orch. (1965); *Divertimento* for piano and orch. (1967); *Balladino* for cello, and orch. or piano (1968); *Variazioni "I due orsini"* for orch. (1968); *The Old Familiar Faces* for bass and chamber orch. (1969); *L'Homme désarmé*, cantata (1970–71; posthumous, Leyden, Sept. 25, 1973); 2 piano sonatinas (1928, 1942); Piano Sonata (1940); *Intervallen*, 6 inventions for piano (1942; orchestrated in 1954); Organ Sonata (1942); 2-Piano Sonata (1953); Quintet for clarinet, bassoon, violin, viola, and cello (1957); *De kwink*, ballad for male chorus, bassoon and percussion (1965); *Les Donemoiselles*, punning tribute to the Dutch Society Donemus, 6 small pieces for piano (1968); Trio for 2 violins and double bass (1969).

Mulder, Ernest Willem, Dutch composer; b. Amsterdam, July 21, 1898; d. there, April 12, 1959. He studied at the Toonkunst Cons. in Amsterdam, later taught there; was a lecturer at the Univ. of Utrecht (1938–47), director of the Bussum Music School and conductor of the Toonkunst Musical Society. He specialized in sacred music.
WORKS: opera, *Dafne* (1932–34); *3 Chansons* for soprano and orch. (1921–28); *Sinfonia Sacra I* for 6 soloists, chorus and orch. (1922–32), *II, Dialogue Mystique*, for baritone, chorus and orch. (1936–40), *III, super psalmos*, for orch. (1948) and *IV, super passionem*, for orch. (1949–50); *Requiem (Missa pro Defunctis)* for soloists, chorus and orch. (1927–32); Piano Concerto (1935); *Holland*, for chorus and orch. (1942); *Stabat Mater Dolorosa* for soloists, chorus and orch. (1948); *Te Deum Laudamus* for chorus and orch. (1951); *Symphonietta* for medium voice and orch. (1958); 2 violin sonatas (1920); *Ars contrapunctica*, a collection of 7 small works for various instrumental combinations (1938–40); *Sonata (in modo classico)* for solo violin (1941); Trio for 3 bassoons (1942); String Quartet (1942); Sextet for wind quintet and piano (1946); Quartet for oboe, bassoon, cello and harp (1946); songs.

Mulder, Herman, Dutch composer; b. Amsterdam, Dec. 12, 1894. He studied harmony and voice, had a brief career as a concert singer. A prolific composer, he wrote 12 symphonies: No. 1 (1940), No. 2 (1952), No. 3 (1954), No. 4 (1959–60), No. 5 (1961), No. 6 (1962), No. 7 (1964), No. 8 (1967), No. 9 (1968), No. 10 (1971), No. 11 (1972–73) and No. 12 (1974–75); *Suite* for orch. (1941); Piano Concerto (1943); Concerto for Orch. (1956); Concertino for piano, 9 wind instruments and percussion (1964); Violin Concerto (1964); Concertino for violin and string orch. (1964); Concertino for oboe and orch. (1966); *Music* for violin and chamber orch. (1967); 2-Piano Concerto (1968); *Ouverture* (1967–70); *Capriccio* for orch. (1970); *Funerailles* for orch. (1971); 13 string quartets (Nos. 7–13, 1951–70); 5 sonatas, one each for oboe, flute, clarinet, horn and bassoon, all with piano (1943–45); Piano Quintet (1947); English Horn Sonata (1950); 3

cello sonatinas (1956, 1956, 1967); 2 string quintets with 2 violas (1956, 1972); 2 string sextets (1957, 1973); 5 violin sonatas (1958–75); Viola Sonata (1960); Trio for flute, oboe and bassoon (1960); String Quintet, with 2 cellos (1961); 2 wind quintets (1961, 1966); Piano Trio (1965); Piano Quartet (1965); Violin Sonatina (1972); 2 string trios (1972); *Droomland (Dreamland)*, after Edgar Allan Poe, for baritone (or contralto) and piano (1949; orchestrated 1971); piano pieces; songs.

Mulè, Giuseppe, Italian composer; b. Termini, Sicily, June 28, 1885; d. Rome, Sept. 10, 1951. He studied at the Cons. of Palermo; graduated as a cellist as well as in composition. In 1922 he was engaged as director of the Cons. of Palermo (until 1925); in 1926 he succeeded Respighi as director of Santa Cecilia in Rome. He wrote mostly for the stage, and was particulary successful in providing suitable music for revivals of Greek plays. He composed numerous operas in the tradition of the Italian "verismo": *La Baronessa di Carini* (Palermo, April 16, 1912), *La Monacella della fontana* (Trieste, Feb. 17, 1923), *Dafni* (Rome, March 14, 1928), *Liolà* (Naples, Feb. 2, 1935); the oratorio *Il Cieco di Gerico*; the symph. poems *Sicilia canora* (1924) and *Vendemmia* (1936); also *Tre canti siciliani*, for voice and orch. (1930); a string quartet and other chamber music; songs.

Mule, Marcel, French saxophone player; b. Aube, June 24, 1901. He studied clarinet and saxophone with his father; was a member of the Garde Républicaine (1923–36); in 1929 he formed the Quatuor de Saxophones de Paris; in 1942 was appointed instructor of the newly established saxophone class at the Paris Cons. In 1957–58 he made his first American tour, appearing as soloist with the leading American orchestras in concertos by modern French composers.

Müller, Adolf, Sr., Hungarian opera composer; b. Tolna, Oct. 7, 1801; d. Vienna, July 29, 1886. He began his career as a singer; in 1828 became conductor at the Theater an der Wien, and brought out there a number of Singspiele, musical farces, etc.; also 2 operas: *Domi, der amerikanische Affe* (Jan. 28, 1831; fairly successful) and the comic opera *Das Zauberrütchen* (Dec. 2, 1831).

Müller, Adolf, Jr., Austrian composer and conductor; son of the preceding; b. Vienna, Oct. 15, 1839; d. there, Dec. 14, 1901. After completing his education in Vienna, he was engaged as theater conductor in the provinces; was conductor of the German Opera at Rotterdam (1875–83); after that at the Theater an der Wien, where his father had directed before him. He produced there a number of operas: *Der Pfarrer von Kirchfeld* (Nov. 5, 1870), *Heinrich der Goldschmidt, Waldmeisters Brautfahrt, Van Dyke,* etc.; and the operettas *Der Hofnarr* (Nov. 20, 1886; his greatest success), *Der Teufels Weib* (Nov. 22, 1890), *Der Millionen-Onkel* (Nov. 5, 1892), *General Gogo* (Feb. 1, 1896), and *Der Blondin von Namur* (Oct. 15, 1898).

Müller, August Eberhard, German organist and composer; b. Nordheim, Hannover, Dec. 13, 1767; d. Weimar, Dec. 3, 1817. He was an organist at various churches at Magdeburg and Leipzig; in 1800 he became assistant to Johann Adam Hiller at the Thomasschule in Leipzig, and succeeded him as cantor there in 1804; also was music director of the Thomaskirche and Nikolaikirche. In 1810 he became court conductor in Weimar. He wrote 3 piano concertos, and 18 piano sonatas; 11 flute concertos; 11 church cantatas; a practical piano method (1805; really the 6th ed. of Löhlein's *Pianoforte-Schule,* revised by Müller; Kalkbrenner's method is based on it; Czerny publ. the 8th ed. in 1825); a method for the flute. He also publ. cadenzas for and a guide to the interpretation of Mozart's concertos; arranged piano scores of Mozart's operas (very popular in his time).

BIBLIOGRAPHY: G. Haupt, *A. E. Müller's Leben und Klavierwerke* (Leipzig, 1926).

Müller, Franz (Karl Friedrich), German writer on Wagner and other subjects; b. Weimar, Nov. 30, 1806; d. there, Sept. 2, 1876. He was a government councillor in Weimar; was closely connected with the growing Wagner movement, and publ. a number of pamphlets on Wagner's operas: *Tannhäuser* (1853), *Richard Wagner und das Musikdrama* (1861), *Der Ring des Nibelungen* (1862), *Tristan und Isolde* (1865), *Lohengrin* (1867), and *Die Meistersinger von Nürnberg* (1869), the last three at the express command of King Ludwig II of Bavaria; also *Im Foyer* (1868; on theatrical affairs in Weimar).

Müller, Friedrich, German clarinetist, conductor, and composer; b. Orlamünde, Dec. 10, 1786; d. Rudolstadt, Dec. 12, 1871. In 1803 he entered the royal orch. at Rudolstadt as clarinet player; in 1831, became its conductor; pensioned in 1854. He wrote 2 symphonies; 2 clarinet concertos and other music for clarinet; also clarinet studies; a quartet for clarinet and strings; etc.

Müller, Georg Gottfried (also known as **George Godfrey**), American Moravian minister, violinist, and composer; b. Gross Hennersdorf, Saxony, May 22, 1762; d. Lititz, Pennsylvania, March 19, 1821. He came to America in 1784, and spent the major part of his life at Lititz, as a member of the culturally important group of Moravians in America. His works are listed by A. G. Rau and H. T. David in *A Catalogue of Music by American Moravians* (Bethlehem, 1938), and his music is represented in vol. I of the series, *Music by the Moravians in America,* publ. by the N.Y. Public Library (1938).

Müller, Gottfried, German composer; b. Dresden, June 8, 1914. He studied with Sir Donald Tovey in Edinburgh, Scotland, and with Straube in Leipzig; was instructor at the Hochschule für Musik in Leipzig and, from 1952 to 1961, organist in Berlin. In 1961 he was appointed prof. of composition at the Cons. of Nuremberg. Among his works are a set of orchestral variations on a German folksong, which became popular; *Deutsches Heldenrequiem* (1934); *Capriccio* (1959); *Dürersymphonie* (1962); Concertino for 3 Pianos (1963); String Quartet (1966); Concerto for 2 Pianos and Orch. (1967); Piano Concerto (1969).

Müller, Hans, German musicologist; son of the poet Wolfgang Müller von Königswinter; b. Cologne, Sept. 18, 1854; d. Berlin, April 11, 1897. He was appointed prof. of history of music at the Hochschule für Musik, Berlin, in 1889; publ. *Hucbalds echte und unechte Schriften über Musik* (1884); *Abhandlung über Mensuralmusik in der Karlsruher Handschrift St. Peter Pergamen, 29a* (Leipzig, 1886); etc.

Müller, Heinrich Fidelis, German composer and choral leader; b. Fulda, April 23, 1827; d. there, Aug. 30, 1905. He was for many years choirmaster at the Cologne Cathedral; composed the oratorios *Weihnachtsoratorium, Die heilige Elisabeth, Die Passion unseres Herrn*; several Masses, motets, choruses, etc.

Müller, Hermann, German music editor and ecclesiastic; b. Dortmund, Oct. 1, 1868; d. Paderborn, Jan. 17, 1932. He studied theology (Dr. theol.; 1891, priest), later church music with Haberl and Haller in Regensburg (1894); from 1894, cathedral choirmaster in Paderborn; specialist in church music. He publ. *Der feierliche Gottesdienst der Karwoche* (9th ed., 1928); *Gänge durchs Kirchenlied* (1926); numerous articles on church music in special publications.

Müller, Iwan, clarinetist and instrument maker; b. Reval, Estonia, Dec. 14, 1786; d. Bückeburg, Feb. 4, 1854. He developed the clarinet with 13 keys plus the "Altclarinet" (superseding the basset-horn). In 1809 he went to Paris, where he established a clarinet workshop; although he faced the opposition of conservative instrument makers, his improved clarinet eventually won general popularity. He spent the last years of his life at Bückeburg as court musician; publ. a method for his new instruments; 6 clarinet concertos and 2 clarinet quartets.
BIBLIOGRAPHY: F. G. Rendall, *The Clarinet* (London, 1954; *passim*).

Müller, Joseph, collector of musicians' portraits; b. Frankfurt, April 23, 1877; d. Closter, N.J., May 9, 1939. He studied at the Cons. of Ostend, Belgium, graduating in 1893; settled in N.Y. in 1933, and in 1934 became curator of musical iconography at the N.Y. Public Library; publ. *The Star Spangled Banner: Words and Music issued between 1814–64,* an annotated bibliographical list of the different versions, with many facsimiles (N.Y., 1935); contributed articles on musical iconography to the *Musical Quarterly* and other publications.

Müller, Karl Christian, organist and teacher, b. Saxe-Meiningen, July 3, 1831; d. New York, June 4, 1914. He studied piano and organ with Heinrich Pfeiffer, composition with Andreas Zöllner. He went to New York in 1854; worked in a piano factory, then played violin in the orch. of the Barnum Museum. From 1879 to 1895 he taught harmony at the N.Y. College of Music; transl. Sechter's *Grundsätze der musikalischen Composition* (entitled *Fundamental Harmony,* N.Y., 1871; 9 subsequent eds.); also supplemented it by 4 sets of tables on modulation, chord succession, and harmonization (1882–93).
WORKS: *Pleasant Recollections* and *Golden Hours*

for piano; 3 organ sonatas; Sonata for violin and piano; String Quartet; choruses; songs; *March of the Crusaders* and *Resignation* for organ; several large works in MS.

Müller, Maria, lyric soprano; b. Leitmeritz, Austria, Jan. 29, 1898; d. Bayreuth, March 13, 1958. Studied in Prague; later with Max Altglass, N.Y.; was a member of the Prague Opera (1921–23), Munich Opera (1923–24), and Metropolitan Opera (1924–35; debut as Sieglinde, Jan. 21, 1925). In 1926 she joined the Berlin State Opera; also sang at the Wagner Festivals in Bayreuth.

Müller, Paul, Swiss conductor and composer; b. Zürich, June 19, 1898. He studied at the Zürich Cons. (1917–20); in Paris and Berlin. From 1927 to 1969 he was on the faculty of the Zürich Cons. His early works show Romantic influences; later he turned to a modern contrapuntal style.
WORKS: Viola Concerto (1935); 2 violin concertos (1936, 1957); 2 *Sinfonias* for string orch. (1945, 1953); Cello Concerto (1954); 2 *Sinfoniettas* (1964); Concerto for 2 violins, string orch., and harpsichord (1969); chamber music.
BIBLIOGRAPHY: F. Jakob, *Paul Müller: Biographie und Werkverzeichnis* (Zürich, 1963).

Müller, Peter, German composer; b. Kesselstadt, near Hanau, June 9, 1791; d. Langen, Aug. 29, 1877. He taught music at various schools in Germany; wrote his renowned *Jugendlieder,* male choruses, organ pieces, etc. In 1839 he became pastor at Staden. His opera (after Bulwer-Lytton), *Die letzten Tage von Pompeii,* was produced at Darmstadt, Dec. 25, 1853; he also wrote 7 string quintets and other chamber music.

Müller Quartets. Two famous German string quartets, the first to undertake regular concert tours, their members being:
(1) The brothers **Karl** (1797–1873); **Gustav** (1799–1855); **Theodor** (1802–1875); and **Georg** (1808–1855); they were all born in Brunswick and belonged to the orchestra there, Karl as concertmaster, Theodor as cellist, Gustav as violinist, and Georg as conductor. Their artistic tours included not only all large German cities, but also Vienna and Paris (1833), Copenhagen (1838), St. Petersburg in 1845, and Holland in 1852.
BIBLIOGRAPHY: L. Köhler, *Die Gebrüder Müller und das Streichquartett* (Leipzig, 1858); E. Stier "Das Streichquartett der Gebrüder Müller, " *Braunschweigisches Archiv* (July 1913).
(2) The four sons of Karl, all b. in Brunswick (this quartet was organized in 1855, after the death of two members of the first one); **Karl,** 1st violin, b. April 14, 1829; d. Stuttgart, Nov. 11, 1907; **Hugo,** 2d violin, b. Sept. 21, 1832; d. Brunswick, June 26, 1886; **Bernhard,** viola, b. Feb. 24, 1825; d. Rostock, Sept. 4, 1895; and **Wilhelm,** cello, b. June 1, 1834; d. New York, Sept. 1897. For ten years they held the position of court quartet at Meiningen; then, after extended and successful travels, they settled in Rostock as members of the orch., Karl being appointed music director. The quartet was broken up by the appointment of Wil-

helm (1873) to succeed Sweerts as 1st cello in the Royal Orch. at Berlin, and prof. in the Hochschule. Karl lived from then on at Stuttgart and Hamburg; was also a noted composer.

Müller, Sigfrid Walther, German composer; b. Plauen, Jan. 11, 1905; d. in a Russian prison camp in Baku, Nov. 2, 1946. He studied at the Leipzig Cons. with Karg-Elert and Martienssen; also church music and organ with Straube; taught at the Leipzig Cons. (1929–32) and at the Hochschule für Musik in Weimar (1940–41); then was in the German army on the eastern front. His output comprised 62 op. numbers, mostly chamber music and organ works; also an opera, *Schlaraffenhochzeit* (Leipzig, 1937); *Böhmische Musik,* for orch.; *Gohliser Schlossmusik,* for small orch.; Concerto for Flute and Chamber Orch. (1941).

Müller, Wenzel, Austrian composer; b. Tyrnau, Moravia, Sept. 26, 1767; d. Baden, near Vienna, Aug. 3, 1835. He studied with Dittersdorf; conducted theater orchestras in provincial towns; was director of the Prague Opera from 1808 to 1813; then went to Vienna as conductor at the Leopoldstadt Theater, a post he held almost to the end of his life. He wrote an enormous amount of stage music, and his Singspiele were very popular in their day; among them were the following which he brought out at the Leopoldstadt Theater: *Das Sonnenfest der Braminen* (Sept. 9, 1790); *Kaspar der Fagottist, oder die Zauberzither* (June 8, 1791); *Das Neusonntagskind* (Oct. 10, 1793); *Die Schwestern von Prag* (March 11, 1794); *Die Teufelsmühle am Weinerberg* (an Austrian fairy tale; Nov. 12, 1799; his most popular stage work). A full list of his operas is given in the 2nd supplement to Riemann's *Opernhandbuch* (Leipzig, 1887).
BIBLIOGRAPHY: W. Krone, *Wenzel Müller* (Berlin, 1906); L. Raab, *Wenzel Müller* (Vienna, 1928); R. Haas, "Wenzel Müller," *Mozart-Jahrbuch 1953* (1954).

Müller-Blattau, Joseph Maria, German musicologist; b. Colmar, Alsace, May 21, 1895; d. Saarbrücken, Oct. 21, 1976. He studied music with Friedrich Ludwig at the Univ. of Strasbourg, and also took lessons with Pfitzner in composition and Ernst Münch in piano at the Strasbourg Cons. He was in the German Army during World War I; after the Armistice of 1918 he resumed his studies, taking courses with Wilibald Gurlitt at the Univ. of Freiburg-im-Breisgau; then occupied various teaching posts in Königsberg and Frankfurt; succeeded Wilibald Gurlitt at the Univ. of Freiburg in 1937; then served in military administration (1939–42); gave lectures at Strasbourg Univ. during the last years of World War II. In 1952 he was appointed director of the State Cons. at Saarbrücken, where he remained until his death. He was the editor of the abortive 12th ed. of Riemann's *Musiklexikon* (1937–39) of which only a few issues appeared before the wartime conditions made further publication impossible.
WORKS: *Das Elsass, ein Grenzland deutscher Musik* (1922); *Grundzüge einer Geschichte der Fuge* (1923; 2nd and augmented ed., 1930); *Musikalische Erneuerung* (collected essays; 1928); *Grundlagen der musikalischen Gestaltung* (1928); *Geschiscte der Musik in Ost- und Westpreussen* (1931); *Hamann und Herder in ihren Beziehungen zur Musik* (1931); *Einführung in die Musikgeschichte* (1932); *Das deutsche Volkslied* (1932); *Johannes Brahms* (1933); *G. Fr. Händel* (1933); *J. S. Bach* (1935; 2nd ed., 1950); *Geschichte der deutschen Musik* (1938; 2nd ed., 1953); *Hans Pfitzner* (1940); *Gestaltung-Umgestaltung: Studien zur Geschichte der musikalischen Variation* (1950); *Das Verhältnis von Wort und Ton in der Geschichte der Musik* (1952); *Musikalisches Taschenlexikon* (1952).

Müller-Hartmann, Robert, German composer; b. Hamburg, Oct. 11, 1884; d. Dorking, Surrey, Dec. 15, 1950. He studied at the Stern Cons. in Berlin, was lecturer on music at Hamburg Univ. (1923–33); in 1937 settled in England, where he worked mainly as an arranger and translator. He wrote a number of symph. works, some of which were first performed by Richard Strauss and Karl Muck: a symphony, a symph. ballad, several sets of variations, etc; a trio for flute, violin, and viola; 2 violin sonatas; many organ works; piano pieces.

Müller-Hermann, Johanna, Austrian composer and pedagogue; b. Vienna, Jan. 15, 1878; d. there. April 19, 1941. She studied with Karl Nawratil, Josef Labor, Guido Adler, Zemlinsky, and J. B. Foerster; began to compose at an early age, in a Romantic vein, influenced chiefly by Mahler and Max Reger; was regarded as one of the foremost European women composers of orchestral and chamber music. She wrote an oratorio, *In Memoriam,* to Walt Whitman's words; Symphony for voices with orch.; a symph. fantasy on Ibsen's play *Brand*; String Quartet; String Quintet; Piano Quintet; Violin Sonata; Cello Sonata; Piano Sonata; several song cycles.

Müller-Reuter, Theodor, German conductor and composer; b. Dresden, Sept. 1, 1858; d. there, Aug. 11, 1919. He studied piano with Alwin Wieck in Dresden and Clara Schumann in Frankfurt; also took lessons in composition with E. J. Otto and Meinardus in Dresden. He taught piano at Strasbourg Cons. (1879–87), and at Dresden; subsequently conducted the Concert Society in Krefeld (1893–1918), returning to Dresden shortly before his death. He wrote the operas *Ondolina* (Strasbourg, 1883) and *Der tolle Graf* (Nuremberg, 1887) and many choral works; publ. a valuable *Lexikon der deutschen Konzert-Literatur* (Leipzig, 1909; supplement, 1921); also a volume of reminiscences and essays, *Bilder und Klänge des Friedens; musikalische Erinnerungen und Aufsätze* (Leipzig, 1919).

Müller von Asow, Erich Hermann, German musicologist; b. Dresden, Aug. 31, 1892; d. Berlin, June 4, 1964. He studied at the Univ. of Leipzig with Hugo Riemann (1912–15); during World War I was engaged as military band conductor in the German Army; then was in charge of the Pädagogium der Tonkunst in Dresden (1926–32); in 1936 he went to Austria; was briefly under arrest by the Gestapo in 1943; in 1945, returned to Germany, and lived mostly in Berlin. His publications include several valuable biographical studies, among them, *Angelo und Pietro Mingotti* (Leipzig, 1917); *J. G. Mraczek* (Dresden, 1917); *Heinrich Schütz* (Dresden, 1922); *An die unsterbliche Geliebte: Liebesbriefe berühmter Musiker* (Dresden, 1934; 2nd ed., Vienna, 1942); *The Letters and Writings of G. F. Handel* (in English, London, 1935; in German, 1949); *J. S. Bach, Gesammelte Briefe und Schriften* (Regensburg, 1940; 2nd ed., 1950); *Egon Kornauth* (Leipzig, 1941); *Johannes Brahms und seine Welt* (Vienna, 1943); *Max Reger und seine Welt* (Berlin, 1944); numerous publications on Mozart. He began in 1955 a thematic catalogue of works of Richard Strauss, which was completed by A. Ott and Fr. Trenner (3 vols.; Vienna, 1959–74). Anticipating the ominous *Zeitgeist,* he regrettably publ. a *Handbuch der Judenfrage, Das Judentum in der Musik* (Leipzig, 1932). A Festschrift on the occasion of his 50th birthday was publ. in Salzburg (1942); and a compendium, *Epistolae et Musica,* on his 60th birthday (Hamburg, 1952). For a complete list of his writings, see the article in *Kürschners Deutscher Musiker-Kalender* (1954).

Müller von Kulm, Walter, Swiss composer; b. Kulm, Aug. 31, 1899; d. Arlesheim, near Basel, Oct. 3, 1967. He studied in Basel and Zürich; in 1947 was appointed director of the Basel Cons. He has written a number of stage works, among them an opera, *Der Erfinder* (1944); a ballet, *Die blaue Blume* (1936); an oratorio, *Vater unser* (1945); Symphony (1928); and several works of chamber music. He has also publ. a manual of harmony, *Grundriss der Harmonielehre* (Basel, 1948).

Mumma, Gordon, American avant-garde composer; b. Framingham, Mass., March 30, 1935. He studied piano and French horn at the Univ. of Michigan; began experimenting with electronic music at the age of 19, composing music and sound effects for an experimental theater in Ann Arbor. In 1957 he joined Robert Ashley and the artist Milton Cohen in a revolutionary theatrical art based on projected images; this developed into an esthetic medium called "Manifestations: Light and Sound" and later "Space Theatre;" in 1964 Mumma, Cohen and Ashley gave a memorable presentation of the Space Theatre at the Biennial Exhibition in Venice, becoming pioneers in the electronic light-show. With the development of transistor circuitry in electronics, Mumma began a serious study of its technology. In 1961 Mumma became a founder of the annual contemporary music festival in Ann Arbor called ONCE. Working at the Institute of Science and Technology in Ann Arbor, he developed a skill in seismology; made a study of tape recordings of earthquakes and underground nuclear explosions. In 1966 he joined the Merce Cunningham Dance Company and moved to New York; formed an ensemble called the Sonic Arts Union, which made two European tours. He gave courses in electronic circuitry at Brandeis Univ. (1966–67) and at the Univ. of Illinois in Urbana (1969–70); designed the Sound Modifier Console for the Pepsi Cola Pavilion at EXPO 70 in Osaka, Japan; developed a process of "cybersonic" control of acoustical and electronic media. He also applied computer techniques to composition.

WORKS: for magnetic tape: *Vectors* (1959); *Densities* (1959); *Sinfonia* for 12 instruments with tape (1960); *Mirrors* (1960); *Meanwhile, a Twopiece* for percussion and tape (1961); *Epoxy* (1962); *Megaton for William Burroughs* (1963); *Le Corbusier* for orch., organ, tape and cybersonic concertante (1965). Instrumental works: *A Quarter of Fourpiece* for four instruments (1963); a group of pieces with the punning titles *Very Small Size Mograph, Medium Size Mograph, Large Size Mograph* (1962–64) for piano and instruments; *Mesa* for cybersonic bandoneon with electronic accompaniment (1966), his most significant work); *Diastasis, As in Beer* for two cybersonic guitars with electronic accompaniment (1967); *Swarmer* for violin, concertina, musical saw and cybersonic modifiers (1968); *Digital Process with Poem Field* for tape and film projections (1969); *Communication in a Noisy Environment* (produced in Automation House, New York, by Intermedia Institute, Nov. 19, 1970); also a number of works with the generic title *Conspiracy* for digital computer and several performers intended to illustrate a democratic society in which the living enjoy civil rights on a par with computers; *Telepos* for dancers and telemetry belts and accelerometers (1971); *Phenomenon Unarticulated* for frequency modulated ultrasonic oscillators (1972); *Ambivex* for "surrogate myoelectrical telemetering system with pairs of performing appendages" (1972).

Munch, Charles, eminent Alsatian conductor; b. Strasbourg, Sept. 26, 1891; d. Richmond, Virginia, Nov. 6, 1968. The original spelling of his name was **Münch**; he was a son of **Ernst Münch,** a choral conductor in Alsace. He studied violin at the Strasbourg Cons., then went to Paris where he studied violin with Lucien Capet, and later took further violin lessons with Carl Flesch in Berlin and conducting with Furtwängler in Leipzig. He was sergeant of artillery in the German Army during World War I; was gassed at Peronne, and wounded at Verdun. In 1918, as an Alsatian, he became a French citizen; was concertmaster of the municipal orch. of Strasbourg (1919–26); later joined the Gewandhaus Orch. in Leipzig as concertmaster. He made his professional debut as a symphony conductor in Paris with the Straram Orch. (Nov. 1, 1932); in order to perfect his conducting technique he took some instruction with Alfred Szendrei (Sendrey), a Hungarian conductor then living in Paris (1933–40). Although he began his career as a conductor at the age of 41, he quickly rose to eminence; organized his own orch. in Paris, the Orchestre de la Société Philharmonique (1935–38), performing many French works. In 1938 he was engaged to conduct the Société des Concerts du Conservatoire de Paris, and remained with it during the difficult time of the German occupation. He received the French Legion of Honor in 1945. He made his American debut with the Boston Symph. Orch. on Dec. 27, 1946; in 1948 he made a transcontinental tour of the U.S. with the French Radio Orch. In 1949 he was selected as permanent conductor of the Boston Symph., to succeed Koussevitzky. In 1952 he traveled with the Boston Symph. to Europe on its first European tour; in 1956 the Boston Symph., with Munch and Monteux as conductors, made another European tour which included

Russia. He retired as conductor of the Boston Symph. Orch. in 1962. Returning to Paris he organized there the Orchestre de Paris; it was during an American tour of this orchestra that he collapsed and died in Richmond, Virginia. In his conducting Munch combined a distinct individuality with a fine sense of authentic color and stirring rhythms; in classical works he continued the traditions of the German school, striving mainly for precision and fidelity to the music, while making allowances for appropriate romantic effusions. Modern French music occupied a prominent place on his programs; he brought out new works by Albert Roussel, Milhaud, Honegger and others. He publ. a book, *Je suis chef d'orchestre* (Paris, 1954; in English, *I Am a Conductor*, N.Y., 1955).

BIBLIOGRAPHY: Hope Stoddard, *Symphony Conductors of the U.S.A.* (N.Y., 1957; pp. 136–46).

Münch, Ernst, Alsatian organist and choral conductor; b. Niederbronn, Dec. 31, 1859; d. Strasbourg, April 1, 1928, He was appointed organist at St. Wilhelm (St. Guillaume) Church in Strasbourg in 1882, where he founded a choir which attained a great renown for its performance of Bach's cantatas and passions; Albert Schweitzer served as organist at these performances. His son, **Fritz Münch** (b. Strasbourg, June 2, 1890), succeeded him as conductor of the St. Wilhelm Choir in 1924; his second son, **Charles Münch (Munch),** became a celebrated conductor; his third son was **Hans Münch.**

Münch, Hans, Alsatian conductor; b. Mulhouse, March 9, 1893. He was a nephew of **Ernst Münch** and son of the organist **Eugen Münch** of Mulhouse. He studied organ, composition and conducting at the Basel Cons. He conducted the choral society Liedertafel in Basel (1925–65) and also the subscription concerts of the Allgemeine Musikgesellschaft until 1966. He composed several cantatas, a symphony (1951) and *Symphonische Improvisationen* (1971).

Münchinger, Karl, German conductor; b. Stuttgart, May 29, 1915. He studied with Abendroth in Leipzig; in 1941 he conducted symphony orchestras in Hannover, and in 1945 founded the Stuttgart Chamber Orch. From then on he pursued his conducting career mainly outside of Germany; toured America, Japan and Russia; made his U.S. debut in San Francisco in 1953, and during the following season made a U.S. tour with his Chamber Orch. of Stuttgart; he visited the U.S. again in 1977. In 1966 he organized a "Klassische Philharmonie" in Stuttgart with which he gave regular performances.

Münnich, Richard, German music educator and theorist; b. Berlin, June 7, 1877; d. Weimar, July 4, 1970. He studied piano with his father and cello with Otto Hutschenreuter; then took courses at the Univ. of Berlin with Max Friedlaender and Carl Stumpf (1897–1901). He subsequently devoted himself to music education; held various teaching posts in Berlin and Stettin; for 25 years taught music theory at the Klindworth-Scharwenka Cons. in Berlin (1910–35); in 1935 he was appointed prof. at the Hochschule für Musik in Weimar; he retired in 1949. He publ. a number of practice books for school, among them *Widerholungsbüchlein für den Musikunterricht an höheren Schulen* (4th ed., 1928); *Jale, ein Beitrag zur Tonsilbenfrage und zur Schulmusik-Propädeutik* (Lahr, 1930; new ed., Wolfenbüttel, 1957). In his numerous writings on harmony he followed Riemann's analytical theories. A Festschrift was presented to him on his 70th birthday (1947).

Munsel, Patrice Beverly, American soprano; b. Spokane, Washington, May 14, 1925. She studied in N.Y. with William Herman and Renato Bellini; won an audition at the Metropolitan Opera and made a successful debut there on Dec. 4, 1943 in the minor role of Philine in *Mignon* (the youngest singer ever accepted by the Metropolitan); she remained on the staff until 1958. She subsequently made several European tours. Her best roles are Gilda, Lucia, Rosina, Violetta and Lakmé. She portrayed Melba in a motion picture on Melba's life (1953).

Munz, Mieczyslaw, Polish-American pianist and pedagogue; b. Cracow, Oct. 31, 1900; d. New York, Aug. 25, 1976. He studied piano and composition at the Vienna Academy of Music, and later at the Hochschule für Musik in Berlin; his principal teacher there was Ferruccio Busoni. He made a brilliant debut in Berlin in 1920 as soloist in 3 works on the same program: the Brahms Piano Concerto in D minor, Liszt's Piano Concerto in A and *Variations Symphoniques* by César Franck. His American debut took place in a solo recital in N.Y. on Oct. 20, 1922; he subsequently was soloist with a number of orchestras in the U.S.; also toured Europe, South America, Australia and Japan. He was on the faculty of the Curtis Institute of Music, Philadephia from 1941 to 1963, when he was engaged as prof. of piano at the Juilliard School of Music, N.Y. In 1975 he gave courses in Tokyo. His piano playing was distinguished by a fine romantic flair supported by an unobtrusive virtuoso technique. He was highly esteemed as a teacher.

Münzer, Georg, German writer on music and teacher; b. Breslau, Sept. 4, 1886; d. Berlin, April 24, 1908. He studied in Berlin with Klindworth (piano) and Helmholtz (acoustics); also musicology with Bellermann and Spitta; received his Dr. phil. with the dissertation *Beiträge zur Konzertgeschichte Breslaus;* lived in Breslau and Berlin.

WORKS: *Zur Einführung in Richard Wagners "Ring des Nibelungen"* (1900), *Heinrich Marschner* (1901); numerous essays in music journals.

Muradeli, Vano, Russian composer; b. Gori, Georgia, April 6, 1908; d. Tomsk, Siberia, Aug. 14, 1970. As a child he improvised songs accompanying himself on the mandolin (there was no piano in his home); he did not learn to read music until he was 18, when he entered the Tiflis Cons.; after graduation (1934) he went to the Moscow Cons., where he studied first with Shekhter and then with Miaskovsky. His early compositions were influenced by his native folk music; he wrote a *Georgian Suite* for piano (1935) and incidental music to plays on Caucasian subjects. His first important work was a symphony in memory of the assassinated Soviet dignitary Kirov (Moscow, Nov. 28, 1938); his 2nd Symphony (1946) received a Stalin prize. The performance of his opera *Great Friendship* (Moscow, Nov. 7, 1947) gave rise to an official condemnation of modernistic trends in Soviet music, culminating in the resolution of the Central Committee of the Communist Party of Feb. 10, 1948, which described the opera as "chaotic, inharmonious and alien to the normal human ear." Muradeli's reputation was rehabilitated by his subsequent works, *The Path of Victory* for orch., and a series of choruses (*Stalin's Will Has Led Us; Song of the Fighters for Peace; Hymn to Moscow*, which received a Stalin prize in 1951), and an opera *October* (Moscow, April 22, 1964).

Muratore, Lucien, French tenor; b. Marseilles, Aug. 29, 1876; d. Paris, July 16, 1954. He studied at the Cons. of Marseilles, graduating with honors in 1897, but began his career as an actor. Later he studied opera at the Paris Cons.; made his opera debut at the Opéra–Comique, Dec. 16, 1902, in Hahn's *La Carmélite* with extraordinary success. Muratore also sang in the premières of several operas by Massenet: *Ariane* (1906), *Bacchus* (1909), and *Roma* (1912), Février's *Monna Vanna* (1909), Giordano's *Siberia* (1911), etc. In 1913 he made his American debut with the Boston Opera Co.; on Dec. 15, 1913, he sang Faust with the Chicago Opera Co. In 1914 he joined the French Army; in 1917 sang at the Teatro Colón in Buenos Aires; then returned to the Chicago Opera Co. In 1922 he went back to France; for 7 years he served as mayor of the town of Biot. He was married three times; his first two marriages (to **Marguerite Bériza**, a soprano, and to the famous prima donna **Lina Cavalieri**) ended in divorce; his third wife was Marie Louise Brivaud.

Muris, Johannes (Jean) de, important musical theorist, astronomer, and mathematician; b. (probably in Normandy) c.1290; d. c.1351. He is often confused with a certain Julianus de Muris, rector of the Sorbonne in Paris, who was appointed to that post in 1350. It was also believed that Johannes de Muris was the author of the famous treatises *Speculum musicae* and *Summa musicae*, but it has since been established that the author of the *Speculum musicae* was Jacques de Liège; indeed the conservatism of this treatise is quite inconsistent with the progressive views held by Muris. But he did write the *Musica Speculativa*, which bears the inscription "abbreviata Parisiis in Sorbona A.D. 1323," and another important treatise, *Ars novae musicae*, in which his forward looking ideas are especially manifest (this treatise may be pieced together from material in Gerbert's *Scriptores*, III). In 1344 he was canon of Mezières (near Bourges), and he was one of the astronomers who took part in the reform of the calendar under the auspices of Pope Clement VI at Avignon. He does not appear to have been active as a composer. There is extant a letter of his to Philippe de Vitry.

BIBLIOGRAPHY: Hugo Riemann, *Geschichte der Musiktheorie* (2nd ed., 1921; p. 234 ff.); J. Wolf, *Geschichte der Mensuralnotation von 1250–1460* (1905); W. Grossmann, *Die einleitenden Kapitel des Speculum musicae* (1924; erroneous in ascribing the authorship of *Speculum musicae* to Johannes de Muris); H.

Besseler, "Studien zur Musik des Mittelalters," *Archiv für Musikwissenschaft* 7 (p. 180ff.), and 8 (p. 207ff.). A partial transl. into English of *Ars novae musicae* is found in O. Strunk, *Source Readings in Music History* (N.Y., 1950).

Murphy, Lambert, American tenor; b. Springfield, Mass., April 15, 1885; d. Hancock, N.H., July 24, 1954. He studied at Harvard Univ. (A.B., 1908); took singing lessons with T. Cushman in Boston and Luckstone in N.Y.; was soloist in various Boston churches (until 1910); made tours with the Boston Festival Orch.; appeared at many festivals; from 1910 to 1914, was a member of the Metropolitan Opera.

Murray, Bain, American composer and musicologist; b. Evanston, Illinois, Dec. 26, 1926. He studied at Harvard Univ. with Walter Piston (composition), Otto Gombosi (musicology) and A. Tillman Merritt (theory), obtaining his M.A. in 1952. From 1955 to 1970 he taught at Oberlin Cons.; in 1970 was appointed prof. of music at the Cleveland State Univ. He composed a ballet, *Peter Pan*, some chamber music and a number of songs.

Murrill, Herbert Henry John, English composer; b. London, May 11, 1909; d. there, July 24, 1952. He studied at the Royal Academy of Music in London with York Bowen, Stanley Marchant and Alan Bush; then took courses at Oxford Univ., with Ernest Walker and Sir Hugh Allen. He occupied various posts as organist and choral director; in 1933 he was appointed to the staff of the Royal Academy of Music, remaining at that post until his death. His relatively small output is in a modern vein, exemplified by a "jazz opera," *Man in Cage* (London, 1930). He also wrote 2 cello concertos (1935, 1950) and some chamber music, as well as songs and piano pieces.

Murschhauser, Franz Xaver Anton, German music theorist; b. Zabern, near Strasbourg, June (baptized July 1), 1663; d. Munich, Jan. 6, 1738. He studied with J. K. Kerll in Munich; from 1691 was music director of the Frauenkirche there. He wrote the theoretical treatise *Academia musico-poetica bipartita, oder Hohe Schule der musikalischen Composition*, the first part of which appeared in 1721, provocatively described as being intended "to give a little more light to the excellent Herr Mattheson." The latter retaliated with such devastating effect in his *Melopoetische Lichtscheere* (*Critica musica*, 1722; pp. 1–88) that Murschhauser refrained from publishing the second part of his work. His compositions for organ are reprinted in the *Denkmäler der Tonkunst in Bayern* 30 (18), ed. by M. Seiffert, with a biographical sketch.

BIBLIOGRAPHY: M. Vogeleis, "F. X. A. Murschhauser," *Kirchenmusikalisches Jahrbuch* (1901).

Murska, Ilma di, Croatian soprano; b. 1836; d. (suicide by poison) Munich, Jan. 14, 1889. She studied with Mathilde Marchesi in Vienna, and later in Paris; made her debut in Florence (1862). After a European tour, she was engaged at the Vienna Opera. She made her London appeerence for the first time as Lucia (May 11, 1865) and was favorably received there for several seasons (until 1873); toured America and Australia (1873–76); was again in London in 1879. She taught at the National Cons., N.Y., in 1880. She led a turbulent life; was married 3 times; killed herself in a fit of despondency.

Musard, Philippe, famous French dance composer; b. Tours, Nov. 8, 1792; d. Auteuil (Paris), March 30, 1859. He studied music privately with Reicha; first came into public view at the promenade concerts in Paris, begun in Nov. 1833, in a bazaar of the Rue St. Honoré; there he introduced Dufresne, a remarkable player on the cornet, and wrote special solo pieces for him, which became a great attraction; he also conducted balls at the Paris Opéra (1835–36), at which his orch. of 70 musicians won great acclaim. His quadrilles and galops enjoyed immense popularity, and he earned the sobriquet "le roi des quadrilles." In London he conducted the promenade concerts at Drury Lane during the season of 1840–41, and appeared at other concerts in England. His son **Alfred Musard** (1828–81) was likewise a composer of quadrilles, and a band leader.

Musgrave, Thea, remarkable Scottish composer; b. Edinburgh, May 27, 1928. She studied composition at the Univ. of Edinburgh and in Paris with Nadia Boulanger. From 1955 to 1970 she was active mainly as a choral conductor and accompanist; from 1970 to 1978 she was on the music faculty at the Univ. of California, Santa Barbara. The diatonic lyricism of the initial period of her creative evolution soon gave way to increasingly chromatic constructions, eventually systematized into serial organization. She has described her compositions as "dramatic-abstract" in form, because though they contain no program they reveal some unusual dramatic traits.

WORKS: the operas: *The Abbott of Drimrock,* chamber opera (London, 1955); *The Decision* (1964; London, Nov. 30, 1967); *The Voice of Ariadne,* after *The Last of the Valerii* by Henry James (Aldeburgh, England, Festival, June 11, 1974); *Mary, Queen of Scots* (Edinburgh Festival, Sept. 6, 1977); *A Tale for Thieves,* ballet (1953); *Four Madrigals* for unaccompanied chorus (1953); *A Suite o' Bairnsangs* for voice and piano (1953); *Cantata for a Summer's Day* for vocal quartet, speaker, flute, clarinet, string quartet and double bass (1954); *Song of the Burn* for unaccompanied chorus (1954); *5 Love Songs* for tenor and guitar (1955); *Divertimento* for string orch. (1957); String Quartet (1958); *Obliques* for orch. (1958); *A Song for Christmas* for voice and piano (1958); *Scottish Dance Suite* for orch. (1959); *Triptych* for tenor and orch. (1959); *Colloquy* for violin and piano (1960); Trio for flute, oboe, and piano (1960); *Monologue* for piano (1960); *Serenade* for flute, clarinet, harp, viola and cello (1961); *Perspectives* for orch. (1961); Chamber Concerto No. 1 for 9 instruments (1962); *The Phoenix and the Turtle* for chorus and orch. (1962); *Marko the Miser,* "a tale for children to mime, sing and play" (1962); *Sinfonia* (1963); *The Five Ages of Man* for chorus and orch. (1964); *Excursions* for piano duet (1965); *Festival Overture* (1965); Chamber Concerto No. 2 for 5 instruments (1966); Chamber Concerto No. 3 for 8 instruments (1966); *Nocturnes and Arias* for orch. (1966); *Variations* for brass band (1966); *Sonata for Three* for flute, violin and guitar (1966); *Impromptu No. 1* for flute and oboe (1967); *Concerto for Orchestra* (1967); *Memento Creatoris* for unaccompanied chorus (1967); *Music* for horn and piano (1967); Clarinet Concerto (London, Feb. 5, 1969; a deft, chic virtuoso piece, requiring the soloist to promenade among members of the orchestra); *Beauty and the Beast,* ballet for chamber orch. and electronic tape (1968–69; London, Nov. 19, 1969); *Soliloquy No. 1* for guitar and electronic tape (1969); *Night Music* for chamber orch. (1969); *Memento Vitae* for orch. (1969–70); *Elegy* for viola and cello (1970); *Impromptu No. 2* for flute, oboe and clarinet (1970); *From One to Another* for viola and electronic tape (1970); Viola Concerto (1973); *Space Play,* concerto for 9 instruments (1974).

Musicescu, Gavriil, Rumanian composer of sacred music and folksong arranger; b. Ismail, March 20, 1847; d. Jassy, Dec. 21, 1903. He studied at the Cons. of Jassy and later at the St. Petersburg Cons. In 1872 he was appointed prof. at the Jassy Cons. and became its director in 1901. He composed mainly choral music for the Orthodox Church; published a manual for vocal teachers (Jassy, 1877). His arrangements of Rumanian folksongs have an authentic flavor, thanks to his skill in finding suitable harmonizations of intervallically peculiar melodic patterns.

BIBLIOGRAPHY: G. Breazul, *G. Musicescu* (Bucharest, 1962).

Musin, Ovide, Belgian violinist; b. Nandrin, near Liège, Sept. 22. 1854; d. Brooklyn, N.Y., Nov. 24, 1929. He studied with Heynberg and Léonard at the Liège Cons., taking 1st violin prize at the age of 13; he won the gold medal at 15; toured Europe from 1874 to 1882 with remarkable success. In 1883 he went to America; between 1892 and 1897 he made two world tours. From 1897 to 1908 he taught at the Cons. of Liège; in 1908 he established himself in N.Y., and opened his own school of music. He publ. a number of brilliant violin pieces; also instructive works, *System of Daily Practice* (1899) and *The Belgian School of the Violin* (4 vols.; 1916; a combination of his own methods with those of his teacher Léonard); also a book, *My Memories* (1920). His wife, **Annie Louise Tanner-Musin** (b. Boston, Oct. 3, 1856; d. there, Feb. 28, 1921), was a well-known coloratura soprano. See the article on Musin in the *Dictionary of American Biography.*

Musiol, Robert Paul Johann, German writer on music and pedagogue; b. Breslau, Jan. 14, 1846; d. Fraustadt, Posen, Oct. 19, 1903. He studied in Liebenthal, Silesia; devoted himself to teaching. He published a useful lexicon, *Musikalisches Fremdwörterbuch; Katechismus der Musikgeschichte* (2nd ed., 1888); edited Tonger's *Konversations-Lexikon der Tonkunst* (1881–85) and *Musikerlexikon* (1890).

Mussolini, Cesare, Italian composer and theorist; b. Romagna, 1735; d. probably in London, where he went in 1780; publ. (in English) *A New and Complete Treatise on the Theory and Practice of Music, with Solfeggios* (London, 1795); also canzonets. He was an ancestor of Benito Mussolini.

Mussolini, Romano, Italian jazz pianist; son of Il Duce; b. Carpena, Forli, Sept. 26, 1927. With the rest of Mussolini's family he lived in Ischia after the war; picked up accordion and piano; became a professional jazz band leader in Rome.

Mussorgsky, Modest, great Russian composer; b. Karevo, district of Pskov, March 21, 1839; d. St. Petersburg, March 28, 1881. He received his first instruction on the piano from his mother; at the age of 10 he was taken to St. Petersburg, where he had piano lessons with Anton Herke. In 1852 he entered the cadet school of the Imperial Guard; composed a piano piece entitled *Porte enseigne Polka,* which was published (1852); after graduation, he joined the regiment of the Guard. In 1857, he met Dargomyzhsky, who introduced him to Cui and Balakirev; he also became friendly with the critic and chief champion of Russian national music, Vladimir Stasov. These associations prompted Mussorgsky's decision to become a professional composer. He played and analyzed piano arrangements of works by Beethoven and Schumann; Balakirev helped him to acquire a knowledge of form; he tried to write music in a classical style, but without success; his inner drive was directed towards "new shores," as Mussorgsky himself expressed it. The liquidation of the family estate made it imperative for Mussorgsky to take a paying job; he became a clerk in the Ministry of Communications (1863), resigning 4 years later. During this time, he continued to compose, but his lack of technique compelled him time and again to leave his various pieces unfinished. He eagerly sought professional advice from his friends Stasov (for general esthetics) and Rimsky-Korsakov (for problems of harmony); to the very end of his life, he regarded himself as being only half-educated in music, and constantly acknowledged his inferiority as a craftsman. But he yielded to no one in his firm faith in the future of national Russian music. When a group of composers from Bohemia visited St. Petersburg in 1867, Stasov published an article in which he for the first time referred to the "mighty handful of Russian musicians" pursuing the ideal of national art. The expression was picked up derisively by some journalists, but it was accepted as a challenge by Mussorgsky and his comrades-in-arms, Balakirev, Borodin, Cui, and Rimsky-Korsakov, the "mighty five" of Russian music. In 1869, Mussorgsky once again entered government service, this time in the forestry department. He became addicted to drink, and had epileptic fits; he died a week after his 42nd birthday. The significance of Mussorgsky's genius did not become apparent until some years after his death. Most of his works were prepared for publication by Rimsky-Korsakov, who corrected some of Mussorgsky's harmonic crudities, and reorchestrated the symphonic works. Original versions of Mussorgsky's music were preserved in manuscript, and eventually published. But despite the availability of the authentic scores, Mussorgsky's works continue to be performed in Rimsky-Korsakov's editions, made familiar to the whole musical world. In his dramatic works, and in his songs, Mussorgsky draws a boldly realistic vocal line, in which inflections of speech are translated into a natural melody. His first attempt in this genre was an unfinished opera, *The Marriage,* to Gogol's comedy; here Mussorgsky also demonstrated his penetrating sense of musical humor. His ability to depict tragic moods is revealed in his cycle, *Songs and Dances of Death;* his understanding of intimate poetry is shown in the children's songs. His greatest work is the opera *Boris Godunov* (to Pushkin's tragedy), which has no equal in its stirring portrayal of personal destiny against a background of social upheaval. In it, Mussorgsky created a true national music drama, without a trace of the Italian conventions that had theretofore dominated the operatic works by Russian composers. Mussorgsky wrote no chamber music, perhaps because he lacked the requisite training in contrapuntal technique. Of his piano music, the set of pieces, *Pictures at an Exhibition* (somewhat after the manner of Schumann's *Carnaval*), is remarkable for its vivid representation of varied scenes (it was written to commemorate his friend, the painter Victor Hartmann, whose pictures were the subjects of the music); the work became famous in the brilliant orchestration of Ravel. Although Mussorgsky was a Russian national composer, his music influenced many composers outside Russia, and he came to be regarded as the most potent talent of the National Russian School.

WORKS: OPERAS: *The Marriage* (1864; only the first act completed; produced, Petrograd, Oct. 26, 1917; completed and orchestrated by Alexandre Tcherepnin; performed in this form for the first time, Essen, Sept. 14, 1937); *Boris Godunov* (St. Petersburg, Feb. 8, 1874; revised and reorchestrated by Rimsky-Korsakov in 1896; produced in this new form, St. Petersburg, Dec. 10, 1896, and subsequently all over the world; Mussorgsky's original score, ed. by Paul Lamm, publ. in 1928); *Khovanshchina* (on a historical subject from the time of Peter the Great; completed and orchestrated by Rimsky-Korsakov; first performed, St. Petersburg, Feb. 21, 1886); *The Fair at Sorochinsk* (unfinished, completed by Cui; St. Petersburg, Oct. 26, 1917; also arranged and orchestrated by Nicolas Tcherepnin, and produced at Monte Carlo, March 17, 1923); CHORAL WORKS: *The Destruction of Sennacherib,* after Byron, for chorus and orch. (St. Petersburg, March 18, 1867) and *Joshua,* for contralto, bass, chorus, and piano (1874–77); FOR ORCH.: *Scherzo* (St. Petersburg, Jan. 23, 1860), *Intermezzo in modo classico* (1867), *A Night on the Bald Mountain* (1860–66; reorchestrated by Rimsky-Korsakov and performed posthumously, St. Petersburg, Oct. 27, 1886); FOR PIANO: *Scherzo* (1858), *Jeux d'enfants-les quatre coins* (German subtitle *Ein Kinderscherz;* 1859), *Impromptu passionné* (1859), Sonata, for piano, 4 hands (1860), *Souvenirs d'enfance* (1865), *Rêverie* (1865), *La Capricieuse* (1865), *Intermezzo in modo classico* (piano version of the orch. piece; 1867), *Pictures at an Exhibition* (1874; *Promenade; Gnomus; Il vecchio castello; Tuileries; Bydlo; Ballet des poussins dans leurs coques; Deux juifs, l'un riche et l'autre pauvre; Promenade; Limoges—Le Marché; Catacombae; Cum mortuis in lingua mortua; La Cabane sur des pattes de poule; La Grande Porte de Kiev;* French titles by Mussorgsky), *En Crimée* (1880), *Méditation* (1880), *Une Larme* (1880), piano transcriptions of dances from the opera *The Fair at Sorotchinsk,* many incomplete fragments of youthful works, etc.; SONGS: *King Saul* (1863), *Cradle Song* (1865), *Darling Savishna* (1866), *The Seminarist* (1866), *Hopak* (1866), *On the Dnieper* (1879), *Hebrew Song* (1879), *The Classicist* (satirical; 1867), *The Garden by the Don* (1867), *The Nursery,* children's song cycle (1868-72), *Rayok* (*The Peep-show;* a musical lampoon at assorted contemporaries; 1870), *Sunless,* song cycle (1874), *Forgotten* (1874), *Songs and Dances of Death,* a cycle of 4 songs (1875-77), *Mephistopheles' Song of the Flea* (1879), a number of other songs. In 1928-34 the Soviet State Edition, under the direction of Paul Lamm, undertook the publication of his complete works, including variants, fragments, notations of folksongs, etc.

BIBLIOGRAPHY: V. Stasov, *M.* (St. Petersburg, 1881); V. Baskin, *M.* (Moscow, 1887); Pierre d'Alheim, *M.* (Paris, 3rd ed., 1896); Marie Olénine-d'Alheim, *Le Legs de Mussorgsky* (Paris, 1908); M.-D. Calvocoressi, *M.* (Paris, 1907, 2nd French ed., 1911; English transl., London, 1919); Rosa Newmarch, "M.'s Operas," *Musical Times* (July 1913); M. Montagu-Nathan, *M.* (London, 1916); Oskar von Riesemann, *M.* (Munich, 1925; in English, N.Y., 1935); Alfred Swan, "M. and Modern Music," *Musical Quarterly* (April 1925); Kurt von Wolfurt, *M.* (Stuttgart, 1927); R. Godet, *En marge de Boris Godunov* (Paris, 1927); Igor Glebov, *M.* (Leningrad, 1928); H. van Dalen, *M.* (The Hague, 1930); Y. Keldish, *Lyricism in M.'s Songs* (Moscow, 1933); M. D. Calvocoressi, "M.'s Musical Style," *Musical Quarterly* (Oct. 1932); M. D. Calvocoressi, "M.'s Youth," *Musical Quarterly* (Jan. 1934); V. Fedorov, *M.* (Paris, 1935); Maria Tibaldi Chiesa, *M.* (Milan, 1935); Gerald Abraham and M. D. Calvocoressi, "M.," in *Masters of Russian Music* (London 1936; pp. 178-248); C. Barzel, *M.* (Paris, 1939); G. Orlov, *Chronicle of the Life and Works of Mussorgsky* (Moscow, 1940); G. Gavazzeni, *M. e la musica russa dell' 800* (Florence, 1943); R. Garcia Morillo, *M.* (Buenos Aires, 1943); M. D. Calvocoressi, *M.* (completed by Gerald Abraham, London, 1946); R. Hofmann, *M.* (Paris 1952); M. D. Calvocoressi, *M. M., His Life and Works* (London, 1956; ed. by Gerald Abraham; a completely different book from the earlier ones by Calvocoressi); numerous publications in Russian, pertaining to various aspects of Mussorgsky's life and works; special numbers of Russian magazines. A collection of letters and documents were publ. by A. Rimsky-Korsakov (Moscow, 1932); materials, largely taken from this volume, were transl. and ed. by J. Leyda and S. Bertensson, as *The M. Reader* (N.Y., 1947). The paintings of Victor Hartmann that inspired Mussorgsky's *Pictures at an Exhibition* were reproduced by Alfred Frankenstein in his article on the subject in the *Musical Quarterly* (July 1939); Frankenstein also brought out an illustrated edition of the work (1951).

Mustel, Victor, celebrated French builder of harmoniums; inventor of the celesta; b. Le Havre, June 13, 1815; d. Paris, Jan. 26, 1890. He began as a carpenter; went to Paris in 1844, where he worked in several shops, becoming foreman in Alexandre's harmonium factory; established himself in 1853; the following year invented "the double expression," which won the first prize at the Paris Exposition of 1855; from 1866 the firm became famous as "V. Mustel et ses Fils." He also constructed an instrument consisting of graduated tuning forks in a resonance box, operated by a keyboard; this was patented in 1886 by his son **Auguste** (1842-1919) as "Celesta." Tchaikovsky heard the celesta in Paris, and became so enchanted with it that he used it (for the first time in any score) in his ballet *The Nutcracker.*

Müthel, Johann Gottfried, German organist and composer; b. Möllin, Jan. 17, 1718; d. Riga, Jan. 17, 1788. He studied at Lübeck and became court organist at Schwerin. In 1750 he traveled to Leipzig to see Bach, with whom he remained through several weeks before Bach's death. He then journeyed to Potsdam, where he formed a friendship with Carl Philipp Emanuel Bach. In 1753 he went to Riga as organist at the Lutheran Church there. He had the reputation of a very excellent organist; his compositions for the organ were highly praised. He publ. several piano works in Riga, including a duet, the title of which includes for the first time the word "Fortepiano."

Muti, Lorenzo, Italian singer and conductor; b. Spoleto, Sept. 2, 1951. Menotti chose him for the boy's role in the première of his opera *Maria Golovin* in Brussels in 1958. He was also the boy singer in Britten's *Abraham and Isaac* in 1965; in 1966 he sang Yniold in *Pelléas et Mélisande* in Spoleto. But as his voice was about to break, he decided to study music seriously and academically; took courses at the Curtis Institute in Philadelphia and at the Juilliard School, N.Y., graduating in 1973. He made a successful debut in Spoleto as conductor in Salieri's opera buffa *Prima la musica, poi le parole* in the summer of 1974.

Muti, Riccardo, Italian conductor; b. Naples, July 28, 1941. He studied at the Conservatorio di Musica San Pietro a Majella with Nino Rota and with J. Napoli; then took a course in conducting with Votto at the Milan Cons. and compositon with Bettinelli there. In 1967 he won the international prize for conducting named after Guido Cantelli. In 1967 he was appointed permanent conductor of the Teatro Communale in Florence and of the Maggio Musicale Fiorentino. In 1974 he was also engaged as the principal conductor of the New Philharmonia Orch. in London. He also conducted guest appearances in the U.S., and was particularly praised for his appearances with the Philadelphia Orch.

Muzio, Claudia, Italian dramatic soprano; b. Pavia, Feb. 7, 1889; d. Rome, May 24, 1936. Her baptismal name was **Claudina Muzzio,** but she adopted the altered form Claudia Muzio early in her career. She studied with Mme. Casaloni in Turin; made her debut as Manon at Arezzo (Feb. 7, 1912), then sang in Italy, South America, France, and England; made her first American appearance at the Metropolitan Opera as Tosca (Dec. 4, 1916); from 1922 to 1933 was a member of the Chicago Opera; after returning to the Metropolitan Opera for a season, she went back to Italy in 1934.

BIBLIOGRAPHY: H. M. Barnes, *Claudia Muzio; a Biographical Sketch and Discography* (Austin, Texas, 1947).

Muzio, Emanuele, Italian composer; b. Zibello, Aug. 25, 1825; d. Paris, Nov. 27, 1890. He studied piano with Margherita Barezzi (Verdi's first wife), and composition with Verdi himself, one of the very few pupils Verdi ever had. In 1852 he was engaged as conductor of the Italian Opera in Brussels; later traveled to England and America; settled in Paris in 1875 as a singing teacher. Carlotta Patti and Clara Louise Kellogg were his pupils. He wrote several operas: *Giovanna la pazza* (Brussels, April 8, 1851), *Claudia* (Milan, Feb. 7, 1853), *Le Due Regine* (Milan, May 17, 1856), *La Sorrentina* (Bologna, Nov. 14, 1857); also many songs and piano pieces.
BIBLIOGRAPHY: A. Belforti, *Emanuele Muzio, l'unico alievo di G. Verdi* (Milan, 1896); L. A. Garibaldi, ed., *Giuseppe Verdi nelle lettere di Emanuele Muzio ed Antonio Barezzi* (Milan, 1931).

Mycielski, Zygmunt, Polish composer and musicologist; b. Przeworsk, Aug. 17, 1907. He studied in Cracow, and later in Paris with Nadia Boulanger and Paul Dukas. In 1929–36 he was a member of the Society of Young Polish Composers in Paris. After the end of World War II, he became active as a journalist; edited the principal Polish music magazine *Ruch Muzyczny* (1945–48, 1960–68). His music, couched in a modern idiom, contains elements of Polish folk inflections; but dodecaphonic usages are also encountered.
WORKS: Piano Trio (1934); *Lamento di Tristano* for small orch., in memory of Szymanowski (1937); *5 Symphonic Essays* (1945); *Portrait of a Muse* for narrator, chorus and 15 instruments (1947); 6 symphonies: No. 1 (1947); No. 2 (1960); No. 3, *Sinfonia breve* (1967; Warsaw, Sept. 23, 1972); No. 4 (1972–73; Poznań, April 2, 1976); No. 5 (1977); *Polish Symphony* (1951); *Silesian Overture* (1948); *Brzezina* for soprano and string quartet (1952); *Zabawa w Lipinach* (*Merrymaking at Lipiny*), ballet in 1 scene (1953); Piano Concerto (1954); *Nowy lirnik mazowiecki* (*New Mazovian Bard*), 9 songs and finale for soprano, baritone, chorus and orch. (1955); *5 Préludes* for piano quintet (1967); songs; orchestration of 13 Bach chorale preludes (1964). He publ. 2 collections of musical essays: *Uzieczki z Pieciolinii* (*Flight of the Staff-lines*, Warsaw, 1956) and *Notatki o muzyce i muzykach* (*Notes on Music and Musicians*, Cracow, 1961).

Myer, Edmund J., American teacher of singing; b. York Springs, Pa., Jan. 21, 1846; d. Los Angeles, Jan. 25, 1934. He studied in Philadelphia and N.Y.; founded the National Summer School of Music at Lake Chautauqua and Round Lake, N.Y.; publ. a number of books and pamphlets on the voice: *Truths of Impor-*tance to Vocalists (1883); *The Voice From a Practical Standpoint* (1886); *Voice Training Exercises* (1888); *Vocal Reinforcement* (1891); *Position and Action in Singing* (1897); *The Renaissance of the Vocal Art* (1902); *The Vocal Instructor* (1913); *A Revelation to the Vocal World* (1917).

Myers, Rollo, English writer on music; b. Chislehurst, Kent, Jan. 23, 1892. He studied briefly at the Royal College of Music in London; then was music correspondent for English papers in Paris (1919–34); member of the staff of the BBC in London (1935–44); active as music journalist and editor; publ. the books: *Modern Music: Its Aims and Tendencies* (London, 1923); *Music in the Modern World* (London, 1939); *Erik Satie* (London, 1948); *Debussy* (London, 1949); *Introduction to the Music of Stravinsky* (London, 1950); *Emmanuel Chabrier and His Circle* (London, 1969); *Modern French Music* (Oxford, 1971). He edited an anthology, *Twentieth Century Music* (London, 1960); numerous articles on music.

Mysliveczek, Joseph, Bohemian composer; called "Il Boemo" or "Venatorini" in Italy; b. Ober-Sárka, near Prague, March 9, 1737; d. Rome, Feb. 4, 1781. He studied with Habermann and Seeger in Prague; in 1763, went to Venice in order to perfect himself as a composer. After traveling through Italy, he wrote the opera *Bellerofonte* for Naples, and it was produced there with extraordinary success, on Jan. 20, 1767. This was followed by a mock-exotic opera *Montezuma* (Florence, Jan. 1771) and *Ezio* (Naples, 1775). In 1777 he went to Munich, where he wrote the oratorio *Abramo ed Isacco;* there he fell desperately ill, but survived, and went back to Italy; presented a new opera in Naples, *Olimpiade,* on Nov. 4, 1778; his last opera was *Armida* (Lucca, Aug. 15, 1778); there were at least 25 operas by him in addition to the above; he also wrote a set of 6 symphonies, named after the first six months of the year; concertos, clavier sonatas, etc. Mozart had genuine admiration for him.
BIBLIOGRAPHY: G. de Saint-Foix, "Un ami de Mozart," *Revue Musicale* (March 1928); Paul Nettl, *Mozart in Böhmen* (Prague, 1938); J. Čeleda, *Josef Mysliveček* (Prague, 1946; in Czech).

Mysz-Gmeiner, Lula, Hungarian contralto; b. Kronstadt, Transylvania, Aug. 16, 1876; d. Schwerin, Aug. 7, 1948. She studied violin in her native town, and singing in Berlin with Etelka Gerster and Lilli Lehmann; made her debut there in 1900; then traveled in Europe as concert singer; was greatly praised for her interpretations of German lieder. She married an Austrian officer, Ernst Mysz (1900).

N

Nabokov, Nicolas, distinguished Russian-American composer; b. near Lubcha, Novogrudok district, Minsk region, April 17, 1903; d. New York, April 6, 1978. He was a scion of a distinguished Russian family; his uncle was a liberal member of the short-lived Duma (Russian parliament); the famous writer Vladimir Nabokov was his first cousin. (The name is to be pronounced with stress on the 2nd syllable, Nabókov). Nabokov received his early education in St. Petersburg; after the Revolution he went to Yalta, Crimea, where he took composition lessons with Rebikov; then proceeded to Berlin, where he became a student of Busoni; finally moved to Paris, where he was introduced to Diaghilev, who commissioned him to write a work for the Ballet Russe; this was an auspicious beginning of Nabokov's career. In 1933 he went to the U.S.; taught at Wells College (1936–41) and at the Peabody Cons. of Music, Baltimore (1947–52). From 1952 to 1963 he was secretary-general of the Congress for Cultural Freedom; then served as artistic director of the Berlin Music Festivals (1963–68); lectured on esthetics at the N.Y. State Univ. at Buffalo (1970–71) and at N.Y. Univ. (1972–73). In his music he adopted a cosmopolitan style, with an astute infusion of fashionable bitonality; in works of Russian inspiration, he reverted to melorhythms of Russian folksongs.
WORKS: operas, *The Holy Devil,* on the subject of Rasputin (Louisville, April 18, 1958; revised and expanded, produced in Cologne under the title *Der Tod des Grigori Rasputin,* Nov. 27, 1959); *Love's Labour's Lost,* to a libretto of W. H. Auden after Shakespeare (Brussels, 1973); ballets: *Union Pacific* (Philadelphia, April 6, 1934); *Vie de Polichinelle* (1934); *The Wanderer* (1966); *Don Quichotte* (N.Y., 1966); ballet-cantata, *Ode, or Meditation at Night on the Majesty of God, as revealed by the Aurora Borealis* (Ballet Russe, Paris, June 6, 1928); Symph. No. 1, *Symphonie lyrique* (Paris, Feb. 16, 1930); Symph. No. 2, *Sinfonia biblica* (N.Y., Jan. 2, 1941); Symph. No. 3, *A Prayer* (N.Y., Jan. 4, 1968); incidental music to Milton's *Samson Agonistes* (Wells College, May 14, 1938); *The Return of Pushkin,* for voice and orch. (Boston, Jan. 2, 1948); *Vita Nuova,* for soprano, tenor and orch. (Boston, March 2, 1951); Cello Concerto, subtitled *Les Hommages* (Philadelphia, Nov. 6, 1953); *America was Promises,* cantata (N.Y., April 25, 1950); oratorio, *Job* (1933); *Collectionneur d'échos,* for soprano, bass and 9 percussion instruments (1933); *Symboli Chrestiani* for baritone and orch. (1953); *5 Poems by Anna Akhmatova* for voice and orch. (1964); *Studies in Solitude* (1961); String Quartet (1937); Sonata for bassoon and piano (1941); 2 piano sonatas (1926, 1940); Piano Concerto (1932); Flute Concerto (1948); piano pieces; songs.

Nachbaur, Franz, German tenor; b. Giessen, near Friedrichshafen, March 25, 1830; d. Munich, March 21, 1902. He studied in Stuttgart and was a pupil of Pischek there; sang as a chorister at Basel, then in opera at Mannheim, Hannover, Prague, Vienna, and other musical centers. In 1866 he joined the roster of the Munich Opera, and remained there until his retirement in 1890. He was the first to sing the part of Walther in *Die Meistersinger* (1868); sang Lohengrin in Rome (1878); appeared in London with a German opera company (1882).

Nachez, Tivadar (Theodor Naschitz), Hungarian violinist; b. Budapest, May 1, 1859; d. Lausanne, May 29, 1930. He studied in Berlin with Joachim, and in Paris with Léonard. He lived mostly in London; went to California during World War I; then returned to Europe and presented his farewell concert in London in 1926. He wrote a number of violin pieces derived from Hungarian folksongs.

Nadel, Arno, German composer and writer; b. Vilna, Lithuania, Oct. 3, 1878; d. Auschwitz in March 1943. He studied in Königsberg with Birnbaum and Schwalm; then at the Jewish Seminary in Berlin with Loewengard and L. Mendelssohn; in 1916 became choral conductor of the Jewish Community in Berlin. He compiled several anthologies of Jewish songs, among them *Jontefflieder,* in 10 vols. (1919); *Jüdische Volkslieder,* in 2 vols. (Leipzig, 1921; new ed., 1926). In 1943 he was taken to Auschwitz and put to death in the Nazi concentration camp there.

Nadermann, François Joseph, French harp virtuoso and composer; b. Paris, 1781; d. there, April 2, 1835. He was a pupil of Krumpholtz; from 1816 served at the Royal Chapel; in 1825 was appointed prof. at the Paris Cons. He joined his brother Henri in the management of the harp-making business founded by their father. He composed 2 harp concertos and various other pieces for the instrument.

Nagel, Wilibald, German musicologist; b. Mülheim-am-Ruhr, Jan. 12, 1863; d. Stuttgart, Oct. 17, 1929. He was a pupil of Ehrlich, Spitta, Bellermann, etc., in Berlin. He established himself as instructor at the Univ. of Zürich; lived 1893–96 in London, studying early English music; in 1898 he settled in Darmstadt as lecturer on musical science at the Technical Academy; conducted the Academy Singing Society; 1917, prof. at the Stuttgart Musikhochschule; 1917–21, editor of the *Neue Musikzeitung,* was also a concert pianist.
WORKS: *Geschichte der Musik in England* (2 vols., 1894, 1897; down to Purcell's death); *Annalen der englischen Hofmusik, 1509–1649* (1894); *Geschichte der Musik am Darmstädter Hof, 1570–1800* (1901); *Beethoven und seine Klaviersonaten* (2 vols., 1903, 1905; 2nd ed., 1923, 1924); *Studien zur Geschichte der Meistersänger* (1909); *Christoph Graupner als Sinfoniker* (1912); *Die Klaviersonaten von Brahms* (1915); *Wilhelm Mauke* (1919); *Johannes Brahms* (1923).

Nägeli, Johann (Hans) Georg, Swiss publisher, writer, and composer; b. Wetzikon, near Zürich, May 26, 1773; d. there, Dec. 26, 1836. He was a music publisher at Wetzikon (established 1792); founder and president of the Swiss Association for the Cultivation of Music; singing teacher at a primary school, applying the Pestalozzian system. As a song composer he is best known by *Freut euch des Lebens* (Life let us cher-ish). He wrote *Gesangsbildungslehre nach Pestaloz-zischen Grundsätzen* (with M. Pfeiffer; 1810; popular ed., 1811); *Christliches Gesangbuch* (1828); *Vorlesungen über Musik mit Berücksichtigung der Dilettanten* (1826); *Musikalisches Tabellwerk für Volksschulen zur Herausbildung für den Figuralgesang* (1828); a polemical pamphlet against Thibaut; *Der Streit zwischen der alten und der neuen Musik* (1826); etc. Nägeli publ. (from 1803) a periodical, *Répertoire des clavecinistes*, in which he brought out piano pieces by contemporary composers, including the first publication of Beethoven's sonatas, op. 31. With Beethoven he was on intimate terms, despite disagreements.

BIBLIOGRAPHY: Biographical sketches of Nägeli were written by Ott (1838), Bierer (1844), Keller (1848), and Schneebeli (1873); H. Kling, *Beethoven et ses relations avec Nägeli* (1912); R. Hunziker, *H. G. Nägeli* (Zürich, 1938); A. E. Cherbuliez, *Der unbekannte Nägeli* (Chur, 1938); I. I. Hassan, *Die Welt- und Kunstanschauung Hans Georg Nägelis* (Zürich, 1947). Willi Reich ed. a collection of Nägeli's articles under the title, *Von Bach zu Beethoven* (Basel, 1945).

Naginski, Charles, composer; b. Cairo, Egypt, May 29, 1909; d. by drowning, Lenox, Mass., Aug. 4, 1940. He was brought to America at an early age; studied piano with his father and other teachers; 1928–33, held a fellowship at the Juilliard Graduate School as pupil in composition of Rubin Goldmark.

WORKS: for orch.: *Suite* (1931), 2 symphs. (1935; 1937), *1936*, orchestral poem (1936), *Sinfonietta* (1937), *3 Movements*, for chamber orch. (1937), *The Minotaur*, ballet for orch. (1938), *Nocturne and Pantomime* (1938), *5 Pieces from a Children's Suite* (Boston, 1940), *Movement*, for strings; 2 string quartets (1933); songs.

Nancarrow, Conlon, American composer; b. Texarkana, Ark., Oct. 27, 1912. He studied trumpet and played in jazz orchestras; took courses at Cincinnati Cons.; then in Boston with Nicolas Slonimsky and Walter Piston. In 1937 he joined the Abraham Lincoln Brigade, during the Spanish Civil War; returned to the U.S. in 1939; in 1940 settled in Mexico City. In his music he is preoccupied mainly with problems of rhythm and sonority; in order to make possible faithful execution, he composes music by perforating player-piano rolls according to notes and rhythms; such pieces are not playable except on player pianos. A number of Nancarrow's *Studies for Player Piano*, which could be adequately notated, were publ. in *Soundings*, 4 (1977); this collection also contains a critical study with contributions by Gordon Mumma, Charles Amirkhanian, John Cage, Roger Reynolds and James Tenney.

Nanino (Nanini), Giovanni Bernardino, Italian composer, brother and pupil of **Giovanni Maria Nanino;** b. Vallerano, c.1550; d. Rome, 1623. From 1591 he was maestro di cappella at San Luigi de' Francesi; later at San Lorenzo in Damaso. Proske printed 4 Psalms *a* 4 in *Musica divina.* Nanino publ. 3 books of madrigals *a* 5 (1588–1612); 4 books of motets *a* 1–5, with organ (1608–18); Psalms *a* 4 and 8 (1620); and a *Venite exul-*

temus *a* 3, with organ (1620). Many other works are in manuscript.

Nanino (Nanini), Giovanni Maria, Italian composer; b. Tivoli, c.1545; d. Rome, March 11, 1607. He was a pupil of Palestrina; after completing his studies, he officiated in Vallerano as maestro di cappella; but on Palestrina's resignation as maestro at Santa Maria Maggiore, Rome, he was called there in 1571. Resigning in 1575, he founded the first public school of music opened in Rome by an Italian, in which his brother, **Giovanni Bernardino,** and Palestrina were active instructors. Nanino's compositions were performed at the Sistine Chapel; in 1577 he became a member of the papal choir, and, in 1604, maestro di cappella of the Sistine Chapel. His works are among the best of the Palestrina epoch; the 6-part motet *Hodie nobis coelorum rex* is still sung annually on Christmas morning in the Sistine Chapel. Haberl publ. a sketch of Nanino in the *Kirchenmusikalisches Jahrbuch* for 1891, with 5 hitherto unpubl. Lamentations *a* 4. Other printed works are motets *a* 3–5 in canon form with cantus firmus (1586); 4 books of madrigals *a* 5 (1578–86); canzonets *a* 3 (1587–99); psalms in Constantini's *Psalmi a 8 voci;* other motets and madrigals in collections of the time. 3 motets *a* 3, one *a* 4, and a Miserere are in Proske, *Musica divina*, 4 pieces in L. Torchi, *L'Arte musicale in Italia* (vol. 2); detached numbers in the collections of Rochlitz, Tucher, Lück. An admirable work in MS is the *Cento cinquanta sette contrappunti e canoni a 2–11 voci, sopra del canto fermo, intitolata la base di Costanzo Festa;* also a *Trattato di contrappunto.*

BIBLIOGRAPHY: G. Radiciotti, *Giovanni Maria Nanino, musicista tiburtino . . . Vita ed opere* (Pesaro, 1909); G. Reese, *Music in the Renaissance* (N.Y., 1954).

Napier, William, British music publisher; b. 1740; d. London, 1812. He was a violinist in the Chapel Royal; established a music-publishing business; Haydn arranged 2 books of Scottish songs for him, with accompaniment for piano, violin, and cello (1792).

BIBLIOGRAPHY: F. Kidson, *British Music-publishers* (1900).

Napoli, Gennaro, Italian composer; b. Naples, May 19, 1881; d. there, June 28, 1943. He was a pupil of d'Arienzo and de Nardis at the Royal Cons. in Naples; 1906, won the "Pensionato nazionale per la musica"; 1912, teacher of composition at the Liceo Musicale, Naples; 1915, at the Royal Cons.; 1926, assistant director; editor of *L'Arte pianistica.*

WORKS: the opera *Jacopo Ortis;* the dramatic scene *Armida abbandonata* (1906); *In montagna,* orchestral suite (1906); Symph. in D minor; *Il Sole risorto,* for soli, chorus, and orch. (1909); piano pieces, songs, etc. Author of *Bassi imitati e fugati* (1915).

Napoli, Jacopo, Italian composer; son of **Gennaro Napoli;** b. Naples, Aug. 26, 1911. He studied at the Cons. San Pietro a Maiella, Naples, with his father and S. Cesi; subsequently appointed to the faculty, and eventually became director. He specialized in opera, often with a Neapolitan background, which gave him the opportunity to use Neapolitan songs in his scores. In 1962 he was appointed Director of the Cons. of Milan. The list of his operas includes: *Il Malato immaginario* (Naples, 1939); *Miseria e nobilità* (Naples, 1945); *Un curioso accidente* (Bergamo, 1950); *Masaniello* (1951; won a prize of La Scala, Milan); *I Peccatori* (1954); *Il Tesoro* (Rome, 1958); *Il Rosario* (Brescia, 1962); *Il Povero diavolo* (Triest, 1963); *Il barone avaro* (Naples, 1970).

Napravnik, Eduard, celebrated Russian conductor of Czech origin; b. Býšt, near Hradec Králové, Bohemia, Aug. 24, 1839; d. St. Petersburg (Petrograd), Nov. 23, 1916. He studied music at home, and at Prague; also took lessons with J. B. Kittl. In 1861 he was engaged by the Russian nobleman Yussupov to lead his private orch. in St. Petersburg; in 1863 he became a répétiteur at the Imperial Opera; 2nd conductor in 1867, and chief conductor in 1869. He held this post for 47 years, until his death, and became greatly renowned as a thorough musician, possessing a fabulous sense of pitch and rhythm, and exceptional ability as a disciplinarian. His reputation and influence were very great in Russian operatic affairs; Dostoyevsky in one of his novels uses Napravnik's name as a synonym for a guiding spirit. Napravnik conducted the première of *Boris Godunov* and of many other Russian operas; his interpretations of the Russian repertory established a standard emulated by other Russian conductors; yet he was deficient in emotional inspiration; his performances of symphonic works were regarded as competent but not profound. He was himself a composer of several operas, in the Russian style, imitative of Tchaikovsky; one of them, *Dubrovsky* (St. Petersburg, Jan. 15, 1895), has become part of the active repertory in Russia. Other operas were: *Nizhegorotzy* (St. Petersburg, Jan. 8, 1869); *Harold* (St. Petersburg, Nov. 23, 1886); *Francesca da Rimini* (St. Petersburg, Dec. 9, 1902). He also wrote 4 symphonies, some chamber music, piano pieces, etc.
BIBLIOGRAPHY: P. Weymarn, *E. Napravnik* (St. Petersburg, 1881); N. Findeisen, *E. Napravnik* (St. Petersburg, 1898).

Narayana Menon, Yatakke Kurupath, Indian virtuoso on the vina; b. New Delhi, June 27, 1911. He specialized in comparative musicology; was for many years director of the All India Radio; made many European tours as performer and lecturer.

Nardini, Pietro, Italian violinist; b. Leghorn, April 12, 1722; d. Florence, May 7, 1793. He was a pupil of Tartini at Padua; from 1762–65, solo violinist in the court orch., Stuttgart; lived with Tartini until the latter's death in 1770; then maestro of the court music at Florence. Both Leopold Mozart and Schubart praised his playing. Among his works are 6 violin concertos; 6 sonatas for violin and bass; 6 violin solos; 6 violin duets; 6 string quartets; 6 flute trios. Sonatas are in Alard's *Les Maîtres classiques* and David's *Hohe Schule des Violinspiels;* others in Jensen's *Klassische Violinmusik;* also numerous new eds.
BIBLIOGRAPHY: A. Moser, *Geschichte des Violinspiels* (p. 269 ff.); C. Pfäfflin, *Pietro Nardini* (Stuttgart, 1935; with a thematic catalogue of works).

Nares, James, English composer and organist; b. Stanwell, Middlesex, 1715 (baptized April 19); d. London, Feb. 10, 1783. He was a chorister in the Chapel Royal under Gates; also studied with Pepusch. Deputy organist of St. George's Chapel, Windsor; organist of York Cathedral, 1734; in 1756 he succeeded Greene as organist and composer to the Chapel Royal; Mus. Doc., Cambridge, 1757; Master of the Children at the Chapel Royal, 1757–80. He publ. a dramatic ode, *The Royal Pastoral;* a collection of catches, canons, and glees (1772); methods for harpsichord, organ, and singing; etc. Detached pieces are in Arnold's *Cathedral Music,* Page's *Harmonia Sacra,* and Stevens' *Sacred Music.*
BIBLIOGRAPHY: *Dictionary of National Biography,* XL.

Narváez, Luis de, Spanish guitar virtuoso of the 16th century. He was a native of Granada; chamber musician to Philip II. He publ. *Los seys libros del Delphin de música de cifra para tañer vihuela* (Vallodolid, 1538; in tablature), containing the earliest examples of variation form publ. in Spain; reprinted in modern notation by. E Pujol in *Monumentos de la Música Española* (vol. 3, Barcelona, 1945); some selections in Morphy's *Les Luthistes espagnols du XVIe siècle* (Leipzig, 1902); one in A. T. Davison and W. Apel, *Historical Anthology of Music* (vol. 1, Cambridge, Mass., 1946).
BIBLIOGRAPHY: E. M. Torner, *Collección de Vihuelistas españoles del siglo XVI* (Madrid, 1924) and J. B. Trend, *Luis Milán and the Vihuelistas* (1925).

Nasidze, Sulkhan, Georgian composer; d. Tbilisi, March 17, 1927. He studied piano and composition at the Tbilisi Cons.; in 1963 joined its staff; in 1974 became artistic director of the State Philharmonic of Georgia in Tbilisi. His music is imbued with Georgian melorhythms, and is set in a fairly advanced idiom. He wrote the oratorio *Fatherland mine* (1967); cantata, *Spring, spring!* (1975); 5 symphonies (1958, 1964, 1970, 1972, 1975); *Rhapsody* on themes of old Tbilisi for orch. (1964); 2 piano concertos (1954, 1961); Cello Concerto (1974); Piano Trio (1958); 2 string quartets (1968, 1971); *Polyphonic Sonata* for piano; vocal cycles; choruses.

Nastasijević, Svetomir, Serbian composer; b. Gornje Milanovec, April 1, 1902. He studied engineering and architecture; at the same time he learned to play the violin; wrote music criticism and publ. 2 manuals on music theory. His works include the music drama, *Medjuluško Blago* (*The Treasure of the Medjuluzje;* Belgrade, March 4, 1937); *Durad Branković,* national opera from medieval Serbian history (Belgrade, June 12, 1940); several symphonic poems and choruses. In his operas, he adopts the Wagnerian system of leitmotives.
BIBLIOGRAPHY: V. Peričić, *Muzički Stvaraoci u Srbiji* (Belgrade, 1969; pp. 342–50).

Nat, Yves, French pianist; b. Béziers, Dec. 28, 1890; d. Paris, Aug. 31, 1956. He studied at the Paris Cons. with Diémer; appointed prof. of piano there in 1934. He gave numerous recitals in France, where his reputation was very high; made an American tour as accompanist in 1911 and in 1914 (with Luisa Tetrazzini).

Natanson, Tadeusz, Polish composer; b. Warsaw, Jan. 26, 1927. He studied composition with Wilkomirski, Perkowski and Poradowski at the State College of Music in Wroclaw (1952–56); in 1965 he joined its faculty.
WORKS: opera, *Tamango* (1972); a ballet-pantomime, *Quo Vadis* (1970); *Toccata* for orch. (1956); Piano Concerto (1956); *Rondo Concertante* for violin and orch. (1958); Double Concerto for 2 saxophones and orch. (1959); *3 Pictures* for 7 instruments and percussion (1960); *Satires* for chorus and instrumental ensemble (1960); 5 symphonies: No. 1, *Symphonie Concertante,* for piano and orch. (1961); No. 2 (1962); No. 3, *In Memory of John F. Kennedy* (1965); No. 4 (1969); No. 5 for baritone, chorus and orch. (1975); *Concerto breve* for trombone and orch. (1963); Concertino for Piano, Strings and Percussion (1966); *Vers Libre* for orch. (1966); *6 Pieces* for 6 performers (1967); Viola Concerto (1971); *Triptyque* for orch. (1976); *3 Pieces* for double bass and piano (1976). He published *Contemporary Composers' Techniques,* in 2 vols. (1970, 1972).

Nathan, Hans, German-American musicologist; b. Berlin, Aug. 5, 1910. He took a course in musicology at Berlin Univ. (Dr. phil., 1934); studied piano with Rudolph Schmidt and Claudio Arrau, theory with Grete von Zieritz, and conducting with Michael Taube; was active as a music critic in Berlin (1932–36). In 1936 he went to the U.S.; became an American citizen in 1944; in 1936–38 he did postgraduate study at Harvard Univ. After a year of teaching at Tufts Univ. he joined the faculty of Michigan State Univ. in East Lansing, in 1946; held a Guggenheim Fellowship in 1957. He wrote *Das Rezitativ der Frühopern Richard Wagners* for his dissertation at the Univ. of Berlin (1934); in the U.S. he devoted himself chiefly to subjects of American music; publ. the valuable books *Dan Emmett and the Rise of Early Negro Minstrelsy* (Norman, Oklahoma, 1962) and *William Billings: Data and Documents* (Detroit, 1975). He is the editor of the complete, critical edition of works by William Billings, in 4 vols. (vol. 1, 1976); contributed articles on folk music, history and modern biography to various publications; these include important accounts of Luigi Dallapiccola's works: "Luigi Dallapiccola: Fragments from Conversations," *Music Review* (Nov. 1966) and "Considérations sur la manière de travailler de Luigi Dallapiccola," *Schweizerische Musikzeitung* (Aug. 1975).

Nathan, Isaac, English composer; b. Canterbury, 1790 d. Sydney, Australia, Jan. 15, 1864. He studied under D. Corri.
WORKS: music to the comedy *Sweethearts and Wives* (1823, very popular); an opera, *The Alcaid* (1824); an operetta, *The Illustrious Stranger* (1827); *Hebrew Melodies* (Byron), with Braham (1822, 1861); songs; *Musurgia Vocalis, an essay on the History and Theory of Music, and on the Qualities, Capabilities, and Management of the Human Voice* (1823; 2nd ed.,

1836); *Memoirs of Madame Malibran de Bériot* (3rd ed., 1836).
BIBLIOGRAPHY: Catherine Mackerras, *The Hebrew Melodist; A Life of Isaac Nathan* (Sydney, 1963).

Nathan, Montagu. See **Montague-Nathan, Montagu.**

Natorp, Bernhard Christoph Ludwig, German vocal pedagogue; b. Werden-on-Ruhr, Nov. 12, 1774; d. Münster, Feb. 8, 1846. He studied theology and pedagogics at Halle Univ.; pastor at Essen, 1798; counsellor of the Consistory at Potsdam, 1808; general superintendent at Münster, 1819.
WRITINGS: *Anleitung zur Unterweisung im Singen für Lehrer in Volksschulen* (2 courses, 1813, 1820; often republ.); *Lehrbüchlein der Singekunst* (2 courses, 1816, 1820); *Über den Gesang in den Kirchen der Protestanten* (1817); *Über den Zweck, die Einrichtung und den Gebrauch des Melodienbuchs für den Gemeindegesang in den evangelischen Kirchen* (1822), followed by the *Melodienbuch* (1822); *Choralbuch für evangelische Kirchen* (1829; harmonized in 4 parts with preludes and interludes by Rinck; 4th ed., 1885); and *Über Rincks Präludien* (1834).
BIBLIOGRAPHY: H. Knab, *B. C. L. Natorp* (Kassel, 1933).

Natra, Sergiu, Rumanian-born Israeli composer; b. Bucharest, April 12, 1924. He studied composition with Leon Klepper at the Bucharest Cons. (1945–52); emigrated to Israel in 1961, where he became active mainly as a teacher.
WORKS: *Divertimento in a Classical Style* for string orch. (1943); *March and Chorale* for orch. (1944); String Quartet (1947); *Suite* for orch. (1948); Symph. No. 1 (1952); *4 Poems* for baritone and orch. (1958); *Music* for violin and harp (1959); Sinfonia for strings (1960); *Toccata* for orch. (1963); *Music* for solo harpsichord and 6 instruments (1964); Sonatina for solo harp (1965); *Music* for oboe and strings (1965); *Variations* for piano and orch. (1966); *Song of Deborah* for mezzo-soprano and chamber orch. (1967); *Commentary on Nehemia* for baritone, chorus and orch. (1967); 3 solo sonatinas: for trombone, for trumpet, and for oboe (all 1969); *Environment for an Exhibition,* sound collage on tape (1970); Piano Trio (1971).

Nau, Maria Dolores Benedicta Josefina, operatic soprano; b. New York (of Spanish parentage), March 18, 1818; d. Levallois, near Paris, Jan., 1891. She was a pupil of Cinti-Damoreau at the Paris Cons.; from 1836–42 sang minor parts at the Paris Opéra, then appeared in Brussels and London; from 1844 she sang again at the Opéra, in leading roles; 1849–50 in London; 1850 and 1854–56 in the U.S.; she returned to Paris in 1856 and retired from the stage.

Naudin, Emilio, tenor; b. (of French parentage) Parma, Oct. 23, 1823; d. Boulogne-sur-Mer, May 5, 1890. He was a pupil of Panizza in Milan; debut at Cremona, c.1845; appeared in Vienna, St. Petersburg, London, Madrid, and Paris (from 1862 at the Théâtre Italien). He created the role of Vasco da Gama in *L'Africaine* (in accordance with a stipulation in Meyerbeer's will); retired in 1879.

Naujalis, Juozas, Lithuanian composer; b. Raudondvaris, near Kaunas, April 9, 1869; d. Kaunas, Sept. 9, 1934. He studied at the Warsaw Musical Institute; served as organist in various Lithuanian towns; 1919, director of the Music School, later of the State Musical Institute. His compositions include Masses, a Lithuanian church hymn; also piano and organ works; etc. He edited a collection of contemporary organ masters (6 vols).

Naumann, Emil, German composer and writer, grandson of **Johann Gottlieb Naumann;** b. Berlin, Sept. 8, 1827; d. Dresden, June 23, 1888. He was a pupil of Schnyder von Wartensee at Frankfurt; of Mendelssohn, 1842; studied at the Leipzig Cons., 1843–44; then attended Bonn Univ. In 1848 his oratorio *Christus der Friedensbote* was produced at Dresden; also the opera *Judith*. In 1856 his treatise on *Die Einführung des Psalmengesanges in die evangelische Kirche* procured his appointment as music director in the court church, Berlin, for which he composed motets, psalms, etc., publishing *Psalmen auf alle Sonn- und Feiertage des evangelischen Kirchenjahres* (vols. VIII–X of Commer's *Musica sacra*). The Univ. of Berlin conferred on him the title of Dr. phil. for *Das Alter des Psalmengesangs;* his master work is *Die Tonkunst in ihren Beziehungen zu den Formen und Entwickelungsgesetzen alles Geisteslebens* (2 vols.; 1869, 1870). He went to Dresden in 1873, and lectured on musical history at the Cons. OTHER WRITINGS: *Deutsche Tondichter, von Sebastian Bach bis auf die Gegenwart* (1871; often republ.); *Italienische Tondichter, von Palestrina bis auf die Gegenwart* (1876; 2nd ed., 1883); *Illustrierte Musikgeschichte* (2 vols., 1883–85; English transl. by F. Praeger, 1886; new German ed., brought up to date, by E. Schmitz, 1908). *Musikdrama oder Oper?* (1876; *contra* Wagner); *Zukunftsmusik und die Musik der Zukunft* (1877); etc.

Naumann, Johann Gottlieb, German composer, b. Blasewitz, near Dresden, April 17, 1741; d. Dresden, Oct. 23, 1801. Intended for a school teacher, he was trained in the Dresden Kreuzschule, where he learned singing. In 1757 a Swedish musician named Weeström took him to Italy. He received lessons from Tartini in Padua, and in 1761 he went to Rome and Naples with the violinist Pitscher to study dramatic composition; studied counterpoint later with Padre Martini at Bologna; brought out his first opera, *Il Tesoro insidiato*, in 1763 at the San Samuele Theater, Venice; and returned to Dresden in 1763, receiving next year the appointment of court composer of sacred music, and of "chamber composer" in 1765. On a second Italian tour he brought out several operas; then, after refusing an offer from Frederick the Great, he was appointed Kapellmeister at Dresden (1776). In 1777 he was also invited to Stockholm to reorganize the orch., and brought out operas then and in 1780. In all he produced 24 operas; also a ballet, 11 oratorios, 21 Masses, cantatas and other sacred music (including the fine *Vater unser,* after Klopstock; an elegy, *Klopstocks Grab;* 18 symphonies; sonatas for piano,

violin, and harmonica; songs (complete ed. by Breitkopf & Härtel); etc. H. F. Mannstein publ. a catalogue of Naumann's compositions.

BIBLIOGRAPHY: A. G. Meissner, *Bruchstücke zur Biographie J. G. Naumanns* (2 vols.; Prague, 1803–04; 2nd ed., Vienna, 1814); *Des sächsischen Kapellmeisters Naumann's Leben* (Dresden, 1841); G. Schweizer, *Biographie von Johann Gottlieb Naumann* (3 vols.; Zürich, 1843–45); M. J. Nestler, *Der kursächsische Kapellmeister Naumann aus Blasewitz* (Dresden, 1901); R. Engländer, *Johann Gottlieb Naumann als Opernkomponist* (Leipzig, 1922).

Naumann, Karl Ernst, German organist and music editor, grandson of **Johann Gottlieb Naumann;** b. Freiberg, Saxony, Aug. 15, 1832; d. Jena, Dec. 15, 1910. He studied in Leipzig (1850) under Hauptmann, Richter, Wenzel, and Langer; took the degree of Dr. phil. at the Univ. in 1858 for his dissertation *Über die verschiedenen Bestimmungen der Tonverhältnisse und die Bedeutung des pythagoreischen oder reinen Quinten-Systemes für unsere heutige Musik;* studied for 2 years in Dresden under Johann Schneider (organ), soon afterward being called to Jena as music director and organist; prof. in 1877; retired in 1906. Composed chiefly chamber music; publ. many valuable revisions and arrangements of classical works, especially for the Bach-Gesellschaft.

Naumann, Siegfried, Swedish composer; b. Malmö, Nov. 27, 1919. He studied at the Musical College in Stockholm, and later at the Santa Cecilia Academy in Rome (with Pizzetti and Malipiero); also took courses at the Mozarteum in Salzburg. He wrote 3 symphonies and some other works in a traditionally acceptable infra-modern idiom, but at the age of 40 decided to adopt an austere structural style governed by serial procedures and diversified by aleatory passages. To mark this decisive avatar, he designated his first serial work, *Ruoli (Roles)* for 4 clarinets as op. 1 (1959). His subsequent compositions in this modern style are: 7 *Sonetti de Petrarca* for tenor, harp, vibraphone and 4 cellos (1959); *Phaedri: 4 Fabulae* for soli, chorus and 8 instruments (1961); *Improvviso sopra 28 strutture* for keyboard and percussion instruments (1961); *Transformations* for orch. (1962; Gävleborg, April 29, 1962); *Risposte I* for flute and percussion (1963); *Risposte II* for piano, Hammond organ, electric guitar, trombone and percussion (1963); *Il Cantico del Sole* for soli, chorus, 10 solo instruments and orch. (1963; performed at the Festival of the International Society for Contemporary Music in Stockholm, Sept. 14, 1966); *Cadenza* for 9 players (1964); *Missa in onore della Madonna de Loreto* for chorus, organ and percussion (1964); *Solitude* for harp and percussion (1966); *Spettacolo I* for soprano and orch. (1967); *Spettacolo II* for 3 soli, chorus and orch. (1969); *Estate* for chamber orch. (1968); *Massa vibrante* for percussion (1969); *Ljudposter (Soundposts)* for wind orch. (1970); *Due Cori su testi latini* for chorus, double bass, Hammond organ and percussion (1970); *Teatro strumentale* for chamber ensemble (1971); *Il cielo del ponte a Moriano,* a dialogue for tenor, chorus and chamber orch. (1972); *Bombarda* for organ and percussion (1973); *3 Canti da Cabaret* for soprano and percussion (1973).

Nauwach, Johann, German composer; b. Brandenburg, about 1595; d. about 1630. He was a chamber musician at the Electoral court of Saxony in Torgau; from 1612–18 he studied in Florence and Turin; he was one of the first German followers of Caccini. He publ. *Libro primo di arie passeggiate a una voce per cantar e sonar nel chitarrone* (Dresden, 1623), and *Erster Theil teutscher Villanellen mit 1, 2, und 3 Stimmen auf der Tiorba* (Dresden, 1627).
BIBLIOGRAPHY: A. Einstein, in *Sammelbände der Internationalen Musik-Gesellschaft* XII; H. Kretzschmar, *Geschichte des neuen deutschen Liedes*, I (1912).

Nava, Gaetano, Italian singing master; b. Milan, May 16, 1802; d. there, March 31, 1875. He was taught by his father (**Antonio Maria Nava,** 1775–1826), and Pollini; then at Milan Cons., 1817–24, by Orlandi, Ray, Piantanida, and Frederici. From 1837 prof. of solfeggio at the Cons. and of choral singing from 1848. Wrote a great number of excellent solfeggi and vocalises; also a *Metodo pratico di vocalizzazione*.

Navarro, Juan, Spanish composer; b. Marchena, c.1530; d. Palencia, Sept. 25, 1580. He was perhaps a pupil of Fernández de Castilleja in Seville; in 1554 applied unsuccessfully for the post of *maestro de capilla* at Málaga (F. Guerrero was the successful candidate); *maestro de capilla* at Ávila (1565–66); then at Salamanca (1566–74); and at Ciudad Rodrigo (1574–78); from 1578 at the Cathedral in Palencia. Navarro's *Psalmi, Hymni ac Magnificat totius anni . . . 4, 5 ac 6 v.* were publ. at Rome, 1591. A book, *Liber in quo 4 Passiones Christi Domini continentur . . . 8 Lamentationes: Oratioque Hieremiae Prophetae,* is by another Juan Navarro, a Franciscan monk born in Cádiz and serving in Mexico. Extant MSS: *Antifona a San Sebastian* (in Málaga), part of a Magnificat (in Seville), 8 pieces (in Toledo), *Recuerde el alma dormida*, madrigal *a 5* (in the Collección del Patriarca, Valencia); madrigals: 7 for 4 voices, 1 for 5 voices (Biblioteca Medinaceli and Biblioteca Nacional, Madrid). The madrigal *Ay de mí, sin ventura,* was printed by Pedrell in *Cancionero Musical Popular Español* III: Eslava printed 3 Magnificats and 2 psalms; several motets are in the *Antología Musical,* ed. by Elústiza and Castrillo Hernández (Barcelona, 1933; with biography).
BIBLIOGRAPHY: G. Chase, "Juan Navarro Hispalensis and Juan Navarro Gaditanus," *Musical Quarterly* (April 1945); Robert Stevenson, *Spanish Cathedral Music in the Golden Age* (Berkeley, Calif., 1961).

Navas, Juan, important Spanish composer of the 2nd half of the 17th century; wrote numerous secular works, including some interesting *Pasacalles* with guitar accompaniment; also some sacred music.
BIBLIOGRAPHY: F. Pedrell, *Teatro lírico español anterior al siglo XIX,* vols. III and IV (1897).

Navrátil, Karel, Czech composer; b. Prague, April 24, 1867; d. there, Dec. 23, 1936. He was a pupil of Ondříček (violin) and G. Adler (theory); lived in Prague.
WORKS: the lyric drama *Hermann;* opera, *Salammbô;* the symphonic poems *Der weisse Berg, Lipany, Jan Hus, Žižka,* and *Žalco;* Symph.; Violin Con-

certo; 2 piano concertos; Sonata for violin; Sonata for viola; men's choruses; songs.

Naylor, Bernard, English-born Canadian conductor and composer; b. Cambridge, Nov. 22, 1907. He studied composition with Vaughan Williams, Holst and Ireland at the Royal College of Music in London (1924–26); then served as conductor of the Oxford Univ. Opera Club (1927–31). In 1932 he went to Canada, and was engaged to conduct the Winnipeg Symph. Orch.; returned to England in 1936 and was organist and director of music at Queen's College, Oxford, until 1939; once more in Canada, he conducted the Little Symph. Orch. in Montreal (1942–47); returned again to England and taught at Oxford (1950–52) and Reading Univ. (1953–59). He moved permanently to Canada in 1959. As a composer, he specializes in sacred choral music.
WORKS: *Variations* for small orch. (1960); String Trio (1960); *The Living Fountain,* cycle of 4 songs for tenor and string orch. (1947); *Missa da Camera* for 4 vocal soloists, chorus and chamber orch. (1954–66); *The Resurrection According to Saint Matthew,* Easter cantata (1965); *The Nymph Complaining for the Death of Her Faun* for mezzo-soprano, flute, oboe, clarinet, bassoon and string quartet (1965); *Festal Te Deum* for chorus and orch. (1968); *Scenes and Prophecies* for soprano, chorus, brass and percussion (1968–69); several a cappella choruses, including *9 Motets* (1952), *Magnificat & Nunc Dimittis* (1964) and *Missa sine Credo* (1969); songs.

Naylor, Edward Woodall, English organist and composer, son of **John Naylor;** b. Scarborough, Feb. 9, 1867; d. Cambridge, May 7, 1934. He was a pupil of his father, and from 1888–92, of the Royal College of Music; Mus. Doc., Cambridge, 1897; organist at St. Mary's, Kilburn, 1896–8; from 1908, organist at Emanuel College, Cambridge.
WORKS: an opera, *The Angelus* (London, Jan. 27, 1909; won the Ricordi prize); men's choruses; sacred music; overture, *Tokugawa,* for orch. (Tokyo, 1919); chamber music; etc. Author of *Shakespeare and Music* (London, 1896), *An Elizabethan Virginal Book* (London, 1905), *The Poets and Music* (London, 1928).

Naylor, John, English composer; b. Stanningley, near Leeds, June 8, 1838; d. at sea, May 14, 1897. He was a choirboy at Leeds Parish Church; Mus. Doc., Cambridge, 1872; organist of various churches in England; 1883, organist and choirmaster of York Minster, and also (1892) conductor of the York Musical Society.
WORKS: 4 cantatas: *Jeremiah, The Brazen Serpent, Meribah,* and *Manna;* church services, anthems, hymns, part-songs, organ pieces, and a well-known book of chants.

Naylor, Ruth, Australian soprano; b. Adelaide, Aug. 3, 1908; d. London, Oct. 16, 1976. She studied voice in London, Berlin, Munich and Salzburg. Between 1932 and 1948 she sang regularly with several opera companies in London, eliciting favorable comments for the precision of her fioriture; she excelled particularly in lyric roles in Italian opera.

Nazareth, Ernesto, Brazilian pianist and composer of dance music and songs; b. Rio de Janeiro, March 20, 1863; d. there, Feb. 4, 1934. He was a pioneer in fostering a national Brazilian type of composition, writing pieces in European forms with Brazilian melorhythmic inflections, pointedly entitled *Fado brasileiro, Tango brasileiro, Valsa brasileira, Marcha brasileira,* etc.; he also composed original dances in the rhythms of samba and chôro. In his declining years he became totally deaf. A detailed list of his works is found in *Composers of the Americas,* Vol. X (Washington, 1964).

Neal, Heinrich, composer, son of the American painter David Neal; b. Munich, Sept. 8, 1870; d. Heidelberg, June 9, 1940. He was a pupil of Rheinberger in Munich and Draeseke in Dresden. In 1894 he was co-founder of a cons. in Heidelberg, where he taught until 1920; afterwards he taught privately. His works are mostly for piano: *24 Études* in all keys as an introduction to modern music, op. 75; other études (op. 80, 81); Studies for polyphonic playing, op. 90; several German rhapsodies; *Kinderouvertüre* for 2 pianos, 8 hands, op. 36; etc.

Neate, Charles, English musician; b. London, March 28, 1784; d. Brighton, March 30, 1877. He studied piano with John Field, cello with W. Sharp and composition with Wölff. He started his career as a concert pianist in London; in 1815 he went to Vienna where he succeeded in entering into a friendly relationship with Beethoven. Returning to London, he was one of the founders of the London Philharmonic Society, with which he appeared as performer and conductor. He composed 2 piano sonatas, a quintet for piano, woodwind, and double bass; 2 piano trios; publ. *An Essay on Fingering* (1855). Literature on Beethoven frequently mentions Neate's relationship with him.

Nebra, José de, Spanish composer; b. Catalayud, Zaragoza, Jan. 6, 1702; d. Madrid, July 11, 1768. He was organist at the Convent of the Descalzas Reales in Madrid; was appointed 2nd organist to the Royal Chapel in 1724, and music director there in 1751. Together with Literes he was engaged to reconstruct and compose new music when the archives of the Royal Chapel were destroyed in the fire of 1734. He was a prolific composer; wrote about 20 operas, a great deal of sacred music. His Requiem for Queen Barbara (1758) is reproduced in Eslava's *Lira Sacro-Hispana.*
BIBLIOGRAPHY: M. Soriano-Fuertes, *Historia de la música española,* IV (Madrid, 1859); E. Cotarelo y Mori, *Historia de la Zarzuela,* chap. III (Madrid, 1934).

Nechayev, Vasily, Russian pianist and composer; b. Moscow, Sept. 28, 1895; d. there, June 5, 1956. He studied at the Moscow Cons. with Goldenweiser (piano), graduating in 1917; then took composition lessons with Vasilenko. In 1925 he joined the staff of the Moscow Cons. He made a systematic study of the folksongs of the Ural region and made arrangements of folksongs of other lands. He composed the operas *7 Princesses,* after Maeterlinck (1923), and *Ivan Bolot-*

nikov (1930); a septet, a quartet, violin sonata, cello sonata, songs and a number of piano pieces.

Nedbal, Karel, Czech conductor; nephew of **Oskar Nedbal;** b. Dvur Králové, near Prague, Oct. 28, 1888; d. Prague, March 20, 1964. He studied with Novák in Prague and Foerster in Vienna; conductor at the theater of Moravska-Ostrava, then of the Vinohrady Choral Society in Prague, and in 1914 of the Vinohrady Theater (with Ostrčil); 1921–28, opera director at Olomouc; 1928–38, at Bratislava; 1938–40, at Brno; from 1940 in Prague as radio and opera conductor.

Nedbal, Oskar, Czech composer and conductor; b. Tábor, Bohemia, March 26, 1874; d. (suicide) Zagreb, Dec. 24, 1930. He was a pupil of Bennewitz (violin), Knittl and Stecker (theory), and Dvořák (composition) at the Prague Cons., where he graduated in 1892. From 1891 to 1906 he played viola in the famous Bohemian String Quartet (Karl Hoffmann, Josef Suk, Nedbal, Hans Wihan); 1896–1906 also conducted concerts of Bohemian music in Prague and Vienna; 1906–19, conductor of the Tonkünstler-Orch. in Vienna; also of the Volksoper there for a time; from 1919, guest conductor in Czechoslovakia, Austria, and Yugoslavia.
WORKS: the ballets *Der faule Hans* (1902), *Grossmütterchens Märchenschätze* (1908), *Prinzessin Hyazintha* (1911), *Des Teufels Grossmutter* (1912), *Andersen* (1914); the operettas *Die keusche Barbara* (Prague, 1910), *Polenblut* (Vienna, Oct. 25, 1913; successfully revived, Oct. 10, 1954); *Die Winzerbraut* (Vienna, Feb. 11, 1916), *Die schöne Saskia* (Vienna, Nov. 16, 1917), and *Eriwan* (Vienna, Nov. 29, 1918); an opera, *Sedlák Jakub* (*Farmer James*; Brno, Oct. 13, 1922); also instrumental works.
BIBLIOGRAPHY: J. Květ, *In memoriam Oskar Nedbal* (Bratislava, 1931).

Neefe, Christian Gottlob, German composer and conductor; b. Chemnitz, Feb. 5, 1748; d. Dessau, Jan. 26, 1798. While a law student in Leipzig, he had music lessons with A. Hiller; was conductor at Leipzig and Dresden, then of Seyler's traveling opera troupe, and (1779) of the Grossmann-Hellmuth company at Bonn, where he was appointed deputy organist and succeeded van den Eeden as Electoral music director in 1782, also as Beethoven's teacher. In 1796 he became conductor of the Dessau opera.
WORKS: 8 vaudevilles and operas for Leipzig and Bonn; Klopstock's ode *Dem Unendlichen,* for 4 voices and orch.; Double Concerto for violin, piano, and orch.; sonatas, variations, and fantasias for piano; songs; etc.
BIBLIOGRAPHY: Irmgard Leux, *Christian Gottlob Neefe* (Leipzig, 1925); A. Einstein republ. Neefe's autobiography (originally publ. in *Allgemeine musikalische Zeitung* I).

Neel, Boyd, English conductor; b. Blackheath, Kent, July 19, 1905. He studied medicine and served as an intern at a London hospital before taking up music. In 1933 he organized the Boyd Neel String Orch., with a membership of music students, and succeeded in building it up to a fine ensemble. In 1953 he became

dean of the Royal Cons. of Music in Toronto, Canada. He publ. a book, *The Story of an Orchestra* (London, 1950), in which he recounts his musical adventures.
BIBLIOGRAPHY: Donald Brook, *International Gallery of Conductors* (London, 1951; pp. 125-28).

Nef, Albert, Swiss conductor and composer; brother of **Karl Nef**; b. St. Gall, Oct. 30, 1882; d. Bern, Dec. 6, 1966. He studied at the Leipzig Cons. and with Kretzschmar in Berlin (Dr. phil., 1906); from 1907, opera conductor in Lübeck, Neustrelitz, and Rostock; since 1912 in Bern, also conductor of the Orchestral Society since 1922; from 1920, president of the Swiss Stage Artists Alliance. Author of *Das Lied in der deutschen Schweiz im letzten Drittel des 18. und am Anfang des 19. Jahrhunderts* (1909); also *50 Jahre Berner Theater* (Bern, 1956). He composed a singspiel, *Graf Strapinski* (Bern, 1928); *Appenzeller Tänze* for orch. (1926); *Wanderschaft*, song cycle for tenor, mixed chorus, and orch. (Bern, 1924); choruses; piano pieces; songs.

Nef, Karl, Swiss musicologist; b. St. Gall, Aug. 22, 1873; d. Basel, Feb. 9, 1935. He entered the Leipzig Cons. in 1891, studying with Reckendorf (piano), Julius Klengel (cello), and Jadassohn (theory); attended the lectures on musicology by Kretzschmar at the Univ., and in 1896 became Dr. phil. with his dissertation *Die Collegia musica in der deutschen reformierten Schweiz* (publ. St. Gall, 1897). He settled in Basel in 1897; 1898-1909, editor of *Schweizerische Musikzeitung;* 1900, Privatdozent for musicology at the Univ.; 1909, associate prof.; 1923, prof.
WRITINGS: *Ferdinand Fürchtegott Huber* (1898); "Zur Geschichte der deutschen Instrumentalmusik in der zweiten Hälfte des 17. Jahrhunderts," *Beihefte der Internationalen Musik-Gesellschaft* 5 (1902); *Die Musik im Kanton St. Gallen, 1803-1903* (1903); *Katalog der Musikinstrumente im historischen Museum zu Basel* (1906); *Schriften über Musik und Volksgesang* (1908), bibliography of books and essays by Swiss writers); *Einführung in die Musikgeschichte* (1920; 3rd ed., 1945; in French 1925, 2nd ed., 1931; in English as *Outline of the History of Music*, N.Y., 1935); *Geschichte der Sinfonie und Suite* (1921); *Geschichte unserer Musikinstrumente* (1926; new ed., 1949); *Die 9 Sinfonien Beethovens* (1928); *Aufsätze* (posthumous; Basel, 1936). A dedicatory vol., *Karl Nef zum 60. Geburtstag*, was publ. at Basel in 1933.

Neff, Fritz, German composer, b. Durlach, Baden, Nov. 20, 1873; d. Munich, Oct. 3, 1904. He was a pupil of Thuille and Mottl in Karlsruhe; a composer of great promise unfulfilled. Publ. choral works: *Ein schön teutsch Reiterlied, Chor der Toten, Schmied Schmerz, Die Weihe der Nacht;* songs (*Die Polenschänke*, etc.).

Negrea, Marţian, Rumanian composer; b. Vorumloc, Transylvania, Feb. 10, 1893; d. Bucharest, July 13, 1973. He studied with Timotei Popovici at the Andréien Seminary in Sibiu (1910-14); then took courses with Franz Schmidt and Mandyczewski in Vienna (1918-21). Returning to Rumania, he became prof. of composition at the Cons. in Cluj (1921-41) and harmony at the Cons. in Bucharest (1941-63). His music is marked by a romantic quality; almost all of his compositions are programmatic in intent and folkloric in content. Thematically, he applies elements of Transylvanian melorhythms.
WORKS: a 2-act opera, *Marin Pescarul* (1933; Cluj, Oct. 3, 1934); *Fantezie simfonică* (1921); *2 Rapsodia română* for orch. (1938, 1950); *Poveşti din Grui (Fairytale from Grui)*, symph. poem (1940); *Divertissement* for orch. (1951); *Prin Munţii Apuseni (Through the Western Mountains)*, suite for orch. from music to the film (1952); *Recrutul (The Recruit)*, symph. suite (1953); *Simfonia primăverii (Spring Symphony,* 1956); *Sărbătoarea muncii (Celebration of Work)*, symph. poem (1958); Concerto for Orch. (1963); *Requiem* for soloists, chorus and orch. (1957); *Oratoriul patriei* for narrator, soloists, chorus and orch. (1959); *Prelude and Fugue* for string quartet (1920); *4 Pieces* for harp (1945); string quartet (1949); *4 Rumanian Sketches* for clarinet and piano (1958); *Suite* for clarinet and piano (1960); Piano Sonata (1921); Piano Sonatina (1922); choruses; songs.

Negri, Gino, Italian composer; b. Milan, May 25, 1919. He studied at the Milan Cons. with Renzo Bossi, graduating in 1942. In 1959 he was appointed artistic director of the Teatro del Popplo in Milan. He wrote a number of light operas, all to his own libretti, among them *Vieni qui, Carla* (Milan, Feb. 28, 1956); *Massimo* (Milan, April 12, 1958); *Il tè delle tre* (Como, Sept. 12, 1958); *Il Circo Max* (Venice, Sept. 23, 1959); *Publicità, ninfa gentile* (Milan, 1970).

Neidhardt (Neidhart, Nithart) von Reuenthal, a German Minnesänger; b. c.1180; d. c.1240. He was in all probability the earliest German musician whose songs are extant. These are found in manuscript collections of the late 14th century; a complete list of sources is given in Hagen's *Minnesinger* (vol. 4; 1838). An edition of Neidhardt's songs, with facsimile reproductions and transcriptions in modern notation, was brought out by Wolfgang Schmieder in the *Denkmäler der Tonkunst in Österreich* 71 (37.i). Another collection, *Neidhardt-Lieder*, ed. by F. Gennrich, was publ. as no. 9 in the series *Summa musica medii aevi* (Darmstadt, 1962).
BIBLIOGRAPHY: L. Erk and F. M. Böhme, *Deutscher Liederhort* (Leipzig, 1894); H. Rietsch, *Die deutsche Liedweise* (1904); D. Boueke, *Materialien zur Neidhart-Überlieferung* (Munich, 1967); K. H. Kohrs, "Zum Verhältnis von Sprache und Musik in den Liedern Neidharts von Reuental," *Deutsche Vierteljahrsschrift für Literaturwissenschaft und Geistesgeschichte* XLIII/4 (1969).

Neidlinger, William Harold, American choral conductor and music pedagogue; b. Brooklyn, July 20, 1863; d. East Orange, N.J., Dec. 5, 1924. He studied with Dudley Buck in New York and with Dannreuther in London; was active as a choral leader and a singing teacher. He published *Small Songs for Small Singers* (1896), which became a standard work for kindergartens; he himself composed attractive, if not musically distinguished, children's songs, among them *Earth, Sky and Air in Song, Little Folks' Song Book*, etc.

Neitzel, Otto, German composer and writer; b. Falkenburg, Pomerania, July 6, 1852; d. Cologne, March 10, 1920. He was a pupil at Kullak's Academy, Berlin; studied also at the Univ. (Dr. phil., 1875); then made a concert tour, as pianist, with Pauline Lucca and Sarasate; in 1878 became conductor of the Musikverein at Strasbourg, where (1879-81) he likewise conducted in the City Theater. Until 1885 he taught at the Moscow Cons.; then at the Cologne Cons.; from 1887, also critic for the *Kölnische Zeitung;* visited the U.S. in 1906-07 as lecturer, pianist, and conductor; 1919, member of the Academy of Arts, Berlin.

WORKS: the operas *Die Barbarina* (Wiesbaden, Nov. 15, 1905) and *Der Richter von Kaschau* (Darmstadt, March 31, 1916); Piano Concerto (1900), etc. He wrote *Führer durch die Oper des Theaters der Gegenwart* (3 vols., 1890-93; 4th ed., 1908); *Beethovens Symfonien nach ihrem Stimmungsgehalt erläutert* (1891; 6th ed., 1924); *Saint-Saëns* (1899); *Aus meiner Musikantenmappe* (1914).

BIBLIOGRAPHY: A. Dette, *Die Barbarina* (Fulda, 1913; guide to Neitzel's opera; contains biographical sketch).

Nejedlý, Vít, Czech composer, son of **Zdeněk Nejedlý;** b. Prague, June 22, 1912; d. Dukla, Slovakia, Jan. 1, 1945. He studied composition with Jeremiáš and conducting with Talich at the Charles Univ. in Prague, obtaining his Ph.D. in 1936; after the occupation of Czechoslovakia by the Nazis in 1939 he went to the Soviet Union where he was an editor of Czech programs for Radio Moscow foreign broadcasts; in 1943 joined the Czechoslovak contingent of the Red Army, and moved with it to the borders of Czechoslovakia, when he died of typhoid fever.

WORKS: an opera, *Tkalci (The Weavers),* after Hauptmann (1938; completed by Jan Hanuš; Pilsen, May 7, 1961); a melodrama, *The Dying* (1933); 3 symphonies: No. 1 (1931); No. 2, *Bídy a smrti (Poverty and Death,* 1934); No. 3, *Španělská (Spanish,* 1937-38; dedicated to the Spanish Loyalist Army fighting Franco); *Overture to Verhaeren's Dawn* (1932); *Commemoration* for orch. (1933); Sinfonietta (1937); *Dramatic Overture* (1940); *Lidová Suita (Popular Suite)* for orch. (1940); 2 cantatas, *Den (The Day,* 1935) and *To You—the Red Army* (1943); *2 Compositions* for wind quintet (1934); *2 Compositions* for nonet (1934); *Small Suite* for violin and piano (1935); String Quartet (1937); Concertino for nonet (1940); *Fantasy* for piano (1937); many songs, military marches and choruses.

BIBLIOGRAPHY: J. Jiránek, *Vít Nejedlý* (Prague, 1959).

Nejedlý, Zdeněk, Czech music scholar, historian and socialist politician; b. Litomysl, Feb. 10, 1878; d. Prague, March 9, 1962. He studied music with Zdenko Fibich in Prague and musicology with Hostinský at Charles Univ. in Prague. From 1899 to 1909 he was employed as an archivist of the National Museum in Prague; from 1909 to 1939 he was prof. at Charles Univ. where he organized the dept. in musicology. Intensely involved in political activities, he joined the Communist Party of Czechoslovakia in 1929. After the Nazi invasion of 1939 he went to Russia, where he was prof. of the history dept. at Moscow Univ. In 1945

he returned to Czechoslovakia; served as Minister of Education (1948-53) and deputy premier (1953). He publ. a number of books on the history of Czech music; of these the most original is a history of Bohemian music, in the form of catechism, in 3 vols. (Prague, 1904, 1907, 1913); he further publ. several monographs on Czech composers and their works, among them *Smetana's Operas* (1909), *The Modern Bohemian Opera since Smetana* (1911), *Vítězslav Novák* (1921), and also biographies of Mahler (1912) and Wagner (1917).

BIBLIOGRAPHY: J. Teichmann, *Zdeněk Nejedlý* (Prague, 1938); V. Pekárek, *Zdeněk Nejedlý* (Prague, 1948); J. Jiránek, *Zdeněk Nejedlý* (Prague, 1952); F. Cervinka, *Zdeněk Nejedlý* (Prague, 1959).

Nelhybel, Vaclav, Czech-American composer; b. Polanka, Sept. 24, 1919. He studied composition and conducting with Rídký at the Prague Cons. (1938-42) and musicology at the Univ. of Prague (also 1938-42); in 1942 went to Switzerland and took courses in medieval and Renaissance music at the Univ. of Fribourg; was affiliated with the Swiss National Radio (1947-50); then became musical director of Radio Free Europe in Munich (1950-57). In 1957 he settled in the U.S., and became a citizen in 1962; subsequently evolved energetic activities as a lecturer and guest conductor at American colleges and high schools. As a composer, he is especially notable for his fine pieces for the symphonic band. His harmonic idiom is of a freely dissonant texture, with melorhythmic components gravitating toward tonal centers.

WORKS: In 1976 he accomplished the setting for organ, brass and timpani of 52 hymns and 6 church pieces, published in a collection entitled *Festival Hymns and Processionals.* His other works include 2 operas: *A Legend* (1953-54) and *Everyman,* a medieval morality play (Memphis, Oct. 30, 1974) and 3 ballets: *morality de Feux* (1942), *In the Shadow of a Lime Tree* (1946) and *The Cock and the Hangman* (Prague, Jan. 17, 1947). FOR ORCH.: Symph. No. 1 (1942); *Ballade* (1946); *Étude symphonique* (1949); Concertino for Piano and Chamber Orch. (1949); *Sinfonietta Concertante* (1960); Viola Concerto (1962); *Houston Concerto* (1967); *Concertino da Camera* for cello, 15 winds and piano (1971); *Polyphonies* (1972); *Toccata* for solo harpsichord, 13 winds and percussion (1972); *Cantus and Ludus* for piano, 17 winds and percussion (1973); *Polyphonic Variations* for strings and trumpet (1975); *Slavonic Triptych* (1976). FOR SYMPH. BAND: *Caucasian Passacaglia* (1963); *Concerto Antiphonale* for 14 brasses (1964); *Symphonic Requiem,* with baritone in the last of its 4 movements (1965); *Estampie,* with antiphonal brass sextet (1965); *Yamaha Concerto* (1971); *Introit,* with solo chimes (1972); *Dialogues,* with piano solo (1976). FOR VOICE: *Caroli Antiqui Varii,* 7 a cappella choruses for 7 voices (1962); *Epitaph for a Soldier* for soloists and a cappella chorus (1964); *Peter Piper* for chorus, and clarinet choir or piano (1965); *Cantata Pacis* for 6 soloists, chorus, winds, percussion and organ (1965); *Dies Ultima* for 3 soloists, mixed chorus, speaking chorus, orch. and jazz band (1967); *Sine Nomine* for 4 soloists, chorus, orch. and tape (1968); *America Sings* for solo baritone, chorus and band

(1974); *Estampie Natalis* for double chorus, piccolo, viola, cello and percussion (1976). CHAMBER MUSIC: *3 Organa* for 4 bassoons (1948); 2 string quartets (1949, 1962); 2 wind quintets (1948, 1958, 1960); Quartet for 4 horns (1957); Quartet for piano and 3 brass instruments (1959); *4 Miniatures* for string trio (1959); *Numismata* for brass septet (1961); Brass Trio (1961); 2 brass quintets (1961, 1965); *Impromptus* for wind sextet (1963); 9 clarinet trios (1963); *Scherzo Concertante* for horn and piano (1963); *3 Pieces* for saxophone quartet (1965); *Quintetto Concertante* for violin, trombone, trumpet, xylophone and piano (1965); Concerto for Percussion (1972); *Concerto Spirituoso No. 1* for 12 flutes, electric harpsichord and solo voice (1974), *No. 2* for 12 saxophones, electric harpsichord and solo voice (1974), *No. 3* for electric violin, English horn, horn, tuba, vibraphone, winds, percussion and solo voice (1975), *No. 4* for voice, string quartet and chamber orch. (1977); *Oratio No. 1* for piccolo, solo trumpet, chimes, and string quartet or string orch. (1974) and *No. 2* for solo oboe and string trio (1976); *Music* for 6 trumpets (1975); *Ludus* for 3 tubas (1975); bassoon quartet (1976); *Variations* for solo harp (1977). FOR PIANO: *103 Short Pieces* (1965). FOR ORGAN: *3 Danses Liturgiques* (1964); *26 Short Preludes* (1972); *Preambulum*, with timpani (1977).

Nelle, Wilhelm, German authority on church music; b. Schwöbber, near Hameln, May 9, 1849; d. Münster, Oct. 15, 1918. He studied theology in Halle and Tübingen, where he also studied music with Robert Franz and Otto Scherzer. From 1872 he was active as a priest in various German cities. In 1895 he founded the Evangelischer Kirchengesang-Verein für Westfalen. He was prominent in the reform and organization of Evangelical church music in Germany.
WRITINGS: *Das Evangelische Gesangbuch von 1835* (1883); *Liederbüchlein, 25 geistliche und weltliche Lieder* (1891); *Choralbuch zum Rheinisch-Westfälischen Evangelischen Gesangbuch* (with Hollenberg, 1892; 3rd ed., 1908); *Die Festmelodien des Kirchenjahres charakterisiert* (1895; 2nd ed., 1904, as *Aus dem Evangelischen Melodienschatz*, I); *Geschichte des deutschen evangelischen Kirchenliedes* (1904; 3rd ed., 1928); *Chorbuch* (with J. Plath, 1917).

Nelson, John, American conductor; b. San José, Costa Rica (of American missionary parents), Dec. 6, 1941. He received his primary musical training with local teachers in Costa Rica; then went to New York where he studied conducting with Jean Morel at the Juilliard School of Music (1963–67). He began making professional appearances while still a student; conducted the Pro Arte Chorale in N.Y., eliciting high praise for his performance of *Les Troyens* of Berlioz. He subsequently made guest appearances with major American and European orchestras; also led the Jerusalem Symph. Orch. He revisited Costa Rica to conduct the National Symph. Orch. in San José. In 1977 he was appointed conductor and music director of the Indianapolis Symph. Orch.

Nelson, Oliver E., black American composer and arranger; b. St. Louis, June 4, 1932; d. Los Angeles, Oct. 27, 1975. He studied piano, saxophone, taxidermy, dermatology and embalming; interrupting his courses in mortuary science, he took private lessons in composition with Elliott Carter in New York and George Tremblay in Los Angeles; in the 1950s and 1960s he played saxophone in several jazz orchestras, among them those led by Wild Bill Davis, Louis Bellson, Duke Ellington, and Count Basie; then devoted himself chiefly to composing, conducting and arranging.
WORKS: *Blues and the Abstract Truth* (1960); *Afro-American Sketches* (1961); *Divertimento* for 10 woodwind instruments (1962); *Soundpiece for Jazz Orchestra* (1964); *Patterns* for orch. (1965); *A Study in 5/4* for wind ensemble (1966); Concerto for Xylophone, Marimba and Vibes (1967); *The Kennedy Dream Suite* for jazz combo (1967); *Jazzhattan Suite* for jazz combo (1967). In 1967 he moved to Hollywood, where he specialized in writing music for films and television (*It Takes a Thief, Ironside,* etc.).

Nelson, Robert U., American musicologist; b. Brush, Colorado, Sept. 16, 1902. He studied at the Univ. of Calif., Berkeley (A.B., 1923); later worked with Gaston Déthier and Percy Goetschius at the Institute of Musical Art, N.Y. (diplomas in piano and organ, 1925), and with Walter Piston and Willi Apel at Harvard Univ. (M.A., 1937; Ph.D., 1944). He also studied composition with Gustav Holst and Eugene Zador. From 1925 to 1937 he was member of faculty at Washington State Univ.; in 1938 became instructor at the Univ. of Calif., Los Angeles; prof. since 1955. He publ. a valuable study, *The Technique of Variation* (Berkeley, California, 1948); contributed numerous articles to music magazines.

Nelson, Ron, American composer; b. Joliet, Illinois, Dec. 14, 1929. He studied composition with Howard Hanson, Bernard Rogers, Louis Mennini and Wayne Barlow at the Eastman School of Music, Rochester, N.Y. (1947–56); in the interim went to Paris where he took courses with Tony Aubin at the École Normale de Musique (1954–55). In 1963 he joined the music staff at Brown Univ. at Providence, Rhode Island.
WORKS: the opera *The Birthday of the Infanta* (Rochester, N.Y., May 14, 1956); *Savannah River Holiday* for orch. (1957); *The Christmas Story*, cantata (1959); *This is the Orchestra* for orch. (1963); oratorio, *What is Man?* (1964); orchestral *Trilogy JFK-MLK-RKF* commemorating John F. Kennedy, Martin Luther King and Robert Kennedy (1969); also liturgical music; solo songs; piano pieces.

Nelsova, Zara, brilliant Canadian cello player; b. Winnipeg, Dec. 24, 1924, of Russian extraction. She studied first with Herbert Walenn in London, and at the age of 13 was soloist with the London Symph. Orch.; gave a series of concerts with her two older sisters, a pianist and a violinist, in England, Australia and South Africa, billed as the "Canadian Trio." In 1942 she went to the U.S. and took lessons with Feuermann in N.Y.; in 1946 received additional instruction with Casals in Prades. In 1953 she toured in South America, in 1954 gave concerts in Israel, and in 1966 played in Russia. In 1962 she joined the faculty of the Juilliard School of Music in N.Y. She received rapturous reviews from European and American music critics for her poetic interpretations of classical and modern cello music.

Němeček, Franz Xaver. See **Niemtschek, Franz Xaver.**

Nemescu, Octavian, avant-garde Rumanian composer; b. Pascani, March 29, 1940. He studied with Jora, Alfred Mendelsohn, Vieru, Ciortea, Vancea and with Paul Constantinescu at the Bucharest Cons. (1956–63); attended the summer courses of new music held in Darmstadt (1972); taught asymptotic approximations from infinitude to infinitesimality.
WORKS: Clarinet Sonata (1961–62); *Poliritmii* for clarinet, piano and prepared piano (1962–63); *Triunghi (Triangle)* for orch. (1964; Bucharest, Dec. 3, 1967); *4 Patru dimensiuni în timp (4 Dimensions in Time): I* for orch. (1965), *II* for chorus and orch. (1966), *III* for orch. (1967) and *IV* for orch. (1968); *Combinaţii în cercuri (Combinations of Circles)* for cello, tape and multi-media action (1965); *Plurisens,* cycle for variable group and multimedia action (1965–68); *Memorial I–V* for various combinations of instruments, tape and multimedia action (1968–70); *Concentric* and *Efemeride,* both for variable ensemble, tape and multimedia action (1968–69); *Ego,* multimedia spectacle (1970); *Le roi va mourir* for an instrumentalist, clock, tape and multimedia action (1971–72); *Ulysse* for variable group, tape and multimedia action (1972–73); *Jeu des sens,* music for a pair of ears, eyes, hands, a nose, and a mouth (1973–74); *Pourras-tu seul?* and *Cromoson,* both "imaginary music" (1973–74); *Natural!!,* space music (1973–74); *Kalendrier,* permanent music for the atmosphere of a room (1974).

Nemiroff, Isaac, American composer; b. Cincinnati, Feb. 16, 1912; d. New York, March 5, 1977. He studied at the Cincinnati Cons.; and with Stefan Wolpe at the N.Y. College of Music; taught at various music schools in N.Y. and Brooklyn.
WORKS: Duo for Violin and Cello (1939); Concerto for oboe and string orch. (1955); Concertino for flute solo, violin and string orch. (1958); *Lorca* Solo cantata for voice, flute and strings (1963); Woodwind Quintet (1968); Quintet for Flute, Clarinet, Cello, Voice and Piano (1969); *Atomyriades* for solo oboe (1972); Duo for Oboe and Bass Clarinet (1973); 2 String Quartets; 2 Violin Sonatas; Saxophone Sonata.

Nemtin, Alexander, Soviet composer; b. Perm, July 13, 1936. He studied at the Moscow Cons., graduating in 1960. He writes music in different genres, but his most notable creation is an intimately plausible reification of Scriabin's *Acte préalable,* the "preliminary act" of the planned *Mysterium.* Nemtin put together the score from sketches left by Scriabin after death, supplemented by materials from his late opus numbers, endeavoring to recreate Scriabin's symphonic textures. The first part of this work was performed in Moscow on March 16, 1973.

Nenna, Pomponio, Italian madrigalist; b. Bari, near Naples, c.1550; d. Rome, c.1618. Held in high regard by his contemporaries, he was created a Knight of the Golden Spur in 1603; publ. 8 books of madrigals for 5 voices from 1582 to 1618, and a book of madrigals *a* 4 (1613; 2nd ed., 1621). Several responds are printed in *Istituzione e monumenti dell'arte musicale italiana,* vol. 5 (pp. LIII–LX); madrigals, ed. by E. Dagnino, in *Pubblicazioni dell'Istituto italiano per la storia della musica* (Rome, 1942).

Nenov, Dimiter, Bulgarian composer and pianist; b. Razgrad, Jan. 1, 1902; d. Sofia, Aug. 30, 1953. He studied piano and composition at the Cons. in Dresden; returning to Bulgaria, he taught piano at the Sofia Music Academy (1937–43).
WORKS: Symph. No. 1 (1922); *Ballad* for orch. (1926); Piano Concerto (1932–36); 2 ballads for piano and orch. (1942, 1943); *Rhapsodic Fantasy* for orch. (1943); Violin Sonata (1921); Piano Sonata (1922).

Nepomuceno, Alberto, important Brazilian composer; b. Fortaleza, July 6, 1864; d. Rio de Janeiro, Oct. 16, 1920. He studied in Rome, Berlin, and Paris, returning to Brazil in 1895. In 1902 he was appointed director of the Instituto Nacional de Musica in Rio de Janeiro, holding this post until 1916. In 1910 he conducted Brazilian music at the International Exposition in Brussels. In some of his music he introduced thematic material from Brazilian folk music.
WORKS: the operas *Artemis* (Rio de Janeiro, June 14, 1898), *O Garatuja* (Rio de Janeiro, Oct. 26, 1904), *Abul* (Buenos Aires, June 30, 1913); Symphony (early work; publ. posthumously, 1937); *Suite Brasileira* for orch. (contains a popular *Batuque*); songs; piano pieces.

Neri, Saint Donna Filippo, one of the greatest spiritual leaders of the Renaissance; b. Florence, July 21, 1515; d. Rome, May 25, 1595. He went to Rome as a youth and in 1551 took holy orders. He began by giving lectures on religious subjects and holding spiritual exercises in the oratory of the church of San Girolamo della Carità, and soon attracted a large following. These meetings invariably ended with the singing of hymns, or *laudi spirituali,* for which the poet Ancina wrote many of the texts, while Giovanni Animuccia, maestro di cappella at the Vatican, and music director of the Oratory, set them to music. In 1575 the Congregation of the Oratory, as a seminary for secular priests, was officially recognized by Pope Gregory XIII, and in 1578 the Congregation transferred its headquarters to the church of Santa Maria in Vallicella. But the founder himself remained at S. Girolamo until 1583; from 1578 the great Spanish polyphonist Victoria lived with him there, as chaplain at this church. Another Spanish musician who was prominently associated with the Oratorio was Francisco Soto de Langa. S. Filippo was friendly with Palestrina, whose spiritual adviser he was, but there is no evidence that the latter succeeded Animuccia as music director of the Oratory. From the musical practice of the Oratory there eventually developed the form that we know as "oratorio." Contrary to general belief, this form did not make its first appearance in Cavalieri's *Rappresentazione di anima e di corpo,* performed at S. Maria in Vallicella in 1600, but in Giov. Francesco Anerio's *Teatro Armonico spirituale di madrigali a*

5, 6, 7 e 8 voci, dating from 1619 and consisting of musical settings of the Gospels and of stories from the Bible. It was not until about 1635–40 that this form actually began to receive the title of "oratorio," from the place where the performances were given.
BIBLIOGRAPHY: P. G. Bacci, *Vita di San F. Neri* (Naples, 1855; English transl. 2 vols., St. Louis, 1903); L. Ponnelle and L. Bourdet, *St. Ph. Neri et la société romaine de son temps* (Paris, 1918; English transl., London, 1932); P. Pasquetti, *L'Oratorio musicale in Italia* (Florence, 1906), chapters 4–8; L. Pastor, *Geschichte des Päpste* (Freiburg, 1886–1930; in English, London, 1930, vol. 19, chapter 4); D. Alaleona, *Storia dell'Oratorio Musicale in Italia* (Milan, 1945); C. Gasbarri, *L'oratorio filippino* (Rome, 1957).

Nerini, Émile, French composer; b. Colombes, near Paris, Feb. 2, 1882; d. Paris, March 22, 1967. Son of a piano manufacturer, he studied with Decombes, Diémer, Lenepveu, and Caussade at the Paris Cons.
WORKS: the lyric dramas *Manoël* (Paris, May 11, 1905), *Le Soir de Waterloo* (Paris, April 17, 1910), *L'Épreuve dernière* (Monte Carlo, March 16, 1912), *Mazeppa* (Bordeaux, 1925); operetta *Mademoiselle Sans-Gêne* (1944; Bordeaux, 1966); *Bacchus,* for chorus and orch.; programmatic pieces for orch. (*Parmi les roses, Solitude, Rêve oriental,* etc.); chamber music; instrumental sonatas; songs; etc.; publ. a *Traité d'Harmonie.*

Neruda, Franz Xaver, Bohemian cellist, brother of **Wilma Maria Francisca Neruda;** b. Brünn, Dec. 3, 1843; d. Copenhagen, March 20, 1915. At an early age he appeared in concerts with his father and sister; 1864–76, member of the Royal Orch. in Copenhagen, where in 1868 he founded the Society for Chamber Music; succeeded Gade in 1892 as conductor of a similar organization in Stockholm. He composed 5 cello concertos; *Aus dem Böhmerwald* and *Slovakische Märsche* for orch.; string quartets; pieces for cello, for piano, for organ; songs.

Neruda (Lady Hallé), Wilma Maria Francisca, Czech violinist; b. Brünn, March 21, 1839; d. Berlin, April 15, 1911. Her father was an organist; her brother, **Franz Xaver Neruda,** a cellist. She first played in public in Vienna when she was 7 years old, with her sister **Amalie,** a pianist; then made a tour with her father, sister, and brother through Germany. On June 11, 1849, she played at a Philharmonic concert in London; after prolonged travels on the Continent, including Russia, she married the Swedish conductor **Ludvig Norman** from whom she was divorced in 1869; she returned to London the same year. On July 26, 1888, she married **Sir Charles Hallé,** and with him made tours to Europe, Australia, and South Africa until her husband's death in 1895. When she announced her intention of retiring, a number of admirers, headed by the Prince of Wales (Edward VII), raised a subscription and presented to her a palace at Asolo, near Venice. In 1899 she made an American tour. In 1901 Queen Alexandra conferred upon her the title of "Violinist to the Queen." Her instrument, a Stradivarius dated 1709, considered one of the finest in existence, was presented to her in 1876 jointly by the Duke of Saxe-Coburg and Gotha, Earl Dudley, and Earl Hardwicke.
BIBLIOGRAPHY: *Dictionary of National Biography* (Supplement, 1901–11), II, p. 190.

Nessler, Victor E., Alsatian composer; b. Baldenheim, Jan. 28, 1841; d. Strasbourg, May 28, 1890. He studied in Strasbourg, where he produced his first opera, *Fleurette* (1864). In 1870 he became conductor of the Caroltheater in Leipzig and produced there his opera *Der Rattenfänger von Hameln* (Leipzig, March 19, 1879), which established his reputation as an opera composer. An even greater success was achieved by his opera *Der Trompeter von Säkkingen* (Leipzig, May 4, 1884), which entered the repertory of many European opera houses. In both operas Nessler adroitly appealed to the romantic tastes of the German audiences, even though from a purely musical standpoint these productions offered little originality. His other operas, none of which achieved a comparable success, included *Dornröschens Brautfahrt* (1867), *Irmingard* (1876), *Der wilde Jäger* (1881), *Otto der Schütz* (1886) and *Die Rose von Strassburg* (1890). He also wrote several operettas: *Die Hochzeitsreise* (1867), *Nachtwächter und Student* (1868) and *Am Alexandertag* (1869).
BIBLIOGRAPHY: C. Schneider, "Victor Nessler, compositeur alsacien du *Trompette de Säkkingen,*" *La Musique en Alsace hier et aujourd'hui* (Strasbourg, 1970).

Nestyev, Izrail, Russian musicologist; b. Kerch, April 17, 1911. He studied at the Moscow Cons., graduating in 1937; during the war of 1941–45 served as a military correspondent; subsequently was in charge of the programs of the Moscow Radio (1945–48); in 1956, joined the staff of the Moscow Cons., conducting seminars on European music. He is the author of the standard biography of Prokofiev (Moscow, 1946; in English, N.Y., 1946; new revised edition, Moscow, 1957; in English, Stanford, Cal., 1960, with a foreword by N. Slonimsky); other books are *Popular Song as Foundation of Musical Creativity* (Moscow, 1961); *How to Understand Music* (Moscow, 1962); *Hanns Eisler and his Songs* (Moscow, 1962); *Puccini* (Moscow, 1963); *Béla Bartók, Life and Works* (Moscow, 1969). He was a co-editor of the symposium, *Sergei Prokofiev; Articles and Materials* (Moscow, 1962); and *European Music of the 20th Century; Materials and Documents* (Moscow, 1975).

Nettl, Bruno, American musicologist, son of **Paul Nettl;** b. Prague March 14, 1930. He was brought to the U.S. in 1939; studied at Indiana Univ. (A.B., 1950; M.A., 1951; Ph.D., 1953); in 1960–64 was on the staff of Wayne State Univ., Detroit; then at the Univ. of Illinois in Urbana. He published *North American Indian Musical Styles,* (Philadelphia, 1954); *Music in Primitive Culture* (Cambridge, Mass., 1956); *Theory and Method in Ethnomusicology* (N.Y., 1964); *Folk and Traditional Music of the Western Continents* (Englewood Cliffs, N.J., 1965; 2nd ed., 1973); *Reference Materials in Ethnomusicology* (2nd ed., Detroit, 1967).

Nettl, Paul, eminent American musicologist; b. Hohenelbe, Bohemia, Jan. 10, 1889; d. Bloomington, Indiana, Jan. 8, 1972. He studied jurisprudence at the Univ. of Prague (LL.D., 1913) and musicology with H. Rietsch (Dr. phil., 1915); from 1920 to 1937 he was instructor of the Musicological Institute at the German Univ. in Prague; in 1939 emigrated to the U.S.; taught at the Westminster Choir School, Princeton, N.J. In 1946 he was appointed to the faculty of the Univ. of Indiana, Bloomington. He publ. a number of valuable books and pamphlets, among them *Über den Ursprung der Musik* (Prague, 1920); *Alte jüdische Spielleute und Musiker* (Prague, 1923); *Musik und Tanz bei Casanova* (Prague, 1924); *Das Wiener Lied in Zeitalter des Barock* (Vienna, 1934); *Mozart in Böhmen,* after Prochazka's *Mozart in Prag* (Prague, 1938); *The Story of Dance Music* (N.Y., 1947); *Luther and Music* (Philadelphia, 1948); *The Book of Musical Documents* (N.Y., 1948); *Casanova und seine Zeit* (Esslingen, 1949); *The Other Casanova* (1950); *Forgotten Musicians* (N.Y., 1951); *National Anthems* (1952); *Beethoven Encyclopedia* (N.Y., 1956); revised in 1967 as *Beethoven Handbook*); *Mozart and Masonry* (N.Y., 1957); *Beethoven und seine Zeit* (Frankfurt, 1958); G. F. *Händel* (1958); *Mozart und der Tanz* (1960); *The Dance in Classical Music* (1963). A bio-bibliographical brochure, *Ein Musikwissenschaftler in zwei Welten: Die musicwissenschaftlen und literarischen Arbeiten von Paul Nettl,* compiled by Thomas Atcherson, was publ. as part of a Festschrift in Vienna, 1962.

Neubauer, Franz Christoph, Czech violinist and composer; b. Melník, March 21, 1750; d. Bückeburg, Oct. 11, 1795. He was taught violin by the village schoolmaster; led a wandering life; produced an operetta, *Ferdinand und Yariko,* in Munich (1784); then proceeded to Vienna where he met Mozart and Haydn; from 1790 to 1794 he served as Kapellmeister to Prince Weilburg; in 1795 succeeded Johann Christoph Friedrich Bach as court Kapellmeister at Bückeburg. He was a prolific composer; wrote 12 symphonies; the 11th symph. was entitled *La Bataille,* and included in the score some imitative sounds of battle.

BIBLIOGRAPHY: F. von Schlichtegroll, *Musiker-Nekrologe* (ed. R. Schaal, Kassel, 1953).

Neuendorff, Adolf, German conductor; b. Hamburg, June 13, 1843; d. New York, Dec. 4, 1897. He went to America in 1854 and studied violin with Matzka and Weinlich, and piano with Schilling. He appeared both as a concert violinist and pianist; gave violin concerts in Brazil in 1861. In 1863 he went to Milwaukee, then a center of German music, and served as music director of the German theater there; subsequently moved to N.Y. where he conducted German opera, including the first American performances of *Lohengrin* (April 3, 1871) and *Die Walküre* (April 2, 1877); in 1884 he moved to Boston and became the first conductor of the Music Hall Promenade Concerts (later Boston Pops); he then followed his wife, the singer **Georgine von Januschowsky,** to Vienna where she was prima donna at the Imperial Opera (1893-95); finally returned to N.Y., and in 1897 became conductor of the Metropolitan Permanent Orch., succeeding Seidl.

BIBLIOGRAPHY: *Dictionary of American Biography* XIII.

Neuhaus, Heinrich, eminent Russian pianist and pedagogue; b. Elizabetgrad, April 12, 1888; d. Moscow, Oct. 10, 1964. He studied piano with his father, **Gustav Neuhaus** (1847-1938); other musical members of the family were his uncle, pianist and composer **Felix Blumenfeld,** and his first cousin, the Polish composer **Karol Szymanowski.** He began giving concerts at the age of 9; made a concert tour in Germany in 1904; then studied composition with Paul Juon in Berlin; in 1912-14 he took piano lessons with Leopold Godowsky in Vienna. Returning to Russia, he taught piano at the Kiev Cons. (1918-22); then was prof. from 1922 to his death at the Moscow Cons. Among his students were Gilels and Sviatoslav Richter. Neuhaus published *The Art of Piano Playing* (Moscow, 1958).

BIBLIOGRAPHY: V. Delson, *Heinrich Neuhaus* (Moscow, 1966).

Neukomm, Sigismund Ritter von, Austrian composer and conductor; b. Salzburg, July 10, 1778; d. Paris, April 3, 1858. He was a pupil of the organist Weissauer, and of Michael Haydn for composition; at 15, Univ. organist; at 18, chorusmaster at the opera. From 1798 he studied at Vienna under Joseph Haydn, who showed him fatherly care. in 1806 he passed through Stockholm, where he was elected a member of the Academy, to St. Petersburg, there becoming conductor of the German opera. 1809 found him in Paris, an intimate of Grétry and Cherubini, and pianist to Talleyrand after Dussek. For his Requiem in memory of Louis XVI (Vienna, 1814), Louis XVII ennobled him in 1815, decorating him with the cross of the Legion of Honor. In 1816 he went to Rio de Janeiro, and was appointed court music director by Emperor Dom Pedro, whom he accompanied to Lisbon on the outbreak of the revolution in 1821. He was in Talleyrand's service until 1826; then traveled for many years; and finally resided alternately in London and Paris. Despite his almost continuous travels, he was a most industrious composer. Besides much church music, he produced 10 German operas; a symphony, 5 overtures, and 7 fantasias for orch.; chamber music; a piano concerto and many piano pieces; 57 organ pieces; about 200 French, English, Italian, and German songs; etc. His autobiography was publ. as *Esquisses biographiques de Sigismond Neukomm* (Paris, 1859).

BIBLIOGRAPHY: Gisela Pellegrini, *Sigismund Ritter von Neukomm: ein vergessener Salzburger Musiker* (Salzburg, 1936); L. H. Corrêa de Azevedo, "S. Neukomm, an Austrian Composer in the New World," *Musical Quarterly* (Oct. 1959).

Neumann, Angelo, Austrian tenor; b. Vienna, Aug. 18, 1838; d. Prague, Dec. 20, 1910. He began a mercantile career, but deserted it after vocal lessons from Stilke-Sessi, and after his debut as a lyric tenor in 1859; sang at theaters in Cracow, Ödenburg, Pressburg, Danzig, and the Vienna court opera (1862-76); from 1876-82 he was manager of the Leipzig opera under Förster; then gathered together a traveling company for producing Wagner operas, journeying as far as Italy; from 1882 to 1885 he was manager of the Bremen opera; then until his death, of the German opera in Prague (Landestheater). He publ. *Erinnerungen an Richard Wagner* (1907; English transl. by E. Livermore, 1908).

Neumann, Franz (František), Czech conductor and composer; b. Přerov, Moravia, June 16, 1874; d. Brno, Feb. 24, 1929. He was a pupil at the Leipzig Cons.; répétiteur in Karlsruhe and Hamburg; Kapellmeister in Regensburg, Linz, and Reichenberg; 1904, 2nd Kapellmeister in Frankfurt; 1919, 1st conductor of the Czech National Opera, Brünn; 1925, its director. He composed the operas *Die Brautwerbung* (Linz, 1901), *Liebelei* (Frankfurt, Sept. 18, 1910), *Herbststurm* (Berlin, April 9, 1919), *Beatrice Caracci* (Brno, April 29, 1922; in Czech), and *Leyer und Schwert* (publ. 1901; not produced); 2 ballets; men's choruses; etc.

Neumann, Věroslav, Czech composer; b. at Citoliby, near Louny, May 27, 1931. He studied theory with Jaroslav Řídký at the Prague Cons. After a few works in a traditional style, he adopted the 12-tone method of composition. He wrote *Panoráma Prahy (Panorama of Prague)* for baritone and orch. (1962); a *Peace Symphony* (1964); *Ode* for orch. (1966); *Pozvánka na koktejl (Invitation to Cocktails)* for orch. (1969); *Omaggio a Prokofieff* for 2 violins (1969); children's choral cycle *Intervals* (1971).

Neumark, Georg, German hymn-writer; b. Langensalza, March 3, 1621; d. Weimar, July 8, 1681. He was the author of the words and music of the hymn *Wer nur den lieben Gott lässt walten,* used by Bach in several of his cantatas, and by Mendelssohn in the oratorio *St. Paul.* Neumark publ. several vols. of verse, some with his own tunes; the most important is *Poetisch-musikalisches Lustwäldchen* (Jena, 1652; enlarged ed., as *Fortgepflanztes Lustwäldchen,* 1657).
BIBLIOGRAPHY: Franz Knauth, *Georg Neumark, Leben und Dichten* (Langensalza, 1881).

Neupert, Edmund, Norwegian-American pianist and pedagogue; b. Christiania, April 1, 1842; d. New York, June 22, 1888. He studied at Kullak's Academy in Berlin; then taught there. In 1868 he went to Denmark, where he taught piano at the Copenhagen Cons.; for 2 years he was piano instructor at the Moscow Cons. (1881–83); then emigrated to the U.S. and settled in N.Y. as a piano teacher. His collections of piano studies were much in use by American teachers.

Nevada, Emma, stage name of **Emma Wixom,** operatic soprano; b. Alpha, near Nevada City, Calif., Feb. 7, 1859; d. Liverpool, June 20, 1940. She studied from 1877 with Marchesi in Vienna. Made her debut in London, May 17, 1880, in *La Sonnambula;* sang at Trieste in the autumn; then in Florence, Leghorn, Naples, Rome, and Genoa, and at La Scala, Milan. Her first appearance in Paris was at the Opéra-Comique, May 17, 1883, as Zora in F. David's *Perle du Brésil.* During the season of 1884–85 she was a member of Col. Mapleson's company at the old Academy of Music in New York, singing on alternate nights with Patti. She sang in Chicago at the Opera Festival, 1885, and again in 1889. She then sang mostly in Europe (ret'd. 1910).
BIBLIOGRAPHY: T. Williams, *Notable American Women,* II (N.Y., 1971); G. Jellinek, *Dictionary of American Biography,* Supplement II.

Nevada, Mignon Mathilde Marie, daughter of **Emma Nevada;** operatic soprano; b. Paris, Aug. 14, 1886; d. Long Melford, England, June 1971. She made her debut at the Costanzi Theater, Rome, as Rosina in *Il Barbiere di Siviglia;* then sang a season at the San Carlos in Lisbon; after a season at the Pergola Theater in Florence, she made her London debut in Covent Garden as Ophelia (Oct. 3, 1910), and sang there in subsequent seasons; also appeared at La Monnaie, Brussels, and (1923) at La Scala, Milan; during World War II she engaged in war work at Liverpool, England; 1954, lived in London.

Neveu, Ginette, French violinist; b. Paris, Aug. 11, 1919; d. in an airplane disaster at the Azores Islands, Oct. 28, 1949. She was a grandniece of **Widor;** studied with her mother, and later with Carl Flesch; first played in public with the Colonne Orch. in Paris at the age of 7. After graduating from the Paris Cons. with a 1st prize, she won the Wieniawski Grand Prize at the International Contest in Warsaw in 1934. Her American debut took place with the Boston Symph., Oct. 24, 1947; her success was immediate and unmistakable. She was at the height of her career when she perished on her way to the U.S. for her third annual tour.
BIBLIOGRAPHY: M. J. Ronze-Neveu, *Ginette Neveu; la fulgurante carrière d'une grande artiste* (Paris, 1952; in English, London, 1956).

Nevin, Arthur Finley, American composer and pedagogue, brother of **Ethelbert Nevin;** b. Edgworth, Penn., April 27, 1871; d. Sewickley, Penn., July 10, 1943. He received a musical training at home, mainly from his father; then studied at the New England Cons. in Boston; in 1893 went to Berlin where he studied piano with Klindworth and composition with Boise. Returning to the U.S. he devoted himself to teaching and conducting; was prof. of music at the Univ. of Kansas (1915–20) and director of the municipal music dept. of Memphis, Tenn. (1920–22); lived for a time on the Montana Indian reservations studying Indian music. He was unable to secure a performance for his "Indian" opera *Poia,* but succeeded in making arrangements with the Berlin State Opera to produce it; it was staged on April 23, 1910, but only four performances were given; the composer attributed the failure to the hostile anti-American Berlin group; another opera, *A Daughter of the Forest,* was produced in Chicago, January 5, 1918; among his other works were 2 orchestral suites, *Lorna Doone* and *Love Dreams;* some chamber music and a number of piano pieces.
BIBLIOGRAPHY: E. E. Hipsher, *American Opera and Its Composers* (Philadelphia, 1934; pp. 334–43).

Nevin, Ethelbert Woodbridge, popular American composer; brother of **Arthur Finley Nevin;** b. Edgeworth, Pennsylvania, Nov. 25, 1862; d. New Haven,

Feb. 17, 1901. After receiving preliminary musical studies in America, he went to Germany where he took lessons in singing and piano with Franz Böhme (1877-78); returning to the U.S. he studied piano with Benjamin J. Lang and harmony with Stephen A. Emery in Boston. In 1884 he went again to Germany to study piano with Karl Klindworth (1884-86); then lived in Berlin, Paris and Florence, before finally settling in New Haven. He had a natural talent for melodious songs and piano pieces in a semi-Classical manner. His *Narcissus* for piano became a perennial favorite with sentimental piano teachers; his songs, *The Rosary* and *Mighty Lak' a Rose*, achieved tremendous popularity in women's clubs. His pantomime *Lady Floriane's Dream* was produced in N.Y. in 1898.

BIBLIOGRAPHY: V. Thompson, *The Life of Ethelbert Nevin* (Boston, 1913); F. Rogers, "Some Memories of Ethelbert Nevin," *Musical Quarterly* (July 1917); J. T. Howard, *Ethelbert Nevin* (N.Y., 1935).

Nevin, Gordon Balch, American composer; b. Easton, Penn., May 19, 1892; d. New Wilmington, Penn., Nov. 15, 1943. He studied organ and theory in N.Y.; was organist at various churches in Pennsylvania; also in Cleveland; publ. numerous songs (*In Memoriam, Song of Sorrow, Moonlight Serenade,* etc.); contributed to music magazines.

Neway, Patricia, American soprano; b. Brooklyn, Sept. 30, 1919. She studied at the Mannes College of Music in N.Y. After several appearances in minor roles, she achieved her first significant success as Magda in Menotti's opera *The Consul* (Philadelphia, March 1, 1950); appeared in another Menotti opera, *Maria Golovin,* at the Brussels World's Fair on Aug. 30, 1958. Her repertoire includes parts in operas by Alban Berg, Benjamin Britten and Menotti.

Newcomb, Ethel, American pianist; b. Whitney Point, N.Y., Oct. 30, 1875; d. there, July 3, 1959. She went to Vienna in 1895, and studied with Leschetizky until 1903; served as his assistant from 1904 to 1908; made her debut on Feb. 28, 1903, with the Vienna Philharmonic Orch.; returning to America, she appeared in recitals; then settled at her home in Whitney Point.

Newlin, Dika, American writer on music and composer; b. Portland, Oregon, Nov. 22, 1923. She studied piano and theory at Michigan State Univ., East Lansing (B.A., 1939) and at the Univ. of California, Los Angeles (M.A., 1941); later took courses at Columbia Univ., N.Y. (Ph.D., 1945); in the interim she attended the classes of Schoenberg in Los Angeles, acquiring a thorough knowledge of the method of composition with 12 tones; also had some sessions with Sessions, and took additional instruction in piano playing with Serkin and Schnabel. She taught at Western Maryland College (1945-49); at Syracuse Univ. (1949-51); at Drew Univ. in Madison, N.J. (1952-65); and at North Texas State Univ. in Denton (1965-75). In 1977 she joined the faculty of the New School for Social Research in N.Y. She published a valuable study in comparative musical styles *Bruckner-Mahler-Schoenberg* (N.Y., 1947; totally revised edition, N.Y., 1977);

she translated into English Schoenberg's *Style and Idea* (N.Y., 1951), Rufer's *Das Werk A. Schönbergs* (London, 1962) and Leibowitz's *Schoenberg et son école* (N.Y., 1949). Her compositions follow the Schoenbergian idiom; she wrote a *Sinfonia* for piano (1947); Piano Trio (1948); Chamber Symph. (1949); *Fantasy on a Row* for piano (1958); *Study in 12 Tones* for viola d'amore and piano (1959); *Atone* for chamber ensemble (1976); *Second-Hand Rows* for voice and piano (1977-78).

Newman, Alfred, American film composer; b. New Haven, March 17, 1901; d. Hollywood, Feb. 17, 1970. He studied piano with Sigismund Stojowski and composition with Rubin Goldmark; also attended a Schoenberg seminar at the Univ. of California, Los Angeles. He began his career as a pianist in vaudeville shows; in 1930 went to Hollywood and devoted himself entirely to composition for the motion pictures; wrote 300-odd scores, 44 of which were nominated for awards of the Motion Picture Academy, and 8 were winners; among his most successful were *All About Eve, The Egyptian* and *Love Is a Many-Splendored Thing.* Stylistically he followed an eclectic type of median Romanticism, mimicking the most popular works of Tchaikovsky, Rachmaninoff, Wagner and Liszt, and amalgamating these elements in an iridescent free fantasia; in doing so he created a *sui generis* form of art that is described as "movie music."

Newman, Ernest, English music critic; b. Liverpool, Nov. 30, 1868; d. Tadworth, Surrey, July 7, 1959. His real name was **William Roberts;** he assumed his *nom de plume* to symbolize an "earnest new man." He prepared himself for the Indian Civil Service, but entered business in Liverpool, pursuing his musical studies as a favorite avocation. In 1903 he accepted an instructorship in the Midland Institute, Birmingham, and took up music as a profession; 1905, in Manchester as critic of the *Guardian;* 1906-19, in Birmingham as critic for the *Daily Post;* 1919-20, in London as critic for the *Observer;* from March 1920 on the staff of the *London Sunday Times;* from 1923, also contributor to the *Glasgow Herald;* 1924-25, guest critic of the *New York Evening Post.* One of the best equipped and most influential of the English music critics. He continued to write his regular column in the *Sunday Times* in his 90th year.

WRITINGS: *Gluck and the Opera* (1895); *A Study of Wagner* (1899); *Wagner* (1904); *Musical Studies* (1905; 3rd ed., 1914); *Elgar* (1906); *Hugo Wolf* (1907; German transl., 1910); *Richard Strauss* (1908); *Wagner as Man and Artist* (1914); *A Musical Motley* (1919); *The Piano-Player and Its Music* (1920); *A Musical Critic's Holiday* (1925); *The Unconscious Beethoven* (1927); *What to Read on the Evolution of Music* (1928); *Stories of the Great Operas* (3 vols., 1929-31); *Fact and Fiction about Wagner* (1931); *The Man Liszt* (1934); *The Life of Richard Wagner* in 4 vols. (1933; 1937; 1941; 1946); *Opera Nights* (1943; U.S. ed. as *More Stories of Famous Operas*); *Wagner Nights* (1949; U.S. ed. as *The Wagner Operas*); *More Opera Nights* (1955; U.S. ed. as *17 Famous Operas*); *From the World of Music: Essays from "The Sunday Times"* (selected by F. Aprahamian, London, 1956);

More Musical Essays (2nd selection from *The Sunday Times*, London, 1958). Newman translated Felix Weingartner's book *Über das Dirigieren* (Leipzig, 2nd ed., 1925), Schweitzer's *J. S. Bach* (Leipzig, 1911), and Rolland's *Beethoven the Creator* (London, 1929; New York, 1937); for Breitkoph & Härtel's complete ed. of Wagner's works he wrote entirely new and remarkably fine translations. He edited *Fifty Songs of Hugo Wolf* (with critical introduction); editor of *The New Library of Music* (historical and bibliographical monographs); editor of a new revised ed. (in English) of Berlioz's *Memoirs* (1932); a collection of his essays under the title *Testament of Music* (London, 1963); contributor to numerous English and American journals.

BIBLIOGRAPHY: H. van Thal, ed., *Fanfare for Ernest Newman* (London, 1955); Vera Newman, *Ernest Newman: A Memoir* (London, 1963).

Newman, William S., distinguished American music scholar; b. Cleveland, April 6, 1912. He studied piano with Riemenschneider and Arthur Loesser; composition with Elwell and Shepherd, in Cleveland; received his Ph.D. at Western Reserve Univ. in 1939; then took courses in musicology with Paul Henry Lang at Columbia Univ. in 1940; during World War II served in the U.S. Army Air Force Intelligence. In 1946 he joined the staff of the Univ. of North Carolina at Chapel Hill (Emeritus, 1976). He focused most of his research on the evolution of the instrumental sonata. His chief project was *A History of the Sonata Idea* in 3 vols.: *The Sonata in the Baroque Era* (Chapel Hill, 1959); *The Sonata in the Classic Era* (Chapel Hill, 1963); *The Sonata Since Beethoven* (Chapel Hill, 1969). His other publications include 3 critical editions of works in sonata forms (*13 Keyboard Sonatas of the 18th and 19th Centuries; 6 Keyboard Sonatas from the Classic Era; 3 Keyboard Sonatas by the Sons of Bach*); he further contributed articles on the sonata to the *Enciclopedia della musica, Die Musik in Geschichte und Gegenwart,* and *Grove's Dictionary of Music and Musicians.* He publ. *Performance Practices in Beethoven's Sonatas* (N.Y., 1971), and contributed numerous articles to American and European music magazines on various aspects of Classical sonata form. He began his musical career as a pianist, appearing in solo recitals and also with orchestras (until 1970); publ. a useful manual *The Pianist's Problems* (N.Y., 1950; 3rd expanded ed., 1974). He composed an operetta *Freddy and His Fiddle* (1936); *An American Tragedy,* concert overture (1941); several pieces for band and some chamber music.

Newmarch, Rosa Harriet (*née* **Jeaffreson**), English writer on musical subjects; b. Leamington, Dec. 18, 1857; d. Worthing, April 9, 1940. Growing up in an artistic atmosphere, she entered the Hetherley School of Art to study painting, but after a time abandoned that career for literary pursuits; settled in London in 1880 as contributor to various journals. There she married Henry Charles Newmarch in 1883. She visited Russia in 1897 and many times afterwards; established contact with foremost musicians there; her enthusiasm for Russian music, particularly that of the Russian National School of Composition, was unlim-

ited, and she published several books on the subject which were of importance to the appreciation of Russian music in England, though her high-pitched literary manner was sometimes maintained to the detriment of factual material.

WRITINGS: *Tchaikovsky* (1900); *Songs to a Singer* (1906); *Poetry and Progress in Russia* (1907); *The Russian Opera* (1914; in French, 1922); *The Russian Arts* (1916); *The Devout Russian* (1919); *The Concert-Goer's Library* (collection of program notes; 6 vols., London, 1928–48); she translated *The Life and Letters of Tchaikovsky* (1908; abridged from Modest Tchaikovsky's biography).

Newmark, John, Canadian pianist; b. Bremen, Germany, June 12, 1904. He studied in Leipzig; made a career as an accompanist; traveled all over the world with celebrated singers, violinists and cellists, among them Kathleen Ferrier, Elisabeth Schumann, Richard Tucker, George London, Szymon Goldberg and Maurice Eisenberg. He settled in Montreal.

Newsom, Hugh Raymond, American concert manager and composer; b. Cawnpore, India, Dec. 20, 1891; d. Baltimore, May 21, 1978. He was brought to America as an infant, and studied music at the Oberlin Cons., Ohio; later had some lessons with George Chadwick at the New England Cons. in Boston. He became a successful concert manager; in 1937 married the harpist **Marjorie Brunton.** In the meantime, he composed industriously; wrote an oratorio-drama *The Divine Tragedy;* several other oratorios and a number of character pieces for piano and song cycles; also wrote a harp concerto, which was first performed by his wife in New York on Nov. 6, 1968. His style of composition is disarmingly euphonious in an attractive lyric vein.

Ney, Elly, German pianist; b. Düsseldorf, Sept. 27, 1882; d. Tutzing, March 31, 1968. She was a piano student of Leschetizky and Sauer in Vienna; made her debut in Vienna in 1905; gave successful recitals in Europe and America; then devoted herself mainly to teaching; lived mostly in Munich. She was married to Willem van Hoogstraten (1911–27); in 1928 she married P. F. Allais of Chicago. She published an autobiography, *Ein Leben für die Musik* (Darmstadt, 1952; 2nd ed. as *Erinnerungen und Betrachtungen; mein Leben aus der Musik,* 1957).

BIBLIOGRAPHY: C. von Pidoll, *Elly Ney* (Leipzig, 1942); Zenta Maurina, *Begegnung mit Elly Ney* (Memmingen, 1956); E. Valentin, *Elly Ney, Symbol einer Generation* (Munich, 1962).

Nezhdanova, Antonina, Russian soprano; b. Krivaya Balka, near Odessa, June 16, 1873; d. Moscow, June 26, 1950. She studied at the Moscow Cons.; in 1902 joined the staff of the Bolshoi Theater. She was equally successful as a lyric, dramatic and coloratura soprano; her range extended to high G. In 1912 she made an appearance as Gilda in *Rigoletto* at the Grand Opéra in Paris. Her best roles were Tatiana in *Eugene Onegin;* Marguerite in *Faust* and Elsa in *Lohengrin.* In 1943 she became prof. of voice at the Moscow Cons.

BIBLIOGRAPHY: G. Polyanovsky, *A. Nezhdanova* (Moscow, 1970).

Nibelle, Adolphe-André, French composer of operettas; b. Gien, Loiret, Oct. 9, 1825; d. Paris, March 11, 1895. His numerous light operas had considerable vogue in Paris. Among the most successful were *Le Loup-Garou* (1858), *Les Filles du Lac* (1858), *L'Arche-Marion* (1868), *La Fontaine de Berny* (1869), *Le 15 Août* (1869), *Les Quatre Cents Femmes d'Ali-Baba* (1872), *L'Alibi* (1873); also publ. *Heures musicales* (24 songs).

Nicholl, Horace Wadham, English organist and composer; b. Tipton, near Birmingham, March 17, 1848; d. New York, March 10, 1922. He studied music with his father and with the local organist Samuel Prince; then served as church organist in the vicinity; in 1871 received an offer to go to Pittsburgh as organist at St. Paul's Cathedral; in 1878 he went to N.Y. where he was engaged as teacher. He wrote several biblical oratorios, 2 symphonies and *Hamlet*, a "psychic sketch" for orch.; numerous piano pieces.

Nicholl, Joseph Weston, English composer; b. Halifax, Yorkshire, May 7, 1875; d. there, May 1925. He studied in Berlin, Munich and Paris; returning to England he led the Yorkshire Military Band. He wrote a symph. poem *In English Seas* and a number of pieces for band.

Nicholls, Agnes, English soprano; b. Cheltenham, July 14, 1877; d. London, Sept. 21, 1959. She studied singing with Visetti at the Royal College of Music in London; made her operatic debut in Manchester on Nov. 20, 1895 as Dido in a revival of Purcell's opera; on May 14, 1901 she sang the role of the Dewman in *Hänsel und Gretel* at Covent Garden, London. On July 15, 1904 she married the conductor **Hamilton Harty.** She was quite successful in Wagnerian roles; in 1908 she sang Sieglinde in *Die Walküre* at Covent Garden under the direction of Hans Richter.

Nichols, Ernest Loring ("Red"), American cornetist and band leader; b. Ogden, Utah, May 8, 1905; d. Las Vegas, June 28, 1965. He received his early training from his father, a clarinet player; joined various bands in New York; then cut a swath in the world of popular music with his own band, "Red Nichols and his Five Pennies" (actually, the number of "Pennies" was ten); among his players were Jimmy Dorsey, Benny Goodman and Glenn Miller. A maudlin motion picture, *The Five Pennies*, was made in 1959 and catapulted Red Nichols into top ranks of jazzmen. Heuristic exegetes of European hermeneutics lamented the commercialization of his style, giving preference to his earlier, less slick, jazzification.

BIBLIOGRAPHY: G. Johnson, *The 5 Pennies: The Biography of Jazz Band Leader Red Nichols* (N.Y., 1959).

Nicodé, Jean-Louis, German pianist and composer; b. Jerczik, near Posen, Aug. 12, 1853; d. Langebrück, near Dresden, Oct. 5, 1919. He was taught by his father and the organist Hartkäs; entered Kullak's Academy in Berlin, 1869, where he studied piano with Kullak, harmony with Wüerst, and counterpoint and composition with Kiel. He made a concert tour (1878) with Mme. Artôt through Galicia and Rumania; 1878–85, piano teacher at Dresden Cons.; till 1888, conductor of the Philharmonic Concerts; established the "Nicodé Concerts" in 1893, and, in order to enlarge their scope by the production of larger choral works formed the "Nicodé Chorus" in 1896. In 1900 he abandoned these concerts, retired to Langebrück, and devoted himself to composition. He wrote a symph.; symphonic poems; 2 sonatas for cello and piano; many piano pieces; songs.

BIBLIOGRAPHY: Th. Schäfer, *Jean-Louis Nicodé. Ein Versuch kritischer Würdigung und Erläuterung seines Schaffens* (Berlin, 1907); O. Taubmann, "Jean-Louis Nicodé," *Monographien moderner Musiker III,* (Leipzig, 1909).

Nicolai, Otto, famous German opera composer; b. Königsberg, June 9, 1810; d. Berlin, May 11, 1849. A piano pupil of his father, a singing teacher, he escaped from parental tyranny at the age of 16, and found a protector in Justizrat Adler of Stargard, who sent him to Berlin in 1827 to study under Zelter and Klein. He had developed excellent ability as a teacher, when the Prussian Ambassador at Rome, von Bunsen, appointed him (1833) organist of the embassy chapel at Rome, where he also studied the old Italian masters under Baini, Going to Vienna in 1837, he was Kapellmeister at the Kärnthnerthor Theater till Oct. 1838, when he returned to Rome and took up Italian opera composition. He had a great vogue, bringing out *Rosmonda d'Inghilterra* (Turin, 1838; at Trieste, 1839, as *Enrico II d'Inghilterra*), *Il Templario* (after *Ivanhoe*; Turin, Feb. 11, 1840; at Naples, autumn, 1843, as *Teodosia;* at Vienna as *Der Templer*), *Odoardo e Gildippe* (Turin, 1841), and *Il Proscritto* (Milan, March 13, 1841; in Vienna as *Die Heimkehr des Verbannten,* Feb. 3, 1844). Succeeding Kreutzer as court Kapellmeister at Vienna, 1841–47, he founded the Philharmonic Society in 1842. He began to compose *Die lustigen Weiber von Windsor,* the opera upon which his fame rests, in Vienna; but was called to Berlin (1847) as Kapellmeister of the Opera and of the newly established Domchor. His last-mentioned opera (in English *The Merry Wives of Windsor*) came out in Berlin, March 8, 1849, only two months before his death by a stroke of apoplexy. Nicolai's other works are a Mass (dedicated 1843 to Friedrich Wilhelm IV); a Festival Overture on *Ein' feste Burg* (1844); a piano concerto; piano pieces; 2 symphonies; a string quartet; a cello sonata; a Requiem; a *Te Deum;* songs.

BIBLIOGRAPHY: H. Mendel, *Otto Nicolai: eine Biographie* (Berlin, 1866); G. R. Kruse, *Otto Nicolai, Ein Künstlerleben* (Berlin, 1911); B. Schroeder, *Otto Nicolais Tagebücher, nebst biographischen Ergänzungen* (Leipzig, 1892); "Otto Nicolais Briefe aus den Jahren 1832–48," *Deutsche Rundschau* (Jan. 1897); G. R. Kruse, "Otto Nicolai als Symphoniker," *Allgemeine Musik-Zeitung* (1908); G. R. Kruse, "Otto Nicolais italienische Opern," *Sammelbände der Internationalen Musik-Gesellschaft* XII/2 (1911); G. R. Kruse, *Otto Nicolais musikalische Aufsätze* (Regensburg, 1913); *Otto Nicolai: Briefe an seinen Vater,* ed. by W.

Altmann (Regensburg, 1924); *Otto Nicolais Tage-bücher,* ed. by W. Altmann (Regensburg, 1937).

Nicolau, Antonio, Catalan composer and conductor; b. Barcelona, June 8, 1858; d. there, Feb. 26, 1933. He studied in Barcelona with Balart and Pujol; also in Paris, where he lived for 8 years; then became conductor of the Sociedad de Conciertos de Barcelona, with which he gave many important 1st performances in Spain; was director of the Barcelona Municipal Music School from 1896 and teacher of many of the leading Catalan musicians, including Lamote de Grignon.
WORKS: the operas *El Rapto* (Madrid, 1887) and *Constanza* (Barcelona); the dramatic scene *La Tempestad* (Barcelona); the symph. poems *El Triunfo de Venus* (Paris, 1882) and *Spes; choral works: Captant* (1904), *La Mort del Escolà, Entre flors, La Mare de deu;* songs.
BIBLIOGRAPHY: R. Mitjana, *Para música vamos!* (Valencia, 1909).

Nicolini, stage name of **Ernest Nicolas,** French dramatic tenor; b. Saint-Malo, Feb. 23, 1834; d. Pau, Jan. 19, 1898. He studied at the Paris Cons.; made his debut in July 1857, in Halévy's *Mousquetaires de la Reine,* at the Opéra-Comique, where he was engaged till 1859; then went to Italy, and sang as "Nicolini" with moderate success. From 1862-70 he sang at the Salle Ventadour, Paris, visiting London in 1866. In 1871 he sang opera at Drury Lane; from 1872 for several years at Covent Garden. After touring with **Adelina Patti,** he married her, on Aug. 10, 1886.

Niculescu, Stefan, Rumanian composer and musicologist; b. Moreni (Ploesti), July 31, 1927. He studied at the Bucharest Cons. with Mihail Jora, Ion Dumitrescu, Tudor Ciortea, Theodor Rogalski and others; attended the summer courses on advanced music in Darmstadt; also worked in an electronic studio in Munich (1966); from 1963 on he was on the staff of the Bucharest Cons. In his music he follows the median course of serialism, without excluding tonality.
WORKS: a children's opera *Le Livre avec Apolodore* (1975); Clarinet Sonata (1954-55); Symphony (1955-56); String Trio (1957); *Inventions* for clarinet and piano (1964); *Inventions* for viola and piano (1965); *Hétéromorphie* for orch. (1967; Bucharest, April 12, 1968); *Formants* for 17 string soloists (1968); *Tastenspiel* for piano (1968); *Aphorisms by Heraclitus* for a cappella chorus (1968-69); Wind Sextet (1970); *Unisonos I* for orch. (Mainz, Germany, Sept. 26, 1970; a revised version, *Unisonos II,* 1971-72; Graz Festival, Oct. 17, 1972); *Triplum I* for flute, cello and piano (1971); *Ison I,* variations for 14 instrumental soloists (1971); *Triplum II* for clarinet, cello and piano (1972). He published a monograph on George Enesco (Bucharest, 1971), and several analytic articles on the music of Webern, Xenakis, Boulez, Ligeti and Cage.

Niecks, Friedrich (Frederick), German pedagogue and writer on music; b. Düsseldorf, Feb. 3, 1845; d. Edinburgh, June 24, 1924. He studied the violin under Langhans, Grünewald, and Auer, and piano and composition with J. Tausch; debut (as violinist) at Düsseldorf in 1857; until 1867 he was a member of the orch.

there, the last years as concertmaster; in 1868, organist at Dumfries, Scotland, and viola player in a quartet with A. C. Mackenzie. After 2 terms in Leipzig Univ. (1877), and travels in Italy, he won a position in London as critic for the *Monthly Musical Record* and *Musical Times;* in 1891, appointed Reid Prof. of Music at Edinburgh Univ. In 1901 Niecks founded the Music Education Society. He was made Mus. Doc. (*honoris causa*) by Dublin Univ. in 1898; LL.D. by Edinburgh Univ. After his retirement in 1914 he lived in Edinburgh.
WRITINGS: *A Concise Dictionary of Musical Terms* (2nd ed., 1884); *Frédéric Chopin as a Man and Musician* (1888; 3rd ed., 1902; German ed., 1890); *Programme Music in the Last Four Centuries* (1907); *R. Schumann* (posthumous, 1925).

Niedermeyer, Louis, Swiss composer; b. Nyon, April 27, 1802; d. Paris, March 14, 1861. He was a pupil in Vienna of Moscheles (piano) and Förster (composition); in 1819, of Fioravanti in Rome, and Zingarelli in Naples. He lived in Geneva as an admired song composer, and settled in Paris in 1823; there he brought out four unsuccessful operas (*La Casa nel bosco,* May 28, 1828; *Stradella,* March 3, 1837; *Marie Stuart,* Dec. 6, 1844; *La Fronde,* May 2, 1853). He then bent his energies to sacred composition, and reorganized Choron's Institute for Church Music as the École Niedermeyer, which eventually became a flourishing institution with government subvention; he also founded (with d'Ortigue) a journal for church music, *La Maîtrise;* and publ. with him a *Méthode d'accompagnement du plain-chant* (1856; 2nd ed., 1876; English transl. by W. Goodrich, N.Y., 1905). His Masses, motets, hymns, etc. were well received; his romances (*Le Lac; Le Soir; La Mer; L'Automne;* etc.) are widely known; he also publ. organ preludes, piano pieces, etc.
BIBLIOGRAPHY: A. Niedermeyer, *Louis Niedermeyer, Son œuvre et son école* (Paris, no date); Anon., *Vie d'un compositeur moderne* (by Niedermeyer's son; Fontainbleau, 1892; reprinted Paris, 1893, with preface by Saint-Saëns); M. Galerne, *L'École Niedermeyer* (Paris, 1928)

Nielsen, Alice, American soprano; b. Nashville, Tenn., June 7, 1876; d. New York, March 8, 1943. She was of partly Danish, partly Irish extraction; sang in a church choir in Kansas City; then joined the Burton Stanley Opera Co. where she sang operettas; she made her debut as a grand opera singer in Naples as Marguerite in *Faust* (Dec. 6, 1903); made her first American appearance in N.Y. (Nov. 10, 1905). In 1908 she toured with the San Carlo Co. in the U.S.; then achieved the status of a prima donna with the Boston Opera Co. (1909-13) and also sang with the Metropolitan Opera. She settled eventually in New York as a singing teacher.

Nielsen, Carl (August), greatly significant Danish composer; initiator of the modern Danish school of composition; b. Nørre-Lyndelse, near Odense, on the island of Fyn (Funen), June 9, 1865; d. Copenhagen, Oct. 3, 1931. As a boy, he received violin lessons from his father; then played second violin in his village orch. and took trumpet lessons; at the age of 14 be-

came a trumpeter in the Odense military band. While in Odense he made his first efforts at composing, producing a few chamber pieces; a string quartet he wrote qualified him for admission to the Royal Cons. in Copenhagen, where he studied composition with O. Rosenhoff, violin with V. Tofte, and music history with Gade (1884–86). He played violin in the Royal Chapel Orch. in Copenhagen (1889–1905); later conducted at the Royal Opera in Copenhagen (1908–14) and led the *Musikföreningen* (Music Society) in Copenhagen (1915–27); also conducted concerts in Germany, Holland, Sweden and Finland; a few months before his death was appointed director of the Royal Cons. in Copenhagen. The early style of his music, romantic in essence, was determined by the combined influences of Gade, Grieg, Brahms and Liszt, but later on he experienced the powerful impact of modern music, particularly in harmony, which grew more and more chromatic and dissonant; yet he reserved the simple diatonic progressions, often in folksong manner, for his major climaxes; in his orchestration he applied opulent sonorities and colorful instrumental counterpoint; there are instances of bold experimentation in some of his works, as for instance, the insertion of a snare-drum solo in his Fifth Symphony playing independently of the rest of the orchestra; he attached somewhat mysterious titles to his 3rd and 4th symphonies (*Expansive* and *Inextinguishable*). Nielsen is sometimes described as the Sibelius of Denmark, despite obvious dissimilarities in idiom and sources of inspiration; while the music of Sibelius is deeply rooted in national folklore, both in subject matter and melodic derivation, Nielsen seldom drew on Danish popular modalities; Sibelius remained true to the traditional style of composition, while Nielsen sought new ways of modern expression. It was only after his death that Nielsen's major works entered the world repertory; festivals of his music were organized on his centennial in 1965, and his symphonies in particular were played and recorded in England and America, so that Nielsen finally emerged as one of the most important composers of his time.

WORKS (all premières in Copenhagen, except where otherwise noted). FOR THE STAGE: 2 operas: *Saul og David,* after E. Christiansen (*Saul and David,* 1898–1901; Nov. 28, 1902) and *Maskarade,* after V. Andersen (1904–06; Nov. 11, 1906); incidental music to 14 plays, including *Aladdin* (1918–19; Feb. 15, 1919) and *Moderen* (*The Mother,* 1920; Jan. 30, 1921). FOR ORCH.: 6 symphonies: No. 1 (1891–92; March 14, 1894); No. 2, *De Fire Temperamenter* (*The Four Temperaments,* 1901–02; Dec. 1, 1902); No. 3, *Sinfonia Espansiva* (1910–11; Feb. 28, 1912); No. 4, *Det Uudslukkelige* (*The Inextinguishable,* 1915–16; Feb. 1, 1916); No. 5 (1921–22; Jan. 24, 1922); No. 6, *Sinfonia Semplice* (1924–25; Dec. 11, 1925); *Little Suite* for strings (1888; Sept. 8, 1888); *Symphonic Rhapsody* (1888; Feb. 24, 1893; lost); *Helios,* overture (1903; Oct. 8, 1903); *Saga-Drøm* (*Dream of Saga,* 1908; April 6, 1908); *Ved en ung Kunstners Baare* (*At the Bier of a Young Artist); Andante lamentoso* for string orch. (1910); Violin Concerto (1911; Feb. 28, 1912); paraphrase on *Naermere Gud til dig"* ("*Nearer My God to Thee")* for wind orch. (1912; Aug. 22, 1915); *Pan og Syrinx,* a pastorale (*Pan and Syrinx,* 1917–18; Feb. 11,

1918); Flute Concerto (1926; Paris, Oct. 21, 1926); *Rhapsodic Overture, En Fantasirejse til Faerøerne* (*A Fantasy-Journey to the Faroe Islands,* 1927; Nov. 27, 1927); Clarinet Concerto (1928; Humlebaek, Sept. 14, 1928); *Bøhmisk-Dansk Folketone* (*Bohemian and Danish Folktunes),* paraphrase for string orch. (1928; Nov. 1, 1928). FOR VOICE: 10 cantatas for various ceremonial occasions; *Hymnus amoris* for soprano, tenor, baritone, bass, chorus and orch. (1896–97; April 27, 1897) *Søvnen (Sleep)* for chorus and orch. (1903–04; March 21, 1905); *Fynsk Foraar (Springtime in Funen),* lyrical humoresque for soprano, tenor, bass-baritone, chorus and orch. (1921; Odense, July 8, 1922); *3 Motets* for chorus a cappella (1929; April 11, 1930); numerous original songs to Danish words; harmonizations of Danish folksongs. CHAMBER MUSIC: String Quintet (1888); 4 string quartets: No. 1 (op. 13, 1888; revised 1897), No. 2 (op. 5, 1890), No. 3 (op. 14, 1898) and No. 4 (op. 44, 1906; originally titled *Piacevolezza,* op. 19); *2 Fantasias* for oboe and piano (1889); 2 violin sonatas (1895, 1912); *Serenata in Vano* for clarinet, bassoon, horn, cello and bassoon (1914); from incidental music to *Moderen: Faith and Hope are Playing* for flute and viola, *The Fog is Lifting* for flute and harp, and *The Children are Playing* for solo flute (all 1920); Wind Quintet (1922; Oct. 9, 1922); *Prelude and Theme with Variations* for solo violin (1923); *Praeludio e Presto* for solo violin (1928); *Canto Serioso* for horn or cello, and piano (1928); *Allegretto* for 2 recorders (1931). FOR PIANO: *5 Pieces* (1890); *Symphonic Suite* (1894), 6 *Humoreske-Bagateller* (1894–97), *Festpraeludium* (1900), *Chaconne* (1916), *Theme with Variations* (1916), *Suite (Den Luciferiske) (Lucifer Suite,* 1919–20), *3 Pieces* (1928), *Klavermusik for Smaa og Store (Piano Music for Young and Old),* 24 short 5-tone pieces in all keys in 2 volumes (1930). FOR ORGAN: *29 Short Preludes* (1929), *2 Posthumous Preludes* (1929), *Commotio* (1930–31). Nielsen publ. the books *Levende Musik* (Copenhagen, 1925; in English as *Living Music,* London, 1953) and *Min Fynske Barndom* (reminiscences of his childhood, Copenhagen, 1927; in English under the title *My Childhood,* London, 1953).

BIBLIOGRAPHY: Hugo Seligmann, *Carl Nielsen* (Copenhagen, 1931); Knud Jeppesen, "Carl Nielsen: A Danish Composer," *Music Review* (1946); T. Meyer and F. S. Petersen, *Carl Nielsen* (2 vols.; Copenhagen, 1947–48); L. Dolleris, *Carl Nielsen* (Odense, 1949); H. Madsen, *Carl Nielsens Fyn* (Odense, 1950); R. Simpson, *Carl Nielsen, Symphonist, 1865–1931* (London, 1952); R. Simpson, *Sibelius and Nielsen* (London, 1965); D. Fog (with T. Schousboe), *Carl Nielsen, Kompositioner; en bibliografi* (Copenhagen, 1965); A. M. Telmanyi, *Mit Barndomschjem* (Copenhagen, 1965); *Carl Nielsen: Centenary Essays* (London, 1966).

Nielsen, Ludolf, Danish violinist and composer; b. Nørre-Tvede, Jan. 29, 1876; d. Copenhagen, May 11, 1939. He was a pupil at the Copenhagen Cons. of V. Tofte (violin), A. Orth (piano), Bondesen (harmony), O. Malling and F. P. E. Hartmann (composition); as winner of the Ancker stipend traveled in 1907 in Germany, Austria, and Italy; then lived in Copenhagen as teacher and composer.

WORKS: the operas *Isabella* (Copenhagen, Oct. 8,

1915), *Uhret (The Clock),* and *Lola* (Copenhagen, 1920); the ballet *Reisekameraden;* 3 symphonies; other orchestral works; chamber music; choruses; songs; piano pieces; etc.

Nielsen, Riccardo, Italian composer; b. Bologna, March 3, 1908. He studied with Alfredo Casella and Carlo Gatti; began composing in the Italian Baroque manner but eventually made a decisive turn towards the 12-tone technique of composition. He occupied various administrative and teaching positions; from 1946 to 1950 was director of the Teatro Communale in Bologna; in 1954 became director of the Liceo Frescobaldi in Ferrara, where he also taught composition. WORKS: *Sinfonia concertante* for piano and orch. (1932); Violin Concerto (1933); *Sinfonia in G* (1934); *Divertimento* for clarinet, bassoon, trumpet, violin, viola and cello (1934); Concerto for Orch. (1935); *Musica per archi* (1946); monodrama, *L'Incubo* (Venice, 1948); radio opera, *La via di Colombo* (1953); *Variations* for orch. (1956); *Requiem nella miniera* (1957); *Invenzioni e sinfonie* for soprano and orch. (1959); *Varianti* for orch. (1965); *6 + 5 fasce sonore* for strings (1968); Piano Quartet (1961); *7 Aforismi* for clarinet and piano (1958); Cello Sonata (1958); *Cadenza a due* for cello and piano (1967); Chamber Cantata for voice, women's chorus and instruments (1969); *Ganymed* for soprano, clarinet, cello and piano (1958); *4 Poesie di Apollinaire* for voice and piano (1961). He publ. a theoretical work, *Le forme musicali* (Bologna, 1961).

Nielsen, Svend, Danish composer; b. Copenhagen, April 20, 1937. He studied music theory with Vagn Holmboe at the Copenhagen Cons., graduating in 1967; then continued to take lessons in advanced composition with Per Norgaard; in 1969 he became music instructor at the Copenhagen Cons. Among his works are *Duetter* for soprano, contralto, flute, cello, vibraphone and percussion (1964); *Prisma-suite* for contralto, flute, viola and strings (1965); *Metamorfoser* for 23 solo strings (1968); *Nuages* for orch. (1972); a chamber opera, *Bulen* (1968).

Nielsen, Tage, Danish composer; b. Fredericksborg, Jan. 16, 1929. He studied musicology at the Univ. of Copenhagen (1948-55); then was program director of the Danish Radio (1957-63); in 1963 he was appointed rector at the Cons. of Aarhus. WORKS: String Quartet (1947); Sonatina for 2 bassoons (1948); Piano Sonata (1950); *Intermezzo gaio* for orch. (1952); *4 Miniatures* for string orch. (1963); *Bariolage* for orch. (Aarhus, Feb. 7, 1966); *Variants* for solo flute (1966); *Il Giardino magico* (Aarhus, March 24, 1969); *Elegy* for guitar solo (1975); organ pieces; songs; music for schools.

Niemann, Albert, German opera tenor; b. Erxleben, near Magdeburg, Jan. 15, 1831; d. Berlin, Jan. 13, 1917. He began his career as an actor and dramatist; then sang in a chorus in Dessau; had lessons with F. Schneider and the baritone Nusch; then went to Paris where he studied with Duprez. In 1866 he was engaged at the Royal Court Opera in Berlin, and remained on the staff until 1887. Wagner thought highly of him and asked him to create the role of Tannhäuser in Paris (March 13, 1861) and of Siegmund at the Bayreuth Festival in 1876. From 1886 to 1888 he was a member of the Metropolitan Opera Co. in N.Y.; his debut there was in his star role as Siegmund (Nov. 10, 1886); then he sang Tristan at the American première of *Tristan und Isolde* (Dec. 1, 1886) and Siegmund in *Götterdämmerung* (Jan. 25, 1888). BIBLIOGRAPHY: R. Sternfeld, *Albert Niemann* (Berlin, 1904); Niemann's correspondence with Wagner was publ. by W. Altmann (Berlin, 1924).

Niemann, Walter, German writer on music and composer; b. Hamburg, Oct. 10, 1876; d. Leipzig, June 17, 1953. He was a pupil of his father, Rudolf Niemann, and of Humperdinck (1897); 1898-1901, studied at the Leipzig Cons. with Reinecke and von Bose, and at the Univ. with Riemann and Kretzschmar (musicology); Dr. phil. in 1901, with the dissertation *Über die abweichende Bedeutung der Ligaturen in der Mensuraltheorie der Zeit vor Johannes de Garlandia* (publ. Leipzig, 1902; reprint, Wiesbaden, 1971); 1904-06, editor of *Neue Zeitschrift für Musik,* in Leipzig; 1906-07, teacher at the Hamburg Cons.; 1907-17, again in Leipzig as writer and critic of the *Neueste Nachrichten,* then gave up this position to devote himself to composition. Besides a violin sonata and a few works for orch. and string orch., he wrote numerous piano pieces (over 150 opus nos.). WRITINGS: *Musik und Musiker des 19. Jahrhunderts* (1905); *Die Musik Skandinaviens* (1906); *Das Klavierbuch* (1907; 5th ed., 1920); *Edvard Grieg* (1908; with G. Schjelderup); *Die musikalische Renaissance des 19. Jahrhunderts* (1911); *Taschenlexikon für Klavierspieler* (1912; 4th ed., 1918); *Die Musik seit Richard Wagner* (1913; later editions as *Die Musik der Gegenwart*); *Jean Sibelius* (1917); *Klavier-Lexikon* (1917); *Die nordische Klaviermusik* (1918); *Die Virginalmusik* (1919); *Meister des Klaviers* (1919); *Brahms* (1920; English transl. N.Y., 1929; reprint, N.Y., 1969).

Niemtschek (Niemetschek, Němeček), Franz Xaver, Czech writer on music; b. Sadská, near Poděbrady, July 24, 1766; d. Vienna, March 19, 1849. He was prof. of philosophy at the Univ. of Prague from 1802, and is known in musical annals for his biography of Mozart, whom he greatly admired and evidently knew personally: *Leben des k. k. Kapellmeisters Wolfgang Gottlieb Mozart* (Prague, 1798; 2nd ed., 1808; in English, London, 1956).

Niessen-Stone, Matja von, American soprano; b. Moscow, Dec. 28, 1870; d. New York, June 8, 1948. At the age of 6 she was taken to Germany where she studied singing with Adolf Jansen in Dresden and in Berlin with Lilli Lehmann and others; after a successful debut in Dresden in 1890 she toured Europe; in 1906 she went to the U.S. and sang at the Metropolitan Opera House, N.Y., during the season 1908-09. From 1910 to 1917 she taught voice at the Institute of Musical Art, N.Y. In 1922 she went back to Europe and taught singing in Berlin until 1938, when she returned to New York.

Nietzsche, Friedrich, the celebrated philosopher; b. Röcken, near Lützen, Oct. 15, 1844; d. Weimar, Aug. 25, 1900, after 11 years of insanity. Prof. of classical philology at the Univ. of Basel 1869–79; he was at first a warm partisan of Wagner, whom he championed in *Die Geburt der Tragödie aus dem Geiste der Musik* (1872; 2nd ed., 1874) and *Richard Wagner in Bayreuth* (1876). In *Der Fall Wagner* and *Nietzsche contra Wagner* (both 1888) and *Götzendämmerung* (1889) he turned against his former idol and became a partisan of Bizet. Nietzsche was also a trained musician; he publ. 17 songs (1864) and *An das Leben* for chorus and orch. (1887); in MS are piano pieces (2 and 4 hands) and songs. His lieder have been edited by G. Göhler (Leipzig, 1924), and Complete Works by Curt Paul Jang (Basel, 1976).

BIBLIOGRAPHY: E. Förster-Neitzsche, *Das Leben F.N.s* (2 vols., Leipzig, 1895–1904; English transl. [condensed], N.Y., 1912–15); J. Zeitler, *N.s Ästhetik* Leipzig, 1900); Th. Lessing, *Schopenhauer, Wagner, N.* (Munich, 1906); H. Bélart, *F.N. und Richard Wagner* (Berlin, 1907); P. Lasserre, *Les Idées de N. sur la musique. La Période Wagnérienne (1871–9)* (Paris, 1907; new ed., 1930); E. Eckertz, *N. als Künstler* (Munich, 1930); H. Bélart, *F. N.s Freundschaftstragödie mit R. Wagner* (Dresden, 1912); E. Förster-Nietzsche, *Wagner und N. zur Zeit ihrer Freundschaft* (Munich, 1915); "Wagner and N. The Beginning and End of Their Friendship," *Musical Quarterly* (July 1918; selection from E. Förster-Nietzsche's book, transl. by C. V. Kerr); W. Dahms, *Die Offenbarung der Musik. Eine Apotheose F. N.s* (1922); L. Griesser, *N. und Wagner* (1923); K. Hildebrandt, *Wagner und N., ihr Kampf gegen das 19. Jahrhundert* (Breslau, 1924); H. Baugh, "N. and His Music," *Musical Quarterly* (April 1926); J. M. Verweyen, *Wagner und N.* (Stuttgart, 1926); E. Gürster, *N. und die Musik* (1929); J. G. Huneker, *Essays* (N.Y., 1929); G. B. Foster, *F. N.* (N.Y., 1931); P. G. Dippel, *N. und Wagner* (1934); E. Ruprecht, *Der Mythos bei Wagner und N.* (Berlin, 1938). See also *F. N.s gesammelte Briefe* (Berlin, 1900–1908; vol. III, 2, contains letters to Bülow, H. von Senger, and M. von Meysenbug; vol. IV, letters to P. Gast) and H. Daffner's ed. of *N.s Randglossen zu Bizets "Carmen"* (Regensburg, 1912). P. Gast's letters to N. were publ., in 1924 (vol. I).

Niewiadomski, Stanislaw, Polish composer and music critic; b. Soposzryn, Galicia, Nov. 4, 1859; d. Lwow, Aug. 15, 1936. He studied in Lwow (with Mikuli), Vienna (F. Krenn), and Leipzig (Jadassohn); 1886–87 and 1918–19, manager of the Lwow Opera; 1885–1914, music critic there; 1887–1914, teacher at the Lwow Cons.; 1918–21, editor of *Gazeta Muzyczna;* from 1919, music critic in Warsaw and teacher at the Cons. there; 1929, director of the Warsaw Music Institute. He composed numerous songs and piano pieces (about 500 works), and published biographies of Chopin and Moniuszko.

Nigg, Serge, French composer; b. Paris, June 6, 1924. He studied composition with Messiaen and Simone Pié at the Paris Cons. (1941–46); and privately with René Leibowitz, mainly on the Schoenbergian method of composition with 12 tones. Nigg became one of the earliest representatives of dodecaphony in France; however, under the influence of his political convictions, he abandoned the 12-tone method and began writing in a manner accessible to the large public. In 1959 he formed, with Durey and others, the Association of Progressive Musicians, advocating socialist realism in music.

WORKS: a symph. poem, *Timour* (1944); *Variations* for piano and 10 instruments (Paris, Jan. 29, 1947); *3 Mouvements symphoniques* (1947); *Pour un poète captif,* an appeal to the liberation of a radical poet imprisoned for political disturbances (1950); Piano Concerto No. 1 (Paris, Jan. 10, 1955); Violin Concerto No. 1 (1957); Violin Concerto No. 2 (Paris, May 27, 1960); *Hieronymus Bosch Symphony* (Strasbourg, June 21, 1960); Flute Concerto (1961); *Histoire d'œuf* for 2 speakers, percussion and piano (1961); *Visages d'Axel* (1967); *Fulgur* for band, percussion, 2 harps, piano, celesta and tubular chimes (Paris, Oct. 9, 1969); Piano Concerto No. 2 (1971); ballets, *Billard* (1951) and *L'Étrange Aventure de Gulliver à Lilliput* (1958); choral works: *Le Fusillé inconnu* (1949); cantata, *Les Vendeurs d'indulgences* (1953); *Le Chant de dépossédé* for speaker, baritone and orch. (1964); 2 piano sonatas and other piano works; songs.

BIBLIOGRAPHY: J. Roy, *Présences contemporaines de la musique française* (Paris, 1962; pp. 425–38).

Niggli, Arnold, Swiss writer and editor; b. Aarburg, Dec. 20, 1843; d. Zürich, May 30, 1927. He studied law at Heidelberg, Zürich, and Berlin. 1875–1909, secretary to the town council at Aarau; 1890–98, editor of the *Schweizerische Musikzeitung;* later, lived in Zürich. He publ. a valuable work, *Die Schweizerische Musikgesellschaft; eine musik- und kulturgeschichtliche Studie* (1886), a *Geschicte des Eidgenössischen Sängervereins, 1842–92,* and short studies of a number of great composers and performers (some of them in Waldersee's *Sammlung musikalischer Vorträge*).

Nikisch, Arthur, celebrated Hungarian conductor; b. Szent-Miklós, Oct. 12, 1855; d. Leipzig, Jan. 23, 1922. His father was head bookkeeper to Prince Lichtenstein. Nikisch attended the Vienna Cons., studying with Dessoff (composition) and Hellmesberger (violin), graduating in 1874. While still a student he had the honor of playing among the first violins under Wagner's direction at the laying of the cornerstone of the Bayreuth Theater (1872). He was at first engaged as a violinist in the court orch. (1874); then as second conductor at the Leipzig Theater. From 1882 to 1889 he was first conductor there. In 1889 he was engaged as conductor of the Boston Symph. Orch., with excellent success, remaining at this post until 1893. Returning to Europe he was music director of the Budapest Opera (1893–95); also conducted the Philharmonic Concerts there; from 1895, conductor of the Gewandhaus Concerts, Leipzig, succeeding Reinecke, and of the Philharmonic Concerts, Berlin. From 1897 he was in constant demand as visiting conductor, and made a number of extended tours with the Berlin Philharmonic Orch.; directed many of the concerts of the London Philharmonic Society, and works of Wagner and Richard Strauss at Covent Garden; in 1912 he made a tour of the U.S. with the entire London Symphony Orch. (85 performers). 1902–07, he was director of studies at the Leipzig Cons.; 1905–06, general director of the Stadttheater. As symphonic conductor he possessed an extraordinary romantic power of musical inspiration; he was the first of his profession that opened the era of "the conductor as hero," exercising a peculiar magnetism on his audiences equal to that of virtuoso artists; his personal appearence, a poetic-looking beard and flowing hair, contributed to his success.

BIBLIOGRAPHY: F. Pfohl, *Arthur Nikisch als Mensch und als Künstler* (Leipzig, 1900; new ed., 1925); I. Lipaiev, *Arthur Nikisch* (Moscow, 1904; in Russian); E. Segnitz, *Arthur Nikisch* (1920); A. Dette, *Arthur Nikisch* (1922); H. Chevalley, *Arthur Nikisch, Leben und Wirken* (1922; 2nd ed., 1925). His son **Mitja Nikisch** (b. Leipzig, May 21, 1899; d. Venice, Aug. 5, 1936) was an excellent pianist; toured South America in 1921; U.S. debut in New York, Oct. 23, 1923.

Nikolaidi, Elena, contralto; b. Izmir, Turkey, of Greek parents, June 13, 1909. She studied voice with Thanos Mellos, whom she married on April 27, 1936; made her operatic debut at the Vienna State Opera, Dec. 16, 1936; later sang in Salzburg, London, Prague, and Cairo; American debut (in a concert), N.Y., Jan. 20, 1949.

Nikolais, Alwin, American choreographer, stage director and composer of electronic ballet scores; b. Southington, Conn., Nov. 25, 1912. He studied piano; played in movie houses for the silent films. In 1929 he began to study dance with a pupil of Mary Wigman; became director of the Hartford Parks Marionette Theater and later chairman of the dance dept. of the Hartt School of Music in Hartford. In 1942–46 he served in military counterintelligence in Europe; then studied with Hanya Holm in New York. In 1948 he joined the dance faculty of the Henry Street Settlement and in 1949 became co-director of the Henry Street Playhouse in N.Y. His principal choreographic innovation is the technique of body extension by tubular projections and disks attached to the head, upper and nether limbs, so that a biped dancer becomes a stereogeometrical figure; often in his productions clusters of dancers form primitivistic ziggurats. His portrayal of extraterrestrial creatures in Menotti's children's opera *Help, Help, the Globolinks!* was acclaimed for its imaginative quality at its première at the Hamburg State Opera (Dec. 19, 1968).

Nikolayev, Leonid, Russian pianist and pedagogue; b. Kiev, Aug. 13, 1878; d. Tashkent, Oct. 11, 1942. He was a pupil of Sergei Taneyev and Ippolitov-Ivanov at the Moscow Cons.; then settled in St. Petersburg, where he became prof. of piano at the Cons. in 1906, achieving a fine reputation as a teacher; among his piano pupils was Shostakovich. Nikolayev went to Tashkent, Central Asia, after the German invasion of Russia in 1941, and died there shortly afterwards. He composed several symph. works; a *Hymn to Beauty* for soli, chorus, and orch.; a cello sonata; a violin sonata; a number of piano works (sonata, *Tarantella,* etc.); also a suite for 2 pianos; made arrangements for piano of organ works by Buxtehude and Pachelbel.

BIBLIOGRAPHY: S. Savshinsky, *Leonid Nikolayev* (Moscow, 1950).

Nikolayeva, Tatiana, Russian pianist and composer; b. Bezhitz, May 4, 1924. She studied at the Moscow Cons. with Goldenweiser (piano) and Golubev (compostion). After a highly successful series of concerts in Russia, she appeared in Prague (1948); at the bicentennial Bach festival in Leipzig (1950) she won 1st prize for her playing of Bach's clavier works. In 1953 she visited Iceland as a member of the Soviet delegation; in the same year also toured Siberia. Among her works are 2 piano concertos; Piano Sonata; *24 Concert Etudes,* for piano; Symphony; *Song of Happiness,* a cantata (1949); a vocal cycle, *Iceland* (1953); many piano pieces.

Nikolov, Lazar, Bulgarian composer; b. Burgas, Aug. 26, 1922. He studied composition with Vladigerov at the Bulgarian State Cons. in Sofia (1942–46); in 1961 joined its faculty. An experimenter by nature, he was one of the few composers in Bulgaria who adopted modern procedures of composition, melodically verging on atonality and harmonically on polytonality.

WORKS: 2 operas: *Prometheus Bound,* chamber opera (1963–69; Ruse, March 24, 1974) and *Uncles* (1975); 2 piano concertos: No. 1 (1947–48; Ruse, Nov. 21, 1949) and No. 2 (1954–55; Sofia, Feb. 28, 1963); Concerto for String Orch. (1949; Ruse, Nov. 30, 1951); Violin Concerto (1951–52; Varna, March 25, 1955); 2 symphonies: No. 1 (1953; Varna, Feb. 16, 1956) and No. 2, with 2 pianos (1960–61); Piano Concertino (1964); *Symphonies* for 13 strings (1965); *Divertimento concertante* for chamber orch. (1968); Cello Concertino (1973); *Chants* for soloists, chorus and chamber instrumental group (1969); Violin Sonata (1953–54); Viola Sonata (1955); Piano Quintet (1958–59); Flute Sonata (1962); Cello Sonata (1962); Clarinet Sonata (1962); 2 string quartets (1965; 1970); Sonata for 2 harps (1971); Double Bass Sonata (1972); Bassoon Sonata (1976); Oboe Sonata (1976); 4 piano sonatas (1950, 1952, 1955, 1964); 2-Piano Sonata (1952).

Niles, John Jacob, American folk singer and authority on folk music; b. Louisville, Kentucky, April 28, 1892. He studied at the Cincinnati Cons. and in France (Univ. and Cons. of Lyons; Schola Cantorum, Paris); made a special study of the music of the Southern Appalachians; made arrangements of some 1,000 folksongs and wrote choral works in folk style; published *7 Kentucky Mountain Songs* (1929); *7 Negro Exultations* (1929); *Songs of the Hill Folk* (1934); *10 Christmas Carols* (1935); *More Songs of the Hill Folk* (1936); *Ballads and Tragic Legends* (1937); *The Anglo-American Ballad Study Book* (1945); *The Anglo-American Carol Study Book* (1948); *The Shape-Note Study Book* (1950); etc. Also the song collections *Singing Soldiers* (1927) and *Songs My Mother Never Taught Me* (with Douglas Moore, 1929).

Nilius, Rudolf, Austrian conductor; b. Vienna, March 23, 1883; d. Bad Ischl, Dec. 31, 1962. He studied cello; was a member of the Vienna Philharmonic (1904–12); conducted the Tonkünstlerorchester in Vienna

(1912-21). In 1921 he founded in Vienna the Philharmonic Chamber Orch. Concerts.

Nilson, Leo, Swedish composer of electronic music; b. Malmö, Feb. 20, 1939. He studied organ and piano at the Music Academy in Stockholm; was briefly an organist of the Swedish church in Paris, where he was exposed to *musique concrète;* upon return to Sweden began writing electronic music for films, television, and various avant-garde exhibitions. His works include *Skorpionen* (1965), *Skulpturmusik I, II* and *III* (1966, 1967, 1968), *Satellitmusik* (1967), *That Experiment H₂S* (1968); *Sirrah* (1971), *Star-75,* multimedia work with dancers and sculptor (1975).

Nilsson, Birgit, celebrated Swedish dramatic soprano; b. near Karup, May 17, 1918. She studied singing in Stockholm. In 1947 she joined the Royal Opera; sang Elsa at the Bayreuth Festival in 1954, and Isolde in 1957 and 1959; she also appeared at La Scala, Milan. She made her U.S. debut at the Hollywood Bowl on Aug. 9, 1956; sang Wagnerian roles with the San Francisco Opera and the Chicago Lyric Opera. In London she sang Brünnhilde in a complete cycle of Wagner's tetralogy in 1957. She made her long-delayed debut with the Metropolitan Opera as Isolde in N.Y., on Dec. 18, 1959. At the peak of her career she was acclaimed as one of the greatest Wagnerian singers of all time.

Nilsson, Bo, Swedish composer of ultramodern tendencies; b. Skellefteaa, May 1, 1937. Largely autodidact, he experimented with techniques of serial compostion, the phonetic possibilities of vocal music and electronic sonorities; attended seminars on modern techniques in Cologne and Darmstadt. His works are constructed on precise quasi-mathematical, serial principles, and are often given abstract titles in German.

WORKS: *Frequenzen* for piccolo, flute, percussion, guitar, xylophone, vibraphone and double bass (1955-56); *Bewegungen (Movements)* for piano (1956); *Schlagfiguren* for piano (1956); *Buch der Veränderungen (Book of Changes)* for orch. (1957); *Zeiten im Umlauf (Times in Transit)* for 8 woodwinds (1957); *Kreuzungen (Crossings)* for flute, vibraphone, guitar and xylophone (1957); *Audiogramme* for tape (1957-58); *Ett blocks timme (Stunde eines blocks),* chamber cantata for soprano and 6 instrumentalists (1957-58); *20 Gruppen* for piccolo, oboe, and clarinet, or any three instruments (1958); *Quantitäten* for piano (1958); *Plexus* for orch. (1959); *Stenogramm* for percussion or organ (1959); *Reaktionen* for 1-4 percussionists (1960); *Szenes I-IV: I* for 2 flutes, 2 trumpets, piano, harp, and 2 percussionists (1960); *II* for 6 trumpets, 6 violins, 4 percussionists, piano, harp, celesta and vibraphone (1961); *III* for chamber orch. (1961); *IV* for saxophone, orch. and chorus (1974-75); *Versuchungen (Temptations)* for 3 orch. groups (1961); *La Bran* for chorus and orch. (1961); *Entrée* for tape and orch. (1963); *Litanei über das verlorene Schlagzeug (Litany for the Lost Drum)* for orch. without percussion, to conform to the title (1965); *Déjà-vu* for wind quartet (1967); *Revue* for orch. (1967); *Attraktionen* for string quartet (1968); *Design* for violin,

clarinet and piano (1968); *Rendez-vous* for piano (1968); *Quartets* for 36 winds, percussion and tape (1969); *Caprice* for orch. (1970); *Exit* for tape and orch. (1970); *Eurythmical Voyage* for piano, tape and orch. (1970); *Déjà-connu (Already Known)* for wind quintet (1973); *Nazm* for speakers, vocal soloists, chorus, orch. and tape (1972-73). He published an autobiography, under the title *Spaderboken* (Stockholm, 1966).

Nilsson, Kristina (Christine), Swedish soprano; b. Sjöabol, near Vexiö, Aug. 20, 1843; d. Stockholm, Nov. 22, 1921. Her teachers were Baroness Leuhausen, and F. Berwald at Stockholm; with him she continued study in Paris, and on Oct. 27, 1864, made her debut, as Violetta in *La Traviata,* at the Théâtre Lyrique, where she was engaged for three years. After successful visits to London, she was engaged 1868-70 at the Paris Opéra; then made long tours with Strakosch in America (1870-72), and sang in the principal Continental cities. In 1872 she married Auguste Rouzaud (d. 1882); her second husband (married 1887) was the Spanish count Angel Vallejo y Miranda. She revisited America in the winters of 1873, 1874, and 1884. Her voice was not powerful, but brilliant. She excelled as Marguerite and Mignon.

BIBLIOGRAPHY: B. Carlsson, *Kristina Nilsson* (Stockholm, 1922); T. Norlind, *Kristina Nilsson* (Stockholm, 1923); H. Headland, *Christine Nilsson, the Songbird of the North* (Rock Island, Ill., 1943).

Nilsson, Torsten, Swedish organist and composer; b. Höör, Jan. 21, 1920. He studied church music at the Royal College of Music in Stockholm (1938-42); served as church organist in Köping (1943-53), Hälsingborg (1953-62), and from 1962 in the Oscar Church in Stockholm. He excels in liturgical works; in his organ music he introduces many innovations, such as static tone-clusters and specified periods of thematic improvisation.

WORKS: 5 church opera-oratorios: *Ur jordens natt (Out of the Night of the Earth)* for improvising soli and vocal groups, with organ (Stockholm, April 12, 1968); *Dantesvit (Dante Suite)* for soli, vocal group, percussion, organ, harpsichord and tape (Stockholm, April 23, 1969); *Skapelse (The Creation)* for narrator, chorus, organ and instruments (Stockholm, May 11, 1970); *Ur jordens natt. Del 2 (Out of the Night of the Earth, Part 2;* Stockholm, April 12, 1974); *Den sista natten (The Last Night)* for 2 actors, mixed and children's chorus, flute, harp, organ and percussion (Stockholm, Nov. 25, 1973); Concerto for organ and 7 woodwinds (1963); *Caresser,* after Pablo Neruda, for baritone, chorus and instrumental ensemble (1969); *Verwerfungen* for organ and 13 percussion instruments (1970); *Non est Deus?* chamber oratorio on a Biblical text (1971-72); *Baltassan* for soli, chorus and organ (1972); *Steget over Troskelm (Over the Threshold),* concerto for piano, wind instruments, and percussion (1975); many songs.

Nin (y Castellanos), Joaquín, Spanish composer and pianist; b. Havana, Sept. 29, 1879; d. there, Oct. 24, 1949. He studied piano with Carlos Vidiella in Barcelona, and M. Moszkowski in Paris; composition with d'Indy at the Schola Cantorum; 1906–08, prof. there; 1908–10, in Berlin; then briefly in Havana and Brussels; lived for many years in Paris; member of the French Legion of Honor, Spanish Academy, etc. He was especially noted as an interpreter of early piano music.

WORKS: "mimodrama," *L'Autre;* for piano: *Suite de valses lyriques, Danza Ibérica, Message à Claude Debussy, "1830": Variations on a Frivolous Theme,* etc.; for violin and piano: *En el jardín de Lindaraja, Suite espagnole,* etc.; *Chants d'Espagne,* for cello; etc.; publ. several essays on general problems of esthetics, among them *Pour l'art* (Paris, 1909; English transl., London, 1915, as *In the Service of Art), Idées et commentaires* (1912), *Clavecin ou piano* (1921), and *Las Tres Grandes Escuelas.* He edited 2 valuable collections of Spanish keyboard music: *16 sonatas anciennes d'auteurs espagnols* (Paris, 1925) and *17 sonates et pièces anciennes d'auteurs espagnols* (Paris, 1929); also 10 violin pieces by Herrando, etc.

BIBLIOGRAPHY: R. Villar, *Músicos Españoles* (vol. II); H. Collet, *L'Essor de la musique espagnole au XXᵉ siècle* (Paris, 1929).

Nin-Culmell, Joaquín, Cuban-Spanish pianist and composer, son of **Joaquín Nin;** b. Berlin, Sept. 5, 1908. He studied piano in Paris at the Schola Cantorum, and later took private lessons with Alfred Cortot and composition at the Paris Cons. with Paul Dukas; in 1930–34 he had lessons in Granada with Manuel de Falla. He emigrated to the U.S. in 1936; was prof. of music and chairman of the music dept. of Williams College, Williamstown, Mass. (1940–49); in 1950 he was appointed to the faculty of the Univ. of California at Berkeley; emeritus in 1974. His music retains its national Spanish element, the main influence being that of Manuel de Falla, but he employs modern harmonies and characteristic asymmetrical rhythms of the cosmopolitan modern school. He was soloist in his own Piano Concerto at a concert of the Rochester, N.Y., Philharmonic in Williamstown, Mass. (Dec. 5, 1946); other works are the opera *La Celestina;* Cello Concerto (1963); Piano Quintet (1938); *Tonadas* for piano (4 books); *Dedication Mass* for mixed chorus and organ; *Jorge Manrique* for soprano and string quartet (1963); also several song cycles.

Nisard, Théodore, pen name of **Abbé Théodule-Eléazar-Xavier Normand,** French authority on Gregorian Chant; b. Quaregnon, near Mons, Jan. 27, 1812; d. Jacqueville, Seine-et-Marne, Feb. 29, 1888. He was a chorister at Cambrai, and also studied music at Douay; attended the priests' seminary at Tournai; and in 1839 was appointed director of Enghien Gymnasium, occupying his leisure with the study of church music. In 1842 he became 2nd chef de chant and organist at St. Germain des Prés, Paris; but soon devoted himself wholly to literary work; he publ. the first transcription of the Antiphonary of Montpellier (neumes and Latin letter notation from A to P), discovered by Danjou in 1847. Of his numerous books on plainchant the most important are a revised ed. of Jumilhac's *La Science et la pratique du plain-chant* (1847; with Le Clercq) and *Dictionnaire liturgique, historique et pratique du*

plain-chant et de musique d'église au moyen âge et dans les temps modernes (1854; with d'Ortigue). He also publ. *De la notation proportionelle au moyen âge* (1847); *Études sur les anciennes notations musicales de l'Europe* (1847); *Études sur la restauration du chant grégorien au XIXᵉ siècle* (1856); *Du rythme dans le plain chant* (1856); *Les Vrais Principes de l'accompagnement du plain-chant sur l'orgue d'après les maîtres des XVᵉ et XVIᵉ siècles* (1860); *Des chansons populaires chez les anciens et chez les Français* (1867); *L'Archéologie musicale et le vrai chant grégorien* (1890; 2nd ed., 1897).

Nissen, Georg Nikolaus, Danish Councillor of State; b. Hadersleben, Jan. 22, 1761; d. Salzburg, March 24, 1826. He married Mozart's widow in 1809, and collected materials for a biography of Mozart publ. by his widow in 1828 as *Biographie W. A. Mozarts nach Originalbriefen.*

Nissen, Hans Hermann, German baritone; b. Zippnow, near Marienwerder, West Prussia, May 20, 1893. He studied voice with Raatz-Brockmann in Berlin; made his debut in 1920 as concert singer; then sang opera at the Berlin Volksoper; in 1924 joined the staff of the Munich Opera; in 1930 went to the U.S., where he was a member of the Chicago Civic Opera (1930–32); on Nov. 23, 1938 made his debut at the Metropolitan Opera House as Wotan; he continued his professional career as a singer in Munich; was a member of the Bavarian State Opera in Munich until 1967, and remained there as a voice teacher.

Nixon, Roger, American composer; b. Tulare, California, Aug. 8, 1921. He studied clarinet with a local teacher; in 1940 attended a seminar in composition with Arthur Bliss at the Univ. of California, Berkeley, and in 1941 with Ernest Bloch. In 1942–46 he was in the U.S. Army; returned to Berkeley in 1947, where he had fruitful sessions with Sessions (Ph.D., 1952); in the summer of 1948 took private lessons with Schoenberg. Subsequently he joined the staff of San Francisco State College. A prolific composer, he writes in a consistent modern idiom anchored in fluctuating tonality and diversified by atonal protuberances. His music is marked by distinctly American melorhythms; his miniature opera, *The Bride Comes to Yellow Sky,* is an exemplar of adroit modernistic Westernism fashioned in non-ethnomusicological manner.

WORKS: String Quartet No. 1 (1949); *Air for Strings* (1952); Violin Concerto (1956); *The Wine of Astonishment,* cantata for baritone solo and mixed chorus (1960); *Reflections* for symphonic band (1962); *Elegiac Rhapsody* for viola and orch. (1962); *Three Dances* for orch. (1963); *Nocturne* for symph. band (1965); opera, *The Bride Comes to Yellow Sky* (Eastern Illinois Univ., Feb. 20, 1968; revised and performed by the San Francisco State College Opera Workshop, March 22, 1969); Viola Concerto (San Francisco, April 29, 1970); *A Solemn Processional* for symph. band (San Francisco, May 9, 1971); various pieces of chamber music; choruses; songs; piano pieces.

Noack, Friedrich, German musicologist; b. Darmstadt, July 10, 1890; d. there, Jan. 21, 1958. He studied musicology in Berlin with Kretzschmar, Stumpf, and J. Wolf. After World War I he studied at the Institute für Kirchenmusik in Berlin; then taught music subjects at the Univ. of Darmstadt; from 1947 until his death he taught at the Musikhochschule in Frankfurt. He was also on the staff of the Cons. of Mainz (1926-39) and at the Musikhochschule in Mannheim (1939-45) and at the Landesmusikschule in Darmstadt (1945-54). His publications include *Chr. Graupners Kirchenmusiken* (Leipzig, 1926); and numerous bibliographical articles in various German publications. He edited vols. 51 and 52 of *Denkmäler deutscher Tonkunst* and vol. 10 of the works of Telemann (Kassel, 1955); also revised vol. 1 (on the symphony) of Kretzschmar's *Führer durch den Konzertsaal* (1932).

Nobel, Felix de, Dutch pianist and choral conductor; b. Haarlem, May 27, 1907. He studied piano with Martha Autengruber and composition with Sem Dresden at the Amsterdam Cons. (1925-30); from 1930 to 1940 served as solo pianist for the Amsterdam Concertgebouw Wind Quintet; from 1939 to 1973 conducted The Netherlands Chamber Choir and taught song interpretation at the Amsterdam and The Hague Conservatories; in 1974 was appointed musical director of the Kurt Thomas Foundation in The Hague. He was chiefly known as an excellent accompanist for singers. He made arrangements of Dutch, Irish and Jewish folksongs for women's chorus. In 1965 he received the Elizabeth Sprague Colledge Memorial Medal.

Noble, Ray, English bandleader, composer, and arranger; b. near London, Dec. 17, 1903; d. Santa Barbara, California, April 3, 1978. He received a thorough musical training at Cambridge; formed a band in London, assembled mostly from hotel orchestra groups. Most of his arrangements were of English folk tunes; then he began to compose; among his most popular songs was *Goodnight, Sweetheart,* which subsequently became his theme song on American radio shows. In 1934 he went to the U.S.; Glenn Miller helped him to assemble musicians for his band, and he opened at the Rainbow Room in N.Y. on June 1, 1935, seated at a white grand piano on a rotating platform, making a tour among the guests at the floorside, and returning to the bandstand at the end of the number. He became extremely successful on network radio shows, appearing not only as a bandleader and composer but also as an actor, usually in the role of a comical Englishman. Besides his theme song—*Goodnight, Sweetheart*—he composed *The Very Thought of You, By the Fireside, The Touch of Your Lips,* and several other hit songs. His *Cherokee,* originally a section of an American Indian Suite, became a perennial favorite. Ray Noble demonstrated, in a chorus he wrote for 5 saxophones, his expertise in purely contrapuntal writing with a jazz flavor.

Noble, Thomas Tertius, English organist and composer; b. Bath, May 5, 1867; d. Rockport, Mass., May 4, 1953. He studied organ with Parratt at the Royal College of Music in London, where he also took courses in music theory with Bridge and Stanford. He was subsequently employed as a church organist in Colchester and Cambridge. In 1898 he organized the York Symph. Orch. which he conducted until 1912; then emigrated to America and served as organist at St. Thomas' Episcopal Church, N.Y., until 1947; he gave his final organ recital, playing his own works, in N.Y., Feb. 26, 1947. He published *The Training of the Boy Chorister* (N.Y., 1943).

Nobre, Marlos, Brazilian composer; b. Recife, Feb. 18, 1939. He studied piano and theory at the Pernambuco Cons. (1946-54); in 1960 went to Rio de Janeiro where he took composition lessons with H. J. Koellreutter; later studied with Camargo Guarnieri at the São Paulo Cons. (1963-64) and with Alberto Ginastera in Buenos Aires (1963-64); took a course in electronic music with Ussachevsky at Columbia Univ. (1969); Nobre was musical director of the National Symph. Orch. of Brazil (1971-76). Despite a somewhat quaquaversal efflux of styles and idioms to which he was exposed during his student days, he succeeded in forming a strongly individual manner of musical self-expression, in which sonorous and structural elements are effectively combined with impressionistic, pointillistic and serial techniques, supplemented by restrained aleatory procedures. He is one of the few contemporary Latin American composers who does not disdain to make use of native melo-rhythmic inflections, resulting in ingratiating harmoniousness. WORKS: Concertino for Piano and Strings (1959); *Variations* for solo oboe (1960); Piano Trio (1960); *Theme and Variations* for piano (1961); *16 Variations* for piano (1962); Solo Viola Sonata (1963); *Divertimento* for piano and orch. (Rio de Janeiro, Nov. 10, 1965); *Rhythmic Variations* for piano and percussion (1963); *Ukrínmakrinkrín* for soprano, wind instruments, and piano, to a text derived from primitive Brazilian Negro and Indian rituals (Buenos Aires, Nov. 20, 1964); *Modinha* for voice, flute and viola (1966); *Sonata breve* for piano (1966); *Canticum Instrumentale* for flute, harp, piano and timpani (1967); String Quartet No. 1 (1967); *Rhythmetron* for 32 percussion instruments (1968; choreographed, 1969); *Convergencias* for orch. (Rio de Janeiro, June 11, 1968); Wind Quintet (1968); *Tropicale* for flute, clarinet, piano and percussion (1968); *Desafio* for viola and string orch. (1968; Recife, Oct. 30, 1974); *Concerto breve* for piano and orch. (Rio de Janeiro, May 27, 1969); *Ludus Instrumentalis* for chamber orch. (1969); *Mosaico* for orch. (1970; Rio de Janeiro, May 12, 1970); *Biosfera* for string orch. (1970; Lisbon, Jan. 27, 1971); *Sonancias* for piano and percussion (1972); *O Canto Multiplicado* for voice and string orch. (1972); *In memoriam* for orch. (Rio de Janeiro, Sept. 18, 1976); Concerto for String Orch. (1975-76).

Nobutoki, Kiyoshi, Japanese composer and pedagogue; b. Osaka, Dec. 29, 1887; d. Tokyo, Aug. 1, 1965. He studied music in Japan and in Germany; composed a cantata, *Kaido Tosei* (Tokyo, Nov. 26, 1940) and other choral works; was primarily engaged in educational work in Tokyo.

Noda, Ken, a fantastically precocious Japanese-American pianist and composer; b. New York, Oct. 5, 1962. He studied piano with Adele Marcus in N.Y.; made his professional debut at 14 as soloist with the Minnesota Orch. in Beethoven's 3rd Piano Concerto (Minneapolis, May 14, 1977); later played with the New York Philharmonic, the St. Louis Symph., and the Baltimore Symph.; in the meantime he took composition lessons with Sylvia Rabinof and Thomas Pasatieri in N.Y. He was only 10 years old when his one-act opera, *The Canary,* was performed (to piano accompaniment) at the Music Festival in Brevard, North Carolina, on Aug. 18, 1973; the following year, it received 1st prize in the National Young Composers' Contest sponsored by the National Federation of Music Clubs; he wrote another one-act opera, *The Swing,* in 1974. So impressive were his achievements that in 1976 he was awarded a National Endowment of the Arts grant to write an opera titled *The Rivalry,* to his own libretto based on a story of Andrew Jackson. He also composed *A Zoo Suite* for piano (1973); Piano Sonatina (1974); *Prelude and Canon* for piano (1974); *An Emily Dickinson Song Cycle, A Christina Rossetti Song Cycle* and *A Cycle of German Poems* (all in 1977). With commendable modesty he acknowledges influences of Mozart, Verdi, Puccini, Rachmaninoff, Menotti, Barber and Pasatieri.

Noda, Teruyuki, Japanese composer; b. Mie Prefecture, June 15, 1940. He studied at the Tokyo Univ. of Arts with Tomojiro Ikenouchi and Akio Yashiro.
Works: *Symphony in One Movement* (1963); Trio for violin, horn and piano (1963); Quartet for horn, cello, timpani and piano (1965); *Choral Symphony* (Tokyo, July 10, 1968); *Mattinata (Morning Song)* for marimba, 3 flutes and contrabass (1968; Tokyo, Oct. 4, 1968); *A Mirror or A Journey,* symphonic radio piece with monologue (1968); 2 Quartets for Japanese instruments (1969, 1973); *Dislocation* for orch. Tokyo, Feb. 10, 1971); *Mutation* for 4 Japanese instruments and orch. (1971); *Shi-sha-no-Sho (Livre de Mort)* for mixed chorus (1971); Quartet No. 2 for Japanese instruments (1973).

Nodermann, Preben (Magnus Christian), Danish composer; b. Hjörring, Jan. 11, 1867; d. Lund, Nov. 14, 1930. He was a pupil of O. Malling in Copenhagen (1888–90); 1899–1903, organist in Malmö; then Kapellmeister at the Cathedral in Lund.
Works: the operas *King Magnus* (Hamburg, 1898), *Gunnlögs Saga* (publ. but not produced), *Rokoko* (Leipzig, 1923); an operetta, *Prinz Inkognito* (Copenhagen, 1909; publ. as *Die Jungfernstadt*); motets; sacred and secular choruses; pieces for violin and piano; organ preludes; etc. He made a new vocal score of Gluck's *Orfeo* (1906). Publ. *Tragedien om Orpheus och Eurydice af J. Celcius* (1901) and *Studier i svensk hymnologi* (1911).

Noelte, A. Albert, German-American music pedagogue and composer; b. Starnberg, March 10, 1885; d. Chicago, March 2, 1946. He went to the U.S. in 1901 and studied music and literature in Boston; in 1908 returned to Germany but frequently visited the U.S.; in 1931 settled there and was appointed prof. at Northwestern Univ., Evanston, Illinois. He earned a fine reputation as a teacher; many American scholars and composers were his pupils. He composed an orchestral piece, *Prologue to a Romantic Drama,* which was performed in Chicago on Jan. 16, 1941 and a number of other pieces of little consequence. His opera *François Villon* was produced in Karlsruhe in 1920.

Nohl, (Karl Friedrich) Ludwig, German writer on music; b. Iserlohn, Westphalia, Dec. 5, 1831; d. Heidelberg, Dec. 15, 1885. He studied jurisprudence at Bonn (1850), Heidelberg, and Berlin; entered the legal profession against his own desire, to please his father. In music he was instructed by Dehn, later (1857) by Kiel, in Berlin,. Having embraced music as his profession, he became lecturer at Heidelberg, 1860; associate prof. at Munich, 1865–8; retired to Badenweiler till 1872, when he settled in Heidelberg as a private lecturer, becoming prof. in 1880.
WRITINGS: (several also in English): *Mozarts Briefe* (1865; 2nd ed., 1877); *Briefe Beethovens* (1865); *Musikalisches Skizzenbuch* (1866); *Musiker-Briefe* (1867); *Beethovens Leben* (3 vols., 1867–77); *Neues Skizzenbuch* (1869); *Gluck und Wagner* (1870); *Die Beethoven-Feier und die Kunst der Gegenwart* (1871); *Beethoven, Liszt, Wagner* (1874); *Beethoven nach den Schilderungen seiner Zeitgenossen* (Stuttgart, 1877; in English as *Beethoven as Depicted by His Contemporaries,* London, 1880); *Mozart nach den Schilderungen seiner Zeitgenossen* (1880); *Richard Wagners Bedeutung für die nationale Kunst* (1883); *Das moderne Musikdrama* (1884); *Die geschichtliche Entwickelung der Kammermusik* (1885). For Reclam's *Universal-Bibliothek* he wrote *Allgemeine Musikgeschichte* and biographies of Beethoven, Mozart, Wagner, Haydn, Weber, Spohr, and Liszt.

Nolte, Ewald Valentin, American music educator; b. Utica, Nebraska, Sept. 21, 1909. He studied music with Albert Noelte (not related to Nolte) at Northwestern Univ., Evanston, Illinois (M. Mus., 1945; Ph.D., 1954), and with Paul Hindemith and Leo Schrade (1950–51) at Yale Univ. His professional career was devoted mainly to education and to conducting church choruses. From 1944 to 1964 he was on the music faculty of Northwestern Univ.; then at Salem College; from 1964–72, Director of the Moravian Music Foundation. He published a series of anthologies *Music for Young Americans;* arranged American folksongs; supplied accompaniments to hymns; composed choral sacred music; edited numerous works from the Moravian Foundation Archives.

Nono, Luigi, prominent Italian composer of the musical and political avant-garde; b. Venice, Jan. 29, 1924. He studied jurisprudence at the Univ. of Padua, graduating in 1946; then took lessons in composition with Malipiero at the Cons. of Venice; later studied advanced harmony and counterpoint with Bruno Maderna and Hermann Scherchen. During the final years of World War II he was a participant in the Italian Resistance movement against the Nazis. He became a member of the Italian Communist Party and in 1975 was elected to its Central Committee. In his compositions he adopted Schoenberg's method of 12-tone technique; his devotion to Schoenberg's ideas was strengthened by his marriage to Schoenberg's daughter Nuria. As a resolutely "engaged" artist Nono mitigates the antinomy between the modern idiom of his music and the conservative Soviet ideology of Socialist Realism by his militant political attitude and his emphasis on revolutionary subjects in his works, so that even extreme dissonances may be dialectically justified as representing the horrors of Fascism. Nono made 3 visits to the Soviet Union (1963, 1973, 1976) but his works are rarely, if ever, performed there. Nono makes use of a variety of techniques: serialism, "sonorism" (employment of sonorities for their own sake), aleatory and concrete music, electronics. Perhaps his most militant composition, both politically and musically, is *Intolleranza 1960*, to texts by Brecht, Éluard, Sartre and Mayakovsky, a protest against imperialist policies and social inequities; at its production in Venice on April 13, 1961, a group of neo-Fascists showered the audience with leaflets denouncing Nono for his alleged contamination of Italian music by alien doctrines, and even making a facetious allusion to his name as representing a double negative.

WORKS (besides *Intolleranza*): *Variazioni canoniche* for orch. based on the 12-tone row of Schoenberg's *Ode to Napoleon Buonaparte* (Darmstadt, Aug. 27, 1950); *Polifonica, Monodia, Ritmica* for flute, clarinet, bass clarinet, saxophone, horn, piano, and percussion (Darmstadt, July 10, 1951); *España en el corazón* (to words by F. G. Lorca) for voices and instruments (Darmstadt, July 21, 1952); ballet *Der rote Mantel* (Berlin, Sept. 20, 1954); *La Victoire de Guernica* for voices and orch. (1954); *Canti* for 13 instruments (Paris, March 26, 1955); *Incontri* for 24 instruments (Darmstadt, May 30, 1955); *Varianti*, for violin solo, strings, and woodwinds (Donaueschingen, Oct. 20, 1957); *La Terra e la compagna*, for soli, chorus, and instruments (Hamburg, Jan. 13, 1958); *Il Canto sospeso* for solo voices, chorus and orch., to texts from letters by young men and women condemned to death by the Fascists (Cologne, Oct. 24, 1956); *Sarà dolce tacere* for 8 solo voices to texts from "La Terra e la Morte" by Cesare Pavese (Washington, Feb. 17, 1961); *La fabbrica illuminata* for voice and magnetic tape (1964); music for the documentary play *Die Ermittlung* by Peter Weiss, dealing with the trial of Nazi guards (Frankfurt, Oct. 19, 1965); *Sul ponte di Hiroscima*, commemorating the victims of the atomic attack on Hiroshima, for soloists and orch. (1962); *A Floresta é jovem e cheja de vida*, oratorio to texts from declarations by the Vietnam guerrilla fighters (1966); *Per Bastiana* for electronic tape and 3 orchestral groups (1967); *Non consumiano Marx* for electronic sound (1968); *Voci destroying Muros* for women's voices and instruments in mixed media, featuring a machine gun pointed towards the audience (1970); *Y entonces comprendió* for voices and magnetic tape, dedicated to Ché Guevara (1970); *Ein Gespenst geht um in der Welt (A Spectre Rises Over Europe)*, to words from the Communist Manifesto, for voice and orch. (Cologne, Feb. 11, 1971); *Como una ola de fuerza y luz* for singer, piano, magnetic tape and orch. (1972); 2 piano concertos (1972, 1975).

Nordal, Jón, Icelandic composer; b. Reykjavik, March 6, 1926. He studied with Jón Thórarinsson at the Reykjavik School of Music; then in Zürich with Willy Burkhard (1949–51), and finally in Paris and Rome (1955–57). He taught at the Reykjavik School of Music before becoming its director in 1959, a post he still holds. He is a member of the modern group "Musica Nova," and in 1968 became a member of the Royal Swedish Academy. His early works are in the neo-Classical mold; in the course of time he adopted colorism in the French Impressionist vein.

WORKS: *Concerto Grosso* for orch. (1950); *Sinfonietta seriosa* (1954); Piano Concerto (1957); Concerto for Orch.; *Brotaspil (A Play of Fragments)* for orch. (1963); *Adagio* for flute, harp, piano and string orch. (1965); *Stiklur* for orch. (1969); *Canto elegiaco* for cello and orch. (1971); *Epitafion* for orch. (1974); *Langnaetti (The Long Night)* for orch. (1976); Violin Sonata; *Rórill* for flute, oboe, clarinet and bass clarinet.

Norden, Norris Lindsay, American composer and theorist; b. Philadelphia, April 24, 1887; d. there, Nov. 3, 1956. He studied with C. Rybner at Columbia Univ. (Mus. Bac., 1910; M.A., 1911); held various positions as church organist in Philadelphia, and conducted choral societies.

WORKS: He wrote several large works for chorus and orch.: *Thanatopsis* (1922); *Te Deum* (1923); *Charity* (1928); overtures; symph. poems, *Silver Plume* (1924), *The White Swan* (1936), etc.; publ. about 150 choral arrangements of sacred works by Russian and Scandinavian composers; also articles on music theory.

Nordgren, Pehr Henrik, Finnish composer; b. Saltvik, Jan. 19, 1944. He studied music with Joonas Kokkonen; traveled to Japan and took courses in Japanese music at the Tokyo Univ. of Arts and Music (1970–73). In his compositions he makes use of both advanced and traditional harmonies.

WORKS: *Euphonie I* for orch (1966–67); *Epiphrase* for orch. (1967); *Euphonie II* for orch. (1967); *Nattlig vaka (Nightly Wake)*, suite from music to the radio play by Nelly Sachs, for chamber ensemble (1967); *Minore* for orch. (1968); *Neljä kuolemankuvaa (4 Scenes of Death)* for chamber ensemble (1968); *The Turning Point* for orch. (Helsinki, March 14, 1974); *Autumnal Concerto* for Japanese instruments and orch. (Helsinki, Aug. 27, 1974); Symphony (1974); 2 string quartets (1967, 1968); *Sonatina per sestetto* for flute, clarinet, violin, cello, piano and percussion (1969); *Kolme Maanitusta (3 Enticements)* for wind quintet (1970); *Ritornello* for violin and piano (1970); *Hoichi the Earless* for piano (1972).

Nordheim, Arne, significant Norwegian composer; b. Larvik, June 20, 1931. He studied at the Oslo Cons. (1948–52) with Karl Andersen and Bjarne Brustad; in 1955 he took additional instruction with Holmboe in Copenhagen. Returning to Oslo, he joined the avant-garde circles; experimented in pointillistic tone color; adopted a motivic method of melorhythmic structures without formal development. He was a music critic for the Oslo daily *Dagbladet* and in 1968 visited the U.S. as a lecturer and composer.

WORKS: *Epigram* for string quartet (1954); String Quartet (1956); *Aftonland (Evening Land)*, song cycle for soprano and chamber ensemble (1957); *Canzona per Orchestra* (Bergen, June 11, 1961); *Katharsis*, ballet based on the legend of St. Anthony, for orch. and tape (1962); *Kimaere*, ballet (1963); *Partita* for viola, harpsichord and percussion (1963); *Epitaffio* for orch. and tape (1963); *Favola*, musical play for soloists, chorus, orch. and tape (1965); the electronic pieces, *Evolution* (1966), *Warsawa* (1967-68), *Solitaire* (1968), *Pace* (1970) and *Lux et tenebrae* (1971); 3 *Responses* for percussion groups and tape (1967); *Eco* for soprano, chorus, and orch. (1967-68); *Colorazione* for Hammond organ, 2 percussionists and tape (1967-68); *Signaler* for accordion, percussion and electric guitar (1967); incidental tape music for Ibsen's *Peer Gynt* (1969); *Floating* for orch. (Graz, Oct. 20, 1970); *Dinosaurus* for accordion and tape (1971); *Listen* for piano (1971); *Partita II* for electric guitar (1971); *Greening* for orch. (Los Angeles, April 12, 1973); *Zimbel* for orch. (1974); *Spur* for accordion and orch. (1974); *Doria* for tenor and orch. (1974-75).

Nordica, Lillian (real name **Lillian Norton**), distinguished American soprano; b. Farmington, Maine, Dec. 12, 1857; d. Batavia, Java, May 10, 1914. She studied with John O'Neill at the New England Cons., Boston; made her concert debut in Boston, 1876, and toured with the Handel and Haydn Society. In 1878 traveled to Europe as soloist with Gilmore's band. She then studied operatic roles with Antonio San Giovanni in Milan, who suggested the stage name Nordica, which she used for her operatic debut there on March 8, 1879, as Elvira in *Don Giovanni*. In St. Petersburg, she sang for Czar Alexander II a week before he was assassinated in March, 1881. After making appearances in several German cities, she made her Paris debut on July 22, 1882, as Marguerite, at the Opéra; on Jan. 22, 1883 she married Frederick A. Gower. With him she returned to America and made her American debut with Colonel Mapleson's company in N.Y. on Nov. 23, 1883. In 1884 she began proceedings for divorce from her first husband, but he mysteriously disappeared while attempting to cross the English Channel in a balloon. She first sang at the Metropolitan Opera House, N.Y., on March 27, 1890. She was heard for the first time as Isolde at the Metropolitan Opera House on Nov. 27, 1895, scoring an overwhelming success. From then on she sang chiefly Wagner roles; she remained at the Metropolitan Opera House until 1909, when she began to make extended concert tours. Her farewell appearance was in Reno, Nevada, June 12, 1913. In 1896 she married the Hungarian tenor Zoltan Doeme, from whom she was divorced in 1904; in 1909, she married the banker George W. Young in London. She died while on a trip around the world.
BIBLIOGRAPHY: Ira Glackens, *Yankee Diva; Lillian Nordica and the Golden Days of Opera* (N.Y., 1963).

Nordoff, Paul, American composer; b. Philadelphia, June 4, 1909; d. Herdecke, West Germany, Jan. 18, 1977. He studied piano with Olga Samaroff and composition with Rubin Goldmark at the Juilliard School of Music in New York (1928-33). He subsequently taught composition classes at the Philadelphia Cons. (1937-42), at Michigan State College (1945-49) and at Bard College (1949-59); afterwards devoted himself mainly to music therapy and work with mentally retarded children, in Germany, Finland, and England. He held two Guggenheim Fellowships (1933, 1935).
WORKS: *The Masterpiece*, opera in one act (Philadelphia, Jan. 24, 1941); a secular Mass for mixed chorus and orch. (1934); *The Sun*, cantata with eurhythmic ballet (1945); *Winter Symphony* (1955); *The Frog Prince* for narrator and orch. to his own text (1955); Violin Concerto; 2 piano concertos; Piano Quintet; string quartets and other chamber music; song cycles and piano pieces. He published *Music Therapy for Handicapped Children* (with C. Robbins; N.Y.; 2nd edition, London, 1971, with a preface by Benjamin Britten) and *Music Therapy in Special Education* (N.Y., 1971).

Nordquist, Johan Conrad, Swedish conductor; b. Vänersborg, April 11, 1840; d. there, April 16, 1920. He was a pupil of the Music Academy in Stockholm (1856); joined the court orch. in 1859 as viola player; 1864, regimental bandmaster; 1876, chorus master at the Royal Opera; 1885, court conductor; 1888-92, general director. From 1870 to 1872 and again from 1880 to 1900 he taught at the Stockholm Cons.; then occupied various posts as organist and conductor. He wrote a funeral march for the obsequies of Charles XV (1872) and a festival march for the golden wedding anniversary of Oscar II (1897), besides piano pieces and songs.

Nordraak, Rikard, the composer of the Norwegian national hymn, *Ja, vi elsker;* b. Christiania, June 12, 1842; d. Berlin, March 20, 1866. He was a pupil of Kiel and Kullak in Berlin; composer of strong Norwegian nationalist tendency; a close friend of Grieg, upon whom he exerted a considerable influence and who wrote a funeral march in his memory. His death at the age of 23 was a grievous loss to Norway's music. Besides the Norwegian national anthem, he wrote music to Björnson's *Mary Stuart in Scotland;* also songs and piano pieces.
BIBLIOGRAPHY: L. Greni, *Rikard Nordraak* (Oslo, 1941); A. van E. Sein, *Rikard Nordraak* (Oslo, 1942); also articles by Ö. Anker in *Norsk Musikkgranskning* for 1940.

Noren, Heinrich Gottlieb (real name **Heinrich Suso Johannes Gottlieb**—in 1916 he added his wife's name Noren to his own), Austrian composer; b. Graz, Jan. 5, 1861; d. Rottach, Bavaria, June 6, 1928. He studied violin with Vieuxtemps in Brussels (1878) and with Massart in Paris (1883); music theory with Bussler in Berlin; in 1895 he settled in Krefeld, where he founded his own music school. He then taught at Stern's Cons. in Berlin (1902-07); in 1915 he moved to Rottach. His name attracted attention with the performance of his orchestral variations *Kaleidoskop* (Dresden, July 1, 1907), in which the last movement, dedicated to "a famous contemporary," was a variation on a theme from *Ein Heldenleben* by Richard Strauss. The publishers of Strauss instituted a lawsuit against Noren, which created a ripple of excitement in musical circles. He also composed an opera, *Der Schleier der Beatrice;* a symphony; violin concerto and some chamber music.

Norena, Eide (real name **Kaja Hansen Eide**), Norwegian soprano; b. Horten, April 26, 1884; d. Switzerland, Nov. 19, 1968. She studied voice in Oslo, then in Weimar, London, and Paris; pupil of Raimund von Zur Mühlen; began her career as a concert singer in Scandinavia, later joining the Oslo Opera Co.; sang at La Scala, Milan, then at Covent Garden; 1926-32, member of the Chicago Civic Opera; from 1932, of the Metropolitan Opera Company (debut as Mimi, Feb. 9, 1933); from 1935, of the Paris Opéra; toured the U.S. in concert.

Nørgaard, Per, prominent Danish composer; b. Gentofte, near Copenhagen, July 13, 1932. He studied music theory at the Royal Danish Music Cons. in Copenhagen with Holmboe, Høffding and Hjelmborg (1952-56) and also took courses with Nadia Boulanger in Paris (1956-57). Returning to Denmark, he taught at the Funen Cons. (1958-60), the Royal Cons. (1960-65) and since 1965 at the Aarhus Cons. After a period of adolescent emulation of Sibelius, he plunged into the mainstream of cosmopolitan music making, exploring the quasi-mathematical serial techniques based on short tonal motives, rhythmic displacement, metrical modulation, pointillism, graphic notation and a "horizontal" invariant fixing certain notes to specific registers; then shifted to a pointillistically impressionistic colorism evolving in a tonal bradykinesis.

WORKS: 2 operas: *The Labyrinth* (1963; Copenhagen, Sept. 2, 1967) and *Gilgamesh* (1971-72; Aarhus, May 4, 1973); 3 ballets: *Le Jeune Homme à marier* (*The Young Man Is to Marry,* after Ionesco, 1964; Danish television, April 2, 1965; first stage performance, Copenhagen, Oct. 15, 1967), *Tango Chicane* (Copenhagen, Oct. 15, 1967) and *Trio* for 3 dancers and percussion (Paris, Dec., 1972); 3 oratorios: *It Happened in Those Days,* Christmas oratorio for youth (1960); *Dommen (The Judgement),* Easter oratorio for youth (1962); *Babel* (1964; Stockholm, Sept. 15, 1966); *Metamorphose* for strings (1952); 3 symphonies: No. 1, *Sinfonia austera* (1954; Danish Radio, Aug. 19, 1958); No. 2 (1970; Aarhus, April 13, 1970); No. 3, with chorus and organ (1972-75; Copenhagen, Sept. 2, 1976); *Triptychon* for mixed voices, and wind instruments or organ (1957); *Constellations,* concerto for 12 solo strings or 12 string groups (Copenhagen, Nov. 3, 1958); *Lyse Danse* for chamber orch. (1959); *Fragment VI* for 6 orch. groups: winds, brass, percussion, harp, pianos, timpani (1959-61; Aarhus, Feb. 12, 1962); *Nocturnes,* suite for soprano, and piano or 19 instruments (1961-62); *3 Love Songs* for contralto and orch. (1963); *Prism* for 3 vocalists and instrumental ensemble (1964); *Composition* for small orch. (1966); *Iris* for orch. (Copenhagen, May 19, 1967); *Luna, 4 Phases,* for orch. (Danish Radio, Sept. 5, 1968); *Recall* for accordion and orch (1968); *Voyage Into the Golden Screen* for chamber orch. (Copenhagen, March 24, 1969); *Mosaic* for 16 winds (1969); *Doing* for wind orch. (1969); *Lilá* for 11 instruments (1972); Quintet for flute, violin, viola, cello and piano (1951-52); *Suite* for flute and piano (1952); *Solo intimo* for solo cello (1953); *Diptychon* for violin and piano (1953); 2 trios for clarinet, cello and piano (1955, 1974); *Songs from Aftonland* for contralto, flute, harp, violin, viola and cello (1956); 3 string quartets: No. 1, *Quartetto Brioso* (1958); No. 2, *In 3 Spheres* (1965); No. 3, *Inscape* (1969); *Miniatures* for string quartet (1959); 2 piano sonatas (1952, 1957); *Trifoglio* for piano (1953); *4 Sketches* and *9 Studies* for piano (1959); *Travels* for piano (1969); electronic pieces; incidental music; songs.

Nørholm, Ib, Danish composer; b. Copenhagen, Jan. 24, 1931. He studied with Bjørn Hjelmborg and Vagn Holmboe at the Royal Danish Cons. in Copenhagen (1950-54); became a church organist in Elsinore (1957-63) and then in Copenhagen; taught at the Royal Cons. and later at the Funen Cons. in Odense; wrote music criticism. His musical idiom is permeated with Scandinavian lyricism, even when he introduces modernistic devices.

WORKS: opera, *Invitation to a Beheading,* after Vladimir Nabokov's novel (1965, Danish Television, Oct. 10, 1967); chamber opera, *Den unge Park* (*The Young Park;* Aarhus, Oct. 14, 1970); 3 symphonies: No. 1 (Danish Radio, Aug. 13, 1959); No. 2, *Isola Bella* (Copenhagen, April 27, 1972); No. 3, *Day's Nightmare* (Copenhagen, Oct. 9, 1973); *Fluctuations* for 34 solo strings, 2 harps, harpsichord, mandolin and guitar (1962); *Relief I* and *II* for chamber ensemble (both 1963) and *III* for orch. (1964); *Serenade of Cincinnatus* for chamber orch. (1964); *Exile* for orch. (Copenhagen, Sept. 8, 1966); *Efter Ikaros (After Icarus),* suite for orch. (1967); *Heretic Hymn,* fresco for orch. (1974); *Jongleurs-69* for soloists, chorus, ensembles, loudspeaker voice and orch. (Odense, Nov. 25, 1969); *Tys og lovsang (Light and Hymn of Thanksgiving)* for solists, chorus, organ and instrumental ensemble (Copenhagen Cathedral, Dec. 5, 1972); *Day's Nightmare II* for soloists, chorus and orch. (Copenhagen, Nov. 29, 1973); *Rhapsody* for viola and piano (1955); 4 string quartets: No. 1, *In Vere* (1955), No. 2, *5 Impromptus* (1965), No. 3, *From My Green Herbarium* (1966) and No. 4, *September—October—November* (1966); *Tombeau* for cello and piano (1956); Violin Sonata (1956-57); Trio for clarinet, cello and piano (1957); *Mosaic Fragments* for flute and string trio (1958); Piano Trio (1959); *Signature from a Province* for piano (1970); songs.

Norlind, (Johan Henrik) Tobias, Swedish musicologist; b. Hvellinge, May 6, 1879; d. Uppsala, Aug. 13, 1947. He studied piano and music in Lund; then went to Germany where he took courses in composition with Jadassohn at the Leipzig Cons. (1897-98) and with Thuille in Munich (1898-99), also studied musicology with Sandberger at the Munich Univ., and subsequently with Friedlaender at the Univ. of Berlin. Returning to Sweden in 1900, he attended the universities of Uppsala and Lund, obtaining the degree of Dr. phil. in 1909. He then held several positions as instructor in colleges and universities; in 1921 he was appointed prof. of music history at the Royal Academy of Music, Stockholm.

WRITINGS: *Svensk musikhistoria* (Stockholm,

1901; German translation, abridged, 1904); *Musiken vid svenska skolor under 1600 talet* (1906); *Beethoven* (1907); *Allmänt Musiklexikon* (2 vols., 1916; new ed., 1927; exceedingly valuable for Scandinavian and Finnish music); *Jenny Lind* (1919); *Wagner* (1923); *Svensk Folkmusik och folkdans* (1930); *Bilder ur svenska musikens historia*, in 4 vols. (1947); numerous articles on Swedish music in various European publications.

Norman, (Fredrik Vilhelm) Ludvig, Swedish conductor; b. Stockholm, Aug. 28, 1831; d. there, March 28, 1885. He studied piano and composition at the Leipzig Cons. with Moscheles, Hauptmann, and Rietz (1848–52); returning to Stockholm, he became in 1859 conductor of the newly formed Philharmonic Society. He married the violinist **Wilma Neruda** in 1864 (divorced, 1869). He composed 4 symphonies; Piano Concerto; String Octet; Piano Sextet; 11 books of songs; and piano pieces; also published *Musikaliska Uppsatser och Kritiker* (posthumous; Stockholm, 1888).

North, Alex, American composer and conductor; b. Chester, Pa., Dec. 4, 1910. He studied at the Curtis Institute in Philadelphia and at the Juilliard School of Music in New York; also took private lessons with Ernst Toch in Los Angeles. He began his career as a composer for documentary films and gradually established himself as a composer of imaginative cinema music; wrote the scores for *Death of a Salesman, Viva Zapata!, A Streetcar Named Desire, The Bad Seed, The Sound and the Fury, Spartacus, The Misfits, Cleopatra, The Agony and the Ecstasy* and *Who's Afraid of Virginia Woolf?* His song *Unchained Melody* acquired great popularity. Apart from these lucrative tasks, he composed grand symphonies, modernistic concertos and unorthodox cantatas.
WORKS: *Rhapsody* for piano and orch. (N.Y., Nov. 11, 1941); *Revue* for clarinet and orch. (N.Y., Nov. 20, 1946, Benny Goodman soloist, Leonard Bernstein conducting); Symph. No. 1 (1947); *Morning Star Cantata* (N.Y., May 18, 1947); *Little Indian Drum* for narrator and orch. (N.Y., Oct. 19, 1947); *Negro Mother Cantata* (N.Y., May 17, 1948); *Holiday Set* for orch. (Saratoga, N.Y., July 10, 1948); Symph. No. 2 (1968); Symph. No. 3 (1971; incorporating parerga & paralipomena from the score originally written for the film *2001, a Space Odyssey*, which was not used in the actual production).

North, Roger, English musician; b. Tostock, Suffolk, Sept. 3, 1653; d. Rougham, March 1, 1734. He was a solicitor; rose to be named Attorney-General to King James II; music was his avocation. He publ. *Memoires of Musick* and *Musicall Gramarian*, containing comments on the musical mores of his era.
BIBLIOGRAPHY: J. Wilson, ed., *Roger North on Music; Being a Selection from His Essays Written During the Years c.1695–1728* (London, 1959).

Noskowski, Sigismund (Zygmunt von), significant Polish conductor and composer; b. Warsaw, May 2, 1846; d. there, July 23, 1909. He studied at the Warsaw Musical Institute; then became an instructor in a school for the blind, and devised a music notation for the blind. He subsequently went to Germany where he studied composition with Kiel in Berlin. After a brief period of professional activities in western Europe he returned to Warsaw and was director of the Music Society there (1881–92); in 1888 he was appointed prof. of the Warsaw Cons.; later conducted at the Warsaw Opera and led some concerts of the Warsaw Philharmonic Society. He wrote the operas *Livia Quintilla* (Lemberg, 1898), *Wyrok* (Warsaw, 1906) and *Zemsta* (Warsaw, 1909); 3 symphonies (1875, 1880, 1903); and several symph. poems, of which *Step* (1897) became quite popular in Poland; also chamber music and songs. He publ. 2 collections of folk melodies and was co-author with M. Zawirski of a book on harmony and counterpoint (Warsaw, 1909).

Notker (Balbulus), a monk at the Monastery of St. Gall; b. Elgg, near Zürich (or Jonschwyl, near St. Gall), c.840; d. April 6, 912. He was one of the earliest and most important writers of sequences. Several short musical treatises in Latin and German are traditionally ascribed to him; but these should be more correctly attributed to a certain **Notker Labeo,** who was also a monk at St. Gall, but who flourished about a century later than Notker "Balbulus" (a nickname meaning "the stammerer"). It has also been established that he was not the author of the *Media in vita in morte sumus* (cf. P. Wagner, "Das Media vita," in *Schweizerisches Jahrbuch für Musikwissenschaft* I). Gerbert (*Scriptores* I) publ. 4 of the abovementioned treatises, together with a commentary on the so-called "Romanian" letters (this is probably a forgery). Two of these treatises, also a fifth one (presumably also by N. Labeo), are included in Riemann's *Studien zur Geschichte der Notenschrift*. All 5 treatises were publ. by Piper in 2 vols. as part of the projected collected edition of Notker Labeo's works.
BIBLIOGRAPHY: A. K. Henschel, *Zehn Sequenzen des Notker Balbulus, aus den ältesten Quellen übertragen und mit der Überlieferung verglichen* (dissertation, Erlangen, 1924); R. van Doren, *Étude sur l'influence musicale de l'Abbaye de St. Gall* (1925); H. Husmann, "Die St. Galler Sequenztradition bei Notker und Ekkehard," *Acta Musicologia* 26 (1954).

Nottebohm, Martin Gustav, German musicologist; b. Lüdenscheid, Westphalia, Nov. 12, 1817; d. Graz, Oct. 29, 1882. He was a pupil of Berger and Dehn at Berlin, 1828–29; of Schumann and Mendelssohn at Leipzig, 1840; and 1846 of Sechter at Vienna, where he settled as a music teacher and writer.
WRITINGS: *Ein Skizzenbuch von Beethoven* (1865); *Thematisches Verzeichniss der im Druck erschienenen Werke von Beethoven* (2nd ed., 1868; reprint 1913); *Beethoveniana* (2 vols., 1872, 1887); *Beethovens Studien* (vol. I, 1873; Beethoven's exercises, etc., under Haydn, Albrechtsberger, and Salieri); *Thematisches Verzeichniss der im Druck erschienenen Werke von Franz Schubert* (1874); *Mozartiana* (1880); *Ein Skizzenbuch von Beethoven aus dem Jahre 1803* (1880). Paul Mies republished 2 of Nottebohm's eds. of Beethoven's sketchbooks as *Zwei Skizzenbücher von Beethoven aus den Jahren 1801 bis 1803* (Leipzig, 1924).

Nouguès, Jean, French composer; b. Bordeaux, April 25, 1875; d. Auteuil, Aug. 28, 1932. He showed remarkable precocity as a composer, having completed an opera, *Le Roi du Papagey,* before he was 16. After regular study in Paris he produced his opera *Yannha* at Bordeaux in 1897. The next two operas, *Thamyris* (Bordeaux, 1904) and *La Mort de Tintagiles* (Paris, 1905), were brought out without much success; but after the production of his spectacular *Quo Vadis* (text by H. Cain after Sienkiewicz's famous novel; Nice, Feb. 9, 1909) he suddenly found himself famous. The work was given in Paris on Nov. 26, 1909, in New York on April 4, 1911; had numerous revivals in subsequent years. His later operas failed to measure up to *Quo Vadis;* they included *L'Auberge rouge* (Nice, Feb. 21, 1910), *La Vendetta* (Marseilles, 1911), *L'Aiglon* (Rouen, Feb. 2, 1912), and *Le Scarabée bleu* (1931).

Nourrit, Adolphe, celebrated French tenor; b. Montpellier, March 3, 1802; d. (suicide) Naples, March 8, 1839. His father **Louis Nourrit** (1780–1831) was a leading opera tenor in France; Adolphe Nourrit studied voice with the famous teacher Manuel García; at the age of 19 he made his debut as Pylaides in Gluck's opera *Iphigénie en Tauride* at the Paris Opéra (Sept. 10, 1821) with excellent success. He soon became known in Paris as one of the finest tenors of his generation, and famous opera composers entrusted him with leading roles at the premières of their works; thus he appeared in the title role of Meyerbeer's *Robert le Diable* (Paris, Nov. 21, 1831) and as Raoul in *Les Huguenots* (Paris, Feb. 29, 1836); in the title role in Rossini's *Le Comte Ory* (Paris, Aug. 20, 1828) and as Arnold in his *Guillaume Tell* (Paris, Aug. 3, 1829); as Masaniello in Auber's *La Muette de Portici* (Paris, Feb. 29, 1828); as Eléazar in Halévy's *La Juive* (Paris, Feb. 23, 1835), and others. He then traveled in Italy, and was particularly successful in Naples. His career seemed to be assured, but despite all these successes he fell into a state of depression and killed himself by jumping from the roof of his lodging in Naples.

BIBLIOGRAPHY: L.M. Quicherat, *Adolphe Nourrit* (3 vols., Paris, 1867); E. Boutet de Monvel, *Un Artiste d'autrefois, Adolphe Nourrit* (2 vols. Paris, 1903); F. Rogers, "Adolphe Nourrit," *Musical Quarterly* (Jan. 1939).

Nováček, Ottokar, American violinist and composer of Czech descent; b. Weisskirchen, Hungary, May 13, 1866; d. New York, Feb. 3, 1900. He studied violin with his father, Martin Joseph Nováček, and Brodsky at the Leipzig Cons., graduating in 1885. In 1891 he was engaged by Nikisch to join the Boston Symph. Orch., of which Nikisch was the musical director. In America Nováček began to compose; his name became known chiefly through his brilliant violin piece *Perpetuum mobile;* he also wrote a piano concerto; 3 string quartets; 8 *Concert-Caprices* for violin and piano; *Bulgarian Dances* for violin and piano; and songs.

Nováček, Rudolf, Czech violinist and composer; b. Bela Crkva, April 7, 1860; d. Prague, Aug. 12, 1929. He lived mostly in Temesvár; also held occasional positions as violin teacher and conductor in Rumania, Bulgaria and Russia. His *Sinfonietta* for wind instruments (first performed in Prague, Nov. 11, 1888) became popular.

Novaes, Guiomar, Brazilian concert pianist; b. São João da Boã Vista, Feb. 28, 1896. She began to play the piano as a small child and made her first public appearance at the age of 8. In 1909 she entered the competition for a scholarship at the Paris Cons., winning over 380 rivals. In Paris she studied with Isidor Philipp, graduating in 1911 with first prize. Still very young, she embarked on a successful concert career; made her debut in N.Y. on Nov. 11, 1915. In 1922 she married the Brazilian composer **Octavio Pinto.** She subsequently settled permanently in New York.

Novák, Jan, Czech composer; b. Nová Říše, April 8, 1921. He studied piano with local teachers, and composition with Petrželka at the Brno Cons. (1940–46) and with Bořkovec at the Prague Academy of Musical Arts (1946–47); during the summer of 1947 he attended the composition classes of Aaron Copland at the Berkshire Music Center at Tanglewood, Mass., and also took lessons with Martinu in N.Y. (1947–48). Returning to Czechoslovakia he lived in Brno; but left the country in the wake of the political events of 1968; moved to Denmark (1968–70) and in 1970 settled in Rovereto, Italy, where he taught piano at the municipal music school.

WORKS: Oboe Concerto (1952); *Balletti* for nonet (1955); Concerto for 2 Pianos and Orch. (1955); *Toccata chromatica* for piano (1957); Concertino for wind quintet (1957); *Capriccio* for cello and orch. (1958); *Musica Caesariana* for wind orch. (1960); *Passer Catulli* for bass singer and 9 instruments (1961); *Ioci vernalis* for bass, 8 instruments and bird songs on tape (1964); *Testamentum* for chorus and 4 horns (1956); *Dido,* oratorio (1967); *Ignis pro Ioanne Palach,* cantata (1968; Prague, April 15, 1969); *Mimus magicus* for soprano, clarinet and piano (1969); *Rondini,* 8 rondos for piano (1970); *Concentus Eurydicae* for guitar and string orch. (1970); *Orpheus et Eurydice* for soprano, viola d'amore and piano (1971); *Invitatio pastorum,* cantata (1971) *Panisci fistula,* 3 preludes for 3 flutes (1972); *Rosarium,* exercise for 2 guitars (1972); choruses; songs.

Novák, Johann Baptist, Slovenian composer; b. Ljubljana, 1756; d. there, Jan. 29, 1833. He served as a government clerk and at the same time studied music; was music director of the Philharmonic Society in Ljubljana (1808–25), and gave concerts as a singer and violinist. A close contemporary of Mozart, he composed in a Mozartean manner. His historical importance lies in his incidental music to *Figaro,* a play in the Slovenian language based on the same comedy by Beaumarchais that served for Mozart's great opera. Novák's music forms a striking parallel to Mozart's procedures and yet contains some original traits.

BIBLIOGRAPHY: Dragotin Cvetko, "J. B. Novák— Ein slowenischer Anhänger Mozarts," *Bericht über den Internationalen Musikwissenschaftlichen Kongress Wien, Mozartjahr, 1956.*

Novák, Milan, Slovak composer; b. Trahovice, Aug. 12, 1927. He studied piano with Kafenda; composition with Alexander Moyzes and conducting with Talich at the Bratislava Cons. In 1955 he was appointed conductor of the Military Artistic Ensemble in Bratislava.

WORKS: 2 ballets: *Where the Play Ends* (1964) and *Ballad about a Tree* (1967); Concertino for trumpet, strings, piano 4 hands, and percussion (1964); *Reminiscences* for cello and orch. (1969); Concerto for Harp and Chamber Orch. (1972); *Mountains and the Heart,* song cycle for bass and orch. (1973); *Thirty Happy Years,* cantata for children's chorus and orch. (1975); *So That There is Life on Earth,* cantata (1976); Clarinet Sonatina (1959); Cello Sonatina (1961); String Quartet (1975); *Music* for flute and string quartet (1975); music for theater and films.

Novák, Vítězslav, eminent Czech composer; b. Kamenitz, Dec. 5, 1870; d. Skuteč, July 18, 1949. He studied jurisprudence and philosophy at the Univ. of Prague and music at the Cons. there where his teachers were Jiránek, Stecker and Dvořák. From 1909 to 1920 he taught at the Prague Cons., and from 1918 to 1939 was prof. of composition at the Master School of the Czech State Cons. Brahms was the first to discover the extraordinary talent of Novák and recommended him to his own publisher Simrock. Novák's early works follow the general line of German romantic composition, but in his operas and symphonic poems he showed a profound feeling for national elements in Czech music. In 1946 he received the title of National Artist of the Republic of Czechoslovakia.

WORKS: OPERAS: *Zvikovský rarášek (The Imp of Zvikov;* Prague, Oct. 10, 1915); *Karlštejn* (Prague, Nov. 18, 1916); *Lucerna* (Prague, May 13, 1923); *Děduv Odkaz (Old Man's Bequest;* Brno, Jan. 16, 1926); TWO BALLETS: *Signorina Gioventù* and *Nikotina* (both performed in Prague on Feb. 10, 1929); FOR ORCH.: *Slovácka Suite* (Prague, Feb. 4, 1906); *Lady Godiva,* overture (Prague, Nov. 24, 1907); *V Tatrach (In the Tatra Mountains;* Prague, Dec. 7, 1907); *Toman a lesní panna* (Prague, April 5, 1908); *Podzimni Symfonie (Autumn Symphony;* Prague, Dec. 18, 1934); *De Profundis* (Brno, Oct. 9, 1941); *Majova Sinfonie (May Symphony,* in celebration of the liberation of Prague by the Soviet Army in May, 1945; dedicated to Stalin; Prague, Dec. 5, 1945); the cantata, *Boure* (Brno, April 14, 1910); *12 Ukolébavek (12 Lullabies),* variations on a poem for women's voices (Prague, 1938; CHAMBER MUSIC: Piano Trio; Piano Quartet; Piano Quintet; 2 string quartets; *Trio quasi una ballata;* Sonata for viola, cello and piano; numerous piano pieces, among them *Ballade, Czech Dances, Sonata eroica, Pan, Suite exoticon,* 6 sonatinas, etc. *St. Wenceslas Triptych* for organ; songs.

BIBLIOGRAPHY: Z. Nejedlý, *Vítězslav Novák* (Prague, 1921); K. Hoffmeister, *Tvorba V. Nováka, z let 1941–1948* (Prague, 1949); Bohumir Štědroň, *Vítězslav Novák v obrazech* (Prague, 1967); Vladimir Lebl, *Vítězslav Novák,* in English (Prague, 1968).

Novello, Clara Anastasia, daughter of **Vincent Novello;** English soprano; b. London, June 10, 1818; d. Rome, March 12, 1908. Having studied piano and singing in London, she entered the Paris Cons. in 1829, but returned home the following year because of the revolution. After a successful debut on Oct. 22, 1832, at Windsor, she was engaged for the Philharmonic Society, the Antient Concerts, and the principal festivals. In 1837 Mendelssohn engaged her for the Gewandhaus concerts; she then sang in Berlin, Vienna, and St. Petersburg. She made her operatic debut in Padua (July 6, 1841); sang with great success in the principal Italian cities. On Nov. 22, 1843, she married Count Gigliucci, withdrawing to private life for several years; reappeared in 1850, singing in concert and opera (chiefly in England and Italy). After her farewell appearance in London in 1860, she retired to Rome. Schumann greatly admired Clara Novello, and coined the term Novelette for some of his pieces as an affectionate homage to her.

BIBLIOGRAPHY: Valeria Gigliucci, *Clara Novello's Reminiscences, compiled by her daughter* (London, 1910; with memoir by A. D. Coleridge); Averil Mackenzie-Grieve, *Clara Novello* (London, 1955).

Novello & Co., prominent firm of music publishers, founded 1811 in London by Vincent Novello. Under the management of his eldest son, **Joseph Alfred Novello,** the business increased enormously, and after the latter's retirement in 1856 **Henry Littleton** (d. London, May 11, 1888), who for some years had been a partner, assumed the general management, becoming sole proprietor in 1866. The following year he acquired the business of Ewer and Co., and in 1867 changed the name of the firm to **Novello, Ewer & Co.** On his retirement in 1887 he was succeeded by his sons, **Alfred H.** and **Augustus J. Littleton,** and his sons-in-law, **George T. S. Gill** and **Henry W. Brooke.** In 1898 the house was formed into a limited company, under the name of Novello & Co., Ltd. In 1846 they acquired *Mainzer's Musical Times* (established 1844), which they have publ. since then as the *Musical Times.* The New York branch, established in 1850, was taken over in 1906 by H. W. Gray & Co.

BIBLIOGRAPHY: J. Bennett, *A Short History of Cheap Music as Exemplified in the Records of the House of Novello, Ewer & Co.* (1887); "The Novello Centenary," *Musical Times* (June 1911).

Novello-Davies, Clara, Welsh singing teacher and choral conductor; b. Cardiff, April 7, 1861; d. London, March 1, 1943. Her real surname was Davies; her father (who was also her first teacher) called her "Clara Novello" after the celebrated singer of that name, and she adopted the combined name professionally. She sang at concerts; in 1881 she turned to choral conducting; organized a Royal Welsh Ladies' Choir, with which she traveled with fine success in Great Britain, France, America, and South Africa; at the World's Fair in Chicago (1893) and at the Paris Exposition of 1900 the chorus was awarded 1st prize. She was commended by Queen Victoria (1894) and by King George and Queen Mary (1928). She publ. a number of successful songs (*A Voice from the Spirit Land, The Vigil, Comfort,* etc.). Author of the book *You Can Sing* and an autobiography, *The Life I Have Loved* (London, 1940). Her son, **Ivor Novello** (b. Cardiff, Jan. 15, 1893; d. London, March 6, 1951), wrote (at her request) the song *Keep the Home Fires Burning*, immensely popular during the World War of 1914–18.

Novello, Joseph Alfred, English music publisher, son of **Vincent Novello**; b. London, Aug. 12, 1810; d. Genoa, July 16, 1896. He was also a bass singer, organist, and composer; choirmaster at Lincoln's Inn Chapel. He entered his father's business at 19. He inaugurated an important innovation, the printing of separate vocal parts for choir use; did much to popularize classical music in England by publishing cheap oratorio scores. After retirement he lived in Genoa.

Novello, Vincent, English music publisher; b. London, Sept. 6, 1781; d. Nice, Aug. 9, 1861. He was a chorister in the Sardinian Chapel, Duke St.; later deputy organist to Webbe and Danby, and 1797–1822 organist at the chapel of the Portuguese Embassy. He was pianist to the Italian Opera, 1812; co-founder of the Philharmonic Society, sometimes conducting its concerts; 1840–43, organist at the Roman Catholic Chapel, Moorfields. In 1811 he founded the great London music publishing firm of Novello & Co. Himself a composer of sacred music (Masses, motets, anthems, Kyries, etc), he gathered together and published excellent collections: *A Collection of Sacred Music* (1811; 2 vols.); *Purcell's Sacred Music* (1829; 5 vols.); *Croft's Anthems; Greene's Anthems; Boyce's Anthems; Masses* by Haydn, Mozart, Beethoven; etc. He retired to Nice in 1849. See **Novello & Co.**
BIBLIOGRAPHY: Mary Cowden-Clarke, *Life and Labours of Vincent Novello* (London, 1862); W. Barclay Squire, "Some Novello Correspondence," *Musical Quarterly* (April 1917); *Dictionary of National Biography*, vol. XLI; also N. Medici and R. Hughes. *A Mozart Pilgrimage* (London, 1955; travel diaries of Vincent Novello and his wife).

Noverre, Jean-Georges, the French dancer who introduced the dramatic action into the ballet (ballet-pantomime); b. Paris, April 29, 1727; d. St.-Germain-en-Laye, Nov. 19, 1810. He was a solo dancer at Berlin; ballet master at the Opéra-Comique, Paris, 1749; at London, 1757–75; at Lyons, Stuttgart, Vienna, Milan, and (1775–80) at the Grand Opéra, Paris. He publ. *Lettres sur la danse, et sur les ballets* (1760, several eds.; English transl., London, 1782, 1930, 1951).
BIBLIOGRAPHY: C.E. Noverre, *Life and Works of the Chevalier Noverre* (London, 1882); H. Abert, "Jean Georges Noverre und sein Einfluss auf die dramatische Ballet-Komposition," *Jahrbuch Peters* (1908); H. Niedecken, *J. G. Noverre; sein Leben und seine Beziehungen zur Musik* (Halle, 1914); D. Lynham, *The Chevalier Noverre* (London, 1950).

Novikov, Anatoly, Russian composer; b. Skopin, Oct. 30, 1896. He studied at the Moscow Cons. with Glière, Vasilenko and Catoire; devoted himself to organizing chorus groups in the Soviet Military Academy; composed a number of patriotic songs which entered the Soviet popular repertory, among them *Five Bullets*; wrote the political cantata *We Need Peace* (1954), *Hymn of the Democratic Youth of the World; My Fatherland, Russia; March of Communist Brigades*; etc.; also some lively musical comedies. On the occasion of

his 80th birthday in 1976 he was awarded the order of Hero of Socialist Labor, the order of Lenin and the gold medal, Sickle and Hammer.

Novotná, Jarmila, Czech soprano; b. Prague, Sept. 23, 1903. She studied with Emmy Destinn; made her debut in *La Traviata* (Prague, June 27, 1926); in 1928 joined the roster of the Berlin State Opera. She made her American debut at San Francisco, in *Madama Butterfly* (Oct. 18, 1939); first sang at the Metropolitan Opera, N.Y., in *La Bohème*, Jan. 5, 1940; remained on its staff until 1956; then retired to Vienna.

Novotný, Václav Juda, Bohemian composer; b. Wesetz, near Počatek, Sept. 17, 1849; d. Aug. 1, 1922. He studied at the Prague Organ School with Skuhersky; for many years editor of the Bohemian musical paper *Dalibor*; composed pieces for violin and songs; made a large collection of Bohemian folksongs; transl. into Czech about 100 opera texts, among them all the dramatic works of Wagner.

Nowak, Leopold, eminent Austrian music bibliographer; b. Vienna, Aug. 17, 1904. He studied at the Univ. of Vienna (Dr. phil., 1932); in 1932 he joined the staff there; from 1946 to 1969 he was director of the music division of the National Library in Vienna; in 1954 he became the editor of the collected works of Bruckner. A Festschrift was presented to him in 1964 on his 60th birthday. He published a number of valuable monographs on music; these include *Grundzüge einer Geschichte des Basso ostinato in der abendländischen Musik* (Vienna, 1932); *Franz Liszt* (1936); *Te Deum laudamus* (on the music of Bruckner; Vienna, 1947); *Joseph Haydn* (Zürich, 1951; 3rd ed., 1959); *Anton Bruckner* (Vienna, 1964); *Gegen den Strom. Leben und Werk von E. N. von Reznicek* (with Reznicek's daughter; Zürich, 1960); he was the compiler of valuable catalogues at special exhibitions in Vienna, among them one on Haydn and one on Bruckner.

Nowak, Lionel, American composer and pianist; b. Cleveland, Sept. 25, 1911. He studied piano with Beryl Rubinstein and Edwin Fischer; composition with Herbert Elwell and Quincy Porter; also had fruitful sessions with Sessions. Upon graduation from the Cleveland Institute of Music in 1936 he was music director for the Humphrey-Weidman Dancers; then taught at Converse College, South Carolina (1942–46) and at Syracuse Univ. (1946–48); in 1948 he was appointed to the faculty of Bennington College, and was still prof. of piano there in 1978.
WORKS: Concertino for Piano and Orch. (1944); Oboe Sonata (1949); 3 cello sonatas (1950, 1951, 1960); *Diptych* for string quartet (1951); Trio for Clarinet, violin and cello (1951); Quartet for oboe and strings (1952); Sonata for solo violin unaccompanied (1952); Piano Trio (1954); *Concert Piece* for kettledrums and string orch. (1961).

Nowowiejski, Felix, Polish composer; b. Wartenburg, Feb. 7, 1877; d. Poznań, Jan. 18, 1946. He studied with Bussler at Stern's Cons. in Berlin; won the Paderewski Prize in 1903. He lived mostly in Berlin; after World War I he taught organ and church music at the State

Cons. in Poznań (1920–27). A competent composer, he followed the line of German romanticism.

WORKS: an opera *Legenda Baltyku (Baltic Legend)*, which was produced in Poznan in 1924; 5 symphonies; 3 symph. poems; Piano Concerto (1941); Cello Concerto (1938) and a considerable amount of chamber music. His best known work was the oratorio *Quo vadis* (1907) after Sienkiewicz's novel.

BIBLIOGRAPHY: Jan Boehm, *F. Nowowiejski* (Olsztyn, 1968).

Nucius (Nucis), Johannes, German composer and theorist; b. Görlitz, c.1563; d. Himmelwitz, March 25, 1620. In 1591 he became a Cistercian monk in the monastery of Rauden; from 1609, abbot of the monastery of Himmelwitz in Silesia. He published *Modulationes sacrae,* 5–6 voices (1591), and 2 books of *Sacrae cantiones* (1609); 2 of his Masses are in MS. Also publ. a theoretical work, *Musices poeticae sive De compositione cantum praeceptiones ultissimae* (1613).

BIBLIOGRAPHY: B. Widmann, *Johannes Nucius, Abt von Himmelwitz* (Bregenz, 1921); E. Kirsch, *Von der Persönlichkeit und dem Stil des Johannes Nucius* (1926).

Nuitter (real name **Truinet**), **Charles Louis Etienne,** French writer on music; b. Paris, April 24, 1828; d. there, Feb. 23, 1899. He was a lawyer by profession; then became interested in the theater; was custodian of the archives of the Paris Opéra. He changed his real name, **Truinet,** to Nuitter by anagrammatic transposition of letters, and under that name wrote librettos for many operas and operettas, including some by Offenbach; also translated librettos of operas by Weber, Mozart, Wagner, and Verdi; wrote scenarios for Delibes (*Coppélia*) and others. He publ. *Le Nouvel Opéra* (1875); *Les Origines de l'opéra français* (1886; with Thoinan); many articles in music magazines.

Nunn, Edward Cuthbert, English organist, conductor, and composer; b. Bristol, Feb. 23, 1868; d. London, Nov. 26, 1914. He studied at the Royal Academy of Music; then served as organist at various churches, and conducted opera. He composed the children's operas: *Kamar-al-Zaman, The Fairy Slipper, The Shepherdess and the Sweep, The Garden of Paradise, The Wooden Bowl;* also cantatas and other choral works.

Nunó, Jaime, Spanish bandmaster; composer of the Mexican national anthem; b. San Juan de las Abadesas, Sept. 8, 1824; d. Auburndale, N.Y., July 18, 1908. He studied with Mercadante in Italy; in 1851 went to Cuba, and in 1853 to Mexico, where he was appointed chief of military bands; was commissioned to write a national anthem for Mexico; it was sung for the 1st time on Sept. 15, 1854. Subsequently he was active as impresario for Italian opera companies in Cuba, Mexico, and the U.S.

Nussio, Otmar, Italian composer; b. Grosseto, Oct. 23, 1902. He studied flute, piano and composition at the Cons. in Milan and with Respighi in Rome. He conducted concerts of light music and wrote a number of overtures and orchestral suites, among them

Escapades musicales (1949); *Tzigana* (1954); *Portraits musicaux* (1955); *Episodio* (1958); *Monologhi di vita e di morte* (1958) and *Alborada* (1971); also a Flute Concerto (1936); Piano Concerto (1960); *Passatempo donchisciottesco* for clarinet and orch. (1971); *Cantata ticinese* for voices and orch. (1962). His suite for harpsichord, flute, violin solo, and strings, *Rubensiana,* was performed for the first time in the Rubens House in Antwerp, on May 21, 1950.

Nyiregyházi, Erwin, remarkable Hungarian pianist; b. Budapest, Jan. 19, 1903. He absorbed music by a kind of domestic osmosis, from his father, a professional tenor, and his mother, an amateur pianist. An exceptionally gifted wunderkind, he had perfect pitch and a well-nigh phonographic memory as a very small child; played a Haydn sonata, pieces by Grieg, Chopin and some of his own at a concert in Fiume at the age of 6. In 1910 he entered the Budapest Academy of Music, studying theory with Albert Siklós and Leo Weiner and piano with István Tomán. In 1914 the family moved to Berlin, where he became a piano student of Ernst von Dohnányi. He made his debut in Germany playing Beethoven's 3rd Piano Concerto with the Berlin Philharmonic (Oct. 14, 1915). In 1916 he began studying with Frederick Lamond, a pupil of Liszt, who was instrumental in encouraging Nyiregyházi to study Liszt's music, which was to become the most important part of his concert repertoire. In 1920 he went to the U.S.; his American debut (N.Y., Carnegie Hall, Oct. 18, 1920) was sensationally successful; the word "genius" was freely applied to him by critics usually restrained in their verbal effusions. Inexplicably, his American career suffered a series of setbacks; he became involved in a lawsuit with his manager; he married his next manager, a Mrs. Mary Kelen, in 1926, but divorced her a year later. He then went to California where he became gainfully employed as a studio pianist in Hollywood; in 1930 he made a European tour; then lived in New York and in Los Angeles. Beset by personal problems, he fell into a state of abject poverty, but resolutely refused to resume his concert career; he did not even own a piano. He married frequently, and as frequently divorced his successive wives. In 1972 he married his 9th wife, a lady 10 years his senior; she died shortly afterwards. Attempts were made in vain by friends and admirers in California to induce him to play in public; a semi-private recital was arranged for him in San Francisco in 1974; a recording of his playing Liszt was issued in 1977; it was greeted with enthusiastic reviews, all expressing regret of his disappearance from the concert stage. Nyiregyházi composed several hundred works, mostly for piano; they remain in manuscript. As a child, Nyiregyházi was the object of a "scientific" study by Dr. Géza Révész, director of the Psychological Laboratory in Amsterdam, who made tests of his memory, sense of pitch, ability to transpose into different keys at sight, etc.; these findings were published in German as *Psychologische Analyse eines musikalisch hervorragenden Kindes* (Leipzig, 1916) and in English as *The Psychology of a Musical Prodigy* (London, 1925), but the examples given and the tests detailed in the book proved to be no more unusual than the capacities of thousands of similarly gifted young musicians.

Nystedt, Knut, Norwegian composer, organist and choral conductor; b. Oslo, Sept. 3, 1915. He studied organ with A. Sandvold, conducting with Fjeldstad, and composition with Per Steenberg and Bjarne Brustad at the Oslo Cons. (1931–43); then organ with E. White and composition with Aaron Copland in New York (1947). Returning to Norway, he became organist at the Torshov Church in Oslo; in 1950 he organized the Norwegian Soloist Choir and took it on a series of successful tours in Europe and in the U.S. He gave lectures on Norwegian music in Long Beach, California, in 1962; conducted a musical seminar in Minneapolis in 1964; was composer-in-residence at Berea College, Kentucky, in 1968 and at Augsburg College, Minnesota, in 1969. As a composer, he continues the tradition of Scandinavian romanticism.

WORKS: Christmas opera, *Med krone og stjerne (With Crown and Star,* 1971); *Høgfjell (The Mountains),* suite for orch. (1940–41); *Naadevegen,* oratorio (1943–46); *Norge, mitt land (Norway, My Country)* for chorus and orch. (1944); *Concerto Grosso* for 3 trumpets and strings (1946); *Spenningens land (Land of Suspense),* symph. fantasy (1947; Oslo, Sept. 29, 1948); *Festival Overture* (1950); *Symphony for Strings* (1950; 2 earlier symphonies were withdrawn); Concertino for clarinet, English horn and strings (1952); *De syv segl (The Seven Seals),* visions for orch. (1958–60); *Collocations* for orch. (1963); *Lucis Creator Optime* for soloists, chorus, organ and orch. (1968); *Spes mundi,* Mass for chorus, church play group, Orff school instruments, trumpet, organ liturgist and congregation (1970); *Mirage* for orch. (1974); 4 string quartets (1938, 1948, 1956, 1966); Violin Sonata (1941); numerous organ pieces; *The Moment* for soprano, celesta and percussion (1962); *Suoni* for flute, marimba and female chorus (1970); *Pia memoria,* requiem for 9 winds (1971); church motets; a hymn *De Profundis,* his most popular work (1964).

Nystroem, Gösta, Swedish composer; b. Silvberg, Oct. 13, 1890; d. Särö, near Göteborg, Aug. 9, 1966. He studied piano with his father and theory with Hallen. In 1919 he went to Paris, where he took courses with Vincent d'Indy, Chevillard, and the Russian musician Leonid Sabaneyev, then living in France. In 1932 he returned to Sweden. His music is marked with Romantic tendencies, tinged with Impressionism.

WORKS: radio drama, *De Blinda (The Blind,* 1949); ballet, *Ungersvennen och de sex Prinsessorna (The Young Lad and the 6 Princesses,* 1951); radio opera, *Herr Arnes Penningar (Sir Arne's Hoard),* based on a novel by Selma Lagerlöf (Swedish Radio, Nov. 26, 1959). FOR ORCH.: *Rondo capriccioso* for violin and orch. (1917); symph. poem, *Is havet (The Arctic Ocean,* 1924); symph. poem, *Babels torn (The Tower of Babel,* 1928); 2 concertos for string orch. (1930, 1955); 6 symphonies with subtitles: No. 1, *Sinfonia breve* (1931; Göteborg, Oct. 19, 1932); No. 2, *Sinfonia espressiva* (1932–35; Göteborg, Feb. 18, 1937); No. 3, *Sinfonia del Mare,* with soprano solo (1947–48; Stockholm, March 24, 1949); No. 4, *Sinfonia Shakespeareana* (1952; Göteborg, Nov. 5, 1952); No. 5, *Sinfonia seria* (1963; Stockholm, Oct. 9, 1963); No. 6, *Sinfonia Tramontana* (1965; Stockholm, Oct. 30, 1966); 4 suites of incidental music: No. 1, *Konungen (The King,* 1933), after Lagerkvist; No. 2, *The Tempest* (1934), after Shakespeare; No. 3, *Bödeln (The Hangman,* 1935); No. 4, *The Merchant of Venice* (1936), after Shakespeare; *Suite* for small orch. (1950); *Partita* for flute, strings and harp (1953); Violin Concerto (1954); *Concerto ricercante* for piano and orch. (1959; Stockholm, May 15, 1960); *Summer Music* for soprano and orch. (1964); 2 string quartets (1956, 1961); 3 *Havsvisioner (Visions of the Sea)* for a cappella chorus (1956); piano pieces, among them the sentimental *Regrets* (1923; also for orch.); songs.

O

Oakeley, Sir Herbert Stanley, English composer; b. Ealing, Middlesex, July 22, 1830; d. London, Oct. 26, 1903. He studied at Oxford; later attended the Leipzig Cons.; also took organ lessons in Dresden and Bonn. In 1865 he was appointed prof. of music at Edinburgh Univ., and held this post until 1891; was influential in the musical affairs of Scotland in general. He wrote a cantata, *Jubilee Lyric; Suite in the Olden Style,* for orch.; many pieces of church music; choruses, arrangements of Scottish national melodies, etc.

BIBLIOGRAPHY: E. M. Oakeley, *The Life of Sir H. S. Oakeley* (London, 1904).

Oberhoffer, Emil Johann, German conductor; b. near Munich, Aug. 10, 1867; d. San Diego, Calif., May 22, 1933. He received his musical training from his father, an organist; learned to play violin and organ; later studied piano in Paris with Isidor Philipp. He then came to the U.S.; in 1897 settled in St. Paul, Minnesota; became conductor of the Philharmonic Choral Society in Minneapolis (1901); succeeded in securing an endowment for the establishment of a permanent orch.; gave his first concert with the newly organized Minneapolis Symph. Orch. on Nov. 5, 1903; led it until 1923; then retired, and lived in California. See J.T. Howard in *Dictionary of American Biography,* Supplement I.

Oberthür, Karl, German harp player and composer; b. Munich, March 4, 1819; d. London, Nov. 8, 1895. He studied with Elise Brauchle and G. V. Röder in Munich; after playing at various theaters in Switzerland and Germany, he went to London in 1844; established himself as a teacher in London. He wrote 2 operas; several cantatas; a symph. legend, *Lorelei,* for harp and orch.; a nocturne for 3 harps; many elegant soli for harp (*Élégie, Pensées musicales, Réveil des elfes, Miranda, Le Sylphe,* etc.).

Obin, Louis-Henri, French bass singer; b. Ascq, near Lille, Aug. 4, 1820; d. Paris, Nov. 11, 1895. From 1844 till 1869 he was a renowned singer at the Paris Opéra; after his retirement from the stage, he taught at the Paris Cons. (1871–91).

Oborin, Lev, Russian pianist; b. Moscow, Sept. 11, 1907; d. Moscow, Jan. 5, 1974. He studied at the Moscow Cons. with Igumnov, graduating in 1926; in 1928, was appointed instructor in piano there; received various prizes as pianist, but dedicated himself mainly to teaching.

Obouhov, Nicolas, remarkable Russian composer; b. Moscow, April 22, 1892; d. Paris, June 13, 1954. He studied at the St. Petersburg Cons. with Nicolas Tcherepnin and Maximilian Steinberg; after the revolution he emigrated to France and lived in Paris, where he had some instruction from Ravel. As early as 1914 he began experimenting with harmonic combinations containing 12 different notes without duplication (he called his system "absolute harmony"). In 1915 he devised a special notation for this type of harmony, entirely enharmonic, with crosses indicating sharps or flats; several composers, among them Honegger,

wrote pieces in Obouhov's notation. He gave a demonstration of his works written and notated in this system in Petrograd at a concert organized by the editors of the review *Muzykalny Sovremennik* on Feb. 3, 1916. He devoted his entire life to the composition of his magnum opus, *Le Livre de Vie,* for solo voices, chorus, 2 pianos and orch. The manuscript score, some 2000 pages long, was deposited after his death at the Bibliotèque Nationale in Paris. A mystic, Obouhov signed his name "Nicolas l'illuminé" and used his own blood to mark sections in the score; the finale represented the spiritual and religious apotheosis in which both the old and the new Russian societies and political factions become reunited. In this and some other scores Obouhov introduced shouting, screaming, sighing and groaning sounds for the voice parts. A section of *Le Livre de Vie* was performed by Koussevitzky in Paris on June 3, 1926. In quest of new sonorities Obouhov devised an electronic instrument "croix sonore" in the form of a cross and composed works for it, which were performed by Mme. Aussenac de Broglie. He published *Traité d'harmonie tonale, atonale et totale* (Paris, 1946), which presents an exposition of his system.

BIBLIOGRAPHY: Boris de Schloezer, "Nicolas Obouhov," *Revue Musicale* (1921); C. Laronde, *Le Livre de vie de Nicolas Obouhow* (Paris, 1932).

Oboussier, Robert, Swiss composer; b. Antwerp (of Swiss parents), July 9, 1900; d. (stabbed to death by his roommate), Zürich, June 9, 1957. He studied at the Cons. of Zürich, with Volkmar Andreae and Philipp Jarnach (composition); then with Siegfried Ochs in Berlin (conducting). He then lived in Florence (1922–28); was music editor of the *Deutsche allgemeine Zeitung* but in 1938 political conditions in Germany impelled him to leave for Switzerland; in 1942 he became director of the Central Archive of Swiss Music. Of cosmopolitan background, he combined in his music the elements of both Germanic and Latin cultures. His collection of critical reviews, *Berliner Musik-Chronik 1930–38* was publ. posthumously in 1969.

WORKS: opera, *Amphitryon* (Berlin, March 13, 1951); *Trilogia sacra,* for chorus and orch. (1929); Piano Concerto (1933; rev., 1944); Symphony (1936); *Antigone,* cantata (1939); Violin Concerto (1953); *3 Psalms,* for soli, chorus, and orch. (1947); *Vie et mort,* song cycle for contralto; piano pieces.

BIBLIOGRAPHY: K. H. Wörner, "Robert Oboussier," *Musica* (Oct. 1954).

Obradović, Aleksandar, Serbian composer; b. Bled, Aug. 22, 1927. He studied composition with Logar at the Belgrade Academy of Music, graduating in 1952; had advanced studies with Lennox Berkeley in London (1959–60); traveled to Russia in 1963; spent a year in the U.S. studying at the Columbia Univ. electronic music center in N.Y. (1966–67); in 1969 he was appointed prof. at the Belgrade Academy of Music. Formally, his music adheres to the architectonic Classical design with strongly discernible tonal centers, but he experiments with atonal thematics and polytonal harmonies; in some of his works he applies explicit dodecaphonic formulas.

WORKS: a ballet, *Prolećni uranak* (*Spring's Awakening*, 1949); 5 symphonies: No. 1 (1952; Belgrade, March 11, 1953), No. 2 (1959–61; Belgrade, Jan. 22, 1965), No. 3, *Mikrosimfonija*, for tape and orch. (1967; Opatija, Oct. 27, 1968), No. 4 (1972; Belgrade, May 24, 1972) and No. 5 (1973); *Symphonic Kolo* (1949); *Symphonic Scherzo* (1955); *Plameni Vjetar* (*Flaming Wind*), song cycle for baritone and orch. (1955; Belgrade, Jan. 13, 1959); Concertino for Piano and String Orch. (1956); Concerto for Clarinet and String Orch. (1958; Belgrade, May 26, 1959); *Symphonic Epitaph* for narrator, chorus and orch. (1959; Belgrade, May 21, 1959); *Scherzo-Overture* (1959); *Kroz svemir* (*Through the Universe*), suite for orch. (1961); *Scherzo in modo dodecaphonico* for orch. (1962; Belgrade, May 24, 1962); *Prelude and Fugue* for voice and string orch. (1963); *Epitaph H* for orch. and tape (1965; Berlin, Oct. 6, 1965); *Sutjeska* for narrator, chorus and orch. (1968); *Dramatična fuga* for wind orch. (1972; Belgrade, Nov. 17, 1972); Quintet for flute, clarinet and string trio (1950); *Platani* for chamber ensemble (1964); *Microsonata I* for solo clarinet (1969); *Microsonata II* for solo bassoon (1971); choruses; songs; electronic pieces.

BIBLIOGRAPHY: V. Peričić, *Muzički Stvaraoci u Srbiji* (Belgrade, 1969; pp. 351–363).

Obraztsova, Elena, Russian mezzo-soprano; b. Leningrad, July 7, 1937. Her father was an engineer who played the violin. She studied voice and academic subjects at the Leningrad Cons.; graduated in 1964. She possesses a remarkably even tessitura, brilliant in all registers, as well as great skill in handling her natural resources; she received 1st prize at the Tchaikovsky Competition in Moscow in 1970; was awarded the Lenin prize in 1976. Her success came rapidly, first in Russia, then in Europe, Japan and in June 1975 at the Metropolitan in the U.S. where she was acclaimed as a superlative opera singer. Her roles include virtually the entire Russian opera repertory; she also excels as Carmen, Azucena, etc. Her U.S. debut was in the role of Marina in *Boris Godunov;* she returned to the U.S. in 1976 and sang Amneris in *Aida* and Delilah in *Samson et Delilah.*

Obrecht (Hobrecht, Obreht, Obertus, Hobertus), Jacob, famous Netherlands contrapuntist; b. Berg-op-Zoom, Nov. 22, 1450 (or 1451); d. Ferrara, 1505 (of the pestilence). The son of a city trumpeter, he received his rudimentary musical training in his native town; he entered the Univ. of Louvain on Aug. 17, 1470; then returned to Berg-op-Zoom; took holy orders, and said his first Mass as ordained priest there on April 23, 1480. He was named *maître des enfants* at Cambrai on July 28, 1484; was in Bruges from 1485 to 1487; at the request of the Duke of Ferrara, he obtained a leave of absence for 6 months to travel to Italy; arrived in Ferrara in Dec. 1487; returned to Bruges in 1488, and remained there until 1491, when he became music director at Notre-Dame in Antwerp; he visited Berg-op-Zoom in 1496–97, after which he went again to Bruges; at various times was also in Antwerp. In 1504 he once more entered the service of the ducal court at Ferrara, where he remained until his death. He was a prolific composer; his Masses, motets, hymns, etc., are found in various collections of the period, and also in the Archives of the Papal Chapel. He was well known in Italy during his lifetime; Petrucci publ. a collection *Missae Obrecht* (1503), containing the Masses *Je ne demande, Grecorum, Fortuna desperata, Malheur me bat, Salve diva parens;* the collection *Missae diversorum* (vol. I) includes Obrecht's Mass *Si dedero.* The extensive edition of Obrecht's works in 7 vols., edited by Johannes Wolf (1908–21, Amsterdam and Leipzig), contains 24 Masses, 22 motets, chansons, and the famous 4-part Passion according to St. Matthew, the oldest known polyphonic setting of this text. Since the publication of this edition, additional works by Obrecht have been brought to light. On the other hand, some works formerly attributed to him have been proved to be spurious; thus another Passion, long thought to have been by Obrecht, was apparently by a chapel singer in the court of King Louis XII of France, named Longueval. A new *Opera omnia,* edited by A. Smijers, began publication in 1953 (Vereeniging voor Nederlandse Muziekgeschiedenis, Amsterdam), reaching 9 vols. by 1977.

BIBLIOGRAPHY: O. J. Gombosi, *Jakob Obrecht. Eine stilkritische Studie* (Leipzig, 1925); E. H. Juten, "Obrecht," *Annales of the Académie Royale d'Archéologie de Belgique* (ser. 7, vol. 7, Antwerp, 1930); A. W. Ambros, *Geschichte der Musik* (vol. III, p. 182ff.; vol. V contains 6 examples); Anny Piscaer, *Jacob Obrecht* (Berg-op-Zoom, 1938); article on Obrecht in *Dictionnaire des musiciens,* ed. by René Vannes (Brussels, 1947); Gustave Reese, *Music in the Renaissance* (N.Y., 1954); Bain Murray, "New Light on Jacob Obrecht's Development," *Musical Quarterly* (Oct. 1957); C. Dahlhaus, "Zu Marcus van Crevels neuer Obrecht-Ausgabe," *Die Musikforschung* (Oct.–Dec. 1967); L. G. van Hoorn, *Jacob Obrecht* (The Hague, 1968).

Obretenov, Svetoslav, Bulgarian composer; b. Provadia, Nov. 25, 1909. He studied at the Sofia Cons.; was active as choral conductor. He has written mostly for chorus; his oratorio *The Partisans* was performed for the first time in Sofia on June 25, 1949.

BIBLIOGRAPHY: V. Krstev, *Svetoslav Obretenov* (Sofia, 1959).

O'Brien, Charles, Scottish composer; b. Edinburgh, Sept. 6, 1882; d. there, June 27, 1968. He studied with H. MacCunn; later devoted himself to teaching. Among his compositions are a symphony, 3 overtures, 2 piano trios, a clarinet sonata, a number of piano pieces and songs.

Obrist, Aloys, Italian conductor and music editor; b. San Remo, March 30, 1867; d. (by suicide, after having killed the singer Anna Sutter out of jealousy) Stuttgart, June 29, 1910. He studied at the Univ. of Berlin; received his Dr. phil. (1892) with the dissertation *Melchior Franck.* He filled posts as conductor in Rostock, Augsburg, etc.; then became court conductor at Stuttgart; from 1900, was custodian of the Liszt Museum in

Weimar, and chairman of the editorial board for the publication of Liszt's works. He was a connoisseur of old instruments, and owned a valuable collection, which passed to the Bach Museum in Eisenach.

Očenáš, Andrej, Slovak composer; b. Selce, near Banská Bystrica, Jan. 8, 1911. He studied composition with Alexander Moyzes at the Bratislava Academy, graduating in 1937; then took a course with Vitĕzslav Novák at the Prague Cons., graduating in 1939. He worked at the Czech Radio in Bratislava after 1938 and was director of musical programs there (1957-62); taught at the Bratislava Cons. (1945-54). His music is imbued with a Slovak ethos.
WORKS: a musical play, *Rok na dedine* (*Year in a Village;* Bratislava, Dec. 11, 1948); 3 ballets: *At the Brigand's Ball* (1941), *Highlander's Songs* (1954-56), and *The Romance of the Rose,* a "stage symphony" with a narrator, solo singers, chorus and orch. (1969-71); *Tales of My Native Land,* suite for orch. (1943); *Resurrection,* symph. trilogy (1946); *To My Nation,* symph. poem (1947); Cello Concerto (1952); *Ruralia Slovaca* for string orch., 2 flutes, 2 clarinets, 2 trumpets, horns and piano (1957); Piano Concerto (1959); *Concertino rustico* for cimbalom, strings and piano (1963); Sinfonietta (1967); *O zemi a človeku* (*About Earth and Man*), symph. for chorus and small orch. (1970); *May Overture* (1972); Violin Concerto (1974); *Margarita and Besná,* cantata (1939); *Prophecies,* oratorio (1949-50); *Monuments of Glory,* symph. tetralogy for tenor, children's and mixed choruses, and orch. (1963); *Pastorale of Orava* for soloists, chorus and orch. (1961); *I Loved You,* laudatorium for soloists, chorus, organ and orch. (1974); 2 string quartets (*Pictures of the Soul,* 1942; *Etude,* 1970); Concertino for Flute and Piano (1961-62); Piano Trio (1967); *Frescoes* for violin and piano (1967); *Poem of the Heart* for solo violin (1968); *Don Quixote,* duo for violin and cello (1969); *Zvony* (*The Bells*), piano sonata (1972); the piano pieces, *Rainstorm* (1946), *New Spring* (1954), *Youth* (1956), *Pictures of Legends* (1957); *Pastels* for organ (1961); choruses; songs.

Ochs, Siegfried, German choral conductor and composer; b. Frankfurt, April 19, 1858; d. Berlin, Feb. 5, 1929. He studied medicine and chemistry before turning to music; took private lessons with Friedrich Kiel and Heinrich Urban. In 1882 he organized in Berlin a choral union, under his own name, working in close collaboration with the Berlin Philharmonic under the direction of Hans von Bülow. In 1920 it was merged with the chorus of the Berlin Hochschule für Musik and earned a reputation as one of the best choral ensembles in Germany. Ochs was also a composer; he wrote a comic opera, *Im Namen des Gesetzes* (Hamburg, 1888), 2 operettas and several song cycles; publ. an autobiography, *Geschehenes, Gesehenes* (Leipzig, 1922); compiled a valuable history of German choral singing, *Der deutsche Gesangverein* (4 vols., Berlin, 1923-28); published *Über die Art, Musik zu Hören* (Berlin, 1926); edited Bach's cantatas and publ. choral arrangements of German folksongs.
BIBLIOGRAPHY: M. Stappenbeck, *Chronik des Philharmonischen Chores in Berlin* (Berlin, 1932); K.

Singer, *Siegfried Ochs, der Bergründer des Philharmonischen Chors* (Berlin, 1933).

Ockeghem (or **Okeghem, Okenghem, Ockenheim,** etc.), **Johannes** (or **Jean de**), great Flemish contrapuntist and teacher; b. c.1420 in East Flanders; d. Tours, Feb. 6, 1496 (old style calendar), according to an entry in the Archives Nationales, Paris. He was probably a pupil of Binchois; boy chorister at Antwerp Cath., 1443-44; chorister in the chapel of Duke Charles of Bourbon, 1446-48; in 1449, pupil of Dufay in Cambrai; in 1452-53, chorister in the royal chapel; from 1454, composer and first chaplain to three successive kings of France: Charles VII, Louis XI, and Charles VIII; was treasurer of the Abbey of St.-Martin at Tours; 1465, "maître de la chapelle du roy"; in 1469 he traveled to Spain, and in 1484 to Flanders, at the King's expense. Upon Ockeghem's death, Guillaume Crétin wrote a poetic "Déploration," and Josquin Des Prez (his greatest pupil) and Lupi composed musical epitaphs. Important both as teacher and composer, Ockeghem was the leader of the 2nd generation of the great Franco-Flemish school of the 15th century (which includes Busnois, Regis and Caron). His art expresses the mysticism of the Netherlands in the late Middle Ages; his technical skill in the development of purely formal resources, while very important, is not the most prominent characteristic of his style, as most historians have asserted. At the same time, Ockeghem's achievements in the art of imitative counterpoint unquestionably make his music a milestone on the way to the a cappella style of the coming generations.
WORKS: 16 Masses and individual sections of Masses; 9 motets; a ninefold canon-motet, *Deo gratias,* in 36 parts (of doubtful authenticity); about 20 chansons, and 1 canon (*Fuga a 3 in epidiatessaron*=the chanson *Prenez sur moi*). Burney, Forkel, Kiesewetter, Schlecht, Ambros-Kade, Wooldridge, and P. Wagner have printed fragments of the Mass *Cujusvis toni* (*ad omnem tonum*); Bellermann (*Die Mensuralnoten und Taktzeichen*), a fragment of the *Missa Prolationum;* Riemann, in *Musikgeschichte in Beispielen* (1912; no. 16) and in *Handbuch der Musikgeschichte* (II, 1), fragments of the Mass *Pour quelque peine* (probably not by Ockeghem); the Masses *Caput* and *Le Serviteur* (which is probably a work of V. Faugues, according to Tinctoris [Coussemaker, *Scriptores* IV, 146a]) are publ. in entirety in *Denkmäler der Tonkunst in Österreich* 38 (19.i); the Mass *Mi mi* (ed. for practical use by H. Besseler), is in F. Blume's *Das Chorwerk* #4 (1928); 2 sections of the Mass *L'Homme armé* are in A. T. Davison and W. Apel, *Historical Anthology of Music* (Cambridge, Mass., 1947); a motet, *Alma redemptoris mater,* in *Altniederländische Motetten* (Kassel, 1929), ed. by H. Besseler; another motet, *Ut heremita solus,* in Schering's *Geschichte der Musik in Beispielen* (1931; no. 52); the "Déploration" on the death of Binchois, *Mort tu as navré,* in J. Marix's *Les Musiciens de la cour de Bourgogne au XVe siècle* (1937; no. 54); the motet *Intemerata Dei Mater* in Smijers's *Muziekgeschiedenis in Voorbeelden,* I (1939); the canon-motet in 36 parts, in Riemann's *Handbuch der Musikgeschichte* II, 1. Regarding the chansons, there are 4 in Ambros-Kade's *Geschichte,*

V; 4 in O. Gombosi's *Jacob Obrecht* (1925); 1 in J. Wolf's *Sing- und Spielmusik aus älterer Zeit* (1926); 8 in *Trois Chansonniers français du XVᵉ siècle*, I (1927), ed. by Droz-Rokseth-Thibault; 2 in K. Jeppesen's *Der Kopenhagener Chansonnier* (1927); and 2 in Davison and Apel, *Historical Anthology of Music*. A 3-part chanson, *O rosa bella*, by Hert, with a new discantus added to it by Ockeghem, is in *Denkmäler der Tonkunst in Österreich* 14/15 (7). The *Fuga in epidiatessaron* has been discussed, reprinted, and solved with more or less success by innumerable writers; reprints are to be found in Jeppesen, Droz-Rokseth-Thibault, and J. S. Levitan (see below). A complete ed. of Ockeghem's works, edited by D. Plamenac, was begun in 1927 in the *Publikationen älterer Musik* of the Deutsche Musikgesellschaft, with a vol. containing 8 Masses; new ed. of this vol., N.Y., 1958; vol. 2, containing 8 Masses and Mass sections, N.Y., 1947 (rev. 1966).

BIBLIOGRAPHY: L. de Burbure, *J. de Ockeghem* (1853; 2nd ed. 1868); E. Thoinan, *Déploration de Guillaume Crétin sur le trépas de J. Ockeghem* (Paris, 1864); M. Brenet, *J. de Ockeghem* (Paris, 1893; 2nd ed. in *Musique et musiciens de la vieille France*, 1911; with bibliography); A. Schering, "Ein Rätseltenor Ockeghems" (Kretzschmar-Festschrift, 1918); D. Plamenac, *J. Ockeghem als Motetten- und Chansonkomponist* (Vienna, 1924); M. Cauchie, "Les Véritables Nom et prénom d'Ockeghem," *Revue de Musicologie* (1926); W. Stephan, *Die burgundisch-niederländische Motette zur Zeit Ockeghems* (Heidelberg, 1937); J. S. Levitan, "Ockeghem's Clefless Compositions," *Musical Quarterly* (Oct. 1937); Ernst Krenek, *J. Ockeghem* (N.Y., 1953); Gustave Reese, *Music in the Renaissance* (N.Y., 1954); several important essays in *Essays in Music in Honor of Dragan Plamenac*, ed. by G. Reese and R. J. Snow (Pittsburgh, 1969); *Johannes Ockeghem en zÿm tÿd* (Dendermonde, 1970).

O'Connell, Charles, American conductor and music executive; b. Chicopee, Mass., April 22, 1900; d. New York, Sept. 1, 1962. He studied at the Catholic School and College of the Holy Cross (B.A., 1922); also organ in Paris with Widor. From 1930 to 1944 he was head of the artist and repertory dept. of the RCA Victor Co., then music director of Columbia Masterworks (1944–47). He publ. *The Victor Book of the Symphony* (1934; new ed., 1948); *The Victor Book of the Opera* (1937); *The Other Side of the Record* (relating personal experiences in dealing with musical celebrities; N.Y., 1947); *The Victor Book of Overtures, Tone Poems and Other Orchestral Works* (1950).

Odak, Krsto, Croatian composer; b. Siverić, Dalmatia, March 20, 1888; d. Zagreb, Nov. 4, 1965. He studied composition with P. Hartmann in Munich (1911–13) and in Prague with Novák. Upon his return to Yugoslavia he was prof. of composition at the Music Academy of Zagreb, retiring in 1961. He wrote 4 symphonies (1940, 1953, 1961, 1965); the operetta, *Dorica pleše* (*Dorrit Dances;* 1934); the radio opera, *Majka Margarita* (*Mother Margaret;* Zagreb, 1955); Piano Concerto (1963); 4 string quartets (1925, 1927, 1934, 1957); 2 Masses in the old Slavonic language; other sacred works; song cycles.

Odaka, Hisatada. See **Otaka, Hisatada.**

Oddone Sulli-Rao, Elisabetta, Italian composer; b. Milan, Aug. 13, 1878; d. there, March 3, 1972. She studied at the Milan Cons.; composed a one-act opera *A gara colle rondini* (Milan, 1920) and a children's opera, *Petruccio e il cavallo cappuccio* (Milan, 1916); several oratorios; chamber music and a number of songs. She did some valuable work on dissemination of Italian folksongs; published *Canzoniere popolare italiano, Canzoncine per bimbi, Cantilene popolari dei bimbi d'Italia,* etc.

Odington, Walter (Walter of Evesham), a Benedictine monk at the monastery of Evesham; he was at Oxford in 1316, and at Merton College there in 1330. He is one of the chief medieval writers on mensural notation; his *De speculatione musices* (MS in Corpus Christi College, Cambridge) was printed by Coussemaker in 1864 (*Scriptores* I). This work is particularly valuable for the light it throws on musical rhythm as practiced in the late 13th century; it also discusses intervals, notation, musical instruments, and musical forms (rondellus, motet, etc.). His views on consonance and dissonance are interesting for their acceptance of thirds and sixths as legitimate consonances. He was also noted as an astronomer.

BIBLIOGRAPHY: J. Wolf, "Early English Musical Theorists," *Musical Quarterly* (Oct. 1939); G. Reese, *Music in the Middle Ages* (N.Y., 1940).

Odnoposoff, Adolfo, Argentine cellist, brother of **Ricardo Odnoposoff;** b. Buenos Aires, Feb. 22, 1917. He studied with Alberto Schiuma; then went to Berlin where he took lessons with Feuermann and to Paris where he became a student of Diran Alexanian. He was subsequently active as a concert cellist in Palestine (1936–38), in Peru (1938–40), in Chile (1940–44), in Havana (1944–58) and in Mexico City, where he also taught at the Cons. Nacional de Música (1958–64); then was prof. of cello and chamber music at the Cons. of Music in San Juan, Puerto Rico. In 1975 he became prof. of cello at North Texas State Univ. in Denton. Several Latin American composers (Roque Cordero, Rodolfo Halffter, Eduardo Mata, Floro Ugarte, Antonio Tauriello and others) wrote special works for him.

Odnoposoff, Ricardo, Argentine violinist, brother of **Adolfo Odnoposoff;** b. Buenos Aires, Feb. 24, 1914. He studied with Aaron Klasse in Buenos Aires (1919–26), Rudolph Deman in Berlin (1927–28), and Carl Flesch in Berlin (1928–32). A precocious musician, he played in public as an infant; was soloist with the Berlin Philharmonic at 17; won 1st prize at the International Contest for Violinists in Vienna at 18. He evolved a brilliant career as a concert violinist, appearing in all parts of the world; eventually settled in Vienna as prof. of the Music Academy.

Odo de Cluny (Saint), important musical theorist of the 10th century; b. near Le Mans, 879; d. Tours, Nov. 18, 942. A pupil of Rémy d'Auxerre in Paris, he took holy orders at 19, and in 899 was canon and choir singer at Tours; in 909 he entered the Benedictine monastery at Baume, near Besançon, and then was successively abbot at Aurillac, Fleuri, and (from 927) Cluny. The famous medieval treatise *Dialogus de musica* (also known as *Enchiridion musices*) is attributed to him without foundation (it is printed in Gerbert's *Scriptores* and, in English translation, in Oliver Strunk's *Source Readings in Music History*, N.Y., 1950). In the development of pitch notation through letter-names, he was the first to give a complete series (2 octaves and a fifth) of letter-names (G, A, B, C, D, E, F, G, etc.) corresponding to our modern series; but whereas we change from capital to lower-case letters at *c* to designate the pitches of the 2nd octave, in Odo's system the change was made at *a*. He was also the first to add the sign *gamma* (Greek 'G') to designate the note corresponding to G on the first line of our bass clef. He distinguished between b flat and b natural (b *rotundum* and b *quadratum*), but only at one point in the gamut, namely, the note lying one degree below middle C in our system.

BIBLIOGRAPHY: Th. Nisard, *St.-Odo de Cluny* (Paris, 1866); M. Huglo, "L'Auteur du *Dialogue sur la musique* attribué à Odo," *Revue de Musicologie* (1969).

O'Dwyer, Robert, English-Irish composer and conductor; b. Bristol, Jan. 27, 1862; d. Dublin, Jan. 6, 1949. He was a conductor of the Carl Rosa Opera Co. in London and on tour (1891); then with the Arthur Rousbey Opera Co. in England and Ireland (1892–96); in 1899, became musical director at the Univ. of Ireland, Dublin; from 1914 to 1939, prof. of Irish music there; musical director (from 1901) of the Gaelic League choir, for which he arranged many Irish songs. He wrote one of the earliest operas with a Gaelic text, *Eithne,* produced in Dublin on May 16, 1910; also composed songs with Gaelic words; organ pieces. He left a book in manuscript, *Irish Music and its Traditions.*

Oesterlein, Nikolaus, Austrian music scholar; b. Vienna, May 4, 1842; d. there, Oct. 8, 1898. An ardent admirer of Wagner, he amassed an enormous collection of materials relating to Wagner's life and works. This collection, known as the "Wagner Museum," was subsequently given to the town of Eisenach; the catalogue, publ. by Breitkopf & Härtel (1882–95), fills 4 vols. Oesterlein also publ. a volume, entitled *Bayreuth,* on the inauguration of the festival plays in 1876, and *Über Schicksale des Wagner-Museums in Wien* (1892).

Oetting, William H., American organist and pedagogue; b. Pittsburgh, Oct. 14, 1875; d. there, Oct. 29, 1969. He studied in Berlin with Riemann, Egidi, Boise, and Hutcheson; while there, he taught at the Klindworth-Scharwenka Cons. In 1901 he returned to the U.S., and for half a century was organist at various churches in Pittsburgh. He publ. *Preparatory Exercises for Manuals and Pedals* (2nd ed., 1953).

Oettingen, Arthur Joachim von, German physicist and musical theorist; b. Dorpat, Russia, March 28, 1836; d. Leipzig, Sept. 6, 1920. He studied physics at the Univ. of Dorpat; then in Paris and Berlin; from 1863 to 1893, was prof. of physics at the Univ. of Dorpat; from 1894 to 1919, at the Univ. of Leipzig. He publ. *Das Harmoniesystem in dualer Entwicklung* (1866; revised ed. as *Das duale Harmoniesystem,* 1913), reconciling and developing the systems of Helmholtz and Hauptmann; *Die Grundlage der Musikwissenschaft* (Leipzig, 1916); etc.

Offenbach, Jacques, the creator of French burlesque opera; b. Cologne, June 20, 1819; d. Paris, Oct. 5, 1880. He was the son of a Jewish cantor, whose original surname was Eberst; Offenbach was the town where his father lived. He went early to Paris; studied cello with Vaslin at the Cons. (1833–34); then played the cello in the orch. of the Opéra-Comique; composed various pieces for his instrument. In 1849 he was engaged as conductor at the Théâtre Français; wrote a *Chanson de Fortunio* for the production of Alfred de Musset's *Chandelier* (1850); the song proved tremendously popular; he then undertook the composition of operettas, a genre in which he became a master.

WORKS: He wrote a 1-act operetta, *Pepito* (Théâtre des Variétés, Oct. 28, 1853); in 1855 he ventured to open a theater of his own, the old Théâtre Comte, in the Passage Choiseul, which under a new name, Bouffes-Parisiens, became celebrated; he carried on the enterprise until 1866, producing a number of his most popular pieces, among them *Les Deux Aveugles,* for the opening of the Bouffes-Parisiens (July 5, 1855), *Le Violoneux* (Aug. 31, 1855), *Madame Papillon* (Oct. 3, 1855), *Ba-ta-clan* (Dec. 29, 1855), *La Bonne d'enfants* (Oct. 14, 1856), *Les Trois Baisers au diable* (Jan. 15, 1857), *Le Mariage aux lanternes* (Oct. 10, 1857), *Mesdames de la Halle* (March 3, 1858), *Orphée aux enfers* (one of his most celebrated pieces; Oct. 21, 1858), *Geneviève de Brabant* (Nov. 19, 1859), *Daphnis et Chloé* (March 27, 1860), *Barkouf* (Dec. 24, 1860), *La Chanson de Fortunio* (a new operetta to Musset's *Chandelier*), *Le Pont des soupirs* (March 23, 1861), *Monsieur et Madame Denis* (Jan. 11, 1862), etc. Having abandoned the management of the Bouffes-Parisiens, he produced several operettas in Ems, Germany; and an opera-ballet *Die Rheinnixen,* in Vienna (Feb. 8, 1864); then returned to Paris, where he staged, at the Variétés, one of his most spectacular successes, *La Belle Hélène* (Dec. 17, 1864), an operetta that was soon taken over by theater enterprises all over the world; another fabulously successful operetta was *La Vie parisienne* (Palais Royal, Oct. 31, 1866); subsequent productions were *La Grande Duchesse de Gérolstein* (Variétés, April 12, 1867), *La Périchole* (Variétés, Oct. 6, 1868; one of the most enduringly popular operas of Offenbach; recurring revivals in many countries), and *Les Brigands* (Variétés, Dec. 10, 1869). In 1870, the Franco-Prussian War interrupted his activities in Paris; he resumed the production of operettas with *Boule-de-neige* (Bouffes-Parisiens, Dec. 14, 1871); in 1873 he took over the management of the Théâtre de la Gaîté, and produced there a new enlarged version of *Orphée aux enfers,* as an "opéra-féerique" (Feb. 7, 1874). In 1877 he undertook a tour in America, which was not wholly successful; he described his impressions in *Notes d'un musicien en voyage* (Paris, 1877) and in *Offenbach en Amérique* (Paris, 1877; in English, 1877, as *Offenbach in America;* republished as *Orheus in America* by the Indiana Univ. Press, Bloomington, Indiana, 1957). His last operetta produced in his lifetime was *La Fille du tambour-major* (Paris, Folies-Dramatiques, Dec. 13, 1879). A posthumous work, *La Belle Lurette,* was revised by Delibes, and staged in Paris on Oct. 30, 1880. His only grand opera, and his true masterpiece, *Les Contes d'Hoffmann,* remained unfinished at his death; recitatives were added by Ernest Guiraud. The famous barcarolle was taken from Offenbach's opera-ballet *Die Rheinnixen* (1864), where the tune was used for a ghost song. *Les Contes d'Hoffmann* was produced at the Opéra-Comique on Feb. 10, 1881 with immediate and decisive success; presented in N.Y. on Oct. 16, 1882; also all over Europe. Offenbach's music is characterized by an abundance of flowing, rollicking melodies, seasoned with ironic humor, suitable to the extravagant burlesque of the situations. His irreverent treatment of mythological characters gave Paris society a salutary shock; his art mirrored the atmosphere of precarious gaiety during the Second Empire.

BIBLIOGRAPHY: E. de Mirecourt, *Offenbach* (Paris, 1867); A. Martinet, *Offenbach* (Paris, 1887); H. Berlioz, *Les Musiciens et la Musique* (ed. by A. Hallays, Paris, 1903); P. Bekker, *Offenbach* (Berlin, 1909); E. Rieger, *Offenbach und seine Wiener Schule* (Vienna, 1920); L. Schneider, *Offenbach* (Paris, 1923); R. Brancour, *Offenbach* (Paris, 1929); A. Henseler, *Jakob Offenbach* (Berlin, 1930); H. Kristeller, *Der Aufstieg des Kölners Jacques Offenbach* (Berlin, 1931); S. Kracauer, *Jacques Offenbach* (Paris, 1937; in English, London, as *Offenbach and the Paris of His Time;* N.Y., as *Orpheus in Paris,* 1938); S. Sitwell, *La Vie Parisienne: a Tribute to Offenbach* (London, 1937); J. Brindejont-Offenbach, *Offenbach, mon grand-père* (Paris, 1940). For details of productions see A. Loewenberg, *Annals of Opera* (Cambridge, 1943; 2nd ed., 1955); A. Decaux, *Offenbach, Roi du Second Empire* (Paris, 1958).

Ogdon, John (Andrew Howard), English pianist; b. Manchester, Jan. 27, 1937. He studied at the Royal Manchester College of Music; made appearances in recitals and as soloist with orchestras. In 1962 he won the world's most prestigious contest, the Tchaikovsky Competition in Moscow. A man of massive physique, he handles the piano with masculine power, but is also capable of the finest quality of lyricism.

Ogihara, Toshitsugu, Japanese composer; b. Osaka, June 6, 1910. He studied composition with Yoritsuné Matsudaira at Nihon Univ.; took private lessons with Alexander Tcherepnin during the latter's stay in Japan. His music follows the classical models.

WORKS: ballet, *Springtime* (1973); *2 Movements* for percussion and orch. (1942); *Sôshun no Hiroba,* symph. poem (1955); Symph. No. 1 (1958); *Rhapsody* for orch. (1960); 2 violin concertos (1962, 1963); Violin Concertino (1962); *Capriccio* for string orch. (1964); *4 Pieces* for horn and string orch. (1972); 4 string quartets (1940, 1949, 1953, 1969); 2 string trios (1947, 1961); Violin Sonata (1959); Concerto for Clarinet and String Quartet (1955); *Capriccio* for woodwinds and strings (1958); Trio for clarinet, cello and piano (1962);

English Horn Sonata (1962); Quartet for 4 flutes (1963); Trio for flute, violin and Piano (1965); Piano Quintet (1970); Trio for clarinet, violin and cello (1970); Trio for oboe, cello and Piano (1970); Trio for cello, bassoon and piano (1971); *Serenade* for Cello, Violin and Clarinet (1972); *4 Pieces* for tuba, 3 tenor trombones, and bass trombone (1972); *2 Suites* for flute and piano (1974); piano pieces; songs.

Oginski, Prince Michael Cleophas, Polish composer; b. Guzow, near Warsaw, Sept. 25, 1765; d. Florence, Oct. 15, 1833. He was a Polish nobleman of a musical family; his uncle, Michael Casimir Oginski (1731–1803), was an amateur composer of some talent. He pursued the career of diplomacy; as a Polish patriot, he left Poland after its partition, and agitated in Turkey and France for the Polish cause. In 1799 he wrote an opera, *Zelis et Valcour ou Bonaparte au Caire,* to ingratiate himself with Napoleon; it was revived in a radio performance in Cracow on June 29, 1953. Of historical interest are his polonaises, many of which were publ.; the one in A minor, known as *Death Polonaise,* became extremely popular; he also wrote mazurkas and waltzes for piano, and a patriotic Polish march (1825).

Ogura, Roh, Japanese composer; b. Kyushu, Jan. 19, 1916. He studied with Fukai, Sugawara, and Ikenouchi; then was engaged in teaching.

WORKS: an opera, *Neta* (1957); *Orly—A Bugbear at Sea,* for narrator and orch. (1963); Symph. in A (1941); Piano Concerto (Tokyo, March 24, 1946); Symph. in F (Tokyo, April 25, 1951); *5 Movements on Japanese Folk Songs* for orch. (1957); Symph. in G (1968); Violin Concerto (1971); 3 string quartets (1941, 1946, 1954); Violin Sonata (1950); Violin Sonatina (1960); *Divertimento* for 7 winds (1964); *Divertimento* for 8 winds (1972); *Dance Suite* for 2 pianos (1953); choruses; songs.

Ohana, Maurice, French composer and pianist; b. Casablanca, June 12, 1914, of Spanish parentage. He studied piano with Lazare Lévy in Paris and composition with Daniel Lesur; subsequently took lessons with Alfredo Casella in Rome. He settled in Paris.

WORKS: the operas *Syllabaire pour Phèdre* (Avignon, 1969) and *Autodafé,* for puppet theater (Lyon, 1972); a ballet *Etudes chorégraphiques* (1955); *Synaxis* for percussion, 2 pianos and orch. (1966); *Chiffres de clavecin* for harpsichord and 21 instruments (1968); *Silenciaire* for percussion and 12 strings (1969); *Signes* for flute, piano, guitar and percussion (1965); *Cinq séquences* for string quartet (1962–64); *Syrtes* for cello and piano (1972); 24 Preludes for piano (1973); the oratorios, *Llanto por Ignacio Sanchez Mejias* (1950) and *Récit de l'an Zéro* (1959); numerous choral pieces; film scores.

BIBLIOGRAPHY: J. Roy, *Présences contemporaines, Musique française* (Paris, 1962).

O'Hara, Geoffrey, American song composer; b. Chatham, Ontario, Canada, Feb. 2, 1882; d. St. Petersburg, Florida, Jan. 31, 1967. He settled in the U.S. in 1904; became an American citizen in 1922. He studied with

Homer Norris and J. Vogler; played the Chatham Episcopal Church; then acted in vaudeville as pianist, singer, and composer; wrote the song *Your eyes have told me* for Caruso. In 1913 he was appointed instructor in American Indian music as part of the program of the Secretary of Interior; in 1917, became an army song leader; was instructor in community singing at Teachers College, Columbia Univ. (1936–37); charter member of the American Society of Composers, Authors and Publishers (1914).

WORKS: He wrote several operettas, among them *Peggy and the Pirate, Riding Down the Sky, The Count and the Co-ed, The Smiling Sixpence*; about 300 songs, of which the following were extremely popular: *K-K-K-Katy, I Love a Little Cottage, Wreck of the Julie Plante, Leetle Bateese, The Living God, I Walked Today Where Jesus Walked, Give a Man a Horse He Can Ride, Where Heaven Is, Tomasso Rotundo, A Little Close Harmony, The Old Songs, Sing Awhile Longer, Forward to Christ, One World,* etc.; publ. a collection of Canadian folksongs.

Ohlsson, Garrick, American pianist; b. Bronxville, N.Y., April 3, 1948. He entered the preparatory division of the Juilliard School of Music in 1961 as a student of Sascha Gorodnitzki; in 1968 he enrolled in the master class of Rosina Lhévinne. He came to public notice in 1969 when he won the International Busoni competition in Bolzano and the Montreal contest for pianists. A giant leap in his career was made when he became the first American pianist to win the prestigious quinquennial Chopin International Piano Competition in Warsaw in 1970, contending against top-notch Polish and Russian performers. A Polish writer described Ohlsson as a "bear-butterfly" for his ability to traverse the entire spectrum of 18 dynamic degrees discernible on the modern pianoforte, from the thundering fortissimo to the finest pianississimo, with reference also to his height (6 foot, 4 inches), weight (225 lbs.) and stretch of hands (an octave and a fifth in the left hand and an octave and a fourth in the right hand). His interpretations are marked by a distinctive Americanism, technically flawless and free of romantic mannerisms.

Oistrakh, David, famous Russian violinist; b. Odessa, Sept. 30, 1908; d. Amsterdam, Oct. 24, 1974. He studied violin as a child with Stolarsky in Odessa, then entered the Odessa music school, graduating in 1926; appeared as soloist in Glazunov's Violin Concerto under the composer's direction in Kiev in 1926. In 1928 he went to Moscow; his name attracted universal attention in 1937 when he won 1st prize at the International Competition in Brussels in which 68 violinists from 21 countries took part. He played in Paris and London in 1953 with extraordinary success; made his 1st American appearances in 1955, as soloist with major American orchestras and in recitals, winning enthusiastic acclaim; his playing was marked, apart from a phenomenal technique, by stylistic fidelity to works by different composers of different historical periods. Soviet composers profited by his advice as to technical problems of violin playing; he collaborated with Prokofiev in making an arrangement for violin and piano of his flute sonata. (He also played a chess match with Prokofiev.) A whole generation of Soviet violinists numbered among his pupils, first and foremost his son Igor Oistrakh (b. Odessa, April 27, 1931) who has had a spectacular career in his own right; he won 1st prize at the International Festival of Democratic Youth in Budapest (1949) and the Wieniawski Contest in Poznan (1952); some critics regarded him as equal to his father in virtuosity.

BIBLIOGRAPHY: V. Bronin, *David Oistrakh* (Moscow, 1954); I. Yampolsky, *David Oistrakh* (Moscow, 1964); D. Naberin, *David und Igor Oistrakh* (Berlin, 1968); V. Josefowitsch, *D. Ostrach* (Stuttgart, 1977).

Okeghem, Johannes. See **Ockeghem, Johannes.**

Oki, Masao, Japanese composer; b. Shizuoka, Oct. 3, 1901; d. Kamakura, April 18, 1971. He studied engineering and music; then devoted himself mainly to teaching and composition. He wrote 6 symphonies of which the 5th was subtitled *Atomic Bomb*; it was performed in Tokyo, Nov. 6, 1953; the 6th Symph. (1970) was entitled *Vietnam*. His other works included a cantata, *Take Back the Human* (1961–63); a String Quartet, and some choral works.

Olah, Tiberiu, Rumanian composer; b. Arpasel, Jan. 2, 1928. He studied at the Cons. in Cluj (1946–49), then went to Russia where he studied at the Moscow Cons. (1949–54); in each of the years 1966–69, he attended the summer courses in new music at Darmstadt. In 1958 he was appointed to the staff of the Bucharest Cons. In his music Olah adopts a strong contrapuntal style, with some excursions into the atonal domain and dodecaphonic organization.

WORKS: Piano Sonatina (1950); String Quartet (1952); Trio for violin, clarinet and piano (1954); Symph. No. 1 (1955); Violin Sonatina (1955); Cantata for female chorus, 2 flute, strings and percussion (1956); *Prind visele arpii (Dreams Become Reality,* 1959); *Lumina lui Lenin (The Light of Lenin,* 1959); and *Constelaţia omului (The Galaxy of Man,* 1960); a cycle of 5 works inspired by the works of the Rumanian sculptor Constantin Brâncuşi: *Coloana fără sfîrşit (Endless Column),* symph. poem (1962); *Poarta sărutului (Archway of the Kiss),* symph. poem and *Masa tăcerii (The Table of Silence),* symph. poem (1967–68); 5 Pieces for orch. (1966); Sonata for solo clarinet (1963); *Spaţiu şi ritm (Space and Rhythm),* etude for 3 percussion groups (1964); *Translations* for 18 strings (1968); *Perspectives* for 13 instruments (1969); Sonata for solo cello (1971); *Invocation* for 5 instruments (1971); *Crescendo* for orch. (1972); *Evenimente 1907* for orch. (1972); *The Time of Memory* for chamber ensemble (1973); N.Y., Dec. 6, 1974): songs.

Olczewska, Maria (real name **Marie Berchtenbreitner;** German mezzo-soprano; b. Augsburg, Aug. 12, 1892; d. Klagenfurt, Austria, May 17, 1969. She sang in operetta in Hamburg; then was engaged at the Leipzig Opera (1920–23); subsequently was a member of the Vienna State Opera (1923–36) and Covent Garden in London (1924–32) where she sang Wagnerian

operas with excellent success; she was then engaged at the Chicago Opera and at the Metropolitan Opera, N.Y., making her debut as Brangäne (Jan. 16, 1933), remaining on its staff until 1935. In 1947 she returned to Vienna, where she taught at the Cons. She had a powerful voice, which made it possible for her to master the Wagner roles; but she was also excellent in dramatic parts, such as Carmen. Furthermore, she had a genuine talent as a stage actress.

Oldberg, Arne, American composer; b. Youngstown, Ohio, July 12, 1874; d. Evanston, Illinois, Feb. 17, 1962. He studied composition with Middelschulte; then went to Vienna where he was a piano pupil of Leschetizky (1893-95); also took courses with Rheinberger in Munich. Returning to America in 1899, he became head of the piano dept. at Northwestern Univ.; retired in 1941. Most of his orchestral works were performed by the Chicago Symph. Orch., among them Paolo and Francesca (Jan. 17, 1908); At Night (April 13, 1917), Symph. No. 4 (Dec. 31, 1942); Symph. No. 5 (Jan. 19, 1950), and St. Francis of Assisi, for baritone and orch. (Ravinia Festival, July 16, 1954). Other works are: Academic Overture (1909); The Sea, symph. poem (1934); 2 piano concertos, of which the second won the Hollywood Bowl prize and was performed there (Aug. 16, 1932); Violin Concerto (1933; Chicago, Nov. 7, 1946); 2 rhapsodies for orch.; chamber music; piano pieces.

Oldham, Arthur, English composer; b. London, Sept. 6, 1926. He studied at the Royal College of Music with Herbert Howells, and privately with Benjamin Britten. From 1945 he was active as musical director of various London theaters. He has written the ballets Mr. Punch (1946), The Sailor's Return (1947); Circus Canteen (1951), and Bonne-Bouché (1952); a symph. poem, The Apotheosis of Lucius (1952); musical for children, The Land of Green Ginger (1964); Hymns for the Amusement of Children for voices and organ (1962); various sacred and secular works.

Oldman, Cecil Bernard, English music librarian; b. London, April 2, 1894; d. there, Oct. 7, 1969. He studied at Exeter College, Oxford; in 1920 received an appointment in the Dept. of Printed Books in the British Museum; from 1948 to 1959 was Principal Keeper. His specialty was documentation on Mozart; he publ. and annotated the Letters of Constanze Mozart to J. A. André, in the 3rd vol. of Emily Anderson's Letters of Mozart and his Family (1938); contributed numerous valuable papers to British, German, and Dutch publications. In 1951 he became chairman of the Council of the British Union Catalogue of Music.

Oldroyd, George, English organist and composer; b. Healey, Yorkshire, Dec. 1, 1886; d. London, Feb. 26, 1951. He studied organ and music theory with Eaglefield Hull; violin with Frank Arnold. After a year in Paris as organist of the English Church there (1915), he played at various London churches; taught at the Trinity College; in 1949 succeeded Stanley Marchant as prof. at London Univ. He wrote a number of sacred works, of which a Stabat Mater is notable; publ. The Technique and Spirit of Fugue: An Historical Study (London, 1948); Polyphonic Writing for Voices, in 6 and 8 Parts (London, 1953); and some essays on Gregorian Chant.

Olds, Gerry, American composer; b. Cleveland, Feb. 26, 1933. He studied at the Cleveland Institute and at the Chicago Cons. (M.A. 1957). His works include a Short Symphony (1957); Violin Concerto (1956); Toccata for string orch. (1958); Wind Quintet (1958); 2nd Symph. in one movement (1958); String Trio (1959), and Piano Concerto (1960).

Olenin, Alexander, Russian composer, brother of the singer Olénine d' Alheim; b. Istomino, district of Riazan, June 13, 1865; d. Moscow, Feb. 15, 1944. He studied with P. Pabst and with Erdmannsdörfer; lived most of his life in Moscow. He wrote an opera in a folk style, Kudeyar (Moscow, Nov. 26, 1915); a symph. poem, After the Battle; Preludes prairiales, for 2 oboes, violin, and piano (1927); a piano sonata; violin sonata; several song cycles (The Street, The Peasant's Son, The Autumn Home, etc.), and 52 songs to texts by Heine.

BIBLIOGRAPHY: V. Belaiev, "Olenin's Reminiscences of Balakirev," Musical Quarterly (Jan. 1930).

Olénine d'Alheim, Marie, Russian soprano; b. Istomino, Riazan district, Oct. 2, 1869; d. Moscow, Aug. 27, 1970, at the age of 100. She studied in Russia and later in Paris. Through her brother, the composer Alexander Olenin, she met Stasov, Balakirev, and Cui, and became interested in Russian vocal music. In 1893 she married the French writer Pierre d'Alheim (1862-1922), translator of the text of Boris Godunov; together they organized, in Moscow and in Paris, numerous concerts and lectures on Russian music, particularly on Mussorgsky; she was an outstanding interpreter of Russian songs; publ. a book, Le Legs de Mussorgsky (Paris, 1908). In 1935 she settled in Paris as voice teacher; in 1949 she joined the French Communist party; in 1959 she returned to Russia.

Oliphant, Thomas, British composer; b. Condie, Perthshire, Dec. 25, 1799; d. London, March 9, 1873. Of Scottish birth, he settled in London in 1830 and became a member of the Madrigal Society of London; publ. A Brief Account of the Madrigal Society (1835), A Short Account of Madrigals (1836), and La Musa Madrigalesca (1837; the words of 400 madrigals, chiefly of the Elizabethan period); also wrote English words for Italian madrigals; publ. several collections of glees, catches, and rounds. See the article on him in the Dictionary of National Biography.

Olitzka, Rosa, German contralto; b. Berlin, Sept. 6, 1873; d. Chicago, Sept. 29, 1949. She studied with Desirée Artôt and Julius Hey; sang at Berlin (1891); then was engaged at the Hannover Opera (1892-93); at Covent Garden, London (1894), and in New York with Damrosch's German Opera Co., conducted by Damrosch (1895-97); later also with the Metropolitan Opera. After a season with the Chicago Opera Co. (1910-11), she left the stage and was active as vocal teacher in Chicago.

Olitzki, Walter, German baritone; b. Hamburg, March 17, 1903; d. Los Angeles, Aug. 2, 1949. After a career in Germany, he appeared as Beckmesser at the Metropolitan Opera, N.Y. (Dec. 2, 1939); specialized in Wagnerian roles; was with the Metropolitan Opera until 1947. He was a nephew of **Rosa Olitzka.**

Oliveira, Jocy de, Brazilian pianist and avant-garde composer; b. Curitiba-Parana, Brazil, on April 11, 1936, of French and Portuguese origin. She studied piano in São Paulo with J. Kliass and in Paris with Marguerite Long; then traveled to the U.S.; obtained her M.A. at Washington Univ. at St. Louis in 1968. She appeared as a piano soloist with major orchestras in Europe and America, specializing in modern repertory; in 1966 she played the piano part in Stravinsky's *Capriccio* in St. Louis, under Stravinsky's direction. As a composer, she occupies the aphelion of ultramodernism, experimenting in electronic, environmental, theatrical, cinematic and television media, as exemplified by *Probabilistic Theater* I, II and III for musicians, actors, dancers, television and traffic conductor, and other environmental manifestations. Her *Polinteracões I, II, III* present the culmination of "total music" involving the visual, aural, tactile, gustatory and olfactory senses, with an anatomic chart serving as a score for guidance of the participants, supplemented by a phonemic table indicating the proper verbalization of vocal parts. (Complete score and illustrations were reproduced in *Source,* No. 7, Sacramento, California, 1970.) A performance of *Polinteracões* was attempted on the occasion of the Catalytic Celebration of the 10th Anniversary Festival of the New Music Circle in St. Louis on April 7, 1970, but was stopped by the management as a noisy, noisome nuisance. Jocy de Oliveira is also active in belles-lettres; she wrote a sociological fantasy *0 3° Mundo* (*The Third World*), a utopian, optimistic vision of the future); a controversial play, *Apague meu* (*Spotlight*), first produced in São Paulo in 1961; poetical works, etc. She also composed a number of advanced sambas, precipitating the vogue of the Brazilian "bossa nova." She is the wife of the Brazilian conductor **Eleazar de Carvalho.**

Oliver, Henry Kemble, American composer of hymn tunes; b. Beverly, Mass., Nov. 24, 1800; d. Salem, Aug. 12, 1885. He was a chorister at Park Street Church in Boston; graduated from Dartmouth College in 1818; played the organ in various churches in Salem and Boston; in 1826, founded and managed the Salem Mozart Association; subsequently went to Lawrence, Mass., where he was mayor in 1859; later was also mayor of Salem; 1861-65, was treasurer of the State of Massachusetts. He was given B.A. and M.A. degrees by Harvard Univ. (1862) and was made Mus. Doc. by Dartmouth College (1883). He wrote many well-known hymn tunes (*Federal Street, Morning, Harmony Grove, Beacon Street, Hudson*), motets, chants, and a *Te Deum;* publ. *The National Lyre* (1848; with Tuckerman and Bancroft; contains many of his own compositions), *Oliver's Collection of Hymn and Psalm Tunes* (1860), and *Original Hymn Tunes* (1875).
BIBLIOGRAPHY: F. J. Metcalf, *American Writers and Compilers of Sacred Music* (1925; pp. 230-33); *Dictionary of American Biography* (vol. XIV).

Oliver, Joseph ("King"), black American jazz cornetist and bandleader; b. on a plantation near Abend, Louisiana, May 11, 1885; d. Savannah, Georgia, April 8, 1938. In 1907 he was working in Storyville (the brothel district of New Orleans) with the Melrose Brass Band; in subsequent years he was with a number of other "brass bands" there, and in 1915 formed his own group, eventually known as the Creole Jazz Band; in 1917 he acquired the nickname "King," traditionally reserved for the leading jazz musicians. Also in 1917, the government closed the bordellos in Storyville, putting most of the musicians (among others) out of work; the following year Oliver moved his band to Chicago, leading a migration of jazz musicians to that city that was largely responsible for the dispersion of the black New Orleans jazz style throughout the country; in 1922 Louis Armstrong, whom he had known in New Orleans, joined the band, helping to make it the most polished exponent of New Orleans collectively improvised jazz; the group's 1923 recordings were the most influential early jazz recordings ever made; they have been reissued by the Smithsonian Institution. Subsequent bands formed by Oliver remained a potent force in jazz until around 1928. Oliver is the uncle of composer **Ulysses Kay.**
BIBLIOGRAPHY: W. C. Allen, *King Joe Oliver* (London, 1958); M. Williams, ed., *Jazz Panorama* (contains essays on Oliver by Edmond Souchon and Larry Gushee; N.Y., 1964); F. Ramsey, Jr., in *Dictionary of American Biography,* Supplement II.

Olivero, Magda, Italian soprano; b. Saluzzo, near Turin, March 25, 1912. She studied at the Turin Cons.; made her debut in Turin in 1933; then sang in the Italian provinces. She temporarily retired from the stage when she married in 1941, but resumed her career in 1951; made successful appearances at La Scala, Milan, in Paris and London. In 1966 she made her American debut in Dallas in the title role of Cherubini's *Medea;* she was 63 years old when she made her first appearance with the Metropolitan Opera, N.Y., in April 1975 as Tosca, an unprecedented occurrence in the opera annals; on Dec. 5, 1977 she gave a highly successful recital in a program of Italian art songs at Carnegie Hall, N.Y. Among her operatic roles were Violetta, Mimi and Tosca; she was praised mainly for her dramatic penetration of each character and her fine command of dynamic nuances.

Oliveros, Pauline, American avant-garde composer; b. Houston, May 30, 1932. She received the rudiments of musical education from her mother and grandmother; studied composition at the Univ. of Houston (1949-52), at San Francisco State College (1954-56), and privately with Robert Erickson. In 1967 she joined the faculty of the Univ. of California at San Diego. She cultivates total music in mixed media.
WORKS: *Trio* for flute, piano and page turner (1961); *Outline* for flute, percussion and string bass (1963); *Duo* for accordion and bandoneon with optional mynah bird obbligato, see-saw version (1964); *Variation for Sextet* (1964); *Pieces of Eight* for wind

octet, cash register and magnetic tape (1965); *Rock Symphony* for electronic tape (1965); *Seven Sets of Mnemonics* for multimedia (1965); *Bye Bye Butterfly* for oscillators, amplifiers, and assorted tapes (1965); *Particle Dangling in Honor of Gertrude Stein* for tape, mobile and work crew (1966); *Engineer's Delight* for piccolo and 7 conductors (1967); *Evidence for Computing Bimolecular and Termolecular Mechanism in the Hydrochlorination of Cyclohexene,* for inter-media (1968); *Double-Basses at 20 Paces* (1968); *The Dying Alchemist* for multimedia (1968); *Night Jar* for viola d'amore (1968); *The Wheel of Fortune,* improvisation suggested by the trump cards of the Tarot deck (1969); *One Sound* for string quartet, an invariant quadritone monody; *Apple Box Orchestra with Bottle Chorus* (1970). In her later avatar she embraced Tibetan Buddhism and adopted a static type of composition with no perceptible tonal variation; typical of this style is her *Rose Mountain* for vocal monotone and accordion (1977; renamed *Horse Sings From Cloud,* after a dream about flying horses). She is a member of the militant feminist group SCUM (acronym for "Society for Cutting Up Men").

d'Ollone, Max (full name, **Maximilien-Paul-Marie-Félix**), French composer and writer on music; b. Besançon, June 13, 1875; d. Paris, May 15, 1959. He studied with Lavignac, Massenet, and Lenepveu at the Paris Cons.; received the Grand Prix de Rome in 1897 with his cantata *Frédégonde;* was active as opera conductor in Paris and the French provinces. A prolific composer, he wrote 5 operas: *Le Retour* (Angers, Feb. 13, 1913), *Les Uns et les autres* (Paris, Nov. 6, 1922), *L'Arlequin* (Paris, Dec. 24, 1924), *George Dandin,* after Molière (Paris, March 19, 1930), and *La Samaritaine* (Paris, June 25, 1937); *Dans la cathédrale,* for orch. (1906); *Fantaisie* for piano and orch. (1899); chamber music; many songs; contributed to French magazines on musical subjects; publ. a book, *Le Théâtre lyrique et le public* (Paris, 1955).

Olmeda de San José, Federico, Spanish musicologist and composer; b. Burgos de Osma, 1865; d. Madrid, Feb. 11, 1909. He studied violin and music theory at Burgos; was appointed organist at the Cathedral of Burgos in 1888; in 1908 went to Madrid as choirmaster of the Convent of Las Descalzas Reales; founded and edited the review *La Voz de la Música* (1907); publ. manuals of solfeggio; the essays, *Folklore de Burgos* (Burgos, 1902), *Pio X y el canto romano* (Burgos, 1904), etc. and an important study on the 12th-century Codex of Calixtus II, in *Viaje Musical a Santiago de Galicia* (1895). He wrote 4 symphonies; a symph. poem, *Paraíso perdido;* an *Oda* for string orch.; several church works: *32 Rimas* for piano (1890–91); organ pieces, etc. (altogether some 350 works).

BIBLIOGRAPHY: H. Collet, *L'Essor de la musique espagnole au XXᵉ siècle* (Paris, 1929).

Olsen, Ole, Norwegian composer; b. Hammerfest, July 4, 1850; d. Oslo, Nov. 10, 1927. He studied with J. Lindeman; was active as organist and theater conductor in Trondhjem and other provincial towns; in 1870 went to Leipzig, where he studied with Richter and Reinecke; returning to Norway in 1874, he became a piano teacher in Oslo; was conductor of the Music Society there (1878–81), instructor of music at the Military Academy (1887–1903), and inspector of military music (1899–1919). He wrote the operas *Stig Hvide* (1876), *Stallo* (1902), *Klippeøerne* (1905), which were not produced, and *Lajla* (Oslo, Oct. 8, 1908); also some incidental music; Symph. (1878); the symph. poems *Aasgaardsreien* (1878) and *Alfedans (Elf Dance;* 1880); Concerto for Horn and Orch. (Oslo, April 1, 1905); numerous choruses; songs; piano music.

Olsen, Poul Rovsing, Danish composer and ethnomusicologist; b. Copenhagen, Nov. 4, 1922. He studied law at the Univ. of Aarhus (1940–42) and Univ. of Copenhagen (1942–48); concurrently, took lessons in composition with Knud Jeppesen at the Royal Cons. of Music in Copenhagen (1943–46); later studied with Nadia Boulanger in Paris (1948–49). Between 1958 and 1963 he took part in ethnomusicological expeditions to Arabia, India, Greece and East Greenland and wrote numerous valuable papers on the folklore and musical cultures of the areas he visited. He served as chairman of the Danish Society of Composers (1962–67); taught ethnomusicology at the Univ. of Lund, Sweden (1967–69) and subsequently at the Univ. of Copenhagen. In 1977 he was elected president of The International Folk Music Council. He was a music critic for the newspapers *Morgenbladet* (1945–46), *Information* (1949–54) and *Berlingske Tidende* (1954–74). Much of his music embodies materials of the Eastern countries where he traveled. His *Elegy* for organ (1953) is the first piece in the serial system by a Danish composer.

WORKS: opera, *Belisa* (1964; Copenhagen, Sept. 3, 1966); 4 ballets: *Ragnarök (Twilight of the Gods,* 1948; Copenhagen, Sept. 12, 1960); *La Création* (1952; Copenhagen, March 10, 1961); *Brylluppet (The Wedding,* 1966; Copenhagen, Sept. 15, 1969); *Den Fremmede (The Stranger;* 1969; Copenhagen, July 17, 1972); *Symphonic Variations* (1953); Piano Concerto (1953–54); *Sinfonia I* (1957–58; Copenhagen, April 13, 1959); *Sinfonia II, Susudil,* based on Arab and Turkish modes (1966; Copenhagen, Oct. 31, 1966); *Capriccio* for orch. (1961–62); *Kejseren (The Emperor)* for tenor, male chorus and orch. (1963; Copenhagen, Sept. 5, 1964); *Et russisk bal (The Russian Ball)* for orch. (1965); *Au Fond de la Nuit* for chamber orch. (1968); *Randrussermarchen* for orch. (1977); *2 Pieces* for clarinet and piano (1943); *Romance* for cello and piano (1943); Violin Sonata (1946); 2 string quartets (1948, 1969); Serenade for Violin and Piano (1949); 2 piano trios (1950, 1976); *Schicksalslieder,* after 4 Hölderlin poems, for soprano or tenor, and 7 instruments (1953); *Evening Songs* for mezzo-soprano and flute (1954); *Prolana* for clarinet, violin and piano (1955); Cello Sonata (1956); *Alapa-Tarana,* vocalise for mezzo-soprano and percussion (1959); *The Dream of Pan* for solo flute (1959); *Nouba,* 6 movements for harp (1960); *Passacaglia* for flute, violin, cello and piano (1960); *Á l'inconnu* for soprano or tenor, and 13 instruments (1962); *Patet* for 9 musicians (1966); *Fantasy* for 2 accordions (1967); *Arabesk* for 7 musicians (1968); *Shangri-La* for flute, viola d'amore and piano (1969); *Pour une Viole d'Amour* (1969); *Recontres* for cello and percussion (1970); *A Song of Mira Bai* for chorus, 3 trumpets and percussion (1971); *Poème* for accordion, guitar and percussion (1973); *Concertino* for clarinet, violin, cello and piano (1973); *Partita* for solo cello (1974); *Nostalgie* for guitar (1976); for piano: 3 sonatinas (1941, 1951, 1967); *Rondo* (1947); 2 sonatas for 4 hands (1948, 1967); *12 Preludes* (1948); 2 sonatas (1950, 1952); *3 Nocturnes* (1951); *5 Inventions* (1957); *Bagatelles* (1962); *Images* (1965); *4 Innocent Sonatas* (1969); *Many Happy Returns* (1971). He published 2 books: *Musiketnologi* (Copenhagen, 1974) and *Music and Musical Instruments in the World of Islam* (with Jean Jenkins, London, 1976).

Olsen, Sparre, Norwegian composer; b. Stavanger, April 25, 1903. He studied composition with Valen in Oslo (1925–30), then with Max Butting in Berlin, and with Percy Grainger in London; was violinist with the Oslo Symph. Orch. (1923–33) and in Bergen (1933–40); in 1936 became a recipient of the State Salary of Art (a government life pension); in 1968 was awarded the Order of St. Olav. His music is in the national tradition.

WORKS: *Variations on a Norwegian Folk Song* for orch. or piano (1930); *Little Overture* (1931); *2 Edda Songs* for voice, and orch. or piano (1931); *2 Modelle für Musik als Hörkulisse* for orch. (1931); *Gneisten (The Spark)* for male chorus and orch. (1933); *Cantata for Bergen* (1934); *Røystene (The Voices)* for soloists, chorus and chamber orch. (1935); *Prelude and Fugue* for orch. (1935); *Draumkvedet (The Dream Ballad)* for narrator, soloists, chorus and orch. (Bergen, April 19, 1937); *3 Symphonic Fantasias:* No. 1 (1938–39; Oslo, Sept. 21, 1939), No. 2 (1957; Oslo, Oct. 6, 1957), No. 3 (1973; Bergen, Nov. 28, 1974); *Nidarosdomen (The Nidaros Cathedral),* fugue and chorale for orch. (1940); *From Telemark,* suite for small orch. or piano (1940–41); *Ver Sanctum* for chorus and orch. (1941); *De Profundis Sursum Corda,* peace cantata (1945; Bergen, May 1946); *Music for Orchestra* (Oslo, Nov. 3, 1948); *Pastoral and Dance* for orch. (1949); *Leitom Suite* for orch. or piano (1951); *Serenade* for flute and string orch. (1954); *Intrada* for orch. with choral finale (1956); *Canticum* for orch. (1972); *Suite* for flute, oboe and clarinet (1933); *Wind Quintet* (1946); *3 Pieces* for flute and viola (1970); *String Quartet* (1972); songs; sacred choruses.

Olsson, Otto Emanuel, eminent Swedish organist and composer; b. Stockholm, Dec. 19, 1879; d. Stockholm, Sept. 1, 1964. He studied with Lagergren and Dente at the Stockholm Cons. (1897–1901); from 1908 until 1945, taught there; was organist of the Gustav Vasa Church in Stockholm (1908–56); became a member of the Royal Academy of Music in 1915.

WORKS: *Requiem* for soli, chorus and orch. (1903); 3 string quartets (1903, 1906, 1947); 2 organ symphonies (1903, 1918); 3 sets of *Preludes and Fugues* for organ (1910–11, 1918, 1935); *6 Latin Hymns* for a cappella chorus (1911–13); solo songs.

Ondříček, Emanuel, Czech violinist; son of **Jan Ondříček** and brother of **Franz Ondříček,** b. Pilsen, Dec. 6, 1882; d. Boston, Dec. 30, 1958. He studied with his father and with Ševčik at the Prague Cons.; after a series of concerts in Europe, he settled in the U.S. in 1912; became an eminent teacher in Boston and N.Y.; publ. a manual, *Mastery of Tone Production and Expression on the Violin.*

Ondříček, Franz, Czech violinist; b. Prague, April 29, 1857; d. Milan, April 12, 1922. He studied with his father, **Jan Ondříček,** and later with Bennewitz at the Prague Cons., winning 1st prize (1876–79); and with Massart at the Paris Cons., where he also won 1st prize (1879–81). He undertook extensive concert tours of Europe, America, Siberia, and the Far East before settling in Vienna (1907), where he founded the celebrated Ondříček Quartet (with Silbiger, Junck, and Jelinek); was prof. at the Neues Wiener Kons. (1910–19); from 1919 taught at the Prague Cons. In 1885 he married **Anna Hlavaček,** a singer at the National Theater of Prague. As a concert player, he impressed his audiences with his fiery temperament, but in his later years developed a grand Classical style, marked by dignified repose. He publ. *Rapsodie bohème,* for violin and orch.; a cadenza to the Violin Concerto of Brahms; numerous pieces for violin with piano. In collaboration with S. Mittelmann, he brought out *Neue Methode zur Erlangung der Meistertechnik des Violinspiels auf anatomisch-physiologischer Grundlage* (2 parts, 1909) with 15 of his own études.

Ondříček, Jan, Czech violinist; b. Bělec, near Bratronice, May 6, 1832; d. Prague, March 13, 1900. He was the son of a village violinist, and studied with him; played in various orchestras, and also conducted; was a friend of Dvořák. He had 9 children, all of whom were musicians.

Onégin, Sigrid (*née* **Hoffmann;** full name **Elizabeth Elfriede Emilie Sigrid**), contralto; b. Stockholm (of a German father and a French mother), June 1, 1889; d. Magliaso, Switzerland, June 16, 1943. She studied in Frankfurt with Resz, in Munich with E. R. Weiss, and with di Ranieri in Milan. She made her first public appearance, using the name **Lilly Hoffmann,** in Wiesbaden, Sept. 16, 1911, in a recital, accompanied by the Russian pianist and composer **Eugene Onégin** (b. St. Petersburg, Oct. 10, 1883; d. Stuttgart, Nov. 12, 1919; real name Lvov; he was a grandnephew of Alexis Lvov, author of the Russian Tsarist hymn), whom she married on May 25, 1913; after his death, she married a German doctor, Fritz Penzoldt (Nov. 20, 1920). She made her first appearance in opera, as Carmen, in Stuttgart, on Oct. 10, 1912; American operatic debut at the Metropolitan Opera House, N.Y., as Amneris, on Nov. 22, 1922; revisited America several times, her last tour (in recitals) being in 1938. From 1931 she lived mostly in Switzerland.

BIBLIOGRAPHY: Fritz Penzoldt, *Alt-Rhapsodie; Sigrid Onegin, Leben und Werk* (Neustadt, 1953; includes several chapters written by Sigrid Onégin herself, originally publ. 1939, Magdeburg).

O'Neill, Norman, English conductor and composer; b. London, March 14, 1875; d. there, March 3, 1934. He was a direct descendant of the notable English musician **John Wall Callcott;** his father was a painter. He studied in London with Arthur Somervell, and later with Knorr in Frankfurt. Returning to London in 1899, he married the pianist **Adine Rückert** (1875–1947). He wrote incidental music for the Haymarket Theatre, of which he was musical director from 1908 to 1919; also produced the ballets *Before Dawn* (1917); *Punch and Judy* (1924), *Alice in Lumberland* (1926), etc.

BIBLIOGRAPHY: D. Hudson, *Norman O'Neill: A Life of Music* (London, 1945).

Onofri, Alessandro, Italian organist and composer; b. Spoleto, May 29, 1874; d. Varese, Aug. 27, 1932. He studied in Rome with Mascagni, Rossi, and others; in 1904 settled in Boston, where he was church organist. He wrote the operas *Biancospino* (Venice, March 31, 1910) and *Assiuolo* (Rome, Sept. 25, 1912); the light operas *La Famiglia modello* (Leghorn, 1913) and *Il Bocciuolo di rosa* (Rome, 1916). During his stay in the U.S., he wrote a set of American dances for piano.

Onslow, George (full name **André Georges Louis Onslow**), noted French composer; b. Clermont-Ferrand, July 27, 1784; d. there, Oct. 3, 1853. He was the grandson of the first Lord Onslow, studied in London with Hüllmandel, Dussek, and Cramer (piano) and in Paris with Reicha (composition). He wrote 3 comic operas, produced in Paris: *L'Alcalde de la Vega* (Aug. 10, 1824), *Le Colporteur* (Nov. 22, 1827), and *Le Duc de Guise* (Sept. 8, 1837); 4 symphonies, and some other orchestral music. However, these works failed to maintain interest; Onslow's real achievement was the composition of a great number of chamber works, in which he demonstrated an uncommon mastery of counterpoint; he wrote 34 string quintets; 36 string quartets; 6 piano trios; a sextet for flute, clarinet, horn, bassoon, double bass, and piano (the double-bass part was expressly written for the famous virtuoso Dragonetti); a nonet, for violin, viola, cello, double bass, flute, oboe, clarinet, bassoon, and horn; a septet, for flute, oboe, clarinet, horn, bassoon, double bass, and piano; violin sonatas; cello sonatas; piano sonatas 4 hands; a number of piano pieces. As a result of a hunting accident in 1829, when a stray bullet injured him, he became deaf in one ear; his Quintet No. 15, subtitled *Le Quintette de la balle (Quintet of the bullet)*, was the musical rendering of this episode.

BIBLIOGRAPHY: L. Halévy, *Notice sur George Onslow* (Paris, 1855).

Oosterzee, Cornelie van, Dutch composer; b. Batavia, Java, Aug. 16, 1863; d. Berlin, Aug. 8, 1943. She studied in Berlin, and settled there in 1890; her opera *Das Gelöbnis* was produced in Weimar on May 1, 1910.

Opieński, Henryk, eminent Polish music scholar and composer; b. Cracow, Jan. 13, 1870; d. Morges, Switzerland, Jan. 21, 1942. He studied with Zelenski in Cracow, with Vincent d'Indy in Paris, and with H. Urban in Berlin; then went to Leipzig, where he studied musicology with Riemann and conducting with Nikisch. In 1907 he was appointed instructor at the Warsaw Musical Society; from 1908 to 1912 he conducted the Warsaw Opera; in 1912, went again to Germany, where he took his degree of Dr. phil. (Leipzig, 1914). He spent the years of World War I at Morges, Swit-

zerland; returning to Poland, he was director of the Cons. of Poznań (1919–26); then settled again in Morges.

WORKS: the operas *Maria* (1904; Poznań, April 27, 1923) and *Jakub lutnista (Jacob the Lutenist*; 1916–18; Poznań, Dec. 21, 1927); the oratorio *The Prodigal Son* (1930); the symph. poems *Lilla Weneda* (1908) and *Love and Destiny* (1912); *Scènes lyriques en forme de quatuor,* for string quartet; violin pieces; songs; an album of 15 Polish songs (with French words; 1928) and another album of 15 Polish songs publ. with English words (1936). He publ. several books and essays on Chopin (Lwow, 1910; 2nd ed., 1922; Warsaw, 1911; Warsaw, 1912, etc.); also the collected letters of Chopin, in Polish, German, French, and English (1931); other writings include a history of music in Polish (Warsaw, 1912; 2nd ed., 1922); *La Musique polonaise* (Paris, 1918; 2nd ed., 1929); a valuable monograph on Moniuszko (Warsaw, 1924); a monograph on Paderewski (Lwow, 1910; 2nd ed., Warsaw, 1928; in French, Lausanne, 1928; 2nd ed., 1948).

BIBLIOGRAPHY: A. Fornerod, *H. Opieński* (Lausanne, 1942).

Orbón, Julián, Spanish-born composer; b. Avilés, Aug. 7, 1925. He received the rudiments of musical education from his father, a professional pianist. After the Spanish Civil War the family emigrated to Cuba; he studied music theory with José Ardevol, with whom he also formed a "Grupo de Renovació Musical" (1942–49). After the revolution of 1959 in Cuba Orbón went to Mexico, and in 1963 he settled in N.Y. In his music he follows a neo-Classical mode of composition; among his works are: Symphony in C (1945); *Danzas sinfónicas* (1955); Concerto Grosso (1958); *Oficios de 3 días* for chorus and orch. (1970); String Quartet (1951); numerous piano pieces and choruses.

Orchard, William Arundel, Australian pianist, conductor and composer; b. London, April 13, 1867; d. during a voyage in the South Atlantic, off the coast of South Africa (23°49′ latitude south; 09°33′ longitude east), April 17, 1961. He studied in London and Durham; in 1903 went to Australia and lived in Sydney, where he was active as conductor and music educator; served as director of the New South Wales State Cons. (1923–34); later taught at the Univ. of Tasmania. He wrote an opera *The Picture of Dorian Gray,* after Oscar Wilde; a violin concerto; a string quartet; a string quintet; choruses; songs. He publ. 2 books dealing with Australian music: *The Distant View* (Sydney, 1943) and *Music in Australia* (Melbourne, 1952).

Ordoñez, Carlos, Austrian composer of Spanish extraction; b. Vienna, April 19, 1734; d. there, Sept. 1786. He was employed as a clerk, but studied violin and performed successfully at chamber music concerts. He wrote numerous singspiele and much instrumental music, some of which was publ. still in his lifetime. His singspiel *Diesmal hat der Mann den Willen* was performed in Vienna on April 22, 1778; his marionette opera *Alceste* was introduced by Haydn in Esterház in 1775. He developed an excellent métier, and several of his symphonies possessed enough merit to be misattributed to Haydn. For further details see H. C. Robbins Landon's article on Ordoñez in *Die Musik in Geschichte und Gegenwart.*

Orefice, Giacomo, Italian composer; b. Vicenza, Aug. 27, 1865; d. Milan, Dec. 22, 1922. He studied with Mancinelli and Busi in Bologna; in 1909, became prof. at the Verdi Cons. in Milan; also wrote music criticism.
WORKS: operas: *Mariska* (Turin, Nov. 19, 1889), *Consuelo* (Bologna, Nov. 27, 1895); *Il Gladiatore* (Madrid, March 20, 1898), *Chopin* (Milan, Nov. 25, 1901), *Cecilia* (Vicenza, Aug. 16, 1902), *Mosè* (Genoa, Feb. 18, 1905), *Il Pane d'altrui* (Venice, Jan. 19, 1907), *Radda* (Milan, Oct. 25, 1912), *Castello dei sogni* (unfinished); a ballet, *La Soubrette* (Milan, 1907); a symph; the orchestral suites *Sinfonia del bosco* (1898), *Anacreontiche,* and *Laudi francescane* (1920); chamber music; piano pieces; etc. He arranged Monteverdi's *Orfeo* (produced, Milan, Nov. 30, 1909); publ. a monograph on his teacher Mancinelli (Rome, 1921).

Orel, Alfred, Austrian musicologist; b. Vienna, July 3, 1889; d. there, April 11, 1967. He studied law in Vienna; then musicology with Guido Adler; 1919, Dr. phil. (dissertation: *Die Hauptstimme in den Salve Regina der Trienter Codices*); from 1918, librarian of the music division of the municipal library, Vienna, and of the Musicological Institute of the Univ.; later (1936) also associate prof. at the Univ.
WRITINGS: *Ein Wiener Beethoven-Buch* (1921); *Unbekannte Frühwerke Anton Bruckners* (with a reprint of the G minor Overture; Vienna, 1921); *Anton Bruckner: Das Werk—Der Künstler—Die Zeit* (Vienna, 1925); *Beethoven* (Vienna, 1927); *Der junge Schubert* (Vienna, 1940); *Mozarts deutscher Weg; Eine Deutung aus Briefen* (Vienna, 1940; 2nd ed., 1943); *Grillparzer und Beethoven* (Vienna, 1941); *Mozart in Wien* (Vienna, 1944); *Hugo Wolf* (Vienna, 1947); *Johannes Brahms* (Olten, 1948); *Goethe als Operndirektor* (Bregenz, 1949); *Bruckner-Brevier: Briefe, Dokumente, Berichte* (Vienna, 1953); *Musikstadt Wien* (Vienna, 1953); *Mozart, Gloria Mundi* (Salzburg, 1956). He edited (with R. Ficker) selections from the Trent Codices, in *Denkmäler der Tonkunst in Österreich* 53 (27.i), and the collected works of Bruckner (with R. Haas). He also brought out pictorial biographies of Beethoven, Schubert, and Brahms. A Festschrift in honor of his 70th birthday was publ. in Vienna in 1960.

Orel, Dobroslav, Czech ecclesiastical music scholar; b. Ronov, near Prague, Dec. 15, 1870; d. Prague, Feb. 18, 1942; studied music with Novák and Hostinský in Prague, later musicology with Guido Adler in Vienna; 1914, Dr. phil. there (dissertation: *Der Mensuralkodex Speciálník, ein Beitrag zur Geschichte der Mensuralmusik und der Notenschrift in Böhmen bis 1540);* ordained priest; prof. at the Prague Cons. (1907-19); 1909-18, ed. of the Prague church music periodical *Cyrill;* 1921-38, prof. of musicology at the Komensky Univ., Bratislava; conductor of various choral societies in Bratislava. His writings, some in Czech, some in German, include: *Handbook of the Roman Plainchant* (1899); *The Franus Cantional of 1505* (1921);

Czech Hymnal (1921); *Old Czech Rorate Songs* (1922); *J. L. Bella,* a biography (1924). He edited (with M. Springer) the liturgical works: *Graduale parvum* (Regensburg, 1912) and *Proprium Provinciae Pragensis ad Grad. Rom.* (1913); and (with Hejčl) *Marian Folk-Vespers* (1912).

Orem, Preston Ware, American composer, conductor, and teacher; b. Philadelphia, 1865; d. there (while conducting a school orch.), May 26, 1938. He studied at the Univ. of Pennsylvania; taught at Combs Cons., Philadelphia (1896-1905); in 1900, became editor for the Theodore Presser Co. and conductor of the Presser Choral Society. He publ. a harmony book for beginners; composed an *American Indian Rhapsody* for piano; a symph. sketch, *Out of the West;* chamber music; piano pieces; songs.

Orff, Carl, outstanding German composer; b. Munich, July 10, 1895. He studied at the Academy of Music in Munich, and with Heinrich Kaminski; from 1950, prof. at the Hochschule für Musik in Munich. In his music he sought to revive the old monodic forms, and adopt them to modern tastes by means of dissonant counterpoint, with lively rhythm in asymmetrical patterns. Apart from his compositions, Orff initiated a highly important method of musical education, which was adopted not only in Germany but in England, America and Russia; it stemmed from the Günther School for gymnastics, dance and music which Orff founded in 1924 with Dorothee Günther in Munich, with the aim of promoting instrumental playing and understanding of rhythm among children; he commissioned the piano manufacturer Karl Maendler to construct special percussion instruments that are extremely easy to play; the "Orff instruments" became widely adopted in American schools. Orff's ideas of rhythmic training owe much to the eurhythmics of Jaques-Dalcroze, but he simplified them to reach the elementary level; as a manual, he compiled a set of musical exercises, *Schulwerk* (1930-35, revised, 1950-54).
WORKS: His most famous work is the scenic oratorio, *Carmina Burana* (Frankfurt, June 8, 1937; numerous productions in Europe and America); the words (in Latin and German) are from 13th-century student poems found in the monastery of Benediktbeuren in Bavaria ("Burana" is the Latin adjective of the locality). Other works: *Der Mond,* opera, after a fairy-tale by Grimm (Munich, Feb. 5, 1939; revised version, Munich, Nov. 26, 1950); *Die Kluge,* opera after a fairy tale by Grimm (Frankfurt, Feb. 20, 1943); *Catulli Carmina,* scenic cantata after Catullus (Leipzig, Nov. 6, 1943); *Die Bernauerin,* a musical play (Stuttgart, June 15, 1947); *Antigonae,* musical play after Sophocles (Salzburg, Aug. 9, 1949); *Trionfo di Afrodite* (3rd part of a triology under the general title *Trionfi,* the 1st and 2nd parts being *Carmina Burana* and *Catulli Carmina;* Milan, Feb. 13, 1953); *Astutuli,* opera-ballet (Munich, Oct. 20, 1953); *Comoedia de Christi Resurrectione,* Easter cantata (Munich, March 31, 1956); *Oedipus der Tyrann,* musical play after Sophocles (Stuttgart, Dec. 11, 1959); *Ludus de nato infante mirificus,* a nativity play (Stuttgart, Dec. 11, 1960); *Prometheus,* opera (Stuttgart, March 24, 1968); *Rota* for voices and instruments, after the canon *Su-*

mer is icumen in, composed as a "salute to youth" for the opening ceremony of the Munich Olympics (1972); stage play *De temporum fine comoedia* (Salzburg, 1973). He further wrote a dance play, *Der Feuerfarbene* (1925); *Präludium* for orch. (1925); Concertino for wind instruments and harpsichord (1927); *Entrata,* for orch., based on melodies of William Byrd (1928; revised 1940); festival music for chamber orch. (1928); *Bayerische Musik* for small ensemble (1934); *Olympischer Reigen,* for various instruments (1936); revised versions of Monteverdi's *Orfeo* (Mannheim, April 17, 1925; 2nd version, Munich, Oct. 13, 1929; 3rd version, Dresden, Oct. 4, 1940) and Monteverdi's *Ballo delle Ingrate, Lamento d'Arianna,* and *L'Incoronazione di Poppea.*

BIBLIOGRAPHY: A. Liess, *Carl Orff (Zürich, 1955);* E. Helm, "Carl Orff," *Musical Quarterly* (July 1955); I. Kiekert, *Die Musikalische Form in den Werken Carl Orffs* (Regensburg, 1957); A. Liess, *Carl Orff: His Life and His Music* (N.Y., 1966); M. Devreese-Papgnies, *Sur les traces du Schulwerk de Carl Orff, Méthodologie pour l'usage des instruments d'orchestre scolaire* (Brussels, 1968); R. B. Glasgow and G. H. Dale, *Study to Determine the Feasibility of Adapting the Carl Orff Approach to Elementary Schools in America* (Washington, 1968); L. Barenboim, ed., *Carl Orff's System of Musical Education of Children* (Leningrad, 1971).

Orgad, Ben-Zion, German-born Israeli composer; b. Gelsenkirchen, Aug. 21, 1926. He came to Palestine in 1933; studied composition with Ben-Haim (1940–46); made several trips to America and took courses in composition with Copland at Tanglewood (1949, 1952, 1961) and with Irving Fine and Harold Shapero at Brandeis Univ. (1960–61); lectured on Israeli music in the U.S. (1970). Returning to Israel, he worked in the Ministry of Culture in Jerusalem.

WORKS: *Tóccata* for piano (1946); *Ballade* for solo flute (1947); *Hatsvi Israel (The Beauty of Israel),* symph for baritone and orch. (1949); Biblical cantata *Isaiah's Vision* (1952); *Min He'afar (Out of the Desert),* quintet for mezzo-soprano or contralto, flute, bassoon, viola and cello (1956); *Building the King's Stage* for orch. (1957); *Monolog* for solo viola (1957); Septet for clarinet, bassoon, horn, violin, viola, cello and double bass (1959); *Music* for orch. with solo horn (1960); String Trio (1961); *7 Variations on C* for piano (1961); *Tak'sim* for solo harp (1962); *Movement on A* for orch. (1965); *Kaleidoscope* for orch. (1965); *Mizmorim,* cantata on psalms (1966–67); *Songs of an Early Morning* for mezzo-soprano, baritone and chamber orch. (1968); *Landscapes* for wind quintet (1969); *First Watch* for string orch. (1969); *Melodic Dialogues on 3 Scrolls* for violin, oboe, percussion, string quartet and string orch. (1969); *Songs without Words,* sextet for violin, cello, flute, clarinet, percussion and piano (1970); *Ballade* for orch. (1971); *A Tale of a Pipe* for soloists, female chorus and 19 instruments (1971); *The Second Watch* for chamber orch. (1973); Duo for violin and cello (1973).

Orgeni, Aglaja (real name **Görger St. Jorgen**), Hungarian coloratura soprano; b. Roma Szombat, Dec. 17, 1841; d. Vienna, March 15, 1926. She was a pupil of Mme. Viardot-Garcia at Baden-Baden; made her de-but on Sept. 28, 1865, as Amina, at the Berlin Opera; first appearance in London, April 7, 1866, as Violetta, at Covent Garden; she sang later in Vienna, Dresden, Berlin, Copenhagen, etc.; from 1886, taught singing at the Dresden Cons.; was made "Royal Professor" in 1908 (the first case of the title being conferred on a woman). In 1914 she settled in Vienna. Among her distinguished pupils were Erika Wedeking and Edyth Walker.

BIBLIOGRAPHY: Erna Brand, *Aglaja Orgeni* (Munich, 1931).

Orlov, Nikolai, Russian pianist; b. Eletz, Feb. 26, 1892; d. Grantown-on-Spey, Scotland, May 31, 1964. He studied at the Moscow Cons. with Igumnov; also privately with Taneyev; in 1921, left Russia and gave concerts throughout Europe; also appeared in the U.S.; made his headquarters mainly in Paris.

Ormandy, Eugene (real name **Blau**), outstanding conductor; b. Budapest, Nov. 18, 1899; studied violin with his father; entered the Royal Academy of Music in Budapest at the age of 5; began studying with Hubay at 9; received an artist's diploma for violin in 1914; received a teacher's certificate at the Royal Academy in 1917; then was concertmaster of the Blüthner Orch. in Germany; also gave recitals and played with orchestras as soloist; in 1921, came to the U.S., obtained the position of concert-master of the Capitol Theater Orch., N.Y., and remained there for 2½ years; made his debut as conductor with that orch. in Sept. 1924; in 1925, became its associate music director; 1929, conducted the N.Y. Philharmonic at Lewisohn Stadium; 1930, guest conductor with the Robin Hood Dell Orch., Philadelphia; on Oct. 30, 1931, conducted the Philadelphia Orch. In 1931, he was appointed permanent conductor of the Minneapolis Symph. Orch.; in 1936, engaged as associate conductor of the Philadelphia Orch. (with Stokowski); in 1938, permanent conductor; traveled with it on transcontinental tours in 1937, 1946, and in 1948; in 1949, made an extended tour in England; in the spring of 1955, presented concerts with the Philadelphia Orch. in 10 European countries; in the summer of 1958 he led it on another European tour (including Russia). He appeared on numerous occasions as guest conductor with European orchestras; in Australia (summer of 1944); South America (summer of 1946), etc. In 1973 he took the Philadelphia Orch. to China and led it in several cities there; this was the first appearance of an American symphony orchestra in the People's Republic of China. Ormandy is an officer of the French Legion of Honor (1952); Knight of the Order of the White Rose of Finland (1955); holder of the medal of the Bruckner Society (1936); honorary Mus. Doc., Univ. of Pennsylvania; in 1976 he was named honorary Knight Commander of the British Empire by Queen Elizabeth in honor of the American Bicentennial. In his interpretations, Ormandy reveals himself as a Romanticist; he excels in the works of Beethoven, Schumann, and Richard Strauss; his renditions of music by Debussy and of the moderns are marked by color without extravagance; he conducts all his scores from memory.

BIBLIOGRAPHY: Hope Stoddard, *Symphony Con-*

ductors of the U.S.A. (N.Y., 1957; pp. 147–59); H. Kupferberg, *Those Fabulous Philadelphians* (N.Y., 1969).

Ornithoparchus (Greek form of his real name, **Vogelsang**), **Andreas,** German music scholar; b. Meiningen, c.1485; d. Münster, c.1535; led a wandering life; about 1516, *magister artium* at Tübingen. He was the author of a valuable theoretical treatise, *Musice active micrologus* (1517; 6th ed., 1540; English transl. by Dowland, London, 1609).
BIBLIOGRAPHY: J. W. Lyra, *Andreas Ornithoparchus und dessen Lehre von den Kirchenakzenten* (Gütersloh, 1877).

Ornstein, Leo, remarkable Russian pianist and composer; b. Kremenchug, Dec. 11, 1892. The son of a synagogal cantor, he studied music at home; then with Vladimir Puchalski in Kiev; at the age of 10 he was accepted as a pupil at the St. Petersburg Cons. As a consequence of anti-Semitic disturbances in Russia, the family decided to emigrate to the U.S. in 1907. Ornstein studied piano with Mrs. Bertha Feiring Tapper at the New England Cons., Boston, and with Percy Goetschius; also attended the Institute of Musical Art, N.Y. He gave his first concert in N.Y., as pianist, on March 5, 1911; then played in Philadelphia and other cities. About 1910 he began to compose; experimented with percussive sonorities, in dissonant harmonies; made a European tour in 1913; played in Norway, Denmark, and in Paris; appeared in London on March 27, 1914, in a piano recital announced as "futuristic music" and featuring his sonata and other works. Returning to the U.S. early in 1915, he gave a series of recitals at the Bandbox Theater, N.Y., comprising works by Debussy, Ravel, Schoenberg, Scriabin, and other modern composers; also his own music; his *Danse sauvage* excited his audiences by its declared wildness. Ornstein was hailed as the prophet of a new musical era, but soon ceased to attract attention. He continued to compose, although the titles of his works were no longer wild and provocative; in 1974 he completed his major work, *Biography in Sonata Form.* In 1978 he was living in Texas.
WORKS: for orch.: *3 Moods: Anger, Peace, Joy* (1914); *The Fog,* symph. poem (1915); Piano Concerto (Philadelphia Orch., Feb. 13, 1925, composer soloist); *Lysistrata Suite* (1933); Symphony (1934); *Nocturne and Dance of Fates* (St. Louis, Feb. 12, 1937); *3 Russian Choruses,* a cappella (1921); Piano Quintet; String Quartet; Violin Sonata; Cello Sonata; *Nocturne* for clarinet and piano; 4 piano sonatas; many pieces for piano: *À la chinoise; Suicide in an Airplane* (1913); *Danse sauvage* (1915); *Suite russe;* songs (*The Corpse,* etc.).
BIBLIOGRAPHY: Carl Van Vechten, *Music and Bad Manners* (N.Y., 1916; pp. 229–43); Ch. L. Buchanan, "Ornstein and Modern Music," *Musical Quarterly* (April 1918); F. H. Martens, *Leo Ornstein: The Man, His Ideas, His Work* (N.Y., 1918); Paul Rosenfeld, in *Musical Chronicle, 1917–1923* (N.Y., 1923); Paul Rosenfeld, in *An Hour with American Music* (N.Y., 1929); Vivian Perlis, "The Futurist Music of Leo Ornstein," *Notes* (June 1975).

Orr, Charles Wilfred, English composer; b. Cheltenham, July 31, 1893, d. Stroud, Gloucestershire, Feb. 24, 1976. He studied at the Guildhall School of Music in London; wrote songs in the manner of German lieder, to words by English poets; his set of 7 songs to texts from Housman's *A Shropshire Lad* is notable.
BIBLIOGRAPHY: S. Northcote, "The Songs of C. W. Orr," *Music & Letters* (1937).

Orr, Robin, Scottish composer; b. Brechin, June 2, 1909. He studied organ and composition at the Royal College of Music in London and at Cambridge Univ. (1929–32); subsequently took courses with Edward J. Dent in London, with Alfredo Casella in Siena and with Nadia Boulanger in Paris. From 1938 to 1950 he was active as organist and music instructor in Cambridge; then taught at the Royal College of Music in London (1950–56), and at the Univ. of Glasgow (1956–65); in 1965 was appointed prof. of music at Cambridge Univ. His works include *Symphony in One Movement* (London, Dec. 12, 1963); *Full Circle,* opera (Perth, Scotland, April 10, 1968); *Journeys and Places* for mezzo-soprano and string quintet (1971); string quartet; choral pieces. He edited *The Kelvin Series of Scots Songs.*

Orrego-Salas, Juan, Chilean composer and music educator; b. Santiago, Jan. 18, 1919. He studied at the School of Architecture of the Catholic Univ. of Santiago (1938–42); studied composition with Humberto Allende and Domingo Santa Cruz, at the National Cons. of Music at the Univ. of Chile (1936–43); came to the U.S. and attended classes in musicology with Paul Henry Lang and George Herzog at Columbia Univ. in N.Y. (1944–45); subsequently studied composition with Randall Thompson at Princeton Univ. (1945–46) and with Aaron Copland at Tanglewood, Mass. (summer, 1946); in 1953 received the diploma as Professor Extraordinario de Composición (Ph.D.) from the Univ. of Chile and the honorary degree of Doctor Scientiae from the Catholic Univ. of Santiago (1971). From 1942 to 1961 he taught at the Univ. of Chile; in 1961 was engaged as prof. of composition and Latin American music history at the Indiana Univ. in Bloomington and Director of the Latin American Music Center there.
WORKS: opera-oratorio *El Retablo del Rey Pobre* for 3 sopranos, mezzo-soprano, contralto, tenor, baritone, chorus and small orch. (1950–51); 3 ballets: *Juventud* (after Handel's *Solomon,* 1948); *Umbral del Sueño* (1951); *The Tumbler's Prayer* (1960); an oratorio *The Days of God* (Washington, Nov. 2, 1976); 2 cantatas: *Cantata de Navidad* for soprano and orch. (1946) and *América, no en vano invocamos tu nombre* (1966); *Missa, in tempore discordiae* for tenor, chorus and orch. (1968–69); *Psalms* for narrator and wind orch. (1962); *Songs,* in 3 movements, for medium voice and string quartet (1945); *Canciones Castellanas* for soprano and 8 instruments (1948); *Cantos de Advenimeinto* for medium voice, cello and piano (1948); *Words of Don Quixote* for baritone and chamber ensemble (Washington, Oct. 31, 1970); numerous songs and choruses. FOR ORCH.: *Escenas de Cortes y Pastores,* suite (1946); *Obertura Festiva* (1948); 4 symphonies: No. 1 (1949; Santiago, July 1950); No. 2, *a la*

memoria de un vagabundo (1954; Minneapolis, Feb. 17, 1956); No. 3 (1961; Washington, April 22, 1961); No. 4, *de la respuesta lejana* (Bloomington, Indiana, 1967); Piano Concerto (1950); *Concerto da Camera* for woodwind quartet, 2 horns, harp and strings (1952); *Serenata Concertante* (1954–55; Louisville, May 3, 1955); *Jubileaus Musicus* (1956); *Concerto a Tre* for violin, cello; piano and orch. (Washington, May 7, 1965); Concerto for Wind Orch. (1963–64); *Volte* for piano, 15 winds, harp and percussion (1971); *Variaciones Serenas* for string orch. (1971). CHAMBER MUSIC: Violin Sonata (1945); *Sonata a duo* for violin and viola (1945); *Suite* for solo bandoneon (1952); Sextet for clarinet, string quartet and piano (1954); *Duo Concertante* for cello and piano (1955); *Pastorale and Scherzo* for violin and piano (1956); 2 *Divertimentos* for flute, oboe and bassoon (1956); String Quartet No. 1 (1957); Concertino for brass quartet (1963); *Sonata a Quattro* for flute, oboe, harpsichord and double bass (1964); Piano Trio (1966); *Quattro Liriche Breve* for saxophone and piano (1967); *Mobili* for viola and piano (1967); *Esquinas* for solo guitar (1971); *Serenata* for flute and cello (1972); *Sonata de Estío* for flute and piano (1972); *Presencias* for flute, oboe, clarinet, violin, viola, cello and harpsichord (1972). FOR PIANO: 2 *suites* (1946, 1951), *Variaciones y fuga sobre un pregón* (1946), *Diez Prezas Simples* (1951), *Canción y Danza* (1951), *Rústica* (1952), Sonata (1967).

Orsi, Romeo, Italian clarinetist and manufacturer of wind instruments; b. Como, Oct. 18, 1843; d. Milan, June 11, 1918. He studied at the Royal Cons. of Milan (1856–64); in 1873 became prof. of clarinet there; for 40 years was 1st clarinetist of La Scala (1871–1911); gave concerts in Italy and in Paris. In 1881 he constructed a combination clarinet capable of performing both B-flat and A clarinet parts; it had a temporary acceptance among orchestral players; also manufactured a bass clarinet in A for use in Verdi's *Otello;* publ. a method for the saxophone.

Orth, John, American organist and composer; b. Annweiler, Bavaria, Dec. 2, 1850; d. Boston, May 3, 1932. His parents settled in Taunton, Mass., when he was a year old; he studied organ with his father; then went to Germany, where he took courses with Kullak and Deppe (piano); also had lessons with Liszt; studied composition with Faiszt, Weitzmann, Kiel, and P. Scharwenka. In 1875 he settled in Boston as pianist and teacher; became a propagandist for Liszt's music in America, in lecture-recitals. In 1883, he married his pupil, Lizette E. Blood, known as **L. E. Orth** (d. Boston, Sept. 14, 1913), who was herself a composer of songs and piano pieces. Orth publ. a number of teaching pieces for piano.

Orthel, Léon, Dutch composer and pianist; b. Roosendaal, North Brabant, Oct. 4, 1905. He studied composition with Johan Wagenaar at the Royal Cons. of The Hague (1921–26); a government fellowship enabled him to study with Paul Juon at the Hochschule für Musik in Berlin (1928–29). From 1941 to 1971 he taught piano and theory at the Royal Cons. at The Hague; concurrently taught composition at the Amsterdam Cons. (1949–71); was chairman of the Com-

posers' Section of the Royal Dutch Society of Musicians (1947–70). He gave concerts as a pianist in Holland. As a composer, he followed the romantic trends.

WORKS: Among his best lyric works are 13 separate song cycles to the poems of Rainer Maria Rilke (1934–72). Other works include a *Concertstuk* for violin and orch. (1924); *Scherzo* for piano and orch. (1927); Cello Concerto (1929); *Concertino alla Burla* for piano and orch. (1930); 6 symphonies: No. 1 (1931–33); No. 2, *Piccola sinfonia* (1940; Rotterdam, Oct. 31, 1941; his finest work and one of the most frequently played); No. 3 (1943); No. 4, *Sinfonia concertante*, for piano and orch. (1949); No 5, *Musica Iniziale* (1959–60); No. 6 (1960–61); *Nonnen-Klage* for soprano, and orch. or piano (1943); 2 *Scherzos* for orch. (1954–55, 1956–57); 3 *movimenti ostinati* for orch. (1971–72; Amsterdam, Sept. 1, 1973); trumpet concerto (1973–74); *Une Martyre (Dessin d'un maître inconnu)* for high voice, and orch. (1974–75); 2 violin sonatas (1924, 1933); 2 cello sonatas (1925, 1958); *Burleske* for cello and piano (1926); *Ballade* for cello and piano (1927); 5 *Pezzettini* for clarinet and piano (1963); String Quartet (1964); Viola Sonata (1964–65); *Ballade* for flute and piano (1970); *Otto Abbozzi* for flute, cello and piano (1971); 5 *Bagatelles* for solo harp (1973); organ sonata (1973). FOR PIANO: sonata (1923); 4 *Pieces* (1923–24); 8 sonatinas (1924; *Minatuure sonatine,* 1942; 1945; 1953; for the left hand, 1959; 1974; *Uit 1920 en 1922,* 1975; *Sonatina capricciosa,* 1975); *Preludes* (1925); *Epigrams* (1938); 5 *Études-Caprices* (1957); 2 *Hommages en forme d'Étude* (1958); 3 *Pezzettini* (1958); 3 *Exempelkens* (1963); pieces for children.

d'Ortigue, Joseph-Louis, French musicologist; b. Cavaillon, Vaucluse, May 22, 1802; d. Paris, Nov. 20, 1866. He studied law in Aix-en-Provence; in 1829, settled in Paris, where he wrote articles on music for various journals. In 1857 he founded *La Maîtrise* (with Niedermeyer) and in 1862 the *Journal des Maîtrises* (with F. Clément), both periodicals for church music; in 1863 he became editor of *Le Ménestrel;* succeeded Berlioz as critic for the *Journal des Débats.* In his various positions he exercised considerable influence on musical life in Paris.

WRITINGS: *Le Balcon de l'opéra* (Paris, 1833; a book of essays); *De l'École musicale italienne et de l'administration de l'académie Royale de Musique* (1839; republ. 1840 as *Du Théâtre italien et de son influence . . .*); *Abécédaire du plain-chant* (1844); *Dictionnaire liturgique,* etc. (1854); *Introduction à l'étude comparée des tonalités, et principalement du chant grégorien et de la musique moderne* (1853); *La Musique à l'église* (1861); *Traité théorique et pratique de l'accompagnement du plain-chant* (with Niedermeyer; 1856; English transl. by W. Goodrich, N.Y., 1905).

BIBLIOGRAPHY: M. Barber, *Joseph-Louis d'Ortigue* (Paris, 1919).

Ortiz, Diego, Spanish composer; b. Toledo, c.1525; date of death unknown; in the service of the Duke of Alba at the vice-regal court in Naples from 1555 until 1570. He was one of the earliest masters of variations (divisions). His greatest work is *Tratado de glosas sobre clausulas y otros géneros de puntos en la música de violones* (Rome, 1553; modern ed. by M. Schneider, Berlin, 1913; 2nd ed., Kassel, 1936), containing early examples of instrumental variations and ornamental cadenzas (for viola da gamba alone with harpsichord). An Italian version of this work was also publ. at Rome in 1553 (*Il primo libro de Diego Ortiz Toletano*, etc.). In addition, Ortiz publ. a vol. of sacred music at Venice in 1565 (hymns, motets, psalms, etc., for 4-7 voices). Some motets by him (in lute tablature) were included in Valderrábano's *Silva de Sirenas* (1547). Modern reprints of his sacred music are in the collections of Proske, Eslava, and Pedrell.

BIBLIOGRAPHY: J. Subirá, *La Música en la Casa de Alba* (Barcelona, 1927).

Ortmann, Otto Rudolph, American music educator; b. Baltimore, Jan. 25, 1889. He studied piano and composition at the Peabody Cons. of Music, Baltimore; in 1913 was appointed to its faculty; from 1928 to 1942 served as its director. He then taught at Goucher College (1942-57), where he was Chairman of Music Dept. (1948-57). He was co-founder of the American Musicological Society. Upon retirement he continued to give private instruction in piano, voice and corrective speech, despite advanced age and almost total blindness.

WRITINGS: *The Physical Basis of Piano Touch and Tone* (1925); *The Psychological Mechanics of Piano Technique* (1929; 2 edition, 1962); numerous articles in *Psychological Review, Journal of Comparative Psychology* and the *Musical Quarterly.*

Orto, Marbriano (Marbrianus) de, Netherlands composer and singer; b. Ortho, near Laroche; d. Nivelles, Feb. 1529. As a young man he was a singer in the papal choir at Rome (1484-89); then went to Nivelles, and lived there most of his life; in 1505 he was in the service of Philip the Fair of Burgundy; went to Spain with him in 1506, and was ennobled. In 1515, he was in the chapel of Archduke Charles (later Emperor Charles V). Petrucci publ. a book of 5 Masses by him (1505), also 11 chansons for 4 voices in the *Odhecaton* (1500-1503), and a Lamentation in *Lamentationum Jeremias prophetae liber I* (1506); several MSS are in the Vienna Library and the Univ. of Jena; Ambros reproduced an *Agnus* from the so-called "Mi-mi" Mass (based on the theme of 2 notes, E, A) in the supplement of his *Geschichte der Musik.*

BIBLIOGRAPHY: G. van Doorslaer, *La Chapelle de Philippe le Beau;* K. E. Roediger, *Die geistlichen Musikhandschriften der Universitäts-Bibliothek Jena* (2 vols.; 1935); G. Reese, *Music in the Renaissance* (N.Y., 1954).

Osborn-Hannah, Jane, American soprano; b. Wilmington, Ohio, July 8, 1873; d. New York, Aug. 13, 1943. She received her first singing lessons from her mother; then went to Europe where she studied with Marchesi and Sbriglia in Paris; was engaged at the Leipzig Opera (1904-07); then sang in Dresden, Berlin, and Munich; appeared in London in 1908; made her American debut at the Metropolitan Opera House as Elisabeth (Jan. 5, 1910); was a member of the Chi-

cago Opera Co. (1910-14); was particularly notable in Wagnerian roles; after 1914 lived mostly in N.Y. She was married to Frank Hannah, American consul at Magdeburg.

Osborne (real name **Eisbein**), **Adrienne,** American contralto; b. Buffalo, Dec. 2, 1873; d. Zell am Ziller, Austria, June 15, 1951. She studied with August Götze and Max Stägemann in Leipzig; later with **Felix von Kraus,** whom she married in 1899. She sang at the Municipal Opera in Leipzig; in 1908 settled in Munich, where she received the rank of Royal Chamber Singer. After the death of her husband in 1937, she went to live in Zell am Ziller, and remained there until her death.

Osborne, Nigel, English composer; b. Manchester, 1948. He studied at Oxford Univ. with Egon Wellesz and Kenneth Leighton; then traveled to Poland and worked with Witold Rudziński and at the Polish Radio Experimental Studio in Warsaw (1970-71). In his compositions he strives to present the olden modalities of remote musical eras with the aid of modern techniques, including electronic sound.

WORKS: *Beautiful Thing I* and *Beautiful Thing II* for chamber ensemble (1969-70); *Byzantine Epigrams* for chorus a cappella (1969); *7 Words,* a cantata (1969-71); *Charivari* for orch. (1973); *Chansonnier* for chamber ensemble (1975); *Passers By* for bass recorder, cello, electronic synthesizer, and diapositive (1976); *I am Goya* for bass baritone and 4 instruments (1977); *Concert piece* for cello and orch. (1977).

Osghian, Petar, Serbian composer; b. Dubrovnik, April 27, 1932. He studied in Belgrade; adopted a free neo-Romantic style of composition.

WORKS: *Poema eroico* for orch. (Belgrade, Dec. 8, 1959); *Symphoniette* for strings (Belgrade, Dec. 20, 1960); Concerto for Orchestra (Belgrade, Feb. 25, 1964); *Sigogis* for orch. (Zagreb, May 12, 1967); *Meditation* for 2 pianos, numerous other piano pieces.

Osgood, George Laurie, American singer and vocal teacher; b. Chelsea, Mass., April 3, 1844; d. Godalming, England, Dec. 12, 1922. He studied at Harvard Univ.; led the Glee Club there; then went to Germany, where he studied singing and interpretation with Haupt and Robert Franz; gave concerts in Germany; in 1872 returned to the U.S., and settled in Boston as a successful vocal teacher. He subsequently lived in Switzerland and England. He publ. *Guide in the Art of Singing,* which went through 8 editions; also anthems, choruses, and some 50 songs.

BIBLIOGRAPHY: *Dictionary of American Biography* (vol. XIV).

Osgood, Henry Osborne, American music journalist; b. Peabody, Mass., March 12, 1879; d. New York, May 8, 1927. He was educated in Boston; also studied music in Germany, Italy, and France; was correspondent in Munich and Paris for the *Musical Courier* of N.Y.; returning to the U.S. in 1914, he became associate editor of the *Musical Courier.* He publ. *So This Is Jazz* (N.Y., 1926); composed *The Rouge Bouquet* (words by Joyce Kilmer) for men's chorus; also songs.

Osterc, Slavko, Yugoslav composer; b. Verzej, June 17, 1895; d. Ljubljana, May 23, 1941. He studied at the Prague Cons. with Jirák and Novák (1925–27); took a course in the quarter-tone system with Alois Hába; returning to Yugoslavia, he became prof. at the Cons. of Ljubljana. He was associated with the modern movement in Europe; experimented with various techniques, including quarter-tone writing.
WORKS: ballets, *The Masque of the Red Death* (after Edgar Allan Poe; 1930), *Illegitimate Mother* (1940), *Illusions* (1941); symph. poem, *Mermaid* (1924); *Nocturne,* for strings (1940); Sonata for 2 clarinets (1929); Quintet for wind instruments (1932); Saxophone Sonata (1941); a number of piano pieces. The following works by him were performed at the festivals of the International Society for Contemporary Music: Concerto for Piano and Wind Instruments (Prague, Sept. 1, 1935), *Mouvement symphonique* (London, June 24, 1938), and *Passacaglia-Chorale* for orch. (Warsaw, April 14, 1939).

Osthoff, Helmuth, German musicologist; b. Bielefeld, Aug. 13, 1896. He studied at the Univ. of Berlin with Johannes Wolf, with Kretzschmar and Schünemann, and at the Stern Cons. with Brecher, Klatte and Kwast. In 1922 he obtained his Dr. phil.; was employed as choral rehearsal conductor at the Leipzig Opera (1923–25); then became assistant to Arnold Schering in Halle (1926–28) and in Berlin (1928–35). In 1938 he joined the faculty of the Univ. of Frankfurt. He publ. a number of valuable biographical and historical studies, among them *Der Lautenist Santino Garsi da Parma* (Leipzig, 1926); *Adam Krieger; neue Beiträge zur Geschichte des deutschen Liedes in 17. Jahrhundert* (Leipzig, 1929); *Die Niederländer und das deutsche Lied* (Berlin, 1938); *Josquin Desprez* (2 vols., Tutzing, 1962–65). A *Festschrift* was publ. in Tutzing in 1961 to honor his 65th birthday, and another in 1969 for his 70th birthday (contains a bibliography of his writings).

Ostrčil, Otakar, eminent Czech conductor and composer; b. Smichov, near Prague, Feb. 25, 1879; d. Prague, Aug. 20, 1935. He studied languages at the Univ. of Prague, and then taught at a school there (until 1920); at the same time took courses in piano with Adolf Mikeš (1893–95); and composition privately with Fibich (1895–1900). From 1909 till 1922 he conducted an amateur orch. in Prague; also conducted opera there (1914–19); in 1920 he succeeded Karel Kovařovic as principal conductor at the Prague National Theater. In his compositions, Ostrčil continued the Romantic tradition of Czech music, with some modern elaborations revealing the influence of Mahler.
WORKS: the operas: *Vlasty Skon* (*The Death of Vlasta;* Prague, Dec. 14, 1904); *Kunálovy oči* (*Kunala's Eyes;* Prague, Nov. 25, 1908); *Poupě* (*The Bud;* Prague, Jan. 25, 1911); *Legenda z Erinu* (*The Legend of Erin;* Brno, June 16, 1921); *Honzovo královstvi* (*Johnny's Kingdom;* Brno, May 26, 1934); Symph. (1905); Sinfonietta (1921); *Summer,* 2 symph. movements (1926); *Calvary,* a set of variations (1928); several cantatas; a string quartet; a trio for violin, viola, and piano; several song cycles.

BIBLIOGRAPHY: J. Bartoš, *Otakar Ostrčil* (Prague, 1936).

O'Sullivan, Patrick, American pianist and pedagogue; b. Louisville, Kentucky, Aug. 23, 1871; d. Los Angeles, March 18, 1947. He studied piano with Harold Bauer in Paris and Ph. Scharwenka in Berlin; composition with Wilhelm Berger in Berlin; returning to America, he occupied various posts as choral conductor and teacher; was prof. at the Louisville Cons. (1915–39) and at the Cons. of Memphis, Tenn., conducted by Roman Catholic sisters. Among his works are: *Heraklius,* for orch.; *Fantaisie irlandaise,* for piano and orch.; *Epithalamium,* for chorus and string quartet; also publ. a collection of 65 Irish melodies for 2 voices.

Otaka, Hisatada, Japanese composer; b. Tokyo, Sept. 26, 1911; d. there, Feb. 16, 1951. He went to Europe in 1931 and studied music theory with Richard Stöhr and Joseph Marx in Vienna; also took lessons in conducting with Felix Weingartner at the Vienna Academy (1934–38); returned to Japan in 1940; conducted Nippon Symph. Orch. (1942–51) in Tokyo.
WORKS: 2 *Japanese Suites* for orch.: No. 1 (Budapest, Nov. 8, 1938) and No. 2 (Vienna, Nov. 3, 1939); Sinfonietta for Strings (1937); *Midare* for orch. (Berlin, Dec. 10, 1939); Cello Concerto (Tokyo, May 23, 1943); *Rhapsody* for piano and orch. (Tokyo, Dec. 10, 1943); *Fatherland* for orch (Tokyo, Oct. 22, 1945); Symph. (1948); Flute Concerto (Tokyo, March 5, 1951); Violin Sonata (1932); 2 string quartets (1938, 1943); Piano Trio (1941); many piano pieces and songs.

Otaño, (José María) Nemesio, Spanish composer and musicologist; b. Azcoitia, Dec. 19, 1880; d. San Sebastián, April 29, 1956. He studied with V. Arregui and V. Goicoechea; became a Jesuit priest; founded the Schola Cantorum at Comillas and, in 1907, the journal *Música Sacro-Hispana,* of which he was editor until 1922. He supported energetically the study of Spanish folk music; made a study of the Spanish villancico; from 1940 till 1951 was director of the Madrid Cons. He publ. an important collection of old and new Spanish organ music, *Antología de organistas españoles;* an essay on folklore, *El Canto popular montañés;* a collection of Spanish military music of the 18th century (Burgos, 1939); also composed a number of sacred works; wrote a book, *La Música religiosa y la legislación eclesiástica* (Barcelona, 1912).

Otescu, Ion Nonna, Rumanian composer and conductor; b. Bucharest, Dec. 15, 1888; d. there, March 25, 1940. He studied at the Bucharest Cons. with Kiriac and Castaldi (1903–07); then with Widor at the Paris Cons. and with Vincent d'Indy at the Schola Cantorum (1908–11). He was a prof. of composition at the Bucharest Cons. (1913–40) and its director (1918–31). He also conducted opera at the National Theater (1921–39); from 1927 led the concerts of the Bucharest Philharmonic; was a founding member (1920) of the Society of Rumanian Composers.
WORKS: a musical comedy, *Bubi* (1903); 2 operas; *Ilderim* (libretto by Queen Marie of Rumania, 1920;

Bucharest, 1920) and *De la Matei cetire* (1938; revised and completed by Aurel Stroe; posthumous premiere, Cluj, Dec. 27, 1966); 2 ballets, *Ileana Cosînzeana* (1918); and *Rubinul miraculos* (1919); *Idilă* for string orch. (1908); the symph. poems *Templul din Gnid* (1908), *Legenda trandafirului roşu* (1910), *Narcis* (1911) and *Vrăjile Armidei* (1915); *Din bătrîni,* symph. sketch (1912); *Peisaj de iarnă,* symph. tableau (1913); *Scherzo* for orch. (1923); songs.

Othegraven, August von, German composer; b. Cologne, June 2, 1864; d. Wermelskirchen, March 11, 1946. He studied at the Cons. of Cologne; from 1889 taught there; prof., 1914. He composed chiefly for chorus; his oratorio *Marienleben* (Cologne, 1919) was fairly successful; also wrote a musical fairy tale *Die schlafende Prinzessin* (Cologne, 1907) and an operetta, *Poldis Hochzeit* (Cologne, 1912).
BIBLIOGRAPHY: B. Voss, *August von Othegraven, Leben und Werk* (Cologne, 1961).

Othmayr, Caspar, German composer; b. Amberg, March 12, 1515; d. Nuremberg, Feb. 4, 1553. He studied at the Univ. of Heidelberg; in 1536 became "magister" and then rector of the monastery school at Heilsbronn near Ansbach; in 1548 became provost in Ansbach. He was celebrated not only for his sacred works, but also for his ingenious polyphonic settings of secular songs; of the latter, the most important are *Reuterische und jegerische Liedlein,* for 4 voices (1549). Sacred works include: *Cantilenae* (1546); *Epitaphium Lutheri* (1546); *Bicinia sacra* (1547); *Symbola Principum* (1547; new ed. by H. Albrecht, 1941); *Trincina* (1549).
BIBLIOGRAPHY: H. Albrecht, *Caspar Othmayr, Leben und Werk* (Kassel, 1950).

Otis, Philo Adams, American writer and composer of sacred music; b. Berlin Heights, Ohio, Nov. 24, 1846; d. Chicago, Sept. 23, 1930. He studied music with Dudley Buck in N.Y., and with Clarence Eddy in Chicago. He served as chorusmaster at the First Presbyterian Church in Chicago (1905-12); publ. *The First Presbyterian Church, 1833-1913* (a history, 1913); *Impressions of Europe, 1873-1874. Music, Art and History* (1922); *The Chicago Symphony Orchestra* (a history, 2 vols., 1925); *The Hymns You Ought to Know* (1928); composed 2 sacred cantatas: *Wondrous Words of Love* and *The Risen Christ;* a *Pastorale,* for violin, cello, double bass, harp, and organ; many hymns and anthems.

Otterloo, Willem van, Dutch conductor and composer; b. Winterswijk, Dec. 27, 1907. He studied cello with Orobio de Castro and composition with Sem Dresden at the Amsterdam Cons.; played the cello in the Utrecht Orch.; 1933, assistant conductor there; 1937, associate conductor. From 1949 to 1972 he was conductor of the Residente Orch. at The Hague, bringing it to a fine state of prefection; also filled in numerous guest appearances, especially with the Melbourne, Australia, Symph., which he conducted annually. In 1974 he was appointed conductor of the Düsseldorf Symph. Orch.
WORKS: String Trio (1932); Sinfonietta for wind orch. (1943; his most frequently played work); *Serenade (Divertimento)* for brass, celesta, piano and percussion (1944; Holland Festival, The Hague, June 5, 1952); *Uilenspiegel Variaties* for orch. (1950); *Intrada* for wind orch. (1958); choral works; piano pieces; songs.

Ottman, Robert W., American music theorist and pedagogue; b. Fulton, N.Y., May 3, 1914. He studied music theory with Bernard Rogers at the Eastman School of Music, Rochester, N.Y. (M. Mus., 1943). During World War II he served in the Infantry in the U.S. Army (1943-46); after the war took lessons in composition with Alec Rowley at Trinity College of Music in London; in 1946 was engaged as lecturer in music at the North Texas State Univ., from which he also received his Ph.D. (1956); continued at his post as prof. of music in 1977-78. He published a number of excellent school manuals: *Music for Sight Singing* (N.Y., 1956); *Elementary Harmony, Theory and Practice* (N.Y., 1961; 2nd ed., 1970); *Advanced Harmony, Theory and Practice* (N.Y., 1961; new ed., 1972); *The 371 Chorales of J.S. Bach* (with Frank Mainous; very successful, N.Y., 1966); *Workbook for Elementary Harmony* (N.Y., 1974); *Programmed Rudiments of Music* (with Frank Mainous; N.Y., 1978).

Otto, (Ernst) Julius, German choral conductor and composer; b. Königstein, Sept. 1, 1804; d. Dresden, March 5, 1877. He studied with Weinlig in Dresden; then was a teacher there. In 1830 he was appointed cantor at the Kreuzkirche, and held this position for 45 years; his choir became one of the most celebrated in Germany; he also conducted several choral societies. His best works are the excellent male choruses in his collection *Ernst und Scherz,* which became extremely popular (*Burschenfahrten, Gesellenfahrten, Soldatenleben, Der Spinnabend, Der Sängersaal,* etc.); 2 grand operas and 4 comic operas for amateur performance (*Die Mordgrundbruck bei Dresden* is the best); 3 oratorios; many songs for solo voice (*In die Ferne, Des deutschen Rheines Braut,* etc.); piano sonatas, rondos, etc.
BIBLIOGRAPHY: A. R. Scheumann, *Julius Otto* (Dresden, 1904).

Oudin, Eugène (Espérance), American baritone; b. New York, Feb. 24, 1858; d. London, Nov. 4, 1894. He was of French extraction; studied law at Yale Univ.; was an amateur singer, and made his debut in N.Y., on Aug. 30, 1886, in an operetta. On Jan. 31, 1891, he created the role of Ivanhoe in Arthur Sullivan's opera of that name, and won immediate acclaim. He remained in England most of his life, but also made several appearances in Europe, including Russia; scored notable successes in Wagnerian roles (Wolfram, Telramund, etc.).

Oudrid (y Segura), Cristóbal, Spanish composer; b. Badajoz, Feb. 7, 1825, d. Madrid, March 12, 1877. He studied music with his father; acquired his craft by arranging works of Haydn and Mozart for wind instruments; in 1844 went to Madrid, where he took lessons with Saldoni. He showed a decided talent for writing melodious zarzuelas, among them *Buenas* *noches, Señor Don Simon* (Madrid, April 16, 1852), *El Postillon de la Rioja* (Madrid, June 7, 1856), *El último mono* (Madrid, May 30, 1859), and *El Molinero de Subiza* (1870).

BIBLIOGRAPHY: A. Pena y Goni, *La Opera española en el siglo XIX* (Madrid, 1881).

Oulibicheff, Alexander, Russian official and music amateur; b. Dresden, April 13, 1794; d. Nizhny-Novgorod, Feb. 5, 1858. He studied violin at home in Dresden, where his father was Russian ambassador; was educated in Germany. When the family returned to Russian after 1812, he was employed in the Ministry of Finance, and later in that of Foreign Affairs (1816-30). He was the editor of the French periodical, *Journal de St. Petersbourg* (1812-30); retired to his estate in Nizhny-Novgorod in 1841. His greatest admiration was for Mozart; his magnum opus is *Nouvelle Biographie de Mozart, suivie d'un aperçu sur l'histoire générale de la musique* (3 vols., Moscow, 1843; 2nd German ed., 1859; Russian transl. by Modest Tchaikovsky, Moscow, 1890). By way of praising Mozart, he inserted deprecating remarks on Beethoven's later style; when he was taken to task for this lack of appreciation (by Lenz and others), he publ. *Beethoven, ses criques et ses glossateurs* (Leipzig and Paris, 1857), in which he emphatically reiterated his sharp critcism of Beethoven's harmonic and formal procedures.

Oury, Anna Caroline (*née* **Belleville**), German pianist; b. Landshut, June 24, 1808; d. Munich, July 22, 1880. Her father, a French nobleman named Belleville, was director of the Munich Opera. She studied with Czerny in Vienna; made her debut there; then gave concerts in Munich and in Paris; settled for many years in London, where she married the violinist **Antonio James Oury** (b. London, 1880; d. Norwich, July 25, 1883) in 1831; toured with him in Russia, Germany, Austria, and France. She wrote a number of piano pieces in the salon style, of which nearly 200 were published.

Ouseley, Sir Frederick Arthur Gore, English composer and theorist; b. London, Aug. 12, 1825; d. Hereford, April 6, 1889. He was the son of Sir Gore Ouseley, ambassador to Persia; studied at Oxford Univ. (B.A., 1846; M.A., 1849). He was ordained priest in 1849; was curate of St. Paul's, Knightsbridge (1849-51). In 1855 he succeeded Sir Henry Bishop as prof. of music at Oxford Univ. He was a fine organist, and excelled in fugal improvisation.

WORKS: 2 oratorios, *The Martyrdom of St. Polycarp* (1855) and *Hagar* (1873); 11 church services; 70 anthems; *The Psalter, Arranged for Chanting, with Appropriate English Chants, Anglican Psalter Chants, Cathedral Services by English Masters* (2 vols.). He also publ. *Treatise on Harmony* (1868), *Counterpoint, Canon and Fugue,* after Cherubini (1868), *Musical Form and General Composition* (1875). He left his fine music library to St. Michael's College, Tenbury.

BIBLIOGRAPHY: F. T. Havergal, *Memorials of F. A. G. Ouseley, Bart.* (London, 1889); F. W. Joyce, *Life of Rev. Sir F. A. G. Ouseley, Bart, etc.* (London, 1892; revised, 1896, with an appendix by J. S. Bumpus, containing a list of all of Ouseley's extant works); M. F. Alderson and H.C. Colles, *History of St. Michael's College, Tenbury* (London, 1943).

Ovchinnikov, Viacheslav, Soviet composer; b. Voronezh, May 29, 1936. He studied with Khrennikov at the Moscow Cons., graduating in 1962. Among his works are 4 symphonies, a piano concerto, a violin concerto and some chamber music. He also wrote for the films.

Overton, Hall, American composer; b. Bangor, Michigan, Feb. 23, 1920; d. New York, Nov. 24, 1972. He studied piano at the Chicago Musical College; served in the U.S. Army overseas (1942-45). After the war, he studied composition with Persichetti at the Juilliard School of Music, N.Y., graduating in 1951; also took private lessons with Wallingford Riegger and Darius Milhaud. At the same time he filled professional engagements as jazz pianist and contributed to the magazine *Jazz Today.*

WORKS: the operas, *The Enchanted Pear Tree,* after Boccaccio's *Decameron* (Juilliard School of Music, N.Y., Feb. 7, 1950); *Pietro's Petard* (N.Y., June, 1963); *Huckleberry Finn,* after Mark Twain (Juilliard American Opera Center, N.Y., May 20, 1971); 2 symphonies (1955, 1962); 2 string quartets; String Trio; Viola Sonata; Cello Sonata; *Pulsations* for chamber ensemble (his last work; 1972).

Ozawa, Seiji, glamorous Japanese conductor of extraordinary accomplishments; b. Hoten, China, of Japanese parents, Sept. 1, 1935. He was taken back to Japan when he was 6 years old; studied with Hideo Saito at the Toho School of Music in Tokyo, graduating in 1959; upon Saito's advice he went to Europe, where he took conducting lessons with Eugène Bigot in Paris; was also accepted by Herbert von Karajan as a pupil. In 1960 he was invited by Charles Munch to take courses in conducting at Tanglewood; there he sang in the chorus, and was also given opportunity to conduct the student orchestra, and won the Koussevitzky Prize at the Berkshire Music Center. Progressing rapidly in his profession, he was engaged in 1960 as an assistant conductor of the N.Y. Philharmonic, and made an auspicious conducting debut at Carnegie Hall on April 14, 1961. Immediately afterwards he accompanied Leonard Bernstein, then music director of the N.Y. Philharmonic, on its tour of Japan. In Tokyo he was invited to conduct the orchestra of the Japan Broadcasting Corporation, but trouble developed between him and the players, who objected to being commanded in an imperious manner by one of their own countrymen; still Ozawa obtained engagements with other Japanese orchestras which he conducted on his periodic visits to his homeland. In the meantime he advanced significantly in his American career; in 1964 he took over the Summer Ravinia Festival with the Chicago Symph. Orch., and conducted it for several seasons; from 1965 to 1969 he was principal conductor of the Toronto Symph. Orch. with which he also toured Europe. From 1969 to 1974 he was music director of the San Francisco Symph. Orch., but even before completing his engagement with it he accepted the prestigious invitation to become permanent conductor and music director of the Boston Symph. Orch., an astonishing event in the American music world, marking the first time when an Oriental musician was elected by the notoriously conservative trustees of that great orchestra as successor to such German, French and Russian luminaries as Karl Muck, Pierre Monteux, Koussevitzky, Charles Munch and others; he was also the youngest conductor to head the Boston Symph. In March, 1978 Ozawa made a triumphant return to Japan with the Boston Symph. Orch. as its music director; this time his former detractors in the press and those among Japanese musicians who had been skeptical about his abilities greeted him with national pride in his march to fame. Equally brilliant in classical and romantic repertory, and astonishingly adept in the works of the modern school, Ozawa has shown his exceptional ability in conducting with superlative ease such formidable scores as the 4th Symphony of Ives and compositions of the extreme avant-grade of American and European music; all these works he invariably conducts from memory, an extraordinary feat in itself. In 1976, and again in 1978, he traveled to China and conducted concerts in programs of classical music; for sentimental reasons he also revisited his childhood house there.

P

Paap, Wouter, Dutch writer on music and composer; b. Utrecht, May 7, 1908. He studied piano with local teachers, but was largely self-taught in composition. He dedicated himself mainly to contemporary Dutch music; in 1945 he became editor-in-chief of the most important periodical in the Dutch language *Mens en Melodie;* continued as its editor until 1974. Among his publications, all in Dutch, are monographs on Anton Bruckner (Bilthoven, 1936), Eduard van Beinum (Baarn, 1956), Willem Mengelberg (in the collection, *Music in Holland,* Amsterdam, 1958); *Moderne Kerkmuziek in Nederland* (Amsterdam, 1948); *De Symphonieën van Beethoven* (Utrecht, 1947); *De Kunst van het Moduleren* (Utrecht, 1948); *De Symphonie* (Bilthoven, 1957); *Muziek, modern en klassiek* (Utrecht, 1961); *Mozart* (Utrecht, 1962). He was a co-editor of the valuable encyclopedia in the Dutch language *Algemene muziekencyclopedie* (6 vols.; Amsterdam, 1957-63). His compositions include *De Drukkunst* for speaker and orch.; an oratorio, *Sterre der Zee;* piano works and pieces for carillon.

Pablo, Luis de, Spanish composer; b. Bilbao, Jan. 28, 1930. He studied jurisprudence at Madrid Univ., receiving a law degree in 1952. He attended the Cons. of Madrid; traveled to Paris where he received musical advice from Messiaen and Boulez; also took courses at the summer seminars for new music at Darmstadt. Returning to Spain, he organized the modern performance groups "Tiempo y Música" and "Alea." Like most Spanish composers, he followed in his youth the precepts of the national school, with the music of Manuel de Falla as principal influence, but soon he adopted hyperserial techniques, in which whole tonal complexes, chords, or groups of chords become thematic units; similarly, dynamic processes assume the role of compositional determinants, eventually attaining the ultimate libertarianism in promiscuous cross-fertilization of all media, all styles, and all techniques of musical composition. WORKS: *Coral* for woodwinds (1953); *Comentarios* for soprano, piccolo, vibraphone, and double bass (1956); Clarinet Quintet (1954); 2 string quartets (1955, 1957); *Elegía* for string orch. (1956); Harpsichord Concerto (1956); Piano Sonata (1958) *Movil I* and *Movil II* for 2 pianos (1958, 1968); *Radial* for 24 instruments (1960); *Polar* for voice, saxophone, bass clarinet, and percussion (1961); *4 Inventions* for orch. (1955-62); *Tombeau* for orch. (1963); 6 *Modulos:* No. 1, for chamber ensemble (1965); No. 2, for double orch. (1966); No. 3, for 17 instruments (1967); No. 4, *Ejercicio* for string quartet (1965); No. 5, for organ (1967); No. 6, *Parafrasis* for 24 instruments (1968); *Sinfonías* for 17 wind instruments (1955-66); *Cesuras* for double trio of woodwinds and strings (Festival of American and Spanish Music, Madrid, Oct. 22, 1964); *Imaginario I* for harpsichord and 3 percussionists (1967); *Imaginario II* for orch. (1967); *Heterogéneo* for 2 narrators, Hammond organ, and orch. (1968; Donaueschingen, Oct. 18, 1970); *Protocolo,* opera (1968; Paris, Oct. 23, 1970); *Quasi una Fantasia* for string sextet and orch. (1968; Paris, April 17, 1972); *Por diversos motivos* for voice, projected images and chamber orch. (1969); *Oroitaldi* for orch. (1971); *Éléphants ivres (Drunken Elephants),* in 4 parts, for differing orch. formations (1972-73); *Je mange, tu manges* for small orch. and tape (1972; Royan, April 14, 1973); *Masque* for flute, clarinet, piano, and percussion (1973). He published *Aproximación a una estética de la música contemporánea* (Madrid, 1968).

Pabst, Louis, German pianist and composer; b. Königsberg, July 18, 1846; d. Moscow, 1903. He made his first appearance as pianist in his native city in 1862; was in England from 1867 to 1869; then established a music school in Riga, Russia (1869-75); subsequently toured Australia; there he founded the Academy of Music of Melbourne (1887); revisited London in 1894; in 1897 went to Russia; became instructor at the music school of the Philharmonic Society in Moscow in 1899; 1903, court councillor of the Ministry of the Interior. He publ. a number of piano pieces.

Pabst, Paul, German pianist; brother of **Louis Pabst;** b. Königsberg, May 27, 1854; d. Moscow, June 9, 1897. He studied with Liszt; went to Russia, and taught at the Moscow Cons. He made a number of effective paraphrases for piano of operatic works; particularly well known is the one on *Eugene Onegin.*

Pacchiarotti, Gaspare, famous Italian male soprano; b. Fabriano, near Ancona, 1740; d. Padua, Oct. 28, 1821. He studied under Bertoni at St. Mark's in Venice; from 1769, sang at the principal Italian theaters with brilliant success; 1778, went to London with Bertoni, returning there in 1780-84 and 1790. In 1792 he retired and settled in Padua; sang for Napoleon when the latter passed through Padua in 1796. A. Calegari publ. *Modi generali del canto* (1836), based on Pacchiarotti's method.
BIBLIOGRAPHY: G. C. Pacchiarotti (his adopted son) *Cenni biografici intorno a Gaspare Pacchiarotti* (Padua, 1844); R. Sassi, *Un celebre musico fabrianese Gaspare Pacchiarotti* (Fabriano, 1935); A. Heriot, *The Castrati in Opera* (London 1956; pp. 163-71).

Pacchierotti, Ubaldo, Italian composer and conductor; b. Cervarese-Croce (Padua), Oct. 30, 1875; d. Milan, April 18, 1916. He studied at the Cons. S. Pietro a Majella in Naples; conducted in Leghorn and Buenos Aires.
WORKS: the operas *La Lampada* (Buenos Aires, 1899), *L'Albatro* (Milan, 1905), *Eidelberga mia!* (Genoa, Feb. 27, 1908; in N.Y. as *Alt Heidelberg,* 1910), *Il Santo* (Turin, 1913); and other works.
BIBLIOGRAPHY: C. M. Rietmann, "Ubaldo Pacchierotti," *Pensiero Mus.* (Nov.-Dec. 1926).

Pache, Joseph, German pianist and conductor; b. Friedland, Silesia, June 1, 1861; d. Baltimore, Dec. 7, 1926. He studied piano with Klindworth in Berlin (1883-85); composition with Max Bruch in Breslau (1885-86); then studied voice with J. Hey in Berlin. He emigrated to the U.S. in 1891; from 1894, conductor of the Oratorio Society in Baltimore.

Pachelbel, Carl Theodorus, son of **Johann Pachelbel;** b. Stuttgart, Nov. 24, 1690; d. Charleston, S.C., Sept. 14, 1750. He emigrated to Boston in the 1730s and in 1733 assisted in the erection of the organ in Trinity Church, Newport, R.I., of which he became organist for about a year. On Jan. 21, 1736 he advertised a concert in N.Y., the first there of which details have been recorded, and on March 8, a second one. He then moved to Charleston, became organist of St. Philip's Church, and on Nov. 22, 1737 gave a public concert in his home. An 8-part Magnificat, the only known composition of Pachelbel, is in the State Library, Berlin (publ. N.Y., 1937).

BIBLIOGRAPHY: O. G. Sonneck, *Early Concert-Life in America (1731-1800)* (in English, Leipzig, 1907); J. T. Howard, *Our American Music* (N.Y., 1939 and later eds.); V. L. Redway, "A New York Concert in 1736," *Musical Quarterly* (April 1936); V. L. Redway: "C. T. Pachelbel, Musical Emigrant," *Journal of the American Musicological Society* (Spring 1952).

Pachelbel, Johann, celebrated German organist and composer; b. Nuremberg (baptized Sept. 1), 1653; d. there, March 3, 1706. He studied at Nuremberg, Altdorf, and Regensburg; organist at St. Stephen's Cathedral in Vienna, 1674; court organist at Eisenach, 1677; of the Predigerkirche at Erfurt, 1678; court organist at Stuttgart, 1690; at Gotha, 1692. Organist at St. Sebald's, Nuremberg, 1695. Several organ pieces by Pachelbel are printed by Commer in *Musica sacra,* vol. I; others by G. W. Körner in *Der Orgelvirtuose;* by Winterfield in *Evangelischer Kirchengesang,* vol. II; by Trautwein (a chaconne with 13 variations, a fugue, and a fughetta, for clavier, Berlin, 1860); by A. Schering in *Geschichte der Musik in Beispielen* (no. 243); by A. Einstein in the vol. of examples to his *Geschichte der Musik;* by A. G. Ritter in *Geschichte des Orgelspiels im 14.-18. Jahrhundert;* J. Bonnet in *Historical Organ Recitals* (vol. I); etc. H. Botstiber and M. Seiffert publ. 94 fugues on the Magnificat in the *Denkmäler der Tonkunst in Österreich* 17 (8.ii), with biography; M. Seiffert edited *Hexachordon Apollinis,* 4 arias with variations, *Musikalische Sterbensgedanken,* 6 chaconnes, 4 fantasies, 19 suites, and 7 fugues in *Denkmäler der Tonkunst in Bayern* 2 and 6 (2.i and 4.i), with introduction and biography by A. Sandberger; K. Matthaei publ. a practical ed. of Pachelbel's organ works, in 4 vols. (1930–36). His *Kanon in D,* which is the first part of a *Kanon* and *Gigue in D* for organ, became extremely popular in America around 1960, and has been published and republished in numerous arrangements for various instruments.

BIBLIOGRAPHY: G. Beckmann, "J. Pachelbel als Kammerkomponist," *Archiv für Musikwissenschaft* I/2 (1919); M. Seiffert, "Pachelbels Sterbensgedanken," *Sammelbände der Internationalen Musik Gesellschaft* V; M. Seiffert, *Geschichte des Klavierspiels* (p. 196ff.); Ph. Spitta; *J. S. Bach* (vol. I, p. 106ff.); E. Born, *Die Variation als Grundlage handwerklicher Gestaltung im musikalischen Schaffen Johann Pachelbels* (Berlin, 1941); H. H. Eggebrecht, "J. Pachelbel als Vokalcomponist," *Archiv für Musikwissenschaft* XI (1954).

Pachelbel, Wilhelm Hieronymus, German musician son of **Johann Pachelbel;** b. Erfurt, 1686 (baptized, Aug. 29, 1686); d. Nuremberg, 1764. He was an organist, from 1706, at the Jakobkirche in Nuremberg; from 1725, at St. Sebald's there. Publ. *Musikalisches Vergnügen* (1725; prelude, fugue, and fantasia for organ or clavier); also a prelude and fugue in C; all reprinted by M. Seiffert in *Denkmäler der Tonkunst in Bayern* 2 and 6 (2.i and 4.i),), as supplement to his father's works.

Pachler-Koschak, Marie Leopoldine, Austrian pianist; b. Graz, Oct. 2, 1792; d. there, April 10, 1855. She was an enthusiastic admirer of Beethoven, who wrote to her in 1817: "I have found no one, not excepting the great pianists, who interprets my compositions as well as you." In 1816 she married Dr. Karl Pachler, a lawyer in Graz. In their house Franz Schubert spent several weeks in the summer of 1827. Schubert wrote a little four-hand march for their son, Faust Pachler, who publ. *Beethoven und M. Pachler-Koschak* (Berlin, 1866), which contains valuable details concerning Beethoven's last days.

Pachmann, Vladimir de, eccentric Russian pianist; b. Odessa, July 27, 1848; d. Rome, Jan. 6, 1933. He received his primary music education at home from his father, an Austrian violinist; then went to Vienna where he enrolled in the piano class of Prof. Dachs at the Vienna Cons. He began his concert career with a tour of Russia in 1869; he was 40 years old before he made a decisive impact on the international scene; his first American tour in 1891 was sensationally successful, and it was in America where he began exhibiting his curious eccentricities, some of them undoubtedly calculated to produce shock effect; he made grimaces when he did not like his own playing and shouted "bravo!" when he played a number to his satisfaction; even more bizarre was his crawling under the grand piano after the concert claiming that he was looking for the wrong notes he had accidentally hit; all this could be explained as an idiosyncratic behavior; but he also allowed himself to mutilate the music itself, by inserting arpeggios between phrases and extra chords at the end of a piece. Most American critics were outraged by his shenanigans, but some, notably Philip Hale, found mitigation in the poetic quality of his interpretations. Pachmann was particularly emotional in playing Chopin, when his facial contortions became quite obnoxious; James Huneker dubbed him "Chopinzee." Pachmann did not lack official honors; in 1885, on his tour of Denmark, he was made Knight of the Order of Danebrog; in 1916 the London Philharmonic Society awarded him the Beethoven Medal. His personal life was turbulent; he married frequently (the exact number of his wives is in dispute). His first wife was Maggie Oakey, whom he married in 1884; she edited several Chopin *Études* indicating Pachmann's own fingering; they were divorced in 1895.

BIBLIOGRAPHY: H. C. Schonberg, *The Great Pianists* (N.Y., 1963).

Pacini, Giovanni, Italian composer; b. Catania, Feb. 17, 1796; d. Pescia, Dec. 6, 1867. He was a pupil of Marchesi and Padre Mattei at Bologna, and of Furlanetto at Venice; his first opera was *Annetta e Lucinda* (Milan, 1813); up to 1835 he had produced over 40 operas on various Italian stages, when the failure of *Carlo di Borgogna* at Venice temporarily checked the flow of dramatic composition; he went to Viareggio, near Lucca, and established a very successful school of music there, for which he wrote several short treatises—*Corso teoretico-pratico di lezioni di armonia* (1863), *Cenni storici sulla musica e trattato di contrappunto* (1864)—and built a private theater. Later he removed the school to Lucca. In 1840 Pacini, who prided himself on rapid work, wrote his dramatic masterpiece, *Saffo*, in 28 days (Naples, Nov. 29, 1840; enthusiastically received). Forty more operas followed up to 1867; the best were *Medea* (Palermo, Nov. 28, 1843), *La Regina di Cipro* (Turin, Feb. 7, 1846), and *Niccolò de' Lapi* (Florence, Oct. 29, 1873; posthumous production). Pacini also wrote numerous oratorios, cantatas, Masses, etc.; a *Dante* symphony; an octet; 6 string quartets; other chamber music vocal duets and arias. He was an active contributor to several musical papers; and publ. memoirs, *Le mie memorie artistiche* (Florence, 1865; enlarged by Cicconetti, 1872; rev. by F. Magnani, 1875). His brother, **Emilio Pacini,** b. 1810; d. Neuilly, near Paris, Dec. 2, 1898, was a distinguished librettist.

BIBLIOGRAPHY: Anon., *G. Pacini* (Pescia, 1896); M. Davini, *Il Maestro Pacini* (Palermo, 1927); A. Cametti, *Il Corsaro di Pacini* (1913).

Pacini, Leonardo, Italian composer; b. near Pistoia, May 26, 1885; d. Viareggio, April 13, 1937. He was pupil of Pizzetti at Florence; in 1921, graduated from the Liceo Martini of Bologna. He was a Franciscan friar.

WORKS: the operas *Alla Muda* (1924; Viareggio, 1925) and *Mirta;* the operetta *Il Pirata* (Viareggio, 1927); the oratorios *Transitus Divi Dominici* (Bologna, 1921) and *Frate Francesco* (Viareggio, 1929); the cantatas *La Sagra dei Caduti* (1922), *Portiuncola Pia,* and *Clara Discipula* (Viareggio, 1924); *Sinfonia del giglio,* for chorus and orch.; psalms, motets, and other church music; chamber music; songs; etc.

Paciorkiewicz, Tadeusz, Polish composer and organist; b. Sierpc, Oct. 17, 1916. He studied organ with Rutkowski and composition with Sikorski at the Warsaw Cons. (1936–43). He taught in music schools in Plock (1945–49), Lódź (1949–54) and Warsaw (from 1954).

WORKS: opera, *Romanza from Gdańsk* (1964); 2 radio operas: *Ushiko* (1962) and *Ligea* (1964); a ballet *Legenda Warszawy* (1959); an oratorio, *De revolutionibus* (1972–73; Olsztyn, Feb. 19, 1973); 2 piano concertos (1952, 1954); 2 symphonies (1953, 1957); Violin Concerto (1955); *Duet koncertujacy* for organ and orch. (1962); Organ Concerto (1967); *Divertimento* for clarinet and string orch. (1968); Trombone Concerto (1971); Viola Concerto (1976); Wind Quintet (1951); Violin Sonata (1954); Bassoon Sonatina (1954); String Quartet (1960); *4 Capriccios (Quasi una sonata)* for clarinet and piano (1960); Trio for oboe, clarinet and bassoon (1963); Trio for flute, viola and harp (1966); *6 Miniatures* for 4 trombones (1972); Piano Quintet (1972); *Duet Concertante* for clarinet and piano (1973); *Missa brevis* for chorus and organ (1973–74); Cello Sonata (1975); *3 Pieces* for harp (1976); Organ Sonata (1946); 2 piano sonatinas (1952, 1953); songs.

Pacius, Fredrik (Friedrich), German-born Finnish composer; b. Hamburg, March 19, 1809; d. Helsingfors, Jan. 8, 1891. He studied violin with Spohr and composition with Hauptmann. He served as violinist in the Royal Chapel in Stockholm (1828–34); then went to Helsingfors, where he organized a choral society (1835) and later (1845) established regular symphony concerts there. Pacius wrote the first Finnish opera *Kung Karls jakt* (to a Swedish libretto); it was staged in Helsingfors on March 24, 1852. He was the author of the Finnish national anthem *Maamme laulu,* set to the words of the Swedish poem *Vartland,* later translated into Finnish (1848); he also wrote many other songs of a Swedish-Finnish inspiration. Among his other works are the opera *Loreley* (Helsingfors, April 28, 1887); a Violin Concerto (1845); numerous choral works and songs.

BIBLIOGRAPHY: M. Collan-Beaurain, *F. Pacius* (Helsinki, 1921); Otto E. Andersson, *Den unge Pacius* (Helsinki, 1938); J. Rosas, *F. Pacius som tonsättare* (Abo, 1949).

Paderewski, Ignace Jan, celebrated Polish pianist and composer; b. Kurylówka, Podolia (Russian Poland), Nov. 18, 1860; d. New York, June 29, 1941. His father was administrator of some large estates, and was artistically inclined; his mother died soon after his birth. From the age of 3 he began to be attracted by the piano, and about that time received his first music lessons from an itinerant violinist. His second teacher was a certain Peter Sowinski, who taught him some operatic arrangements for 4 hands, which he played with his sister. He also filled a notebook with his own childish compositions. His first public appearance was in a charity concert with his sister, at the age of 12. His playing aroused the interest of wealthy patrons, who took him to Kiev, where he heard his first concerts. He was then sent to the Cons. at Warsaw; there his first teacher discouraged him from taking up the piano; he studied various instruments and played the trombone in the Cons. orchestra. Nevertheless, he continued his piano studies under Schlozer, Strobl, and Janota. Owing to a dispute about rehearsals, he was expelled from the Cons. after a year; in 1877 he made a tour of some of the smaller Russian towns with a violinist. He was then readmitted to the Cons., studied piano, counterpoint, and composition, and after his graduation, in 1878, was engaged as instructor of piano there. In 1880 he married a young student named Antonina Korsak, who died in childbirth a year later. In 1881 he went to Berlin to study composition with Kiel; there he met Rubinstein, who encouraged his attempts at composition. In 1883 he gave up his position at Warsaw and returned to Berlin, studying orchestration with Urban. While on a vacation in the Tatra Mountains in Slovakia (which inspired his *Tatra Album* for piano), he met the famous actress Modjeska, who urged him to take up a pianistic career and provided him with funds to begin study in Vienna under Leschetizky, with whom he remained for several years. His first important appearance as a pianist was at a concert with Pauline Lucca at Vienna in 1887. In March, 1888, he gave his first recital in Paris, and was enthusiastically received. He made his debut as soloist in Vienna in 1889, with great success. He was also obtaining recognition as a composer, for Mme. Essipov played his Piano Concerto under the baton of Hans Richter in Vienna. His English debut took place in London on May 9, 1890; his American debut in New York on Nov. 17, 1891, was followed by a series of 117 concerts. He had made a tour of Germany in 1890, and, in spite of critical hostility in Berlin, soon won over the public of that country also. His subsequent numerous tours of Europe, North and South America, South Africa, and Australia were an uninterrupted succession of triumphs. In 1909 he accepted the directorship of the Warsaw Cons. (succeeding Mlynarski). In 1913 he came to the U.S. and acquired a ranch in Paso Robles, California. Paderewski was a great Polish patriot; during World War I he gave the entire proceeds of his concerts for the benefit of Polish populations caught in the war between Russia and Germany. After the establishment of the new Polish state, Paderewski served as its representative in Washington; in 1919 he became the Prime Minister of the Polish Republic, the first professional musician to occupy such a post. He participated in the Versailles treaty conference (during which the famous, but possibly apocryphal colloquy ensued between Clemenceau and Paderewski, when the former remarked: "You, a famous pianist, and now Prime Minister—what a come-down!" In 1920 he withdrew from politics and resumed his career. In 1939 he made his last American tour. Once more during his lifetime Poland was invaded, this time by both Germany and Russia. Once more Paderewski returned to politics. He joined the Polish government in exile in France and was appointed president of its parliament on Jan. 23, 1940. He returned to the U.S. Nov. 6, 1940, and immediately resumed his efforts in behalf of his native country. At the order of President Roosevelt, he was given state interment at the Arlington National Cemetery. Paderewski received the following honorary degrees: Dr. phil. from the Univs. of Lwow (1912), Cracow (1919), Poznan (1924); LL.D. from Columbia (1922), Southern Calif. (1923), Glasgow (1925); Mus. Doc. from the Univs. of Yale (1917) and Cambridge (1926); D.C.L. from Oxford Univ. (1920). He held the Grand Cross of the French Legion of Honor (1922) and many other decorations. In 1936 he played in a motion picture entitled *The Moonlight Sonata*. No other instrumentalist up to that time, not even Paganini or Liszt, earned such large sums of money. In 1898 he bought the beautiful Châlet de Riond-Bosson on Lake Geneva, near Morges, where he spent time when not on tour, and in that year he married Helena Gorska, Baroness von Rosen. In 1900, by a deed of trust, Paderewski established a fund of $10,000 (original trustees were Wm. Steinway, Major H. L. Higginson, and Dr. Wm. Mason), the interest to be devoted to triennial cash prizes "to composers of American birth without distinction as to age or religion," in the following forms: symph. works for orchestra; compositions for solo instruments with orchestra; chamber music. An outstanding trait of the artist was his ar-

dent patriotism. In the year of the Chopin centenary (1910) he donated $60,000 to the Chopin Memorial Hall in Warsaw, and in the same year he unveiled a colossal statue of King Jagiello, commemorating the latter's victory over the Teuton Knights in 1410, which he had erected at a cost of $100,000. A postage stamp with his picture was issued in Poland in 1919, and 2 stamps were issued in the U.S. in his honor in the series "Men and Liberty" in 1960.

WORKS: Paderewski began to compose in his seventh year, and his earliest ambition—and one that never left him—was to win laurels as a composer. His Menuet in G (one of a set of *6 Humoresques* for piano) has attained extraordinary popularity. His opera *Manru* (1897–1900), dealing with life in the Tatra Mountains, was successfully produced at Dresden on May 29, 1901 (Metropolitan Opera, N.Y., Feb. 14, 1902). His Symphony in B minor was first performed at Boston on Feb. 12, 1909 (inspired by the 40th anniversary of the revolution of 1863).

OTHER WORKS: FOR PIANO: *Prelude and Capriccio, Minuetto* in G minor; *Three Pieces (Gavotte, Mélodie, Valse mélancolique); Élégie; 3 Polish Dances; Introduction and Toccata; Chants du Voyageur* (5 pieces); *6 Polish Dances; Album de mai* (5 pieces); Variations and Fugue in A minor; *Tatra Album* (also for 4 hands); *6 Humoresques de Concert* (with the famous Menuet in G); *Dans le désert,* toccata; Sonata in E-flat minor; FOR ORCH.: Piano Concerto in A minor; *Fantaisie polonaise* for piano and orch.; Paderewski's Sonata for violin and piano; songs. Paderewski ed. the complete works of Chopin for the Chopin Institute (Warsaw, 1949–58). A complete list of compositions was publ. in the *Bollettino bibliografico musicale* (Milan, 1932).

BIBLIOGRAPHY: H. T. Finck, *Paderewski and His Art* (N.Y., 1895); E. A. Barghan, *I. J. Paderewski* (London, 1908); J. C. Hadden, *Modern Musicians* (Boston, 1913); *To I. J. Paderewski* (Kosciusko Foundation; N.Y., 1928); J. F. Cooke, *I. J. Paderewski* (Philadelphia, 1928); H. Opienski, *Paderewski* (Lausanne, 1928; new ed., 1948); A. Henderson, *Contemporary Immortals* (N.Y., 1930); C. Philips, *Paderewski* (N.Y., 1933); R. Landau, *Paderewski* (N.Y., 1934); L T. Wolkowicz, *Paderewski's Diamond Anniversary* (N.Y., 1936); Mary Lawton, in collaboration with Paderewski, publ. *The Paderewski Memoirs* (to 1914 only; N.Y., 1938); A. Gronowicz, *Paderewski Pianist and Patriot* (Edinburgh, 1943); S. Giron, *Le Drame Paderewski* (Geneva, 1948); A. Baumgartner, *Le Vérité sur le prétendu drame Paderewski* (Geneva, 1948); A. Strakacz, *Paderewski As I Knew Him* (New Brunswick, N.J., 1949); C. Kellogg, *Paderewski* (N.Y., 1956); R. F. and P. Hume, *The Lion of Poland. The Story of Paderewski* (N.Y., 1962); Cz. R. Halski, *Paderewski* (in Polish; London, 1964).

Padilla, Lola Artôt de, Spanish soprano; daughter of the baritone **Mariano Padilla y Ramos;** b. Sèvres, near Paris, Oct. 5, 1885; d. Berlin, April 12, 1933. She was trained solely by her mother, **Désirée Artôt.** After singing in *salons* and concerts, she was engaged by Albert Carré for the Opéra-Comique in 1903. Later toured as concert singer through Europe; engaged at the Komische Oper, Berlin, 1905–08, as prima donna;

1909–27, member of the Royal Opera, Berlin; then retired.

Padilla y Ramos, Mariano, Spanish baritone; b. Murcia, 1842; d. Paris, Nov. 23, 1906. He studied with Mabellini in Florence; made his debut in Messina; sang in opera with great success in Italy, Austria, Germany, and Russia. In 1869 he married the singer **Désirée Artôt.**

Paër, Ferdinando, significant composer; b. Parma, June 1, 1771; d. Paris, May 3, 1839. He was a pupil of Fortunati and Ghiretti. His career as an opera composer began in 1792, when he produced the operas *Circe* (Venice) and *Le Astuzie amorose* (Parma). In that year he was also appointed honorary maestro di cappella to the court of Parma. In Vienna, 1797–1802, his style underwent a change, both harmony and orchestration showing increased variety and fullness; *Camilla, ossia il sotterraneo* (Vienna, Feb. 23, 1799) is considered his best opera. Paër succeeded Naumann as court Kapellmeister at Dresden in 1802; *Leonara, ossia l'amore conjugale* (Dresden, Oct. 3, 1804) is identical in subject with Beethoven's *Fidelio*. In 1807 he went to Paris, becoming "maître de chapelle" to Napoleon and conductor of the Opéra-Comique; later (1812) he succeeded Spontini at the Italian Opera, where he remained, through the vicissitudes of Catalini's domination and the joint conductorship of Rossini (1824–26), his successful rival on the stage, until his forced resignation in 1827 (he was held to blame for the poor financial condition of the theater). In 1828 he received the cross of the Legion of Honor; was elected to the Institut in 1831; and in 1832 was appointed conductor of the royal chamber music. Although some of his 43 operas were successful—e.g., *Sargino* (Dresden, May 26, 1803) and *Agnese* (first performed privately, near Parma, Oct., 1809)—they have all disappeared from the repertory, except for *Le Maître de chapelle* (Paris, March 29, 1821), occasionally performed in France; he also wrote 2 oratorios and a Passion, 10 cantatas, and much other vocal music; a *Symphonie bacchante* and variations on *Vive Henri IV*, for full orch.; 4 grand military marches; many piano variations; etc.
BIBLIOGRAPHY: T. Massé and A. Deschamps, *Paër et Rossini* (Paris, 1820); C. de Colobrano, *Funérailles de F. Paër* (Paris, 1893).

Paganelli, Giuseppe Antonio, Italian composer; b. Padua, March 6, 1710; d. Madrid, c.1762. He was employed as a cembalo player in an Italian opera company; was in Venice (1732); then at Bayreuth (1737–39). In 1755 he went to Madrid. He wrote several operas; but his historical importance lies in his works for the harpsichord. His *Divertisement de le Beau Sexe* (6 sonatas) was publ. by Gino Tagliapietra (Milan, 1936).
BIBLIOGRAPHY: F. Torrefranca, "Poeti minori del clavicembalo," *Rivista Musicale Italiana* (1910); E. Schenk, *G. A. Paganelli* (Salzburg, 1928).

Paganini, Niccolò, most famous of violin virtuosos; b. Genoa, Oct. 27, 1782; d. Nice, May 27, 1840. His father, a poor shopkeeper with little musical knowledge, but loving the art, taught him to play on the mandolin, and then procured abler teachers for his gifted son; under G. Servetto, and after him the maestro di cappella G. Costa, Niccolò's progress in violin playing was rapid; at 8 he composed a sonata for violin; in 1793 he appeared in public; from 1795 he studied with Ghiretti and began to compose seriously. His career as an independent virtuoso dates from 1798, when he ran away from his father after a concert at Lucca, and made a tour by himself to Pisa and other places. Though only 16, he was passionately fond of gambling, and addicted to all forms of dissipation; at Leghorn he had to part with his violin to pay a gambling debt, but a French merchant named Levron lent him a fine Guarnerius violin, and was so charmed with his playing that he made him a present of it. In 1804 he went home, and spent a year in assiduous practice; set out again on his travels in 1805, arousing unbounded enthusiasm; was soon appointed court solo violinist at Lucca (where his novel performances on the G string began), and stayed there until 1808; then up to 1827 he traveled throughout Italy, his renown spreading from year to year, and his vast technical resources maturing and augmenting so that victory over would-be rivals (Lafont at Milan, 1816, and Lipinski at Piacenza, 1817) was easy. When he left Italy for the first time in 1828, his opening concert, at Vienna, was a veritable triumph; from the municipality he received the great gold medal of St. Salvator; from the Emperor the (honorary) title of court virtuoso. He reached Berlin in March, 1829, Paris in March, 1831; played for the first time in London on June 3, 1831. Within a year he accumulated a fortune in Britain. The winter of 1833–34 was passed in Paris; he then retired for a time to his villa at Parma, though often visiting Paris. He spent the winter of 1838 in Paris, where his chief disorder, laryngeal phthisis, was aggravated by the climate. In search of sun and fresh air he went to Nice, but soon died there.
Paganini's stupendous technique (in double stops, left-hand pizzicato, staccato, harmonics), great power and perfect control of tone, the romantic passion and intense energy of his style, quite apart from mere tricks of virtuosity (such as tuning up the A string by a semitone or playing the *Witches' Dance* on one string after severing the other three on the stage, in sight of the audience, with a pair of scissors), made him the marvel of his time. He was an artist quite *sui generis,* whose dazzling genius held his audiences spellbound, and impressed musicians and amateurs alike.
WORKS: 24 *Capricci per violino solo* (op. 1; piano transcriptions by Schumann and Liszt); 6 *Sonate per violino e chitarra* (op. 2); do. (op. 3); 6 *Gran quartetti a violino, viola, chitarra e violoncello* (op. 4, 5); Concerto in B minor, *La Campanella*, with rondo 'à la clochette' (op. 7); *Le Streghe,* variations on theme by Süssmayr (op. 8); Variations on *God Save the King* (op. 9); *Il Carnevale di Venezia,* 20 variations (op. 10); Concert Allegro *Moto perpetuo* (op. 11); Variations on *Non più mesta* (op. 12); Variations on *Di tanti palpiti* (op. 13); *Variazioni di bravura* on airs from *Mosè*; 60 Studies in 60 Progressive Variations on the Air *Barucabà*. Of these only op. 1–5 were publ. during his life (the others posthumously). A number of works are

still in MS. A piece for violin and guitar, written by Paganini in 1815, was published in 1977 as his Concerto No. 6, edited by Ruggiero Ricci. His Collected Works are being published in an Edizione Nazionale, ed. by L. Ronga et al. (1976–   ).

BIBLIOGRAPHY: J. M. Schottky, *Paganinis Leben und Treiben als Künstler und als Mensch* (Prague and Hamburg, 1830; reprinted 1909); L. F. L'Héritier, *Notice sur le célèbre violiniste N. Paganini* (Paris, 1830; English transl., London, 1830); F. C. J. Schuetz, *Leben, Charakter und Kunst des Ritters N. Paganini* (Illmenau, 1830); K. F. Guhr, *Über Paganinis Kunst, die Violine zu spielen* (Mainz, 1831; English transl. by S. Novello, London, 1831); F. J. Fétis, *Notice biographique sur N. Paganini* (Paris, 1851; English transl., London, 1852); G. Conestabile, *Vita di N. Paganini* (Perugia, 1851; new ed., Milan, 1936); O. Bruni, *N. Paganini, Racconto storico* (Florence, 1873; new ed., 1903); A. Niggli, "N. Paganini," in Waldersee's *Sammlung musikalischer Vorträge* (Leipzig, 1882); S. S. Stratton, *N. Paganini: His Life and Work* (London, 1907); J.-G. Prod'homme, *Paganini* (Paris, 1907; English transl., N.Y., 1911); A. Bonaventura, *N. Paganini* (Modena, 1911); J. Kapp, *N. Paganini* (Berlin, 1913; rev. ed., 1928); E. Istel, *Paganini* (1919); J. Siber, *Paganini* (Berlin, 1920); G. Kinsky, "Paganinis musikalischer Nachlass," in the *Heyer Catalogue IV* (pp. 402–47); L. Day, *Paganini* (N.Y., 1929); A. Günther, *Paganini in Lucca* (Munich, 1929); A. Montanelli, *Paganini a Forlì* (Forlì, 1930); E. Istel, "The Secret of Paganini's Technique," *Musical Quarterly* (Jan. 1930); A. Codingola, *Paganini intimo* (a very important documentary compilation; Genoa, 1935); J. Pulver, *Paganini, the Romantic Virtuoso* (London, 1936); R. de Saussine, *Paganini le magicien* (Paris, 1938; English transl., N.Y., 1954); I. Pizzetti, *N. Paganini* (Turin, 1940); N. Podenzani, *Il Romanzo di N. Paganini* (Milan, 1944); M. Tibaldi Chiesa, *Paganini, la vita e l'opera* (3rd ed., Milan, 1944); H. Spivacke, *Paganiniana* (Washington, 1945); T. Valensi, *Paganini* (Nice, 1950); A. Mell, "Paganiniana in the Muller Collection of the New York Public Library," *Musical Quarterly* (Jan. 1953); G. I. C. de Courcy, *Paganini: the Genoese* (Norman, Okla., 1957); R. de Saussine, *Paganini* (Milan, 1958); A. Codignola, *Arte e magia di Niccolò Paganini* (Milan, 1960); W. G. Armando, *Paganini: eine Biographie* (Hamburg, 1960); D. F. Botti, *Paganini e Parma* (Parma, 1961); P. Berri, *Paganini: Documenti e testimonianze* (Genoa, 1962); L. Day, *Paganini of Genoa* (London, 1966).

Page, John, English tenor and anthologist; b. c.1760; d. London, Aug. 16, 1812. He was a lay clerk at St. George's, Windsor, Gentleman of the Chapel Royal; Vicar-choral at St. Paul's, 1801. He compiled *Harmonica sacra* (1800; 3 vols.; a collection of 74 anthems in score, by eminent English composers of the 16th-18th centuries; new ed. by Rimbault); *Festive Harmony* (1804; 4 vols.; madrigals, glees, and elegies); *Collection of Hymns* (1804); *The Burial Service, Chant, Evening Service, Dirge and Anthems App. to be Perf. at the Funeral of Lord Nelson* (1806); anthems, psalms, etc.

Page, Kate Stearns, American piano pedagogue; b. Brookline, Mass., Aug. 21, 1873; d. New York, Jan. 19, 1963. She taught at the Denison House Settlement in Boston for 10 years and at the Parke School, Brookline, Mass., for 5 years; from 1933 piano teacher at the Diller-Quaile School of Music, N.Y. Publ. valuable pedagogical material, some of it in collaboration with Angela Diller.

Page, Nathaniel Clifford, American music editor, b. San Francisco, Oct. 26, 1866; d. Philadelphia, May 12, 1956. He was a pupil of E. Stillman Kelley; 1905–09, editor for O. Ditson Co. in Boston; from 1909, for C. C. Birchard & Co., Carl Fischer, Theo. Presser, etc.; then again for O. Ditson Co.; 1921–29, conducted summer classes in orchestration at Columbia Univ. He made a special study of Oriental music.

WORKS: a light opera, *The First Lieutenant* (San Francisco, 1889); other stage works; many band and orchestral pieces; cantatas; songs; etc. He publ. over 400 vocal and instrumental arrangements of popular pieces.

Pahissa, Jaime, Catalan composer; b. Barcelona, Oct. 7, 1880; d. Buenos Aires, Oct. 27, 1969. He was a practicing architect for 4 years before turning to music as a profession; studied composition with Morera in Barcelona. He associated himself with the Catalan nationalist movement in art, obtaining his first important success with the romantic opera *La Presó de Lleida (The Prison of Lérida)* in 1906, which had 100 consecutive performances in Barcelona; it was later rewritten and produced in Barcelona on Feb. 8, 1928 under the title *La Princesa Margarita*, again obtaining a notable success. Other operas produced in Barcelona were *Gala Plácida* (Jan. 15, 1913) and *Marinela* (March 31, 1923). Among his orchestral works the most remarkable is *Monodía*, written in unisons, octaves, double octaves, etc., without using any other intervals, and depending for its effect only on instrumental variety (Barcelona, Oct. 12, 1925); in a different vein is his *Suite Intertonal* (Barcelona, Oct. 24, 1926), based on his own method of free tonal and polytonal composition. In 1935 Pahissa emigrated to Argentina, settling in Buenos Aires, where he continued to compose; also established himself as a teacher and writer there. He published in Buenos Aires several books: *Espíritu y cuerpo de la música* (1945); *Los grandes problemas de la música* (1945; new ed., 1954); *Vida y obra de Manuel de Falla* (Buenos Aires, 1947; also in English, London, 1954); *Sendas y cumbres de la música española* (1955). A detailed account of Pahissa's career in Barcelona is found in the *Diccionario de la Música Ilustrado* (1930).

Pahlen, Kurt, Austrian writer on music; b. Vienna, May 26, 1907. He studied at the Vienna Cons., and also at the Univ. of Vienna (with Guido Adler, Lach, and Orel), graduating in 1929. In 1939 he settled in Buenos Aires, where he became a successful teacher and writer on musical subjects; publ. a music history: *Historia gráfica universal de la música* (Buenos Aires, 1944; in English as *Music of the World,* N.Y., 1949); also a general manual of musical knowledge, *Síntesis del saber musical* (Buenos Aires, 1948); *Ins Wunder-*

land der Musik (Zürich, 1948); *Manuel de Falla und die Musik in Spanien* (Olten, 1953); *Musiklexikon der Welt* (Zürich, 1956).

Paik, Nam June, Korean-American avant-garde composer and experimenter in the visual arts; b. Seoul, July 20, 1932. He studied first at the Univ. of Tokyo; then went to Germany where he took courses in music theory with Thrasybulos Georgiades in Munich and with Wolfgang Fortner in Freiburg-im-Bresigau. Turning towards electronics, he did experimental work at the Electronic Music Studio in Cologne (1958–60); attended the summer seminars for new music at Darmstadt (1957–61). In his showings he pursues the objective of total art as the sum of integrated synesthetic experiences, involving all sorts of actions, walking, talking, dressing, undressing, drinking, smoking, moving furniture, engaging in quaquaversal commotion, intended to demonstrate that any human, or inhuman, action becomes an artistic event through the power of volitional concentration of an ontological imperative. Paik attracted attention at his duo recitals with the topless cellist Charlotte Moorman, at which he acted as a surrogate cello, with his denuded spinal column serving as the fingerboard for Ms. Moorman's cello bow, while his bare skin provided an area for intermittent pizzicati. About 1963 Paik began experimenting with video tape as a medium for sounds and images; his initial experiment in this field was *Global Groove*, a high-velocity collage of intermingled television bits, which included instantaneous commercials, fragments from news telecasts, and subliminal extracts from regular programs, subjected to topological alterations. His list of works (some of them consisting solely of categorical imperatives) includes *Ommaggio a Cage* for piano demolition, breakage of raw eggs, spray painting of hands in jet black, etc. (Düsseldorf, Nov. 13, 1959); *Symphony for 20 Rooms* (1961); *Variations on a Theme of Saint-Saëns* for cello and piano, with the pianist playing *Le Cygne* while the cellist dives into an oil drum filled with water (N.Y., Aug. 25, 1965, composer at the keyboard, cellist Charlotte Moorman in the oil drum); *Performable Music*, wherein the performer is ordered to make an incision with a razor of no less than 10 centimeters on his left forearm (Los Angeles, Dec. 2, 1965); *Opéra sextronique* (1967); *Opéra électronique* (1968); *Creep Into the Vagina of a Whale* (c.1969); *Young Penis Symphony*, a protrusion of 10 erectile phalluses through a paper curtain (c.1970; produced for the first time at "La Mamelle" in San Francisco, Sept. 21, 1975, under the direction of Ken Friedman who also acted as one of the 10 performers). Of uncertain attribution is a symphony designated as No. 3, which Paik delegated to Ken Friedman who worked on it in Saugus, California, the epicenter of the earthquake of Feb. 9, 1971, and of which the earthquake itself constituted the finale.
BIBLIOGRAPHY: Calvin Tomkins, "Video Visionary," *New Yorker* (May 5, 1975); autobiographical note in *Source* 11 (1973).

Paine, John Knowles, American composer and teacher; b. Portland, Me., Jan. 9, 1839; d. Cambridge, Mass. April 25, 1906. His father kept a music store in Portland, and conducted the local band. His first music teacher was H. Kotzschmar. He then went to Berlin and studied under Haupt (counterpoint), Fischer (singing), and Wieprecht (instrumentation), 1858–61. After organ concerts in Berlin and various American cities, he settled in Boston as organist of the West Church, Cambridge St. In 1862 he became teacher of music at Harvard Univ., and organist at Appleton Chapel, Cambridge, Mass.; from 1875 until his death he occupied the newly created professorship of music at Harvard, the first in any American university. In 1866–67 he toured Germany and conducted his Mass at Berlin. He was awarded the honorary degrees of M.A., Harvard, 1869; Mus. Doc., Yale, 1890. He was one of the most notable pioneers in American musical development. Among his many pupils were J. A. Carpenter, A. Foote, E. B. Hill, F. S. Converse, H. T. Finck, D. G. Mason.
WORKS: *Domine salvum fac,* for men's chorus and orch. (1863); Mass in D for soli, chorus, and orch.; oratorio, *St. Peter; Centennial Hymn* for chorus and orch.; (Philadelphia, 1876); music to *Œdipus tyrannus* (Sophocles), for men's voices and orch.; *The Realm of Fancy,* cantata for soprano solo, chorus and orch.; *Phœbus, arise; The Nativity,* cantata for soli, chorus, and orch.; *Song of Promise,* cantata for soprano, chorus, and orch.; incidental music to *The Birds* of Aristophanes; *Columbus March and Hymn,* for the Chicago Exposition (1893); *Hymn of the West,* for the St. Louis Exposition (1904); 2 symphonies, in C minor, and in A (*Spring Symphony;* Cambridge, Mass., March 10, 1880); 2 symphonic poems, *The Tempest,* and *An Island Fantasy;* overture to *As You Like It; Duo concertante* for violin and cello with orch.; String Quartet; Piano Trio; Larghetto and Scherzo for piano, violin, and cello; Romanza and Scherzo for piano and cello; Sonata for piano and violin; characteristic pieces for piano; variations and fantasias for organ; motets, part-songs, and songs. An opera, *Azara* (text by himself), was publ. in 1901, and had a concert performance in Boston in 1907. He wrote *The History of Music to the Death of Schubert* (posthumous, 1907). His *Lecture Notes* were publ. in 1885.
BIBLIOGRAPHY: G. T. Edwards, *Music and Musicians of Maine* (1928); M. A. DeW. Howe, "J. K. Paine," *Musical Quarterly* (July 1939); see also *Dictionary of American Biography,* vol. XIV.

Paisible, Louis Henri, French violinist and composer; b. Paris, 1745; d. St. Petersburg, April 10, 1782 (suicide). He studied with Gaviniès; played in the orch. of the Concert Spirituel in Paris; then traveled through Europe; in 1778 was engaged at the Russian court in St. Petersburg. Although well received at first, he was unable to make headway with a series of concerts for which he solicited subscriptions; deprived of resources, he shot himself. Twelve of his string quartets and 2 violin concertos have been publ. in Paris and London.
BIBLIOGRAPHY: A. Mooser, *Annales de la musique et des musiciens en Russie au XVIIIᵉ siècle* (Geneva, 1950; vol. II, pp. 274–78).

Paisiello, Giovanni, famous Italian composer; b. Taranto, May 9, 1740; d. Naples, June 5, 1816. From the age of 5 he studied at the Jesuit school in Taranto, where he was taught by a priest, Resta, and where his singing so delighted Guaducci, maestro at the Capuchin church, that he advised the boy's father to place him in the Cons. di S. Onofrio at Naples. There he studied under Durante, Cotumacci, and Abos, from 1754 to 1759, remaining 4 years longer as a teacher, and occupying himself with sacred composition (Masses, oratorios, etc.). But a comic intermezzo performed at the Cons. in 1763 disclosed such dramatic talent that he was commissioned to write an opera for the Marsigli Theater at Bologna; here his first comic opera was produced, *La Pupilla, ossia Il Mondo alla rovescia* (1764). For 12 years, during which he brought out some 50 operas, his successes were many and reverses few, even in rivalry with Piccinni and Cimarosa. Important works of this period are *Le finte Contesse* (Rome, Feb., 1766), *L'Idolo cinese* (Naples, spring, 1767), and *La Frascatana* (Venice, Nov., 1774). Invited to St. Petersburg by Empress Catherine II in 1776, he lived there 8 years on a princely salary, produced several operas, including *Il Barbiere di Siviglia* (St. Petersburg, Sept. 26, 1782), which became so popular in Italy that it still stood as a rival to Rossini's masterpiece in 1816. During the next 15 years he acted as maestro di cappella to Ferdinand IV of Naples (1784–99); *Il Re Teodoro in Venezia* (Vienna, Aug. 23, 1784; perhaps his best opera), *Le Gare generose* (Naples, spring, 1786), *L'Amor contrastato* (later called *La Molinara*; Naples, summer, 1788); *Nina, o La Pazza per amore* (Caserta, June 25, 1789; a charming "opera semiseria," a genre in which Paisiello excelled), and *I Zingari in fiera* (Naples, Nov. 21, 1789) are especially noteworthy. During the revolutionary period of 1799–1801 Paisiello stood well with the republican government, but lost the favor of the King, together with his place and salary. From 1802–03 he was Napoleon's maître de chapelle at Paris. From 1803 to the Bourbon restoration of 1815, he held his former position at Naples, and other posts of importance, all of which later he lost on Ferdinand's return in 1815, being retained solely as maestro di cappella. Paisiello was an extraordinarily productive composer, and one of the most popular of his time; yet of his 100 or more operas only a few are ever revived nowadays. His vein of melody was original, fresh, and natural; although he introduced instrumental effects that were novel in Italy, he carefully avoided the over-elaborate numbers common to the period, obtaining his effect by the grace, beauty, and dramatic truthfulness of his melody.

WORKS: OPERAS: *Il Marchese di Tulipano, La Serva padrona, Il Barbiere, Il Re Teodoro, La Molinara, Nina,* and *Proserpine.* CHURCH MUSIC: a Passion oratorio (Warsaw, 1784); 3 solemn Masses for double choir and 2 orchestras; *Te Deum* for the same; Requiem for 4 voices and orch. (performed at his own funeral); 30 Masses for the same; two 5-part Masses; *Dixit, Magnificat, Miserere,* about 40 motets with orch.; etc. INSTRUMENTAL MUSIC: 12 symphonies; funeral march for Gen. Hoche; 6 piano concertos; 12 piano quartets; 6 string quartets; sonata and concerto for harp; 2 vols. of sonatas, caprices, etc. for piano.

BIBLIOGRAPHY: I. F. Arnold, *G. Paisiello: seine kurze Biographie* (Erfurt, 1810); J. F. Lesueur, *Notice sur Paisiello* (Paris, 1816); Gagliardo, *Onori funebri . . . di Paisiello* (Naples, 1816); Quatremère de Quincy, *Notice historique de Paisiello* (Paris, 1817); F. Schizzi *Della vita a degli studi di G. Paisiello* (Milan, 1833); C. G. Pupino, *Paisiello* (Naples, 1908); S. Panareo, *Paisiello in Russia* (Trani, 1910); H. Abert, "Paisiellos Buffokunst und ihre Beziehungen zu Mozart" *Archiv für Musikwissenschaft* I/3 (1919); A. Della Corte, *Settecento italiano: Paisiello* (Turin, 1922); F. Barberio, "I primi dieci anni di vita artistica di Paisiello," *Rivista Musicale Italiana* (1922); A. Cametti, *Paisiello e la corte di Vienna* (Rome, 1929); G. C. Speciale, *G. Paisiello* (Naples, 1931); P. Petrosellini, *Il Barbiere di Siviglia di G. Paisiello* (1932); A. Loewenberg, "Paisiello's and Rossini's *Barbiere di Siviglia,*" *Music & Letters* (April 1939); E. Faustini-Fasini, *Opere teatrali, oratori e cantate di G. Paisiello* (Bari, 1940); M. F. Robinson, *Naples and Neapolitan Opera* (London, 1972).

Pakhmutova, Alexandra, Soviet composer; b. Stalingrad, Nov. 9, 1929. She studied at the Moscow Cons. with Shebalin, graduating in 1953. Her music is unpretentious and melodious; its thematic resources are derived from Russian folksongs. Her most successful work is a Concerto for Trumpet and Orch. (Moscow, June 11, 1955); she also wrote songs, some of which became popular.

BIBLIOGRAPHY: Y. Dobrynina, *Alexandra Pakhmutova* (Moscow, 1959).

Paladilhe, Émile, French composer; b. Montpellier, June 3, 1844; d. Paris, Jan. 6, 1926. He entered the Paris Cons. in 1853; pupil of Marmontel (piano), Benoist (organ), and Halévy (counterpoint); 1st prize for piano and organ, 1857; won the Grand Prix de Rome in 1860 with the cantata *Le Czar Ivan IV* (Opéra, 1860). He brought out the 1-act comedy-opera *Le Passant,* at the Opéra-Comique (April 24, 1872), followed by *L'Amour africain* (May 8, 1875), *Suzanne* (Dec. 30, 1878), *Diana* (Feb. 23, 1885), the 5-act opera *Patrie* (Opéra, Dec. 20, 1886); and *Les Saintes Maries de la mer,* a sacred lyric drama (Montpellier, 1892). He also produced 2 Masses, Symph. in E-flat, some sacred music, and numerous songs (*Mandolinata, Premières pensées, Mélodies écossaises*). In 1892 he succeeded Guiraud as member of the Institut de France.

Palange, Louis Salvador, American conductor, composer and arranger, of Italian descent; b. Oakland, Cal., Dec. 17, 1917. He played the clarinet and bassoon in school bands; in 1936 went to Los Angelos, where he took lessons with Wesley La Violette. In 1955 he became conductor of the Beach Cities Symph. Orch.; in 1965 formed the Southeast Symph. Continuing to accumulate orchestral groups, he assumed in 1967 the direction of 3 more orchestras: Downey Symph. Orch., Hollywood-Wilshire Symph. Orch. and the Metropolitan Symph. Orch. of Los Angeles.

WORKS: *Symphony in Steel* for band (Los Angeles, March 8, 1941); Symph. No. 1 (*Invasion Symphony,* 1946); Violin Concerto (1950); String Quartet (1950); *Hollywood Panorama,* tone poem (Burbank, Sept. 21, 1952); *A Romantic Piano Concerto* (Cleveland, May 13, 1954); *Poker Deck Ballet Suite* for orch.

(Redondo Beach, Cal., Dec. 9, 1960); Symph. No. 2 (Los Angeles, March 22, 1968).

Palau, Manuel, Spanish composer and conductor; b. Valencia, Jan. 4, 1893; d. Valencia, Feb. 18, 1967. He studied first at the Cons. of Valencia; later in Paris, where he took lessons from Koechlin and Ravel. Returning to Valencia, he established himself as teacher, conductor, and composer. Most of his thematic material is inspired by Catalan folksongs; his instrumental music usually bears programmatic content; his technique of composition follows the French Impressionist procedures.

WORKS: zarzuelas: *Beniflors, Amor torna,* etc.; *Gongoriana,* orch. suite (1927); 2 symphonies; *Concierto levantino,* for guitar and orch.; *Homenaje a Debussy,* for orch.; sonata for guitar solo; numerous songs of a popular nature; piano pieces: *Valencia, Levantina, Sonatina Valenciana, Tres Impresiones fugaces, Campanas y paisaje balear, Danza hispalense, Danza iberica, Evocación de Andalucía,* etc.

BIBLIOGRAPHY: A. Mingote, *Manuel Palau* (Valencia, 1946); F. J. León Tello, *La Obra pianística de Manuel Palau* (Valencia, 1956).

Páleníček, Josef, Czech composer and pianist; b. Travnik, July 19, 1914. He studied with Otakar Šín and Vítězslav Novák at the Prague Cons.; then went to Paris and took lessons with Albert Roussel (1936–37). He traveled as pianist in the Czech Trio; in 1963 appointed to the staff of the Prague Cons. In 1977 he received the State Prize for his interpretations of Janáček's piano works, his specialty.

WORKS: 3 piano concertos: No. 1 with string orch. and timpani (1939), No. 2 (1953) and No. 3, for young pianists, with small orch. (1961); Saxophone Concerto (1944); Concertino for Orch. (1937–45); Flute Concerto (1955); *Concertino da camera* for clarinet and orch. (1957); *Symphonic Variations on an Imaginary Portrait of Ilya Erenburg* for orch. (1971); Cello Concerto (1973); an oratorio, *Song of Man* (1952–58); Piano Quintet (1933); *Preludium a Capriccio* for violin and piano (1935); Clarinet Sonatina (1936); *Choral Variations* for cello and piano (1942); *Little Suite* for clarinet and piano (1943); String Quartet No. 1 (1954); *Masks,* 2 pieces for saxophone and piano (1957); *Little Suite* for violin and piano (1958); *Trio Sonata* for mezzo-soprano, oboe and piano (1965); *Variations* for cello and piano (1972); *Rondo Concertante* for cello and piano (1972); *In modo antico,* suite for cello and guitar (1973); Piano Sonata (1936); *Piano Sketchbook,* cycle of 5 pieces (1939); instructive works for children.

Palester, Roman, Polish composer; b. Śniatyń, Dec. 28, 1907. He studied with Soltys at the Cons. of Lwów and with Sikorski at the Warsaw Cons.; he went to France in 1925, and after a brief visit in Poland, he settled in Paris. In his music Palester adopted the modernistic devices of the French school, but preserved elements of Polish folksongs in the thematic structure of his works; harmonically he did not choose to transcend the limits of enhanced tonality. Several of his works were performed at festivals of the International Society for Contemporary Music: *Symphonic Music* (London, July 27, 1931), *Danse po-*lonaise, for orch. (Barcelona, April 22, 1936), Violin Concerto (London, July 14, 1946). Other works are: 4 symphonies (1936; 1942; 1947; 1952; newly revised in 1971); *Requiem* (1948); Sonatina for 3 clarinets (1936); Concertino for Piano and Orch. (1942); *Serenade* for 2 flutes and string orch. (Cracow, Nov. 9, 1947); Concertino for Harpsichord and Chamber Ensemble (1958); Piccolo Concerto for chamber orch. (1959); *Variations* for orch. (1963); *Metamorphosen* for orch. (1968); Trio for flute, viola and harp (1969); Piano Sonata (1970); Duo for 2 violins (1972); *Suite à quatre* for oboe and string trio (1973); a one-act opera, *La Mort de Don Juan* (Brussels, 1965).

Palestrina (Giovanni Pierluigi, called da Palestrina), the greatest composer of the Catholic Church and of the Roman School, b. Palestrina, near Rome, c.1525; d. Rome Feb. 2, 1594. He was a chorister at the Cathedral of his native town c.1532; in 1534, when Cardinal della Valle, Bishop of Palestrina, was made Archbishop of S. Maria Maggiore in Rome, he took Palestrina with him and entered him in the choir school of that church. In 1537 we find him listed as an elder choir boy; in 1539, his voice having broken, he left the choir and returned home. But by 1540, or soon after, he was back in Rome, studying music; his teacher may have been Firmin Le Bel, choirmaster of S. Maria Maggiore. In 1544 he was appointed organist and choirmaster at the Cathedral of St. Agapit in Palestrina; the bishop there was Cardinal del Monte, who in 1550 became pope under the name of Julius III, and who in 1551 bestowed upon Palestrina the post of maestro of the Cappella Giulia. Meanwhile, Palestrina had married (June 12, 1547) and had become father of two sons. In 1554 he publ. his first book of Masses, dedicated to Julius III, who rewarded him by making him a member of the Pontifical Choir (Jan., 1555); this aroused much resentment, for Palestrina was admitted without taking the entrance examination, and it is said that he had a poor voice. A few months later he was dismissed with a small pension by the new pope, Paul V, on the ground that he was a married man. He then received the appointment of maestro of the church of St. John Lateran, for which he wrote his celebrated *Lamentations.* In 1560 he resigned this post, and in March of the following year he became maestro of S. Maria Maggiore. In 1563 his first book of motets was published. About this time the Council of Trent concerned itself with the reform of church music, decreeing the exclusion of all profane and impure elements; contapuntal music, which lent itself to many abuses, might also have been forbidden, had it not been for the determined opposition of the Emperor Ferdinand I. Palestrina's role in influencing the decisions of the Council, especially as regards the proposed exclusion of contrapuntal music, has been grossly exaggerated and misrepresented by most historians, beginning with Baini. Palestrina's famous *Missa Papae Marcelli* is undoubtedly a model of the purest religious style; but there is no evidence that it played much part in shaping the fate of church music at that time. From 1565 to 1571 Palestrina was music director at the new Roman Seminary, where his elder sons were students. In 1567 he resigned his post at S. Maria Maggiore and entered the service of Cardinal

Ippolito d'Este (d. 1572). In 1568 the Emperor Maximilian offered him the post of maestro at the court of Vienna, but Palestrina demanded so high a salary that the matter was dropped. In 1571 he resumed his old post as maestro of the Cappella Giulia, retaining this office until his death. In 1576 Pope Gregory XIII issued a decree for the revision of the Gradual, which was to be carried out by Palestrina and Annibale Zoilo; but the revised version, known as the "Medicean Gradual," was not printed until 20 years after Palestrina's death (1614). In 1580, having suffered several family bereavements, including the death of his wife, Palestrina decided to enter the priesthood; but soon he changed his mind, and on March 28, 1581, he married the widow of a prosperous furrier. He then took a partner and successfully carried on the fur business. In 1583 he was invited to become maestro at the court of Mantua, but again his terms were rejected as too high. In 1584 he brought out his settings of the *Song of Solomon,* and in 1589 his harmonized version of the Latin Hymnal was published. At his death he was buried in the Cappella Nuova of old St. Peter's Church.

In his music Palestrina aimed at technical smoothness and beauty of sound rather than at forceful expression and originality. In the "Motu Proprio" of Pope Pius X, on sacred music (1903), Palestrina's works are recommended as "of excellent quality from a liturgical and musical standpoint."

WORKS: A monumental edition of his complete compositions was publ. by Breitkopf & Härtel in 33 volumes (1862–1907), comprising 181 motets, 113 hymns and offertories, 93 Masses, 9 Lamentations, 10 litanies, 4 psalms, 35 Magnificats, 83 secular madrigals, 56 Italian sacred madrigals, miscellaneous compositions, and documents. After the completion of this great edition the same firm began the separate publication of several of the most famous works. Breitkopf & Härtel also publ. a special catalogue. A new collected edition was begun in 1939 under the editorship of R. Casimiri, reaching 32 vols. as of 1977.

BIBLIOGRAPHY: G. Baini, *Memorie storico-critiche della vita e delle opere di G. P. a Palestrina* (Rome, 1828, 2 vols.; German transl., abridged, Leipzig, 1834); K. von Winterfeld, *Joh. P. von Palestrina* (Breslau, 1832); W. Bäumker, *Palestrina* (Freiburg, 1887); correspondence with the Duke of Mantua, in *Kirchenmusikalisches Jahrbuch* (1886); P. Wagner, *Palestrina als weltlicher Komponist* (Strasbourg, 1890); F. X. Haberl, "Die Kardinals-Kommission von 1564 und Palestrinas *Missa Papae Marcelli,*" *Kirchenmusikalisches Jahrbuch* (1892); Ph. Spitta, "Palestrina im 16. und 19. Jahrhundert," *Deutsche Rundschau* (July 1894); F. X. Haberl, *G. P. da Palestrina e il Graduale romanum officiale dell'editio medicaea (1614)* (Regensburg, 1894); A. Cametti, *Cenni biografici di G. P. da Palestrina* (Milan, 1895); G. Félix, *Palestrina et la musique sacrée (1594–1894)* (Lille, 1896); C. Respighi, *Nuovo studio su G. P. da Palestrina e l'emendazione del Graduale romano* (Rome, 1899); A. Cametti, "Un nuovo documento sulle origini di G. P. da Palestrina," *Rivista Musicale Italiana* (1903); Michel Brenet, *Palestrina* (Paris, 1905); J. Gloger, *Die "Missa Prima." Eine Studie über den Palestrinastil* (Leobschütz, 1910); E. Schmitz, *G. P. Palestrina* (Leipzig, 1914); K. Weinmann, *Palestrinas Geburtsjahr* (Regensburg,

1915); R. Casimiri, *G. P. da Palestrina. Nuovi documenti biografici* (Rome, 1918); id., *Il "Codice 59" dell'archivio musicale lateranense* (Rome, 1919); Zoë K. Pyne, *G. P. da Palestrina. His Life and Times* (London, 1922); A. Cametti, *G. P. da Palestrina e il suo commercio di pelliccerie* (Rome, 1922); id., "G. P. da Palestrina e le sue alleanze matrimoniali," *Rivista Musicale Italiana* (1923); id., *Le Case dei Pierluigi in Palestrina* (Rome, 1925); id., *Palestrina* (Milan, 1925); id., "Bibliografia palestriniana," *Bollettino Bibliografico Musicale* (Sept. 1926); K. Jeppesen, *The Style of Palestrina and the Dissonance* (Danish, 1923; German, 1925; English, 1927; 2nd English ed., 1946); id., in the P. Wagner-Festschrift (1926), Adler-Festschrift (1930), and Liège Kongress-Bericht (1931); L. P. Manzetti, "Palestrina," *Musical Quarterly* (July 1928); K. G. Fellerer, *Palestrina* (Regensburg, 1930; 2nd ed., Düsseldorf, 1960); F. Raugel, *Palestrina* (Paris, 1930); W. Widmann, "Die 6-stimmigen Messen Palestrinas," *Kirchenmusikalisches Jahrbuch* (1930–31); O. Ursprung, *Die katholische Kirchenmusik* (1933); H. Coates, *Palestrina* (London, 1938); O. Strunk, "Guglielmo Gonzaga and Palestrina's *Missa Dominicalis,*" *Musical Quarterly* (April 1947); J. Samson, *Palestrina ou La poésie de l'exactitude* (Geneva, 1950); K. Jeppesen, "The Recently Discovered Mantova Masses of Palestrina," *Acta Musicologica* (1950); A. I. M. Kat, *Palestrina* (Haarlem, 1951); G. Reese, *Music in the Renaissance* (N.Y., 1954); H. K. Andrews, *An Introduction to the Technique of Palestrina* (London, 1958); K. Jeppesen, "Palestrina," in *Die Musik in Geschichte und Gegenwart;* R. L. Marshall, "The Paraphrase Technique of Palestrina in His Masses Based on Hymns," *Journal of the American Musicological Society* (1963); T. Day, "Echoes of Palestrina's *Missa ad fugam* in the Eighteenth Century," *Journal of the American Musicological Society* (Fall, 1971); L. Lockwood, Norton Critical Score edition of *Pope Marcellus Mass,* containing score, backgrounds, and analyses (N.Y., 1975).

Palisca, Claude Victor, American musicologist; b. Fiume, Nov. 24, 1921. He came to the U.S. in 1930; attended public schools in N.Y. and Florida; studied composition at Queens College with Karol Rathaus (B.A., 1943) and at Harvard Univ. with Walter Piston and Randall Thompson (composition) and with Otto Kinkeldey, Gombosi and Davison (musicology); obtained his M.A. in 1948; Ph.D. in 1954. He was a member of the faculty at the Univ. of Illinois, Urbana, (1953–59); in 1959 joined the staff of Yale Univ. He held the John Knowles Paine Traveling Fellowship (1949–50); Fulbright Grant for Italy (1950–52); Guggenheim Fellowship (1960–61).

WRITINGS: *Girolamo Mei: Letters on Ancient and Modern Music to Vincenzo Galilei and Giovanni Bardi* (Rome, 1960); *17th-Century Science and the Arts* (with others; Princeton, 1961); *Musicology* (with others; Englewood Cliffs, N.J., 1963); *Baroque Music* (Englewood Cliffs, N.J., 1968); transl. (with G. A. Marco) of Gioseffo Zarlino's *Le istitutioni harmoniche* (Part 3, 1558; New Haven, 1968).

Palkovský, Oldřich, Czech composer; b. Brušperk, Feb. 24, 1907. He studied composition with Petrželka at the Brno Cons. (1926–31) and with Suk at the Prague Cons. (1931–33); was director of the State Testing Commission for Music (1939–54) and taught at the Kroměříž branch of the Brno Cons.

WORKS: 6 symphonies (1933–34, 1939, 1944, 1947, 1956–57, 1962); Concerto for Cimbalom and Small Orch. (1952–53); *Scherzo capriccio* for orch. (1953); *Morvarian Dances* for orch. (1956); *Variations and Fugue* for cimbalom, string orch. and timpani (1959); Flute Concerto (1959); Oboe Concerto (1961); Accordion Concerto (1961); *3 Symphonic Movements* (1971); 6 string quartets (1931, 1933, 1937, 1957, 1962, 1970); 2 piano trios (1940, 1968); Violin Sonata (1942); Viola Sonata (1944); Concertino for Winds (1945); Cello Sonata (1946); Clarinet Sonata (1947); 2 wind quintets (1949, 1958); Quartet for flute, violin, viola, and cello (1950); Horn Sonata (1963); *Chamber Music for 8 instruments* (1964); *Balladic Sonata* for bassoon and piano (1969); *Sonnets* for flute, bass clarinet, and piano (1969); piano pieces; songs.

Palkovský, Pavel, Czech composer, son of **Oldřich Palkovský;** b. Zlín, Dec. 18, 1939. He studied composition with Schaefer at the Brno Cons., graduating in 1960, and with Kapr at the Janáček Academy of Music in Brno, graduating in 1964.

WORKS: Cello Sonata (1963); 2 symphonies: No. 1 (1964) and No. 2 for piano and orch. (1968–69); *Chamber Music I* for strings, piano and percussion (1964); *Chamber Music II* for piano, organ, celesta and percussion (1968); Horn Sonata (1967); *3 Studies* for accordion and 9 winds (1969); Trio for 3 accordions (1969).

Pallantios, Menelaos, Greek composer and pedagogue; b. Piraeus, Jan. 29, 1914. He studied with Mitropoulos in Greece and with Alfredo Casella in Rome; in 1936 became an instructor at the Cons. of Athens, and in 1962 was appointed its director. In 1969 he was elected to the Athens Academy. He wrote music to several ancient Greek tragedies endeavoring to recreate the classical modes in modern investiture. Among his works are: Symphony (1948); *Divertimento* for orch. (1952); Piano Concerto (1961); *5 Character Pieces* for oboe, clarinet and bassoon (1962).

Pallavicini, Carlo, Italian composer; b. Salò, near Brescia, 1630; d. Dresden, Jan. 29, 1688. He served as an organist at S. Antonio in Padua in 1665–66 and in 1673–74 was Maestro dei concerti there; then went to Venice; in 1687 he was appointed music director of the new Italian Opera at Dresden; wrote several operas for it. A scene from *Le Amazoni nell'isole fortunate* (Piazzola, near Padua, Nov. 11, 1679) was publ. in the *Sammelbände der Internationalen Musik-Gesellschaft* (vol. 2), and the complete score of *La Gerusalemme liberata* (Venice, Jan. 3, 1687) was edited by Abert in the *Denkmäler deutscher Tonkunst* (vol. 55).

Pallavicino, Benedetto, Italian composer; b. Cremona, 1551; d. Mantua, May 6, 1601. He was a court singer in Mantua from 1582 and maestro di cappella to the Duke from 1596. Monteverdi mentions Pallavicino's death in a letter applying for his post to the Duke of Mantua in Nov. 1601. Pallavicino publ. 1 book of madrigals *a* 4 (1579), 8 books *a* 5 (1581, ?, 1585, 1588, 1593, 1600, 1604, 1612), 1 book *a* 6 (1587) and other madrigals in collections; also a book of motets *a* 8, 12, and 16 (1595).

BIBLIOGRAPHY: D. de Paoli, *Monteverdi* (Milan, 1945); G. Sartori, "Monteverdiana," *Musical Quarterly* (July 1952); P. Flanders, *A Thematic Index to the Works of Benedetto Pallavicino* (N.Y., 1971).

Pallemaerts, Edmundo, Belgian composer; b. Malines, Dec. 21, 1867; d. Buenos Aires, April 20, 1945. He studied music with De Greef and Kufferath at the Brussels Cons.; settled in Buenos Aires in 1889, and founded there the Conservatorio Argentino, of which he was the first director (1894). He wrote a *Fantasia Argentina* for orch.; many minor works for piano; also songs.

Palma, Athos, Argentine composer; b. Buenos Aires, June 7, 1891; d. Miramar, Argentina, Jan. 10, 1951. He studied with C. Troiani (piano) and other teachers in Buenos Aires; in 1904, went to Europe, returning to Buenos Aires in 1914. There he was busily engaged as a teacher. His music follows the Italian tradition, although the subject matter is derived from South American history and literature. He wrote the operas *Nazdah* (Buenos Aires, June 19, 1924) and *Los Hijos del Sol (The Sons of the Sun,* after an Inca legend; Buenos Aires, Nov. 10, 1928); *Cantares de mi tierra,* for strings (1914); the symph. poems *Jardines* and *Los Hijos del Sol;* a violin sonata; a cello sonata; a piano sonata; many songs; pedagogical works: *Teoría razonada de la música* and *Tratado completo de armonía.*

BIBLIOGRAPHY: N. Lamuraglia, *Athos Palma: vida, arte, educación* (Buenos Aires, 1954).

Palmer, Horatio Richmond, American music pedagogue; b. Sherburne, N.Y., April 26, 1834; d. Yonkers, N.Y., Nov. 15, 1907. He was taught by his father and sister, later by various teachers in New York, Berlin, and Florence. He settled in Chicago after the Civil War; from 1873 he had charge of the New Church Choral Union there, giving concerts with as many as 4,000 singers; from 1877–91 dean of the Summer School of Music at Chautauqua. Of his collections, *The Song Queen, The Song King, The Song Herald,* and *Concert Choruses* had great success; also publ. *Theory of Music, Class Method* (of elementary teaching), *Manual for Teachers* (in public schools), etc.

BIBLIOGRAPHY: *Dictionary of American Biography,* vol. XIV (1934).

Palmer, Robert, American composer; b. Syracuse, N.Y., June 2, 1915. He studied at the Eastman School of Music, Rochester, N.Y., with Howard Hanson and Bernard Rogers; then had lessons with Roy Harris and Aaron Copland; he taught music at the Univ. of Kansas (1940–43); in 1943 appointed to the faculty of Cornell Univ., Ithaca. He adheres to the neo-Classical mold in most of his works; in his melodic progressions he frequently employs a scale of alternating whole tones and semitones, known as the "Rimsky-Korsakov scale" because of its many occurrences in his operas and symphonic works.

WORKS: *Poem* for violin and chamber orch. (1938); Concerto for Orch. (1943); *K 19,* symph. elegy for Thomas Wolfe (1945); Chamber Concerto No. 1 for violin, oboe, and strings (1949); Symphony (1953); 4 string quartets (1939, 1947. 1954, 1959); Concerto for 5 instruments (1943); Piano Quartet (1947); Piano Quintet (1950); Viola Sonata (1951); Wind Quintet (1951); Quintet for clarinet, piano, and strings (1952); Violin Sonata (1956); *Memorial Music* for chamber orch. (1959); numerous choral works; 2 piano sonatas (1946, 1948); Sonata for Piano 4-hands (1952); Sonata for 2 pianos (1944); songs.

BIBLIOGRAPHY: W. Austin, "The Music of Robert Palmer," *Musical Quarterly* (Jan. 1956).

Palmgren, Selim, eminent Finnish composer; b. Pori (Bjorneborg), Feb. 16, 1878; d. Helsinki, Dec. 13, 1951. He studied piano and composition at the Cons. of Helsinki (1895–99); then went to Berlin where he continued his piano studies with Ansorge, Berger and Busoni. Returning to Finland, he became active as a choral conductor in Helsinki (1902–04); from 1909–12 he was director of the Music Society in Turku. In 1921 he made a tour of the U.S. as pianist; from 1923 to 1926 taught piano and composition at the Eastman School of Music, Rochester, N.Y.; then returned to Helsinki. He was married to the Finnish soprano **Maikki Pakarienen** in 1910, after her divorce from Armas Järnfelt; after her death Palmgren married Minna Talwik. He excelled in piano compositions, often tinged with authentic Finnish colors; some of his pieces are marked by effective impressionistic devices, such as whole-tone scales and consecutive mild dissonances. Among his piano miniatures, *May Night* enjoys considerable popularity with music students and their teachers.

WORKS: 5 piano concertos: No. 1 (1903); No. 2, *Virta (The Stream,* 1913); No. 3, *Metamorphoses* (1915); No. 4, *Huhtikuu (April,* 1924–26); No. 5 (1939–41); 2 operas, *Daniel Hjort* (April 15, 1910; revised version, Helsinki, 1938) and *Peter Schlemihl; Pastorale* for orch. (1920); *Turun lilja (The Lily of Turku),* cantata (1929); *Ballet Music* for orch. (1944); *Concert Fantasy* for violin and orch. (1945); for piano: 2 sonatas; *Fantasia; 24 Preludes; Ballade* (in the form of a theme with variations); *Finnische Lyrik* (12 pieces); *Finnische Suite (The Seasons); Maskenball,* suite; *24 Etudes* (1921–22); etc.; songs and men's choruses. He publ. a book, *Minusta Tuli Muusikko* (Helsinki, 1948).

Palombo, Paul Martin, American composer; b. Pittsburgh, Sept. 10, 1937. He was trained in electronics; studied composition at Peabody Cons. in Baltimore and at the Eastman School of Music, Rochester, N.Y., with Wayne Barlow and Bernard Rogers (1963–69); in 1969 appointed to the faculty of the Univ. of Cincinnati College-Cons. of Music; in 1973 assumed the direction of the electronic music studio there.

WORKS: *Serenade* for string orch. (1964); Piano Sonata (1965); Sinfonietta for chamber orch. (1965); Cello Sonata (1966); String Quartet No. 1 (1966–67); *Movement* for orch. (1967); *Variations* for orch. (1967–68); *Proteus,* ballet for tape and orch. (1969); *Morphosis,* electronic ballet (1970); *Metatheses* for flute, oboe, double bass and harpsichord (1970); *Montage* for violin and piano (1971); *Crystals,* electronic multimedia score (1971); *Ritratti Anticamente* for viola and piano (1972, revised 1974); 4 *Sonos: I* for harpsichord and tape (1972), *II* for harp and tape (1972), *III* for double bass and tape (1973) and *IV* for string trio and tape (1974); *Etcetera,* electronic ballet (1973); *Stegowagenvolkssaurus,* electronic music for a sculpture (1973–74).

Pálsson, Páll P., Austrian-born Icelandic composer and conductor; b. Graz, May 9, 1928. He studied with Michl, Mixa and Brugger in Graz; settled in Iceland in 1949 and was first trumpet player in the Icelandic Symph. Orch. In 1964 he was appointed director of the Reykjavik Male Choir and later became one of the conductors of the Icelandic Symph. Orch. and the Reykjavik Chamber Ensemble.

WORKS: Divertimento for 18 winds (1963); *Hringspil I* for violin, viola, clarinet and bassoon (1964), and *II* for 2 trumpets, horn and trombone; *Crystals* for string quartet and wind quintet (1970); *Requiem* for a cappella chorus (1970); *Dialog* for orch. (1973); *Mixed Things* for flute and piano (1977).

Panassié, Hugues, French music critic, expert on jazz; b. Paris, Feb. 27, 1912; d. Montauban, France, Dec. 8, 1974. He founded the "Hot Club de France" (1932); lectured on jazz at the Sorbonne in 1937, and in America in 1938; publ. *Le Jazz Hot* (basic treatise on the subject, Paris, 1934; in English, as *Hot Jazz,* N.Y., 1936); *The Real Jazz* (N.Y., 1942; in French, *La Véritable Musique de Jazz,* Paris, 1946); *La Musique de jazz et le swing* (Paris, 1945); *Douze années de Jazz (1927–1938)* (Paris, 1946); *Louis Armstrong* (Paris, 1947); *Jazz panorama* (Paris, 1950); *Discographie critique* (Paris, 1951); *Dictionnaire du jazz* (with Madeleine Gautier; Paris, 1954; in English as *Dictionary of Jazz,* London, 1956; American ed., Boston, 1956, as *Guide to Jazz).*

Panizza, Ettore, Argentine conductor and composer of Italian extraction; b. Buenos Aires, Aug. 12, 1875; d. Milan, Nov. 28, 1967. He studied at the Cons. of Milan, Italy, graduating in 1898 with prizes for piano and composition; began his career as operatic conductor in Italy in 1899, and continued successfully for more than half a century. From 1907 to 1913 he conducted Italian operas at Covent Garden, London; then at La Scala, Milan (1916–26) and at the Metropolitan Opera, N.Y. (1934–42). He publ. an autobiography, *Medio siglo de vida musical* (Buenos Aires, 1951).

WORKS: operas: *Il Fidanzato del mare* (Buenos Aires, Aug. 15, 1897); *Medio evo latino* (Genoa, Nov. 17, 1900); *Aurora* (Buenos Aires, Sept. 5, 1908); *Bisanzio* (Buenos Aires, July 25, 1939); also *Il Re della foresta,* for soli, chorus, and orch.; *Tema con Variaciones,* for orch.; violin sonata; cello sonata; string quartet; piano pieces; songs.

Pannain, Guido, distinguished Italian musicologist and composer; b. Naples, Nov. 17, 1891; d. there, Sept. 6, 1977. He studied composition with C. de Nardis at Naples; upon graduation, devoted himself mainly to research, into both old and new aspects of music.

WRITINGS: *La Teoria musicale di G. Tinctoris* (1913); *Le Origini della scuola musicale napoletana* (1914); *Le Origini e lo sviluppo dell' arte pianistica in Italia dal 1500 al 1700 circa* (1917); *Lineamenti di storia della musica* (1922; 9th ed., 1970); *Musica e musicisti in Napoli nel secolo XIX* (1922); *Storia del Conservatorio di Napoli* (1942); *La Vita del linguaggio musicale* (1947); *Ottocento musicale italiano* (1952); collaborated with A. Della Corte in *Storia della musica*, in 3 vols. (1936; 3rd ed., 1952). Beginning in 1928, he was one of the chief contributors to the *Rassegna musicale* (essays on modern composers; publ. as *Musicisti dei tempi nuovi*, Turin, 1932; English transl. by Bonavia, London, 1932, as *Modern Composers*); *Ottocento musicale italiano* (Milan, 1952); *L'opera e le opere ed altri scritti di letteratura musicale* (Milan, 1958); *Verdi* (Turin, 1964); *Wagner* (Milan, 1964).

WORKS: the operas *L'Intrusa* (1926; Genoa, 1940 and *Beatrice Cenci* (Naples, Feb. 21, 1942); *Madame Bovary* (Naples, April 16, 1955); 2 Violin Concertos (1930, 1960); Viola Concerto (1955); Harp Concerto (1968); Piano Concerto (1968); *Requiem* (1955).

Panofka, Heinrich, German singing teacher; b. Breslau, Oct. 3, 1807; d. Florence, Nov. 18, 1887. He began his career as a violinist, and after playing some concerts in Germany he went to Paris in 1832 and began taking singing lessons with Bordogni. With Bordogni he organized, in 1842, the Académie de Chant, which failed to prosper. In 1844 he went to London where he became a fashionable singing teacher; eventually he went to Florence, spending his last days there. He published a manual *L'Art de chanter* (Paris, 1853), which had a considerable vogue.

Panseron, Auguste-Mathieu, French singing teacher; b. Paris, April 26, 1795; d. there, July 29, 1859. His father, who orchestrated many operas for Grétry, taught him until he entered the Paris Cons. in 1804; he studied under Gossec, Levasseur, and Berton, winning the Prix de Rome in 1813. After study in Bologna, Rome, Naples, Vienna (with Salieri), and Munich, he returned to Paris in 1818, taught singing, was accompanist at the Opéra-Comique, and wrote three 1-act operas; became prof. of solfeggio at the Cons. in 1826, prof. of vocalisation in 1831, and prof. of singing in 1836. From 1825-40 he brought out some 200 *romances;* he also composed church music, but attained real eminence as a vocal teacher and as a writer of instructive works on singing.

Panufnik, Andrzej, eminent Polish composer and conductor; b. Warsaw, Sept. 24, 1914. His mother was an Englishwoman who studied violin in Warsaw, his father a manufacturer of string instruments. Panufnik studied composition with Sikorski at the Warsaw Cons. (1932-36); then took lessons in conducting with Weingartner at the Vienna Academy (1937-38) and briefly with Philippe Gaubert in Paris. He returned to Warsaw in 1939, and remained there during the Nazi occupation of the city; had an underground performance in 1942 of his *Tragic Overture.* In 1945 he conducted the Cracow Philharmonic; then conducted the

Warsaw Orch. (1946). In 1954 he went to England, and in 1961 became a British subject. From 1957 to 1959 he was conductor and music director of the Birmingham Symph. Orch., and frequently a guest conductor in London. In his youth, before the war, he belonged to the vanguard group among Polish composers; he made use of advanced techniques, including quarter-tones, which he employed in the instrumental *Berceuse (Lullaby).* Even in the matter of notation he was an innovator; in several of the orchestral scores he left blank spaces instead of rests in the inactive instrumental parts. In his music of the later period he adopted a more circumspect idiom, expressive, direct and communicative. He constantly revised his old scores for better effect.

WORKS: Piano Trio (1934; recomposed 1945 and revised 1967); *5 Polish Peasant Songs* for treble chorus, 2 flutes, 2 clarinets and bass clarinet (1940, recomposed 1945; London Festival of the International Society for Contemporary Music, July 12, 1946; revised 1959); *Tragic Overture* (1942; score lost in Warsaw fires; recomposed 1945; first public performance, N.Y., March 24, 1949; revised 1955); *Lullaby* for 29 string instruments, and 2 harps (1947; Paris, April 26, 1948; revised 1955); *Nocturne* for orch. (1947, revised 1955); *12 Miniature Studies* for piano (1947, revised 1955); *Sinfonia Rustica* (1948; Warsaw, May 13, 1949; revised 1955); *Hommage à Chopin* in 2 versions; for soprano and piano (1949), and for flute and string orch. (1966); *Old Polish Suite* for string orch. (1950, revised 1955); *Concerto in modo antico (Gothic Concerto)* for orch. (1951, revised 1955); *Heroic Overture* (1952; Helsinki Olympiad, July 27, 1952; revised 1965); *Rhapsody* for orch. (1956; first public performance, London, Aug. 26, 1957); *Sinfonia Elegiaca* (1957, revised 1966; first and third sections arranged as a ballet, *Elegy,* N.Y., 1957); *Polonia,* suite for orch. (1959; London, Aug. 21, 1959); *Autumn Music* for orch. (1962); Piano Concerto (1962; revised 1972); *Sinfonia Sacra* (1963; Monaco, Aug. 12, 1964; as a ballet, *Cain and Abel,* West Berlin, Nov. 1968); *Landscape* for string orch. (London, Nov. 13, 1965); *Divertimento* for string orch. (London, Sept. 24, 1966); *Jagiellonian Triptych* for strings (London, Sept. 24, 1966); *Epitaph for the Victims of Katyń* for woodwinds, string, and timpani (N.Y., Nov. 17, 1968; Stokowski conducting); *Reflections* for piano (1968); *Universal Prayer,* a setting of Alexander Pope's poem, for 4 soloists, chorus, 3 harps and organ (Cathedral Church of St. John the Divine, N.Y., May 24, 1970; Stokowski conducting); *Thames Pageant,* cantata for young players and singers (1969); a ballet, *Miss Julie* (Stuttgart, March 8, 1970); Concerto for Violin and String Orch. (1972; London, July 18, 1972); *Invocation for Peace* for youth chorus and youth orch. (Southampton, Nov. 28, 1972); *Winter Solstice* for soprano, baritone, chorus and instruments (London, Dec. 16, 1972); *Sinfonia Concertante* for flute, harp and string orch. (1973; London, May 20, 1974); *Sinfonia di Sfere (Symphony of Spheres,* 1975; London, April 13, 1976).

BIBLIOGRAPHY: Scarlett Panufnik (his wife), *Out of the City of Fear* (recounting Panufnik's flight from Poland; London, 1956).

Panula, Jorma, Finnish conductor and composer; b. Kauhajoki, Aug. 10, 1930. He studied at the Helsinki School of Church Music, at the Sibelius Academy in Helsinki with Leo Funtek, and with Dean Dixon at Lund. As conductor, he has appeared with the Helsinki Philharmonic Orchestra and also with several European orchestras. In his works he often explores modernistic ideas and idioms, as exemplified by his *Jazz capriccio* for piano and orch. (1965) and *Teräs-sinfonia* (*Steel Symphony,* 1969). He also composed a Violin Concerto (1954).

Panum, Hortense, Danish musicologist; b. (of Danish parents) Kiel, March 14, 1856; d. Copenhagen, April 26, 1933. Her father, a prof. of physiology at Kiel Univ., returned to Copenhagen in 1864. She studied history of music with W. Tappert in Berlin (1886–87). After her return she devoted herself to historical studies (especially concerning old instruments).

WRITINGS: *Illustreret Musikhistorie* (1895–1905; Part II by W. Behrend); *Musiken og musiklivet i Danmark för anno 1880* (1904); *Musiken og musiklivet i Danmark efter anno 1800* (1906); *Haydn, Mozart, og Beethoven* (1908); *Middelalderens Strengeinstrumenter og dares Forlöbere i Oldtiden* (profusely illustrated; I, 1915; II, 1928; III, 1931; English edition in 1 vol., by J. Pulver, as *The Stringed Instruments of the Middle Ages, their Evolution,* etc., London, 1939; reprinted N.Y., 1972); *Af Musikhistoriens Billedbog* (1916; 2nd ed., 1930); *Langelegen som dansk Folkeinstrument* (1918); *Illustreret Musiklexikon* (Copenhagen, 1924–26; with W. Behrend and O. M. Sandvik; new ed., 1940).

Panzéra, Charles, French baritone; b. Hyères, Feb. 16, 1896; d. Paris, June 6, 1976. He studied at the Paris Cons.; made his debut at the Opéra-Comique in 1919; then gave concerts in Europe and America; also taught at the Juilliard School, N.Y. In 1949 he was appointed prof. at the Paris Cons. He publ. a manual, *L'Art de chanter* (Paris, 1945).

Panzner, Karl, German conductor; b. Teplitz, Bohemia, March 2, 1866; d. Düsseldorf, Dec. 17, 1923. He studied piano and composition at the Dresden Cons.; then private pupil of Anton Rubinstein, who advised him to adopt the career of a concert pianist. Instead, he became a theater conductor; in 1893 he succeeded E. Paur as Kapellmeister at the Leipzig Stadttheater, where he remained 6 years. In 1899 he was called to Bremen to conduct the Philharmonic and (in 1904) also the "Lehrer Gesangverein," with which he made several successful tours (notably to Paris in 1907); from 1907 to 1909 he filled numerous engagements as visiting conductor in Barcelona, Paris, St. Petersburg, Moscow, Rome, and New York. From 1909 he was municipal music-director in Düsseldorf; also conductor of the Philharmonic Society concerts at Hamburg.

BIBLIOGRAPHY: W. Gareiss, *Karl Panzner* (Leipzig, 1909).

Papaioannou, Yannis, Greek composer; b. Kavala, Jan. 6, 1911. He studied piano and music theory at the "Hellenic Odeon" in Athens (1929-34); then had some composition lessons with Honegger in Paris (1949). In 1953 he was appointed to the staff of his alma mater; introduced into his courses a study of modern techniques of composition. His own music traversed from a fairly conservative neo-Classical idiom to dodecaphony and eventually integral serialism.

WORKS: *Daphnis and Chloe* for chorus and orch. (1934); *Idyll* for orch. (1938); *Choreographic Prelude* for orch. (1939); the symph. poems *The Corsair* (1940), *Poem of the Forest* (1942), *Vassilis the Albanian* (1945), *Matins of Souls* (1947), *Pygmalion* (1951), *Hellas* (1956) and *Symphonic Tableau* (1968); 5 symphonies (1946, 1951, 1953, 1963, 1964); *Triptych* for strings (1947); Piano Concerto (1950); *Concerto for Orch.* (1954); 3 suites for orch. (Nos. 1 & 2, *Pictures from Asia*; No. 3, *Egypt,* 1961); Concertino for Piano and String Orch. (1962); *Sarpidon's Funeral,* cantata (1965); *3 Byzantine Odes* for soprano and chamber ensemble (1966); *Electra Monologues* for soprano and instrumental ensemble (1968); *Footsteps* for mezzo-soprano, narrator, chorus and instrumental ensemble (1969); *India,* suite for orch. (1969); *4 Orphic Hymns* for narrator and instrumental ensemble (1971); Concerto for Violin and Chamber Orch. (1971); Concerto for Violin, Piano and Orch. (1972-73); Violin Sonata (1947); *Winter Fantasy,* ballet for flute, clarinet, violin, cello and piano (1950); String Quartet (1959); *Suite* for guitar (1960); Sonatina for flute and guitar (1962); Quartet for flute, clarinet, guitar and cello (1962); Trio for oboe, clarinet and bassoon (1962); *Archaic* for 2 guitars (1962); String Trio (1963); Trio for flute, viola and guitar (1967); Quartet for oboe, clarinet, viola and piano (1968); *5 Characters,* brass quintet (1970); *Aphigissis* (*Narration*) for solo violin (1970); *The Harlequin's Prattling* for solo tuba (1971); *Portrait* for solo tuba (1972); *Syneirmoi* (*Associations*) for 9 instruments (1973); *Echomorphes* (*Sound-figures*) for solo violin (1975); *Rhythms and Colors* for solo cello (1976); *Puck* for solo cello (1976); Piano Trio (1977); Piano Sonata (1958) and other pieces for piano: *Odalisque* (1937), *24 Preludes* (1938), 2 suites (1948, 1959), *Partita in Modo Antico* (1957), *12 Inventions* (1958), *Oraculum* (1965), *7 Piano Pieces* (1969) and *Enigma* (1969); choruses; songs; theater music.

Papandopulo, Boris, Croatian conductor and composer; b. Honef-on-the-Rhine, Feb. 25, 1906. He studied in Zagreb and Vienna; in 1959 he was appointed conductor of the National Theater in Zagreb; from 1964 to 1968 he conducted in Split and Rijeka; later filled engagements as a guest conductor in Yugoslavia. His operas and most of his instrumental works are written in a national Croatian idiom; but he also experimented with the 12-tone techniques, as exemplified by his pointedly titled *Dodekafonski Concert* for 2 pianos (1961).

WORKS: the operas, *Amphytrion* (1940), *Sunflower* (1942) and *Rona* (Rijeka, May 25, 1956); *Marulova Pisan* (Split, Aug. 14, 1970), dedicated to the town of Split and dealing with the seige of neighboring town by the Turks around 1500 and its liberation by Spalatines; a "fantastic opera," *Madame Buffault* (1972); the ballets *Zlato* (*Gold,* Zagreb, 1931); *Žetva* (*The Harvest*; Serayevo, 1950); *Beatrice Cenci* (Gelsenkirchen, 1959); *Gitanella* (1965); *Dr. Atom,* subtitled $Qu + H^3 + H^2 = He^4 + n + 9$ (Rijeka, 1966); *Ljudi u hotelu* (performed in Vienna, as *Menshen im Hotel*, 1967); *Teuta* (1973); the cantata, *Legend of Comrade Tito* (Zagreb, May 10, 1962); 2 symphonies: No. 1 (1930); No. 2 (Zagreb, May 8, 1946, composer conducting; String Symphonietta (his most frequently performed work); 4 piano concertos (1938, 1942, 1947, 1958); Concerto for 4 Timpani and Orch. (1969); Concerto for Harpsichord and String Orch. (1962); Double-Bass Concerto (1968); 5 string quartets (1927, 1933, 1945, 1950, 1970); many choral works and piano pieces.

BIBLIOGRAPHY: Kovačević, *Hrvatski Kompozitori i Njihova Djela* (Zagreb, 1960).

Papi, Gennaro, Italian-American conductor; b. Naples, Dec. 21, 1886; d. New York, Nov. 29, 1941. He studied with de Nardis at the S. Pietro a Majella Cons. in Naples (graduated, 1904); assistant conductor in Warsaw (1909-10), Turin (1911), London (Covent Garden, 1911-12), Milan, Odessa, and Buenos Aires; 1913-16, assistant to Toscanini at the Metropolitan Opera House; 1916-25, conductor of Russian and Italian opera there; 1925-32, conductor of the Chicago Civic Opera; then made appearances in Milan, Mexico City, and Buenos Aires until 1935, when he was reengaged at the Metropolitan.

Papier, Rosa, Austrian mezzo-soprano; b. Baden, near Vienna, Sept. 15, 1858; d. Vienna, Feb. 9, 1932. She sang at the Imperial Opera, Vienna; later taught at the Vienna Cons. In 1881 she married the pianist **Hans Paumgartner.**

Papineau-Couture, Jean, Canadian composer; b. Outremont (part of metropolitan Montreal), Nov. 12, 1916. He studied piano with Léo-Pol Morin (1939-40) and theory with Gabriel Cusson in Montreal (1937-40); then in the U.S. (1940-45) with Quincy Porter at the New England Cons. in Boston and Nadia Boulanger at the Longy School in Cambridge, Mass., and also in California. Upon return to Montreal, he devoted himself to teaching and musical organization; was founding president of the Société de Musique Contemporaine du Québec (1966-73) and Dean of the music faculty at the Univ. of Montreal (1968-73). His music underwent an evolution, common to many Canadian composers, from a neo-Baroque idiom to Expressionism, with judicious excursions into serial techniques.

WORKS: *Concerto Grosso* for small orch. (1943, revised 1955); Symphony (1947-48, revised 1956); *Papotages (Tittle-Tattle),* ballet (1949; Montreal, Nov. 20, 1950); Concerto for Violin and Chamber Orch. (1951); *Poème* for orch. (1952); *Prélude* for orch. (1953); *Psaume CL* for soprano, tenor, chorus, wind ensemble and one or two organs (1954); 5 *Pièces Concertantes:* No. 1, *Repliement (Folding Back),* for piano and string orch. (1956); No. 2, *Eventails,* for cello and chamber orch. (1959); No. 3, *Variations,* for flute, clarinet, violin, cello, harp and string orch. (1959); No. 4, *Additions,* for oboe and string orch. (1959); No. 5, *Miroirs (Mirrors),* for orch. (1963); *3 Pieces* for orch. (1961); Piano Concerto (1965; Toronto, Feb. 6, 1966); *Paysage* for 8 narrators, 8 singers, wind quintet, string quintet,

piano, harp and percussion (1968; Zagreb, May 9, 1969); *Oscillations* for orch. (1969); *Contraste* for voice and orch. (1970); *Obsession* for 16 players (1973); *Eglogues* for alto, flute and piano (1942); *Suite* for piano (1942); Violin Sonata (1944, revised 1953); *Suite* for flute and piano (1944-45); *Rondo* for piano, 4 hands (1945); *Aria* for solo violin (1946); *Quatrains* for soprano and piano (1947); *Suite* for flute, clarinet, bassoon, horn and piano (1947); 2 string quartets (1953, 1967); *Suite* for solo violin (1956); *Eclosion,* stage music for a mime, violin, piano and tape (1961); *3 Caprices* for violin and piano (1962); *Fantaisie* for wind quintet (1963); *Canons* for brass quintet (1964); *Dialogues* for violin and piano (1967); Sextet for oboe, clarinet, bassoon, violin, viola and cello (1967); *Nocturnes* for flute, clarinet, violin, cello, harpsichord, guitar and percussion (1969); *Complémentarité* for piano (1971); *Dyarchie* for harpsichord (1971); *Chanson de Rahit* for voice, clarinet and piano (1972); Trio for clarinet, viola and piano (1974); *Départ* for solo alto flute (1974); *Versegère* for solo bass flute (1975); *Slano* for string trio (1975); *J'aime les tierces mineures* for solo flute (1976); *Le Débat du cœur et du corps* for narrator, cello and percussion (1977).

Pâque, Désiré, a remarkable Belgian composer; b. Liège, May 21, 1867; d. Bessancourt, France, Nov. 20, 1939. He began to compose as a child; wrote a Mass at the age of 12; studied at the Liège Cons.; lived in Sofia, Athens, Lisbon, and Geneva, settling in Paris in 1914. He wrote 144 op. numbers, among them: one-act opera *Vaima* (1903); 8 symphonies (1895; 1905; 1912; 1916; 1919; 1927; 1934; 1936); 2 piano concertos (1888; 1935); Cello Concerto (1893); *Ouverture sur 3 themes bulgares* (Ostende, Aug. 17, 1895); *Ouverture libre* (1899; Munich, Dec. 29, 1911); Requiem (1900); 10 string quartets (1892-1939); 3 piano quintets (1896; 1924; 1938); 2 sextets (1909; 1919); 5 suites for piano, violin, and viola (1891-96); 3 piano trios (1903-30); 4 violin sonatas (1890-1934); 4 piano sonatas (1911); Viola Sonata (1915); 13 albums of piano pieces; choral works. His production falls into 3 periods: cosmopolitan and formal (1886-1908); freely episodic, in an "adjonction constante" of recurrent themes (1909-18); atonal and polytonal (1919-39). His last manner is exemplified by *10 pièces atonales pour la jeunesse* for piano (1925). Only a few of his works are published; the bulk of his music remains in MS.

Paradies (originally **Paradisi**), **Pietro Domenico,** Italian composer and harpsichordist; b. Naples, 1707; d. Venice, Aug. 25, 1791. He was a pupil of Porpora; brought out several operas in Italy; went to London in 1747 where he earned a living mainly as a teacher of harpsichord playing, but also produced an opera *Fetonte* (1747); publ. *12 Sonate di gravicembalo* (London, 1754). Towards the end of his life he returned to Italy. Some of his manuscript works are preserved in the Fitzwilliam Museum at Cambridge; his sonatas were brought out by G. Benvenuti and D. Cipollini in Milan (1920).

Paradis, Maria Theresia von, Austrian pianist and composer; b. Vienna, May 15, 1759; d. there, Feb. 1, 1824. Blind from her fifth year, she was taught by

Richter and Koželuh (piano), Salieri and Righini (singing), and Friberth and Abbé Vogler (composition), becoming an excellent pianist and organist; played in Paris in 1784, and made a tour to London, Brussels, and German capitals in 1786. By the aid of a system of notation invented by a friend, she became a skillful composer, her chief works being a melodrama, *Ariadne und Bacchus* (Vienna, 1791), an operetta, *Der Schulkandidat* (1792), the fairy opera *Rinaldo und Alcina* (Prague, summer, 1797), a funeral cantata on the death of Louis XVI (1794), a piano trio, sonatas and variations for piano, songs, etc. In her last years she taught singing and piano playing.

BIBLIOGRAPHY: F. Niecks, in the *Monthly Musical Record* (Jan. 1913); H. Ullrich, "M. T. Paradis and Mozart," *Music & Letters* (Oct. 1946); E. Komorzynski, "Mozart und M. T. Paradis," *Mozart-Jahrbuch* (Salzburg, 1952).

Paranov, Moshe, American pianist and conductor; b. Hartford, Conn., Oct. 28, 1895. He studied piano with Julius Hartt and Harold Bauer, composition with Ernest Bloch and Rubin Goldmark. He married Julius Hartt's daughter, Pauline; was co-founder of the Julius Hartt School of Music, Hartford, in 1920; in 1957, was named president of the Julius Hartt Musical Foundation of the Univ. of Hartford.

Paray, Paul, French conductor; b. Le Tréport, May 24, 1886. He received his musical education from his father, a church organist; in 1904 he entered the Paris Cons. where he studied with Leroux, Causade, Lenepveu, and Vidal; received the 1st Grand Prix de Rome with his cantata *Yanitza* (1911). He was drafted into the French Army during World War I and was taken prisoner by the Germans; after the armistice he returned to Paris where he made his debut as conductor on Feb. 29, 1920; served as assistant conductor of the Concerts Lamoureux, and succeeded Chevillard as 1st conductor in 1923. He was subsequently conductor of the symph. concerts in Monte Carlo; from 1944 to 1952 he conducted the Colonne Orch. in Paris; in 1952 he was engaged to conduct the Detroit Symph. Orch., and on Oct. 18, 1956 inaugurated the new Ford Auditorium in Detroit, in a program which included his own *Mass of Joan of Arc*; resigned in 1963 and returned to France. In July 1977, at the age of 91, he conducted an orchestral concert in honor of Marc Chagall's 90th birthday celebration in Nice. Paray's compositions include a ballet, *Artémis troublée* (Paris Opéra, April 28, 1922); *Fantaisie,* for piano and orch. (Paris, March 25, 1923); 2 symphonies; chamber music; piano pieces.

BIBLIOGRAPHY: W. L. Landowski, *Paul Paray* (Lyons, 1956); Hope Stoddard, *Symphony Conductors of the U.S.A.* (N.Y., 1957; pp. 160-70).

Parelli, Attilio (real last name **Paparella**), Italian conductor and composer; b. Monteleone d'Orvieto, near Perugia, May 31, 1874; d. there, Dec. 26, 1944. He studied at the Santa Cecilia in Rome; graduated in 1899; held various posts as conductor in Italy and France; went to the U.S. as assistant conductor to Campanini at the Manhattan Opera, N.Y. (1906); also conducted for the Chicago Grand Opera Company. In

1925 he returned to Europe. He wrote the operas *Hermes* (Geneva, Nov. 8, 1906), *I dispettosi amanti* (Philadelphia, March 6, 1912) and *Fanfulla* (Trieste, Feb. 11, 1921); a symphony; an orchestral suite, *Rapsodia umbra;* a symph. poem, *La Chimera;* songs.

Parent, Armand, Belgian violinist; b. Liège, Feb. 5, 1863; d. Paris, Jan. 19, 1934. He was a pupil at the Liège Cons. of L. Massart (violin) and S. Dupuis (harmony). From 1883 to 1889, concertmaster with the Colonne Orch.; from 1900 prof. of violin at the Schola Cantorum. In 1892 he founded (with Loiseau, Vieux, and Fournier) the "Quatour Parent," which for many years enjoyed an excellent reputation. Parent wrote 2 string quartets, a string quintet, a violin sonata, and a number of minor pieces for violin and piano; also *Gymnastique du violon, 20 Études de virtuosité, Études pour violon, Exercises pour le violon d'après les 17 quatuors de Beethoven,* and a 5-part *Méthode complète.*

Parepa-Rosa (*née* **Parepa de Boyescu**), **Euphrosyne,** English soprano; b. Edinburgh, May 7, 1836; d. London, Jan. 21, 1874. Her father was a native of Bucharest; her mother, **Elizabeth Seguin,** was a well-known singer. She made her operatic debut at the age of 16 in Malta; then sang in principal Italian music centers, in Madrid, and in Lisbon. She made her first London appearance as Elvira in *I Puritani* on May 21, 1856, and became a great favorite of the English public. She married the impresario Carlo Rosa in 1867 during an American tour. She returned to England in 1873 and remained there until her death.

BIBLIOGRAPHY: *Dictionary of National Biography,* vol. XLIII.

Paribeni, Giulio Cesare, Italian teacher and critic; b. Rome, May 27, 1881; d. Milan, June 13, 1960. He studied at Rome Univ. and at the Liceo di S. Cecilia; was first a conductor, then, from 1911-15, head of the publishing firm of Sonzogno; from 1914 teacher of composition and harmony at the Royal Cons., Milan; from 1922 opera critic of *L'Ambrosiano,* Milan. Author of *Storia e teoria della antica musica greca* (Milan, 1912) and *Muzio Clementi,* a biography (Milan, 1921). Composer of orchestral works, chamber music, and church music.

Parík, Ivan, Slovak composer; b. Bratislava, Aug. 17, 1936. He studied composition with Očenáš at the Bratislava Cons.; then with Cikker and Alexander Moyzes at the Bratislava Academy of Music, graduating in 1962; was then appointed to its faculty. In his music he utilizes a wide range of contemporary resources, from serialism to pointillistic minimalism and expressionistic abstractions.

WORKS: *Music* for 4 string instruments (1958); *2 Songs,* to Japanese poetry, for mezzo-soprano, violin, clarinet, xylophone and gong (1960); Sonata for Flute Solo (1962); *Epitaph* for flute, viola and cello (1962); *Music for Three* for flute, oboe and clarinet (1964); *Koláže (Collage)* for a variable chamber ensemble (1968); *Exercises* for solo trumpet (1968); *Vežová hudba (Tower Music)* for 12 brasses, 2 tapes, and bells (1969); *Sonata-Canon* for flute and tape (1971); *Medi-*

tation for viola and piano (1975); *Epitaph* for flute and guitar (1975); electronic pieces.

Parish-Alvars, Elias, English harpist; b. Teignmouth, Feb. 28, 1808; d. Vienna, Jan. 25, 1849. He studied harp with Bochsa; from 1831-36 gave concerts in Germany. While in Leipzig he was associated with Mendelssohn. In 1847 he settled in Vienna. His compositions for harp enjoyed a certain popularity during his lifetime.

Parker, Charlie, nicknamed **"Yardbird"** or **"Bird"** (real Christian name **Charles Christopher**), black American jazz saxophonist, the leading exponent of bebop; b. Kansas City, Aug. 29, 1920; d. New York, March 12, 1955. He was self-taught, on an alto saxophone given to him at age 11 by his mother; at 15 left school and became a professional musician; in 1939 went to N.Y., and in 1941 was in the big band of Jay McShann, with which he made his first recordings. In 1943 he played tenor sax (his only extended period on that instrument) in Earl Hines' band; met Dizzy Gillespie and other young musicians dissatisfied with the prevailing big band swing style; after work they would meet in a club called "Minton's," and there gradually evolved the new style of *bebop*. Parker became the acknowledged leader of this style as he developed an improvising technique characterized by virtuosic speed, intense tone, complex harmonies, and florid melodies having irregular rhythmic patterns and asymmetric phrase lengths. After the mid-1940s he usually worked in small combos led either by himself or by one of the other members of the small, close-knit circle of bopsters; occasionally he also worked with larger ensembles (including a string orchestra, for which he wrote the arrangements). As a composer he usually worked with the 12-bar blues patterns (but always in an unstereotyped manner; he made 175 blues recordings, all markedly different), or with chord progressions of well-known "standard" tunes: his *Ornithology,* for instance, is based on the progressions of *How High the Moon.* He achieved a prominence that made him a living legend (a leading N.Y. club, Birdland, was named after him); his life, though, in addition to being tragically short, was plagued by the consequences of narcotics addiction (acquired when he was in his mid-teens) and alcoholism. He had a nervous breakdown in 1946 and was confined at Camarillo State Hospital, Calif., for 6 months; because of suspected narcotics possession, the N.Y.C. police rescinded his cabaret license in 1951, thereby denying him the right to work in N.Y. clubs; he attempted suicide twice in 1954, and subsequently entered Bellevue Hospital, N.Y. He died in the N.Y. apartment of a fervent admirer, Rothschild Baroness Pannonica de Konigswarter.

BIBLIOGRAPHY: M. Harrison, *Charlie Parker* (London, 1960); R. G. Reisner, *Bird: The Legend of Charlie Parker* (N.Y., 1962); J. G. Jepsen, *A Discography of Charlie Parker* (Copenhagen, 1968); T. Williams, "Charlie Parker Discography," *Discographical Forum* (1968-70; 13 installments); R. Russell, *Bird Lives!* (N.Y., 1973); P. Koster and D. M. Bakker, *Charlie Parker* (discography, 4 vols.,; Alphen aan den Rijn, Holland, 1974); L. O. Koch, "Ornithology: A Study of

Charlie Parker's Music," *Journal of Jazz Studies* (Dec. 1974 and June 1975); J. Patrick, "Charlie Parker and Harmonic Sources of Bebop Composition," *Journal of Jazz Studies* (June 1975).

Parker, Henry Taylor, American critic and writer on music; b. Boston, April 29, 1867; d. there, March 30, 1934. He attended Harvard Univ.; then served as N.Y. correspondent of the *Boston Evening Transcript* and later as its London correspondent; in 1905 he became the paper's principal drama and music critic, holding this position until his death. Although not trained as a musician (he could not read notes), Parker possessed an extraordinary sense of esthetic values and often gave unstinted praise to composers of the modern school who were disdained by the musical establishment; he was equally capable of appreciation of fresh talents among performers. He wrote a curiously antiquated prose, employing archaic turns of phrase, but his articles, often very long, were uniquely artistic. He signed his name H.T.P. which was facetiously deciphered by some as an acronym for "Hard To Please," or "Hell To Pay." He publ. a collection of essays on music, *Eighth-Notes* (N.Y., 1922).

BIBLIOGRAPHY: D.T.W. McCord, *H.T.P.; Portrait of a Critic* (N.Y., 1935).

Parker, Horatio William, eminent American composer and pedagogue; b. Auburndale, Mass., Sept. 15, 1863; d. Cedarhust, N.Y., Dec. 18, 1919. He studied piano with John Orth, theory with Emery and composition with Chadwick in Boston; subsequently went to Germany where he took courses in organ and composition with Rheinberger in Munich (1882-85); under his tutelage he wrote a cantata, *King Trojan* (1885). Returning to America he became an organist and prof. of music at the Cathedral School, Garden City, Long Island; in 1888, became organist at the Church of the Holy Trinity in Boston. He attracted attention with the first performance of his oratorio *Hora Novissima* (N.Y., May 3, 1893), in which he demonstrated his mastery of choral writing, while his harmonic and contrapuntal style remained securely tied to German practices. In 1894 he was engaged as chairman of the music department at Yale Univ., where he remained until his death. Many American composers received the benefit of his excellent instruction; among them was Charles Ives who kept his sincere appreciation of Parker's teaching long after he renounced Parker's conservative traditions. Parker conducted performances of his works in England in 1900 and 1902; received an honorary degree of Mus. Doc. at Cambridge Univ. in 1902. Returning to the U.S. he continued to compose industriously, without making any concessions to the emerging modern schools of composition; his choral works are particularly notable. In 1911 his opera *Mona* won the $10,000 prize offered by the Metropolitan Opera Co. in N.Y., and was produced there on March 14, 1912; he also won a prize offered by the National Federation of Women's Clubs for his 2nd opera *Fairyland,* which was produced in Los Angeles on July 1, 1915. Neither of the two operas possessed enough power to survive in the repertory. Besides the two operas and the oratorio *Hora Novissima,* Parker wrote a masque, *Cupid and Psyche,* for the 50th anniversary of the founding of the Yale Art School (New Haven, June 16, 1916); Concerto for Organ and Orch. (Boston, Dec. 26, 1902); 2 string quartets; piano trio and other pieces of chamber music; a great number of choral works, for which he is mainly distinguished: *The Lord Is My Shepherd, The Ballad of a Knight and His Daughter, King Trojan, Blow, Blow, Thou Winter Wind, The Norsemen's Raid, Morning and Evening Service, Harald Harfager, Dream-King and His Love, 6 Part-Songs, The Holy Child, The Legend of St. Christopher, Adstant Angelorum Chori, A Wanderer's Psalm, Hymnos Andron, A Star Song, King Gorm the Grim, A Song of Times, Morven and the Grail, The Dream of Mary,* etc.; numerous songs, with orchestral or piano accompaniments; patriotic odes, such as *Union and Liberty* for the inauguration of Theodore Roosevelt in 1905 and the World War I song *The Red Cross Spirit Speaks;* he also wrote a sonata for organ and other organ pieces of various dimensions; published the educational vols. *The Progressive Music Series* (8 vols.) and *Music and Public Entertainment* (1911).

BIBLIOGRAPHY: G. W. Chadwick, *Horatio Parker* (N.Y., 1921); D. S. Smith, "A Study of Horatio Parker," *Musical Quarterly* (April 1930); Isabel Parker Semler, with Pierson Underwood *Horatio Parker, A Memoir for His Grandchildren* (N.Y., 1942; with complete list of works).

Parker, James Cutler Dunn, American organist and composer; b. Boston, June 2, 1828; d. Brookline, Mass., Nov. 27, 1916. He studied law in Boston, and music in Leipzig (1851–54) under Moscheles (piano), Hauptmann and Richter (composition); then lived in Boston; was organist and choir director of Trinity Church (1864–91) and prof. at the Boston Univ. College of Music. His choral works include *Redemption Hymn* (1877); cantata *The Blind King* (1886); *St. John: The Life of Man* (oratorio); several church services. He publ. a *Manual of Harmony* (1855) and *Theoretical and Practical Harmony* (1870).

BIBLIOGRAPHY: *Dictionary of American Biography,* vol. XIV.

Parkhurst, Howard Elmore, American organist; b. Ashland, Mass., Sept. 13, 1848; d. (accidentally drowned) Lavalette, N.J., Aug. 18, 1916. He publ. *A Complete System of Harmony* (1908), *A Complete Method for the Modern Organ* (1911), *The Church Organist* (1913), *The Beginnings of the World's Music* (1915), *Rambles in Music-Land* (1914); wrote an oratorio, an orchestral overture, and church music.

Parlow, Kathleen, Canadian violinist; b. Calgary, Sept. 20, 1890; d. Oakville, Ontario, Aug. 19, 1963. Her family moved to San Francisco when she was a child, and she had her early instruction in violin there; in 1906 she was sent to St. Petersburg, Russia, where she was accepted by Leopold Auer in his violin class at the St. Petersburg Cons. She subsequently developed an extensive concert career; played in England, Scandinavia, the U.S. and in the Orient. In 1929–36 she was violin instructor at Mills College, Oakland, California; in 1941 joined the faculty of the Royal Cons. of Music in Toronto; there she organized in 1942 the Parlow String Quartet.

BIBLIOGRAPHY: M. P. French, *Kathleen Parlow, A Portrait* (Toronto, 1967).

Parodi, Lorenzo, Italian pedagogue and composer; b. Genoa, Aug. 10, 1856; d. there, March 28, 1926. He studied in Genoa and with Guiraud and Massenet in Paris. He taught esthetics and history of music at the Liceo Amilcare Zanella in Genoa, of which he was also director.

WORKS: the oratorios *Joannes Baptista* and *Calvario;* Masses and hymns; cantatas; a *Stabat Mater; Suite greca* and *Ouverture triomphale* for orch.; pieces for violin, and for piano; songs. Also publ. *Musicologia, L'Estetica del canone,* and a treatise on instrumentation.

Parratt, Sir Walter, English organist, b. Huddersfield, Feb. 10, 1841; d. Windsor, March 27, 1924. He was a pupil of his father; at 7 played his first church service; at 11, organist at Armitage Bridge, and passed through successive similar positions to Magdalen College, Oxford (1872) and St. George's Chapel, Windsor (1882), succeeding Elvey. Mus. Bac., Oxon., 1873; organ prof. at Royal College of Music, 1883; knighted in 1892; Master of Music in Ordinary to the Queen, 1893, to King Edward VII (1901), and King George V (1910); from 1908, prof. of music at Oxford (resigned on Jan. 1, 1918); from 1916 dean of music at London Univ.; Mus. Doc. *(hon. c.),* Oxford, 1894; Commander of the Victorian Order; etc.

WORKS: music to Aeschylus' *Agamemnon* and *Orestes; Elegy to Patroclus* (1883); anthems, songs, music for organ and piano.

BIBLIOGRAPHY: *Musical Times* (July 1902); *Dictionary of National Biography* (Suppl., 1922–30; pp. 655–7); Sir Donald Tovey and G. Parratt, *Walter Parratt, Master of Music* (London, 1941).

Parris, Hermann M., American physician and prolific composer; b. Ekaterinoslav, Russia, Oct. 30, 1903; was brought to America in 1905, the family settling in Philadelphia. He studied medicine at the Jefferson Medical College, Philadelphia, obtaining his M.D. in 1926. He received his musical training at the Univ. of Pennsylvania, graduating in 1924.

WORKS: symphonies (1946, 1947, 1949, 1952); 8 piano concertos (one each year between 1946 and 1953); 4 string quartets (1946, 1948, 1960, 1964); 22 piano sonatas (at least one each year between 1946 and 1965); 115 piano preludes (on the average of 5 a year between 1946 and 1967); *Hebrew Rhapsody* for orch. (1949); 4 rhapsodies for brass ensemble (1949); *Rhapsody No. 2* for orch., subtitled *Heart* (1950); *Images* for brass octet (1950); *Lament* for string orch., dedicated to the memory of Olin Downes (1956); *Viola Sonata; Cello Sonata;* 2 violin sonatas; songs. His orchestral piece entitled *Hospital Suite,* portraying events in the sick room, brought out, congenially so, by the Doctors' Orchestral Society (N.Y., May 13, 1948), attracted considerable attention in medical circles.

Parris, Robert, American composer; b. Philadelphia, May 21, 1924. He studied composition with Peter

Mennin at the Juilliard School of Music, N.Y. (1946–48); at Tanglewood with Ibert (1950) and Copland (1951) and in Paris with Honegger (1952–53). He settled in Washington; in 1963 was appointed to the faculty of George Washington Univ. His music is distinguished by strong formal structure and tonal cohesion; when pragmatically justifiable, he applies serialistic techniques with deliberate circumspection. His composition that had the greatest repercussion was a percussion piece, Concerto for 5 kettledrums and orch. (1955; Washington, March 25, 1958). Other works are: Sextet for brass (1948); *Night* for baritone, clarinet and string quartet (1951); Symphony (1952); Piano Concerto (1954); Viola Concerto (1956); Quintet for flute, oboe, bassoon, violin and cello (1957); Violin Concerto (1959); *The Raids: 1940* for soprano, violin and piano (1960); *Lamentations and Praises* for 8 instruments and percussion (1962); Viola Concerto (5th Inter-American Music Festival, Washington, May 20, 1971); Violin Sonata; Viola Sonata; Sonatina for flute, oboe, clarinet, horn and bass; 2 string quartets; 2 string trios; Trio for clarinet, cello and piano; songs.

Parrish, Carl, American musicologist and composer; b. Plymouth, Pa., Oct. 9, 1904; d. as a result of injuries in an automobile accident, Valhalla, N.Y., Nov. 27, 1965. After receiving his Ph.D at Harvard (1939), he taught at Wells College (1939–41), Fisk Univ. (1941–45), Westminster Choir College (1945–49), Pomona College (1949–53); from 1953 prof. at Vassar College. Publ. *The Notation of Medieval Music* (N.Y., 1957), and *A Treasury of Early Music* (N.Y., 1958). In collaboration with John F. Ohl, he publ. *Masterpieces of Music before 1750* (N.Y., 1951); wrote choral settings of folksongs; a string quartet; a song cycle; piano pieces.

Parrott, Ian, British composer; b. London, March 5, 1916. He studied at the Royal College of Music and at Oxford Univ. where he received his degrees of B. Mus. and Dr. Mus. During World War II he served in the Royal Corps of Signals in the Middle East and North Africa; after the war he was lecturer in music at Birmingham Univ. (1947–50) and from 1950 prof. at the Univ. of Aberystwyth. He wrote the opera *The Black Ram* (in the Welsh language, Aberystwyth, March 9, 1966); a ballet, *Maid in Birmingham* (1951); 3 symphonies (1946, 1960, 1966); a symph. prelude, *El Alamein* (1944); a symph. impression, *Luxor* (1948); Piano Concerto (1948); Wind Quintet (1948); *Fantasy Trio* for piano, violin and cello (1950; *Solemn Overture* (1956); Concerto for English Horn and Orch. (1956); Concerto for Trombone and Wind Instruments (1967); 4 string quartets. He publ. a number of useful manuals: *Pathway to Modern Music* (London, 1947); *A Guide to Musical Thought* (London, 1955); *Method in Orchestration* (London, 1957); and a monograph, *Elgar* (London, 1971).

Parry, Sir Charles Hubert Hastings, eminent English composer and pedagogue; b. Bournemouth, Feb. 27, 1848; d. Knight's Croft, Rustington, Oct. 7, 1918. While at Eton, from 1861, he studied composition with G. Elvey; took part in the concerts of the Musical Society as a pianist, organist, violinst, and composer. At 19, while still a student at Eton, he took the degree

of Mus. Bac. at Oxford. Entered Exeter College, Oxford, in 1867. There he began to study music in earnest under Bennett and Macfarren, also taking piano lessons from Dannreuther (1872–79). His public career as a composer began with the production of an *Intermezzo religioso* for strings at the Gloucester Festival of 1868. In 1883 Perry was appointed Choragus of Oxford Univ.; in that year Cambridge conferred on him the hon. degree of Mus. Doc., followed by Oxford (1884) and Dublin (1891). In 1894 he succeeded Sir George Grove as director of the Royal College of Music, which post he held until his death; 1899–1908, prof. of music at Oxford Univ.; knighted in 1898.

WORKS: the opera *Guinevere* (1885–86); for orch.: 4 symphonies (1878–82; 1883; 1889; 1889), overture *Guillem de Cabestanh* (1878–79), *Overture to an Unwritten Tragedy* (1893), Piano Concerto in F-sharp (1878–79), *Suite moderne* (1886), *Lady Radnor's Suite,* for strings (1894), *An English Suite* (publ. posthumously, 1921), symph. fantasy in B minor, *1912* (1912), symph. poem, *From Death to Life* (1914), etc.; choral works: the oratorios *Judith* (Birmingham, 1888), *Job* (Gloucester, 1892; his best work), and *King Saul* (Birmingham, 1894), *Scenes from Shelley's Prometheus Unbound* (Gloucester, 1880), choral song *Jerusalem* (publ. 1916), many anthems, hymns, motets, odes part-songs, etc.; chamber music: 3 string quartets (1867; 1868; 1878–80), 3 piano trios (1878; 1884; 1884–90), String Quintet (1884), Piano Quartet (1879), Nonet for winds (1877), Fantasy-Sonata for violin and piano (1878), Cello Sonata (1883), etc.; songs; organ pieces; piano pieces.

WRITINGS: His published writings include numerous excellent articles in *Grove's Dictionary, Studies of Great Composers* (1886; 8th ed., 1904), *The Art of Music* (1893; enlarged as *The Evolution of the Art of Music,* 1896; new rev. ed. by H. C. Colles, N.Y., 1930), *Summary of the History and Development of Medieval and Modern European Music* (1893), *The Music of the 17th Century* (vol. III of the *Oxford History of Music,* 1902; 2nd ed., 1938, ed. by E. J. Dent), *J. S. Bach* (1909; rev. ed., 1934), *Style in Musical Art* (1911). His college addresses were publ. by H. C. Colles (1920).

BIBLIOGRAPHY: R. O. Morris, "H. Parry," *Music & Letters* (April 1920); Ch. L. Graves, *H. Parry, His Life and Works* (2 vols., London, 1926); G. M. Greene, *Two Witnesses* (N.Y., 1930); J. A. Fuller-Maitland, *The Music of Parry and Stanford* (Cambridge, 1934).

Parry, John (called **"Bardd Alaw,"** master of song), Welsh musician; b. Denbigh, Feb. 18, 1776; d. London, April 8, 1851. He played clarinet in a band; then was bandmaster; composer for Vauxhall, 1809; conductor of "Eisteddfodau" in Wales for years; was critic for the *Morning Post* (1834–48), and treasurer of the Royal Society of Musicians (1831–49).

WORKS: *The Welsh Harper* (1839–48; collection of Welsh music, with a historical introduction); various other collections; also much original music (incidental music to several plays, harp sonatas, glees, songs, part-songs, etc.).

BIBLIOGRAPHY: *Dictionary of National Biography,* vol. XLIII (1895).

Parry, John, blind Welsh bard; b. Nevin, South Caernarvonshire, North Wales, 1710; d. Wynnstay, Denbighshire, Oct. 7, 1782. He served as harper to Sir W. W. Wynne. He collected several vols. of folksongs: *Antient British Music* (tunes of Cambro-Britons, 1742); *Collection of Welsh, English and Scotch Airs* (1760–65); *Cambrian Harmony: a Collection of Antient Welsh Airs* (1781).

Parry, Joseph, Welsh composer; b. Merthyr Tydvil, May 21, 1841; d. Penarth, near Cardiff, Feb. 17, 1903. His parents emigrated to America, but he returned to Britain, won Eisteddfod prizes for songs, and entered the Royal Academy of Music in 1868, studying under Bennett, Garcia, and Steggall. Mus. Bac., Cambridge, 1871; then appointed prof. of music at the Univ. College, Aberystwyth.
WORKS: 5 operas: *Blodwen* (Aberdare, 1878); *Virginia* (Aberdare, 1883); *Arianwen* (Cardiff, 1890); *Sylvia* (Cardiff, 1895); *King Arthur* (finished 1897); the oratorios *Emmanuel* (1880) and *Saul of Tarsus* (1892); the cantatas *The Prodigal Son, Nebuchadnezzar, Cambria,* and *The Maid of Cefu Idfa; Druids' Chorus;* an orchestral ballade, overtures, a string quartet, piano music, anthems, songs.
BIBLIOGRAPHY: *Dictionary of National Biography* (Suppl., 1901–11; vol. III, pp. 73–74.

Parsch, Arnošt, avant-garde Czech composer; b. Bučovice, Moravia, Feb. 12, 1936. In 1967 he joined in Brno a modern group of composers, organized by Alois Piňos.
WORKS: Concerto for instruments, percussion and piano (1964); Trio for clarinet, violin and viola (1965); Sonata for chamber orch. and tape (1966); *Didacticas 1; Didacticas 2* for double bass and piano (1966–68); *Didacticas 3* for violin, piano and percussion (1969); *4 Poetics* for various instrumental combinations and tape (1966–69); 2 symphonies (1967; 1970–72); *Structures* for bass clarinet and piano (1967); *Transpositions* for wind quintet (1967); Concertino for violin, piano, guitar and percussion (1968); 2 string quartets (1969, 1973); *Rota* for violin and double bass (1971); *Esercizii per uno, due, tre e quattro* for 2 flutes, cello and guitar (1971); *Contraposizioni per Due Boemi* for bass clarinet and piano (1972); *Znamení touhy (Sign of Desire),* melodramatic cantata (1972); *4 Pezzi* for clarinet, violin, double bass and piano (1972); *Útěk (Escape),* symph. poem (1973; Prague, March 30, 1974); *Night of Fire* for children's chorus, organ and piano (1975); *Les Fleurs* for bass clarinet and piano (1976); Double Concerto for flute, trombone and orch. (1976); *Sitting Bull,* jazz cantata (1975).

Parsley (Parseley, Persleye, Parcele, etc.), **Osbert,** English church music composer; b. 1511; d. 1585. Lay clerk at Norwich Cathedral for about 50 years. *Tudor Church Music* (vol. 10) contains reprints of 5 of his works; MSS in the British Museum include several motets; *Perslis clocke,* for 5 voices; etc.
BIBLIOGRAPHY: *Dictionary of National Biography,* vol. XLIII (1895).

Parsons, Albert Ross, American piano pedagogue; b. Sandusky, Ohio, Sept. 16, 1847; d. Mt. Kisco, N.Y., June 14, 1933. He studied with F. L. Ritter in N.Y.; then went to Germany where he took piano lessons with Moscheles, Reinecke, Wenzel and Papperitz at the Leipzig Cons. and music theory with Richter and Paul there; later he received additional instruction with Tausig, Kullak, Weitzmann and Wüerst in Berlin. In 1871 he settled in N.Y. where he earned the reputation of a piano teacher according to the best German traditions of the art. He publ. the manuals *Science of Pianoforte Practice* (1886); *The Virtuoso Handling of the Pianoforte* (1917) and wrote some choral and piano music.
BIBLIOGRAPHY: *Dictionary of American Biography,* vol. XIV.

Pärt, Arvo, Estonian composer; b. Paide, Sept. 11, 1935. He studied with Heino Eller at the Tallinn Cons., graduating in 1963. His youthful works are in a traditional style, but soon he adopted a distinctly aggressive type of the modern avant-garde, making use of tone-clusters, dodecaphonic techniques and improvisational devices of the aleatory type. He was the first Estonian composer to employ the 12-tone method in his curiously thanatological orchestral work *Nekrolog,* written in 1960. His other compositions include: String Quartet (1959), *Meie Aed (Our Garden),* cantata for children's chorus and orch. (1959); *Maailma samm (The World's Stride),* oratorio (1961); Symph. No. 1, *Polyphonic* (1963); *Perpetuum mobile* for orch. (1963); *Solfeggio* for mixed chorus (1963); a satirical *Quintettino* for winds (1964); the aleatory *Diagrams* for piano (1964); *Syllabic Music* for 13 instruments (1964); *Collage on B-A-C-H* for strings, oboe, and harpsichord (1964); *Pro et Contra,* short concerto for cello and orch. (1964); Symph. No. 2 (1966); *Credo* for chorus and orch. (1968); Symph. No. 3 (1971).

Partch, Harry, remarkable American composer; b. Oakland, California, June 24, 1901; d. San Diego, California, Sept. 3, 1974. Largely autodidact, he began experimenting with instruments capable of producing fractional intervals, which led him to the formulation of a 43-tone scale; he expounded his findings in his book, *Genesis of a Music* (1949). Among new instruments constructed by him are elongated violas, a chromelodeon, kitharas with 72 strings, harmonic canons with 44 strings, boos (made of giant Philippine bamboo reeds), cloud-chamber bowls, blow-boys (a pair of bellows with an attached automobile horn), etc. Seeking intimate contact with American life, he wandered across the country; collected indigenous expressions of folkways, inscriptions on public walls, etc., for texts in his productions.
WORKS: *8 Hitchhiker Inscriptions from a California Highway Railing* and *U.S. Highball, a Musical Account of a Transcontinental Hobo Trip* for chorus and instruments (both performed for the first time in Carnegie Chamber Hall, N.Y., April 22, 1944); *The Letter, a Depression Message from a Hobo Friend,* for voices and instrumental ensemble (1944); *Oedipus,* music drama (Mills College, Oakland, Calif., March 14, 1952); *The Bewitched,* a dance satire (Univ. of Illinois, Urbana, Ill., March 26, 1957); *Revelation in the Courthouse Park,* a musical tragedy (Univ. of Illinois, Ur-

bana, April 11, 1961); *Water, Water* an American ritual (Univ. of Ill., March 9, 1962).

BIBLIOGRAPHY: Peter Yates, "Genesis of a Music," *High Fidelity* (July 1963); P. Earls, "Harry Partch: *Verses* in Preparation for *Delusion of the Fury*," *Inter-American Institute for Musical Research: Yearbook III* (1967).

Partos, Oedoen, Hungarian-born Israeli composer and violist b. Budapest, Oct. 1, 1907; d. Tel Aviv, July 6, 1977. He studied violin with Hubay and composition with Kodály at the Royal Academy of Music in Budapest (1918–25). In 1938 he went to Palestine; was first violist in the Palestine Philharmonic (later Israel Philharmonic) from 1938 to 1956. In 1951 he was appointed director of the Israel Rubin Academy of Music in Tel Aviv; from 1961, member of the faculty of the Tel Aviv Univ. He was the soloist for the premières of his 3 viola concertos. His early works followed the rhythmical and melodic patterns of the Oriental tradition, emphasized the chromatic melodic turns, and developed a free accumulation of variations on a theme that is never stated in its entirety. In 1971 Partos went to Holland and experimented with the possibilities of 31-tone scales proposed by the 17th-century Dutch physicist and mathematician Christiaan Huygens.

WORKS: 2 string quartets: No. 1, *Concertino* (1932, revised 1939; N.Y., May 24, 1941); No. 2, *Tehilim* (*Psalms*, 1960; also for string orch. without double basses, 1960); *4 Folk Songs* for alto and string quartet (1939); *Yizkor (In memoriam)* for viola or violin or cello, and string orch. (1947); *Rondo* for violin and piano (1947); *4 Israeli Tunes* for violin or viola or or cello, and piano (1948); 3 viola concertos: No. 1, *Songs of Praise* (Tel Aviv, Jan. 22, 1949); No. 2 (1957); No. 3, *Sinfonia Concertante* (Jerusalem, 1963); *Ein Gev*, symph. fantasy (1951–52; Ein Gev, Oct. 1, 1953; UNESCO Prize, 1952; Israel State Prize, 1954); *Oriental Ballad* for viola and cello, and orch. or piano (1956); Violin Concerto (1958); *Maqamat* for flute and string quartet (1959); *Agada (A Legend)* for viola, piano and percussion (1960; London Festival of the International Society for Contemporary Music, June 6, 1962); *Iltur (Improvisation)* for 12 harps (1960); *Prelude* for piano (1960); *Dmuyoth (Images)* for orch. (1960); *Cantata* (1961); *5 Israeli Songs* for tenor, oboe, piano and cello (1962); *Symphonic Movements* (1966); *Arpiliyot (Nebulae)* for wind quintet (1966); *Netivim (Paths)*, symph. elegy (1969); *Shiluvim (Fuses)* for viola and chamber orch. (Tel Aviv, June 21, 1970); Concertino for Flute and Piano (1970); *Metamorphoses* for piano (1971); *Music* for chamber orch. (1971); *3 Fantasies* for 2 violins (1972); composed in the 31-tone system); *Arabesque* for oboe and chamber orch. (1975); Ballad, piano quartet (1977); *Fantasy*, piano trio (1977); *Invenzione a tre (Homage à Debussy)* for flute, harp and viola (1977).

Pasatieri, Thomas, talented American opera composer; b. New York, Oct. 20, 1945. He began to play the piano by spontaneous generation, and picked up elements of composition, particularly vocal, by a similar subliminal process; between the ages of 14 and 18 he wrote some 400 songs. He persuaded Nadia Bou-

langer to take him as a student by correspondence between Paris and New York when he was 15; at 16 he entered the Juilliard School of Music, where he became a student of Vittorio Giannini and Vincent Persichetti; also took a course with Darius Milhaud in Aspen, Colorado, where his first opera *The Women*, to his own libretto, was performed when he was only 19. It became clear to him that opera was his natural medium, and that the way to achieve the best results was by following the evolutionary line of Italian operatic productions characterized by the felicity of *bel canto*, facility of harmonic writing and euphonious fidelity to the lyric and dramatic content of the subject. In striving to attain these objectives, Pasatieri ran the tide of mandatory inharmoniousness; while his productions were applauded by hoi polloi they shocked music critics and other composers (one of them described Pasatieri's music as "a stream of perfumed urine.") This attitude is akin to that taken by some towards Vittorio Giannini and Gian Carlo Menotti (interestingly, all three are of Italian genetic stock). A list of Pasatieri's operas follows (and it grows with every passing year): *The Women* (Aspen, Colorado, Aug. 20, 1965); *La Divina* (N.Y., March 16, 1966); *Padrevia* (Brooklyn, Nov. 18, 1967); *Calvary* (Seattle, April 7, 1971); *The Trial of Mary Lincoln* (television opera; Boston, Feb. 14, 1972); *Black Widow* (Seattle, March 2, 1972); *The Seagull*, after Chekhov's play (Houston, Texas, March 5, 1974); *Signor Deluso*, after Molière's comedy *Sganarelle* (Greenway, Virginia, July 1974); *The Penitentes* (Aspen, Colorado, Aug. 3, 1974); *Ines de Castro* (Baltimore, March 30, 1976); *Washington Square*, after Henry James (Detroit, Oct. 3, 1976). He further wrote *Héloïse and Abelard* for soprano, baritone and piano (1971); *Rites de passage* for voice and strings (1974); *3 Poems of James Agee* for voice and piano (1974); 2 piano sonatas and other piano pieces.

BIBLIOGRAPHY: Peter G. Davis, "They Love Him in Seattle," *N.Y. Times Magazine* (March 21, 1976).

Pasdeloup, Jules-Étienne, famous French conductor; b. Paris, Sept. 15, 1819; d. Fontainebleau, Aug. 13, 1887. He was a piano pupil, at the Conservatoire, of Laurent and Zimmerman; 1841, *répétiteur* of a solfeggio class; 1847–50, teacher of a piano class, which he gave up to organize the celebrated symphony concerts of the "Société des jeunes élèves du Cons." (1851), developing (1861) into the "Concerts populaires de musique classique" at the "Cirque d'hiver," a pioneer series of good, inexpensive, popular concerts which were a success from the start. Pasdeloup also taught a vocal ensemble class at the Cons. (1855–68). His popular concerts gradually lost ground in competition with Colonne and Lamoureux, ceasing in 1884; he revived them just before his death, in 1886–87. A grand popular music festival at the Trocadéro, instituted for his benefit, netted him nearly 100,000 francs.

Pashchenko, Andrei, prolific Russian composer; b. Rostov, Aug. 15, 1883; d. Moscow, Nov. 16, 1972. He studied with Vitols and Steinberg at the St. Petersburg Cons., graduating in 1917; occupied various clerical positions; was librarian of the Leningrad Philharmonic; in 1961 he went to live in Moscow. An exceptionally fertile composer, he wrote some 14 operas and 15 symphonies; the style of his music is a natural continuation of the traditions of the Russian National School; in his later works he allowed a certain influx of Impressionistic harmonies and unresolved dissonant combinations.

WORKS: operas: *Eagles in Revolt* (Leningrad, Nov. 7, 1925), *King Maximilian* (1927), *The Black Cliff* (Leningrad, June 12, 1931), *The Pompadours* (1939), *Jester Balakirev* (1949), *The Capricious Bride* (1956), *Radda and Loyko* (1957), *Nila Snishko* (1961), *Great Seducer* (1966), *Woman, This Is the Devil* (1966), *African Love* (1966), *The Horse in the Senate* (1967), *Portrait* (1968), *Master and Margarita* (1971); 15 symphonies (1915, 1929, 1933, 1938, 1952, 1954, 1956, 1957, 1958, 1963, 1964, 1966, 1969, 1970); 4 sinfoniettas (1943, 1945, 1953, 1964); *Volga Fantasy* for orch. (1961); *Ukrainiada*, symph. poem (1963); *Icarus*, symph. poem (1964); *Dance Triptych* for orch. (1965); *The Voice of Peace*, symph. poem (1971); *Poem of Stars*, symph. poem (1971); Cello Concerto (1964); 9 string quartets; numerous works for chorus. He publ. *Essays on the History and Theory of Music* (Leningrad, 1939).

BIBLIOGRAPHY: Y. Meylikh, *Andrei Pashchenko* (Leningrad, 1960).

Pashkalov, Viacheslav, Russian ethnomusicologist; b. Moscow, May 14, 1873; d. Leningrad, Dec. 26, 1951. He studied literature and music in Moscow; in 1919 was appointed head of the ethnographic division of the Moscow State Library. He publ. the valuable treatises: *Survey of the Musical Structure of the Russian Songs of the Province of Voronezh* (1914); *The Musical Structure of the Songs of Crimea* (1924); *Songs of the Orient* (1925). He was also a composer; wrote a number of songs in a national Russian style.

Pashkevich, Vassily, Russian violinist and composer; b. c.1740; d. March 20, 1800. In 1763 he was admitted as a violinist to the 2nd court orch. in St. Petersburg; in 1779 was engaged as a theater conductor there. His Russian opera *A Carriage Accident* was performed in St. Petersburg on Nov. 7, 1779; in 1782 he presented 2 comic operas in Russian: *The Miser* (Moscow) and *The Pasha of Tunis* (St. Petersburg). In 1783 he was transferred to the 1st court orch.; in 1786 was commissioned by Catherine the Great to write a comic Russian opera, *Fevey*, for which the Empress herself wrote the libretto. It was produced in St. Petersburg on April 19, 1786, and Pashkevich received an award of 1,000 rubles. In 1789 he was appointed chief of ball music at the Imperial Palace, and simultaneously was elevated to the rank of concertmaster of the 1st court orch. In 1790 he collaborated with Sarti and Canobbio in another Russian opera to a text of Catherine the Great, *The Early Reign of Oleg*, which was first produced at the palace, and publicly performed in St. Petersburg on Nov. 2, 1790. In collaboration with Martín y Soler, he wrote still another comic opera to a text by the Empress, *Fedul and His Children* (performed at the palace, Jan. 27, 1791; publicly, St. Petersburg, March 2, 1791). He was given the honorary rank of colonel. A Mass according to the Russian Orthodox liturgy by him was publ. in Moscow in 1796.

BIBLIOGRAPHY: R.-Aloys Mooser, *Annales de la Musique et des Musiciens en Russie au XVIIIe siècle* (Geneva, 1950; vol. II, pp. 55–57).

Pasmore, Henry Bickford, American singing teacher and composer; b. Jackson, Wisconsin, June 27, 1857; d. San Francisco, Feb. 23, 1944. He studied in San Francisco; then went to Leipzig and London, where he took courses in singing with various teachers. Returning to America, he taught singing at the Univ. of the Pacific, San José; at Stanford Univ., and at Mills College. He wrote an exotic opera, *Lo-ko-rah;* another opera on a libretto based on Californian history, *Amor y Oro;* an overture, *Miles Standish;* a symph. poem, *Gloria California;* a Mass; several cantatas; church music; songs.

Pasquali (Pascale, Paschali), Francesco, Italian composer, one of the earliest musicians to write instrumental pieces with figured bass; b. Cosenza, c.1590; d. after 1633. He studied in Rome, and remained there for most of his life. Between 1615 and 1633 he brought out 3 books of madrigals for 4 and 5 voices, and several vols. of secular and sacred songs for 1, 2, 3, 4, and 5 voices.

Pasquali, Nicolò, Italian violinist and composer; b. c.1718; d. Edinburgh, Oct. 13, 1757. He settled in Edinburgh in 1740; was in Dublin between 1748 and 1752; then briefly in London, before returning to Edinburgh. He publ. sonatas for violin with accompaniments, 12 overtures, and an instructive book, *Thorough-bass Made Easy* (Edinburgh, 1757).

Pasquini, Bernardo, Italian organist and composer; b. Massa di Valdinievole, Tuscany, Dec. 7, 1637; d. Rome, Nov. 21, 1710. He came to Rome in 1650 and studied with Vittori and Cesti; was employed as a church organist at Chiesa Nuova (1661–63), at Santa Maria in Aracoeli (1664), at Santa Maria Maggiore (1665–67), at S. Luigi dei Francesi (1673–75); served as 1st organist at the Oratory of SS. Crocifisso (1644–85), and was at one time in the employ of Prince Giambattista Borghese as a chamber musician. He was renowned as a teacher; Durante, G. Muffat and Della Ciaja were his pupils. He wrote about 15 oratorios, 14 operas (1672–97) and chamber cantatas, but was distinguished mainly for his keyboard composition; his toccatas and suites were published during his lifetime in the collection *Toccates et suites pour le clavecin de MM. Pasquini, Poglietti et Gaspard Kerle* (Paris, 1704). Other clavier works were brought out by L. Torchi in *L'Arte Musicale in Italia,* Cesi, Tagliapietra in *Antologia di musica antica e moderna per pianoforte* and other anthologies. His vocal pieces were published by F. Boghen (1923, 1930). His collected works for keyboard, ed. by M. B. Haynes, are publ. in 7 vols. (Rome, 1964–68); a sonata for 2 claviers was brought out by W. Danckert (Kassel, 1971).

BIBLIOGRAPHY: V. Virgili, *Bernardo Pasquini* (Pescia, 1908); A. Bonaventura, *Bernardo Pasquini* (Ascoli Piceno, 1923); F. Boghen, *L'Arte di Bernardo Pasquini* (1931); G. Roncaglia, "Il Tirinto di Bernardo Pasquini e i suoi intermezzi," *Rassegna Musicale*

(Nov., 1931); W. S. Newman, *The Sonata in the Baroque Era* (Chapel Hill, North Carolina, 1966).

Pasquini, Ercole, Italian organist and composer; b. Ferrara; d. Rome, between 1608 and 1620. He studied with Alessandro Milleville; was organist in Ferrara and later at St. Peter's in Rome, retiring in 1608. His set of *Canzone francese per cembalo* is reprinted by Torchi in *L'Arte Musicale in Italia* (vol. III).

BIBLIOGRAPHY: Fr. Superbi, *Apparato degli Huomini illustri della città di Ferrara* (1620).

Passereau, Pierre, French composer of the first half of the 16th century. He was chapel singer to the Duke of Angoulême (Francis I). 23 of his chansons appear in various anthologies published between 1533 and 1547; 2 of them reprinted in F. Lesure, ed., *Anthologie de la Chanson parisienne au XVIe siècle* (Monaco, 1953); his *Opera omnia*, ed. by G. Dottin, was issued by the American Institute of Musicology (1967).

Passy, (Ludvig Anton) Edvard, Swedish pianist and pedagogue; b. Stockholm, Sept. 4, 1789; d. Drottningholm, Aug. 16, 1870. He received his first music instruction from his brother; then studied with L. Piccinni (who was Kapellmeister in Stockholm from 1796–1801), with John Field in St. Petersburg, and with Eggert in Stockholm. After several successful tours of Germany he settled in his native city as a highly esteemed teacher, and organist of the court chapel.

WORKS: 2 piano concertos; Fantasy for piano and orch.; 3 string quartets; 2 piano trios; organ fugues; piano pieces, songs; etc.

Pasta (*née* **Negri**), **Giuditta,** famous Italian dramatic soprano; b. Saronno, near Milan, Oct. 28, 1797; d. at her villa on Lake Como, April 1, 1865. She studied with Asioli at the Milan Cons. and made her debut in 1815; after indifferent appearances in London and Paris she returned to Italy for further vocal study with Scappa. At her appearances in Paris in 1822 she was acclaimed as a vocal phenomenon; the range of her voice was from A in the low register to D in the high treble; but what contributed chiefly to her success was her extraordinary dramatic power, so that she won out with the audiences and critics against all her possible rivals. So great was her fame at the peak of her career that renowned composers wrote roles to suit her voice in their operas; Bellini did so in *La Sonnambula* and *Norma*, Donizetti composed *Anna Bolena* and Pacini produced his *Niobe* for her.

BIBLIOGRAPHY: Maria Ferranti Giulini, *Giuditta Pasta e i soui tempi* (Milan, 1935).

Pasternack, Josef Alexander, Polish-American conductor; b. Czenstochowa, Poland, July 1, 1881; d. Chicago, April 29, 1940. He studied at the Warsaw Cons. with Michalowski (piano) and Noskowski (composition); came to America in 1895; played the viola in the Metropolitan Opera orch. (1900–10); was assistant conductor there during the season of 1909–10; then was conductor of various opera companies in New York and Chicago; composed popular orchestral pieces and songs; made numerous arrangements.

Pasterwitz, Georg von, German church composer; b. Bierhütten, near Passau, June 7, 1730; d. Kremsmünster, Jan. 26, 1803. He studied music with Eberlin in Salzburg; after touring Europe, entered the order of the Benedictines in 1755; was choirmaster at the monastery in Kremsmünster (1767–82); lived in Vienna (1782–95); in 1795 resumed his post in Kremsmünster. He publ. 24 organ fugues and 300 *Themata und Versetten zum Präambulieren.* In MS: about 20 Masses, numerous psalms, offertories, vespers, motets, etc.; also several operas, intermezzi, and detached arias interpolated in various operas of other composers.

BIBLIOGRAPHY: G. Huemer, *Die Pflege der Musik im Stifte Kremsmünster* (Wels, 1877); A. Kellner, *Musikgeschichte des Stiftes Kremsmünster* (Kassel, 1956).

Pastou, Étienne-Jean Baptiste, French vocal educator; b. Vigan, Gard, May 26, 1784; d. Ternes, near Paris, Oct. 8, 1851. He founded a singing school in Paris in 1819; was made prof. at the Paris Cons. in 1836; publ. a method for ensemble singing, *École de la lyre harmonique* (Paris, 1822).

Patachich, Iván, Hungarian composer; b. Budapest, June 3, 1922. He studied composition with Szabó, Siklós and Viski at the Budapest Academy; was active mainly as a theater conductor; in 1952 became musical director of the Budapest Film Studio.

WORKS: 2 operas: *Theomachia* (1962) and *Fuente Ovejuna* (1969); 3 ballets: *Black and White* (1958), *Sunday Romance* (1963) and *Mngongo and Mlaba* (1965); 2 cantatas: *Country of Cliffs* (1953) and *Music of the Bible* (1968); 2 harp concertos (1956, 1968); Double-Bass Concertino (1957); Flute Concerto (1958); Viola Concerto (1959); Oboe Concerto (1959); *3 Pieces* for clarinet and orch. (1961); Guitar Concerto (1961); *Concerto Breve* for cello and orch. (1962); 2 divertimentos for orch. (1962, 1969); 2 piano concertos (1963, 1968); *Sinfonietta Savariensis* (1964); Violin Concerto (1964); *Quadri di Picasso* for orch. (1965); Bassoon Concerto (1965); 2 symphonies (1965, 1966); Percussion Concerto (1966); *Colori 67* for orch. (1967); *3 Schizzi* for orch. (1969); Concerto for Violin, Piano and Orch. (1969); *2 Pezzi* for trumpet and chamber orch. (1969); *2 Pezzi* for trombone and chamber orch. (1969); Organ Concerto (1972); Concertino for Piano and Wind Orch. (1972); 2 violin sonatas (1948, 1964); Wind Quintet (1960); Double-Bass Sonatina (1961); 2 piano trios (1962, 1967); Sonata for harp and horn (1964); *Canzone moro e caccia* for horn and piano (1971); *Ritmi pari e dispari* for 2 horns (1971); *Proporzioni* for percussion (1972); *Quartettino* for saxophones (1972); *Aquarelli* for 2 trombones (1972); Piano Sonata (1965); Piano Sonatina (1966); *4 Pezzi piccoli* for piano (1971).

Patanè, Giuseppe, talented Italian conductor; b. Naples, Jan. 1, 1932. He was a son of **Franco Patanè** (1908–68), a noted opera conductor; studied at the Cons. S. Pietro a Majella in Naples; made his debut as conductor at the age of 19 when he led a performance of *La Traviata* at the Teatro Mercadante in Naples; he was subsequently 2nd conductor at the Teatro San Carlo in Naples (1951–56); became principal conductor of the Linz Opera in 1961, and in 1962 conductor of the Berlin Opera; he further filled engagements at La Scala, Milan, at the Vienna Opera and in Copenhagen, with excellent acclaim; he also showed his fine musicianship as an orchestral conductor with the Vienna Philharmonic, Radio Orch. of Berlin, the Orchestre de la Suisse Romande in Switzerland, etc. In 1978 he conducted Italian opera at the Metropolitan Opera in New York, receiving extraordinary praise in the press.

Patey, Janet Monach (*née* **Whytock**), English contralto; b. London, May 1, 1842; d. Sheffield, Feb. 28, 1894. She was married to the bass singer **John Patey** (1835–1901). After singing at various English festivals, she made an American tour in 1871; also sang in Australia (1890). In her prime she was regarded as the foremost English contralto.

Patiño, Carlos, Spanish cleric and composer; b. Santa Maria del Campo; d. Madrid, Sept 5, 1675. In 1632 he received a grant from King John IV of Portugal; from 1633 to 1648 he was maestro di cappella at the Spanish court; in 1660 he was appointed to a similar position at the Royal Cloister of the Incarnation. He was one of the most important composers of sacred music of his time; particularly excelled in polyphonic works for 8–12 voices; most of his music is preserved in manuscript in the archives of El Escorial and in Salamanca. His *Missa in Devotione* for double chorus is reproduced in Eslava's *Lira sacro-hispana;* Felipe Pedrell transcribed some of Patiño's *Tonos humanos* in vols. 3 and 4 of *Teatro Lirico Espanol anterior al siglo XIX.*
BIBLIOGRAPHY: Varela Silvari, *Galería biográfica de músicos gallegos* (Coruña, 1874); V. Torres, *Galeria de gallegos ilustres* (Madrid, 1875; vol. 5).

Paton, Mary Ann, Scottish soprano; b. Edinburgh, Oct., 1802; d. Bulcliffe Hall, Chapelthorpe, July 21, 1864. Of a musical family, she sang in concerts as a child; made her first operatic appearance as Susanna in the *Marriage of Figaro* (London, Aug. 3, 1822). She sang the part of Rezia in the première of Weber's *Oberon* in London (April 12, 1826) and was praised by Weber himself. She had a very fine voice, and could sing lyric and coloratura parts with equal brilliance. She was married to **Joseph Wood,** the tenor.
BIBLIOGRAPHY: "Miss Paton," *Quarterly Music Magazine and Review* (London, 1823); *Memoir of Mr. and Mrs. Wood* (Philadelphia, 1840).

Patterson, Annie Wilson, Irish collector of folksongs and writer on music; b. Lurgan, Oct. 27, 1868; d. Cork, Jan. 16, 1934. She studied organ at the Royal Irish Academy of Music with Sir R. Stewart; was organist at various churches in Dublin; in 1909, settled in Cork; was awarded the degree of Mus. Doc. by the National Univ. of Ireland. She organized the "Feis Ceoil," Irish Music Festival, held annually since 1897.
WORKS: *6 Original Gaelic Songs; Rallying Song of the Gaelic League* (with orch.); *The Bells of Shandon,* for chorus; *Invernia,* arrangement of Irish airs; 2 Irish operas, *The High-King's Daughter* and *Oisin;* cantatas; symph. poems; etc. Writings: *The Story of Oratorio* (1902); *Schumann* (1903; in Master Musician Se-

ries; new rev. ed., 1934); *Chats with Music-Lovers* (1908); *How to Listen to an Orchestra* (1913; new ed., 1928); *Great Minds in Music; Beautiful Song and the Singer; The Music of Ireland; The Profession of Music* (1926).

Patterson, Franklin Peale, American composer; b. Philadelphia, Jan. 5, 1871; d. New Rochelle, N.Y., July 6, 1966. He studied at the Univ. of Pennsylvania, and later in Munich with Thuille and Rheinberger.
WORKS: His opera, *The Echo,* produced in Portland, Oregon, on June 9, 1925, was awarded the David Bispham Memorial Medal and the medal award of the National Federation of Music Clubs. Other works: the short operas *Beggar's Love (A Little Girl at Play), Mountain Blood,* and *The Forest Dwellers;* the grand operas *Through the Narrow Gate* and *Caprice.* He also publ. various instructive pamphlets: *How to Write a Good Tune* (1924), *Practical Instrumentation* (1923), *Leit-Motives of the Nibelungen Ring* (1896), *The Perfect Modernist* (1921), etc.
BIBLIOGRAPHY: E. Hipsher, *American Opera and Its Composers* (Philadelphia, 1934; pp. 355–58).

Patti, Adelina (Adela Juana Maria), one of the greatest coloratura singers of the 19th century, both in opera and concert; b. Madrid, Feb. 10, 1843; d. Brecknock, Wales, Sept. 27, 1919. Daughter of two Italian singers, she was taken to New York at an early age; from 1851–55 sang in many concerts there. She was taught piano by her sister **Carlotta,** and singing by her half-brother Ettore Barili; her formal debut was made at New York on Nov. 24, 1859, as Lucia (under the stage name of "the little Florinda"). In London she first appeared in *La Sonnambula* on May 14, 1861, at Covent Garden, her success rivaling that of the Grisi; her Paris debut was in the same role, at the Théâtre Italien, on Nov. 19, 1862. In Paris she married the Marquis de Caux in 1868, from whom she separated in 1877, and was divorced in 1885. She sang for the first time in Italy at La Scala, Milan, Nov. 3, 1877, Violetta in *La Traviata* being the role selected. She sang in all the chief cities of Europe, and was everywhere received with enthusiasm. She commanded very large fees. She retired from the stage in 1895, but continued to appear in concerts, giving an official "farewell" concert at Albert Hall, London, on Dec. 1, 1906. Her last public appearance was at a benefit concert for the Red Cross in the same hall, on Oct. 20, 1914. Her second husband, the tenor **Nicolini,** whom she married in 1886, died in 1898; she married a Swedish nobleman, Baron Cederström, in 1899. Although her voice was not powerful, it possessed a wide range (c^1–f^3), wonderful flexibility, and perfect evenness throughout; it probably excelled that of any other singer in voluptuous sweetness and bell-like purity. Her vocalization and technical skill were above all criticism, and the ease with which she took the highest notes was astonishing. But she was a poor actress, she lacked temperment, and her musical intelligence was ordinary. Her operatic repertory included about 30 roles in the operas of Rossini, Bellini, Donizetti, Meyerbeer, Gounod, Auber, and Verdi (earlier works).
BIBLIOGRAPHY: Th. de Grave, *Biographie d'A. Patti* (Paris, 1865); G. de Charnacé, *A. Patti* (Paris,

(1868); G. M. Dalmazzo, *A. Patti's Life* (London, 1877); L. Lauw, *Fouteen Years with A. Patti* (London, 1884); E. Hanslick, "A. Patti," in *Musikalische Stationen* (Berlin, 1885; English transl. in Hanslick, *Vienna's Golden Years of Music*, N.Y., 1950, pp. 187–208); A. Weismann, *Die Primadonna* (1919); H. Klein, *The Reign of Patti* (N.Y., 1920).

Patti, Carlotta, sister of **Adelina Patti;** b. Florence, Oct. 30, 1835; d. Paris, June 27, 1889. Her father and mother were her first teachers in singing; she had piano lessons with Henri Herz, at Paris. Her early youth was spent in New York. Lameness prevented success on the stage, but she was more fortunate as a concert singer, making her debut in New York in 1861, followed by an American tour with the impresario Ullmann. Here, and in Europe, she became a favorite on the concert stage, more especially as a coloratura vocalist of exquisite technique united with great sentiment. In 1871 she married the cellist **De Munck.**

Pattison, John Nelson, American pianist and composer; b. Niagara Falls, Oct. 22, 1845; d. New York, July 27, 1905. He studied piano in Germany with celebrated teachers (Thalberg, Henselt, Hans von Bülow) and also had lessons from Liszt. He gave a series of concerts in the U.S., and toured as accompanist for Parepa-Rosa, Louise Kellogg, Albani, Pauline Lucca, and others. He wrote a symph. work, *Niagara;* marches and overtures for military band; a concerto-fantasia for piano and orch.; some 200 pieces for piano solo. He published *Memoir of J. N. Pattison* (N.Y., 1868).

Pattison, Lee, American pianist; b. Grand Rapids, Wis., July 22, 1890; d. Claremont, Calif., Dec. 22, 1966. He first studied at the New England Cons. of Music; later in Berlin with Schnabel. In 1917 he formed a duo piano team with Guy Maier; they gave a number of successful concerts, until 1931, when the partnership was dissolved. From 1932 till 1937 he was head of the piano dept. of Sarah Lawrence College; also taught at the Juilliard Summer School; lived mostly in N.Y. His compositions include *Florentine Sketches* for piano and a piano suite of 7 pieces, *Told in the Hills.*

Patton, Willard, American singer and composer; b. Milford, Maine, May 26, 1853; d. Minneapolis, Dec. 12, 1924. He studied with Dudley Buck and others in N.Y.; was active as a tenor in oratorios; in 1883 settled in Minneapolis as vocal teacher. WORKS: an oratorio, *Isaiah* (1897); the operettas *The Gallant Garroter* (1882) and *La Fianza* (1889); a grand opera, *Pochontas* (Minneapolis, Jan. 4, 1911); 2 musical "epics," *The Star of Empire* (1900) and *Foot-Stones of a Nation* (1906); a symph. fantasy, *The Spirit of 1861* (1915).

Patzak, Julius, Austrian tenor; b. Vienna, April 9, 1898; d. Rottach-Egern, Bavaria, Jan. 26, 1974. He studied at the Univ. of Vienna where he attended the classes of Guido Adler and Mandyczewski; made his debut in 1926; sang at the State Opera in Munich from 1928 to 1945; then was on the staff of the Vienna Opera (1946–59); continued to fill guest engagements in Berlin. He was also distinguished as a singer in oratorio and in recitals. He retired from the stage in 1966 and lived in Rottach-Egern.

Pauer, Ernst, Austrian pianist; b. Vienna, Dec. 21, 1826; d. Jugenheim, near Darmstadt, May 9, 1905. He studied piano with Mozart's son, W. A. Mozart, Jr. and composition with Sechter. In 1851 he went to London; taught at the Royal Academy of Music (1859–64); in 1861 he began a series of historical performances of harpsichord and piano music in chronological order, which attracted considerable attention. After a number of concerts in Germany and Austria he was appointed pianist to the Austrian court (1866). He continued his activities until 1896, when he retired and lived in Jugenheim. He publ. in English a number of educational works of some value, among them *The Art of Pianoforte-playing* (1877); *Musical Forms* (1878); *The Elements of the Beautiful in Music* (1877); and also *The Birthday Book of Musicians and Composers* (London, 1881) and *A Dictionary of Pianists and Composers for the Pianoforte* (1895); he further brought out collections for piano students: *The New Gradus ad Parnassum; Classical Companion: Celebrated Concert-studies* and *Cultures of the Left Hand.* He made excellent arrangements of symphonies by Beethoven and Schumann, for piano solo, piano 4 hands and piano 8 hands; also arranged Mendelssohn's orchestral works for piano 4 hands and 8 hands; these arrangements were widely used in the 19th century and were extremely useful for young pianists until the advent of the phonograph administered a lethal blow to this type of musical activity.

Pauer, Jiří, Czech composer; b. Libušín, near Kladno, central Bohemia, Feb. 22, 1919. He studied composition with Otakar Šín; then with Alois Hába at the Prague Cons. (1943–46) and with Bořkovec at the Prague Academy of Music (1946–50). He occupied various administrative posts with the Ministry of Education and Culture and the Czech Radio; was artistic director of the Opera of the National Theater in Prague (1953–55); then taught at the Prague Academy. His music follows the pragmatic precepts of Socialist Realism in its modern application, broadly lyrical and tensely dramatic by turns. WORKS: 5 operas: *Žvanivý Slimejš* (The Talkative Snail, 1949–50; Prague, April 5, 1958); *Zuzana Vojířová* (1954–57; (Prague, May 11, 1958); *Červená Karkulka* (Little Red Riding Hood; 1958–59; Olomouc, 1960); *Manželské kontrapunkty* (Marital Counterpoints, 1961, 3 operatic satirical sketches, Ostrava, 1962; 2nd version as 5 satires, Liberec, 1967); *Zdravý nemocný* (Le Malade imaginaire, after Molière, 1966–69; Prague, May 22, 1970); a children's ballet, *Ferdy the Ant* (1974; Prague, 1976); *Comedy Suite* for orch. (1949); *Bassoon Concerto* (1949); *Youth Suite* for orch. (1951); *Scherzo* for orch. (1951); *Children's Suite* for chamber orch. (1953); *Rhapsody* for orch. (1953); *Oboe Concerto* (1954); *Horn Concerto* (1958); *Symph.* (1963); *Panychide,* symph. picture (1969); *Canto festivo* for orch. (1970–71); *Trumpet Concerto* (1972); *Initials* for orch. (1974); *Canto Triste,* cycle for medium voice and orch. (1971); *Swan Song,* monodrama for male voice and orch. (1973); *Tragédie o* *vose a nose (Tragedy of Wasp and Nose)* for bass and orch. (1976); chamber music: *Partita* for solo harp (1947); *Divertimento* for 3 clarinets (1949); *Capriccio* for flute or oboe, clarinet or bassoon, and piano (1952); *Violin Sonatina* (1953); *Cello Sonata* (1954); 3 string quartets (1960, 1969, 1970); *Divertimento* for nonet (1961); *Wind Quintet* (1961); *Piano Trio* (1963); *Monologues* for solo clarinet (1964); *Interpolations* for solo flute (1969); *Rhapsody* for solo cello (1969); *Musica da concerto* for 13 winds (1971); *Trompetina* for trumpet and piano (1972); for piano: *My Notebook* (1942–43), *For a Happy Journey* (1950) and *Bagatelles* (1968); also songs and choruses.

Pauer, Max, eminent English pianist and teacher; son of **Ernst Pauer;** b. London, Oct. 31, 1866; d. Jugenheim, May 12, 1945. He studied with his father; embarked on several successful concert tours in Germany; in 1880 was appointed prof. of piano at the Cologne Cons.; in 1897 became prof. at Stuttgart Cons.; in 1908 was appointed director of the Hochschule für Musik in Mannheim; retired in 1934. He made an American tour in 1913–14. Following his father's excellent example in arranging Classical symphonies for piano, he made transcriptions of symphonies by Mozart and Haydn for piano solo and piano 4 hands. He published an ironic autobiography, *Unser seltsames Ich* (Stuttgart, 1942).

Paul, Oscar, German music theorist; b. Freiwaldau, April 8, 1836; d. Leipzig, April 18, 1898. He studied theology; then took private lessons in piano with Plaidy and theory with Hauptmann and Richter. He adapted Hauptmann's *Lehre von der Harmonik* for practical usages and publ. the result under the title *Lehrbuch der Harmonik* (1880; in English, N.Y., 1885). He also publ. *Geschichte des Klaviers* (Leipzig, 1868); *Handlexikon der Tonkunst* (Leipzig, 1873); *Musikalische Instrumente* (Braunschweig, 1874).

Paull, Barberi, American composer of the avant-garde; b. New York, July 25, 1946. She began to play piano as an infra-adolescent, in private and in public; with the awakening of consciousness, opted for jazz and multimedia forms of self-expression, but went through the motions of academic training at the Juilliard School of Music in N.Y., where she studied composition with Hall Overton and Jacob Druckman (1970–71); later took courses with Charles Wuorinen at the Manhattan School of Music (1972) and attended the Musical Theatre Workshop conducted by Lehman Engel (1973). Then, in a dash of feminist self-assertion, she founded the Barberi Paull Musical Theatre, Inc., and presented with it a series of mixed-media events. In her compositions she elevates eclecticism to an article of democratic faith, embracing jazz, pop tunes and electronic sound in the context of ostentatious and unapologetic cosmic sentimentality.

WORKS: an electronic ballet *Time*, (1971); *Earth Pulse*, choreographic cantata, making use of musique concrète (1971); *The Mass* for tape, percussion and visual projections (1974); *A Land Called The Infinity of Love* for multimedia (1975); *Sheer Silver Sheen Flower Sky* for chorus (1971–74); *O Wind* for mezzo-soprano and string quartet (1975); *Song for Orchestra* (1977); *A Christmas Carol* after Dickens, for chorus and instrumental trio (1977; also in a jazz version); many unabashed pop tunes.

Paulli, Holger Simon, Danish conductor; b. Copenhagen, Feb. 22, 1810; d. there, Dec. 23, 1891. He studied violin with Schall and Wexschall; at the age of 18 entered the court orch. in Copenhagen; then became concertmaster, and principal conductor (1864–83). In 1866 he was appointed co-director with Gade and Hauptmann of the newly founded Copenhagen Cons. He was an admirer of Wagner, and conducted the first performances in Denmark of *Lohengrin* (1870); *Die Meistersinger* (1872) and *Tannhäuser* (1875). He composed a singspiel *Lodsen (The Pilot),* produced in Copenhagen on Sept. 25, 1851; also wrote some ballet music, violin pieces and songs.

BIBLIOGRAPHY: F. Bendix, *Af en Kapelmusikers Erindringer* (Copenhagen, 1913).

Paulson, Gustaf, Swedish composer and organist; b. Hälsingborg, Jan. 22, 1898; d. there, Dec. 17, 1966. He studied composition in Copenhagen with Peder Gram; from 1929 until his death, served as church organist in Hälsingborg. He was an extraordinarily prolific composer; wrote 13 symphonies and 19 concertos for every instrument of the orchestra. His music reflected the type of Scandinavian Romanticism associated with Sibelius and Nielsen, pervaded by streaks of coherent polyphony.

WORKS: 13 symphonies: No. 1 (1928); No. 2 (1933); No. 3, *Sinfonia da chiesa* (1945); No. 4, *Uppstandelse (The Resurrection,* 1947); No. 5, *Aron Bergenson in memoriam* (1948); No. 6 (1952); No. 7 (1953); No. 8 (1954); No. 9 (1956); No. 10 (1957); No. 11, *Stabat Mater* (1959; Hälsingborg, March 26, 1961); No. 12 (1963; Hälsingborg, Nov. 28, 1963); No. 13 (1966); 2 sinfonias for string orch. (1953, 1954); 19 concertos: 2 for piano (1940, 1961); 2 for cello (1944, 1957); 2 for oboe (1950, 1957); 2 for English horn, with strings (1958, 1959) 2 for clarinet (1958, 1959); for bassoon (1959); for saxophone (1959); for violin (1960); for flute, with female choir, subtitled *Arets tider* (1962); for horn (1964); for trombone (1965); for trumpet (1965); for viola (1965); for double bass (1965–66); *Symphonic Variations* (1934); *Metamorphoses on a Theme by Clementi* for orch. (1951); *Passion* for cello and orch. (1961); *Stabat Mater* for soli, female chorus, strings and percussion (1956; Hälsingborg, March 17, 1957); *Vid korset,* oratorio (1957); 5 string quartets; Violin Sonata (1958); Cello Sonata (1960); piano pieces; organ pieces; songs.

Paulus, Olaf, Norwegian composer; b. Christiania, Jan. 25, 1859; d. Stavanger, June 29, 1912. Pupil of C. Cappelen and J. Svendsen, and at the Leipzig Cons.; from 1889 he was organist at the Cathedral in Stavanger; made a trip to the U.S. in 1902, directing choral concerts in Minneapolis and St. Paul. In his native country he is highly esteemed as a national composer; his men's choruses are in the repertory of all Norwegian societies; also wrote songs and piano pieces, and ed. a collection of songs, *De 1,000 hjems sange (Home Songs;* 1888).

Pauly, Rosa, Hungarian dramatic soprano; b. Eperjes, March 15, 1894; d. Herzlia, Israel, Dec. 14, 1975. She studied voice with Rosa Papier-Paumgartner in Vienna, and made her operatic debut at the Vienna Opera as Desdemona in Verdi's *Otello* in 1918. She subsequently sang in Hamburg, Cologne and Mannheim. From 1927-31 she was a member of the staff at the Kroll Opera in Berlin; she was also on the staff of the Vienna State Opera (1929-1935); in 1934 she sang the challenging role of Elektra in Strauss's opera in Salzburg, gathering encomiums; in 1935 she appeared at La Scala, Milan. She made her American debut as Elektra in a concert performance with the N.Y. Philharmonic on March 21, 1937; sang it again at her first appearance with the Metropolitan Opera on Jan. 7, 1938. She sang at the Teatro Colón in 1939. In 1946 she went to Palestine, and devoted herself to teaching in Tel Aviv, Israel. She was reputed to be one of the best dramatic sopranos of her era.

Paumann, Conrad, German organist; b. Nuremberg, between 1410 and 1415; d. Munich, Jan 24, 1473; He was born blind, but achieved mastery as organist, harpist, flutist and player on theorbo-lute. He was the chief contributor to the oldest extant organ book, *Fundamentum organisandi,* containing preludes and other pieces; it was publ. by Arnold in Chrysander's *Jahrbücher* (1867; reprints, Leipzig, 1926 and Wiesbaden, 1969); a facsimile reprint was brought out by K. Ameln in 1925. A specimen, in tablature with 7 lines for the right hand and letters for the left hand, is included in Schering's *Geschichte der Musik in Beispielen.* The oldest text of the *Fundamentum organisandi* (Anno 1492) is found at the Berlin Library.
BIBLIOGRAPHY: H. Abele, *Erinnerungen an einen grossen Münchener Tonmeister* (Munich, 1910); A. Schering, *Studien zur Musikgeschichte der Frührenaissance* (1914); Gustave Reese, *Music in the Renaissance* (N.Y., 1954).

Paumgartner, Bernhard, eminent Austrian musicologist and conductor; b. Vienna, Nov. 14, 1887; d. Salzburg, July 27, 1971. He was a son of **Hans Paumgartner** (1843-96) who was for many years a chorusmaster of the Vienna Court Opera, and of **Rosa Papier,** a well-known singer. He studied with Bruno Walter; in 1917 was engaged as director of the Mozarteum in Salzburg, which he headed until 1938, and again from 1945 to 1959. Shortly before his death he was elected an Honorary President of the Salzburg Festival. A versatile musician, he was active as conductor, composer and writer on musical subjects. He wrote an opera *Rossini in Neapel* (Zürich, March 27, 1936) and some other stage music, including the ballets *Pagoden* (Munich, 1927); *Ballo Medico* (Vienna, 1943); *Salzburger Divertimento* (Salzburg, 1955, using Mozart's music); *Ouvertüre zu einem ritterlichen Spiel,* for orch.; various instrumental pieces in a Baroque manner. Among his publications were *Mozart* (Berlin, 1927; revised edition, 1957); *Schubert* (Zürich, 1943); *J. S. Bach* (Zürich, 1950); contributed numerous articles on Mozart and on music in Salzburg. He published an autobiographical memoir *Erinnerungen* (Salzburg, 1969). A collection of his articles and essays was published posthumously (Kassel, 1973).

Paunović, Milenko, Serbian composer; b. Šajkaš, Nov. 28, 1889; d. Belgrade, Oct. 1, 1924. He studied in Leipzig with Max Reger and Hugo Riemann; became a choral conductor in Novi Sad. In his music he followed Wagnerian concepts, and wrote several music dramas to his own texts. He also composed a *Yugoslav Symphony* (Ljubljana, March 17, 1924).

Paur, Emil, Austrian conductor; b. Czernowitz, Bukovina, Aug. 29, 1855; d. Mistek, Bohemia, June 7, 1932. He was trained in the rudiments of music by his father, and played the violin and piano in public at the age of 8; at 11 he entered the Vienna Cons. where he studied violin with Hellmesberger and composition with Dessoff, graduating in 1870. He achieved an excellent reputation as a competent drillmaster, and in 1893 was engaged as conductor of the Boston Symph. Orch. to succeed Nikisch; he held this post for 5 seasons; from 1898 to 1902 he conducted the N.Y. Philharmonic Society; during the season of 1899-1900 he led the Wagner repertory at the Metropolitan Opera, N.Y.; from 1899 to 1902 he served as director of the National Cons. in N.Y., succeeding Dvořák; from 1902 to 1904 he filled engagements in Europe; in 1904 he was again engaged in the U.S., as conductor of the Pittsburgh Symph. Orch. (until 1910). In 1912 he returned to Berlin, but failed to impress the fastidious concert audiences there; for the rest of his life he conducted occasional engagements. He was married to the pianist **Maria Bürger** (1862-99).

Payne, Albert, German music publisher; b. Leipzig, June 3, 1842; d. there, April 1, 1921. From 1858-61, pupil at the Leipzig Cons. of David (violin), Dreyshock (piano), E. Fr. Richter and Hauptmann (theory); then for a short time of Massart in Paris. In 1862 he entered the publishing firm of his father; under the title *Payne's Kleine Kammermusik Partiturausgabe* he began in 1886 the publication of a low-priced pocket edition of chamber music of the Classical masters, which immediately met with pronounced favor, so that he soon added the works of the Romanticists; in 1892 he sold the edition (212 numbers) to Ernst Eulenburg, who enlarged its scope still futher.

Payne, Anthony, English composer; b. London, Aug. 2, 1936. He studied first at Dulwich College; read music at Durham Univ. (1958-61); then wrote music criticism for the *Daily Telegraph.* He is married to soprano **Jane Manning.** His style of composition follows the lines of intellectual neo-Classicism, peppered with dashes of modernistic atonalities and polytonalities.
WORKS: *Phoenix Mass* for chorus, 3 trumpets and 3 trombones (1965-72); *Paraphrases and Cadenzas* for clarinet, viola and piano (1969); *2 Songs Without Words* for 5 male voices a cappella (1970); *Sonatas and Ricercars* for wind quintet (1970-71); *Concerto for Orch.* (London, Jan. 8, 1975).

Payne, John, American composer; b. New York, May 23, 1941. He studied psychology at Brown Univ. (B.A., 1962); played in jazz bands. Bypassing the traditional forms of conventional modernism, he devoted his energies to total environmental art. He collaborated with Carol Law and Charles Amirkhanian in producing a live-electronic theater event *Ode to Gravity* (San Francisco, Sept. 21, 1968); staged the audience participation happenings *Thursday Mix* (San Francisco, March 27, 1969, a Thursday) and *Friday Mix* (San Francisco, May 2, 1969, a Friday). He also programmed a number of electronic scores, among them *Elevator Music* and *Toot le fromage*, making use of inchoate concrete noises.

Paz, Juan Carlos, significant Argentine composer; b. Buenos Aires, Aug. 5, 1901; d. there, Aug. 25, 1972. He studied composition with Constantino Gaito; in 1929, with several young composers of radical tendencies, he organized in Buenos Aires the "Grupo Renovación," and in 1937 inaugurated a series of concerts of new music. His early works are marked by strong polyphony, in a neo-Classical style; about 1927, he adopted atonal and polytonal procedures; in 1934 he began to compose almost exclusively in the 12-tone idiom; after 1950 he moderated his musical language, and even wrote pieces in simplified harmony.
WORKS: FOR ORCH.: *Movimiento sinfónico* (1930); Passacaglia, for 12 violas, 10 cellos, 10 double basses (1936; Paris Festival of the International Society for Contemporary Music, June 25, 1937); *Rítmica constante* (1951); *6 superposiciones* (1954); *Estructuras* (1962). CHAMBER MUSIC: *Tema y transformaciones*, for 11 wind instruments (1929); Wind Octet (1930); *Concierto No. 1*, for flute, oboe, clarinet, bassoon, trumpet, and piano (1932); *Concerto No. 2*, for oboe, trumpet, 2 French horns, bassoon, and piano (1934); *Composición dodecafónica* for flute and piano (1935); *Composición dodecafónica* for clarinet and piano (1937); Trio for flute, clarinet, and bassoon (1937); Trio for clarinet, trumpet, and saxophone (1937); Trio for flute, oboe and bass clarinet (1940); 3 string quartets (1938, 1942, 1961); *Dédalus 1950*, for flute, clarinet, violin, cello and piano (1951); *Continuidad* for percussion ensemble (1954); *Concreción* for 7 wind instruments (1964). FOR PIANO: 3 sonatas; *3 movimientos de jazz; 10 piezas sobre una serie dodecafónica*, etc. He publ. *Arnold Schoenberg o el fin de la era tonal* (Buenos Aires, 1954); *Introduccion a la música de nuestro tiempo* (Buenos Aires, 1955); also published an autobiographical volume, *Alturas, tensiones, ataques, intensidades* (Buenos Aires, 1972).
BIBLIOGRAPHY: J. C. Beschinsky, *Juan Carlos Paz*, (Buenos Aires, 1964); Hector J. Galla, "La Obra Musical de Juan Carlos Paz," *Boletín Latino-Americano de Música*, and F. C. Lange, "Juan Carlos Paz" (ibidem, vol. IV).

Peace, Albert Lister, English organist and composer; b. Huddersfield, Jan. 26, 1844; d. Liverpool, March 14, 1912. He played organ in the parish church as a child; in 1865, he became organist in Glasgow; then studied at Oxford Univ. (Mus. Bac., 1870; Mus. Doc., 1875). From 1879 to 1897 he was organist at Glasgow Cathedral; in 1897, became successor to W. T. Best as organist of St. George's Hall in Liverpool. He wrote a cantata, *St. John the Baptist; Psalm 138* for soli, chorus, and orch.; many organ pieces; anthems; church services.

Pearce, Stephen Austen, English-American organist and composer; b. London, Nov. 7, 1836; d. Jersey City, N.J., April 9, 1900. He was a graduate of Oxford Univ. (Mus. Bac., 1859; Mus. Doc., 1864). In 1872 he settled in America; taught vocal music at Columbia College, N.Y.: also at the Peabody Institute, Baltimore. He wrote an opera, *La Belle Américaine;* a dramatic oratorio, *Celestial Visions;* a church cantata, *The Psalm of Praise;* piano pieces; songs; compiled *A Pocket Dictionary of Musical Terms* in 21 languages (N.Y., 1889).

Pears, Sir Peter, English tenor; b. Farnham, June 22, 1910. He studied at the Royal College of Music in London; during the season of 1936–37 toured the U.S. as a member of the New English Singers. In 1938 he joined Benjamin Britten in a series of recitals devoted mainly to contemporary English composers, with Britten acting as his accompanist. In 1948 he was a co-founder with Britten of the Aldeburgh Festival. Pears sang leading tenor parts in almost all of Britten's operas: *Peter Grimes, The Rape of Lucretia, Albert Herring, Billy Budd, Gloriana, The Turn of the Screw* and *Death in Venice;* he also sang the tenor solo part in Britten's *War Requiem*. He was knighted by Queen Elizabeth II in 1978.

Pearsall, Robert Lucas de, English composer; b. Clifton, March 14, 1795; d. Wartensee, on Lake Constance, Aug. 5, 1856. He studied law and music; as a boy of 13 wrote a cantata, *Saul and the Witch of Endor.* He lived many years in Germany, where he publ. many of his compositions; was in London on several extended visits; in 1842, purchased a castle on Lake Constance, and remained there for the rest of his life. As a composer, he was at his best in many ingenious madrigals; particularly popular were his part-songs, *Sir Patrick Spens, The Hardy Norseman,* and *O who will o'er the downs so free;* he edited old church music in Germany; publ. an *Essay on Consecutive Fifths and Octaves in Counterpoint.*
BIBLIOGRAPHY: W. Barclay Squire, "Letters of R. L. Pearsall," *Musical Quarterly* (April 1919).

Pechner, Gerhard, German baritone; b. Berlin, 1903; d. New York, Oct. 21, 1969. He made his first appearance as an opera singer in Berlin in 1927; was compelled to leave Germany in 1933; from 1933 till 1939 he was on the staff of the German Opera House in Prague. In 1940 he was engaged by the San Francisco Opera, and in 1941 made his debut at the Metropolitan Opera in New York. He particularly distinguished himself in Wagnerian roles.

Pedrell, Carlos, Uruguayan composer; b. Minas, Uruguay, Oct. 16, 1878; d. Montrouge, near Paris, March 3, 1941. He studied in Madrid with his uncle, **Felipe Pedrell;** later went to Paris, where he took lessons with Vincent d'Indy and Bréville at the Schola Cantorum. Returning to South America, he was inspector of music in the Buenos Aires schools; lectured at the Univ. of Tucumán; in 1921 he went to Paris, where he remained for the rest of his life. His works are cast in French style, but the rhythmic elements are related to Spanish and South American sources; his songs, with richly developed accompaniments, are the best among his works.

WORKS: the operas *Ardid de Amor* (Buenos Aires, June 7, 1917), *Cuento de Abril*, and *La Guitare* (Madrid, 1924); the ballets *La Rose et le gitan* (Antwerp, 1930) and *Alleluia* (Buenos Aires, 1936); for orch.: *Une Nuit de Schéhérazade* (1908), *Danza y canción de Aixa* (1910), *En el estrado de Beatriz* (1910), *Fantasia Argentina* (1910), *Ouverture Catalane* (1912), *Pastorales*, for voice and orch. (Paris, 1928); choruses; songs.

BIBLIOGRAPHY: A. Suarès, "Carlos Pedrell," *Revue Musicale* (June 1931).

Pedrell, Felipe, eminent Spanish musicologist and composer; b. Tortosa, Feb. 19, 1841; d. Barcelona, Aug. 19, 1922. A chorister in the Cathedral of Tortosa, his musical studies were guided by J. A. Nin y Serra. His prolific literary career began in 1867, with articles in various mus. reviews; his first opera, *El último Abencerrage*, was produced at Barcelona in 1874. After a visit to Italy and a sojourn in Paris, he settled in Barcelona (1882), where he founded the *Salterio Sacro-Hispano* for the publication of contemporary religious music, and the weekly review *Notas Musicales y Literarias*, both of which ceased publication in 1883. In 1888 he founded the *Ilustración Musical Hispano-Americana*, which he edited until its demise in 1896. In 1889–91 he composed his great dramatic trilogy, *Los Pirineos*, and as a sort of introduction to this work he wrote his famous pamphlet *Por nuestra música*, a plea for the creation of a national lyric drama on the basis of the national folksong. In 1891–92, critic for the *Diario de Barcelona*; in 1894 he went to Madrid, where he was made a member of the Royal Academy of Fine Arts; also prof. at the Madrid Cons. (1895–1903) and lecturer on music history at the Madrid Ateneo. He was also invited to direct the reform of religious music in Spain; ed. the review *Música religiosa*, 1896–99. At the end of 1904 he returned to Barcelona as artistic director for the publishing firm of Vidal y Llimona, which revived the *Salterio Sacro-Hispano*. There he spent the rest of his life, writing, teaching, and composing. Among his pupils were Albéniz, Granados, Manuel de Falla, and Gerhard. Though highly praised by contemporary critics, his music has not obtained recognition outside of Spain; but the importance of his achievement in bringing to light the treasures of Spain's musical past is universally recognized, and he is considered the leading spirit of the modern Spanish nationalist revival in music. On his 70th birthday Pedrell was honored by the publication of a Festschrift, *Al Maestro Pedrell: Escritos heortásticos*, with contributions from the foremost musical scholars throughout the world.

WORKS: OPERAS: *El último Abencerrage* (Barcelona, April 14, 1874); *Quasimodo* (Barcelona, April 20, 1875); *Mazeppa* and *Tasse à Ferrare* (both on 1-act French texts, Madrid, 1881); *Cléopâtre* (4-act, French text); *Los Pirineos*, his most ambitious effort, a trilogy consisting of a Prologue and the 3 dramas *El Conde de Foix*, *Rayo de Luna*, and *La Jornada de Panissars* (the Prologue produced separately in Venice, March 12, 1897; the entire work, Barcelona, Jan. 4, 1902); *La Celestina* (not produced); *Matinada* (really a dramatic

cantata; produced scenically, Barcelona, Oct. 27, 1905). FOR ORCH.: the symph. poems *Excelsior* (after Longfellow); *El Conde Aranau* and *Glosa* (both with chorus); *Cant de la Montanya*, 'symph. scenes'; *I Trionfi*, suite after Petrarch; *Marcia a Mistral*. VOCAL WORKS: *Canço latina* for chorus and orch.; *Messa di Gloria* for soli, chorus, organ, and orch.; Requiem a cappella; *Hymne à Ste. Thérèse;* motets and antiphons; songs (from V. Hugo's *Les Orientales*, Th. Gauthier's *Consolations*, etc.). Also string quartet, etc.; 302 opus numbers in all. He edited the collections *Hispaniae Schola musica sacra*, works of Morales, Guerrero, Victoria, Cabezón, Ginés Pérez, Diego Ortiz (8 vols.); *Teatro lírico español anterior al siglo XIX* (5 vols., 1897–98); *Salterio Sacro-Hispano* (1905); *Antología de organistas clásicos de España* (2 vols., 1905, 1908); the complete works of Victoria (8 vols., 1903–13; with biography in vol. VIII); *Cancionero popular español* (Barcelona, 1919–20, 4 vols.; new ed., 2 vols., 1936).

WRITINGS: *Diccionario técnico de la música* (1894); *Teatro lírico español anterior al siglo XIX* (1897–98; 5 vols. in 1); *Prácticas preparatorias de instrumentación* (1902); *Emporio científico e histórico de organografía musical antigua española* (1901); *Musicalerías* (1906); *Catálech de la Biblioteca musical de la Diputació de Barcelona* (2 vols., 1908, 1909); *Jean I. d'Aragon, compositeur de musique* (1909; in Riemann-Festschrift); *Tomás Luis de Victoria* (1918; reprinted from vol. VIII of collected works); *P. Antonio Eximeno* (1921). Of a valuable *Diccionario biográfico y bibliográfico de músicos y escritores de música españoles, portugueses y hispano-americanos antiguos y modernos*, only vol. I appeared (A-G; 1894–97). He publ. a book of reminiscences, *Jornadas de Arte* (Paris, 1911). His collected essays and critical writings were publ. in Paris in 3 vols., *Orientaciones, Musiquerías, Lírica nacionalizada* (1911–13). A complete list of Pedrell's works was publ. by A. Reiff in *Archiv für Musikwissenschaft* III/1 (1921).

BIBLIOGRAPHY: G. Tebaldini, *Felipe Pedrell ed il dramma lirico spagnuolo* (Turin, 1897); R. Mitjana, *La Música contemporanea en España y Felipe Pedrell* (Málaga, 1901); H. de Curzon, *Felipe Pedrell et "Les Pyrénées"* (Paris, 1902); "Felipe Pedrell," *La Nouvelle Revue* (Jan. 1912); A. Reiff, "Felipe Pedrell," *Zeitschrift für Musikwissenschaft* (Feb. 1921); Manuel de Falla, "Felipe Pedrell," *Revue Musicale* (Feb. 1923); E. Istel, "Felipe Pedrell," *Musical Quarterly* (April 1925).

Pedrollo, Arrigo, Italian composer; b. Montebelli, near Vicenza, Dec. 5, 1878; d. Vicenza, Dec. 23, 1964. He studied at the Cons. of Milan (1891–1900); at his graduation wrote a symphony, which was performed by Toscanini. In 1914 he won the Sonzogno competition with his opera *Juana*. His other operas include *Terra promessa* (Cremona, 1908); *La Veglia* (Milan, Jan. 2, 1920); *L'Uomo che ride* (Rome, March 6, 1920); *Maria di Magdala* (Milan, 1924); *Delitto e castigo*, after Dostoyevsky's *Crime and Punishment* (La Scala, Milan, Nov. 16, 1926); *L'Amante in trappola* (Verona, Sept. 22, 1936); *Il Giglio di Ali* (1948).

Pedrotti, Antonio, Italian conductor and pedagogue; b. Trento, Aug. 14, 1901; d. there, May 16, 1975. He was a student of Respighi in composition at the Conservatorio di Santa Cecilia in Rome; in 1929 returned to Trento, his native town, where he became director of the local conservatory. He conducted the Augusteum Orch. in Rome from 1938 to 1944.

Pedrotti, Carlo, Italian composer and conductor; b. Verona, Nov. 12, 1817; d. there, Oct. 16, 1893 (suicide). He was a pupil of Domenico Foroni; obtained an excellent success with his first opera, *Lina* (Verona, 1840); was then engaged as conductor of the Italian Opera at Amsterdam; he wrote 2 operas there, *Mathilde* (1841) and *La Figlia del Arciere* (1844). He returned to Verona in 1845 and presented there his operas *Romea di Monfort* (1846), *Fiorina* (1851), *Il Parrucchiere della reggenza* (1852), and *Tutti in maschera* (Nov. 4, 1856; his principal work; also performed in Paris); the following were given in Milan: *Gelmina* (1853), *Genoveffa del Brabante* (1854), *La Guerra in quattro* (1861); also *Isabella d'Arragona* (Turin, 1859), *Mazeppa* (Bologna, 1861), *Marion Delorme* (Trieste, 1865), *Il Favorito* (Turin, 1870), and *Olema la schiava* (Modena, 1872).

Peellaert, Augustin-Philippe-Marie-Ghislain, Baron de, Belgian composer; b. Bruges, March 12, 1793; d. Brussels, April 16, 1876. He studied in Paris with Momigny; in 1832, became a member of the executive board of the Brussels Cons. He wrote Masses and other sacred works; chamber music; songs; several operas, of which the following were produced in Brussels: *L'Heure du rendez-vous* (1821), *Agnès Sorel* (Aug. 30, 1823), *Le Barmècide* (1824), *Teniers ou La Noce flamande* (Feb. 21, 1825), *L'Exilé* (1827), *Faust* (1834), *Le Coup de pistolet* (1836), *Louis de Male* (1838); publ. an autobiography, *Cinquante ans de souvenirs* (Brussels, 1867).

Peerce, Jan (real name **Jacob Pincus Perelmuth**), American tenor; b. New York, June 3, 1904. He played the violin in dance bands, and sang at various entertainment places in N.Y. In 1933 he was engaged as a singer at the Radio City Music Hall, N.Y.; made his operatic debut in Philadelphia as the Duke in *Rigoletto* (May 14, 1938), and gave his first solo recital in N.Y. on Nov. 7, 1939. His lyrical voice attracted attention and he was engaged by the Metropolitan Opera Co.; made his debut there as Alfredo in *La Traviata* on Nov. 29, 1941; sang also the parts of Cavaradossi in *Tosca*, Rodolfo in *La Bohème* and Faust in Gounod's opera; remained on the staff of the Metropolitan until 1962; continued to appear as a solo singer in his early 70s.
BIBLIOGRAPHY: Alan Levy, *The Bluebird of Happiness: The Memoirs of Jan Peerce* (N.Y., 1977).

Peeters, Flor, outstanding Belgian organist and composer; b. Thielen, July 4, 1903. He studied with J. Brandt and Mortelmans. From 1923 to 1952 he was prof. of organ at the Lemmens Institute in Malines; from 1948 to 1968 he was a prof. of organ at the Antwerp Cons.; in 1968 he inaugurated a series of international master courses in organ at the Cathedral of Malines. He became renowned as a master improviser on the organ; he wrote nearly 500 works for organ, which were publ. in several collections with titles in English: *60 Short Pieces* (1955); *30 Short Chorale-Preludes* (1959); *213 Hymn Preludes for the Liturgical Year* (in 24 installments, 1959–67); *6 Lyrical Pieces* (1960);. He further wrote several cantatas and numerous choruses a cappella. Other publications include *Ars Organi; Little Organ Book* and *Antologia pro organo.*
BIBLIOGRAPHY: Piet Visser, *Flor Peeters, Organist* (Turnhout, 1950; in Flemish).

Peiko, Nicolai, Russian composer; b. Moscow, March 25, 1916. He studied with Miaskovsky at the Moscow Cons., graduating in 1939. He then was commissioned to collect folksong materials in the remote Yakutsk district of Siberia; wrote a *Suite on Yakutsk Themes* for orch. (1941); then investigated Bashkir music, and composed a Bashkir opera, *Aykhylu;* also a Tartar ballet, *Spring Winds* (1950). Other works include 3 symphonies (1944; 1946; 1950) and a *Suite on Russian Themes* for orch. (1949); *Festive Overture* on Kabardin themes (1951); a *Concert Fantasy* on Finnish themes, for violin and orch. (1953); Piano Concerto (1954); piano pieces; songs. His most successful work is a *Moldavian Suite,* for orch. (Moscow, Dec. 14, 1950).

Peixinho, Jorge, avant-garde Portuguese composer; b. Montijo, Jan. 20, 1940. He studied piano at the Lisbon Cons. (1951–58); then went to Italy where he took lessons with Goffredo Petrassi at the Santa Cecilia Academy in Rome (1959–61) and with Luigi Nono in Venice; later attended the seminars of Boulez and Stockhausen at the Basel Cons. (1962–63); in addition, worked at the electronic studio in Ghent, Belgium (1972–73). In 1974 he was appointed to the music faculty at the New Univ. of Lisbon.
WORKS: *Alba* for soprano, contralto, female chorus and 11 instruments (1959); *Fascinação* for soprano, flute and piano (1959); *Políptico* for chamber orch. (1960); *Sobreposições* for orch. (1960); *Episodes* for string quartet (1960); Saxophone Concerto (1961); *Sucessões simétricas* for piano (1961); *Collage I* for 2 pianos (1962); *Diafonia* for harp, celesta, piano, harpsichord, metal percussion and 12 strings (1963); *Morfocromia* for 2 instrumental groups (1963); *Dominó* for flute and 3 percussion groups (1964); *Sequência* for flute in G, celesta, vibraphone and percussion (1964); *Kinetofonias* for 25 strings (1965); *Situação 66* for flute, clarinet, trumpet, harp and viola (1966); *Harmónicos* for piano and 2 tapes (1967); *Nomos* for orch. (1967); *Eurídice Reamada* for 5 soloists, chorus and orch. (1968); *As Quatro Estações* for trumpet, cello, harp, piano and tape (1968); *CDE* for clarinet, violin, cello and piano (1970); *A Idade do Ouro* for clarinet, violin, harp, piano, organ and tape (1970); *A Lira Destemperada* for soprano, trombone and percussion (1972); *Voix* for soprano and chamber orch. (1972); *Morrer em Santiago* for 6 percussionists (1973); *Elegia a Amílcar Cabral* for 4-track tape (1973); incidental and film music.

Pekov, Mihail, Bulgarian composer; b. Vidin, Aug. 6, 1941. He studied composition with Veselin Stoyanov at the Bulgarian State Cons., graduating in 1967; then went to Leningrad where he took courses with Salmanov at the Leningrad Cons.

WORKS: Piano Concerto (1965); Violin Concerto (1965); Concerto for Orch. (1970); *Double Concerto* for violin, cello and orch. (1970); *Music for Chamber Ensemble No. 1* (1970) and *No. 2* (1973); *Partita* for flute, viola, harp and harpsichord (1971); 3 string quartets (all 1973); Symph. (1974); Overture (1975).

Pelemans, Willem, Belgian composer; b. Antwerp, April 8, 1901. He studied music history at the Cons. of Malines; then engaged in music journalism. A highly prolific composer, he adopted an attractive idiom of writing music in a romantic manner.

WORKS: a comic opera *De mannen van Smeerop* (1952; Brussels, 1963); 3 chamber operas: *La Rose de Bakawali* (1938), *Le Combat de la vierge et du diable* (1949) and *De nozem en de nimf* (1960); a musical tale *Het Tinnen Soldaatje (Le Petit Soldat de plomb),* after Andersen (1945); a lyrical drama *Floris en Blancefloer* (1947); 3 ballets: *Miles gloriosus* (1945), *Herfstgoud (Automnal,* 1959) and *Pas de quatre* (1969); an oratorio *De wandelende jood* (1929); the cantatas *Diederik en Katrina* (1957), *De vogel van sneeuw* (1964), *Piet en de pijp (Pierre et la pipe,* 1963; for children) and *'t Pelske* (1976); 6 symphonies (1936, 1937, 1937, 1938, 1938, 1939); 8 ballades for orch. (1933–35); 5 concertos for orch. (1948, 1955, 1957, 1961, 1966); 5 concertinos for chamber orch. (1948; 1949; 1950; for strings, 1958; 1966); *Schetsen voor een buffa-opera* for chamber orch. (1952); *Ouvertura Buffa* for orch. (1959); *Petite Suite* for orch. (1962); concertos for harpsichord (1931), 3 for piano (1945, 1950, 1967), violin (1954), viola (1963) 2 trumpets (with strings, 1963), organ (1965), 2 pianos (1973) and saxophone (1976); Concertino for Cello and Strings (1961); Sextet for brasses (1968); *Petite Suite* for string sextet (1967); 2 wind quintets (1948, 1968); Quintet for flute, clarinet, violin, viola and cello (1950); Quintet for harp, flute, violin, viola and cello (1962); 8 string quartets (1942, 1943, 1943, 1943, 1944, 1955, 1961, 1970); 2 quartets for 4 clarinets (1961, 1976); Saxophone Quartet (1965); Wind Quartet (1965); Piano Quartet (1967); 3 piano trios (1932, 1942, 1972); *Pas de trois* for piano trio; 3 trios for oboe, clarinet and bassoon (1940, 1941, 1960); 2 sonatas for flute, oboe, and piano (1955, 1956); String Trio (1945); Trio for 2 violins and piano (1957); Brass Sonata for trumpet, horn and trombone (1955); Trio for 2 oboes and English horn (1971); 3 violin sonatas (all 1942); Solo Violin Sonata (1955); Viola Sonata (1945); *Walssonate* for viola and piano (1949); Cello Sonata (1959); Solo Cello Sonata (1947); Sonata for cello and bassoon (1946); Sonata for flute, oboe, and harpsichord or piano (1959); Sonata for flute and harp (1967); Clarinet Sonata (1961); Clarinet Sonatina (1961); *Concertstuk* for clarinet and piano (1967); *Suite* for trumpet and piano (1944); Sonata for 2 guitars (1967); *Suite* for 2 guitars (1968); *6 Etudes* for 2 guitars (1974); *6 Nocturnes* for harpsichord (1930); 7 *Personages van James Ensor* for harpsichord (1933); *Studie* for harpsichord (1966); for piano: 19 sonatas (1935–69); Sonata for 4 hands (1961); 3 toccatas (1948, 1951, 1951); 4 suites (1932–33); *10 Banalities* (1944); 2 sonatas for 2 pianos (1947, 1954); for voice: *3 Liederen* for vocal quartet and wind quintet (1944); *Japanese*

verzen for soprano, alto, baritone and piano (1958); *Haikai* for middle voice, flute *(ad lib.)* and harp (1967). Among his publications are the brochures *Architectonische muziek* (1927), *Muziek beluisteren* (1932), *Geest en Klank* (1943) and *De Vlaamse muziek en P. Benoit* (1971).

Pelissier, Victor, horn virtuoso and composer. His name appears first in 1792 on Philadelphia concert programs as "first horn of the Theatre in Cape François." In 1793 he went to New York, where he lived for many years, and became the principal horn player, also composer and arranger, of the Old American Co.

WORKS: the operas *Edwin and Angelina or The Banditti* (N.Y., John Street Theater, Dec. 19, 1796), *Ariadne Abandoned by Theseus in the Isle of Naxos* (N.Y., 1797), and *Sterne's Maria or The Vintage* (1799); incidental music to about 18 plays performed in N.Y. (mostly in 1794–96), including *Fourth of July or Temple of American Independence* (1799), *Castle of Otranto* (adaptation of *Sicilian Romance*), etc.; various pantomimes performed in Philadelphia; a quartet; and a few separate pieces. In 1811 he publ. the collection *Columbian Melodies,* which contains 3 songs from *Sterne's Maria.*

BIBLIOGRAPHY: O. G. Sonneck, *Early Opera in America* (N.Y., 1915); J. T. Howard, *Our American Music* 4th ed.; N.Y., 1965; *Sammelbände der Internationalen Musik-Gesellschaft* VI, 475.

Pellegrini, Vincenzo, Italian composer and organist; b. Pesaro, late 16th century; d. Milan, 1636. He was a canon at Pesaro (1603) and maestro di cappella at the cathedral of Milan (1611–31). His extant works include *Canzoni da intavolatura d'organo fatte alla francese* (Venice, 1599); *Missarum a 4 e 5 voci* (Venice, 1603); sacred vocal pieces with organ accompaniment, published under the title *Concerti ecclesiastici da 1, 2, 3, 5 e 6 voci* (Venice, 1619); other compositions are in the collections *Parnassus musicus Ferdinandoeus* (Venice, 1615); 2 canzone (*La Serpentina* and *La Capricciosa*) in Torchi's *L'Arte Musicale in Italia* (vol. III).

Pelletier, Wilfrid, Canadian conductor; b. Montreal, June 20, 1896. Of a musical family, he received his primary music education at home; in 1914 went to Paris where he studied piano with Isidor Philipp and composition with Widor. Returning to America in 1917, he was engaged as opera coach at the Metropolitan Opera, N.Y.; in 1950 he became a principal conductor there, specializing particularly in the French repertory; at the same time he filled conducting engagements at the Ravinia Opera and the San Francisco Opera; in 1942 became director of the Cons. in Montreal, and from 1951 to 1962 was conductor of the Orchestre Symphonique in Quebec; in 1968 became artistic consultant to the Canadian Ministry of Culture and settled in Montreal. He was married to the singer **Queena Mario** (1925–36); in 1937 he married the soprano singer **Rose Bampton.** He published an autobiographical sketch *Une Symphonie inachevée* (Quebec, 1972).

Pelton-Jones, Frances, American harpsichordist; b. Salem, Oregon, Dec. 6, 1863; d. New York, April 24, 1946. She studied piano with Carl Faelten at the New England Cons. in Boston; organ with Dudley Buck and William C. Carl in N.Y.; became interested in harpsichord playing and attained considerable proficiency at it; presented a special series of harpsichord recitals in New York under the name "Salons Intimes," which she continued for 20 years.

Pembaur, Joseph, Jr., Austrian pianist; son of **Joseph Pembaur, Sr.;** b. Innsbruck, April 20, 1875; d. Munich, Oct. 12, 1950. He was a pupil of his father; then studied with Rheinberger and Thuille at the Munich Academy of Music; was prof. of piano at the Munich Musikschule (1897–1900); subsequently was on the faculty of the Leipzig Cons. (1902–21); in 1921, appointed prof. at the Munich Academy of Music. He wrote a violin sonata; a number of songs; publ. *Von der Poesie des Klavierspiels* (1910; 2nd ed., 1911).
BIBLIOGRAPHY: C. Werner, *Joseph Pembaur zum 60. Geburtstag* (Berlin, 1935).

Pembaur, Joseph, Sr., Austrian composer and teacher; b. Innsbruck, May 23, 1848; d. there, Feb. 19, 1923. He studied at the Vienna Cons. with Bruckner and in Munich with Rheinberger and others. In 1874 he was appointed director of the Innsbruck Music School; retired in 1918.
WORKS: opera, *Der Bauer von Langwall* (Innsbruck, May 2, 1898); a symph. tableau, *In Tirol;* a Requiem (in memory of the Tyrolese fallen in World War I; 1916); an organ sonata; numerous male choruses a cappella; also publ. *Harmonie- und Modulatinonslehre* (1910) and *Über das Dirigieren* (1892).

Pembaur, Karl Maria, Austrian organist and conductor; son of **Joseph Pembaur, Sr.;** b. Innsbruck, Aug. 24, 1876; d. Dresden, March 6, 1939. He studied with his father; then with Rheinberger at the Munich Academy of Music. In 1901 he went to Dresden, where he became court organist and choral conductor; also conducted at the Dresden Opera. He wrote the Singspiel *Seien Sie vorsichtig; Geistliche Sonette* for 5 solo voices and piano; *Bergbilder,* for woodwind quintet and piano; marches; songs; publ. *Drei Jahrhunderte Kirchenmusik am sächsischen Hofe* (Dresden, 1920).

Peña Costa, Joaquín, Spanish musicologist; b. Barcelona, March 1, 1873; d. there, June 25, 1944. He studied law at the Univ. of Barcelona, but devoted himself mainly to musical journalism; translated librettos of Wagner's operas into Catalan; arranged vocal scores of *Tristan und Isolde, Lohengrin, Tannhäuser,* and *Die Meistersinger;* ed. 5 vols. of songs of Beethoven, Schubert, Fauré, etc. under the title *Canconer selecte.* In 1940 he began work on a large music dictionary in Spanish; it was completed by H. Anglès, and publ. as *Diccionario de Música Labor* (Barcelona, 1954; 2 vols.; of limited value owing to a multitude of errors).

Peña y Goñi, Antonio, Spanish writer on music; b. San Sebastián, Nov. 2, 1846; d. Madrid, Nov. 13, 1896. He studied at the Cons. of Madrid; for 30 years was music critic of the periodical *Imparcial,* in which he carried on earnest propaganda for Wagner, whom he knew personally. He composed a cantata, *Viva Hernani* (1875), and some minor choral and piano works; publ. the important historical book, *La Opera española y la música dramática en España en el siglo XIX* (1881); also *La Obra maestra de Verdi* (1875), *Impressiones musicales* (1878), *Charles Gounod* (1879), guides to Wagner's operas, etc.

Penderecki, Krzysztof, foremost Polish composer of the 20th-century avant-garde; b. Debica, Nov. 23, 1933. (His name is pronounced Krzhysh'-tof Pende-rets'-kee, not Penderekee). He studied theory with Arthur Malawski and Stanislaw Wiechowicz at the Superior School of Music in Cracow, matriculating in 1958; after graduation he taught there (1958–66); went to West Germany and taught at the Folkwang Hochschule für Musik in Essen (1966–72); in 1973 became a part-time member of the faculty at Yale Univ.; also gave courses at Aspen, Colorado (1977). He rapidly acquired a reputation as one of the most original composers of his generation. In 1975 he was made an honorary member of the Royal Academy of Music in London, the Arts Academy of West Berlin, the Arts Academy of the German Democratic Republic, and the Royal Academy of Music in Stockholm. After a few works of an academic nature, he developed a hyper-modern technique of composition in a highly individual style, in which no demarcation line is drawn between consonances and dissonances, tonal or atonal melody, traditional or innovating instrumentation; an egalitarian attitude prevails towards all available resources of sound. While Penderecki's idiom is naturally complex, he does not disdain tonality, even in its overt triadic forms. In his creative evolution, he has bypassed orthodox serial procedures; his music follows an athematic course, in constantly varying metrical and rhythmic patterns. He utilizes an entire spectrum of modern sonorities, expanding the domain of tone to unpitched elements, making use of such effects as shouting, hissing and verbal ejaculations in vocal parts, at times reaching a climax of aleatory glossolalia; tapping, rubbing or snapping the fingers against the body of an instrument; striking the piano strings by mallets, etc. For this he designed an optical notation, with symbolic ideograms indicating the desired sound; thus a black isosceles triangle denotes the highest possible pitch; an inverted isosceles triangle, the lowest possible pitch; a black rectangle for a sonic complex of white noise within a given interval; vertical lines tied over by an arc for arpeggios below the bridge of a string instrument; wavy lines of varying amplitudes for extensive vibrato; curvilinear figures for aleatory passages; dots and dashes for repetitions of a pattern; sinusoidal oscillations for quaquaversal glissandos; etc. He applies these modern devices to religious music, including masses in the orthodox Roman Catholic ritual.
WORKS: *Psalmy Dawida (Psalms of David)* for chorus, 2 pianos, celesta, harp, 4 double basses and percussion (1958; Cracow, June 26, 1962); *Emanacje (Emanations)* for 2 orchestras of string instruments (1958–59); *Strofy (Strophes)* for soprano, narrator and 10 instruments (1959; Warsaw Sept. 17, 1959); *3 Min-*

iatures for violin and piano (1959); *Anaklasis* for 42 strings and percussion (1959–60; Baden-Baden, Oct. 16, 1960); *Wymiary czasu i ciszy (Dimensions of Time and Silence)* for wordless chorus, strings and percussion (1960; Warsaw, Sept. 18, 1960); *Tren pamieci ofiarom Hiroszimy (Threnody in Memory of Victims of Hiroshima)* for 52 string instruments, Penderecki's most impressive and most frequently performed work, rich in dynamic contrasts and ending on a tone cluster of two octavefuls of icositetraphonic harmony (1959–60; Warsaw Radio May 31, 1961); String Quartet No. 1 (1960); *Fonogrammi* for 3 flutes, strings and percussion (1961); *Psalmus*, electronic music (1961); *Polymorphia* for 48 string instruments (1961; Hamburg, April 16, 1962; perf. as a ballet under the title *Noctiphobie*, Amsterdam, 1970); *Stabat Mater* for 3 choruses a cappella (1962; an independent section of the *St. Luke Passion*); *Kanon* for 52 string instruments and tape (1962; Warsaw, Sept. 20, 1962); *Fluorescences* for orch. (1962; Baden-Baden, Oct. 21, 1962); *Cantata in Honorem Almae Matris Universitatis Jagellonicae* for chorus and orch. (1964); *Mensura Sortis* for 2 pianos (1964); Sonata for cello and orch. (1964); *Capriccio* (No. 1) for oboe and 11 strings (1965); *Passio et mors Domini Nostri Jesu Christi secundum Lucam (Passion According to St. Luke)* for narrator, soprano, baritone, bass, boys' chorus, 3 mixed choruses, and orch. (1962–65; Cathedral in Münster, West Germany, March 30, 1966; a specially commissioned work); *De Natura Sonoris* (No. 1) for orch. (1965–66; Royan, April 7, 1966); *Dies Irae*, oratorio for soprano, tenor, bass, chorus and orch. (1966–67; Cracow April 14, 1967; also performed two days later as a commemorative service at the site of the Nazi concentration camp at Oświecim-Brzezinka); Concerto for Violino Grande and Orch. (1967; Östersund, Sweden, July 1, 1967; revised version, Hanover, N.H., Aug. 4, 1968; the solo instrument is specially constructed with 5 strings); *Capriccio* (No. 2) for violin and orch. (1967; Donaueschingen, Oct. 22, 1967); *Pittsburgh Overture* for wind ensemble (1967; commissioned by the American Wind Symphony Orch. in Pittsburgh); *Capriccio per Siegfried Palm* for solo cello (1968); String Quartet No. 2 (1968); *De Natura Sonoris No. 2* for winds, percussion and strings (1968; Juilliard School of Music, N.Y., Dec. 3, 1971); a 3-act opera, *Die Teufel von Loudun (The Devils of Loudon)*, dealing with a *furor uterinus* among nuns of Loudun struck by a multifutuent incubus personified by a neighboring monastic youth (1968–69; Hamburg, June 20, 1969); *Utrenja (Morning Prayer)* in 2 parts (1969–71): *Grablegung Christi (The Entombment of Christ)* for soprano, contralto, tenor, bass, basso profundo, 2 choruses and orch., to a text in old Slavonic (Cathedral in Altenberg, April 8, 1970) and *Auferstehung Christi (Resurrection of Christ)* for the same soloists, boys' chorus, 2 mixed choruses and orch. (Münster Cathedral, May 28, 1971); *Kosmogonia* for soprano, tenor, bass, chorus and orch., commissioned by the United Nations and performed for the first time at its New York headquarters building (1970; Oct. 24, 1970); *Actions* for jazz ensemble (1971; Donaueschingen, Oct. 17, 1971); *Prélude* for winds, percussion and double basses (1971; Holland Festival, Amsterdam, July 4, 1971); *Partita*, concerto for harpsichord, 4 oth-er electronically amplified solo instruments, and chamber orch. (1971; Eastman School of Music, Rochester, N.Y., Feb. 11, 1972); Cello Concerto (1972; Edinburgh Festival, Sept. 2, 1972); *Ecloga VIII* for 6 male voices a cappella (1972; Edinburgh Fest., Aug. 21, 1972); *Ekecheireia* for tape (1972); *Canticum Canticorum Salomonis (Song of Songs)* for 16-voice chorus, chamber orch. and *ad lib.* dance pair (1970–73; Lisbon, June 5, 1973); Symphony No. 1 (1973; London, July 19, 1973); *Intermezzo* for 24 strings (1973); *Magnificat* for bass solo, vocal group, 2 choruses, boys' chorus and orch. (1973–74; Salzburg, Aug. 17, 1974); *Als Jakob erwachte* for voices, orch. and 12 ocarinas (1974; Monte Carlo, Aug. 14, 1974); an opera *Raj utracony (Paradise Lost)*, after Milton (1976–78); *De Profundis* for chorus and orch. (1977; Graz, Oct. 16, 1977).

Penfield, Smith Newell, American organist and teacher; b. Oberlin, Ohio, April 4, 1837; d. New York, Jan. 7, 1920. After preliminary study of the piano in N.Y., he went to Leipzig, where he took lessons from Moscheles, Reinecke, Plaidy, and Papperitz (piano), Richter (organ), and Hauptmann (theory). Returning to America, he conducted various choral societies; from 1882 was active in N.Y. as church organist and teacher. He wrote a piano sonata, subtitled *Poem of Life;* some sacred music; songs; piano pieces.

Penherski, Zbigniew, Polish composer; b. Warsaw, Jan. 26, 1935. He studied composition with Poradowski and Szeligowski at the Warsaw Cons., graduating in 1959.

WORKS: an opera, *The Waning of Perin* (1971–72; Poznań, Oct. 6, 1974); *Studies in Color* for piano (1961); *Musica humana* for baritone, chorus and orch. (1963); *Chamber Primer* for instrumental ensemble (1964); *Street Music* for clarinet, trumpet, percussion, accordion and 4 pianists on 2 pianos (1966); *Missa abstracta* for narrator, tenor, chorus and orch. (1966); String Quartet (1966); *3 Recitativi* for soprano, piano and percussion (1968); *Hymnus laudans* for chorus and orch. (1970; Wroclaw, Feb. 24, 1972); *Incantations* for percussion sextet (1972); *Mazurian Chronicles* for orch. and tape (1973); *Radio Symphony* for flute and percussion (1974); *Anamnesis* for orch. (1975).

Penn, Arthur, English-born American composer; b. London, Feb. 13, 1875; d. New London, Conn., Feb. 6, 1941. He received his primary education in England; in 1903 he emigrated to America and was active as a teacher in New London. He composed several comic operas, for which he wrote his own librettos: *Yokohama Maid, Your Royal Highness, The Lass of Limerick Town, Captain Crossbones, Mam'zelle Taps, The China Shop;* and a number of songs in a popular manner, among them *Carissima, The Magic of Your Eyes* and *Sunrise and You.*

Penna, Lorenzo, Italian composer; b. Bologna, 1613; d. there, Oct. 31, 1693. He studied at the Univ. of Ferrara; was maestro di cappella at S. Cassiano in Imola (1667–69); then entered the Carmelite Order in Mantua; subsequently was director of music at the Carmelite Church in Parma (1672–73). In 1676 he became a member of the Accademia dei Filarmonici in Bologna, where he remained until his death.

WORKS: *Messe e salmi concertati* in 5 voices (1656); *Psalmorum totius anni modulatio* in 4 and 5 voices (1669); *Correnti francesi a quattro* with string instruments (1673, designated as "Sonate" in the dedication); *Il sacro Parnaso delli salmi festivi* for 4 to 8 voices (1677); *Reggia del sacro Parnaso* for 4 to 8 voices (1677); *Galeria del sacro Parnaso* for 4 to 8 voices, with instrumental accompaniment ad libitum (1678); he also publ. didactic editions: *Li primi albori musicali per li principianti della musica figurata* (1672); *Albori musicali per li studiosi della musica figurata* (1678); *Direttorio del canto fermo* (Modena, 1689).

BIBLIOGRAPHY: J.-H. Lederer, *Lorenzo Penna und seine Kontrapunkttheorie* (dissertation; Graz. 1970).

Pennario, Leonard, brilliant American pianist; b. Buffalo, July 9, 1924. He was taken to California as a child and studied piano there; appeared in public at the age of 7, and was soloist with the Los Angeles Philharmonic at 15. He then took piano lessons with Guy Maier; served in the U.S. Army Air Corps during World War II; then resumed his career; was the pianist with Heifetz and Piatigorsky in trio concerts; made several European tours; also was active as a teacher.

Penny, George Barlow, American organist and composer of sacred music; b. Haverstraw, N.Y., June 30, 1861; d. Rochester, N.Y., Nov. 15, 1934. He studied in N.Y. with Dudley Buck (organ) and Percy Goetschius (composition); from 1890 to 1911 filled various positions as teacher and organist in Kansas; in 1911 was appointed director of the Rochester Cons., connected with the Eastman School of Music there. He made 9 European and 2 Oriental tours as organist, lecturer, and conductor; publ. several services for the Episcopalian Church, and other sacred music.

Pente, Emilio, Italian violinist and music editor; b. Padua, Oct. 16, 1860; d. Sachsa, Germany, May 14, 1929. He studied at the Cons. of Milan; did research on Tartini and recovered about 40 Tartini manuscripts, which he arranged for publication in Germany; from 1909 to 1928 he taught at the Guildhall School of Music in London; then went to Germany. He edited and arranged a number of violin works by Tartini, and also pieces by Albinoni, Geminiani, Giardini, Nardini and Vivaldi. He himself composed 17 opus numbers of violin music.

Pentenrieder, Franz Xaver, German composer; b. Kaufbeuren, Bavaria, Feb. 6, 1813; d. Munich, July 17, 1867. He studied with Kalcher and Stunz; became conductor at the court opera; wrote a successful opera, *Die Nacht zu Paluzzi* (Munich, Oct. 2, 1840; performed widely in Germany), and a comic opera, *Das Haus ist zu verkaufen* (Leipzig, 1846); a number of church works; songs. As the result of an accident, he became insane, and spent the last few years of his life in an asylum.

Pentland, Barbara, Canadian composer; b. Winnipeg, Jan. 2, 1912. After taking piano lessons at a Montreal boarding school she went to N.Y., and studied with Frederick Jacobi and Bernard Wagenaar at the Juilliard School of Music, (1936–39); also took summer courses with Aaron Copland at the Berkshire Music Center in Tanglewood (1941 and 1942). She was an instructor at the Toronto Cons. (1943–49) and with the music department of the Univ. of British Columbia in Vancouver (1949–63). In her compositions she adopts a pragmatic method of cosmopolitan modernism, employing dissonant linear counterpoint and dodecaphonic melodic structures within the framework of classical forms.

WORKS: a chamber opera, *The Lake* (1952; Vancouver, March 3, 1954); a ballet-pantomime, *Beauty and the Beast,* for 2 pianos (1940); *Concert Overture* (1935); *2 Pieces* for strings (1938); *Lament* for orch. (1939); *Holiday Suite* for chamber orch. (1941); *Arioso and Rondo* for orch. (1941); Concerto for Violin and Small Orch. (1942); 4 symphonies: No. 1 (1945–48); No. 2 (1950), No. 3, *Symphony in Ten Parts,* for chamber ensemble (1957) and No. 4 (1959); *Colony Music* for piano and strings (1947); *Variations on a Boccherini Theme* for orch. (1948); Concerto for Organ and Strings (1949); *Ave Atque Vale* for orch. (1951); *Ricercar* for strings (1955); Concerto for Piano and String Orch. (1956); *Strata* for string orch. (1964); *Ciné scene* for chamber orch. (1968); *News,* to a text from the news media, for virtuoso voice and orch. (1970); *Variations Concertante* for piano and small orch. (1970); *Res Musica* for string orch. (1975); Piano Quartet (1939); Cello Sonata (1943); 3 string quartets (1944, 1953, 1969); *Vista* for violin and piano (1945); Violin Sonata (1946); Wind Octet (1948); *Weekend Overture* for resort combo of clarinet, trumpet, piano and percussion (1949); Solo Violin Sonata (1950); Solo Flute Sonatina (1954); Duo for viola and piano (1960); *Canzona* for flute, oboe and harpsichord (1961); Piano Trio (1963); *Variations* for solo viola (1965); *Trio con Alea* for string trio (1966); Septet for horn, trumpet, trombone, violin, viola, cello and organ (1967); *Reflections* for solo free-bass accordian (1971); *Interplay* for accordion and string quartet (1972); *Mutations* for cello and piano (1972); *Occasions* for brass quintet (1974); *Disasters of the Sun* for mezzo-soprano, 9 instruments and tape (1976); songs; for piano: *Studies in Line* (1941); Variations (1942); Sonata (1945); *Sonata Fantasy* (1947); 2 sonatinas (1951), *Mirror Study* (1952); 2-Piano Sonata (1953), *Toccata* (1958); *3 Duets after Pictures by Paul Klee* (1959); *Fantasy* (1962); *Puppet Show* (1964); *Shadows* (1964); *Signs* (1964); *Suite Borealis* (1966); *Space Studies* (1967); *Arctica* for young pianists (1971–73); *Vita Brevis* (1973).

Pépin, Clermont, Canadian composer; b. St.-Georges-de-Beauce, May 15, 1926. He studied piano in Quebec and harmony in Montreal, with Claude Champagne. He went to Philadelphia in 1941, where he studied composition with Rosario Scalero. From 1949 to 1955 he lived in Paris and took composition lessons with Jolivet, Honegger and Messiaen. Returning to Canada, he joined the staff of the Montreal Cons. (1955–64; director, 1967–72).

WORKS: 3 ballets: *Les Portes de l'enfer* (1953),

L'Oiseaux-Phénix (1956) and *Le Porte-rêve* (1957–58); 2 piano concertos (1946, 1949); *Variations Symphoniques* for orch. (1947); 4 symphonies: No. 1 (1948); No. 2 (Montreal, Dec. 22, 1957); No. 3, *Quasars* (Montreal, Feb. 7, 1967); No. 4, *La Messe sur le monde*, for narrator, chorus and orch. (1975); *Guernica*, symph. poem after Picasso's painting (Quebec, Dec. 8, 1952); *Le Rite de soleil noir*, symph. poem (1955; Luxembourg, Sept., 1955); *Hymne au vent du nord*, cantata (1960); *Monologue* for chamber orch. (1961); *Nombres* for 2 pianos and orch. (Montreal, Feb. 6, 1963); *Monade* for string orch. (1964); *Prismes et Cristaux* for string orch. (Montreal, April 9, 1974); *Monade* for violin and orch. (1972); *Chroma* for orch. (Guelph, Ontario, May 5, 1973); Piano Sonata (1947); 4 string quartets (1948, 1955, 1956, 1960); *Cycle Éluard* for soprano and piano (1949); *Musique pour Athalie* for woodwinds and brass (1956); Suite for piano trio (1958); *Sequences* for flute, oboe, violin, viola and cello (1972); *Réseaux* for violin and piano (1973–74); piano pieces; incidental music.

BIBLIOGRAPHY: *34 Biographies of Canadian Composers* (Canadian Broadcasting Co., Montreal, 1964).

Pepöck, August, Austrian operetta composer; b. Gmunden, May 10, 1887; d. there, Sept. 5, 1967. He studied in Vienna with Heuberger and R. Fuchs; then was active as a conductor of theater music in various provincial towns in Germany; then lived mostly in Vienna. He scored great success with his operettas *Mädel ade!* (Vienna, Oct. 5, 1930) and *Der Reiter de Kaiserin* (Vienna, April 30, 1941). He also wrote some chamber music, and songs.

Pepping, Ernst, German composer; b. Duisburg, Sept. 12, 1901. He studied in Berlin with Gmeindl; afterwards was a teacher at the Church Music School in Berlin-Spandau; in 1953 became prof. of composition at the Berlin Hochschule für Musik. By virtue of his lifelong association with Lutheran Church culture, he acquired a profound understanding of German polyphonic music, both sacred and secular, and is generally regarded as the most significant representative of modern German choral writing; he also made arrangements of German folksongs.

WORKS: *Deutsche Choralmesse* (1930); *Choralbuch* (1931); *Spandauer Chorbuch*, a collection of choral works for the entire church year, in 20 vols. (1934-41); *Te Deum* (1956); *Grosses Orgelbuch* in 3 parts (1939); *Kleines Orgelbuch* (1940); *Das Weltgericht* for 4 voices (1958); *Die Weihnachtsgeschichte des Lukas*, set for 4-7 voices (1959); numerous psalms and motets, of which the most significant are the adventmotettes *Aus hartem Weh die Menschheit klagt* for 3-4 voices (1964); *Deines Lichtes Glanz* for 4-6 voices (1967); 3 symphonies (1939, 1943, 1947); *Partita* for orch. (1934); *Suite* for trumpet, saxophone and trombone (1926); Piano Concerto (1951); 2 string quartets; String Trio; 4 piano sonatas; numerous secular works for chorus; 33 folksongs for children's voices (1947). He publ. an important collection, *Der polyphone Satz* in 2 vols. (1943, 1957). A complete list of his works is included in a Festschrift presented to him on his 70th birthday (Berlin, 1971).

BIBLIOGRAPHY: Karl Laux, "Ernst Pepping," in *Musik und Musiker der Gegenwart* (Essen, 1949; pp. 193-201).

Pepusch, John Christopher (Johann Christoph), German-English opera composer; b. Berlin, 1667; d. London, July 20, 1752. He was taught by Klingenberg (theory) and Grosse (organ). He had a position at the Prussian court in 1681-97; then went to Holland, and (1700) to London, joining the Drury Lane orch. as violinist, later as cembalist and composer, adapting Italian airs to English operas, adding recitatives and songs. In 1710 he founded (with Needler, Gates, Galliard, and others) the Academy of Ancient Music, famous for the revival of 16th-century compositions; 1712, organist and composer to the Duke of Chandos, preceding Handel; 1713, Mus. Doc., Oxford; for many years director of Lincoln's Inn Theatre, for which he wrote the masques *Venus and Adonis* (1715), *Apollo and Daphne* (1716), *The Death of Dido* (1716), *The Union of the Three Sister-Arts* (1723), and arranged music to the ballad-operas *The Beggar's Opera*, *Polly*, and *The Wedding*. In 1730 a fortune brought him by marriage with the singer **Marguerite de l'Épine** rendered him independent. From 1737 until death he was organist of the Charterhouse. Pepusch was a learned, though conservative, musician who enjoyed a high renown in England. He published a *Treatise on Harmony* (1731; repr. Hildesheim, 1970); various odes and cantatas, instrumental concertos and sonatas are of slight importance, and his name is preserved in music history mainly for his original music and some arranged numbers in *The Beggar's Opera*.

BIBLIOGRAPHY: *Dictionary of National Biography* (vol. 44); F. Kidson, "*The Beggar's Opera*," *Its Predecessors and Successors* (Cambridge, 1922; repr. N.Y., 1969); C. W. Hughes, "J. C. Pepusch," *Musical Quarterly* (Jan. 1945); M. Boyd, "English Secular Cantatas in the 18th Century," *Music Review* (May 1969).

Perabo, (Johann) Ernst, German-American pianist; b. Wiesbaden, Nov. 14, 1845; d. Boston, Oct. 29, 1920. The family moved to New York in 1852. He studied with his father; then at the Leipzig Cons. with Moscheles (piano), Reinecke (composition), and others. Returning to America in 1865, he established himself as a concert pianist, and a highly successful teacher in Boston; had nearly 1,000 pupils, among them well-known musicians (Mrs. H. H. A. Beach was one of his pupils). He publ. a number of piano pieces: *Moment musical; Scherzo; Prelude; Waltz; Pensées; Circumstance, or Fate of a Human Life; Prelude, Romance, and Toccatina.*

Peragallo, Mario, Italian composer; b. Rome, March 25, 1910. He was a student of Alfredo Casella, and in his early works followed the line of the Italian Baroque characteristic for its modern but euphonious polyphony; later he adopted a radical quasi-dodecaphonic idiom, with frequent reversions to diatonic structures.

WORKS: Operas, *Ginevra degli Almieri* (Rome, Feb. 13, 1937), *Lo Stendardo di S. Giorgio* (1941), *La Gita in campagna* (La Scala, Milan, March 24, 1954); a scenic cantata, *La Collina* (1947); Concerto for Orch. (1940); 2 piano concertos (1949, 1951); Violin

Concerto (1954); *Forme sovrapposte* for orch. (1959); *Vibrazioni* for flute, "tiptofono" and piano (1960); 3 string quartets; Piano Quartet; numerous choral works and songs.

Perahia, Murray, talented American pianist; b. New York, April 19, 1947. He studied piano with Jeannette Haien and Mieczyslaw Horszowski; conducting with Carl Bamberger at the Mannes College of Music, receiving his bachelor's degree in conducting in 1969. In 1972 he won the Leeds International Pianoforte Competition; in 1975 he was the first recipient of the Avery Fisher Artist Award; made solo appearances with major American orchestras; also was soloist with the Berlin Philharmonic; gave numerous recitals in Europe; in 1977 made a tour of Japan; also played in Israel. He excels particularly in the Romantic repertory, to which his fiery temperament is suited best.

Perceval, Julio, Argentinian composer; b. Brussels, July 17, 1903; d. (in a traffic accident), Santiago, Chile, Sept. 7, 1963. He studied organ at the Brussels Cons.; subsequently with Marcel Dupré in Paris. Emigrating to Argentina in 1926, he became active as organist in Buenos Aires; then was prof. of organ playing at the Univ. of Cuyo (1939-59). In 1959 he went to Chile where he taught at the National Cons. of Santiago. He composed a number of songs and organ pieces; also some chamber music.

Pereira-Salas, Eugenio, Chilean musicologist; b. Santiago, May 19, 1904. He studied at the Univ. of Chile in Santiago; in 1926 went to Europe where he took lessons at the Sorbonne in Paris and at the Univ. of Berlin; then took courses at the Univ. of California, Berkeley on a Guggenheim Fellowship (1933-34); returning to Chile he was lecturer in geography and history at the Univ. of Chile; in 1938 he organized there a department of Chilean folklore; publ. a number of important books on Chilean music, among them *Los Orígenes del arte musical en Chile* (Santiago, 1941); *La Canción nacional de Chile* (Santiago, 1947); *Juegos y alegrías coloniales de Chile* (Santiago, 1947); *Historia de la música en Chile* (Santiago, 1957).

Peress, Maurice, American conductor; b. New York, March 18, 1930. He studied music at N.Y. Univ. (B.A., 1951) and at Mannes College of Music, N.Y., (1955-57); was a member of the faculty of N.Y. Univ. (1957-61) and for a season assistant conductor of the N.Y. Philharmonic (1961-62); then held the post of music director and conductor of the Corpus Christi, Texas, Symph. Orch. (1962-74); in 1974 was appointed conductor of the Kansas City Philharmonic. In 1971 he conducted the world premiere of Leonard Bernstein's *Mass* at the Kennedy Center, Washington.

Pérez Casas, Bartolomeo, Spanish conductor and composer; b. Lorca, near Murcia, Jan. 24, 1873; d. Madrid, Jan. 15, 1956. He studied at the Madrid Cons.; played the clarinet in various military bands; also was a bandmaster. He then established himself in Madrid as a teacher at the Cons.; from 1915 to 1936 conducted the Orquesta Filarmónica de Madrid. He wrote a lyric drama in one act, *Lorenzo;* an orchestral suite,

A mi tierra (an early work, which became fairly popular); a string quartet; pieces for band.

Pérez, David, Italian composer of operas; b. Naples (of Spanish parents), 1711; d. Lisbon, Oct. 30, 1778. He was a pupil of Galli (violin) and Mancini (theory) at the Cons. di Loreto in Naples; presented his first opera, *Siroe,* at the San Carlo in Naples, on Nov. 4, 1740; in 1741 went to Palermo as maestro of the court orch., remaining there until 1748. He then lived the life of a traveling composer, visiting various cities in Italy, until 1752, when he was engaged as maestro di cappella at the royal chapel in Lisbon. In 1755 he visited London. Among his best operas are *Alessandro nell'Indie* (Genoa, Dec. 26, 1745), *Demetrio* (Venice, Spring, 1751), and *Solimano* (Lisbon, 1757; his most important dramatic work). As an opera composer, he was considered a worthy rival of Jommelli. He also wrote several Masses; a Miserere for 5 voices with bassoons obbligati and organ; *Mattutino de' morti,* for chorus and orch. (London, 1774); etc.

BIBLIOGRAPHY: E. Soares, *David Pérez, Subsídios para a biografia do célebre mestre* (Lisbon, 1935); H. Kretzschmar, *Geschichte der Oper* (pp. 188-89).

Perfall, Karl von, German composer and conductor; b. Munich, Jan. 29, 1824; d. there, Jan. 14, 1907. He took music lessons with Hauptmann in Leipzig (1848-49); became conductor of the Munich "Liedertafel" (1850); founded the Oratorio Society (1854); in 1864 was appointed intendant of the court music and abandoned his activites as conductor. From 1867 to 1893 he was intendant of the court theater in Munich. Of his operas (all produced in Munich), *Raimondin* (March 27, 1881) and *Junker Heinz* (April 9, 1886) were successful. He publ. *25 Jahre Münchener Hoftheater-Geschichte* (1892; covering the period from 1867); *Ein Beitrag zur Geschichte des königlichen Theaters in München* (1894); *Die Entwickelung des modernen Theaters* (1899).

Pergament, Moses, Finnish-born Swedish composer and conductor; b. Helsinki, Sept. 21, 1893; d. Stockholm, March 5, 1977. He studied violin at the St. Petersburg Cons. and conducting at Berlin. In 1915 he settled in Sweden; from 1923 to 1966 he was active as a music critic in Swedish newspapers; published 4 books on music. His musical style was initially circumscribed by Russian paradigms; later he was influenced by Sibelius; still later he adopted some modernistic procedures. Several of his compositions reflect an ancestral strain of Jewish melos.

WORKS: the chamber opera *Himlens hemlighet* (*The Secret of Heaven,* 1952); the radio opera, *Eli* (1958; Swedish Radio, March 19, 1959); the opera-oratorio, *Abrams Erwachen* (1970-73); the ballets, *Vision* (1923) and *Krelantems and Eldeling* (1920-28); *Romance* for violin and orch. (1914); *Adagio* for clarinet and strings (1915); *Rapsodia ebraica* for orch. (1935); *Concerto romantico* for strings (1935); *Dibbuk,* fantasy for violin and orch. (1935); *Almquistiana,* 2 suites for orch. (1936, 1938); *Nedanförmänskliga visor* (*Subhuman Songs*) for narrator, soli, chorus and orch. (1936); *Swedish Rhapsody* for orch. (1941); *Den judiska sången* (*The Jewish Song*), choral symphony

(1944); Violin Concerto (1948); *Kol Nidré* for cello and orch. (1949); Piano Concerto (1951); Concerto for 2 violins and orch. (1954); Cello Concerto (1955); *Canto lirico* for violin and orch. (1956); *Pezzo intimo* for 16 solo cellos (1957); *De sju dödssynderna* (*The Seven Deadly Sins*), oratorio (1963); Viola Concerto (1964–65); *4 Poems by Edith Södergran* for soprano and orch. (1965–66); *Årstider,* 4 songs for baritone and orch. (1968); *Drömmen om mullen och vindarna* (*The Dream of the Earth and the Winds*) for baritone and orch. (1969); *Fantasia differente* for cello and strings (1970); Piano Trio (1912–13, revised 1940); Violin Sonata (1918–20); 3 string quartets (1922, 1952, 1956); Solo Violin Sonata (1961); Flute Sonata (1968); *Little Suite* for woodwinds (1970); Sonatina for flute and string orch. (1973); *Biblical Cantata* for chorus and orch. (1974); over 100 solo songs; theater and film music.

Perger, Richard von, Austrian composer and conductor; b. Vienna, Jan. 10, 1854; d. there, Jan. 11, 1911. He studied cello and theory; was in the Austrian army during the campaign in Bosnia (1878); then received a stipend, and took lessons with Brahms (1880–82); was director of the Cons. of Rotterdam, Holland (1890–95); returning to Vienna, conducted the Gesellschaftskonzerte; from 1899 to 1907 was director of the Vienna Cons. His music bears unmistakable evidence of the profound influence of Brahms.
WORKS: The text and music of a comic opera, *Der Richter von Granada* (Cologne, 1889); the Singspiel *Die 14 Nothhelfer* (Vienna, 1891); the musical fairy tale, *Das stählerne Schloss* (Vienna, 1904); Violin Concerto; some chamber music; songs. He published a biography of Brahms (1908; new ed. by Hernried, 1934); his *Geschichte der K. K. Gesellschaft der Musikfreunde in Wien* was published posthumously (1912).

Pergolesi, Giovanni Battista, remarkable Italian composer; b. Jesi, near Ancona, Jan. 4, 1710; d. Pozzuoli, March 16, 1736. The family's original name was **Draghi;** the surname Pergolesi was derived from the town of Pergola, where Pergolesi's ancestors lived. He was the only surviving child of his parents, three having died in their infancy. He studied music with Francesco Santi, choir director at Jesi Cathedral; was given a stipend by the Marchese Cardolo Pianetti, which enabled him to enter the Conservatorio dei Poveri at Naples; there, he was a pupil of Domenico de Matteis (violin) and Gaetano Greco (theory); later also studied with Durante and Feo. He became proficient as a violinist, and played on various occasions during the carnivals. His first performed work was an oratorio, *La Conversione di S. Guglielmo d'Aquitania* (which included a comic section in the Neapolitan dialect), presented at the monastery of S. Agnello Maggiore in Naples in the summer of 1731; another oratorio, *La Fenice sul rogo,* was performed in the same year; this was followed by a serious opera, *Salustia,* and an opera buffa, *Lo Frate 'nnamorato* (Naples, Sept. 23, 1732). In Dec. 1732 he was commissioned by the municipal authorities of Naples to write a solemn Mass as a votive offering after a series of severe earthquakes. On Aug. 28, 1733 Pergolesi presented a serious opera, *Il Prigionier superbo;* it contained a comic intermezzo, *La Serva padrona,* which was to become his most celebrated work. After a brief sojourn in Rome (May, 1734) to conduct his Mass at the San Lorenzo Church, he returned to Naples; there his new opera *Adriano in Siria* was produced, on Oct. 25, 1734, with an intermezzo, *Livietta e Tracollo* (performed at various times under different titles, *La Contadina astuta, La finta Polacca,* etc.). During another trip to Rome he performed his serious opera *L'Olimpiade* (Jan. 8, 1735), directing from the harpsichord, but it had little success. His last opera was a comic play, *Il Flaminio* (Naples, autumn, 1735). At that time his health was undermined by consumption; early in 1736 he went to Pozzuoli, where he died at the age of 26; he was buried in the common grave. His last completed work was a masterpiece of sacred music, *Stabat Mater.* Several dramatic works ascribed to Pergolesi and published under his name, notably *Il Maestro di musica* and *Il Geloso schernito,* are spurious. The revival of his comic intermezzo *La Serva padrona* in Paris (1752) precipitated the so-called *querelle des bouffons* between the supporters of the Italian and the French factions. Pergolesi's instrumental music is less known, and there are grave doubts as to the authenticity of many of these works published under his name: 14 trio sonatas (of these, 3 were ed. by Riemann, Berlin, 1900); 6 concertini for strings (publ. in London as works by Carlo Ricciotti); 3 "sinfonie" (string quartets); 2 concertos for flute and strings; sonata for violin and strings; 5 harpsichord sonatas. Stravinsky used some of these instrumental works for his ballet *Pulcinella,* but most of the borrowed material is not by Pergolesi. *La Serva padrona* was publ. in new editions by Abert (1911), Karl Geiringer, and others; *Flaminio* was ed. by Mortari (1942); the spurious *Il Maestro di musica* (which is in reality a pasticcio publ. in Paris in 1753) was orchestrated and ed. by Schering (1924); the intermezzo *La finta Polacca* was issued by Radiciotti (1914); the *Stabat Mater* was publ. by Eulenburg in Alfred Einstein's edition. Among other extant works attributed to Pergolesi are the oratorios, *Il Pentimento, La Morte d'Abel,* and *Septem verba;* 10 chamber cantatas; at least 5 Masses; still doubtful is the authenticity of many arias, including the popular *Tre giorni son che Nina.* A complete ed. of Pergolesi's works, *Opera Omnia,* was brought out in Rome (1940–42), in 5 vols. (148 works, of which 129 publ. for the first time; many are spurious). The chaotic entanglement of spurious and authentic works is marvelously unraveled in M. Paymer's *Pergolesi: A Thematic Catalogue of the Opera Omnia* (N.Y., 1977).
BIBLIOGRAPHY: P. Boyer, "Notices sur la vie et les ouvrages de Pergolèse," *Mercure de France* (July 1772); Marchese di Villarosa, *Lettera biografica intorno alla patria ed alla vita di G. B. Pergolesi* (Naples, 1831; 2nd ed., 1843); F. Villars, *La Serva padrona, son apparition à Paris en 1752, son influence, son analyse* (Paris, 1863); A. Gianandrea, *Pergolesiana* (Jesi, 1885); E. Faustini-Fasini, *G. B. Pergolesi attraverso i suoi biografi e le sue opere* (Milan, 1900); G. Radiciotti, *G. B. Pergolesi: vita, opere ed influenza su l'arte* (Rome, 1910; 2nd ed., Milan, 1935; in German, Zürich, 1954); A. Della Corte, "G. B. Pergolesi,"

in *L'Opera comica italiana nel 1700* (vol. I, pp. 49–75; Bari, 1923); G. Radiciotti, "Tre giorni," *Musica d'Oggi* (July 1925); A. Della Corte, *Pergolesi* (Turin, 1936); R. Giraldi, *G. B. Pergolesi* (Rome, 1936); G. de Saint-Foix, "Le Deuxième Centenaire de Pergolesi," *Revue de Musicologie* (1936); special issues of *Rassegna Musicale* (1936) and *Musica d'Oggi* (1936); L. Reichenburg, *Contribution à l'histoire de la Querelle des Bouffons* (Philadelphia, 1937; a complete list of pamphlets publ. in Paris during the *querelle des bouffons*); H. Claydon, "Three String Quartets Attributed to Pergolesi," *Music & Letters* (Oct. 1938); F. Schlitzer, *G. B. Pergolesi* (Turin, 1940); S. A. Luciani, *G. B. Pergolesi: note e documenti* (Siena, 1942); E. J. Luin, *Fortuna e influenza della musica di Pergolesi in Europa* (Siena, 1943); F. Walker, "Two Centuries of Pergolesi Forgeries and Misattributions," *Music & Letters* (Oct. 1949); C. L. Cudworth, "Notes on the Instrumental Works Attributed to Pergolesi," *Music & Letters* (Oct. 1949); F. Walker, "Pergolesi Legends," *Monthly Musical Record* (1952); F. Walker, "Orazio: The History of a Pasticcio," *Musical Quarterly* (July 1952); A. Loewenberg, *Annals of Opera* (Cambridge, 1943; new ed., 1955); H. Hucke, "Die musikalischen Vorlagen zu Igor Stravinskys *Pulcinella*," in W. Stauder *et al.*, eds., *Frankfurter musikhistorische Studien* (Osthoff Festschrift; Tutzing, 1969); M. Paymer, *The Instrumental Music Attributed to Giov. B. Pergolesi: A Study in Authenticity* (City Univ. of N.Y., 1977).

Peri, Jacopo, Italian composer; called "Il Zazzerino" from his abundant hair, b. Rome, Aug. 20, 1561; d. Florence, Aug. 12, 1633. Of noble family, he studied at Lucca under Cristoforo Malvezzi; was maestro at the court of Ferdinando I and Cosimo II de' Medici, and from 1601 at the court of Ferrara. A participant in the Florentine circle at the houses of Counts Bardi and Corsi, where the revival of ancient Greek musical declamation was planned, Peri set to music Rinuccini's text of *Dafne* (1597). It was first performed at Corsi's palace in Florence, and played again at Pitti's palace. Peri followed it with a setting of Rinuccini's *Euridice* for the wedding of Maria de' Medici with Henry IV of France (produced Oct. 6, 1600; publ. Florence, 1600; repr. in *Monuments of Music and Music Literature in Facsimile I/8*). *Dafne* was the first "opera" or drama set to music in monodic style (i.e., vocal soli supported by instruments); this style was termed *stile rappresentativo*. In 1608 Peri wrote for Mantua the recitatives of *Ariadne* (text by Rinuccini), while Monteverdi composed the arias. In the same year he submitted in Mantua an opera *Tetide* (text by Cini), which, however, was not produced. With Grazie, Signorini, and del Turco he wrote *Guerra d'amore* (Florence, 1615). No records are available showing that *Adone* (text by Cicognini), composed 1620, ever had a public performance. *La Precedenza delle dame* was produced at Florence in 1625, and Peri also collaborated with Gagliano on *La Flora* (Florence, Oct. 11, 1628). He published in 1609 *Le varie musiche* in 1–3 parts, some to be sung with harpsichord or chitarrone, others to be played on the organ. Kiesewetter printed 3 madrigals *a* 4 in *Schicksale und Beschaffenheit des weltlichen Gesanges* (1841). Fragments from *Euridice* are in several histories of music; a complete ed. was

publ. by Guidi in Florence, and by Torchi in vol. VI of *L'Arte Musicale in Italia*; a facsimile reprint was publ. in Milan, 1934; A. Schering's *Geschichte der Musik in Beispielen* contains 3 excerpts (nos. 171a-c). BIBLIOGRAPHY: G. O. Corazzini, "Commemorazione della Riforma melodrammatica," in the annual report of the Reale Instituto di Musica (Florence, 1895); A. Solerti, *Le Origini del melodramma* (3 vols., Florence, 1905); O. G. Sonneck, "Dafne, the First Opera," *Sammelbände der Internationalen Musik-Gesellschaft* 15 (1913); M. Mila, "J. Peri," *Rassegna Musicale* 4 (1933). For details of productions of Peri's operas, see A. Loewenberg, *Annals of Opera* (Cambridge, 1943; 2nd ed., 1955).

Peričić, Vlastimir, Serbian composer and musicologist; b. Vršac, Dec. 7, 1927. He studied in Vienna with Uhl; became active as a pedagogue in Belgrade; publ. manuals on harmony and form.
WORKS: String Quartet (1950); *Symphonic Movement* (Belgrade, Oct. 14, 1952); *Fantasia quasi una sonata* for violin and piano (1954); Sinfonietta for strings (Zagreb, Nov. 13, 1957); piano pieces. He compiled a valuable reference work on Serbian composers, *Muzički Stvaraoci u Srbiji* (Belgrade, 1969).

Périer, Jean, French tenor; b. Paris, Feb. 2, 1869; d. there, Nov. 3, 1954. He studied at the Paris Cons., obtaining 1st prize for singing (1892); was engaged at the Opéra-Comique. He created the role of Pelléas at the première of Debussy's opera (1902), and sang the leading tenor parts in several other premières of French operas; a talented comedian, he also appeared in variety shows in Paris. He publ. an instructive album, *Mes Exercises, tirés des chansons populaires de France* (Paris, 1917).

Perinello, Carlo, Italian music editor; b. Trieste, Feb. 13, 1877; d. Rome, Jan. 6, 1942. He studied music in Trieste and Leipzig; then taught at the Trieste Cons. (1904-14) and at the Milan Cons. He served on the staff of the Istituto Editoriale Italiano, and collaborated in the preparation of its publications.

Perkins, Charles Callahan, American musician and painter; b. Boston, March 1, 1823; d. Windsor, Vermont, Aug. 25, 1886. He was educated at Harvard Univ.; also studied in Italy and in Paris. In 1850 he became the head of the Handel and Haydn Society, in which position he exercised considerable influence on musical affairs in Boston; compiled (with John S. Dwight) vol. I of *History of the Handel and Haydn Society of Boston* (Boston, 1883).

Perkins, Francis Davenport, American music critic; b. Boston, Nov. 18, 1897; d. New York, Oct. 8, 1970. He studied at the New England Cons., at Trinity College, Cambridge, England, and at Harvard Univ. (B.A. *cum laude,* 1918). In 1919 he became exchange editor (later music editor) of the *N.Y. Tribune;* contributed numerous articles to various musical publications.

Perkins, Henry Southwick, American vocal teacher; b. Stockbridge, Vermont, March 20, 1833; d. Chicago, Jan. 20, 1914. He studied voice at the Boston Music

School (graduated in 1861). He filled various administrative and educational posts in Iowa, Kansas, and Illinois; in 1890 founded the Chicago National College of Music; was active as director of music festivals and conventions across the country, from Maine to California. He was one of the organizers of the Music Teachers National Association in 1876; edited 30 song books, hymn books, class books; etc.; composed vocal quartets and songs.

Perkins, John MacIvor, American composer and pedagogue; b. St. Louis, Aug. 2, 1935. He studied music at Harvard Univ. (B.A., 1958), and at Brandeis Univ. (M.F.A., 1962); also took lessons with Nadia Boulanger in Paris and with Roberto Gerhard and Edmund Rubbra in London. He was instructor in music at the Univ. of Chicago (1962–64); lecturer on music at Harvard Univ. (1965–70). In 1970 he was appointed head of the music department of Washington Univ. in his native St. Louis.

WORKS: *Canons* for 9 instruments (1957); *Three Miniatures* for string quartet (1960); *Variations* for flute, clarinet, trumpet, piano and percussion (1962); *Music for 13 Players* (1964); *Music for Orchestra* (1965); choral works and piano pieces.

Perkins, (David) Walton, American pianist and music critic; b. Rome, N.Y., Nov. 16, 1847; d. Chicago, Feb. 6, 1929. He was a pupil of Th. Kullak and Anton Rubinstein in Berlin; upon his return to America, he settled in Chicago; with William H. Sherwood, organized the Sherwood Music School in Chicago (1897); was its director until 1901. He composed piano pieces and songs; edited collections of choruses, and composed choral works.

Perkins, William, American composer; b. Dallas, April 28, 1941. He studied at the Univ. of Colorado, Boulder, with Cecil Effinger (B.A. 1971) and at the New England Cons. of Music, Boston (M.M. 1974).

WORKS: *Textures* for musical saw and percussion (1970); *Twilight Music* for musical saw and harpsichord (1970); *Chamber Symphony* (1971); *Contrast* for woodwind trio and percussion (1972); 2 Preludes for vibraphone and electric guitar (1973); String Quartet (1974).

Perkins, William Oscar, American vocal teacher and composer; brother of **Henry Southwick Perkins**; b. Stockbridge, Vermont, May 23, 1831; d. Boston, Jan. 13, 1902. He studied voice in Milan; lived in Boston as a teacher; publ. about 40 collections of songs, anthems, etc., including many of his own pieces.

Perkowski, Piotr, Polish composer; b. Oweczacze, Ukraine, March 17, 1901. He studied composition with Statkowski at the Warsaw Cons. (1923–25); then took private lessons with Szymanowski in Warsaw and with Albert Roussel in Paris. He subsequently devoted himself to teaching; was director of the Toruń Cons. (1936–39); taught composition at the Warsaw Cons. (1947–51, 1955–73); was artistic director of the Cracow Philharmonic (1949–51) and dean of the Music Academy in Wroclaw (1951–55); served as coun-

cilor for cultural development for the city of Warsaw (1965–74). In his earlier years he followed the fashionable cosmopolitan trend of absolute music without reference to national or general programmatic subjects, but under the influence of social changes he began introducing concrete, historic and pictorial representations.

WORKS: opera, *Garlands* (Warsaw, 1962); 5 ballets: *Swantewit* (1930; revised 1945–47; Pozań, June 19, 1948), *Clémentine* (1960–63); *Rhapsody* (1949); *Fantasia* (1950); and *Balladyna* (1960–64; Warsaw, 1965); 2 symphonies: No. 1, with chorus (1925, score lost; reconstructed 1955) and No. 2 (1949); *Geometric Suite* for orch. (1930); 2 violin concertos (1933, 1960); *Warsaw Overture* (1954); *Sinfonia drammatica* (1963); *Scottish Impressions* for orch. (1968); 5 cantatas: *Wisla* (1951), *Épitaphe pour Nicos Belojannis* (1952), *Suita weselna (Merry Suite)* for soprano, tenor, chorus and orch. (1952), *Suita epicka* (1953); and *Alexiares*, with narrator and tape (1966–69); *Niebo w plomieniach (The Sky in Flames)*, a song cycle with orch. (1969); String Quartet (1930); *Elegia* for cello and organ (1945); Trumpet Sonatina (1954); Flute Sonata (1954); piano pieces.

Perle, George, American composer and theorist; b. Bayonne, New Jersey, May 6, 1915. He studied composition with Wesley La Violette at DePaul Univ. in Chicago (1935–38) and also took private lessons with Ernst Krenek (1939–41); obtained his degree of M.Mus. from the American Cons. of Music in Chicago in 1942; received his Ph.D. in 1956 at N.Y. Univ. with the dissertation *Serial Composition and Atonality* (in book form, publ. at Berkeley, 1962; 4th ed., 1977); also wrote *Twelve-Tone Tonality* (Berkeley, 1977). In 1961 he joined the faculty of Queens College; Guggenheim Fellowships in composition 1966–67, 1974–75; many other grants, commissions, and awards. He is one of the most important American theorists and practitioners of the method of composition with 12 tones; he has contributed numerous analytic essays on the works of Schoenberg, Berg and Webern; co-founder and director of the International Alban Berg Society, City Univ. of N.Y.

WORKS: 2 symphonies; *Rhapsody* for orch. (1953); Cello Concerto (1966); String Quintet (1958); 3 wind quintets (1959, 1960, 1967); 7 string quartets (1938–73); *Sonata quasi una fantasia* for clarinet and piano (1972); sonatas for viola solo (1942), for clarinet solo (1943), for cello solo (1947), for violin solo (1959 and 1963); *Monody I* for flute (1960); *Monody II* for double bass (1962); *Short Sonata* for piano (1964); *Solo Partita* for violin and viola (1965); Wind Quintet No. 2 (1966–67); *Dodecatonal Suite* for piano (1970); choruses and songs. A list of his early works is found in Vol. 15 of *Composers of the Americas* (Washington, D.C., 1959).

BIBLIOGRAPHY: L. Kraft, "The Music of George Perle," *Musical Quarterly* (July 1971); B. Saylor, "String Quartets by Babbitt, Perle, and Seeger," *Contemporary Music Newsletter* (May-June 1973).

Perlea, Jonel, Rumanian-American conductor and composer; b. Ograda, Dec. 13, 1900; d. New York, July 29, 1970. He studied piano and composition in Munich

(1918–20) and conducting in Leipzig (1920–23). He made his conducting debut in Bucharest in 1919; held posts as conductor in Leipzig (1922–23) and Rostock (1923–25); then returned to Rumania and conducted the Bucharest Opera (1929–32 and 1934–36) and Bucharest Radio Orch., of which he was a founder (1936–44). He led conducting classes at the Bucharest Cons. (1941–44); during the last year of World War II he was interned in a German concentration camp. After the war he conducted opera in Rome (1945–47); in 1950 conducted at La Scala, Milan. He made his American debut at the Metropolitan Opera, N.Y., Dec. 1, 1949, conducting *Tristan und Isolde;* appeared at the San Francisco Opera and Lyric Opera of Chicago; from 1955 to 1970 was conductor of the Connecticut Symph. Orch. He taught conducting at the Manhattan School of Music from 1952 until shortly before his death; became a naturalized U.S. citizen in 1960. He suffered a heart attack in 1957 and a stroke in 1958 as a result of which he lost the use of his right arm, but continued to conduct with his left hand.

WORKS: *2 Sketches* for orch. (1919); Piano Sonata; String Quartet (1921); *Symphonic Variations on an Original Theme* (1930); *Don Quixote,* symph. poem (1946); *Symphony Concertante* for violin and orchestra (1968); *3 Studies* for orch. (1969).

Perlman, Itzhak, Israeli-American violinist; b. Tel Aviv, Aug. 31, 1945. He was struck with polio as a child of 4, and his legs were paralyzed. His parents, immigrants from Russia, encouraged him to play the violin despite his handicap, and he gave his first public concert in Tel Aviv at the age of 9. When he was 13, he went to New York where he studied at the Juilliard School of Music in N.Y. with Ivan Galamian and his assistant Dorothy Delay. In 1963 he played at Carnegie Hall; in 1964 he received first prize at the Leventritt competition. This was the beginning of a brilliant career; he played with great success in Europe, America and Japan, while making his home in New York.

Perne, François Louis, French music scholar; b. Paris, Oct. 4, 1772; d. Laon (Aisne), May 26, 1832. He studied with Abbé d'Haudimont at the maîtrise of St.-Jacques-de-la-Boucherie; was chorus singer at the Paris Opéra in 1792; double-bass player in the orch. there, 1799. His profound skill in composition was illustrated by his writing a triple fugue, to be sung backwards on reversing the page; his knowledge of old music was extraordinary. In 1813 he became prof. of harmony at the Paris Cons., as successor to Catel; he became inspector-general of the Cons. in 1816, and librarian in 1819. In 1822 he went into retirement, at an estate near Laon; returned to Paris shortly before his death. He publ. *Exposition de la séméiographie, ou notation musicale des Grecs* (1815), *Cours d'harmonie et d'accompagnement* (1822), *Chansons du Châtelain de Coucy* (1830), and a great number of articles on Greek and medieval music publ. in vols. I-IX of the *Revue Musicale,* edited by Fétis. He also wrote several pieces of sacred music.

Perosi, Don Lorenzo, distinguished Italian composer of church music; b. Tortona, Dec. 21, 1872; d. Rome, Oct. 12, 1956. He studied at the Cons. of Milan (1892–93); also took courses at Haberl's School for Church Music at Regensburg (1894); became maestro di cappella at Imola, and then at San Marco in Venice. He was ordained priest in 1896; in 1898 became musical director of the Sistine Chapel, and leader of the papal choir; he resigned this post in 1915 owing to a severe mental disturbance; spent some time in a sanitarium (1922–23). Regaining his health after treatment, he returned to active service as choral conductor and composer. Shortly after his 80th birthday, he led a performance of his oratorio *Il Natale del Redentore* at the Vatican, before Pope Pius XII (Dec. 28, 1952). He was a self-denying and scholarly worker for the cause of the cultivation of a pure church style, both in composition and in performance, and was esteemed above all others as a church musician at the Vatican. His *magnum opus,* the sacred trilogy *La Passione di Cristo* (I. *La Cena del Signore;* II. *L'Orazione al monte;* III. *La Morte del Redentore*), was produced in Milan, Dec. 2, 1897, at the Italian Congress for Sacred Music, and had numerous performances elsewhere in Europe and America. Other oratorios are: *La Trasfigurazione del Nostro Signore Gesù Cristo* (Venice, March 20, 1898); *La Risurrezione di Lazaro* (Venice, July 27, 1898), in La Fenice Theater, by special permission); *La Risurrezione di Cristo* (Rome, Dec. 13, 1898); *Il Natale del Redentore* (Como, Sept. 12, 1899); *L'Entrata di Cristo in Gerusalemme* (Milan, April 25, 1900); *La Strage degli innocenti* (Milan, May 18, 1900); *Mosè* (Milan, Nov. 16, 1901); *Dies Iste* (Rome, Dec. 9, 1904); *Transitus Animae* (Rome, Dec. 18, 1907); *In Patris memoriam* (Naples, May 15, 1919); *Giorni di Tribulazione* (Milan, Oct. 1916). He wrote further some 40 Masses with organ; a Requiem with instrumental accompaniment; a *Stabat Mater* for solo voices, chorus, and orch.; *Vespertina Oratio,* for solo voices, chorus, and orch.; about 150 motets, Psalms, etc.; 2 symph. poems, *Dovrei non piangere* and *La Festa del villaggio;* a series of 8 orchestral pieces, each named after an Italian city: *Roma, Firenze, Milano, Venezia, Messina, Tortona, Genoa, Torina;* other orchestral works; a piano concerto; a violin concerto; chamber music; many organ works.

BIBLIOGRAPHY: I. Seytre, *L'Abbé Perosi: sa biographie, son œuvre* (Nice, 1901); Romain Rolland, *Don Lorenzo Perosi,* in *Musiciens d'aujourd'hui* (Paris, 1914; in English, N.Y., 1915); A. Damerini, *Lorenzo Perosi* (Rome, 1924); A. Della Corte, *Lorenzo Perosi* (Turin, 1936); A. Paglialunga, *Lorenzo Perosi* (Rome, 1952); M. Glinski, *Lorenzo Perosi* (Milan, 1953); M. Rinaldi, *Lorenzo Perosi* (Rome, 1967).

Perotin (called **Perotinus Magnus**), celebrated composer of the 12th century; putative dates of life are: born between 1155 and 1160; died between 1200 and 1250. He was the greatest master (after Leonin) of the Notre Dame School, representing the flowering of the Ars antiqua. He was maître de chapelle at Beatae Mariae Virginis (before the erection of Notre-Dame), Paris. Among his extant works are organa in 2, 3, and 4 parts. His melodic writing differs from the practice of Leonin in that he employs triadic progressions; there is also a suggestion of rudimentary canonic procedures. His most famous quadruple organum, *Sederunt principes,* was publ. by R. Ficker in 1930, and appears in several collections of medieval music. Other works are in Coussemaker's *L'Art harmonique au Xii^e et XIIIe siècles;* vol. I of *Oxford History of Music;* Y. Rokseth, *Motets du XIIIe siècle* (1936); Davison and Apel, *Historical Anthology of Music* (vol. 1, 1946). A complete edition is edited by E. Thurston (N.Y., 1970).

BIBLIOGRAPHY: R. Ficker, in *Neue Musikzeitung* 2 (1928); J. Handschin, in *Schweizerisches Jahrbuch für Musikwissenschaft* 2; F. Ludwig, in the Riemann-Festschrift (1909), the *Archiv für Musikwissenschaft* 3, the *Zeitschrift für Musikwissenschaft* 5, Guido Adler's *Handbuch der Musikgeschichte* (1930), and the Adler-Festschrift (Vienna, 1930); H. Besseler, *Die Musik des Mittelalters und der Renaissance* (Potsdam, 1931-35); G. Reese, *Music in the Middle Ages,* chap. 11 (N.Y., 1940); Hans Tischler, *The Motet in 13th-Century France* (New Haven, 1942); J. Chailley, *Histoire musicale du moyen-âge* (Paris, 1950); W. Waite, *The Rhythm of Twelfth-Century Polyphony* (New Haven, 1954).

Perrault, Michel, Canadian composer; b. Montreal, July 20, 1925. He studied harmony, oboe and timpani at the Montreal Cons. (1943-46); went to Paris where he took lessons with Honegger and Nadia Boulanger (1946-47). Returning to Canada he was percussion player and assistant conductor of the Montreal Symph. Orch. (1957-60); then became associated with the Minute Opera Company. He founded in Montreal a jazz organization, La Société de Concerts de Musique de Chambre Noire, and his own publishing house, Publications Bonart.

WORKS: 3 ballets: *Commedia del arte* (1958), *Sea Gallows* (1958) and *Suite canadienne* (1965); *Les Trois Cones* for cello and orch. (1949); *La Belle Rose* for cello and orch. (1952); *Fête et parade* for trumpet and orch. (1952); *Esquisses en plein air* for soprano and string orch. (1954); *Monologues* for string orch. (1954); *Margoton* for harp and orch. (1954); *Le Saucisson canadien* for 4 saxophones and string orch. (1955); *Pastiche espagnol* for trumpet and orch. (1956); *Pastiche tzigane* for 2 trumpets and orch. (1957); *Berubée* for piano and orch. (1959); *Jeux de quartes* for harp and orch. (1961); *Serenata per tre fratelli* for 3 horns and orch. (1962); Double Bass Concerto (1962); *Homage,* overture (1966); Concerto for horn and orch. without brasses (1967); Violin Sonata (1946); Saxophone Quartet (1953); Piano Trio (1954); Sextet for clarinet, harp and string quartet (1955); incidental music; works for jazz ensemble; songs.

Perrin, Harry Crane, British organist and pedagogue; b. Wellingborough, Aug. 19, 1865; d. Exeter, England, Nov. 6, 1953. Pupil in Dublin of Sir R. Stewart, Dr. C. W. Pearce, and Dr. F. Bates; Mus. Bac., Dublin, 1890; F.R.C.O., 1892; Mus. Doc., 1901; 1892-98, organist and choirmaster at St. Michael's Coventry; 1898-1908, at Canterbury Cathedral, and conductor of the Cathedral Musical Society; 1908-30, prof. of music and director of the Cons., McGill Univ., Montreal, Canada (from 1920, dean of the faculty there); 1930, retired as dean-emeritus, and returned to England. He composed cantatas; overture and suite for orch.; numerous church services and anthems; song cycles, part-songs, etc.

Perrin, Pierre, French poet; b. Lyons, c.1620; d. Paris, April 25, 1675. Author of the librettos for the first French operas (so called): Cambert's *La Pastorale* (1659), *Pomone* (1671), and *Ariane* (1672). The privilege obtained from Louis XIV by Perrin and Cambert to organize the Académie de Musique (1668) was revoked in Lully's favor (1672).

BIBLIOGRAPHY: A. Pougin, *Les vrais créateurs de l'opéra français, Perrin et Cambert* (Paris, 1881); H. Prunières, "Lully and the Académie de Musique et de Danse," *Musical Quarterly* (Oct. 1925).

Perry, Edward Baxter, American pianist; b. Haverhill, Mass., Feb. 14, 1855; d. Camden, Maine, June 13, 1924. He became nearly blind in childhood, but was able to go to Germany where he took lessons with Kullak, Pruckner, and also with Clara Schumann and Liszt. Returning to America he originated an innovative type of "lecture-recital" with which he traveled all over the U.S.; he also did some teaching, composed a number of semi-attractive piano pieces and publ. *Descriptive Analyses of Piano Works* (1902) and *Stories of Standard Teaching Pieces* (1910).

Perry, George, English composer; b. Norwich, 1793; d. London, March 4, 1862. He was a choirboy at the Cathedral of Norwich; moved to London in 1822, and became director of the music at the Haymarket Theatre; then organist of Quebec Chapel; 1832-47, concertmaster of the Sacred Harmonic Society orch.

WORKS: the oratorios *Elijah and the Priests of Baal* (1818), *The Fall of Jerusalem* (1830), *The Death of Abel* (1846), *Hezekiah* (1847); a cantata, *Belshazzar's Feast* (1836); 2 operas, *Morning, Noon and Night* (1822), *Family Quarrels* (1830); overture to *The Persian Hunters;* anthems, songs, piano pieces.

Perry, Julia, American composer; b. Lexington, Kentucky, March 25, 1924. After studying at the Westminster Choir College, she went to Europe where she took lessons with Luigi Dallapiccola and Nadia Boulanger. Her opera, *The Cask of Amontillado* was produced at Columbia Univ. on Nov. 20, 1954. She also wrote symphonic works and much chamber music.

Persiani (*née* **Tacchinardi**), **Fanny,** Italian coloratura soprano; b. Rome, Oct. 4, 1812; d. Neuilly-sur-Seine, May 3, 1867. Her father, the tenor **Nicola Tacchinardi,** was her teacher. After a successful debut at Leghorn in 1832, she sang in the principal cities of Italy; from 1837-47 she appeared in London and Paris with brilliant success; also visited Holland and Russia, but returned to Paris in 1858. In 1830 she married the composer **Giuseppe Persiani.**

BIBLIOGRAPHY: G. Tebaldini, "G. Persiani e F. Tacchinardi, memorie ed appunti," *Rivista Musicale Italiana* 12.

Persiani, Giuseppe, Italian opera composer; b. Recanati, Sept. 11, 1799; d. Paris, Aug. 13, 1869. As a youth he played violin in theater orchestras in Rome and Naples, where he studied with Zingarelli. In 1830 he married the singer **Fanny Tacchinardi,** who became known as "La Persiani"; her illustrious name completely eclipsed his; yet he was a notable composer whose dramatic opera *Ines de Castro,* produced in Naples on Jan. 27, 1835, scored great success and was performed all over Europe; the celebrated soprano Malibran sang the title role, and Czerny wrote a piano paraphrase on themes of the opera. Persiani's other operas are *Attila* (Parma, Jan. 31, 1827); *Il Solitario* (Milan, April 26, 1829), *Il Fantasma* (Paris, Dec. 14, 1843), and *Eufemio di Messina* (Lucca, Sept. 20, 1829; performed also under the alternative titles *La distruzione di Catania* and *I Saraceni a Catania*).

BIBLIOGRAPHY: G. Tebaldini, "Giuseppe Persiani e Fanny Tacchinardi," *Rivista Musicale Italiana* (1905).

Persichetti, Vincent, outstanding American composer; b. Philadelphia, June 6, 1915. He studied piano with Alberto Jonás and Olga Samaroff; took lessons in composition with Nordoff and Roy Harris, and conducting with Fritz Reiner. He served as head of the composition dept. at the Philadelphia Cons. (1942–48); in 1948 was appointed to the staff of the Juilliard School of Music, N.Y., and in 1952 became director of publications of the Elkan-Vogel Co. in Philadelphia. Persichetti's music is remarkable for its polyphonic skill in fusing the seemingly incompatible idioms of Classicism, Romanticism and stark modernism, but the melodic lines maintain an almost Italianate diatonicism, in a lyrical manner.

WORKS: A prolific composer, he wrote 9 symphonies: No. 1 (1942; Rochester, Oct. 21, 1947); No. 2 (1942); No. 3 (Philadelphia, Nov. 21, 1947); No. 4 (Philadelphia, Dec. 17, 1954); No. 5 (Louisville, Aug. 28, 1954); No. 6 for band (St. Louis, April 16, 1956); No. 7, *Liturgic* (St. Louis, Oct. 24, 1959); No. 8 (Berea, Ohio, Oct. 29, 1967); No. 9, *Janiculum* (Philadelphia, March 5, 1971); a series of serenades for various instrumental groups: No. 1, for 10 wind instruments (1929); No. 2, for piano (1929); No. 3, for violin, cello and piano (1941); No. 4, for violin and piano (1945); No. 5, for orch. (Louisville, Nov. 15, 1950); No. 6, for trombone, viola and cello (1950); No. 7, for piano (1952); No. 8, for piano, 4 hands (1954); No. 9, for soprano and recorders (1956); No. 10, for flute and harp (1957); No. 11, for band (1960); No. 12, for tuba (1960); No. 13, for 2 clarinets (1963); Concertino for Piano and Orch. (Rochester, Oct. 23, 1945); *Dance Overture* (Tokyo, Feb. 7, 1948); *Fables,* for narrator and orch. (Philadelphia, April 20, 1945); *The Hollow Men,* for trumpet and string orch. (Germantown, Dec. 12, 1946); *Divertimento* for band (N.Y., June 16, 1950); *Pageant,* for band (Miami, March 7, 1953); *King Lear,* ballet music for 7 instruments (Martha Graham Co., Montclair, N.J., Jan. 31, 1949); *Spring Cantata* for women's chorus and piano (1963); *Winter Cantata* for women's chorus, flute and marimba (1964); *The Pleiades* for chorus, trumpet and string orch. (1967); *The Creation,* oratorio (N.Y., April 17, 1970); *Lincoln Address* for narrator and orch., to the excerpts from Lincoln's second inaugural address (originally scheduled for performance for President Nixon's inaugural concert, Jan. 19, 1973, but cancelled because of the ominous threat in the text to the "mighty scourge of war" to be brought down on the unyielding foe, which might have been misinterpreted in the light of the then raging war in Vietnam; the work was finally per-

formed by the St. Louis Symph. Orch. at Carnegie Hall, N.Y., on Jan. 25, 1973); Concerto for English Horn and String Orch. (N.Y., Nov. 17, 1977); Piano Concerto (Dartmouth College, Hanover, N.H., Aug. 2, 1964); 5 parables: No. 1 for flute solo (1965), No. 2, for woodwind quintet (1968), No. 3, for oboe (1968), No. 4, for bassoon (1969), No. 5, for glockenspiel (1969); 3 string quartets (1939, 1944, 1959); *Suite* for violin and cello (1940); Sonata for Solo Violin (1940); 2 piano quintets: No. 1 (1940); No. 2 (his most remarkable chamber music work; Library of Congress, Washington, D.C., Feb. 4, 1955); Violin Sonata (1941); *Pastoral* for woodwind quintet (Philadelphia, April 20, 1945); *Vocalise* for cello and piano (1945); Sonata for Unaccompanied Cello (1952); 11 piano sonatas (1939–65); 6 piano sonatinas (1950–54); Sonata for 2 pianos; Concerto for Piano 4-Hands; Sonatina for organ pedals; numerous other works of organ music; choruses; songs. He published a manual, *Twentieth-Century Harmony: Creative Aspects and Practice* (N.Y., 1961); *Essays on Twentieth-Century Choral Music* (Norman, Oklahoma, 1963).

BIBLIOGRAPHY: Robert Evett, "The Music of Vincent Persichetti," *Juilliard Review* (Spring 1955).

Persinger, Louis, eminent American violinist and teacher; b. Rochester, Illinois, Feb. 11, 1887; d. New York, Dec. 31, 1966. He was a student of Hans Becker at the Leipzig Cons., where he made his debut on March 23, 1904; then undertook further study with Ysaÿe in Brussels and Thibaud in Paris. He toured Germany, Austria and Scandinavia as a concert violinist; served as concertmaster of the Berlin Philharmonic (1914–15); returning to the U.S. he was director of the Chamber Music Society of San Francisco (1916–28); then devoted himself mainly to teaching; in 1930 he joined the staff of the Juilliard School of Music, N.Y. He achieved a great reputation as a teacher who subordinated technical demands to the paramount considerations of formal balance and expressiveness of the melodic line. Among his pupils were Yehudi Menuhin and Ruggiero Ricci.

Perti, Jacopo (Giacomo) Antonio, greatly significant Italian composer; b. Crevalcore, near Bologna, June 6, 1661; d. there, April 10, 1756. A pupil of Padre Petronio Franceschini, as early as 1680 he brought out a Mass, and next year was elected a member of the Accademia Filarmonica, of which he was five times the president. After spending several years as an opera composer at Parma, he became maestro at San Pietro in Bologna (1690), and in 1696 maestro at San Petronio. He wrote 24 operas, the most successful of which was *Il Furio Camillo* (Venice, 1692), and 19 oratorios; publ. the oratorio *Abramo vincitor de' propri affetti* (1687), *Cantate morali e spirituali* (1688), and *Messe e salmi concertati* (1735). His MSS were dispersed; Abbate Santini possessed a valuable collection. Extant works include 4 Passions and 8 oratorios at Bologna, an *Adoramus Te* in the Fitzwilliam Museum, Cambridge, 2 fine choruses in Novello's *Sacred Music,* and other compositions in various collections.

BIBLIOGRAPHY: L. Mancini, *J. A. Perti* (Bologna, 1813); G. Atti, *Orazione in lode di I. A. Perti* (1844); an extended biography of Perti is found in L. Busi's *Il*

Padre Giambatt. Martini (Bologna, 1891; vol. I, p. 61 et seq.); F. Giegling, "G. A. Perti," *Die Musikforschung* 4 (1955).

Pertile, Aureliano, Italian operatic tenor; b. Montagnara, Nov. 9, 1885; d. Milan, Jan. 11, 1952. He made his debut in 1911; was for a season (1921–22) a member of the Metropolitan Opera, N.Y.; then at La Scala, Milan (1922–37); also sang in London. After retirement, he settled down in Milan as voice teacher.

Perusso, Mario, Argentine composer; b. Buenos Aires, Sept. 16, 1936. He began his music career by singing in an opera chorus at the Teatro Colón in Buenos Aires; then began to compose. His one-act opera *La Voz del Silencio* was produced at the Teatro Colón in Buenos Aires, Nov. 23, 1969. Other works include *3 symphonic Movements* (1954); *Elegía* for orch. (1964); *Invenzioni* for string quartet (1967); *La eternidad y el viento* for orch. (1968).

Pessard, Émile-Louis-Fortuné, French composer; b. Paris, May 29, 1843; d. there, Feb. 10, 1917. Pupil in the Paris Cons. of Bazin (harmony), Laurent (piano), Benoist (organ), and Carafa (composition); won the 1st harmony-prize in 1862, and the Grand Prix de Rome in 1866 with the cantata *Dalila* (Opéra, 1867). In 1881 he was appointed professor of harmony at the Paris Cons. He enjoyed considerable regard as a composer of fine songs. Debussy copied Pessard's song *Chanson d'un fou,* and the manuscript in Debussy's handwriting was publ. erroneously as Debussy's own. WORKS: *La Cruche cassée* (Opéra-Comique, 1870); *Le Char* (Opéra-Comique, 1878); *Le Capitaine Fracasse* (1878); *Tabarin* (Opéra, 1885); *Tatarin sur les Alpes* (1888); *Don Quichotte* (1889); *Les Folies amoureuses* (Opéra-Comique, April 15, 1891; his most successful comic opera); *Une Nuit de Noël* (1893); *Mlle. Carabin* (1893); *Le Muet* (1894); *La Dame de trèfles* (1898); *L'Armée des Vierges* (1902); *L'Épave* (1903); etc.

Pestalozzi, Heinrich, Swiss composer; b. Wädenswil, near Zürich, Aug. 26, 1878; d. Zürich, Aug. 9, 1940. He studied theology and music in Berlin; was singing teacher there (1902–12); then pastor in Arosa, Switzerland; in 1917 was appointed voice teacher at the Zürich Cons. His many songs and choral works have enjoyed great popularity in Switzerland; a full list is found in Refardt's *Musikerlexikon der Schweiz.* Pestalozzi publ. several manuals on singing: *Individuelle Stimmbildung; Kehlkopfgymnastik; Die deutsche Bühnenaussprache im Gesang; Geheimnisse der Stimmbildung; Der Weg zu einer schönen Stimme.*

Petchnikov, Alexander, Russian violinist; b. Elets, Jan. 20, 1873; d. Buenos Aires, Nov. 3, 1949. He was a pupil of Hřimalý at the Moscow Cons., where he won the Gold Medal; subsequently lived in Germany; from 1913 to 1921 taught at the Royal Academy in Munich; founded a string quartet in Berlin in 1924, and taught at the Stern Cons. there. After the advent of the Nazi regime, he was compelled to leave Germany, and in 1936 went to Argentina.

Peter, Johann Friedrich (John Frederick), American Moravian organist and composer; b. Heerendijk, Holland (of German parentage), May 19, 1746; d. Bethlehem, Pa., July 13, 1813. He was educated in Holland and Germany; came to America in 1770. He served the Moravian church in various capacities in Nazareth, Bethlehem, and Lititz, Pa., and in Salem, N.C. (1779–89), where he married. He spent the rest of his life mostly in Bethlehem as organist of the church. He is widely considered the greatest of the American Moravian composers. His collection of copies of instrumental works by Stamitz, J. C. F. Bach, and J. Ch. Bach, Abel, Boccherini, and Haydn (preserved in the Archives of the Moravian Church) proves his knowledge of contemporary music. He began to compose in 1770. While at Salem he wrote (in 1789) a set of six quintets for 2 violins, 2 violas, and cello (his only secular works), which appear to be the oldest preserved examples of chamber music composed in America; they were publ., under the editorship of H. T. David, in 1955, for the N.Y. Public Library series, *Music of the Moravians in America.* His solo arias and choral anthems (more than 100) for strings and organ, or with woodwinds, strings and organ, are well written, often quite expressive, and evidently constitute the finest and most elaborate concerted church music written in America at that time. Those preserved in the Archives of the Moravian Church at Bethlehem are listed in A. G. Rau's and H. T. David's *A Catalogue of Music by American Moravians* (Bethlehem, Pa., 1938).
BIBLIOGRAPHY: A. G. Rau, "J. F. Peter," *Musical Quarterly* (July 1937); H. T. David, "Musical Life in the Pennsylvania Settlements of the *Unitas Fratrum,*" *Transactions of the Moravian Historical Society* (Bethlehem, 1942; repr. as Moravian Music Foundation Publication No. 6, 1959); E. Nolte, "The Paradox of the Peter Quintets," *Moravian Music Foundation Bulletin* (Fall 1967); J. S. Ingram, "Reflections of the Salem *Collegium Musicum,*" ibid. (Spring-Summer 1975).

Peter, Simon, American Moravian composer; brother of **Johann Friedrich Peter;** b. Heerendijk, Holland (of German parentage), April 2, 1743; d. Salem, N.C., May 29, 1819. With his brother, he was educated at Moravian Brethren's schools in Holland and Germany; came to America in 1770. His ministry was spent in both the Northern and Southern Provinces of the Moravian Church (i.e., both Pennsylvania and North Carolina). From 1784 to 1819 he lived in North Carolina as pastor of several congregations, and was a member of the governing board of the Church. He composed only a few sacred anthems, but one of these, *O Anblick, der mirs Herze bricht,* may well be one of the most expressive of all Lenten songs written in America.
BIBLIOGRAPHY: H. T. David, "Musical Life in the Pennsylvania Settlements of the *Unitas Fratrum,*" *Transactions of the Moravian Historical Society* (1942).

Peters, Carl Friedrich, German music publisher; b. Leipzig, March 30, 1779; d. there, Nov. 20, 1827. In 1814 Peters purchased Kühnel & Hoffmeister's Bureau de Musique (established in 1800; Hoffmeister left the firm in 1805; Kühnel was the sole owner from 1805 to his death in 1813). The firm was thenceforward known as "C. F. Peters, Bureau de Musique." Its rich catalogue contained the first edition of collected works of J. S. Bach; it also included music by Beethoven, who entrusted to the Bureau de Musique the publication of his 1st Symph., Piano Concerto, op. 19, Septet, op. 20, Piano Sonata, op. 22, and other works. Later C. F. Peters acquired works by Weber, Spohr, Czerny, Chopin, Schumann, Wagner, Liszt, and Brahms. In more recent times the works of Mahler, Grieg, Hugo Wolf, Max Reger, Richard Strauss (his 7 symph. poems), and others were publ. From 1868, classical works were publ. in the inexpensive and reliable "Edition Peters." Its large and important musical library was opened to the public in 1893 as the "Bibliothek Peters." Scholarly annual books *(Peters Jahrbuch)* were publ. until 1941, containing articles by eminent musicologists, current bibliography, etc. Dr. Max Abraham was sole proprietor from 1880 to 1900. After his death in 1900, his nephew, Heinrich Hinrichsen (b. Hamburg, Feb. 5, 1868; d. Belgium, Sept., 1942), became head of the firm; from 1927 to 1932 he shared the ownership with his son, Max Hinrichsen (b. Leipzig, July 6, 1901); soon afterwards, two other sons joined the firm—in 1933 Walter Hinrichsen (b. Leipzig, Sept. 23, 1907), and in 1934 Hans Hinrichsen (b. Leipzig, Aug. 22, 1909; d. Perpignan, France, 1941). The Litolff catalogue was acquired by Peters in 1938. Heinrich Hinrichsen was still in charge in 1939, when the Nazi regime finally forced him into exile, and Johannes Petschull was appointed manager in his stead. After World War II the firm was divided into three separate but closely affiliated companies: Peters Edition, London, under the direction of Max Hinrichsen; C. F. Peters Corporation, New York, owned by Walter Hinrichsen; and the German firm, since 1950 in Frankfurt, under the management of Johannes Petschull.

Peters, Roberta, American soprano; b. New York, May 4, 1930. She studied singing with William Pierce Herman; made her operatic debut with the Metropolitan Opera, N.Y., as Zerlina in *Don Giovanni* on Nov. 17, 1950 (as a substitute on short notice) and subsequently remained on the roster, singing with excellent success such roles as Rosina in *Il Barbiere di Siviglia,* Susanna in *Le Nozze di Figaro,* and Gilda in *Rigoletto.*

Petersen, Wilhelm, German composer; b. Athens, March 15, 1890; d. Darmstadt, Dec. 18, 1957. He studied in Germany and worked as a theater conductor; served in the German army during World War I; in 1922 settled in Darmstadt as a teacher. He wrote the opera *Der goldne Topf* (Darmstadt, March 29, 1941); 5 symphonies (1921, 1923, 1934, 1941, 1957); 3 violin sonatas; 3 string quartets and other chamber music; several sacred choruses and songs. He was highly regarded in Darmstadt as a musician and pedagogue. In 1972 a Wilhelm Petersen Society was founded to memorialize his work.
BIBLIOGRAPHY: A. Petersen, *Wilhelm Petersen, Skizze seines Wesens und Lebens* (Darmstadt, 1962).

Petersilea, Carlyle, American pianist and teacher; b. Boston, Jan. 18, 1844; d. Tropico, near Los Angeles, June 11, 1903. He studied at the Leipzig Cons. with Moscheles, Reinecke, and others, winning a prize. After a tour in Germany, he returned to Boston; established there the Petersilea Academy of Music (1871); after 15 years, he closed his own school to become a teacher at the New England Cons. (1886); in 1892, went to California. He spent the spring of 1884 with Liszt at Weimar. He publ. technical studies and various pieces for piano.

Peterson-Berger, (Olof) Wilhelm, Swedish composer; b. Ullånger, Feb. 27, 1867; d. Frösön, Dec. 3, 1942. He studied with J. Dente and O. Bolander at the Stockholm Cons. (1886–89); then in Dresden with Scholtz (piano) and Kretschmer (composition); eventually settled in Stockholm, where he became active as a pedagogue and music critic of *Dagens Nyheter* (1896). A symposium of articles was publ. in Stockholm on the occasion of his 70th birthday (1937).
WORKS: *Sveagaldrar,* a festival play for the silver jubilee of the accession of Oscar II (1897); a fairy opera, *Lyckan* (*Luck;* Stockholm, 1903); the music dramas, all produced in Stockholm, *Ran* (1899–1900; May 20, 1903), *Arnljot* (1907–09; April 13, 1910), *Domedagsprofeterna* (*The Prophets of Doom,* 1912–17), and *Adils och Elisiv* (1921–24; Feb. 27, 1927); 5 symphonies with programmatic subtitles: No. 1, *Baneret* (1889–1903; Stockholm, Feb. 23, 1904); No. 2, *Sunnanfärd* (1910; Göteborg, March 22, 1911); No. 3, *Same Ätnam* (1913–15; Stockholm, Dec. 11, 1917); No. 4, *Holmia* (1929; Stockholm, April 9, 1930); No. 5, *Solitudo* (1932–33; Stockholm, April 11, 1934); *Romance* for violin and orch. (1915); Violin Concerto (1928; Stockholm, Feb. 6, 1929); orch. suites, *I Somras* (1903), *Earina* (1917), and *Italiana* (1922); cantatas, *Norrbotten* (1921), *Operakantaten* (1922, revised 1935–36), and *Soluppgång* (1929); 2 violin sonatas (1887, 1910); *Suite* for violin and piano (1896); 40 songs for mixed choir; nearly 100 solo songs; over 100 piano pieces.
WRITINGS: *Svensk Musikkultur* (1911); *Richard Wagner som kulturföreteelse (Wagner as a Phenomenon of Civilization,* 1913; in German as *Richard Wagner als Kulturerscheinung,* 1917). A selection of his essays was publ. in Stockholm in 2 vols. (1923); another, in 1 vol., in Östersund (1951). His reminiscences were publ. posthumously (Uppsala, 1943).
BIBLIOGRAPHY: B. Carlberg, *Peterson-Berger* (Stockholm, 1950).

Petin, Nikola, Serbian composer; b. Belgrade, Dec. 19, 1920. He studied with Slavenski and others; became teacher at Novi Sad. His music is romantically colored. Among his works are *3 Symphonic Portraits: Hamlet, Ophelia, Polonius; Symphonia brevis; Ballade* for bassoon and piano; incidental music for the theater.

Petit, Raymond, French music critic and composer; b. Neuilly-sur-Seine, July 6, 1893. He studied music with Tournemire in Paris; lived there most of his life; contributed numerous articles on modern music to the *Revue Musicale* and criticism to *Le Ménestrel* as well as to some American publications.

WORKS: an opera, *La Sulamithe; Suite grave* for orch. (1920); *2 Méditations* for string quartet (1921); *Dialogue* for 2 violins; *Hymnus* for voice and flute (1924); *Il Cantico del sole*, for voice and wind instruments (Frankfurt Festival of the International Society for Contemporary Music, July 3, 1927); songs.

Petkov, Dimiter, Bulgarian composer and conductor; b. Smolyan, May 4, 1919. He studied composition with Veselin Stoyanov at the Bulgarian State Cons., graduating in 1950; then went to Moscow for postgraduate studies in music theory at the Moscow Cons. (1952-54). Returning to Bulgaria he became director of the National Opera Theater in Sofia (1954-62 and again since 1975).

WORKS: a musical comedy, *Restless Hearts* (1960; Sofia, 1976); a children's operetta, *The Winding Path* (1956; Michailovgrad, Oct. 29, 1975); an oratorio, *Rozhan Comes Down from Rhodopa* (1965); 5 cantatas: *September Legend* (1953), *Communists* (1956), *Requiem for a Sailor* (1967), *Cantata about Paissy* (1973) and *Festive Cantata* (1974); *The Sparks of October*, suite for soloists, children's chorus and orch. (1967); *3 Polyphonic Pieces* for flute, clarinet and bassoon (1953); choruses; arrangements of folk songs.

Petra-Basacopol, Carmen, Rumanian composer; b. Sibiu, Sept. 5, 1926. She studied with P. Constantinescu, Jora, Ciortea and Rogalski at the Bucharest Cons. (1949-56); then taught at her alma mater. Her music is lyrical; her instrumentation is colorful and effective.

WORKS: a ballet, *Fata şi masca* (1969); Symph. No. 1 (1955); *Land of the Stone*, symph. poem (1959); Piano Concerto (1961); *Symphonic Triptych* (1962); 2 violin concertos (1963, 1965); *The Death of the Doe*, ballad for solo baritone, clarinet, piano, strings and percussion (1966); *Song of the Supreme Sacrifices and of the Light*, cantata (1967); *Suite* for flute and piano (1950); *Cello Sonata* (1952); *Violin Sonata* (1954); *3 Sketches* for oboe and bassoon (1956); *Piano Trio* (1958); *Sonata* for flute and harp (1960); *Concertino* for harp, wind quintet, double bass and xylophone (1969); *Elegy* for violin and piano (1971); *Primavera*, poem for soprano, clarinet and piano (1971); *Impressions of the Village Museum*, concert suite for piano (1960); songs.

Petrassi, Goffredo, outstanding Italian composer; b. Zagarolo, near Rome, July 16, 1904. He worked as a clerk in a music store in Rome, studying musical compositions in his leisure time; began taking regular lessons in composition with Vincenzo di Donato and with Alessandro Bustini at the S. Cecilia Academy in Rome; in 1939 was himself appointed to its faculty as prof. of composition. In 1956 he conducted composition classes at the Berkshire Music Center in Tanglewood. Despite the late beginning, Petrassi acquired a solid technique of composition; the chief influence in his music was that of Casella; later he became interested in 12-tone procedures.

WORKS: OPERAS: *Il Cordovano* (1944-48; La Scala, Milan, May 12, 1949) and *La Morte dell'Aria* (1949-50; Rome, Oct. 24, 1950). BALLETS: *La Follia di Orlando* (1942-43; La Scala, Milan, April 12, 1947) and *Il Ritratto di Don Quixote* (1945; Paris, Nov. 21, 1947). FOR ORCH.: *Divertimento* (1930); *Overture da concerto* (1931); *Passacaglia* (1931); *Partita* (1932; Rome, April 2, 1933); 8 *Concertos for Orchestra*: No. 1 (1933-34; Rome, March 31, 1935); No. 2 (1951; Basel, Jan. 24, 1952); No. 3, *Récréation concertante* (1952-53; Aix-en-Provence Festival, July 23, 1953); No. 4, for string orch. (1954; Rome, April 28, 1956); No. 5 (1955; Boston, Dec. 2, 1955); No. 6, *Invenzione concertata*, for brass, strings and percussion (1956-57; London, Sept. 9, 1957); No. 7 (1961-64; Bologna, March 18, 1965); No. 8 (1970-72; Chicago, Sept. 28, 1972); Piano Concerto (1936-39; Rome, Dec. 10, 1939; Walter Gieseking soloist); Flute Concerto (1960; Hamburg, March 7, 1961); *Estri*, chamber symph. for 15 performers (1966-67; Dartmouth College, Hanover, N.H., Aug. 2, 1967; as a ballet, Spoleto, July 11, 1968). VOCAL WORKS: *3 Choruses*, with small orch. (1932); *Psalm IX* for chorus, strings, brass, 2 pianos and percussion (1934-36); *Magnificat* for soprano, chorus and orch. (1939-40); *Coro di morti*, dramatic madrigal for male chorus, brass, double basses, 3 pianos and percussion (1940-41; Venice, Sept. 28, 1941); *2 Liriche di Saffo* for voice, and piano or 11 instruments (1941); *Quattro Inni Sacri* for tenor, baritone and organ (1942; version with orch., Rome, Feb. 22, 1950); *Noche Oscura*, cantata (1950-51; Strasbourg, June 17, 1951); *Nonsense*, to words by Edward Lear, for chorus a cappella (1952); *Propos d'Alain* for baritone and 12 performers (1960); *Sesto non-senso*, after Lear, for chorus a cappella (1964); *Mottetti per la Passione* for chorus a cappella (1966); *Beatitudines*, chamber oratorio in memory of Martin Luther King, Jr., for baritone and 5 instruments (1969; Fiuggi, July 17, 1969); *Orationes Christi* for chorus, brass, 8 violins and 8 cellos (1974-75; Rome, Dec. 6, 1975). CHAMBER MUSIC: *Sinfonia, siciliana e fuga* for string quartet (1929); *Siciliana e marcetta* for 2 pianos (1930); *Introduzione e allegro* for violin and piano (1933; also with 11 instruments); *Toccata* for piano (1933); *Preludio, aria e finale* for cello and piano (1933); *Invenzioni* for 2 pianos (1944); *Sonata da camera* for harpsichord and 10 instruments (1948); *Dialogo angelico* for 2 flutes (1948); *Musica a due* for 2 cellos (1952); *String Quartet* (1958); *Serenata* for flute, viola, double bass, harpsichord and percussion (1958); *String Trio* (1959); *Serenata II*, trio for harp, guitar and mandolin (1962); *Musica di Ottoni* for brass and timpani (1963); *Tre per sette* for 3 performers on 7 wind instruments (1966); *Ottetto di Ottoni* for 4 trumpets and 4 trombones (1968); *Souffle* for one performer on 3 flutes (1969); *Elogio per un'Ombra* for solo violin (1971); *Nunc* for solo guitar (1971); *Ala* for flute and harpsichord (1972); *Quattro Odi* for string quartet (1973-75); *Oh les Beaux Jours!* for piano (1976); *Fanfare* for 3 trumpets (1944-76); *Petite pièce* for piano (1976).

Petrauskas, Kipras, Lithuanian tenor; b. Vilna, Nov. 23, 1885; d. there, Jan. 17, 1968. He studied with his brother, the composer **Mikas Petrauskas**; appeared in his brother's opera, *Birute* (Vilna, Nov. 6, 1906); then became a singer at the Imperial Opera, St. Petersburg (1911-20); also appeared in Berlin, Paris, Milan, and made a tour of the U.S. He returned to Lithuania before World War II, and remained there; in 1950 received the Stalin Prize.

Petrauskas, Mikas, Lithuanian composer; b. Kaunas, Oct. 19, 1873; d. there, March 23, 1937. He studied organ with his father; was church organist at the age of 15; then went to St. Petersburg, where he studied with Rimsky-Korsakov at the Cons. During the abortive revolution of 1905 he became implicated in various political activities and was imprisoned; he was briefly in Vilna, where he produced his opera *Birute* (Nov. 6, 1906); in 1907 he emigrated to America; settled in Boston in 1914, and founded the Lithuanian Conservatory in South Boston; with the aid of a Lithuanian chorus there, he produced his operas *The Devil Inventor* (3 acts; South Boston; May 20, 1923) and *Egle, Queen of the Snakes* (6 acts; South Boston, May 30, 1924; Petrauskas himself sang the part of the King of the Snakes); cantatas; etc. The Lithuanian Conservatory publ. the piano scores of his operas *The King of the Forest* (1918) and *Egle;* he also publ. arrangements of Lithuanian songs in the periodical *Kankles* (Boston, 1917–21); further publ. a brief dictionary of musical terms in Lithuanian (Boston, 1916) and an album of Lithuanian songs (Boston, 1922). In 1930 he went back to Lithuania.

Petrella, Errico, Italian opera composer; b. Palermo, Dec. 10, 1813; d. Genoa, April 7, 1877. He studied at the Naples Cons. (Collegio di S. Sebastiano) as a pupil of Costa, Bellini, Ruggi, and Zingarelli. His first theatrical attempt was the 2-act opera buffa *Il Diavolo color di rosa* (Naples, 1829). Being successful, it was followed by some 20 operas, both comic and serious; *Le Miniere di Freibergh* (Naples, 1839) was his first buffo work; *Elnava, o l'Assedio di Leida* (Milan, March 4, 1856), the best in the serious style. *Marco Visconti* (Naples, Feb. 9, 1854) obtained immediate popularity in Italy, and *La Contessa d'Amalfi* (Turin, March 8, 1864) also had a notable success. Other operas were *Ione,* after Bulwer Lytton's novel, *The Last Days of Pompeii* (Milan, Jan. 26, 1858), *Giovanni II di Napoli* (Naples, Feb. 27, 1869), *I promessi sposi* (Lecco, Oct. 2, 1869), and *Bianca Orsini* (Naples, April 4, 1874). During a quarter of a century he vied with Verdi in Italian favor, but his lack of a true sense of dramatic development and his dependence on Bellini and Donizetti as models caused his operas to appear old-fashioned without a redeeming freshness. Despite his many productions, he died in poverty.

BIBLIOGRAPHY: F. Guardione, *Di Errico Petrella e della traslazione della salma da Genova a Palermo* (Palermo, 1908); G. Siciliano, *Di Errico Petrella, musicista palermitano* (Palermo, 1913).

Petrelli, Eleanora (*née* **Wigström**), Swedish soprano; b. Simtuna, April 9, 1835; d. Chicago, Feb. 21, 1904. While touring Finland as a member of a small theatrical company, she married a wealthy Russian named Petrov, and Italianized her married name to Petrelli. She studied in Milan with Lamperti, and in Paris with Mme. Viardot-Garcia. After her husband died in 1869, she virtually abandoned the stage, but continued to give concerts in Russia, Germany, and Scandinavian countries. In 1886 she settled in Stockholm, but soon went to Chicago, where she established a school for vocal culture. She published a number of songs.

Petri, Egon, distinguished pianist; b. Hannover, March 23, 1881; d. Berkeley, Calif., May 27, 1962. He was educated in a musical family; his father was the Dutch violinist, **Henri Wilhelm Petri** (1856–1914). He studied violin before he began to take piano lessons with Teresa Carreño. As a boy he played 2nd violin in a string quartet organized by his father in Dresden. He then went to Berlin, where he became a pupil of Busoni, who influenced Petri's own conception of piano playing as the fullest representation, by a single instrument, of the sonorities of an orchestra; he played with Busoni in London in 1921, in a concert for 2 pianos; made an extensive tour in Russia in 1923. He established himself as an eminent pedagogue in Europe; was teacher of piano at the Hochschule für Musik in Berlin (1921–26); presented a series of concerts in the U.S. (American debut, N.Y. Jan. 11, 1932); then taught at Cornell Univ. (1940–46) and at Mills College, Oakland, California.

Petrić, Ivo, Slovenian composer; b. Ljubljana, June 16, 1931. He studied composition with Skerjanc and conducting with Švara at the Ljubljana Music Academy (1953–58). In 1962 he became artistic leader of a group dedicated to the promotion of new music; in 1969 was appointed to the secretariat of the Union of Slovenian Composers. His compositions are romantic in their inspiration, and agreeably modernistic in technical presentation.

WORKS: 3 symphonies (1954; 1957; 1960); *Concerto Grosso* for string orch. (1955); *Divertimento* for orch. (1956); Concerto for Flute and Chamber Orch. (1955–57); Concerto for Clarinet and Chamber Orch. (1958); *Concertante Suite* for bassoon and strings (1959); *Concertante Overture* (1960); *Concertante Music* for wind quintet, timpani and strings (1962); *Croquis sonores* for harp and chamber ensemble (Warsaw Fest., Sept. 27, 1963); *Mosaics* for clarinet and chamber ensemble (1964); *Symphonic Mutations* (1964); *Epitaph* for harp, clarinet, violin, cello, strings and percussion (1965); *Integrali v barvah* (Integrals in Colors) for orch. (1968); *Burlesque pour les temps passés* for trombone and orch. (1969); *Music Concertante* for piano and orch. (1970); *Dialogues concertants* for cello and orch. (1972); *3 Images* for violin and orch. (1973); *Nocturnes and Games* for orch. (1973); *Fresque symphonique* for orch. (1973); *Episodes lyriques* for oboe and orch. (1974); *Gemini Concerto* for violin, cello and orch. (1975); a cantata, *Pierre de la mort* (The Stone of Death, 1962); 2 wind quintets (1953, 1959); Bassoon Sonata (1954); Oboe Sonata (1955); Flute Sonata (1955); Clarinet Sonata (1956–57); *3 Sketches* for flute and string quartet (1961); Horn Sonatina (1961); *3 Contrasts* for violin and piano (1961); *7 Movements* for 7 instruments (1963); *Jeux à 3* for cello, percussion and harp (1965); *Jeux à 4* for flute, piano, harp and cello (1966); *Little Chamber Concerto* for solo oboe, English horn, bass clarinet, horn, harp, piano, and string quartet (1966); *5 Movements* for oboe, and harp or string quartet (1967); *Intarzije* (Inlaid Work) for wind trio, horn, trumpet, trombone, percussion and string quintet

(1968); *Lirizmi* for horn and piano (1969); *Quatuor 69* for string quartet (1969); *Gemini Music* for cello and piano (1971); *Les Paysages*, poetic sketches for piano (1972); *Mosaïques* for percussion (1973); *Capriccio* for solo cello and small ensemble (1974).

Petridis, Petro, eminent Greek composer; b. Nigdé, Asia Minor, July 23, 1892. He studied at the American College in Constantinople and at the Univ. of Paris (political science); participated in the Balkan war of 1911–12 as a member of the Greek army; then returned to Paris, where he took lessons with Albert Wolff and Albert Roussel. He first essayed composition in 1917, with his songs, *Le Rayon* and *Berceuse;* continued to live in Paris, but also visited London and other European centers. In 1939 he went back to Athens; wrote there the oratorio *Saint Paul,* to celebrate the 1900th anniversary of St. Paul's sojourn in Greece.
WORKS: opera, *Zemphyra* (1923–25); oratorio, *St. Paul* (Athens, June 29, 1951, composer conducting); *A Byzantine Requiem* (1952); 5 symphonies (1928, 1940, 1941, 1943, 1951); Concerto for 2 pianos and orch. (1972); Violin Concerto (1972); *Panighiri,* suite of Greek tableaux for orch.; *Suite grecque; Suite ionienne;* Piano Concerto; chamber music; a number of songs.

Petrov, Andrei, Soviet composer; b. Leningrad, Sept. 2, 1930. He studied at the Leningrad Cons. with Evlakhov. When still a student he wrote a number of works that were successfully performed: the ballets *The Magic Apple Tree* (Leningrad, Nov. 8, 1953); *The Station Master* (after Pushkin; Leningrad, May 9, 1955); symph. poem *Radda and Loiko* (after Maxim Gorky; Leningrad, Dec. 12, 1954); *The Shores of Hope* (1959); a song cycle with orch., *For Peace* (Leningrad, Dec. 20, 1951); *Pioneer Suite* for orch. (1951; quite successful); *Sport Suite* for orch., written for the International Festival of Democratic Youth in Bucharest (1953); *Pathetic Poem* for voices, 2 pianos and percussion (1969). In his music Petrov maintains an ambiance of lyric melodiousness and harmonious simplicity.
BIBLIOGRAPHY: A. Kenigsberg, *Andrei Petrov* (Moscow, 1959).

Petrov, Ivan, Russian operatic bass; b. Irkutsk, Feb. 29, 1920. He made his debut at the Bolshoi Theater, Moscow, in 1943; his most celebrated interpretation is in the title role of *Boris Godunov,* inviting comparisons with Chaliapin. He made several tours as a member of the Opera of the Bolshoi Theater in Europe, in Japan and in the U.S.
BIBLIOGRAPHY: I. Nazarenko, *Ivan Petrov* (Moscow, 1957).

Petrov, Ossip, celebrated Russian basso; b. Elizavetgrad, Nov. 15, 1806; d. St. Petersburg, March 11, 1878. The intendant of the Imperial Opera accidentally heard him in 1830, singing with an inferior company at a fair in Kursk, and immediately engaged him. Petrov made his debut in St. Petersburg as Sarastro in *The Magic Flute.* The enormous compass of his voice, its extraordinary power and beautiful quality, combined with consummate histrionic skill, secured for

him recognition as one of the greatest of Russian bassos; this place he held throughout his long career (he appeared on the stage for the last time March 10, 1878, 4 days before his death). He created the roles of Susanin in Glinka's *Life for the Tsar* (1836), Ruslan in *Ruslan and Ludmila* (1842); the Miller in Dargomyzhsky's *Russalka* (1856), and Varlaam in Mussorgsky's *Boris Godunov* (1874).
BIBLIOGRAPHY: *Recollections of the 50th Anniversary of O. A. Petrov* (St. Petersburg, 1976); V. Stassov, *O. A. Petrov,* in vol. III of his collected works (St. Petersburg, 1894); A. Kompaneisky, "A Great Russian Singer," *Russkaya Muzykalnaya Gazeta* 9 (1903); E. Lastotchkina, *Ossip Petrov* (Moscow, 1950).

Petrović, Radomir, Yugoslav composer; b. Belgrade, May 13, 1923. He studied in Belgrade, and subsequently became active as a teacher there. His works are in a classical tradition, but he often makes use of national thematic elements; of these, his *Moto sinfonico* (Belgrade, March 3, 1959) is the most successful.

Petrovics, Emil, Serbian-born Hungarian composer; b. Nagybecskerek (now Zrenjanin), Feb. 9, 1930. He lived in Belgrade until 1941; came to Budapest; studied at the Cons. there with Sugár (1949–51), with Viski (1951–52) and Farkas (1952–57). He was musical director of the Petöfi Theater in Budapest (1960–64); then taught at the Academy of Dramatic Arts.
WORKS: satirical one-act opera, *C'est la guerre* (1961; Budapest Radio, Aug. 17, 1961; first stage performance, Budapest, March 11, 1962; highly successful; was awarded the Kossuth Prize in 1966); *Lysistrate,* comic opera after Aristophanes (1962); opera, *Bün és bünhödés (Crime and Punishment),* after Dostoyevsky (1969; Budapest, Oct. 26, 1969); 2 oratorios, *Jónás könyve (The Book of Jonah,* 1966), and *Ott essem el én (Let Me Die There)* for male chorus and orch. (1972); Flute Concerto (1957); Symphony for string orch. (1962); *Cassazione* for brass (1953); String Quartet (1958); *4 Self-Portraits in Masks* for harpsichord (1958); Wind Quintet (1964); *Passacaglia in Blues* for bassoon and piano (1964; as a ballet, Budapest, 1965).

Petrucci, Ottaviano dei, Italian music publisher, the first to print a complete collection of part-songs from movable type; b. Fossombrone, June 18, 1466; d. there, May 7, 1539. In 1498 he received from the Council of the Republic of Venice the privilege of printing music by this new method for 20 years, and worked there industriously 1501–11, then ceding the business to A. Scotto and N. da Rafael, and removing to Fossombrone, with a 15-year privilege for printing within the Papal States. His editions, printed with great neatness, are rare and highly prized specimens of early presswork. In Fossombrone he labored from 1513–23. His publications appeared at the most flourishing epoch of the Netherlands School, and his first work, *Odhecaton A* (1501), contains 96 numbers (modern ed. by Helen Hewitt, Cambridge, Mass., 1942), *Canti B.* (1502), and *Canti C.* (1504), 49 and 137, repetively, by famous composers before 1501. Petrucci's last publications were 3 books of Masses (1520–23) printed in folio as chorus books. Books I and IV of the 9 books of *frottole* publ. in Venice from 1504–08 by Petrucci were ed. by R. Schwartz in Jg. 8 of Th. Kroyer's *Publikationen älterer Musik* (Leipzig, 1933–35).

BIBLIOGRAPHY: A. Schmid, *O. d. Petrucci* (Vienna, 1845; contains full list of works known at the time; Italian by B. Revel, in *Bollettino bibliografico Musicale*, Milan, 1931–33); A. Vernarecci, *O. d. Petrucci* (Bologna; 2nd ed., 1882); J. B. Weckerlin, *Petrucci Harmonice musices odhecaton* (Paris, 1885); E. Vogel, "Der erste Notendruck für Figuralmusik," *Jahrbuch Peters* (1895; full list of contents of *Odhecaton*); M. Cauchie, "L'Odhecaton, recueil de musique instrumentale," *Revue de Musicologie* (Nov. 1925) and "A propos des trois receuils instrumentaux de la série de l'Odhecaton," ib. (May 1928); J. Marix, "Harmonice Musices Odhecaton A," ib. (Nov. 1935); K. Jeppesen, "Die neuentdeckten Bücher der Lauden des O. d. Petrucci," *Zeitschrift für Musikwissenschaft* (Nov. 1929); G. Reese, "The First Printed Collection of Part-Music: The *Odhecaton*," *Musical Quarterly* (Jan. 1934); A. Catelani, "Due stampe ignote di O. Petrucci" (1856; reprinted in *Bollettino Bibliografico Musicale*, 1932); C. Sartori, "A Little-Known Petrucci Publication," *Musical Quarterly* (April 1948); C. Sartori, *Bibliografia delle opere musicali stampate da O. Petrucci* (Florence, 1948). A facsimile ed. of the *Odhecaton A* was publ. by the *Bollettino Bibliografico Musicale* (1932).

Petrushka, Shabtai, German-born Israeli composer; b. Leipzig, March 15, 1903. He studied at the Institute of Technology in Berlin-Charlottenburg, and received an engineering diploma; studied music at the Leipzig Cons. He was an orchestral leader in various theaters in Berlin (1928–33); after the Nazi advent in 1933 he was a member of the orch. of the Jewish *Kulturbund*, for which he wrote incidental music. He emigrated to Palestine in 1938; served as an arranger and conductor of the Palestine Broadcasting Service (1938–48); then was assistant director of music of the Israel Broadcasting Service (1948–58) and head of the music division of the Israel Broadcasting Authority (1958–68); in 1970 joined the faculty of the Rubin Academy of Music in Jerusalem.

WORKS: *The Broken Blackboard*, a musical for children (1969); String Trio (1939); *4 Movements* for symph. band (1953); *5 Oriental Dances* for orch. (1954); *Piccolo Divertimento* for symph. band (1970); *3 Jewish Melodies* for 2 flutes and 3 clarinets (1972); *Hebrew Melodies* for wind quintet (1974); Wind Quartet (1975); *Jewish Melodies* for brass quintet (1974); *3 Sephardic Songs* for female chorus (1976).

Petrželka, Vilém, noted Czech composer and music pedagogue; b. Královo Pole, near Brno, Sept. 10, 1889; d. Brno, Jan. 10, 1967. He studied with Janáček at the Brno Organ School (1905–08) and in 1910 became Janáček's assistant at the school; subsequently took private lessons in Prague with Vítězslav Novák; taught at the Philharmonic Society School in Brno (1914–19) and in 1919 became a prof. at the newly formed Brno Cons. In his compositions he continued the national tradition of modern Moravian music; he was mainly influenced by Janáček, but he expanded his resources and on occasion made use of jazz rhythms, quarter-tones and other modernistic procedures.

WORKS: an opera, *Horník Pavel* (*The Miner Paul*, 1935–38); a cantata *Modlitba k slunci* (*A Prayer to the Sun*, 1921; Brno, Feb. 13, 1922); a symph. drama *Námořník Mikuláš* (*Mariner Nicholas*) for narrator, soli, chorus, organ, jazz band, and orch., employing quarter-tones (1928; Brno, Dec. 9, 1930); *Věčný návrat* (*Eternal Return*), symph. poem (1922–23; Brno, Feb. 10, 1924); *Suite* for string orch. (1924–25); *Dramatic Overture* (1932; Brno, March 26, 1933); *Partita* for string orch. (1934); a one-movement Sinfonietta (1941; Brno, Jan. 22, 1942); Violin Concerto (1943–44; revised 1946); *Pastoral Sinfonietta* (1951–52); Symphony (1956); 2 song cycles with orch.: *Živly* (*The Elements*, 1917) and *Cesta* (*The Way*, 1924; also with piano); 5 string quartets (1909; 1914–15; *Fantasy*, Op. 19, 1927; *Suite*, 1932; 1947); *Z intimních chvil* (*From Intimate Moments*) for violin and piano (1918); *Štafeta* (*The Courier*), 4 songs for voice and string quartet (1926–27); Solo Cello Sonata (1930); Violin Sonata (1932); Piano Trio (1936–37); *4 Impromptus* for violin and piano (1939–40); *Divertimento* for wind quintet (1941); *Serenade* for nonet or chamber orch. (1945); *2 Pieces* for cello and piano (1947); Violin Sonatina (1953); *Miniatures* for wind quintet (1953); *2 Pieces* for viola and piano (1959); *Fantasy* for string quartet, Op. 59 (1959); *Suite* for string trio (1961); Piano Sonata (1908); *Songs of Poetry and Prose* for piano (1917); *Suite* for piano (1930); *5 nálad* (*5 Moods*) for piano (1954); a number of choruses; of these, the patriotic part-song for male chorus *To Je Má Zem* (*This Is My Land*), written and performed in 1940, is well known; also arrangements of folksongs.

BIBLIOGRAPHY: L. Firkušný, *Vilém Petrželka* (Prague, 1946).

Pettersson, Gustaf Allan, Swedish composer; b. Västra Ryd, Sept. 19, 1911. He studied violin and viola with J. Ruthström and counterpoint with H. M. Melchers at the Royal Academy of Music in Stockholm; later took courses in composition with Blomdahl. From 1939 to 1951 he was a violist in the Stockholm Philharmonic Orch.; he was 40 years old when he went to Paris for private lessons with René Leibowitz and Arthur Honegger. Returning to Sweden, he concentrated his vital energies on composition, producing 12 symphonies, each one in a compact single movement. His music is characterized by an intense motoric drive; stylistically, it represents the modern type of Scandinavian hyper-romanticism.

WORKS: 12 symphonies: No. 1 (1951; withdrawn); No. 2 (1952–53; Swedish Radio, May 9, 1954); No. 3 (1954–55; Göteborg, Nov. 21, 1956); No. 4 (1958–59; Stockholm, Jan. 21, 1961); No. 5 (1960–62; Stockholm, Nov. 8, 1963); No. 6 (1963–66; Stockholm, Jan. 21, 1968); No. 7 (1966–67; Stockholm, Oct. 13, 1968); No. 8 (1969; Stockholm, Feb. 23, 1972); No. 9 (1970; Göteborg, Feb. 18, 1971); No. 10 (1972; Stockholm, Jan. 14, 1974); No. 11 (1973; Bergen, Norway, Oct. 24, 1974); No. 12, with chorus, after Pablo Neruda subtitled *De döda på torget* (1974). He also wrote 24 *Barfotasånger* (*Barefoot Songs*) for voice and piano (1943–45; from these is drawn a suite for mixed chorus); Concerto for

Violin and String Quartet (1949); 3 concertos for string orch.: No. 1 (1949-50), No. 2 (1956; Stockholm, Dec. 1, 1968), No. 3 (1956-57; Stockholm, March 14, 1958; the *Mesto* movement from it has become popular as a separate piece); 7 sonatas for 2 violins (1951-52); *Symphonic Movement* (1973); *Vox Humana*, 14 songs for soprano, alto, tenor, baritone, bass, chorus and string orch., to texts by Latin-American poets (1974; Stockholm, March 19, 1976).

Petyrek, Felix, Czech composer; b. Brno, May 14, 1892; d. Vienna, Dec. 1, 1951. He studied piano with Godowsky and Sauer; composition with Schreker at the Vienna Univ. (graduated in 1919). He taught piano at the Salzburg Mozarteum (1919-21); then at the Berlin Hochschule für Musik (1921-23); lived in Italy (1923-26); taught composition at the Odeon Athenon, in Athens (1926-30); from 1930 to 1939, at the Stuttgart Akademie für Musik; after 1945, settled in Vienna. Among modern composers, he occupied a fairly advanced position; in his melodic writing, he adopted the scale of alternating whole tones and semitones as a compromise between tonality and atonality.

WORKS: *Der Garten des Paradieses,* opera after Andersen (1923-41; Leipzig, Nov. 1, 1942); *Die arme Mutter und der Tod,* fairy play after Andersen with small orch. (Winterthur, 1923); the pantomimes *Tahi* and *Komödie; Die Litanei,* for boys' chorus, 2 trumpets, 2 harps, and percussion (Zürich Festival of the International Society for Contemporary Music, June 21, 1926); Sinfonietta; Divertimento for 8 wind instruments; Piano Trio; *Tänze,* for 2 flutes, Sextet for clarinet, string quartet, and piano (Donaueschingen Festival, July 30, 1922); Piano Trio; songs; piano pieces.

Petz (Pez), Johann Christoph, German composer; b. Munich, Sept. 9, 1664; d. Stuttgart, Sept. 25, 1716. He was a chorister in Munich (1676-86); then resided in Liège and in Bonn (until 1705); in 1706 was appointed court conductor at Stuttgart, where he remained until his death. He publ. a set of 12 sonatas (Augsburg, 1696) under the title *Duplex Genius sive Gallo-italus Instrumentorum Concentus;* also a Psalm. Two of his operas were produced in Bonn. Instrumental and vocal works were publ. by B. A. Wallner in the *Denkmäler der Tonkunst in Bayern* 35 (27/28).

Petzel, Johann Christoph. See **Pezel, Johann Christoph.**

Petzet, Walter, German pianist, composer, and music editor; b. Breslau, Oct. 10, 1866; d. Dresden, Aug. 13, 1941. He studied with Kleffel in Augsburg; later at the Munich Academy with Rheinberger and others; in 1887 went to Minneapolis, where he taught piano until 1890; from 1891 to 1896 taught piano at the Scharwenka Cons. in N.Y.; in 1896 succeeded Busoni as prof. at the Helsingfors Cons.; from 1898 to 1910, was prof. at the Cons. of Karlsruhe; subsequently taught at the Weimar Cons. (1910-13), at the Klindworth Scharwenka Cons. in Berlin (1913-16), and at the Dresden Cons. (1917-21); lived mostly in Dresden. He wrote 2 piano concertos, numerous piano pieces, etc.; wrote music criticism for the *Signale für die musikalische Welt.*

Petzold, Rudolf, English composer and teacher; b. Liverpool, (of a German father and English mother), July 17, 1908. He studied composition with Jarnach in Cologne, where he later became teacher of composition at the Hochschule für Musik (1958-70). He wrote a number of instrumental and choral works in a compact polyphonal style, among them 3 symphonies (1942, 1953, 1956); 4 string quartets (1932, 1948, 1955, 1972); Concerto for Violin and String Orch. (1960); Piano Trio (1961); Cello Sonata (1964); Sonata for violin unaccompanied (1965); Piano Sonata (1967); Violin Sonata (1969); several sacred cantatas and other choral music.

Petzoldt, Richard, German musicologist; b. Plauen, Nov. 12, 1907; d. Leipzig, Jan. 14, 1974. He studied at the Univ. of Berlin where his teachers were Abert, Schering, Moser, Sachs, Hornbostel, Schünemann, and Blume; receiving his Dr. phil. with the dissertation *Die Kirchenkompositionen und weltlichen Kantaten Reinhard Keisers* (Düsseldorf, 1935). He edited the *Allgemeine musikalische Zeitung* (1935-39) and the periodical *Musik in der Schule* (1949-54); was prof. of music history at the Univ. of Leipzig (1952-67). He publ. a number of informative books and other editions mainly concerned with classical German music. His publications include *Beethoven* (1938); *Schubert* (1940); *Schumann* (1941); *Mozart* (1948); *J. S. Bach und Leipzig* (1950); *Die Oper in ihrer Zeit* (1956); compiled iconographies of Bach (1950), Schubert (1953), Beethoven (1953), Tchaikovsky (1953), Handel (1955), Glinka (1955), Schumann (1956), Mozart (1956); for Beethoven's bicentennial he publ. the pictorial volume *Ludwig van Beethoven* (Leipzig, 1970; 2nd ed., 1973); also a pictorial book on Schütz, *Heinrich Schütz und seine Zeit in Bildern* (Kassel, 1972).

Peuerl (Peurl, Bäwerl, Bäurl, Beurlin), Paul, Austrian organist; b. c.1570; d. after 1625. He was organist at Horn, Lower Austria (1602) and of the Protestant church school in Steyer (1609-24). He is generally acknowledged to be the originator of the German variation-suite; following the example of the lutenists, he expanded the earlier combination of pavane and galliard into a new 4-movement suite form for strings. He edited *Newe Padouan, Intrada, Däntz und Galliarda* (1611); *Weltspiegel, das ist: Neue teutsche Gesänge* (1613); *Ettliche lustige Padovanen, Intrada, Galliard, Couranten und Däntz sampt zweyen Canzon zu 4 Stimmen* (1620); *Gantz neue Padouanen, Auffzüg, Balletten, Couranten, Intraden und Däntz* (1625). Selections from his works, ed. by Karl Geiringer, appear in the *Denkmäler der Tonkunst in Österreich* 70 (36.ii).

BIBLIOGRAPHY: E. Noack, "Ein Beitrag zur Geschichte der älteren deutschen Suite," *Archiv für Musikwissenschaft* II/2; P. Nettl, "Zur Lebensgeschichte Paul Peuerls," *Bulletin de la Société Musicologique* V/1; K. Geiringer, "Paul Peuerl," *Studien zur Musikwissenschaft* (vol. XVI; Vienna, 1929; pp. 32-69); E. Mohr, *Die Allemande* (Zürich, 1932; p. 70 ff.); H. J. Moser, *Die Musik im frühevangelischen Österreich* (Kassel, 1953; p. 37ff.).

Pevernage, Andries, Flemish composer; b. Harelbeke, near Courtrai, 1543; d. Antwerp, July 30, 1591. He was a boy chorister in Courtrai; then was chorusmaster at Bruges (1563); returned to Courtrai and held the post of chorusmaster at a church there from 1564 until 1585, when he went to Antwerp as master of the choristers at the Cathedral. He was greatly honored there, and was buried in the Cathedral itself. He wrote a number of vocal works, sacred and secular. Three books of his spiritual chansons were publ. in 1589, 1590, and 1591; other collections were publ. posthumously.
BIBLIOGRAPHY: J. A. Stellfeld, *Andries Pevernage* (Louvain, 1943).

Peyser, Herbert Francis, American music critic; b. New York, Aug. 6, 1886; d. there, Oct. 19, 1953. He studied in Germany and France; returning to America, he was assistant to Henry T. Finck on the *N.Y. Evening Post* and (from 1924 to 1940) associate music critic of the *N.Y. World Telegram.* He collaborated with L. Biancolli on the book *Masters of the Orchestra* (N.Y., 1953).

Peyser, Joan, American musicologist, editor, author, and journalist; b. New York, June 12, 1931. She played piano in public at 13; majored in music at Barnard College (B.A., 1951); studied musicology with Paul Henry Lang at Columbia University (M.A., 1956); then devoted herself mainly to musical journalism; enlivened the music pages of the Sunday *N.Y. Times* with book reviews and breezy colloquies with composers; wrote scripts for the television series *The World of Music;* acted as musical adviser to the N.Y. City Board of Education. She published the popular book, *The New Music: The Sense Behind the Sound* (N.Y., 1971); created considerable excitement in the music world with her biography, *Boulez: Composer, Conductor, Enigma;* (N.Y., 1976); trying to penetrate the eponymous enigma, she undertook a journey to the interior of France, where she interviewed family and friends of her subject, as though Boulez were indeed the Fourth B of Music. In 1977 she became editor of *The Musical Quarterly,* the first woman to be editor of this prestigious journal. She intends to retain the highest level of scholarship, eschewing the theretofore mandatory sesquipedalian polysyllabification in favor of plain American speech.

Pezel (Petzold, Petzel, Pezelius, etc.**), Johann Christoph,** German musician; b. Calau, 1639; d. Bautzen, Oct. 13, 1694. He was a municipal trumpeter in Leipzig (1664–81) and Bautzen; publ. several collections of pieces for wind instruments: *Musica vespertina Lipsica* (1669); *Hora decima* (1670); *Intraden* (1676); *Deliciae musicales* (1678), etc. His most interesting work is *Fünffstimmigte blasende Musik* (Frankfurt, 1685; 3 pieces arranged for modern brass ensemble by Robert D. King, and publ. in Wakefield, Mass.). Selections from various of his works, ed. by A. Schering, are in *Denkmäler deutscher Tonkunst* 63.

Pfannstiehl, Bernhard, German organist; b. Schmalkalden, Dec. 18, 1861; d. Freiberg, Oct. 21, 1940. He became blind in infancy, and was educated at the Institute for the Blind in Leipzig; studied piano at the Leipzig Cons.; was thrice winner of the Mendelssohn Prize. Following Liszt's advice, he made a specialty of the organ; was church organist in Leipzig (1896–1903), in Chemnitz (1903–11), and at the Kreuzkirche, Dresden (1912–34). He enjoyed a great reputation as an interpreter of Bach.
BIBLIOGRAPHY: K. Hasse, "Bernhard Pfannstiehl," *Die Orgel* (1910).

Pfatteicher, Carl Friedrichs, American specialist in church music and pedagogue, of German parentage; b. Easton, Pennsylvania, Sept. 22, 1882; d. Philadelphia, Sept. 29, 1957. He studied theology in Germany and at Harvard Univ. (Th.D., 1912); taught Latin and German at various schools; then was prof. of music at Philips Academy, Andover (1912–47); from 1949 on he was lecturer in musicology at the Univ. of Pennsylvania. He publ. a number of useful school manuals and collections of sacred music, among them *The Christian Church Year in Chorals* (1917); *The Christian Church Year in Part Songs* (1915); *Thesaurus musicae sacrae* (1920); *The Oxford American Hymnal* (1930); was co-editor of *The Office Hymns of the Church in Their Plainsong Settings* and *The Church Organist's Golden Treasury.*

Pfeiffer, Georges-Jean, French composer; b. Versailles, Dec. 12, 1835; d. Paris, Feb. 14, 1908. He began his career as a pianist; then was active as music critic in Paris; was a member of the firm Pleyel, Wolff et Cie., piano makers at Paris.
WORKS: operetta, *Capitaine Roche* (1862); 1-act opera, *L'Enclume* (Paris, 1884); comic opera, *Le Légataire universel* (Paris, 1901); an oratorio, *Hagar;* a symph. poem, *Jeanne d'Arc; Légende,* symph. fantasy for piano and orch.; many pieces of chamber music; also piano pieces.

Pfeiffer, Theodor, German pianist and pedagogue; b. Heidelberg, Oct. 20, 1853; d. Baden-Baden, Nov. 9, 1929. He studied piano with Hans von Bülow at Raff's Cons. in Frankfurt. In 1889 he settled in Baden-Baden as private teacher. He publ. a number of valuable studies: *Studien nach Kreutzerschen Violin-Etüden gebildet; Tonleiterschule; Virtuosen-Studien* (in part preparatory studies for Bülow's editions); also wrote a Mass, songs, men's choruses, and piano pieces (*Albumblatt, Dryadenspiel, Mazurka-Caprice, Konzert-Etüde,* etc.). His recollections of Bülow's remarks in teaching specific works were publ. as *Studien bei Hans von Bülow* (1894; 6th ed., 1909).

Pfitzner, Hans (Erich), eminent German composer; b. Moscow (of German parents), May 5, 1869; d. Salzburg, May 22, 1949. He studied at Hoch's Cons. in Frankfurt with James Kwast (piano) and Iwan Knorr (composition); married Kwast's daughter in 1899. He taught piano and theory at the Cons. of Coblenz (1892–93); was assistant conductor of the Municipal Theater in Mainz (1894–96); teacher at Stern's Cons. in Berlin (1897–1906); conductor in the Theater des Westens (1903–06). During the 1907–08 season he led the renowned Kaim Concerts in Munich. From 1908 to 1916 he was in Strasbourg as municipal music director and director of the Cons.; from 1910 to 1916, he was conductor at the Strasbourg Opera; conducted some concerts of the Munich Konzertverein (1919–20); then led a master class at the Berlin Academy of Arts (1920–29); prof. of composition at the Akademie der Tonkunst in Munich (1930–33); after that he devoted himself chiefly to composition, appearing frequently as guest conductor of his own works, and accompanist in recitals of his songs. In 1944 he went to Vienna; stricken by poverty and illness, he was taken to a home for the aged in Munich, and later to Salzburg. Charged with active participation in the cultural propaganda of the Nazi regime, he appeared before the Denazification Court in Munich in 1948, but was exonerated.

Pfitzner enjoyed great esteem in Germany as a national composer. When he presented a concert of his works in Berlin on May 12, 1893, he was hailed by the press as a talent of the first magnitude. After the 1st performance of his opera, *Der arme Heinrich*, in Mainz on April 2, 1895, the critics (Humperdinck among them) praised the work in extravagant terms; even more successful was his opera *Palestrina* (to his own libretto), produced in Munich on June 12, 1917. A Pfitzner Society was formed in Munich as early as 1904, and a Hans Pfitzner Association, in Berlin in 1938, with Furtwängler as president. Although his music is traditional in style and conservative in harmony, he was regarded as a modernist, a comrade-in-arms of Richard Strauss; very soon, however, his fame began to dwindle; there were fewer performances of his operas, and still fewer of his instrumental works; he himself bitterly complained of this lack of appreciation.

WORKS: OPERAS: *Der arme Heinrich* (Mainz, April 2, 1895), *Die Rose vom Liebesgarten* (Elberfeld, Nov. 9, 1901), *Das Christelflein* (Munich, Dec. 11, 1906; revised version, Dresden, Dec. 11, 1917), *Palestrina* (Munich, June 12, 1917), *Das Herz* (Munich, Nov. 12, 1931); FOR ORCH.: 3 preludes from *Palestrina* (1917), Symph. No. 1, in C-sharp minor (arranged from String Quartet No. 2, 1933), *Kleine Sinfonie* (1939), *Elegie und Reigen* (1940), Symph. No. 2, in C major (1940), *Fantasie* (1947), Piano Concerto (1922), Violin Concerto (1923), 2 cello concertos (1935; 1944); CHAMBER MUSIC: Cello Sonata (1890), Piano Trio (1896), 3 string quartets (1903; 1925; 1942), Piano Quartet (1908), Violin Sonata (1918), Sextet for clarinet, violin, viola, cello, double bass, and piano (1945); VOCAL WORKS: *Der Blumen Rache*, ballad for contralto, women's voices, and orch. (1888), *Columbus*, for chorus a cappella (1905), *Gesang der Barden*, for men's chorus with instruments (1906), *Von deutscher Seele*, cantata for soli, chorus, orch., and organ (1921), *Das dunkle Reich*, for soprano, baritone, chorus, orch., and organ (1929), *Fons salutifer* for chorus and orch. (1942), *Herr Oluf*, ballad for baritone and orch. (1891), *Die Heinzelmännchen*, for baritone and orch. (1903); *Zwei deutsche Gesänge*, for baritone, men's chorus, and orch. (1916), *Lethe*, for baritone and orch. (1926), 106 songs for voice and piano. He further publ. arrangements and new editions of musical works by E. T. A. Hoffmann, Schumann, Marschner, and Loewe; also numerous essays and pamphlets, polemical in nature, with virulent attacks against modern ideas in theory; these were publ. as *Gesammelte Schriften* (Augsburg, 1926; 2 vols.; new ed. in 3 vols., Munich, 1929); also *Eindrücke und Erinnerungen* (Hamburg, 1947); *Über musikalische Inspiration* (Berlin, 1940); *Philosophie und Dichtung in meinem Leben* (Berlin, 1944). A list of Pfitzner's works was publ. by A. Berrsche (Munich, 1919; 2nd ed., 1926).

BIBLIOGRAPHY: P. N. Cossmann, *Hans Pfitzner* (Munich, 1904); R. Louis, *Hans Pfitzners "Die Rose vom Liebesgarten"* (Munich, 1904); R. Louis, *Hans Pfitzner* (Leipzig, 1907); A. Berrsche, *Hans Pfitzners "Der arme Heinrich"* (1910); A. Seidl, *Hans Pfitzner* (1921); C. Wandrey, *Hans Pfitzner, seine geistige Persönlichkeit und das Ende der Romantik* (1922); W. Lütge, *Hans Pfitzner* (1924); E. Kroll, *Hans Pfitzner* (1924); *Pfitzner-Festschrift* (1930); W. Abendroth, *Hans Pfitzner* (1935); E. Valentin, *Hans Pfitzner: Werk und Gestalt eines Deutschen* (Regensburg, 1939); J. Müller-Blattau, *Hans Pfitzner* (Potsdam, 1940); H. Lindlar, *Hans Pfitzners Klavierlied* (Würzburg, 1940); W. Abendroth, *Hans Pfitzner: sein Leben in Bildern* (Leipzig, 1941); J. Bahle, *Hans Pfitzner und der geniale Mensch* (Constance, 1949); Hans Rutz, *Hans Pfitzner: Musik zwischen den Zeiten* (Vienna, 1949); a symposium of articles, *Hans Pfitzner zum 75. Geburtstag* (Cologne, 1944); *Hans Pfitzner, ein Bild in Widmungen, anlässlich seines 75. Geburtstages*, ed. by W. Abendroth (Leipzig, 1944); *In Memoriam Hans Pfitzner* (Vienna, 1950); J. Müller-Blattau, *Hans Pfitzner: Lebensweg und Schaffensernte* (Frankfurt, 1969); *Festschrift aus Anlass des 100 Geburtstag*, ed. by W. Abendroth (Munich, 1969).

Pflughaupt, Robert, German pianist; b. Berlin, Aug. 4, 1833; d. Aix-la-Chapelle, June 12, 1871. He studied with Dehn in Berlin, Henselt in St. Petersburg, and Liszt in Weimar. He wrote a number of agreeable piano pieces (*Petite valse, Mazurka, Galop de concert, Invitation à la Polka*, etc.). His wife, **Sophie Pflughaupt** (*née* **Shtchepin;** b. Dvinsk, Russia, March 15, 1837; d. Aix-la-Chapelle, Nov. 10, 1867), was also an excellent pianist, a pupil of Henselt and Liszt.

Pfohl, Ferdinand, German writer on music; b. Elbogen, Bohemia, Oct. 12, 1862; d. Hamburg, Dec. 16, 1949. He studied law in Prague; in 1885, went to Leipzig, where he took private lessons in music with Oscar Paul. In 1892 he became the music critic of the influential *Hamburger Nachrichten*, holding this important post until his retirement in 1932; also taught music theory at Vogt's Cons. in Hamburg.

WRITINGS: *Die moderne Oper* (1894); *Die Nibelungen in Bayreuth* (1897); *Arthur Nikisch als Mensch und Künstler* (Leipzig, 1900; 2nd ed., 1925); *Karl Grammann. Ein Künstlerleben* (Berlin, 1910); *Richard Wagner. Sein Leben und Schaffen* (1911; 4th ed., 1924); *Beethoven* (1922); also descriptions of African music: *Quer durch Afrika* (1891) and *West-Östliche Fahrten* (1902); publ. guides to Wagner's operas. His original compositions include the symph. poems *Die versunkene Glocke, Pierrot lunaire,* and *Frau Holle;* a symph. fantasy, *Das Meer;* piano pieces.

Pfordten, Hermann Ludwig von der, German writer on music; b. Munich, July 5, 1857; d. there, Nov. 16,

1933. He was the son of a Bavarian minister; studied in Munich and in Leipzig; became prof. of music history at the Univ. of Munich; he specialized in writing about Wagner's music.

WRITINGS: *Handlung und Dichtung der Bühnenwerke Richard Wagners* (1893; 8th ed., 1922); *Musikalische Essays* (2 vols.; 1897; 1899); *Deutsche Musik* (1917; 3rd ed., 1922); *Der Musikfreund,* an introductory book on music (1923; 8th ed., 1928); *Einführung in Wagners Werke und Schriften* (3rd ed., 1925); popular biographies of Beethoven (1907; 4th ed., 1922), Mozart (1908; 3rd ed., 1926), Schubert (1916; 3rd ed., 1928), Weber (1919), Schumann (1920), and Robert Franz (1923).

Pfrogner, Hermann, Austrian musicologist; b. Graz, Jan. 17, 1911; studied law at the Univ. of Vienna; held various positions in financial institutions; studied musicology with E. Schenk (1945–47); in 1948 settled in Stuttgart. He contributed numerous articles on modern harmony to various periodicals; publ. a fundamental essay dealing with 12-tone composition, *Die Zwölfordnung der Töne* (Zürich, 1953); also *Musik, Geschichte ihrer Deutung* (Freiburg, 1954); *Lebendige Tonwelt: zum Phänomen Musik* (Munich, 1976).

Pfundt, Ernst Gotthold Benjamin, celebrated German timpani player; b. Dommitzsch, near Torgau, June 17, 1806; d. Leipzig, Dec. 7, 1871. He studied theology, and at the same time developed an extraordinary ability as a drummer; was called by Mendelssohn in 1835 to join the Gewandhaus Orch., and remained there as drummer until his death; achieved legendary fame for his rhythmic skill. He was the inventor of the pedal kettledrums; publ. a method for drums (1849; 3rd ed., enlarged by H. Schmidt, 1894).

Phalèse, Pierre (Petrus Phalesius), Flemish music publisher; b. Louvain, c.1510; d. there, c.1573. He established a music publishing business in 1545; the printing was done elsewhere, and it was not until 1553 that Phalèse began to print on the premises in Louvain. From 1570 he worked in association with Jean Bellère of Antwerp. After the death of Pierre Phalèse, the business was moved to Antwerp (1581), and was managed by his sons, Pierre Jr. and Corneille; continued under the management of the heirs until about 1674. Two compositions by Pierre Phalèse, the elder, are found in A. Schering's *Geschichte der Musik in Beispielen* (no. 134).

BIBLIOGRAPHY: A. Goovaerts, *Notice biographique sur Phalèse* (1869); A. Goovaerts, *Histoire et bibliographie de la typographie musicale dans le Pays-Bas* (1880).

Phelps, Ellsworth C., American organist and composer; b. Middletown, Conn., Aug. 11, 1827; d. Brooklyn, N.Y., Nov. 29, 1913. Self-taught in music, he became organist in New London at the age of 19; settled in Brooklyn in 1857; held various positions as organist and taught in the public schools. He wrote several symphonic works in a programmatic genre, usually on American subjects: *Hiawatha* (1878), *Emancipation* (1880), etc.; pieces for military band (performed by Gilmore and Sousa), etc.; more than 200 pieces in all.

Phile (Fyles, Pfeil, Phyla), Philip, violinist and teacher; b. Germany, c.1734; d. Philadelphia, between Aug. 1 and Nov. 9, 1793, in a yellow-fever epidemic. He served in the Pennsylvania German Regiment during the Revolutionary War; was transferred in July 1778 to the Invalid Regiment; discharged on Jan. 4, 1783; pension granted, July 11, 1785. He was active in Philadelphia and New York; gave concerts; played in theater orchestras; conducted the orchestra of the Old American Co. of Comedians. He was probably the composer of the music of the *President's March,* to which Joseph Hopkinson (son of Francis Hopkinson) wrote the words *Hail Columbia.* He also wrote a piece entitled *Harmony Music* for the series of summer concerts at Gray's Gardens in Philadelphia.

BIBLIOGRAPHY: O. G. Sonneck, *Report on the "Star Spangled Banner," "Hail Columbia,"* etc. (Washington, 1909).

Philidor (real name **Danican**), famous family of French musicians. (1) **Jean Danican-Philidor;** b. c.1620; d. Paris, Sept. 8, 1679, as "Fifre de la Grande Écurie" (piper in the King's military band). (2) **André Philidor** (*l'aîné*), son of Jean; d. Dreux, Aug. 11, 1730. As a youth he played the cromorne in the King's military band; later played the oboe, bassoon and trompette marine, in addition to the cromorne, in the King's private band. He served as a librarian of the Royal Music Library at Versailles, and accumulated a collection of manuscripts of old instrumental pieces performed at the French court since the time of François I; the bulk of this collection, numbering some 350 manuscript volumes, is at St. Michael's College, Tenbury, Worcester; 59 vols. are in the library of the Paris Cons., 35 vols. in the city library of Versailles, and 35 vols. in the collection of the Library of Congress, Washington. Among his published works are *Mascarade des Savoyards* (1700); *Mascarade du roi de la Chine* (1700); *Suite de danses pour les violons et hautbois* (1699); *Pièces à deux basses de viole, basse de violon et basson* (1700); *Marches et batteries de tambour avec les airs de fifres et de hautbois.* (3) **Jacques** (*le cadet*), brother of André (*l'aîné*); b. Paris, May 5, 1657; d. Versailles, May 27, 1708. He was a bassoonist in the Royal Chapel and later chamber musician to Louis XIV. (4) **Anne Danican-Philidor,** son of André (*l'aîné*); b. Paris, April 11, 1681; d. there, Oct. 8, 1728. A flute player, he composed pastoral operas (*L'Amour vainqueur,* 1697; *Diane et Endymion,* 1698; *Danaë,* 1701), and music for flutes, violins and oboes. He was the founder of the famous Paris concert series, the Concert Spirituel (1725). (5) **Pierre Danican-Philidor,** son of Jacques (*le cadet*); b. Paris, Aug. 22, 1681; d. there, Sept. 1, 1731. Was a flute player; published 3 books of suites for 2 transverse flutes (1717, 1718), and flute trios. (6) **François André Danican-Philidor,** the last and greatest in the line of musicians in the family, the youngest son of André; b. Dreux, Sept. 7, 1726; d. London, Aug. 31, 1795. He achieved distinction not only in music but in chess; a famous chess opening was named after him. He defeated a number of celebrated chessmasters of his time; brought out a fundamental treatise on chess, *L' Analyse des échecs* (London, 1749; new ed., under the title *Analyse du jeu des échecs,* 1777; altogether there were more than 100 editions of this famous book). As a member of the London Chess Club, he was guaranteed a sum of money in exchange for his availability to play with other members of the club. In 1756 he began a surprisingly successful career as a composer for the theater. His first stage work was *Le Diable à quatre,* a *comédie en vaudevilles,* which was the predecessor of opéra-comique; it was produced at the Opéra-Comique on Aug. 19, 1756; his next production was a ballet with music by Charpentier for which Philidor made some revisions, and which was produced under the title *Le Retour du printemps;* these were succeeded by several one-act pieces: *Blaise le savetier* (1759), *L'Huitre et les plaideurs* (1759), *Le Quiproquo ou Le Volage fixé* (1760), *Le Soldat magicien* (1760), *Le Jardinier et son seigneur* (1761); but his most successful production of this period was *Le Maréchal ferrant,* in 2 acts (1761), which was performed more than 200 times; there followed a group of one-act pieces: *Sancho Pança* (1762), *Le Bûcheron, ou Les Trois Souhaits* (1763), *Le Sorcier,* in 2 acts (Jan. 2, 1764), and *Tom Jones,* in 3 acts (Feb. 27, 1765), which enjoyed great success, and incidentally contained an interesting novelty, a vocal quartet a cappella. Philidor's finest production, the grand opera *Ernelinde, princesse de Norvège,* was staged on Nov. 24, 1767; it was revised in 1769 and produced under the title *Sandomir, prince de Danemark,* but was revived in 1773 under its original title. Continuing his successful opera productions, Philidor staged *Le Jardinier de Sidon* (1768), *L'Amant déguisé* (1769), *La Nouvelle École des femmes* (1770) and *Le Bon Fils* (1773). His next opera, *Sémire et Mélide,* was given at Fontainebleau on Oct. 30, 1773, but it was published under the title *Mélide ou Le Navigateur.* There followed *Berthe* (Brussels, 1775), *Les Femmes vengées* (1775), and *Le Puits d'Amour* (1779), a play adapted from a novel originally published in 1765, for which Philidor composed six ariettes, which were published with the novel and then were used in the production of the play. Further works were *Persée* (1780), *L'Amitié au village* (1785), *Thémistocle* (first given at Fontainebleau on May 23, 1786 and then produced the following year at the Paris Opéra), *La Belle Esclave* (1787) and *Le Mari comme il les faudrait tous* (1788). A posthumous opera, *Bélisaire,* completed by Berton, was produced in 1796.

François André Philidor eclipsed his famous rivals Grétry and Monsigny in the richness of harmony and skill in orchestration, but he yielded to Grétry, if not to Monsigny, in the power of dramatic expression and melodic invention. Philidor was greatly admired by the Parisians, but his love for chess often distracted him from Paris in favor of frequent trips to London to play at the chess club there. Apart from his operas, he wrote church music; chamber pieces, among them quartets for 2 violins, oboe and continuo. He set to music Horace's *Carmen saeculare,* a sort of secular oratorio that enjoyed notable success; in alternation with Jean-Claude Trial, he issued a series of publications, *12 Ariettes périodiques.*

BIBLIOGRAPHY: J. Lardin, *Philidor peint par lui-même* (Paris, 1847); G. Allen, *The Life of Philidor, Musician and Chess Player* (Philadelphia, 1858; reprint, N.Y., 1971); A. Pougin, "Philidor," *Chronique Musicale* (1874-75); Ch. Piot, "Particularités inédites concernant les œuvres musicales de Gossec et de Philidor," *Bulletins de l'Académie Royale de Belgique* (Brussels, 1875); G. E. Bonnet, "L'œuvre de Philidor," *Revue Musicale* (Oct. 1921); G. E. Bonnet, *Philidor et l'évolution de la musique française au XVIIIe siècle* (1921); *Dictionary of National Biography* XLV. For details of productions of Philidor's operas, consult A. Loewenberg's *Annals of Opera.*

Philip, Achille, French composer; b. Arles, Oct. 12, 1878; d. Béziers (Hérault), Oct. 12, 1959. He studied at the Paris Cons. with Guilmant (organ) and Vincent d'Indy (composition); from 1905 to 1950 taught organ at the Schola Cantorum in Paris. He wrote an opera *L'or du Menhir* (Rouen, 1934); the symphonic poems, *Les Djinns* (1913); *Dans un parc enchanté* (1917) and *Nymphes et Naiades* (1920); a number of sacred works; chamber music; songs.

Philipp, Isidor, eminent French pianist; b. Budapest, Sept. 2, 1863; d. Paris, Feb. 20, 1958 (as a result of injuries received from a fall in the Paris Métro). He was brought to Paris as an infant; studied piano with Georges Mathias at the Paris Cons., winning first prize in 1883; then took lessons with Saint-Saëns, Stephen Heller and Ritter. His concert career was brief, but he found his true vocation in teaching; in 1903 he was appointed prof. of piano at the Paris Cons.; many famous musicians, among them Albert Schweitzer, were his pupils. In Paris he continued to perform, mostly in chamber music groups; formed a concert trio with Loeb and Berthelier, with which he gave a number of successful concerts. After the outbreak of World War II he went to the U.S.; arrived in N.Y. in 1941; despite his advanced age he accepted private students, not only in N.Y., but also in Montreal. At the age of 91, he played the piano part in Franck's Violin Sonata (N.Y., March 20, 1955); then returned to France. He published some technical studies for piano, among them *Exercises journaliers; École d'octaves; Problèmes techniques; Études techniques basées sur une nouvelle manière de travailler; La Gamme chromatique;* made arrangements for 2 pianos of works by Bach, Mendelssohn, Saint-Saëns, and others; also brought out *La Technique de Liszt* (2 vols., Paris, 1932).

BIBLIOGRAPHY: Henry Bellamann, "Isidor Philipp," *Musical Quarterly* (Oct. 1943).

Philippe de Vitry. See **Vitry, Philippe de.**

Philippot, Michel, French composer; b. Verzy, Feb. 2, 1925. He first took courses in mathematics; then studied music at the Paris Cons. (1945-47); also took private lessons with René Leibowitz (1945-49); was a sound engineer at the French Radio-Television Network (1949-59); became its president in 1973.

WORKS: 2 Piano Sonatas (1946, 1973); Overture for chamber orch. (1948); Piano Trio (1953); Variations for 10 instruments (1957); *Trois compositions* for piano (1958); *Composition* for string orch. (1959); *Composition* for double orchestra (1959); *Pièce pour* dix for chamber ensemble; *Transformations triangulaires* for 12 instruments (1962); *Pieces* for solo violin (1967); Organ Sonata (1971); *Scherzo* for solo accordion (1972); *Commentariolus copernicae* for flute, clarinet, bassoon, horn, trumpet, violin, cello, piano and percussion (1972; Paris, Oct. 22, 1973); *Trio inacheve* for flute, clarinet and trombone (1973); Octet (1974).

Philips, Peter, important English composer and organist; b. 1561; d. Brussels, 1628. He belonged to a Catholic family; was probably a chorister at St. Paul's Cathedral; was befriended by a Catholic almoner, Sebastian Westcote, and received a bequest upon the latter's death in 1582. In that year, Philips left England; on Aug. 18, 1582 he arrived at Douai, where he presented himself at the English College; then proceeded to Rome, where he entered the service of Cardinal Alessandro Farnese; also was for 3 years organist at the English College in Rome (1582–85). In the autumn of 1585 Philips joined the household of Lord Thomas Paget in Rome, and subsequently traveled with him through Spain, France, and the Netherlands. From early 1587 until June 1588, Philips was with Paget in Paris; then went to Antwerp, remaining there until early 1589; also made visits to Brussels. After Paget's death in 1590, Philips settled in Antwerp, and was active there as teacher of keyboard playing. In 1593 Philips went to Amsterdam, where he met Sweelinck. On his return trip to Antwerp, he was detained at Middelburgh, was charged with planning the assassination of Queen Elizabeth, and was alleged to have participated with Lord Paget in the act of burning the Queen in effigy in Paris. He stood trial in The Hague in Sept. 1593, but was released for lack of evidence. Late in 1593 he was back in Antwerp. In 1597 he moved to Brussels, entering the service of the Archduke Albert, as organist of the Royal Chapel. After Albert's marriage to Isabella of Spain (1599) Philips was officially designated as "Organist to their Serene Highnesses the Archduke Albert and Isabella." On March 9, 1610 he received a canonry at Soignies, but continued to reside in Brussels. On Jan. 5, 1621 he exchanged his title at Soignies for a chaplainship at Tirlemont; in 1623 he is also described as canon of Béthune. However, he continued to be designated canon of Soignies for many years afterwards, even in posthumous editions of his works, possibly because he was best known in that nominal post. Philips was highly esteemed in his day, and his works were printed in many collections; his music shows mixed Italian and Netherlandish characteristics; he excelled in madrigals and motets; his pieces for the virginals reveal a kinship with Sweelinck.

WORKS: 4 madrigals in *Melodia Olympica di diversi eccellentissimi musici* (Antwerp, 1591); 2 vols. of madrigals for 6 voices (1596; 1603); 1 vol. of madrigals for 8 voices (1598); motets for 5 voices (1612); motets for 8 voices (1613); *Gemmulae sacrae,* for 2-3 voices, with continuo (1613); *Les Rossignols spirituels,* for 2-4 voices (1616); *Deliciae sacrae,* for 2-3 voices (1622); litanies for 4-9 voices (1623); *Paradisus sacris cantionibus conditus* (1628); other works listed in the catalogue of the library of King João IV of Portugal, publ. by Vasconcellos in 1873. W. B. Squire

edited the madrigals *Amor che vuoi* for 4 voices (London, 1890), *Dispiegate guancie amate,* for 8 voices in *Ausgewählte Madrigale* (Leipzig, 1906), the motets *Hodie Sanctus Benedictus* for 5 voices (London, 1899), and *Ego sum panis vivus* (London, 1902); Sir Richard Terry, who contributed greatly to a revival of the music by Philips, publ. 4 motets for 5 voices in the collection *Downside Motets* (London, 1904–05). 19 keyboard pieces are included in the *Fitzwilliam Virginal Book,* vol. 1 (1889); other keyboard pieces are found in various anthologies.

BIBLIOGRAPHY: P. Bergmans, *L'Organiste des archiducs Albert et Isabelle, Peter Philips* (Ghent, 1903); C. Hughes, "Peter Philips: An English Musician in the Netherlands," *Papers of the American Musicological Society, 1940* (1946).

Phillipps, Adelaide, English contralto; b. Stratford-on-Avon, Oct. 26, 1833; d. Karlsbad, Oct. 3, 1882. Her family took her to America as a child; she was trained as a dancer, and made her first appearance at Tremont Theater in Boston on Jan. 12, 1842 in a variety show. She also displayed an early gift as a vocalist, and was introduced to Jenny Lind, who encouraged her to study singing; accordingly she was sent to London where she took lessons with Manuel García; made her professional debut in Milan as Rosina (Dec. 17, 1854). Returning to Boston in 1855, she sang light opera in English; her first appearance on the grand opera stage in America was as Azucena in Verdi's *Il Trovatore* (N.Y., March 17, 1856). After a long and successful tour in Europe she joined the Boston Ideal Opera Company, making her first appearance with it on Nov. 30, 1880. She was advised to go to Karlsbad for her health in 1882, but died shortly after her arrival there. During her European engagements she sang under the name **Signorina Filippi.**

BIBLIOGRAPHY: A. C. L. Waterston, *Adelaide Phillipps* (Boston, 1883); V. F. Yellin, in *Notable American Women,* III (N.Y., 1971).

Phillips, Burrill, American composer; b. Omaha, Nov. 9, 1907. He studied music with Edwin Stringham in Denver; then with Howard Hanson and Bernard Rogers at the Eastman School of Music in Rochester, N.Y. After graduation he held numerous teaching posts: at the Eastman School of Music (1940-49), at the Univ. of Illinois, Urbana (1949-64), and as guest lecturer at the Juilliard School of Music, N.Y. (1968-69). His music is cast in a neo-Classical style.

WORKS: Ballets: *Play Ball* (Rochester, April 29, 1938) and *Step into My Parlor* (1941); for orch.: *Selections from McGuffey's Reader* (Rochester, May 3, 1934), *Sinfonia Concertante* (Rochester, April 3, 1935), *American Dance,* for bassoon and strings (Rochester, April 25, 1940), *3 Satiric Fragments* (Rochester, May 2, 1941), Piano Concerto (1943), *Scherzo* (1944), *Tom Paine Overture* (N.Y., May 15, 1947), *La Piñata* (1960), *Perspectives in a Labyrinth* for 3 string orchs. (1963); chamber music: Trio for trumpets (1937), 2 string quartets (1939, 1959), Violin Sonata (1942), Cello Sonata (1946), *Partita* for violin, viola, cello and piano (Rochester, May 7, 1948), *4 Figures in Time,* for flute and piano (1953), *5 Pieces* for woodwind quintet (1965), Quartet for oboe and strings (1966), 4 piano sonatas, *Nine by Nine,* a set of 9 variations, each one in a meter of 9 beats (1942), *Toccata* (1944), *3 Informalities* (1945), *3 Divertimenti* (1946), *5 Various and Sundry* (1961); organ pieces; several choruses; also an opera *Don't We All* (Rochester, N.Y., May 9, 1949).

Phillips, Harvey, American bass tuba virtuoso; b. Aurora, Missouri, Dec. 2, 1929, in a family of farmers and artisans. He learned to play tuba in high school; got a job in a circus band; was with Ringling Brothers and Barnum and Bailey Circus until 1950, when he received a scholarship to study at the Juilliard School of Music in N.Y.; played with the N.Y. City Opera; was subsequently a member of the N.Y. Brass Quintet; also filled engagements with the N.Y. Philharmonic and the Metropolitan Opera Orch. In the interim he commuted to Boston to teach at the New England Cons. and later joined the faculty of Indiana Univ. In 1974 he organized in N.Y. a Christmas concert of 250 tuba players performing carols; also gave 5 solo concerts on the tuba at Carnegie Recital Hall, with a small jazz band, a string quartet, a woodwind quintet, several pianists, horn players, percussion and 3 tuba players in a program that included Gunther Schuller's *Capriccio* for tuba and chamber orch., the Bass Tuba Concerto by Vaughan Williams and Hindemith's Sonata for Tuba and Piano.

Phillips, Montague Fawcett, English composer and pedagogue; b. London, Nov. 13, 1885; d. Esher, Jan. 4, 1969. He studied with F. Corder at the Royal Academy of Music in London; subsequently taught there. He wrote a light opera, *The Rebel Maid* (London, March 12, 1921), which enjoyed some success, and numerous choral works and orchestral overtures, mostly on subjects from British history; during World War II he wrote *Empire March* for orch. (1941) and an overture, *In Praise of My Country* (1944).

Phillips, Philip, American hymn-tune writer; b. on a farm in Chautauqua County, N.Y., Aug. 13, 1834; d. Delaware, Ohio, June 25, 1895. He sang in a choir as a child; was a cheesemaker by trade; then traveled as an itinerant singer; published gospel song books. His best known hymn is *Home of the Soul.*
BIBLIOGRAPHY: R. G. McCutchan, *Our Hymnody* (N.Y., 1937).

Piaf, Edith, French chanteuse; b. Paris, Dec. 19, 1915; d. there, Oct. 11, 1963. Her real name was **Giovanna Gassion;** she took her first name from Edith Cavell, Belgian nurse shot by the Germans in World War I. Her childhood was tragic; she was abandoned by her mother, an Italian café singer; traveled with her father, a circus contortionist, taking part in his act as an acrobat. She then became a street singer in Paris, earning the nickname Piaf (Parisian argot for sparrow) on account of her ragged and emaciated appearance. She was befriended by a cabaret owner; when he was murdered she was held by the French police as a material witness. During the war and German occupation she entertained French prisoners in Germany; as a result, she was accused of collaboration, but was exonerated. In 1954 she made her first American tour.

Although untutored, she developed a type of ballad singing that was infused with profound sentiment and expressive artistry, eliciting enthusiastic response from nightclub audiences and sophisticated music critics alike. She composed chansonnettes, among which *La Vie en rose* became popular; publ. a book of memoirs *Au Bal de la chance* (Paris, 1958).

Piastro, Josef, Russian-American violinist; b. Kerch, Crimea, March 1, 1889; d. Monrovia, Calif., May 14, 1964. He studied with Leopold Auer at the St. Petersburg Cons.; came to the U.S. in 1920; was concertmaster of the Los Angeles Philharmonic and conducted children's concerts in Hollywood. In America he assumed the pseudonym **Borissoff,** to avoid confusion with his brother, also a violinist, **Michel Piastro.** He composed *Crimean Rhapsody* for violin and piano (1920).

Piastro, Michel, Russian-American violinist; brother of **Josef Piastro;** b. Kerch, Crimea, July 1, 1891; d. New York, April 10, 1970. Like his brother, he studied with Leopold Auer at the St. Petersburg Cons.; in 1920 came to the U.S.; was concertmaster of the San Francisco Symph. Orch. (1925–31) and of the N.Y. Philharmonic under Toscanini (1931–37). In 1941 he conducted a radio series "Longines Symphonette" sponsored by the Longines Wittnauer Watch Co.

Piatigorsky, Gregor, great Russian cellist; b. Ekaterinoslav, April 17, 1903; d. Los Angeles, Aug. 6, 1976. He received his first music lessons from his father, a violinist; then took cello lessons with Alfred von Glehn; played in various orchestras in Moscow. In 1921 he left Russia and proceeded to Berlin, where he took cello lessons with Julius Klengel. From 1924 to 1928 he was the first cellist of the Berlin Philharmonic; then devoted himself entirely to the concert career. He played the solo part in *Don Quixote* by Richard Strauss under the composer's direction many times in Europe, and was probably unexcelled in this part; Strauss himself called him "mein Don Quixote." He went to America in 1929 and made his American debut at Oberlin, Ohio on Nov. 5, 1929; played the Dvořák Concerto with the N.Y. Philharmonic eliciting great praise (Dec. 29, 1929). He was regarded as the world's finest cello player after Casals; continued giving solo recitals and appearing with major European and American orchestras for many years; gave first performances of several cello concertos commissioned by him to Hindemith, Dukelsky, Castelnuovo-Tedesco, and others. He taught advanced classes at the Curtis Institute in Philadelphia and later at the Univ. of Southern California, Los Angeles; presented a series of trio concerts with Heifetz and Pennario. He was the recipient of honorary degrees of D. Mus. from Temple Univ., Columbia Univ., Univ. of California in Los Angeles, etc. He publ. an autobiographical volume, *Cellist* (N.Y., 1965).

Piatti, Alfredo Carlo, Italian cellist and composer; b. Borgo Canale, near Bergamo, Jan. 8, 1822; d. Crocetto di Mozzo, July 18, 1901. He received his primary music education from his father, the violinist **Antonio Piatti;** then studied cello at the Milan Cons.; began his concert career in 1838, and in 1843 played with Liszt in Munich; obtained excellent success in England, where he gave annual concerts; from 1859 to 1898 he was a regular performer in Saturday Popular Concerts of chamber music in London. He combined an excellent technical skill with profound musicianship; in the cello world he occupied the position of artistry and authority comparable with that of Joachim among violinists. He wrote 2 cello concertos; 6 cello sonatas and a number of solo pieces for cello; also ed. 6 string sonatas by Boccherini and Locatelli and brought out editions of cello methods by Kummer and others.

BIBLIOGRAPHY: M. Latham, *Alfredo Piatti* (London, 1901).

Picchi, Silvano, Argentine composer; b. Pisa, Italy, Jan. 15, 1922. His family emigrated to Argentina while he was a child; he studied composition with Constantino Gaito, Alberto Ginastera, Arturo Luzzatti, Gilardo Gilardi and Floro M. Ugarte in Buenos Aires. He is the music critic of *La Prensa* in Buenos Aires.

WORKS: *Suite irreverente* for orch. (1949); *Música para caballos* for orch. (1952); Piano Concerto (Buenos Aires, July 23, 1967); Violin Concerto (Buenos Aires, Aug. 12, 1968); *Discantus* for guitar and bassoon (1968); *Euè,* funeral chant for string orch. on an African theme (Buenos Aires, March 18, 1969); *Sinfonia breve* (1970); *Mozartiana* for strings (1971); 2 trios for oboe, violin and piano; guitar pieces; songs.

Piccinni (Piccini), Niccolò, Italian opera composer; b. Bari, Jan. 16, 1728; d. Paris, May 7, 1800. Piccinni's father was a violinist at the Basilica di San Nicola in Bari, and his maternal uncle, **Gaetano Latilla** (1713-83), a well-known operatic composer. The innate ability of young Piccinni attracted the attention of the Archbishop of Bari, Muzio Gaeta, who arranged for him to enroll at the Cons. di Sant' Onofrio in Naples; there, at the age of 14, he began studying under the celebrated masters Leo and Durante; continued as a student for 13 years, and then became instructor at the same Cons. His first work, *Le Donne dispettose,* an opera buffa in the style made popular in Naples by Logroscino, was produced at the Teatro dei Fiorentini in 1754. He wrote 139 operas; in 1761 alone he produced 10 operas; 7 more followed in 1762. An instinct for the theater made him select librettos rich in dramatic content. His melodic invention was fresh and his arias were written in a pleasing style eminently suitable to the voice. He elaborated the conventional climactic scenes so that dramatic interest was sustained to the end. He varied the tempos and the harmonies in the ensembles, which further contributed to the general effect. After modest successes in Naples with *Le Gelosie* (1755) and *Il Curioso del proprio danno* (1756), he went to Rome, where he produced his opera *Alessandro nelle Indie* (Jan. 21, 1758); later wrote another setting to the same subject (Naples, Jan. 12, 1774). Piccinni's greatest success in Rome was his comic opera *La buona figliuola,* to Goldoni's libretto based on Richardson's *Pamela* (Feb. 6, 1760; also produced in Italy as *La Cecchina nubile*); Piccinni wrote a sequel to it, *La buona figliuola maritata* (Bologna, June 10, 1761). Other operas produced in

Rome were: *Le Contadine bizarre* (Feb. 10, 1763); *Gli Stravaganti* (Jan. 1, 1764; also performed under the title *La Schiava riconosciuta*); *Il Barone di Torreforte* (Jan. 10, 1765); *La Pescatrice* (Jan. 9, 1766); *Antigone* (1770); and *Le finte gemelle* (Jan. 2, 1771). Piccinni's fortunes declined with the rising popularity in Rome of a powerful rival, Anfossi; not wishing to compete, Piccinni returned to Naples, where he staged his opera *I Viaggiatori* with excellent success. Piccinni's historical role was destined to be played on the international scene in Paris, where he went with his family in Dec. 1776. His arrival in Paris precipitated one of the most famous controversies in music history, the "querelle célèbre," which was in essence a continuation of the "Guerre des Bouffons" of 1752. In the later case, the Parisian public was sharply divided into two warring factions, one supporting the Italian operatic art as practiced by Piccinni, and the other championing the operatic realism of Gluck. Piccinni himself had the highest regard for Gluck, and never encouraged the frenzied outbursts of the "Piccinnists." Gluck left Paris in 1780; at his death in Vienna (1787) Piccinni made plans to organize annual concerts in Paris in Gluck's memory, but failed to find financial support for his project. Piccinni's first opera in French, *Roland* (Jan. 27, 1778), had considerable success; he continued to use French librettos, producing several operas in close succession, of which the following were fairly well received: *Le Fat méprisé* (Paris, May 16, 1779); *Atys* (Paris, Feb. 22, 1780); *Iphigénie* (Paris, Jan. 23, 1781; fairly successful, despite the fact that Gluck's masterpiece on the same subject was produced 2 years before); *Didon* (Fontainebleau, Oct. 16, 1783; his most enduring work; separate arias have been reprinted many times); *Le Dormeur éveillé* (Paris, Nov. 14, 1783); *Le Faux Lord* (Paris, Dec. 6, 1783); and *Pénélope* (Fontainebleau, Nov. 2, 1785). In 1778 Piccinni became director of the Italian troupe in Paris; in 1784 he was appointed *maître de chant* at the newly founded École Royale de Chant et de Déclamation Lyrique in Paris, but lost this position after the Revolution and returned to Naples, where he subsisted on a small pension granted him by the King of Naples; went back to Paris in 1798, where he was received with public honors, and given a purse of 5,000 francs for immediate necessities; an honorary position of a 6th inspector was granted to him by the Paris Cons. (formerly the École Royale de Chant). But Piccinni was too ill for active life; he retired to Passy, where he spent the last months of his life. *La Cecchina* was revived in Bari on his bicentenary, Feb. 7, 1928. A complete list of Piccinni's operas is given by A. Cametti under the title "Saggio cronologico delle opere teatrali di Niccolò Piccinni," in *Rivista Musicale Italiana* 8 (also separately, Turin, 1901).

BIBLIOGRAPHY: Ph. Coquéau, *Entretiens sur l'état actuel de l'opéra de Paris* (Paris, 1779; a discussion of the relative merits of Piccinni and Gluck in dialogue form); P. L. Ginguené, *Notice sur la vie et les ouvrages de Nicolas Piccinni* (Paris, 1800); G. Desnoiresterres, *Gluck et Piccinni* (Paris, 1872); E. Thoinan, *Notes bibliographiques sur la guerre musicale des Gluckistes et Piccinnistes* (Paris, 1878); H. Curzon, *Les Dernières Années de Piccinni à Paris* (Paris, 1890); H. Abert, "Piccinni als Buffokomponist," *Jahrbuch Pe-*

ters (1913); G. de Napoli, "Nicola Piccinni nel secondo centenario della nascità," *Rivista Musicale Italiana* (1928); A. Parisi, "Intorno al soggiorno di Nicola Piccinni in Francia," *Rivista Musicale Italiana* (1928); A. Della Corte, *Piccinni* (Bari, 1928); P. La Rotella, *Niccolò Piccinni* (Bari, 1928); N. Pascazio, *L'Uomo Piccinni e la "Querelle célèbre"* (Bari, 1951). See also A. Loewenberg, *Annals of Opera.*

Pichl, Wenzel, Bohemian violinist and composer; b. Bechin, Sept. 23, 1741; d. Vienna, Jan. 23, 1805. He studied violin with Pokorny and composition with Seeger in Prague. In 1775 he was appointed chamber composer to Archduke Ferdinand at Milan; went with him to Vienna in 1796; also supplied musical entertainment to Viennese noblemen; he died during a concert at the palace of Prince Lobkowitz. He wrote about 700 works, including 12 operas, some 20 Masses, 89 symphonies (of which 66 were publ.), 13 serenades (3 of which were publ.), a great number of concertos for violin and other instruments with orch., 7 octets, 7 septets, 6 sextets, 21 quintets, 172 string quartets (of which 163 were publ.) 148 works for baryton, piano pieces, etc. His 6 fugues with a fugal prelude for violin alone became fairly popular (reprint, ed. by Kocian and Gardavsky, Prague, 1951).
BIBLIOGRAPHY: R. Kolisko, *Wenzel Pichls Kammermusik* (Vienna, 1918).

Pick-Mangiagalli, Riccardo, Italian composer; b. Strakonice, Bohemia, July 10, 1882; d. Milan, July 8, 1949. He was of mixed Italian and Bohemian parentage; studied at the Cons. Giuseppe Verdi in Milan with Appiani (piano) and Ferroni (composition). He began his career as a successful concert pianist, but later turned exclusively to composition. In 1936 he succeeded Pizzetti as director of the Cons. Giuseppe Verdi, and held this post until his death.
WORKS: OPERAS: *Basi e Bote* (Rome, March 3, 1927), *Casanova a Venezia* (La Scala, Milan, Jan. 19, 1929; an orchestral suite from it, entitled *Scene carnevalesche,* was performed in Milan, Feb. 6, 1931), *L'Ospite inatteso* (Milan-Turin-Genoa Radio network, Oct. 25, 1931; the first opera to be given a world première by radio anywhere), *Il Notturno romantico* (Rome, April 25, 1936). FOR THE DANCE: *Il Salice d'oro,* mimodrama (Milan, Sept. 18, 1918), *Sumitra* (Frankfurt, 1922), *Mahit,* ballet-fable with singing (La Scala, Milan, March 20, 1923), *La Berceuse* (San Remo, Feb. 21, 1933), *Variazioni coreografiche* (San Remo, April 13, 1935). FOR ORCH.: *Sortilegi,* symph. poem for piano and orch. (Milan, Dec. 13, 1917), *Notturno e rondo fantastico* (Milan, May 6, 1919), *Due preludi* (Rome, March 1, 1921), *Quattro poemi* (Milan, April 24, 1925), *Piccola suite* (Milan, June 12, 1927), *Preludio e fuga* (Rome, March 11, 1928), *Preludio e scherzo sinfonico* (Milan, Oct. 22, 1938); Violin Sonata; String Quartet; piano pieces; songs.
BIBLIOGRAPHY: G. M. Gatti, *Musicisti moderni d'Italia e di fuori* (2nd ed., Bologna, 1925).

Picka, František, Czech organist, conductor, and composer; b. Strašice, near Hořovice, May 12, 1873; d. Prague, Oct. 18, 1918. Of a musical family, he received a solid education in Prague; held several posts as cho-

rus master and opera conductor. His opera, *Malíř Reiner (The Painter Reiner),* was produced in Prague (April 28, 1911); the bulk of his works consists of church music, including 9 Masses and many other works in effective contrapuntal style.

Pierné, (Henri-Constant-) Gabriel, French composer, conductor, and organist; b. Metz, Aug. 16, 1863; d. Ploujean, near Morlaix, July 17, 1937. He studied at the Paris Cons. (1871-82), where his teachers were Marmontel (piano), César Franck (organ), and Massenet (composition); won 1st piano prize (1879); 1st prize for counterpoint and fugue (1881), and 1st prize for organ (1882); awarded the Grand Prix de Rome (1882) with the cantata *Édith;* succeeded César Franck as organist at Ste.-Clothilde, where he remained until 1898. In 1903 he was appointed assistant conductor to Colonne, and in 1910 his successor (until 1932); elected a member of the Académie des Beaux-Arts in 1925. He was a prolific composer, but of his many works only the oratorio *La Croisade des Enfants* and the piano piece, *Marche de petits soldats de plomb,* became popular.
WORKS: OPERAS: *La Coupe enchantée* (Royan, Aug. 24, 1895; revised version, Opéra-Comique, Paris, Dec. 26, 1905), *Vendée* (Lyons, March 11, 1897), *La Fille de Tabarin* (Opéra-Comique, Paris, Feb. 20, 1901), *On ne badine pas avec l'amour* (Opéra-Comique, Paris, May 30, 1910), *Sophie Arnould,* 1-act lyric comedy, based on episodes from the life of the famous singer (Opéra-Comique, Feb. 21, 1927). BALLETS AND PANTOMIMES: *Le Collier de saphirs* (1891), *Les Joyeuses Commères de Paris* (1892), *Bouton d'or* (1893), *Le Docteur Blanc* (1893), *Salomé* (1895), *Cydalise et le chèvre-pied* (1919; Paris Opéra, Jan. 15, 1923; as an orchestral suite, 1926), *Impressions de Music-Hall,* "ballet à l'Américaine" (Opéra, April 6, 1927), *Giration* (1934), *Fragonard* (1934), *Images* "divertissement sur un thème pastoral" (Opéra, June 19, 1935); the oratorios *La Croisade des enfants,* for mixed choir of children and adults (Paris, Jan. 18, 1905), *Les Enfants à Bethléem,* for soloists, children's chorus, and orch. (Amsterdam, April 13, 1907), and *Les Fioretti de St. François d'Assise* (1912). FOR ORCH.: *Suite de concert* (1883), *Première suite d'orchestre* (1883), *Ouverture symphonique* (1885), *Marche solonnelle* (1889), *Pantomime* (1889), *Ballet de cour* (1901), *Paysages franciscains* (1920), *Gulliver au pays de Lilliput* (Paris Festival of the International Society for Contemporary Music, June 23, 1937), Piano Concerto (1887), *Scherzo-Caprice* for piano and orch. (1890), *Poème symphonique* for piano and orch. (1901), *Konzertstück* for harp and orch. (1901), *L'An mil,* symph. poem with chorus (1897). CHAMBER MUSIC: *Pastorale variée dans le style ancien,* for wind instruments (also for piano), *Berceuse* for violin and piano, *Caprice* for cello and piano, *Canzonetta* for clarinet and piano, *Solo de concert* for bassoon and piano, *Variations libres et Finale* for flute, violin, viola, cello and harp; FOR PIANO: *15 Pièces* (1883); *Étude de concert; Album pour mes petits amis,* containing the famous *Marche des petits soldats de plomb; Humoresque; Rêverie; Ariette dans le style ancien; Pastorale variée; Sérénade à Colombine; Sérénade vénitienne; Barcarolle* for 2 pianos. SONG CYCLES: *Contes* (1897), *3 Adapta-*

tions musicales (1902), and *3 Mélodies* (1904); 38 other songs; harp music, folksong arrangements, etc. He contributed the section "Histoire de l'instrumentation" to Lavignac's *Encyclopédie de la musique*.

BIBLIOGRAPHY: W. Weber, *Gabriel Pierné*; H. Eymieu, "Gabriel Pierné," *Revue Illustrée* (Paris, March 15, 1897); L. Schneider, "Gabriel Pierné," *Le Théâtre* (Paris, March, 1901); O. Séré, *Musiciens français d'aujourd'hui* (Paris, 1921).

Pierné, Paul, French composer, cousin of **Gabriel Pierné**; b. Metz, June 30, 1874; d. Paris, March 24, 1952. He studied at the Paris Cons. with Lenepveu and Caussade; wrote a number of works, which were occasionally performed in Paris: the operas *Le Diable galant* (1913), *Emilde*, and *Mademoiselle Don Quichotte*, a ballet, *Le Figurinaï*; 2 symphonies and several symph. poems of a programmatic nature (*Jeanne d'Arc, Cléopâtre, De l'ombre à la lumière, Nuit évocatrice, Rapsodie Lorraine*, etc.); choral works; organ pieces; a song cycle, *Schéhérazade*; piano pieces.

Pierpont, James, American composer; b. Boston, 1822; d. Winter Haven, Florida, 1893. In 1857 he published a ballad entitled *One Horse Open Sleigh* (composed in 1850); in 1859 it was published under the title *Jingle Bells, or the One Horse Open Sleigh* (the original music is reprinted in facsimile in Richard Jackson's *Popular Songs of 19th-Century America*, N.Y., 1976); however, while the original words and the music to the verse are the same as known today, the original music to the chorus is different. This song did not acquire its wide popularity as a Christmas song until the 20th century; during the 19th century, Pierpont's most popular works were *The Little White Cottage, or Gentle Nettie Moore* (1857), *We Conquer or Die* (1861) and *Strike for the South* (1863), the last 2 being rallying songs for the confederacy during the Civil War (his father, in contrast, was a fiery abolitionist minister). He was the uncle of millionaire financier John Pierpont Morgan.

BIBLIOGRAPHY: F. W. Lovering, "Jingle Bells: Its Author Was a Rover," *Musical Courier* (Dec. 1959).

Pierre, Constant, French writer on music; b. Paris, Aug. 24, 1855; d. there, Jan., 1918. He was a pupil at the Paris Cons.; played the bassoon in various Paris orchestras; from 1881 devoted himself mainly to musical journalism; was for many years editor of *Le Monde musical*.

WRITINGS: essays on *Les Noëls populaires* (1866) and *La Marseillaise* (1887); *La Facture instrumentale à l'Exposition universelle de 1889* (1890); *Les Facteurs d'instruments de musique, les luthiers* (1893); *L'École de chant de l'Opéra (1672–1807)* (1895); *B. Sarrette et les origines du Conservatoire national de musique et de déclamation* (1895); *Notes inédites sur la musique de la Chapelle Royale (1532–1790)* (1899); *Le Conservatoire national de musique et de déclamation* (1900); *Le Concert Spirituel 1725–1790* (compiled in 1900, but left in manuscript form until published in Paris in 1975; very valuable); *Les Hymnes et chansons de la Révolution* (1904); compiled *Musique des fêtes et cérémonies de la Révolution française* (1899; of documentary value).

Pierson (Pearson), Henry Hugh, English composer; b. Oxford, April 12, 1815; d. Leipzig, Jan. 28, 1873. He was educated at Cambridge; in 1839 went to Germany, where he studied music with Tomaschek and Reissiger; entered the circle of Mendelssohn in Leipzig; after a brief term as prof. of music at the Univ. of Edinburgh (1844), he returned to Germany where he remained for the rest of his life; married **Caroline Leonhardt**, who wrote the German librettos for his operas. He changed his name from the original form Pearson to Pierson in order to secure proper pronunciation by Germans; used the pen name **Edgar Mansfeldt** for his published music.

WORKS: operas: *Leila* (Hamburg, Feb. 22, 1848) and *Contarini oder Die Verschwörung zu Padua* (Hamburg, April 16, 1872; revived in Dessau, April 24, 1883, under the title *Fenice*); oratorio *Jerusalem* (Norwich Festival, Sept. 23, 1852); incidental music to the 2nd part of Goethe's *Faust*; overtures to Shakespeare's *Macbeth, As You Like It*, and *Romeo and Juliet*. His music was totally submerged in Mendelssohn's style.

BIBLIOGRAPHY: H. G. Sear, "*Faust* and Henry Hugo Pierson," *Music Review* (1949).

Pietri, Giuseppe, Italian composer; b. Sant'Ilario, Elba, May 6, 1886; d. Milan, Aug. 11, 1946. He studied at the Cons. of Milan and became a successful composer of operettas; the most popular among them were *Addio giovinezza* (Leghorn, 1915); *Acqua cheta* (Rome, 1920); *La donna perduta* (Rome, 1923); *Primarosa* (Milan, 1926); and *Casa mia* (Rome, 1930).

BIBLIOGRAPHY: R. Carli, *Giuseppe Pietri, cantore dei goliardi* (Leghorn, 1956).

Pijper, Willem, renowned Dutch composer; b. Zeist, Sept. 8, 1894; d. Leidschendam, March 18, 1947. He received rudimentary education from his father, an amateur violinist; then went to the Toonkunst School of Music in Utrecht, where he studied composition with Johan Wagenaar and piano with Mme. H. J. van Lunteren-Hansen (1911-1916); from 1918 to 1923, was music critic of *Utrecht Dagblad* and from 1926 to 1929, co-editor of the monthly *De Muziek*. He taught composition at the Amsterdam Cons. (1925-30) and served as director of the Rotterdam Cons. from 1930 until his death. In his music Pijper continued the romantic tradition of Mahler, and also adopted the harmonic procedures of the modern French School. He postulated a "germ-cell theory," in which an opening chord or motif is the source of all succeeding harmonic and melodic development; he also cultivated the scale of alternating whole tone and semitones, regarding it as his own, not realizing that it was used abundantly by Rimsky-Korsakov (in Russian reference works it is termed the Rimsky-Korsakov scale); the "Pijper scale," as it became known in Holland, was also used by Anton von der Horst and others. During the German bombardment of Rotterdam in May, 1940, nearly all of Pijper's manuscripts were destroyed by fire, including the unpublished reduced scoring of his large Second Symphony (restored in 1961 by Pijper's student Karel Mengelberg); also destroyed was the unpublished *Divertimento* for piano and string orch.

WORKS: FOR THE STAGE: 2 operas ("symphonic dramas"): *Halewijn* (1932-33; Amsterdam, June 13, 1933; revised 1934) and *Merlijn* (1939-45, incomplete; posthumous, Rotterdam, June 7, 1952). INCIDENTAL MUSIC: Sophocles' *Antigone* (1920, revised 1922 and 1926), Euripides' *Bacchantes* (1924) and *The Cyclops* (1925), Shakespeare's *The Tempest* (1930) and Vondel's *Phaëton* (1937). FOR ORCH.: 3 symphonies: No. 1, *Pan* (1917; Amsterdam, April 23, 1918); No. 2 for large orch. (1921; Amsterdam, Nov. 2, 1922; reduced scoring accomplished by Karel Mengelberg, 1961); No. 3 (1926; Amsterdam, Oct. 28, 1926; his most frequently performed work); *6 Symphonic Epigrams* (1928; Amsterdam, April 12, 1928); *6 Adagios* (1940; posthumous, Utrecht, Nov. 14, 1951); *Orchestral Piece with Piano* (1915; Utrecht, Dec. 11, 1915); Pijper originally titled this "Piano Concerto No. 1," which caused confusion with his later and only Piano Concerto (1927; Amsterdam, Dec. 22, 1927), which in turn was sometimes incorrectly referred to as "Piano Concerto No. 2" in some catalogues; Cello Concerto (1936; Amsterdam, Nov. 22, 1936; revised in 1947); Violin Concerto (1938-39; Amsterdam, Jan. 7, 1940). CHAMBER MUSIC: 2 piano trios (1913-14; 1921); 5 string quartets (1914; 1920; 1923; 1928; 1946, unfinished); Septet for wind quintet, double bass and piano (1920); Sextet for wind quintet and piano (1922-23); Trio for flute, clarinet and bassoon (1926-27); Wind Quintet (1928-29); 2 violin sonatas (1919; 1922); 2 cello sonatas (1919, 1924); Flute Sonata (1925); Sonata for solo violin (1931). FOR PIANO: *Theme with 5 Variations* (1913); *3 Aphorisms* (1915); 3 sonatinas (1917, 1925, 1925); *3 Old Dutch Dances* (1926); Sonata (1930); 2-Piano Sonata (1935). FOR VOICE AND ORCH.: *Fêtes galantes*, after Verlaine, with mezzo-soprano (1916; Schweningen, Aug. 2, 1917); *Romance sans paroles*, after Verlaine, with mezzo-soprano (1919; Amsterdam, April 15, 1920); *Hymne*, after Boutens, with bass-baritone (1941-43; Amsterdam, Nov. 1945). FOR VOICE AND PIANO: *8 Vieilles Chansons de France* (1918); *8 Noëls de France* (1919); *8 Old Dutch Love Songs* (1920; revised 1943); *8 Old Dutch Songs*, in 2 sets (1924, 1935). FOR A CAPPELLA CHORUS: *Heer Halewijn* (1920) and *Heer Danielken* (1925). He also wrote a *Passepied* for carillon (1916) and made orchestrations and arrangements of Haydn, Mozart, etc.; published two collections of articles, *De Quinten-Cirkel* (Amsterdam, 1929) and *De Stemvork* (Amsterdam, 1930).

BIBLIOGRAPHY: M. D. Calvocoressi, "Willem Pijper," *Monthly Musical Record* (1924); Cor Backers, *Nederlandse Componisten van 1400 tot op onze tijd* (The Hague, 1941; new ed., 1948; pp. 123-31); A. L. Ringer, "Willem Pijper and the Netherlands School of the 20th Century," *Musical Quarterly* (Oct. 1955); W. C. M. Kloppenburg, *Thematisch-bibliografische Catalogus van de Werken van Willem Pijper* (Amsterdam, 1960); J. Wouters, "Willem Pijper," *Sonorum Spectrum* 30 (Spring 1967); M. Flothuis, "Willem Pijper: An Unharmonious Figure in an Unharmonious Age," *Key Notes* 3 (1976).

Pilarczyk, Helga, German soprano; b. Schöningen, March 12, 1925. She studied piano and aspired to a concert career; then took voice lessons and sang in operetta. She found her true vocation in opera; was a member of the Hamburg State Opera from 1954 until 1967. She made a specialty of modern music; sang Schoenberg's dramatic monologue *Erwartung*, and the leading parts in Alban Berg's *Wozzeck* and *Lulu* as well as in works by Stravinsky, Prokofiev, Dallapiccola, Honegger, Krenek and others. She appeared as a guest artist at the Bavarian State Opera in Munich, Vienna State Opera, La Scala in Milan, Paris Opéra, Covent Garden Opera in London and the Metropolitan Opera, N.Y.; publ. an interesting essay, *Kann man die moderne Oper singen?* (Hamburg, 1964).

Pilati, Mario, Italian composer; b. Naples, Oct. 16, 1903; d. there, Dec. 10, 1938. He studied at the Naples Cons.; was instructor there (1930-38).

WORKS: *Notturno* for orch. (1923); *La Sera* for women's voices and orch. (1926); Flute Sonata (1926); *Il Battesimo di Cristo* for soli, chorus, and orch. (1927); Piano Quintet (1928); Violin Sonata (1929); Cello Sonata (1929); String Quartet (1930); piano pieces; also transcriptions for piano of works by Pizzetti and Casella.

BIBLIOGRAPHY: G. Gavazzeni, "M. Pilati," in his *Il Suono è stanco* (Bergamo, 1950).

Pilkington, Francis, English composer; b. c.1562; d. Chester, 1638. He received a B. Mus. degree at Lincoln College in Oxford; was successively lay clerk (1602), minor canon (1612), curate (1616), and precentor of the Chester Cathedral (1623). He publ. *The First Booke of Songs or Ayres of 4 parts* (1604), reprinted by Arkwright in the *Old English Edition* (nos. 18-20) and by Fellowes in *The English School of Lutenist Song Writers* (vols. 7, 15); *The First Set of Madrigals and Pastorals of 3, 4, and 5 parts* (1614) and *The Second Set of Madrigals and Pastorals of 3, 4, 5, and 6 parts* (1624), reprinted by Fellowes in *The English Madrigal School* (vols. 25, 26). Pilkington also contributed 2 songs to Sir William Leighton's collection, *The Teares or Lamentacions of a Sorrowful Soule* (1614).

BIBLIOGRAPHY: E. H. Fellowes, *The English Madrigal Composers* (London, 1921; 2nd ed., 1948).

Pillois, Jacques, French-American composer and pedagogue; b. Paris, Feb. 14, 1877; d. New York, Jan. 3, 1935. He was a student of Widor and Vierne at the Paris Cons.; upon graduation taught at various schools in Paris. In 1927 he went to the U.S. and was on the faculty of the N.Y. Univ. (1927-30) and later at Smith College. He wrote some attractive pieces of chamber music and songs, under the pen name **Jacques Desky.**

Pimsleur, Solomon, American pianist and composer; b. Paris, Sept. 19, 1900, of Austrian-Jewish parents; d. New York, April 22, 1962. He was taken to the U.S. as a child in 1903; studied piano privately; took music courses at Columbia Univ., but graduated in English literature (M.A., 1923); also studied with Rubin Goldmark. He gave numerous piano recitals in the U.S. His compositions, in a romantically flavored and technically competent idiom, include *Ode to Intensity,* a "symphonic ballad" (N.Y., Aug. 14, 1933); *Overture to Disillusionment; Meditative Nocturne* for orch.; 3

string quartets; Piano Trio; Piano Quintet; Violin Sonata; Cello Sonata; many piano pieces with imaginative titles (*Impulsive Sonata, Tranquil Sonata, Reflective Sonata, Mournful Prelude and Melodious Fugue,* etc.); a *Shakespearean Sonnet Symphony* for chorus and orch. His projected opera, *Diary of Anne Frank,* remains unfinished.

Pincherle, Marc, noted French musicologist; b. Constantine, Algiers, June 13, 1888; d. Paris, June 20, 1974. He studied music in Paris with Pirro, Laloy, and Rolland; served in both world wars; was taken prisoner of war in June, 1940 and was interned in Germany until March, 1941. He taught the history of violin playing at the École Normale; was artistic director of the Société Pleyel (1927–55) and President of the Société Française de Musicologie (1948–56). As a musicologist he devoted his energy mainly to the history of violin music.
WRITINGS: *Les Violonistes compositeurs et virtuoses* (Paris, 1922); *Feuillets d'histoire du violon* (ib., 1927; 2nd ed., 1935); *Corelli* (Paris, 1933); *Les Musiciens peints par eux-mêmes* (160 letters of famous composers from his own autograph collection; Paris, 1939); *Antonio Vivaldi et la musique instrumentale* (2 vols., Paris, 1948); *Les Instruments du quatuor* (Paris, 1948); *L'Orchestre de chambre* (Paris, 1948); *Jean-Marie Leclair l'aîné* (Paris, 1952); *Petit lexique des termes musicaux d'usage courant* (Paris, 1953); *Corelli et son temps* (Paris, 1954; English transl. as *Corelli, His Life, His Work,* N.Y., 1956); *Vivaldi* (Paris, 1955; English transl., N.Y., 1957); *Albert Roussel* (Geneva, 1957); *Histoire illustrée de la musique* (Paris, 1959; in English, N.Y., 1959); *Le Monde des virtuoses* (Paris, 1961; in English, N.Y., 1963; also in German, Rumanian and Japanese); *Le Violon* (Paris, 1966; 2nd updated ed., 1974).

Pingoud, Ernest, Russian-born Finnish composer; b. St. Petersburg, Oct. 14, 1888; d. Helsinki, June 1, 1942. He studied piano in St. Petersburg with Siloti; then went to Leipzig where he took courses in music history with Hugo Riemann and in composition with Max Reger. In 1918 he settled in Finland where he served as managing director of the Helsinki Symph. Orch. (1924-42). In his music he was influenced by the Russian modern school, particularly by Scriabin, from whom he acquired his predilection for mystical titles, often in French (*La Flamme éternelle, Le Chant d'espace,* etc.).
WORKS: For orch.: *Prologue* (1916); *Confessions* (1916); *La dernière aventure de Pierrot* (1916); *Diableries galantes "Le fétiche"* (1917); 3 piano concertos (1917, 1921, 1922); *Hymnjä yölle* (Hymns to the Night, 1917); *Kuolemantanssi* (*Danse Macabre*) for chorus and orch. (1918); 5 *Sonnets* for chamber orch. (1918); *Ritari Peloton ja moitteeton* (*The Knight Without Fear or Reproach*), an "adventure" for orch. (1918); *Mysterium* (1919); *Flambeaux éleints* (1919); *Chantecler* (1919); *Le Sacrifice* (1919); 3 symphonies (1920, 1920, 1923-27); *Profeetta* (The Prophet, 1921); *Cor ardens* (1927); *Narcissos* (1930); *Le Chant d'espace* (1931, revised 1938); *Suurkaupungin kasvot* (*The Face of the Big City*), ballet for piano and orch. (1936); *La Flamme éternelle* (1938-39); *Epäjumala*

(*The Idol*), ballet; chamber music; piano works; songs.
BIBLIOGRAPHY: A. Rudnev, "Ernest Pingoud," in *Suomen Saveltajia* (Helsinki, 1945; pp. 487-500).

Pinkham, Daniel, American composer; b. Lynn, Mass., June 5, 1923. He studied organ and music theory at Phillips Academy in Andover (1937–40), and at Harvard Univ. with A. Tillman Merritt, Walter Piston, and Archibald T. Davison (A.B., 1943; M.A., 1944); had harpsichord lessons with Putnam Aldrich and Wanda Landowska, and organ with E. Power Biggs; took summer courses in composition at the Berkshire Music Center in Tanglewood, with Aaron Copland, Arthur Honegger and Nadia Boulanger; subsequently was music director of King's Chapel in Boston and member of the faculty of the New England Cons. of Music. The formal design of his music is compact and contrapuntally cohesive; the rhythmic element is propulsive; now and then he astutely applies modernistic devices without disrupting the tonal fabric of the music.
WORKS: Piano Concertino (Cambridge, Mass., May 3, 1950); Concertante No. 1 for violin and harpsichord soli, strings, and celesta (Boston, Dec. 16, 1954); Concerto for celesta and harpsichord soli (N.Y., Nov. 19, 1955); Violin Concerto No. 1 (Falmouth, Mass., Sept. 8, 1956); Concertante No. 2 for violin and strings (Boston, May 9, 1958); *Cantilena and Capriccio,* for violin and harpsichord; Divertimento for oboe and strings; other chamber music; 2 cantatas: *Wedding Cantata* (Cambridge, Mass., Sept. 22, 1956) and *Christmas Cantata* (*Sinfonia Sacra;* Boston, Dec. 10, 1957); Symph. No. 1 (1960); *Catacoustical Measures,* composed to test the acoustics at Lincoln Center in N.Y. (1962); Symph. No. 2 (Lansing, Michigan, Nov. 23, 1963); *Signs of the Zodiac* for speaker and orch. (1964); *Eclogue* for flute, harpsichord and handbells (1965); Violin Concerto No. 2 (1968); sacred choruses; motets; several dozens of briskly selling arrangements for chamber orch. of well-known Christmas songs.

Piños, Alois Simandl, Czech composer; b. Vyškov, Oct. 2, 1925. He studied forestry at the Brno Univ. (graduating in 1953) and music with Petrželka at the Brno Cons. (1948-49) and at the Janáček Academy of Music with Kvapil and Schaeffer (1949-53); attended the summer courses of new music at Darmstadt (1965) and an electronic music seminar in Munich (1966). In 1953 he joined the faculty of the Janáček Academy of Music in Brno. In 1967 he founded in Brno a modern music group with which he produced a number of works of the local avant-garde, some composed collectively.
WORKS: chamber opera, *The Criers* (1970); the audio-visual works, *The Lattice* for piano and film (1970); *The Genesis* for chamber orch. and film (1970); and *Static Music for Tape* with slides (1970); *Czech Dances* for orch. (1951); *Wedding Suite* for orch. (1952); Horn Concerto (1953); Concertino for orch. (1963); *Abbreviations,* 10 pieces for orch. (1963); Concerto for Orch. and Tape (1964); *Double Concerto* for cello, piano, winds and percussion (1965–66; Prague, March 7, 1967); *Chamber Concerto* for strings (1967); a cantata, *Ars amatoria* (1967); *Concerto on the*

Name B-A-C-H for bass clarinet, cello, piano, strings and percussion (1968); a symphony, *Apollo XI* (1970); *Symphonic Diptych* (1973-74); Cello Sonata (1950); 2 wind quintets (1951, 1959); Sonata for viola and cello (1960); Piano Trio (1960); Suite for string trio (1961); *Monologues* for solo bass clarinet (1962); *Caricatures* for flute, bass clarinet and piano (1962); string quartet (1962); *Hunting Music* for baritone and 4 horns (1963); *Conflicts* for violin, bass clarinet, piano and percussion (1964); *2 Lyrical Sketches* for narrator, flute and violin (1964); *4 Lyrical Sketches* for narrator, flute, bass clarinet and piano (1965); *3 Pieces* for bass clarinet and piano (1965); *Pulsus intermissi* for solo percussionist (1965); *Ludus floralis*, 5 songs for baritone, female chorus, percussion and tape (1966); *Hyperboles*, 7 pieces for solo harp (1966); *Gesta Machabaeorum* for chorus, flute, trumpet, harp and percussion (1967-68); *16 January 1969* for piano quintet and kettledrums (1969); *Dialogues* for solo bass clarinet (1969); *2 campanari* for bass clarinet, piano and ringing instruments (1971); *Be Beaten* for solo percussionist (1972); *Sonata Concertante* for cello and piano (1974); *Power of Love* for baritone and string quartet (1974); *Composition for 3* for flute, clarinet and marimbaphone (1975); *Acquaintance*, to advertising texts, for soprano, bass-baritone, and guitar or harpsichord (1975); *Paradoxes* for piano (1965); *2-3-1*, 3 pieces for piano (1969); *Esca* for prepared piano (1971); several tape pieces, including *Home* (1972-73) and *Speleophony* (1976); songs; choruses. Piños published *Tónové skupiny* (The Tone Groups, Prague, 1971; contains a German-language résumé), intended as a preamble to a projected work, *Composition and Tone Groups*.

Pinsuti, Ciro, celebrated Italian singing teacher and composer; b. Sinalunga, near Florence, May 9, 1829; d. Florence, March 10, 1888. His talent developed so rapidly that at 11 he was elected an honorary member of the Accademia Filarmonica, Rome. Taken to England soon after by Henry Drummond, he studied the piano under C. Potter, and the violin under Blagrove; returned to Bologna, 1845, and studied at the Liceo, also privately with Rossini, soon becoming assistant teacher of a piano class. In 1848 he went back to England; appointed prof. of singing at the Royal Academy of Music in 1856. He divided his time between London and Italy; brought out an opera, *Il Mercante di Venezia*, at Bologna (Nov. 9, 1873), another, *Mattia Corvino*, at Milan (1877), and a third, *Margherita*, at Venice (1882). In 1871 he represented Italy at the opening of the London Exhibition, for which he composed the hymn *O people of this favoured land*. As a recipient of the order of the Italian Crown, he was styled "Cavaliere" Pinsuti. Besides his operas, he wrote some 200 songs to English and Italian texts.

Pinto, Alfredo, Italian-Argentine composer; b. Mantua, Oct. 22, 1891; d. Buenos Aires, May 26, 1968. He studied piano with Longo and composition with De Nardis in Naples; then went to Buenos Aires where he became active as pianist and conductor. He wrote the operas *La última esposa, o Sheherazade* and *Gualicho* (Buenos Aires, 1940); symph. poems *Nostalgias*

(1929); *Eros* (1930); *Rebelión* (1939); numerous piano pieces, choruses and songs.

Pinto, Octavio, Brazilian composer; b. São Paulo, Nov. 3, 1890; d. there, Oct. 31, 1950. He was trained as an architect; built apartment houses in Brazil; also studied piano with Isidor Philipp. In 1922 he married the Brazilian pianist, **Guiomar Novaës**; Villa-Lobos wrote his suite, *Prole do Bébé* for their children. Pinto publ. a number of effective piano miniatures, of which the *Scenas Infantis* (1932) and *Children's Festival* (1939) are best known.

Pinza, Ezio (baptismal name **Fortunio**), celebrated Italian bass; b. Rome, May 18, 1892; d. Stamford, Conn., May 9, 1957. The family moved to Ravenna when he was an infant; he studied engineering; also was active in sports. He began to study voice at the age of 18 with Ruzza and Vizzani, at the Cons. of Bologna; served in the Italian artillery during World War I; made his opera debut as King Mark in *Tristan und Isolde* at the Teatro Reale in Rome (1920); then sang for 3 seasons at La Scala, Milan; was selected by Toscanini for the leading part in the world première of Boito's *Nerone* (May 1, 1924). He made his American debut at the Metropolitan Opera House as Pontifex Maximus in Spontini's *La Vestale* (Nov. 1, 1926) and remained on its staff until 1943; appeared also in San Francisco, Chicago, etc.; sang in Europe and in South America; his most celebrated roles were Méphistophélès in Gounod's *Faust*, Don Giovanni, and Boris Godunov. In 1949 he appeared as a musical comedy star in *South Pacific*, and immediately became successful in this new career; also appeared in films.

Pipelare, Matthaeus, Flemish composer; b. about 1450; d. about 1512. He was active in Antwerp; was engaged as master of the choirboys in 's-Hertogenbosch (1498–1500). His style has a certain affinity to that of Pierre de la Rue. His extant works include 9 Masses and a number of motets and chansons.

BIBLIOGRAPHY: R. Cross, "The Life and Works of Matthaeus Pipelare," *Musica Disciplina* (1963).

Pipkov, Lubomir, noted Bulgarian composer; b. Lovec, Sept. 19, 1904; d. Sofia, May 9, 1974. He studied piano at the Bulgarian State Cons. in Sofia (1923–26); then took courses in composition with Nadia Boulanger and Paul Dukas at the École Normale de Musique in Paris (1926–32). Returning to Bulgaria, he occupied several administrative posts, including the directorship of the Sofia Opera Theater (1944–47). His style of composition is determined by the inherent asymmetry of Bulgarian folksongs; there is a similarity in his compositions with those of Bartók, resulting from common sources in Balkan and Macedonian music; his harmonic investiture is often polytonal or polymodal.

WORKS: 3 operas: *The Nine Brothers of Yanina* (1932; Sofia, Sept. 19, 1937), *Momchil* (1939–44; Sofia, April 24, 1948) and *Antigone 43* (1961–62; Ruse, Dec. 23, 1963); *Oratorio for Our Time* (1959; Plovdiv, Dec. 18, 1959); 2 cantatas: *The Wedding* (1934) and *Cantata of Friendship* (1958); Concerto for Winds, Percussion and Piano (1930); 4 symphonies: No. 1

(1939–40), No. 2 (1954), No. 3 for strings, trumpet, 2 pianos and percussion (1965) and No. 4 for string orch. (1970); *Heroic Overture* (1950); *Journey through Albania,* variations for string orchestra (1950); Violin Concerto (1951); Piano Concerto (1954); *Symphony-Concerto* for cello and orch. (1963; Moscow, April, 20, 1964); Concerto for Clarinet and Chamber Orch. (1966); *The Partisan's Grave* for trombone and string orch. (1970); 3 string quartets (1928, 1948, 1966); 2 violin sonatas (1929, 1969); Piano Trio (1930); Piano Quartet (1939); Sonata for solo violin (1969); *Tableaux et études métrorythmiques* for piano (1972); *Suggestions printanieres* for piano (1972); choruses; songs.

BIBLIOGRAPHY: K. Iliev, *Lubomir Pipkov* (Sofia, 1958).

Pirani, Eugenio, Italian pianist and composer; b. Bologna, Sept. 8, 1852; d. Berlin, Jan. 12, 1939. A pupil of Colinelli at the Bologna Liceo Musicale, he graduated in 1869; then studied in Berlin with Th. Kullak (piano) and Kiel (composition); taught in Kullak's Academy 1870–80, also touring Italy (1873, 1876), England and Germany, France and Russia. He lived in Heidelberg till 1895, and then settled in Berlin. He publ. concert studies and many pieces for piano solo; songs; duets; etc.; also *Die Hochschule des Klavierspiels,* op. 88 (in German and English) and *Secrets of the Success of Great Musicians* (Philadelphia, 1922).

Pires, Filipe, Portuguese composer; b. Lisbon, June 26, 1934. He studied piano with Mendes and composition with Croner de Vasconcelos at the Lisbon Cons. (1946–54); then went to Germany where he attended classes at the College of Music and Theater in Hannover (1957–60). Returning to Portugal, he taught composition at the Oporto Cons. (1960–70) and at the Lisbon Cons. (1972–75); subsequently worked in an electronic studio in Paris under the direction of Pierre Schaeffer. His own music hews resolutely to the tenets of the cosmopolitan avant-garde.

WORKS: String Quartet (1958); Piano Trio (1960); *Eternal Return* for baritone and orch. (1961); *Perspectivas* for 3 groups of instruments (1965); *Metromonie* for flute, viola and harp (1966); *Portugaliae Genesis* for baritone, chorus and orch. (1968; Lisbon, May 21, 1969); *Homo Sapiens* for magnetic tape (1972); *Dialogues* for 8 instrumentalists and tape (1975). He published a school manual, *Elementos teóricos de contraponto e cánon* (Lisbon, 1968).

Pirogov, Alexandr, Russian operatic bass; b. Moscow, July 4, 1899; d. there, June 18, 1964. He was engaged as a member of the Bolshoi Theater in 1924, and appeared in Russian operas; his dramatic portrayal of the title role of *Boris Godunov* was particularly notable.

Pironkov, Simeon, Bulgarian composer; b. Lom, June 18, 1927. He studied composition with Veselin Stoyanov and Khadjiev at the Bulgarian State Cons. in Sofia, graduating in 1953; in 1961 was appointed director of the Theater for Youth in Sofia. His music is rhythmically animated, harmonically tense, melodically modal and instrumentally coloristic.

WORKS: an opera after Brecht, *The Good Man from Sechwan* (1967); Sinfonietta (1952); Symph. for string orch. (1961); *The Apology of Socrates* for solo bass, string orch. and percussion (1966); *Movements* for 13 strings (1967); *Requiem for an Unknown Young Man* for 13 strings (1968); *Night Music* for orch. (1968); *3 Songs to Ancient Greek Lyrics* for voice and orch. (1971); *Ballet Music in Memory of Igor Stravinsky* for chamber orch. (1972); *Music* for 2 pianos and orch. (1973; Nuremberg, Jan. 17, 1974); Trio for flute, clarinet and piano (1949); String Trio (1950); Solo Violin Sonata (1955); 2 string quartets (1960, 1966); *16 Preludes* for piano (1949).

Pirro, André, distinguished French musicologist; b. St.-Dizier, Haute-Marne, Feb. 12, 1869; d. Paris, Nov. 11, 1943. Pupil of his father, an organist; from 1896 prof. at the Schola Cantorum, and member of the board of directors; from 1904 also lecturer on the history of the theory of music at the École des Hautes Études Sociales; in 1912 he succeeded R. Rolland as prof. of the history of music at the Sorbonne.

WORKS: *L'Orgue de J.-S. Bach* (1897; won prize of the Académie des Beaux-Arts; preface by Widor; English transl. by J. W. Goodrich, N.Y., 1902); *J. S. Bach* (1906; 6th ed., 1924; English translation, N.Y., 1957); *Descartes et la musique* (1907); *L'Esthétique de J.-S. Bach* (1907; a most valuable work); *Dietrich Buxtehude* (1913); *Heinrich Schütz* (1913); *Les Clavecinistes* (1925); *La Musique à Paris 1380–1422* (Strasbourg, 1930); "Leo X and Music," *Musical Quarterly* (Jan. 1935); *Histoire de la musique de la fin du XIV siècle à la fin du XVI* (Paris, 1940). For Guilmant's *Archives des Maîtres de l'Orgue* he wrote a number of biographies of early French organists (Titelouze, Daquin, Couperin, Marchand, etc.); contributed valuable essays to various musical publications.

Pirrotta, Nino, eminent Italian musicologist; b. Palermo, June 13, 1908. He studied at the Conservatorio V. Bellini in Palermo and at the Univ. of Florence; served as librarian and lecturer in music history at the Cons. of Palermo (1936–48) and chief librarian at Santa Cecilia in Rome. He then went to the U.S.; was visiting prof. at Princeton Univ. (1954–55), and at Columbia Univ. (1956), and at Harvard Univ. (1956–72); was subsequently on the staff of the Univ. of Rome. His principal fields of research are Renaissance polyphony and Baroque opera; his publications include *Il Sacchetti e la tecnica musicale del trecento italiano* (with E. Li Gotti; Florence, 1935); *Il Codice Estense lat. 568 e la musica francese in Italia al principio dell '400* (Palermo, 1946); *Li due Orfei. Da Poliziano a Monteverdi* (Turin, 1969); "Gesualdo, Ferrara e Venezia," and "Monteverdi e i problemi dell'opera," in *Studi sul teatro veneto fra Rinascimento ed età barocca* (Florence, 1971).

Pisa, Agostino, Italian music scholar; flourished in Rome c.1600, in which year he was *Dr. jur.* there. He publ. the earliest known treatise on conducting, *Breve dichiariazione della battutta musicale* (Rome, 1611); a 2nd augmented ed. was publ. in the same year, also in Rome, as *Battuta della musica dichiarata.*

BIBLIOGRAPHY: R. Schwartz, "Zur Geschichte des

Taktschlagens," *Jahrbuch Peters* (1907); G. Schünemann, *Geschichte des Dirigierens* (Leipzig, 1913).

Pisador, Diego, Spanish lutenist; b. Salamanca, c.1509; d. after 1557. In 1526 he entered the priesthood; in 1552 he publ. in Salamanca a *Libro de música de vihuela,* containing madrigals, a set of Spanish ballads, and transcriptions of secular and sacred works by Josquin Des Prez and others; the collection is reprinted by A. Morphy in *Les Luthistes espagnols du XVIᵉ siècle.*

Pisari (Pizari), Pasquale, Italian composer; b. Rome, 1725; d. there, March 27, 1778. He was a pupil of Giovanni Biordi; in 1752 he was taken into the papal chapel, being a fine bass singer; he wrote most of his sacred works for it, and the MSS are preserved in the archives of the papal chapel; they include several Masses, motets, 2 Te Deums for 8 voices, one Te Deum for 4 voices (his most remarkable work); also a *Dixit* in 16 parts, for 4 choirs, and a series of motets for the entire year, written for the Lisbon court. Padre Martini called Pisari the "Palestrina of the 18th century."

Pischna, Josef, famous Bohemian pianist and pedagogue; b. Erdischowitz, June 15, 1826; d. Prague, Oct. 19, 1896. He was a pupil at the Prague Cons.; taught for many years in Moscow; then at the Prague Cons. His pedagogical work, *60 Exercises* for piano, became a standard method in Europe and has been reprinted in many editions.

Pisendel, Johann Georg, German violinist and composer; b. Kadolzburg, Dec. 26, 1687; d. Dresden, Nov. 25, 1755. He studied violin with Torelli at Ansbach, and music theory with Pistocchi; later (1716) took lessons in Venice from Vivaldi, who dedicated several works to him. In 1710 he succeeded Melchior Hoffmann as leader of the Collegium musicum in Leipzig; then held the post of violinist in the Dresden court chapel orch. (1712); traveled with the Elector of Saxony to Paris, Berlin, Italy, and Vienna (1714-18); in 1728 became concertmaster in Dresden; 1731, appointed to a similar post in the orch. of the Dresden Opera. It seems certain that Bach wrote his partitas for unaccompanied violin for Pisendel. In his own works, Pisendel combined characteristics of German, French, and Italian music; many of his MSS are extant in the Dresden archives, among them 8 violin concertos, 3 concertos for oboes and string orch., 2 concerti grossi, a symphony, and 2 solo pieces for violin with bass; a violin concerto is reprinted in *Denkmäler deutscher Tonkunst* 29/30.
BIBLIOGRAPHY: A. Moser, *Geschichte des Violin-Spiels* (p. 316ff.); H. R. Jung, "J. G. Pisendel," *Musica* (Nov. 1955).

Pisk, Paul Amadeus, eminent Austrian composer, musicologist and teacher; b. Vienna, May 16, 1893. He studied piano with J. Epstein and composition with Schreker and Schoenberg; also took courses in conducting with Hellmesberger and in musicology with Guido Adler; obtained his Dr. phil. in 1918; wrote music criticism for the socialist newspaper the *Wiener Arbeiterzeitung* and was co-editor (with Paul Stefan) of the progressive periodical *Musikblätter des Anbruch.* In 1936 he emigrated to the U.S. and occupied various teaching posts: at the Univ. of Redlands, California (1937-51), at the Univ. of Texas, Austin (1951-62), at Washington Univ., St. Louis (1963-72); also gave courses at the summer schools of the Univ. of Southern California, Los Angeles (1966), Univ. of Cincinnati (1969) and Dartmouth College (1972). In 1973 he settled in Los Angeles. In his music he follows the precepts of Schoenberg and the New Vienna School, but also writes utilitarian music for amateurs and workers.
WORKS: monodrama *Schattenseite* (1931); *American Suite,* ballet (Redlands, Calif., Feb. 19, 1948); *Die neue Stadt,* a "cantata for the people" (Vienna, Nov. 1926; on the occasion of completion of a workers' settlement); *Der grosse Regenmacher,* scenic ballad for narrator and orch. (1931); *Requiem* for baritone and orch. (1942). FOR ORCH.: *Partita* (Prague Festival of the International Society for Contemporary Music, May 17, 1925); *Suite on American Folksongs* for 24 instruments (1944); *Bucolic Suite* for string orch. (Saratoga Springs, Sept. 10, 1946); *Rococo Suite,* for viola and orch. (1953); *Baroque Chamber Concerto* for violin and orch. (1953); *Canzona* for chamber orch. (1954); *3 Ceremonial Rites* (1957-58); *Elegy* for string orch. (1958); *Sonnet* for chamber orch. (1960). CHAMBER MUSIC: 3 Songs with string quartet (Salzburg, Aug. 10, 1922); String Quartet (1924); 3 violin sonatas (1921, 1927, 1939); *Fantasy* for clarinet and piano (1925); *Rondo* for violin and piano (1932); *Variations on a Waltz by Beethoven* for violin, viola and guitar (1933); Piano Trio (1933-35); *Moresca Figures* for violin, clarinet and piano (1934); *Berceuse slave* for oboe and piano (1939); *Bohemian Dance Rondo* for bassoon and piano (1939); Suite for 4 clarinets (1939); *Shanty-Boy Fantasy* for oboe and piano (1940); *Variations on an Old Trumpet Tune* for brass sextet (1942); *Little Woodwind Music* (1945); *Cortege* for brass choir (1945); *Variations and Fugue on an American Theme* for violin and cello (1946); Clarinet Sonata (1947); Suite for oboe and piano (1947); *Introduction and Rondo* for flute and piano (1948); 1st Suite for flute solo (1950); *Intermezzo* for clarinet and piano (1950); *Elegy and Scherzino* for oboe, 2 clarinets and bassoon (1951); Quartet for 2 trumpets, horn and trombone (1951); Sonata for horn and piano (1953); Suite for 2 flutes (1953); Flute Sonata (1954); Suite for oboe, clarinet and piano (1955); *Eclogue* for violin and piano (1955); *Idyll* for oboe and piano (1957); String Trio (1958); Woodwind Quintet (1958); Woodwind Trio (1960); *Music* for violin, clarinet, cello and bassoon (1962); *Envoi* for 6 instruments (1964); Duo for clarinet and bassoon (1966); *Perpetuum mobile* for organ and brass quartet (1968); 2nd suite for flute solo (1969); Suite for woodwind and piano (1970); *Variables* for clarinet and piano (1973); *Discussions* for oboe, clarinet, bassoon, viola and cello (1974); Brass Quintet (1976); piano pieces; songs. He published (with Homer Ulrich) *History of Music and Musical Style* (N.Y., 1963); edited Masses by Jacobus Gallus for *Denkmäler der Tonkunst in Österreich.*
BIBLIOGRAPHY: Boris Kremenliev, "Paul A. Pisk,"

Music of the West Magazine (July 1952); *Paul A. Pisk, Essays in his Honor* J. Glowacki, ed., (Univ. of Texas Press, Austin, 1966).

Pistocchi, Francesco Antonio, founder of the famous School of Singing at Bologna; b. Palermo, 1659; d. Bologna, May 13, 1726. Taken to Bologna very young, his first work was publ. there in 1667, when he was but 8 years old: *Capricci puerili saviamente composti e passeggiati in 40 modi sopra un Basso da un balletto, per il clavicembalo ed altri instrumenti.* His teacher in theory was G. A. Perti; he studied singing under Padre Vastamigli and B. Monari. As a lad he became maestro at the church of San Giovanni in Monte; later a priest in the Oratorian order; from 1697–99 was Kapellmeister at the court of Ansbach; and returned to Bologna, *via* Vienna and Venice, about 1700. There he founded, soon after his return, the first school of music in which vocal instruction was given systematically in the several classes. In this school were trained many eminent singers (Bernacchi, Bertolino da Faenza, Minelli, Pio Fabri, etc.); similar institutions soon sprang up in other Italian cities. Pistocchi was twice elected president of the Accademia Filarmonica (1708 and 1710).

Piston, Walter (Hamor), outstanding American composer; b. Rockland, Maine, Jan. 20, 1894; d. Belmont, Mass., Nov. 12, 1976. The family name was originally Pistone; his paternal grandfather was Italian. He received his primary education in Boston; studied painting at the Massachusetts Normal Art School, graduating in 1916; then took piano lessons with Harris Shaw and studied violin with Fiumara, Theodorowicz and Winternitz; played in restaurants and places of public entertainment as a youth. During World War I he was in the U.S. Navy; after the armistice he entered Harvard Univ. graduating in musical subjects *summa cum laude* in 1924; while at Harvard he conducted concerts of the univ. orch., the Pierian Sodality. For a time he was employed as a draftsman for Boston Elevated Railway. In 1924 he went to Paris, on a John Knowles Paine Fellowship, and became a student of Nadia Boulanger; also took courses with Paul Dukas at the École Normale de Musique (1925); returning to the U.S. in 1926 he was appointed to the faculty of Harvard Univ.; in 1944 became prof. of music; emeritus in 1960. As teacher, he was greatly esteemed, not alone because of his consummate knowledge of music and pedagogical ability, but also because of his immanent humanity in instructing students whose esthetics differed from his own; among his grateful disciples was Leonard Bernstein. As a composer, Piston followed a cosmopolitan course, adhering to classical forms, while extending his harmonic structures towards a maximum of tonal saturation; he was particularly expert in contrapuntal writing. Beginning about 1965, Piston adopted, for the first time, a modified system of 12-tone composition, particularly in initial thematic statements; his Symph. No. 8 and *Variations* for cello and orch. are explicitly dodecaphonic. Piston rejected the narrow notion of ethnic Americanism in his music, and stated once that an artist could be as American working in the Library of the Boston Atheneum as roaming the Western prairie; yet he employed upon occasion the syncopated rhythms of jazz. He received the Pulitzer Prize for his Symph. No. 3 and Symph. No. 7, and a N.Y. Music Critics Circle Award for his Symph. No. 2. He held the degree of Doctor of Music *honoris causa* of Harvard Univ.; was elected a member of the National Institute of Arts and Letters, the American Academy of Arts and Letters and the American Academy of Arts and Sciences. He traveled little and declined invitations to go to South America and to Russia under the auspices of the State Dept., preferring to live in his house in suburban Belmont, near Boston. His working habits were remarkably methodical; he rarely altered or revised his music once it was put on paper, and his handwriting was calligraphic. With the exception of a Harvard Glee Club chorus or two he never wrote for voices. WORKS: Ballet *The Incredible Flutist* (Boston Pops, May 30, 1938; his only stage work; very popular as an orchestral suite). FOR ORCH.: 8 symphonies: No. 1 (Boston, April 8, 1938, composer conducting); No. 2 (Washington, March 5, 1944; received the N.Y. Music Critics Circle Award, 1945); No. 3 (Boston, Jan. 9, 1948; received the Pulitzer Prize); No. 4 (Minneapolis, March 30, 1951); No. 5 (commissioned by the Juilliard School of Music for its 50th anniversary; N.Y., Feb. 24, 1956); No. 6 (Boston, Nov. 25, 1955); No.7 (Philadelphia, Feb. 10, 1961; won the Pulitzer Prize); No. 8 (Boston, March 5, 1965); *Symphonic Piece* (Boston, March 23, 1928), *Suite* (Boston, March 28, 1930, composer conducting), Concerto for Orchestra (Cambridge, Mass., March 6, 1934, composer conducting), *Prelude and Fugue* (Cleveland, March 12, 1936), Concertino for Piano and Chamber Orch. (N.Y., June 20, 1937), Violin Concerto (N.Y., March 18, 1940), Sinfonietta (Boston, March 10, 1941), *Prelude and Allegro* for organ and strings (Boston, Oct. 29, 1943), *Fanfare for the Fighting French* (Cincinnati, Oct. 23, 1942), *Fugue on a Victory Tune* (N.Y., Oct. 21, 1944), *Symphonic Suite* (Dallas, Feb. 29, 1948), *Toccata* (Orchestre National de France, Munch conducting, Bridgeport, Conn., Oct. 14, 1948), *Fantasy* for English horn, strings, and harp (Boston, Jan. 1, 1954), *Serenata* (Louisville, Oct. 24, 1956); Viola Concerto (Boston, March 7, 1958); Concerto for 2 Pianos and Orch. (1959); *Three New England Sketches* for orch. (Worcester, Mass., Music Festival, Oct. 23, 1959); Violin Concerto No. 2 (Pittsburgh, Oct. 28, 1960); *Symphonic Prelude* (Cleveland, April 20, 1961); *Lincoln Center Festival Overture* (N.Y., Sept. 25, 1962); *Capriccio* for harp and string orch. (1963; Washington, 3rd Inter-American Music Festival, May 8, 1965); *Pine Tree Fantasy* (1965), *Variations* for cello and orch. (N.Y., March 2, 1967, with Rostropovitch as soloist); Clarinet Concerto (Dartmouth College, Hanover, N.H., Aug. 6, 1967); *Ricercare* (N.Y., March 7, 1968); Flute Concerto (1971). CHAMBER MUSIC: *3 Pieces* for flute, clarinet and bassoon (1926); Flute Sonata (1930); *Suite* for oboe and piano (1931); Piano Trio (1935); Viola Sonata (1939); *Interlude* for viola and piano (1942); Quintet for flute and strings (1942); *Partita* for violin, viola and organ (1944); Sonatina for violin and harpsichord (1945); *Divertimento* for 9 instruments (N.Y., May 18, 1946); Duo for viola and cello (1949); Quintet for horn and woodwinds (1956); Sextet for stringed instruments (1964); Piano Quartet

(1964); 5 string quartets (1933, 1935, 1947, 1951, 1962); *Carnival Song,* for men's chorus and 11 brass instruments (Harvard Glee Club, Cambridge, Mass., March 7, 1940); Concerto for string quartet, wind instruments, and percussion (Portland, Maine, Oct. 26, 1976).

BIBLIOGRAPHY: N. Slonimsky, "Walter Piston," in Henry Cowell's *American Composers on American Music* (1933); Israel Citkowitz, "Walter Piston—Classicist," *Modern Music* (Jan.-Feb. 1936); Elliott Carter, "Walter Piston," *Musical Quarterly* (July 1946); Madeleine Goss, *Modern Music Makers* (N.Y., 1952); W. Austin, "Piston's Fourth Symphony," *Music Review* (May 1955).

Pitfield, Thomas Baron, English composer; b. Bolton, April 5, 1903. He studied at the Royal Manchester College of Music; became instructor there in 1947; also studied engineering and painting; was a book illustrator; wrote verse. In his music, he adopts a simple style, in folksong manner. His works include a cantata, *The Rhyming Shopman;* a piano concerto; various pieces of chamber music; a set of piano pieces under the general title *Ballet in Education;* also various pieces of humorous content, among them "a zoological sequence in space," *Planibestiary* for voices, piano and percussion (1966); "Morality with Music," *Adam and the Creatures* for speaker, chorus, organ and percussion (1968).

BIBLIOGRAPHY: A. K. Holland, "T. B. Pitfield," *Monthly Musical Record* (May 1939).

Pitoni, Giuseppe Ottavio, Italian composer of church music; b. Rieti, March 18, 1657; d. Rome, Feb. 1, 1743. He began music studies at 5, under Pompeo Natale in Rome; at 8 was chorister at S. Giovanni de' Fiorentini, later at the S. S. Apostoli, and studied counterpoint under Foggia. In 1673, maestro di cappella at Terra di Rotondo; in 1674, at Assisi; in 1676, at Rieti; finally, in 1677, he became maestro at the Collegio di S. Marco, Rome, retaining this post until death, though simultaneously engaged at San Apollinare (1686), San Lorenzo in Damaso (1686), San Giovanni in Laterano (1708-19), and St. Peter's (1719); also in some minor Roman churches. He was an excellent teacher, and taught after the same method by which he himself rose to eminence as a composer, e.g., the writing out in score of Palestrina's works to study his style. Durante, Leo, and Feo were his greatest pupils. As a composer, he cultivated a distinct feature of the Roman school, the writing in many parts.

WORKS: His finest works are a *Dixit a 16* (for 4 choirs), still sung yearly at St. Peter's during Holy Week, and 3 Masses based on popular airs, *Li Pastori a Maremme, Li Pastori a Montagna,* and *Mosca.* Of Masses and psalms he composed over 40 *a 12* (for 3 choirs) and over 20 *a 16* (for 4 choirs), psalms and motets *a 24* and 36; and left an unfinished Mass *a 48.* He also wrote for St. Peter's a set of Masses, vespers, etc., for the entire year, besides motets *a 3-8,* hymns, etc. Only one book of motets, *a 2,* was publ. (Rome, 1697) during his lifetime, probably because he insisted that music written for one church should not be performed in any other. Proske, in his *Musica divina* (1855-61), printed a Mass, a Requiem, 6 motets, a

psalm, a hymn, and a *Christus factus est.* In the Vatican Library is a MS work by Pitoni, *Notizie dei maestri di cappella sì di Roma che oltramontani,* 1500-1700; and a fragmentary *Guida armonica* (108 printed pages).

BIBLIOGRAPHY: M. Tiberti, "G. O. Pitoni," *Musica d'Oggi* (1941).

Pitt, Percy, English conductor and composer; b. London, Jan. 4, 1870; d. there, Nov. 23, 1932. He studied in Germany with Jadassohn and Reinecke at the Leipzig Cons. and with Rheinberger at the Akademie der Tonkunst in Munich. Returning to England in 1893, he became active primarily as a theater conductor; was conductor of the Beecham Opera Co. (1915-18), artistic director of the British National Opera Co. (1920-24) and musical director of the British Broadcasting Corporation (1922-30). He wrote some instrumental music; his *Ballade* for violin and orch. (1900) was performed by Ysaÿe.

BIBLIOGRAPHY: J. D. Chamier, *Percy Pitt of Covent Garden and the BBC* (London, 1938).

Pittaluga, Gustavo, Spanish composer; b. Madrid, Feb. 8, 1906. He studied law at the Univ. of Madrid and composition with Oscar Esplá; was a member of the "Grupo de los 8" in Madrid and of the Paris group of modern musicians, "Triton" (1935); from 1936 to 1939 was a member of the staff of the Spanish Embassy in Washington (for the Loyalist Government); then remained in the U.S.; was in charge of the film library at the Museum of Modern Art, N.Y. (1941-43).

WORKS: *La Romería de los Cornudos,* ballet, after F. G. Lorca (Madrid, 1933); a zarzuela, *El Loro* (Madrid, 1933); *Concerto militaire* for violin and orch. (Barcelona, 1933); *Petite suite* for 10 instruments (Paris, 1935; also for piano as *3 Pièces pour une espagnolade); Capriccio alla romantica,* for piano and orch. (Paris, 1936); *6 Danses espagnoles en suite* for piano (1935); *Vocalise-étude,* for voice and piano (1932); *Berceuse* for violin and piano (1935); *Ricercare,* for violin, clarinet, bassoon, and trumpet (1934); *5 Canciones populares* for chorus and 10 instruments (1939); *Habanera* for violin and piano (1942); *Lament* for Federico García Lorca, for narrator and orch. (1942).

Pittrich, George Washington, German composer; b. Dresden, Feb. 22 (on Washington's birthday; hence the selection of Christian names), 1870; d. Nuremberg, April 28, 1934. He studied at the Dresden Cons. with Draeseke and others; was active as conductor in Dresden (1890-98), Hamburg (1898), Cologne (1899-1901), Frankfurt (1901-04), Dresden (1904-12), and Berlin (from 1912). He wrote a 1-act opera, *Marga* (Dresden, Feb. 8, 1894); incidental music to Shakespeare's *As You Like It* and to several classical German plays; Christmas musical plays *Der Stern von Bethlehem, Der Zauberschleier, Mäusekönigin;* Clarinet Concerto; Fantasia for piano with string orch.; many songs.

Pitzinger, Gertrude, Bohemian contralto; b. Mährisch-Schönberg, Aug. 15, 1904. She studied music with Joseph Marx at the Vienna Singakademie, and voice with various teachers. After several concert tours in central Europe she went to the U.S., and gave a N.Y. recital on Jan. 17, 1938 with excellent success; she specialized in German lieder; her repertory included some 400 songs. She taught singing at the Hochschule für Musik in Frankfurt (1960–73) before retiring.

Piutti, Karl, German composer; b. Elgersburg, April 30, 1846; d. Leipzig, June 17, 1902. He studied at the Leipzig Cons.; in 1880 became organist at the Thomaskirche. He wrote a great number of organ works, including a *Hochzeit Sonata;* about 200 organ preludes; psalms and motets a cappella; songs. He also publ. *Regeln und Erläuterungen zum Studium der Musiktheorie.*

Pixis, Johann Peter, German pianist; b. Mannheim, Feb. 10, 1788; d. Baden-Baden, Dec. 22, 1874. Of a musical family (his father and his brother were good musicians), he received his primary education at home; went to Munich in 1809, and to Paris in 1825; established himself as a teacher, and was greatly esteemed in the Paris musical world. In 1845 he settled in Baden-Baden, where he continued to teach.

WORKS: operas: *Almazinde, oder Die Höhle Sesam* (Vienna, April 11, 1820), *Bibiana, oder Die Kapelle im Walde* (Aachen, Oct. 8, 1829), etc.; Piano Concerto; Piano Quartet; Piano Quintet; String Quintet; 7 piano trios; sonatas, variations, transcriptions, etc. for piano solo; altogether about 150 opus numbers. Together with Liszt, Chopin, Thalberg, Czerny, and Herz, he wrote *Hexaméron* (a series of brilliant variations on the march from Bellini's opera, *I Puritani*).

BIBLIOGRAPHY: R. Batka, "Aus J. P. Pixis Memoiren," in *Kranz. Gesammelte Blätter über Musik* (Leipzig, 1903).

Pizzetti, Ildebrando, eminent Italian composer; b. Parma, Sept. 20, 1880; d. Rome, Feb. 13, 1968. He studied piano with his father Odvardo Pizzetti in Parma and composition with Tebaldini at the Cons. of Parma, graduating in 1901; then devoted himself to composition and teaching; was on the faculty of the Cons. of Parma (1907–08), at the Cons. of Florence (1908–24), Cons. of Milan (1924–36) and at the Accademia di Santa Cecilia in Rome (1936–58). In 1914 he founded (with G. Bastianelli) in Florence a modernistic periodical, pointedly named *Dissonanza,* to promote the cause of new music. In 1930 he made a trip to the U.S. to attend the performance of his *Rondo Veneziano,* conducted by Toscanini with the N.Y. Philharmonic; in 1931 Pizzetti conducted his opera *Fra Gherardo* at the Teatro Colón in Buenos Aires. Pizzetti's music represents the Romantic trend in modern Italy; in his many works for the theater, he created the modern counterpart of medieval mystery plays; the mystical element is very strong in his own text for his operas. He employed astringent chromatic harmony, but the mainstream of his melody flows along pure diatonic lines.

WORKS: OPERAS: *Fedra* (Milan, March 20, 1915), *Debora e Jaele* (1915–21; Milan, Dec. 16, 1922), *Lo Straniero* (1922–25; Rome, April 29, 1930), *Fra Gherardo* (1925–27; Milan, May 16, 1928; his most famous work; N.Y., March 21, 1929, at the Metropolitan Opera), *Orsèolo* (Florence, May 5, 1935), *L'Oro* (1938–42; Milan, Jan. 2, 1947), *Vanna Lupa* (Florence, May 4, 1949), *Ifigenia* (1950; Turin Radio, Sept. 18, 1950; 1st stage performance, Florence, May 4, 1951), *Cagliostro* (La Scala, Milan, Jan. 24, 1953), *La Figlia di Jorio* (Naples, Dec. 4, 1954), *Assassinio nella cattedrale,* after T. S. Eliot's *Murder in the Cathedral* (Milan, La Scala, March 1, 1958; highly acclaimed), *Il Calzare d'argento,* sacred play (Milan, La Scala, March 23, 1961), *Clitennestra,* music drama (La Scala, Milan, March 1, 1965). INCIDENTAL MUSIC: to the tragedy by Gabriele d'Annunzio *La Nave* (1905), to d'Annunzio's *La Pisanella* (Paris, June 11, 1913), *La sacra rappresentazione di Abram e d'Isaac,* mystery play (Florence, 1917; expanded and produced in Turin, March 11, 1926), to *Agamemnon,* by Aeschylus (Greek Theater at Syracuse, 1930), *The Trachiniae,* by Sophocles (Greek Theater, Syracuse, 1936), *As You Like It* by Shakespeare (Florence, May, 1938). CHORAL WORKS: *Requiem* (1922), *De Profundis* (1938), *Cantico di gloria,* for a treble chorus, 24 wind instruments, 2 pianos, and percussion (1948). FOR ORCH.: *Ouverture per una farsa tragica* (1911), *Concerto dell'estate* (N.Y., Toscanini conducting; Feb. 28, 1929), *Rondo veneziano* (N.Y., Feb. 27, 1930; as a ballet, La Scala, Milan, Jan. 8, 1931), Cello Concerto (Venice, Sept. 11, 1934), Symph. in A (1940), Violin Concerto (Rome, Dec. 9, 1945), *Canzone di beni perduti* (Venice, Sept. 4, 1950). CHAMBER MUSIC: 2 string quartets (1906; 1933), Piano Trio (1925), Violin Sonata (1919), Cello Sonata (1921); for piano: *Da un autunno già lontano* (1911; 3 pieces), *Sonata 1942;* songs: *Tre liriche* (1904), *Sera d'inverno* (1906), *I Pastori* (his most remarkable song; poem by Gabriele d'Annunzio; 1908), *La Madre al figlio lontano* (1910), *Erotica* (1911), *Due canti popolari greci* (1912), *Tre sonetti di Petrarca* (1922), *E il mio dolore io canto* (1940); transcriptions of madrigals by Gesualdo, of Veracini's sonatas for violin and continuo, etc.

WRITINGS: *La Musica dei Greci* (Rome, 1914), *Musicisti contemporanei* (Milan, 1914), *Intermezzi critici* (Florence, 1921), *Paganini* (Turin, 1940), *Musica e dramma* (Rome, 1945), *La Musica italiana dell' 800* (Turin, 1946); numerous articles in Italian magazines.

BIBLIOGRAPHY: R. Fondi, *I. Pizzetti e il dramma musicale italiano d'oggi* (Rome, 1919); G. M. Gatti, "I. Pizzetti," *Musical Quarterly* (Jan., April 1923); M. Pilati, *"Fra Gherardo" di Pizzetti* (Milan, 1928); M. Rinaldi, *L'Arte di Pizzetti e "Lo Straniero"* (Rome, 1930); G. Tebaldini, *I. Pizzetti* (Parma, 1931); G. M. Gatti, *I. Pizzetti* (Turin, 1934; in English, London, 1951; a basic biography, with a list of works; new Italian ed., 1955); G. Bastianelli, "Pizzetti," *Il Convegno* (March-April 1921); M. Castelnuovo-Tedesco, "I. Pizzetti e la sua musica corale," *Il Pianoforte* (Aug. 15, 1921; a Pizzetti issue); G. Gavazzeni, *Tre studi su Pizzetti* (Como, 1937); a special Pizzetti number of the *Rassegna Musicale* (Oct. 1940); M. Castelnuovo-Tedesco, "I. Pizzetti," in David Ewen's *The Book of Modern Composers* (N.Y., 1945); a symposium, *Firenze a I. Pizzetti* (Florence, 1947); M. LaMorgia, *La città d'annunziana a Ildebrando Pizzetti: saggi e note* (Milan, 1958).

Pizzi, Emilio, Italian composer; b. Verona, Feb. 1, 1861; d. Milan, Nov. 27, 1940. He studied at the Instituto Musicale of Bergamo and at the Cons. of Milan (with Ponchielli and Bazzini); received 1st prize for his opera, *Lina* (1885); in 1897, was appointed director of the Instituto Musicale at Bergamo; from 1900 lived for some time in London.
WORKS: operas: *Guglielmo Ratcliff* (Bologna, Oct. 31, 1889), *Gabriella* (world première, Boston, Nov. 25, 1893, with Adelina Patti in the title role), *La Rosalba* (Turin, May 31, 1899), *Vendetta* (in German, Cologne, Dec. 1, 1906; in Italian, as *Ivania*, Bergamo, Sept. 14, 1926), a comic opera in English, *Bric-à-Brac Will* (London, 1895); a *Messa solenne* for soli, chorus, and orch.; a Requiem; violin pieces; piano pieces; songs.

Pizzini, Carlo Alberto, Italian composer; b. Rome, March 22, 1905. He studied electrical engineering; then took a course in composition with Respighi at the Accademia di Santa Cecilia in Rome, graduating in 1929. In 1938 he became a member of the staff of the Italian Radio; and was inspector of auditions (1968–70). He wrote an opera *Dardanio* (Rome, 1928) and several orchestral works, among them *Sinfonia in istile classico* (1930); *Il Poema delle Dolomiti* (1931); *Strapaese*, a symph. suite (1932); *Al Piemonte*, symph. triptych (1941); *Grotte di Postumia*, divertimento in variation form (1941); *Concierto para tres hermanas* for guitar and orch. (1969); also chamber music and piano pieces.

Plaidy, Louis, famous German piano teacher; b. Wermsdorf, Nov. 28, 1810; d. Grimma, March 3, 1874. He began his professional career as a violinist, and performed in public in Dresden and Leipzig; at the same time he took piano lessons from Agthe, and became greatly proficient as pianist, so that Mendelssohn engaged him in 1843 as piano teacher at the Leipzig Cons. Plaidy concentrated on the technical problems of piano pedagogy; taught at the Leipzig Cons. until 1865; then continued to give private lessons. He publ. a number of instructive piano studies which are still widely used; his *Technische Studien für das Pianoforte-Spiel* is a standard manual; he also publ. a booklet, *Der Klavierlehrer* (1874; British ed. as *The Pianoforte Teacher's Guide;* American ed., transl. by J. S. Dwight, as *The Piano-Teacher*).

Plamenac, Dragan, eminent Croatian-American musicologist; b. Zagreb, Feb. 8, 1895. He studied jurisprudence at the Univ. of Zagreb and at Vienna Univ.; then took a course in composition with Franz Schreker at the Vienna State Academy of Music with Vítězslav Novák in Prague; in 1919 went to France on a scholarship and studied there with André Pirro at the Sorbonne; then took a course with Guido Adler at the Univ. of Vienna, receiving his Dr. phil. there (1925); taught musical subjects at the Univ. of Zagreb (1928–39); after the outbreak of war he came to the U.S.; in 1946 became a naturalized American citizen; in 1947 received a Guggenheim Fellowship; then taught at the Univ. of Illinois, Urbana (1955–63). A Festschrift on his 70th birthday, *Essays in Musicology,* edited by Gustave Reese and R. J. Snow, was published in Pittsburgh in 1969. Plamenac's chief accomplishment in musicology is his painstaking and fruitful research into the sources of the music of the Renaissance; his writings on Ockeghem, beginning with his doctoral dissertation, *Joh. Ockeghem als Motetten- und Chansonkomponist* (1925) are particularly valuable. He contributed a section on the music of the southern Slavs to Gustave Reese's book *Music in the Renaissance* (N.Y., 1954).

Planchet, Dominique-Charles, French composer and pedagogue; b. Toulouse, Dec. 25, 1857; d. Versailles, July 19, 1946. He studied at the École Niedermeyer in Paris; was for many years organist at the Cathedral in Versailles; in 1898 appointed organist at the Ste.-Trinité, Paris; taught at the École Niedermeyer; was active as general secretary of the Société des Compositeurs; in 1905, won the Prix Chartier for chamber music. He wrote an opera, *Le Fils du Croisé* (privately performed in Versailles, 1885); 2 cello concertos; *Esclavage africain*, cantata for male voices; much sacred music; organ pieces; a piano trio; a violin sonata; songs; contributed the section "L'Art du maître de chapelle" to Lavignac's *Encyclopédie de la musique.* On his chamber music, see the entry in *Cobbett's Cyclopedic Survey of Chamber Music* (London, 1930).

Plançon, Pol (-Henri), famous French bass; b. Fumay, June 12, 1851; d. Paris, Aug. 12, 1914. He was destined by his parents for a commercial career in Paris, but showed a natural vocal ability, and began to study singing with Sbriglia; made his operatic debut in Lyons (1877); then appeared in Paris (Feb. 11, 1880); after a season in Monte Carlo, he made a highly successful appearance at the Paris Opéra as Méphistophélès in Gounod's *Faust* (June 23, 1883); sang that role more than 100 times during his 10 seasons at the Opéra, and was regarded as unrivaled in his dramatic delivery and vocal power. On June 3, 1891, he sang Méphistophélès in London; his American debut, in the same role, took place at the Metropolitan Opera House on Nov. 29, 1893. He then resigned from the Paris Opéra and remained a member of the Metropolitan Opera until his retirement in 1906. He had an imposing physique, mobile features, and an innate acting ability. His repertory consisted of about 50 roles in French, Italian, German, and English. In some operas he sang more than 1 part, as in *Roméo et Juliette* (Capulet and Friar), *Aida* (Ramfis and King), *Les Huguenots* (St.-Bris and Marcel), etc. Of Wagnerian roles, he sang the Landgrave, King Henry, and Pogner.

Planquette, Jean–Robert, French composer of operettas; b. Paris, July 31, 1848; d. there, Jan. 28, 1903. He studied at the Paris Cons. with Duprato; wrote chansonnettes and "saynètes" for the cafés-concerts in Paris; then composed a 1-act operetta, *Paille d'avoine* (1874); and others. He achieved his first great success with the production of *Les Cloches de Corneville,* a comic opera in 3 acts (Folies-Dramatiques, April 19, 1877); it was performed for the 1000th time there in 1886, and became one of the most popular works of its genre; in English, given as *The Chimes of Normandy* (N.Y., Oct. 22, 1877; London, Feb. 23, 1878). Other operettas were *Le Chevalier Gaston* (Monte

Carlo, Feb. 8, 1879), *Rip Van Winkle* (London, Oct. 14, 1882; very successful), *Nell Gwynne* (1884), *Surcouf* (Oct. 6, 1887; in English as *Paul Jones*), *La Cocarde tricolore* (1892), *Le Talisman* (1893), *Panurge* (1895), *Mam'zelle Quat'Sous* (1897). A posthumous operetta, *Le Paradis de Mahomet* (orchestrated by Louis Ganne), was produced at the Variétés in Paris in 1906.

Plantade, Charles-Henri, French composer; b. Pontoise, Oct. 14, 1764; d. Paris, Dec. 18, 1839. As a child, he studied singing and the cello in the Royal School for the "pages de musique"; afterwards he took lessons with Honoré Langlé (theory), Hüllmandel (piano), and Petrini (harp). In 1797 he became singing teacher at the Campan Institute at St.-Denis, where Hortense de Beauharnais, the future queen of Holland, was his pupil. He subsequently was in the service of Queen Hortense as her representative in Paris; was prof. at the Paris Cons. from 1799 to 1807, and again in 1815–16 and 1818–28. From 1812 he also held the post of *maître de chambre* at the Paris Opéra. He received the ribbon of the Legion of Honor from Louis XVIII (1814). Losing his various positions after the revolution of 1830, he retired to Batignolles. He wrote several operas, of which *Le Mari de circonstances* (Opéra-Comique, March 18, 1813) was the most successful; 2 other operas, *Palma, ou Le Voyage en Grèce* (1798) and *Zoé, ou La Pauvre Petite* (1800), were also performed. He further composed Masses, motets, etc. for the Chapelle Royale; publ. 20 sets of *romances*, 3 books of vocal duets (nocturnes), and a harp sonata.

Planté, Francis, French pianist; b. Orthez, Basses-Pyrénées, March 2, 1839; d. St. Avit, near Mont-de-Marsan, Dec. 19, 1934. From 1849 he was a pupil of Marmontel at Paris Cons.; won 1st prize after 7 months' tuition. After a course in harmony in Bazin's class (1853), he retired for private study during ten years, and then reappeared as a pianist of finished technique and style. About 1900 he suddenly vanished from concert life, vowing that he would "never be seen again in public." He created a sensation in 1915 when he was heard again in several concerts in Paris; but, in order to keep his strange vow, he was hidden from the view of the audience by a screen.
BIBLIOGRAPHY: O. Comettant, *Francis Planté* (Paris, 1874); A. Dandelot, *Francis Planté* (Paris, 1920; 3rd ed., 1930); A. Lenoir and Jean de Nahuque, *Francis Planté: Doyen des pianistes* (Paris, 1931).

Plass, Ludwig, German trombonist and historian of military music; b. Osterode, March 13, 1864; d. Berlin, Sept. 16, 1946. He studied trombone at the Hochschule für Musik in Berlin; in 1893 became solo trombonist of the Royal Chapel; in 1905, court bandleader; collected materials on military music in Germany; wrote 28 pieces for wind instruments; publ. interesting historical essays on the German post horn; also *Bachs Clarintrompeter* (1927); *Was bliesen unsere Reiter?* (1934); etc.

Platania, Pietro, Italian composer; b. Catania, April 5, 1828; d. Naples, April 26, 1907. He studied with P. Raimondi at the Naples Cons.; was director of the Pa-

lermo Cons. (1863); later maestro di cappella at Milan, and director of the Royal College of Music at Naples (1888).
WORKS: operas: *Matilde Bentivoglio* (Palermo, 1852); *Piccarda Donati* (Palermo, March 3, 1857); *La Vendetta slava* (Palermo, Feb. 4, 1865); *Spartaco* (Naples, March 29, 1891); a symphony, *L'Italia;* a festival symphony with choruses to welcome King Umberto in 1878; *Pensiero sinfonico;* a Requiem; Psalm 67 for chorus and orch.; etc.; and *Trattato d'Armonia* (1872).
BIBLIOGRAPHY: F. Guardione, *Pietro Platania* (Milan, 1908).

Plato, the great Greek philosopher (427–347 B.C.); formulated in his *Timaeus* a system of musical harmony, eruditely interpreted by Th.-Henri Martin in his *Études sur le Timée de Platon* (Paris, 1841). R. von Westphal, in his *Harmonik und Melopöie der Griechen* (Leipzig, 1865), von Jan in "Die Harmonie der Sphären" (in *Philogus,* vol. LII), and H. Abert's *Die Lehre vom Ethos in der griechischen Musik* (Leipzig, 1899) may also be consulted. Plato's thoughts on music are collected in an essay by Deyk in Weber's *Cäcilia* (1828). Plato likened the movements of music to those of the soul, whose development may therefore be influenced by musical art.
BIBLIOGRAPHY: J. Regner, *Platos Musik-Theorie* (Halle, 1923).

Platti, Giovanni, Italian composer; b. Padua, July 9, 1697; d. Würzburg, Jan 11, 1763. He was attached to the Würzburg court in 1724; was active there as tenor, violinist, composer, and teacher; regarded by some music historians as the first composer to employ the classical sonata form, but this contention is debatable.
WORKS: 12 keyboard sonatas by Platti were edited by L. Hoffmann-Erbrecht (Leipzig, 1953–54); one is included in W. S. Newman, *13 Keyboard Sonatas of the 18th and 19th Centuries* (Chapel Hill, N.C., 1947); a *Miserere* was transcribed by Molinari and performed in Rome (March 15, 1936); a flute sonata was edited by Jarnach (1936).
BIBLIOGRAPHY: F. Torrefranca, "La Creazione della sonata drammatica moderna rivendicata all'Italia: Giovanni Platti, il grande," *Rivista Musicale Italiana* 17; O. Kaul, *Geschichte der Würzburger Hofmusik im 18. Jahrhundert* (Würzburg, 1924); Fausto Torrefranca, *G. B. Platti e la sonata moderna* (Milan, 1963).

Playford, Henry, English music publisher, son of **John Playford;** b. London, May 5, 1657; d. there, 1720. He continued his father's trade; his most important publications were *The Theatre of Musick* (with R. Carr; 4 books, 1685–87, described as "the newest and best songs"); *Banquet of Music* (6 books; 1688–92); Purcell's *Orpheus Britannicus* (1698–1702) and his *Ten Sonatas* with a *Te Deum* and *Jubilate* for St. Cecilia's Day (1697); Blow's *Amphion Anglicus* (1700); and an ode on Purcell's death (1695).

Playford, John, English music publisher; b. Norfolk, 1623; d. London, Nov. 1686. He was in business for 36 years (1648–84); his publishing firm was responsible for the most important music editions of the 17th century; he publ. *The Dancing Master* (1651; 12th ed., 1703; modern ed. by M. Dean-Smith, London, 1958); Hilton's *Catch that catch can* (1652); *Musick's Recreation on the Lyra-Violl* (1652; facsimile edition by N. Dolmetsch was published in London, 1960); *Select Musical Ayres and Dialogues* (1653); *Briefe Introduction to the Skill of Musick for Song and Violl* (1654; enlarged ed., 1655, with an essay on "The Art of Descant" by Dr. Thos. Campion, which was revised by Purcell in the 10th ed. of 1683; this very popular work, written by John Playford himself, ran through 19 numbered editions up to 1730, besides 6 unnumbered editions); *Psalms and Hymns in Solemn Musick of four parts* (1671); *The Whole Book of Psalms, with the usual Spiritual Song* (1673; 20th ed., 1757); *The Musical Companion* (1673; Book I, catches and rounds; Book II, dialogues, glees, ayres and songs); *Choice Ayres, Songs and Dialogues to be sung to the theorbo* (5 books, 1676–84); *Musick's Delight on the Cithern* (1666); *The Division-Violin* (variations for violin over a basso ostinato; 2nd ed., 1685).

BIBLIOGRAPHY: F. Kidson, "John Playford and the 17th-Century Music Publishing," *Musical Quarterly* (Oct. 1918): J. Pulver, "John Playford," *Music News and Herald* (May 1927); C. L. Day and Eleanor Murrie, *English Song-Books, 1651-1702 and Their Publishers* (London, 1936; reprinted from *Transactions of the Bibliographical Society,* March 1936).

Plaza, Juan Bautista, Venezuelan composer; b. Caracas, July 19, 1898; d. there, Jan. 1, 1964. He went to Rome in 1920 to study at the Pontifical Institute of Sacred Music; upon returning to Venezuela, became organist of the Cathedral of Caracas. He wrote a number of sacred choral works; also the symph. poems, *El Picacho abrupto, Vigilia, Campanas de Pascua, Las Horas,* etc.; *Fuga criolla* for orch.; *Sonatina venezolana* for piano; songs.

Plé-Caussade, Simone, French composer and pianist; b. Paris, Aug. 14, 1897. She studied piano at the Paris Cons. with Alfred Cortot and composition with Georges Caussade, whom she later married; in 1928 she was appointed prof. of harmony and counterpoint at the Paris Cons.; among her students were Gilbert Amy and Betsy Jolas. She wrote a number of orchestral and chamber music works in a fine impressionistic manner.

Pleshakov, Vladimir, American pianist; b. Shanghai, of Russian parents, Oct. 4, 1934. He studied piano with Russian teachers in Shanghai; in 1949 went to Sydney, Australia, where he took piano lessons with Alexander Sverjensky. In 1955 he emigrated to the U.S. and studied medicine at the Univ. of California, Berkeley (A.B., 1958). Turning back to music, he entered Stanford Univ. in the graduate school of music (Ph.D., 1973). He made especial study of piano manufacture of Beethoven's era, and performed on reconstructed pianos at his concerts of classical music.

Plessis, Hubert du, South African composer; b. Malmesbury, Cape Province, June 7, 1922. He studied music with W. H. Bell at Gordonsbai (1942–44) and later at the Rhodes Univ. College in Cape Town; in 1951 he went to London and took courses in composition with Alan Bush and Ferguson at the Royal Academy of Music; returning to South Africa in 1955 he was lecturer on music at the College of Music in Cape Town and, from 1958, at the Univ. of Stellenbosch. As a composer he cultivates mainly vocal music; many of his songs are based on South African motifs; among them are the cycles *In den ronde* (1948), *Die vrou* (1960; to words in Afrikaans, Dutch and German); he also wrote *Suid-Afrik, nag en daeraad* for chorus and orch., in Afrikaans (1966).

Pleyel, Camille, French pianist, son of **Ignaz Pleyel;** b. Strasbourg, Dec. 18, 1788; d. Paris, May 4, 1855. He was a pupil of his father; had some success as a composer, but is chiefly noteworthy as a piano manufacturer, entering his father's firm in 1821. Kalkbrenner was his partner for a time; Auguste Wolff, his successor. His wife, **Marie-Félicité-Denise** (b. Paris, Sept. 4, 1811; d. St.-Josse-ten-Noode, March 30, 1875), was a pianist; pupil of Henri Herz, Moscheles, and Kalkbrenner. In her fifteenth year, as Mlle. Moke, her virtuosity created a sensation in Belgium, Austria, Germany, and Russia. Before her marriage, Berlioz was in love with her (1830). From 1848–72 she was prof. of piano at the Brussels Cons.

Pleyel, Ignaz Joseph, remarkable pianist, composer, and piano manufacturer; b. Ruppertsthal, near Vienna, June 18, 1757; d. on his estate near Paris, Nov. 14, 1831. He was the 24th of 38 children in an impoverished family of a school teacher; however, he received sufficient education, including music lessons, to qualify for admittance to the class of Wanhal; thanks to the generosity of a princely patron he was apprenticed to Haydn with whom he lived 5 years, and was later enabled to go to Rome. In 1783 he became second Kapellmeister at the Strasbourg Cathedral; was advanced to the rank of first Kapellmeister in 1789 but lost his position during the turbulent times of the French Revolution. He conducted the "Professional Concerts" in London during the season 1791–92, and honored his teacher Haydn by playing a work of Haydn at his opening concert (Feb. 13, 1792). After several years he returned to Strasbourg to liquidate his estate; in 1795 he went to Paris, where he opened a music store which was in business until 1834, and in 1807 founded a piano factory, which manufactured famous French pianos; the firm eventually became known as "Pleyel et Cie.," and continued to prosper for over a century and a half. The name Pleyel is mainly known through his piano manufacture, but he was a prolific and an extremely competent composer. His productions are so close in style to those of Haydn that specialists are still inclined to attribute certain works in Haydn's catalogues to Pleyel. He composed fully 60 symphonies, of which 33 were published; more than 60 string quartets, 8 instrumental concertos and numerous duos, trios and quintets for strings, as well as 6 quartets for flute and strings, a number of piano and violin sonatas, some songs and 2 operas, *Ifigenia in Aulide* (produced in Naples in 1785) and *Die Fee Urgele* for puppet theater, staged in Eszterháza in 1776. The attribution of Haydn's *6 Feld-*

partien to Pleyel remains moot. As music publisher, Pleyel brought out an English translation of J. L. Dussek's *Klavierschule,* under the title *Instructions on the Art of Playing the Pianoforte or Harpsichord* (London, 1796); in French as *Méthode pour piano-forte par Pleyel et Dussek;* a German edition appeared in Leipzig in 1804 under Pleyel's name.

BIBLIOGRAPHY: L. de Fourcaud, *La Salle Pleyel* (Paris, 1893); Rita Benton, "À la recherche de Pleyel perdu" *Fontes Artis Musicae* (1970).

Plishka, Paul Peter, American bass; b. Old Forge, Penn., Aug. 28, 1941. He studied at the Montclair, New Jersey, State College; was a member of the Patterson, New Jersey, Lyric Opera (1961–66); in 1967 he joined the staff of the Metropolitan Opera, N.Y.; also makes frequent appearances as soloist with major American orchestras.

Plonsky, Peter, intransigent American composer and singer of the uncompromising avant-garde; b. Brooklyn, N.Y., April 23, 1943. He studied composition with Morton Feldman and Earle Brown who inculcated in him the ultramodern notions of musical indeterminacy within static harmony and relentless monotony. In search of musical timelessness he studied Eastern instruments; traveled in Europe and America collecting symbolic souvenirs; took a handful of earth from the grave of Anton von Webern. At his audio-visual séances, held usually in claustrophiliac emporia, he practiced mental arts; in 1970 he knocked a small radio station off the air by telekinesis of thunderclouds; explored the inner space of his organism to bring about calculated epilepsy by producing a variety of groans, moans, sneezes, wheezes and tongue clicks; he calls these exhibitions "Mind Emission Vocal Trances" operating "within the astral causality."

WORKS: *Innards* for 9 performers and 9 colored cans of spray paint (1963); *Ear Rub* performed by rubbing the ears to produce sound (1973); autokinetic and hyperkinetic actions.

Plotnikov, Eugene, Russian conductor; b. Odessa, Aug. 29, 1877; d. New York, Sept. 28, 1951. He studied at the Moscow Cons.; was coach and assistant conductor at the Moscow Opera; also conducted at the Paris Opéra (1921). In 1922 he settled in the U.S.; conducted Russian operas in N.Y. and other American cities.

Plüddemann, Martin, German composer; b. Kolberg, Sept. 29, 1854; d. Berlin, Oct. 8, 1897. He studied at the Leipzig Cons.; later took singing lessons with Hey in Munich; in 1889 was engaged as singing teacher at the Styrian Music School in Graz. He wrote a number of popular male choruses and ballads; publ. pamphlets of Wagnerian tendency.

BIBLIOGRAPHY: R. Batka, *M. Plüddemann und seine Balladen* (Prague, 1896); L. Schemann, *M. Plüddemann und die deutsche Ballade* (1930).

Plutarch, famous Greek writer; b. Chæronea, Bœotia, 50 A.D.; d. there, 120. Among his treatises ("Moralia") one, *De musica,* contains important historical data concerning music (Latin transl. by R. Volkmann; Ger-

man transl., with parallel Greek text, and commentary, by R. Westphal, 1865; also by Weil and Reinach, with commentary, 1900).

Pocci, Franz, Graf von, composer; b. (of an old Italian noble family) Munich, March 7, 1807; d. there, May 7, 1876. Possessing versatile talents, he wrote plays with music for a puppet theater in Munich, for which he also designed the scenery. He was at his best in pieces for children (*Blumenlieder, Bildertöne für Klavier, Soldatenlieder, Jägerlieder, Alte und neue Kinderlieder,* etc.). His 2 piano sonatas were praised by Schumann for their poetic expression and fine romantic spirit. An opera, *Der Alchemist,* was produced in Munich (1840); his grandson F. Pocci publ. a collection: *Franz Poccis Lustiges Komödienbüchlein* (Munich, 1921).

BIBLIOGRAPHY: K. Pastor, *Franz Pocci als Musiker* (Munich, 1932); L. Hirschberg, "F. Pocci, der Musiker," *Zeitschrift für Musikwissenschaft* (1918).

Pochon, Alfred, Swiss violinist; b. Yverdon, July 30, 1878; d. Lutry, Switzerland, Feb. 26, 1959. He made his first public appearance at the age of 11; then went to Liège to study with César Thomson, who engaged him as second violin in his string quartet. In 1902 the philanthropist E. de Coppet asked Pochon to organize a string quartet, later to become famous as Flonzaley Quartet, so named after Coppet's summer residence near Lausanne. He was at his best in pieces playing 2nd violin, until it was disbanded in 1929. In 1938 Pochon returned to Switzerland; was director of the Cons. of Lausanne until 1957, when he retired. He published *A Progressive Method of String-Quartet Playing* (N.Y., 1924).

Podéšť, Ludvík, Czech composer; b. Dubňany, Dec. 19, 1921; d. Prague, Feb. 27, 1968. He studied composition with Jaroslav Kvapil at the Brno Univ., graduating in 1948; worked at the Brno Radio (1947–51); was music director of the Vit Nejedlý Army Artistic Ensemble (1953–56) and of the music department of the Czech Television (1958–60).

WORKS: 2 operas: *Tři apokryfy (3 Apocryphas),* to Čapek short stories (1957–58; No. 1, *Staré zlaté časy;* No. 2, *Svatá noc;* No. 3, *Romeo a Julie*) and *Hrátky s čertem (Frolics with the Devil,* 1957–60; Liberec, Oct. 12, 1963); *Smrt (Death),* a cantata (1942); *Písně z koncentráku (Songs from the Concentration Camp)* for baritone and orch. (1946); *Měsíce (Months)* for soprano and orch. (1948, revised 1957–58); symphony (1947–48, revised 1964) *Raymonda Dienová,* symph. poem (1950–51); 4 suites for orch. (1951, 1954, 1956, 1960); 2 piano concertos (1951–53; 1958–59); *Jarní Serenáda,* violin concerto (1953); *Advent Rhapsody* for orch. (1956–57); Concertino for Cimbalom and Orch. (1963); *The Seconds of a Day,* symph. variations (1965); Concertino for 2 Cellos and Chamber Orch. (1965); *Partita* for strings, guitar and percussion (1967); 2 string quartets (1942; *5 Spring Days,* 1948); *Litanie* for string quartet (1944); Wind Quintet (1946); Violin Sonata (1947); Cello Sonata (1947); *Hojačky* for 2 clarinets and piano (1947); *Suite* for viola and piano (1955–56); Piano Sonatina (1945); Piano Sonata (1946).

Podešva, Jaromír, Czech composer; b. Brno, March 8, 1927. He studied composition with J. Kvapil at the Janáček Academy in Brno (1947–55); on an American visit attended classes of Aaron Copland at the Berkshire Center in Tanglewood; then had lessons with Dutilleux in Paris; wrote a book of impressions. In 1969 he was appointed to the staff of the Cons. of Ostrava. His music is marked by contrapuntal density and dynamic intensity.

WORKS: an opera *Opuslíš-li mne (If You Leave Me,* 1962–63); an opera-buffa *Bambini di Praga* (1968); Piano Concerto (1949); 6 symphonies: No. 1, (1950–51); No. 2, for strings and flute (1960–61); No. 3, *Kulminace—Perla na dně: Dvě symfonické paralely myšlenek M. Kundery a B. Hrabala (Culmination—The Pearl at the Bottom: 2 Symph. Parallels to Ideas by M. Kundera and B. Hrabal,* 1966); No. 4 for chamber orch. (1966); No. 5, after poems by Evtushenko and Halas, for voices and orch. (1967); No. 6 (1970); *Cesta vlasti (Throughout My Homeland,* 1952–53), a 3-part cycle of symph. poems: *Kounicovy koleje (Kounic College;* Brno site of a Nazi concentration camp), *V kraj vešla Rudá armáda (The Red Army Enters the Country),* and *Veliký pochod (Great March); Setkání mládeže (Meeting of Youth)* for orch. (1956); *Triple Concerto* for violin, cello, piano and orch. (1956–57); *Suita Notturna* for orch. (1957); Sinfonietta for string orch. (1959); *Slavnost l'Humanité,* overture for strings and brasses in celebration of the Paris organ of the Communist Party (1961); Flute Concerto (1965); *Dotazník srdce,* chamber cantata for narrator, baritone and 9 instruments (1965); Concerto for String Quartet and Orch. (1971); 5 string quartets (1950; *You Shall Live in Peace,* 1951; 1955; *From the Life of Contemporary Man,* 1959–60; 1965); Clarinet Sonatina (1947–48); 2 violin sonatas (1948, 1958); Piano Trio (1948); Sextet for 2 violins, viola, cello, clarinet and horn (1949); *Poetic Trio* for violin, cello and piano (1954); *O šťastných dětech (Happy Children),* a nonet (1955); Cello Sonatina (1960); Cornet Sonatina (1960); *3 Sonata Studies* for flute and piano (1964); Sonata for soprano and piano (1967); *5 Pieces* for violin and piano (1968); *Suite* for viola and piano (1969); Wind Quintet No. 1 (1969–70); *How the Flood Came to Earth* for 5 children's choirs, flute, trumpet, cello and piano (1971); 2 piano sonatas (1951; *Březen,* 1953, 1953); *4 Miniatures* for piano (1953); *Rhapsodiettas* for piano (1955); numerous a cappella choruses, including *Long Live the Universe,* a quasi sinfonietta (1959–60) and *Sinfonietta to Nature* (1962).

Poglietti, Alessandro, Italian composer; from 1661 court organist in Vienna; killed in July 1683 at the siege of Vienna by the Turks. His compositions include 12 ricercari, suites for harpsichord (*On the Hungarian Rebellion, Nightingale Suite,* etc.), and other instrumental pieces, some of which appear in *Toccates et Suites,* publ. by Roger (Amsterdam); also church music. H. Botstiber publ. some reprints in the *Denkmäler der Tonkunst in Österreich* 27 (13.ii).

BIBLIOGRAPHY: A. Koczirz, "Zur Lebensgeschichte Alexander Pogliettis," *Studien zur Musikwissenschaft* (1916).

Pohl, Carl Ferdinand, German writer on music; b. Darmstadt, Sept. 6, 1819; d. Vienna, April 28, 1887. During his stay in London (1863–66) he gathered all available facts concerning the residence there of Mozart and Haydn, embodying this information in his publication *Mozart und Haydn in London* (1867; 2 vols.). Pohl also began an extended biography of Haydn, but publ. only one vol. (in 2 parts: 1875, 1882); the work was finished by Hugo Botstiber. Other publications: *International Exhibition of 1862. Cursory Notices on the History of the Glass Harmonica* (London, 1862); an interesting historical review, *Die Gesellschaft der Musikfreunde ... und ihr Conservatorium* (1871); *Denkschrift aus Anlass des 100 jährigen Bestehens der Tonkünstler-Sozietät in Wien* (1871); *Bibliographie der Musiksammelwerke des 16. und 17. Jahrhunderts* (with R. Eitner and A. Lagerberg; 1877).

Pohl, Richard, German writer on music; b. Leipzig, Sept. 12, 1826; d. Baden-Baden, Dec. 17, 1896. He studied natural sciences, and philosophy in Karlsruhe, Göttingen and Leipzig; in 1854 he went to Weimar where he established a personal friendship with Liszt, and became an ardent advocate of the new German school of music. After Liszt's temporary absence from Weimar, Pohl went to Baden-Baden, where he remained until his death. He was the joint editor of the *Neue Zeitschrift für Musik,* to which he contributed a number of articles under the pseudonym **Hoplit.** He also publ. *Bayreuther Erinnerungen* (1877); *Autobiographisches* (1881); *Franz Liszt* (1883); *Hector Berlioz, Studien und Erinnerungen* (1884); *Die Höhenzüge der musikalischen Entwickelung* (1888). He possessed a fine literary gift and wrote some poetry; when his first wife Johanna, a harpist, died in 1870 he wrote a heartfelt memoir *Meiner theuren Gattin zum Gedächtnis;* then married again; his second wife, Luise, compiled Pohl's materials on Berlioz and published *Hector Berlioz Leben und Werke* (1900); also a fictional life of Wagner under the title *Richard Wiegand. Episoden aus dem Leben eines grossen Meisters* (1904).

Pohlig, Karl, German conductor; b. Teplitz, Feb. 10, 1858; d. Brunswick, June 17, 1928. A pupil of Liszt in Weimar, Pest, and Rome, he began his career as a pianist, touring Germany, Austria, Russia, Scandinavia, and Italy; became 1st Kapellmeister at Graz, then assistant conductor to Mahler at the Vienna court opera, and conductor at Covent Garden (1897, 1898); until 1900 1st Kapellmeister at the Hoftheater in Coburg; 1900–07, at the Hoftheater in Stuttgart, and conductor of the symph. concerts; in 1907, engaged as conductor of the Philadelphia Orch.; directed it for 5 seasons, emphasizing the German repertory, and particularly Wagner, of whom he was an impassioned admirer.

Poirée, (Élie-Émile-) Gabriel, French writer on music; b. Villeneuve-St.-Georges, near Paris, Oct. 9, 1850; d. Paris, May 25, 1925. He was librarian of the Ste. Geneviève library.

WRITINGS: *L'Évolution de la musique* (1884); an essay on *Tannhäuser* (1895; with Alfred Ernst); *Essais de technique et d'esthétique musicales* (No. 1, Wagner's *Meistersinger,* 1898; No. 2, *Étude sur le discours musical,* 1899; new ed. 1922); *Le Chant gnostico-ma-*

gique des sept voyelles (1901; with Ch.-E. Ruelle); *Une Nouvelle Interprétation du second hymne delphique* (1901); *Chopin* (1907); *Wagner* (1921); also publ. a string quartet (1908).

Poise, (Jean Alexandre) Ferdinand, French composer of comic operas; b. Nîmes, June 3, 1828; d. Paris, May 13, 1892; studied at the Paris Cons. with A. Adam and Zimmerman, taking 2nd Grand Prix de Rome in 1852.
WORKS: light operas, all produced in Paris: *Bonsoir, voisin* (Sept. 18, 1853); *Le Thé de Polichinelle* (May 4, 1856); *Don Pèdre* (April 30, 1858); *Le Jardinier galant* (March 4, 1861); *Le Corricolo* (Nov. 28, 1868); *Les Deux Billets* (Feb. 19, 1870); *Les Trois Souhaits* (Oct. 29, 1873); *La Surprise de l'amour* (Oct. 31, 1877); *L'Amour médicin* (Dec. 20, 1880); *Joli Gilles* (Oct. 10, 1884).

Poissl, Johann Nepomuk, German composer; b. Haukenzell, Bavaria, Feb. 15, 1783; d. Munich, Aug. 17, 1865. He was a pupil of Danzi in Munich; from 1825 to 1848 was in charge of the court music. He wrote about 12 operas; of these the following had a modicum of success: *Athalia* (Munich, June 3, 1814), *Der Wettkampf zu Olympia* (Munich, April 21, 1815), and *Nittetis* (Darmstadt, June 29, 1817); also several oratorios, a Mass, and other works for the church.
BIBLIOGRAPHY: E. Reipschläger, *Schubaur, Danzi und Poissl* (Berlin, 1911); L. Schrott in *Die Musik* (1940; pp. 299–303).

Pokorný, Franz Xaver, Czech composer; b. Königstadt (Mestec Kralove), Dec. 20, 1728; d. Regensburg, July 2, 1794. He joined the court orchestra in Oettingen-Wallerstein in 1753; then went to Mannheim, where he studied with Stamitz, Holzbauer and Richter, returning to Wallerstein after a few months. In 1767 he became a court musician in Thurn and Taxis. In the light of recent research, Pokorný appears as a pioneer in symphonic writings; fully 165 symphonies have been discovered that are probably his; they are all written in a characteristic style of the Mannheim School. The Symphony in E flat, often credited to G. M. Monn, has been definitely identified as a work by Pokorný.
BIBLIOGRAPHY: J. Murray Barbour, "Pokorný Vindicated," *Musical Quarterly* (Jan. 1963).

Pokrass, Dimitri, Russian composer of popular music; b. Kiev, Nov. 7, 1899. He studied piano at St. Petersburg Cons. (1913–17); in 1919 he joined the Soviet Cavalry during the Civil War, and wrote the song, *The Red Cavalry.* This was the first of a series of many songs that have acquired great popularity, among them *If War Comes Tomorrow* (1938), *March of the Tank Brigade, Farewell,* etc. He also wrote music for films.

Polacco, Giorgio, Italian conductor; b. Venice, April 12, 1873; d. New York, April 30, 1960. Taught at first in St. Petersburg; he continued in Venice at the Liceo B. Marcello, and graduated from the Cons. G. Verdi in Milan. After conducting in various Italian cities, he was 4 seasons at the Teatro Colón in Buenos Aires, and 7 in Rio de Janeiro. On Nov. 11, 1912, he made his debut at the Metropolitan Opera House; following Toscanini's resignation (1915), Polacco was principal conductor of the Italian, French, and Russian works until 1917; 1918–30, chief conductor of the Italian repertory of the Chicago Opera Co.

Poldini, Ede (Eduard), Hungarian composer; b. Budapest, June 13, 1869; d. Corseaux, Switzerland, June 28, 1957. He studied at the Budapest Cons., and later with Mandyczewski (theory) and Julius Epstein (piano) in Vienna. In 1908 he went to live at Vevey. In 1935 he received the order of the Hungarian Cross; in 1948 was awarded the Hungarian Pro Arte Prize.
WORKS: the comic operas *The Vagabond and the Princess* (Budapest, Oct. 17, 1903), *The Carnival Marriage* (Budapest, Feb. 16, 1924; produced in London under the title, *Love Adrift,* 1926), and *Himfy* (Budapest, 1938); wrote in all 156 opus numbers, most of them for piano; his *Poupée valsante* became an international favorite; other popular piano pieces are *Arlequinades, Morceaux pittoresques, Images, Moments musicaux, Marionnettes,* etc.

Poldowski (pen name of **Irene Regine Wieniawska;** by marriage, **Lady Dean Paul**), Polish-English composer; b. Brussels, March 18, 1879; d. London, Jan. 28, 1932. She was a daughter of the Polish violinist **Henryk Wieniawski;** her mother was an Englishwoman. She studied at the Brussels Cons. with Gevaert, and later in London with Percy Pitt; married Sir Aubrey Dean Paul; took additional courses in composition with Gédalge and Vincent d'Indy in Paris; began writing songs to French words, in the Impressionist style; set 21 poems by Paul Verlaine, and 8 poems by others; her songs have been frequently performed at recitals. She also composed *Caledonian Market,* a suite of 8 pieces for piano; *Berceuse de l'enfant mourant* for violin and piano; *Tango* for violin and piano; *Suite miniature de chansons à danser* for woodwind instruments; 2 symph. sketches (*Nocturnes* and *Tenements*); and an operetta, *Laughter.*

Pole, William, English writer on music; b. Birmingham, April 22, 1814; d. London, Dec. 30, 1900. He was a prof. of civil engineering at University College, London; also a student of music (Mus. Doc., Oxon., 1864), and examiner in music for London Univ., 1876–90. Publ. *Philosophy of Music* (1879; 6th ed., 1924); contributor to the original ed. of *Grove's Dictionary.*

Polgar, Tibor, Hungarian-born Canadian composer and conductor; b. Budapest, March 11, 1907. He studied with Kodály at the Liszt Academy in Budapest, graduating in 1925; lived in West Germany in 1962–64; then emigrated to Canada and in 1966 became a staff member of the Univ. of Toronto Opera department.
WORKS: 4 operas: *Kérök (The Suitors,* 1954), *A European Lover,* a satire (1965) and 2 comic operas, *The Troublemaker* (1968) and *The Glove* for coloratura soprano, tenor, baritone, actress-dancer, actor-dancer, and piano (1973); *Improvisazione* for 4 horns (1962); *In Private* for violin and viola (1964); a cantata, *The Last Words of Louis Riel* (1966–67); *Variations on a Hungarian Theme* for solo harp, or for

harp, strings and timpani (1969); *Ilona's Four Faces* for saxophone and piano (1970); Sonatina for 2 flutes (1971); *Notes on Hungary* for concert band (1971); *How Long Shall the Ungodly Triumph?*, psalm for 6 voices and organ (1974); *Annabel Lee* for voice, flute and harp (1974); arrangements for children's choir and orch.; songs.

Polignac, Armande de, French composer; b. Paris, Jan. 8, 1876; d. Neauphle-le-Vieux (Seine-et-Oise), April 29, 1962. She studied with Gabriel Fauré and Vincent d'Indy; composed the operas *Morgane* and *L'Hypocrite sanctifié;* a dramatic scene, *Judith de Béthulie* (Paris Opéra, March 23, 1916); *La Source lointaine,* Persian ballet (Paris, 1913); *Les Mille et Une Nuits,* Arabian ballet (Paris, 1914); *Chimères,* Greek ballet (Paris Opéra, June 10, 1923); *Urashima,* Japanese ballet; also a Chinese ballet for small orch., *La Recherche de la vérité; Petite suite pour le clavecin* (1939).

Poliński, Alexander, Polish music historian, b. Wlostow, June 4, 1845; d. Warsaw, Aug. 13, 1916. He was a pupil of Noskowski, Zelenski, and Minchejmer in Warsaw; 1899, music critic for the *Warsaw Courier;* from 1904, prof. of history of music at the Warsaw Cons. He published (in Polish) *Concerning Church Music and Its Reform* (1890), *The Song "Bogarodzica" from the Viewpoint of Music* (1903), *History of Polish Music* (1907).

Polívka, Vladimír, Czech pianist and composer; b. Prague, July 6, 1896; d. there, May 11, 1948. He studied piano at the Prague Cons. and took lessons in composition from Vitězslav Novák at the Master School there (1912–18); traveled in Europe, America and Japan with the violinist Jaroslav Kocián; from 1923 to 1930 taught piano in Chicago. In 1938 he returned to Prague and taught at the Cons. there; was chairman of "Přítomnost," an association for contemporary music.
WORKS: chiefly for piano, including *Dni v Chicagu* (*Days in Chicago,* 1926); *3 Impromptus* (1930); *Merry Musik* (1932–33); a tragically colored piano suite, titled *Krajiny z let okupace* (*Landscapes in the Years of Occupation,* 1941); also an opera *Polobůh* (*The Demi-God,* 1930); a melodrama, *A Ballad of a Deaf-Mute* (1936); a symph. poem *Jaro* (*Spring,* 1918); *Little Symphony* (1921); *Suite* for viola and small orch. (1934); Concerto for Piano and Small Orch. (1934); *Overture* (1942); 2 violin sonatas (1918, 1919); *Suite* for viola and wind quintet (1934); String Quartet (1937); *Divertimento* for wind quintet (1939); *Giacona* for viola and piano (1944); Viola Sonata (1945); choruses; songs; incidental music. He published several collections of children's pieces, collaborated on a book about Smetana (Prague, 1941) and wrote a book of travels, describing his world tour (Prague, 1945).

Polko (*née* **Vogel**), **Elise,** German singer; b. Leipzig, Jan. 13, 1822; d. Munich, May 15, 1899. She studied with Manuel García in Paris; married a railway engineer Eduard Polko, under whose name she became professionally known. She published a number of semi-fictional stories about music which became astonishingly popular in Germany during her lifetime.
WRITINGS: *Musikalische Märchen* (3 vols., 1852; also translated into English); *Faustina Hasse,* a novel about the famous singer (2 vols., 1860); *Alte Herren* (1865, about Bach's predecessors at the Thomaskirche in Leipzig); *Verklungene Akkorde* (1868; several editions); *Erinnerungen an Felix Mendelssohn-Bartholdy* (1868; in English, 1869); *Nicolò Paganini und die Geigenbauer* (1876); *Vom Gesange* (1876); *Aus der Künstlerwelt* (1878); *Der Klassiker der Musik* (1880); *Meister der Tonkunst* (1897).

Pollack, Ben, American drummer and bandleader; b. Chicago, June 22, 1903; d. (suicide by hanging) at Palm Springs, Calif., June 7, 1971. He was a drummer with a New Orleans band; in 1924 he organized his own group, with 16-year-old Benny Goodman as clarinetist and Glenn Miller as trombonist and arranger; later he engaged Harry James as trumpeter; he himself presided at the drums. With this stellar personnel he cut a deep swath through the jazzland and was dubbed "The Father of Swing." When his career declined, he entered entertainment business; ran a restaurant in Hollywood; later managed a night club in Palm Springs. He left a suicide note, explaining his act by despondency over personal and financial problems.

Pollack, Egon, Austrian conductor; b. Prague, May 3, 1879; d. there (of a heart attack during a performance), June 14, 1933. He studied with Knittl at the Prague Cons.; then conducted at the Bremen Opera (1905–10), at the Leipzig Opera (1910–12) and at the Frankfurt Opera (1912–17); from 1922 to 1931 he was general music director at the Hamburg Opera. He was generally regarded as the foremost interpreter of the works of Richard Strauss.

Pollak, Robert, Austrian violinist; b. Vienna, Jan. 18, 1880; d. Brunnen, Switzerland, Sept. 7, 1962. He studied violin with Carl Flesch and Henri Marteau. In 1906 he went to Geneva where he taught violin; at the outbreak of World War I he happened to be in Russia, and was interned as an enemy alien. After the war he taught violin at the Moscow Cons.; in 1926 went to the U.S. and taught at the San Francisco Cons.; then went to Japan and taught violin at the Imperial Cons. of Tokyo (1930–37); in 1937 returned to California and in 1943 became an American citizen.

Pollarolo, Antonio, Italian composer; son of **Carlo Francesco Pollarolo;** b. Venice, 1680; d. there, May 4, 1746. He studied with his father, and became his assistant at San Marco in Venice, 1702; in 1723 he was 2nd maestro di cappella there; in 1740, 1st maestro. He wrote the operas *Aristeo* (Venice, 1700) and *Leucippo e Teonoe* (1719), among others.

Pollarolo, Carlo Francesco, Italian organist and composer; b. Brescia, 1653; d. Venice, 1722. He was a pupil of Legrenzi. In 1665 he became a chorister at San Marco, Venice; in 1690, 2nd organist; in 1692, 2nd maestro di cappella.
WORKS: the oratorios *Jefte, La Rosinda,* and *Jesabel;* over 85 operas, among them *La Forza della virtù*

(1693), *Ottone* (1694), *Gl'Inganni felici* (1695), *Faramondo* (1699), *Semiramide* (1714), and *Ariodante* (1716). His *Sonata per organo o cembalo* is reprinted in Torchi's *L'Arte musicale in Italia* (vol. III).

Pollini, Bernhard (real name **Baruch Pohl**), German impresario; b. Cologne, Dec. 16, 1838; d. Hamburg, Nov. 27, 1897. A tenor, he made his debut at Cologne, 1858, as Arturo in Bellini's *I Puritani;* later sang baritone roles in an Italian opera troupe, of which he subsequently became manager and artistic director. He then undertook the management of the Italian opera at St. Petersburg and Moscow. In 1874 he became director of the Hamburg City Theater; in 1876 he also became manager of the Altona Theater and in 1894 of the Thalia Theater in Hamburg.

Pollini, Cesare, Cavaliere de', Italian writer on music; b. Padua, July 13, 1858; d. there, Jan. 26, 1912. After legal studies at the Univ. of Padua, he took a 2-year course in music with Bazzini in Milan (1881–83); from 1883–85 director of the chief Cons. at Padua; resigned to devote himself to writing and composition. Publ. *Terminologia musicale tedesco-italiana; Teoria generale della musica; La Musica italiana nelle sue principali fasi storiche;* etc.
BIBLIOGRAPHY: G. Sacerdoti, *C. Pollini* (Padua, 1912); S. Leoni, *C. Pollini nella vita e nell'arte* (Padua, 1917).

Pollini, Francesco (Giuseppe), Austrian pianist; b. Laibach (Ljubljana), of Italian parents, March 25, 1762; d. Milan, Sept. 17, 1846. He was a pupil of Mozart (who dedicated a violin rondo to him) at Vienna, later of Zingarelli at Milan, where he was appointed prof. of piano shortly after the opening of the Cons. (1809). He was the first to write piano music on 3 staves, imitated by Liszt, Thalberg, and others; a specimen of this style being one of his *32 Esercizi in forma di toccata* (op. 42), a central melody surrounded by passagework for both hands; publ. a method and many pieces for piano; wrote an opera buffa, *La Casetta nei boschi* (Milan, Feb. 25, 1798).

Pollini, Maurizio, Italian pianist; b. Milan, Jan. 5, 1942. He studied at the Verdi Cons. in Milan with Carlo Vidusso; played in public at the age of 11; at 15 won the second prize in a Geneva contest; at 18 won first prize at the Chopin Contest in Warsaw, the youngest of 89 contestants. Returning to Italy, he took a course of study with Benedetti Michelangeli. Because of his signal success in winning the Warsaw Prize, he became known as a Chopin specialist, but later enlarged his repertoire to include not only the classics, but also the moderns; he has in his repertory the complete works of Schoenberg, as well as many piano pieces by Prokofiev and Stravinsky.

Pollitt, Arthur W., English organist; b. Liverpool, Nov. 27, 1878; d. there, Feb. 3, 1933. He studied at the Royal College of Music in Manchester, where he became assistant organist at the Cathedral; 1900–17, organist at the Liverpool Church, and at the School for the Blind; 1918, chorus director of the Liverpool Philharmonic Society. Publ. *The Necessity of Music in a School Curriculum; The Self-reliant Musician; The Enjoyment of Music;* etc.

Pollock, Robert, American composer; b. New York, July 8, 1946. He studied at Swarthmore College and at Princeton Univ. In 1972 he received a Guggenheim Foundation Grant. He adopted the serial method of composition early in the game, and became particularly interested in correlating the duration of a note with its pitch; this is the principle on which he built his *Geometrics* for string quartet and other pieces with abstract titles.

Pololáník, Zdeněk, Czech composer; b. Tišnov, Oct. 25, 1935. He studied organ with J. Černocký and composition with Petrželka and Theodor Schaefer at the Brno Cons. (1957–61). Much of his music represents a curious revival of medieval polyphonic forms, made astringent by abrasive dissonance.
WORKS: an opera-oratorio, *Sheer hush-sheereem* (*Song of Songs,* 1969); 2 ballets: *Mechanism* (1964) and a puppet ballet, *Popelka* (*Cinderella,* 1966); Sinfonietta (1958); *Toccata* for double bass, brass, percussion, 2 harps, harpsichord and piano (1959); *Divertimento* for string orch. and 4 horns (1960); 5 symphonies: No. 1 (1961), No. 2 for 11 wind instruments (1962), No. 3 for organ and percussion orchestra (1963), No. 4 for strings (1963) and No. 5 for chamber orch. (1968); *Concentus resonabilis* for 19 solo instruments and tape (1963); *Concerto Grosso* for flute, guitar, harpsichord and string orch. (1966); Piano Concerto (1966). CHAMBER MUSIC: Sonatina for cello and double bass (1956); *Suite* for violin and piano (1957); String Quartet (1958); Double-Bass Sonata (1959); *Scherzo contrario* for violin, bass clarinet, and xylophone (1961); *Little Mythological Exercises* for narrator and string quartet (1961); *Musica spingenta I* for double bass and wind quintet (1961), *II* for harpsichord and string quartet (1962) and *III* for bass clarinet and 13 percussion instruments (1962); *Musica concisa* for flute, bass clarinet, harpsichord, piano and percussion (1963); *Sonata eccentrica* for solo violin (1963); *Preludii dodici (12 Preludes)* for 2 pianos and organ (1963); horn sonata (1965); *Musica transcurata* for bass clarinet and harpsichord (1967); *Pulsazione* for percussion (1967). FOR VOICE: Mass for chorus, brasses, harp and organ (1956); *Nebuchadnezzar* for chorus, 3 trumpets and 4 timpani (1960); *Song of the Dead Children* for chorus, 3 trumpets and percussion (1963); *Vávra* for children's chorus and piano (1964); *Rumor letalis* for chorus a cappella (1966); *Cantus psalmorum* for bass, organ, harp and percussion (1966; Northwestern Univ., Evanston, Illinois, April 13, 1969); *Missa brevis* for children's chorus and organ (1970); songs. FOR PIANO: *Preludes* (1957) and *Variations on 2 Moravian Songs* (1957). FOR ORGAN: *Sonata bravura* (1959), *Sonata gaudia* (1962), *Allegro affanato* (1963).

Polovinkin, Leonid, Russian composer; b. Kurgan, Aug. 13, 1894; d. Moscow, Feb. 8, 1949. He studied at the Moscow Cons. with Glière and Vassilenko; began his career as a composer by writing theater music in Moscow after the revolution of 1917; adopted a modernistic idiom, emphasized the element of humor. Later he devoted more time to abstract instrumental music; wrote 9 symphonies, 4 string quartets, 2 piano trios, several overtures on folk themes; 5 piano sonatas; 24 postludes for piano; songs.

Ponc, Miroslav, Czech violinist, conductor and composer; b. Vysoké Mýto, Dec. 2, 1902; d. Prague, April 1, 1976. He studied organ with Wiedermann at the Prague Cons. (1920–22) and quarter-tone composition with Alois Hába (1922–24); then went to Berlin and took lessons with Schoenberg. Upon returning to Prague he studied violin with Josef Suk at the Cons., graduating in 1930; subsequently took lessons in conducting with Scherchen in Strasbourg (1933). After the war he was active mainly as a theater conductor in Prague; wrote a number of scores of incidental music for plays.

WORKS: *5 Polydynamic Compositions* for piano, xylophone and string quartet (1923); the song cycles *A Bad Dream* (1925) and *A Black Swan* (1926); *3 Merry Pieces* for wind quintet (1929); *Little Pieces* for flute or cello, and piano (1930); Piano Concertino (1930); *Overture to an Ancient Tragedy* with the application of quarter-tones in the Greek enharmonic mode (Prague, Feb. 18, 1931); Nonet (1932); the 2 antique ballet pictures, *Osudy* (*The Fates*, 1935); *Suite* for piano with 2 manuals tuned in quarter-tones (1935); String Trio (1937); *3 Intermezzi* from Molière's play *Le Malade imaginaire* (1938).

Ponce, Manuel María, distinguished Mexican composer; b. Fresnillo, Dec. 8, 1882; d. Mexico City, April 24, 1948. He studied piano with his older sister; in 1905, went to Europe, where he took lessons in composition with Enrico Bossi at Bologna and in piano with Martin Krause in Berlin. Upon his return to Mexico, he taught piano at the National Cons. He gave a concert of his compositions in Mexico on July 7, 1912, which included a piano concerto. During World War I he lived in N.Y. and in Havana; then went to Paris for additional study, and took lessons with Paul Dukas. His contact with French music wrought a radical change in his style of composition; his later works are more polyphonic in structure and more economical in form. He possessed a great gift of melody; one of his songs, *Estrellita*, became a universal favorite, often mistaken for a folksong. In 1941 he made a tour in South America, conducting his own works. He was the first Mexican composer of the 20th century to employ an identifiably modern musical language; his place in the history of Mexican music is a very important one. His works are often performed in Mexico; a concert hall was named after him in the Instituto de Bellas Artes.

WORKS: FOR ORCH.: *Estampas nocturnas* (1923), *Canto y danza de los antiguos Mexicanos* (1933), *Chapultepec,* symph. triptych (Mexico, Aug. 25, 1929; revised version, Mexico, Aug. 24, 1934), *Suite en estilo antiguo* (1935), *Poema elegiaco* (Mexico, June 28, 1935), *Ferial* (Mexico, Aug. 9, 1940), *Concierto del Sur,* for guitar and orch. (Montevideo, Oct. 4, 1941), Violin Concerto (Mexico, Aug. 20, 1943); Piano Trio (1911), *4 Miniaturas,* for string quartet (1929), *Pequeña suite en estilo antiguo,* for violin, viola, and cello (1933), Sonata for violin and viola (1935), Cello So-

nata (1922); numerous piano pieces, some based on Mexican rhythms; about 30 songs; 34 arrangements of Mexican folksongs. A collection of his articles was publ. posthumously in 1948.

BIBLIOGRAPHY: Otto Mayer-Serra, *Música y músicos de Latino-América,* (Mexico, 1947; vol. 2, pp. 782–86); D. López Alonso, *Manuel M. Ponce: ensayo biográfico* (Mexico, 1950); J. C. Romero, "Efemérides de Manuel Ponce," *Nuestra Música* 2 (1950).

Ponchielli, Amilcare, celebrated Italian composer; b. Paderno Fasolaro, Cremona, Aug. 31, 1834; d. Milan, Jan. 16, 1886. He studied at the Milan Cons. (1843–54); his first dramatic work (written with 3 other students) was the operetta *Il Sindaco Babbeo* (Milan, March 3, 1851). Leaving the Cons., he was organist at St. Ilario in Cremona; then became bandmaster. In 1883 he became prof. at the Cons. of Milan. Puccini and Mascagni were among his pupils. He brought out the opera *I promessi sposi* at Cremona (Aug. 30, 1856), followed by *La Savoiarda* (Cremona, Jan. 19, 1861; revised as *Lina,* Milan, Nov. 17, 1877), and *Roderico, re de' Goti* (Piacenza, Dec. 26, 1863). His first striking success was achieved with a revised version of *I promessi sposi* (Milan, Dec. 5, 1872); continuous good fortune attended the production of his operas *I Lituani* (La Scala, March 7, 1874; revised and revived in 1884 as *Aldona*), *La Gioconda* (his most famous work; Milan, April 8, 1876), *Il Figliuol prodigo* (Milan, Dec. 26, 1880), and *Marion Delorme* (Milan, March 17, 1885). An unfinished opera, *I Mori di Venezia,* in the orchestration by A. Cadore, was produced posthumously in Monte Carlo (March 17, 1914). Ponchielli also brought out a musical farce, *Il Parlatore eterno* (Lecco, Oct. 18, 1873) and the ballets *Le due gemelle* and *Clarina* (both in 1873); a cantata in honor of Donizetti; a funeral march, *Il 29 Maggio,* for Manzoni; a patriotic hymn, *Inno in memoria di Giuseppe Garibaldi.* Of his operas, *La Gioconda* established itself in the repertory everywhere; the ballet number from it, *Dance of the Hours,* is extremely popular at concerts of light orchestral music. Ponchielli also wrote sacred music, for use at the Cathedral of Bergamo, where he was maestro di cappella from 1881 to 1886.

BIBLIOGRAPHY: A. Mandelli, *Le Distrazioni di A. Ponchielli* (Cremona, 1897); G. Cesari, *A. Ponchielli nell'arte del suo tempo* (Cremona, 1934); G. de Napoli, *A. Ponchielli* (Cremona, 1936); A. Damerini, *A. Ponchielli* (Turin, 1940).

Pond, Sylvanus Billings, American music publisher and composer; b. Milford, Vt., April 5, 1792; d. Brooklyn, March 12, 1871. He was a prominent musician of his time; conducted the N.Y. Sacred Musical Society and the N.Y. Academy of Sacred Music; wrote songs for Sunday School; ed. and publ. *Union Melodies* (1838), *The U.S. Psalmody* (N.Y., 1841), and *The Book of Praise,* for the Reformed Dutch Church in America (N.Y., 1866); composed the hymn tunes *Armenia* (1835) and *Franklin Square* (1850). Early in life, he went to Albany; established a piano workshop; from 1820, was partner of the publishing house of Meacham and Pond there; in 1832 he joined Firth & Hall of N.Y., and the firm's name became Firth, Hall & Pond;

1848, reorganized as Firth, Pond & Co., one of the principal publishers of Stephen Foster's songs; in 1850, S. B. Pond retired, and his son, **William A. Pond,** became the owner; upon the withdrawal of Firth in 1863, the firm became known as William A. Pond & Co.; W. A. Pond's eldest son, **William A. Pond Jr.,** was taken into partnership, but died in 1884; William A. Pond Sr. died the following year, and his 2 other sons, **Albert Edward** and **George Warren Pond,** succeeded him. In 1934, Joseph Fletcher acquired the catalogue; in 1946, it was purchased by Carl Fischer, Inc. For the dealings of Firth, Pond & Co. with Stephen Foster, see J. T. Howard, *Stephen Foster, America's Troubadour* (N.Y., 1931; 4th ed., 1965); consult also H. Dichter and E. Shapiro, *Early American Sheet Music, Its Lure and Its Lore, 1768–1889* (N.Y., 1941).

Pongrácz, Zoltán, Hungarian composer; b. Diószeg, Feb. 5, 1912. He studied with Kodály at the Budapest Academy of Music (1930–35); then took lessons in conducting from Rudolf Nilius in Vienna and Clemens Krauss in Salzburg. During World War II he served as director of the music department of the Hungarian Radio (1943–44); after the end of the war conducted the Philharmonic Orch. in Debrecen (1946–49); later taught at the Cons. there (1954–64); in 1968 was appointed a supervisor of vocal music in Budapest.

WORKS: an opera, *Odysseus and Nausikaa* (1949–50; Debrecen, 1960); a ballet, *The Devil's Present* (1936); *Christmas Cantata* (1935); *St. Stephen Oratorio* (1938); a cantata, *Apollo musagètes* (1958); *Negritude* for speaking chorus, chorus and percussion (1962); *Ispirazioni* for chorus, orch. and tape (1965); *Music from Nyírség* for soloists, chorus and folk orch. (1965); *Pastorale* for clarinet, organ, 6 winds and percussion (1941); *Javanese Music*, on a South Asiatic motive, for chamber ensemble (1942); Symphony (1943); *Ballo ongaro* for youth orch. (1955); *3 Orchestral Etudes* (1963); *Hangok és zörejek (Tones and Noises),* aleatory music for orch. (1966); *Szinek és vonalak (Colors and Lines)* for youth orch. (1971); *Music for 5 cellos* (1954); *Wind Quintet* (1956); *Toccata* for piano (1957); *3 Small Pieces* for Orff ensemble (1966); *Phonothèse* for tape (1966); *Sets and Pairs,* electronic variations for piano and celesta (1968); *3 Improvisations* for piano, percussion and 3 tape recorders (1971); *3 Bagatelles* for percussion (1972); *Zoophonia,* concrete music synthesized from animal sounds (1973); incidental music for magnetic tape.

Poniatowski, Josef (Michal Xawery Franciszek Jan), Prince of Monte Rotondo, Polish composer; b. Rome, Feb. 20, 1816; d. Chislehurst, England, July 3, 1873. He was a member of the Polish nobility; his uncle was a marshal in Napoleon's army. He studied in Florence, and appeared on the stage as a tenor; then wrote operas (to Italian and French librettos); in 1848 he went to Paris and was elevated to the rank of Senator by Napoleon III; after the fall of the Second Empire, he went to England.

WORKS: OPERAS: *Giovanni da Procida* (Florence, 1838); *Don Desiderio* (Pisa, Dec. 26, 1840); *Ruy Blas* (Lucca, 1843); *Malek-Adel* (Genoa, June 20, 1846); *Esmeralde* (Florence, June 27, 1847); *Pierre de Médicis* (Paris, March 9, 1860); *Au travers du mur* (Paris, May 9, 1861); *L'Aventurier* (Paris, Jan. 26, 1865); *La Contessina* (Paris, April 28, 1868); *Gelmina* (London, June 4, 1872).

Poniridis, Georges, distinguished Greek composer and violinist; b. Constantinople, of Greek parents, Oct. 8, 1892. He studied violin with Ysaÿe at the Brussels Cons. and composition with Vincent d'Indy and Albert Roussel at the Schola Cantorum in Paris, where he remained until the outbreak of World War II; then returned to Athens and served in the Music Division of the Greek Ministry of Education (1954–58). In his music he makes use of authentic Greek motives, at times endeavoring to emulate the simple monody of ancient Greek chants and the rhythms of classical prosody.

WORKS: *Triptyque symphonique* (Athens, Nov. 22, 1937); 2 symphonies (1935, 1942); *3 Symphonic Preludes* (1938); Chamber Symph. for strings and percussion; *Petite Symphonie* (1956); Flute Sonata (1956); String Quartet (1959); Clarinet Sonata (1962); Quartet for oboe, clarinet, bassoon and xylophone (1962); Trio for xylophone, clarinet and bassoon (1962); Trio for flute, oboe and clarinet (1962); Piano Concerto (1968); Violin Concerto (1969); 2 violin sonatas; Viola Sonata (1967); Cello Sonata (1967); 3 piano sonatas; scores of incidental music to ancient Greek plays; arrangements of Greek folksongs.

Pons, Charles, French composer; b. Nice, Dec. 7, 1870; d. Paris, March 16, 1957. He studied organ, and earned his living as church organist in his youth; then turned to theater music, and produced a long series of operas: *L'Épreuve* (Nice, 1904), *Laura* (Paris, 1906), *Mourette* (Marseilles, 1909), *Le Voile du bonheur* (Paris, April 26, 1911), *Françoise* (Lyons, 1913), *Loin du bal* (Paris, 1913), *Les Fauves* (Paris, 1917), *Le Drapeau* (Paris, 1918), *Le Passant de Noël* (Nice, 1935), *L'Envol de la Marseillaise* (Marseilles, 1947); an overture, *Pyrrhus;* a symph. poem, *Heures vendéennes;* a *Symphonie tragique;* several orchestral suites; an oratorio, *La Samaritaine* (Nice, 1900); other vocal works with orch.: *La Mort de Démosthène* (Paris, 1928) and *Dans la forêt normande* (1934); chamber music; songs.

Pons, Lily (baptismal names **Alice Joséphine**), glamorous French coloratura soprano; b. Draguignan, April 12, 1898; d. Dallas, Texas, Feb. 13, 1976. She studied piano as a child; took voice lessons with Albert di Gorostiaga. She made her debut as an opera singer in Mulhouse in 1928 in the title role in *Lakmé;* sang in provincial theaters in France; then was engaged at the Metropolitan Opera, N.Y. and sang Lucia at her debut there on Jan. 3, 1931, with excellent success; she remained on its roster until 1940. While in New York, she continued her vocal studies, with Maria Gay and Giovanni Zenatello. Her fame as an extraordinary dramatic singer spread rapidly; she was engaged to sing at the Grand Opéra and the Opéra-Comique in Paris, at Covent Garden in London, the Teatro Colón in Buenos Aires, in Mexico and in Cuba. She went to Hollywood and appeared in motion pictures, among them *That Girl from Paris* (1936), *Hitting a New High* (1938). During World War II she toured the battlefronts in North Africa, India, China and Burma; received numerous honors. So celebrated did she become that a town in Maryland was named Lillypons in her honor. She was married twice and divorced both times, to August Mesritz, a publisher, and to the conductor **André Kostelanetz.** She possessed an expressive coloratura voice, which she used with extraordinary skill.

Ponse, Luctor, Swiss-born Dutch composer; b. Geneva, Oct. 11, 1914. He studied at the Cons. in Valenciennes, France, winning the "Prix d'Excellence" for theory in 1930 and for piano in 1932; after a further study in Geneva (1933–35), he went to Holland, and in 1964 became a member of the staff of the Institute of Sonology at Utrecht Univ.; also taught at the Groningen Cons.
WORKS: *Divertissement* for string orch. (1946); Piano Concerto (1951–55); 3 sinfoniettas (1952, 1959, 1961); 2 symphonies (1953, 1957); *Feestgericht* ballet for orch. (1957); 2-Piano Concerto (1961–62); *Concerto da Camera* for oboe and string orch. (1962); 2 violin concertos (1963, 1965); Trio for flute, clarinet and piano (1940–41); 2 string quartets (1941, 1947); 2 cello sonatas (1943, 1950); *2 Pieces* for wind quintet (1943); Duo for violin and cello (1946); Violin Sonata (1948); Quintet for flute, oboe, violin, viola and cello (1956); *2 Caprices* for flute and piano (1956); Sextet for flute, oboe, violin, viola, cello and harpsichord (1958); *Variations* for flute and harpsichord (1962); *Euterpe Suite* for 11 instruments (1964); piano pieces.

Ponselle (real name **Ponzillo**), **Carmela,** American mezzo-soprano, sister of **Rosa Ponselle;** b. Schenectady, N.Y., June 7, 1892; d. New York, June 13, 1977. She began to study singing rather late in life; made her professional debut in 1923; first appearance at the Metropolitan Opera House as Amneris in *Aida* (Dec. 5, 1925; remained on its roster until 1928; was reengaged for the seasons 1930–35; then devoted most of her time to teaching.

Ponselle (real name **Ponzillo**), **Rosa,** American soprano; b. Meriden, Conn., Jan. 22, 1897. She sang in various entertainment places in New Haven; then appeared with her sister **Carmela** in vaudeville in Pittsburgh. She made her first appearance as an opera singer at the Metropolitan Opera, N.Y., in the role of Leonora in *La Forza del Destino*, opposite Caruso (Nov. 15, 1918); remained with the Metropolitan Opera until 1936; received praise for her opulent voice, with fine low tones; her interpretations of the Italian roles were particularly impressive. In 1936 she married Carl Jackson, son of the former Baltimore mayor, and retired to the Baltimore suburb of Green Spring Valley. Her 80th birthday was celebrated there by friends in January 1977.
BIBLIOGRAPHY: Oscar Thompson, *The American Singer* (N.Y., 1937; pp. 335–46).

Pontécoulant, Louis-Adolphe le Doulcet, Marquis de, French writer on music; b. Paris, 1794; d. Bois-Colombe, near Paris, Feb. 20, 1882. After an adventurous career, he began the study of music history and the construction of instruments; publ. the following: *Essai*

sur la facture musicale considérée dans ses rapports avec l'art, l'industrie, et le commerce (1857; 2nd augmented ed., as *Organographie* in 2 parts, 1861); *Musée instrumental du Conservatoire de musique* (1864); *La Musique à l'Exposition universelle de 1867* (1868); and *Les Phénomènes de la musique* (1868).

Pontoglio, Cipriano, Italian composer; b. Grumello del Piano, Dec. 25, 1831; d. Milan, Feb. 22, 1892. He was a pupil of Ant. Cagnoni in Milan, and P. Serrao in Naples; then opened a music school in Milan. He composed 5 operas: *Lamberto Malatesta* (Pavia, 1857), *Tebaldo Brusato* (Brescia, 1865; rewritten as *L'Assedio di Brescia,* Rome, June 15, 1872), *La Schiava greca* (Bergamo, 1868), *La Notte di Natale* (Bergamo, Aug. 29, 1872), and *Edoardo Stuart* (Milan, May 21, 1887); publ. songs, piano pieces, etc.

Poole, Elizabeth, English mezzo-soprano; b. London, April 5, 1820; d. Langley, Bucks, Jan. 14, 1906. She made her debut at Drury Lane in 1834; sang in Italian opera in the U.S. (appearing with Malibran). Until her retirement in 1870 she was immensely popular as a ballad singer. Balfe wrote for her *'Tis gone, the past is all a dream,* which she introduced into *The Bohemian Girl.*

Poot, Marcel, remarkable Belgian composer; b. Vilvorde, near Brussels, May 7, 1901. He received his first musical training from his father; then studied at the Brussels Cons. with Sevenants, Lunssens and de Greef (1916–20) and at the Flemish Cons. of Antwerp with Lodewijk Mortelmans (1921–23); in the interim he also received guidance from Paul Gilson, and in 1925, with 7 other Gilson pupils (René Bernier, Gaston Brenta, Francis de Bourguignon, Theodore Dejoncker, Robert Otlet, Maurice Schoemaker and Jules Strens) founded the "Groupe des Synthétistes," dedicated to propaganda of new musical ideas; (the group disbanded in 1930). Also in 1925, Poot was co-founder, with Gilson, of *La Revue Musicale Belge,* to which he contributed until its dissolution in 1938. He was on the staff of the Brussels Cons. from 1938 to 1966, and its director from 1949 until his retirement. The most striking element of his music is its rhythmic vivacity; his harmony is well within the tonal sphere.
WORKS: a chamber opera, *Moretus* (1943; Brussels, 1944); radio plays (1933–36); 3 ballets: *Pâris et les trois divines* (1933), *Camera* (1937) and *Pygmalion* (1952); 2 oratorios: *Le Dit du routier* (1943) and *Icare* (1945). FOR ORCH.: *Variations en forme de danses* (1923); *Charlot,* 3 sketches inspired by Charlie Chaplin films (1926); *Rondo* for piano and small orch. (1928); *Capriccio* for oboe and orch. (1928); 4 symphonies (1929; *Triptyque symphonique,* 1938; 1952; 1970); *Poème de l'Espace,* symph. poem inspired by Lindbergh's flight (1929; Liège ISCM Fest., Sept. 4, 1930); *Jazz Music* (1930; Brussels, Feb. 21, 1932); *Fugato* (1931); *Ouverture joyeuse* (1934); *Allegro symphonique* (1935); *Fantaisie Rythmique* (1936); *Danse laudative* (1937); *Ballade* for string quartet and orch. (1937); *Impromptu en forme de rondo* (1937); *Légende épique* for piano and orch. (1938); *Suite* for small orch. (1940); *Ballade* for clarinet and orch. (1941); *Concertstück* for cello and orch. (1942); *Fantasia*

(1944); *3 Danses* (1945); Sinfonietta (1946; Chicago, Oct. 22, 1946); *Musique légère* (1946); *Mouvement symphonique* for wind orch. (1946); *Rhapsodie* (1947); *Divertimento* for small orch. (1952); *Ouverture Rhapsodique* for wind orch. (1952); *Mouvement perpétuel* (1953); *Ballade* for violin and orch. (1955); *Rondo Diabolique,* scherzo (1958); Piano Concerto (1959; Brussels, May 25, 1960; compulsory work for finalists of 1960 Queen Elisabeth piano competition won by Malcolm Frager); *2 Mouvements symphoniques* (1960); *Suite en forme de variations* (1962); *Concertstück* for violin and orch. (1962); *Concerto Grosso* for 11 strings (1962); *Music* for string orch. (1963); *Suite Anglaise* (1966); *Concerto Grosso* for piano quartet and orch. (1969); Cello Concertino (1971); Oboe Concertino (1972); Trumpet Concerto (1973). CHAMBER MUSIC: Viola Sonatina (1926); Piano Quartet (1932); *3 Pièces en trio* for piano trio (1935); *5 Bagatelles* for string quartet (1939); *Scherzo* for 4 saxophones (1941); *Divertimento* for oboe, clarinet and bassoon (1942); Octet for winds and strings (1948); String Quartet (1952); *Sarabande* for horn and piano (1953); *Ballade* for oboe, clarinet and bassoon (1954); *Fantaisie* for 6 clarinets (1955); Concertino for Wind Quintet (1958); *Légende* for horn and piano (1958); Concertino for Flute, Violin and Cello (1963); Concertino for 4 Saxophones (1963); *Musique* for wind quintet (1964); *Legende* for 4 clarinets or saxophones (1967); Quartet for 4 horns (1969); *Mosaïque* for 8 winds (1969); *Musique de chambre* for piano trio (1971); several *Ballades* and other pieces for solo instruments, with piano. FOR PIANO: Sonata (1927); *6 petites pièces* (1927); *6 petites pièces faciles* (1936); *6 petites pièces récréatives* (1937); *Suite* (1942); Sonatina (1945); *Variations* (1952); choral works and songs; film music.

Popov, Alexander, Bulgarian composer; b. Kolarovgrad, July 14, 1927. He studied composition with Veselin Stoyanov, at the Bulgarian State Cons., graduating in 1954; played viola in the orch. of the National Opera in Sofia; is a member of the "Sofia Soloists" Chamber Ensemble.
WORKS: 2 cantatas: *Cantata about the April Uprising* (1952) and *Land of Songs* (1969); *Suite* for orch. (1956); *Native Land,* variations for orch. (1958); *The Artist,* suite for string quartet and string orch. (1961); Sinfonietta (1964); *Concerto Grosso* for string orch. (1966); *Prelude and Dance* for orch. (1972); *Adagio* for orch. (1973); *Variants* for 13 strings (1973); 2 string quartets; choruses; songs.

Popov, Gavriil, outstanding and original Russian composer; b. Novocherkask, Sept. 12, 1904; d. Repino, near Leningrad, Feb. 17, 1972. He studied at the St. Petersburg Cons. with Nikolayev (piano) and Vladimir Shcherbachev (composition). From his student days, he adopted the procedures of modern music; his Septet (Moscow, Dec. 13, 1927) was written in a system of dissonant counterpoint then fashionable in Western Europe; his 1st Symph. (1927–34) was in a similar vein. When modern music became the target of attack in Russia, Popov modified his style towards a more popular conception, following the tenets of "socialist realism"; wrote several film scores, among them *Communist Youth Union, Leader of Electrifica-*

tion (1932); other works: Symph. No. 2, subtitled *Fatherland* (Moscow, Feb. 15, 1944); Symph. No. 3, for string orch., on Spanish themes (Moscow, Jan. 31, 1947); Symph. No. 4, *Glory Be to the Fatherland* (1949); Symph. No. 5 (1965); Symph. No. 6 (Moscow, Jan. 23, 1970); Organ Concerto (1970).

Popovici, Doru, Rumanian composer and musicologist; b. Reşiţa (Banat), Feb. 17, 1932. He studied at the Bucharest Cons. with P. Constantinescu, Negrea, Andricu, Rogalski, Jora and Vancea (1950–55); attended the annual, international summer courses in new music at Darmstadt; in 1968 was appointed director of the Rumanian Radio and Television.
WORKS: 2 one-act operas: *Prometeu* (*Prometheus,* 1958; Bucharest, Dec. 16, 1964) and *Mariana Pineda,* after García Lorca (1966; Bucharest, Dec. 22, 1966); cantatas, *Porumbeii morţii* (1957), *Noapte de August* for baritone and orch. (1959) and *Omagiu lui Palestrina* for female chorus and orch. (1966); *Triptyque* for orch. (1955); *2 Symphonic Sketches* (1955); Concertino for String Orch. (1956); Concerto for Orch. (1960); 4 symphonies: No. 1 (1962); No. 2, *Spielberg* (1966); No. 3, *Bizantina,* for chorus and orch. (1968); and No. 4, for chorus and orch. (1973); *Poem bizantin* for orch. (1968); *Codex Cajoni* for string orch. (1968); Cello Sonata (1952); Violin Sonata (1953); String Quartet No. 1 (1954, revised 1964); *Fantasy "Orphée"* for string trio (1955); Sonata for 2 cellos (1960); Sonata for 2 violas (1965); *Omagiu lui Tuculescu,* quintet for piano, violin, viola, cello and clarinet (1967); *Musique solennelle* for violin and piano (1969); Piano Sonatina (1953); choruses; songs. He publ. 6 books, all in Bucharest: *Muzica corală românească* (1966), *Începuturile muzicii culte româneşti* (with Miereanu, 1967), *Gesualdo di Venosa* (1969), *Muzica românească contemporană* (1970), *Cîntec flamand. Şcoala muzicală neerlandeză* (1971) and *Muzica elisabethană* (1972).

Popper, David, famous Czech cellist and composer; b. Prague, Dec. 9, 1843; d. Baden, near Vienna, Aug. 7, 1913. He studied cello with Goltermann at the Prague Cons.; began his career with a highly successful appearance as soloist at the Karlsruhe Music Festival on March 29, 1865; from 1868 to 1873 he was 1st cellist of the Vienna Court Orch. In 1872 he married the famous pianist **Sophie Menter,** but they were divorced 14 years later. From 1896 until his death he taught cello at the Budapest Cons. He wrote a number of extremely attractive and marvelously idiomatic pieces for the cello, which remained in the international repertoire, among them *Sérénade orientale, Gavotte, Tarentelle, Elfentanz, Im Walde, Ungarische Rhapsodie;* also a *Requiem* for 3 cellos (performed by him, with Delsart and Howell in London, Nov. 25, 1891); he also published the cello studies, *Hohe Schule des Violoncellspiels* (40 studies) and, as a preparatory book of easy pieces, *10 mittelschwere grosse Etüden.*

Poradowski, Stefan, Polish composer and music pedagogue; b. Wloclawek, Aug. 16, 1902; d. Poznań, July 9, 1967. He studied composition with Opieński at the Poznań Cons. (1922–26); then took private lessons with Rezniček in Berlin (1929). Returning to Poland, he taught composition and theory at the Poznań Cons. (1930–39 and 1945–67); also gave courses (after 1956) at the Cons. in Wroclaw.

WORKS: Opera, *Flames* (1966); a Passion play, *Odkupienie (Redemption)* for mezzo-soprano, chorus and orch. (1941); *Koń Światowida (The Horse of Sviatovid)*, fantastic poem for tenor, baritone, chorus and orch. (1931); *Spring Song,* cantata (1926); Sinfonietta (1925); *Concerto antico* for viola d'amore and orch. (1925); *Triptych* for string orch. (1926); 7 symphonies (1928; 1930; 1932; 1934; 1938; 1952; 1958); Double Bass Concerto (1929); *Capriccio on a Theme by Kreutzer* for string orch. (1930); *Serenada klasyczna* for string orch. (1949); *Rapsodia polska* for violin and orch. (1944); *Ratusz poznański (The Townhall of Poznań)*, symph. poem (1950); Concerto for Flute, Harp and String Orch. (1954); 4 string quartets (1923; 1923; 1936; 1947); Violin Sonata (1925); 5 trios: *I* and *II* for violin, viola and double bass (1929, 1930), *III* for string trio (1935), *IV* for 3 double basses (1952) and *V* for string trio (1955). He publ. the textbooks *Nauka harmonii (Science of Harmony,* Poznań, 1931); 5th ed., Warsaw, 1964); *Sztuka pisania kanonów (Art of Writing Canons,* Poznań, 1965).

Porcelijn, David, Dutch composer; b. Friesland, Jan. 7, 1947. He studied flute with Frans Vester (1964–68) and composition with Kees van Baaren and Jan van Vlijmen (1966–70) at the Royal Cons. of The Hague; later took lessons in conducting with Michel Tabachnik in Geneva. A modernist par excellence, Porcelijn makes explorations in every direction, his music ranges from the infraclassical to ultramathematical.

WORKS: *4 Interpretations* for various instruments (1967–69); *Continuations* for 11 wind instruments (1968); *Combinations* for 26 solo instruments (1969–70); *Requiem,* in memory of Varèse, for percussion ensemble (1969–70); *Zen* for solo flute (1970); *1000 Frames* for 1+ wind instruments and/or 1+ pianos (1970); *Confrontation and Indoctrinations* for jazz band and 19 instruments (Scheveningen, June 23, 1972); *Cybernetic Object* for orch. (The Hague, June 18, 1971); *Amoeba* for x flutes (1971); *Pole,* ballet for 26 instruments (1971–72); *10-5-6-5(a)* for 2 string quartets, wind quintet and 2 vibraphones (1972); *Pulverizations I* for 52 strings (1972); *Pulverizations* for wind quintet (1972); *Pulverizations II* for alto saxophone, 22 winds, 5 percussion groups and 52 strings (1973); Concerto for Flute, Harp and Orch. (1973); Flute Concerto (1975); *Shades* for flute, violin and viola (1975); *Rhythm Song* for male chorus and percussion (1976); *Into the Earth* for 14 brass and 2 percussionists (1976).

Porges, Heinrich, writer on music; b. Prague, Nov. 25, 1837; d. Munich, Nov. 17, 1900. He was a pupil of Cölestin Müller (piano) and Zwonař (theory). In 1863 he became co-editor (with Brendel) of the *Neue Zeitschrift für Musik,* and was in close contact with Wagner; in 1867 he was called to Munich by King Ludwig II, for whom he had written a study on *Tristan und Isolde* (publ. 1906 by Hans von Wolzogen).

WRITINGS: *Die Aufführung von Beethovens 9. Symphonie unter Richard Wagner in Bayreuth* (1872), *Die Bühnenproben zu den 1876er Festspielen* (1877), and other essays on Wagner in German periodicals.

Porpora, Nicola Antonio, famous Italian composer and singing teacher; b. Naples, Aug. 17, 1686; d. there, March 3, 1768. The son of a bookseller, he entered the Cons. dei Poveri at Naples at the age of 10 and studied with Gaetano Greco, Matteo Giordano, and Ottavio Campanile. Porpora's first opera, *Agrippina,* was presented at the Royal Palace of Naples (Nov. 4, 1708); Cardinal Grimani attended the performance and wrote a libretto on the same subject for Handel. This episode gave rise to the incorrect statement (by Fétis and others) that Handel heard Porpora's opera in Rome in 1710. Porpora produced in Naples 2 more operas: *Flavio Anicio Olibrio* (1711) and *Basilio, re d'oriente* (1713). From 1711 until 1725, he held the title of maestro di cappella to Philip, Landgrave of Hesse-Darmstadt. He gained a great reputation as a singing teacher, and numbered among his pupils the famous castrati Farinelli, Caffarelli, Antonio Uberti (who called himself "Porporino" out of respect for his teacher), and Salimbeni. Metastasio, who wrote librettos for several of Porpora's operas, was also his pupil. Porpora's career as a singing teacher was divided between Naples and Venice. In Naples he taught at the Conservatories of Sant' Onofrio (1715–22 and 1760–61) and Santa Maria di Loreto (1739–41 and 1760–61); in Venice he gave lessons at the Ospedali degli Incurabili (1726–33 and 1737–39), the Ospedali della Pietà (1742–46), and the Ospedaletto (1746–47). In 1718 Porpora collaborated with Domenico Scarlatti in the writing of the opera *Berenice, regina d'Egitto,* produced in Rome (1718). At about this time he succeeded in obtaining support from the Austrian court. His opera *Temistocle* was produced in Vienna on the Emperor's birthday (Oct. 1, 1718); his next opera, *Faramondo,* was staged in Naples (Nov. 19, 1719). He continued to write operas for theaters in Naples and Rome: *Eumene* (Rome, 1721); *Adelaide* (Rome, 1723); *Semiramide, regina dell'Assiria* (Naples, 1724); *Didone abbandonata* (his first opera to a libretto by Metastasio; produced at Reggio, 1725). In 1726 he settled in Venice. He wrote the following operas during the next 8 years: *Meride e Selinunte* (Venice, 1726); *Siroe, re di Persia* (Milan, 1726); *Semiramide riconosciuta* (Venice, 1729); *Mitridate* (Rome, 1730); *Tamerlano* (1730); *Poro* (Turin, 1731); *Germanico in Germania* (Rome, 1732); *Issipile* (Rome, 1733). In 1733 he applied for the post of maestro di cappella at San Marco in Venice, but failed to obtain it. In the same year he was engaged by the directors of the "Opera of the Nobility" in London (organized as a rival company to that of Handel). For this venture Porpora wrote 5 operas: *Arianna in Nasso* (Dec. 29, 1733), *Enea nel Lazio* (May 11, 1734), *Polifemo* (Feb. 1, 1735), *Ifigenia in Aulide* (May 3, 1735), and *Mitridate* (Jan. 24, 1736; a different score from the earlier opera of the same title). For a while he competed successfully with Handel, but soon the "Opera of the Nobility" began to falter, and Porpora left London on the eve of the company's collapse. From 1747–51, he was in Dresden as singing teacher to the Electoral Princess. There he became Hasse's competitor for the position of musical director. Although Hasse himself conducted Porpora's "pastoral drama" *Filandro* (Dresden, July 18, 1747), their relationship was made difficult by the intrigues of Hasse's wife, the singer Faustina Bordoni. In 1751 Porpora left Dresden for Vienna, where he became the teacher of Haydn, who paid for his lessons by serving Porpora as accompanist and personal helper. Porpora returned to Naples in 1758. His last stage work, *Il Trionfo di Camilla* (Naples, May 30, 1760; a revision and adaptation to a new text of an earlier opera of the same title produced in Naples on Jan. 20, 1740), was unsuccessful. He wrote, all told, 44 operas, 11 oratorios, and numerous Masses and motets. His instrumental music includes 6 *sinfonie da camera* (London, 1735), 12 violin sonatas (Vienna, 1754), a cello concerto, and a cello sonata. The fugues in Clementi's *Practical Harmony* are from Porpora's violin sonatas, some of which have been published by A. Schering, F. David, D. Alard, and A. Moffat. A trio sonata was publ. in Riemann's *Collegium Musicum* (no. 23).

BIBLIOGRAPHY: Marchese di Villarosa, *Memorie dei compositori di musica del regno di Napoli* (Naples, 1840); F. Clément, *Les Musiciens célèbres depuis le XVIe siècle* (Paris, 1868); S. Fassini, *Il Melodramma italiano a Londra* (Turin, 1914); S. di Giacomo, *I quattro antiche Conservatorii di musica di Napoli* (Palermo, 1925); F. Walker, *A Chronology of the Life and Works of Nicola Porpora*, in *Italian Studies* (vol. 6, Cambridge, 1951); U. Prota-Giurleo, "Per una esatta biografia di Nicolo Porpora," *La Scala* (Jan. 1957; establishing for the first time his dates of birth and death).

Porrino, Ennio, Italian composer; b. Cagliari, Sardinia, Jan. 20, 1910; d. Rome, Sept. 25, 1959; studied at the Santa Cecilia in Rome with Mulè, and later took an additional course with Respighi. He subsequently taught at Santa Cecilia; in 1954 became prof. of composition at the Naples Cons.

WORKS: 1-act opera *Gli Orazi* (Milan, 1941); the ballet *Altair* (Naples, 1942); for orch.: *Tartarin de Tarascon*, overture (Rome, 1933), *Sardegna*, symph. poem, based on Sardinian folk themes (Rome, 1933; his most popular work), *3 Canzoni italiane*; *Sonata drammatica* for piano and orch.; *I Canti della Sardegna* for voice and orch. (1948); songs.

Porro, Pierre-Jean, famous French guitar virtuoso; b. Béziers, 1750; d. Montmorency, May 31, 1831. Through his influence the guitar became a fashionable instrument in Paris; he had a class of pupils there; also was editor and publisher of *Journal de Guitarre* (1787-1803). He publ. a guitar method, *Tableau Méthodique*, numerous divertissements, sonatas, canzonets, for guitar solo and with other instruments; also *Collection de musique sacrée* for 4 mixed voices and organ.

BIBLIOGRAPHY: F. Donnadieu, *Porro, compositeur et éditeur de musique* (Béziers, 1897).

Porsile, Giuseppe, Italian composer; b. Naples, May 5, 1680; d. Vienna, May 29, 1750. He served as maestro di cappella in Naples and later in Barcelona; from 1720 to 1749, was singing master at the Vienna court, and composer to the Austrian Empress Amalia. He wrote the operas *Meride e Selinunte* (performed at Laxenburg, near Vienna, Aug. 28, 1721), *Spartaco* (Vienna, Feb. 21, 1726), and 4 others; 12 oratorios, various cantatas; instrumental pieces.

Porta, Costanzo, important Italian composer; b. Cremona, c.1529; d. Padua, May 19, 1601. He studied with Willaert in Venice; was chorusmaster at Osimo, near Ancona, from 1552 to 1564. In 1565 he became choirmaster at the Basilica of St. Anthony in Padua; in 1567 received a similar post at the Cathedral of Ravenna; in 1575 was in Loreto, returning to Padua in 1574. He was highly esteemed as a master contrapuntist; wrote not only sacred music but also madrigals; combined great technical skill with a characteristically Italian grace of melodic line.

WORKS: Books of motets *a* 4 (1559), *a* 5 (1555), *a* 6 (1585), *a* 4-8 (1580); 1 book of Masses for 4, 5, 6 voices (1578); 2 books of Introits for 5 voices (1566, 1588); 4 books of madrigals for 4, 5 voices (1555-85); hymns for 4 voices (posthumous, 1602); vesper psalms and canticles for 8 voices (1605); in MS are various madrigals, Lamentations, a treatise on counterpoint, etc. Reprints are in Torchi's *L'Arte musicale in Italia* (vol. 1), Einstein's *The Golden Age of the Madrigal* (N.Y., 1942), etc.

BIBLIOGRAPHY: G. Reese, *Music in the Renaissance* (N.Y., 1954); A. Garbelotto, *Il Padre Costanzo Porta da Cremona* (Rome, 1955; a documented biography).

Porter, Cole, remarkable American composer of popular music; b. Peru, Indiana, June 9, 1891; d. Santa Monica, Calif., Oct. 15, 1964. He was educated at Yale Univ. (B.A. 1913); then took academic courses at the Harvard Law School, and later at the Harvard School of Music. While at Yale Univ., he wrote football songs (*Yale Bull Dog Song, Bingo Eli Yale*, etc.); also composed music for college functions. His first production in N.Y. was *See America First* (1916). There followed a cascade of musical comedies for which he wrote both the lyrics and the music, that placed him in the front rank in the American Musical Theater. He was a master of subtle expression without sentimentality, a kinetic dash without vulgarity and a natural blend of word poetry with the finest of harmonious melodies.

WORKS: *Kitchy-Koo* (1919), *50 Million Frenchmen* (1929), *Gay Divorcee* (1932), *Anything Goes* (1934), *Jubilee* (1935), *Red Hot and Blue* (1936), *Leave It to Me* (1938), *Dubarry Was a Lady* (1939), *Panama Hattie* (1940), *Let's Face It* (1941), *Something for the Boys* (1943), *Mexican Hayride* (1944), *Kiss Me, Kate* (1948), *Out of This World* (1950), *Can-Can* (1954), and *Silk Stockings* (1955). Of his many songs, at least half a dozen became great favorites: *Begin the Beguine, It's De-Lovely, Night and Day, My Heart Belongs to Daddy, Don't Fence Me In, Wunderbar*, etc.

BIBLIOGRAPHY: G. Eells, *The Life That Late He Led. A Biography of Cole Porter* (N.Y., 1967); R. Kimball and B. Gill, *Cole* (a pictorial biography; N.Y., 1971); L. Siebert, *Cole Porter: An Analysis of 5 Musical Comedies and a Thematic Index of the Complete Works* (City Univ. of N.Y., 1975); Charles Schwartz, *Cole Porter* (N.Y., 1977; a "candid" biography; conclusively debunks the story that Cole Porter ever served in the French Army, let alone the French Legion, as was claimed for him). *Night and Day,* a motion picture musical biography of Cole Porter, starring Cary Grant in the role of Porter, was produced by Warner Bros. in 1946.

Porter, Quincy, American composer; b. New Haven, Conn., Feb. 7, 1897; d. Bethany, Conn., Nov. 12, 1966. He was brought up in an intellectual atmosphere; his father and his grandfather were professors at Yale Univ. He studied with David Stanley Smith and Horatio Parker at the Yale School of Music (Mus. Bac., 1921); submitted a violin concerto for the American Prix de Rome, received an honorable mention; also won the Steinert and Osborne prizes. After graduation he went to Paris, where he took courses with Lucien Capet (violin) and Vincent d'Indy (composition). Returning to America, he earned a living as a violinist in theater orchestras in N.Y.; then took an additional course in composition with Ernest Bloch. He taught at the Cleveland Institute of Music (1922–28 and 1931–32); played the viola in the Ribaupierre String Quartet there; spent 3 years in Paris on a Guggenheim Fellowship (1928–31); was prof. at Vassar College, and conductor of the Vassar Orch. (1932–38); in 1938 succeeded Frederick Converse as dean of the New England Cons., Boston; from 1942 to 1946 was its director. In 1946 he was appointed prof. at Yale Univ. His music is built on strong contrapuntal lines, with incisive rhythms; his harmonic procedures often reach stridently polytonal sonorities; the general idiom combines the influences of both the modern German and the modern French styles.
WORKS: *Ukrainian Suite,* for string orch. (Rochester, N.Y., May 1, 1925); Suite in C minor for orch. (1926); *Poem and Dance,* for orch. (Cleveland, June 24, 1932, composer conducting); *Dance in Three-Time,* for chamber orch. (St. Louis, July 2, 1937); Symph. No. 1 (N.Y., April 2, 1938, composer conducting); *Music for Strings* (1941); *Fantasy on a Pastoral Theme,* for organ and string orch. (1942); Viola Concerto (Columbia Univ. Festival, N.Y., May 16, 1948); *Fantasy* for cello and small orch. (1950); *The Desolate City,* for baritone and orch. (1950); *Concerto Concertante* for 2 pianos and orch. (Louisville, March 17, 1954; awarded the Pulitzer Prize); *New England Episodes,* symph. suite (commissioned for the Inter-American Music Festival, Washington, D.C., April 18, 1958); Symph. No. 2 (Louisville, Jan. 14, 1964); 10 string quartets (1923, 1925, 1930, 1931, 1935, 1937, 1943, 1950, 1955, 1965); *In Monasterio,* for string quartet (1927); Quintet for clarinet and strings (1929); *Quintet on a Childhood Theme,* for flute and strings (1940); String Sextet on Slavic folk tunes (1947); 2 violin sonatas (1926, 1929); *Little Trio,* for flute, violin, and viola (1928); Suite for viola alone (1930); Sonata for French horn and piano (1946); 4 pieces for violin and piano (1947); Duo for violin and viola (1954); Duo for flute and harp (1957); Piano Sonata (1930); *Canon and Fugue* for organ (1941); *6 Miniatures* for piano (1943); *Day Dreams* for piano (1957); several songs.
BIBLIOGRAPHY: H. Elwell, "Quincy Porter," Modern Music XXIII/1; H. Boatwright, "Quincy Porter," *American Composers Alliance Bulletin* (1957).

Portugal (Portogallo), Marcos Antonio da Fonseca (real name **Ascenção**), Portuguese composer; b. Lisbon, March 24, 1762; d. Rio de Janeiro, Feb. 7, 1830. A pupil at the ecclesiastical seminary at Lisbon, his musical education was continued under the operatic singer Borselli (singing and composition), by whose influence he was appointed cembalist at the Madrid opera in 1782. Between 1784 and 1791 he wrote for Lisbon 17 stage works, mostly ephemeral. His reputation was made in Italy, where, with the exception of a short visit to Lisbon, he lived from 1793 to 1799, bringing out 22 Italian operas. From 1799 to 1810 he acted as conductor at the San Carlos Theater, Lisbon, producing Italian and Portuguese operas. His *Il Filosofo seducente, ossia Non irritar le donne* (Venice, Dec. 27, 1798), was selected by Napoleon for opening the Théâtre Italien at Paris in 1801. In 1807 the royal family fled to Brazil before the French invasion; Portugal remained until the San Carlos Theater was closed in 1810, and then followed the court to Rio de Janeiro, where he was made general music director. The royal theater of São João, after its inauguration in 1813, produced several new operas by Portugal. In that year he became director of the new Cons. at Vera Cruz, jointly with his brother **Simão;** visited Italy in 1815, returned to Rio de Janeiro, and passed his last years there as an invalid. His masterpiece is generally assumed to be *Fernando nel Messico* (Venice, Jan. 16, 1798; written for the famous English singer Elizabeth Billington; produced in London, in Italian, March 31, 1803); other Italian operas that had a favorable reception were *Demofoonte* (Milan, Feb. 8, 1794); *Le Donne cambiate* (Venice, Oct. 22, 1797); of Portuguese operas, *A Castanheira (The Chestnut Seller),* produced in Lisbon in 1790, enjoyed considerable popular success. He further wrote about 100 sacred works.
BIBLIOGRAPHY: Manoel Carvalhães, *Marcos Portugal na sua musica dramatica* (Lisbon, 1910).

Porumbescu, Ciprian, Rumanian composer; b. Sipote, Oct. 14, 1853; d. Stupca, Bukovina, June 6, 1883. After preliminary studies in Rumania, he went to Vienna where he became a student of Bruckner; published a collection of "social songs of Rumanian students" (Vienna, 1880); composed an operetta *Cral Nou (The New King)* to a Rumanian libretto, and many songs. His death at the age of 29 deprived Rumania of the country's first national composer, but he is greatly revered as such. The town of Stupca where he died has been renamed Ciprian Porumbescu, and his name is attached to the official designation of several Rumanian conservatories.

Pospíšil, Juraj, Slovak composer; b. Olomouc, Jan. 14, 1931. He first studied music in his home town; then with Petrželka at the Janáček Academy in Brno and later with Alexander Moyzes and Cikker at the Bratislava Music Academy.
WORKS: *Mountains and People,* symph. poem (1955); *Margita and Besná,* ballad for soloists, chorus and orch. (1955); Cello Sonata (1956); 2 symphonies: No. 1 (1957) and No. 2, *Nebula in Andromeda* (1963); Sonata for Strings (1961); Trombone Concerto (1962); *Passacaglia and Fugue* for organ (1962); *Mikropoviedky (Micro-stories)* for soprano, flute, violin and

cello (1963); *Glosy (Marginal Notes)* for wind quintet (1964); *Protirečenia (Contradictions)* for piano quartet (1964); *Music* for 12 strings (1965); Double Bass Sonata (1966); Solo Violin Sonata (1966); *Trojversia (3 Verses)* for 9 instruments (1966); String Quartet (1970); Flute Quartet (1971); *Bagatelles* for trombone and piano (1972); *Concerto Eroico* for horn and orch. (1975); *Fragment* for orch. (Košice, Oct. 4, 1976); *Symphonic Fresco* (1976); *Little Pieces* for clarinet and piano (1976).

Posselt, Ruth, American violinist; b. Medford, Mass., Sept. 6, 1914. She studied with Emanuel Ondricek; has given numerous recitals in America and Europe; gave the world premières of violin concertos by Walter Piston, Vladimir Dukelsky, Edward Burlingame Hill, and others. On July 3, 1940 she married **Richard Burgin.**

Poston, Elizabeth, English pianist and composer; b. Highfield, Hertfordshire, Oct. 24, 1905. She studied piano with Harold Samuel; during World War II was in charge of music in the European Service of the BBC in London. She has a strong predilection for the Elizabethan period; her stylizations of old song patterns are adroitly made and preserve an authentic modality of the originals.
WORKS: *The Holy Child,* for chorus, vocal soloists, and string orch. (1950); *Concertino da Camera on a Theme of Martin Peerson* for ancient instruments (1950); *The Nativity* for chorus, vocal soloists, and string orch. or organ (1951); Trio for flute, clarinet or viola, and piano (1958); *Peter Halfpenny's Tunes* for recorder and piano (1959); *Lullaby* and *Fiesta,* 2 pieces for piano (1960); *Magnificat* for 4 solo voices and organ (1961); *3 Scottish Carols* for chorus, and strings or organ (1969); *Harlow Concertante* for string quartet and string orch. (1969); *An English Day Book* for mixed voices, and harp (1971); Sonatina for cello and piano (1972); she compiled several books of hymn tunes and Christmas carols.

Pothier, Dom Joseph, learned authority on Gregorian chant, b. Bouzemont, near Saint-Dié, Dec. 7, 1835; d. Conques, Belgium, Dec. 8, 1923. He became a Benedictine monk in 1859 at Solesmes; 1862, sub-prior; 1866, prof. of theology at the Solesmes Monastery; 1895, prior at the Benedictine monastery of St.-Wandrille; 1898, abbot there. When the religious orders were banned from France, he moved to Belgium. In 1904 he was appointed by Pius X president of the publication committee of the *Editio Vaticana.*
WRITINGS: *Les Mélodies grégoriennes* (highly important source book, based on the study of original MSS; Tournai, 1880; 3rd ed., 1890; in German, 1881; in Italian, 1890); *Méthode du chant grégorien* (Paris, 1902). Was a chief editor of *Liber Gradualis* (Tournai, 1883; *Hymni de Tempore et de Sanctis* (Solesmes, 1885); *Processionale Monasticum* (Solesmes, 1888); *Liber Antiphonarius* (Solesmes, 1891); *Liber Responsorialis* (Solesmes, 1895); *Cantus Mariales* (Paris, 1902). He contributed many valuable articles to the *Revue du Chant Grégorien.*
BIBLIOGRAPHY: F. Velluz, *Étude bibibliographique sur les mélodies grégoriennes de Dom Joseph Pothier* (Grenoble, 1881); N. Rousseau, *L'École grégorienne de Solesmes* (Tournai, 1911); A. Le. Guennant, *Précis de rythmique grégorienne d'après les principes de Solesmes* (Paris, 1948); M. Blanc, *L'Enseignement musical de Solesmes* (Paris, 1953; chap. 2).

Potter, Philip Cipriani Hambly, English pianist and composer; b. London, Oct. 2, 1792; d. there, Sept. 26, 1871. He studied music first with his father; then with Attwood, Callcott, and Crotch; also took piano lessons with Woelffl during the latter's sojourn in England. In 1817 he went to Vienna, where he studied composition with Aloys Förster; he met Beethoven, who gave him good advice. He traveled in Germany and Italy; returned to London in 1821; the following year he became piano teacher at the Royal Academy of Music; succeeded Crotch as principal in 1832; retired in 1859. From 1855 to 1870 he was conductor of the Madrigal Society. He frequently appeared in London as pianist; introduced 3 of Beethoven's concertos (Nos. 1, 3, 4) to England. He publ. a number of piano pieces, including a set of variations under the title *The Enigma* comprising "variations in the style of 5 eminent artists." This early anticipation of the famous work by Elgar was not known to Elgar himself. He wrote 10 symphonies, 4 overtures, 3 piano concertos, 4 piano sonatas and other pieces. Wagner conducted one of Potter's symphonies during his engagement with the London Philharmonic Society in 1855. Potter ed. for Novello a series of Mozart's piano works.
BIBLIOGRAPHY: *Dictionary of National Biography* (vol. 46).

Poueigh, Jean (Marie-Octave-Géraud), French composer and writer on music; b. Toulouse, Feb. 24, 1876; d. Olivet (Loiret), Oct. 14, 1958. After music study in his native city, he entered the Paris Cons. as a student of Caussade, Lenepveu, and Gabriel Fauré; also received advice from Vincent d'Indy; settled in Paris. He harmonized and edited a number of folksongs of Languedoc and Gascogne in *Les Chansons de France* (1907–08), *3 Chansons des Pays d'Oc,* and *14 Chansons anciennes;* also ed. the collection *Chansons populaires des Pyrénées françaises* (vol. 1, 1926). His original compositions include the operas *Les Lointains* (1903), *Le Meneur de louves* (1921), *Perkin,* a Basque legend (Bordeaux, Jan. 16, 1931), *Le Roi de Camargue* (Marseilles, May 12, 1948), *Bois-brûlé* (1956); ballets: *Fünn* (1906), *Frivolant* (Paris Opéra, May 1, 1922), and a Moroccan ballet, *Chergui;* a symph. tableau, *La Basilique aux vainqueurs;* piano pieces and songs. Under the pen-name of **Octave Séré** he publ. *Musiciens français d' aujourd'hui* (Paris, 1911; 7th ed., 1921); contributed numerous articles to various French periodicals.

Pougin, Arthur (pen name of **François-Auguste-Arthur Paroisse-Pougin**), French writer and critic; b. Châteauroux, Indre, Aug. 6, 1834; d. Paris, Aug. 8, 1921. He was a pupil of Alard (violin) and Reber (harmony) at the Paris Cons.; 1855, conductor of the Théâtre Beaumarchais; 1856–59, assistant conductor of the Folies-Nouvelles; till 1863, violinist in the Opéra-Comique orch.; then devoted himself to musical journalism; in his articles he fulminated against Debussy and other "anarchistes de musique," as he described the modern French composers; but he was brilliant even at his most outrageous stolidity of judgment. He was music critic for *Le Ménestrel, Le Soir, La Tribune, L'Evénement,* and the *Journal Officiel.* He started the *Revue de la Musique* in 1876, but it ran for only 6 months; published many biographical sketches and essays: *André Campra* (1861), *Gresnick* (1862), *Dezèdes* (1862), *Floquet* (1863), *Martini* (1864), *Devienne* (1864; all six are collected as *Musiciens français du XVIIIᵉ siècle*); *Verdi* (1886; in English, 1887); edited an *Almanach de la musique* (1866, 1867, 1868; the last two with necrological supplements); *Dictionnaire historique et pittoresque théâtre* (1885); *Méhul* (1889; 2nd ed., 1893); *L'Opéra-Comique pendant la Révolution* (1891); *Essai historique sur la musique en Russie* (1896; 2nd ed., 1904; in English, 1915); *J.–J. Rousseau, musicien* (1901); *Musiciens du XIXᵉ siècle* (1911); *Marie Malibran* (in English, 1911); *Marietta Alboni* (1912); *Massenet* (1914); *Giuseppina Grassini* (1920); *Le Violon, les violonistes, et la musique de violon du XVIᵉ au XVIIIᵉ siècle* (posthumous, 1924). Pougin wrote for Larousse's *Grand Dictionnaire Universel* all the articles on music. He likewise edited the supplement to Fétis' *Biographie universelle* (2 vols., 1878–80), and the new edition of the *Dictionnaire lyrique, ou histoire des opéras* of Félix Clément and P. Larousse (Paris, 1898; with supplement up to 1904).

Poulenc, Francis, brilliant French composer; b. Paris, Jan. 7, 1899; d. there, Jan. 30, 1963. He studied piano with Ricardo Viñes and composition with Koechlin; at the age of 18 he joined a group of progressive French musicians, which presented concerts as "Nouveaux Jeunes," out of which developed the "Groupe des Six." Poulenc was mainly influenced by Satie and Ravel; his early works pursued the aim of sophisticated entertainment; a professional pianist himself, he developed in his piano pieces a highly idiomatic style in a modern vein; like Ravel, he successfully revived the classical keyboard style in a new guise. His songs are also notable; the melodic line is always lucid, while the accompaniments, although elaborate, are never obtrusive. He frequently appeared in joint recitals with the tenor Pierre Bernac, in Europe and in America.

WORKS: *Le Gendarme incompris,* comédie-bouffe (1920); *Les Mamelles de Tirésias,* opéra-bouffe (Opéra-Comique, June 3, 1947); *Les Dialogues des Carmélites,* religious opera (La Scala, Milan, Jan. 26, 1957); *La Voix humaine,* one-act lyric tragedy for soprano solo (Paris, Feb. 9, 1959); *La Dame de Monte Carlo,* lyric scene for voice and orch. (Paris, Dec. 5, 1961); *Les Biches,* ballet (Diaghilev's Ballets Russes, Monte Carlo, Jan. 6, 1924); *Animaux modèles,* ballet (Paris Opéra, Aug. 8, 1942); *Figure humaine,* cantata (London, March 25, 1945); *Rapsodie nègre,* for small orch. (1917); *Aubade,* for piano and 18 instruments (Paris, June 19, 1929); *Deux marches et un intermède,* for chamber orch. (BBC, London, June 6, 1938); *Concert champêtre,* for harpsichord and small orch. (Paris, May 3, 1929); Concerto for 2 Pianos and Orch. (1932); Concerto for Organ, String Orch., and Kettledrums (Paris, June 10, 1941); Piano Concerto (Boston, Jan. 6, 1950, composer soloist); *Sept répons des*

ténèbres, for soprano, chorus, and orch. (N.Y., April 11, 1963). CHAMBER MUSIC: Sonata for 2 clarinets (1918), *Le Bestiaire,* for voice, flute, clarinet, bassoon, and string quartet (1919); Sonata for clarinet and bassoon (1922), Sonata for horn, trumpet, and trombone (1922), Trio for oboe, bassoon, and piano (1926), Sextet for flute, oboe, clarinet, bassoon, horn, and piano (1930–32), *Le Bal masqué,* for voice with instruments (1932), String Quartet (1946), Violin Sonata (1943); Cello Sonata (1948); Flute Sonata (1956); Oboe Sonata (1962); Clarinet Sonata (1962). CHORAL WORKS: Sécheresses for chorus and orch. (1937); 2 books of traditional French songs, arranged for chorus a cappella (1945), *Stabat Mater,* for chorus a cappella (Strasbourg Festival, June 13, 1951); *Gloria,* for soprano, chorus and orch. (Boston, Jan. 20, 1961; one of his most famous and most frequently performed compositions); incidental music for plays; film scores; many piano pieces, of which the earliest, *Mouvements perpétuels* (1918), is the most popular; other piano pieces are *Promenades, 12 Improvisations, Suite française,* etc.; Sonata for 2 pianos (1918). SONG CYCLES: *Le Bestiaire* (1919), *Cocardes* (1919), *Poèmes de Ronsard* (1925), *Chansons gaillardes* (1926), *Airs chantés* (1928), *8 Chansons polonaises* (1934), *4 Chansons pour enfants* (1935), *Tel jour telle nuit* (1937), *Fiançailles pour rire* (1939), *Banalités* (1940), *Chansons villageoises* (1942); separate songs: *Épitaphe, Ronsard à sa guitare, Miroirs brûlants, Le Portrait, La Grenouillère, Priez pour paix, Ce donc petit visage, Bleuet, Les Chemins d'amour, Montparnasse et Hyde Park; Histoire de Babar le petit éléphant,* for narration and piano (1940); etc. He wrote a monograph on Chabrier (Paris, 1961); his reminiscences, *Moi et mes amis,* were published posthumously (Paris, 1963); another posthumous publication was *Journal de mes mélodies* (Paris, 1964).

BIBLIOGRAPHY: A. Schaeffner, "Francis Poulenc, musicien français," *Contrepoints* 1 (1946); C. Rostand, *Francis Poulenc: Entretiens avec Claude Rostand* (Paris, 1954); Henri Hell, *Poulenc, musicien français* (Paris, 1958); Pierre Bernac, *Francis Poulenc* (N.Y., 1977).

Poulet, Gaston, French violinist and conductor; b. Paris, April 10, 1892; d. Draveil (Essonne), April 14, 1974. He studied violin at the Paris Cons., gaining 1st prize; organized a string quartet and gave concerts in Europe; from1927 to 1936 conducted the Concerts Poulet at the Théâtre Sarah-Bernhardt in Paris; also taught at the Paris Cons.; in 1932 became director of the Cons. of Bordeaux and conducted the Orchestre Philharmonique there; from 1940 to 1945 conducted the Concerts Colonne in Paris; guest conductor with the London Symph. (1947) and in Germany (1948); also in South America. He played the violin in the 1st performance of Debussy's Violin Sonata with Debussy himself at the piano.

Poulet, Gérard, French violinist, son of **Gaston Poulet;** b. Bayonne, Aug. 12, 1938. He entered the Paris Cons. at the age of 11 in the class of André Asselin, and won 1st prize at 12; in the same year (1950) he played 3 violin concertos with the Orchestre Colonne, under his father's direction; then appeared with other

Paris orchestras; subsequently gave concerts and played with orchestras in England, Holland, Germany, Italy, Austria, and Holland. In 1956 he won 1st Grand Prix at the Paganini competition of Genoa, and was given the honor of performing on Paganini's own violin, the famous Guarneri del Jesù.

Pouplinière. See **La Pouplinière.**

Pourtalès, Guy de (complete name **Guido James de Pourtalès**), French writer on music; b. Berlin, Aug. 4, 1881; d. Lausanne, June 12, 1941; studied in Bonn, Berlin, and Paris; was in the French army during World War I; then settled in Paris as a music critic. He publ. a number of successful biographies of composers: *La Vie de Franz Liszt* (1925); *Chopin, ou le poète* (1927; 2nd ed., 1946; in English, as *Chopin: A Man of Solitude*, London, 1930); *Wagner, histoire d'un artiste* (1932; revised and augmented ed., 1942); *Berlioz et l'Europe romantique* (1939).

Pousseur, Henri, Belgian composer of the ultramodern school; b. Malmédy, June 23, 1929. He studied at the Liège Cons. (1947–52) and the Brussels Cons. (1952–53); had private lessons in composition from André Souris and Pierre Boulez; worked in Cologne and Milan electronic music studios until 1959, where he came in contact with Stockhausen and Berio; was a member of the avant-garde group of composers "Variation" in Liège. He taught music in various Belgian schools (1950–59); was founder (1958) and director of the Studio de Musique Electronique APELAC in Brussels, now a part of the Centre de Recherches Musicales in Liège; gave lectures at new music summer courses in Darmstadt (1957–67), Cologne (1962–68), Basel (1963–64), the State Univ. of N.Y. in Buffalo (1966–69), and at the Cons. in Liège. In his music he tries to synthesize all expressive powers of which man, as a biological species *Homo sapiens* (or even *Homo insipiens*) is capable in the domain of art (or non-art); the technological resources of the subspecies *Homo habilis* (magnetic tape, electronics/synthesizers, aleatory extensions, the principle of indeterminacy, glossolalia, self-induced schizophasia), all form part of his rich musical (or non-musical) vocabulary for multimedia (or nullimeda) representations. The influence of his methods (or non-methods) of composition (or non-composition) is pervasive.

WORKS: Piano Sonatina (1949); *3 Chants sacrés* for soprano and string trio (1951); *Seismogrammes* for tape (1953); *Symphonies* for 15 solo instruments (1954–55); *Quintet to the Memory of Webern* for violin, cello, clarinet, bass clarinet and piano (1955); *Exercices for piano: Variations I* and *Impromptu et Variations II* (1956); *Scambi* for tape (1957); *Mobile* for 2 pianos (1956–58); *Madrigal I* for solo clarinet (1958); *Madrigal II* for flute, violin, viola da gamba and harpsichord (1961); *Madrigal III* for clarinet, violin, cello, 2 percussionists and piano (1962); *Rimes pour différentes sources sonores* for 3 orchestral groups and tape (1958–59; Donaueschingen Fest., Oct. 17, 1959); *Électre,* "musical action" (1960); *Répons* for 7 musicians (1960; revision with actor added, 1965); *Ode* for string quartet (1960–61); *Caractères* for piano (1961); *Trois visages de Liège* and *Prospective* for tape (1961);

Votre Faust, an aleatory "fantasy in the manner of an opera" for 5 actors, vocal quartet, 12 musicians and tapes, for which the audience decides the ending (in collaboration with Michel Butor, 1961–67; Milan, 1969; concert version, titled *Portail de Votre Faust,* for 4 voices, tape, and 12 instruments); *Trait* for 15 strings (1962); *Miroir de Votre Faust* for piano, and soprano *ad lib* (*Caractères II,* 1964–65); *Caractères madrigalesques* for solo oboe (*Madrigal IV* and *Caractères III,* 1965); *Apostrophe et six réflexions* for piano (1964–66); *Phonèmes pour Cathy* for solo voice (*Madrigal V, 1966); Echoes I* for solo cello (1967); *Echoes II, de Votre Faust* for mezzo-soprano, flute, cello and piano (1969); *Couleurs croisées (Crossed Colors)* for orch., a series of crypto-musical variations on the civil rights song, *We Shall Overcome* (1967; Brussels Radio, Dec. 20, 1968); *Mnemosyne I,* monody, after Hölderlin, for solo voice, or unison chorus, or one instrument (1968); *Mnemosyne II,* an instrumental recreation of *Mnemosyne I,* with ad libitum scoring (1969); *Croisées des couleurs croisées (Crosses of Crossed Colors;* an intensified sequel to *Couleur croisées)* for female voice, 2–5 pianos, tape recorders and 2 radio receivers dialed aleatorily, to texts from Indian and Negro materials and political speeches (N.Y., Nov. 29, 1970); *Icare apprenti* for an undetermined number of instruments (1970); *Les Éphémerides d'Icare 2* for piano and instruments (Madrid, April 20, 1970); *Invitation à l'Utopie* for narrator, 2 female voices, 4-voice chorus, and instruments (Brussels Radio, Jan. 25, 1971); *L'Effacement de Prince Igor,* scene for orch. (Brussels, Feb. 28, 1972); *Le Temps des Paraboles* (1972); *Die Erprobung des Petrus Hebraïcus,* chamber opera (Berlin Festival, Sept. 12, 1974); *Vue sur les jardins interdits* for organ or saxophone quartet (1974); *19√8/4* for solo cello (1975). He published *Fragments théoriques I. Sur la musique expérimentale* (Brussels, 1970).

Powell, Earl "Bud," black American jazz pianist, the originator of the most prevalent bebop piano style; b. New York, Sept. 27, 1924; d. there, Aug. 1, 1966. In 1943 he worked with Cootie Williams's big band; also with various combos; became associated with Dizzy Gillespie, Charlie Parker and others involved in the emerging bebop revolution of the period; was a frequent participant of the formative jam sessions at Minton's Playhouse. He gradually discarded the stride piano style, with its rhythmically regular left hand, developing a style in which the left hand supplies irregular punctuation to long, rapid, saxophone-like melodies played by the right hand. His career was repeatedly interrupted by hospitalizations for alcoholism, tuberculosis, and mental illness.

Powell, John, American pianist, composer and ethnomusicologist; b. Richmond, Va., Sept. 6, 1882; d. Charlottesville, Virginia, Aug. 15, 1963. His father was a school teacher, his mother an amateur musician; he received his primary musical education at home; then studied piano with F. C. Hahr, a pupil of Liszt; subsequently entered the Univ. of Virginia (B.A., 1901) and then went to Vienna where he studied piano with Leschetizky (1902–07) and composition with Navrátil (1904–07); gave successful piano recitals in Paris and

London; returning to the U.S., he toured the country as a pianist, playing some of his own works. His most successful piece was *Rapsodie nègre*, inspired by Joseph Conrad's *Heart of Darkness*, for piano and orch.; Powell was the soloist in its first performance with the Russian Symph. Orch. (N.Y., March 23, 1918). The titles of some of his works disclose a whimsical propensity; perhaps his most important achievement lies in ethnomusicology; he methodically collected rural songs of the south; was the organizer of the Virginia State Choral Festivals and of the annual White Top Mountain Folk Music Festivals. A man of versatile interests, he was also an amateur astronomer, and discovered a comet.

WORKS: Symphony in A (Detroit, April 23, 1947); 2 piano concertos; Violin Concerto; *Rapsodie nègre* for piano and orch.; *In Old Virginia*, overture (1921); *Natchez on the Hill*, 3 Virginian country dances for orch. (1932); *A Set of Three*, for orch. (1935); *Virginia Symphony* (Richmond, Nov. 5, 1951); String Quartet; *Sonate Virginianesque*, for violin and piano (1919); 3 piano sonatas; *Sonate psychologique, Sonate noble, Sonata Teutonica;* piano suite *In the South;* piano suite (also for orch.) *At the Fair; In the Hammock,* for 2 pianos 8 hands; an opera, *Judith and Holofernes.*

Powell, Laurence, British-American composer and conductor; b. Birmingham, England, Jan. 13, 1899. He studied at Ratcliffe College, Leicester (1909–15), Ushaw College, Durham (1915–17); was in the British Army and the Royal Air Force during World War I; then studied music at the Birmingham and Midland Institute School of Music (1919–22); under Sir Granville Bantock; his examiner was Sir Donald Francis Tovey. While there, he won a full scholarship to Birmingham Univ., where he carried on his studies concurrently with Bantock, gaining a Mus. Bac. degree with first class honors. In 1923 he went to the U.S.; became a naturalized citizen in 1936; took courses at the Univ. of Wisconsin (M.A. 1926); subsequently held various teaching positions; at the Univ. of Wisconsin (1924–26), Univ. of Arkansas (1926–34), Little Rock Junior College (1934–39); was organist at St. Mary's Church, Victoria, Texas (1947–52); organist and choirmaster at St. Francis Cathedral, Santa Fe (1952–68); a choir director and organist at Assumption Church in Albuquerque (1968–70); organist and choirmaster at Our Lady of Victory Church, Victoria, Texas (1970–75); upon retirement in 1975 was honored by a plaque "for Laurence Powell for demonstrating beauty in God and man through music and song." As conductor, he was the organizer and musical director of the Little Rock Symph. Orch. (1934–39); conductor of the Grand Rapids, Michigan, Federal Symphony (1939–41), founder and conductor of the Santa Fe Orch., later renamed Rio Grande Symphony (1953–55).

WORKS: for orch: *The Ogre of the Northern Fastness* (1921), *Keltic Legend* (Bournemouth, England, Aug. 27, 1924, composer conducting; revised version, Madison, Wis., May 20, 1931); *Charivari,* suite (1925); 2 symphonies (1929, 1943); *Deirdre of the Sorrows* (1933; Little Rock, March 18, 1937, composer conducting), *The County Fair,* suite (1936); *Suite,* for string orch. (1931; Grand Rapids, May 9, 1940, com-

poser conducting); *Picnic* an "Arkansas pastoral" for string orch. (Oklahoma City, March 21, 1936); *Variations* (Rochester, N.Y., Oct. 28, 1941); *Duo Concertante* for recorders and orch. (1941); *The Santa Fe Trail,* for baritone, narrator, and orch. (Rio Grande Symph. Orch., Santa Fe, New Mexico. (April 22, 1958); *Penny Overture* (1960); *Overture on French Folk Tunes* (1970); *Oracle* for orch. (1975). *Halcyone,* dramatic poem for chorus and orch. (1923), *Alleluya,* cantata for chorus and orch. (1926); *The Seasons* (after poems by Blake) for chorus a cappella (1928); Piano Quartet (1933); Quartet for clarinets (1936); 3 sonatinas for recorders unaccompanied, one each for soprano, alto and tenor (1977); several Masses; songs. All of his works are deposited in the Library of the Univ. of Arkansas at Fayetteville.

Powell, Maud, American violinist; b. Peru, Illinois, Aug. 22, 1868; d. Uniontown, Pennsylvania, Jan. 8, 1920. She received her primary instruction at home; then went to Europe where she took violin lessons with Schradieck in Leipzig and theory with Charles Dancla in Paris. Returning to the U.S. in 1885 she gave concerts and acquired a sort of automatic celebrity since the female species among violinists was a *rara avis* in her time. Thus, when the Arion Society of New York rigged a musical expedition to Germany in 1892 for the quadricentennial of the discovery of America, she went along as a "representative American violinist." She also played at the Chicago World's Fair in 1893. See A. R. Coolidge in *Notable American Women* (N.Y., 1971) III.

Powell, Mel, American composer; b. New York, Feb. 12, 1923. As a youth he made arrangements for the Benny Goodman Band and played piano in radio orchestras; concurrently took lessons with Bernard Wagenaar and Joseph Schillinger in N.Y. (1937–39) and later with Ernst Toch in Los Angeles (1946–48). In 1948 he entered the Yale School of Music, where he studied with Hindemith (B.M., 1952). From 1957 to 1969 he was on the staff of Yale Univ.; in 1969 was appointed Dean of Music at the California Institue of the Arts. In his works he cultivates the minutiae of rhythmic and intervallic units, with quick changes of tonal and temporal articulation, without venturing into the outer space of musical entropy.

WORKS: *Divertimento* for flute, clarinet, oboe, bassoon and trumpet (1955); *Stanzas* for orch. (1957); *Miniatures* for baroque ensemble (1957); *Filigree Setting* for string quartet (1959); *Haiku Settings* for voice and piano (1961); *Setting* for cello and orch. (1961); *Improvisation* for clarinet, viola and piano (1962); *Events* for tape (1963); *2 Prayer Settings* for tenor, oboe, violin, viola and cello (1963); *Cantilena* for soprano, violin and electronic tape (1970); several groups of pieces for magnetic tape, *Analogs, Immobiles,* etc.

BIBLIOGRAPHY: Leslie Thimmig, "The Music of Mel Powell," *Musical Quarterly* (Jan. 1969).

Power, Lionel (Lionel, Leonell Polbero, Powero, etc.), English composer; date of birth unknown; d. Winchester, 1445. He was a contemporary of Dunstable, whose style he so closely approximated that authorship of works of the two composers has often been confused (some authorities claim, without foundation, that Power and Dunstable were identical). He wrote a treatise "Upon the Gamme" (c.1450, transcribed by J. Wylde, in the British Museum; reprinted by Hawkins in *History of the Science and Practice of Music* vol. 2; also by S. B. Meech in *Speculum,* July, 1935; pp. 242–58; and in part by M. Bukofzer, *Geschichte des englischen Diskants und des Fauxbourdons,* 1936).

WORKS: *2 Ave Reginas,* a *Salve Regina,* a *Mater ora filium* and 21 pieces (mostly parts of Masses) for 3-4 voices appear in the *Denkmäler der Tonkunst in Österreich* 14/15 (7), *Sammelbände der Internationalen Musik-Gesellschaft* (vol. 2, p. 378), Stainer's *Early Bodleian Music,* and *The Old Hall Manuscript* (3 vols., ed. by A. Ramsbotham; Burnham, Bucks, 1933–38; see also A. Schering, *Geschichte der Musik in Beispielen* (no. 37) and Davison and Apel, *Historical Anthology of Music* (vol. 1, no. 63). Other pieces preserved in MS at Bologna, Modena, Oxford, Vienna, and London (British Museum), include a *Missa Rex Saeculorum* (with *Kyrie*), a 4-voiced *Ave Regina* and part of a *Kyrie.* 2 Masses attributed to Power were publ. in the *Documenta polyphoniae liturgicae S. Ecclesiae Romanae* (ser. 1, nos. 2 and 9). The *Complete Works,* ed. by C. Hamm, is issued by the American Institute of Musicology (1969).

BIBLIOGRAPHY: H. Riemann, *Geschichte der Musiktheorie,* p. 143; W. Korte, *Die Harmonik des 15. Jahrhunderts* (1929; p. 23); C. Hamm, "The Motets of Lionel Power," in H. S. Powers, *Studies in Music History: Essays for Oliver Strunk* (Princeton, N.J., 1968).

Pownall, Mary Ann, English actress and singer, b. 1751; d. Charleston, S.C., Aug. 11, 1796. She was known first as **Mrs. Wrightson** (her 1st husband was a prompter in a London theater); made her debut in 1770 in *The Recruiting Officer,* in London; from 1776 to 1788 was a Vauxhall favorite. In 1792 she first appeared in Boston with the Old American Co., of which she was a leading artist; later sang in subscription concerts in N.Y., and joined John Henry's New York Co. She composed the text and music of numerous songs—including *Advice to the Ladies of Boston, Washington* (in honor of George Washington), and *Primroses*—some of which appeared in a book of songs that she compiled with J. Hewitt (publ. in N.Y.). Her 2nd husband was A. Pownall.

BIBLIOGRAPHY: J. T. Howard, *Our American Music* (N.Y., 1931, and later eds.).

Pozdro, John Walter, American composer; b. Chicago, August 14, 1923. He studied at the American Cons. in Chicago, at Northwestern Univ. and at the Eastman School of Music (with Howard Hanson and Bernard Rogers), graduating in 1958 with a Ph.D. in composition. He subsequently joined the faculty of the Univ. of Kansas. His music may be described as pragmatically modern, with resources ranging from modal counterpoint in an attractive neo-archaic manner to euphoniously dissonant superpositions of harmonic groups.

WORKS: *Malooley and the Fear Monster,* a "family opera" in one act (Lawrence, Kansas, Feb. 6, 1977); *Overture* (1948); Symph. No. 1 (1949); *A Cynical*

Overture (1952; Univ. of Texas Southwestern Symposium of Contemporary Music, March 24, 1953); Symph. No. 2 (1957; Rochester, N.Y., May 4, 1958); Symph. No. 3 (1960; Oklahoma City, Dec. 12, 1960); *Waterlow Park* for orch. (Lawrence, Kansas, May 8, 1972); *Rondo gioioso* for string orch. (1964); *Music for a Youth Symphony* (1969); chamber music: Quintet for woodwinds and piano (1947); Sextet for flute and strings (1948); 2 string quartets (1947, 1952); *Elegy* for trumpet and piano (1953); *Trilogy* for clarinet, bassoon, trumpet and piano (1960); Sonata for brasses and percussion (1966); Violin Sonata (1971). 4 piano sonatas (1947, 1963, 1964, 1976); 8 Piano Preludes (1950–74); for chorus: *They That Go Down to the Sea* (1967); *The Creation* for children's voices (1967); solo songs: *Landscape I and II* for carillon (1964, 1969).

Pozniak, Bronislaw, German pianist and pedagogue; b. Lwow, Aug. 26, 1887; d. Halle, April 20, 1953. He studied at the Cons. of Cracow; then in Berlin with Barth; established a trio, and traveled in Germany; then settled in Breslau as piano teacher; in 1946 moved to Leipzig, and eventually to Halle. He publ. *ABC des Klavierspielers* (1939; 2nd ed., 1948); *Praktische Anweisungen für das Studium der Chopinschen Werke* (Halle, 1949); was editor of a new edition of Chopin's piano works for Peters.

Praetorius, Ernst, German musicologist; b. Berlin, Sept. 20, 1880; d. Ankara, March 27, 1946. He studied violin in Breslau and Halle; history and theory in Berlin with Friedlaender, Fleischer, and Stumpf; 1905, Dr. phil. with his dissertation, *Die Mensuraltheorie des Franchinus Gafurius* (Leipzig, 1905); in 1906, appointed director of the famous Heyer Museum in Cologne; held this post until 1909, when he joined the staff of the Cologne Opera. Subsequently, he held similar positions in Bochum (1912), Leipzig (1913), Lübeck (1914), Breslau (1915), and Berlin (1922). From 1924 until 1933 he was general musical director in Weimar; in 1934 went to Turkey, where he was active in the educational field and on the radio; remained in Ankara until his death.

Praetorius (Latinized from **Schulz** or **Schulze**), **Hieronymus,** German composer, b. Hamburg, Aug. 10, 1560; d. there, Jan. 27, 1629. He studied with his father, **Jacobus Schulze,** organist of the Jacobikirche; then in Cologne. He became town cantor in Erfurt in 1580; assistant organist to his father in 1582, and his successor in 1586. He brought out a *Hamburger Melodeyen-Gesangbuch* (1604; with his son **Jacobus,** J. Decker, and D. Scheidemann). His works were publ. in 5 collections in 1622–25, under the general title, *Opus musicum novum et perfectum:* I, *Cantiones sacrae a 5-12;* II, *Magnificats a 8-12;* III, *Liber missarum,* 6 Masses *a 5-8;* IV, *Cantiones variae, a 5-20,* containing Latin and German motets; V, *Cantiones novae officiosae, a 5-15,* also containing Latin and German motets. A selection of his works (a Mass, a Magnificat, and some motets) was publ. by Hugo Leichtentritt in the *Denkmäler deutscher Tonkunst* 23.

BIBLIOGRAPHY: Hugo Leichtentritt, *Geschichte*

der Motette (1908; page 309ff.); B. Friedrich, *Der Vokalstil des Hieronymus Praetorius* (Hamburg, 1932).

Praetorius, Jacobus, German composer and organist; son of **Hieronymus Praetorius;** b. Hamburg, Feb. 8, 1586; d. there, Oct. 22, 1651. He studied with Sweelinck in Amsterdam; in 1603 was appointed organist at the Peterskirche in Hamburg. He contributed several motets to his father's collection, *Hamburger Melodeyen-Gesangbuch.*

Praetorius, Michael, great German musician, composer, and theorist; b. Kreuzberg, Thuringia, Feb. 15, 1571; d. Wolfenbüttel, Feb. 15, 1621. His real family name was **Schultheiss** (German for magistrate, or praetor), which he Latinized as Praetorius. He was the son of a preacher; attended the Latin school of Torgau; studied organ in Frankfurt; then was in the service of the Duke of Braunschweig (from 1604); was also prior of the Ringelheim monastery, although without actual residence there. In 1612 he succeeded Mancinus as Kapellmeister in Wolfenbüttel and remained there until his death. WORKS: *Musae Sioniae,* a collection of 1244 vocal numbers in 9 parts, in note-against-note counterpoint (1605-10; 2nd ed. of Part IX, as *Bicinia et tricinia,* 1611); *Musarum Sioniarum motetae et psalmi 4-16 vocae* (1607); *Eulogodia Sionia* (1611); 60 motets *a* 2-8 for the "close of the Divine Service"; *Missodia Sionia* (1611); *Hymnodia Sionia* (1611; hymns *a* 2-8); *Megalynodia* (1611; madrigals and motets *a* 5-8); *Terpsichore* (1612; dance pieces *a* 4-6, by Praetorius and some French composers); *Polyhymnia caduceatrix et panegyrica* (1619; songs of peace and rejoicing *a* 1-21); *Polyhymnia exercitatrix* (1620; *a* 2-8); *Uranodia* or *Uranochordia* (1613; 19 songs *a* 4); *Kleine und grosse Litaney* (1613); *Epithalamium* (1614); *Puericinium* (1621; 14 church songs *a* 3-12). REPRINTS: organ works by W. Gurlitt, in the *Archiv für Musikwissenschaft* (1921); also by K. Matthäi (Brunswick, 1930); *Psalm 116,* by R. Holle (Mainz, 1933); 2 pieces by A. Schering in *Geschichte der Musik in Beispielen* (nos. 161, 162); various numbers reprinted by G. Tucher, L. Schöberlein, F. Riegel, K. Ameln, etc. WRITINGS: *Syntagma musicum,* his major work, of which 3 volumes were printed: vol. I, part 1, Wolfenbüttel, 1614, in 2 parts, is a historical and descriptive treatise in Latin on ancient and ecclesiastical music, and ancient secular instruments; vol. II, Wolfenbüttel, 1618 (appendix, 1620), written in German, in 5 parts and an Appendix (1620), is the most important extant source of information on musical instruments of the period, describing their form, compass, tone quality, etc., the organ, in particular, being treated at great length; the Appendix contains 42 woodcuts of the principal instruments enumerated (vol. II has been reprinted as vol. XIII of the publications of the Gesellschaft für Musikforschung; facsimile reprint, with introduction by W. Gurlitt, Kassel, 1929); vol. III, Wolfenbüttel, 1618, contains a valuable and interesting account of secular composition at that time, and a treatise on solmisation, notation, etc. A reprint of vol. III was publ. by E. Bernouilli (1916). A complete ed. of Praetorius' works was issued in 21

vols. under the editorship of Friedrich Blume (1928-41).
BIBLIOGRAPHY: W. Gurlitt, *Michael Praetorius (Creuzburgensis), sein Leben und sein Werke* (Leipzig, 1915); F. Blume, *Michael Praetorius Creuzburgensis* (Wolfenbüttel, 1929); P. Zimmermann, "Zur Biographie des Michael Praetorius," *Braunschweigischer Geschichtsverein Jahrbuch* (1930); R. Unger, *Die mehrchörige Aufführungspraxis bei Michael Praetorius und die Feiergestaltung der Gegenwart* (Wolfenbüttel, 1941); G. Ilgner, *Die lateinischen liturgischen Kompositionen von Michael Praetorius Creuzburgensis* (Kiel, 1944).

Pratella, Francesco Balilla, Italian composer and writer of radical tendencies; b. Lugo, Romagna, Feb. 1, 1880; d. Ravenna, May 18, 1955. He studied with Ricci-Signorini, then at the Liceo Rossini in Pesaro with Cicognani and Mascagni; taught in Cesana (1908-09); director of the Istituto Musicale, Lugo (from 1910), of the Liceo Musicale G. Verdi, Ravenna (1927-45). He joined the Italian futurist movement in 1910 (Russolo's manifesto of 1913 was addressed to "Balilla Pratella, grande musicista futurista"), and in 1913 wrote his first composition in a "futurist" idiom, the choral *Inno alla vita.* His other works are the operas *Lilia* (won honorable mention in the Sonzogno Contest, 1903; performed in Lugo, Nov. 13, 1905), *La Sina d'Vargöun,* to his own libretto (Bologna, Dec. 4, 1909), *L'Aviatore Dro* (also to his own libretto; Lugo, Nov. 4, 1920), *La Ninna nanna della bambola,* children's opera (Milan, May 21, 1923), *Dono primaverile,* comedy with music (Bologna, Oct. 17, 1923), *Fabiano,* opera (Bologna, Dec. 9, 1939); incidental music; for orch.: *Romagna, La Guerra, 5 Poemi musicali;* chamber music; etc.
WRITINGS: *Cronache e critiche* (1905-17); *Evoluzione della musica* (1910-18); *Saggio di gridi, canzoni, cori e danze del popolo italiano* (1919); *Il Canzoniere dei canterini romagnoli* (1923); *Scritti vari di pensiero, di arte e di storia musicale* (Bologna, 1932); *Luci ed ombre* (1933); *Il Vino e la musica* (1937); *Linee di storia della musica* (1946).
BIBLIOGRAPHY: A. Toni, "La Sina d'Vargöun di Francesco Balilla Pratella," *Rivista Musicale Italiana* (1910); G. Bastianelli, *Musicisti d'oggi e di ieri* (Milan, 1914); G. M. Gatti, *Musicisti moderni d'Italia e di fuori* (Bologna, 1920); A. Ghigi, *F. B. Pratella* (Ravenna, 1929); F. B. Pratella, *Appunti biografici e bibliografici* (Ravenna, 1931).

Pratt, Silas Gamaliel, American composer, b. Addison, Vt., Aug. 4, 1846; d. Pittsburgh, Oct. 30, 1916. Both his parents were church singers. The family moved to Chicago when he was a child, and he received his primary music education there; at 22 he went to Berlin, where he studied piano with Kullak and theory with Kiel (1868-71). He then returned to Chicago, where he served as organist of the Church of the Messiah; in 1872, established the Apollo Club. In 1875 he went to Germany once more; studied orchestration with Heinrich Dorn, and also took some piano lessons with Liszt. On July 4, 1876, he conducted in Berlin his *Centennial Overture,* dedicated to President Grant; also at the Crystal Palace in London, when

President Grant was visiting there; another work that he presented in London was a *Homage to Chicago March.* Returning to Chicago, he conducted his opera, *Zenobia, Queen of Palmyra* (to his own libretto) in concert form, on June 15, 1882 (stage performance, Chicago, March 26, 1883; New York, Aug. 21, 1883). The opera was received in a hostile manner by the press, partly owing to the poor quality of the music, but mainly as a reaction to Pratt's exuberant and immodest proclamations of its merit in advance of the production. Nothing daunted, Pratt unleashed a vigorous campaign for native American opera; organized the Grand Opera Festival of 1884, which had some support. The following year he visited London again, and conducted there his symph. work, *The Prodigal Son* (Oct. 5, 1885). Returning to Chicago, he revised his early lyric opera *Antonio,* renamed it *Lucille,* and produced it on March 14, 1887. In 1888 he moved to N.Y.; there he presented, during the quadricentennial of the discovery of America, his opera, *The Triumph of Columbus* (in concert form, Oct. 12, 1892); also produced a scenic cantata *America,* subtitled *Four Centuries of Music, Picture, and Song* (Nov. 24, 1894; with stereopticon projections). Other works: *Lincoln Symphony;* a symph. poem, *The Tragedy of the Deep* (1912; inspired by the Titanic disaster); a cantata, *The Last Inca;* also pub. a manual, *Pianist's Mental Velocity* (N.Y., 1903). In 1906 he settled in Pittsburgh; established there the Pratt Institute of Music and Art, and remained its director until his death. Pratt was a colorful personality; despite continuous and severe setbacks, he was convinced of his own significance. The story of his salutation to Wagner at their meeting: "Herr Wagner, you are the Silas G. Pratt of Germany" may be apocryphal, but is very much in character.

BIBLIOGRAPHY: E. E. Hipsher, *American Opera and Its Composers* (Philadelphia, pp. 361–63); *Dictionary of American Biography* (vol. 15).

Pratt, Waldo Selden, distinguished American music historian and pedagogue; b. Philadelphia, Nov. 10, 1857; d. Hartford, Conn., July 29, 1939. He studied at Williams College and at Johns Hopkins Univ., specializing in classical languages; was practically self-taught in music. After completing his studies, he was assistant director of the Metropolitan Museum of Art, N.Y. (1880–82); in 1882 he was appointed to the faculty of Hartford Theological Seminary, where he taught hymnology; then taught music history at Smith College (1895–1908), and later at the Institute of Musical Art, N.Y. He publ. a manual *The History of Music* (1907; several subsequent editions; still in use in American colleges); *Musical Ministries in the Church* (1901; several subsequent editions); *The Music of the Pilgrims* (1921, commenting on Ainsworth's Psalter as brought to Plymouth in 1620, with the tunes in full; reprinted, N.Y., 1971); *The Music of the French Psalter of 1562* (N.Y., 1939; reprint, 1966).

BIBLIOGRAPHY: Otto Kinkeldey, "Waldo Selden Pratt," *Musical Quarterly* (April 1940); J. T. Howard, in *Dictionary of American Biography,* Supplement II.

Predieri, Luca Antonio, Italian composer; b. Bologna, Sept. 13, 1688; d. there, Jan. 3, 1767. He was of a musical family; served as maestro di cappella at S. Paolo in Bologna (1725–29) and at S. Pietro (1729–31). In 1737 he went to Vienna as Kapellmeister, remaining there until 1765; then returned to Bologna. His opera *Il Sogno di Scipione* was performed at the Emperor's palace in Laxenburg, near Vienna, on Oct. 1, 1735. He also wrote oratorios and instrumental works for festive occasions.

Preger, Leo, Corsican composer; b. Ajaccio, Jan. 27, 1907; d. there, Dec. 25, 1965. He studied with Nadia Boulanger in Paris, and acquired considerable mastery of antique counterpoint; subsequently devoted himself mainly to sacred choral music. He wrote the choral works *La Reine Isaure, Cantate de l'arc, Arrestation de Jésus, Cantique de St. Jean de la Croix;* psalms; etc.

Preindl, Joseph, Austrian composer; b. Marbach, Jan. 30, 1756; d. Vienna, Oct. 26, 1823. He was a pupil of Albrechtsberger; in 1809 was appointed cantor at St. Stephen's. He publ. 5 Masses and other church works; brought out a *Gesanglehre* (singing manual) and a book of melodies by old German composers; wrote pieces for organ. His method, *Wiener Tonschule,* was publ. after his death, ed. by Seyfried (Vienna, 1827; 2nd ed., 1832).

Preiss, Cornelius, Austrian writer on music; b. Troppau, May 20, 1884; d. Linz, April 1, 1944. He studied in Olmütz and Graz (Dr. phil., 1907); taught in Graz (1908–24) and Linz (from 1924). He publ. the valuable survey, *Zur Geschichte der Operette* (1908); the monographs, *K. Millöcker* (1905); *L. C. Seydler* (1908), *Meyerbeer-Studien* (1907–14), *J. Drechsler* (1910), *R. Volkmann* (1912), *R. Stöhr* (1914), *K. Zeller* (1928), *F. X. Süssmayr* (1933); a collection of Austrian folksongs, *Österreichischer Liederquell* (3 vols., 1930–32); and the manual, *Sing- und allgemeine Musiklehre* (1933). Preiss was also a composer; wrote mainly vocal music.

Preobrazhensky, Anton, Russian specialist in Russian sacred music; b. Syzran, Feb. 28, 1870; d. Leningrad, Feb. 17, 1929. He studied at the Kazan Seminary; upon graduation went to Moscow where he taught at the Synod School (1898–1902); then was librarian at the Court Chapel in St. Petersburg; from 1920 to his death, he taught the history of Russian church music at the Cons. of Leningrad. He published a number of valuable reference works on Russian hymnody: *Dictionary of Russian Hymns* (Moscow, 1896); *Bibliography of Hymns* (Moscow, 1900); *The Monodic Hymn in the Russian Church of the 17th Century* (St. Petersburg, 1904); *Liturgic Music in Russia* (1924); also a biography of Lvov (St. Petersburg, 1908).

Presley, Elvis, fantastically popular American rock 'n' roll singer and balladeer; b. Tupelo, Mississippi, Jan. 8, 1935; d. Memphis, Tennessee, Aug. 16, 1977. He was employed as a mechanic and furniture repairman in his early youth; picked up guitar playing in his leisure hours; sang cowboy ballads at social gatherings. With the advent of rock 'n' roll he revealed himself as the supreme genius of the genre; almost effortlessly he captivated multitudes of adolescents by the hallucinogenic monotone of his vocal delivery enhanced by rhythmic pelvic gyrations (hence the invidious appellation "Elvis the Pelvis"); made recordings that sold millions of albums. He made America conscious of the seductive inanity of rock ballads; his rendition of such songs aroused primitive urges among his multitudinous admirers; these were "Don't Be Cruel," "Hound Dog," "Love Me Tender," "All Shook Up," "Jailhouse Rock," "Heartbreak Hotel," "Rock Around The Clock," "It's Now Or Never"; his audience responded by improvising songs about him: "My Boy Elvis," "I Wanna Spend Christmas with Elvis" and "Elvis for President." He also appeared as an actor in sentimental motion pictures. His art was the prime inspiration for the famous Liverpudlian quartet, The Beatles. An International Elvis Presley Appreciation Society was organized by 1970. Elvis Presley was indeed The King of Kings of rock. His death (of cardiac arrhythmia aggravated by an immoderate use of tranquilizers and other drugs) precipitated the most extraordinary outpouring of public grief over an entertainment figure since the death of Rudolph Valentino. His entombment in the family mausoleum in Memphis was the scene of mob hysteria during which two people were run over and killed by an automobile; two men were arrested for the alleged plot to spirit away his body and hold it for ransom. Entrepreneurs avid for gain put out a mass of memorial literature, souvenirs and gewgaws, sweatshirts emblazoned with Presley's image in color, Elvis dolls and even a lifesize effigy, as part of a multi-million dollar effort to provide solace to sorrowing humanity; the only discordant note was sounded by Presley's own bodyguards who authored a book provocatively titled *Elvis, What Happened?*, with murky insinuations that the King of Rock was a drug addict, but it was providentially providential before Presley's death.

BIBLIOGRAPHY: T. Saville, compiler, *The International Elvis Presley Appreciation Society Handbook* (Heanor, Derbyshire, England, 1970); J. Hopkins, *Elvis, A Biography* (N.Y., 1971); A. Hand, compiler, *Elvis Special* (Manchester, England, 1973); G. Peellaert, N. Cohn and L. Schober, *Rock Dreams, Die Geschichte der Popmusik* (Munich, 1973); posthumous publications, put out in 1977, include such contemptible maculature as *The Boy Who Dared Rock; Starring Elvis; The Illustrated Elvis* and *Elvis Presley Scrapbook*.

Presser, Theodore, American music publisher; b. Pittsburgh, Pa., July 3, 1848; d. Philadelphia, Oct. 27, 1925. He studied music at the New England Cons. in Boston with S. Emery, G. E. Whiting, J. C. D. Parker, and B. Lang; then at the Leipzig Cons. with Zwintscher and Jadassohn; in 1883 he founded in Philadelphia *The Etude,* a well-known music monthly of which he was the editor until 1907; James F. Cooke was its editor from 1908 to 1949; it discontinued publication in 1957. Shortly after the foundation of *The Etude,* Presser established a publishing house, Theo. Presser Co., for music and books about music, which has come to be one of the important firms in the U.S. In 1906 he founded the Presser Home for Retired Music Teachers, which in 1908 moved to fine new quar-

ters in Germantown (accommodations for 65 guests). In 1916 he established the Presser Foundation to administer this Home, also to provide for the relief of deserving musicians and to offer scholarships in more than 75 colleges and universities in the U.S. James Francis Cooke was president of the Foundation from 1918. Presser wrote instructive pieces and studies for piano; was a co-founder of the Music Teachers National Association (1876).

BIBLIOGRAPHY: *Dictionary of American Biography* (vol. 15).

Prêtre, Georges, French conductor; b. Waziers, Aug. 14, 1924. He studied at Douai and in Paris; in 1946 made his debut at the Opéra-Comique; also conducted the Pasdeloup Concerts. In 1965 he made an American tour; appeared as guest conductor with the Philadelphia Orch. By temperament he is an ebullient interpreter of Romantic music, indulging in eloquent bodily movements and projecting musical rhetorics with an imperious hand; but he can be superlatively restrained in Classical repertory.

Previn, André, brilliant American pianist, conductor and composer; b. Berlin, April 6, 1929, of Jewish parents. He showed his musical gift as a small child; his father, a lawyer, was an amateur musician who gave him his early training; they played piano 4-hands together at home. At the age of 6, André Previn was accepted as a pupil at the Berlin Hochschule für Musik, in the class of Prof. Breithaupt, but soon was compelled to leave school as a Jew. In 1938 the Previns went to Paris; in 1939 the family emigrated to America, settling in Los Angeles, where André's grand-uncle Charles Previn was head of music at the Universal Studios in Los Angeles. He took lessons in composition with Joseph Achron, Ernst Toch and Castelnuovo-Tedesco; later studied conducting with Pierre Monteux in San Francisco. He served in the U.S. Army (1950–52); played in various jazz groups; also appeared as piano soloist with orchestras; wrote music for films, among them, *Bad Day at Black Rock* (1955); *Subterraneans,* a documentary on the "beatnik" movement (1960) and *Two for the Seesaw* (1962); adapted Borodin's music from the opera *Prince Igor* for the ballet *Kismet* (1955); arranged the musicals *Irma La Douce, My Fair Lady,* and *West Side Story;* scored the film music for *Gigi* (1958) and *Porgy and Bess* (1959), which received Academy Awards. In the meantime he concentrated his energies on conducting, which soon became his principal vocation. He was engaged as principal conductor of the Houston Symph. Orch. (1967–68); then became director of the London Symph. Orch., with which he traveled in Russia, Japan, South Korea and Hong Kong in 1971. Among his original works are *Overture to a Comedy* (1963); Cello Concerto (1967); Horn Concerto (1968); Violin Sonata, and other chamber music; many piano pieces and songs. He was married thrice; to the jazz singer Betty Bennett, to the jazz poet Dory Langdon (who subsequently made a career of her own as composer and singer of pop songs of lament) and finally to the actress Mia Farrow.

BIBLIOGRAPHY: Edward Greenfield, *André Previn* (N.Y., 1973).

Previtali, Fernando, Italian conductor; b. Adria, Feb. 16, 1907. He studied cello, piano and composition at the Cons. of Turin; from 1936 to 1953 conducted the Rome Radio Orch.; from 1953 to 1973 he was artistic director of the Accademia di Santa Cecilia. In 1971 he was appointed music director of the Teatro Regio in Parma. He made several appearances as guest conductor in the U.S. (debut with the Cleveland Orch., Dec. 15, 1955); also conducted in Russia. He wrote a ballet *Allucinazioni* and other music; publ. an instructive manual *Guida allo studio della direzione d'orchestra* (Rome, 1951).

Prévost, André, Canadian composer; b. Hawkesburg, Ontario, July 30, 1934. He studied piano and bassoon at the Montreal Cons. (1951–60); composition with Pépin and Papineau-Couture; then went to Paris where he studied with Messiaen and Dutilleux. In 1964 he returned to America and took summer courses at the Berkshire Music Center in Tanglewood under the direction of Schuller, Copland and Kodály; in 1965 he joined the staff of the music faculty of the Univ. of Montreal.
WORKS: *Poème de l'infini,* symph. poem (1960); *Scherzo* for string orch. (1960); *Fantasmes* for orch. (1963; Montreal, Nov. 22, 1963; posthumously dedicated to John F. Kennedy); *Pyknon,* pièce concertante for violin and orch. (1966); *Célébration* for orch. (1966); *Terre des hommes (Man and His World)* for 2 narrators, 3 choirs and orch. (1967; Montreal, April 29, 1967; opening of Expo '67); *Diallèle* for orch. (1968; Toronto, May 30, 1968); *Evanescance* for orch. (1970; Ottawa, April 7, 1970); *Hommage (à Beethoven)* for 14 strings (1970–71); *Psaume 148* for chorus, brass and organ (1971; Guelph, Canada, May 1, 1971); *Chorégraphie I (. . . Munich, September 1972 . . .)* for orch. (1972–73; Toronto, April 22, 1975; inspired by the Munich Olympics tragedy) and *II (E = MC²)* for orch. (1976); *Pastorale* for 2 harps (1955); *Fantasie* for cello and piano (1956); 2 string quartets (1958; *Ad pacem,* 1971–72); *Mobiles* for flute, violin, viola and cello (1959–60); Violin Sonata (1960–61; arranged as a ballet under the title *Primordial,* 1968); Cello Sonata (1962; arranged for violin, and piano or Ondes Martenot, 1967); *Triptyque* for flute, oboe and piano (1962); *Mouvement* for brass quintet (1963); *Ode au St. Laurent* for optional narrator and string quartet (1965); *Suite* for string quintet (1968); *Missa de Profundis* for chorus and organ (1973); *4 Preludes* for 2 pianos (1961); *5 Variations sur un thème grégorien* for organ (1956); songs; choruses.

Prévost, Eugène-Prosper, French conductor and composer; b. Paris, April 23, 1809; d. New Orleans, Aug. 19, 1872. He studied at the Paris Cons. with Lesueur, winning the Grand Prix de Rome in 1831 with the cantata, *Bianca Cappello.* He conducted theatrical music in Le Havre (1835–38), then went to New Orleans, where he conducted until 1862; was active in Paris (1862–67) before returning to New Orleans as a singing master. He produced several operas in Paris, of which *Cosimo* (Opéra-Comique, Oct. 13, 1835) was the most successful, and one *(Blanche et René)* in New Orleans; also wrote oratorios and Masses.

Prey, Claude, French composer; b. Fleury-sur-Andelle, May 30, 1925. He studied at the Paris Cons. with Milhaud and Messiaen; then with Mignone in Rio de Janeiro and with Frazzi in Siena; completed studies at the Laval Univ. in Quebec, Canada in 1958.
WORKS: an opera, *Le Phénix* (1957); an "opéra épistolaire," *Lettres perdues* (1960); *La dictée,* lyrical monodrama (1961); a chamber opera after Edgar Allan Poe, *Le coeur révélateur (The Tell-Tale Heart,* 1962); an opera in 12 variations, *L'homme occis* (1963); *Métamorphose d'Echo,* 9 variations for female voice and 24 strings (1965); *Les Mots croisés (Jeu concertante)* for contralto, tenor and 2 instrumental groups (1965); a theater-music piece, *Donna Mobile,* for 8 actresses and 3 instrumentalists (1965; Avignon Fest., July 15, 1972); an "opéra-test," *La noirceur du lait* (Strasbourg, 1967); an opera-oratorio, *Jonas* (1966; scenic version, Lyon, Dec. 2, 1969); an opera-parody in 2 trials, *On veut la lumière? allons-y!* for 5 cast members and 8 instruments (1967; Angers, 1968); an opera, *Fêtes de la faim,* for 5 comedians, cello and 2 percussionists (Avignon, 1969); a short opera, *Le jeu de l'oie* (Paris, 1970); *Théâtrophonie* for 12 voices and piano (1971).

Prey, Hermann, German baritone; b. Berlin, July 11, 1929. He studied at the Berlin Hochschule für Musik; in 1952 won the first prize in a singing contest organized by the U.S. Army and went on an American tour. Returning to Europe, he sang in Vienna, Berlin, Munich and at La Scala in Milan; appeared as Wolfram in *Tannhäuser* with the Metropolitan Opera, N.Y. He is successful also on the concert stage.

Preyer, Carl Adolph, German pianist, composer, and teacher; b. Pforzheim, Baden, July 28, 1863; d. Lawrence, Kansas, Nov. 16, 1947. He studied at the Stuttgart Cons.; then with Navrátil in Vienna, and with H. Urban and H. Barth in Berlin. In 1893 he settled in the U.S.; became piano teacher at the School of Fine Arts, Univ. of Kansas, and remained with that institution throughout his life. He publ. several instructive collections for piano, *20 Progressive Octave Studies, Melodious Pieces in the Form of Etudes, 12 Wrist Studies, 12 Etudes for the Left Hand;* also some character pieces.
BIBLIOGRAPHY: Howard F. Gloyne, *Carl A. Preyer: The Life of a Kansas Musician* (Lawrence, Kansas, 1949).

Preyer, Gottfried von, Austrian organist and composer; b. Hausbrunn, March 15, 1807; d. Vienna, May 9, 1901. He studied with Sechter; in 1835 became organist of the Lutheran Church in Vienna; in 1838, prof. of music theory at the Vienna Cons., of which he was director from 1844 to 1848. In 1853 he became music director at St. Stephen's; pensioned in 1876. He wrote 3 operas; the oratorio, *Noah* (often performed in Vienna); a symph.; several Masses and other church music.

Price, Enrique (Henry), English conductor; b. London, May 5, 1819; d. New York, Dec. 12, 1863. He settled in Columbia, and established the Philharmonic

Orch. of Bogotá (Nov. 11, 1846); was its first conductor.

Price, Florence B. (*née* **Smith**), black American pianist and composer; b. Little Rock, Arkansas, April 9, 1888; d. Chicago, June 3, 1953. She studied with Chadwick and Converse at the New England Conservatory in Boston, graduating in 1906. She had been publishing her compositions since she was 11 (1899); in 1928 she won a prize from G. Schirmer for *At the Cotton Gin*, for piano; around this time she was also writing musical jingles for radio commercials. Her first notable success came in 1932 with her Symphony in E minor (winner the Wanamaker Award; performed by the Chicago Symphony at the Century of Progress Exhibition in 1933); she became known as the first black woman to write symphonies. She also wrote *Concert Overture on Negro Spirituals; Piano Concerto in One Movement* (many performances); *Negro Folk Songs in Counterpoint* for string quartet; for piano: *Arkansas Jitter, Three Little Negro Dances*, the suite *From the Canebrakes*; many other works for piano and for organ.
BIBLIOGRAPHY: B. G. Jackson, "Florence Price, Composer," *Black Perspective in Music* (Spring 1977).

Price, Jorge Wilson, Colombian musician, son of **Enrique Price**; b. Bogotá, May 20, 1853; d. there, Oct. 9, 1953 (at the age of 100). He was educated in New York; returning to Columbia, he founded the National Academy (1882) and taught violin.
BIBLIOGRAPHY: J. I. Perdomo Escobar, *Historia de la Música en Colombia* (Bogotá, 1945).

Price, Leontyne, black American soprano; b. Laurel, Mississippi, Feb. 10, 1927. She studied at Central State College at Wilberforce, Ohio, and at the Juilliard School of Music, N.Y. (1949–52), with Florence Page Kimball. She achieved her first successes in the role of Bess in Gershwin's opera *Porgy and Bess*, which she sang on tour in the U.S. in 1952–54 and in Europe in 1955. In 1956 she gave concerts in India. In 1957 she joined the San Francisco Opera Co.; was also a member of the Lyric Opera in Chicago. In 1958 she sang *Aida* at the Vienna State Opera, and in 1960 she appeared in the same role at La Scala, Milan, with exceptional acclaim. On Jan. 27, 1961, she made her debut with the Metropolitan Opera Co., N.Y., as Leonora in *Il Trovatore;* subsequently sang the principal parts in *Madama Butterfly, Don Giovanni, Turandot* and *La Fanciulla del West* with unfailing musical, theatrical and popular success. She married the baritone **William C. Warfield** in 1952. On July 4, 1964 she was awarded the Medal of Freedom by the U.S. Government.
BIBLIOGRAPHY: H. L. Lyon, *Leontyne Price: Highlights of a Prima Donna* (1973).

Price, Margaret, British operatic soprano; b. Tredegar, Wales, April 13, 1941. She studied at Trinity College of Music in London; made her debut in 1962 at the Welsh National Opera as Cherubino in *Le nozze di Figaro*, and in 1963 sang the same role at Covent Garden in London. She established herself as a foremost performer of soprano roles in Mozart's operas, excelling as Donna Anna in *Don Giovanni*, the Countess in *Le nozze di Figaro* and Pamina in *Die Zauberflöte*; she also distinguished herself as Desdemona in Verdi'a *Otello*. She made appearances, invariably successful, with the operas at Cologne, Munich, Hamburg, Chicago and San Francisco. She joined the cast of the Paris Opéra during its American tour in 1976, eliciting extraordinary praise from the public and critics. Her voice is essentially a lyric soprano, but is capable of technically brilliant coloratura.

Prieberg, Fred K., German writer on music; b. Berlin, June 3, 1928. He took music courses at the Univ. of Freiburg-im-Breisgau (1950-53); from 1953 to 1969 lived in Baden-Baden. He published a number of informative books on modern music, among them *Musik unterm Strich* (Freiburg, 1956); *Musik des technischen Zeitalters* (Zürich, 1956); *Lexikon der neuen Musik* (Freiburg, 1958); *Musica ex machina* (Berlin, 1960); *Musik in der Sowjetunion* (Cologne, 1965); *Musik im anderen Deutschland* (Cologne, 1968).

Priestman, Brian, English conductor; b. Birmingham, England, Feb. 10, 1927; received his musical education at the Univ. of Birmingham (M.A., 1952); was music director of the Royal Shakespeare Theatre, Stratford-on-Avon, England (1960-63); conductor of Edmonton, Alberta, Canada Symph. (1964-68); from 1970 to 1978 he was music director of the Denver Symphony Orchestra; in 1978 he became music director and conductor of the Miami Philharmonic.

Příhoda, Váša, noted Czech violinist; b. Vodnany, Aug. 22, 1900; d. Vienna, July 26, 1960. He received his first instructions from his father, a professional violinist; made his public debut at the age of 13 in Prague; made a successful Italian tour in 1920; in 1921 appeared in the U.S.; in 1927, in England; then played in recitals throughout Europe. During World War II he taught at the Mozarteum in Salzburg; after the war, resumed his career as a concert artist giving recitals in Paris and London.

Prill, Emil, eminent German flutist; brother of **Karl** and **Paul Prill;** b. Stettin, May 10, 1867; d. Berlin, Feb. 28, 1940. He studied with his father; finished his musical education at the Hochschule für Musik in Berlin; in 1888 taught in Kharkov, Russia; then played 1st flute with the Hamburg Philharmonic; in 1892 became 1st flutist at the Berlin Opera; in 1903 was appointed instructor at the Hochschule. He publ. the methods *Schule für die Böhm-Flöte* and *Flötenschule;* also a valuable practical collection of flute passages from orchestral works, *Orchesterstudien* (7 books).

Prill, Karl, German violinist; brother of **Emil** and **Paul Prill;** b. Berlin, Oct. 22, 1864; d. Vienna, Aug. 18, 1931. He studied violin with Joachim at the Berlin Hochschule für Musik; played in various orchestras, including that of the Gewandhaus (1891-97); in 1897 became concertmaster of the court opera in Vienna; also taught violin at the Vienna Academy. He organized the Prill String Quartet, which was famous in his day.

Prill, Paul, German cellist and conductor; brother of **Emil** and **Karl Prill**; b. Berlin, Oct. 1, 1860; d. Bremen, Dec. 21, 1930. He studied with Manecke (cello) and Sturm (theory); was solo cellist in various German orchestras; conducted opera in Rotterdam (1886-89), in Hamburg (1889-92), in Nuremberg (1901-06); conducted the Mozart Orch. in Berlin (1906-08); then settled in Munich as conductor of the Konzertverein.

Primrose, William, pre-eminent Scottish viola virtuoso; b. Glasgow, Aug. 23, 1903. He studied violin in Glasgow with Camillo Ritter; then had lessons with Eugène Ysaÿe in Belgium (1925-27), who advised him to become a viola player; accordingly he accepted the position of violist in the London String Quartet, with which he made several American tours (1930-35). In 1937 he was engaged by Toscanini as first viola player in the NBC Symphony Orch. in N.Y., holding this post until 1942; in 1939 he established the William Primrose Quartet; in recognition of his services to English music he received the Order of Commander of the British Empire (1953); in 1956 he became violist in the Festival Piano Quartet; from 1961 to 1965 he taught at the Univ. of Southern California, Los Angeles; from 1965 to 1972 he was on the faculty of the School of Music of Indiana Univ. in Bloomington. In 1972 he inaugurated a master class at the Tokyo Univ. of Fine Arts and Music. Primrose published a didactic volume *Technique Is Memory. A Method for Violin and Viola Players* (London, 1960). He commissioned a viola concerto from Béla Bartók, but the work was not completed at the time of Bartók's death, and the task of reconstructing the score from Bartók's sketches was accomplished by Tibor Serly; Primrose gave the first performance of the work with the Minneapolis Symph. on Dec. 2, 1949.

Pringsheim, Klaus, German conductor and composer; b. Feldafing, near Munich, July 24, 1883; d. Tokyo, Dec. 7, 1972. A scion of a highly cultured family, he studied mathematics with his father, prof. at Munich Univ. and physics with Röntgen, the discoverer of X-rays. His twin sister Katherine was married to Thomas Mann. In Munich, Pringsheim took piano lessons with Bernard Stavenhagen, a student of Liszt, and composition with Ludwig Thuille. In 1906 he went to Vienna and was engaged as assistant conductor of the Vienna Opera, under tutelage of Gustav Mahler who took him as a pupil in conducting and composition, a relationship that developed into profound friendship. Mahler recommended him to the management of the German Opera in Prague; Pringsheim conducted there from 1909 to 1914; then was engaged as conductor and stage director at the Opera of Bremen (1915-18) and musical director of the Max Reinhardt theaters in Berlin (1918-25). In 1923-24 he conducted in Berlin a Mahler cycle of 8 concerts, featuring all of Mahler's symphonies and songs with orchestra. In 1927 he became the music critic of the socialist newspaper *Vorwärts*. A turning point in Pringsheim's life came in 1931 with an invitation to teach music at the Imperial Academy of Music in Tokyo, where he taught until 1937; several of his Japanese students became prominent composers. From 1937 to 1939 Pringsheim served as music adviser to the Royal Dept. of Fine Arts in Bangkok, Thailand. In 1939 he returned to Japan; was briefly interned in 1944 as an opponent of the Axis policies. In 1946 he went to California; after some intermittent activities, he returned to Japan in 1951; was appointed director of the Musashino Academy of Music in Tokyo; continued to conduct; also wrote music reviews for English-language Tokyo newspapers. As a composer, Pringsheim followed the neo-Romantic trends, deeply influenced by Mahler. His compositions include Concerto for Orchestra (Tokyo, Oct. 13, 1935); Japanese radio opera *Yamada Nagasama* (1953); Concertino for Xylophone and Orch. (1962); *Theme, Variations and Fugue* for wind orch. (his last compostion, 1971-72) and a curious album of 36 2-part canons for piano (1959). A chapter from his theoretical work, *Pythagoras, die Atonalität und wir* was published in *Schweizerische Musikzeitung* (1957). His reminiscences "Mahler, My Friend" were published posthumously in the British periodical *Composer* (1973-74). Pringsheim was a signatory of a letter of protest by surviving friends of Mahler against the motion picture *Death in Venice*, after a novelette of Thomas Mann, in which the central character, a famous writer who suffers a homosexual crisis, was made to resemble Mahler.

Printz, Wolfgang Caspar, German composer and writer; b. Waldthurn, Oct. 10, 1641; d. Sorau, Oct. 13, 1717. Originally a theological student, he later led a roving life, and then was cantor successively at Promnitz, Triebel, and (from 1665) Sorau. He brought out *Historische Beschreibung der edelen Sing- und Kling-Kunst* (Dresden, 1690), a work of some importance for the history of music of the 17th century. His other theoretical writings include *Anweisung zur Singkunst* (1666; 2nd ed., 1671; 3rd ed., 1685); *Compendium ad Oden componendam* (1668); *Musica modulationis vocalis* (1678); *Exercitationes . . . de concordantiis* (1687–89); also a curious satire on music theory, *Phrynis Mytilenaeus oder Satyrischer Componist* (1676-77; 2nd ed., 1696); also wrote 3 musical stories, characterizing different types of musicians. According to his own statement, the MSS of his numerous compositions were destroyed in a fire. A complete edition of his works, in 3 vols., was initiated in 1974, with publication of *Musikerromane* (Berlin, 1974).

BIBLIOGRAPHY: E. Schmitz, "Studien über W. Printz als Musikschriftsteller," *Monatshefte für Musik-Geschichte* (1904).

Proch, Heinrich, Austrian conductor, composer, and singing teacher; b. Böhmisch-Leipa. July 22, 1809; d. Vienna, Dec. 18, 1878. He studied law and at the same time took violin lessons; became conductor of the Josephstadt Theater, Vienna, in 1837; from 1840 to 1870 conducted at the Vienna Opera. He wrote many songs that were popular for a time; his set of variations for coloratura soprano with flute obbligato was particularly well known; also brought out in Vienna a comic opera, *Ring und Maske* (Dec. 4, 1844), and 3 one-act operas, *Die Blutrache* (Dec. 5, 1846), *Zweiter und dritter Stock* (Oct. 5, 1847), and *Der gefährliche Sprung* (Jan. 5, 1849).

Procházka, Rudolf, Bohemian writer on music and composer; b. Prague, Feb. 23, 1864; d. there, March 24, 1936. He studied violin with Wittich and composition with Fibich; then devoted himself mainly to music education; in 1911 he organized a commission for the licensing of music teachers in Bohemia. He published several monographs: *Dei böhmischen Musikschulen* (1890); *Mozart in Prag* (1892; very valuable; revised by Paul Nettl in 1939 as *Mozart in Böhmen*); *Robert Franz* (1894); *Arpeggien: Musikalisches aus alten und neuen Tagen* (1897; 2nd ed. as *Musikalische Streiflichter,* 1901); *Johann Strauss* (1900; 2nd ed., 1903); *Das romantische Musik-Prag* (1914); *Der Kammermusikverein in Prag* (1926). He also was a composer; wrote an allegorical opera, *Das Glück* (Prague, 1898); some orchestral pieces; *Deutsch-böhmische Reigen* for piano 4-hands; solo piano pieces; many choruses and songs.
BIBLIOGRAPHY: C. Hunnius, *Rudolf von Procházka, Ein deutscher Tondichter Böhmens* (Leipzig, 1902); E. Janetschek, "Rudolf von Procházka," *Neue Zeitschrift für Musik* (Dec. 1915).

Procter, Alice McElroy, American pianist; b. Albany, New York, April 18, 1915. She studied composition at Smith College and at the Eastman School of Music in Rochester, where she received her Ph.D. Subsequently, she taught piano in Boston and environs. She published some ingratiating teaching pieces for piano, among them the *Jumping Cat* and *Footsteps in the Night.* She is the wife of the composer **Leland Procter.**

Procter, Leland, American composer and teacher; b. Newton, Mass., March 24, 1914. He studied composition at the Eastman School of Music in Rochester, with Howard Hanson and Bernard Rogers, and later at the Univ. of Oklahoma. Returning to Boston he taught at the New England Cons. He published some teaching pieces for piano and wrote symphonic works. He is the husband of the pianist **Alice McElroy Procter.**

Prod'homme, Jacques-Gabriel, industrious French librarian and music critic; b. Paris, Nov. 28, 1871; d. there, June 17, 1956. He studied philology and music history at the École des Hautes Études Sociales (1890–94); then became a writer on musical and other subjects in the socialist publications, among them *La Revue Socialiste, Droits de l'Homme, Messidor,* etc. An ardent believer in the cause of peace, he edited in Munich the *Deutsch-französische Rundschau,* dedicated to the friendship between the French and German peoples (1897–1900). His hopes for peace were shattered by two devastating wars within his lifetime.
WRITINGS: Among his publications are *Le Cycle Berlioz,* in 2 vols.: *La Damnation de Faust* (1896) and *L'Enfance du Christ* (1898); *Hector Berlioz. Sa vie et ses œuvres* (1905); *Les Symphonies de Beethoven* (1906; 15th ed., 1938; awarded a prize by the French Academy); *Paganini* (1907; in English, 1911); *Écrits de musiciens* (1912); *La Jeunesse de Beethoven* (1921); *Richard Wagner et la France* (1921); *L'Opéra, 1669–1925* (1925); *Pensées sur la musique et les musiciens* (1926); *Beethoven raconté par ceux qui l'ont vu*

(1927); *Mozart raconté par ceux qui l'ont vu* (1928); *Schubert raconté par ceux qui l'ont vu* (1928); *Wagner raconté par ceux qui l'ont vu* (1929); *Les Sonates pour piano de Beethoven* (1937); *L'Immortelle bien-aimée de Beethoven* (1946); *Gluck* (1948); *Gossec* (1949); contributed a number of articles to the *Musical Quarterly.* In collaboration with Ch. Bertrand, he publ. *Guide musical et étude analytique de la Götterdämmerung* (1902); with A. Dandelot, *Gounod. Sa vie et ses œuvres d'après des documents inédits* (2 vols., 1911); with E. Crauzat, *Les Menus plaisirs du roi; l'École royale et le Conservatoire de Paris* (1929). Together with Fr. Holl, F. Caille, and L. van Vassenhove he transl. Wagner's prose works in 13 vols. (1908–25).

Profe, Ambrosius, German organist and music editor; b. Breslau, Feb. 12, 1589; d. there, Dec. 27, 1661. He studied theology at Wittenburg; then was cantor in Silesia; from 1663, he was church organist in Breslau. He edited important collections of German sacred music: *Geistliche Concerte und Harmonien,* for 1-7 voices (1641-46); *Corollarium geistlicher Collectaneorum* (a supplement to the previous vol.; 1649); a collection of Christmas songs, *Cunis solennibus Jesuli recens-nati sacra genethliaca* (11946); also brought out Heinrich Albert's *Arien* (1657).

Profeta, Laurenţiu, Rumanian composer; b. Bucharest, Jan. 12, 1925. He studied with P. Constantinescu, A. Mendelsohn, and Chirescu at the Bucharest Cons. (1945-49); later took courses at the Moscow Cons. (1954-56). He served as director of music for the Ministry of Culture (1952-60) and secretary of the Rumanian National Committee of the International Music Council (1960-70). His music is marked by rhapsodic expansiveness in romantically rich harmonies.
WORKS: 3 ballets: *Soţia căpitanului (The Captain's Wife,* 1946) *Prinţ şi cereştor (The Prince and the Beggar,* 1963-66) and *Marinarul visător (The Dreaming Sailor,* 1972); *Cîntece de tabără (Songs of Bivouac),* suite for soloists, children's chorus and orch. (1957); *Întîmplarea din grădină (The Adventures of the Gardener),* oratorio (1958); *Cantata patriei (Cantata of the Fatherland)* for narrator, mezzo-soprano, chorus and orch. (1959); *Brăduţul singuratic (The Singular Spruce Tree),* musical tale (1960); *6 Humorous Pieces* for children soloists, children's chorus and orch. (1966); *Suite for Marionnettes* for chamber orch. (1951); *Poemul Patriei* for orch. (1952); *Zile de vacanţă (Vacation Days),* symph. suite (1956); *Carnival* for 2 pianos (1957); film music; choruses; songs.

Prohaska, Carl, Austrian composer; b. Mödling, near Vienna, April 25, 1869; d. Vienna, March 28, 1927. He studied piano with Anna Assmayr in Vienna and with Eugen d'Albert in Berlin; composition with Franz Krenn; musicology with Mandyczewski in Vienna. In 1908 he joined the faculty of the Akademie der Tonkunst in Vienna, where he taught piano and theory. He wrote an opera *Madeleine Guinard;* an oratorio, *Frühlingsfeier* (1913); String Quartet; Piano Trio; Quintet for 2 violins, viola, cello and double bass; a group of piano pieces.

Prohaska, Felix, Austrian conductor, son of **Carl Prohaska;** b. Vienna, May 16, 1912. He received his primary music education at home with his father; then studied piano with Steuermann, and theory with Egon Kornauth and Hanns Gál. He then served as chorus conductor at the Graz Opera (1936–39); conducted opera in Duisburg (1939–41) and in Strasbourg 1941–43); then was principal conductor at the Vienna State Opera (1945–56) and at the Frankfurt Opera (1956–61); subsequently became instructor in conducting and director of the Hochschule für Musik in Hannover (1961–69); also filled in guest engagements in Europe and South America.

Prokofiev, Sergei, great Russian composer; b. Sontzovka, near Ekaterinoslav, April 23, 1891; d. Moscow, March 5, 1953. His mother was an amateur pianist, and he received his first training from her. He improvised at the piano; in June 1900, at the age of 9, he completed the piano score of an opera, *The Giant;* then wrote an overture and 3 tableaux for an opera entitled *On Desert Island* (1902); in 1904 he embarked on the composition of another opera *Ondine,* which he completed in 1907. He then went to Moscow where he began taking regular lessons from Glière, under whose guidance he composed a Symphony in G, and the opera, *Feast During the Plague,* after Pushkin (1903). At the age of 13 he entered the St. Petersburg Cons., where he studied composition with Rimsky-Korsakov, Wihtol, and Liadov; piano with Mme. Essipova, and conducting with Nicolas Tcherepnin. He graduated from the Cons. in 1914; received the Anton Rubinstein Prize (a grand piano) as a pianist-composer for his 1st Piano Concerto. Even before graduation, he appeared before various modern music societies in St. Petersburg, playing his own piano pieces, and soon earned a reputation as a youthful "futurist." He developed a novel piano idiom, explicitly demonstrated in his *Sarcasms* and *Visions fugitives,* percussive and sharp, yet not without a lyric charm. Grotesquerie and irony animated Prokofiev's early works; he also felt a strong attraction towards subjects of elemental or primitive character. His first important orchestral composition, the *Scythian Suite,* or *Ala and Lolly,* draws upon the ancient Russian sun-worship. While a parallel with Stravinsky's *Le Sacre du printemps* may exist, there is no similarity between the styles of the two works. Another score, primitivistic in its inspiration, was *Seven, They Are Seven,* an incantation from an old Sumerian ritual. During the same period, Prokofiev wrote his famous *Classical Symphony,* which he completed at the age of 26. In it he successfully recreated the formal style of the 18th century; while the structure was indeed classical, the sudden modulatory shifts and a subtle element of grotesquerie betrayed a 20th-century hand. He conducted the first performance of the *Classical Symphony* in the spring of 1918, and then left Russia, proceeding through Siberia and Japan to America; gave concerts of his music in New York, Chicago, and other cities. In 1920 he went to Paris, where he became associated with Diaghilev, who produced Prokofiev's ballets *Chout* (French transliteration of the Russian word for buffoon), *Le Pas d'acier,* and *L'Enfant prodigue.* Koussevitzky, who became Prokofiev's

publisher, commissioned several works from him for his concerts in Paris, and subsequently in Boston. In 1921 Prokofiev again visited the U.S. for the production by the Chicago Opera Co. of his opera, *Love for Three Oranges.* In 1927 he played a series of concerts in Russia; visited Russia again in 1929; then after a stay in Paris and other European cities, he went to Russia in December 1932 and remained permanently, with the exception of concert engagements in Europe and America. He had never relinquished Soviet citizenship, and was not officially an émigré. He visited the U.S. for the last time in 1938. In Russia he wrote some of his most popular works: the symph. fairy tale, *Peter and the Wolf* (for a children's theater in Moscow), the cantata *Alexander Nevsky* (originally for a film), the ballet *Romeo and Juliet,* the opera *War and Peace,* the 5th, 6th, and 7th symphonies; several piano sonatas; songs; etc. Although Prokofiev was the target of sharp criticism on the part of the Soviet press for his "decadent" practices in adopting certain modernistic procedures, his status on the whole remained very high; virtually all of his works were published; his music became a major influence on the young generation of Soviet composers. Outside Russia, too, Prokofiev enjoyed enduring fame; his *Classical Symphony,* his 3rd Piano Concerto, *Peter and the Wolf,* the march from *Love for Three Oranges,* the suite from *Lieutenant Kijé,* and many of the piano works have become repertory pieces all over the world. Prokofiev never departed from the tonal system despite occasional excursions into modernistic practices (polytonality, atonality). He had an innate sense of sharp rhythm, often in asymmetrical patterns; in his melodic writing he was equally adept in simple lyricism, along modal lines, and in a modern manner spanning large intervals; he was a master of instrumentation, developing an individual method of treating orchestral sonorities. Above all, his music shows a professional care for the performer, never reaching beyond the practicable limits of execution. In 1923, he married **Lina Llubera,** a Spanish soprano. Her real name was **Carlina Codina;** she was born in Madrid in 1898, Catalan on her father's side, and Polish and French on her mother's side. She assumed the stage name Lina Llubera; made her debut in Milan as Gilda in *Rigoletto.* About 1940 Prokofiev went to live with Myra Mendelson, a young Komsomol writer, but was not legally divorced from Lina Llubera. In 1946, the latter was sent to a concentration camp in Central Asia on a political charge, and spent 8 years there. She left Russia in 1976, and in 1977 was in the U.S.

WORKS: OPERAS: *Magdalena* (1913); *The Gambler,* after Dostoyevsky (1915-16; revised 1927; première, Brussels, April 29, 1929); *Love for Three Oranges,* after Carlo Gozzi (Chicago, Dec. 30, 1921, composer conducting); *The Flaming Angel,* (1919; 2 fragments performed at a Koussevitzky concert, Paris, June 14, 1928; complete performance in concert form was given in Paris on Nov. 25, 1954; its stage première was given in Venice on Sept. 14, 1955); *Simeon Kotko* (1939; Moscow, June 23, 1940); *Betrothal in a Convent,* after Sheridan's *Duenna* (1940; Leningrad, Nov. 3, 1946); *War and Peace,* after Tolstoy (1941–52; 1st version, Leningrad, June 12, 1946; 2nd version, Leningrad, April 1, 1955); *A Tale about a*

Real Man (1947–48; privately performed, Leningrad, Dec. 3, 1948; severely censured by Soviet critics and not produced in public; revived posthumously at the Bolshoi Theater in Moscow on Oct. 8, 1960).

BALLETS: *A Tale of a Buffoon Who Outwitted Seven Buffoons,* (usually performed outside Russia as *Chout;* 1920; Paris, May 17, 1921); *Le Pas d'acier* (1924; Paris, June 7, 1927); *L'Enfant prodigue* (1928; Paris, May 21, 1929); *Sur le Borysthène* (1930; Paris, Dec. 16, 1932); *Romeo and Juliet* (1935–36; Leningrad, Jan. 11, 1940); *Cinderella* (1940–44; Moscow, Nov. 21, 1945); *A Tale of the Stone Flower* (1948–50; Moscow, Feb. 12, 1954).

INCIDENTAL MUSIC: to *Egyptian Nights,* op. 61 (1933); *Boris Godunov* (1936), *Eugene Onegin* (1936), *Hamlet* (1937–38; first performed in connection with the opening of the Leningrad Theater, May 15, 1938). Film music: *Lieutenant Kijé* (1933); *The Queen of Spades* (1938); *Alexander Nevsky* (1938); *Lermontov* (1941); *Tonya* (1942); *Kotovsky* (1942); *Partisans in the Ukrainian Steppes* (1942); *Ivan the Terrible* (1942–45).

CHORAL WORKS: 2 poems for women's chorus with orch. *The White Swan* and *The Wave* (1909); *Seven, They Are Seven,* cantata for tenor, chorus, and orch. (1917–18; Paris, May 29, 1924); cantata for the 20th anniversary of the October Revolution, for 2 choruses, military band, accordions, percussion, to texts by Marx, Lenin, and Stalin (1937; not performed at the time; was finally brought to a performance in Moscow on April 5, 1966, but not in its entirety; the section which used a text from Stalin was eliminated); *Songs of Our Days* op. 76, suite for solo voices, mixed chorus, and orch. (Moscow, Jan. 5, 1938); *Alexander Nevsky,* cantata for mezzo-soprano, mixed chorus, and orch. (Moscow, May 17, 1939); *Salute,* cantata for mixed chorus and symph. orch., for Stalin's 60th birthday (Moscow, Dec. 21, 1939); *Ballad of a Boy Who Remained Unknown,* cantata for soprano, tenor, chorus, and orch. (Moscow, Feb. 21, 1944); *Hymn to the Soviet Union* (1943; submitted to the competition for a new Soviet anthem but failed to win; a song by Alexander Alexandrov was selected); *Flourish, Powerful Land,* cantata for the 30th anniversary of the October Revolution (Moscow, Nov. 12, 1947); *Winter Bonfire,* suite for narrators, boys' chorus, and symph. orch. (Moscow, Dec. 19, 1950); *On Guard for Peace,* oratorio for mezzo-soprano, narrators, mixed chorus, boys' chorus, and symph. orch. (Moscow, Dec. 19, 1950).

FOR ORCH: Sinfonietta (1914; Petrograd, Nov. 6, 1915; new version, 1929; Moscow, Nov. 18, 1930); *Rêves,* symph. tableau (St. Petersburg, Dec. 5, 1910); *Autumn,* symph. tableau (Moscow, Aug. 1, 1911); 1st Piano Concerto (Moscow, Aug. 7, 1912, composer soloist); 2nd Piano Concerto (Pavlovsk, Sept. 5, 1913, composer soloist; 2nd version, Paris, May 8, 1924, composer soloist); 1st Violin Concerto (1916–17; Paris, Oct. 18, 1923); *Scythian Suite* (1914; Petrograd, Jan. 29, 1916); *Chout,* symph. suite from the ballet (Brussels, Jan. 15, 1924); *Classical Symphony* (1916–17; Petrograd, April 21, 1918, composer conducting); 3rd Piano Concerto (1917–21; Chicago, Dec. 16, 1921, composer soloist); *Love for Three Oranges,* symph. suite from the opera (Paris, Nov. 29, 1925);

Symph. No. 2, (1924; Paris, June 6, 1925; 2nd version, not completed); *Le Pas d'acier,* symph. suite from the ballet (1926; Moscow, May 27, 1928); Overture for chamber orch. (Moscow, Feb. 7, 1927; also for large orch., 1928; Paris, Dec. 18, 1930); *Divertissement,* (1925–29; Paris, Dec. 22, 1929); Symph. No. 3 (1928; Paris, May 17, 1929); *L'Enfant prodigue,* symph. suite from the ballet (1929; Paris, March 7, 1931); Symph. No. 4 (Boston, Nov. 14, 1930; a new version radically revised in 1947); *4 Portraits,* symph. suite from the opera *The Gambler* (1931; Paris, March 12, 1932); *On the Dnieper,* symph. suite from the ballet (1933); 4th Piano Concerto, for left hand alone (1931; Berlin, Sept. 5, 1956); 5th Piano Concerto (Berlin, Oct. 31, 1932, composer soloist); *Symphonic Song* (Moscow, April 14, 1934); 1st Cello Concerto (1933–38; Moscow, Nov. 26, 1938; revised and performed for the first time in Moscow on Feb. 18, 1952, as Cello Concerto No. 2, but later retitled *Sinfonia-Concertante;* this final version was performed posthumously in Copenhagen on Dec. 9, 1954); *Lieutenant Kijé,* symph. suite from film music (1934; Paris, Feb. 20, 1937, composer conducting); *Egyptian Nights,* symph. suite (1934; Moscow, Dec. 22, 1938); 2nd Violin Concerto (1935; Madrid, Dec. 1, 1935); *Romeo and Juliet,* 1st suite from the ballet (Moscow, Nov. 24, 1936); *Romeo and Juliet,* 2nd suite from the ballet (Leningrad, April 15, 1937); *Peter and the Wolf,* symph. fairy tale (Moscow, May 2, 1936); *4 Marches,* for military band (1935–37); *Russian Overture,* (Moscow, Oct. 29, 1936); *Symphonic March* (1941); *The Year 1941* (Sverdlovsk, Jan. 21, 1943); *March* for military orch. (Moscow, April 30, 1944); Symph. No. 5 (1944; Moscow, Jan. 13, 1945); *Romeo and Juliet,* 3rd suite from the ballet (Moscow, March 8, 1946); *Ode on the End of the War,* for 8 harps, 4 pianos, military band, percussion ensemble, and double basses (1945; Moscow, Nov. 12, 1945); *Cinderella,* 3 suites from the ballet (1946); *Waltzes,* suite for orch. (1946; Moscow, May 13, 1947); Symph. No. 6 (1945–47; Leningrad, Oct. 11, 1947); *Festive Poem* (Moscow, Oct. 3, 1947); *Ivan the Terrible,* suite for orch. (1942–45); *Pushkin Waltzes* (1949); *Summer Night* symph. suite on themes from the opera, *Betrothal in a Convent* (1950); *Wedding Scene,* suite from the ballet, *A Tale of the Stone Flower* (Moscow, Dec. 12, 1951); *Gypsy Fantasy,* from the ballet, *A Tale of the Stone Flower* (Moscow, Nov. 18, 1951); *Ural Rhapsody,* from the ballet, *A Tale of the Stone Flower* (1951); *The Mistress of the Copper Mountain,* suite from the ballet, *A Tale of the Stone Flower* (incomplete); *The Meeting of the Volga with the Don River* (for the completion of the Volga-Don Canal; 1951; Moscow, Feb. 22, 1952); Symph. No. 7 (1951–52; Moscow, Oct. 11, 1952); Concertino for Cello and Orch. (1952; unfinished); Concerto for 2 Pianos and String Orch. (1952; incomplete).

CHAMBER MUSIC: *Humorous Scherzo* for 4 bassoons (1912; London, Sept. 2, 1916); *Ballade* for cello and piano (1912); *Overture on Hebrew Themes* for clarinet, 2 violins, viola, cello, and piano (N.Y., Jan. 26, 1920); Quintet for oboe, clarinet, violin, viola, and double bass (1924; Moscow, March 6, 1927); 1st String Quartet (Washington, April 25, 1931); Sonata for 2 violins (Moscow, Nov. 27, 1932); 1st Violin Sonata (1938–46; Moscow, Oct. 23, 1946); 2nd String Quartet (1941;

Moscow, Sept. 5, 1942); Sonata for flute and piano (Moscow, Dec. 7, 1943); 2nd Violin Sonata (transcription of the Flute Sonata; Moscow, June 17, 1944); Sonata for violin unaccompanied (1947); Cello Sonata (1949; Moscow, March 1, 1950).

PIANO MUSIC: 9 sonatas: No. 1 (1909); No. 2 (1912); No. 3 (1917); No. 4 (1917); No. 5 (1923); No. 6 (1940); No. 7 (1942); No. 8 (1944); No. 9 (1947); No. 10 remains in sketches (1953); 2 sonatinas (1931–32); 4 Études (1909); 4 Pieces (1911); 4 Pieces (1912); Toccata (1912); 10 Pieces (1913); *Sarcasms*, a suite of 5 pieces (1912–14); *Visions fugitives*, a suite of 20 pieces (1915–17); *Tales of an Old Grandmother*, 4 pieces (1918); *Schubert's Waltzes*, transcribed for 2 pianos (1911); March and Scherzo from the opera, *Love for Three Oranges* (1922); *Things in Themselves* (1928); 6 Pieces (1930–31); 3 Pieces (1934); *Pensées* (1933–34); *Children's Music*, 12 easy pieces (1935); *Romeo and Juliet*, 10 pieces from the ballet (1937); 3 pieces from the ballet *Cinderella* (1942); 3 Pieces (1941–42); 10 pieces from the ballet *Cinderella*, op. 97 (1943); 6 pieces from the ballet *Cinderella* (1944).

SONGS: 2 *Poems* (1911); *The Ugly Duckling* after Andersen (1914); 5 *Poems* (1915); 5 *Poems* (1916); 5 *Songs without Words* (1920; also for violin and piano); 5 *Poems* (1921); 6 *Songs* (1935); 3 *Children's Songs* (1936); 3 *Poems* (1936); 3 songs from the film *Alexander Nevsky* (1939); 7 *Songs* (1939); 7 *Mass Songs* (1941–42); 6 transcriptions of folksongs (1944); 2 duets (1945); *Soliders' March Song* (1950).

BIBLIOGRAPHY: M. Montagu-Nathan, "S. Prokofiev," *Musical Times* (Oct. 1916); M. Montagu-Nathan, "Prokofiev's First Pianoforte Concerto," *Musical Times* (Jan. 1917); M. Montagu-Nathan, *Contemporary Russian Composers* (N.Y., 1917); L. Sabaneyev, *Modern Russian Composers* (N.Y., 1927); N. Slonimsky, "S. Prokofiev," *Quarterly on the Soviet Union* (N.Y., April 1939); Gerald Abraham, *8 Soviet Composers* (London, 1943); S. Prokofiev, "The War Years," *Musical Quarterly* (Oct. 1944); I. Nestyev, *S. Prokofiev* (Moscow, 1946; in English, N.Y., 1946; enlarged Russian ed., Moscow, 1957; in English with a foreword by Nicolas Slonimsky; Stanford, California, 1961); Rena Moisenko, *Realist Music: 25 Soviet Composers* (London, 1949; pp. 173–87); N. Nabokov, *Old Friends and New Music* (Boston, 1951; pp. 141–83); S. Schlifstein, ed., *S. Prokofiev, Materials, Documents, Reminiscences* (Moscow, 1956; of prime documentary value; contains Prokofiev's autobiography and a complete catalogue of Prokofiev's works, with exhaustive commentaries and dates); F. Streller, *Prokofiev* (Leipzig, 1960); C. Samuel, *Prokofiev* (Paris, 1960); L. Gakkel, *Piano Works of S. Prokofiev* (Moscow, 1960); I. V. Nestyev and G. Edelman, eds., *Sergey Prokofiev, Articles and Materials* (Moscow, 1962); L. Berger, ed., *Traits of Prokofiev's Style* (Moscow, 1962); M. Hofmann, *Prokofiev* (Paris, 1963); L. and E. Hanson, *Prokofiev, The Prodigal Son* (London, 1964); S. Slonimsky, *The Symphonies of Prokofiev* (Leningrad, 1964); S. Schlifstein, ed., *Prokofiev*, album of pictures annotated in Russian and English (Moscow, 1965); V. Serov, *S. Prokofiev, a Soviet Tragedy* (N.Y., 1968); V. M. Blok, *Cello Works by Prokofiev* (Moscow, 1973). A complete text of Prokofiev's autobiography was published in Moscow in 1973.

Proksch, Josef, Bohemian pianist and pedagogue; b. Reichenberg, Aug. 4, 1794; d. Prague, Dec. 20, 1864. He studied with Koželuch; in 1811 he lost his eyesight, but still learned Logier's system, and in 1830 founded a "Musikbildungsanstalt" (school of piano playing) in Prague. He publ. a useful piano manual, *Versuch einer rationellen Lehrmethode im Pianofortespiel;* also a *Musikalisches Vademecum; Aphorismen über katholische Kirchenmusik; Allemeine Musiklehre;* made for his pupils transcriptions, for 2, 3, 4, and even 8 pianos, of orchestral works; composed a concerto for 3 pianos, sonatas and other works; also vocal music. His son, **Theodor Proksch** (1843–76), and a daughter, **Marie Proksch** (1836–1900), managed the school after his death; the last director of the Proksch school was **Robert Franz Proksch,** a great-grandnephew of Josef Proksch; he died in 1933.

BIBLIOGRAPHY: R. Müller, *Josef Proksch* (Prague, 1874); H. P. Kraus, *Musikbibliothek Josef Proksch* (Vienna, 1934).

Prony, Gaspard-Claire-François-Marie-Riche, Baron de, French harpist and music theorist; b. Chamelot, Rhône, July 12, 1755; d. Paris, July 29, 1839. As a member of the Académie, he was in charge of educational information; publ. a report on Érard's double-pedal harp, *Rapport sur la nouvelle harpe à double mouvement* (1815); other reports are: *Note sur les avantages du nouvel établissement d'un professorat d'harpe à l'école royale de musique* (1825); *Instruction élémentaire sur les moyens de calculer les intervalles musicaux* (1832; employing Euler's system of logarithms).

Prošev, Toma, Macedonian composer; b. Skopje, Nov. 10, 1931. He studied with Škerjanc at the Zagreb Academy of Music, graduating in composition in 1961; then made a musical pilgrimage to Nadia Boulanger in Paris (1964); thus musically replenished returned to Zagreb and devoted himself to teaching. His music is moderately modern.

WORKS: 2 operas: *Paučina (The Cobweb,* 1957) and *Mali princ (The Little Prince,* 1964); 2 ballets: *Okviri i odjeci (Frames and Echoes,* 1961) and *Pjesma nad pjesmama (Song of Songs,* 1967); 3 oratorios: *Jama (The Pit,* 1961), *Skopje* (1965) and *Sonce na prastarata zemja (Sun of the Ancient Country,* 1967); Piano Concertino (1958); *Makete (Dummies)* for orch. (1960); *Concertante Music* for cello and string orch. (1960); *Improvisations concertante* for violin and string orch. (1962); 2 symphonies (1962, 1963); 2 violin concertos (1963, 1964); *Tempera I–IV* for strings (1963–70); *Metastasis* for orch. (1963); Concerto for Ondes Martenot and orch. (1964); *Relations* for orch. (1964); *Morphographie* for chamber orch. (1965); *Diametry* for voice and chamber orch. (1966); *3 Movements* for clarinet and string orch. (1966); *Colors* for 6 solo voices and ensemble (1967); *Chamber Music* (1971); *Intergrali* for piano and chamber ensemble (1971); Violin Sonata (1953); String Quartet (1959); *Intima* for piano (1962).

Proske, Carl, German authority on sacred music; b. Gröbnig, Feb. 11, 1794; d. Regensburg, Dec. 20, 1861. He was a medical student, regimental physician during the war of 1813-15; took the degree of M.D. at Halle in 1817, and practiced at Oberglogau and Oppeln. In 1823 he renounced medicine for theology, and studied at Regensburg; was ordained in 1826, became vicar-choral in 1827, and canon and Kapellmeister of the Church of Our Lady at Regensburg in 1830. After diligent research in Germany and Italy, he began his lifework, the publication of sacred classics, the first being Palestrina's *Missa Papae Marcelli* (Palestrina's original version, and arrangements by Anerio *a* 4 and Suriano *a* 8), followed by the famous collection *Musica divina*, containing chiefly Italian masterworks of the 16th-17th centuries: vol. I, 12 Masses *a* 4 (1853); vol. II, motets for the entire church year (1855); vol. III, fauxbourdons, psalms, Magnificats, hymns, and antiphons (1859); vol. IV, Passions, Lamentations, responses, Te Deums, litanies (1863; edited by Wesselack); publication continued by Schrems and Haberl; also *Selectus novus missarum a 4-8* (1855-59). His valuable library was purchased for the Episcopal Library at Regensburg; in 1909, when Dr. Karl Weinmann was appointed librarian, it was opened to musicians and music students.

BIBLIOGRAPHY: Dom. Mettenleiter, *Carl Proske* (Regensburg, 1868; 2nd ed., 1895); K. Weinmann, *Carl Proske, der Restaurator der klassischen Kirchenmusik* (Regensburg, 1909); K. Weinmann, "Die Proskesche Musikbibliothek in Regensburg," in the Riemann Festschrift (Leipzig, 1909).

Prosniz, Adolf, Austrian pianist and pedagogue; b. Prague, Dec. 2, 1829; d. Vienna, Feb. 23, 1917. He was a pupil of Proksch and Tomaschek; 1869-1900, prof. of piano at the Vienna Cons.; then retired and lived in Vienna.

WRITINGS: *Kompendium der Musikgeschichte* (vol. I, 1889; 3rd ed., 1920; vol. II, 1900; vol. III, 1915); *Handbuch der Klavierliteratur* (vol. I, 1450-1830, 1884; 2nd ed., 1908; vol. II, 1830-1904, 1907); *Elementarmusiklehre* (6 eds.); *Historische Klavierliteratur aus dem 16., 17. und 18. Jahrhundert. Ausgewählte Beispiele zu jedem Handbuch der Klavierliteratur* (9 vols.).

Prota-Giurleo, Ulisse, Italian musicoligist; b. Naples, March 13, 1886; d. Perugia, Feb. 9, 1966. At first an art critic, he took up the study of musicology and devoted himself chiefly to Neapolitan music. His publications (all printed in Naples) are valuable for their documentation.

WRITINGS: *Musicisti napoletani alla corte di Portogallo* (1923); *Musicisti napoletani in Russia* (1923); *Paisiello ed i soui primi trionfi a Napoli* (1923); *Nicola Logroscini, "il dio dell'opera buffa"* (1927); *La grande orchestra del R. Teatro San Carlo nel settecento* (1927); *La Famiglia e la giovinezza di Salvator Rosa* (containing 52 unpublished documents; 1929); "Notizie sul musicista belga Jean Macque," *Report of the First Congress of the International Society for Musical Research* (Burnham, 1930); *Sacchini non nacque a Pozzuoli* (1952); *Nouvi contributi alla biografia di Domenico Cimarosa* and *Nuovi contributi alle biografie di Nicola Porpora e Giuseppe Porsile* (both published serially in *La Scala* during 1955-56); *I Treatri di Napoli nel '600; la commedia e le maschere*

(Naples, 1962); numerous essays publ. in the Italian periodicals *Samnium, Vita Musicale Italiana, Nostro Tempo,* etc.

Protheroe, Daniel, American conductor and composer; b. Ystradgynlais, S. Wales, Nov. 24, 1866; d. Chicago, Feb. 24, 1934. From 1884-86, conductor of the Choral Society at Ystradgynlais; choral conductor in Scranton, Pa., 1886-94; singer and teacher in Milwaukee, 1894-1909; then lived in Chicago as music director of the Central Church. He wrote a symph. poem, *In The Cambrian Hills;* a string quartet; works for men's chorus; songs; a *Course in Harmony and Choral Conducting.*

Prout, Ebenezer, eminent English music theorist and teacher; b. Oundle, Northamptonshire, March 1, 1835; d. London, Dec. 5, 1909. Excepting some piano lessons as a boy, and later a course with Charles Salaman, he was wholly self-taught. His father had him trained for a school teacher, and he took the degree of B.A. at London Univ. in 1854; but in 1859 went over definitely to music; was organist at Union Chapel, Islington, 1861-73; prof. of piano at the Crystal Palace School of Art, 1861-85; prof. of harmony and composition at the National Training School from 1876, and took Sullivan's class at the Royal Academy of Music in 1897; also conducted the Hackney Choral Association 1876-90, bringing it to a high state of efficiency; edited the *Monthly Musical Record* 1871-74, was critic on the *Academy* 1874-79, and on the *Athenaeum* 1879-89. In 1894 he was called to Dublin Univ. as prof. of music, succeeding Sir R. Stewart; in 1895 both Dublin and Edinburgh Universities conferred on him the degree of Mus. Doc. (honoris causa). His valuable theoretical works are the following: *Instrumentation* (Novello primer 1876; 3rd ed., 1904); *Harmony, Its Theory and Practice* (1889; 20th ed., entirely rewritten, 1903); *Counterpoint, Strict and Free* (1890); *Double Counterpoint and Canon* (1891); *Fugue* (1891); *Fugal Analysis* (1892); *Musical Form* (1893); *Applied Forms* (1895); all of which have passed through many editions; *The Orchestra* (2 vols., 1898-99; in German, 1905-06); and *Some Notes on Bach's Church-Cantatas* (1907). He was also a competent composer of useless works, among them 4 symphonies; 2 overtures; 2 organ concertos; a piano quintet; 2 string quartets; 2 piano quartets; clarinet sonata; the cantatas *Hereward, Alfred, The Red Cross Knight;* a considerable amount of church music; *Freedom,* ode for baritone solo and orch.; organ arrangements.

Provenzale, Francesco, one of the founders of the Neapolitan Opera School; b. Naples, 1627; d. there, Sept. 6, 1704. From 1663 he was maestro at the Cons. di Santa Maria di Loreto; 1673-1701, director of the Cons. della Pietà de' Turchini; c.1680 associate conductor of the Royal Chapel; 1686-99, conductor at the Tesoro di San Gennaro, Naples. Romain Rolland believed him to be identical with Francesco della Torre.

WORKS: operas (all performed in Naples): *Ciro* (1653), *Serse* (1955), *Artemisia* (1657), *Teseo o L'Incostanza triofante* (1658), *L'Eritrea* (1659), *Lo Schiavo di sua moglie* (1671), *La Stellidaura vendicata o Diffendere l'offensore* (1674), and *Candaule re di Lidia*

(1679); also oratorios; motets; a 9-voiced hymn with instrumental accompaniment, *Pange lingua;* and cantatas.

BIBLIOGRAPHY: R. Rolland, *Histoire de l'opéra avant Lully et Scarlatti* (1895); H. Riemann, *Handbuch der Musikgeschichte* II, 2, p. 385ff.; H. Goldschmidt, "F. Provenzale als Dramatiker," *Sammelbände der Internationalen Musik-Gesellschaft* VII/4; G. Pannain, "F. Provenzale e la lirica del suo tempo," *Rivista Musicale Italiana* (1925).

Prudent, Émile, French pianist; b. Angoulême, Feb. 3, 1817; d. Paris, May 13, 1863. Early orphaned, he was adopted by a piano tuner; studied at the Paris Cons. with Zimmerman (piano) and Laurent (harmony), taking 1st prize in 1833. He made tours as a pianist in France, Belgium, England, and Germany; then settled in Paris, and was greatly esteemed there as a teacher. He wrote a number of piano works; contemporary critics ranked him between Thalberg and Döhler; his paraphrase of *Lucia di Lammermoor* enjoyed considerable success; he publ. *6 études de salon,* and other effective piano pieces (*L'Hirondelle, La Berceuse, Chanson sicilienne, Le Réveil des fées,* etc.).

Pruett, James W., American librarian and music educator; b. Mt. Airy, North Carolina, Dec. 23, 1932. He studied music and comparative literature at the Univ. of North Carolina, Chapel Hill (B.A., 1955; M.A., 1957; Ph.D., 1962). After serving as music librarian at the Univ. of North Carolina (1955–76) and assistant prof. of music (1963–74) and prof. of music (1974–76), he was appointed chairman of the music dept. there in 1976; in 1974–77 was the editor of *Notes,* the quarterly journal of the Music Library Association. His specialty is the music of the late Italian Rennaissance and American musical biography; he contributed valuable papers on musical bibliography to various scholarly journals; published an interesting essay, "Charles Butler: Musician, Grammarian, Apiarist," in the *Musical Quarterly* (1963).

Prüfer, Arthur, German musicologist; b. Leipzig, July 7, 1860; d. Würzburg, June 3, 1944. He was a law student; then turned to music; studied at the Leipzig Cons. (1887–88), also attending the lectures on musicology of Paul and Kretzschmar at the Univ.; studied further in Berlin (1888–89) with Spitta and Bargiel; took the degree of Dr. phil. (Leipzig, 1890), with the dissertation *Über den ausserkirchlichen Kunstgesang in den evangelischen Schulen des 16. Jahrhunderts;* qualified 1895 as lecturer at Leipzig Univ. with the essay *Johann Hermann Schein;* 1902 as associate prof., with the lecture *J. S. Bach und die Tonkunst des 19. Jahrhunderts.* Further publications: *Die Bühnenfestspiele in Bayreuth* (1899; 2nd ed., completely rewritten and greatly enlarged, as *Das Werk von Bayreuth,* 1909); *Joh. Herm. Schein und das weltliche deutsche Lied des 17. Jahrhunderts* (1908); *R. Wagner in Bayreuth* (1910); *Die Musik als tönende Faust-Idee* (1920); *Tristan und Isolde* (3rd ed., 1928); *Deutsches Leben im Volkslied und Wagners Tannhäuser* (1929); *Tannhäuser und der Sängerkrieg* (1930). He edited the first collected ed. of Schein's works, publ. 1901–23 by Breitkopf & Härtel (8 vols. appeared); publ. separately

selections of 20 "weltliche Lieder" and instrumental pieces of Schein.

Prumier, Antoine, French harpist; b. Paris, July 2, 1794; d. there, Jan. 20, 1868. He studied at the Paris Cons.; played the harp in the orch. of the Opéra-Comique (from 1835); succeeded Nadermann as harp prof. at the Cons. He wrote about 100 fantasies, rondos, and airs with variations, for harp. His son **Ange-Conrad Prumier** (b. Paris, Jan. 5, 1820; d. there, April 3, 1884), succeeded him at the Opéra-Comique, and became prof. at the Cons. in 1870. He publ. études for harp; nocturnes for harp and horn; sacred songs.

Prunières, Henry, eminent French musicologist; b. Paris, May 24, 1886; d. Nanterre, April 11, 1942. He studied history of music with R. Rolland; *Dr. ès lettres,* 1913; 1909–14, instructor at the École des Hautes Études Sociales in Paris; 1920, founded the important journal *La Revue Musicale,* of which he was editor-in-chief until 1939; 1921, organized the concerts at the Théâtre du Vieux Colombier; was head of the French section of the International Society for Contemporary Music.

WRITINGS: *Lully* (1910; 2nd ed., 1927), *L'Opéra italien en France avant Lully* (1913); *Le Ballet de cour en France avant Benserade et Lully* (1914), *Monteverdi* (1924, enlarged 1926; 2nd ed., 1931; also in English, N.Y., 1926; reprint, 1972); *La Vie illustre et libertine de J.-B. Lully* (1929), *Cavalli et l'opéra vénitien au XVIIᵉ siècle* (1931), *Nouvelle histoire de la musique* (2 vols., 1934, 1936; in English, 1 vol., 1943; reprint, N.Y., 1972); and the following valuable essays: "La Musique de la Chambre et de l'Écurie sous le règne de François I," *Année Musicale* 1 (1911), "Jean de Cambefort, Surintendant de la musique de la chambre de roy," *Année Musicale* 2 (1913). He was general editor of a complete ed. of Lully's works (10 vols., Paris, 1930–39).

BIBLIOGRAPHY: special issue of the *Revue Musicale* (1952–53), dedicated to Prunières.

Prüwer, Julius, Austrian conductor; b. Vienna, Feb. 20, 1874; d. New York, July 8, 1943. He studied piano with Friedheim and Moriz Rosenthal, and theory with R. Fuchs and Krenn; also profited greatly by his friendly association with Brahms. He studied conducting with Hans Richter; began his career as conductor in Bielitz; then conducted at the Cologne Opera (1894–96) and at the Municipal Theater in Breslau (1896–1923), where he distinguished himself by conducting numerous new works. From 1924 to 1933 he conducted popular concerts of the Berlin Philharmonic. In 1933 he was compelled to leave Germany owing to the barbarous racial laws of the Nazi regime; conducted in Russia and in Austria; eventually reached New York where he remained until his death.

Pryor, Arthur (Willard), Ameican trombonist, bandleader and composer of band music; b. St. Joseph, Missouri, Sept. 22, 1870; d. Long Branch, New Jersey, June 18, 1942. He began his professional career in 1889 as a performer on the slide trombone. When J. P. Sousa formed his own band in 1892 he hired Pryor as his trombone soloist, and from 1895 until he left to form his own band in 1903, Pryor was assistant conductor for Sousa. Pryor's Band gave its first major concert at the Majestic Theatre in N.Y. on Nov. 15, 1903, but beginning in 1904 it initiated series of summer outdoor concerts at Asbury Park, Coney Island, and other amusement parks. From 1903 to 1909 it made 6 coast-to-coast tours. Unlike Sousa, who would have nothing to do with "canned music," Pryor was quick to take advantage of the developing record industry; he made some 1,000 acoustic records, before 1930. He likewise entered upon a series of commercial radio broadcasts. He composed about 300 works, including operettas, ragtime and cakewalk tunes, and novelties such as "The Whistler and His Dog," Pryor's best-known work. He was a charter member of ASCAP in 1914 and of the American Bandmasters Assn. in 1929. In 1933 he retired to Long Branch, New Jersey.

BIBLIOGRAPHY: *Dictionary of American Biography* (Suppl. II, pp. 610-611).

Przyblski, Bronislaw, Polish composer; b. Lódź, Dec. 11, 1941. He studied music theory with Kiesewetter at the Lódź Cons.; then joined its faculty. In his music he experiments with mathematical notions, except in straightforward Polish pieces.

WORKS: *Circulus* for percussion (1971); *Canon enigmaticus per fiati* for 2 to 50 arbitrarily selected wind instruments (1971); *Rotazioni per tre* for 3 selected instruments (1971); *Polish Dance Suite* for orch. (1971); *Omaggio a Nicolaus Copernicus* for orch. (1972; Lódź, May 25, 1973); *Scherzi musicali* for string ensemble (1973); *Voices* for 3 narrators and instruments ensemble (1974); *Polish Symphony* (1974).

Ptaszyńska, Marta, Polish composer and percussionist; b. Warsaw, July 29, 1943. She studied piano and timpani at the Music Lyceum in Warsaw (1957-62); then took courses in composition with Dobrowolski and Rudziński at the Warsaw Cons. (1962-68) and worked out problems of electronic music with Kotoński in his studio; had supplementary practice in percussion at the Cons. of Pozań (1963-67); in 1969 traveled to Paris where she, like everybody, had lessons with Nadia Boulanger. In 1972 she received a grant of the Kosciuszko Foundation to travel to the U.S., and studied percussion at the Cleveland Institute of Music (1972-74). From 1974 till 1977 she taught percussion at Bennington College in Vermont; in 1977 became instructor in composition at the Univ. of California, Berkeley. She played with the "Percussions de Strasbourg"; was a composer and percussionist at the Claremont Music Festival in California, and at the 4th New York Festival of Contemporary American Music. Her music is entirely free of any strictures, whether academically traditional or fashionably modern. Being a virtuoso drummer, she naturally gives a prominent place to percussion in her scores; she also makes use of stereophony by spatial separation of players or groups of instruments.

WORKS: *Oscar from Alva,* opera for television, with libretto by the composer, based on Byron's poem, scored for a large ensemble, including a raucous rock group (1972); *Improvisations* for orch. (1968; Cracow, March 26, 1971); oratorio, *Chant for All the People on Earth* (1969); *Helio, Centricum, Musicum,* multi-media spectacle for voices, dancers and instrumentalists (1973); *Spectri Sonori* for orch. (1973; Cleveland, Jan. 22, 1974); *Crystallites* for orch. (1973; Bydgoszcz, Poland, Jan. 24, 1975); Concerto for Percussion Quartet and Orch. (1974; Bennington College, Vermont, Oct. 20, 1974); *Chimes, Bells, Wood, Stones* for wind and string instruments and percussion (Bennington College, June 9, 1977); *Preludes* for vibraphone and piano (1965); *Variations* for solo flute (1967); *Scherzo* for xylophone and piano (1967; received the Polish State Prize); *A Tale of Nightingales* for baritone and 6 instruments (1968); *Projections Sonores* for chamber ensemble (1970); *Madrigals,* in memory of Stravinsky, for wind instruments, string quartet, trumpet, trombone, and gong (1971); *Space Model* for solo percussion (1971); *Sonospheres No. 1* for clarinet, trombone, cello and piano (1971); *Sonospheres No. 2* for 8 instruments (1971); *Sonospheres No. 3* for flute, clarinet, trombone, cello, piano and percussion (1972); *Siderals* for 2 percussion quintets, with light projections (Univ. of Illinois, Urbana, Nov. 21, 1974); *Recitative, Arioso, Toccata* for solo violin (1969-75); *2 Poems* for solo tuba (1973-75); *Mobile* for 2 players (1975); *Ornaments in Wood* for flute, clarinet, bass clarinet and bassoon (1975); *Classical Variations* for 4 timpani and string quartet (1976); *Quodlibet* for solo double bass (1976); *Epigrams* for 20 women's voices, flute, harp, piano and percussion (1976-77); *Inventions* for solo percussionists (1972-77); *Linear Constructions in Space* for percussion quartet (1977); *3 Interludes* for 2 pianos (1969); *Touracou* for harpsichord (1974); *Farewell Souvenir* for piano (1975); percussion music for children.

Ptolemy, Claudius, great Alexandrian astronomer, geographer, and mathematician who flourished early in the 2nd century A.D. Wrote an important treatise on music, a good Latin version of which was made by Gogavinus (1562); Wallis publ. the original Greek text in 1682; O. Paul gives a fragment in Greek, with German transl., in his *Boëtius*. A new ed. of this work was publ. by Ingemar Düring (Göteborg, 1930), with excellent commentary and explanation.

BIBLIOGRAPHY: I. Düring, *Ptolemaios und Porphyrios über die Musik* (Göteborg, 1934); M. Shirlaw, "Claudius Ptolemy as Musical Theorist," *Music Review* (Aug. 1955).

Puccini, Giacomo, celebrated Italian composer; b. Lucca, Dec. 22, 1858; d. Brussels, Nov. 29, 1924. Beginning with his great-great-grandfather, Giacomo (1712-81), all of his ancestors in the direct line were musicians of local prominence: **Antonio** (1747-1832), **Domenico** (1771-1815), **Michele** (1813-64). As a child Puccini showed neither inclination nor special talent for music; but his mother, determined to continue family tradition, sent him to the Istituto Musicale of Lucca (founded by Pacini), where Carlo Angeloni, a pupil of Michele Puccini, became his teacher. After Angeloni's untiring patience had aroused interest, and then enthusiasm, in his pupil, progress was rapid and Puccini soon was a good pianist and organist. About 1875 he became organist at the church in a nearby village, Muligliano, and soon after was also appointed organist at San Pietro in Somaldi. In 1877 he submitted a cantata, *Juno*, to a competition held at Lucca, but failed to win the prize. Nevertheless, he produced the work, which won considerable local success, so that the young composer brought out, also with success, a motet for the feast of Santa Paolina. These successes fired his ambition, and when he became acquainted about that time with *Aida* he resolved to win laurels as a dramatic composer. Assistance from a grand-uncle and a stipend granted by Queen Margherita enabled him to enter the Milan Cons., where he spent 3 years (1880–83) in serious study with Antonio Bazzini and Amilcare Ponchielli. For his graduation he wrote a *Capriccio sinfonico*, which at its performance at one of the Cons. concerts, and later by Faccio, elicited unstinted praise from the critics. In the same year Ponchielli introduced Puccini to the librettist Fontana, who furnished him the text of a 1-act opera; in a few weeks the score was finished and sent to the Sonzongo competition. It did not win the prize, but on May 31, 1884, *Le Villi* was produced at the Teatro dal Verme, in Milan, with gratifying success. Ricordi, who was present, considered the work sufficiently meritorious to commission the young composer to write a new opera for him; but 5 years elapsed before this work, *Edgar* (3 acts, text by Fontana), was produced at La Scala (April 21, 1889), scoring only a moderate success. By this time Puccini had become convinced that, in order to write a really effective opera, he needed a better libretto than Fontana had provided. Accordingly, he commissioned Domenico Oliva to write the text of *Manon Lescaut;* during the composition, however, Puccini and Ricordi practically rewrote the entire book, and in the publ. score Oliva's name did not mention. With *Manon Lescaut* (4 acts), first produced at the Teatro Regio in Turin on Feb. 1, 1893, Puccini won a veritable triumph, which was even surpassed by the next work, *La Bohème* (4 acts; text by Illica and Giacosa), produced at the same theater on Feb. 1, 1896. These two works not only carried their composer's name throughout the world, but also have found and maintained their place in the repertory of every opera house. With fame came wealth, and in 1900 he built at Lago del Torre, where he had been living since 1891, a magnificent villa. The next opera, *Tosca* (3 acts; text by Illica and Giacosa), produced at the Teatro Costanzi in Rome on Jan. 14, 1900, is Puccini's most dramatic work; it has become a fixture of the standard repertory and contains some of Puccini's best-known arias. At its première at La Scala on Feb. 17, 1904, *Madama Butterfly* (2 acts; text by Illica and Giacosa) was hissed. Puccini thereupon withdrew the score and made some slight changes (division into 3 acts, and addition of the tenor aria in the last scene). This revised version was greeted with frenzied applause in Brescia on May 28 of the same year. Puccini was now the acknowledged ruler of the Italian operatic stage, his works rivaling those of Verdi in the number of performances. The first performance of *Madama Butterfly* at the Metropolitan Opera House (Feb. 11, 1907) took place in the presence of the composer, whom the management had invited especially for the occasion. It was then suggested that he write an opera on an American subject, the première to take place at the Metropolitan Opera House.

He found his subject when he witnessed a performance of Belasco's *The Girl of the Golden West;* he commissioned C. Zangarini and G. Civinini to write the libretto, and in the presence of the composer the world première of *La Fanciulla del West* occurred, amid much enthusiasm, at the Metropolitan Opera House on Dec. 10, 1910; while it never equaled the success of Puccini's *Tosca* or *Madama Butterfly,* it returned to favor in the 1970's as a period piece. Puccini then brought out *La Rondine* (3 acts; Monte Carlo, March 27, 1917) and the 3 1-act operas *Il Tabarro* (after Didier Gold's *La Houppelande),* *Suor Angelica,* and *Gianni Schicchi* (all performed at the Metropolitan Opera House, Dec. 14, 1918). His last opera, *Turandot* (after Gozzi), was left unfinished; the final scene was completed by Franco Alfano and the work performed at La Scala, Milan, on April 25, 1926; it was also given at the Metropolitan Opera House, Nov. 16, 1926. All operas by Puccini have been performed in the U.S.: *Le Villi* (Metropolitan Opera House, Dec. 17, 1908); *Manon Lescaut* (Hinrichs Co., Philadelphia, Aug. 29, 1894); *La Bohème* (Los Angeles, Oct. 18, 1897); *Tosca* (Metropolitan Opera House, Feb. 4, 1901); *Madama Butterfly* (Washington, Oct. 15, 1906).

BIBLIOGRAPHY: M. Virgilio, *Della Decadenza dell'opera in Italia* (Milan, 1900); A. Brüggemann, *Madama Butterfly e l'arte di G. Puccini* (Milan, 1904); Wakeling Dry, *G. Puccini* (London, 1906); F. Torrefranca, *G. Puccini e l'opera internazionale* (Turin, 1912); D. C. Parker, "A View of G. Puccini," *Musical Quarterly* (Oct. 1917); A. Weismann, *G. Puccini* (Munich, 1922); A. Cœuroy, *La Tosca* (Paris, 1924); A. Bonaventura, *G. Puccini: L'Uomo, l'artista* (Leghorn, 1924); A. Fraccaroli, *La Vita di G. Puccini* (Milan, 1925; also in German); G. Marotti and F. Pagni, *G. Puccini intimo* (Florence, 1926); G. Adami, letters of Puccini (Milan, 1928; in English, London, 1931); A. Neisser, *Puccini* (Leipzig, 1928); F. Salerno, *Le Donne pucciniane* (Palmero, 1928); G. M. Gatti, "The Works of G. Puccini," *Musical Quarterly* (Jan. 1928); R. C. Merlin, *Puccini* (Milan, 1930); R. Specht, *Puccini* (Berlin, 1931; in English, N.Y., 1933); W. Maisch, *Puccinis musikalische Formgebung* (Neustadt, 1934); G. Adami, *Puccini* (Milan, 1935; in German, 1943); M. Carner, "The Exotic Element in Puccini," *Musical Quarterly* (Jan. 1936); K. G. Fellerer, *G. Puccini* (Potsdam, 1937); V. Seligman, *Puccini Among Friends* (correspondence; N.Y., 1938); G. Marotti, *Giacomo Puccini intimo* (Florence, 1942); F. Thiess, *Puccini, Versuch einer Psychologie seiner Musik* (Berlin, 1947); A. Bonaccorsi, *Giacomo Puccini e i suoi antenati musicali* (Milan, 1950); G. Marek, *Puccini: A Biography* (N.Y., 1951); Dante del Fiorentino, *Immortal Bohemian: an Intimate Memoir of Giacomo Puccini* (N.Y., 1952); V. Terenzio, *Ritratto di Puccini* (Bergamo, 1954); A. Machard, *Une Vie d'amour: Puccini* (Paris, 1954); L. Ricci, *Puccini interprete di se stesso* (Milan, 1954); E. Greenfield, *Puccini: Keeper of the Seal* (London, 1958); C. Sartori, *Puccini* (Milan, 1958); M. Carner, *Puccini* (London, 1958); W. Sandelewski, *Puccini* (Cracow, 1963); C. Hopkinson, *A Bibliography of the Works of Giacomo Puccini* (N.Y., 1968); S. Jackson *Monsieur Butterfly: The Story of Giacomo Puccini* (1974); *Letters of G. Puccini* (London, 1974).

Puchalsky, Vladimir, Russian pianist and composer; b. Minsk, April 2, 1848; d. Kiev, Feb. 23, 1933. He studied at the St. Petersburg Cons. with Leschetizky (piano) and Zaremba (theory); in 1876 appointed instructor at the Kiev Cons.; remained in Kiev until his death. He wrote an opera, *Valeria;* piano pieces and songs.

Puchat, Max, German composer and pianist; b. Breslau, Jan. 8, 1859; d. (killed in a fall in the Karwendel Alps) Aug. 12, 1919. He studied with Kiel in Berlin, winning the Mendelssohn Prize in 1884. From 1886 to 1903 he was active as choral conductor in German provinces; then went to Milwaukee, where he conducted the local Musikverein (1903–05); in 1910, settled in Breslau, where he established his own music school. He wrote several symph. works: *Euphorion* (1888), *Leben und Ideal* (1892), *Tragödie eines Künstlers* (1894), *Ouvertüre über ein nordisches Thema,* etc.; Piano Concerto; String Quartet; songs.

Pucitta, Vincenzo, Italian composer; b. Civitavecchia, 1778; d. Milan, Dec. 20, 1861. He studied with Fenaroli in Naples; traveled through Europe, and was successful as an opera composer in Italy, Austria, France, and England; wrote about 30 operas, of which the best were *La Burla fortunata* (Venice, April 9, 1804) and *La Vestale* (London, May 3, 1810).

Puente, Giuseppe Del, baritone; b. Naples, Jan. 30, 1841; d. Philadelphia, May 25, 1900. He first studied cello at the Naples Cons. but later began to cultivate his voice, making his operatic debut at Jassy; was then engaged for the Teatro San Carlo in Naples, and for appearances in France, Germany, Russia, Spain, and England (debut Covent Garden, 1873; became very popular there); first American engagement under Strakosch at the N.Y. Academy of Music in 1873–74; became a member of the first Metropolitan Opera company and sang the role of Valentin in the inaugural performance of *Faust* on Oct. 22, 1883. In 1885 he returned to the Academy of Music under Mapleson's management, taking part in the American première of *Manon* on Dec. 23 of that year; he was also a member of the opera troupes of Patti and Hinrichs; with the latter's company he sang in the American première of *Cavalleria Rusticana* (Philadelphia, Sept. 9, 1891). He married the mezzo-soprano **Helen Dudley Campbell.**

Puget, Paul-Charles-Marie, French composer; b. Nantes, June 25, 1848; d. Paris, March 14, 1917. He studied at the Paris Cons. with Marmontel (piano) and Massé (composition); won 1st Grand Prix de Rome in 1873 with the cantata *Mazeppa;* wrote much theater music; his opera *Beaucoup de bruit pour rien,* after Shakespeare (Paris, March 24, 1899), had a moderately good reception.

Pugnani, Gaetano, celebrated Italian violinist and composer; b. Turin, Nov. 27, 1731; d. there, July 15, 1798. He studied violin with G. B. Somis; on April 19, 1748 he was appointed violinist in the Royal Chapel of Turin; in 1794 he went to Rome to study with Ciampi; subsequently travelled in Europe as a concert violinist; he was particularly successful in London, and served as concertmaster of the Italian Opera at King's Theatre in London (1767–70). In 1770 he was back in Turin, where he founded a school of his own; among his pupils were Viotti, Conforti, Bruni and Polledro. He continued his concert career in Europe, including Russia. His own style of composition approximates that of Tartini; his violin music is of a virtuoso quality. Fritz Kreisler publ. a purported arrangement for violin and piano of a piece by Pugnani, *Preludio e Allegro e Tempo di Minuetto,* but this proved to be a brilliant imitation of the Italian style by Kreisler himself, who admitted his deception in the end, giving as a reason his desire to attach a famous name to his music as a chance for success.

WORKS: 9 violin concertos; 12 octets (*sinfonie*) for strings, 2 oboes, and 2 horns; 6 quintets for 2 violins, 2 flutes and cello; 6 string quartets; 3 sets of trios for 2 violins and cello; 2 sets of violin duets; 18 violin sonatas; several operas: *Nanetta e Lubino* (London, 1769), *Issea* (Turin, 1771), *Aurora* (Turin, 1775), *Adone e Venere* (Naples, 1784), *Demetrio a Rodi* (Turin, 1879); an instrumental suite *Werther* (1759; not connected with Goethe's famous work).

BIBLIOGRAPHY: F. Fayolle, *Notices sur Corelli, Tartini, Gaviniès, Pugnani et Viotti* (Paris, 1810); Dom. Carutti, "Della famiglia de Gaetano Pugnani," *Miscellanea di storia italiana* (3rd series, vol. II, Turin, 1895); S. Cordero di Pamparato, *Gaetano Pugnani* (Turin, 1930); A. Della Corte, *Notizie di Gaetano Pugnani, musicista torinese* (Turin, 1931); E. M. von Zschinsky-Troxler, *Gaetano Pugnani* (Berlin, 1939; contains a thematic catalogue); A. Müry, *Die Instrumentalwerke Gaetano Pugnanis* (Basel, 1941).

Pugni, Cesare, Italian composer; b. Genoa, May 31, 1802; d. St. Petersburg, Jan. 26, 1870. He studied violin with Alessandro Rolla and composition with Asioli at the Cons. of Milan; began his career as composer for the stage with the ballet *Elerz e Zulmida* (Milan, May 6, 1826) and the opera *Il Disertore svizzero* (Milan, May 28, 1831), followed by several other operas: *La Vendetta* (Milan, Feb. 11, 1832), *Ricciarda di Edimburgo* (Trieste, Sept. 29, 1832), *Il Contrabbandiere* (Milan, June 13, 1833), *Un Episodio di S. Michele* (Milan, June 14, 1834), etc.; also wrote an ingenious *Sinfonia a canone* for 2 orchestras playing the same music, but with 2nd orch. coming in one measure later than the first (this musical legerdemain amused Meyerbeer); he then lived in Paris, where he produced the ballets *La Fille de marble* (Oct. 20, 1847), *Le Violon du diable* (Jan. 19, 1849), etc. In 1851 he was appointed ballet composer for the Imperial Theater in St. Petersburg; wrote about 300 ballet scores; of these *Esmeralda* (originally produced in Milan, 1845) and *Konyok-Gorbunok (Le Cheval enchanté,* St. Petersburg, 1864) still retain their popularity in Russia.

Pugno, Raoul, celebrated French pianist; b. (of an Italian father) Montrouge, Seine, June 23, 1852; d. (while on a concert tour) Moscow, Jan 3, 1914. He studied at the Paris Cons. with G. Mathias (piano) and Ambroise Thomas (composition). He began a career as organist at the St.-Eugène Church in 1871; taught harmony at the Paris Cons. (1892–96) and subsequently was prof. of piano there (1896–1901). In the meantime he gave numerous recitals, and gradually rose to the rank of a great virtuoso; appeared in England in 1894; in America, in 1897–98. He was equally remarkable as an ensemble player; his sonata recitals with Ysaÿe became world-famous. Pugno was also a composer; wrote several operas: *Ninetta* (Paris, Dec. 23, 1882), *Le Sosie* (Oct. 7, 1887), *Le Valet de cœur* (April 19, 1888), *Le Retour d'Ulysse* (Paris, Feb. 1, 1889), *La Vocation de Marius* (March 29, 1890), etc.; ballet, *La Danseuse de corde* (Paris, Feb. 5, 1892); piano pieces; songs. His scores for *La Ville morte* (after Gabriele d'Annunzio), left incomplete at his death, was finished by Nadia Boulanger.

Pujol, Francesc, Catalan composer; b. Barcelona, May 15, 1878; d. there Dec. 24, 1945. He studied at the Barcelona Cons., also with Millet; was assistant conductor (1900–41), then musical director (1942–45) of the Orfeó Catalá, Barcelona. He wrote many sardanas, church music, orchestral works, etc. Publ. valuable studies on Catalan songs: *Chant de la Sibila; L'Œuvre du "Chansonnier populaire de la Catalogne"* (Report of the International Musicological Congress, Vienna, 1927); *Observacions, apéndix i notes al Romancerillo catalán de Manuel Milá y Fontanals* (with Joan Punti; 1927ff.); Catalan folksongs with piano accompaniment (Madrid, 1921).

Pujol, Juan, Catalan church musician; b. Barcelona, c.1573; d. there, May, 1626. From 1593 to 1595 he was *maestro de canto* in Tarragona; 1595–1612, maestro at Nuestra Señora del Pilar in Saragossa; then at Barcelona Cathedral until his death. His Masses, motets, Passions, psalms, and villancicos are preserved in manuscript. A collected ed. of Pujol's works was undertaken by H. Anglès, of which 2 vols. appeared (1926 and 1932).

Puliti, Leto, Italian music scholar; b. Florence, June 29, 1818; d. there, Nov. 15, 1875. He published the valuable historical account, *Cenni storici della vita del serenissimo Ferdinando de' Medici* (1884), with information concerning Cristofori, the inventor of the piano.

Pulver, Jeffrey, English violinist and musicologist; b. London, June 22, 1884; studied with Ševčik (Prague), Heermann (Frankfurt), Marteau (Geneva), and A. Moser (Berlin). He made a speciality of old English music, and played the viola d'amore, the tenor viola, and other old string instruments.
WRITINGS: *A Dictionary of Musical Terms* (1913); *A Dictionary of Old English Music and Musical Instruments* (1923); *Johannes Brahms* (1926); *A Biographical Dictionary of Old English Music* (1927); *Paganini, the Romantic Virtuoso* (London, 1936; reprint, N.Y., 1970); *The Ancient Dance Forms* (2 parts; 1912, 1914); *The Intermezzi of the Opera* (1917); *The Viols in England* (1920); *The Music of Ancient Egypt* (1921); etc.

Puppo, Giuseppe, Italian violinist; b. Lucca, June 12, 1749; d. Florence, April 19, 1827. He was a successful violin virtuoso at an early age; traveled in Spain; was

in England until 1784, when he settled in Paris; was a fashionable teacher there; in 1811, abandoned his family in Paris, went to Naples, and then to Florence, dying in poverty. He publ. 3 violin concertos, 8 études for the violin, and 6 piano fantasias.

Purcell, Daniel, brother of **Henry Purcell;** b. London, c.1660; d. there (buried, Nov. 26), 1717. He became organist of Magdalen College, Oxford, in 1688; took his brother's place as dramatic composer in 1695, and was organist of St. Andrew's, Holborn, from 1713.
WORKS: incidental music to 30 dramas; several odes (e.g., funeral ode for his brother); *The Psalm Tunes set full for the Organ or Harpsichord* appeared posthumously (London, 1718).

Purcell, Henry, one of the greatest of English composers; b. London (?), c.1659; d. Dean's Yard, Westminster, Nov. 21, 1695. Until recently it was believed that his father was Henry Purcell (d. 1664), Gentleman of the Chapel Royal and Master of the choristers at Westminster Abbey. But the latest evidence indicates that he was the son of Henry's brother, Thomas Purcell, who was also a Gentleman of the Chapel Royal and held other important posts at the court. From 1669 he was a chorister of the Chapel Royal under Cooke and Humfrey, also receiving instruction from Dr. Blow. When his voice broke in 1673, he was appointed Assistant Keeper of the Instruments. In 1677 he was appointed composer to the King's band, and in 1679 he succeeded Blow as organist of Westminster Abbey. In 1682 he became one of the 3 organists of the Chapel Royal as Lowe's successor; in 1683, Keeper of the King's Wind Instruments. His first printed composition is a song in vol. I (1675) of Playford's *Choice Ayres;* vol. II (1679) contains several other songs, and an elegy on the death of Matthew Locke. In 1680 Purcell wrote the first of 29 "odes" and "welcome songs." His first publ. chamber music dates from 1683, *Sonatas of III Parts: two violins and bass: to the Organ or Harpsichord* (with engraved portrait), 12 numbers, based on Italian models, each having an Adagio, a Canzone (fugue), a slow movement, and an air. *The Yorkshire Feast Song,* called by D'Urfey, the author, "one of the finest compositions he ever made," was composed and produced in 1690. This is one of 29 "welcome songs," which he wrote (on an average of 2 annually) in his capacity of "composer-in-ordinary." Although the texts are almost invariably stupid or bombastic, Purcell wrote some of his finest music for these occasional odes. During the last five years he developed extraordinary activity in theatrical composition, to which he had given some attention since 1680, when he began to write some incidental dances and occasional airs for various dramas. In spite of this close connection with the stage, he wrote only one opera, *Dido and Aeneas,* produced in 1689. He lies in the north aisle of Westminster Abbey, and his burial tablet well expresses contemporary estimation of his worth: "Here lyes Henry Purcell, Esq.; who left this life, and is gone to that blessed place where only his harmony can be exceeded." His church music shows an original melodist, and a master of form, harmony, and all contrapuntal devices; his music for the stage is equally rich in invention, dramatic instinct, and power of characterization; his chamber works surpass those of his predecessors and contemporaries.

WORKS: Besides the compositions mentioned, there were publ. during Purcell's life a theoretical treatise, *The Art of Descant*, in the 10th ed. of Playford's *Briefe Introduction of the Skill of Musick* (1683); Playford also publ. several airs and "symphonies" (written for various dramas) in *The Theatre of Musick* (1685), anthems and sacred songs in *Harmonia Sacra* (1688), and pieces for harpsichord in *Musick's Handmaid* (part II, 1689); of the incidental music to plays there appeared *Amphitryon* (1690; the airs in the text, the instrumental pieces in *Ayres for the Theatre*), *Dioclesian* (1691), and "Select ayres" from the *Fairy Queen* (1692). The stage pieces for which Purcell wrote music include the following: 1680, Lee's *Theodosius*, D'Urfey's *The Virtuous Wife* (1694?); 1681, Tate's arrangement of Shakespeare's *Richard II*, D'Urfey's *Sir Barnaby Whigg*; 1682, Beaumont and Fletcher's *The Double Marriage* (1685?); 1685, Davenant's *Circe*, Lee's *Sophonisba*; 1688, D'Urfey's *A Fool's Preferment*; 1689, Betterton's *Dioclesian*, Settle's *Distressed Innocence*, Southerne's *Sir Anthony Love*, Dryden's *Amphitryon*, Lee's *The Massacre of Paris*; 1691, Dryden's *King Arthur*, *The Gordian Knot Untyed* (author unknown), Dryden's *The Indian Emperor*, Southerne's *The Wives' Excuse*; 1692, Dryden's *Cleomenes*, *The Fairy Queen* (an arrangement of the *Midsummer Night's Dream*), D'Urfey's *The Marriage-hater Matched*, Crowne's *Regulus*, Shadwell's *The Libertine*, Bancroft's *Henry II*, Dryden's *Aureng-Zebe*, Dryden and Lee's *Oedipus*; 1693, Congreve's *The Old Bachelor*, D'Urfey's *The Richmond Heiress*, Southern's *The Maid's Last Prayer*, Wright's *The Female Virtuosos* (after Molière), Congreve's *The Double Dealer*, Shadwell's *Epsom Wells*, Fletcher's *Rule a Wife and Have a Wife*; 1694, D'Urfey's *Don Quixote* (part I), Dryden's *Love Triumphant*, Crowne's *The Married Beau*, Southerne's *The Fatal Marriage*, Ravenscroft's *The Canterbury Guests*, D'Urfey's *Don Quixote* (part II), Shadwell's arr. of *Timon of Athens*, Dryden's *The Spanish Friar*, Dryden's *Tyrannic Love*; 1695, Behn's *Andelazer*, Beaumont and Fletcher's *Bonduca*, Howard and Dryden's *Indian Queen*, Scott's *The Mock Marriage*, Norton's *Pausanias*, Gould's *The Rival Sisters*, Southerne's *Oroonoko*, Davenant and Dryden's arrangement of *The Tempest*, D'Urfey's *Don Quixote* (part III). In this list only *Dioclesian*, *The Fairy Queen*, *The Indian Queen*, and *King Arthur* are provided with sufficient music to be possibly classed as "semi-operas"; the music for other dramas usually includes overtures, airs, and instrumental dances. Purcell's widow, who survived him till 1706, publ. *A Choice Collection of Lessons for the Harpsichord or Spinet* (1696), *Ten Sonatas in Four Parts* (1697), *Orpheus Britannicus: A Collection of the choicest Songs . . . with Symphonies for Violins or Flutes . . .* (Part I, 1698, 2nd ed., 1706; Part II, 1702; 2nd ed., 1711; both parts in 1 vol., with the addition of several new numbers, 1721). Many compositions were publ. in Playford's *Harmonia Sacrae* (1688–93), Walsh's *The Catch Club, or Merry Companions* (c.1730), Boyce's *Cathedral Music* (3 vols., 1760–73), Arnold's continuation of the same (4 vols., 1790), Page

and Sexton's *Harmonia Sacra* (3 vols., 1800). Vincent Novello collected all services, anthems, hymns, and sacred songs, and publ. them as *Purcell's Sacred Music* (4 vols., 1829–32; very inaccurate). The Musical Antiquarian Society publ. *Dido and Aeneas* (ed. G. A. Macfarren, 1840), *Bonduca* (ed. E. F. Rimbault, 1842; with historical sketch of dramatic music in England), *King Arthur* (ed. E. Taylor, 1843), *Ode for St. Cecilia's Day* (ed. E. F. Rimbault, 1847). In 1876 the Purcell Society was formed in London for the purpose of publishing the first complete ed. of Purcell's works; 26 vols. were brought out from 1878–1928; in 1957 publication resumed, with the set being extended to 32 vols. by 1977. The Purcell Society also began to publ. a *Popular Edition of Selected Works* (vol. 1: *15 Songs and Airs;* London, 1939). Various selections have been publ. by P. Warlock (*Fantasias* in 3, 4, and 5 parts; some publ. for the 1st time; London 1927), G. Jensen, A. Egidi, A. Moffat and H. David (trio sonatas), W. Barclay Squire (harpsichord pieces), A. Schering in *Geschichte der Musik in Beispielen* (nos. 246–48a). F. Blume in *Das Chorwerk* (5 sacred choruses), E. Dent (*Let the Dreadful Engines*), W. Gillies Whittaker (22 sonatas; Eds. de l'Oiseau-Lyre, Paris), etc. The so-called *Trumpet Voluntary*, ascribed to Purcell, and made popular through an orchestral transcription by Sir Henry Wood, is not Purcell but by Jeremiah Clarke; for details, see C. L. Cudworth, "Some New Facts About the Trumpet Voluntary," *Musical Times* (Sept. 1953).

BIBLIOGRAPHY: W. H. Cummings, *Purcell* (London, 1881; 3rd ed., 1911; abridged ed., 1923); W. Barclay Sqire, "Purcell's Dramatic Music," *Sammelbände der Internationalen Musik-Gesellschaft* V/4 (1904); J. F. Runciman, *Purcell* (London, 1909) G. E. Arkwright, "Purcell's Church Music," *Musical Antiquary* (July 1910); P. A. Scholes, "H. Purcell: Sketch of a Busy Life," *Musical Quarterly* (July 1916); W. Barclay Squire, "Purcell's *Dido and Aeneas,*" *Musical Times* (June 1918); H. Dupré, *Purcell* (Paris, 1927; in English, N.Y., 1928); D. Arundell, *H. Purcell* (London, 1927; in German, 1929); E. Dent, *Foundations of the English Opera* (1928); A. K. Holland, *H. Purcell, the English Musical Tradition* (London, 1932); F. de Quervain, *Der Chorstil H. Purcells* (Leipzig, 1935); J. A. Westrup, *Purcell* (London, 1937); S. Favre-Lingorow, *Der Instrumentalstil von Purcell* (Bern, 1950); S. Demarquez, *Purcell* (Paris, 1951); G. van Ravenzwaÿ, *Purcell* (Haarlem, 1954); R. Sietz, *Henry Purcell: Zeit, Leben, Werk* (Leipzig, 1955); Imogen Holst, ed. *Henry Purcell, 1659–1695; Essays on His Music,* (London, 1959); F. B. Zimmerman, *Henry Purcell: An Analytical Catalogue of His Music* (N.Y., 1963); F. B. Zimmerman, *Henry Purcell, His Life and Times* (N.Y., 1967); F. B. Zimmerman, *Henry Purcell, Melodic and Intervallic Indexes to His Complete Works* (1975).

Puschmann, Adam, German meistersinger; b. Görlitz, 1532; d. Breslau, April 4, 1600. He was a pupil of Hans Sachs; brought out *Gründlicher Bericht des deutschen Meistergesanges* (1571; new ed., Halle, 1888); his songs were publ. by Georg Münzer in 1906. His brother **Zacharias Puschmann** (with whom he is often confused) was a cantor in Gölitz.

Pustet, Friedrich, German publisher; b. Hals, near Passau, Feb. 25, 1798; d. Munich, March 6, 1882. In 1826 he founded a music publishing firm, mainly for church music, in Regensburg; for 30 years he had the exclusive right of printing, with the privilege of the Holy See, the chant books according to the Editio Medicaea, which, however, was superseded by the newer Vaticana Edition. In 1921 Pustet's firm merged with the publishing house of Kösel, retaining, however, the original name; the firm thus lasted through 5 generations of the family, and was directed in the 1970's still in Regensburg, by **Friedrich Pustet** (b. Munich, Nov. 26, 1927). Pustet published Proske's *Musica divina;* Peter Wagner's *Elemente des gregorianischen Gesanges;* Johner's *Cantus ecclesiastici; Kirchenmusikalisches Jahrbuch* (from its founding in 1886 through the vol. for 1935); etc. A Festschrift was compiled by H. Bohatta, on the centenary of the foundation of the firm (Regensburg, 1926).

Pyamour, John, English composer; date of birth unknown; d. 1431. He was a clerk of the Chapel Royal in 1419, and Master of Children in 1420; was commissioned to find boys with good voices for the royal service; traveled with King Henry V and the chapel on the Continent, and probably remained in Normandy for several years. His motet *Quam pulchra es* is extant in MS.
BIBLIOGRAPHY: John Harvey, *Gothic England* (London, 1947).

Pycard, English singer and composer, who flourished c.1400. The *Old Hall Manuscript* contains 6 works by him; his contrapuntal skill was out of the ordinary, and he used complicated canonic forms in sections of the Mass.
BIBLIOGRAPHY: M. Bukofzer, *Studies in Medival and Renaissance Music* (N.Y., 1950).

Pylkkänen, Tauno Kullervo, Finnish composer; b. Helsinki, March 22, 1918. He studied composition with Palmgren and Madetoja at the Sibelius Academy in Helsinki, while also attending the Helsinki Cons. (1937–41). He subsequently worked at the Finnish Broadcasting Company (1942–61) and was artistic director of the Finnish National Opera (1960–70); then lectured in opera history at the Sibelius Academy. He is primarily an opera composer; his idiom is basically Romantic, with sporadic excursions into modernity.
WORKS: operas: *Bathsheba Saarenmaalla (Bath-sheba at Saarenmaa;* 1940, revised 1958); *Mare ja hänen poikansa (Mare and Her Son,* 1943); *Simo Hurtta* (1948); *Sudenmorsian (The Wolf's Bride),* radio opera (1950); *Varjo (The Shadow,* 1952); *Opri and Oleksi* (1957); *Ikaros* (1956-60); *Vangit (The Prisoners,* 1964); *Tuntematon sotilas* (The Unknown Soldier, 1967); a ballet, *Kaarina Maununtytär (Kaarina, Maunu's Daughter,* 1960); for orch.: *Introduction and Fugue* (1940); *Lapin kesä (Summer in Lapland,* 1941); *Kullervon sotaanlähtö (Kullervo Leaves for War,* 1942); Sinfonietta (1944); Symph. No. 1 (1945); *Suite* for oboe and strings (1946); *Marathon,* overture (1947); *Symphonic Fantasy* (1948); *Ultima Thule* (1949); Cello Concerto (1950); *Symphonic Prelude* (1952); chamber music: *Notturno* for violin and piano (1943); String Quartet (1945); *Fantasia appassionata* for cello and piano (1954); several canatas and songs.
BIBLIOGRAPHY: *Suomen Säveltäjiä* (Helsinki, 1945; pp. 726–31).

Pyne, James Kendrick, English organist; b. Bath, Feb. 5, 1852; d. Ilford, Essex, Sept. 3, 1938. Pupil of his father, **James K. Pyne** (for 53 years organist at Bath Abbey); then of Dr. S. S. Wesley, organist at Winchester Cathedral. He held positions as church organist at the Manchester Cathedral (1876–98); in 1877 became organist of Town Hall Corporation, Manchester; celebrated his 50 years of tenure (1927) by giving 3 organ recitals on the jubilee day. He composed organ music; also a Comminion Service and sacred works.
BIBLIOGRAPHY: S. Lucas, "J. K. Pyne," *Musical Opinion* (Nov. 1927).

Pythagoras, the Greek philosopher and mathematician; b. Samos, c.582 B.C.; d. Metapontum, c.500 B.C. His doctrines on the musical ratios are preserved in the writing of his followers, no books by Pythagoras himself having come down to us. The Pythagoreans (Archytas, Didymos, Eratosthenes, Euclid, Ptolemy, etc.) reckoned only the fifth and octave as pure consonances (the fourth being the fifth below); their system recognized only intervals reached by successive skips of pure fifths, the major third being the 4th fifth above (ratio 64:81, instead of the modern 64:80, or 4:5), their minor third the 3rd fifth below; etc. Their thirds and sixth were, consequently, dissonant intervals.
BIBLIOGRAPHY: Klaus Pringsheim, "Pythagoras, die Atonalität und wir," *Schweizerische Musikzeitung* (1957); I. Focht, "La Notion pythagoricienne de la musique," *The Esthetics and Sociology of Music* 3 (1972).

Q

Quagliati, Paolo, Italian composer and excellent cembalist; b. Chioggia, c.1555; d. Rome, Nov. 16, 1628. He publ. *Carro di fedeltà d'amore,* one of the earliest music dramas, containing not only monodies, but ensemble numbers up to 5 voices (Rome, 1611); also motets and "dialogues" *a* 2–8 (3 vols.; 1612, 1620, 1627); etc. Reprints are found in H. Riemann's *Musikgeschichte in Beispielen* and L. Torchi's *L'Arte Musicale in Italia* III.

BIBLIOGRAPHY: A. Cametti, "Paolo Quagliati, organista e compositore," *Rassegna Dorica* (Dec. 20, 1930; pp. 28–34).

Quaile, Elizabeth, American piano pedagogue; b. Omagh, Ireland, Jan. 20, 1874; d. South Kent, Conn., June 30, 1951. She came early to N.Y. and studied with Franklin Robinson; then devoted herself to teaching; from 1916 to 1919 she was head of the piano dept. of the David Mannes School; then went to Paris where she studied piano with Harold Bauer. Returning to N.Y. in 1921 she founded, with Angela Diller, the Diller-Quaile School of Music. She published a number of highly successful piano teaching materials, some of it written by her alone (*First Book of Technical Exercises, A Pre-Czerny Book,* etc.), and some in collaboration with Angela Diller. The books proved to be standard guides for piano students.

Quantz, Johann Joachim, famous German flutist and composer; b. Oberscheden, Hannover, Jan. 30, 1697; d. Potsdam, July 12, 1773. Naturally musical, at 8 he played the double bass at village festivals. His father died when he was but 10, and Quantz was apprenticed to an uncle, then 'Stadtmusikus' at Merseburg, in 1708, learning various instruments, among them the harpsichord with Kiesewetter. His apprenticeship ended, he went to Radeburg, Pirna, and in 1716 joined the town orch. of Dresden, under Heine. In 1717, during 3 months' leave of absence, he studied counterpoint with Zelenka and Fux at Vienna; in 1718 he became oboist in the Royal Polish orch. of Warsaw and Dresden, but soon took up the flute, which he studied under Buffardin. In 1724 he was sent to Italy in the suite of the Polish ambassador; studied counterpoint under Gasparini at Rome; went to London *via* Paris in 1726; and returned to Dresden in 1727, resuming his position as orchestral flute player in 1728. In this year he played before Frederick the Great (then Crown Prince) at Berlin, and so pleased him that he engaged Quantz to teach the flute, and to make two long yearly visits to Berlin for the purpose. Frederick ascended the throne in 1740, and next year called Quantz to Berlin and Potsdam as chamber musician and court composer at a salary of 2,000 Thaler, besides an honorarium for each composition furnished, and 100 ducats for each flute supplied by Quantz. Here he remained until his death.

WORKS: He left in MS 300 concertos for one and two flutes, and some 200 other flute pieces (solos, duets, trios, and quartets). He published *Sei sonate* with bass (1734); *Sei duetti* (1759); *Neue Kirchenmelodien* (1760; settings of 22 odes by Gellert as chorales); *Versuch einer Anweisung, die Flöte traversiere zu spielen* (1752; this famous flute method also contains valuable information on 18th-century performance practices; 2nd and 3rd eds., 1780, 1789; French, 1752; Dutch, 1755; English translation by E. R. Reilly, N.Y., 1966); *Application pour la flûte traversière à deux clefs* (an account of his invention of a 2nd key applied to the flute for just intonation, and also of the tuning barrel for the instrument).

BIBLIOGRAPHY: Quantz's autobiography is in Marpurg's *Historisch-kritische Beyträge zur Aufnahme der Musik* (Berlin, 1755; reprinted in Willi Kahl, *Selbstbiographien deutscher Musiker des XVIII. Jahrhunderts,* Cologne, 1948); A. Quantz, *Leben und Werke des Flötisten J. J. Quantz* (Berlin, 1877); R. Schäfke, "Quantz als Ästhetiker. Eine Einführung in die Musikästhetick des galanten Stils," *Archiv für Musikwissenschaft* VI/2 (1924); Everett Helm, *Music at the Court of Frederick The Great* (Norman, Okla., 1960); E. R. Reilly, *Quantz and His "Versuch." Three Studies* (American Musicological Society Studies and Documents 5, 1971).

Quarenghi, Guglielmo, Italian cellist; b. Casalmaggiore, Oct. 22, 1826; d. Milan, Feb. 4, 1882. Pupil at Milan Cons., 1839–42; from 1850, 1st cello at La Scala Theater; 1851, prof. of cello at the Cons.; from 1879, maestro di cappella at Milan Cathedral.

WORKS: an excellent cello method, and original pieces and transcriptions for cello; church music; and an opera, *Il Di di S. Michele* (Milan, 1863).

Quarles, James Thomas, American organist and educator; b. St. Louis, Nov. 7, 1877; d. Saugus, Calif., March 4, 1954. He studied organ with local teachers; then with Widor in Paris. He was church organist in St. Louis (1897–1913); then taught at Cornell Univ. (1913–23) and at the Univ. of Missouri (1923–43). He gave nearly 1000 organ recitals in various parts of the U.S.; composed anthems, organ pieces, and songs.

Quatremère de Quincy, Antoine-Chrysostome, French writer; b. Paris, Oct. 28, 1755; d. there, Dec. 28, 1849. Secretary of the Académie des Arts. Publ. *De la nature des opéras bouffons italiens* (Paris, 1789; pamphlet) and eulogies of Catel, Boieldieu, Gossec, Méhul, Monsigny, Paisiello, and other deceased members of the Académie (in *Recueil de notices historiques,* 1834–37, 2 vols.; also printed separately).

Quef, Charles, French organist and composer; b. Lille, Nov. 1, 1873; d. there, July 2, 1931. He studied at the Lille Cons. and at the Paris Cons. with Guiraud, Th. Dubois, Guilmant, and Widor (1898, won 1st prize for organ and improvisation); organist in Paris at Ste. Marie, St. Laurent, and (from 1901) of La Trinité, succeeding Guilmant; concertized in France and England. Publ. sacred choruses and other works.

Querol Gavaldá, Miguel, Spanish musicologist; b. Ulldecona, Tarragona, April 22, 1912. He studied music at the Benedictine Monastery of Monserrat (1926–36) and later in Barcelona with Juan Lamote de Grignon. He published *La Música en las obras de Cervantes*

(Barcelona, 1948), *La Escuela estética catalana contemporánea* (doctoral dissertation; Madrid, 1953); edited the *Cancionero musical de la casa de Medinaceli* (2 vols.; Barcelona, 1949-50; *Breve historia de la música* (Madrid, 1955); also wrote some church music; chamber music; a *Sonata romántica catalana* for piano; etc.

Quilter, Roger, English composer; b. Brighton, Nov. 1, 1877; d. London Sept. 21, 1953. He received his primary education at Eton College; then went to Germany where he studied with Iwan Knorr. He is particularly noted for his fine settings of Shakespeare's poems.

WORKS: incidental music for Shakespeare's play *As You Like It* (1922); *The Sailor and His Lass,* for soprano, baritone, chorus and orch. (1948) numerous song cycles, among them *7 Elizabethan Lyrics, 3 Songs of the Sea, 4 Shakespeare Songs,* etc. He also wrote a light opera *Julia* (London, Dec. 3, 1936).

BIBLIOGRAPHY: L. Woodgate, "Roger Quilter," *Musical Times* (Nov. 1953).

Quinault, Jean-Baptiste-Maurice, French singer and actor; b. Paris, c.1685; d. Gien, 1744. He was an actor at the Théâtre Français, in Paris (1712-33). He set to music about 20 *intermèdes,* ballets, etc. and also produced a grand ballet *Les Amours des déesses* (Paris, 1729).

Quinault, Philippe, b. Paris, June 3, 1635; d. there, Nov. 26, 1688; French dramatic poet; was Lully's librettist.

BIBLIOGRAPHY: G. A. Crapelet, *Notice sur la vie et les ouvrages de Quinault* (Paris, 1824); E. Richter, *Philippe Quinault. Sein Leben, seine Tragödien, seine Bedeutung für das Theater Frankreichs und des Auslandes* (Leipzig, 1910); Etienne Gros, *Philippe Quinault, sa vie et son œuvre* (Paris, 1926); J. B. A. Buijtendorp, *Philippe Quinault, sa vie, ses tragédies et ses tragi-comédies* (Amsterdam, 1928).

Quinet, Fernand, Belgian cellist, conductor and composer; b. Charleroi, Jan. 29, 1898; d. Liège, Oct. 24, 1971. He studied music theory in Charleroi, then enrolled at the Brussels Cons., where he studied cello with Édouard Jacobs and composition with Léon Du Bois. After graduation he devoted his time to teaching and conducting. He served as director of the Cons. in Charleroi (1924-38); in 1938 he succeeded François Rasse as director of the Liège Cons., and held this post until 1963; founded the Liège Symph. Orch. and was its principal conductor. He composed relatively little.

WORKS: the songs: *Recueillement, Les chevaux de bois; 4 Mélodies; En bateau; La Légende de sœur Béatrice,* cantata (1920); *La Guerre,* cantata (1921; received the Belgian Grand Prix de Rome); Violin Sonata (1923); *Charade,* 4 pieces for piano trio (1927); Viola Sonata (1928); *Moralités-non-légendaires* for voice and 18 instruments (1930); *L'École buissonnière* for string quartet (1930); *3 Symphonic Movements* (London Festival of the International Society for Contemporary Music, July 28, 1931); *Suite* for 3 clarinets (1930).

Quinet, Marcel, Belgian composer; b. Binche, July 6, 1915. He studied at the Conservatories of Mons and Brussels with Léon Jongen, Raymond Moulaert and Marcel Maas (1934-42); also took private composition lessons with Jean Absil (1940-45). He then devoted himself to music pedagogy; was on the staff of the Brussels Cons. (from 1943) and also taught at the Chapelle Musicale Reine Elisabeth (1956-59, 1968-71). His music is moderately modernistic in the amiable manner of the French School, with some euphoniously dissonant excrescences.

WORKS: *La Vague et le Sillon,* cantata (1945; Belgian Grand Prix de Rome, 1945); *3 Esquisses concertantes* for violin and orch. (1946); *Divertissement* for orch. (1946); *3 Pièces* for orch. (1951; performed at the Salzburg International Festival of the Society for Contemporary Music, June 21, 1952); Sinfonietta (1953); *Variations élégiaques sur un thème de Rolland de Lassus* for orch. (1955); 3 piano concertos (1955; 1964; 1966); Variations for Orch. (1956); *Serenade* for string orch. (1956); *Impressions Symphoniques* (1956); *Allegro de concert* for orch. (1958); *Divertimento* for chamber orch. (1958); Concertino for Flute, Celeste, Harp and Strings (1959); Symphony (1960); Concertino for Oboe, Clarinet, Bassoon and String Orch. (1960); *Ballade* for clarinet, and string orch. (1961); Viola Concerto (1962-63); *Concerto Grosso* for 4 clarinets and strings (1964); *Les Deux Bavards,* chamber opera (1966); *Overture for a Festival* (1967); *La Nef des fous,* ballet (1969); *Music* for strings and timpani (1971); *Mouvements* for chamber orch. (1973); *Lectio pro Feria Sexta,* cantata (1973); *Esquisses symphoniques* (1973); *Gorgone* for orch. (1974); *Croquis,* 8 piano pieces (1946); *8 petites pièces* for wind quintet (1946); 2 string trios (1948, 1969); *2 Impromptus* for piano (1949); Wind Quintet (1949); Violin Sonatina (1952); *Passacaille* for piano (1954); Piano Quartet (1957); String Quartet (1958); *Petite Suite* for 4 clarinets (1959); *Toccata* for piano (1961); *Sonate à trois* for trumpet, horn and trombone (1961); *Hommage à Scarlatti* for piano (1962); *Ballade* for violin and wind quintet (1962); Wind Quartet (1964); Sonata for 2 violins and piano (1964); *Partita* for piano (1965); *Ballatella* for trumpet, or horn, or trombone, and piano (1966); *Pochades* for 4 saxophones (1967); Trio for oboe, clarinet and bassoon (1967); Flute Sonata (1968); *3 Preludes* for piano (1970); *Polyphonies* for 3 performers on 8 wind instruments (1971); *Novelettes* for 2 pianos (1973); *Dialogues* for 2 pianos and chamber orch. (1975); *Tableautins* for piano (1974); songs.

Quintanar, Hector, Mexican composer; and conductor; b. Mexico City, April 15, 1936. He had lessons in music theory with Carlos Chávez, Rodolfo Halffter and Galindo at the National Cons. in Mexico City (1959-64); also worked on the problems of electronic music in New York (1964), Paris (1967) and Mexico City (1968). Upon return to Mexico, he supervised the construction of the first electronic laboratory, at the National Univ. (1968). In his compositions he employs traditional instruments as well as electronic sound.

WORKS: 3 symphonies (1961, 1962, 1964); *Sinfonia modal* (1961-62); *El viejo y el mar,* symph. poem after Hemingway (1936); *Fábula* for chorus and orch. (1964); Double Quartet for string quartet and wind quartet (1964–65); String Trio (1965–66); Violin Sonata (1967); *Aclamaciones* for chorus, tape and orch. (1967); Sonata for 3 trumpets (1967); *Galaxias* for orch. (1968; Mexico City, July 7, 1968); *Sideral I* for tape (1968), *Sideral II* for orch. (1969; Mexico City, July 7, 1969); *Sideral III* for tape (1971); *Solutio?* for soprano and piano (1969); *Símbolos* for violin, clarinet, saxophone, horn, trumpet, trombone, piano, tape, optical slides and lights (1969); *Ilapso* for clarinet, bassoon, trumpet, trombone, percussion, violin, and double bass (1970); *Voz* for soprano and tape (1971); Quintet for piano, violin, double bass, flute and trumpet (1973); *Diálogos* for piano and tape (1973).

Quiroga, Manuel, Spanish violinist; b. Pontevedra, April 15, 1890; d. there, April 19, 1961. He studied at the Royal Cons. in Madrid and at the Paris Cons.; toured in Europe and in the U.S. with great success. He suffered a street accident in N.Y. in 1937 during one of his American tours and was compelled to abandon public appearances; returned to Spain and retired to Pontevedra. He composed some violin pieces and a "sainete," *Los Amos del Barrio* (Madrid, Sept. 7, 1938).

Quittard, Henri Charles Étienne, French musicologist, b. Clermont-Ferrand, May 13, 1864; d. Paris, July 21, 1919. He was a student of César Franck, but did not elect to pursue a career as a composer or a performer; instead, he wrote music criticism in *Le Matin* and *Le Figaro;* in 1912 he was appointed archivist at the Paris Opera.

WRITINGS: *Henry du Mont: un musicien en France au XVIIᵉ siècle* (1906); *Les Couperins* (1913); also contributed articles on 17th-century French music to various scholarly publications.

R

Raabe, Peter, German conductor and writer on music; b. Frankfurt-am-Oder, Nov. 27, 1872; d. Weimar, April 12, 1945. He studied with Bargiel at the Hochschule für Musik in Berlin; in 1894 began a career as theater conductor; in 1899 was appointed conductor of the Netherlands Opera in Amsterdam; then conducted the Kaim Orch. in Munich (1903–06) and the newly established Kaim Orch. in Mannheim (1906–07); in 1907 he became principal conductor in Weimar; in 1910 he was appointed custodian of the Liszt Museum in Weimar; from 1920 to 1934 he conducted the Municipal Orch. in Aachen. In 1935 he became head of the Reichsmusikkammer and the Deutscher Tonkünstlerverein; in these offices he was called upon to perform administrative tasks for the Nazi regime, including the racial restrictions of musicians. His co-workers presented him with an honorary *Festschrift zu Peter Raabes 70. Geburtstag* (Leipzig, 1942). Raabe died just before the total collapse of the Third Reich which he tried to serve so well. He left some scholarly and valuable writings, among them: *Grossherzog Karl Alexander and Liszt* (Leipzig, 1918); *Franz Liszt: Leben und Schaffen* (Stuttgart, 1931; 2 vols., with an annotated catalogue of Liszt's works); *Die Musik im dritten Reich* (Berlin, 1935; an exposition of the musical ideology of the Third Reich); *Kulturwille im deutschen Musikleben* (Berlin, 1936); *Deutsche Meister* (Berlin, 1937); *Wege zu Weber* (Regensburg, 1942); *Wege zu Liszt* (Regensburg, 1943); *Wege zu Bruckner* (Regensburg, 1944).

Raaff, Anton, German singer, a friend of Mozart; b. Gelsdorf, near Bonn, May 6, 1714; d. Munich, May 27, 1797. He studied with Ferrandini in Munich and Bernacchi in Bologna; sang in Italy; then in Bonn, Vienna, and at various German courts (1742–52); in Lisbon (1753–55), Madrid (1755–59), and Naples, returning in 1770 to Germany, where he was attached to the court of the Elector Karl Theodor at Mannheim. In 1778 he went to Paris with Mozart; in 1779 was in Munich. Mozart wrote the role of Idomeneo for him, and also the aria, *Se al labbro mio non credi,* K. 295.
BIBLIOGRAPHY: H. Freiberger, *Anton Raaff: sein Leben und Wirken* (Cologne, 1929).

Raalte, Albert van, Dutch conductor; b. Amsterdam, May 21, 1890; d. there, Nov. 23, 1952. He studied at the Cologne Cons. with Bram Eldering (violin) and Waldemar von Baussnern (theory); later in Leipzig with Nikisch and Max Reger; was theater conductor in Brussels (1911) and Leipzig (1912); conducted Wagner's operas at the Municipal Opera in Leipzig (1914–15); then at the Dutch National Opera in The Hague (1915–22); then formed his own opera enterprise there. He remained in Holland during the German Occupation, conducted the radio orch. at Hilversum; was sent to a concentration camp as a person with Jewish associations; after the Liberation in 1945, he returned to his post at Hilversum, building the radio orch. to a high degree of efficiency.

Raasted, Niels Otto, Danish organist and composer; b. Copenhagen, Nov. 26, 1888; d. there, Dec. 31, 1966.

He studied at the Copenhagen Cons. (1909–12); then at the Cons. of Leipzig, with Max Reger, Karl Straube, and R. Teichmüller (1913–14); returning to Denmark, he became cathedral organist; also conducted the Bach Society (1925–46).
WORKS: 3 symphonies (1914, 1938, 1944); several orch. suites, among them *Pictures from Finland* (1928) and *Hans Christian Andersen Suite* (1940); *Sinfonia da chiesa* (1944); 3 string quartets (1914, 1918, 1920); 5 violin sonatas; 6 organ sonatas; an oratorio, *Saul* (1923); cantatas (all performed on the Copenhagen Radio); *Sangen om København* (June 27, 1934), *Thylands pris* (May 12, 1941); *Kong Vaar* (Oct. 20, 1947).

Rääts, Jaan, Estonian composer; b. Tartu, Oct. 15, 1932. He studied with Heino Eller at the Tallinn Cons. (1952–57); was director of the music division of the Estonian Radio (1955–66); then served as music director of Estonian Television. His music possesses firm thematic lines animated by a motoric pulse.
WORKS: 7 symphonies (1957, 1958, 1959, 1959, 1966, 1967, 1973); Concerto for String Orch. (1961); Violin Concerto (1963); a "declamatorio," *Karl Marx* (Tallinn, June 6, 1964); Nonet (1966); *24 Preludes* for piano (1968); 3 piano quintets; Piano Sextet (1972); 5 string quartets; 4 piano sonatas.

Rabaud, Henri, eminent French composer and conductor; b. Paris, Nov. 10, 1873; d. there, Sept. 11, 1949. The son of Hippolyte Rabaud (1839–1900), professor of cello at the Paris Cons., he was a pupil of Gédalge and Massenet; won the Premier Grand Prix de Rome in 1894 with his cantata *Daphné;* in 1908 he became conductor at the Paris Opéra and at the Opéra-Comique; from 1914 to 1918, director of the Opéra. In 1918 he was engaged to conduct the Boston Symph. Orch., succeeding Karl Muck; conducted only one season (1918–19) and was followed by Pierre Monteux; returned to Paris and was appointed director of the Paris Cons. in 1922 (following Gabriel Fauré's resignation); he held this post until 1941.
WORKS: the operas *La Fille de Roland* (Opéra-Comique, March 16, 1904), *Le Premier Glaire* (Bézièrs, 1908), *Marouf, Savetier du Caire* (Opéra-Comique, May 15, 1914; his most successful opera), *Antoine et Cléopâtre,* after Shakespeare (1916–17), *L'Appel de la mer* (1 act; Opéra-Comique, April 10, 1924; in German, Leipzig, May 6, 1927), *Le Miracle des loups* (Opéra-Comique, Nov. 14, 1924), *Rolande et le mauvais garçon* (Opéra, May 28, 1934), *Le Jeu de l'Amour et du Hasard* (1948; produced posthumously at Monte Carlo, 1954); an oratorio, *Job* (1900); Psalm 4 for soli, chorus, and orch.; *Hymne à la France éternelle* (1916); *L'Été,* for 4-voice choir; also for orch.; 2 symphonies; *La Procession nocturne,* symph. poem after Lenau's *Der nächtliche Zug* (his most famous orchestral work; first performed Paris, Jan. 15, 1899); *Églogue,* "poème virgilien"; *Divertissement sur des chansons russes; Suite anglaise,* for string quartet; Concertino for Cello and Piano; *Allegro de concert,* for cello and piano; piano pieces; songs; etc.

BIBLIOGRAPHY: Max d'Ollone, *Rabaud* (Paris, 1958).

Rabe, Folke, Swedish composer; b. Stockholm, Oct. 28, 1935. He studied composition with Blomdahl and Lidholm at the Royal College of Music in Stockholm (1957–64); also took lessons with Ligeti (1961–64). In 1965 he worked at the Tape Music Center in San Francisco; in 1968 he joined the staff of the Swedish Foundation for Nationwide Concerts. An accomplished jazz musician, he was a founder, with Jan Bark, of the Culture Quartet of 4 trombones. He experimented with multimedia techniques; produced pieces of "vocal theater" with nonsemantic texts.

WORKS: *Notturno* for mezzo-soprano, flute, oboe and clarinet (1959); *7 Variations* for piano (1957–60); *Piece* for speaking chorus, with nonsense verses by Lasse O'Månsson (1961); *Impromptu* for clarinet, trombone, cello, piano and percussion (1962); 2 works for the Culture Quartet, composed in collaboration with Jan Bark: *Bolos* (1962) and *Polonaise* (1965); *Medea*, theater music for speaking or singing female chorus, oboe, prepared piano and percussion (1963; Stockholm, March 22, 1963); *Pajazzo* for 8 jazz musicians, conductor and audience (1963); *Rondes-fragment* for chorus (1964); *Hep-Hep* for orch. (1966); *Hommage à Mesmer*, electronic music; *Joe's Harp* for chorus (1970).

Rabich, Ernst, German choral conductor and composer; b. Herda, May 5, 1856; d. Gotha, Feb. 1, 1933. After study with local teachers, he became in 1880 church organist and conductor of the Liedertafel (900 singers) in Gotha; from 1897, editor of *Blätter für Haus- und Kirchenmusik* and later of the *Musikalisches Magazin* (a large collection of excellent monographs to which he contributed); retired in 1918. He composed several choral works with orch.: *Die Martinswand; Die Frühlingsfeier; Des Volkes Gruss; Das hohe Lied der Arbeit; Dornröschen;* etc.; brought out *Psalter und Harfe*, a collection of motets (5 books); *Thüringer Liederkranz*.

Rabin, Michael, American violinist; b. New York, May 2, 1936; d. there, Jan. 19, 1972. He was of a musical family; his father was a violinist in the N.Y. Philharmonic; his mother a pianist. He studied with Ivan Galamian in N.Y. and made excellent progress; in his early youth he appeared as soloist with a number of American orchestras; made several European tours as a concert violinist, and also played in Australia. His sudden death at the age of 35 was a shock to American music lovers.

Rabinof, Benno, American violinist; b. New York, of Russian-Jewish parents, Oct. 11, 1910; d. Brevard, North Carolina, July 2, 1975. He studied privately with Victor Küzdö, Franz Kneisel and Leopold Auer. He made his debut in 1927, playing the Tchaikovsky Violin Concerto with members of the N.Y. Philharmonic conducted by Leopold Auer. In 1930 he played Glazunov's Violin Concerto, with Glazunov himself leading the Boston Symph. Orch. as guest conductor. With his wife, the pianist **Sylvia Smith-Rabinof,** he traveled extensively in Europe and America.

Rabinovich, David, Russian musicologist; b. Kharkov, Aug. 8, 1900. He studied piano at the St. Petersburg Cons. with Essipova, and first appeared in public at the age of 13; then entered classes in composition with Glière and piano with Igumnov at the Moscow Cons., graduating in 1930. He subsequently abandoned his concert career as pianist, and devoted himself to musicology, specializing in monographs on Soviet composers. He published *D. Shostakovich, Composer* (Moscow, 1959, in an English translation); *Portraits of Pianists* (Moscow, 1962); numerous articles in Soviet music periodicals.

Rabl, Walter, Austrian conductor and composer; b. Vienna, Nov. 30, 1873; d. Klagenfurt, July 14, 1940. He was a pupil of J. F. Hummel, and later of Navratil in Vienna; studied musicology with Guido Adler in Prague (Dr. phil., 1897). He conducted at the Düsseldorf Opera (1903–06), and at the municipal theaters in Essen, Dortmund, and Magdeburg (1915–24); wrote an opera, *Liane* (Strasbourg, 1903); a symphony; Quartet for clarinet, violin, cello, and piano; Violin Sonata; several song cycles.

BIBLIOGRAPHY: A. Eccarius-Sieber, "Walter Rabl," in vol. II of *Monographien moderner Musiker* (Leipzig, 1907).

Rachmaninoff, Sergei, great Russian composer and superb pianist; b. on his father's estate at Oneg, district of Novgorod, April 1, 1873; d. Beverly Hills, Calif., March 28, 1943. He was of a musical family; his grandfather was an amateur pianist, a pupil of John Field; his father also played the piano; Rachmaninoff's *Polka* was written on a theme improvised by his father. After financial setbacks, the family estate was sold, and in 1882 Rachmaninoff was taken to St. Petersburg; became a piano pupil of Demiansky at the Cons. there (1882–85); acting on the advice of his cousin, the well-known pianist and conductor Alexander Siloti, Rachmaninoff went to Moscow and studied piano with Zverev (1885–88) at the Moscow Cons.; in 1888 he began to study piano with Siloti and composition with Taneyev and Arensky. He met Tchaikovsky, who appreciated Rachmaninoff's talent, and gave him friendly advice. At the age of 19 he wrote his Prelude in C-sharp minor, which became one of the most celebrated piano pieces in the world. He graduated as pianist in 1891, and as composer in 1892, receiving the gold medal for his opera in one act, *Aleko*, after Pushkin (1892). His 1st Symph. was given in Moscow in 1897, with little success. Discouraged, Rachmaninoff destroyed the manuscript; however, the orchestral parts were preserved, and after Rachmaninoff's death the score was restored and performed in Moscow (1945). He toured with the Italian violinist Teresina Tua in Russia (1895); gave his own piano recitals, and soon became known as a piano virtuoso; in 1899 he gave a concert of his orchestral works with the Philharmonic Society of London. He continued to compose for orch., for piano, and for voice; in 1901 he gave the 1st performance of his 2nd Piano Concerto in Moscow, at a concert conducted by Siloti; this concerto became the most celebrated work of its genre written in the 20th century, and its singular charm has never abated since; it is no exaggeration to say that it became a model for piano concertos by a majority of modern Russian composers, and also of semi-popular virtuoso pieces for piano and orch. written in America. In 1902 Rachmaninoff married his cousin Natalie Satina; they spent some months in Switzerland; then returned to Moscow. Rachmaninoff was engaged to conduct opera at the Bolshoi Theater for two seasons (1904–06), and proved himself a very efficient conductor. From 1906 to 1909 he lived mostly in Dresden; spent the summers in his Russian country home near Novgorod. In 1909 he made his 1st American tour; his initial public appearance in the U.S. took place at Smith College, Northampton, Mass., on Nov. 4, 1909. His fame was such that the Boston Symph. Orch. offered him the post of permanent conductor, but he declined; the offer was repeated in 1918, but then, too, Rachmaninoff decided against acceptance. From 1910 to 1917 he lived in Moscow; conducted the Philharmonic Society Orch. there (1911–13). After the October Revolution of 1917, he left his native country, never to return; lived on his small estate on Lake Lucerne, Switzerland; made annual tours in Europe and in the U.S.; in 1935 made N.Y. his home; later settled in Los Angeles. He became an American citizen a few weeks before his death.

Among Russian composers Rachmaninoff occupies a very important place. The sources of his inspiration lie in the Romantic tradition of 19th-century Russian music; the link with Tchaikovsky's lyrical art is very strong; melancholy moods prevail, and minor keys predominate in Rachmaninoff's compositions, as in Tchaikovsky's; but there is an unmistakable stamp of Rachmaninoff's own individuality in the broad, rhapsodic sweep of the melodic line, and particularly in the fully expanded sonorities and fine resonant harmonies of his piano writing; its technical resourcefulness is unexcelled since Liszt. Despite the fact that Rachmaninoff was an émigré, and stood in avowed opposition to the Soviet regime (until the German attack on Russia in 1941 impelled him to modify his stand), his popularity never wavered in Russia; after his death Russian musicians paid spontaneous tribute to him. Rachmaninoff's music is much less popular in Germany, France, and Italy; on the other hand, in England and America it constitutes a potent factor on the concert stage.

WORKS: OPERAS: *Aleko,* after Pushkin's *The Gypsies* (Moscow, May 9, 1893); *The Miserly Knight* (Moscow, Jan. 24, 1906, composer conducting); *Francesca da Rimini* (Moscow, Jan. 24, 1906, composer conducting). FOR ORCH.: Symph. No. 1 (St. Petersburg, March 27, 1897); Symph. No. 2 (St. Petersburg, Feb. 8, 1908, composer conducting); Symph. No. 3 (Philadelphia, Nov. 6, 1936); *Andante and Scherzo* for string orch. (Moscow, Feb. 24, 1891); *Prince Rostislav,* symph. poem (1891); *Intermezzo* (Moscow, Oct. 31, 1892); *The Rock,* symph. fantasy (1893; Moscow, March 20, 1896); *Caprice bohémien,* for orch. (1894); *The Isle of the Dead,* symph. poem, inspired by Böcklin's painting (Moscow, May 1, 1909, composer conducting); *Symph. Dances* (Philadelphia, Jan. 3, 1941); 4 piano concertos: No. 1, in F-sharp minor (1890–91; revised, 1917); No. 2, in C minor, one of his most famous

works (Moscow, Nov. 9, 1901, composer soloist); No. 3, in D minor (N.Y., Nov. 28, 1909, composer soloist); No. 4, in G minor (Philadelphia, March 18, 1927); *Rhapsody on a Theme* by Paganini, for piano and orch. (Baltimore, composer soloist with the Philadelphia Orch., Nov. 7, 1934). CHAMBER MUSIC: *Trio élégiaque,* in memory of Tchaikovsky (1893); *Romance* and *Danse hongroise,* for violin and piano (1893); Cello Sonata (1901). CHORAL WORKS: *The Spring,* for baritone, chorus, and orch. (Moscow, March 24, 1902); *Liturgy of St. John Chrysostom,* for chorus a cappella (Moscow, Nov. 25, 1910); *The Bells,* after Edgar Allan Poe, for orch., chorus, and soloists (St. Petersburg, Dec. 13, 1913, composer conducting); Vesper Mass, for chorus a cappella (Moscow, March 10, 1915); *3 Russian Songs,* for chorus and orch. (Philadelphia, March 18, 1927). FOR PIANO: *5 Morceaux de fantaisie,* op. 3: *Élégie, Prélude* (the famous one, in C-sharp minor), *Mélodie, Polichinelle, Sérénade* (1892); *7 Morceaux de salon,* op. 10 (1894); *6 Moments musicaux,* op. 16 (1896); *Variations on a Theme by Chopin,* op. 22 (1903); *10 Preludes,* op. 23 (1904); Sonata No. 1, in D minor, op. 28 (1907); *13 Preludes,* op. 32 (1910); *6 Études-Tableaux,* op. 33 (1911); *Polka V.R.,* on a theme by the composer's father, Vassily Rachmaninoff (1911); Sonata No. 2, in B-flat minor (1913); *9 Études-Tableaux,* op. 39 (1916–17; orchestrated by Respighi, 1931); *Variations on a Theme by Corelli* for piano, op. 42 (1931); *6 Duets for piano, 4 hands,* op. 11 (1894); *Fantasy* (Suite No. 1) for 2 pianos, op. 5 (1893); Suite No. 2, op. 17 (1901); arrangements for piano of *Prelude, Gavotte,* and *Gigue* from Bach's Violin Partita in E major; of Mendelssohn's *Scherzo* from *A Midsummer Night's Dream,* Mussorgsky's *Hopak,* Rimsky-Korsakov's *Flight of the Bumble-Bee,* Fritz Kreisler's *Liebesfreude* and *Liebeslied,* and of his own song, *Lilacs.* SONGS: (all written before 1916): 6 Songs, op. 4; 6 Songs, op. 8; 12 Songs, op. 14, of which *Spring Waters* is best known; 12 Songs, op. 21 (including *Fate,* on Beethoven's 5th Symph., and *Lilacs*); 15 Songs, op. 26 (including *Christ is Risen*); 14 Songs, op. 34 (including *Vocalise*); 6 Songs, op. 38.

BIBLIOGRAPHY: Ivan Lipayev, *S. R.* (in Russian; Saratov, 1913); V. Belaiev, *R.* (Moscow, 1924); V. Belaiev, "S. R.," *Musical Quarterly* (July 1927); Oskar von Riesemann, *R.'s Recollections* (N.Y., 1934; reprint, 1970); Watson Lyle, *R.: a Biography* (London, 1939); Alfred and Katherine Swan, "R.: "Personal Reminiscences," *Musical Quarterly* (Jan. and April 1944); A. Gronowicz, *R.* (N.Y., 1946); Sophie Satin, ed., *In Memory of R.* (N.Y., 1946, in Russian); Igor Boelza, ed., *R. and Russian Opera* (Moscow, 1947); A. Solovtsov, *S. R.* (Moscow, 1947); J. Culshaw, *S. R.* (London, 1949); J. Andriessen, *R.* (Amsterdam, 1950); V. Seroff, *R.* (N.Y., 1950; in French, Paris, 1954); A. Alexeyev, *S. R.* (Moscow, 1954); S. Bertensson and J. Leyda, *S. R.* (N.Y., 1956); Z. Apetian, ed., *Reminiscences about R.* (Moscow, 1957); R. Threlfall, *S. R., His Life and Music* (London, 1973).

Rachmilovich, Jacques, Russian conductor; b. Odessa, Oct. 8, 1895; d. on board the S.S. Giacomo en route to Italy, Aug. 7, 1956, and was buried at sea. He studied at the St. Petersburg Cons.; emigrated to America in 1925 and settled in California, where he organized the Santa Monica Symph. Orch. (1945). He made numerous appearances as guest conductor, specializing in modern music.

Radecke, Ernst, German musicologist, son of **Robert Radecke;** b. Berlin, Dec. 8, 1866; d. Winterthur, Switzerland, Oct. 8, 1920. He studied music with his father; then took courses in musicology at the Universities of Jena, Munich and Berlin; received his Dr. phil. at the Univ. of Berlin with his dissertation *Das deutsche weltliche Lied in der Lautenmusik des 16. Jahrhunderts* (publ. Leipig, 1891). In 1893 he went to Winterthur, Switzerland, and devoted himself mainly to teaching; in 1908 became lecturer on musicology at the Univ. of Zürich. He published a number of analytic essays of classical works.

Radecke, Robert, German conductor and composer; b. Dittmannsdorf, Oct. 31, 1830; d. Wernigerode, June 21, 1911. He was a brother of the conductor **Rudolf Radecke;** studied at the Leipzig Cons., with Ferdinand David (violin) and Moscheles (piano); also took a course in composition with Hauptmann; appeared first as a violinist; then went to Berlin where he conducted Court Opera (1863–87); also taught at the Royal Institute for Church Music there (1892–1907). He wrote a "Liederspiel," *Die Mönkgüter* (Berlin, May 1, 1874); several overtures; 2 piano trios; choruses and piano works, but became known to the general public mainly for his song *Aus der Jugendzeit,* which obtained extraordinary popularity in Germany and was commonly mistaken for a folksong.

Radecke, Rudolf, German conductor, pedagogue, and composer; brother of **Robert Radecke;** b. Dittmannsdorf, Sept. 6, 1829; d. Berlin, April 15, 1893. He studied at the Leipzig Cons.; in 1859 went to Berlin where he organized the Radecke Choral Society (1868), and a music school (1869); also taught music at the Stern Cons. (1864–71). He wrote a number of part-songs.

Radenković, Milutin, Serbian composer; b. Mostar, April 6, 1921. He studied at the Belgrade Music Academy, where he subsequently became a teacher; also active as music critic. His works are couched in a neo-Classical idiom; of these, the most significant are Concertino for Piano and Orch. (1958) and *Dramatic Overture* (1960); he also composed chamber music; 2 piano sonatas; piano etudes and preludes; song cycles.

Radić, Dušan, Serbian composer; b. Sombor, April 10, 1929. He studied at the Music Academy of Belgrade; then went to Paris where he had private lessons with Milhaud and Messiaen. His music follows the cosmopolitan modernistic manner, Baroque in formal structure, dissonant in contrapuntal intricacies and hedonistic in its utilitarian appeal.

WORKS: *Symphoniette* (1954); *Spisak (Inventory),* song cycle of 13 numbers for 13 performers (2 female voices and 11 instruments; Belgrade, March 17, 1954); *Balada o mesecu lutalici (Ballad of the Errant Moon),* ballet (Belgrade, Oct. 19, 1960); Concertino for Clarinet and Strings (1956); *Sinfonia* (1965–66); Piano Quintet; several cantatas; songs; theater music.

BIBLIOGRAPHY: V. Peričić, *Muzički Stvaraoci u Srbiji* (Belgrade, 1969; pp. 407–21).

Radica, Ruben, Croatian composer; b. Split, May 19, 1931. He studied with Kelemen in Zagreb, with Frazzi in Siena and with Leibowitz in Paris. In 1963 he was appointed to the faculty of the Music Academy in Zagreb. He belongs to the avant-garde of Slovenian music; in 1961 he adopted the 12-tone method of composition.

WORKS: *Concerto grosso* (1957); *4 Dramatic Epigrams* for piano and string quartet (1959); *Concerto abbreviato* for cello and orch. (1960); *Lyrical Variations* for strings (1961); *Formacije (Formations)* for orch. (1963); *19 and 10, Interferences* for narrator, chorus and orch. (1965); *Sustajarnje (Prostration)* for electric organ and orch. (1967); *Composition* for Ondes Martenot and chamber orch. (Graz, Sept. 26, 1968); *Extensio* for piano and orch. (1973).

Radiciotti, Giuseppe, Italian writer on music; b. Jesi, Le Marche, Jan. 25, 1858; d. Tivoli, April 4, 1931. He was a music pupil of his uncle, G. Faini; after finishing a course of studies at the Univ. of Rome, he taught in secondary schools there; in 1895 appointed prof. at the Liceo in Tivoli.

WRITINGS: *Teatro, musica e musicisti in Sinigaglia* (1893); *Contributi alla storia del teatro e della musica in Urbino* (1899); *Il Teatro e la musica in Rome nel secondo quarto del secolo XIX* (1904); *Teatro, musica e musicisti in Recanati* (1904); *L'Arte musicale dei Marchigiani* (1905); *L'Arte musicale in Tivoli nei secoli XVI, XVII e XVIII* (1907); *G. B. Pergolesi* (1910; in German, 1954); *Rossini* (1914); *La Cappella musicale del duomo di Pesaro* (1914); *G. Rossini: Vita documentata, opere ed influenza sul'arte* (a monumental biography in 3 vols., 1927–29); *Aneddoti rossiniani autentici* (Rome, 1929); also numerous essays in various journals.

BIBLIOGRAPHY: L. Parigi, "G. Radiciotti," in *Critica Musicale* (1918); V. Scotti, "G. Radiciotti" in the *Bollettino Bibliografico Musicale* (1931).

Radnai, Miklós, Hungarian composer; b. Budapest, Jan. 1, 1892; d. there, Nov. 4, 1935. He studied violin, piano, and composition at the Academy of Music; in 1925 was appointed director of the Budapest Opera. He wrote a ballet, *The Birthday of the Infanta,* after Oscar Wilde (Budapest, April 26, 1918); *Symphony of the Magyars,* for chorus and orch.; Violin Concerto; some chamber music; a textbook of harmony; contributed critical essays to Hungarian publications.

Radó, Aladár, Hungarian composer; b. Budapest, Dec. 26, 1882; killed in battle near Belgrade, Sept. 7, 1914. He studied in Budapest and Berlin; wrote 2 operas: *The Black Knight* (1911) and *Golem* (1912); Symphony (1909); *Hungarian Concerto* for cello and orch. (1909); 2 string quartets; String Quintet; publ. several albums of piano pieces and song cycles.

Radoux, Charles, Belgian composer, writer on music, and pedagogue; son of **Jean-Théodore Radoux;** b. Liège, July 30, 1877; d. there, April 30, 1952. He studied with his father; in 1907 received the Belgian Prix de Rome with the cantata *Geneviève de Brabant;* in 1911, appointed prof. at the Liège Cons.; wrote music criticism for the *Journal de Liège;* was active in folksong research.

WORKS: the operas *Les Sangliers des Ardennes* (Liège, 1905) and *Oudelette* (Brussels, April 11, 1912); choral compositions with orch.: *Adieu-Absence-Retour, Chanson d'Halewyn, Les Fées;* orch. sketches: *Danse tzigane, Burlesque, Vision, Triptique champêtre; Scène grecque* for cello and orch.; *Variations* for violin and orch.; *Lamentation* (on a Bach prelude) for English horn and piano; piano pieces; folksong albums (*5 Noëls liégeois, 7 Chansons populaires de l'ancien Hainaut, Cramignons liégeois,* etc.). He used the surname **Radoux-Rogier** in his works.

Radoux, Jean-Théodore, Belgian composer and pedagogue; b. Liège, Nov. 9, 1835; d. there, March 21, 1911. He studied bassoon with Daussoigne-Méhul at the Cons. of Liège, where he became teacher of bassoon in 1856; won the Belgian Prix de Rome with the cantata *Le Juif errant* (1859); then went to Paris for additional study with Halévy. In 1872 he was appointed director of the Cons. of Liège.

WORKS: the operas *Le Béarnais* (Liège, March 14, 1866) and *La Coupe enchantée* (Brussels, 1872); oratorio, *Cain* (1877); symph. poems, *Ahasvère* and *Le Festin de Balthasar;* a patriotic overture, *Épopée nationale;* church music; publ. a monograph, *Vieuxtemps. Sa vie, ses œuvres* (1891).

Radovanović, Vladan, Serbian composer; b. Belgrade, Sept. 5, 1932. He studied at the Music Academy in Belgrade. His early works are set in a neo-Classical style; later he annexed ultramodern techniques, including electronic effects. His *Urklang* for mezzo-soprano and chamber orch. (Belgrade, March 14, 1962) deploys a counterpoint of instrumental colors, with the soloist singing wordlessly. Similarly wordless is his suite, *Chorales, Intermezzi e Fuga* for women's chorus (Belgrade, May 16, 1962). His experimental period includes such innovative works as *Sphaeroön* in 26 vocal parts, singing detached vowels (Belgrade, March 14, 1962) and *Pentaptych,* suite for voice and 6 instruments (Belgrade, April 22, 1964).

BIBLIOGRAPHY: V. Peričić, *Muzički Stvaraoci u Srbiji* (Belgrade, 1969; pp. 422–29).

Radziwill, Prince Anton Heinrich, Polish music amateur and patron of the arts; b. Vilna, June 13, 1775; d. Berlin, April 7, 1833. He played the cello and possessed a fine singing voice; he also wrote incidental music for Goethe's *Faust,* but his name is retained in music history solely because of his associations with Beethoven and Chopin. Beethoven dedicated to him his *Namensfeier* overture, op. 115, and Chopin inscribed to him his op. 8.

Rae, Allan, Canadian composer; b. Blairmore, Alberta, July 3, 1942. He studied arranging and music theory at the Berkeley School of Music in Boston, graduating in 1965; then took courses in electronic music at the Royal Cons. in Toronto (1970–73); subsequently joined its faculty as an instructor in electronic music.

WORKS: 2 string quartets (1966, 1967); *A Day in the Life of a Toad* for brass quintet (1970); *Trip* for orch. (1970); *Impressions* for wind quintet (1971); *Sleep Whispering* for vibraphone, flute and piano (1971); *Wheel of Fortune* for winds and strings (1971); *Symphony, In the Shadow of Atlantis* (1972); *The Hippopotamus* for orch. (1972); *Like Gods, Like Gods Among Them,* dance drama (1973); *Listen to the Wind,* suite for chorus and orch. (1973); *Poems for Trio* for piano trio (1974); *A Crack in the Cosmic Turtle* for jazz group and orch. (1975); *4 Brass Quartets* for 2 trumpets and 2 trombones (1975); *Image* for orch. (1975); *Rainbow Sketches* for flute, oboe, violin, piano and 2 percussionists (1976).

Raeli, Vito, Italian musical journalist; b. Tricase, July 8, 1880; d. there, May 7, 1970. He studied music privately; in 1905 he moved to Rome; in 1920 he founded the *Rivista Nazionale di Musica,* which he edited until it discontinued publication in 1943. He published numerous valuable monographs and essays on Italian composers, among them *Da V. Ugolini a O. Benevoli: nella cappella, 1603–1646* (Rome, 1920) and *Maestri compositori pugliesi* (Tricase, 1928).

Raff, Joseph Joachim, greatly renowned German composer and pedagogue; b. Lachen, near Zürich, May 27, 1822; d. Frankfurt, June 24, 1882. He was educated at the Jesuit Lyceum in Schwyz; then became a school teacher; at the same time he studied music; in 1843 he sent some of his piano pieces to Mendelssohn, who was sufficiently impressed to recommend them for publication by Breitkopf & Härtel. Mendelssohn's early death made it necessary for Raff to seek other associations; in 1850 he joined Liszt at Weimar and became an ardent propagandist of the new German school. Liszt produced Raff's opera *König Alfred* (Weimar, March 9, 1851). In 1854 Raff published a highly partisan pamphlet *Die Wagnerfrage,* in which he took up the cause of Wagner, then a center of fierce debate. In 1859 he married the actress Doris Genast. Raff's 2nd opera, *Dame Kobold,* was produced in Weimar on April 9, 1870; he wrote 4 more operas but they were never staged. In 1877 he was appointed director of Hoch's Cons. in Frankfurt; his teaching was extremely successful; musicians from many countries enrolled in his classes; among them was MacDowell. Raff was a composer of prodigious fecundity, a master of all technical aspects of composition. He wrote 214 opus numbers which were published, and many more that remained in manuscript. In spite of his fame, his music fell into lamentable desuetude after his death; some examples of his contrapuntal skill are quoted in school manuals. He wrote 11 symphonies, some of them furnished with romantic subtitles indicating the nature of the music: No. 1, *An das Vaterland,* op. 96; No. 2, op. 140; No. 3, *Im Walde,* op. 153; No. 4, op. 167; No. 5, *Leonore,* op. 177; No. 6, *Gelebt, gestrebt; gelitten, gestritten; gestorben, umworben* (an epigraph that might well be applied to Raff's own destiny); No. 7, *In den Alpen,* op. 201; No. 8, *Frühlingsklänge,* op. 205; No. 9, *Im Sommer,* op. 208; No. 10, *Zur Herbstzeit,* op. 213; No. 11, *Der Winter,* op. 214 (left unfinished, completed by M. Erdmannsdörfer); *Symphonietta* for 8 woodwinds and 2 horns; Piano Concerto; 2 violin concertos; Cello Concerto; 8 string quartets; 3 piano trios; 5 violin sonatas; about 120 piano pieces of various descriptions and 9 pieces for piano 4 hands; numerous transcriptions of orchestral and other works.

BIBLIOGRAPHY: A. Schäfer, *Chronologisch-systematisches Verzeichnis der Werke Joachim Raffs* (Wiesbaden, 1888); Helen Raff, *Joachim Raff. Ein Lebensbild* (Regensburg, 1925); J. Kälin and A. Marty, *Leben und Werk des Komponisten Joachim Raff* (Zürich, 1972).

Rago, Alexis, Venezuelan composer; b. Caracas, May 25, 1930. He studied in Caracas and later at the Peabody Cons. in Baltimore; then went for further studies to Vienna and Rome, where he took courses in piano and composition. Returning to Venezuela he became Director of the Cons. of the state of Aragua.

WORKS: *Tres Escenas de Rítos Prohibidos* for piano (1959); *Autantepuy,* symph. poem (1962); *5 Instantes* for orch. (1968); *Mítica de Sueños y Cosmogonías* for wind quintet (commissioned by the 4th Inter-American Festival in Washington, and performed there on June 25, 1968); *Guri,* symph. poem on indigenous themes (1968); *Sincronismos, Audio-Sonorrítmicos* (1969); several piano suites; songs.

Rahlwes, Alfred, German conductor and composer; b. Wesel, Oct. 23, 1878; d. Halle, April 20, 1946. He studied with Wüllner, G. Hollaender and W. Hess at the Cologne Cons.; upon graduation was active as choral conductor in Halle. He wrote an opera, *Frau Potiphar* (Essen, 1907); numerous men's choral pieces; chamber music; songs.

BIBLIOGRAPHY: M. Soupe, "Alfred Rahlwes zum Gedächtnis," in *Handel Festival Program Book* (Halle, 1956).

Raichev, Alexander, Bulgarian composer; b. Lom, April 11, 1922. He studied composition with Vladigerov and orchestration with Goleminov at the Sofia Cons. (1943–47); later took courses at the Budapest Cons. (1949–50); returning to Bulgaria he was appointed to the faculty of the Sofia Cons. His music is marked by Balkan melorhythms and asymmetrical time periods.

WORKS: 3 operas: *The Bridge* (Ruse, Oct. 2, 1965), *Your Presence* (1968) and *Alarm* (1974); an operetta-revue, *The Orchid's Glory* (1962; Sofia, March 6, 1963); 3 oratorios: *Friendship* (1954), *Dimitrov Is Alive* (1954) and *October 50* (1967); *September Requiem* (1973); Piano Concerto (1947); 5 symphonies: (1949, 1958, 1966, 1968, 1972); *Sonata-Poem* for violin and orch. (1955); *Bright Day,* overture (1966); *Leninist Generations,* symph. eulogy (1970); *Flaming Dawn,* overture (1971); *Academic Overture* (1973); *Festival Overture* (1975); chamber music; songs; choruses.

Raichl, Miroslav, Czech composer; b. Náchod, Feb. 2, 1930. He studied composition with Bořkovec at the Prague Academy of Music, graduating in 1953; subsequently devoted himself mainly to teaching and administrative work in the Union of Czechoslovak Composers.

WORKS: *Fuente Ovejuna,* opera after Lope de

Vega (1957; Prague, 1959); 2 symphonies (1955; 1960); Cello Concerto (1956); *Revolutionary Overture* (1958); *Someone Was Playing on the Oboe* for female chorus a cappella (1970).

Raida, Karl Alexander, German composer; b. (of German parents) Paris, Oct. 4, 1852; d. Berlin, Nov. 26, 1923. He studied at the Conservatories of Stuttgart and Dresden; was Kapellmeister from 1878–92 at the Viktoria Theater in Berlin, where he founded the Akademie für dramatischen Gesang (1882) and the Gesellschaft der Opernfreunde (1887); 1895–97 director of the new Deutsches Theater in Munich; a successful composer of light operas, operettas, ballets, farces, etc.

Raimann, Rudolf, Hungarian composer; b. Veszprem, May 7, 1861; d. Vienna, Sept. 26, 1913. He entered the service of Prince Esterházy as music director; wrote an opera, *Enoch Arden,* after Tennyson (Budapest, May 8, 1894), and about a dozen operettas, produced in Vienna: *Das Waschermädel* (April 19, 1905); *Paula macht alles* (March 27, 1909), *Die Frau Gretl* (April 7, 1911), *Unser Stammhalter* (Nov. 15, 1912), etc.

Raimondi, Gianni, Italian tenor; b. Bologna, April 17, 1923. He made his debut in 1947 in Bologna; appeared at La Scala, Milan, as Alfredo in *La Traviata,* with Maria Callas as Violetta. In 1957 he made his first American tour; on Sept. 29, 1965 appeared as Rodolfo in *La Bohème* at the Metropolitan Opera in N.Y.; among his other parts were Cavaradossi in *Tosca,* the Duke in *Rigoletto* and Faust in Gounod's opera.

Raimondi, Ignazio, Italian composer; b. Naples, c.1737; d. London, Jan. 14, 1813. He left Italy about 1770; conducted concerts in Amsterdam; then went to Paris, and eventually (1790) to London, where he remained until the end of his life.

WORKS: a symphony titled *Les Aventures de Télémaque* (Amsterdam, Jan. 15, 1777); opera, *La Muta* (Paris, Nov. 12, 1789); a symphony titled *The Battle* (1785; very popular in England); several string quartets; string trios; various other instrumental pieces.

Raimondi, Pietro, inventive Italian composer; b. Rome, Dec. 20, 1786; d. there, Oct. 30, 1853. He studied with La Barbara and Tritto at the Cons. della Pietà de' Turchini, Naples; in 1807 brought out an opera buffa, *Le Bizzarie d'amore,* at Genoa; it was followed by about 60 other dramatic works and 21 ballets, for whose production he traveled from place to place (Florence, Naples, Rome, Messina, Milan, etc.); was director of the royal theaters at Naples (1824–32) and prof. of Palermo Cons. (1832–52); in 1852 became maestro di cappella at St. Peter's, Rome. Raimondi was a contrapuntist of remarkable skill; he published 4 fugues *a* 4, which could be combined as a quadruple fugue *a* 16; 6 fugues *a* 4, to be combined as a sextuple fugue *a* 24; in the *24 Fughe a 4, 5, 6 e 8 voci* publ. by Ricordi, there is one such quadruple fugue *a* 16, and a quintuple fugue *a* 20; further, 6 fugues *a* 4, performable as a sextuple fugue *a* 24; and a fugue *a* 64, for 16 choirs *a* 4. His most astounding feat in combination, however, was the sacred trilogy *Giuseppe* (Joseph), comprising 3 oratorios, *Potifar, Giuseppe, Giacobbe,* performed at the Teatro Argentina, Rome, Aug. 7, 1852, at first separately, and then simultaneously, the ensemble of 400 musicians on the stage and in the orchestra presenting a most striking effect, and arousing great curiosity among professional musicians.

BIBLIOGRAPHY: F. Cicconetti, *Memorie intorno a Pietro Raimondi* (Rome, 1867); Cecil Gray, "Pietro Raimondi," *Music Review* (Jan. 1940).

Rainger, Ralph, American composer of popular songs, pianist and arranger; b. New York, Oct. 7, 1901; d. Beverly Hills, Calif., Oct. 23, 1942. He received solid training in music, and even attended Schoenberg's lectures at the Univ. of California in Los Angeles. He became a professional accompanist; in 1930 went to Hollywood where he prospered as a film composer. Among the many songs he wrote, *Thanks for the Memories* received an Academy Award in 1938 and became a perennial favorite as the theme song of the comedian Bob Hope.

Rainier, Priaulx, South African-born English composer; b. Howick, Natal, Feb. 3, 1903. She studied violin at the South African College of Music; in 1920 went to London, where she studied violin and took courses with McEwen at the Royal Academy of Music; studied briefly with Nadia Boulanger in Paris (1939); in 1942, was appointed prof. at the Royal Academy of Music.

WORKS: *Incantation* for clarinet and orch. (1933); *3 Greek Epigrams* for soprano and piano (1937); String Quartet (1939); *Suite* for clarinet and piano (1943); *Sinfonia da camera* for string orch. (1947; revised version, London, Feb. 21, 1958); *Dance of the Rain* for tenor and guitar (1948); *Barbaric Dance Suite* for piano (1949); *Ballet Suite* for orch. (1950); *Cycle for Declamation* for solo soprano, tenor or baritone (1953); *6 Pieces* for wind quintet (1954); *Requiem* for solo tenor and chorus (1955–56); *Trio-Suite* for piano trio (1959); *Pastoral Triptych* for solo oboe (1960); *Dance Concerto "Phala-phala"* for orch. (1960–61; London, Jan. 17, 1961); *Quanta* for oboe quartet (1961–62); *Suite* for solo cello (1963–65); Cello Concerto (1963–64; London, Sept. 3, 1964); String Trio (1965–66); *Aequora Lunae (The Seas of the Moon)* for double orch., percussion and solo winds (1966–67; Cheltenham Festival, July 18, 1967); *Trios and Triads* for 10 trios and percussion (1969–73); *The Bee Oracles,* after Sitwell, for tenor or baritone solo, flute, oboe, violin, cello and harpsichord (1970); *Quinque* for harpsichord (1971); *Ploërmel* for winds and percussion (1973; London, Aug. 13, 1973); *Prayers from the Ark* for tenor and harp (1976); Violin Concerto (1976–77; Edinburgh Festival, Sept. 6, 1977); songs.

Rains, Leon, American operatic bass; b. New York, Oct. 1, 1870; d. Los Angeles, June 11, 1954. He studied with Saenger in N.Y. (1891–96) and with Bouhy in Paris; made a concert tour with Melba in the U.S. (1898); then was a member of the court opera at Dresden (from 1899); made his first appearance with the Metropolitan Opera Company in 1908; then returned to Dresden, and continued to sing there for several years, eventually returning to America.

Raisa, Rosa, soprano; b. Bialystok, Poland, May 30, 1893; d. Los Angeles, Sept. 28, 1963. In order to escape the horrors of anti-Semitic persecutions she fled to Naples at the age of 14; on Lombardi's advice she entered the Cons. San Pietro a Maiella, where she studied under Barbara Marchisio; debut at Parma, Sept. 6, 1913, in Verdi's *Oberto, Conte di San Bonifacio* (revived for the Verdi centenary); then sang 2 seasons at the Costanzi in Rome; 1914 at Covent Garden; 1914–15, with the Chicago Opera Co.; sang with increasing success in Rio de Janeiro, Montevideo, São Paulo, and Milan; on her reappearance with the Chicago company she scored a trumph as Aida (Nov. 13, 1916).

Raison, André, French composer and organist, active in Paris 1687–1719. He received instruction at Nanterre; was organist of the Jacobins and at the church of Ste. Geneviève in Paris; publ. 2 books of organ pieces (1688, 1714), of which the first was reprinted by Guilmant in *Archives des maîtres de l'orgue* 2 (Paris, 1899).

Raitio, Väinö, Finnish composer; b. Sortavala, April 15, 1891; d. Helsinki, Sept. 10, 1945. He studied in Helsinki with Melartin and Furuhjelm and in Moscow with Ilyinsky; also in Berlin (1921) and Paris (1925–26). His music is programmatic in the Romantic manner, but there is a more severe strain in his pieces derived from Finnish legends.

WORKS: 5 operas to Finnish librettos: *Jeftan tytär (Jephtha's Daughter,* 1929; Helsinki, 1931); *Prinsessa Cecilia* (1933; Helsinki, 1936); *Väinämöisen kosinta (Väinämöisen's Courtship)* (1935); *Lyydian kuningas (The King of Lydia,* 1937; Helsinki, 1955); *Kaksi kuningatarta (Two Queens;* Helsinki, 1945); Piano Concerto (1915); *Poem* for cello and orch. (1915); *Symphonic Ballad* (1916); Symphony (1918–19); *Joutsenet (The Swans)* for orch. (1919); *Fantasias estatica,* symph. poem (1921); *Antigone* for orch. (1921–22); *Kuutamo Jupiterissa (Moonlight on Jupiter),* symph. tableau (1922); *Fantasia poetica,* symph. poem (1923); *Pyramid* for chorus and orch. (1924–25); *Vesipatsas (Waterspout),* ballet (1929); *Felis domestica,* scherzo for orch. (1935); Concerto for Violin, Cello and Orch. (1936); *Nocturne* for violin and orch. (1938); *Fantasy* for cello, harp and orch. (1942); *Le Ballet grotesque* (1943); String Quartet; Piano Quintet; Violin Sonata; works for piano and organ.

BIBLIOGRAPHY: Sulho Ranta, ed., *Suomen Säveltäjiä* (Helsinki, 1945; pp. 514–21).

Rajičić, Stanojlo, Serbian composer; b. Belgrade, Dec. 16, 1910. He studied music in Vienna and Berlin; upon return to Serbia, he joined the faculty of the Belgrade Academy of Music. His early compositions are set in a radical idiom of atonal music, verging on dodecaphony, but later he adopted a national style derived from melorhythms of Serbian folksongs.

WORKS: 2 operas: *Simonida* (1956; Sarajevo, May 24, 1957) and *Karadjordje* (1973); a ballet, *Pod zemljom (Under the Earth,* 1940); 6 symphonies (1935; 1941; 1944; 1946; 1959; 1967); 3 piano concertos (1940, 1942, 1950); 3 violin concertos (1941, 1946, 1950); 2 clarinet concertos (1943, 1962); Cello Concerto (1949);

Bassoon Concerto (1969); *Magnovenja (Moments),* a song cycle for mezzo-soprano and orch. (1964); Piano Trio (1934); 2 string quartets (1938, 1939); piano pieces.

BIBLIOGRAPHY: V. Peričić, *Muzički Stvaraoci u Srbiji* (Belgrade, 1969; pp. 430–52).

Rakov, Nicolai, Russian composer; b. Kaluga, March 14, 1908. He studied violin in Moscow and composition at the Moscow Cons. with Glière; in 1935 joined its staff as teacher of orchestration. He was also active as a violinist and conductor. In his compositions he pursues the romantic and nationalistic line of Russian music.

WORKS: 2 symphonies (1940, 1957); Sinfonietta (1958); *Little Symphony* for strings (1962); 2 violin concertos (1944, 1955); Concertino for Violin and String Orch. (1959); Violin Sonata (1951); Oboe Sonata (1951); Flute Sonata (1970); 2 piano sonatinas; numerous pieces for Russian folk instruments.

BIBLIOGRAPHY: A. Solovtsov, *Nicolai Rakov* (Moscow, 1958).

Raksin, David, American composer, conductor and teacher; b. Philadelphia, Aug. 4, 1912. He learned to play piano and woodwind instruments from his father, a bandleader; organized his own jazz band at the age of 12; then entered the Univ. of Pennsylvania (Mus. B., 1934); studied composition privately with Isadore Freed (1934–35). In 1935 he went to Hollywood and was engaged by Charlie Chaplin to arrange the score for his film *Modern Times;* attended the classes of Arnold Schoenberg at the Univ. of California, Los Angeles (1937–38). He wrote more than 100 film scores, among them *Laura, Forever Amber, The Secret Life of Walter Mitty, Carrie, Separate Tables,* and *The Bad and the Beautiful;* also incidental music for plays, including *Mother Courage* by Brecht; made an orchestration of Stravinsky's *Circus Polka* for George Balanchine's production with the Barnum & Bailey Circus; composed numerous orchestral works in a light vein, among them, *Toy Concertino* which became popular. In 1956 he was appointed lecturer in composition at the Univ. of Southern California, Los Angeles.

Ralf, Richard, German composer; b. Karlsruhe, Sept. 30, 1897. He studied piano as a child with his father, the choirmaster at the Karlsruhe Opera; later attended the Scharwenka Cons. in Berlin, graduating in 1914. Drafted into the German Army, he suffered a severe shell shock at the French front; returning to Berlin, he studied composition with Hugo Kaun. In 1946 he emigrated to the U.S., eventually settling in Los Angeles. His music follows the florid and emotional trend of post-Wagnerian romanticism.

WORKS: *Transcendental,* ballet (1921); Violin Sonata (1923); String Quartet (1924); Violin Concerto (1925); *Brothers Arise,* cantata (1959); *Symphonic Songs* for mezzo-soprano and orch. (1968).

Ralf, Torsten, Swedish tenor; b. Malmö, Jan. 2, 1901; d. Stockholm, April 27, 1954. He studied at the Stockholm Cons. and in Berlin. Made his debut as Cavaradossi in Stettin (1930); then sang in Frankfurt

(1933–35), Dresden (1935–44), London (1935–39), New York (Metropolitan Opera House, 1945), and Buenos Aires (1946).

Ramann, Lina, German writer on music; b. Mainstockheim, near Kitzingen, June 24, 1833; d. Munich, March 30, 1912. She was a pupil of Franz and Frau Brendel at Leipzig; founded (1858) a music seminary for women teachers, at Glückstadt, Holstein; in 1865, with Ida Volkmann, a music school at Nuremberg, which they sold in a most flourishing condition to August Göllerich in 1890; from then until her death she lived in Munich, devoting herself entirely to literary work.

WRITINGS: *Die Musik als Gegenstand der Erziehung* (1868); Aus der Gegenwart (1868); *Allgemeine Erzieh- und Unterrichtslehre der Jugend* (1869; 3rd ed., 1898); *Bach und Händel* (1869); *Fr. Liszts Oratorium "Christus"; eine Studie zur zeit- und musikgeschichtlichen Stellung desselben* (1880); *Franz Liszt als Künstler und Mensch* (3 vols., 1880–94; vol. 1 in English, 1882); *Franz Liszt als Psalmensänger* (1886); she transl. and ed. Liszt's literary works, *Gesammelte Schriften* (6 vols., 1880–83); also wrote a *Grundriss der Technik des Klavierspiels,* in 12 books. Composed 4 sonatinas (op. 9) and other piano music; ed. *Liszt-Pädagogium* (5 vols. of Liszt's piano compositions with Liszt's own changes, additions, remarks, etc.

BIBLIOGRAPHY: M. Ille-Beeg, *Lina Ramann* (1914).

Ramboušek, Joseph, Czech double-bass virtuoso and pedagogue; b. Mníšek, Nov. 16, 1845; d. Moscow, March 10, 1901. He studied with Josef Hrabět at the Prague Cons.; then was in Stuttgart and Göteborg, and finally went to Moscow where he was engaged as double-bass player at the Moscow Opera. He taught at the Philharmonic Institute in Moscow; among his pupils was Koussevitzky.

Rameau, Jean-Philippe, great French composer, the creator of the modern science of harmony, b. Dijon, Sept. 25, 1683; d. Paris, Sept. 12, 1764. Of a musical family, he learned to play the harpsichord as a small child; from 10 to 14 he attended the Jesuit College at Dijon; then devoted himself to music, and in 1701 was sent to Italy; after a brief stay at Milan he joined the orchestra of a traveling French opera troupe as violinist. In 1702 he was assistant organist at Notre-Dame in Avignon; in June of that year he became organist at Clermont-Ferrand. In 1706 he publ. his first *Livre de pièces de clavecin* in Paris, where he probably had been living since the spring of 1705. Until 1708 he remained in Paris as church organist. In 1709 he became his father's successor at the Cathedral in Dijon; in 1714 he was organist in Lyons. Then he became organist of the Cathedral at Clermont-Ferrand, where he wrote his famous *Traité de l'Harmonie* (Paris, 1722). This epoch-making work, though little understood at the time, attracted considerable attention and roused opposition, so that when he settled definitely in Paris (1723) he was by no means unknown. The fact that he failed in 1727 in a competition for the position of organist at St.-Vincent-de-Paul did not injure his reputation, for it was generally known that Marchand (probably out of jealousy) had exerted his powerful influence in favor of Daquin, who was in every respect inferior to Rameau. He became organist at Sainte-Croix-de-la-Bretonnerie, and soon was recognized as the foremost organist in France. In 1726 appeared his *Nouveau système de musique théorique,* an introduction to the *Traité.* The leading ideas of his system of harmony are (1) chord-building by thirds; (2) the classification of a chord and all its inversions as one and the same, thus reducing the multiplicity of consonant and dissonant combinations to a fixed and limited number of root chords; (3) his invention of a fundamental bass ("basse fondamentale"), which is an imaginary series of root tones forming the real basis of the varied chord progressions employed in a composition. The stir that these novel theories occasioned, and his reputation as the foremost French organist, by no means satisfied Rameau's ambition; his ardent desire was to bring out a dramatic work at the Opéra. He had made a modest beginning with dramatic music in 1723, when he wrote some dances and divertissements for Alexis Piron's fairy burlesque *L'Endriague,* which was produced at the Théâtre de la Foire St.-Germain. In 1726 he brought out at the same theater two light operas by the same poet, *L'Enrôlement d'Arlequin* (Feb. 28) and *La Robe de dissension, ou Le Faux Prodigue* (autumn). He then became music master to the wife of the "fermier-général" La Pouplinière, and the latter obtained of Voltaire a libretto on *Samson,* which Rameau set to music; but it was rejected on account of its biblical subject. A second libretto, by Abbé Pellegrin, was accepted, and *Hippolyte et Aricie* was produced at the Opéra in 1733; its reception was cool, despite undeniable superiority (over the operas of Lully and his following) in the rich and varied harmony and instrumentation, and Rameau almost renounced dramatic composition. But the persuasions of his friends, who also influenced public opinion in his favor, were effective; in 1735 he brought out the successful opera-ballet *Les Indes galantes,* and in 1737 his masterpiece, *Castor et Pollux,* a work that for years held its own beside the operas of Gluck. A career of uninterrupted prosperity commenced; he was recognized as the leading theorist of the time, and his instruction was eagerly sought; for the next 30 years his operas dominated the French stage; he was named composer of the King's chamber music, and just before his death he was granted a patent of nobility. From the beginning of his dramatic career Rameau roused opposition, and at the same time found ardent admirers. The first war of words was waged between the "Lullistes" and the "Ramistes." This had scarcely been ended by a triumphant revival of *Pygmalion* in 1751, when the production of Pergolesi's *La Serva padrona* (1752) caused a more prolonged and bitter controversy between the adherents of Rameau and the "Encyclopédistes," a struggle known as "La Guerre des Bouffons," in which Rameau participated by writing numerous essays defending his position. Practically the same charges were made against him as a century later against Wagner: unintelligible harmony, lack of melody, preponderance of discords, noisy instrumentation, etc. But when 25 years later the war between Gluckists and Piccinnists was raging, Rameau's

works were praised as models of beauty and perfection. It is a matter for regret that Rameau was indifferent to the quality of his librettos; he relied so much upon his musical inspiration that he never could be brought to a realization of the importance of a good text; hence the inequality of his operas. Nevertheless, his operas mark a decided advance over Lully's in musical characterization, expressive melody, richness of harmony, variety of modulation, and expert and original instrumentation.

WRITINGS: *Traité de l'harmonie* (1722; English transl. with commentary by P. Gossett, 1971); *Nouveau système de musique théorique* (1726); *Plan abrégé d'une nouvelle méthode d'accompagnement* (1730); *Les Différentes Méthodes d'accompagnement pour de clavecin ou pour l'orgue* (1732); *Génération harmonique* (1737); *Démonstration du principe de l'harmonie* (1750); *Nouvelles réflexions de M. Rameau sur sa démonstration du principe de l'harmonie* (1752); *Réflexions sur la manière de former la voix* (1752); *Observations sur notre instinct pour la musique* (1754); *Code de musique pratique* (1760). The publications of 1722, 1726, 1737, 1750, 1752, 1754, and 1760 have been reissued in the series *Monuments of Music and Music Literature in Facsimile.*

WORKS: Theatrical entertainments to which Rameau contributed music: *L'Endriague* (Paris, Feb. 3, 1723); *L'Enrôlement d'Arlequin* (Paris, Feb., 1726); *La Robe de dissension* (1726); *Les Jardins de l'Hymen ou La Rose* (1726; Paris, March 5, 1744); *Les Courses de Tempé* (1734). Operas: *Hippolyte et Aricie* (Paris, Oct. 1, 1733); *Les Indes galantes,* "ballet héroïque" (Paris, Aug. 23, 1735); *Castor et Pollux* (Paris, Oct. 24, 1737); *Les Fêtes d'Hébé,* ballet (Paris, May 21, 1739); *Dardanus* (Paris, Nov. 19, 1739); *La Princesse de Navarre,* ballet (Versailles, Feb. 23, 1745); *Platée* (Versailles, March 31, 1745); *Les Fêtes de Polymnie,* ballet (Paris, Oct. 12, 1745); *Le Temple de la Gloire,* ballet (Versailles, Nov. 27, 1745); *Les Fêtes de l'Hymen et de l'Amour,* "ballet héroïque" (Versailles, March 15, 1747); *Zaïs,* "pastorale héroïque (Paris, Feb. 29, 1748); *Pygmalion,* ballet (Paris, Aug. 27, 1748); *Les Surprises de l'Amour,* ballet (Versailles, Nov. 27, 1748); *Naïs,* "pastorale héroïque" (Paris, April 22, 1749); *Zoroastre* (Paris, Dec. 5, 1749); *La Guirlande,* ballet (Paris, Sept. 21, 1751); *Acante et Céphise,* "pastorale héroïque" (Paris, Nov. 9, 1751); *Daphnis et Églé* (Fontainebleau, Oct. 30, 1753); *Les Sybarites,* ballet (Fontainebleau, Nov. 13, 1753); *La Naissance d'Osiris,* ballet (Fontainebleau, Oct. 12, 1754); *Anacréon,* ballet (Fontainebleau, Oct. 23, 1754); *Les Paladins* (Paris, Feb. 12, 1760); *Abaris ou Les Boréades* (1764). Most of the above were publ. in short score (voice, violin, and bass, with the ritornelli in full). Other publ. music: *Premier livre de pièces de clavecin* (1706); *Pièces de clavecin avec une méthode pour la mécanique des doigts* (n.d.; with important notes); *Pièces de clavecin avec une table pour les agréments* (1731); and *Nouvelles suites de pièces pour clavecin avec des remarques sur les différents genres de musique* (n.d.; Farrenc publ. these last two in his *Trésor des pianistes,* 1861); *Pièces de clavecin en concerts* (1741; with accomp. of violin, flute, and viola or 2nd violin); detached numbers of the above are in Pauer's *Old French Composers* and *Popular Pieces by Rameau;*

Hugo Riemann edited a complete ed. of the clavecin compositions (publ. by Steingräber). In 1895 Durand & Cie. began the publication of a monumental edition under the editorship of C. Saint-Saëns and Ch. Malherbe; after the latter's death (1911) his part of the work was divided between M. Emmanuel and M. Teneo. 18 vols. appeared up to 1924: I, *Pièces de clavecin;* II, *Musique instrumentale;* III, *Cantates;* IV, *Motets* (1st series); V, *Motets* (2nd series); VI, *Hippolyte et Aricie;* VII, *Les Indes galantes;* VIII, *Castor et Pollux;* IX, *Les Fêtes d'Hébé;* X, *Dardanus;* XI, *La Princesse de Navarre, Les Fêtes de Ramire, Nélée et Myrthis, Zéphire;* XII, *Platée;* XIII, *Les Fêtes de Polymnie;* XIV, *Le Temple de la Gloire;* XV, *Les Fêtes de l'Hymen et de l'Amour;* XVI, *Zaïs;* XVII, in 2 parts: Part I, *Pygmalion, Les Surprises de l'Amour;* Part II, *Anacréon, Les Sybarites;* XVIII, *Naïs.*

BIBLIOGRAPHY: BIOGRAPHY: Ch. Poisot, *Notice biographique sur J.-P. Rameau* (Paris, 1864); Th. Nisard, *Monographie de J.-P. Rameau* (Paris, 1867); A. Pougin, *Rameau* (Paris, 1876); R. Garraud, *Rameau* (Paris, 1876); H. Grigne, *Rameau* (Dijon, 1876); M. Brenet, "Notes et croquis sur J.-P. Rameau," *Guide Musical* (1899) and "La Jeunesse de Rameau," *Rivista Musicale Italiana* (1902–03); H. Quittard, "Les Années de jeunesse de Rameau," *Revue d'Histoire et de Critique Musicale* (1902); L. de La Laurencie, *Quelques documents sur J.-P. Rameau et sa famille* (Paris, 1907) and *Rameau* (Paris, 1908); L. Laloy, *Rameau* (Paris, 1908); L. de la Laurencie, "Rameau et ses descendants," *Sammelbände der Internationalen Musik-Gesellschaft* (1911); M. M. Mayer, *J.-P. Rameau; J. S. Bach* (Chambéry, 1946); Y. Tiénot, *J.-P. Rameau, esquisse biographique* (Paris, 1954); H. Charlier, *J.-P. Rameau* (Lyons, 1955); P. Berthier, *Rameau* (Paris, 1957); C. Girdlestone, *Rameau* (London, 1957).

CRITICISM AND HISTORY: L. Danjou, *Rameau, son influence sur l'art musical* (Paris, 1866); J. Carlez, *Grimm et la musique de son temps* (Paris, 1872); R. de Récy, "La Critique musicale au siècle dernier; Rameau et les Encyclopédistes," *Revue des Deux Mondes* (July 1886); A. Jullien, *La Musique et les philosophes au XVIIIᵉ siècle* (Paris, 1873); E. Newman, *Gluck and the Opera* (London, 1895); H. Imbert, "L'Œuvre de J.-P. Rameau," *Guide Musical* (1896); H. Riemann, *Geschichte der Musiktheorie* (2nd ed., 1921; p. 459ff); E. Dacier, "L'Opéra au XVIIIᵉ siècle," *Revue Musicale* (1902); E. Hirschberg, *Die Encyklopädisten und die französische Oper im 18. Jahrhundert* (Leipzig, 1903); R. Rolland, *Musiciens d'autrefois* (Paris, 1908); A. Jullien, *Musiciens d'hier et d'aujourd'hui* (Paris, 1910); P.-M. Masson, "Lullistes et Ramistes," *L'Année Musicale* (1911); J. Rivière, *Études* (Paris, 1911); J.-G. Prod'homme, *Écrits de musiciens, XVᵉ au XVIIIᵉ siècle* (Paris, 1912); L. Striffling, *Le Goût musical en France au XVIIIᵉ siècle* (Paris, 1913); G. Cucuel, *La Pouplinière et la musique de chambre au XVIIIᵉ siècle* (Paris, 1913); M. Shirlaw, *The Theory of Harmony* (London, 1917); J. Tiersot, "Rameau," *Musical Quarterly* (Jan. 1928); P. Lasserre, *Philosophie de goût musical* (Paris, 1928; new ed., 1931); P. M. Masson, *L'Opéra de Rameau* (1930; 2nd ed., 1932); "Rameau et Beethoven," in the Liège *Kongressbericht* (1930), and "Rameau and Wagner," *Musical Quarterly* (Oct. 1939); G. Migot, *Rameau et le génie de la musique française* (Paris, 1930); J. Gardien, *J.-P. Rameau* (Paris, 1949); P. M. Masson, "Les Deux Versions du *Dardanus* de Rameau," *Acta Musicologica* (Jan.–July 1954); J. Malignon, *Rameau* (Paris, 1960); H. Charlier, *J. Ph. Rameau* (Lyon, 1960); Sr. M. M. Keane, *The Theoretical Writings of J. Ph. Rameau* (Washington, 1961).

Ramin, Günther, German conductor, organist and composer; b. Karlsruhe, Oct. 15, 1898; d. Leipzig, Feb. 27, 1956. He studied organ with Karl Straube, piano with Robert Teichmüller and theory with Stephan Krehl at the Leipzig Cons. In 1918 he was appointed organist at the Thomaskirche; from 1935 to 1943 he conducted the Philharmonic Chorus in Berlin. His compositions include an *Orgelchoral-Suite* and many other organ pieces, as well as chamber music and songs. He edited several collections of organ works and published the manual *Gedanken zur Klärung des Orgelproblems* (Kassel, 1929; new enlarged edition; 1955).

BIBLIOGRAPHY: L. von Koerber, *Der Thomanerchor und sein Kantor* (Hamburg, 1954).

Ramírez, Luis Antonio, Puerto Rican composer; b. San Juan, Feb. 10, 1923. He studied piano and harmony with Alfredo Romero in San Juan (1954–57); then went to Spain and studied composition with Cristóbal Halffter and Daniel Bravo, and piano with Juan Molinari at the Madrid Cons. (1957–60). Returning to San Juan, he taught at the Univ. of Puerto Rico.

WORKS: *Sonata elegiaca* for cello and piano (1970); *Fantasia sobre un Mito Antillano* for double bass, guitar, horn, percussion and strings (1970); *3 Piezas Breves* for horn, 2 trumpets, trombone, piano, percussion, and strings (1972); *Fragmentos* for orch. (1973).

Ramos (Ramis) de Pareja, Bartolomé, Spanish theorist; b. Baeza, c.1440; d. after 1491. After lecturing at Salamanca, he went to Bologna in 1472; published in 1482 his Latin treatise *Musica practica* (modern ed. by Joh. Wolf, Leipzig, 1901; extract in English in O. Strunk, *Source Readings in Music History,* N.Y., 1950), one of the important landmarks in the science of harmony. In 1491 he was in Rome. He established the mathematical ratios 4:5 and 5:6 for the intervals of the major and minor third, thus completing the definition of the consonant triad and laying the basis of our harmonic system. He was also the first to set forth the theory of equal temperament, probably based on the practice of the early Spanish guitarists (vihuelistas), since the frets on the guitar were placed a semitone apart.

BIBLIOGRAPHY: J. Haar, "Roger Caperon and Ramos de Pareia," *Acta Musicologia* (1969).

Ramous, Gianni, Italian pianist and composer; b. Milan, April 12, 1930. He studied piano with Carlo Zecchi; autodidact in composition. In 1964 he became a member of the faculty at the Cons. of Genoa. He wrote *Polimorfia* for orch. (1966); Piano Concerto (1964); *Prismi* for solo violin, winds and drums (1969); 3 string quartets (1948, 1949, 1959); oratorio *La crucifissione* (1961); cantata *Lettera alla madre* (1963); a comic opera-farce, *Le fatiche del guerriero* (Triest, Nov. 23, 1963).

Ramovš, Primož, Slovenian composer; b. Ljubljana, March 20, 1921. He studied composition with Slavko Osterc at the home town Academy of Music (1935–41), with Vito Frazzi in Siena (1941), and privately with Casella and Petrassi in Rome (1941–43). Since 1945 he has worked at the library of the Slovene Academy of Sciences and Art (director since 1952) and taught at the Ljubljana Cons. (1948–64). The framework of his style of composition is neo-Classical, distinguished by great contrapuntal skill and ingenious handling of rich, dissonant sonorities; dodecaphony and aleatorality are sometimes employed.
WORKS: 3 numbered symphonies (1940, 1943, 1948); 3 divertimentos for orch. (1941, 1942, 1944); Piano Concerto (1946); Concertino for Piano and String Orch. (1948); Concerto for 2 Pianos and String Orch. (1949); *Suite* for 2 violins, cello and string orch. (1950); Sinfonietta (1951); *Musique funèbre* for orch. (1955); *Chorale and Toccata* for orch. (1955); *Adagio* for cello and string orch. (1958); *Concerto piccolo* for bassoon and string orch. (1958); Trumpet Concertino (1960); *7 Compositions* for strings (1960); Concerto for Violin, Viola and Orch. (1961); *Koncertantza glasba (Concertante Music)* for percussion and orch. (1961; his most remarkable work); *Intrada* for orch. (1962); *Profiles* for orch. (1964); *Vzporedja (Parallels)* for piano and string orch. (1965); *Odmevi (Echoes)* for flute and orch. (1965); *Antiparallels* for piano and orch. (1966; Zagreb, May 15, 1967); *Finale* for orch. (1966); *Portret* for harp, winds, strings and percussion (1968); *Symphony 68* (1968; Ljubljana, Oct. 27, 1968); *Nasprotja (Contrasts)* for flute and orch. (1969); Symph. for piano and orch. (1970). CHAMBER MUSIC: Quartet for 4 horns (1939); Wind Trio (1942); Trio for flute, trumpet, and bassoon (1952); Sonatina for clarinet, piano and trumpet (1953); *Kontrasti* for piano trio (1961); *Aphorisms* for viola and piano (1961); *Zvučna slika* for horn and piano (1962); *Eneafonia* for 9 instruments (1963); *Fluctuations* for chamber ensemble (1964); *Prolog—Dialog—Epilog* for flute, clarinet and bassoon (1966); *Nihanja (Oscillations)* for solo flute, harp, percussion and strings (1969); *Con sordino* for trumpet, trombone and piano (1969); *Siglali* for piano and 8 instruments (1973); many compositions for solo instruments; piano pieces; choruses; songs.

Rampal, Jean-Pierre, eminent French flutist; b. Marseille, Jan. 7, 1922. He took flute lessons with his father, Joseph Rampal; attended courses in medicine; then enrolled in the Paris Cons. He played flute in the orchestra of the Vichy Opera (1947–51) and later was first flutist at the Paris Opéra. In 1968 he was appointed professor at the Paris Cons. At the peak of his career, he combined his pedagogical activities with world-wide tours as a soloist with major orchestras and in recitals, achieving extraordinary success, considering that flute recitals rarely attract large audiences. His playing is remarkable for its virtuoso technique and an uncanny ability to graduate subtle dynamics of flute sonorities in all registers. Several French composers, among them Poulenc and Jolivet, wrote special works for him.

Ramsey, Robert, English organist and madrigalist; b. about 1595. He took his Mus. B. at Cambridge in 1616; was organist of Trinity College (1628–44) and Master of the Children (1637–44). He wrote numerous church services, anthems and madrigals, which remained in manuscript until 1962, when an *Evening Service* and some madrigals were published in England.
BIBLIOGRAPHY: E. Thompson, "Robert Ramsey," *Musical Quarterly* (April 1963).

Ran, Shulamit, Israeli composer; b. Tel Aviv, Oct. 21, 1949. She studied piano; took composition lessons from Paul Ben-Haim (1960–63). A scholarship enabled her to go to the U.S., where she enrolled in the Mannes College of Music in N.Y. (1963–67), studying piano with Nadia Reisenberg and composition with Dello Joio; in 1963 attended the seminars of Aaron Copland and Lukas Foss at the Berkshire Music Center. In 1973 she joined the faculty of the Univ. of Chicago.
WORKS: *Capriccio* for piano and orch. (N.Y., Nov. 30, 1963, composer soloist); *Symphonic Poem* for piano and orch. (Jerusalem, Oct. 17, 1967, composer soloist); *10 Children's Scenes* for piano, 4-hands (1967); *Structures* for piano (1968); *7 Japanese Love Poems* for voice and piano (1969); *O The Chimneys,* after poems by Sachs, for voice, flute, clarinet, bass clarinet, cello, percussion, piano and tape (N.Y., Jan. 19, 1970); *Concert Piece* for piano and orch. (1971; Tel Aviv, July 12, 1971, composer soloist); *3 Fantasy Pieces* for cello and piano (1972); *Ensembles for 17,* for high female voice and 16 instrumentalists (Chicago, April 11, 1975); *Sonata Brevis* for harpsichord (1975); *Double Vision* for 2 quintets and piano (Chicago, Jan. 21, 1977); Piano Concerto (1977).

Randall, James, American composer; b. Cleveland, June 16, 1929. He studied at Columbia Univ. (B.A., 1955), at Harvard Univ. (M.A., 1956) and at Princeton (M.F.A., 1958); in 1957 he was appointed to the music faculty of Princeton Univ.
WORKS: *Pitch-derived Rhythm: 5 Demonstrations* (1961); *Mudgett: Monologues of a Mass Murderer* for tape (1965); *Lyric Variations* for violin and computer (1968). He dabbled in mathematics; the structure of much of his music shows an interrelation between seemingly unrelated categories, such as pitch and rhythm, much in the manner that the transcendental number pi is mathematically placed in relation with an imaginary number i and the transcendental base of natural logarithms.

Randegger, Alberto, Jr., Italian violinist and composer; nephew of **Alberto Randegger, Sr.;** b. Trieste, Aug. 3, 1880; d. Milan, Oct. 7, 1918. He accompanied his uncle to London and appeared as a violinist at an orchestral concert conducted by the latter; took courses at the Royal Cons. of Music; then returned to Italy and lived in Milan. He composed a short opera *L'Ombra di Werther* (Trieste, 1899); a violin concerto; piano pieces and songs.

Randegger, Alberto, Sr., Italian conductor; b. Trieste, April 13, 1832; d. London, Dec. 18, 1911. He studied piano and composition in Italy; in 1854 went to England and became successful as a singing teacher. In 1868 he was appointed prof. of singing at the Royal Academy of Music in London. From 1879 to 1885 he conducted the Carl Rosa Company; then was opera conductor at Drury Lane and Covent Garden (1887-98).

Randegger, Giuseppe Aldo, Italian pianist and pedagogue; b. Naples, Feb. 17, 1874; d. New York, Nov. 30, 1946. He studied in Naples; in 1893 he went to America and was active mainly as a teacher; he composed an opera *The Promise of Medea,* and a number of songs.

Randolph, Harold, American pianist and music educator; b. Richmond, Virginia, Oct. 31, 1861; d. Northeast Harbor, Maine, July 6, 1927. He studied at the Peabody Cons. of Music in Baltimore; in 1898 he succeeded Asger Hamerik as director of the Peabody Cons., and enjoyed an excellent reputation as a teacher and administrator.
BIBLIOGRAPHY: D. Leedy, "Harold Randolph, the Man and Musician," *Musical Quarterly* (April 1944).

Rands, Bernard, English composer; b. Sheffield, March 2, 1934. He studied at the Univ. of Wales (B. Mus., 1956; M. Mus., 1958); then went to Italy where he took a course in musicology with Roman Vlad in Rome and composition with Luigi Dallapiccola in Florence (1958-60); also attended the International Teaching Festivals in Darmstadt, taking composition and conducting in the seminars of Pierre Boulez and Bruno Maderna; in 1962 consulted Luciano Berio in Milan on problems of electronic music. He received grants from the Arts Council of Great Britain which enabled him to travel to Sydney, Australia (1972), and to accompany the BBC Symph. Orch. on its European tour (1974). In 1976 he was engaged as prof. of music at the Univ. of California at San Diego. His music reaches the utmost limits of structural abstraction; he uses graphic notation in most of his works for instrumental groups; some titles of his works connote abstract constructions, as *Formants, Metalepsis* and *Sound Patterns* of variable durations, or suggest a concrete task to be performed, as in *Agenda* and *Memos,* or else an engineering blueprint, as in the *3 Wildtracks;* other works reflect his preoccupation with Hinduism, as in *Aum (Om),* a Mantric word interpreted as having 3 sounds representing Brahma, Vishnu, and Siva.
WORKS: (virtually all published by Universal Edition): for orch.: *Refractions* for 24 players (1961); *Per esempio* (1968); *Wildtrack 1* (1969), *Wildtrack 2* (1973), *Wildtrack 3* (1975); *Agenda* (1970); *Mesalliance* for piano and orch. (1972); *Ology* for jazz orch. (1973); *Aum* for harp and orch. (London, BBC Symph. Orch., Boulez conducting, April 17, 1974); *Agenda* for orch. (1970); for various instrumental ensembles: *Actions for 6* (1963); *Tableau* (1970); *Formants I* for solo harp (1965); *Formants 2* (1970); *déjà* (1972); *"As All Get Out"* for variable ensemble and variable duration (1972); *Cuadema* for string quartet (1975); *Scherzi* (1974); *Metalepsis* with soprano solo (1971); *3 Ballads* for voice, accompanied by instruments, piano or tape (1970-73); 4 pieces under the generic title *Sound Pat-*

terns (1967-69), of variable duration; 5 piano pieces under the generic title *Espressione;* 5 pieces, each for a solo instrument (double bass; trombone; cello; organ; piano) under the generic title *Memo* (1971-75); *Serena* for singing actress, 2 mimes, and instruments (1972).

Rangström, Ture, remarkable Swedish composer; b. Stockholm, Nov. 30, 1884, d. there, May 11, 1947. He studied singing in Berlin and Munich with Julius Hey (1905-07); then composition with Lindegren in Stockholm and Pfitzner in Munich. Returning to Sweden, he became music critic of the *Stockholms Dagblad* (1910-14) and the *Svenska Dagbladet* (1907-09, and after 1927). From 1922 to 1925 he was conductor of the Göteborg Symph. Orch.; then became stage director at the Stockholm Opera. His music is permeated with a lyrical sentiment, and his forms are rhapsodic; in his symphonies he achieves great intensity by a concentrated development of the principal melodic and rhythmic ideas; his songs are also appreciated.
WORKS: OPERAS: *Kronbruden (The Crown Bride),* after Strindberg (première, Stuttgart, in German, as *Die Kronbraut,* Oct. 21, 1919), *Middelalderlig* (Stockholm, 1921), *Gilgamesh* (left incomplete; finished and orchestrated by John Fernström; Stockholm, Nov. 20, 1952). FOR ORCH.: 4 symphonies (I, *In memoriam A. Strindberg,* 1915; II, *My Country,* 1919; III, *Song Under the Stars,* 1931; IV, *Invocatio,* 1936); the symph. poems *Dithyramb* (1909; revised in 1949 by Atterberg), *En höstsang (Ode to Autumn,* 1912), *Havet sjunger (The Sea Sings,* 1914), *Gamla Stockholm* (1939); *Festpreludium 1944,* for the 50th anniversary of the Stockholm Opera Theater (1944); *Divertimento elegiaco,* for strings (1918); *Un Petit Rien,* for string orch. (1937); *Ballad* for piano and orch. (1937); *Poem-Capriccio amoroso,* for violin and orch. (1944); *Ein Nachtstück in E.T.A. Hoffmanns Manier,* for string quartet (1909); other chamber music; piano pieces; about 60 fine songs, to Swedish texts.
BIBLIOGRAPHY: the special issue of *Musikrevy* 25 (1970).

Ránki, György, Hungarian composer; b. Budapest, Oct. 30, 1907. He studied composition with Kodály at the Budapest Academy of Music (1926-30); won the Erkel Prize twice (1952, 1967) and the Kossuth Prize (1954); in 1963 was awarded the title "Merited Artist of the Hungarian People's Republic." His music derives its inspiration chiefly from Hungarian folksongs.
WORKS: *Hóemberek (Snow Men;* London, 1939); a musical comedy *A csendháborító (The Rioter,* 1950; Budapest Radio, 1950; stage version, Budapest, 1959); the opera *Pomádé király új ruhája* (after Andersen's *The Emperor's New Clothes;* Budapest, June 6, 1953); children's musical comedy *A győztes ismeretlen (The Winner is Unknown,* 1961); operetta *Hölgyválasz (Spoon Dance,* 1961); children's opera *Muzsikus Péter új kalandjai (New Adventures of Peter Musician,* 1962); a symph. dance drama *Cirkusz (The Circus,* 1965); opera, *The Tragedy of Man* (Budapest, Dec. 4, 1970); 4 cantatas: *A város peremén (At the Outskirts of the City,* 1947), *In the Year 1848* (1948), *Freedom Song* (1950) and *Battle in Peace* (1951); 2 oratorios: *1944* (1967) and *Cantus Urbis* (1972); *Kardtánc*

(*Sword Dance*) for orch. (1949; version for violin and piano, 1957); *Hungarian Dances from the 16th Century* for orch. (1950); *1514*, fantasy for piano and orch. depicting the Hungarian peasant uprising of 1514 (1959; version for 2 pianos and percussion, 1962); *Don Quijote and Dulcinea*, 2 miniatures for oboe and small orch. (1960; version for oboe and piano, 1961); *Aurora Tempestuosa*, prelude for orch. (1967); *Aristophanes*, suite for violin and piano (1947); Sonata for recorder and cimbalom (1948); *Serenata all'antiqua* for violin and piano (1956); *Pentaerophonia* for wind quintet (1958); *Lament*, in memoriam Kodály, for voices, chorus and cimbalom (1971); piano pieces; music for radio plays and some 80 motion pictures.

Rankl, Karl, Austrian conductor and composer; b. Gaaden, near Vienna, Oct. 1, 1898; d. Salzburg, Sept. 6, 1968. He was a pupil of Schoenberg and Anton von Webern in Vienna; from them he acquired a fine understanding of the problems of modern music. He occupied various positions as a chorusmaster and opera coach in Vienna; served as assistant to Klemperer at the Kroll Opera House in Berlin (1928–31); then conducted opera in Graz (1932–37) and at the German Theater in Prague (1937–39). At the outbreak of war he went to England; was consecutively music director at Covent Garden Opera (1946–51), of the Scottish National Orch. in Glasgow, and of the Elizabethan Opera Company, Sydney, Australia; eventually returned to Austria. He composed an opera *Deirdre of the Sorrows*, which received a prize at the Festival of Britain in 1951; other works include 8 symphonies, an oratorio *Der Mensch*, and many other choral works.

BIBLIOGRAPHY: Donald Brook, *International Gallery of Conductors* (London, 1951; pp. 140–44).

Ranta, Sulho, eminent Finnish composer and writer on music; b. Peräseinäjoki, Aug. 15, 1901; d. Helsinki, May 5, 1960. He studied at the Helsinki Cons. with Melartin, and later in Germany, France and Italy. Returning to Finland, he taught at the Sibelius Academy in Helsinki (1934–56); was also active as a music critic. He was editor of a comprehensive biographical dictionary of 90 Finnish composers, *Suomen Säveltäjiä* (Helsinki, 1945), and of a general biographical survey of performers, *Sävelten Taitureita* (Helsinki, 1947).

WORKS: 4 symphonies: *Sinfonia programmatica* (1929–31); *Sinfonia piccola* (1931–32); *Sinfonia semplice* (1936); *Sinfonia dell'arte* (1947); *Oratorio volgare* for solo voices, chorus and orch. (1951); *Tuntematon maa* (*The Unknown Land*) for piano and orch. (1930); Concertino No. 1 for piano and strings (1932); *Kainuun kuvia* (*Images boréales*), suite for orch. (1933); Concertino No. 2 for flute, harp, viola and strings (1934); Concerto for Orchestra (1938); *Kansansatu* (*Folk Story*), symph. variations (1940); *Sydärnen tie* (*The Way of the Heart*), cantata (1945–46); *Eksyneitten legioonalaisten rukous* (*Prayer of the Lost Legionnaires*) for 8 soloists, chorus and orch. (1956); Piano Trio (1923); *Suite Symphonique* for flute, clarinet, horn, string quartet and piano (1926–28); Concertino for String Quartet (1935); piano pieces.

Rapee, Erno, conductor; b. Budapest, June 4, 1891; d. New York, June 26, 1945. He studied piano with Emil Sauer at the National Academy in Budapest; gave concerts as pianist; appeared as conductor with various European orchestras; in 1912 came to America as accompanist; in 1913 was engaged as musical director of the Hungarian Opera Co., N.Y.; then became conductor for S. L. Rothafel (Roxy) at his motion picture theaters in N.Y.; after several years at the Roxy Theater (1926–31) he became music director of the N B C; then at the Radio City Music Hall, again under Rothafel's management. He introduced classical works into his programs, mostly in the form of potpourris, but upon occasion also in full version; brought out a collection of music to accompany silent movies, *Motion Picture Moods for Pianists and Organists, Adapted to 52 Moods and Situations* (N.Y., 1924; reprint 1974), containing pieces of light music by famous and obscure composers depicting the emotions and excitements of joy, melancholy, passion, frustration, and also typical movie scenes, such as love making within permissible limits (kisses not to exceed 7 seconds in duration), costumed bacchanalia, fights to the death, etc.

Rapf, Kurt, Austrian pianist, organist and composer; b. Vienna, Feb. 15, 1922. He studied at the Vienna Music Academy; was later instructor there (1949–53). He was then music director in Innsbruck (1953–60). In 1970 he was elected president of the Austrian Composers' Union.

WORKS: *8 Miniaturen* for orch. (1965); *Aphorismen* (1968); Concerto for Violin and Orch. (1971); chamber music: *4 Impressionen* for 9 performers (1966); *Music for 7 Instruments* (1965); 6 pieces for wind instrument quintet (1963); Quintet for harp and 4 wind instruments (1968); miscellaneous pieces for organ and for piano.

Raphael, Günther, German composer; b. Berlin, April 30, 1903; d. Herford, Oct. 19, 1960. He was the son of the organist **Georg Raphael**; studied in Berlin with Max Trapp (piano), Walter Fischer (organ), and Robert Kahn (composition). He then taught at the Leipzig Cons. (1926–34). Suspected of fractional Jewish ancestry, he was deprived of the right to teach by the Nazi regime, and went to Sweden. After the war he taught at Laubach (1945–48) and at the State Hochschule für Musik in Cologne.

WORKS: 5 symphonies (1926, 1932, 1942, 1947, 1953); 2 violin concertos (1928, 1960); *Symphonic Fantasy* for violin and orch. (1940); Concertino for Saxophone and Orch. (1951); Concertino for Flute and Orch. (1956); *Zoologica*, character study for orch. (1958); numerous pieces of chamber music.

BIBLIOGRAPHY: *In memoriam Günther Raphael* (Wiesbaden, 1961).

Raphling, Sam, American composer; b. Fort Worth, Texas, March 19, 1910. He studied piano in Chicago and, as an exchange fellowship student, in Germany. Returning to the U.S., he was active in Chicago as a teacher and pianist; publ. a number of compositions in various genres: *Abraham Lincoln Walks at Midnight*, for orch.; *Cowboy Rhapsody*, for violin and orch.;

American Album, for two pianos (1946); sonatina, for 2 clarinets (1948); *Prelude and Toccata,* for trumpet and trombone (1949); *Lyric Prelude,* for trombone and piano (1950); *Dance Suite,* for 2 trumpets (1950); *Variations* for 2 flutes unaccompanied (1955; also for flute and clarinet); sonatina for 2 trombones (1955; also for 2 bassoons); *Sonata, Variations, Introduction and Workout,* for French horn unaccompanied (1955); *Nocturnal Prelude,* for piano (1955); *Duograms,* for 2 oboes (1955); Trio for 3 oboes (1955); *Pastorale,* for oboe and piano (1955); etc.

Rappold, Marie (*née* **Winterroth**), English dramatic soprano; b. London, of German parents, c.1873; d. North Hollywood, California, May 12, 1957. The family moved to America when she was a child. She studied with Oscar Saenger in N.Y.; made her opera debut in 1905 at the Metropolitan Opera on Nov. 22, 1905; remained on its roster until 1909; then went to Europe. She was married to Dr. Julius Rappold, but divorced him and married the tenor **Rudolf Berger.** She had another period of singing at the Metropolitan Opera (1910–20); then settled in Los Angeles as a singer.

Rappoldi, Eduard, Austrian violinist and composer; b. Vienna, Feb. 21, 1831; d. Dresden, May 16, 1903. He studied at the Vienna Cons.; then played violin in opera orchestras in Vienna and Rotterdam; conducted opera in Lübeck and Prague; was 2nd violinist in the Joachim Quartet in Berlin (1871–77); concertmaster of the Court Opera in Dresden (1878–98); from 1893 till his death, prof. of violin at the Dresden Cons. He publ. 2 violin sonatas; chamber music; piano pieces; songs. His wife, **Laura Rappoldi-Kahrer** (b. Mistelbach, near Vienna, Jan. 14, 1853; d. Dresden, Aug. 2, 1925), was an excellent pianist, a pupil of Liszt; from 1890 taught piano at the Dresden Cons.

Rasbach, Oscar, American composer; b. Dayton, Ky., Aug. 2, 1888; d. Pasadena, California, March 24, 1975. He studied academic subjects in Los Angeles; music with Ludwig Thomas, Julius Albert Jahn, José Anderson, and A. J. Stamm. He was first engaged in business; then went to Vienna, where he took piano lessons with Leschetizky and studied theory with Hans Thornton. He returned to the U.S. in 1911 and settled in San Marino, Calif. He wrote 2 operettas, *Dawn Boy* and *Open House,* and a number of songs, of which *Trees,* to Joyce Kilmer's dendrological poem, became enormously popular.

Rascher, Sigurd M., German-American saxophone virtuoso; b. Elberfeld, May 15, 1907. He studied at the Stuttgart Cons., and became proficient on the saxophone. In 1939 he went to the U.S., where he developed a fine concert career playing works written especially for him by celebrated composers, among them Jacques Ibert, Frank Martin and (most importantly) Glazunov, who composed a saxophone concerto for him in 1934.

Raselius (Rasel), Andreas, German composer and theorist; b. Hahnbach, near Amberg, c.1563; d. Heidelberg, Jan. 6, 1602. Son of a Lutheran preacher; from 1581–84 studied at Leipzig Univ.; then appointed cantor at the Gymnasium in Regensburg; remained there till 1600, when he returned to Heidelberg as Hofkapellmeister to the Elector Palatine Frederick IV. In 1589 he publ. a music instruction book, *Hexachordum seu Quaestiones musicae practicae.* Other publ. works: *Teutsche Sprüche* (2 vols.: *a* 5, 1594; *a* 5–9, 1595); *Regensburgischer Kirchenkontrapunkt* (5-voiced Lutheran chorales; 1599); in MS: motets and Magnificats. A selection of his Latin and German motets was ed. by L. Roselius in the *Denkmäler der Tonkunst in Bayern* 36 (29/30).

BIBLIOGRAPHY: J. Auer, *A. Raselius* (1892); L. Roselius, *A. Raselius als Motettenkomponist* (Berlin, 1924).

Raskin, Judith, American soprano; b. New York, June 21, 1928. She studied at Smith College; sang minor parts at various theaters, and made her first impact as a modern singer in the title role in Douglas Moore's *The Ballad of Baby Doe* at Central City, Colorado. She then became the leading soprano singer with the New York City Opera; made her Metropolitan Opera debut in 1962 as Susanne in *Le Nozze di Figaro.*

Rasmussen, Karl Aage, Danish composer; b. Kolding, Dec. 13, 1947. He studied composition with Norgaard and Gudmundsen-Holmgreen at the Aarhus Cons., graduating in 1970. In 1972 he was appointed editor of the weekly program "Resonance" at the Danish Radio. His music follows the cosmopolitan trends of pragmatic hedonism within neo-Classical formal structures.

WORKS: opera, *Jefta,* for 9 singers, 7 musicians and tape (1976); radio opera, *Crapp's Last Tape,* after Beckett, for baritone, solo instruments and chamber orch. (Aarhus, Nov. 1, 1968); *Canto Serioso* for string quartet (1965); *Mass* for chorus, solo horn and bell chimes (1966); *This Moment* for 3 sopranos, flute and percussion (1966); *Coralis Constantinus* for chamber orch. (1967); *Symphony for Young Lovers,* 6 movements for orch. (1967); *Repriser—fristelser og eventyr (Recapitulations—Temptations and Fairy-tales)* for orch. (1968); *Symphonie Classique* for chamber orch. (1969); *Afskrift (Transcript)* for flute, violin, viola, cello and piano (1971); *Protokol og Myte* for accordion, electric guitar and percussion (1971); *Als kind (As a Child)* for string quartet (1972); *Music* for solo accordion (1972); *Genklang (Echo)* for piano 4 hands, prepared piano, mistuned ("honky-tonk") piano, and celesta (1972); *Anfang und Ende (Beginning and End)* for orch. (1970–73; Aarhus, Feb. 11, 1976); *Love is in the World* for soprano, guitar and percussion (1974); *Lullaby* for flute and piano (1976); *Berio-Mask,* palimpsest for chamber ensemble (1977); *Le Tombeau de Père Igor* for clarinet, cello and piano (1977); *Vladimir Mayakovsky,* "Konzertstück" for a stage performance (1977); *Schein,* polyphony for orch. (1977).

Rasse, François, Belgian composer; b. Helchin, near Ath, Jan. 27, 1873; d. Brussels, Jan. 4, 1955. He studied violin with Eugène Ysaÿe at the Brussels Cons., winning the Belgian Grand Prix de Rome in 1899; from 1925 to 1938 was director of the Liège Cons.

WORKS: operas, *Déidamia* (1905) and *Sœur Bé-*

atrice (1938); ballet, *Le Maître à danser* (1908); for orch.: *Symphonie romantique* (1901), *Symphonie mélodique* (1903), *Symphonie rythmique* (1908), tone poems, *Douleur* (1911), *Joie* (1925), *Aspiration* (1946), Violin Concerto (1906), *La Dryade* for clarinet and orch. (1943), *Lamento* for cello and orch. (1952); 2 string quartets (1906; 1950); Piano Quartet (1941); numerous piano pieces; choral works; songs. A catalogue of his works was publ., with a biographical sketch, by the Centre Belge de Documentation Musicale (1954).

Rastrelli, Joseph, German composer and conductor; b. Dresden, April 13, 1799; d. there, Nov. 15, 1842. He was a pupil of his father, the Italian musician Vincenzo Rastrelli (1760-1839); then studied with Mattei in Bologna. In 1830 he was appointed court conductor in Dresden; was Wagner's predecessor in this post. His opera, *Salvator Rosa, oder Zwey Nächte in Rom* (Dresden, July 22, 1832), was the first new German opera produced in Dresden after the disbanding of the Italian Opera Co. there.

Rasumovsky. See **Razumovsky.**

Ratez, Émile-Pierre, French composer; b. Besançon, Nov. 5, 1851; d. Lille, May 19, 1934. He studied at the Paris Cons. with Bazin and Massenet (1872-81); played the viola in the orch. of the Opéra-Comique; in 1891 was appointed director of the Lille branch of the Paris Cons.; also conducted popular concerts there (1893-1906). He wrote the operas *Lydéric* (Lille, 1895) and *Paula* (Besançon, 1904); a ballet, *La Guivre* (Paris, 1925); a cantata, *Scènes héroïques* (1899); chamber music; publ. *Traité élémentaire de contrepoint et de fugue* and *Traité d'harmonie théorique et pratique.*

Rath, Felix vom, German composer; b. Cologne, June 17, 1866; d. Munich, Aug. 25, 1905. He studied piano with Reinecke in Leipzig and composition with Thuille in Munich, where he settled. A composer of more than ordinary abilities, he publ. a piano concerto, a piano quartet, a violin sonata, and a number of piano pieces.

Rathaus, Karol, Polish-American composer; b. Tarnopol, Sept. 16, 1895; d. New York, Nov. 21, 1954. He studied composition with Schreker in Berlin and in Vienna; taught in Berlin; in 1932 went to Paris, and in 1934 to London. In 1938 he settled in New York; in 1940 was appointed to the faculty of Queens College, and remained in that capacity until his death. His music is distinguished by a firm sense of contrapuntal development; the harmonies are maintained within a general tonal framework; the esthetic attitude is that of late Romanticism. Several of his works were performed at festivals of the International Society for Contemporary Music.
WORKS: ballet, *Der letzte Pierrot* (Berlin, May 7, 1927); opera, *Fremde Erde* (Berlin, Dec. 10, 1930); 3 symphonies (1922; 1923; 1942); Suite for Orch. (Liège Festival, Sept. 6, 1930); Piano Concerto (Berkeley, Calif., Festival, Aug. 1, 1942); *Jacob's Dream* for orch. (1941); Adagio for strings (1941); *Polonaise sympho-*

nique (N.Y., Feb. 26, 1944); *Vision dramatique,* a symph. movement (Tel Aviv, April 4, 1948); 5 string quartets; *Serenade* for clarinet, violin, viola, cello, and piano; *Eine kleine Serenade* for 4 wind instruments and piano; Clarinet Sonata; Violin Sonata; 4 piano sonatas; *Psalm 23; Diapason,* for mixed chorus, baritone solo, and orch., to texts by Dryden and Milton.
BIBLIOGRAPHY: Boris Schwartz, "Karol Rathaus," *Musical Quarterly* (Oct. 1955).

Rathburn, Eldon, Canadian composer; b. Queenstown, New Brunswick, April 21, 1916. He studied composition with Willan, organ with Peaker, and piano with Godden at the Royal Cons. in Toronto; in 1947 was appointed a staff composer with the National Film Board of Canada and supplied musical scores for many notable documentaries, including *The Romance of Transportation* (1952), *City of Gold* (1957) and *Labyrinth* (1967); in 1972 became instructor at the Univ. of Ottawa. His music is extremely amiable, aiming to please everybody.
WORKS: *Symphonette* (1943, revised 1946); 2 *Cartoons* for orch. (1944, 1946); *Images of Childhood* for orch. (1949-50); *Overture to a Hoss Opera* (1952); *Nocturne* for piano and small orch. (1953); *Overture Burlesca* (1953); *Milk Maid Polka* for orch. (1956); *Gray City* for orch. (1960); *City of Gold,* suite for orch. from music to the film (1967); *Aspects of Railroads* for orch. (1969); *3 Ironies* for solo brass quintet and orch. (Hamilton, Oct. 15, 1975) and *Steelhenge,* concerto for steel band and orch. (1975); *5 Short Pieces* for differing combinations of winds, each piece having a separate title (1949-56); *Bout in 3 rounds,* for guitar and double bass (1971); *The Metamorphic Ten* for accordion, mandolin, banjo, guitar, double bass, harp, piano, celeste and 3 percussionists (1971); *2 Interplays* for saxophone quartet (1972); *Rhythmette* for 2 pianos and rhythm band (1973); *The Nomadic Five,* brass quintet (1974); *Silhouette* for 2 pianos (1936); *Black and White* for piano (1970); songs.

Raţiu, Adrian, Rumanian composer; b. Bucharest, July 28, 1928. He studied with Paul Constantinescu, Negrea and Rogalski at the Bucharest Cons. (1950-56); attended the summer courses in new music at Darmstadt (1969). He was editor of the Rumanian music journal, *Muzica* (1959-63); in 1962 appointed to the staff of the Bucharest Cons. His music is pleasantly atonal and euphoniously dissonant.
WORKS: Symph. No. 1 (1956, revised 1961); Concerto for Oboe, Bassoon and String Orch. (1963); *Diptych* for orch. (1965); *Studi* for strings (1968); *6 Images* for orch. (1971); *Poem* for cello and orch. (1972); Piano Concerto (1973); *Oda păcii (Ode to Peace),* cantata (1959); String Quartet (1956); *Viziune nocturnă* for viola and piano (1964); *Partita* for wind quintet (1966); *Concertino per la "Musica Nova"* for clarinet, violin, viola, cello and piano (1967; Musica Nova is a Rumanian chamber ensemble); *Impresii* for chamber ensemble (1969); *Diaphonie* for 2 flutes (1972); *Improvisation* for oboe and piano (1972); *Sonata a cinque* for 2 trumpets, horn, trombone and tuba (1973); *Monosonata I* and *II* for piano (1968, 1969); *Constelaţii (Constellations)* for piano (1970); choruses; songs.

Ratner, Leonard Gilbert, American musicologist and composer; b. Minneapolis, July 30, 1916. He studied composition with Arnold Schoenberg at the Univ. of Calif., Los Angeles, and musicology with Manfred Bukofzer and Albert Elkus at Berkeley (Ph.D., 1947). He also had composition lessons with Ernest Bloch and Frederick Jacobi. In 1947 he was appointed to the staff of Stanford Univ.; held a Guggenheim Fellowship in 1962–63.

WORKS: chamber opera, *The Necklace;* Symph.; an overture, *Harlequin;* 2 string quartets; Violin Sonata; Cello Sonata; Piano Sonata; etc.

WRITINGS: *Music: The Listener's Art* (N.Y., 1957); *Harmony: Structure and Style* (N.Y., 1962); *Classic Music: Expression, Form, and Style* (N.Y., 1979).

Rattenbach, Augusto, Argentine composer; b. Buenos Aires, Feb. 5, 1927. After a study of elementary music theory in Argentina, he went to Hamburg where he learned modern techniques. Most of his mature compositions are in a serial idiom, with the formative elements determined in advance.

WORKS: Piano Concerto (1956); *Passacaglia* (1957); Wind Quintet (1957); ballet, *Un Episodio Vulgar* (1961); *Serenata* for flute, clarinet, trumpet and cello (1962); *Obstinaciones* for orch. (1965); a series of *Microvariaciones* for various ensembles.

Ratzenberger, Theodor, German pianist; b. Grossbreitenbach, April 14, 1840; d. Wiesbaden, March 8, 1879. He was a pupil of Liszt (piano) and Cornelius (composition); publ. some salon pieces for piano.

Rauchenecker, Georg Wilhelm, German violinist and composer; b. Munich, March 8, 1844; d. Elberfeld, July 17, 1906. He studied violin with Joseph Walter; filled various posts as a theater violinist in France; then lived in Switzerland; conducted the Berlin Philharmonic for a season (1884). In 1889 he established a music school in Elberfeld, and conducted an orchestral society there until his death.

WORKS: operas (all produced in Elberfeld): *Die letzten Tage von Thule* (1889), *Ingo* (1893), *Don Quixote* (1897), *Sanna* (1898), *Zlatorog* (1903), *Der Florentiner* (posthumous; Strasbourg, 1910); Symphony; *Orientalische Fantasie* for solo violin with string quintet; 6 string quartets; String Sextet; Octet for woodwind instruments.

Raudenbush, George King, American violinist and conductor; b. Jersey Shore, Pennsylvania, March 13, 1899; d. San Diego, California, May 26, 1956. He studied in Detroit and in Boston, where he was a pupil of Chadwick; made his debut as a violinist in N.Y., in 1921; then played the violin in the N.Y. Symph. Orch.; in 1929 he founded the Harrisburg Symph. Orch. and conducted it until 1950.

Raugel, Félix, French musicologist; b. Saint-Quentin, Nov. 27, 1881; d. Paris, Dec. 30, 1975. While attending the Lycée at Lille he studied music with Ch. Queste and F. Lecocq; continued his studies in 1900 in Paris with H. Libert and at the Schola Cantorum with Vincent d'Indy. Together with E. Borrel he founded in 1908 the Société Haendel for the cultivation of early music.

WRITINGS: *Les Orgues de l'abbaye de St. Mihiel* (1919); *Recherches sur quelques maîtres de l'ancienne facture d'orgues française; Le Cantique français* (Tourcoing, 1920); *Les Organistes* (1923); *Les Grandes Orgues des églises de Paris et du département de la Seine* (1927); *Palestrina* (1930); *Les Grandes Orgues de Notre Dame* (1934); *Le Chant choral* (1948); *L'Oratorio* (1948); ed. organ works of Handel, Scarlatti, Buxtehude, etc.

Rautavaara, Einojuhani, Finnish composer; b. Helsinki, Oct. 9, 1928. He studied composition with Merikanto at the Sibelius Academy in Helsinki (1948–54); in New York and at Tanglewood with Copland, Persichetti and Sessions (1955–56); in Switzerland for dodecaphonic studies with Vogel (1957); and in Cologne with Rudolf Petzold (1958). In 1966 he was appointed to the faculty of the Sibelius Academy in Helsinki. He adopted in his works an eclectic modern idiom, with occasional dodecaphonic excursions. In 1975 he began a series of chamber operas based on the *Kalevala,* the Finnish national epic.

WORKS: FOR THE STAGE: an opera *Kaivos* (The Mine, 1958–61; Finnish television, 1963); a ballet *Kiusaukset* (The Temptations, 1969; Helsinki, Feb. 8, 1973); a comic opera *Apollon contra Marsyas* (1970; Helsinki, Aug. 30, 1973). VOCAL WORKS: *Die Liebenden (The Lovers)* for voice and orch. (1959); *Itsenäisyys-kantaatti (Independence Cantata,* 1967); *Daughter of the Sea,* for soprano, chorus and orch. (Helsinki, Dec. 4, 1971); *Vigilia (The Mass)* for soloists and chorus (1971); *True and False Unicorn* for chorus, tape and chamber ensemble (1971); *The Water Circle* for chorus, piano and orch. (Copenhagen, Dec. 4, 1972). FOR ORCH.: 4 symphonies (1956, 1957, 1961, 1964–70); *Arabescata* (1963); *Anadyomene* (1968); *Sotilasmessu (Soldier's Mass)* for winds and percussion (1968); Cello Concerto (1968); Piano Concerto (1969); *Dithyrambos* for violin and orch. (1970); *Regular Sets of Elements in a Semiregular Situation* for 3 flutes, 3 horns, trumpet, percussion, piano, 4 violins and 4 cellos (1971); *Cantus Arcticus,* concerto for birds (on tape) and orch. (Oulu, May 26, 1972); *A Portrait of the Artist at a Certain Moment,* for strings (Jyvskyla, May 28, 1972); flute concerto (1973); *Ballad* for harp and strings (1973). CHAMBER MUSIC: 3 string quartets (1952, 1958, 1965); *A Requiem in Our Time* for 13 brasses and percussion (1953); *2 Preludes and Fugues* for cello and piano (1955); Wind Octet (1964); Quartet for oboe and string trio (1965); Bassoon Sonata (1965–68); *Sonetto* for clarinet and piano (1969); Solo Cello Sonata (1969); *Music* for upright piano and amplified cello (1976). PIANO MUSIC: *Pelimannit (The Fiddlers),* suite (1952); *Ikonit (Icons),* suite (1956); *Partita* (1958); *Etudes* (1969); 2 sonatas: No. 1, *Christus und die Fischer* (1969) and No. 2, *The Fire Sermon* (1970); *Toccata* for organ (1971); solo songs.

Rautio, Matti, Finnish composer; b. Helsinki, Feb. 25, 1922. He studied composition and piano at the Sibelius Academy in Helsinki; until 1970 was director of the school music department of the Sibelius Academy; then became a lecturer on music theory there. In his works he follows a median line of modern music, programmatic and utilitarian in the use of advanced techniques.

WORKS: *Divertimento 1* for cello and orchestra or piano (1955); *Sininen haikara (The Blue Heron)*, suite from the ballet (1957); *Tanhumusiikkia (Folk Dance Music)* for soprano, baritone, chorus and orch. (1960); Piano Concerto (1968–71); *Divertimento 2* for cello and piano (1972).

Ravanello, Oreste, Italian composer; b. Venice, Aug. 25, 1871; d. Padua, July 2, 1938. He studied with Agostini and Girardi in Venice; in 1893 became an organist at San Marco; in 1898 was appointed maestro di cappella at San Antonio in Padua; in 1914 became director of the Istituto Musicale. He composed about 30 masses; numerous pieces for organ; published several useful guides for organ playing, among them *Cento Studi ed Esercizi per il Organo.*

BIBLIOGRAPHY: A. Garbelotto and M. Cicogna, *Oreste Ravanello* (Padua, 1939).

Ravasenga, Carlo, Italian composer; b. Turin, Dec. 17, 1891; d. Rome, May 6, 1964. He studied violin, piano and composition in Turin; then became active as a teacher and music editor. He wrote the operas *Una Tragedia fiorentina*, after Oscar Wilde (Turin, 1916) and *Il Giudizio di Don Giovanni* (1916); the orchestral suite, *Un Giorno di festa* (1916); symph. suite, *Giuditta e Oloferno; Variazioni pittoresche* for string quartet; *Contrasto burlesco-sentimentale,* for piano; Violin Sonata; Piano Sonata.

Ravel, Maurice (Christian names **Joseph Maurice**), great French composer; b. Ciboure, Basses-Pyrénées, March 7, 1875; d. Paris, Dec. 28, 1937. His father was a Swiss engineer, and his mother of Basque origin. The family moved to Paris when he was an infant. He began to study piano at the age of 7 with Henri Ghis and harmony at 12 with Charles-René. In 1889 he entered the Paris Cons.; studied piano with Anthiome; won 1st medal in 1891, and passed to the advanced class of Charles de Bériot; studied harmony with Émile Pessard. Still as a student he wrote and publ. a *Menuet antique* for piano and *Habanera* for 2 pianos (later included in the *Rapsodie espagnole* for orch.); these pieces, written at the age of 20, already reveal great originality in the treatment of old modes and of Spanish motifs; however, he continued to study; in 1897 he entered the class of Gabriel Fauré (composition) and Gédalge (counterpoint and fugue); his well-known *Pavane pour une Infante défunte* for piano was written during that time (1899). On May 27, 1899, he appeared in public as conductor, in a performance of his overture *Shéhérazade* with the Société Nationale in Paris. The work was never published, but some elements were incorporated in Ravel's song cycle of the same title (1903). In 1901 he won the 2nd Prix de Rome with the cantata *Myrrha;* but the ensuing attempts to win the Grand Prix de Rome were unsuccessful; at his last try (1905) he was eliminated in the preliminaries, and so was not allowed to compete; the age limit then set an end to his further effort to enter. Since 6 prizes all went to pupils of Lenepveu, suspicion was aroused of unfair discrimination; Jean Mar-

nold published an article, "Le Scandale du Prix de Rome," in the *Mercure de France* (June 1905) in which he brought the controversy into the open; this precipitated a crisis at the Paris Cons.; its director, Théodore Dubois, resigned, and Gabriel Fauré took his place. By that time, Ravel had written a number of his most famous compositions, and was regarded by most French critics as a talented disciple of Debussy. No doubt Ravel's method of poetic association of musical ideas paralleled that of Debussy; his employment of unresolved dissonances and the enhancement of the diatonic style into pandiatonicism were techniques common to Debussy and his followers; but there were important differences: whereas Debussy adopted the scale of whole tones as an integral part of his musical vocabulary, Ravel resorted to it only occasionally; similarly, augmented triads appear much less frequently in Ravel's music than in Debussy's; in his writing for piano Ravel actually anticipated some of Debussy's usages; in a letter addressed to Pierre Lalo and publ. in *Le Temps* (April 9, 1907) Ravel pointed out that at the time of the publication of his piano piece *Jeux d'eau* (1902) Debussy had brought out only his suite *Pour le Piano* which had contained little that was novel. In Paris, in France, and soon in England and other European countries, Ravel's name became well known, but for many years he was still regarded as an ultramodernist. A curious test of audience appreciation was a "Concert des auteurs anonymes" presented by the Société Indépendante de Musique on May 9, 1911; the program included Ravel's *Valses nobles et sentimentales,* a set of piano pieces in the manner of Schubert; yet Ravel was recognized as the author. Inspired evocation of the past was but one aspect of Ravel's creative genius; in this style are written the *Pavane pour une Infante défunte, Le Tombeau de Couperin,* and *La Valse;* luxuriance of exotic colors marks his ballet *Daphnis et Chloé,* his opera *L'Heure espagnole,* the song cycles *Shéhérazade* and *Chansons madécasses* and his virtuoso pieces for piano, *Miroirs* and *Gaspard de la nuit;* other works are deliberately austere, even ascetic in their pointed Classicism: the piano concertos, the Piano Sonatina, and some of his songs with piano accompaniment. His association with Diaghilev's Ballets Russes was most fruitful; for Diaghilev he wrote one of his masterpieces, *Daphnis et Chloé;* another ballet, *Boléro,* commissioned by Ida Rubinstein and performed at her dance recital at the Paris Opéra on Nov. 22, 1928, became Ravel's most spectacular success as an orchestral piece.

Ravel never married, and lived a life of semi-retirement, devoting most of his time to composition; he accepted virtually no pupils, although he gave friendly advice to Vaughan Williams and to others; he was never on the faculty of any school. As a performer, he was not brilliant; he appeared as pianist only in his own works, and often accompanied singers in programs of his songs; although he accepted engagements as conductor, his technique was barely sufficient to secure a perfunctory performance of his music. When the war broke out in 1914, he was rejected because of his frail physique, but he was anxious to serve; his application for air service was denied, but he was received in the ambulance corps at the front; his health gave way, and in the autumn of 1916 he was compelled to enter a hospital for recuperation. In 1922 he visited Amsterdam and Venice, conducting his music; in 1923 he appeared in London; in 1926 he went to Sweden, England, and Scotland; in 1928 he made an American tour as conductor and pianist; in the same year he received the degree of D. Mus. *honoris causa* at Oxford Univ. In 1929 he was honored at his native town of Ciboure by the inauguration of the Quai Maurice Ravel. Shortly afterwards, he began to experience difficulties in muscular coordination, and suffered from attacks of aphasia, symptoms indicative of a cerebral malady; a brain operation was performed on Dec. 19, 1937, but was not successful, and he died 9 days later.

WORKS: 1-act opera, *L'Heure espagnole,* text by Franc-Nohain (Paris, Opéra-Comique, May 19, 1911; Metropolitan Opera House, N.Y., Nov. 7, 1925); the "fantaisie lyrique" *L'Enfant et les sortilèges,* libretto by Colette (Monte Carlo, March 21, 1925); the ballets *Daphnis et Chloé* (Paris, June 8, 1912), *Adélaide ou le langage des fleurs,* after the *Valses nobles et sentimentales* (Paris, April 22, 1912), *Ma Mère l'Oye,* elaborated from the piano suite (Paris Opéra, March 11, 1915), *Le Tombeau de Couperin,* choreographic poem from the orchestral suite (Ballets Suédois, Paris, Nov. 8, 1920), *La Valse* (Paris, Dec. 12, 1920), *Boléro* (Ida Rubinstein's dance recital, Paris, Nov. 22, 1928). FOR ORCH.: overture *Shéhérazade* (1898; publ. Paris, 1975); *Pavane pour une Infante défunte* (1899); *Alborada del gracioso (Serenade of a Clown;* 1905); *Rapsodie espagnole* (Paris, March 15, 1908); *Daphnis et Chloé,* 2 suites from the ballet (1909–11); *Ma Mère l'Oye,* after the piano duet (1912); *Le Tombeau de Couperin* (1917); *La Valse* (1920); *Tzigane,* for violin and orch. (also with piano accompaniment; 1924); *Boléro* (1928; 1st American performance, N.Y., Nov. 14, 1929); Piano Concerto in D for left hand alone, written for the one-armed pianist Paul Wittgenstein, who gave its first performance (Vienna, Jan. 5, 1932); Piano Concerto in G (Paris, Jan. 14, 1932, Ravel conducting, Marguerite Long, pianist). CHAMBER MUSIC: Sonata in one movement for violin and piano (1897; publ. Paris, 1975); String Quartet in F (1903); *Introduction et Allegro,* for harp, string quartet, flute, and clarinet (Paris, Feb. 22, 1907); Piano Trio (1914); Sonata for violin and cello (1920–22); *Berceuse sur le nom de Fauré,* for violin and piano (1922); Violin Sonata (1923–27); *Tzigane,* for violin and piano (London, April 26, 1924, Jelly d'Aranyi, violinist; Ravel at the piano, in a concert of Ravel works). VOCAL WORKS: *Shéhérazade,* song cycle for solo voice and orch. (Paris, May 17, 1904); *Trois poèmes de Mallarmé,* for voice, piano, 2 flutes, 2 clarinets, and string quartet (1913); *Trois chansons,* for mixed chorus a cappella (1916); *Chansons madécasses,* for voice, flute, cello, and piano (1926); *Don Quichotte à Dulcinée,* 3 songs with orchestral accompaniment (Paris, Dec. 1, 1934). Songs: *Ballade de la Reine morte d'aimer* (1894); *Un Grand Sommeil noir* (1895); *Sainte* (1896); *Deux épigrammes de Clément Marot* (1896); *Si morne* (1898; publ. 1975, Paris); *Manteau de fleurs* (1903); *Le Noël des jouets,* text by Ravel (1905); *5 Mélodies populaires grecques* (1905; another Greek melody was publ. in the *Revue Musicale,* Dec. 1938); *Les Grands Vents ve-* *nus d'outre-mer* (1906); *Histoires naturelles* (1906); *Sur l'herbe* (1907); *Vocalise en forme d'habanera* (1907); *4 Chants populaires* (1910); *2 Mélodies hébraïques* (1914); *Ronsard à son âme* (1924); *Rêves* (1927). FOR PIANO: *Sérénade grotesque; Menuet antique* (1895); *Pavane pour une Infante défunte* (1899); *Jeux d'eau* (1901); *Miroirs* (5 pieces): *Noctuelles, Oiseaux tristes, Une Barque sur l'océan, Alborada del Gracioso, La Vallée des cloches* (1905); *Sonatine* (1903–5); *Gaspard de la nuit: Ondine, Le Gibet, Scarbo* (1908); *Menuet sur le nom d'Haydn* (1909); *Valses nobles et sentimentales* (1911); *Prélude* (1913); *À la manière de . . . Borodine, Chabrier* (1913); *Le Tombeau de Couperin* (1914–17); *Sites auriculaires,* for 2 pianos (1895–97): *Habanera* and *Entre cloches; Ma Mère l'Oye,* 5 'pièces enfantines' for piano 4 hands, written for Christine Verger, age 6, and Germaine Durant, age 10, and performed by them (Paris, April 20, 1910); *Frontispiece* for 2 pianos, 5 hands (1918). Ravel was commissioned by Koussevitzky to make an orchestration of Mussorgsky's *Pictures at an Exhibition;* it was first performed by Koussevitzky at one of his concerts (Paris, Oct. 19, 1922) and subsequently became one of the most popular orchestral suites; Ravel also orchestrated Chabrier's *Menuet pompeux,* arranged Debussy's *Prélude à l'après-midi d'un faune* for 2 pianos, etc.

BIBLIOGRAPHY: O. Séré, *Musiciens français d'aujourd'hui* (1911); Roland-Manuel, *Maurice Ravel et son œuvre* (1914; rev. ed., 1926; in English, London, 1941); M. O. Morris, "Maurice Ravel," *Music & Letters* (July 1921); A. Cœuroy, *La Musique française moderne* (1922); E. Vuillermoz, *Musiques d'aujourd'hui* (1923); E. B. Hill, *Modern French Music* (N.Y., 1924); F. H. Shera, *Debussy and Ravel* (London, 1925); special Ravel issue of *Revue Musicale* (April 1925); Cecil Gray, *A Survey of Contemporary Music* (London, 1925); Roland-Manuel, *Ravel et son œuvre dramatique* (1928); M. D. Calvocoressi, *Music and Ballet* (London, 1933); Roland-Manuel, *À la gloire de Ravel* (1938); special Ravel issue of *Revue Musicale* (Dec. 1938); V. Jankélévitch, *Maurice Ravel* (Paris, 1939); R. Wild, ed., *Ravel par quelques-uns de ses familiers* (Paris, 1939); P. Landormy, "Maurice Ravel," *Musical Quarterly* (Oct. 1939); M. Goss, *Bolero: The Life of Maurice Ravel* (N.Y., 1940); M.D. Calvocoressi, "Ravel's Letters to Calvocoressi," *Musical Quarterly* (Jan. 1941); K. Akeret, *Studien zum Klavierwerk von Maurice Ravel* (Zürich, 1941); H. Jourdan-Morhange, *Ravel et nous* (Geneva, 1945); A. Machabey, *Maurice Ravel* (Paris, 1947); N. Demuth, *Ravel* (London, 1947); Roland-Manuel, *Ravel* (Paris, 1948; a new work); W.-L. Landowski, *Maurice Ravel, sa vie, son œuvre* (Paris, 1950); L. La Pegna, *Ravel* (Brescia, 1950); José Bruyr, *Maurice Ravel, ou le Lyrisme et les sortilèges* (Paris, 1950); W. Tappolet, *Maurice Ravel: Leben und Werk* (Olten, 1950); V. Perlemuter, *Ravel d'après Ravel* (Lausanne, 1953); V. Seroff, *Maurice Ravel* (N.Y., 1953); Marcelle Gerar and René Chalupt, eds., *Ravel au miroir de ses lettres* (Paris, 1956); R. de Fragny, *Maurice Ravel* (Lyon, 1960); R. H. Myers, *Ravel: Life and Works* (London, 1960); H. H. Stuckenschmidt, *Maurice Ravel: Variationen über Person und Werk* (Frankfurt, 1966; in English, Philadelphia, 1968); Arbie Orenstein, "L'Enfant et les sortilèges: Correspondence inédit de Ravel et Colette," *Revue de Musicolo-gie* LII/2 (1966); A. Orenstein, "Maurice Ravel's Creative Process," *Musical Quarterly* (Oct. 1967); R. Petit, *Ravel* (Paris, 1970); A. Orenstein, "Some Unpublished Music and Letters by Maurice Ravel," *Music Forum* 3 (1973); Arbie Orenstein, *Ravel, Man and Musician* (N.Y., 1975; contains an amplified list of works, including early unpublished compositions).

Ravenscroft, John (Giovanni), English composer; b. London, d. there, c.1708. In 1695 he was in Rome, where he publ. a set of 'sonate a trè' under the Italianized name Giovanni Ravenscroft. He apparently was a pupil of Corelli, whose style he imitated. His op. 2, containing 6 sonatas for 2 violins with continuo, was publ. posthumously in London.
BIBLIOGRAPHY: W. S. Newman, "Ravenscroft and Corelli," *Music & Letters* (Oct. 1957).

Ravenscroft, Thomas, English composer and music editor; b. c.1590; d. c.1633. He was a chorister at St. Paul's Cathedral under Edward Pearce; in 1607 received his Mus. B. at Cambridge; from 1618 to 1622 he was music master at Christ's Hospital, London.
WORKS: *Pammelia: Musick's Miscellanie: or Mixed Varietie of Pleasant Roundelayes and Delightful Catches of 3–10 Parts in one* (1609; the first collection of rounds, catches, and canons printed in England; 2nd ed., 1618); *Deuteromelia: or the Second Part of Musick's Melodie* (1609); *Melismata: Musicall Phansies, Fitting the Court, Citie, and Countrey Humours, to 3, 4 and 5 Voyces* (1611); *A Briefe Discourse of the true (but neglected) use of Charact'ring the De-grees by their Perfection, Imperfection, and Diminu-tion in Mensurable Musicke: Harmony of four voyces concerning the pleasure of five usuall recreations, 1. Hunting, 2. Hawking, 3. Dancing, 4. Drinking, 5. Ena-mouring* (1614); and *The Whole Booke of Psalmes: With the Hymnes Evangelicall and Songs Spirituall Composed into 4 parts by Sundry Authors* (1621; 2nd ed., newly corrected and enlarged, 1633; his best-known and most valuable work, containing numbers by 15 leading British composers, and some by Ravenscroft himself).

Ravina, Jean-Henri, French composer; b. Bordeaux, May 20, 1818; d. Paris, Sept. 30, 1906. He studied at the Paris Cons. with Zimmerman (piano) and Laurent (theory); taught at the Cons. (1834–36); then made a concert tour as pianist in Russia (1858); later traveled in Spain; lived chiefly in Paris. He wrote elegant and attractive salon pieces for piano, which enjoyed considerable vogue, and eventually became part of the piano repertory: *Nocturne; Douce pensée; Jour de bonheur; Petit boléro; Câlinerie;* also *Études de style et de perfectionnement; Études harmonieuses;* etc.; a piano concerto. He made 4-hand arrangements of all of Beethoven's symphonies.

Rawsthorne, Alan, important English composer; b. Haslingden, May 2, 1905; d. Cambridge, July 24, 1971. He went to a dentistry school; did not begin to study music until he was 21, when he entered the Royal Manchester College of Music; later studied piano with Egon Petri in Berlin (1930–31). Returning to England

in 1932, he occupied various teaching posts; then devoted himself mainly to composition, and succeeded brilliantly in producing music of agreeable, and to some ears even delectable music. In 1961 he was made a Commander of the British Empire. His music is essentially a revival of the contrapuntal style of the past, without much harmonic elaboration; but the rhythms are virile, and the melodies fluid, emanating from a focal point of tonality.
WORKS: a ballet, *Madame Chrysanthème* (London, April 1, 1955); Concerto for Clarinet and Strings (1936); *Symphonic Studies* (1938; International Society for Contemporary Music Festival, Warsaw, April 21, 1939); 2 piano concertos: No. 1 (originally for strings and percussion, 1939; rescored for full orch., 1942; London, 1942) and No. 2 (1951; London, June 17, 1951); 4 overtures: *Street Corner* (1944); *Cortèges,* fantasy overture (1945); *Hallé,* for the centennial of the Hallé Orch. (1958) and *Overture for Farnham* (1967); 2 violin concertos: No. 1 (1940, sketches lost in an air raid; reconstructed 1943–48; Cheltenham Festival, July 1, 1948) and No. 2 (London, Oct. 24, 1956); Concerto for Oboe and Strings (1947); Concerto for String Orch. (1949); 3 symphonies: No. 1 (1950; London, Nov. 15, 1950); No. 2, *Pastoral,* with solo soprano (1959; Birmingham, Sept. 29, 1959); No. 3 (1964; Cheltenham Fest., July 8, 1964); *Concertante Pastorale* for flute, horn and strings (1951); *A Canticle of Man,* chamber cantata for baritone, chorus, flute and strings (1952); *Practical Cats,* an entertainment for children, after T. S. Eliot, for narrator and orch. (Edinburgh, Aug. 26, 1954); *Improvisations on a Theme of Constant Lambert* for orch. (1960); Concerto for 10 instruments (1962); *Medieval Diptych* for baritone and orch. (1962); *Divertimento* for chamber orch. (1962); *Carmen Vitale,* cantata (1963; London, Oct. 16, 1963); *Elegiac Rhapsody* for strings (1964); Cello Concerto (London, April 6, 1966); *The God in the Cave* for chorus and orch. (1967); Concerto for 2 Pianos and Orch. (1968); *Theme, Variations and Finale* for orch. (1968); *Triptych* for orch. (1970); Trio for flute, oboe and piano (1936); *Theme and Variations* for 2 violins (1937); Viola Sonata (1938); *Theme and Variations* for string quartet (1939); 3 string quartets (1939, 1954, 1965); Clarinet Quartet (1948); Cello Sonata (1949); Violin Sonata (1959); Piano Trio (1962); *Concertante* for violin and paino (1935–62); Quintet for piano, oboe, clarinet, horn and bassoon (1963); *Tankas of the 4 Seasons* for tenor, oboe, clarinet, bassoon, violin and cello (1965); Quintet for piano and strings (1968); Oboe Quartet (1970); *Suite* for flute, viola and harp (1970); Quintet for piano, clarinet, horn, violin and cello (1971); *Elegy* for solo guitar (1971; completed from composer's sketches by Julian Bream); *Baga-telles* for piano (1938); *The Creel* for 2 pianos (1940); Piano Sonatina (1948); *4 Romantic Pieces* for piano (1953); *Ballade* for piano (1967); *Theme with 4 Studies* for piano (1971); choruses; several song cycles, to French and English words.
BIBLIOGRAPHY: K. Avery, "Alan Rawsthorne," *Music & Letters* (Jan. 1951); A. E. F. Dickinson, "The Progress of Alan Rawsthorne," *Music Review* (May 1951); A. Frank, *Modern British Composers* (London, 1954; pp. 74–79); F. Routh, *Contemporary British Mu-*

sic: *The Twenty-five Years from 1945 to 1970* (London, 1972; pp. 44–55).

Raxach, Enrique, Spanish-born Dutch composer; b. Barcelona, Jan. 15, 1932. He studied composition in Barcelona with Nuri Aymerich (1949–52); in 1958 moved to Paris, where he had contacts with Boulez; lived successively in Zürich, Munich and Cologne before settling in Holland in 1962. In his music he explores purely structural potentialities.
WORKS: *Estudios* for string orch. (1952); *Cantata* for tenor and chamber ensemble (1952); *Polifonias* for string orch. (1953–54); *6 Movements* for orch. (1955); *3 Metamorphoses: I* for orch. (1956); *II* for orch. (1958); and *III* for 15 instruments (1959); *Prometheus* for orch. (1957–58); 2 string quartets (*Fases*, 1961; with electronic sound, 1971); *Estrofas* for 6 instruments (1962); *Fluxion* for chamber orch. (1962–63); *Syntagma* for orch. (1964–65); *Textures* for orch. (1966); *Summer Music* for cello and piano (1967); *Equinoxial* for orch. (1967–68); *Imaginary Landscape* for flute and percussion (1968); *Paraphrase* for contralto and 11 instruments (1969); *Inside Outside* for orch. and tape (1969); *Scattertime* for 6 instruments (1971); *Interface from the Esoteric Garden* for chorus and orch. (1971–72); *Figures in a Landscape* for orch. (1972–74); *Chimaera* for bass clarinet and tape (1974); *Ad marginem* for flute, violin, viola and orch. (1974–75).

Ray, Don Brandon, American conductor and composer; b. Santa Maria, Calif., June 7, 1926. He studied composition with John Vincent at the Univ. of Calif., Los Angeles (B.A., 1948) and with Ernst Kanitz at the Univ. of Southern Calif.; conducting with Roger Wagner and Richard Lert. In 1960 he was engaged as conductor of the Committee on The Arts (COTA) Symph. Orch. and Chorale in the San Fernando Valley. He composed orchestral pieces, Protestant church services, incidental music to theatrical plays.

Razumovsky, Count (from 1815, **Prince**) **Andrei,** Russian diplomat and music lover; b. St. Petersburg, Nov. 2, 1752; d. Vienna, Sept. 23, 1836. He was the Russian ambassador at Vienna from 1793 to 1809; from 1808 to 1816 he maintained the celebrated Razumovsky Quartet (1st violin, Schuppanzigh; 2nd violin, Louis Sina, whose part was occasionally taken over by Razumovsky; viola, Weiss; cello, Lincke), later known as the Schuppanzigh Quartet (without Razumovsky). Razumovsky's name was immortalized through the dedication to him of Beethoven's 3 string quartets, op. 59, and (with Prince Lobkowitz) Fifth and Sixth Symphonies. He was a munificent and prodigal patron of art, but after the destruction by fire of his Vienna palace (Dec. 31, 1814) he gave up the quartet, and disappeared from musical history.

Razzi, Fausto, Italian composer; b. Rome, May 4, 1932. He studied composition with Goffredo Petrassi at the Santa Cecilia in Rome; then devoted himself to teaching. Among his works is a String Quartet (1958); *Movimento* for piano and orch. (1966); *Improvvisazione* for viola, 18 wind instruments and timpani

(1966); *4 invenzioni* for 7 instruments (1968); *Musica* for 10 wind instruments (1969).

Rea, John, Canadian composer; b. Toronto, Jan. 14, 1944. He studied composition with Ruth Wylie at Wayne State Univ. in Detroit and with Weinzweig at the Univ. of Toronto (M.M., 1959); then took a postgraduate course at Princeton Univ.
WORKS: opera, *The Prisoner's Play* (Univ. of Toronto, May 22, 1973); ballet, *Les Jours* (1969; ballet suite, Toronto, July 11, 1974); *Jeux de Scène: Fantasie-Hommage à Richard Wagner,* musical-theater work for 6 performers on blacksmith's anvil, English horn, oboe, cello, piccolo, flute, piano, marimba and 3 glockenspiels (1976; Vancouver, Feb. 27, 1977); Clarinet Sonatina (1965); *Sestina* for flute, clarinet, trumpet, cello, harpsichord and percussion (1968); *Prologue, Scene and Movement* for soprano, viola and 2 pianos (1968); *Tempest* for any combination of voices and/or instruments (1969); *What You Will,* set of 12 single pieces of 6 polytonal duets for piano (1969); *Fantaisies et Allusions* for saxophone quintet (1969); 4 pieces of miscellaneous instrumentation, each named *Anaphora* (1970–75).

Read, Daniel, American composer; b. Attleboro, Mass., Nov. 16, 1757; d. New Haven, Dec. 4, 1836. He worked on a farm as a youth; studied mechanics, and was employed as surveyor at 18; began to compose at 19. He served in the Continental Army as a private; at 21 he settled at New Stratford, then going to New Haven. In 1782–83, he maintained a singing school on the North River. He also was a combmaker. At his death, he left a collection of some 400 tunes by him and other composers. He published *The American Singing Book, or a New and Easy Guide to the Art of Psalmody, devised for the use of Singing Schools in America* (New Haven, 1785; subsequent eds., 1786, 1792, 1793, 1795); *The American Musical Magazine* (containing New England church music; compiled with Amos Doolittle, New Haven, 12 numbers, May 1786 to Sept. 1787; repr. Scarsdale, N.Y., 1961); *Supplement to The American Singing Book* (New Haven, 1787); *The Columbian Harmonist,* in 3 books: no. 1 (New Haven, 1793), no. 2 (New Haven, 1794; 2nd ed., with numerous additions, 1798; 3rd ed., with further additions, 1801), no. 3 (New Haven, 1795); all 3 books in 1 vol. (New Haven, 1795; 2nd ed. completely revised, Dedham, 1804; 3rd ed., Boston, 1807; 4th ed., Boston, 1810). Shortly before his death he completed the compilation, *Musica Ecclesia, or Devotional Harmony,* but it remained unpublished. Many of his tunes—e.g., *Sherburne, Windham,* and *Lisbon*—achieved great popularity.
BIBLIOGRAPHY: G. Hood, "Daniel Read," *Musical Herald* (N.Y., Oct. 1882); F. J. Metcalf, *American Composers and Compilers of Sacred Music* (N.Y., 1925); I. Lowens, "Daniel Read's World," *Notes* (March 1952); *Dictionary of American Biography.*

Read, Gardner, outstanding American composer and erudite music scholar; b. Evanston, Ill., Jan. 2, 1913. He studied theory at the Northwestern Univ. School of Music; conducting with Bakaleinikoff, and composition at the Eastman School of Music with Paul

White, Bernard Rogers, and Howard Hanson (Mus. Bac., 1936; M.M., 1937); he studied with Aaron Copland at the Berkshire Music Center; taught composition at the St. Louis Institute of Music (1941–43), at the Kansas City Cons. of Music (1943–45), and at the Cleveland Institute of Music (1945–48); appointed composer-in-residence and prof. of composition, Boston Univ. College of Music, in 1948; retired in 1978. A composer of extraordinary fecundity, he excels in instrumental music; his idiom of composition is basically Romantic, but the harmonic and contrapuntal textures are intense and dense with polytonal encounters.

WORKS: An opera, *Villon* (1967). FOR ORCH.: *The Lotus-Eaters* (Interlochen, Mich., Aug. 12, 1932); *Sketches of the City*, symph. suite after Carl Sandburg (Rochester, April 18, 1934); *The Painted Desert* (Interlochen, Mich., July 28, 1935); Symph. No. 1 (1936; N.Y., Nov. 4, 1937; awarded 1st Prize in the American Composer's Contest sponsored by the N.Y. Philharmonic); *Fantasy*, for viola and orch. (Rochester, April 22, 1937); *Prelude and Toccata* (Rochester, April 29, 1937); *Suite* for string orch. (N.Y., Aug. 5, 1937); *Passacaglia and Fugue* (Chicago, June 30, 1938); *The Golden Journey to Somarkand*, for chorus, soloists, and orch. (1936–39); *Pan e Dafni* (1940); *American Circle* (Evanston, March 15, 1941); *First Overture* (Indianapolis, Nov. 6, 1943); Symph. No. 2 (awarded 1st Prize of the Paderewski Fund Competition, 1942; Boston, Nov. 26, 1943, composer conducting); *Night Flight*, tone poem after Antoine de St.-Exupéry (Rochester, April 27, 1944); Cello Concerto (1945); *Threnody*, for flute and strings (Rochester, Oct. 21, 1946); *A Bell Overture* (Cleveland, Dec. 22, 1946); *Partita* for small orch. (Rochester, May 4, 1947); *Pennsylvaniana Suite* (Pittsburgh, Nov. 21, 1947); Symph. No. 3 (1948); *Quiet Music for Strings* (Washington, May 9, 1948); *Dance of the Locomotives* (Boston, June 26, 1948); *Sound Piece*, for brass and percussion (Boston, May 11, 1949); *The Temptation of St. Anthony*, dance-symph. after Flaubert (Chicago, April 9, 1953); *Toccata Giocosa* (Louisville, March 13, 1954); *Vernal Equinox* (Brockton, Mass., April 12, 1955); Symph. No. 4 (1958; Cincinnati, Jan. 30, 1970); *Jeux des timbres* for orch. (1963). VOCAL WORKS: *4 Nocturnes* for voice and orch. (Rochester, April 3, 1935); *From a Lute of Jade*, for voice and orch. (Rochester, March 15, 1937); *Songs for a Rainy Night*, for voice and orch. (Rochester, April 27, 1942); *The Prophet*, oratorio, after Kahlil Gibran (1960; Boston, Feb. 23, 1977); *The Reveille* for chorus, winds, percussion, and organ (1962); an opera, *Villon* (1967) (1960); *Chants d'Auvergne* for chorus and instruments (1962); many songs and choruses. CHAMBER MUSIC: *Suite* for string quartet (1936); *Piano Quintet* (1945), *Sonata Brevis*, for violin and piano (1948); *Nine by Six* for wind sextet (1951); String Quartet No. 1 (1957); *Sonoric Fantasia No. 1* for celesta, harp, and harpsichord (1958); *Sonoric Fantasia No. 2* for violin and orch. (1965); *Sonoric Fantasia No. 3* for viola and small orch. (1970); *Sonoric Fantasia No. 4* for organ and percussion (1975–76); Piano Concerto (1975–78). *Los Dioses aztecos*, a suite of 7 movements for percussion ensemble (1959); *Petite suite* for recorders and harpsichord (1963). FOR ORGAN: *Passacaglia and Fugue* (1937);

Suite for Organ (co-winner, 1st prize of Pennsylvania College for Women, Pittsburgh, 1950); *8 Preludes on Old Southern Hymns* (1951). PIANO MUSIC: *3 Satirical Sarcasms* (1941); *Driftwood Suite* (1943); *Dance of the Locomotives* (1944); *Sonata da Chiesa* (1948); *Touch Piece* (1949); *5 Polytonal Studies* for piano (1964).

BOOKS: *Thesaurus of Orchestral Devices* (N.Y., 1953); *Music Notation: A Manual of Modern Practice* (Boston, 1964); *Style and Orchestration* (N.Y., 1975).

Reading, John, English organist; d. Winchester, 1692. Lay vicar of Lincoln Cathedral, 1667, and Master of the Choristers, 1670; organist of Winchester Cathedral, 1675–81; then of Winchester College, for which he composed the well-known song *Dulce Domum* (publ. in Hayes's *Harmonia Wiccamica*).

Reading, John, son of preceding; b. 1677; d. London, Sept. 2, 1764. Chorister of the Chapel Royal, under Blow; organist of Dulwich College, 1700–02; lay vicar at Lincoln Cathedral 1702, and Master of the Choristers, 1703; later organist in several London churches. He published *A Book of New Anthems* and *A Book of New Songs with Symphonies and a Thorough Bass fitted to the Harpsichord.*

Reardon, John, American baritone; b. San Francisco, April 8, 1930. He studied voice with Martial Singher and Margaret Harshaw; then appeared with several American opera companies in the secondary roles; among his leading parts were Escamillo in *Carmen* and Count Almaviva in *Le Nozze di Figaro.* He also sang in operettas.

Rebel, François, French composer; b. Paris, June 19, 1701; d. there, Nov. 7, 1775. He became an excellent violinist under the tutelage of his father, Jean-Féry Rebel. He was in charge of the "24 violins" of the King and master of the royal chamber music. From 1757 to 1767 Rebel and his lifelong friend and collaborator, François Francœur, were directors of the Académie Royale de Musique (the Opéra). The operas composed jointly by Rebel and Francœur and produced at Paris include *Pirame et Thisbé* (Oct. 17, 1726) and *Scanderberg* (Oct. 27, 1735).

BIBLIOGRAPHY: L. de La Laurencie, "Une Dynastie de musiciens aux XVIIᵉ et XVIIIᵉ siècles: Les Rebel," *Sammelbände der Internationalen Musik-Gesellschaft* 7.

Rebello, João Lourenço (João Soares), Portuguese composer; b. Caminha, 1610; d. San Amaro, Sept. 16, 1661. He was maestro to King John IV of Portugal, who dedicated to Rebello his *Defensa de la música moderna* (1649). Psalms *a* 16, Magnificats, Lamentations, and Misereres by Rebello were publ. in Rome (1657).

Reber, Napoléon-Henri, French composer; b. Mulhouse, Alsace, Oct. 21, 1807; d. Paris, Nov. 24, 1880. He studied with Reicha and Le Sueur at the Paris Cons.; became prof. of harmony in 1851, succeeded Halévy as prof. of composition in 1861 (being succeeded in turn by Saint-Saëns in 1880), and was also inspector of the branch conservatories from 1871).

WORKS: ballet, *Le Diable amoureux* (1840); the comic operas *La Nuit de Noël* (1848), *Le Père Gaillard* (1852), *Les Papillottes de M. Benoist* (1853), and *Les Dames capitaines* (1857), all produced at the Opéra-Comique; 4 symphonies; chamber music; piano pieces for 2 and 4 hands; 33 songs; vocalises for soprano or tenor (op. 16), etc.; and a *Traité d'harmonie* (1862, and several later eds.)

BIBLIOGRAPHY: Saint-Saëns, *Notice sur Henri Reber* (Paris, 1881).

Řebiček, Josef, Czech conductor and composer; b. Prague, Feb. 7, 1844; d. Berlin, March 24, 1904. He studied violin at the Prague Cons.; was violinist in the court orch. in Weimar; then played in theater orchestras in Prague and Wiesbaden; conducted opera in Warsaw, Budapest, etc.; from 1897 till 1903 was conductor of the Berlin Philharmonic, succeeding Franz Mannstädt. He wrote *Huldigungsfestklänge* (on old Dutch themes) for orch.; a symphony; a violin sonata; many pieces for violin.

Rebikov, Vladimir, Russian composer; b. Krasnoyarsk, Siberia, May 31, 1866; d. Yalta, Aug. 4, 1920. He studied at the Moscow Cons. with Klenovsky; then in Berlin and Vienna. He then went to Odessa, where his first opera, *In the Thunderstorm,* was produced in 1894. In 1898 he moved to Kishinev, Bessarabia, where he organized a branch of the Imperial Russian Musical Society. In 1901 he settled in Moscow, remaining there until 1919; he spent his last year of life in the Crimea. His early works were under the influence of Tchaikovsky, but beginning with *Esquisses* for piano he made a decisive turn towards a modern style; he became particularly fond of the whole-tone scale and its concomitant, the augmented triad; claimed priority in this respect over Debussy and other European composers; his piano piece *Les Démons s'amusent* is based entirely on the whole-tone scale. He declared that music is a language of emotion, and therefore could not be confined to set forms, or to arbitrarily defined consonances. An entirely new departure is represented by his *Mélomimiques,* short lyric pieces for piano, in which mimicry and suggestion are used in an Impressionistic manner. He also wrote several vocal "melomimics," 3 "rhythmo-declamations" for piano (op. 32), and 20 for voice and piano. In these compositions he abandoned cohesive form in favor of a free association of melodic and rhythmic phrases, sparingly harmonized; prevalence of esthetic theories over musical substance made his experiments ephemeral. A melodious waltz from his children's opera, *The Christmas Tree,* is his most popular composition.

WORKS: the operas *In the Thunderstorm* (Odessa, Feb. 27, 1894) and *The Christmas Tree* (Moscow, Nov. 1, 1903); a musico-psychological pantomime, *Little Snow White* (Tiflis, 1909); a 2-act fairy opera, *Prince Charming;* scenic fables after Krylov: *The Grasshopper and the Ant, A Dinner with a Bear, The Ass and the Nightingale, The Funeral, The Liar* (Moscow, Dec. 27, 1903); several "musico-psychological tableaux": *Slavery and Freedom, Songs of the Harp, The Night-*

mare, etc.; numerous piano pieces (*Scènes bucoliques, Silhouettes, Dans la Forêt, Chansons blanches, Idylles, Les Danses, Les Démons s'amusent,* etc.) etc. He publ. numerous articles on musical esthetics, particularly relating to modern music; translated into Russian Gevaert's *Traité d'Instrumentation.*

BIBLIOGRAPHY: M. Montagu-Nathan, *Contemporary Russian Composers* (N.Y., 1917); N. Nabokov, *Old Friends and New Music* (Boston, 1951; pp. 148–50).

Rebling, Gustav, German organist; b. Barby, July 10, 1821; d. Magdeburg, Jan. 9, 1902. He was a pupil of Fr. Schneider at Dessau (1836–39); in 1847 became organist of the French church in Magdeburg; in 1858, organist of the Johanniskirche; retired in 1897. He wrote pieces for organ and piano; choruses and songs; 2 cello sonatas; other chamber music.

Rebner, Adolf, Austrian violinist; b. Vienna, Nov. 21, 1876; d. Baden-Baden, June 19, 1967. He was a pupil of Grün at the Vienna Cons.; settled in Frankfurt in 1896, and after 1904 taught violin at Hoch's Cons. In 1921 he organized the Rebner String Quartet, with Hindemith as the violist, and gave numerous concerts with it obtaining excellent success; with the advent of the Nazi regime in Germany he went to Vienna; after the *Anschluss* lived briefly in the U.S.; eventually returned to Europe and lived in Baden-Baden.

Rebner, Wolfgang Edward, German pianist; son of **Adolf Rebner;** b. Frankfurt, Dec. 20, 1910. He studied at Hoch's Cons. in Frankfurt; served as accompanist to the cellist Feuermann in the U.S. (1935–37) and South America. In 1955 he returned to Germany, and taught at the Richard Strauss Cons. in Munich. He composed some excellent chamber music and the orchestral suites *Persönliche Noten* (1961) and *Aus Südamerika* (1964).

Redford, John, English organist, composer, and poet; d. London, 1547. He was one of the vicars-choral of St. Paul's Cathedral in London. Surviving in MS are a number of fantasias on plainsong melodies (2 of which are printed in Davison and Apel, *Historical Anthology of Music,* vol. I, Cambridge, Mass., 1946) and 3 motets.

BIBLIOGRAPHY: C. F. Pfatteicher, *John Redford* (Kassel, 1934); *Grove's Dictionary* 5th ed.

Redhead, Richard, English composer of church music; b. Harrow, March 1, 1820; d. Hallingley, April 27, 1901. He served as organist in various churches in London; wrote much vocal music; edited the collections *Cathedral and Church Choir Book, Parochial Church Tune Book,* and *The Universal Organist.*

Redlich, Hans Ferdinand, distinguished Austrian musicologist and conductor; b. Vienna, Feb. 11, 1903; d. Manchester, England, Nov. 27, 1968. He studied piano and conducting, but devoted his energies mainly to biographical and analytical books on composers; he was only 16 when he published an essay on Mahler. After taking courses at the universities of Vienna and Munich, he obtained his Dr. phil. at the Univ. of

Frankfurt with the dissertation, *Das Problem des Stilwandels in Monteverdis Madrigalwerk* (publ. Leipzig, 1931; in a revised edition in Berlin, 1932). He conducted opera at the Municipal Theater of Mainz (1925-29); then lived in Mannheim. In 1939 he emigrated to England; from 1941 to 1955 he conducted the Choral and Orchestra Society in Letchworth; also was lecturer at the Extra Mural Board of the Univ. of Cambridge (1942-55); from 1955 to 1962 he was lecturer at the Reid School of Music at the Univ. of Edinburgh; then was at the Univ. of Manchester. He published *Gustav Mahler: eine Erkenntnis* (Nuremberg, 1919); *Claudio Monteverdi: Leben und Werk* (Olten, 1949; in English, London, 1952); *Bruckner and Mahler* (London, 1955; revised ed. 1963); *Alban Berg: The Man and His Music* (London, 1957; a fundamental work).

Redman, Harry Newton, American organist and composer; b. Mount Carmel, Illinois, Dec. 26, 1869; d. Boston, Dec. 26, 1958. He studied organ and composition with Chadwick; from 1897 taught at the New England Cons., Boston; 2 string quartets, 2 violin sonatas, an *Octave Method* and studies for piano; 2 albums of songs, etc. About 1925 he abandoned music and devoted himself chiefly to painting; exhibited in Boston as late as 1957.

Rée, Anton, Danish pianist and pedagogue; b. Aarhus, Oct. 5, 1820; d. Copenhagen, Dec. 20, 1886. He studied with Karl Krebs in Hamburg; had a few lessons with Chopin in Paris. In 1842 he returned to Denmark and settled in Copenhagen as a teacher. He publ. *Musikhistoriske Momenter* and a book of exercises, *Bidrag til Klaverspillets Teknik; Danses caractéristiques* for piano; etc.

Rée, Louis, pianist; cousin of **Anton Rée;** b. Edinburgh, Oct. 15, 1861; d. Vienna, Feb. 28, 1939. He was a pupil of Leschetizky in Vienna; settled there as a teacher; gave duo-piano concerts with his wife, **Susanne Pilz-Rée** (1865-1937). He wrote a concerto for 2 pianos (1925); publ. transcriptions for 2 pianos and various other works.

Reed, Herbert Owen, American composer and educator; b. Odessa, Missouri, June 17, 1910. He studied with Howard Hanson and Bernard Rogers at the Eastman School of Music, Rochester, N.Y. (Ph.D., 1939); upon graduation he was appointed to the faculty of Michigan State Univ., retiring in 1976.
WORKS: a "folk opera" *Michigan Dream* (East Lansing, Michigan, May 13, 1955); a short opera-legend *Earth Trapped* (East Lansing, Feb. 24, 1962); ballet-pantomime, *The Mask of the Red Death*, after Edgar Allan Poe (1936); symph. poem *Evangeline* (Rochester, N.Y., March 30, 1938); Symph. No. 1 (Rochester, April 27, 1939); Cello Concerto (1949); *La Fiesta Mexicana* for concert band (1949); *The Turning Mind* for orch. (1968); oratorio *A Tabernacle for the Sun* (1963); chamber opera-dance, *Living Solid Face* (South Dakota Univ., Brookings, Nov. 28, 1976); chamber music; piano pieces; choruses; solo songs. He publ. several teaching manuals: *A Workbook in the Fundamentals of Music* (N.Y., 1946); *Basic Music* (N.Y., 1954); *Composition Analysis Chart* (N.Y.,

1958); *Basic Contrapuntal Technique* (with P. Harder; N.Y., 1964); *Scoring for Percussion* (with J. T. Leach, Englewood Cliffs, N.J., 1969).

Reed, Peter Hugh, American music critic and journalist; b. Washington, June 14, 1892; d. Wingdale, N.Y., Sept. 25, 1969. He studied voice in Italy, preparing for an operatic career, which was frustrated when he entered the U.S. Army in World War I and was gassed. His speaking voice was, however, unimpaired; he became a pioneer of radio reviews of phonograph records. In 1935 he founded *The American Music Lover*, a monthly magazine devoted to serious music on records; in 1944 the name was changed to *The American Record Guide*. Reed remained its editor and publisher until 1957.

Reed, Thomas German, versatile English musician; b. Bristol, June 27, 1817; d. London, March 21, 1888. Under the guidance of his father, he appeared in Bath as a child of 10 in the various capacities of singer, pianist, and actor. In 1844 he married **Priscilla Horton** (b. Birmingham, Jan. 1, 1818; d. Bexley Heath, March 18, 1895), an actress and a singer. Together they started the celebrated series "Mr. and Mrs. German Reed's Entertainment" (1855), which included productions of operettas by Offenbach, Balfe, Clay, Sullivan, etc. These entertainments enjoyed great success, and were continued by his son **Alfred German Reed,** who died in London on March 10, 1895, a few days before the death of his mother.

Reed, William Henry, English violinist and composer; b. Frome, July 29, 1876; d. Dumfries, July 2, 1942. He studied at the Royal Academy of Music in London; was a violinist in the London Symph. Orch. at its foundation in 1904; then taught violin at the Royal College of Music; was concertmaster of the London Symph. Orch. from 1912 to 1935. He was a close friend of Elgar, and published a book, *Elgar As I Knew Him* (1936). His works include the orchestral sketches *The Lincoln Imp* (Hereford Festival, 1921) and *Aesop's Fables* (Hereford Festival, 1924); Violin Concerto; *Rhapsody* for violin and orch.; 5 string quartets; violin pieces; songs; etc.

Reed, William Leonard, English composer; b. London, Oct. 16, 1910. He studied at the Guildhall School of Music in London (1917-26), at Oxford Univ. (1929-33), and at the Royal College of Music (1934-36) where his teachers were Constant Lambert and Howells. He traveled to Scandinavia and the U.S., where he stayed for several years.
WORKS: the operas *The Vanishing Island* (Santa Barbara, California, 1955), *The Crowning Experience* (Detroit, 1958); the operettas, *Annie* (London, 1967), *High Diplomacy* (London, 1969); several orchestra pieces in a light vein; various pieces of chamber music; choruses; piano works. He publ. *The Golden Book of Carols* (London, 1947); *The Treasury of Christmas Music* (London, 1950); *Music of Britain* (London, 1952); *The Treasury of Eastern Music* (London, 1963); *The Treasury of English Church Music* (with G. Knight, 5 vols.; London, 1965); *The Second Treasury of Christmas Music* (London, 1967).

Reese, Gustave, eminent American musicologist; b. New York, Nov. 29, 1899; d. Berkeley, California, Sept. 7, 1977. He studied jurisprudence at N.Y. Univ. (LL.B., 1921) and music (Mus. Bac., 1930); subsequently joined its faculty and taught there during the periods 1927–33, 1934–37, and 1945–74; concurrently he worked with G. Schirmer, Inc., publishers (1924–45; from 1940 to 1945 was director of publications); then was director of publications for Carl Fischer, music publishers (1944–55). From 1933 to 1944 he was associate editor, and in 1944–45, editor of the *Musical Quarterly.* In 1934 he was a co-founder of the American Musicological Society; was its President from 1950 to 1952, and remained its honorary president until his death. He gave numerous lectures at American universities; also gave courses at the Juilliard School of Music, N.Y. An entire generation of American music scholars numbered among his students; he was widely regarded as a founder of American musicology as a science. He held a chair at the Graduate School of Arts and Science at N.Y. Univ., which gave him its "Great Teacher Award" in 1972 and its presidential citation on his retirement from active teaching in 1974; he then became a visiting prof. at the Graduate Center of the City Univ. of N.Y. He died while attending the congress of the International Musicological Society in Berkeley, California. Gustave Reese contributed a great number of informative articles to various American and European publications and music encyclopedias, but his most lasting achievement lies in his books, *Music in the Middle Ages* (N.Y., 1940; also in Italian, Florence, 1960), and *Music in the Renaissance* (N.Y., 1954; revised 1959), which have become classics of American music scholarship; he also brought out an interesting book that describes selected early writings on music not available in English, *Fourscore Classics of Music Literature* (N.Y., 1957). On his 65th birthday, he was honored with an offering of a collection of articles by his colleagues and students, *Aspects of Medieval and Renaissance Music,* edited by Jan LaRue (N.Y., 1966).

Reeve, William, English composer; b. London, 1757; d. there, June 22, 1815. Pupil of Richardson; organist at Totness, Devon, 1781–83; returned to London, and composed operettas, pantomimes, and incidental music for plays, for Astley's Circus and Covent Garden (1791); in 1792, organist of St. Martin's, Ludgate Hill; from 1802, part-proprietor of Sadler's Wells Theatre. Besides music to some 40 plays, he composed glees and songs; the song "I am a friar in orders grey," in the play of *Merry Sherwood,* was very popular.

Reeves, David Wallace, American bandmaster; b. Owego, N.Y., Feb. 14, 1838; d. Providence, Rhode Island, March 8, 1900. As a boy he began to play cornet in circus and minstrel bands; later was in Union Army bands; his career as bandmaster began in 1866 when he became the leader of the American Band of Providence, which is said to trace its roots back to the War of 1812; during its 35 years under the direction of Reeves it became a model of excellence among American municipal bands; Reeves succeeded in standardizing the instrumentation of the ordinary parade and outdoor-concert band; he wrote some 80 marches, of which the best is *The Second Connecticut Regiment March,* known to have been a favorite of Charles Ives. Reeves was a great friend of Patrick Sarsfield Gilmore, conductor of the band of the N.Y. 22nd Regiment, and it was Gilmore who popularized Reeves's marches. Upon Gilmore's death, Reeves took over the 22nd Regiment Band for the 1892–93 season, until it was taken over by Victor Herbert in the fall of 1893. J. P. Sousa called Reeves "the father of band music in America."

Reeves, John Sims, English tenor; b. Shooter's Hill, Kent, Sept. 26, 1818; d. Worthing, London, Oct. 25, 1900. Learned to play several instruments; had lessons with J. B. Cramer (piano) and W. H. Callcott (harmony). Debut (as a baritone) at Newcastle-on-Tyne, in the role of Rodolfo (*Sonnambula*), in 1839. Studied further and sang minor tenor parts at Drury Lane, 1842–43; studied in Paris under Bordogni, and in Milan under Mazzucato, appearing at La Scala, 1846, as Edgardo (*Lucia*). He retired in 1891, but reappeared in concerts in 1893, and even made a successful tour in South Africa in 1896. Publ. *Sims Reeves; His Life and Recollections Written by Himself* (London, 1888); *My Jubilee, or Fifty Years of Artistic Life* (London, 1889); *Sims Reeves On the Art of Singing* (1900).
BIBLIOGRAPHY: H. S. Edwards, *The Life and Artistic Career of Sims Reeves* (London, 1881); Ch. E. Pearce, *Sims Reeves: Fifty Years of Music in England* (1924); *Modern English Biography,* vol. VI.

Refardt, Edgar, eminent Swiss musicologist and bibliographer; b. Basel, Aug. 8, 1877; d. there, March 3, 1968. He studied law; obtained the degree of Dr. jur.; in 1915 was appointed librarian and cataloguer of the musical collection of the Municipal Library of Basel; publ. valuable bibliographical works on Swiss music; also essays on various literary and musical subjects.
WRITINGS: *Verzeichnis der Aufsätze zur Musik in den nichtmusikalischen Zeitschriften der Universitätsbibliothek Basel* (Leipzig, 1925); *Historisch-biographisches Musikerlexikon der Schweiz* (Zürich, 1928; basic source of information on Swiss music and musicians); *Hans Huber: Leben und Werk eines Schweizer Musikers* (1944; definitive biography of Huber; supersedes Refardt's previous writings on Huber); *Johannes Brahms, Anton Bruckner, Hugh Wolf: drei Wiener Meister des 19. Jahrhunderts* (1949); *Musik in der Schweiz* (collection of articles; 1952); *Thematischer Katalog der Instrumentalmusik des 18. Jahrhunderts in den Handschriften der Universitätsbibliothek Basel,* ed. by Hans Zehntner (Basel, 1957); etc.

Refice, Licinio, Italian composer of sacred music; b. Patrica, near Rome, Feb. 12, 1883; d. Rio de Janeiro, Sept. 11, 1954 (while conducting his mystery play, *Santa Cecilia*). He studied with Falchi and Renzi at Santa Cecilia in Rome; in 1910 became teacher of church music at the Scuola Pontifica Superiore di Musica Sacra. In 1947 he toured the U.S. as director of the Roman Singers of Sacred Music (99 concerts).
WORKS: the operas *Cecilia* (Rome, 1934) and *Margherita da Cortona* (Milan, 1938); the cantatas *La Ve-*

dova di Naim (1912), *Maria Magdalena* (Rome, 1917), and *Il Martirio di S. Agnese* (Rome, 1919); *Stabat Mater* (1917); *Te Deum* (1918); *Missa Jubilaei* (1925), *Missa Italica* (1944); the choral symph. poems *Dantis poetae transitus* (Ravenna, 1921) and *Il Trittico francescano* (Assisi, 1925); a Requiem; the sacred play *Santa Cecilia* (Rome, Feb. 15, 1934); the oratorios *Cananea* and *La Samaritana;* hymns; motets; etc.

Regamey, Constantin, Russian-born Swiss composer; b. Kiev, Jan. 28, 1907. He went to Poland in 1920; studied piano with Turczyński, but devoted himself mainly to philology; took courses in Sanskrit at the Univ. of Warsaw and later at L'École des Hautes Études in Paris, graduating in 1936; returning to Poland, he taught Sanskrit at the Univ. of Warsaw (1937-39). During the war he was seized by the Germans and deported to Switzerland in 1944; taught Slavic and Oriental languages at the Univ. of Lausanne; was editor of the review *Feuilles musicales* (1954-62) and was president of the Association of Swiss Musicians (1963-68). As a composer, he adopted an eclectic idiom, with a juxtaposition of tonal and atonal elements. Works: opera buffa *Mio, mein Mio* (1973); 7 *Chansons persanes,* after Omar Khayyam, for baritone and chamber orch. (1942); Sonatina for flute and piano (1944); Quintet for clarinet, bassoon, violin, cello and piano (1944); String Quartet (1948); *Variazioni e tema* for orch. (1948); 5 *Etudes* for female voice and orch. or piano (1955-56); *4 × 5,* concerto for 4 quintets (Basel, May 28, 1964); *Autographe* for chamber orch. (1963-66); *Symphonie des Incantations* for soprano, baritone and orch. (1967); *3 Lieder des Clowns* for baritone and orch. (1968); *Alpha,* cantata for tenor and orch., to a Hindu text (1970). He published a survey, *Musique du XXᵉ siècle* (Lausanne, 1955).
BIBLIOGRAPHY: H. Jaccard, *Initiation à la musique contemporaine: Trois compositeurs vaudois: Raffaele d'Allessandro, Constantin Regamey, Julien-François Zbinden* (Lausanne, 1955).

Reger, Max, pre-eminent German composer; b. Brand, Bavaria, March 19, 1873; d. Leipzig, May 11, 1916. In 1874 his father, a school teacher and good organist (d. 1905 in Munich), removed to Weiden, where Reger attended the Realschule. Although he was intended for the schoolmaster's career, he received thorough instruction on the piano and harmonium from his father, and on the organ and in theory from Lindner. At an early age he began to write piano pieces and chamber music, and after hearing *Die Meistersinger* and *Parsifal* in Bayreuth (1888) he gave expression to the emotions created in him by those masterpieces in an ambitious symphonic poem, *Héroïde funèbre.* In 1889 he passed the entrance examination for the teachers' seminary. But by that time music had taken such complete possession of him that he submitted a number of his manuscripts to Hugo Riemann, who immediately recognized Reger's exceptional talent. Accordingly, Reger became Riemann's pupil at the Sondershausen Cons. in April, 1890, and in 1891 followed him to the Wiesbaden Cons., where he continued his studies till 1895, and also taught piano and organ (till 1896). Having served

a year in the army, he settled in Weiden as composer, writing the works up to about op. 50. However, he did not attract general attention until 1901, when he removed to Munich, whence he undertook pianistic tours through Germany, Austria, and Switzerland. During the academic year of 1905-06 he was prof. of counterpoint at the Königliche Akademie der Tonkunst, and conductor of the Gesangsverein; in 1907 he was called to Leipzig as Musikdirektor at the Univ. (also conductor of the Univ. chorus St. Pauli) and prof. of composition at the Cons.; the former post he resigned in 1908, but the latter he retained till his death in 1908; he was made Dr. phil. (*honoris causa,* Univ. of Jena); in 1911 Hofrat, and in 1913 General-Musikdirector; 1911-15, Hofkapellmeister in Meiningen; then in Jena and Leipzig. He died suddenly of paralysis of the heart. A German Max Reger Society was founded in 1920, with branches in many cities; another society was established in Austria. The Max Reger Archives (containing most of his manuscripts) are at Weimar. A complete ed. of Reger's works was begun in 1954 by Breitkopf & Härtel, reaching 38 vols. by 1977. W. Altman publ. a catalogue of Reger's works (1917; 2nd ed., 1926); Fritz Stein ed. a thematic catalogue: *Thematisches Verzeichnis der im Druck erschienen Werke von Max Reger* (Leipzig, 1934; 1953).
WORKS: FOR ORCH.: op. 90, *Sinfonietta;* op. 95, *Serenade;* op. 100, *Variationen und Fuge über ein lustiges Thema von J. A. Hiller;* op. 108, *Symphonischer Prolog zu einer Tragödie;* op. 120, *Eine Lustspielouvertüre;* op. 123, *Konzert im alten Stil;* op. 125, *Romantische Suite;* op. 128, *Vier Tondichtungen nach Böcklin;* op. 130, *Ballet-Suite;* op. 132, *Variationen und Fuge über ein Thema von Mozart;* op. 140, *Eine vaterländische Ouvertüre;* p. 50, *Zwei Romanzen* for violin and orch.; op. 101, *Violin Concerto in A;* op. 114, Piano Concerto in F minor.
VOCAL WORKS: with orch.: op. 21, *Hymne an den Gesang* (men's chorus); op. 71, *Gesang der Verklärten* (mixed chorus *a* 5); op. 106, *Psalm 100* (mixed chorus and organ); op. 112, *Die Nonnen* (mixed chorus and organ); op. 119, *Die Weihe der Nacht* (alto solo and mixed chorus); op. 124, *An die Hoffnung* (also solo); op. 126, *Römischer Triumphgesang* (men's chorus); mixed choruses a cappella, opp. 6, 39 (*a* 6); men's choruses a cappella, opp. 38, 83; women's choruses a cappella, op. 111b; duets, opp. 14, 111a; about 300 songs, opp. 3, 4, 5, 12, 15, 23, 31, 35, 37, 43, 48, 51, 55, 62, 66, 68, 70, 75, 76 (60 *Schlichte Weisen*), 88, 97, 98, 104; op. 19, *Zwei geistliche Gesänge;* op. 61, *Leicht ausführbare Kompositionen zum gottesdienstlichen Gebrauch in der katholischen Kirche* (38 motets for mixed voices); op. 105, *Zwei geistliche Lieder;* op. 110, Motets for mixed chorus a cappella (*a* 5); op. 137, *Zwölf geistliche Lieder; Der evangelische Kirchenchor* (I. 40 mixed choruses for all festivals [4 series]; II, Cantata *O wie selig* for mixed chorus, string orch., and organ; III, Cantata, *O Haupt voll Blut und Wunden* (for alto and tenor soli, mixed chorus, violin and oboe soli, and organ). Men's and mixed choruses, and songs (sacred and secular), without opus numbers.
CHAMBER MUSIC: op. 118, String Sextet in F; op. 64, Piano Quintet in C minor; op. 113, Piano Quartet in D minor; 5 string quartets: op. 54 (G minor and A), op. 74 (D minor), op. 109 (E-flat, op. 121 (F-sharp minor);

2 piano trios: op. 2 (B minor, for piano, violin, and viola), op. 102 (E minor); op. 77a, *Serenade* for flute, violin, and viola; op. 77b, Trio for flute, violin, and viola; op. 103a, *Suite* for violin and piano (A minor); 9 violin sonatas: op. 1 (D minor), op. 3 (D), op. 41 (A), op. 72 (C), op. 84 (F-sharp minor), op. 103b (*Zwei kleine Sonaten*, D minor and A), op. 122 (E minor), op. 139 (C minor); op. 93, *Suite im alten Stil* for violin and piano; 4 cello sonatas: op. 5 (F minor), op. 28 (G minor), op. 78 (F), op. 116 (A minor); 3 clarinet sonatas: op. 49 (A-flat major and F-sharp minor), op. 107 (B-flat); op. 42, 4 sonatas for violin solo; op. 117, *Präludien und Fugen* for violin solo; op. 131, 3 suites for cello solo; op. 91, 7 sonatas for unaccompanied violin; op. 131a, 6 Preludes and Fugues for unaccompanied violin; op. 131b, 3 duos for 2 violins; op. 133, Piano Quartet in A minor; op. 141a, *Serenade*, in G major for flute, violin and cello; op. 141b, Trio in D minor for violin, viola and cello; op. 143, *Träume am Kamin*, 12 pieces for piano solo; op. 146, Clarinet Quintet in A major without op. number: Piano Quintet in C minor.

FOR ORGAN: op. 16, *Suite* in E minor; op. 27, Fantasy on *Ein' feste Burg*; op. 29, *Fantasie und Fuge* in C minor; op. 30, Fantasy Sonata on *Freu dich sehr, o meine Seele*; op. 33, Sonata in F-sharp minor; op. 40, 2 Fantasies on *Wie schön leucht' uns der Morgenstern* and *Straf mich nicht in deinem Zorn*; op. 46, *Fantasie und Fuge über BACH*; op. 52, 3 Fantasies on *Alle Menschen müssen sterben, Wachet auf! ruft uns die Stimme*, and *Hallelujah! Gott zu loben*; op. 57, *Symphonische Phantasie und Fuge*; op. 60, Sonata in D minor; op. 67, 52 *Vorspiele* to the chorales in general use; op. 73, *Variationen und Fuge über ein Originalthema*; op. 92, *Suite* in G minor; op. 127, *Introduktion, Passacaglia und Fuge* in E minor; numerous minor pieces: opp. 7, 56, 59, 63, 65, 69, 79, 80, 85, 129; also organ transcriptions of Bach clavier pieces.

FOR PIANO: 4 hands: op. 9, *Walzer-Capricen;* op. 10, *Deutsche Tänze;* op. 22, *Sechs Walzer;* op. 34, *Cinq pièces pittoresques;* op. 58, *Sechs Burlesken;* op. 94, *Sechs Stücke;* for 2 pianos: op. 86, *Variatonen und Fuge über ein Thema von Beethoven;* op. 96, *Introduktion, Passacaglia und Fuge;* for piano solo: op. 17, *Aus der Jugendzeit* (20 pieces); op. 18, *Improvisationen* (8 pieces); op. 20, *Fünf Humoresken;* op. 24, *Six Morceaux;* op. 25, *Aquarellen;* op. 26, *Sieben Fantasiestücke;* op. 32, *Sieben Charackterstücke;* op. 36, *Bunte Blätter* (9 pieces); op. 44, *Zehn kleine Vortragsstücke;* op. 45, *Sechs Intermezzi;* op. 53, *Silhouetten* (7 pieces); op. 81, *Variationen und Fuge über ein Thema von Bach;* op. 82, *Aus meinem Tagebuche* (35 pieces); op. 89, 4 *Sonatinen* (E minor, D, F, A minor); op. 99, *Sechs Präludien und Fugen;* op. 115, *Episoden* (2 books); op. 134, *Variationen und Fuge über ein Thema von Ph. Telemann;* 2 books of canons in all major and minor keys; 4 *Spezialstudien für die linke Hand allein;* minor pieces. Transcriptions for piano, 4 hands: Bach's Prelude and Fugue in D, Toccata and Fugue in D minor, Fantasia in G, Prelude and Fugue in G, Prelude and Fugue in A minor, Fantasia and Fugue in G minor, Toccata and Fugue in E, Prelude and Fugue in E minor; Bach's orchestral suites and *Brandenburg Concertos;* Hugo Wolf's symphonic poem *Penthesilea* and the overture *Italienische Serenade;*

songs of Jensen, Brahms, Hugo Wolf and Richard Strauss.

BIBLIOGRAPHY: R. Braungart, *Max Reger,* in vol. II of Monographien moderner Musiker (Leipzig, 1907); G. Robert-Tornow, *Max Reger und Karl Straube* (Göttingen, 1907); V. Junk, *Max Reger als Orchesterkomponist* (Leipzig, 1910); W. Fischer, *Über die Wiedergabe der Orgelkompositionen Max Regers* (Cologne, 1911); M. Hehemann, *Max Reger. Eine Studie über moderne Musik* (Munich, 1911; 2nd ed., 1917); F. Rabich, *Regerlieder: Eine Studie* (Langensalza, 1914); H. Grace. "The Late Max Reger as Organ Composer," *Musical Times* (June 1916); H. Poppen, *Max Reger* (1917); E. Isler, *Max Reger* (Zürich, 1917); R. Würz, ed., *Max Reger: eine Sammlung von Studien* (4 vols.; Munich, 1920–23); H. Unger, *Max Reger* (1921 and 1924); K. Hasse, *Max Reger* (1921); E. Segnitz, *Max Reger* (1922); E. Brennecke, "The Two Reger-Legends," *Musical Quarterly* (July 1922); A. Lindner (his teacher), *Max Reger, Ein Bild seines Jugendlebens und künstlerischen Werdens* (Stuttgart, 1922; 3rd ed., 1938); G. Bagier, *Reger* (Stuttgart, 1923); A. Spemann, *Max Reger-Brevier* (1923); H. Unger, *Max Reger* (Bielefeld, 1924); E. Gatscher, *Die Fugentechnik Regers in ihrer Entwicklung* (Stuttgart, 1925); S. Kallenberg, *Max Reger* (1929); E. C. Ebert-Stockinger, *Max Reger* (1930); G. R. Dejmek, *Der Variationszyklus bei Max Reger* (Essen, 1930); Elsa Reger (his widow), *Mein Leben für und mit Max Reger* (1930); P. Coenen, *Max Regers Variationsschaffen* (Berlin, 1935); R. Huesgen, *Der junge Max Reger und seine Orgelwerke* (Schramberg, 1935); H. E. Rahner, *Regers Choralfantasien für die Orgel* (Kassel, 1936); E. Brand, *Max Reger im Elternhaus* (Munich, 1938); F. W. Stein, *Max Reger* (Potsdam, 1939); F. W. Stein, *Max Reger. Sein Leben in Bildern* (1941); E. H. Müller von Asow, *Max Reger und sein Welt* (Berlin, 1945); K. Hasse, *Max Reger: Entwicklungsgang eines deutschen Meisters* (Leipzig, 1946); H. M. Poppen, *Max Reger* (Leipzig, 1947); R. Braungart, *Freund Reger; Erinnerungen* (Regensburg, 1949); A. Kalkoff, *Das Orgelschaffen Max Regers* (Kassel, 1950); *Max Reger. Festschrift* (contains articles about Reger; Leipzig, 1953); special Reger issue of the *Zeitschrift für Musik* (March 1953); G. Wehmeyer, *Max Reger als Liederkomponist* (Regensburg, 1955); E. Otto, *Max Reger: Sinnbild einer Epoche* (Wiesbaden, 1957); Reger-Festkomitee, ed., *Max Reger; Beiträge zur Regerforschung* (Meiningen, 1966); O. Schreiber & G. Sievers, ed., *Max Reger Zum 50. Todestag* (Bonn, 1966); G. Sievers, *Die Grundlagen Hugo Riemanns bei Max Reger* (Wiesbaden, 1967); E. Brand-Selter, *Max Reger; Jahre der Kindheit* (Wilhelmshaven, 1968); H. Wirth, *Max Reger in Selbstzeugnissen und Bilddokumenten* (Reinleh, 1973); K. Röhring, ed. *Max Reger: ein Synposion* (Wiesbaden, 1974).

Regis, Johannes, noted Flemish composer and organist; b. Flanders, c.1430; d. Soignies, c.1485. He was "magister puerorum" at the Cathedral of Antwerp (1460–64); then was clerk to Dufay at Cambrai, and finally canon at Soignies. He wrote 2 Masses on the melody of *L'Homme armé;* a 5-part motet, *O admirabile commercium,* and other choral pieces. His collected works were publ. in 2 vols. by the American

Institute of Musicology in Rome (1956), under the editorship of C. W. H. Lindenburg.
BIBLIOGRAPHY: C. W. H. Lindenburg, *Het Leven en de werken van Johannes Regis* (Amsterdam, 1938).

Regli, Francesco, Italian lexicographer; b. Milan, 1802; d. Turin, March 10, 1866. He founded a theatrical publication, *Il Pirata*, in 1835; publ. a *Dizionario biografico dei più celebri poeti ed artisti melodrammatici che fiorirono in Italia dal 1800 al 1860* (Turin, 1860); *Storia del violino in Piemonte* (Turin, 1863); *Elogio a G. Rossini* (Turin, 1864); *Elogio a Felice Romani* (Turin, 1865).

Regnart, Jacob, one of five brothers active as musicians; b. probably in or near Douai, c.1540; d. Prague, Oct. 16, 1599. He was trained as a chorister, was alumnus at the Imperial Chapel in Vienna, and was a tenor there from 1564; in 1568-70 he was in Italy; from 1576 second Kapellmeister at the Imperial Court in Prague; from 1582-95 Vice Kapellmeister to the Archduke Ferdinand of Innsbruck, and then in Prague again as Vice Kapellmeister. Publ. (1574-1611) a great number of Masses, motets, canzone, villanelle, and German songs (many books of these last went through 7 editions; in a collection of 1590 are some songs by his brothers, **Franz, Karl,** and **Pascasius**). In the *Monatshefte für Musikgeschichte* (vol. XII, p. 97) is a list of his works; also W. Pass, *Thematischer Katalog Sämtlicher Werke Jacob Regnarts* (Vienna, 1969). Reprints have been publ. by L. Lechner (villanelle), R. Eitner (in *Publikation älterer Musikwerke*, vol. 19), H. Osthoff (5-voiced German songs), A. Schering in *Geschichte der Musik in Beispielen* (no. 139), A. Einstein (a madrigal), etc.
BIBLIOGRAPHY: H. Osthoff, *Die Niederländer und das deutsche Lied* (Berlin, 1938, pp. 343-422).

Regt, Hendrik de, Dutch composer; b. Rotterdam, July 5, 1950. He studied composition with Otto Ketting in The Hague (1968-72).
WORKS: *Canzoni e Scherzi* for soprano, flute and harp (1972); *Proteus,* music for flute, viola and harp (1974); *Metamorfosen* for oboe and English horn (1974); *Silenus en Bacchanten* for flute, oboe and guitar (1974); *Pastorale* for flute and oboe (1974-75); *Circe* for clarinet, violin and piano (1975); *Mond im Zenit verharrend,* after Goethe, for chorus and orch. (1976); about 30 works, each entitled *Musica,* written for different instrumental combinations: for wind quintet (1969); oboe, cello, harp and percussion (1970); 4 saxophones (1971); flute, percussion and narrator (1970-72); flute, viola, cello, guitar and percussion (1972); 2 trumpets, horn and trombone (1971-72); flute, guitar and percussion (1972); 4 clarinets (1972-73); 4 horns (1974).

Rehberg, Walter, Swiss pianist and writer; b. Geneva, May 14, 1900; d. Zürich, Oct. 22, 1957. He studied with his father, Willy Rehberg (1863-1937); then in Berlin with Ernst Toch and Eugen d'Albert; began a career as pianist; in 1934 appointed prof. at the Music Academy in Zürich. Publ. (with his wife Paula Rehberg) popular biographies of Brahms (1944), Schubert (1946), Chopin (1949), and Schumann (1954).

Reich, Steve, American composer; b. New York, Oct. 3, 1936. He studied philosophy at Cornell Univ. (B.A. 1957) and composition at the Juilliard School of Music (1958-61) and at Mills College, with Luciano Berio and Darius Milhaud (M.A. 1963). He moved back to New York in 1965; formed a performing ensemble with Arthur Murphy and Jon Gibson; in 1970 made a trip to Ghana to study African drumming. His music explores the potentialities of mixed media, electronics and ethnic resources.
WORKS: *Pitch Charts* for an instrumental ensemble (1963); *Music for Piano and Tapes* (1964); *Livelihood* for tape (1965); *It's Gonna Rain* for tape (1965); *Come Out* for tape (1966); *Melodica* for tape (1966); *Reed Phase* for a reed instrument and tape (1966); *Piano Phase* for two pianos (1967); *My Name Is* for several performers, tape recorders and audience (1967); *Violin Phase* for violin and tape (1967); *Pendulum Music* for microphone, amplifiers, speakers and performers (1968); *Pulse Music* for the phase shifting pulse gate, an electronic device built by Reich (1969); *Four Log Drums* for four log drums and phase shifting pulse gate (1969); *Four Organs* for four electric organs and maracas (1970); *Clapping Music* for 2 musicians clapping hands in an interlocking rhythmic pattern (1972); *Music for Pieces for Wood* (1973); *Music for Mallet Instruments, Voices and Organ* (1973); *Music for 18 Musicians* (1975).

Reich, Willi, Austrian writer on music; b. Vienna, May 27, 1898. He studied at the Univ. of Vienna; Ph.D. (1934) with the dissertation *Padre Martini als Theoretiker und Lehrer;* also studied privately with Alban Berg; ed. a modern music magazine, *23.* In 1938 he settled in Switzerland; in 1948, became music critic of the *Neue Zürcher Zeitung.*
WRITINGS: *Alban Berg* (Vienna, 1937; basic biography); *Bekenntnis zu Mozart* (Lucerne, 1945); *Joseph Haydn* (Lucerne, 1946); *Hugo Wolf-Rhapsodie* (Zürich, 1947); *Richard Wagner* (Olten, 1948); *Anton Bruckner: ein Bild seiner Persönlichkeit* (Basel, 1953); edited *Arthur Honegger Nachklang: Schriften, Photos, Dokumente* (Zürich, 1957); *Gustav Mahler im eigenen Wort, im Wort der Freunde* (Zürich, 1958); *Felix Mendelssohn im Spiegel eigener Aussagen und zeitgenössischer Dokumente* (Zürich, 1970).

Reicha, Anton, Czech composer; b. Prague, Feb. 26, 1770; d. Paris, May 28, 1836. Nephew and pupil of **Joseph Reicha** (*recte* **Rejcha;** composer and violinist, leader and later Kapellmeister, of the Electoral orch. at Bonn). From 1788, flutist in the Bonn orch., in which Beethoven was a viola player; 1794-99, piano teacher in Hamburg, writing an opera, and going to Paris in hopes in producing it; but had to content himself with the successful performance of two symphonies. From 1801-08 he lived in Vienna, intimate with Beethoven, and associating with Haydn, Albrechtsberger, and Salieri. After the French invasion he went to Paris; brought out the moderately successful comic operas *Cagliostro* (1810), *Natalie* (1816), and *Sapho* (Dec. 16, 1822); also gained a high reputation as a theorist and teacher (some of his pupils were Liszt, Elwart, Gounod, Lefebvre, and Dancla), and as an instrumental composer. Among his best works are 4

sets of 6 woodwind quintets each (op. 88, 91, 99, 100).
In 1818 he succeeded Méhul as prof. of counterpoint
and fugue at the Paris Cons.; was naturalized in 1829;
succeeded to Boieldieu's chair in the Académie française in 1835.

WRITINGS: *Études ou théories pour le pianoforte,
dirigées d'une manière nouvelle* (1800); *Traité de mélodie, abstraction faite de ses rapports avec l'harmonie* (1814; 2nd ed., 1832); *Cours de composition
musicale* (1818); *Traité de haute composition musicale* (1824, 1826; 2 vols.; edited 1834 by Czerny together with the *Cours de composition musicale* in
German as *Vollständiges Lehrbuch*, 4 vols.); *Art du
compositeur dramatique* (1833); *Petit traité d'harmonie pratique* (n.d).

BIBLIOGRAPHY: J. A. Delaire, *Notice sur Reicha*
(Paris, 1837); E. Bücken, *Anton Reicha; sein Leben
und Kompositionen* (Munich, 1912) and "Beethoven
und A. Reicha," *Die Musik* (March 1913); A. Hnilička,
Portraite (Prague, 1922); J. G. Prod'homme, "From
the Unpublished Autobiography of A. Reicha," *Musical Quarterly* (July 1936); M. Emmanuel, *A. Reicha*
(Paris, 1937).

Reichardt, Johann Friedrich, German composer and
writer; born Königsberg, Nov. 25, 1752; d. Giebichenstein, near Halle, June 27, 1814. A pupil of C. G. Richter (piano and composition) and Veichtner (violin), he
later studied philosophy at the Univs. of Königsberg
and Leipzig; in 1775 obtained the post of Kapellmeister to Frederick the Great. He founded (1783) the
Concerts Spirituels for the performance of new
works, for which he wrote short analytical programs.
Dismissed in 1794 because of his sympathy with the
French Revolution, Reichardt lived in Altona till 1797;
was then appointed inspector of the salt works at Giebichenstein. The French invasion drove him to Danzig
in 1806, and on Jerome Bonaparte's threat to confis-
cate his property Reichardt joined him at Kassel, and
became his court conductor. For Berlin and Potsdam
Reichardt composed numerous Italian and German
operas, incidental music to plays, and German Singspiele, the latter exercising considerable influence on
the development of German opera. As a song composer (cf. Lindner, *Geschichte des deutschen Liedes*)
he ranks high (he set about 60 of Goethe's lyrics to
music); his instrumental music includes 7 symphonies, 14 piano concertos, 2 piano quartets, 6 string
trios, a violin concerto, 11 violin sonatas, 12 piano sonatas, etc. An extremely diligent writer, he edited a
number of musical periodicals and published several
books: *Über die deutsche komische Oper* (1774), *Über
die Pflichten des Ripienviolinisten* (1776), *Briefe eines
aufmerksamen Reisenden, die Musik betreffend* (2
parts; 1774, 1776), *Schreiben über die Berlinische Musik* (1775), *Vertraute Briefe aus Paris* (1804, 1805; 3
parts), *Vertraute Briefe, geschrieben auf einer Reise
nach Wien* (2 vols.; 1810). His autobiography is in the
Berlinische musikalische Zeitung, nos. 55–89 (1805).
His wife **Juliane** (*née* **Benda**; b. Potsdam, May 4, 1752;
d. there, May 11, 1783) was a fine pianist, who also
publ. a number of songs.

BIBLIOGRAPHY: H. M. Schletterer, *J. F. Reichardt.
Sein Leben und seine musikalische Tätigkeit* (Augsburg, 1865; only vol. I publ.); C. Lange, *J. F. Reichardt*

(Halle, 1902); W. Pauli, *J. F. Reichardt. Sein Leben
und seine Stellung in der Geschichte des deutschen
Liedes* (Berlin, 1902); M. Faller, *Reichardt und die Anfänge der musikalischer Journalistik* (Kassel, 1929);
P. Sieber, *Reichardt als Musikästhetiker* (Strasbourg,
1930); H. Dennerlein, *Reichardt und seine Klavierwerke* (Münster, 1930); J. Müller-Blattau, "Musik zur
Goethezeit," *Euphorion* (1930); F. Flössner, *Beiträge
zur Reichardt-Forschung* (Frankfurt, 1933); E. Neuss,
*Das Giebichensteiner Dichterparadies; J. F. Reichardt
und die Herberge der Romantik* (Halle, 1949).

Reichardt, Luise, daughter of **Johann Reichardt;** b.
Berlin, April 11, 1779; d. Hamburg, Nov. 17, 1826. She
composed a number of songs, of which a selection
was publ. by G. Rheinhardt (Munich, 1922).

BIBLIOGRAPHY: M. G. W. Brandt, *Leben der Luise
Reichardt* (Karlsruhe, 1858).

Reichel, Friedrich, German composer; b. Oberoderwitz, Jan. 27, 1833; d. Dresden, Dec. 29, 1889. He studied with Wieck and Rietz in Dresden. Chief among his
32 published works is a *Frühlingssymphonie;* he also
wrote an operetta, *Die geängsteten Diplomaten;* part-
songs for men's voices; and some motets.

Reicher-Kindermann, Hedwig, German dramatic soprano; b. Munich, July 15, 1853; d. Trieste, June 2,
1883. She was a daughter of the baritone **August Kindermann** (1817–91); began her career as a contralto
but later sang soprano. The Wagnerian impresario
Neumann engaged her for his Wagner troupe, and she
successfully performed the roles of Fricka and Brünnhilde. She was married to the playwright Emanuel
Reicher, and adopted a hyphenated name Reicher-
Kindermann in her professional activities. Her early
death was lamented.

BIBLIOGRAPHY: A. Neumann, *Erinnerungen an
Richard Wagner* (Leipzig, 1907; in English, N.Y.,
1908).

Reichert, Arno Julius, German writer on music; b.
Dresden, May 31, 1866; d. there, Feb. 10, 1933. After
studying at the Dresden Cons. he was appointed
teacher of music at the Freimaurer-Institut, Dresden;
1894–1904, taught at R. L. Schneider's Musikschule;
from 1904 head of the music divison of the Dresden
Royal Library. He arranged about 450 folksongs for
chorus; publ. *50 Jahre Sinfonie-Konzerte* (a record of
the works produced in Dresden from 1858–1908) and
*Die Original-Musik-Handschriften der sächsischen
Landesbibliothek* (Leipzig, 1923).

Reichert, Johannes, German conductor and composer; b. Dresden, June 19, 1876; d. Teplitz, Feb. 15,
1942. He was a pupil of Draeseke (1893), and of Ni-
code and Buchmayer (1894–98); in 1896–1900, conductor of the orch. class at the Dresden Musikschule;
1902–06, also répétiteur at the court theater; founded
in 1899 the Volkssingakademie (a mixed chorus recruited exclusively from the working classes);
1905–13, private teacher of the crown prince of Saxony; 1906–22, municipal Musikdirektor in Teplitz-
Schönau; then lived in retirement in Teplitz.

Reichmann, Theodor, German baritone; b. Rostock March 15, 1849; d. Marbach, on Lake Constance, May 22, 1903. He studied voice with Lamperti in Milan; returning to Germany he made his operatic debut in Magdeburg; subsequently sang in Berlin, Strasbourg, Hamburg, and Munich; also made guest appearances at the Metropolitan Opera, N.Y. (1889–91) and at Covent Garden Opera in London. In 1893 he was engaged at the Court Opera in Vienna.

Reichwein, Leopold, Austrian conductor; b. Breslau, May 16, 1878; d. (suicide) Vienna, April 8, 1945. He was theater conductor in Breslau, Mannheim, and Karlsruhe; then on the staff of the Vienna Opera (1913–21); music director of the Gesellschaft der Musikfreunde in Vienna (1921–26); music director in Bochum (1926–38); returned to Vienna in 1938; conducted at the State Opera, and taught conducting at the Vienna Academy. He committed suicide at the end of the war, when he was accused of Nazi affiliations. He was also a composer; wrote the operas *Vasantasena* (Breslau, 1903) and *Die Liebenden von Kandahar* (Breslau, 1907); incidental music to Goethe's *Faust;* songs.

Reid, General John, b. Straloch, Perthshire, Feb. 13, 1721; d. London, Feb. 6, 1807. A musical amateur, he left £52,000 to found a chair of music in Edinburgh Univ., also providing that an annual concert of his own compositions should be given. The "Reid" professors since the foundation (1839) have been John Thomson; Sir Henry Bishop, 1842; Henry Hugh Pearson, 1844; John Donaldson, 1845; Sir Herbert Stanley Oakeley, 1865; Frederick Niecks, 1891; and Donald Francis Tovey, from 1914 until his death in 1940.

Reif, Paul, Czech-American composer; b. Prague, March 23, 1910; d. New York, July 7, 1978. He played violin as a child; studied composition in Vienna with Richard Stöhr and Franz Schmidt, and conducting with Franz Schalk and Bruno Walter; also had lessons with Richard Strauss. In 1941 he emigrated to the U.S., and in 1942 joined the U.S. Intelligence Corps; while with the U.S. Army in North Africa he set to music the soldiers' song *Dirty Gertie from Bizerte,* which was introduced by Josephine Baker in Algiers in April, 1943. Upon his discharge in 1945 he was awarded the Croix de Guerre and the Purple Heart. Returning to the U.S., he was active as an arranger in Hollywood; wrote a number of lightweight pieces (*Petticoat Waltz, Dream Concerto,* etc.); also several song cycles, among them *5 Finger Exercises,* to poems by T. S. Eliot; *Reverence for Life* and *Monsieur le Pélican* as a tribute to Albert Schweitzer; etc. WORKS: *Triple City* for chorus and brass ensemble (N.Y., April 16, 1963); *Requiem to War* for mixed chorus and percussion (N.Y., May 20, 1963); *Birches,* to Robert Frost's words, for voice and orch. (N.Y., Feb. 2, 1965); *Letter from a Birmingham Jail* for mixed chorus and piano, to words by Martin Luther King, Jr. (Howard Univ., Washington, D.C., March 2, 1965); *Philidor's Defense* for chamber orch., inspired by the famous Philidor chess opening: 1. P-K4, P-K4; 2. N-KB3, P-Q3 (N.Y., April 10, 1965); the operas, *Mad Hamlet* (1965) and *Portrait in Brownstone* (N.Y., May

15, 1966); *Pentagram* for piano (1969); *The Artist* (N.Y., April 17, 1972); *The Curse of Mauvais-Air* (N.Y., May 9, 1974); *5 Divertimenti* for 4 strings (1969); *Episodes* for string orch. (1972); Quintet for clarinet, viola, piano, percussion and folk singer (1974); *Duo for Three* for clarinet, cello and mezzo-soprano (1974); *America 1776–1876–1976* for orch., solo guitar, banjo, electric guitar, and vocal quartet (Metropolitan Museum, N.Y., Jan. 24, 1976).

Reimann, Aribert, German pianist and composer; b. Berlin, March 4, 1936. He studied with Blacher and Pepping; then took music courses at the German Academy in Rome; subsequently became active as accompanist. He composed a *Quasimodo Cantata;* an opera *Traumspiel* after Strindberg (Kiel, June 20, 1965); 2 piano concertos: No. 1 (Berlin, Oct. 26, 1962); No. 2 (Nuremberg, Jan. 12, 1973); Cello Concerto (1959); *Nenia* for women's voices (Sprechstimme) and orch. (1968); *Inane,* monologue for soprano and orch. (Berlin, Jan. 8, 1969); *Loqui* for orch. (Saarbrücken, Dec. 5, 1969); *Vogelscheuchen,* ballet (Berlin, Oct. 7, 1970); *Melusine,* opera (Schwetzinger, April 29, 1971); *King Lear,* opera after Shakespeare (Munich, July 9, 1978).

Reimann, Heinrich, German writer on music, son of **Ignaz Reimann;** b. Regersdorf, Silesia, March 14, 1850; d. Berlin, May 24, 1906. He studied music with his father; conducted singing societies in Silesia; in 1887 went to Berlin where he was engaged as a librarian, organ teacher and music critic. He publ. several biographical monographs: *Johannes Brahms* (Berlin, 1897; several subsequent printings); *Hans von Bülow* (Berlin, 1909; posthumous); *Johann Sebastian Bach* (posthumous; Berlin, 1912; completed by Schrader); also brought out an informative memoir, *Musikalische Rückblicke* (2 vols., Berlin, 1900) published a valuable collection of old German songs, arranged for concert performance, *Das deutsche Lied* (4 vols.), the collection *Internationales Volksliederbuch* (3 vols.) and *Das deutsche geistliche Lied* (6 vols.).

Reimann, Ignaz, German church composer; b. Albendorf, Silesia, Dec. 27, 1820; d. Regensdorf, June 17, 1885. Publ. 18 Masses, 4 Requiems, 3 Te Deums, 48 offertories, 40 graduals; many others, also instrumental works, in manuscript.

Reimers, Paul, German tenor; b. Lunden, Schleswig-Holstein, March 14, 1878; d. New York, April 14, 1942. He studied with Georg Henschel in England; made his stage debut as Max in *Der Freischütz* in Hamburg (1903), but did not pursue his operatic career and sang mainly in oratorio. In 1913 he went to America; gave several concerts in programs of German Lieder, and also performed songs of the modern French school.

Rein, Walter, German composer and pedagogue; b. Stotternheim, near Erfurt, Dec. 10, 1893; d. Berlin, June 18, 1955. He studied composition with Erwin Lendvai; joined the Jöde youth movement in music, and wrote many instructive choral works; in 1935 became prof. at the Hochschule für Musik-Erziehung in Berlin (until 1945). His folksong arrangements were publ. in Jöde's *Musikant* and the *Lobeda-Chorbuch.*

Reinach, Théodore, French musicologist; b. St. Germain-en-Laye, July 3, 1860; d. Paris, Oct. 28, 1928. He studied jurisprudence and philology, specializing particularly in Greek studies; was editor of the *Revue des Études Grecques* (1888-1907); his investigations of the nature of Greek music are of importance. He publ. *La Musique grecque* (Paris, 1926); brought out Plutarch's treatise on music (with H. Weil; Paris, 1900) and *Le Second Hymne delphique à Apollon* (with L. Boëllmann; Paris, 1897).

Reinagle, Alexander, important American musician; b. Portsmouth, England (of Austrian parents), baptized April 23, 1756; d. Baltimore, Sept. 21, 1809. He studied in Edinburgh with Raynor Taylor; in London for a time; also visited Lisbon and other Continental cities. From his correspondence he appears to have been an intimate friend of C. P. E. Bach. Came to New York early in 1786, settling in the same year in Philadelphia, where he taught, managed subscription concerts (also in N.Y.), and was active as singer, pianist, conductor, and composer; 1787, introduced 4-hand piano music to America; associated, possibly as harpsichordist, with the Old American Co., and most likely took part in their 1788-89 season in N.Y.; in 1793 he was engaged as musical director of a stock company for the production of plays and comic operas, with Thomas Wignell as general director; also built the New Theatre, which opened on Feb. 2, 1793, with Reinagle acting as composer, singer, and director; later also managed a company in Baltimore. WORKS: *Collection of Most Favorite Scots Tunes with Variations for Harpsichord* (London; probably issued in Glasgow); *6 Sonatas with Accompaniment for Violin* (London, c.1780); *Miscellaneous Quartets* (Philadelphia, 1791); *Concerto on the Improved Pianoforte with Additional Keys* (1794); *Preludes* (1794); accompaniments and incidental music to *The Sicilian Romance* (1795), *The Witches of the Rock,* pantomime (1796), and various English plays; *Masonic Overture* (1800); 4 piano sonatas (in Library of Congress, Washington; Sonata No. 2 publ. in abridged form by J. T. Howard in *A Program of Early American Piano-Music,* N.Y., 1931); *Collection of Favorite Songs;* music to Milton's *Paradise Lost* (incomplete); S. R. Duer, *An Annotated Edition of 4 Sonatas by Alexander Reinagle* (Peabody Cons., 1976). BIBLIOGRAPHY: J. R. Parker, "Musical Reminiscences," *Euterpeiad* (Jan. 19, 1822); O. G. Sonneck, *Early Concert Life in America* (Leipzig, 1907; in English); O. G. Sonneck, *Early Opera in America* (N.Y., 1915); E. C. Krohn, "A. Reinagle As Sonatist," *Musical Quarterly* (Jan. 1932); J. T. Howard, *Our American Music* (N.Y., 1939 and later eds.); O. G. Sonneck and W. T. Upton, *Bibliography of Early Secular American Music* (Washington, 1945); *Sammelbände der Internationalen Musik-Gesellschaft* 11; *Dictionary of American Biography;* C. A. Horton, *Serious Art and Concert Music for Piano in the 100 Years from Alexander Reinagle to Edward MacDowell* (Univ. of North Carolina, 1965).

Reinecke, Carl (Heinrich Carsten), renowned German pianist and composer; b. Altona, June 23, 1824; d. Leipzig, March 10, 1910. He was a pupil of his father, a music teacher. His first concert tour was to Denmark and Sweden in 1843; he then went to Leipzig, learned much through meetings with Mendelssohn and Schumann, made a second tour through North Germany, and was from 1846-48 court pianist to Christian VIII at Copenhagen. Then, after spending some years in Paris, he became teacher at the Cologne Cons. in 1851, music director at Barmen 1854-59, at Breslau, 1859-60, and from 1860-95 conductor of the Gewandhaus Concerts at Leipzig. At the same time he was prof. of piano playing and free composition at the Leipzig Cons. An eminent pianist, he excelled as an interpreter of Mozart, made concert tours almost yearly, and was enthusiastically welcomed in England, Holland, Scandinavia, Switzerland, and throughout Germany; among his pupils were Grieg, Riemann, Sinding, Arthur Sullivan, Karl Muck, and Cosima Wagner. As a composer, and teacher of composition, Reinecke was the leader in Leipzig for a quarter of a century; his numerous works , in every genre, are classic in form and of a refined workmanship. WORKS: the operas *König Manfred* (Wiesbaden, July 26, 1867), *Ein Abenteuer Händels* (Schwerin, 1874), *Auf hohen Befehl* (Hamburg, 1886), *Der Gouverneur von Tours* (Schwerin, 1891); several musical fairy tales, for solos, chorus, and piano: *Nussknacker und Mausekönig, Schneewittchen, Dornröschen, Aschenbrödel, Die wilden Schwäne, Glückskind und Pechvogel,* etc.; the oratorio *Belsazar;* several choral works with orch.: *Sommertagsbilder, Schlachtlied, Der deutsche Sang,* etc.; numerous choruses for mixed voices; for orch.: 3 symphonies, 9 overtures, smaller works; 4 piano concertos; Violin Concerto; Cello Concerto; Harp Concerto; Flute Concerto; chamber music: Octet for wind instruments; Sextet for wind instruments; 6 string quartets; Piano Quintet; 2 piano quartets; 6 piano trios; Trio for piano, oboe, and horn; Trio for piano, clarinet, and horn; Violin Sonata; 3 violin sonatinas; 3 cello sonatas; Sonata for flute and piano; numerous character pieces for piano; Sonata for piano, left hand; a suite, *Biblische Bilder;* 3 sonatas for 2 pianos; altogether about 300 op. numbers. He wrote cadenzas to 42 movements of piano concertos by Bach, Mozart, Beethoven, and Weber; some of these cadenzas are often used. He also wrote the following books: *Was sollen wir spielen?* (1886), *Zur Wiederbelebung der Mozartschen Klavierkonzerte* (1891), *Die Beethovenschen Klaviersonaten* (1896; 9th ed., 1924; in English, 1898), *Und manche liebe Schatten steigen auf* (1900), *Meister der Tonkunst* (1903), *Aus dem Reich der Töne* (1907). BIBLIOGRAPHY: J. von Wasielewski, *Carl Reinecke. Ein Künstlerbild* (Leipzig, 1892); E. Segnitz, *Carl Reinecke* (Leipzig, 1900); M. Steinitzer, *Das Leipziger Gewandhaus im neuen Heim unter Carl Reinecke* (Leipzig, 1924); N. Topusov, *Carl Reinecke; Beiträge zu seinem Leben* (dissertation; Berlin 1943).

Reiner, Fritz, eminent Hungarian conductor; b. Budapest, Dec. 19, 1888; d. New York, Nov. 15, 1963. He studied piano with Thomán and composition with Koessler at the Music Academy in Budapest; concurrently took courses in jurisprudence. He was conductor of the People's Opera in Budapest (1911-14) and of the Court Opera in Dresden (1914-21); subsequently conducted in Hamburg, Berlin, Vienna, Rome and Barcelona. In 1922 he was engaged as music director and conductor of the Cincinnati Symph. Orch.; held this position until 1931 when he became prof. of conducting at the Curtis Institute of Music in Philadelphia; among his students were Leonard Bernstein, Lukas Foss and several other well-known American musicians. In 1936–37 he made guest appearances at Covent Garden Opera, London; between 1935 and 1938 was guest conductor at the San Francisco Opera; from 1938 to 1948 he was conductor and music director of the Pittsburgh Symph. Orch.; in the interim filled engagements at the Metropolitan Opera, N.Y. He achieved the peak of his success as conductor with the Chicago Symph. Orch., which he led from 1953 to 1962; and which he brought up to the point of impeccably fine performance, both in classical and modern music. His striving for perfection created for him the reputation of a ruthless master of the orchestra; he was given to explosions of temper, but musicians and critics agreed that it was because of his uncompromising drive towards the optimum of orchestral playing that the Chicago Symph. Orch. achieved a very high rank among American symphonic organizations.

Reiner, Karel, prominent Czech composer and pianist; b. Žatec, June 27, 1910. He studied law in Prague (Dr. jur., 1933); then attended classes in quarter-tone and sixth-tone composition with Alois Hába at the Prague Cons. (1934–35); was associated with E. F. Burian's improvisational theater in Prague (1934–38). Unable to leave Central Europe when the Nazis invaded Czechoslovakia, he was detained at Terezín, and later sent to the dread camps of Dachau and Auschwitz, but survived, and after liberation resumed his activities as composer and pianist. His earliest works were atonal and athematic; in 1935–36 he wrote a *Suite* and a *Fantasy* for quarter-tone piano, and a set of 5 quarter-tone songs; after 1945 he wrote mostly traditional music; then returned to ultramodern techniques.
WORKS: 2 operas: *Pohádka o zakleté písen (Tale of an Enchanted Song,* 1949) and *Schustermärchen (The Cobbler's Tale* or *The Horrible Dragon, the Princess and the Cobbler),* fairy-tale opera for puppets, 5 singers and chamber ensemble (1972); a ballet, *Jednota (Unity,* 1933); a cantata, *Bylo jim tisíc let (It Was a Thousand Years Since Then,* 1962); Piano Concerto (1932); Violin Concerto (1937); *Concertante Suite* for winds and percussion (1947); *Divertimento* for clarinet, harp, strings and percussion (1947); *3 Czech Dances* for orch. (1949); *Spring Prelude* for orch. (1950); *Motýli tady nežijí (Butterflies Don't Live Here Anymore),* 6 Pictures for orch., based on music to the film (1959–60; depicts the fate of Jewish children in the Terezin concentration camp); Symphony (1960); *Symphonic Overture* (1964); Concerto for Bass Clarinet, Strings and Percussion (1966); *Concertante Suite* for orch. (1967); Bassoon Concertino (1969); *Promluvy (Utterances)* for chamber orch. (1975); *Music for strings* (1975); *Introduction and Allegro* for orch. (1976); 3 string quartets (1931, 1947, 1951); *7 Miniatures* for wind quintet (1931); *Dvanáct (The Twelve),* suite for piano and wind quintet (1931); 2 nonets (Concerto, 1933; *Preambule,* 1974); *Sonata Brevis* for

cello and piano (1946); *4 Compositions* for clarinet and piano (1954); *3 Compositions* for oboe and piano (1955); *Elegie and Capriccio* for cello and piano (1957); Double-Bass Sonata (1957); Violin Sonata (1959); *Small Suite* for 9 wind instruments (1960); *6 Bagatelles* for trumpet and piano (1962); *2 Compositions* for oboe and harp (1962); *4 Compositions* for solo clarinet (1963); *6 Studies* for flute and piano (1964); Trio for flute, bass clarinet and percussion (1964); Piano Trio (1965); *Suite* for bassoon and piano (1965); *Music* for 4 clarinets (1965); *Črty (Sketches)* for piano quartet (1966–67); *Concert Studies* for solo cymbalom (1967); *2 Compositions* for saxophone and piano (1967); *Concertante Sonata* for percussion (1967); *Prolegomena* for string quartet (1968); *4 Abbreviations* for brass quintet (1968); *Dua,* 5 compositions for 2 flutes, 2 oboes, 2 clarinets and 2 trumpets, in any combination (1969); *Volné listy (Loose Leaves)* for clarinet, cello and piano (1969); *Formulas* for trombone and piano (1970); *Recordings* for solo bassoon (1970); *Drawings* for clarinet, horn and piano (1970); *Maxims* for flute quartet (1970); *Tercetti* for oboe, clarinet and bassoon (1971); *Talks* for wind quintet (1971–72); *Akrostichon a Allegro* for bass clarinet and piano (1972); *Duo* for 2 quarter-tone clarinets (1972); *Replicas* for flute, viola and harp (1973); *Sujets* for solo guitar (1973); *Overtura ritmica* for solo guitar (1974); *Strophes* for viola and piano (1975); *9 Merry Improvisations* for piano (1928–29); *5 Jazz Studies* for piano (1930); 3 piano sonatas (1931, 1942, 1961); *Minda-Minda,* 7 compositions for piano (1937); songs.

Reinhardt, Heinrich, Austrian operetta composer; b. Pressburg, April 13, 1865; d. Vienna, Jan. 31, 1922. He studied with Bruckner and Mocker in Vienna; was music critic for several papers.
WORKS: the operettas *Das süsse Mädel* (Vienna, Oct. 25, 1901, his greatest success), *Der liebe Schatz* (Vienna, Oct. 30, 1902), *Der General-Konsul* (Vienna, Jan. 28, 1904), *Krieg im Frieden* (Vienna, Jan. 20, 1906), *Die süssen Grisetten* (Vienna, 1907), *Ein Märchen für alles* (Munich, 1908), *Die Sprudelfee* (Vienna, 1909), *Napoleon und die Frauen* (Vienna, April 28, 1911), *Prinzessin Gretl* (Berlin, 1914), *Des Königs Gäste* (Vienna, 1916), *Die erste Frau* (Munich, 1918); 2 operas, *Die Minnekönigin* and *Der Schuster von Delft;* author of *Die Entwicklung der Operette* and *Virtuosentum und Künstlerschaft.*

Reinhold, Hugo, Austrian composer; b. Vienna, March 3, 1854; d. there, Sept. 4, 1935. He studied piano with Julius Epstein and composition with Bruckner at the Vienna Cons., graduating in 1874; then was engaged as piano teacher at the Akademie der Tonkunst in Vienna. He composed a number of attractive piano pieces, a violin sonata, and songs.

Reinken, Jan Adams, Alsatian organist; one of the foremost among the German masters of his time; b. Wilshausen, April 26, 1623; d. Hamburg, Nov. 24, 1722. In 1654 Reinken studied with Scheidemann in Hamburg; became his assistant and, in 1663, successor as organist at the Katharinenkirche in Hamburg. He composed *Hortus musicus* for 2 violins, viola, and bass (1687), and *Partite diverse.* Some of his pieces were republished by R. Buchmayer, by Seiffert in *Organum,* and by others.

BIBLIOGRAPHY: A. Pirro, "Notes pour servir, éventuellement, à la biographie de Reinken," in the Scheuerleer-Festschrift (1925); id., "Reinken et la musique en Alsace au XVIIᵉ siècle," in *Annuaire* of the Club vosgien (Strasbourg, vol. 3, 1935).

Reinthaler, Karl (Martin), German composer; b. Erfurt, Oct. 13, 1822; d. Bremen, Feb. 13, 1896. He studied with G. A. Ritter and Marx in Berlin, and for 3 years in Rome; taught singing at the Cologne Cons. (1853); from 1857, municipal music director in Bremen.

WORKS: 2 operas, *Edda* (Bremen, 1875) and *Käthchen von Heilbronn* (Frankfurt, 1881); an oratorio, *Jephtha,* repeatedly performed in Germany and elsewhere; the famous *Bismarck Hymne;* choral works; a symph.; songs; psalms.

Reisenauer, Alfred, German pianist and composer; b. Königsberg, Nov. 1, 1863; d. (on a concert tour) Libau, Latvia, Oct. 3, 1907. He was a pupil of Liszt, with whom he was on friendly terms in Rome. Reisenauer traveled as a concert pianist almost in every region of the globe, including Siberia. He published a number of attractive songs to words by Heine, Uhland and Goethe.

BIBLIOGRAPHY: J. Schwerin, *Erinnerungen an Alfred Reisenauer* (Königsberg, 1909).

Reiss, Albert, German dramatic tenor; b. Berlin, Feb. 22, 1870; d. Nice, June 19, 1940. He was an actor before making his debut as a singer in Königsberg (Sept. 28, 1897); then sang in various German towns; on Dec. 23, 1901, made his American debut at the Metropolitan Opera House in the minor roles of the Sailor and Shepherd in *Tristan und Isolde;* then sang more important parts in Wagner's operas. In 1919 he returned to Berlin; in 1938 retired from the stage and lived in Nice.

Reiss, Jósef Wladyslaw, Polish musicologist; b. Dembica, Aug. 4, 1879; d. Cracow, Feb. 22, 1956. He studied musicology with Guido Adler at the Univ. of Vienna; received his Dr. phil. with a dissertation on the Polish composer Gomólka (1912); in 1922 he went to Cracow, where he was prof. of music at Cracow Univ., remaining at that post until 1942. He wrote (in Polish): *The Problem of Meaning in Music* (1915); *A History of Music* (1919); *Beethoven* (1920); *Henryk Wieniawski* (1931); also a manual on form, *Formenlehre,* which appeared in German (Leipzig, 1917).

Reisserová, Julie, Czech composer; b. Prague, Oct. 9, 1888; d. there, Feb. 25, 1938. She studied with J. B. Foerster; also with Albert Roussel in Paris. Among her works are *Pastorale maritime* for orch. (1933); *Esquisses* for piano; several albums of songs.

BIBLIOGRAPHY: J. Vacková, *Julie Reisserová* (Prague, 1948).

Reissiger, Carl Gottlieb, German composer; b. Belzig, near Wittenberg, Jan. 31, 1798; d. Dresden, Nov. 7, 1859. He studied with Schicht at the Thomasschule, Leipzig, from 1811; went to Vienna in 1821 and thence to Munich (1822), pursuing his studies of composition under Winter; taught at the Berlin Royal Institute for Church Music, and in 1826 he succeeded Marschner as music director of the German Opera at Dresden; soon after was appointed court Kapellmeister as Weber's successor. Reissiger was a prolific composer (over 200 op. numbers), writing with great facility, but with little originality. The waltz for piano, *Weber's Last Thought,* long misattributed to Weber, was proved to be a composition by Reissiger; many of his songs also became popular.

BIBLIOGRAPHY: H. Pfiel, *C. G. Reissiger* (1879); K. Kreiser, *C. G. Reissiger* (Dresden, 1918).

Reissmann, August, German writer on music; b. Frankenstein, Silesia, Nov. 14, 1825; d. Berlin, July 13, 1903. He studied in Breslau; in 1850 he went to Weimar where he became a student and an associate of Liszt. He then devoted himself mainly to musical commentary; lived in Berlin (1863–80), where he gave lectures on music history at the Stern Cons.

WRITINGS: *Von Bach bis Wagner* (1861); *Das deutsche Lied in seiner historischen Entwicklung* (Kassel, 1861); *Robert Schumann* (1865; in English, 1886); *Felix Mendelssohn-Bartholdy* (1867); *Schubert* (1873); *Joseph Haydn* (1879); *J. S. Bach* (1881); *Händel* (1882); *Gluck* (1882); *Weber* (1886); contributed to German music encyclopedias. He was also a composer; wrote 3 operas; *Gudrun* (Leipzig, 1871); *Die Bürgermeisterin von Schorndorf* (Leipzig, 1880) and *Gralspiel* (Düsseldorf, 1895); several cantatas; a violin concerto; chamber music; many songs.

BIBLIOGRAPHY: Göllrich, *August Reissmann als Schriftsteller und Komponist* (Leipzig, 1884).

Reiter, Josef, Austrian composer; b. Braunau, Jan. 19, 1862; d. Bad Reichenhall, June 2, 1939. He received his first instruction in music from his father, a town organist; in 1886 went to Vienna, where he became active as a choral conductor; then was director of the Mozarteum in Salzburg (1908–11). He wrote 4 operas: *Der Bundschuh* (Troppau, 1894); *Klopstock in Zürich* (Linz, 1894); *Der Totentanz* (Dessau, 1908); and *Der Tell* (Vienna, 1917); also numerous choruses and solo songs.

BIBLIOGRAPHY: M. Morold, *Josef Reiter* (Vienna, 1904); L. Etzmannsdorfer, *Josef Reiter* (Vienna, 1924).

Reizenstein, Franz, German pianist and composer; b. Nuremberg, June 7, 1911; d. London, Oct. 15, 1968. He studied piano with Leonid Kreutzer and composition with Hindemith at the Hochschule für Musik in Berlin (1930–34); with the advent of the anti-Semitic Nazi regime he went to England; entered the Royal College of Music in London and studied with Lambert and Vaughan Williams (1934–36); also took private piano lessons with Solomon (1938–40). He was then instructor in piano at the Royal Academy (1958–64), and from 1964 to his death at the Royal Manchester College. He wrote music of fine neo-Romantic quality.

WORKS: 2 radio operas: *Men Against the Sea* (1949) and *Anna Kraus* (1952); *Genesis,* oratorio (1958); *Voices of Night,* cantata (1950–51); Cello Concerto (1936); *Prologue, Variations and Finale* for violin and orch. (1938; originally for violin and piano); 2 piano concertos: No. 1 (1941) and No. 2 (1956–61; London, June 7, 1961; composer as soloist); *Cyrano de Bergerac,* overture (1951); *Serenade in F* for wind ensemble and double bass, or for small orch. (1951); Violin Concerto (1953); Concerto for string orch. (1966–67; London, Jan. 17, 1969); Sonata for cello solo (1931; revised in 1967); *Theme, Variations and Fugue* for clarinet quintet (1932, revised 1960); Wind Quintet (1934); *Divertimento* for string or brass quartet (1936–37); Oboe Sonatina (1937); *Partita* for flute and string trio (1938); Violin Sonata (1945); Cello Sonata (1947); Piano Quintet (1948); Trio for flute, oboe, and piano (1949); *Fantasia Concertante* for violin and piano (1956); Trio for flute, clarinet, and bassoon (1963); *Concert Fantasy* for viola and piano (1956); Sonata for viola solo (1967); Sonata for violin solo (1968); 2 piano sonatas (1944, 1964).

Relfe, John, English theorist and composer; b. Greenwich, 1763; d. London, c.1837. Member of the King's Band, 1810; also an esteemed teacher of piano and harmony.
WORKS: airs, sonatas, lessons, divertimentos, etc., for harpsichord or piano; songs; *Guida Armonica* (3 parts, 1798; 2nd ed. as *The Principles of Harmony* 1817); *Remarks on the Present State of Musical Instruction* (1819); *Lucidus ordo* (1821). He proposed a reformed thoroughbass figuring, marking the root chord *r.,* and the inversions *'* and *".*

Rellstab, Johann Karl Friedrich, German writer on music; b. Berlin, Feb. 27, 1759; d. there, Aug. 19, 1813. Pupil of Agricola and Fasch; succeeded his father as head of a printing establishment, adding a music printing and publishing department and a circulating library of music; founded short-lived amateur concerts in 1787; lost his property in the war of 1806, and gave music lessons, lectured on harmony, and wrote criticisms for the *Vossische Zeitung.* His compositions are unimportant.
WRITINGS: *Versuch über die Vereinigung der musikalischen und oratorischen Deklamation* (Vienna, 1785); *Anleitung für Klavierspieler, den Gebrauch der Bach'schen Fingersetzung, die Manieren und den Vortrag betreffend* (1790); a polemical pamphlet, *Über die Bemerkungen eines Reisenden* [Reichardt], *die Berlinischen Kirchenmusiken, Konzerte, Opern und die königliche Kammermusik betreffend* (1789).
BIBLIOGRAPHY: O. Guttmann, *J. K. F. Rellstab* (Berlin, 1910).

Rellstab (Heinrich Friedrich) Ludwig, the noted novelist, son of **Johann Karl Friedrich Rellstab;** b. Berlin, April 13, 1799; d. there, Nov. 27, 1860. Artillery officer, teacher of mathematics and history in the Brigade School, Berlin, retired from the army in 1821, and lived as a writer in Berlin from 1823. Editor and music critic of the *Vossische Zeitung* (1826–48). Publ. the satirical pamphlets *Henriette, oder die schöne Sängerin, eine Geschichte unserer Tage von Freimund Zuschauer* (1826; on Henriette Sontag's triumphs), and *Über mein Verhältniss als Critiker zu Herrn*

Spontini als Componisten und General-Musikdirector in Berlin, nebst einem vergnüglichen Anhang (1827; directed against Spohr's truckling to virtuosity in *Agnes von Hohenstaufen*), for each of which he suffered a period of imprisonment, though his opinions were eventually upheld in official circles and by the public. Between 1830 and 1841 Rellstab edited a musical periodical, *Iris im Gebiet der Tonkunst;* he also contributed to several other papers. In his *Gesammelte Schriften* are biographies of Liszt, Ludwig Berger, Bernhard Klein, Nanette Schechner, and others; vol. I contains criticisms, on opera and concert, which came out in the *Vossische Zeitung* 1826–48. He wrote an autobiography, *Aus meinem Leben* (1861, 2 vols.).
BIBLIOGRAPHY: L. R. Blengert, *L. Rellstab* (Leipzig, 1918).

Remenkov, Stefan, Bulgarian composer; b. Silistra, April 30, 1923. He studied piano with Nenov and composition with Pantcho Vladigerov and Veselin Stoyanov at the Bulgarian State Cons. in Sofia, graduating in 1950; later took a course with Khachaturian at the Moscow Cons.
WORKS: an operertta, *The Errors are Ours* (1966); 2 children's operettas, *Ghanem* (1967) and *The Prince and the Pauper* (1973); a ballet, *The Unvanquished* (1960); 2 piano concertos (1953, 1970); *Prelude and Dance* for string orch. (1957); 4 symphonies: No. 1, *Children's Symphony* (1961), No. 2, *Symphony in the Classical Style* (1962), No. 3 (1965); and No. 4 (1968); Cello Concerto (1964); Concertino for Flute and String Orch. (1973); *Fantasy* for violin and orch. (1974); Violin Sonata (1955); Nonet; 3 piano sonatas (1944, 1948, 1949).

Reményi, Eduard, eminent Hungarian violinist; b. Miskolc, July 17, 1830; d. San Franciso, May 15, 1898. He studied with Böhm at the Vienna Cons. (1842–45). Banished from Austria for participation in the Hungarian Revolution of 1848, he began the career of a wandering violinist in America; returned to Europe in 1853, and in 1854 became solo violinist to Queen Victoria. In 1860 he was amnestied, and appointed solo violinist to the Austrian Count; in 1865, commenced a brilliant tour, visiting Paris, Germany, Belgium, and Holland; then proceeded to London (1877), and to America in 1878, traveling in the U.S., Canada, and Mexico; in 1886 he began a new concert tour around the world, visiting Japan, China, and South Africa. Some notes on his trip to the Far East are in the N.Y. Public Library. He collapsed suddenly while playing the pizzicato from the *Sylvia* suite of Delibes at a San Francisco concert, and died of apoplexy. His technique was prodigious; in vigor, passion, and pathos he was unexcelled. He made skilful transcriptions of Chopin's Waltzes, Polonaises, and Mazurkas, and pieces by Bach, Schubert, etc.; these are united under the title of *Nouvelle École du violin.* He was also a natural performer of Gypsy music; Liszt profited very much by his help in supplying and arranging authentic Gypsy tunes. He composed a violin concerto, and some solos for violin.
BIBLIOGRAPHY: G. Kelley and G. Upton, *Eduard Reményi. Musician, Littérateur, and Man* (Chicago, 1906); E. Sas, *Reményi* (Budapest, 1934).

Remoortel, Edouard van, Belgian conductor; b. Brussels, May 30, 1926; d. Paris, May 16, 1977. He studied at the Brussels Cons., and took a course in conducting with Josef Krips. From 1951 on he was the principal conductor of the Belgian National Orch.; in 1958 was appointed music director and conductor of the St. Louis Symph. Orch., retaining this post until 1963. In 1965 he went to Monte Carlo as artistic consultant to the Orchestre National de l'Opéra of Monaco.

Rémusat, Jean, French flutist; b. Bordeaux, May 11, 1815; d. Shanghai, Sept. 1, 1880. He studied with Tulou. After successful concert giving, he became 1st flutist at the Queen's Theatre, London; from 1853 was flutist at the Théâtre-Lyrique, Paris. He publ. a flute method and solo pieces for flute.

Remy, Alfred, American music lexicographer; b. Elberfeld, Germany, March 16, 1870; d. New York, Feb. 26, 1937. He emigrated to the U.S. in 1882; studied piano and violin; lectured on music history and on languages at various schools in N.Y. and Brooklyn; from 1906 to 1915 was on the music staff of Columbia Univ. He contributed articles to various American reference works and was editor-in-chief of the 3rd edition of *Baker's Biographical Dictionary of Musicians* (N.Y., 1919).

Rémy, Guillaume, Belgian violinist; b. Ougrée, Aug. 26, 1856; d. Nantes, France, June 16, 1932. He studied at the Cons. of Liège; graduated in 1873 sharing the first prize with Ysaÿe; continued his studies under Massart at the Paris Cons.; awarded first prize in 1878. Settling in Paris, he became concertmaster of the Colonne Orch., frequently appearing as a soloist. From 1885 to 1930 he was prof. at the Paris Cons.; played recitals with Saint-Saëns and Gabriel Fauré at the piano. He also formed a string quartet. During the last years of his life he was head of the violin department of the American Cons. at Fontainebleau.

Renaud, Maurice, French baritone; b. Bordeaux, July 24, 1861; d. Paris, Oct. 16, 1933. He studied in Paris and Brussels; sang at the Théâtre de la Monnaie, Brussels (1883-90); at the Opéra-Comique, Paris (1890-91); and the Paris Opéra (1891-1902). He made his American debut in New Orleans, on Jan. 4, 1893. From 1906 till 1909 he sang at the Manhattan Opera House, where he became a favorite; then appeared in Chicago for a season, and at the Metropolitan Opera House (1910-12); thereafter, was active chiefly in France. He sang baritone and bass parts in some 60 operas.

Renié, Henriette, eminent French harpist and composer; b. Paris, Sept. 18, 1875; d. there, March 1, 1956. She studied with Alphonse Hasselmans at the Paris Cons.; received 1st prize for harp at the age of 11; then entered the classes of Lenepveu and Dubois in harmony and composition. She performed her own Concerto for Harp and Orch. at the Concerts Lamoureux, Paris, on March 24, 1901; further wrote *Pièce symphonique*, for harp and orch.; *Légende et Danse caprice*, for harp and orch.; publ. numerous pieces for harp solo: *Promenades matinales, Feuilles d'au-*tomne, Ballade fantastique, Légende, Contemplation, Défile lilliputien, Danse des lutins*, etc.; Trio for harp, violin, and cello; Trio for harp, flute, and bassoon; several songs. She taught for many years at the Paris Cons.; among her students was Marcel Grandjany.

Renner, Josef, German choral conductor; b. Schmatzhausen, near Landshut, Bavaria, April 25, 1832; d. Regensburg, Aug. 11, 1895. He received his primary music education from his father; was a choral conductor in Regensburg (1858-92) and organized the Regensburg Madrigal Quartet with the purpose of reviving authentic performances of German part-songs of the Renaissance. He published several valuable collections of German madrigals: *Auswahl deutscher Madrigale von Meistern des 16. Jahrhundert, Neue Regensburger Sängerhalle, Regensburger Oberquartette, Mutter Donau*, and *Männerquartette von der Donau* (242 numbers in all).

Resinarius, Balthasar, German composer; b. Tetschen, c.1486; d. Böhmisch-Leipa, April 12, 1544. He was a choirboy in the court chapel of Emperor Maximilian; then became Bishop of Leipa, Bohemia. He was one of most important early Protestant composers of sacred music. He brought out 118 "Responsories" (Wittenberg, 1543; 80 printed by Rhaw and reprinted by Bärenreiter and Concordia, 1957); 30 choral pieces in Rhaw's *Neue deutsche geistliche Gesenge für die gemeinen Schulen* (1544; edited by J. Wolf in *Denkmäler deutscher Tonkunst* 39); 4 motets in *Offices* collected by Rhaw; 3 bicinia, in Rotenbucher's *Diphona amoena et florida* (Nuremberg, 1549).

BIBLIOGRAPHY: I. M. Schröder, *Die Responsorienvertonungen des Balthasar Resinarius* (Kassel, 1954).

Resnik, Regina, American soprano; b. New York, Aug. 30, 1922. She studied in New York; made her concert debut at the Brooklyn Academy of Music (Oct. 27, 1942); sang in opera in Mexico (1943); won an annual audition at the Metropolitan Opera in 1944, and appeared there in *Il Trovatore* (Dec. 6, 1944); sang the leading part in Beethoven's *Fidelio* (March 17, 1945). In 1953 she appeared in Bayreuth as Sieglinde. Later, she sang mezzo-soprano parts; appeared as Marina in *Boris Godunov* at the Metropolitan Opera, on Feb. 15, 1956. She married Harry W. Davis, a lawyer, in New York, on July 16, 1946.

Respighi, Ottorino, eminent Italian composer; b. Bologna, July 9, 1879; d. Rome, April 18, 1936. He studied violin with F. Sarti at the Liceo Musicale of Bologna; composition with L. Torchi and G. Martucci. In 1900 he went to Russia, and played 1st viola in the orch. of the Imperial Opera in St. Petersburg; there he took lessons with Rimsky-Korsakov, which proved a decisive influence in Respighi's coloristic orchestration. From 1903 to 1908 he was active as a concert violinist; also played the viola in the Mugellini Quartet of Bologna. In 1913 he was engaged as prof. of composition at the Santa Cecilia in Rome; in 1923, appointed its director, but resigned in 1925, retaining only a class in advanced composition; subsequently devoted himself to composing and conducting. He was elected a member of the Italian Royal Academy on March 23, 1932. In 1925–26 and again in 1932 he made tours of the U.S. as pianist and conductor.

His style of composition is a highly successful blend of songful melodies with full and rich harmonies; he was one of the best masters of modern Italian music in orchestration. His power of evocation of the Italian scene and his ability to sustain interest without prolixity is incontestable. Although he wrote several operas, he achieved his greatest success with 2 symph. poems, *Le Fontane di Roma* and *I Pini di Roma*, each consisting of 4 tone paintings of the Roman lanscape; a great innovation for the time was the insertion in the score of *I Pini di Roma* of a phonograph recording of a nightingale.

WORKS: OPERAS: *Re Enzo* (Bologna, March 12, 1905); *Semirama*, lyric tragedy in 3 acts (Bologna, Nov. 20, 1910); *La bella addormentata nel bosco*, musical fairy tale (Rome, April 13, 1922, performed by Vittorio Podrecca's marionettes, Teatro dei Piccoli, with singers off stage); *Belfagor*, lyric comedy (Milan, April 26, 1923); *La Campana sommersa*, after Hauptmann's *Die versunkene Glocke* (Hamburg, Nov. 18, 1927); *Maria Egiziaca*, mystery play in 1 act (N.Y., March 16, 1932); *La Fiamma* (Rome, Jan. 23, 1934); a free transcription of Monteverdi's *Orfeo* (Milan, March 16, 1935); *Lucrezia* (posthumous, Milan, Feb. 24, 1937). BALLETS: *La Boutique Fantasque*, on themes by Rossini (London, June 5, 1919); *Scherzo veneziano* (Rome, Nov. 27, 1920); *Belkis, regina di Saba* (Milan, Jan. 23, 1932). FOR ORCH.: *Notturno* (1905); *Sinfonia drammatica* (1915); *Fontane di Roma*, symph. poem in 4 movements (Rome, March 11, 1917); *Antiche arie e danze per liuto*, 3 sets, the 3rd for string orch. (1916; 1923; 1931); *Ballata delle gnomidi* (Rome, April 11, 1920); *I Pini di Roma*, symph. poem in 4 movements (Rome, Dec. 14, 1924); *Rossiniana*, suite from Rossini's piano pieces (1925); *Vetrate di chiesa*, symph. impressions in 4 movements (Boston, Feb. 25, 1927); *Impressioni brasiliane*, symph. suite (1927; composed for Respighi's Brazilian tour and conducted by him for the first time in São Paulo, June 16, 1928); *Trittico Botticelliano*, for chamber orch. (commissioned by E. S. Coolidge; 1927); *Gli Uccelli*, suite for small orch. on themes by Rameau, B. Pasquini, and others (1927); *Feste romane*, symph. poem in 4 movements (N.Y. Philharmonic, Toscanini conducting, Feb. 21, 1929); *Metamorphoseon modi XII*, theme and variations (commissioned by the Boston Symph.; Boston, Nov. 7, 1930); *Concerto gregoriano*, for violin and orch. (Rome, Feb. 5, 1922); *Concerto in modo misolidio*, for piano and orch. (N.Y., Dec. 31, 1925, composer soloist); *Concerto a cinque*, for violin, oboe, trumpet, double bass, piano and strings (1932). CHORAL WORKS: *La Primavera*, cantata for soloists, chorus, and orch. (Rome, March 4, 1923) and *Lauda per la Natività del Signore*, for soloists, chorus, and orch. (1930). CHAMBER MUSIC: 11 pieces for violin and piano (1904–07); String Quartet in D major (1907); *Quartetto dorico*, for string quartet (1924); *Il Tramonto*, after Shelley, for mezzo-soprano and string quartet (1917); Violin Sonata (1917). Also *Huntingtower Ballad*, for band (Sousa memorial concert, Washington, April 17, 1932); 45 songs; 3 vocalises without words; arrangements of works by Monte-

verdi, Vitali, Pergolesi, Cimarosa, Marcello, etc., and of several *Etudes Tableaux* by Rachmaninoff; co-author, with S. A. Luciani, of *Orpheus: iniziazione musicale, storia della musica* (Florence, 1925).

His wife, **Elsa Olivieri Sangiacomo Respighi** (b. Rome, March 24, 1894), was his pupil; wrote a fairy opera, *Fior di neve*, the symph. poem *Serenata di maschere*, and numerous songs; was also a concert singer herself. She publ. Respighi's biography, *Ottorino Respighi: Dati biografici ordinati* (Milan, 1954; in English; London, 1962).

BIBLIOGRAPHY: S. A. Luciani, in the *Bolletino Bibliografico Musicale* (1926); M. Saint-Cuy, "Ottorino Respighi," in *Musicisti contemporanei* (1932); M. Mila, "Probleme di gusto ed arte in Ottorino Respighi," *Rassegna Musicale* (1933); R. de Rensis, *Ottorino Respighi* (Turin, 1935).

Restori, Antonio, Italian musicologist; b. Pontremoli, Massa Carrara, Dec. 10, 1859; d. Genoa, June 30, 1928. He studied philology at the Univ. of Bologna, and taught in secondary schools in various Italian cities; from 1897 prof. of Romance languages at the Univ. of Messina. He publ. *Notazione musicale dell'antichissima Alba bilingue* (1892); *Musica allegra di Francia nei secoli XII e XIII* (1893); *La Gaîé de la Tor, aubade del secolo XIII* (1904); "La Musique des chansons françaises," in Juleville's *Histoire de la langue et de la littérature françaises* (1895).

Reszke, Édouard de. See **De Reszke, Édouard.**

Reszke, Jean de. See **De Reszke, Jean.**

Rethberg, Elisabeth (real name **Elisabeth Sättler**), German soprano; b. Schwarzenberg, Sept. 22, 1894; d. Yorktown Heights, N.Y., June 6, 1976. She studied piano and voice in Dresden; joined the Dresden State Opera at the age of 21, and was on its staff from 1915 to 1922; then went to the U.S. and made her American debut as Aida at the Metropolitan Opera, N.Y. (Nov. 22, 1922), remaining on its staff until 1942. She subsequently embarked on a grand concert tour with Ezio Pinza in the U.S., Europe and Australia; their close association resulted in a lawsuit for alienation of affection brought by Ezio Pinza's wife against her, but the court action was not pursued. Elisabeth Rethberg was married twice: first to Ernst Albert Dormann, from whom she was divorced, and then to **George Cehanovsky**, the singer, whom she married in 1956.

BIBLIOGRAPHY: H. Henschel and E. Friedrich, *Elisabeth Rethberg* (Schwarzenberg, 1928).

Réti, Rudolf, outstanding American composer and theorist; b. Užice, Serbia, Nov. 27, 1885; d. Montclair, N.J., Feb. 7, 1957. He studied at the Cons. of Vienna; took early interest in new music and was one of the founders of the International Society for Contemporary Music (Salzburg, 1922). In 1938 he came to the U.S.; in 1943 married the Canadian pianist, **Jean Sahlmark;** in 1950 they settled in Montclair, N.J. His compositions are marked by precise structure and fine stylistic unity. Among his works are *Symphonia mystica* (1951); *Triptychon* for orch. (1953); Concertino for Cello and Orch. (1953); 2 piano concertos; Violin

Sonata; several choruses and solo songs; piano pieces. An original music analyst, he published several books which contributed to the development of logical theory of modern music: *The Thematic Process in Music* (N.Y., 1952); *Tonality, Atonality, Pantonality* (posthumous, N.Y., 1958); *Thematic Patterns in Sonatas of Beethoven* (posthumous; brought out by D. Cooke, London, 1965).

Rettich, Wilhelm, German composer and conductor; b. Leipzig, July 3, 1892. He studied at the Leipzig Cons. with Max Reger; was in the German Army in World War I and was taken prisoner by the Russians; sent to Siberia, he made his way to China after the Russian Revolution and eventually returned to Leipzig; occupied various posts as theater conductor; was music director of the local synagogue until 1933, when the advent of the Nazi regime forced him to leave Germany; he went to Holland and became a naturalized Dutch citizen. In 1964 he returned to Germany and lived in Baden-Baden. As a composer he excelled in symphonic and chamber music; wrote 3 symphonies; Violin Concerto; Piano Concerto; much chamber music for various combinations; piano pieces and songs.

Reubke, Adolf, German organ builder at Hausneindorf, near Quedlinburg; b. Halberstadt, Dec. 6, 1805; d. there, March 3, 1875. He built the great organ in the cathedral of Magdeburg, with 88 stops, and one at the Jacobikirche with 53 stops. His son **Emil Reubke** (1836–1885) inherited his firm and introduced various improvements, such as pneumatic tubes. Another son of Adolf Reubke, **Julius** (b. Hausneindorf, March 23, 1834; d. Pillnitz, June 3, 1858) was a fine pianist and a favorite pupil of Liszt; his death at the age of 24 was a great loss to music. His few compositions show considerable talent; his organ sonata is still played. **Otto Reubke,** the youngest son of Adolf Reubke (b. Hausneindorf, Nov. 2, 1842; d. Halle, May 18, 1913), was a pupil of Hans von Bülow; for many years he directed the Robert Franz Singakademie in Halle (1867–1911).

Reuchsel, Amédée, French organist; b. Lyons, March 21, 1875; d. Montereau (Loire), July 10, 1931. He studied organ with J. Dupont and harmony with A. Mailly and E. Tinel at the Brussels Cons.; then went to Paris where he became a student of Gabriel Fauré. He published *Théorie abrégée de la musique* and *L'Éducation musicale populaire,* and edited the collection *Solfège classique et moderne* for the Paris Cons. (18 books).

Reuchsel, Maurice, French violinist and composer, brother of **Amédée Reuchsel;** b. Lyons, Nov. 22, 1880; d. there, July 12, 1968. He studied with his father; after concerts in France and Italy, he returned to Lyons, where he taught violin. He published *La Musique à Lyon* (1903), *L'École classique du violon* (1905); and *Un Violoniste en voyage* (1907).

Reuling, (Ludwig) Wilhelm, German conductor and composer; b. Darmstadt, Dec. 22, 1802; d. Munich, April 19, 1879. He studied with Rinck and Seyfried; was theater conductor in Vienna (1829–54). He composed 37 operas and operettas, and 17 ballets, produced mostly in Vienna; in addition, he wrote overtures, chamber music, and songs. A complete list of his operas produced in Vienna, with dates of premières, is found in Anton Bauer, *Opern und Operetten in Wien* (Vienna, 1955).

Reusner (Reussner), Esajas, German lute player and composer; b. Löwenberg, Silesia, April 29, 1636; d. Berlin, May 1, 1679. He was a pupil of his father, a lutenist, and at the age of 15 was engaged as musician to Countess Radziwill in Breslau; at 19, lutenist at Brieg; in 1674 became lutenist at the court of the Elector of Brandenburg in Berlin. He publ. several suites for the lute: *Deliciae testudinis* (1667; new ed., 1697, as *Erfreuliche Lautenlust); Neue Lautenfrüchte* (1676); a book of 100 religious melodies arranged for the lute, and publ. in tablature (1678). Reprints of suites and chorale settings by Reusner are in the *Reichsdenkmale,* vol. 12.

BIBLIOGRAPHY: A. Sparmann, *Esaias Reusner und die Lautensuite* (dissertation, Berlin, 1926); K. Koletschka, "E. Reussner der Jüngere und seine Bedeutung für die deutsche Lautenmusik des XVII. Jahrhunderts," *Studien zur Musikwissenschaft* (1928).

Reuss, August, German composer; b. Liliendorf, Moravia, March 6, 1871; d. Munich, June 18, 1935. Pupil of L. Thuille in Munich; after a brief activity as Kapellmeister in Augsburg (1906) and Magdeburg (1907) he lived in Berlin; then in Munich; 1927, co-director of the Trapp Music School; 1929, prof. at the Akademie der Tonkunst. His works include a comic opera, *Herzog Philipps Brautfahrt* (Graz, 1909); a piano concerto; a string quartet; etc.

Reuss, Eduard, German music pedagogue and critic; b. New York, Sept. 16, 1851; d. Dresden Feb. 18, 1911. He went to Germany as a child, and became a student of Liszt in Weimar; also studied composition with Savard in Paris (1876–77); from 1880 to 1896 he was a music teacher at Karlsruhe, and from 1896 to 1902 in Wiesbaden. He was married to the singer **Luise Reuss-Belce** whom he accompanied on her American tour during the season 1902–03; then returned to Dresden. He published several books on Liszt: *Franz Liszt. Ein Lebensbild* (1898), *Liszts Lieder* (1906); and *Franz Liszt in seinen Briefen* (1911).

Reuss, Wilhelm Franz, German conductor; son of **Eduard Reuss** and **Luise Reuss-Belce;** b. Karlsruhe, March 17, 1886; d. in a Russian prisoner-of-war camp, Königsberg, May 15, 1945. He studied music theory with Draeseke and Max von Schillings; filled in conducting engagements in Berlin (1923–27) and Kassel (1927–33); in 1935 went to Königsberg.

Reuss-Belce, Luise, Austrian soprano; b. Vienna, Oct. 24, 1860; d. Aibach, Germany, March 5, 1945 (was found dead in a refugee train during the last months of the war). She studied voice in Vienna; made her debut as Elsa in *Lohengrin* in Karlsruhe (1881); then sang in Bayreuth (1882) and in Wiesbaden (1896–99); her subsequent appearances were at Covent Garden, London (1900) and at the Metropolitan Opera House in N.Y., where she sang Wagner parts (1902–03); from

1903 to 1911 she was an opera singer in Dresden. In 1885 she married **Eduard Reuss;** after his death in 1911 she moved to Berlin where she established a singing school. In 1913 she was appointed stage manager at the festival opera performances in Nuremberg; she was the first woman to occupy such a post in Germany.

Reuter, Florizel von, American composer and violinist; b. Davenport, Iowa, Jan. 21, 1890; He studied violin with César Thomson in Brussels and Henri Marteau in Geneva; after a brief concert career, he settled in Munich (1934). His opera *Postmaster Wynn*, after Pushkin's tale, was produced in Berlin in 1947. He eventually returned to America, where he was active as a composer and writer; among his works are a *Rumanian Rhapsody* for orch. (1966) and some chamber music. He published a manual, *Führer durch die Solo-Violinmusik* (Berlin, 1926), and *Psychical Experiences of a Musician* (London).

Reutter, (Johann Adam Karl) Georg von, Jr., Austrian composer; son of **Georg von Reutter, Sr.;** b. Vienna, April 6, 1708; d. there, March 11, 1772. He studied with his father, and upon the latter's death (1738) succeeded him as Kapellmeister at St. Stephen's Cathedral in Vienna. He became 2nd court Kapellmeister in 1746 (the 1st being Antonio Predieri), and acting 1st Kapellmeister in 1751 (after Predieri's retirement). In 1740 he was ennobled by Maria Theresa with the title "Edler von Reutter." He wrote several operas, oratorios, and much church music; a Mass, a Requiem, etc. are in the *Denkmäler der Tonkunst in Österreich* 88; a symphony, *Servizio di tabula,* in vol. 31 (15.ii). Reutter was the choir leader who engaged young Haydn as a chorister at St. Stephen's and who, according to some accounts, treated him harshly.
BIBLIOGRAPHY: N. Hofer, *Die beiden Reutter als Kirchenkomponisten* (Vienna, 1915).

Reutter, Georg von, Sr., Austrian organist and composer; b. Vienna, 1656; d. there, Aug. 29, 1738. He was a pupil of Johann Casper Kerll; in 1686, became organist at St. Stephen's Cathedral in Vienna; from 1697 to 1703, theorbo player at the Imperial Court Chapel. In 1700 he became court and chamber organist, and in 1715, 1st Kapellmeister at St. Stephen's Cathedral, a post that he held until his death. The ricercar and 6 capriccios publ. under his name in the *Denkmäler der Tonkunst in Österreich* 27 (13.ii) are really by Strungk.
BIBLIOGRAPHY: N. Hofer, *Die beiden Reutter als Kirchenkomponisten* (Vienna, 1915); G. Frotscher, *Geschichte des Orgelspiels* (Berlin, 1934–35; vol. I).

Reutter, Hermann, outstanding German composer; b. Stuttgart, June 17, 1900. He studied piano and cello in Stuttgart and singing and composition at the Munich Academy of Arts; in 1923 began a concert career as a pianist; made numerous concert tours with the singer Sigrid Onegin (1930–40) including 7 separate tours in the U.S. Returning to Germany, he dedicated himself to composition and teaching. He was for many years (1932–66) prof. of composition at the Hochschule für

Musik in Stuttgart; conducted a seminar in song composition; gave similar courses in Scandinavia. In 1971 he traveled as visiting prof. in the U.S. and Japan. In appreciation of his service to music he received a "Festschrift der Freunde," *Hermann Reutter, Werk und Wirken* (Mainz, 1965), on his 65th anniversary. As a composer, Reutter follows the traditional line of German neo-Classicism, in which the basic thematic material, often inspired by German folk music, is arranged along strong contrapuntal lines, wherein a dissonant intervallic fabric does not disrupt the sense of immanent tonality.
WORKS: OPERAS: *Saul* (Baden-Baden, July 15, 1928), *Der verlorene Sohn,* after André Gide (Stuttgart, March 20, 1929), *Doktor Johannes Faust* (Frankfurt, May 26, 1936), *Odysseus* (Frankfurt, Oct. 7, 1942), *Der Weg nach Freundschaft,* subtitled *Ballade der Landstrasse* (Göttingen, Jan. 25, 1948), *Don Juan und Faust* (Stuttgart, June 11, 1950), *The Bridge of San Luis Rey,* after Thornton Wilder's novel (Frankfurt Radio, June 20, 1954), *Die Witwe von Ephesus* (Cologne, June 23, 1954), *Der Tod des Empedokles,* scenic concerto in one act (Schwetzinger, May 29, 1966). VOCAL WORKS: oratorio, *Der grosse Kalender* (1933), *Der glückliche Bauer,* canata (1944), *Pandora* (1949), *Die Rückkehr des verlorenen Sohnes,* chamber oratorio after André Gide, being a new version of the opera *Der verlorene Sohn* (Munich, Feb. 15, 1952); *Spanischer Totentanz* for 2 voices and orch., after García Lorca (1953); *Ein kleines Requiem* for bass, cello and piano (1961); a triptychon, *St. Sebastian* (1968); *Der Himmlische Vagant,* a lyrical portrait of François Villon, for 2 voices and instruments (Donaueschingen Music Festival, Oct. 6, 1951). FOR ORCH.: *Prozession,* for cello and orch. (Wiesbaden, Dec. 6, 1957); 5 piano concertos; Violin Concerto; String Quartet; Violin Sonata; Cello Sonata; *Fantasia apocalyptica,* for piano; *Antagonismus,* for 2 pianos; 3 vols. of Russian songs, arranged and harmonized; other minor pieces. He brought out an anthology of contemporary art songs, *Das zeitgenössische Lied* (4 vols., Mainz, 1969).
BIBLIOGRAPHY: Karl Laux, *Musik und Musiker der Gegenwart* (Essen, 1949; pp. 203–15).

Revelli, William D., American band leader and prime developer of modern U.S. university bands; b. Spring Gulch, near Aspen, Colorado, Feb. 12, 1902. The family moved to Southern Illinois, near St. Louis, when he was an infant; he began to study the violin at the age of 5; later he was a pupil of Dominic Sarli. He was graduated from the Chicago Musical College in 1919. After playing violin professionally in the Chicago area, he became in 1925 the leader of the Hobart, Indiana, High School Band, which he in time built to national prominence, winning the high school band championship for 6 consecutive years. In 1935 he was made Director of the Univ. of Michigan Band at Ann Arbor, and was also in charge of its Wind Instruments Dept. Over the next 36 years he developed his band into 7 independent groups of players and the Wind Dept. into a body of 14 specialist teachers. Revelli's Symphony Band toured the country many times and made several trips abroad under State Department auspices, most notably a 16-week tour in early 1961 that took it to the Soviet Union, Bulgaria, Turkey, Egypt, and other countries in the Mid-East. In 1971 Revelli became Director Emeritus of the Univ. of Michigan Bands. As instructor and promoter of bands within the U.S. academic system, Revelli continued the tradition of Fillmore and A. A. Harding. He was the recipient of many awards, and was active as editor, adviser, and administrator of the various undertakings in the American band field; he was also founder of the College Band Directors National Association (1941) and was its honorary Life President; received honorary doctoral degrees from 5 American universities.

Révész, Géza, Hungarian specialist in musical psychology; b. Siófek, Dec. 9, 1878; d. Amsterdam, Aug. 19, 1955. He studied experimental psychology at the Univ. of Göttingen (Dr. phil., 1905); taught psychology at the Univ. of Budapest (1910–20). In 1921 he settled in Holland, where he became director of the Psychological Institute of the Univ. of Amsterdam.
WRITINGS: *Zur Grundlegung der Tonpsychologie* (Leipzig, 1913); *Das frühzeitige Auftreten der Begabung und ihre Erkennung* (Leipzig, 1921); *Musikgenuss bei Gehörlosen* (with prof. Katz; Leipzig, 1926); *Inleiding tot de muziekpsychologie* (Amsterdam, 1944; in German, Bern, 1946; in English, as *Introduction to the Psychology of Music,* N.Y., 1953). A book that attracted most attention, and also put in doubt the efficacy of the author's method, was *Erwin Nyiregyházi. Psychologische Analyse eines musikalisch hervorragenden Kindes* (Leipzig, 1916; in English as *The Psychology of a Musical Prodigy,* London, 1925) which analyzes the case of a talented Hungarian child pianist who had perfect pitch, could transpose at sight and commit to memory short musical phrases instantly; but examples cited in the book do not go beyond the capabilities of thousands of other musically gifted children.

Revueltas, Silvestre, remarkable Mexican composer; b. Santiago Papasquiaro, Dec. 31, 1899; d. Mexico City, Oct. 5, 1940. He studied violin at the Mexico Cons.; with Felix Borowski in Chicago (1916) and with Ševčík in N.Y. (1922); conducted theater orchestras in Texas (1926–28); in 1929 returned to Mexico City and became assistant conductor to Carlos Chávez of the Orquesta Sinfónica de Mexico; only then did he begin to compose. In 1937 he went to Spain, where he was active in the cultural affairs of the Loyalist Government during the civil war. His health was ruined by exertions and irregular life, and he died of pneumonia. His remains were deposited in the Rotonda de los Hombres Ilustres in Mexico City on March 23, 1976 to the music of his *Redes* and the funeral march from Beethoven's *Eroica*. He possessed an extraordinary natural talent and intimate understanding of Mexican music, so that despite a lack of academic training in composition, he succeeded in creating works of great originality, melodic charm, and rhythmic vitality.
WORKS: the ballets *El Renacuajo paseador* (Mexico City, Oct. 4, 1940) and *La Coronela* (left unfinished at his death; completed by Galindo and Huízar; produced posthumously, Nov. 20, 1941); for orch.: *Es-*

quinas (Mexico City, Nov. 20, 1931), *Ventanas* (Nov. 4, 1932), *Cuauhnahuac* (June 2, 1933), *Janitzio* (Oct. 13, 1933), *Colorines* (N.Y., Nov. 4, 1933), *Planos,* "geometric dance" for orch. (Mexico City, Nov. 5, 1934), *Homenaje a Federico García Lorca* (Madrid, Sept. 22, 1937, composer conducting), *Redes* (Barcelona, Oct. 7, 1937), *Sensemayá* for voice and orch. (Mexico City, Dec. 15, 1938), La Noche de las Mayas, film score (1939), symph. suite; 3 string quartets; for piano: *Canción* and *Allegro;* songs.
BIBLIOGRAPHY: O. Mayer-Serra, "Silvestre Revueltas," *Musical Quarterly* (April 1941); N. Slonimsky, *Music of Latin America* (N.Y., 1945; pp. 247–51); G. Contreras, *S. Revueltas* (Mexico, 1954).

Revutsky, Lev, Ukrainian composer; b. Irshavetz, near Poltava, Feb. 20, 1889; died in Kiev, March 31, 1977. He studied in Kiev with Glière; then was engaged as instructor at the Musico-Dramatic Institute in Kiev (1924–41). During the occupation of Kiev by the Germans he went to Tashkent; in 1944 returned to Kiev; in 1957 he was elected to the Ukrainian Academy of Sciences. His works include 2 symphonies (1915, 1926); 2 piano concertos (1914; 1934); a number of choral pieces to Ukrainian words.
BIBLIOGRAPHY: G. Kisselev, *Lev Revutsky* (Kiev, 1949); V. Klein, *Lev Revutsky, Composer, Pianist* (Kiev, 1972).

Rey, Cemal Reshid, Turkish composer; b. Istanbul, Oct. 25, 1904. Of a distinguished family (his father was a poet and also served twice as Minister of the Interior in the Turkish government), he studied in Paris with Laparra (composition) and Marguerite Long (piano); returning to Istanbul in 1923, he taught at the Cons.; from 1949 to 1969 he was principal conductor of the Istanbul Radio Orch. His music is imbued with Turkish melorhythms; many of his works are written on Turkish subjects.
WORKS: the operas *Yann Marek* (1922), *Sultan Cem* (1923), *Zeybek* (1926), *Tchelebi* (1945), *Benli Hürmüz* (1965), operetta, *Yaygara* (1969); 3 symphonies (1941, 1950, 1968); *La Légende du Bebek,* for orch. (Paris, Dec. 15, 1929); *Karagueuz,* symph. poem (Paris, Feb. 14, 1932; composer conducting); *Scènes turques,* for orch. (Paris, March 6, 1932); *Concerto chromatique* for piano and orch. (Paris, March 12, 1933, composer soloist); Violin Concerto (1939); *L'Appel,* symph. poem (Paris, April 3, 1952, composer conducting); *Fatih* for orch. (1956); 3 symph. Scherzos (1958); *Colloque instrumental* for flute, 2 horns, harp and strings (1957); *Variations on an Istanbul Folksong* for piano and orch. (1966); numerous arrangements of Turkish folksongs for various instrumental combinations; choruses; piano pieces.

Rey, Jean-Baptiste, French conductor and composer; b. Tarn-et-Garonne, Dec. 18, 1734; d. Paris, July 15, 1810. He studied at Toulouse and became a theater conductor in the provinces. In 1776 he was appointed court musician to Louis XVI, as "surintendant de la chapelle." He conducted the Concert Spirituel (1782–86); then was in charge of the musical performances at the Paris Opéra. In 1799 he became prof. at the Paris Cons. He taught according to the principles of Rameau and became embroiled in an academic controversy with the followers of the more modern method of Catel. He played an important role in producing operas by Gluck, Grétry, and others; wrote some stage music himself.

Rey, Louis Charles Joseph, French composer and cellist; brother of **Jean–Baptiste Rey;** b. Lauzerte, Oct. 26, 1738; d. Paris, May 12, 1811. He was trained as a cellist, and was in the orch. of the Paris Opéra from 1766 until 1806; composed music for cello and other instruments.

Reyer, Louis-Étienne-Ernest, French composer; b. Marseilles, Dec. 1, 1823; d. Le Lavandou, near Hyères, Jan. 15, 1909. An ardent admirer of Wagner, he added the German suffix "er" to his real name **Rey.** He studied in the free municipal school of music; then took a place in the government financial bureau at Algiers, and while there composed a Solemn Mass (for the arrival of the French governor in Algiers; performed 1847) and publ. several songs. He definitely embarked upon a musical career in 1848, studying at Paris with his aunt, **Louise Dumont,** the wife of Aristide Farrenc. In 1866 he became librarian at the Opéra, and followed d'Ortigue as music critic of the *Journal des Débats;* his collected essays were publ. in 1875 as *Notes de musique;* also in *Quarante ans de musique* (posthumous, 1909). He was elected to David's chair in the Institut in 1876; chevalier of the Legion of Honor, 1862; Grande-Croix, 1906. Although Reyer was an avowed admirer of Wagner, his music does not betray specific Wagnerian influences; both in form and in harmonic progressions Reyer adheres to the classical French school of composition, with a certain tendency towards exoticism in his choice of librettos.
WORKS: for the stage: *Le Sélam,* text by Gautier (labeled a "symphonie orientale," but actually a 4-act opera; Paris, April 5, 1850), *Maître Wolfram,* 1-act opera (Paris, May 20, 1854), *Sacountale,* ballet pantomime (Paris, July 14, 1858), *La Statue,* opera (in 3 acts, Paris, April 11, 1861; recast in 5 acts, Feb. 27, 1903), *Erostrate,* opera (Baden-Baden, Aug. 21, 1862, by the Paris Opéra troupe), *Sigurd,* opera (Brussels, Jan. 7, 1884; his most popular work; 300 performances up to 1925 in Paris and many abroad), *Salammbô,* opera (Brussels, Feb. 10, 1890); a cantata, *Victoire* (1859); a hymn, *L'Union des arts* (1862); men's choruses: *L'Hymne de Rhin, Le Chant du paysan, Chœur des buveurs, Chœur des assiégés;* a dramatic scene, *La Madeleine au désert* (1874); also some church music.
BIBLIOGRAPHY: A Jullien, *E. Reyer* (Paris, 1909); H. Roujon, *Notice sur la vie et les travaux de E. Reyer* (Paris, 1911); H. de Curzon, *E. Reyer, sa vie et ses œuvres* (Paris, 1923).

Reynolds, Roger, American composer; b. Detroit, July 18, 1934. He studied engineering at the Univ. of Michigan (B.S.E., 1957) and composition (M.M., 1961); spent a year in Cologne on a Fulbright Grant for work on electronic music (1962); was in Paris in 1963 and in Italy on a Guggenheim Fellowship, in 1964–65. In his early scores he used serial methods, but later expanded his resources to include the entire spectrum of multimedia expression, enhanced by the mathematical concepts of sets and matrices and Gestalt psychology. In 1960 he was one of the founders of the avant-garde festival ONCE in Ann Arbor, Michigan. In 1966 he went to Japan at the invitation of the Institute of Current World Affairs. In 1969 he staged there the festival Cross Talk Intermedia, featuring experimental works by Japanese and American composers. In 1970 he joined the faculty of the Univ. of California in San Diego. Reynolds uses graphic notation in his scores, suggesting the desired sounds by pictorial shapes.
WORKS: *Epigram and Evolution* for piano (1959); *Sky,* a song cycle for soprano, alto flute, bassoon and harp, to Japanese Haiku poems (1960); *Wedge* for chamber orch. (1961); *Acquaintances* for flute, double bass, and piano (1961); *4 Etudes for flute quartet* (1961); *Mosaic* for flute and piano (1962); *The Emperor of Ice Cream,* his major work, to a poem of Wallace Stevens, scored for 8 voices, piano, percussion, and double bass (1962); *A Portrait of Vanzetti* for narrator, wind instruments, percussion, and magnetic tape (1963); *Graffiti* for orch. (1964); *Fantasy* for pianists (1964); *Quick Are the Mouths of Earth* for chamber orch. (1965); *Ambages* for solo flute (1965); *Masks* for orch. and mixed chorus, to a text by Melville (1965); *Blind Men* for mixed choir, brass, percussion, and slide projection, to a text by Melville (1966); *Threshold* for orch. (1967); *. . . between . . .* for chamber orch. and electronics (1968); *Traces* for piano, flute, cello, tapes, and electronics (1969); *Ping,* inspired by a story of Samuel Beckett, scored for flute (multiphonic), piano (motorized by agitating strings), harmonium, bowed cymbal and tam-tam, electronic sound distribution, film, ring modulator, 35 slides and magnetic tape (1969); *I/O* (for "In and Out"), for 9 female vocalists, 9 male mimes, 2 flutes, clarinet, electronics and projections (1969), based on a concept of Buckminster Fuller with relation to the synergetic antonyms of the opposite sexes; *Compass,* a collage of video projections, taped voices, cello, and double bass, to words by Jorge Luis Borges (1973); *Promises of Darkness,* for 11 instruments (N.Y., Jan. 8, 1976); *Fiery Winds* for orch. (N.Y., Feb. 13, 1978).

Reynolds, Verne, American horn player and composer; b. Lyons, Kansas, July 18, 1926. He studied composition at the Cincinnati Cons. (B.M., 1950); at the Univ. of Wisconsin with Cecil Burleigh (M.M., 1951) and at the Royal College of Music in London with Herbert Howells. He played the horn in the Cincinnati Symph. Orch. and in the Rochester Philharmonic; appointed prof. of horn at the Eastman School of Music.
WORKS: Violin Concerto (1951); overture, *Saturday with Venus* (1953); *The Hollow Men* for baritone, male chorus, brass choir and percussion (1954); *Music for 5 Trumpets* (1957); *Serenade* for 13 winds (1958); 48 Etudes for horn (1959); *Celebration Overture* for orch. (1960); *Partita* for horn and piano (1961); Sonata for flute and piano (1962); Suite for 4 horns (1962); Suite for brass quintet (1963); Woodwind Quintet (1964); *Serenade* for horn and strings (1966); String Quartet (1967); *Concertare I* for brass quintet and percussion (1968); *Concertare II* for trumpet and strings (1968); Sonata for tuba and piano (1968); *Concertare*

III for woodwind quintet and piano (1969); Sonata for horn and piano (1970); 48 Etudes for trumpet (1970); Violin Sonata (1970); *Concertare IV* for brass quintet and piano (1971); *Scenes* for wind instruments and percussion (1971). He has made many transcriptions for various instrumental combinations of works by Handel, Kreutzer, J. J. Fux, Schumann, etc.

Řezáč, Ivan, Czech composer; b. Řevnice, Nov. 5, 1924; d. Prague, Dec. 26, 1977. He studied piano with Rauch and composition with Šín, Janeček and Dobiáš at the Prague Academy, graduating in 1953; in 1966 he joined its faculty. In his music he follows the type of optimistic lyricism made popular by Shostakovich.

WORKS: 3 piano concertos (1955, 1964, 1972); 2 symphonies (1958, 1961); *Návrat (The Return)* for cello and orch. (1962); 2 string quartets (1955, 1971); Cello Sonata (1956); Piano Trio (1958); *Nocturnes* for violin and piano (1959); *Torso of a Schumann Monument* for viola and piano (1963); Duo for violin and piano (1964); *Variations on a Czech Folk Song* for cello and piano (1965); *6 Tales* for cello and guitar (1973); *Musica da camera* for flute, oboe, violin, viola and cello (1973); opera, *Mr. Theodor Mundstock* (1974); *Quadrature of the Heart* for string quartet and orch. (1975); *Vivace* for 67 musicians (1977); *Montage* for orch. (1977); 2 piano sonatas (1954, 1957); 2 piano sonatinas (1959, 1966), *Dry Points* for piano (1962); *Sisyfona neděle (Sisyphus Sunday)* for piano (1972).

Reznicek, Emil Nikolaus von, Austrian composer; b. Vienna, May 4, 1860; d. Berlin, Aug. 2, 1945. He studied law at Graz and music with Wilhelm Mayer (W. A. Rémy); later took a brief course with Reinecke and Jadassohn at the Leipzig Cons. He was subsequently engaged as theater conductor in Graz, Zürich, Berlin, Jena, Mainz, Stettin, and Weimar; was Kapellmeister at the court theater in Mannheim (1896–99). After a short residence in Wiesbaden, he settled in Berlin, and in 1902 established there a very successful series of concerts for chamber orch., Orchester-Kammerkonzerte; in 1906 he was appointed prof. at the Scharwenka Cons. in Berlin; conducted the Warsaw Opera during the 1907–08 season; then became the conductor of the Komische Oper, Berlin (1909–11); from 1920 to 1926, he taught at the Hochschule für Musik; retired from teaching in 1919.

WORKS: operas: *Donna Diana,* to his own libretto (Prague, Dec. 16, 1894; very successful; the overture frequently performed in concerts); *Till Eulenspiegel* (Karlsruhe, Jan. 12, 1902); *Ritter Blaubart* (Darmstadt, Jan. 29, 1920); *Holofernes* (Berlin, Oct. 27, 1923); *Spiel oder Ernst* (Dresden, Nov. 11, 1930); *Der Gondoliere des Dogen* (Stuttgart, Oct. 29, 1931); 5 symphonies; 3 symph. poems; a *Symphonietta* (also known as the *Ironische Symphonie;* Berlin, March 30, 1905, composer conducting); Violin Concerto (Berlin, Feb. 26, 1925); *Nachtstück,* for cello, harp, 4 horns, and string quartet; piano pieces; songs.

BIBLIOGRAPHY: O. Taubmann, *Emil Nikolaus von Reznicek* (Leipzig, 1907); Max Chop, *E. N. von Reznicek: sein Leben und seine Werke* (Vienna, 1920); R. Specht, *E. N. von Reznicek: eine vorläufige Studie* (Leipzig, 1923).

Rhaw (Rhau), Georg, German publisher and composer; b. Eisfeld, Franconia, 1488; d. Wittenberg, Aug. 6, 1548. Cantor of the Thomsschule, Leipzig, from 1518 to 1520, bringing out a Mass *a* 12 and a Te Deum at the disputation of Luther and Eck, then settled in Eisleben as a schoolmaster; later, went to Wittenberg, where in 1524 he established a publishing business, issuing many first eds. of Luther's writings and numerous collections of musical works, mostly Protestant, including *Sacrorum Hymnorum Liber Primus* (1542; modern ed. by R. Gerber in *Das Erbe deutscher Musik,* vols. 21, 25); *Newe deutsche Gesenge für die gemeinen Schulen* (1544; reprinted by Joh. Wolf as vol. 34 of the *Denkmäler deutscher Tonkunst), Bicinia gallica, latina et germanica* (1545, contains the earliest known version of the *Ranz des vaches;* selections were republ. in F. Jöde's *Musikantengilde,* 1926; also ed. by K. Ameln, Kassel, 1934), etc. He was the author of an *Enchiridion musices,* in 2 parts (1517, 1520).

BIBLIOGRAPHY: W. Wölbing, *Georg Rhaw* (Berlin, 1922); H. Albrecht, ed., *Georg Rhaw* Musikdrucke *aus den Johren 1538 bis 1545* (Kassel, 5 vols., 1955–70).

Rheinberger, Joseph (Gabriel), eminent German organist, composer and pedagogue; b. Vaduz, Liechtenstein, March 17, 1839; d. Munich, Nov. 25, 1901. He played piano and organ as a child; then took regular lessons in organ playing with J. G. Herzog, piano with J. E. Leonhard, and composition with J. J. Maier, at the Munich Cons.; subsequently studied composition with Franz Lachner, while earning his living as a piano accompanist at the Munich Gesangverein. From 1864 to 1877 he served as principal conductor of the Munich Oratorio Society. In 1859 he succeeded his teacher Leonhard as prof. of piano at the Munich Cons., and also taught composition there. His loyalty to the cultural and musical institutions in Munich earned him many honors from the Bavarian government; King Ludwig II made him Knight of St. Michael; towards the end of his life in 1894 he was given the rank of "Zivilverdienstorden," equivalent of nobility; in 1899 he was made Dr. phil. (*honoris causa*) by the Univ. of Munich. Rheinberger's reputation as a teacher of organ was without equal during his lifetime; students flocked to him from all parts of the world. As a composer, he created a number of works remarkable for their dignity, formal perfection and consummate technical mastery, if not for inventive power. His organ sonatas are unquestionably among the finest productions of organ literature.

WORKS: a romantic opera, *Die sieben Raben* (Munich, 1869); comic opera, *Des Türmers Töchterlein* (Munich, 1873); for orch.: *Florentiner Symphonie;* symph. poem, *Wallenstein;* Piano Concerto; oratorio, *Der Stern von Bethlehem;* 12 Masses; 3 Requiems; motets and hymns; 2 organ concertos; 20 organ sonatas; chamber music: Nonet; 2 string quintets; Piano Quintet; 4 piano trios; Violin Sonata; Cello Sonata; Horn Sonata; for piano: *Symphonische Sonata, Romantische Sonata;* numerous Lieder.

BIBLIOGRAPHY: P. Molitor, *Joseph Rheinberger und seine Kompositionen für die Orgel* (Leipzig, 1904); T. Kroyer, *Joseph Rheinberger* (Regensburg, 1916); Harvey Grace, *The Organ Works of Rheinberger* (London, 1925); Hans-Josef Irmen, *Joseph Rhein-*

berger als Antipode des Cäcilanismus (Regensburg, 1970); *J. Rheinberger. Thematisches Verzeichnis* (1974).

Rhené-Baton (real name **René Baton**), French conductor; b. Courseulles-sur-Mer, Calvados, Sept. 5, 1879; d. Le Mans, Sept. 23, 1940. He studied piano at the Paris Cons. and music theory privately with Gédalge. He began his conducting career as a chorus director at the Opéra-Comique in Paris; then conducted various concert groups in Angers and Bordeaux; from 1916 to 1932 he was principal conductor of the Concerts Pasdeloup. He composed orchestral pieces, chamber music and a number of songs.
BIBLIOGRAPHY: D. Sourdet, *Douze chefs d'orchestre* (Paris, 1924).

Rhodes, Willard, American pianist, opera conductor, music educator and a foremost ethnomusicologist; b. Dashler, Ohio, May 12, 1901. He earned his A.B. and B. Mus. degrees from Heidelberg College in Tiffin, Ohio, both in 1922; then studied at the Mannes School of Music in N.Y. (1923-25) and at Columbia Univ. (M.A. 1925); went to Paris where he took lessons in piano with Alfred Cortot and in composition with Nadia Boulanger (1925-27). From 1927 to 1935 he served as conductor with the American Opera Co., the Cincinnati Summer Opera Co., and with his own Rhodes Chamber Opera Co. He then turned to educational music; was director of music in the public schools of Bronxville, N.Y. (1935-37). In 1937 he was appointed to the faculty at Columbia Univ.; became Professor Emeritus in 1969. He held the post of music consultant to the U.S. Bureau of Indian Affairs beginning in 1937, and a founding member (1953) and first president (1956-58) of the Society for Ethnomusicology. It was in this connection that he accumulated a most valuable collection of Amerindian folk music, both notated and recorded (many pressings released by the Library of Congress). In 1961 he was elected President of the Society for Asian Music, and in 1968 of the International Folk Music Council; was also a Fellow of the African Studies Association and numerous other ethnomusicological organizations. He did field work in Rhodesia and Nyasaland (1957-58) and in South India (1965-66); was visiting professor at the Juilliard School of Music, N.Y., Brigham Young Univ., Utah; the Univ. of Hawaii and Ahmadu Bello Univ. in Nigeria. In 1978 he accepted an appointment as visiting prof. at the Univ. of Arizona.
BIBLIOGRAPHY: *Ethnomusicology*, special issue dedicated to Rhodes, with lists of his published writings and recordings, May 1969.

Riadis, Emile, Greek composer; b. Salonica, May 13, 1885; d. there, July 17, 1935. He studied in Munich with Felix Mottl; in 1910, went to Paris, where he appeared as composer under the name Riadis, formed from the ending of his mother's maiden name, Elefteriadis (his father's real name was **Khu).** In 1915 he became piano teacher at the Cons. of Salonica. He wrote a number of songs, distinguished by an expressive melodic line, somewhat Oriental in its intervallic pattern; his harmonizations are in the French manner.
WORKS: a Byzantine Mass; an orch. suite; *Biblical Dances;* a symph. poem, *Sunset in Salonica;* String Quartet; Piano Quartet; Cello Sonata; *3 Greek Dances,* for piano; and several sets of songs: *Jasmins et minarets, Les Étranges pèlerinages,* etc.

Riaño, Juan Facundo, an authority on old Spanish and Moorish musical notation; b. Granada, Nov. 24, 1828; d. Madrid, Feb. 27, 1901. He was the founder and director of the Museo de Reproducciones Artísticas. He publ. (in English) *Critical and Bibliographical Notes on Early Spanish Music* (London, 1887), a valuable work containing many reproductions of old Spanish instruments. He developed the theory that the neumes of the Mozarabic notation were derived from the characters of the Visigothic alphabet.

Ribári, Antal, Hungarian composer; b. Budapest, Jan. 8, 1924. He studied composition at the Budapest Academy of Music (1943-47); later took lessons with Ferenc Szabó.
WORKS: 2 operas: *Lajos Király Válik (The Divorce of King Louis,* 1959) and *Liliom* (1960); a ballet *Fortunio* (1969); 6 cantatas: *The Wounded Pigeon and the Fountain* (1962); *The Well of Tears* (1964); *Hellas* (1964); *Clown* (1967); *Dylan Thomas* (1971); *Requiem for the Lover,* after Blake, Shelley and Swinburne (1973); *Sinfonietta* (1956); Cello Concerto (1958); 3 symphonies (1960, 1964, 1970); *Musica per archi* (1961); *Pantomime* for orch. (1962); Violin Concertino (1965); *Metamorphosis* for soprano, 3 woodwinds, piano, vibraphone, 3 bongos, 3 gongs and strings (1966); *Dialogues* for viola and orch. (1967); *Sinfonia Festiva* (1972); 3 violin sonatas (1953, 1954, 1972); 2 string quartets (1955, 1964); String Quintet (1956); Viola Sonata (1958); 2 cello sonatas (1948, revised 1973; 1968); *9 Miniatures* for string quartet (1966); *5 Miniatures* for wind trio (1969); *Chamber Music* for 5 instruments (1970); *Dialogues* for flute and piano (1971); *Fantasia* for string trio (1971); *All'antica,* Suite for piano (1968); 2 piano sonatas (1947, 1971); songs.

Ribera (Maneja), Antonio, Spanish conductor; b. Barcelona, May 3, 1873; d. Madrid, March 4, 1956; studied with Riemann and Mottl in Leipzig and Munich; conducted the Wagner Society in Barcelona (1901-04); then theater conductor in Lemberg (1905-12); again in Barcelona (1912-25), and finally in Madrid (from 1925).

Ribera (y Tarragó), Julián, Spanish scholar and musicologist; b. Carcagente, near Valencia, Sept. 19, 1858; d. there, May 2, 1934. He was for many years prof. of Hispanic-Arabic literature at the Univ. of Madrid. His magnum opus is *La Música de las cantigas. Estudio sobre su origen y naturaleza* (Madrid, 1922; in English, as *Music in Ancient Arabia and Spain,* London 1929), in which he maintains that the famous cantigas of Alfonso the Wise are derived from the metrical forms of the Arabs; he further published *La Música andaluza medieval en las canciones de trovadores, troveros y minnesinger* (3 vols., Madrid, 1923-25); *Historia de la música árabe medieval y su influencia en la española* (Madrid, 1927; published in English as *Music in Ancient Arabia and Spain,* London, 1929;

reprint, N.Y. 1970); *La Música de la jota aragonesa* (1928).

BIBLIOGRAPHY: H. Spanke, "Die Theorie Riberas über Zusammenhänge zwischen frühromanischen Strophenformen und andalusisch-arabischer Lyrik des Mittelalters," in *Volkstum und Kultur der Romanen*, III, pp. 258–78; V. Castañeda, "Don J. Ribera y Tarragó," *Boletín de la Academia de la Historia* 104 (Madrid, 1934; pp. 401–16).

Ricci, Corrado, Italian librettist; b. Ravenna, April 18, 1858; d. Rome, June 5, 1934. From 1906 to 1919 he served as general director of the dept. of Fine Arts in the Italian Ministry of Education in Rome; he was instrumental in having a concert hall established at the Augusteo. Besides several librettos, he published *Figure e figuri del mondo teatrale* (Milan, 1920); *Arrigo Boito* (Milan, 1919); *Burney, Casanova e Farinelli in Bologna* (Milan, 1890).

Ricci, Federico, Italian composer; brother of **Luigi Ricci;** b. Naples, Oct. 22, 1809; d. Conegliano, Dec. 10, 1877. He studied with Zingarelli and Raimondi. In collaboration with his elder brother he produced 4 operas: *Il Colonnello* (Naples, March 14, 1835), *Il Disertore per amore* (Naples, Feb. 16, 1836), *L'Amante di richiamo* (Turin, 1846), and *Crispino e la comare* (Venice, Feb. 28, 1850). Subsequently he had excellent success with his own operas *La Prigione d'Edimburgo* (Trieste, March 13, 1838) and *Corrado d'Altamura* (La Scala, Milan, Nov. 16, 1841). In 1853 he received the appointment as musical director of the imperial theaters in St. Petersburg, Russia; upon his return he produced another successful opera *Una Follia a Roma* (Paris, 1869); he retired in 1876.

BIBLIOGRAPHY: F. de Villars, *Notice sur Luigi et Federico Ricci* (Paris, 1866); L. de Rada, *I Fratelli Ricci* (Florence, 1878).

Ricci, Luigi, Italian composer; brother of **Federico Ricci;** b. Naples, July 8, 1805; d. Prague, Dec. 31, 1859. He wrote about 30 operas, at least 4 of them in collaboration with his brother Federico. He was only 18 when his first opera *L'Impresario in angustie* was performed at the Cons. di S. Sebastiano, where he was a student (1823). In 1836 he was appointed maestro di cappella of the cathedral at Trieste and chorusmaster at the city theater there. In 1844 he married Lidia Stolz, of Prague; in 1855 when he was about 50 he developed symptoms of insanity, and was committed to an asylum in Prague, where he died.

WORKS: operas: *Il Colombo* (Parma, June 27, 1829), *L'Orfanella di Ginevra* (Rome, 1829), *Chiara di Rosemberg* (Milan, Oct. 11, 1831), *Il nuovo Figaro* (Parma, Feb. 15, 1832), *Chi dura vince* (Rome, Dec. 27, 1834), *Il Birraio di Preston* (Florence, Feb. 4, 1847), *Crispino e la comare* (in collaboration with his brother Federico; Venice, Feb. 28, 1850; Metropolitan Opera, N.Y., Jan. 18, 1919), *La Festa di Piedigrotta* (Naples, 1852), and *Il Diavolo a quattro* (Trieste, 1859). His son (by his wife's identical twin sister Francesca Stolz), **Luigi Ricci, Jr.** (b. Trieste, Dec. 27, 1852; d. Milan, Feb. 10, 1906), was also a composer of operas.

BIBLIOGRAPHY: F. de Villars, *Notice sur Luigi et Frederico Ricci* (Paris, 1866); L. de Rada, *I Fratelli Ricci* (Florence, 1878); C. de Incontrera, *Luigi Ricci* (Trieste, 1959).

Ricci, Ruggiero, celebrated American violinist; b. San Francisco, July 24, 1918. His musical education was lovingly fostered by his father, along with 6 of his siblings, every one of whom started out as a musician, and 2 of whom, the cellist **Giorgio Ricci** and the violinist **Emma Ricci** achieved the rank of professional performers. Ruggiero Ricci studied violin with Louis Persinger, and made a sensational appearance at the public concert in San Francisco on Nov. 15, 1928, when he was 10 years old, with his teacher accompanying him at the piano. On Oct. 20, 1929 he played in N.Y.; he embarked on an international concert tour in 1932. He successfully negotiated the perilous transition from child prodigy to serious artist; he accumulated a formidable repertory of about 60 violin concertos, including all violin works of Paganini; edited the newly discovered manuscript of Paganini's early Violin Concerto, presumed to have been composed around 1815, and gave its first N.Y. performance with the American Symph. Orch. on Oct. 7, 1977; he also gave the first performances of violin concertos by several modern composers, among them Alberto Ginastera (1963) and Gottfried von Einem (1970). During World War II he served as "entertainment specialist" with the U.S. Army Air Force. After the end of the war, he returned to the concert stage; made several world tours which included South America, Australia, Japan and Russia; he also gave master courses at the North Carolina School of the Arts, Indiana Univ. and the Juilliard School of Music, N.Y. He owns a 1734 Guarnerius del Gesù violin. In 1978 he celebrated a "Golden Jubilee," marking half a century of his professional career.

Riccitelli, Primo, Italian composer; b. Campli, Aug. 9, 1875; d. Giulianova, March 27, 1941; pupil of Mascagni at the Liceo Rossini, Pesaro. He wrote the operas *Maria sul Monte* (1911; Milan, July 8, 1916), *I Compagnacci* (1-act; Rome, April 10, 1923; Metropolitan Opera, N.Y., Jan. 2, 1924), and *Madone Oretta* (Rome, Feb. 3, 1932); also songs.

Riccius, August Ferdinand, German composer; b. Bernstadt, Feb. 26, 1819; d. Karlsbad, July 5, 1886. He was conductor of the Euterpe Concerts in Leipzig (from 1849); then at the City Theater there (1854–64); in 1864 went to Hamburg, where he conducted opera, and wrote music criticism for the *Hamburger Nachrichten*. He composed an overture to Schiller's *Braut von Messina;* a cantata, *Die Weihe der Kraft;* piano music; choruses; songs.

Riccius, Karl August, German violinist, conductor, and composer, nephew of **August Ferdinand Riccius;** b. Bernstadt, July 26, 1830; d. Dresden, July 8, 1893. He studied in Dresden with Wieck, and in Leipzig with Mendelssohn, Schumann, and Ferdinand David. In 1847 he became violinist in the Dresden Court Orchestra, and later also conductor. He wrote a comic opera, *Es spukt* (Dresden, 1871); several ballets; music to various plays; publ. piano pieces and songs.

Rice, William Gorham, American writer on music; b. Albany, N.Y., Dec. 23, 1856; d. there, Sept. 10, 1945. His writings include *Carillons of Belgium and Holland; The Carillon in Literature;* "Tower Music of Belgium and Holland," *Musical Quarterly* (April 1915); etc.

Richafort, Jean, Flemish composer; b. c.1480; d. 1548. Probably a pupil of Josquin, he was chapelmaster at St. Rombaut, in Mechlin, from 1507 to 1509; in 1531, in the service of Mary of Hungary, regent of the Netherlands; 1542–47, chapelmaster at St. Gilles in Bruges. Surviving are Masses, Magnificats, motets, and chansons.
BIBLIOGRAPHY: G. Van Doorslaer, "Jean Richafort," *Bulletin de l'Académie Royale d'Archéologie de Belgique* (1930; p. 103ff.); G. Reese, *Music in the Renaissance* (N.Y., 1954); M. E. Kabis, *The Works of Jean Richafort, Renaissance Composer* (2 vols.; N.Y. Univ., 1957).

Richards, (Henry) Brinley, British composer and pianist; b. Carmarthen, Wales, Nov. 13, 1817; d. London, May 1, 1885. He was a pupil of the Royal Academy of Music; resided in London, and was highly esteemed as a concert pianist and teacher. He wrote the popular hymn *God bless the Prince of Wales* (1862).

Richards, Lewis Loomis, American pianist and music educator; b. St. Johns, Michigan, April 11, 1881; d. East Lansing, Michigan, Feb. 15, 1940. He studied at the Brussels Cons.; in 1927 became head of the dept. of music at Michigan State College; was also director of Michigan State Institute of Music and Allied Arts.

Richardson, Alfred Madeley, English organist; b. Southend-on-Sea, Essex, June 1, 1868; d. New York, July 23, 1949. He received his classical education at Keble College, Oxford (A.M., 1892), and studied at the Royal College of Music under Sir C. H. H. Parry, Sir W. Parratt and E. Pauer; then went to the U.S., and in 1912 was appointed instructor in theory at the institute of Musical Art, N.Y. He published *The Psalms; Their Structure and Musical Rendering* (1903); *Church Music* (1904); *The Choir-Trainer's Art* (1914); *Extempore Playing* (1922); *The Medieval Modes* (1933); *Fundamental Counterpoint* (1936).

Richault, Charles-Simon, French publisher; b. Chartres, May 10, 1780; d. Paris, Feb. 20, 1866. In 1805 he founded a music publishing house, the first issues of which were Mozart's concertos and Beethoven's symphonies in score. His sons **Guillaume-Simon** (1806–77) and **Léon** (1839–95) carried on the business, publishing works by French composers, and also excellent editions of German classics. In 1898 the stock was bought by the publisher Costallat of Paris.

Richter, Alfred, German pedagogue, son of **Ernst Friedrich Richter;** b. Leipzig, April 1, 1846; d. Berlin, March 1, 1919. He was trained by his father and became a competent music teacher; was a member of the faculty of the Leipzig Cons. (1872–82); then lived in London, but returned to Germany in 1897. He brought out a number of music school manuals, among them, a supplement to his father's *Lehrbuch der Harmonie* (Leipzig, 1853), *Aufgabenbuch* (1879; went through 64 editions before 1952; published in English as *Additional Exercises;* N.Y., 1882); *Die Elementarkenntnisse der Musik* (1895; 6th ed., 1920); *Die Lehre von der thematischen Arbeit* (1896); *Das Klavierspiel für Musikstudierende* (1898; 2nd ed., 1912); *Die Lehre von der Form in der Musik* (1904; 2nd ed., 1911). He also composed piano pieces, songs and choruses.

Richter, Ernst Friedrich (Eduard), eminent German theorist and composer; b. Gross–Schönau, Oct. 24, 1808; d. Leipzig, April 9, 1879. A son of a schoolmaster, he was educated in Zittau; matriculated in 1831 as a student of theory at the Univ. of Leipzig; when the Leipzig Cons. was founded in 1843 he became Hauptmann's coadjutor as teacher of harmony; conducted the Leipzig Singakademie (1843–47); and was organist of the Petrikirche (from 1851), at the Neukirche (from 1862) and in 1868 became music director of the Nikolaikirche and cantor of the Thomaskirche. He composed several sacred cantatas, masses, psalms, etc., and also wrote chamber music, piano pieces and organ compositions. But he became primarily known as the compiler of practical and useful manuals on harmony, counterpoint and fugue, which went into numerous editions and translations into all European languages, among them, *Lehrbuch der Harmonie* (Leipzig, 1853; 36th ed., 1953; in English, N.Y., 1867; newly translated by Theodore Baker from the 25th German edition, N.Y., 1912; also publ. in Swedish, Russian, Polish, Italian, French, Spanish and Dutch); *Lehrbuch des einfachen und doppelten Kontrapunkts* (Leipzig, 1872; 15th ed., 1920; in English, London, 1874 and N.Y., 1884; also in French and Russian); *Lehrbuch der Fuge* (Leipzig, 1859; in English, London, 1878; also in French); these 3 manuals were brought out together as *Die praktischen Studien zur Theorie der Musik* (Leipzig, 1874–76); Richter's son, **Alfred Richter,** compiled a supplement to the *Lehrbuch der Harmonie* as *Aufgabenbuch,* which also went into a number of editions.

Richter, Ferdinand Tobias, Austrian organist and composer; b. Würzburg, 1651 (baptized July 22, 1651); d. Vienna, Nov. 3, 1711. He was court organist in Vienna from 1683; enjoyed a great reputation as a theorist and teacher. The following works are extant in Vienna in manuscript: 2 stage pieces: *L'Istro ossequioso* (Vienna, Jan. 6, 1694) and *Le Promesse degli dei* (Vienna, June 9, 1697); *5 Sepulcri* (a special type of Viennese oratorio performed in semi-operatic manner during Holy Week); an oratorio; sonata for 7 instruments; 2 sonatas for 8 instruments. Modern reprints of his suites, toccatas, and versets are found in *Denkmäler der Tonkunst in Österreich* 27 (13. ii).

Richter, Francis William, American organist; nephew of **Hans Richter;** b. Minneapolis, Feb. 5, 1888; d. Los Angeles, Dec. 25, 1938. He became blind at the age of 3; showed musical ability, and was sent to Vienna, where he studied with the blind pianist Joseph Labor; also took lessons with Leschetizky (piano) and Karl Goldmark (theory); subsequently studied organ with

Guilmant in Paris. Returning to the U.S., he was active as church organist and teacher. In 1930 he settled in Portland, Oregon; then moved to Los Angeles.

Richter, Franz Xaver, German composer; b. Holleschau, Moravia, Dec. 1, 1709; d. Strasbourg, Sept. 12, 1789. In 1740 he was a member of the chapel of the Prince–Abbot at Kempten; in 1747 he joined the electoral orch. at Mannheim; 1769 till his death, Kapellmeister at Strasbourg Cathedral. A prolific composer of decided originality, he was one of the chief representatives of the new instrumental style of the Mannheim school.

WORKS: In the library of Strasbourg Cathedral are the manuscripts of 28 Masses, 2 Requiems, 16 psalms, 38 motets, 2 cantatas, 2 Passions, Lamentations for Holy Week, etc. (the greater part with orch.). An oratorio, *La Deposizione della Croce,* was produced in Mannheim (1748). Publ. works: 69 symphonies (4 reprinted by Riemann in *Denkmäler der Tonkunst in Bayern* 4 and 13 [3.i and 7.ii]), 6 string quartets (reprinted in vol. 27 [15]), 8 trios for flute (or violin), cello, and piano (G minor reprinted in vol. 28 [16]; A in *Collegium musicum);* 12 trio sonatas for 2 violins with basso continuo; 6 duets for flute; 6 sonatas for flute with basso continuo; 6 piano concertos with string orch. Almost all the chamber music was originally publ. in London. A treatise, *Harmonische Belehrung oder gründliche Anweisung zur musikalischen Tonkunst* (MS in library of Brussels Cons.), was publ. in transl. by Ch. Kalkbrenner as *Traité d'harmonie et de composition* (1804).

BIBLIOGRAPHY: F. X. Mathias, "Thematischer Katalog der im Strassburger Münsterarchiv aufbewahrten kirchenmusikalischen Werke Fr. X. Richters," in *Reimann Festschrift* (Leipzig, 1909).

Richter, Hans, eminent German conductor; b. Raab, Hungary, April 4, 1843; d. Bayreuth, Dec. 5, 1916. He studied theory with Sechter, violin with Heissler and French horn with Kleinecke at the Vienna Cons.; from 1862 to 1866 he was employed as horn player in the orch. at the Kärnthnerthor–Theater in Vienna. The turning point in his career was his contact with Wagner at Triebschen in 1866, when Wagner asked him to make a fair copy of the score of *Die Meistersinger;* obviously satisfied with Richter's work, Wagner recommended him to Hans von Bülow as a chorusmaster at the Munich Opera (1867); in 1868–69 Richter was also given an opportunity to assist Bülow as conductor of the court orch. in Munich. Subsequently Richter became a favorite conductor of Wagner and prepared rehearsals of Wagner's operas, among them the Brussels performance of *Lohengrin* (March 22, 1870). From 1871 to 1875 he was conductor of the Pest National Theater; then conducted the Imperial Opera in Vienna and became its first principal conductor in 1893; concurrently he conducted the concerts of the Vienna Philharmonic (1875–97). He was selected by Wagner to conduct the entire *Ring des Nibelungen* at the Bayreuth Festival in 1876; received the Order of Maximilian from the King of Bavaria and the Order of the Falcon from the Grand Duke of Weimar. When Wagner went to London in 1877, he took Richter along with him, and let him conduct several concerts

of the Wagner Festival in Albert Hall. In May, 1879 Richter conducted a second Wagner Festival in London, which led to the establishment of an annual series of May concerts known as "Orchestral Festival Concerts" and later simply "Richter Concerts," which he conducted regularly until 1897; then he was engaged as conductor of the Hallé Symph. Orch. in Manchester. He was also regular conductor of the Birmingham Festival (1885–1909) and of the Wagner operas at Covent Garden (1903–10). He conducted his farewell concert with the Manchester Symph. Orch. on April 11, 1911. His popularity in England was immense; his corpulent bear-like figure and an imposing Germanic beard imparted an air of authority; his technique was flawless. Besides Wagner's music, Richter gave repeated performances of symphonies of Brahms; among English composers he favored Elgar.

BIBLIOGRAPHY: F. Klickmann, "Dr. Hans Richter," *Windsor Magazine* (Sept. 1896); L. Karpath, *Wagners Briefe an Hans Richter* (Vienna, 1924).

Richter, Nico Max, Dutch composer; b. Amsterdam, Dec. 2, 1915; d. there, Aug. 16, 1945. He studied conducting with Scherchen; directed a student orchestra; in February 1942 he was arrested by the Nazis as a member of the Dutch Resistance, and spent three years in the Dachau concentration camp, which fatally undermined his health; he died shortly after liberation.

WORKS: *Amorijs,* a chamber opera; *Kannitverstan,* ballet; *Serenade,* sinfonietta for flute, oboe, guitar and strings (1931–34); *Concertino* for clarinet, horn, trumpet, piano and 2 violins (1935); Trio for flute, viola and guitar (1935); *Sinfonia* for chamber orch. (1936); *Serenade* for flute, violin and viola (1945; 2 extant movements reconstructed by Lex van Delden).

Richter, Sviatoslav, outstanding Russian pianist; b. Zhitomir, March 20, 1915. Both his parents were pianists; the family moved to Odessa when he was a child. He was engaged as a piano accompanist at the Odessa Opera, and developed exceptional skill in playing orchestral scores at sight. He made his debut as a concert pianist at the Sailors' Collective Circle in Odessa in 1935. In 1937 he entered the Moscow Cons., where he studied piano with Neuhaus, graduating in 1947; was awarded the Stalin Prize in 1949. During the Russian tour of the Philadelphia Orch. in 1958, Richter was soloist, playing Prokofiev's 5th Piano Concerto in Leningrad; subsequently he made several international concert tours, including China (1957) and the U.S. (1960). Both in Russia and abroad he earned a reputation as a piano virtuoso of formidable attainments; was especially praised for his impeccable sense of style, with every detail of the music rendered with lapidary perfection.

Ricketts, Frederick J., English bandmaster and composer who used the pseudonym **Kenneth J. Alford;** b. London, Feb. 21, 1881; d. Redgate, Surrey, May 15, 1945. Trained first as an organist, Ricketts graduated from Kneller Hall, the school for British bandmasters, afterwards serving his longest stint as bandmaster of the Royal Marines (1928–44). In February, 1914 he published, under his pseudonym "Alford" (not to be confused with the American bandmaster and composer Harry L. Alford) his popular march *Col. Bogey,* epitomizing the steadily swinging and moderately paced English military march. *Col. Bogey* reached its height of fame when it was introduced into the motion picture *The Bridge on the River Kwai* (1958).

Ricordi & Co., G., famous music publishing firm of Milan; founded by **Giovanni Ricordi,** b. Milan, 1785; d. there, March 15, 1853. As first violinist and conductor at the old Fiando theater, he also earned small sums as a music copyist, and in 1807 went to Leipzig to learn music engraving in Breitkopf & Härtel's establishment. Returning, he opened a little shop and began publishing in 1808, the first works being engraved by himself. He was an intimate of Rossini, whose operas he published; also recognized Verdi's genius when the latter was still unknown. His son **Tito Ricordi** (b. Milan, Oct. 29, 1811; d. there, Sept. 7, 1888) succeeded to the business. In 1845 he established the *Gazzetta Musicale,* one of the most important Italian musical papers; also introduced the Edizioni Economiche, and under his administration the house became the largest music publishing firm in Italy. With Verdi he was on terms of intimate friendship, and that composer's works (especially *Aida*) made a fortune for both publisher and author. Owing to ill health he withdrew from active management in 1887. His successor was his son **Guilio Ricordi** (b. Milan, Dec. 19, 1840; d. there, June 6, 1912), a man of extraordinary business ability, who continued the policy of expansion. In 1888 he bought, and consolidated with his own, the important firm of Francesco Lucca. It was he who discovered Puccini. A trained musician, he publ., under the pseudonym of **J. Burgmein,** much elegant salon music (160 opus numbers). Until his death (when it ceased publication) he was ed. of the *Gazzetta Musicale.* His son **Tito** (b. May 17, 1865; d. Milan, March 30, 1933), a remarkable pianist, was the subsequent head of the house. The catalogue contains over 120,000 numbers, and in the archives are the autograph scores of more than 550 operas by the most famous Italian composers. The firm has branches in New York, Canada, Australia, and South America.

BIBLIOGRAPHY: E. di S. M. Valperga, *Ricordi,* (Rome, 1943); G. Adami, *G. Ricordi, l'amico dei musicisti italiani* (Milan, 1945); O. Vergani, *Piccolo viaggo in un archivio* (Milan, 1953); C. Sartori, *Casa Ricordi, 1808–1958: profilo storico* (Milan, 1958).

Rider-Kelsey, Mme. Corinne, American soprano; b. on a farm near Batavia, N.Y., Feb. 24, 1877; d. Toledo, Ohio, July 10, 1947. She attended Oberlin College; then studied voice in Chicago and N.Y.; made her professional debut in Handel's *Messiah* (St. Louis, Nov. 24, 1904); made her first operatic appearance as Micaëla in *Carmen,* at Covent Garden, London, on July 2, 1908. In 1926 she married the violinist **Lynell Reed,** who wrote her biography under the title *Be Not Afraid* (N.Y., 1955). See V. L. Scott in *Notable American Women* (N.Y., 1971), III.

Řídký, Jaroslav, eminent Czech composer, conductor and teacher; b. Františkov, near Liberec, Aug. 25, 1897; d. Poděbrady, Aug. 14, 1956. He took courses in composition at the Prague Cons. with Jaroslav Křička and E. B. Foerster; simultaneously studied the harp; was first harpist in the Prague Philharmonic (1924–38); later became its conductor. He taught theory at the Prague Cons. (1928–48); in 1948 was appointed prof. of composition at the Music Academy in Prague, remaining at this post until his death.

WORKS: 7 symphonies: No. 1 (1924); No. 2, with cello obbligato (1925); No. 3 (1927); No. 4, with chorus (1928); No. 5 (1930–31); No. 6, *The Year 1938* (1938; unfinished); No. 7 (1955); Sinfonietta for full orch. (1923); Violin Concerto (1926); *Overture* (1928–29); 2 cello concertos (1930, 1940); 2 cantatas: *A Winter Fairytale* (1936) and *To My Fatherland* (1941); *Serenade* for string orch. (1941); Chamber Sinfonietta (1944–45); Piano Concerto (1952); *Slavonic March* for orch. (1954); 2 cello sonatas (1923, 1947–48); Clarinet Quintet (1926); 5 string quartets (1926, 1927, 1931, 1933, 1937); *Serenata appassionata* for cello and piano (1929); 2 nonets (1933–34, 1943); Wind Quintet (1945); *Joyous Sonatina* for violin and piano (1947); Piano Trio (1950–51); piano pieces; choruses.

Ridout, Godfrey, Canadian composer; b. Toronto, May 6, 1918. He studied piano, organ, conducting and composition at the Toronto Cons. and at the Univ. of Toronto, where he became a member of the faculty in 1948. His music is tuneful and winsome. In 1963–64 he reconstructed a comic opera, *Colas et Colinette,* the earliest known North American work in this form, composed by the French-Canadian musician Joseph Quesnel in 1788, for which only vocal parts and a second violin part were extant.

WORKS: television opera, *The Lost Child* (1975); a ballet *La Prima Ballerina* (1966; Montreal Expo '67); *Ballade* for viola and string orch. (1938; Toronto, May 29, 1939); *Festal Overture* (1939); *Comedy Overture* (1941); *Dirge* for orch. (1943); 2 *Etudes* for string orch. (1946, revised 1951); *Esther,* dramatic symphony for soprano, baritone, chorus and orch. (1951–52; Toronto, April 29, 1952); *Cantiones Mysticae:* No. 1, after Donne, for soprano and orch. (1953; N.Y., Oct. 16, 1953, Stokowski conducting), No. 2, *The Ascension,* for soprano, trumpet and strings (1962; Toronto, Dec. 23, 1962) and No. 3, *The Dream of the Rood,* for baritone or tenor, chorus, orch., and organ (1972); *Music for a Young Prince,* suite for orch. (1959); *Fall Fair* for orch. (performed at the United Nations on U.N. Day, Oct. 24, 1961); 4 *Sonnets* for chorus and orch. (1964); *In Memoriam Anne Frank* for soprano and orch. (Toronto, March 14, 1965); *When Age and Youth Unite* for chorus and orch. (1966); 4 *Songs of Eastern Canada* for soprano and orch. (1967); *Partita Academica* for concert band (1969); *Frivolités Canadiennes,* based on melodies by Joseph Vézina, for small orch. (1973); *Jubilee* for orch. (1973); *Concerto Grosso* for solo piano, solo violin, and string orch. (1974; Toronto, Jan. 18, 1975); *George III His Lament,* variations on an old British tune, for small orch. (1975); *Tafelmusik* for wind ensemble (1976); *Folk Song Fantasy* for piano trio (1951); *Introduction and Allegro* for flute, oboe, clarinet, bassoon, horn, violin and cello (1968); choruses; songs.

Riechers, August, German violin maker; b. Hannover, March 8, 1836; d. Berlin, Jan. 4, 1893. He was trained in the making and repairing of violins by Bausch of Leipzig; Joachim entrusted his violins to Riechers' hands. He publ. a valuable pamphlet, *Die Geige und ihr Bau* (1893; in English as *The Violin and the Art of its Construction; a Treatise on the Stradivarius Violin,* 1895), with 4 plates of full-size diagrams exhibiting the structure and exact dimensions of the model Stadivarius violin.

Riedel, Karl, German choral conductor; b. Kronenberg, near Elberfeld, Oct. 6, 1827; d. Leipzig, June 3, 1888. He was a silk-dyer by trade; owing to revolutionary perturbations of 1848, he abandoned his trade and decided to study music; took lessons with Carl Wilhelm at Krefeld; then enrolled in the Leipzig Cons. In 1854 he organized a singing society which he named after himself, the "Riedelverein," which specialized in programs of old church music; it became extremely successful and continued its activities long after Riedel's death. In 1868 Riedel was elected president of the Allgemeiner deutscher Musikverein, and founded its Leipzig branch; he also became president of the Wagnerverein. He published the collections, *Altböhmische Hussiten- und Weihnachtslieder* and *12 altdeutsche Lieder;* made a skillful reduction of Schütz's 4 Passions to one; edited Schütz's *Sieben Worte,* J. S. Franck's *Geistliche Melodien,* Eccard's *Preussische Festlieder,* and Praetorius' *Weihnachtslieder.*
BIBLIOGRAPHY: A. Göhler, *Der Riedelverein zu Leipzig* (Leipzig, 1904; includes a brief biographical sketch of Riedel).

Riedt, Friedrich Wilhelm, German flutist; b. Berlin, Jan. 24, 1710; d. there, Jan. 5, 1783. He studied with Graun; in 1741 became chamber musician to Frederick the Great; 1749, director of the "Musikübende Gesellschaft" in Berlin. He wrote 6 trios for 2 flutes and continuo; sonatas for 2 flutes; a sonata for flute and cello; published the *Versuch über die musikalischen Intervalle* (Berlin, 1753); contributed various articles (critical and polemical) to Marpurg's *Historisch-kritische Beyträge zur Aufnahme der Musik.*

Riegel (Rigel), Heinrich (Henri) Joseph, French composer; b. Wertheim, Franconia, Feb. 9, 1741; d. Paris, May 2, 1799. He was of German extraction; studied with F. X. Richter in Mannheim and with Jommelli in Stuttgart. In 1767 he went to Paris; from 1783 to 1786 belonged to a group of composers associated with the Concert Spirituel. On the title page of several of his works published in Paris his name appears as Rigel, and this gallicized form was adopted by his son **Henri-Jean,** who was born in Paris. Riegel was one of the earliest composers who wrote ensemble music with piano, published as "symphonies" for 2 violins, cello, 2 horns, and piano. He was a fairly voluminous composer; he wrote several short operas in the manner of the German singspiel, all of which were produced in Paris: *Le Savetier et le financier* (1778), *L'Automat* (1779), *Rosanie* (1780), *Blanche et Vermeille* (1781), *Lucas* (1785), *Les Amours du Gros-Caillou* (1786), and *Alix de Beaucaire* (1791). His other works include 6 symphonies, 5 piano concertos, 6 string quartets, several *Sonates de clavecin en quattuor,* a number of piano sonatas, some with violin obbligato, and 3 *Sonates en symphonies* for piano. During the revolutionary period in France he composed various pieces celebrating the events. A "symphonie" in D was republished by R. Sondheimer (1923). A sonata is included in W. S. Newman's *Six Keyboard Sonatas from the Classical Era* (1965).
BIBLIOGRAPHY: G. de Saint-Foix, "Rigel," *Revue Musicale* (June 1925); R. Sondheimer, "H. J. Rigel," *Music Review* (Aug. 1956).

Riegger, Wallingford, outstanding American composer; b. Albany, Georgia, April 29, 1885; d. New York, April 2, 1961. He received his primary education at home; his mother was a pianist; his father a violinist. The family moved to New York in 1900, and Riegger began serious study with Percy Goetschius (theory) and Alwin Schroeder (cello) at the Institute of Musical Art; after graduation (1907), he went to Berlin, where he took courses at the Hochschule für Musik; conducted opera in Würzburg and Königsberg (1915–16); also led the Bluethner Orch. in Berlin (1916–17). He returned to America in 1917 and became teacher of theory and cello at Drake Univ., Des Moines (1918–22); in 1922 received the Paderewski Prize for his Piano Trio; in 1924 he was awarded the E. S. Coolidge Prize for his setting of Keats's *La Belle Dame sans Merci;* in 1925 he was given the honorary degree of Dr. of Music by the Cincinnati Cons. He taught at the Institute of Musical Art, N.Y. (1924–25) and at the Ithaca Cons. (1926–28); then settled in N.Y., where he became active as composer and participant in various modern music societies; took part in the development of electronic instruments (in association with Theremin), and learned to play an electric cello. His music is of a highly advanced nature; a master craftsman, he wrote in disparate styles with an equal degree of proficiency; he used numerous pseudonyms for certain works (**William Richards, Walter Scotson, Gerald Wilfring Gore, John H. McCurdy, George Northrup, Robert Sedgwick, Leonard Gregg, Edwin Farell, Edgar Long,** etc.). After a long period of neglect on the part of the public and the critics, he began to receive recognition; his 3rd Symph. was the choice of the N.Y. Music Critics Circle (1948).
WORKS: for orch.: *American Polonaise* (1923); *Rhapsody* (N.Y., Oct. 29, 1931); *Fantasy and Fugue* for organ and orch. (1931); *Passacaglia and Fugue* (Washington, March 19, 1944); Symph. No. 1 (1944); Symph. No. 2 (1946); Symph. No. 3 (N.Y., May 16, 1948); Symph. No. 4 (Univ. of Illinois, April 12, 1957); *Scherzo* (N.Y., Jan. 30, 1933); *Dichotomy* (Berlin, March 10, 1932); *Variations* for piano and orch. (1953; Louisville, Feb. 13, 1954); Concerto for Piano and Woodwinds (Washington, Feb. 19, 1954); *Dance Rhythms* (Atlanta, March 4, 1955); *Music for Orchestra* (Cleveland, March 22, 1956); *Sinfonietta* (1959); *Duo* for piano and orch. (1960). *Overture* (1956); *Preamble and Fugue* (1956); *La Belle Dame sans Merci,* for 4 solo voices and chamber orch. (Pittsfield, Mass., Sept. 19, 1924); *Study in Sonority,* for 10 violins or multiples of 10 (1927); Suite for solo flute (1929); 3 Canons for flute, oboe, clarinet, and bassoon (1930);

Divertissement for flute, harp, and cello (N.Y., Dec. 11, 1933); *Music for Brass Choir;* duos for 3 woodwind instruments; 2 string quartets; *Whimsy,* for cello and piano; Sonatina for violin and piano; Piano Quintet (1950); Nonet for brass (1951); *New and Old,* 12 pieces for piano in various styles; several stage works for dance, scored for various instrumental ensembles (*Theater Piece, Chronicle, Case History, Trojan Incident,* etc.); *Suite for Younger Orchestras; The Dying of the Light,* song to words by Dylan Thomas (1956); *Quintuple jazz* (Iowa City, May 20, 1959); *Variations for violin and orch.* (Louisville, April 1, 1959).
    BIBLIOGRAPHY: H. Cowell, ed., *American Composers on American Music* (1933); R. F. Goldman, "The Music of Wallingford Riegger," *Musical Quarterly* (Jan. 1950; with a list of works).

Riehl, Wilhelm Heinrich von, German writer on music; b. Biebrich-on-Rhine, May 6, 1823; d. Munich, Nov. 16, 1897. He studied at the Univ. of Munich, where he became (1854) prof. of political economy; also lectured on music history. He publ. the valuable compendium, *Musikalische Charakterköpfe* (3 vols., 1853-61; 6th ed., 1879; 3rd vol. contains the essays "Die Kriegsgeschichte der deutschen Oper" and "Die beiden Beethoven"), and 2 vols. of original songs, *Hausmusik* (1856; 1877). Posthumous publications: *Zur Geschichte der romantischen Oper* (Berlin, 1928); *Musik im Leben des Volkes,* a collection of Riehl's articles, compiled and ed. by J. Müller-Blattau (Kassel, 1936).
    BIBLIOGRAPHY: H. Simonsfeld, *Heinrich Riehl als Kulturhistoriker* (Munich, 1899); V. von Geramb, *W. H. Riehl, Leben und Wirken* (Salzburg, 1954).

Riem, Friedrich Wilhelm, German organist and composer; b. Kölleda, Thuringia, Feb. 17, 1779; d. Bremen, April 20, 1857. He was a pupil of J. A. Hiller in Leipzig; organist at the Thomaskirche (1807-14), then in Bremen. He wrote an oratorio, *Der Erlöser;* a string quintet, a piano quartet, 3 string quartets, 4 violin sonatas, 6 piano sonatas; also publ. a collection of organ pieces for concert and church.

Riemann, (Carl Wilhelm Julius) Hugo, pre-eminent German musicologist; b. Grossmehlra, near Sondershausen, July 18, 1849; d. Leipzig, July 10, 1919. He was trained in theory by Frankenberger at Sondershausen, studied the piano with Barthel and Ratzenberger; took the gymnasial course in the Rossleben Klosterschule, 1865-68, and studied first law, then philosophy and history, at Berlin and Tübingen; then entered the Leipzig Cons. In 1873 he took the degree of *Dr. phil.* at Göttingen with the dissertation *Musikalische Logik;* was active as a conductor and teacher at Bielefeld until 1878, when he qualified as University lecturer on music at Leipzig; taught music at Bromberg (1880-81), then at the Hamburg Cons. till 1890, at the Sondershausen Cons. for a short time, and at the Weisbaden Cons. until 1895, when he resumed his lectures at Leipzig. In 1905 he was made prof.; in 1908, director of the newly established Collegium Musicum, and in 1914 also director of the newly established Forschungsinstitut für Musikwissenschaft. He was made Mus. Doc. (*honoris causa*) by the Univ. of

Edinburgh (1899). On his 60th birthday he was honored by the publication of a Festschrift (ed., Karl Mennicke) containing contributions from the world's foremost scholars, many of whom were Riemann's pupils. The second Riemann Festschrift was publ., after his death in 1919.
    The mere bulk of Riemann's writings, covering every branch of musical science, constitutes a monument of indefatigable industry, and is proof of enormous concentration and capacity for work. When one takes into consideration that much of this work is the result of painstaking research and of original, often revolutionary, thinking, one must share the great respect and admiration in which Riemann was held by his contemporaries. Although many of his ideas are now seen in a different light, his works treating of harmony were considered to constitute the foundation of modern musical theory. His researches in the field of music history have solved a number of vexed problems, and thrown light on others. And, finally, in formulating the new science of musicology, the labors of Riemann have been a most important factor.
    WRITINGS: THEORY: *Musikalische Syntaxis* (1877); *Skizze einer neuen Methode der Harmonielehre* (1880); rewritten as *Handbuch der Harmonielehre* (1887; 8th ed., 1920); *Elementarmusiklehre* (1882); *Neue Schule der Melodik* (1883); *Vergleichende Klavierschule* (1883); *Musikalische Dynamik und Agogik* (1884); *Praktische Anleitung zum Phrasierung,* (1886; rewritten as *Vademecum der Phrasierung,* 1900); *Systematische Modulationslehre* (1887); *Lehrbuch des einfachen, doppelten und imitierenden Kontrapunkts* (1888; 6th ed., 1921; in English, 1904); *Die Elemente der musikalischen Ästhetik* (1900); *Grosse Kompositionslehre* (vol. I, *Der homophone Satz,* 1902; vol. II, *Der polyphone Satz,* 1903; vol. III, *Der Orchestersatz und der dramatische Vokalstil,* 1913); *System der musikalischen Rhythmik und Metrik* (1903); *Grundriss der Musikwissenschaft* (1908; 4th ed. edited by J. Wolf, 1928); *Analyse von Beethovens Klaviersonaten* (3 vols. 1915-19). HISTORY: *Studien zur Geschichte der Notenschrift* (1878); *Die Entwickelung unserer Notenschrift* (1881); *Die "Martyriai" der byzantinischen liturgischen Notation* (1882); *Notenschrift und Notendruck* (1896); *Geschichte der Musiktheorie im 9-19. Jahrhundert* (1898); *Epochen und Heroen der Musikgeschichte* (1900); *Geschichte der Musik seit Beethoven* (1901); *Handbuch der Musikgeschichte* (5 vols., 1904-13); as supplement to this, *Musikgeschichte in Beispielen* (1912; a collection of 150 compositions, 13th-18th century; 4th ed., with introduction by A. Schering, 1929); *Die byzantinische Notenschrift im 10.-15. Jahrhundert* (vol. I, 1909; vol. II, 1915); *Kompendium der Notenschriftkunde* (1910); *Folkloristische Tonalitätsstudien* (1916). LEXICOGRAPHY: *Musik-Lexikon,* one of the standard reference works on music; published in Leipzig, 1882, following editions appeared in 1884, 1887, 1894, 1900, 1905, 1909, 1916; the 9th, 10th, and 11th editions were brought out in 1919, 1922, and 1929, under the editorship of Alfred Einstein; the 12th edition, under Wilibald Gurlitt, was published in 3 vols. (Mainz, 1959, 1961, 1967); to these was added a supplement in 2 vols. (Mainz, 1972, 1973), edited by Carl Dahlhaus; *Opern-Handbuch* (Leipzig, 1887; sup-

plement, 1893). Riemann contributed to Schlesinger's *Meisterführer* analyses of Beethoven's string quartets (vol. XII, 1910), and some of the orchestral works of Brahms (vol. III, 1908), Schumann (vol. XIII, 1911), and Tchaikovsky (vol. XIV, 1911); revised Marx's *Lehre von der musikalischen Komposition* (4 vols.; 1887-90); ed. vols. IV (1907) and V (1908) of Deiters's transl. of Thayer's *Beethoven,* and revised vols. II and III (1910, 1911). He publ. in various journals innumerable articles and essays; of these some were collected and publ. as *Präludien und Studien* (3 vols., 1895, 1900, 1901); edited works of early composers in the *Denkmäler deutscher Tonkunst in Bayern* and in the *Denkmäler deutscher Tonkunst;* also the collections *Alte Kammermusik* (4 vols.), *Collegium musicum* (50 books), *Hausmusik aus alter Zeit* (96 madrigals, canzone, etc., of the 14th and 15th centuries), etc. He composed many instructive piano pieces; also chamber music, choruses, and songs.
BIBLIOGRAPHY: biographical sketch by K. Mennicke in the Riemann–Festschrift (Leipzig, 1909); R. Heuler, "Dr. H. Riemann als Volksschulgesangpädagod," *Sonde* (Würzburg, 1910); Riemann issue of the *Zeitschrift für Musikwissenschaft* (July 1919); H. Grabner, *Die Funktionstheorie Riemanns* (Munich, 1923); H. L. Denecke, *Die Kompositionslehre Hugo Riemanns* (Kiel, 1937); W. Gurlitt, *Hugo Riemann* (Wiesbaden, 1951).

Riemann, Ludwig, German writer on music; b. Lüneburg, March 25, 1863; d. Essen, Jan. 25, 1927. Pupil of his father; also of O. von Königslöw and H. Schröder (violin), H. Grüters and A. Löschhorn (piano), J. Alsleben, A. Haupt, and W. Bargiel (composition) at the Königliche Institut für Kirchenmusik in Berlin; from 1889, teacher of singing at the Gymnasium in Essen; 1918, prof.
WRITINGS: *Populäre Darstellung der Akustik in Beziehung zur Musik* (1896), *Über eigentümliche, bei Natur- und orientalischen Kulturvölkern vorkommende, Tonreihen und ihre Beziehungen zu den Gesetzen der Harmonie* (1899), *Das Wesen des Klavierklanges und seine Beziehungen zum Anschlag* (1911; valuable), *Das Erkennen der Ton- und Akkordzusammenhänge in Tonstücken klassischer und moderner Literatur* (1925), *Kurzgefasste praktische Modulationsübungen* (2nd ed., 1924), etc.

Riemenschneider, Albert, American organist and music editor; b. Berea, Ohio, Aug. 31, 1878; d. Akron, July 20, 1950. He studied at Baldwin Wallace College (B.A., 1899) and in Cleveland; then went to Vienna where he took lessons with R. Fuchs and H. Reinhold, and proceeded to Paris where he continued his organ study with Widor and Guilmant. Returning to America in 1905, he became a choral director of Baldwin Wallace Cons., and later president of the College. His main contribution to American musicology is a number of fine editions of Bach's vocal works, among them *Liturgical Year* (the *Orgelbüchlein;* 1933); *Chorales* (120 chorales in original clefs and with the original orchestral parts; 2 vols., 1939; with Ch. N. Boyd) and *371 Harmonized Chorales and 69 Chorale Melodies with Figured Bass* (1941).

Riepel, Joseph, Austrian theorist; b. Hörschlag, Jan., 1709 (baptized Jan. 22); d. Regensburg, Oct. 23, 1782. He studied in Linz; then took a course with Zelenka in Dresden (1740-45); in 1751 he settled in Regensburg. He published several vols. dealing with theory, harmony and rhythm, which are valuable fron the historical point of view: *De rhythmopoeia oder von der Tactordnung* (Augsburg, 1752); *Harmonisches Sylbenmass* (Regensburg, 1776), etc.; also composed symphonies, piano concertos, violin concertos and sacred choral music.
BIBLIOGRAPHY: W. Twittenhoff, *Die musiktheoretischen Schriften J. Riepels* (Halle, 1935); E. Schwarzmaier, *Die Takt- une Tonordnung J. Riepels* (Wolfenbüttel, 1936); J. Markl, *J. Riepel als Komponist* (Kallmünz, 1937).

Ries, Ferdinand, German pianist and composer; b. Bonn, Nov. 28, 1784; d. Frankfurt, Jan. 13, 1838. He was the son of **Franz Anton Ries,** "der alte Ries," a close friend of Beethoven; thanks to this relationship, Ferdinand Ries was accepted by Beethoven as a piano pupil and studied with him in Vienna from 1801 to 1805; also in Vienna he took a course in music theory with Albrechtsberger. He made successful tours as a concert pianist in Germany, Scandinavia and Russia; then went to London, where he remained fron 1813 to 1824, and acquired prominence as a piano teacher. From 1830 he stayed mainly in Frankfurt. He was an excellent pianist and prolific composer.
WORKS: the operas *Die Räuberbraut* (Frankfurt, 1828), *Liska* (produced in London, 1831, under the title *The Sorceress);* 2 oratorios; 6 symphonies; 9 piano concertos; chamber music; 52 piano sonatas and other pieces for his instrument. His music reflects both the spirit and the technique of composition of Beethoven, the fateful distance between them being that of genius which Ries never possessed. His reminiscences of Beethoven were published posthumously under the title *Biographische Notizen über L. von Beethoven* (Koblenz, 1828; numerous later editions in all European languages; the work was partly dictated by Ries to Wegeler during the last years of Ries's life, and inevitably contains stories that could not be trusted.
BIBLIOGRAPHY: L. Überfeldt, *Ferdinand Ries' Jugendentwicklung* (Bonn, 1915).

Ries, Franz, German publisher; son of **Hubert Ries;** b. Berlin, April 7, 1846; d. Naumberg, June 20, 1932. He studied violin with his father and later with Massart at the Paris Cons. His career as a concert violinist was brief, and in 1875 he entered the music publishing business; from 1882 to 1924 was director of the firm Ries & Erler in Berlin; in 1924 his son **Robert Ries** became the proprietor; after the death of Robert Ries the firm was taken over by his 2 daughters.

Ries, Franz Anton, German violinist; b. Bonn, Nov. 10, 1755; d. Godesberg, Nov. 1, 1846. He was known as "der alte Ries," to distinguish him from his son **Ferdinand.** Franz Anton Ries was music director of the Margrave Max Franz of Cologne and Bonn, and was a close friend of Beethoven in Bonn.

Ries, Hubert, German violinist; brother of **Ferdinand Ries**; b. Bonn, April 1, 1802; d. Berlin, Sept. 14, 1886. Studied at Kassel under Spohr (violin) and Hauptmann (composition); in 1836, concertmaster of the royal orch., Berlin; in 1851 teacher at the Royal Theaterinstrumentalschule; pensioned 1872. Publ. excellent instructive works for violin: *Violinschule* (also in English); *Erzählungen aus alter Zeit* (30 instructive duets); *15 Violinstudien von mässiger Schwierigkeit*, op. 26; *30 Violinstudien für den ersten Unterricht*, op. 28; *50 Intonationsübungen, 12 Violinstudien in Form von Konzertstücken*, op. 9; duets, exercises, etc., also 2 violin concertos (op. 13 and 16).

Riesemann, Oscar, Russian–Germann musicologist; b. Reval, Estonia, Feb. 29, 1880; d. St. Niklausen, near Lucerne, Switzerland, Sept. 28, 1934. He studied music theory with Sanberger and Thuille at the Royal Academy in Munich; then took courses in philology and jurisprudence at the Univ. of Moscow; subsequently went to Germany again and took courses with Friedlaender in Berlin and with Hugo Riemann in Leipzig, where he obtained his Dr. phil. with the dissertation *Die Notation des alt-russischen Kirchengesanges* (publ. in Moscow, in German, 1908). He then was active as a music critic in Moscow, and during World War I served on the Russian side in the sanitary corps, but made his way to Germany once more during the Russian Revolution; he described this turbulent period in an autobiographical publication *Fluchten* (Stuttgart, 1925). He subsequently lived in Munich and then in Switzerland. He published a monograph on Mussorgsky (Munich, 1926; in English, N.Y., 1929), and, in English, *Rachmaninoff's Recollections* (N.Y., 1934), a loyal but not always accurate account, which was gently repudiated by Rachmaninoff himself.

Rieter-Biedermann, J. Melchior, Swiss publisher; b. Winterthur, May 14, 1811; d. there, Jan. 25, 1876. He founded a successful music publishing house in 1849 in Winterthur, with a branch at Leipzig in 1862, which gradually became more important than the original house, so that the latter was dissolved in 1884. After the death of the last proprietor, Robert Astor (d. Leipzig, April 14, 1917), the firm was bought by C. F. Peters. Brahms was the most famous composer in their catalog.

Rieti, Vittorio, Italian–American composer; b. Alexandria, Egypt, Jan. 28, 1898. He studied with Frugatta in Milan; then took courses with Respighi and Casella in Rome, where he lived until 1939, when he emigrated to the U.S. (became an American citizen June 1, 1944). He taught at the Peabody Cons. in Baltimore (1948–49), Chicago Musical College (1950–53), Queen's College, N.Y. (1958–60) and at the Hunter College of Music in N.Y. (1960–64). His style of composition represents an ingratiating synthesis of cosmopolitan modern tendencies.
WORKS: operas: *Orfeo*, a lyric tragedy (1928); *Teresa nel bosco* (Venice Festival, Sept. 15, 1934); *Don Perlimplin* (Univ. of Illinois, Urbana, March 30, 1952); *The Pet Shop* (N.Y., April 14, 1958); *The Clock* (1960); *Maryam the Harlot* (1966); ballets: *L'Arca di Noè*

(1922), *Barabau*, with chorus (Ballets Russes, London, Dec. 11, 1925), *Le Bal* (Monte Carlo, 1929); *David triomphant* (Paris, 1937), *Waltz Academy* (Boston, 1944), *The Mute Wife*, on themes by Paganini (N.Y., 1944), *Trionfo di Bacco e Arianna* (N.Y., 1948), *Unicorn* (1950); oratorio, *Viaggio d'Europa* (Rome, 1954); for orch.: 6 symphonies; of these No. 4 is subtitled *Sinfonia Tripartita* (St. Louis, Dec. 16, 1944); No. 6 was first performed in N.Y., Dec. 11, 1974; *Concerto du Loup* (named after the Loup River in Southern France) for chamber orch. (Los Angeles, Aug. 8, 1942); Concerto for 5 wind instruments and orch. (Prague Festival, May 31, 1924); 3 piano concertos (1926; 1937, 1960); Violin Concerto (1928); Harpsichord Concerto (1930); 2 cello concertos; Concerto for 2 pianos and orch. (Cincinnati, 1952); Sonata for flute, oboe, bassoon and piano (1924); 4 string quartets (1926; 1942; 1953; 1960); Woodwind Quartet (1958); *Madrigal* for 12 instruments; *5 Fables of La Fontaine* for orch. (1968); Triple Concerto for violin, viola, piano and orch. (1971); Octet for flute, oboe, piano, bassoon, viola, violin, cello and piano (1971); Piano Trio (1972). Concerto for String Quartet and Orch. (N.Y., Feb. 1, 1978). See *Notes* (Dec. 1972) for a list of his works.

Rietsch, Heinrich, Czech musicologist and composer; b. Falkenau-on-Eger, Sept. 22, 1860; d. Prague, Dec. 12, 1927. He studied in Vienna under Krenn and R. Fuchs (composition) and Hanslick (music history). In 1900 he became instructor at the German Univ. in Prague. He edited Muffat's *Florilegium* for the *Denkmäler der Tonkunst in Österreich;* also J. J. Fux's *Concentus musico-instrumentalis* (ibid.). He publ. *Die Tonkunst in der 2 Hälfte des 19. Jahrhunderts* (Leipzig, 1900); *Die deutsche Liedweise* (Leipzig, 1904); *Die Grundlagen der Tonkunst* (Leipzig, 1907); several of his publications were reprinted. His autobiographical sketch was published in *Neue Musikzeitung* (1915).
BIBLIOGRAPHY: Paul Nettl, "Verzeichnis der wissenschaftlichen und künstlerischen Arbeiten von Rietsch bis 1920," *Zeitschrift für Musikwissenschaft* II (p. 736).

Rietschel, Georg Christian, German organist and theologian; b. Dresden, May 10, 1842; d. Leipzig, June 13, 1914. After filling several pastorates in various German cities, he became prof. of theology at Leipzig Univ. (1899). He published *Die Aufgabe der Orgel im Gottesdienste bis in das 18. Jahrhundert* (1892) and *Lehrbuch der Liturgik* (2 vols., 1900, 1909).

Rietz, Julius, German conductor and editor; b. Berlin, Dec. 28, 1812; d. Dresden, Sept. 12, 1877. He was of a musical family; his father was a court musician, and his brother was a friend of Mendelssohn. Julius Rietz studied cello and played in theater orchestras in Berlin. In 1834 he became 2nd conductor of the Düsseldorf Opera; from 1847 to 1854 he was a theater conductor in Leipzig; in 1848 became conductor of the Gewandhaus Concerts; later he was appointed artistic director of the Dresden Cons. A scholarly musician and competent orchestral conductor, Rietz was also an excellent music editor; he prepared for publication the complete edition of Mendelssohn's works for Breitkopf & Härtel (1874–77), and also edited Mozart's operas and symphonies, Beethoven's overtures, etc. As a composer, he followed the musical style of Mendelssohn.

BIBLIOGRAPHY: "Pauline Viardot-Garcia to Julius Rietz, Letters of Friendship," *Musical Quarterly* (July 1915 to Jan. 1916); H. Zimmer, *Julius Rietz* (dissertation; Berlin, 1943).

Riezler, Walter, German musicologist; b. Munich, Oct. 2, 1878; d. there, Jan. 22, 1956. He studied music with Max Reger and Felix Mottl (1904–06). He was first interested principally in art; he was director of the Stettin Museum of Fine Arts (1910–33); in 1934 he reutrned to Munich; after 1946 taught music history at the Univ. of Munich. He publ. an excellent monograph on Beethoven (1936) which went through 7 German editions up to 1951 and was also translated into English (N.Y., 1938).

Rigel, Henri–Jean, French composer; son and pupil of **Heinrich Joseph Riegel** (he changed his name from its German form to French); b. Paris, May 11, 1772; d. Abbeville, Dec. 16, 1852. He conducted the French Opera in Cairo (1798–1800); in 1808 was attached to Napoleon's court as a chamber musician. He wrote the operas *Les deux meuniers* (Cairo, 1799) and *Le Duel nocturne* (Paris, 1808); 4 piano concertos and numerous minor piano pieces.

Righini, Vincenzo, Italian composer; b. Bologna, Jan. 22, 1756; d. there, Aug. 19, 1812. Pupil of Bernacchi (singing) and Padre Martini (counterpoint). Stage debut as a tenor at Parma, 1775; went to Prague in 1776, where he also began composing; in 1780 he became singing master to the Archduchess Elizabeth at Vienna, and conductor of the Opera Buffa; from 1788 to 1793 he was Electoral Kapellmeister at Mainz; in 1793, after the successful production of his opera *Enea nel Lazio* at Berlin, he was appointed Kappelmeister at the Court Opera.

WORKS: some 20 operas, including *Il Convitato di pietra* (Vienna, Aug. 21, 1777; one of the early settings of the Don Giovanni story) and *Gerusalemme liberata* and *La Selva incantata* (a single work consisting of 2 2-act operas; Berlin, Jan. 7, 1803); a series of fine vocal exercises (1806).

Rignold, Hugo, English conductor; b. Kingston-on-Thames, May 15, 1905; d. London, May 30, 1976. His father was a theatrical conductor; his mother an opera singer. He was taken to Canada as a child, and studied violin in Winnipeg; in 1920 he returned to England on a scholarship to the Royal Academy of Music. During World War II he was stationed in Cairo, where he trained a radio orch. in performances of symph. music. Returning to England, he was a ballet conductor at Covent Garden (1947); from 1948 to 1950 was conductor of the Liverpool Philharmonic.

BIBLIOGRAPHY: Donald Brook, *International Gallery of Conductors* (Bristol, 1951; pp. 151–54).

Riisager, Knudåge, prominent Danish composer; b. Port Kunda, Estonia, March 6, 1897; d. Copenhagen, Dec. 26, 1974. He attended courses in political science at the Univ. of Copenhagen (1916–21); concurrently studied music with Peter Gram, Peter Møller and Otto Malling (1915–18); then went to Paris and took private lessons with Albert Roussel and Paul le Flem (1923–24); subsequently studied counterpoint with Herman Grabner in Leipzig (1932). He held a position in the Ministry of Finance of Denmark (1925–47); was chairman of the Danish Composers' Union (1937–62) and director of the Royal Danish Cons. (1956–67). A fantastically prolific composer, he wrote music in quaquaversal genres, but preserved a remarkable structural and textural consistency while demonstrating an erudite sense of modern polyphony. He also had a taste for exotic and futuristic subjects.

WORKS: (all premières are in Copenhagen unless stated otherwise): FOR THE STAGE: opera buffa, *Susanne* (1948; Royal Danish Opera, Jan. 7, 1950); 14 ballets: *Benzin* (1927; Dec. 26, 1930), a "ballet-bouffonnerie" *Cocktails-Party* (1929), *Tolv med Posten* (*Twelve by the Mail*, after H. C. Andersen, 1939; Feb. 21, 1942); *Slaraffenland* (*Fool's Paradise*, 1940; Feb. 21, 1942; originally an orchestral piece, 1936), *Qarrtsiluni*, on Eskimo themes (1942; Feb. 21, 1942; originally an orchestral piece, 1938), *Fugl Fønix* (*Phoenix*, 1944–45; May 12, 1946), *Etude*, based on Czerny's studies (1947; Jan. 15, 1948), *Månerenen* (*The Moon Reindeer;* 1956; Nov. 22, 1957), *Stjerner* (1958), *Les Victoires de l'Amour* (1958; March 4, 1962), *Fruen fra havet* (*Lady from the Sea*, 1959; N.Y., April 20, 1960), *Galla-Variationer* (1966; March 5, 1967), *Ballet Royal* (May 31, 1967), and *Svinedrengen* (*The Swineherd;* Danish television, March 10, 1969). FOR ORCH.: *Erasmus Montanus*, overture (1920; Göteborg, Sweden, Oct. 15, 1924); *Suite Dionysiaque* for chamber orch. (1924); 5 symphonies: No. 1 (1925; July 17, 1926); No. 2 (1927; March 5, 1929); No. 3 (1935; Nov. 21, 1935); No. 4, *Sinfonia Gaia* (1940; Oct. 24, 1940); No. 5, *Sinfonia Serena*, for strings and percussion (1949–50; Nov. 21, 1950); *Introduzione di traverso*, overture (1925); *Variations on a Theme of Mezangean* (1926); *T-DOXC*, "poème mécanique" (1926; Sept. 3, 1927); *Klods Hans* (1929); *Fastelavn* (*Shrovetide*), overture (1929–30); *Suite* for small orch. (1931); Concerto for Orch. (1931; Dec. 7, 1936); Concertino for trumpet and string orch. (1933; March 2, 1934); *Primavera*, overture (1934; Jan. 31, 1935); *Slaraffenland*, 2 suites (1936, 1940; as a ballet, 1940); *Sinfonia concertante* for strings (1937); *Partita* (1937); *Basta* (1938); *Qarrtsiluni* (1938; as a ballet, 1940); *Torgutisk dans* (1939); *Tivoli-Tivoli!* (1943; Aug. 15, 1943); *Sommer-Rhapsodi* (1943; Jan. 30, 1944); *Bellman-Variationer* for small orch. (1945); *Sinfonietta* (1947; Stockholm, Oct. 1, 1947); *Chaconne* (1949); *Archaeopteryx* (1949); *Variations on a Sarabande of Charles, Duke of Orleans, 1415* for string orch. (1950); Violin Concerto (1950–51; Oct. 11, 1951); *Toccata* (1952); *Pro fistulis et fidibus* for woodwinds and string orch. (1952; March 2, 1953); *Rondo giocoso* for violin and orch. (1957; June 18, 1957); *Burlesk Ouverture* (1964); *Entrada-Epilogo* (May 19, 1971); *Bourrée*, ballet-variations (Danish Radio, March 7, 1972); *Trittico* for woodwinds, brass, double bass and percussion (Danish Radio, March 3, 1972); *Apollon* (Nov. 11, 1973); incidental music. FOR VOICE: *Dansk Salme* for chorus and orch. (1942; April 13, 1943); *Sang til Solen* for mezzo-soprano, baritone, chorus, and orch. (1947; Sept. 25,

1947); *Sangen om det Uendelige (Canto dell'Infinito)* for chorus and orch. (1964; Sept. 30, 1965); *Stabat Mater* for chorus and orch. (1966; Danish Radio, Nov. 9, 1967); choruses; songs. CHAMBER MUSIC: 2 violin sonatas (1917, 1923); 6 string quartets (1918, 1920, 1922, 1925–26, 1932, 1942–43); Sonata for violin and viola (1919); Wind Quintet (1921); *Variations* for clarinet, viola and bassoon (1923); Sinfonietta for 8 wind instruments (1924); *Divertimento* for string quartet and wind quintet (1925); Sonata for flute, violin, clarinet, and cello (1927); *Music* for wind quintet (1927); *Conversazione* for oboe, clarinet and bassoon (1932); Concertino for 5 violins and piano (1933); *Serenade* for flute, violin and cello (1936); Quartet for flute, oboe, clarinet, and bassoon (1941); *Divertimento* for flute, oboe, horn and bassoon (1944); Sonatina for piano trio (1951); 2-violin sonata (1951); String Trio (1955). FOR PIANO: *4 Épigrammes* (1921); Sonata (1931), *2 Morceaux* (1933); Sonatina (1950); *4 Børneklaverstykker* (1964). He published a collection of essays, *Det usynlige Mønster (The Unseemly Monster;* Copenhagen, 1957) and a somewhat self-deprecatory memoir, *Det er sjovt at være lille (It Is Amusing to Be Small;* Copenhagen, 1967).

BIBLIOGRAPHY: Sigurd Berg, *Knudåge Riisagers Kompositioner,* an annotated catalogue of works (Copenhagen, 1967).

Riley, John, American composer and cellist; b. Altoona, Pennsylvania, Sept. 17, 1920. He studied cello and composition in the U.S., and also in London; received his Mus. B. at the Eastman School of Music, Rochester, in 1951; studied composition on a Fulbright Grant with Arthur Honegger in Paris (1952–53); at Yale Univ. with Quincy Porter (Mus. M., 1955). His works include a *Rhapsody* for cello and orch. (1951); *Apostasy* for orch. (1954); *Fantasy* for oboe and string orch. (1955); Sinfonietta (1955); 2 string quartets (1954, 1959).

Riley, Terry, American composer of the avant-garde; b. Colfax, California, June 24, 1935. He studied at the Univ. of California at Berkeley with Seymour Shifrin, William Denny and Robert Erikson, obtaining his M.A. in composition in 1961; went to Europe and played piano and saxophone in cabarets in Paris and in Scandinavia. In 1970 he was initiated in San Francisco as a disciple of Pandit Pran Nath, the North Indian singer, and followed him to India. In his music Riley explores the extremes of complexity and gymnosophistical simplicity. His ascertainable works include *Spectra* for 6 instruments (1959), String Trio (1961), and *In C,* for orchestra, notated in fragments to be played any number of times at will in the spirit of aleatory latitudinarianism, all within the key of C major, with an occasional F sharp providing a *trompe l'oreille* effect; it was first performed in San Francisco, May 21, 1965. His other compositions are *Poppy Nogoods Phantom Band* (1966), *A Rainbow in Curved Air* (1968), and *Genesis '70,* a ballet (1970). Riley's astrological signs are Sun in Cancer (euphemistically known in Southern California as Moon Children so as to exorcise middle-aged fear of malignancy), Scorpio Rising and Aries Moon.

Rimbault, Edward Francis, English writer and editor; b. London, June 13, 1816; d. there, Sept. 26, 1876. Son of **Stephen Francis Rimbault,** organist and composer (1773–1837); pupil of his father, of Samuel Wesley and Dr. Crotch; organist of the Swiss Church, Soho, in 1832. He began giving lectures on English musical history in 1838; in 1840 he founded, with E. Taylor and W. Chappell, the Musical Antiquarian Society; received the degree of Dr. phil. from Göttingen. He composed various songs, of which *Happy Land* became a popular favorite.

WRITINGS: *Bibliotheca Madrigaliana* (1847; English poetry and compositions publ. during the reigns of Elizabeth and James I); *The Organ, Its History and Construction* (1855 and other eds.; it is the first part of the Appendix to Hopkins's *The Organ: Its History); The Pianoforte: Its Origin, Progress and Construction* (1860); *The Early English Organ-builders and Their Works* (1864); *J. S. Bach* (after Hilgenfeldt and Forkel; 1869); *Singing Tutor* (after Lablache), etc. He edited collections of sacred and secular music, particularly those by English composers of the 16th, 17th, and 18th centuries.

Rimsky-Korsakov, Andrei, son of **Nicolai Rimsky-Korsakov**; b. St. Petersburg, Oct. 17, 1878; d. there, (Leningrad), May 23, 1940. He studied philology at the Univ. of St. Petersburg and later at Strasbourg and Heidelberg (Dr. phil., 1903); returning to Russia he devoted his energies to Russian music history. In 1915 he began the publication of an important magazine *Musikalny Sovremennik (The Musical Contemporary),* but the revolutionary events of 1917 forced suspension of its publication. He edited the first 4 vols. of the complete biography of his father, *N. A. Rimsky-Korsakov; Life and Works* (Moscow, 1933, 1935, 1936, 1937; an additional vol., No. 5, was completed and edited by his younger brother **Vladimir Rimsky-Korsakov**); other publications were *M. P. Mussorgsky, Letters and Documents* (1932; extremely valuable); he further edited and annotated his father's *Chronicle of My Musical Life* (Moscow, 1935); compiled the catalogue, *Musical Treasures of the Manuscript Dept. of the Leningrad Public Library* (1938). He was married to the composer **Julia Weissberg.**

Rimsky-Korsakov, Georgi, grandson of **Nicolai Rimsky-Korsakov** and nephew of **Andrei Rimsky-Korsakov**; b. St. Petersburg, Dec. 26, 1901; d. Leningrad, Oct. 10, 1965. He studied at the St. Petersburg Cons.; in 1923 founded a society for the cultivation of quarter-tone music; composed some works in that system; publ. the articles "Foundations of the Quarter-Tone System" (Leningrad, 1925) and "The Deciphering of the 'Luce' Part in Scriabin's Prometheus," in the Russian magazine *De musica* (1927); then became active in work on electronic musical instruments; was co-inventor of the "Emeriton" (1930), capable of producing a complete series of tones at any pitch and of any chosen or synthetic tone color; wrote solo pieces for it; also an Octet for 2 emeritons, 2 clarinets, bassoon, violin, viola, and cello (1932). From 1927 to 1962 he was on the faculty of the Cons. of Leningrad.

Rimsky-Korsakov, Nikolai, great Russian composer; b. Tikhvin, near Novgorod, March 18, 1844; d. Liubensk, near St. Petersburg, June 21, 1908. He remained in the country until he was 12 years old; in 1856 he entered the Naval School in St. Petersburg, graduating in 1862. As a child he took piano lessons with provincial teachers, and later with a professional musician, Théodore Canillé, who introduced him to Balakirev; he also met Cui and Borodin. In 1862 he was sent on the clipper Almaz on a voyage that lasted 2½ years; returning to Russia in the summer of 1865, he settled in St. Petersburg, where he remained most of his life. During his travels he maintained contact with Balakirev, and continued to report to him the progress of his musical composition. He completed his First Symphony (which was also the earliest work in this form by a Russian composer), and it was performed in St. Petersburg under Balakirev's direction on Dec. 31, 1865, at a concert of the Free Music School in St. Petersburg. In 1871 Rimsky-Korsakov was engaged as prof. of composition and orchestration at the St. Petersburg Cons., even though he was aware of the inadequacy of his own technique. He remained on the faculty until his death, with the exception of a few months in 1905, when he was relieved from his duties as prof. for his public support of the rebellious students during the revolution of that year. As a music educator, Rimsky-Korsakov was of the greatest importance to the development and maintenance of the traditions of the Russian national school; among his students were Glazunov, Liadov, Arensky, Ippolitov-Ivanov, Gretchaninov, Nicolas Tcherepnin, Maximilian Steinberg, Gnessin, and Miaskovsky. Igor Stravinsky studied privately with Rimsky-Korsakov from 1903 on.

In 1873 Rimsky-Korsakov abandoned his naval career, but was appointed to the post of inspector of the military orchestras of the Russian Navy, until it was abolished in 1884. From 1883 to 1894 he was also assistant director of the Court Chapel and led the chorus and the orchestra there. Although he was not a gifted conductor, he gave many performances of his own orchestral works; made his debut at a charity concert for the victims of the Volga famine, in St. Petersburg, March 2, 1874; the program included the 1st performance of his 3rd Symph. From 1886 until 1900 he conducted the annual Russian Symphony concerts organized by the publisher Belaieff; in June 1889 he conducted 2 concerts of Russian music at the World Exposition in Paris; in 1890 he conducted a concert of Russian music in Brussels; led a similar concert there in 1900. His last appearance abroad was in the spring of 1907, when he conducted in Paris 2 Russian historic concerts arranged by Diaghilev; in the same year he was elected corresponding member of the French Academy to succeed Grieg. These activities, however, did not distract him from his central purpose as a national Russian composer. His name was grouped with those of Cui, Borodin, Balakirev, and Mussorgsky as the "Mighty Five," and he maintained an intimate friendship with most of them; at Mussorgsky's death he collected his manuscripts and prepared them for publication; he also revised Mussorgsky's opera *Boris Godunov*; it was in Rimsky-Korsakov's version that the opera became famous. Later some criticism was voiced against Rimsky-Korsakov's reduction of Mussorgsky's original harmonies and melodic lines to an academically acceptable standard. He had decisive influence in the affairs of the Belaieff publishing firm and helped publish a great number of works by Russian composers of the St. Petersburg group; only a small part of these sumptuously printed scores represents the best in Russian music, but culturally Rimsky-Korsakov's solicitude was of great importance. Although he was far from being a revolutionary, he freely expressed his disgust at the bungling administration of Czarist Russia; he was particularly indignant about the attempts of the authorities to alter Pushkin's lines in his own last opera, *Le Coq d'or,* and refused to compromise; he died, of angina pectoris, with the situation still unresolved; the opera was produced posthumously, with the censor's changes; the original text was not restored until the revolution of 1917.

Rimsky-Korsakov was one of the greatest masters of Russian music. His source of inspiration was Glinka's operatic style; he made use of both the purely Russian idiom and coloristic Oriental melodic patterns; such works as his symph. suite *Scheherazade* and *Le Coq d'or* represent Russian Orientalism at its best; in the purely Russian style the opera *Snow Maiden* and the *Russian Easter Overture* are outstanding examples. The influence of Wagner and Liszt in his music was small; only in his opera, *The Legend of the Invisible City of Kitezh,* are there perceptible echoes from *Parsifal.* In the art of orchestration Rimsky-Korsakov had few equals; his treatment of instruments, in solo passages and in ensemble, was invariably idiomatic. In his treatise on orchestration he selected only passages from his own works to demonstrate the principles of practical and effective application of registers and tone colors. Although Rimsky-Korsakov was an academician in his general esthetics, he experimented boldly with melodic progressions and ingenious harmonies that pointed towards modern usages. He especially favored the major scale with the lowered submediant and the scale of alternating whole tones and semi-tones (which in Russian reference works came to be termed as "Rimsky-Korsakov's scale"; in the score of his opera-ballet *Mlada* there is an ocarina part tuned in this scale); in *Le Coq d'or* and *Kashchei the Immortal* he applied dissonant harmonies in unusual superpositions; but he set for himself a definite limit in innovation, and severely criticized Richard Strauss, Debussy, and Vincent d'Indy for their modernistic practices.

WORKS: OPERAS: *Pskovityanka (The Maid of Pskov;* 1868–72; revised, 1891; St. Petersburg, Jan. 13, 1873; last version, St. Petersburg, April 18, 1895); *Maiskaya Noch (May Night;* St. Petersburg, Jan. 21, 1880); *Snegurotchka (Snow Maiden;* St. Petersburg, Feb. 10, 1882); *Mlada* (St. Petersburg, Nov. 1, 1892); *Noch pered Rozhdestvom (Night Before Christmas;* St. Petersburg, Dec. 10, 1895); *Sadko* (Moscow, Jan. 7, 1898; Metropolitan Opera, N.Y., Jan. 29, 1929); *Mozart i Salieri,* on Pushkin's play dealing with Salieri's supposed poisoning of Mozart (Moscow, Dec. 7, 1898); *Boyarynia Vera Sheloga* (Moscow, Dec. 27, 1898; originally written as a prologue to *Pskovityanka;* N.Y., May 9, 1922); *Tsarskaya Neviesta (The*

Tsar's Bride; Moscow, Nov. 3, 1899); *Tsar Saltan* (Moscow, Nov. 3, 1900); *Servilia* (St. Petersburg, Oct. 14, 1902); *Kashchei Bezsmertny (Kashchei the Immortal;* Moscow, Dec. 25, 1902); *Pan Voyevoda (The Commander;* St. Petersburg, Oct. 16, 1904); *Skazanie o nevidimom grade Kitezhe (The Legend of the Invisible City of Kitezh;* St. Petersburg, Feb. 20, 1907); *Zolotoy Pietushok (The Golden Cockerel;* usually performed under the French title, *Le Coq d'or;* posthumous; Moscow, Oct. 7, 1909; the only opera of Rimsky-Korsakov often produced abroad).

FOR ORCH.: op. 1, Symph. No. 1 in E minor (originally in E-flat minor; later rewritten and transposed); op. 5, *Sadko,* symph. poem (1867; revised 1869 and 1891); op. 6, *Fantasy on Serbian Themes* (1867; revised 1888); op. 9, Symph. no. 2, *Antar* (1868; revised 1876 and 1897; also as a symph. suite); op. 28, *Overture on Russian Themes* (1866; revised 1880); op. 29, *Conte féerique* (1880); op. 30, Piano Concerto in C-sharp minor (1882–83); op. 31, *Symphoniette* in A minor (on Russian themes; 1879); op. 32, symph. no. 3 in C major (1873–74; revised 1885–86); op. 33, *Fantaisie de concert sur des thèmes russes* for violin and orch. (1886); op. 34, *Capriccio espagnol* (1887); op. 35, *Scheherazade,* symph. suite (St. Petersburg, Nov. 3, 1888); op. 36, *Grande pâque russe (Russian Easter Overture;* 1888); suite from the opera, *Tsar Saltan* (1903; includes the famous musical tableau, *The Flight of the Bumblebee);* op. 59, *Pan Voyevoda,* suite from the opera (1903); op. 61, *Nad mogiloi (At the Grave;* in memory of Belaieff; 1904); op. 62, *Chanson russe (Dubinushka,* 1905, with chorus *ad lib.);* without op. numbers: *Night on Mount Triglav,* from the opera, *Mlada* (1907); suite from the opera, *Le Coq d'or* (1907).

CHAMBER MUSIC: op. 12, String Quartet in F (1875); op. 37, *Serenade* for cello and piano (1903); without op. numbers: String Sextet in A (1876); Quintet in B-flat for flute, clarinet, horn, bassoon, and piano (1876); first movement of a string quartet on B-la-f (Belaieff; other movements by Liadov, Borodin, and Glazunov; 1886); String Quartet in G (1897); Trio in C minor, for violin, cello, and piano (1897).

VOCAL WORKS WITH ORCH.; op. 20, *Stikh ob Alexeye (Poem about Alexis),* folksong for mixed chorus (1877); op. 21, *Slava (Glory),* for mixed chorus (1876–80); op. 44, *Svitezyanka,* cantata for soprano and tenor solo and mixed chorus (1897); op. 53, *Strekozy (Dragonflies)* for women's voices (1897); op. 58, *Piesnia o veshchem Olegye (Poem of Oleg the Wise),* for men's chorus; op. 60, *From Homer,* for women's voices (1899); op. 49, 2 ariosos for bass, *Anchar (The Upas Tree)* and *Prorok (The Prophet)* (1897); choruses a cappella, opp. 13, 14, 16, 18, 19, 23; 77 songs; 5 vocal duets; a vocal trio.

PIANO PIECES: op. 10, 6 *Variations on BACH;* op. 11, 4 pieces; op. 15, 3 pieces; op. 17, 6 fugues.

ARRANGEMENTS AND EDITIONS: He edited a collection of 100 Russian folksongs, op. 24 (1876); harmonized 40 folksongs. After Dargomyzhsky's death, he orchestrated his posthumous opera, *Kamennyi Gost (The Stone Guest);* also orchestrated Borodin's *Prince Igor;* his greatest task of musical reorganization was the preparation for publication and performance of Mussorgsky's works; he reharmonized the cycle, *Songs and Dances of Death,* the symph. picture, *Night*

on the Bald Mountain; orchestrated the opera, *Khovanshchina;* revised *Boris Godunov* (in melody and harmony, as well as in orchestration).

WRITINGS: Among his pedagogical works, the book on harmony (St. Petersburg, 1884; numerous subsequent eds. in Russian; in English, N.Y., 1930) is widely used in Russian music schools; publ. *Foundations of Orchestration* (2 vols., St. Petersburg, 1913; ed. by Maximilian Steinberg; also available in French and in English); collected articles were publ. in 1911, ed. by M. Gnessin. His autobiographical book, *The Chronicle of My Musical Life* (posthumous, 1909; 5th ed. by his son Andrei, supplemented and annotated, 1935) is a valuable document of the most important period of Russian music; it is publ. also in English (N.Y., 1924; new ed., 1942), in French (Paris, 1938), etc. A complete edition of Rimsky-Korsakov's works was begun in 1946; 49 vols. were published by 1970.

BIBLIOGRAPHY: V. Yastrebtzev, *R.-K.* (1900; 2nd ed. with a complete list of works, 1908); N. Findeisen, *R.-K.* (1908); I. Lapshin, *Philosophical Motives in the Works of R.-K.* (1911); N. van Gilse van der Pals, *R.-K.* (Leipzig, 1914); M. Montagu-Nathan, *History of Russian Music* (London, 1915; pp. 179–236); Rosa Newmarch, *The Russian Opera* (London, 1915; pp. 281–333); M. Montagu-Nathan, *R.-K.* (London, 1916); Igor Glebov, *R.-K.* (1922); E. Istel, "R.-K., the Oriental Wizard," *Musical Quarterly* (July 1929); N. van Gilse van der Pals, *R.-K.s Opernschaffen* (Leipzig, 1929); A. Rimsky-Korsakov, *R.-K., Life and Works* (fundamental biography; 5 fascicles; Moscow, 1933, 1935, 1936, 1937, 1946; last vol. ed. by Vladimir Rimsky-Korsakov); Igor Markevitch, *R.-K.* (Paris, 1935); G. Abraham and M. D. Calvocoressi, *Masters of Russian Music* (London, 1936); A. Solovtzov, *R.-K.* (Moscow, 1948; 2nd ed., 1957); G. Abraham, *R.-K.; a Short Biography* (London, 1949); M. O. Yankovsky, *R.-K. and the Revolution of 1905* (Moscow, 1950); V. Kisselev, *R.-K.; Documents* (Moscow, 1951); D. Kabalevsky, ed., *R.-K., Materials and Letters* (Moscow, 2 vols., 1953 and 1954); M. F. Gnessin, *Reflections and Reminiscences about N.A. R.-K.* (Moscow, 1956); I. Kunin, *R.-K.* (Moscow, 1964); S. Evseyev, *R.-K. and Russian National Songs* (Moscow, 1970); numerous monographs on individual operas and other works.

Rinaldo di Capua, Italian opera composer; b. Capua, c.1710; d. Rome, after 1770. He came from the vicinity of Naples and seems to have been active chiefly in Rome, where Burney knew him in 1770, and where most of his operas were given (others were produced in Florence, Venice, London, and Paris). His career as a dramatic composer probably began in 1737. Thereafter he produced about 30 theatrical works with varying success, among them, *Ciro riconosciuto* (Rome, 1737), *Vologeso re de' Parti* (Rome, 1739), and *La Zingara* (Paris, June 19, 1753; his best work). He also composed a *Cantata per la Natività della Beata Vergine* (1747).

BIBLIOGRAPHY: Charles Burney, *Present State of Music in France and Italy* (1771); Ph. Spitta's study of Rinaldo di Capua in *Vierteljahrsschrift für Musikwissenschaft* III (1887); G. Radiciotti, in *Musica d'Oggi* (July 1925); A. Loewenberg, *Annals of Opera* (Cambridge, 1943); R. L. Bostian, *The Works of Rinaldo di*

Capua, dissertation (2 vols.; Univ. of North Carolina, Chapel Hill, 1961).

Rinck, Johann Christian Heinrich, famous German organist; b. Elgersburg, Feb. 18, 1770; d. Darmstadt, Aug. 7, 1846. He studied under Bach's pupil Kittel in Erfurt (1786-89); was town organist at Giessen (1790), and at Darmstadt (1805); became court organist there in 1813, and chamber musician in 1817. One of the foremost players of the time, he made frequent concert tours. He wrote many organ works.
BIBLIOGRAPHY: His *Selbstbiographie* (Breslau, 1833); M. J. Fölsing, *Züge aus dem Leben und Wirken des Dr. C. H. Rinck* (Erfurt, 1848); F. Clément, *Musiciens célèbres* (Paris, 1868; 4th ed., 1887); F. W. Donat, *C. H. Rinck und die Orgelmusik seiner Zeit* (1933).

Ringbom, Nils-Eric, Finnish violinist and composer; b. Turku, Dec. 27, 1907. He studied at the Turku Academy, and took private lessons with Leo Funtek; played violin in the municipal orch. of Turku; then moved to Helsinki and became director of the annual Sibelius Festival (1951-60) and managing director of the Helsinki Philharmonic (1942-70).
WORKS: *Little Suite* for orch. (1933); *Till livet (To Life)* for chorus and string orch. (1936); 5 symphonies (1939, 1944, 1948, 1962, 1970); *Vandrerska (The Wanderer)* for soprano and orch. (1942); Duo for violin and viola (1945); *Hymn to Helsinki* for chorus and orch. (1949); Wind Sextet (1951; first work by a Finnish composer ever performed at the International Festival for Contemporary Music, Salzburg, 1952). He published *Helsingfors Orkesterföretag* (a history of the Helsinki Orch., 1932; in Swedish and Finnish); *Sibelius* (in Swedish and Finnish, Helsinki, 1948; also published in German and English).

Ringer, Alexander L., American musicologist; b. Berlin, Feb. 3, 1921, of Dutch parentage. He attended the Hollander Cons. in Berlin; in 1939 went to Amsterdam where he studied composition with Henk Badings. In 1946 he emigrated to the U.S.; was on the staff of the City College of N.Y. (1948-52), Univ. of Pennsylvania (1952-55), Univ. of Calif., Berkeley (1955-56) and Univ. of Oklahoma (1956-58). In 1958 he was appointed to the faculty of the Univ. of Illinois, Urbana; also regular guest lecturer at the Hebrew Univ. in Jerusalem.
WRITINGS: *The Chasse: Historical and Analytical Bibliography of a Musical Genre* (Ann Arbor, Michigan Univ. Microfilm, 1955); *An Experimental Program in the Development of Musical Literacy Among Musically Gifted Children in the Upper Elementary Grades* (Washington, 1970).

Rinuccini, Ottavio, great Italian poet and librettist; b. Florence, Jan. 20, 1563; d. there, March 28, 1621. He wrote several librettos for the Florentine creators of opera: the text of the intermezzo *Apollo e il pitone,* set to music by Marenzio in 1589, and subsequently the famous *La favola di Dafne* set to music by Peri in 1597, a work that is usually regarded as the first true opera. Rinuccini's *Euridice,* with music by Peri, was performed in 1600; another setting by Caccini, in 1602. He also wrote the libretto of Monteverdi's *Arianna* (1608). These texts were republished by A. Solerti in vol. II of *Gli Albori del melodramma* (Milan, 1905) and by A. Della Corte, *Drammi per musica dal Rinuccini allo Zeno* (Turin, 1958).
BIBLIOGRAPHY: F. Meda, *Ottavio Rinuccini* (Milan, 1894); A. Civita, *Ottavio Rinuccini ed il sorgere del melodramma in Italia* (Mantua, 1900); F. Raccamadoro-Ramelli, *Ottavio Rinuccini, studio biografico e critico* (1900); A. Solerti, *Le Origini del melodramma* (Turin, 1903); A. Solerti, *Musica, ballo e drammatica alla corte medicea dal 1600 al 1637* (Florence, 1905); O. G. Sonneck, "Dafne, the first Opera," *Sammelbände der Internationalen Musik-Gesellschaft* (1913); A. Della Corte, *Ottavio Rinuccini librettista* (Turin, 1925); U. Rolandi, "Didascalie sceniche in un raro libretto dell'Euridice del Rinuccini," *Rivista Musicale Italiana* (1926); M. Schild, *Die Musikdramen Ottavio Rinuccinis* (Würzburg, 1933).

Riotte, Philipp Jakob, German conductor and composer; b. St. Mendel, Trier, Aug. 16, 1776; d. Vienna, Aug. 20, 1856. He studied with André in Offenbach; in 1808 settled in Vienna, where he conducted at the Theater an der Wien; produced there 48 works of his own, including operas, ballets, and minor pieces; also wrote a symphony, 9 piano sonatas, 6 violin sonatas, etc. He was the author of the "tone picture," *Die Schlacht bei Leipzig (The Battle of Leipzig)* for piano, which achieved extraordinary popularity in Germany.
BIBLIOGRAPHY: G. Spengler, *Der Komponist Ph. J. Riotte,* dissertation (Saarbrücken, 1973).

Ripa, Alberto da (called **Alberto Mantovano**), Italian lutenist; b. Mantua, c.1480; d. there, 1551. Little is known about his life, except that he was in the service of Francis I of France from about 1525. His *Tablature de Luth* was brought out posthumously by his pupil Guillaume Morlaye (6 books; Paris, 1553-1562); individual pieces by him are found in the publications of Phalèse (1546 and 1574) and also in Francesco da Forli's *Intavolatura di liuto* (1536).
BIBLIOGRAPHY: J. G. Prod'homme, "Guillaume Morlaye, éditeur d'Albert de Ripe," *Revue de Musicologie* (1925).

Rischbieter, Wilhelm Albert, German music theorist and pedagogue; b. Brunswick, July 20, 1834; d. Dresden, Feb. 11, 1910. He studied with Hauptmann; was violinist in Leipzig, Bremen, Nuremberg, and Liegnitz. In 1862 he was appointed teacher of harmony and comp. at the Dresden Cons. and held this position for nearly 40 years, until 1900. He publ. *Über Modulation, Quartsextakkord und Orgelpunkt* (1879); *Erläuterungen und Aufgaben zum Studium des Kontrapunkts* (1885); and *Die Gesetzmässigkeit der Harmonik* (1888).

Riseley, George, English organist and conductor; b. Bristol, Aug. 28, 1845; d. there, April 12, 1932. He was a chorister at the Bristol Cathedral from the age of 7, and studied with the cathedral organist, John Davis Corfe; in 1876 succeeded him at that post; in 1877 he organized a series of orchestral concerts in Bristol which contributed greatly to Bristol's musical life;

also conducted the Bristol Festival (1896–1911). In 1898 he was appointed conductor of the Queen's Hall Choral Society in London. He wrote a Jubilee Ode (Bristol, 1887), part-songs, and pieces for organ. For an account of his career see the *Musical Times* (Feb. 1899).

Risler, Édouard, French pianist; b. Baden-Baden (of a German mother and Alsatian father), Feb. 23, 1873; d. Paris, July 22, 1929. He studied piano with Diémer at the Paris Cons. and continued his studies with Klindworth, Stavenhagen and Eugène d'Albert in Germany. In 1923 he was appointed prof. of the Paris Cons. He gave concert recitals all over Europe and acquired a high reputation as a fine musician as well as a virtuoso pianist; he made a specialty of presenting cycles of one composer's works; he played Beethoven's 32 sonatas, Chopin's complete piano works, and both books of Bach's *Well-Tempered Clavier.*

Rist, Johann, German poet and composer; b. Ottensen, near Hamburg, March 8, 1607; d. Wedel-on-Elbe, Aug. 31, 1667. He studied theology at the universities of Hamburg and Bremen; later became a pastor in Mecklenburg and Wedel. In 1644 he was made poet-laureate by the Emperor, and in 1653 elevated to the rank of nobleman. He organized in Hamburg a Liederschule, for which he secured the cooperation of many important composers of the day, among them Schiedemann and Thomas Selle. He has been described as the "organizer of the German Parnassus" and indeed his role in the development of a purely national type of secular song, of German folk inspiration, was historically significant. He also wrote a number of sacred songs: *O Ewigkeit, du Donnerwort; O Traurigkeit; O Herzeleid; Werde munter, mein Gemüte;* etc., which are still sung in Lutheran churches in Germany. He compiled valuable collections of German sacred songs.
    BIBLIOGRAPHY: Th. Hansen, *Johann Rist und seine Zeit* (Halle, 1872; reprint, Leipzig, 1973); W. Krabbe, *Johann Rist und das deutsche Lied* (Bonn, 1910); O. Kern, *Johann Rist als weltlicher Lyriker* (Marburg, 1919); O. Heins, *Johann Rist und das niederdeutsche Drama des 17. Jahrhunderts* (1930).

Ristić, Milan, Serbian composer; b. Belgrade, Aug. 31, 1908. He studied in Belgrade with Slavenski and in Prague with Alois Hába. A prolific composer, he writes mostly instrumental music; his style ranges from neo-Romantic grandiosity to economic neo-Classicism, from epically declamatory diatonicism to expressionistically atonal melos. Some of his works are written in an explicit dodecaphonic technique; in some, he makes use of quarter-tones.
    WORKS: 6 symphonies (1941, 1951, 1961, 1966, 1967, 1968); Violin Concerto (1944); Piano Concerto (1954); *Suite giocosa* for orch. (1956); *Symphonic Variations* (1957); *Burleska* for orch. (1957); *7 Bagatelles* for orch. (1959); Concerto for Orch. (1963); Clarinet Concerto (1964); 2 string quartets; Wind Quintet; Septet; Violin Sonata; Viola Sonata; 24 fugues for various instrumental combinations; Suite for 4 trombones in quarter-tones.

BIBLIOGRAPHY: V. Peričić, *Muzički Stvaraoci u Srbiji* (Belgrade, 1969; pp. 453–73).

Ristori, Giovanni Alberto, Italian composer; b. Bologna, 1692; d. Dresden, Feb. 7, 1753. He received his education from his father, a violinist in an Italian opera company; with him he went to Dresden (1715) and obtained the post of director of the Polish chapel there; then was appointed chamber organist to the court of Saxony (1733), church composer (1746), and assistant conductor (1750). He wrote a number of operas for the Italian Opera in Dresden. His *Calandro,* staged at Pillnitz, near Dresden, on Sept. 2, 1726, was one of the earliest Italian comic operas produced in Germany, and so possesses historical significance beyond its intrinsic worth; other operas produced in Dresden and in court theaters near Dresden were *Don Chisciotte* (Feb. 2, 1727), *Cleonice* (Aug. 15, 1718), *Le Fate* (Aug. 10, 1736), *Arianna* (Aug. 7, 1736), etc. He also wrote 3 oratorios, 16 cantatas, 11 Masses; some instrumental music; many of his MSS were destroyed during the siege of Dresden (1760).
    BIBLIOGRAPHY: C. R. Mengelberg, *G. A. Ristori* (Leipzig, 1916).

Ritter, Alexander, German composer and poet; b. Narva, Estonia (of German parents), June 27, 1833; d. Munich, April 12, 1896. He was taken to Dresden in 1841; there he studied violin with Franz Schubert (namesake of the great composer), who was concertmaster of the Dresden opera; then studied at the Leipzig Cons. (1849–51) with Ferdinand David (violin) and E. F. Richter (theory). In 1854 he married Wagner's niece, **Franziska Wagner,** and settled in Weimar, where he entered into a close association with Liszt, von Bülow, Cornelius, Raff, and others. He was conductor at the opera in Stettin (1856–58), where his wife was engaged as soprano; he then lived in Dresden (1858–60), Schwerin (1860–62), and Würzburg (1863–82). When Bülow became conductor at the Hofkapelle in Meiningen (1882) Ritter settled there and played the violin in the orch.; after Bülow's departure from Meiningen in 1886, Ritter moved to Munich. He wrote 2 operas, *Der faule Hans* (Munich, Oct. 15, 1885) and *Wem die Krone?* (Weimar, June 8, 1890), to his own librettos, and several symph. poems in an intensely Romantic manner (*Seraphische Phantasie, Erotische Legende, Karfreitag und Frohnleichnam,* and *Kaiser Rudolfs Ritt zum Grabe*); a string quartet; about 60 songs; piano pieces. Ritter's significance derives, however, not from these well-made but ephemeral compositions, but from his profound influence on young Richard Strauss in the creation of a new type of philosophical tone poem along the lines of "Musik als Ausdruck" (music as expression), a modern development of the art of Liszt, Wagner, and Berlioz. Ritter wrote the poem printed in the score of *Tod und Verklärung.*
    BIBLIOGRAPHY: S. von Hausegger, *Alexander Ritter. Ein Bild seines Charakters und Schaffens* (Berlin, 1907).

Ritter, August Gottfried, German organist; b. Erfurt, Aug. 25, 1811; d. Magdeburg, Aug. 26, 1885. He was a pupil of Fischer at Erfurt, Hummel at Weimar, and

Rungenhagen at Berlin; filled various posts as organist at Erfurt, Merseburg, and Magdeburg; edited the *Urania* (1844–48); was co-editor of the *Orgelfreund* and *Orgelarchiv*; publ. a valuable book, *Zur Geschichte des Orgelspiels im 14. bis zum Anfange des 18. Jahrhunderts* (1884), and *Die Kunst des Orgelspiels* (2 vols., in English, N.Y., 1874); also organ pieces; 4 books of chorales; a piano concerto, a piano quartet, 2 symphonies, 3 overtures, etc.

Ritter, Frédéric Louis, German-American music historian and choral conductor; b. Strasbourg, June 22, 1834; d. Antwerp, July 4, 1891. He was of Spanish extraction, his original family name being Caballero, which was translated into German as Ritter (knight). He studied in Strasbourg with Schletterer and in Paris with J. G. Kastner. In 1856 he went to Cincinnati, where he organized the Philharmonic Orch., but left for New York in 1861; was active mainly as a choral conductor; in 1867 became prof. of music at Vassar College. He publ. several manuals and music histories; *History of Music* (2 vols.; Boston, 1870, 1874; 2nd ed., 1880); *Music in England* (N.Y., 1883); *Music in America* (N.Y., 1883; 3rd ed., 1893); *Music in Its Relation to Intellectual Life* (N.Y., 1891); etc. His wife, **Fanny Raymond Ritter** (b. Philadelphia, 1840; d. Poughkeepsie, N.Y., Oct. 26, 1890), was the author of *Woman as a Musician: An Art-Historical Study* (1876), *Some Famous Songs* (1878), etc.

Ritter, Hermann, German violist, inventor of the viola alta; b. Wismar, Sept. 16, 1849; d. Würzburg, Jan. 22, 1926. He studied at the Hochschule für Musik in Berlin; attended courses at the Univ. of Heidelberg; turning his attention to musical instruments, he began a series of experiments for the purpose of improving the muffled tone of the ordinary viola; profiting by some practical hints in A. Bagatella's book, *Regole per la Costruzione di Violini* (Padua, 1786), he constructed a slightly larger model possessed of better resonance and a more brilliant tone. Exhibiting this new "viola alta" in 1876, he attracted the attention of Wagner, who invited his cooperation for the Bayreuth festival; after that engagement he made successful tours of all Europe as viola virtuoso; from 1879, prof. of viola and history of music at the Musikschule in Würzburg; in 1905 he founded the "Ritterquartett" (violin, W. Schulze-Prisca; viola alta, Ritter; viola tenore, E. Cahnbley; viola bassa, H. Knöchel). WRITINGS: *Die Geschichte der Viola alta und die Grundsätze ihres Baues* (Leipzig, 1876; 2nd ed., 1877, was reprinted, Wiesbaden, 1969); *Repetitorium der Musikgeschichte* (1880); *Aus der Harmonielehre meines Lebens* (1883); *Elementartheorie der Musik* (1885); *Ästhetik der Tonkunst* (1886); *Studien und Skizzen aus Musik-und Kulturgeschichte, sowie Musikästhetik* (Dresden, 1892); *Katechismus der Musikästhetik* (2nd ed., 1894); *Katechismus der Musikinstrumente* (1894); *Volksgesang in alter und neuer Zeit* (1896); *Schubert* (1896); *Haydn, Mozart, Beethoven* (1897); *Die fünfsaitige Geige und die Weiterentwicklung der Streichinstrumente* (1898); *Allgemeine illustrierte Encyklopädie der Musikgeschichte* (6 vols., 1901–02). He publ. numerous original compositions and transcriptions for viola and piano, and *Elementartechnik der Viola alta.*
  BIBLIOGRAPHY: G. Adema, *Hermann Ritter und seine Viola alta* (Würzburg, 1881; 2nd ed., 1894).

Ritter, Peter, German composer; b. Mannheim, July 2, 1763; d. there, Aug. 1, 1846. He studied violin and cello with his father; completed his theoretical studies under Abbé Vogler. He entered the Mannheim court orch. as a cellist; later became its concertmaster, and, in 1803, conductor. He brought out in Mannheim his first opera, *Der Eremit auf Formentera* (Dec. 14, 1788; text by the celebrated poet A. von Kotzebue), which attained considerable vogue in Germany; some 20 more operas and Singspiele followed, but were not successful. In 1787 he married the famous actress Katharina Baumann (to whom Schiller had proposed); in 1790 both were employed at the Hoftheater; his wife retired on a pension in 1819, and Ritter himself in 1823. Besides his operas, he wrote a fine chorale, *Grosser Gott dich loben wir* (1792); an oratorio, *Das verlorene Paradies*; and much chamber music (selections publ. by Riemann in vol. 28(16), of the *Denkmäler der Tonkunst in Bayern*). 24 autograph scores, including 2 symphonies, several concertos, etc., are in the Library of Congress in Washington.
  BIBLIOGRAPHY: W. Schulze, *Peter Ritter* (Berlin, 1895).

Ritter (real name **Bennet**), **Théodore,** French pianist and composer; b. near Paris, April 5, 1841; d. Paris, April 6, 1886. He was a pupil of Liszt; made successful European tours; publ. numerous solo pieces for piano, of which *Les Courriers* was a favorite; his operas, *Marianne* (Paris, 1861) and *La Dea risorta* (Florence, 1865), were unsuccessful.

Rivé-King, Julie, American pianist; b. Cincinnati, Oct. 30, 1854; d. Indianapolis, July 24, 1937. She received her primary instruction from her mother; then studied in New York with William Mason and in Leipzig with Reinecke; also was a pupil of Liszt. She played Liszt's Piano Concerto No. 1 at her American debut, with the N.Y. Philharmonic (April 24, 1875); this was the beginning of an active career; she gave about 4,000 concerts in the U.S., retiring only a year before her death. In 1876 she married Frank King of Milwaukee. From 1905 till 1936 she was piano instructor at the Bush Cons. in Chicago. She wrote some attractive piano pieces (*Impromptu, Polonaise héroïque, Bubbling Spring*, etc.). See A. R. Coolidge in *Notable American Women* (N.Y., 1971) III.

Rivier, Jean, French composer; b. Villemomble, July 21, 1896. He was in the French army in World War I, and did not begin his musical studies until 1918, when he entered the Paris Cons. and studied with Caussade; participated in various modern music societies in Paris; formed a style of composition that combined the elements of French Classicism and Impressionism. He was also esteemed as a teacher; was on the faculty of the Paris Cons. from 1947 to 1966. WORKS: opera, *Vénitienne* (Paris, July 8, 1937); for orch.: 7 symphonies: No. 1 (Paris, Jan. 29, 1933); No. 2, for strings (1937); No. 3 (1937; Paris, Nov. 25,

1940); No. 4 (Paris, 1947); No. 5 (Strasbourg, June 24, 1951); No. 6, *Les Présages* (Paris, Dec. 11, 1958); No. 7, *Les Contrastes* (Paris, Jan. 9, 1962); Piano Concerto (1941); Violin Concerto (1942); *3 Pastorales* (Paris, Feb. 7, 1929); *Adagio,* for string orch. (Paris, March 1, 1931); *Ouverture pour une opérette imaginaire* (Paris, Dec. 13, 1931); Concertino for Viola and Orch. (Paris, Feb. 15, 1936); *Jeanne d'Arc à Domrémy,* symph. tableau (Paris, Jan. 31, 1937); *Ballade des amants désespérés,* for orch. (1945); *Rapsodie provençale* (Aix-en-Provence, July 22, 1949); *Résonances* (1965); *Brillances* for 7 woodwind instruments (1971); *Triade* for string orch. (1967); *Climats* for celesta, vibraphone, xylophone, piano, and strings (1968); Clarinet Concerto (1960); Bassoon Concerto (1965); Oboe Concerto (1966); Trumpet Concerto (1972); Duo for flute and clarinet (1968); 2 string quartets; violin pieces; piano pieces; song cycles; choruses.

Roberton, Sir Hugh S., Scottish composer and choral conductor; b. Glasgow, Feb. 23, 1874; d. there, Oct. 7, 1952. In 1906 he founded the Glasgow Orpheus Choir, which contributed to a large extent to the cultivation of choral music in Scotland. He disbanded it in 1951. He publ. about 300 vocal pieces, including *The Faux Bourdon Series of Psalm Tunes; Songs of the Isles,* and *Concert Edition of Scottish Songs;* also a pamphlet, *Prelude to the Orpheus* (London, 1947).

Roberts, Megan, American composer of the avant-garde; b. Hempstead, N.Y., Oct. 12, 1952. She was taken to California as a babe-in-arms, and flourished there; took lessons with Robert Ashley at Mills College in Oakland, and with Emma Lou Diemer at the Univ. of California, Santa Barbara. She experimented with unimedia arts of audio, video, dance and theater; then switched to rock 'n' roll. Her most mind-boggling contribution to the unichoreovideoelectrobiosonic School of California Calisthenics is *Suite for a Small Chamber* (1976), in which the movements of dancers trigger electronic devices and tape-loop playback machines. In her video piece *Factory* (1976) she utilizes the technique of strobosonic photophonoscopy. On Jan. 14, 1977 she presented in San Francisco a multimedia study in violence free of moral redeeming value. Her major work, *I Could Sit Here All Day* (1976), is scored for birds, drums and disembodied human voices, and tends to represent the ante-human and anti-human predecessors of rock 'n' roll.

Robertson, Leroy, American composer; b. Fountain Green, Utah, Dec. 21, 1896; d. Salt Lake City, July 25, 1971. He studied in Provo; then in Boston with Chadwick and Converse at the New England Cons.; subsequently went to Europe, where he took courses with Ernest Bloch in Switzerland and with Hugo Leichtentritt in Berlin. Returning to America, he became instructor of music at Brigham Young Univ. at Provo; in 1948, was appointed head of the music dept., Univ. of Utah. In 1947 his symph. work *Trilogy* received the 1st prize of $25,000 in a contest sponsored by Henry H. Reichhold of Detroit; it was performed by the Detroit Symph. Orch. on Dec. 11, 1947, but despite the attendant publicity, the work was not successful, and there were few subsequent performances. In 1963 he retired as chairman of the music dept. of the Univ. of Utah. Other works: *The Book of Mormon,* oratorio (Salt Lake City, Feb. 18, 1953); *Prelude, Scherzo, Ricercare,* for orch. (1940); *Rhapsody,* for piano and orch. (1944); *Punch and Judy Overture* (1945); Violin Concerto (1948); Piano Concerto (Salt Lake City, Nov. 30, 1966); Piano Quintet (1933); String Quartet (1940; N.Y. Music Critics Circle Award, 1944); *American Serenade,* for string quartet (1944); other chamber music; piano pieces; songs.

Robertson, Rae, pianist; b. Ardersier, Scotland, Nov. 29, 1893; d. Los Angeles, Nov. 4, 1956. He studied with F. Niecks at Edinburgh Univ.; then at the Royal Academy of Music, London, with Matthay and F. Corder; married **Ethel Bartlett,** pianist, with whom he gave numerous concerts in Europe and America as duo-pianists. With her he edited an Oxford Univ. Press series of works for 2 pianos.

Robeson, Lila, American contralto; b. Cleveland, April 4, 1880; d. Euclid, Ohio, Dec. 7, 1960. She studied singing with Isidor Luckstone and Oscar Saenger in N.Y.; made her operatic debut as Ortrud with the Aborn Opera Co. (Boston, April 4, 1911); from 1912 till 1920 she was a member of the Metropolitan Opera Co.; then devoted herself mainly to teaching; in 1953 taught voice at Western Reserve Univ., Cleveland.

Robeson, Paul, great black American bass; b. Princeton, N.J., April 9, 1898; d. Philadelphia, Jan. 23, 1976. He first studied law (1919, B.A., Rutgers Univ.; 1923, LL.B, Columbia Univ.); when his talent for singing and acting was discovered, he appeared in plays in the U.S. and England; acted the part of Emperor Jones in Eugene O'Neill's play and of Porgy in the Negro folk play by Du Bose and Dorothy Heyward. In 1925 he gave his first Negro spiritual recital in N.Y.; then toured in Europe. In 1930 he appeared in the title role of Shakespeare's *Othello* in London. Returning to the U.S., he continued to give recitals, but his radical political beliefs interfered with the success of his career. In 1952 he was awarded the International Stalin Peace Prize ($25,000). During the summer of 1958 he made an extensive European tour.

BIBLIOGRAPHY: E. G. Robeson, *Paul Robeson, Negro* (N.Y., 1930); S. Graham, *Paul Robeson* (N.Y., 1946); Marie Seton, *Paul Robeson* (London, 1958); autobiography, *Here I Stand* (London, 1958); Dorothy Butler Gilliam, *Paul Robeson, All American* (N.Y., 1977).

Robinson, Earl, American composer; b. Seattle, Wash., July 2, 1910; studied at the Univ. of Washington (B.M., 1933); then took lessons with Aaron Copland. In 1934 he joined the Federal Theater Project, for which he wrote incidental music for several plays; his *Ballad for Americans* from the revue *Sing for Your Supper* became nationally famous (1939).

Robinson, Franklin Whitman, American organist and teacher; b. New York, June 27, 1875; d. Northeast Harbor, Maine, Sept. 16, 1946. He studied with MacDowell and Rybner at Columbia Univ. (M.A., 1907); in 1908 became instructor at the Institute of Musical Art,

N.Y.; publ. *Anthems and Chant Forms* (1908–14) and *Aural Harmony* (N.Y., 1914; revised ed., 1936).

Robinson, Stanford, English conductor; b. Leeds, July 5, 1904. He played piano in hotel orchestras in London before entering the Royal College of Music; there he studied conducting under Sir Adrian Boult; organized the London Wireless Chorus, and conducted its programs for many years. In 1936 he became a director of the opera dept. of the BBC; in 1949 he was put in charge of the BBC Opera Orch. for broadcasting symph. music.

BIBLIOGRAPHY: Donald Brook, *International Gallery of Conductors* (Bristol, 1951; pp. 155–58).

Robles, Daniel Alomias, Peruvian composer and folksong collector; b. Huánuco, Jan. 3, 1871; d. Chosica, near Lima, July 17, 1942. He was of Indian blood; traveled through Indian villages of Peru, Bolivia, and Ecuador and collected many hundreds of melodies, of which the *Himno al Sol* was notated by him as sung by a 117-year-old Indian. From 1919 to 1934 he lived mostly in the U.S.; then returned to Lima. He had no formal education and little musical technique; his melodic and rhythmic material was arranged by various composers for performances. In this manner he brought out an operetta, *El Condor Pasa;* several orchestral suites (*El Resurgimiento de los Andes, El Indio, Danza Huanca,* etc.). 5 melodies collected by Robles are reproduced in *La Musique des Incas et ses survivances* by Raoul and Marguerite d'Harcourt (Paris, 1925).

BIBLIOGRAPHY: N. Slonimsky, *Music of Latin America* (N.Y., 1945; p. 275).

Robyn, Alfred George, American pianist, organist, and composer; b. St. Louis, April 29, 1860; d. New York, Oct. 18, 1935. He studied with his father, an organist; traveled with Emma Abbott at the age of 16, as pianist and accompanist; filled numerous posts as church organist in N.Y. He wrote the light operas, *The Yankee Consul* (1903), *The Gypsy Girl* (1905), *The Yankee Tourist* (1907), *Fortune Land* (1907), *All for the Ladies* (1912); etc.; the oratorios *The Ascension, Love Unending, Praise and Thanksgiving;* a symph. poem, *Pompeii;* Piano Concerto; Piano Quintet; 4 string quartets; numerous piano pieces; songs. Some of his songs and piano pieces sold extremely well.

Rocca, Lodovico, Italian composer; b. Turin, Nov. 29, 1895. He studied with Orefice at the Cons. of Milan; also attended the Univ. of Turin; from 1940 to 1966 he was director of the Cons. of Turin.

WORKS: operas: *In Terra di leggenda* (Milan, Sept. 28, 1933), *Il Dibuc* (Milan, March 24, 1934), *La Morte di Frine* (Milan, April 24, 1937), *Monte Ivnor* (Rome, Dec. 23, 1939), *L'Uragano* (Milan, Feb. 8, 1952); for orch: *Contrasti* (1919), *Aurora di morte* (1920), *La Foresta delle samodive* (1921), *L'Alba del malato* (1922), *Le Luci* (1923), *Chiaroscuri* (1924), *La Cella azzurra* (1925); *Biribù, occhi di rana,* for voice and string quartet (1937); *Schizzi francescani,* for tenor and 8 instruments (1942); *Antiche Iscrizioni* for soloists, *chorus,* and orch. (1952; Rome, Feb. 6, 1953).

BIBLIOGRAPHY: G. Bas, in *Musica d'Oggi* (1925 and 1927); M. Castelnuovo-Tedesco in *Il Pianoforte* (1925); A. Damerini, in *Il Pianoforte* (1927).

Rochberg, George, significant American composer; b. Paterson, New Jersey, July 5, 1918. He studied theory and composition with George Szell in N.Y. (1939–41); served in the U.S. military forces during World War II; after the war enrolled in the classes of composition at the Curtis Institute with Rosario Scalero and Gian Carlo Menotti (B. Mus., 1947). In 1950 he was in Rome on a Fulbright Fellowship; in 1951 was appointed music editor for the Theodore Presser Co.; also taught classes at the Curtis Institute; in 1960 he joined the music faculty of the Univ. of Pennsylvania. In his style he pursues the ideal of tonal order and logically justifiable musical structures; the most profound influence he experienced was that of Schoenberg and Anton von Webern; many of his works follow the organization in 12 different notes; at the same time he does not deny himself the treasures of the sanctified past, and even resorts to overt quotations in his works of recognizable fragments from music by composers as mutually unrelated as Schütz, Bach, Mahler and Ives, treated by analogy with the "objects trouvés" in modern painting and sculpture.

WORKS: *Capriccio* for 2 pianos (1949); Symph. No. 1 (Philadelphia, March 28, 1958); *Night Music* (1952; won the George Gershwin Memorial Award); *Cantio Sacra* for chamber orch. (1953); *Fantasia* for violin and piano (1955); *Sinfonia Fantasia* (1956); *Waltz Serenade* for orch. (Cincinnati, Feb. 14, 1958); *Cheltenham Concerto* (1958); Symph. No. 2 (Cleveland, Feb. 26, 1959); *Time-Span,* symph. movement (St. Louis, Oct. 22, 1960); Symph. No. 3 for solo voices, chamber chorus, double chorus and orch. (using quotations from works by Schütz, Bach, Mahler and Ives; N.Y., Nov. 24, 1970); Violin Concerto (Pittsburgh, April 4, 1975); Symph. No. 4 (Seattle, Nov. 15, 1976); *Dialogues* for clarinet and piano (1958); String Quartet No. 1 (1952); String Quartet No. 2, with soprano (1961); String Quartet No. 3 (1972); *Black Sounds* for wind instruments and percussion (1965); *Contra mortem et tempus* for violin, flute, clarinet and piano; containing phrases from works by Boulez, Varèse and Ives (1965); *Tableaux* for soprano and 11 players (1968); Piano Quintet (1975); a number of piano pieces and songs. He published a theoretical essay *The Hexachord and Its Relation to the 12-Tone Row* (Bryn Mawr, 1955), and several magazine articles dealing with 12-tone techniques.

BIBLIOGRAPHY: A. L. Ringer, "The Music of George Rochberg," *Musical Quarterly* (Oct. 1966).

Rochlitz, Johann Friedrich, German writer on music; b. Leipzig, Feb. 12, 1769; d. there, Dec. 16, 1842. A pupil of Doles in the Thomasschule, he entered the Univ. of Leipzig as a theological student; publ. some novels and sketches; his 2 pamphlets, *Blicke in das Gebiet der Kunst* and *Einige Ideen über Anwendung des guten Geschmacks* (both 1796), treat in part of music. In 1798 he founded the *Allgemeine musikalische Zeitung,* which he edited till 1818, and contributed to until 1835. From 1805 he was a director of the Gewandhaus Concerts. His best-known work is *Für Freunde der Tonkunst* (4 vols., 1824–32; 3rd ed.,

1868), which contains biographies, essays, analyses of compositions, etc.; vol. IV has an outline *Geschichte der Gesangmusik*, which Rochlitz supplemented by a *Sammlung vorzüglicher Gesangstücke* in 3 vols., from Dufay to Vallotti. Müller-Blattau compiled Rochlitz's essays on Bach under the title *Wege zu Bach* (1926). Rochlitz composed songs for men's chorus; also a setting of the 23rd Psalm; wrote texts for operas, oratorios, cantatas, etc.

BIBLIOGRAPHY: Ernst Rychnovsky, *L. Sphor und F. Rochlitz* (Prague, 1904); J. Gensel, *Aus Rochlitzs Briefen an Henriette Voigt* (Leipzig, 1906); H. Ehinger, *J. F. Rochlitz als Musikschriftsteller* (Leipzig, 1929).

Rockstro (real name **Rackstraw**), **William Smyth,** English music scholar; b. North Cheam, Surrey, Jan. 5, 1823; d. London, July 2, 1895. He studied at the Leipzig Cons. under Mendelssohn, Plaidy, and Hauptmann. Returning to London, he taught piano and singing; wrote a popular ballad, *Queen and Huntress;* publ. piano arrangements of numerous operas; devoted himself to a close study of ecclesiastical music, and became an acknowledged authority on plainchant; became a Roman Catholic in 1876.

WRITINGS: *History of Music for Young Students* (1879); *Practical Harmony* (1881); *Rules of Counterpoint* (1882); *Life of G. F. Handel* (1833); *Mendelssohn* (1884); *General History of Music* (1886; 3rd ed., 1897); *Jenny Lind, the Artist* (1891; with Canon Scott Holland); *Jenny Lind, Her Vocal Art and Culture* (1894; with Otto Goldschmidt); also publ. *Festival Psalter, Adapted to the Gregorian Tones; Accompanying Harmonies to the Ferial Psalter;* and *Harmonies for Additional Chants and the Ambrosial Te Deum.*

Roda y López, Cecilio de, Spanish writer on music; b. Albuñol, near Granada, Oct. 24, 1865; d. Madrid, Nov. 27, 1912. From 1904 he was president of the music division of the Ateneo in Madrid; elected member of the Academy in 1906. He was the author of *Los Instrumentos, las Danzas y las Canciones en el Quijote* (1905), *La Evolución de la Música* (1906), *Un Quaderno di autografi di Beethoven del 1825* (Turin, 1907), etc.

Rode, (Jacques-) Pierre (Joseph), French violinist; b. Bordeaux, Feb. 26, 1774; d. Château-Bourbon, near Damazan, Nov. 25, 1830. He was a pupil of Fauvel; from 1787, of Viotti at Paris; made his debut in 1790 in a concerto by Viotti, at the Théâtre Feydeau; after tours in Holland and Germany and a short visit to London he was appointed prof. of violin at the newly opened Paris Cons. During a visit to Spain in 1799 he met Boccherini, who wrote concertos for him. In 1800 he was court violinist to Napoleon; from 1803 to 1808 was in Russia with Boieldieu; became 1st violinist to the court of Alexander I; then spent 3 years in Paris, after which he toured Germany and Austria (at Vienna Beethoven wrote for him the G major Sonata, op. 96, which Rode performed with Archduke Rudolph in Vienna, on Dec. 29, 1812); lived for a time in Berlin, where he married in 1814; then retired and lived in Bordeaux.

WORKS: 13 violin concertos; the famous *24 Caprices en forme d'études, dans les 24 tons de la gamme;* 12 études; 3 books of violin duos; etc.; and a *Méthode du violon* (with Baillot and Kreutzer).

BIBLIOGRAPHY: A. Pougin, *Notice sur Rode* (Paris, 1874); H. Ahlgrimm, *Pierre Rode* (Vienna, 1929).

Rodeheaver, Homer Alvan, American composer of hymn tunes who described himself as a "musical missionary"; b. Union Furnace, Ohio, Oct. 4, 1880; d. New York, Dec. 18, 1955. Taken to Jellicoe, Tennessee, as a child, he grew up helping in his father's lumber business and learning to play the trombone from a local musician. During the Spanish-American War he enlisted as trombonist in the 4th Tennessee Regimental Band. After the war he became interested in gospel songs and evangelism; accompanied the evangelist Billy Sunday on his tours (1910–30), leading the singing with his trombone. He composed the music for many gospel songs, of which the best known is *Then Jesus Came.* His theme song was *Brighten the Corner,* composed by Charles H. Gabriel. Rodeheaver was the founder of the Summer School of Sacred Music at Winona Lake, Indiana, and was connected with the Rodeheaver-Hall-Mack Music Publishing Co. there. Besides a dozen or so collections of hymn poems and homilies, he published *Song Stories of the Sawdust Trail* (N.Y., 1917), *20 Years with Billy Sunday* (Nashville, 1936), and *Letter from a Missionary in Africa* (Chicago, 1936). With his predecessor Ira D. Sankey, he was a leading figure in American musical evangelism.

Röder, Carl Gottlieb, German printer of music; b. Stötteritz, near Leipzig, June 22, 1812; d. Gohlis, Oct. 29, 1883. He founded the great Leipzig establishment for engraving and printing music, starting in 1846 with one engraver's apprentice; the business became one of the largest in the world. A book printing department was added later. In 1872 Röder's sons-in-law C. L. H. Wolff and C. E. M. Rentsch became partners in the firm; Röder himself retired in 1876. After Rentsch's death (Feb. 19, 1889) his heirs withdrew from the firm, but a son-in-law of Wolff, Karl Johannes Reichel (b. Aug. 15, 1853; d. Leipzig, Sept. 9, 1927), became a partner, and after Wolff's death (1915), head of the firm. On the 50th anniversary of its foundation the firm issued a Festschrift, to which Hugo Riemann contributed a valuable essay, *Notenschrift und Notendruck;* a second Festschrift (on the 75th anniversary), took the form of a study by W. von zur Westen entitled *Musiktitel aus 4 Jahrhunderten* (1921).

Röder, Martin, German composer and singing teacher; b. Berlin, April 7, 1851; d. Boston, June 7, 1895. After studying music in Berlin, he went to Milan, where he organized the Società del Quartetto Corale (1875), giving performances of vocal quartets; then occupied various posts as singing teacher in Berlin (1881–87), Dublin (1887–92), and finally at the New England Cons. in Boston (1892). He wrote 3 operas, of which only one, *Vera,* was performed (Hamburg, 1881); 2 symph. poems, *Azorenfahrt* and *Leonore;* the overture *Attila;* chamber music; publ. *Studi, critici, raccolti* (Milan, 1881) and *Dal Taccuino di un diret-*

tore di orchestra (1881; in German as *Aus dem Tage-buche eines wandernden Kapellmeisters*, 1884).

Rodgers, Jimmie, American singer of country music; b. Mendoza, Mississippi, Sept. 8, 1897; d. New York, May 26, 1933. Known as "the Singing Brakeman" because he worked on the railroad, he made early recordings in a western-style of country music in the 1920's, but his career was dogged by tuberculosis and an inability to control his spendthrift life style. In 1961 his name was the first to be placed in the Country Music Hall of Fame in Nashville, Tennessee, and in 1977 a U.S. postage stamp was issued to commemorate his 80th birthday.

Rodgers, Richard, celebrated American composer of popular music; b. Hammels Station, Long Island, N.Y., June 28, 1902. He studied at Columbia Univ. (1919–21) and at the Institute of Musical Art in N.Y. (1921–23). He collaborated for 18 years with the lyricist Lorenz Hart in a series of inspired and highly popular musical comedies: *The Girl Friend* (1926), *A Connecticut Yankee* (1927), *On Your Toes* (1936), *Babes in Arms* (1937), *I Married an Angel* (1938), *The Boys From Syracuse* (1942). *The Rodgers and Hart Song Book* (N.Y., 1951) contains their most famous songs. After Hart's death in 1943 Rodgers became associated with Oscar Hammerstein II. Together they wrote the greatly acclaimed musical *Oklahoma!* (1943; Pulitzer Prize, 1944), followed by a number of no less successful productions: *Carousel* (1945), *Allegro* (1947), *South Pacific* (1948; Pulitzer Prize, 1950); *The King and I* (1951), *Me and Juliet* (1953), *Pipe Dream* (1955), *The Flower Drum Song* (1958), *The Sound of Music* (1959), *No Strings* (1962), *Do I Hear a Waltz?* (1965). Rodgers wrote the music for the television shows *Victory at Sea* (1952) and *Winston Churchill: The Valiant Years* (1960). Individual songs from his musical comedies have become perennial favorites: *Some Enchanted Evening, Getting to Know You, Do-Re-Mi,* etc., etc., etc.
BIBLIOGRAPHY: Deems Taylor, *Some Enchanted Evenings: The Story of Rodgers and Hammerstein* (N.Y., 1953); David Ewen, *Richard Rodgers* (N.Y., 1957; 2nd ed., N.Y., 1963); *Richard Rodgers Fact Book* (N.Y., 1965; new ed. with supplement, 1968); Rodgers published *Musical Stages: An Autobiography* (N.Y., 1975).

Rodio, Rocco, contrapuntist of the early Neapolitan school; b. Calabria, c.1530; d. c.1615. He publ. *Regole per far contrapunto solo e accompagnato nel canto fermo* (1st ed., 1600; 3rd ed., 1626); also a collection (Naples, 1580) of 9 Masses; the last, *Missa de Beata Virgine* (a 5) is remarkable, because it can also be sung by 4 or 3 voices, by omitting the *quintus,* the *quintus* and *superius* (soprano), or the *quintus* and *bassus.*

Rodolphe, Jean Joseph, French composer; b. Strasbourg, Oct. 14, 1730; d. Paris, Aug. 18, 1812. He studied the French horn with his father; then the violin with Leclair *(l'aîné)* in Paris; composition with Traetta in Parma, and with Jommelli in Stuttgart; wrote ballet music for Jommelli's productions there. In 1764 he was in Paris once more; brought out his 1st opera, *Le Mariage par capitulation* (Comédie-Italienne, Dec. 3, 1764); another opera, *L'Aveugle de Palmyre* (Comédie-Italienne, March 5, 1767), obtained considerable success. The famous balletmaster Noverre produced several of Rodolphe's ballets at the Paris Opéra. Mozart met Rodolphe in Paris in 1778, and spoke of him highly. 3 of Rodolphe's ballets are printed in the *Denkmäler deutscher Tonkunst* 43/44. From 1784 to 1802 Rodolphe taught composition and solfège at the Paris Cons.; publ. the manuals, *Solfèges* and *Théorie d'accompagnement.*

Rodrigo, Joaquín, Spanish composer; b. Sagunt, Valencia, Nov. 22, 1902. He lost his sight as a child; revealed an innate talent for music and was sent to Paris where he studied with Paul Dukas; in 1939 he returned to Spain. His music is profoundly imbued with Spanish melorhythms; his *Concierto de Aranjuez,* for guitar and orch. (Barcelona, Nov. 9, 1940) became famous. He further composed *Juglares* for orch. (1923); *Concierto heroico,* for piano and orch. (Lisbon, April 5, 1943); *Concierto de estio,* for violin and orch. (Lisbon, April 11, 1944); *Concierto in modo galante* for cello and orch. (Madrid, Nov. 4, 1949); Concerto for Harp and Orch. (1954); *Fantasia para un gentilhombre* for guitar and orch. (1955); *Sones en la Giralda* for harp and orch. (1963); *Concierto Andaluz* for 4 guitars (1967); *Concierto-madrigal* for 2 guitars and orch. (1968); *Sonata Pimpante* for violin and piano (1966); *Sonata a la española* for guitar (1969); *Pájaros de primavera* for guitar (1972); choruses; piano pieces.
BIBLIOGRAPHY: F. Sopeña, *Joaquín Rodrigo* (Madrid, 1946); A. Iglesias, *Joaquín Rodrigo* (Orense, 1965).

Rodrigo de Ledesma, Mariano, Spanish composer; b. Zaragoza, Dec. 14, 1779; d. Madrid, March 28, 1848. He served as a chorister at the Cathedral of Zaragoza; was organist and chorusmaster at Vinaroz (1799–1802); then tenor in Madrid; in 1807 he was appointed conductor of the Madrid opera theater, but the French invasion forced him to flee, and he took refuge in Seville. In 1812 he was in Cádiz; there he composed an anti-Bonaparte hymn, *En tan infausto día,* while Joseph Bonaparte was king of Spain; fled to England, where he established himself as a singing teacher in London. With the restoration of legitimate monarchy in Spain, he returned there, and received a court appointment; publ. *40 Ejercicios de vocalización* (Madrid, 1820; Paris, 1827; also in English). He was again in England from 1823 to 1831; heard Weber conduct his operas in London, and was profoundly impressed; thenceforth he tried to emulate Weber, writing music in a Romantic manner. Back in Spain once more, he became maestro to Queen María Cristina. He wrote chiefly church music: 3 Solemn Masses, 9 Lamentations, a Stabat Mater; also some secular songs and instrumental pieces. Eslava reprinted 5 motets for 4 voices and orch. by Rodrigo in the *Lira sacro-hispana.*
BIBLIOGRAPHY: R. Mitjana, *El Maestro Rodrigo de Ledesma y sus Lamentaciones de Semana Santa* (Málaga, 1909).

Rodriguez, Augusto, Puerto Rican composer; b. San Juan, Feb. 9, 1904. He studied literature at the Univ. of Puerto Rico; music at Harvard with E. B. Hill and Walter Piston; since 1934, professor at the Univ. of Puerto Rico; organized a chorus, which achieved a high degree of excellence; gave a concert with it in New York in 1949. He published several songs, and dance suites.

Rodriguez, Felipe, Spanish composer; b. Madrid, May 1, 1759; d. there, May, 1814. He was a member of the Monserrat School; ordained priest, 1778; served as organist in Madrid. He wrote organ pieces, some of which are printed in *Música instrumental,* ed. by D. Pujol (vol. 2, Montserrat, 1946), and church music; his *Rondo* for piano is printed by J. Nín in the collection *17 Sonates et pièces anciennes d'auteurs espagnols* (Paris, 1929).

Rodriguez, Vicente, Spanish organist and composer; b. Valencia, about 1685; d. there, 1761. He was a cleric, served as organist of the Valencia Cathedral from 1716 to his death; wrote several Masses; also keyboard music; his Sonata in F (1744), printed by Joaquín Nín in his collection, *17 Sonates et pièces anciennes d'auteurs espagnols* (Paris, 1929), is in the style of Domenico Scarlatti.

Rodríguez de Hita, Antonio, Spanish composer; b. 1724; d. Madrid, Feb. 21, 1787. In 1757 he was chorusmaster at the Cathedral of Palencia, where he publ. a book of advice to his pupils, *Consejos que a sus discípulos da don Antonio Rodriguez de Hita.* Then he became music director at the Convent of the Incarnation in Madrid. From 1768 he collaborated with the dramatist Ramón de la Cruz in a series of notable stage works impregnated with Spanish atmosphere; the best are the comic operas (zarzuelas) *Las Segadoras de Vallecas* (Madrid, Sept. 3, 1768) and *Las Labradoras de Murcia* (Madrid, Sept. 16, 1769). He also composed the Spanish opera *Briseida* (Madrid, July 11, 1768), various hymns for 4 and 8 voices; etc.
BIBLIOGRAPHY: E. Cotarelo y Mori, *Don Ramón de la Cruz* (with music examples); E. Cotarelo y Mori, *Historia de la Zarzuela* (Madrid, 1934).

Rodzinski, Artur, eminent Polish conductor; b. Spalato, Dalmatia, Jan. 1, 1892; d. Boston, Nov. 27, 1958. He studied jurisprudence at the Univ. of Vienna; at the same time took piano lessons with Emil Sauer, composition with Schreker and conducting with Schalk. He made his conducting debut in Lwów in 1921; subsequently conducted Polish operas in Warsaw. In 1926 he was appointed assistant conductor to Leopold Stokowski with the Philadelphia Orch.; in 1929 he was appointed permanent conductor of the Los Angeles Philharmonic; after 4 seasons there he was engaged as conductor of the Cleveland Orch., where he introduced the novel custom of presenting operas in concert form; on Jan. 31, 1935 he conducted the American prèmiere of Shostakovich's controversial opera, *Lady Macbeth of the District of Mtzensk.* In 1943 he received his most prestigious appointment as conductor and music director of the N.Y. Philharmonic, but his independent character and tempera-

mental ways of dealing with the management forced him to resign amid raging controversy in the middle of his 4th season (Feb. 3, 1947); almost immediately he was engaged as conductor and music director of the Chiago Symph. Orch., but there, too, a conflict rapidly developed, reaching such a point of mutual outrage that he was summarily dismissed by the management during his first season (Jan. 13, 1948). After these distressing American experiences Rodzinski conducted mainly in Europe; in the autumn of 1958 he received an invitation to conduct at the Lyric Opera in Chicago, but a heart ailment forced him to cancel his plans, and he died in a Boston hospital.
BIBLIOGRAPHY: His widow, Halina Rodzinski, published a scrupulously documented and startlingly candid biography, *Our Two Lives* (N.Y., 1976). See also Donald Brook, *International Gallery of Conductors* (Bristol, 1951; pp. 159–64).

Roeckel, August, Austrian writer on music; b. Graz, Dec. 1, 1814; d. Budapest June 18, 1876. He studied music with his father Joseph August Roeckel (1783–1870), who was a singer and impresario; he also took lessons with J. N. Hummel, who was his uncle. He served as a theater conductor in Weimar (1838–43) and music director in Dresden (1843–49); became involved in the revolutionary activities in Saxony in 1848 and was arrested and sentenced to death; however, his sentence was commuted and he spent 13 years in the prison in Waldheim; upon release he engaged in literary activities. He maintained an active correspondence with Wagner, whose music and ideas he admired; Wagner's letters to him were published by La Mara, *Richard Wagners Briefe an August Roeckel* (Leipzig, 1894; in English, Bristol, 1897).

Roesgen-Champion, Marguerite, famous Swiss harpsichordist and composer; b. Geneva, Jan. 25, 1894; d. there, 1976. She was a student of Ernest Bloch and Jaques-Dalcroze at the Cons. of Geneva; made a specialty of harpsichord playing, and gave numerous recitals on that instrument in France and elsewhere; lived mostly in Paris. She composed a number of attractive pieces in a romantic genre, among them *Faunesques* for orch. (Paris, 1929); *Concerto moderne* for harpsichord and orch. (Paris, Nov. 15, 1931, composer soloist); symph. suite *Aquarelles* (Paris, Nov. 26, 1933); Harp Concerto (Paris, March 28, 1954); 5 concertos for harpsichord and orch. (1931–59); *Concerto romantique* for piano and orch. (1961); a number of pieces for flute in combination with the harpsichord and other instruments; a curious piece for piano 4-hands, entitled *Spoutnik* (1971).

Rogalski, Theodor, Rumanian composer and conductor; b. Bucharest, April 11, 1901; d. Zürich, Feb. 2, 1954. He studied at the Bucharest Cons. with Castaldi and Cuclin; at the Leipzig Cons. with Karg-Elert (1920–22); and in Paris with Vincent d'Indy (1922–25). Returning to Rumania, he was music director of the Bucharest Radio (1939–44) and chief conductor of the Bucharest State Philharmonic (1950–54). His music is permeated with the spirit of Rumanian folklore, while his harmony and orchestration reveal Impressionistic traits.

WORKS: *Trei dansuri romîneşti (3 Rumanian Dances;* Bucharest, May 27, 1951; attained great popularity and had numerous performances in Europe and America); *2 Capricci* for orch. (1932); String Quartet (1925); violin pieces and songs.

Rogatis, Pascual de, Italian-Argentine composer; b. Teora, May 17, 1880. He was taken to Buenos Aires as a child; studied piano and composition with Alberto Williams and violin with Pietro Melani and Rafael Albertini; after completing his education he established himself as a violin teacher and practicing composer. His following operas were performed in Buenos Aires: *Anfión y Zeto,* Greek tragedy (Aug. 18, 1915), *Huémac,* to a story of ancient Mexico (July 22, 1916), *La Novia del hereje (The Heretic's Bride;* June 13, 1935). He further composed a symph. poem, *Atipac* (Buenos Aires, April 7, 1928) and numerous vocal pieces on Argentine themes. He was still alive and active in Buenos Aires in 1976.

Rogel, José, Spanish composer of light opera; b. Orihuela, Alicante, Dec. 24, 1829; d. Cartagena, Feb. 25, 1901. At a very early age he was taught music by the organist J. Cascales, and at 10 composed a Mass, which he conducted himself. After he finished his law studies in Valencia, he studied counterpoint with Pascual Pérez; subsequently conducted at various theaters in Madrid, and in 1854 began his unusually successful career as composer of zarzuelas, of which he wrote about 75 (some in collaboration). Among the best are *El Joven Telémaco, Las Amazones del Tormes, El Rey Midas, Los Infiernos de Madrid, Genoveva de Brabante, Pablo y Virginia.*

Roger, Gustave-Hippolyte, famous French tenor; b. La Chapelle St.-Denis, near Paris, Dec. 17, 1815; d. Paris, Sept. 12, 1879. He was a pupil of Morin at the Paris Cons.; made his debut at the Opéra-Comique in 1838; then at the Paris Opéra, where he created the role of the Prophète in Meyerbeer's opera (1848); later toured in Germany. While hunting in the fall of 1859 the accidental discharge of his gun injured his right arm so severely that it had to be amputated. An artificial arm proved ineffective, and he was obliged to retire from the stage in 1861. From 1868 until his death he was prof. of singing at the Cons. He published his memoirs as *Le Carnet d'un Ténor* (Paris, 1880).

BIBLIOGRAPHY: A. Laget, *G.-H. Roger* (Paris, 1865).

Roger, Victor, French composer of operettas; b. Montpellier, July 21, 1854; d. Paris, Dec. 2, 1903. He studied at the École Niedermeyer; wrote light music; composed some 30 operettas, of which the following were brought out in Paris with considerable success: *Joséphine vendue par ses sœurs* (March 20, 1886); *Oscarine* (Oct. 15, 1888); *Le Fétiche* (March 13, 1890); *Samsonnet* (Nov. 26, 1890); *Miss Nicol-Nick* (Jan. 23, 1895); *Le Voyage de Corbillon* (Jan. 30, 1896); *Sa Majesté l'Amour* (Dec. 23, 1896); *Les Fêtards* (Oct. 28, 1897); *L'Auberge du Tohu-Bohu* (1897); *L'Agence Crook & Co.* (1898); *La Petite Tâche* (1898); *Poule*

blanche (1899); *Le Jockey malgré lui* (Dec. 2, 1902). After his death 3 completely finished scores were found: *La Fille de Fra Diavolo, La Princesse de Babylone,* and *Adélaïde.*

Roger-Ducasse, Jean-Jules Aimable, French composer; b. Bordeaux, April 18, 1873; d. Le-Taillan-Médoc, near Bordeaux, July 19, 1954. He studied at the Paris Cons. with Fauré (composition), Pessard (harmony), Gédalge (counterpoint) and with de Bériot. In 1902 he won the 2nd Prix de Rome for the cantata *Alcyone;* in 1909, appointed inspector of singing in the Paris schools; subsequently prof. of ensemble at the Paris Cons.; from 1935 to 1945 taught composition there; then retired to Bordeaux. His 1st work to be played in public was a *Petite Suite* for orch. (Paris, March 5, 1898). He adopted a pleasing style of Impressionism; his symph. pieces enjoyed considerable success, without setting a mark for originality.

WORKS: comic opera, *Cantegril* (Opéra-Comique, Feb. 9, 1931); a mimodrama, *Orphée* (St. Petersburg, Jan. 31, 1914); for orch.: *Variations plaisantes sur un thème grave* (Paris, Jan. 24, 1909), *Suite française* (1909), *Prélude d'un ballet* (1910), *Le Joli Jeu de furet,* orchestral scherzo (1911), *Nocturne de printemps* (Paris, Feb. 14, 1920), *Symphonie sur la Cathédrale de Reims* (never completed), *Le Petit Faune* (Bordeaux, May 22, 1954), etc.; *Sarabande,* symph. poem with voices (1911); *Au Jardin de Marguerite,* for soloists, chorus, and orch. (1901–05); *Sur quelques vers de Virgile,* for chorus and orch.; Piano Quartet (1899–1912); String Quartet (1900–09); songs (*Le Cœur de l'eau, Noëls des roses, 7 Préludes,* études, arabesques, etc.); pedagogic works (*Solfèges,* 3 vols.; *Dictée musicale,* 4 vols.; *Exercices de piano,* 3 vols.; etc.). His autobiography was publ. in *L'Écran des musiciens* (1930).

BIBLIOGRAPHY: L. Ceillier, *Roger-Ducasse* (Paris, 1920); A. Cœuroy, *La Musique française moderne* (Paris, 1922); *Catalogue de l'œuvre de Roger-Ducasse* (Bordeaux, 1955).

Rogers, Bernard, American composer; b. New York, Feb. 4, 1893; d. Rochester, N.Y., May 24, 1968. He studied architecture before devoting himself to music. His first teacher was Arthur Farwell; he subsequently studied with Ernest Bloch in Cleveland. His symph. composition, *To the Fallen,* was performed by the N.Y. Philharmonic on Nov. 13, 1919; on the strength of it, he won a Pulitzer Traveling Scholarship and went to Europe for further study; in 1927 he received a Guggenheim Fellowship; took courses with Nadia Boulanger in Paris and Frank Bridge in London. When he returned from Europe in 1929 he was engaged as instructor at the Eastman School of Music, Rochester, N.Y.; remained there, teaching orchestration and composition. His lyric drama, *The Marriage of Aude,* was brought out in a festival of American music at the Eastman School, on May 22, 1931. The Metropolitan Opera Co. produced his 1-act opera, *The Warrior* (to the story of Samson and Delilah), on Jan. 11, 1947, but it was not successful; another opera, *The Veil,* was produced at the Univ. of Indiana on May 18, 1950. Other works: for orch.: *The Faithful* (1918), *Adonais* (Rochester, April 29, 1927), *Prelude to Hamlet* (1928), Symph. No. 2 (Rochester, Oct. 24, 1930), *3 Japanese*

Dances (Rochester, May 3, 1934), *Once Upon a Time,* 5 fairy tales for small orch. (Rochester, April 4, 1935), *The Supper at Emmäus* (Rochester, April 29, 1937), Symph. No. 3 (Rochester, Oct. 27, 1937), *The Colors of War* (Rochester, Oct. 25, 1939), *The Song of the Nightingale* (Cincinnati, March 21, 1940), *The Dance of Salome* (Rochester, April 25, 1940), *The Plains,* "landscapes for orch." (N.Y., May 3, 1941), *Invasion* (N.Y., Oct. 17, 1943); *Characters from Hans Christian Andersen* (Rochester, April 28, 1945), *In Memory of Franklin Delano Roosevelt* (N.Y., April 11, 1946), *Amphitryon,* symph. overture (N.Y., March 10, 1947), Symph. No. 4 (Rochester, May 4, 1948), *Dance Scenes* (Louisville, Oct. 28, 1953), *Fantasy,* for flute, viola, and orch. (Rochester, April 25, 1938), *Africa* (Cincinnati, Jan. 30, 1959); *Soliloquy,* for bassoon and string orch. (Rochester, Oct. 18, 1938), *The Silver World,* for flute, oboe, and strings (1950), *Leaves from the Tale of Pinocchio,* suite for narrator and small orch. (1950); vocal works: *The Passion,* oratorio in 6 scenes, for soloists, mixed chorus, and orch. (Cincinnati, May 12, 1944; his most significant work); *Apparitions* for orch. (1967); *The Raising of Lazarus,* for soloists, chorus, and orch. (1928), *The Exodus,* sacred poem, for soloists, chorus, and orch. (1932); *Fantasia* for horn, kettledrums, and string orch. (Rochester, Feb. 20, 1955); a string quartet and other chamber music. He publ. a valuable manual, *The Art of Orchestration* (N.Y., 1951).

BIBLIOGRAPHY: E. E. Hipsher, *American Opera and Its Composers* (Philadelphia, 1934; pp. 369–70); David Diamond, "Bernard Rogers," *Musical Quarterly* (April 1947).

Rogers, Clara Kathleen (née **Barnett**), English soprano; b. Cheltenham, Jan. 14, 1844; d. Boston, March 8, 1931. She was the daughter of the composer **John Barnett**; studied at the Leipzig Cons. with Moscheles and Plaidy (piano), Papperitz and Richter (theory), David and Rietz (ensemble playing); singing with Goetz in Berlin and with Sangiovanni in Milan. She made her debut in Turin (1863) as Isabella in *Robert le Diable* (stage name "Clara Doria"); came to America in 1871 with the Parepa-Rosa Co.; debut, N.Y., in *Bohemian Girl* (Oct. 4, 1871); later settled in Boston as a teacher; from 1902 was prof. of singing at the New England Cons.; married a Boston lawyer, Henry M. Rogers, in 1878. She publ. *The Philosophy of Singing* (1893); *Dreaming True* (1899); *My Voice and I* (1910); *English Diction in Song and Speech* (1912); *The Voice in Speech* (1915); *Memories of a Musical Career* (Boston, 1919) and its sequel, *The Story of Two Lives* (Norwood, Mass., 1932); songs.

Rogers, Francis, American baritone; b. Roxbury, Mass., April 14, 1870; d. New York, May 15, 1951. He studied singing with W. L. Whitney in Boston, Vannuccini in Florence, Bouhy in Paris, and Luckstone in N.Y.; from 1924 member of the faculty of the Juilliard Graduate School, N.Y. He publ. *Some Famous Singers of the 19th Century* (N.Y., 1914).

Rogers, James Henderson, American organist and song composer; b. Newark, N.Y., 1852; d. St. Petersburg, Fla., May 30, 1933. He studied music in N.Y.;

was a church organist; composed a quantity of anthems and other church pieces, later collected in a book under the title, *The Church Chorus Series.*

Rogers, James Hotchkiss, American organist and composer; b. Fair Haven, Conn., Feb. 7, 1857; d. Pasadena, Calif., Nov. 28, 1940. He studied with Clarence Eddy in Chicago; in Berlin under Loeschhorn and Ehrlich (piano), Rohde (theory), and Haupt (organ); in Paris under Fissot (piano), Guilmant (organ), and Widor (theory). Returning to the U.S., he settled in Cleveland (1883) as organist; eventually retired to California. He publ. about 150 works: a Lenten cantata, *The Man of Nazareth;* an Easter cantata, *The New Life;* anthems, secular part-songs, songs, piano pieces, studies for piano and organ. Among his most popular songs are *The Star* and *At Parting.*

Roget, Henriette, French composer and organist; b. Bastia, Corsica, Jan. 9, 1910. She studied organ with Marcel Dupré and composition with Henri Busser at the Paris Cons.; received the Premier Second Prix de Rome in 1933. She was director in charge of voice training at the Paris Opéra until 1959; served as organist at the Oratoire du Louvre and prof. of piano accompanying and score reading at the Paris Cons. She wrote a great number of piano books for children, among them *Adroits petits doigts* (1957), *Abécédaire* (1958) and *Méthode* (1970).

WORKS: *Montanyas del Rosello,* for organ and orch. (Paris, April 6, 1933, composer soloist); *Sinfonia andorrana,* for orch. (1936); *Concerto classique* for cello and orch. (1944); *Concerto sicilien* for piano and orch. (1943); *Symphonie pour rire* (1947); *Cathérinettes,* ballet (1937); *Hymne à l'aviation* (1937; awarded a prize at the Paris Exhibition); *3 Ballades françaises* for orch. (Paris, Jan. 11, 1936); *Rythmes* for orch. (Paris, Jan. 23, 1937); a number of effective organ pieces.

BIBLIOGRAPHY: A. Machabey, *Portraits de trente musiciens français* (Paris, 1949).

Rogister, Jean, Belgian violist and composer; b. Liège, Oct. 25, 1879; d. there, March 20, 1964. He studied violin, viola, horn and composition at the Liège Cons.; played viola in local orchestral groups. His style of composition followed the precepts of César Franck, but upon occasion he introduced into his music some modernistic Impressionistic sonorities.

WORKS: lyric drama, *Lorsque minuit sonna* (1930); *Requiem* (1944; with orch. and full chorus, Liège, March 24, 1946); an oratorio, *The Bells,* after Edgar Allan Poe, for soprano and 8 instruments (1924); 3 symphonies: No. 1 (1927); No. 2, *Symphonie wallonne* (1931–32); No. 3, with solo string quartet (1942–43); *Symphonie intime* for string quartet, double bass, flute, clarinet, and bassoon (1929); *Fantaisie concertante* for viola and orch. (1910); *Viola Concerto* (1914); *Cello Concerto* (1917); *Trombone Concerto* (1919); *Poème* for violin and orch. (1920); *Impression de mai* for violin and orch. (1935); *Suite* for flute and chamber orch. (1949); symph. poems, *Destin* (1919); *La Fiancée du lutin* (1920); *Nuit d'Avril* (1921); *Paysage* (1923); *Fantaisie burlesque sur un thème populaire* (1928); *La Lune et les peupliers* (1932); *Jeux symphoniques* (1952); *Hommage à César Franck* (1955); *Adagio* for 2 string ensembles (1960); 8 string quartets (1902, 1914, 1921, 1926, 1927, 1928, 1931, 1940); *Esquisse dramatique* for string quartet (1935); Quintet for ancient instruments (clavecin, 2 quintons, viola d'amore, and viola da gamba, 1934); Wind Quintet (1947); choruses; songs.

Rogowski, Ludomir, Polish composer; b. Lublin, Oct. 3, 1881; d. Dubrovnik, Yugoslavia, March 14, 1954. Of a musical family, he received his early training at home; in 1906 went to Leipzig and took a course with Hugo Riemann. Returning to Poland, he conducted the Vilna Symph. Orch., which he founded (1910); in 1911 was in Paris; from 1912 to 1914, was a theater conductor in Warsaw. He was again in France (1917–19); in Poland (1919–26), finally settling in Dubrovnik (1927), where he remained for the rest of his life, with only occasional engagements as conductor in Warsaw (1935 and 1938).
WORKS: operas: *Tamara* (1918), *Un Grand Chagrin de la petite Ondine* (1919), *La Sérénade inutile* (1921), *Królewicz Marko* (1930); the ballets *Bajka* (1922) and *Kupala* (1925); 6 symphonies: No. 1, *Offering* (1921), No. 2, *Rejoicing* (1936), No. 3 (1940), No. 4 (1943), No. 5 (1947), No. 6 (1949); other symphonic works: *Images ensoleillées* (1918), *Villafranca* (1919), *Les Saisons* (1933), *Les Sourires* (1933), *Poème du travail* (1936), *Fantômes* (1937), 4 rhapsodies on Slavonic themes (1945), *Dubrovnik Impressions* (1950); 6 works for violin and orch.; 2 string quartets; short pieces for various instruments; numerous arrangements of Slavonic songs for chorus. In some of his works he made use of the so-called Slavonic scale (Lydian mode with the lowered 7th) and the scale of alternating whole tones and semitones, known as Rimsky-Korsakov's scale.

Roguski, Gustav, Polish composer and pedagogue; b. Warsaw, May 12, 1839; d. there, April 5, 1921. He studied in Germany with Kiel; then went to Paris, where he became a pupil of Berlioz. Returning to Warsaw in 1873, he was appointed prof. at the Cons. He wrote a symphony, 2 string quartets, a quintet for wind instruments and piano, many piano pieces, choruses, and songs; publ. a manual of harmony in Polish (with L. Zelenski). He was greatly esteemed as a teacher of composition; Paderewski was his pupil.

Rohde, (Friedrich) Wilhelm, Danish violinist and composer; b. Altona, Dec. 11, 1856; d. Gentofte, near Copenhagen, April 6, 1928; pupil at the Leipzig Cons. of H. Schradieck and F. David (violin), J. Röntgen (piano), E. F. Richter (composition), and H. Kretzschmar. He lived in Chicago (1878–85); after one season as violist in the Boston Symph. Orch. he returned to Germany; lived in Schwerin; from 1914, in Copenhagen. He composed several symph. poems; a serenade for strings; *Höller-Galopp* for violin, cello, flute, horn, and piano; a number of male choruses; piano pieces.

Rohloff, Ernst, German music historian; b. Graudenz, April 17, 1899. He studied in Leipzig with Straube (organ), Schering and Abert (musicology), received his

Dr. phil. for the dissertation *Studien zum Musiktraktat des Johannes de Grocheo* (Leipzig, 1925); settled in Weissenfels as teacher and organist. He published several valuable papers on medieval music.

Röhr, Hugo, German conductor and composer; b. Dresden, Feb. 13, 1866; d. Munich, June 7, 1937. He studied composition with Wüllner at the Dresden Cons.; began his career as conductor in Augsburg; after filling several engagements in Breslau, Prague and Mannheim he was appointed conductor at the court opera in Munich (1896); from 1924 to 1934 he taught conducting at the Munich Academy of Music. He wrote several short operas: *Das Vaterunser* (Munich, 1904), *Frauenlist* (Leipzig, 1917), *Cœur-Dame* (1927); a dramatic poem *Ekkehard*, for soli, chorus, and orch.; chamber music; songs.

Röhrig, Emil, German composer; b. Rettert, Oct. 31, 1882; d. Aachen, July 22, 1954. After studying violin in Chemnitz, he became engaged as violinist and conductor in Krefeld and Aachen. He wrote much music for brass; also concertos for double bass, viola, trumpet, etc.; cantatas and other choral works.

Roig, Gonzalo, Cuban conductor and composer; b. Havana, July 20, 1890; d. there, June 13, 1970. He played violin in theater orchestras; in 1922 organized the Orquesta Sinfónica de la Habana. He also wrote zarzuelas, among which *Cecilia Valdés* enjoyed considerable success. In 1912 he wrote the song *Quiereme mucho*, which became a popular hit.

Rojo, Casiano, Spanish authority on Gregorian Chant; b. Acinas, near Burgos, Aug. 5, 1877; d. at the monastery of Santo Domingo de Silos, Burgos, Dec. 4, 1931. He was employed as organist and chorus leader; received his training in the proper interpretation of Gregorian Chant from Dom Pothier; published a valuable manual *Método de canto gregoriano* (Valladolid, 1906); *Antiphonarium Mozarabicum de la Catedral de León* (with G. Prado; León, 1928); and *El Canto mozárabe* (with G. Prado; Barcelona, 1929).

Rokseth, Yvonne (*née* **Rihouët**), French musicologist and organist; b. Maisons-Laffitte, near Paris, July 17, 1890; d. Paris, Aug. 23, 1948. She studied at the Paris Cons.; with d'Indy and Roussel at the Schola Cantorum; and with Pirro at the Sorbonne; *Dr. ès lettres* (dissertation: *La Musique d'orgue au XVe siècle et au début du XVIe*; Paris, 1930); held various positions as organist in Paris (1920–25); was later librarian at the Paris Cons. and prof. of musicology at the Univ. of Strasbourg (from 1937); publ. a biography of Grieg (Paris, 1933); edited *Deux livres d'orgue parus chez P. Attaingnant en 1531*, in the series Publications de la Société française de musicologie (1925); *Polyphonies du XIIIe siècle: Le Manuscrit Montpellier H 196* (facsimile, transcription, and commentary, 4 vols., 1935–39); also organ works of Marc Antonio da Bologna of 1523; etc.; co-editor of *Trois Chansonniers français du XVe siècle* (Paris, 1927).
BIBLIOGRAPHY: G. Thibault "Yvonne Rokseth," *Revue de Musicologie* (1948).

Roland, Claude-Robert, Belgian composer, organist and conductor; b. Pont-de-Loup, Dec. 19, 1935. He studied composition at the Music Academy in Châtelet and at the Conservatories of Mons, Liège, Paris and Brussels with Froidebise, C. Schmit, R. Bernier, Messiaen and Defossez; also took a course in conducting with Scherchen. He was an organist in churches in various Belgian cities (1955–67); director of the Music Academy at Montignies-le-Tilleul (1966–75); in 1972 appointed to the staff of the Brussels Cons.

WORKS: *Sonance* for string quartet (1956); 2 *Sonances* for piano (1956, 1960); *Recherche* for orch. (1956); *Indicatif 1* for 12 strings (1957); *Sonance* for clavichord (1959); *Sinfonia scolastica pour les bouffons de la Reine* (1961); *Serenade* for chamber orch. (1961); *Chansons et reveries* for violin and piano (1962); Organ Concerto (1963); *Ballade* for violin and piano (1966); *Prelude, Fugue et rondo a cinq* for wind quintet (1967); *Sonancelle* for solo guitar (1967); *Rossignolet du bois* for orch. (1971); *Prélude, fugue et commentaires* for 4 clarinets (1971).

Roland-Manuel, Alexis (real name **Roland Alexis Manuel Lévy**), French composer and writer; b. Paris, March 22, 1891; d. there, Nov. 1, 1966. He was a pupil of Albert Roussel and Vincent d'Indy; also studied privately with Ravel. In 1947 he became prof. at the Paris Cons. In his compositions he adopted the French neo-Classical style, close to Roussel's manner; however, it is not as a composer but as a perspicacious critic that he became chiefly known. He publ. 3 books on Ravel: *Maurice Ravel et son œuvre* (1914), *Maurice Ravel et son œuvre dramatique* (1928), *Maurice Ravel* (1938; in English, London, 1947); also monographs on Honegger (1925) and Manuel de Falla (1930).

WORKS: *Isabelle et Pantalon,* opéra-bouffe (Paris, Dec. 11, 1922); *Le Diable amoureux,* light opera (1929); *L'Écran des jeunes filles,* ballet (Paris Opéra, May 16, 1929); *Elvire,* ballet on themes of Scarlatti (Paris Opéra, Feb. 8, 1937); Piano Concerto (1938); *Cantique de la sagesse,* for chorus and orch. (1951); oratorio, *Jeanne d'Arc* (1937).

Roldán, Amadeo, Cuban violinist and composer; b. Paris (of Cuban parents), July 12, 1900; d. Havana, March 2, 1939. He studied violin at the Madrid Cons. with Fernández Bordas, graduating in 1916; won the Sarasate Violin Prize; subsequently studied composition with Conrado del Campo in Madrid and with Pedro Sanjuán. In 1921 he settled in Havana; in 1924, became concertmaster of the Orquesta Filarmónica there; 1925, assistant conductor; from 1932, conductor. In his works he employed with signal success the melorhythms of Afro-Cuban popular music; as a mulatto, he had an innate understanding of these elements.

WORKS: *La Rebambaramba,* a ballet, employing a number of Cuban percussion instruments in the score; a suite from this ballet was performed in Havana on Aug. 12, 1928; *Obertura sobre témas cubanos* (Havana, Nov. 29, 1925); *El Milagro de Anaquillé* (Havana, Sept. 22, 1929); *Danza Negra,* for voice and 7 instruments (1929); *Motivos de Son,* for voice and 9 instruments (1930); 3 *Toques* for chamber orch. (1931); 6 *Ritmicas:* Nos. 1–4 for piano and wind quintet; Nos. 5 and 6 for a percussion ensemble.

Rolla, Alessandro, Italian violinist, Paganini's teacher; b. Pavia, April 6, 1757; d. Milan, Sept. 15, 1841. He was a pupil of Renzi and Conti; from 1782 till 1802 he was concertmaster of the ducal orch. in Parma; Paganini studied with him there. In 1805 he was appointed violinist to the French Viceroy Eugène Beauharnais, in Milan; prof. at the Cons. of Milan from its foundation in 1807.

WORKS: several ballets: *Adelasia* (Milan, 1779), *Iserbeck* (Padua, 1802), *Eloisa e Roberto* or *Il Conte d'Essex* (Rome, 1805), *Pizzarro* (Milan, 1807), *Abdul* (Vienna, 1808), *Achilles auf Skyros* (Vienna, 1808); symphonies; 3 violin concertos; 4 viola concertos; 6 string quartets; trios for violin, viola, and cello; also for 2 violins and cello; other chamber music.

Rolla, Antonio, Italian violinist; son of **Alessandro Rolla;** b. Parma, April 18, 1798; d. Dresden, May 19, 1837. He studied with his father; was concertmaster of the orch. of the Italian Opera Co. in Dresden (1823–35); composed a number of violin pieces.

Rolland, Romain, famous French author and musicologist; b. Clamecy, Nièvre, Jan. 29, 1866; d. Vézelay, Yonne, Dec. 30, 1944. He was educated at the École de Rome; *Dr. ès lettres* (1895) with two theses, *Cur ars picturae apud Italos XVI saeculi deciderit* and the very valuable *Les Origines du théâtre lyrique moderne* (*Histoire de l'opéra en Europe avant Lully et Scarlatti;* 3rd ed., 1931); the latter was awarded the Prix Kastner-Bourgault by the Academy in 1896, and at the same time won him the professorship in the history of music at the École Normale. In 1900 he organized the 1st international congress for the history of music in Paris, and read a paper on *Les Musiciens italiens en France sous Mazarin et "l'Orfeo" de Luigi Rossi* (publ. 1901); with J. Combarieu he ed. the transactions and the papers read as *Documents, mémoires et vœux* (1901). In Oct., 1901, he founded, with J. Combarieu (editor), P. Aubry, M. Emmanuel, L. Laloy, and himself as principal contributors, the fortnightly *Revue d'Histoire et Critique Musicales.* In 1903 the Univ. of Paris commissioned him to organize the music section of the newly founded École des Hautes Études Sociales, of which he was the 1st president, and where he lectured on the history of music; resigned in 1909, devoting his entire time to literary work. From 1913 he resided in Switzerland, but in 1938 returned to France and took up his residence at Vézelay.

Rolland's writings exhibit sound scholarship, broad sympathy, keen analytical power, well-balanced judgment, and intimate acquaintance with the musical milieu of his time. The book by which he is most widely known is *Jean-Christophe,* a musical novel remarkable for its blending of historical accuracy, psychological and esthetic speculation, subtle psychological analysis, and romantic interest; for it he received the Nobel Prize (1915). The 1st volume was publ. in 1905, the last (10th) in 1912; English translation, N.Y., 1910–13. Rolland's other works include *Paris als Mu-*

sikstadt (1904; in Strauss's series *Die Musik;* rewritten and publ. in French as *Le Renouveau* in *Musiciens d'aujourd'hui); Beethoven* (1903; English translation with brief analyses of the symphs., quartets, and sonatas by A. E. Hull, 6th ed., 1927); *Haendel* (1910; English translation, 1916); *Voyage musical au pays du passé* (1920; in English, 1922); *Beethoven: Les Grandes Époques créatrices* (1928; English transl. by Ernest Newman entitled *Beethoven the Creator,* 1929); *Goethe et Beethoven* (1930; in English, 1931); *Beethoven: Le Chant de la Résurrection* (1937; on the *Missa solemnis* and the last sonatas); essays in various journals he collected and publ. in 2 vols. as *Musiciens d'autrefois* (1908; 6th ed., 1919; in English, 1915) and *Musiciens d'aujourd'hui* (1908; 8th ed., 1947; in English, 1914); *Essays on Music* (a selection from some of the above books; N.Y., 1948).
BIBLIOGRAPHY: P. Seippel, *Romain Rolland: l'Homme et l'œuvre* (Paris, 1913); Stefan Zweig, *Romain Rolland: der Mann und das Werk* (Frankfurt, 1921; in English, N.Y., 1921); J. Bonnerot, *Romain Rolland, sa vie, son œuvre* (Paris, 1921); E. Lerch, *Romain Rolland und die Erneuerung der Gesinnung* (Munich, 1926); M. Lob, *Un Grand Bourguignon, Romain Rolland* (Auxerre, 1927); Chr. Sénéchal, *Romain Rolland* (Paris, 1933); M. Doisy, *Romain Rolland* (Brussels, 1945); R. Argos, *Romain Rolland* (Paris, 1950); W. T. Starr, *A Critical Bibliography of the Published Writings of Romain Rolland* (Evanston, Ill., 1950). *Richard Strauss and Romain Rolland: Correspondence,* ed. by R. Myers (London, 1968).

Rolle, Johann Heinrich, German composer; b. Quedlinburg, Dec. 23, 1716; d. Magdeburg, Dec. 29, 1785. He played the viola and the organ in the Berlin court orch. (1741); went to Magdeburg in 1746 as church organist; in 1752 became his father's successor as town music director there. He wrote 4 Passions, 20 oratorios, several church services for the entire year; *Odes of Anacreon* for voice and harpsichord; etc.
BIBLIOGRAPHY: W. Kawerau, *J. H. Rolle. Ein musikalisches Characterbild* (Magdeburg, 1885); H. von Hase, "J. H. Rolle," *Zeitschrift für Musikwissenschaft* 2; R. Kaestner, *J. H. Rolle* (Kassel, 1932).

Röllig, Carl Leopold, Austrian composer and inventor; b. Vienna, c.1735; d. there, March 4, 1804. He was a harmonica player; invented the "Orphika" and "Xänorphika" (pianos with bows instead of hammers), and made many tours, in an attempt to popularize them. In 1797 he settled in Vienna. He wrote a comic opera, *Clarisse* (Hamburg, Oct. 10, 1771); publ. the pamphlets *Über die Harmonika* (1787) and *Über die Orphika* (1795).

Rollin, Jean, French composer; b. Paris, Aug. 3, 1906. He studied composition at the Paris Cons. with Noël Gallon and musicology with Pirro and Masson. His works include Concerto for Piano and Strings (1947); Violin Concerto (1950); Concerto for Double Bass and Orch. (1951); 2 symphonies (1953, 1958); the opera *Gringoué* (1965); chamber music; songs.

Rolón, José, Mexican composer; b. Ciudad Gusmán, Jalisco, June 22, 1883; d. Mexico City, Feb. 3, 1945. He studied in Paris with Moszkowski, and later with Nadia Boulanger and Dukas. In Mexico he was active as a teacher. He composed a symph. poem *Cuauhtémoc* (Mexico City, Jan. 10, 1930); symph. suite *Zapotlán* (Mexico City, Nov. 4, 1932); Piano Concerto (Mexico City, Sept. 4, 1942); many effective piano pieces.

Roman, Johan Helmich, significant Swedish composer; b. Stockholm, Oct. 26, 1694; d. Haraldsmala, near Kalmar, Nov. 20, 1758. He was of Finnish ethnic origin; began playing the violin as a mere child, and at 16 was already a member of the court orchestra, where his father **Johan Roman** was concertmaster. In 1715 he traveled to England where he took lessons with Ariosti and Pepusch in London; returned to Stockholm in 1721. In 1727 he was appointed conductor of the court orch.; from 1735 to 1737 he traveled in Europe; in 1740 he was named a member of the Swedish Academy, and in 1745 retired from active work. Roman was the first Swedish composer to write instrumental and choral music that could compare favorably with German and Italian works, and for that reason called "the father of Swedish music." His style shows the influence of Handel, with whom he became personally acquainted in England.
WORKS: Two sets of Roman's numerous compositions were published during his lifetime, *12 Sonate a flauto traverso, violone e cembalo* (1727) and *Assaggio a violino solo* (1740). A great number of his works in manuscript are preserved in various Swedish libraries, among them 21 *sinfonie,* 2 *sinfonie da chiesa,* 6 overtures, 5 suites, 2 concerti grossi, 5 violin concertos, about 20 violin sonatas, 17 trio sonatas, etc.; of these several were published in modern times; an edition of his collected works was begun in Stockholm in 1965 in the series of *Monumenta musicae Svecicae.*
BIBLIOGRAPHY: P. Vretblad, *J. H. Roman Svenska musikens fader* (2 vols., Stockholm, 1914; vol. II contains complete thematic catalogue); C. A. Moberg, *J. H. Roman* (Stockholm, 1944); I. Bengtsson, *J. H. Roman och hans Instrumentalmusik* (Uppsala, 1955); G. Carleberg, *Buxtehude, Telemann och Roman* (Stockholm, 1965).

Romani, Carlo, Italian composer; b. Avelino, May 24, 1824; d. Florence, March 4, 1875. He studied with Palafuti (piano) and Picchianti (composition); completed his studies under his uncle, **Pietro Romani;** set to music the recitatives of *Der Freischütz* for its first Italian performance (Florence, Feb. 3, 1843); wrote the operas (all produced at Florence); *Tutti amanti* (1847), *Il Mantello* (1852; successful), *I Baccanali di Roma* (1854), *Ermellina ossia Le Gemme della corona* (1865); an oratorio, *San Sebastiano* (1864); various patriotic songs.

Romani, Felice, renowned Italian librettist; b. Genoa, Jan. 31, 1788; d. Moneglia, Jan. 28, 1865. He wrote about 100 librettos for Mayr, Winter, Vaccai, Rossini, Bellini, Donizetti, Pacini, Ricci, etc.
BIBLIOGRAPHY: F. Regli, *Elogio a Felice Romani* (Turin, 1865); L. Lianovosani, *Saggio bibliografico relativo ai melodrammi di Felice Romani* (Milan, 1878); E. Branca (Romani's wife), *Felice Romani ed i più ri-*

putati maestri di musica del suo tempo (Turin, 1882); C. Paschetto, *Felice Romani* (Turin, 1907).

Romani, Pietro, Italian composer; b. Rome, May 29, 1791; d. Florence, Jan. 6, 1877. He studied with Fenaroli; became conductor at the Teatro della Pergola in Florence; taught singing at the Istituto Musicale there. He wrote 2 operas, *Il Qui pro quo* (Rome, 1817) and *Carlo Magno* (Florence, 1823); also ballet music; he is remembered chiefly for his aria *Manca un foglio,* for Bartolo in *Il Barbiere de Siviglia,* which he wrote for the production of the opera in Florence in 1816 as a substitute for Rossini's original aria *A un dottor della mia sorte,* which presented some vocal difficulties. Romani's aria was long retained in many productions of the opera.

Romberg, Andreas (Jacob), German violinist and composer; b. Vechta, near Münster, April 27, 1767; d. Gotha, Nov. 10, 1821. He was the son of the clarinetist and music director **Gerhard Heinrich Romberg** (1745-1819); played in public at 7; in 1784 made a concert tour with his cousin **Bernhard Romberg** through Holland and France, remaining in Paris as soloist for the Concert Spirituel during that season. From 1790 to 1793 he played in the Electoral orch. at Bonn with Bernhard; toured in Italy with him; lived many years in Hamburg (1801-15), and then succeeded Spohr as court Kapellmeister at Gotha.
WORKS: Operas: *Der Rabe* (Hamburg, April 7, 1794), *Die Ruinen zu Paluzzi* (Hamburg, Dec. 27, 1811), *Die Grossmut des Scipio* (Gotha, 1816); Singspiele; choral works with orch.; church music; 10 symphonies; 23 violin concertos; 33 string quartets; 8 flute quintets with strings; 1 clarinet quintet; 2 string quintets; piano quartet; 3 violin sonatas; 11 rondos and caprices for violin; a concertante for violin and cello with orch., etc. His *Toy Symphony* was popular for a time, as was his setting of Schiller's *Lied von der Glocke.*
BIBLIOGRAPHY: J. F. Rochlitz, *Für Freunde der Tonkunst* (vol. 1, Leipzig, 1824); K. Stephenson, *Andreas Romberg* (Hamburg, 1938).

Romberg, Bernhard, German cellist and composer; b. Dinklage, Nov. 11, 1767; d. Hamburg, Aug. 13, 1841. He was the son of **Anton Romberg,** famous bassoonist (1742-1814), who took him to Paris in 1781; he remained there for 2 years; played in the court orch. at Bonn (1790-93); then traveled in Spain; was the constant companion of his cousin **Andreas Romberg; in** 1796 they played at a concert with Beethoven in Vienna. Romberg was appointed prof. of cello playing at the Paris Cons. in 1801, but resigned in 1803. He was then in Hamburg and Berlin; in 1807 toured in Russia; paid a visit to England (1814); then was court Kapellmeister in Berlin (1815-19); was subsequently in Vienna (1822-25) and again in Russia (1825); lived in Paris (1839-40) before retiring to Hamburg.
WORKS: For the cello he wrote 9 concertos, 3 concertinos, a fantasia with orch., 4 sets of Russian airs with orch., caprices and fantasias on Swedish, Spanish, and Rumanian airs, and polonaises. In Berlin he publ. a cello method (1840); also brought out several operas: *Ulysses und Circe* (Berlin, July 27, 1807), *Rit-*

tertreue (Berlin, Jan. 31, 1817), *Alma* (Copenhagen, May 15, 1824), etc.; 11 string quartets; other chamber music.
BIBLIOGRAPHY: H. Schäfer, *Bernhard Romberg* (Münster, 1931).

Romberg, Sigmund, famous operetta composer; b. Nagy Kaniza, Hungary, July 29, 1887; d. New York, Nov. 9, 1951. He studied at the Univ. of Bucharest and in Vienna (with Heuberger); in 1909 came to the U.S. as an engineer, later turning to composition; settled in N.Y. in 1913. He composed over 70 operettas, including *The Midnight Girl* (Feb. 23, 1914; his first success); *The Blue Paradise* (with E. Eysler; N.Y., Aug. 5, 1915); *Maytime* (N.Y., Aug. 16, 1917); *Blossom Time* (on Schubert's melodies; N.Y., Sept. 29, 1921); *The Rose of Stamboul* (March 7, 1922); *The Student Prince* (N.Y., Dec. 2, 1924); *The Desert Song* (N.Y., Nov. 30, 1926); *My Maryland* (N.Y., Sept. 12, 1927); *The New Moon* (Sept. 19, 1928); *Up in Central Park* (N.Y., Jan. 27, 1945).
BIBLIOGRAPHY: E. Arnold, *Deep in My Heart* (a biography in the form of a novel, N.Y., 1949). See R. Crawford in *Dictionary of American Biography,* Supplement V.

Romero, Mateo (real name **Matthieu Rosmarin**), Spanish composer; b. Liège, 1575; d. Madrid, May 10, 1647. He was a soldier and was often called "El Maestro Capitán." After serving with the Spanish Army in Flanders he became cantor of the Chapel Royal in Madrid (1593), and maestro in 1598; in 1605 he was ordained a priest. In 1638 he went to Portugal as emissary to the Duke of Braganza (the future Emperor João IV). He enjoyed the reputation as one of the finest composers of both sacred and secular music of his time. 22 works by Romero for 3-4 voices are included in the *Cancionero de Sablonara* (modern ed. by J. Arcoa, Madrid, 1918); other compositions are found in Diego Pizarro's collection, *Libro de tonos humanos* and in Pedrell's *Teatro lírico español* III (La Coruña, 1896-98); a motet, *Libera me,* was included by Eslava in his collection *Lira sacro-hispana.*
BIBLIOGRAPHY: R. A. Pelinski, *Die weltliche Vokalmusik Spaniens am Anfang des 17. Jahrhunderts, der Cancionero de la Sablonara* (Tutzing, 1971).

Romeu, Luis, Spanish composer; b. Vich, near Barcelona, June 21, 1874; d. there, Sept. 23, 1937. A priest, he was first choirmaster, then organist, at the cathedral in Vich. His works, which show the influence of Catalan folksong, include a Mass for the *Mare de Deu de Nuria* and *Cants catequistics et Marianes* (3 collections). He publ. a book on Catalan church music, *La Versio autética dels Goigs del Roser de tot l'any* (vol. I of *Obra del Cançoner popular de Catalunya;* Barcelona, 1928). The total number of his works, secular and sacred, is 331.

Römhildt, Johann Theodor, German organist and composer; b. Salzungen, Sept. 23, 1684; d. Merseburg, Oct. 26, 1757. He studied with Johann Jakob Bach in Ruhla; in 1697 entered the Thomasschule in Leipzig where he was a pupil of Schelle and Kuhnau; subsequently served as cantor at Spremberg, Freystadt and Merseburg; in 1731 was appointed court musician in

Merseburg, and in 1735 cathedral organist there. He composed 238 church cantatas, 19 secular cantatas, 2 oratorios, 2 Masses, a *St. Matthew Passion* (which was publ. in 1921 in Leipzig), motets and some instrumental works.

BIBLIOGRAPHY: Karl Paulke, "J. Th. Römhildt," *Archiv für Musikwissenschaft* 1 (1919).

Ronald, Sir Landon (real name **L. R. Russell**), English conductor; b. London, June 7, 1873; d. there, Aug. 14, 1938. He was a son of the composer **Henry Russell, Sr.** and brother of the impresario **Henry Russell, Jr.** He entered the Royal College of Music where he studied composition with Sir Charles Parry and also attended the classes of Sir Charles Stanford and Sir Walter Parratt. He first embarked on a concert career as a pianist, but soon turned to conducting light opera and summer symph. concerts. In 1908 he was appointed conductor of the New Symph. Orch. in London (later named Royal Albert Hall Orch.); from 1910 until his death he was principal of the Guildhall School of Music. He was knighted in 1922. He composed an operetta, *A Capital Joke;* a ballet, *Britannia's Realm* (1902; for the coronation of King Edward VII) and a scenic spectacle *Entente cordiale* (1904; to celebrate the triple alliance of Russia, France and England); about 300 songs. He published 2 autobiographical books, *Variations on a Personal Theme* (London, 1922) and *Myself and Others* (London, 1931).

Roncaglia, Gino, Italian musicologist; b. Modena, May 7, 1883; d. there, Nov. 27, 1968. He studied with Sinigaglia; devoted himself to musical biography.

WRITINGS: *Giuseppe Verdi* (Naples, 1914); *La Rivoluzione musicale italiana* (Milan, 1928); *Rossini l'Olimpico* (Milan, 1946); *Invito alla musica* (Milan, 1947; 4th ed., 1958); *Invito all' opera* (Milan, 1949; 2nd ed., 1954); *L'Ascensione creatrice di Giuseppe Verdi* (Florence, 3rd ed., 1951); *La Cappella musicale del Duomo di Modena* (Florence, 1957); *Galleria verdiana: studi e figure* (Milan, 1959).

Ronconi, Domenico, famous Italian tenor and singing teacher; b. Lendinara, July 11, 1772; d. Milan, April 13, 1839. He was a successful opera tenor; sang in Italy, France, Germany, and Russia. In 1829 he opened a singing school in Milan; publ. vocal exercises that were widely used. His son, **Giorgio Ronconi** (b. Milan, Aug. 6, 1810; d. Madrid, Jan. 8, 1890), was a well-known baritone; spent some years in New York (from 1867).

Ronga, Luigi, eminent Italian musicologist; b. Turin, June 19, 1901. He studied at the Univ. of Turin and in Dresden; in 1926 became prof. at the Cons. of Palermo; later joined the faculty of Santa Cecilia, Rome.

WRITINGS: He publ. an excellent monograph on Frescobaldi (Turin, 1930); also one on Rossini (Florence, 1939) and essays on other Italian composers; *Bach, Mozart, Beethoven; tre problemi critici* (Venice, 1956); *Arte e gusto nella musica, dell'ars nova a Debussy* (Milan, 1956); *The Meeting of Poetry and Music* (N.Y., 1956); *La musica nell'età barocca* (Rome, 1959); *Il linguaggio musicale romantico* (Rome, 1960);

La musica europea nella seconda metà dell'Ottocento (Rome, 1961).

Rongé, Jean-Baptiste, Belgian composer and translator; b. Liège, April 1, 1825; d. there, Oct. 28, 1882. He was a pupil at the Liège Cons.; won the 2nd Belgian Prix de Rome (1851); wrote occasional cantatas and other pieces; a meeting with the poet André van Hasselt directed his interests towards literary work; in collaboration they translated into French the librettos of *Don Giovanni, Zauberflöte, Freischütz, Barbiere di Siviglia,* and other famous operas. After van Hasselt's death (1874), Rongé returned to composing, producing a comic opera, *La Comtesse d'Albany* (Liège, 1877); also wrote some choruses and songs, and *24 Études rythmiques* (for voice).

Ronnefeld, Peter, German composer and conductor; b. Dresden, Jan. 26, 1935; d. Kiel, Aug. 6, 1965. He studied with Blacher in Berlin and Messiaen in Paris; was chorus conductor at the Vienna Opera (1957–59); then was active in Kiel. As a conductor, he specialized in modern music, but he also excelled in the romantic repertory; his own opera *Die Ameise* (Düsseldorf, Oct. 21, 1961) had a fine reception. He further wrote Concertino for flute, clarinet, horn, bassoon, and string orch. (1950); *Sinfonie '52* (1952); *Rondo* for orch. (1954), 2 *Episodes* for chamber orch. (1956); a cantata *Quartär* (1958); a ballet, *Die Spirale* (1961). His early death was lamented.

Röntgen, Julius, important German-Dutch composer; b. Leipzig, May 9, 1855; d. Utrecht, Sept. 13, 1932. He studied music with his father, Engelbert Röntgen (1829–97); later with Plaidy and Reinecke in Leipzig and Fr. Lachner in Munich. In 1878 he settled in Amsterdam as teacher; was conductor of the Society for the Promotion of Music (1886–98); was a co-founder (1885) of the Amsterdam Cons., and its director from 1914 to 1924. He was a friend of Brahms and Grieg; edited the letters of Brahms to Th. Engelmann (1918); publ. a biography of Grieg (1930). An astonishingly industrious composer, he wrote an enormous amount of music in every genre, cast in an expansive Romantic style: 12 symphonies; 3 piano concertos; 3 operas *(Agnete, Samum,* and *Der lachende Kavalier);* much chamber music; etc.; edited old Dutch keyboard compositions (vol. 37 of the *Vereeniging voor Nederlandsche Muziekgeschiedenis*) and 14 songs by Adrianus Valerius. His correspondence was publ. by his widow (1934).

Roos, Robert de, Dutch composer; b. The Hague, March 10, 1907; d. there, March 18, 1976. He studied composition with Johan Wagenaar at his local Royal Cons.; then went to Paris, where he studied composition with Koechlin, Roland-Manuel and Milhaud, piano with Isidor Philipp, and conducting with Monteux (1926–34); returning to Holland, he worked with Sem Dresden. He served as a cultural attaché at the Netherlands Embassy in Paris (1947–56); then was First Secretary for Press and Cultural Affairs in Caracas (1957–62), London (1962–67) and, in 1967, in Buenos Aires.

WORKS: a chamber oratorio after Omar Khayyám

(1928); *5 Etudes* for piano and small orch. (1929); *Mouvement symphonique* (1930); a ballet, *Kaartspel (Card Game,* 1934); a dance pantomime, *Landelijke Comedie (Pastoral Comedy)* for orch. (1937–39); *Lyrische Suite* for chorus and small orch. (1938); Violin Concertino (1939); *Danses* for flute and small orch. (1940); Viola Concerto (1941–42); Sinfonietta (1943); *Sinfonia romantica (Museum-Symphonie)* for chamber orch. (1943); Piano Concerto (1943–44); *Adam in ballingschap* for 2 narrators, 2 flutes, 2 horns and strings (1944); *Quo Vadis,* suite for orch. (1947); *Variations sérieuses sur un thème ingénu* for orch. (1947); *De getemde Mars* for chorus and orch. (1948); 2 violin concertos (1949–50, 1956–58); Sinfonia No. 2 (1952); *Suggestioni* for orch. (1961); *Composizioni* for orch. (1962); *Sinfonia in due moti* for string orch. (1968); a cantata, *Postrema Verba,* for baritone, chorus and 25 instruments (1969); *2 Songs* for baritone and instruments (1971); *Musica* for violins, cellos and double basses (1971); *Rapsodie e Danza* for 2 flutes and orch. (1972–73); *3 Romantic Songs* for soprano and orch. (1975); Sextet for piano and winds (1935); 7 string quartets (1941; 1942; 1944–45; 1945–49; 1951; 1969–70; *Quartettino,* 1971); Solo Violin Sonata (1943); *Introduction, Adagio and Allegro* for 2 violins (1945); Violin Sonata (1946); *Capriccio* for clarinet and piano (1952); *Distrazioni* for violin and piano (1953); *3 Pezzi senza nome* for piano quartet (1958); Trio for 2 violins and cello (1965); *Quattro per due* for oboe and viola (1966); *Incidenze* for flute, cello or viola da gamba, and harpsichord (1966–67); *Incontri* for wind quintet (1966); Piano Trio (1968); *2 moti lenti* for 2 violins and cello (1970); *4 Pezzi* for wind trio (1970–71); incidental music for classical dramas.

Root, Frederick Woodman, American organist and writer on music, son of **George Frederick Root;** b. Boston, June 13, 1846; d. Chicago, Nov. 8, 1916. He was taught by his father, then by Dr. B. C. Blodgett and William Mason in New York. In 1863 became organist of the Third Presbyterian Church, Chicago; in 1865, of the Swedenborgian Church. In 1869–70 traveled in Europe, studying singing with Vannuccini in Florence. He published *The Technic and Art of Singing, Methodical Sight-Singing, Introductory Lessons in Voice Culture, The Polychrome Lessons in Voice Culture, Resources of Musical Expression, A Study of Musical Taste, The Real American Music;* composed anthems, cantatas, songs.

Root, George Frederick, American composer and publisher; b. Sheffield, Mass., Aug. 30, 1820; d. Bailey's Island, Maine, Aug. 6, 1895. He was a pupil of George J. Webb in Boston; then lived in New York; was organist of the Church of the Strangers. Going to Chicago in 1859, he joined the music publishing firm of Root and Cady established in 1858 by his elder brother, Ebenezer Towner Root, and Chauncey Marvin Cady; it was dissolved in 1871. He wrote many popular songs (*Battlecry of Freedom; Tramp, tramp, tramp; Just before the battle, Mother);* publ. numerous collections of church music and school songs. For some of his earlier compositions he used the German translation of his name, **Friedrich Wurzel,** as a pseudonym.

BIBLIOGRAPHY: his autobiography, *The Story of a Musical Life* (Cincinnati, 1891); D. J. Epstein, "Music Publishing in Chicago before 1871: The Firm of Root and Cady, 1858–1871," *Notes* (June 1944 through June 1946; reprinted in one vol., *Detroit Studies in Music Bibliography* 14, Detroit, 1969).

Rootham, Cyril Bradley, English organist and composer; b. Bristol, Oct. 5, 1875; d. Cambridge, March 18, 1938. He studied music with his father, Daniel Rootham (1837–1922); won classical and musical scholarships at St. John's College (Mus. Bac., 1900; A. M., 1901; Mus. Doc., 1910); finished at the Royal College of Music under Sir Charles Stanford and Sir Walter Parratt. From 1901 till his death he was organist at St. John's College, Cambridge; also conductor of the Univ. Musical Society there (1912–36).

WORKS: His career as composer was also bound with the musical life in Cambridge; he brought out there his opera *The Two Sisters,* on Feb. 14, 1922; *For the Fallen* for chorus and orch. (1919); *Brown Earth* (performed by the musical societies of Oxford and Cambridge Universities, Albert Hall, London, March 14, 1923). His 2nd symph. (with a choral ending) was performed posthumously by the BBC, March 17, 1939. Other works include *Pan,* rhapsody for orch. (1912); String Quintet (1909); String Quartet (1914); Septet for viola, flute, oboe, clarinet, bassoon, horn, and harp (1930); Piano Trio (1931).

Ropartz, (Joseph) Guy (Marie), French composer; b. Guingamp, Côtes-du-Nord, June 15, 1864; d. Lanloup-par-Plouha, Nov. 22, 1955. He entered the Paris Cons. as pupil of Dubois and Massenet; then took lessons in organ and composition from César Franck, who remained his chief influence in composition; from 1894 until 1919, director of the Cons. and conductor of the symph. concerts at Nancy; from 1919 to 1929 conducted the Municipal Orch. in Strasbourg; after that lived in retirement in Lanloup-par-Plouha (Côtes-du-Nord).

WORKS: the 3-act opera *Le Pays* (Nancy, Feb. 1, 1912; Paris Opéra, April 14, 1913; his most important stage work); incidental music for Pierre Loti's *Pêcheur d'Islande* (1889–91) and *Le Mystère de Saint Nicolas,* a legend in 13 scenes (1905). FOR ORCH.: 5 symphonies: No. 1 (1895), No. 2 (1900), No. 3, with chorus (1906), No. 4 (1910), No. 5 (1945); *La Cloche des morts* (1887); *Les Landes* (1888); *Marche de Fête* (1888); *5 Pièces brèves* (1889); *Carnaval* (1889); *Sérénade* (1892); *Dimanche breton* (1893); *À Marie endormie* (1912); *La Chasse du prince Arthur* (1912); *Soir sur les Chaumes* (1913); *Divertissement* (1915); *Sérénade champêtre* (Paris, Feb. 24, 1934); *Pastorale et danse,* for oboe and orch. (1907); *Romanza e scherzino,* for violin and orch. (1926); *Rapsodie* for cello and orch. (Paris, Nov. 3, 1928). Sacred music for chorus: 5 motets a cappella (1900); 3 Masses; Requiem for soloists, chorus, and orch. (Paris, April 7, 1939; *De Profundis* for solo voice, chorus, and orch. (1942); etc. CHAMBER MUSIC: 6 string quartets (1893, 1912, 1925, 1934, 1940, 1951); Piano Trio (1918); String Trio (1935); 3 violin sonatas; 2 cello sonatas. FOR PIANO: *Dans l'ombre de la montagne* (1913); *Musiques au jardin* (1917); *Croquis d'été* (1918); *Croquis d'automne* (1929); *Jeunes filles* (1929); *3 Nocturnes,* etc.; many organ pieces. SONGS: *Chrysanthèmes, La Mer, Paysage, Tes yeux, De tous les temps, Poème d'adieu, En mai, Chanson de bord, Il pleut, Au Bord d'un ruisseau, Douloureux mensonge, La vieille maison,* etc. PEDAGOGIC WORKS AND OTHER WRITINGS: *Enseignement du Solfège, Leçons d'harmonie,* etc.; *Notations artistiques* (essays; Paris, 1891); also 3 vols. of poems and a play, *La Batte.*

BIBLIOGRAPHY: A. Cœuroy, *La Musique française moderne* (1922); M. Boucher, "Guy Ropartz," *Revue Musicale* (1924); F. Lamy, *J. G. Ropartz, l'homme et l'œuvre* (Paris, 1948); L. Kornprobst, *J. G. Ropartz* (Strasbourg, 1949); *Livre du centenaire de J. G. Ropartz* (Paris, 1966).

Rore, Cipriano (Cyprian) de, celebrated composer; b. Mechlin or Antwerp, 1516; d. Parma, 1565. He was a pupil of Willaert, maestro at San Marco, Venice; and in 1542 publ. his 1st book of madrigals *a* 5. From about 1547 to 1558 he was in the service of the Duke of Ferrara, Ercole II; visited Antwerp in 1558, and in 1561 was appointed maestro di cappella to Duke Ottavio Farnese at Parma. Upon Willaert's death in 1562, Rore was appointed his successor as maestro di cappella at St. Mark's in Venice, but soon resigned and returned to the court of Parma (July, 1564).

WORKS: publications: 8 books of madrigals, 3 of motets, a Passion according to St. John, *Fantasie* and *ricercari.* Motets and madrigals are in collections by Susato, Phalèse, and others. In MS (Munich Library) are 3 Masses: *Vivat Felix Hercules a 5, Praeter rerum seriem a 7,* and a *Missa a note nere a 5;* also motets and madrigals. Reprints in A. Einstein's *The Italian Madrigal* (5 madrigals in vol. 3); A. Schering's *Vier Meister-Madrigale aus dem 16. Jahrhundert* (Leipzig, 1916); Davison's and Apel's *Historical Anthology of Music* (vol. 1, no. 131); F. Blume's *Das Chorwerk* (madrigals ed. by W. Wiora in vol. 5; 1930); Madrigals *a* 3 and *a* 4, ed. by Gertrude P. Smith (Northampton, Mass., 1943); G. Tagliapietra's *Antologia di musica antica e moderna per pianoforte* (Milan, 1931); Ph. de Monte's complete works: vols. 4 (1928), 8 (1929), 23 (1933); A. Schering's *Geschichte der Musik in Beispielen* (no. 106); A. Einstein's *The Golden Age of the Madrigal* (1942); reprints of motets by Commer, Burney, Hawkins, Kiesewetter, Dehn, etc. The *Opera Omnia,* ed. by B. Meier, is issued by The American Institute of Musicology: motets, vols. 1, 6, and 8; madrigals, vols. 2, 3, and 4; Masses, vol. 7; Magnificats and chansons, vol. 8.

BIBLIOGRAPHY: R. van Aerde, *Notice sur la vie et les œuvres de Cipriano de Rore* (Mechlin, 1909); J. Musiol, *Cipriano de Rore, ein Meister der venezianischen Schule* (Breslau, 1932); A. Einstein, *The Italian Madrigal* (Princeton, 1949; vol. 1, p. 384ff.); A. Johnson, "The Masses of Cipriano de Rore," *Journal of the American Musicological Society* (Fall 1953); B. Meier, "Staatskompositionen von Cyprian de Rore," *Tijdschrift van de Vereniging voor Nederlandse Musiekgeschiedenis* XXI/2 (1969); D. Harrán, "Rore and the *Madrigale Cromatico,*" *Music Review* (Feb. 1973).

Rorem, Ned, brilliant American composer; b. Richmond, Indiana, Oct. 23, 1923. He received his musical training in Chicago, where he studied with Leo Sowerby at the American Cons.; subsequently attended Northwestern Univ. (1940–42), the Curtis Institute in Philadelphia (1943) and the Juilliard School of Music, N.Y. (1946); in N.Y. he also took lessons with Virgil Thomson and Aaron Copland. From 1949 to 1951 he lived in Morocco; then moved to Paris where he stayed until 1957; he entered the circle of modern Parisian composers, and the French influence, particularly in his songs, remains the most pronounced characteristic of his music. Returning to the U.S., he was composer-in-residence at the Univ. of Buffalo (1959–61) and at the Univ. of Utah (1966–67). Rorem is regarded as one of the finest song composers in America; he has a natural feeling for the vocal line and for the prosody of the text. A born linguist, he has mastered the French language to perfection; he is also an elegant stylist in English. He published a succession of personal journals, recounting with gracious insouciance his encounters in Paris and New York.

WORKS: the operas, *A Childhood Miracle,* for 6 voices and 13 instruments (N.Y., Punch Opera Co., May 10, 1955); *The Robbers* (N.Y., April 15, 1958); *Miss Julie* (N.Y., Nov. 4, 1965); *Bertha* (N.Y., Nov. 26, 1973); Symph. No. 1 (Vienna, 1951); Symph. No. 2 (La Jolla, Calif., Aug. 5, 1956); Symph. No. 3 (N.Y., April 19, 1959); *Design,* for orch. (Louisville, May 28, 1955); 3 piano concertos (1950, 1951, 1970); *Sinfonia* for woodwinds and percussion (Pittsburgh, July 14, 1957); *The Poets' Requiem,* for chorus, soprano solo, and orch., on 8 contemporary poems (N.Y., Feb. 15, 1957); *Eagles,* symph. poem (Philadelphia, Oct. 23, 1959); Trio for flute, cello and piano (1960); *Lovers,* a "narrative" for harpsichord, oboe, cello and percussion (1964); *Sun* for orch. (N.Y., July 1, 1967); *10 Variations* for orch. (Cincinnati, Dec. 5, 1975); *Assembly and Fall,* symph. poem (1975); *Air Music,* a Bicentennial commission from the Cincinnati Symph. Orch. (1976; received the Pulitzer Prize, 1976); *Book of Hours* for flute and harp (1976); 8 piano etudes (1976); *Serenade* for voice, viola, violin and piano (1976); *Sky Music* for solo harp (1976); *Women's Voices,* a set of songs (1976); 2 string quartets; 3 piano sonatas; *A Quiet Afternoon,* a set of 9 piano pieces; *Sicilienne,* for 2 pianos; *From an Unknown Past,* a cycle of 7 choruses; *5 Prayers for the Young,* for chorus; an organ suite, *A Quaker Reader* (N.Y., Feb. 2, 1977); many songs.

WRITINGS: *Paris Diary* (N.Y., 1966); *New York Diary* (N.Y., 1967); *Critical Affairs* (N.Y., 1970); *The Final Diary* (N.Y., 1974); and *Pure Contraption: A Composer's Essays* (N.Y., 1974).

Rosa, Carl (real name **Karl Rose**), famous opera impresario; b. Hamburg, March 21, 1842; d. Paris, April 30, 1889. At 12 he made tours as violinist in England, Denmark, and Germany; studied further in the Conservatories of Leipzig (1859) and Paris; was concertmaster at Hamburg (1863–65); gave a concert at the Crystal Palace, London (March 10, 1866), and toured in the U.S. with Mr. Bateman, meeting the singer **Euphrosyne Parepa** and marrying her in New York in 1867. They organized an English opera company and toured America until 1871; then returned to London. After his wife's death in 1874, he produced opera in English in various London theaters, forming the Carl Rosa Opera Co., which under various managements continued to be an important factor in English musical life for many years.

Rosa, Salvatore, Italian painter, poet, and musician; b. Arenella, near Naples, June 21, 1615; d. Rome, March 15, 1673. He studied music and became an expert lute player; from 1635 to 1640 he divided his time between Rome and Naples, and from 1640 to 1649 was court painter to the Medici at Florence; then lived in Rome. The pieces credited to Rosa by Burney and others have been proved to be spurious; it is doubtful whether Rosa ever composed music. His *Satire,* written about 1640 and containing sharp criticism of Italian church music of his day, was publ. posthumously in 1695, and was reprinted several times; Mattheson attacked Rosa's views in his *Mithridat, wider den Gift einer welschen Satyre des Salvator Rosa* (1749).
BIBLIOGRAPHY: N. d'Arienzo, "S. Rosa musicista," *Rivista Musicale Italiana* (1894); D. Battesti, *Saggio sulla vita e le satire di Salvatore Rosa* (Bourges, 1913); F. Gerra, *Salvatore Rosa e la sua vita romana dal 1650 al 1672* . . . (a summary of 200 letters written by Rosa; Rome, 1937); Frank Walker, "Salvatore Rosa and Music," *Monthly Musical Record* (Oct. 1949 and Jan.-Feb. 1950).

Rosbaud, Hans, eminent Austrian conductor; b. Graz, July 22, 1895; d. Lugano, Dec. 29, 1962. He studied at the Hoch Cons. in Frankfurt; was director of the municipal music school in Mainz (1923-30); then radio conductor in Frankfurt and Münster; was active in Strasbourg during World War II; in 1945 was appointed director of the Munich Konzertverein; in 1948 he became music director of Baden-Baden; also conducted concerts in Switzerland and elsewhere in Europe. He particularly distinguished himself as a conductor of modern works. He conducted the first stage performance of Schoenberg's *Moses und Aron* (Zürich, 1957).

Rösch, Friedrich, German composer; b. Memmingen, Dec. 12, 1862; d. Berlin, Oct. 29, 1925. He was a law student at Munich; studied music with Rheinberger; lived in Berlin, St. Petersburg, and Munich. In 1898 he, with Hans Sommer and Richard Strauss, organized the Genossenschaft deutscher Tonsetzer (dissolved in 1937).
WORKS: *Antonius,* a burlesque oratorio; numerous choral pieces in a humorous vein; 4-part madrigals for men's chorus; songs; a book, *Musikästhetische Streitfragen* (Leipzig, 1897).

Rosé, Arnold (Josef), distinguished violinist; b. Jassy, Rumania, Oct. 24, 1863; d. London, Aug. 25, 1946. He studied under Karl Heissler at the Vienna Cons.; made his professional debut at the Gewandhaus, Leipzig, Oct. 30, 1879; in 1881 was appointed concertmaster of the Vienna Philh. and Opera orch.; held this post for 57 years, until 1938, when he was forced to leave Vienna; spent his last years in London. In 1882 he founded the Rosé Quartet, which won a high reputation throughout Europe; the Quartet made its American debut at the Library of Congress, Washington, on April 28, 1928. In 1902 Rosé married Justine Mahler, a sister of Gustav Mahler.

Rose, Leonard, brilliant American cellist; b. Washington, D.C., July 27, 1918. He studied at the Curtis Institute of Music with Felix Salmond; then was engaged by the NBC Symph. Orch. under Toscanini (1938-39); subsequently was the first cellist in the Cleveland Orch. (1939-43) and with the N.Y. Philharmonic (1943-51); was on the staff of the Curtis Institute of Music, Philadelphia (1951-62); gave numerous cello recitals in America and Europe.

Roseingrave, Thomas, English organist and composer; b. Winchester, 1690; d. Dunleary, June 23, 1766. He was the son and pupil of the organist **Daniel Roseingrave** (1650-1727); went to Italy in 1710 on a stipend from the Chapter of St. Patrick's Cathedral in Dublin, and at Venice met Alessandro and Domenico Scarlatti; traveled with the latter to Rome and Naples. In 1720 he was at London, where he produced Domenico Scarlatti's opera *Narciso;* from 1725 to 1737 he was organist at St. George's, Hanover Square; then lived at Hampstead, and about 1749 returned to Dublin.
WORKS: *15 Voluntarys and Fugues, made on Purpose for the Organ or Harpsichord* (1730); *12 Solos for the German Flute, with a Thorough Bass for the Harpsichord; 8 Suites of Lessons for Harpsichord; 6 Double Fugues* for organ or harpsichord (1750); etc.
BIBLIOGRAPHY: V. Butcher, "Thomas Roseingrave," *Music & Letters* (July 1938).

Rösel, Artur, German violinist and composer; b. Münchenbernsdorf, Aug. 23, 1859; d. Weimar, April 3, 1934. He studied violin and composition in Weimar; was violinist in various theater orchestras in Hamburg, Lugano, and Rotterdam. In 1888 he became concertmaster of the Weimar court orch. He wrote a "lyric stage play" *Halimah* (Weimar, 1895); symph. poem, *Frühlingsstürme;* 2 violin concertos; viola concerto, 2 string quartets; violin pieces.

Roselius, Ludwig, German composer and musicologist; b. Kassel, Aug. 2, 1902; d. Bremen, Feb. 6, 1977. He studied in Berlin; took courses in composition with Georg Schumann at the Prussian Academy of the Arts, and musicology with H. Abert and J. Wolf at the Univ. of Berlin; received his Dr. phil. for his dissertation, *Andreas Raselius als Motettenkomponist* (1924); he also edited motets by Raselius for the *Denkmäler der Tonkunst in Bayern* 36 (29/30). He served as rehearsal conductor for the chorus of the German Opera House in Berlin (1921-23); lived in Berlin and Bremen (1928-40); remained in Bremen as music critic. He wrote the operas *Doge und Dogaressa* (Dortmund, Nov. 14, 1928), *Godiva* (Nuremberg, Aug. 17, 1933), *Gudrun* (Graz, April 29, 1939); also many choruses for schools.

Rosell, Lars-Erik, Swedish composer; b. Nybro, Aug. 9, 1944. He studied composition (with Lidholm) and organ at the State College of Music in Stockholm

(1968–72). In his music, he often requires improvisation from performers.

WORKS: *Moments of a Changing Sonority* for harpsichord, Hammond organ and strings (1969); *Terry Riley* for 3 pianos (1970); *Twilight* for chamber ensemble (1970); *Dorian Mode* for piano, vibraphone, clarinet, cello and trombone (1971); *3 Psaltarpsalmer* for chorus and instruments (1971); *Poem in the Dark,* after Sachs, for mezzo-soprano, flute, trombone, double bass and percussion (1972); *Efter syndafallet,* dramatic scene after Arthur Miller's play *After the Fall,* for soprano, alto, baritone and instrumental ensemble (Stockholm, Feb. 15, 1973); a chamber opera, *Nattesang* (1974; Copenhagen, Dec. 15, 1974); *Visiones prophetae,* Biblical scene for soloists, 3 choruses, wind orch., harp, organ and 2 double basses (Lund, June 27, 1974); *Musik* for cello and string orch. (Stockholm, March 4, 1975); *Expando* for orch. (1976).

Rosellen, Henri, French pianist and composer; b. Paris, Oct. 13, 1811; d. there, March 18, 1876. He studied at the Paris Cons. with Zimmerman (piano) and Halévy (composition); later became a pupil of Henri Herz, under whose influence he began to compose salon music for piano. His *Rêverie* was fantastically popular for many years; he further composed *Nocturne et Tarentelle;* 12 *Études brillantes;* 76 fantasias on operatic airs; variations for piano; chamber music. He was a highly successful teacher in Paris, and publ. a *Manuel des pianistes.*

Rosen, Charles, erudite American pianist and musicologist; b. New York, May 5, 1927. He studied piano with Moriz Rosenthal and music theory with Karl Weigl, then took a course in music history at Princeton Univ., receiving his B.A. *summa cum laude* in 1947, M.A. in 1949; also holds the degree of Ph.D. in French literature (1951). He made his New York debut as pianist in 1951; was assistant professor in modern languages at the Massachusetts Institute of Technology (1953–55); in 1971, appointed prof. of music at the State Univ. of N.Y. at Stony Brook. He is equally adept as a virtuoso pianist, particularly in the modern repertoire, and as a brilliant writer on musical, philosophical and literary subjects. In 1972 he received the National Book Award for his volume *The Classical Style: Haydn, Mozart, Beethoven* (N.Y., 1971).

Rosen, Jerome, American composer; b. Boston, July 23, 1921. He studied composition with William Denny at the Univ. of California, Berkeley (M.A., 1949); also had sessions with Sessions there; then went to Paris, where he obtained a diploma as a clarinetist (1950). Upon his return to the U.S., he became prof. of music at the Univ. of California, Davis. He wrote a Sonata for clarinet and cello (1954); String Quartet (1955); Saxophone Concerto (Sacramento, Jan. 24, 1958); Clarinet Quintet (1959); *Petite suite* for 4 clarinets (1962); *Elegie* for percussion (1967); *5 Pieces* for violin and piano (1970); songs.

Rosen, Jerome, American violinist, pianist, poet, physicist, and polymath nonpareil; b. Detroit, Nov. 16, 1939. He began to play the violin at the age of 5, and piano at 6; studied violin with Josef Gingold in Cleve-

land and Ivan Galamian at the Curtis Institute of Music in Philadelphia (1955–58); took piano lessons with Arthur Loesser in Cleveland; composition with Herbert Elwell and Marcel Dick in Cleveland and Wallingford Riegger in Stockbridge, Mass.; studied chamber music playing with Alexander Schneider and conducting with George Szell, Louis Lane and James Levine in Cleveland. He subsequently worked in the Cleveland Orch. as violinist and pianist (1959–66); then played violin in the Detroit Symph. Orch. (1968–72). In 1972 he joined the Boston Symph. as a violinist and in 1974 as a pianist, harpsichordist and celesta player. Concurrently he gave violin recitals in Detroit, N.Y. and other American cities, and played chamber music. He also took a hand in conducting, in Detroit and Cleveland; in 1973–77 was conductor of the Boston Univ. Repertoire Orch. He taught chamber music playing at the Berkshire Music Center (1973–74 and 1977); served as rehearsal pianist for Seiji Ozawa, Rostropovich, Casals and George Szell. Besides music, he took courses in physics and mathematics at Western Reserve Univ.; wrote heavy and light poetry. He is not related to his namesakes Jerome Rosen, the composer, or Charles Rosen, pianist.

Rosen, Max, American violinist; b. Dorohoi, Rumania, April 11, 1900; d. New York, Dec. 17, 1956. He was brought to the U.S. as an infant and studied with David Mannes in N.Y. In 1912 he went to Germany, where he had lessons with Leopold Auer; made his concert debut in Dresden, Nov. 16, 1915, and his American debut as soloist with the N.Y. Philharmonic (Jan. 12, 1918); he subsequently settled in N.Y. as a violin teacher.

Rosenberg, Hilding (Constantin), eminent Swedish composer; b. Bosjökloster, June 21, 1892. He studied organ and served as church organist in the provinces. In 1914 he enrolled at the Royal Academy of Music in Stockholm, where he took courses in composition with Ellberg and Stenhammar. In 1920 he obtained a stipend for further studies; took courses in piano with Buchmayer in Dresden, and attended classes in conducting with Striegler and Scherchen. Returning to Sweden, he became an assistant conductor at the Stockholm Opera (1932–34). In 1948 he visited the U.S. and conducted the first American performance of his Fourth Symphony. His music continues the traditional lines of Scandinavian romanticism, but injects a strong element of neo-Classical polyphony. In his string quartets Nos. 8–12 he makes use of the 12-tone technique. His imposing mastery of composition contributed to his stature as one of the most prestigious figures in modern Swedish music. As a pedagogue, he formed an important group of disciples.

WORKS: 7 operas: *Resan till Amerika* (*Journey to America;* Stockholm, Nov. 24, 1932; also an orch. suite); *Marionetter* (*Marionettes,* 1937–38; Stockholm, Feb. 14, 1939; also an orch. suite); *De tvà Konungadöttrarna* (*The Two Princesses;* Swedish Radio, Sept. 19, 1940); *Lycksalighetens ö* (*The Isle of Bliss,* Stockholm, Feb. 1, 1945); a chamber opera, *Kaspers fettisdag* (*Kasper's Shrove Tuesday,* 1953; Stockholm, Jan. 28, 1954); a radio opera, *Porträttet* (*The Portrait,* 1955, after Gogol's short story; Swedish Radio, March

22, 1956); a lyric comedy, *Hus med dubbel ingång* (*The House with Two Doors,* libretto after Calderón's *Casa con dos puertas;* Stockholm, May 24, 1970); also the 4-part opera-oratorio, *Josef och hans bröder* (*Joseph and His Brothers,* 1945–48, based on Thomas Mann's novel; last part of the oratorio performed in Stockholm, March 23, 1948; shortened version for concert performance, 1951). 6 ballets: *Yttersta domen* (*The Last Judgment,* 1929; also an orch. suite); *Orfeus i stan* (*Orpheus in Town,* 1938; Stockholm, 1938; also an orch. suite); *Eden* (1961; produced by Birgit Cullberg from *Music for String Orchestra,* 1946); *Salome* (1963; Stockholm, Feb. 28, 1964); *Sönera* (*The Sons,* 1963–64); *Babels Torn* (*The Tower of Babel,* 1966; Swedish TV, Jan. 8, 1968); 9 symphonies: No. 1 (1917, revised 1919; first performed in Göteborg, April 5, 1921; a second revision, in progress since 1922, first performed in Stockholm, May 18, 1974); No. 2 *Sinfonia Grave* (1928, revised 1935; Göteborg, March 27, 1935); No. 3 (1939; Swedish Radio, Dec. 11, 1939), originally a symph. drama for radio subtitled *De fyra livsåldrarna* (*The Four Ages of Man),* with words from Romain Rolland's *Jean Christoph* read before each movement, text and subtitle were later discarded; No. 4, *Johannes uppenbarelse* (*The Revelation of St. John),* with baritone and chorus (1940; Swedish Radio, Dec. 6, 1940); No. 5, *Örtagårdsmästaren* (*The Gardener),* with contralto and chorus (1944; Swedish Radio, Oct. 17, 1944); No. 6, *Sinfonia Semplice* (1951; Gävle, Jan. 24, 1952); Symphony for wind orch. and percussion (the same music as his ballet *Babels Torn;* first concert perf., Göteborg, Oct. 27, 1972); No. 7 (1968; Swedish Radio, Sept. 29, 1968); No. 8, with chorus, subtitled *In candidum* (1974; Malmö, Jan. 24, 1975). OTHER WORKS FOR ORCH.: *Sinfonia da chiesa* Nos. 1 and 2 (1923; 1924); 2 violin concertos (1924, 1951); *Suite* for strings (1927); Trumpet Concerto (1928); *Suite* for violin and orch. (1929); *5 Pieces* for piano and strings (1933, revised 1965); *Sinfonia Concertante* for violin, viola, oboe, bassoon and orch. (1935); *Bergslagsbilder* (*Pictures from Bergslagen,* 1937); *Taffel-musik* (*Table Music,* 1939); 2 cello concertos (1939, 1953); *Djufar,* suite (1942); Viola Concerto (1942); *Overtura bianca-nera* for strings (1946); Concerto No. 1, for string orch. (1946); Concerto No. 2 (1949); Piano Concerto (1950); Concerto No. 3, *Louisville Concerto* (1954; Louisville, March 12, 1955); *Riflessioni* Nos. 1–3 for string orch. (1959–60); *Metamorfosi I-III* (1963–64). VOCAL WORKS: *Den heliga natten* (*The Holy Night),* a Christmas oratorio (1936); *Huvudskalleplats* (*Calvary),* a Good Friday oratorio (1938, revised 1965); *14 Chinese Poems* for soprano and piano (1945–51); *Åt Jordgudinnan* (*To the Earth Goddess)* for mezzo-soprano, flute, clarinet, violin, viola, cello and lute (1959); *Dagdrivaren,* 6 songs for baritone and orch. (1962–63); small solo songs; motets. CHAMBER MUSIC: 12 string quartets: Nos. 1–7 (1920, 1924, 1926, 1939, 1949, 1953, 1956), Nos. 8–12 (1957); Trio for flute, violin and viola (1921); 3 solo violin sonatas (1921, revised 1966; 1953; 1963); 2 violin sonatas (1926, 1941); Trio for oboe, clarinet and bassoon (1927); Wind Quintet (1959, revised 1965); Solo Flute Sonata (1959); Solo Clarinet Sonata (1960); *6 Moments Musicaux* for string quartet (1972). FOR PIANO: 4 sonatas: No. 1 (1923), No. 2 (1925; Stock-

holm, Sept. 4, 1970), No. 3 (1926), No. 4 (1927); *11 Studies* (1924); *Improvisations* (1939–41); *Theme and Variations* (1941); *6 Polyphonic Studies* (1945); Sonatina (1949). FOR ORGAN: *Fantasia e Fuga* (1941); *Preludio e Fuga* (1948); *Toccata, Aria Pastorale e Ciaconna* (1952).

Rosenbloom, Sydney, British pianist and composer; b. Edinburgh, June 25, 1889; d. East London, South Africa, July 22, 1967; studied at the Royal Academy of Music in London; after teaching in the English provinces, he went to South Africa (1920); in 1921 was appointed prof. at the Harrison Cons. in Johannesburg. In 1930 he visited the U.S., and gave piano recitals in California. Upon returning to South Africa, he settled in East London. His works are mostly for piano, written in an ingratiating and highly pianistic manner, along Romantic lines: *Caprice Impromptu, Valse-Etude, 3 Concert Studies, 6 Preludes, 2 Scherzos, Romance Triste, Etchings, From My Sketch Book, Falling Snow,* etc.

Rosenboom, David, American composer of the avantgarde; b. Fairfield, Iowa, Sept. 9, 1947. He studied piano with his mother; also played violin, viola, trumpet and drums. He attended the Univ. of Illinois where he took courses in composition with Salvatore Martirano and Gordon Binkerd; worked with Lejaren Hiller in the Experimental Music Studio there (1965–67). In 1968–69 he served as artistic coordinator for the Electric Ear mixed-media series at the Electric Circus in New York. In 1970 he participated in research in neurophysics and biofeedback systems at the State Univ. of N.Y. at Stony Brook. With this esthetic background, his music was bound to be experimental in nature; however, he also composed in classical forms. His scores are notated in diagrams and engineering blueprints, with special symbols for dynamics, tempi, etc.

WORKS: *Contrasts* for violin and orch. (1963); Septet for strings, brass and piano (1964); Sextet for bassoon, flute and string quartet (1965);Trio for clarinet, trumpet and string bass (1966); *Caliban Upon Setebos,* after Robert Browning, for orch. (1966); *The Thud, Thud, Thud, of Suffocating Blackness* for saxophone, electric cello, piano, celesta, percussion, tape and lights (1966); *mississippippississim* for 33 musicians, speaker and tape (1968); *How Much Better If Plymouth Rock Had Landed on the Pilgrims* for electronic and traditional instruments (1969); *Ecology of the Skin,* a demonstration in biofeedback experience with audience participation (1970). His zodiac sign is Virgo.

Rosenfeld, Gerhard, German composer; b. Königsberg, Feb. 10, 1931. He studied music theory at the Hochschule für Musik in East Berlin (1952–57); had private lessons in composition with Wagner-Régeny (1955–57), Hanns Eisler (1958–60) and Leo Spies (1960–61).

WORKS: *Divertimento* for chamber orch. (1962); Sinfonietta (1964); 2 violin concertos (1963, 1973); Nonet (1967); Cello Concerto (1967–69); Piano Concerto (1969); 2 *Quartettinos* for string quartet (1969, 1973); *Fresken* for orch. (1969); Piano Sonata (1969); *Sona-*

tine for orch. (1971); Concerto for Harp, Double Bass and Orch. (1971); *Reger-Variationen* for string quartet, wind quintet, 3 trumpets, 3 trombones, tuba, percussion and string orch. (1973).

Rosenfeld, Leopold, Danish composer and writer on music; b. Copenhagen, July 21, 1850; d. there, July 19, 1909. He studied at the Copenhagen Cons. and was for some years music critic of *Musikbladet;* wrote several choral works with orch., of which *Henrik og Else* (Copenhagen, Feb. 7, 1885) had considerable success; he also publ. a number of piano pieces and about 200 songs to German and Danish texts.

Rosenfeld, Paul, American author and music critic; b. New York, May 4, 1890; d. there, July 21, 1946. He studied at Yale Univ. (B.A., 1912) and at Columbia Univ. School of Journalism (Litt. B., 1913). He then associated himself with progressive circles in literature and music; wrote music criticisms for *The Dial* (1920–27); contributed also to other literary and music magazines. Although not a musician by training, Rosenfeld possessed a penetrating insight into musical values; he championed the cause of modern American music. He collected the most significant of his articles in book form: *Musical Portraits* (on 20 modern composers; 1920); *Musical Chronicle,* covering the New York seasons 1917–23 (1923); *An Hour with American Music* (1929); *Discoveries of a Music Critic* (1936). Analects from his articles were published as *Musical Impressions* (N.Y., 1969).
BIBLIOGRAPHY: J. Mellquist and L. Wiese, ed., *Paul Rosenfeld, Voyager in the Arts* (N.Y., 1948); H. A. Leibowitz, "Remembering Paul Rosenfeld," *Salmagundi* (Spring 1969); B. Mueser, *The Criticism of New Music in N.Y.: 1919–1929* (City Univ. of N.Y., 1975).

Rosenhain, Jacob (Jacques), German pianist and composer; b. Mannheim, Dec. 2, 1813; d. Baden-Baden, March 21, 1894. He was a child prodigy; made his 1st public appearance at the age of 11 in Mannheim; studied there with Schmitt, and in Frankfurt with Schnyder von Wartensee. In 1837 he went to Paris and London; continued to travel until 1870, when he settled as a teacher in Baden-Baden. His brother **Eduard Rosenhain** (b. Mannheim, Nov. 16, 1818; d. Frankfurt, Sept. 6, 1861) was also a noteworthy pianist and teacher; he wrote a serenade for cello and piano, and piano pieces.
WORKS (by J. Rosenhain): the operas *Der Besuch im Irrenhause* (Frankfurt, Dec. 29, 1834), *Le Démon de la nuit* (Paris, March 17, 1851), *Le Volage et jaloux* (Baden-Baden, Aug. 3, 1863); 3 symphonies; 3 string quartets; 4 piano trios; many piano pieces; *12 Études caractéristiques* for piano; etc. He publ. *Erinnerungen an Paganini* (1893).
BIBLIOGRAPHY: E. Kratt-Harveng, *Jacques Rosenhain* (Baden-Baden, 1891).

Rosenman, Leonard, American composer; b. Brooklyn, Sept. 7, 1924. He studied with local teachers; later took courses with Roger Sessions, Luigi Dallapiccola and briefly with Arnold Schoenberg. His main mundane occupation is that of a movie composer; he

wrote the scores for such commercially notable films as *East of Eden, Rebel Without a Cause* and *The Chapman Report* (dealing with sexual statistics); also compiled music for television programs, among them *The Defenders* and *Marcus Welby, M.D.* But he is also the composer of a number of highly respectable and even elevated musical works, among them a Violin Concerto and the challenging score *Foci* for 3 orchestras. His *Threnody on a Song of K. R.* (written to the memory of his wife Kay Rosenman), a set of orchestral variations on her original melody, was performed by the Los Angeles Philharmonic, under the composer's direction, May 6, 1971.

Rosenmüller, Johann, German composer; b. Ölsnitz, c.1619; d. Wolfenbüttel, Sept. 10, 1684. He graduated from the Univ. of Leipzig in 1640; from 1642 was master at the Thomasschule; later deputy cantor for Tobias Michael; in 1651 he was appointed organist of the Nikolaikirche. Imprisoned for a moral offense in 1655, he escaped and fled to Hamburg, thence to Venice; but in 1674 he was appointed ducal Kapellmeister at Wolfenbüttel.
WORKS: *Kernsprüche mehrenteils aus Heiliger Schrift,* for 3 to 7 parts with continuo (2 vols., 1648, 1652); *Studentenmusik mit 3 und 5 Violen* (dance music; 1654); *12 Sonate da camera a 5 stromenti* (Venice, 1670; reprinted by Karl Nef in the *Denkmäler deutscher Tonkunst* 18); *Sonate a 2-5 stromenti d'arco* (Nuremberg, 1682); 6 Mass sections; 2 Magnificats; many sacred choruses. Rosenmüller's setting of *Welt ade* was used by Bach in his church cantata No. 27, *Wer weiss wie nahe mir mein Ende.*
BIBLIOGRAPHY: A. Horneffer, *Johann Rosenmüller* (Berlin, 1898); F. Hamel, *Die Psalmkompositionen Johann Rosenmüllers* (Strasbourg, 1933).

Rosenstock, Joseph, Polish-American conductor; b. Cracow, Jan. 27, 1895. He studied at the Cracow Cons.; then with Schreker in Vienna; graduated from the Vienna Academy of Music in 1920; conducted opera in Darmstadt (1922–25), Wiesbaden (1925–27), and Mannheim (1930–33); his American debut was at the Metropolitan Opera, conducting *Die Meistersinger* (Oct. 30, 1929); in 1933 he was disqualified in Germany as a Jew; conducted operatic performances of the Jewish Kulturbund in Berlin until 1936, when he was appointed conductor of the Nippon Philharmonic Orch. in Tokyo; was successful there until 1941; then went to the U.S.; conducted in Tokyo again in 1945–46; from 1948 to 1955 he was conductor and music director of the N.Y. City Opera. In 1965 he settled in Salt Lake City, Utah, conducting occasional concerts and teaching.

Rosenthal, Harold, English music editor and critic; b. London, Sept. 30, 1917. He received his B.A. degree from the Univ. of London in 1940; served in the British Army during World War II; in 1950 launched, with Earl of Harewood, the magazine *Opera* and became its editor in 1953; also issued *Opera Annuals* (1954–60). He was archivist of the Royal Opera House, Covent Garden (1950–56); contributed to many European and American music journals. His publications include: *Sopranos of Today* (London,

1956); *Two Centuries of Opera at Covent Garden* (London, 1958); *A Concise Oxford Dictionary of Opera* (with John Warrack; London, 1964). He also edited *The Mapleson Memoires* (London, 1965).

Rosenthal, Manuel, French composer and conductor; b. Paris, June 18, 1904, of a Russian mother and French father. He studied violin and composition at the Paris Cons., graduating in 1924; also took some lessons with Ravel. He was mobilized in 1939, and taken prisoner of war; remained in Germany for a year, returning to France in March, 1941. After conducting various orchestras in Europe, he made a tour of the U.S. in the autumn of 1946; in 1948, appointed instructor in composition at the College of Puget Sound, Tacoma, Wash. In 1949 he was engaged as conductor of the Seattle Symph. Orch.; was dismissed summarily for moral turpitude in Oct., 1951 (the soprano who appeared as soloist with the Seattle Symph. Orch. under the name of Mme. Rosenthal was not his legal wife). In 1962 he was appointed prof. of orchestral conducting at the Paris Cons.; was conductor of the Liège Symph. Orch. (1964–67). He composed a number of works in an entertaining manner, expertly orchestrated.
WORKS: *Bootleggers,* a satirical operetta (Paris, May 2, 1933); *La Poule noire,* 1-act operetta (Paris, 1937); *Les Petits métiers,* for orch. (St. Louis, March 3, 1936); *La Fête du vin,* choreographic poem (1937; N.Y., Dec. 5, 1946, composer conducting); *St. Francis of Assisi,* for chorus, orch. and vibraphone (Paris, Nov. 1, 1944, composer conducting); *Musique de table,* symph. suite (N.Y., Oct. 10, 1946); *Aeolus* for wind quintet and strings (1970); *2 Etudes en camaïeu* for strings and percussion (1971). He arranged for L. Massine, choreographer, a ballet, *Gaîté Parisienne* (based on music from various Offenbach operettas; Monte Carlo, April 5, 1938; highly successful).

Rosenthal, Moriz, famous Polish pianist; b. Lwow, Dec. 17, 1862; d. New York, Sept. 3, 1946. He studied piano at the Lwow Cons. with Karol Mikuli who was a pupil of Chopin; in 1872, when he was 10 years old, he played Chopin's Rondo in C for 2 pianos with his teacher in Lwow. The family moved to Vienna in 1875, and Rosenthal became the pupil of Joseffy, who inculcated in him a passion for virtuoso piano playing, which he taught according to Tausig's method. Liszt accepted Rosenthal as a student during his stay in Weimar and Rome (1876–78). After a hiatus of some years, during which Rosenthal studied philosophy at the Univ. of Vienna, he returned to his concert career in 1884, and established for himself a reputation as one of the world's greatest virtuosos; was nicknamed (because of his small stature and great pianistic power) "little giant of the piano." Beginning in 1888 he made 12 tours of the U.S., where he became a permanent resident in 1938. He publ. (with L. Schytte) a *Schule des höheren Klavierspiels* (Berlin, 1892). His wife, **Hedwig Kanner-Rosenthal,** was a distinguished piano teacher.

Rosetti, Francesco Antonio (real name **Franz Anton Rösler**), Bohemian composer; b. in the region of Leitmeritz, c.1750; d. Schwerin, June 30, 1792. For many years Rosetti was confused with a Bohemian cobbler, named Rösler, who was born in Niemes in 1746 and whose date of birth was erroneously listed as that of Rosetti. He was a theological student; was engaged as a string player in court orchestras; in 1789 he became music director in Ludwigslust. He was a prodigiously fertile composer who wrote in the manner of Haydn and Boccherini, and even dubbed "a German Boccherini." He wrote 3 Requiems; one of these was composed in memory of Mozart; it was performed in Prague shortly after Mozart's death in 1791; its score is unfortunately lost. His other works include an opera *Das Winterfest der Hirten* (1789) and nearly 90 "symphonies"; 9 string quartets; 4 flute concertos; 5 oboe concertos; 3 clarinet concertos; 4 bassoon concertos; 5 horn concertos; 5 concertos for 2 horns; etc., etc. Oskar Kaul publ. 5 symphonies in vol. 22 (12.i) and chamber music in vol. 33 (25) of the *Denkmäler der Tonkunst in Bayern.*
BIBLIOGRAPHY: Oskar Kaul, *Die Vokalwerke Anton Rosettis* (Munich, 1911).

Rosier, Carl, Netherlandish organist and composer; b. Liège, Dec., 1640; d. Cologne, Dec., 1725. He served as organist at the Cologne Cathedral and City Hall (1699–1725); wrote much sacred music; publ. 14 sonatas for oboe with violins (Amsterdam, 1700).
BIBLIOGRAPHY: Ursel Niemöller, *Carl Rosier, Kölner Dom- und Ratskapellmeister* (Cologne, 1957).

Rosing, Vladimir, Russian-American tenor and opera director; b. St. Petersburg, Jan. 23, 1890; d. Los Angeles, Nov. 24, 1963. He studied voice with Jean de Reszke; made his debut as tenor in St. Petersburg in 1912; gave a successful series of song recitals in programs of Russian songs in London between 1913 and 1921. In 1923 he was appointed director of the opera department at the Eastman School of Music in Rochester, N.Y.; founded an American Opera Co. which he directed in a series of operatic productions in the English language. In 1939 he went to Los Angeles as organizer and artistic director of the Southern California Opera Association. He staged several pageants: *The California Story* in Hollywood Bowl in 1950; *The Oregon Story* in 1959; *The Kansas Story* in 1960.

Roslavetz, Nikolai, remarkable Russian composer; b. Suray, near Chernigov, Jan. 5, 1881; d. Moscow, Aug. 23, 1944. He studied violin with Jan Hřimalý, and composition with Ilyinsky and Vassilenko, at the Moscow Cons., graduating in 1912; won the Silver Medal for his cantata *Heaven and Earth,* after Byron. A composer of advanced tendencies, he published an atonal violin sonata in 1913, the first of its kind by a Russian composer; his 3rd String Quartet exhibits 12-tone properties. He edited a short-lived journal *Muzykalnaya kultura* in 1924, and became a leading figure in the modern movement in Russia. But with a change of Soviet cultural policy toward Socialist Realism and nationalism, Roslavetz was subjected to severe criticism in the press for persevering in his aberrant ways. To conciliate the authorities he tried to write operettas; then was given an opportunity to redeem himself by going to Tashkent to write ballets based on Uzbek folksongs; he failed in all these pursuits. But interest in his music became pronounced abroad, and posthumous performances were arranged in West Germany.

WORKS: Symphony (1922); the symph. poems *Man and the Sea*, after Baudelaire (1921) and *End of the World*, after Paul Lafargue (1922); Cello Sonata (1921); Violin Concerto (1925); cantata, *October* (1927); *Nocturne* for harp, oboe, 2 violas and cello (1913); 3 string quartets (1913, 1916, 1920); 3 piano trios; 4 violin sonatas; *3 Dances* for violin and piano (1921); cello sonata (1921); 5 piano sonatas.

BIBLIOGRAPHY: D. Gojowy, "N. A. Roslavetz, ein früher Zwölftonkomponist," *Die Musikforschung* (1969; includes a detailed list of the location, dates of publication, etc., of extant works).

Rösler, Franz Anton. See **Rosetti, Francesco.**

Rösler, Johann Josef, Hungarian composer; b. Chemnitz, Aug. 22, 1771; d. Prague, Jan. 29, 1813. He served as Kapellmeister for Prince Lobkowitz in Prague; brought out an opera, *Elisene, Prinzessin von Bulgarien* (Prague, Oct. 18, 1807), which was the first original stage work to be produced at the German Opera Theater in Prague; wrote a great amount of instrumental music. A movement from one of his piano concertos was erroneously attributed to Beethoven.

BIBLIOGRAPHY: H. Engel, "Der angeblich Beethovensche Klavierkonzertsatz," *Neues Beethovenjahrbuch* (1925).

Rosner, Arnold, American composer, b. New York, Nov. 9, 1945. He studied mathematics at N.Y. Univ.; then went to the Univ. of Buffalo where he took courses in composition with Leo Smit and Henri Pousseur (Ph.D. 1971). He subsequently taught at the Univ. of Western Ontario, and at Brooklyn College.

WORKS: 6 symphonies (1961, 1961, 1963, 1964, 1974, 1976); 6 string quartets (1962, 1963, 1965, 1965, 1972, 1977); *5 Mystical Pieces* for English horn, harp and strings (1967); *6 Pastoral Dances* for woodwinds and strings (1968); *A Gentle Musicke* for flute and strings (1969); Concerto Grosso for orch. (1975); *Reponses, Hosanna and Fugue* for harp and string orch. (1977); Sonata for flute and cello (1962); Violin Sonata (1963); Wind Quintet (1964); Concertino for harp, harpsichord, celesta and piano (1968); Cello Sonata (1968); Sonata for oboe, violin, and piano (1972); 2 piano sonatas (1963, 1970); *Musique de clavecin* for harpsichord (1974); choruses; songs.

Rosowsky, Solomon, Jewish-American music scholar and composer; b. Riga, Latvia. March 27, 1878; d. New York, July 30, 1962. He studied law at the Univ. of Kiev, and composition at the St. Petersburg Cons. with Liadov, Rimsky-Korsakov and Glazunov. He was a co-founder of the Society for Jewish Folk Music in St. Petersburg in 1909; in 1920 he went back to Riga, and organized there the first Jewish Cons. of Music; in 1925 he emigrated to Palestine. He settled in New York in 1947, devoting himself mainly to the music of biblical times, culminating in the publication of an important volume, *The Cantillation of the Bible* (N.Y., 1957). His compositions include a piano trio (1909) and several scores of incidental music for plays in Yiddish.

Ross, Hugh, choral conductor and organist; b. Langport, England, Aug. 21, 1898. He studied at the Royal College of Music, where he won 1st prize in organ and was made a Fellow in 1915; went to Canada; became conductor of the Winnipeg Male Voice Choir (1921); organized and conducted the Winnipeg Symph. Orch. (1923–27); in 1927, appointed conductor of the Schola Cantorum, N.Y.; conducted many modern works.

Ross, Walter, American composer; b. Lincoln, Nebraska, Oct. 3, 1936. He studied music at the Univ. of Nebraska, receiving an M.M.A. in 1962; then composition with Robert Palmer and conducting with Husa at Cornell Univ. (D.M.A., 1966). In 1967 he was appointed to the music faculty of the Univ. of Virginia. Much of his music is inspired by American themes.

WORKS: a one-act chamber opera *In the Penal Colony* (1972); *The Silent Firefly* for mezzo-soprano and instruments (1965); Concerto for Brass Quintet and Orch. (1966); *Cryptical Triptych* for trombone and piano (1968); *5 Dream Sequences* for percussion quartet and piano (1968); *Old Joe's Fancy* for saxophone quartet and concert band (1969); 2 trombone concertos (1971, 1977); Trombone Quartet (1972); *Fancy Dances* for 3 bass tubas (1972); Concerto for Tuba and Concert Band (1973); *Divertimento* for wind quintet (1974); *Concerto Basso* for tuba and euphonium ensemble (1974); *Piltdown Fragments* for tuba and tape (1975); *A Jefferson Symphony* for chorus and orch. (Charlottesville, April 13, 1976); Concerto for Wind Quintet and String Orch. (1977).

Rosseau, Norbert, Belgian composer; b. Ghent, Dec. 11, 1907; d. there, Nov. 1, 1975. He played violin as a child; his family emigrated to Italy in 1921, and he studied piano with Silvestri and composition with Respighi. His early works are cast in a traditional style of European modernism; later he half-heartedly experimented with dodecaphony and electronics; some of his music bears pseudo-scientific titles, as, e.g., the symphonic poem entitled H_2O.

WORKS: OPERAS: *Sicilenne* (1947); *Les Violons du prince* (1954); *Juventa*, ballet (1957). VOCAL MUSIC: *Inferno*, oratorio after Dante (1940); *L'An mille*, dramatic ode (1946); *Incantations*, cantata (1951); *Maria van den Kerselare*, Flemish oratorio (1952); *Zeepbellen*, chamber cantata with children's chorus (1958); *Il Paradiso terrestre*, oratorio after Dante (1968). FOR ORCH.: *Suite Agreste* (1936); H_2O, symph. poem (1938; Liège, June 24, 1939); 2 concertos for orch. (1948, 1963); 2 symphonies: No. 1 (1953); No. 2, *Sinfonia Sacra*, for soloists, chorus and orch. (1960–63); *Suite Concertante*, for string quintet, winds, harpsichord and timpani (1959); Concerto for Wind Quintet and Orch. (1961); *Variations*, for orch. (1963); Viola Concerto (1964); *Sonata a quattro*, for 4 violins and strings (1966); Horn Concerto (1967). CHAMBER MUSIC: Violin Sonatina (1949); *Trois jouets*, for oboe, clarinet and bassoon (1955); Wind Quintet (1955); Clarinet Sonatina (1956); String Quartet (1956); Trio for flute, cello and piano (1956); *Rapsodie* for flute, bassoon and piano (1958); *Serenade à Syrinx*, for flute, violin, cello and harp (1959); Concertino for piano, double string quartet and double bass (1963); *Pentafonium* for viola, cello, flute, oboe and harpsichord (1964); *Diptique*, for string quartet (1971); *Dialogue* for flute, oboe, viola and piano (1971); Piano Quartet (1975).

Rossellini, Renzo, Italian composer; b. Rome, Feb. 2, 1908. He studied composition with Sallustio and Setaccioli; taught at the Liceo Musicale in Pesaro and at the Cons. in Rome. In 1973 he was named artistic director of the Opera at Monte Carlo.

WORKS: the operas, *Alcassino e Nicoletta* (1928–30); *La Guerra,* to his own libretto (Rome, Feb. 25, 1956); *Il Vortice* (Naples, Feb. 8, 1958); *Uno Sguardo del Ponte,* after Arthur Miller's play (Rome, March 11, 1961); *L'Avventuriere* (Monte Carlo, Feb. 2, 1968); *La reine morte* (Monte Carlo, 1973); the ballets, *La Danza di Dássine* (San Remo, Feb. 24, 1935); *Poemetti pagani* (Monte Carlo, 1963); *Il ragazzo e la sua ombra* (Venice, 1966); for orch.: *Suite in tre tempi* (1931); *Ut Unum Sint* (Miami, Oct. 20, 1963); *Stornelli della Roma bassa* (1946); film music. He published 2 books of autobiographical content, *Pagine di un musicista* (Bologna, 1964) and *Addio del passato* (Milan, 1968).

Rossi, Abbate Francesco, Italian composer; b. Bari, about 1645; canon there, 1680. He composed the operas *Bianca di Castiglia* (Milan, 1674), *Il Sejano moserno della Tracia* (Venice, 1680), *La Pena degli occhi* and *La Clorilda* (both in Venice, 1688), *Mitrane* (Venice, 1689); oratorio *La Caduta degli angeli;* Requiem; psalms; etc.

Rossi, Giovanni Gaetano, Italian composer; b. Borgo S. Donnino, Parma, Aug. 5, 1828; d. Genoa, March 30, 1886. He studied at the Milan Cons.; from 1851 was concertmaster at the Teatro Regio, Parma; also court organist and (1864–73) director of the Istituto Musicale. From 1873 to 1879 he conducted at the Teatro Carlo Felice in Genoa; then was director of the Liceo Musicale. He composed 4 operas; an oratorio, *Le sette parole;* overture, *Saulo;* a Requiem, 3 Masses, etc.

Rossi, Giulio, Italian bass; b. Rome, Oct. 27, 1865; d. Milan, Oct. 9, 1931. He had a tenor voice until he was 19, when an unintentional plunge into the Tiber in December induced an illness, after which his voice lowered to the range of *basso profondo.* He then began vocal study under Oreste Tomassoni; made his debut at Parma, Oct. 20, 1887. In 1889 he toured South America with Adelina Patti, and made 2 tours of Mexico and California with Luisa Tetrazzini; from 1908 till 1913 sang at the Metropolitan Opera. His repertory included about 80 Italian operas.

Rossi, Lauro, Italian dramatic composer; b. Macerata, Feb. 19, 1810; d. Cremona, May 5, 1885. He was a pupil of Furno, Zingarelli, and Crescentini at Naples, bringing out a comic opera, *Le Contesse villane* there (1829) with fair success. He became maestro at the Teatro Valle, Rome, in 1832; with his tenth opera, *La Casa disabitata* o *I falsi monetari,* produced at La Scala, Milan, Aug. 16, 1834, he won a veritable triumph; it made the rounds of Italy and was given in Paris. In 1835 he went to Mexico as conductor and composer to an Italian opera troupe, becoming its director in 1837, and going to Havana (1839) and New

Orleans (1842), returning to Italy in 1844. He brought out a new opera, *Il Borgomastro di Schiedam* (Milan, June 1, 1844), with indifferent success; his opera *Il Domino nero* (Milan, Sept. 1, 1849) fared a little better. His most successful opera was *La Contessa di Mons* (Turin, Jan. 31, 1874). He wrote 29 operas in all. In 1850 he was given the post of director of the Milan Cons.; in 1870 he succeeded Mercadante as director of the Naples Cons.; resigned in 1878, and retired to Cremona in 1882.

BIBLIOGRAPHY: F. Florimo, *La Scuola musicale di Napoli* (1882).

Rossi, Luigi (Latinized as **Aloysius Rubeus**), Italian composer and singer; b. Torremaggiore, Foggia, 1598; d. Rome, Feb. 19, 1653. He studied in Naples with G. de Macque; then went to Rome, where his opera *Il Palazzo d'Atlante incantato* was produced (Feb. 22, 1642). In 1646 he was called by Mazarin to Paris with 20 other singers, and there staged his most important work, *Orfeo* (March 2, 1647), the 1st Italian opera expressly written for a Paris production. He wrote besides the oratorio *Giuseppe* and some 100 cantatas; reprints of some of these appear in Gevaert's *Les Gloires de l'Italie,* Riemann's *Kantatenfrühling* and Landshoff's *Alte Meister des Bel Canto.* Riemann also publ. several da capo arias by Rossi in the *Handbuch der Musik-Geschichte* (Vol. II/2).

BIBLIOGRAPHY: A. Wotquenne, *Étude bibliographique sur Luigi Rossi* (Brussels, 1909); Henry Prunières, "Notes sur la vie de Luigi Rossi," *Sammelbände der Internationalen Musik-Gesellschaft* 12; Henry Prunières, "Les Réprésentations du Palazzo d'Atlante," and A. Cametti, "Alcuni documenti inediti su la vita di Luigi Rossi," *Sammelbände der Internationalen Musik-Gesellschaft* 14; Henry Prunières, "Notes bibliographiques sur les cantates de Luigi Rossi au Conservatoire de Naples," *Zeitschrift der internationalen Musik-Gesellschaft* 14; Henry Prunières, *L'Opéra italien en France avant Lulli* (Paris, 1913; pp. 86–150); Romain Rolland, "Le Premier Opéra joué à Paris: l'Orféo de Luigi Rossi," *Musiciens d'autrefois* (1912); A. Cametti, "Luigi Rossi: Organista a S. Luigi dei Francesi," *La Critica Musicale* (1919); A. Ghislanzoni, *Luigi Rossi* (Rome, 1954).

Rossi, Michel Angelo, Italian composer; b. Genoa, 1602; d. Rome, July 7, 1656. He was a pupil of Frescobaldi; in 1638 was attached to the court of the Duke of Este in Modena; in 1640 he went to Rome. Among his works are an opera *Erminia sul Giordano* (Rome, 1635) and a set of *Toccate e Correnti per organo o cembalo* (2nd ed., Rome, 1657). The complete keyboard works of Rossi were published by A. Toni (Milan, 1920); the 1657 edition of *Toccate e Correnti* are included in L. Torchi, *L'Arte Musicale in Italia,* and 10 *correnti* published by F. Boghen (Milan, 1923); 2 toccatas and 3 *correnti* were edited by Béla Bartók (N.Y., 1930).

BIBLIOGRAPHY: Alceo Toni, "Michel Angelo Rossi," *Bollettino Bibliografico Musicale* (June 1927).

Rossi, Salomone (Salamone), Italian composer of Jewish origin (called himself **Ebreo**); b. Mantua, 1570; d. there, c.1630. Nothing is known of the circumstances of his life, except that he was in the service of the court of Mantua, and publ. 13 books of madrigals and instrumental works. He also wrote some synagogue music. As composer of instrumental works, he demonstrated technical procedures in advance of his time; particularly notable are his variations on popular Italian melodies.

WORKS: canzonettas for 3 voices (1589); madrigals (5 books; 1600, 1602, 1603, 1610, 1622); sonatas (4 books: I, II, *Sinfonie e gagliarde a 3–5,* 1607, 1608; III, IV, *Varie sonate, sinfonie,* etc. 2nd ed., 1623, 1622, 2nd ed., 1636); madrigals for 4–5 voices (1614); *cantici,* psalms, hymns, and *laudi* for 3–8 voices (1620); *madrigaletti* for 2–3 voices, with basso continuo (1628). His *Salmi e cantici ebraici* were publ. under its original Hebrew title *Hashirim asher lish'lomo* in Venice, 1623. He also wrote an intermezzo to the drama *L'Idropica* (1608) and music to a sacred play, *Maddalena.* Naumbourg and Vincent d'Indy prepared a new ed. of selected sacred and secular works by Rossi (2 vols.; Paris, 1877); examples of Rossi's instrumental music appear in Reimann's *Alte Kammermusik, Musikgeschichte in Beispielen* (no. 81), and *Handbuch der Musikgeschichte* (II/2); 6 duets are reprinted in Landshoff's *Alte Meister des Bel Canto;* F. Rikko and J. Newman edited *Sinfonie, Gagliarde, Canzone* (N.Y., 1965). Lazare Saminsky remodelled Rossi's *Adon Olam* in conformity with modern choral sonorities, retaining his harmonic texture, as part of his *Sabbath Evening Service* (N.Y., 1930). The *Complete Works* were begun in 1967, edited by Fritz Rikko (N.Y.). A complete list of works, locations of manuscripts and 17th century publications, reprints, etc. are included in J. Newman and F. Rikko, *A Thematic Index to the Works of Salomon Rossi* (Music Indexes and Bibliographies 6, Hackensack, N.J., 1972).

BIBLIOGRAPHY: D. Maggid, *Die Dreihundertjahrfeier des Salomon de Rossi* (1887); E. Birnbaum, "Jüdische Musiker am Hofe zu Mantua von 1542–1628," in *Kalendar für Israeliten für das Jahr 5654* (Vienna, 1893); Paul Nettl, *Alte jüdische Spielleute und Musiker* (Prague, 1923); B. Selwyn, *The Gonzaga Lords of Mantua* (London, 1927); A. Einstein, "S. Rossi as Composer of Madrigals," *Hebrew Union College Annual* 23 (Cincinnati, 1950/51); N. Zaslaw, "Synagogue Music Rediscovered. I. Salomon Rossi: The Songs of Solomon," *American Choral Review* (April 1972).

Rossi-Lemeni, Nicola, Italian bass; b. Istanbul, Nov. 6, 1920, of an Italian father and a Russian mother. He was educated in Italy; studied law and planned a diplomatic career. In 1943 he decided to become a professional singer, but the war interfered with his plans, and his debut did not take place until 1946. He first appeared in America as Boris Godunov, with the San Francisco Opera (Oct. 2, 1951); also sang Mefistofele (Boito), William Tell, etc.; in 1955, he was engaged at La Scala, Milan. Besides the regular operatic repertory, he sang a number of parts in modern works, such as Wozzeck.

Rossignol, Felix Ludger. See **Joncières, Victorin de.**

Rossini, Gioacchino (Antonio), great Italian composer; b. Pesaro, Feb. 29, 1792; d. Paris, Nov. 13, 1868.

His father was a town trumpeter at Pesaro, and also played the horn and trumpet in provincial theaters; his mother sang opera as *seconda donna.* For a time Rossini was left in a home in Bologna while his parents performed in various theaters in Italian cities; there he acquired some knowledge of music, and learned to play the harpsichord and to sing; he studied with Angelo Tesei; at the age of 14 he entered the Liceo Comunale of Bologna, where he took courses with Padre Mattei (theory) and Cavedagni (cello); at that time he had already written a number of pieces of chamber music, and on Aug. 8, 1808, his cantata *Il Pianto d'armonia per la morte d'Orfeo* was performed at the Liceo, and also won a prize. After relinquishing his studies, he wrote his first opera buffa, *La Cambiale di matrimonio;* after its production in Venice (Nov. 3, 1810) he returned to Bologna, and brought out there a 2-act opera buffa, *L'Equivoco stravagante.* Two more comic operas were ordered by the San Moisè theater in Venice, and produced there in 1812, and there were further commissions from other theaters. In 1813 he obtained his first grand success, with the opera *Tancredi* at the Fenice Theater in Venice, followed by *L'Italiana in Algeri,* another opera buffa, produced at the San Benedetto Theater in Venice. Encouraged by a steady demand, Rossini ventured to set to music an Italian version of the famous play of Beaumarchais, *Le Barbier de Séville,* despite the fact that an opera on the same subject by Paisiello, *Il Barbiere di Siviglia,* produced as early as 1782, was still enjoying great success. Rossini's opera was brought out at the Argentina Theater in Rome on Feb. 20, 1816, under the title *Almaviva ossia l'inutile precauzione;* he himself stated that he wrote the score in 13 days, using the overture from his earlier opera, *Elisabetta, regina d'Inghilterra.* Rossini himself conducted; the opera was hissed on the first night, but the second performance was very favorably received, and the opera became Rossini's greatest triumph. From 1815 to 1823 he was under contract to write 2 operas annually for the famous impresario Barbaja, who managed the theaters of Naples, La Scala of Milan, and the Italian opera in Vienna. During these 8 years he composed no fewer than 20 operas, beginning with *Elisabetta, regina d'Inghilterra;* in that opera he replaced the traditional *recitativo secco* by *recitativo stromentato.* On March 16, 1822, he married Barbaja's mistress, the Spanish soprano **Isabella Colbran.** He spent the next season in Vienna; then returned with his wife to Bologna. In 1823, disappointed at the cool reception in Venice of his opera *Semiramide,* in which his wife sang, he accepted a favorable offer from Benelli, the manager of the King's Theatre in London. After a brief stay in Paris, Rossini arrived in London and was received by the king. During the 5 months in London he earned large sums from concerts given for the nobility at generous fees. He then agreed to undertake the management of the Théâtre-Italien in Paris, and produced several operas of his own as well as one by Meyerbeer. After the expiration of his contract he was given a more or less nominal post as "premier compositeur du roi," and another of "inspecteur-général du chant en France" at the combined salary of 20,000 francs. He produced at the Paris Opéra several French versions of his earlier Italian pieces; the glorious culmination of his Paris seasons was the production of his great dramatic work *Guillaume Tell,* presented at the Opéra on Aug. 3, 1829, with a magnificent cast, winning immense applause. With this grand work, Rossini abruptly closed his career as a composer of operas, at the age of 37. The reasons for this decision were never made clear, but rumors flew around Paris that he was unhappy about the cavalier treatment he received from the management of the Opéra, and decided to yield the operatic field to "the Jews" (Meyerbeer and Halévy), whose operas gradually captivated the audiences. The Revolution of 1830 invalidated Rossini's contract for five more operas, and it was only after a difficult litigation that Rossini was granted a pension by the government of the new King Charles X.

In 1837 Rossini separated from his wife, and after her death in 1845, married Olympia Descuilliers (Aug. 16, 1846). He lived in Bologna from 1836 till 1848, and accepted the honorary presidency of the Liceo Musicale, where he also taught singing to some exceptionally talented pupils; was briefly in Paris in 1843 to undergo corrective surgery of the urinary tract for gonorrhea; in 1848 he settled in Florence, and in 1855, decided to return to Paris, where he remained for the rest of his life. His villa in Passy became the magnet of the artistic world in Paris; Rossini and his wife entertained gladly and lavishly. He was a great gourmet, and invented recipes for Italian food that were enthusiastically adopted by French chefs. His wit was fabulous, and his sayings were eagerly collected and reported. He did not abandon composition entirely during his last years of life; in 1864 he wrote a *Petite Messe Solennelle;* as a token of gratitude to the government of the Second Empire, he composed a *Hymne à Napoléon III;* of greater interest are the numerous piano pieces, songs, and instrumental works which Rossini called *Péchés de vieillesse (Sins of Old Age).*

Rossini's melodies have been used by many composers as themes for various works: Respighi utilized Rossini's *Quelques Riens* in his ballet *La Boutique fantasque,* and other themes in his orchestral suite *Rossiniana.* An opera entitled *Rossini in Neapel* was written by Bernhard Paumgartner (1936). Benjamin Britten made use of Rossini's music in his orch. suites, *Soirées musicales* and *Matinées musicales.* The most famous arrangement of his music is the Prayer from *Mosè in Egitto* transcribed for violin by Paganini.

WORKS: OPERAS: *La Cambiale di matrimonio* (Venice, Nov. 3, 1810); *L'Equivoco stravagante* (Bologna, Oct. 26, 1811); *L'Inganno felice* (Venice, Jan. 8, 1812); *La Scala di seta* (Venice, May 9, 1812); *Demetrio e Polibio* (Rome, May 18, 1812); *La Pietra del paragone* (Milan, Sept. 26, 1812); *L'Occasione fa il ladro, ossia Il Cambio della valigia* (Venice, Nov. 24, 1812); *Ciro in Babilonia* (Ferrara, 1812); *Il Signor Bruschino, ossia Il Figlio per azzardo* (Venice, Jan., 1813); *Tancredi* (Venice, Feb. 6, 1813); *L'Italiana in Algeri* (Venice, May 22, 1813); *Aureliano in Palmira* (Milan, Dec. 26, 1813); *Il Turco in Italia* (Milan, Aug. 14, 1814); *Sigismondo* (Venice, Dec. 26, 1814); *Elisabetta, regina d'Inghilterra* (Naples, Oct. 4, 1815); *Torvaldo e Dorliska* (Rome, Dec. 26, 1815); *Il Barbiere di Siviglia* (1st performed in Rome, Feb. 20, 1816, as *Almaviva ossia L'Inutile precauzione;* 1st performed

under the title *Il Barbiere di Siviglia* at Bologna, Aug. 10, 1816); *La Gazzetta* (Naples, Sept. 26, 1816); *Otello, ossia Il Moro di Venezia* (Naples, Dec. 4, 1816); *Cenerentola, ossia La Bontà in trionfo* (Rome, Jan. 25, 1817); *La Gazza ladra* (Milan, May 31, 1817); *Armida* (Naples, Nov. 11, 1817); *Adelaida di Borgogna* (Rome, Dec. 27, 1817); *Mosè in Egitto* (Naples, March 5, 1818); *Adina, o Il Califfo di Bagdad* (Lisbon, June 22, 1826); *Ricciardo e Zoraide* (Naples, Dec. 3, 1818); *Ermione* (Naples, March 27, 1819); *Edoardo e Cristina* (Venice, April 24, 1819); *La Donna del lago* (Naples, Sept. 24, 1819); *Bianca e Falliero, ovvero Il Consiglio dei tre* (Milan, Dec. 26, 1819); *Maometto II* (Naples, Dec. 3, 1820); *Matilde di Shabran, ossia Bellezza e cuor di ferro* (Rome, Feb. 24, 1821); *Zelmira* (Naples, Feb. 16, 1822); *Semiramide* (Venice, Feb. 3, 1823); *Il Viaggio a Reims* (Paris, June 19, 1825); *Le Siège de Corinthe* (new version of *Maometto II;* Paris, Oct. 9, 1826); *Moïse* (new version of *Mosè in Egitto;* Paris, March 26, 1827); *Le Comte Ory* (Paris, Aug. 20, 1828); *Guillaume Tell* (Paris, Aug. 3, 1829).

CANTATAS: *Il Pianto d'armonia sulla morte d'Orfeo* (1808); *La Morte di Didone* (1811); *Egle ed Irene* (1814); *Inno agli Italiani* (1815); *Le Nozze di Teti e Peleo* (1816); *Igea* (1819); *Partenope* (1819); *Voto filiale* (1820); *La Riconoscenza* (1821); *La santa alleanza* (1822); *Il vero omaggio* (1822); *L'Augurio felice* (1822); *Il Bardo* (1822); *Omaggio pastorale* (1823); *Il Pianto delle muse in morte di Lord Byron* (1824); *I Pastori* (1825); *Il Serto votivo* (1829); *Giovanna d'Arco* (1832); *Inno popolare* (1846); *Inno nazionale* (1848); *Inno alla pace* (1848); *Il Fanciullo smarrito* (1861); *Coro di cacciatori* (1861).

FOR ORCH.: an early overture (1808); Variations for clarinet and orch. (1809); marches; fanfares.

CHAMBER MUSIC: 5 string quartets (1804); *Tema con variazioni,* for flute, clarinet, bassoon, and horn (1812); *Rondeau fantastique,* for horn and piano (1856).

The Rossini Foundation in Pesaro began publication of all the works of Rossini in 1954, in the series *Quaderni Rossiniani;* 19 vols. appeared by 1977.

BIBLIOGRAPHY: Stendhal, *Vie de Rossini* (Paris, 1824; often republished; German ed. with corrections and additions, Leipzig, 1824; 3rd ed., 1929; in English, London, 1824, 1956); G. Carpani, *Le Rossiniane* (Padua, 1824); J. d'Ortigue, *De la guerre des dilettanti ou de la révolution opérée par Rossini dans l'opera français* (Paris, 1829); H. Blaze de Bury, *Vie de Rossini* (Paris, 1854); M. and L. Escudier, *Rossini* (Paris, 1854); E. de Mirecourt, *Rossini* (Paris, 1855); A. J. Azevedo, *G. Rossini* (Paris, 1864); F. Hiller, "Plaudereien mit Rossini," in *Aus dem Tonleben unserer Zeit* (Leipzig, 1868); H. S. Edwards, *Life of Rossini* (London, 1869; condensed in *Great Musicians,* 1881); A. Pougin, *Rossini: Notes, impressions, souvenirs, commentaires* (Paris, 1870); O. Moutoz, *Rossini et son Guillaume Tell* (Bourg, 1872); S. Silvestri, *Della vita e delle opere di G. Rossini* (Milan, 1874); A. Zanolini, *Biografia di G. Rossini* (Bologna, 1875); J. Sittard, *G. A. Rossini* (Leipzig, 1882); C. Thrane, *Rossini og operaen* (Copenhagen, 1885); A. Kohut, *Rossini* (Leipzig, 1892); G. Mazzatinti, *Lettere inedite e rare di Rossini* (Pesaro, 1892); E. Checchi, *Rossini* (Florence,

1898); G. Tebaldini, *Da Rossini a Verdi* (Naples, 1901); G. Mazzatinti and G. Manis, *Lettere di G. Rossini* (Florence, 1902); L. Dauriac, *Rossini* (Paris, 1906); E. Michotte, *Souvenirs personnels* (Paris, 1906); E. Corradi, *G. Rossini* (Rome, 1909); A. Testoni, *G. Rossini: Quattro episodi della sua vita* (Bologna, 1909); F. Cowen, *Rossini* (N.Y., 1912); H. de Curzon, *Rossini* (Paris, 1920; 2nd ed., 1930); R. Fauchois, *Rossini* (Lyons, 1922); G. M. Gatti, *Le "Barbier de Séville" de Rossini* (Paris, 1926); G. Radiciotti, *G. Rossini: vita documentata, opere ed influenza su l'arte* (3 vols.; Tivoli, 1927–29; basic biography); G. Radiciotti, *Aneddoti Rossiniani autentici* (Rome, 1929); H. de Curzon, *Une heure avec Rossini* (Paris, 1930); Lord Derwent, *Rossini and Some Forgotten Nightingales* (London, 1934); F. Toye, *Rossini: A Study in Tragi-Comedy* (London, 1934); H. Gerigk, *Rossini* (Potsdam, 1934); A. Bonaventura, *Rossini* (Florence, 1934); G. Monaldi, *Rossini nell'arte, nella vita, negli aneddoti* (Milan, 1936); L. d'Amico, *Rossini* (Turin, 1938); A. Fraccaroli, *Rossini* (Milan, 1941; 4th ed., 1944); R. Bacchelli, *G. Rossini* (Turin, 1941; 2nd ed., 1945); F. Bonavia, *Rossini* (London, 1941); G. Roncaglia, *Rossini, l'olimpico* (Milan, 1946); K. Pfister, *Das Leben Rossinis: Gesetz und Triumph* (Vienna, 1948); C. van Berkel, *Rossini* (Haarlem, 1950); special issue of *Rassegna Musicale* (Sept. 1954) devoted to the collection of 1100 pages of Rossini's manuscript works in the Pesaro archives; F. Schlitzer, *Rossiniana: contributo all'epistolario di G. Rossini* (Siena, 1956); Luigi Rognoni, *Rossini* (Modena, 1956); F. Schlitzer, *Rossini e Siena e altri scritti rossiniani* (Siena, 1958); R. Bacchelli, *Rossini e esperienze rossiniane* (Milan, 1959); P. Ingerslev-Jensen, *Rossini* (Copenhagen, 1959); H. Weinstock, *Rossini* (N.Y., 1968).

Rostand, Claude, French writer on music; b. Paris, Dec. 3, 1912; d. Villejuif, Oct. 9, 1970. He studied with N. Dufourck. In 1958 he organized a modern music society in Paris, Musique d'Aujourd'hui.
WRITINGS: *L'œuvre de Gabriel Fauré* (Paris, 1945); *Richard Strauss* (Paris, 1949); *La Musique française contemporaine* (Paris, 1952); dialogues with Milhaud, Poulenc, Markevitch and others; biographies of Brahms (2 vols., Paris, 1954–55), Liszt (Paris, 1960); Hugo Wolf (Paris, 1967) and Webern (1969); *Dictionnaire de la musique contemporaine* (Lausanne, 1970).

Rostropovich, Leopold, Russian cellist, father and teacher of **Mstislav Rostropovich;** b. Voronezh, March 9, 1892; d. Orenburg, July 31, 1942. He studied cello with his father Vitold Rostropovich; gave concerts; from 1925 to 1931 was prof. at the Cons. of Azerbaijan in Baku; then lived in Moscow; after the outbreak of the Nazi-Soviet war in 1941 he moved to Orenburg.

Rostropovich, Mstislav, eminent Russian cellist and conductor; b. Baku, March 27, 1927. His father and grandfather were cello players; he took lessons with his father; in 1937 entered the Moscow Cons., where he studied with Kozolupov, and took courses in composition with Shebalin; graduated in 1948 and joined the faculty of the Moscow Cons.; concurrently taught classes at the Leningrad Cons. In 1950 he won the

International Competition of Cellists in Prague; then embarked on a highly successful career as a cello virtuoso, achieving a high rank among master cellists, next to Casals and Piatigorsky. Prokofiev, Shostakovich, Benjamin Britten, Walter Piston, Lukas Foss and others wrote special works for him. He also revealed himself as an excellent pianist, and played accompaniments (from memory) to his wife, the singer **Galina Vishnevskaya.** Still another achievement in his versatile career was that of a fine conductor, both in opera and in symphony concerts. He received the Lenin Prize in 1963. But despite all these distinctions and official honors, he began having difficulties with the Soviet authorities, owing chiefly to his spirit of uncompromising independence; he let the dissident author Solzhenitsyn stay at his *dacha* near Moscow; also dared to criticize the bureaucrats of the Soviet Ministry of Culture, which was in charge of handling artistic engagements. As a result, he found himself hampered in his professional activities and was denied the opportunity to play and conduct as often as he wished. In 1974 he decided to take a leave of absence and went abroad, while still keeping his Soviet citizenship. His wife and two daughters followed him to the U.S. In 1975 he accepted the offer to conduct the National Symph. Orch. in Washington, and made a brilliant debut with it in the fall of 1977. In March 1978 he and his wife were stripped of their citizenship by the Soviet government as "ideological renegades."
BIBLIOGRAPHY: Tatiana Gaidamovich, *Mstislav Rostropovich* (Moscow, 1969); "The Magnificent Maestro," *Time* (Oct. 24, 1977; the cover story).

Roswaenge, Helge, Danish tenor; b. Copenhagen (of German parents), Aug. 29, 1897; d. Munich, June 19, 1972. He studied engineering and took voice lessons; then made a grand tour through Scandinavia, Germany and Austria in concert and in opera. From 1949 he was attached principally to the Berlin State Opera. In his prime, his voice was often compared in quality of bel canto with that of Caruso. He published 3 booklets of an autobiographical nature, *Skratta Pajazzo (Ridi, Pagliaccio;* Copenhagen, 1945); *Mach es besser, mein Sohn* (Leipzig, 1962), and *Leitfaden für Gesangsbeflissene* (Munich, 1964).

Rota, Nino, brilliant Italian composer; b. Milan, Dec. 3, 1911. He was a precocious musician; at the age of 11 he wrote an oratorio which had a public performance, and at 14 composed a lyric comedy in 3 acts, *Il Principe porcaro,* after Hans Christian Andersen (1926); he then undertook a serious study of composition with Alfredo Casella and Ildebrando Pizzetti at the Academy of Santa Cecilia in Rome, graduating in 1930; then went to the U.S.; enrolled in the Curtis Institute of Philadelphia, where he studied composition with Rosario Scalero and conducting with Fritz Reiner. Returning to Italy, he was on the staff of the Liceo Musicale in Bari, and in 1950 became its director. His music demonstrates a great facility, and even felicity, with occasional daring incursions into the arcane regions of dodecaphony.
WORKS: the short operas *Ariodante* (Parma, 1942), *I due timidi* (1950); *Il Cappello di paglia di Firenze* (Palermo, 1955); the opera-buffa, *La notte di un*

nevrastenico (Turin, Nov. 19, 1959); *Aladino e la lampada magica* (Naples, 1968); *La visita meravigliosa* (Palermo, Feb. 6, 1970); the ballets, *La rappresentazione di Adamo ed Eva* (Perugia, 1957) and *La strada* (after the Fellini film of the same name, produced in 1954; Milan, 1965); Piano Concerto (1960); Trombone Concerto (1967); *Concerto soirée* (1961); *Fantasia su 12 note del Don Giovanni di Mozart* for piano and orch. (1962); oratorios, *Mysterium* (1962) and *La vita di Maria* (1970); numerous successful film scores: *Rocco e i suoi fratelli* (1960) and *Il gattopardo*, by Visconti (1963), *Romeo e Giulietta*, by Zeffirelli (1968) and several films by Fellini, among them *La dolce vita* (1960) and *Otto e mezzo* (1963).

Roters, Ernst, German composer; b. Oldenburg, July 6, 1892; d. Berlin, Aug. 25, 1961. He studied at the Klindworth-Scharwenka Cons. in Berlin with Moritz Mayer-Mahr (piano), Hugo Leichtentritt (theory), and Georg Schumann (composition); was in the German army during World War I; then worked in the films; was again in the German army during the last year of World War II (1944–45); after the cessation of hostilities, he returned to Berlin, where he conducted the Deutsches Theater (1945–47). A highly prolific composer (150 op. numbers before 1955), he wrote an opera, *Die schwarze Kammer* (Darmstadt, 1928); incidental music for 15 plays; about 50 radio works; 3 piano concertos; numerous pieces of chamber music and songs.

Roth, Bertrand, Swiss pianist; b. Degersheim, Feb. 12, 1855; d. Bern, Jan. 25, 1938. He studied at the Leipzig Cons. and later in Weimar with Liszt; from 1884 to 1900, taught at the Cons. of Dresden; in 1901 he established there the Musiksalon Bertrand Roth, Sunday matinées at which were performed works by contemporary composers.

Roth, Feri, eminent Hungarian violinist; b. Zvolen, Czechoslovakia, July 18, 1899; d. Los Angeles, May 7, 1969. He studied at the State Academy in Budapest; organized a string quartet with which he toured Europe and Africa; then emigrated to the U.S. and formed the Roth Quartet (with Jenö Antal, Ferenc Molnar, and Janos Scholz), which made an American debut at the Pittsfield Music Festival, Sept. 21, 1928. In 1946 he was appointed prof. of violin and chamber ensemble at the Univ. of California at Los Angeles, a post he held until his death.

Roth, Herman, German musicologist; b. Hornberg, Baden, Feb. 15, 1882; d. Berlin, Feb. 1, 1938. He studied philology and philosophy; then took courses in music with Philipp Wolfrum in Heidelberg (1902) and Hugo Riemann in Leipzig (1905). He was music critic in Leipzig (1907–10) and Munich (1910–21); taught at the Cons. of Baden (1921–24) and at the Hochschule für Musik at Stuttgart (1925–32); then settled in Berlin. He publ. the books *Heinrich Kasper Schmid* (Munich, 1921) and *Elemente der Stimmführung* (Stuttgart, 1926); edited works by Bach, Handel, etc.

Rothenberger, Anneliese, German lyric soprano; b. Mannheim, June 19, 1924. She studied at the Mann-

heim Musikhochschule; made her operatic debut in Koblenz in 1948; in 1949–56 sang at the Hamburg State Opera; in 1958 joined the staff of the Vienna Opera, while continuing to fill guest engagements in opera and recital in Europe, including Russia; made her American debut at the Metropolitan Opera on Nov. 18, 1960, and sang there until 1963. She was particularly successful in the soubrette roles; was also praised as an actress. She published an autobiography, *Melodie meines Lebens* (Munich, 1972).

Rothier, Léon, French bass; b. Reims, Dec. 26, 1874; d. New York, Dec. 6, 1951. He studied at the Paris Cons. with Crosti (singing), Lhérie (opéra-comique), and Melchissedec (opera), winning 1st prizes in all 3 classes upon graduation. He made his operatic debut as Jupiter in Gounod's *Philémon et Baucis* at the Opéra-Comique, where he remained until 1903; then was active at Marseilles (1903–07), Nice (1907–09), and Lyons (1909–10). On Dec. 10, 1910, he made his American debut at the Metropolitan Opera, N.Y. as Méphistophélès; after retirement (1939), he remained in N.Y. as a teacher.

Rothmüller, Marko, Yugoslav baritone; b. Trnjani, Dec. 31, 1908. He studied in Zagreb; then took lessons in singing with Franz Steiner in Vienna, and also had lessons in composition with Alban Berg. He made his operatic debut as Rigoletto at the Hamburg State Opera in 1932; was a member of the opera in Zagreb (1932–34) and Zürich (1935–47); then was with the Covent Garden Opera in London (1948–55). He sang for a season with the N.Y. City Opera (1948–49); remained in N.Y. as a singing teacher. He was distinguished in Wagner roles; also sang leading roles in modern works, including Wozzeck in Alban Berg's opera. He wrote some chamber music and songs; published an interesting volume, *Die Musik der Juden* (Zürich, 1951; in English, London, 1953).

Rothwell, Walter Henry, British-American conductor; b. London, Sept. 22, 1872; d. Santa Monica, Calif., March 12, 1927. He studied at the Vienna Cons. (1881–88) with J. Epstein (piano), R. Fuchs (theory), and Bruckner (composition); took further courses in Munich with Thuille and Schillings. In 1895 he became assistant conductor to Mahler at the Hamburg Opera; then conducted the German opera in Amsterdam (1903–04) and (1904–08) the Savage Opera Co. in the U.S., with which he gave performances of *Parsifal* in English. He then was conductor of the St. Paul Symph. Orch. (1908–14); after several years in N.Y. as teacher, he was engaged (1919) to organize and conduct the Los Angeles Philh. Orch., which he led until his death. He was married (Sept. 10, 1908) to the soprano **Elisabeth Wolff.**

Rottenberg, Ludwig, Austrian conductor and composer; b. Czernowitz, Bukovina, Oct. 11, 1864; d. Frankfurt, May 6, 1932. He studied music with A. Hřimalý, R. Fuchs, and E. Mandyczewski in Vienna; was Kapellmeister at the Stadttheater in Brünn (1891–92) and at the Frankfurt opera (1893–1926); retired in 1927. In 1912 and 1913 he conducted the Wagner performances at Covent Garden, London. He publ. a collection of 30 songs, a violin sonata, and piano variations; his opera, *Die Geschwister,* was produced in Frankfurt on Nov. 30, 1915. Rottenberg was the father-in-law of **Paul Hindemith.**

Rouart-Lerolle & Cie., French publishing house, founded in 1905 at Paris by **Alexander Rouart** (1869–1921), through the purchase of the firms of Meuriot and Baudoux. When, in 1908, **Jacques Lerolle,** son of the famous painter, became his associate, the firm acquired the catalogue of the publ. house of Gregh (founded in 1840). After the death of Rouart in 1921, Lerolle became director, Mme. Rouart, the founder's widow, a partner, and François Hepp (1887–1965), son-in-law of Rouart, co-director. In 1942, the entire stock of Rouart-Lerolle & Cie. was sold to Salabert.

Rouget de l'Isle, Claude-Joseph, composer of the *Marseillaise;* b. Lons-le-Saulnier, Jura, May 10, 1760; d. Choisy-le-Roy, June 27, 1836. He composed the famous national hymn in 1792, while stationed in Strasbourg as a military engineer. The original title of the *Marseillaise* was *Le Chant de guerre de l'armée du Rhin,* and it was designed to be a patriotic song at the time of the war with Austria; it was taken up by the Marseilles soldiers marching towards Paris, and so assumed its universally known title. Rouget de l'Isle was himself not a revolutionary; he was in fact imprisoned for refusing to take the oath against the crown. He went to Paris after Robespierre's downfall, and composed a *Hymne dithyrambique sur la conjuration de Robespierre* (1794), *Chant des vengeances* (1798), and a *Chant du combat* for the army in Egypt (1800). He publ. 50 *Chants français* in 1825; wrote several opera librettos. Maurice de La Fuye and Émile Guéret, in their book *Rouget de l'Isle, inconnu* (Paris, 1943), argued that he wrote only the words and not the music of the *Marseillaise,* and suggested that the composer was Ignace Pleyel. A. Loth, in his pamphlet *Le Chant de la Marseillaise* (Paris, 1886), claimed that the composer was one Grisons.

BIBLIOGRAPHY: J. Tiersot, *Rouget de l'Isle: son œuvre, sa vie* (Paris, 1892); A. Köckert, *Rouget de l'Isle* (Leipzig, 1898); A. Lanier, *Rouget de l'Isle* (Besançon, 1907); J. Tiersot, *Histoire de la Marseillaise* (Paris, 1915); R. Brancour, *La Marseillaise et le Chant du départ* (1916); E. Istel, "Is the Marseillaise a German Composition?" *Musical Quarterly* (April 1922); V. Helfert, "La Marseillaise," *Rivista Musicale Italiana* (1922); A. Becker, *La Marseillaise* (Brunswick, 1930); G. de Froidcourt, *Grétry, Rouget de Lisle et la Marseillaise* (Liège, 1945).

Rousseau, Jean-Jacques, great philosopher and author; b. Geneva, June 28, 1712; d. Ermenonville, near Paris, July 2, 1778. Without other musical training than desultory self-instruction, Rousseau made his debut as a music scholar at the age of 29, reading a paper before the Académie in Paris (1724), which was received and publ. as a *Dissertation sur la musique moderne* (1743). His opera *Les Muses galantes* had only one private representation, at the house of La Pouplinière in 1745; his revision of the intermezzo *La Reine de Navarre* (by Voltaire and Rameau) was a

failure in Paris; but his opera *Le Devin du village* (Fontainebleau, Oct. 18, 1752; Paris Opéra, March 1, 1753) was very successful and remained in the repertory for 75 years. In the meantime his musical articles for the *Encyclopédie* had evoked scathing criticism from Rameau and others; improved by revision and augmentation, they were republished as his *Dictionnaire de musique* (Geneva, 1767; the existence of this edition cannot be proved; first known edition, Paris, 1768). In 1752 commenced the dispute, known as the "guerre des bouffons," between the partisans of French and Italian opera; Rousseau sided with the latter, publishing a *Lettre à M. Grimm au sujet des remarques ajoutées à sa lettre sur Omphale* (1752), followed by the caustic *Lettre sur la musique française* (1753, to which the members of the Opéra responded by burning him in effigy and excluding him from the theater), and *Lettre d'un symphoniste de l'Académie royale de musique à ses camarades* (1753). He wrote 2 numbers for the melodrama, *Pygmalion* (1770; Paris, Oct. 30, 1775). Publ. posthumously were six new arias for *Le Devin du village,* and a collection of about 100 *romances* and duets, *Les Consolations des misères de ma vie* (1781), and fragments of an opera, *Daphnis et Chloé* (1780). All his writings on music have been often republished in eds. of his *Collected Works* (1782; many subsequently editions).

BIBLIOGRAPHY: A. Jensen, *J.-J. R. Fragments inédits, recherches biographiques* (Paris, 1882); A. Jansen, *J.-J. R. als Musiker* (Berlin, 1884); A. Pougin, *J.-J. R., musicien* (Paris, 1901); E. Istel, *J.-J. R. als Komponist seiner lyrischen Szene "Pygmalion"* (Leipzig, 1901); F. Hellouin, "J.-J. R. et la psychologie de l'orchestre," in *Feuillets d'histoire musicale française* (Paris, 1903); E. Schütte, *J.-J. R. Seine Persönlichkeit und sein Stil* (Leipzig, 1910); J. Tiersot, *J.-J. R.* (Paris, 1912); E. Faguet, *Rousseau artiste* (Paris, 1913); A. L. Sells, *The Early Life of Rousseau: 1712–40* (London, 1929); R. Gérin, *J.-J. R.* (Paris, 1930); M. Moffat, *Rousseau et le théâtre* (Paris, 1930); J. Tiersot, "Concerning J.-J. R., the Musician," *Musical Quarterly* (July 1931); H. V. Somerset, "J.-J. R. as a Musician," *Music & Letters* (1936); L. Richebourg, *Contributions à l'histoire de la "querelle des bouffons"* (Paris, 1937); A. Pochon, *J.-J. R., musiciens et le critique* (Montreux, 1940); E. Kisch, "Rameau and Rousseau," *Music & Letters* (1941); A. R. Oliver, *The Encyclopaedists as Critics of Music* (N.Y., 1947); Jean Senelier, *Bibliographie générale des œuvres de J. R.* (Paris, 1949); A. Lowenberg, *Annals of Opera* (Cambridge, 1943; 2nd ed., 1955). *Correspondance générale de Jean-Jacques Rousseau,* ed. by Dufour and Plan was publ. in 20 vols. (Paris, 1924–34). The Institut of Musée Voltaire, brought out the *Correspondance complète de J.-J. R.,* ed. by R. A. Leigh (18 vols., Geneva, 1965–73).

Rousseau, Marcel (-Auguste-Louis), French composer; b. Paris, Aug. 18, 1882; d. there, June 11, 1955. He studied with his father, **Samuel Rousseau;** then entered the Paris Cons. as a student of Lenepveu; won the Deuxième Premier Grand Prix de Rome with the cantata *Maïa* (1905). Later in his professional career he added his father's first name to his own, and produced his works as **Samuel-Rousseau.**

WORKS: the operas (all produced in Paris) *Tarass*

Boulba, after Gogol (Nov. 22, 1919), *Le Hulla* (March 9, 1923), *Le Bon Roi Dagobert* (Dec. 5, 1927; his most successful work), *Kerkeb* (April 6, 1951); the ballets *Promenade dans Rome* (Paris, Dec. 7, 1936) and *Entre deux rondes* (Paris, April 27, 1940); orchestral tableaux, *Solitude triste* and *Impression dolente;* etc. In 1947 he was elected to the Académie des Beaux-Arts.

Rousseau, Samuel-Alexandre, French composer; father of **Marcel Samuel-Rousseau;** b. Neuve-Maison, Aisne, June 11, 1853; d. Paris, Oct. 1, 1904. He studied at the Paris Cons. with César Franck (organ) and Bazin (composition); won the Grand Prix de Rome with the cantata *La Fille de Jephté* (1878); also the Prix Cressent with the 1-act comic opera *Dianora* (Opéra-Comique, Dec. 22, 1879). His opera *Mérowig* was awarded the Prize of the City of Paris, and was performed in concert form at the Grand Théâtre there on Dec. 12, 1892. In 1892 he was appointed conductor at the Théâtre-Lyrique; was for 10 years chorusmaster at the Société des Concerts du Conservatoire; also taught harmony at the Paris Cons. On June 8, 1898, his lyric drama *La Cloche du Rhin* was staged at the Paris Opéra with considerable success, but had only 9 performances in all; this was followed by the music dramas *Milia* (Opéra-Comique, 1904) and *Léone* (Opéra-Comique, March 7, 1910).

Roussel, Albert (Charles Paul), outstanding French composer; b. Tourcoing, Département du Nord, April 5, 1869; d. Royan, Aug. 23, 1937. Orphaned as a child, he was educated by his grandfather, mayor of his native town, and after the grandfather's death, by his aunt. He studied academic subjects at the Collège Stanislas in Paris; music with the organist Stoltz; then studied mathematics in preparation for entering the Naval Academy; at the age of 18 he began his training in the navy; from 1889 to Aug., 1890 he was a member of the crew of the frigate Iphigénie, sailing to Indo-China. This voyage was of great importance to Roussel, since it opened for him a world of Oriental culture and art, which became one of the chief sources of his musical inspiration. He later sailed on the cruiser Dévastation; received a leave of absence then for reasons of health, and spent some time in Tunis; was then station in Cherbourg, and began to compose there. In 1893 he was sent once more to Indo-China. He resigned from the navy in 1894 and went to Paris, where he began to study music seriously with Eugène Gigout. In 1898 he entered the Schola Cantorum in Paris as a pupil of Vincent d'Indy; continued this study until 1907, when he was already 38 years old, but at the same time he was entrusted with a class in counterpoint, which he conducted at the Schola Contorum from 1902 to 1914; among his students were Erik Satie, Stan Golestan, Paul Le Flem, Roland-Manuel, Guy de Lioncourt, and Varèse. In 1909 Roussel and his wife Blanche Preisach-Roussel undertook a voyage to India, where he became acquainted with the legend of the queen Padmâvatî, which he selected as a subject for his famous opera-ballet. His choral symph. *Les Évocations* was also inspired by this tour. At the outbreak of war in 1914, Roussel applied for active service in the navy but was rejected and volunteered as an ambulance driver. After the Armistice of 1918, he settled in Normandy and devoted himself to composition. In the autumn of 1930 he visited the U.S.

Roussel began his work under the influence of French Impressionism, with its dependence on exotic moods and poetic association. However, the sense of formal design asserted itself in his symphonic works; his *Suite en fa* (1927) signalizes a transition towards neo-Classicism; the thematic development is vigorous, and the rhythms are clearly delineated, despite some asymmetrical progressions; the orchestration, too, is in the Classical tradition. Roussel possessed a keen sense of the theater; he was capable of fine characterization of exotic or mythological subjects, but also knew how to depict humorous situations in lighter works. An experiment in a frankly modernistic manner is exemplified by his *Jazz dans la nuit* for voice and piano.

WORKS: FOR THE STAGE: *Le Marchand de sable qui passe,* incidental music (Le Havre, Dec. 16, 1908); *Le Festin de l'araignée,* ballet-pantomime in 1 act (Paris, April 3, 1913); *Padmâvatî,* opera-ballet in 2 acts (1914–18; Paris, June 1, 1923); *La Naissance de la lyre,* lyric opera in 1 act (Paris, July 1, 1925); *Bacchus et Ariane,* ballet in 2 acts (Paris, May 22, 1931); *Le Testament de la tante Caroline,* opéra-bouffe (1932–33; Olomouc, Czechoslovakia, Nov. 14, 1936; Paris, March 11, 1937); *Aeneas,* ballet with chorus, in 1 act (Brussels, July 31, 1935). FOR ORCH.: 4 symphonies: No. 1, *Le Poème de la forêt* (1904–06; Brussels, March 22, 1908), No. 2, *Symphonie en si bémol* (1919–21; Paris, March 4, 1922), No. 3, *Symphonie en sol mineur* (commissioned by the Boston Symph. Orch.; performed there by Koussevitzky, Oct. 24, 1930), No. 4, *Symphonie en la majeur* (1934; Paris, Oct. 19, 1935); *Suite en fa* (Boston, Jan. 21, 1927); *Sinfonietta* for strings (Paris, Nov. 19, 1934); *Résurrection,* symph. poem (Paris, May 17, 1904); *Évocations,* suite in 3 movements (Paris, May 18, 1912); *Pour une fête de printemps* (Paris, Oct. 29, 1921); *Rapsodie flamande* (Brussels, Dec. 12, 1935); *Concert pour petit orchestre* (Paris, May 5, 1927); *Petite suite pour orchestre* (Paris, Feb. 6, 1930); Piano Concerto (Paris, June 7, 1928); Concertino for cello and orch. (Paris, Feb. 6, 1937); *Le Bardit de Francs,* for male chorus, brass, and percussion (Strasbourg, April 21, 1928); *Psaume LXXX,* for tenor, chorus, and orch. (Paris, April 25, 1929); symph. suites from theater works: *Le Festin de l'araignée* (1912), *Padmâvatî* (1914–18), *La Naissance de la lyre* (1922–24), *Bacchus et Ariane* (1930). CHAMBER MUSIC: Piano Trio (1902); *Divertissement* for flute, oboe, clarinet, bassoon, horn, and piano (1906); *Sérénade,* for flute, violin, viola, cello, and harp (1925); Trio for flute, viola, and cello (1929); String Quartet (1932); Trio for violin, viola, and cello (1937); 2 violin sonatas (1908; 1924); *Joueurs de flûte,* suite for flute and piano (1924); *Andante et Scherzo,* for flute and piano (1934). FOR PIANO: *Des Heures passent,* a cycle of 4 pieces (1898); *Rustiques,* a cycle of 3 pieces (1904–06); suite of 3 pieces (1910); Sonatina (1912); *Petit canon perpétuel* (1913); *Prélude et fugue (Hommage à Bach);* etc. SONGS: *Adieux* (1907); *Jazz dans la nuit* (1928); *Deux idylles* (1931); 3 sets of *Poèmes chinois* (1908; 1927; 1932); etc. A complete catalogue of works, with a biographical notice and annotations, was publ. in Paris, 1947, and constitutes a primary source of information.

BIBLIOGRAPHY: Roland-Manuel, "A. R.," *Revue Musicale* (Nov. 1922); L. Vuillemin, *A. R. et son œuvre* (Paris, 1924); Roussel issue of *Revue Musicale* (May-June 1929); H. Prunières, "A. R. and the 80th Psalm," *Musical Quarterly* (Jan. 1930); R. Dumesnil, "L'Œuvre symphonique de A. R.," *Musique Française* (Feb. 1933); R. Petit, "A. R.," *Modern Music* (Nov.-Dec. 1937); A. Hoérée, *A. R.* (Paris, 1938); P. Landormy, "A. R.," *Musical Quarterly* (Oct. 1938); N. Demuth, *A. R.: A Study* (London, 1947); R. Bernard, *A. R.: sa vie, son œuvre* (Paris, 1948); Marc Pincherle, *A. R.* (Paris, 1957); Basil Deane, *Albert Roussel* (London, 1961); Dom Angelico Surchamp, *Albert Roussel: l'homme et son œuvre* (Paris, 1967).

Roussier, Abbé Pierre-Joseph, French writer on music; b. Marseilles, 1716; d. as canon at Ecouis, Normandy, c.1790.

WRITINGS: *Observations sur différents points d'harmonie* (1765); *Traité des accords, et de leur succession* (1764; supplemented by *L'harmonie pratique*, 1775); *Mémoire sur la musique des anciens* (1770); *Notes et observations sur le mémoire du P. Amiot concernant la musique des chinois* (1779); *Mémoire sur la nouvelle harpe de M. Cousineau* (1782); *Mémoire sur le clavecin chromatique* (1782); *Lettre sur l'acceptation des mots "basse fondamentale"* (1783; *Journal encyclopédique*, vol. I); etc.

Rovelli, Pietro, Italian violinist; b. Bergamo, Feb. 6, 1793; d. there, Sept. 8, 1838. He studied with R. Kreutzer; then played in various orchestras in Italy; was concertmaster of the court orch. in Munich (1817-19). He publ. excellent études and caprices for violin; also *Variazioni* for violin and orch.

Rowbotham, Rev. John Frederick, British music historian; b. Edinburgh, April 18, 1854; d. Sutton-Cheney, Oct. 20, 1925. He studied music in Oxford, Berlin, Dresden, Paris, and Vienna; held various appointments as vicar and rector until 1910, when he founded *The Bard,* of which he was editor. He traveled on the Continent to collect materials for his *History of Music,* publ. in 3 vols. (London, 1885-87); also publ. *How to Write Music Correctly* (1889); *A Short History of Music* (1891); *Private Life of the Great Composers* (1892); *The Troubadours, and the Courts of Love* (1895); *A History of Music to the Time of the Troubadours* (1899); *Story Lives of Great Musicians* (1908); etc.

Rowen, Ruth Halle, American musicologist and educator; b. New York, April 5, 1918. She studied at Horace Mann High School (graduated 1935), at Barnard College (B.A., 1939), and at the Columbia University Graduate Faculties (William Mason Scholar, M.A., 1941; Clarence Barker Scholar, Ph.D., 1948), where she took courses with William John Mitchell, Paul Henry Lang, Erich Hertzmann, and Douglas Stuart Moore; 1954-63 directed education dept. of Carl Fischer, Inc.; in 1963 was appointed musicologist at the inception of the M.A. program in music at The City College of New York (chairman 1966-75); in

1967 became one of the 12 original faculty members of the Ph.D. program in music at the Graduate School of the City University of N.Y. She served as musicianship chairman of the National Federation of Music Clubs (1962-74). She wrote *Early Chamber Music* (N.Y., 1949; New preface and supplementary bibliography, 1974); *Music through Sources and Documents* (Englewood Cliffs, N.J., 1978); co-author of *Hearing—Gateway to Music* (Evanston, Ill., 1959); co-composer of *Choral Program Favorites* (N.Y., 1956).

Rowicki, Witold, Russian-born Polish conductor and composer; b. Taganrog, Feb. 26, 1914. He studied violin with Malawski and composition with Piotrowski at the Cracow Cons., graduating in 1938; during the war he was in Germany, where he took private conducting lessons with Paul Hindemith's brother, Rudolf (1942-44). After the end of the war he was a founder of the Katowice Radio Symph. Orch. (1945-50) and of the Warsaw Philharmonic (1950-55); became its music director in 1958; subsequently directed the Wielki Theater Opera Center in Warsaw (1965-70). He achieved a fine reputation for his promotion of modern Polish music. He is also a composer; his works include a Symphony (1957) and a *Warsaw Concerto* for orch. (Warsaw, Nov. 6, 1976).

BIBLIOGRAPHY: L. Terpilowski, *Witold Rowicki* (Cracow, 1961).

Rowley, Alec, English composer; b. Weybridge, Surrey, March 13, 1892; d. London, Jan. 12, 1958. He studied at the Royal Academy of Music; upon graduation, became a teacher. Among his works are a pantomime, *The Princess Who Lost a Tune;* 2 piano concertos; *Rhapsody* for viola and orch.; Concerto for Oboe and Orch.; *Phyllis and Corydon,* for string quartet; *From Faerie,* for string quartet; *Little Jesus,* for voice, piano, and string quartet; *Water-colours,* for piano, violin, viola, and cello; *Pastel Portraits,* for piano, violin, and cello; 3 little trios for piano, violin, and cello; *The Puppet Show, 4 Contrasts, A Short Suite;* also piano pieces for children.

Royce, Edward, American composer and teacher; b. Cambridge, Mass., Dec. 25, 1886; d. Stamford, Conn., July 7, 1963. He studied at Harvard Univ. (B.A., 1907), later at the Stern Cons. in Berlin; 1913, founded the music dept. at Middlebury College, Vermont; then head of the theory dept. at the Ithaca Cons. (1916-21); from 1923 till 1947 prof. of theory at the Eastman School of Music, Rochester, N.Y.

WORKS: He composed 2 tone poems, *The Fire Bringers* (Rochester, April 23, 1926) and *Far Ocean* (Rochester, June 3, 1929); piano pieces, songs.

Royer, Étienne, French composer; b. Grenoble, April 12, 1882; d. Paris, March 2, 1928. He studied with Vincent d'Indy and Sérieyx at the Schola Cantorum in Paris; was a cello pupil of L. Revel; wrote music criticism and publ. pedagogical works. He composed a *Danse mystique* for orch.; *Cantus memorialis,* for violin and orch.; *Pour le temps de la moisson* and *Pour les fêtes de mai,* for string quartet (based on French folk tunes); songs; piano pieces, etc.

Royer, Joseph-Nicolas-Pancrace, French composer; b. 1700; d. Paris, Jan. 11, 1755. He was a native of Burgundy, and settled in Paris in 1725. In 1739 he became a member of the court orch.; 1748, lessee and director of the Concert Spirituel; 1753, inspector of the Paris Opéra and "maître de musique de la chambre du roy." WORKS: the operas *Pyrrhus* (Paris, 1730), *Zaide* (1739), *Le Pouvoir de l'amour* (1743), *Almasis* (1747), *Myrtil* (1750); *Pandore,* after Voltaire (not produced). He publ. sonatas and a book of pieces for the clavecin. BIBLIOGRAPHY: M. Brenet, *Les Concerts en France sous l'ancien régime* (Paris, 1900).

Rôze, Marie-Hippolyte (née **Roze-Ponsin**), famous French soprano; b. Paris, March 2, 1846; d. there, June 21, 1926. She studied at the Paris Cons. with Mocker and later with Auber, winning 2 prizes in 1865; made her debut at the Opéra-Comique in the title role of Hérold's *Marie* (Aug. 16, 1865); sang there for 3 seasons; then appeared at the Paris Opéra as Marguerite in Gounod's *Faust* (Jan. 2, 1879); made her London debut as Marguerite (1872); continued to sing in England for many years. She visited America twice, in 1877–78 and 1880–81. In 1874 she married an American bass, **Julius E. Perkins,** who died the following year; later she married the impresario, **Col. J. H. Mapleson,** but the marriage ended in divorce. In 1890 she settled in Paris as a teacher.

Rôze, Raymond (J. H. Raymond Rôze-Perkins), English composer; son of **Marie Rôze;** b. London, 1875; d. there, March 31, 1920. He studied at the Brussels Cons., where he won 1st prize; wrote overtures and incidental music to many plays. In 1913 he conducted at Covent Garden a season of opera in English, during which he brought out his own opera *Joan of Arc* (Oct. 31, 1913); another opera by him, *Arabesque,* was produced at the Coliseum, London, in 1916.

Rozkošný, Josef Richard, Czech composer; b. Prague, Sept. 21, 1833; d. there, June 3, 1913. He studied painting and music in Prague; his teachers were Tomaschek (piano) and Kittl (composition). His songs and choruses became popular, and he successfully attempted the composition of operas to Czech librettos; 8 operas were produced in Prague, among them: *Svatojanské proudy* (*The Rapids of St. John;* Oct. 3, 1871), *Popelka* (*Cinderella;* May 31, 1885), *Černé jezero* (*The Black Lake;* Jan. 6, 1906). He also publ. a number of piano pieces.

Rózsa, Miklós, brilliant Hungarian-American composer; b. Budapest, April 18, 1907. He studied piano and composition in Leipzig, with Hermann Grabner; musicology with Theodor Kroyer. In 1932 he settled in Paris, where he became successful as a composer; his works were often performed in European music centers. In 1935 he went to London as a writer for the films; in 1939 emigrated to the U.S., and settled in Hollywood. His orchestral and chamber music is cast in the advanced modern idiom in vogue in Europe between the two wars; neo-Classical in general content, it is strong in polyphony and incisive rhythm; for his film music, he employs a more Romantic and diffuse style, relying on a Wagnerian type of grandiloquence. WORKS: for orch.: *Nordungarische Bauernlieder und Tänze* (1929); Symphony (1930); *Serenade* for small orch. (1932); *Scherzo* (1933); *Thema, Variationen und Finale* (1933); *Capriccio, pastorale e danza* (1938); *Variations on a Hungarian Peasant Song* (N.Y., Nov. 14, 1943); Concerto for string orch. (Los Angeles, Dec. 28, 1944); Violin Concerto (Dallas, Jan. 5, 1956, Jascha Heifetz soloist); *Sinfonia concertante* for violin, cello, and orch. (1966); Piano Concerto (Los Angeles, April 6, 1967); Cello Concerto (1969); *Tripartita* for orch. (1973). He has won Oscars for 3 film scores: *Spellbound* (1945), *A Double Life* (1947), and *Ben Hur* (1959); other notable film scores are *Quo Vadis* (1951), *Ivanhoe* (1952), *Julius Caesar* (1953), *Lust for Life* (1956), and *El Cid* (1961). BIBLIOGRAPHY: Christopher Palmer, *Miklós Rózsa: A Sketch of his Life and Work* (with a foreword by Eugene Ormandy; N.Y., 1975).

Różycki, Ludomir, Polish composer; b. Warsaw, Nov. 6, 1884; d. Katowice, Jan. 1, 1953. He studied piano with his father, a teacher at the Warsaw Cons.; theory with Noskowski at the Cons., graduating with honors in 1903. He then went to Berlin, where he took lessons with Humperdinck; in 1908 he was appointed conductor of the opera theater in Lwow; then undertook a European tour; settled in Berlin, where he remained through the years of World War I. In 1920 he returned to Warsaw; after 1945, lived mostly in Katowice. He was highly regarded in Poland as a national composer of stature; his style of composition was a successful blend of German, Russian, and Italian ingredients, yet the Polish characteristics were not obscured by the cosmopolitan harmonic and orchestral dress. WORKS: the operas *Boleslaw smialy* (*Boleslaw the Bold;* Lwow, Feb. 11, 1909), *Meduza* (Warsaw, Oct. 22, 1912), *Eros und Psyche* (Breslau, March 10, 1917; in German), *Casanova* (Warsaw, June 8, 1923), *Beatrice Cenci* (Warsaw, Jan. 30, 1927), *Mlyn diabelski* (*The Devilish Mill,* Poznan, Feb. 21, 1931), *Lili chce spiewac,* comic opera (Poznan, March 7, 1933); the ballets: *Pan Twardowski* (Warsaw, May 9, 1921; his most successful work; more than 800 performances in Warsaw) and *Apollon et la belle* (1937); for orch.: the symph. poems *Stanczyk* (1903), *Anhelli* (1909), *Warszawianka* (1910), *Mona Lisa Gioconda* (1910), *Pietà* (1942), *Warszawa wyzwolona* (*Warsaw Liberated;* 1950); 2 piano concertos (1918; 1942); Violin Concerto (1944); Piano Quintet (1913); String Quartet (1916); Violin Sonata (1903); Cello Sonata (1906); a number of piano pieces; several song cycles. BIBLIOGRAPHY: A. Wieniawski, *Ludomir Różycki* (Warsaw, 1928); M. Kaminski, *Ludomir Różycki* (Katowice, 1951).

Rubbra, Edmund, notable English composer; b. Northampton, May 23, 1901. His parents were musical, and he was taught to play the piano by his mother. He left school as a young boy and was employed in various factories; at the same time he continued to study music by himself, and attempted some composition; organized a concert devoted to the works of his favorite composer, Cyril Scott (Northampton, 1918); subsequently took lessons from him in

London; in 1919 he studied with Holst; his other teachers in composition were John Ireland, Eugene Goossens, and Vaughan Williams. He compensated for a late beginning in composition by an extremely energetic application to steady improvement of his technique; finally elaborated a style of his own, marked by sustained lyricism and dynamic Romanticism; his harmonic language often verges on polytonality. Taught at Oxford Univ. 1947–68.

WORKS: 1-act opera, *Bee-Bee-Bei* (1933); ballet, *Prism* (1938); for orch.: *Double Fugue* (1924), *Triple Fugue* (1929), Symph. No. 1 (London, April 30, 1937), Symph. No. 2 (London, Dec. 16, 1938), Symph. No. 3 (Manchester, Dec. 15, 1940), Symph. No. 4 (London, Aug. 14, 1942), Symph. No. 5 (London, Jan. 26, 1949), Symph. No. 6 (London, Nov. 17, 1954), Symph. No. 7 (Birmingham, Oct. 1, 1957), Symph. No. 8 (London, Jan. 5, 1971); Symph. No. 9, *The Resurrection,* for soloists, chorus, and orch. (1973); Chamber Symphony (Middlesborough, Jan. 8, 1975). *Sinfonia Concertante,* for piano and orch. (London, Aug. 10, 1943), *Soliloquy,* for cello and orch. (London, Jan. 1, 1945), Viola Concerto (London, April 15, 1953); chamber music: *Fantasy* for 2 violins and piano (1925), *Lyric Movement,* for piano quintet (1929), 2 string quartets (1933; 1952), Piano Trio (1950), 2 violin sonatas (1925; 1931), Cello Sonata (1946); choral works: *The Sacred Hymnody* (1921), *La Belle Dame sans merci* (1925), *The Morning Watch* (1941), *Te Deum* (1951); a number of madrigals and motets for unaccompanied chorus; songs with orch. (*Ballad of Tristram, 4 Medieval Latin Lyrics, 5 Sonnets,* etc.); songs with piano; miscellaneous pieces for various instruments. He published *Counterpoint. A Survey* (London, 1960).

BIBLIOGRAPHY: Edwin Evans, "Edmund Rubbra," *Musical Times* (Feb.-March 1945; with a list of works); Colin Mason, "Rubbra's 4 Symphonies," *Music Review* (Jan. 1941); Alan Frank, *Modern British Composers* (London, 1953; pp. 53–57).

Rubens, Paul Alfred, English composer of light music; b. London, April 29, 1875; d. Falmouth, Feb. 5, 1917. He was educated at Oxford; in 1899 he contributed some numbers to the famous musical revue *Floradora,* and this success induced him to devote himself to the composition of light operas. The following stage works by him were produced: *Lady Madcap* (1904), *Miss Hook of Holland* (1907), *My Mimosa Maid* (1908), *Dear Little Denmark* (1909), *The Balkan Princess* (1910), *The Sunshine Girl* (1912); he also wrote numerous songs and ballads.

Rubenson, Albert, Swedish composer; b. Stockholm, Dec. 20, 1826; d. there, March 2, 1901. He studied at the Leipzig Cons. (1844–48) with Ferdinand David (violin), Hauptmann (counterpoint), and Gade (composition). Returning to Stockholm, he wrote music criticism; in 1872 became inspector at the Stockholm Cons., and from 1888 till his death was its director. He wrote an overture, *Julius Cæsar;* a symph.; several orchestral suites; a string quartet; many songs. His style was derived from Mendelssohn and Schumann, but he attempted to inject some elements of Swedish folksong into his music, and in doing so contributed to the rise of musical nationalism in Sweden.

Rubin, Marcel, Austrian composer; b. Vienna, July 7, 1905. He studied piano with Richard Robert, theory of composition with Richard Stöhr and counterpoint and fugue with Franz Schmidt at the Vienna Music Academy; simultaneously attended courses in law. In 1925 he went to Paris where he took private lessons with Darius Milhaud. He was back in Vienna in 1931 to complete his studies in law, and in 1933 received his degree of Dr. juris. After the Nazi *Anschluss* of Austria in 1938, Rubin, being a non-Aryan, fled to Paris, but was interned as an enemy alien in France; after France fell in 1940, he made his way to Marseille. Convinced that only the Communists could efficiently oppose Fascism, he became a member of the illegal Austrian Communist party in exile; in 1942 he went to Mexico and remained there until 1946; he returned to Vienna in 1947. His music follows the modernistic models of Parisianized Russians and Russianized Frenchmen, with a mandatory hedonism in "new simplicity." Although Rubin studied works of Schoenberg, Berg and Anton von Webern with great assiduity and wrote articles about them, he never adopted the method of composition with 12 tones in his own music.

WORKS: comic opera, *Kleider machen Leute* (Vienna Volksoper, Dec. 14, 1973); "dance piece," *Die Stadt* (1948); 6 symphonies (1927–28, 1937, 1939, 1945, 1965, 1974); Concerto for Double Bass and Orch. (1970); Trumpet Concerto (1972); *Ballade* for orch. (1948); *Rondo-Burleske* for orch. (1960); *3 Komödianten,* for orch. (1963); Sonatina for orch. (1965); Sinfonietta for string orch. (1966); *Pastorale* for strings (1970); 3 piano sonatas (1925, 1927, 1928); String Quartet (1926; revised 1961); String Trio (1927; revised 1962); Sonatina for oboe and piano (1927); Cello Sonata (1928); *Divertimento* for piano, violin and cello (1967); *Serenade* for flute, oboe, clarinet, horn and bassoon (1971); Violin Sonata (1974); oratorio *Die Albigenser* (1957–61); song cycles to poems by Clément Marot, Guillaume Apollinaire, Rimbaud, Goethe, François Villon, etc.

BIBLIOGRAPHY: Hartmut Krones, *Marcel Rubin* (Vienna, 1975).

Rubini, Giovanni Battista, celebrated Italian tenor; b. Romano, near Bergamo, April 7, 1794; d. there, March 3, 1854. His teacher was Rosio of Bergamo; after an auspicious debut in Pavia (1814), he sang for a time in Naples; there he married (1819) a singer, **Mlle. Chomel,** known under the professional name of **La Comelli.** On Oct. 6, 1825 he sang in Paris, where he scored his first triumphs in Rossini's operas at the Théâtre-Italien; his performances of the leading parts in the operas of Bellini and Donizetti were also very successful, and there is reason to believe that Rubini's interpretations greatly contributed to the rising fame of both of those composers. Between 1831 and 1834 he sang in Paris and London; in 1843 he undertook a tour with Liszt, traveling with him in Holland and Germany; in the same year he sang in Russia with tremendous acclaim; visited Russia again in 1844; then returned to Italy, bought an estate near his native town, and remained there until his death; for some years he gave singing lessons. He publ. *12 Le-*

zioni di canto moderno per tenore o soprano and an album of 6 songs, *L'Addio.*

BIBLIOGRAPHY: C. Traini, *G. B. Rubini* (Romano, 1954).

Rubinstein, Anton, celebrated Russian composer and pianist; brother of **Nicholas Rubinstein;** b. Vykhvatinetz, Podolia, Nov. 28, 1829; d. Peterhof, near St. Petersburg, Nov. 20, 1894. He was of a family of Jewish merchants who became baptized in Berdichev in July, 1831. His mother gave him his first lessons in piano; the family moved to Moscow, where his father opened a small pencil factory. A well-known Moscow piano teacher, Alexandre Villoing, was entrusted with Rubinstein's musical education, and was in fact his only piano teacher. In 1839 Villoing took him to Paris, where Rubinstein played before Chopin and Liszt; remained in Paris until 1841; then made a concert tour in Holland, Germany, Austria, England, Norway, and Sweden, returning to Russia in 1843. Since Anton's brother Nicholas evinced a talent for composition, the brothers were taken to Berlin in 1844, where, on Meyerbeer's recommendation, Anton too studied composition, with Dehn; subsequently he made a tour through Hungary with the flutist Heindl. He returned to Russia in 1848 and settled in St. Petersburg. There he enjoyed the enlightened patronage of the Grand Duchess Helen, and wrote 3 Russian operas, *Dmitri Donskoy* (1852), *Sibirskie Okhotniki (The Siberian Hunters;* 1853), and *Fomka Durachok (Thomas the Fool;* 1853). In 1854, with the assistance of the Grand Duchess, Rubinstein undertook another tour in Western Europe. He found publishers in Berlin, and gave concerts of his own works in London and Paris, exciting admiration as both composer and pianist; on his return in 1858, he was appointed court pianist and conductor of the court concerts. He assumed the direction of the Russian Musical Society in 1859; in 1862 he founded the Imperial Cons. in St. Petersburg, remaining its director until 1867. For 20 years thereafter held no official position; from 1867 until 1870 he gave concerts in Europe, winning fame as a pianist second only to Liszt. During the season of 1872–73, he made a triumphant American tour, playing in 215 concerts, for which he was paid lavishly; appeared as soloist and jointly with the violinist Wieniawski. He produced a sensation by playing without notes, a novel procedure at the time. Returning to Europe, he elaborated a cycle of historical concerts, in programs ranging from Bach to Chopin; the last concert of a cycle he usually devoted to Russian composers. In 1887 he resumed the directorship of the St. Petersburg Cons., resigning again in 1891, when he went to Dresden (until 1894). He returned to Russia shortly before his death.

In 1890 Rubinstein established the Rubinstein Prize, an international competition open to young men between 20 and 26 years of age. Two prizes of 5,000 francs each were offered, one for composition, the other for piano playing. Quinquennial competitions were held in St. Petersburg, Berlin, Vienna, and Paris.

Rubinstein's role in Russian musical culture is of the greatest importance. He introduced European methods into education, and established high standards of artistic performance. He was the first Russian musician who was equally prominent as composer and interpreter. According to contemporary reports, his playing possessed extraordinary power (his octave passages were famous) and insight, revealed particularly in his performance of Beethoven's sonatas. His renown as a composer was scarcely less. His *Ocean Symphony* was one of the most frequently performed orchestral works in Europe and in America; his piano concertos were part of the standard repertory; his pieces for piano solo, *Melody in F, Romance, Kamennoi Ostrow,* became perennial favorites. After his death, his orchestral works all but vanished from concert programs, as did his operas (with the exception of *The Demon,* which is still performed in Russia); his piano concerto No. 4, in D minor, is occasionally heard.

WORKS: FOR THE STAGE: operas: *Dmitri Donskoy* (St. Petersburg, April 30, 1852), *Sibirskie Okhotniki (The Siberian Hunters;* 1853), *Fomka Durachok (Thomas the Fool;* St. Petersburg, May 23, 1853), *Die Kinder der Heide,* 5-act German opera (Vienna, Feb. 23, 1861), *Feramors,* after the poem *Lalla Rookh* of Th. Moore (Dresden, Feb. 24, 1863), *The Demon,* after Lermontov (St. Petersburg, Jan. 25, 1875), *Die Makkabäer* (Berlin, April 17, 1875), *Nero* (Hamburg, Nov. 1, 1879), *Kupets Kalashnikov (The Merchant Kalashnikov;* St. Petersburg, March 5, 1880), *Sulamith* and *Unter Räubern* (both performed Hamburg, Nov. 8, 1883), *Der Papagei (The Parrot;* Hamburg, 1884), *Goriusha* (St. Petersburg, Dec. 3, 1889); ballet, *Die Rebe (The Vine;* 1885). VOCAL WORKS: oratorios: *Paradise Lost* (Weimar, 1858; revised and arranged as a sacred opera, Düsseldorf, 1875), *The Tower of Babel* (Königsberg, 1870), *Moses* (1892), *Christus* (1893); 2 cantatas, *Die Nixe,* for alto solo and female chorus, and *Der Morgen,* for male chorus; scene and aria for soprano, *E dunque ver?;* 2 scenes for alto and orch., *Hecuba* and *Hagar in der Wüste;* about 100 songs (of these, *Asra* is popular). INSTRUMENTAL WORKS: for orch.: 6 symphonies (No. 2, *Ocean;* No. 4, *Dramatic;* No. 5, *Russian); Ouverture triomphale; Ouverture de concert;* 3 "character pictures": *Faust, Ivan the Terrible, Don Quixote;* a 'morceau symphonique' *La Russie;* 5 piano concertos; *Fantaisie* for piano and orch.; *Konzertstück,* for piano and orch.; Violin Concerto; 2 cello concertos; chamber music: Octet for piano, strings, and winds; Sextet for strings; Quintet for piano, flute, clarinet, horn, and bassoon; String Quintet; Piano Quintet; 10 string quartets; Piano Quartet; 5 piano trios; 2 violin sonatas; 2 cello sonatas; piano works: 4 sonatas; *Kamennoi Ostrow; Soirées à St. Petersburg; Album de Péterhof; Soirées musicales;* 6 *Barcarolles; Sérénade russe;* polkas, mazurkas, etc.

WRITINGS: *Memoirs* (St. Petersburg, 1889; in English, as *Autobiography of Anton Rubinstein,* Boston, 1890); *Music and its Representatives* (Moscow, 1891; in English, N.Y., 1892; also publ. as *A Conversation on Music); Leitfaden zum richtigen Gebrauch des Pianoforte-Pedals* (posthumous; Leipzig, 1896; in French, Brussels, 1899); *Gedankenkorb, Litterarischer Nachlass* (posthumous; Stuttgart, 1896); *Die Meister des Klaviers* (posthumous; Berlin, 1899).

BIBLIOGRAPHY: A. McArthur, *Anton Rubinstein* (London, 1889); E. Zabel, *Anton Rubinstein* (Leipzig, 1892); A. Soubies, *Anton Rubinstein* (Paris, 1895); I.

Martinov, *Épisodes de la vie de Rubinstein* (Brussels, 1895); J. Rodenberg, "Meine persönlichen Erinnerungen an Anton Rubinstein, nebst Briefen," *Deutsche Rundschau* 21 (Berlin, 1895; in English in *Music 8,* Chicago, 1905); E. Wessel, *Some Explanations, Hints and Remarks of Anton Rubinstein from his Lessons in the St. Petersburg Cons.* (St. Petersburg, 1901; in German, Leipzig, 1904); N. Findeisen, *Anton Rubinstein* (Moscow, 1907); La Mara, *Anton Rubinstein,* in the series, *Musikalische Studienköpfe* (vol. 3, 7th ed., Leipzig, 1909; separately, Leipzig, 1911); N. Bernstein, *Anton Rubinstein* (Leipzig, 1911); A. Hervey, *Anton Rubinstein* (London, 1913); K. Preiss, *Anton Rubinsteins pianistische Bedeutung* (Leipzig, 1914); Igor Glebov, *Anton Rubinstein in His Musical Activities and Opinions of His Contemporaries* (Moscow, 1929); C. D. Bowen, *"Free Artist": The Story of Anton and Nicholas Rubinstein* (N.Y., 1939; fictionalized account, but accurate as to actual events; with a complete list of works and a detailed bibliography, compiled by Otto E. Albrecht); O. Bennigsen, "The Brothers Rubinstein and Their Circle," *Musical Quarterly* (Oct. 1939); L. Barenboym, *A. G. Rubinstein,* vol. I (Moscow, 1957).

Rubinstein, Artur, celebrated pianist; b. Lódź, Poland, Jan. 28, 1887. He performed in public at a very early age; after taking lessons with A. Różycki in Warsaw, he was sent to Berlin, where he studied with Heinrich Barth (piano) and with Robert Kahn and Max Bruch (theory). He made his European debut playing a Mozart concerto in Berlin, with Joachim as conductor; then toured in Russia with Koussevitzky's orch. In 1906 he made his American debut with the Philadelphia Orch. During World War I he played recitals in England with Eugène Ysaÿe; in 1916 toured Spain, and later gave concerts in South America. In 1932 he married a daughter of Emil Mlynarski. Rubinstein is one of the finest interpreters of Chopin's music, for which his fiery temperament and poetic lyricism are particularly suitable. After his concerts in Spain and South America, he became one of the most ardent exponents of Spanish music. His popularity with audiences continued through the last decades of his career; he was equally successful in France, Spain, the U.S., and South America, appearing in recitals and with major symph. orchestras. His style of playing tends towards bravura in Classical compositions, but he rarely indulges in mannerisms. He appeared in several films made in Hollywood, as pianist, representing himself. In 1946 he became an American citizen. He published an autobiography, *My Young Years* (N.Y., 1973). On April 1, 1976 he received the U.S. Medal of Freedom, the highest honor awarded to a civilian, presented by President Ford. His 90th birthday was celebrated in 1977.

BIBLIOGRAPHY: B. Gavoty, *Artur Rubinstein* (Geneva, 1955; in English, 1956).

Rubinstein, Beryl, American pianist and composer; b. Athens, Ga., Oct. 26, 1898; d. Cleveland, Dec. 29, 1952. He studied piano with his father and Alexander Lambert; toured the U.S. as a child (1905–11); then went to Berlin to study with Busoni and Vianna da Motta. He was appointed to the faculty of the Cleveland Institute of Music in 1921; became its director in 1932. He wrote an opera, *The Sleeping Beauty,* to a libretto by John Erskine (Juilliard School of Music, N.Y., Jan. 19, 1938); 32 piano studies; 3 dances for piano; transcriptions from Gershwin's *Porgy and Bess.* He conducted his orchestral *Scherzo* with the Cleveland Orch. on March 17, 1927; performed his Piano Concerto in C with the same orch. on Nov. 12, 1936.

Rubinstein, Joseph, Russian pianist; b. Starokonstantinov, Feb. 8, 1847; d. (committed suicide) Lucerne, Sept. 15, 1884. He studied in Vienna with Dachs; later took lessons with Liszt in Weimar. He was an ardent admirer of Wagner, whom he knew personally; in 1874 he was the pianist at the preliminary rehearsals of *Der Ring des Nibelungen* at Bayreuth; made piano transcriptions of it and also of *Parsifal.*

Rubinstein, Nicolai, Russian pianist and pedagogue; brother of **Anton Rubinstein;** b. Moscow, June 14, 1835; d. March 23, 1881. He began to study piano with his mother at the age of 4, when his brother, 6 years older than he, was already on the road to fame as a child prodigy; was taken to Berlin with his brother, and there studied with Kullak (piano) and Dehn (composition). The brothers met Mendelssohn and Meyerbeer; returning to Moscow in 1846, he began to take lessons with Alexandre Villoing. He also studied law, and received a degree from the Univ. of Moscow (1855); subsequently was a minor functionary in the government; earned his living by giving private lessons. In 1858 he began his concert career; appeared in Russia, and also in London. In 1859, when he was only 24 years old, he became head of the Moscow branch of the Russian Music Society; in 1866 this Society opened the Moscow Cons., of which Nicolai Rubinstein was director until his death. From 1860 he was the regular conductor of the Moscow concerts of the Imperial Russian Musical Society. In 1878 he conducted 4 Russian concerts at the Paris Exposition; at the first and the fourth of the series he performed Tchaikovsky's Piano Concerto No. 1 (which he had criticized so sharply when Tchaikovsky first submitted it to him in 1874). Anton Rubinstein declared that Nicolai was a better pianist than himself, but this generous appreciation was not accepted by the public. As an educator, however, Nicolai Rubinstein played perhaps a greater role than his famous brother. Among his pupils were Taneyev, Siloti, and Emil Sauer.

BIBLIOGRAPHY: N. Findeisen, "Nicolai Rubinstein," *Russkaya Muzÿkalnaya Gazeta* 10 (1901); C. D. Bowen, *"Free Artist": The Story of Anton and Nicholas Rubinstein* (N.Y., 1939); Olga Bennigsen, "The Brothers Rubinstein and Their Circle," *Musical Quarterly* (Oct. 1939).

Rubio Piqueras, Felipe, Spanish musicologist; b. Valera de Arriba, Sept. 13, 1881; d. Toledo, 1936. He was ordained priest in 1904, and served as organist at the Cathedral of Badajoz until 1917; then went to Toledo as church organist. He publ. valuable works on music in Toledo: *Códices polifónicos toledanos* and *Música y Músicos toledanos* (1923); wrote some church music.

Rûbner, Cornelius. See **Rybner, Cornelius.**

Rubsamen, Walter (Howard), renowned American musicologist; b. New York, July 21, 1911; d. Los Angeles, June 19, 1973. He studied flute with Georges Barrère in N.Y.; musicology at Columbia Univ. with Paul Henry Lang (B.A., 1933); then went to Germany, where he attended classes of Otto Ursprung and Rudolph von Ficker at the Univ. of Munich; received his doctorate there with the dissertation *Pierre de la Rue als Messenkomponist* (1937). Returning to the U.S. he was appointed to the music faculty at the Univ. of California, Los Angeles, obtaining full professorship in 1955; in 1965 he was appointed chairman of the music dept. there, remaining in this capacity until his death.
WRITINGS: *Literary Sources of Secular Music in Italy c. 1500* (Berkeley, Calif., 1943; reprint, N.Y., 1972); *Chanson and Madrigal, 1480-1530* (with D. Heartz and H. M. Brown; Cambridge, Mass., 1964); "Mr. Seedo, Ballad Opera and the Singspiel," in *Miscelánea en Homenaje a Mons. Higinio Anglés* (Barcelona, 1958–61); he edited *Opera Omnia* of Pierre de La Rue for the American Institute of Musicology and brought out a German 16th-century *Magnificat on Christmas Carols* (N.Y., 1971); contributed a number of informative articles on ballad opera in England and on Renaissance composers to various American and European publications.

Rückauf, Anton, outstanding composer of German songs; b. Prague, March 13, 1855; d. Schloss Alt-Erla, Austria, Sept. 19, 1903. He studied with Proksch in Prague and with Nottebohm and Nawrátil in Vienna; published about 80 songs, which were made popular by the singer Gustav Walter at his recitals, with Rückauf himself at the piano; he also wrote an opera *Die Rosenthalerin*, which was produced in Dresden in 1897.

Ruckers, Hans, known as "the eldest" of the family of celebrated Flemish harpsichord makers; b. Mechlin, c.1550; d. Antwerp, c.1598. He was the first of the family to make instruments; in 1579 was admitted to the Guild of St. Luke. His second son, **Hans Ruckers,** also known as **Jean** (baptized Antwerp, Jan. 15, 1578; d. there, early in 1643) was greatly esteemed by his contemporaries, and was exempted from Civic Guard duties in appreciation of his artistry. **Andreas Ruckers** the elder (baptized Antwerp, Aug. 30, 1579; d. c.1654) manufactured harpsichords between 1601 and 1644. **Andreas Ruckers** the younger, son of the elder Andreas (baptized Antwerp, March 31, 1607; d. after 1667), made instruments between 1637 and 1667. Another member of the same family was **Christoffel Ruckers,** who flourished about 1600. He constructed 2 virginals.
BIBLIOGRAPHY: For a list of surviving instruments and other particulars, see Donald H. Boalch, *Makers of the Harpsichord and Clavichord, 1440 to 1840* (N.Y., 1956); also, Georg Kinsky, "Die Familie Ruckers, *Zeitschrift für Musikwissenschaft* IV; André M. Pols, *De Ruckers en de klavierbouw in Vlaanderen* (Antwerp, 1942); J. Lambrechts-Douillez, "Documents Dealing with the Ruckers Family and Antwerp Harpsichord-Building," in E. M. Ripin, *Keyboard Instruments* (Edinburgh, 1971).

Rüdel, Hugo, German horn player and choral conductor; b. Havelberg, Feb. 7, 1868; d. Berlin, Nov. 27, 1934. He studied in Berlin, and was engaged as horn player in the orchestra of the Berlin Opera; in 1906 he became choral conductor at the Bayreuth Festivals; in 1909 he took over the famous Domchor, in Berlin; also conducted other singing societies.

Rudel, Julius, outstanding Austrian-American conductor; b. Vienna, March 6, 1921. He studied at the Vienna Academy of Music; in 1938 emigrated to the U.S. (naturalized citizen, 1944). In 1943 he made his American debut as conductor of the N.Y. City Opera; in 1957 became its music director. He also appeared as guest conductor of the Philadelphia Orch. and of several operatic companies; received numerous awards from American cultural organizations. In 1961 the Austrian government bestowed on him honorary insignia for arts and sciences. He championed the cause of American opera; gave first performances of several new stage works by American composers.
BIBLIOGRAPHY: *Current Biography* for July 1965.

Rudersdorff, Hermine, Russian dramatic soprano; b. Ivanovsky, Ukraine, Dec. 12, 1822; d. Boston, Feb. 26, 1882. A pupil of Bordogni at Paris and of Micherout at Milan, she sang at first in Germany (1840–54); then in London (1854–65). Engaged at the Boston Jubilee of 1869, she settled in Boston, becoming renowned as a teacher (Emma Thursby was her pupil). In 1844 she married Dr. Küchenmeister, from whom she was divorced, then married in 1850 an English merchant, Maurice Mansfield. Their son was the famous actor, Richard Mansfield (1857–1907).

Rudhyar, Dane, American composer, painter and mystical philosopher; b. Paris, March 23, 1895. His parental name was **Daniel Chennevière;** he changed it in 1917 to Rudhyar, derived from an old Sanskrit root conveying the sense of dynamic action and the color red, astrologically related to the Zodiacal sign of his birth and the red-colored planet Mars. He studied philosophy at the Sorbonne, in Paris, receiving his baccalauréat in 1911, and took music courses at the Paris Cons. In composition he was largely self-taught; he also achieved a certain degree of proficiency as a pianist; developed a technique which he called "orchestral pianism." In 1913 the French publisher Durand commissioned him to write a short book on Debussy, with whom he briefly corresponded. At the same time he joined the modern artistic circles in Paris. In 1916 he went to America; became a naturalized American citizen in 1926. His "dance poems" for orch., *Poèmes ironiques* and *Vision végétale,* were performed at the Metropolitan Opera House, N.Y., April 4, 1917. In 1918 he visited Canada; in Montreal he met the pianist Alfred Laliberté, who was closely associated with Scriabin, and through him Rudhyar became acquainted with Scriabin's theosophic ideas. In Canada he also published a collection of French poems, *Rapsodies* (Toronto, 1918). In 1920 he went to Hollywood to write scenic music for the *Pilgrimage Play, The Life*

of Christ, and also acted the part of Christ in the prologue of the silent film version of *The Ten Commandments* produced by Cecil B. DeMille. In Hollywood he
initiated the project of "Introfilms" depicting inner
psychological states on the screen through a series of
images, but it failed to receive support and was abandoned. Between 1922 and 1930 he lived part-time in
Hollywood and part-time in N.Y.; he was one of the
founding members of the International Composers
Guild in N.Y. In 1922 his orchestral tone poem *Soul
Fire* won the $1000 prize of the Los Angeles Philhar-
monic; in 1928 his book *The Rebirth of Hindu Music*
was published in Madras, India. After 1930 Rudhyar
devoted most of his time to astrology. His first book
on the subject, *The Astrology of Personality*, was published in 1936 and became a standard text in the field;
it was described by the pioneer in the publishing of
popular astrological magazines, Paul Clancy, as "the
greatest step forward in astrology since the time of
Ptolemy." A new development in Rudhyar's creative
activities took place in 1938 when he began to paint,
along nonrepresentational symbolistic lines; the titles
of his paintings (*Mystic Tiara, Cosmic Seeds, Soul
and Ego, Avatar,* etc.) reflect theosophic themes. His
preoccupations with astrology left him little time for
music; about 1965 he undertook a radical revision of
some early compositions, and wrote several new ones;
in 1978 he lived in Palo Alto, California, and continued an active schedule of lecturing.

The natural medium for Rudhyar's musical expression is the piano; his few symphonic works are mostly
orchestrations of original piano compositions. In his
writing for piano Rudhyar builds sonorous chordal
formations supported by resonant pedal points, occasionally verging on polytonality; a kinship with Scriabin's piano music is clearly felt, but Rudhyar's harmonic idiom is free from Scriabin's Wagnerian
antecedents. Despite his study of oriental religions
and music, Rudhyar does not attempt to make use of
eastern modalities in his own music.
WORKS: FOR ORCH.: *3 Poèmes ironiques* (1914);
Vision végétale (1914); *The Warrior,* symph. poem for
piano and orch. (1921; performed 55 years later, Palo
Alto, Dec. 10, 1976); *Sinfonietta* (1927); *Syntonies* in 5
sections: *To the Real* (1920), *The Surge of Fire* (1921),
Ouranos (1927), *The Human Way* (1927); *Tripthong*
for piano and orch. (1948; revised, 1977); *Thresholds*
(1954). CHAMBER MUSIC: *3 Melodies* for flute, cello and
piano (1919); *3 Poems* for violin and piano (1920);
Solitude for string quartet (1950); Piano Quintet
(1950); *Barcarolle* for violin and piano (1955). SONGS:
3 Chansons de Bilitis (1919); *3 Poèmes tragiques*
(1918); *3 Invocations* (1939). FOR PIANO: *3 Poèmes*
(1913); *Mosaics,* a tone cycle in 8 movements on the
life of Christ (1918); *Syntony* (1920–54; revised 1968);
3 Paeans (1925); *Granites* (1929); *9 Tetragrams*
(1920–67); *Pentagrams* (1924–26); *Transmutation*
(1976); *Theurgy* (1976).
WRITINGS: *Claude Debussy* (Paris, 1913); *Art as
Release of Power* (N.Y., 1930); *The Astrology of Personality* (N.Y., 1936; revised, 1970); *The Practice of
Astrology* (Amsterdam, 1967; N.Y., 1970); *The Plane-
tarization of Consciousness* (Amsterdam, 1970; N.Y.,
1972); *The Astrological Houses* (N.Y., 1972).
BIBLIOGRAPHY: Paul Rosenfeld, *An Hour with
American Music* (N.Y., 1929; pp. 71–78); A. Morang,
Dane Rudhyar, Pioneer in Creative Synthesis (N.Y.,
1939); *Dane Rudhyar. A Brief Biography* (Berkeley,
Calif., 1972); a special issue of the magazine *Human
Dimensions,* dedicated to Rudhyar (Buffalo, N.Y.,
1975).

Rüdinger, Gottfried, German composer; b. Lindau,
Aug. 23, 1886; d. Gauting, near Munich, Jan. 17, 1946.
He was a student in theology; at the same time he
took courses in composition with Max Reger at the
Leipzig Cons. (1907–09); in 1910 he settled in Munich
where he taught at the Academy. He composed industriously in many genres; brought out a "peasant play-
opera," *Tegernseer im Himmel* and the children's operas *Benchtesgadener Sagenspiel, Musikanten-
komödie, König Folkwart,* etc.; wrote much choral
and chamber music; his pieces for small brass ensembles, in the style of old townpiper music, are especially attractive; he also brought out a number of instructive piano pieces.

Rudnick, Wilhelm, German organist and composer;
b. Damerkow, Dec. 30, 1850; d. there, Aug. 7, 1927. He
studied at Kullak's Akademie der Tonkunst in Berlin;
subsequently occupied various posts as church organist in Landsberg and Liegnitz; was also active as choral conductor. He wrote numerous organ works of excellent quality; a fantasy on *Ein' feste Burg, Trinitatis-
Sonate, Pfingsten-Sonate, Konzert-Phantasie, Choralvorspiele;* vocal works.

Rudnicki, Marian Teofil, Polish conductor and composer; b. Cracow, March 7, 1888; d. Warsaw, Dec. 31,
1944. He conducted operetta in Cracow (1916–19) and
later at the Warsaw Municipal Opera. He wrote
mostly theater music; also composed choral works
and solo songs.

Rudnytsky, Antin, Polish pianist, conductor, and
composer; b. Luka, Galicia, Feb. 7, 1902; d. Toms
River, New Jersey, Nov. 30, 1975. He studied piano
with Schnabel and Petri in Berlin, composition with
Schreker and musicology with Curt Sachs; received
his Dr. phil. at the Univ. of Berlin in 1926. In 1927 he
went to Russia where he conducted opera in Kharkov
and Kiev; then was again in Poland, as conductor of
the Muncipal Opera in Lwow (1932–37). In 1937 he
emigrated to the U.S.; toured with his wife, the singer
Maris Sokil, as her piano accompanist. He composed
3 symphonies (1936, 1941, 1942); a cello concerto
(1942); an opera, *Dovbush* (1937); some ballet music,
and miscellaneous pieces for instrumental ensembles
and piano works.

Rudolf, Max, eminent German conductor; b. Frankfurt, June 15, 1902. He studied piano with Eduard
Jung and composition with Bernhard Sekles at the
Hoch Cons. in Frankfurt; was employed as coach and
conductor in various provincial opera houses in Germany; then was active as conductor in Prague
(1929–35); in 1935 he went to Göteborg, Sweden,
where he served as a regular guest conductor with the
Göteborg Symph. Orch., the Swedish Broadcasting
Co., and director of the Oratorio Society. In 1940 he
emigrated to the U.S.; became naturalized as an

American citizen in 1946. In 1945 he joined the conductorial staff of the Metropolitan Opera Co., N.Y., and a year later became a member of its management; gave many distinguished performances of standard operas. In 1958 he was appointed principal conductor and music director of the Cincinnati Symph. Orch., and took it on a world tour in 1966, and on a European tour in 1969; from 1963 to 1970 was the musical director of the Cincinnati May Festival; in 1970 he moved to Philadelphia where he conducted the opera class at the Curtis Institute of Music (until 1973). In 1976 he was appointed musical adviser to the New Jersey Symph. Orch. He published *The Grammar of Conducting* (N.Y., 1950), which also appeared in a Japanese translation.

Rudorff, Ernst Friedrich Karl, German pianist; b. Berlin, Jan. 18, 1840; d. there, Dec. 31, 1916. He studied with Bargiel in Berlin and with Moscheles, Plaidy, and Reinecke in Leipzig. After a few years of teaching in Cologne (1865–68), he was appointed head of the piano dept. at the Hochschule für Musik in Berlin, and held this post for 41 years (1869–1910). He was a friend of Brahms, whose letters to him were publ. in vol. III of the Brahms correspondence (Berlin, 1907); Rudorff's correspondence with Joachim was publ. in vol. III of *Briefe von und an Joseph Joachim* (1913). He composed 3 symphonies; piano pieces.
BIBLIOGRAPHY: Elisabeth Rudorff, ed., *Aus den Tagen der Romantik, Bildnis einer deutschen Familie* (Leipzig, 1938).

Rudziński, Witold, Polish composer; b. Siebież, Lithuania, March 14, 1913. He studied piano at the Cons. of Vilna (1931–36); went to Paris, where he took composition lessons with Nadia Boulanger and Charles Koechlin (1938–39); upon return, he taught at the Vilna Cons. (1939–42) and the Lódź Cons. (1945–47); settled in Warsaw and became active mainly as a musical administrator and pedagogue; in 1957 became a member of the faculty of the Superior School of Music in Warsaw.
WORKS: 5 operas: *Janko Muzykant (Janko the Musician,* 1948–51; Bytom, June 20, 1953), *Komendant Paryza (The Commander of Paris,* 1955–58; Poznań, 1960), *Odprawa poslów greckich (The Departure of Greek Emissaries;* Cracow, 1962), *Sulamita (The Shulamite,* 1964) and *Chlopi (The Peasants,* 1972; Warsaw, June 30, 1974); 2 oratorios: *Gaude Mater Polonia* for narrator, 3 soloists, chorus and orch. (1966) and *Lipce* for chorus and chamber orch. (1968); a cantata, *Chlopska droga (Peasants' Road,* 1952); *Dach świata (The Roof of the World)* for narrator and orch. (1960); *The Nike of the Vistula,* war ballads and scenes for narrator, 4 soloists, chorus and orch. (1973); Piano Concerto (1936); 2 symphonies (1938, 1944); *Divertimento* for string orch. (1940); *Uwertura baltycka (Baltic Overture,* 1948); *Parades,* suite for orch. (1958); *Music Concertante* for piano and chamber orch. (1959); *Musica profana* for flute, clarinet, trumpet and strings (1960); *Obrazy Świętokrzyskie (Pictures from the Holy-Cross Moutains)* for orch. (1965); Concerto Grosso for percussion and 2 string orch. (1970; Poznań, March 29, 1973); *Uwertura Góralska (Mountain Overture)* for orch. (1970); Trio for

flute, oboe and piano (1934); Clarinet Sonatina (1935); 2 string quartets (1935, 1943); Violin Sonata (1937); Viola Sonata (1946); Nonet (1947); Quintet for flute and strings (1954); *Deux portraits de femmes* for solo voice and string quartet (1960); *Variations and Fugue* for percussion (1966); *Preludes* for clarinet, viola, harp and percussion (1967); *Polonaise-Rapsodie* for cello and piano (1969); *Fantazja Góralska (Mountain Fantasia)* for guitar (1970); *To Citizen John Brown,* concertino for soprano, flute, horn, cello, piano and percussion (1972); *Proverbia latina* for harpsichord (1974); *Suite* for 2 pianos (1937); songs. He published a biography of Moniuszko in 2 vols. (Cracow, 1955, 1961) and *The Technique of Béla Bartók* (Cracow, 1965).

Rudziński, Zbigniew, Polish composer; b. Czechowice, Oct. 23, 1935. He studied composition with Perkowski at the Warsaw State College of Music (1956–62); traveled to Paris on a French government grant (1965–66); upon return to Poland, was music director of the Warsaw Documentary Film Studio (1960–67).
WORKS: Sonata for 2 string quartets, piano and kettledrums (1960); *4 Songs* for baritone and chamber ensemble (1961); *Epigrams* for flute, 2 female choruses and 6 percussionists (1962); *Contra Fidem* for orch. (1964); String Trio (1964); *Study in C* for variable ensemble (1964); *Moments Musicaux I, II and III* for orch. (1965, 1967, 1968); *Impromptu* for 2 pianos, 3 cellos and percussion (1966); Symph. for textless bass, chorus and orch. with strings (1969); Quartet for 2 pianos and percussionists (1969); *Muzyka noca (Night Music)* for chamber orch. (1970); *Requiem* for narrator, chorus and orch. (1971); *Tutti e solo* for soprano, flute, horn and piano (1973); Piano Sonata (1975).

Ruelle, Charles Émile, French musicologist, authority on Greek music; b. Paris, Oct. 24, 1833; d. there, Oct. 15, 1912. He was chief librarian of the Bibliothèque de Ste.-Geneviève, Paris, from 1898 to 1905; translated into French the treatises of Aristoxenus (1871), Nicomachus (1881), etc.; publ. the valuable treatises *Études sur l'ancienne musique grecque* (1875 and 1900); *Le Monocorde* (1891); *Sextus Empiricus* (1899); *De la musique des Grecs modernes et en particulier de leur musique ecclésiastique* (1876); contributed to the *Dictionnaire des antiquités grecques.*

Rufer, Josef, Austrian music scholar; b. Vienna, Dec. 18, 1893. He studied composition with Zemlinsky and Schoenberg in Vienna (1919–22); later was assistant to Schoenberg at the Prussian Academy of Arts in Berlin; from 1929 was also active as a music critic. From 1947 to 1950 he edited (with Stuckenschmidt) the monthly music magazine *Stimmen;* then was teacher of theory and 12-tone method of composition at the Hochschule für Musik in Berlin (1956–69). He published a number of valuable books dealing with 12-tone music: *Die Komposition mit zwölf Tönen* (Berlin, 1952; English translation by Humphrey Searle as *Composition with 12 Notes Related Only to One Another,* London, 1954); *Musiker über Musik* (Darmstadt, 1955), and, most importantly, an annotated catalogue of Schoenberg's works *Das Werk Arnold Schönbergs* (Kassel, 1959; in English, *The Works of Arnold Schoenberg;* London, 1962).

Rüfer, Philippe (-Barthélemy), German pianist and composer; b. Liège, June 7, 1844 (of German parents); d. Berlin, Sept. 15, 1919. He studied at the Cons. of Liège; in 1871, settled in Berlin, where he taught piano at Stern's Cons., Kullak's Akademie der Tonkunst, and (from 1881) at Scharwenka's. He wrote the operas *Merlin* (Berlin, Feb. 28, 1887) and *Ingo* (Berlin, Feb. 1896); a symphony; 3 overtures; piano music; songs.

BIBLIOGRAPHY: P. Magnette, *Philippe Rüfer. Étude biographique et critique* (Liège, 1910).

Ruff, Willie, American jazz musician; b. Sheffield, Alabama, Jan. 9, 1931. He studied at Yale Univ. (M.M., 1954); played the French horn and string bass. He formed a duo with pianist Dwike Mitchell, and together they filled a series of highly successful engagements in intellectual nightclubs. In 1959 they gave a series of jazz concerts in Russia, triumphantly overriding Soviet scruples regarding the allegedly decadent nature of jazz, and scoring a popular success. They were equally triumphant as part of President Johnson's goodwill entourage to Mexico in April 1966.

Ruffo, Titta, famous Italian baritone; b. Pisa, June 9, 1877; d. Florence, July 5, 1953. His real name was **Ruffo Cafiero Titta,** but he found it convenient to transpose his first and last names for professional purposes. He studied with Persichini at the Santa Cecilia in Rome, then with Cassini in Milan. He made his operatic debut in Rome as the Herald in *Lohengrin* (1898); then sang in Rio de Janeiro; returning to Italy, he appeared in all the principal theaters; also sang in Vienna, Paris, and London. He made his American debut in Philadelphia as Rigoletto (Nov. 4, 1912) with the combined Philadelphia-Chicago Opera Co.; 1st appearance with the Metropolitan Opera, as Figaro in *Il Barbiere di Siviglia* (N.Y., Jan. 19, 1922). He left the Metropolitan in 1929 and returned to Rome. In 1937 he was briefly under arrest for opposing the Mussolini regime; then went to Florence, where he remained until his death. He publ. a book of memoirs, *La mia parabola* (Milan, 1937).

BIBLIOGRAPHY: M. A. Barrenechea, *Titta Ruffo; notas de psicología artística* (Buenos Aires, 1911).

Ruggi, Francesco, Italian composer, b. Naples, Oct. 21, 1767; d. there, Jan. 23, 1845. He studied at the Cons. di S. Loreto in Naples under Fenaroli; became prof. of composition at the Cons. di San Pietro a Maiella; Bellini and Carafa were his pupils there. He wrote the operas *L'Ombra di Nino* (Naples, 1795), *La Guerra aperta* (Naples, 1796), and *Sofì tripponi* (Milan, 1804); much sacred music.

Ruggles, Carl (real Christian names **Charles Sprague**), remarkable American composer; b. Marion, Massachusetts, March 11, 1876; d. Bennington, Vermont, Oct. 24, 1971. He learned to play violin as a child; then went to Boston where he took violin lessons with Felix Winternitz and theory with Josef Claus; later enrolled as a special student at Harvard Univ., where he attended composition classes of John Knowles Paine. Impressed with the widely assumed supremacy of the German school of composition (of which Paine was a notable representative), Ruggles germanized his given name from Charles to Carl. In 1907 he went to Minnesota, where he organized the Winona Symph. Orch. and conducted it for several years (1908–12). In 1917 he went to New York, where he became active in promotion of modern music; was a member of the International Composers Guild and of the Pan American Association of Composers. He wrote relatively few works, which he was in the habit of constantly revising and rearranging, and they were mostly in small forms. He did not follow any particular modern method of composition, but instinctively avoided needless repetition of thematic notes, which made his melodic progressions atonal; his use of dissonances, at times quite strident, derived from the linear proceedings of chromatically inflected counterpoint. A certain similarity resulted from this process with the 12-tone method of composition of Schoenberg, but Ruggles never adopted it explicitly. In his sources of inspiration, he reached for spiritual exaltation with mystic connotations, scaling the heights and plumbing the depths of musical expression. Such music could not attract large groups of listeners and repelled some critics; one of them remarked that the title of *Sun-Treader* of Ruggles ought to be changed to "Latrine-Treader." Unable and unwilling to withstand the prevailing musical mores, Ruggles removed himself from the musical scene; he went to live on his farm in Arlington, Vermont, and devoted himself exclusively to his avocation, painting; his pictures, mostly in the manner of abstract expressionism, were occasionally exhibited in New York galleries. In 1966 he moved to a nursing home in Bennington, Vermont, where he died at the age of 95. A striking revival of interest in his music took place during the last years of his life, and his name began to appear with increasing frequency on the programs of American orchestras and chamber music groups. His manuscripts were recovered and published; virtually all of his compositions have been recorded.

WORKS: *Men and Angels,* symph. suite for 5 trumpets and bass trumpet (N.Y., Dec. 17, 1922; revised for brass instruments or strings and renamed *Angels*); *Men and Mountains,* symph. suite in 3 movements: *Men, Lilacs, Marching Mountains* (N.Y., Dec. 7, 1924; revised for larger orch.; N.Y., March 19, 1936); *Portals* for string orch. (N.Y., Jan. 24, 1926); *Sun-Treader,* after Browning, for large orch. (Paris, Feb. 25, 1932); *Polyphonic Composition* for 3 pianos (1940); *Evocations,* piano suite (1945; an orchestral version was performed, N.Y., Feb. 3, 1971); *Organum,* for large orch. (N.Y., Nov. 24, 1949); song cycle, *Vox clamans in deserto* for voice and chamber orch. (1923); *Exaltation* for "congregation in unison" and organ (1958); *Symphonia dialectica* for orch., begun in 1923, remained unfinished.

BIBLIOGRAPHY: Paul Rosenfeld, *An Hour with American Music* (N.Y., 1929; pp. 101–06); Charles Seeger, "Carl Ruggles," *Musical Quarterly* (Oct. 1932); Lou Harrison, "Carl Ruggles," *Score* (June 1955); Lou Harrison, *About Carl Ruggles* (Yonkers,

N.Y., 1946); John Kirkpatrick, "The Evolution of Carl Ruggles. A Chronicle Largely in His Own Words," *Perspectives of New Music* (1967/68).

Rühlmann, (Adolf) Julius, German writer on music; b. Dresden, Feb. 28, 1816; d. there, Oct. 27, 1877. He played the trombone in the court orch. of Dresden, where he founded the Dresden Tonkünstlerverein (1855); taught piano and music history at the Dresden Cons. He prepared a valuable *Geschichte der Bogeninstrumente,* which was publ. posthumously by his son, Richard Rühlmann (1882); he also wrote *Die Urform der Bogeninstrumente* (1874).

Rühlmann, Frans, Belgian conductor; b. Brussels, Jan. 11, 1868; d. Paris, June 8, 1948. He studied at the Cons. of Brussels; filled engagements as conductor at the Théâtre de la Monnaie in Brussels, and also in Liège, Antwerp, etc. In 1905 he was engaged at the Opéra-Comique in Paris; in 1914 conducted at the Paris Opéra; also led a series of popular concerts in Antwerp.

Rühlmann, Franz, German musicologist; b. Chemnitz, Dec. 7, 1896; d. in a camp for prisoners of war, Landsberg (Gorzów Wielkopolski, in northwestern Poland), June 15, 1945. He was in the German army in both wars; studied in Leipzig with Kiel; Dr. phil., 1924, with the dissertation, *Richard Wagner und die deutsche Opernbühne;* was instructor of theater music at the Hochschule für Musik in Berlin (from 1933). He brought out vocal scores of *Der Freischütz,* Mozart's *Requiem,* Gluck's operas, etc.

Ruiter, Wim de, Dutch composer and organist; b. Heemstede, Aug. 11, 1943. He studied organ with Piet Kee in Amsterdam (1963–69) and composition with Ton de Leeuw there (1968–74); taught 20th-century music theory at the Cons. in Zwolle (1973–77) and at the Sweelinck Cons. (formerly Amsterdam Cons.) since 1973. With another Dutch organist he gave successful concerts of duo-organ music, 4-hands, 4-feet.
WORKS: *Solo* for flute (1969); *Music* for 2 double basses (1969); Quartet for 2 violas and 2 cellos (1970); Quartet for flute, bass clarinet, vibraphone and piano (1970); *Two Quartets Together* (1970; a joining together of the previous 2 quartets); *Situations* for 16 voices (1970); 2 string quartets (1972, 1974); *Hoplopoia* for chorus and orch. (1973); *Re* for orch. (Utrecht, Sept. 14, 1975); *Thick & Thin* for organ, 4-hands, 4-feet (1975); *Tall & Small* for treble recorder (1975); *Off & On* for 4 bass clarinets (1976); *To be or not to be* for 12 wind instruments and vibraphone (1976); Quintet for 5 flutes and tape (1976; in collaboration with Jacques Bank); Quartet for recorders (1977); *3 Pieces* for orch. (1977).

Rummel, Christian, German composer and conductor; b. Brichsenstadt, Nov. 27, 1787; d. Wiesbaden, Feb. 13, 1849. He was an able performer on the piano, violin, and clarinet; served as municipal conductor in Wiesbaden from 1815 until 1841; publ. a clarinet concerto, 2 quintets, etc. His son **Joseph Rummel** (b. Wiesbaden, Oct. 6, 1818; d. London, March 25, 1880) was court pianist to the Duke of Nassau, and publ.

piano music; another son, **August Rummel** (b. Wiesbaden, Jan. 14, 1824; d. London, Dec. 14, 1886), also was a good pianist.

Rummel, Franz, pianist, son of **Joseph Rummel,** grandson of **Christian Rummel;** b. London, Jan. 11, 1853; d. Berlin, May 2, 1901. He studied with Louis Brassin at the Brussels Cons., winning the 1st prize in 1872; toured in America 3 times (1878, 1886, 1898). He married a daughter of S. F. B. Morse, inventor of the telegraph.

Rummel, Walter Morse, distinguished pianist, son of **Franz Rummel,** and grandson of S. F. B. Morse, inventor of the telegraph; b. Berlin, July 19, 1887; d. Bordeaux, May 2, 1953. He studied piano with Leopold Godowsky, and composition with Hugo Kaun. In 1908 he went to Paris, where he became acquainted with Debussy, and devoted himself to promoting Debussy's piano works, of which he became a foremost interpreter. He was married twice, to the pianist **Thérèse Chaigneau,** with whom he appeared in 2-piano recitals (later divorced), and to Sarah Harrington (also divorced).

Runciman, John F., English music critic; b. 1866; d. London, April 7, 1916. He was a church organist before he joined the staff of the *Saturday Review* in London, 1894, as music critic; held this position till his death; also was editor of *The Chord* (quarterly) and the *Musician's Library.* His critical reviews were remarkable for their unabashed violence in denouncing composers and performers whom he did not like; on some occasions he became involved in libel suits. He publ. selected essays in 1899 under the title of *Old Scores and New Readings,* a biographical study of Haydn (1908), one of Purcell (1909), and *Richard Wagner, Composer of Operas* (1913).

Rung, Frederik, Danish composer, son of **Henrik Rung;** b. Copenhagen, June 14, 1854; d. there, Jan. 22, 1914. He studied with his father; became conductor at the Copenhagen Opera (1884); also led the Cecilia Society (founded by his father); taught at the Copenhagen Cons. from 1881 till 1893.
WORKS: the operas: *Det hemmelige Selskab (The Secret Party;* Copenhagen, Feb. 9, 1888) and *Den trekantede Hat (The Three-cornered Hat;* Copenhagen, Nov. 7, 1894); Symph.; Rhapsody for orch.; *Danse des papillons* for orch.; Serenade for 9 instruments; Piano Quintet; 2 string quartets; Violin Sonata; piano pieces; songs.

Rung, Henrik, Danish conductor and composer; father of **Frederik Rung;** b. Copenhagen, March 3, 1807; d. there, Dec. 13, 1871. He founded the Cecilia Society in 1891; wrote a number of choral works and popular songs.
BIBLIOGRAPHY: C. Thrane, *Caeciliaföreningen og dens Stifter* (Copenhagen, 1901).

Runge, Paul, German musicologist; b. Heinrichsfeld, Posen, Jan. 2, 1848; d. Colmar, Alsace, July 4, 1911. Studied with J. Schneider and at the Royal Institute for Church Music in Berlin; lived from 1873 as organist and teacher in Colmar. His writings, which are of importance especially in connection with the music of the Minnesingers and Mastersingers, are *Die Sangesweisen der Colmarer Handschrift und die Liederhandschrift Donaueschingen* (1896), *Die Lieder und Melodien der Geissler des Jahres 1349* (1900), *Die Lieder des Hugo von Montfort mit den Melodien des Burk Mangolt* (1906), "Die Notation des Mastergesanges" (1907; in the report of the Basel Congress of the Internationale Musik-Gesellschaft); with R. Batka he published *Die Lieder Mülichs von Prag* (1905).

Rungenhagen, Carl Friedrich, German conductor and composer; b. Berlin, Sept. 27, 1778; d. there, Dec. 21, 1851. He was a pupil of Benda; in 1815, 2nd conductor of the Singakademie, succeeding Zelter in 1833 as first conductor; member of the Berlin Academy, and teacher in the School of Composition. He composed 4 operas, 3 oratorios, a *Te Deum,* 30 motets, 30 4-part songs, over 100 sacred and 1,000 secular songs; also symphonies, quartets, etc.

Runolfsson, Karl Otto, Icelandic composer; b. Reykjavik, Oct. 24, 1900; d. there, Nov. 29, 1970. He played the trumpet in the radio orchestra in Reykjavik; in 1939, appointed teacher at the Cons. there. He wrote a set of Icelandic songs for voice and orch. (1938); a symphony (1968); choral works on Icelandic themes; a trumpet sonata; a violin sonata.

Runze, Maximilian, German writer on music and editor; b. Woltersdorf, Pomerania, Aug. 8, 1849; d. Berlin, May 9, 1931. He studied philosophy and theology at the Univs. of Greifswald and Berlin; from 1882, rector of St. Johannis-Moabit, Berlin, and lecturer at the Humboldt-Akademie. His writings on the life and works of Karl Loewe are valuable: *Karl Loewe, eine ästhetische Beurteilung* (1884), *Loewe redivivus* (1888), *Ludwig Giesebrecht und Karl Loewe* (1894), *Goethe und Loewe* (1901), *Karl Loewe* (1905; a biography); also *Die musikalische Legende* (1902), *Volkslied und Ballade* (1907). He edited *Arien aus ungedruckten Opern und Oratorien Loewes* (1892; 3 vols.), *Loewe-Hohenzollern Album* (1898; 2 vols.), *Gesamtausgabe der Balladen, Legenden und Gesänge Loewes* (1899–1903; 17 vols.).

Ruolz-Montchal, Henri (-Catherine-Camille), Comte de, French composer; b. Paris, March 5, 1808; d. there, Sept. 30, 1887. He was a pupil of Berton, Lesueur, Paër, and Rossini; he won some success as a composer, but the loss of his family fortune in 1840 induced him to abandon music and devote himself to the more practical study of chemistry.
WORKS: the operas *Attendre et courir* (with F. Halévy; 1830), *Lara* (Naples, Nov. 22, 1835; was highly praised by Alexandre Dumas in the *Gazette Musicale de Paris*), *La Vendetta* (Paris, 1839), *La Jolie Fille de Perth,* and *Manfred;* a Requiem; *Cantate en honneur de Jeanne d'Arc;* a string quartet; 2 piano trios; motets; songs.

Rupnik, Ivan, Serbian composer; b. Belgrade, Aug. 29, 1911. He studied in Ljubljana; later in Vienna with Alban Berg. His early works are in a neo-Romantic

vein, with Expressionistic overtones; later he abjured modern devices and began writing music for the masses, in conformity with socialist ideology. His cantata, *Song of the Dead Proletarians,* which he conducted in Belgrade on Dec. 14, 1947, is an epitome of programmatic realism. He further wrote 2 symphonies, several overtures (*Romantic Overture, Youth Overture*), ethnic symphonic works (*Musical Impressions from Istria, A Peasant Evening Party*) and a *Hymn of Peace.*

Rusca, Francesco, Italian composer of church music; was Maestro di Cappella of the Como Cathedral from 1659 until 1699. He wrote about 100 Masses, psalms, cantatas, etc., in a highly developed polyphonic style, containing as many as 16 independent vocal and instrumental parts. His 5 keyboard toccatas are included in vol. III of *I Classici* (Como, 1961).

Rusconi, Gerardo, Italian composer; b. Milan, Feb. 1, 1922; d. there, Dec. 23, 1974. He studied at the Cons. of Parma; began his career as a composer by writing light music for the stage, radio and the films; then undertook more serious genres of music. He composed *La moglie di Lot* for soprano, horn and piano (1962); *Concerto breve* for horn and strings (1965); *Tre musiche* for flute and piano (1967); *Moments* for orch. in memory of Martin Luther King (1968); *L'Appuntamento,* one-act opera (1971); numerous transcriptions and harmonizations of popular songs.

Rush, Loren, American composer; b. Fullerton, Calif., Aug. 23, 1935, He studied piano, bassoon and the double bass; played the bassoon in the Oakland Symphony and the double bass in the Richmond Symphony; also was a drummer. He studied composition with Robert Erickson at San Francisco State College (B.A., 1957); upon graduation organized the Loren Rush Jazz Quartet; enrolled at the Univ. of California at Berkeley studying composition with Andrew Imbrie, Seymour Shifrin, William Denny and Charles Cushing (M.A. 1960). He applies a whole spectrum of modern techniques, including serialism, spatial distribution, controlled improvisation and pointillistic exoticism.
WORKS: *Five Japanese Poems* for soprano, flute, clarinet, viola and piano (1959); *Serenade* for violin and viola (1960); *Mandala Music,* improvisation for a group, inspired by the Oriental geometrization of the Cosmos and an important symbol in Jungian psychology (1962); *Hexahedron* for piano, notated on all six surfaces of a large cube (1964); *Nexus 16* for chamber orch. (1964); *soft music, HARD MUSIC* for two amplified pianos (1969); *The Cloud Messenger* for orch. (1970).

Russell, George Alexander, American organist and song composer; b. Franklin, Tenn., Oct. 2, 1880; d. Dewitt, N.Y., Nov. 24, 1953. The son of a Presbyterian minister, he studied at home; his mother, Felicia Putnam Russell (a direct descendant of General Israel Putnam of Revolution fame), taught him piano; the family moved to Texas, where he studied academic subjects; entered the College of Fine Arts, Syracuse Univ., studying organ with George A. Parker and composition with William Berwald; subsequently studied in Europe with Leopold Godowsky and Harold Bauer (piano), and with Widor (organ). Returning to America in 1908, he toured as accompanist to various artists; in 1910 he became director of the Auditorium concerts at Wanamaker's in N.Y.; in 1917 was appointed prof. in the newly-founded chair of music at Princeton Univ.; assembled the famous Rodman Wanamaker Collection of old Italian string instruments. He wrote the songs *Sunset, The Sacred Fire, In Fountain Court, Lyric from Tagore, Expectation, Puer Redemptor,* etc.; the piano pieces *Theme and Variations, Contrapuntal Waltz,* etc.

BIBLIOGRAPHY: J. T. Howard, *Alexander Russell* (N.Y., 1925).

Russell, Henry, English singer and composer; b. Sheerness, Dec. 24, 1812; d. London, Dec. 8, 1900. He studied in Italy as a young boy; took a few lessons from Rossini in Naples; was in London in 1828; then in Canada (1833); served as organist of the First Presbyterian Church of Rochester, N.Y. (1833–41). He returned to England in 1841 and became extremely popular there as a composer and singer of dramatic and topical songs, of which *Woodman, Spare that Tree* attained immense popularity; other songs were *Old Arm Chair, Oh, Weep Not!, A Life on the Ocean Wave* (official march of the Royal Marines), *Cheer, Boys, Cheer, Ivy Green, The Gambler's Wife, Old Bell, The Maniac,* etc. He published a book of reminiscences, *Cheer, Boys, Cheer* (London, 1895) and *L'Amico dei cantanti,* a treatise on singing. He was the father of **Henry Russell,** the impresario, and of **Sir Landon Ronald,** the composer and conductor, whose real name was **L. R. Russell.**

Russell, Henry, English impresario; son of **Henry Russell** the singer and composer; b. London, Nov. 14, 1871; d. there, Oct. 11, 1937. He studied singing at the Royal College of Music, and devised an original method of vocal instruction, which attracted the attention of Mme. Melba, who sent him a number of her good pupils. Owing to his wide acquaintance with singers, he was invited in 1903 to manage a season of opera at Covent Garden; in 1905 he brought his company to the U.S., where Boston was the principal field of his operations; his success there resulted, in 1909, in the formation of the Boston Opera Co., of which he was general manager until its dissolution in 1914. Just before the outbreak of World War I, he had taken the entire Boston troupe to Paris, where he gave a successful spring season at the Théâtre des Champs-Élysées. He then lived mostly in London. He published a book of memoirs, *The Passing Show* (London, 1926).

Russell, Louis Arthur, American organist and pianist; b. Newark, N. J., Feb. 24, 1854; d. there, Sept. 5, 1925. He studied singing with William Shakespeare and George Henschel in London. Returning to America in 1878, he was active as church organist in Newark; founded the College of Music there (1885) and organized the Newark Symph. Orch. (1893). He published several instructive books: *The Embellishments of Music; How to Read Modern Music; Problems of Time and Tune; Development of Artistic Pianoforte Touch;* etc.

Russo, William Joseph, American composer; b. Chicago, June 25, 1928. He played trombone in various jazz bands, including the Stan Kenton Band (1950–54), for which he also became a composer-arranger; studied privately in Chicago with John Becker (1953–55) and Karel Jirák (1955–57). He then went to New York where he organized his own band (1958–61); proceeded to London and conducted a jazz orch. (1962–65). Returning to America, he was affiliated with the Center for New Music in Chicago (1965–76), where he directed the Chicago Jazz Ensemble and the Free Theater, for which he composed 4 rock cantatas; subsequently moved to San Francisco, where he found a congenial environment for his type of sophisticated jazz and blues. Learned counterpoint lends distinction to his own compositions even when they reach the never-never land of decibel-laden rock.

WORKS: opera, *John Hooton,* for jazz orch, soloists, strings, piano and chorus (1961); opera, *Antigone,* for 4 soloists and chamber orch. (1967); a rock opera, *Aesop's Fables,* for 6 to 10 soloitst and rock band (1971); 2 comic operas, *Isabella's Fortune* (1974) and *Pedrolino's Revenge* (N.Y., Sept. 11, 1974); a ballet, *Les Deux Errants (The Seekers)* (1955); 4 rock cantatas: *The Civil War* (1968), *David* (in collaboration with Robert Perrey, 1968), *Liberation* (1969), and *Joan of Arc* (1970); *The English Suite* for jazz orch. (1955); 2 symphonies: No. 1 (1955), and No. 2, *Titans* (1957; N.Y. Philharmonic, April 19, 1959); Concerto Grosso for saxophone quartet and concert band (1960); *Variations on an American Theme* for orch. (1961); Cello Concerto (1962); *The Island* for 6 soloists and jazz orch. (1963); *The English Concerto* for violin and orch. (1963; Bath Festival, June, 1963; Yehudi Menuhin, soloist); *In Memoriam* for 2 soloists, small chorus, and jazz orch. (1966); *America 1966,* concerto grosso for jazz orch. (1966); *3 Pieces* for blues band and orch. (1967–68; Ravinia Festival, Chicago Symph., July 7, 1968); *Songs of Celebration* for 5 soloists, chorus, and orch. (1971); *Song of Songs* for 6 soloists, chorus, and modified jazz band-orch. (1972); *Carousel Suite* for narrator, dancers, and chamber orch. (1975); *Street Music,* blues concerto for piano, harmonica and orch. (1975). He wrote the books *Composing for the Jazz Orchestra* (Chicago, 1961) and *Jazz Composition and Orchestration* (Chicago, 1968).

Russolo, Luigi, Italian futurist composer; b. Portogruaro, May 1, 1885; d. Cerro, Feb. 4, 1947. In 1909 he joined the futurist movement of Marinetti; formulated the principles of "art of noises" in his book, *L'Arte dei rumori* (Milan, 1916); constructed a battery of noise-making instruments ("intonarumori"), with which he gave concerts in Milan (April 21, 1914) and Paris (June 18, 1921), creating such a commotion in the concert hall that on one occasion a group of outraged concert-goers mounted the stage and physically attacked Russolo and his fellow noise-makers. The titles of his works sing the glory of the machine and of urban living: *Convegno dell'automobili e dell'aeroplani, Il Risveglio di una città, Si pranza sulla terrazza* *dell'Hotel.* In his "futurist manifesto" of 1913 the noises are divided into 6 categories, including shrieks, groans, clashes, explosions, etc. In 1929 he constructed a noise instrument which he called "Russolophone." Soon the novelty of machine music wore out, the erstwhile marvels of automobiles and airplanes became commonplace, and the future of the futurists turned into a yawning past; Russolo gradually retreated from cultivation of noise and devoted himself to the most silent of all arts, painting. His pictures, influenced by the modern French school, and remarkable for their vivid colors, had several successful exhibitions in Paris and New York. The text of Russolo's manifesto is reproduced, in an English translation, in N. Slonimsky's *Music Since 1900.*

Rust, Friedrich Wilhelm, German violinist and composer; b. Wörlitz, near Dessau, July 6, 1739; d. Dessau, March 28, 1796. He was a pupil of the violinist Höckh at Zerbst and (1763) of Franz Benda at Berlin, under the patronage of Prince Leopold III of Anhalt-Dessau, whom he accompanied to Italy (1765–66), and who appointed him court music director in 1775. He brought out several stage pieces, wrote incidental music to plays and considerable instrumental music. Davis Singer and Wilhelm Rust published several of his violin pieces. His son **Wilhelm Karl Rust** (b. Dessau, April 29, 1787; d. there, April 18, 1855), was organist at Vienna (1819–27); then teacher in Dessau. Publ. pieces for piano and organ.
BIBLIOGRAPHY: W. Hosäus, *F. W. Rust und das Dessauer Musikleben* (Dessau, 1882); E. Prieger, *F. W. Rust* (Cologne, 1894; with list of works); R. Czach, *F. W. Rust* (Essen, 1927).

Rust, Wilhelm, German organist and editor; b. Dessau, Aug. 15, 1822; d. Leipzig, May 2, 1892. Pupil of his uncle, **W. K. Rust** (piano and organ); later of Fr. Schneider (1843–46). He went to Berlin in 1849, taught there, and entered the Singakademie; joined the Leipzig Bach-Verein in 1850, played in numerous concerts, became organist of St. Luke's in 1861, conductor of the Berlin Bach-Verein from 1862–74, "Royal Music Director" in 1864; in 1870, teacher of theory and composition at the Stern Cons.; in 1878, organist of the Thomaskirche at Leipzig, and teacher in the Cons. there; in 1880 he succeeded Richter as cantor of the Thomasschule. As editor of several vols. of the Bach edition prepared by the Bach-Gesellschaft, he displayed great erudition.

Ruthardt, Adolf, German piano pedagogue and music editor; b. Stuttgart, Feb. 9, 1849; d. Leipzig, Sept. 12, 1934. He studied music with his father Friedrich Ruthardt; then enrolled at the Stuttgart Cons.; subsequently was active as piano teacher, first in Geneva (1868-85) and then at the Leipzig Cons. (1887-1914). He wrote a number of attractive piano pieces and useful student exercises, among them *Trillerstudien, Oktavenstudien, Terzen-Etüden, Sexten-Etüden,* etc.; also published an *Elementär-Klavierschule.* He brought out a selection of Cramer's *Studies* (1909), a collection of *Old Dances* (2 vols., 1913) and *Klavierbuch nordischer Komponisten* (2 vols., 1913); further published *Das Klavier: ein geschichtlicher Abriss* and edited various manuals of piano literature.

Ruthström, (Bror Olaf) Julius, Swedish violinist; b. Sundsvall, Dec. 30, 1877; d. Stockholm, April 2, 1944. He studied at the Stockholm Cons. (1894–99) and the Berlin Hochschule für Musik (1901–03); pupil of A. Moser, J. Joachim, and W. Burmester; toured Scandinavia and Central Europe; publ. valuable pedagogic works for the violin: *Mechanics of Passage-Playing* (1914); *The Art of Bowing* (1921); *Double-Note Studies* (1924); *Violin School* (1928).

Rutz, Ottmar, German singing teacher, b. Fürth, July 15, 1881; d. Garmisch, Sept. 8, 1952. He was the son of Josef Rutz and Klara Rutz, vocal teachers in Munich, whose ideas on various physiological aspects of singing (especially as regards the position of pectoral muscles in singing different types of songs) he expounded in several books: *Neue Entdeckungen von der menschlichen Stimme* (Munich, 1908); *Musik, Wort und Körper als Gemütsausdruck* (Leipzig, 1911); *Typenstimmbildung, zugleich die neue Ausdruckskunst für Bühne und Konzert* (with Klara Rutz; 1920); *Menschheitstypen und Kunst* (1921) and *Vom Ausdruck des Menschen* (1926).

Ruygrok, Leo (Leonard Petrus), Dutch cellist, conductor and composer; b. Utrecht, May 8, 1889; d. Hilversum, Jan. 3, 1944. He studied composition with Johan Wagenaar and cello with Ed. Ferrée; was active as cellist; then conductor at Arnhem (1915-19) and in the Hague (1919-40). He wrote 2 symphonies, 4 overtures, and cello pieces.

Ruyneman, Daniel, Dutch composer; b. Amsterdam, Aug. 8, 1886; d. there, July 25, 1963. He began his study of music relatively late; took composition lessons with Zweers at the Amsterdam Cons. (1913–16); in 1918 was co-founder of the Society of Modern Dutch Composers; in 1930, organized the Netherlands Society for Contemporary Music, serving as president until 1962; edited its magazine, *Tijdschrift voor Hedendaagse Muziek* (1930–40) until it was suppressed during the Nazi occupation of Holland. Ruyneman made a special study of Javanese instruments and introduced them in some of his works. He was naturally attracted to exotic subjects with mystic connotations and coloristic effects; also worked on restoration of old music; in 1930 he orchestrated fragments of Mussorgsky's unfinished opera *The Marriage,* and added his own music for the missing acts of the score.
WORKS: FOR THE STAGE: opera, *The Brothers Karamazov* (1928); music for the "psycho-symbolic" play, *De Clown,* for vocal and instrumental orch. (1915). FOR ORCH.: 2 symphonies: No. 1, *Symphonie Brève* (1927) and No. 2, *Symphony 1953* (1953; Utrecht, March 14, 1956); *Musica per orchestra per una festa Olandese* (1936); Concerto for Orch. (1937); Piano Concerto (1939); Violin Concerto (1940; Amsterdam, Feb. 23, 1943); *Partita* for string orch. (1943); *Amphitryon,* overture (1943); *Amatarasu (Ode to the Sun Goddess),* on a Japanese melody, for chamber ensemble (1953); *Gilgamesj,* Babylonian epos for orch. (1962). VOCAL WORKS: *Sous le Pont Mirabeau*

for female chorus, flute, harp and string quartet (1917); *De Roep (The Call),* a color spectrum of wordless vowel sounds for 5-part a cappella mixed chorus (1918); *Sonata,* on wordless vowel sounds, for chamber a cappella chorus (1931); *4 Liederen* for tenor and small orch. (1937); *Die Weise von Liebe und Tod des Kornets Christoph Rilke* for narrator and piano (1946; orchestrated, 1951); *Ancient Greek Songs* for baritone or bass, flute, oboe, cello and harp (1954); *5 Melodies* for voice and piano (1957); *3 Chansons de Maquisards Condamnés* for alto or baritone, and orch. (1957); *Réflexions I* for soprano, flute, guitar, viola, vibraphone, xylophone and percussion (1958–59). CHAMBER MUSIC: *Réflexions: II* for flute, viola and guitar (1959), *III* for flute, violin, viola, cello and piano or harpsichord (1960–61; reconstructed by Rob du Bois) and *IV* for wind quintet (1961); 3 violin sonatas (Nos. 2–3, 1914 and 1956); *Klaaglied van een Slaaf* for violin and piano (1917); *Hiëroglyphs* for 3 flutes, celesta, harp, cupbells, piano, 2 mandolins and 2 guitars (1918; the unique cup-bells, which some claim were cast by J. Taylor & Co., Loughborough, England, and which others claim were found by the composer in a London junk shop, were destroyed in a Rotterdam air raid in 1940, and performances of the work since then have substituted a vibraphone); Sonata for violin (1925); *Divertimento* for flute, clarinet, horn, violin and piano (1927); Clarinet Sonata (1936); *4 Tempi* for 4 cellos (1937); *Sonatina in modo antiquo* for cello and piano (1939); *Sonata da camera* for flute and piano (1942); String Quartet (1946); *Nightingale Quintet* for winds (1949); *4 Chansons Bengalies* for flute and piano (1950); Sonatina for flute, and piano or harpsichord (1951); Oboe Sonatina (1952); *3 Fantasies* for cello, and piano or harpsichord (1960). FOR PIANO: *3 Pathematologieën* (1915), 2 sonatinas (1917, 1954), Sonata (1931), *Kleine Sonata* (1938) and *5 Sonatines mélodiques pour l'enseignement moderne du piano* (1947).

BIBLIOGRAPHY: A. Petronio, *Daniel Ruyneman et son œuvre* (Liège, 1922); C. Bérard, "Daniel Ruyneman," *Chesterian* (1928); A. Hoérée, "Daniel Ruyneman," *Revue Musicale* (March 1949); Wouter Paap, "Daniel Ruyneman," *Mens en Melodie* 5 (1962); Jos Wouters, "Daniel Ruyneman," *Sonorum Speculum* 11 (1962); Rob du Bois, "Daniel Ruyneman: on the Barracades," *Key Notes* (1976).

Ruzicka, Peter, German composer; b. Düsseldorf, July 3, 1948. He studied piano, oboe and counterpoint at the Hamburg Cons. (1963–68); then took lessons in composition with Henze in Rome and Otte in Bremen. Ruzicka's admiration for Mahler is revealed through frequent use of material from Mahler's symphonies in his music.

WORKS: *3 Szenen* for solo clarinet (1967); *Esta noche,* funeral music for the victims of war in Vietnam, for alto flute, English horn, viola and cello (1967); Concerto for Beat Band and Orch. (1968); *desfuge,* scene with text by Paul Celan for alto and Cello Sonata (1969); 2 string quartets (1969, 1970); *Antifone-strofe* for 25 solo strings and percussion (1970); *Metastrofe,* subtitled "an attempt at a breakout" for 87 instruments (Berlin, May 4, 1971); *Epigenesis* for orch. (1971); *Sinfonia* for solo strings, 16 vocalists and percussion (1970–71); *Experience,* musical theater (1971–72); *In processo di tempo,* an "anti-cello concerto" for 26 instruments and non-anticello (Hilversum, Sept. 11, 1972); *Torso* for orch. (1973); *Versuch,* 7 pieces for string orch. (Utrecht, Sept. 19, 1975).

Růžička, Rudolf, Czech composer; b. Brno, April 25, 1941. He studied at the Janáček Academy of Music in Brno; then taught electronic music there. In 1967, he, along with A. Parsch and M. Štědroň, joined a composing collective group originally founded by Alois Piňos, and named, in English, "Teamwork." It was modeled after the Soviet "Production Collective" (Procoll) of 1925; together, the "Teamwork" produced some pieces of utilitarian music. Růžička's individual compositions include a *Sonata aleatorica* for organ and percussion (1964); *Melodrama I* and *II* for 3 narrators, chorus and 7 instruments (1965); *Elektronika A* for alto, chamber orch. and electronic sound (1965); *Elektronika B* for chamber orch. and electronic sound (1966) and *Elektronika C* for tape (1967); *Musica à 5* for viola, bass clarinet, harpsichord, flute and percussion (1966); *Timbres* for wind quintet and tape (1968); *Deliciae* for double bass and *musique concrète* (1969); *Conteminationi* for bass clarinet and piano (1969); *Sonata Nuova* for cello and piano (1970); *Cantata ai ai a* (1970); 2 tape pieces, *Discordia* and *Mavors* (both 1970); *Sinfonia cosmica* for orch. and organ (1971); *Sonate triste* for trombone and piano (1971); 2 string quartets.

Ryan, Thomas, American musician; b. Ireland, 1827; d. New Bedford, Mass., March 5, 1903. He settled in the U.S. in 1844, and in 1849 was a co-founder of the Mendelssohn Quintette Club, playing the viola (and upon occasion, the clarinet), with August Fries (1st violin), Francis Riha (2nd violin), Eduard Lehmann (viola and flute), and Wulf Fries (cello). With this club he traveled all over the U.S., doing missionary work in bringing good music to remote communities; he also acted as its manager; arranged classical sonatas and other works for it; after half a century, Ryan was the sole remaining original member of the organization. He published his memoirs, *Recollections of an Old Musician* (N.Y., 1899).

Ryba, Jan Jakub, Czech composer; b. Přeštice, Oct. 26, 1765; d. Rožmitál, April 8, 1815. He studied academic subjects in Prague; in 1788 was appointed rector at a school in Rožmitál; remained there until his death (suicide). A very prolific composer, he left about 120 Masses, 100 motets, 30 pastorals (Christmas cantatas to Latin and Czech texts); also many songs to Czech words; of these latter, 2 albums were published during his lifetime; other works were a symphony, several string quartets, sonatas. There is a growing realization in Czechoslovakia of Ryba's importance as an early representative of the national art song.

BIBLIOGRAPHY: J. Němeček, *Jan Jakub Ryba* (Prague, 1947).

Rybner, (Peter Martin) Cornelius, pianist, conductor, and composer; b. Copenhagen, Oct. 26, 1855; d. New York, Jan. 21, 1929. His original name was **Rübner,**

but he changed it to Rybner about 1920. He studied at the Copenhagen Cons. with Gade and J. P. Hartmann; then at the Leipzig Cons. with Ferdinand David (violin) and Reinecke (piano); finished his pianistic studies under Hans von Bülow and Anton Rubinstein. After a series of concerts in Europe as pianist, he settled in Karlsruhe; succeeded Mottl in 1892 as conductor of the Philharmonic Society there, and held this position until 1904, when he emigrated to the U.S., succeeding MacDowell as head of the music dept. at Columbia Univ. (1904-19). His works include a ballet, *Prinz Ador* (Munich, 1902); a symph. poem, *Friede, Kampf und Sieg;* a violin concerto; numerous choruses; piano pieces; songs; also some chamber music.

Rychlík, Jan, Czech composer; b. Prague, April 27, 1916; d. there, Jan. 20, 1964. He studied with Jaroslav Řídký at the Prague Cons. A practical musician, he played in dance orchestras, experimented with modern techniques, and was active as a music critic; he wrote a book on jazz and one on valveless brass instruments.

WORKS: *Symphonic Overture* (1944); *Suite* for wind quintet (1946); *Concert Overture* (1947); *Partita Giocosa* for wind orch. (1947); Trio for clarinet, trumpet, and bassoon (1948); *Divertimento* for 3 double basses (1951); *Etudes* for English horn and piano (1953); String Trio (1953); *4 Partitas* for solo flute (1954); *Chamber Suite* for string quartet (1954); *Arabesques* for violin and piano (1955); *Burlesque Suite* for solo clarinet (1956); *Serenade* for wind octet (1957); Wind Quintet (1960); *Hommagi gravicembalistici* for harpsichord (1960); *African Cycle I-V* for 8 winds and piano (1961); first complete performance, Prague, June 29, 1962); *Relazioni* for alto flute, English horn, and bassoon (1964); music for 55 films and 8 plays.

Rychlík, Józef, Polish composer; b. Cracow, May 12, 1946. He graduated in composition from the Cracow High School of Music. He composed *Symphonic Music I* for 2 string quartets and 2 pianos (1969); *Symphonic Music II* for chamber ensemble (1969); *Ametrio* for flute, violin and cello (1971); *Spatial Sequences* for 22 players (1971); *"000"* for chamber group and any wind instrument solo (1972); *Sketches* for organ and orch. (1972); *Plenitudo temporis* for orch. (1974); *Peut-être,* graphic composition for any solo instrument, or voice, or dancer, or ballet group, with *ad lib* tape (1974).

Rychnovsky, Ernst, Czech music critic; b. Janovice, June 25, 1879; d. Prague, April 25, 1934. He studied law in Prague; then music with Rietsch; became music critic of the *Prager Tageblatt.* He published monographs on Spohr and Rochlitz (1904), Kittl (2 vols.; 1904, 1905), Blech (1905), Haydn (1909), Schumann (1910), Liszt (1911), Smetana (1924), etc.; compiled a bibliography on German intellectual life in Bohemia (1906-09).

Ryder, Arthur Hilton, American organist and composer; b. Plymouth, Mass., April 30, 1875; d. Newton, Mass., July 18, 1944. He studied at Harvard Univ. with Walter Spalding (theory) and J. K. Paine (composition); subsequently was church organist and choir director in Boston and neighboring towns. In 1935 he developed a system of "Radical Harmony" which he taught at extension courses at Boston Univ.; also composed songs and organ pieces.

Ryder, Thomas Philander, American organist and composer; b. Cohasset, Mass., June 29, 1836; d. Somerville, Mass., Dec. 2, 1887. He was for many years organist at Tremont Temple in Boston; publ. a number of piano pieces in a light vein.

Rydman, Kari, Finnish composer; b. Helsinki, Oct. 15, 1936. He attended music classes at the Univ. of Helsinki; then developed energetic activities as composer, music critic and school teacher. In his music he reveals himself as a blithe spirit, writing ultramodern pieces, but also turning out some fetching Finnish pop tunes.

WORKS: 5 string quartets (1959, 1963, 1964, 1964, 1966); Piano Quintet (1960); Trio for violin, cello and percussion (1961); *Sonata 1* for 3 violins, viola, cello, piano and percussion (1962); *Sonata 2* for violin, viola, guitar and percussion (1962); *Sonata 4* for violin, clarinet, guitar and percussion (1963); *Sonata 6* for cello and percussion (1964); *Khoros 1* for 3 flutes, oboe, percussion, harp, violin, viola, cello, and double bass (1964); *Khoros 2* for orch. (1966); *Rondeaux des nuits blanches d'été* for orch. (1966); *Sonata 8* for viola and harpsichord (1967); *Symphony of the Modern Worlds,* commissioned by the Swedish Broadcasting Corp. (1968), which contains blues, beat rhythms, political songs and the Chinese Communist anthem, *Dong Fang Hong (The East Is Red); Sonata 9* for small orch. (1969); *DNA* for orch. and electronic organ (1970); *Suite* for narrator and orch. (1971).

Ryelandt, Joseph, Belgian composer; b. Bruges, April 7, 1870; d. there, June 29, 1965. He studied composition with Edgar Tinel. Thanks to a personal fortune (he was a Baron) he did not have to earn a living by his music, but he taught at the Cons. of Ghent (1929-39) and served as director of the Municipal Cons. in Bruges (1924-45). He lived a very long life *(obiit aet. 95)* and composed much music.

WORKS: *La Parabole des vierges,* spiritual drama (1894); *Sainte Cécile,* lyrical drama (1902); 5 oratorios: *Purgatorium* (1904); *De Komst des Heren (The Coming of the Lord,* 1906-07); *Maria* (1910); *Agnus Dei* (1913-15); *Christus Rex* (1921-22); *Te Deum* for soli, chorus and orch. (1927); 5 symphonies (1897, 1904, 1908, 1913, 1934); *Gethsemani,* symph. poem (1908); *Patria,* overture (1917); 11 piano sonatas; 4 string quartets; horn sonata (1897); 2 piano quintets; 2 piano trios; 7 violin sonatas; 3 cello sonatas; viola sonata; 7 cantatas; organ pieces; songs.

Rysanek, Leonie, Austrian soprano; b. Vienna, Nov. 14, 1926. She studied at the Academy of Music and Dramatic Art in Vienna with **Rudolf Grossmann,** whom she later married. She made her debut at Innsbruck in 1949; then sang at Saarbrücken (1950-52) and at the Munich State Opera (1952-54). In 1954 she joined the staff of the Vienna State Opera; in subsequent years also sang at La Scala in Milan, at Covent

Garden in London, and at the Paris Opéra. She made a spectacular American appearance at the Metropolitan Opera House, N.Y., on Feb. 5, 1959, when she replaced Maria Callas in the role of Lady Macbeth in Verdi's opera on short notice; she remained on its staff until 1966, and sang the roles of Aida, Desdemona and Tosca, as well as several Wagner parts (Elsa in *Lohengrin,* Elisabeth in *Tännhauser,* Sieglinde in *Die Walküre).* Her younger sister **Lotte Rysanek** (b. Vienna, March 18, 1928) attained a fine reputation in Vienna as a lyric soprano.

Rytel, Piotr, Polish composer; b. Vilna, Sept. 20, 1884; d. Warsaw, Jan. 2, 1970. He studied with Michalowski and Noskowski at the Warsaw Cons.; in 1911, appointed a prof. of piano and in 1918, a prof. of harmony there. In 1948 he conducted at the Warsaw Opera House.

WORKS: operas, *Ijola* (1927; Warsaw, Dec. 14, 1929), *Koniec Mesjasza* (1935–36), *Krzyzowcy* (1940–41) and *Andrzej z Chelmna* (1942–43); a ballet, *Śląski pierścień* (*The Silesian Ring,* 1956); the symph. poems, *Grazyna* (1908, revised 1954), *Poemat* (1910), *Korsarz,* after Byron (*The Corsair,* 1911), *Sen Dantego* (*The Dream of Dante,* 1911), *Legenda o św. Jerzym* (*The Legend of St. George,* 1918); 3 symphonies: No. 1 (1909), No. 2, *Mickiewiczowska* (in honor of the Polish poet Mickiewicz) for tenor, chorus and orch. (1949) and No. 3 for tenor and orch. (1950–51); Piano Concerto (1907); Violin Concerto (1950); *Sinfonia concertante* for flute, clarinet, horn, harp, and orch. (1960); *Romance* for clarinet and piano (1948); *Variations* for clarinet and piano (1957).

Ryterband, Roman, Polish pianist and composer; b. Łódź, Aug. 2, 1914. He lived mostly in Switzerland; acquired a cosmopolitan knowledge of various European cultures; eventually came to America where he occupied teaching posts in Montreal and Chicago; became an American citizen in 1964; settled in Palm Springs, California in 1967. His *Suite polonaise* for piano is an artful stylization of Polish dance tunes. He also composed an "opera grotesque," *Fantômes rebelles;* a music drama, *A Border Incident;* Sonata for 2 flutes and harp; Concertino for piano, strings and harp; *Sonata Breve* for violin and harp; *Toccata* for harpsichord and chamber orch.; Quintet for 2 flutes, viola, cello and harpsichord; *Russian Rhapsody* for orch.; various works for violin, cello, flute, marimba, harp, saxophone and trombone.

Rzewski, Frederic, American avant-garde composer; b. Westfield, Mass., April 13, 1938, of Polish parentage. He attended Harvard Univ. (1954–58) and Princeton Univ. (1958–60); was active in modern music circles in Italy (1960–62) where he stayed on a Fulbright scholarship; subsequently he received a Ford Foundation grant which enabled him to spend two years in Berlin (1963–65); while in Rome, he organized, with other similarly futuroscopic musicians, the MEV (*Musica Elettronica Viva*). In the interim he played concerts with the topless cellist Charlotte Moorman. From 1971 he lived mostly in New York. As a composer, he pursues the shimmering distant vision of optimistic, positivistic anti-music. He is furthermore a granitically overpowering piano technician, capable of depositing huge boulders of sonoristic material across the keyboard without actually wrecking the instrument.

WORKS: *For Violin,* for violin solo (1962); *Nature morte* for instruments and percussion groups (1965); *Composition for Two* (1964); *Zoologischer Garten* (1965); *Spacecraft* (his magnum opus, 1967; "plan for spacecraft" published in *Source 3,* 1968); *Impersonation,* audiodrama (1967); *Requiem* (1968); *Symphony for Several Performers* (1968); *Last Judgement* for trombone (1969); *Falling Music* for piano and tape (1971); *Coming Together* for speaker and instruments (1972); Piano Variations on the song *No Place to Go But Around* (1974); *The People United Will Never Be Defeated,* a set of 36 variations for piano on the Chilean song, *¡El Pueblo Unido Jamás Será Vencido!* (1975).

S

Saar, Louis Victor (Franz,), Dutch pianist and teacher; b. Rotterdam, Dec. 10, 1868; d. St. Louis, Missouri, Nov. 23, 1937. He studied with Rheinberger in Munich (1886–89); lived in Vienna, Leipzig and Berlin; in 1894 he went to the U.S.; taught music at various schools in N.Y.; was member of the faculty at the Cincinnati College of Music (1906–17), at the Chicago Musical College (1917–33), and from 1934 until his death, at the St. Louis Institute of Music. He was also a composer; wrote about 150 opus numbers, including musico-geographic orchestral pieces such as *From the Mountain Kingdom of the Great North West* (1922); *Along the Columbia River* (1924); also published arrangements of folksongs for men's chorus, and *Album of Church Classics.*

Sabaneyev, Leonid, Russian writer on music; b. Moscow, Oct. 1, 1881; d. Antibes, France, May 3, 1968. He studied with Taneyev at the Moscow Cons.; also took a course in mathematics at the Univ. of Moscow. In 1920 he joined the board of the newly-organized Moscow Institute of Musical Science. In 1926 he left Russia and lived in France. He was an energetic promoter of modern music, and a friend of Scriabin, about whom he wrote a monograph, which would have been important if his account of Scriabin's life and ideology could be trusted; he compromised himself when he wrote a devastating review of Prokofiev's *Scythian Suite* at a concert that never took place.

WRITINGS (all in Russian): *Richard Wagner and the Synthesis of Arts* (1913); *The Development of the Harmonic Idea* (1913); *Medtner* (1913); *Scriabin* (1916; 2nd revised ed., 1923); *History of Russian Music* (Moscow, 1924; also in German, 1926); *Modern Russian Composers* (in English, N.Y., 1927); *Sergei Taneyev* (Paris, 1930; in Russian); *Music for the Films* (in English; London, 1935). He wrote 2 piano trios (1907; 1923), a violin sonata, and some other music.

Sabata, Victor de, outstanding Italian conductor and composer; b. Trieste, April 10, 1892; d. Santa Margherita Ligure, Dec. 11, 1967. He studied with Saladino and Orefice at the Milan Cons. (1901–11); devoted himself mainly to conducting; led symph. concerts at La Scala, Milan, and at the Augusteo, Rome. In 1927 he made his American debut as guest conductor of the Cincinnati Symph. Orch., and visited the U.S. frequently thereafter. He was regarded as the best conductor, after Toscanini, of Verdi's operas; he was also praised for his fine performances of Beethoven's symphonies. He composed an opera, *Il Macigno* (La Scala, Milan, March 31, 1917); the symph. poems *Juventus* (1919), *La Notte di Platon* (1924), and *Gethsemani* (1925; N.Y., Jan. 21, 1926); some chamber music.

BIBLIOGRAPHY: R. Mucci, *Victor de Sabata* (Lanciano, 1937).

Sabbatini, Galeazzo, Italian composer and theorist; b. Pesaro, c.1595; d. there, Dec. 6, 1662. He was maestro di cappella in Pesaro 1626; from 1630–36 maestro to the Duke of Mirandola. His last publ. work appeared in 1639 (Venice); author of a treatise on thoroughbass, *Regola facile e breve per sonare sopra il basso con-* *tinuo* (Venice, 1628; 3rd ed., Rome, 1669). He published 2 books of madrigals *a* 2–4 (1625, 1626; other eds.); 2 books of *Sacrae laudes a* 2–5 (1637, 1641); 1 with organ (1642); 3 books of *Madrigali concertati a* 2–5 (with instruments; 1627, 1630, 1636); Hymns to the Virgin Mary *a* 3–6 (1638); *Sacri laudi e motetti a voce sola* (1639).

Sabbatini, Luigi Antonio, Italian theorist; b. Albano Laziale, near Rome, Oct. 24, 1732; d. Padua, Jan. 29, 1809. Pupil of Padre Martini at Bologna, and Vallotti at Padua, succeeding the latter as maestro at the Antonius Basilica in 1780. He published *Elementi teorici della musica colla pratica de' medesimi in duetti, e terzetti a canone* (1789; part transl. into French by Choron); *La vera idea delle musicali numeriche segnature* (1799; gives an epitome of Vallotti's system); *Trattato sopra le fughe musicali* (1802; with fine examples by Vallotti); and *Notizie sopra la vita e le opere del R. P. Fr. A. Vallotti* (1780).

Sabin, Robert, American music critic and editor; b. Rochester, Feb. 21, 1912; d. New York, May 17, 1969. He studied at the Eastman School of Music in Rochester before going to New York; was editor of *Musical America* (1945–50); edited the 9th edition of Oscar Thompson's *International Cyclopedia of Music and Musicians* (1964).

Sabin, Wallace Arthur, English organist; b. Culworth, Dec. 15, 1860; d. Berkeley, Calif., Dec. 8, 1937. He studied with M. J. Monk at Banbury and T. W. Dodds at Oxford. Emigrated to the U.S. and settled in San Francisco, where he was organist at St. Luke's (1894–1906), at Temple Emanu-El (from 1895), and at the First Church, Scientist (from 1906). His settings of the Hebrew liturgy were publ. in Stark's Service Book. He composed many part-songs for men's voices.

BIBLIOGRAPHY: R. R. Rinder, *Tribute to W. A. Sabin* (San Francisco, 1938).

Sacchetti, Liberius, Russian writer on music and pedagogue; b. Kenzar, near Tambov, Aug. 30, 1852; d. St. Petersburg, March 11, 1916. He studied with Rimsky-Korsakov and others at the St. Petersburg Cons.; in 1878 was appointed to its faculty as lecturer on musical esthetics. He publ. an *Outline of General Music History* (St. Petersburg, 1882); *A Brief Anthology of Musical History* (St. Petersburg, 1896); manuals on esthetics for use at the St. Petersburg Cons., etc. He was highly regarded as a scholar and teacher in Russia.

Sacchi, Don Giovenale, Italian scholar; b. Barzio, Como, Nov. 22, 1726; d. Milan, Sept. 27, 1789. He was a member of the Barnabite monastic order, and an assiduous student of ancient music; also was distinguished as a biographer.

WRITINGS: *Del numero e delle misure delle corde musiche e loro corrispondenze* (1761); *Della divisione del tempo nella musica, nel ballo e nella poesia* (1770); *Della natura e perfezione dell'antica musica de' Greci* (1778); *Della quinte successive nel contrappunto e delle regole degli accompagnamenti* (1780); *Vita del Cav. Don Carlo Broschi, detto Farinelli* (1784); *Don Placido, dialogo dove cercasi se lo studio della musica al religioso convenga o disconvenga* (1786); etc.; translated Cardinal Fontana's *Vita di Benedetto Marcello* (1788).

Sacchini, Antonio (Maria Gasparo Gioacchino), Italian opera composer; b. Florence, June 14, 1730; d. Paris, Oct. 6, 1786. He entered the Cons. of Santa Maria di Loreto at Naples as a pupil of Francesco Durante (composition), Nicola Fiorenza (violin), and Gennaro Manna (singing). His intermezzo *Fra Donato* was performed at the Cons. in 1756; he subsequently wrote music for various stage productions in Naples; then proceeded to Rome, where his opera *Semiramide* was successfully produced in 1762. This success marked the beginning of his career as an operatic composer; thereafter he produced operas every year: *Alessandro nell'Indie* (Venice, 1763), *Lucio Vero* (Naples, Nov. 4, 1764), *La Contadina in corte* (Rome, 1765), and *L'Isola d'amore* (Rome, 1766). In 1768 he succeeded Traetta as director of the Cons. dell'Ospedaletto in Venice; his oratorio *Caritas omnia vincit* was brought out there on April 16, 1769. He then went to Munich and produced there his operas *L'Eroe cinese* (1769) and *Scipione in Cartagena* (1770). In 1772 he traveled to London with Venanzio Rauzzini, and while there presented the following operas: *Tamerlano* (1773), *Montezuma* (1775), *Erifile* (1776), *L'Amore soldato* (May 5, 1778), *Il Calandrino e l'avaro deluso* (1778), and *Enea e Lavinia* (1779). In 1781 he received an invitation from Marie Antoinette, through the "intendant des menus-plaisirs," to come to Paris. His name was already known in France, since his opera *Isola d'amore,* arranged as *La Colonie* ("comic opera imitated from the Italian"), had been produced in Paris on Aug. 16, 1775. He arrived in Paris in August, 1781, and was forthwith commissioned to write 3 works at a fee of 10,000 francs each. For this purpose he adapted his Italian opera *Armida e Rinaldo* (Milan, 1772) to a French text as *Renaud,* "tragédie lyrique" in 3 acts (produced at the Académie Royale de Musique, Feb. 25, 1783), and his opera *Il cidde* (Rome, 1764) as *Chimène* (Fontainebleau, Nov. 18, 1783); the 3rd opera, *Dardanus,* was a new work; it was staged at the Trianon, Versailles, Sept. 18, 1784, in the presence of Louis XVI and Marie Antoinette. In Paris Sacchini found himself in unintended rivalry with Piccinni as a representative of Italian music in the famous artistic war against the proponents of the French operas of Gluck; Sacchini's most successful opera, however, was to the French text, *Oedipe à Colonne,* first presented at Versailles (Jan. 4, 1786) and produced at the Paris Opéra (Feb. 1, 1787) after Sacchini's death. It held the stage for half a century, and there were sporadic revivals later on. His last opera, also to a French libretto, *Arvire et Evelina,* was left unfinished, and was produced posthumously (Paris Opéra, April 29, 1788; 3rd act added by J. B. Rey). Sacchini's music is a typical product of the Italian operatic art of his time. It possesses melodious grace, but lacks dramatic development. The undistinguished style of Sacchini's productions is probably the reason for the disappearance of his operas from the active repertory; Piccinni fared much better in comparison.

BIBLIOGRAPHY: A. Jullien, *La Cour et l'opéra sous Louis XVI: Marie Antoinette et Sacchini* (Paris, 1878); J.-G. Prod'homme, *Écrits de musiciens des XVe–XVIIIe siècles* (Paris, 1912); J.-G. Prod'homme, "Un Musicien napolitain à la cour de Louis XVI," *Le Ménestrel* (Dec. 11 and Dec. 18, 1925); V. Morelli, "Antonio Sacchini," *Vita Musicale Italiana* 7–8 (1926); U. Prota-Giurleo, *Sacchini non nacque a Pozzuoli* (Naples, 1952, proving that Sacchini was born in Florence and not in the vicinity of Naples); F. Schlitzer, *Antonio Sacchini: schede e appunti per una sua storia teatrale* (Siena, 1955); A. Loewenberg, *Annals of Opera* (Cambridge, 1943; 2nd ed., Geneva, 1955).

Sacco, P. Peter, American composer of Italian descent; b. Albion, N.Y., Oct. 25, 1928. Virtually his whole family consisted of tenors: his father, a brother and couple of uncles. Peter Sacco followed the family tradition and became a tenor himself. He also studied piano and exhibited himself in public as a keyboard prodigy; he also studied trumpet and tuba. After 3 years of preparatory school in music in Rochester, N.Y., he entered Fredonia State Univ. (B.M., 1950); he was drafted into the U.S. Army, and was stationed in Frankfurt, Germany (1950–52); there he studied music theory with a local teacher and also played church organ and piano programs for the officer's club. In 1953 he enrolled in the Eastman School of Music, Rochester, N.Y., as a student of Bernard Rogers and Howard Hanson (M.M., 1954). He continued to perform as a tenor; sang in various school performances of classical operas and oratorios. In 1959 he was appointed to the music faculty of San Francisco State Univ.; in 1970–71 he was visiting prof. at the Univ. of Hawaii, where he taught composition and gave vocal recitals. As a composer, he adheres to traditional harmony, but diversified into the ingenious chromatic developments, approximating a euphonious type of dodecaphony.

WORKS: opera, *Mr. Vinegar* (Redding, California, May 12, 1967); oratorio, *Jesu* (Grand Rapids, Mich., Dec. 3, 1956, composer conducting); oratorio, *Midsummer Dream Night* (San Francisco, June 25, 1961, composer conducting); *Solomon,* oratorio (San Francisco, Dec. 12, 1976, composer as tenor soloist); Symph. No. 1 (Oklahoma City, Dec. 17, 1958); Symph. No. 2 (*The Symphony of Thanksgiving;* San Francisco, March 23, 1976); Symph. No. 3 (*The Convocation Symphony;* Redding, Ca., June 1, 1968); *Moab Illuminations* for orch. (1972); Piano Concerto (1964; San Francisco, April 4, 1968); Violin Concerto (1969; Walnut Creek, California, April 24, 1974).

Sacher, Paul, Swiss conductor; b. Basel, April 28, 1906. He studied with Karl Nef (music theory) and Weingartner (conducting). In 1926 he founded the Kammer Orchester in Basel; commissioned special works from a number of celebrated contemporary composers (among them Richard Strauss, Hindemith, Honegger, etc.) and presented them for the first time with his ensemble; in 1933 founded the Schola Cantorum Basiliensis; from 1941, was leader of the Collegium Musicum in Zürich; publ. *Alte und Neue Musik*

(Zürich, 1951), annotated catalogue of the 25 years of the Basel Kammer Orchester. Sacher made his American debut in N.Y. on April 3, 1955, conducting a concert of the Collegiate Chorale at Carnegie Hall.

BIBLIOGRAPHY: *30 Jahre Collegium musicum* (Zürich, 1972).

Sachs, Curt, eminent German musicologist and authority on musical instruments; b. Berlin, June 29, 1881; d. New York, Feb. 5, 1959. While attending the Gymnasium in Berlin, he studied piano and composition with L. Schrattenholz and clarinet with Rausch; entered Berlin Univ.; studied history of music with Oskar Fleischer, and also history of art; Dr. phil., 1904; after some years as art critic, he turned to musicology, and studied with Kretzschmar and Joh. Wolf; specialized in the history of musical instruments; in 1919 appointed curator of the Museum of Musical Instruments in Berlin, and in 1920, prof. of the National Academy of Music there; also prof. at the Univ. of Berlin. In 1933 he was compelled to leave Germany; went to Paris as Chargé de Mission at the Musée de l'Homme; was visiting prof. at the Sorbonne. In 1937 he settled in the U.S.; was lecturer at the Graduate School of Liberal Arts of N.Y. Univ. (1937-38); consultant to the N.Y. Public Library (1937-52); adjunct prof., Columbia Univ. (from 1953); president of the American Musicological Society (1948-50). In 1956, he was made Dr. phil. (*honoris causa*) of West Berlin Univ.

WRITINGS: *Musikgeschichte der Stadt Berlin bis zum Jahre 1800* (1908); *Musik und Oper am kurbrandenburgischen Hof* (1910); *Reallexikon der Musikinstrumente* (1913; very valuable); *Handbuch der Musikinstrumentenkunde* (1920; 2nd ed., 1930; very valuable); *Die Musikinstrumente des alten Ägyptens* (1921); *Katalog der Staatlichen Instrumentensammlung* (1922); *Das Klavier* (1923); *Die modernen Musikinstrumente* (1923); *Geist und Werden der Musikinstrumente* (1929); *Vergleichende Musikwissenschaft in ihren Grundzügen* (1930); *Eine Weltgeschichte des Tanzes* (1933; in English as *World History of the Dance*, N.Y., 1937); *Les Instruments de musique de Madagascar* (Paris, 1938); *The History of Musical Instruments* (N.Y., 1940); *The Rise of Music in the Ancient World* (N.Y., 1943); *The Commonwealth of Art* (N.Y., 1946); *Our Musical Heritage* (N.Y., 1948; 2nd ed., 1955); *Rhythm and Tempo: A Study in Music History* (N.Y., 1953); valuable essays in various European and American periodicals; compiled and edited *The Evolution of Piano Music* (N.Y., 1944).

BIBLIOGRAPHY: E. Hertzmann, "Alfred Einstein and Curt Sachs," *Musical Quarterly* (April 1941); K. Hahn, "Verzeichnis der wissenschaftlichen Arbeiten von Curt Sachs," *Acta Musicologica* 29.

Sachs, Hans, foremost poet of the Meistersinger; b. Nuremberg, Nov. 5, 1494; d. there, Jan. 19, 1576. He wrote over 4,000 poems *(Meisterschulgedichte),* 1,700 tales, etc., and 208 dramatic poems; also invented numerous melodies *(Weisen).* He is the central figure in Wagner's opera, *Die Meistersinger von Nürnberg.* The original melodies of a large number of the poems are preserved in *Das Singebuch des Adam Puschmann* (ed. by G. Münzer, 1907).

BIBLIOGRAPHY: Ch. Schweitzer, *Un Poète allemand au XVIᵉ siècle: Étude sur la vie et les œuvres de H. Sachs* (Nancy, 1889); K. Drescher, *Studien zu H. Sachs* (Marburg, 1891); R. Genée, *H. Sachs und seine Zeit* (Leipzig, 1894; 2nd ed., 1901); B. Suphan, *H. Sachs: Humanitätszeit und Gegenwart* (Weimar, 1895); K. Drescher, *Nürnberger Meistersinger-protokolle von 1575-1689* (2 vols.; Tübingen, 1898); K. Mey, *Der Meistergesang* (1901); H. Holzschuher, *H. Sachs in seiner Bedeutung für unsere Zeit* (Berlin, 1906); E. Mummenhoff, *Musikpflege und Musikaufführungen im alten Nürnberg* (Leipzig, 1908); H. Nutzhorn, *Meistersangeren H. Sachs* (Copenhagen, 1911); F. H. Ellis, *H. Sachs Studies* (Bloomington, Ind., 1941).

Sachs, Léo, composer; b. Frankfurt, Germany, April 3, 1856; d. Paris, Nov. 13, 1930. He was active in the field of modern music in Paris; composed several symph. poems *(Retour des cloches; Sur l'eau; Lamento);* a piano quintet; 2 string quartets; a piano trio; 3 violin sonatas; a viola sonata; a cello sonata; *Petite suite* for string quartet; 24 preludes for piano. His total output amounts to nearly 200 op. numbers. His style of composition was mildly modernistic.

Sachse, Leopold, opera stage director; b. Berlin, Jan. 5, 1880; d. Englewood, N.J., April 4, 1961. Studied at the Cons. of Cologne; then in Vienna; in 1902 joined the Strasbourg Opera as baritone; in 1907, general manager of the Stadttheater in Münster; in 1913 organized the Sachse Opera in Berlin; from 1922 to 1933 was with the Hamburg Staatsoper. In 1935 he was engaged as stage director of Wagner's operas at the Metropolitan Opera House, N.Y., retiring in 1943; in 1945 became stage director of the N.Y. City Opera; in 1951 organized the Opera in English Co. at Cooper Union, N.Y. From 1936 to 1943 he taught stage technique at the Juilliard Graduate School, N.Y.

Sack, Erna, German coloratura soprano; b. Spandau-Berlin, Feb. 6, 1898; d. Mainz, March 2, 1972. She studied in Prague and in Berlin; made her 1st operatic appearance at the Municipal Theater in Bielefeld; sang in Austria at the Salzburg festivals, in Italy, and in England; made her first American appearance as concert singer in 1937-38, and revisited the U.S. in 1954. In 1953 she gave a series of concerts in Australia.

Sacks, Stuart, American composer; b. Albany, N.Y., Feb. 28, 1941. He studied at Boston Univ. with Hugo Norden; developed a neo-Romantic style couched in emotional tonality. The CBS Television network presented on April 11, 1965, in N.Y., performances of his *Saul* for mezzo-soprano, oboe, percussion and strings and *Poème* for violin and piano. His other works include an overture; *Arioso* for strings; *Divertissement* for winds and strings; *Elegy* for solo cello and orch.

Sacrati, Francesco (Paolo), Italian composer; b. Parma, c.1600; d. Modena, May 20, 1650. He was one of the earliest composers for the opera theaters that opened in Venice after 1637; was also a pioneer of opera buffa before the rise of the Neapolitan school. He wrote an opera, *La Delia,* for the opening of the

Teatro Crimani dei Santi Giovanni e Paolo in Venice (Jan. 20, 1639); there followed *La finta pazza* (Teatro Novissimo, Venice; Jan. 14, 1641); this was also one of the earliest Italian operas performed in Paris (Salle du Petit Bourbon, Dec. 14, 1645); other operas by Sacrati were: *Bellerofonte* (1642), *Venere gelosa* (Padua, 1643), *Ulisse errante* (1644), *Proserpina rapita* (1644), *La Semiramide in India* (1648), *L'Isola d'Alcina* (Bologna, 1648). In 1649 he was appointed maestro di cappella at the court of Modena, but died a few months after the appointment.

BIBLIOGRAPHY: Henry Prunières, *L'Opéra italien en France avant Lully* (Paris, 1913); A. Loewenberg, *Annals of Opera* (Cambridge, 1943; 2nd ed., 1955).

Sadai, Yizhak, Bulgarian-born Israeli composer; b. Sofia, May 13, 1935. He emigrated to Israel in 1949; studied with Haubenstock-Ramati and Roscovich at the Tel Aviv Academy of Music (1951–56); then devoted himself to teaching; in 1966 joined the music staff of the Univ. of Tel Aviv.

WORKS: *Divertimento* for alto, flute, viola and piano (1954); 3 cantatas: *Ecclesiastes* (1956), *Hazvi Israel* (1957), and *Psychoanalysis* (1958); *Ricercare Symphonique* for orch. (1956); *Serenade* for winds (1956); *Interpolations* for harpsichord and string quartet (1960); *Nuances* for chamber orch. (1964); *Aria da Capo* for 6 instruments and 2 tape recorders (1965); *Registers* for violin and piano (1967); *Préludes à Jérusalem* for voice and instruments (1968); *From the Diary of a Percussionist* for percussion player and tape (1971); *La prière interrompue* for tape (1975).

Sadie, Stanley, eminent English writer on music and lexicographer; b. London, Oct. 30, 1930. He studied music privately with Bernard Stevens (1947–50) and then with Dart, P. Hadley and Cudworth in Cambridge (M.A., Mus. B.); received his Ph.D. in 1958 for the dissertation *British Chamber Music, 1720–90.* He was then on the staff of Trinity College of Music in London (1957–65); from 1964 was engaged as music critic of the *Times,* and from 1967 was an editor of the *Musical Times.* A scholar of the loftiest category, he brought out the monographs on Handel (London, 1962; 3rd ed., 1966), Mozart (London, 1966; also published in Japanese, Tokyo, 1970), Beethoven (London, 1967), *Handel Concertos* (London, 1972) and published numerous individual articles in British and American music journals. With Arthur Jacobs he edited *The Pan Book of Opera* (London, 1964; new ed., as *Opera. A Modern Guide,* N.Y., 1972). In 1970 he was entrusted with the formidable task of preparing for publication, as editor-in-chief, the 6th edition of *Grove's Dictionary of Music & Musicians,* in 20 vols., about 15,000 pages and 22,500 articles by world-wide contributors, to be published in 1979; the auguries are most propitious for its becoming a worthy rival of that monument of German musicographical endeavor, *Die Musik in Geschichte und Gegenwart.*

Saenger, Gustav, American music editor and arranger; b. New York, May 31, 1865; d. there, Dec. 10, 1935. He studied violin with Leopold Damrosch and others; was an orchestral violinist; then conducted theater orchestras in N.Y.; in 1897 was engaged as arranger for Carl Fischer, Inc., and in 1909 became editor-in-chief of Fischer's publications; also edited the Fischer periodicals, *Metronome* (from 1900) and the *Musical Observer* (1904–29). Besides a vast number of arrangements, he publ. pieces for violin and piano (*5 Silhouettes; 3 Concert Miniatures;* etc.); also a *New School of Melody.*

Saenger, Oscar, American singing teacher; b. Brooklyn, Jan. 5, 1868; d. Washington, April 20, 1929. He sang in church as a boy; studied voice with J. Bouhy at the National Cons. in N.Y., and taught there from 1889 to 1897; made his debut with the Hinrichs Grand Opera Co. in 1891; after a brief tour in Germany and Austria returned to America and devoted himself entirely to teaching. Among his students were many well-known singers (Marie Rappold, Paul Althouse, Mabel Garrison, etc.).

Saenz, Pedro, Argentine composer; b. Buenos Aires, May 4, 1915. He studied piano with Alberto Williams, and theory with Arturo Palma. In 1948 he went to Paris where he took lessons with Arthur Honegger, Darius Milhaud and Jean Rivier. Returning to Buenos Aires, he occupied numerous teaching and administrative posts in educational institutions.

WORKS: *Movimentos Sinfónicos* for orch. (1963); Piano Quintet (1942); String Trio (1955); *Divertimento* for oboe and clarinet (1959); *Capriccio* for harpsichord and string quartet (1966); numerous piano pieces and songs.

Saerchinger, César, German-American editor and writer; b. Aachen, Oct. 23, 1884; d. Washington, Oct. 10, 1971. He studied singing with his mother (a pupil of G. B. Lamperti); settled in America in 1902, and continued his musical education in N.Y. Still as a young man, he began writing biographical articles for various American encyclopedias; was managing editor and contributor to *The Art of Music* (14 vols., 1915–17); from 1919 to 1930 was foreign correspondent of the *N.Y. Evening Post* and the *Musical Courier;* lived in Berlin (1920–25) and London (1925–37); then returned to N.Y. He edited *International Who's Who in Music and Musical Gazetteer* (N.Y., 1918); publ. *Voice of Europe* (N.Y., 1937); *Artur Schnabel* (London, 1957).

Saeverud, Harald, prominent Norwegian composer; b. Bergen, April 17, 1897. He studied music theory at the Bergen Music Academy with B. Holmsen (1915–18) and with F. E. Koch at the Hochschule für Musik in Berlin (1920–21); took a course in conducting with Clemens Krauss in Berlin (1935). In 1953 he received the Norwegian State Salary of Art (a government life pension for outstanding artistic achievement). He began to compose very early, and on Dec. 12, 1912, at the age of 15, conducted in Bergen a program of his own symph. pieces. His music is permeated with characteristically lyrical Scandinavian Romanticism, with Norwegian folk melos as its foundation; his symphonic compositions are polyphonic in nature, and tonal in essence, with euphonious dissonant textures imparting a peculiarly somber character to the music.

WORKS: a ballet, *Ridder Blåskjeggs mareritt (Bluebeard's Nightmare,* 1960; Oslo, Oct. 4, 1960); 9 symphonies: No. 1, in 2 symph. fantasias (1916-20; first complete performance, Bergen, 1923); No. 2 (1922; Bergen, Nov. 22, 1923; revision, 1934; Oslo, April 1, 1935); No. 3 (1925-26; Bergen, Feb. 25, 1932); No. 4 (1937; Oslo, Dec. 9, 1937); No. 5, *Quasi una fantasia* (1941; Bergen, March 6, 1941); No. 6, *Sinfonia Dolorosa* (1942; Bergen, May 27, 1943); No. 7, *Salme (Psalm,* 1944-45; Bergen, Sept. 1, 1945); No. 8, *Minnesota* (1958; Minneapolis, Oct. 18, 1958); No. 9 (1965-66; Bergen, June 12, 1966); *Ouverture Appassionata* (1920; retitled second fantasia of his *First Symphony,* often played independently); *50 Small Variations* for orch. (1931); *The Rape of Lucretia,* incidental music for Shakespeare's play (1935; also a *Lucretia Suite* for orch., 1936); Oboe Concerto (1938); *Divertimento No. 1* for flute and strings (1939); *Syljetone (The Bride's Heirloom Brooch)* for chamber orch. or piano (1939); *Rondo Amoroso* for chamber orch. or piano (1939); *Gjaetlevise-Variasjoner (Shepherd's Tune Variations)* for chamber orch. (1941); *Siljuslåtten (Countryside Festival Dance,* 1942; also for piano); *Galdreslåtten (The Sorcerer's Dance,* 1942); *Romanza* for violin, and orch. or piano (1942); *Kjempeviseslåtten (Ballad of Revolt,* 1943; also for piano); *Peer Gynt,* incidental music to a revised production of Ibsen's verse drama (1947; Oslo, March 2, 1948; also exists as 2 orch. suites and as a piano suite); *Olav og Kari,* dance scene for 2 singers, chorus and orch. (1948); Piano Concerto (1948-50); Violin Concerto (1956); *Vade mors (Get Thee Behind Me, Death,* 1955); *Allegria (Sinfonia Concertante,* 1957); Bassoon Concerto (1963); *Mozart-Motto-Sinfonietta* (1971); *5 Capricci* for piano (1918-19); Piano Sonata (1921); *Tunes and Dances from "Siljustøl,"* 5 vols. for piano (1943-45); 6 piano sonatinas (1948-50); *20 Small Duets* for violins (1951); 2 string quartets (1970, 1975); *Fabula gratulatorum* for piano (1973).

Saeverud, Ketil, Norwegian composer, son of **Harald Saeverud;** b. Fana, near Bergen, July 19, 1939. He studied organ at the Cons. in Bergen, composition with Blomdahl and Lidholm in Stockholm and with Jersild in Copenhagen. Returning to Norway, he became a teacher at the Cons. in Bergen.
WORKS: Clarinet Quartet (1962); Sinfonietta (1963); Piano Concertino (1964); Wind Quintet (1964); *Guitar Suite* for solo guitar (1966); *Ariseturo,* concerto for percussion and 8 winds (1966-67); *Duets for Bassoons* (1966); Trumpet Concerto (1968-69; Bergen, April 22, 1972); 2 string quartets (1969, 1973); *Rondo con Variazione* for piano (1970); *Flauto Solo* (1970); *So einsam ist der Mensch,* after Nelly Sachs, for vocal quartet (1971); *Tromba Solo* (1971); *Or "Håvamål"* for chorus and orch. (1971); *Mi-Fi-Li,* symph. poem (Oslo, Sept. 4, 1972); Sextet for violin, cello, oboe, bassoon, trumpet and trombone (1972); Double-Bass Concerto (Oslo, Sept. 6, 1973); *Variations* for organ (1973); Quartet for voice, recorder, guitar and piano (1974); Trio for soprano, alto and piano (1974); *Collage* for narrator, violin and guitar (1975).

Safonov, Vassily, eminent Russian pianist, conductor, and pedagogue; b. Ishcherskaya, Caucasus, Feb.

6, 1852; d. Kislovodsk, Feb. 27, 1918. He studied at the Cons. of St. Petersburg with Leschetizky and Brassin (piano) and Zaremba (theory); made his debut as pianist with the Imperial Russian Music Society in St. Petersburg, on Nov. 22, 1880; then taught piano at the St. Petersburg Cons. (1881-85); in 1885 was appointed to the piano faculty of the Moscow Cons., and in 1889 became its director, resigning in 1905; among his pupils were Scriabin and Medtner. He conducted the symph. concerts of the Imperial Russian Music Society in Moscow; was the first modern conductor to dispense with the baton; achieved international fame as a forceful and impassioned interpreter of Russian music; conducted in almost all the capitals of Europe; on March 5, 1904, was engaged as guest conductor of the N.Y. Philharmonic, obtaining sensational success; as a consequence, was appointed regular conductor for 3 seasons (1906-09; was succeeded by Gustav Mahler); at the same time he was also director of the National Cons. in N.Y. After his return to Russia, he was appointed permanent conductor of the Imperial Russian Music Society in St. Petersburg. He publ. *A New Formula for the Piano Teacher and Piano Student* (Moscow, 1916; in English).
BIBLIOGRAPHY: V. Safonov (Moscow, 1959).

Safranek-Kavić, Lujo, Croatian composer; b. Zagreb, Oct. 12, 1882; d. there, July 18, 1940. He wrote a symph. suite for violin and orch., *Guslar* (inspired by the playing of the gusle, the South Slav national instrument), 2 operas (*Hasanaginica* and *The Queen of Medvedgrad*), chamber music, and songs.

Sagaev, Dimiter, Bulgarian composer; b. Plovdiv, Feb. 27, 1915. He studied composition with Stoyanov and Vladigerov at the Bulgarian State Cons. in Sofia, graduating in 1940; then became instructor at the Bulgarian Cons. His music is Romantic in essence and is national in its thematic resources with its rhythmical pulse derived from Bulgarian folksongs.
WORKS: 2 operas: *Under the Yoke* (1965) and *Samouil* (1975); a ballet, *The Madara Horseman* (1960); an oratorio, *In the Name of Freedom* (1969); a cantata-poem, *The Shipka Epic* (1977; commemorating the centennial of the crucial battle between the Russian and the Turkish forces in the Balkans); *Youth Suite* for orch. (1952); *Sofia,* symph. poem (1954); *3 Bulgarian Symphonic Dances* (1956); 2 violin concertos (1963, 1964); Viola Concerto (1963); Oboe Concerto (1964); Symph. No. 1 for narrator, singer, 2 female choruses and orch. (1964); Bassoon Concerto (1973; Burgas, March 26, 1974); Flute Concerto (1974); 7 string quartets (1945, 1962, 1962, 1963, 1966, 1967, 1968); 2 wind quintets (1961, 1962); Trio for flute, violin and piano (1974); Quartet for flute, viola, harp, and piano (1975); songs; incidental music. Sagaev published several theoretical texts, including *Textbook of Wind Orchestration* (Sofia, 1957), *How to Work with Student Brass Bands* (Sofia, 1962) and *A Practical Course of Symphony and Orchestration* (Sofia, 1966).

Sagittarius. See **Schütz, Heinrich.**

Saikkola, Lauri, Finnish composer; b. Viipuri (Vyborg), March 31, 1906. He studied violin at the Viipuri School of Music (1919–28) and then took private composition lessons from Akimov and Funtek (1930–34); was a violinist in the Viipuri Philh. (1923–34) and the Helsinki Philh. Orch. (1934–65). His music is rooted in the Romantic tradition.

WORKS: 2 operas: *Ristin* (Helsinki, 1959) and *The Master's Snuff Box,* chamber opera (1970); *3 Symphonic Scenes* (1932); *1500-Meter Race,* a parody for orch. (1933); *Partita* for orch. (1935); *Pastorale* for orch. (1936); 5 symphonies: No. 1, *Sinfonia campale* (1938); No. 2, *Sinfonia tragica* (1946); No. 3 (1949); No. 4 (1951); No. 5 (1958); *Karelian Scenes* for orch. (1940); *Karelia in Flames,* for orch. (1940); *Nocturno* for cello and orch. (1944); *Taivaaseen menijä (Going to Heaven),* folk story for narrator, soloists, chorus and orch. (1950); *Violin Concerto* (1952); *Concerto di miniatura* for cello and chamber orch. (1953); *Concerto da camera* for piano and chamber orch. (1957); *Pezzi* for strings (1965); *Musica Sinfonica* (1966); *The Well of Dreams* for baritone, chorus and chamber orch. (1968); *Clarinet Concerto* (1969); *Raasepori Fantasia* for orch. (1971); 3 string quartets (1931–68); *Divertimento* for wind quartet (1949); Wind Quintet (1968); 2 suites for clarinet and piano (1955, 1968); *Suite* for oboe and piano (1968); Viola Sonatina.

Saint-Foix, Georges (du Parc Poullain, Comte) de, eminent French musicologist, specialist in Mozart research; b. Paris, March 2, 1874; d. Aix-en-Provence, May 26, 1954. He studied jurisprudence, and also attended classes in music theory with Vincent d'Indy at the Schola Cantorum in Paris. His principal, and most important, publication was W. A. Mozart, Sa vie musicale et son œuvre de l'enfance à la pleine maturité (2 vols., 1912; with T. de Wyzewa; 3rd vol., by Saint-Foix alone, published 1937; 4th vol., published 1940; 5th vol., published 1946; of no less importance is his book Les Symphonies de Mozart (Paris, 1932; 2nd ed., 1948; in English, London, 1947; reprint, N.Y., 1968). He contributed a number of informative articles, dealing with Mozart's contemporaries; in several instances, in collaboration with T. de Wyzewa and L. de La Laurencie.

Saint-George, George, notable player on the viola d'amore; b. (of English parents) Leipzig, Nov. 6, 1841; d. London, Jan. 5, 1924. He studied piano, violin, and theory in Dresden and Prague; his violin teacher, Moritz Mildner of Prague, had a fine viola d'amore, which he lent to Saint-George for practicing; he made such progress on this little-used instrument that he decided to adopt it as a specialty. About 1862 he settled in London and became a manufacturer of string instruments; gave performances on the Welsh crwth for the "Hon. Soc. Cymmrodorion"; also played the viola d'amore in duos with his son, **Henry Saint-George,** who assisted him on the viola da gamba.

Saint-George, Henry, son of **George Saint-George;** b. London, Sept. 26, 1866; d. there, Jan. 30, 1917. He studied the violin with his father, with whom he subsequently gave concerts, playing works for early instruments; was editor of *The Strad* for 4 years; publ.

The Bow: Its History, Manufacture and Use (1895; 3rd ed., 1922); *The Place of Science in Music* (1905); *Fiddles: Their Selection, Preservation and Betterment* (1910).

Saint-Georges, Joseph Boulogne, Chevalier de, West Indian composer and violinist; b. near Basse Terre, Guadeloupe, 1739, the son of a wealthy Frenchman and a Negro slave; d. Paris, June 10, 1799. He was raised in Santo Domingo; went to Paris with his father in 1749 (his mother joined them in 1760); as a youth he studied boxing and fencing, and became one of the leading fencers of Europe; he also studied music, with Jean-Marie Leclair, *l'aîné,* and with François Gossec (1763–66); the latter dedicated his op. 9 string trios to Saint-Georges. In 1771 Saint-Georges became concertmaster of the Concerts des Amateurs in Paris, led by Gossec; in 1772 he appeared as violin soloist in his 2 violin concertos, op. 2; in 1773, succeeded Gossec as director of the Concerts des Amateurs. He continued his activities as a fencer, and in this capacity went to London twice, in 1785 and 1789; in 1792 he became colonel of a Negro regiment, the Légion Nationale des Américains et du Midi (among his 1,000 troops was the father of Dumas *père*); he left the service in 1797 and spent the last two years of his life in Paris.

WORKS: operas (performed at the Comédie Italienne, Paris): *Ernestine* (July 1777), *La Chasse* (Oct. 12, 1778), *L'Amant anonyme* (March 8, 1780), *La Fille Garçon* (1788), *La Marchand des marrons* (Théâtre des Petits Comédiens, Paris, 1789), *Le Droit du seigneur* (1789); *Guillaume tout Cœur* (1790); 10 violin concertos; 6 *symphonies concertantes* for 2 violins and orch.; 2 symphonies; 6 string quartets (1778); 3 violin sonatas (1781); 118 songs with keyboard accompaniment; other instrumental and vocal music.

BIBLIOGRAPHY: Roger de Beauvoir, *Le Chevalier de Saint-Georges* (Paris, 1810); L. de La Laurencie, "The Chevalier de Saint-Georges, Violinist," *Musical Quarterly* 5 (1919); L. de La Laurencie, *L'École française de violon* (vol. 2, 1923; reprint, Geneva, 1971); B. S. Brook, *La Symphonie française dans la seconde moitié du XVIIIᵉ siècle* (Paris, 1962); D.-R. de Lerma, "Two Friends within the Saint-Georges Songs," *Black Perspective in Music* (Fall 1973); D.-R. de Lerma, "The Chevalier de Saint-Georges," *Black Perspective in Music* (Spring 1976).

Saint-Lubin, Léon de, violinist and composer; b. Turin, July 5, 1805; d. Berlin, Feb. 13, 1850. After filling various positions as a theater violinist, he pursued further studies with Spohr; was concertmaster at the Josephstadt Theater in Vienna (1823–30); then held a similar position at the Königstadt Theater in Berlin (1830–47). He composed 2 operas, *König Branors Schwert* and *Der Vetter des Doctor Faust;* 5 violin concertos; 2 string quintets, 2 piano trios, a violin sonata, and 19 string quartets.

Saint-Marcoux, Micheline Coulombe, Canadian composer; b. Notre-Dame-de-la-Doré, Quebec, Aug. 9, 1938. She studied with François Brassard in Jonquière; in Montreal with Claude Champagne at the École Vincent d'Indy, graduating in 1962, and later with Gilles Tremblay and Clermont Pépin at the Cons.

there (1963–67). She went to Paris in 1969 and studied composition with Gilbert Amy and Jean-Paul Guézec and electronic music with members of the Groupe de Recherches Musicale; she was a co-founder in Paris of the Groupe International de Musique Electroacoustic, along with 5 other composers from different countries. She returned to Montreal in 1971; became active as a teacher.

WORKS: Flute Sonata (1964); *Kaléidoscope* for piano, left hand (1964); String Quartet (1965–66); *Equation I* for 2 guitars (1967); *Modulaire* for orch. (1967; Montreal, March 31, 1968); *Séquences* for 2 Ondes Martenots and percussion (1968); *Assemblages* for piano (1969); *Doréanes* for piano (1969); *Hétéromorphie* for orch. (Montreal, April 14, 1970); *Bernavir* for tape (1970); *Trakadie* for tape and percussion (1970); *Makazoti* for 8 voices and instrumental group (1971); *Arksalalartôq* for tape (1971); *Contrastances* for tape (1971); *Moustières* for tape (1971); *Zones* for tape (1972); *Alchéra* for mezzo-soprano, flute, clarinet, trombone, violin, cello, percussion, harpsichord or Hammond organ and tape (1973); *Ishuma* for soprano, instrumental group, Ondes Martenot and Synthi A (1973–74); *Genesis* for wind quintet (1975); *Miroirs* for tape and harpsichord (1975); *Moments* for soprano, flute, viola, and cello (1977).

Saint-Requier, Léon, French composer, conductor, and music editor; b. Rouen, Aug. 8, 1872; d. Paris, Oct. 1, 1964; studied with Vincent d'Indy, Guilmant, and Charles Bordes; taught harmony at the Schola Cantorum (1900–34) and at the École César Franck (1934–44); was active as choral conductor at various Paris churches; edited the collection *Palestrina* (sacred songs of the 16th, 17th, and 18th centuries). He composed a Christmas motet *Il est né le divin enfant* (using some folk melodies; 1924); the oratorio, *La Mort du doux Jésus* (1932); *Messe de grande louange* (1946); *Le Sermon sur la montagne* (1949); *Messe de St. Jean Apôtre* (1957); other religious works.

Saint-Saëns, (Charles-) Camille, celebrated French composer; b. Paris, Oct. 9, 1835; d. Algiers, Dec. 16, 1921. His widowed mother sent him to his great-aunt, Charlotte Masson, who taught him to play piano. He proved exceptionally gifted, and gave a performance in a Paris salon before he was 5; at 6 he began to compose; at 7 he became a private pupil of Stamaty; so rapid was his progress that he made his pianistic debut at the Salle Pleyel on May 6, 1846, playing a Mozart concerto and a movement from Beethoven's C minor concerto, with orch. After studying harmony with Pierre Maleden, he entered the Paris Cons., where his teachers were Benoist (organ) and Halévy (composition). He won the 2nd prize for organ in 1849, and the 1st prize on 1851. In 1852 he competed unsuccessfully for the Grand Prix de Rome, and failed again in a second attempt in 1864, when he was already a composer of some stature. His *Ode à Sainte Cécile* for voice and orch. was awarded the 1st prize of the Société Sainte-Cécile (1852). On Dec. 11, 1853, his 1st Symph. was performed; Gounod wrote him a letter of praise, containing a prophetic phrase regarding the "obligation de devenir un grand maître." From 1853 to the end of 1857 Saint-Saëns was organist at

the church of Saint-Merry in Paris; in 1858 he succeeded Lefébure-Wély as organist at the Madeleine. This important position he filled with distinction, and soon acquired a great reputation as virtuoso on the organ and a master of improvisation. He resigned in 1877, and devoted himself entirely to composition and conducting; also continued to appear as pianist and organist. From 1861 to 1865 he taught piano at the École Niedermeyer; among his pupils were André Messager and Gabriel Fauré. Saint-Saëns was one of the founders of the Société Nationale de Musique (1871), established for the encouragement of French composers, but withdrew in 1886 when Vincent d'Indy proposed to include works by foreign composers in its program. In 1875 he married Marie Truffot; their 2 sons died in infancy; they separated in 1881, but were never legally divorced; Madame Saint-Saëns died in Bordeaux on Jan. 30, 1950, at the age of 95. In 1891 Saint-Saëns established a museum in Dieppe (his father's birthplace), to which he gave his manuscripts and his collection of paintings and other art objects. On Oct. 27, 1907, he witnessed the unveiling of his own statue (by Marqueste) in the court foyer of the opera house in Dieppe. He received many honors: in 1868 he was made Chevalier of the Legion of Honor; in 1884, Officer; in 1900, Grand-Officer; and in 1913, Grand-Croix (the highest rank); in 1881 he was elected to the Institut de France; was also a member of many foreign organizations; received an honorary Mus. D. degree at Cambridge Univ. He visited the U.S. for the 1st time in 1906; was a representative of the French government at the Panama-Pacific Exposition in 1915 and conducted his choral work, *Hail California* (San Francisco, June 19, 1915), written for the occasion. In 1916, at the age of 81, he made his 1st tour of South America; continued to appear in public as conductor of his own works almost to the time of his death. He took part as conductor and pianist in a festival of his works in Athens, Greece, in May, 1920. He played a program of his piano pieces at the Saint-Saëns museum in Dieppe on Aug. 6, 1921. For the winter he went to Algiers, where he died.

The position of Saint-Saëns in French music was very important. His abilities as a performer were extraordinary; he aroused the admiration of Wagner during the latter's stay in Paris (1860–61) by playing at sight the entire scores of Wagner's operas; curiously, Saint-Saëns achieved greater recognition in Germany than in France during the initial stages of his career. His most famous opera, *Samson et Dalila*, was produced in Weimar (in 1877), under the direction of Edouard Lassen, to whom the work was suggested by Liszt; it was not performed in France until nearly 13 years later, in Rouen. He played his 1st and 3rd piano concertos for the first time at the Gewandhaus in Leipzig. Solidity of contrapuntal fabric, instrumental elaboration, fullness of sonority in orchestration, and a certain harmonic saturation are the chief characteristics of his music, qualities that were not yet fully exploited by French composers at the time, and the French public preferred the lighter type of music. However, Saint-Saëns overcame this initial opposition, and towards the end of his life was regarded as an embodiment of French traditionalism. The shock of the German invasion of France in World War

I made him abandon his former predilection for German music, and he wrote virulent articles against German art. He was unalterably opposed to modern music, and looked askance at Debussy; he regarded later manifestations of musical modernism as outrages, and was outspoken in his opinions. That Saint-Saëns possessed a fine sense of musical characterization, and true Gallic wit, is demonstrated by his ingenious suite, *Carnival of the Animals*, which he wrote in 1886 but did not allow to be published during his lifetime. He also possessed a considerable literary talent; publ. 2 books of poetry.

WORKS: FOR THE THEATER: operas: *La Princesse jaune* (Paris, June 12, 1872), *Le Timbre d'argent* (Paris, Feb. 23, 1877), *Samson et Dalila* (Weimar, Dec. 2, 1877; Paris Opéra, Nov. 23, 1892; Metropolitan Opera, N.Y., Feb. 8, 1895), *Étienne Marcel* (Lyons, Feb. 8, 1879), *Henry VIII* (Paris, March 5, 1883), *Proserpine* (Paris, March 16, 1887), *Ascanio* (Paris, March 21, 1890), *Phryné* (Paris, May 24, 1893), *Les Barbares* (Paris, Oct. 23, 1901), *Hélène* (Monte Carlo, Feb. 18, 1904), *L'Ancêtre* (Monte Carlo, Feb. 24, 1906), *Déjanire* (Monte Carlo, March 14, 1911). Incidental music: *Antigone* (Paris, Nov. 21, 1893), *Andromaque*, by Racine (Paris, Feb. 7, 1903), *On ne badine pas avec l'amour*, by Alfred de Musset (Paris, Feb. 8, 1917). Ballet, *Javotte* (Lyons, Dec. 3, 1896).

FOR ORCH. Symph. No. 1 (Paris, Dec. 18, 1853); Symph. No. 2 (Leipzig, Feb. 20, 1859); Symph. No. 3 (with organ, London, May 19, 1886); *Le Rouet d'Omphale*, symph. poem (1869; Paris, Jan. 9, 1872); *Marche héroïque* (Paris, Dec. 10, 1871); *Phaéton*, symph. poem (Paris, Dec. 7, 1873); *Danse macabre*, symph. poem (one of his most successful works; Paris, Jan. 24, 1875); *La Jeunesse d'Hercule*, symph. poem (Paris, Jan. 28, 1877); *Suite algérienne* (Paris, Dec. 19, 1880); *Une Nuit à Lisbonne* (Paris, Jan. 23, 1881); *Le Carnaval des Animaux* (contains, as its 13th section, the popular *Swan*; Paris, Feb. 26, 1922); 5 piano concertos (all 1st performed by Saint-Saëns): No. 1, D (Leipzig, Oct. 26, 1865), No. 2, G minor (Paris, May 6, 1868), No. 3, E-flat (Leipzig, Nov. 25, 1869), No. 4, C minor (Paris, Oct. 31, 1875), No. 5, F (Paris, June 3, 1896); 3 violin concertos: No. 1 (*Concertstück*), A major (Paris, April 4, 1867); No. 2, C (1858); No. 3, B minor (Paris, Jan. 2, 1881); *Introduction et Rondo Capriccioso*, for violin and orch. (1863; arranged for violin and piano by Bizet, and performed for the first time in Paris, Nov. 6, 1913); 2 cello concertos: No. 1, A minor (Paris, Jan. 19, 1873; still extremely popular); No. 2, D minor (1902); *Africa*, fantasy for piano and orch. (Paris, Oct. 25, 1891).

CHAMBER MUSIC: Piano Quintet (1858), 2 piano trios (1869; 1892), Piano Quartet (1875), Septet for trumpet, strings, and piano (1881), 2 string quartets (1899; 1919), 2 violin sonatas (1885; 1896), 2 cello sonatas (1873; 1905), Oboe Sonata (1921), Clarinet Sonata (1921), Bassoon Sonata (1921).

VOCAL WORKS: for chorus: *Oratorio de Noël* (1863), *Le Déluge*, oratorio (Paris, March 5, 1876), *Hail California*, for chorus and orch. (1915), *Hymne à la Paix*, for chorus and orch. (1919); numerous choruses a cappella. Song cycles: *Mélodies persanes* (1870) and *La Cendre rouge* (1915); about 100 other songs; *La Fian-*

cée du timbalier, for voice and orch. (Paris, Feb. 19, 1888).

FOR PIANO: études and various other pieces for piano; also duets for piano, 4 hands and 2 pianos.

ARRANGEMENTS: completed Guiraud's opera *Frédégonde* (Paris Opéra, Dec. 18, 1895); publ. numerous arrangements of works by Classical and Romantic composers; edited Gluck's *Armide*, *Orphée*, and *Écho et Narcisse* in the Pelletan edition (1875–1902), the Durand ed. of Rameau's works (from 1895), and Mozart's piano sonatas (1915).

Durand published *Catalogue général et thématique des œuvres de C. S.-S.* (1897; rev. ed., 1907).

WRITINGS: *Notice sur H. Reber* (1881); *Matérialisme et musique* (1882); *Harmonie et mélodie* (1885; a collection of essays, chiefly on Wagner); *Notes sur les décors de théâtre dans l'antiquité romaine* (1886); *Ch. Gounod et le Don Juan de Mozart* (1894); *Problèmes et mystères* (1894); *Portraits et souvenirs* (1899); *Essai sur les Lyres et Cithares antiques* (1902); *École buissonnière* (1913; in English, as *Musical Memories*, N.Y., 1919; reprint, N.Y., 1969 and 1971); *Au Courant de la vie* (1914); *Germanophilie* (1916); *Les Idées de M. Vincent d'Indy* (1919); *Outspoken Essays on Music* (London and N.Y., 1922; translation of assorted articles; reprint, Westport, Conn., 1969).

BIBLIOGRAPHY: C. Kit and P. Loanda, *Musique savante. Sur la musique de M. S.-S.* (Lille, 1889); Blondel, *C. S.-S. et son cinquantenaire artistique* (Paris, 1896); C. Bellaigue, *C. S.-S.* (Paris, 1899); E. Solenière, *C. S.-S.* (Paris, 1899); O. Neitzel, *C. S.-S.* (Berlin, 1899); P. Locard, *Les Maîtres contemporains de l'orgue* (Paris, 1900); special S.-S. issue of *Le Monde Musical* (Oct. 31, 1901); A. Hervey, *French Music in the 19th Century* (London, 1903); E. Baumann, *Les Grandes Formes de la musique: L'Œuvre de S.-S.* (Paris, 1905; new ed., 1923); special S.-S. issue of *Musica* (June 1907); L. Aubin, *Le Drame lyrique* (Tours, 1908); R. Rolland, *Musiciens d'aujourd'hui* (Paris, 1908; English transl., 1914); A. Jullien, *Musiciens d'hier et d'aujourd'hui* (Paris, 1910); O. Sérè, *Musiciens français d'aujourd'hui* (rev. ed., 1921); J. Bonnerot, *C. S.-S.* (Paris, 1914; 2nd ed., 1922); L. Augé de Lassus, *S.-S.* (Paris, 1914); J. Montargis, *C. S.-S.* (Paris, 1919); *Funerailles de S.-S.* (collection of speeches, Paris, 1921); J. Chantavoine, *L'Œuvre dramatique de C. S.-S.* (Paris, 1921); A. Hervey, *S.-S.* (London, 1921); W. Lyle, *C. S.-S., His Life and Art* (London, 1923); G. Servières, *S.-S.* (Paris, 1923; 2nd ed., 1930); J. Handschin, *C. S.-S.* (Zürich, 1930); J. Normand, *S.-S.* (1930); L. Schneider, *Une Heure avec S.-S.* (1930); J. Langlois, *C. S.-S.* (Moulins, 1934); R. Dumanine, *Les Origines normandes de C. S.-S.* (Rouen, 1937); René Fauchois, *La Vie et l'œuvre prodigieuse de C. S.-S.* (Paris, 1938); D. Brook, *Five Great French Composers* (London, 1946); J. Chantavoine, *C. S.-S.* (Paris, 1947); James Harding, *Saint-Saëns and His Circle* (London, 1965).

Sainton, Prosper, violinist; b. Toulouse, June 5, 1813; d. London, Oct. 17, 1890. He was a pupil of Habeneck at the Paris Cons., winning 1st prize for violin in 1834; was prof. at the Cons. of Toulouse (1840–44); went to

England in 1844; appointed prof. at the Royal Academy of Music in 1845; became concertmaster of the London Philharmonic (1846–54), at Covent Garden (1847–71), and at Her Majesty's Theatre (1871–80). He married (1860) **Charlotte Helen Dolby**, a contralto (b. London, May 17, 1821; d. there, Feb. 18, 1885). Sainton wrote 2 violin concertos and several violin solos; his wife composed some songs and choruses.

Saito, Hideo, Japanese cellist, conductor and music educator; b. Tokyo, May 23, 1902; d. there, Sept. 18, 1974. He went to Germany for music study; was a cello student of Julius Klengel in Leipzig (1923–27) and of Feuermann in Berlin (1930). Returning to Japan, he played cello in the Nihon Symph. Orch., and studied conducting with Rosenstock, then resident in Japan. He was a co-founder of the Toho Music School in Tokyo, where he taught cello, conducting and academic music courses. Among his students was Seiji Ozawa, who came to regard Saito's influence as a major factor in his own career.

Sakač, Branimir, Croatian composer; b. Zagreb, June 5, 1918. He graduated in composition from the Zagreb Music Academy in 1941; later taught there. In his music he adopted a purely structural method, using highly dissonant contrapuntal combinations within strict neo-Classical forms.

WORKS: *Serenade* for string orch. (1947); *Simfonija o mrtvom vojniku (Symphony of the Dead Soldiers,* 1951); Chamber Symphony (1953); Solo Violin Sonata (1953); *3 sintetskim poemama (Synthetic Poems,* 1959); *Aleatory Prelude* for piano and tape (1961); *2 Miniatures* for flute, harp and percussion (1963); *Episode* for orch. and tape (1963); *Study I* for piano and percussion (1963); *Study II* for piano (1964); *Structure I* for chamber ensemble (1965); *Prostori (Spaces)* for orch; *Solo I* for violin and chamber orch.; *Doppio* for string quartet; *Canto dalla Commedia,* after Dante, for solo violin, percussion and chorus (1969); *Turm-Musik (Tower Music)* for orch. (1970); *Ad Litteram* for piano (1970); *Barasou (Ballad of Rats and Mice)* for voice and chamber ensemble (1971); *Matrix Symphony* for 3 voices and orch. (1972); *Syndrome* for chamber ensemble (1974); tape pieces.

Sala, Nicola, Italian composer and theorist; b. Tocco-Gaudio, near Benevento, April 7, 1713; d. Naples, Aug. 31, 1801. He was a pupil of Fago, Abos, and Leo at the Cons. della Pietà de' Turchini, Naples; apparently was not engaged as a teacher there until his old age; was appointed 2nd maestro when he was 74, in 1787, and 1st maestro 6 years later; continued to teach until 1799. It was during his tenure at the Cons. that he publ. his most celebrated theoretical work, *Regole del contrappunto prattico* (3 vols., 1794; reprinted by Choron in Paris, 1808, as *Principii di composizione delle scuole d'Italia*). He brought out several operas: *Vologeso* (Rome, 1737), *Zenobia* (Naples, Jan. 12, 1761), *Demetrio* (Naples, Dec. 12, 1762), and *Merope* (Naples, Aug. 13, 1769); also an oratorio, *Giuditta* (1780), Masses, litanies, and other religious works.

Salabert, Francis, French music publisher; b. Paris, July 27, 1884; d. in an airplane accident at Shannon, Ireland, Dec. 28, 1946. The Editions Salabert was founded by his father, **Édouard Salabert,** in 1896; at the latter's death in 1903, Francis Salabert took over the management. A professional musician and composer in his own right, he made a series of practical arrangements for small orch. of numerous classical and modern works, which were widely used. Editions Salabert expanded greatly through the purchase of the stock of orchestral and other music of the firms Gaudet (1927), Mathot (1930), Senart (1941), Rouart-Lerolle (1942), and Deiss (1946). On the death of Francis Salabert, his widow assumed the directorship.

Salaman, Charles Kensington, English pianist; b. London, March 31, 1814; d. there, June 23, 1901. He studied with Charles Neate in London and with Henri Herz in Paris. Returning to London, he took active part in musical affairs; in 1853 he founded, with Lucas Blagrove and others, the Concerti da Camera; from 1837 to 1855 was an associate of the Philharmonic Society; in 1849 he was a founder of an amateur choral society in London; co-founder, in 1858, of the Musical Society of London; was one of the founders of the Musical Association in 1874. He wrote a comic opera, *Pickwick* (London, 1889); about 100 choral works for the synagogue; many anthems, part-songs, piano pieces; also many songs to English, Latin, Greek, and Hebrew texts.

Salas Viú, Vicente, Spanish-Chilean musicologist; b. Madrid, Jan. 29, 1911; d. Santiago, Chile, Sept. 2, 1967. He studied academic subjects at the Univ. of Madrid; music with Rodolfo Halffter; wrote for various literary and musical publications until 1939, when he emigrated to Chile; settled in Santiago. He published a very valuable book, *La Creación musical en Chile 1900–1951* (Santiago, 1952), in 2 sections, embracing a general account of musical activities in Chile and detailed biographies of 40 Chilean composers; also *La última luz de Mozart* (Santiago, 1949); *Momentos decisivos en la música* (Buenos Aires, 1957).

Salazar, Adolfo, eminent Spanish musicologist; b. Madrid, March 6, 1890; d. Mexico City, Sept. 27, 1958. He studied with Manuel de Falla and Pérez Casas. In 1914 he became editor-in-chief of the *Revista Musical Hispano-Americana* (until 1918); from 1918 to 1936 was music critic of the influential Madrid daily *El Sol;* was founder and later secretary of the Sociedad Nacional de Música (1915–22). During the final period of the Spanish Civil War he was cultural attaché at the Spanish embassy in Washington (1938–39); then settled in Mexico City as writer and teacher.

WRITINGS: *Música y músicos de hoy* (Madrid, 1928), *Sinfonía y ballet* (Madrid, 1929); *La Música contemporánea en España* (Madrid, 1930), *La Música actual en Europa y sus problemas* (Madrid, 1935), *El Siglo romántico* (Madrid, 1935; new ed. as *Los grandes compositores de la época romántica,* 1955); *La Música en el siglo XX* (Madrid, 1936); *Música y sociedad en el sigo XX* (Mexico, 1939), *Las grandes estructuras de la música* (Mexico, 1940), *La Rosa de los vientos en la música europea* (Mexico, 1940; reissued in 1954 as *Conceptos fondamentales en la his-*

toria de la música); *Forma y expresión en la música: ensayo sobre la formación de los géneros en la música instrumental* (Mexico, 1941), *Introducción en la música actual* (Mexico, 1941), *Los grandes periodos en la historia de la música* (Mexico, 1941), *Poesía y música en lengua vulgar y sus antecedentes en la edad media* (Mexico, 1943), *La Música en la sociedad europea* (Mexico, 1942–46; a monumental work; 4 vols.; covers the entire period of music history until modern times), *La Música moderna* (Buenos Aires, 1944; in English as *Music in Our Time*, N.Y., 1946), *Música, instrumentos y danzas en las obras de Cervantes* (Mexico, 1948), *La Danza y el ballet* (Mexico, 1949), *La Música, como proceso histórico de su invención* (Mexico, 1950), *J. S. Bach* (Mexico, 1951), *La Música de España* (Buenos Aires, 1953); several other smaller works, brochures and pamphlets on a variety of subjects. Salazar was also a composer; wrote 3 symphonic works: *Paisajes, Estampas,* and *Don Juan de los Infernos;* songs to words by Verlaine; piano pieces.

Saldoni, Baltasar, Spanish composer and lexicographer; b. Barcelona, Jan. 4, 1807; d. Madrid, Dec. 3, 1889. He was a pupil of Mateo Ferrer at Montserrat and of Carnicer in Madrid. In 1826 he produced in Madrid his light opera, *El Triunfo del amor,* and a series of Italian operas: *Saladino e Clotilde* (1833), *Ipermestra* (1838), and *Cleonice regina di Siria* (1840); also 2 Spanish operas, *Boabdil* (1845) and *Guzmán el Bueno* (1855). He achieved his best successes with zarzuelas *El Rey y la costurera* (1853), *La Corte de Mónaco* (1857), and *Los Maridos en las máscaras* (1864). In 1840 he was appointed prof. of singing at the Madrid Cons. His *magnum opus* as a scholar was the *Diccionario biográfico-bibliográfico de efemérides de músicos españoles,* in 4 vols. (Madrid, 1868–81), to which a supplementary volume was added, in the form of a chronology of births and deaths of Spanish musicians, day by day, year by year, with exhaustive biographical notes. This monumental compilation, upon which Saldoni worked nearly 40 years, contains (inevitably) a number of errors, but in the absence of other musicographical works on Spanish musicians, it still retains considerable documentary value.

Sales, Pietro Pompeo, Italian composer; b. Brescia, 1729; d. Hanau, Germany, Nov. 21, 1797. Little is known about his early life; when a devastating earthquake destroyed his home in Italy, he went to Germany; in 1760 was in the service of the Prince-Bishop of Augsburg as Kapellmeister; was in Stuttgart in 1766–69; from 1770 was Kapellmeister with the Elector at Koblenz, where Burney met him in 1772. After the French invasion of 1797 he fled to Hanau, where he died shortly afterwards. He also visited London. His operas had performances in Germany and Italy, as well as in London; he also composed oratorios, church music, instrumental works; a piano sonata is reprinted in Haffner's *Raccolta Musicale.*
BIBLIOGRAPHY: F. Collignon, *Pietro Pompeo Sales* (Bonn, 1923).

Saleski, Gdal, Russian cellist; b. Kiev, Feb. 11, 1888; d. Los Angeles, Oct. 8, 1966. He sang in a Kiev synagogue; then went to Germany where he took lessons in cello with Julius Klengel at the Leipzig Cons.; also played in the cello section of the Gewandhaus Orch. under Nikisch; subsequently was in Scandinavia (1915–21); then went to the U.S.; played cello in the NBC Orch. under Toscanini (1937–48). He published a compilation, *Famous Musicians of a Wandering Race* (N.Y., 1927; revised ed. under the title *Famous Musicians of Jewish Origin,* N.Y., 1949); biographical data in it are often inaccurate; both editions include Bizet, Ravel, and Saint-Saëns, in the mistaken belief that since they wrote music on Jewish subjects, they must have been Jews.

Saléza, Albert, French tenor; b. Bruges, near Bayonne, Oct. 18, 1867; d. Paris, Nov. 26, 1916. He studied at the Paris Cons., taking the 1st prize in singing, 2nd in opera; made his debut at the Opéra-Comique on Sept. 19, 1888, as Mylio in *Le Roi d'Ys* by Lalo; then sang at Nice (1892–94), at the Paris Opéra (1892–94), at Monte Carlo (1895–97), returning to the Paris Opéra in 1897; sang at the Théâtre de la Monnaie, Brussels (1898–99); also appeared at Covent Garden, London; was engaged at the Metropolitan House, N.Y., from 1899 to 1901; returned to sing in Paris in 1901. In 1911 he became prof. of singing at the Paris Cons.
BIBLIOGRAPHY: H. de Curzon, *Croquis d'artistes* (Paris, 1898).

Salieri, Antonio, illustrious Italian composer; b. Legnago, near Verona, Aug. 18, 1750; d. Vienna, May 7, 1825. He studied music with his brother, Francesco, who was a violinist, and also took lessons from the organist Simoni. His father died in 1765, and Salieri was taken to Venice by a wealthy patron; there he studied harmony with Pescetti and singing with Pacini. Gassmann, the Viennese composer, who was in Venice at the time, took Salieri to Vienna in 1766, and provided there for his education. While Gassmann was in Rome (1770), Salieri took his place as conductor at the Burg Theater in Vienna, and brought out there his 1st opera, *Le Donne letterate,* with marked success. From that time until 1774 he produced 9 more operas of his own, all in the Italian style, the last being *La Calamità dei cuori.* When Gassmann died in 1774, Salieri became his successor as court composer. He began a serious study of Gluck's style under the master's own direction; Gluck recommended Salieri to the administration of the Académie de Musique in Paris for the composition of a French opera; this was produced in Paris as *Les Danaïdes,* based on an Italian libretto, *Ipermestra,* by Calzabigi; the opera was advertised as composed by Gluck in collaboration with Salieri, but after the 12th performance Gluck declared that the work was entirely by Salieri; it remained in the repertory of the Paris Opéra for many years. Salieri then returned to Vienna, where he produced a comic opera, *La Grotta di Trofonio* (Oct. 12, 1785), with much success. His French opera, *Les Horaces,* was produced in Paris on Dec. 7, 1786, and proved a failure, but his next French opera, *Tarare* (Paris Opéra, June 8, 1787), made a sensation, and was performed on all the principal stages of Europe; Lorenzo Da Ponte made a revised Italian version of it as *Axur, Re d'Ormus,* which was produced in Vienna on Jan. 8, 1788, with enormous acclaim. In 1788 Salieri succeeded Bonno as court Kapellmeister at Vienna, retaining this post until 1824, but he did not conduct operatic performances after 1790, confining himself to the concerts of the Hofsängerkapelle; was also conductor of the Tonkünstler-Sozietät (founded in 1771 by Gassmann) until 1818. In Vienna he enjoyed great renown as a teacher; Beethoven studied with him, and acknowledged himself willingly as Salieri's pupil; Schubert and Liszt were also his pupils. Salieri was undoubtedly a master of the Italian method of composition, and his technique in harmony and counterpoint was of the highest. He had a reputation for intrigue, and this gave rise to the fantastic story of his poisoning of Mozart (Pushkin publ. a drama, *Mozart and Salieri,* based on this story, and Rimsky-Korsakov set it to music). In all, Salieri wrote 39 operas, of which 6 remained unproduced; 11 cantatas, 6 Masses, 4 Te Deums, a Requiem, many other pieces of church music; 2 symphonies; 2 piano concertos; various other instrumental works.

BIBLIOGRAPHY: I. von Mosel, *Über das Leben und die Werke des Anton Salieri* (Vienna, 1827); A. von Hermann, *Antonio Salieri* (Vienna, 1897); C. Serini, "Antonio Salieri," *Rivista Musicale Italiana* (1926); R. Nützlader, "Salieri als Kirchenmusiker," *Studien zur Musikwissenschaft* 14 (Vienna, 1927); G. Magnani, *Antonio Salieri* (Legnago, 1934); A. Della Corte, *Un Italiano all'estero, Antonio Salieri* (Turin, 1936); E. J. Juin, "Documenti inediti sul Salieri come maestro di F. Liszt e di altri," *Rivista Musicale Italiana* (1936); R. Angermüller, *Antonio Salieri* (3 vols.; vol. 1, Salzburg, 1970; vol. 3, Munich, 1971).

Salinas, Francisco de, Spanish organist and theorist; b. Burgos, March 1, 1513; d. Salamanca, Jan. 13, 1590. He became blind at the age of 10; was taught organ playing, and studied languages at the Univ. of Salamanca. In 1538 he was taken to Italy by Cardinal Sarmiento; in 1553-58, was organist to the Duke of Alba at the vice-regal court of Naples, where Diego Ortiz was maestro. In 1561 Salinas returned to Spain, and from 1567 until his retirement in 1587 was prof. of music at the Univ. of Salamanca. He wrote the theoretical treatise *De musica libri septem* (Salamanca, 1577; English translation by A. M. Daniels, Univ. of Southern California, 1962), chiefly valuable for the examples of Spanish folk music it contains. It was to Salinas that Luis de León dedicated his famous *Ode to Music.*

BIBLIOGRAPHY: Otto Kinkeldey, *Orgel und Klavier in der Musik des 16. Jahrhunderts* (Leipzig, 1910); F. Pedrell, *Lírica nacionalizada* (Paris, 1913; pp. 211-63; contains musical examples); J. B. Trend, "Francisco de Salinas," *Music & Letters* (Jan. 1927).

Sallinen, Aulis, Finnish composer; b. Salmi, April 9, 1935. He studied under Aarre Merikanto and Joonas Kokkonen at the Sibelius Academy (1955-60); was managing director of the Finnish Radio Symph. (1960-70); taught at the Sibelius Academy (1963-76); appointed Arts Professor by the Finnish State for the years 1976-81. In his music he uses modern techniques, with a prevalence of euphonious dissonance and an occasional application of serialism.

WORKS: an opera, *Ratsumies* (*The Horseman,* 1973-74; Savonlinna Opera Fest., July 17, 1975); a ballet, *Variations sur Mallarmé* (1967; Helsinki, 1968); *2 Mythical Scenes* for orch. (1956); Concerto for Chamber Orch. (1959-60); *Variations* for cello and orch. (1960-61); *3 Lyrical Songs About Death* for baritone, male chorus and orch. (1962); an orch. elegy, *Mauermusik* (*Wall Music*), subtitled "In memory of a certain young German" killed at the Berlin Wall (1962); *14 Juventas Variations* for orch. (1963); *Metamorphoses* for piano and chamber orch. (1964); Violin Concerto (1968); *Chorali* for 32 wind instruments, percussion, harp and celesta (1970); 3 symphonies: No. 1 (1970-71), No. 2, *Symphonic Dialogue,* for solo percussionist and orch. (1972) and No. 3 (1974-75); *Suita grammaticale* for children's choir, strings, kantele and school instruments (1971-72); *Chamber Music I* for chamber string orch. (1975); *Chamber Music II* for alto flute and chamber string orch. (1975-76); Cello Concerto (1976); 4 string quartets: No. 1 (1958); No. 2, *Canzona* (1960); No. 3, *Some Aspects of Peltoniemi Hintrik's Funeral March* (1969); No. 4, *Quiet Songs* (1971); *Serenade* for 2 wind quartets (1963); *Elegy for Sebastian Knight* for solo cello (1964); *Quattro per quattro* for violin, cello, oboe and harpsichord (1964-65); *4 Etudes* for violin and piano (1970); *Chaconne* for organ (1970); Solo Cello Sonata (1971); *Metamorfora* for cello and piano (1974); *Canto and Ritornello* for solo violin (1975); *4 Dream Songs* for solo voice and piano (1972).

Salmanov, Vadim, Russian composer; b. St. Petersburg, Nov. 4, 1912. He studied piano with his father; theory with Akimenko; composition at the Leningrad Cons. with Gnessin; in 1952 he was appointed prof. there. His early works are marked by broad Russian melodism, with the harmonic structure following the models of Prokofiev and Shostakovich; during his last period he adopted more advanced techniques; his Violin Sonata (1962) is written in the 12-tone idiom. He also wrote Symph. No. 1 (1952); *Poetic Pictures,* symph. suite (1955); *The Twelve,* oratorio to the text by Alexander Blok (1957); Symph. No. 2 (1959).

BIBLIOGRAPHY: M. Aranovsky, *V. N. Salmanov* (Leningrad, 1960).

Salmenhaara, Erkki, Finnish composer; b. Helsinki, March 12, 1941. He studied at the Sibelius Academy with Kokkonen; then went to Vienna, where he took lessons with Ligeti. His music is often inspired by literary works; he favors unusual combinations of instruments, including electronics; makes use of serial techniques in dense, fastidious sonorities.

WORKS: opera, *Portugalin nainen* (*The Woman of Portugal,* 1972); *9 Improvisations,* concerto for piano, strings and timpani; Symph. No. 1; Symph. No. 2 (1963, revised 1966); Symph. No. 3 (1964); *Le Bateau ivre* (after Rimbaud), for orch. (1966); *BFK-83* for orch. (1967); *La Fille en mini-jupe,* poem for orch. (1967); *Suomi-Finland,* an "unsymphonic poem" for orch. (1967); *Requiem profanum* for soprano, alto, baritone, strings and piano (1968-69); *Illuminations* (after Rimbaud), poem for orch. (1971); Symph. No. 4, *Nel mezzo del cammin di nostra vita,* after Dante (1971); Horn Concerto (Oslo, Oct. 3, 1974); Cello Sonata (1960); String Trio (1961); *La Clarté vibrante,* cantata for soprano, 4 cellos and percussion; *Pan and Echo* for 4 suspended cymbals, tam-tam and amplifier; Concerto for 2 violins with amplifiers and loudspeakers; *Composition* for string quartet (1963); *Elegia I* for 3 flutes, 2 trumpets and double bass (1963); *Elegia II* for 2 string quartets (1963); *Composition 3* for violin, clarinet, guitar and percussion (1963); Wind Quintet (1964); *Elegia III* for cello (1965); 3 Piano Sonatas (1966, 1973, 1975); *Elegia IV* for viola (1967); *Etude* for harpsichord (1969); *Trois Scènes de nuit* for violin and piano (1970); *Quartetto* for flute, violin, viola and cello (1971); *Prelude, Pop Tune and Fugue* for flute; *And the Fire and the Rose Are One* for 2 violins (1972); songs.

Salmhofer, Franz, Austrian composer; b. Vienna, Jan. 22, 1900; d. there, Sept. 2, 1975. He was a chorister at the Admont Monastery in Styria until 1914; then studied composition with Schreker at the Vienna Academy, and musicology with Guido Adler at the Vienna Univ. In 1923 he married the pianist **Margit Gál.** In 1929 he became conductor at the Hofburg Theater, for which he composed incidental music, ballets, and operas; he resigned in 1939; from 1945 to 1955 he was conductor at the Vienna State Opera.

WORKS: operas: *Dame in Traum* (Vienna, Dec. 26, 19365), *Iwan Sergejewitsch Tarassenko* (Vienna, March 9, 1938), *Das Werbekleid* (Vienna, June 25, 1946); ballets: *Das lockende Phantom, Der Taugenichts in Wien, Weihnachtsmärchen, Österreichische Bauernhochzeit;* 2 symphonies (1947; 1955); the overtures *Der Ackermann und der Tod* and *Heroische Ouvertüre;* Trumpet Concerto; Cello Concerto; *Der geheimnisvolle Trompeter,* symph. poem for narrator and orch., after Walt Whitman's *The Mystic Trumpeter* (1924); *Kammersuite,* for 16 instruments; (Vienna, May 10, 1923); String Quartet; Piano Quartet; Viola Sonata; Cello Sonata; songs; piano pieces.

Salmon, Alvan Glover, American composer and pianist; b. Southold, N.Y., Sept. 23, 1868; d. Boston, Sept. 17, 1917. He studied at the New England Cons. in Boston, graduating in 1888; then with Goetschius and MacDowell in N.Y.; went to Russia, where he took lessons from Glazunov and became deeply interested in Russian music; collected a valuable library of works by Russian composers (about 3000 vols.) and an extensive collection of autographs; publ. numerous essays. His compositions are chiefly for piano (*Valse arabesque, Scherzo, Novelette, Fileuse, Impromptu, Tarentelle fantastique,* etc.).

Salmond, Felix, distinguished English cellist; b. London, Nov. 19, 1888; d. New York, Feb. 19, 1952. He studied at the Royal College of Music with W. E. Whitehouse, and in Brussels with Édouard Jacobs; made his debut in London (1909), accompanied at the piano by his mother, Mrs. Norman Salmond. He gave the world première of Elgar's Cello Concerto under Elgar's direction, on Oct. 27, 1919; after a European tour, he settled in America (debut, N.Y., March 29, 1922); was head of the cello dept. at the Curtis Institute of Music in Philadelphia (1925–42) and taught cello at the Juilliard Graduate School of Music in N.Y.

from its opening in 1924. He enjoyed the reputation of a fine chamber music player and an excellent teacher.

Salò, Gasparo da. See **Gasparo da Salò.**

Saloman, Siegfried, composer; b. Tondern, Schleswig, Oct. 2, 1816; d. Stockholm, July 22, 1899. He studied composition with J. P. Hartmann in Copenhagen, and violin with Lipinski in Dresden. He lived in Copenhagen for many years and produced 2 operas there, *Tordenskjold I Dynekilen* (May 23, 1844) and *Diamantkorset* (*The Diamond Cross;* March 20, 1847); toured Russia and Holland (1847–50); married the singer **Henriette Nissen,** and traveled with her; in 1859, settled in Russia; one of his operas, to a German libretto, was produced in Russian as *Karpatskaya Roza* in Mosocw, Jan. 7, 1868; several other operas were produced in Stockholm, where he went in 1879 after the death of his wife. Some of his violin pieces and songs have been published.

Salomon (Salomonis). See **Elias Salomon.**

Salomon, Johann Peter, German violinist, composer, and impresario; b. Bonn (baptized Feb. 20), 1745; d. London, Nov. 25, 1815. He was a member of the Electoral orch. at Bonn (1758–62); after a successful concert tour he was engaged as concertmaster and composer to Prince Heinrich of Prussia at Rheinsberg (1764). When the orch. was disbanded Salomon went to Paris and then to London, where he settled in 1781; made himself known as a violinist and conductor; introduced symphonies by Haydn and Mozart in a series of concerts he gave in 1786. In 1790 he went to Italy to engage singers for the Italian Opera in London, and from there went to Vienna, where he saw Haydn and persuaded him to accept an engagement in London. At Salomon's behest Haydn wrote the works familiarly known as his "Salomon Symphonies"; it is through his association with Haydn's 2 visits to England, in 1791 and 1794, that Salomon's name remains in the annals of music. He was a founder of the Philharmonic Society in London (1813). His own works are of merely antiquarian interest; they include the operas *Les Recruteurs* (Rheinsberg, 1771), *Le Séjour du bonheur* (Rheinsberg, 1773), *Titus* (Rheinsberg, 1774), *La Reine de Golconde* (Rheinsberg, 1776), *Windsor Castle,* or *The Fair Maid of Kent* (London, 1795); also violin sonatas.

BIBLIOGRAPHY: "Memoir of Johann Peter Salomon," *Harmonicon* (London, Feb. 1830).

Salonen, Sulo, Finnish composer; b. Pyhtää, Jan. 27, 1899; d. Porvoo, May 21, 1976. He was a pupil of Furuhjelm and Palmgren; devoted himself mainly to the composition of sacred music; structurally, they continue the tradition of Lutheran services of the 19th century.

WORKS: *Passion Cantata* (1942); *Viisauden ylistys (In Praise of Wisdom)* for narrator, voices and instruments (1961); *Requiem* (1962); Wind Quintet (1962); String Trio (1971); 2 string quartets (1971, 1972); *Cum jubilo* for chorus, organ and percussion (Helsinki, Jan. 24, 1974); about 50 motets; numerous organ pieces.

Salter, Mary Elizabeth Turner (Mrs. Sumner Salter), American soprano; b. Peoria, Ill., March 15, 1856; d. Orangeburg, N.Y., Sept. 12, 1938. She studied in Burlington, Iowa, and Boston; from 1874 to 1893, sang in churches in Boston and N.Y.; she married **Sumner Salter** in 1881, and settled with him in Williamstown, Mass.

WORKS: She publ. a number of song cycles, and was still composing at the age of 80 (*Christmas Song,* 1936). Song cycles: *Love's Epitome, A Night in Naishapur, Lyrics from Sappho, From Old Japan;* about 80 songs publ. separately (*The Cry of Rachel, The Pine Tree, Für Musik, Die stille Wasserrose,* etc.); duets, some part-songs, and church music.

Salter, Sumner, American organist and arranger; b. Burlington, Iowa, June 24, 1856; d. New York, March 5, 1944. After graduating from Amherst College he studied at the New England Cons.; then taught at various schools in Boston and elsewhere; from 1905 to 1923, was director of music at Williams College; then retired. He edited *The Pianist and Organist* (official organ of the American Guild of Organists) from 1895 to 1898; publ. church music and numerous organ arrangements of various works. In 1881 he married **Mary E. Turner,** the singer and composer.

Salva, Tadeáš, Slovak composer; b. Lucky, near Ruzomberok, Oct. 22, 1937. He studied with Ján Zimmer in Bratislava; then with Cikker and A. Moyzes in Prague and with Szabelski and Lutoslawski in Warsaw (1960-65); was manager of the music dept. of the radio at Košice (1965-68); then was a dramaturgist for the TV studio in Bratislava. He occasionally uses jazz elements.

WORKS: television opera, *Margita a Besné (Margaret and the Wild,* 1972); *Cantiliniae* for chamber chorus (1961); *Canticum Zachariae* (1963); Concerto for clarinet, narrator, 4 voices and percussion (1965); *Symfónia lásky (Symphony of Love)* for narrator, chorus, 3 oboes, horn, double bass, piano and percussion (1965); *Requiem* for 3 narrators, 3 choruses, brass, 6 kettledrums, percussion and organ (1966); Concerto for cello and chamber orch. (1967); *Mša glagolskaja (Glagolitic Mass)* for solos, chorus, 2 harps, 3 oboes, brass, percussion and organ (1969); *Aliquoten* for tape (1971); Nonet (1971); *Music per Archi* (1971); *War and the World,* poem for baritone, women's chorus, double bass, organ and chamber orch. (1972); *Ballad-Fantasy* for soprano, piano and orch. (1972); *Burlesque* for violin and chamber orch. (1972); *Elegies* for narrator, soprano, chorus and chamber orch. (Bratislava, Oct. 5, 1974); *Ballad* for 2 clarinets (1974); 3 string quartets; other chamber music songs.

Salvayre, (Gervais-Bernard-) Gaston, French composer; b. Toulouse, June 24, 1847; d. St. Ague, near Toulouse, May 17, 1916. He was a pupil at the Cons. of Toulouse; then entered the Paris Cons., studying organ with Benoist and composition with Ambroise Thomas. After failing to win the Prix de Rome for 5 consecutive years, he finally obtained it in 1872 with the cantata *Calypso.* He was subsequently chorusmaster at the Opéra-Populaire in 1877.

WORKS: operas: *Le Bravo* (Paris, April 18, 1877), *Richard III* (St. Petersburg, Dec. 21, 1883), *Egmont* (Paris, Dec. 6, 1886), *La Dame de Monsoreau* (Paris, Jan. 30, 1888), *Solange* (Paris, March 10, 1909); ballets: *Le Fandango* (Paris, Nov. 26, 1877), *La Fontaine des fées* (Paris, 1899), *L'Odalisque* (Paris, 1905); for orch.: *Le Jugement dernier* (Paris, Dec. 3, 1876, under the title *La Résurrection*), *Ouverture symphonique* (Paris, March 22, 1874), *Air et Variations* for string orch. (1877).

Salviucci, Giovanni, Italian composer; b. Rome, Oct. 26, 1907; d. there, Sept. 5, 1937. He studied with Respighi and Casella; developed a fine style of instrumental writing; his works were performed by Italian orchestras with increasing frequency, but his early death cut short his promising career. His *Ouverture* in C-sharp minor (1932) received a national prize.

WORKS: the symph. poem *La Tentazione e la preghiera* (1931); *Sinfonia italiana* (1932; Rome, Feb. 25, 1934); *Introduzione, Passacaglia e Finale* (1934); *Serenata* for 9 instruments (1937); also *Psalm of David,* for soprano and chamber orch. (Rome, 1935); *Alcesti,* after Euripides, for chorus and orch. (1937).

BIBLIOGRAPHY: F. Ballo, "Giovanni Salviucci," *Rassegna Musicale* (Jan. 1937).

Salzedo (originally **Salzédo**), **Carlos,** eminent harpist and composer; b. Arcachon, France, April 6, 1885; d. Waterville, Maine, Aug. 17, 1961. He studied at the Cons. of Bordeaux (1891-94), winning 1st prize in piano; then entered the Paris Cons., where his father, **Gaston Salzédo,** was prof. of singing; studied with Charles de Bériot (piano), gaining 1st prize in 1901, and with Hasselmans (harp), also receiving 1st prize. He began his career as a concert harpist upon graduation; traveled all over Europe (1901-05); was solo harpist of the Association des Premiers Prix de Paris in Monte Carlo (1905-09); in 1909 settled in N.Y.; was 1st harpist in the orch. of the Metropolitan Opera Co. (1909-13). In 1913 he formed the Trio de Lutèce (from Lutetia, ancient name for Paris), with Georges Barrère (flute) and Paul Kéfer (cello). In 1921 he was cofounder, with Edgard Varèse, of the International Composers' Guild in N.Y., with the aim of promoting modern music; this organization presented many important contemporary works; in the same year he founded a modern music magazine, *Eolian Review,* later renamed *Eolus* (discontinued in 1933). He became an American citizen in 1923; was elected president of the National Association of Harpists; held teaching positions at the Institute of Musical Art, N.Y., and the Juilliard Graduate School of Music; organized and headed the harp dept. at the Curtis Institute of Music in Philadelphia. In 1931 he established the Salzedo Harp Colony at Camden, Maine, for teaching and performing during the summer months. Salzedo introduced a number of special effects, and publ. special studies for his new techniques; designed a "Salzedo Model" harp, capable of rendering novel sonorities (Eolian Flux, Eolian chords, gushing chords, percussion, etc.). His own compositions are rhythmically intricate and contrapuntally elaborate and require a virtuoso technique.

WORKS: *Terres enchantées,* for orch. with harp solo (performed under the title *The Enchanted Isle* by

Salzedo with the Chicago Symph. Orch., Nov. 28, 1919); *5 Poetical Studies* for harp solo (1918); *3 Poems* for soprano, 6 harps, and 3 wind instruments (1919); *Bolmimerie* for 7 harps (1919); *4 Preludes to the Afternoon of a Telephone,* for 2 harps (1921); *Sonata* for harp and piano (1922); *3 Poems by Mallarmé,* for soprano, harp, and piano (1924); Concerto for harp and 7 wind instruments (N.Y., April 17, 1927; composer soloist); *Pentacle,* 5 pieces for 2 harps (1928); *Préambule et Jeux,* for harp, 4 wind instruments, and 5 string instruments (Paris, 1929); *Scintillation* for harp solo (1936); *Panorama,* suite for harp solo (1937); *10 Wedding Presents,* for harp solo (1946–52); etc.; many transcriptions for harp of various works by Bach, Corelli, Rameau, Haydn, Brahms, etc. He publ. *Modern Study of the Harp* (N.Y., 1921), *Method for the Harp* (N.Y., 1929); *The Art of Modulating* (in collaboration with Lucile Lawrence; N.Y., 1950).

Salzer, Felix, distinguished Austrian-American theorist and pedagogue; b. Vienna, June 13, 1904. He studied theory and composition with Schenker and Weise; musicology with Guido Adler; in 1926 received his Dr. phil. at the Univ. of Vienna; then taught at the New Vienna Cons.; emigrated to the U.S. in 1939; naturalized citizen, 1945. He was on the faculty of the Mannes College of Music in N.Y. (1940–56); in 1956 was appointed to the faculty of Queens College of the City Univ. of N.Y. He is a leading "Schenkerian" theorist and was instrumental in bringing the views of Heinrich Schenker to the attention of American musicians; his own contribution has been in the expansion and application of Schenker's concepts—previously restricted to a narrow range of tonal music—to Remaissance, Medieval, and some 20th-century music. He published a number of important books on music theory: *Sinn und Wesen der abendländischen Mehrstimmigkeit* (Vienna, 1935); *Structural Hearing* (2 vols., N.Y., 1952; new ed., N.Y., 1962); *Counterpoint in Composition: the Study of Voice Leading* (with C. Schachter, N.Y., 1969); edited (with William Mitchell) *Music Forum* (N.Y., 1967–), a hardcover periodical.

Salzman, Eric, American composer and musicologist; b. New York, Sept. 8, 1933. He studied composition at Columbia Univ., with Otto Luening, Vladimir Ussachevsky, William Mitchell and Jack Beeson (B.A., 1954) and at Princeton Univ. with Roger Sessions and Milton Babitt (M.F.A., 1956); in addition he took courses in musicology with Oliver Strunk, Arthur Mendel and Nino Pirotta. In 1957 he went to Europe on a Fulbright Fellowship to study with Goffredo Petrassi in Rome; also attended courses of Karlheinz Stockhausen at Darmstadt. Returning to the U.S., he became a music critic for the *N.Y. Times* (1958–62) and for the *N.Y. Herald Tribune* (1963–66). He taught at Queens College of the City of N.Y. (1966–68); then was director of "New Images of Sounds," a series of concerts given at Hunter College, N.Y. In his compositions he follows the most advanced techniques in mixed media.

WORKS: String Quartet (1955); Flute Sonata (1956); *Partita* for solo violin (1958); *Inventions* for orch. (1959); *The Owl and the Cuckoo,* for soprano, guitar and chamber ensemble (1963); *Verses and Cantos* for 4 voices and instruments, with electronic extensions (N.Y., Nov. 30, 1967); *Larynx Music,* magnetic tape piece for dance (1968); *Feedback,* "environment piece" for magnetic tape and film (1968); *The Nude Paper Sermon* for actor, Renaissance consort, chorus, and electronics (1968–69); *The Conjurer,* multimedia spectacle (with Michael Sahl, 1975); *Noah,* spectacle (N.Y., Feb. 10, 1978); aleatory pieces for electronic and mixed media under the general title *The Electric Ear* for performance at the Electric Circus in Greenwich Village in New York. He publ. *Twentieth Century Music: An Introduction* (Englewood Cliffs, N.J., 1967).

Samara, Spiro, Greek composer; b. Corfu, Nov. 29, 1861; d. Athens, March 25, 1917. He was a pupil of Enrico Stancampiano in Athens; later of Léo Delibes at the Paris Cons. He won considerable success with his 1st opera, *Flora Mirabilis* (Milan, May 16, 1886), and devoted himself almost exclusively to dramatic compositions. Other operas were *Medgè* (Rome, 1888), *Lionella* (Milan, 1891), *La Martire* (Naples, May 23, 1894), *La Furia domata* (Milan, 1895); *Storia d'amore* (Milan, 1903; in Gotha, 1906, as *La Biondinetta*), *Mademoiselle de Belle-Isle* (Genoa, Nov. 9, 1905), *Rhea* (Florence, April 11, 1908), *La Guerra in tempo di guerra* (Athens, 1914). He publ. *Scènes orientales,* suite for piano (4 hands); many pieces for piano solo; songs.

Samaroff, Olga (née **Hickenlooper**), American pianist and educator; b. San Antonio, Texas, Aug. 8, 1882; d. New York, May 17, 1948. She studied as a child with her mother and grandmother (Mrs. L. Grünewald, a former concert pianist); subsequently studied in Paris (with Delaborde), Baltimore (with Ernest Hutcheson), and Berlin (with Ernst Jedliczka). She made her concert debut in N.Y. (Jan. 18, 1905) with the N.Y. Symph. Society; appeared with other orchestras in the U.S. and Europe; gave joint recitals with Fritz Kreisler, Zimbalist, and other violinists. In 1911 she married **Leopold Stokowski;** divorced in 1923; for 2 seasons was music critic for the *N.Y. Evening Post* (1927–29); taught at the Juilliard Graduate School and at the Philadelphia Cons. of Music; from 1930, gave master courses in N.Y.; lectured extensively on music appreciation. See *Notable American Women,* III (Cambridge, Mass., 1971).

WRITINGS: *The Layman's Music Book* (N.Y., 1935); *The Magic World of Music* (N.Y., 1936); *A Music Manual* (N.Y., 1937); *An American Musician's Story* (autobiography; N.Y., 1939); *The Listener's Music Book* (N.Y., 1947; enlarged and revised ed. of *The Layman's Music Book*).

Samazeuilh, Gustave, French composer; b. Bordeaux, June 2, 1877; d. Paris, Aug. 4, 1967. He studied music with Chausson and at the Schola Cantorum with Vincent d'Indy; also took some lessons from Paul Dukas. In his music he absorbed the distinct style of French Impressionism, but despite its fine craftsmanship, performances were few and far between.

WORKS: for orch.: *Étude symphonique* (1907), *Nuit* (Paris, March 15, 1925), *Naïades au soir* (Paris, Oct. 18, 1925), *L'Appel de la danse* (1946); for orch.

with chorus: *Le Sommeil de Canope* (1908), *Chant d'Espagne* (Paris, Jan. 10, 1926), *Le Cercle des heures* (Paris, Feb. 17, 1934); String Quartet (1911); *Suite en trio,* for strings (1938); etc.; many transcriptions for piano of orchestral works by d'Indy, Debussy, Franck and Fauré. He was known also as a writer on musical subjects; publ. *Un Musicien français: Paul Dukas* (Paris, 1913; augmented ed., 1936); *Musiciens de mon temps: chroniques et souvenirs* (Paris, 1947).

Saminsky, Lazare, Russian-American composer, conductor, and writer on music; b. Odessa, Nov. 8, 1882; d. Port Chester, N.Y., June 30, 1959. He studied mathematics and philosophy at the Univ. of St. Petersburg; composition with Rimsky-Korsakov and Liadov, conducting with Nicolas Tcherepnin at the St. Petersburg Cons. (graduated, 1910). He emigrated to the U.S. in 1920, settling in N.Y.; in 1923 was a co-founder of the League of Composers; in 1924 appointed music director of Temple Emanu-El, N.Y.; established an annual Three-Choir Festival there in 1936, presenting old and new music. In his compositions he followed the Romantic tradition; Hebrew subjects and styles play an important part in some of his music. He was married to an American writer, Lillian Morgan Buck, who died in 1945; in 1948 married the American pianist **Jennifer Gandar.**
WORKS: operas: *Gagliarda of a Merry Plague,* chamber opera (N.Y., Feb. 22, 1925), *The Daughter of Jephta* (1929), *Julian, the Apostate Caesar* (1923–38); 5 symphonies: No. 1, *Of the Great Rivers,* in "E-Frimoll" (free minor mode; Petrograd, Feb. 25, 1917, composer conducting), No. 2, *Symphonie des Sommets* (1918; Amsterdam, Nov. 16, 1922), No. 3, *Symphony of the Seas* (Paris, June, 1925, composer conducting), No. 4 (Berlin, April 19, 1929, composer conducting), No. 5, *Jerusalem, City of Solomon and Christ,* with chorus (1929–30; performed many years later, N.Y., April 29, 1958); *Vigiliae,* a symph. triptych (Moscow, Feb. 20, 1913, composer conducting); *Lament of Rachel,* suite from a ballet (Boston, March 3, 1922); *Litanies of Women,* for voice and chamber orch. (Paris, May 21, 1926); *Venice,* a "poem-serenade" for chamber orch. (Berlin, May 9, 1928); *Ausonia,* orch. suite (Florence, Feb. 24, 1935); *Three Shadows,* poems for orch. (N.Y., Feb. 6, 1936); *Pueblo, a Moon Epic* (Washington, Feb. 17, 1937); *Stilled Pageant,* for orch. (Zürich, Aug., 1938); *Eon Hours,* suite of 4 rondos for 4 voices and 4 instruments (N.Y., Nov. 28, 1939); *Requiem,* in memory of Lillian M. Saminsky (N.Y., May 20, 1946); *A Sonnet of Petrarch,* for 3 voices and 3 instruments (1947); *To a New World,* for orch. (1932; N.Y., April 16, 1951); several Hebrew services; piano pieces. Books: *Music of Our Day* (N.Y., 1932); *Music of the Ghetto and the Bible* (N.Y., 1934); *Living Music of the Americas* (N.Y., 1949); *Essentials of Conducting* (N.Y., 1958); *Physics and Metaphysics of Music and Essays on the Philosophy of Mathematics* (The Hague, 1957).
BIBLIOGRAPHY: *Lazare Saminsky, Composer and Civic Worker,* a collection of essays by Domenico de Paoli, Leigh Henry, L. Sabaneyev, Joseph Yasser, and Léon Vallas (N.Y., 1930). See also Wayne Shirley, *Modern Music . . . Analytic Index,* edited by W. and C. Lichtenwanger (N.Y., 1976; pp. 183-84).

Sammarco, (Giuseppe) Mario, Italian baritone; b. Palermo, Dec. 13, 1868; d. Milan, Jan. 24, 1930. He studied singing with Antonio Cantelli, making a successful debut at Milan (1894); then sang in Brescia, Madrid, Lisbon, Brussels, Moscow, Warsaw, Berlin, and Vienna. After his London appearance as Scarpia in *Tosca* at Covent Garden (Oct. 19, 1905) he sang there every season until the outbreak of World War I. He made his American debut as Tonio (Feb. 1, 1908) at the Manhattan Opera House, N.Y.; in 1910 joined the Chicago Opera Co. He sang in Russian, Spanish, Italian, French, and English.

Sammartini (or **San Martini**), **Giovanni Battista,** significant Italian composer; younger brother of **Giuseppe Sammartini;** b. Milan, 1701; d. there, Jan. 15, 1775. He served as church organist in Milan; in 1728 he was appointed maestro di cappella at the Santissimo Entierro in Milan; in 1768 held a similar position at S. Gottardo. His historical significance lies not so much in his own music as in his authority as a teacher; Gluck was his student between 1737 and 1741. His own works are important mainly in the evolution of the sonata form, in which he introduced extensive thematic development, but the claim that he anticipated Haydn in the formulation of symphonic form cannot be sustained; a chamber symphony in 4 movements, supposedly written by Sammartini in 1734 and often cited as the earliest work in symphonic form, is apparently nonexistent. But Sammartini was a prodigiously industrious composer; among his works are 3 operas, of which 2 were produced in Milan: *L'Ambizione superata dalla virtù* (1734) and *Agrippina* (1743); an oratorio, *Gesù bambino adorato;* about 20 symphonies; 6 trio sonatas for flute, 2 violins and bass; string quartets; harpsichord sonatas; sacred and secular church music. Four symphonies were brought out by N. Jenkins (*Collegium musicum,* VI, New Haven, 1963); other symphonies were edited by B. D. Churgin (Vol. 1, *The Early Symphonies;* Harvard Publications in Music; Cambridge, Mass., 1968); several concertos were brought out by H. Töttcher (Hamburg, 1968) and by H. Illy (Kassel, 1971).
BIBLIOGRAPHY: Fausto Torrefranca, "Le origini della Sinfonia," *Rivista Musicale Italiana* (1913); G. de Saint-Foix, "La Chronologie de l'œuvre instrumentale de Giovanni Sammartini," *Sammelbände der Internationalen Musik-Gesellschaft* (1914); R. Sondheimer, "G. B. Sammartini," *Zeitschrift für Musikwissenschaft* (1920); H. G. Mishkin, "5 Autograph String Quartets by G. B. Sammartini," *Journal of the American Musicological Society* (Summer 1953); H. G. Mishkin, "The Published Instrumental Works of G. B. Sammartini," *Musical Quarterly* (1959); W. S. Newman, *The Sonata in the Classical Era* (Chapel Hill, N.C., 1963); N. Jenkins and B. Churgin, *Thematic Catalogue of the Works of G. B. Sammartini* (1976).

Sammartini (San Martini), Giuseppe, called "il Londinese" (because he lived in London), to distinguish him from his brother **Giovanni Battista Sammartini;** b. Milan, c.1693; d. London, c.1750. In 1727 he went to London; played the oboe at King's Theatre; then became director of chamber music in the household of the

Prince of Wales. He gave concerts with Arrigoni at Hickford's Rooms in 1732; Burney heard him play in 1744. He contributed a "Sinfonia" and an aria to an oratorio *La calumnia delusa* (1724), a pasticcio by several Italian composers. He further wrote sonatas for 2 flutes, 12 *concerti grossi*, 12 violin sonatas, 8 overtures, harpsichord pieces, etc. A sonata was edited by Riemann in his *Collegium musicum.*

Sammons, Albert Edward, English violinist and composer; b. London, Feb. 23, 1886; d. there, Aug. 24, 1957. He studied with his father and other teachers in London; was 1st violinist of the London String Quartet (1907-16); also concertmaster of the London Philharmonic; edited the Violin Concerto by Delius; composed a *Phantasy Quartet* for strings and other works; taught violin at the Royal College of Music.

Samosud, Samuil, Russian opera conductor; b. Odessa, May 14, 1884; d. Moscow, Nov. 6, 1964. He conducted opera in Leningrad (1917-36); then moved to Moscow, conducting at Bolshoi Theater (1936-43) and at the Stanislavsky Musical Theater (1943-50); also appeared as a symph. conductor.

Sampson, George, English organist and conductor; b. Clifton, July 24, 1861; d. Brisbane, Australia, Dec. 23, 1949. He studied with George Riseley and Harford Lloyd; was organist at various churches in Bristol; in 1898, went to Australia; in 1907 he organized and conducted the Sampson Orch. there, which later became the Queensland State and Municipal Orch. His works include a *Berceuse* for organ and strings, church music, and a *Romance* for violin and piano. Author of *The Pianoforte; Rhythm; Elements of Music; Queensland Manual of Music; A Day with Felix Mendelssohn,* (1910); *Seven Essays* (Cambridge, 1947).

Sams, Eric, English music critic; b. London, May 3, 1926. He was educated at Cambridge Univ.; became active in broadcasting and in musical journalism; contributed regularly to the *Musical Times;* pub. valuable monographs, *The Songs of Hugo Wolf* (London, 1961) and *Songs of Robert Schumann* (London, 1969).

Samuel, Adolphe, Belgian composer; b. Liège, July 11, 1824; d. Ghent, Sept. 11, 1898. He was educated at the Cons. of Liège and that of Brussels, winnning the Belgian Grand Prix de Rome (1845); taught harmony at the Brussels Cons. (1860-70); in 1871 was appointed director of the Ghent Cons. He founded the Brussels Popular Concerts in 1865; in 1869 organized the 1st annual musical festivals, with an orch. of 450 and a chorus of 1200.
WORKS: 5 operas: *Il a rêvé* (1845), *Giovanni da Procida* (1848), *Madeleine* (1849), *Les Deux Prétendants* (1851), *L'Heure de la retrainte* (1852); 7 symphonies; overtures; string quartets; piano pieces; publ. *Cours d'harmonie pratique et de basse chiffrée; Livre de lecture musicale* (400 national airs).
BIBLIOGRAPHY: E. L. V. Mathieu, *Notice sur Adolphe Samuel* (1922).

Samuel, Gerhard, German-American conductor and composer; b. Bonn, April 20, 1924. He studied violin as a child; his family emigrated to America in 1938. He performed menial jobs as a dishwasher and shoe salesman in New York before winning a scholarship at the Eastman School of Music in Rochester, N.Y.; there he studied conducting with Hermann Gerhard and composition with Howard Hanson (B.S., 1945); also played violin with the Rochester Philharmonic (1941-45). In 1945 he enrolled at Yale Univ., studying composition with Paul Hindemith (M.M., 1947); attended for two summers the conducting sessions with Koussevitzky at the Berkshire Music Center in Tanglewood. From 1949 to 1959 he was violinist and assistant conductor of the Minneapolis Symph. Orch.; from 1959 to 1970 he conducted the Oakland Symph. Orch.; then was associate conductor of the Los Angeles Philharmonic Orch. In 1976 he was appointed to the faculty of the Cincinnati College. He composed a number of choral and symphonic works in a fine modernistic idiom, inter alia, *Twelve on Death and No* for tenor, small chorus and orch. (1968); *Looking at Orpheus Looking* for orch. (1971); *To an End* for chorus and orch. (1972); *Into Flight From* for orch. (1973); *Requiem for Survivors* for orch. (1974).

Samuel, Harold, famous English pianist; b. London, May 23, 1879; d. there, Jan. 15, 1937. He studied at the Royal College of Music with Dannreuther (piano) and Stanford (composition); later was on its faculty. He was particularly distinguished as an interpreter of Bach; in 1921 gave 6 successive Bach recitals in London and a similar cycle in New York; toured the U.S. regularly from 1924. He wrote a musical comedy, *Hon'ble Phil,* and some piano pieces.

Samuel-Rousseau, Marcel. See **Rousseau, Marcel.**

Sanborn, (John) Pitts, American music critic; b. Port Huron, Mich., Oct. 19, 1879; d. New York, March 7, 1941. He studied at Harvard Univ. (B.A., 1900; M.A., 1902); was music editor of the *N.Y. Globe* (1905-23), *N.Y. Evening Mail* (1924-31), and *N.Y. World Telegram* (from 1931). He publ. *Prima Donna—A Novel of the Opera* (London, 1929); *The Metropolitan Book of the Opera* (with Emil Hilb; N.Y., 1937); a pamphlet, *Beethoven and His Nine Symphonies* (1939); etc.

Sanchez de Fuentes, Eduardo, important Cuban composer and educator; b. Havana, April 3, 1874; d. there, Sept. 7, 1944. He studied music with Ignacio Cervantes and Carlos Anckermann. He occupied an influential position in the artistic affairs of Cuba; wrote 6 operas and many other works, but is known outside Cuba chiefly by his popular song, *Tú,* which he publ. at the age of 18.
WORKS: operas (all produced in Havana): *El Náufrago,* after Tennyson's *Enoch Arden* (Jan. 31, 1901), *Dolorosa* (April 23, 1910), *Doreya* (Feb. 7, 1918), *Kabelia,* to his own libretto after a Hindu legend (June 22, 1942); *Bocetos cubanos,* for orch., women's chorus, and soprano solo (Barcelona, 1922); *Temas del patio,* symph. prelude; songs (*Mírame así,* etc.); piano pieces; publ. *El Folk-lore en la música cubana* (1923), *Folklorismo* (1928), *Viejos rítmos cubanos* (1937), etc.
BIBLIOGRAPHY: O. Martínez, *Eduardo Sánchez du*

Fuentes: in Memoriam (Havana, 1944); M. Guiral, *Un grand musicógrafo y compositor cubano: Eduardo Sánchez de Fuentes* (Havana, 1944); A. Carpentier, *La Música en Cuba* (Mexico, 1946; pp. 213-17).

Sandberg, Mordecai, American composer; b. Rumania, Feb. 4, 1897; d. North York, Ontario, Dec. 28, 1973. He studied in Vienna; from 1922 to 1938 he lived in Jeruslem; in 1940 emigrated to America. A musican of grandiose visions, he set out to write a musical score for the entire Bible, and composed a tetralogy *Shelomo* for soloists, chorus and orch.; other works are 2 oratorios, *Ruth* (N.Y., May 22, 1949) and *Ezkerah* (N.Y., April 22, 1952); 2 symphonies, chamber music and piano pieces.

Sandberger, Adolf, eminent German musicologist; b. Würzburg, Dec. 19, 1864; d. Munich, Jan. 14, 1943. He studied composition in Würzburg and Munich; musicology at the Univ. of Berlin, with Spitta; obtained his Dr. phil. in 1887; in 1889 he was appointed custodian of the music department of the Munich Library; also lectured at the Univ. of Munich (1894–1930). He was editor of the *Denmäler der Tonkunst in Bayern* and of Breitkopf & Härtel's monumental edition of the complete works of Roland de Lassus. Sandberger was one of the most important teachers of musicology in Germany, who formulated the basic principles of contemporary muscial bibliography. He was also composer; he wrote an opera *Ludwig der Springer;* 2 string quartets; piano trio; violin sonata; various piano pieces; choruses; songs. Among his writings were *Leben und Werke des Dichtermusikers Peter Cornelius* (1887; dissertation); *Beiträge zur Geschichte der bayerischen Hofkapelle unter Orlando di Lasso* (planned in 3 vols.; Vol. I, 1894; Vol. III, 1895; Vol. II was not published); *Zur Geschichte des Haydnschen Streichquartetts* (1899); *Lasso und die geistigen Strömungen seiner Zeit* (Munich 1926). His collected essays were issued in 3 vols.: I, Biography of Lassus (1921); II, Beethoven (1924); III, History of Opera (1934). A Sandberger Festschrift was published in his honor in 1918, edited by Kroyer; a 2nd Festschrift appeared in 1929.
    BIBLIOGRAPHY: L. Schiedermair, "Adolf Sandberger," *Zeitschrift für Musikwissenschaft* (Jan. 1935); E. I. Luin, "In memoria di Adolf Sandberger," *Rivista Musicale Italiana* (1943, pp. 418-23).

Sandby, Herman, Danish cellist and composer; b. Kundby, near Holbaek, March 21, 1881; d. Copenhagen, Dec. 14, 1965. He studied cello with Hugo Becker and composition with Iwan Knorr in Frankfurt (1895–1900); gave concerts in Scandinavia, England, and Germany; in 1912 settled in America as 1st cellist of the Philadelphia Orch.; moved to N.Y. in 1916; returned to Denmark in 1930.
    WORKS: Cello Concerto (Philadelphia, Feb. 5, 1916); *The Woman and the Fiddler,* symph. suite; 3 symphonies (1930, 1938, 1942); *Serenade,* for strings (1940); 3 string quartets; String Sextet; String Quintet; Piano Quintet; Piano Trio; etc.

Sanders, Paul F., Dutch composer; b. Amsterdam, Dec. 21, 1891. He studied with Sem Dresden and Willem Pijper; contributed to various Dutch publications; was co-founder (with Willem Pijper) of the magazine *De Muziek;* in 1947 was N.Y. correspondent of Dutch newspapers.
    WORKS: *Pierrot aan de lantaarn,* ballet for recitation and chamber orch. (1923); *Rataplan,* ballet for chamber orch. (1925); *Mara,* for chorus and orch.; String Quartet; Sonata for solo violin (1933); *Little Suite,* for piano 4 hands; songs; etc. He publ. *De Piano* (Amsterdam, 1926); *Moderne Nederlandsche Componisten* (The Hague, 1933).

Sanders, Robert L., American composer; b. Chicago, July 2, 1906; d. Delray Beach, Florida, Dec. 26, 1974. He studied at the Bush Cons. of Music (later named Chicago Cons.; Mus. B., 1924; Mus. M., 1925); in 1925 went to Rome on a fellowship of the American Academy there, and studied composition with Respighi; later was in Paris where he took lessons with Guy de Lioncourt. Returning to America in 1929 he joined the faculty of the Chicago Cons.; was also organist at the 1st Unitarian Church; from 1938 to 1947 was dean of the School of Music at Indiana Univ., Bloomington; from 1947 to 1973 taught at Brooklyn College of Music. He wrote a number of orchestral and other pieces, among them, a choreographic suite for orch., *Scenes of Poverty and Toil* (performed under the title *The Tragic Muse,* Chicago, Jan. 30, 1936, with composer conducting); 3 "little symphonies" (1939, 1954, 1963); Symphony in A (1954-55); *The Mystic Trumpeter* for baritone, speaker, chorus and speaking chorus with orch., to texts by Walt Whitman (1941); *Song of Myself,* cantata, to words by Walt Whitman (Brooklyn, April 19, 1970); other choral works; chamber music; *Variations on an Original Theme* for pipe organ, pedals only (1956).

Sanderson, Sibyl, American soprano; b. Sacramento, Calif., Dec. 7, 1865; d. Paris, May 15, 1903. She was educated in San Francisco, where her musical talent attracted attention; taken to Paris by her mother at the age 19, she studied at the Cons. with Massenet; also with Sbriglia and Mathilde Marchesi. Massenet was charmed with her voice and her person; wrote the leading part in *Esclarmonde* for her; she created it at the Opéra-Comique, on May 14, 1889; the role of Thaïs (Paris Opéra, March 16, 1889) was also written by Massenet for her. Other French composers were equally enchanted with her; Saint-Saëns wrote *Phryné* for her (1893). She made her American debut at the Metropolitan Opera, N.Y., as Manon (Jan. 16, 1895), but had little successs with the American public. In 1897 whe married a wealthy Cuban, Antonio Terry, who died in 1900.
    BIBLIOGRAPHY: J. Massenet, *Mes Souvenirs* (Paris, 1912); T. Wilkins, in *Notable American Women,* III (Cambridge, Mass., 1971).

Sandi, Luis, Mexican composer; b. Mexico City, Feb. 22, 1905. He studied violin with Rocabruna (1923–30) and composition with Campa and Mejía (1925–31) at the National Cons. of Mexico City. He conducted a chorus at the Cons. (1922–35); in 1937 he founded the Coro de Madrigalistas and conducted it until 1965. He was a prof. of music in primary schools (1924–32) and

Chief of the Music Section of the Secretariat of Public Education (1933–65).

WORKS: 2 operas: *Carlota* (Mexico City, Oct. 23, 1948) and *La Señora en su Balcón* (1964); 3 ballets: *Día de Difuntos (Day of the Dead,* 1938), *Bonampak* (1948; Mexico City, Nov. 2, 1951), and *Coatlicue* (1949); *El Venado* for orch. (1932; Mexico City, Oct. 28, 1938); *Sonora* for orch. (1933); *Suite Banal* for small orch. (1936); *Norte* for orch. (Mexico City, Aug. 15, 1941); Concertino for flute and orch. (1944); *Tema y Variaciones* for orch. (1944); *Esbozos Sinfónicos* (1951); *4 Miniatures* for orch. (1952); *América,* symph. poem (1965); *Las Troyanas* for chorus and instruments (1936); *Gloria a los Héroes,* cantata (1940); *La Suave Patria,* cantata (1951); String Quartet (1938); *La Hoja de Plata* for instruments (1939); *Fátima,* suite for guitar (1948); *Cuatro Momentos* for string quartet (1950); *Hoja de Album* for cello and piano (1956); Cello Sonatina (1958); Quintet (1960); Sonatina for solo violin (1967); Violin Sonata (1969); *Cuatro Piezas* for recorders (1977); numerous choruses; songs; piano pieces. He published a booklet *De música y otras cosas* (Mexico City, 1969).

BIBLIOGRAPHY: Carlos Chávez, "Luis Sandi," *Nuestra Música* (July 1949); a list of works is found in Vol. 14 of *Compositores de América* (Washington, D.C., 1968).

Sándor, Arpád, Hungarian pianist; b. Budapest, June 5, 1896; d. there, Feb. 10, 1972. Studied there with Bartók and Kodály at the Royal Academy, graduating in 1914; after several years in Berlin, he toured the U.S. as accompanist in 1922; then returned to Germany, and wrote art criticism in the *Berliner Tageblatt.* In 1933 he settled permanently in the U.S.; was accompanist to Jascha Heifetz, Lily Pons, and other celebrated artists. He became an American citizen in 1943.

Sándor, György, Hungarian pianist; b. Budapest, Sept. 21, 1912. He studied at the Royal Academy of Music there, with Bartók (piano) and Kodály (composition). After a series of concerts in Europe (1930–38), he settled in the U.S. in 1939; was soloist in the première of Bartók's posthumous Piano Concerto No. 3, with the Philadelphia Orch. (Feb. 8, 1946); traveled in Australia in 1951. He made brilliant transcriptions of several modern orchestral works, including *L'Apprenti sorcier* by Paul Dukas.

Sandoval, Miguel, pianist, conductor, and composer; b. Guatemala City, Nov. 22, 1903; d. New York, Aug. 24, 1953. He settled in the U.S. in 1925; was active as conductor and pianist; wrote a symph. poem, *Recueridos en un paseo,* and publ. numerous piano works and songs in the Latin American vein.

Sandström, Sven-David, Swedish composer; b. Motala, Oct. 30, 1942. He studied in Stockholm at the Univ. (1963–67) and at the Royal College of Music (1968–72); also took courses in advanced techniques of composition with Norgaard and Ligeti. In his own works he pursues the techniques of expansive serialism, making use of modern resources, including quarter-tone divisions, aleatory procedures, etc.

WORKS: *Music* for 5 strings (1968); Sonata for solo flute (1968); *Bilder (Pictures)* for percussion and orch. (Norrköping, April 17, 1969); *Combinations* for solo clarinet (1969); *Concertato* for clarinet, trombone, cello and percussion (1969); *Intrada* for winds, strings and percussion (1969); *Invention* for 16 voices (1969); *17 Bildkombinationer (17 Picture Combinations)* for winds, percussion and strings (1969); String Quartet (1969); *Disturbances* for 6 brass (1970); *Disjointing* for solo trombone (1970); *In the Meantime* for chamber orch. (1970); *Jumping Excursions* for clarinet, cello, trombone and cymbal (1970); *Mosaic* for string trio (1970); *Sounds* for 14 strings (1970); *To You* for orch. (1970); *Around a Line* for winds, piano, percussion and strings (1971); *Concentration* for 8 winds and 4 double basses (1971); *Lamento* for 3 choral groups and 4 trombones (1971); *Visst?* for soprano, 2 choruses, winds, pop orch. and violin group (1971; Mellerud, April 23, 1972); *Concentration II* for 2 pianos (1972); *Through and Through* for orch. (1972); *Convergence* for solo bassoon (1973); *Birgitta-music I* for speaking and singing groups, orch., Renaissance ensemble, organ, and folk musicians and dancers (Vadstena, June 23, 1973); *Inside* for bass trombone and piano (1974); *Utmost* for wind quintet, trumpet, trombone, tuba, and percussion (1975).

Sandt, Maximilian van de, Dutch pianist and composer; b. Rotterdam, Oct. 18, 1863; d. Cologne, July 14, 1934. He was a pupil of Liszt in the last year of the master's life; toured in Europe with conspicuous success; was on the faculty of the Cons. of Cologne (1896–1906); from 1910 taught at Bonn. He composed many brilliant piano pieces in a romantic vein.

Sandvik, Ole Mörk, Norwegian musicologist; b. Hedemarken, May 9, 1875; d. Oslo, Aug. 5, 1976, at the age of 101. He studied theology; taught liturgy at the Theological Seminary of the Univ. of Oslo, (1916–45). He continued his activities as a writer and lecturer, working at the Oslo Library on various research projects until very old age.

WRITINGS: *Norsk Kirkemusic* (1918); *Folkemusikk i Gudbrandsdalen* (1919; 2nd ed., 1948), *Norsk Folkemusikk* (1921), *Norges Musikkhistorie* (1921, with G. Schjelderup); *Norsk Koralhistorie* (1930); *Østerdalsmusikken* (1943); *Gregoriansk sang* (1945); a centennial biography of Agathe Backer-Gröndahl (1948); a monograph on L. M. Lindeman (1950); compiled the Gradual for the Norwegian Church; publ. albums of regional folksongs, etc. A symposium of articles in his honor was publ. on the occasion of his 70th birthday (Oslo, 1945).

Sanford, Harold Bryant, American conductor and arranger; b. Florence, Mass., Sept. 5, 1879; d. Springfield, Mass., Jan. 19, 1945. He studied violin with Emil Mollenhauer in Boston, and theory with Goetschius; was employed as a violinist, conductor, and arranger by Victor Herbert in N.Y. (1906–24); conducted recordings for various phonograph companies; also on the radio.

Sanford, Samuel Simons, American pianist; b. Bridgeport, Conn., 1849; d. New York, June 6, 1910.

He studied with William Mason; went to Europe in 1868, where he took lessons with Anton Rubinstein, who had a high opinion of Sanford's abilities. However, Sanford did not undertake a pianistic career; in 1894 he became prof. of applied music at Yale Univ., developing the music dept. in collaboration with Horatio Parker.

Sangiovanni, Antonio, celebrated Italian singing teacher; b. Bergamo, Sept. 14, 1831; d. Milan, Jan. 6, 1892. He studied at the Cons. of Milan; in 1854, was appointed prof. of singing there, and acquired considerable fame as a builder of voices. Two generations of Italian and foreign singers were his pupils.

Sanjuán, Pedro, Spanish composer and conductor; b. San Sebastian, Nov. 15, 1886; d. Washington, D.C., Oct. 18, 1976. He studied composition with Turina; after conducting in Europe, he went to Havana, where he organized the Havana Philharmonic (1926); was also teacher of composition there; Roldán, Caturla, and other Cuban composers were his pupils; in 1932 he went back to Spain; was in Madrid (1932–36); from 1939 until 1942, he was again conductor of the Havana Philharmonic; in 1942 was appointed prof. of composition at Converse College, Spartanburg, S.C.; American citizen, 1947.

WORKS: *Rondo fantástico* (Havana, Nov. 29, 1926); *Castilla,* suite for orch. (Havana, June 12, 1927); *Sones de Castilla,* for small orch.; *La Macumba,* a "ritual symphony" (St. Louis, Dec. 14, 1951, composer conducting); *Antillean Poem* for band (N.Y., Aug. 11, 1958, composer conducting); *Symphonic Suite* (Washington, May 9, 1965); choral works; piano pieces.

Sankey, Ira David, American composer of gospel songs and evangelical singer; b. Edinburg, Pennsylvania, Aug. 28, 1840; d. Brooklyn, Aug. 13, 1908. As a youth of 17, he became choir leader in the Methodist Church of New Castle, Pennsylvania; served for a year with the N.Y. 12th Infantry Regiment at the time of the Civil War. In 1870 he was a delegate to the YMCA convention at Indianapolis, where his forceful singing attracted the attention of the evangelist preacher Dwight L. Moody. He joined Moody as music director and remained at this post for some 30 years, until approaching blindness forced his retirement in 1903. Of his many gospel tunes, the most popular has proved to be *The Ninety and Nine,* which he improvised at a moment's notice during a service in Edinburgh, Scotland. His chief publications were *Sacred Songs and Hymns* (London, 1873) and 6 vols. of *Gospel Hymns* issued between 1875 and 1891. He also published *My Life and the Story of the Gospel Hymns and of the Sacred Songs and Solos* (Philadelphia, 1907). He is not to be confused with another gospel song writer, Ira Allan Sankey, a lesser light than Ira David Sankey.

BIBLIOGRAPHY: E. J. Goodspeed, *A Full History of the Wonderful Career of Moody and Sankey, in Great Britain and America* (1876; reprint, N.Y., 1971); G. C. Stebbins, *Reminiscences and Gospel Hymn Stories* (N.Y., 1924; reprint, N.Y., 1971); R. G. McCutchan, *Our Hymnody* (N.Y., 1937).

San Martini. See **Sammartini.**

Sanromá, Jesús María, brilliant Puerto Rican pianist; b. Carolina, Puerto Rico (of Catalonian parents), Nov. 7, 1902. At the age of 14 he was sent to the U.S. by the governor of Puerto Rico; studied piano with Antoinette Szumowska at the New England Cons.; 1920, won the Mason & Hamlin piano prize; then went to Europe, where he studied with Alfred Cortot (in Paris) and Artur Schnabel (in Berlin); from 1926 till 1944 he was pianist of the Boston Symph. Orch.; taught at the New England Cons.; gave annual concerts in the U.S., Canada, and South America; also played in Europe. In 1951 he was appointed chairman of the music dept. at the Univ. of Puerto Rico. He excels particularly in the works of modern composers, and has given several world premières of contemporary concertos (by Hindemith, etc.).

BIBLIOGRAPHY: E. S. Belava, *El Niño Sanromá* (San Juan, Puerto Rico, 1952).

San Sebastián, Padre José Antonio de. See **Donostia, Jose Antonio de.**

Santa Cruz (Wilson), Domingo, foremost Chilean composer; b. La Cruz, near Quillota, July 5, 1899. He studied jurisprudence at the Univ. of Chile; then entered diplomatic service; was second secretary of the Chilean legation in Spain (1921–24); received his musical training with Enrique Soro in Santiago and with Conrado del Campo in Madrid. Returning to Chile, he devoted himself to musical administration, teaching and composition; in 1928 he became prof. at the National Cons. in Santiago, and in 1933 was appointed dean of the faculty of fine arts at the Univ. of Chile. His role in the promotion of musical culture in Chile was of great importance; he traveled in Europe and the U.S. as a lecturer. In his works he follows the cosmopolitan traditions of neo-Classical music, and made use of identifiable Chilean melodies in but a few of his compositions.

WORKS: *Cantata de los rios de Chile* for chorus and orch. (Santiago, Nov. 27, 1942); *5 Piezas breves* for string orch. (Santiago, May 31, 1937); *Variaciones* for piano and orch. (Santiago, June 25, 1943); *Sinfonia concertante* for flute, piano and strings (Santiago, Nov. 29, 1945); Symph. No. 1 for strings, celesta and percussion (Santiago, May 28, 1948); Symph. No. 2 for strings (Santiago, Nov. 26, 1948); *Egloga* for soprano, chorus and orch. (Santiago, Nov. 24, 1950); *Cantares de la Pascua,* for chorus a cappella (Santiago, Dec. 7, 1950); *Canciones del mar,* song cycle (1955); *Endechas* for tenor and 8 instruments (1957); 3 string quartets; Symph. No. 3 with contralto solo (Washington, D.C., May 9, 1965); Symph. No. 4 (1968); *Oratorio Ieremieae prophetae* (1969); many songs and choruses; piano pieces.

BIBLIOGRAPHY: Otto Mayer-Serra, *Música y músicos de latinoamérica* (Mexico City, 1947; vol. 2, pp. 892–99); special issue of the *Revista Musical Chilena* (Dec. 1951); Vicente Salas Viú, *La Creación musical en Chile 1900–1951* (Santiago, 1951; pp. 367–422).

Santa María, Fray Tomás de, important Spanish organist and composer; b. Madrid, c.1510; d. Valladolid,

1570. A Dominican monk, and a pupil of Antonio de Cabezón; publ. *Libro llamado Arte de tañer fantasía* (Valladolid, 1565), a treatise on playing fantasias on keyboard instruments and on the guitar or lute (German transl., with critical and biographical introduction, by E. Harich-Schneider and R. Boadella, Leipzig, 1937).

BIBLIOGRAPHY: F. Pedrell, *Hispaniae schola musica sacra* (vol. 6); Villalba, *Antología de organistas clásicos españoles*, I; O. Kinkeldey, *Orgel und Klavier in der Musik des 16. Jahrhunderts* (Leipzig, 1910; with mus. examples); H. Collet, *Le Mysticisme musical espagnol au XVIe siècle* (Paris, 1913); J. Bonnet, *Historical Organ Recitals* VI (1940); G. Reese, *Music in the Renaissance* (N.Y., 1954).

Santelmann, William Henry, German-American violinist and band conductor; b. Offensen, Sept. 24, 1863; d. Washington, D.C., Dec. 17, 1932. He studied at the Leipzig Cons.; in 1887 settled in America; played the baritone in the U.S. Marine Band in Washington (1887–95); was its conductor from 1898 until 1927, when he retired. He wrote the suite *Pocahontas*, for band; marches and dances; made numerous transcriptions.

Santi, Padre Angelo de, Italian Jesuit priest and music scholar; b. Trieste, July 12, 1847; d. Rome, Jan. 28, 1922. He took a leading part in the reform of Catholic church music, his views being embodied in the *Motu proprio* of Pius X on sacred music (1903). He founded the Schola Cantorum of the Vatican Seminary. He published *Il Maestro Filippo Capocci e le sue composizioni per organo* (1888); *L'Origine delle feste natalizie* (1907); also articles in *Rassegna Gregoriana*, etc.

Santini, Abbate Fortunato, Italian music scholar and composer; b. Rome, Jan. 5, 1778; d. there, Sept. 14, 1861. He was noted as the collector of one of the finest music libraries ever formed; ordained priest in 1801; as early as 1820 he publ. a catalogue of the manuscripts then in his possession, *Catalogo della musica antica, sacra e madrigalesca*, listing 1,000 titles by more than 700 composers. His original compositions include a Requiem, a *Stabat Mater*, many motets.

BIBLIOGRAPHY: V. Stassov, *L'Abbé Santini et sa collection musicale à Rome* (Florence, 1854; biography and summary of Santini's own catalogue); Mendelssohn's *Reisebriefe* (Leipzig, 1861; 5th ed., 1882; English transl. by Lady Wallace as *Letters from Italy and Switzerland*, London, 1862); J. Killing, *Kirchenmusikalische Schätze der Bibliothek des Abbate F. Santini* (Düsseldorf, 1910); K. Fellerer, "Verzeichnis der kirchenmusikalischen Werke der santinischen Sammlung," *Kirchenmusikalisches Jahrbuch* (Regensburg, 1931).

Santley, Sir Charles, English baritone; b. Liverpool, Feb. 28, 1834; d. Hove, near London, Sept. 22, 1922. He studied with Nava in Milan; then with Garcia in London; made his professional debut as Adam in Haydn's *Creation*, on Nov. 16, 1857. His stage debut was at Covent Garden, Oct. 1, 1859; he joined the Carl Rosa Company in 1875, and toured with it for several years; visited America in 1871 and 1891; Australia in

1889–90. In 1887 he was made Commander of the Order of St. Gregory by Pope Leo XIII; in 1907, was knighted. His songs were publ. under the pseudonym "Ralph Betterton"; he also publ. *Student and Singer* (London, 1892; a vol. of reminiscences); *The Singing Master* (2 parts; London, 1900); *The Art of Singing and Vocal Declamation* (London, 1908); *Reminiscences of My Life* (London, 1909).

BIBLIOGRAPHY: J. J. M. Levien, *Sir Charles Santley* (London, 1930).

Santoliquido, Francesco, Italian composer; b. San Giorgio a Cremano, Naples, Aug. 6, 1883; d. Anacapri, Italy, Aug. 26, 1971. He studied at the Santa Cecilia in Rome; graduated in 1909; in 1912 he went to live in Hammamet, a village in Tunisia, spending part of each year in Rome; about 1950 made his home in Anacapri. Many of his compositions contain melodic inflections of Arabian popular music.

WORKS: the operas *La Favola di Helga* (Milan, Nov. 23, 1910), *Ferhuda* (Tunis, Jan. 30, 1919), *La Bajadera dalla maschera gialla* (Rome, 1923), *La Porte verde*, musical tragedy in 4 acts (Bergamo, Oct. 15, 1953); for orch.: *Crepuscolo sul mare* (Nuremberg, Jan. 19, 1909; composer conducting), *Il Profumo delle oasi sahariane* (Tunis, April 17, 1918; also in Rome, March 5, 1922), *Acquarelli* (Rome, April 11, 1923), Symph. in F (1924), *La Sagra dei morti*, heroic elegy for the victims of World War I (Rome, 1929), *Tre miniature per i piccoli* (1933), *Preludio e Burlesca*, for string orch. (Rome, 1938), *Alba di gloria*, symph. prelude (Rome, Nov. 13, 1940), *Grotte di Capri*, 5 pieces for orch. (1943), *Santuari asiatici*, symph. sketches (Naples, 1952); String Quartet; Violin Sonata; *Aria antica*, for cello and piano; *Chiarità lunare*, for violin and piano; 2 *Pezzi* for 5 wind instruments; *Piccola ballata* for piano; 2 *Acqueforti tunisine* for piano; a cycle of songs to words by Pierre Louys; *Messa facile* for chorus; publ. *Il Dopo-Wagner; Claudio Debussy e Richard Strauss* (Rome, 1909); also books of verse; wrote short stories in English.

Santoro, Claudio, Brazilian composer and conductor; b. Manaos, Nov. 23, 1919. He studied at the Cons. of Rio de Janeiro and later in Paris with Nadia Boulanger. Returning to Brazil, he taught music in various schools; conducted concerts in South America and Europe, including Russia. He wrote music in an advanced idiom as a youth, mostly in the 12-tone style; but later he decided to compose works accessible to the masses, and this attitude was strengthened by his acceptance of the Russian tenets of socialist realism in art; however, he returned to the avant-garde type of composition (including aleatory practices) in his music of the 1960's. In 1970 he went to Germany and became prof. of composition at the Hochschule für Musik in Heidelberg.

WORKS: the ballets: *A fábrica* (The Factory, 1947); *Anticocos* (1951); *O café* (1953); *Icamiabas* (1959); *Zuimaaluti* (1960); *Prelúdios* (1962); *Ode to Stalingrad* for chorus and orch. (1947); 8 symphonies: No. 1 (1940); No. 2 (1945); No. 3 (Rio de Janeiro, Dec. 20, 1949); No. 4, subtitled *Da paz* (Symphony of Peace; Rio de Janeiro, Oct. 30, 1945); No. 5 (Rio de Janeiro, March 28, 1956); No. 6 (Paris, May 1, 1963); No. 7, surnamed *Brasília* (1960); No. 8 (1963); *Variations on a 12-tone Row* for orch. (1945); *Chôro* for saxophone and orch. (Rio de Janiero, June 20, 1952); *Ponteio* for string orch. (Rio de Janeiro, June 19, 1945); *Abertura trágica* for orch. (1958); 2 violin concertos (1951, 1958); 3 piano concertos (1953, 1959, 1960); Cello Concerto (1961; Washington, D.C., May 12, 1965); 7 string quartets (1943–65); 5 violin sonatas (1940–57); 4 cello sonatas (1943–63); String Trio (1941); Flute Sonata (1941); Oboe Sonata (1943); Trumpet Sonata (1946); *Diagrammas cíclicos* for piano and percussion (1966); 6 pieces for various instruments, entitled *Mutations* (1968–72); *Antistruktur* for harp and cello (1970); 25 Preludes for piano (1957–63); oratorio, *Berlin, 13 de agôsto* for narrator, chorus and orch. (1962); *Agrupamento à 10* for voice and chamber orch. (1966); *Aleatorius I-III*, in graphic notation (1967). For list of works prior to 1963, consult vol. 9 of *Composers of America* (Washington, D.C., 1963).

Santos, (Jóse Manuel) Joly Braga, Portuguese composer; b. Lisbon, May 14, 1924. He studied composition with Luís de Freitas Branco at the Lisbon Cons. (1934–43), then conducting with Scherchen at the Venice Cons. (1948), electronic music at the Gavessano (Switzerland) Acoustic Experimental Stadium (1957–58) and composition with Mortari at the Rome Cons. (1959–60). He conducted the Oporto Radio Symph. Orch. (1955–59); in 1961 joined the staff, as conductor. His music represents a felicitous fusion of Portuguese Renaissance modalities and folk rhythms.

WORKS: 3 operas: radio opera *Viver ou Morrer (To Live or to Die,* 1952); *Mérope* (Lisbon, May 15, 1959); *Trilogia das Barcas* (1969; Lisbon, May, 1970); 3 ballets: *Alfama* (1956), *A nau Catrineta* (1959) and *Encruzilhada* (1968); 3 symphonic overtures (1945, 1947, 1954); 6 symphonies: No. 1 (1946); No. 2 (1948); No. 3 (1949); No. 4 (1950); No. 5, *Virtus Lusitaniae* (1966); No. 6, with solo soprano and chorus (1972); *Nocturno* for string orch. (1947); Concerto for String Orch. (1951); *Variações Sinfónicas sobre un theme de l'Alentejano* (1952); Viola Concerto (1960); *Divertimento* for chamber orch. (1961); *Três Esboços Sinfónicos (3 Symphonic Sketches,* 1962); Sinfonietta for string orch. (1963); *Double Concerto* for violin, cello, string orch. and harp (1965); *Variações concertantes* for string orch. and harp (1967); Piano Concerto (1973); *Variações* for orch. (1976); *Requiem à memória de Pedro de Freitas Branco* for soloists, chorus and orch. (1964); *Ode à Música* for chorus and orch. (1965); *Nocturno* for violin and piano (1942); 2 string quartets (1944, 1956); Violin Sonata (1945); Piano Quartet (1957); choruses.

Santucci, Marco, Italian composer; b. Camajore, Tuscany, July 4, 1762; d. Lucca, Nov. 29, 1843. He was Anfossi's successor (1797–1808) maestro at S. Giovanni in Laterano, Rome; in 1808 was appointed canon at the Cathedral of Lucca. A motet *a* 16, for 4 choirs, received a prize from the Accademia Napoleone in 1806 because of the "entirely new and original" combination of voices. Baini publ. an energetic protest against this award, pointing out that such polyphonic writing was common in works by Italian composers of the 16th and 17th centuries. Santucci

also wrote Masses, motets, psalms, canons in up to 7 parts, symphonies, organ sonatas, etc.; publ. a treatise *Sulla melodia, sull'armonia e sul metro* (1828).

BIBLIOGRAPHY: G. Rinuccini, *Biografia di Marco Santucci* (Milan, 1851).

Sanz, Gaspar, Spanish 17th-century guitarist; b. Calanda (Aragón); studied at Salamanca Univ., taking degrees in theology and philosophy; became maestro to the Spanish Viceroy at Naples. He was guitar teacher to Don Juan of Austria, for whom he wrote an *Instrucción de música sobre la guitarra española* (Zaragoza, 1674; 2nd ed., 1697), containing examples of contemporary Spanish dance music and folksong.

Sanzogno, Nino, Italian conductor and composer; b. Venice, April 13, 1911. He studied composition with Malipiero in Venice; took conducting lessons with Scherchen in Brussels in 1935; after playing violin in a string quartet, he was appointed opera conductor at the Teatro La Fenice in Venice; from 1962 to 1965 conducted at La Scala, Milan; also toured in South America. He became favorably known as an excellent conductor of modern opera in Italy; he also gave courses on conducting in Darmstadt. He composed a Viola Concerto, Cello Concerto, Octet for strings and woodwinds, and some orchestral pieces.

Sapelnikov, Vassily, Russian pianist; b. Odessa, Nov. 2, 1867; d. San Remo, March 17, 1941. He was a pupil of L. Brassin and Sophie Menter at the St. Petersburg Cons.; in 1888, made his debut at Hamburg with Tchaikovsky's 1st Piano Concerto, under the composer's direction; then made tours throughout Europe; lived chiefly in Germany, also for a time in Florence; 1916, returned to Russia, remaining there until 1922; from 1923, again in Germany and Italy. He wrote an opera, *Der Khan und sein Sohn,* and pieces for piano (*Petite Mazourka, Danse des elfes, Valse-Caprice, Impromptu, Solitude*).

Saperstein, David, American composer; b. New York, March 6, 1948. He studied at the Juilliard School of Music, and took courses with Elliott Carter, Walter Piston and Vincent Persichetti at the Dartmouth College Summer Sessions (1963–64), and with Milton Babbitt at Princeton Univ., receiving his A.B. degree in 1969. His works, written in an advanced idiom, include Wind Quintet (1963); Duo for violin and percussion (1965); Brass Quartet (1966); *Etudes* for piano (1967); *Variations* for 8 instruments (1969); Sextet (1970).

Saperton, David, American pianist; b. Pittsburgh, Oct. 29, 1889; b. Baltimore, July 5, 1970. He received his first instruction on the piano from his grandfather, a former tenor at the Brünn Opera, while his father, a physician and former concert bass, superintended his theoretical studies. At the age of 10 he made his first public appearance with orch. in Pittsburgh; in 1905 he gave a recital in New York; in 1910–12, toured Germany, Austria, Hungary, Italy, Russia, and Scandinavia; then returned to the U.S.; in 1924, joined the piano faculty of the Curtis Institute, Philadelphia.

Sapio, Romualdo, Italian singing teacher; b. Palermo, Sept. 8, 1858; d. New York, Sept. 22, 1943; studied at the Palermo Cons.; made his debut as conductor in Milan (1883); conducted Patti's tours of North and South America; also operatic and concert tours of Albani and Nordica; in 1892 settled in New York, as teacher of singing; the same year he married the concert singer **Clementine de Vere.**

Sapp, Allen Dwight, American composer; b. Philadelphia, Dec. 10, 1922. He studied piano and theory privately in Philadelphia; then entered Harvard Univ., taking courses in composition with Walter Piston and orchestration with E. B. Hill (A.B., 1942; A.M., 1949); then did graduate work there with A. T. Davison, A. T. Merritt, Irving Fine and Randall Thompson; also attended classes of Aaron Copland and Nadia Boulanger in Cambridge (1942–43). During the war he was employed as chief cryptanalyst in the Civil Censorship Division of the U.S. Army, and chief of Code Research; in 1949 was appointed to the faculty of Harvard Univ. His music is cast in a neo-Classical idiom, with contrapuntal and harmonic elements coalescing in a free design.
    WORKS: for orch.: *The Double Image* (1957); *The Septagon* (1957); *Colloquies* for piano and orch. (1963); Piano Trio; String Trio; 3 violin sonatas; Viola Sonata; 4 piano sonatas; *A Maiden's Complaint in Springtime* for women's chorus and chamber ensemble (1960); *Canticum novum pro pace* for men's chorus and wind instruments (1962).

Sárai, Tibor, Hungarian composer; b. Budapest, May 10, 1919. He studied composition with Pál Kadosa; taught at the Béla Bartók Cons. (1953–59) and at the Budapest Academy of Music. In his compositions he adheres to the national Hungarian tradition, enhanced by a free use of euphonious dissonances.
    WORKS: an oratorio, *Variations on the Theme of Peace* (1961–64); *Serenade* for string orch. (1946); *Tavaszi Concerto (Spring Concerto)* for flute, viola, cello and string orch. (1955); *6 Scenes* from the dance play "János vitéz" (1956–57); Symph. No. 1 (1965–67); Symph. No. 2, with soprano solo (1972–73); *Diagnosis '69* for tenor and orch. (1969); *Musica* for 45 strings (1970–71); *Jövöt faggató ének (Future Questioning)* for alto, baritone, male chorus and orch. (1971); 2 string quartets (1958, 1971); *Lassú és friss* for violin and piano (1958); Quartet for flute, violin, viola and cello (1961–62); *Studio* for flute and piano (1964); *De profundis*, solo cantata for tenor and wind quintet (1968); Piano Sonatina (1959); *8 Small Piano Pieces* (1965).

Saran, Franz Ludwig, German writer on music; b. Altranstädt, near Lützen, Oct. 27, 1866; d. Erlangen, April 24, 1931. He studied languages in Halle, Leipzig, and Freiburg; 1896, instructor in German language and literature at the Halle Univ.; 1905, prof.; from 1913, prof. at the Univ. of Erlangen. His works having to do with music include the revision and editing of R. Westphal's *Aristoxenos von Tarent Melodik und Rhythmik* (2 vols., 1893) and the editing and transcription of the famous Jena MS of *Minnelieder* (2 vols., with G. Holz and E. Bernouilli, 1901; vol. 2 includes a systematic treatise on the rhythm of medieval songs); also publ. *Der Rhythmus des französischen Verses* (1904).

Sarasate, Pablo de (Pablo Martín Melitón Sarasate y Navascuez), celebrated Spanish violin virtuoso; b. Pamplona, March 10, 1844; d. Biarritz, Sept. 20, 1908. He studied at the Paris Cons. under Alard, taking 1st prize in the violin class in 1857, and a "premier accessit" in 1859. In 1866 he acquired a Stradivarius violin. His playing was noted for its extraordinary beauty of tone, impeccable purity of intonation, perfection of technique, and grace of manner; but his repertory consisted almost exclusively of fantasies on operatic airs (mostly arranged by himself). Later his taste changed, and he turned to the masterpieces of violin literature. His tours, extending through all Europe, North and South America, South Africa, and the Orient, were an uninterrupted succession of triumphs. He bequeathed to his native city the gifts that had been showered upon him by admirers throughout the world; the collection was placed in a special museum. For him Saint-Saëns wrote his *Rondo Capriccioso*, Lalo his *Symphonie espagnole;* Bruch, the *Schottische Fantasie;* Mackenzie, the *Pibroch* suite. Sarasate's compositions, exclusively for violin, are pleasing and effective.
    WORKS: for violin and orch.: *Zigeunerweisen* (his best and most popular work); *Navarra*, for 2 violins; *Jota de San Fermin*, for orch.; Spanish dances for violin and piano, etc.
    BIBLIOGRAPHY: M. L. van Vorst, "Sarasate," *Scribner's Magazine* (March 1896); Julio Altadill, *Memorias de Sarasate* (Pamplona, 1909); A. Hartmann, "The Perfect Virtuoso," *Musical America* (March 25, 1940); León Zárate, *Sarasate* (Barcelona, 1945); G. Woolley, "Pablo Sarasate: His Historical Significance," *Music & Letters* (July 1955); Angel Sagardia, *Pablo Sarasate* (Palencia, 1956).

Sargeant, Winthrop, American music critic; b. San Francisco, Dec. 10, 1903. He studied violin in San Francisco with Arthur Argiewicz and with Lucien Capet in Paris; took composition lessons with Albert Elkus in San Francisco and with Karl Prohaska in Vienna. He played the violin in the San Francisco Symph. Orch. (1922–24), in the N.Y. Symph. (1926–28), and in the N.Y. Philharmonic (1928–30). He then devoted himself to musical journalism; was on the editorial staff of *Musical America* (1931–34); was music critic of the *Brooklyn Daily Eagle* (1934–36); served as music editor of *Time* magazine (1937–39); also wrote essays on various subjects for *Time* (1939–45); subsequently was roving correspondent for *Life* magazine (1945–49), and music critic for *The New Yorker* (1947–72); from 1972 reviewed records for it. He evolved a highly distinctive manner of writing; professionally solid, stylistically brilliant, and ideologically opinionated; he especially inveighed against the extreme practices of the cosmopolitan avant-garde. He published *Jazz: Hot and Hybrid* (N.Y., 1938; 3rd ed., N.Y., 1975); *Geniuses, Goddesses, and People* (N.Y., 1949); *Listening to Music* (N.Y., 1958); *In Spite of Myself: A Personal Memoir* (N.Y.,

1970); *Divas: Impressions of Today's Sopranos* (N.Y., 1973).

Sargent, Sir (Harold) Malcolm (Watts), eminent English conductor; b. Ashford, Kent, April 29, 1895; d. London, Oct. 3, 1967. He studied organ at the Royal College of Organists in London; then was articled to Dr. Keeton, organist of the Peterborough Cathedral (1911–14); served in the infantry during World War I; after the armistice he took piano lessons with Moiseiwitsch. He made his conducting debut in 1921 in London, in a performance of his own composition *Impression on a Windy Day;* then filled various engagements with the D'Oyly Carte Opera Co., Diaghilev's Ballet Russe, the Royal Choral Society, etc. In 1945 he made his American debut, conducting a series of concerts with the NBC Symph.; in the following season he toured Australia for the Australian Broadcasting Commission. He was knighted in 1947. From 1950 to 1957 he was conductor of the BBC Symph. Orch.
BIBLIOGRAPHY: Donald Brook, *International Gallery of Conductors* (Bristol, 1951; pp. 159–64); Ph. Matthewman, *Sir Malcolm Sargent* (London, 1959); Charles Reid, *Malcolm Sargent: A Biography* (London, 1968).

Sari, Ada (real name **Jadwiga Szajerowa**), Polish soprano; b. Wadowice, near Cracow, June 29, 1886; d. Ciechocinek, July 12, 1968. She studied in Milan; after appearances in Rome, Naples, Trieste and Parma, she joined the staff of the Warsaw Opera; made extensive tours in Europe, in South America and in the U.S. Eventually she returned to Warsaw, devoting herself mainly to teaching.

Sárközy, István, Hungarian composer; b. Pesterzsébet, Nov. 26, 1920. He studied composition with Kodály, Farkas and Viski at the Budapest Academy of Music; in 1959 was appointed to its faculty.
WORKS: cantatas: *Ode to Stalin* (1949), *Julia Songs* (1958), and *The Earthquake Approaches* (1958); a comedy oratorio "*Y*" *War,* for 10 solo voices, vocal quintet and 8 instruments (1971); *Concerto Grosso* (1943–44; revised with an added subtitle, *Ricordanze I,* 1969); *Small Suite* for orch. (1951); *Fantasy and Dance* for gypsy orch. (1952); *To Youth,* overture (1953); *Sinfonia Concertante* for clarinet and orch. (1963); *Concerto Semplice (Ricordanze II)* for violin and orch. (Budapest, Oct. 11, 1974); *12 Variations* for piano (1945); *Sonatina* for 2 pianos (1950); *Sonata da camera* for flute and piano (1964); *Ciaccona* for solo cello (1967); *Chamber Sonata* for clarinet and piano (1969); *Psaume et Jeu,* quartet for wind instruments (1970); *4 Etudes* for solo clarinet (1972); *Ricordanze III* for string quartet (1977); scores of incidental music; songs.

Sarly, Henry, Belgian composer; b. Tirlemont, Dec. 28, 1883; d. Brussels, Dec. 3, 1954. He studied with his father and with Huberti, Tinel, Gilson and Du Bois at the Brussels Cons.; in 1921 became inspector of musical education in Belgian schools. He composed a number of attractive pieces, among them *Scènes brabançonnes,* for orch.; Piano Quintet; *Poème* for piano trio; Violin Sonata; numerous piano pieces and songs. He

also published a manual, *Cours théorique et pratique d'harmonie.*

Sarnette, Eric Antoine Joseph André, French inventor of musical instruments; b. Tarbes, Hautes-Pyrénées, Nov. 28, 1898. He studied at Marseilles, and later at the Paris Cons.; also took lessons with Adolphe Sax, the son of the inventor of the saxophone. He became interested in acoustical problems; was active on the staff of the French Radio; manufactured new musical instruments (the sax trumpet, alto clarinet, etc.); publ. *La Musique et le micro* (Paris, 1934) and *L'Orchestre moderne à la Radio* (Paris, 1940).

Saro, J. Heinrich, German bandmaster and composer; b. Jessen, Jan. 4, 1827; d. Berlin, Nov. 27, 1891. In 1859 he became bandmaster in Berlin; in 1867 his band won the international competition at the Paris Exposition; in 1872 he was awarded a gold medal for his performance at the Boston Jubilee. He wrote a number of brilliant pieces of military music, and also some symph. works; publ. *Lehre vom musikalischen Wohlklang und Tonsatz,* and *Instrumentationslehre für Militärmusik.*

Sarrette, Bernard, founder of the Paris Conservatoire; b. Bordeaux, Nov. 27, 1765; d. Paris, April 11, 1858. A captain in the national guard at Paris, he brought together, after the 14th of July, 1789, 45 musicians to form the nucleus of the Parisian band of the national guard. In 1790 the City of Paris assumed the expenses of this band, which was increased to 70 members, among them artists of distinction. In 1792 the financial embarrassments of the Commune led to the suspension of payment; but Sarrette held the band together and, with the aid of the municipality, established a free school of music employing all the members as teachers. From this school came the musicians employed in the fourteen armies of the Republic. Its energetic principal soon had it converted into a national Institute of Music; and in Sept., 1795, it was definitely organized as a Conservatory. Sarrette, having gained his end, assumed the captaincy of the 103rd Regiment; but the board of directors (5 inspectors and 4 professors) proved so incompetent that he was recalled to the directorship of the Conservatoire in 1796. By introducing advanced methods of instruction, establishing the school of declamation, the concert hall, the grand library, etc., he raised the Cons. to an institution of the first rank. At the Restoration in 1814 he was deprived of his position; nor would he accept it after the revolution of 1830, not wishing to oust his friend Cherubini.
BIBLIOGRAPHY: Pierre Constant, *B. Sarrette et les origines du Conservatoire national de musique et de déclamation* (Paris, 1895).

Sarti, Giuseppe, important Italian composer (nicknamed "Il Domenichino"); b. Faenza (baptized Dec. 1), 1729; d. Berlin, July 28, 1802. He was a pupil of Padre Martini at Bologna. As a young man he was organist in the Cathedral of his native town (1748–50); appointed director of a theater there in 1752; produced there his earliest opera, *Pompeo in Armenia*

(1752); in the following year he brought out a new opera, *Il Rè pastore*, in Venice, with excellent success. In 1755 he was engaged as conductor of an Italian opera company in Denmark. The opera performances were terminated after 2 seasons, but Sarti received the appointment of court conductor, and remained in Copenhagen. In 1765 he was sent by the Danish government to Italy in order to engage singers for a new opera season in Copenhagen, but the project was put off; Sarti remained in Italy until 1768; returned to Copenhagen, and conducted at the Danish court theater (1770–75). As a result of political intrigue in the palace, Sarti was dismissed. He returned to Italy with his wife, the singer **Camilla Pasi,** whom he had married in Copenhagen. He was director of the Cons. dell'Ospedaletto at Venice (1775–79); then entered the competition for the post of maestro di cappella at the Cathedral of Milan, and won it, defeating a number of competitors, including Paisiello. He assumed his position at the Milan Cathedral in 1778; his prestige as a scholar and composer was very high; he was also renowned as a teacher; Cherubini was one of his students; his operas were produced in rapid succession in Copenhagen, Venice, Rome, Florence, and Vienna. In 1784 he was engaged by Catherine the Great as court musician. On the way to Russia he passed through Vienna, where he was received with honors by the Emperor Joseph II; he also met Mozart, who quoted a melody from Sarti's opera *Fra i due litiganti il terzo gode* in *Don Giovanni.* His greatest success in St. Petersburg was *Armida e Rinaldo* (1786; remodelled from an earlier opera, *Armida,* originally produced in Copenhagen, 1759); the leading part was sung by the celebrated Portuguese mezzo-soprano, Luiza Todi, but she developed a dislike of Sarti, and used her powerful influence with Catherine the Great to prevent Sarti's re-engagement. However, he was immediately engaged by Prince Potemkin, and followed him to southern Russia and Moldavia during the military campaign against Turkey; on the taking of Otchakov, Sarti wrote an ode to the Russian liturgical text of thanksgiving, and it was performed in January 1789 at Jassy, Bessarabia, with the accompaniment of cannon shots and church bells. Potemkin gave him a sinecure as head of a musical academy in Ekaterinoslav, but the academy was never established. After Potemkin's death in 1791, his arrangements with Sarti were honored by the court of St. Petersburg; in 1793 Sarti was reinstated as court composer. He retained his position during the reign of the Emperor Paul, and only after Paul's violent death at the hands of the palace guard, decided to leave Russia. He died on his way to Italy, in Berlin. Although Sarti enjoyed a great reputation during his lifetime, and wrote music comparing favorably with that by other Italian composers, his productions sank into oblivion after his death.

WORKS: operas: *Pompeo in Armenia* (Faenza, 1752); *Il Rè pastore* (Venice, 1753); *Vologeso* (Copenhagen, 1754); *Gram og Signe* (Copenhagen, Feb. 21, 1757); *Impermestra* (Rome, 1766); *La Contadina fedele* (Vienna, 1771); *La Successione in Sidone* (Copenhagen, April 4, 1771); *Deucalio e Pyrrha* (Copenhagen, March 19, 1772); *Le Gelosie villane* (Venice, Nov., 1776); *Medonte, Rè di Epiro* (Florence, Sept. 8, 1777); *I Contrattempi* (Venice, Nov., 1778); *Giulio*

Sabino (Venice, Jan., 1781); *Fra due litiganti il terzo gode* (Milan, Sept. 14, 1782); *I finti eredi* (St. Petersburg, Oct. 19, 1785); *Armida e Rinaldo* (St. Petersburg, 1786); *Ena nel Lazio* (Gatchina, near St. Petersburg, Oct. 15, 1799); contributed some numbers to the Russian opera *The Early Reign of Oleg* (St. Petersburg, Oct. 22, 1790), for which Catherine the Great wrote the libretto.

BIBLIOGRAPHY: G. Pasolini-Zanelli, *Giuseppe Sarti* (Faenza, 1883); A. Untersteiner, "Giuseppe Sarti," *Gazetta Musicale de Milano* (July 24, 1902); C. Rivalta, *Giuseppe Sarti, musicista faentino del secolo XVIII* (Faenza, 1928); G. Fesetchko, "Giuseppe Sarti," *Sovietskaya Musica* (Dec. 1950); R.-Aloys Mooser, *Annales de la Musique et des Musiciens en Russie au XVIIIᵉ siècle* (vol. II; Geneva, 1951; pp. 415–50, 463–79).

Sartori, Claudio, eminent Italian music scholar and encyclopedist; b. Brescia, April 1, 1913. He studied music with Th. Gérold in Strasbourg; was a librarian at the Cons. of Bologna (1938–42); in 1943 was appointed librarian at the Cons. of Milan; in 1965 he became the head of the Biblioteca Nazionale Braidense in Milan, which conducts a thorough codification of Italian musical sources. He published a number of informative reference works: *Bibliografia delle opere musicali stampate da Ottaviano Petrucci* (Florence, 1948); *Bibliografia della musica strumentale stampata in Italia fino al 1700* (2 vols.; Florence, 1952, 1968); *Monteverdi* (Brescia, 1953); *La Cappella musicale del Duomo di Milano* (Milan, 1957); *Casa ricordi* (Milan, 1958); *Dizionario degli editori musicali italiani* (Florence, 1958); *Puccini* (Milan, 1958); *Giacomo Carissimi: Catalogo delle opere attribute* (Milan, 1975). He was editor-in-chief of *Dizionario Ricordi della musica e dei musicisti* (Milan, 1959).

Sartorio, Antonio, Italian composer; b. Venice, c.1620; d. there, Jan. 5, 1681. He was attached to the court of Hannover (1666–75); in 1676 was appointed maestro di cappella at San Marco in Venice, a post held until his death. He was a leading representative of the Venetian school; produced 14 operas, of which the best known were *Seleuco* (Venice, Jan. 16, 1666), *L'Adelaide* (Venice, Feb. 19, 1672), and *Orfeo* (Venice, Dec. 14, 1672). He published a Psalm for 8 voices (Venice, 1680).

Sartorius, Paul, German organist and composer; b. Nuremberg, Nov. 16, 1569; d. Innsbruck, Feb. 28, 1609. His real name was **Schneider,** Sartorius being its Latin translation (tailor). He studied with Lechner in Nuremberg; then went to Rome for further study; then was organist at the court chapel of Duke Maximilian II of Austria in Mergentheim (1594–1602); in 1602 he went to Innsbruck. He published *Missae tres octonis v. decantandae* (Munich, 1599); *Madrigali a cinque voci* (Venice, 1600); *Sonetti spirituali a 6 voci* (Nuremberg, 1601); *Neue Teutsche Liedlein mit vier Stimmen nach art der Welschen Canzonette* (Nuremberg, 1601); *Sacrae cantiones sive motecta* (Venice, 1602); he further wrote Masses and motets in a polyphonic style similar to Palestrina's, and some choral works to German texts.

BIBLIOGRAPHY: W. Senn, *Musik und Theater am Hof zu Innsbruck* (Innsbruck, 1954).

Sáry, László, Hungarian composer; b. Györ, Jan. 1, 1940. He studied at the Budapest Academy with Endre Szervánszky; after graduation in 1966, he joined the Budapest New Music Studio. In his music he strives to attain the ultimate "total sound."

WORKS: 3 vocal quintets: *Lamento 65* (1965), *3 Madrigals* (1966) and *Incanto* (1969); *Variations* for clarinet and piano (1966); *Catacoustics* for 2 pianos (1967); *Cantata No. 1* for soprano, chamber chorus and chamber ensemble (1967–68; the middle movement is often played separately as *Quartetto* for soprano, flute, violin and cimbalom); *Musica da camera* for flute and percussion (1968); *Fluttuazioni* for violin and piano (1968–69); *Versetti* for organ and percussion (1966–69); *Hommage aux ancêtres* for vocal sextet (1969); *Improvisations '69* for vocal sextet and chamber ensemble (1969); *Pezzo concertato* for flute and piano (1969–70); 3 *Sonanti*: No. 1 for harpsichord, No. 2 for flute and percussion, and No. 3 for cimbalom (all 1970); *Canzone solenne* for orch. (1971); *Immaginario No. 1* for orch. (1971); *Psalmus* for voice and 2 string instruments plucked with a plectrum (1972); Trio for flute, piano and gongs (1972); *Pentagram* for 5 instrumental ensembles, with mixed voices and 6 articulators (1972); *Image* for clarinet, cello and piano (1972); *Sounds* for any soloist or any kind of ensemble or orch. (1972–73); *String* for 1 or more keyboard instruments or chamber ensemble (1973); *Drop by Drop*, in 2 versions: No. 1 for string orch., No. 2 for 2 prepared pianos (1975); *Snowdrops* for optional instruments (1975).

Sás, Andrés, Peruvian composer; b. Paris, April 6, 1900, of French-Belgian parents; d. Lima, Peru, July 25, 1967. He studied at the Brussels Cons. with Marchot (violin), Ernest Closson (music history), and Maurice Imbert (counterpoint). In 1924 he was engaged by the Peruvian government to teach violin at the National Academy of Music in Lima; in 1928 he returned temporarily to Belgium; the following year, settled in Lima permanently; married the Peruvian pianist Lily Rosay, and with her established the Sás-Rosay Academy of Music. He became profoundly interested in Peruvian folk music, and collected folk melodies; made use of many of them in his own compositions.

WORKS: incidental music to Molière's *La Malade imaginaire* (1943); the ballets, *La Señora del pueblo* (Viña del Mar, Chile, Jan. 20, 1946), *El Hijo prodigo* (1948); for orch.: *Canción India* (1927), *Tres Estampas del Perú* (1936) *Poema Indio* (1941), *Sueño de Zamba* (1943), *Danza Gitana* (1944), *La Patrona del pueblo* (1945), *La Parihuana* (1946), *Las Seis Edades de la Tía Conchita* (1947), *La Leyenda de la Isla de San Lorenzo* (1949); *Recuerdos*, for violin and piano (also for orch.; 1927); *Rapsodia Peruana*, for violin and piano (also for orch.: 1928); *Sonata-Fantasía* for flute and piano (1934); String Quartet (1938); *Cantos del Perú*, for violin and piano (1941); for piano: *Aires y Danzas del Perú* (2 albums; 1930 and 1945), *Suite Peruana* (1931), *Himno y Danza* (1935), *Sonatina Pe-*

ruana (1946); *Fantasía romántica* for trumpet and orch. (1950); numerous choruses and songs.

BIBLIOGRAPHY: N. Slonimsky, *Music of Latin America* (N.Y., 1945; pp. 275–76).

Saslavsky, Alexander, Russian-American violinist; b. Kharkov, Russia, Feb. 8, 1876; d. San Francisco, Aug. 2, 1924. He studied in his native town with local violin teachers; then with Jakob Grün in Vienna; after a Canadian tour in 1893 he joined the N.Y. Symph. Orch.; in 1903 became its concertmaster; in 1919, became concertmaster of the newly organized Los Angeles Philharmonic.

BIBLIOGRAPHY: *Dictionary of American Biography.*

Sassòli, Ada, Italian harpist; b. Bologna, Sept. 25, 1886; d. Rome, Dec. 3, 1946. She studied at the Cons. of Bologna; then entered the class of A. Hasselmans at the Paris Cons., winning 1st prize for harp playing in 1902. She toured with Mme. Melba in England and Australia (1904–05); made several tours of the U.S.; appeared as soloist with the Boston Symph. and other American orchestras; returned to Europe in 1916; was appointed prof. of harp at the Santa Cecilia in Rome, and lived there until her death.

Satie, Erik (Alfred-Leslie), celebrated French composer who elevated his eccentricities and verbal virtuosity to the plane of high art; b. Honfleur, May 17, 1866; d. Paris, July 1, 1925. He received his early musical training from a local organist Vinot, who was a pupil of Niedermeyer; at 13 he went to Paris where his father was a music publisher, and attended Paris Cons. (1879–86); took organ lessons with Guilmant, but soon relinquished systematic study of music; played in various cabarets in Montmartre; in 1884 he published a piano piece which he numbered, with malice aforethought, opus 62. His whimsical ways and Bohemian manner of life attracted many artists and musicians; he met Debussy in 1891; joined the Rosecrucian Society in Paris in 1892 and began to produce short piano pieces with eccentric titles intended to ridicule modernistic fancies and classical pedantries alike. Debussy thought highly enough of him to orchestrate 2 numbers from his piano suite, *Gymnopédies* (1888). He was 40 years old when he decided to learn something about the technique of composition, and entered the Schola Cantorum in Paris, in the classes of Vincent d'Indy and Albert Roussel. In 1898 he moved to Arcueil, a suburb of Paris; there he held court for poets, singers, dancers and musicians, among whom he had ardent admirers. Milhaud, Sauguet and the conductor Desormière organized a group, which they called only half-facetiously "École d'Arcueil," in honor of Satie as master and leader. But Satie's eccentricities were not merely those of a Parisian poseur; rather they were adjuncts to his esthetic creed which he enunciated with boldness and total disregard for professional amenities; he was once brought to court for sending an insulting letter to a music critic. Interestingly enough, he attacked modernistic aberrations just as assiduously as reactionary pedantry, publishing "manifestos" in prose and poetry. Although he was dismissed by most serious musicians as an uneducated person who tried to conceal his ignorance of music with persiflage, he exercised a profound influence on the young French composers of the first quarter of the 20th century; moreover, his stature as an innovator in the modern idiom grew after his death, so that the avant-garde musicians of the later day accepted him as inspiration for their own experiments; thus "space music" could be traced back to Satie's *musique d'ameublement* in which players were stationed at different parts of a hall playing different pieces in different tempi. The instruction in his piano piece *Vexations*, to play it 840 times in succession, was carried out literally in New York on Sept. 9, 1963, by a group of 5 pianists working in relays overnight, thus setting a world's record for duration of any musical composition. When critics accused Satie of having no idea of form, he published *Trois Morceaux en forme de poire*, the eponymous pear being reproduced in color on the cover; other pieces bore self-contradictory titles, such as *Heures séculaires et instantanées, Crépuscule matinal de midi; other titles were *Pièces froides, Embryons desséchés, Prélude en tapisserie, Préludes flasques (Pour un chien), Descriptions automatiques,* etc. In his ballets he introduced jazz for the first time in Paris; at the performance of his ballet *Relâche* (Paris, Nov. 29, 1924); the curtain bore the legend, "Erik Satie is the greatest musician in the world; whoever disagrees with this notion will please leave the hall." Other ballets were *Parade* (Paris, May 18, 1917, produced by Diagilev's Ballet Russe), and *Mercure* (Paris, June 15, 1924); further works, the symphonic drama *Socrate* for 4 sopranos and chamber orch. (Paris, Feb. 14, 1920); incidental music to Péladan's *Le Fils des étoiles* (1891; prelude orchestrated by Ravel) and for *Le Prince de Byzance* (1891); stage music to H. Mazel's *Le Nazaréen* (1892), to J. Bois' *La Porte heroïque au ciel* (1893), to M. de Féraudy's *Pousse l'Amour* (1905); many pieces were produced posthumously, as *Jack in the Box* and the mockingly titled *Cinq grimaces pour le "Songe d'une nuit d'été,"* orchestrated by Milhaud, etc. In 1912 Erik Satie published a facetious autobiographic notice, *Mémoirs d'un amnésique.*

BIBLIOGRAPHY: G. Jean-Aubry, *La Musique française d'aujourd'hui* (Paris, 1916); Carl van Vechten, "Erik Satie," in *Interpreters and Interpretations* (N.Y., 1917); R. D. Chennevière, "Erik Satie and the Music of Irony," *Musical Quarterly* (Oct. 1919); A. Coeuroy, *La Musique française moderne* (Paris, 1922); W. W. Roberts, "The Problem of Satie," *Music & Letters* (Oct. 1923); 2 special issues of the *Revue Musicale* (March 1924; June 1952); G. M. Gatti, *Musicisti moderni d'Italia e di fuori* (Bologna, 1925); W. Dankert, "Der Klassizismus Erik Saties und seine geistesgeschichteliche Stellung," *Zeitschrift für Musikwissenschaft* (Nov. 1929); P. -D. Templier, *Erik Satie* (Paris, 1932); D. Milhaud, "Notes sur Erik Satie," in *Les Œuvres nouvelles* (vol. 6, N.Y., 1946); W. H. Mellers, *Studies in Contemporary Music* (London, 1947); Rollo H. Myers, *Erik Satie* (London, 1948); Anne Rey, *Erik Satie* (Paris, 1974); Grete Wehmeyer, *Erik Satie* (Berlin, 1974).

Sato, Keijirō, Japanese composer; b. Tokyo, June 6, 1927. He studied medicine; music became his avocation. Most of his works are modernistic miniatures for piano or strings, e.g. a group of pieces under the generic title *Calligraphy* for 9, 10, and 11 string instruments (1962–65); he also wrote an *Electronic Raga* (1967).

Satter, Gustav, pianist and composer; b. Vienna, Feb. 12, 1832; d. Savannah, Ga., 1879. He studied in Vienna and Paris; undertook a pianistic tour in the U.S. and Brazil (1854–60) with surprising success; went back to Paris, where Berlioz warmly praised his music; then lived in Vienna, Dresden, Hannover, and Stockholm.

WORKS: an opera, *Olanthe;* the overtures *Lorelei, Julius Cæsar, An die Freude;* 2 symphonies; a symph. poem, *George Washington;* much chamber music; 3 sonatas, studies, waltzes, etc., for piano; about 160 opus numbers in all.

BIBLIOGRAPHY: *The Life and Works of Gustav Satter* (by an anonymous ex-Confederate admirer; Macon, Georgia, 1879).

Sattler, Heinrich, German organist and teacher; b. Quedlinburg, April 3, 1811; d. Oct. 17, 1891. He devoted himself mainly to teaching; from 1861, was on the staff of the Oldenburg Seminary. He publ. a treatise, *Die Orgel* (5 eds.); a book, *Erinnerung an Mozarts Leben und Werke* (1856); composed an oratorio, *Die Sachsentaufe;* and 2 cantatas, *Triumph des Glaubens und Pfingstkantate;* sacred works; chamber music; many organ pieces.

Satz, Ilya, Russian composer; b. Tchernobyl, Kiev district, April 30, 1875; d. St. Petersburg, Dec. 12, 1912. He studied cello in Kiev; then took lessons in composition with Taneyev in Moscow; his general education was desultory. He traveled in Europe in 1900; then made a tour as a cellist through Siberia. He returned to Moscow in 1903; in 1905 became music director of the Studio of the Moscow Art Theater, and wrote incidental music for new plays, including Maeterlinck's *Blue Bird* and Andreyev's *A Man's Life;* also composed ballet music for Salome's dance; the ballet *The Goat-Footed (The Dance of the Satyrs,* was reorchestrated and prepared for performance by Glière). Satz had a talent for the grotesque; a lack of technique prevented his development into a major composer. A memorial volume, *Ilya Satz,* with articles by Glière and several members of the Moscow Art Theater, was publ. at Moscow in 1923.

Sauer, Emil von, eminent pianist; b. Hamburg, Oct. 8, 1862; d. Vienna, April 27, 1942. He studied with Nicholas Rubinstein in Moscow (1879–81), and Liszt in Weimar (1884–85); made numerous European tours; played in the U.S. in 1898–99 and 1908. From 1901 till 1907, and again from 1915, was prof. at the Meisterschule für Klavierspiel in Vienna; from 1908 till 1915 he lived in Dresden; appeared in concerts until 1936, and then retired to Vienna. He wrote 2 piano concertos, 2 piano sonatas, many studies for piano; edited complete works of Brahms and pedagogical works of Pischna, Plaidy, Kullak, etc. He publ. an autobiography, *Meine Welt* (1901).

Sauguet, Henri, French composer; b. Bordeaux, May 18, 1901. His real name is **Henri-Pierre Poupard;** he assumed his mother's maiden name, Sauguet. He was a pupil of Joseph Canteloube; in 1922 he went to Paris, where he studied with Koechlin; became associated with Erik Satie, and formed a group designated as the École d'Arcueil (from the locality where Satie lived near Paris). In conformity with the principles of utilitarian music, he wrote sophisticated works in an outwardly simple manner; his first conspicuous success was the production of his ballet, *La Chatte,* by Diaghilev in 1927.

WORKS: operas: *Le Plumet du colonel* (Paris, April 24, 1924), *La Contrebasse,* after Chekhov (Paris, 1932), *La Chartreuse de Parme* (Paris, March 16, 1939), *La Gageure imprévue* (Paris, July 4, 1944), *Les Caprices de Marianne* (Aix-en-Provence, July 20, 1954); ballets: *La Chatte* (Monte Carlo, April 30, 1927), *Paul et Virginie* (Paris, April 15, 1943), *Les Mirages* (Paris, Dec. 15, 1947), *Cordelia* (Paris, May 7, 1952); *L'as de cœur* (1960); *Paris* (1964); *L'imposteur ou Le Prince et le mendiant* (1965); for orch.: *Les Saisons et les jours,* "allegoric symph." (Paris, Dec. 15, 1946); *Symphonie expiatoire,* in memory of innocent war victims (Paris, Feb. 8, 1948); Symph. No. 3 (1955); *Symphonie des marches* (Paris, June 4, 1966); Symph. No. 4, *Troisième âge* (1971); 3 Piano Concertos (1933, 1948, 1963); *Orphée* for violin and orch. (Aix-en-Provence, July 26, 1953); *Mélodie concertante* for cello and orch. (1963); *The Garden Concerto* for harmonica and orch. (1970); oratorio, *Chant pour une ville meurtrie* (1967); *Alentours saxophoniques* for alto saxophone, wind ensemble and piano (1976); 2 String Quartets (1926, 1948); piano pieces; songs.

Sauret, Émile, French violinist; b. Dun-le-Roi (Cher), May 22, 1852; d. London, Feb. 12, 1920. He studied with Vieuxtemps at the Paris Cons. and with Bériot in Brussels; was a child prodigy, and made his London debut at the age of 14. He was 20 when he was engaged for an American tour (1872); gave concerts in America again in 1874, 1876, 1877, and 1895. From 1903 till 1906 he taught at the Chicago Musical College; returning to Europe, he lived in Geneva and Berlin; was at various times a prof. of violin in London and Berlin. In 1873 he married the pianist **Teresa Carreño** (divorced in 1876). He was a typical representative of the French school of violin playing, distinguished by grace, elegance, and excellent taste.

WORKS: He composed for violin and orch. *Souvenir de Moscou, Rapsodie russe, Rapsodie suédoise, Farfalla,* and *Elégie et rondo;* for violin and piano, *Feuilles d'album, Pensées fugitives, Scènes champêtres, 20 grandes études, 12 Études artistiques, 24 Études-caprices;* publ. a method, *Gradus ad Parnassum du violoniste* (in 4 parts, with annotations in French and German); also made about 25 transcriptions.

Sauveur, Joseph, French acoustician; b. La Flèche, March 24, 1653; d. Paris, July 9, 1716. A deaf-mute, learning to speak in his 7th year, he became a remarkable investigator in the realm of acoustics; in 1696, member of the Académie. He was the first to calculate absolute vibration numbers, and to explain scientifically the phenomenon of overtones.

WRITINGS: (all publ. in the *Mémoires* of the Académie): *Principes d'acoustique et de musique* (1700–01); *Application des sons harmoniques à la composition des jeux d'orgue* (1702); *Méthode générale pour former des systèmes tempérés . . .* (1707); *Table générale des systèmes tempérés* (1711); *Rapports des sons des cordes d'instruments de musique aux flèches des cordes* (1713).

BIBLIOGRAPHY: H. Scherchen, *Vom Wesen der Musik,* chap. I (Zürich, 1946; in English as *The Nature of Music,* Chicago, 1950).

Sauzay, (Charles-) Eugene, French violinist and composer; b. Paris, July 14, 1809; d. there, Jan. 24, 1901. He studied with Baillot at the Paris Cons., and was a member of the Baillot's string quartet; taught violin at the Paris Cons. from 1860 to 1892. He publ. *Symphonie rustique; Études harmoniques,* for violin; numerous transcriptions; also the books *Haydn, Mozart, Beethoven, étude sur le quatuor* (Paris, 1861; 2nd ed., 1884), and *L'École de l'accompagnement* (Paris, 1869).

Savage, Henry Wilson, American impresario; b. New Durham, N. H., March 21, 1859; d. Boston, Nov. 29, 1927. He started in business as a real estate operator in Boston, where he built the Castle Square Theater; later went into theatrical enterprise himself and in 1897 opened a season of opera in English. His Castle Square Opera Co. flourished, and he undertook tours of other cities. In 1900 he formed the English Grand Opera Cp. and engaged several artists from the Carl Rosa Co. of London. In 1904–05 he organized a special troupe, producing *Parsifal* in English in the principal cities of the East and Middle West; in 1906–07 the same company made a tour with Puccini's *Madama Butterfly;* he also produced light opera with another company, which, among other operttas, introduced Lehár's *The Merry Widow* to the U.S. (1906).

BIBLIOGRAPHY: *Dictionary of American Biography.*

Savard, (Marie-Gabriel-) Augustin, French music educator; b. Paris, Aug. 21, 1814; d. there, June 7, 1881. He studied with Leborne and Bazin; in 1843 he was appointed prof. of solfège at the Paris Cons., and later taught harmony and thoroughbass. He was an excellent teacher; among his many foreign students was MacDowell. He published the manuals, *Cours complet d'harmonie théorique et pratique* (2 vols., Paris, 1853, 1856); and *Principes de la musique* (Paris, 1861; very popular; 14th ed., 1913); its abridged version, *Premières notions de musique* (Paris, 1866) also went into numerous editions.

Savard, Marie-Emmanual-Augustin, French composer and pedagogue; son of **Marie-Gabriel-Augustin Savard;** b. Paris, May 15, 1861; d. Lyons, Dec. 6, 1942. He studied at the Paris Cons. with Durand, Taudou, and Massenet; won the Prix de Rome in 1886 with the cantata *La Vision de Saul;* in 1892–93 was chorusmaster at the Opéra; director of the Cons. in Lyons from 1902 until 1921, when he retired.

WORKS: a lyric drama, *La Forêt* (Paris Opera, 1910); 2 symphonies; an overture, *Roi Lear; Poème* for voice and orch.; String Quartet; Violin Sonata; etc.

Savart, Félix, French acoustician; b. Mézières, June 30, 1791; d. Paris, March 17, 1841. He was prof. of acoustics at the Collège de France; in 1821, was elected member of the Académie.

WRITINGS (publ. in the *Annales de physique et de chimie*): *Mémoire sur la construction des instruments à cordes et à archet* (1819, separate reprint; in German, 1844); *Sur la communication des mouvements vibratoires entre les corps solides* (1820); *Sur les vibrations de l'air* (1823); *Sur la voix humaine* (1825); *Sur la communication des mouvements vibratoires par les liquides* (1826); *Sur la voix des oiseaux* (1826); etc.

Saville, Frances, American soprano; b. San Francisco, Jan. 6, 1863; d. Burlingame, Calif., Nov. 8, 1935. She went early to Australia, where she made her debut in oratorio; continued her studies in Paris with Marchesi; in 1892 made her operatic debut in Brussels; also appeared with Carl Rosa Co. in England, at the Paris Opéra-Comique, in Vienna, Berlin, St. Petersburg, Warsaw, etc.; on Nov. 18, 1895, she made her debut as Juliette (with Jean de Reszke) at the Metropolitan Opera House, on whose roster she remained through the season 1899–1900; later she appeared at the Vienna Opera; then lived in retirement in California.

Savín, Francisco, Mexican conductor and composer; b. Mexico City, Nov. 18, 1929. He studied piano in Mexico City with José Velásquez (1944–53) and took conducting lessons with Scherchen and composition with Rodolfo Halffter (1955–56). He then went to Europe; studied at the Music Academy in Prague, and composition with Karel Janeček (1957–59). Returning to Mexico, he was an assistant conductor of the Mexican National Symph. Orch. (1959–62) and principal conductor of the Xalapa Symph. Orch. (1963–67); was then director of the National Cons. of Music in Mexico City (1967–70); in 1973 was appointed director of the conducting workshop at the National Cons.

WORKS: *Quetzalcoátl*, symph. poem for 2 narrators and orch. (1957); *Metamorfosis* for orch. (1962); *2 Formas plásticas* for wind quintet (1964, 1965); *3 Líricas* for mezzo-soprano, flute, clarinet, viola, percussion, and piano (1966); *Concreción* for electronic organ and orch. (1969); *Monología de las Delicias* for 4 female voices and orch. (1969); *Quasar 1* for eletronic organ, tape, and percussion (1970).

Savine, Alexander, American conductor, composer, and singing teacher; b. Belgrade, April 26, 1881; d. Chicago, Jan. 19, 1949. He studied in Belgrade with S. Mokranjac, and later at the Vienna Cons. (singing with Pauline Lucca). He then was engaged as opera conductor in Berlin (1905–07); taught singing at the Musical Academy in Winnepeg, Canada (1908–12); later settled in the U.S.; was director of the opera dept. at the Institute of Musical Art, N.Y. (1922–24); in 1929 moved to Chicago. He married in 1914 the soprano **Lillian Blauvelt.** He wrote the opera *Xenia*

(Zürich, May 29, 1919); 4 symph. poems; choruses; songs.

Sawallisch, Wolfgang, German conductor; b. Munich, Aug. 23, 1923. He studied piano and composition at the Cons. of Munich, graduating in 1946. He made his conducting debut in Augsburg in 1947; subsequently occupied posts as music director in Aachen (1953–57), Wiesbaden (1957–59) and Cologne (1959–63). In 1964 he toured the U.S. with the Vienna Symph. Specializing in opera, he has achieved some of his finest successes in the Wagnerian repertory, conducting in Bayreuth since 1957.

Sax, (Antoine-Joseph-) Adolphe, inventor of the saxophone; b. Dinant, Belgium, Nov. 6, 1814; d. Paris, Feb. 7, 1894. He was the son of **Charles-Jospeh Sax,** the instrument maker, and acquired great skill in manipulating instruments from his early youth; his practical and imaginative ideas led him to undertake improvements of the clarinet and other wind instruments. He studied the flute and clarinet at the Brussels Cons.; in 1842 he went to Pairs with a wind instrument of his invention, which he called the "saxophone," made of metal, with a single-reed mouthpiece and conical bore. He exhibited brass and woodwind instruments at the Paris Exposition of 1844, winning a silver medal; his father joined him in Paris, and together they continued the manufacture of new instruments; evolved the saxhorns (improved over the bugle-horn and ophicleide by replacing the keys by a valve mechanism), and the saxo-tromba, a hybrid instrument producing a tone midway between the bugle and the trumpet. Conservative critics and rival instrument makers ridiculed Sax's innovations, but Berlioz and others warmly supported him; he also won praise from Rossini. His instruments were gradually adopted by French military bands. Sax won a gold medal at the Paris Industrial Exposition of 1849. Financially, however, he was unsuccessful, and was compelled to go into bankruptcy in 1852. He exhibited his instruments in London (1862) and received the Grand Prix in Paris (1867) for his improved instruments. In 1857 the Paris Cons. engaged him as instructor of the saxophone; with some interruptions, saxophone instruction was continued at the Paris Cons. for a whole century. He publ. a method for his instrument. Although Wieprecht, Červený, and others disputed the originality and priority of his inventions, legal decisions gave the rights to Sax; the saxophone became a standard instrument; many serious composers made use of it in their scores (Bizet's *L'Arlésienne*, etc.). The instrument fell into desuetude after Sax's death; but about 1918 a spectacular revival of the saxophone took place, when it was adopted in jazz bands; its popularity became world-wide; numerous methods were publ. and special schools established; and there appeared saxophone virtuosos for whom many composers wrote concertos.

BIBLIOGRAPHY: O. Comettant, *Histoire d'un inventeur au XIXᵉ siècle* (Paris, 1860); Th. Lajarte, *Instruments Sax et fanfares civiles* (Paris, 1876); J. Kool, *Das Saxophone* (Leipzig, 1931); Albert Remy, *La Vie tourmentée d'Adolphe Sax* (Brussels, 1939); L. Kochnitzky, *Adolphe Sax and His Saxophone* (N.Y.,

1949); M. Perrin, *Le Saxophone, Son histoire, sa technique et son utilisation dans l'orchestre* (Paris, 1955); J. M. Londeix, *125 ans de musique pour saxophone* (Paris, 1971).

Sax, Charles-Joseph, Belgian instrument maker; b, Dinant-sur-Meuse, Feb. 1, 1791; d. Paris, April 26, 1865. He established an instrument factory at Brussels in 1815, manufacturing not only wind instruments, but also pianos, harps, and guitars; his specialty, however, was brass instruments. He joined his son **Adolphe Sax** in Paris, and helped him to launch his revolutionary inventions.

Sayão, Bidú, Brazilian soprano; b. Niteroi, near Rio de Janeiro, May 11, 1902. She studied with Jean de Reszke in Nice (1923–25); sang at the Opéra-Comique in Paris, at the Royal Opera in Rome, and at La Scala, Milan, In 1935 she made her American debut in a recital in N.Y.; opera debut with the Metropolitan Opera Co. on Feb. 13, 1937, as Manon; also made several South American tours.

Saygun, Ahmed Adnan, Turkish composer; b. Izmir, Sept. 7, 1907. He studied composition in Paris with Le Flem and Vincent d'Indy at the Schola Cantorum. Returning to Turkey in 1931, he was active as teacher and composer; in 1946 he was appointed prof. at the Cons. of Ankara. He visited the U.S. in 1950 and in 1957-58.
WORKS: 3 operas on Turkish themes: *Tas Bebek* (Ankara, Dec. 27, 1934); *Kerem* (Ankara, March 1, 1953); *Köroglu* (Ankara, 1973); the oratorio, *Yunus Emre* (Ankara, May 25, 1946); Piano Concerto (1956); 4 symphonies (1953, 1955, 1961, 1973); Violin Concerto (1967); Wind Quintet (1968); 3 String Quartets (1947, 1958, 1967); Quartet for clarinet, saxophone, percussion, and piano; an orchestral suite of national dances, *Zeybek, Interlude and Horon* (Ankara, April 14, 1951); Cello Sonata; Violin Sonata; songs.

Sayn-Wittgenstein-Berleburg, Count Friedrich Ernst, German composer; b. Castle Sannerz, Fulda, June 5, 1837; d. Meran, April 16, 1915. He pursued a military career; also studied music with Julius Rietz in Leipzig; publ. *Szenen aus der Frithjofsage* for voice and orch., and songs; wrote 2 operas, *Die Wolfenbraut* (Graz, 1879) and *Antonius und Kleopatra* (Graz, 1883).

Sayve, Lambert de, Flemish composer; b. Sayve, near Liège, 1594; d. Prague, Feb. 1614. As a youth he went to Vienna, where he became singer in the Imperial chapel; in 1569 he was choirmaster at the monastery of Melk, near Linz, a post he retained until 1577 (made a trip to Spain in 1570). In 1582 he entered the service of the Archduke Charles in Graz; in 1583 he joined the retinue of Archduke Matthias, King of Bohemia, and lived in Prague. He publ. during his lifetime *Il primo libro delle canzoni a la Napolitana a 5 voci* (Vienna, 1582); *Teutsche Liedlein mit 4 Stimmen* (Vienna, 1602); and (his most important works) a collection *Sacrae Symphoniae* (1612), containing 141 pieces *a* 4 to 16 in 12 books. Modern reprints by F. Blume in *Das Chorwerk* 51 by A. Einstein in *Denk-*

mäler der Tonkunst in Österreich 77 (41). 6 Masses by Sayve (*a* 5 to 16) are in Austrian libraries.
BIBLIOGRAPHY: R. Bragard, *Lambert de Sayve* (Liège, 1934); H. Osthoff, *Die Neiderländer und das deutsche Lied* (Berlin, 1938); H. Federhofer, "L. de Sayve an der Grazer Hofkapelle," *Revue Belge de Musicologie* 3 (1949).

Sbriglia, Giovanni, celebrated singing teacher; b. Naples, June 23, 1832; d. Paris, Feb. 20, 1916. He sang as a tenor at the San Carlo Theater in Naples; was heard in Italy by Maretzek, the impresario, who engaged him for a season at the Academy of Music, N.Y., where Sbriglia appeared with Adelina Patti (1860); he then made a grand tour of the U.S. with Parodi and Adelaide Phillipps; also sang in Mexico and Havana. He returned to Europe in 1875 and settled in Paris, where he became a highly successful vocal teacher. Jean, Joséphine, and Édouard de Reszke studied with him when they already professional artists; Sbriglia trained the baritone voice of Jean de Reszke, enabling him to sing tenor roles. Pol Plançon, Nordica, and Sibyl Sanderson were among his pupils.

Scacciati, Bianca, Italian soprano; b. Florence, July 3, 1894; d. Brescia, Oct. 15, 1948. She studied in Milan; made her debut there as Marguerite in *Faust* in 1917. She rapidly asserted herself as one of the most impressive dramatic sopranos in Italy; sang for many seasons at La Scala, Milan; also made successful appearances at Covent Garden, London, at the Paris Opéra and at the Teatro Colón in Buenos Aires. She was particularly noted for her interpretation of the title role of Puccini's *Turandot.*

Scala, Francis Maria, Italian-born American bandleader; first leader of the U.S. Marine Band so designated; b. Naples, 1819 (or 1820); d. Washington, D.C., April 18, 1903. Beginning his musical career on the clarinet, he enlisted in the U.S. Navy as a Musician Third-Class on the frigate Brandywine when it was anchored at Naples in 1841. Following the ship's return to Washington, Scala left the Navy for the Marine Corps, and in 1843 was designated fife-major of the fife corps associated with Marine Corps headquarters. On Sept. 9, 1855 he became *de facto* the leader of the Marine Band; in 1861 he was made "Principal Musician," and on Sept. 4, 1868, was for the first time, referred to as "Leader of the Band." John Philip Sousa was one of his apprentice bandsmen. Retiring in 1871, Scala continued to reside in Washington until his death. In Sept. 1945 his son Norman P. Scala made the first of several gifts to the Library of Congress honoring his father; these materials contain a large amount of manuscripts and printed music, chiefly band arrangements made by or for Scala, that represent in essence the library of the Marine Band during the Civil War; included is a note in the hand of Abraham Lincoln, then Scala's Commander-in-Chief.

Scalchi, Sofia, celebrated Italian mezzo-soprano; b. Turin, Nov. 29, 1850; d. Rome, Aug. 22, 1922. She made her debut at Mantua in 1866 as Ulrica in Verdi's *Ballo in Maschera;* then sang throughout Italy; appeared in concert in London (Sept. 16, 1868) and at

Covent Garden (Nov. 5, 1868) as Azucena, obtaining enormous success. She visited the U.S. for the first time in 1882 with Mapleson's opera company; sang in the opening season of the Metropolitan Opera (1883–84) and again in 1891–96. She then toured with unfailing success in Russia, Austria, Spain, and South America. She married Count Luigi Lolli in 1875; in 1896 she retired to her estate in Turin; in 1921 went to Rome, where she remained until her death. Her voice had a range of 2½ octaves; it was essentially a contralto voice, but with so powerful a high register that she sucessfully performed soprano parts.

Scalero, Rosario, eminent Italian pedagogue and composer; b. Moncalieri, near Turin, Dec. 24, 1870; d. Settimo Vittone, near Turin, Dec. 25, 1954. He studied violin with Sivori in Genoa, and in London with Wilhelmj; general subjects with Mandyczewski in Vienna. In 1896 he was engaged as violin teacher in Lyons, France; then was instructor at Santa Cecilia, Rome, and examiner at the Naples Cons., and later at the Cons. of Parma. In 1919 he came to the U.S., and was head of the composition classes at the David Mannes School, N.Y.; in 1928 joined the faculty of the Curtis Institute of Music, Philadelphia; among his students there were Samuel Barber, Gian Carlo Menotti, and Lukas Foss. He wrote a violin concerto; *Neapolitan Dances,* for violin and piano; chamber music; sacred songs; etc.

Scaria, Emil, Austrian bass; b. Graz, Sept. 18, 1838; d. Blasewitz, near Dresden, July 22, 1886. He studied with Netzer at Graz, with Lewy at Vienna, and with Garcia in London. After singing in opera in Dessau (1862), Leipzig (1863), and Dresden (1964), he acquired a fine reputation; in 1872 he was engaged as a member of the Court Opera of Vienna. He excelled in Wagner's operas; created the role of Gurnemanz in *Parsifal.*
  BIBLIOGRAPHY: A. Neumann, *Erinnerungen an Richard Wagner* (Leipzig, 1907; English transl., N.Y., 1908).

Scarlatesco, Ion, Rumanian composer; b. Bucharest, 1872; d. there, Sept. 19, 1922. A versatile musician, he began his career as pianist; also wrote plays and was active as music critic and harmony teacher. He composed about 50 ballads for voice and piano; a string quartet; a *Rumanian Rhapsody* for orch.; several other pieces in the Rumanian style, among which *Bagatelle* for violin became popular.

Scarlatti, Alessandro, founder of the "Neopolitan School" of music; b. Palermo, May 2, 1660; d. Naples, Oct. 24, 1725. He was brought to Rome in 1672, and was a pupil there of Carissimi; in 1679 he conducted his first known opera, *L'Errore innocente,* at Rome; then followed a performance there of *L'Onestà negli amori* at the palace of Queen Christina of Sweden (Feb. 6, 1680); on the score of another opera, *Il Pompeo* (Rome, Jan. 25, 1683), he is styled maestro di cappella to the Queen. In 1694 he was maestro to the Viceroy at Naples. In 1703 he became assistant maestro to Foggia at S. Maria Maggiore, Rome, and succeeded him as 1st maestro in 1707, resigning in 1709

and returning to Naples, where he subsequently became maestro of the royal chapel. He also taught music; was briefly engaged at the Cons. di Santa Maria di Loreto, Naples (1689), but never had prolonged tenure; among his private pupils was Hasse, who studied with him in 1724. Scarlatti wrote approximately 115 operas (about 50 are extant); *La Rosaura* (Rome, 1690), ed. by Eitner, was printed by the *Gesellschaft für Musikforschung,* vol. XIV; in *Teodora Augusta* (Rome, Jan. 3, 1693) he used an incipient *recitativo obbligato* accompanied by the entire orchestra; also several arias with the first part sung *da capo,* a style that was later generally adopted by opera composers. An aria and a duet from *Laodicea e Bernice* (Naples, 1701) have been publ. by J. J. C. Maier, also a terzet and quartet from *La Griselda* (Rome, 1721), with German transl. by Wolzogen; in *Il Tigrane,* his most celebrated opera, marked in the libretto as his 106th work for the stage (Naples, Feb. 16, 1715), the orch. comprises violins, violas, cellos, double basses, 2 flutes, 2 oboes, 2 bassoons, and 2 horns; *Il Trionfo dell'onore,* his only comic opera (Naples, Nov. 26, 1718), was transl. into English by Geoffrey Dunn (London, July 23, 1937). Other important operas are: *Olimpia vendicata* (Naples, Dec. 23, 1685); *La Statira* (Rome, Jan. 5, 1690); *Pirro e Demetrio* (Naples, Jan. 28, 1694); *Il Prigioniero fortunato* (Naples, Dec. 14, 1698). 14 oratorios are also known; he is said to have written over 200 Masses (up to ten parts), besides much other sacred music (*Concerti sacri,* motets *a* 1–4, with 2 violins, viola, and organ, were publ. at Amsterdam as op. 1 and 2; a few separate numbers are in the collections of Choron, the Prince of Moskowa, Commer [a *Tu es Petrus*], Dehn, Proske, and Rochlitz; Choron also publ. a Requiem, and Proske a Mass); his secular vocal music includes madrigals (one *a* 4 is in Padre Martini's *Esempli di contrappunto fugato*), serenatas, duets, some 800 cantatas. He also composed 12 symphonies (concertos) for small orch., a string quartet, a sonata for 3 flutes and one for 2 flutes, 2 violins, and continuo, one for flute, 2 violins, and continuo, 2 suites for flute and harpsichord, variations on Corelli's *La Follia,* toccatas for harpsichord, etc. Some of his works have been publ. by G. Bas and F. Nekes (a 4-voiced *Missa ad voces aequales*), Lenzewski (*concertos for strings continuo*), Tebaldini (sonata for flute and strings), J. S. Shedlock (toccatas for harpsichord; 9 vols.), Tagliapietra, Longo (keyboard compositions), etc. Harvard Publications in Music began in 1974 issuing a series of the operas, edited by D. J. Grout.
  BIBLIOGRAPHY: E. J. Dent, "The Operas of A. S. " *Sammelbände der Internationalen Musik-Gesellschaft* IV/1; id., *A. S. His Life and Works* (London, 1905; new ed. with preface and notes by F. Walker, London, 1960); Ch. Van den Borren, *A. S. et l'esthétique de l'opéra napolotain* (1922); A. Lorenz, "A. S.s Opern in Wien," *Zeitschrift für Musikwissenschaft* IX/2 (1926); id., *A. S.s Jugendopern* (2 vols., Augsburg, 1927); E. Jaloux, *Sur un air de S.* (Maastricht, 1928); A. Cametti, in *Musica d'Oggi* (Feb. 1931); P. Fienga, "La Véritable Patrie et la famille d'Alessandro Scarlatti," *Revue Musicale* (Jan. 1929); *Gli Scarlatti* (Siena, 1940); O. Tiby, *La Famiglia Scarlatti: nuove ricerche e documenti* (Rome, 1947); M. Fabbri, *Alessandro Scarlatti e il principe Ferdinando de' Medici*

(Florence, 1961); R. Pagano & L. Bianchi, *A. Scarlatti. Catalogue of Works* (Turin, 1972).

Scarlatti, (Giuseppe) Domenico, famous Italian composer and harpsichordist; son of **Alessandro Scarlatti;** b. Naples, Oct. 26, 1685. d. Madrid, July 23, 1757. A pupil of his father, he was named organist and composer at the royal chapel in Naples when he was 16; two years later his first operas, *Ottavia restituita al trono* and *Il Giustino*, were produced in Naples (Dec. 19, 1703). In 1705 he was sent by his father to Venice, where he studied with Gasparini. In 1709 he was back in Rome, where he engaged in a friendly contest with Handel, who was adjudged his superior on the organ, while Scarlatti held his own on the harpsichord. From 1709–14 he was maestro di cappella to Queen Maria Casimira of Poland, for whose private theater (in her palace in Rome) he composed 7 operas and an oratorio. He had been appointed in 1713 assistant to Bai, the maestro di cappella at the Vatican, and upon the latter's death in 1714 succeeded him as maestro; resigned in 1719. During this time was also maestro to the Portuguese Ambassador to the Holy See. There is no evidence that Scarlatti went to London in 1720, as is usually stated. But in that year his opera *Amor d'un ombra e gelsoia d'un'aura* (rewritten as *Narciso*) was produced there at the Haymarket Theatre under Roseingrave's direction (May 30), and his brother **Francesco** gave a concert there in September. Scarlatti went to Lisbon about 1719, where he was engaged as maestro of the royal chapel and music teacher to the Princess Maria Barbara, for whom he composed his famous *Esercizi per gravicembalo*, of which the first were publ. in 1738. In 1729 the princess married the heir to the Spanish throne and Scarlatti accompanied her to Madrid, where he spent the rest of his life. When Maria Barbara became queen in 1746, he was appointed her *maestro de cámara*. After leaving Italy he returned only twice, once for a brief visit to his father at Naples in 1724, and the other time to marry Maria Catalina Gentili on May 15, 1728, in Rome. In Madrid, Scarlatti does not appear to have composed operas, but he founded an instrumental school in Spain, the chief representative being P. Antonio Soler, his pupil. He composed over 600 sonatas and pieces for harpsichord, besides operas, cantatas, and sacred music (2 Misereres *a* 4; a Stabat Mater; a Salve Regina for soprano and strings [1756], his last work); his *Fuga estemporanea per orchestra* (MS) is in the library of the Univ. of Münster. The principal MS source for the harpsichord works of Scarlatti is the collection of the Biblioteca Marciana at Venice, which belonged originally to the Queen of Spain and at her death was brought to Italy by Farinelli. Domenico Scarlatti's special claim to renown rests upon his harpsichord music; he studied the characteristics of the instrument, and adapted his compositions to them, being one of the finest writers in the "free style" (a homophonic style with graceful ornamentation, in contrast to the former contrapuntal style). He also obtained effects by the frequent crossing of the hands; runs in thirds and sixths; leaps wider than an octave; broken chords in contrary motion; tones repeated by rapidly changing fingers; etc. During Scarlatti's lifetime some of his keyboard pieces were printed in various eds. in London and Paris. Later editions include a collection by Czerny, of 200 pieces; Breitkopf, 60; Pauer, 50; Köhler, 12 sonatas and fugues; Tausig, 3 sonatas; Bülow, 18 pieces in suite form; Schletterer, 18; André, 28; Banck, 30; Farrenc, 100 (in *Trésor des pianistes);* Sauer, 25; Barth, 70; Gerstenberg, 5 sonatas (not included in the Longo ed.); Buonamici, 22 (in Schirmer's Library, vol. 73). Ricordi publ. Scarlatti's "complete" harpsichord works, ed. by A. Longo, in 11 vols. (1 vol. as supplement; 1906ff.), also a Thematic Index (Milan, 1937). 60 sonatas ed. by Ralph Kirkpatrick were publ. by G. Schirmer. A complete edition of the sonatas is in vols. 31–41 of *Le Pupitre* series; the *Complete Keyboard Works*, in a fine facsimile edition of 18 vols., was put out by Ralph Kirkpatrick in 1971.

BIBLIOGRAPHY: E. J. Dent, in the *Monthly Musical Record* (1906), and in *Auftakt* (1922); A. Longo, *D. Scarlatti e la sua figura nella storia della musica* (Naples, 1913); G. F. Malipiero, "D. Scarlatti," *Musical Quarterly* (July 1927); F. Torrefranca, *Le Origini italiane del romanticismo musicale* (Turin, 1930); W. Gerstenberg, *Die Klavierkompositionen D. Scarlattis* (1933); S. Sitwell, *A Background for D. Scarlatti* (London, 1935); U. Rolandi, "Per una biobibliografia di Scarlatti," *Bolletino dei Musicisti* (Nov. 1935); C. Valabrega, *D. Scarlatti, il suo secolo, la sua opera* (with 233 musical examples; Modena, 1937); S. A. Luciani, "D. Scarlatti" (biographical and bibliographical notes; valuable), *Rassegna Musicale* (Dec. 1938; Jan. and Feb. 1939; also reprinted separately); *Gli Scarlatti* (Siena, 1940); A. Solar Quintes, "Documentos sobre la familia de Domenico Scarlatti," *Anuario Musical* (Barcelona, 1949); H. Keller, *D. Scarlatti* (Leipzig, 1957); G. Pestelli, *Le Sonate di Domenico Scarlatti; Proposta di un ordinamento cronologico* (Turin, 1967); R. Kirkpatrick, "Who Wrote the Scarlatti Sonatas," *Notes* (March 1973). The most important publication dealing with his life and works is *Domenico Scarlatti* by Ralph Kirkpatrick, published in Princeton and London in 1953. Apart from clearing up biographical data, Kirkpatrick gives a new chronological numbering of works, which has been widely accepted and has superseded Longo's catalogue.

Scarlatti, Giuseppe, Italian composer, grandson of **Alessandro Scarlatti;** nephew of **Domenico Scarlatti;** b. Naples, c.1718; d. Vienna, Aug. 17, 1777. He was in Rome in 1739, and later in Lucca, where he married **Barbara Stabili**, a singer (1747). He went to Vienna in 1757, and remained there for 20 years until his death. He wrote 31 operas, produced in Rome, Florence, Lucca, Turin, Venice, Naples, Milan, and Vienna; of these the most successful was *L'Isola disabitata* (Venice, Nov. 20, 1757). Another **Giuseppe Scarlatti** (a nephew of Alessandro Scarlatti), whose name appears in some reference works, was not a musician.

BIBLIOGRAPHY: H. Springer, "Das Partitur-Autograph von Giuseppe Scarlattis bisher verschollener Clemenza di Tito," *Beiträge zum Bibliotheks- und Buchwesen* (1913); *Gli Scarlatti* (Siena, 1940); O. Tiby, *La Famiglia Scarlatti: nuove ricerche e documenti* (Rome, 1947); Frank Walker, "Some Notes on the Scarlattis," *Music Review* (Aug. 1951).

Scarmolin, (Anthony) Louis, American conductor and composer; b. Schio, Italy, July 30, 1890; d. Union City, New Jersey, July 13, 1969. He came to the U.S. as a boy; graduated from the N.Y. College of Music in 1907; served in the U.S. Army during World War I; then lived in Union City, New Jersey. He wrote 6 operas and several symphonic poems and overtures; also *Miniature Symphony* (Cleveland, Feb. 7, 1940); altogether he composed some 200 opus numbers.

Scarpini, Pietro, Italian pianist; b. Rome, April 6, 1911. He studied at the Cons. di Musica Santa Cecilia in Rome; made his concert debut in 1936; then gave recitals in Europe and in the U.S.; from 1940 to 1967 he taught at the Cons. of Florence; in 1967 joined the faculty of the Milan Cons. He specializes in the modern repertory of piano music; wrote a piano concerto and a piano quintet; also made an arrangement for 2 pianos of the 10th Symphony of Mahler.

Scelsi, Giacinto, remarkable Italian composer; b. La Spezia, Jan. 8, 1905. He studied composition with Respighi and Casella in Rome; then went to Vienna, where he became interested in the Schoenbergian method of writing music outside the bounds of traditional tonality; at the same time he became deeply immersed in the study of the musical philosophy of the East, in which the scales and rhythms are perceived as functional elements of the human psyche. As a result of these multifarious absorptions of ostensibly incompatible ingredients, Scelsi formulated a style of composition that is synthetic in its sources and pragmatic in its artistic materialization. WORKS: FOR ORCH.: *Rotative* for 3 pianos, wind instruments and percussion (1930); *Rapsodia romantica* (1931); *Sinfonietta* (1932); *Preludio e fuga* (1938); *Balata* for cello and orch. (1945); *La Nascità del verbo* (1948; International Festival for Contemporary Music, Brussels, June 28, 1950); *4 Pezzi su una nota sola* (1959); *Hurqualia* for orch. and amplified instruments (1960); *Aion* (1961); *Nomos* for 2 orchestras, and organ (1963); *Chukrim* for string orch. (1963); *Amahit* for violin and 18 instruments (1965); *Anagamin* for 12 string instruments (1965); *Ohoi* for 16 string instruments (1966); *Uaxuctum* for chorus, orch. and Ondes Martenot (1966); *Natura renovatur* for 11 string instruments (1967); *Konx-om-pax* for chorus, orch. and organ (1969); *Pfhat* for chorus and orch. (1974). CHAMBER MUSIC: 4 string quartets (1944, 1961, 1963, 1964); *Piccola Suite* for flute and clarinet (1953); *Hyxos* for alto flute, gong and bells (1955); String Trio (1958); *Elegia* for viola and cello (1958); *Rucke di Guck* for piccolo and oboe (1958); *I Presagi* for 10 instruments (1958); *Kya* for solo clarinet and 7 instruments (1959); *Khoom* for soprano and 6 instruments (1962); *Duo* for violin and cello (1965); *Ko-lho* for flute and clarinet (1966); *Okanagon* for harp, tam-tam, and double bass (1968); *Duo* for violin and double bass (1977); *5 Divertimenti* for violin solo (1952-56); *Pwill* for flute solo (1954); *Coelocanth* for viola solo (1955); *3 Studies* for viola solo (1956); *Trilogy*, 3 pieces for cello solo (1957-65); *Ko-Tha* for guitar solo (1967); *Praham II* for 9 instruments (1973); *3 Pezzi* for clarinet; *3 Pezzi* for trumpet; *3 Pezzi* for saxophone; *3 Pezzi* for French horn; *3 Pezzi* for trombone; other pieces for solo instruments. VOCAL WORKS: *Taiagaru*, 5 invocations for soprano solo (1962); *20 Canti del Capricorno* for solo voice (1962-72); *Manto per quattro* for voice, flute, trombone and cello (1972); *Praham I* for voice, 12 instruments and tape (1972); piano pieces: 24 Preludes (1936-40); *Hispania* (1939); 10 suites; 3 sonatas.

Schaab, Robert, German organist and composer; b. Rötha, near Leipzig, Feb. 28, 1817; d. Leipzig, March 18, 1887. He studied with C. F. Becker and Mendelssohn; became organist of the Johanniskirche in Leipzig; publ. a great number of works for organ; his 60 *Choralvorspiele* (op. 118, 119, 121) are valuable.

Schaaf, Edward Oswald, American composer; b. Brooklyn, Aug. 7, 1869; d. Newark, N.J., June 25, 1939. He was a physician; M.D., Bellevue Hospital Medical College, N.Y., 1894; studied at the Univ. of Vienna (1894-96); musically an autodidact, through intensive study of classical masterworks. He wrote a grand opera, 8 smaller operas, 2 symphonies, 4 string quartets, 2 Masses, 70 songs, 20 military band pieces, and 90 works for player-piano. He publ. *A Study of Modern Operatic Art; The Art of Playing Piano Transcriptions;* etc.; lived most of his life in Newark.

Schachner, Rudolf Joseph, German pianist and composer; b. Munich, Dec. 31, 1821; d. Reichenhall, Aug. 15, 1896. He was a pupil of J. B. Cramer; appeared in concert in Vienna, Paris, Leipzig, etc.; in 1853, settled in London as a teacher; later went to Vienna. He composed 2 piano concertos and a number of pieces for piano solo: *Poésies musicales, Romance variée, Ombres et rayons, La Chasse,* etc.

Schacht, Matthias Henriksen, Danish music lexicographer; b. Visby, Jütland, April 29, 1660; d. Kerteminde, Aug. 8, 1700. He was a pedagogue; served as rector; left in manuscript a music dictionary, *Bibliotheca musica* (publ. by G. Skjerne as *Musicus danicus,* Copenhagen, 1928), which Gerber utilized for his lexicon.

Schacht, Theodor von, German composer; b. Strasbourg, 1748; d. Regensburg, June 20, 1823. He studied in Stuttgart with Jommelli; then went to Regensburg (1773), where he became music director of the town theater; wrote numerous operas in German and Italian; also symphonies, concertos, and chamber music. He was a minor master of the contrapuntal art; wrote an amusing series of 84 canons, under the title *Divertimento del bel sesso nel soggiorno di Baden* (1811).
BIBLIOGRAPHY: S. Färber, *Das Regensburger fürstlich Thurn und Taxissche Hoftheater und seine Oper* (Regensburg, 1936).

Schack (Žak), Benedikt, Bohemian tenor and composer; b. Mirotitz, 1758 (baptized Feb. 7); d. Munich, Dec. 10, 1826. He studied in Prague and Vienna; made his operatic debut in Salzburg (1786); became acquainted with Mozart's librettist Schikaneder, and through him met Mozart in Vienna (1789) and became friendly with him; he was the singer (if contemporary reports are to be trusted) who sang passages from the Requiem for the dying composer. Mozart wrote piano variations (K. 613) on an aria from Schack's opera *Die verdeckten Sachen*. Among Schack's theatrical pieces the following were performed in Vienna: *Der dumme Gärtner aus dem Gebirge* (July 12, 1789), *Die wiener Zeitung* (Jan. 12, 1791), *Die Antwort auf die Frage* (Dec. 16, 1792), *Die beiden Nannerin* (July 26, 1794).

Schad, Joseph, German pianist and composer; b. Steinach, Germany, March 6, 1812; d. Bordeaux, July 4, 1879. He studied at the Würzburg Cons. and later with Aloys Schmitt at Frankfurt. In 1834 he became organist at Morges, Switzerland; in 1847, settled in Bordeaux, where he gained high repute as a piano teacher. He publ. a great number of melodious piano pieces which enjoyed some success during his lifetime: *Le Soupir, La Gracieuse, La Rose des Alpes, Fleur des Alpes, Tarentelle,* etc.; fantasias, transcriptions.

Schadewitz, Carl, German composer; b. St. Ingbert, Jan. 23, 1887; d. Reppendorf, near Kitzingen, March 27, 1945. He studied in Würzburg, and lived there most of his life as choral conductor and teacher. He was a prolific composer; his works include a musical fairy tale, *Johannisnacht;* a "Romantic" oratorio, *Kreislers Heimkehr;* an opera, *Laurenca;* a tone poem, *Heldengedenken* (1943); a number of songs, of which the cycle *Die Heimat* (1934) is outstanding; much chamber music; choruses.
BIBLIOGRAPHY: A. Maxsein, *Carl Schadewitz* (Würzburg, 1954).

Schaefer, Karl Ludolf, German physiologist, physicist, and acoustician; b. Rostock, July 2, 1866; d. Berlin, Feb. 12, 1931. He obtained his M.D. diploma in 1889; then studied with Carl Stumpf; taught vocal physiology at the Berlin Hochschule. He publ. *Musikalische Akustik* (1902; 2nd ed., 1912), *Einführung in die Musikwissenschaft auf physikalischer, physiologischer und psychologischer Grundlage* (Leipzig, 1915); and numerous other studies on acoustics and tone psychology.

Schaefer, Theodor, Czech composer; b. Telč, Jan. 23, 1904; d. Brno, March 19, 1969. He studied with Jaroslav Kvapil at the Brno Cons. (1922–26) and with Novák at the Prague Cons. (1926–29). Upon graduation he taught at the Palacký Univ. at Olomouc, the Brno Cons., and, until his death, at the Janáček Academy in Brno. He was an advocate of a so-called diathematic principle of constructing themes using fragments of preceding thematic units.
WORKS: a children's opera, *Maugli* (1932); ballet, *Legenda o štestí (Legend of Happiness,* 1952); 2 unnumbered symphonies (1926; 1955–61); Violin Concerto (1932–33); *Wallachian Serenade* for orch. (1936); Piano Concerto (1937–43); *Jánošík,* balladic overture (1939); *Winter Cantata* for soprano, chorus and orch. (1943–45); *Diathema* for viola and orch. (1955–56); *The Barbarian and the Rose* for piano and orch. (1957–58); *Diathema* for orch. (1957–58); *Rhapsodic Reportage* for orch. (1960); 3 string quartets (1929, 1941, 1944–45); Wind Quintet (1935–36); *Divertimento mesto* for wind quintet and String Trio (1946); *Cikánovy housle (Gypsy Violin);* 4 movements for violin and piano (1960); *Etudes* for piano (1936–37); *Theme with Variations* for piano (1936); choruses; songs, including *Milostné balady (Love Ballads),* for voice and piano commemorating the destruction of the village of Lidice by the Nazis (1943); *Bithematikon* for baritone and orch. (1967).

Schaeffer, Pierre, French acoustician and inventor; b. Nancy, Aug. 14, 1910. Working in a Paris radio studio he conceived the idea of a musical montage composed of random sounds, and, on April 15, 1948, formulated the theory of *musique concrète*. When the magnetic tape was perfected, Schaeffer made ingenious use of it by rhythmic acceleration and deceleration, changing the pitch and dynamics and modifying the nature of the instrumental timbre. He made several collages of elements of "concrete music," among them *Concert de bruits* (1948) and (with Pierre Henry) *Symphonie pour un Homme Seul* (1950) and an experimental opera *Orphée 53* (1953); he also wrote *Variation sur une flûte mexicaine* (1949). He publ. *A la recherche de la musique concrète* (Paris, 1952) and *Traité des objets sonores* (Paris, 1966).
BIBLIOGRAPHY: Marc Pierret, *Entretiens avec Pierre Schaeffer* (Paris, 1969).

Schaeffner, André, French musicologist; b. Paris, Feb. 7, 1895. He studied archaeology at the École du Louvre and ethnography and theology at the Institut d'Ethnologie at the École des Hautes Etudes; also took courses in music at the Schola Cantorum with Vincent d'Indy; from 1929 to 1965 he headed the department of ethnology at the Musée de l'Homme in Paris. Between 1931 and 1958 he conducted 6 scientific excursions in central and western Africa; from 1958 to 1967 he was president of the Société Française de Musicologie. His musical interests were wide ranging, from folk songs to modern music. He published *Le Jazz* (with A. Cœuroy, Paris, 1926); a monograph on Stravinsky (Paris, 1931); *Les Instruments de musique en pays Kissi* (Paris, 1949); *Les Kissi. Une Société noire et ses instruments de musique* (Paris, 1951). He was the editor of the French edition of Riemann's *Musiklexikon* (Paris, 1931).

Schäfer, Dirk, eminent Dutch composer, pianist and pedagogue; b. Rotterdam, Nov. 23, 1873; d. Amsterdam, Feb. 16, 1931. He studied in Rotterdam and Cologne; after a European concert tour he settled in Amsterdam where he was acting as pianist and teacher; he composed several piano works on exotic themes; also *Rapsodie javanaise* for orch. (1904); 2 violin sonatas; piano quintet; cello sonata and songs. A book of reminiscences about him, *Herinnering aan Dirk Schäfer* was published in Amsterdam, the year after his death.
BIBLIOGRAPHY: Cor Backers, *Nederlandse Componisten van 1400 tot op onze tijd* (Amsterdam, 1942; pp. 110–12).

Schafer, R. Murray, Canadian composer; b. Sarnia, Ontario, July 18, 1933. He studied at the Royal Cons. of Music on Toronto with John Weinzweig (1954–55); went to Vienna in 1956 and then on to England as a journalist. Returning to Canada in 1962, he became associated with the Canadian Broadcasting Corp., explored the nature of physical sound for an "inventory of world soundscapes." He developed a *sui generis* system of topological transmutation, exemplified by his satire/tribute for orchestra and tape *The Son of Heldenleben* (Montreal, Nov. 13, 1968), in which he systematically distorted the thematic materials of *Ein Heldenleben* by Richard Strauss, retaining the essential motivic substance of the original score.

WORKS: 2 operas: *Loving/Toi,* with electronic sound (stage première, Toronto, March 11, 1978); *Patria,* a trilogy-in-progresss, of which *Patria II* is complete (Stratford, Ontario, Aug. 23, 1972); Concerto for harpsichord and 8 wind instruments (1954); *Minnelieder* for mezzo-soprano and wind quintet (1956); *Protest and Incarceration,* 2 songs for mezzo-soprano and orch. (1960); *St. Jean de Brebeuf,* cantata for baritone and orch. (1961); *Canzoni for Prisoners* for orch. (1961–62); *5 Studies on Texts by Prudentius* for soprano and 4 flutes (1962); 2 educational works of variable duration for youth orch.: *Invertible Material* (1963) and *Statement in Blue,* in aleatory notation (1964); *Untitled Composition* for orch. (1963); *Requiems for the Party Girl* for soprano and 9 instruments (1966); *Threnody* for 5 young narrators, youth chorus and orch., with tape (1966); *Gita,* piece for chorus, brass ensemble and tape (Lenox, Mass., Aug. 10, 1967); *From the Tibetan Book of the Dead* for soprano, chorus, flute, clarinet and tape (1968); *The Son of Heldenleben* (1968); *No Longer Than Ten Minutes* for orch. (1970; the title derives from the stipulation of the maximum length of the piece; Toronto, Feb. 16, 1971); *Sappho* for mezzo-soprano, harp, piano, guitar and percussion (1970); String Quartet (1970); *Okeanos* for tape (1971); *Enchantress* for soprano, flute and 8 cellos (1971); *In Search of Zoroaster* for male voice, chorus, percussion played by chorus members, and organ (1971); *East* for orch. (1972); *Tehillah* for chorus and percussion (1972); *Arcana* for voice and instruments (1972); the trilogy *Lustro* (1969–72), consisting of 3 separately composed works: *Divan i Shams i Tabriz* for 7 singers, tape and orch. (1969); *Music for the Morning of the World* for voice and tape (1970), and *Beyond the Great Gate of Light* for 7 singers, tape and orch. (1972; premiere as a trilogy, Toronto, May 31, 1973); *North/White* for orch. (1973; Vancouver, Aug. 17, 1973; a protest to government and industry's "rape of the Canadian North"); String Quartet No. 2, *Waves* (1976); *Train* for youth orch. (1976); *Adieu Robert Schumann* for contralto and orch., derived from Clara Schumann's diaries chronicling Schumann's madness (1976; Ottawa, March 14, 1978); *Apocalypsis* for 500 professional and amateur performers (1976).

WRITINGS: *British Composers in Interview* (London, 1963), *The Composer in the Classroom* (Toronto, 1965); *Ear Cleaning* (Toronto, 1967); *The New Soundscape* (Toronto, 1969); *When Words Sing* (N.Y., 1971); *E.T.A. Hoffmann and Music* (Toronto, 1975); *The Tuning of the World* (N.Y., 1977); *Ezra Pound and Music: the Complete Criticism* (N.Y., 1977).

Schäffer, August, German composer; b. Rheinsberg, Aug. 25, 1814; d. Baden-Baden, Aug. 7, 1879. Pupil, from 1833, of Mendelssohn at Berlin, where he spent most of his life. His humorous duets and quartets won great popularity; he also composed symphonies, string quartets, piano pieces, etc., and produced a few operas: *Emma von Falkenstein* (Berlin, 1839), *José Riccardo* (Hanover, 1857), *Junker Habakuk* (Hanover, 1861).

Schäffer, Boguslaw, remarkable Polish composer and music theoretician of great originality; b. Lwów, June 6, 1929. After studies in violin at Opole, he studied composition with Arthur Malawski at the State High School of music in Cracow, and musicology with Jachimecki at the Jagello Univ. in Cracow (1949–53); in 1959 took lessons with Nono; in 1963, he became prof. of composition at the Cons. of Cracow. In 1967 he started a periodical devoted to new music, *Forum Musicum.* Schäffer's early compositions are inspired by the melorhythms of Polish folksongs but he made a decisive turn in 1953 with his *Music for Strings: Nocturne,* which became the first serial work by a Polish composer; he devised a graphic and polychromatic optical notation indicating intensity of sound, proportional lengths of duration, and position of notes in melodic and contrapuntal lines, with the components arranged in binary code; he has also written music in the "third stream" style, combining jazz with classical procedures. He makes use of the entire spectrum of musical resources, including the antigenic type of "decomposed" music. He is married to Mieczyslawa Janina Hanuszewska (b. Borszow, Oct. 1, 1929), a learned musicographer.

WORKS: Concerto for 2 pianos (1951); *3 Short Pieces* for chamber orch. (1952); Sonatina for piano (1952); *2 Studies* for solo flute (1953); *Music* for string quartet (1954); *Composition* for piano (1954); *2 Studies* for solo saxophone (1954); Sonata for solo violin (1955); *Study in Diagram* for piano (1956); *Permutations* for 10 instruments (1956); *10 Models* for piano (1954, 1957, 1961, 1963, 1965, 1970, 1971, 1972, 1976, 1977); *Extremes* for 10 instruments, a score without notes (1957); 4 string quartets (1957, 1964, 1971, 1973); *Quattro Movimenti* for piano and orch. (1957); *Tertium datur,* treatise for harpsichord and chamber orch. (1958; Warsaw, Sept. 18, 1960); *8 Pieces* for piano (1954–58); *Variations* for piano (1958); *Monosonata* for 6 string quartets subdivided in 3 uneven groups (1959); International Society for Contemporary Music, Festival, June 19, 1961); *Equivalenze sonore,* concerto for percussion chamber orch. (1959); *3 Studies, Articulation* and *Linear Construction* for piano (1959); *Concerto breve* for cello and orch. (1959); Concerto for string quartet (1959); *Joint Constructions* for strings (1960); *Negatives* for solo flute (1960); *Montaggio* for 6 players (1960); *Topofonica* for 40 instruments (1960); *Little Symphony: Scultura* (1960; Warsaw, Sept. 29, 1965); *Configurations, Points of Departure* and *Non-Stop,* for piano (1960); *Non-Stop* was first performed by a relay team of 2 pianists at the first Polish Happening in Cracow, Aug. 27-28, 1964, with a total duration of 8 hours); *Concerto per sei e tre* for a changing solo instrument (clarinet, saxophone, violin, cello, percussion, and piano) and 3 orchestras (1960; Katowice, Nov. 7, 1962); *Musica* for harpsichord and instruments (1961); *Kody (Codes)* for chamber orch. (1961); *Azione a due* for piano and 11 instruments (Warsaw, Sept. 19, 1961); *Imago musicae* for violin and 9 interpolating instruments (1961); *Sound Forms* for solo saxophone (1961); *3 Compositions for MJQ* (Modern Jazz Quartet), third-stream music (1961); *Constructions* for solo vibraphone (1962); *4 Pieces* for string trio (1962); *Course "J"* for jazz ensemble and chamber symph. orch. (Warsaw, Oct. 28, 1962); *Musica Ipsa* for an orch. of deep instruments (Warsaw, Sept. 20, 1962); *TIS-MW-2*, metamusical audio-visual spectacle for actor, mime, ballerina and 5 musicians (1962–63; Cracow, April 25, 1964); *Expressive aspects* for soprano and flute (1963); *Contours* for piano (1963); *Collage and Form* for 8 jazz musicians and orch. (1963); Violin Concerto (1961–63) *TIS GK*, stage work (1963); *Scenario* for a non-existent but possible instrumental actor (1963); *Music for MI* for voice, vibraphone, 6 narrators, jazz ensemble and orch. (1963); *S'alto* for saxophone and chamber orch. of soloists (1963); *Audiences I-V* for various performers (1964); *Sfumato* for solo harpsichord (1964); *2 Pieces* for violin and piano (1964); *Collage* for chamber orch. (1964); Quartet for 2 pianists and 2 optional performers (1965); *Przeslanie (Transmissions)* for cello and 2 pianos (1965); *Symphony: Electronic Music* for tape (1964–66); *Howl*, monodrama, after Allen Ginsberg's poem, for narrator, 2 actors, and ensemble of instrumentalists and ensemble of performers (1966); *Visual Music* for 5 optional performers (1966); Trio for flute, harp, and viola (1966); Quartet for oboe and string trio (1966); *Composition* for harp and piano (1966); *Decet* for harp and 9 instruments (1966); *Assemblage* for tape (1966); *4H/1P* for piano, 4 hands (1966); *Quartet* for 4 actors (1966); Piano Concerto (1967); *Hommage à Strzeminski* for tape (1967); *Media* for voices and instruments (1967); *Symfonia: Muzyka orkiestrowa* (1967); *Quartet SG* (1968); *Lecture* for 6 performers (1968); *Fragment* for 2 actors and cello player (1968); *Concerto* for tape (1968); *Jazz Concerto* for jazz ensemble of 12 instruments and an orch. of flutes, bassoons, trumpets, trombones and low strings (1969; International Society for Contemporary Music Festival, Boston, Oct. 30, 1976); Piano Trio (1969); *Scena otwarta* for 3 players (1969); *Heraklitiana* for 10 optional solo instruments and tape (1970); *Synetics* for 3 performers (1970); *Comunicazione audiovisiva* for 5 players (1970); *Thema* for tape (1970); *Texts* for orch. (1971); *Mare*, concertino for piano and 9 instruments (1971); *Estratto* for string trio (1971); *15 Elements* for 2 pianos (1971); *Experimenta* for a pianist (on 2 pianos) and orch. (1971; Poznán, April 27, 1972); *Variants* for solo oboe (1971); *Variants* for wind quintet (1971); *Sgraffito* for flute, cello, harpsichord and 2 pianos (1971); *Contract* for soprano, cello and percussion (1971); *Confrontations* for solo instrument and orch. (1972); *Conceptual Music* (1972); *Interview* for solo violin (1972); Concerto for 3 Pianos (1972); *Free Form No.* 1 for 5 instruments (1972) and No. 2, *Evocazioni*, for solo double bass (1972); *blueS No.* 1 for 2 pianos and tape (1972); *blueS No.* 2 for instrumental ensemble (1972); *blueS No.* 3 for 2 pianos (1978); *Bergsoniana* for soprano, flute, piano, horn, double bass and piano (1972); *Dreams of Schäffer*, after Ionesco, for an ensemble of performers (1972; Cracow, April 14, 1975); *Hommage à Czyżewski* for an ensemble of

stage and musical performers (1972); *19 Micropieces* for cello and 6 concurrent performers (1972); *Negative Music* for any instrument (1972); *Neues* for 3 violins (1972); *21 VI 1972, Twilight*, situational composition (1972); Symphony in 9 movements for large orch. and 6 solo instruments (1973); *Tentative Music* for 159 instruments (1973); *aSa* for harpsichord (1973); *aDieu* for trombone solo (1973); *Synthistory* for tape (1973); *Algorhythms* for 7 performers (1975).

WRITINGS: He publ. several informative music books in the Polish language: *Almanach wspólczesnej kompozytorów polskich (Almanac of Modern Polish Composers*, Cracow, 1956); *Maly informator muzyki XX wieku (Little Lexicon of Music of the 20th Century*, Cracow, 1958; new edition, 1967); *Nowa Muzyka, problemy wspólczesnej techniki kompozytorskiej (New Music: Problems of Contemporary Technique in Composing*, Cracow, 1958; new edition, 1969); *Klasycy dodekafonii (Classics of Dodecaphonic Music*, in 2 vols., Cracow, 1961, 1964); *Leksykon kompozytorów XX wieku (Lexicon of 20th Century Composers*, in 2 vols., Cracow, 1963, 1965); *W kruge nowej muzyki (In the Sphere of New Music*, Cracow, 1967); *Dźwieki i znaki (Sounds and Signs: Introduction to Contemporary Composition*, Warsaw, 1969); *Wstęp do kompozycji (Introduction to Composition;* Cracow, 1976; in Polish and English).

Schäffer, Julius, German choral conductor and writer; b. Krevese, near Osterburg, Sept. 28, 1823; d. Breslau, Feb. 10, 1902. He studied theology at Halle, where friendship with Franz, and musicians in the nearby city of Leipzig, won him over to music. In 1850 he went to Berlin to study under Dehn; in 1855, to Schwerin, where he founded and conducted the Schlosskirchenchor, modelled after the Berlin cathedral choir. In 1860 he became conductor of the Singakademie, Breslau. He published chorale books (1866; 1880); songs and part-songs. In defence of Franz's "additional accompaniments" to scores by Bach and Handel, Schäffer wrote, *versus* Chrysander, *Zwei Beurteiler Robert Franzs* (1863), *Fr. Chrysander in seinen Klavierauszugen zur deutschen Händel-Ausgabe* (1876), and *R. Franz in seinen Bearbeitungen älterer Vokalwerke* (1877); also *Die Breslauer Singakademie* (1875).

BIBLIOGRAPHY: E. Bonn, *Julius Schäffer* (Breslau, 1903).

Schaffrath, Christoph, German composer; b. Hohenstein-on-Elbe, 1709; d. Berlin, Feb. 17, 1763. As harpsichordist he entered the service of Frederick the Great in 1735 (while the latter was still Crown Prince) at Rheinsberg, and in 1740 followed that monarch to Berlin. He wrote concertos and sonatas for harpsichord, chamber music, etc.

Schafhäutl, Karl Franz Emil von, German acoustician; b. Ingolstadt, Feb. 16, 1803; d. Munich, Feb. 25, 1890, as prof. of mining, etc., custodian of the State geological collections, etc. He was also a student of acoustics, and worked in close cooperation with Theobald Böhm, whom he advised and aided in the construction of his instruments.

WRITINGS: "Theorie gedackter, zylindrischer und

konischer Pfeifen und der Querflöten," and "Über Schall, Ton, Knall und einige andere Gegenstände der Akustik," both in *Neue Annalen der Chemie* (1833; 1834; both also separately printed); *Über Phonometrie* (1854); *Abt Georg Jos. Vogler; Sein Leben, Charackter und musikalisches System* (1888); also, in the *Allegemeine musikalische Zeitung*, 1879, investigations into the phenomena of *Klangfarbe* (tone color), with results at variance with Helmholtz's theory.

BIBLIOGRAPHY: "Errinerungen an K. Ett und K. von Schafhäutl," *Kirchenmusikalisches Jahrbuch* (1891).

Schalk, Franz, Austrian conductor; b. Vienna, May 27, 1863; d. Edlach, Sept. 2, 1931. He studied with Bruckner; 1888, Kapellmeister in Reichenbach; 1889–95, in Graz; 1895–98, in Prague; guest conductor at Covent Garden, London, in 1898, 1907, and 1911; succeeded Seidl in 1898 as conductor at the Metropolitan Opera House; 1899, conductor of the Berlin Royal Opera; from 1900 at the Vienna Hofoper; 1904–21, also conductor of the Vienna Gesellschaft der Musikfreunde and prof. of the classes in conducting at the Royal Academy of Music; from 1918 director of the Vienna State Opera (succeeded Gregor; 1919–24, co-director with R. Strauss; thereafter sole director). A tireless worker, he contributed much to the high artistic standards of the Vienna Opera. His book, *Briefe und Betrachtungen,* was brought out posthumously (Vienna, 1935).

Schalk, Josef, Austrian pianist and writer on music; brother of **Franz Schalk;** b. Vienna, March 24, 1857; d. there, Nov. 7, 1900. He studied with Bruckner and Epstein; piano teacher at the Vienna Cons. His arrangements of the Bruckner symphonies for piano 4 hands did much to make these works known, and his book, *Anton Bruckner und die moderne Musikwelt* (1885), effectively upheld Bruckner's music. He was also a friend of Hugo Wolf, whom he championed.

Schall, Claus, Danish composer; b. Copenhagen, April 28, 1757; d. Copenhagen, Aug. 10, 1835. He was a violinist and theater conductor; wrote many instrumental pieces and 7 operas to Danish librettos, of which the following (all produced in Copenhagen) were the most successful: *Claudine af Villa Bella* (Jan. 29, 1787), *Kinafarerne* (March 2, 1792), *Domherren i Milano* (March 16, 1802), and *De tre Galninger* (March 19, 1816).

Scharfe, Gustav, German singing teacher; b. Grimma, Saxony, Sept. 11, 1835; d. Dresden, June 25, 1892. He was a baritone at the Dresden Court Opera for 11 years; teacher of singing at the Cons. (1874); professor (1880). He wrote *Die methodische Entwickelung der Stimme,* a standard work; also choruses and songs.

Scharfenberg, William, German-American music editor; b. Kassel, Feb. 22, 1819; d. Quogue, Long Island, N.Y., Aug. 8, 1895. He studied with Hummel at Weimar; played 2nd violin in Spohr's quartet in Kassel; in 1838 went to N.Y., where he became a popular piano teacher. He was successively secretary, vice-president, treasurer and president of the N.Y. Philhar-

monic Society; for many years he served as music editor and adviser to the firm of G. Schirmer, and did excellent editorial work in this capacity.

Scharrer, August, German composer and conductor; b. Strasbourg, Aug. 18, 1866; d. Weiherhof, near Fürth, Oct. 24, 1936. He studied music in Strasbourg and Berlin; then became a theater conductor in Karlsruhe (1897–98) and Regensburg (1898–1900); then was second conductor of the Kaim Orch. (1900–04) and conductor of the Berlin Philharmonic (1904–07); from 1914 to 1931 he conducted the Philharmonic Society of Nuremberg. He wrote an opera *Die Erlösung* (Strasbourg, Nov. 21, 1895); several orchestral overtures; some chamber music, choruses and songs.

Scharrer, Irene, English pianist; b. London, Feb. 2, 1888; d. there, Jan. 11, 1971. She studied with Tobias Matthay at the Royal Academy of Music; toured as a concert pianist in the U.S.; returning to London she taught at the Matthay School.

Scharwenka, Philipp, German composer and pedagogue; b. Samter, Posen, Feb. 16, 1847; d. Bad Nauheim, July 16, 1917. He studied with Wüerst and Dorn at the Kullak Academy of Music in Berlin; in 1870 was appointed teacher of composition there; with his brother **Xaver** he founded in 1881 the Scharwenka Cons. in Berlin; together they made an American trip in 1891; in 1893 the Scharwenka Cons. was amalgamated with the Klindworth Cons., which acquired an excellent reputation for its teaching standards. He was an excellent composer in a Romantic vein, greatly influenced by Schumann; his *Arkadische Suite* for orchestra, the symphonic poem *Frühlingswogen,* and the orchestral *Dramatische Fantasie* were performed many times until they inevitably lapsed into innocuous desuetude; he also wrote a symphony, a violin concerto, much chamber music and piano pieces.

Scharwenka, Xaver, German pianist, composer and pedagogue; brother of **Philipp Scharwenka;** b. Samter, Posen, Jan. 6, 1850; d. Berlin, Dec. 8, 1924. He studied with Kullak and Wüerst at Kullak's Academy of Music in Berlin, graduating in 1868; then joined its faculty. Apart from teaching, he established an annual series of chamber music concerts in Berlin; in 1881 he founded with his brother the Scharwenka Cons.; in 1891 he went to the U.S.; appeared as soloist with his own piano concerto (N.Y., Jan. 24, 1891). Returning to Berlin in 1898, he became co-director of the newly amalgamated Klindworth-Scharwenka Cons.; in 1914 established his own course of master classes for piano. As a composer, he was undoubtedly superior to his brother, although both were faithful imitators of Schumann and other German Romantics. He wrote an opera *Mataswintha* (Weimar, Oct. 4, 1896; Metropolitan Opera, N.Y., April 1, 1907); 4 piano concertos; numerous effective piano pieces, of which *Polish Dances* became favorites with American piano teachers and students. He also published technical studies for piano, *Beiträge zur Fingerbildung; Studien im Oktavenspiel;* a collection of famous études arranged according to progressive difficulty, under the title

Meisterschule des Klavierspiels; Methodik des Klavierspiels (1907; with A. Spanuth) and a book of memoirs, *Klänge aus meinem Leben: Erinnerungen eines Musikers* (Leipzig, 1922).

Schat, Peter, Dutch composer; b. Utrecht, June 5, 1935. He studied composition with Kees van Baaren and piano with Jaap Callenbach at The Hague Cons.; then traveled to England and took private lessons in England with M. Seiber; also received instruction with Boulez in Zürich. Upon returning to Holland he became active in connection with the Studio for Electro-Instrumental Music in Amsterdam. From his earliest steps in composition, he adopted the serial method; also experimented with electronic sonorities. With Louis Andriessen and Misha Mengelberg, he organized in 1968 a series of Political-Demonstrative Experimental Concerts and also formed the Amsterdam Electric Circus, an itinerant troupe of musicians. WORKS: His most notorious production was *Labyrinth*, a "total theater" spectacle in mixed media (1961-65; Amsterdam, June 23, 1966), which spawned a series of excerpts: *Choirs from the "Labyrinth"* for chorus and orch. (1962-63); *Voices from the "Labyrinth"* for 3 voices and orch. (1962-63); *Dances from the "Labyrinth"* for orch. (1962); *Scenes from the "Labyrinth"* for speaking voices, soprano, tenor, bass, chorus and orch. (1961-64); *Improvisations from the "Labyrinth"* for 3 voices, bass clarinet, double bass, piano and percussion (1964); *Tapes from the "Labyrinth"* for 4 tapes (1964-65). OTHER WORKS: a "circus opera," *Houdini* (1974-76; Amsterdam, Sept. 29, 1977); *Introduction and Adagio in Old Style* for string quartet (1955); Septet for flute, oboe, horn, bass clarinet, piano, cello and percussion (1957); *2 Pieces* for flute, violin, trumpet and percussion (1959); Wind Octet (1959); *Inscripties* for piano (1959); *Mosaics* for orch. (1959); *Crytogamen* for baritone and orch. (1959); *Concerto da Camera* for 2 clarinets, piano, strings and percussion (1960); *Improvisations and symphonies* for wind quintet (1960); *The Fall*, after James Joyce, for chorus a cappella (1960); *Entelechie I* for 5 instrumental groups (1961); *Entelechie II*, scenes for 11 musicians (1961); *Signalement* for 6 percussionists and 3 double basses (1961); *Sextet*, fragment for 3 actors and 3 musicians (1961); *First Essay on Electrocution* for violin, guitar and metal guitar (1966); *Clockwise and anti-clockwise* for 16 wind instruments (1967); *Anathema* for piano (1968); *On Escalation* for 6 solo percussionists and orch. (Amsterdam, May 30, 1968); *Hypothema* for recorders (1969); *Thema* for solo electrified oboe, 4 electric guitars, Hammond organ and 18 wind instruments (Amsterdam, July 5, 1970); *To You* for solo voice, 6 guitars, 3 bass guitars, 4 pianos, 2 Hammond organs, 6 humming tops and electronics (1970-72; Amsterdam, June 20, 1972); *Canto General*, dedicated to the memory of the slain socialist President of Chile, Salvador Allende, for mezzo-soprano, violin and piano (1974); *May 75*, a song of liberation for 2 soloists, chorus and orch. (1975; 10th scene from the opera *Houdini*); *Houdini Symphony* for 4 soloists, chorus and orch. (1976); *I am Houdini*, ballet for tenor, 2 pianos and chorus (1976). He also collaborated with Louis Andriessen, Reinbert de Leeuw, Misha Mengelberg and Jan van Vlijmen on the anti-imperialist opera *Reconstructie* (1968-69; Holland Fest., Amsterdam, June 29, 1969). BIBLIOGRAPHY: Reinbert de Leeuw, "Labyrinth: An Opera of Sorts," *Sonorum Speculum* 27 (Summer 1966); "Peter Schat about To You," *Sonorum Speculum* 55 (1974); "Interview with Peter Schat," *Key Notes* 4 (1976/2).

Schatz, Albert, German music collector; b. Rostock, May 19, 1839; d. there, Oct. 18, 1910. From his early youth he became interested in the history of opera and began to collect materials on this subject. He made an extensive trip to America and spent 7 years in San Francisco; returning to Rostock in 1873, he purchased the music business of Ludwig Trutschel. In 1908 he sold his valuable collection of librettos and the accompanying card catalogs and other records to the Library of Congress in Washington, where the whole collection is retained as a separate unit and is made available from the Library on positive microfilm. BIBLIOGRAPHY: O. G. Sonneck, editor, *Catalogue of Opera Librettos printed before 1800* (2 vols., Washington, 1914).

Schaub, Hans Ferdinand, (properly **Siegmund Ferdinand**), German composer, conductor, and teacher; b. Frankfurt, Sept. 22, 1880; d. Hanstedt, near Marburg, Nov. 12, 1965. He studied at the Hoch Cons. there with Iwan Knorr (theory) and Carl Friedberg (piano); with Arnold Mendelssohn in Darmstadt, and with Humperdinck in Berlin; also took lessons with Richard Strauss. He then became instructor at the Cons. of Breslau (1903-06); in 1906, settled in Berlin as teacher at Benda's Cons. and editor of the *Deutsche Musikerzeitung*. In 1916 he moved to Hamburg as music critic and pedagogue. After 1951 he lived in Hanstedt. WORKS: *Passacaglia*, for orch. (1928); *3 Intermezzi*, for small orch.; *Capriccio*, for violin and piano; the cantata *Den Gefallenen* (1940); oratorio, *Deutsches Te Deum* (1942).

Schauffler, Robert Haven, American writer on music; b. Brünn, Moravia (of American parents), April 8, 1879; d. New York, Nov. 24, 1964. He was educated at Princeton Univ., and also took courses at the Univ. of Berlin; studied cello with B. Steindel, A. Schroeder, and A. Hekking. WRITINGS: *The Musical Amateur* (Boston, 1911); *Fiddler's Luck. The Gay Adventures of a Musical Amateur* (Boston, 1920); *Beethoven: The Man who Freed Music* (N.Y., 1929; abridged ed. 1932 as *The Mad Musician*; new ed., 1937); *The Unknown Brahms* (N.Y., 1933); *The Magic of Music; An Anthology* (N.Y., 1935); *Fiddler's Folly and Encores* (N.Y., 1942); *Florestan: The Life and Work of Robert Schumann* (N.Y., 1945); *Franz Schubert: The Ariel of Music* (N.Y., 1949); various smaller publications.

Schaum, John W., American piano pedagogue; b. Milwaukee, Jan. 27, 1905; studied at Milwaukee State Teachers College, at Marquette Univ. (B.M., 1931), and Northwestern Univ. (M.M., 1934). He established a successful piano teaching class in Milwaukee and publ. several piano methods and many collections of piano pieces that sold an enormous number of copies: *The Schaum Piano Course* (9 vols.); *The Schaum Adult Piano Course* (3 vols.); *The Schaum Duet Albums* (2 vols.); also theory books, *The Schaum Theory Lessons* (2 vols.) and *The Schaum Note Spellers* (2 vols.).

Schebek, Edmund, Bohemian writer on music; b. Petersdorf, Moravia, Oct. 22, 1819; d. Prague, Feb. 11, 1895, as Imperial councillor and secretary of the Chamber of Commerce. He wrote the official (Austrian) report on the musical instruments at the Paris Exposition of 1855 (separate reprint 1858); *Der Geigenbau in Italien und sein deutscher Ursprung* (1875; in English, London, 1877); and *Zwei Briefe über J. J. Froberger* (1874).

Schebest, Agnese, Austrian mezzo-soprano; b. Vienna, Feb. 10, 1813; d. Stuttgart, Dec. 22, 1869. She studied at Dresden, and sang in the opera there; publ. an autobiography, *Aus dem Leben einer Künstlerin* (1857).

Scheel, Fritz, German conductor; b. Lübeck, Nov. 7, 1852; d. Philadelphia, March 13, 1907. His grandfather and father were orchestral conductors, and at 10 the boy played the violin in his father's orch.; 1864–69, pupil of F. David in Leipzig. At 17 he began his career as concertmaster and conductor at Bremerhaven; in 1873, solo violin and conductor of the summer concerts in Schwerin; succeeded Hans Sitt in 1884 as conductor of the Chemnitz municipal orch.; 1890–93, conductor of orchestral concerts in Hamburg. Came to America in 1893, and after conducting some orchestral concerts in New York went to Chicago in 1894 as conductor of the Trocadero concerts at the Columbian Exposition; in 1895 he established the San Francisco Symph. Orch., which he conducted for 4 seasons; then accepted an engagement to conduct a series of summer concerts at Woodside Park, Philadelphia. His playing of Beethoven's symphonies induced influential music lovers to organize the Philadelphia Orchestral Association, which established in the fall of 1900 the Philadelphia Orchestra, of which Scheel was conductor until his death.
BIBLIOGRAPHY: Frances A. Wister, *25 Years of the Philadelphia Orchestra 1900–1925* (Philadelphia, 1925); John H. Mueller, *The American Symphony Orchestra* (Bloomington, Ind., 1951, pp. 125-27); H. Kupferberg, *Those Fabulous Philadelphians* (N.Y., 1969; pp. 15-26); *Dictionary of American Biography* XVI.

Scheff, Fritzi, Austrian soprano; b. Vienna, Aug. 30, 1879; d. New York, April 8, 1954. She studied singing with her mother, Hortense Scheff, of the Vienna Opera, and adopted her last name, having previously appeared under her father's name, **Yager.** She made her operatic debut in Frankfurt (1899); appeared at the Metropolitan Opera, N.Y., as Marzelline in *Fidelio* (Dec. 28, 1900), and continued for 3 seasons as a member of the company. Later she shifted to light opera, and it was in this field that she became famous. She created the role of Fifi in Victor Herbert's operetta *Mlle. Modiste* (Trenton, N.J., Oct. 7, 1905); her singing of Fifi's waltz song *Kiss Me Again* became a

hallmark of her career. Her 3 marriages (to Baron Fritz von Bardeleben, the American writer John Fox Jr., and the singer George Anderson) ended in divorce.

Scheffler, Siegfried, German composer; b. Ilmenau, May 15, 1892; d. Hamburg, June 5, 1969. He studied with his father; then took courses at the Leipzig Cons. with Max Reger, Stephan Krehl, Hans Sitt and others; also attended classes in musicology at the Univ. of Leipzig with Hugo Riemann and Arnold Schering and in Berlin with Humperdinck and Kretzschmar. In 1924 he settled in Hamburg; wrote music criticism and supervised music programs at the Hamburg Radio. He composed *Wunderhorn Lieder* (1914); *Rokoko-Novelle* for orch. (1923); and incidental music for various plays. He published *Richard Wagner* (2 vols.; Hamburg, 1928) and *Melodie der Welle* (Berlin, 1933).

Scheibe, Johann Adolf, German theorist and composer; b. Leipzig, May 3, 1708; d. Copenhagen, April 22, 1776. He studied law at Leipzig, but on his father's death had recourse to his musical training to support himself; failing to obtain the post of organist at the Thomaskirche in the competition (adjudicated by Bach, among others) with Görner, he traveled for a time, and settled in Hamburg; published a paper, *Der critische Musicus* (1737–40; No. 6 contains a sharp attack on Bach). In 1740 he became Kapellmeister to the Margrave of Brandenburg-Culmbach; 1744, court conductor at Copenhagen; was pensioned in 1748. In 1745 he had reprinted in Leipzig the previous issues of *Der critische Musicus*, with the addition of polemical exchanges that ensued in the interim.
WORKS: a Danish opera, *Thusnelda* (Copenhagen, 1749); tragic cantatas *a* 2, with clavier; songs; *Musikalische Erquickungstunden* (6 sonatas for flute with continuo); 3 sonatas for flute with harpsichord. In MS he left 2 oratorios, about 200 church works, 150 flute concertos, 30 violin concertos, etc. He also wrote *Abhandlung vom Ursprung und Alter der Musik, insonderheit der Vocalmusik* (1754; maintains that partsongs originated with Northern peoples); an *Abhandlung über das Recitativ* (1764–65); *Über die musikalische Composition* (only vol. 1, of the 4 projected, was publ. in 1773); etc.
BIBLIOGRAPHY: E. Riechel, "Gottsched und J. A. Scheibe," *Sammelbände der Internationalen Musik-Gesellschaft* 2 (1901); E. Rosenkaimer, *J. A. Scheibe als Verfasser seines "Critischen Musicus"* (dissertation, Bonn, 1923); K. A. Storch, *J. A. Scheibes Anschauungen von d. musikalischen Historie, Wissenschaft und Kunst* (diss., Leipzig, 1923).

Scheibler, Johann Heinrich, inventor and writer on music; b. Montjoie, near Aix-la-Chapelle, Nov. 11, 1777; d. Krefeld, Nov. 20, 1837. A silk manufacturer at Krefeld, he became interested in acoustic phenomena, and invented an apparatus consisting of 56 tuning forks, for tuning fixed-tone instruments according to the equally tempered scale. He publ. several pamphlets to explain his invention: *Der physikalische und musikalische Tonmesser* (1834); *Anleitung, die Orgel vermittelst der Stösse (vulgo Schwebungen) und des Metronoms correct gleichschwebend zu stimmen*

(1834); etc., all united as *Schriften über physikalische und musikalische Tonmessung* (1838). His system is more clearly explained by Töpfer (1842), Vincent (1849), and Lecomte (1856). At the Stuttgart Congress of physicists in 1834, Scheibler proposed the pitch of $a^1 = 440$ (vibrations) at 69 degrees Fahrenheit, which was adopted (hence called the "Stuttgart pitch").

BIBLIOGRAPHY: J. J. Löhr, *Über die Scheibler'sche Erfindung überhaupt und dessen Pianoforte- und Orgel-Stimmung insbesondere* (Krefeld, 1836).

Scheidemann, Heinrich, German composer; b. Hamburg, c.1596; d. there, 1663. Important organist; pupil and successor of his father, Hans Scheidemann, organist of the Katherinenkirche; also studied under Sweelinck at Amsterdam. His successor was Reinken. Of his works very little was publ., but many works for organ and harpsichord were preserved in MS. Modern eds. by M. Seiffert in his *Organum* (15 preludes and fugues for organ), K. Straube and F. Dietrich (other organ works), R. Buchmayer, and G. Tagliapietra.

BIBLIOGRAPHY: M. Seiffert's essay in *Vierteljahrsschrift für Musikwissenschaft* (1891); R. Buchmayer, "Musikgeschichtliche Ergebnisse einer Reise nach Lüneburg," *Dresdener Anzeiger* (July 5-26, 1903).

Scheidemantel, Karl, German baritone; b. Weimar, Jan. 21, 1859; d. there, June 26, 1923. He was a pupil of Bodo Borchers, and sang at the court theater in Weimar, 1878–86; also studied voice with Julius Stockhausen in the summers of 1881–83. Member of the Dresden court opera from 1896–1911; 1911–20, prof. at the Grossherzogliche Musikschule in Weimar; 1920–22, director of the Landesoper in Dresden. In 1909 the Dresden Opera brought out Mozart's *Cosi fan tutte* with an entirely new text by Scheidemantel (as *Dame Kobold*). His new transl. of *Don Giovanni* won the prize of the Deutscher Bühnenverein (1914). He publ. *Stimmbildung* (1907; 4th ed. as *Gesangsbildung*, 1913; in English, 1910); also ed. a collection of songs, *Meisterweisen* (1914; 6 parts).

BIBLIOGRAPHY: P. Trede, *K. Scheidemantel* (Dresden, 1911).

Scheidt, Samuel, famous German organist and composer; b. Halle-on-Saale (baptized Nov. 3, 1587); d. there, March 24, 1654; pupil of Sweelinck in Amsterdam; organist of the Moritzkirche, and Kapellmeister to Margrave Christian Wilhelm of Brandenburg, at Halle. He was among the first to treat the chorale artistically, in true organ style.

WORKS: *Tabulatura nova* (1624, 3 vols.; republ., 1892, as vol. I of *Denkmäler deutscher Tonkunst*; contains figured chorales, toccatas, fantasias, passamezzi, a Mass, Magnificats, psalms, hymns); *Tabulaturbuch* (1650); 100 psalms *a* 4; *Cantiones sacrae a* 8 (1620); *Concerti sacri 2-12 voc., adjectis symphonis et choris instrumentalibus* (1621; 1622); *Ludi musici* (2 parts, 1621, 1622; Paduane, Gagliarde, etc.); *Liebliche Kraft-Blümlein* (1635); *Newe geistliche Conzerten a 2-3* with figured bass (1631); the same, Part II (1634); Part III (1635); Part IV (1640); *70 Symphonien auf Conzerten-Manier a 3* with figured bass (1644). The collected ed. of Scheidt's works, begun by G. Harms

in 1923 and continued by others, consists of 15 vols. as of 1977.

BIBLIOGRAPHY: M. Seiffert in *Vierteljahrsschrift für Musikwissenschaft* 7(1891); A. Werner, "Samuel und Gottfried Scheidt," *Sammelbände der Internationalen Musik-Gesellschaft* (1900); C. Mahrenholz, *S. Scheidt* (1924); R. Hünicken, *S. Scheidt* (Halle, 1934); W. Serauky, *S. Scheidt in seinen Briefen* (ib., 1937); a Festschrift, issued in honor of his 350th birthday (Wolfenbrittel, 1937); C. Mahrenholz, "Aufagabe und Bedeutung der Tabulatura nova," *Musica* (March 1954); E. Gessner, *Samuel Scheidts Geistliche Konzert: Ein Beitrag zur Geschichte der Gattung* (Berlin, 1961).

Schein, Johann Hermann, important German composer; born Grünhain, Saxony, Jan. 20, 1586; d. Leipzig, Nov. 19, 1630. On the death of his father, the pastor at Meissen, in 1599, he entered the Electoral Chapel at Dresden as a soprano; studied at Schulpforta from 1603–07, then at Leipzig Univ. (jurisprudence); became "Praeceptor" and "Hausmusikmeister" to Captain von Wolffersdorf at Weissenfels; court Kapellmeister at Weimar in 1615, and succeeded Calvisius as cantor of the Thomasschule at Leipzig in 1616. He was among the first to make artistic adaptations of the chorales for the organ; together with Praetorius and Schütz he shares the distinction of being among the pioneers to introduce into German music the newly developed monodic and instrumental style of the Italians.

WORKS: His most important work is *Cantional oder Gesangbuch Augspurgischer Confession a 4-6* (1627; 2nd ed., 1645; 312 German and Latin sacred songs and psalms). He also wrote other church music, sacred and secular madrigals, and 20 suites for strings (*Banchetto musicale*, 1617; among the earliest instrumental ensemble works in Germany). The complete edition of his works in 7 vols., ed. by Arthur Prüfer, was publ. by Breitkopf & Härtel (1901–23); a new edition, edited by A. Adrio and published by Barenreiter, has been in process since 1963 and, as of 1977, consists of 10 vols.

BIBLIOGRAPHY: A. Prüfer, *J. H. Schein* (Leipzig, 1895); A. Prüer, "J. H. Schein und das weltliche deutsche Lied des 17. Jahrhunderts," *Beihefte der Internationalen Musik-Gesellschaft* (1908); A. Adrio, *Johann Hermann Schein* (Berlin, 1959).

Scheinpflug, Paul, German violinist and composer; b. Loschwitz, near Dresden, Sept. 10, 1875; d. Memel, March 11, 1937. He studied violin with Rappoldi and composition with Draeseke at the Dresden Cons.; in 1898 went to Bremen as concertmaster of the Philharmonie and conductor of the Leiderkranz; then was conductor of the Musikveren in Königsberg (1909–14); conducted the Blüthner Orch. in Berlin (1914–19); was music director in Duisburg (1920–28); in 1930 settled in Berlin but continued to fill engagements as guest conductor.

WORKS: a symph. poem, *Frühling*; an *Ouvertüre zu einem Lustspiel*; piano quartet; string quartet; violin sonatas; many male choruses; *Worpswede*, song cycle for voice, piano, violin, and English horn, many song albums.

BIBLIOGRAPHY: F. Dubitzky, *Paul Scheinpflug* (Leipzig, 1907).

Schelble, Johann Nepomuk, German singer and pedagogue; b. Hüfingen, Black Forest, May 16, 1789; d. Frankfurt, Aug. 6, 1837. He studied with Weisse in Donaueschingen, with Volger in Darmstadt, and with Krebs in Stuttgart. From 1813 to 1816 he was in Vienna and became an intimate friend of Beethoven; then settled in Frankfurt, where he founded the famous Cäcilien-Verein (1818). His methods for teaching the musical rudiments and training the sense of absolute pitch were much admired; he enjoyed the esteem of many musicians of his time; Mendelssohn paid tribute to him in his correspondence.

BIBLIOGRAPHY: K. Lanz, *Die Gehörsentwicklungs-Methode von Schelble* (Brunswick, 1873); O. Bormann, *J. N. Schelble* (dissertation; Frankfurt, 1926).

Schelle, Karl Eduard, German music critic; b. Biesenthal, near Berlin, May 31, 1816; d. Vienna, Nov. 16, 1882. In 1864 he succeeded Hanslick as music critic for the Vienna *Presse*; also lectured on music history at the Vienna Cons. He publ. *Der Tannhäuser in Paris* (1861) and a valuable monograph, *Die papstliche Sängerschule in Rom, genannt die Sixtinische Kapella* (1872).

Schelling, Ernest (Henry), American conductor, composer, and pianist; b. Belvidere, N.J., July 26, 1876; d. New York, Dec. 8, 1939. He first appeared in public as a child prodigy playing the piano at the age of 4½ at the Academy of Music in Philadelphia. He was then sent to Paris, where he studied, still as a small child, with Mathias (a pupil of Chopin) in Paris, and also with Moszkowski; his other teachers were Leschetizky, Hans Huber, Barth, and finally Paderewski at Morges, Switzerland (1898–1902). Extended tours in Europe (from Russia to Spain) followed; he also toured in South America; returned permanently to the U.S. in 1905, and devoted most of his energies to conducting and composing. He conducted the young people's symph. concerts in N.Y. (from 1924), in Philadelphia, Boston, Cincinnati, Los Angeles, San Francisco, etc.; for 2 seasons (1936–38) he was regular conductor of the Baltimore Symph. Orch.; also made frequent appearances as conductor in Europe.

WORKS: *A Victory Ball,* orchestral fantasy after the poem by Alfred Noyes (his most successful work; first performed by Stokowski with the Philadelphia Orch., Feb. 23, 1923); *Légende Symphonique* (Philadelphia, Oct. 31, 1913); *Suite Fantastique,* for orch. (Amsterdam, Oct. 10, 1907); *Impressions from an Artist's Life,* symph. variations for piano and orch. (Boston, Dec. 31, 1915, composer soloist); Violin Concerto (Boston Symph., Providence, R. I., Oct. 17, 1916, Fritz Kreisler soloist); *Morocco,* symph. tableau (N.Y., Dec. 19, 1927, composer conducting). For further details see William Lichtenwanger, *Dictionary of American Biography,* Supplement II.

Schenck, Jean (Johann), German virtuoso on the viola da gamba; b. Amsterdam (baptized June 3, 1660); d. c.1715, he became chamber musician to the Elector-

Palatine at Düsseledorf; later at Amsterdam, where he published *Kunst-Oeffeningen; Il Giardino armonico,* sonatas for 2 violins, gamba, and continuo (1692); *Scherzi musicali* for gamba; 18 sonatas for violin with continuo (1693); etc.; also *Sang-Arien van d'opera Ceres en Bacchus.*

BIBLIOGRAPHY: A. Einstein, *Zur deutschen Literatur für Viola da Gamba im 16. und 17. Jahrhundert* (Leipzig, 1905, pp. 32–35); K. H. Pauls, *Die Musikforschung* (1962, pp. 157–171 and 1966, pp. 288–289).

Schenck, Johann, Austrian composer; b. Wiener-Neustadt, Nov. 30, 1753; d. Vienna, Dec. 29, 1836. He studied with Wagenseil in Vienna. In 1778 he had a Mass performed, which made his reputation; it was followed by other pieces of sacred music; then he began composing light operas, some of which enjoyed great popularity. It was from Schenck that Beethoven took surreptitious lessons while studying with Haydn.

WORKS: operettas (all produced in Vienna): *Die Weinlese* (Oct. 12, 1785); *Die Weihnacht auf dem Lande* (Dec. 14, 1786); *Im Finstern ist nicht gut tappen* (Oct. 12, 1787); *Das unvermutete Seefest* (Dec. 9, 1789); *Das Singspiel ohne Titel* (Nov. 4, 1790); *Der Erntekranz* (July 9, 1791); *Achmet und Almanzine* (July 17, 1795); *Der Dorfbarbier* (Vienna, Oct. 30, 1796; his most popular work; originally staged as a comedy, June 18, 1785); *Die Jagd* (May 7, 1799); *Der Fassbinder* (Dec. 17, 1802). In 1819 he wrote his last works, the canatas *Die Huldigung* and *Der Mai.* He also wrote 6 symphonies, string quartets, string trios, and songs. The score of *Der Dorfbarbier* was publ. by R. Haas in the *Denkmaler der Tonkunst in Österreich* 66 (34).

BIBLIOGRAPHY: F. Staub, *Johann Schenck. Eine Skizze seines Lebens* (Vienna, 1901). A short biographical sketch was published in *Studien zur Musikwissenschaft* (1924).

Schenck, Pyotr, Russian composer; b. St. Petersburg, Feb. 28, 1870; d. Perkiarvy, Finland, July 5, 1915. He studied piano and theory at the Cons. of St. Petersburg; gave concerts as pianist; then devoted himself to conducting; appeared in several European countries. His music was entirely under the influence of Tchaikovsky.

WORKS: 2 operas: *Acteya,* from Etruscan life, which had a concert performance, conducted by the composer, in St. Persburg (Dec. 3, 1899), and *The Miracle of Roses* (St. Petersburg, Oct. 7, 1913); also ballet music; 3 symphonies; an orchestral fantasy, *Dukhy (Ghosts);* a symph. poem, *Hero and Leander;* instrumental pieces; choruses; songs.

Schenk, Erich, eminent Austrian musicologist; b. Salzburg, May 5, 1902; d. Vienna, Oct. 11, 1974. He took courses with Sandberger in Munich, at the Akademie der Tonkunst and at the Univ.; Dr. phil., 1925; in 1929 became lecturer at the Univ. of Rostock; in 1940, prof. of musicology at the Univ. of Vienna; settled there as music editor and pedagogue. A Festschrift, edited by O. Wessely, was publ. in honor of his 60th birthday (Vienna, 1962).

WRITINGS: *G. A. Paganelli* (diss., Salzburg, 1928);

Johann Strauss (Potsdam, 1940); *Musik in Kärnten* (Vienna, 1941); *Beethoven zwischen den Zeiten* (Bonn, 1944); *950 Jahre österreichishe Musik* (Vienna, 1946); *Kleine wiener Musikgeschichte* (Vienna, 1946); *W. A. Mozart: Eine Biographie* (Vienna, 1955; N.Y., 1959); 2nd augmented edition, 1975, as *Mozart: Sein Leben, seine Welt;* in English, N.Y., 1959).

Schenker, Heinrich, outstanding Austrian theorist; b. Wisniowczyki, Galicia, June 19, 1868; d. Vienna, Jan. 14, 1935. He studied with Anton Bruckner at the Vienna Cons.; composed songs and piano pieces; Brahms liked them sufficiently to recommend Schenker to the publisher Simrock; for a while Schenker toured as accompanist of Messchaert, the baritone; then returned to Vienna and devoted himself entirely to the development of his theoretrical research; gathered around him a group of enthusiastic disciples (Otto Vrieslander, Hermann Roth, Hans Weisse, Anthony van Hoboken, Oswald Jonas, Felix Salzer, John Petrie Dunn, and others). He endeavored to derive the basic laws of musical composition from a penetrating analysis of the standard masterworks. The result was the contention that each composition is a horizontalization, through various stages, of a single triad. Schenker brought out editions for piano of works by Bach and Handel and the complete piano sonatas of Beethoven (also separately, special analytical editions of the last five sonatas). WRITINGS: *Neue musikalische Theorien und Fantasien:* I. *Harmonielehre* (1906; in English, ed. by O. Jonas, Chicago, 1954); II. *Kontrapunct,* in 2 vols.: *Cantus Firmus und zweistimmiger Satz* (1910); *Drei- und mehrstimmiger Satz, Übergänge zum freien Satz* (1920); III, *Der freie Satz* (1935; new ed. by O. Jonas, 1956); *Ein Beitrag zur Ornamentik* (based on C. P. E. Bach; 1908; new ed., 1954); a monograph on Beethoven's Ninth Symphony (1912) and one on his Fifth Symphony (1925); *Der Tonwille* (a periodical containing articles and analyses by Schenker and appearing at irregular intervals from 1921 to 1924); *Das Meisterwerk in der Musik* (a continuation of *Der Tonwille* in the form of an annual; 3 vols., 1925, 1926, 1930); *5 Urlinie-Tafeln* (N.Y., 1932); *Johannes Brahms: Oktaven und Quinten* (Vienna, 1933). BIBLIOGRAPHY: W. Riezler, "Die Urlinie," *Die Musik* (April 1930); I. Citkowitz, "The Role of H. Schenker," *Modern Music* 11 (1933); O. Jonas, *Das Wesen des musikalischen Kunstwerkes; eine Einführung in die Lehre H. Schenkers* (Vienna, 1934); R. Sessions, "H. Schenker's Contribution, *Modern Music* 12 (1953); A. T. Katz,; "H. Schenker's Method of Analysis," *Musical Quarterly* (July 1935); A. Waldeck and N. Broder, "Musical Synthesis as Expounded by H. Schenker," *Musical Mercury* (Dec. 1935); A. T. Katz, *Challenge to Musical Tradition* (N.Y. 1945); F. Salzer, *Structural Hearing* (N.Y. 1952; 2nd ed. 1962; a development of the Schenker theories); F. Salzer and C. Schachter, *Counterpoint in Composition. The Study of Voice Leading* (N.Y., 1969; a textbook based on Schenkerian principles). A periodical that places heavy emphasis on the application of Schenkerian ideas is *The Music Forum* (1967–).

Scherchen, Hermann, eminent German conductor; b. Berlin, June 21, 1891; d. Florence, June 12, 1966. He was self-taught in music; played the viola in the Berlin Philharmonic (1907-10); in 1911-12, toured with Arnold Schoenberg. In 1914 he obtained an engagement as symph. conductor in Riga; at the outbreak of World War I he was interned in Russia; after the Armistice he returned to Berlin; founded and directed the Neue Musikgesellschaft there (1918); edited the music periodical *Melos* (1920–21); conducted numerous concerts at modern music festivals in Donaueschingen, Frankfurt, etc.; conducted symph. concerts of the Collegium Musicum in Winterthur, Switzerland (1932-38); from 1928 till 1933 was in charge of the music of the Königsberg Radio. In 1933 he left Germany; edited the periodical *Musica Viva* in Brussels (1933-36); conducted at music festivals in Barcelona (1936), and Paris. On Oct. 30, 1964, he conducted a concert of the Philadelphia Orch. He distinguished himself as a scholarly exponent of modern music; conducted many world premières of ultramodern works; publ. the valuable manual on conducting, *Lehrbuch des Dirigierens* (Leipzig, 1929; in English as *Handbook of Conducting,* London, 1933; 6th ed., 1949); *Vom Wesen der Musik* (Zürich, 1946; in English as *The Nature of Music,* London, 1947; Chicago, 1950); *Musik für Jedermann* (Winterthur, 1950).

Scheremetiev, Alexander. See **Sheremetiev, Alexander.**

Schering, Arnold, eminent German musicologist; b. Breslau. April 2, 1877; d. Berlin, March 7, 1941. Having completed the course at the Gymnasium in Dresden, he matriculated at Berlin Univ., continuing his musical studies there with Joachim (violin) and Succo (composition); then took courses at the Univs. of Munich and Leipzig; Dr. phil. (Leipzig, 1902) with the dissertation *Geschichte des Instrumentalkonzerts* (as far as Vivaldi; continuation, 1905; 2nd ed., 1927); instructor for esthetics and history of music at Leipzig Univ. in 1907; associate prof., 1915; from 1903-06 ed. of *Neue Zeitschrift für Musik.* From 1909-23 prof. of music at the Leipzig Cons.; 1920, prof. of the Univ. of Halle; 1928, prof. at the Univ. of Berlin and head of the Board of the German *Denkmäler;* 1933, president of the German Musicological Society. A noted Bach scholar, he edited the *Bach-Jahrbuch* from its inception in 1904 through 1939. In 1908 he discovered in Uppsala Schütz's long-lost work, *Weihnachtsoratorium* (publ. as supplement to Spitta's complete ed., 1909). He was the first to develop the theory that in early *a cappella* music the "tenor" was performed by the organ. In his history of the oratorio he emphasized the importance of the *lauda* as one of the sources. WRITINGS: *Bachs Textbehandlung* (1900); *Geschichte des Instrumentalkonzerts bis auf die Gegenwart* (1905; 2nd ed., 1927); *Die Anfänge des Oratoriums* (1907); *Geschichte des Oratoriums* (1911); *Musikalische Bildung und Erziehung zum musikalischen Hören* (1911; 4th ed., 1924); *Die niederländische Orgelmesse im Zeitalter des Josquin* (1912); *Studien zur Musikgeschichte der Frührenaissance* (1914); *Tabellen zur Musikgeschichte* (1914; 4th ed., 1934); *Deutsche Musikgeschichte im Umriss* (1917); *Die me-*

trisch-rhythmische Grundgestalt unserer Choralmelodien (1924); 2 additional vols. to R. Wustmann's *Musikgeschichte Leipzigs* (1927, 1941); *Geschichte der Musik in Beispielen* (1931); *Aufführungspraxis alter Musik* (1931); *Beethoven in neuer Deutung* (1934; aroused a considerable controversy because of its attempt to explain some of Beethoven's compositions as related to modern political trends); *Beethoven und die Dichtung* (1936); *J. S. Bachs Leipziger Kirchenmusik* (1936); *Von grossen Meistern der Musik* (1940); *Das Symbol in der Musik* (1941); *Über Kantaten J. S. Bachs* (posthumous, 1942); *Vom musikalischen Kunstwerk* (posthumous, 1949); also prepared a new ed. of von Dommer's *Handbuch der Musikgeschichte* (1914). He ed. about 12 vols. of works by early composers (Hasse, Quantz, Schütz, etc.); also composed music to Goethe's *Faust* and a violin sonata.

BIBLIOGRAPHY: *Festschrift Arnold Schering zum 60. Geburtstag* (Berlin, 1937).

Scherman, Thomas, American conductor; b. New York, Feb. 12, 1917; son of Harry Scherman, founder and president of the Book-of-the-Month Club. He attended Columbia Univ. (B.A., 1937); then studied piano with Isabelle Vengerova, theory with Hans Weisse, and conducting with Carl Bamberger and Max Rudolf. He served in the army (1941–45), entering as a private and reaching the rank of captain in the Signal Corps. In 1947 he organized in New York the Little Orchestra Society for the purpose of presenting new works and reviving forgotten music of the past, and conducted it successfully for a number of seasons.

Schermerhorn, Kenneth DeWitt, American conductor; b. Schenectady, N.Y., Nov. 20, 1929. He studied music at the New England Cons. (grad. 1950). His first important engagement was as conductor of the American Ballet Theater (1956–65); he subsequently conducted the New Jersey Symph. Orch. (1962–68); in 1968 he was appointed the conductor of the Milwaukee Symph. Orchestra.

Scherzer, Otto, German violinist and composer; b. Ansbach, March 24, 1821; d. Stuttgart, Feb. 23, 1886. After studying with Molique, he became violinist in the Stuttgart court orch. (1838–54); was music director at Tübingen Univ. (1860–77); publ. a number of songs and piano pieces.

BIBLIOGRAPHY: Anon., *Otto Scherzer. Ein Künstlerleben* (Stuttgart, 1897).

Schetky, Johann Georg Christoff, German cellist and composer; b. Darmstadt, 1740; d. Edinburgh, Nov. 29, 1824. The original family name was **Von Teschky;** Schetky's ancestors were from Transylvania. He traveled in Germany; in 1768 was in Hamburg; in 1772, settled in Edinburgh, where he was 1st cellist of the concerts in St. Cecilia's Hall. He married Maria Anna Teresa Reinagle, sister of Alexander Reinagle. He publ. 6 string quartets; 6 string trios; 6 duos for violin and cello; 6 cello sonatas with bass; 6 flute duos; 6 cello duos; 6 sonatas for violin and cello; harpsichord sonatas; songs. In manuscript he left 3 symphonies, 4 cello concertos, and an oratorio. His son, **J. George**

Schetky (b. Edinburgh, June 1, 1776; d. Philadelphia, Dec. 11, 1831), was the 2nd of 11 children; emigrated to America in 1792; naturalized in Philadelphia on Nov. 19, 1806. He appeared as a cellist in Philadelphia; about 1800, entered into partnership with Benjamin Carr in the music publ. business; was a co-founder of the Musical Fund Society in Philadelphia. His arrangement for military band of Kotzwara's *Battle of Prague* was much played.

BIBLIOGRAPHY: Madeira, *Music in Philadelphia* (Philadelphia, 1896); O. G. Sonneck, *Bibliography of Early American Secular Music* (Washington, 1905); O. G. Sonneck, *Early Concert Life in America* (Leipzig, 1907; in English); Laurance Oliphant Schetky, *The Schetky Family; A Compilation of Letters, Memoirs and Historical Data* (privately publ., Portland, Ore., 1942; of great documentary value, establishing correct factual data from family archives; the author was a grandson of J. George Schetky).

Scheurleer, Daniel François, Dutch musicologist; b. The Hague, Nov. 13, 1855; d. there, Feb. 6, 1927. Although a banker, he took an active part in musical affairs; was president, for many years, of the Vereeniging voor Nederlandsche Muziekgeschiedenis; made Dr. phil. *(honoris causa)* by the Univ. of Leyden in 1910; he was the owner of a valuable musical library (catalogue publ. in 1885; 2 supplements 1903 and 1910) and collection of instruments (catalogue publ. 1885 and 1887; now in the Museum of The Hague); 1921, founded the Union Musicologique. He publ. *Het Muziekleven in Nederland in de tweede helft der 18e eeuw* (The Hague, 1909) and other studies; ed. Fruytier's *Ecclesiasticus* (1563), etc.

BIBLIOGRAPHY: *Gedenkboek aangeboden aan Dr. D. F. Scheurleer op zijn 70sten Verjaardag* (1925; contains a complete bibliography of his works).

Schibler, Armin, Swiss composer; b. Kreuzlingen, Nov. 20, 1920. He studied with Willy Burkhard in Zürich; since 1944, music director at the Kanton Gymnasium there. Much of his music is cast in neo-Classical forms; some works employ a modified form of the 12-tone technique.

WORKS: OPERAS: *Der spanische Rosenstock* (Bern, April 9, 1950), *Der Teufel im Winterpalais* (1950–53), *Das Bergwerk von Falun* (1953), *Die Füsse im Feuer* (Zürich, April 25, 1955; aroused considerable interest), *Blackwood & Co.,* burlesque opera (Zürich, June 3, 1962); the symph. oratorio *Media in vita* (Zürich, April 26, 1963); FOR ORCH.: *Concertino* for piano and chamber orch. (1943); *Fantasy* for viola and small orch. (1945); *Fantasy* for oboe, harp, and small orch. (1946); Symph. No. 1 (1946); *Passacaglia* (1949); *Symph. Variations* (1950); *Concertante Fantasie* for cello and orch. (1951); Symph. No. 2 (1953); *Concerto for Amateur Orchestra* (1953); Symph. No. 3 (Winterthur, Nov. 13, 1957); *Metamorphoses Ebrietatis,* symph. poem (Montreux, Sept. 6, 1966); Horn Concerto (1956); Trombone Concerto (1957); *Concerto breve* for cello and orch. (1958–59); Violin Concerto (1960); Trumpet Concerto (1960–61); Concerto for Percussion and Orch. (Zürich, Jan. 6, 1961); Piano Concerto (1962–68); Concerto for Piano, Percussion and String Orch. (1963); Double Concerto for Flute,

Harp and Chamber Orch. (1966); Bassoon Concerto (1967); *6 Pieces* for orch. (1969); CANTATAS: *Die Hochzeit* (1946); *Gefährten* (1946); *Weil Alles erneut sich begibt* (1949); *Mondlicht* (1950); CHAMBER MUSIC: Solo Sonata for Flute (1944); Suite for cello alone (1945); *Little Concerto* for viola alone (1947); 4 string quartets (1945, 1951, 1958, 1960); *Trio Concertante* for trumpet, violin, and piano (1948); *Duo Concertante* for violin and piano (1950); *Dodecaphonic Studies* for piano.

BIBLIOGRAPHY: K. H. Wörner, *Armin Schibler; Werk und Persönlichkeit* (Amriswil, 1953); several works for speaking and singing voices.

Schicht, Johann Gottfried, German composer; b. Reichenau, Saxony, Sept. 29, 1753; d. Leipzig, Feb. 16, 1823. In 1776, already well trained as an organist and pianist, he matriculated at Leipzig as a law student, but became pianist at Joh. Adam Hiller's Liebhaber-Konzerte, and at the Gewandhaus Concerts evolved from them in 1781, succeeding Hiller as conductor in 1785. In 1810 he became cantor at the Thomasschule. WORKS: the oratorios *Die Feier der Christen auf Golgotha, Moses auf Sinai,* and *Das Ende des Gerechten;* Masses, motets, Te Deums, the *100th Psalm;* several chorale-motets (*Nach einer Prüfung kurzer Tage, Jesus meine Zuversicht, Herzlich lieb hab' ich dich, o Herr,* etc.); 9 settings of Leo's Miserere *a* 4–8; an excellent book of chorales (1819; of 1,285 melodies, 306 are original); a concerto, sonatas, caprices, etc., for piano; and *Grundregeln der Harmonie* (Leipzig, 1812).

BIBLIOGRAPHY: P. Langer, *Chronik der Leipziger Singakademie* (Leipzig, 1902).

Schick, George, American conductor; b. Prague, April 5, 1908. He studied at the Prague Cons.; was assistant conductor at the Prague Opera from 1927 until 1938. He settled in the U.S. in 1939; was conductor of the San Carlo Opera (1943); then conducted in Chicago; from 1948 to 1950 was conductor of the Little Symph. of Montreal; from 1950 to 1956, associate conductor of the Chicago Symph. Orch.

Schick (*née* **Hamel**), **Margarete Luise,** noted German soprano; b. Mainz, April 26, 1773; d. Berlin, April 29, 1809. She studied with Steffani at Würzburg, later with Righini at Mainz, where her stage debut took place in 1791. Her favorite roles were Susanna *(Figaro)* and Zerlina *(Don Giovanni).* From 1794 she sang at the Royal Opera, Berlin, having great success in operas by Gluck. Her contemporaries regarded her as the equal of the famous Mara. In 1791 she married the violinist **Ernst Schick.**

BIBLIOGRAPHY: K. Levezow, *Leben und Kunst der Frau Margarete Luise Schick* (Berlin, 1809).

Schickele, Peter, American composer; b. Ames, Iowa, July 17, 1935. He studied at the Juilliard School of Music, with Vincent Persichetti and William Bergsma. After quaquaversal professional gyrations, he rocketed to fame in the rollicking role of a roly-poly character P. D. Q. Bach, the mythical composer of such outrageous travesties as *The Civilian Barber, Gross Concerto for Divers Flutes* (featuring a nose flute and a wiener whistle to be eaten during the performance), *Concerto for Piano vs. Orchestra, Iphigenia in Brooklyn, The Seasonings, Pervertimento for Bagpipes, Bicycles & Balloons, No-No Nonette, Schleptet, Fuga Meshuga, Missa Hilarious, Sanka Cantata, Fantasie-Shtick,* etc., all perpetrated in a clever pseudo-Baroque style. He publ. *The Definitive Biography of P. D. Q. Bach (1807–1742?),* (N.Y., 1976).

Schidlowsky, León, Chilean composer; b. Santiago, July 21, 1931. He studied philosophy and psychology at the Univ. of Chile (1948–52) and had private lessons in composition with Free Focke and in harmony with Juan Allende; then went to Germany for further studies (1952–55). Returning to Chile, he organized an avant-garde group "Tonus" for the propagation of new techniques of composition; was a music teacher at the Hebrew Institute in Santiago (1955–61), director of the music archives of the Institute of Musical Extension of the Univ. of Chile (1961–65) and director of the Institute and a member of the faculty of the Cons. Nacional de Música in Santiago (1965–69). In 1969 he emigrated to Israel, where he was appointed to the faculty of the Ruben Academy in Tel Aviv. In his music he adopts a serial technique, extending it into fields of rhythms and intensities; beginning in 1964 he superadded aleatory elements, using graphic notation.

WORKS: an opera, *Die Menschen* (1970); *Requiem* for soprano and chamber orch. (1954); *Caupolicán,* epic narrative for narrator, chorus, 2 pianos, celeste and percussion orch. (1958); *Tríptico* for orch. (1959); *Oda a la Tierra* for 2 narrators and orch. (1958–60); *La Noche de Cristal,* symph. for tenor, male chorus, and orch., commemorating the martyrdom of Jews on the Nazi "crystal night" (1961); *Eróstrato* for percussion orch. (1963); *Invocación* for soprano, narrator, percussion and string orch. (1964); *Nueva York* for orch., dedicated to "my brothers in Harlem" (1965; Third Inter-American Music Festival, Washington, May 9, 1965); *Jeremias* for 8 mixed voices and string orch. (1966); *Kadish* for cello and orch. (1967); *Epitaph for Hermann Scherchen* for orch. (1967); *Babi Yar* for string orch., piano and percussion (1970); *Serenata* for chamber orch. (1970); *Arcanas* for orch. (1971); *Constellation II* for string orch. (1971); *Rabbi Akiba,* scenic fantasy for narrator, 3 soloists, children's and mixed chorus, and orch. (1972); *Amereida* (consisting of *Memento, Llaqui* and *Ecce Homo*) for narrator and orch. (1965–72); chamber vocal music: 2 *Psalms* for contralto, clarinet, bass clarinet, violin and cello (1954); *6 Japanese Songs* for soprano and 9 instruments (1954); *Cantata Negra* for contralto, piano, xylophone and 3 percussionists (1957); *Amatorias* for tenor and instrumental ensemble (1962–63); *De Profundis* for soprano, contralto, tenor, flute, oboe, bass clarinet, saxophone, trumpet, trombone and strings (1963); *Lament* for chorus a cappella (1966); *Requiem* for 12 soloists a cappella (1968); *Espergesia* for tenor and percussion (1968); *Monodrama* for actress and percussion (1970); *In memoriam* for narrator, flute, oboe, clarinet, cello and percussion (1971); *Canticas* for 2 sopranos, countertenor, tenor, baritone and brass (1971); *Verrà la morte* for solo soprano (1972); *Hommage à Picasso* to a text by Gertrude Stein, for soprano, alto, tenor and bass (1973); chamber instrumental music: *Elegía* for clarinet and string quartet (1952); Trio for flute, cello and piano (1955); *Cuarteto Mixto* for flute, clarinet, violin and cello (1956); Concerto for 6 instruments (1957); *In memoriam* for clarinet and percussion (1957); *4 Miniatures* for flute, oboe, clarinet and bassoon (1957); *Soliloquios* for 8 instruments (1961); *Visiones* for 12 strings (1967); String Quartet (1967); Wind Quintet (1968); *Eclosión* for 9 instruments (1967); *6 Hexáforos* for 6 percussionists (1968); Sextet (1970); *Kolot* for solo harp (1971); *Meshulash (Triangle)* for piano trio (1971); for piano: *6 Miniatures*, to paintings by Klee (1952), *8 Structures* (1955), *5 Pieces* (1956) and *Actus* (1972).

BIBLIOGRAPHY: M. E. Grebe, "León Schidlowsky, síntesis de su trayectoria creativa," *Revista Musical Chilena* (1968; contains a list of works).

Schiedermair, Ludwig, eminent German musicologist; b. Regensburg, Dec. 7, 1876; d. Bensberg, near Cologne, April 30, 1957. He studied in Munich with Sandberger and Beer-Walbrunn; 1901, Dr. phil., for the dissertation *Künstlerische Bestrebungen am Hofe des Kurfürsten Ferdinand Maria von Bayern;* studied further with Riemann in Leipzig and with Kretzschmar in Berlin. In 1906 he became instructor of musicology at the Univ. of Marburg; in 1912, lecturer at the Univ. of Bonn (1920, prof.). In 1927, on the occasion of the Beethoven centennial, he was appointed director of the Beethoven-Haus Research Institute in Bonn.

WRITINGS: *Gustav Mahler* (Leipzig, 1901); *Beiträge zur Geschichte der Oper um die Wende des 18. und 19. Jahrhunderts* (2 vols., Leipzig, 1907, 1910); *Bayreuther Festspiele im Zeitalter des Absolutismus* (Leipzig, 1908); *Die Briefe Mozarts und seiner Familie* (5 vols.; Munich, 1914; vol. 5 is an iconography); *W. A. Mozarts Handschrift* (facsimiles, Bückeburg, 1919); *Einführung in das Studium der Musikgeschichte* (Munich, 1918; new ed., Bonn, 1947); *Mozart* (Munich, 1922; 2nd ed., Bonn, 1948); *Der junge Beethoven* (Leipzig, 1925; 3rd ed., Bonn, 1951); *Beethoven: Beiträge zum Leben und Schaffen* (Leipzig, 1930); *Die deutsche Oper* (Leipzig, 1930); *Die Gestaltung weltanschaulicher Ideen in der Vokalmusik Beethovens* (Leipzig, 1934); *Musik am Rheinstron* (Cologne, 1947); *Musikalische Begegnungen; Erlebnis und Erinnerung* (Cologne, 1948); *Deutsche Musik im Europäischen Raum* (Münster, 1954). A Festschrift, *Beethoven und die Gegenwart*, was publ. in honor of Schiedermair's 60th birthday (Berlin, 1937).

BIBLIOGRAPHY: J. Schmidt-Görg, "Ludwig Schiedermair," *Die Musikforschung 2* (1957).

Schiedermayer, Johann Baptist, German composer; b. Pfaffenmünster, Bavaria, June 23, 1779; d. Linz, Austria, Jan. 6, 1840, as cathedral organist. He wrote the Singspiele *Wellmanns Eichenstämme* (Linz, 1815), *Das Glück ist kugelrund* (Linz, 1816), *Die Rückkehr ins Vaterhaus* (Linz, 1816); 16 Masses and much other sacred music; also symphonies, string trios, organ pieces, etc.; a *Theoretisch-praktische Chorallehre zum Gebrauch beim katholischen Kirchenritus* (1828); an abridged ed. of Leopold Mozart's violin method.

Schiedmayer. The name of 2 well-known firms of piano makers in Stuttgart, i.e., "Schiedmayer & Söhne" and "Schiedmayer Pianofortefabrik." **Balthasar Schiedmayer** (1711–81) began manufacturing musical instruments in Erlangen about 1740; at his death in 1781, his son **Johann David Schiedmayer** (1753–1805) assumed the management; he was succeeded by his 19-year-old son **Johann Lorenz Schiedmayer** (1786–1860), with whom he had moved about 1800 from Erlangen to Nuremberg. Johann Lorenz ended the business at Nuremberg after 2 years, and went to Vienna for a brief time; in 1809 he was in Stuttgart, where he set up business in partnership with a young piano maker, Karl Dieudonné (d. 1825); from 1825, he carried on the business alone, until 1845, when his eldest sons, **Adolf Schiedmayer** (1819–90) and **Hermann Schiedmayer** (1820–91), entered the firm, which was then called "J. L. Schiedmayer & Söhne." In 1853 Johann Lorenz Schiedmayer provided his two younger sons, **Julius** (1822–78) and **Paul** (1829–90), with their own separate factory, producing harmoniums. After their father's death they turned to piano making, and their business became known as "Schiedmayer Pianofortefabrik." Upon Paul Schiedmayer's death in 1890, his son, **Max Julius,** became head of the firm.

BIBLIOGRAPHY: A. Eisenmann, *Schiedmayer und Söhne* (Stuttgart, 1909).

Schifrin, Lalo (Boris), American composer; b. Buenos Aires, June 21, 1932. He studied music at home with his father who was concertmaster at the Teatro Colón; took composition lessons with Argentinian dodecaphonist Juan Carlos Paz. In 1950 he went to Paris where he attended the classes of Olivier Messiaen. He became interested in jazz and represented Argentina at the International Jazz Festival in Paris in 1955; returning to Buenos Aires he formed his own jazz band, adopting the bebop style. In 1958 he went to New York as arranger for Xavier Cugat; then was pianist with Dizzy Gillespie's band (1960–62); composed for it several exotic pieces, such as *Manteca*, *Con Alma* and *Tunisian Fantasy*, based on Gillespie's *Night in Tunisia*. In 1963 he wrote a ballet *Jazz Faust*. In 1964 he went to Hollywood, where he rapidly found his métier as composer for the films and television; among his motion picture scores are *The Liquidator*, *The Fox* and *The Cincinnati Kid*. He also experimented with applying the jazz idiom to religious texts, as, for instance, in his *Jazz Suite on Mass Texts* (1965). He achieved his greatest popular success with the theme-motto for the television series *Mission: Impossible,* in 5/4 time, for which he received two "Grammy" awards. His adaptation of modern techniques into mass media placed him in the enviable position of being praised by professional musicians. His oratorio *The Rise and Fall of the Third Reich,* featuring realistic excerpts and incorporating an actual recording of Hitler's speech in electronic amplification, was brought out at the Hollywood Bowl in Aug. 3, 1967. His other works include a Suite for trumpet and brass orch. (1961); *The Ritual of Sound* for 15 instruments (1962); *Pulsations* for eletronic keyboard, jazz band orch. (Los Angeles, Jan. 21, 1971); *Madrigals for the*

Space Age, in 10 parts for narrator and chorus (Los Angeles, Jan. 15, 1976).

Schikaneder, Emanuel (Johann), Mozart's librettist; b. Straubing, Sept. 1, 1751; d. Vienna, Sept. 21, 1812. His baptismal names were Johannes Joseph; he assumed the name Emanuel later in life. He was a member of a troupe of itinerant players when he met Mozart at Salzburg. In 1784 he reached Vienna, where he was an actor and an impresario. He was not successful until he persuaded Mozart to set to music his play *Die Zauberflöte,* which recouped his fortunes; it was produced on Sept. 30, 1791, shortly before Mozart's death; Schikaneder himself took the part of Papageno. He wrote 55 theater pieces and 44 librettos for operas, and Singspiele; with Zitterbarth he was the manager of the Theater an der Wien, which he directed from its foundation (1801) until 1806. He died insane after a series of financial setbacks.
BIBLIOGRAPHY: O. E. Deutsch, *Das Freihaustheater auf der Wieden, 1787–1801* (Vienna, 1937); Egon von Komorzynski, *Der Vater der Zauberflöte: Emanuel Schikaneders Leben* (Vienna, 1948); Egon von Komorzynski, *Emanuel Schikaneder: ein Beitrag zur Geschichte des deutschen Theaters* (Vienna, 1951). For a complete list of his librettos see Anton Bauer, *Opern und Operetten in Wien* (Vienna, 1955).

Schiller, Friedrich von, great German poet; b. Marbach, Nov. 10, 1759; d. Weimar, May 9, 1805. Many musicians have turned to his works for inspiration.
BIBLIOGRAPHY: M. Berendt, *Schiller bis Wagner* (Berlin, 1901); J. Baltz, *Beethoven und Schiller* (Arnsberg, 1905); A. Kohut, *F. Schiller in seinen Beziehungen zur Musik* (Stuttgart, 1905); H. Knudsen, *Schiller und die Musik* (Greifswald, 1908); G. Adler, *Schiller und Schubert* (Vienna, 1910).

Schilling, Gustav, German musical lexicographer; b. Schwiegershausen, near Hannover, Nov. 3, 1803; d. Nebraska, March, 1880. He studied theology at Göttingen and Halle; in 1857 he emigrated to America; lived in N.Y., later was in Montreal; finally settled in Nebraska.
WRITINGS: His most important work was the *Enzyklopädie der gesammten musikalischen Wissenschaften oder Universal-Lexikon der Tonkunst* (6 vols.; 1835–38; 2nd ed., 7 vols., 1840–42). Other publications are *Versuch einer Philosophie des Schönen in der Musik* (1838); *Lehrbuch der allgemeinen Musikwissenschaft* (1840); *Geschichte der heutigen oder modernen Musik* (1841); *Die musikalische Europa* (1842); *Musikalische Dynamik; oder, Die Lehre vom Vortrage in der Musik* (1843); *Der Pianist* (1843); *Franz Liszt* (1844); *Sicher Schlüssel zur Klaviervirtuosität* (1844); *Die schöne Kunst der Töne* (1847); *Musikalische Didaktik* (1851); *Allgemeine Volksmusiklehre* (1852); *Akustik oder die Lehre vom Klange* (2nd ed., 1856).

Schillinger, Joseph, Russian composer and theorist; b. Kharkov, Aug. 31, 1895; d. New York, March 23, 1943. He studied at the St. Petersburg Cons. with Tcherepnin, Wihtol, and others; from 1918 to 1922, taught at the State Academy of Music in Kharkov; also conducted an orch. there; from 1922 to 1928 was active in Leningrad as teacher and composer. In 1928 he came to America, settling in N.Y.; taught at the New School for Social Research; then established private classes, teaching his own system of composition, based on rigid mathematical principles. He became highly successful as instructor; George Gershwin took lessons from him; many other composers of popular music became his students. After Schillinger's death, Lyle Dowling and Arnold Shaw edited and published his magnum opus, under the title *The Schillinger System of Musical Composition* (2 vols.; N.Y., 1946); this was followed by *The Mathematical Basis of the Arts* (N.Y., 1947); a short volume of musical patterns, *Kaleidophone,* was publ. previously (N.Y., 1940). Schillinger was also a composer in his own right; his works include a *March of the Orient,* for orch. (Leningrad, May 12, 1926); *First Airphonic Suite,* for the theremin with orch. (Cleveland, Nov. 28, 1929; Leo Theremin, the inventor, as soloist); piano pieces; etc.
BIBLIOGRAPHY: Frances Schillinger, *Joseph Schillinger: A Memoir by His Wife* (N.Y., 1949); Vernon Duke, "Gershwin, Schillinger, and Dukelsky," *Musical Quarterly* (Jan. 1947).

Schillings, Max von, renowned German composer and conductor; b. Düren, April 19, 1868; d. Berlin, July 24, 1933. While attending the Gymnasium at Bonn he studied violin with O. von Königslöw, and piano and composition with K. J. Brambach. He then entered the Univ. of Munich, where he studied law, philosophy, literature, and art. He became associated with Richard Strauss and under his influence decided to devote himself entirely to music. In 1892 he was engaged as assistant stage director at the Festival Theater in Bayreuth; in 1902 became chorusmaster; in 1908 he moved to Stuttgart as general music director; on the occasion of the inauguration of the new opera theater there, he was given the rank of nobility, and added the nobiliary particle "von" to his name; he remained in Stuttgart until 1918; was intendant of the Berlin State Opera (1919–25). He made several visits as conductor to the U.S. In 1923 he married the soprano **Barbara Kemp.** As a composer, he trailed in the path of Wagner, barely avoiding direct imitation.
WORKS: operas: *Ingwelde* (Karlsruhe, Nov. 13, 1894), *Der Pfeifertag* (Schwerin, Nov. 26, 1899), *Moloch* (Dresden, Dec. 8, 1906), *Mona Lisa* (Stuttgart, Sept. 26, 1915; enjoyed considerable success; produced by the Metropolitan Opera, N.Y., March 1, 1923); incidental music to *Orestie* of Aeschylus (1900) and to Part I of Goethe's *Faust;* a symph. prologue to *Oedipus Rex* of Sophocles; also several melodramas with orch.: *Kassandra, Das eleusische Fest, Das Hexenlied,* and *Jung Olaf;* 2 symph. fantasies, *Meergruss* and *Seemorgen;* Violin Concerto; String Quartet; String Quintet; pieces for violin and piano; men's choruses a cappella; songs; piano pieces. A complete catalogue of his works, compiled by J. Beck, was publ. at Berlin in 1934.
BIBLIOGRAPHY: R. Louis, *Max Schillings* (Leipzig, 1909); A. Richard, *Max Schillings* (Munich, 1922); W. Raupp, *Max von Schillings* (Hamburg, 1935).

Schimon, Adolf, Austrian singing teacher and composer; b. Vienna, Feb. 29, 1820; d. Leipzig, June 21, 1887. He studied with Berton, Halévy, and others at the Paris Cons.; studied the Italian method in Florence, bringing out his opera, *Stradella*, there in 1846; was *maestro al cembalo* at Her Majesty's Theatre, London (1850–52), then at the Italian Opera in Paris. In 1858 Flotow brought out Schimon's comic opera *List um List* at Schwerin. His works futher included Italian and French songs; German leider; 2 string quartets; a piano trio; a violin sonata; piano music; etc. He was married to the soprano **Anna Regan (Schimon-Regan).**

Schimon-Regan, Anna, distinguished German soprano; b. Aich, near Karlsbad, Sept. 18, 1841; d. Munich, April 18, 1902. In 1859 she had her first singing lessons from Mme. Schubert in Karlsbad; the next year her aunt, the famous **Caroline Unger,** took her to Florence and taught her till 1864; she was then engaged at the court opera in Hannover (1864–67); during the winter of 1867–68 she sang in Berlioz's concerts in St. Petersburg. She made her first visit to England in 1869, appearing in concerts with Caroline Unger; gave song recitals there every winter till 1875. In 1872 she married **Adolf Schimon,** and settled in Munich.

Schindelmeisser, Ludwig, German composer; b. Königsberg, Dec. 8, 1811; d. Darmstadt, March 30, 1864. He studied with A. B. Marx in Berlin and also with Dorn in Leipzig, where he met Wagner and became friendly with him. He worked as an opera conductor in Berlin, Budapest, Frankfurt and Hamburg, and himself wrote several operas: *Peter von Szapáry* (Budapest, 1839); *Malvina* (Budapest, 1841); *Der Rächer,* after Corneille's *Le Cid* (Budapest, 1846); *Melusine* (Darmstadt, 1861); a ballet *Diavolina*; the orchestral overtures, *Rule Britannia*; *Loreley*; numerous piano pieces and songs.

Schindler, Anton Felix, Beethoven's faithful friend and biographer; b. Medlov, in the district of Olomouc, June 13, 1795; d. Bockenheim, near Frankfurt, Jan. 16, 1864. He was the son of a schoolteacher; studied law at the Univ. of Vienna, and at the same time learned to play violin. He was a violinist and conductor at the Josephstadt Theater and at the Kärtnertor Theater in Vienna (1825); conducted performances of several of Beethoven's symphonies. He met Beethoven in 1814; in 1819 became Beethoven's secretary and helper, and lived in the same house with him until their break in 1824, when Beethoven unjustly accused him of disloyalty. A few months before Beethoven's death, Schindler was called back and never left him again. He was present at Beethoven's death, and received from the estate the bulk of Beethoven's writings and correspondence, as well as some 400 conversation books, but for personal reasons he destroyed a major part of this material. From 1831 till 1835 Schindler was Kapellmeister at the Cathedral of Münster; from 1835 to 1837 at Aachen; later moved to Bockenheim, remaining there until his death. His intimacy with Beethoven lends peculiar value to his *Biographie Ludwig van Beethovens* (Münster, 1840; 2nd, enlarged ed., 1845;

3rd ed., 1960). The biography was publ. in English, transl. by Moscheles (London, 1841); modern German eds. were brought out by Kalischer (1909) and Fritz Volbach (1927). His diaries of his sojourns in Paris and Berlin (1841–43) were edited by Marta Becker (Frankfurt, 1939). His pamphlet, *Beethoven in Paris* (1842), is an account of the production of Beethoven's works at the Concert Spirituel; it formed an appendix to the 2nd ed. of his biography. After Schindler's death, his papers, comprising the invaluable conversation books and sketch books of Beethoven that survived, as well as a vast amount of personal notes of all kinds, passed on to the Royal Library of Berlin.

BIBLIOGRAPHY: E. Hüffer, *A. F. Schindler, der Biograph Beethovens* (diss., Münster, 1909) R. Zimmermann, in *Allgemeine Musikzeitung* 38–39 (1925).

Schindler, Kurt, German conductor and music editor; b. Berlin, Feb. 17, 1882; d. New York, Nov. 16, 1935. He studied piano with Ansorge and composition with Bussler and others in Berlin; took additional theory lessons in Munich with Thuille. He then was briefly assistant conductor to Richard Strauss in Berlin and to Mottl in Munich; in 1904 he emigrated to America and, after serving as an assistant chorusmaster at the Metropolitan Opera House, was engaged as reader and music editor for G. Schirmer, Inc. In 1909 he founded in N.Y. the MacDowell Chorus, which became in 1910 the Schola Cantorum. Schindler conducted it until 1927 in programs including his choral arrangements of folksongs of various nations. His editions of arrangements of folksongs are valuable; among them are *6 Old French Christmas Carols* (1908); *Century of Russian Song from Glinka to Rachmaninov* (50 songs, with English translation; 1911); *The Developement of Opera* (examples of various periods; 1912); *Songs of the Russian People* (1915); *10 Student Songs of Finland* (1915); *A Cappella Choruses from the Russian Liturgy* (1913–17); *Masters of Russian Song* (2 vols., 1917); *Old Spanish Sacred Motets* (1918); *Modern Spanish Choral Works* (1918); *60 Russian Folk-Songs* (3 vols., 1918–19); *Folk Music and Poetry of Spain and Portugal* (N.Y., 1941; posthumous; about 1,000 musical examples; text in English and Spanish).

Schiøler, Victor, prominent Danish pianist; b. Copenhagen, April 7, 1899; d. there, Feb. 17, 1967. He studied with his mother, Augusta Schiøler (1868–1946); then with Ignaz Friedman and Artur Schnabel; made his piano debut in 1914; from 1919 toured in Europe; first American tour, 1948–49. He was also active as a conductor in Denmark.

Schiøtz, Aksel, Danish tenor; b. Roskilde, Sept. 1, 1906; d. Copenhagen, April 19, 1975. He studied languages at the Univ. of Copenhagen; then was a school teacher. It was not until 1939 that he made his debut as an opera singer; in 1942 he began to give concerts and became known in Denmark as a singer of lieder. In 1946 he made appearances in England, and in 1948 was in the U.S. In 1958 was appointed to the faculty of the Royal Cons. of Music in the Univ. of Toronto. He publ. *The Singer and His Art* (N.Y., 1969).

BIBLIOGRAPHY: G. Schiøtz, *Kunst og Kamp: Gerd og Aksel Schiøtz* (Copenhagen, 1951).

Schipa, Tito (baptismal names **Raffaele Attilio Amadeo),** famous Italian tenor; b. Lecce, Jan. 2, 1889; d. New York, Dec. 16, 1965; studied composition with A. Gerunda, and began his career as a composer of piano pieces and songs; then turned to singing, and in 1911 made his debut at Vercelli. After numerous appearences in Europe, he was engaged by the Chicago Civic Opera (1920–32); made his first appearance with the Metropolitan Opera on Nov. 23, 1932 as Nemorino in *L'Elisir d'amore;* made extensive tours of Europe and South America, as well as in the U.S.; lived in California until 1941, when he went back to Italy. On Sept. 28, 1946, he married Teresa Borgna of São Paulo, Brazil. He toured the U.S. again in 1947. He wrote an operetta, *La Principessa Liana* (1935); a Mass (1929), and several songs.

Schippers, Thomas, greatly gifted American conductor; b. Kalamazoo, Michigan, March 9, 1930; d. New York, Dec. 16, 1977. He played piano in public at the age of 6, and was a church organist at 14. He studied piano at the Curtis Institute of Music, Philadelphia (1944–45) and privately with Olga Samaroff (1946–47); subsequently attended Yale Univ.; there he took some composition lessons from Paul Hindemith. In 1948 he won 2nd prize in the contest for young conductors organized by the Philadelphia Orch. He then took a job as organist in the Greenwich Village Presbyterian Church, N.Y.; joined a group of young musicians in an enterprise called the Lemonade Opera, and conducted this group for several years. On March 15, 1950, he conducted in New York the premiere of Menotti's opera *The Consul* and the television premiere of his *Amahl and the Night Visitors* (N.Y. Dec. 25, 1951). In 1951 he became staff member of the N.Y. City Opera Co. On March 26, 1955 he led the N.Y. Philharmonic as guest conductor, the youngest musician to conduct the orchestra. In the fall of 1955 he made his debut as an opera conductor at the Metropolitan Opera in N.Y., also the youngest to do so; in 1955 he was guest conductor at La Scala, Milan. From 1958 to 1976 he was associated with Menotti in the Spoleto Festival of Two Worlds. Other engagements included appearances with the N.Y. Philharmonic, which he accompanied in 1959 to the Soviet Union as an alternate conductor with Leonard Bernstein. In 1962 he conducted at La Scala, Milan, the world premiere of Manuel de Falla's cantata *Atlantida*. In 1964 he conducted at the Bayreuth Wagner Festival. He was favorite conductor for new works at the Metropolitan Opera; conducted the first performance of Menotti's opera *The Last Savage* and the opening production of the Metropolitan Opera House of Samuel Barber's *Antony and Cleopatra* (Sept. 16, 1966); he also conducted the first production at the Metropolitan of the original version of Mussorgsky's *Boris Godunov* (1974). In 1970 he was appointed conductor and music director of the Cincinnati Symph. Orch., one of the few American-born composers to occupy a major symphony orchestra post. There was an element of tragedy in his life; rich, handsome and articulate, he became a victim of lung cancer, and was unable to open the scheduled season of the Cincinnati Orch. in the fall of 1977; in a grateful gesture the management gave him the title of Conductor Laureate. He bequeathed a sum of 5 million dollars to the orchestra. He was happily married but his wife died of cancer in 1973. When he conducted a production of *La Forza del destino* at the Metropolitan Opera on March 4, 1960, the baritone Leonard Warren collapsed and died on the stage.

Schirmer, the family of music publishers. The first of the family to be connected with music was **Johann Georg Schirmer,** who settled in Sondershausen and was married there on July 18, 1781. He was a cabinet-maker, a native Gäuroden, and made musical instruments. His son, **Ernst Ludwig Rudolf Schirmer** (b. Sondershausen, May 8, 1784), emigrated to New York with his wife and children in 1840. There his son **(Friedrich) Gustav (Emil) Schirmer** (b. Königsee, Thuringia, Sept. 19, 1829; d. Eisenach, Aug. 5, 1893) found employment in the music store of Scharfenberg & Luis, and after several years entered the employ of Kerksieg & Breusing, music dealers, becoming manager in 1854. In 1861 he took over the business with a partner, and acquired sole control in 1866, establishing the house of **G. Schirmer Inc.** He was an enlightened and progressive publisher; he entered into personal relations with noted European composers, and was among the original patrons of Wagner's Bayreuth Festival. He was an amateur pianist and had a real love for music. The diary of Tchaikovsky's visit to N.Y. in 1891 makes repeated mention of Schirmer and his family. Schirmer married an American, Mary Fairchild, by whom he had 5 daughters and 2 sons. The younger of these sons, **Gustave Schirmer** (b. New York, Feb. 18, 1864; d. Boston, July 15, 1907), organized in 1885 the Boston Music Company, which gained prominence especially through the publication of Ethelbert Nevin's music. Shortly afterwards, with his brother, he became a partner in the firm founded by his father in N.Y., and after the latter's death in 1893 he managed the business jointly with his brother, retaining independent control of the Boston Music Co. His brother, **Rudolph Edward Schirmer** (b. New York, July 22, 1859; d. Santa Barbara, Calif., Aug. 19, 1919), was educated in N.Y. public schools and from 1873 to 1875 lived at Weimar with his mother, brother, and 4 sisters; studied violin and piano there with Helene Stahl and came in contact with the Liszt circle; in 1876 entered the College of New Jersey (later Princeton Univ.), and after graduation in 1880 studied law for 4 years at Columbia College, being admitted to the bar in 1884. In 1885 he took the place of his brother Gustave in his father's music publishing business. Later he was rejoined by Gustave, and upon their father's death in 1893, became president of the firm, assuming sole control from 1907. In 1915 he founded the *Musical Quarterly.* He was a director of the N.Y. Oratorio Society and the N.Y. Symph. Society, and a trustee of the Institute of Musical Art, N.Y. **Gustave Schirmer, 3rd** (b. Boston, Dec. 29, 1890; d. Palm Beach, Florida, May 28, 1965), son of Gustave Schirmer and grandson of the founder of G. Schirmer. Inc., inherited the Boston Music Co. from his father and acquired the Willis Music Co. of Cincinnati. He was president of G. Schirmer, Inc., 1919–21 and 1944–57. Rudolf E. Schirmer's son, also named **Rudolph Edward Schirmer** (b. Santa Barbara, Calif., June 8, 1919), in 1949 became vice-president of G. Schirmer, Inc.

Schirmer, Ernest Charles, American music publisher; b. Mt. Vernon, N.Y., March 15, 1865; d. Waben, Massachusetts, Feb. 15, 1958. His father, Edward Schirmer (1831–85), a native of Thuringia, Saxony, was a brother of the famous music publisher, **Gustav Schirmer** of New York, the brothers emigrating to the U.S. in 1840. Ernest Schirmer entered apprenticeship in the music store of Gustav Schirmer, N.Y., in 1878. In Oct., 1891, he became business manager of the Boston Music Co.; admitted to partnership in Jan., 1902. In 1917 he withdrew from the Boston Music Co., and in 1921 founded the E. C. Schirmer Music Co., with the stated purpose of promoting good music. In 1956 he was still active in the affairs of the E. C. Schirmer Co. The publications of the firm include the Concord Series, the Choral Repertory of the Harvard Univ. Glee Club, Radcliffe, Vassar, and Wellesley College Choral Music, the Polyphonic and "A Cappella" Libraries, the St. Dunstan Edition of Sacred Music, and treatises on harmonic analysis, musical theory, and music appreciation. The firm enjoys a world market for its publications with agencies in London and Berlin.

G. Schirmer, Inc., one of the greatest music publishing houses in America. It was an outgrowth of the business founded in New York in 1848 by Kerksieg & Breusing, of which **Gustav Schirmer** became manager in 1843. With another employee, Bernard Beer, Schirmer took over the business in 1861, and the firm became known as "Beer & Schirmer." In 1866 Schirmer became the sole owner, establishing the house of "G. Schirmer, Music Publishers, Importers and Dealers." Until 1880 the business was located at 701 Broadway in New York; then it was moved to 35 Union Square, and in 1909 was transferred to a 7-story building at 3 East 43rd St. It remained at that address until 1960, when it was moved to 609 Fifth Avenue, and its retail store relocated at 4 East 49th Street. In 1969, G. Schirmer, Inc. was acquired by Macmillan Inc. and in 1973 the executive offices were moved to 866 Third Avenue. In 1973 Schirmer Books was founded as a division of Macmillan Publishing Co., Inc., taking over the publication of books on music for college, trade and professional/reference markets, while G. Schirmer continued publication of musical works. The New York firm also maintained branches in Cleveland (until 1962) and in Los Angeles (until 1967). After the death of the founder Gustav Schirmer in 1893, the firm was incorporated under the management of his sons, **Rudolph Edward Schirmer** and **Gustave Schirmer.** Rudolph Schirmer died in 1919 and was succeeded by his nephew **Gustav Schirmer,** who was President until 1921. Then W. Rodman Fay became president, with O. G. Sonneck as vice-president. On May 7, 1929, Carl Engel was made president and continued in that office (except for one year, 1933, when his place was taken by Hermann Irion) until his death in 1944, when **Gustave Schirmer, 3rd,** became president again, retiring in 1957. He was succeeded by Ru-

dolph Tauhert, who was president from 1957 to 1972. Robert A. Barton is currently (1978) president and Edward Murphy is vice-president and general manager. In 1892 the firm began publication of the *Library of Musical Classics,* notable for careful editing and general typographical excellence; with its didactic Latin motto "Musica laborum dulce lenimen" it became a familiar part of musical homes. In the same year was launched the *Collection of Operas,* a series of vocal scores with original text and English translation; another series, *The Golden Treasury* was begun in 1905. *Schirmer's Scholastic Series* containing pedagogical works began publishing in 1917. Among other laudable initiatives was the *American Folk-Song Series* offering authentic folk material. An expansion into the field of lexicography followed with the publication of *Baker's Biographical Dictionary of Musicians,* first issued in 1900, under the editorship of its original author Theodore Baker; its 6th edition was published in 1978, edited by Nicolas Slonimsky, who also took care of the 5th edition in 1958. Theodore Baker also compiled and edited *A Dictionary of Musical Terms* (G. Schirmer, N.Y., 1895; many reprints) and *Pronouncing Pocket-Manual of Musical Terms* (1905; more than a million copies sold). In 1915 *The Musical Quarterly* was founded under the editorship of O. G. Sonneck; its subsequent editors have been Carl Engel (1929–44), Gustave Reese (1944–45), Paul Henry Lang (1945–72), and Christopher Hatch (1972–77); in 1977 its editorship was entrusted to Joan Peyser. *The Musical Quarterly* has published through the years articles by the foremost scholars of Europe and America; it occupies the pre-eminent place among music journals in the English language. The music catalog of G. Schirmer, Inc. comprises tens of thousands of publications, ranging from solo songs to full orchestral scores. Particularly meritorious is the endeavor of the publishers to promote American music; the firm has published works by Ernest Bloch, Charles Loeffler, Charles Griffes, Walter Piston, Roy Harris, William Schuman, Samuel Barber, Gian Carlo Menotti, Paul Creston, Leonard Bernstein, Elliott Carter, Henry Cowell, Norman Dello Joio, Morton Gould, Virgil Thomson, Milton Babbitt, Gunther Schuller and many others; it also took over some works of Charles Ives. Among European composers, the works of Arnold Schoenberg, Gustav Holst and Benjamin Britten are included in the Schirmer catalogue as well as a number of works by Soviet composers.

Schiske, Karl, significant Austrian composer; b. Györ (Raab), Hungary, Feb. 12, 1916; d. Vienna, June 16, 1969. He studied music theory privately with Ernst Kanitz in Vienna (1932–38) and musicology with Orel and Schenk at the Univ. of Vienna (Dr. phil., 1942). In 1952 was appointed to the faculty of the Vienna Musikakademie; in 1967 he received the Great Austrian State Prize. In 1966–67 he was visiting prof. at the Univ. of California, Riverside. His technique of composition is curiously synthetic, and yet invariably logical, containing elements of medieval counterpoint and the serial methods of composition.

WORKS: 5 symphonies (1942, 1948, 1951, 1955, 1965); Piano Concerto (1939); Violin Concerto (1952); *Divertimento* for chamber orch. (1963); Sextet for clarinet, string quartet and piano (1937); Wind Quintet (1945); Violin Sonata (1948); 2 string quartets (1936, 1945); *Synthese* for "4 x 4" instruments (1958); *Vom Tode*, oratorio (1946); sacred and secular choruses; piano pieces and songs.

BIBLIOGRAPHY: Karlheinz Roschitz, *Karl Schiske* (Vienna, 1970).

Schiuma, Alfredo, Argentine composer; b. Buenos Aires, July 1, 1885; d. there, July 24, 1963. He studied with Romaniello in Buenos Aires, and later established his own music school there. He wrote several operas in a singable Italianate idiom; the following were produced in Buenos Aires: *Amy Robsart*, based on Walter Sott's novel *Kenilworth* (April 24, 1920); *La Sirocchia* (April 23, 1922); *Tabaré* (Aug. 6, 1925); *Las Virgenes del Sol* (June 20, 1939); *La Infanta* (Aug. 12, 1941); 4 symphonies (1928–57); a symph. tableau, *Pitunga* (Buenos Aires, March 31, 1929); and a symph. sketch, *Los Incas* (Buenos Aires, April 26, 1931); also choruses, chamber music and songs.

Schjelderup, Gerhard, Norwegian composer and writer; b. Christiansand, Nov. 17, 1859; d. Benediktbeuren, Bavaria, July 29, 1933. He went to Paris in 1878, and studied with Franchomme (cello) and Massenet (composition); in 1888 settled in Germany; lived in Dresden (from 1896); then moved to Benediktbeuren, where he remained till his death. He wrote music influenced partly by Wagner, partly by Grieg.
WORKS: operas: *Sonntagmorgen* (Munich, May 9, 1893), *Norwegische Hochzeit* (Prague, March 17, 1900), *Frühlingsnacht* (Dresden, May 1, 1908; in Norwegian, as *Vaarnat*, Oslo, Aug. 31, 1915), *Sturmvögel* (Schwerin, Sept. 19, 1926); musical fairy tale, *Sampo; Weihnacht-Suite*, for orch.; 2 symph. poems, *Eine Sommernacht auf dem Fjord* and *Brand* (after Ibsen); *In Baldurs Hain* for violin and piano; *Fantasiestück* for cello and piano; songs. He publ. a biography of Grieg (in Norwegian, 1903; German ed., with Walter Niemann, 1908) and a monograph on Wagner (in Norwegian, 1908; in German, 1913).
BIBLIOGRAPHY: O. M. Sandvik, "G. Schjelderup," *Schweizerische Musikzeitung* (Oct. 1948).

Schladebach, Julius, German physiologist and musician; b. Dresden, 1810; d. Kiel, Sept. 21, 1872. He publ. vol. 1 of a *Neues Universal-Lexikon der Tonkunst* (1854), completed by Bernsdorf; also *Die Bildung der menschlichen Stimme zum Gesang* (1860).

Schläger, Hans, Austrian composer; b. Felskirchen, Dec. 5, 1820; d. Salzburg, May 17, 1885. He was a pupil of Preyer at Vienna; chorusmaster of the Männergesangverein (1844–61); then Kapellmeister of Salzburg Cathedral, and director of the Mozarteum, resigning on his marriage with Countess Zichy in 1867. He wrote the operas *Heinrich und Ilse* (Salzburg, 1869) and *Hans Haidekukuk* (Salzburg, 1873); the symph. tone picture *Waldmeisters Brautfahrt*; symphonies; string quartets; etc.

Schlegel, Leander, Dutch composer; b. Overveen, near Haarlem, Feb. 2, 1844; d. there, Oct. 20, 1913. He studied at the Cons. in The Hague; then went to Leip-

zig where he was a student of Reinecke; toured with Wilhelmj as his accompanist; then returned to Holland; was director of a music school in Haarlem (1871–98); in 1898 he moved to Overveen where he continued to teach. He was a composer of solid attainments; in his music he tried to emulate Brahms; wrote a symphony, a piano quartet, a string quartet and a number of piano pieces in a romantic mood; also many melodious songs.

Schleinitz, Heinrich Conrad, German musician; b. Zschaitz, near Döbeln, Oct. 1, 1803; d. Leipzig, May 13, 1881. He studied at the Thomasschule in Leipzig; then became a member of the Gewandhaus managing board, and was instrumental in engaging Mendelssohn as conductor and director of the Leipzig Conservatorium; after Mendelssohn's death, he took over the administration of the school.

Schlesinger, Adolf Martin, German music publisher; b. Sülz, Silesia, Oct. 4, 1769; d. Berlin, Nov. 11, 1838. About 1795 he founded a music store in Berlin; it became known under the name of "Schlesinger'sche Buch- und Musikalienhandlung" in 1821. He was one of Beethoven's German publishers. The firm was carried on after his death by his son, **Heinrich Schlesinger,** who began publishing in 1851 the influential music periodical *Echo*. In 1864 the business was sold to R. Lienau (1838-1920), whose sons tooks it over after his death. The firm was further enlarged and enriched by the acquisition of several other music publishing firms, among them Haslinger of Vienna (1875), Krentzlin of Berlin (1919), Vernthal of Berlin (1925) and Köster of Berlin (1928). Schlesinger was the original publisher of *Der Freischütz* by Carl Maria von Weber, Beethoven's op. nos. 108–111, 132, 135; also works by Mendelssohn, Chopin, Liszt and Berlioz.

Schlesinger, Kathleen, British musicologist; b. Hollywood, near Belfast, Ireland, June 27, 1862; d. London, April 16, 1953. She was educated in Switzerland; then settled in England; became interested in musical instruments; publ. *The Instruments of the Modern Orchestra* (2 vols., London, 1910). Her chief work is *The Greek Aulos* (London, 1939), containing not only a description of ancient Greek instruments, but also propounding an original theory of the formation of Greek modes, which aroused much controversy; the weight of learned opinion inclined against her hypotheses.

Schlesinger, Maurice, music publisher; son of **Adolf Martin Schlesinger;** b. Berlin, Oct. 3, 1797; d. Baden-Baden, Feb. 25, 1871. He moved to Paris in 1819, and was at first engaged in book selling. In 1822 he established a music publishing business, and launched the publication of the *Gazette Musicale*, soon united with the *Revue Musicale* (continued publication until 1880). He became one of the most important Paris publishers; publ. full scores of operas by Meyerbeer, Donizetti, and others; also Berlioz's *Symphonie fantastique* and much of Chopin's music. In 1846 he sold the catalogue to Brandus and Dufour; later it was acquired by Joubert.

Schlesinger, Sebastian Benson, German composer; b. Hamburg, Sept. 24, 1837; d. Nice, Jan. 8, 1917. He went to the U.S. at the age of 13; studied music at Boston, chiefly under Otto Dresel; was for 17 years German Consul at Boston; then lived for a time in London, and during his last years in Paris. He was a gifted composer; published about 120 songs which received praise from Max Bruch and Robert Franz; wrote several piano pieces in a Romantic vein (*Novelette, Albumblatt, Impromptu-Caprice,* etc.).

Schletterer, Hans Michel, German conductor and writer on music; b. Ansbach, May 29, 1824; d. Augsburg, June 4, 1893. He studied with Spohr at Kassel and Ferdinand David in Leipzig. After filling a number of teaching posts in provincial towns, he taught at the Univ. of Heidelberg (1854-58); then was choral conductor and singing teacher in Augsburg, where he founded an oratorio society and a music school. He publ. 17 books of choral music a cappella; a selection of Lutheran church music, *Musica sacra* (2 vols., 1887; 3rd ed., 1927); *Das deutsche Singspiel* (1863); *J. Fr. Reichardt* (1865); *Geschichte der geistlichen Dichtung und kirchlichen Tonkunst* (1869); *Studien zur Geschichte der französischen Musik* (3 vols.; 1884-85; mostly borrowed from Castil-Blaze); etc.

Schlick, Arnolt, the elder, blind organist and lutenist; b. in Bohemia, c.1460; d. Heidelberg, c.1525. He was organist to the Count Palatine at Heidelberg from 1485; since he bore the title of Imperial organist, he may have also served at one time at the court of Friedrich III.
WORKS: *Spiegel der Orgelmacher und Organisten* (1511; reprinted by R. Eitner as a supplement to *Monatschefte für Musik-Geschichte,* 1869; by E. Flade, 1932; by P. Smets, 1937, and Flade again, 1951); *Tablaturen etlicher Lobgesang und Lidlein uff die Orgeln und Lauten* (1512; new ed. by G. Harms, 1924; reprints by R. Eitner in *Monatshefte für Musik-Geschichte,* 1869; A. G. Ritter, *Zur Geschichte des Orgelspiels* II/96, 1884; and Wm. Tappert, *Sang und Klang aus alter Zeit,* Berlin, 1906).
BIBLIOGRAPHY: R. Eitner, in *Monatschefte für Musik-Geschichte* XXI; F. Stein, *Zur Geschichte der Musik in Heidelberg* (containing index of *Spiegel der Orgelmacher;* 1912; 2nd ed., 1921); A. Pirro, "Orgues et organistes de Haguenau," *Revue de Musicologie* (1926); R. Kendall, "Notes on A. Schlick," *Acta Musicologica* (1939); A. Mendel "Pitch in the 16th and Early 17th Centuries," *Musical Quarterly* (Jan. 1948); H. H. Lenneberg, "The Critic Criticized: Sebastian Virdung and His Controversy with A. Schlick," *Journal of the American Musicological Society* (Spring 1957).

Schlieder, Frederick William, American organist and composer; b. Foreston, Ill., Jan. 22, 1873; d. New York, Jan. 13, 1953. He studied at Syracuse Univ. (M.M., 1895); later took organ lessons in Paris with Guilmant; returning to America in 1905, he was active as concert organist; from 1910 till 1923, was organist at the Collegiate Church of St. Nicholas, N.Y.; also taught harmony at the Philadelphia Cons. He publ. *Lyric Composition through Improvisation: First Year's Training in Formal Self-expression* (Boston, 1927); a sequel was publ. by the Schlieder Book Foundation, Decatur, Ill. (1946); he further publ. *Beyond the Tonal Horizon of Music,* a collection of aphorisms (Decatur, Ill., 1948).

Schloezer, Boris de, renowned Russian-French writer on music; b. Vitebsk, Dec. 8, 1881; d. Paris, Oct. 7, 1969. He studied music in Brussels and Paris; returning to Russia he devoted himself to a profound study of philosophy, esthetics and music theory. His sister, Tatiana Schloezer was the second wife of Scriabin, and Schoelzer became an intimate friend of Scriabin, who confided to him his theosophic and musical ideas. In 1920 he emigrated to France, where he continued his literary activities in the Russian émigré press and in French literary magazines. He published a monograph on Scriabin (vol. 1, Berlin, 1923, in Russian; vol. 2 was planned but not completed; vol. 1, covering Scriabin's ideology and commentary on his music, was published in a French translation, with an introduction by Scriabin's daughter Marina, Paris, 1975); other publications in French: *Igor Stravinsky* (Paris, 1929); *Introduction à J. S. Bach* (Paris, 1947; in Spanish, Buenos Aires, 1961; in German under the title *Entwurf einer Musikasthetik,* Hamburg, 1964). Schoelzer also wrote a philosophical fantasy, *Mon nom est personne (My Name Is Nobody)* and *Rapport secret,* depicting a distant planet whose inhabitants achieved immortality and divinity through science.

Schlögel, Xavier, Belgian composer; b. Brillonville, Famène, July 14, 1854; d. Ciney, near Namur, March 23, 1889. He studied with Ledent at the Liège Cons. He composed *Scènes champêtres* for orch.; *Ballade des épées* for voice and orch.; *Messe solennelle* for male chorus, organ, and orch.; string quartets and piano trios.

Schlösser, (Karl Wilhelm) Adolf, German pianist, son and pupil of **Louis Schlösser;** b. Darmstadt, Feb. 1, 1830; d. Great Bookham, England, Nov. 10, 1913. He made his debut at Frankfurt in 1847; after concert tours in Germany, France, and England, he settled in London (1854); taught (until 1903) at the Royal Academy of Music. He composed piano quartet; piano trio; 24 studies and many other pieces for piano.

Schlösser, Louis, German composer; b. Darmstadt, Nov. 17, 1800; d. there, Nov. 17, 1886. He was pupil of Rinck at Darmstadt; Seyfried, Mayseder, and Salieri at Vienna, and Le Sueur and Kreutzer at the Paris Cons.; was court conductor in Darmstadt.
WORKS: about 70 opus numbers publ.: the operas *Granada* (Vienna, 1826), *Das Leben ein Traum* (1839), *Die Jugend Karls II. von Spanien* (1847), *Die Braut des Herzogs* (1847), and *Benvenuto Cellini;* an operetta, *Kapitän Hector;* the melodrama *Die Jahreszeiten;* music to *Faust;* ballets, entr'actes, symphonies, overtures, string quartets, concertino for horn with orch., piano pieces, songs, etc.

Schlottmann, Louis, German pianist and composer; b. Berlin, Nov. 12, 1826; d. there, June 13, 1905. He studied with Taubert and Dehn; gave successful concerts in London and elsewhere and settled in Berlin as a teacher.

WORKS: overtures to *Romeo and Juliet* and *Wallensteins Lager; Trauermarsch, Rezitativ und Finale,* symph. scene for orch.; *Concerstück* for piano; chamber music; piano pieces *(3 Capricettes; Polonaise de concert; Andantino; Jugendspiegel);* choruses and songs.

Schlusnus, Heinrich, German baritone; b. Braubach, Aug. 6, 1888; d. Frankfurt, June 18, 1952. He studied with Louis Bachner in Berlin; was a member of the Nuremberg Opera (1915–17); on the roster of the Berlin State Opera (from 1917); made appearances with the leading opera companies of Europe; also with the Chicago Opera Co.; toured the U.S. as concert singer.

Schmedes, Erik, Danish tenor; b. Gentofte, near Copenhagen, Aug. 27, 1868; d. Vienna, March 21, 1931. He studied piano, then turned to singing; studied with Mme. Artôt in Paris; made his operatic debut as baritone in Wiesbaden (Jan. 11, 1891), as the Herald in *Lohengrin;* then sang baritone roles in Nuremberg and Dresden (1894–97). After a course of study with A. Iffert in Dresden, he developed a definite tenor voice, and appeared as Siegfried at the Vienna Opera (Feb. 11, 1898); remained as a tenor with the Vienna Opera until 1824. He was a member of the Metropolitan Opera Co. during the season of 1908–09; made his debut as Siegmund (Nov. 18, 1908).

Schmelzer, Johann Heinrich, Austrian composer; b. Scheibbs, c.1623; d. Prague, 1680. In 1649–70, violinist at the Vienna court chapel; 1671 assistant conductor; 1679; first conductor. He may have been the teacher of the famous violinist, Henrich Biber. Composed valuable chamber music, including *Duodena selectarum sonatarum* (12 trio sonatas, 1659; repr. in *Denkmäler der Tonkunst in Österreich* 105); *Sacro-profanus concentus musicus* (sonatas, for 2–8 instruments, 1662; repr. ibid, vols. 111/112); *Sonate unarum fidium* (6 solo violin sonatas, 1664; repr. ibid, vol. 93; also one reprinted in the supplement to G. Beckermann's *Das Violinspiel in Deutschland vor 1700*); also the trumpet fanfares to Bertali's Festspiel, *La Contesa dell'aria* (1667), publ. as *Arie per il balletto a cavallo* (ed. by P. Nettl in *Denkmäler der Tonkunst in Österreich* 56 [28.ii]) and a *Missa nuptialis* (ed. by G. Adler in *Denkmäler der Tonkunst in Österreich* 49). Other MSS of vocal and instrumental works by Schmelzer are in Vienna, Kromeriz, Paris, and Uppsala.

BIBLIOGRAPHY: E. Wellesz, *Die Ballett-Suiten von J. H. und A. A. Schmelzer* (Vienna, 1914); A. Moser, *Geschichte des Violinspiels* (p. 126ff.); P. Nettl, in *Studien zur Musikwissenschaft* VIII.

Schmelzl (Schmeltzl, Schmaelzl), Wolfgang, Austrian musician; b. Kennath, c.1500; d. St. Lorenz at Steinfeld, c.1561. He was a Protestant cantor at Amberg; then, c.1540, a teacher in Vienna and singer at the S. Salvator Chapel, and finally a Catholic priest at St. Lorenz at Steinfeld, near Vienna, where he died. He is known for a collection of 4–5 voiced quodlibets and folksongs of the period, published in 1544. Re-

print by Schering in *Geschichte der Musik in Beispielen* (no. 111).

BIBLIOGRAPHY: Elsa Bienenfeld, "W.S., sein Liederbuch (1544) und das Quodlibet des XVI. Jahrhunderts," *Sammelbände der Internationalen Musik-Gesellschaft* VI/1 (1904); R. Eitner, in *Monatschefte für Musik-Geschichte* III.

Schmid, Adolf, Austrian conductor and arranger; b. Hannsdorf, Nov. 18, 1868; d. Englewood, New Jersey, Feb. 12, 1958. He studied at the Vienna Cons.; went to London in 1901 where he became music director of His Majesty's Theatre; in 1915 he emigrated to the U.S.; conducted ballet performances, including the Pavlova Ballet Russe (1916–18); then became arranger for radio and schools; also wrote some picturesque music for orch., such as *Caravan Dance, A Bacchanal Dance,* etc. He published *The Language of the Baton* (N.Y., 1937).

Schmid, Anton, Austrian writer on music; b. Pihl, near Leipa, Bohemia, Jan. 30, 1787; d. Baden, near Vienna, July 3, 1857. After serving as a choirboy he went to Vienna, where he was employed as librarian and custodian at the Vienna Library (1819–44). He published the valuable monographs *Ottaviano dei Petrucci da Fossombrone, der erste Erfinder des Musiknotendruckes mit beweglichen Metalltypen, und seine Nachfolger in 16. Jahrhundert* (1845); *J. Haydn und N. Zingarelli* (1847; to prove that Haydn composed *Gott erhalte Franz den Kaiser*); *Christoph Willibald, Ritter von Gluck* (1854); and "Beiträge zur Literatur und Geschichte der Tonkunst" (in Dehn's *Cäcilla,* 1842–46).

Schmid, Ernst Fritz (Friedrich), eminent German musicologist; b. Tübingen, March 7, 1904; d. Augsburg, Jan. 20, 1960. He studied natural science in Göttingen, music at the Munich Academy with Courvoisier (composition) and Sandberger (musicology), and in Vienna (under Lach and Robert Haas); Dr. phil. (Tübingen, 1929). In 1934 he went to Graz, where he organized a seminar in musicology; then was prof. at the Univ. of Tübingen (1935–37). During World War II he served in the German Army; in 1948 he settled in Augsburg.

WRITINGS: *C. Ph. E. Bach und seine Kammermusik* (Kassel, 1931); *Joseph Haydn: ein Buch von Heimat und Vorfahren* (Kassel, 1934); *W. A. Mozart* (Lübeck, 1934); ed. of *Ein schwäbisches Mozartbuch* (Stuttgart, 1947). A memorial volume, containing a complete list of publications, was brought out anonymously in 1961.

Schmid, Heinrich Kaspar, German composer; b. Landau, Sept. 11, 1874; d. Munich, Jan. 8, 1953. He studied with Thuille and Bussmeyer at the Munich Academy; in 1903 he went to Athens where he taught music at the Odeon; in 1905 returned to Munich and was on the faculty at the Munich Academy until 1921; then was director of the Karlsruhe Cons. (1921–24) and of the Augsburg Cons. (1924–32). His eyesight failed him and he was totally blind during the last years of his life. As a composer he followed the Romantic tradition of the Bavarian School; he wrote a great number of lieder, and composed Singspiele in a folklike manner, as well as choruses and chamber music.

BIBLIOGRAPHY: H. Roth, *H. K. Schmid* (Munich, 1921); W. Zentner, "H. K. Schmid," *Neue Musikzeitschrift* (Aug.-Sept. 1949).

Schmid, Otto, German music editor and critic; b. Dresden, May 6, 1858; d. there, Sept. 12, 1931. He studied music privately with Kretschmer in Dresden; taught music history at the Dresden Cons. (1912–24) and wrote music criticism. Among his publications are monographs on Koschat (1887) and Kretschmer (1890); published a valuable history of music in Dresden: *Die Heimstätten der Sächsischen Landestheater* (Dresden, 1919); *Richard Wagners Opern und Musikdramen in Dresden* (Dresden, 1919); *Der Mozart-Verein zu Dresden* (Dresden, 1921); etc.; he edited the important collections *Musik am sächsischen Hofe* (10 vols.; compositions by Hasse, J. C. Schmidt, J. A. and C. S. Binder, Naumann, Petzold, ect., and members of the royal house); *Orgelwerke altböhmischer Meister* (2 vols.).

Schmidl, Carlo, Italian music publisher and lexicographer; b. Trieste, Oct. 7, 1859; d. there, Oct. 7, 1943. He was the son and pupil of the Hungarian composer **Antonio Schmidl** (1814–80). In 1872 he entered the employ of the music publisher Vicentini, and in 1889 he established his own business at Trieste; also directed the Leipzig branch of the Ricordi Co. (1901–06). He compiled and publ. an important biographical music dictionary, *Dizionario universale dei musicisti* (Milan, 1887–89; 2nd ed., 1926–29; supplement, 1938), containing scrupulously accurate data on Italian musicians, exact dates of performance of major works, and other information testifying to independent research. Schmidl also wrote biographies of Schumann (1890) and G. S. Mayr (1901).

Schmidt, Arthur Paul, German-American music publisher; b. Altona, Germany, April 1, 1846; d. Boston, May 5, 1921. He settled in Boston in 1866, and entered the music firm of George D. Russell & Co. In 1876 he established a business of his own; for some years maintained branches in New York and Leipzig. Henry R. Austin became president of the firm in 1949. The A. P. Schmidt Co. won prominence by publication of the works of MacDowell; brought out virtually the complete output of Arthur Foote (more than 150 items); also works by Chadwick, Hadley, Paine, Mrs. Beach, and other composers of the "New England School."

Schmidt, Franz, important Austrian composer; b. Pressburg, Dec. 22, 1874; d. Perchtoldsdorf, near Vienna, Feb. 11, 1939. He studied organ, piano, and cello at the Vienna Cons.; a pupil of Anton Bruckner (composition) and Robert Fuchs (theory); also took piano lessons with Leschetizky. From 1896 to 1911 he played cello in the Vienna Philharmonic Orch.; also taught at the Cons. (both cello and piano). From 1925 till 1927 he was director of the Vienna Academy of Music, and from 1927 to 1931, rector of the Hochschule für Musik; retired in 1937. While engaged in pedagogical activites he continued to compose; his

music is steeped in Viennese Romanticism, and the influence of Bruckner is particularly pronounced. Although he is regarded in Austria as a very important symphonic composer, his music is almost totally unknown elsewhere.

WORKS: operas, *Notre Dame* (Vienna, April 1, 1914; an orchestral suite from it entitled *Zwischenspiel aus einer unvollständigen romantischen Oper* was performed by the Vienna Philharmonic, Dec. 6, 1903); *Fredigundis* (Berlin, Dec. 19, 1922); oratorio, *Das Buch mit sieben Siegeln* (Vienna, June 15, 1938); 4 symphonies: No. 1 (Vienna, Jan. 25, 1902); No. 2 (Vienna, Dec. 3, 1913); No. 3 (Vienna, Dec. 2, 1928); No. 4 (Vienna, Jan. 10, 1934); *Konzertante Variationen über ein Thema von Beethoven* (Piano Concerto No. 1), for piano, left hand alone, and orch. (Vienna, Feb. 2, 1924, Paul Wittgenstein soloist); Piano Concerto No. 2, left hand alone (Vienna, Feb. 10, 1935, Wittgenstein soloist); *Chaconne,* for orch. (Vienna, Jan. 29, 1933); 2 string quartets; Piano Quintet; 2 clarinet quintets; several works for organ.

BIBLIOGRAPHY: Andreas Liess, *Franz Schmidt. Leben und Schaffen* (Graz, 1951); Carl Nemeth, *Franz Schmidt. Ein Meister nach Brahms und Bruckner* (Vienna, 1957).

Schmidt, Gustav, German conductor and composer; b. Weimar, Sept. 1, 1816; d. Darmstadt, Feb. 11, 1882. While theater conductor at Frankfurt he produced his operas *Prinz Eugen* (1845) and *Die Weiber von Weinsberg* (1858); other operas were *La Réole* (Breslau, 1863) and *Alibi.* He also wrote songs, ballads, and popular male choruses.

Schmidt, Heinrich, German music editor; b. Kirchenlamitz, near Bayreuth, April 30, 1861; d. Bayreuth, May 23, 1923. Pupil of Rheinberger, Kellermann, and Riehl at the Königliche Akademie der Tonkunst in Munich; Dr. phil. (Univ. of Munich, 1897) with the dissertation *Joh. Mattheson, ein Förderer der deutschen Tonkunst, im Lichte seiner Werke* (Leipzig, 1897); from 1898 teacher at the seminary in Bayreuth. He ed. *Streichorchester für Mittelschulen* (8 vols.; selections of classical pieces), *Der Männerchor auf natürlicher Grundlage* (1913), *Der Chorgesang für Mittelschulen* (1918), and a new ed. of Hohmann's *Violinschule.* Publ. *Die Orgel unserer Zeit in Wort und Bild* (1904; 2nd ed., 1922) and *Richard Wagner in Bayreuth* (1909; with U. Hartmann).

Schmidt, Johann Philipp Samuel, German composer; b. Königsberg, Sept. 8, 1779; d. Berlin, May 9, 1853. He wrote operas for Königsberg and Berlin; many cantatas; 9 oratorios and Masses; symphonies; quintets and quartets for strings, etc.; also contributed to musical periodicals of Berlin and Leipzig.

Schmidt, John Henry, German organist, composer, and singing teacher; lived in Radevormwald, near Düsseldorf until Dec., 1783, when he arrived in Gouda, Holland; was appointed organist of the Cathedral of St. John at Schiedam on Oct. 23, 1785; held this office until 1790, when he sailed for Rio de Berbice, British Guiana. In 1796 he arrived in New York; in June, 1796 he appeared in Charleston and advertised as a singing teacher and piano manufacturer; towards the end of 1796 he settled in Philadelphia, where he became orgaenst of St. Peter's Church (1797); also announced concerts in Baltimore (1796) and Albany (1797). He composed a *Sonata for Beginners.*

BIBLIOGRAPHY: O. G. Sonneck, *Bibliography of Early Secular American Music* (Washington, 1905); O. G. Sonneck, *Early Concert Life in America* (Leipzig, 1907; in English).

Schmidt, Joseph, Rumanian tenor; b. Bavideni, Bukovina, March 4, 1904; d. Zürich, Nov. 16, 1942. He studied at the Berlin Cons.; in 1928 began his career as a radio singer and won great popularity in Germany. In 1933 he went to Belgium; in 1938 was briefly in America; then settled in Switzerland. His voice was regarded as of great lyric expressiveness, but being almost a dwarf (he stood only 4 feet 10 inches in height), he was unable to appear in opera.

Schmidt, Karl, German music scholar; b. Friedberg (Hesse), July 10, 1869; d. there, Feb. 28, 1948. He studied in Leipzig; was active in school music in Laubach and Friedberg; publ. the valuable paper, *Quaestiones de musicis scriptoribus romanis imprimis Cassiodoro et Isidoro* (Leipzig, 1898).

Schmidt, Leopold, German writer on music; b. Berlin, Aug. 2, 1860; d. there, April 30, 1927. He studied philosophy at the Univ. of Berlin, and at the same time attended musical courses at the Royal Hochschule. He subsequently held numerous positions as a theater conductor in Berlin and in the provinces; then taught at the Klindworth-Scharwenka Cons. in Berlin and wrote music criticism for the *Berliner Tageblatt.* He published a number of competently written monographs on Meyerbeer (1898), Haydn (1898; 3rd ed., 1914), Mozart (1909), Beethoven (1914); also wrote several analytic guides for classical and modern operas; edited *Beethovenbriefe* in 2 vols. (1909, 1922) and *Brahms Briefwechsel* (1910). His collected criticism were published in 3 vols. (1909, 1913, 1922).

Schmidt, Ole, Danish conductor and composer; b. Copenhagen, July 14, 1928. He attended the Royal Danish Cons.; had conducting lessons from Rafael Kubelik and Sergui Celibidache. He made his conducting debut at the Copenhagen Academy of Music in 1955; was conductor of the Royal Opera in Copenhagen (1958–65) and Hamburg Symph. Orch. (1970–71); in 1971 was appointed conductor of the Danish Radio Symphony. In 1975 he received the Carl Nielsen Prize. His music follows the vigor and the lyrical sentiment of Scandinavian Romanticism, while sustaining the Classical symmetry of form.

WORKS: opera: *Edstillingen (The Exhibition;* Copenhagen, Dec. 5, 1969); a ballet, *Fever* (Copenhagen, Oct. 18, 1957); Symph. No. 1 (1955); *Chamber Concerto* for piano and strings (1955); *Pièce concertante* for trumpet, trombone, harp, piano, celesta, percussion and strings (1956); *Chamber Symphony* for wind quintet and strings (1958); *Symphonic Fantasy and Fugue* for accordion and chamber orch. (1959); *Pastel* for chamber orch. (1961); *Briol,* symph. sketch (1962); Concerto No. 2 for accordion, wind orch. and percus-

sion (1963–64); Horn Concerto (Copenhagen, Sept. 8, 1966); Violin Concerto (Dortmund, May 19, 1971); Tuba Concerto (1973); *Divertimento* for violin, viola, cello and piano (1957); 4 string quartets (1962–69); *Improvisation* for piano, double bass and drums (1961); *Painting and Plugging* for harp, strings and piano (1963).

Schmidt, William, American composer; b. Chicago, March 6, 1926. He moved to Los Angeles in 1952 and studied composition with Halsey Stevens and Ingolf Dahl at the Univ. of Southern California; at the same time was active as jazz arranger. He composed a *Concerto Breve for Brass and Band* (1957); pieces for orch. and numerous works for various chamber ensembles; 6 bassoon duets (1957); *Serenade* for tuba and piano (1958); *Rondino* for trombone and piano (1959); Viola Sonata (1959); Woodwind Quintet (1959); *Percussive Rondo* for percussion quartet (1957); etc.

Schmidt-Görg, Joseph, German musicicologist; b. Rüdinghausen, near Dortmund, March 13, 1897. He studied musicology with Schiedermair in Bonn; Dr. phil., 1926 at the Univ. of Bonn; in 1927, on the centennial of Beethoven's death, he became Schiedermair's assistant in the Beethoven Archives; then became director of the Archives (1945–72); taught musicology at the Univ. of Bonn (1930–65). On his 70th birthday in 1967 a Festschrift was published in his honor, *Colloquium amicorum* (Bonn, 1967; contains a catalogue of his writings). He published numerous books connected with Beethoveniana: *Unbekannte Manuskripte zu Beethovens weltlicher und geistlicher Gesangsmusik* (Bonn, 1928); *Katalog der Handschriften des Beethoven-Hauses und Beethoven-Archivs* (Bonn, 1935); *Ludwig van Beethoven* (with H. Schmidt; Bonn, 1969; in English, London, 1970; in Italian, Rome, 1970). He also published *History of the Mass* (in English, N.Y., 1968, and a compendious monograph, *Nicolas Gombert: Leben und Werk* (Tutzing, 1971).

Schmidt-Isserstedt, Hans, German conductor; b. Berlin, May 5, 1900; d. Hamburg, May 28, 1973. He studied composition with Franz Schreker; then devoted himself mainly to conducting. After a series of appointments as opera conductor in Germany he was engaged at the Hamburg State Opera in 1935; was conductor of the Staatsoper in Berlin in 1943; conducted at Glyndebourne in 1958, and in London, at Covent Garden, in 1962. In 1963 he made his American debut as symphonic conductor.

Schmieder, Wolfgang, German musicologist; b. Bromberg, May 29, 1901. He studied at the Univ. of Heidelberg, graduating in 1927; then served as assistant in a musicological seminar there (1927–30); subsequently occupied various positions as music librarian; served as archivist for Breitkof & Härtel in Leipzig; in 1946 he founded the music dept. of the university library in Frankfurt, and continued to direct it until 1963; then lived mainly in Freiburg im Breisgau. He was presented a Festschrift on his 70th anniversary in 1971, *Quellenstudien zur Musik,* edited by K. Dorf-müller and G. von Dadelsen. Among his numerous publications are *Thematisch-systematisches Verzeichnis der musikalischen Werke von J. S. Bach* (Wiesbaden, 1950; of fundamental importance; 6th edition 1969); *Musikalische alte Drücke bis etwa 1750* (with G. Hartwieg; 2 vols., Wolfenbüttel, 1967).

Schminke, Oscar Eberhard, American organist and composer; b. New York, Dec. 12, 1881; d. Liberty, N.Y., Feb. 22, 1969. He suffered from partial deafness since childhood, and after taking piano lessons decided to change his profession; entered the N.Y. College of Dentistry, graduating in 1903; however, he continued to study music; took organ lessons with Gaston Déthier in N.Y. He published several works for organ (*Marche russe, Poème exotique,* etc.); piano pieces (*Chameleon, Moods,* etc.); about a dozen songs.

Schmitt, Aloys, German pianist and composer; b. Erlenbach, Aug. 26, 1788; d. Frankfurt, July 25, 1866. He studied composition with André at Offenbach; in 1816 went to Frankfurt where he remained all his life. He composed 4 operas, *Der Doppelgänger* (Hannover, 1827), *Valeria* (Mannheim, 1832), *Das Osterfest zu Paderborn* (Frankfurt, 1843), and *Die Tochter der Wüste* (Frankfurt, 1845); 2 oratorios, *Moses* and *Ruth;* church music; etc. But he is principally known and appreciated for his numerous piano compositions, including 4 piano concertos, several piano quartets, piano trios, a number of attractive character pieces for piano, and studies for school.
BIBLIOGRAPHY: H. Henkel, *Leben und Wirken von Dr. Aloys Schmitt* (Frankfurt, 1873).

Schmitt, Camille, Belgian composer; b. Aubange, March 30, 1908; d. Limelette, May 11, 1976. He studied at the Brussels Cons. (1928–37); was an organist in France and Belgium (1923–48), prof. at the Liège Cons. (1947–66) and director of the French Section of the Brussels Cons. (1966–73). His wife was the composer **Jacqueline Fontyn.**
WORKS: *Triptyque angevin* for orch. (1941); *Psaume* for orch. (1942); Sinfonietta (1943); *Rapsodie* for orch. (1944); *Préludes joyeux* for orch. (1945; International Society for Contemporary Music Festival, Copenhagen, June 2, 1946); Piano Concerto (1955); *Métamorphoses* for orch. (1963); *Contrepoints* for orch. (1965); *Polyphonies* for orch. (1966); *Alternances* for orch. (1970); Wind Quintet (1943); Trio for oboe, clarinet and bassoon (1945); String Quartet (1948); *Prélude* for clarinet and piano (1952); *Dialogue* for violin and piano (1953); *Métamorphoses* for cello and piano (1961); Quartet for 4 clarinets (1964); *Burlesques* for flute, oboe, clarinet and bassoon (1965); *Contrepoints* for wind quintet (1965); *Polyphonies* for wind quintet (1969); *Polyphonies* for saxophone quartet (1970); *Psautier* for alto, piano, oboe, clarinet and bassoon (1946); *La Halte des Heures,* cantata for solo voice and piano (1959); *Polyphonies* for piano (1966); *Histoire pour Pierre* for piano (1970); chourses.

Schmitt, Florent, outstanding French composer; b. Blâmont, Sept. 28, 1870; d. Neuilly, near Paris, Aug. 17, 1958. He had his first music lessons from H. Hess

(piano) and G. Sandré (harmony) in Nancy. In 1889 he went to Paris, where he studied with Dubois and Lavignac (harmony), Massenet and Fauré (composition). He won the 2nd Prix de Rome in 1897 with the cantata *Frédégonde* and the 1st prize in 1900 with the cantata *Sémiramis,* which was performed at a Colonne concert on Dec. 11, 1900. He spent the years 1901–04 in the Villa Medicis in Rome, sending to the Académie several important instrumental and choral works; then spent 2 years traveling in Germany, Austria, Hungary, and Turkey. In 1906 he settled permanently in Paris, devoting himself entirely to composition. He served as a member of the executive committee of the Société Musicale Indépendante since its foundation in 1909; was also a member of the Société Nationale de Musique. His formative years were spent in the ambience of French symbolism in poetry and Impressionism in music, and he followed these directions in his programmatically conceived orchestral music; but he developed a strong, distinctive style of his own, mainly by elaborating the contrapuntal fabric of his works and extending the rhythmic design to intricate asymmetrical combinations; he also exploited effects of primitivistic percussion, in many respects anticipating the developments of modern Russian music. The catalogue of his works is very long; he continued to compose until his death at the age of 87; attended the première of his Symphony, given at the Strasbourg Festival of the International Society for Contemporary Music, June 15, 1958. He visited the U.S. in 1932 as soloist in his *Symphonie concertante* with the Boston Symph. He was an influential music critic, writing regularly for *Le Temps* (1919–39).
WORKS: BALLETS: *La Tragédie de Salomé* (Paris, Nov. 9, 1907); *Le Petit Elfe Ferme-l'œil,* after Hans Christian Andersen (Opéra-Comique, Feb. 29, 1924); *Oriane la sans-égale* (Paris Opéra, Jan. 7, 1938); incidental music to *Antoine et Cléopâtre,* after Shakespeare (Paris Opéra, June 14, 1920); *Reflets* (Opéra-Comique, May 20, 1932). VOCAL MUSIC WITH ORCH.: *Musique sur l'eau* (1898); *Psaume XLVII,* for soprano, chorus, orch., and organ (1904; Paris, Dec. 27, 1906); *Danse des Devadasis,* for solo voice, chorus, and orch. (1900–08); *Tristesse au Jardin* (1897–1908); *Chant de Guerre,* for tenor, male chorus, and orch. (1914); *Kerob-Shal,* for tenor and orch. (1920–24); *Fête de la lumière,* for soprano, chorus, and orch. (1937); *L'Arbre entre tous,* for chorus and orch. (1939); *À contre-voix,* for mixed chorus (1943); motets and choruses a cappella. FOR ORCH.: *En été* (1894); *Feuillets de voyage* (1903–13); *Reflets de l'Allemagne,* suite of waltzes (1905); *Puppazzi,* suite in 8 movements (1907); *Musiques de plein-air* (1897–99); *Sélamlik,* symph. poem for military band (1906); *Le Palais hanté,* symph. study after Poe (1900–04); *Trois Rapsodies* (1903–04); *Scherzo vif,* for violin and orch. (1903–10); *La Tragédie de Salomé,* from the ballet of the same title (Paris, Jan. 8, 1911); *Légende,* for viola (or saxophone) and orch. (1918); *Mirages: Tristesse de Pan, La tragique Chevauchée* (1921); *Fonctionnaire MCMXII: Inaction en Musique* (1924; Paris, Jan. 16, 1927); *Danse d'Abisag* (1925); *Salammbô,* 6 symph. episodes after Flaubert, from film music (1925); *Ronde burlesque* (1927; Paris, Jan. 12, 1930); *Çançunik* (humorous phonetic spelling of *Sens unique,* i.e., one-way street;

Paris, Feb. 15, 1930); *Symphonie Concertante,* for piano and orch. (Boston, Schmitt soloist, Nov. 25, 1932); *Suite sans esprit de suite* (Paris, Jan. 29, 1938); *Branle de sortie* (Paris, Jan. 21, 1939); *Janiana,* for strings (1941); *Habeyssée,* for violin and orch. (phonetic representation of ABC, as pronounced in French; Paris, March 14, 1947); Symphony (1957; Strasbourg, June 15, 1958). CHAMBER MUSIC: *Scherzo-pastorale,* for flute and piano (1889); *Quatre pièces,* for violin and piano (1901); *Andante et Scherzo,* for harp and string quartet (1906); Piano Quintet (1901–08); *Lied et Scherzo,* for double wind quintet (1910); *Sonate libre en deux parties enchaînées,* for violin and piano (1919); *Suite en rocaille,* for flute, violin, viola, cello, and harp (1934); *Sonatine en trio,* for flute, clarinet, and harpsichord (1935); *Minorités,* for flute, violin, and piano (1938); *Hasards,* for violin, viola, cello, and piano (1939); *À tours d'anches,* for flute, clarinet, bassoon, and piano (1939); Quartet for saxophones (1941); String Trio (1944); Quartet for flutes (1944); String Quartet (1945–48). FOR PIANO: *Soirs* (10 preludes); *Ballade de la neige* (1896); *Musiques intimes* (2 sets; 1890–1900 and 1898–1904); *Nuits romaines* (1901); *Puppazzi,* 8 pieces (1907; also for orch.); *Pièces romantiques* (6 pieces; 1900–08); *Trois Danses* (1935; also for orch.); *Feuillets de voyage* (1903; also for orch.); *Suite sans esprit de suite* (1938; also for orch.); *Clavecin obtempérant,* suite (1945); etc. *Reflets de l'Allemagne,* 8 waltzes for piano, 4 hands (1905; also for orch.). SONGS: *Soir sur le lac* (1898); *Quatre lieds,* to words by Richepin, Maeterlinck, etc.; *Kerob-Shal,* 3 songs (also voice and orch.).

BIBLIOGRAPHY: M. D. Calvocoressi, "Œuvres de Florent Schmitt," *L'Art Moderne* (Jan. 6, 1907); O. Séré, *Musiciens français d'aujourd'hui* (rev. ed., Paris, 1921); G. Jean-Aubry, *La Musique française d'aujourd'hui* (Paris, 1916); A. Cœuroy, *La Musique française moderne* (Paris, 1922); P. O. Ferroud, *Autour de Florent Schmitt* (Paris, 1927); Eric Blom, "Florent Schmitt," *Chesterian* (March 1932); Yves Hucher, *Florent Schmitt, l'homme et l'artiste* (Paris, 1953).

Schmitt, Georg Aloys, German pianist, conductor and composer; son and pupil of **Aloys Schmitt;** b. Hannover, Feb. 2, 1827; d. (suddenly, during a rehearsal) Dresden, Oct. 15, 1902. He studied theory of music with Vollweiler in Heidelberg; then went on a European tour as a pianist; subsequently devoted himself mainly to theatrical conducting; he was court conductor at Schwerin (1857–92); in 1893 was appointed director of the Mozartverein in Dresden, which had a multitudinous choral ensemble (some 1,400 members) and its own orch. Schmitt wrote the opera *Trilby;* several concert overtures; much chamber music, and piano pieces. He orchestrated keyboard works of Handel and Mozart.

Schmitt, Hans, piano teacher; b. Koben, Bohemia, Jan. 14, 1835; d. Vienna, Jan. 14, 1907. At first an oboist at Bucharest and Vienna, throat trouble compelled him to give up that instrument, and he studied the piano under Dachs at the Vienna Cons., 1860–62, taking the silver medal, and being appointed teacher at the Cons. His instructive works for piano include *300*

Studies without Octave-stretches; Vademecum; Fundament der Klaviertechnik; Zirkelübungen in Skalen und Akkorden; 120 kleine Vortragsstücke; Repertoirestudien; Das Pedal des Klaviers (1875, after Louis Köhler; in English, 1893).

Schmitt, Jacob (Jacques), German pianist, brother and pupil of **Aloys Schmitt;** b. Obernburg, Bavaria, Nov. 2, 1803; d. Hamburg, May 24, 1853. He was a reputable piano teacher, and composed about 370 piano pieces; among his works are sonatinas for 2 and 4 hands, and numerous studies, rondos and nocturnes; especially useful is his *Musikalisches Schatzkästlein,* a collection of 133 short piano pieces.

Schmitz, Arnold, German musicologist; b. Sablon, near Metz, July 11, 1893. He studied with Schiedermair in Bonn; then took courses in Munich and Berlin with Kaun and Beer-Walbrunn; was on the faculty of the Univ. of Bonn (1921–28), of Breslau (1929–39); during World War II he was in the German Army; from 1947 to 1961 was prof. at the Univ. of Mainz; in 1965–67 he occupied the chair of musicology at the Univ. of Basel, Switzerland. He published the following: *Beethovens "zwei Prinzipe"* (Berlin, 1923), *Das romantische Beethovenbild* (Berlin, 1927), *Die Bildlichkeit der wortgebundenen Musik J. S. Bachs* (Mainz, 1950).

Schmitz, Elie Robert, eminent French pianist; b. Paris, Feb. 8, 1889; d. San Francisco, Sept. 5, 1949. He studied at the Paris Cons. with Diémer, winning 1st prize in piano; in 1908 toured as accompanist of Slezak, Emma Eames, and other celebrated singers; in 1912, organized the Association des Concerts Schmitz in Paris, which he led until 1914; in 1919 toured the U.S. as pianist; in 1920 founded the Franco-American Music Society in N.Y. (incorporated in 1923 as Pro Musica), of which he was president from its inception; toured again in the U.S. and Europe (1921–29), and the Orient (1929–30 and 1932–33); eventually settled in San Francisco as a teacher. He publ. a book on his system of piano study, *The Capture of Inspiration* (N.Y., 1935; 2nd ed., 1944) and a valuable technical analysis with commentary, *The Piano Works of Claude Debussy* (N.Y., 1950).

Schmitz, Eugen, German musicologist; b. Neuburg, Bavaria, July 12, 1882; d. Leipzig, July 10, 1959. He studied musicology with Sandberger and Kroyer at the Univ. of Munich; obtained his Dr. phil. in 1905 with the dissertation *Leben und Wirken des Nürnberger Komponisten Johann Staden* (published 1906). He wrote music criticism in Dresden; taught music at the Dresden Technische Hochschule. From 1939 to 1953 he was director of the Musikbibliothek Peters in Leipzig. Among his publications are *Hugo Wolf* (Leipzig, 1906); *Richard Strauss als Musikdramatiker* (Munich, 1907); *Richard Wagner* (Leipzig, 1909; 2nd ed., 1918); *Harmonielehre als Theorie* (Munich, 1911); *Geschichte der Kantate und des geistlichen Konzerts* (Leipzig, 1914; 2nd ed., 1955); *Palestrina* (Leipzig, 1914; 2nd ed., 1954); *Musikästhetik* (Leipzig, 1915; 2nd ed., 1925); *Orlando di Lasso* (Leipzig, 1915; 2nd ed., 1954); *Klavier, Klaviermusik und Klavierspiel*

(Leipzig, 1919); *Richard Wagner: wie wir ihn heute sehen* (Dresden, 1937); he was an editor for the *Denkmäler der Tonkunst in Bayern* 12 and 14 (7.i and 8.i).

Schmuller, Alexander, violinist; b. Mozyr, Russia, Dec. 5, 1880; d. Amsterdam, March 29, 1933. Pupil of Ševčik, Hřimaly, and Auer; from 1908 he taught at the Stern Cons. in Berlin, and from 1914 at the Amsterdam Cons. For several years he gave concerts with Max Reger, whose music he was one of the first to champion; made many concert tours in Europe and the U.S.

Schnabel, Artur, celebrated Austrian pianist and pedagogue; b. Lipnik, April 17, 1882; d. Morschach, Canton Schwyz, Switzerland, Aug. 15, 1951. After taking lessons for two years from Hans Schmitt, he studied in Vienna with Leschetizky (1891–97); appeared in public as a child prodigy; lived many years in Berlin, where he gave joint recitals with the violinist Carl Flesch; formed (1912) a trio with A. Wittenberg (violin) and A. Hekking (cello); from 1925 until 1933 he taught at the Hochschule für Musik in Berlin; after the advent of the Nazi regime he went to Switzerland, where he organized his famous master classes during summer seasons. He made his American debut in 1921, and revisited the U.S. several times; lived in N.Y. after 1939, but eventually returned to Europe. It was as an interpreter of Beethoven that he reached his greatest heights; he was distinguished also in his performances of the piano music of Brahms. His pedagogical method was strict in the observance of every detail of the music, but at the same time he inspired his pupils by encouraging an individual treatment in the matter of dynamics and formal concept. Schnabel was also a composer; in his works he pursued an uncompromisingly modernistic idiom, thriving on dissonance, and tracing melodic patterns along atonal lines. WORKS: Symph. No. 1 (1938–40; Minneapolis, Dec. 13, 1946); *Rhapsody* for orch. (Cleveland, April 15, 1948); Piano Concerto; chamber music. He publ. *Reflections on Music* (Manchester, 1933; N.Y., 1934) and *Music and the Line of Most Resistance* (Princeton, 1942); *My Life and Music* (London, 1961); edited the piano sonatas of Beethoven.
BIBLIOGRAPHY: César Saerchinger, *Artur Schnabel* (London, 1957).

Schnabel, Joseph Ignaz, German composer of sacred music; b. Naumburg-on-Queiss, Silesia, May 24, 1767; d. Breslau, June 16, 1831. He was appointed Kapellmeister at the Cathedral of Breslau (1804) and remained in Breslau for the rest of his life; from 1812 taught at the Roman Catholic Seminary and was director of the Royal Institute for Church Music. He wrote many sacred works; publ. 5 Masses, 4 Graduals, 2 offertories, hymns, also wrote marches for military band; a quintet for guitar and strings; and a clarinet concerto. His brother, **Michael Schnabel** (b. Naumburg, Sept. 23, 1775; d. Breslau, Nov. 6, 1842), founded a piano factory in Breslau (1814); his son, **Karl Schnabel** (b. Breslau, Nov. 2, 1809; d. there, May 12, 1881), who was an excellent pianist and composer

of operas and piano music, carried on the business after Michael Schnabel's death.
BIBLIOGRAPHY: H. E. Guckel, *Joseph Ignaz Schnabel*, part 2 of *Katholische Kirchenmusik in Schlesien* (Leipzig, 1912).

Schnabel, Karl Ulrich, German pianist and composer; son of **Artur Schnabel;** b. Berlin, Aug. 6, 1909. He studied piano with Leonid Kreutzer and composition with Paul Juon in Berlin; after a series of appearances as soloist in Europe, including Russia, he made an American tour (debut, N.Y., Feb. 23, 1937); played 2-piano recitals with his father; also gave duo-piano concerts (4 hands at 1 piano) with his wife, **Helen Fogel.**

Schneerson, Grigory, eminent Russian musicologist and critic; b. Eniseisk, Siberia, March 13, 1901. He studied piano at the Moscow Cons. with Medtner and Igumnov. In 1931 he joined the International Music Bureau in Moscow; from 1939 to 1948 was in charge of the Music Dept. of the VOKS (All-Union Society for Cultural Relations with Foreign Nations); from 1948 to 1961 was head of the foreign section of Sovietskaya Musica, and from 1954 to 1966 edited the bibliographic series *Foreign Literature of Music.* A gifted linguist, he mastered all European languages and undertook a study of Chinese. In his polemical writings he attacks with devastating sarcasm the extreme manifestations of Western modernism, but he preserves scholarly impartiality in his monographs on foreign music. He is Member Correspondent of the Academy of the Arts of the German Democratic Republic (1968); Honorary Member of the Accademia di Scienze, Lettere, Arti (1976); recipient of the Bernier Prize of the Académie des Beaux-Arts, Paris (1976). WRITINGS (all publ. in Moscow): *Musical Culture in China* (1952); *Aram Khachaturian* (1957; also in English, 1959); *Music, Living and Dead* (in praise of the state of music in the nations of the Socialist bloc, and in condemnation of Western trends, 1960; revised and mitigated, 1964); *Ernst Busch* (1962; revised, 1964); *French Music of the 20th Century* (1964; revised, 1970); *Music and Times* (Moscow, 1970); *Articles on Foreign Music: Essays, Reminiscences* (Moscow, 1974); *American Song* (Moscow, 1977); *Portraits of American Composers* (Moscow, 1977); edited *D. Shostakovich: Articles and Materials* (Moscow, 1976).

Schnéevoigt, Georg Lennart, Finnish conductor; b. Viborg, Finland, Nov. 8, 1872; d. Malmö, Nov. 28, 1947. He studied cello with Karl Schröder in Sondershausen and Julius Klengel in Leipzig; appeared as cellist; in 1900 began his career as conductor; from 1904 to 1908 conducted the Kaim Orch. in Munich; from 1909 to 1920, the Riga Symph.; in 1912, founded a symph. orch. in Helsinki, which became known as the Municipal Orch. In 1914; from 1915 to 1924 he led the Konsertförening in Stockholm; in 1919 founded the Oslo Symph. Orch.; also conducted in Germany; conducted the Los Angeles Philharmonic (1927–29); was general director of the National Opera in Riga (1929–32); then went to Malmö, Sweden. In 1907 he married the pianist, **Sigrid Sundgren.**

Schneider, Alexander, Russian-American violinist; b. Vilna, Oct. 21, 1908. He went to study in Germany as a youth; took violin lessons with Adolph Rebner at the Frankfurt Cons. and with Carl Flesch in Berlin; served as concertmaster of the Frankfurt Symph. Orch. Upon the advent of the anti-Semitic Nazi regime, he emigrated to the U.S.; joined the Budapest Quartet as 2nd violin, and made with it a world tour. In 1950 he established, with Pablo Casals, annual summer music festivals in Prades, France, and was a close collaborator with Casals in arranging the spring music festivals in Puerto Rico. He took part, in association with Rudolf Serkin, in the Marlboro, Vermont, music festivals. In 1945 he received the Elizabeth Sprague Coolidge medal for eminent services to chamber music. He also appeared as conductor with world orchestras (Israel Philharmonic, Los Angeles Philharmonic, as well as the Casals orch. in Puerto Rico); was active as a teacher; played sonata recitals with Eugene Istomin and other pianists.

Schneider, Edward Faber, American pianist, composer and pedagogue; b. Omaha, Nebraska, Oct. 3, 1872; d. Santa Clara, California, July 1, 1950. He studied piano with Xaver Scharwenka in N.Y. during the latter's residence there; then went to Germany, where he took piano lessons with Heinrich Barth in Berlin; eventually settled in San Francisco; taught piano at Mills College for 25 years. He wrote several unnecessary symphonic pieces in a mandatory Romantic vein (*In Autumn Time; Sargasso Sea; Thus Spake the Deepest Stone,* which all were performed in San Francisco for the first and last time); some quite acceptable piano pieces and, inevitably, songs.

Schneider, Friedrich, German organist and composer; b. Alt-Waltersdorf, Saxony, Jan. 3, 1786; d. Dessau, Nov. 23, 1853. He was son and pupil of **Johann Gottlob Schneider;** being brought up in a musical atmosphere he began composing early in life, and published 3 piano sonatas at the age of 17; in 1820 he wrote an oratorio, *Das Weltgericht,* that was extremely successful; the following year he was called to Dessau as court Kapellmeister; there he founded a celebrated school of music, which he directed from 1829 to his death; it attracted pupils from all over Germany. Besides *Das Weltgericht,* he wrote the oratorios, *Die Sündflut* (1823), *Das verlorene Paradies* (1824), and *Das befreite Jerusalem* (1835); also a series of oratorios tracing the life of Jesus, from his birth to crucifixion; he further wrote 25 cantatas, 7 operas, 23 symphonies; numerous pieces of chamber music, choruses and piano sonatas for 2- and 4-hands. He also published theoretical works: *Elementarbuch der Harmonie und Tonsetzkunst* (1820; etc.; in English, 1828); *Vorschule der Musik* (1827); *Handbuch des Organisten* (1829–30; in 4 parts).
BIBLIOGRAPHY: F. Kempe, *Friedrich Schneider als Mensch und Künstler* (Dessau, 1859; 2nd ed., Berlin, 1864); K. Hoede, *Friedrich Schneider und die Zerbster Liedertafel zur Hundertjahrfeier 1927* (Zerbst, 1927).

Schneider, Georg Abraham, German horn virtuoso and composer; b. Darmstadt, April 19, 1770; d. Berlin, Jan. 19, 1839. He was a member of the royal orch. at Berlin; from 1820 was Kappellmeister of the Court Opera and "Musikmeister" of all regiments of the Guards.
WORKS: the operettas *Der Orakelspruch, Aucassin und Nicolette, Die Verschworenen, Der Traum, Der Währwolf;* 13 ballets; music to numerous plays, melodramas, etc.; 2 oratorios; cantatas, orchestral Masses; 54 entr'actes for orch.; overtures; concertos for horn, flute, oboe, English horn, bassoon, etc.; quintets, quartets, and other chamber music.

Schneider, Johann, outstanding German organist; son of **Johann Gottlob Schneider** and brother of **Friedrich Schneider;** b. Alt-Gersdorf, near Zittau, Oct. 28, 1789; d. Dresden, April 13, 1864. He studied jurisprudence and organ; in 1812 became a church organist at Görlitz, and in 1825 was appointed court organist at Dresden. He was praised by Mendelssohn as one of the finest organ virtuosos of the period; he was also greatly renowned as a teacher. He composed a number of organ pieces and songs with organ obbligato.

Schneider, Johann Gottlob, German organist and composer; b. Alt-Waltersdorf, Saxony, Aug. 1, 1753; d. Gersdorf, May 3, 1840. He was apprenticed as a weaver but subsequently decided to study music; his principal achievement consists of giving a fine musical upbringing to his sons, **Friedrich Schneider** and **Johann Schneider.**

Schneider, Julius, German organist and composer; b. Berlin, July 6, 1805; d. there, April 3, 1885. He studied composition with Bernhard Klein; organ and piano with various teachers in Berlin. In 1829 he became organist of the Friedrichwerder church in Berlin, and in 1854 was appointed teacher of organ at the Berlin Institute of Church Music. He composed a variety of organ pieces; a piano concerto, and some chamber music.

Schneider, Karl Ernst, German writer on music; b. Aschersleben, Dec. 29, 1819; d. Dresden, Oct. 25, 1893. He wrote *Das musikalische Lied in geschichtlicher Entwickelung* (1863–65; in 3 vols.); *Zur Periodisierung der Musikgeschichte* (1863); and *Musik, Klavier und Klavierspiel* (1872).

Schneider, Louis, French writer on music; b. Lyons, June 3, 1861; d. Grenoble, Aug. 21, 1934. He settled in Paris; wrote music criticism; published several books on music: *Schumann, sa vie et ses œuvres* (1905; in collaboration with Mareschal); *Massenet* (1908; 2nd ed., 1926); *Monteverdi* (1921); *Offenbach, Hervé, Charles Lecocq, maîtres de l'opérette française* (2 vols., 1924); also humorous musical chronicles under the pen name "Le Pompier de service."

Schneider, Marius, Alsatian musicologist; b. Hageneau, July 1, 1903. He studied in Strasbourg, Paris and Berlin; was a member of the staff at the Ethnological Museum in Berlin (1931–39); lived in Barcelona between 1944 and 1951; returned to Germany and became a member of the faculty of the Univ. of Cologne (1951–68). His publications include *Die Ars nova des 14. Jahrhunderts in Frankreich und Italien* (diss.,

Wolfenbüttel, 1931); *Geschichte der Mehrstimmigkeit* (2 vols., Berlin, 1934, 1935); *El origen musical de los animales-símbolos en la mitología y la escultura antigua* (Barcelona, 1946); *La Danza de espadas y la tarantela* (Barcelona, 1948); *Singende Steine* (1955); *Il significato della musica* (Rome, 1970); numerous valuable contributions to ethnomusicology, philosophy of music and history of musical structures.

Schneider, Max, eminent German musicologist; b. Eisleben, July 20, 1875; d. Halle, May 5, 1967. He studied at the Leipzig Cons. with Riemann and Kretzschmar (musicology) and harmony and composition with Jadassohn. Upon graduation he was librarian at the Univ. of Berlin (1904–07); then served in the music division of the Royal Library (1907–14); subsequently taught at the Univ. of Breslau (1915–28); then was prof. at the Univ. of Halle (1928–60). He did useful work in compiling miscellaneous bio-bibliographical materials in music; published *Die Anfänge des Basso continuo* (Leipzig, 1918; reprint, Farmborough, 1971); *Beiträge zu einer Anleitung Clavichord und Cembalo zu spielen* (Strasbourg, 1934); *Beiträge zur Musikforschung* (Vol. I, Halle, 1935). He edited numerous important bibliographical surveys; also edited the works of Heinrich Schütz. He enjoyed a well-merited reputation in Germany as a thorough scholar. Twice during his lifetime he was the object of honorary Festschrifte: *Festschrift Max Schneider zum 60. Geburtstag* (Halle, 1935); *Festschrift Max Schneider zum 80. Geburtstag* (Leipzig, 1955).

Schneider, Theodor, German cellist and conductor; son of **Friedrich Schneider;** b. Dessau, May 14, 1827; d. Zittau, June 15, 1909. He studied with his father, and with Drechsler (cello); in 1845 was cellist in the Dessau court orch.; 1854, cantor and choir director of the court and city churches; from 1860–96 served as cantor and music director at the Jakobikirche in Chemnitz; also conductor of the Singakademie and of a Männergesangverein which he founded in 1870. He retired in 1898.

Schneider-Trnavsky, Mikuláš, Slovak composer; b. Trnava, May 24, 1881; d. Bratislava, May 28, 1958. He studied in Budapest, Vienna and Prague; returned to Bratislava in 1918, and served as inspector of music schools in Slovakia. He published several valuable collections of Slovak folksongs, arranged with piano accompaniment: *Sbierka slovenských ludových piesní* (2 vols., 1905–10); *Sbierka slovenských národných piesní* (5 sections; Bratislava, 1930; new edition, Prague, 1935–40) and *50 Slovakische Volkslieder* (Bratislava, 1943). He published a book of memoirs, *Usmevy a slzy (Smiles and Tears,* Bratislava, 1959). In 1956 he received the title of National Artist from the government of Czecholovakia.

WORKS: operetta, *Bellarosa* (Bratislava, 1941); *Dumka and Dance* for orch. (1905); *Comedy Overture* (1930–31); *Symphony of Recollections* (1956); Violin Sonata (1905); *Slovak Sonatina* for piano (1938); church music, including several Masses.

Schneitzhoeffer, Jean, French composer; b. Toulouse, Oct. 13, 1785; d. Paris, Oct. 4, 1852. He studied with

Catel at the Paris Cons.; after serving as timpanist at the Paris Opéra (1815–23) he was appointed *chef du chant* there; from 1831 to 1850 he was in charge of choral classes at the Paris Cons. He composed several ballet scores for the Paris Opéra; of these *La Sylphide* (1832), which he wrote for the famous dancer Maria Taglioni, became a perennial favorite. His other ballets are *Proserpine* (1818), *Zémire et Azor* (1824), and *Mars et Vénus;* also *Sinfonia dei gatti,* several concert overtures, and a Requiem.

Schnerich, Alfred, Austrian musicologist; b. Tarvis, Carinthia, Oct. 22, 1859; d. Vienna, April 29, 1944. He studied history of art at the Institut für österreichisches Geschichtsforschung in Vienna; Dr. phil. in 1888; from 1889, librarian at Vienna Univ.; 1921, Hofrat; retired in 1923. He was a member of the editorial commission of the *Denkmäler der Tonkunst in Österreich.*

WRITINGS: *Der Messentypus von Haydn bis Schubert* (1892); *Messe und Requiem seit Haydn und Mozart* (1909); *Jos. Haydn und seine Sendung* (1922; 2nd ed., 1926); *Die kirchliche Tonkunst* (1927).

Schnitger (Schnitker), Arp, German organ builder; b. Golzwarden, Oldenburg, July 2, 1648; d. Neuenfelde, July 24, 1719. His organs are in the Nikolai- and Jakobikirche, Hamburg; the Cathedral and Stephanskirche at Bremen; the Johanniskirche at Magdeburg; the Nikolaikirche at Berlin; etc. His son **Franz Kaspar** (d. 1729) worked with an elder brother at Zwolle, Holland, building the organ at Zwolle (63 stops), and that at Alkmar (56 stops).

BIBLIOGRAPHY: P. Rubardt, *Arp Schnitger* (Freiberg, 1928); G. Fock, *Schnitger und seine Schule* (Kiel, 1931).

Schnittke, Alfred, Russian composer of avant-garde tendencies; b. Engels, in the German Volga Republic, near Saratov, Nov. 24, 1934, to a German-born father and ethnic German mother. He had his first piano lessons in Vienna (1946–48) where his father was stationed as correspondent of a German-language Soviet newpaper. Returning to Moscow he studied composition with Golubev and instrumentation with Rakov at the Moscow Cons. (1953–58); in 1961 was appointed to its faculty. After writing in a conventional manner, he became acutely interested in the new Western techniques, particularly serialism and "sonorism," in which dynamic gradations assume thematic significance; soon he became known as one of the boldest experimenters in modernistic composition in Soviet Russia.

WORKS: 2 violin concertos (1957, 1966); an oratorio *Nagasaki* (1958); *Songs of War and Peace,* oratorio, with thematic materials from contemporary Russian folksongs (1959); Piano Concerto (1960); 2 violin sonatas (1963, 1968); *Poem about Cosmos* for orch. (1961); *Music* for piano and chamber orch. (1964); *3 Poems* for mezzo-soprano and piano (1965); *Dialogues* for cello and 7 instrumentalists (1965); *Variations on a Chord* for piano (1966); String Quartet (1966); *... pianissimo ...* for orch. (Donaueschingen, Oct. 19, 1969); *Serenade for 5 Musicians* for clarinet, violin, double bass, percussion and piano (1968); an electronic *Study* (1969); Concerto for Oboe, Harp and String Orch. (1970); *Canon in Memoriam Igor Stravinsky* for string quartet (1971); *Sinfonia* (1972); *Der gelbe Klang,* scenic composition after the poetic drama by the abstract painter Wassily Kandinsky, for 9 instruments, tape, chorus, pantomime and light projection (1973); *Hymnus I* for cello, piano and percussion; *Hymnus II* for cello and double bass; *Hymnus III* for violin, recorder, celesta and bells (all 1974); *Praeludium in memoriam Dmitri Shostakovich* for violin and tape (1975); *Requiem* for chorus, soloists and ensemble (1975); Piano Quintet (1976); Concerto Grosso for 2 violins, piano, harpsichord, and strings (1977); *Mozart à la Haydn* for 2 violins and 11 string instruments (1977); *Suite in the Old Style* for violin and piano (1977).

Schnoor, Hans, German writer on music; b. Neumünster, Oct. 4, 1893; d. Bielefeld, Jan. 15, 1976. He studied with H. Riemann and A. Schering at the Univ. of Leipzig; became a music critic in Dresden (1926–45); in 1949 settled in Bielefeld.

WRITINGS: *Die Musik der germanischen Völker im XIX. und XX. Jahrhundert* (Dresden, 1926); *Weber auf dem Welttheater* (Dresden, 1942); *Weber: ein Lebensbild aus Dresdner Sicht* (Dresden, 1947); *400 Jahre deutscher Musikkultur; zum Jubiläum der Staatskapelle und zur Geschichte der Dresdner Oper* (Dresden, 1948); *Geschichte der Musik* (1953); *Weber; Gestalt und Schöpfung* (1953); *Oper, Operette, Konzert; ein praktisches Nachschlagsbuch* (1955).

Schnorr von Carolsfeld, Ludwig, German tenor; b. Munich, July 2, 1836; d. Dresden, July 21, 1865. Son of the noted painter; pupil of J. Otto at Dresden, and of the Leipzig Cons.; then of Ed. Devrient at Karlsruhe, making his debut there, followed by engagement in 1858. From 1860, leading tenor at Dresden. He created the role of Tristan in Wagner's *Tristan und Isolde* at Munich, June 10, 1865, his wife, **Malwine Schnorr von Carolsfeld,** singing Isolde. He died shortly afterwards, of heart failure, at the age of 29.

BIBLIOGRAPHY: R. Wagner, *Meine Erinnerungen an Ludwig Schnorr von Carolsfeld,* in vol. VIII of *Gesammelte Schriften und Dichtungen;* C. H. N. Garrigues, *Ein ideales Sängerpaar, Ludwig Schnorr von Carolsfeld und Malwine Schnorr von Carolsfeld* (Copenhagen, 1937).

Schnorr von Carolsfeld (*née* **Garrigues**), **Malwine,** soprano; wife of **Ludwig Schnorr von Carolsfeld;** b. Copenhagen, Dec. 7, 1832; d. Karlsruhe, Feb. 8, 1904. She created Isolde on June 10, 1865, in Munich, her husband singing Tristan; after his death she sang in Hamburg, and later in Karlsruhe; after her retirement from the stage she taught. In 1867 she publ. a volume of poems by her husband and herself.

BIBLIOGRAPHY: C. H. N. Garrigues, *Ein ideales Sängerpaar, Ludwig Schnorr von Carolsfeld und Malwine Schnorr von Carolsfeld* (Copenhagen, 1937).

Schnyder von Wartensee, Xaver, composer; b. Lucerne, April 16, 1786; d. Frankfurt, Aug. 27, 1868. A pupil at Vienna of J. C. Kienlen; joined the campaign against the French in 1815; taught at the Pestalozzian Institute, Yverdun; in 1817 settled in Frankfurt. His works include cantatas; sacred and secular songs; Swiss songs for men's chorus; etc.; *System der Rhythmik* (posthumous publ. by B. Widmann).

BIBLIOGRAPHY: *Lebenserinnerungen von X. Schnyder von Wartensee* (Zürich, 1887; contains an autobiography and a complete list of works; new ed. by Willi Schuh, Berlin, 1940).

Schoberlechner, Franz, pianist and composer; b. Vienna, July 21, 1797; d. Berlin, Jan. 7, 1843. He studied with Hummel and E. A. Förster at Vienna, and at 10 played in public Hummel's 2nd Concerto, written for him. On a pianistic tour to Italy he produced his opera *I Virtuosi teatrali* at Florence (1814), and the next year became maestro di cappella to the Duchess of Lucca, producing there a second opera, *Gli Arabi nelle Gallie* (1816); returned to Vienna in 1820, where he brought out an opera in German, *Der junge Onkel* (Jan. 14, 1823); made a trip to Russia in 1823, and there married the singer **Sophie dall'Occa** (1807–63), with whom he made further tours to Italy and Vienna. He purchased a villa in Florence in 1831, and retired to it some years later. Besides his operas, he composed overtures, string quartets, a piano trio and many piano pieces (sonatas, variations, fantasias, etc.).

Schobert, Johann, important composer; b. Silesia, c.1740; d. Paris, Aug. 28, 1767 (with his entire family, except one child, from eating poisonous mushrooms). From 1760, he was chamber musician to the Prince de Conti in Paris. His works show the general characteristics of the Mannheim school, although it cannot be proved that he ever was in that city. The slow movement of Mozart's Clavier Concerto, K. 39, is based on music by Schobert.

WORKS: opp. 1, 2, 3, sonatas for clavecin and violin; opp. 4, 5, 16, 17, sonatas for clavecin solo; opp. 6, 8, clavecin trios; opp. 9, 10, 11, 12, 18, clavecin concertos; op. 13, *Concerto pastoral* for clavecin; opp. 14, 15, 6, symphonies for clavecin, violin, and 2 horns. (The same works reprinted by Hummel in Amsterdam with different op. numbers.) A Singspiel, *Le Garde-chase et le braconnier,* was produced in Paris (1765) with little success. A selection of Schobert's works (with thematic catalogue) was publ. by H. Riemann in vol. 39 of *Denkmäler deutscher Tonkunst* (1909).

BIBLIOGRAPHY: G. de Saint-Foix "J. Schobert," *Revue Musicale* III/10 (1922); K. Schalscha, *Zur Würdigung Schoberts* (1923); H. T. David, *J. Schobert als Sonatenkomponist* (1928).

Schoeck, Othmar, eminent Swiss composer and conductor; b. Brunnen, Sept. 1, 1886; d. Zürich, March 8, 1957. He was the son of a painter; studied at the Zürich Cons. with Nägeli and Freund; later, with Reger in Leipzig; from 1909 to 1915, conducted the men's chorus "Aussersihl" in Zürich; from 1917 to 1944 led the symph. concerts at St. Gall. Schoeck is acknowledged as a foremost song composer of Switzerland.

WORKS: the operas *Don Ranudo de Colibrados* (Zürich, April 16, 1919); *Das Wandbild,* pantomime (libretto by Busoni; Halle, Jan. 2, 1921); *Venus* (Zürich, May 10, 1922); *Penthesilea* (Dresden, Jan. 8,

1927); *Massimilla Doni* (Dresden, March 2, 1937); *Das Schloss Dürande* (Berlin, April 1, 1943); orch. works: Violin Concerto (1911–12), Cello Concerto (1947), Horn Concerto (1951), *Festlicher Hymnus* for orch. (1950), etc.; chamber music (2 string quartets, 2 violin sonatas, etc.). Song cycles: op. 36, *Elégie* (voice and chamber orch.; 1924); op. 38, *Gaselen* (voice and chamber orch.); op. 40, *Lebendig begraben* (bass and large orch.; 1927); op. 45, *Wanderung im Gebirge* (voice and piano; 1930); op. 47, *Notturno* (bass and string quartet); over 120 songs. A thematic index of his works was publ. by W. Vogel (Zürich, 1956).

BIBLIOGRAPHY: W. Schuh, "Der harmonische Stil O. Schoecks," *Neue Musikzeitung* (1928); E. Isler, *Führer durch "Penthesilea"* (1928); H. Corrodi, *O. Schoeck* (Frauenfeld, 1931; new edition, much enlarged, 1936); W. Schuh, *O. Schoeck* (Zürich, 1934); also aritcles in the *Schweizerische Musikzeitung* (special Schoeck issue, March 1943), *Festgabe der Freunde zum 50. Geburtstag* ed. by W. Schuh (Erlenbach-Zürich, 1936); W. Vogel, *Wesenszüge von Othmar Schoecks Liedkunst* (Zürich, 1950).The Schoeck Society, organized for the purpose of making his music better known, issued a valuable annotated catalogue of his works (Bern, 1961); W. Vogel published 2 companion vol., *Othmar Schoeck im Wort* (St. Gall, 1957) and *Othmar Schoeck im Gespräch* (Zürich, 1965).

Schœlcher, Victor, French statesman and music amateur; b. Paris, July 21, 1804; d. Houilles, Dec. 24, 1893. During the Second Empire he lived in England because of his radical politics, and became an enthusiastic admirer of Handel's music; publ. *The Life of Handel* (1857) in an inadequate English translation (the first 4 chapters in the oringial French were publ. in *La France Musicale,* 1860–62; the entire manuscript was bought for the library of the Paris Cons. in 1881). Schœlcher accumulated a fine collection of Handel materials, which he donated to the Paris Conservatory.

Schoemaker, Maurice, Belgian composer; b. Anderlecht, near Brussels, Dec. 27, 1890; d. Brussels, Aug. 24, 1964. He studied theory with Théo Ysaÿe, Martin Lunssens and Paul Gilson; was one of eight Gilson pupils to form, in 1925, the "Groupe des Synthétistes," whose aim was to promote modern music. He held administrative posts in various Belgian musical organizations.

WORKS: the operas, *Swane* (1933); *Arc-en-ciel* (1937); *De Toverviool* (1954); 3 radio plays: *Sire Halewijn* (1935), *Médée la magicienne* (1936); and *Philoctetes* (1942); 2 ballets: *Breughel-Suite* (1928) and *Pan* (1937); *Le Facétieux Voyage* for orch. (1914); *Récit, Aria et Final* for violin and orch. (1920); *Pan,* prelude for orch. (1921); *Feu d'artifice* for wind orch. (1922); *2 Fantasques* for orch. (1924); *Sinfonia da camera* (1929); *Légende de Sire Halewijn,* symph. poem (1930); *Rapsodie flamande* for orch. (1931); *Variations on a Popular Song* for orch. (1937); *Sinfonia Breve* (1938); *Pièce concertante* for trombone and orch. (1939); *Variazioni* for horn and orch. (1941); *Mouvement symphonique* (1942); *Scènes Espagnoles* for orch. (1943); *2 Danses flamandes* for orch. (1944);

Symphony (1946); Bassoon Concerto (1947); *Ouverture Romane* (1947); *Marillac l'Épée,* dramatic prologue (1949); Piano Trio (1934); Piano Sonata (1934); Solo Cello Sonata (1940); *Suite champêtre* for oboe, clarinet and bassoon (1940); String Quartet (1945); *Variations Miniatures* for string trio (1949); *Morceau de concert* for trombone and piano (1949); *Tombeau de Chopin* for 2 pianos (1949); *Sonata du souvenir* for cello and piano (1953); *La Cage des Oiseaux (Birdcage)* for 4 clarinets (1961).

Schoenberg (Schönberg), Arnold, greatly renowned Austrian composer; b. Vienna, Sept. 13, 1874; d. Los Angeles, July 13, 1951. As a pupil of the Realschule, in Vienna, he learned to play the violin and also the cello. His father's death left him in needy circumstances at the age of 16; he eked out his existence as a bank clerk, but continued to study music. When he was 20 he began taking lessons in counterpoint with Alexander von Zemlinsky, whose sister he married in 1901; played the cello in Zemlinsky's orchestral group Polyhymnia. He also accepted various jobs of arranging operettas and popular songs. His first original work to obtain public performance was a string quartet in D major (1897), which was favorably received in Vienna; but when his early songs, cast in more individual style, were presented in public (1898) there were outbursts of protest in the hall, premonitory of the opposition that increased in vehemence throughout his career as a composer. In 1899 he wrote his string sextet *Verklärte Nacht* (Vienna, March 18, 1902), a fine work, deeply imbued with the spirit of Romantic poetry, and in its harmonic idiom stemming from Wagner; it remains Schoenberg's most frequently performed composition. About 1900 Schoenberg was engaged as conductor of several amateur choral groups in Vienna suburbs; this increased his interest in vocal music. He then began work on a choral composition, *Gurre-Lieder,* after the poem of the Danish writer Jens Peter Jacobsen. For sheer dimensions, it surpassed the most formidable orchestral edifices of Mahler and Strauss; it calls for 5 solo voices, a speaker, 3 male choruses, an 8-part mixed chorus, and a very large orchestra. To write out the score, he had to order special music paper of 48 staves. He completed the first 2 parts of *Gurre-Lieder* in the spring of 1901; only the conducting chorus remained unfinished; this was delayed by 10 years; since the prospect of a performance was remote, there was no compelling reason to have the work ready. In 1901 Schoenberg moved to Berlin; joined E. von Wolzogen, F. Wedekind, and O. Bierbaum, who launched an "Überbrettl" (a sort of artistic cabaret), which created a brief sensation; Schoenberg conducted light music there, and himself composed a cabaret song with trumpet obbligato; later he met Richard Strauss, through whom he obtained the Liszt stipendium (1902) and a position as teacher at the Stern Cons. In the summer of 1903 he returned to Vienna, where he found the support of Mahler, who became a sincere advocate of Schoenberg's music; Mahler's influence was then at its zenith, and performers were aroused sufficiently to give Schoenberg a hearing. In March, 1904, Schoenberg organized the Vereinigung schaffender Tonkünstler with Alexander Zemlinsky and others, for the purpose of promoting modern music; under the auspices of this society Schoenberg conducted the 1st performance of his symph. poem *Pelleas und Melisande* (Jan. 26, 1905); in this work is found the first example of a trombone glissando. His *Kammersymphonie* was performed in Vienna on Feb. 8, 1907, producing much consternation, because of the decided departure from traditional tonal harmony, the use of chords built on fourths, and the cultivation of dissonances without immediate resolution. In the same year Schoenberg also turned to painting; in his art, as in his music, he adopted the tenets of Expressionism. His fame as a leading modernist attracted progressively minded students, among them Alban Berg, Anton von Webern, and Egon Wellesz, whose own music developed according to Schoenberg's precepts. Schoenberg's String Quartet No. 2 (with soprano solo), finished in 1908, was his last work with a designated key signature (F-sharp minor), except for the *Suite* for strings, in G major, written for school use in 1934. In 1910 Schoenberg was appointed teacher of composition at the Vienna Academy; in 1911 he completed his important book, *Harmonielehre*, dedicated to the memory of Mahler; this manual presents a traditional exposition of chords and progressions, but also offers illuminating ideas regarding new musical developments. In 1911 he was again in Berlin, where he lectured at the Stern Cons. and taught privately; a small but enthusiastic group of admirers and disciples followed him there. In 1912 he brought out two works that aroused much controversy: *5 Orchester-Stücke*, first performed by Sir Henry Wood in London, and a cycle of 21 songs with instrumental accompaniment, *Pierrot Lunaire*, in which Schoenberg used the "Sprechstimme," substituting a gliding speech-song for precise pitches; the work was given, after some 40 rehearsals, in Berlin, on Oct. 16, 1912, and the reaction was startling, the critics drawing upon the strongest invective in their vocabulary. On Feb. 23, 1913, the *Gurre-Lieder* was finally performed in Vienna under the direction of Franz Schreker. Meanwhile, Schoenberg was appearing as conductor of his own works in various European cities (Amsterdam, 1911; St. Petersburg, 1912; London, 1914). During World War I he was engaged in periods of military service; in 1918 he settled in Mödling, near Vienna, holding a composition seminar, which attracted many new pupils. In Nov., 1918, Schoenberg organized in Vienna the Verein für musikalische Privataufführungen (Society for Private Musical Performances), from which newpaper critics were excluded and which forbade applause (the English translation of a statement of aims is found in N. Slonimsky, *Music Since 1900*, N.Y., 1971; pp. 1307–11). In 1925 Schoenberg was appointed prof. of a master class at the Prussian Academy of Arts in Berlin, but was dismissed from that post in May, 1933, by order of the German Ministry of Education under the Nazi regime; he then went to Paris, where, in a symbolic gesture, he reassumed his original Jewish faith, which he had abandoned in 1921. On Oct. 31, 1933, he arrived in the U.S. at the invitation of Joseph Malkin, to direct a master class at the Malkin Cons. in Boston. After teaching in Boston for a season, he settled in Hollywood; in 1935 he became prof. of music at the Univ. of

Southern California, and in 1936 accepted a similar position at the Univ. of California in Los Angeles. He became an American citizen on April 11, 1941; in 1947 he received the Award of Merit for Distinguished Achievement from the National Institute of Arts and Letters. In the U.S. he changed the original spelling of his name, Schönberg, to Schoenberg.

In 1924 Schoenberg's creative evolution reached the all-important point where he found it necessary to establish a new governing principle of tonal relationship; a "method of composing with 12 tones," adumbrated in Schoenberg's music as early as 1914 and used partly in *5 Klavierstücke*, op. 23, and *Serenade*, op. 24, was employed for the first time throughout a work in the *Suite for Piano*, op. 25 (1924), in which the thematic material is based on a group of 12 different notes stated in a certain order; such a "tone row" was henceforth Schoenberg's mainspring of thematic invention; development was provided by presenting the basic series in inversion, retrograde, and retrograde inversion; allowing for transposition, 48 forms were obtainable in all, with counterpoint and harmony, as well as melody, derived from the basic tone row; the realm of rhythm remained free, and immediate repetition of single notes was freely admitted. As with many revolutionary innovations the 12-tone technique was not the creation of Schoenberg alone, but rather a result of many currents of musical thought. Josef Matthias Hauer specifically claimed priority in laying the foundations of the 12-tone method; among others who had essayed similar ideas simultaneously with Schoenberg was Jef Golyscheff in his "12 Tondauer-Musik." Instances of themes composed of 12 different notes are found in Liszt (in the *Faust Symphony*) and Strauss (*Also sprach Zarathustra*, in the section *On Science*). Schoenberg's great accomplishment was to establish the 12-tone row and its changing forms as fundamentals of a new musical language, and to write music of great expressiveness and power, which, in spite of the difficulties of performance and slowness of public comprehension, has become one of the strongest influences in the art. In Europe the 12-tone method is often termed "dodecaphony." The most explicit works of Schoenberg couched in the 12-tone idiom are *Begleitungsmusik zu einer Lichtspielscene* (1930), the Violin Concerto (1936), Piano Concerto (1942), and *Klavierstück*, op. 33a (1929). Among adherents to Schoenberg's method were Alban Berg, Anton von Webern, Egon Wellesz, Ernst Krenek, René Leibowitz, Roberto Gerhard, Humphrey Searle, and Luigi Dallapiccola. These and many other composers all over the world adapted the 12-tone technique to their own creative purposes; even in Russia, where Schoenberg's theories are unacceptable on ideological grounds, several composers, including Shostakovich in his last works, made use of 12-tone themes, albeit without integral development. Stravinsky, when he was about 70 years old, turned to the 12-tone method of composition in its total form, with retrograde, inversion, and retrograde inversions. Schoenberg's manuscripts were placed by him in a special collection at the Library of Congress; the remaining part of his manuscripts was installed after his death at the Schoenberg Institute at the Univ. of Southern California, Los Angeles. His centennial in 1974 was commemorated in Los Angeles and many other cities. The publication of the *Journal of the Arnold Schoenberg Institute* was begun in 1976, edited by Leonard Stein.

WORKS: FOR THE STAGE: *Erwartung,* monodrama, op. 17 (1909; Prague, June 6, 1924); *Die glückliche Hand,* drama with music, to Schoenberg's own libretto, op. 18 (1910–13; Vienna, Oct. 14, 1924); *Von Heute auf Morgen,* opera in 1 act, op. 32 (1928; Frankfurt, Feb. 1, 1930); *Moses und Aron,* biblical drama to the composer's libretto (2 acts completed, 1932; resumed 1951, but not finished; radio performances of 2 acts, Hamburg, March 12, 1954; stage performance, Zürich Festival of the International Society for Contemporary Music, June 6, 1957).

FOR ORCH: *Pelleas und Melisande,* symph. poem after Maeterlinck, op. 5 (1902; Vienna, Jan. 26, 1905); *Kammersymphonie,* for 15 instruments, op. 9 (1906; Vienna, Feb. 8, 1907; 2nd version for large orch., 1935); *5 Orchester-Stücke,* op. 16 (1909; London, Sept. 3, 1912; revised, 1949); *Variations,* op. 31 (Berlin, Dec. 2, 1928); *Begleitungsmusik zu einer Lichtspielscene (Accompaniment to a Cinema Scene),* op. 34 (1930); *Suite* in G for strings (1934; Los Angeles, May 18, 1935); *Violin Concerto,* op. 36 (1936; Philadelphia, Dec. 6, 1940); Second Chamber Symph., op. 38 (N.Y., Dec. 15, 1940); Piano Concerto, op. 42 (1942; N.Y., Feb. 6, 1944); *Theme and Variations,* op. 43 (1943; Boston, Oct. 20, 1944; also and originally for band).

FOR CHORUS: *Gurre-Lieder,* for soli, mixed chorus, and orch. (1901; Vienna, Feb. 23, 1913); *Friede auf Erden,* op. 13, (1907); 4 pieces for mixed chorus, op. 27 (1925); *3 Satires,* op. 28 (1925); 6 pieces for men's chorus, op. 35 (1930); *Kol Nidre,* for speaker, chorus, and orch., op. 39 (1938); *A Survivor from Warsaw,* cantata for narrator, chorus, and orch., op. 46 (1947; Albuquerque, Nov. 4, 1948); *3 German Folksongs,* for chorus a cappella, op. 49 (1948); *Dreimal Tausend Jahre,* for chorus a cappella, op. 50a (1949); *De Profundis,* for chorus a cappella, to Hebrew text, op. 50b (1951). The oratorio *Die Jacobsleiter,* begun in 1913, remained unfinished; fragments were performed for the first time in Vienna, June 1, 1961.

CHAMBER MUSIC: String Quartet in D major (1897; not numbered; presumed lost, but brought to the U.S. by Schoenberg; revived at the Library of Congress, Washington, Feb. 8, 1952); *Verklärte Nacht (Transfigured Night),* sextet for strings, op. 4 (1899; arranged for string orch., 1917; revised, 1943); String Quartet No. 1, in D minor, op. 7 (1904; Vienna, Feb. 15, 1907); String Quartet No. 2, in F-sharp minor, op. 10, with voice (1907); *Serenade* for clarinet, bass clarinet, mandolin, guitar, violin, viola, and cello, op. 24 (4th movement with a sonnet by Petrarch for baritone; 1923; Donaueschingen, July 20, 1924); Quintet for flute, oboe, clarinet, horn, and bassoon, op. 26 (1924); *Suite* for 2 clarinets, bass clarinet, violin, viola, cello, and piano, op. 29 (1927); String Quartet No. 3, op. 30 (Vienna, Sept. 19, 1927); String Quartet No. 4, op. 37 (1936); *Ode to Napoleon,* after Byron, for speaker, strings, and piano, op. 41 (1942; N.Y., Nov. 23, 1944); String Trio, op. 45 (1946); *Fantasia,* for violin and piano (1949).

SONGS: op. 1, 2 songs; op. 2, 4 songs; op. 3, 6 songs; op. 6, 8 songs (1905); op. 8, 6 songs (with orch.; 1904);

op. 12, 2 ballads (1907); op. 14, 2 songs; op. 15, cycle of 15 poems from Stefan George's *Das Buch der hängenden Gärten* (1908); op. 20, *Herzgewächse,* after Maeterlinck, for soprano with celesta, harmonium, and harp (1915); op. 21, *Pierrot lunaire,* 1 poems by Albert Giraud, for "Sprechstimme" with piano, flute (interchangeable with piccolo), clarinet (interchangeable with bass clarinet), violin, (interchangeable with viola), and cello (Berlin, Oct. 16, 1912); op. 22, 4 songs (with orch., 1914–15); op. 48, 3 songs.

FOR KEYBOARD: piano: op. 11, *3 Klavierstücke* (1909); op. 19, *6 kleine Klavierstücke* (1911); op. 23, *5 Klavierstücke* (1923); op. 25, *Suite* (1924); op. 33a, *Klavierstück* (1929); op. 33b, *Klavierstück* (1932); for organ: op. 40, *Variations on a Recitative* (1940).

ARRANGEMENTS AND TRANSCRIPTIONS: 2 chorale preludes, by Bach, for large orch.; organ prelude and fugue in E-flat major, by Bach, for orch.; Piano Quartet in G minor by Brahms, for orch.; Cello Concerto, transcribed from a Harpsichord Concerto by G. M. Monn; Concerto for string quartet and orch. after Handel's Concerto Grosso, op. 6, no. 7. The *Sämtliche Werke,* ed. by J. Rufer et al., began publication in 1966.

WRITINGS: *Harmonielehre* (Vienna, 1911; abridged English transl., N.Y., under the title *Theory of Harmony,* 1947); *Models for Beginners in Composition* (N.Y., 1942); *Style and Idea* (N.Y., 1950); numerous essays in German and American publications.

BIBLIOGRAPHY: *A. S.,* a collection of essays by 11 admirers (Munich, 1912); E. Steinhard, "Die Kunst A. S.s," *Neue Musikzeitung* 18 (1912); J. G. Huneker, "S.," in *Ivory Apes and Peacocks* (N.Y., 1915); Egon Wellesz, "S. and Beyond," *Musical Quarterly* (Jan. 1916); Egon Wellesz, *A. S.* (Leipzig, 1921; English transl. London, 1925); C. Gray, "A. S., a Critical Study," *Music & Letters* (Jan. 1922); E. Stein, *Praktischer Leitfaden zu S.s Harmonielehre* (Vienna, 1923); S. issue of *Anbruch* (1924); Paul Stefan, *A. S.* (Vienna, 1924); K. Westphal, "A. S.s Weg zur Zwölftöne-Musik," *Die Musik* (July 1929); Carl Engel, "S.'s Pierrot Lunaire," in *Discords Mingled* (N.Y., 1931); *A. S. zum 60. Geburtstag,* a collection of articles by friends and pupils (Vienna, 1934); H. E. Wind, *Die Endkrise der bügerlichen Musik und die Rolle A.S.s* (Vienna, 1935); R. S. Hill, "S.'s Tone-Rows and the Tonal System of the Future," *Musical Quarterly* (Jan. 1936); D. J. Bach, "A Note on A. S.," *Musical Quarterly* (Jan. 1936); M. Armitage (ed.), *A. S.* (N.Y., 1937; contains essays by Sessions, Krenek, E. Stein, Carl Engel, Otto Klemperer, Paul Pisk, Paul Stefan, etc., also 2 by Schoenberg himself: "Tonality and Form" and "Problems of Harmony"); Darius Milhaud, "To A. S. on His 70th Birthday," *Musical Quarterly* (Oct. 1944); H. Jalowetz, "On the Spontaneity of S.'s Music," *Musical Quarterly* (Oct. 1944); R. Leibowitz, *S. et son école* (Paris, 1947; English transl., N.Y., 1949); Dika Newlin, *Bruckner, Mahler, S.* (N.Y., 1947); R. Leibowitz, *Introduction à la musique de douze sons; les Variations pour orchestre, op. 31, d'A. S.* (Paris, 1949); W. H. Rubsamen, "S. in America," *Musical Quarterly* (Oct. 1951); H. H. Stuckenschmidt, *A. S.* (Zürich, 1951); J. Rufer, *Die Komposition mit zwölf Tönen* (Berlin, 1952; English transl., by Humphrey Searle, as *Composition with 12 Notes Related to One Another,* London,

1954); Roman Vlad, *Storia della dodecafonia* (Milan, 1958); Egon Wellesz, *The Origin of S.'s 12-Tone System* (Washington, 1958); E. Stein, ed. *Arnold Schönberg, Briefe* (Mainz, 1958); J. C. Paz, *Arnold Schönberg: El fin de la era tonal* (Buenos Aires, 1958); Karl H. Wörner, *Gotteswort und Magie: die Oper "Moses und Aron"* (Heidelberg, 1959); M. Kassler, *The Decision of Arnold Schoenberg's Twelve-Note-Class-System and Related Sytstems* (Princeton, 1961); J. Meyerowitz, *Arnold Schönberg* (Berlin, 1967); Georg Krieger, *Schönbergs Werke für Klavier* (1968); Reinhold Brinkmann, *Arnold Schönberg: Drei Klavierstücke Op. 11* (1969); René Leibowitz, *Schoenberg, oder Der Konservative Revolutionär* (Vienna, 1969); C. Rosen, *Arnold Schoenberg* (1975); H. H. Stuckenschmidt, *Schönberg: Leben, Umwelt, Werk* (Zürich, 1974; in English, as *Schoenberg, His Life, World and Work*, London, 1976). For a complete survey of Schoenberg's works, see the annotated catalogue compiled by Josef Rufer, *Das Werk Arnold Schönbergs* (Kassel, 1959; also in English).

Schoenefeld, Henry, American pianist and composer; b. Milwaukee, Oct. 4, 1857; d. Los Angeles, Aug. 4, 1936. He studied at the Leipzig Cons.; upon his return to America he conducted a German male chorus in Chicago (1891–1902) and subsequently conducted various German choral societies in California. He merits consideration in American music because he was one of the earliest American composers to use authentic Indian musical sources. The result of his striving in this direction was a "grand opera," *Atala, or The Love of Two Savages* (which was never produced); *Suite caractéristique,* for string orch. (based on Indian themes); *Wachicanta,* an Indian pantomime; *2 Indian Legends,* for orch.; *Rural Symphony* (won a $500 prize offered by the National Cons. of N.Y., 1892); *Danse américaine,* for piano; many other piano pieces in the salon style (*Little Soldier's March, Valse élégante, Mystics of the Woods, Valse noble,* etc.).
BIBLIOGRAPHY: Rupert Hughes, *Contemporary American Composers* (Boston, 1900; pp. 128–35).

Schoen-René, Anna E., noted German singer and teacher; b. Coblenz, Germany, Jan. 12, 1864; d. New York, Nov. 13, 1942. She studied singing with Pauline Viardot-Garcia, and sang in opera before coming to America in 1895; she devoted herself to teaching in the U.S., first in Minneapolis and then in N.Y., where she joined the faculty of the Juilliard School of Music. She publ. a book of memoirs, *America's Musical Heritage* (N.Y., 1941).

Schoffler, Paul, German operatic bass; b. Dresden, July 15, 1897; d. Amersham, England, Nov. 22, 1977. He was engaged at the State Opera in Dresden in 1925; in 1937 became a member of the Vienna State Opera. He made his American debut with the Metropolitan Opera, N.Y. on Jan. 26, 1950 as Jokanaan in *Salome;* continued on its staff for 2 years; sang at the Metropolitan again in 1963 as the Music Master in *Ariadne auf Naxos* by Strauss; then went to live in England. His best roles were Don Giovanni and Hans Sachs in *Die Meistersinger.*

Scholes, Percy Alfred, eminent English writer on music; b. Leeds, July 24, 1877; d. Vevey, Switzerland, July 31, 1958. (He pronounced his name *Skoles.*) He took his B. Mus. at Oxford in 1908 and later the M.A., D. Litt., and Hon. D. Mus., as also the Hon. Litt. D., Leeds; *Dr. ès lettres,* Univ. of Lausanne (1934); was organist at various churches until 1905; extension lecturer at the Univs. of Oxford, Cambridge, London, and Manchester; in 1908 founded the Home Music Study Union, and until 1921 edited its organ, the *Music Student* and *Music and Youth;* toured the U.S. as lecturer in 1915 and on 4 later occasions; was music critic of the *London Evening Standard* and the *Observer* (1920–27), and for the BBC (1923–29); 1925–30, edited the Audiographic Series of Pianola and Duo Art Rolls; 1928, organized the Anglo-American Music Education Conferences (Lausanne, 1931, 1933); music editor of *Radio Times* (1932–36); lived in Oxford, and for periods in Switzerland, where he later settled permanently. A writer of great literary attainments and stylistic grace, he succeeded in presenting music "appreciation" in a manner informative and stimulating to the layman and professional alike. His *Oxford Companion to Music* is unique in the lexicographical field in its vividness of presentation and its comprehensiveness. His scholarly biographies of Burney and Hawkins are among the finest of the genre.
WRITINGS: *Everyman and His Music* (1917); *An Introduction to British Music* (1918); *The Listener's Guide to Music* (1919; 10th ed., 1942); *Music Appreciation: Why and How?* (1940; 4th ed., 1925); *The Book of the Great Musicans* (3 vols., 1920; many eds.); *New Works by Modern British Composers* (2 series; 1921, 1924); *The Beginner's Guide to Harmony* (1922; several further eds.); *The Listener's History of Music* (3 vols.; 1923–28; 4th ed., 1933); *Crotchets* (1924); *Learning to Listen by Means of the Gramophone* (1925); *Everybody's Guide to Broadcast Music* (1925); *The Appreciation of Music by Means of the Pianola and Duo Art* (1925); *A Miniature History of Music* (1928); *The Columbia History of Music Through Eye and Ear* (5 albums of records with accompanying booklets; 1930–39; eds. in Japanese and Braille); *Music and Puritanism* (Vevey, 1934); *The Puritans and Music in England and New England* (London, 1934); *Music: The Child and the Masterpiece* (1935; American ed.: *Music Appreciation: Its History and Technics*); *Radio Times Music Handbook* (1935; 3rd ed., 1936; American ed. as *The Scholes Music Handbook,* 1935); *The Oxford Companion to Music* (encyclopedia; London and N.Y., 1938; 9th completely revised ed., 1955; contains a pronouncing glossary and over 1,100 portraits and pictures; the 10th edition was edited by John Owen Ward, N.Y., 1970); *God Save the King: Its History and Romance* (London, 1942; new ed. as *God Save the Queen! The History and Romance of the World's First National Anthem,* London, 1954); *The Mirror of Music, 1844–1944, A Century of Musical Life in Britain as Reflected in the Pages of the "Musical Times"* (London, 1947); *The Great Dr. Burney* (2 vols.; London, 1948); *Sir John Hawkins: Musician, Magistrate, and Friend of Johnson* (London, 1952); *The Concise Oxford Dictionary of Music* (London, 1952); *The Oxford Junior Companion to Music* (London, 1954); various pamphlets, e.g., *Song of Sup-*

per, publ. by the London Vegetarian Society (1948); innumerable articles in the musical press; contributions to encyclopedias and dictionaries, etc.

Schollum, Robert, Austrian composer, musicologist and critic; b. Vienna, Aug. 22, 1913. He studied piano and organ at the Vienna Music Academy; composition with Joseph Marx. After World War II he settled in Linz as organist and educator. In 1959 he was appointed prof. of singing at the Vienna Academy of Music. In 1961 he received the Austrian State Prize for composition and in 1971 obtained the prize of the City of Vienna.
WORKS: 5 symphonies (1955, 1959, 1962, 1967, 1969); Violin Concerto (1961), 2 string quartets (1949, 1966); *Mosaik* for oboe, percussion and piano (1967); *Die Ameisen* for cello and piano (1974). He published several books: *Musik in der Volksbildung* (Vienna, 1962); *Egon Wellesz* (Vienna, 1964); *Die Wiener Schule. Entwicklung und Ergebnis* (Vienna, 1969); *Das kleine Wiener Jazzbuch* (Salzburg, 1970); *Singen als menschliche Kundgebung* (Vienna, 1970).

Scholtz, Herrmann, German pianist and composer; b. Breslau, June 9, 1845; d. Dresden, July 13, 1918. He studied in Breslau; then with Plaidy in Leipzig, with Hans von Bülow and Rheinberger in Munich; taught at the Munich Hochschule für Musik (1870–75); then went to Dresden. He was an accomplished pianist and a fine teacher; also wrote a number of piano pieces in a fashionable style: *Albumblätter, Mädchenlieder, Lyrische Blätter, Stimmungsbilder, Ballade,* etc. He edited Chopin's works for Peters; also edited the Piano Concerto, op. 15, of Brahms.

Scholz, Bernard E., German conductor and composer; b. Mainz, March 30, 1835; d. Munich, Dec. 26, 1916. He studied with Ernst Pauer in Mainz and with Dehn in Berlin; after teaching in Munich, he was engaged as court Kapellmeister in Hannover (1859–65); then conducted the Cherubini Society in Florence (1865–66); led the concerts of the Breslau Orch. Society (1871–82), and in the spring of 1883 succeeded Raff as director of the Hoch Cons. in Frankfurt; retired in 1908.
WORKS: the operas *Carlo Rosa* (Munich, 1858), *Ziethen'sche Husaren* (Breslau, 1869), *Morgiane* (Munich, 1870), *Golo* (Nuremberg, 1875), *Der Trompeter von Säkkingen* (Wiesbaden, 1877), *Die vornehmen Wirte* (Leipzig, 1883), *Ingo* (Frankfurt, 1898), *Anno 1757* (Berlin, 1903), and *Mirandolina* (Darmstadt, 1907); a great many choral works with orch.; 2 symphonies; Piano Concerto; 2 string quartets; String Quintet; Piano Quartet; 2 piano trios; 3 violin sonatas; 5 cello sonatas; numerous piano pieces and songs.
WRITINGS: *Lehre vom Kontrapunkt und der Nachahmung* (1897); *Wohin treiben wir?* (1897; collection of essays); *Musikalisches und Persönliches* (1899); *Verklungene Weisen* (1911); edited Dehn's *Lehre vom Kontrapunkt, dem Kanon und der Fuge* (1859; 2nd ed., 1883).

Schönbach, Dieter, German composer of the avant-garde; b. Stolp-Pommern, Feb. 18, 1931. He studied at the Freiburg Hochschule für Musik with Wolfgang Fortner; in 1959 he was appointed music director at the municipal theater in Bochum. His style of composition is quaquaversal. He wrote the first genuine multimedia opera *Wenn die Kälte in die Hütten tritt, um sich bei den Frierenden zu wärmen, weiss einer "Die Geschichte von einem Feuer"* (Kiel, 1968); a multimedia show *Hymnus 2* (Munich, 1972); *Farben und Klänge* in memory of Kandinsky for orch. (1958); Piano Concerto (1958); *Kammermusik* for 14 instruments (1964); *Hoquetus* for 8 wind instruments (1964); 4 chamber music pieces each titled *Canzona da sonar* (1966–67); *Atemmusik* for fifes, whistles and some other "breath" instruments (1969); also several liturgical cantatas to Latin texts. His *Canticum Psalmi Resurrectionis* was performed at the International Festival of Contemporary Music in Rome on June 13, 1959.

Schönberg, Arnold. See **Schoenberg, Arnold.**

Schonberg, Harold C., American music critic; b. New York, Nov. 29, 1915. He studied at Brooklyn College (B.A., 1937) and at N.Y. Univ. (M.A., 1938). He served in the army (1942–46); then was on the staff of the *N.Y. Sun* (1946–50); he was appointed to the music staff of the *N.Y. Times;* became its principal critic in 1960. In 1971 he received the Pulitzer Prize "for distinguished criticism." In his concert reviews and feature articles he reveals a profound knowledge of music and displays a fine journalistic flair without assuming a posture of snobbish aloofness or descending to colloquial vulgarity. His intellectual horizon is exceptionally wide; he is well-versed in art, and can draw and paint; is a chess aficionado and covered knowledgeably the Spassky-Fischer match in Reykjavik in 1972 for the *New York Times.* He published *Chamber and Solo Instrument Music* (N.Y., 1955); *The Collector's Chopin and Schumann* (N.Y., 1959); *The Great Pianists* (N.Y., 1963); *The Great Conductors* (N.Y., 1967); *Lives of the Great Composers* (N.Y., 1970).

Schönberg, Stig-Gustav, Swedish composer; b. Norrköping, May 13, 1933. He studied organ at the Royal College of Music in Stockholm (1953–60) and later with Flor Peeters in Belgium; took courses in composition with Larsson, Blomdahl and Erland von Koch.
WORKS: *Toccata Concertante* Nos. 1–4 for organ (1954, 1968, 1970, 1972); *Intermezzo* for orch. (1958); *Introduction and Allegro* for string orch. (1958–59); *Lacrimae Domini* for organ (1958); *5 Pieces* for clarinet and cello (1959); *Dialogues* for flute and clarinet (1960); 6 string quartets (1961, 1963, 1968, 1969, 1970, 1971–72); Concerto for Organ and String Orch. (Linköping, June 28, 1963); *Il dolce piano,* 10 preludes for piano (1964); *Sinfonia aperta* (1965, revised 1971); 3 concertinos for string orch. (1966); *Impressions* for piano (1966); *Madeleine och Konrad,* ballet (1967, revised 1972); *Partita* for clarinet and piano (1968); *Concitatio* for orch. (1968, revised 1971); *Impromptu visionario* for orch. (1972); *Regina coeli* for soprano, chorus, orch. and organ (1973); *Sonate pastorale* for oboe and organ (1973); *Cantata gloriae* (1974).

Schönberger, Benno, pianist and composer; b. Vienna, Sept. 12, 1863; d. Wisborough Green, Sussex, March 9, 1930. He studied with Anton Door (piano), Bruckner and Volkmann (composition) at the Vienna Cons.; then took lessons with Liszt. After a European concert tour, he went to London, where he taught at the Royal Academy of Music and appeared in chamber music concerts. He wrote 3 sonatas, 3 rhapsodies, a bolero, and a polonaise, for piano, and about 40 songs.

Schondorf, Johannes, German choral conductor and composer; b. Röbel, July 1, 1833; d. Güstrow, Oct. 4, 1912. He studied at the Stern Cons. in Berlin; then was a singing teacher at the Cathedral School in Güstrow; also conducted a choral society there. He publ. *Vaterländische Gesänge,* for mixed voices; many school songs; also piano pieces.

Schönstein, Karl, Austrian singer and government official; b. Ofen, June 26, 1797; d. Vienna, July 16, 1876. Before he assumed office, he had a career as a concert singer; was one of the earliest interpreters of Schubert's songs; Schubert's song cycle *Die schöne Müllerin* is dedicated to him.

Schoop, Paul, Swiss-American composer; b. Zürich, July 31, 1909; d. Los Angeles, Jan. 1, 1976. He studied piano in Paris with Alfred Cortot, Robert Casadesus, and in Berlin with Artur Schnabel; comp. with Paul Dukas and with Hindemith and Schoenberg in the U.S. He settled in Los Angeles, and wrote music for films; also composed a comic opera, *The Enchanted Trumpet,* a symphonic poem *Fata Morgana,* and a number of ballet scores for productions of his sister, a modern dancer, Trudi Schoop.

Schopenhauer, Arthur, the great German philosopher; b. Danzig, Feb. 22, 1788; d. Frankfurt, Sept. 21, 1860. Although his excursions into the realm of music are neither remarkable nor very valuable, they are stimulating, and have inspired a number of valuable contributions by modern investigators, especially in the field of musical esthetics. Wagner was influenced to a considerable extent by Schopenhauer's philosophical system.
BIBLIOGRAPHY: K. Fuchs, *Präliminarien zu einer Kritik der Tonkunst* (Greifswald, 1870); F. von Hausegger, *Richard Wagner und Arthur Schopenhauer* (Leipzig, 1878; 2nd ed., 1892); H. Dinger, *Die Weltanschauung Wagners in den Grundgedanken ihrer Entwickelung* (Leipzig, 1893; traces especially the influence of Hegel and Schopenhauer); M. Seydel, *Arthur Schopenhauers Metaphysik der Musik* (Leipzig, 1895); E. Zoccoli, *L'Estetica di Schopenhauer* (Milan, 1901); G. Melli, *La Filosofia di Schopenhauer* (Florence, 1905; treats the relations between Schopenhauer and Wagner); Th. Lessing, *Schopenhauer, Wagner, Nietzsche* (Munich, 1906); A. Mäcklenburg, "Schopenhauer und seine Stellung zur Musik," *Die Musik* (Dec. 1908); F. J. Wagner, *Beiträge zur Würdigung der Musiktheorie Schopenhauers* (dissertation, Bonn, 1910); A. von Gottschalk, *Beethoven und Schopenhauer* (Blanckenburg, 1912); L. Dunton Green,

"Schopenhauer and Music," *Musical Quarterly* (April 1930).

Schorr, Friedrich, baritone; b. Nagyvárad, Hungary, Sept. 2, 1888; d, Farmington, Conn., Aug. 14, 1953. He studied law at the Univ. of Vienna, and also took private lessons in singing; appeared with the Chicago Opera Co. (1911–12); then was a member of the opera companies in Graz (1914–16), Prague (1916–18), Cologne (1918–23), and of the Berlin State Opera (1923–31). He sang Wolfram at the Metropolitan Opera on Feb. 14, 1924, and continued as a member till the season 1942–43; sang Wotan at the Bayreuth Festivals in 1925, 1927, 1928, and 1930; specialized in Wagnerian opera. He sang the leading roles of the American premières at the Metropolitan Opera of Krenek's *Jonny Spielt Auf* (1929) and Weinberger's *Schwanda* (1931).

Schott, Anton, German tenor; b. Castle Staufeneck, June 24, 1846; d. Stuttgart, Jan. 6, 1913. He was in the Prussian army; after the Franco-Prussian War, he sang at the Munich Opera (1871) and the Berlin Opera (1872–75); then in London and in Italy; made his American debut at the Metropolitan Opera, N.Y., as Tannhäuser (Nov. 17, 1884). He excelled as an interpreter of Wagnerian roles. He publ. a polemical brochure, *Hie Welf, hie Waibling* (1904).

Schott, Bernhard, the founder of the German music publishing firm, **B. Schotts Söhne;** b. Eltville (baptized Aug. 19, 1748); d. Heidesheim, April 26, 1809. He founded the firm in 1770; after his death the business was carried on by his sons **Andreas Schott** (1781–1840) and **Johann Joseph Schott** (1782–1855) under the firm name of B. Schotts Söhne. The 2 sons of Andreas Schott, **Franz Philip Schott** (b. July 30, 1811; d. May 8, 1874) and **Peter Schott** (d. Paris, Sept. 20, 1894), succeeded to the business; Peter Schott was manager of the Paris and Brussels branches; subsequently **Peter Schott, Jr.,** took over the directorship, together with Ludwig Strecker and Franz von Landwehr. B. Schotts Söhne published the journals *Cäcilia* (1824–48), *Süddeutsche Musikzeitung* (1852–69), and *Melos* (1920–34 and from 1946). Dr. Ludwig Strecker, son of the director of the same name, and Heinz Schneider Schott, Dr. Strecker's son-in-law, are the present directors (1958); the main office is at Mainz, and a principal branch is at London. (Schott Frères at Brussels is now an entirely different firm.) The catalogue of Schott is one of the richest in the world; it includes works by Beethoven (last quartets, 9th Symph.), operas by Donizetti, Rossini, etc.; Wagner's *Meistersinger, Ring des Nibelungen,* and *Parsifal;* virtually all works by Hindemith and a great number of other contemporary works. Schott is the publisher of the Riemann Musik-Lexikon.
BIBLIOGRAPHY: W. Altmann, *Richard Wagners Briefwechsel mit seinen Verlegern* (Leipzig, 1911; vol. II contains correspondence with Schott); L. Strecker, *Richard Wagner als Verlagsgefährte* (Mainz, 1951); *Der Musikverlag B. Schott* (Mainz, 1954).

Schouwman, Hans, Dutch pianist and composer; b. Gorinchem, Aug. 8, 1902; d. The Hague, April 8, 1967.

He was a pupil of Peter van Anrooy; developed a singing voice and gave recitals accompanying himself on the piano.

WORKS: *3 Danswijzen (3 Dance Tunes)* for voice, 2 flutes, strings and percussion (1938); *5 Sketches* for clarinet and small orch. (1942); *Friesland,* 4 songs for voice and orch. (1945); *Memento mori* for alto, chorus and small orch. (1947); *Suite* for amateur orch. (1958); *De Prinses op de erwt* for orch. (1965); 2 oboe sonatinas (1940, 1944); *Aubade en Barcarolle* for clarinet and piano (1944); Trio for clarinet, bassoon and piano (1944); *Romance en Humoreske* for bassoon and piano (1944); *4 Pieces* for flute and piano (1944); *2 Legends* for horn and piano (1944); *Notturno* for mezzo-soprano, cello and piano (1949); *Nederlandse Suite* for wind quintet (1953); *Om de kribbe* for soprano, contralto, female chorus and piano (1952); *3 Preludes* for piano left hand (1959); 2 series of old Dutch songs, with string accompaniment; arrangements of folksongs for various instruments; vocal duets; solo songs.

Schrade, Leo, eminent German musicologist; b. Allenstein, Dec. 13, 1903; d. Spéracédès (Alpes-Maritimes), Sept. 21, 1964. He studied with Hermann Halbig at the Univ. of Heidelberg (1923-27), with Adolf Sandberger at the Univ. of Munich and with Theodor Kroyer at the Univ. of Leipzig; Dr. phil., 1927, with the dissertation *Die ältesten Denkmäler der Orgelmusik* (Münster, 1928); held teaching positions in music at the Univ. of Königsberg (1928-32); then at the Univ. of Bonn (from 1932). In 1937 he emigrated to the U.S.; was on the faculty of Yale Univ. (1938-58) where he taught music history; in 1958 he was appointed to the music faculty of the Univ. of Basel. During the academic season 1962-63 he was Charles Eliot Norton Lecturer at Harvard; his lectures were published under the title, *Tragedy in the Art of Music* (Cambridge, Mass., 1964). He published a number of books and articles of prime documentary value, promulgating some important musico-historical theories.

WRITINGS: *Die handschriftliche Überlieferung der ältesten Instrumentalmusik* (Lahr, 1931); *Beethoven in France* (New Haven and London, 1942); *Monteverdi* (N.Y., 1950); *Bach: The Conflict between the Sacred and the Secular* (N.Y., 1954); *W. A. Mozart* (Bern, 1964). He edited Luis Milán's *Libro de música de vihuela* (Leipzig, 1927); Virdung's *Musica getutscht* (Kassel, 1931) and others collections. His edition of the complete *Polyphonic Music of the 14th Century* began to appear in 1956; at his death the first 4 vols. were published: I: *The "Roman de Fauvel"; The Works of Philippe de Vitry; French Cycles of the "Ordinarium Missae";* II-III: *The Works of Guillaume de Machaut;* IV: *The Works of Francesco Landini.* Schrade's "Commentary Notes" to these vols. were published in Monaco. By 1978, 8 more vols. had appeared under the editorship of Frank Lloyd Harrison, W. Thomas Marrocco, Kurt von Fischer, F. Alberto Gallo, and Ernest H. Sanders, with 12 more vols. announced as in progress under the editorship of Kurt von Fischer. A Festschrift for Schrade was published on his 60th birthday: *Music and History: Leo Schrade on the Occasion of his 60th Birthday* (Cologne, 1963; London, 1965).

Schradieck, Henry, German-American violinst; b. Hamburg, April 29, 1846; d. Brooklyn, March 25, 1918. He studied violin as a child with Léonard in Brussels (1854-58), and later with Ferdinand David in Leipzig (1859-61). He then served as concertmaster of the Philharmonic Concerts in Hamburg (1868-74) and of the Gewandhaus Orch. in Leipzig (1874-83). In 1883 he emigrated to America, where he was active as a violin teacher in Cincinnati and N.Y. He published valuable technical studies for the violin: *25 grosse Studien für Geige allein; Scale-studies; Technical Studies; Guide to the Study of Chords; Finger Exercises; Schule der Violintechnik* (3 parts; also adapted for viola).

Schreck, Gustav, German composer and teacher; b. Zeulenroda, Sept. 8, 1849; d. Leipzig, Jan. 22, 1918. He studied at the Leipzig Cons. with Plaidy, Papperitz, and Jadassohn; after a few years of teaching in Finland, he returned to Leipzig and joined the faculty of the Cons. there in 1887. His works are mostly vocal; he wrote an oratorio, *Christus der Auferstandene,* and other sacred works; also Sonata for bassoon and piano; Sonata for oboe and piano; *Divertimento* for 9 woodwinds; piano pieces; songs.

Schreiber, Frederick C., Austrian-American organist and composer; b. Vienna, Jan. 13, 1895. He studied piano, cello and composition in Vienna; was on the faculty of the Vienna Cons. of Music (1927-38). In 1939 he emigrated to the U.S. and settled in N.Y., where he served as chorus director and organist at the Reformed Protestant Church (1939-58). A prolific composer, he wrote a great number of works in various genres, among them 7 symphonies (1927-57); *The Beatitudes,* a symph. trilogy for orch. and chorus (1950); *Christmas Suite* for orch. (1967); *Images* for orch. (1971); *Contrasts* for orch. (1971); 2 piano concertos; Cello Concerto; 2 violin concertos; *Variations on a German Folksong* (1974); numerous choral pieces; chamber music, including 2 string quintets, 7 string quartets, Piano Quartet and 3 piano trios; a great many organ compositions.

Schreiber, Friedrich Gustav, German organ teacher and composer; b. Bienstedt, Aug. 5, 1817; d. Mühlhausen, July 14, 1889. He studied with E. Kast and L. Gebhardt in Erfurt; taught organ in Prague (1840-47); settled at Erfurt in 1851 as municipal music director and cantor at St. Balsius's; founded and conducted a choral society with which he produced oratorios. Among his works are *Borussia* for male chorus and orch.; *Pestalozzi-Kantate* and *Der deutsche Geist* for soli, male chorus, and orch.; songs.

Schreker, Franz, eminent composer and teacher; b. Monaco, March 23, 1878; d. Berlin, March 21, 1934. He spent his early childhood in Monaco, where his father, a native of Austria, was court photographer. He was 10 when his father died, and the family moved to Vienna; there he studied violin with Rosé and theory with Robert Fuchs. In 1908 he organized the Vienna Philharmonic Chorus and conducted many new works with it. In 1912 he was appointed prof. of composition at the Akademie der Tonkunst. In 1920 he went to Berlin, where he was director of the Hochschule für Musik (until 1932); there he had many talented pupils who later became well-known composers (Krenek, Rathaus, Alois Hába, and others). In 1932 became prof. of a class for advanced students at the Prussian Academy of Arts, but lost this post with the advent of the Nazi regime (1933), when he was forced to resign; he died a year later. As a composer, he led the neo-Romantic movement in the direction of Expressionism, emphasizing psychological conflicts in his operas; in his harmonies he expanded the basically Wagnerian sonorities to include many devices associated with Impressionism. He exercised considerable influence on the German and Viennese schools of his time, but with the change of direction in modern music towards economy of means and away from mystical and psychological trends, Schreker's music suffered an irreversible decline.

WORKS: operas (all to his own librettos): *Der ferne Klang* (Frankfurt, Aug. 18, 1912), *Das Spielwerk und die Prinzessin* (Vienna, March 15, 1913; revised and produced as a mystery play, *Das Spielwerk*, Munich, Oct. 30, 1920), *Die Gezeichneten* (Frankfurt, April 25, 1918), *Der Schatzgräber* (Frankfurt, Jan. 21, 1920; very successful), *Irrelohe* (Cologne, March 27, 1924), *Der singende Teufel* (Berlin, Dec. 10, 1928), *Der Schmied von Gent* (Berlin, Oct. 29, 1932), *Christophorus* (not produced); ballet, *Der Geburtstag der Infantin,* after Oscar Wilde (Vienna, 1908); *Rokoko,* dance suite (1908); *Der Wind,* pantomime (1908); *Ekkehard,* overture for orch. and organ (1903); *Romantische Suite* for orch. (1903); *Phantastische Ouvertüre* (1903); *Vorspiel zu einem Drama* (1913; used as a prelude to his opera *Die Gezeichneten*); *Kammersymphonie* (Vienna, March 12, 1917); *Kleine Suite* for small orch. (Breslau, Jan. 17, 1929); *Vom ewigen Leben,* for soprano and orch., after Walt Whitman (1929); 23 songs.

BIBLIOGRAPHY: Paul Bekker, *Franz Schreker* (Berlin, 1919); R. S. Hoffmann, *Franz Schreker* (Leipzig, 1921); J. Kapp, *Franz Schreker* (Munich, 1921); special issues of *Musikblätter des Anbruch* 1928, in honor of Schreker's 50th birthday); F. X. Bayerl, *Franz Schrekers Opernwerk* (Erlangen, 1928); H. Bures-Schreker (daughter of Schreker), *El caso Schreker* (Buenos Aires, 1968); H. Bures-Schreker, H. H. Stuckenschmidt, W. Oehlmann, *Franz Schreker* (Vienna, 1970).

Schrems, Joseph, German music scholar and choral leader; b. Warmensteinach, Oct. 5, 1815; d. Regensburg, Oct. 25, 1872. He was appointed Kapellmeister of the Cathedral at Regensburg in 1839, and held this position almost until his death; revived much early church music in performance; succeeded Proske as editor of *Musica divina.* Through his efforts the library of the Regensburg Cathedral became one of the largest collections of early church music in existence.

Schröder, Alwin, cellist; brother of **Carl** and **Hermann Schröder;** b. Neuhaldensleben, June 15, 1855; d. Boston, Oct. 17, 1928. He studied piano with his father, and violin with De Ahna; then devoted himself to the cello; became successor to his brother as 1st cellist in the Gewandhaus orch. in Leipzig. In 1891 he

went to America; joined the Boston Symph. Orch. (until 1925). He was also for a time the cellist in the Kneisel Quartet. His publications include *Violoncello Studies, Technical Studies, New Studies in Scaleplaying,* as well as collections of classical pieces adapted for cello.

Schröder, Carl, German cellist and composer; brother of **Alwin Schröder;** b. Quedlinburg, Dec. 18, 1848; d. Bremen, Sept. 22, 1935. He studied with Drechsler and Kiel; in 1871 he formed a string quartet with his brothers **Hermann, Franz,** and **Alwin.** He was solo cellist in the Gewandhaus orch. in Leipzig (1874–81); afterwards held 8 successive posts as conductor in Germany and Holland, finally settling in Berlin as cello teacher at Stern's Cons. (1911–24). He then retired and lived in Bremen. Among his works are 2 operas, *Aspasia* (1892) and *Asket* (1893), 2 string quartets, and other chamber music. He compiled 3 pedagogical manuals, *Katechismus des Dirigierens und Taktierens* (1889), *Katechismus des Violinspiels* (1889), and *Katechismus des Violoncellspiels* (1890), which were also publ. in English (1893, 1895, 1896). His collections of classical works for the cello, especially *Vortragstudien* (60 pieces), are of value.

Schröder, Hanning, German composer; b. Rostock, July 4, 1896. He was a medical student; concurrently he took violin lessons with Havemann in Berlin and composition with Weismann in Freiburg im Breisgau; then took a course in musicology with W. Gurlitt. In 1929 he married the musicologist **Cornelia Auerbach** (b. Breslau, Aug. 24, 1900); they remained in Germany under the Nazi regime, but were barred from professional work for their act of human charity in giving shelter to a Jewish couple in their Berlin apartment. After the war, they took up residence in West Berlin.

WORKS: *Musik* for recorder solo (1954), and similar works for solo viola, solo cello, solo violin and solo bassoon; *Hänsel und Gretel,* Singspiel for children (Berlin, Dec. 23, 1952); *Divertimento* for 5 wind instruments (1957); *Divertimento* for viola and cello (1963); *Metronome 80* for violin solo (1969); Nonet for wind quintet, violin, viola, cello and double bass (1970); *Varianten* for solo flute and orch. (1971).

Schröder, Hermann, German violinist and composer; brother of **Carl** and **Alwin Schröder;** b. Quedlinburg, July 28, 1843; d. Berlin, Jan. 30, 1909. He studied with A. Ritter at Magdeburg; from 1885 was teacher at the Royal Institute for Church Music in Berlin; also had a music school of his own. He publ. *Untersuchung über die sympathischen Klänge der Geigeninstrumente* (1891); *Die symmetrische Umkehrung in der Musik* (1902); *Ton und Farbe* (1906); chamber music for instructive purposes: *6 instruktive Quartette, 3 kleine Trios,* etc.; a violin method, *Die Kunst des Violinspiels* (1887); etc.

Schröder-Devrient, Wilhelmine, celebrated German soprano; b. Hamburg, Dec. 6, 1804; d. Coburg, Jan. 26, 1860. She received an early training for the stage from her father, a baritone, and from her mother, Antoinette Sophie Bürger, a well-known actress; she herself played children's parts and was an actress until her

17th year. After the death of her father in 1818, she followed her mother to Vienna, where she studied with Mazatti; made her debut as Pamina in Mozart's *Zauberflöte;* then sang Agathe in *Der Freischütz* under the direction of Weber himself (Vienna, March 7, 1822). She sang Leonore when *Fidelio* was revived in Vienna (1822) in the presence of Beethoven. In 1823 she was engaged at the Court Opera in Dresden; there she married the actor Karl Devrient (divorced 1828). She sang in Paris in 1831 and 1832 with spectacular success; in the summer of 1832 she appeared in London. She returned to Germany in 1837; continued to sing in Dresden until 1847; also appeared as a concert singer, evoking praise from critics and musicians alike; Wagner expressed his admiration for her; she created the roles of Adriano Colonna in *Rienzi* (Oct. 20, 1842), Senta in *Der fliegende Holländer* (Dresden, Jan. 2, 1843), and Venus in *Tannhäuser* (Dresden, Oct. 19, 1845). She contracted 2 more marriages: to Döring (divorced) and von Bock (1850).
BIBLIOGRAPHY: C. von Glümer, *Erinnerungen an Wilhelmine Schröder-Devrient* (Leipzig, 1862; reprinted in Reclam's ed., 1905); A. von Wolzogen, *Wilhelmine Schröder-Devrient* (Leipzig, 1863); G. Bonacci, "G. Schröder-Devrient e Gasparo Spontini," in *Nuova Antologia* (Rome, 1903); C. Hagemann, *Wilhelmine Schröder-Devrient* (Berlin, 1904); E. Schuré, *Précurseurs et revoltés* (Paris, 1904). A purported autobiography, publ. anonymously in many editions since about 1870 as *Aus den Memoiren einer Sängerin* or *Memoires d'une chanteuse allemande,* is in fact a pornographic fantasy whose real author is unknown. A novel based on her life, by Eva von Baudissin, *Wilhelmine Schröder-Devrient: Der Schicksalsweg einer grossen Künstlerin,* was publ. in Berlin, 1937. See also Richard Wagner's *Über Schauspieler und Sänger* (dedicated to her memory), in vol. IX of his *Gesammelte Schriften und Dichtungen,* and his numerous references to her in *Mein Leben.*

Schröter, Christoph Gottlieb, German organist and music theorist; b. Hohenstein, Aug. 10, 1699; d. Nordhausen, May 20, 1782. He served as a chorister in Dresden; in 1717 he went to Leipzig where he studied theology, but turned to music when he became Lotti's copyist in Dresden; then traveled in Germany, Holland and England; returning to Saxony, he obtained the position of a lecturer at Jena Univ.; then served as organist in Minden (1726–32); in 1732 he was appointed organist at Nordhausen and held this position for half a century until his death. He wrote mainly choral sacred music; he composed 7 sets of church cantatas for the entire church year; a Passion; *Die sieben Worte Jesu,* for which he wrote the verses; also instrumental music, including overtures, concertos, and sonatas, as well as fugues and preludes for organ. He claimed priority for the invention of a hammer action for keyed stringed instruments, anticipating Cristofori's invention of the pianoforte; his argument is expounded with polemical passion in his paper "Umständliche Beschreibung eines neuerfundenen Clavierinstruments, auf welchem man in unterschiedenen Graden stark und schwach spielen kann," which was published in 1763 in Marpurg's *Kritische Briefe;* however, music historians rejected his arguments as choronologically invalid. In the field of music theory he published an important paper *Deutliche Anweisung zum Generalbass in beständiger Veränderung des uns angebohrnen harmonischen Dreyklanges* (1772), in which he expounds the thesis that the major and minor triads are the sole fundamental chords in harmony; he also published *Letzte Beschäftigung mit musikalischen Dingen; nebst sechs Temperatur-Planen und einer Notentafel* (1782) and some other theoretical articles in an egotistically assertive vein.

Schröter, Corona (Elisabeth Wilhelmine), celebrated German soprano; b. Guben, Jan. 14, 1751; d. Ilmenau, Aug. 23, 1802. She was trained in music by her father, **Johann Friedrich Schröter,** who was an oboe player. About 1764 she appeared in a "grand concert" in Leipzig and was engaged there till 1771. On Nov. 23, 1776 she sang at the court of Weimar, and was appointed Kammersängerin to the Dowager Duchess of Weimar. She was also active on the dramatic stage; Goethe esteemed her highly as an actress. She composed some songs, publ. in 2 vols. (1786 and 1794); among them, the first setting of Goethe's *Erlkönig.*
BIBLIOGRAPHY: R. Keil, *Corona Schröter. Eine Lebensskizze* (Leipzig, 1875); H. Düntzer, *Charlotte von Stein und Corona Schröter* (Ilmenau, 1902); H. Stümcke, *Corona Schröter* (Bielefeld, 1904).

Schröter, Johann Samuel, pianist and composer; brother of Corona Schröter; b. Warsaw between 1750 and 1753; d. London, Nov. 1, 1788. He traveled with his father and sister to London, where they gave concerts together. He remained in London, and in 1782 was appointed successor of John Christian Bach as music master to the Queen. 12 piano concertos and 7 trios were publ. in London, also in Paris. His widow became attached to Haydn during the latter's stay in London (1790–91) and sent him many impassioned letters, of which copies made by Haydn are extant.
BIBLIOGRAPHY: Konrad Wolff, "Johann Samuel Schroeter," *Musical Quarterly* (July 1958).

Schröter, Leonhart, German contrapuntist; b. Torgau, c.1532; d. Magdeburg, c.1601. From 1561 to 1576 he was cantor at Saalfeld; then librarian at Wolfenbüttel (1572–73); cantor of the Old Latin School in Magdeburg (1576–95). He was an important composer of Lutheran church music; publ. *55 geistliche Lieder* (1562), a German Te Deum for 8 voices (1571; publ. 1576; reprinted by Kade in vol. V of Ambros' *Geschichte der Musik*); also a Latin Te Deum (1584); 16 *Weihnachtsliedlein* for 4–8 voices (1587; reprinted by Engelke in 1914 for Peters); 28 *Hymni sacri* (1587). 4 *Weihnachtsliedlein* are found in Schlesinger's *Musica sacra* (no. 11), other pieces in Jöde's *Das Chorbuch* I and IV; further reprints by W. Ehmann (Göttingen, 1932), G. Hormann (1933), and E. Lendvai (1934).
BIBLIOGRAPHY: G. Hofmann, *Leonhart Schröter, ein lutherischer Kantor zu Magdeburg* (dissertation; Altdorf, 1934).

Schryock, Buren, American composer and conductor; b. Sheldon, Iowa, Dec. 13, 1881; d. San Diego, Jan. 20, 1974. At the age of 7 moved to West Salem, Oregon, where he studied music and played organ in a church; occupied various teaching posts in Michigan, Texas, Nebraska, and California; was conductor of the San Diego Symph. Orch. (1913–20) and of the San Diego Opera Co. (1920–36); then settled in National City, near San Diego.

WORKS: 5 operas to his own librettos: *Flavia* (1930–46), *Mary and John* (1948), *Nancy and Arthur* (1951), *Malena and Nordico* (1954), *Tanshu and San-chi* (1955); a symphony; chamber music; piano pieces.

Schubart, (Christian Friedrich) Daniel, German poet and musician; b. Sontheim, March 13, 1739; d. Stuttgart, Oct. 10, 1791. Organist at Ludwigsburg in 1768; founded a paper, the *Deutsche Chronik,* in 1774; from 1777–87 imprisoned at Hohenasperg for political reasons. After his release, he was made music director of the Stuttgart theater and court poet. He was the author of the words of Schubert's famous song *Die Forelle.* His own compositions are unassuming, but he was historically important in contributing to the creation of the German lied of the folk-like type; his song, *Schlaf wohl, du Himmelsknabe du,* rivalled real folk-songs in popularity. He also wrote piano pieces. His son, **Ludwig Schubart,** edited his philosophical disquistion, *Ideen zu einer Aesthetik der Tonkunst* (1806; new ed., 1924), written in the extravagant vein characteristic of his whole life.

BIBLIOGRAPHY: *Schubarts Leben und Gesinnungen von ihm selbst, im Kerker, aufgesetzt* (2 vols.; Stuttgart, 1791–93); F. D. Strauss, *Schubarts Leben in seinen Briefen* (2 vols.; Berlin, 1849); G. Hauff, *Schubart in seinen Leben und seinen Werken* (Stuttgart, 1885); H. Solcher, *Schubart der Gefangene auf dem Hohenasperg* (Bamberg, 1895); E. Holzer, *Schubart als Musiker* (Stuttgart, 1905); H. Hesse and K. Isenberg, *Schubart: Dokumente seines Lebens* (Berlin, 1927); R. Hammerstein, *Schubart, ein Dichter-Musiker der Goethe-Zeit* (Freiburg-im-Breisgau, 1943); E. Thorn, *Genius in Fesseln: Schubarts Leben* (2nd ed., Geislingen, 1956).

Schubaur, Johann Lukas, German composer; b. Lechfeld, Dec. (baptized 23), 1749; d. Munich, Nov. 15, 1815. While studying medicine in Vienna he earned his livelihood by giving music lessons; began to practice in 1775 in Neuburg but soon moved to Munich, where he became physician to the court and president of the medical commission. He was one of the earliest and most successful composers of German Singspiele. The following were produced in Munich: *Melida* (1781); *Die Dorfdeputierten* (1783); *Das Lustlager* (1784); *Die treuen Köhler* (1786); also composed *Psalm 107,* and a cantata, *Il Sacrifizio.*

BIBLIOGRAPHY: E. Reipschläger, *Schubaur, Danzi und Poissl als Opernkomponisten* (Berlin, 1911).

Schubert, Ferdinand, brother of the great composer **Franz Schubert;** b. Lichtenthal, near Vienna, Oct. 18, 1794; d. Vienna, Feb. 26, 1859, as director of the Normal School of St. Anna. He was devoted to his gifted brother, and inherited the latter's literary remains. He composed a *Tantum ergo,* a *Regina coeli,* a German Requiem *a* 4 with organ, part-songs, etc.; wrote much other church music, a Requeim for Franz, 2 children's operas, etc. (most in MS).

Schubert, Franz (Peter), great Viennese composer; b. Lichtenthal (then a suburb of Vienna; now a part of that city), Jan. 31, 1797; d. Vienna, Nov. 19, 1828. He came of Moravian and Silesian peasant stock. By his father, the schoolmaster at Lichtenthal and an amateur cellist, the gifted boy was taught violin playing at the age of 8; by choirmaster Holzer, the piano, organ, singing, and thoroughbass, becoming first soprano in the church choir in his tenth year. In 1808 he was admitted into the Vienna court choir as a singer, and also entered the "Konvict," the training school for the court singers. His teachers in theory were Ruzicka and Salieri (the latter from 1812 until at least 1816). He also played in the school orchestra, finally as 1st violin. His earliest extant song, *Hagars Klage* (dated March 30, 1811), and several others of the period, show that Zumsteeg was his model at this time; he also cultivated instrumental composition, especially chamber music; his First Symphony was written in 1813. In this year, his voice having broken, he left the "Konvict." His first Mass was completed in 1814 and successfully performed. Meantime he fitted himself for the post of elementary teacher in his father's school, and taught there until 1816. During these three years, the future supreme exponent of the German lied devoted his leisure to obtaining a thorough mastery of vocal expression. His usual method of composition was to jot down the melody with a sketch of the harmony, and then to write out the piece in full, following this first version by a second for the elimination of faults; when the second failed to satisfy him, the song was subjected to a third, or even a fourth, revision (e.g., *Erlkönig* and *Die Forelle*). Such masterworks as *Gretchen am Spinnrade* (Oct. 19, 1814) and *Erlkönig* (1815) mark the swift and unique development of his genius. In the year 1815 he composed as many as 144 songs; in one day (Oct. 15) he wrote eight. From 1814–16 he also composed 2 operettas, 3 Singspiele, and 3 other (fragmentary) stage pieces, none of which were then performed, 4 Masses, other church music, etc. In 1816 his application for the musical directorship of the new State Normal School at Laibach was rejected. The following year he left his place in the Lichtenthal school, and from 1818 made Vienna his home, with the exception of two summers (1818 and 1824) spent at Zelész, Hungary, as music teacher in Count Esterházy's family. From 1817 his friend Franz von Schober (1796–1882) generously aided him, often sharing lodgings and purse with the struggling artist. Through him, Schubert became acquainted with the famous baritone Michael Vogl, one of the first and greatest interpreters of his songs; through his influence Schubert's musical farce, *Die Zwillingsbrüder,* was brought out at the Kärnthnerthor Theater (June 14, 1820), but made little impression. In 1821, however, when he had already written over 600 compositions, his *Erlkönig* was sung at a public concert of the Musikverein with great applause, and others followed at other concerts; Cappi & Diabelli were induced to publish on commission 20 songs (*Erlkönig* was the first), which were so successful that Diabelli assumed the risk of further publications; from 1826 his songs and piano music had good sales. Efforts to obtain a salaried post were unsuccessful; that of vice-Kapellmeister to the court, for which he applied in 1826, was given to Weigl; his friends failed to obtain a similar position for him in Hamburg; and the conductorship of the Kärnthner-thor Theater was also refused him in 1827. Not until March 26, 1828, did he give a public concert of his own works (the E-flat Trio, a movement from the D minor Quartet, songs, etc.), which was an artistic and pecuniary success. Excepting such occasional and momentary good fortune, his life was a continual battle for the daily means of subsistence; although his genius was fully recognized by musicians like Salieri, Weigl, and the singer Vogl, and his songs were highly praised by Beethoven, he was wretchedly underpaid by his publishers, and his greatest works were almost totally neglected. His wonderful gifts and genial and buoyant disposition won many friends; chief among them the poet Mayrhofer, the family von Sonnleithner (at whose house Schubert's compositions were often performed long before their introduction to the public), Baron von Schönstein (whose singing aided in bringing Schubert's lyrical songs into vogue), Moritz Schwind, and Anselm Hüttenbrenner. Two visits which Schubert paid to Beethoven are recorded; but they were never intimate. For months previous to his death, Schubert had been failing; his final illness was brought to a fatal termination by an attack of typhus. He was buried, at his own desire, in the Ostfriedhof at Währing, his grave being the third from Beethoven's. When, in 1888, the remains of both masters were transferred to the Zentralfriedhof, the new graves also were only a few feet apart. In 1897 Brahms was buried close by.

Schubert was the least "schooled" of all great German musicians. For this lack of training, his keen musical intuition and inexhaustible resources of melody amply compensated. The spontaneity and fecundity of his song compositions are not more astounding than the perfection with which the music—melody and accompaniment—fits the poem. He is regarded as the creator of the modern German lied. His known songs for solo voice with piano accompaniment number 634. As to his alleged carelessness in choice of subjects for musical setting, the fact is that he took 72 poems by Goethe, 46 by Schiller, 44 by Wilhelm Müller, 28 by Matthison, 23 by Hölty, 22 by Kosegarten, 13 by Körner, etc.—that is, the best at his command. He also set 47 poems by Mayrhofer and 12 by Schober, both his warm personal friends. Of Heine (then a newcomer) he composed only 6 numbers (in the Schwanengesang). Equally inspired is his transfernece of the "Liedform" to the piano in the Moments musicaux and Impromptus—a miniature form of piano composition extensively copied. In larger forms, his Symphony in C (1828) and the "Unfinished" Symphony in B minor are equal to the best after Beethoven—and Schubert was but 31 when he died.

WORKS: OPERAS AND OTHER STAGE MUSIC: Die Zauberharfe, 3-act melodrama (Vienna, Aug. 19, 1820); Alfonso und Estrella, 3-act opera (1821–22; first produced Weimar, June 24, 1854, by Liszt); Die Verschworenen, later called Der häusliche Krieg, 1-act operetta (1823; Frankfurt, Aug. 29, 1861); Fierabras, 3-act opera (1823; Karlsruhe, Feb. 9, 1897); incidental music to the drama Rosamunde von Cypern (overture from Die Zauberharfe) (Vienna, Dec. 20, 1823); Die Bürgschaft (1816); etc.

CHORAL WORKS: 6 Latin Masses; Deutsche Messe (for 4-part mixed chorus with organ); oratorio Lazarus (fragment); Psalm 92 (for baritone solo and mixed chorus); 2 Tantum ergo (for 4-part mixed chorus with orch.); 2 Stabat Mater (4 voices with orch.); several Salve regina; Miriams Siegesgesang (for soprano solo, chorus, and orch.); prayer Vor der Schlacht (for soli, mixed chorus, and piano); hymn Herr unser Gott (for 8-part men's chorus with wind instruments); Hymne an den Heiligen Geist (for 8-part men's chorus with orch.); Morgengesang im Walde (for 4-part men's chorus with orch.); Nachtgesang im Walde and Nachthelle (for 4-part men's chorus and horns); Schlachtlied (8-part men's chorus with piano); Glaube, Hoffnung und Liebe (for mixed chorus and wind); numerous part-songs.

FOR ORCH.: 8 symphonies, the last being No. 9; the uncounted symphony is No. 7, which exists only in sketches; the "Unfinished" Symphony, consisting of 2 complete movements, is No. 8; Schubert is supposed to have written another symphony, the "Gastein," in 1825, but no trace of it has been found; 7 overtures (2 in "the Italian style"); Concertstück for violin with orch.; etc.

CHAMBER MUSIC: Octet for strings, horn, bassoon, and clarinet, op. 166; Piano Quintet in A, op. 144 (the "Forellenquintet," with double bass); String Quintet in C, op. 163 (with 2 cellos); 15 string quartets; 2 piano trios; String Trio in B-flat; for piano and violin: Rondo brillant in B minor, op. 70; Phantasie in C, op. 159; Sonata in A, op. 162; 3 sonatinas, op. 137; Introduction and Variations for flute and piano, op. 160; etc. For Piano (2 hands): 22 sonatas (including op. 42, in A minor; op. 53, D; op. 78 (fantasia), G; op. 120, A; op. 122, E-flat; op. 143, A minor; op. 147, B; op. 164, A minor; and 3 grand posthumous sonatas in C minor, A, and B-flat); 8 Impromptus, opp. 90, 142; 6 Moments musicaux, op. 94; Adagio and Rondo, op. 145; Fantasia in C, op. 15; sets of variations (op. 10, E minor, on a French air; op. 35, in A-flat; on a Diabelli waltz; op. 2, in C, on Hérold's Marie; etc.); many waltzes (opp. 9, 18, 33, 50 [34 Valses sentimentales], 67 [Hommage aux belles Viennoises], 77 [10 Valses nobles], 91 [12 Grätzer Walzer], etc.); Wanderer-Fantasie in C, op. 15 (arr. for piano and orch. by Liszt); 2 Scherzos; 5 Klavierstücke; etc. For piano 4 hands: 2 sonatas (op. 30, B-flat; op. 140, C); Divertissement à l'hongroise, op. 54; Divertissement in E minor, op. 63; Fantasia in F minor, op. 103; Grand rondo in A, op. 107; Notre amitié, rondo in D, op. 138; Andantino and rondo, op. 84; Lebensstürme, allegro caractéristique, op. 144; Fugue in E minor, op. 52; Polonaises, opp. 61, 75; Variations, opp. 10, 35, 82; 3 Waltzes, op. 33; 4 Ländler; Marches (opp. 27, 40, 51, 55 [Trauermarsch], 66 [héroïque], 121.

SONGS: Erlkönig, op. 1; Gretchen am Spinnrade, op. 2; Heidenröslein, op. 3; Der Wanderer and Der du von dem Himmel bist, in op. 4; 3 Gesänge des Harfners, op. 12; Erster Verlust, Der Fischer, and Es war ein König in Thule, in op. 5; the Suleika songs, opp. 14, 31; An Schwager Kronos, in op. 19; Mignon's songs, op. 62; Über allen Gipfeln ist Ruh', in op. 96 (all the above by Goethe); the grand song cycles by Wilhelm Müller,

Die schöne Müllerin, op. 25, and *Die Winterreise,* op. 89, containing 20 and 24 numbers respectively; 7 songs from Scott's *Lady of the Lake (Fräulein vom See),* op. 52; 9 songs from Ossian; *Der Tod und das Mädchen; Nähe des Geliebten; Des Mädchens Klage; Gruppe aus dem Tartarus; Nur wer die Sehnsucht kennt; Frühlingsglaube; Die Forelle; Du bist die Ruh';* the Barcarolle *Auf dem Wasser zu singen;* 6 songs by Heine, in the *Schwanengesang;* and many more of surpassing beauty.

A complete critical edition of Schubert's works in 40 vols. (21 series), edited by E. Mandyczewski (assisted by Brahms, Brüll, Hellmesberger, J. N. Fuchs, etc.), was publ. from 1888–97 by Breitkopf & Härtel. Since the publication of the monumental edition Max Friedlaender discovered the MSS of about 100 lost songs, which were first publ. in Peters's complete edition of the songs (7 vols.). A new critical edition, the *Neue Ausgabe Samtliche Werke,* under the direction of the Internationalen Schubert-Gesellschaft, was begun in 1964. The thematic index is by O. E. Deutsch and D. R. Wakeling, *Schubert: Thematic Catalogue of all His Works in Chronological Order* (N.Y., 1951).

BIBLIOGRAPHY: BIOGRAPHY: H. Kreissle von Hellborn, *F. S., eine biographische Skizze* (Vienna, 1861; 2nd, greatly enlarged, ed. as *F. S.,* 1865; in English, London, 1866); H. Barbedette, *F. S. Sa vie, ses œuvres, son temps* (Paris, 1865); La Mara, *F. S.,* in vol. I of *Musikalische Studienköpfe* (Leipzig, 1868; 9th ed., 1894; reprinted separately, 1912); A. Audley, *F. S., sa vie et ses œuvres* (Paris, 1871); A. Reissmann, *F. S. Sein Leben und seine Werke* (Berlin, 1873); G. L. Austin, *The Life of F. S.* (Boston, 1873); H. F. Frost, *S.* (N.Y., 1881); M. Friedlaender, *Beiträge zu einer Biographie F. S.s* (Rostock, 1887); A. Niggli, *S.* (Leipzig, 1890); H. Ritter, *S.* (Bamberg, 1896); F. Skalla, *F. S.* (Prague, 1897); H. Frost, *S.* (London, 1899); M. Zenger, *F. S.s Wirken und Erdenwallen* (Langensalza, 1902); R. Heuberger, *S.* (Berlin, 1902; 2nd ed., 1908); E. Duncan, *S.* (London, 1905); W. Klatte, *S.* (Berlin, 1907); L.-A. Bourgault-Ducoudray, *S.* (Paris, 1908; new ed., 1926); H. Antcliffe, *S.* (London, 1910); W. Dahms, *S.* (Berlin, 1912); O. E. Deutsch, *F. S. Die Dokumente seines Lebens und Schaffens* (3 vols. planned; only 2 publ.; Munich, 1913–14); R. Heuberger, *F. S.* (vol. 14 of Riemann's *Berühmte Musiker;* 1921); K. Kobald, *S. und Schwind* (Zurich, 1921); Th. Gerold, *S.* (Paris, 1923); O. Bie, *F. S.* (Berlin, 1925; in English, N.Y., 1929); M. Friedlaender, *S.: Skizze seines Lebens und Wirkens* (Leipzig, 1928); A. Weiss, *F. S.* (Vienna, 1928); P. Stefan, *F. S.* (Berlin, 1928; new ed., Vienna, 1947); P. Landormy, *La Vie de S.* (Paris, 1928); J.-G. Prod'homme, *S.* (Paris, 1928); J.-G. Prod'homme, *S. raconté par ceux qui l'ont vu* (Paris, 1928); C. Whitaker-Wilson, *F. S.* (London, 1928); E. Roggeri, *S.* (Turin, 1928); E. H. Bethge, *F. S.* (Leipzig, 1928); H. Eulenberg, *S. und die Frauen* (Hellerau, 1928); N. Flower, *F. S.* (London and N.Y., 1928; new ed., 1949); K. Kobald, *F. S. und seine Zeit* (Zürich, 1928; new ed., in English, N.Y., 1928); G. R. Kruse, *F. S.* (Bielefeld, 1928); R. Pitrou, *F. S.* (Paris, 1928); A. K. Glazunov, *S.* (Leningrad, 1928); R. Pecio Agüero, *S.* (in Spanish; Paris, 1929); M. Tibaldi Chiesa, *S.* (Milan, 1932; 2nd ed., 1936); R. Bates, *F. S.* (London, 1934); W. Vetter, *F. S.* (Potsdam, 1934); E. Duncan, *S.* (revised ed. N.Y., 1934); G. Schünemann, *Erinnerungen an S.* (Berlin, 1936); E. Buenzod, *F. S.* (4th ed., Paris, 1937); J. Bruyr, *F. S.* (Brussels, 1938); A. Silvestrelli, *F. S.* (Salzburg, 1939); A. Orel, *Der junge S.* (Vienna, 1940); A. Kolb, *F. S., sein Leben* (Stockholm, 1941); K. Höcker, *Wege zu S.* (Regensburg, 1942); R. Tenschert, *Du holde Kunst: Ein kleiner S.-Spiegel* (Vienna, 1943); B. Paumgartner, *F. S.* (Zürich, 1943; 2nd ed., 1947); W. & P. Rehberg, *F. S.* (Zürich, 1946); O. E. Deutsch, *S.: A Documentary Biography* (London, 1946; a transl. and revision of *F. S. Die Dokumente seines Lebens;* a work of fundamental importance; American ed. as *The S. Reader,* N.Y., 1947); A. Hutchings, *S.* (London, 1947; 3rd ed., 1956); C. Weingartner, *F. S.* (Alten, 1947); R. H. Schauffler, *F. S.: The Ariel of Music* (N.Y., 1949); H. Malherbe, *F. S., son amour, ses amitiés* (Paris, 1949); A. Einstein, *S.: A Musical Portrait* (N.Y., 1951); H. Rutz, *S., Dokumente seines Lebens und Schaffens* (Munich, 1952); H. Goldschmidt, *F. S.* (Berlin, 1954); P. Mies, *F. S.* (Leipzig, 1954); O. E. Deutsch, ed., *S.: Die Erinnerungen seiner Freunde* (Leipzig, 1957; in English, as *S.: Memoirs by His Friends,* N.Y., 1958); M. J. E. Brown, *S.: A Critical Biography* (London, 1958); J. Reed, *S.: The Final Years* (London, 1972); J. Wechsberg, *S.* (N.Y., 1977).

CRITICISM, APPRECIATION: J. Rissé, *S. in seinen Liedern* (2 vols.; Hannover, 1872); E. Mandyczewski, "F. S.s Werke," in series XX of B. & H.'s complete ed. (Leipzig, 1895); M. Friedlaender, *F. S. zu seinen 100. Geburtstage* (Berlin, 1897); H. de Curzon, *Les Lieder de F. S.* (Brussels, 1899); O. E. Deutsch, *S.-Brevier* (Berlin, 1905); M. Vancsa, *S. und seine Verleger* (Vienna, 1905); L. Scheibler, "S.s einstimmige Lieder mit Texten von Schiller," *Die Rheinlande* (1905); A. Nathansky, *Bauernfeld und S.* (Trieste, 1906); D. G. Mason, *The Romantic Composers* (N.Y., 1906); M. Gallet, *S. et le Lied* (Paris, 1907); A. Schnerich, *Messe und Requiem seit Haydn und Mozart* (Vienna, 1909); O. Wissig, *F. S.s Messen* (Leipzig, 1909); G. H. Clutsam, *S.* (N.Y., 1912); M. Bauer, *Die Lieder F. S.s* (Leipzig, 1915); H. von der Pfordten, *S. und das deutsche Lied* (1916; 2nd ed., Leipzig, 1920); W. Kahl, "Das lyrische Klavierstück S.s," *Archiv für Musikwissenschaft* 3 (1921); O. E. Deutsch, *Die Originalausgaben von S.s Goethe-Lieder* (Vienna, 1926); H. Költzsch, *F. S. in seinen Klaviersonaten* (Leipzig, 1927); Felicitas von Kraus, *Beiträge zur Erforschung des malenden und poetisierenden Wesens in der Begleitung von F. S.s Liedern* (Mainz, 1927); P. Mies, *S., der Meister des Liedes* (Berlin, 1928); F. Günther, *S.s Lied* (Stuttgart, 1928); F. V. Damian, *F. S.s Liederkreis, Die schöne Müllerin* (Leipzig, 1928); K. Kobald, *Der Miester des deutschen Liedes, F. S.* (Vienna and Leipzig, 1928); F. Weingartner, *S. und sein Kreis* (Zürich, 1928); C. Lafite, *Das Schubertlied und seine Sänger* (Vienna, 1928); R. Capell, *S.'s Songs* (London, 1928); K. Huschke, *Das 7 Gestirn der grossen S.'schen Kammermusikwerke* (Pritzwalk, 1928); H. Biehle, *S.s Lieder als Gesangsproblem* (Langensalza, 1929); A. Farinelli, *Beethoven und S.* (Turin, 1929); Th. Werner, "S.s Tod," in "Joh. Wolf-Festschrift" (1929); *Bericht über den Internationalen Kongress für Schubertforschung* (Augsburg, 1929); H. Bosch, *Die Entwicklung des Romantischen in S.s Liedern* (Leipzig, 1930); H. J. Therstappen, *Die Entwicklung der Form bei S.* (Leipzig,

1931); E. Laaff, *F. S.s Sinfonien* (Wiesbaden; Part I, 1933); T. Archer, "The Formal Construction of *Die schöne Müllerin,*" *Musical Quarterly* (Oct. 1934); H. Eschmann, *S.-Beethoven* (Cologne, 1934); P. Egert, *Die Klaviersonate im Zeitalter der Romantik* (Berlin, 1934); E. G. Porter, *The Songs of S.* (London, 1937); E. Schaeffer, "S.'s *Winterreise,*" *Musical Quarterly* (Jan. 1938); G. Abraham, ed., *The Music of S.* (N.Y., 1947); O. E. Deutsch, "The Discovery of S.'s Great C Major Symphony: a Story in 15 Letters," *Musical Quarterly* (Oct. 1952); W. Vetter, *Der Klassiker S.* (2 vols., Leipzig, 1953); M. J. E. Brown, "S.'s *Winterreise,* Part I," *Musical Quarterly* (April 1953); E. Schmitz, *S.s Auswirkung auf die deutsche Musik bis zu Hugo Wolf und Bruckner* (Leipzig, 1954); M. J. E. Brown, *Essays on Schubert* (London, 1966); T. G. Georgiades, *Schubert: Musik und Lyrik* (Göttingen, 1967); H. Gal, *F. S. oder Die Melodie* (Frankfurt, 1970; in English as *F. S. and the Essence of Melody,* London, 1974); D. Fischer-Dieskan, *Auf den Spuren der Schubert-Lieder; Werden-Wesen-Wir* (Weisbaden, 1971; in English as *S. A Biographical Study of the Songs,* London, 1976). Gerald Moore, *The Schubert Song Cycles, with Thoughts on Performance* (1974).

CORRESPONDENCE, ETC.: O. E. Deutsch, *F. S.s Briefe und Schriften* (Munich, 1922; 4th ed., Vienna, 1954; English transl. with foreword by E. Newman, London, 1928); O. E. Deutsch, *S.s Tagebuch* (1928).

CATALOGUES, ICONOGRAPHY, ETC.: G. Nottebohm, *Thematisches Verzeichniss der im Druck erschienenen Werke von F. S.* (Vienna, 1874); A. Trost, *F. S.-Bildnisse* (Vienna, 1893); H. de Curzon, *Bibliographie critique de F. S.* (Brussels, 1900); W. Kahl, *Verzeichnis des Schrifttums über F. S., 1828-1928* (Regensburg, 1938); A. Orel, *F. S. Sein Leben in Bildern* (Leipzig, 1939).

E. Decsey dramatized Schubert's life in a play entitled *Der unsterbliche Franz* (music by J. Bittner; Vienna, 1930). The musical score of the popular operetta *Blossom Time* (Romberg) is based on melodies by Schubert.

Schubert, Franz, German violinist; b. Dresden, July 22, 1808; d. there, April 12, 1878. He was son and pupil of the Konzertmeister **Franz Anton Schubert** (1768-1827); also took lessons with Rottmeier and L. Haase; then went to Paris where he studied with Lafont. Upon return to Dresden he joined the royal orch. (1823) and in 1861 succeeded Lipinski as 1st Konzertmeister. He was often confused with his great namesake, much to his distress, for he regarded himself as superior. He wrote a celebrated violin piece *L'Abeille;* also composed violin etudes; a fantasia for violin with orch. and numerous other violin pieces.

Schubert, Louis, German violinist; b. Dessau, Jan. 27, 1828; d. Dresden, Sept. 17, 1884. He went to St. Petersburg at the age of 17; then was concertmaster of the City Theater in Königsberg for 6 years; eventually settled in Dresden and became a singing teacher. He produced the operettas *Aus Sibirien* (Königsberg, 1865), *Die Rosenmädchen* (Königsberg, 1860), *Die Wahrsagerin* (Dresden, 1864), *Die beiden Geizigen* (Altenburg, 1879), and *Faustina Hasse* (Altenburg,

1879); publ. a method for violin and a *Gesangschule in Liedern.*

Schuberth, Julius (Ferdinand Georg), founder of the firm of "J. Schuberth & Co." of Leipzig and New York; b. Magdeburg, July 14, 1804; d. Leipzig, June 9, 1875. Established the Hamburger business in 1826; opened a branch at Leipzig, 1832, and at New York, 1850. His brother, **Fritz Wilhelm** (1817-1890), took over the Hamburg house in 1853 (firm name, "Fritz Schuberth"). Schuberth publ. the *Kleine Hamburger Musikzeitung* (1840-50), the *New Yorker Musikzeitung* (from 1867), and *Schuberth's kleine Musikzeitung* (1871-72). In 1872 he founded the music library at Weimar known as the Liszt-Schuberth-Stiftung. In 1891 the business was purchased by Felix Siegel (d. Leipzig, July 4, 1920), the originator of the *Musikalische Universalbibliothek.* In 1943 the entire stock of the Schuberth Publishing House was destroyed in an air raid; after World War II it was re-established in Wiesbaden.

Schuberth, Karl, German cellist; b. Magdeburg, Feb. 25, 1811; d. Zürich, July 22, 1863. He studied in Magdeburg and Dessau; after a European tour, which included Russia (1835), was engaged as court musician in St. Petersburg, and remained there for 20 years. He then went to Switzerland. He publ. 2 cello concertos, Variations for cello with orch.; String Octet; 2 string quintets; 4 string quartets; Cello Sonata.

Schubiger, Anselm (baptismal names **Josef Allis**), learned Swiss writer on music; b. Uznach, March 5, 1815; d. at the Monastery of Einsiedeln, March 14, 1888. He took holy orders in 1839 and assumed the clerical name Anselm. He wrote *Die Sängerschule St. Gallens* (Einsiedeln, 1858); *Die Pflege des Kirchengesanges und der Kirchenmusik in der deutschen katholischen Schweiz* (Einsiedeln, 1873); *Musikalische Spicilegien* (Berlin, 1876; a collection of miscellaneous essays on medieval music); also various papers publ. in journals.

Schuch, Ernst von, eminent Austrian conductor; b. Graz, Nov. 23, 1846; d. Kötzschenbroda, near Dresden, May 10, 1914. He studied violin; in 1867 he became theater conductor in Breslau; then conducted in Würzburg, Graz, and Basel; in 1872 he obtained a position with Pollini's Italian Opera House in Dresden, and in 1873 was engaged as court conductor, remaining with the Dresden Court Opera for 40 years. In 1897 he was given the rank of hereditary nobility, which entitled him to add the nobiliary particle "von" to his name. He was a worthy successor to the traditions established in Dresden by Weber and Wagner, and earned the reputation of one of the finest opera conductors. He was moreover a man of great general culture and of progressive ideas. He brought out about 50 new operas, and conducted the world premiere of the operas *Feuersnot, Salome, Elektra* and *Der Rosenkavalier* by Richard Strauss; also included in his repertory operas by Puccini, which were new to Germany at the time. He seldom left Dresden; his most extensive journey was a trip to New York where he conducted 3 orchestral concerts in 1900. In 1875 he married the opera singer **Klementine Proska** (real name **Procházka;** b. Ödenburg, Feb. 12, 1850; d. Kötzschenbroda, June 8, 1932), who was the principal coloratura soprano during Schuch's tenure at the Dresden Opera until her retirement in 1904. Their daughter **Liesel von Schuch** (b. Dresden, Dec. 12, 1891) was also a coloratura soprano at the Dresden Opera from 1914 to 1935; then taught voice at the Dresden Musikhochschule (until 1967).

BIBLIOGRAPHY: L. Hartmann, "Ernst Schuch und das moderne Kapellmeistertun," *Nord und Süd* (May 1896; Breslau); P. Sakolowski, *Ernst von Schuch* (Leipzig, 1901); F. von Schuch, *Richard Strauss, Ernst von Schuch und Dresdens Oper* (2nd ed., Leipzig, 1953).

Schucht, Jean F., German writer on music; b. Holzthalleben, Thuringia, Nov. 17, 1822; d. Leipzig, March 30, 1894. He studied with Hauptmann and Spohr at Kassel, and with Schnyder von Wartensee at Frankfurt; from 1868 was in Leipzig as critic for the *Neue Zeitschrift für Musik*. He publ. *Wegweiser in der Tonkunst* (1859); *Kleines Lexikon der Tonkunst; Partiturenkenntniss; Meyerbeers Leben und Bildungsgang* (1869); *Grundriss einer praktischen Harmonielehre* (1876); a biography of Chopin (1880); wrote piano pieces and songs.

Schudel, Thomas, American-born Canadian composer; b. Defiance, Ohio, Sept. 8, 1937. He studied composition and bassoon at Ohio State Univ. (1955–59), receiving an M.A. in both subjects there in 1961; then joined the composition classes with Bassett and Finney at the Univ. of Michigan (1961–64). He subsequently was principal bassoonist with the Regina, Canada, Symph. Orch. (1964–74) and taught at the Univ. of Regina (1964–67 and 1972–78); became a Canadian citizen in 1974.

WORKS: *4 Movements* for flute, bassoon and percussion (1963); *4 Movements* for cello and piano (1964); *Set No. 1* for violin, cello, flute, oboe and percussion (1965); *Set No. 2* for wind quintet and brass quintet (1966); *Violin Sonata* (1966); *String Quartet* (1967); *Symph. No. 1* (1971; Trieste, Italy, Oct. 20, 1972; won the Trieste International Competition for symphonic composition); *Mosaic* for flute, 3 percussionists and tape (1974); *Variations* for orch. (1976–77); *Nocturne and Dance* for oboe and piano (1977); *The Dream* for piano (1977).

Schuecker, Edmund, Austrian harpist; b. Vienna, Nov. 16, 1860; d. Bad Kreuznach, Nov. 9, 1911. After studying with Zamara at the Vienna Cons. he played the harp in various orchestras; taught at the Leipzig Cons. (1884). In 1891 he went to America as harpist of the newly organized Chicago Symph.; was a member of the Pittsburgh Symph. (1903–04) and of the Philadelphia Orch. (1904–09). He wrote pieces for harp, of which a *Mazurka* became popular; also published the harp manuals *Etüden- und Melodien-Album* (4 books), *Etüdenschule* (3 books), *6 Virtuosenetüden, Orchestra-Studies* (5 books), *The Most Important Parts from Wagner's Operas* (2 books).

Schuecker, Heinrich, Austrian-American harpist, brother of **Edmund Schuecker;** b. Vienna, Nov. 25, 1867; d. Boston, April 17, 1913. He studied at the Vienna Cons. (1878–84) with Zamara. In 1885 he was engaged as 1st harpist of the Boston Symph. Orch., and held this position until his death. He also taught harp at the New England Cons., Boston.

Schuecker, Joseph E., harpist, son of **Edmund Schuecker;** b. Leipzig, May 19, 1886; d. Los Angeles, Dec. 9, 1938. He studied with his father, and later at the Vienna Cons. with Zamara. From 1904 to 1909 he was 1st harpist of the Pittsburgh Symph. Orch.; in 1909 succeeded his father as harpist in the Philadelphia Orch.; from 1915 till 1920 taught at the Carnegie Institute at Pittsburgh; from 1926 till 1930, again played in the Pittsburgh Symph.; then lived in California. He was the author of a *History of the Harp.*

Schueller, Rudolf, Austrian conductor; b. Böhmisch-Leipz, July 31, 1884; d. Cleveland, Aug. 1, 1949. He studied at the Univ. of Prague; conducted opera in Berlin (1909–14); after World War I was engaged at the Rumanian Opera at Cluj (1920–24); in 1925 he settled in America; was head of the Opera School of the Cleveland Institute of Music; wrote operas and orchestral works.

Schuh, Willi, eminent Swiss musicologist; b. Basel, Nov. 12, 1900. He studied in Munich with Courvoisier, Sandberger, and Beer-Walbrunn; then took courses with Ernst Kurth in Bern; Dr. phil., 1927; was active mainly as music critic and editor; wrote music criticism for the *Neue Zürcher Zeitung* (1928–65); also was editor of the *Schweizerische Musikzeitung* (1928–68); in 1969 he was elected an honorary member of the Swiss Union of Composers. For his 70th birthday he was honored by a Festschrift, *Umgang mit Musik* (Zürich, 1970; contains a list of his publications). His books include *Das Volkslied in der Schweiz* (1932); *Othmar Schoeck* (Zürich, 1934); *Über Opern von Richard Strauss* (Zürich, 1947); *Zeitgenössische Musik* (Zürich, 1947); *Schweizer Musik der Gegenwart* (Zürich, 1948); *Richard Strauss, Betrachtungen und Erinnerungen* (Zürich, 1949; English, London, 1953; enlarged ed., Zürich, 1957); *Richard Strauss, Hugo von Hofmannsthal. Briefwechsel* (Zürich, 1964; enlarged ed., 1970). He was one of the editors of the *Schweizer Musiklexikon* (Zürich, 1964).

Schulhoff, Erwin, Czech composer and pianist; great-grandnephew of **Julius Schulhoff;** b. Prague, June 8, 1894; d. in a concentration camp, Wülzburg, Bavaria, Aug. 18, 1942. He studied music in Prague and Vienna; then went to Leipzig, where he studied piano with Teichmüller and composition with Max Reger (1908–10); continued his studies in Cologne (1910–14). Returning to Prague, he was active as a piano teacher; traveled as a concert pianist in Russia and France. He was an eager propagandist of modern music; together with Alois Hába he worked on the problems of quarter-tone music. In 1933 he was a delegate at the International Congress of Revolutionary Musicians in Moscow. Convinced of the necessity of social revolution, he became a member of the Communist Party; after the Nazi occupation of Czechoslovakia in 1939 he was granted Soviet citizenship to protect him from arrest; however, after the Nazi invasion of Russia in 1941, he was taken to the concentration camp, where he died in the following year. As a composer, he followed the modern trends of the period between the two wars, including the European species of jazz. He was the first to set to music the original German text of the Communist Manifesto of 1848; the manuscript disappeared, but was eventually retrieved, and the work was finally performed in Prague on April 5, 1962.

WORKS: FOR THE STAGE: *Ogelala*, ballet (Dessau, Nov. 21, 1925); *La Somnambule*, ballet dance-grotesque (1925; Oxford ISCM festival, July 24, 1931); *Bartipanu*, ballet scenes for Molière's *Le Bourgeois Gentilhomme* (1926; also an orchestral suite); *Plameny (Flames)*, opera (1927-28; Brno, Jan. 27, 1932). FOR ORCH.: 2 piano concertos (1913, 1923); *32 Variations on an Original Theme* (1919); *Suite* for chamber orch. (1921); 8 symphonies: No. 1 (1925); No. 2 (1932; Prague, April 24, 1935); No. 3 (1935); No. 4, *Spanish*, for baritone and orch. (1936-37); No. 5 (1938); No. 6, *Symphony of Freedom*, with choral finale (1940-41; Prague, May 5, 1946); No. 7, *Eroica* (1941; unfinished); No. 8 (1942; unfinished); *Double Concerto* for flute, piano, string orchestra and 2 horns (Prague, Dec. 8, 1927); Concerto for String Quartet and Wind Orch. (1930; Prague, Nov. 9, 1932). CHAMBER MUSIC: 2 violin sonatas (1913, 1927); cello sonata (1915); *5 Pieces* for string quartet (1923); String Sextet (1924); 2 string quartets (1924, 1925); Duo for violin and cello (1925); *Concertino* for flute, viola and double bass (1925); *Divertissement* for oboe, clarinet, and bassoon (1926); Sonata for solo violin (1927); Flute Sonata (1927); *Hot Sonata* for saxophone and piano (1930). VOCAL MUSIC: *Landschaften (Landscapes)*, vocal symph. for mezzo-soprano and orch. (1918); *Menschheit (Humanity)*, vocal symph. for alto and orch. (1919); *H.M.S. Royal Oak*, jazz oratorio (radio performance, Brno, Feb. 12, 1935); *The Communist Manifesto*, cantata to the German text of the famous declaration of Marx and Engels (1932, Prague, April 5, 1962); *1917*, cycle of 12 songs (1933). FOR PIANO: *Variations on an Original Theme* (1913); *5 Grotesken* (1917); 4 sonatas (1918, 1924, 1926, 1927); *5 Arabesken* (1919); *Ironies* (1920); *Rag Music* (1922); *Partita* (1922); *Ostinato* (1923); *5 Etudes de Jazz* (1926); *6 Esquisses de Jazz* (1927); *Hot Music* (1928); *Suite Dansante en Jazz* (1931).

BIBLIOGRAPHY: E. Schulhoff, *Vzpomniky, studie a dokumenty* (collection of articles and documents; Prague, 1958).

Schulhoff, Julius, noted pianist and composer; b. Prague, Aug. 2, 1825; d. Berlin, March 13, 1898. He studied in Prague; proceeded to Paris, where he gave concerts under the patronage of Chopin, to whom he dedicated his first composition, an *Allegro brillant*. He made a long tour through Austria, England, Spain, and Southern Russia; returning to Paris, he was a successful teacher; after the outbreak of the Franco-Prussian War (1870) he settled in Dresden; moved to Berlin shortly before his death. He publ. excellent salon music for piano; his *Galop di bravura* and *Impromptu Polka* were great favorites.

Schuller, Gunther, significant American composer, conductor and educator; b. New York, Nov. 22, 1925. He played the French horn in the Cincinnati Symph. Orch., and appeared as soloist in his own horn concerto (April 6, 1945); was 1st horn player in the orchestra of the Metropolitan Opera (1945-59); then was prof. of composition at the School of Music at Yale Univ. (1964-66); from 1966 to 1977 was president of the New England Cons. in Boston; also taught composition at the Berkshire Music Center in Tanglewood, Mass. In his performance, works, writings, and various pronouncements he has endeavored to establish a link between serious music and jazz; in 1950 he played French horn in the jazz ensemble led by Miles Davis that established the new style of "cool jazz" (recorded as *Birth of the Cool*); in 1957 he launched the slogan "Third Stream" to designate the combination of classical forms with improvisatory elements of jazz as a synthesis of disparate, but not necessarily incompatible, entities; in this effort he worked especially closely with John Lewis of the Modern Jazz Quartet, and composed several pieces specifically for the MJQ. As part of his investigation of the roots of jazz, he became interested in early ragtime and formed, in 1972, the New England Conservatory Ragtime Ensemble; a recording *(The Red Back Book)* made by this group of Scott Joplin piano rags in band arrangement was instrumental in bringing about the "ragtime revival" of the 1970s.

WORKS: *Suite* for woodwind quintet (1945); Cello Sonata (1946); *Fantasia Concertante* for 3 oboes and piano (1947); *Fantasia Concertante* for 3 trombones and piano (1947); Quartet for 4 double basses (1947); Trio for oboe, horn and viola (1948); Quintet for 4 horns and bassoon (1949); Symph. for brass and percussion (1950); 5 pieces for 5 horns (1952); Quartet for flute and strings (1953); *12 by 11* for chamber orch. and jazz group (1955); *Contours* for chamber orch. (1956); *Seven Studies on Themes of Paul Klee* for orch. (Minneapolis, Nov. 27, 1959); *Spectra* for orch. (N.Y., Jan. 15, 1960); *Variants*, a jazz ballet (N.Y., Jan. 4, 1961); *Contrasts* for orch. (Donaueschingen, Oct. 22, 1961); Piano Concerto (Cincinnati, Oct. 29, 1962); Symph. No. 1 (Dallas, Texas, Feb. 8, 1965); *American Triptych: Three Studies in Texture*, for orch. (New Orleans, March, 1965, composer conducting); Concerto for Orch. (1965; Chicago, Jan. 20, 1966; originally titled *Gala Music*); *The Visitation*, opera (Hamburg, Oct. 12, 1966); *Diptych* for brass quintet and orch., symphonic amplification of the original brass quintet (Boston, March 31, 1967); *Triplum* for orch. (N.Y., June 28, 1967); *Vertige d'Éros*, symph. poem (Madison, Wisconsin, Oct. 15, 1967); Concerto for Double Bass and Orch. (N.Y., June 27, 1968); *Shapes and Designs* for orch. (1968); *The Fisherman and His Wife*, children's opera after a Grimm fairy tale (Boston, May 8, 1970); *Tre Invenzione* for chamber ensemble (1972); Violin Concerto (1975-76). He published a manual, *Horn Technique* (N.Y., 1962) and a very valuable study, *Early Jazz: Its Roots and Musical Development* (N.Y., 1968).

Schulthess, Walter, Swiss conductor and composer; b. Zürich, July 24, 1894; d. there, June 23, 1971. He studied with Andreae in Zürich, with Courvoisier in

Munich, with Ansorge in Berlin; in 1918 settled in Zürich. As a composer, he excelled in lyric songs, in a style resembling Othmar Schoeck's. He also wrote 2 violin sonatas; *Variationen* for cello and orch.; Concertino for Piano and Orch.; piano pieces. He was married to the violinist **Stefi Geyer** (1888–1956).

Schultz, Edwin, German baritone and song composer; b. Danzig, April 30, 1827; d. Tempelhof, near Berlin, May 20, 1907. He studied singing with Brandstätter in Berlin; conducted choral societies and concerts. In 1880 the Prussian Ministry of War commissioned him to compile a book of soldiers' songs. He publ. many male choruses, songs, duets, and the collection *Meisterstücke für Pianoforte.*

Schultz, Helmut, German musicologist; b. Frankfurt, Nov. 2, 1904; killed in battle, Waldburg, April 19, 1945. He studied musicology with Kroyer in Leipzig; in 1933 was appointed to the faculty of the Univ. of Leipzig. He publ. several books: *Johann Vesque von Püttlingen* (Regensburg, 1930); *Instrumentenkunde* (Leipzig, 1931), *Das Madrigal als Formideal* (Leipzig, 1939); edited (with Robert Haas) the works of Hugo Wolf; also was editor of works by Haydn, Rosetti, etc.

Schultz, Svend, Danish composer and choral conductor; b. Nykøbing, Dec. 30, 1913. He studied at the Royal Cons. in Copenhagen (1933–38); became active as a piano teacher and choral conductor; was music critic of *Politiken*, the Copenhagen newspaper (1942–49). In his music, he evolved a neo-Classical style characterized by simplicity of form and a cumulative rhythmic drive.
  WORKS: 10 operas: *Bag Kulisserne* (*Behind the Scenes*, 1946; Copenhagen, May 26, 1949); *Solbadet* (*The Sunbath*, 1947; Aarhus, Nov. 26, 1949), *Kaffehuset* (*The Coffee House*, 1948), *Høst* (*Harvest*, 1950), *Bryllupsrejsen* (*The Honeymoon*, 1951), *Tordenvejret* (*The Thunderstorm*, 1954), *Hosekraemmeren* (*The Stocking Peddler*, 1955), *Dommer Lynch* (*Judge Lynch*, 1959), the comic television opera *Konen i Muddergrøften* (*The Woman in the Muddy Ditch*, 1964; Danish television, April 18, 1965) and the children's opera *Lykken og Forstanden* (1973); 2 marionette operas: *Hyrdinden og skorstensfejeren* (*The Shepherdess and the Chimney-Sweep*, 1953) and *The Marionettes* (1957); a chamber operetta, *Den kåde Donna* (Copenhagen, Aug. 30, 1957); a musical church play, *Eva* (1968); an oratorio, *Job* (1945); *Sankt Hans Nat* for soloists, chorus, and orch. (1953); *Hymn* for chorus and orch. (Copenhagen, March 13, 1957); *Hr. Mortens klosterrov* (*Morten's Pillage of the Monastery*) for soloists, chorus, and chamber orch. (1958; Copenhagen, Oct. 13, 1960); *3 Pastorales* for soloists, chorus, and orch. (Danish Radio, May 28, 1962); *The 4 Temperaments* for female and male choruses, and orch. (Hillerød, Nov. 15, 1974); *Serenade* for string orch. (1940); 5 symphonies: No. 1, *Sinfonia piccola* (1941), No. 2 (1949), No. 3 (1955), No. 4 (1958) and No. 5 (1962); Piano Concerto (1943); *Storstrømsbroen* (*The Storstroem Bridge*), symph. vision (1951); *Introduction and Rondo* for piano and orch. (Danish Radio, Nov. 8, 1964); *2 Variations: Nocturne and Aubade* for orch. (1965); *Sinfonia Piccola No. 2* (1973); *Northern*

Overture (1975); 5 string quartets (1939, 1940, 1960, 1961, 1962); Flute Quartet (1961); *Romantic Trio* for piano trio (1961); Quartet for flute, violin, viola and cello (1962); 2 piano trios (1942, 1963); Clarinet Quintet (1965); *Music for Wind Players* for flute, trumpet, clarinet, percussion, vibraphone, and piano (1966); piano sonata (1931); 2 piano sonatinas (1940, 1950).

Schultze, Norbert, German composer; b. Braunschweig, Jan. 26, 1911. He studied music and theatrical arts in Cologne and in Munich, and took lessons in piano and composition; during the season 1931–32 he acted in a student cabaret *Vier Nachrichter* under the name of **Frank Norbert;** then was theater conductor, arranger and composer in Munich. He wrote several operas, *Schwarzer Peter* (Hamburg, 1936); *Das kalte Herz* (Leipzig, 1943); the television opera, *Peter der dritte* (1964); operetta, *Regen in Paris* (Nuremberg, 1957); the pantomimes *Struwwelpeter* (Hamburg, 1937), *Max und Moritz* (Hamburg, 1938), *Maria im Walde* (Vienna, 1940); but his chief claim to fame was a sentimental song *Lili Marleen*, which he wrote in 1938, and which became immensely popular after it was broadcast from the German-occupied Belgrade in 1941; it became a hit throughout the war not only on the German side, but also among Allied soldiers on all fronts; it was translated into 27 languages.

Schulz, August, German vioinist, conductor, and composer; b. Lehre, near Brunswick, June 15, 1837; d. Brunswick, Feb. 12, 1909. He studied violin with Joachim; was violinist in the court orch. at Brunswick; then concertmaster at Detmold; returned to Brunswick as conductor of symphony concerts and choral societies. He wrote an opera, *Der wilde Jäger* (Brunswick, 1887); for chorus and orch.: *Eine Sommernacht, Prinzessin Ilse*, etc.; many male choruses; altogether nearly 200 opus numbers.

Schulz, Ferdinand, German choral conductor and composer; b. Kossar, near Krossen, Oct. 21, 1821; d. Berlin, May 27, 1897. He was pupil of A. W. Bach and Dehn in Berlin; after serving as chorister, he became conductor of the Cäcilien-Verein in 1856. He wrote motets and other church music; publ. male choruses, songs, and piano pieces.

Schulz, Johann Abraham Peter, German composer; b. Lüneburg, March 31, 1747; d. Schwedt, June 10, 1800. He studied with Kirnberger in Berlin; from 1768 to 1773 was music master to a Polish princess; from 1776 to 1778 was music director of the French theater in Berlin; then was Kapellmeister to Prince Heinrich at Rheinsberg (1780–87); from 1787 to 1795 he was court conductor at Copenhagen; finally returned to Germany, where he was director of an opera troupe.
  WORKS: A song composer of marked ability, he publ. in 1779 *Gesänge am Clavier*, in 1782 *Lieder im Volkston*, both printed together, with augmentations, as *Lieder im Volkston* in 1785; a 3rd book was publ. in 1790. His sacred songs are *Uzens lyrische Gedichte* (1784) and *Religiöse Oden und Lieder* (1786). *Chansons italiennes* (1782), *4 Lieder* with piano, and a *Rundgesang* (round) for mixed voices were also publ. Among his stage works are: *Das Opfer der*

Nymphen (Berlin, 1774); operetta, *La Fée Urgèle* (1782; in German as *Was den Damen gefällt*); operetta, *Clarisse, oder das unbekannte Dienstmädchen* (1783); tragic melodrama, *Minona* (1786; publ.); *Le Barbier de Séville* (Rheinsberg, 1786); the opera, *Aline, reine de Golconde* (Rheinsberg, 1787); the following were produced in Copenhagen: *Høstgildet* (*The Harvest Home*, Sept. 16, 1790); *Indtoget* (*Entry*; Feb. 26, 1793); *Peters Bryllup* (*Peter's Wedding*; Dec. 12, 1793). He further wrote church music, small instrumental works, a piano sonata, and various other pieces for piano (*Musikalische Belustigung, Musikalische Badinage, Musikalischer Luftball*, etc.); publ. *Entwurf einer neuen und leichtverständlichen Musiktablatur . . .* (1786; merely the old organ tablature); *Gedanken über den Einfluss der Musik auf die Bildung eines Volks* (1790); and claimed authorship of *Wahre Grundsätze zum Gebrauch der Harmonie* (1773; publ. as Kirnberger's).

BIBLIOGRAPHY: K. Klunger, *J. A. P. Schulz in seinen volkstümlichen Liedern* (Leipzig, 1909); O. K. Riess, *J. A. P. Schulz Leben* (dissertation, Leipzig, 1913); J. F. Reichardt, *J. A. P. Schulz* (new ed., Kassel, 1948).

Schulz, Johann Philipp Christian, German conductor and composer; b. Langensalza, Feb. 1, 1773; d. Leipzig, Jan. 30, 1827. He studied with Schicht at Leipzig; from 1810 was conductor of the Gewandhaus concerts. He published overtures to *Faust* and *Die Jungfrau von Orleans;* dances interpolated into *Faust* (arraged for piano); *Salvum fac regem* for 4 voices with brass; marches, etc.; songs with piano.

Schulz, Leo, German-American cellist; b. Posen, March 28, 1865; d. La Crescenta, Calif., Aug. 12, 1944. He was a child prodigy, and appeared in public at the age of 5; then studied at the Hochschule für Musik in Berlin; was 1st cellist with the Berlin Philharmonic (1885) and the Gewandhaus Orch. in Leipzig (1886–89); then settled in America; was 1st cellist of the Boston Symph. (1889–98), of the N.Y. Philharmonic (1899–1906); taught in various schools; wrote overtures, string quartets, and some cello music; edited *Cello Classics* (2 vols.), *Cello Album* (2 books), and *Cello Composers* (2 vols.).

Schulz-Beuthen, Heinrich, German composer; b. Beuthen, June 19, 1838; d. Dresden, March 12, 1915. He was destined for the career of civil engineer; while a student at the Univ. of Breslau, he learned to play the piano and attempted composition; produced a Singspiel, *Fridolin* (Breslau, 1862), then went to study at the Leipzig Cons., with Moscheles (piano) and Hauptmann (composition). In 1866 he went to Zürich, where he remained until 1880; then lived in Dresden (1880–93) and Vienna 1893–95); finally settled in Dresden, where he became prof. at the Cons. He was an ardent disciple of Liszt and Wagner; during his lifetime he was regarded as a significant composer.

WORKS: 8 symphonies: No. 1, *Dem Andenken Haydns;* No. 2, *Frühlingsfeier;* No. 3, *Sinfonia maestosa;* No. 4, *Schön Elsbeth;* No. 5, *Reformationssymphonie* (with organ); No. 6, *König Lear* (with male chorus); No. 7 (expanded from a string quartet); No. 8,

Siegessymphonie; the symph. poems *Mittelalterliche Volksszene, Des Meeres und der Liebe Wellen, Beethoven-Hymnus, Ein Pharaonenbegräbnis, Wilhelm Tell, Sturmesmythe;* overtures; orch. suites; *Symphonisches Konzert* for piano and orch.; String Quintet; Wind Octet; String Trio; etc.; a number of piano works (*Heroica Sonata, Erinnerung an die Jugendzeit, Präludium und Fuge);* several sacred choral works; the opera *Aschenbrödel* (Zürich, 1879; text by Mathilde Wesendonk) and 4 other operas.

BIBLIOGRAPHY: K. Mey, *H. Schulz-Beuthen* (Leipzig, 1909); A. Zosel, *H. Schulz-Beuthen* (Würzburg, 1931).

Schulz-Dornburg, Rudolf, German conductor; b. Würzburg, March 31, 1891; d. Gmund-am-Tegernsee, Aug. 16, 1949. He studied in Cologne, where he became a choral director; then conducted opera in Mannheim, Münster, and Essen; in 1934 settled in Berlin as radio conductor; from 1945 till 1948 was general music director in Lübeck.

Schulz-Evler, Andrei, Polish pianist; b. Radom, Dec. 12, 1852; d. Warsaw, May 15, 1905. He studied at the Warsaw Cons., and later with Tausig in Berlin; was prof. of piano at the Kharkov Music School (1888–1904); publ. 52 piano pieces and songs; his transcription of the *Blue Danube Waltz* was very popular with pianists for a time.

Schulz-Schwerin, Karl, German pianist; b. Schwerin, Jan. 3, 1845; d. Mannheim, May 24, 1913. He studied at the Stern Cons. in Berlin (1862–65) with Hans von Bülow, Stern, and Weitzmann. He was court pianist to the Grand Duke of Mecklenburg,; then taught at Stern's Cons. in Berlin (1885–1901); from 1901 lived in Mannheim. He composed a symphony, overtures to *Torquato Tasso* and *Die Braut von Messina; Serenata giocosa, In Memoriam,* and *Jubiläums-Festmarsch* for orch.; *Sanctus, Osanna, Benedictus, Ave Maria,* etc., for soli, chorus, and orch.; piano pieces.

Schuman, William Howard, eminent American composer, educator and music administrator; b. New York, Aug. 4, 1910. He studied harmony with Max Persin; then took lessons in composition with Charles Haubiel; in 1933 he entered Teacher's College at Columbia Univ. (B.S., 1935; M.A., 1937); attended the Mozarteum Academy in Salzburg during the summer of 1935; returning to N.Y., he became instructor at Sarah Lawrence College; took composition lessons with Roy Harris at a summer session of the Juilliard School of Music in 1936; on March 27, 1936 he married Frances Prince. He attracted the attention of Koussevitzky who gave the first performance of his *American Festival Overture* with the Boston Symph. Orch. in 1939, and later conducted his 3rd and 5th symphonies; his 4th Symphony was performed by Rodzinski in Cleveland in 1942, and the Coolidge String Quartet gave a performance of Schuman's String Quartet in 1940. He continued to teach at Sarah Lawrence College until 1945; then served as director of publications for G. Schirmer, Inc. (1945–52); in 1945, also, he was appointed president of the Juilliard School of Music, a post he held until 1962. Continuing his astonishing advance as an executive, he became president of Lincoln Center, N.Y., from 1962 to 1969; his career in this respect was unique among American composers. He was 1st recipient of the Pulitzer Prize in music in 1943; received the Composition Award of the American Academy of Arts and Letters; also held 2 successive Guggenheim Fellowship Awards (1939, 1940). His music is characterized by great emotional tension which is maintained by powerful asymmetric rhythms; the contrapuntal structures in his works reach a great degree of complexity and are saturated with dissonance, without, however, losing the essential tonal references. In several of his works he employs American melorhythms, but his general style of composition is cosmopolitan, exploring all viable techniques of modern composition.

WORKS: a "baseball opera" *The Mighty Casey* (Hartford, Conn., May 4, 1953; revised as a cantata, retitled *Casey at the Bat,* and produced in this version in Washington, April 6, 1976); BALLETS: *Undertow* (choreographer: Antony Tudor; N.Y., April 10, 1945), *Night Journey* (Martha Graham, Cambridge, Mass., Feb. 17, 1948), *Judith,* choreographic poem for orch. (Martha Graham, Louisville, Ky., Jan. 4, 1950); FOR ORCH. : Symph. No. 1 (N.Y., Oct. 21, 1936); Symph. No. 2 (N.Y., May 25, 1938); Symph. No. 3 (Boston, Oct. 17, 1941); Symph. No. 4 (Cleveland, Jan. 22, 1942); Symph. No. 5 (*Symphony for Strings;* Boston, Nov. 12, 1943); Symph. No. 6 (Dallas, Texas, Feb. 27, 1949); Symph. No. 7 (Boston, Oct. 21, 1960); Symph. No. 8 (N.Y., Oct. 4, 1962); Symph. No. 9, subtitled *Le Fosse Ardeatine,* in memory of Italian civilians murdered by the Germans in a cave in Rome in retaliation for resistance activities (Philadelphia, Jan. 10, 1969); Symph. No. 10, subtitled *American Muse,* dedicated to the U.S. Bicentennial (Washington, April 6, 1976); *American Festival Overture* (Boston, Oct. 6, 1939); Concerto for Piano and Small Orch. (N.Y., Jan. 13, 1943); *Prayer in Time of War* (Pittsburgh, Feb. 13, 1943); *William Billings Overture* (N.Y., Feb. 17, 1944); *Circus Overture* (Philadelphia, July 20, 1944); Violin Concerto (1947; Boston, Feb. 10, 1950, Isaac Stern soloist; revised 1954 and 1958); *Credendum* (Cincinnati, Nov. 4, 1955); *New England Triptych* (Miami, Oct. 28, 1956); *Song of Orpheus* for cello and orch. (N.Y., Sept. 26, 1962); *Voyage for Orchestra* (1971; N.Y., Nov. 9, 1975); FOR BAND: *Newsreel* (1941); *George Washington Bridge* (1950); *Chester,* overture (1956); CHORAL WORKS: *4 Canonic Choruses* (original title, *Chorale Canons*) for mixed voices (1932–33); *Pioneers!* for 8-part mixed chorus, after Walt Whitman (1937); *Choral Etude,* for mixed chorus (1937); *Prologue,* for mixed chorus and orch. (1939); *Prelude* for women's voices (1939); *This Is Our Time* secular cantata for mixed chorus and orch. (1940); *Requiescat,* for women's chorus (1942); *Holiday Song,* for mixed chorus (1942); *A Free Song,* secular cantata for mixed chorus and orch., after Walt Whitman (Boston, March 26, 1943); won the 1st Pulitzer Prize awarded for a musical work); *Truth Shall Deliver,* for men's voices (1946); *4 Rounds on Famous Words* (1957); *The Lord Has a Child,* hymn (1957); *In Praise of Shahn,* canticle for orch., in memory of the American painter Ben Shahn (N.Y., Jan. 30, 1970); *The Young Dead Soldiers* for soprano, horn, woodwinds and strings to a text of Archibald MacLeish (Washington, April 6, 1976); *Concerto on Old English Rounds* for viola, women's chorus and orch. (N.Y., April 15, 1976); *The Earth is Born,* music for a film (1957); 4 string quartets (1936, 1937, 1939, 1950); *Quartettino* for 4 bassoons (1939); *3-Score Set* for piano (1943); *Voyage,* a cycle of 5 pieces for piano (1953); songs.

BIBLIOGRAPHY: N. Broder, "The Music of William Schuman," *Musical Quarterly* (Jan. 1945); F. R. Schreiber and V. Persichetti, *William Schuman* (N.Y., 1954). See also *Modern Music . . . Analytic Index,* compiled by Wayne Shirley, ed. by Wm. and C. Lichtenwanger (N.Y., 1976, p. 196).

Schumann, Camillo, German organist and composer, brother of **Georg Schumann;** b. Königstein, March 10, 1872; d. Gottleuba, Dec. 29, 1946. He learned the rudiments of music from his father; then studied with Jadassohn and Reinecke at the Leipzig Cons. After further study with Adolf Bargiel in Berlin (1894–96) he became organist at the church in Eisenach. For some years before his death he lived in retirement at Gottleuba. He was a prolific composer, especially noted for his organ works; he also wrote 6 cantatas, 3 piano trios, 5 cello sonatas, 2 clarinet sonatas, 2 violin sonatas, and 30 albums of piano pieces.

Schumann, Clara (*née* **Wieck**), famous pianist, wife of **Robert Schumann;** b. Leipzig, Sept. 13, 1819; d. Frankfurt, May 20, 1896. She was the daughter of **Friedrich Wieck;** trained by her father from her fifth year; played in public for the 1st time on Oct. 20, 1828; made tours from 1832, and during a sojourn in Vienna (1836) received the title of Imperial Chamber Virtuoso. At Paris she had great success in 1839. On Sept. 12, 1840, she was married to Schumann, despite the stubborn opposition of her father to this union. With Schumann she made a tour of Russia as a pianist (1844); appeared with Jenny Lind in Vienna (1846). After Schumann's death (1856) she went with her children to Berlin, living for some years with her mother, who had been divorced from Wieck and had married the music teacher Adolf Bargiel (d. Feb. 4, 1841). From 1856 till 1888 she played regularly in England. In 1863 she moved to Lichtenthaler, near Baden-Baden. In 1878–79 she taught piano in Hoch's Cons. at Frankfurt. She was a masterly and authoritative interpreter of Schumann's compositions; later she became an equally admirable interpreter of Brahms, her lifelong friend. She was completely free of all mannerisms, and impressed her audiences chiefly by the earnestness of her regard for the music she played. She was a composer in her own right; wrote a piano concerto and numerous character pieces for piano; also some songs; Schumann made use of her melodies in several of his works. She wrote cadenzas to Beethoven's concertos in C minor and G major; edited the Breitkopf & Hartel ed. of Schumann's works, and some of his early correspondence; also edited finger exercises from Czerny's piano method.

BIBLIOGRAPHY: A. von Meichsner, *Friedrich Wieck und seine Töchter Clara und Marie* (Leipzig, 1875); La Mara, *Clara Schumann,* in vol. V of *Musikalische Studienköpfe* (Leipzig, 1882; 3rd ed., 1902); B. Litzmann, *Clara Schumann, Ein Künstlerleben nach*

Tagebüchern und Briefen (3 vols., Leipzig, 1902–08; English transl. in 2 vols., abridged, London, 1913); W. Kleefeld, *Clara Schumann* (Bielefeld, 1910); Florence May, *The Girlhood of Clara Schumann* (London, 1912); F. Schumann, "Brahms and Clara Schumann," *Musical Quarterly* (Oct. 1916); Eugenie Schumann, *Erinnerungen* (1925; English transl., 1927); B. Litzmann, *Letters of Clara Schumann and Johannes Brahms* (2 vols.; Leipzig, 1927; English transl., N.Y., 1927); K. Höcker, *Clara Schumann* (1938); J. N. Burk, *Clara Schumann* (N.Y., 1940); A. De Lara, "Clara Schumann's Teaching," *Music & Letters* (Jan. 1945); L. Henning, *Die Freundschaft Clara Schumanns mit Johannes Brahms* (Zürich, 1952); W. Quednau, *Clara Schumann* (Berlin, 1955); Margaret and Jean Alley, *A Passionate Friendship; Clara Schumann and Brahms* (London, 1956; contains a selection of letters); R. Pitron, *Clara Schumann* (Paris, 1961). See also the bibliography under Robert Schumann.

Schumann, Elisabeth, noted German soprano; b. Merseburg, June 13, 1885; d. New York, April 23, 1952. She studied in Berlin and Hamburg; made her debut at the Hamburg Opera in 1910; on Nov. 20, 1914 she made her American debut as Sophie in *Der Rosenkavalier* at the Metropolitan Opera, N.Y.; then returned to Germany; sang in Munich in 1919; in 1921 she toured with Richard Strauss in the U.S.; subsequently was engaged at the Vienna Opera. In 1938 she settled in the U.S.; taught at the Curtis Institute of Music, Philadelphia; became an American citizen in 1944. She publ. *German Song* (London, 1948).

Schumann, Georg (Alfred), German composer and choral conductor; b. Königstein, Oct. 25, 1866; d. Berlin, May 23, 1952. He studied with his father, the town music director, and with his grandfather, a cantor; then took courses in Dresden and at the Leipzig Cons. with Reinecke and Jadassohn; received the Beethoven Prize in 1887. He conducted a choral society in Danzig (1890–96) and the Bremen Philharmonic Orch. (1896–99). In 1900 he became conductor of the Singakademie, Berlin; in 1934 he was elected president of the Berlin Akademie der Künste.

WORKS: for orch.: *Zur Karnevalszeit* suite; *Liebesfrühling*, overture; *Lebensfreude*, overture; 2 symphonies; chamber music: 2 violin sonatas, 2 piano quintets, Cello Sonata, Piano Trio, Piano Quartet; choral works with orch.: the oratorio *Ruth* (1909), *Amor und Psyche, Totenklage, Sehnsucht, Das Tränenkrüglein*; numerous songs; for piano: *Stimmungsbilder, Traumbilder, Fantasie-Etüden, Harzbilder*.

BIBLIOGRAPHY: P. Hielscher, *Georg Schumann*, in vol. 1 of *Monographien moderner Musiker* (Leipzig, 1906); H. Biehle, *Georg Schumann* (Münster, 1925).

Schumann, Robert (Alexander), great German composer; b. Zwickau, Saxony, June 8, 1810; d. Endenich, near Bonn, July 29, 1856. He was the youngest son of a book seller; his first music lessons (about 1818) were on the piano from the organist of the Zwickau Marienkirche. His attempts at composition date from his seventh year; in his eleventh, without instruction, he wrote choral and orchestral works. He attended the Zwickau Gymnasium from 1820–28, toward the end

of his term developing a marked predilection for the romantic works of Byron and Jean Paul Richter. In 1826 his father wished him to study under Carl M. von Weber, but Weber died, as did Schumann's father shortly thereafter. In 1828 Schumann matriculated at Leipzig Univ. as *studiosus juris*, though he gave more attention to the philosophical lectures. In 1829 he went to Heidelberg, drawn there chiefly by the fame of Thibaut (prof. of law, but a profound student of music), and began to apply himself seriously to musical study, aided by his dexterity as a pianist. In the autumn of 1830 he obtained his mother's permission to return to Leipzig in order to devote himself to music. He lived with Friedrich Wieck, under whom he studied the piano; and also took a course in composition under H. Dorn, though his industry was principally concentrated on piano practice. An unfortunate experiment (the endeavor to obtain independence of the fingers by suspending the fourth finger of the right hand in a sling while practicing with the others) ended in 1832 his bright prospects as a piano virtuoso. Thenceforward he gave himself up to composition and literary work. As a composer, his published works (op. 1-23) up to the beginning of 1840 are exclusively for the piano; Liszt, Henselt, and **Clara Wieck** (his future wife; the daughter of his instructor and host) played them in public. In 1834 Schumann founded, with J. Knorr, L. Schunke, and Wieck, the *Neue Zeitschrift für Musik*, which Schumann edited alone from 1835–44. It entered the field as an exponent of liberal and progressive musical art, in opposition to the vapid productions of the Italian stage, to the then fashionable pianists, and to all shallow or retrograde tendencies. Schumann's numerous essays and criticisms (signed Florestan, Eusebius, Meister Raro, or with the numerals "2" and "12") show what musical journalism can be when actuated by the loftiest motives and based on real and intimate knowledge of the subjects treated. During the succeeding decades it exercised a potent influence; Schumann was among the first to herald Chopin's genius (1831), and one of his last papers was the famous "Neue Bahnen" (1853) on Brahms. In the meantime he had fallen in love with Clara Wieck; owing to her father's determined opposition their marriage did not take place until 1840, the year in which the degree of Dr. phil. was conferred upon Schumann by the University of Jena. He had spent one year, 1838–39, in Vienna, hoping to better his fortunes by establishing himself and his paper in that city, an attempt which failed. From his marriage year, too, dates the beginning of his career as a song composer, and some of his finest lyrical gems were then produced, including the song cycles to poems by Heine (op. 24) and Eichendorff (op. 39), the *Frauenliebe und Leben* (op. 42), and the *Dichterliebe* to Heine's words (op. 48). In 1841 he wrote his First Symphony, speedily followed by three string quartets, op. 41, the Piano Quintet, op. 44, the Piano Quartet, op. 47, and his most beautiful choral work, *Das Paradies und die Peri* (1843). In 1843 he was invited by Mendelssohn to assume the position of teacher (piano, composition, and playing from score) at the newly found Conservatorium in Leipzig; Schumann introduced the pedal-piano, for preparatory organ practice, into the Cons., which possessed no organ for ten years. In January, 1844, he undertook a concert tour to Russia with his wife; in the autumn of the same year he moved to Dresden; his duties in the Leipzig Cons. were uncongenial, and it is probable that Mendelssohn, whom Schumann greatly admired, did not fully appreciate the latter's genius. Schumann likewise retired from the editorship of the *Neue Zeitschrift*, being succeeded in 1845 by K. F. Brendel. In Dresden he lived until 1850, giving private lessons and composing industriously; to this period belong the great C major Symphony, op. 61 (1846), the opera *Genoveva* (1848), and the Piano Trio, op. 80 (1847; one of the finest of its class). In 1847 he became the conductor of the Liedertafel, and in 1848 organized the Chorgesang-Verein. He was called to Düsseldorf in 1850 to succeed Ferdinand Hiller as town musical director (conductor of the Subscription Concerts and the Musical Society). He held this position until the autumn of 1853, when signs of insanity, which had appeared as far back as 1833, and still more alarmingly in 1845, compelled him to resign; for some time his assistant (and successor) Tausch had relieved him of much of the work. On Feb. 6, 1854, the disorder reached a climax; he abruptly left the room in which some friends were assembled, and threw himself into the Rhine; rescued from drowning, he had to be conveyed to an asylum at Endenich, near Bonn, remaining here, with but few lucid intervals, until the end. In 1880 a monument was erected on his grave in the churchyard at Bonn, opposite the Sterneentor. Schumann was a leader of the German Romantic school, and perhaps its most powerful promoter as both a composer and a writer. At the very outset, his individuality found full expression. His mastery of detail, his concentrated passion and profound emotion, are displayed to best advantage in the smaller forms, the piano pieces and songs—the most suitable mediums for presenting the subtle shadings and artistic refinements characteristic of his lyrical genius. Yet—to name but a few—the first two symphonies and the piano concerto are unsurpassed in the post-Beethoven epoch; the Piano Quintet, the *Études symphoniques*, the C major Fantasie, the F-sharp minor and the G minor piano sonatas, rank with the grandest works of their kind. Together with Chopin and Liszt he must be regarded as the founder of the modern piano technique, exploiting the utmost possibilities of the instrument.

WORKS: FOR THE STAGE: opera, *Genoveva*, op. 81 (Leipzig, June 25, 1850); music to Byron's *Manfred*, op. 115; scenes from Goethe's *Faust*. VOCAL WORKS WITH ORCH.: cantata *Das Paradies und die Peri*, op. 50, for solo, chorus, and orch. (after T. Moore's *Lalla Rookh*); *Adventlied*, op. 71, for soprano, chorus, and orch.; *Beim Abschied zu singen*, op. 84, for chorus with woodwind or piano; *Requiem für Mignon*, op. 98b; *Nachtlied*, op. 108, for chorus and orch.; for soli, chorus, and orch.: cantata *Der Rose Pilgerfahrt*, op. 112; ballade *Der Königssohn*, op. 116; ballade *Des Sängers Fluch*, op. 139; four ballades *Vom Pagen und der Königstochter*, op. 140; ballade *Das Glück von Edenhall*, op. 143, for men's chorus and orch.; *Neujahrslied*, op. 144, for chorus and orch.; Missa sacra, op. 147, with orch.; Requiem Mass, op. 148, with orch. CHORUSES A CAPPELLA: 6 4-part songs for men's

voices, op. 33; 5 songs (Burns) for mixed chorus, op. 55; 4 songs for mixed chorus, op. 59; 3 songs for men's chorus, op. 62; 7 *Ritornelle* in canon form, for men's voices, op. 65; 5 Romances and Ballades for chorus (2 sets), op. 67 and 75; 6 Romances for women's voices (2 sets), op. 69 and 91; motet (Rückert) *Verzweifle nicht im Schumerzenstal*, for double men's chorus, op. 93 (revised with orch., 1852); 5 *Jagdlieder* (Laube) for men's chorus, op. 137; 4 songs for double chorus, op. 141.

SONGS: 3 poems by Geibel, op. 29 (No. 1, for 2 sopranos; No. 2, for 3 sopranos; No. 3, for small chorus); 4 duets for soprano and tenor, op. 34, and 4 duets, op. 78; 3 2-part songs, op. 43; *Spanisches Liederspiel* for one voice or S.A.T.B., op. 74; *Minnespiel* from Rückert's "Liebesfrühling," for one or several voices, op. 101; *Mädchenlieder*, for 2 sopranos, op. 103; 3 songs for 3 women's voices, op. 114; ten *Spanische Liebeslieder* for one or several voices, with 4-hand accompaniment, op. 138; the ballads *Belsazar* (op. 51), *Der Handschuh* (op. 87), *Schön Hedwig* (op. 106; for declamation with piano), and *Zwei Balladen*, op. 122 (No. 1, *Ballade vom Haideknaben*; No. 2, *Die Flüchtlinge*; both for declamation with piano); *Liederkreis* (Heine), song cycle, op. 24, and *Liederkreis*, 12 poems by Eichendorff, op. 39; *Myrthen*, op. 25; *Lieder und Gesänge*, 5 sets (op. 27, 51, 77, 96, 127); 3 poems by Geibel, op. 30; 3 songs, op. 31; 12 poems (Kerner), op. 35; 6 poems (Rückert), op. 36; 12 poems (Rückert), composed with Clara Schumann, op. 37; 5 songs for low voice, op. 40; *Frauenliebe und -Leben*, op. 42; *Dichterliebe*, op. 48; *Romanzen und Balladen*, 4 sets (op. 45, 49, 53, 64); *Liederalbum für die Jugend*, op. 79; 6 songs, op. 89; 6 poems by Lenau, and *Requiem*, op. 90; 6 songs from Byron's "Hebrew Melodies," op. 95 (with piano or harp); nine *Lieder und Gesänge* from Goethe's *Wilhelm Meister*, op. 98a; 7 songs, op. 104; 6 songs, op. 107; 4 *Husarenlieder* for baritone, op. 117; 3 *Waldlieder*, op. 119; 5 *heitere Gesänge*, op. 125; *Gedichte der Königin Maria Stuart*, op. 135; 4 songs, op. 142; *Der deutsche Rhein* (no opus number).

FOR ORCH.: 4 symphonies: No. 1, op. 38, in B-flat; No. 2, op. 61, in C; No. 3, op. 97, in E-flat ("Rhenish" Symphony); No. 4, op. 120, in D minor; *Ouvertüre, Scherzo und Finale*, op. 52; 4 concert overtures (*Die Braut von Messina*, op. 100; *Festouvertüre*, op. 123; *Julius Caesar*, op. 128; *Hermann und Dorothea*, op. 136); Piano Concerto in A minor, op. 54; *Konzertstück* (Introduction and Allegro appassionato) in G, for piano and orch., op. 92; *Konzert-Allegro* for piano and orch., in D minor, op. 134; *Konzertstück* for 4 horns, op. 86; Cello Concerto, op. 129; *Fantasia* for violin with orch., op. 131; Violin Concerto (1853; publ. 1937).

CHAMBER MUSIC: Piano Quintet in E-flat, op. 44; 3 string quartets, in A minor, F, and A, op. 41; Piano Quartet in E-flat, op. 47; 3 piano trios (No. 1, in D minor, op. 63; No. 2, in F, op. 80; No. 3, in G minor, op. 110); 4 *Fantasiestücke* for piano, violin, and cello, op. 88; Adagio and Allegro for piano and horn, op. 70; 3 *Fantasiestücke* for piano and clarinet, op. 73; 3 *Romanzen* for piano and oboe, op. 94; 5 *Stücke im Volkston* for piano and cello, op. 102; 2 sonatas for piano and violin (No. 1, in A minor, op. 105; No. 2, in D minor, op. 121); 4 *Märchenbilder* for piano and viola (or violin), op. 113; 4 *Märchenerzählungen* for piano, viola and clarinet (or violin), op. 132.

FOR ORGAN (or pedal-piano): 6 studies in canon form, op. 56; *Skizzen für den Pedalflügel*, op. 58; six fugues on B-A-C-H, op. 60.

FOR PIANO: op. 1, *Variations on A-B-E-G-G*; op. 2, *Papillons*; op. 3, *Studies after Paganini's Caprices*; op. 4, *Intermezzi*; op. 5, *Impromptus* on theme by Clara Wieck; op. 6, *Davids-bündlertänze*; op. 7, *Toccata*; op. 8, *Allegro*; op. 9, *Carnaval*; op. 10, six *Studies on Paganini's Caprices*; op. 11, Sonata No. 1, in F-sharp minor; op. 12, *Fantasiestücke* (2 books); op. 13, *Études symphoniques*; op. 14, Sonata No. 2, in F minor; op. 15, thirteen *Kinderscenen*; op. 16, *Kreisleriana*; op. 17, *Fantasie* in C; op. 18, *Arabeske*; op. 19, *Blumenstück*; op. 20, *Humoreske*; op. 21, *Novelletten* (4 books); op. 22, Sonata No. 3, in G minor ("Concert sans orchestre"); op. 23, *Nachtstücke*; op. 26, *Faschingsschwank aus Wien*; op. 28, three *Romanzen*; op. 32, *Scherzo, Gigue, Romanze und Fughette*; op. 68, *Album für die Jugend*; op. 72, four *Fugues*; op. 76, four *Marches*; op. 82, *Waldscenen*; op. 99, *Bunte Blätter*; op. 111, three *Fantasiestücke*; op. 118, three *Sonatas* for the Young; op. 124, *Albumblätter*; op. 126, seven pieces in fughetta form; op. 133, *Gesänge der Frühe*; also a *Scherzo* (original in Sonata op. 14), a *Presto passionato* (original finale of Sonata op. 22); and a canon on *An Alexis*.

PIANO 4 HANDS: op. 66, *Bilder aus dem Osten*; op. 85, *12 vierhändige Klavierstücke für kleine und grosse Kinder*; op. 109, *Ballszenen*; op. 130, *Kinderball*; op. 46, Andante and Variations in B-flat (for 2 pianos, 4 hands).

WRITINGS: *Gesammelte Schriften über Musik und Musiker*, a collection of his articles in the *Neue Zeitschrift* (1854; 4 vols.; 5th ed. revised by M. Kreisig, 1914; English transl., London, 1877). A judicious selection from the complete writings, edited by H. Simon, was publ. under the same title as the original ed. (3 vols.; Leipzig, 1888–89); a selection of Schumann's critical reviews, transl. into English by P. Rosenfeld, was publ. in N.Y., 1946.

A complete edition of his compositions, in 34 vols., edited by Clara Schumann, was publ. by Breitkopf & Härtel (1881–93); in 1893 Brahms edited a supplementary volume. A new edition, *Sammelbande der Robert-Schumann-Gesellschaft*, began publication in 1961. See also A. Dörffel, *Thematischer Katalog der Werke R. S.s* (Leipzig, 1870), and H. S. Drinker, *Texts of the Vocal Works of R. S. in English Translation* (N.Y., 1947).

BIBLIOGRAPHY: BIOGRAPHY: J. W. von Wasielewski, *R. S.* (Dresden, 1858; 4th ed., 1906; English transl., Boston, 1871); A. Reissmann, *R. S. Sein Leben und seine Werke* (Berlin, 1865; 3rd ed., 1879; English transl., London, 1886); La Mara, *S.*, in vol. I of *Musikalische Studienköpfe* (Leipzig, 1868; 10th ed., reprinted separately, 1911); A. Niggli, *R. S.* (Basel, 1879); P. Spitta, *Ein Lebensbild R. S.s* (Leipzig, 1882); J. A. Fuller-Maitland, *S.* (London, 1884; new ed., 1913); H. Erler, *R. S.s Leben aus seinen Briefen*, 2 vols. (Berlin, 1887; 2nd ed., 1912); H. Reimann, *R. S.* (Leipzig, 1887); R. Batka, *S.* (Leipzig, 1893); H. Abert, *R. S.* (Berlin, 1903; 3rd ed., 1918); A. W. Paterson, *S.* (London, 1903; revised ed., 1934); L. Schneider and M. Mareschal, *S. Sa vie et ses œuvres* (Paris, 1905); E. J. Oldmeadow, *S.* (London, 1905); C. Mauclair, *S.* (Paris, 1906); E. Wolff, *R. S.* (Berlin, 1906); P. J. A. Möbius, *Über R. S.s Krankheit* (Halle, 1906); J. Hartog, *R. A. S. en sijne werken* (Haarlem, 1910); A. Steiner, *S.* (Zürich, 1911); M. D. Calvocoressi, *S.* (Paris, 1912); W. Dahms, *S.* (Berlin, 1916); H. v. d. Pfordten, *R. S.* (1920); F. Niecks, *R. S.* (London, 1925; valuable); H. Bedford, *R. S.* (N.Y., 1925); R. Pitrou, *La Vie intérieure de R. S.* (Paris, 1925); Eugenie Schumann, *Erinnerungen* (1925; in English, London, 1927); V. Basch, *S.* (Paris, 1926); V. Basch, *La Vie douloureuse de S.* (Paris, 1928; in English, N.Y., 1931); H. Tessmer, *R. S.* (Stuttgart, 1930); Eugenie Schumann, *R. S. ein Lebensbild meines Vaters* (Leipzig, 1931); A. Colling, *La Vie de R. S.* (Paris, 1931); M. Kreisig, *Stammbaum der Familie Sch.* (genealogy; 1931); M. Beaufils, *S.* (Paris, 1932); C. Valabrega, *S.* (Modena, 1934); W. Gertler, *R. S. sein Leben in Bildern* (Leipzig, 1936); W. Korte, *R. S.* (Potsdam, 1937); E. Bücken, *R. S.* (Cologne, 1940); W. Boetticher, *R. S., Einführung in Persönlichkeit und Werk* (Berlin, 1941); W. Boetticher, *R. S. in seinen Schriften und Briefen* (Berlin, 1942); R. H. Schauffler, *Florestan: The Life and Works of R. S.* (N.Y., 1945); R. Petzoldt, *R. S.* (Leipzig, 1947); J. Chissell, *S.* (London, 1948); P. Sutermeister, *R. S., sein Leben nach Briefen* (Zürich, 1949); K. H. Wörner, *R. S.* (Zürich, 1949); A. Cœuroy, *R. S.* (Paris, 1950); E. Müller, *R. S.* (Olten, 1950); P. & W. Rehberg, *R. S.* (Zürich, 1954); M. Brion, *S. et l'âme romantique* (Paris, 1954; in English as *S. and the Romantic Age*, London, 1956); R. Petzoldt, *R. S., sein Leben in Bildern* (Leipzig, 1956); G. Eismann, *R. S. ein Quellenwerk über sein Leben und Schaffen* (2 vols., Leipzig, 1956); R. Münnich, *Aus R. S.s Briefen und Schriften* (Weimar, 1956); Percy M. Young, *Tragic Muse: The Life and Works of R. S.* (London, 1957); A. Boucourechliev, *Robert Schumann in Selbstzeugnissen und Bilddokumenten* (Hamburg, 1958).

CRITICISM, APPRECIATION: A. W. Ambros, *R. S.s Tage und Werke*, in *Kultur-historische Bilder aus dem Musikleben der Gegenwart* (Leipzig, 1860); H. Deiters, "S. als Schriftsteller," *Allgemeine musikalische Zeitung* 47–49 (1865); L. Mesnard, *Un Successeur de Beethoven: Étude sur R. S.* (Paris, 1876); S. Bagge, "R. S. und seine Faustszenen," in Waldersee's *Sammlung* (Leipzig 1879); P. Graf von Waldersee, "Über S.s Manfred," in Waldersee's *Sammlung* (Leipzig, 1880); F. G. Jansen, *Die Davidsbündler. Aus R. S.s Sturm- und Drangperiode* (Leipzig, 1883); J. W. von Wasielewski, *Schumanniana* (Bonn, 1883); B. Vogel, *R. S.s Klaviertonpoesie* (Leipzig, 1886); E. David, *Les Mendelssohn-Bartholdy et R. S.* (Paris, 1887); V. Joss, *Fr. Wieck und sein Verhältniss zu R. S.* (Dresden, 1900); M. d'Albert, *R. S. son œuvre pour piano* (Paris, 1904); F. Kerst, *S.-Brevier* (Berlin, 1905); H. Kretzschmar, "R. S. als Ästhetiker," *Jahrbuch Peters* (1906); D. G. Mason, *The Romantic Composers* (New York, 1906); M. Katz, *Die Schilderung des musikalischen Eindrucks bei S.* (Giessen, 1910); Marie Wieck, *Aus dem Kreise Wieck-S.* (Dresden, 1912; 2nd ed., 1914); L. Hirschberg, *R. S.s Tondichtungen balladischen Charakters* (Langensalza, 1913); E. V. Wolff, *R. S.s Lieder in ersten und späteren Fassungen* (Leipzig, 1914); R. Pugno, *Leçons écrites sur S.* (Paris, 1914); R. Hohenemser, "Formale Eigentümlichkeiten in R. S.s Klaviermusik," in "Sandberger Festschrift" (1919); W. H. Hadow, *Studies in Modern Music*, 1st series (London, 1892; 11th ed., 1926); P. Frenzel, *R. S. und Goethe* (Leipzig, 1926); G. Minotti, *Die Enträtselung des Sch.schen Sphinx-Geheimnisses* (Leipzig, 1926); G. Minotti, "Die Enträtselung des Sch.schen Abegg-Geheimniss," *Zeitschrift für Musik* (July-Aug. 1927); O. Bie, *Das deutsche Lied* (Berlin, 1926; pp. 75–131); J. A. Fuller-Maitland, *S.'s Piano Works* (London, 1927); J. A. Fuller-Maitland, *S.'s Concerted Chamber Music* (London, 1929); M. Ninck, *S. und die Romantik in der Musik* (Heidelberg, 1929); H. H. Rosenwald, *Geschichte des deutschen Liedes zwischen Schubert und S.* (Berlin, 1930); W. Schwarz, *R. S. und die Variation* (Kassel, 1932); H. Kötz, *Der Einfluss Jean Pauls auf R. S.* (Weimar, 1933); G. Wilcke, *Tonalität und Modulation im Streichquartett Mendelssohns und S.s* (Leipzig, 1933); G. Minotti, *Die Geheimdokumente der Davidsbündler* (Leipzig, 1934); R. Hernried, "Four Unpublished Compositions by R. S.," *Musical Quarterly* (Jan. 1942); G. Abraham, ed., *S.* (N.Y., 1951); G. Abraham, "Schumann's Jugendsinfonie in G minor," *Musical Quarterly* (Jan. 1951); M. Beaufils, *La Musique de piano de S.* (Paris, 1951); L. B. Plantinga, *Schumann as Critic* (New Haven, 1967); T. A. Brown, *The Aesthetics of Robert Schumann* (N.Y., 1968); Eric Sams, *The Songs of Robert Schumann* (London, 1969).

CORRESPONDENCE: Clara Schumann, *S.s Jugendbriefe. Nach den Originalen mitgeteilt* (Leipzig, 1885; 4th ed., 1912; in English, London, 1888); F. G. Jansen, *R. S.s Briefe* (Leipzig, 1886; augmented ed., 1904; in English, London, 1890); J. Gensel, *S.s Briefwechsel mit Henriette Voigt* (Leipzig, 1892); K. Storck, *S.s Briefe in Auswahl* (Stuttgart, 1906; in English, London, 1907); M. Crémieux, *Lettres choisies de R. S.* (Paris, 1909); A. Schumann, *Der junge S., Dichtungen und Briefe* (Leipzig, 1910); "Aus S.s Kreisen" (unpubl. letters from and to S.) *Die Musik* 14 (1914).

Schumann, Walter, American composer of applied music; b. New York, Oct. 8, 1913; d. Minneapolis, Aug. 21, 1958. He studied law and music at the Univ. of Southern California in Los Angeles; became associated with radio shows and composed music for films; wrote an opera, *John Brown's Body* (Los Angeles, Sept. 21, 1953). He contributed the famous ominously syncopated theme to the television serial *Dragnet*, based on the initial three notes of the minor scale.

Schumann-Heink (*née* **Rössler**), **Ernestine,** famous contralto; b. Lieben, near Prague, June 15, 1861; d. Hollywood, Calif., Nov. 17, 1936. Her father was an officer in the Austrian Army; her mother an Italian amateur singer. In 1872 she was sent to the Ursuline Convent in Prague, where she sang in the church choir; after lessons from Marietta von Leclair in Graz, she made her first public appearance, singing the contralto solo in Beethoven's 9th Symphony (1876); made her opera debut at the Dresden Court Opera (Oct. 13, 1878) as Azucena; continued her studies with Karl Krebs and Franz Wüllner. In 1883 she was engaged to sing at the Hamburg City Opera; when the company was taken to Covent Garden, London, in 1892, she sang Erda; subsequently specialized in the Wagnerian

roles; took part in the Bayreuth Festivals from 1896 until 1903, in 1905 and 1906; also sang with the Berlin Opera. She made her American debut as Ortrud on Nov. 7, 1898 in Chicago; appeared in the same role with the Metropolitan Opera, N.Y., on Jan. 9, 1899; cancelled her contract with the Berlin Opera in order to remain a member of the Metropolitan Opera Co. (until 1904); created the role of Klytemnestra in *Elektra* (Dresden, Jan. 25, 1909); made her last operatic appearance as Erda at the Metropolitan Opera on March 11, 1932. She became an American citizen in 1908. During the last years of her life she was active mainly as a teacher. Her operatic repertory included about 150 parts; her voice, of an even quality in all registers, possessed great power, making it peculiarly suitable to Wagnerian roles. She was married in 1882 to Ernst Heink of Dresden, from whom she was later divorced; in 1893 she married the actor Paul Schumann in Hamburg; he died in 1904; she assumed the names of both Schumann and Heink. Her 3rd husband was a Chicago lawyer, William Rapp, Jr., whom she married in 1905 (divorced 1914).

BIBLIOGRAPHY: M. Lawton, *Schumann-Heink, the Last of the Titans* (N.Y., 1928). See also A. T. Zwart in *Notable American Women* (Cambridge, Mass., 1971).

Schünemann, Georg, eminent German musicologist; b. Berlin, March 13, 1884; d. there, Jan. 2, 1945. He studied flute and played in various orchestras in Berlin; then took courses in musicology with Kretzschmar at the Univ. of Berlin; obtained his degree of Dr. phil. in 1907 with the dissertation *Zur Frage des Taktschlagens in der Mensuralmusik*. He then taught at the Univ. of Berlin and at the Hochschule für Musik there; subsequently was chief of the music division of the Prussian State Library (1935–44). He committed suicide during the darkest time of the war.

WRITINGS: *Geschichte des Dirigierens* (1913; a standard work); *Das Lied der deutschen Kolonisten in Russland* (1923); *Geschichte der deutschen Schulmusik*, in 2 parts (Leipzig, 1928–32); *C. Fr. Zelter, der Begründer der preussischen Musikpflege* (Berlin, 1932); *Führer durch die deutsche Chorliteratur* (2 vols., 1935–36); *Geschichte der Klaviermusik* (Berlin, 1940; 2nd ed. by H. Gerigk, 1953); *Die Violine* (1940); *Die Singakademie zu Berlin* (Regensburg, 1941); numerous essays in German music magazines.

Schunke, Karl, German pianist; b. Magdeburg, 1801; d. Paris (suicide), Dec. 16, 1839. He studied music with his father, the horn player **Michael Schunke** (1778–1821); then took some lessons with Ferdinand Ries, whom he accompanied to London. In 1828 he went to Paris where he became a fashionable piano teacher; nevertheless he suffered from some sort of malaise and killed himself. He composed a number of brilliant salon pieces à la mode and transcriptions of operatic arias for piano.

Schunke, Ludwig, German pianist; b. Kassel, Dec. 21, 1810; d. Leipzig, Dec. 7, 1834. He was a cousin of **Karl Schunke;** studied with his father, **Gottfried Schunke** (1777–1861), who was, like Karl Schunke's father, a horn player; also like his cousin, he went to Paris where he studied piano with Kalkbrenner and Reicha;

settled in Leipzig in 1833 and became an intimate friend of Schumann, of whom he was an exact contemporary, and with whom he became associated in founding the *Neue Zeitschrift für Musik*. His early death at not quite the age of 24 was greatly mourned, for his piano pieces were full of promise; among them were a sonata, a set of variations; *2 Caprices* and a set of *Charakterstücke*. Schumann wrote a heartfelt appreciation of Schunke's talent, which was reprinted in his *Gesammelte Schriften*.

Schuppanzigh, Ignaz, Austrian violinist, friend of Beethoven; b. Vienna, Nov. 20, 1776; d. there, March 2, 1830. He learned to play the violin and the viola; in 1798 became conductor of the Augarten concerts; Beethoven played several times at these concerts. In 1794–95 he was 1st violin in the quartet that played regularly for Prince Lichnowsky. In 1808 he founded the private quartet of Prince Razumovsky (with Mayseder, Linke, and Weiss), interpreting the Beethoven quartets under the master's eye, and also playing quartets of Haydn and Mozart. After a fire in Razumovsky's palace (Dec. 31, 1814) he left Vienna, returning in 1824. Schuppanzigh then became a member of the court orch.; also was director of the German Opera in 1828. He publ. a *Solo brillant* for violin with string quartet; solo variations on a Russian theme; 9 variations for 2 violins.
BIBLIOGRAPHY: G. Kinsky, "Beethoven und das Schuppanzigh-Quartette," *Rheinische Musik- und Theater-Zeitung* XXI (p. 235ff.). See also the literature on Beethoven.

Schuré, Édouard, Alsatian writer on music; b. Strasbourg, Jan. 21, 1841; d. Paris, April 7, 1929. He studied law and philology in Strasbourg; lived in Bonn, Berlin, and Munich; in 1867 settled in Paris. In his writings (in French) he was an avowed propagandist of German music, and particularly Wagner.
WRITINGS: *Histoire du Lied; ou, La Chanson populaire en Allemagne* (Paris, 1868; new ed. with a study *Le Réveil de la poésie populaire en France*, 1903); *Le Drame musical* (Paris, 1875; 12th ed., 1914; German transl. by Hans von Wolzogen as *Das musikalische Drama*; 3rd ed., 1888; part II is devoted to an appreciation of Wagner); *Souvenirs sur Richard Wagner* (Paris, 1900); *Précurseurs et révoltés* (Paris, 1904); *The Musical Idea in Wagner* (English transl. from French, Hampstead, 1910).
BIBLIOGRAPHY: J. Mainor, *Édouard Schuré* (Angers, 1905); A. Roux and R. Veyssié, *Édouard Schuré, son œuvre et sa pensée* (Paris, 1913); R. A. Schuler, *Édouard Schuré à travers son écriture* (Paris, 1928); A. Roux, *In memoriam Schuré* (Paris, 1931).

Schuricht, Carl, German conductor; b. Danzig, July 3, 1880; d. Corseaux-sur-Vevey, Switzerland, Jan. 7, 1967. He studied at home, his father being an organ manufacturer and his mother a pianist. He then took lessons with Humperdinck at the Hochschule für Musik in Berlin, and later in Leipzig with Max Reger. He subsequently conducted theater orchestras in Germany; in 1912 he became municipal music director in Wiesbaden, and held this post until 1944, when he moved to Frankfurt as choral conductor. In 1953 he

conducted in France and Switzerland. He composed some piano music and an orchestral suite, *Drei Herbststücke*.
BIBLIOGRAPHY: B. Gavoty, *Carl Schuricht* (Geneva, 1955).

Schurig, Arthur, German writer on music; b. Dresden, April 24, 1870; d. there, Feb. 15, 1929. He studied in Dresden, Berlin, and Leipzig; followed a military career; upon retirement, devoted much of his leisure to writing on music; publ. an excellent biography of Mozart: *W. A. Mozart; sein Leben und sein Werk* (2 vols.; 1913; 2nd ed., 1923); edited Leopold Mozart's *Reise-Aufzeichnungen* (1920) and Constanze Mozart's *Briefe, Aufzeichnungen, Dokumente* (1922).

Schurig, Volkmar (Julius Wilhelm), German organist and composer; b. Aue-on-the-Mulde, March 24, 1822; d. Dresden, Jan. 31, 1899. He studied in Dresden, where he played organ in the English Church (1844–56); subsequently filled various other posts as organist, singing teacher, and cantor. He publ. organ fantasias, organ preludes, sacred choruses to English texts; children's songs; brought out a useful collection, *Liederperlen deutscher Tonkunst*.

Schürmann, Georg Caspar, German composer; b. Hannover, c.1672; d. Wolfenbüttel, Feb. 25, 1751. He was a singer (alto-falsetto) at the Hamburg Opera (1693–97); was then engaged as court Kapellmeister to the Duke of Brunswick in Wolfenbüttel; traveled in Italy for further study; from 1703 to 1706 was court Kapellmeister in Meiningen; returned to Wolfenbüttel in 1707 and remained there most of his life. He wrote about 20 operas for the Duke of Brunswick, produced in Wolfenbüttel and Hamburg; only a few fragments are extant; his church music is also lost. The following were produced in Brunswick: *Heinrich der Vogler* (Part I, Aug. 1, 1718; Part II, Jan. 11, 1721); *Die getreue Alceste* (1719); *Ludovicus Pius* (1726); this last opera, under the German title, *Ludwig der Fromme*, is partly reproduced in Eitner's *Publikationen älterer Musikwerke;* a suite from *Alceste* and 3 books of arias was publ. by G. F. Schmidt (Wolfenbüttel, 1934).
BIBLIOGRAPHY: G. F. Schmidt, *Die frühdeutsche Oper und die musikdramatische Kunst G. C. Schürmanns* (2 vols.; Regensburg, 1933–34; expanded from dissertation, Munich, 1913).

Schürmann, Gerard, English composer; b. Kertosono, Indonesia, Jan. 19, 1928. He studied piano with his mother; at the outbreak of the war in the Pacific in 1941 he was sent to England; studied piano with Kathleen Long at the Royal College of Music in London, and composition with Alan Rawsthorne. At the same time he served as a Netherlands Cultural Attaché to Great Britain. In 1951 he was appointed conductor at the Dutch Radio in Hilversum; in 1953 he returned to England and devoted himself mainly to composition. His music is set in an advanced neo-Baroque style with application of serial techniques.
WORKS: 2 string quartets (1948, 1964); *Intrada* for strings (1950); *Nine Poems of Blake*, a song cycle (1955); Wind Quintet (1963); *Fantasia* for cello and piano (1965); *Chuench'i* for voice and orch. (1967); *Six*

Studies of Francis Bacon for orch. (1968); Sonatina for flute and piano (1968); *Serenade* for solo violin (1969); *Variants* for chamber orch. (1970); Piano Concerto (1970).

Schuster, Bernhard, German publisher and composer; b. Berlin, March 26, 1870; d. there, Jan. 13, 1934. He studied piano, organ, and violin; was active for a time as a theater conductor. In 1901 he founded the fortnightly review *Die Musik,* which from its inception ranked with the foremost musical journals of Germany; was its editor-in-chief until 1933. In 1905 he founded the publ. house "Schuster und Loeffler" (Berlin and Leipzig), which brought out a number of important works on music (the business was acquired by the Stuttgart Deutsche Verlags-Anstalt in 1922). Schuster publ. 2 books of songs; also composed the operas *Der Jungbrunnen* (Karlsruhe, 1920) and *Der Dieb des Glücks* (Wiesbaden, March 10, 1923); a symphony; a string quartet; sacred choruses.

Schuster, Josef, German composer; b. Dresden, Aug. 11, 1748; d. there, July 24, 1812. He spent 4 years in Italy (1765–69) for study, and after 5 years in Dresden, went to Italy again; took lessons with Padre Martini at Bologna; wrote Italian operas, and was made honorary maestro to the King of Naples; after another 2 years in Dresden, he made a third visit to Italy (1778–81), finally establishing himself in Dresden as theatrical conductor; from 1787 he was associated with Seydelmann as court Kapellmeister. He composed a number of operas, mostly to Italian texts; also cantatas; oratorios, symphonies, etc.; publ. piano pieces for 2 and 4 hands, divertissements for piano and violin, etc.

BIBLIOGRAPHY: R. Engländer, "Die Opern Josef Schusters," *Zeitschrift für Musikwissenschaft* (1928); R. Engländer, "Les Sonates de violon de Mozart et les 'Duetti' de J. Schuster," *Revue de Musicologie* (1939).

Schuster, Joseph, cellist; b. Constantinople, May 23, 1903; d. Los Angeles, Feb. 16, 1969. He studied at the St. Petersburg Cons. and later at the Hochschule für Musik in Berlin; was 1st cellist in the Berlin Philharmonic (1926–31); emigrated to America in 1934; made his concert debut in N.Y. on March 15, 1935; from 1936 to 1944 was 1st cellist of the N.Y. Philharmonic.

Schütt, Eduard, Russian-born Austrian pianist and composer; b. St. Petersburg, Oct. 22, 1856; d. Obermias, near Merano, Italy, July 26, 1933. After studying piano at the St. Petersburg Cons. he went to Germany where he took courses with Richter, Jadassohn and Reinecke at the Leipzig Cons.; then proceeded to Vienna where he became a private pupil of Leschetizky. He wrote the comic opera *Signor Formica* (Vienna, Nov. 19, 1892); 2 piano concertos; Piano Quartet; 2 piano trios; numerous character pieces for piano, some of which retained popularity for a long time (*Scènes de bal, Thème varié et Fugato, Silhouetten-Portraits, Poésies d'Automne, Carnaval mignon,* etc.).

Schütz, Franz, Austrian organist; b. Vienna, April 15, 1892; d. there, May 19, 1962. He was on the staff of the Cons. of the Gesellschaft der Musikfreunde in Vienna from 1921; gave organ recitals; composed organ pieces.

Schütz (Sagittarius), Heinrich, great German composer; b. Köstritz, Oct. 8, 1585; d. Dresden, Nov. 6, 1672. In 1599 he became a choirboy in the court chapel at Kassel, also studying at the Collegium Mauricianum there, and entering Marburg Univ. in 1609, at his parents' desire, to study law; but was sent to Venice in the same year, by Landgrave Moritz of Hesse-Kassel, to study under Giovanni Gabrieli, remaining there till after the latter's death in 1612. Returning to Kassel, he became court organist; in 1617 he was appointed Kapellmeister to the Elector of Saxony at Dresden, after having acted in that capacity since 1615. He repeatedly revisited Italy; from 1631, amid the distractions of the 30 Years' War, he made protracted visits to Copenhagen (in 1633–35, 1637–38, and 1642–45), where he officiated as court conductor, the Dresden court orch. having been wholly dissolved during 6 years (1633–39), and then reorganized with only ten instrumentalists and singers; after 1645 it attained its former standard of efficiency.

Standing at the parting of the ways between Palestrina and Bach, Schütz was of peculiar importance in German art through having applied the grand Italian choral style, and the new dramatico-monodic style (of Monteverdi and his predecessors), to the development of a semi-dramatic church music which is not merely of historical interest as preparing the mightier Bach epoch, but of pleasing and powerful effect in its own right. Schütz was also the composer of the first German opera, *Dafne,* set to Opitz's translation of Rinuccini's libretto (produced at Hartenfels Castle in Torgau, April 23, 1627, at the wedding of Princess Sophie of Saxony), and of a ballet, *Orpheus and Eurydice* (1638, on the wedding of Johann Georg II, of Saxony); the music of both is lost. Karl Riedel did much to awaken appreciation of Schütz's merits by publishing and producing *Die 7 Worte Christi am Kreuz,* and by bringing out other works, notably a Passion consisting of selections from Schütz's *Historia des Leidens Jesu Christi.* Between 1885 and 1894 Breitkopf & Härtel publ. a complete edition of Schütz's works in 16 vols., ed. by Philipp Spitta: Vol. I, *Die evangelischen Historien und die Sieben Worte Jesu Christi;* the Historien being (1) *Die Historia des Leidens und Sterbens unsers Heylandes Jesu Christi* (4 Passions after the Evangelists) and (2) *Historia der fröhlichen und siegreichen Auferstehung unsers einigen Erlösers und Seligmachers Jesu Christi* (first publ. 1623; similar to the Passions); vols. II-III, *Mehrchörige Psalmen mit Instrumenten,* with continuo (first publ. 1619); vol. IV, *Cantiones sacrae a 4* with continuo; vol. V, *Symphoniae sacrae,* Part I; vol. VI, *Kleine geistliche Konzerte a 1-5;* vol. VII, *Symphoniae sacrae,* Part II; vol. VIII, sacred choral music, containing *Musicalia ad chorum sacrum,* with continuo (1648); vol. IX, *Italienische Madrigale,* containing his first publ. work, sent home from Italy, and dedicated to the Landgrave, *Il primo libro dei Madrigali* (1611; 18 madrigals a 5 and a Dialog a 8); vol. X-XI, *Symphoniae sacrae,* Part III; vol. XII-XV, *Gesammelte Motetten, Konzerte, Madrigale und Arien;* vol. XVI, *Psalmen Davids deutsch durch Cornelium Beckern in 4 Stimmen gestellt;* index, etc.

A supplementary vol. was publ. in 1909, containing the long-lost Christmas Oratorio *(Historia von der Geburt Jesu Christi),* discovered in 1908 by Schering in the Univ. of Uppsala (new ed. by A. Mendel, N.Y., 1950); a 2nd supplementary vol. (1927), containing motets, madrigals, and arias, was ed. by Heinrich Spitta. A new ed. of Schütz's complete works, the Neuen Schütz-Gesellschaft edition, in 38 vols., began to appear in 1955 (Bärenreiter, Kassel). Another edition, the Stuttgarter Schütz-Ausgabe, was begun in 1971.

BIBLIOGRAPHY: W. Schäfer, *H. S.* (1854); F. Chrysander, "Geschichte der Braunschweig-Wolffenbüttelschen Kapelle und Oper," *Jahrbuch für musikalische Wissenschaft* I (1863); Fr. Spitta, *Gedächtnisrede auf S.* (1886); Fr. Spitta, *Die Passionen nach den 4 Evangelien von H. S.* (1886); Ph. Spitta, "S.," in *Allgemeine deutsche Biographie* and *Musikgeschichtliche Aufsätze* (1894); M. Seiffert, "Anecdota Schütziana," *Sammelbände der Internationalen Musik-Gesellschaft* I; A. Werner, *Städt. und fürstliche Musikpflege in Weissenfels* (1911); A. Pirro, *S.* (Paris, 1913; 2nd ed., 1924; German transl. by W. Gurlitt, 1914); A. Schering, "Zur Metrik der Psalmen von S.," in "Kretzschmar-Festschrift" (1918); E. H. Müller, *H. S. Leben und Werke* (tabulated; Dresden, 1922); E. H. Müller, *H. S.* (Leipzig, 1925); Fr. Spitta, *H. S., ein Meister der Musica sacra* (1925); J. Müller-Blattau, *Die Kompositionslehre H. Schützens in der Fassung seines Schülers Christoph Bernhard* (1926); F. Blume, *Das monodische Prinzip in der protestantischen Kirchenmusik* (1925); W. Schuh, *Formprobleme bei H. S.* (Leipzig, 1928); A. Einstein, *S.* (Kassel, 1928); R. Gerber, *Das Passionsrezitativ bei S.* (Gütersloh, 1929); E. H. Müller, *Gesammelte Briefe und Schriften* (Regensburg, 1931); H. Birtner, "Zur S.-Bewegung," *Musik und Kirche* (1932); W. Dilthey, *H. S.* (1932); H. Hoffmann, *H. S. in unserer Zeit* (Leipzig, 1933); W. Kreidler, *H. S. und der stile concitato von Claudio Monteverdi* (Stuttgart, 1934); A. A. Abert, *Die stilistischen Grundlagen der "Cantiones sacrae" von H. S.* (Berlin, 1935); H. J. Moser, *H. S.* (Kassel, 1936; 2nd ed., 1954); K. Gudewill, *Das sprachliche Urbild bei S.* (Kassel, 1936); L. Reitter, *Doppelchortechnik bei H. S.* (Derendingen, 1937); J. Piersig, *Das Weltbild des H. S.* (Kassel, 1949); A. Adrio, *Bekenntnis zu H. S.* (a collection of articles; Kassel, 1954); *Festschrift zur Ehrung von H. S.* (Weimar, 1954); H. J. Moser, *Heinrich Schütz: His Life and Work* (translated from 2nd rev. ed. by Carl G. Pfatteicher; St. Louis, 1959); H. H. Eggebrecht, *Heinrich Schütz, Musicus poeticus* (Göttingen, 1959); G. Kirchner, *Der Generalbass bei Heinrich Schütz* (Kassel, 1960); W. S. Huber, *Motivsymbolik bei Heinrich Schütz* (Kassel, 1961).

Schützendorf, four brothers, all baritones: (1) **Gustav** (b. Cologne, 1883; d. Berlin, April 27, 1937), the best known, studied singing in Milan; sang at the Munich Opera, in Berlin, and in Leipzig; made his American debut as Faninal in *Der Rosenkavalier* at the Metropolitan Opera, N.Y., Nov. 17, 1922, and remained on its roster until 1935; then returned to Germany. In 1929 he married the soprano **Grete Stückgold.** (2) **Alfons** (b. Vught, Holland, May 25, 1882; d. Weimar,

Aug. 1946) was distinguished as a Wagnerian singer, and took part in the Bayreuth Festivals; in 1932 settled in Berlin as a singing teacher. (3) **Guido** (b. Herzogenbusch, April 22, 1880; d. Germany, April 1967) sang with the German Opera Co. on its tour in the U.S. in 1929–30. (4) **Leo** (b. Cologne, May 7, 1886; d. Berlin, Dec. 18, 1931) was a member of the Berlin State Opera from 1920 to 1929, and made numerous appearances abroad.

Schuyt (Schuijt), Cornelis, Netherlands composer; b. Leyden, 1557; d. there (buried June 12), 1616; studied at first with his father, an organist, and then in Italy. In 1593 was appointed organist in his native city. Publ. madrigals *a* 5 (1600) and *a* 6 (1611); 12 pavans and galliards in the 12 modes and 2 *canzone alla francese* (1611). The 5-part madrigals were reprinted by A. Smijers (2 vols., 1937–38).

BIBLIOGRAPHY: M. Seiffert, "Cornelis Schuijt," *Tijdschrift der Vereeniging voor Noord-Nederlands Musiekgeschiedenis* 5 (1897).

Schuyt, Nicolaas (Nico), Dutch composer; b. Alkmaar, Jan. 2, 1922. He studied piano with Jacob van Domselaar and Eberhard Rebling; composition with Bertus van Lier. In 1964 he joined the Foundation Donemus for publication of contemporary Dutch music in Amsterdam. He composed many pieces for performance by youth groups.

WORKS: school opera *De Varkenshoeder (The Little Pig Boy,* 1951); a ballet, *De Kast van de oude chinees (The Old Chinese Cupboard);* a cantata for student performance *Wij zullen een muur bouwen* (1952); Concerto for youth orch. (1952–53); *Sonata a tre* for oboe, bassoon and piano (1953–54); *5 Dramatic Nocturnes* for flute and piano (1954); *Sonatina in due pezzi* for piano (1955); *Réveil* for orch. (1955); *Corteggio* for orch. (1958); *Sinfonia divertente* for small orch. (1958); Sonatina for youth chamber orch. (1961); *Quatuor de ballet* for clarinet, trumpet, percussion and piano (1962); *De belevenissen van Strip-Thijs* for clarinet, trumpet, percussion and piano (1962); Sonata for orch. (1964); *Discorsi capricciosi* for small orch. (1965); *Allegro and passacaglia* for violin and piano (1965); *Arkadia* for mezzo-soprano, viola and cello (1966); *Hymnus* for small orch. (1966); *Naar de maan (To the Moon),* for female chorus, mixed chorus and orch. (1967–68); *Greetings from Holland* for small orch. (1970); *Alla notturna* for 2 oboes, oboe d'amore and English horn (1971); *Quasi in modo de valzer* for orch. (1973); *3 Preludes* for strings and piano (1973); *Furies for Four,* piano quartet (1975).

Schwalm, Oskar, German music critic and composer; b. Erfurt, Sept. 11, 1856; d. Berlin, Feb. 11, 1936. He studied at the Leipzig Cons. with Reinecke, Jadassohn, and others; was engaged in music publishing; wrote an overture, *König Drosselbart;* piano pieces; etc.; publ. collections of school songs.

Schwalm, Robert, German composer; brother of Oskar Schwalm; b. Erfurt, Dec. 6, 1845; d. Königsberg, March 6, 1912. He studied at the Leipzig Cons.; in 1875 settled in Königsberg, where he conducted several choral societies.

WORKS: opera *Frauenlob* (Leipzig, 1885); male choruses with orch.: *Morgengrauen, Bismarck-Hymne, An Deutschland, Mila, Wikingerfahrt, Gotenzug, Festgesang, Der Goten Todesgesang, Abendstille am Meer, Thermopylae*, etc.; several biblical cantatas; piano pieces; songs.

Schwanenberg, Johann Gottfried, German composer; b. c.1740; d. Braunschweig, March 29, 1804. He was educated in Italy; upon return to Germany he produced 12 operas to Italian librettos; also wrote concertos for piano and violin; 3 piano sonatas, etc.; also wrote several critical papers on music theory, in one of which he argued for the deletion of H. from the German musical scale.

Schwann, William, American organist and musicographer; b. Salem, Illinois, May 13, 1913. He studied at the Louisville, Kentucky, School of Music at the Univ. of Louisville (A.B., 1935). He began his musical career as an organist and choir director in Louisville churches (1930–35); then went to Boston, where he studied organ with E. Power Biggs; also attended classes of Hugo Leichtentritt, Wallace Woodworth and A. T. Merritt at Harvard Univ.; wrote music criticism. In 1939 he set up a retail shop of phonograph records in Cambridge; in 1949 he launched his *Schwann Record Catalog*. In 1953 the title was changed to *Schwann Long Playing Record Catalog*. In 1971 he added 8-track cartridge tape and cassette tape listings under the new title *Schwann Record and Tape Guide*. He also publishes a semiannual *Supplementary Record & Tape Guide*, an annual *Children's Record Catalog*, an annual *Country and Western Record & Tape Catalog* and a quadrennial *Artist Issue* which lists classical music indexed alphabetically by the names of performing artists. The *Schwann Catalog* is generally regarded as the most authoritative and the most comprehensive compilation of its kind.

Schwartz, Elliott, American composer, teacher and commentator; b. Brooklyn, Jan. 19, 1936. He studied composition with Otto Luening, Jack Beeson and Paul Creston at Columbia Univ.; also attended classes of Varèse, Wolpe, Henry Brant and others at the Bennington Composers Conference, Vermont (summers, 1961–66). He was instructor in music at the Univ. of Massachusetts, Amherst (1960–64); in 1964, appointed to the faculty of Bowdoin College, Brunswick, Maine. He published *The Symphonies of Ralph Vaughan Williams* (Amherst, Mass., 1964); edited (with Barney Childs) *Contemporary Composers on Contemporary Music* (N.Y., 1967) and compiled *Electronic Music: A Listener's Guide* (N.Y., 1973). In his compositions he develops the Satiesque notions of unfettered license in music leading to their completely unbuttoned state.
WORKS: *Texture* for chamber orch. (1966); *Dialogue* for double bass (1967); *Elevator Music* for anybody riding in an elevator (1967); *Signals* for trombone and double bass (1968); *Magic Music* for piano and orch. (1968); *Music for Napoleon and Beethoven* for trumpet, piano, and tape (1969); *Music for Soloists and Audience*, a free-for-all with 4 conductors (1970); *Eclipse I* for 10 players (1971); *Dream Overture* for orch. and recorded music (1972); *Eclipse III* for chamber orch. (1975); *The Harmony of Maine* for solo synthesizer and orch. (1975); all kinds of miscellaneous pieces, involving toys, music boxes, and various noise makers.

Schwartz, Francis, American composer; b. Altoona, Pennsylvania, March 10, 1940. He studied at the Juilliard School of Music (B.S., 1961; M.S., 1962); piano with Lonny Epstein, music theory with Vittorio Giannini and chamber music with Louis Persinger. In 1966 he was appointed to the music faculty of the Univ. of Puerto Rico, San Juan. In his works he cultivates multimedia compositions, in which music, stage, and electronics are combined. The most dramatic theater work was *Auschwitz*, staged in San Juan on May 15, 1968. Other works are *Yo protesto* (Casals Festival, San Juan, March 23, 1974); *Caligula* (N.Y., March 3, 1975); and *Time, Sound, and the Hooded Man* (Buenos Aires, July 16, 1975).

Schwartz, Rudolf, German musicologist; b. Berlin, Jan. 20, 1859; d. Halle, April 20, 1935. He studied philosophy at the Univ. of Berlin, where he also took courses in musicology with Philipp Spitta; he graduated from Leipzig Univ. (Dr. phil., 1892). In 1901 he became librarian of the *Musikbibliothek Peters* and editor of the *Peters Jahrbuch*, to which he contributed numerous valuable essays. A memorial issue of the *Jahrbuch* of 1936 contains a complete list of his writings.

Schwarz, Boris, eminent Russian-American violinist, musicologist and pedagogue; b. St. Petersburg, March 26, 1906. He went to Germany as a youth; studied violin with Carl Flesch in Berlin and with Jacques Thibaud in Paris; attended courses in musicology with Curt Sachs, Schering, and Johannes Wolf. He made his debut as violinist at the age of 14 in Hannover. In 1936 he emigrated to the U.S.; was concertmaster of the Indianapolis Symph. Orch. (1937–38) and played in the violin section of the NBC Symph. (1938–39). In 1941 he was appointed to the faculty of Queens College; was chairman of the music dept. from 1949 to 1956; prof. emeritus, 1976. He is trilingual as a writer, being equally fluent in Russian, German and English; has contributed informative articles, principally on Russian music, to music encyclopedias and journals. His book *Music and Musical Life in Soviet Russia* (N.Y., 1972) attracted attention for its highly critical account of the musical situation in Russia.

Schwarz, Rudolf, Austrian conductor; b. Vienna, April 29, 1905. He studied piano and violin; played viola in the Vienna Philharmonic; then conducted opera in Düsseldorf and Karlsruhe. With the advent of the Nazi regime in 1933 he was, as a Jew, forbidden to engage in professional activities, and became music director of the Jüdischer Kulturbund in Berlin. He was sent to the Belsen concentration camp but survived, and after liberation went to England; was conductor of the Bournemouth Municipal Orch. (1947–50), Birmingham Orch. (1950–57) and BBC Symph. Orch. (1957–62); then was music director of the Northern Sinfonia Orch. in Newcastle-upon-Tyne.

Schwarz, Vera, Austrian soprano; b. Zagreb, July 10, 1889; d. Vienna, Dec. 4, 1964. She studied voice and piano in Vienna; appeared in operettas there; went to Hamburg in 1914 and to Berlin in 1917; toured in South America. In 1939 she went to Hollywood where she became a vocal instructor; in 1948 she returned to Austria; gave courses at the Mozarteum in Salzburg. Her best roles were Carmen and Tosca.

Schwarz, Wilhelm, German singing teacher; b. Stuttgart, May 11, 1825; d. Berlin, Jan. 4, 1878. He taught singing in Hannover and Berlin; publ. *System der Gesangkunst nach physiologischen Gesetzen* (1857) and *Die Musik als Gefühlssprache im Verhältniss zur Stimm- und Gesangbildung* (1860).

Schwarzkopf, Elisabeth, German soprano; b. Jarotschin, near Poznan, Dec. 9, 1915. She studied in Berlin with Maria Ivogün; made her debut in 1938 at the Berlin Opera; then sang at the Vienna Opera, at Covent Garden, London, and at La Scala, Milan. She sang the part of Anna Trulove in the world première of Stravinsky's *The Rake's Progress* (Venice, Sept. 11, 1951). In 1971 she offically retired from the stage; in 1976 joined the staff of the Juilliard School of Music, N.Y.; with her husband Walter Legge gave a course in vocal interpretation.

Schwedler, (Otto) Maximilian, German flutist; b. Hirschberg, March 31, 1853; d. Leipzig, Jan. 16, 1940. He studied in Dresden; played flute in various German orchestras; in 1881 joined the Gewandhaus Orch. in Leipzig; also taught at the Leipzig Cons. He was the inventor of the "Schwedler flute" (1885), fully described in his *Katechismus der Flöte und des Flötenspiels* (Leipzig, 1897); made numerous transcriptions for flute, and publ. a flute method.

Schweitzer, Albert, great humanitarian, physician, and organist, and an authority on Bach; b. Kaysersberg, Alsace, Jan. 14, 1875; d. in his jungle hospital at Lambaréné, Gabon, Sept. 4, 1965, at the age of 90. He was the son of a Günsbach vicar; studied organ with Eugen Münch at Mulhouse, with Ernst Münch at Strasbourg, and with Widor in Paris (from 1893); was organist of the Bach Concerts in Strasbourg from 1896; studied theology and philosophy at the Universities of Strasbourg, Paris, and Berlin; in 1902 joined the faculty of the Univ. of Strasbourg; while teaching there he completed the full medical course (M.D., 1912), with the intention of becoming a medical missionary in Africa, to which task he subsequently devoted most of his time and energy, making occasional concert tours as organist in Europe to raise funds for his hospital work among the African natives. In 1952 he was awarded the Nobel Peace Prize, the only professional musician to hold this prestigious award. His philosophical and theological writings had established his reputation as one of the foremost thinkers of our time. In the field of music he distinguished himself as the author of one of the most important books on Bach, greatly influencing the interpretation of Bach's music, and contributing to the understanding of Bach's symbolic treatment of various musical devices. In 1906 he became organist of the "Société J. S. Bach"

in Paris; in 1909 he presided over the conferences on organ building at the Congress of the International Music Society in Vienna, which led to the adoption of international regulations, and read a paper, "Die Reform unseres Orgelbaues," urging the simplification of the modern organ to correct faulty tone quality caused by extreme wind pressure (full report in the *Wiener Kongressbericht der Internationalen Musik-Gesellschaft*, 1909, pp. 581–679). With Widor, he edited the first 5 vols. of the Schirmer critico-practical edition of Bach's organ works (editions in English, French, and German) and with Édouard Nies-Berger, the remaining 3 vols. He held the degrees of Dr. theol. and Dr. phil.; also the honorary degrees of D.D. (Oxon.) and Litt. D. (St. Andrews).

WRITINGS: *Deutsche und französische Orgelbaukunst und Orgelkunst* (Leipzig, 1906; 2nd ed., 1927); *Jean Sébastian Bach, le musicien-poète* (Paris, 1905; German enlarged ed., 1908; English transl. by Ernest Newman, Leipzig, 1911; re-issued, 1923); publ. an autobiography, *Aus meinem Leben und Denken* (Leipzig, 1931; English transl. as *My Life and Thought*, London, 1933; revised ed., as *Out of My Life and Thought*, N.Y., 1949; selections in German publ. as a school textbook, with an introduction in English, N.Y., 1949); also *African Notebook* (N.Y., 1939); *On the Edge of the Primeval Forest* (combined ed. of various previous vols. in German and English; N.Y., 1948). See also C. R. Joy, ed., *Music in the Life of A. S.* (selections from his writings; N.Y., 1951); R. Grabs, ed., *Gesammelte Werke* (5 vols.; Munich, 1974).

BIBLIOGRAPHY: C. T. Campion, *A. S.: Philosopher, Theologian, Musician, Doctor* (N.Y., 1928); Jan Eigenhuis, *A. S.* (Haarlem, 1929); H. Christaller, *A. S.* (1931); John D. Regester, *A. S.: The Man and His Work* (N.Y., 1931); Magnus C. Ratter, *A. S.* (London, 1935; revised ed., 1950); A. A. Roback, ed., *The A. S. Jubilee Book* (Cambridge, Mass., 1946; a collection of essays); G. Seaver, *A. S.: The Man and His Mind* (London, 1947); O. Kraus, *A. S.: His Work and His Philosophy* (N.Y., 1947); H. Hagedorn, *Prophet in the Wilderness: The Story of A. S.* (N.Y., 1947); R. Grabs, *A. S.: Weg und Werk eines Menschenfreundes* (Berlin, 1953); R. Sonner, *S. und die Orgelbewegung* (Colmar, 1955); Werner Picht, *The Life and Thought of Albert Schweitzer* (N.Y., 1965).

Schweitzer, Anton, German composer; b. Coburg (baptized June 6), 1735; d. Gotha, Nov. 23, 1787. He was a chorister and later viola player in Hildburghausen; in 1764 went to Italy for serious study; returning to Germany, he was appointed (in 1766) music director of the ducal theater in Weimar; in 1769 became conductor of Seyler's operatic troupe, which was engaged by the Duke of Weimar in 1772. After the destruction by fire of the Weimar Theater in 1774, Schweitzer went to Gotha; there he was appointed court conductor in 1778. Schweitzer was one of the earliest composers to write serious operas to German texts. He produced in Weimar his operas *Die Dorfgala* (June 30, 1772) and *Alceste* (May 28, 1773; libretto by Wieland); there followed another opera, *Rosamunde* (Mannheim, Jan. 20, 1780); Mozart expressed appreciation of Schweitzer's operas. But it was as a composer of Singspiele that Schweitzer achieved popularity in his day; he was also important historically as the first composer of a melodrama in German, after Rousseau's *Pygmalion* (Weimar, 1772).

BIBLIOGRAPHY: J. Maurer, *Anton Schweitzer als dramatischer Komponist* (Leipzig, 1912); A. Loewenberg, *Annals of Opera* (1943; 2nd ed., 1955).

Schwencke, Christian Friedrich Gottlieb, German composer; son of the bassoonist **Johann Gottlieb Schwencke** (1744–1823); b. Wachenhausen, Harz, Aug. 30, 1767; d. Hamburg, Oct. 27, 1822. He studied with Marpurg and Kirnberger; succeeded C. P. E. Bach as town cantor and music director at the Katharinenkirche, Hamburg. Wrote cantatas, sacred and secular; 2 oratorios; church music; 6 organ fugues; 3 violin sonatas; piano sonatas. He rescored Handel's *Messiah* and Bach's Mass in B minor; wrote for the Leipzig *Allgemeine Zeitung*.

Schwencke, Friedrich Gottlieb, pianist and organist; son and pupil of **Johann Friedrich Schwencke**; b. Hamburg, Dec. 15, 1823; d. there, June 11, 1896. He gave organ concerts in Paris (1855); succeeded his father in 1852 as organist of the Nikolaikirche in Hamburg. He wrote 3 fantasies for organ, trumpet, trombone, and kettledrums; sacred songs for female chorus with organ; in 1886 he publ. a new and unabridged ed. of his father's chorale preludes.

Schwencke, Johann Friedrich, German organist and composer; son and pupil of **Christian Friedrich Gottlieb Schwencke;** b. Hamburg, April 30, 1792; d. there, Sept. 28, 1852. He was organist at the Nikolaikirche in Hamburg; composed numerous cantatas; over 500 chorale preludes and postludes for organ; a septet for 5 cellos, double bass, and kettledrums; harmonized about 1,000 chorales and 73 Russian folksongs; publ. the popular *Hamburgisches Choralbuch;* made many transcriptions; orchestrated Beethoven's *Adelaide,* and various works by other composers.

Schwerké, Irving, American writer on music; b. Appleton, Wisconsin, July 21, 1893. He received his education at the Univ. of Wisconsin; in 1921 went to Paris; was music correspondent to the *Chicago Tribune* and the *Musical Courier* (1921–40); during the war he lived in Switzerland; then returned to his home town of Appleton, Wisconsin. He wrote the books *Kings Jazz and David* (Paris, 1927); *Tansman, compositeur polonais* (Paris, 1931); *Views and Interviews* (Paris, 1936).

Schwieger, Hans, German conductor; b. Cologne, June 15, 1906. He studied in Cologne; was assistant conductor at the Berlin State Opera (1927–30), at the Kassel Opera (1930–31), in Mainz (1932–43) and in Danzig (1936–37). In 1937 he went to Japan, where he conducted the Tokyo Symph. Orch. In 1938 he settled in the U.S.; organized and conducted the Southern Symph. Orch. at Columbia, S. C. (1938–41); then was conductor of the Fort Wayne Symph. (1944–48). From 1948 to 1971 he was conductor of the Kansas City Philharmonic; then filled engagements as guest conductor in Europe.

BIBLIOGRAPHY: Hope Stoddard, *Symphony Conductors of the U. S. A.* (N.Y., 1957; pp. 182–89).

Schytte, Ludvig (Theodor), Danish composer; b. Aarhus, April 28, 1848; d. Berlin, Nov. 10, 1909. He was a pharmacist as a young man; then began to study piano with Anton Rée and composition with Gade, finishing under Taubert in Berlin and Liszt in Weimar. He settled in Vienna in 1887 as a teacher; moved to Berlin in 1907; taught there at Stern's Cons. A master of the miniature forms, he wrote a number of attractive piano pieces, some of which became extremely popular; about 200 were publ.

WORKS: for piano: *Promenades musicales, Rapsodie norwégienne, Aus froher Kinderzeit, Spanische Nächte, Valse piquante, Waldbilder, Aus der Heimat und Fremde;* numerous piano studies (*6 brillante Vortragsetüden, Melodische Spezialetüden, Studien in Ornamentik und Dynamik);* for piano 4 hands: *Bajaderntänze, Kindersymphonie, Musikalische Wandelbilder, Reiseblätter, Kindersuite,* etc.; also a 1-act opera, *Hero* (Copenhagen, Sept. 25, 1898); the operetta *Der Mameluk* (Vienna, Dec. 22, 1903); a piano concerto; chamber music; a song cycle, *Die Verlassene.*

Sciammarella, Valdo, Argentine composer; b. Buenos Aires, Jan. 20, 1924. He studied composition with Julián Bautista; subsequently engaged in pedagogy. In 1965 he was appointed head of the Music Department at the National School of Fine Arts in Buenos Aires. He wrote a one-act lyric comedy *Marianita Limena* (Buenos Aires, Nov. 11, 1957); *Variaciones Concertantes* for piano and orch. (1952); *Scherzino* for oboe, clarinet and bassoon (1956); *Galeria humana,* chamber ballet (1962); piano pieces.

Sciutti, Graziella, Italian soprano; b. Turin, April 17, 1932. She studied singing in Rome, and became particularly successful in soubrette roles. She was associated with the Glyndebourne Festivals in England between 1954 and 1959; later sang at the Piccola Scala in Milan.

Scontrino, Antonio, Italian composer and teacher; b. Trapani, May 17, 1850; d. Florence, Jan. 7, 1922. He studied at the Palermo Cons.; was a virtuoso on the double bass and gave concerts; went to Munich for a special study of German music at the Musikschule (1872–74); after various engagements as an orch. player and teacher, he settled in Florence in 1892 and taught composition at the Istituto Musicale there.

WORKS: 5 operas: *Matelda* (Milan, June 19, 1879), *Il Progettista* (Rome, Feb. 8, 1882), *Il Sortilegio* (Turin, June 21, 1882), *Gringoire* (Milan, May 24, 1890), and *La Cortigiana* (Milan, Jan. 30, 1896); incidental music to Gabriele d'Annunzio's *Francesca da Rimini; Sinfonia marinaresca; Sinfonia romantica;* Concerto for Double Bass and Orch.; 3 string quartets; church music; songs.

BIBLIOGRAPHY: A biographical brochure, *Antonio Scontrino nella vita e nell'arte,* was publ. in his native town of Trapani in 1935. A detailed analysis of his instrumental works is found in Cobbett's *Cyclopedic Survey of Chamber Music.*

Scott, Charles Kennedy, English choral conductor and composer; b. Romsey, Nov. 16, 1876; d. London, July 2, 1965. He studied organ at the Brussels Cons., taking 1st prize (1897). In 1898, he settled in London; in 1904 he established the Oriana Madrigal Society there, in 1919 the Philharmonic Choir, and in 1922 the Euterpe String Players. He publ *Madrigal Singing* (London, 1907; new enlarged ed., 1931); a vocal method, *Word and Tone* (London, 1933; 2 vols.); *The Fundamentals of Singing* (N.Y., 1954); edited old carols and choral music of the 16th century.

BIBLIOGRAPHY: S. de B. Taylor, "C. K. Scott," *Musical Times* (Nov. 1951).

Scott, Cyril (Meir), remarkable English composer; b. Oxton, Cheshire, Sept. 27, 1879; d. Eastbourne, Dec. 31, 1970. He was a scion of a cultural family; his father was a classical scholar, his mother a fine amateur musician. Having displayed a natural penchant for music as a child, he was sent to Frankfurt, where he studied piano and theory with Iwan Knorr; returning to England in 1898, he continued to study music and began to compose. In 1900 Hans Richter conducted in Liverpool and Manchester Scott's *Heroic Suite;* also in 1900, his First Symphony was played in Darmstadt; his overture *Pelléas and Mélisande* was performed in Frankfurt. His 2nd Symph. was given at a Promenade Concert in London on Aug. 25, 1903. (It was later converted into *3 Symphonic Dances.*) His setting of *La Belle Dame sans Merci* (Keats) for chorus and orch. was produced in London in 1916, and revived at the Leeds Festival in 1934. His opera *The Alchemist,* for which he wrote his own libretto, was produced in Essen, Germany, on May 28, 1925. In 1920 Scott traveled to the U.S. and played his 1st Piano Concerto with the Phildelphia Orch. under Stokowski (Nov. 5, 1920). But he acquired fame mainly as composer of some exotically flavored piano pieces, of which *Lotus Land* became a perennial favorite; Fritz Kreisler arranged it for violin and piano and played it repeatedly at his concerts. Other popular piano pieces were *Danse nègre, Chinese Serenade, Russian Dance, Sphinx, Autumn Idyll, Berceuse, Little Russian Suite, Indian Suite, Spanish Dance,* and most particularly the ingratiating suite *Impresssons of the Jungle Book,* after Kipling. He also wrote over 100 songs. In all these pieces, Scott showed himself a master of musical miniature; he wrote in a distinctly modern idiom, very much in the style of French Impressionism; employed sonorous parallel progressions of unresolved dissonant chords; made frequent use of the whole-tone scale. His writing for piano is ingratiating in its idiomatic mastery; his harmonious modalities exude an aura of perfumed euphony. Among his other works are: *Christmas Overture* (London, Nov. 13, 1906); *La Princesse Maleine,* symph. poem (London, Aug. 22, 1907); 2 piano concertos (1915, 1950); Violin Concerto (Birmingham, Jan. 27, 1928); Cello Concerto (1937); Concerto for Oboe and String Orch. (London, Sept. 13, 1948); Symph. No. 3, subtitled *The Muses* (1939); *Neopolitan Rhapsody* for orch. (1960); 4 string quartets; 2 string trios; 2 piano trios; *Rapsodie arabesque* for flute, violin, viola, cello and harp; Clarinet Quintet (1951); *Sonata melodica* for violin and piano (1951); Piano Quintet; Piano Quartet; 4 violin sonatas; Trio

for flute, cello and piano; Flute Sonata; *Rondo serioso* for viola d'amore. From his early youth Cyril Scott was attracted to occult sciences and was a believer in the reality of the supernatural; he published books and essays on music as a divinely inspired art and inveighed violently against jazz as the work of Satan. He published the following books: *My Years of Indiscretion* (London, 1924); *The Philosophy of Modernism in Its Connection with Music* (London, 1917); *The Influence of Music on History and Morals: A Vindication of Plato* (London, 1928); *Music: Its Secret Influence Throughout the Ages* (London, 1933; 5th ed., 1952); *An Outline of Modern Occultism* (N.Y., 1935); *The Christian Paradox* (N.Y., 1942); an autobiographical volume, *Bone of Contention* (London, 1969); 2 publications on medical matters: *Medicine, Rational and Irrational* (London, 1946) and *Cancer Prevention* (London, 1968).

BIBLIOGRAPHY: Arthur Eaglefield Hull, *Cyril Scott: Composer, Poet and Philosopher* (London, 1918; 3rd ed. 1921).

Scott, Francis George, Scottish composer; b. Hawick, Roxburghshire, Jan. 25, 1880; d. Glasgow, Nov. 6, 1958. He studied humanities at the Univ. of Edinburgh; later at Durham Univ. (B.M., 1909); also took theory lessons with a local organist. As a composer, he cultivated Scottish art music; publ. a number of songs at his own expense; of these the most significant are *Scottish Lyrics* (5 vols., 1921–39). His more ambitious works include *The Ballad of Kynd Kittok* for baritone and orch.; *Lament for the Heroes* for string orch.; and a concert overture, *Renaissance* (Glasgow, Jan. 14, 1939). Scott had a number of ardent admirers in England, among them the poet Hugh MacDiarmid and the composer Kaikhosru Sorabji, who in their exuberant encomiums place him in the ranks of Schubert and Schumann as a song writer.

Scott, Marion Margaret, English writer on music; b. London, July 16, 1877; d. there, Dec. 24, 1953. She studied at the Royal College of Music in London. In 1911 she organized, with Gertrude Eaton, the Society of Women Musicians. She specialized in Haydn research and compiled a complete catalogue of Haydn string quartets, which she published in *Music & Letters* (July 1930). She also published monographs on *Beethoven* (London, 1934; revised ed., 1951) and *Mendelssohn* (London, 1938).

Scott, Tom (Thomas Jefferson), American folk singer and composer; b. Campbellsburg, Ky., May 28, 1912; d. New York, Aug. 12, 1961. He studied violin with an uncle; played in dance bands; wrote songs; then went to Hollywood, where he took theory lessons with George Antheil; subsequently studied with Harrison Kerr and Wallingford Riegger.

WORKS: opera, *The Fisherman* (1956); for orch.: *Song with Dance* (1932); *Plymouth Rock* (1938); *Hornpipe and Chantey* (1944); Symph. No. 1 (Rochester, N.Y., Oct. 22, 1946); *From the Sacred Harp* (1946); *Ballad of the Harp Weaver,* for narrator, harp, chorus, and string quartet (N.Y., Feb. 22, 1947); *Johnny Appleseed* (N.Y., March 1, 1948); *Lento* for saxophone and strings (1953); chamber music: 2 string quartets

(1944; 1956); *Emily Dickinson Suite,* for violin and harp (1955); chanteys for chorus; a number of solo songs; arrangements of folksongs; etc.

BIBLIOGRAPHY: J. Ringo, "Some Notes on Tom Scott's Music," *American Composers Alliance Bulletin* (Winter 1957; with a list of works).

Scotti, Antonio, celebrated Italian baritone; b. Naples, Jan. 25, 1866; d. there, Feb. 26, 1936. He studied with Francesco Lamperti; made his debut as Amonasro in Malta (Nov. 1, 1889); then sang in Italy, Russia, Spain, and South America; made his London debut at Covent Garden on June 8, 1899, as Don Giovanni, and appeared in the same role with the Metropolitan Opera, N.Y., (Dec. 27, 1899). He remained with the Metropolitan Opera for 33 years; made his farewell appearance on Jan. 20, 1933. He also toured in America with his own company. He possessed great histrionic ability, and was especially noted for his dramatic roles (Scarpia, Rigoletto, Falstaff, Don Giovanni).

Scotto, Renata, Italian soprano; b. Savona, Feb. 24, 1934. She studied in Milan, where she made her operatic debut as Violetta in *La Traviata,* at La Scala, Milan; subsequently sang in England with excellent success.

Scotus (Scot), Joannes (called **Erigena**), noted philosopher; b. c.815; d. c.881. His work *De divisione naturae* contains a definition of music, with a description of musical practice in his day.

BIBLIOGRAPHY: J. Handschin, "Die Musikanschauung des Johannes Scotus (Erigena)," *Deutsche Vierteljahrsschrift für Literaturwissenschaft und Geistesgeschichte* V/2; D. M. Cappuyns, *Jean Scot Érigène* (Brussels, 1964).

Scriabin, Alexander, remarkable Russian composer whose solitary genius had no predecessors and left no disciples; b. Moscow, Jan. 6, 1872; d. there, April 27, 1915. His mother died when he was a child, and his father remarried; he received his musical education from his aunt; at the age of 12 he began to take regular piano lessons with George Conus and with Zverev. In 1885 he studied composition with Taneyev. He entered the Moscow Cons. in 1888 as a piano student of Safonov. He practiced assiduously, but never became a virtuoso pianist; at his piano recitals he performed mostly his own works. Graduating with a gold medal from Safonov's class, Scriabin remained at the Moscow Cons. to study fugue with Arensky, but failed to pass the required test and never received a diploma for composition. By that time he had already written several piano pieces in the manner of Chopin; the publisher Belaieff heard him play and offered him a contract; he also financed Scriabin's European tour; on Jan. 15, 1896 Scriabin gave a concert of his own music in Paris. Returning to Russia, he completed his first major work, a piano concerto, and was soloist in its first performance on Oct. 23, 1897 in Odessa. In the same year he married the pianist **Vera Isakovich.** They spent some time abroad; on Jan. 31, 1898 they gave a joint recital in Paris in a program of Scriabin's works. From 1898 to 1903 Scriabin taught piano

classes at the Moscow Cons. His first orchestral work, *Reverie,* was conducted in Moscow by Safonov on March 24, 1899; he also conducted the first performance of Scriabin's 1st Symph. (March 29, 1901). Scriabin's 2nd Symph. was brought out by Liadov in St. Petersburg (Jan. 25, 1902). After the death of his original publisher Belaieff in 1904, Scriabin received an annual grant of 2,400 rubles from the wealthy Moscow merchant Morosov, and went to Switzerland where he began work on his 3rd Symph., *Le Poème divin;* it had its first performance in Paris on May 29, 1905 under the direction of Arthur Nikisch. At that time Scriabin separated from Vera Isakovich and established a household with Tatiana Schloezer, sister of the music critic Boris Schloezer who subsequently became Scriabin's close friend and biographer. In December, 1906, Scriabin went to America at the invitation of Modest Altschuler, who at that time had organized the Russian Symph. Society in N.Y.; Scriabin appeared as soloist at Altschuler's concerts in N.Y. and also gave piano recitals of his own works in N.Y., Chicago, Detroit and other American music centers. Tatiana Schloezer joined him in N.Y. in January, 1907, but they were warned by friends familiar with American mores of the time that charges of moral turpitude might be brought against them since Scriabin had never obtained a legal divorce from his first wife and Tatiana Schloezer was his common-law wife. There was no evidence that such charges were actually contemplated, but to safeguard themselves against such a contretemps, they left America in March, 1907, and went to Paris. In the meantime Altschuler continued to express interest in Scriabin's music and on Dec. 10, 1908 he gave the world première with his Russian Symph. Orch. of Scriabin's great work *Le Poème de l'extase;* the first Russian performance of this work came later in St. Petersburg (Feb. 1, 1909). In the spring of 1908 Scriabin met Serge Koussevitzky, who became one of his most ardent supporters, both as conductor and as publisher. He gave Scriabin a 5-year contract with his newly established publishing firm Éditions Russes, with a generous guarantee of 5,000 rubles annually. In the summer of 1910 Koussevitzky engaged Scriabin as soloist on a tour in a chartered steamer down the Volga River, with stopovers and concerts at all cities and towns of any size along the route. Scriabin wrote for Koussevitzky his most ambitious work, *Promethée,* or *Poème du feu,* with an important piano part, which Scriabin performed at the world première of the work in Moscow on March 15, 1911. The score also included a color keyboard (*clavier à lumière*) or, in Italian, *luce,* intended to project changing colors according to the scale of the spectrum, which Scriabin devised (for at that time he was deeply immersed in the speculation about parallelism of all arts in their visual and auditory aspects). The construction of such a color organ, was, however, entirely unfeasible at the time, and the world première of the work was given without *luce.* A performance with colored lights thrown on a screen was attempted by Altschuler at Carnegie Hall, N.Y., on March 20, 1915, but it was a total failure. Another attempt was made in Moscow by Safonov after Scriabin's death, but that, too, was completely unsuccessful. The crux of the problem was that the actual notes written on a special staff in the score had to be translated into a color spectrum according to Scriabin's visualization of corresponding colors and keys (C major was red, F-sharp major was bright blue, etc.). Perhaps the nearest approximation to Scriabin's scheme was the performance of *Prométhée* by the Iowa University Symph. Orch. on Sept. 24, 1975, under the direction of James Dixon, with a laser apparatus constructed by Lowell Cross; previously, the American pianist Hilde Somer made use of the laser to accompany her solo piano recitals of Scriabin's works, without attempting to follow the parallelism of sounds and colors envisioned by Scriabin, but nonetheless conveying the idea underlying the scheme. The unique collaboration between Scriabin and Koussevitzky came to an unfortunate end shortly after the production of *Prométhée;* Scriabin regarded Koussevitzky as the chief apostle of his messianic epiphany, while Koussevitzky believed that it was due principally to his promotion that Scriabin reached the heights in musical celebrity; to this collision of two mighty egotisms was added a trivial disagreement about financial matters. Scriabin left Koussevitzky's publishing firm and in 1913 signed a contract with the Moscow publisher Jurgenson, who guaranteed him 6,000 rubles annually. In 1914 Scriabin visited London and was soloist in his Piano Concerto and in *Prometheus* at a concert led by Sir Henry Wood (March 14, 1914); he also gave a recital of his own works there (March 20, 1914). His last public appearance was in a recital in Petrograd on April 15, 1915; upon his return to Moscow an abscess developed in his lip, leading to blood poisoning; he died after a few days' illness. His 3 children (of the union with Tatiana Schloezer) were legitimized at his death. His son **Julian,** an exceptionally gifted boy, was accidentally drowned at the age of 11 in the Dnieper River at Kiev (June 22, 1919); Julian's 2 piano preludes, written in the style of the last works of his father, were publ. in a Scriabin memorial volume (Moscow, 1940). His daughter **Marina** is a scholar and composer.

Scriabin was a genuine innovator in harmony. After an early period of strongly felt influences (Chopin, Liszt, and Wagner), he gradually evolved in his own melodic and harmonic style, marked by extreme chromaticism; in his piano piece *Désir,* op. 57 (1908), the threshold of polytonality and atonality is reached; the key signature is dispensed with in his subsequent works; chromatic alterations and compound appoggiaturas create a harmonic web of such complexity that all distinction between consonance and dissonance vanishes. Building chords by fourths rather than by thirds, Scriabin constructed his "mystic chord" of 6 notes (C, F-sharp, B-flat, E, A, and D), which is the harmonic foundation of *Prométhée.* In his 7th Piano Sonata (1913) appears a chordal structure of 25 notes (D-flat, F-flat, G, A, and C, repeated in 5 octaves) which was dubbed "a 5-story chord." These harmonic extensions were associated in Scriabin's mind with theosophic doctrines; he aspired to a universal art in which the impressions of the senses were to unite with religious experience. He made plans for the writing of a "Mysterium," which was to accomplish such a synthesis, but only the text of a preliminary poem (*L'Acte préalable*) was completed at his

death. Scriabin dreamed of having the "Mysterium" performed as a sacred action in the Himalayas, and actually made plans for going to India when the outbreak of World War I in 1914 put an end to such a project. Scriabin's fragmentary sketches for *L'Acte préalable* were arranged in 1973 by the Soviet musician Alexander Nemtin, who supplemented this material with excerpts from Scriabin's 8th Piano Sonata, *Guirlandes,* and Piano Preludes, op. 74; the resulting synthetic score was performed in Moscow on March 16, 1973 under the title *Universe;* a species of color keyboard was used at the performance, projecting colors according to Scriabin's musical spectrum.

WORKS: FOR ORCH.: Concerto for Piano and Orch., op. 20 (1897); *Rêverie,* op. 24 (1899); Symph. No. 1, op. 26 (1900); Symph. No. 2, op. 29 (1901); Symph. No. 3 *(The Divine Poem),* op. 43 (1905); *The Poem of Ecstacy,* op. 54 (1908); *Prometheus (The Poem of Fire),* op. 60 (1911). FOR PIANO: 10 sonatas (opp. 6, 19, 23, 30, 53, 62, 64, 66, 68, 70); 79 preludes in 15 sets (opp. 11, 13, 15, 16, 17, 22, 27, 31, 33, 35, 37, 39, 48, 67, 74); 24 etudes in 4 sets (opp. 2, 8, 42, 65); 6 impromptus (opp. 10, 12, 14); 21 mazurkas (opp. 3, 25, 40); 2 nocturnes (op. 5); *Prelude and Nocturne* for left hand alone (op. 9); *Polonaise* (op. 21); *Fantaisie* (op. 28); *Poème tragique* (op. 34); *Poème satanique* (op. 36); *3 Morceaux* (op. 49); *4 Morceaux* (op. 51); *3 Morceaux* (op. 52); *4 Morceaux* (op. 56); *2 Morceaux* (op. 57); *Feuillet d'album* (op. 58); *2 Morceaux* (op. 59); *Poème-Nocturne* (op. 61); *2 Poèmes* (op. 63); *Vers la flamme* (op. 72); *2 Danses* (op. 73).

BIBLIOGRAPHY: A. E. Hull, *Modern Harmony* (London, 1914; chap. IV has an exposition of Scriabin's principles); *Musikalnyi Sovremennik,* special Scriabin number (Petrograd, 1915); J. L. Dunk, *Hyperacoustics* (London, 1916; discusses Scriabin's harmonic principles); L. Sabaneyev, *S.* (Moscow, 1916; 2nd ed., 1923); A. E. Hull, *S.* (London, 1916); A. E. Hull, "A Survey of the Pianoforte Works of S.," *Musical Quarterly* (Oct. 1916); A. E. Hull, "The Pianoforte Sonatas of S.," *Musical Times* (Nov.-Dec. 1916); M. Montagu-Nathan, *A Handbook of the Pianoforte Works of S.* (Boston, 1916); M. Montagu-Nathan, *Contemporary Russian Composers* (London, 1917); A. E. Hull, "S.'s Scientific Derivation of Harmony Versus Empirical Methods," *Proceedings of the Musical Association* (London, 1917); Paul Rosenfeld, *Musical Portraits* (N.Y., 1920); Igor Glebov, *S.* (Petrograd, 1921); Boris de Schloezer, "A. S.," *Revue Musicale* (1921); O. von Riesemann, "A. S. im Lichte eigener Jugendbriefe," *Die Musik* (1923); Boris de Schloezer, *S.* (Berlin, 1923; in Russian; vol. 1 only; in French, Paris, 1975); A. J. Swan, *S.* (London, 1923); C. Gray, *A Survey of Contemporary Music* (London, 1924); V. Yakovlev, *S.* (Moscow, 1925); Georg Rimsky-Korsakov, "The Deciphering of the 'Lumière' Part in Scriabin's *Promethus*," *De Musica* (Leningrad, 1927; in Russian); R. H. Hill, "A. S.," *Fortnightly Review* (1928); A. J. Swan, *Music 1900-1930* (N.Y., 1929); L. Sabaneyev, "S. and the Idea of Religious Art," *Musical Times* (1931); P. Dickenmann, *Die Entwicklung der Harmonik bei A. S.* (Leipzig, 1935); M. D. Calvocoressi and G. Abraham, *Masters of Russian Music* (N.Y., 1936); *S.: Symposium on the 25th Anniversary of His Death* (Moscow, 1940); N. Slonimsky, "A. S.," in *Great Modern Composers*, ed. by O. Thompson (N.Y., 1941); D. Brook, *Six Great Russian Composers* (London, 1946); L. Danilevich, *S.* (Moscow, 1953); Faubion Bowers, *Scriabin: A Biography of the Russian Composer* (2 vols., Palo Alto, 1969); S. Pavchinsky and V. Zuckerman, eds., *A. N. Scriabin*, collection of essays (Moscow, 1973); Faubion Bowers, *The New Scriabin: Enigma and Answers* (N.Y., 1975). Scriabin's correspondence, ed. by L. Sabaneyev, was publ. in Moscow, 1923.

Scriabine, Marina, Russian-French music scholar and composer; daughter of **Scriabin;** b. Moscow, Jan. 30, 1911. After her father's death, she lived with her mother in Kiev and Moscow; when her mother died, she went to Belgium to live with her maternal grandmother; in 1927 she settled in Paris. She studied at the École Nationale des Arts Décoratifs and designed art posters; studied music theory with René Leibowitz. In 1950 she joined the Radiooffusion Française and worked in electronic techniques; composed a *Suite radiophonique* (1951); also a ballet *Bayalett* (1952) and some chamber music. In 1967 she received a doctorate in esthetics for her thesis, *Représentation du temps et de l'intemporalité dans les arts plastiques figuratifs*. She publ. *Problèmes de la musique moderne* (in collaboration with her uncle, Boris de Schloezer; Paris, 1959; also in Spanish, 1960); *Le Langage musical* (Paris, 1963); *Le Miroir du temps* (Paris, 1973). She contributed the biographical entry on Scriabin for the *Encyclopédie de la musique*, publ. by Fasquelle (Paris, 1961); wrote an introduction to her uncle Boris de Schloezer's book on Scriabin, in French (Paris, 1975).

Scribe, Eugène, famous French dramatist and author of many opera librettos; b. Paris, Dec. 25, 1791; d. there, Feb. 21, 1861. He was the writer of the finest librettos set to music by Auber (*La Muette de Portici, Fra Diavolo, Le Domino noir*, etc.) and Meyerbeer (*Robert le Diable, Les Huguenots, Le Prophète, L'Africaine*). For Boieldieu he wrote *La Dame blanche;* for Halévy, *Manon Lescaut* and *La Juive;* he also wrote for less celebrated composers. In the complete edition of his *Œuvres dramatiques* (Paris, 1874–85; 76 vols.), 26 vols. are filled by his opera librettos.
BIBLIOGRAPHY: J. G. Prod'homme, "Wagner, Berlioz and Monsieur Scribe," *Musical Quarterly* (July 1926).

Scudo, Pierre, French music critic; b. Venice, June 8, 1806; d. Blois, Oct. 14, 1864. He was brought up in France; studied at Choron's school in Paris; was for a time an opera singer; played clarinet in military bands; then turned to journalism; publ. several political pamphlets; became music critic of the influential *Revue des Deux Mondes*. A writer of considerable talent, he held reactionary views; violently attacked Berlioz, Liszt, and Wagner. He became deranged and died in an insane asylum. His articles were publ. in book form: *Critique et littérature musicale* (2 series; 1850; 1859); *L'Art ancienne et l'art moderne* (1854); *L'Année musicale, ou Revue annuelle des théâtres lyriques et des concerts* (3 vols., 1860–62); etc. He also wrote a musical novel, *Le Chevalier Sarti* (1857; not

connected with the composer Giuseppe Sarti); its sequel *Frédérique* was publ. in the *Revue des Deux Mondes*. He publ. some songs (*Le Fil de la Vierge, La Baigneuse*, etc.).

Sculthorpe, Peter, Australian composer; b. Launceston, Tasmania, April 29, 1929. He studied piano and theory of music at the Melbourne Univ. Cons. (1946–50); then went to England and took courses in composition with Egon Wellesz and Edmund Rubbra at the Wadham College of Oxford Univ. (1958–60); returning to Australia he was appointed lecturer in music at the Univ. of Sydney in 1963; was a visiting Fellow at Yale Univ. (1965–67) and a visiting prof. of music at the Univ. of Sussex (1971–72). In his music he frequently utilizes Indonesian, Japanese and Aboriginal Australian modalities; in a later development he applied the entire arsenal of modern musical sounds, including serialism, sonorism and electronics; he also unites visual images to music in mixed media compositions.
WORKS: an opera, *Rites of Passage* (1971–73); 2 ballets: *Manic Espresso* (1958); and *Sun Music Ballet* (Sydney, 1968; incorporates music from the 4 separate *Sun Music* pieces); music for a farce, *Ulterior Motifs* (1956) and several revues, including *Cross Section* (1957); a mixed media score, *Love 200*, for female pop singer, pop group and orch., with lighting effects (1969–70; Sydney, Feb. 14, 1970); a score for radio, *The Fifth Continent*, for narrator, string orch., harp, percussion, oboe, trumpet and tape sounds of howling wind and a didjeridu (1963; uses narrated selections from D. H. Lawrence's novel *Kangaroo*); *Chamber Suite* for high voice, bassoon and piano (1946); *Suite* for 2 violins and cello (1946); *Bassoon Sonatina* (1946); 6 numbered string quartets: No. 3 (1949), No. 4 (1950), No. 5 (*Irkanda II*, 1955) and No. 6 (1965); *The Loneliness of Bunjil*, a string trio (1954, revised 1960); *Piano Sonatina* (1954); 4 works titled *Irkanda* (Aboriginal for "a remote and lonely place"): *I*, solo violin sonata (1955); *II* (string quartet No. 5, 1955), *III* (originally for piano trio; 1961), and *IV* for string orch. and percussion (1965); *King's Cross Overture* (1963); *Night* for piano (1965–70); 4 works titled *Sun Music: I* for orch. (1965), *II* for orch. (1969), *III* for orch. (1966), *IV* for orch. (1967); *Canto 1520* for voices and percussion (1966); *Night Piece* for chorus and piano (1966); *Morning Music for the Christ Child* for a cappella, 4-part chorus (1966); *Red Landscape* for string quartet (1966); *Tabuh Tabuhan* for wind quintet and 2 percussionists (1968); *String Quartet Music* for string quartet (1969); *Overture for a Happy Occasion* for orch. (1970); *Music for Japan* for orch. (1970); *The Stars Turn* for voice and orch. (1970); *Dream* for any number of performers (1970); *Rain* for orch. (1970); *Snow, Moon and Flowers* for piano (1971); *Stars* for piano (1971); *How the Stars Were Made* for 5 percussionists (1971); *Left Bank Waltz* for piano (1962–71); *Ketjak* for 6 male voices and feedback (1972); *Music of Early Morning* (1974); choruses, including *Autumn Song* and *Sea Chant* (both 1968).

Seagle, Oscar, American baritone; b. Chattanooga, Tenn., Oct. 31, 1877; d. Dallas, Dec. 19, 1945. He sang in concerts in the U. S. from 1896 until 1905; then went to Paris for further study, with Jean de Reszke; made his Paris debut in 1907, and also sang in England; returned to America at the outbreak of World War I in 1914 and settled in N.Y. as a singing teacher.

Searle, Humphrey, significant English composer; b. Oxford, Aug. 26, 1915. He studied classical literature at Oxford Univ. and music at the Royal College of Music in London, where his teachers were John Ireland and R. O. Morris. In 1937 he went to Vienna where he took private lessons with Anton von Webern; this study proved to be a decisive influence in Searle's own compositions, which are imbued with the subtle coloristic processes peculiar to the modern Vienna School of composition. He served in the British Army during World War II, and was stationed in Germany in 1946. Returning to London he engaged in various organizations promoting the cause of modern music. Although his own method of writing includes some aspects of the 12-tone method, he does not renounce tonal procedures, and sometimes applies purely national English melodic patterns. He published a manual, *Twentieth-Century Counterpoint* (London, 1954), and contributed numerous articles to British, American and German publications. He was honorary secretary of the Liszt Society (1950–62); acted as an adviser in music for Sadler's Wells Ballet in England (1946–57). In 1964–65 he was composer-in-residence at Stanford Univ., California; then occupied a similar post at the Univ. of Southern California, Los Angeles (1976–77); from 1965 to 1976 he was prof. at the Royal College of Music in London.

WORKS: 2 suites for strings (1942, 1944); 2 piano concertos (1944, 1955); Quintet for bassoon and strings (1945); *Intermezzo* for 11 instruments (1946); *Put Away the Flutes,* for tenor and 6 instruments (1947; in memory of Anton von Webern); *Fuga Ciocosa,* for orch. (1948); Quartet for violin, viola, clarinet and bassoon (1948); *Gold Coast Customs,* to Edith Sitwell's poem, for speakers, men's chorus and orch. (1948); *The Shadow of Cain,* to Edith Sitwell's poem for speakers, men's chorus and orch. (1952); 5 symphonies: No. 1 (1953), No. 2 (1958), No. 3 (Edinburgh, Sept. 3, 1960), No. 4 (Birmingham, England, Nov. 8, 1962), No. 5 (Manchester, Oct. 7, 1964); *Passacaglietta in nomine Arnold Schoenberg* for string quartet (1949); *Gondoliera* for English horn and piano (1950); Suite for clarinet and piano (1956); *3 Cat Poems* for speaker, flute, cello, and guitar (1953); *Burn-Up* for speaker and instruments (1962); *Scherzi* for orch. (1964); *Zodiac Variations* for orch. (1973); *3 Movements* for string quartet (1959); *Sinfonietta* for 9 instruments (1969); *Jerusalem* for speaker, tenor, chorus and orch. (1970); *Counting the Beats* for voice and piano (1963); 2 ballets: *Dualities* (1963); *The Great Peacock* (1958); *Oxus* for voice and orch. (1967); the operas: *The Diary of a Madman* after Gogol (Berlin Music Festival, Oct. 3, 1958); *The Photo of the Colonel* (Frankfurt, Germany, June 3, 1964); *Hamlet,* to a German libretto (Hamburg, March 5, 1968); *Labyrinth* for orch. (1971); *Les Fleurs du Mal* for tenor, horn and piano (1972).

WRITINGS: *The Music of Liszt* (London, 1954; 2nd ed., N.Y., 1966); *Twentieth-Century Counterpoint* (London, 1954); *Ballet Music: An Introduction* (London, 1958).

BIBLIOGRAPHY: M. Schafer, *British Composers in Interview* (London, 1963).

Seashore, Carl Emil, American psychologist and musician; b. Mörlunda, Sweden, Jan. 28, 1866; d. Lewiston, Idaho, Oct. 16, 1949. He was brought to the U.S. as a child; studied at Yale Univ. (Ph. D., 1895); taught psychology at Yale (until 1902), then at Iowa State Univ.; dean of the Graduate College there in 1908; dean emeritus, 1938. He devised a widely used method for measuring musical talent ("Seashore Test") through special measurements of his own invention (audiometer, tonoscope, chronograph, etc.).

WRITINGS: *The Voice Tonoscope* (1903); *Localisation of Sound* (1903); *A Sound Perimeter* (1903); *The Tonoscope and Its Use in the Training of the Voice* (1906); *The Measure of a Singer* (1912); *Seeing Yourself Sing* (1916); *Vocational Guidance in Music* (1916); *The Measurement of Musical Memory* (1917); *The Psychology of Musical Talent* (1919); *Psychology of the Vibrato* (1936); *Psychology of Music* (1938); *Pioneering in Psychology* (1942); *In Search of Beauty in Music* (N.Y., 1947) etc.

BIBLIOGRAPHY: the special Seashore issue of the *Univ. of Iowa Studies in Psychology* 21 (1928).

Sebastian, Georges (original name **György Sebestyén**), Hungarian conductor; b. Budapest, Aug. 17, 1903. He studied composition with Leo Weiner and Kodály at the State Academy of Music in Budapest, graduating in 1921; then took private lessons in conducting with Bruno Walter in Munich (1922–23); subsequently active as opera coach at the Munich State Opera, at the Metropolitan Opera, N.Y., at the Hamburg Municipal Opera, in Leipzig and in Berlin. In 1931 he went to Russia, where he conducted at the Moscow Radio. In 1938 he went to the U.S.; was conductor of the Scranton Philharmonic Orch (1940–45). In 1946 he went back to Europe, and lived mainly in Paris; continued to fill orchestral and operatic engagements in Europe.

Sebastiani, Johann, German composer; b. Weimar, Sept. 30, 1622; d. Königsberg, 1683. He was in the service of the Elector of Brandenburg at Königsberg; appointed Kapellmeister to the palace church in 1663; pensioned in 1679. He wrote a Passion, *Das Leiden und Sterben Jesu Christi* (1672), employing a 5-part chorus with 6 instruments. It is noteworthy for the devotional chorales therein introduced, as in Bach's Passions. It was reprinted by Zelle in vol. 17 of the *Denkmäler deutscher Tonkunst.* Sebastiani's *Parnass-Blumen, Geistliche und weltliche Lieder* were publ. in Hamburg in 2 vols. (1672, 1675); 13 Funeral Songs for several voices were issued separately at Königsberg between 1664 and 1680.

Šebor, Karl, Bohemian conductor and composer; b. Brandeis, Aug. 13, 1843; d. Prague, May 17, 1903. He was a pupil of Kittl; was conductor of the National Opera (1864–67), and military bandmaster in Vienna (from 1871). He wrote the Czech operas (all produced in Prague): *The Templars in Moravia* (Oct. 19, 1864),

Drahomira (1867), *The Hussite's Bride* (Sept. 28, 1868), *Blanka* (1870), *The Frustrated Wedding* (Oct. 25, 1879); cantatas; overtures; songs.

Sechter, Simon, Austrian composer and teacher; b. Friedberg, Bohemia, Oct. 11, 1788; d. Vienna, Sept. 10, 1867. He studied with Koželuh and Hartmann in Vienna; in 1810 he obtained the position of organ instructor at the Vienna Institute for the Blind; was also active as court organist; in 1851 he became prof. of harmony and composition at the Vienna Cons. The excellence of his teaching attracted to him a number of students from all over Europe, among them Henselt, Bruckner, Nottebohm, Vieuxtemps, Thalberg, and Pauer. So great was his renown even before he held an official teaching position, that Schubert, some weeks before his death (1828), expressed a desire to study with him. He was a master contrapuntist and wrote a vast amount of church music; publ. many fugues and preludes for organ; several intricate piano pieces (Dances in Counterpoint; 12 Contrapuntal Pieces; 4 books of amusing fugues for 4 hands on national and operatic airs; etc.); string quartets; songs. He also wrote an opera *Ali Hitsch-Hatsch,* which was produced in Vienna on Nov. 12, 1844. His most important pedagogical work is the treatise *Die Grundsätze der musikalischen Komposition* (3 vols.; Vienna, 1853–54), on the lines of Rameau's "basse fundamentale"; the 1st vol. was publ. in English transl. (N.Y., 1871; 12th ed., 1912). He also publ. a *Generalbass-Schule,* and a new ed. of Marpurg's *Abhandlung von der Fuge.*
BIBLIOGRAPHY: K. F. Pohl, *Simon Sechter* (Vienna, 1868); G. Capellen, *Ist des System S. Sechters ein geeigneter Ausgangspunkt für die theoretische Wagnerforschung?* (Leipzig, 1902).

Seckendorff, Carl Siegmund von, German composer; b. Erlangen, Nov. 26, 1744; d. Ansbach, April 26, 1785. He was an officer in the Austrian and Sardinian armies (1761–74); then in the diplomatic service in Weimar (1776–84); shortly before his death he was appointed Prussian ambassador in Ansbach (1784). At Weimar he was on intimate terms with Goethe, who allowed him to write music for a number of his poems before their publication (*Der Fischer, Der König in Thule,* etc.); in these songs Seckendorff caught the characteristic inflections of folk melodies. He publ. 3 collections of *Volk- und andere Lieder* (1779–82); wrote 12 string quartets, 8 divertimentos for violin and piano, 3 piano trios, and 2 piano sonatas for 3 hands (probably the earliest example of such trimanual settings); 3 Singspiele: *Lila* (1776), *Prosperpine* (1778), and *Jery und Bätely* (1780).
BIBLIOGRAPHY: V. Knab, *K. S. von Seckendorff* (Ansbach, 1914); Max Friedlaender, *Gedichte von Goethe in Kompositionen seiner Zeitgenossen* (1896 and 1916); E. Herrmann, *Das Weimarer Lied in der 2. Hälfte des 18. Jahrhunderts* (dissertation, Leipzig, 1925).

Seedo (Sydow), German musician active in London between 1720 and 1736; d. Potsdam, c.1754. He was one of the earliest composers of English ballad-operas in London; contributed airs to a number of operatic and choreographic productions in Drury Lane, London (*The Boarding-School, The Devil of a Duke, The Judgment of Paris, The Lottery,* etc.).
BIBLIOGRAPHY: Walter H. Rubsamen, "Mr. Seedo, Ballad Opera, and the Singspiel," in *Miscelánea en Homenaje a Monseñor Higinio Anglés,* vol. II (Barcelona, 1958–61).

Seefried, Irmgard, German soprano; b. Köngetried, Bavaria, Oct. 9, 1919. She received her early musical instruction from her father; then studied voice at the Augsburg Cons.; made her first important stage appearance at the Vienna Opera on May 2, 1943, as Eva in *Die Meistersinger;* then sang in Paris, London, Zürich and Stockholm; made her American debut at the Metropolitan Opera House, N.Y., as Susanna in *The Marriage of Figaro* (Nov. 20, 1953). She returned to Vienna and remained a member of the state opera until 1972, when she was named honorary member.
BIBLIOGRAPHY: F. Fassbind, *Irmgard Seefried* (Bern, 1960).

Seeger, Charles, eminent American ethnomusicologist, composer and teacher; b. (of American parents), Mexico City, Dec. 14, 1886. He studied at Harvard Univ., graduating in 1908; then taught music at the Univ. of California (1912–19), at the Institute of Musical Arts, N.Y. (1921–33), at the New School for Social Research, N.Y. (1931–35); assistant director of the Federal Music Project, W.P.A. (1938–40); was chief music director, Pan American Union, Washington, D.C. (1941–53); visiting prof., Yale Univ. (1949–50); lecturer, Univ. of California, Los Angeles (1957–61); member of the Society of Ethnomusicology (1960; honorary president, 1972); holder of various honorary degrees; in 1972 was decorated Commander al Mérito, Chile. His work in the field of ethnomusicology is of the greatest significance; no less important was his work as a pedagogue; among his students was Henry Cowell. His second wife was the renowned American composer **Ruth Crawford; Pete Seeger** was the son of his first marriage. His 90th birthday was celebrated in several sessions presented at the Univ. of California, Berkeley, in Aug., 1977. His publications include (in collaboration with E. G. Stricklen): *An Outline Course in Harmonic Structure and Musical Invention* (1913) and *Harmonic Structure and Elementary Composition* (1916). A collection of his articles, *Studies in Musicology 1935-1975,* was published in Berkeley, California (1977).
BIBLIOGRAPHY: Henry Cowell, ed., *American Composers on American Music* (Stanford Univ., 1933).

Seeger, Joseph (also known as **Seegr, Segert, Zeckert,** etc.), Bohemian organist; b. Repin, March 21, 1716; d. Prague, April 22, 1782. He was a pupil of Czernohorsky and Franz Benda in Prague; played the violin in a Prague church before being appointed organist at the Kreuzherrenkirche (1745); retained this position until his death. He was greatly esteemed as a teacher; among his pupils were J. A. Koželuh, Kuchar, Mašek, Mysliveček, etc. His most celebrated organ works, *8 Toccatas and Fugues,* were publ. posthumously

(1793); his organ preludes were included in Guilmant's collection *École classique de l'orgue.*

Seeger, Pete, American folk singer; son of **Charles Seeger;** nephew of the poet Alan Seeger; b. New York, May 3, 1919. After a brief study of social sciences at Harvard Univ., he became a traveling singer; formed two folksong groups, "Almanac Singers" and "Weavers"; served in the U.S. Army in 1942–45, and entertained U.S. troops in the Pacific. In 1963 he undertook a world-wide tour visiting Australia and many countries in Europe, including Russia where he was spectacularly successful. He publ. a manual, *How to Play the 5-String Banjo* (1948), and compiled several songbooks.

Seeger, Ruth. See **Crawford, Ruth.**

Seeling, Hans, Bohemian pianist; b. Prague, 1828; d. there, May 26, 1862. He went to Italy in 1852; then traveled in the East, returning to Europe in 1857; was in Paris in 1859; then in Germany; finally went back to Prague. He publ. many salon pieces which were successful (*Barcarolle, Lorelei,* etc.).

Segerstam, Leif, Finnish conductor and composer; b. Vaasa, March 2, 1944. He studied composition in Helsinki with Fougstedt, Kokkonen and Englund; violin, piano and conducting at the Sibelius Academy in Helsinki, graduating in 1963. He then went to the U.S.; enrolled at the Juilliard School of Music, N.Y., and studied violin with Louis Persinger, composition with Hall Overton and Vincent Persichetti, and conducting with Jean Morel (1963–65); also had a summer conducting course in 1964 at Aspen, Colorado with Walter Susskind. Returning to Europe, he conducted the Finnish National Opera and Ballet; in 1968 joined the staff of the Stockholm Royal Opera and became its artistic director in 1971.
    WORKS: *Legend* for string orch. (1960); 7 string quartets (1962; 1964; 1965–66; 1966; 1970; 1974; 1975); *5 Pedagogical Duets* for 2 violins (1963); *Pandora,* ballet (1967); *Youth Cantata* (1967); *Three Leaves of Grass,* after Whitman, for soprano and piano (1967); *Seitsemän punaista hetkeä (7 Red Moments),* after Viola Renwall and Gunnar Björling, for soprano and orch. (1967); *Concerto Serioso* for violin and orch. (1967); *Capriccio* for sopranino and chamber ensemble (1968); *Tre plus eller fyra Nnnuuu-r (Three Plus or Four Nnnows),* after Björling, for mezzo-soprano and chamber orch. (1968); *7 Questions to Infinity* for piano (1970); *3 Pictures* for chamber chorus, flute, bass clarinet, viola, vibraphone and glockenspiel (1970); *6 Songs of Experience,* after Blake and Auden, for soprano and stereophonically placed orchestra without conductor (1970–71; Stockholm, April 27, 1974); *Prolonged Moments* for 3 sopranos, wind ensemble and percussion (Stockholm, Oct. 14, 1973); *A Nnnnooowww* for wind quintet (1973); *3 Moments of Parting* for violin and piano (1973); *Patria* for orch. (1973; Stockholm, April 27, 1974); *Two; onwards: inwards, outwards (upwards, downwards) . . . aroundwards . . . towards . . .* for 2 pianos and orch. (1974; Helsinki, April 29, 1975).

Seghers, François-Jean-Baptiste, Belgian violinist; b. Brussels, Jan. 17, 1801; d. Margency, near Paris, Feb. 2, 1881. He studied in Brussels with Gensse, and at the Paris Cons. with Baillot; founded in Brussels the Société Ste.-Cécile in 1848, and conducted it until 1854. Its concerts of orchestral and choral works were famous; after the founder's death it rapidly declined and was soon dissolved.

Segnitz, Eugen, German musicologist; b. Leipzig, March 5, 1862; d. Berlin, Sept. 25, 1927. He studied privately with Papperitz; wrote music criticism; published valuable biographical studies: *Carl Reinecke* (1900), *Wagner und Leipzig* (1901), *Liszt und Rom* (1901), *Goethe und die Oper in Weimar* (1908), *Franz Liszts Kirchenmusik* (1911), *Arthur Nikisch* (1920), *Max Reger* (1922).

Segovia, Andrés, famous Spanish guitar virtuoso; b. Linares, near Jaen, Feb. 21, 1893. He improvised on the guitar as a child; gave his first public concert in Granada at the age of 14; then played in Barcelona (1916) and Madrid; subsequently undertook a grand tour of South America. On April 7, 1924 he gave his first concert in Paris, beginning his international career; he traveled all over the world, arousing admiration for his artistry wherever he went. He made his American debut in New York on Jan. 13, 1928 and 50 years later, a week before his 85th birthday, played his "golden jubilee" concert (N.Y., Feb. 13, 1978). He did much to reinstate the guitar as a concert instrument capable of a variety of expressions; several modern composers wrote works especially for him, among them Castelnuovo-Tedesco, Manuel Ponce and Turina; Albert Roussel wrote a solo piece for guitar entitled simply *Segovia,* which Segovia played in Madrid on April 25, 1925. A commemorative plaque was affixed in 1969 to the house where he was born, honoring him as the "hijo predilecto de la ciudad." He published *An Autobiography of the Years 1893–1920* (N.Y., 1977).
    BIBLIOGRAPHY: V. Borri, *The Segovia Technique* (N.Y., 1972).

Seiber, Mátyás, significant Hungarian-born English composer; b. Budapest, May 4, 1905; d. in an automobile accident, Krueger National Park, Johannesburg, South Africa, Sept. 24, 1960. Of a musical family, he learned to play the cello at home; later entered the Budapest Academy of Music, where he studied with Kodály (1919–24). During the following years he traveled as a member of a ship's orch. on a transatlantic liner; visited Russia as a music journalist. From 1926 to 1933 he taught composition at the Frankfurt Cons.; was the cellist in the Lenzewski Quartet, which specialized in modern music; then was again in Budapest. The catastrophic events in Central Europe and the growing Nazi influence in Hungary forced him to emigrate to England, where he quickly acquired a group of loyal disciples; was co-founder of the Society for the Promotion of New Music; in 1942 was appointed to the faculty of Morley College. His early music followed the national trends of the Hungarian School; later he expanded his melodic resources to include oriental modes and also jazz, treated as folk music; by the time he arrived in England he had added dodecaphony to his œuvre, though he used it in a very personal, lyrical manner, as in his cantata *Ulysses* and the Third String Quartet.

WORKS: an opera *Eva spielt mit Puppen* (1934); 2 operattas; *Besardo Suite* No. 1 for orch. (1940); *Besardo Suite* No. 2 for string orch. (1941); *Transylvanian Rhapsody* for orch. (1941); *Pastorale and Burlesque* for flute and string orch. (1941–42); *Fantasia Concertante* for violin and string orch. (1943–44; London, Dec. 3, 1945); *Notturno* for horn and string orch. (1944); a cantata, *Ulysses*, after Joyce, for tenor, chorus and orch. (1946–47; London, May 27, 1949); *4 French Folksongs* for soprano and strings (1948); *Faust* for soprano, tenor, chorus and orch. (1949); *Cantata secularis* for chorus and orch. (1949–51); Concertino for Clarinet and String Orch. (1951; London, May 11, 1954); *Elegy* for viola and small orch. (1955); *3 Pieces* for cello and orch. (1956); a chamber cantata, *Three Fragments from "A Portrait of the Artist as a Young Man,"* after Joyce, for narrator, wordless chorus and instrumental ensemble (1957); *Improvisations* for jazz band and symph. orch. (in collaboration with Johnny Dankworth, 1959; London, June 2, 1959); a ballet *The Invitation* (1960; posthumous, London, Dec. 30, 1960); 3 string quartets (1924; 1934–35; *Quartetto Lirico*, 1948–51); *Sarabande and Gigue* for cello and piano (1924); *Sonata da camera* for violin and cello (1925); *Serenade* for 2 clarinets, 2 bassoons and 2 horns (1925); *Divertimento* for clarinet and string quartet (1928); 2 *Jazzolettes* for 2 saxophones, trumpet, trombone, piano and percussion (1929, 1933); *4 Hungarian Folksongs* for 2 violins (1931); *Fantasy* for cello and piano (1940); *Fantasia* for flute, horn and string quartet (1945); *Andantino and Pastorale* for clarinet and piano (1949); *Concert Piece* for violin and piano (1953–54); *Improvisation* for oboe and piano (1957); *More Nonsense*, after E. Lear, for baritone, violin, guitar, clarinet and bass clarinet (1957); *Permutazioni a Cinque* for wind quintet (1958); Violin Sonata (1960); *Rhythmical Studies* for piano (1933); *Scherzino capriccioso* for piano (1944); arrangements of folksongs; songs with instrumental or orchestral accompaniment. He also wrote scores for over 25 films, including that for Orwell's *Animal Farm*, England's first feature-length animated film (1954); wrote a handbook on jazz percussion playing, *Schule für Jazz-Schlagzeug* (1929) and publ. *The String Quartets of Béla Bartók* (London, 1945).

BIBLIOGRAPHY: H. Keller, "Mátyás Seiber," *The Musical Times* (Nov. 1955); H. Wood, "The Music of Mátyás Seiber," ibid. (Sept. 1970).

Seidel, Friedrich Ludwig, German organist and composer; b. Treuenbrietzen, July 14, 1765; d. Charlottenburg, May 8, 1831. He studied with Benda in Berlin; served as organist of the Marienkirche; was music director of the royal orch. (1808) and court Kapellmeister (1822). He composed the operas *Der Dorfbarbier* (1817) and *Lila* (1818); incidental music to dramas; an oratorio, *Die Unsterblichkeit* (1797); Masses, motets, songs, piano music.

Seidel, Jan, Czech composer; b. Nymburk, Dec. 25, 1908. He was first attracted to architecture and graphic art; attended Alois Hába's classes in quarter-tone composition in the Prague Cons. (1936–40); then took private lessons in music theory with J. B. Foerster for a more traditional musical training. He was a composer, conductor and pianist in E. F. Burian's Theater (1930–45); acted as artistic advisor to the recording firm Esta (1938–45) and the Gramophone Corporation (1945–53); was chief of the Opera of the National Theater (1958–64); then served as dramatic advisor there. His String Quartet No. 2 is in the quarter-tone system, but most of his music is based on folksong tradition according to the doctrine of social realism.

WORKS: an opera, *Tonka Šibenice* (1964); *Symphonic Prologue* (1942); symph. No. 1 (1943); 2 oboe concertos (1955); 2 orch. suites from the film *The Piper of Strakonice* (1956, 1958); *Lovecká Sinfonietta (Hunting Sinfonietta)* for horn and small orch. (1965–66; Prague, March 14, 1973); Concerto for Flute, Strings and Piano (1966); *Giocosa* for chamber orch. (1972); the cantatas: *Call to Battle* (1946), *May Prelude* (1952) and *Message to the Living* (1953); 4 string quartets: No. 1 (with solo soprano, 1930), No. 2 (with narration, 1940), No. 3, *Chrysanthemums* (1943) and No. 4 (1944); 2 wind quintets (1941, 1946); Violin Sonata (1950); numerous patriotic choruses and songs.

Seidel, Johann Julius, German organist; b. Breslau, July 14, 1810; d. there, Feb. 13, 1856. He was organist at St. Christopher's Church; published *Die Orgel und ihr Bau* (Breslau, 1843; 4th ed. by B. Kothe, 1885; reprinted with an appendix by H. Schmidt, 1907; in English, London, 1852).

Seidel, Toscha, Russian violinist; b. Odessa, Nov. 17, 1899; d. Rosemead, California, Nov. 15, 1962. He began to play the violin as a small child; took lessons from Max Fiedelmann in Odessa; subsequently became a pupil of Leopold Auer at the Cons. of St. Petersburg (graduated in 1912); then went to America; debut in N.Y. (April 14, 1918); made many tours in Europe and the U.S.; also played in Australia. He suffered an irreversible mental illness and was confined to a sanitarium in California for several years before his death.

Seidl, Anton, famous Hungarian conductor; b. Budapest, May 7, 1850; d. New York, March 28, 1898. He studied at the Leipzig Cons.; then was engaged by Hans Richter as chorusmaster at the Vienna Opera; Richter in turn recommended him to Wagner to assist in preparing the score and parts of the *Ring* tetralogy for the forthcoming Bayreuth Festival; Seidl worked in Bayreuth until 1879, when he was engaged by the impresario Angelo Neumann for a grand tour of Wagner's operas. After Wagner's death in 1883 he conducted the Bremen Opera; in 1885 was engaged to conduct the German opera repertory at the Metropolitan Opera House, N.Y. He made his American debut with *Lohengrin* (N.Y., Nov. 23, 1885); also conducted the American premières of *Die Meistersinger* (Jan. 4, 1886) and *Tristan und Isolde* (Dec. 1, 1886). During the week of March 4–11, 1889 he conducted in N.Y. the entire *Ring des Nibelungen*. In 1891 he was engaged as permanent conductor of the N. Y. Philharmonic, and led it until his sudden death (of ptomaine poisoning). Seidl was an excellent technician of the baton and established a standard of perfection rare in American orchestral playing of that time; he introduced many unfamiliar works by German composers and conducted the world première of Dvořák's Symphony *From the New World* (1893).

BIBLIOGRAPHY: H. E. Krehbiel, *Anton Seidl* (N.Y., 1898); H. T. Finck, ed., *Anton Seidl. A Memorial by His Friends* (N.Y., 1899).

Seidl, Arthur, German writer on music; b. Munich, June 8, 1863; d. Dessau, April 11, 1928. He studied with Spitta and Bellermann; Dr. phil., Leipzig, 1887 (dissertation: *Vom Musikalisch-Erhabenen. Prolegomena zur Ästhetik der Tonkunst;* 1887; 2nd ed., 1907). From 1890 to 1893 he was in Weimar; from 1893 to 1897, in Dresden. In 1899 he went to Munich as critic for the *Neueste Nachrichten.* From 1903 to his death, was active mostly at Dessau.

WRITINGS: *Zur Geschichte des Erhabenheitsbegriffs seit Kant* (1889); *Hat Richard Wagner eine Schule hinterlassen?* (1892); *Richard Strauss. Eine Charakterstudie* (with W. Klatte; 1896); *Moderner Geist in der deutschen Tonkunst* (1901; 2nd ed., 1913); *Wagneriana* (3 vols., 1901–02); *Moderne Dirigenten* (1902); *Kunst und Kultur* (1902); *Die Hellerauer Schulfeste und die "Bildungsanstalt Jacques-Dalcroze"* (1912); *Straussiana* (1913); *Ascania. Zehn Jahre in Anhalt* (1913); *Richard Wagners "Parsifal"* (1914); *Neue Wagneriana* (3 vols., 1914); *Hans Pfitzner* (1921); *Neuzeitliche Tondichter und zeitgenössische Tonkünstler* (2 vols., Regensburg, 1926).

BIBLIOGRAPHY: L. Frankenstein, *Arthur Seidl* (Regensburg, 1913); B. Schuhmann, ed., *Musik und Kultur. Festschrift zum 50. Geburtstag Arthur Seidls* (1913).

Seifert, Uso, German organist and composer; b. Römhild, Feb. 9, 1852; d. Dresden, June 4, 1912. He studied with Wüllner and Nicodé at the Dresden Cons.; taught there for 25 years, and was later organist of the Reformed Church. He publ. a piano method; numerous piano pieces *(Capriccietto, Valse-Impromptu, Polacca graziosa, Polonaise,* etc.); choruses; organ works *(Präludium und Doppelfuge, Einleitung und Doppelfuge, Zwanzig Orgelvorspiele,* etc.); edited classic instructive works.

Seiffert, Max, eminent German musicologist; b. Beeskow-on-Spree, Feb. 9, 1868; d. Schleswig, April 13, 1948. He studied musicology with Ph. Spitta at the Univ. of Berlin; took the degree of Dr. phil. with the dissertation *J. P. Sweelinck und seine direkten deutschen Schüler* (Leipzig, 1891). In 1914 he was elected member of the Prussian Academy of the Arts. He devoted himself chiefly to the editing of works by German composers; published *Geschichte der Klaviermusik* (Berlin, 1899–1901; nominally the 3rd ed. of Weitzmann's history, but actually a new and valuable book); compiled numerous catalogues of keyboard works; edited materials for the *Denkmäler deutscher Tonkunst, Denkmäler der Tonkunst in Bayern, Denkmäler der Tonkunst in Österreich,* and edited the complete works of Sweelinck for the *Vereeniging voor Nederlandsche Muziekgeschiedenis;* also prepared many works by Bach and Handel for modern performance. A Festschrift for him was published for his 70th birthday (1938), and another for his 80th birthday (1948).

Seifriz, Max, German violinist and composer; b. Rottweil, Württemberg, Oct. 9, 1827; d. Stuttgart, Dec. 20, 1885. He served as court Kapellmeister to Prince Hohenzollern in Löwenberg (1854–69); then moved to Stuttgart and was acitve there as a municipal music director. He published, with E. Singer, a *Grosse theoretisch-praktische Violinschule* (2 vols., 1884–97); composed a number of choruses and a symphony.

Seinemeyer, Meta, German soprano; b. Berlin, Sept. 5, 1895; d. Dresden, Aug. 19, 1929. She studied voice with Ernst Grenzebach; was on the staff of the German Opera in Berlin from 1918 to 1925. In 1926 she toured South America; then sang at the Vienna Opera in 1927, and at Covent Garden in London (1929). She died of a rare blood disease; on her death bed she married the conductor **Frieder Weissmann.** Her voice possessed a silken quality and a natural expressiveness which was particularly effective in the romantic repertory.

Seiss, Isodor (Wilhelm), German composer and teacher; b. Dresden, Dec. 23, 1840; d. Cologne, Sept. 25, 1905. He studied piano with Friedrich Wieck and music theory with J. Otto. In 1870 he was appointed to the faculty of the Cons. of Cologne, where he conducted the concerts of the Musikalische Gesellschaft (1873–1900); among his students was Willem Mengelberg. He published a number of useful piano studies in the bravura style *(Bravourstudien, Fantasie in Form einer Tokkata,* etc.). He also composed an opera *Der Vierjährige Posten.*

Seitz, Robert, German music publisher and piano manufacturer; b. Leipzig, April 8, 1837; d. there, Sept. 26, 1889. He was a music publisher from 1866 till 1878; then, selling out, he established a piano factory, which failed in 1884, when his interesting paper, *Das musikalische Centralblatt,* ceased to appear.

Seixas, (José Antonio) Carlos de, important Portuguese composer of keyboard music; b. Coimbra, June 11, 1704; d. Lisbon, Aug. 25, 1742. He received his primary musical education from his father, a church organist; then became himself a church organist in Lisbon. He wrote a great number of keyboard sonatas (sometimes designated as "toccatas") of which about 100 are preserved. He knew Domenico Scarlatti personally, but was not demonstrably influenced by the Italian style of keyboard composition. Eighty keyboard sonatas by Seixas were brought out in a modern edition by Santiago Kastner, in the series of *Portugaliae musica* (Lisbon, 1965); an overture and a sinfonia were published in the same series in 1969, edited by P. Salzmann.

BIBLIOGRAPHY: Santiago Kastner, *Carlos de Seixas* (Coimbra, 1947).

Séjan, Nicolas, French composer and organist; b. Paris, March 19, 1745; d. there, March 16, 1819. He was a pupil of Forqueray; organist of St.-André-des-Arts in 1760, of Notre Dame in 1772, of St.-Sulpice in 1783; in 1789, of the royal chapel, and teacher at the École Royale de Chant. He lost his post in the Revolution, but in 1807 became organist at the Invalides, and in 1814 (after the restoration of the monarchy) of the royal chapel. He publ. 6 violin sonatas, piano sonatas, 3 piano trios, and music for piano and for organ.
BIBLIOGRAPHY: C. Bouvet, "Nicolas Séjan et G.-F. Couperin, organistes de l'Opéra," *Musique et Théâtre* (1926).

Sekles, Bernhard, German conductor, composer, and teacher; b. Frankfurt, June 20, 1872; d. there, Dec. 15, 1934. He studied with Iwan Knorr at the Hoch Cons. in Frankfurt, where he became prof. of theory in 1896; from 1924 till 1933 he was director of the Cons.
WORKS: 2 operas, *Scheherazade* (Mannheim, Nov. 2, 1917) and *Die zehn Küsse* (Frankfurt, 1926); the ballets *Der Zwerg und die Infantin,* after Oscar Wilde (Frankfurt, 1913) and *Die Hochzeit des Faun* (Weisbaden, 1921); a symph. poem, *Aus den Gärten der Semiramis; Serenade* for 11 solo instruments; *Kleine Suite* for orch.; *Passacaglia und Fuge* for string quartet; Trio for clarinet, cello, and piano; Violin Sonata; several albums of piano music.

Selby, Bertram Luard, English organist, composer, and teacher; b. Ightham, Kent, Feb. 12, 1853; d. Winterton, Dec. 26, 1918. He studied with Reinicke and Jadassohn at the Leipzig Cons.; filled various organ positions in London; was organist at the Rochester Cathedral.
WORKS: 2 operas: *The Ring* (1886) and *Adela* (1888); an operetta ("duologue") *Weather or no* (London, Aug. 10, 1896; very successful; also produced in Germany as *Das Wetterhäuschen);* 2 piano quintets; a violin sonata; piano pieces; organ works.

Selby, William, organist and composer; b. England, c.1738; d. Boston, Dec., 1798. In 1760 he was appointed organist at Holy Sepulcher Church, London; from 1765 to 1770 he published both sacred and secular music there. He settled in the U.S. in 1771, becoming organist at King's Chapel in Boston; in 1773-74 was organist at Trinity Church in Newport, R.I.; in 1776 returned to Boston as organist at Trinity Church, and from 1778, at the Stone Chapel (formerly King's Chapel). He led an extremely active musical life in Boston as organist and conductor, giving many concerts of secular music as well as religious, and generally raising the musical standards of the area. He composed and published 9 psalms and hymns for solo voice, 8 religious and secular choral works, 6 songs, 9 pieces for guitar, and 3 for keyboard.
BIBLIOGRAPHY: O. G. Sonneck, *Bibliography of Early Secular American Music* (1905; 2nd ed., revised by W. T. Upton, 1945); D. McKay, "William Selby, Musical Émigré in Colonial Boston," *Musical Quarterly* (Oct. 1971).

Seligmann, Hippolyte-Prosper, French cellist; b. Paris, July 28, 1817; d. Monte Carlo, Feb. 5, 1882. He studied at the Paris Cons., taking 1st prize in 1836; made extensive tours. He publ. *6 Études caractéristiques,* fantasies, caprices, etc., for cello with piano; and 2 albums of songs.

Selle, Thomas, German composer; b. Zörbig, March 23, 1599; d. Hamburg, July 2, 1663. He was a rector in Wesselburen (1625); cantor in Itzehoe (1634); cantor at the Johanneum and music director of the 5 principal churches in Hamburg (from 1641). He publ. sacred and secular songs (including settings of poems by Rist), and left in manuscript numerous madrigals, motets, and Passions. He was an early member of the Hamburg school of German song writing. His collections include: *Concertatio Castalidum* (1624); *Deliciae pastorum Arcadiae* (1624); *Hagiodecamelhydrion* (1627–31); *Deliciorum juvenilium decas* (1634); *Monophonetica* (1636). His *Johannes-Passion* of 1642 was brought out in modern ed. by R. Gerber (1934); reprints of separate songs publ. by H. J. Moser.
BIBLIOGRAPHY: A. Arnheim, "Thomas Selle als Schulkantor in Itzehoe und Hamburg," in the "Liliencron Festschrift" (1910); H. J. Moser, "Aus der Frühgeschichte der deutschen Generalbasspassion," *Jahrbuch Peters* (1920); L. Krüger, *Die Hamburgische Musikorganisation im 17. Jahrhundert* (1933; p. 64ff.); S. Günther, *Die geistliche Konzertmsuik von Thomas Selle nebst einer Biographie* (Giessen, 1935).

Sellner, Joseph, German oboe player and teacher; b. Landau, Bavaria, March 13, 1787; d. Vienna, May 17, 1843. He played the oboe in an Austrian army regiment; then at Prague in Weber's orch. (from 1811); from 1817 at the Court Opera in Vienna. He taught at the Vienna Cons. from 1821, and conducted the student concerts there until 1838. His *Theoretischpraktische Oboen-Schule* is a fine method for oboe; he also publ. a concerto and 3 concertinos for oboe with orch., and a concerto for 2 oboes.

Selmer, Johan Peter, Norwegian composer; b. Oslo, Jan. 20, 1844; d. Venice, July 22, 1910. After studying law in Norway he went to Paris, where he took a course under Ambroise Thomas at the Paris Cons. (1868–70) and later at the Leipzig Cons. with Richter (1871–74). From 1883 till 1886 he conducted the Oslo Philharmonic. He was greatly influenced by Berlioz and Wagner; his symph. pieces bear the imprint of late Romanticism; like Grieg, he made use of Norwegian folk material.
WORKS: for orch. (all performed in Oslo): *Scène funèbre* (Sept. 30, 1871), *Alastor,* after Shelley (Oct. 24, 1874), *Karneval in Flandern* (Nov. 8, 1890), *In den Bergen,* suite (1892), *Prometheus,* symph. poem (his most important work; Oct. 29, 1898); choral works with orch.: *Nordens Aand (The Spirit of the North); Hilsen til Nidaros,* cantata; *Nogle politiske Sange og andre Viser (Some Political Songs and Other Airs)* for chorus in unison, and orch.; numerous male choruses a cappella; arrangements for folk melodies; songs for solo voice with piano.
BIBLIOGRAPHY: P. Merkel, *Der norwegische Komponist Johan Selmer. Ein Lebensbild* (Leipzig, 1904).

Selva, Blanche, French pianist and teacher; b. Brive, Jan. 29, 1884; d. St. Amand, Tallende, Puy-de-Dome, Dec. 3, 1942. She studied piano at the Paris Cons., and took courses in composition with Vincent d'Indy at the Schola Cantorum, where she became a teacher. She was one of the strongest propagandists of modern French music early in the century; she presented programs of piano works by Debussy, Ravel and other masters of modern French music at the time when they were not yet universally recognized. She also published several books dealing with piano technique; her compendium, *L'Enseignement musical de la technique du piano* (4 vols.; Paris, 1922, ff.) is valuable. She further published the disquisitions on musical form, *La Sonate* (Paris, 1913); *Quelques mots sur la sonate* (Paris, 1914); *Les Sonates de Beethoven* (Barcelona, 1927); also published a monograph on Déodat de Séverac (Paris, 1930).

Selvaggi, Rito, Italian composer and pedagogue; b. Noicattaro di Bari, May 22, 1898; d. Zoagli (Genoa), May 19, 1972. He studied piano and composition at the Liceo Musicale in Pesaro, and later took lessons with Busoni. He devoted himself mainly to teaching; was prof. at the Cons of Parma (1934–38); then was director of the Palermo Cons. (1938–58) and director of the Cons. in Pesaro (1959–68). He composed the operas *Maggiolata veneziana* (Naples, 1929) and *Santa Caterina de Siena* (1947), the music drama *Eletta* (1947); the oratorio, *Estasi francescana* (1926); "trittico sinfonico" *La natività di Gesù* (1935); *Sonata Drammatica* for viola and piano (1954); *Elegie* for cello, chorus and orch., in memory of Toscanini (1957); numerous choruses and piano transcriptions of classical symphonies.

Sembrich, Marcella (real name **Praxede Marcellina Kochańska**; Sembrich was her mother's maiden name), famous coloratura soprano; b. Wisniewczyk, Galicia, Feb. 15, 1858; d. New York, Jan. 11, 1935. From the age of 4 her father, Kasimir Kochański, gave her piano lessons; violin lessons were soon added. At 10 she appeared in public as a performer on both instruments. At the age of 11 she entered the Lemberg (Lwów) Cons., where she studied with Wilhelm Stengel. In 1874 she played and sang for Liszt, who urged her to train her voice. She then studied singing with Viktor Rokitansky in Vienna, and with G. B. Lamperti, Jr., in Milan. On May 5, 1877, she married her former teacher, **Wilhelm Stengel** (b. Lemberg, Aug. 7, 1846; d. New York, May 15, 1917), and with him went to Athens, where she made her operatic debut on June 3, 1877, as Elvira in Bellini's *Puritani*; returning to Vienna, she studied the German repertory with Richard Lewy. From 1878 to 1880 she sang at Dresden. On June 12, 1880, she made her London debut as Lucia; American debut, at the Metropolitan Opera House, on Oct. 24, 1883. Thereafter she sang at the principal opera houses of Germany, Austria, France, Spain, Scandinavia, and Russia until 1898, then becoming a regular member of the Metropolitan Opera Company. Her farewell appearance in opera was at the Metropolitan, Feb. 6, 1909. He repertory included 40 operatic parts, of which Violetta was the favorite. Of Wagnerian roles, she sang only Eva in *Die Meistersinger*. In 1924 she joined the faculty of the newly-founded Curtis Institute, Philadelphia; also taught at the Juilliard School, N.Y.

BIBLIOGRAPHY: G. Armin, *Marcella Sembrich und Herr Prof. Julius Hey* (Leipzig, 1898); H. G. Owen, *A Recollection of Marcella Sembrich* (N.Y., 1950).

Semet, Théophile (-Aimé-Émile), French composer; b. Lille, Sept. 6, 1824; d. Corbeil, near Paris, April 15, 1888. He studied with Halévy; was a percussionist at the Opéra; wrote popular songs before attempting operatic composition. The following operas by Semet were produced in Paris: *Nuits d'Espagne* (Dec. 30, 1857); *Gil Blas* (March 23, 1860); *Ondine* (Jan. 7, 1863); and *La petite Fadette* (Sept. 11, 1869).

Semkow, Georg (Jerzy), Polish conductor; b. Radomsko, Oct. 12, 1928. He studied at the Cracow Cons.; in 1950 was apprenticed to Eugene Mravinsky, conductor of the Leningrad Philharmonic; also conducted opera at the Bolshoi Theater in Moscow. In the meantime he continued studies in conducting with Tullio Serafin in Rome and Bruno Walter in Vienna. After serving as conductor of the National Polish Opera in Warsaw he received the conductorship of the Royal Opera House in Copenhagen. In the interim, he was guest conductor with numerous European orchestras; toured Japan with the London Philharmonic Orch. He made his U.S. debut in 1968 with the Boston Symph. Orch.; there followed appearances with the N.Y. Philharmonic, Chicago Symph. Orch., Cleveland Orch., etc. In 1976 he was appointed music director of the St. Louis Symph. Orch. A conductor of the Romantic school, he gives impassioned performances of the Vienna classics, Russian and Polish compositions; he is also adept in precise projections of modern scores.

Semmler, Alexander, German-American composer and arranger; b. Dortmund, Nov. 12, 1900; d. Kingston, N.Y., April 24, 1977. He studied at Munich Univ.; emigrated to the U.S. in 1923; became a naturalized American citizen in 1930. A highly competent musician, he readily adapted himself to the demands of the American music market, especially in films, and was able to write film scores of different connotations in various styles. Among his works are *Times Square Overture, American Indian Suite,* and a Piano Trio (1964).

Senaillé (Senaillié), Jean Baptiste, French violinist and composer; b. Paris, Nov. 23, 1687; d. there, Oct. 15, 1730. Although the spelling "Senaillé" is widely used, he signed his name "Senallié," as did his father; contemporary editions of his music invariably used the form "Senaillié." He studied first with his father, a member of the "24 violins du roi"; later was a pupil of Jean Baptiste Anet; then went to Italy, where he studied with Vitali. He returned to Paris in 1720; gave many performances at the Concert Spirituel. His playing was in the Italian tradition; in his music, also, he was influenced by the Italian school of Corelli and Vitali. He publ. 50 violin sonatas (with continuo) in 5 books (1710–27); modern reprints by Moffat, Jensen, Alard, etc.

BIBLIOGRAPHY: L. de la Laurencie, *L'École fran-*

çaise de violon (Paris, 1922; vol. 1, pp. 165–79); A, Moser, *Geschichte des Violinspiels* (1923; p. 179).

Senart, Maurice, French music publisher; b. Paris, Jan. 29, 1878; d. there, May 23, 1962. In 1908 he founded a music publishing enterprise in partnership with Roudanez; in 1912, became sole head of the firm, which bears his name. Among his early publications was the important collection edited by Henry Expert, *Maîtres musiciens de la Renaissance française;* there followed several other collections; many editions of classical music; collected works of Chopin, edited by Alfred Cortot. Senart was also a decided supporter of modern French music; publ. many works by Honegger and Milhaud, and works by composers of other nationalities resident in Paris (Tansman, Harsanyi, etc.). His publishing firm was acquired by Salabert in 1941.

Sendrey, Albert Richard, American composer, son of Aladár Szendrei; b. Chicago, Dec. 26, 1911. He studied in Leipzig, Paris, and London; was arranger for film companies in Paris (1935–37) and London (1937–44) before settling in Hollywood in 1944. Among his original works are: *Oriental Suite* for orch. (1935); 3 symphonies; piano pieces; cello pieces.

Sendrey, Alfred. See **Szendrei, Aladár.**

Senesino, Francesco (real name **Bernardi;** called Senesino after his birthplace), Italian male mezzo-soprano; b. Siena, c.1680; d. c.1750. He studied in Bologna with Bernacchi; in 1917 was engaged to sing at the court theater in Dresden; Handel heard him there, and engaged him for his Italian opera company in London. He began his London appearances in Bononcini's opera *Astarto* (Nov. 30, 1720), and his success was enormous from the start. For 15 consecutive seasons he enjoyed the favor of the London public; was associated with Handel's company until 1733, when a rival organization, the "Opera of the Nobility," engaged him and several other celebrated Italian singers to sing under the direction of Porpora. In 1735 he returned to Siena; in 1739, he was in Florence. It is not known where or exactly when he died.

BIBLIOGRAPHY: F. Haböck, *Die Kastraten und ihre Gesangskunst* (Stuttgart, 1927); A. Heriot, *The Castrati in Opera* (London, 1956, p. 91ff.).

Senff, Barthol (Wilhelm), German music publisher and editor; b. Friedrichshall, near Coburg, Sept. 2, 1815; d. Badenweiler, June 25, 1900. As a young man he entered Kistner's music publishing house in Leipzig, advancing to the position of managing clerk; here he already began publishing the *Signale für die musikalische Welt,* a trial number appearing in Dec. 1842; 1st regular number was issued on Jan. 1, 1843. This was one of the most important German music periodicals of the 19th century; it includes reports of musical events, special articles, and correspondence from the music centers of the world; many celebrated musicians contributed to it, among them Hans von Bülow. Senff remained editor of the *Signale* until his death, and publication continued (with a brief interruption in 1917-18) until 1941. Senff founded his own publishing

business in 1847; his catalogue included original publications of works by Schumann, Liszt, Anton Rubinstein, Raff, Franz, etc. His niece, Marie Senff, managed the firm until 1907, when she sold it and the *Signale* to Simrock of Berlin.

Senfl, Ludwig, important church composer of the Renaissance; b. Basel, c.1486; d. Munich, 1543. His father was a singer from Freiburg-im-Breisgau; the family name may have been **Senffl, Sänftli, Sänfly, Senfel,** etc., and the ultimate origin undoubtedly German, although Ludwig Senfl was known under the appellation "Schweizer" (the Swiss). As a small child, from 1495, he sang in the imperial court chapel; from 1504 he was in Zürich, and shortly afterwards, went to Constance, where he was a pupil of Isaac; he was Isaac's assistant at St. Ann's Church, Augsburg, and also sang in the court chapel of Maximilian I; after Isaac's death (1517), Senfl completed his teacher's *Choralis Constantinus* and became his successor as chamber composer; remained in Augsburg for some time after Maximilian's death (1519), and received a stipend from Charles V; edited the historically important *Liber selectarum cantionum* (1520), which was one of the earliest books with musical notation publ. in Germany. In 1523 he settled in Munich as "intonator" at the Bavarian court chapel; his fame grew; he was referred to by an early contemporary as "prince of all German music." There is extant a letter written to Senfl by Martin Luther, dated Oct. 4, 1530, containing high praise of the composer (reprinted in F. A. Beck's *Dr. M. Luthers Gedanken über die Musik,* Berlin, 1828).

WORKS: *5 Salutationes Domini nostri Hiesu Christi* (motets in 4 voices, Nuremberg; 1526); *Varia carminum genera, quibus tum Horatius tum alii egreii poetae harmoniis composita,* for 4 voices (Nuremberg, 1534; 9 Odes are in P. Hofhaimer's *Harmonie poeticae,* 1539); *Magnificat octo tonorum,* for 4–5 voices (Nuremberg, 1537); 81 numbers by Senfl are in the collection *121 newe Lieder* (Nuremberg, 1534), and 64 numbers in *115 guter newer Liedlein* (Nuremberg, 1544); single compositions in various collections of the period (for a list, see Eitner's *Bibliographie,* Berlin, 1877, and vol. IV of the *Publikationen älterer Musikwerke*). Magnificats and a selection of 12 motets are in *Denkmäler der Tonkunst in Bayern* 5 (3.ii). Many MSS (sacred and secular vocal works) are in the Munich Library. Some songs have been publ. in Jöde's *Chorbuch,* and in *Denkmäler deutscher Tonkunst* (vol. 34, ed. by J. Wolf); *Weltliche Lieder* for 4-part mixed chorus were publ. by Willi Schuh (Zürich, 1929); motets are in Schering's *Geschichte der Musik in Beispielen* (nos. 74, 84–86); etc. 7 Masses were edited by E. Löhrer and O. Ursprung for the *Reichsdenkmale deutscher Musik* (Leipzig, 1936), and this was taken over the following year by the Schweizerische Musikforschende Gesellschaft as vol. I of the collected works of Senfl; as of 1977, there were 11 vols.

BIBLIOGRAPHY: Th. Kroyer, *Ludwig Senfl und sein Motettenstil* (Munich, 1902); H. J. Moser, "Instrumentalismen bei Ludwig Senfl," in "J. Wolf Festschrift" (1929); H. J. Moser, "Der Altmünchner Tonmeister Ludwig Senfl," *Süddeutsche Monatshefte*

(1930); E. Löhrer, *Die Messen von Ludwig Senfl* (Lichtensteig, 1938); H. Birtner, "Sieben Messen von Ludwig Senfl," *Archiv für Musikforschung* (1942); G. Reese, *Music in the Renaissance* (N.Y., 1954).

Senilov, Vladimir, Russsian composer; b. Viatka, Aug. 8, 1875; d. Petrograd, Sept. 18, 1918. He was a student of jurisprudence at the Univ. of St. Petersburg; went to Leipzig, where he studied with Hugo Riemann (1895–1901); returning to Russia, he studied composition with Rimsky-Korsakov and Glazunov at the St. Petersburg Cons., graduating in 1906. His works include a lyric drama, *Vassily Buslayev;* 1-act opera *Hippolytus,* after Euripides; *In Autumn,* symph. poem; *Mtziri,* symph. poem after Lermontov; *Pan,* symph. poem; *The Scythians,* symph. poem; 3 string quartets; choral pieces and songs.

Serafin, Tulio, Italian conductor; b. Rottanova di Cavarzere, Venice, Sept. 1, 1878; d. Rome, Feb. 3, 1968. He studied at the Cons. of Milan; made his debut as conductor in Ferrara in 1900; then he conducted opera in Italian provincial towns; in 1909 he became conductor of La Scala in Milan; from 1924 to 1935 he was on the staff of the Metropolitan Opera, N.Y. He returned to Italy in 1935 and continued to fill engagements in Rome, Milan and elsewhere; also conducted opera in London and Paris; in 1952 he was guest conductor at the N.Y. City Opera Co. He published (with A. Toni) 2 volumes on history of Italian opera, *Stile, tradizioni e convenzioni del melo dramma italiano del Settecento e dell'Ottocento* (Milan, 1958–64).

Serafino, Santo, celebrated Italian violin maker; b. Udine, c. 1650; d. Venice, c.1740. He was a pupil of Niccolo Amati, and probably worked in Cremona; signed his name on the labels as "Sanctus Seraphinus Nicolai Amati Cremonensis Alumnus." His instruments contained elements characteristic of Stainer and of Niccolo Amati. His nephew **Giorgio Serafino** worked in Venice in the 1st half of the 18th century.

Serassi, Giuseppe ("il Vecchio"), the founder of a celebrated house of Italian organ builders; b. Gordano, 1694; d. Crema, Aug. 1, 1760. His son **Andrea Luigi** (1725–1799) carried on the business; built the cathedral organs of Crema, Parma, and Fossano. A younger member of the family, **Giuseppe ("il Giovane";** b. Bergamo, Nov. 16, 1750; d. there, Feb. 19, 1817) upheld the reputation of the firm, and built many organs in Lombardy. His catalogue of 1815 lists 345 instruments. He publ. a description of the new organ at Como (1808), with a short history of the organ, and good rules for registration; also brought out a pamphlet, *Sugli organi* (1816). The catalogue publ. in 1852 by his sons, **Carlo** and **Giuseppe Serassi,** shows a total of 654 organs constructed.

Serato, Arrigo, Italian violinist; b. Bologna, Feb. 7, 1877; d. Rome, Dec. 27, 1948. He received his musical training from his father, a cellist. He was mainly active as a chamber music player; formed the Trio Bolognese with Federico Sarti and Gustavo Tofano and the Quartetto Bolognese with Sarti, Massarenti and Angelo Consolini; then settled in Berlin where he took a course in violin study with Joachim, and was also a member of Joachim's string quartet. He returned to Italy in 1915 and taught master classes in violin at the Santa Cecilia Academy in Rome until his death. Concurrently he resumed his career as a chamber music player; in 1925 he organized a trio with Pizzetti (piano) and Mainardi (cello); also gave recitals with the pianist Ernesto Consolo.
BIBLIOGRAPHY: A. Della Corte, *Arrigo Serato violinista* (Siena, 1950).

Serauky, Walter, eminent German musicologist; b. Halle, April 20, 1903; d. there, Aug. 20, 1959. He studied at Leipzig Univ. with Schering, H. J. Moser, and Prüfer; Dr. phil. at the Univ. of Halle, 1928, with the dissertation *Die musikalische Nachahmungsästhetik im Zeitraum von 1700 bis 1850* (publ. Münster, 1929); joined the faculty of the Univ. of Halle; in 1949, appointed prof. at the Leipzig Univ. He contributed valuable essays to various German publications; brought out a music history of the city of Halle (5 vols.; 1935–43). In 1956 he began publication of an extensive study of Handel, *G. F. Händel; sein Leben, sein Werk;* also edited works by Handel, Türk, and Reichardt.

Serebrier, José, Uruguayan-American conductor and composer; b. Montevideo, Dec. 3, 1938. He began to conduct at the age of 12; went to the U.S. in 1950; studied composition with Vittorio Giannini at the Curtis Institute, Philadelphia (1956–58) and conducting with Antal Dorati in Minneapolis; also took conducting lessons with Monteux at his summer residence in Maine. He subsequently conducted guest engagements in the U.S., South America and Europe; gave the first performance in Poland of the 4th Symph. of Charles Ives.
WORKS: Quartet for saxophones (1955); *Pequeña música* for wind quintet (1955); Symph. No. 1 (1956); *Momento psicologico* for string orch. (1957); *Suite canina* for wind trio (1957); Symph. for percussion (1960); *The Star Wagon* for chamber orch. (1967); *Nueve* for double bass and orch. (1970); *Colores mágicos,* variations for harp and chamber orch. with "Synchrona" images (5th Inter-American Music Festival, Washington, May 20, 1971).

Serendero-Proust, David, Chilean composer and conductor; b. Santiago, July 28, 1934. He studied violin and composition at the National Cons. of Music in Santiago; then went to Germany where he studied conducting in Stuttgart. From 1967 to 1972 he was appointed conductor of the Orquestra Sinfónica de Chile in Santiago. In 1972 he moved to West Germany, where he became active as conductor in Wiesbaden.
WORKS: String Trio (1952); *Duo heterogéneo* for flute, and clarinet (1953); *El Ensayo,* a melodrama for soprano and 14 instruments (1962); *Estratos* for orch. (Mexico City, March 28, 1969, composer conducting).

Seress, Rezsö, Hungarian composer of popular songs; b. Budapest, Nov. 3, 1899; d. there, Jan. 12, 1968. He earned his living by playing piano and singing in restaurants and nightclubs; acquired fame in

1936 by his song *Gloomy Sunday*, which was banned in Hungary and several other countries because its morbid tune precipitated a wave of Sunday suicides among the young. Seress jumped out of a window from the second floor of his Budapest apartment on Jan. 8, 1968 (a Monday, not a Sunday), and died 4 days later.

Sérieyx, Auguste, French composer and writer on music; b. Amiens, June 14, 1865; d. Montreux, Switzerland, Feb. 19, 1949. He studied in Paris, at the Schola Cantorum with Gédalge and Vincent d'Indy; taught composition there (1900–14), and collaborated with Vincent d'Indy in his monumental *Cours de Composition* (3 vols., Paris, 1897–1933); publ. a biography of d'Indy (Paris, 1913) and a short treatise, *Les Trois États de la tonalité* (Paris, 1910). His compositions include *La Voie lactée*, for solo voice and orch.; the cantata *Salvete cedri libani;* violin sonata; piano pieces; songs.

Sering, Friedrich Wilhelm, German composer; b. Fürstenwalde, near Frankfurt-on-the-Oder, Nov. 26, 1822; d. Hannover, Nov. 5, 1901. From 1871 he was head teacher in the Seminary at Strasbourg, where he organized a Gesangverein. He composed an oratorio, *Christi Einzug in Jerusalem; Psalm 72,* for mixed chorus with piano; wrote the manuals, *Gesanglehre für Volksschulen* and *Die Choralfiguration, theoretisch-praktisch,* and an elementary violin method.

Serini, Giovanni Battista, Italian composer; b. Cremona, c.1724; date and place of death unknown. He was in the service of Robert d'Arcy, British ambassador in Venice (1744–46); subsequently was court musician in Bückeburg (1750–56). A collection of his instrumental and vocal works was found in the library at York Minster. Three keyboard sonatas are included in vol. 29 of *I Classici della Musica Italiana.*
BIBLIOGRAPHY: Jack Pilgrim, "A Note on G. B. Serini, *Musical Times* (Aug. 1964).

Serkin, Peter, American pianist, son of **Rudolf Serkin;** b. New York, July 24, 1947. He made his public debut at the age of 10 as a student of his father, and at the age of 14 appeared with his father in Mozart's Concerto for 2 pianos and orch. with the Cleveland Orch. (April 19, 1962); then he started on a brilliant career of his own, specializing in ultramodern music.

Serkin, Rudolf, eminent Austrian pianist; b. Eger, Bohemia, March 28, 1903 (of Russian parentage). He studied in Vienna with Richard Robert (piano), Joseph Marx and Arnold Schoenberg (composition). After an early debut at the age of 12, he began his serious concert career in 1920; appeared frequently in joint recitals with the violinist Adolf Busch (whose daughter he married); made his American debut with Busch at a Coolidge Festival concert in Washington (1933); in 1939 he was appointed to the faculty of the Curtis Institute, Philadelphia; then served as its director (until 1977). Subsequently he took the lead in establishing in Marlboro, Vermont, a summer center for festivals and schooling. His performances of the Vien-

nese classics are unexcelled in authority, faithfulness of treatment, and technical virtuosity.

Serly, Tibor, Hungarian violinist, composer and conductor; b. Losonc, Nov. 25, 1900. He studied with his father (a theater conductor in Budapest); from 1922, with Kodály and Bartók (composition) at the Royal Academy of Music, Budapest; violin with Hubay. After graduating, he went to the U.S.; played viola in the Cincinnati Symph. Orch., the Philadelphia Orch., and the NBC Symph. Orch. In 1937 he settled in N.Y. as a teacher.
WORKS: Viola Concerto (1929); Symph. No. 1 (Budapest, May 13, 1935, composer conducting); *6 Dance Designs* (Budapest, May 13, 1935); *Colonial Pageant,* symph. suite (1937); *Elegy,* for orch. (1945); *Rhapsody,* for viola and orch. (N.Y., Feb. 27, 1948); Trombone Concerto (Chautauqua, Aug. 17, 1952); *Modus Lascivus,* a series of etudes for piano (40 of them were performed by Serly's wife **Miriam Molin,** N.Y., May 4, 1977); songs; etc. Serly completed and orchestrated Bartók's unfinished Viola Concerto (1945).

Sermilä, Jarmo, Finnish composer; b. Hämeenlinna (Tavastehus), Aug. 16, 1939. He studied under Tauno Marttinen and Joonas Kokkonen in Finland and under František Kovařiček in Czechoslovakia. Returning to Finland, he organized a group of composers of electronic music. In his music he pursues an experimental line, particularly in instrumentation.
WORKS: *Monody* for horn and percussion (1970); *Homage* for 3 trumpets, 3 trombones, 2 horns and percussion (1971; Helsinki, April 19, 1972; *Pentagram* for trumpet solo, 2 bassoons, 4 horns, 6 cellos, 2 double basses, and percussion (1972; Turku, Jan. 18, 1973); *Early Music* for 2 flutes and strings (1972); *Tavastonia* for double bass and piano (1973); *Crisis* for clarinet and string quartet (1973); 2 electronic works *The Myth Is Weeping Again* and *A Doll's Cry* (1973); *Electrocomposition* (1976); *The Lions and the Bear* for soprano and percussion (1974); *Perception* for 2 cellos and 2 flutes (1974); *Mimesis 2* for orch. (1974; Helsinki, Jan. 27, 1976); *Counterbass* for double bass and string orch. (1975); *Cornologia* for 22 to 44 horns (1975); *Colors and Contrasts* for flute, violin and piano (1976); *Love-Chain Songs* for soprano, wind quintet, string quintet and 2 percussionists (1976); *Contemplation 1* for fluegelhorn and tape (1976).

Sermisy, Claude (Claudin) de, French composer; b. c.1490; d. Paris, Sept. 13, 1562. In 1508 he was appointed "clerc musicien" of the Sainte-Chapelle at Paris; accompanied Francis I to Italy in 1515; was present at the meeting between Francis and Henry VIII at the Field of the Cloth of Gold (1520). Sermisy composed chansons, motets, and Masses, which were printed in collections of the time and frequently republished after his death, indicating a wide popularity. Attaingnant's *31 chansons* (1529) contains 11 songs by Sermisy, which are reprinted in Expert's *Les Maîtres musiciens;* other modern reprints include 3 chansons in Eitner's *Publikationen älterer Musikwerke* (vol. 23; Leipzig, 1899); 3 chansons in Commer's *Collectio operum musicorum* (vol. 12); 2 chansons in Bordes, *Chansonnier du XIVe siècle;* 4

chansons in Expert's *Anthologie chorale des maîtres musiciens de la Renaissance française.*
BIBLIOGRAPHY: O. Kade, *Die ältere Passionskomposition* (Gütersloh, 1893; deals fully with Sermisy's Passion music); M. Brenet, *Les Musiciens de la Sainte-Chapelle du Palais* (Paris, 1910); G. Reese, *Music in the Renaissance* (N.Y., 1954).

Serocki, Kazimierz, prominent Polish composer and pianist; b. Toruń, March 3, 1922. He studied piano in Lódź; also took a course in composition there with Sikorski. In 1947, following the path of many other composers of his generation, he went to Paris to study with the fabled Nadia Boulanger. Returning to Poland, he formed, with Tadeusz Baird and Jan Krenz, the modernistic "Group '49," dedicated to the cause of the avant-garde; in 1956 was one of the organizers of the audaciously futuristic "Warsaw Autumn" Festivals. In the interim he toured as a concert pianist. In his early music he fell into the fashionable neo-Classical current strewn with tolerable dissonances and spiked with spermatogenic atonalities; experimented with Webernized dodecaphonies before molding his own style of composition, an amalgam of pragmatic serialism and permissible aleatory procedures, while maintaining an air of wellnigh monastic nominalism in formal strictures and informal structures; in some pieces he makes an incursion into the alien field of American jazz.
WORKS: *Symphonic Scherzo* (1948); *Triptych* for chamber orch. (1949); *4 tańce ludowe (People's Dances)* for chamber orch. (1949); *Romantic Concerto* for piano and orch. (1950); 2 symphonies: No. 1 (1952); No. 2, *Symphony of Songs,* for soprano, baritone, chorus, and orch. (1953, Warsaw, June 11, 1953); Trombone Concerto (1953); Sinfonietta for 2 string orchestras (1956); *Musica concertante* for chamber orch. (1958); *Episodes* for strings and 3 groups of percussion (1958-59); *Segmenti* for 12 winds, 6 strings, piano, celesta, harpsichord, guitar, mandolin, and 58 percussion instruments (1960-61); *Symphonic Frescoes* (1963); *Forte e Piano,* music for 2 pianos and orch. (1967; Cologne, March 29, 1968); *Dramatic Story* for orch. (1968-71; Warsaw, Sept. 23, 1971); *Fantasia elegiaca* for organ and orch. (1971-72; Baden-Baden, June 9, 1972); Sonatina for trombone and orch. (1972-73; Strasbourg, Dec. 19, 1975); *Concerto alla Cadenza* for recorder and orch. (1975); *Ad Libitum,* 5 pieces for orch. (1976; Hamburg, Sept. 17, 1977); *3 melodie Kurpiowskie (Melodies from Kurpie)* for 6 sopranos, 6 tenors and chamber orch. (1949); 2 cantatas: *Mazowsze* (1950) and *Murarz warszawski* (1951); *Serce nocy (Heart of the Night),* cycle for baritone and piano (1956); *Oczy powietrza (Eyes of the Wind),* cycle for soprano and orch. or piano (1957-58); *Niobe* for 2 narrators, chorus and orch. (1966); *Poezje (Poems)* for soprano and chamber orch. (1968-69); *Suite* for 4 trombones (1953); *Continuum,* sextet for 123 percussion instruments manipulated by 6 multimanual percussionists (1965-66); *Swinging Music* for clarinet, trombone, cello or double bass, and piano (1970); *Phantasmagoria* for piano and percussion (1970-71); *Impromptu fantastique* for 6 flutes, mandolins, guitars, percussionists, and piano

(1973-74); Piano Sonatina (1952); Piano Sonata (1955); *A piacere* for piano (1963).

Seroff, Victor, American writer on music; b. Batum, Caucasus, Oct. 14, 1902; studied law at the Univ. of Tiflis; then took piano lessons with Moriz Rosenthal in Vienna and Theodore Szanto in Paris; eventually settled in New York and became an American citizen.
WRITINGS: *Dmitri Shostakovich: The Life and Background of a Soviet Composer* (N.Y., 1943); *The Mighty Five: The Cradle of Russian National Music* (N.Y., 1948); *Rachmaninoff* (N.Y., 1950); *Maurice Ravel* (N.Y., 1953); *Debussy, Musician of France* (N.Y., 1956); *Hector Berlioz* (N.Y., 1967); *Prokofiev: A Soviet Tragedy* (N.Y., 1968); *Mussorgsky* (N.Y., 1968); *Franz Liszt* (N.Y., 1970).
BIBLIOGRAPHY: M. R. Werner, *To Whom It May Concern: The Story of V. I. Seroff* (N.Y., 1931).

Serov, Alexander, important Russian composer; b. St. Petersburg, Jan. 23, 1820; d. there, Feb. 1, 1871. He was trained in a law school; also took cello lessons with Karl Schuberth; became a functionary in the Ministry of Justice; served in St. Petersburg (1840-45); then in Simferopol, Crimea (1845-48); in 1849 turned definitely to music, and abandoned government employ. He never took lessons in composition, except a correspondence course in counterpoint, but achieved a certain mastery in harmony and orchestration by studying the classics. In 1851 he began writing critical articles on music and soon became an important figure in Russian journalism; in 1856 he became editor of the *Musical and Theatrical Monitor.* In 1858 he made his first trip abroad, visiting Germany and Bohemia; the following year made another German visit, and also traveled in Austria and Switzerland; during this journey he met Wagner, whose ardent admirer he became and remained to the end of his career; expounded Wagner's ideas in Russian publications and engaged in bitter polemics with those who did not subscribe to his views, including his old friend and schoolmate Vladimir Stasov. He started very late in the field of composition; inspired by the performance of a biblical play, *Judith,* by an Italian troupe at St. Petersburg in 1861, he resolved to write an opera on this subject, essaying an Italian libretto, but later deciding on a Russian text. *Judith* was produced in St. Petersburg on May 28, 1863 with excellent success, but although Serov intended to emulate Wagner in the music, the style of *Judith* was closer to Meyerbeer. Quite different was Serov's 2nd opera, *Rogneda,* written on a Russian subject, in a distinctly national idiom, with plentiful use of Russian folksongs. *Rogneda* was staged in St. Petersburg on Nov. 8, 1865, and won a spectacular success; the Tsar Alexander II attended a subsequent performance and granted Serov an annual stipend of 1000 rubles for it. He then began the composition of another Russian opera, *Vrazhya Sila (Malevolent Power),* but death (of a sudden heart failure) overtook him when the 5th act was still incomplete; the opera was finished by N. T. Solovyev, and produced posthumously in St. Petersburg on May 1, 1871. All 3 operas of Serov retain their popularity in Russia, but are unknown elsewhere. Serov wrote further an Ave Maria for Adelina Patti

(1868); a Stabat Mater; incidental music to *Nero; Plyaska Zaporozhtsev (Dance of the Zaporozh Cossacks)* for orch. (1867); *Ouverture d'une comédie* for piano 4 hands, and a few other small pieces. A selection from his writings was publ. in 4 vols. (St. Petersburg, 1892–95). In 1863 Serov married a young Conservatory pupil, **Valentina Bergmann** (1846–1924), who was the first Russian woman to compose operas: *Uriel Acosta* (Moscow, 1885) and *Ilya Murometz* (Moscow, March 6, 1899; with Chaliapin in the title role). She helped to edit and publish Serov's posthumous works; wrote essays; published a number of piano pieces and a book of memoirs (St. Petersburg, 1914) under the name **Valentina Serova.**

BIBLIOGRAPHY: N. Findeisen, *A. N. Serov. His Life and Work* (St. Petersburg, 1900; 2nd ed., 1904); Valentina Serova, *A. N. Serov* (St. Petersburg, 1914); G. Abraham and M. D. Calvocoressi, *Masters of Russian Music* (N.Y., 1936); G. Khubov, *The Life of A. N. Serov* (Moscow, 1950).

Serpette, Gaston, French composer; b. Nantes, Nov. 4, 1846; d. Paris, Nov. 3, 1904. He studied with Ambroise Thomas at the Paris Cons., taking the 1st Grand Prix de Rome in 1871 with the cantata *Jeanne d'Arc.* From 1874 he produced in Paris a steady progression of light operas of which the following enjoyed a modicum of success: *La Branche cassée* (Jan. 23, 1874); *Le Manoir du pic tordu* (May 28, 1875); *Le Moulin du vert galant* (April 12, 1876); *La Petite Muette* (Oct. 3, 1877); *Le Petit Chaperon rouge* (Oct. 10, 1885); *Adam et Eve* (Oct. 6, 1886); *Mademoiselle du téléphone* (May 2, 1891); *Shakespeare* (Nov. 23, 1899).

Serrano, Emilio, Spanish composer of light operas; b. Vitoria, March 13, 1850; d. Madrid, April 8, 1939. He studied at the Madrid Cons., and taught piano and composition there for half a century (1870–1920); also conducted symph. concerts in Madrid. He wrote 5 operas: *Mitridates* (Madrid, 1882), *Doña Juana la Loca* (Madrid, 1890), *Irene de Otranto* (Madrid, Feb. 17, 1891), *Gonzalo de Córdoba* (Madrid, Dec. 6, 1898), and *La Maja de Rumbo* (Buenos Aires, Sept. 24, 1910).

Serrao, Paolo, Italian composer; b. Filadelfia, Catanzaro, 1830; d. Naples, March 17, 1907. He studied with Mercadante at the Cons. of Naples, and taught there from 1863. He brought out his first opera, *Pergolesi,* in 1857, followed by *La Duchessa di Guisa* (1865) and *Il Figliuol prodigo* (1868); also composed an oratorio, *Gli Ortonesi in Scio;* a funeral symph. for Mercadante, *Omaggio a Mercadante;* a cantata with orch. *Le tre ore d'agonia,* and much church music.

Serres, Louis (Arnal) de, French composer and teacher; b. Lyons, Nov. 8, 1864; d. Néronde (Loire), Dec. 25, 1942. He studied at the Paris Cons. with Taudou (harmony) and César Franck (organ); joined the faculty of the Schola Cantorum; taught there from 1900; when the institution was reorganized in 1935 as the École César Franck, he became its director. His compositions include *Les Heures claires* for voice and orch.; *Les Caresses* for orch.; choruses, motets, and songs.

Servais, (Adrien-) François, famous Belgian cellist; b. Hal, near Brussels, June 6, 1807; d. there, Nov. 26, 1866. He studied at the Brussels Cons.; played in a theater orch. there; then went to Paris, where he gave a concert in 1834, with brilliant success; on May 25, 1835, he played his own cello concerto with the London Philharmonic; subsequently made a grand tour of Europe; spent several years in Russia as a concert player, even reaching Siberia. He was appointed prof. at the Brussels Cons. in 1848, and taught many pupils who became distinguished artists. He wrote 3 concertos and 16 fantasias for cello with orch.; 6 études and 14 duos for cello with piano (with Gregoir); 3 duos for violin and cello (with Léonard).

Servais, François (Franz), French composer and conductor; b. St. Petersburg, Russia, c.1847; d. Asnières, near Paris, Jan. 14, 1901. It was claimed for him that he was an illegitimate son of Liszt and Princess Carolyne Sayn-Wittgenstein, but nothing in her voluminous correspondence with Liszt indicates that she was an expectant mother. However it might be, he was adopted by **François Servais** and assumed his name. He studied cello with Kufferath at the Brussels Cons., and won the Belgian Prix de Rome in 1873 with the cantata *Le Tasse.* From the outset of his career as a conductor he was a Wagner enthusiast, and gave the first Belgian performances of several Wagner operas, in Brussels. His own Opera *Ión* (originally entitled *L'Apollonide*) was produced in Karlsruhe in 1899.

BIBLIOGRAPHY: E. Michotte, *Au souvenir de François Servais* (Paris, 1907).

Servais, Joseph, Belgian French cellist; son of **Adrien-François Servais;** b. Hal, near Brussels, Nov. 23, 1850; d. there, Aug. 29, 1885. He was a pupil of his father; made his debut in a joint recital with him in Warsaw (1867); then went to Weimar, where he played in the orch. (1868–70); in 1872 returned to Belgium, where he was prof. at the Brussels Cons. until his early death.

Servières, Georges, French writer on music; b. Fréjus, Oct. 13, 1858; d. Paris, July 25, 1937. He publ. a number of informative books: *Richard Wagner jugé en France* (1887); *Le "Tannhäuser" à l'Opéra 1861* (1895); *La Musique française moderne* (1897); *Weber* (1906); *Emmanuel Chabrier* (1912); *Épisodes d'histoire musicale* (1914); *Saint-Saëns* (1923); *Documents inédits sur les organistes français des XVIIe et XVIIIe siècles* (1923); *Édouard Lalo* (1925); *La Décoration artistique des buffets d'orgues* (1928); *Gabriel Fauré* (1930).

Sessions, Roger, eminent American composer; b. Brooklyn, Dec. 28, 1896. He studied music at Harvard Univ. (B.A., 1915); then took a course in composition with Horatio Parker at the Yale School of Music (B.M., 1917); then took private lessons with Ernest Bloch in Cleveland and N.Y.; this association was of great importance for Sessions; his early works were strongly influenced by Bloch's rhapsodic style and rich harmonic idiom verging on polytonality. Sessions taught music theory at Smith College (1917–21); then was appointed to the faculty of the Cleveland Institute of Music, first as assistant to Ernest Bloch, then as head of the department. He held 2 consecutive Guggenheim Fellowships (1926, 1927); a fellowship of the American Academy in Rome (1928–31) and a Carnegie Fellowship (1931–32). He lived mostly in Europe from 1926 to 1933; in the interim he presented with Aaron Copland a series of concerts of modern music in N.Y. (called Copland-Sessions Concerts) which played an important cultural role at the time. His subsequent teaching posts included Boston Univ. (1933–35), the New Jersey College for Women (1935–37), Princeton Univ. (1935–45), and the Univ. of California at Berkeley (1945–51); taught again at Princeton (1953–65), at Berkeley (1966–67), and at Harvard Univ. (1968–69); also gave courses at the Juilliard School of Music, N.Y. Among American composers who had fruitful sessions with Sessions during his years of professorship were David Diamond, Paul Bowles, Leon Kirchner, Milton Babbitt, and Hugo Weisgall. In his compositions, Sessions evolved a remarkably compact polyphonic idiom, rich in unresolvable dissonances and textural density, and yet permeated with true lyricism. In his later works he adopted a *sui generis* method of serial composition. The music of Sessions is decidedly in advance of his time; the difficulty of his idiom, both for performers and listeners, creates a paradoxical situation in which he is recognized as one of the most important composers of the century, while actual performances of his works are exasperatingly infrequent.

WORKS: for the stage: *The Black Masters*, incidental music to Leonid Andreyev's play (Smith College, Northampton, June, 1923); *The Trial of Lucullus*, 1-act opera (Berkeley, Calif., April 18, 1947); *Montezuma*, 3-act opera (1962; West Berlin, April 19, 1964); 8 symphonies: No. 1 (Boston, April 22, 1927); No. 2 (San Francisco, Jan. 9, 1947); No. 3 (Boston, Dec. 6, 1957); No. 4 (Minneapolis, Jan. 2, 1960); No. 5 (Philadelphia, Feb. 7, 1964); No. 6 (Newark, N.J., Nov. 19, 1966); No. 7 (Ann Arbor, Michigan, Oct. 1, 1967); No. 8 (N.Y., May 2, 1968); symph. suite from *The Black Masters* (Cincinnati, Dec. 5, 1930); Violin Concerto (Chicago, Jan. 8, 1940); *Idyll of Theocritus* for soprano and orch. (Louisville, Jan. 14, 1956); Piano Concerto (N.Y., Feb. 10, 1956); 2 string quartets (1936, 1951); Duo for violin and piano (1942); Sonata for solo violin (1953); String Quintet (1958); *Divertimento* for orch. (1960); *Psalm 140* for soprano and orch. (1963); *6 Pieces* for cello (1966); *When Lilacs Last in the Dooryard Bloom'd*, cantata for vocal soloists, chorus and orch. (1967–70; Univ. of Calif., Berkeley, May 23, 1971); *Rhapsody* for orch. (Baltimore, March 18, 1970); Concerto for violin, cello and orch. (1970–71); Concertino for chamber orch. (1971–72; Chicago, April 14, 1972); *3 Biblical Choruses* for chorus and chamber orch. (1971); 3 piano sonatas (1930, 1946, 1965); *Pages from a Diary* for piano (1939); *3 Chorale Preludes* for organ (1925); *Mass* for unison chorus and organ (1956); *5 Pieces* for piano (1975). Sessions published the books *The Musical Experience of Composer, Performer, Listener* (Princeton, 1950), *Harmonic Practice* (N.Y., 1951), *Reflections on the Music Life in the United States* (N.Y., 1956), and *Questions about Music* (Cambridge, Mass., 1970).

BIBLIOGRAPHY: N. Slonimsky, in *American Composers on American Music*, ed. by Henry Cowell (Stanford, Calif., 1933; reprint, N.Y., 1962); Mark Brunswick, "Roger Sessions," *Modern Music* (1933); Aaron Copland, *Our New Music* (N.Y., 1941, p. 176ff.) M. A. Schubart, "Roger Sessions," *Musical Quarterly* (April 1946); L. A. Wright and A. Bagnall, "Roger H. Sessions: A Selective Bibliography and a Listing of His Compositions," *Current Musicology* 15 (1973).

Šesták, Zdeněk, Czech composer; b. Citoliby, Dec. 10, 1925. He studied composition with Hlobil and Krejčí at the Prague Cons. (1945–50) and music history at Charles Univ. (1945–49); in 1970 he joined as an active member the Czech Performing Rights Organization.

WORKS: *To Fallen Warriors,* symph. prelude (1949); *Pantomime* for orch. (1959); *Rhapsodic Fantasy* for cello and orch. (1960); 4 numbered symphonies: No. 1, *Epitaph* (1961), No. 2 (1970), No. 3 (1971) and No. 4 for string orch. (1973); *Vocal Symphony* for chorus and orch. (1962); *Balladic Intermezzo* for orch. (1964); *Symphonic Fantasy*, variations for orch. (1966); Concerto for String Orch. (1974); *Auschwitz*, melodrama to a text by Quasimodo (1959); *Hommage à Apollinaire*, for 12 mixed choruses (1972); *The Death of Manon Lescaut*, 4 dramatic fragments for soprano, tenor, chorus, solo viola and piano (1974); *Cassation* for 5 wind instruments (1958); *Suite* for flute and piano (1959); *2 Pieces* for violin and piano (1960); Concertino for Wind Quintet (1964); *Divertimento concertante* for wind quintet (1966); *5 Virtuoso Inventions* for solo bassoon (1966); Sonata for 2 clarinets (1967); *Music* for solo oboe (1967); Concertino No. 1 for horn and piano (1967); *3 Metamorphoses* for solo flute (1968); *Musica Partita* for solo clarinet (1968); Concertino No. 2 for horn and piano (1972); numerous songs; children's pieces.

Setaccioli, Giacomo, Italian composer and teacher; b. Corneto, Tarquinia, Dec. 8, 1868; d. Siena, Dec. 5, 1925. He studied at the Accademia di Santa Cecilia in Rome; after teaching there (1922–25) he was appointed director of the Conservatorio Cherubini in Florence. He wrote the operas *La Sorella di Mark* (Rome, May 7, 1896) and *L'ultimo degli Abenceragi* (Rome, 1893) and *Il Mantelaccio* (posthumous; Rome, 1954); several symphonic pieces; a *Requiem;* chamber music; songs; piano pieces. He published *Debussy è un innovatore?* (Rome, 1910) and *Studi e conferenze di critica musicale* (Rome, 1923).

Seter, Mordecai, Russian-born Israeli composer; b. Novorossiysk, Feb. 26, 1916. He went to Palestine in 1926; then traveled to Paris and studied composition with Nadia Boulanger and Paul Dukas (1932–37); returning to Palestine he taught at the Israeli Academy of Music. He writes music in the Eastern Mediterranean style.

WORKS: 5 ballets: *Pas de deux* or *Women in Tent* (ballet version of the 1956 *Ricercar;* N.Y., 1956), *Midnight Vigil—Rhapsody on Yemenite Themes* (1958; Jerusalem, 1958), *The Legend of Judith* (1962), *Part*

Real, Part Dream (ballet version of the *Fantasia Concertante*, 1964; N.Y., 1965) and *Jephthah's Daughter* (ballet version of symph. score, 1965); a radiophonic oratorio, *Midnight Vigil* (1962; concert version, Jerusalem, July 16, 1963); *Elegy* for viola or clarinet, and orch. or piano (1954); *Ricercar* for violin, viola, cello and string ensemble (1956); *Variations* for orch. (1959); *Fantasia Concertante* for chamber orch. (1965); *Jephthah's Daughter* for orch. (1965); Sinfonietta (1966; revised version of the 1957 *Divertimento*); *Yemenite Suite* for chamber orch. with optional voice (1966); *Meditation* for orch. (1967); *Rounds* for chamber orch. (1967–68); *Requiem* for oboe or violin, piano, and string orch. (1970); *Sabbath Cantata* for soloists, chorus, and string orch. or organ (1940); *Jerusalem*, symph. for chorus and orch. (1966); *Sapei*, music for youth, for chorus, percussion, piano and strings (1968); *Partita* for violin or flute, and piano (1951); Sonata for 2 violins (1952); Sonata for solo violin (1953); *Diptyque* for wind quintet (1955); *Chamber Music 1970*, 6 works for different instrumental combinations (1970); *Concertante* for violin, oboe, horn and piano (1973); Piano Trio (1973); Woodwind Trio (1974); Quintet for violin, cello, flute, horn and piano (1975); *Ensemble* for 6 instruments (1975); 3 string quartets (all 1976); *Solo and Tutti* for clarinet and string quartet (1976); piano pieces; choruses.

Ševčik, Otakar, noted Czech violinist and pedagogue; b. Horaždowitz, March 22, 1852; d. Pisek, Jan. 18, 1934. He studied violin with his father; then at the Prague Cons. with Anton Bennewitz. From 1870 to 1873 he was concertmaster of the Mozarteum in Salzburg; held a similar post in the Theater an der Wien, Vienna. He then went to Russia, where he became prof. at the Cons. of Kiev (1875); also gave concerts in Russia, achieving great success there. In 1892 he returned to Prague; became head of the violin dept. at the Prague Cons. (1901–06); in 1909 he became head of the master school for violin at the Vienna Academy of Music; from 1919 to 1924 he taught again in Prague; also visited abroad as a teacher in the U.S. (1920; 1924; 1931); London (1932), etc. His method, in contradistinction to the usual diatonic system, is founded on chromatic progressions, especially valuable in securing both accuracy and facility. In various parts of the world he had hundreds of pupils, among them Jan Kubelík, Kocian, Marie Hall, Baloković, Erica Morini, and Efrem Zimbalist. He publ. the following pedagogical works (in German, Bohemian, French, and Russian; most of them also printed in English): *Schule der Violintechnik* (4 parts); *Schule der Bogentechnik* (6 parts); *Violinschule für Anfänger* (7 parts); *Triller-Vorstudien und Ausbildung des Fingeranschlags* (2 parts); *Lagenwechsel-Übungen; Doppelgriff-Vorstudien;* also *Böhmische Tänze und Weisen*, for violin and piano.
BIBLIOGRAPHY: Paul Stoeving, *A Key to Ševčik's Works* (London, 1914); V. Nopp, *Otakar Ševčik* (Prague, 1948); J. Dostál, ed., *Otakar Ševčik* (collection of essays on him; Prague, 1953).

Séverac, Déodat de, French composer; b. Saint-Félix-de-Caraman, Lauraguais, July 20, 1872; d. Céret, March 24, 1921. He received his first lessons on the piano from his father, a painter and ardent lover of music. He studied music at the Cons. of Toulouse; in 1890 entered the Schola Cantorum in Paris, where he remained till 1907, studying with Magnard and Vincent d'Indy. He resided alternately in Paris and his native town.
WORKS: the operas *Le Cœur du moulin* (Paris, Dec. 8, 1909) and *Les Princesses d'Hokifari* (not produced); incidental music to L. Damard's *Le Mirage* (1905), E. Sicard's *Héliogabale* (1910), M. Navarre's *Muguetto* (1911), E. Verhaeren's *Hélène de Sparte* (Paris, May 5, 1912); the symph. poems *Nymphes au Crépuscule, Tryptique, Les Grenouilles qui demandent un Roi, Nausikaa; Les Muses sylvestres*, suite for double string quintet and piano; *Le Parc aux cerfs*, suite for oboe, string quintet, and piano; *Suite* in E for organ; for piano; *Petite Suite; En Languedoc*, suite; *La Nymphe émue ou le Faune indiscret; En Vacances*, album of little pieces; sonata; several collections of folksongs; solo songs.
BIBLIOGRAPHY: O. Séré, *Musiciens français d'aujourd'hui* (Paris, 1921); L. Moulin, *Déodat de Séverac* (1922); Blanche Selva, *Déodat de Séverac* (Paris, 1930); A. Cortot, *La Musique française de piano* (vol. 2, Paris, 1932); P. Landormy, "Déodat de Séverac," *Musical Quarterly* (April 1934); G. Soula and I. Girard, *Hommage à Déodat de Séverac* (Toulouse, 1952).

Severn, Edmund, composer and teacher; b. Nottingham, England, Dec. 10, 1862; d. Melrose, Mass., May 14, 1942. In 1866 his father, a violinist, settled in Hartford, Conn.; Severn studied violin with him and with Bernhard Listemann in Boston; composition with Chadwick in Boston and with Ph. Scharwenka in Berlin. His works include 2 symph. poems, *Lancelot and Elaine* (1898) and *Eloise and Abelard* (1915); a suite, *From Old New England* (originally for violin and piano, 1912; orchestrated and conducted by the composer at the Springfield, Mass., Music Festival, May 17, 1919); *Song Celestial*, for orch. (1912); Violin Concerto (N.Y. Philharmonic, Jan. 7, 1916); choral works; songs.

Sevitzky, Fabien, Russian conductor; b. Vishny Volochok, Russia, Sept. 29, 1891; d. Athens, Greece, Feb. 2, 1967; nephew of **Serge Koussevitzky.** He began a career as concert player on the double bass, under his original name, Koussevitzky; his uncle, who was already a celebrated double-bass player himself, suggested that he adopt a truncated form of the last name, and Sevitzky complied to avoid a family quarrel. He made his appearances as conductor in Russia under the name Sevitzky; lived in Moscow until 1922; spent a year in Poland as double-bass player in the Warsaw Philharmonic; with his wife, a Russian singer, **Maria Koussevitzky** (who retained her legal name), he went to Mexico in 1923; then emigrated to the U.S.; joined the Philadelphia Orch., and in 1925 organized the Philadelphia Chamber String Sinfonietta; he led the People's Symph. Orch. in Boston (1934–36); then was permanent conductor of the Indianapolis Symph. Orch. (1937–55) and music director of the Univ. of Miami Symph. Orch., Florida

(1959–65). He died during a guest appearance as a conductor in Athens.

Seybold, Artur, German composer; b. Hamburg, Jan. 6, 1868; d. Weissenfels, near Leipzig, Dec. 15, 1948. He studied at the Hamburg Cons.; traveled as violinist with Laube's orch. in Russia (1888); lived in Hamburg as teacher and conductor of choral societies (from 1890). His numerous compositions for violin and piano and his male choruses won considerable popularity; he also publ. a violin method, *Das neue System,* and instructive pieces.

Seydelmann, Franz, German composer; b. Dresden, Oct. 8, 1748; d. there, Oct. 23, 1806. He was the son of a player in the court orch., which he joined as a youth; studied in Italy with Josef Schuster (1765–69). In 1772 both he and Schuster were appointed composers of church music to the Elector in Dresden; later both became conductors at the court church, cembalists at the Italian Opera in Dresden, and in 1787, conductors there.
WORKS: 7 Italian operas, and a German opera, *Arsene* (Dresden, March 3, 1779); the piano score of *Arsene* is publ.; also publ. are several numbers from his operas *Il Capriccio corretto* and *La Villanella di Misnia;* 6 piano sonatas for 4 hands; 3 sonatas for piano solo; 3 flute sonatas; 3 violin sonatas. In MS are the other Italian operas, 36 Masses, 40 psalms, 37 offertories, a Requiem, numerous other vocal works, both sacred and secular.
BIBLIOGRAPHY: R. Cahn-Speyer, *Franz Seydelmann als dramatischer Komponist* (Leipzig, 1909).

Seyffardt, Ernst Hermann, German choral conductor and composer; b. Krefeld, May 6, 1859; d. Partenkirchen, Dec. 1942. He studied at the Cologne Cons. with F. Hiller and G. Jensen, and at the Berlin Hochschule für Musik with Kiel; conducted the Liedertafel in Freiburg (1887–92); in 1892 was appointed conductor of the Neuer Singverein in Stuttgart; also taught at the Stuttgart Cons.; retired in 1929.
WORKS: dramatic scene *Thusnelda;* Symphony; Violin Sonata; Piano Quartet; String Quartet; *Schicksalsgesang* for alto solo, chorus, and orch.; *Zum Gedächtniss,* for baritone solo, male chorus, and orch.; a patriotic cantata, *Aus Deutschlands grosser Zeit;* a song cycle, *Vom Schwarzwald bis zum Rhein;* other vocal works. His opera, *Die Glocken von Plurs,* was produced at Krefeld in 1912.

Seyfried, Ignaz Xaver, Ritter von, Austrian composer; b. Vienna, Aug. 15, 1776; d. there, Aug. 27, 1841. He was a close friend of Mozart, and had some piano lessons with him; studied also with Koželuh and Haydn; afterwards with Albrechtsberger. In 1797 he became conductor at Schikaneder's theater in Vienna; then at the new Theater an der Wien, when it opened in 1801, retaining this post until 1827. He was an extremely prolific composer, and some of his Singspiele were very successful; one of them, *Die Ochsenmenuette,* based on Haydn's music (Vienna, Dec. 31, 1823), gave rise to the well-known anecdote about Haydn's composing an Ox Minuet for a butcher and receiving an ox as a gift. Seyfried also wrote the opera

Der Wundermann am Rheinfall (Vienna, Oct. 26, 1799), which elicited praise from Haydn. He further wrote numerous melodramas, ballets, oratorios, motets, symphonies, quartets, etc. He publ. Beethoven's exercises in thoroughbass, counterpoint, and composition (1832), with some unwarranted additions (see Thayer's *Beethoven,* III, 80); edited a complete ed. of Albrechtsberger's theoretical works; also edited Preindl's *Wiener Tonschule* (1827; 2nd ed., 1832). For a complete list of Seyfried's theatrical works and dates of performances see Anton Bauer, *Opern und Operetten in Wien* (Graz, 1955).

Seymour, John Laurence, American composer; b. Los Angeles, Jan. 18, 1893. He studied piano with Fannie Charles Dillon; then went to Europe and took lessons in composition with Pizzetti in Italy and with Vincent d'Indy in Paris. Returning to America, he devoted himself mainly to teaching. He was one of the few American composers to have an opera performed by the Metropolitan Opera House, N.Y.; it was an exotic piece entitled *In the Pasha's Garden* (N.Y., Jan. 24, 1935). Another opera, *Ramona,* was produced at the Brigham Young Univ., in Provo, Utah (Nov. 11, 1970); he further wrote the operas, *The Devil and Tom Walker* (1926); *The Snake Woman; The Protégé of the Mistress;* and *The Affected Maids* (after Molière's *Les Précieuses ridicules*); the operettas *The Bachelor Belles, Hollywood Madness,* etc.; a piano concerto; sonatas for various instruments with piano.

Sgambati, Giovanni, celebrated Italian pianist and composer; b. Rome, May 28, 1841; d. there, Dec. 14, 1914. He studied piano with Amerigo Barbieri, and appeared in public at the age of 6; sang in church, and conducted instrumental groups. He then became a pupil of Liszt in Rome; subsequently gave orch. concerts, playing German masterpieces; performed Beethoven's *Eroica* in 1866 for the 1st time in Rome. Historically, Sgambati's concerts were important as the 1st systematic attempt to introduce to the Italian public a varied fare of symph. music. Sgambati appeared also as pianist; after a concert tour in Italy and Germany, he established in 1868 a free piano class annexed to the Accademia di Santa Cecilia in Rome, which in 1877 was formally recognized by the government as the Liceo Musicale; it became the foremost music school in Italy; Sgambati taught piano there until his death. He was an ardent admirer of Wagner, whom he met in 1876; Wagner recommended Sgambati to his own publishers, Schott of Mainz, who subsequently brought out many of Sgambati's works. As pianist and teacher, Sgambati enjoyed a very high reputation in Germany and Italy; his own music betrays strong Germanic influence; unlike most Italian composers of his time, he devoted his energies exclusively to instrumental music, avoiding all service to the theater.
WORKS: Symph. in D (Rome, March 28, 1881); Symph. No. 2; *Epitalamio sinfonico* (1887); overtures; Piano Concerto; *Te Deum* for orch.; *Messa da Requiem;* 2 piano quintets (1876; 1877; his most enduring works); String Quartet (1884); numerous piano pieces: *Fogli volanti, Pièces lyriques, Mélodies poét-*

iques, 6 Nocturnes, etc.; also *Formulario del pianista* (technical exercises); songs.

BIBLIOGRAPHY: Bettina Walker, *My Musical Experiences* (1892; pp. 44–84); R. A. Streatfeild, in *Masters of Italian Music* (1895; pp. 246–56); E. Segnitz, "Sgambatis Klaviermusik," *Musikpädagogische Blätter* 11, 12 (1911); A. de Angelis, "G. Sgambati," *Rivista Musicale Italiana* (Jan. 1912); A. Bonaventura, "G. Sgambati," *La Nuova Musica* (1914); A. Casella, "G. Sgambati," *Music & Letters* (Oct. 1925); A. Casella, in Cobbett's *Cyclopedic Survey of Chamber Music;* A. Bonaventura, "G. Sgambati," *Musica d'Oggi* (1941).

Shafran, Daniel, remarkable Russian cellist; b. Leningrad, Feb. 13, 1923. He studied cello with his father, Boris Shafran, who was an eminent cellist in his own right, and with Alexander Strimer. David Shafran received first prize at the 1937 Moscow competition for string players and at the Prague competition of 1952. He made several concert tours in Europe, and appeared in the U.S. in 1960, 1964 and 1977 with excellent success.

Shakespeare, William, English tenor and singing teacher; b. Croydon, June 16, 1849; d. London, Nov. 1, 1931. He studied at the Royal Academy of Music with Sterndale Bennett; went to Leipzig for study with Reinecke, but soon left for Milan to cultivate his voice; studied with Lamperti there. From 1875, he appeared in England as a tenor; in 1878 appointed prof. of singing at the Royal Academy of Music in London; won a high reputation as vocal teacher. His compositions are entirely in the vein of German Romanticism, his model being Mendelssohn. He publ. *The Art of Singing* (3 parts; 1898–99; several times republ.); *Singing for Schools and Colleges* (1907); *Plain Words on Singing* (1924); and *The Speaker's Art* (1931).

Shanet, Howard, American conductor; b. Brooklyn, Nov. 9, 1918. He studied cello with Evsei Beloussoff; played in the National Orchestral Association, under the direction of Leon Barzin; later studied conducting with Rudolph Thomas, Fritz Stiedry and Koussevitzky at the Berkshire Music Center in Tanglewood; took composition lessons with Hans Weisse, Paul Dessau, Martinu, Lopatnikoff and Arthur Honegger. He completed his academic studies at Columbia Univ. (A.B., 1939; A.M., 1941);. He served in the U.S. Army as Warrant Officer and Bandleader (1942–44); taught at Hunter College, N.Y. between 1945 and 1953; was on the staff at the Berkshire Music Center, Tanglewood, in the summers of 1948 to 1952; in 1953 was appointed to the faculty of Columbia Univ. and as conductor of the Univ. Orch.; in 1972 became chairman of the dept. of music; in 1974 initiated an extensive program in music performance, the first of this nature at Columbia Univ.; served as assistant conductor, N.Y. City Symph. (1947–48), conductor of the Huntington Symph. Orch., West Virginia (1951–52), a guest conductor with the Israel Philharmonic Orch. in 1950, and with the N.Y. Philharmonic (1951, 1959). In 1977 he received the presidential citation of the National Federation of Music Clubs and a certificate of distinguished service at the Institute of International Education. He composed *A War March* for military band

(1944); *Two Canonic Pieces* for 2 clarinets (1947); *Variations on a Bizarre Theme* for orch. (1960); arranged and reconstructed the score *Night of the Tropics* by Gottschalk (1955). He published an "adult education book" *Learn to Read Music* (N.Y., 1956; translated into Norwegian, 1972 and Italian, 1975); a fundamental documentary volume, *Philharmonic: A History of New York's Orchestra* (N.Y., 1975); edited and wrote a critical introduction for *Early Histories of the New York Philharmonic,* containing reprints of books by Krehbiel, Huneker and Erskine (N.Y., 1978).

Shankar, Ravi, Indian sitarist and composer; b. Benares, April 7, 1920. He was trained by his brother, Uday Shankar, and began his career as a musician and a dancer; then engaged in a serious study of the Indian classical instrument, the sitar; in time became a great virtuoso on it. As a consequence of the growing infatuation with Oriental arts in Western countries, he suddenly become popular, and his concerts were greeted with reverential awe by youthful multitudes. This popularity increased a thousandfold when the Beatles went to him to receive the revelation of Eastern musical wisdom, thus placing him on the pedestal usually reserved for untutored guitar strummers. As a composer he distinguished himself by several film scores, including the famous *Pather Panchali;* he also wrote the film scores for *Kabulliwallah* and *Anuradha.* For the Tagore Centenary he wrote a ballet *Samanya Kshati,* based on Tagore's poem of the same name; it was produced in New Delhi on May 7, 1961. He also wrote 2 concertos for sitar and orch. (1970, 1976). He publ. a memoir, *My Music, My Life* (N.Y., 1968).

Shapero, Harold, American composer; b. Lynn, Mass., April 29, 1920. He learned to play piano as a youth; was for several years a pianist in dance orchestras; began serious study in 1936, at the Malkin Cons. in Boston, with Nicolas Slonimsky; then studied with Krenek, with Walter Piston at Harvard Univ., with Paul Hindemith at the Berkshire Music Center, Tanglewood, and with Nadia Boulanger in Cambridge, Mass. He graduated from Harvard Univ. in 1941; received the American Prix de Rome for his *Nine-Minute Overture* (N.Y., June 8, 1941); held a Guggenheim Fellowship in 1946 and 1947; won the Gershwin Prize (1946), etc.; 1949–50, was in Rome; 1952, was appointed prof. at Brandeis Univ., Waltham, Mass. He married the painter Esther Geller in 1945. In his music he adheres to an austere Classical pattern, without excluding a highly emotional melodic line; his exceptional mastery of contrapuntal technique secures clarity of intermingled sonorities in his chamber music. In some of his early compositions he applied the dodecaphonic method.

WORKS: *Serenade in D* for string orch. (1945); *Symphony for Classical Orchestra* (Boston, Jan. 30, 1948); *The Travelers,* overture (1948); *Credo* for orch. (Louisville, Oct. 19, 1955); Concerto for Orch. (1951–58); *3 Pieces for 3 Pieces,* for flute, clarinet, and bassoon (1938); Trumpet Sonata (1939); String Quartet (1940); *4-Hand Piano Sonata* (1941); Violin Sonata (1942); *Partita* for piano and chamber orch. (1960); *3 Improvisations in B flat* (1968) and *3 Studies in C sharp* (1969) for piano and synthesizer; *3 Amateur Sonatas* for piano.

BIBLIOGRAPHY: Madeleine Goss, *Modern Music Makers* (N.Y., 1952; pp. 474–78).

Shapey, Ralph, American conductor and composer; b. Philadelphia, March 12, 1921. He studied violin with Emmanuel Zetlin and composition with Stefan Wolpe. In 1964 he was appointed to the faculty of the Univ. of Chicago, and conductor of the resident Contemporary Chamber Players. His music employs serialistic but uncongested procedures and acrid counterpoint, while formally adhering to neo-Classical paradigms.
WORKS: *Fantasy* for orch. (1951); symph. No. 1 (1952); Concerto for clarinet and small ensemble (1954; Strasbourg Festival, June 9, 1958); *Challenge: The Family of Man* for orch. (1955); *Ontogeny* for orch. (1958); *Invocation-Concerto* for violin and orch. (1959; N.Y., May 24, 1968); *Rituals* for orch. (1959; Chicago, May 16, 1966); *Dimensions* for soprano and 23 instruments (1960); *Incantations* for soprano and 10 instruments (1961); *Convocation* for chamber group (1962); *Chamber Symphony* for 10 solo players (1962); *Partita* for violin and 13 players (1966); *Partita-Fantasy* for cello and 16 players (1967); 7 string quartets (1946; 1949; 1950; 1953; 1957, with voice, 1963; 1972); piano quintet (1946); 2 piano sonatas (1946, 1954); *Evocation* for violin, with piano and percussion (1959; N.Y., March 26, 1960); *Soliloquy* for narrator, string quartet and percussion (1959); *Five for violin and piano* (1960); *Discourse* for 4 instruments (1961); *Seven* for piano, 4 hands (1963); Brass Quintet (1963); String Trio (1965); *Partita* for solo violin (1966); *Mutations No. 2* for piano (1966); *Deux* for 2 pianos (1967); *Songs of Ecstasy* for soprano, piano, percussion and tape (1967); *Reyem,* a "musical offering" for flute, violin and piano (1967); *Praise,* oratorio for bass-baritone, chorus and orch. (1961–71; Chicago, Feb. 28, 1976); solo songs; piano pieces.

Shapleigh, Bertram, American music theorist; b. Boston, Jan. 15, 1871; d. Washington, D.C., July 2, 1940. He studied at the New England Cons.; went to London in 1899, and remained there until 1916; then lived in New York and Washington. He made a specialty of oriental music, and gave numerous lectures on the subject. The Bertram Shapleigh Foundation was established in Washington after his death.

Shaporin, Yuri, significant Russian composer; b. Glukhov, Ukraine, Nov. 8, 1887; d. Moscow, Dec. 9, 1966. He studied law, and graduated from the Univ. of St. Petersburg in 1913; also studied at the St. Petersburg Cons. with Sokolov (composition), graduating in 1918. He wrote theatrical music in Leningrad; moved to Moscow in 1936.
WORKS: opera *The Decembrists* (1930–50; Moscow, June 23, 1953); cantata *A Tale of the Battle for the Russian Land* (Moscow, April 18, 1944); incidental music to *King Lear, Tartuffe, Boris Godunov,* and to Leskov's *The Flea* (also as an orchestral suite); symphony (Moscow, May 11, 1933); symphony-cantata, *On the Field of Kulikov* (Moscow, Nov. 18, 1939); 2 piano sonatas; several song cycles.

BIBLIOGRAPHY: Gerald Abraham, *Eight Soviet Composers* (London, 1942; pp. 89–98); E. A. Grosheva, *Yuri Shaporin* (Moscow, 1957); S. Levit, *Yuri Shaporin* (Moscow, 1964); Ivan Martynov, *Yuri Shaporin* (Moscow, 1966).

Sharp, Cecil James, English editor and collector of folksongs; b. London, Nov. 22, 1859; d. there, June 23, 1924. He studied music privately while attending Cambridge Univ.; in 1882 he went to Australia, settling in Adelaide, where he worked in a bank, and practiced law, becoming associate to the Chief Justice of Southern Australia; in 1889 he resigned from the legal profession and took up a musical career; was assistant organist of the Adelaide Cathedral, and codirector of the Adelaide College of Music. In 1892 he returned to England; was made music instructor of Ludgrove School (1893–1910) and also principal of the Hampstead Cons. (1896–1905). At the same time he became deeply interested in English folksongs; published a *Book of British Songs for Home and School* (1902); then proceeded to make a systematic survey of English villages with the aim of collecting authentic specimens of English songs. In 1911 he established the English Folk Dance Society; also was director of the School of Folk Song and Dance at Stratford-on-Avon. During World War I he was in the U.S., collecting folk music in the Appalachian Mountains, with a view of establishing their English origin. In 1923 he received the degree of M.M. (*honoris causa*) from Cambridge Univ. In 1930 the "Cecil Sharp House" was opened in London as headquarters of the English Folk Dance Society (amalgamated with the Folk Song Society in 1932. Sharp publ. many collections of folksongs and dances: *English Folk Carols* (1911); *Folk-Songs from Various Counties* (1912); *English Folk-Chanteys* (1914); *One Hundred English Folk-Songs* (1916); *Folk-Songs of English Origin* (2 vols.; 1921–23); *English Folk-Songs from the Southern Appalachians* (1917; new enlarged ed., 2 vols., ed. by Maud Karpeles, posthumous, Oxford, 1932; republ. 1952); *American-English Folk-Songs* (1918–21); *The Morris Book,* in 5 parts (1907–13); *Morris Dance Tunes,* in 10 parts (1907–13); *The Country Dance Book,* in 6 parts (1909–22); *Country Dance Tunes,* in 11 parts (1909–22); *The Sword Dances of Northern England,* in 5 parts 1911–13). Books: *English Folk Song* (London, 1907; 3rd ed., revised by Maud Karpeles, London, 1954); *The Dance: An Historical Survey of Dancing in Europe,* with A. P. Oppé (London, 1924).
BIBLIOGRAPHY: W. S. Shaw, "Cecil Sharp and Folk Dancing," *Music & Letters* (Jan. 1921); A. H. Fox Strangways and M. Karpeles, *Cecil Sharp* (London, 1933; 2nd ed., London, 1955).

Sharp, Geoffrey (Newton), English music critic; b. Leeds, June 14, 1914; d. Chelmsford (Essex), March 29, 1974. He studied at Trinity College, Cambridge, and also at the Royal College of Music in London. In 1940 he began publication of the quarterly *Music Review* in Cambridge. He also wrote articles on music for various journals.

Sharpe, Herbert Francis, English pianist and composer; b. Halifax, Yorkshire, March 1, 1861; d. London, Oct. 14, 1925. He studied piano at the National Training School in London; joined the faculty of the Royal College of Music in 1884; gave numerous concerts in London and elsewhere; composed many piano pieces and publ. *Pianoforte School* (with Stanley Lucas).

Shattuck, Arthur, American pianist; b. Neenah, Wis., April 19, 1881; d. New York, Oct. 16, 1951. He studied piano with Leschetizky in Vienna (1895–1902); made his home in Paris, touring extensively in many countries including Iceland and Egypt. Returning to America, he appeared as soloist with many orchestras.

Shaverzashvili, Alexander, Soviet composer; b. Tiflis, Caucasus, July 8, 1919. He studied at the Tiflis Cons. with Andrei Balanchivadze; from 1955, prof. at the Tiflis Cons. He wrote a comic opera, *Grasshopper* (Tiflis, March 18, 1955); Symph. (1945); 2 piano concertos (1946; 1949); Piano Quintet (1955); String Quartet; Piano Trio; Violin Sonata; songs.

Shavitch, Vladimir, American conductor; b. Russia, July 20, 1888; d. Palm Beach, Fla., Dec. 26, 1947. He studied piano with Godowsky and Busoni in Berlin, and composition with Hugo Kaun and Paul Juon (1902–12). Coming to America in 1914, he became conductor of the Syracuse, N.Y., Symph. Orch.; also conducted in Rochester, N.Y. (1923–27); appeared as guest conductor in European capitals.

Shaw, Arnold, American composer, writer, editor, lecturer, and music executive; b. Brooklyn, June 28, 1909. He majored in English literature at Columbia Univ. (M.A., 1931); also studied music; composed a number of snappy piano pieces with a sophisticated tilt (*The Mod Muppet, Bubblegum Waltzes, Stabiles Mobiles*) and singable songs (*Dungaree Doll, Woman is a Five-Letter Word*); edited the mind-boggling books by Joseph Schillinger (*Mathematical Basis of the Arts; Schillinger System of Musical Composition*); lectured at the Juilliard School of Music, New School of Social Research, Univ. of California, Los Angeles; promoted popular singers as general manager of Edward B. Marks Music Corporation, among them Rod McKuen, Burt Bacharach, and Elvis Presley. He lives in Las Vegas; in 1973–74 was named Nevada Composer of the Year. WRITINGS: *Lingo of Tin Pan Alley* (N.Y., 1950); *The Money Song,* a novel (N.Y., 1953); *Belafonte: An Unauthorized Biography* (N.Y., 1960); *Sinatra: 20th Century Romantic* (N.Y., 1968); *The Rock Revolution* (N.Y., 1969); *The World of Soul: Black America's Contribution to the Pop Music Scene* (N.Y., 1970); *The Street That Never Slept* (N.Y., 1971); *The Rockin' 50s* (N.Y., 1974); *Honkers and Shouters: The Rhythm & Blues Years* (N.Y., 1978).

Shaw, Artie (real name **Arthur Arshawsky**), American clarinetist and bandleader; b. New York, May 23, 1910. He played clarinet in bands as a boy; after playing with a variety of radio and dance bands, he formed his own band in 1935, becoming one of the foremost proponents of "big band swing"; his greatest hit, among more than 600 recordings, was that of Cole Porter's song, *Begin the Beguine.* But he considered his fabulous commercial successes as artistically unfulfilling, and throughout his career made attempts for recognition as a "serious" musician. In the 1930s he introduced a group consisting of clarinet, string quartet, and a rhythm section; sporadically, from 1939 to 1954, he led small combos of from 5 to 7 players (but always labeled the "Gramercy 5") in experimental jazz attempts, these groups sometimes including celesta or harpsichord; he also performed as soloist in several clarinet concertos in 1949. He was married consecutively to several movie stars (Lana Turner, Ava Gardner, etc.); in between he also wed the sex authoress Kathleen Winsor. He published a quasi-autobiographical novel *The Trouble with Cinderella* (N.Y., 1952), and a novel, *I Love You, I Hate You, Drop Dead!* (1965).
BIBLIOGRAPHY: Vladimir Simosko, "Artie Shaw and His Gramercy Fives," *Journal of Jazz Studies* (Oct. 1973).

Shaw, Frank Holcomb, American organist and teacher; b. Paxton, Illinois, May 8, 1884; d. Oberlin, Ohio, Sept. 1, 1959. He studied at Oberlin Cons.; then went to Paris where he took organ lessons with Widor; upon returning to the U.S. he filled various teaching posts; from 1924 to 1949 was director of the Oberlin Cons.

Shaw, George Bernard, famous Irish dramatist; b. Dublin, July 26, 1856; d. Ayot St. Lawrence, England, Nov. 2, 1950. Before winning fame as a playwright, he was active as a music critic in London, writing for *The Star* (under the name of "Corno di Bassetto") during the season of 1888–89, and for *The World* from 1890 to 1894. In 1899 he publ. *The Perfect Wagnerite,* a highly individual socialistic interpretation of the *Ring of the Nibelung.* His criticisms from *The World* were reprinted as *Music in London* in 3 vols. (1932; new ed., 1950); those from *The Star* as *London Music in 1888–89* (London and N.Y., 1937); selected criticisms were publ., ed. by Eric Bentley, in N.Y., 1954. Shaw's play *Arms and the Man* was made into an operetta, *The Chocolate Soldier,* by Oskar Straus (1908); his *Pygmalion* was converted into a highly successful musical comedy (1956) under the title *My Fair Lady,* with a musical score by Frederick Loewe.
BIBLIOGRAPHY: W. Irvine, "G. B. Shaw's Musical Criticism," *Musical Quarterly* (July 1946).

Shaw, Martin, English organist and composer; b. London, March 9, 1875; d. Southwald, Sussex, Oct. 24, 1958. He was a pupil at the Royal College of Music in London; played organ in various churches in London. In 1900 he founded the Purcell Society in London; wrote an opera, *Mr. Pepys* (London, Feb. 11, 1926); several masques and ballads; the oratorios *Easter, The Rock* (after T. S. Eliot), *The Redeemer;* sacred choruses; etc. He publ. *The Principles of English Church Music Composition* (1921); edited *The English Carol Book, Songs of Britain, The Motherland Song Book,* and (with his brother, Geoffrey Shaw) *The League of Nations Song Book.* He publ. his autobiography, *Up to Now,* in 1929. His brother **Geoffrey Shaw** (b. London, Nov. 14, 1879; d. there, April 14, 1943) was an organist and composer; also was active in musical education.

Shaw, Mary ((*née* **Postans**), English contralto; b. London, 1814; d. Hadleigh Hall, Suffolk, Sept. 9, 1876. She studied with Sir George Smart; made her debut in London in 1834 with marked success; in 1838 sang in the Gewandhaus, Leipzig, under Mendelssohn's direction, and in other German cities. She made her operatic debut at La Scala, Milan, on Nov. 17, 1839; in 1842 she sang at Covent Garden and the principal festivals in England. In 1844, at the height of her success, her career was suddenly ended when her husband (the painter Alfred Shaw, whom she had married in 1835) became insane and died; the shock affected her vocal cords, so that she was unable to sing. Some time later she remarried and went to live in the country.

Shaw, Oliver, a blind American organist, composer, and singer; b. Middleboro, Mass., March 13, 1779; d. Providence, Dec. 31, 1848. He was a singing teacher and church organist in Providence from 1807; composer of popular psalm tunes and ballads, which he sang in public; some favorites were *Mary's Tears, The Inspiration, Sweet Little Ann,* and *The Death of Perry.* He publ. the collection *The Social Sacred Melodist* (1835).
BIBLIOGRAPHY: T. Williams, *A Discourse on the Life and Death of Oliver Shaw* (Boston, 1851); *Memorial of Oliver Shaw* (Providence, 1884); B. N. Degen, *Oliver Shaw: His Music and Contribution to American Society* (Univ. of Rochester, 1971).

Shaw, Robert, American conductor; b. Red Bluff, Calif., April 30, 1916. He studied at Pomona College, graduating in 1938. In 1941 he founded the Collegiate Chorale in N.Y., giving numerous and highly praised performances of choral works of various periods (until 1954); received a Guggenheim Fellowship in 1944; was choral director at the Berkshire Music Center, Tanglewood (1942–45); on the faculty of the Juilliard School of Music, N.Y. (1946–50); in 1948 founded the Robert Shaw Chorale and toured with it in the U.S.; conductor of the San Diego, Calif., Symph. (summer seasons) from 1953; in 1956, appointed associate conductor of the Cleveland Orch.; also made guest appearances with major American orchestras. In 1967 he was appointed conductor of the Atlanta Symph. Orch.

Shchedrin, Rodion, brilliant Soviet composer; b. Moscow, Dec. 16, 1932. He studied with Shaporin at the Moscow Cons., graduating in 1955. In his music he developed a richly harmonious idiom, diversified by impulsive rhythms.
WORKS: opera *Not Only for Love* (Moscow, 1961); the ballets, *The Humpback Horse* (1955; extremely popular in Russia) and *Anna Karenina* (1972); 3 piano concertos (1954, 1966, 1976); Symph. No. 1 (1958); Symph. No. 2 (1962–65; includes a section which artfully imitates the tuning of an orchestra); *Obstreperous Street Tunes* for orch. (1963; extremely popular); *Chimes* for orch., commissioned by the N.Y. Philhar-

monic (N.Y., Jan. 11, 1968); *Chamber Orchestra Suite* for 20 violins, harp, accordion and 2 double basses (1961); Piano Quintet (1952); 2 string quartets (1951, 1954); *24 Preludes and Fugues* for piano (1969–70); *Polyphonic Album* for piano (1973); oratorio, *Lenin Dwells In the Heart of the People* (1969); *Bureaucratiade* for voices and orch., a satirical work (1963); *Poetorium,* for speaker, chorus and orch. (1969). He made an ingenious arrangement of fragments from Bizet's *Carmen* as a ballet suite, scored for strings and percussion, reducing Bizet's romantic melodies to a coarse but extremely effective ensemble, which he wrote for his wife, the ballerina Maya Plisetskaya (1968).
BIBLIOGRAPHY: N. Rogozhina, *Rodion Shchedrin* (Moscow, 1959).

Shcherbachev, Vladimir, Russian composer; b. Warsaw, Jan. 24, 1889; d. Leningrad, March 5, 1952. He studied at the St. Petersburg Cons. with Maximilian Steinberg and Liadov, graduating in 1914. From 1924 to 1931 he was prof. of composition at the Leningrad Cons. He wrote an opera *Anna Kolosova* (1939); 5 symphonies (1914, 1926, 1932, 1935, 1948); music for films; the orchestral suite from one of them, *The Thunderstorm,* became popular in Russia; he further wrote *A Fairy Tale* for orch. (Petrograd, Dec. 20, 1915); Nonet (1917); numerous piano works.

Shearing, George Albert, English-American jazz pianist; b. London, Aug. 13, 1919. He was blind from birth, learned to read music with Braille notation; for several years he played piano in a blind band; then transferred to the U.S. (naturalized 1955) and organized a quintet, with vibraphone, guitar, drums and bass. In the early 1940s he played a typical stride style of the time; in the late 1940s, influenced by the innovations of bebop, he developed a new manner characterized by surprising, extended harmonies, and a pianistic technique whereby both hands play thick chords in parallel motion ("locked-hand style"). He composed famous tunes, among them *Lullaby of Birdland.*

Shebalin, Vissarion, Russian composer; b. Omsk, June 11, 1902; d. Moscow, May 29, 1963. He studied at the Moscow Cons. with Miaskovsky, graduating in 1928; in 1935, appointed prof. of composition there; from 1942 till 1948 was its director.
WORKS: a musical comedy, *Bridegroom from the Embassy* (Sverdlovsk, Aug. 1, 1942); opera, *The Taming of the Shrew,* after Shakespeare (Moscow, Oct. 1 1955); 5 symphonies (1925, 1929, 1934, 1935, 1962); symph. poem *Lenin,* with chorus and soloists (Moscow, Jan. 21, 1933); *Russian Overture* (1941); Violin Concerto (1940); cantata, *Moscow* (Moscow, Dec. 14, 1946); *Sun Over the Steppes,* opera (Moscow, June 9, 1958); Symph. No. 5 (Moscow, Oct. 9, 1962); Horn Concertino (1930; revised 1959); 9 string quartets; Piano Trio; Viola Sonata; several piano sonatas; song.
BIBLIOGRAPHY: Gerald Abraham, *Eight Soviet Composers* (London, 1943; pp. 61–69); Igor Boelza, *V. Shebalin* (Moscow, 1945).

Shedlock, John South, English writer on music; b. Reading, Sept. 29, 1843; d. London, Jan. 9, 1919. After graduating from London Univ. (1864) he studied composition with Lalo in Paris; upon his return to London, he devoted himself to writing; was music critic of *The Academy* (1879–1901) and of *The Athenæum* (from 1901). He publ. a detailed description of Beethoven's sketch book purchased by the British Museum (*Musical Times*, June 1892–Jan. 1893); this led him to further investigations of Beethoven memorabilia, and in 1893 he discovered in Berlin a copy of Cramer's studies with notations by Beethoven; publ. his findings as *The Beethoven-Cramer Studies* (1893); also publ. 2 vols. of Beethoven's letters in English translation, a short biography of Beethoven in Bell's *Miniature Series* (1905, and a valuable book, *The Pianoforte Sonata, Its Origin and Development* (London, 1895); edited Kuhnau's *Biblical Sonatas* (1895) and harpsichord pieces by Frescobaldi and Froberger.

Shekhter, Boris, Russian composer; b. Odessa, Jan. 20, 1900; d. Moscow, Dec. 16, 1961. He was graduated from the Odessa Cons. in 1922; then entered the Moscow Cons., studying composition with Vassilenko and Miaskovsky; graduated in 1929. In 1940 he went to Turkestan, and became prof. of the Cons. of Ashkhabad.
WORKS: the operas *The Year 1905* (with A. Davidenko, 1935) and *Yusup and Akhmed* (Ashkhabad, June 12, 1942); cantatas, *Volga-Don* (1952) and *A House in Shushenskoye* (1955); 5 symphonies (1929, 1943, 1945, 1947, 1951); an orch. suite, *Turkmenia*, based on Central Asian themes (1932; his best work; given at the Florence Festival of the International Society for Contemporary Music, April 4, 1934); *Rhapsody*, for orch. (1935); piano pieces; songs.

Shelley, Harry Rowe, American organist and composer; b. New Haven, Conn., June 8, 1858; d. Short Beach, Conn., Sept. 12, 1947. He was a pupil of Dudley Buck and Dvořák in New York; from 1899 was active as church organist and teacher.
WORKS: 3 operas: *Leila, Romeo and Juliet,* and *Lotus San;* the symph. poem *The Crusaders;* orch. suite *Souvenir de Baden-Baden;* the cantatas *Vexilla Regis* (N.Y., 1894), *Lochinvar's Ride* (N.Y., 1915), *Death and Life,* and *The Inheritance Divine;* much choral music and some effective piano pieces. His ballads *Minstrel Boy* and *Love's Sorrow* attained considerable success. He also edited the popular collections *Gems for the Organ, The Modern Organist,* and *101 Interludes for Organ.*

Shenshin, Alexander, Russian composer; b. Moscow, Nov. 18, 1890; d. there, Feb. 18, 1944. He studied philology at Moscow Univ.; later took music lessons with Grechaninov and Glière. He subsequently taught music in Moscow, and also conducted occasional symphony concerts. His music is cast in a style reminiscent of Liadov; the elements of exotic musical patterns are noticeable. He composed an opera *O T'ao* (1925); the ballets *Ancient Dances* (1933) and *Story of Carmen* (1935); a song cycle, *From Japanese Anthologies;* and numerous songs to German poems.

BIBLIOGRAPHY: V. Belaiev, *A. A. Shenshin* (Moscow, 1929; in Russian and German).

Shepard, Frank Hartson, American pianist and pedagogue; b. Bethel, Conn., Sept. 20, 1863; d. Orange, N.J., Feb. 15, 1913. He studied music in Boston; then took courses at the Leipzig Cons. (1886–90) with Jadassohn, Reinecke, and others. Returning to America in 1891, he established the Shepard School of Music at Orange, N.J., of which he was director until his death; also was organist at Grace Church there. He publ. *Piano Touch and Scales; Church Music and Choir Training; How to Modulate; Harmony Simplified; Children's Harmony;* etc.

Shepherd, Arthur, eminent American composer and pedagogue; b. Paris, Idaho, Feb. 19, 1880; d. Cleveland, Jan. 12, 1958. He studied with G. Haessel; in 1892, entered the New England Cons., where he studied piano with Dennée and Carl Faelten, and composition with Goetschius and Chadwick. In 1897 he went to Salt Lake City, where he settled as teacher and conductor of the Salt Lake Symph. Orch.; returned to Boston in 1908, and became prof. of harmony and counterpoint at the New England Cons. (until 1917). In 1917 he joined the U.S. Army, and was bandmaster of the 303rd Field Artillery in France. From 1920 to 1926 he was assistant conductor of the Cleveland Orch., and also conducted children's concerts there; was music critic of the Cleveland *Press* (1929–32). In 1927 he became prof. of music at Western Reserve Univ., retiring in 1950; then lived in Boston and Cleveland. A composer of national tendencies, he wrote in a grand Romantic manner, derived from an intense feeling for American melos.
WORKS: FOR ORCH: the overtures *The Nuptials of Attila, Ouverture joyeuse* (Paderewski Prize, 1902), *The Festival of Youth* (1915), and *Overture to a Drama* (1919; Cleveland, March 27, 1924); *Fantaisie Humoresque,* for piano and orch. (Boston, Feb. 8, 1918); *Horizons,* 1st Symph. (Cleveland, Dec. 15, 1927); *Choreographic Suite* (Cleveland, Oct. 22, 1931); 2nd Symph. (Cleveland, March 7, 1940); *Fantasy on Down East Spirituals* (Indianapolis, Nov. 2, 1946); Violin Concerto (1946–47); *Theme and Variations* (Cleveland, April 9, 1953); *Hilaritas,* overture for concert band (1942); FOR CHORUS: *Song of the Sea Wind,* for women's voices and piano (1915); *He Came All So Still,* for women's voices a cappella (1915); *Deck Thyself My Soul,* for mixed chorus and organ (1918); *Ballad of Trees and the Master,* for mixed chorus a cappella (1935); *Song of the Pilgrims,* cantata for tenor solo, mixed chorus, and orch. (1937); *Invitation to the Dance,* for mixed chorus and piano (1937); *Grace for Gardens,* for mixed chorus a cappella (1938); *Build Thee More Stately Mansions,* for women's voices (1938); *Psalm XLII,* for chorus and orch. (1944); *Drive On,* for baritone solo and mixed chorus (1946); CHAMBER MUSIC: 2 violin sonatas (1914, 1927); *Triptych,* for voice and string quartet (1926); 3 string quartets (1927, 1935, 1936); Piano Quintet (1940); *Praeludium Salutatorium,* for flute, oboe, horn, bassoon, violin, viola, and cello (1942); *Divertissement,* for flute, oboe, clarinet, bassoon, and horn (1943); FOR PIANO: 2 sonatas (1907, 1929, both in F minor); songs. He publ. a

valuable handbook, *The String Quartets of Beethoven* (Cleveland, 1937).

BIBLIOGRAPHY: D. Leedy, "Arthur Shepherd," *Modern Music* (1939); W. S. Newman, "Arthur Shepherd," *Musical Quarterly* (April 1950).

Shera, Frank Henry, English writer on music; b. Sheffield, May 4, 1882; d. there, Feb. 21, 1956. He studied at the Royal College of Music in London, where his teachers were Stanford, Parratt, and Walford Davies. He was music director at Malvern College from 1916 to 1926; in 1928 he was appointed prof. of music at Sheffield Univ., retiring in 1950. He publ. *Musical Groundwork* (1922); *Debussy and Ravel* (1925) and *Elgar's Instrumental Works* (1931) in the Musical Pilgrim series.

Sheremetiev, Alexander, Count, Russian nobleman and amateur musician; b. St. Petersburg, March 12, 1859; d. Ste.-Geneviève-des-Bois, near Paris, May 18, 1931. The private choir maintained by his father, Dmitri, attained wide celebrity in St. Petersburg. In 1882 Count Alexander founded a symph. orch. in his own name, and in 1884 a church choir under the direction of Archangelsky. In 1898 he instituted in St. Petersburg a series of symph. concerts at popular prices, conducted by himself and others. Thanks to his inherited wealth, he was able to engage excellent musicians; presented programs of Russian composers, thus contributing to the cause of national music. He also wrote some pieces himself (*Pathetische Fantasie,* for orch.; chamber music; etc.). After the revolution of 1917 he went to Paris, and died in poverty, in a Russian charity institution near Paris.

Sheridan, Frank, American pianist; b. New York, May 1, 1898; d. there, April 15, 1962. He studied piano with Harold Bauer; made his debut with the N.Y. Philharmonic at the Lewisohn Stadium in 1924; toured in Europe in 1929–30; joined the faculty of the Mannes Music School, N.Y., also taught at Columbia Univ.

Sheriff, Noam, Israeli composer; b. Tel Aviv, Jan. 7, 1935. He took private lessons in composition with Ben-Haim (1949–57); studied philosophy at the Hebrew Univ. of Jerusalem (1956–60); then went to Germany and attended classes of Boris Blacher at the Hochschule für Musik in Berlin (1960–62). Returning to Israel, he taught at the Jerusalem Academy of Music and at the National Academy in Tel Aviv. Most of his works are inspired by Jewish folk rhythms and melodic patterns, arranged in modernistic atonal and asymmetrical configurations.
WORKS: *Song of Degrees,* for orch. (1960); *Ashrei (Blessed Is the Man)* for contralto, flute, 2 harps and 2 tom-toms (1961); *Destination Five Minutes* for brass and percussion (1962); *Heptaprisms,* ballet music (1965); *Israel Suite* for orch. (1965); *Confession* for solo cello (1966); *Arabesque* for solo flute (1966); *3 Inventions:* for solo flute (1967); horn (1968), and harp (1968); *2 Epigrams* for chamber orch. (1968); *Cain,* electronic ballet music (1969); String Quartet (1968–69); *A Stone in the Tower of David* for orch. (1972); numerous arrangements of folk songs for the Israeli Broadcasting Authority.

Sherman, Norman, American-born composer and bassoonist living in Canada; b. Boston, Feb. 25, 1926. He studied composition at Boston Univ. (1946–50); then took lessons with Messiaen in Paris (1950). He was principal bassoonist with the Winnipeg Symph. Orch. (1957–61), The Hague Philh. in Holland (1961–69), National Arts Centre Orch. of Ottawa (1969–73), Radio Symph. Orch. of Israel (1973–74) and, since 1974, with the Kingston (Ontario) Symph.; also taught bassoon and chamber music at the Queen's Univ. in Kingston.
WORKS: Concerto for flute, clarinet, horn, bassoon and piano (1948); *Traditions* for wind quintet (1948); a ballet, *The Red Seed* (1950); *Sinfonia Concertante* for bassoon and strings (1950; Winnipeg, Jan. 19, 1961); *Two Pieces* for orch. (No. 1, 1953; No. 2, 1963); *Through the Rainbow and/or Across the Valley* for orch. (1967; Rotterdam, April 25, 1968); *The Reunion* for flute, violin, viola and cello (1967–72); *Thesis* for orch. (1974; Kingston, March 23, 1975); *Canadian Summer* for orch. (1975); *Quadron* for string quartet (1976); *Quintessant* for wind quintet (1977); *Bouquet* for piano or celesta, and clarinet and 3 percussionists (1977).

Sherwood, William Hall, American pianist and pedagogue; b. Lyons, N.Y., Jan. 31, 1854; d. Chicago, Jan. 7, 1911. He was the son of Rev. L. H. Sherwood, the founder of Lyons Music Academy, from whom he received his primary education; spent 5 years in Germany studying with Kullak in Berlin; also took lessons with Liszt in Weimar. He returned to the U.S. in 1876; taught at the New England Cons., and later at the Chicago Cons.; in 1897 established his Sherwood Piano School in Chicago. Among his publ. compositions for piano are 2 suites and 2 sets of *Gypsy Dances.*

Shibata, Minao, Japanese composer; b. Tokyo, Sept. 29, 1916. He attended the Tokyo Univ., graduating from the faculty of science in 1939; took private lessons in composition with Saburo Moroi (1940–43); taught at the Tokyo Univ. of Arts (1959–69).
WORKS: a radio opera, *Strada a Roma* (1961); Piano Sonata (1943); 2 string quartets (1943, 1947); *Classical Suite* for violin and piano (1947); *Symbology* for soprano and chamber orch. (1953); *Black Portrait* for soprano and chamber orch. (1954); *Musique concrète* for stereo tape (1955); 2 *Improvisations* for piano (1957, 1968); *Black Distance* for soprano and chamber orch. (1958); *3 Poems on Katsue Kitazono* for soprano and chamber orch. (1954–58); Sinfonia (1960; Tokyo, Dec. 12, 1960); *Michi (The Street)* for chorus and 4 percussion instruments (1960); *Poem Recited in the Night* for soprano and chamber orch. (1963); *Essay* for 3 trumpets and 3 trombones (1965); *Improvisation for Electronic Sounds* (1968); *Imagery* for marimba (1969); *Display '70 I* and *II* for ryûteki, marimba, percussion and tape (1969, 1970); *Concerto for 8* for 8 flutes (1971).

Shield, William, English violinist and composer; b. Whickham, Durham, March 5, 1748; d. Brightling, Sussex, Jan. 25, 1829. He was taught by his father, a singing master, on whose death he was apprenticed to a ship builder; at the same time he took lessons in music with Charles Avison, at Newcastle-on-Tyne; played violin in various small theaters in the neighborhood; in 1772 he settled in London, as violinist at the Opera; from 1773 to 1791 he played the viola there. He produced his first comic opera, *A Flitch of Bacon,* at the Haymarket Theatre in 1778; it was followed by a great number of theatrical pieces; he held the post of composer to Covent Garden Theatre from 1778 till 1791; then traveled in France and Italy, returning to Covent Garden in 1792, retaining his position until 1797. He was appointed Master of the King's Music in 1817. He wrote about 40 light operas, pantomines, musical farces, ballad operas, etc., of which only separate numbers were ever published; he also wrote 6 string quartets; 6 string trios; 6 duets for 2 violins; other instrumental pieces; publ. *An Introduction to Harmony* (1800) and *Rudiments of Thoroughbass* (c.1815). He had some original ideas, and was not averse to experimentation; e.g., he wrote movements in 5/4 time.

BIBLIOGRAPHY: G. Hauger, "William Shield," *Music & Letters* (Oct. 1950).

Shifrin, Seymour J., American composer; b. New York, Feb. 28, 1926. He studied music at Columbia Univ. (M.A., 1949), and privately with William Schuman and Darius Milhaud. He taught at the Univ. of California, Berkeley (1952–66); in 1966 was appointed to the faculty of Brandeis Univ., at Waltham, Mass. He was twice a recipient of Guggenheim Fellowship grants (1956, 1959).

WORKS: 4 string quartets (1949, 1962, 1966, 1967); Cello Sonata (1948); *Serenade* for 5 instruments (1958); *3 Pieces* for orch. (Minneapolis, Jan. 8, 1960); Chamber Symph. (1961); *Satires of Circumstances* for soprano, flute, clarinet, violin, cello, double bass and piano (1964); *Chronicles* for voices and orch. (1970); song cycles; piano pieces.

Shilkret, Nathaniel, American composer and conductor; b. New York, Jan. 1, 1895. He studied with Pietro Floridia; until the age of 20, he played the clarinet in various orchestras in N.Y.; was also clarinetist in bands led by John Philip Sousa, Arthur Pryor, and Edwin Franko Goldman. In 1916, became music director of the Victor Talking Machine Co., creating the Victor Salon Orch.; held executive posts with Victor until 1935; then went to Hollywood as arranger, but continued to spend part of the season in N.Y.; led thousands of radio broadcasts. He wrote a symph. poem, *Skyward* (1928); Trombone Concerto (1942); numerous descriptive pieces for orch.; popular songs. He commissioned Schoenberg, Stravinsky, Toch, Milhaud, Castelnuovo-Tedesco, and Tansman to write a movement each for a biblical cantata *Genesis,* to which he also contributed (1947). In 1977 he lived in Franklin Square, N.Y.

Shimizu, Osamu, prolific Japanese composer; b. Osaka, Nov. 4, 1911. He studied composition with Hashimoto and Hosokawa at the Tokyo Music Academy, graduating in 1937; was active in the music dept. of the Tokyo Radio Station; wrote articles on music.

WORKS: 10 operas: *The Tale of the Mask-Maker Shuzenji* (Osaka, Nov. 4, 1954), *The Charcoal Princess*

(Osaka, Nov. 1, 1956), *The Man Who Shoots at the Blue Sky* (Osaka, Nov. 26, 1956), *Gauche, the Violoncellist* (Osaka, Oct. 11, 1957), *The Singing Skeleton* (Osaka, March 15, 1962), *Shunkan, the Exile* (Osaka, Nov. 18, 1964), *The Merciful Poet* (operetta, 1965), *Muko Erabi (The Marriage Contest),* comic opera (Los Angeles, Oct. 3, 1968), *Daibutsu-Kaigen (The Great Image of Buddha,* historic opera on the inauguration of the bronze statue of Buddha on April 9, 752 A.D.; Tokyo, Oct. 2, 1970) and *Ikuta Gawa (The River Ikuta;* Tokyo, Nov. 10, 1971); the ballets *The Sun* (1955), *The Crane* (1956), *The Earth* (1957), *Araginu* (1958), *Fire in the Field* (1962) and *Love Poems* (1966); numerous cantatas, including *Ren-nyo* (Tokyo, April 8, 1948), *La Paix* (Tokyo, April 22, 1949) and *Hymn to Dengyō-Daishi* (1966); 3 symphonies: No. 1 (Tokyo, Dec. 8, 1951), No. 2 (1957) and No. 3 (1961); *Dance Suite on the Themes of Flowers* for orch. (1944); *Poème* for flute and orch. (1950); *4 Movements on Indian Melodies* for orch. (1950); *Suite* for orch. (1953); *Taiheiraku,* gagaku for orch. (1971); String Quartet (1940); *Ballad* for flute and piano (1940); *Ballad* for violin and orch. (1941); Quartet for flute, oboe, clarinet and bassoon (1958); *Olympic Hymn* for the opening of the Olympic Games in Japan (Tokyo, Oct. 10, 1964).

Shimoyama, Hifumi, Japanese composer; b. Aomoriken, June 21, 1930. He studied violin with Hiroshi Narita and composition with Yoritsuné Matsudaira; was a member of the "Group 20.5," with the aim of promoting new music, which included works by Yori-Aki Matsudaira, Kenjiro Ezaki and others (1956–62).

WORKS: Violin Sonata (1956); String Quartet (1959); Piano Sonata (1960); *Structure* for 4 players (1961); *Dialog* for cello and piano (1962); *Dialog 1* and *2* for 2 guitarists (1963, 1971); *Reflections* for strings in 3 groups (1967; Hamburg Festival of the International Society for Contemporary Music, June 27, 1969); *Zone* for 16 strings (1970); *2 Ceremonies* for solo cello (1969, 1971); *Exorcism* for 5 strings (1970); *Breath* for chorus, percussion, piano and 3 horns (1971; Tokyo, Nov. 9, 1972); *MSP* for violin and piano (1972); *Wave* for solo cello, strings, harp, piano and percussion (1972); *Transmigration* for percussion and double bass (1973); *Poem* for cello, piano and tape (1974).

Shindo, Tak, American composer; b. Sacramento, Calif. of Japanese parentage, Nov. 11, 1922. He studied music at the Univ. of Southern Calif., orchestration with Miklós Rózsa. As a musicologist he specialized in Japanese music. He became active as composer and arranger in various motion picture studios in Hollywood.

Shinohara, Makota, Japanese composer; b. Osaka, Dec. 10, 1931. He studied composition with Ikenouchi at the Tokyo Univ. of Arts (1952–54); went to France where he took lessons at the Paris Cons. (1954–60); subsequently traveled to Germany and took courses with B. A. Zimmermann at the Hochschule für Musik in Cologne (1962–64) and with Stockhausen at the Cologne State Cons. (1964–65); later worked at the Electronic Music Studio of Utrecht Univ. (1965–66) and at the Columbia-Princeton Electronic Music Studio in

N.Y. (1971–72). Returning to Japan he joined the staff of the Tokyo Radio.

WORKS: Violin Sonata (1958); *3 pièces concertantes* for trumpet and piano (1959); *Obsession* for oboe and piano (1960); *Solitude* for orch. (1961); *Alternance* for 6 percussionists (1961–62); *Tendance* for piano (1962); *Vision* and *Mémoires* for tape (1965, 1966); *Consonance* for flute, horn, cello, harp, vibraphone and marimba (1967); *Personnage* for solo male voice and stereo tape, with optional pantomime and color lighting (1968); *Visione II* for orch. (1970); *Reflexion* for solo oboe (1970); *City Visit* for tape (1971); *Rencontre* for percussion and tape (1972); *Tayutai* for koto (1972); *Kyudo* for shakuhachi and harp (1973).

Shira, Francesco, Italian composer and conductor; b. Malta, Aug. 21, 1808; d. London, Oct. 15, 1883. He studied at the Milan Cons. with Basili; brought out his first opera, *Elena e Malvina,* at La Scala, Milan (Nov. 17, 1832); on the strength of his success he was engaged as conductor of the Santo Carlos Theater in Lisbon (1833–42); also taught at the Lisbon Cons. In 1842, after a brief sojourn in Paris, he became conductor for the English Opera at the Princess's Theatre; then conducted at Drury Lane (1844–47); in 1848 he went over to Covent Garden; returned to Drury Lane in 1852; in later years made a high reputation as a singing teacher, without abandoning composition; wrote the operas *Niccolò de' Lapi* (London, 1863), *Selvaggia* (Venice, Feb. 20, 1875), and *Lia* (Venice, 1876).

Shirinsky, Vassily, Russian composer; b. Ekaterinodar, Jan. 17, 1901; d. Moscow, Aug. 16, 1965. He studied violin with Conus and composition with Catoire and Miaskovsky at the Moscow Cons. As violin soloist he contributed much to early propaganda for modern Russian music, playing the 1st Concerto of Prokofiev and other new works. His own music is characterized by considerable rhythmic complexity, but remains within the confines of traditional harmony. He wrote an opera, *Ivan the Terrible* (1951–54); 2 symphonies; several overtures; Piano Quintet; 4 string quartets; Piano Trio; Violin Sonata; Viola Sonata; Cello Sonata; film music; songs.

Shirley-Quirk, John, English baritone; b. Liverpool, Aug. 2, 1931. (His hyphenated name is composed of Shirley, in Derbyshire, where his ancestors lived, and the Celtic appellation in the language of Manx on the channel Isle of Man). He studied chemistry at the Univ. of Liverpool; taught physics and chemistry in a British Air Force station; at the same time he took lessons in singing. Benjamin Britten engaged him to sing in his church parables at Aldeburgh Festivals; he subsequently sang the multiple role of several individuals in Britten's opera *Death in Venice;* other roles were with the Scottish Opera in the classical repertory.

Shishov, Ivan, Russian composer; b. Novocherkask, Oct. 8, 1888; d. Moscow, Feb. 6, 1947. He studied with Kastalsky and G. Conus; conducted choral groups; taught at the Moscow Cons. (1925–31). He wrote the opera, *Painter Serf* (Moscow, March 24, 1929); 2 symphonies (1925; 1933); several song cycles, arrangements of folksongs.

Shnitke, Alfred., See **Schnittke, Alfred.**

Shore, John, English trumpeter; b. London, 1662; d. there, Nov. 20, 1752. In 1707 he succeeded his uncle **William Shore** as Sergeant Trumpeter to the English Court; in 1711 he was one of the 24 musicians to Queen Anne, and also a lutenist of the Chapel Royal. He is the reputed inventor of the tuning fork. Purcell wrote for Shore trumpet obbligatos to many of his songs.

Shore, Samuel Royle, English music scholar, editor, and composer; b. Birmingham, April 12, 1856; d. Hindhead, Surrey, Feb. 19, 1946. He studied organ with A. R. Gaul, but was mostly self-educated in composition and music history. He became an authority on church music; edited *The Cathedral Series* of music of the 16th-17th centuries; wrote numerous ecclesiastical works, among them a Te Deum, 4 Communion Services, a Requiem, anthems, etc.

Shostakovich, Dmitri, pre-eminent Russian composer of the Soviet generation, whose style and idiom of composition largely defined the nature of new Russian music; b. St. Petersburg, Sept. 25, 1906; d. Moscow, Aug. 9, 1975. He was a member of a cultural Russian family; his father was an engineer employed in the government office of weights and measures; his mother was a professional pianist. Shostakovich grew up during the most difficult period of Russian revolutionary history, when famine and disease decimated the population of Petrograd. Of frail physique, he suffered from malnutrition; Glazunov, the director of the Petrograd Cons., appealed personally to the Commissar of Education Lunacharsky to grant an increased food ration for Shostakovich, essential for his physical survival. Shostakovich received his early musical training from his mother, who taught him piano; in 1919 he entered Petrograd Cons., where he studied piano with Nikolayev and composition with Maximilian Steinberg; graduated in piano in 1923, and in composition in 1925. As a graduation piece, he submitted his First Symphony, written at the age of 18; it was first performed by the Leningrad Philharmonic on May 12, 1926, under the direction of Nikolai Malko, and subsequently became one of Shostakovich's most popular works. His Second Symphony, composed for the 10th anniversary of the Soviet Revolution, bearing the surname *Dedication to October* and ending with a rousing choral finale, was less successful despite its revolutionary sentiment. He then wrote a satirical opera *The Nose,* after Gogol's whimsical story retailing the sudden disappearance of the nose from the face of a government functionary; here Shostakovich revealed his flair for musical satire; the score featured a variety of modernistic devices and included an interlude written for percussion instruments only. *The Nose* was produced in Leningrad on Jan. 12, 1930, with considerable popular acclaim, but was attacked by officious theater critics as a product of "bourgeois decadence," and quickly withdrawn from the stage. Somewhat in the same satirical style was Shostakovich's ballet, *The Golden Age* (1930), which included a celebrated dissonant *Polka*, satirizing the current disarmament conference in Geneva. There followed the Third Symphony, subtitled *May First* (first performed in Leningrad on Jan. 21, 1930), with a choral finale saluting the International Workers' Day. Despite its explicit revolutionary content, it failed to earn the approbation of Soviet spokesmen who dismissed the work as nothing more than a formal gesture of proletarian solidarity. Shostakovich's next work was to precipitate a crisis in his career, as well as in Soviet music in general; it was an opera to the libretto drawn from a short story by the 19th-century Russian writer Leskov, entitled *Lady Macbeth of the District of Mtzensk,* and depicting adultery, murder and suicide in a merchant home under the czars. It was produced in Leningrad on Jan. 22, 1934 and was hailed by most Soviet musicians as a significant work comparable to the best productions of Western modern opera. But both the staging and the music ran counter to growing Soviet puritanism; a symphonic interlude portraying a scene of adultery behind the bedroom curtain, orchestrated with suggestive passages on the slide trombones, shocked the Soviet officials present at the performance by its bold naturalism. After the Moscow production of the opera, *Pravda,* the official organ of the ruling Communist Party, published an unsigned (and therefore all the more authoritative) article accusing Shostakovich of creating a "bedlam of noise." The brutality of this assault dismayed Shostakovich; he readily admitted his faults in both content and treatment of the subject, and declared his solemn determination to write music according to the then emerging formula of "Socialist Realism." His next stage production was a ballet, *The Limpid Brook,* portraying the pastoral scenes on a Soviet collective farm. In this work Shostakovich tempered his dissonant idiom, and the subject seemed eminently fitting for the Soviet theater; but *The Limpid Brook,* too, was condemned in *Pravda,* this time for an insufficiently dignified treatment of Soviet life. Having been rebuked twice for two radically different theater works, Shostakovich abandoned all attempts to write for the stage, and returned to purely instrumental composition. But as though pursued by vengeful fate, he again suffered a painful reverse. His Fourth Symphony was placed in rehearsal by the Leningrad Philharmonic, but withdrawn before the performance when representatives of the musical officialdom and even the orchestral musicians themselves sharply criticized the piece. Shostakovich's rehabilitation finally came with the production of his Fifth Symphony (Leningrad, Nov. 21, 1937), a work of rhapsodic grandeur culminating in a powerful climax; it was hailed, as though by spontaneous consensus, as a model of true Soviet art, classical in formal design, lucid in its harmonic idiom, and optimistic in its philosophical connotations. The height of Shostakovich's rise to recognition was achieved in his Seventh Symphony. He began its composition during the siege of Leningrad by the Nazis in the autumn of 1941; he served in the fire brigade during the air raids; then flew from Leningrad to the temporary Soviet capital in Kuibishev, on the Volga, where he completed the score, which was performed there on March 1, 1942. Its symphonic development is realistic in the extreme, with the theme of the Nazis, in mechanical march time, rising to monstrous loudness, only to be overcome and reduced to a pathetic drum dribble by a victorious Russian song. The work became a musical symbol of the Russian struggle against the overwhelmingly superior Nazi war machine; it was given the subtitle *Leningrad Symphony,* and was performed during the war by virtually every orchestra in the Allied countries. After the tremendous emotional appeal of the *Leningrad Symphony,* the Eighth Symphony, written in 1943, had a lesser impact; the Ninth, Tenth and Eleventh Symphonies followed (1945, 1953, 1957) without attracting much comment; the Twelfth Symphony, dedicated to the memory of Lenin, aroused a little more interest. But it was left for his Thirteenth Symphony (first performed in Leningrad on Dec. 18, 1962) to create a controversy which seemed to be Shostakovich's peculiar destiny; its vocal finale for solo bass and chorus to words by the Soviet poet Evtushenko, expressing the horror of the massacre of Jews by the Nazis during their occupation of the city of Kiev, and containing a warning against residual anti-Semitism in Soviet Russia, met with unexpected criticism by the then-chairman of the Communist Party Nikita Khrushchev, who complained about the exclusive attention in Evtushenko's poem to Jewish victims, and his failure to mention the Ukrainians and other nationals who were also slaughtered. The text of the poem was altered to meet these objections, but the Thirteenth Symphony never gained wide acceptance. There followed the remarkable Fourteenth Symphony in 11 sections scored for voices and orch., to words by Federico García Lorca, Apollinaire, Rilke and the Russian poet Küchelbecker. Shostakovich's Fifteenth Symphony, his last (performed in Moscow under the direction of Shostakovich's son **Maxim Shostakovich,** on Jan. 8, 1971), demonstrated his undying spirit of innovation; the score is set in the key of C major but it contains a dodecaphonic passage and literal allusions to motives from Rossini's *William Tell Overture* and the Fate Motive from Wagner's *Die Walküre.* Shostakovich's adoption, however limited, of themes built on 12 different notes, a procedure that he had himself condemned as anti-musical, is interesting both from the psychological and sociological standpoint; he experimented with these techniques in several other works; his first explicit use of a 12-tone subject occurred in his 12th String Quartet (1968). Equally illuminating is his use in some of his scores of a personal monogram D.S.C.H. (for D, Es, C, H in German notation, i.e., D, E-flat, C, B). One by one, his early works, originally condemned as unacceptable to Soviet reality, were returned to the stage and the concert hall; the objectionable 4th and 13th symphonies were published and recorded; the operas *The Nose* and *Lady Macbeth of the District of Mtzensk* (renamed *Katerina Izmailova,* after the name of the heroine) had several successful revivals.

Shostakovich excelled in instrumental music. Besides the 15 symphonies, he wrote 15 string quartets, a string octet, piano quintet, 2 piano trios, cello sonata, violin sonata, viola sonata, 2 violin concertos, 2 piano concertos, 2 cello concertos, 24 preludes for piano, 24 preludes and fugues for piano, 2 piano sonatas, several short piano pieces; also choral works and song cycles.

What is remarkable about Shostakovich is the unfailing consistency of his style of composition. His entire œuvre, from his first work to the last (147 opus numbers in all) proclaims a personal article of faith. His idiom is unmistakably of the 20th-century, making free use of dissonant harmonies and intricate contrapuntal designs, yet never abandoning inherent tonality; his music is teleological, leading invariably to a tonal climax, often in a triumphal triadic declaration. Most of his works carry key signatures; his metrical structure is governed by a unifying rhythmic pulse. Shostakovich is equally eloquent in dramatic and lyric utterance; he has no fear of prolonging his slow movements in relentless dynamic rise and fall; the cumulative power of his kinetic drive in rapid movements is overwhelming. Through all the peripeties of his career, he never changed his musical language in its fundamental modalities. When the flow of his music met obstacles, whether technical or external, he obviated them without changing the main direction. In a special announcement issued after Shostakovich's death, the government of the Union of Soviet Socialist Republics summarized his work as a "remarkable example of fidelity to the traditions of musical classicism, and above all, to the Russian traditions, finding his inspiration in the reality of Soviet life, reasserting and developing in his creative innovations the art of socialist realism, and in so doing, contributing to universal progressive musical culture." His honors, both domestic and foreign were many: the Order of Lenin (1946, 1956, 1966), People's Artist of the USSR (1954), Hero of Socialist Labor (1966), Order of the October Revolution (1971), honorary membership in the American Institute of the Arts (1943), honorary Doctor of Oxford Univ. (1958), Laureate of the International Sibelius Prize (1958), Doctor of Fine Arts from Northwestern Univ. (1973). He visited the U.S. as a delegate to the World Peace Conference in 1949, as a member of a group of Soviet musicians in 1959, and, to receive the degree of Doctor of Fine Arts from Northwestern Univ., in 1973. A postage stamp of 6 kopecks, bearing his photograph and an excerpt from the *Leningrad Symphony,* was issued by the Soviet Post Office in 1976 to commemorate his 70th birthday. The publication of Shostakovich's collected works in 42 vols., to be completed in 1984, was initiated in 1978.

WORKS: STAGE AND DRAMATIC MUSIC: *The Nose* (Leningrad, Jan. 12, 1930); *Lady Macbeth of the District of Mtzensk* (Leningrad, Jan. 22, 1934; under the title *Katerina Izmailova,* Moscow, Jan. 24, 1934; Metropolitan Opera, N.Y., Feb. 5, 1935; score revised, 1962); *Moskva Cheryomushki* (Moscow, Jan. 24, 1959); ballets: *The Golden Age* (Leningrad, Oct. 26, 1930; contains the celebrated dance number *Polka*); *Bolt* (Leningrad, April 8, 1931); *The Limpid Brook* (Leningrad, April 4, 1935), INCIDENTAL MUSIC: Mayakovsky's comedy, *The Bedbug* (1929); *Rule Britannia* (1931); *Hamlet* (1932); *The Human Comedy,* after Balzac (1934); *Salud, España* (1936); *King Lear* (1940); *Russian River* (1944), FILM SCORES: *New Babylon* (1929); *Alone* (1930); *Golden Mountains* (1931); *The Stranger* (1932); *Love and Hatred* (1934); *Maxim's*

Youth (1935); *Companions* (1935); *Maxim's Return* (1937); *Friends* (1938); *Great Citizen* (1938); *A Man with a Gun* (1938); *Silly Little Mouse* (1939); *Zoya* (1944); *Plain Folks* (1945); *Young Guard* (1948); *Encounter on the Elba River* (1948); *The Fall of Berlin* (1949); *Unforgettable Year 1919* (1951); *Song of the Great Rivers* (1954); *Gadfly* (1955); *The First Echelon* (1956); *Five Days, Five Nights* (1960); *Sophie Perovskaya* (1967), a tribute to one of the executed conspirators in the assassination of Czar Alexander II of Russia in 1881; *King Lear* (1970).

ORCHESTRAL MUSIC: 15 symphonies: No. 1 (Leningrad, May 12, 1926); No. 2, with a choral ending, dedicated to the October Revolution (Leningrad, Nov. 6, 1927); No. 3, subtitled *May First* (Leningrad, Jan. 21, 1930); No. 4 (1936; Moscow, Jan. 20, 1962); No. 5 (Leningrad, Nov. 21, 1937); No. 6 (Leningrad, Nov. 5, 1939); No. 7, *Leningrad Symphony* (Kuibishev, March 1, 1942; 1st American performance, NBC Symph., N.Y., Toscanini conducting, July 19, 1942); No. 8 (Moscow, Nov. 4, 1943); No. 9 (Leningrad, Nov. 3, 1945); No. 10 (Leningrad, Dec. 17, 1953); No. 11 (Moscow, Oct. 30, 1957); No. 12, *The Year 1917,* dedicated to the memory of Lenin (Leningrad, Oct. 1, 1961); No. 13 for orch., chorus and solo bass, to words by Evtushenko (1961; Moscow, Dec. 18, 1962); No. 14, for soprano, bass and chamber orch., in 11 sections (Leningrad, Sept. 29, 1969); No. 15 (Moscow, Jan. 8, 1971); Piano Concerto No. 1, for piano, trumpet and strings (Leningrad, Oct. 15, 1933); Piano Concerto No. 2 (Moscow, May 10, 1957; Maxim Shostakovich, son of the composer, soloist); Violin Concerto No. 1 (Leningrad, Oct. 29, 1955); Violin Concerto No. 2 (Moscow, Sept. 26, 1967); Cello Concerto No. 1 (Leningrad, Oct. 4, 1959); Cello Concerto No. 2 (Moscow, Sept. 25, 1966).

OTHER WORKS FOR ORCH.: *Scherzo* (1919); *Theme and Variations* (1922); *Tahiti Trot,* orchestration of *Tea for Two* by Youmans (1928); *Technically Killed,* a circus piece (1931); *Suite* for jazz orch. (Leningrad, Nov. 28, 1938); orchestration of Mussorgsky's opera *Boris Godunov* (1940); *Festive Overture* (1954); *Overture on Russian and Kirghiz Folk Themes* (1963); *Funeral and Triumphant Prelude in Memory of the Heroes of the Battle of Stalingrad* (1967); *October,* symph. poem (Moscow, Sept. 26, 1967); *March of Soviet Militia* for band (1970); 4 ballet suites (1949, 1951, 1952, 1953).

VOCAL WORKS: 6 songs to words by Japanese poets for voice and orch. (1938–32); *Leningrad* for chorus and orch. (Moscow, Oct. 15, 1942); *Song of the Forests,* cantata (Leningrad, Nov. 15, 1949); *Democratic Vistas,* a cycle of 10 poems by Walt Whitman for chorus and orch. (Moscow, Oct. 10, 1951); 4 songs to texts by Pushkin (1936); 6 songs to words by Burns, Shakespeare, and Walter Raleigh (1942); *Song of the Fatherland* for soloists, chorus, and orch. (1947); *From Jewish Folk Poetry,* vocal cycle with piano (1948); *The Sun Shines Over Our Fatherland,* cantata for boys' chorus, mixed choir and orch. (1952); *4 Monologues* to words by Pushkin for voice and piano (1952); *5 Songs* to words by Dolmatovsky for voice and piano (1954); *Spanish Songs* (1956); *Satires (Scenes from the Past),* 5 songs for voice and piano (1960); *The Death of Stepan Razin* for orch., mixed choir and bass, to words by Evtushenko (Moscow, Dec. 28, 1964); *5 Songs* to texts from the Moscow comic magazine *Crocodile* (1965); *Foreword to My Collected Works and a Brief Meditation Anent This Foreword* for bass voice and orch. (1966); *7 Songs* to words by Alexander Blok, for soprano, violin, cello and piano (1967); *Spring, Spring,* song to words by Pushkin (1967); *Faith,* ballad cycle for men's chorus a cappella (1970); *6 Songs* for contralto and chamber orch. by Marina Tsvetayeva (1974); *Suite* for bass and piano to texts by Michelangelo (1974); *4 Songs* to words from Dostoyevsky for bass and piano (1975).

CHAMBER MUSIC: Piano Trio No. 1 (1923); *3 Pieces* for cello and piano (1924); *2 Pieces* for string octet (1925); Cello Sonata (1934); 15 string quartets (1938, 1944, 1946, 1949, 1952, 1956, 1960, 1960, 1964, 1964, 1966, 1968, 1970, 1973, 1974); Piano Quintet (1940); *2 piano trios* (1923, 1944); Violin Sonata (1968); Viola Sonata (1975).

PIANO MUSIC: *8 Preludes* (1919–20); *3 Fantastic Dances* (1922); *Suite* for 2 Pianos (1922); 2 sonatas (1926, 1942); *Aphorisms* (1927); *24 Preludes* (1932–33); *Children's Album* (1945); *Puppets' Dances* (1946); *24 Preludes and Fugues* (1950–51); Concertino for 2 pianos (1953).

BIBLIOGRAPHY: N. Slonimsky, "Dmitri Shostakovitch," *Musical Quarterly* (Oct. 1942); Victor Seroff, *Dmitri Shostakovitch: The Life and Background of a Soviet Composer* (N.Y., 1943); M. Sahlberg-Vatchadze, *Shostakovich* (Paris, 1945); Ivan Martinov, *Shostakovich* (Moscow, 1946; in English, N.Y., 1947); L. Danilevitch, *Dmitri Shostakovich* (Moscow, 1958); D. Rabinovich, *Dmitri Shostakovich* (Foreign Languages Publ. House; in English, Moscow, 1959); G. Ordzhonokidze, compiler, *Dmitri Shostakovich,* collection of articles (Moscow, 1967); *Dmitri Shostakovich,* articles and materials, edited by Grigory Schneerson (Moscow, 1976); M. Sabinina, *Shostakovich the Symphonist* (Moscow, 1976). See also *Modern Music . . . Analytic Index,* compiled by Wayne Shirley, ed. by Wm. and C. Lichtenwanger (N.Y., 1976; pp. 197–99).

Shtogarenko, Andrei, Ukrainian composer; b. Noviye Kaidaki, near Ekaterinoslav, Oct. 15, 1902. He studied at the Kharkov Cons., graduating in 1936. During World War II he worked in Turkmenia. In 1954 he was appointed director of the Kiev Cons. Virtually all of his music is devoted to Ukrainian subjects.

WORKS: 3 symphonies (1947, 1965, 1968); symph. cantata, *My Ukraine* (1943): cantata *Moscow* (for the 800th anniversary of its foundation: 1948); *Partisan Sketches* for orch. (1957); *The Dawn of Communism Has Come* for chorus, vocal soloists and orch. (1957); a choral symph., *Lenin Walks the Planet* (1958); Violin Concerto (1969); choruses; songs; film scores.

BIBLIOGRAPHY: A. Znosco-Borovsky, *Andrei Shtogarenko* (Kiev, 1947).

Shulman, Alan, American composer; b. Baltimore, June 4, 1915. He studied cello at the Peabody Cons. of Music in Baltimore and with Felix Salmond in N.Y.; took a course in composition with Bernard Wagenaar at the Juilliard School of Music, graduating in 1937;

during World War II was in the U.S. Maritime Service.

WORKS: for orch.: *A Laurentian Overture* (N.Y., Jan. 7, 1952); *Waltzes* (1949); *Popocatepetl,* symph. picture (1952); *Theme and Variations,* for viola and orch. (N.Y., Feb. 17, 1941); *Pastorale and Dance,* for violin and orch. (N.Y., July 15, 1944); Cello Concerto (1948; N.Y., April 13, 1950); chamber music: *Rendezvous,* for clarinet and strings (1946); *Threnody,* for string quartet (1950); *Suite Miniature,* for octet of cellos (1956); *Suite* for solo cello (1950); *Top Brass,* for 12 brass instruments (Portland, Oregon, April 25, 1958); *Four Diversions* for a pride of cellos (Philadelphia, April 6, 1975); numerous short works for violin, for cello, for piano, etc.

Shure, Leonard, American pianist; b. Los Angeles, April 10, 1910. He studied in Berlin with Artur Schnabel; returning to the U.S. in 1933, he taught at the New England Cons. of Music; then was engaged at the School of Music of the Univ. of Texas in Austin. His manner of playing is sweepingly romantic and subjective.

Sibelius, Jean (Johan Julius Christian), great Finnish composer; b. Tavastehus, Dec. 8, 1865; d. Järvenpää, Sept. 20, 1957. The son of an army surgeon, he received an excellent classical education; from childhood, showed a deep absorption in music, and began to compose without a tutor. He had piano lessons from the age of 9, and at 14 began to study the violin with Gustaf Levander, the bandmaster in his native town; soon he took part in amateur performances of chamber music. He was sent to the Univ. of Helsinki in 1885 to study law, but abandoned it before the end of his 1st semester, and entered the Cons., where he studied violin with Vasiliev and Csillag, and composition with Wegelius (1886–89). He had a suite for strings and a string quartet publicly performed in 1889, producing an excellent impression; he was then granted a government stipend for further study in Berlin. He studied with Albert Becker (counterpoint and fugue); after returning to Finland for a short stay, he went to Vienna to complete his musical training; there he was a student of Robert Fuchs and Karl Goldmark (1890–91). At that time his path as a national Finnish composer became determined; the music he wrote was inspired by native legends, with the epic *Kalevala* as a prime source of inspiration. A symph. poem, *Kullervo,* with soloists and chorus, written by Sibelius upon his return to Finland, was performed in Helsinki on April 28, 1892. A little later he completed one of his most famous scores, the symph. poem *En Saga* (revised in 1901). In 1893 he was appointed instructor in theory at the Helsinki Cons. In 1897 the Finnish senate granted him an annual stipend of 2,000 marks for 10 years. On July 2, 1900, the Helsinki Philharmonic gave the première of the most celebrated and the most patriotic symph. work by Sibelius, *Finlandia.* So profoundly moving was the music to Finnish audiences that the Czarist government forbade its performances during times of political unrest. In 1901 Sibelius conducted his own works at the annual festival of the "Allgemeiner deutscher Tonkünstlerverein" at

Heidelberg. In 1904 he moved to a country home at Järvenpää, near Helsinki, where he remained until his death, with only occasional absences. In 1913 Sibelius accepted a commission for a new orchestral work from an American patron of music, Carl Stoeckel, to be performed at the 28th annual Norfolk, Conn., Festival; the completed work was the symph. poem *Aallottaret (The Oceanides),* and Sibelius came to the U.S. to conduct its première on June 4, 1914. The program also included several of his other works. Yale Univ. conferred on him the degree of Mus. Doc. *(honoris causa).* Returning to Finland just before the outbreak of World War I, Sibelius withdrew into seclusion, but continued to work. He made his last public appearance abroad in Stockholm, when he conducted his 7th Symphony on March 24, 1924. He wrote 2 more works after that, a score for Shakespeare's *The Tempest,* and *Tapiola,* a symph. poem. After 1929 he ceased to compose; rumors of his completion of another symphony proved unfounded. Although he was cordial in receiving friends and admirers from abroad, he avoided discussion of his own musical plans. Honors were showered on him; festivals of his music were for years popular events in Helsinki; a postage stamp bearing his likeness was issued by the Finnish government on his 80th birthday; special publications, biographical, bibliographical, and photographic, were issued in Finland. Artistically, too, Sibelius attained the status of universally acknowledged greatness rarely vouchsafed to a living musician; several important contemporary composers paid him homage by acknowledging their debt of inspiration to him, Vaughan Williams among them. Sibelius was the last representative of 19th-century nationalistic Romanticism. He stayed aloof from modern developments, but he was not uninterested in reading scores and listening to performances on the radio of works of such men as Schoenberg, Prokofiev, and Shostakovich.

The music of Sibelius marked the culmination of the growth of national Finnish art, in which Pacius was the protagonist, and Wegelius, the teacher of Sibelius, a worthy cultivator. Like his predecessors, Sibelius was schooled in Germanic tradition, and his early works reflect German lyricism and German dramatic thought. He opened a new era in Finnish music when he abandoned formal conventions and began to write music that seemed inchoate and diffuse, but followed a powerful line of development by variation and repetition; a parallel with Beethoven's late works has frequently been drawn. The thematic material employed by Sibelius is not modelled directly on known Finnish folksongs; rather, he recreated the characteristic melodic patterns of folk music. The prevailing mood is somber, even tragic, with a certain elemental sweep and grandeur. His instrumentation is highly individual, with long songful solo passages, and with protracted transitions that are treated as integral parts of the music. His genius found its most eloquent expression in his symphonies and symph. poems; he wrote relatively little chamber music, and only in his earlier years. His only opera, *The Maid in the Tower* (1896), to a text in Swedish, was never published. He wrote some incidental music for the stage; the celebrated *Valse Triste* was written in 1903 for *Kuolema,* a play by Arvid Järnefelt, brother-in-law of Sibelius.

WORKS: STAGE MUSIC: the opera *Jungfruburen (The Maid in the Tower;* Helsinki, Nov. 7, 1896); *Scaramouche,* a "tragic pantomine" (1913; Copenhagen, May 12, 1922); incidental music to *King Christian II* (1898), *Kuolema* (1903), *Pelléas et Mélisande* (1905), *Belshazzar's Feast* (1906), *Svanevhit* (1908), *Odlan* (1909), *The Language of the Birds* (1911), *Jedermann* (1916), *The Tempest* (1926).

ORCHESTRAL MUSIC: 7 symphonies: No. 1, in E minor, op. 39 (Helsinki, April 26, 1899), No. 2, in D major, op. 43 (Helsinki, March 8, 1902, composer conducting), No. 3, in C major, op. 52 (1904–07; Helsinki, Sept. 25, 1907, composer conducting), No. 4, in A minor, op. 63 (Helsinki, April 3, 1911, composer conducting), No. 5, in E-flat major, op. 82 (Helsinki, Dec. 8, 1915, composer conducting), No. 6, in D minor, op. 104 (Helsinki, Feb. 19, 1923, composer conducting), No. 7, in C major, op. 105 (Stockholm, March 24, 1924, composer conducting); symph. poems: *Kullervo,* op. 7 (Helsinki, April 28, 1892), *En Saga,* op. 9 (Helsinki, Feb. 16, 1893); *Spring Song,* op. 16 (1894), 4 *Legends from the Kalevala,* op. 22: *Lemminkaïnen and the Maidens* (1895), *Lemminkaïnen in Tuonela* (1895), *The Swan of Tuonela* (1893), *The Return of Lemminkaïnen* (1895), *Finlandia,* op. 26 (Helsinki, July 2, 1900), *Pohjola's Daughter,* op. 49 (1906), *Night Ride and Sunrise,* op. 55 (1909), *The Bard,* op. 64 (1913), *Luonnotar,* op. 70 (1913), *Aallottaret (The Oceanides),* op. 73 (Norfolk, Conn., Festival, June 4, 1914, composer conducting), *Tapiola,* op. 112 (commissioned by Walter Damrosch, and 1st performed by him, N.Y., Dec. 26, 1926); symph. suites: *Karelia,* op. 11 (1893), *Rakastava,* for strings and percussion, op. 14 (1911), *Scènes historiques,* op. 25, 1st suite (1899), *Scènes historiques,* op. 66, 2nd suite (1912), *Suite mignonne,* for 2 flutes and strings, op. 98a (1921), *Suite champêtre,* for strings, op. 98b (1921), *Suite caractéristique* for small orch., op 100 (1923); Violin Concerto in D minor, op. 47 (1st version, Helsinki, Feb. 8, 1904; 2nd version, Berlin, Oct. 19, 1905); 6 *Humoresques* for violin and orch., op. 87b and 89 (1917).

CHAMBER MUSIC: string quartet in B-flat major, op. 4 (1882); *Voces intimae,* op. 56, for string quartet (1909); *Malinconia,* for cello and piano, op. 20 (1901); 4 pieces for violin or cello, op. 78 (1915); 6 pieces for violin and piano, op. 79 (1915); Sonatina for violin and piano, op. 80 (1915); 5 pieces for violin and piano, op. 81 (1915); *Novellette,* for violin and piano, op. 102 (1923); 5 *Danses champêtres,* for violin and piano, op. 106 (1925); 4 compositions for violin and piano, op. 115 (1929); 3 compositions for violin and piano, op. 116 (1929); Piano Sonata, op. 12 (1893); 111 piano pieces, grouped in cycles, and composed between 1894 and 1929.

VOCAL MUSIC: *The Origin of Fire,* op. 32, for baritone, male chorus, and orch. (1902); *Oma maa,* cantata for chorus and orch., op. 92 (1918); *Maan virsi,* cantata for chorus and orch., op. 95 (1920); *The Song of Väinö,* for chorus and orch., op. 110 (1926); 85 songs; various early works, without opus numbers.

BIBLIOGRAPHY: K. Flodin, *Finska Musiker* (Helsinki, 1900); Rosa Newmarch, *Jean Sibelius: A Finnish Composer* (Leipzig, 1906); E. G. Furuhjelm, *Jean*

Sibelius (Borgä, 1916); W. Niemann, *Jean Sibelius* (Leipzig, 1917); Cecil Gray, *Sibelius* (London, 1931, 2nd ed., 1938); Cecil Gray, *Sibelius: The Symphonies* (London, 1935; 5th printing, 1947); Karl Ekman, *Jean Sibelius: His Life and Personality* (in English; Helsinki, 1935; 4th Swedish ed., 1956); A. H. Meyer, "Sibelius: Symphonist," *Musical Quarterly* (Jan. 1936); Bengt de Törne, *Sibelius: A Close-Up* (London, 1937); Rosa Newmarch, *Jean Sibelius* (Boston, 1939); H. Askeli, "A Sketch of Sibelius the Man," *Musical Quarterly* (Jan. 1940); Eino Roiha, *Die Symphonien von Jean Sibelius* (Jyväskylä, 1941); E. Arnold, *Finlandia, the Story of Sibelius* (N.Y., 1941); I. Krohn, *Der Formenbau in den Symphonien von Jean Sibelius* (Helsinki, 1942); E. Tanzberger, *Die symphonischen Dichtungen von Jean Sibelius* (Würzburg, 1943); S. Levas, *Jean Sibelius* (in Finnish; Helsinki, 1945); Bengt de Törne, *Sibelius* (in Finnish; Helsinki, 1945); *The Music of Sibelius*, ed. by G. Abraham (N.Y., 1947); I. Hannikainen, *Sibelius and the Development of Finnish Music* (London, 1948); Nils-Eric Ringbom, *Sibelius* (in Swedish; Stockholm, 1948; in English, Norman, Okla., 1954); Veikko Helasvuo, *Sibelius and the Music of Finland* (Helsinki, 1952; in English); O. Andersson, *Jean Sibelius i Amerika* (Åbo, 1955, in Swedish); S. Parmet, *Sibelius symfonier* (Helsinki, 1955); S. Parmet, *The Symphonies of Sibelius: A Study in Musical Appreciation* (London, 1959; transl. from his 1955 monograph); H. E. Johnson, *Jean Sibelius* (N.Y., 1959); E. Tanzberger, *J. Sibelius* (Wiesbaden, 1962).

Siboni, Erik (Anton Waldemar), Danish pianist and composer; b. Copenhagen, Aug. 26, 1828; d. there, Feb. 22, 1892. He was the son of the tenor **Giuseppe Siboni** (b. Forli, Jan. 27, 1780; d. Copenhagen, March 29, 1839, as director of the opera and Cons.); studied with J. P. E. Hartmann; then with Moscheles and Hauptmann at Leipzig and with Sechter at Vienna; returned to Copenhagen, and in 1864 became organist and piano professor at the Royal Academy of Music at Sorö; retired in 1883.
WORKS: operas, *Loreley* (Copenhagen, 1859) and *Carl II's flugt* (Flight of Charles II; Copenhagen, 1862); 2 symphonies; a piano quartet; other chamber music; the choral works *Slaget ved Murten* (Battle of Murten), *Stormen paa København* (Storming of Copenhagen), etc.

Sicilianos, Yorgo, Greek composer; b. Athens, Aug. 29, 1922. He studied composition with Varvoglis (1944–49); then went to Rome where he took a course with Pizzetti at the Santa Cecilia Academy (1951–53); supplemented his music education at the Paris Cons. (1953–54). On a Fulbright Scholarship he traveled to the U.S., where he took a course in composition with Walter Piston at Harvard Univ. and attended the summer class of Boris Blacher at the Berkshire Center in Tanglewood, Mass.; also enrolled for an academic season at the Juilliard School of Music in N.Y., where he studied with Persichetti (1955–56). Upon return to Greece, he occupied various educational and administrative posts; in 1967 he was appointed to the faculty of the Pierce College in Athens. His style of composition is classical in format, pandiatonic in harmony and intricately polyphonic in contrapuntal and fugal developments.
WORKS: *Prelude and Dance* for orch. (1948; Athens Radio, Sept. 1, 1948); *The Revelation of the Fifth Seal,* symph. poem (1951; Athens, May 11, 1952); 4 string quartets (1951, 1954, 1957–61, 1967); Concertino for 5 winds and string orch. (1953; Rome, June 9, 1953); Concerto for Orch. (1953–54; Athens, Nov. 28, 1954); Symph. No. 1 (1955; New York, March 1, 1958); *Tanagra,* ballet for 2 pianos and percussion (1958; Athens, April 21, 1958; orch. version, Athens, Feb. 5, 1962); *Bacchantes,* ballet for women's chorus and orch., after Euripides (1959–60; Athens, Jan. 11, 1960); *Synthesis* for double string orch. and percussion (1962; Athens, Nov. 26, 1962); Cello Concerto (1963); *Miniatures* for piano (1963); *Variations on 4 Rhythmical Patterns* for orch. (1963); *Stasimon B!* for women's chorus, mezzo-soprano and orch. (1965); *Perspectives* for orch. in 4 groups (1966);. *Episodes I,* variations and interludes for chamber orch. (1964–67) and *II* for double chorus, 3 performers and tape (1971); *Epiklesis II,* after Aeschylus, for narrator, male chorus, 4 women's voices and 12 instruments (1968); *Epitaph* for mixed chorus, children's chorus, narrator and orch. (1969–71); *Etudes Compositionnelles* for solo piano (1972–73; orchestrated for piano and orch., 1975); *Medea,* stage music, after Euripides, for women's chorus, flute, tuba, percussion and tape (1973); *Parable,* choreographic picture for chorus, flute, tuba, percussion and tape (1973); *Etude* for solo tuba (1974); *Paysages* for 2 percussionists (1975); *6 Songs* for voice and piano (1975); *Schemata* for 6 percussionists (1976); *Antiphone* for brass, timpani and strings (1976); *The Moonlight Lady,* cantata for mezzo-soprano, narrator, clarinet, viola and guitar (1977).

Sieber, Ferdinand, Austrian singing teacher; b. Vienna, Dec. 5, 1822; d. Berlin, Feb. 19, 1895. He studied with Ronconi; after a brief period of singing in opera, he became a singing teacher in Dresden (1848–54), later settling in Berlin, where he had numerous pupils. He taught in the tradition of the old Italian method. He publ. valuable instructive works; *Die Kunst des Gesangs,* in 2 parts (theoretical and practical studies), with a supplement, *50 Vocalisen und Solfeggien; Vollständiges Lehrbuch der Gesangskunst für Lehrer und Schüler* (1858; 3rd ed., 1878); *Katechismus der Gesangskunst* (1862 and many subsequent eds.); *Die Aussprache des Italienischen im Gesang* (1860; 2nd ed., 1880); and a *Handbuch des deutschen Liederschatzes* (1875), containing a catalogue of 10,000 songs arranged according to vocal range; he also wrote many songs.

Siegel, Carl F. W., German music publisher; was active early in the 19th century; d. Leipzig, March 29, 1869. He founded his firm in 1846, making a specialty of choral music. He was succeeded by Richard Linnemann (b. Leipzig, April 14, 1845; d. there, Dec. 1, 1909), who studied at the Leipzig Cons. and in 1871 acquired control of *Die Sängerhalle* (organ of the German singing society), which continued publication until 1916. Richard Linnemann's sons were Carl Linnemann (b. Leipzig, Sept. 25, 1872; d. there, Dec. 14, 1945) and Richard Linnemann, Jr. (b. Leipzig, Nov. 5,

1874; d. there, April 5, 1932); they entered the business in 1901; bought the stock of E. W. Fritzsch in 1901 and that of K. F. Kistner in 1919. From 1919 to 1927 the firm published the *Archiv für Musikwissenschaft*.

Siegel, Rudolf, German conductor and composer; b. Berlin, April 12, 1878; d. Bayreuth, Dec. 4, 1948. He studied with Humperdinck in Berlin and with Thuille in Munich; in 1910 became conductor of a choral society in Munich; then was in Berlin (1912–14) and Königsberg (1914–17). From 1919 until 1930 he was music director at Krefeld; then moved to Berlin; in 1945 went to Ebing near Bamberg; eventually moved to Munich. He wrote an opera, *Herr Dandolo* (Essen, 1914); *Apostatenmarsch,* for male chorus and orch.; *Heroische Tondichtung,* for orch.; *Dem Vaterlande,* for men's chorus and orch.; made arrangements of German folksongs.

Siegl, Otto, Austrian violinist, conductor and composer; b. Graz, Oct. 6, 1896. He received his first music lessons from his mother, an amateur pianist; then studied violin with a local teacher. In 1915 he was drafted into the Austro-Hungarian Army and served as a Tyrol rifleman in World War I. Still in service he met the musicologist Max Auer, who gave him instruction in the classics. After the Armistice, he was violinist in the Vienna Symph. Orch. (1921–22) and assistant conductor at the Graz Opera (1922–24); also wrote music criticism. In 1926 he went to Germany, where he worked as choral conductor in Bielefeld, Essen and Herford; from 1933 to 1948 he was on the staff of the Cologne Musikhochschule; from 1948 to 1967 he was prof. at the Music Academy in Vienna. In 1957 he was awarded the Great State Prize for Music. A pragmatic musician, he is a master of polyphony; his choral writing is especially meritorious.
WORKS: 2 symphonies (1958, 1959); Cello Concerto (1957); Flute Concerto (1955); Chamber Concerto for piano and orch. (1960); Clarinet Concerto with string orch. (1968); 2 string quintets (1940, 1954); *Quintet-Serenade* for clarinet, bassoon, violin, viola and cello (1961); 5 string quartets (1924–56); Trio for clarinet, cello and piano (1959); 4 cello sonatas (1923, 1923, 1924, 1967); 2 violin sonatas (1925, 1940); 2 viola sonatas (1925, 1938); 2 clarinet sonatas (1965, 1968); Flute Sonata (1968); Sonata for clarinet and cello (1965); oratorio, *Stern des Lebens* (1959); several cantatas; 4 Masses; numerous choruses and about 80 lieder.
BIBLIOGRAPHY: W. Trienes, *Otto Siegl* (Mülheim, 1956); Wolfgang Suppan, *Otto Siegl* (Vienna, 1966).

Siegmeister, Elie, significant American composer; b. New York, Jan. 15, 1909. He took piano lessons as a youth with Emil Friedberger; in 1925 entered Columbia Univ. and studied composition there with Seth Bingham; also took private lessons in composition with Wallingford Riegger. In 1927 he went to Paris where he studied with Nadia Boulanger; returning to N.Y. in 1932 he taught music at various schools; studied conducting at the Juilliard School of Music, N.Y. (1935–38); in 1939 organized a choral group, "American Ballad Singers," for the purpose of performing authentic American folksongs, and traveled as its conductor for several years. He felt strongly that music should express the social values of the people; in his early songs, he selected texts by contemporary American poets voicing indignation at the inequities of the modern world; also gave lectures and conducted choruses at the revolutionary Pierre Degeyter Club in N.Y. From the outset, he adopted an extremely dissonant harmonic idiom and a quasi-atonal melos, with the intervallic stress on minor seconds, major sevenths, and minor ninths. In his symphonies and chamber music he organized this dissonant idiom in self-consistent modern formulations, without, however, espousing any of the fashionable doctrines of composition, such as dodecaphony. The subject matter of the orchestral and vocal of his early period was marked by a strongly national and socially radical character, exemplified by such works as *American Holiday, Ozark Set, Prairie Legend, Wilderness Road* and *Western Suite,* the latter having achieved the rare honor of being performed by Toscanini; he did not ignore the homely vernacular; his clarinet concerto is a brilliant realization of jazz, blues, and swing in a classically formal idiom. Siegmeister achieved an important position as an educator; in 1949 he was appointed to the faculty of Hofstra Univ. in Hempstead, Long Island; became composer-in-residence there in 1966; prof. emeritus in 1976. In 1978 he received the Guggenheim Fellowship award.
WORKS: FOR THE STAGE: *Doodle Dandy of the USA,* play with music, to text by Saul Lancourt (N.Y., Dec. 26, 1942); *Sing Out, Sweet Land,* to text by Walter Kerr (Hartford, Conn., Nov. 10, 1944); *Darling Corie,* 1-act opera, libretto by Lewis Allan (1952; Hofstra Univ., Feb. 18, 1954); *Miranda and the Dark Young Man,* 1-act opera, libretto by Edward Eager (1955; Hartford, Conn., May 9, 1956); *The Mermaid in Lock No. 7,* 1-act opera, libretto by Edward Mabley (Pittsburgh, July 20, 1958); *Dublin Song,* 3-act opera, libretto by Edward Mabley, based on Sean O'Casey's drama *The Plough and the Stars* (1963; St. Louis, May 15, 1963; revised and performed under the title *The Plough and the Stars,* Baton Rouge, Louisiana, March 16, 1969); *Night of the Moonspell,* 3-act opera, libretto by Edward Mabley after Shakespeare's play *Midsummer Night's Dream* (Shreveport, Louisiana, Nov. 14, 1976); *Fables from the Dark Wood,* for ballet (Shreveport, Louisiana, April 25, 1976); film score, *They Came to Cordura* (1959).
FOR ORCH.: *American Holiday* (1933); *Walt Whitman Overture* (N.Y., March 31, 1940); *Ozark Set* (1943; Minneapolis, Nov. 7, 1944); *Prairie Legend* (1944; N.Y., Jan. 18, 1947); *Wilderness Road* (1944; Minneapolis, Nov. 9, 1945); *Western Suite* (1945; N.Y., Nov. 24, 1945; Toscanini conducting NBC Symph. Orch.); *Sunday in Brooklyn* (N.Y., July 21, 1946); *Lonesome Hollow* (1946; Columbus, Ohio, 1948); *Summer Night* (1947; N.Y., Sept. 27, 1952); Symph. No. 1 (1947; N.Y., Oct. 30, 1947; revised in 1972); *From My Window* (1949); Symph. No. 2 (1950; N.Y., Feb. 25, 1952); *Divertimento* (1953; Oklahoma City, March 28, 1954); Concerto for Clarinet and Orch. (Oklahoma City, Feb. 3, 1956); Symph. No. 3 (1957; Oklahoma City, Feb. 8, 1959); Concerto for Flute and Orch. (1960; Oklahoma City, Feb. 17, 1961); *Theater*

Set, drawn from the music for the film *They Came to Cordura* (1960; Rochester, N.Y., May 8, 1969); *Dick Whittington and His Cat,* for narrator and orch. (1966; Philadelphia, Feb. 10, 1968); *Five Fantasies of the Theater* (1967; Hofstra Univ., Oct. 18, 1970); Symph. No. 4 (1970; Cleveland, Dec. 6, 1973); Symph. No. 5, subtitled *Visions of Time* (1971–75; Baltimore, May 4, 1977); Piano Concerto (Denver, Colo., Dec. 3, 1976; Alan Mandel, soloist); *Shadows and Light,* subtitled *Homage to Five Paintings* (Shreveport, Louisiana, Nov. 9, 1975); Double Concerto for violin, piano and orch. (Columbia, Maryland, June 25, 1976); Violin Concerto (1977–78).

VOCAL MUSIC: for voice and orch.: *Strange Funeral in Braddock* (1933; originally for voice and piano; Evergreen, Colo., July 30, 1972); *Abraham Lincoln Walks at Midnight,* for mixed chorus and orc. to a text of Vachel Lindsay (1937); *Funnybone Alley,* for voice and string orch., musical fantasy for children to poems by Alfred Kreymborg (1946); *I Have a Dream,* for mixed chorus, baritone, narrator and orch., to the text by Edward Mabley based on a speech by Martin Luther King, Jr. (1967; Omaha, Nebraska, Oct. 7, 1968); *The Face of War,* for bass voice and orch., to poems by Langston Hughes (N.Y., May 24, 1968); *A Cycle of Cities,* for mixed chorus, soprano, tenor and orch. to poems by Lawrence Ferlinghetti, Langston Hughes and Norman Rosten (Wolf Trap, Virginia, near Washington, D.C., Aug. 8, 1974); many pieces for band.

FOR CHORUS: *Heyura, Ding, Dong, Ding* (1935; revised 1970); *John Henry* (1935), *Song of Democracy* (1938); *Johnny Appleseed,* words by Stephen Vincent Benèt (1940); *American Ballad Singers Series* (1943); *American Folk Song Choral Series* (1953). Songs: *Cortege for Rosenbloom,* to words by Wallace Stevens (1926); *4 Robert Frost Songs* (1930); *The Strange Funeral in Braddock,* to words by Michael Gold (1933); *3 Elegies for García Lorca,* to words by Antonio Machado (1938); *Nancy Hanks,* to words by Rosemary Benèt (1941); *Songs of Experience,* to words by William Blake (1966); 11 songs to words by E. E. Cummings (1970); *Songs of Innocence,* to words by William Blake (1972); *City Songs,* to words by N. Rosten (1977).

CHAMBER MUSIC: *Nocturne* for flute and piano (1927); *Prelude* for clarinet and piano (1927); *Contrasts* for bassoon and piano (1929); 3 string quartets (1935, 1960, 1973); *Down River* for alto saxophone and piano (1939); 5 violin sonatas (1951, 1965, 1965, 1971, 1972); *Song for a Quiet Evening,* for violin and piano (1955); *Fantasy and Soliloquy* for solo cello (1964); Sextet for brass and percussion (1965); *American Harp,* for solo harp (1966); *Declaration,* for brass and timpani (1976); for piano: *Theme and Variations No. 1* (1932); *Toccata on Flight Rhythms* (1937); *American Sonata* (1944); *Sunday in Brooklyn* (1964); Sonata No. 2 (1964); *Theme and Variations No. 2* (1967); *On This Ground* (1971).

WRITINGS: *A Treasury of American Song* (with Olin Downes; N.Y., 1940); *The Music Lover's Handbook* (1943; revised as *The New Music Lover's Handbook,* Irvington-on-Hudson, N.Y., 1973); *Work and Sing* (N.Y., 1944); *Invitation to Music* (Irvington-on-

Hudson, 1961); *Harmony and Melody* (2 vols.; Belmont, California, 1965–66).

BIBLIOGRAPHY: David Ewen, *The World of 20th-Century Music* (Englewood Cliffs, New Jersey, 1968); Grigory Schneerson, *Portraits of American Composers* (Moscow, 1977, pp. 113–34); autobiographical sketch in *The New Music Lover's Handbook* (Irvington-on-Husdon, N.Y., 1973; pp. 561–69).

Siepi, Cesare, Italian bass; b. Milan, Feb. 10, 1923. He made his debut in Schio (Venice) in 1941; in 1946 appeared for the first time at La Scala, Milan. He made his American debut at the Metropolitan Opera, N.Y., Jan. 27, 1951, and sang there in subsequent years. In 1966 he became a member of the Vienna State Opera; also appeared at Covent Garden Opera in London, in Salzburg, and other musical centers. His most successful roles were Mephistophélès in Gounod's *Faust* and Figaro in Mozart's *Marriage of Figaro.*

Sieveking, Martinus, Dutch pianist; b. Amsterdam, March 24, 1867; d. Pasadena, Calif., Nov. 26, 1950. He studied piano with his father; began his career as an accompanist; traveled with Adelina Patti on her tour of England (1891–92); then settled in the U.S.; in 1915 established his own piano school in N.Y. and announced a new method which guaranteed to achieve virtuosity in 24 months; not very successful in N.Y., he went to California, where he found a fertile field for his quick road to virtuosity for everybody.

Siface, Giovanni Francesco, famous Italian male soprano; b. Pescia, Feb. 12, 1653; d. Ferrara, May 29, 1697 (murdered by hired assassins). He was a member of the Papal Chapel in 1675–77; in Modena from 1679 till 1687; later sang at Venice and London.

Sigismondi, Giuseppe, Italian singing teacher and composer; b. Naples, Nov. 13, 1739; d. there, May 10, 1826. He was librarian at the Cons. in Naples (from 1808); wrote an opera, 4 oratorios, vocal music, and pieces for piano and organ; only a few of his works were published.

Sigtenhorst-Meyer, Bernhard van den, Dutch composer; b. Amsterdam, June 17, 1888; d. The Hague, July 17, 1953. He studied at the Amsterdam Cons.; later in Vienna and Paris; settled in The Hague as composer and writer.

WORKS: 2 string quartets (1919, 1944); Sonata for cello solo (1926); 2 violin sonatas (1926, 1938); *6 Miniatures* for oboe and piano (1926–46); 2 piano sonatas (1922, 1925); 3 piano sonatinas (1928, 1930, 1948); other piano pieces: *La Vieille Chine* (1916), *Les Oiseaux* (1917); 2 albums, *Le Monde de contesbleus* (1926–28); edited works by Sweelinck; publ. the valuable treatises, *Jan P. Sweelinck en zijn instrumentale Muziek* (The Hague, 1934; 2nd ed., 1946) and *De vocale Muziek van Jan P. Sweelinck* (1948).

BIBLIOGRAPHY: C. Backers, *Nederlandsche Componisten* (The Hague, 2nd ed., 1948, pp. 131–37); H. Antcliffe, "Sigtenhorst-Meyer: A Personal Impression," *Monthly Musical Record* (Dec. 1953).

Sigurbjörnsson, Thorkell, Icelandic composer; b. Reykjavik, July 16, 1938. He studied violin, piano, organ, theory, and music history at the Reykjavik School of Music (1948-57); then came to the U.S. and studied composition and piano at Hamline Univ. in Minnesota (1957-59) and electronic music with Lejaren Hiller and composition with Gaburo at the Univ. of Illinios (1959-61). Returning to Reykjavik he founded the modern group "Musica Nova"; was assistant director of music for the Iceland State Broadcasting Service (1966-69) and a music critic. In his music he modernizes traditional modalities by an injection of acrid dissonances and vitalizes the fundamentally placid metrical divisions by disruptive rhythmic asymmetries.

WORKS: *Ballade* for tenor, flute, viola, and guitar (1960); *Leikar* for chorus and orch. (1961); *Flökt (Fluctuations)* for orch. (1961); *Víxl (Rotation)* for violin, clarinet, cello, and duplicate instruments on tape (1962); a chamber opera, *Composition in 3 Scenes* (1964); a children's opera. *Apaspil* (1966); *Cadenza and Dance* for violin and orch. (1967); a children's opera, *Rabbi* (1968); *Hässelby-Quartet,* string quartet (1968); *Ymur* for orch. (1969); *Kisum* for clarinet, viola, and piano (1970); *Intrada* for clarinet, viola, and piano (1970); *Ys og Thys (Much Ado),* overture (1970); *Laeti* for orch. and orch. on tape (1971); a ballet, *Thorgeirsboli (The Bull-man,* 1971); *Happy Music* for brass ensemble (1971); *Mistur* for orch. (1972); *Haflög* for orch. (1973); *Dáik* for clarinet, cello, and synthesizer (1973); *Hylling (Homage)* for flute, cello, piano, percussion, tape, and audience (1974); *Nidur,* concerto for double bass and orch. (1974); *Búkolla,* concerto for clarinet and orch. (1974); *Four Better or Worse* for flute, clarinet, cello, and piano (1975); *Albumblatt* for orch. (1975); *Wiblo* for horn, piano, and strings (1976); *Solstice* for soprano, alto, baritone, flute, marimba, and double bass (1976); *Ríma* for orch (1977); *Copenhagen Quartet* for string quartet (1977); *The Pied Piper* for flute and string trio (1978).

Sigwart, Botho (real name **Sigwart Botho, Count of Eulenburg**), German pianist and composer; son of the German diplomat and poet Count Phillip of Eulenburg; b. Berlin, Jan. 10, 1884; d. in Galicia, June 2, 1915 (from wounds received in battle). He studied piano in Vienna and musicology at the Univ. of Munich (Dr. phil., 1907, with the dissertation, *Erasmus Widmann*); completed his studies with Max Reger at Leipzig (1908-09). In 1909 he married the concert singer **Helene Staegemann.** He wrote a number of piano pieces, a string quartet, and several melodramas.

Siklós, Albert, Hungarian composer; b. Budapest, June 26, 1878; d. there, April 3, 1942. His real name was **Schönwald,** but he changed it to Siklós in 1910. He studied law, and later took courses with Koessler at the Budapest Academy of Music, graduating in 1901; he taught at the Academy from 1910, and gradually became one of its most respected teachers. He was a prolific composer, but few of his works were published, and there were virtually no performances outside Hungary. He wrote the opera *The House of the Moons* (Budapest, Dec. 21, 1927); a ballet, *The Mirror* (Budapest, March 28, 1923), and other stage works; 2 symphonies and an interesting *Symphonie aethérique* for 12 double basses (1899); Cello Concerto; Violin Concerto; much chamber music; piano pieces. He publ. a number of instructive books, and also a music dictionary in Hungarian.

Sikorski, Kazimierz, Swiss-born Polish composer and pedagogue; b. Zürich, June 28, 1895 (of Polish parents). He studied at the College of Music in Warsaw; then took a course in musicology with Chybiński in Lwów; completed musical studies in Paris (1925-27). He taught at the State Cons. in Lódź (1947-54); at the State College in Warsaw (1951-57); became its director (1957-66). Many Polish composers of the younger generation were his students, among them Grazyna Bacewicz, Panufnik, Palester and Serocki.

WORKS: 4 symphonies: (1918, 1921, 1953, 1971); *Suite* for string orch. (1917); Clarinet Concerto (1947); Concerto for horn and small orch. (1948); *Popular Overture* (1954); Flute Concerto (1957); Concerto for trumpet, string orch., 4 timpani, xylophone and tam-tam (1959); *6 Old Polish Dances* for small orch. (1963); *Concerto Polyphonique* for bassoon and orch. (1965); Oboe Concerto (1967); Trombone Concerto (1973); 3 string quartets; String Sextet; choruses. He published 3 books; *Instrumentoznawstwo (The Study of Instruments,* Warsaw, 1932; 2nd and 3rd eds., 1950 and 1975; the 3rd ed. includes information on modern percussion); *Harmonia (Harmony,* 3 vols., Cracow, 1948-49; 4th ed., 1972) and *Kontrapunkt (Counterpoint,* 3 vols., Cracow, 1953-57).

Sikorski, Tomasz, Polish composer and pianist, son of Kazimierz Sikorski; b. Warsaw, May 19, 1939. He studied piano with Drzewiecki and composition with his father; then took lessons with Nadia Boulanger in Paris. As a pianist, he emphasizes new music in his programs. His own compositions are also in the advanced idiom.

WORKS: a radio opera, *Przygody Sindbada zeglarza (The Adventures of Sinbad the Sailor,* 1971); *Echoes 2 quasi improvvisazione* for 1-4 pianos, percussion and tape (1961-63); *Antyfony* for soprano without text, piano, horn, chimes, 2 gongs, 2 tamtams and tape (1963); *Prologues* for female chorus, 2 pianos, 4 flutes, 4 horns and 4 percussionists (1964); *Architectures* for piano, winds and percussion (1965); *Concerto breve* for piano, 24 winds and 4 percussionists (1965); *Sequenza I* for orch. (1966); *Sonant* for piano (1967); *Intersections* for 36 percussion instruments (1968); *Homophony* for 4 trumpets, 4 horns, 4 trombones, piano and 2 gongs (1968); *Diafonia* for 2 pianos (1969); *For Strings* for 3 violins and 3 violas (1970); *Vox humana* for chorus, 12 brasses, 2 pianos, 4 gongs and 4 tam-tams (1971); *Zerstreutes Hinausschauen* for piano (1971); *Holzwege* for orch. (1972); *Etude* for orch. (1972); *Bez tytulu (Untitled)* for piano, clarinet, trombone and cello (1972); *Listening Music* for 2 pianos (1973); *Music from Afar* for chorus and orch. (1974); *Other Voices* for winds and percussion (1975).

Silas, Eduard, pianist and composer; b. Amsterdam, Aug. 22, 1827; d. London, Feb. 8, 1909. He studied piano in Frankfurt and in Paris; took courses at the

Paris Cons. with Halévy; won 1st prize for organ playing in competition with Saint-Saëns. In 1850 he settled in England as organist; also taught harmony at the Guildhall School in London. Among his works are 3 symphonies, 3 piano concertos, 2 string quintets, 2 piano trios, numerous piano pieces; also an oratorio, *Joash* (Norwich Festival, 1863), and a Mass.

Silbermann, German family of organ and piano makers. (1) **Andreas Silbermann,** b. Klein-Bobritzsch, Saxony, May 16, 1678; d. Strasbourg, March 16, 1734. He settled in Strasbourg in 1703; was the builder of the organ of the Strasbourg Cathedral (1714–16) and of 29 others. (2) **Gottfried Silbermann,** brother of Andreas, b. Klein-Bobritzsch, Jan. 14, 1683; d. Dresden, Aug. 4, 1753. Apprenticed to a bookbinder, he ran away and joined his brother in Strasbourg, working as his helper. He then lived in Freiberg; built 47 organs, the finest of which is that in the Freiberg Cathedral (1714), having 3 manuals and 45 stops. He owed his fame, however, mainly to the manufacture of pianos in Germany, in which field he was a pioneer; the hammer action in his instruments was practically identical with that of Cristofori, the piano inventor. Silbermann also invented the "cembal d'amour," a clavichord with strings of double length, struck in the middle by the tangents, thus yielding the duplicated octave of the tone of the entire string. He supplied 3 pianos to Frederick the Great for Potsdam, and Bach played on them during his visit there in 1747. (3) **Johann Andreas Silbermann,** eldest son of Andreas; b. Strasbourg, June 24, 1712; d. there, Feb. 11, 1783. He built 54 organs; publ. a *Geschichte der Stadt Strassburg* (1775). (4) **Johann Daniel Silbermann,** brother of Johann Andreas; b. Strasbourg, March 31, 1717; d. Leipzig, May 9, 1766. He worked with his uncle Gottfried at Freiberg, and continued the manufacture of pianos after the latter's death. (5) **Johann Heinrich Silbermann,** brother of Johann Andreas and Johann Daniel; b. Strasbourg, Sept. 24, 1727; d. there, Jan. 15, 1799; made pianos at Strasbourg, similar to those of his uncle Gottfried, and introduced them into France. (6) **Johann Friedrich Silbermann,** son of Johann Heinrich; b. Strasbourg, June 21, 1762; d. there, March 8, 1817. He was an organist in Strasbourg; during the Revolution wrote a *Hymne à la Paix;* also composed some German songs.
BIBLIOGRAPHY: L. Mooser, *Gottfried Silbermann* (Langensalza, 1857); G. Zschaler, *Gottfried Silbermann* (1898); E. Flade, *Der Orgelbauer Gottfried Silbermann* (Leipzig, 1926); H. Hullemann, *Die Tätigkeit des Orgelbauers Gottfried Silbermann im Reussenland* (Leipzig, 1937); R. Gärtner, *Gottfried Silbermann der Orgelbauer* (Dresden, 1938); J. Wörsching, *Die Orgelbauer Familie Silbermann in Strassburg* (Mainz, 1941); E. Flade, *Gottfried Silbermann. Ein Beitrag zur Geschichte des deutschen Orgel- und Klavierbau im Zeitalter Bachs* (Leipzig, 1953); Donald Boalch, *Makers of the Harpsichord and Clavichord 1440–1840* (London, 1956, pp. 112–14; contains genealogy and list of extant instruments made by members of the family).

Silcher, Friedrich, German composer; b. Schnaith, Württemberg, June 27, 1789; d. Tübingen, Aug. 26, 1860. He studied with his father and with Auberlen, an organist at Fellbach; lived for some years in Stuttgart; in 1817 was appointed music director at the Univ. of Tübingen, receiving the honorary degree of Dr. phil. in 1852. He was an influential promoter of German popular singing; publ. several collections of German folksongs, in which he included his own composition; of the latter, *Lorelei* (*Ich weiss nicht, was soll es bedeuten,* to words by Heinrich Heine) became so popular that it was often mistaken for a folksong; his other well-known songs are *Ännchen von Tharau, Morgen muss ich fort von hier, Zu Strassburg auf der Schanz,* etc. He also publ. a *Choralbuch* for 3 voices, 3 books of hymns for 4 voices; *Tübinger Liedertafel* (male choruses). He wrote the books *Geschichte des evangelischen Kirchengesanges* (1844); *Harmonie- und Kompositionslehre* (1851; 2nd ed., 1859).
BIBLIOGRAPHY: A. Köstlin, *F. Silcher und Weber* (Stuttgart, 1877); A. Prümers, *F. Silcher: der Meister des deutschen Volkslieds* (Stuttgart, 1910); G. Brügel, "Kritische Mitteilungen zu Silchers Volksliedern," *Sammelbände der Internationalen Musik-Gesellschaft* (1914); A. Bopp, *F. Silcher* (Stuttgart, 1916); A. Bopp, *Liederbuch aus Schwaben* (1918); H. Kleinert and H. Rauschnabel, eds., *F. Silcher* (Stuttgart, 1935); A. Lämmle, *F. Silcher* (Mühlacker, 1956).

Sills, Beverly (real name **Belle Silverman**), celebrated American soprano; b. Brooklyn, May 25, 1929. At the age of three she appeared on the radio as Bubbles. At the age of 12 she began to study music seriously, singing with Estelle Liebling and piano with Paolo Gallico. From acting soap operas on the radio she gradually progressed to grand opera; appeared with the Philadelphia Civic Opera, and the N.Y. City Opera. On July 7, 1956 she created the role of Baby Doe in Douglas Moore's folk opera *The Ballad of Baby Doe,* at Central City, Colorado. Eventually she launched a brilliantly successful career; appeared at La Scala in Milan; at the Teatro Colón in Buenos Aires; her Met debut was in *The Siege of Corinth* (Rossini), April 8, 1975; was acclaimed by the most fastidious European and American critics as a stellar diva of the first magnitude. She published an autobiography, *Bubbles: A Self-Portrait* (N.Y., 1976).

Siloti, Alexander, eminent Russian pianist, pedagogue and conductor; b. on the family estate near Kharkov, Oct. 9, 1863; d. New York, Dec. 8, 1945. He studied piano with Zverev and Nicholas Rubinstein at the Moscow Cons., and music theory with Tchaikovsky (1876–81), winning the gold medal. He made his debut as pianist in Moscow in 1880; then made a tour in Germany; Liszt accepted him as a student in 1883, and Siloti continued his study with Liszt in Weimar until Liszt's death in 1886. Returning to Russia, he was appointed prof. of piano at the Moscow Cons. (1888–91); among his students was Rachmaninoff (his first cousin). Between 1891 and 1900 he lived in Germany, France and Belgium; returned to Russia in 1901 and conducted the concerts of the Moscow Philharmonic Society during the season 1901–02; in 1903 he organized his own orchestra in St. Petersburg, which he conducted until 1913; these concerts acquired great cultural importance; Siloti invited Mengelberg and Mottl as guest conductors, and Rachmaninoff, Casals and Chaliapin as soloists. In 1915 he began a series of popular free concerts, and in 1916 started a Russian Musical Fund to aid indigent musicians. In 1919 he left Russia; lived in Finland, Germany and England; in 1922 he settled in N.Y., where he was active principally as a teacher, but continued to appear as a soloist with American orchestras; from 1925 to 1942 he was on the faculty of the Juilliard School of Music. He published a collection of piano pieces which he edited, with indications of fingering and pedaling; also arranged and edited concertos by Bach and Vivaldi. He published a book of his reminiscences of Liszt (St. Petersburg, 1911; in English, Edinburgh, 1913). See *Dictionary of American Biography*, III.

Silva, Francisco Manuel da, Brazilian composer of the Brazilian national anthem; b. Rio de Janeiro, Feb. 21, 1795; d. there, Dec. 18, 1865. He was a pupil of Marcos Portugal. In 1833 he founded the Sociedade Beneficente Musical; was active mostly as a music teacher and choral conductor. He wrote an opera *O prestigio da lei,* but he owes his fame to the fact that he was the composer of the Brazilian national anthem, *Ouviram do Ypiranga as margens placidas.*
BIBLIOGRAPHY: A. de Albuquerque, *Ouviram do Ypiranga. Vida de Francisco Manuel de Silva* (Rio de Janeiro, 1959); A. de Andrade, *Francisco Manuel da Silva e seu tempo, 1808-65. Uma fase do passado musical do Rio de Janeiro á luz de novos documentos* (2 vols., Rio de Janeiro, 1967).

Silva, Luigi, American cellist; b. Milan, Nov. 13, 1903; d. New York, Nov. 29, 1961. He was of a musical family; his father was a vocal teacher; his mother a Viennese singer. He studied music at home; then took cello lessons with Arturo Bonucci in Bologna and composition with Respighi in Rome. He played in several string quartets in Italy; in 1939 he emigrated to the U.S.; taught cello and chamber music at the Eastman School of Music, Rochester, N.Y. (1941-49); in 1949 joined the staff of the Juilliard School of Music, N.Y. He made transcriptions for cello of works by Paganini, Boccherini, and other Italian composers; edited Bach's unaccompanied cello suites.

Silva, Oscar da, Portuguese pianist and composer; b. Paranhos, near Oporto, April 21, 1870; d. Oporto, March 6, 1958. He studied at the Lisbon Cons.; in 1892 went to Germany where he had lessons with Reinecke and Clara Schumann. Returning to Portugal in 1910 he devoted himself mainly to teaching, acquiring a very high reputation as a piano pedagogue. From 1932 to 1952 he lived in Brazil; then returned to Portugal. He wrote an opera, *Dona Mecia* (Lisbon, July 4, 1901); a symph. poem, *Alma crucificada;* and a number of effective piano pieces, among them: *Rapsodia portuguesa, Estudos indefinidos, Papillon dans le jardin, Paginas portuguesas;* some chamber music and a number of songs to French words.
BIBLIOGRAPHY: A. Pinto, *Musica moderna portuguesa e os seus representantes* (Lisbon, 1930, pp. 114-29).

Silva, (David) Poll da, French composer; b. St.-Esprit, near Bayonne, March 28, 1834; d. Clermont, Oise, May 9, 1875. He went to Paris as a youth, and was encouraged by Halévy to study music and compose despite his incipient blindness; his mother, who was an educated musician, wrote out his compositions from dictation. Despite his handicap, he wrote 3 operas, 2 oratorios, 2 symphonies, and various other works.

Silver, Charles, French composer; b. Paris, April 16, 1868; d. there, Oct. 10, 1949. He studied with Dubois and Massenet at the Paris Cons., winning the Grand Prix de Rome in 1891 with the cantata *L'Interdit.* He wrote the operas *La Belle au bois dormant* (Marseilles, 1902); *Le Clos* (Paris, 1906); *Myriane* (Nice, 1913); *La Mégère apprivoisée* (Paris, Jan. 30, 1922); *La Grand'-mère* (Oct. 7, 1930); *Quatre-vingt-treize* (Paris, Jan. 24, 1936); also orchestral works, songs, etc.

Silverstein, Joseph, American violinist; b. Detroit, March 21, 1932. He studied with his father and with Efrem Zimbalist at the Curtis Institute of Music in Philadelphia; later with Joseph Gingold and Mischa Mischakoff. He played in the Houston Orch., Denver Orch. and the Philadelphia Orch. In 1955 he joined the Boston Symph. Orch., and in 1961 was appointed its concertmaster. He also appeared as soloist.

Silvestri, Constantin, Rumanian conductor and composer; b. Bucharest, June 13, 1913; d. London, Feb. 23, 1969. He studied composition with Jora at the Bucharest Cons.; toured as a concert pianist (1925-46); then was engaged as conductor of the Bucharest Philh. (1946-55); later conducted the Bucharest Opera (1955-57) and the Rumanian Radio Orch. (1958-59); also taught conducting at the Bucharest Cons. (1948-59). In 1961 he went to England, where he became principal conductor of the Bournemouth Symph. Orch. until his death. He composed mostly in small forms in an unpretentious neo-Baroque manner.
WORKS: Concerto Grosso (1941); 2 string quartets (1935, 1947); *Sonatina a 2 voci* for clarinet and cello (1938); Oboe Sonata (1939); 2 violin sonatas (1939); piano pieces and songs.

Silvestrov, Valentin, Ukrainian composer; b. Kiev, Sept. 30, 1937. He studied with Liatoshinsky at the Kiev Cons.; began to compose in a boldly experimental idiom of Western provenance; wrote piano pieces in the strict 12-tone technique. Although severely reprimanded in the press, he was not forcibly restrained from continuing to write music in a modernistic manner.
WORKS: for piano: *Variations* (1958), Sonatina (1959), Sonata (1960), *Signals* (1962), *Serenade* (1962), Piano Quintet (1961); *Quartetto piccolo* for string quartet (1961); Trio for flute, trumpet and celesta (1962); Symph. No. 1 (1963); *Mysteries* for alto flute and percussion (1964); *Monodia* for piano and orch. (1965); *Projections* for harpsichord, vibraphone and bells (1965); *Spectrum* for chamber orch. (1965); Symph. No. 2 for flute, percussion, piano and strings (1965); Symph. No. 3 (1966); *Drama* for violin, cello and piano (1971); *Meditation* for cello and chamber

orch. (1972); String Quartet (1974); Symph. No. 4 for brass instruments and strings (1976); also children's pieces for piano and songs. Some of his compositions had their world premières at European festivals of modern music.

Simai, Pavol, Czech composer; b. Levice, June 29, 1930. He studied with Pál Kadosa in Budapest, with Alexander Moyzes and Jan Cikker in Bratislava and with Paul Dessau in East Berlin. In 1968 he settled in Sweden.
WORKS: Flute Sonatina (1952); *Zuzuka,* ballet (1954–60); *Mother Speaks,* melodrama for female speaker, flute, clarinet, bassoon, guitar and percussion (1959); *Victory* for orch. (1963); *Meditation* for contralto and string quartet (1965); *5:10* for clarinet, violin, cello and piano (1972); Piano Trio (1974); *Violoncellen* for mezzo-soprano, cello and piano (1975).

Simandl, Franz, double bass player and composer; b. Blatna, Bohemia, Aug. 1, 1840; d. Vienna, Dec. 13, 1912. He was double bass player in the Vienna court orch.; from 1869, taught at the Vienna Cons.; publ. *Neueste Methode des Kontrabass-Spiels* (in 3 parts) and *30 Etüden für Kontrabass; Die hohe Schule des Kontrabass-Spiels,* a collection of concertos, studies, solo pieces, etc. His original compositions include a *Konzertstück, Konzert-Étude,* a concerto, fantasias, and minor pieces for his instrument.

Simić, Borivoje, Serbian conductor and composer; b. Belgrade, Nov. 1, 1920. He studied in Belgrade and became a choral conductor of the Belgrade Radio. His music is modernistic in nature and eclectic in its materials, making use of a dissonant counterpoint and jazz. His *Movimento dinamico* (Belgrade, Sept. 30, 1955) is characteristic in this resepect.

Similä, Martti, Finnish conductor and composer; b. Oulu (Uleaborg), April 9, 1898; d. Lahti, Jan. 9, 1958. He studied in Finland; then in Paris and London; conducted the Helsinki Opera (1927–44) and the Municipal Orch. of Lahti. He made two tours in the U.S. as pianist, in 1923 and 1926; was again in the U.S. in 1957 to lead a memorial concert of the music of Sibelius with the N.Y. Philharmonic (Dec. 8, 1957). He wrote a book *Sibeliana;* also composed orchestral music.

Simionato, Giulietta, Italian contralto; b. Forli, Dec. 15, 1910. She studied voice with Guido Palumbo in Milan; made her operatic debut in Florence in 1938; from 1939 till 1959 she was the leading contralto singer at La Scala, Milan. After the end of the war, she made guest appearances in the major opera houses in Europe; also appeared in South America. She sang at the Metropolitan Opera in New York from 1959 to 1965, and then retired from the stage. Her best roles were Rosina in *The Barber of Seville* and Amneris in *Aida.*

Simon, Abbey, American pianist; b. New York, Jan. 8, 1922. He studied with David Saperton and Josef Hofmann at the Curtis Institute of Music in Philadelphia; also took lessons with Leopold Godowsky in New York. He began his concert career at 18, evolving a grand bravura style of pianistic virtuosity in which no technical difficulties seem to exist, no tempi are too fast, no nuance too subtle. He made successful tours in the U.S., South America, Europe (including Russia), Australia, and Japan.

Simon, Alicia, Polish musicologist; b. Lódź, Nov. 13, 1879; d. there, May 23, 1957. She studied in Warsaw; then went to Germany where she attended the classes of Kretzschmar and Johannes Wolf at the Univ. of Berlin. In 1918 she went to the U.S., and worked on the staff of the Library of Congress in Washington (1924–28); then returned to Poland. She was prof. at the Univ. of Lódź from 1945 to her death. She published some valuable studies on Polish music, among them *Polnische Elemente in der deutschen Musik bis zur Zeit der Wiener Klassiker* (Zürich, 1916); *The Polish Songwriters* (in English; Warsaw, 1936; 2nd ed., 1939).

Simon, Anton, French pianist and composer; b. Paris, Aug. 5, 1850; d. St. Petersburg, Feb. 1, 1916. He studied piano at the Paris Cons.; in 1871 went to Russia, where he became active as a piano teacher. He wrote the operas *Rolla* (Moscow, April 29, 1892), *The Song of Triumphant Love* (Moscow, Dec. 14, 1897), and *The Fishermen* (Moscow, March 7, 1899); a mimodrama, *Esmeralda* (1902); 2 ballets, *The Stars* (1898) and *Living Flowers* (1900); Piano Concerto; Clarinet Concerto; 22 pieces for brass instruments and numerous piano compositions and songs.

Simon, James, German musicologist; b. Berlin, Sept. 29, 1880; d. in the Auschwitz concentration camp, about Oct. 14, 1944. He studied piano with Ansorge and composition with Max Bruch. From 1907 to 1919 he taught at the Klindworth-Scharwenka Cons. in Berlin. He left Germany shortly after the advent of the Nazi regime, and lived in Zürich; then moved to Amsterdam where the Hitlerite wave engulfed him after the Nazi invasion of Holland. He was deported to Theresienstadt on April 5, 1944, and from there, on Oct. 12, 1944, was sent to Auschwitz, where he was put to death a few days later. His opera, *Frau im Stein* was produced in Stuttgart in 1925; he also wrote a symphony, a piano concerto; a sextet for piano and wind instruments; choruses and many songs.

Simonds, Bruce, American pianist and pedagogue; b. Bridgeport, Conn., July 5, 1895. After studying at Yale Univ. (A.B. 1917), he attended the Schola Cantorum in Paris (1919–20) and the Matthay School in London (1920–21). Made his debut as a pianist in Europe in 1921; in the same year returned to the U.S. and embarked on a successful career as concert pianist; also in 1921 joined the teaching staff at Yale; prof. since 1938; dean of the Yale School of Music, 1941–54.

Simoneau, Léopold, Canadian tenor; b. Quebec City, May 3, 1918. He studied singing in N.Y.; he began his career as opera singer in Paris, at La Scala, Milan and in Salzburg. He was particularly praised for his performances of Mozart's roles. In 1971 he went to San

Francisco, where he taught at the Cons. He is married to the Canadian coloratura soprano **Pierrette Alarie.**

Simonetti, Achille, Italian-British violinist; b. Turin, June 12, 1857; d. London, Nov. 19, 1928. He studied violin with Gamba at the Milan Cons. and with Dancla at the Paris Cons.; toured in England with the singer Marie Rôze and the double bass virtuoso Bottesini; settled in London in 1891, but made frequent tours on the Continent. He wrote a cadenza for Brahms's Violin Concerto, which he played for the first time in Dresden (Dec. 11, 1896); composed numerous solo pieces for the violin.

Simonis, Jean-Marie, Belgian composer; b. Mol, Nov. 22, 1931. He studied composition with Stekke, Souris, Louel and Quinet, and conducting with Defossez at the Royal Cons. of Brussels; taught at the Royal Cons. from 1969 and at the Music Academy in Uccles from 1971.
WORKS: a radio opera *Gens de maison* (1962); *3 Motets* for soprano, chorus and orch. (1961); *Introduction et Danse* for chamber orch. (1963); *Trois esquisses symphoniques* (1964); *Sinfonia da camera* for string orch. (1966); *L'Automne,* symph. poem (1967); *Scherzetto* for chamber orch. (1968); *3 Pieces* for 4 clarinets (1965); *Duetti* for viola and piano (1968); *Impromptu* for solo cello (1968–69); *Séquences* for clarinet and piano (1969); *3 Lagu Dolanan* for soprano and percussion (1969); *Suggestions* for flute and 4 percussionists (1970); *Boutades* for 4 saxophones (1971); *Mouvements* for 2 pianos (1971); a number of piano pieces: *Etude de Concert* (1963); *Historiettes* (1972); *Impromptu* (1973); *2 Animations* (1973); *2 Pastourelles* (1973); *Evocations* (1974).

Simpson (or **Sympson**), **Christopher,** English player of the viola da gamba and composer; b. Yorkshire, c.1610; d. Scampton, Lincolnshire, 1669. He fought on the Royalist side in the English civil war (1643) and later entered the service of Sir Robert Bolles as music tutor to the latter's son. Simpson was famous as a composer.
WORKS: *The Division Violist or an Introduction to the Playing Upon a Ground: Divided into 2 parts* (London, 1659; 2nd ed. with title and text in Latin and English, in 3 parts, London, 1665; 3rd ed., 1712, with 2 sonatas for viola da gamba; modern ed. by Nathalie Dolmetsch, London, 1958); *The Principles of Practicle Musick . . . either in Singing or Playing upon an Instrument* (London, 1665; enlarged ed., as *Practicall Musick in 5 Parts teaching by a new and easie Method,* London, 1667); also compiled annotations to Campion's *Art of Discant* (1655). In MS: *Months and Seasons: Fancies, Airs, Galliards,* for 2 basses and a treble; *Fancies* for viola da gamba; etc.

Simpson, George Elliott, American music educator and composer; b. Orange, N.J., Nov. 1, 1876; d. Kansas City, Oct. 8, 1958. He studied with Emil Mollenhauer (violin) in N.Y. (1886–90); then took composition lessons with Carl Busch in Kansas City (1894–1900); subsequently studied at the Leipzig Cons. with Jadassohn and Reinecke (1900–03). He occupied various teaching positions in Kansas City and

in Texas. His works include an *American Symphony* (Kansas City, March 26, 1925); 12 symph. poems; 4 overtures; about 50 piano pieces and 80 songs.

Simpson, Robert, English composer and writer on music; b. Leamington, Warwickshire, March 2, 1921. He studied composition with Howells in London (1941–44); received his Mus. D. from Durham Univ. in 1951; joined the staff of the BBC as a music producer in 1951. He published a valuable monograph, *Carl Nielsen, Symphonist* (London, 1952); also *The Essence of Bruckner* (London, 1966) and 3 BBC booklets: *Bruckner and the Symphony* (1963), *Sibelius and Nielsen* (1965) and *Beethoven's Symphonies* (1970); also edited *The Symphony* (2 vols.; London, 1967). He was awarded the Carl Nielsen Gold Medal of Denmark in 1956 for his valiant work in behalf of Nielsen's music. While occupied with writing and directing radio programs, he composed symphonies, chamber music, and choruses.
WORKS: 5 symphonies: No. 1, in one movement (1951; Copenhagen, June 11, 1953); No. 2 (1955; Cheltenham Festival, July 16, 1957); No. 3 (1962; Birmingham, March 14, 1963); No. 4 (1970–72; Manchester, April 26, 1973); No. 5 (1972; London, May 3, 1973); Violin Concerto (1959; Birmingham, Feb. 25, 1960); Piano Concerto (1967; Cheltenham Festival, July 14, 1967); 6 string quartets (1952, 1953, 1954, 1973, 1974, 1975); *Canzona* for brass (1958); *Variations and Fugue* for recorder and string quartet (1958); Trio for clarinet, cello and piano (1967); Quartet for clarinet and strings (1968); Quartet for horn, violin, cello and piano (1975); *Media morte in vita sumus,* motet for chorus, brass, and timpani (1975); Piano Sonata (1946); *Variations and Finale on a Theme by Haydn* for piano (1948).
BIBLIOGRAPHY: R. Johnson, *Robert Simpson. 50th Birthday Essays* (London, 1971).

Simpson, Thomas, English composer; b. Milton (Kent), 1582 (baptized April 1, 1582); d. after 1625. He went to Germany as a youth; served as viol player at the Heidelberg Court from 1608 to 1611; then was Musicus to the Prince of Holstein-Schaumburg (1616–22) and subsequently was employed in the royal chapel of Copenhagen as court musician to King Christian IV. An excellent composer of court dances and songs, he brought out *Opusculum newer Pavanen* (Frankfurt, 1610); *Pavanen, Galliarden, Courtanten und Volten* (Frankfurt, 1611; reprinted in 1617 under the title *Opus newer Paduanen, Galliarden, Intraden, Canzonen, etc.*); and *Tafel-Consort, allerhand lustige Lieder von 4 Instrumenten und Generalbass* (Hamburg, 1621).
BIBLIOGRAPHY: G. Oberst, *Englische Orchestersuiten um 1600* (Wolfenbüttel, 1929).

Simrock, Nikolaus, founder of the famous German publishing house in Berlin; b. Mainz, Aug. 23, 1751; d. Bonn, June 12, 1832. He played the horn in the Electoral Orchestra in Bonn until 1794. In 1785 he opened a music shop in Bonn, selling musical instruments; in 1793 he established there a music publishing house with its own printing press. During Beethoven's lifetime Simrock's catalogue listed 85 of his works, including the *Kreutzer Sonata* and opus numbers 17, 31, 81b, 102 and 107. His son **Peter Joseph Simrock** (b. Bonn, Aug. 18, 1792; d. Cologne, Dec. 13, 1868) succeeded him and greatly increased the prestige of the house by acquiring the early works of Brahms. Peter was succeeded by his son **Fritz August Simrock** (b. Bonn, Jan. 2, 1837; d. Ouchy, near Lausanne, Aug. 20, 1901), who transferred the firm to Berlin in 1870, published the works of Brahms and, at the suggestion of Brahms, added the works of Dvořák to his catalogue. His nephew **Hans Simrock** (b. Cologne, April 17, 1861; d. Berlin, July 26, 1910) reorganized the firm in 1902 as a stock company and established branches in London and Paris. A grandson of Fritz August Simrock, **Fritz Auckenthaler** (b. Zürich, Nov. 17, 1893; d. Basel, April 19, 1973), headed the firm from 1920 to 1929, when it was sold to A. J. Benjamin in Hamburg; in 1951 the Hamburg firm, which also had a branch in London, resumed its original name, N. Simrock Co.

BIBLIOGRAPHY: W. Ottendorf-Simrock, *Das Haus Simrock* (Ratingen, 1954); K. Stephenson, *Johannes Brahms und Fritz Simrock, weg einer Freundschaft. Briefe des Verlegers an den Komponisten* (Hamburg, 1961).

Sims, Ezra, American composer; b. Birmingham, Alabama, Jan. 16, 1928. He studied at the Birmingham Cons. of Music (1945–48), with Quincy Porter at Yale Univ. (B.M., 1952), and with Darius Milhaud and Leon Kirchner at Mills College (M.A., 1955). He subsequently settled in Cambridge, Mass. His music incorporates experimental techniques, including microtones and electronic collage. In 1977 he developed a polyphonic microtonal keyboard which is capable of switching to any equal temperament expressible by the equation $5x + 7y = 62$, with each degree of the resulting temperament alterable downward by a semitone; the same keyboard can be adjusted to produce an asymmetrical scale of 18 or 19 degrees.

WORKS: *Chamber Cantata on Chinese Poems* (1954); *Cello Sonata* (1957); 3 String Quartets: No. 1 (1959); *Sonate Concertanti* for "demountable octet," consisting of 5 sonatinas for oboe, viola, cello and bass, and 5 sonatas for 2 string quartets numbered as String Quartet No. 2 (1961–62). String Quartet No. 3 is titled, with malice aforethought and intent to mislead, *String Quartet No. 2 (1962)*, but it was actually composed in 1974 and dedicated to Nicolas Slonimsky to help rectify his error in the 1971 Supplement to Baker's in which 3 string quartets are mentioned; furthermore, this confutatious work is not a string quartet at all, but a piece scored for flute, clarinet, violin, viola, and cello. Other works are: *Octet* for strings in quarter-tones and sixth-tones (1964); *Antimatter* for magnetic tape collage (1968); *Real Toads*, musique concrète (1970); *More Overture and Another Interlude* for tape collage with musique concrète (1970); *Elegie nach Rilke* for voice and instruments (1976).

Šín, Otakar, eminent Czech music theorist and composer; b. Rokytno, Moravia, April 23, 1881; d. Prague, Jan. 21, 1943. He studied composition with Vítězslav Novák at the Prague Cons., where he was appointed prof. of theory in 1919. He published the textbooks, *Complete Science of Harmony on the Basis of Melo-*

dies and Rhythm (Prague, 1922); *Science of Counterpoint, Imitation and Fugue* (Prague, 1936) and *General Science of Music as a Preparation for the Study of Harmony, Counterpoint and Musical Forms* (completed and publ. posthumously by František and Karel Janeček in Prague, 1949).

WORKS: 2 symph. poems: *Tillotama* (1908) and *King Menkera* (1916–18); *Radio Overture* (1936); *3 Czech Dances* for orch. (1939; also for nonet); 2 string quartets (1923, 1926–28); *Cello Sonata* (1934); *Small Suite* for violin and piano (1937); *Hunting,* festive greeting for horns (1938); numerous piano pieces; choruses; songs.

Sinatra, Frank (Francis Albert), popular American singer; b. Hoboken, N.J., Dec. 12, 1915, of immigrant Italian parents. He sang in a glee club in school; appeared on amateur radio shows. Inspired by the tone production of Tommy Dorsey's trombone playing, he evolved, by convex inhalation from a corner of the mouth, a *sui generis* "mal canto" in *sotto voce* delivery, employing a Caruso-like *coup-de-glotte* at climactic points. This mode of singing, combined with an engagingly slender physique, stirred the young females of the World War II era to fainting frenzy at his performances. Sinatra's press agents were quick to exploit the phenomenon, dubbing him "Swoonlight Sinatra." He eventually overcame his anesthetic appeal and became a successful baritone crooner; like most of his colleagues, he never learned to read music. He revealed an unexpected dramatic talent as a movie actor, eliciting praise from astonished cinema critics. In May, 1976, the Univ. of Nevada at Las Vegas conferred on him the honorary degree of Literarum Humanitarum Doctor, in appreciation of his many highly successful appearances in the hotels and gambling casinos of Las Vegas.

BIBLIOGRAPHY: E. J. Kahn, *The Voice: The Story of an American Phenomenon* (N.Y., 1947); A. Shaw, *Sinatra: 20th-Century Romantic* (N.Y., 1968); A. I. Lonstein, *The Compleat Sinatra Discography, Filmography, Television Appearances, Motion Picture Appearances, Radio, Concert, Stage Appearances* (Ellenville, N.Y., 1970); Earl Wilson, *Sinatra: An Unauthorized Biography* (N.Y., 1976; Sinatra instituted a suit for 3 million dollars against the publishers for alleged distortion of his life as "boring and uninteresting.")

Sinclair, George Robertson, English organist; b. Croydon, Oct. 28, 1863; d. Birmingham, Feb. 7, 1917. He received his musical education in Dublin; in 1889 was appointed organist of Hereford Cathedral, and also conducted the Three Choirs Festivals (1891–1912). He acquired a reputation as a master organist; the 11th variation of Elgar's *Enigma* is inscribed to Sinclair ("G. R. S.") and portrays vividly Sinclair's virtuosity in the use of the organ pedals.

BIBLIOGRAPHY: *Musical Times* (Oct. 1900; March 1906; March 1917).

Sinding, Christian, celebrated Norwegian composer; b. Kongsberg, Jan. 11, 1856; d. Oslo, Dec. 3, 1941. He studied first with L. Lindeman in Norway; then at the Leipzig Cons. with Schradieck (violin), Jadassohn (theory), and Reinecke (orchestration); after 4 years (1877–81) he returned to Norway, and had his Piano Quartet and a symphony performed in Oslo; a government stipend enabled him to continue his studies in Germany, and he spent 2 years (1882–84) in Munich, Berlin, and Dresden; there he wrote his 1st opera, *Titandros,* much influenced by Wagner. On Dec. 19, 1885, he gave a concert of his works in Oslo; during another stay in Germany, his Piano Quintet was played in Leipzig with Brodsky and Busoni among the performers (Jan. 19, 1889); Erika Lie-Nissen played his Piano Concerto in Berlin (Feb. 23, 1889). He publ. a number of piano pieces in Germany; of these *Frühlingsrauschen* became an international favorite. His opera to a German text, *Der heilige Berg* (1914), was not successful. In 1915 he received a pension for life of 4,000 crowns "for distinguished service"; on his 60th birthday (1916) the Norwegian government presented him with a purse of 30,000 crowns, a mark of appreciation for "the greatest national composer since Grieg." He was invited by George Eastman to teach at the Eastman School of Music in Rochester, N.Y., during the academic season 1921–22; after this journey, he lived mostly in Oslo. He continued to compose, and toward the end of his life wrote in larger forms; his 3rd Symph. was conducted by Nikisch with the Berlin Philharmonic in 1921, and his 4th Symph. was performed on his 80th birthday in Oslo (1936). His works aggregate to 132 opus numbers. Most of his music is of a descriptive nature; his lyric pieces for piano and his songs are fine examples of Scandinavian Romanticism, but the German inspiration of his formative years is much in evidence; he was chiefly influenced by Schumann and Liszt.

WORKS: OPERAS: *Titandros* (1884; not produced); *Der heilige Berg* (Dessau, April 19, 1914). FOR ORCH.: Symph. No. 1 (Oslo, March 25, 1882); Symph. No. 2 (Berlin, March 22, 1907); Symph. No. 3 (Berlin, Jan. 10, 1921); Symph. No. 4, subtitled *Vinter og Vaar* (Oslo, Jan. 11, 1936); *Épisodes chevaleresques,* op. 35 (1888); *Rondo infinito,* op. 42 (1889; revised 1897); Piano Concerto in D-flat (Berlin, Feb. 23, 1889); 3 violin concertos (1898, 1901, 1917); *Legende* for violin and orch., op. 46 (1900); *Romanze* for violin and orch., op. 100 (1910); *Abendstimmung,* for violin and orch., op. 120 (1915). CHAMBER MUSIC: String Quartet, op. 70 (1904); Piano Quintet, op. 5 (1884); 3 piano trios: op. 23 (1893), op. 64 (1902), op. 87 (1908); 4 violin sonatas: op. 12 (1894), op. 27 (1895), op. 73 (1905), op. 99, subtitled *Sonate im alten Stil* (1909); 4 violin suites: op. 10 (1889), op. 14 (1891), op. 96 (1909), op. 123 (1919); *Scènes de la vie* for violin and piano, op. 51 (1900); *Cantus doloris,* variations for violin and piano, op. 78 (1906); 3 capricci for violin and piano, op. 114 (1913); etc.; *Nordische Ballade,* for cello and piano, op. 105 (1911); etc. For piano: Sonata, op. 91 (1909); *Fatum,* variations, op. 94 (1909); *5 Stücke,* op. 24 (1894); 7 *Stücke,* op. 25 (1895); 6 *Stücke,* op. 31 (1896); 6 *Stücke,* op. 32 (1896; No. 3 is the celebrated *Frühlingsrauschen*); 6 *Charakterstücke,* op. 33 (1896; contains *À la Menuetto* and *Ständchen*); 6 *Charakterstücke,* op. 34 (1896; contains *Chanson*); 6 *Klavierstücke,* op. 49 (1899; contains *Humoresque*); *Mélodies mignonnes,* op. 52 (1900); *4 Morceaux de salon,* op. 54 (1900; contains *Sérénade*); etc. VOCAL WORKS: songs:

Alte Weisen, op. 1 (1886), *Lieder und Gesänge,* op. 11 (1888; contains *Viel Träume* and *Ein Weib*), *Galmandssange,* op. 22 (1893; contains *Mainat*), *Nyinger,* op. 90 (1908), etc.; about 250 publ. songs in all; several cantatas and other choral works. A complete list of Sinding's works was publ. by Ö. Gaukstad, in the *Norsk Musikkgranskning* (1938).

Singelée, Jean-Baptiste, Belgian violinist and composer; b. Brussels, Sept. 25, 1812; d. Ostend, Sept. 29, 1875. He publ. 144 works (2 concertos, many solos for violin, fantasias on operatic airs, etc.).

Singer, Edmund, Hungarian violinist; b. Totis, Hungary, Oct. 14, 1830; d. Stuttgart, Jan. 23, 1912. He studied in Budapest, and later at the Paris Cons.; was concertmaster in Weimar (1853–61); later, prof. at the Stuttgart Cons. He wrote a number of attractive violin pieces: *Tarantella, Rapsodie hongroise, Airs variés,* etc.; wrote cadenzas for the violin concertos of Beethoven and Brahms; edited the études of Rode, Kreutzer, Fiorillo, Rovelli, and Gaviniés; with M. Seifriz, compiled the *Grosse theoretisch-praktisch Violinschule* (2 vols., 1884).

Singer, Kurt, German musicologist; b. Berent, Oct. 11, 1885; d. in the Terezin concentration camp, Feb. 7, 1944. He studied musicology with Friedlaender in Berlin; also became a doctor of medicine; wrote criticisms for the socialist newspaper *Vorwärts.* In 1935, deprived of his posts in German organizations, became music director of the Reichsverband jüdischer Kulturbünde. He went to Holland in 1939, but was arrested there by the invading Germans, and eventually perished.

WRITINGS: *Richard Wagner* (Berlin, 1913); *Bruckners Chormusik* (Stuttgart, 1924); *Berufskrankheiten der Musiker* (Berlin, 1927; in English as *Diseases of the Musical Profession,* N.Y., 1932); *Heilwirkung der Musik* (Stuttgart, 1927).

Singer, Otto, German pianist and composer; b. Sora, July 26, 1833; d. New York, Jan. 3, 1894. He studied piano with Moscheles in Leipzig; then became a pupil of Liszt in Weimar; emigrated to America in 1867. He wrote several cantatas including *The Landing of the Pilgrim Fathers* (1876); 2 piano concertos and other piano music. His son, **Otto Singer, Jr.** (b. Dresden, Sept. 14, 1863; d. Leipzig, Jan. 8, 1931) studied music in Munich; was active primarily as a choral conductor in Leipzig and Berlin. Among his compositions are a *Konzertstück* for violin and orch.; a piano quintet; many choruses. He arranged vocal scores of operas by Wagner and Richard Strauss.

Singer, Peter, Austrian composer and music theorist; b. Häselgehr (Lechtal), July 18, 1810; d. Salzburg, Jan. 25, 1882. He was a Franciscan monk; composed 101 Masses, about 600 offertories, etc.; publ. *Cantus choralis in provincia Tirolensi consuetus* (Salzburg, 1862). In 1839 he invented the "Pansymphonikon," a kind of orchestrion with reeds; publ. *Metaphysische Blicke in die Tonwelt, nebst einem neuen System der Tonwissenschaft* (Munich, 1847).

BIBLIOGRAPHY: Pater Hartmann, *Peter Singer* (Innsbruck, 1910).

Singher, Martial, French baritone; b. Oloron-Sainte-Marie, Basses-Pyrénées, Aug. 14, 1904. He studied at the Paris Cons. (Premier Prix, 1929). In 1930–41 he sang at the Paris Opéra; on Jan. 10, 1940 he married Margareta Busch, daughter of conductor Fritz Busch. After the fall of Paris to the Germans he went to the U.S.; made his American debut at the Metropolitan Opera, N.Y. on Dec. 10, 1943 as Dapertutto in *Tales of Hoffmann;* subsequently sang the roles of Figaro in the *Marriage of Figaro* and in the *Barber of Seville,* Scarpia in *Tosca,* etc., remaining with the company with some interruptions until 1959. He taught at the Mannes College of Music in N.Y. (1951–55) and at the Curtis Institute of Music in Philadelphia (1954–68). In 1962 he took over the directorship of the opera dept. at the Music Academy of the West in Santa Barbara, California.

Singleton, Esther, American writer on music; b. Baltimore, Nov. 4, 1865; d. Stonington, Conn., July 2, 1930. She lived most of her life in N.Y.; publ. *A Guide to the Operas* (1899); *A Guide to Modern Opera* (1909); *The Orchestra and Its Instruments* (1917); contributed the chapter on American music to Lavignac's *Encylopédie de la Musique* (1915).

Sinico, Francesco, Italian choral conductor and composer; b. Trieste, Dec. 12, 1810; d. there, Aug. 18, 1865. He studied with G. Farinelli; was organist and conductor in various churches; in 1843 established his own singing school in Trieste, providing excellent training for choral singing. He produced his opera *I Virtuosi di Barcellona* in 1841. His son, **Giuseppe Sinico** (b. Trieste, Feb. 10, 1836; d. there, Dec. 31, 1907), continued the popular singing classes at the Sinico School in Trieste; wrote several operas, which he produced there: *Marinella* (Aug. 26, 1854), *I Moschettieri* (March 26, 1859), *Aurora di Nevers* (March 12, 1861) *Alessandro Stradella* (Lugo, Sept. 19, 1863), and *Spartaco* (Nov. 20, 1886). He publ. a *Breve metodo teoricopratico di canto elementare.*

BIBLIOGRAPHY: *Una Famiglia triestina di musicisti "I Sinico"* (Trieste, 1932).

Sinigaglia, Leone, Italian composer; b. Turin, Aug. 14, 1868; d. there, May 16, 1944. He was a pupil at the Turin Cons., studying with Giovanni Bolzoni; later in Vienna (1895–1900) with Mandyczewski, and in Prague with Dvořák. His first successful work was a violin concerto dedicated to Arrigo Serato (1900), who played it with considerable success in the principal cities of Germany. His early works were much influenced by Brahms and Dvořák; then he turned for inspiration to the music of his native Piedmont, and in this field achieved a lasting reputation. Toscanini conducted in Turin the première of Sinigaglia's suite *Danze Piemontesi* on popular themes (May 14, 1905); later he publ. a collection of songs (6 albums), *Vecchie canzoni popolari del Piemonte;* another work in the folksong manner is the symph. suite *Piemonte* (1909; Utrecht, Feb. 16, 1910); he further wrote *Le Baruffe Chiozzotte,* an overture to Goldoni's comedy (Utrecht, Dec. 21, 1907); *Rapsodia piemontese,* for violin; and orch.; *Romanze,* for violin and orch.; *Variations on a Theme of Brahms,* for string quartet (1901); *Serenade* for string trio (1906); Cello Sonata (1923).

BIBLIOGRAPHY: E. Desderi, "L. Sinigaglia," *Rivista Musicale Italiana* (1946).

Siohan, Robert, French music theorist, writer and composer; b. Paris, Feb. 27, 1894. He studied at the Paris Cons.; in 1929 he founded the Concerts Siohan which he conducted until 1936; then was choral conductor at the Paris Opera (1932–47); from 1948 to 1962 he was instructor in solfège and sight-reading at the Paris Cons.; subsequently served as Inspecteur général de la musique in the Ministry of Culture. He received his doctorate at the Sorbonne in 1954 with his thesis *Théories nouvelles de l'homme* (published under the title *Horizons sonores,* Paris, 1956). Among his compositions are the opera *Le Baladin de satin cramoisi* (1927); *Cantique au frère soleil* (1928); Violin Concerto; Cello Concerto; Piano Concerto; *Gravitations* for viola and piano; quartet with soprano part. He published a monograph on Stravinsky (Paris, 1959; in English, N.Y., 1970); *Histoire du public musical* (Lausanne, 1967); numerous articles in French and German publiications.

Sipilä, Eero, Finnish composer; b. Hailuoto, July 27, 1918; d. Kajaani, May 18, 1972. He studied with Merikanto and Madetoja; wrote relatively few works, mostly in baroque forms, and also sacred choral pieces; the most important are *Partita* for wind quartet (1955); *Super flumina Babylonis* and *Miserere,* 2 motets for chorus (1963); *Te Deum Laudamus* for alto, baritone, chorus and orch. (1969) and *Composition* for orch. (Kajaani, May 8, 1973).

Siqueira, José de Lima, Brazilian composer and conductor; b. Conceição, June 24, 1907. He played saxophone and trumpet, taking instruction from his father; then entered the National School of Music in Rio de Janeiro, where he studied with Burle Marx and Francisco Braga. Upon graduation he founded the Orquesta Sinfónica Brasileira, which he conducted until 1948; in 1949 he organized another orchestra, called Orquesta Sinfónica de Rio de Janeiro; he also filled in engagements as conductor in the U.S. (1944) and in Russia (1955).

WORKS: opera, *A compadecida* (1959; Rio de Janeiro, Dec. 20, 1961); symph. drama, *Gimba* (1960); *O carnaval Carioca,* a festive theater piece to commemorate the centennial of the city of Rio de Janeiro (1965); *Alvorada Brasileira,* symph. poem (1936); *4 Poemas indígenas* for orch. (1944); 4 symphonies (1933, 1951, 1954, 1956); 6 orchestral pieces, each entitled *Dança Brasileira;* 5 symph. suites on Brazilian themes (1955–70); *Candomblé,* oratorio on folkloric texts (Rio de Janeiro, Dec. 20, 1957); *Encantamento da Magia Negra,* a fetishist motet on native themes (1957); Cello Concerto (1952); Piano Concerto (1955); Violin Concerto (1957); 3 string quartets; Piano Trio; 2 violin sonatas; Cello Sonata; numerous songs and piano pieces. A list of his works is found in the *Composers of America* Vol. 16 (Washington, D.C., 1970).

Širola, Božidar, Croatian musicologist and composer; b. Žakanj, Dec. 20, 1889; d. Zagreb, April 10, 1956. He studied musicology with Guido Adler in Vienna receiving his Dr. phil. in 1921 at the Univ. of Vienna. Returning to Yugoslavia, he was on the faculty of the Zagreb Cons. (1935–41); then was director of the Ethnographic Museum in Zagreb. He wrote the operas *Comedy in Stanac* (1916), *Cittern and Drum* (1930), and *The Village Chaplain* (1940); 8 oratorios; 4 Masses; *Symphonie Concertante* for piano and orch. (1952); Violin Concerto (1953); *Spomen iz Slovenije (Reminiscences of Slovenia)* for wind octet (1926); 13 string quartets; Piano Quartet; 3 piano trios; 8 piano sonatas; *24 Inventions* for piano; published (in German) several valuable essays on Croatian music, and (in Croatian) a history of Croatian music (Zagreb, 1922).

Sistermans, Anton, Dutch bass; b. Hertogenbosch, Aug. 5, 1865; d. The Hague, March 18, 1926. He studied with Stockhausen in Frankfurt; from 1895 gave concerts in Europe; his only appearance in opera was as Pogner (Bayreuth, 1899). From 1904 to 1915 he taught singing at the Klindworth-Scharwenka Cons., Berlin; then lived in The Hague.

Sitsky, Larry, China-born Australian pianist and composer; b. Tientsin, Sept. 10, 1934 (to Russian émigré parents). The family went to Australia in 1951. Sitsky studied piano with Winifred Burston at the New South Wales Cons. in Sydney (1951–55); then went to San Francisco where he studied with Egon Petri (1958–61). Returning to Australia, he taught piano at the Queensland State Cons. (1961–65), and since 1966 has taught at the Canberra School of Music. As a concert pianist, he gave recitals at a young age while still in China (1945–51) and has continued concertizing since then throughout Australia.
WORKS: 2 operas: *The Fall of the House of Usher,* after Poe (1965), and *Lenz* (1969–70); a ballet, *Sinfonia (The Dark Refuge)* for 10 players (1964); *Apparitions* for amateur or school orch. (1966); *Prelude (Homage to Stravinsky)* for orch. (1968); Concerto for violin, female chorus and orch. (1970); Concerto for amplified wind quintet and orch. (1970–71; Sydney, April 3, 1971); *Burlesque* for flute, oboe and piano (1958); Solo Violin Sonata (1959); Solo Flute Sonata (1959); Oboe Sonatina (1962); Woodwind Quartet (1963); Sonata for 2 guitars (1968); String Quartet (1969); *Sonata Formalis* for piano (1959); *Fantasia (In Memory of Petri)* for piano (1962); *Dimensions* for piano and 2 tapes (1964); *Improvisations* for harpsichord (1965); Concerto for 2 solo pianos (1967); *5 Improvisations* for chorus and piano (1961); *Song of Love* for orch. (1974); *The Legions of Asmodeus* for 4 Theremins (1975); *Narayana* for piano trio (1975).

Sitt, Hans, German violinist and composer; b. Prague, Sept. 21, 1850; d. Leipzig, March 10, 1922. He studied at the Prague Cons.; held various positions as violinist and conductor of theater orchestras in Breslau, Prague, and Chemnitz. In 1881 he settled in Leipzig; organized a series of popular concerts there; was viola player in the Brodsky Quartet; conducted the Bachverein (1885–1903) and other musical societies there. He wrote 3 violin concertos, a viola concerto, 2 cello concertos; publ. valuable studies for the violin; also *Praktische Violaschule; Schulausgabe neuerer Violinlitteratur* (5 books); and (with Reinecke) *Lyrica,* a collection of 30 classic and romantic pieces for violin and piano.

Sittard, Alfred, German organist; son of **Josef Sittard;** b. Stuttgart, Nov. 4, 1878; d. Berlin, March 31, 1942. He studied with his father, and later with Wüllner at the Cologne Cons.; was organist at the Kreuzkirche in Dresden (1903–12), and then at St. Michael's in Hamburg (1912–25). In 1925 he was appointed prof. of organ at the Berlin Akademie für Kirchen- und Schulmusik, and in 1933 became Kapellmeister of the Berlin Cathedral chorus. He publ. *3 Choralstudien* for organ; also wrote *Das Hauptorgelwerk und die Hilfsorgel der Michaeliskirche in Hamburg* (1912).

Sittard, Josef, German music historian; b. Aachen, June 4, 1846; d. Hamburg, Nov. 24, 1903. He studied at the Stuttgart Cons., and later joined its faculty as instructor in singing and piano; from 1885 was music critic for Hamburg *Correspondent.* He publ. several valuable papers dealing with German city music; *Studien und Charakteristiken* (1889, collected essays); *Geschichte des Musik- und Concertwesens in Hamburg* (1890); *Zur Geschichte der Musik und des Theaters am Württembergischen Hofe* (2 vols., 1890, 1891); etc.; also composed some choral works and songs.

Sivori, Camillo, Italian violinist; b. Genoa, Oct. 25, 1815; d. there, Feb. 19, 1894. He was a child prodigy; as a mere infant he was presented to Paganini, who accepted him as a pupil; later he studied with Paganini's own teacher, Giacomo Costa. He played in Paris and London at the age of 12, producing an understandable sensation; toured Germany and Russia, and in 1846–50 made an extensive tour through North and South America. His manner of playing, if not his bizarre behavior, was modeled after Paganini's. He composed 2 violin concertos and numerous character pieces in the virtuoso manner fashionable in his day: *Tarentelle napolitaine, Carnaval de Chili, Carnaval de Cuba, Carnaval américan, Folies espagnoles,* etc.
BIBLIOGRAPHY: E. James, *Camillo Sivori: A Sketch of His Life, Talents, Travels and Successes* (London, 1845); L. Escudier, *Mes Souvenirs* (Paris, 1863); A. Pierrottet, *Camillo Sivori* (Milan, 1896).

Sixt, Johann Abraham, German organist and composer; b. Gräfenhausen, Württemberg, Jan. 3, 1757; d. Donaueschingen, Jan. 30, 1797. He was the son of a schoolmaster and organist; received his musical training at home; traveled in Germany; was in Vienna in 1784, and received a recommendation from Mozart. He then settled in Donaueschingen, and remained there for 13 years as piano teacher and chamber musician to the court, until his death. He wrote piano trios; sonatas, and other instrumental works; of particular interest are his lieder, with long introductions in the accompaniment, setting the mood of the text.

Sixta, Jozef, Slovak composer; b. Jičín, May 12, 1940. He studied with Očenaš at the Cons. in Bratislava (1955-60) and with Alexander Moyzes at the Music Academy there (1960-64); then went to Paris where he had lessons with Messiaen and Jolivet. Returning to Bratislava, he taught at the Academy of Music there.

WORKS: Quintet for piano and winds (1961); *Fantasia* for piano (1962); Symph. (1964); String Quartet (1965); *Variations* for 13 instruments (1967); *Synchronia* for string orch. (1968); *Asynchronia* for string orch. (1970); Nonet (1970); Quartet for 4 flutes (1976).

Sjöberg, Svante Leonard, Swedish organist, conductor, and composer; b. Karlskrona, Aug. 28, 1873; d. there, Jan. 18, 1935. He studied at the Stockholm Cons. with Nordquist and Dente, and in Berlin with Max Bruch. Returning to Sweden in 1901, he was organist at the Stadskyrka in Karlskrona, and conductor of the Musikförening there (1901-34). He wrote an overture to *Gustaf Vasa* (1901); some chamber music, and songs.

Sjögren, Emil, Swedish composer; b. Stockholm, June 16, 1853; d, there, March 1, 1918. He studied composition at the Stockholm Cons. with H. Berens, in Berlin with Kiel, and in Vienna with Grädener. In 1891 he was appointed organist at St. John's Church in Stockholm. His importance as composer rests chiefly on his songs, of which he wrote about 200, to texts in Swedish, French, and German; he also wrote a festival overture; several choruses; 5 violin sonatas; a cello sonata; 2 piano sonatas; several groups of lyric pieces for piano. Nils Brodén compiled an index of all of Sjögren's publ. compositions (Stockholm, 1918). A complete ed. of his songs was undertaken by the Swedish Academy in 1950-51.

BIBLIOGRAPHY: S. E. Svensson, "Emil Sjögrens vokala lyrik," *Svensk Tidskrift för Musikforskning* (1935).

Skalkottas, Nikos, greatly talented Greek composer; b. Chalkis, island of Euboea, March 8, 1904; d. (of a strangulated hernia), Athens, Sept. 19, 1949. He studied violin with his father, with his uncle, and with a nonrelated violinist at the Athens Cons. (1914-20). In 1921 he went to Berlin, where he continued his violin studies at the Hochschule für Musik (1921-23); then took lessons in theory of music with Philipp Jarnach (1925-27). But the greatest influence on his creative life was Schoenberg, whom he met in Berlin; Schoenberg, in his book *Style and Idea*, mentions Skalkottas as one of his most gifted disciples. Skalkottas eagerly absorbed Schoenberg's instruction in the method of composition with 12 tones related only to one another, but in his own music applied it in a very individual manner without trying to imitate Schoenberg's style. In Berlin Skalkottas also received some suggestions in free composition from Kurt Weill. He returned to Athens in 1933, when Schoenberg was driven out of Germany by the Nazis; in Athens Skalkottas earned his living by playing violin in local orchestras, but continued to compose diligently, until his early death. His music written between 1928 and 1938 reflects Schoenberg's idiom; later works are tonally conceived, and several of them are in the clearly ethnic Greek modalities, set in the typical asymmetric meters of Balkan folk music. After his death a Skalkottas Society was formed in Athens to promote performances and publication of his works; about 110 scores of various genres are kept in the Skalkottas Archives in Athens.

WORKS: *The Mayday Spell,* a "fairy drama" for soprano, speaker, dancers and orch. (1944-49); 2 ballets: *The Maid and Death* (1938) and *La Mer grecque* (1948); 2 suites for orch. (1929, 1944); 3 piano concertos: No. 1 (1931), No. 2 (1937-38); No. 3, with 10 winds and percussions (1939; London, July 9, 1969; due to length of the work, a different soloist was used for each movement); *36 Greek Dances* for orch. (1933-36; also performed in separate sections); 2-Piano Concertino (1937; Oxford, July 1, 1969); Violin Concerto (1938); Concertino for oboe and strings (1961 orchestration by P. Guarino of the original for oboe and piano, 1939); Concerto for Violin, Viola and Wind Orch. (1939-40; London, July 7, 1969); *10 Sketches* for string orch. or string quartet (1940); Double Bass Concerto (1940); *Little Suite* for string orch. (1942); *The Return of Ulysses,* symphony in one movement (1944-45; London, June 23, 1969); Concerto for 2 Violins and Orch. (1944-45); *5 Short Greek Dances* for orch. (1946); *Classical Symphony in A* for wind orch. (1947); Sinfonietta (1948); Piano Concertino (1949); *The Unknown Soldier* for chorus and orch. (1929). Chamber music: Sonata for solo violin (1925); 4 violin sonatinas (1928, 1929, 1935, 1935); 5 string quartets: No. 1 (1928; his first 12-tone work), No. 2 (1929), No. 3 (1935), No. 4 (1940; London, July 13, 1969), and *Easy String Quartet* (1929); 2 violin sonatas (1929, 1940); Octet for 4 woodwinds and string quartet (1930); *Piece* for 8 winds or double string quartet (1931); Piano Trio (1936); *Scherzo* for piano and 3 strings (1936); *March of the Little Soldiers* for violin and piano (1936); *Rondo* for violin and piano (1936); *Little Chorale and Fugue* for violin and piano (1936); *8 Variations on a Greek Folk Tune* for piano trio (1938); *Suite* for cello and piano (1938); Cello Sonata (1938); *9 Greek Dances* for string quartet (1938-47; transcribed from the *36 Greek Dances*); *Gavotta* for violin and piano (1939); Concertino for oboe and piano (1939); Duo for violin and viola (1939-40); *Largo* for cello and piano (1940); 2 quartets for piano, oboe, bassoon and trumpet (1941-43); Concertino for trumpet and piano (1941-43); *Sonata concertante* for bassoon and piano (1943); 2 *Little Suites* for violin and piano (1946, 1949); Duo for violin and piano (1947); *Bolero* for cello and piano (1948-49); *Little Serenade* for cello and piano (1949); Cello Sonatina (1949); *Tender Melody* for cello and piano (1949). For piano: Sonatina (1927); *15 Little Variations* (1927); 4 *Suites* (1936, 1940, 1940, 1940); *32 Pieces* (1940); *4 Etudes* (1940); an unpublished treatise, in Greek, *The Technique of Orchestration* (1940).

BIBLIOGRAPHY: J. Papaioannou, "Nikos Skalkottas," in H. Hartog, ed., *European Music in the Twentieth Century* (N.Y., 1957).

Škerjanc, Lucijan Marija, Slovenian composer; b. Graz, Dec. 17, 1900; d. Ljubljana, Feb. 27, 1973. He studied composition in Vienna with Josef Marx and in

Paris with Vincent d'Indy; returning to Yugoslavia he became prof. of the Academy of Music in Ljubljana. His music reflects neo-Romantic trends with some Impressionistic colors. His works include 5 symphonies; Clarinet Concerto; Harp Concerto; Horn Concerto; String Quintet; *Concertone* for 4 cellos; also published a manual on counterpoint.

Škerl, Dane, Slovenian composer; b. Ljubljana, Aug. 26, 1931. He studied with Škerjanc at the Ljubljana Academy of Music, graduating in 1952; then took courses in electronic music in Cologne. He taught at the Music Academy in Sarajevo (1963–68); in 1970 was appointed to the faculty of the Music Academy of Ljubljana.

WORKS: 2 ballets: *Kontrasti* (*Contrasts*, 1967) and *Grozdanin kikot* (1969); Concertino for violin and string orch. (1948); *Prelude and Scherzo* for clarinet and strings (1948); Concertino for piano and strings (1949); 5 symphonies (1951, 1963, 1965, 1970, 1972); *Serenade* for strings (1952); Concerto for Orch. (1956); *Rolo* for orch. (1959); *Inventions* for violin and strings (1960); *18 Etudes* for strings (1960); *5 Compositions* for clarinet and strings (1961); *Contrasts* for orch. (1962); Clarinet Concerto (1963); *Little Suite* for orch. (1965); *7 Bagatelles* for strings (1966); *Improvvisazione concertante* for horn, viola and chamber orch. (1968); Trombone Concerto (1970); a cantata, *Moj dom* (*My House*, 1962); *4 Miniatures* for flute, bassoon and piano (1957); *Prelude and Scherzo* for violin, clarinet and piano (1959); *Skica* (*Sketch*) for violin and piano (1964); *3 Improvisations* for flute, cello and piano (1966); piano pieces.

Skilton, Charles Sanford, distinguished American composer; b. Northampton, Mass., Aug. 16, 1868; d. Lawrence, Kansas, March 12, 1941. After graduating from Yale Univ. (B.A., 1889) he studied in New York with Harry Rowe Shelley (organ) and Dudley Buck (composition); then went to Germany, where he studied with Bargiel at the Hochschule für Musik in Berlin (1891–93). From 1893 to 1896 he was director of music at the Salem Academy and College, N.C., and conducted the local orchestra there; then filled a similar post at the State Normal School, Trenton, N.J. (1898–1903); in 1903 he was engaged as prof. of organ and theory at the Univ. of Kansas, Lawrence, where he remained most of his life. He made a detailed study of Indian music, and introduced Indian motifs into the traditional forms of a suite or a fantasy.

WORKS: the operas *The Sun Bride* (radio performance, April 17, 1930), *Kalopin* (not produced; received the David Bispham Memorial Medal of the American Opera Society of Chicago, 1930), *The Day of Gayomair* (1936; not produced); for orch.: *Suite Primeval,* on Indian melodies, in 2 parts: *2 Indian Dances* (originally for string quartet, 1915; Minneapolis, Oct. 29, 1916); part II (Minneapolis, Nov. 13, 1921); *Autumn Night* (Detroit, Dec. 11, 1930); *Shawnee Indian Hunting Dance* (Detroit, Dec. 11, 1930); *A Carolina Legend,* symph. poem: *Mt. Oread,* overture; *Sioux Flute Serenade,* for small orch. (1920); cantata *The Witch's Daughter* (1918); *The Guardian Angel,* oratorio (1925); *From Forest and Stream* (1930); *Midnight,* for women's voices; *The Fountain,* for women's voices;

String Quartet; Sonatina for violin and piano; *Sarabande* for wind instruments. Also publ. *Modern Symphonic Forms* (N.Y., 1927).

BIBLIOGRAPHY: J. T. Howard, *Charles Sanford Skilton* (N.Y., 1929).

Skinner, Ernest M., American organ builder; b. Clarion, Pa., Jan. 15, 1866; d. Duxbury, Mass., Nov. 27, 1960. He was the founder of the Ernest M. Skinner Co., organ builders, originally of Dorchester, later of Methuen, Mass. Unitl 1905 the business was carried on by Skinner himself; it was then incorporated, with Skinner as president. From 1917 to 1932 he was technical director of the Skinner Organ Co., which in 1932 was merged with the Aeolian Co. of Garwood, N.J., and became the Aeolian-Skinner Organ Co. Skinner was especially successful in the construction of organ pipes reproducing the exact tone color of the various woodwind instruments and the French horn; among several inportant inventions is the "duplex windchest," by means of which the stops of 2 manuals are made interchangeable, and the arrangement of placing the stops on swinging sides. The Skinner Co. built the organ in the National Cathedral at Washington, D.C. Skinner publ. the valuable books *The Modern Organ* (1915; 6th ed., 1945), and *The Composition of the Organ* (1947).

Sklavos, Georges, Greek composer; b. Brailov, Rumania, of Greek parents, Aug. 20, 1888. He studied with Armand Marsick at the Athens Cons.; was appointed instructor there in 1913. He devoted himself chiefly to the musical theater.

WORKS: operas: *Lestenitza* (Athens, March 14, 1947), *Kassiani* (Oct. 30, 1959), *Amphitryon* (1960); symph. poems: *L'Aigle* (1922); ethnically colored orchestral pieces: *Fantaisie crétoise, Noces insulaires, Suite arcadienne;* choruses; songs.

Sköld, (Karl) Yngve, Swedish composer; b. Vallby, April 29, 1899. He studied piano and composition in Stockholm (1915–18); then in Brno (1921–22) and Prague (1922). From 1938 to 1964 he was librarian of the Swedish Composers' Society. His music blends Nordic Romanticism with subdued modernity.

WORKS: 4 symphonies (1915, 1937, 1949, 1966); 3 piano concertos (1917, 1946, 1969); Cello Sonata (1927); 3 string quartets (1930, 1955, 1965, 1974); *Suite Concertante* for viola and orch. (1936); *Sinfonia de chiesa* for orch. (1939); Violin Concerto (1941); Cello Concerto (1947); *Double Concerto* for violin, cello and orch. (1950); *Divertimento* for orch. (1951); Quintet for 2 flutes, cello and piano (1958); Sonata for viola and organ (1962); Concertino for 5 winds, timpani and strings (1963); 2 piano sonatas (1963); Piano Sonatina (1970); *Divertimento* for violin, viola and cello (1971); *Trio domestico* for piano trio (1974).

Skriabin, Alexander. See **Scriabin.**

Škroup, Franz (František), Czech composer and conductor; b. Osice, near Pardubice, June 3, 1801; d. Rotterdam, Feb. 7, 1862. He studied law in Prague. In 1827 he became conductor at the Bohemian Theater, Prague, and remained at that post until 1857; put into performance several Wagner operas for the 1st time in Prague. He wrote several operas to Czech librettos, which he conducted at the Bohemian Theater: *Dráteník* (Feb. 2, 1826); *Oldřich a Božena* (Dec. 14, 1828); *Libušin snatek (Libusa's Marriage)* (3rd act performed Nov. 6, 1835; first full performance, April 11, 1850); also the German operas *Drahomira* (Nov. 20, 1848) and *Der Meergeuse* (Nov. 29, 1861). In 1860 Škroup took a position offered to him with a German opera troupe in Rotterdam, and died there after 2 seasons. Besides his operas, he wrote some chamber music and many popular Bohemian songs, of which *Kde domov muj* became so famous as to be mistaken for folksong and was made into the Czech national anthem.

BIBLIOGRAPHY: J. Plavec, *František Škroup* (Prague, 1946).

Škroup, Jan Nepomuk, Czech composer, brother of **František Škroup;** b. Osice, near Pardubice, Nov. 15, 1811; d. Prague, May 5, 1892. He was a chorusmaster at the Prague Opera; then served as music director at various churches in Prague and finally at the Cathedral; in 1846, he was appointed teacher of singing at the Theological Seminary. He wrote manuals for church services: *Manuale pro sacris functionibus* and *Musica sacra pro populo;* also a vocal method.

Skrowaczewski, Stanislaw, eminent Polish-American conductor and composer; b. Lwów, Oct. 3, 1923. He studied piano and music theory at the universities of Lwów and Cracow; then he took composition lessons with Nadia Boulanger in Paris. He started brilliantly on his career as a composer; wrote symphonic works in a fine neo-Classical manner, several string quartets and other chamber music, but soon focused his attention primarily on conducting. He led the Wroclaw Philharmonic (1946–47), the Katowice Philharmonic Orch. (1949–54), and the Warsaw Philharmonic (1957–59). On Dec. 4, 1958, he made his first American appearance as conductor with the Cleveland Orch. with immediate success. Subsequently he was guest conductor with the Cincinnati Symph. Orch., the Pittsburgh Symph. Orch., and the N.Y. Philharmonic; also conducted in South America. In 1960 he was appointed conductor and music director of the Minneapolis Symph. Orch., renamed in 1970 as the Minnesota Orch., and asserted his excellence both as a technician of the baton and interpreter of the classic and modern repertory. He resigned as music director of the Minnesota Orch. effective in the fall of 1979.

WORKS: 4 symphonies (1948–55); *Music at Night,* symph. variations (1952); Concerto for English horn and orch. (1969); *Ricercari notturni* for saxophone and orch. (Minneapolis, Jan. 19, 1978).

Skuhersky, František, Czech composer, pianist and organist; b. Opočno, July 31, 1830; d. České Budějovice, Aug. 19, 1892. He first studied medicine; then had music lessons with Kittl in Prague; from 1854 to 1866 he was in Innsbruck where he conducted the Musikverein. Returning to Prague he conducted the court orchestra, gave music courses at the Czech Univ., and became particularly interested in the problem of Bohemian church music. He published several

fundamental texts on music theory in the Czech language: *O formách hudebních* (Prague, 1873); *Nauka o hudebni komposici* (4 vols.; Prague, 1880–84); *Nauka o harmonii* (Prague, 1885). He wrote the operas *Vladimir, Bohuv Zvolenec* (Prague, Sept. 27, 1863), and *Rektor a General* (Prague, March 28, 1873), and a German opera *Der Liebesring* (Innsbruck, 1861; in Czech under the title *Lora,* Prague, 1868); a symph. poem, *May;* 4 Masses; *30 Orgelvorspiele in den Kirchentonarten* (without accidentals) and a similar set of organ pieces with accidentals; many organ studies; piano pieces and songs.

Slatkin, Leonard, American conductor; b. Los Angeles, Sept. 1, 1944. He was reared in a family of musicians; his father was a violinist, his mother a cellist. Slatkin played the violin in infancy; took up viola at puberty; played piano through adolescence; studied composition with Castelnuovo-Tedesco in Los Angeles. He made his conducting debut at the Aspen Music Festival at the age of 19; then studied conducting with Jean Morel at the Juilliard School of Music (Mus.B., 1968). He subsequently held the post of associate conductor of the St. Louis Orchestra and principal guest conductor of the Minnesota Symph. Orch.; also was guest conductor with the N.Y. Philharmonic, Chicago Symph. Orch., the Philadelphia Orch., and with several European orchestras, among them the London Symph. and the Concertgebouw Orch. of Holland. In 1977–79 he was conductor of the New Orleans Philharmonic; then was engaged as conductor of the St. Louis Symph. Orch., effective in 1979–80.

Slaughter, A. Walter, English composer; b. London, Feb., 1860; d. there, April 2, 1908. He was a chorister at St. Andrews, Wells St.; studied with A. Cellier and Jacobi. He was a conductor, successively, of the Royal Theatre, the Olympic, Drury Lane, and St. James's Theatre; wrote a number of musical stage works, among them the 3-act comic opera *Marjorie* (1889), *The Rose and the Ring* (after Thackeray; 1890), and a musical comedy, *The French Maid* (1897).

Slavenski, Josip, outstanding Yugoslav composer; b. Cakovec, May 11, 1896; d. Belgrade, Nov. 30, 1955. His real name was **Štolcer (Stolzer),** but he changed it to the distinctly Slavonic name in about 1930, and used it exclusively in his published works. He studied with Kodály in Budapest and with Novák in Prague. In 1924 he established himself in Belgrade; in 1949 he became professor of composition at the Music Academy there. A musician of advanced ideas, he attempted to combine the Slavic melodic and rhythmic elements with modern ingredients; experimented with nontempered scales and devised a "natural" scale of 53 degrees to the octave. His first such experiment was *Prasimfonia* ("protosymphony") scored for orchestra, organ and piano (1919–26); there followed *Balkanophonia,* suite for orch. (Berlin, Jan. 25, 1929); an oriental cantata entitled *Religiophonia* (1934). Other works are Violin Concerto (1927); 4 string quartets (1923, 1928, 1938, 1940); *Slavenska Sonata* for violin and piano (1924); *Sonata Religiosa* for violin and organ (1925); piano pieces on Balkan themes.

BIBLIOGRAPHY: K. Kovačević, *Hrvatski kompozitori i njihova djela* (Zagreb, 1960).

Slavický, Klement, Czech composer; b. Tovačov, Sept. 22, 1910. He studied composition with Jirák and Suk, and conducting with Děděček and Talich at the Prague Cons. (1927–31) and then at its Master School there (1931–33); was music director of the Czech Radio in Prague (1936–51); then taught privately.
WORKS: *Fantasia* for orch. and solo piano (1931); 3 sinfoniettas (1940, 1962, 1972); *Moravian Dance Fantasies* for orch. (1951); *Rhapsodic Variations* for orch. (1953; Prague, Feb. 17, 1954); String Quartet (1933); *2 Compositions* for cello and piano (1936); Trio for oboe, clarinet and bassoon (1937); *Suite* for oboe and piano (1959); *Partita* for solo violin (1962); *Intermezzi mattutini* for flute and harp (1965); *Trialogo* for violin, clarinet and piano (1966); *Capricci* for horn and piano (1967); *Musica monologica* for harp (1968). For piano: *3 compositions* (1947); a sonata subtitled *Zamyšlení nad životem* (*Contemplation of Life*, 1957–58); *In Black and White* (1958); *12 Little Etudes* (1964); *Etudes and Essays*, 7 pieces (1965); *Suite* for piano 4 hands (1968); *Cycle* (1970); organ pieces; choruses; songs.

Slavík, Josef, Bohemian violinist; b. Jince, March 3, 1806; d. Budapest, May 30, 1833. He studied with Pixis at the Prague Cons.; then went on a concert tour; in 1825 was appointed to the court chapel there, and became a friend of Schubert, who dedicated to him his *Fantasie* for violin and piano, which Slavík performed for the first time in 1828. Among his own compositions are a violin concerto (1823); and a *Grand Potpourri* for violin and orch. (1826).
BIBLIOGRAPHY: J. Pohl, *Josef Slavík* (Prague, 1906); St. Klíma, *Josef Slavík* (Prague, 1956).

Sleeper, Henry Dike, American organist and music educator; b. Patten, Maine, Oct. 9, 1865; d. Winter Park, Florida, Jan. 28, 1948. He studied with J. K. Paine in Boston, and later in London. After teaching at various colleges, he joined the faculty of Smith College in 1898, and was head of the music dept. there from 1904 to 1924. He wrote a number of organ pieces and songs; was co-editor of *The Common Order Choir Book* (1903) and *Hymns of Worship and Service* (college edition).

Slenczynska, Ruth, American pianist of precocious talent; b. Sacramento, California, Jan. 15, 1925. Her father, a violinist, subjected her to severe discipline when her musical talent was revealed in early childhood; she played in public in Berlin when she was 6 years old, and performed with an orchestra in Paris at the age of 11. She made a sensation and was acclaimed by European critics as a prodigy of nature; she took lessons with Egon Petri, Artur Schnabel, Alfred Cortot and others in Europe and America, and even played for Rachmaninoff, who became interested in her destiny. However, she developed psychological difficulties with her father, whose promotion of her career became obsessive, and had to cease public appearances; when she played concerts at the age of 15, the critics characterized her performances as

mechanical reproductions of the music, seemingly without any personal projection. She then engaged in teaching; became prof. of piano at Southern Illinois Univ. in Edwardville, Illinois. She published a book of memoirs (with Louis Biancolli), *Forbidden Childhood* (N.Y., 1957) in which she recounted the troubles of a child prodigy's life; she also brought out a pedagogical edition *Music at Your Fingertips. Aspects of Pianoforte Technique* (with A. M. Lingg; N.Y., 1961).

Slezak, Leo, famous Austrian tenor; b. Mährisch-Schönberg, Moravia, Aug. 18, 1873; d. Egern-on-the-Tegernsee, Bavaria, June 1, 1946. As a youth, he sang in the chorus of the Brünn Opera; made his debut as Lohengrin there (March 17, 1896); the role became one of his outstanding successes. He was with the Berlin Opera for a season (1898–99); in 1901 became a member of the Vienna Opera, where he was active until 1926; also performed frequently in Prague, Milan, and Munich. Not satisfied with his vocal training, he went to Paris, where he studied with Jean de Reszke. He made his London debut with marked acclaim as Otello (June 2, 1909); appeared in America for the first time also as Otello, with the Metropolitan Opera Co., N.Y. (Nov. 17, 1909); sang with the Metropolitan during its spring tour of 1910 and its summer season in Paris; subsequently sang also in Russia; gave recitals presenting distinguished programs, performed with impeccable taste. He also acted in motion pictures. He was a man of great general culture, and possessed exceptionally sharp literary wit, which he displayed in his reminiscences *Meine sämtlichen Werke* (1922) and *Der Wortbruch* (1927); both were later combined in a single volume (1935); English transl. as *Songs of Motley: Being the Reminiscences of a Hungry Tenor* (London, 1938); also publ. *Rückfall* (1940). A final book of memoirs, *Mein Lebensmärchen*, was publ. posthumously (1948). His son, the film actor Walter Slezak, published his letters, *Mein lieber Bub. Briefe eines besorgten Vaters* (Munich, 1966) and *What Time's the Next Swan?* (N.Y., 1962), alluding to the possibly apocryphal story of the swan failing to arrive in time in *Lohengrin*.

Slobodianik, Alexander, brilliant Soviet pianist; b. Kiev, Sept. 5, 1941. He studied at the Moscow Conservatory with Gornostaeva, graduating in 1964. In 1966 he received the fourth prize at the Tchaikovsky Competition in Moscow. He subsequently undertook numerous concert tours in Russia and abroad. He was particularly successful during his American tours during the 1970s. Like most Soviet pianists who venture abroad he astounds by his unlimited technical resources, but he is also appreciated for the romantic élan of his playing.

Slobodskaya, Oda, Russian soprano; b. Vilna, Dec. 12, 1888; d. London, July 29, 1970. She studied voice at the St. Petersburg Cons.; made her opera debut in Petrograd in 1918. In 1922 she went to Paris; in 1931 settled in London, where she appeared as a music hall singer under the pseudonym **Odali Careno** for a few seasons; in 1932 sang Venus in *Tannhäuser* at Covent Garden; also appeared at La Scala in Milan and at the Teatro Colón in Buenos Aires.

Slonimsky, Nicolas, Russian-American musicologist; b. St. Petersburg, April 27, 1894. A failed *wunderkind,* he was given his first piano lesson by his illustrious maternal aunt **Isabelle Vengerova,** on Nov. 6, 1900, according to the old Russian calendar. Possessed by inordinate ambition, aggravated by the endemic intellectuality of his family of both maternal and paternal branches (novelists, revolutionary poets, literary critics, university professors, translators, chessmasters, economists, mathematicians, inventors of useless artificial languages, Hebrew scholars, speculative philosophers), he became determined to excel beyond common decency in all these doctrines; as an adolescent, wrote out his future biography accordingly, setting down his death date in 1967, but survived. He enrolled in the St. Petersburg Cons. and studied harmony and orchestration with two pupils of Rimsky-Korsakov, Kalafati and Maximilian Steinberg; also tried unsuccessfully to engage in Russian journalism. After the Revolution he made his way South; was a rehearsal pianist at the Kiev Opera, where he took some composition lessons with Glière (1919); then was in Yalta, Crimea (1920), where he earned his living as a piano accompanist to displaced Russian singers, and as an instructor at a dilapidated Yalta Cons.; thence proceeded to Turkey, Bulgaria and Paris, where he became secretary and piano-pounder to Serge Koussevitzky. In 1923 came to the U.S.; became coach in the opera dept. of the Eastman School of Music, Rochester, N.Y., where he took an opportunity to study some more composition with the visiting professor Selim Palmgren, and conducting with Albert Coates; in 1925 was again with Koussevitzky in Paris and Boston, but was fired for insubordination in 1927. He learned to speak polysyllabic English and began writing music articles for the *Boston Evening Transcript* and the *Christian Science Monitor;* ran a monthly column of musical anecdotes of questionable authenticity in *Etude* magazine; taught theory at the Malkin Cons. in Boston and at Boston Cons.; conducted the Pierian Sodality at Harvard Univ. (1927–29) and the Apollo Chorus (1928–30). In 1927 he organized the Chamber Orch. of Boston with the purpose of presenting modern works; with it he gave first performances of works by Charles Ives, Edgar Varèse, Henry Cowell, and others; became a naturalized American citizen in 1931. In 1931–32 he conducted special concerts of modern American, Cuban and Mexican music in Paris, Berlin and Budapest under the auspices of the Pan-American Association of Composers, producing a ripple of excitement; repeated these programs at his engagements with the Los Angeles Philharmonic (1932) and at the Hollywood Bowl (1933), which created such consternation that his conducting career came to a jarring halt. In 1945–47 he became, by accident (the head of the dept. had died suddenly of a heart attack), lecturer in Slavonic languages and literatures at Harvard Univ.; in 1962–63 he traveled in Russia, Poland, Yugoslavia, Bulgaria, Rumania, Greece, and Israel under the auspices of the Office of Cultural Exchange at the U.S. State Dept., as a lecturer in native Russian, ersatz Polish, synthetic Serbo-Croatian, Russianized Bulgarian, Latinized Rumanian, archaic Greek, passable French and tolerable German. Returning from his multinational travels, he taught variegated musical subjects at the Univ. of California, Los Angeles; was irretrievably retired after a triennial service (1964–67), ostensibly owing to irreversible obsolescence and recessive infantiloquy; but disdaining the inexorable statistics of the actuarial tables, continued to agitate and even gave long-winded lecture-recitals in institutions of dubious learning. As a composer, he cultivated miniature forms, usually with a gimmick, e.g. *Studies in Black and White* for piano (1928) in "mutually exclusive consonant counterpoint," a song cycle, *Gravestones,* to texts from tombstones in an old cemetery in Hancock, New Hampshire (1945) and *Minitudes,* a collection of 50 quaquaversal piano pieces (1971–77). His only decent orchestra work is *My Toy Balloon* (1942), a set of variations on a Brazilian song, which includes in the score 100 colored balloons to be exploded *f f f* at the climax. He also conjured up a *Möbius Strip-Tease,* a perpetual vocal canon notated on a Möbius band to be revolved around the singer's head; it had its first and last performance at the Arriére-Garde Coffee Concert at UCLA, on May 5, 1965, with the composer officiating at the piano non-obbligato. A priority must be conceded to him for writing the earliest singing commercials to authentic texts from the *Saturday Evening Post* advertisements, among them *Make This a Day of Pepsodent, No More Shiny Nose,* and *Children Cry for Castoria* (1925). More "scholarly," though no less defiant of academic conventions, is his *Thesaurus of Scales and Melodic Patterns* (1947), an inventory of all conceivable and inconceivable tonal combinations, culminating in a mind-boggling "Grandmother Chord" containing 12 different tones and 11 different intervals. Beset by a chronic itch for novelty, he coined the term "pandiatonicism" (1937), which *mirabile dictu* took root and even got into reputable reference works, including the 15th edition of the *Encyclopædia Britannica.* In his quest for trivial but not readily accessible information, he blundered into the muddy field of musical lexicography; published *Music Since 1900,* a chronology of musical events, which actually contains some beguiling serendipities (N.Y., 1937; 4th edition, 1971); took over the vacated editorship (because of the predecessor's sudden death during sleep) of Thompson's *International Cyclopedia of Music and Musicians* (4th to 8th editions; 1946–58), and somehow managed to obtain the editorship of the 5th and 6th editions of the prestigious *Baker's Biographical Dictionary of Musicians* (N.Y., 1958; 1978). Other publications: *Music of Latin America* (N.Y., 1945; several reprints; also in Spanish, Buenos Aires, 1947); *The Road to Music,* ostensibly for children (N.Y., 1947); *A Thing or Two about Music* (N.Y., 1948; inconsequential; also lacking an index); *Lexicon of Musical Invective,* a random collection of pejorative reviews of musical masterpieces (N.Y., 1952); numerous articles for encyclopedias; also a learned paper, *Sex and the Music Librarian,* valuable for its painstaking research; the paper was delivered by proxy, to tumultuous cachinnations, at a symposium of the Music Library Association, at Chapel Hill, N.C., Feb. 2, 1968.

BIBLIOGRAPHY: Henry Cowell, "Nicolas Slonimsky", in *American Composers on American Music* (Stanford, Calif., 1933; cf. reciprocally, Nicolas Slonimsky, "Henry Cowell," ibid.). In 1978 he mobilized his powers of retrospection in preparing an autobiography, tentatively entitled *My Grandfather Invented the Telegraph*. (Indeed, S. grand-père was instrumental in introducing c. 1850 a method of multiple transmission of telegraphic messages. Recently the Soviets claimed for him a priority over American inventors.)

Slonimsky, Sergei, Soviet composer; nephew of **Nicolas Slonimsky;** b. Leningrad, Aug. 12, 1932. He studied with Boris Arapov and Orest Evlakhov at the Leningrad Cons., graduating in 1955; in 1958 he was appointed instructor in theory there. His style of composition is in the tradition of Soviet modernism, evolving towards considerable complexity of texture and boldness of idiom. Some of his works, such as his opera *Virineya*, represent a contemporary evolution of the Russian National School of composition, broadly diatonic and freely songful; others tend towards ultramodernism, including polytonality, dodecaphony, microtonality, tone clusters, prepared piano, electronics, aleatory procedures and spatial music. Of these, the *Concerto* for symph. orch., ensemble of electronically amplified guitars and solo instruments is typical; even more advanced is his *Antiphones* for string quartet, employing non-tempered tuning and "ambulatory" setting, in which performers are placed in different parts of the hall and then walk while playing before assembling on the stage; it is particularly successful at modern music festivals, and has been performed in New York, Tokyo, Warsaw, etc., as well as Leningrad and Moscow.

WORKS: *2 Pieces* for viola and piano (1956); *Carnival Overture* for orch. (1957); *Songs of Freedom,* on Russian folk motives for mezzo-soprano, baritone and piano (1957); Symph. No. 1 (1958; Leningrad, March 11, 1962); *Suite* for viola and piano (1959); Sonata for violin solo (1960); Piano Sonata (1962); *Polish Stanzas,* vocal cycle to words of Antoni Slonimski (1963); *Choreographic Miniatures* for orch. (1964); *3 Pieces* for cello solo (1964); *Dialogues* for wind quintet (1964); *Concerto-Buffo* for small orch. (1964); *Parting from a Friend,* vocal scene for voice and piano (1966); *Virineya,* opera (1967; Leningrad, Sept. 30, 1967); *Monologues* for soprano, oboe, horn and harp (1967); *Antiphones* for string quartet (1968); *Chromatic Poem* for organ (1969); *Northern Landscapes* for chorus a cappella (1969); *Children's Pieces* for piano (1970); *Icarus,* ballet (Moscow, May 30, 1971); *Merry Songs* for voice and piano (1971); *Coloristic Fantasy* for piano (1972); *Choral Games* for children's chorus, boy soloist and 2 drums (1972); *The Master and Margarita,* chamber opera, after a novel by Bulgakov (1973); Concerto for symph. orch., electric guitars and solo instruments (1973); *Dramatic Song* for orch. (1973); *Sonatina-Allegro* for horn and piano (1974); *Monologue and Toccata* for clarinet and piano (1974); *Pesnohorka* for contralto, flute, oboe, trumpet, balalaika, accordion, 3 electric guitars, Russian castanets, and vibraphone, to texts from rural Russian songs (1975). *Songs of the Troubadours,* vocal cycle to old French texts in Russian translation, for soprano, tenor, 4 recorders and lute (1975); *Festive Music* for balalaika, castanets and orch. (1975); *Solo espressivo* for oboe solo (1975); *Song of Songs* for soprano, tenor, chorus, oboe, horn and harp (1975); 2nd Symph. (1977–78). He has contributed a number of articles on Soviet music to periodicals and has published a valuable book, *The Symphonies of Prokofiev* (Leningrad, 1964).

BIBLIOGRAPHY: A. Milka, *Sergei Slonimsky* (Leningrad, 1976).

Slonimsky, Yuri, eminent Russian writer on ballet; b. St. Petersburg, March 13, 1902; d. there (Leningrad), April 23, 1978. He studied law at the St. Petersburg Univ.; at the same time attended the Institute of Arts History; was a co-founder, with Georgi Balanchivadze (George Balanchine), of "Young Ballet," a group organized to promote modern dance. A brilliant ballet critic, Yuri Slonimsky achieved a fine reputation for his penetrating analysis of current productions and historical essays on ballet. He published *Giselle* (Leningrad, 1926; revised 1969); *Masters of Ballet* (Moscow, 1937); *The Soviet Ballet* (in English, N.Y., 1947); *Tchaikovsky and the Ballet Theater of His Time* (Moscow, 1956). He was the author of several ballet librettos, among them *Icarus* by Sergei Slonimsky (no relation).

Slonov, Mikhail, Russian song composer; b. Kharkov, Nov. 16, 1869; d. Moscow, Feb. 11, 1930. He collected Russian folksongs and himself composed a number of songs, some of them popularized by Chaliapin, such as *Farewell*.

Sloper, (Edward Hugh) Lindsay, English pianist and teacher; b. London, June 14, 1826; d. there, July 3, 1887. He studied with Moscheles at London, A. Schmitt at Frankfurt, and Rousselot at Paris; made his debut in London (1846); became a popular concert pianist and teacher there. He wrote many piano pieces; studies and textbooks for piano; songs.

Smallens, Alexander, American conductor; b. St. Petersburg, Russia, Jan. 1, 1889; d. Tucson, Arizona, Nov. 24, 1972. He was brought to the U.S. as a child; studied at the College of the City of N.Y. (B.A., 1909); then took courses at the Paris Cons. (1911). He devoted himself mainly to theatrical conducting; was assistant conductor of the Boston Opera (1911–14); accompanied the Anna Pavlova Ballet Co. on a tour of South America (1915–18); then was on the staff of the Chicago Opera Co. (1919–22) and of the Philadelphia Civic Opera (1924–31); from 1927 to 1934 he was assistant conductor of the Philadelphia Orch., and from 1947 to 1950, was musical director at the Radio City Music Hall in N.Y. He was the original conductor of Gershwin's opera *Porgy and Bess,* and conducted it on a European tour in 1956.

Smalley, Roger, English composer; b. Swinton, near Manchester, July 26, 1943. He studied at the Royal College of Music in London with Antony Hopkins (piano) and Peter Racine Fricker (composition); later attended courses in new music with Stockhausen in Cologne. In 1967 he became Artist-in-Residence at King's College, Cambridge. In 1970 he formed a new ensemble, called "Intermodulation," to promote socially unacceptable music. In this antagonistic manner he wrote *Strata* for 15 string players (1970) and

Beat Music for 55 players (London, Aug. 12, 1971). But he also composed an austere *Missa Brevis*.

Smallwood, Williams, English organist; b. Kendal, Dec. 31, 1831; d. there, Aug. 6, 1897. He studied with Dr. Camidge and H. Phillips; was organist of the Kendal Parish Church from 1847 till his death. He composed didactic piano pieces and salon music; also anthems, hymns, songs, etc. His *Pianoforte Tutor* had an immense sale.

Smareglia, Antonio, Italian composer; b. Pola, Istria, May 5, 1854; d. Grado, near Trieste, April 15, 1929. He was trained in engineering before turning to music; studied composition with Franco Faccio at the Cons. of Milan. He became totally blind about 1905, but continued to compose by improvising on the piano with a musical amanuensis; lived in Milan until 1921, when he was appointed prof. of composition at the Tartini Cons., Trieste.

WORKS: OPERAS: *Preziosa* (Milan, Nov. 19, 1879); *Bianca da Cervia* (Milan, Feb. 7, 1882); *Re Nala* (Venice, Feb. 9, 1887); *Il Vassallo di Szigeth* (Vienna, Oct. 4, 1889); *Cornelio Schutt* (Prague, May 20, 1893); *Nozze istriane* (Trieste, March 28, 1895; very successful); *La Falena* (Venice, Sept. 4, 1897); *Oceana* (Milan, Jan. 22, 1903); *L'Abisso* (Milan, Feb. 9, 1914).

BIBLIOGRAPHY: G. Zuccoli, *A. Smareglia* (Trieste, 1923); G. D. Nacamuli, *A. Smareglia* (Trieste, 1930); A. Smareglia, *Vita ed arte di Antonio Smareglia* (Lugano, 1932); Mario Smareglia, *A. Smareglia* (Pola, 1934); Silvio Benco, *Ricordi di Antonio Smareglia* (Duino, 1968).

Smart, Sir George (Thomas), English organist and conductor; b. London, May 10, 1776; d. there, Feb. 23, 1867. Chorister in the Chapel Royal under Ayrton; pupil of Dupuis (organ) and Arnold (composition). Knighted 1811 at Dublin by the Lord Lieutenant after conducting a series of concerts. Original member of the Philharmonic Society and conductor of its concerts 1813–44, introducing the works of Beethoven and Schumann. Also conducted the Lenten oratorios (1813–25). Publ. a collection of glees and canons (1863), 2 vols. of sacred music, 2 piano sonatinas, etc.; edited Orlando Gibbons's madrigals and Handel's "Dettingen" Te Deum.

BIBLIOGRAPHY: H. B. and C. L. Cox, *Leaves from the Journals of Sir George Smart* (London, 1907); C. Maclean, "Sir George Smart, Musician-Diarist," *Sammelbände der Internationalen Musik-Gesellschaft* X (1909); A. Hyatt King, "The Importance of Sir George Smart," *Musical Times* (Dec. 1950).

Smart, Henry, English organist; son of **Sir George's** brother Henry (1778–1823); b. London, Oct. 26, 1813; d. there, July 6, 1879. He was a pupil of his father and W. H. Kearns; served as organist at several London churches; finally at St. Pancras, Euston Road, in 1864, his sight failing in that year; he received a government pension in 1879. His opera, *Bertha, or the Gnome of the Hartzberg,* was produced at the Haymarket Theatre, May 26, 1855; the cantatas *The Bride of Dunkerron* (1864), *King René's Daughter* (1871), *The Fishermaidens* (1871), and *Jacob* (1873) appeared after he

was blind. He wrote many songs, part-songs, and anthems; Evening Service; organ music; etc.

BIBLIOGRAPHY: Wm. Spark, *Henry Smart, His Life and Works* (London, 1881); W. D. Seymour, *Henry Smart* (London, 1881).

Smetáček, Václav, Czech conductor; b. Brno, Sept. 30, 1906. He studied oboe at the Prague Cons.; was first oboist in the Czech Philharmonic Orch. (1930–33); also studied composition with Jaroslav Křička at Charles Univ. in Prague. In 1934 he embarked on his chief career as conductor; led the choral society Hlahol in Prague; then enlarged his activities into the field of opera and symphonic music; has made numerous appearances as guest conductor all over Europe, in America and in Japan.

Smetana, Bedřich (Friedrich), great Bohemian composer; b. Leitomischl, March 2, 1824; d. insane at Prague, May 12, 1884. (His name is pronounced with a stress on the first syllable; Smetana himself said that the rhythm should be identical with the initial phrase in Beethoven's *Fidelio Overture*.) His talent manifested itself very early, but his father's prejudice against music as a profession precluded systematic instruction. However, a friend of his schooldays, Katharina Kolař, who was studying the piano with Proksch in Prague, introduced Smetana to her master, who accepted him as a pupil (piano and theory). Kittl, the director of the Cons., procured him a position as music teacher in the family of Count Thun. After four years of earnest work Smetana gave up his position and undertook his first concert tour, which resulted in a disastrous financial failure. In despair he turned to Liszt, who helped him open a piano school of his own. This flourished, and a year later (1849) he married **Katharina Kolař,** who had also become a fine pianist. His reputation as a performer, especially as an interpreter of Chopin, grew rapidly, but his first compositions were received coldly. When, therefore, the Philharmonic Society of Göteborg (Sweden) offered him the conductorship in 1856, he immediately accepted. In his first year there he wrote his first three symphonic poems, *Richard III, Wallensteins Lager,* and *Hakon Jarl* (after Öhlenschläger). As conductor and pianist he was highly appreciated. But the cold climate undermined his wife's health. For her sake he spent his vacations regularly in Prague; on the trip there in 1859, she died in Dresden. Meantime, important events were evolving at home. Škroup had made a beginning with national opera, whose chief national element was Bohemian texts, the music being practically devoid of national characteristics. The younger musicians and poets sought the establishment of a national art. After Austria had granted political autonomy to Bohemia in 1860, an agitation was begun for the erection of a national opera house in Prague. Smetana resigned his post in Göteborg, and returned to Prague in May, 1861, assuming a leading role in the new movement. On Nov. 18, 1862, the new opera house was opened, but the dozen Bohemian operas by Škroup, Shuherský, and Šebor could not furnish an important or varied repertory; consequently, Meyerbeer and the Italians were sung in Bohemian. Smetana therefore turned to opera, and finished his first dramatic work, *Braniboři v Čechách (The Branden-burgers in Bohemia)*, in 1863. It was not produced till Jan. 5, 1866; its success, while not overwhelming, was decided. On May 30, 1866, his second opera, *Prodaná nevěsta (The Bartered Bride)*, was received with immense enthusiasm. Smetana was appointed 1st conductor (replacing the Meyerbeer fanatic, Mayer), and acclaimed as Bohemia's greatest composer. This opera has also found success abroad (Austria and Germany, 1892; Scandinavia, 1894; England, 1895; Italy, 1905; Belgium, 1907; U.S., Feb. 19, 1909, at the Metropolitan Opera House). The next opera, *Dalibor* (May 16, 1868), on account of Smetana's employment of leading motifs and more elaborate treatment of the orchestra, caused several critics to charge the composer with attempting to Wagnerize the national opera. In 1871, when there was talk of crowning Emperor Francis Josef as King of Bohemia, Smetana wrote *Libussa* for the coronation festivities. But no coronation took place, and Smetana's enemies found means of preventing a production at the National Opera. Hoping to duplicate the success of his second work, he selected a comedy, *Dvě vdovy (The Two Widows)*, produced on March 27, 1874, with only moderate success. He returned to the symphonic poem, but now found inspiration in national subjects. Thus originated the six masterpieces bearing the collective title *Má Vlast (My Country): Vyšehrad* (the ancient castle of the Bohemian kings) and *Vltava (The Moldau)* in 1874; *Šárka* (a valley north of Prague, named after a mythological character) and *Z českých luhův a hayův (From Bohemia's Meadows and Groves)* in 1875; *Tábor (The Camp;* introducing the Hussite war song) in 1878; and *Blaník* in 1879. To this period also belongs the famous E minor String Quartet *Z mého Života (Aus meinem Leben;* 1876). But Smetana's labors on behalf of national art had already borne fruit; a reaction soon set in, and by the end of 1875 his friends again controlled the opera. Early in 1876 he began a new opera, *Hubička (The Kiss)*, produced with gratifying success on Nov. 7, 1876. *Tajemství (The Secret)*, staged in Prague on Sept. 18, 1878, was hailed as a second *Bartered Bride*, and won even the opposition party. For the opening (June 11, 1881) of the new National Opera, *Libussa* was unanimously chosen, and created a profound impression. His last opera, *Čertova stěna (The Devil's Wall)*, presented on Oct. 29, 1882, was a comparative failure. Meanwhile, an early syphilitic infection affected his hearing, so that he became almost totally deaf and had to cease all public appearances; his brain was affected; he suffered hallucinations, and had to be confined in an asylum. A detailed account of Smetana's illness and death is found in Dieter Kerner's *Krankheiten grosser Musiker* (Stuttgart, 1969; Vol. 2, pp. 77-92). Smetana's other works are: *Richard III*, symph. poem (Prague, Jan. 5, 1862, composer conducting); *Hakon Jarl*, symph. poem (Prague, Feb. 24, 1864, composer conducting); *Píseň Česká (Bohemian Song)*, for vocal quartet and orch. (1868; Prague, March 29, 1875); *Pražský Karneval (The Carnival of Prague)*, symph. poem (Prague, March 2, 1884); *Rybář (The Fisher)*, music to a tableau after Goethe, for harmonium, harp, and string quintet (Žofin, April 12, 1869); a *Festmarsch* for the Shakespeare tercentenary (1864); String Quartet in D minor; Piano Trio; 2 pieces for violin and piano; choruses and songs; piano music (a set of Bohemian dances, 3 sets of polkas, the popular concert étude *Am Seegestade*, etc.).

BIBLIOGRAPHY: B. Wellek, *F. Smetana. Mit einem Anhang von Korrespondenzen Smetanas an Liszt* (Prague, 1895; 2nd ed. as *F. Smetanas Leben und Wirken*, 1899); O. Hostinský, *B. Smetana* (Prague, 1901); R. Batka, *Die Musik in Böhmen* (Berlin, 1906); W. Ritter, *F. Smetana* (Paris, 1907); K. Hoffmeister, *B. Smetana* (Prague, 1914); V. Helfert, *B. Smetana* (Brno, 1924); V. Balthasar, *B. Smetana* (Prague, 1924); E. Rychnovsky, *Smetana* (Stuttgart, 1924); Z. Nejedlý, *B. Smetana*, a monumental biography in 4 vols. (Prague, 1924-33; 2nd ed. in 7 vols., 1950-54); J. Bistron, *F. Smetana* (Vienna, 1924); J. Tiersot, *Smetana* (Paris, 1926); J. Teichmann, *B. Smetana* (Prague, 1944); P. Pražák, *Smetanovy zpěvohry* (on Smetana's operas; 4 vols.; Prague, 1948); H. Boese, *Zwei Urmusikanten: Smetana, Dvořák* (Zürich, 1955); Brian Large, *Smetana* (N.Y., 1970). Documentary vols. containing various materials on Smetana were publ. in Prague by Mirko Očadlik (1950) and F. Bartoš (9th ed., 1954; in English as *Letters and Reminiscences*, Prague, 1955); numerous monographs on Smetana's individual works have also been publ. in Prague.

Smeterlin, Jan, Polish pianist; b. Bielsko, Poland, Feb. 7, 1892; d. London, Jan. 18, 1967. He was a child prodigy; made his first concert appearance at the age of 8; toured widely as a concert pianist, eventually settling in London. He was praised for his congenially romantic interpretations of Chopin's music.

Smijers, Albert Anton, eminent Dutch musicologist; b. Raamsdonksveer, July 19, 1888; d. Huis ter Heide, near Utrecht, May 15, 1957. He studied music with Averkamp at the Cons. of Amsterdam; was trained for the priesthood; ordained in 1912; then entered the school for church music at Klosterneuburg; took a course in musicology with Guido Adler at the Univ. of Vienna (1914-19); Dr. phil. with the dissertation *Karl Luython als Motettenkomponist* (1917; publ. Amsterdam, 1923). Returning to Holland, he was appointed prof. of musicology at the Univ. of Utrecht; formed the Institute of Musicology there. He brought out 7 volumes of the anthology *Van Ockeghem tot Sweelinck* (Amsterdam, 1939-56); in collaboration with Charles Van den Borren and others he publ. *Algemeene Muziekgeschiedenis* (Utrecht, 1938); began an edition of the collected works of Josquin Des Pres and Obrecht.

Smit, Leo, Dutch composer; b. Amsterdam, May 14, 1900; d. in a concentration camp, probably in Poland, in 1943 or 1944. He studied composition with Sem Dresden at the Amsterdam Cons.; taught at the Cons. (1924-27); then lived in Paris. He returned to Amsterdam in 1937; was arrested by the Nazis in 1943 and sent to the concentration camp at Westerbork in northeast Holland; removed to an unknown camp (presumably in Poland) and an equally unknown fate. His music was greatly influenced by the contemporary French school of his time.

WORKS: *Introduction to Teirlinck's play "De Ver-*

traagde Film" for chamber orch. (1923); Quintet for flute, violin, viola, cello and harp (1928); *Schemselnihar,* ballet (1929); *Silhouetten,* suite for orch.; *2 Hommages* (Sherlock Holmes and Remington) for piano (1928–30); Harp Concertino (1933); Sextet for piano and wind quintet (1933); Symphony (1934–36); Concerto for Piano and Wind Orch. (1937); *Forlane en Rondeau* (orchestrated by Godfried Devreese); Concertino for Cello and Small Orch. (1937); *Suite* for oboe and cello (1938); Trio for clarinet, viola and piano (1938); Concerto for Viola and Strings (1940); *Divertimento* for piano, 4 hands (1940); Flute Sonata (1943).

Smit, Leo, American pianist and composer; b. Philadelphia, Jan. 12, 1921. He studied piano with Isabelle Vengerova at the Curtis Institute of Music in Philadelphia; took lessons in composition with Nicolas Nabokov. He made his debut as a pianist at Carnegie Hall, N.Y. in 1939; then taught at various schools and colleges. In 1967 he traveled in Latin America and gave concerts of American music there. His own style of composition is neo-Classical, marked by a strong contrapuntal fabric; the influence of Stravinsky, with whom he had personal contact, is particularly pronounced here. He wrote an opera, *The Alchemy of Love* to a libretto by the astronomer Fred Hoyle (1969); the ballet, *Virginia Sampler* (N.Y., March 4, 1947); *The Parcae,* overture (Boston, Oct. 16, 1953); Symph. No. 1 (Boston, Feb. 1, 1957); *Capriccio* for string orch. (Ojai, California, May 23, 1958); Sextet for clarinet, bassoon and strings (1940); *Academic Graffiti* for voice, clarinet, cello, piano and percussion, to the text by W. H. Auden (1959); Piano Concerto (1968); *In Woods* for Oboe, Harp, and Percussion (1978); choruses and a number of piano pieces.

Smith, Alice Mary (Mrs. Meadows White), English composer; b. London, May 19, 1839; d. there, Dec. 4, 1884. She was a pupil of Sterndale Bennett and G. A. Macfarren; married M. White in 1867.

WORKS: the cantatas *Rüdesheim* (1865), *Ode to the Northeast Wind* (1878), *Ode to the Passions* (1882), *Song of the Little Baltung* (1883), and *The Red King* (1884); Symphony in C minor; 4 overtures: *Endymion, Lalla Rookh, Masque of Pandora,* and *Jason;* 2 piano quartets; 2 string quartets; Piano Trio; Clarinet Concerto; *Introduction and Allegro* for piano and orch.; part-songs; etc.

Smith, Bernard (Bernhard Schmidt), called "Father Smith," organ builder; b. in Germany c.1630; d. London, Feb. 20, 1708. He settled in London in 1660 with 2 nephews; became organ builder to the King and court organ builder to Queen Anne. He built organs for St. Margaret's, Westminster (1675), Durham Cathedral (1683), the Temple (1684), St. Paul's Cathedral (1697), and the Banqueting Hall, Whitehall (1699).

BIBLIOGRAPHY: A. Freeman, *Father Smith* (London, 1926).

Smith, Bessie (Elizabeth), black American "blues" singer; b. Chattanooga, Tennessee, April 15, 1895 (possibly 1894 or 1898); d. in an automobile accident, Sept. 26, 1937, on a highway outside Clarksdale, Miss.

Born in a wretchedly poor family, she joined Rainey's Rabbit Foot Minstrels (blues pioneer Ma Rainey was her teacher) and developed a style of singing that rapidly brought her fame. Her first record, *Down Hearted Blues,* sold 800,000 copies in 1923, and she was billed as the "Empress of the Blues." She was a large, impressive woman—5'9" and weighing over 200 pounds—and had a powerful voice to match; the excellence of her vocal equipment, along with her natural expressive qualities and improvisatory abilities combined to make her the consummate blues singer of her time.

BIBLIOGRAPHY: P. Oliver, *Bessie Smith* (London, 1959); Gunther Schuller, *Early Jazz* (N.Y., 1968); Carman Moore, *Somebody's Angel Child* (N.Y., 1969); C. Albertson, *Bessie* (N.Y., 1973); C. Albertson, *Bessie Smith. Empress of the Blues* (a collection of her songs, with essays by Albertson and Schuller; N.Y., 1975). See also L. Gara in *Notable American Women* (Cambridge, Mass. 1971), III.

Smith, Carleton Sprague, distinguished American musicologist; b. New York, Aug. 8, 1905. He was educated at Harvard Univ. (M.A., 1928) and at the Univ. of Vienna, where he studied History (Dr. phil., 1930). Returning to the U.S., he was instructor in history at Columbia Univ. (1931–34); then served as chief of the Music Division at N.Y. Public Library (1931–43, and 1946–59); a linguist, he lectured in South America, in Spanish and Portuguese, on social history of the U.S.; a skillful flutist, he often took part in concerts of old and new music.

Smith, Cecil, American music critic; b. Chicago, July 12, 1906; d. London, May 28, 1956. He studied with H. Levy (piano) and Sowerby (composition) in Chicago; later at Harvard Univ. with Piston. He taught at the Univ. of Chicago (1929–46); was music critic of the *Chicago Tribune* (1936–42) and editor of *Musical America* (1948–51). He went to England in 1951 and wrote for the London *Daily Express;* remained in London until his death. He wrote the books *Musical Comedy in America* (N.Y., 1950) and *Worlds of Music* (Philadelphia, 1952).

Smith, David Stanley, American composer and music educator; b. Toledo, Ohio, July 6, 1877; d. New Haven, Conn., Dec. 17, 1949. He studied with Horatio Parker at Yale Univ., graduating in 1900. He then went to Europe, where he took courses in composition with Thuille in Munich and Widor in Paris. Upon his return to the U.S. he obtained the Mus. Bac. degree at Yale (1903) and was appointed instructor at the Yale School of Music; in 1916 became prof. there; in 1920 was appointed dean of the School of Music, retiring in 1946. He was conductor of the New Haven Symph. Orch. from 1920 to 1946.

WORKS: Symph. No. 1 (1905); Symph. No. 2 (1917); Symph. No. 3 (Cleveland, Jan. 8, 1931, composer conducting); Symph. No. 4 (Boston, April 14, 1939, composer conducting); *Prince Hal,* overture (New Haven, Dec., 1912); *Impressions,* suite for orch. (1916); *Fête Galante,* fantasy for flute and orch. (N.Y., Dec. 11, 1921); *A Satire,* orch. sketch (N.Y., Nov. 15, 1933); *Epic Poem,* for orch. (Boston, April 12, 1935, composer conducting); *Requiem*, for violin and orch. (1939); *Credo*, symph. poem (1941); 4 Pieces for string orch. (1943); *The Apostle*, symph. poem (1944); *Flowers*, suite of 4 pieces for 10 instruments (1924); *Sinfonietta*, for string orch. (1931); choral works: *Rhapsody of St. Bernard*, for mixed chorus and orch. (1915), *Visions of Isaiah*, for soprano, tenor, chorus, and orch. (1927), *The Ocean*, for bass solo, mixed chorus, and orch. (1945); chamber music: 10 string quartets; *Sonata Pastorale*, for oboe and piano; 2 violin sonatas; piano quintet; cello sonata; piano works; songs (cycle, *Songs of Three Ages*, etc.).

BIBLIOGRAPHY: B. C. Tuthill, "David Stanley Smith," *Musical Quarterly* (Jan. 1942).

Smith, Gerrit, American organist and composer; b. Hagerstown, Md., Dec. 11, 1859; d. Darien, Conn., July 21, 1912. He studied music at the Stuttgart Cons.; began his professional career as organist in Buffalo; settled in N.Y. in 1885 as church organist. He was one of the founders of the Manuscript Society, N.Y.; wrote a cantata, *King David;* many songs of a lyric inspiration; *25 Song-Vignettes* (for children), and an interesting suite, *Aquarelles,* including 8 songs and 8 piano pieces.

BIBLIOGRAPHY: Rupert Hughes, *Contemporary American Composers* (Boston, 1900; pp. 309-17).

Smith, Hale, black American composer; b. Cleveland, June 29, 1925. He studied piano with Dorothy Price and composition with Marcel Dick at the Cleveland Institute of Music (1946–50; M.M., 1952); moved to New York in 1958; was active as arranger for music publishers; in 1963 became a musical consultant for C. F. Peters Corp.; from 1969 was advisor for the Black Music Center of Indiana Univ.; in 1970 joined the music faculty of the Univ. of Connecticut. He wrote musical scores for Dizzy Gillespie, Ahmad Jamal, Eric Dolphy, and Abby Lincoln, and worked in various capacities for Quincy Jones, Clark Terry, Oliver Nelson, Miriam Makeba, and Hugh Masakela.

WORKS: a chamber opera, *Blood Wedding* (Cleveland, 1953); *Orchestral Set* (1952, revised 1968) *Contours* for orch. (Louisville, Oct. 17, 1961); *By Yearning and By Beautiful* for string orch. (1964); *Music for harp and orch.* (1972); *Ritual and Incantations* for orch. (1974); *Innerflexions* for orch. (N.Y., Sept. 2, 1977); Duo for violin and piano (1953); Cello Sonata (1955); *Epicedial Variations* for violin and piano (1956); *3 Brevities* for solo flute (1960); *Introductions, Cadenzas and Interludes* for 8 players (1974); *Variations* for 6 players (1975); *5 Songs* for voice and violin (1956); *2 Love Songs of John Donne* for soprano and 9 instruments (1958); *Comes Tomorrow,* jazz cantata for chorus and accompaniment (1972, revised 1977); *Toussaint L'Ouverture 1803* for chorus and piano (1977); *Evocation* for piano (1966); *Anticipations, Introspections and Reflections* for piano (1971).

Smith, John Chistopher (Johann Christoph Schmidt), organist and composer; b. Ansbach, Germany, 1712; d. Bath, England, Oct. 3, 1795. His father went to England with Handel in 1720 as his agent, and the son became Handel's pupil. When Handel's eyesight began to deteriorate, Smith helped him in playing the organ and harpsichord at performances of Handel's oratorios, and continued to supervise performances of Handel's music after Handel's death; Smith presented Handel's MS scores, and other objects left to him by Handel, to George III in appreciation for a royal pension. He retired about 1770, and settled in Bath. He wrote several English operas, of which 2 Shakespearian pieces, *The Fairies* (1754) and *The Tempest* (1756) were publ.; also wrote the oratorios *Paradise Lost* (1760), *Judith, Redemption,* etc.

BIBLIOGRAPHY: W. Coxe, *Anecdotes of G. F. Handel and J. C. Smith* (London, 1799).

Smith, John Stafford, English organist and composer; b. Gloucester, baptized, March 30, 1750; d. London, Sept. 21, 1836. He studied with his father, Martin Smith, organist at Gloucester Cathedral, and also took lessons with Boyce. In 1784 he was made a Gentleman of the Chapel Royal, and in 1802 succeeded Arnold as organist there; from 1805 to 1817 he was master of the Boy Choristers there; from 1785 served as lay-vicar at Westminster Abbey; was also known as a composer of catches and glees and won several prizes of the Catch Club in London. The importance of John Stafford Smith to American music lies in the fact that he included in his 5th collection of glees, which he issued in 1799, an arrangement of the tune *To Anacreon in Heaven,* to which Francis Scott Key wrote *The Star-Spangled Banner* (1814); but there were several reasons for questioning whether he could not have been the composer, his authorship was doubted by many reputable American scholars. William Lichtenwanger, in his paper, "The Music of *The Star-Spangled Banner:* From Ludgate Hill to Capitol Hill," in *The Quarterly Journal of the Library of Congress* (July 1977), seems to have dispelled these doubts by publishing excerpts from the "Recollections" of Richard John Samuel Stevens, an active member of the Anacreontic Society of London, who states in the rubric for 1777: "The president was Ralph Tomlinson. . . . He wrote the Poetry of the Anacreontic Song; which Stafford Smith set to Music." Smith was an excellent musician; he transcribed into modern notation old manuscripts for *History of Music* by Sir John Hawkins; edited *Musica antiqua,* containing compositions "from the commencement of the 12th to the 18th century" (2 vols., 1812), and published *A Collection of Songs of Various Kinds for Different Voices* (1785).

BIBLIOGRAPHY: O. G. Sonneck, *Report on the Star-Spangled Banner* (1914); numerous other publications dealing with Smith and *The Star-Spangled Banner* are superseded by Lichtenwanger's paper.

Smith, Julia, American pianist, composer and writer on music; b. Denton, Texas, Jan. 25, 1911. She studied piano with Carl Friedberg at the Juilliard School of Music, N.Y.; devoted herself mainly to composition and music criticism. She wrote the operas *Cynthia Parker* (Denton, Texas, Feb. 16, 1940); *The Gooseherd and the Goblin* (N.Y., Feb. 22, 1947); *The Stranger of Manzano* (Dallas, Texas, May 6, 1947); *Cockcrow* (Austin, Texas, April 22, 1954); *The Shepherdess and the Chimney Sweep* (Fort Worth, Texas, Dec. 28, 1967); *Daisy* (Miami, Florida, Nov. 3, 1973); *Folkways*

Symphony (1948); *Remember the Alamo* for speaker, chorus and wind orch. (1964); Piano Trio (1955); String Quartet (1964); Piano Concerto (Dallas, Feb. 28, 1976). She published the monographs *Aaron Copland* (N.Y., 1955); *Master Pianist. The Career and Teaching of Carl Friedberg* (N.Y., 1963); *A Directory of Women Composers* (Chicago, 1970).

Smith, Lawrence, American conductor; b. Portland, Oregon, April 8, 1936. He studied piano with Leonard Shure in N.Y. and with Ariel Rubstein in Portland, Oregon; then enrolled in Portland State Univ. (B.S., 1956) and at Mannes College of Music, N.Y. (B.M., 1959). In 1964 he received first prize at the Mitropoulos International Conducting Competition, N.Y.; was assistant conductor at the Metropolitan Opera (1965-68), music director of Westchester, Conn. Symph. (1967-69); was principal guest conductor, Phoenix, Arizona Symph. (1971-73); music director of Austin, Texas, Symph. (1972-73); in 1973 he was appointed music director and conductor of the Oregon Symph. Orch. in Portland.

Smith, Leland, American composer; b. Oakland, Calif., Aug. 6, 1925. He studied composition at Mills College with Darius Milhaud (1941-43) and at Univ. of California, Berkeley, with Roger Sessions (1946-48), obtaining his A.B. and M.A. degrees; also took courses in musicology there with Manfred Bukofzer. He subsequently attended classes of Olivier Messiaen at the Paris Cons. (1948-49). In 1950 he was appointed to the music faculty of the Univ. of California at Berkeley; other posts included Mills College (summer classes between 1951 and 1961) and Univ. of Chicago (1952-58). In 1958 he joined the faculty at Stanford Univ.; became a professor in 1968. His style of composition is that of liberal modernism marked by a discriminate application of eclectic idioms, not excluding triadic usages. WORKS: Sonata for trumpet and piano (1947); Trio for flute, cello and piano (1947); Trio for violin, trumpet and clarinet (1948); *Divertimento No. 1* for 5 instruments (1949); Symph. No. 1 (1951); Woodwind Quintet (1951); Sonata for heckelphone (or viola) and piano (1954); *Santa Claus,* opera in 5 scenes on the libretto by e. e. cummings (1955); Concerto for Orchestra (1956); Quintet for bassoon and strings (1956); *Divertimento No. 2* for chamber orch. (1957); *3 Pacifist Songs* (1960); Wind Trio (1960); Quartet for horn, violin, cello and piano (1961); *Orpheus* for guitar, harp and harpsichord (1967); *Machines of Loving Grace* for computer, bassoon and narrator (1970). He publ. *Handbook of Harmonic Analysis* (Stanford, 1963).

Smith, Moses, American music critic; b. Chelsea, Mass., March 4, 1901; d. Boston, July 27, 1964. He studied law at Harvard Univ. (graduated 1924) and also music. He was music critic of the *Boston American* (1924-34) and of the *Boston Evening Transcript* (1934-39); then was music director of the Columbia Phonograph Co. (1939-42). In 1947 he published a controversial biography of Koussevitzky, who brought a libel suit for a million dollars against Smith and his publisher, claiming that the book described him as "generally incompetent, brutal to the musi-

cians and a poseur." The suit, however, was dismissed.

Smith, Reed, American educator and writer on folklore; b. Washington, N.C., Jan. 16, 1881; d. Pawley's Island, S.C., July 24, 1943. He was educated at the Univ. of South Carolina and at Harvard Univ. (Ph.D., 1909); in 1910, appointed prof. of English literature at the Univ. of South Carolina; he publ. *South Carolina Ballads* (1928); also various essays on songs of the South.

Smith, Sydney, English pianist and composer; b. Dorchester, July 14, 1839; d. London, March 3, 1889. He studied piano at the Leipzig Cons. with Moscheles and Plaidy; settled in London in 1859 as a teacher; publ. many salon pieces for piano (*La Harpe éolienne, Le Jet d'eau, The Spinning-wheel,* etc.); also arrangements from operas.

Smith, Warren Storey, American music critic; b. Brookline, Mass., July 14, 1885; d. Boston, Oct. 13, 1971. He studied piano in Boston; in 1922 joined the staff of the New England Cons., where he taught until 1960; was mainly active as a music critic; was music editor of the *Boston Post* (1924-53). He was also a composer; wrote a piano trio, piano solo pieces and several songs.

Smith, William O., American composer; b. Sacramento, California, Sept. 22, 1926. He studied clarinet and took courses in composition with Darius Milhaud at Mills College, Oakland, Calif., and with Roger Sessions at the Univ. of Calif., Berkeley (M.A., 1952). He taught clarinet in various institutions in Calif.; in 1960 received a Guggenheim Fellowship. WORKS: Suite for clarinet, flute and trumpet (1947); *Serenade* for flute, violin, trumpet and clarinet (1947); *Schizophrenic Scherzo* for clarinet, trumpet, saxophone and trombone (1947); Clarinet Sonata (1948); Concertino for trumpet and jazz instruments (1948); Quintet for clarinet and string quartet (1950); String Quartet (1952); *Capriccio* for violin and piano (1952); *Suite* for violin and clarinet (1952); *Divertimento* for jazz instruments (1956); Concerto for Clarinet and Combo (1957); Trio for clarinet, violin and piano (1957); Quartet for clarinet, violin, cello and piano (1958); *5 Pieces* for clarinet alone (1958); *Quadrodram* for clarinet, trombone, piano, percussion, dancer and film (Seattle, Dec. 9, 1970).

Smith, Willie "The Lion" (full name **William Henry Joseph Berthol Bonaparte Bertholoff Smith**), black American jazz pianist and composer; b. Goshen, N.Y., Nov. 24, 1897; d. New York, April 18, 1973. He attended Howard Univ. and studied music privately, receiving instruction in piano and theory from Hans Steinke. He played ragtime piano in clubs in Newark, Atlantic City, and New York, and also made appearances in Europe before 1920; in the post-W.W. I period he became one of the creators of "Harlem stride" jazz piano, a style he retained through the rest of his career; worked mostly in New York, toured Europe several times, and Africa in 1949-50; made numerous recordings. His compositions (*Fingerbuster, Echoes of*

Spring, etc.) were primarily for his own use. His autobiography, *Music on My Mind* (written with George Hoefer; N.Y., 1964), is an extremely valuable account of the jazz scene in Harlem.

Smith, Wilson George, American pianist and composer; b. Elyria, Ohio, Aug. 19, 1855; d. Cleveland, Feb. 26, 1929. He studied piano with the Scharwenka brothers in Berlin. Returning to the U.S. in 1882 he settled in Cleveland, where he taught piano. He published a number of salon pieces for piano, such as *Poème d'amour, Homoresque, Menuet moderne, Romanza appassionata* and *Babbling Brook;* about 40 songs. His album of 5 piano pieces, *Hommage à Edvard Grieg,* was commended for its spirit by Grieg himself.

BIBLIOGRAPHY: Rupert Hughes, *Contemporary American Composers* (Boston, 1900; pp. 394–406).

Smither, Howard E., American musicologist and educator; b. Pittsburg, Kansas, Nov. 15, 1925. He studied at Hamline Univ., St. Paul, Minnesota (A.B., 1950), and at Cornell Univ. with Donald J. Grout and William W. Austin (M.A., 1952); in 1953 received a Senior Graduate Fellowship, awarded by Cornell Univ. for study in Germany; attended classes of Rudolf von Ficker in Munich; in 1965–66 studied in Italy on a Fulbright Grant; in 1972 did research in Italy on the history of the oratorio on a fellowship from the National Endowment for the Humanities. He was on the faculties of Oberlin Cons. (1955–60), at the Univ. of Kansas (1960–63), and at Tulane Univ. (1963–68); in 1968 was appointed prof. of music at the Univ. of North Carolina at Chapel Hill. He published an important study: *A History of the Oratorio* (2 vols., Chapel Hill, Univ. of North Carolina, 1977); contributed to the 6th edition of *Grove's Dictionary of Music and Musicians* a major article on the oratorio, as well as biographical articles on Italian composers of oratorios.

Smolensky, Stepan, Russian music scholar b. Kazan, Oct. 20, 1848; d. Vasilsursk, near Nizhny-Novgorod, Aug. 2, 1909. He devoted his efforts mainly to collecting and analyzing Russian manuscripts of old church music; published *A Course of Choral Church Singing* (Kazan, 1885) and numerous papers on specific subjects connected with old Russian musical notation. A list of Smolensky's writings was published in a memorial volume edited by N. Findeisen (St. Petersburg, 1911).

Smolian, Arthur, conductor and writer; b. Riga, Dec. 3, 1856; d. Leipzig, Nov. 5, 1911. He was a pupil of Rheinberger and Wüllner at the Munich Cons.; conducted choruses in Leipzig (from 1884); taught at the Karlsruhe Cons. (1890–1901); in 1901 settled again in Leipzig as music critic and editor. In his writings he was an ardent proponent of Wagner's ideas. He publ. *Vom Schwinden der Gesangskunst* (1903) and *Stella del Monte* (1903; a free narrative of Berlioz's last years).

Smulders, Charles, Belgian composer; b. Maestricht, May 8, 1863; d. Liège, April 21, 1934. He studied at the Liège Cons.; won the Belgian Prix de Rome in 1889;

taught at the Liège Cons. He wrote the symph. poems *Adieu-Absence-Retour; Chant d'Amour; Le Jour; Le Crépuscule;* 2 piano concertos; *Hebrew Melodies* for cello and orch.; Violin Sonata; Piano Sonata; choruses; songs.

BIBLIOGRAPHY: W. Paap, "C. Smulders en A. Diepenbrock," *Mens en Melodie* 1 (1946).

Smyth, Dame Ethel (Mary), foremost English woman composer; b. Rectory (Middlesex), April 22, 1858; d. Woking, Surrey, May 8, 1944. She studied at the Leipzig Cons.; then with Heinrich von Herzogenberg, following him to Berlin; her String Quintet was performed in Leipzig in 1884. She returned to London in 1888; presented her orchestral *Serenade* (April 26, 1890) and an overture *Antony and Cleopatra* (Oct. 18, 1890). Her prestige as a serious woman composer rose considerably with the presentation of her Mass, for solo voices, chorus, and orch., at Albert Hall (Jan. 18, 1893). After that she devoted her energies to the theater. Her first opera, *Fantasio,* to her own libretto in German, after Alfred de Musset's play, was produced in Weimar on May 24, 1898; this was followed by *Der Wald* (Berlin, April 9, 1902), also to her own German libretto; it was produced in London in the same year, and in N.Y. by the Metropolitan Opera, on March 11, 1903. Her next opera, *The Wreckers,* was her most successful work; written originally to a French libretto, *Les Naufrageurs,* it was first produced in a German version as *Strandrecht* (Leipzig, Nov. 11, 1906); the composer herself translated it into English, and it was staged in London on June 22, 1909; the score was revised some years later, and produced at Sadler's Wells, London, on April 19, 1939. She further wrote a comic opera, in English, *The Boatswain's Mate* (London, Jan. 28, 1916), a one-act opera, described as "a dance-dream," *Fête Galante* (Birmingham, June 4, 1923), and *Entente Cordiale* (Bristol, Oct. 20, 1926). Other works are a Concerto for Violin, Horn, and Orch. (London, March 5, 1927); *The Prison,* for soprano and bass solo, chorus, and orch. (London, Feb. 24, 1931); choral pieces (*Hey Nonny No, Sleepless Dreams,* etc.); a group of songs; etc. Her formative years were spent in Germany, and her music never overcame the strong German characteristics, in the general idiom as well as in the treatment of dramatic situations on the stage. At the same time, she was a believer in English national music and its potentialities. She was a militant leader for woman suffrage in England, for which cause she wrote *The March of the Women,* the battle song of the W. S. P. U. After the suffrage was granted, her role in the movement was officially acknowledged; in 1922 she was made a Dame of the British Empire. She publ. a number of books, mostly autobiographical in nature: *Impressions That Remained* (2 vols., 1919; new ed., 1945); *Streaks of Life* (1921); *As Time Went On* (1936); *What Happened Next* (1940); also some humorous essays and reminiscences, *A Three-legged Tour in Greece* (1927); *A Final Burning of Boats* (1928); *Female Pipings in Eden* (1934); *Beecham and Pharaoh* (1935).

BIBLIOGRAPHY: R. Boughton, in *Music Bulletin* (Feb. 1923) R. Capell, in *Monthly Musical Record* (July 1923); R. A. Streatfeild, *Musiciens anglais contemporains* (Paris, 1913); Kathleen Dale, "Dame Ethel

Smyth," *Music & Letters* (July 1944); C. St. John, *Ethel Smyth: A Biography* (N.Y., 1959).

Snel, Joseph-François, Belgian violinist and composer; b. Brussels, July 30, 1793; d. Koekelberg, near Brussels, March 10, 1861. He studied violin with Baillot at the Paris Cons. In 1818 he founded in Brussels the Académie de Musique et de Chant (with Mees); popularized in Belgium the instructional singing methods of Galin and Wilhem; held various positions as inspector of schools. His ballets *Frisac et le page inconstant, L'Enchantement de Polichinelle,* etc. were produced at the Brussels Opera; in 1830; during the Belgian Revolution, he wrote the ballet *Barricades.*

Snetzler (Schnetzler), Johann, Swiss organ builder; b. Schaffhausen, April 6, 1710; d. there, Sept. 28, 1785. He went to London in 1746 and established an organ workshop there; built organs for the Moravian Churches in London and in Leeds, for Chesterfield Church, and (on the recommendation of Burney) for the Church of King's Lynn. He returned to Switzerland shortly before his death. His London factory was purchased by Ohrmann, Nutt, and Eliot. A list of his organs exported to the U.S is found in W. L. Summer's *The Organ* (London, 1952).

Snoer, Johannes, Dutch harpist; b. Amsterdam, June 28, 1868; d. Vienna, March 1, 1936; he studied with Edmund Schuecker when the latter was in Amsterdam; from 1894 to 1910 was first harpist of the Gewandhaus Orch. in Leipzig; traveled as soloist in Europe and America in 1905–06. He publ. several practial pieces for the harp and didactic works: *Praktische Harfenschule, Tägliche Übungen, Studien in Konzertform, Orchesterstudien,* etc.; also *Die Harfe als Orchesterinstrument* (Leipzig, 1898).

Sobolewski, Friedrich Eduard de, German-American composer; b. Königsberg, Oct. 1, 1808, of Polish parents; d. St. Louis, May 17, 1872. He was a pupil of Weber in Dresden; became an opera conductor in Königsberg and Bremen; produced there his operas *Imogen* (1833), *Velleda* (1836), and *Salvator Rosa* (1848); his opera *Komala* was produced by Liszt in Weimar on Oct. 30, 1858. In 1859 he emigrated to the U.S., settling in Milwaukee, then a center of German musical immigrants. There he staged his opera, *Mohega,* on Oct. 11, 1859, to his own libretto in German; he selected an American subject dealing with an Indian girl saved by Pulaski from death. Sobolewski subsequently moved to St. Louis; organized a symphony orch. there, which he led until his death. He futher wrote the oratorios *Johannes der Täufer, Der Erlöser,* and *Himmel und Erde;* 2 symphonies; the symph. poems *Vineta* and *Meeresphantasie;* several male choruses; publ. the pamphlets, *Reaktionäre Briefe* (1854), *Oper nicht Drama* (1858), and *Das Geheimnis der neuesten Schule der Musik* (1859).
    BIBLIOGRAPHY: E. E. Hipsher, *American Opera and Its Composers* (Philadelphia, 1927; 2nd ed., 1934; pp. 382–85).

Socor, Matei, Rumanian composer and pedagogue, b. Jassy, Sept. 28, 1908. He studied music theory with Castaldi at the Bucharest Cons. (1927–29); then went to Germany and took a course in composition with Karg-Elert at the Leipzig Cons. (1930–33). Returning to Rumania, he dedicated himself to teaching music at various schools in Bucharest and elsewhere.
    WORKS: Concerto for Orch. (1939); *Passacaglia* for cello and chamber orch. (1944); Violin Concerto (1955); *Mama,* poem for mezzo-soprano, chorus and orch. (1949); Wind Sextet (1969); Piano Sonata (1932); choruses; songs.

Soderino, Agostino, Italian organist and composer; flourished in the early 17th century. He was church organist in Milan, where he publ. his *Canzoni a 4 & 8 voci . . . Libri I, Op. 2* (1608); 2 keyboard canzonas from this publication (*La Scaramuccia* and *La Ducalina*) are reprinted in L. Torchi, *L'Arte Musicale in Italia* (vol. III).

Söderlind, Ragnar, Norwegian composer; b. Oslo, June 27, 1945. He studied in Oslo with Baden (counterpoint), Hukvari (conducting) and Ulleberg (horn); then studied at the Sibelius Academy in Helsinki with Erik Bergman and Joonas Kokkonen.
    WORKS: a chamber opera, *Esther og den blå ro* (1972); *Nocturne* for orch. (1963); *Prelude* for orch. (1964); *Pietà* for mezzo-soprano and string orch. (1965); *Rokkomborre,* symph. poem (1967); *Polaris,* symph. vision (1967–70); *Trauermusik* for orch. (1968); *Fantasia borealis* for chamber orch. (1969); *Sinfonia minimale* for amateur orch. (1971); *International Rhapsody* for orch. (1971); *Sinfonia* for orch. with solo soprano (1975); *Elegia I* for solo cello and *II* for solo violin (1966; when played simultaneously, they become *Elegia III*); *Dithyrambe,* sketch for bassoon and harp (1967); *Körsbärblommor (Cherry Blossom),* 5 Japanese love poems for baritone, flute, English horn, cello and percussion (1967); *Intermezzo* for percussionist (1968); *La Mort des pauvres* for male chorus, 4 trombones and percussion (1969); *La poema battutta* for 8 percussionists (1973); *2 Pieces from the Desert* for oboe and piano (1973; orchestrated, 1974); String Quartet (1975); *Consolation* for piano (1969); choruses; songs.

Soderlund, Gustav Frederic, Swedish-American music scholar and teacher; b. Göteborg, Jan. 25, 1881; d. Rochester, N.Y., Nov. 28, 1972. He studied piano in Sweden; went to South America in 1908, and taught music at the Cons. of Valparaiso, Chile. In 1915 he settled in the U.S.; was on the faculty of the Univ. of Kansas (1919–27) and at the Eastman School of Music in Rochester, N.Y. (1927–47). He published in the Eastman School Series 2 collections of musical examples for use in teaching; *Examples Illustrating the Development of Melodic Line and Contrapuntal Style* (1932) and *Examples of Gregorian Chant* (1937).

Söderman, (Johan) August, Swedish composer; b. Stockholm, July 17, 1832; d. there, Feb. 10, 1876. He studied piano and composition at the Stockholm Academy of Music (1847–50); then joined, as composer of operettas, a theatrical company on a Scandinavian tour. In 1856 he went to Leipzig, where he studied privately with Richter and acquired an appreciation of German vocal music; he was particularly influenced by the lyric works of Schumann, Wagner, and Liszt, an influence that is combined with Swedish national elements in his theater music.

WORKS: the operettas *Urdur* (1852) and *Hin Ondes första lärospan* (*The Devil's First Lesson;* Stockholm, Sept. 14, 1856); incidental music to about 80 plays by Shakespeare, Schiller, and Swedish writers; *Digte og Sange*, part-songs to words by Bjørnson; several songs to Swedish words; a ballad for solo voice, chorus, and orch., *Die Wallfahrt nach Kevlaar*, after Heine (1859–66); also a *Missa solemnis* (1875).

BIBLIOGRAPHY: G. Jeanson, *A. Söderman: en svensk tondiktares liv och verk* (Stockholm, 1926; includes a complete list of works).

Sodero, Cesare, conductor; b. Naples, Aug. 2, 1886; d. New York, Dec. 16, 1947. He studied with Alessandro Longo (piano) and Martucci (composition) at the Naples Cons.; in 1907 emigrated to the U.S. and settled in N.Y.; was a music director of the Edison Phonograph Co., of the National Broadcasting Co., and of the Mutual Broadcasting Co.; conducted the San Carlo Grand Opera Co. and the Philadelphia Grand Opera. He wrote an opera, *Ombre russe* (Venice, June 19, 1930); ballets; chamber music.

Soffredini, Alfredo, Italian composer; b. Leghorn, Sept. 17, 1854; d. Milan, March 12, 1923. He studied with Mazzucato and Sangalli at the Milan Cons.; was editor of the influential *Gazzetta Musicale* (Milan) from 1896 to 1912; also taught composition; among his students was Mascagni.

WORKS: 8 operas to his own librettos: *Il Saggio* (Leghorn, Feb. 3, 1883), the 2-act childern's opera *Il piccolo Haydn* (Faenza, Nov. 24, 1889; Vienna, 1897; also productions in Russia and elsewhere), *Salvatorello* (Pavia, March 25, 1894), *Tarcisio* (Milan, Nov. 23, 1895), *Aurora* (Pavia, April 21, 1897), *La Coppa d'oro* (Milan, Jan. 27, 1900), *Graziella* (Pavia, Nov. 15, 1902), *Il Leone* (Cesena, 1914). He publ. *Le Opere di Verdi* (Milan, 1901) and contributed essays on Italian music to various publications, as well as to the *Gazzetta Musicale.*

Sofronitzky, Vladimir, Russian pianist; b. Leningrad, May 8, 1901; d. Moscow, Aug. 29, 1961. He studied with Nikolayev at the Leningrad Cons., graduating in 1921; then went on a concert tour in Russia, Poland and France. Returning to Russia he taught piano at the Leningrad Cons. (1936–42) and at the Moscow Cons. from 1942 until his death. He was greatly praised for his interpretations of Chopin, and particularly Scriabin.

BIBLIOGRAPHY: V. Delson, *Vladimir Sofronitzky* (Moscow, 1959); J. Milstein, *Reminiscences of Sofronitzky* (Moscow, 1970).

Sohn, Joseph, American music critic and writer; b. New York, March 22, 1876; d. there, March 15, 1935. After graduation from the College of the City of N.Y. he went to Berlin for further musical studies; upon his return to N.Y. he became music critic of the *N.Y.*

American and *The Forum.* He publ. *Robert Schumann, a Lyrical Poet* (1896), *Lessons of the Opera* (1903), *Music in America and Abroad* (1904), *Joseph Joachim* (1904), *Opera in New York* (1907), *The Mission of Richard Wagner* (1910).

Sokalsky, Pyotr, Russian writer on music; b. Kharkov, Sept. 26, 1832; d. Odessa, April 11, 1887. He studied biology and taught school. His significance in Russian music lies in his being an ardent collector of Russian folksongs; his chief work, *The Russian Folk-Song; Its Melodic Structure and Harmonic Characteristics*, was published posthumously in 1888. He also wrote some piano music and 3 operas, *The Siege of Dubno, Mazeppa,* and *A Night in May.*

Sokola, Miloš, Czech composer; b. Bučovice, Moravia, April 18, 1913. He studied composition with Petrželka, and violin with O. Vávra at the Brno Cons. (1936–38); further composition studies in Prague with V. Novák (1938–39) and J. Křička (1943–45). He was a violinist in the Prague National Theater Orch. (1942–73).

WORKS: an opera, *Marnotratný syn* (*The Prodigal Son*, 1948; Olomouc, 1963); 9 *Variations on a Theme by Vítězslava Kaprálová* for orch. (1952; Prague, Feb. 17, 1957; from Kaprálová's *April Preludes*); Violin Concerto (1952); *Devátý květen* (*The Ninth of May*), Symph. poem (1960); Concerto for Organ and String Orch. (1971); 5 string quartets (1944; with solo tenor, 1946; 1955; 1964; 1971); Violin Sonata (1972); Wind Quintet (1973); for piano: *5 Miniatures* (1931), Sonata (1946), *Valses* (1953), *12 Preludes* (1954), *Suite* for left hand (1972); for organ: *Toccata quasi Passacaglia* (1964), *B-A-C-H Studies* (1972) and *Andante Cantabile* (1973).

Sokoloff, Nikolai, American conductor; b. near Kiev, Russia, May 28, 1886; d. La Jolla, California, Sept. 25, 1965. He was brought to America as a child, and studied violin with Loeffler in Boston; played the violin in the Boston Symph. Orch.; then conducted various symphonic groups. In 1918 he became conductor of the newly organized Cleveland Orch., and to the extent of his limited abilities, he discharged his duties at this post in an acceptable fashion until 1933. He served as music director of the Federal Music Project (1935–38); for 2 seasons conducted the Seattle Symph. Orch. (1938–40); then went to live in La Jolla, California, occasionally filling in guest conducting engagements.

Sokolov, Nikolai, Russian composer and pedagogue; b. St. Petersburg, March 26, 1859; d. there, March 27, 1922. He was a pupil of Rimsky-Korsakov at the St. Petersburg Cons., graduating in 1884; later taught harmony there for many years until his death. He was also a prolific composer in the traditional Russian manner; many of his works were published by Belaieff; among them music for Shakespeare's play *The Winter's Tale;* 3 string quartets; violin pieces and a great number of songs.

Solano, Francisco Ignacio, Portuguese musical theorist; b. Coimbra, c.1720; d. Lisbon, Sept. 18, 1800. He publ. *Nova instrucçao musical* (1764), *Nova arte e breve compendio de musica* (1768; 2nd ed., 1794), *Novo tratado de musica* (1779), *Dissertação sobre o caracter da musica* (1780).

Solares, Enrique, Guatemalan pianist and composer; b. Guatemala City, July 11, 1910. He studied piano with Salvador Ley in Guatemala; composition with Raymond Moulaert in Brussels, with Jaroslav Křička in Prague (1936–39), and Alfredo Casella in Rome (1939–42). He returned to Guatemala in 1943; taught piano, then entered the diplomatic service and was a consular officer in Guatemalan embassies in Rome, Brussels, Madrid and Paris. His compositions are set in Baroque forms; later he experimented with serial techniques.
WORKS: *Ricercare sobre el nombre de BACH* for string orch. (1941); *Toccatina* for guitar (1946); *Partita* for string orch. (1947); Sonata for solo violin (1958); *Fantasia* for guitar (1959); *Idea con 15 Deformaciones* for piano (1962); *7 Traversuras* for piano (1969); *12 Microtransparencias* for piano (1970).

Soldat, Marie, Austrian violinist; b. Graz, March 25, 1863; d. there, Sept. 30, 1955. She first studied in Graz, and from 1879 to 1882 with Joachim at the Hochschule für Musik in Berlin, graduating as winner of the Mendelssohn Prize; made a specialty of the Brahms Violin Concerto, which she performed with great authority. In 1887 she formed in Berlin her own string quartet (all women); in 1899 she married the lawyer Röger, and settled in Vienna, continuing her concert career; there she formed a new string quartet (with Elsa von Plank, Natalie Bauer-Lechner, and Leontine Gärtner); eventually retired in Graz, remaining there until her death at the age of 92.

Solenière, Eugène de, French writer on music; b. Paris, Dec. 25, 1872; d. there, Dec. 4, 1904. After studing music in Germany, he settled in Paris as a writer and lecturer on musical esthetics.
WRITINGS: *La Femme compositeur* (1895); *Rose Caron* (1896); *Notes musicales* (1896); *Massenet; Étude critique et documentaire* (1897); *Musique et religion* (1897); *Camille Saint-Saëns* (1899); *Cent années de musique française 1800-1900* (1901); *Notules et impressions musicales* (1902).

Soler, Josep, Catalan composer; b. Barcelona, March 25, 1935. He studied composition with René Leibowitz in Paris (1959) and with Cristòfor Taltabull in Barcelona (1960–64). In 1977 he was appointed to the staff of the Barcelona Cons.
WORKS: 3 operas: *Agamemnon* (1960); *Edipo y Iocasta* (1972; Barcelona, Oct. 30, 1974); and *Jesús de Nazaret* (1974–78); *Danae* for string orch. (1959, revised 1969; Lisbon, June 23, 1977); *Cantata Ioel Prophetae,* chamber cantata (1960); Trio for 2 violins and piano (1961); Piano Trio (1964); *Orpheus* for piano and orch. (1965; revised 1974); *Quetzalcoatl* for flute and chamber orch. (1966); 2 symphonies: *The Solar Cycle I* and *The Solar Cycle II* (1967; 1969, revised 1977); *Lachrymae* for 11 instruments (1967); *Diaphonia* for 17 wind instruments (1968); String Trio (1968); *Música triste* for guitar (1968); Piano Concerto (1969);

Concerto for harpsichord, oboe, English horn, bass clarinet, viola and cello (1969); *Sounds in the Night* for 6 percussionists (1969); *Inferno* for chamber ensemble (1970); 3 string quartets (1966, 1971, 1975); *Tañido de Falsas* for guitar and percussion (1971); *Noche Oscura* for organ and percussion (1971); Cello Concerto (1973); *Requiem* for solo percussion and orch. (1974–75; Kassel, Germany, Sept. 18, 1977); *Apuntava l'alba* for orch. (1975; Barcelona, Feb. 5, 1976); *3 Erotic Songs* for chorus a cappella (1976); *Shakespeare Lieder* for tenor and orch. (1976–77); *Harmonices Mundi,* in 3 volumes; No. 1 for piano, and Nos. 2 and 3 for organ (1977); songs.

Soler, Padre Antonio, important Spanish composer and organist; b. Olot, Catalonia, 1729 (baptized Dec. 3); d. El Escorial, near Madrid, Dec. 20, 1783. He entered the school of the monastery of Montserrat as a child, and studied organ and harmony there. In 1752 he took Holy Orders at El Escorial, and spent the rest of his life there. For some time between 1752 and 1757 he had an opportunity to take lessons with Domenico Scarlatti, who was then attached to the Spanish court; Scarlatti's influence is apparent in Soler's harpsichord sonatas. Soler was a prolific composer of both sacred and secular music; a catalog of his manuscripts at El Escorial contains 428 separate numbers. 14 harpsichord sonatas by Soler were published by J. Nin in *Classiques espagnols du piano* (2 vols., Paris, 1925, 1929); 100 piano sonatas and a *Fandango,* edited by the pianist F. Marvin, were published in N.Y. (1958–59); 6 concertos for 2 keyboard instruments were edited by Santiago Kastner (Barcelona, 1952); 6 quintets for strings and organ were brought out by Roberto Gerhard for the *Institut d'Estudis Catalans* (Barcelona, 1933, with an introductory essay by H. Anglès); a collection of 27 "*Sonatas para Clave*" was printed in London by T. Birchall; 6 organ concertos were edited by Padre S. Rubrio (Madrid, 1968).
BIBLIOGRAPHY: J. Nin, "The Bicentenary of Antonio Soler," *Chesterian* (1930).

Solerti, Angelo, Italian historiographer; b. Savona, Sept. 20, 1865; d. Massa Carrara, Jan. 10, 1907. His contributions to the early history of opera are valuable: *Le Origini del melodramma* (a collection of contemporary documents and prefaces to the earliest operas; Turin, 1903); *Gli Albori del melodramma,* 3 vols. (Milan, 1904-05); *Musica, ballo e drammatica alla corte medicea dal 1600 al 1637* (Florence, 1905); *Ferrara e la Corte Estense nella second metà del secolo XVI* (contains a chapter on *Musica e canto;* Città di Castello, 1891).

Sollberger, Harvey, American flutist and composer; b. Cedar Rapids, Iowa, May 11, 1938. He studied composition with Philip Bezanson at the Univ. of Iowa and with Jack Beeson and Otto Luening at Columbia Univ. (M.A. 1964). In 1965–71 he was on the staff of Columbia Univ. In his music he employs an imaginatively applied serial method.
WORKS: Trio for flute, cello and piano (1961); *Grand Quartet* for flutes (1962); *Solos* for violin and 5 instruments (1962); *Two Oboes Troping* (1963); *Chamber Variations* for 12 players and conductor (1964);

Musica Transalpina for soprano, baritone and 6 players (1965).

Sollertinsky, Ivan, brilliant Russian music critic; b. Vitebsk, Dec. 3, 1902; d. Novosibirsk, Feb. 11, 1944. He studied philosophy at the Univ. of Petrograd (1919–24); then became a music critic; he showed profound understanding of the problems of modern music and was one of the earliest supporters of Shostakovich; published numerous articles dealing with Soviet music in general; these were assembled in a collection with a biographical sketch and bibliography compiled by M. Druskin (Leningrad, 1946); another collection of his essays was edited by Shostakovich (Leningrad, 1956).

Solomon (real name **Solomon Cutner**), English pianist; b. London, Aug. 9, 1902. He made a sensational debut as a child prodigy at the age of 8, playing Tchaikovsky's Concerto No. 1 in London (June 30, 1911). Later he was sent to Paris for further study, resuming his career as an adult performer in 1923. He appeared under the single name Solomon, without a patronymic; toured all over the world as a concert pianist; also played with orchestras. His interpretation of the classics is particularly fine in that he adheres strictly to the spirit of the music, without superimposing any mannerisms of his own. In 1956 he suffered a stroke, which paralyzed his right arm; as a result, he was forced to withdraw from his concert career; he has since lived in London.

Solomon, Izler, American conductor; b. St. Paul, Minnesota, Jan. 11, 1910. He took violin lessons with Myron Poliakin in Philadelphia and Michael Press in N.Y.; then took courses at the Michigan State College (1928–31). He made his debut as conductor with the Lansing, Michigan, Civic Orch. on March 17, 1932; then conducted the Illinois Symph. (1936–42) and the Columbus, Ohio Philharmonic (1943–46); was guest conductor of the Israel Philharmonic during its American tour in 1951; also filled in engagements with the Buffalo Philharmonic Orch., Chicago Symphony, Los Angeles Philharmonic, Detroit Symphony, Philadelphia Orch., etc. From 1956 to 1975 he was principal conductor and music director of the Indianapolis Symph. Orch.; during his tenure he brought it to a considerable degree of perfection; in his programs he included many works of the modern American school. In 1975 he suffered a stroke, and was unable to continue his career.

Soloviev, Nikolai, Russian composer; b. Petrozavodsk, May 9, 1846; d. St. Petersburg, Dec. 27, 1916. After completing his studies of composition at the St. Petersburg Cons. he was appointed prof. of harmony there (1874). He composed the operas *Cordelia* (St. Petersburg, Nov. 24, 1885) and *Vakula, the Smith* (1880), and completed the score of Serov's opera *The Evil Power.* He further wrote a symph. picture, *Russia and the Mongols* (1882); a choral *Prayer for Russia* (1876); a number of songs and piano pieces. He was known in St. Petersburg principally as a music critic.

Solovyev-Sedoy, Vassily, Russian composer; b. St. Petersburg, April 25, 1907. He studied at the Leningrad Cons., graduating in 1936; occupied various administrative posts. He possessed a peculiar knack in writing songs and choruses in a Russian manner, one of which, *Evenings at Moscow,* became immensely popular. He also wrote a ballet, *Taras Bulba,* after Gogol (Leningrad, Dec. 12, 1940) and the operettas *A Faithful Friend* (Kuibyshev, Oct. 6, 1945) and *The Dearest Thing* (Moscow, Oct. 2, 1952).

BIBLIOGRAPHY: A. Sokhor, *Vassily Solovyev-Sedoy* (Leningrad, 1952); Yuli Kremlev, *Vassily Solovyev-Sedoy* (Leningrad, 1960).

Solti, Sir George, eminent Hungarian conductor; b. Budapest, Oct. 21, 1912. He studied piano with Dohnányi and composition with Kodály at the Budapest Cons. From 1933 to 1939 he conducted at the Budapest Opera; during World War II he lived in Switzerland; was active as pianist and conductor in Zürich; in 1947 he was appointed conductor at the Munich State Opera, in 1951 was engaged at the Frankfurt Opera. He made his American debut with the San Francisco Opera Co. on Sept. 13, 1953; subsequently conducted the Opera Theater Association in Chicago (1956–57); made his first appearance as conductor of the Metropolitan Opera, N.Y. on Dec. 17, 1960. He was then engaged as music director and conductor of the Los Angeles Philharmonic, but the project collapsed when the board of trustees refused to grant him full powers in musical and administrative policy. He was then music director at Covent Garden, London (1961–71). In 1969 he was appointed conductor of the Chicago Symph. Orch., and it was in this capacity that he reached his first achievement as an orchestra builder and interpreter. He showed himself as an enlighted disciplinarian and a master of orchestral psychology, so that he could gain and hold the confidence of the orchestra players while demanding the utmost in their professional performance; under his direction the Chicago Symphony entered the first ranks of American orchestras. In addition to his work with the Chicago Symph. Orch., he was music director of the Orchestre de Paris (1971–75), which he took on a tour of China (1974); was also for several years the musical director of the Paris Opéra. In 1972 he became a British subject and was knighted. Artistically, Solti is distinguished in opera as well as in the symphony; his performances of the Wagner cycles aroused enthusiasm among music scholars and opera-goers for his fidelity to the spirit of the music drama.

BIBLIOGRAPHY: Barry Furlong, *Season with Solti: A Year in the Life of the Chicago Symphony* (1974).

Soltys, Adam, Polish composer; son of **Mieczslaw Soltys;** b. Lwów, July 4, 1890; d. there, July 6, 1968. He studied with his father, and later with Georg Schumann in Berlin; also took courses in musicology at the Univ. of Berlin with Kretzschmar and Johannes Wolf (Dr. phil., 1921). Returning to Poland, he was prof. of composition at the Lwów Cons., was its director from 1930 to 1939, and again after the end of the war. His compositions include 2 symphonies (1927, 1946), symphonic poems, *Slowanie* (1949) *O pokoj* (*About Peace,* 1953) and *Z gór i dolin* (*From Mountains and Valleys,*

1960); also numerous teaching pieces for violin and for piano.

Soltys, Mieczyslaw, Polish composer; b. Lwów, Feb. 7, 1863; d. there, Nov. 12, 1929. He studied music in Vienna and Paris; returning to Poland, he was appointed director of the Lwów Cons. in 1899, retaining this post for 30 years until his death. He wrote the operas *Rzeczpospolita Babinska* (Lwów, April 27, 1905), *Opowiesc ukrainska* (Lwów, March 8, 1910), *Panie Kochanku* (Lwów, May 3, 1924), and *Nieboska komedia* (1925); a symph. poem, *The Fugitive;* Piano Concerto; choruses; piano pieces; songs.

Somer, Hilde, greatly talented Austrian-American pianist; b. Vienna, Feb. 11, 1930. She studied piano with her mother; appeared in public as a child prodigy; in 1938 was taken to the U.S.; at the age of 14 she enrolled at the Curtis Institute of Music in Philadelphia as a student of Rudolf Serkin, and also took private lessons with Moritz Rosenthal, Wanda Landowska and Claudio Arrau. Soon she embarked on an energetic career in recital and with orchestras in Europe and America. While preserving her native sentiment for the Viennese classics, she boldly plunged into the world of modern music; gave the premières of piano concertos by John Corigliano, Jr. (San Antonio, April 7, 1968), Antonio Tauriello (Washington, June 29, 1968), and the Second Piano Concerto of Alberto Ginastera, (Indianapolis, March 22, 1973); further commissioned a concerto by Henry Brant (1977). Of equal merit is her fervent espousal of Scriabin's music; she was the first pianist to make a tour playing Scriabin's music with the accompaniment of colored laser lights projected onto a screen, according to Scriabin's own synesthetic associations of sound and color.

Somers, Harry Stewart, outstanding Canadian composer and pianist; b. Toronto, Sept. 11, 1925. He studied piano with Reginald Godden (1942–43) and Weldon Kilburn (1945–49) at the Royal Cons. in Toronto; attended classes in composition with Weinzweig at the Toronto Cons.; then went to Paris where he took private lessons with Darius Milhaud (1949–50); in 1969 he traveled to Rome on a grant from the Canadian Cultural Institute. Returning to Canada, he eked out a meager living as a music copyist, but in 1971 was named Companion of the Order of Canada, and became active as commentator on new music for Canadian radio and television. His historical opera, *Louis Riel,* was performed at the Kennedy Center in Washington, D.C. on Oct. 23, 1975, as part of America's bicentennial celebration. His musical idiom is quaquaversal, absorbing without prejudice the ancient, national and exotic resources, from Gregorian chant to oriental scales, from simple folkways to electronic sound, all handled with fine expertise.
WORKS: FOR THE STAGE: *The Fool,* one-act chamber opera for 4 soloists and chamber orch. (1953; Toronto, Nov. 15, 1956); *The Homeless Ones,* a television operetta (1955; Canadian television, Toronto, Dec. 31, 1955); *The Fisherman and His Soul,* ballet (Hamilton, Nov. 5, 1956); *Ballad,* ballet (1958; Ottawa, Oct. 29, 1958); *The House of Atreus,* ballet (1963; Toronto, Jan.

13, 1964); *Louis Riel,* historical opera (1966–67; Toronto, Sept. 23, 1967; uses electronic sound); *Improvisation,* theater piece for narrator, singers, strings, any number of woodwinds, 2 percussionists and piano (Montreal, July 5, 1968); *And,* a choreography for dancers, vocal soloists, flute, harp, piano and 4 percussionists (1969; Canadian television, Toronto, 1969); *Enkidu,* chamber opera after the epic of Gilgamesh (Toronto, Dec. 7, 1977). FOR ORCH.: *Scherzo* for strings (1947); 2 piano concertos: No. 1 (Toronto, March, 1949); No. 2 (Toronto, March 12, 1956); *North Country* for string orch. (Toronto, Nov. 10, 1948); *Suite* for harp and chamber orch. (Toronto, Dec. 11, 1952); *The Case of the Wayward Woodwinds* for chamber orch. (1950); Symph. No. 1 (1951; Toronto, April 27, 1953); *Passacaglia and Fugue* (1954); *Little Suite for String Orchestra on Canadian Folk Songs* (1955); *Fantasia* (Montreal Orch., April 1, 1958); *Lyric* (Inter-American Music Festival, Washington, April 30, 1961); *5 Concepts* (1961; Toronto, Feb. 15, 1962); *Movement* (1962; Canadian television, Toronto, March 4, 1962); *Stereophony* (1962–63; Toronto, March 19, 1963); *The Picasso Suite,* light music for small orch. (1964; Saskatoon, Feb. 28, 1965); *Those Silent Awe-filled Spaces,* from a saying by the Canadian artist, Emily Carr, for orch. (1977–78; Ottawa, Feb. 2, 1978). FOR VOICE: *5 Songs for Dark Voice* for contralto and orch. (Stratford, Ontario, Aug. 11, 1956); *At the Descent from the Cross* for bass voice and 2 guitars (1962); *12 Miniatures* for soprano, recorder or flute, viola da gamba and spinet (1963); *Crucifixion* for chorus, English horn, 2 trumpets, harp and percussion (1966); *Kuyas* for soprano, flute and percussion (1967; adapted from *Louis Riel*); *Voiceplay* for male or female singer/actor (Toronto, Nov. 14, 1972; Cathy Berberian, soloist); *Kyrie* for soloists, chorus, flute, oboe, clarinet, cello, 3 trumpets, piano and 6 percussionists (1970–72); *Zen, Yeats and Emily Dickinson* for female narrator, male narrator, soprano, flute, piano and tape (1975); choruses; songs. CHAMBER MUSIC: 3 string quartets (1943, 1950, 1959); *Suite* for percussion (1947); *Mime* for violin and piano (1948); *Rhapsody* for violin and piano (1948); *Wind Quintet* (1948); Trio for flute, violin and cello (1950); 2 violin sonatas (1953, 1955); *Movement* for wind quintet (1957); Sonata for solo guitar (1959); *Theme and Variations* for any combination of instruments (1964); *Music* for solo violin (1974). PIANO MUSIC: *Strangeness of Heart* (1942), *Flights of Fancy* (1944), 5 sonatas (*Testament of Youth,* 1945; 1946; 1950; 1950; 1957), *3 Sonnets* (1946), *Solitudes* (1947), *4 Primitives* (1949) and *12 X 12,* fugues (1951).
BIBLIOGRAPHY: B. Cherney, *Harry Somers* (1975).

Somervell, Sir Arthur, English music educator and composer; b. Windermere, June 5, 1863; d. London, May 2, 1937. He studied the classics at King's College, Cambridge (B.A., 1883), and music with Stanford and Parry at the Royal College of Music; then taught music courses there (1893–1901); subsequently was active as inspector of music. He was knighted in 1929. He composed *Normandy,* symph. variations; *Highland Concerto* for piano and orch.; numerous educational pieces for schools; choruses; song cycles; piano pieces, etc. He edited *Songs of the Four Nations* (50 folksongs of England, Scotland, Ireland, and Wales).

Somis, Giovanni Battista, Italian violinist and composer; b. Turin, Dec. 25, 1686; d. there, Aug. 14, 1763, as maestro at the court. Son and pupil of the court violinist **Francesco Lorenzo Somis** (called "Ardy" or "Ardito"; 1663-1736). In 1696 entered the orch. of the ducal chapel at Turin, and from 1703-06 was a pupil of Corelli in Rome; he then returned to Turin. In 1733 appeared as soloist at the Concert Spirituel in Paris with great success. He was the teacher of Giardini, Guignon, Pugnani, Chabran, and Leclair. He published *Trattenimenti per camera*, op. 5 (trio sonatas for 2 violins and basso continuo; Paris, 1733). Sonatas for violin solo and other works are in MS.
BIBLIOGRAPHY: G. Fino, "Un grande violinista torinense ed una famiglia di violinisti, G. B. Somis," *Il Momento* (Turin, Oct. 25-26, 1927).

Somis, Lorenzo Giovanni, Italian violinist; brother of **Giovanni Battista Somis;** b. Turin, Nov. 11, 1688; d. there, Nov. 29, 1775. He studied in Bologna; from 1724-70 he was 2nd violin in the ducal chapel at Turin. Publ. *8 Sonate da camera a violino solo e violoncello o cimbalo*, op. 2 (publ. in Paris), and *6 Sonate e tre*, op. 3 (1725).

Sommer, Hans (real name **Zincke**), German composer and writer on music; b. Braunschweig, July 20, 1837; d. there, April 28, 1922. He studied mathematics at the Univ. of Göttingen (Dr. phil., 1858); later taught mathematics in Brunswick, while taking active part in musical affairs there. In 1885 he married and settled in Berlin; from 1888 till 1898 he lived in Weimar; then again in Braunschweig. He was one of the original founders of the Genossenschaft deutscher Tonsetzer (performing rights society) with Richard Strauss, Max Schillings, and Friedrich Rösch.
WORKS: the operas *Der Nachtwächter* (Braunschweig, Nov. 22, 1865); *Loreley* (Braunschweig, April 11, 1891); *Saint Foix* (Munich, Oct. 31, 1894); *Der Meermann* (Weimar, April 19, 1896); *Rübezahl* (Braunschweig, May 15, 1904; his strongest opera); *Riquet mit dem Schopf* (Braunschweig, April 14, 1907); *Der Waldschratt* (Braunschweig, March 31, 1912). His operas *Augustin, Münchhausen*, and *Das Schloss der Herzen* were not performed. His lyric songs were greatly appreciated in Germany, and often performed in England; among the best are the cycles *Der Rattenfänger von Hamelin, Der wilde Jäger, Hunold Singuf, Tannhäuser, Sapphos Gesänge, Aus dem Süden, Eliland;* also *Balladen und Romanzen*, etc.
BIBLIOGRAPHY: E. Stier, "Hans Sommer," in vol. 1 of *Monographien moderner Musiker* (Leipzig, 1906); *Erich Valentin, Hans Sommer* (Braunschweig, 1939).

Sommer, Vladimír, Czech composer; b. Dolní Jiřetín, near Most, Feb. 28, 1921. He studied composition with K. Janeček at the Prague Cons. (1942-46) and with Bořkovec at the Prague Academy of Music (1946-50). He was music director of Radio Prague (1952-53) and secretary of the Guild of Czech Composers (1953-56); taught at the Prague Academy (1953-60) and since

then at the Charles Univ. in Prague. His music is crafted in a fine functional manner.
WORKS: Sonata for 2 violins (1948); *Cantata on Gottwald* for baritone, chorus and orch. (Prague, Nov. 20, 1949); Violin Concerto (Prague, June 13, 1950); 3 string quartets (1950; 1955; 1960-66); Piano Sonata (1954-56); *Antigone*, overture (1956-57); 3 symphonies: No. 1, *Vokální Symfonie*, for narrator, mezzo-soprano, chorus and orch., to texts by Dostoyevsky, Kafka and Cesare Pavese (1957-59, revised 1963; Prague, March 12, 1963), No. 2, *Anno mundi ardenti*, for string orch., piano and timpani (1968); No. 3, *Sinfonia concertante*, for 2 violins, viola, cello and chamber orch. (1968); Cello Concerto (1956-59); *Černý Muž (The Black Man)*, symph. poem for tenor, bass and orch. (1964); songs.

Sommerfeldt, Øistein, Norwegian composer; b. Oslo, Nov. 25, 1919. He studied piano, bassoon, music theory and composition in Paris with Nadia Boulanger (1950-56); is currently a music critic in Oslo.
WORKS: *3 Suites* for orch. (1956; based on Grieg's *Dances* for piano, Op. 72); *Miniature Suite* for orch. (1958, revised 1972); *Miniature Overture* (1960); *Adagio, Scherzo and Finale* for orch. (1969); *Hafrsfjord* for narrator, and orch. or military band (1972); *3 Lyric Scenes* for tenor or soprano, and orch. (1972); *Sinfonia "La Betulla"* (1967-74); 5 piano sonatinas (1956; 1960; 1968; 1970; 1972); *Divertimento* for flute (1960, revised 1969); *Divertimento* for bassoon (1960, revised 1973); *Transformation*, audio-visual score for chamber group and tape (1970); *Divertimento* for trumpet (1971); Violin Sonata (1971); *Elegy* for trumpet and organ (1971); *Suite* for piano trio (1973); *Divertimento* for oboe (1974).

Sondheim, Stephen, brilliant American composer and lyricist; b. New York, March 22, 1930. Of an affluent family, he received his academic education in private schools; composed a school musical at the age of 15. He then entered Williams College, where he wrote the book, lyrics and music for a couple of college shows; graduated *magna cum laude* in 1950. In quest of higher musical learning he went to Princeton, where he took lessons in modernistic complexities with Milton Babbitt and acquired sophisticated techniques of composition. He made his mark on Broadway when he wrote the lyrics for Bernstein's *West Side Story* (1957). His first success as a lyricist-composer came with the Broadway musical *A Funny Thing Happened on the Way to the Forum* (1962), which received a Tony Award. His next musical, *Anyone Can Whistle* (1964), proved unsuccessful, but *Company* (1970), for which he wrote both lyrics and music, established him as a major composer and lyricist on Broadway. There followed *Follies* (1971), for which he wrote 22 pastiche songs; it was named as best musical by the New York Drama Critics Circle. His next production, *A Little Night Music*, with the nostalgic score harking back to the turn of the century, received a Tony, and its leading song, "Send in the Clowns," was awarded a Grammy in 1976. This score established Sondheim's characteristic manner of treating musicals; it is almost operatic in conception, and the score boldly introduces dissonant counterpoint *à la moderne*. In

1976 he produced *Pacific Overtures,* based on the story of the western penetration into Japan in the 19th century, and composed in a stylized Japanese manner, modeled after the Kabuki theater.

Sondheimer, Robert, German musicologist; b. Mainz, Feb. 6, 1881; d. Hannover, Dec. 7, 1956. He studied with Engelbert Humperdinck at the Cons. of Cologne; then took courses in musicology in Bonn, Berlin, and Basel; in 1933 he settled in London, where he established the Sondheimer Edition, incorporating the bulk of the Edition Bernoulli which he had headed previously in Berlin. He brought out numerous editions of works by Haydn and the composers of the Mannheim School. He published *Haydn. A Historical and Psychological Study Based on His Quartets* (London, 1951).

Sonneck, Oscar George Theodore, eminent American musicologist; b. Jersey City, N.J., Oct. 6, 1873; d. New York, Oct. 30, 1928. Attended the Gelehrtenschule in Kiel (1883–89) and the Kaiser Friedrich Gymnasium in Frankfurt (1889–93), where he also took piano lessons with James Kwast; from 1893–97 he studied at Munich Univ., musicology with Sandberger and philosophy with Riehl and Lipps; private pupil in composition of M. E. Sachs; 1897–98, pupil of K. Schröder (conducting) at the Sondershausen Cons. and Iwan Knorr (instrumentation) in Frankfurt; spent the greater part of 1899 in research work in Italy; then returned to the U.S., continuing his researches in the principal libraries. On Aug. 1, 1902, he was appointed to be Chief of the Music Division of the Library of Congress in Washington; he resigned on Sept. 5, 1917, to accept a position with the publishing house of G. Schirmer in New York as director of the Publication Department, managing editor of *The Musical Quarterly* (of which he had been editor since its foundation in 1915), and personal representative of the president, Rudolph E. Schirmer; in 1921 he became vice-president of G. Schirmer. He represented the U.S. Government at the international congresses of music held in London and Rome in 1911. He took a leading part in the formation of the Society for the Publication of American Music, and of the Beethoven Association in N.Y. Under Sonneck's administration the Music Division of the Library of Congress became one of the largest and most important music collections in the world. His writings, exhibiting profound and accurate scholarship and embodying the results of original research, laid the real foundation for the scientific study of music in the U.S.; his elaborate catalogues, issued by the Library of Congress, are among the most valuable contributions to musical bibliography. The Sonneck Society, an organization designed to encourage the serious study of American music in all its aspects, was established in 1975 and named after Sonneck in recognition of his achievements in this area. He was also a composer and a poet; wrote a string quartet; symphonic pieces; a *Rhapsody* and *Romanze* for violin and piano; some vocal works and piano pieces. He published 2 vols. of poems in German: *Seufzer* (1895) and *Eine Totenmesse* (1898). WRITINGS: *Francis Hopkins and James Lyon. Two Studies in Early American Music* (1905); *Early*

Concert Life in America (1731–1800) (1907); *Report on "The Star-Spangled Banner," "Hail Columbia," "America," "Yankee Doodle"* (1909); *A Survey of Music in America* (1913) *The Star-Spangled Banner* (1914); *Early Opera in America* (1915); *Suum Cuique* (1916; collection of essays); *Miscellaneous Studies in the History of Music* (1921); *Beethoven. Impressions of Contemporaries* (1926); *Beethoven Letters in America* (1927); *The Riddle of the Immortal Beloved* (1927). Catalogues: *Classification of Music and Literature of Music* (1904; 2nd ed., revised and augmented, 1917); *Bibliography of Early Secular Music* (1905; 2nd ed., revised and enlarged, by W. T. Upton, 1945); *Dramatic Music* (1908); *Orchestral Music* (1912); *Opera Librettos printed before 1800* (2 vols., 1914); *First Editions of Stephen C. Foster* (1915; with W. R. Whittlesey); *First Editions of Edward MacDowell* (1917).
BIBLIOGRAPHY: H. Putnam and R. Goldmark, "Remarks at the Funeral Services for O. G. Sonneck," *Musical Quarterly* (Jan. 1929); C. Engel, "O. G. Sonneck," in *"Adler-Festschrift"* (1930); *Musical Quarterly* (Oct. 1933); H. Wiley Hitchcock, *After 100 [!] Years: The Editorial Side of Sonneck* (booklet; contains a bibliography of Sonneck's writings and musical compositions, compiled by I. Lowens; Library of Congress, 1975).

Sonninen, Ahti, Finnish composer; b. Kuopio, July 11, 1914. He studied with Palmgren, Merikanto, Ranta and Leo Funtek at the Sibelius Academy in Helsinki; from 1938 to 1952 he was a choral and orchestra director for the Finnish Radio. He followed the tenets of international musical modernism in his technique of composition, but also adhered to subjects from Finnish folklore.
WORKS: FOR THE STAGE: *Merenkuninkaan tytär (Daughter of Neptune),* opera (1949); *Pessi and Illusia,* ballet (1952); *Ruususolmu (Wreath of Roses),* ballet (1956); *Karhunpeijaiset (Feast to Celebrate the Killing of a Bear),* ritual opera (1968); *Se (It),* ballet farce (Helsinki, Feb. 24, 1972); *Haavruuva (Lady of the Sea),* opera (1971). VOCAL WORKS: *7 Songs to Hungarian Folk Poems* for soprano and orch. (1939–41); *Midsummer Night* for soprano and orch. (1946); *El amor pasa* for soprano, flute and orch. (1953); *Smith of the Heavens* for baritone and orch. (1957); *The Karelian Wedding* for voice, chorus, flute, accordion, percussion, harpsichord and tape (1965); *Highway Requiem* for soprano, baritone, chorus and orch. (1970); *Forging of the Golden Virgin* for voices, 2 percussionists and tape (1971); *Finnish Messiah* for soloists, mixed and children's chorus and orch. (1972); *In the Court of the Lamb,* suite for soloists, chorus and orch. (1972); about 15 cantatas and 100 choruses a cappella. FOR ORCH.: *East Karelian Suite* (1942); *Violin Concerto* (1943–45); *Piano Concerto* (1944–45); *Symphonic Sketches* (1947); *Preludio Festivo* (1953); *Under Lapland's Sky,* suite (1954); *Pezzo Pizzicato* (1954–55); *Rhapsody* (1957); *4 Partitas* for strings (1958); *Prelude and Allegro* for trumpet, trombone and orch. (1961); *Reactions* for chamber orch. (1961). CHAMBER MUSIC: *Conference* for clarinet, horn, trumpet and trombone (1954); *Theses* for string quartet (1968); *Divertimento* for wind quintet (1970). FOR PIANO: the suites *In the Big City* (1954), *White Pepper*

(1970), *Black Pepper* (1970), *Koli* (1970) and *3 Characters* (1971); about 70 songs with piano; music for films.

Sonnleithner, Joseph, Austrian music amateur, librettist and archivist; b. Vienna, March 3, 1766; d. there Dec. 26, 1835. He was a son of the Austrian composer **Christoph von Sonnleithner** who taught him music. Joseph Sonnleithner was one of the founders of the Gesellschaft der Musikfreunde, to which he bequeathed his books and musical instruments. Publ. the interesting *Wiener Theateralmanach* (1794, 1795, 1796). He wrote some librettos and adapted others, including *Fidelio* for Beethoven and *Faniska* by Cherubini. In 1827 he discovered the famous Antiphonary of St. Gall of the 9th century, in neume notation; probably a copy of the one sent there by Charlemagne in 790. His nephew was **Leopold von Sonnleither,** b. Vienna, Nov. 15, 1797; d. there, March 4, 1873. The staunch friend of Schubert, he procured the publication of the *Erlkönig* (Schubert's first publ. work); at his father's house the *Prometheus,* the *Gesang der Geister über den Wassern,* the *23rd Psalm,* and other important works by Schubert were performed from manuscript.
BIBLIOGRAPHY: A. Fareanu, "Leopold von Sonnleithners Erinnerungen an Franz Schubert," *Zeitschrift für Musikwissenschaft* (1919).

Sontag, Henriette (real name **Gertrud Walburga Sonntag**), celebrated German soprano; b. Coblenz, Jan. 3, 1806; d. Mexico City (on a tour), June 17, 1854. She played children's parts on the stage; then studied at the Prague Cons. with Triebensee, Pixis, Bayer, and Frau Czegka; in 1820 she sang in Italian and German opera at Vienna, and in 1823 created the title role in Weber's *Euryanthe;* on May 7, 1824, she sang in Vienna the soprano solos in Beethoven's *Missa solemnis* and 9th Symph.; made her first Berlin appearance on Aug. 3, 1825 in the part of Isabella in Rossini's *Italiana in Algeri;* her Paris debut as Rosina in *Il Barbiere di Siviglia* (June 15, 1826) was an unqualified success and she was adjudged by many as superior to Catalani; she broke her Berlin contract in order to sing at the Italian Opera in Paris (1827); went to London in 1828, and secretly married the Sardinian ambassador to the Dutch court, Count Rossi; was ennobled by the King of Prussia (as "Fräulein Henriette von Lauenstein"). She then interrupted her career on the stage, and settled with her husband at The Hague; also traveled with him on his diplomatic missions to Germany and Russia. She continued to give concerts as a solo singer, arousing enthusiasm wherever she went. In 1848 she resumed her operatic career; made several tours in England; in the autumn of 1852 she embarked for the U.S., and gave a number of concerts; then went to Mexico (1854), where she sang opera. She died of cholera during an epidemic there.
BIBLIOGRAPHY: Théophile Gautier, *L'Ambassadrice, Biographie de la comtesse Rossi* (Paris, 1850); J. Gundling, *Henriette Sontag* (2 vols.; Leipzig, 1861); W. Berger, *Berühmte Frauen* (Berlin, 1904); H. Stumcke, *Henriette Sontag* (Berlin, 1913); F. Rogers, "Henriette Sontag in New York," *Musical Quarterly* (Jan. 1942); E. Pirchan, *Henriette Sontag* (Vienna,

1946); Frank Russell, *Queen of Song, The Life of Henriette Sontag, Countess de Rossi* (N.Y., 1964).

Sonzogno, Edoardo, Italian music publisher; b. Milan, April 21, 1836; d. there, March 14, 1920. He inherited a printing plant and bookstore founded by his father, and in 1874 began to publish popular editions of French and Italian music with marked success. In 1883 he inaugurated a series of contests for new operas; the 2nd contest, in 1888, was won by Mascagni (then unknown) with *Cavalleria Rusticana.* Sonzogno established his own theater (the Lirico Internazionale) at Milan in 1894. From 1861 until his retirement in 1909 he was sole proprietor of the newspaper *Il Secolo.* He was succeeded by his nephew **Riccardo Sonzogno** (1871–1915); upon the latter's death, the business was taken over by another nephew, **Renzo Sonzogno,** who had previously headed a firm of his own. He died in 1920, and in 1923 control was acquired by a group of Italian industrialists.

Sonzogno, Giulio Cesare, Italian composer; b. Milan, Dec. 24, 1906; d. Milan, Jan. 23, 1976. He was related to the family of the music publishers Sonzogno. He studied cello and composition in Milan; composed mostly for the stage.
WORKS: ballet, *L'Amore delle tre melarancie (Love for Three Oranges),* after Carlo Gozzi, on the same subject that Prokofiev used in his famous opera (La Scala, Milan, Feb. 1, 1936); the operas *Regina Uliva* (Milan, March 17, 1949), *I passaggeri* (Trieste, 1961), *Il denaro del Signor Arne* (1968), *Boule de suif,* after Maupassant (Bergamo, 1970) and *Mirra* (1970).

Sopeña, Federico, Spanish writer on music; b. Valladolid, Jan. 25, 1917. He studied in Bilbao and Madrid; in 1951 became director of the Madrid Cons.; was also the founder and publisher of the music magazine *Música.* He published a number of useful monographs of Spanish composers: *J. Turina* (1943; revised 1956); *Joaquín Rodrigo* (1970); also *Historia de la música en cuadros esquemáticos* (1947), and *La Música europea contemporánea* (1953).

Sopkin, Henry, American conductor; b. Brooklyn, Oct. 20, 1903. He studied violin in Chicago; taught music in high schools there, and conducted college orchestras. In 1944 he was engaged as conductor of the Atlanta Youth Symphony, which became the nucleus of a professional symphony orchestra there; Sopkin brought it up to a considerable degree of professional efficiency. In 1966 he was appointed music instructor at the California Institute of the Arts in Los Angeles.

Soproni, József, Hungarian composer; b. Sopron, Oct. 4, 1930. He was a pupil of János Viski at the Budapest Academy of Music (1949–56); then taught at the Béla Bartók Cons. since 1957 and at the Academy since 1963. His music is marked by a strong polyphonic art, but he also employs the technique of sonorism, or sound for sound's sake.
WORKS: Concerto for String Orch. (1953); *4 Bagatelles* for piano (1957); *Partita* for harpsichord (1957); Viola Sonatina (1958); 4 string quartets (1958, 1960,

1965, 1971); *Meditatio con Toccata* for organ (1959); *Requiem on the Death of a Poet* (1960); *Carmina polinaesiana*, cantata for female chorus and chamber ensemble (1963); *Musica da camera* No. 1 for piano trio (1963); *7 Pieces* for piano (1963); *Ovidii metamorphoses*, cantata for soprano, chorus and orch., with solo violin (1965); *Violin Concerto* (1967); *Cello Concerto* (1967); *De aetatibus mundi carmina*, cantata after Ovidius for soprano, baritone, chorus and orch. (1968); *Eklypsis* for orch. (1969); *Incrustations* for piano (1970); *Invenzioni sul B-A-C-H* for piano (1971); Flute Sonata (1971); *Concerto da camera* for 12 performers (1972); Symph. No. 1 (1975; Budapest, May 19, 1977); *Musica da Camera* No. 2 for clarinet, violin, cello and piano (1976); songs.

Sor (real name **Sors**), **Fernando**, celebrated Spanish guitar virtuoso; b. Barcelona, Feb. 13, 1778; d. Paris, July 8, 1839. At the age of 11 he entered the school of the monastery of Montserrat, where he studied music under the direction of Anselmo Viola; wrote a Mass; then left the monastery and returned to Barcelona, where he presented his only opera, *Telemaco nella isola di Calipso*, on Aug. 25, 1797. A few years later he went to Madrid; there he joined the French army, earning the rank of captain. When Bonapartist rule was defeated in Spain, in 1813, he fled to Paris. There he met Cherubini, Méhul, and other important composers, who urged him to give concerts as a guitarist, and he soon acquired fame. In Paris he produced 2 ballets, *Cendrillon* (1823) and *Le Sicilien, ou L'Amour peintre* (1827). He was then summoned to London by the Duke of Sussex; subsequently traveled in Russia; wrote funeral music for the obsequies of Alexander I of Russia (1825). After another stay in London, he returned to Paris, settling there permanently in 1828. He wrote for the guitar a number of fantasies, minuets, and studies, as well as a method; all these works are modeled after the Classical forms, rather than on popular motifs. Selected works by Sor have been edited by G. Meier.
BIBLIOGRAPHY: M. Rocamora, *Fernando Sor* (Barcelona, 1957); G. Marini, "La música per chitarra di Fernando Sor," *Il convegno musicale* (with a list of works; 1964); Brian Jeffrey, *Fernando Sor, Composer and Guitarist* (N.Y., 1977).

Sorabji, Kaikhosru (real Christian names **Leon Dudley**), remarkable English composer of unique gifts; b. Chingford, Aug. 14, 1892. His father was a Parsi, his mother of Spanish-Sicilian extraction. He was largely self-taught in music, but through sheer perserverance and an almost mystical belief in his demiurgic powers, he developed an idiom of composition of extraordinary complexity, embodying the Eastern types of melodic lines and asymmetrical rhythmic patterns, resulting in a contrapuntal texture somewhat akin to that of Busoni, but enormously more intricate. Virtually the only performances of his works were by himself as a pianist. About 1950 he issued a declaration forbidding any performance of his works by anyone anywhere; however, since this prohibition could not be sustained for works actually published, there were furtive performances of his piano works in England and the United States by a few fearless pianists. His magisterial work is *Opus Clavicembalisticum* for piano solo, completed in 1930, and comprising 3 parts with 12 subdivisions, including a theme with 44 variations, and a passacaglia with 81 variations; the score is characteristically dedicated to "the everlasting glory of those few men blessed and sanctified in the curses and execrations of those many whose praise is eternal damnation." Sorabji performed it for the first time (and last) in Glasgow under the auspices of the Active Society for the Propagation of Contemporary Music on Dec. 1, 1930. He also wrote 4 symphonies for piano with instrumental ensembles (1940, 1954, 1960, 1964); a "Tantric" Symphony (1939); "Dschami" Symphony for baritone, double chorus, piano, organ and orch. (1942-51); 5 piano concertos (1920-50); 3 organ symphonies (1926, 1940, 1953); a characteristically titled *Concerto per suonare da me solo* for piano (1946); *Sequentia cyclica* for piano (1949); *Passeggiata veneziana* (1956); *Opus clavisymphonicum* for piano and orch. (1959); *Gulistan* for piano (1940); *100 Transcendental Studies* for piano (1940-44); 5 piano sonatas (1919-50; 5th sonata bears the title *Opus archimagicum*); several early piano works with French titles: *Fantaisie espagnole* (1922), *Le Jardin parfumé* (1923), *Valse-Fantaisie* (1925); 2 piano quintets; songs to words by Verlaine and Baudelaire. Sorabji was also a brilliant writer of aggressively polemical bent; he published *Around Music* (London, 1932); *Mi contra Fa: The Immoralisings of a Machiavellian Musician* (London, 1947).
BIBLIOGRAPHY: A. G. Browne, "The Music of Kaikhosru Sorabji," *Music & Letters* (Jan. 1930); E. Rubbra, "Sorabji's Enigma," *Monthly Musical Record* (Sept. 1932).

Sörenson, Torsten, Swedish composer; b. Grebbestads, April 25, 1908. He was educated at the Royal College of Music in Stockholm, graduating in 1936; later studied composition with Hilding Rosenberg (1942) and Carl Orff (1949). In 1935 he was appointed a church organist in Göteborg.
WORKS: *Den underbara Kvarnan* for baritone and orch. (1936, revised 1958); *Sinfonietta* for string orch. (1946, revised 1957); 2 trios for flute, clarinet and oboe (1949, 1959); *Hymn om Kristus*, cantata (1950); Concerto for Organ and String Orch. (1952); Symphony for chamber orch. (1956); Sonata for viola solo (1956); Piano Sonata (1956); *Sinfonia da chiesa* Nos. 1 and 2 for string orch. (1958, 1964-69); 3 sonatas for flute solo (1962, 1964, 1966); *Hymnarium*, 56 motets for 1 to 6 voices, and instruments (1957-62); *Per quattro archi*, string quartet (1970); Brass Quintet (1970); *Laudate nomen Domini* for chorus, 17 winds and percussion (1972); *En sang om Herrens boninger* for soprano, 2 choruses and orch. (1975); *Svart-Vitt* (*Black and White*), 24 pieces for piano (1975).

Soresina, Alberto, Italian composer; b. Milan, May 10, 1911. He studied with Paribeni and Bossi at the Milan Cons., graduating in 1933; then took a course in composition in Siena with Frazzi. He subsequently was on the faculty of the Cons. of Milan (1947-60), and later taught singing at the Cons. of Turin (1963-66); in 1967 was appointed teacher of music theory at the Milan Cons.

WORKS: operas, *Lanterna rossa* (Siena, 1942), *Cuor di cristallo* (Bergamo, 1942), *L'Amuleto* (Bergamo, Oct. 26, 1954), *Tre sogni per Marina* (Lecco, 1967); for orch.: *Trittico Wildiano* (1939), *Il Santo,* symph. poem (1940), *2 notturni* for harp and string orch. (1946), *Divertimento* (1956); chamber music: Concertino for viola, cello and piano (1953), *Sonatina serena* for violin and piano (1956); several works for voice and orch., including *La Fanciulla mutata in rio* (1939); piano pieces.

Sorge, Georg Andreas, erudite German composer and theorist; b. Mellenbach, Schwarzburg, March 21, 1703; d. Lobenstein, April 4, 1778. Still as a youth, he was appointed court organist at Lobenstein (1721) and retained this position until his death. In his middle life, he wrote numerous works for piano and organ; music historians regard him as a typical "little master" of Bach's time. His reverence for Bach is demonstrated by his 3 keyboard fugues on B.A.C.H. Among his works published in his lifetime are *Clavierübung aus 18 Sonatinen in 3 Teilen* (1738); *Clavierübung aus 24 Praeludia durch den ganzen Circulum Modorum* and *Clavier-Toccata per omnem circulum Modorum* (both works in emulation of Bach's *Well-Tempered Clavier*). His masterwork remains *Vorgemach der musicalischen Composition* (3 vols., 1745–47), in which he relates his discovery of combinatorial tones before Tartini.
BIBLIOGRAPHY: M. Frisch, *Georg A. Sorge* (Leipzig, 1954); R. Frisius, *Untersuchungen über den Akkordbegriff* (Göttingen, 1970).

Soriano, Alberto, Uruguayan composer and musicologist; b. Santiago del Estero, Argentina, Feb. 5, 1915. He studied violin in Bahia, Brazil; in 1937 went to Montevideo, where he settled. In his music he makes use of South American melorhythms, while retaining fundamental classical forms. From 1953 to 1969 he was prof. of enthnomusicology at the Univ. of Montevideo. Among his scholarly publications is *Algunas de las inmanencias etnomusicológicas* (Montevideo, 1967).
WORKS: Piano Concerto (1952); Guitar Concerto No. 1 (1952); *Sinfonietta* for guitar, cello, bassoon and flute (1952); *4 Rituales sinfónicos* (1953); *Divertimento* for bassoon and string orch. (1954); Cello Sonata (1955); Violin Concerto (1956); Guitar Concerto No. 2 (1957); Violin Sonata (1959); Piano Trio (1961); *Canticos sinfónicos a la Revolución de Cuba* (1961); Concertino for Cello and Orch. (1961); *Pastoral de Sibiu* for flute and orch. (1962); *Tríptico de Praga* for orch. (1962); *Tiempo sinfónico para los caidos en Buchenwald* (1962). A list of his works is found in *Compositores de América*, vol. 16 (Washington, D.C., 1970).

Soriano, Francesco. See **Suriano, Francesco.**

Soriano Fuertes, Mariano, Spanish music historian; b. Murcia, March 28, 1817; d. Madrid, March 26, 1880. Pupil of his father (director of the royal chamber music); 1843, prof. at Madrid Cons.; from 1844, director, successively, of music schools at Córdoba, Seville, and Cádiz; conducted opera at Barcelona, where he founded the *Gaceta Musical*. He composed some zarzuelas. Author of *Música árabe-española* (1853); *Historia de la música española desde la venida de los fenicios hasta el año de 1850* (4 vols., 1855–59; a pioneer work, but quite unscientific and unreliable); *Memoria sobre las sociedades corales en España* (1865); *Calendario histórico musical . . .* (1872).

Sormann, Alfred (Richard Gotthilf), German pianist and composer; b. Danzig, May 16, 1861; d. Berlin, Sept. 17, 1913. He studied at the Hochschule für Musik in Berlin with Barth, Spitta, and Bargiel; in 1885, studied with Liszt. He made his debut in 1886, giving successful concerts in the chief German towns. He composed the operas *Die Sibylle von Tivoli* (Berlin, 1902) and *König Harald* (Stettin, 1909); a piano concerto; 2 string quartets; a piano trio; concert études and other piano pieces; songs.

Soro, Enrique, significant Chilean composer; b. Concepción, July 15, 1884; d. Santiago, Dec. 2, 1954. He was a son of the Italian composer **José Soro,** and was educated by him; played in public as a small child. He was granted a stipend by the government of Chile for study in Italy; entered the Cons. of Milan at 14; graduated in 1904, with a grand prize in composition. Returning to Chile in 1905, he was appointed inspector of musical education in primary schools; in 1907 joined the faculty of the Cons. of Santiago; from 1919 to 1928 he was its director. He traveled as a pianist; gave concerts in Europe and South America; also publ. a number of works. In 1948 he was awarded the Premio Nacional de Arte.
WORKS: For orch.: *Sinfonía romántica* (1920); Piano Concerto (1919); *Suite sinfónica*, no. 1, subtitled *Pensamientos intimos* (1918); *Suite sinfónica*, no. 2 (Santiago, May 9, 1919, composer conducting); *Tres preludios sinfónicos* (Santiago, July 18, 1936); *Aires chilenos*, for orch. (Santiago, 1942); *Suite en estilo antiguo* (Santiago, May 28, 1943). Chamber music: Piano Quintet (1919); *Impresiones líricas*, for piano and strings (1918); String Quartet (1904); Piano Trio (1926); Violin Sonata; Cello Sonata; 3 piano sonatas (1920, 1923, 1942); a number of piano pieces in a salon genre, some of them based of Chilean melorhythms.
BIBLIOGRAPHY: L. G. Giarda, *Analytische Studie über Soros 2. Sonate für Violine und Klavier A moll, das Quartett A dur und das Klavierquintett* (Santiago, 1919); Vicente Salas Viú, *La Creación musical en Chile 1900–1951* (Santiago, 1953; pp. 427–52).

Soto de Langa, Francisco, Spanish composer; b. Langa, c.1534; d. Rome, Sept. 25, 1619. He spent most of his life in Rome, where he was one of the disciples of St. Philip Neri; for Neri's Congregation of the Oratorio he wrote 5 books of "laudi spirituali" (publ. between 1583 and 1598); some specimens are reproduced in Alaleona's *Studi su la storia dell'oratorio musicale in Italia* (Turin, 1908).

Soubies, Albert, French writer in music; b. Paris, May 10, 1846; d. there, March 19, 1918. He studied law and was admitted to the bar; about the same time he became a pupil of Savard, Bazin, and Guilmant at the Paris Cons. In 1876 he became music critic for *Le Soir* and in 1885 began to write for the *Revue de l'Art Dra-matique*. In 1874 he revived the famous old *Alma-nach Duchesne* (publ. between 1752 and 1815), reissuing it as *Almanach des Spectacles* (43 vols. publ. up to 1914).

WRITINGS: *Histoire de la musique* (his principal work; issued in separate sections dealing with music in individual European nations; publ. 1896–1906); *Les Grands Théâtres parisiens*, in 2 parts: *67 ans à l'Opéra: 1826–1893* (1893) and *69 ans l'Opéra-Comique: 1825–1894* (1894); *Histoire de l'Opéra-Comique* (2 vols.; 1892–93; with Charles Malherbe); *Histoire du Théâtre-lyrique 1851–1870* (1899); *L'Œuvre dramatique de Richard Wagner* (1886).

Soubre, Étienne-Joseph, Belgian composer; b. Liège, Dec. 30, 1813; d. there, Sept. 8, 1871. He studied at the Liège Cons., and became its director (1862). He composed the opera *Isoline* (Brussels, 1855); *Symphonie triomphale* (1845); 2 cantatas; a Requiem with orch.; *Stabat Mater* and *Ave Verum*, with orch.; *Hymne à Godefroid de Bouillon*, for male chorus and orch.; church music, choruses, overtures, symphonies, etc.

Souhaitty, Jean-Jacques, Franciscan monk and music theorist; flourished in the middle of the 17th century; lived in Paris. He was the first to employ number notation, indicating by numerals 1 to 7 the degrees of the scale, and used this system for popular teaching. He publ. *Nouvelle méthode pour apprendre le plain-chant et la musique* (Paris, 1665; 2nd ed. as *Nouveaux éléments de chant . . .*, 1677) and an *Essai du chant de l'église par la nouvelle méthode des chiffres* (Paris, 1679).

Šourek, Otakar, Czech writer on music; b. Prague, Oct. 10, 1883; d. there, Feb. 15, 1956. He was trained as an engineer and studied music as an avocation. His principal work is a monumental biography of Dvořák, which was issued under the title *Život a dílo Antonína Dvořáka (Life and Works of Antonin Dvořák; 4 vols.,* 1916, 1917, 1930, 1933); in addition he compiled a thematic catalogue of Dvořák's works, in German and Czech (Berlin, 1917); further published monographs dealing with Dvořák's symphonies (Prague, 1922; 3rd edition, 1948); orchestral music (2 vols.; Prague, 1944–46); chamber music (Prague, 1943); the last 2 works were published together in German (2 vols., Prague, 1954); a Dvořák reader (Prague, 1929; in English, Prague, 1954); an abridged German version of Šourek's Dvořák biography was published as *Dvořák, Leben und Werk* (Vienna, 1935) and in English as *The Life and Work of Dvořák* (N.Y., 1941). Šourek also published monographs on Karel (Prague, 1946) and Suk (Prague, 1954; translated into 8 European languages). Until his death he was the editor of the collected works of Dvořák.

BIBLIOGRAPHY: F. Oeser, "Otakar Šourek," *Musica* (April 1956).

Souris, André, Belgian composer; b. Marchienne-au-Pont, July 10, 1899; d. Paris, Feb. 12, 1970. He studied at the Brussels Cons. (1911–18) with M. Lunssens (harmony), Closson (music history), and privately with Gilson (composition). In 1927 he won the Prix Rubens, and traveled to Italy, France and Austria; conducted the Belgian Radio Orch. (1937–46); from 1946 till his death he taught at the Royal Cons. in Brussels. His first works were in the style of Debussy, but in 1925 he pursued a more advanced quasi-atonal technique of composition. He was the founder of the quarterly music review *Polyphonie* (1947–54).

WORKS: *Scherzo* for orch. (1923); *Burlesque* for small orch. (1931); *Danceries de la Renaissance* for orch. (1932); *Hommage à Babeuf* for wind orch. and percussion (1934; Paris, June 22, 1927); *Symphonies* for orch. (1939); *Pastorales Wallonnes* for vocal quartet and small orch. (1942); *Le Marchand d'images*, rustic cantata on popular Walloon songs, for soli, chorus and orch. (3 versions, 1944, 1954 and 1965); *Cinque Laude* for vocal quartet, chorus and small orch. (1961); *Ouverture pour une Arlequinade* for small orch. (1962); *3 poèmes japonais* for soprano, string quartet and piano (1916); *Bagatelles* for violin and piano (1923); *Berceuse* for violin and piano (1924); *Choral, Marche et Galop* for 2 trumpets and 2 trombones (1925); *Avertissement* for 3 narrators and percussion (1926); *Quelques airs de clarisse Juranville* for mezzo-soprano, string quartet and piano (1928); *Fatrasie* for violin, and harp or piano (1934); *Rengaines* for wind quintet (1937); *Comptines pour enfants sinistres* for soprano, mezzo-soprano, viola, clarinet and piano (1942); *L'Autre Voix* for soprano and 5 instruments; *Triptyque pour un violin* for narrator, 6 soli, organ and percussion (1963); *Concert flamand*, suite for 4 winds (1965); *3 pièces anciennes* for violin and viola (1969); film music; songs. He collaborated with René Vannes on the *Dictionnaire des musiciens* (Brussels, 1946).

BIBLIOGRAPHY: Paul Nougé, *André Souris* (1928); R. Wangermee, *La Musique belge contemporaine* (Brussels, 1959; pp. 82–99); A. Fraiken, "Necrologies: André Souris," *La Vie Musicale Belge* (Jan.-Feb. 1970).

Sousa, John Philip, famous American bandmaster and popular composer; b. Washington, D.C., Nov. 6, 1854; d. Reading, Pa., March 6, 1932. He was the son of a Portuguese father and a Bavarian mother. He studied violin with John Esputa and harmony with G. F. Benkert in Washington (1864–67); also acquired considerable proficiency on wind instruments; played in the Marine Band at the age of 13; led an orch. in a vaudeville theater in Washington before he was 18; in 1877 was engaged as violinist in the special orchestra in Philadelphia that was conducted by Offenbach during his American tour. In 1880 Sousa was appointed leader of the Marine Band; he resigned on Aug. 1, 1892, and organized a band of his own, with which he gave successful concerts throughout the U.S. and Canada; played at the Chicago World's Fair in 1893 and at the Paris Exposition in 1900; made 4 European tours (1900, 1901, 1903, and 1905) with increasing acclaim, and finally a tour around the world in 1910–11. His flair for writing band music was extraordinary; the infectious rhythms of his military marches and the brilliance of his band arrangements earned him the sobriquet of "The March King"; particularly celebrated is his march *The Stars and Stripes Forever*, which became famous all over the world. During

World War I Sousa served as a lieutenant in the Naval Reserve. He continued his annual tours almost to the time of his death. He compiled for the Naval Dept. the *National, Patriotic and Typical Airs of All Lands* (1890); publ. an autobiography, *Marching Along* (Boston, 1928), and wrote 5 novels.

WORKS: His publ. compositions aggregate to several hundred, including the comic operas *The Smugglers* (1897), *Désirée* (1884), *The Queen of Hearts* (1886), *El Capitan* (Boston, April 13, 1896; his most brilliant operetta), *The Charlatan* (1897), *The Bride Elect* (1898), *Chris and the Wonderful Lamp* (1900), *The Free Lance* (1906), *The Glass-Blowers* (1911), *The American Maid* (1913), and *Victory* (1915); suites for orch. and band: *Last Days of Pompeii, Three Quotations, Sheridan's Ride, At the King's Court, Looking Upward, Impressions at the Movies,* etc.; a symph. poem, *The Chariot Race* (from *Ben Hur);* many waltzes, songs, etc.; and numerous popular military marches: *The Stars and Stripes Forever, El Capitan, The Washington Post, The High School Cadets, Thunderer, Semper Fidelis, Liberty Hall, Manhattan Beach, King Cotton, Hands Across the Sea* (a selection of 24 marches are reprinted in facsimile from the original sheet music in Lester S. Levy's *Sousa's Great Marches* [N.Y., 1975]); publ. an instruction book for trumpet and drum, and one for violin.

BIBLIOGRAPHY: *Through the Years with Sousa* (excerpts from his writings; N.Y., 1910); Ann M. Lingg, *J. P. Sousa* (N.Y., 1954); R. F. Goldman, "The Great American Composers: John Philip Sousa," *HiFi Stereo Review* (July 1967); J. R. Smart, *The Sousa Band. A Discography* (Washington, D.C., 1970); W. B. Stacy, *John Philip Sousa and His Band Suites: An Analytic and Cultural Study* (Univ. of Colorado, 1972); P. E. Bierley, *John Philip Sousa: American Phenomenon* (N.Y., 1973); P. E. Bierley, *John Philip Sousa: A Descriptive Catalog of His Works* (Urbana, Ill. 1973).

Souster, Tim, English composer of the extreme avant-garde; b. Bletchley, Buckinghamshire, Jan. 29, 1943. He studied music theory at New College in Oxford; in 1963 attended courses in new music given by Stockhausen and Berio in Darmstadt. Back in England, he became one of the most articulate exponents of serial, aleatory, and combinatorial ideas, in which electronic media are employed in conjunction with acoustical performances by humans; he expounded these ideas in his writings in *The Listener, Tempo,* and other progressive publications. In 1969 he was a co-founder of the Intermodulation Group, with the aim of presenting works by congenial composers and experimenters. In 1969–71 he was composer in residence at King's College in Cambridge.

WORKS: *Songs of the Seasons* for soprano and viola (1965); *Poem in Depression* for soprano, flute, viola, cello and piano (1965); *Parallels* for 2 percussion players (1966); *Metropolitan Games* for piano duet (1967); *Titus Groan Music* for wind quintet, electronics and magnetic tape (1969); *Chinese Whispers* for percussion and 3 electronic synthesizers (1970); *Waste Land Music* for soprano saxophone, modulated piano, modulated organ and electronic synthesizer (London,

July 14, 1970); *Triple Music II* for 3 orchestras (London, Aug. 13, 1970).

Southard, Lucien H., American composer; b. Sharon, Vt., Feb. 4, 1827; d. Augusta, Georgia, Jan. 10, 1881. He studied music in Boston. After serving in the Union Army during the Civil War he conducted the orch. of the Peabody Cons. in Baltimore (1868–71); then lived in Boston (1871–75) and Augusta. He composed an opera, *Omano,* from Indian life, to an Italian libretto (manuscript score in the Boston Public Library); church music, glees, and organ pieces; publ. a harmony manual (1855); edited collections of sacred music.

BIBLIOGRAPHY: F. J. Metcalf, *American Composers and Compilers of Sacred Music* (1925).

Southern, Eileen, black American musicologist; b. Minneapolis, Feb. 19, 1920. The Norwegian pianist Meda Zarbell Steele supervised her studies at Chicago Musical College and helped her obtain scholarships at Univ. of Chicago, where she studied with Scott Goldwaite and Sigmund Levarie (B.A.; M.A., 1941, with the thesis *The Use of Negro Folksong in Symphonic Music).* She then taught at Prairie View College (1941–42), Southern Univ. (1942–45, 1949–51), Clafin Univ. (1946–48), and secondary schools in N.Y. (1954–60). Simultaneously she pursued her own studies of medieval and Renaissance music; enrolled at N.Y. Univ. in the classes of Gustave Reese and Martin Bernstein, and wrote her dissertation on the *Buxheim Organ Book* (Ph.D., 1961). She subsequently gave courses in Renaissance music at Brooklyn College (1960–68) and York College (1968–75); also published a fundamental study on music, *The Music of Black Americans: A History* (N.Y., 1961), with a companion volume, *Readings in Black American Music* (N.Y., 1971); in 1973 she founded the journal *Black Perspective in Music.* In 1976 she was appointed to the staff of Harvard Univ. as prof. of music and chairman of the dept. of Afro-American studies.

Souzay, Gérard (real name **Gérard Marcel Tisserand**), French baritone; b. Angers, Dec. 8, 1920. He studied with Vanni-Marcoux and others at the Paris Cons.; specialized in French art songs and German lieder, but also earned distinction as interpreter of operatic parts, among them Count Almaviva in Mozart's *Le Nozze di Figaro* and Golaud in Debussy's *Pelléas et Mélisande.* He made his American debut as an opera singer in 1960 with the New York City Opera; on Jan. 21, 1965, he appeared with the Metropolitan Opera in N.Y. as Count Almaviva.

Sowande, Fela, Nigerian composer; b. Oyo, Nigeria, May 29, 1905; studied music in Lagos; then went to London where he played in a combo in night clubs; at the same time he took courses at London Univ. and Trinity College of Music. He served in the Royal Air Force during World War II. In 1944 he composed an *African Suite* for strings; returned to Nigeria in 1953; in 1957 he received a grant from the State Dept. to travel in the U.S.; was again in the U.S. in 1961, on a Rockefeller grant, and on June 1, 1961 conducted a group of members of the New York Philharmonic in

Carnegie Hall in a program of his own compositions, among them a *Nigerian Folk Symphony*. Upon returning to Nigeria, he joined the staff of the Univ. College at Ibadan. In his music he pursues the goal of cultural integration of native folk material with western art forms.

Sowerby, Leo, prominent American organist and composer; b. Grand Rapids, Mich., May 1, 1895; d. Port Clinton, Ohio, July 7, 1968. He studied in Chicago with Calvin Lampert (piano) and Arthur Olaf Andersen (theory); after service in the U.S. Army during World War I he received the American Prix de Rome (1921), the first of its kind to be awarded for composition; he stayed at the American Academy in Rome for 3 years (1921–24); served as organist at the Cathedral of St. James, a position which he held from 1927 to 1962, when he became director of the College for Church Musicians at the National Cathedral in Washington, D.C.; from 1925 to 1962 he taught composition at the American Cons. in Chicago. As a composer, Sowerby continued the traditions of the French School, maintaining the clarity of design and transparency of sonorities above sheer experimentation. His choral works are particularly fine. Hindemith's dictum that Sowerby was the 4th B of music is invidious. On Jan. 17, 1917 he presented in Chicago a program of his works, billed "Leo Sowerby: His Music," which included the world premières of his concert overture, *Comes Autumn Time*, an orchestral scherzo entitled *The Irish Washerwoman*, a cello concerto, and a piano concerto with a soprano obbligato, with the composer at the piano. Other works include *A Set of Four* for orch. subtitled "Suite of Ironics" (Chicago, Feb. 15, 1918); Symph. No. 1 (Chicago, April 7, 1922); *King Estmere*, ballad for 2 pianos and orch. (Rome, April 8, 1923); *From the Northland* for orch. (Rome, May 27, 1924); *Money Musk*, for orch. (1924); *Medieval Poem* for organ and orch. (Chicago, April 20, 1926); *Vision of Sir Launfal* for soli and mixed chorus (1926); Symph. No. 2 (Chicago, March 29, 1929); *Prairie*, a symph. poem (Interlochen, Michigan, Aug. 11, 1929); 2nd Cello Concerto (N.Y., April 2, 1935); 2nd Piano Concerto (Boston, Nov. 30, 1936); Organ Concerto (Boston, April 22, 1938); Symph. No. 3 (Chicago, March 6, 1941); *Song for America* for chorus (1942); *The Canticle of the Sun*, after St. Francis, for chorus and orch. (N.Y., April 16, 1945; won the Pulitzer Prize); Symph. No. 4 (Boston, Jan. 7, 1949); *Christ Reborn*, oratorio (Philadelphia, Nov. 1, 1953); *Fantasy-Portrait* for orch. (Indianapolis, Nov. 21, 1953); *The Throne of God* for voices and orch. (Washington, D.C., Nov. 18, 1957); he further wrote 2 jazz pieces for band, *Monotony* and *Syncopata* (Chicago, Oct. 11, 1925); chamber music: 2 string quartets (1923, 1935); 2 violin sonatas (1922, 1924); Wind Quintet (1916); Cello Sonata (1921); *Pop Goes the Weasel*, for flute, oboe, clarinet, bassoon and horn (1927); Clarinet Sonata (1938); Trumpet Sonata (1945); Suite for organ, brass and timpani (1953); also numerous organ pieces and anthems. BIBLIOGRAPHY: B. C. Tuthill, "Leo Sowerby," *Musical Quarterly* (April 1938).

Sowinski, Wojciech (Albert), Polish pianist; b. Lukaszówka, Podolia, 1803; d. Paris, March 5, 1880. He was a pupil of Czerny and Seyfried in Vienna; toured Italy as pianist; in 1830 settled in Paris, and was a successful piano teacher there. He publ. the first dictionary of Polish musicians in a western language, *Les Musiciens polonais et slaves, anciens et modernes. Dictionnaire biographique des compositeurs, chanteurs, instrumentistes, luthiers* (Paris, 1857; in Polish, Paris, 1874), and it is through this publication that his name is remembered. He also wrote 3 operas, *Lenore, Le Modèle,* and *Une Scène sous la ligne;* an oratorio, *Saint Adalbert;* several motets; a symphony; overtures on Polish subjects; a piano concerto; a piano quartet; a piano trio; numerous piano pieces in the salon genre.

Spadavecchia, Antonio, Russian composer of Italian descent; b. Odessa, June 3, 1907. He studied with Shebalin at the Moscow Cons., and also took lessons from Prokofiev.
WORKS: operas, *Ak-Buzat (The Magic Steed;* Ufa, Nov. 7, 1942; in collaboration with Zaimov), *The Inn Hostess,* after Goldoni (Moscow, April 24, 1949), *Pilgrimage of Sorrows,* after Alexei Tolstoi (Perm, Dec. 29, 1953); *The Gadfly* (Perm, Nov. 8, 1957); *Yukki* (1970); ballets, *Enemies* (Moscow, May 20, 1938), *The Shore of Happiness* (Moscow, Nov. 6, 1948); a symph. suite, *Dzangar* (1940); *Heroic Overture on Bashkir Songs* (Ufa, Nov. 6, 1942); Piano Concerto (1944); *Romantic Trio* for violin, cello, and piano (1937).

Spaeth, Sigmund, American writer on music; b. Philadelphia, April 10, 1885; d. New York, Nov. 11, 1965. He studied piano and violin with A. Bachmann; then attended Haverford College (M.A., 1906); Ph.D., Princeton Univ., 1910, with the dissertation, *Milton's Knowledge of Music* (publ. 1913). He was music editor of the *N.Y. Evening Mail* (1914–18); education director of the American Piano Co. (1920–27); president of the National Association of American Composers and Conductors (1934–37); lectured widely on music; gave popular talks on the radio; was active in musical journalism; held various posts in educational organizations.
WRITINGS: *The Common Sense of Music* (1924); *The Art of Enjoying Music* (1933); *Music for Everybody* (1934); *Great Symphonies* (1936); *Stories Behind the World's Great Music* (1937); *Music for Fun* (1939); *Great Program Music* (1940); *At Home with Music* (1945); *A History of Popular Music in America* (N.Y., 1948); *Opportunities in Music* (N.Y., 1950); *Dedication; The Love Story of Clara and Robert Schumann* (N.Y., 1950); edited several annotated songbooks: *Barber Shop Ballads* (1925; reprinted 1940), *Read 'em and Weep* (1926; revised 1945); *Weep Some More, My Lady* (N.Y., 1927); *50 Years of Music* (N.Y., 1959).

Spalding, Albert, American violinist; b. Chicago, Aug. 15, 1888; d. New York, May 26, 1953. He was taken to Europe as a child and studied violin in Florence and Paris; made his public debut in Paris on June 6, 1905, and his American debut as a soloist with the N.Y. Symph. Orch. on Nov. 8, 1908. From 1919 he made annual tours of the U.S. and acquired the reputation of a fine artist, even though not necessarily a contagiously flamboyant one. He wrote a number of pieces for the violin; published an autobiography, *Rise to Follow* (N.Y., 1943), and a fictionalized biography of Tartini, *A Fiddle, a Sword, and a Lady* (N.Y., 1953).

Spalding, Walter Raymond, American pedagogue; b. Northampton, Mass, May 22, 1865; d. Cambridge, Mass., Feb. 10, 1962. Graduate of Harvard Univ. (B.A., 1887; M.A., 1888, with honors in music); taught classics at St. Mark's School, Southborough, Mass., 1889–92; from 1892 to 1895 studied music in Paris (with Guilmant and Widor) and Munich (with Rheinberger); appointed instructor of music at Harvard in 1895, assistant prof. in 1903; and prof. in 1912; also prof. at Radcliffe College. In 1920–21 he lectured at 8 French universities.

WRITINGS: *Tonal Counterpoint* (1940); *Modern Harmony in Its Theory and Practice* (1905; with Arthur Foote); *Music; an Art and a Language* (1920); *Music at Harvard* (1935).

Spangenberg, Heinrich, German composer; b. Darmstadt, May 24, 1861; d. there, Sept. 27, 1925. He studied at Hoch's Cons. in Frankfurt; in 1881 for a short time was a pupil of N. Rubinstein (piano) in Moscow; then studied with Leschetizky (piano) and Grädener (composition) in Vienna. In 1884, Kapellmeister at the opera and instructor at the Cons. in Mainz; in 1886, at Fredenberg's Cons. in Weisbaden, and in 1888 conductor of the Lehrerverein; about 1890 he founded his own Cons. there, of which he was director until 1914. He composed 3 operas; piano pieces; songs and numerous choruses for men's voices.

Spanuth, August, German music editor; b. Brinkum, near Hannover, March 15, 1857; d. Berlin, Jan. 9, 1920. Pupil of Heymann (piano) and Raff (composition) at Hoch's Cons. in Frankfurt; debut as pianist in 1874; then lived as concert pianist and teacher in Koblenz and Bremen; toured the U.S. as pianist in 1886; taught at the Chicago Musical College, 1887–93; from 1893–1906, in N.Y. as teacher and music critic of the *Staatszeitung*; settled in Berlin in 1906 as teacher at Stern's Cons. and (from 1907) ed. of *Signale für die musikalische Welt*. He publ. *Preparatory Piano Exercises* and *Essential Piano Technics*; songs and piano pieces; with X. Scharwenka he wrote *Methodik des Klavierspiels* (1907).

Spark, William, English organist and composer; b. Exeter, Oct. 28, 1823; d. Leeds, June 16, 1897. Chorister in Exeter Cathedral; pupil of S. S. Wesley; from 1850–80, organist at St. George's, Leeds; founder, 1851, of the Leeds Madrigal and Motet Society; borough organist of Leeds, 1860; Mus. Doc., Dublin, 1861; editor of *The Organist's Quarterly Journal*.

WRITINGS: *Memoir of Dr. S. S. Wesley; Henry Smart, His Life and Works* (London, 1881); *Musical Memories* (1888); and *Musical Reminiscences* (1892).

Sparnaay, Harry, prominent Dutch bass clarinet player; b. Amsterdam, April 14, 1944. He played tenor saxophone in the Bohemia Jazz Quintet and later in the Theo Deken Orch.; studied clarinet at the Amster-

dam Cons., where he eventually turned to the bass clarinet. He had over 100 works written for him (as a soloist or for his chamber duo, Fusion Moderne, which was formed in 1971 with the pianist Polo de Haas) by Berio, Goeyvaerts, Hrisanidis, Kunst, Logothetis, Raxach, Straesser and others; played in contemporary music festivals in Amsterdam, Berlin, Bonn, Frankfurt and Zagreb.

Spasov, Ivan, Bulgarian composer; b. Sofia, Jan. 17, 1934. He studied composition with Vladigerov at the Bulgarian State Cons. (1951–56) and later with Sikorski and Wislocki at the Warsaw Cons. In 1962 he became music director of the symph. orch. in Pazardjik and also taught at the Plovdiv Cons.

WORKS: *Sonata Concertante* for clarinet and orch. (1959); 2 symphonies (1960, 1975); *Micro-Suite* for chamber orch. (1963); *Dances* for orch. (1964); *Episodes* for 4 instrumental groups (1965); *Movements I* for 12 strings (1966) and *II* for 12 strings and 3 bagpipes (1968); 2 *Bulgarian Melodies* for orch. (1968, 1970); *Competition* for 22 winds (1969; Plovdiv, May 10, 1973); Cello Concerto (1974); *Monologues of a Woman,* monodrama (1975); Piano Concerto (1976); an oratorio, *Plakat* (1958); Clarinet Sonata (1959); Viola Sonata (1960); *Bagatelles* for flute and harp (1964); *10 Groups* for hunting horn and piano (1965); *Musique pour des amis* for string quartet and jazz quartet (1966); String Quartet No. 1 (1973); *Games* for piano (1964); *The Art of the Seria* in 3 notebooks (1968, 1969, 1970); songs.

Spazier, Johann Gottlieb Carl, German song composer and scholar; b. Berlin, April 20, 1761; d. Leipzig, Jan. 19, 1805. Student of philosophy at Halle and Göttingen; prof. at Giessen; settled in Leipzig, 1800. He wrote many songs, some of which became great favorites.

WRITINGS: the autobiographical *Karl Pilgers. Roman seines Lebens* (3 vols., 1792–96); *Freie Gedanken über die Gottesverehrung der Protestanten* (1788); *Etwas über Gluckische Musik und die Oper "Iphigenia in Tauris"* (1795).

BIBLIOGRAPHY: M. Friedlaender, *Das deutsche Lied im 18. Jahrhundert* (1902).

Speaight, Joseph, English pianist and pedagogue; b. London, Oct. 24, 1868; d. there, Nov. 20, 1947. He studied piano with Ernst Pauer and composition with R. O. Morgan at the Guildhall School of Music; taught there from 1894 to 1919; then on the faculty of Trinity College (1919–39). He wrote 3 symphonies, a piano concerto, piano pieces, and songs.

Speaks, Oley, American baritone and song composer; b. Canal Winchester, Ohio, June 28, 1874; d. New York, Aug. 27, 1948. He studied singing with Emma Thursby and composition with Max Spicker and W. Macfarlane; sang at various churches in N.Y. (1898–1906); then devoted himself entirely to concert singing and composition. He wrote some of the most popular songs in the American repertory: *On the Road to Mandalay, Sylvia, The Prayer Perfect, Morning, Life's Twilight, My Homeland, The Lord Is My Light, To You,* etc.

Specht, Richard, Austrian writer on music; b. Vienna, Dec. 7, 1870; d. there, March 18, 1932. Trained as an architect, he turned to musical criticism at the suggestion of Brahms and Goldmark, writing at first for *Die Zeit* (Vienna daily), and from 1908–15 for *Die Musik.* In 1909 he founded *Der Merker,* which he ed. until 1919 (at first with R. Batka, later with J. Bittner). 1914, Officier de l'Académie (France); 1926, professor.

WRITINGS: *Kritisches Skizzenbuch* (1900); *Gustav Mahler* (1906; enlarged, 1913); *Joh. Strauss* (1909); *Das Wiener Operntheater von Dingelstedt bis Schalk und Strauss* (1919); *Richard Strauss und sein Werk,* in 2 vols. (1921); *Julius Bittner* (1921); *Wilhelm Furtwängler* (1922); *E. N. von Reznicek* (1923); *Brahms* (1928; in English, 1930); *Bildnis Beethovens* (1930; in English as *Beethoven as He Lived,* 1933); *Giacomo Puccini* (1931; in English, 1933).

Speer, Daniel, German composer; b. Breslau, July 2, 1636; d. Göppingen, Oct. 5, 1707. He taught music in Stuttgart (1665–67); in 1675 he settled in Göppingen, where he was employed as town piper; he was dismissed for publishing a pamphlet mocking the authorities, and spent a year and a half in prison; was sent away to Waiblingen in 1690, but was reinstated in 1693 and recalled to Göppingen. He publ. (under assumed names and anagrams) several collections of whimsical songs; also several pieces of chamber music.

BIBLIOGRAPHY: H. J. Moser, "Daniel Speer," *Acta Musicologica* 9 (1937).

Speidel, Wilhelm, German pianist and composer; b. Ulm, Sept. 3, 1826; d. Stuttgart, Oct. 13, 1899. Pupil at Munich of Wänner and W. Kuhe, and of Ignaz Lachner (composition); 1846–48, teacher at Thann, Alsatia; 1848–54, at Munich; 1854, music director at Ulm; 1857, conductor of the Liederkranz at Stuttgart; cofounder of the Cons., and teacher of piano there until he founded his Künstler- und Dilettantenschule für Klavier in 1874. On Lebert's death (1884), Speidel rejoined the Cons., uniting with it his own school.

Spelman, Timothy Mather, American composer; b. Brooklyn, Jan. 21, 1891; d. Florence, Italy, Aug. 21, 1970. He studied music with H. R. Shelley in N.Y., and with W. R. Spalding and E. B. Hill at Harvard Univ. (1909–13); then went to Europe where he took a course with Walter Courvoisier at the Munich Cons. (1913–15); returned to the U.S. in 1915 and was active as director of a military band. After 1918 he went back to Europe with his wife, the poetess Leolyn Everett, settling in Florence. As the specter of a new war loomed, he returned to the U.S.; in 1947 he went back to Florence. His music was performed more often in Europe than in America; indeed, his style of composition is exceedingly European, influenced by Italian Romanticism and French Impressionism.

WORKS: *Snowdrop,* a pantomime (Brooklyn, 1911); *The Romance of the Rose,* a "wordless fantasy" (Boston, 1913; revised version, St. Paul, Minn., Dec. 4, 1915); *La Magnifica,* short music drama to a libretto by Leolyn Everett-Spelman (1920); *The Sunken City,* opera (1930); *The Courtship of Miles Standish,* opera after Longfellow (1943); for orch.: *Saint's Days,* suite

in 4 movements (one movement, *Assisi, the Great Pardon of St. Francis,* was performed in Boston, March 26, 1926); *The Outcasts of Poker Flat,* symph. poem after Bret Harte (1928); Symph. (Rochester, N.Y., Oct. 29, 1936); *Jamboree,* a "pocket ballet" (1945); Oboe Concerto (1954); *5 Whimsical Serenades,* for string quartet (1924); *Le Pavillion sur l'eau* for flute, harp and strings (1925); *Pervigilium Veneris,* for soprano, baritone, chorus, and orch. (Paris, April 30, 1931); a number of choruses and songs.

Spencer, Allen, American pianist and pedagogue; b. Fair Haven, Vt., Oct. 30, 1870; d. Chicago, Aug. 25, 1950. He studied piano in Rochester and Chicago; in 1892 was appointed teacher at the American Cons. in Chicago; then became its dean (1928–48). He published *Foundations of Piano Technique.*

Spencer, Émile-Alexis-Xavier, French composer; b. Brussels, May 24, 1859; d. Nanterre (Seine), May 24, 1921. He studied piano in Brussels; in 1881 went to Paris where he found his métier as a composer for vaudeville; was credited with about 4,000 chansonnettes, which were popularized by famous singers, among them Yvette Guilbert. His chanson *Jambes de bois* was used by Stravinsky in *Pétrouchka* under the impression that it was a folksong; when Spencer brought an action for infringement on his authorship, Stravinsky agreed to pay him part of the royalties for performances.

Spencer, S. Reid, American pianist and teacher; b. Baltimore, July 30, 1872; d. Brooklyn, July 28, 1945. He studied with P. C. Lutkin at the Northwestern Univ. School of Music, and taught there from 1895 to 1900. After teaching in various conservatories, he established his own music school in Brooklyn (1927). He published a textbook on harmony (1915).

Spencer, Vernon, English-American pianist and composer; b. Belmont, Durham, Oct. 10, 1875; d. Los Angeles, Jan. 9, 1949. He studied at the Leipzig Cons., graduating in 1897; in 1903 he settled in the U.S.; was director of the Wesleyan Univ. Cons. of Music at Lincoln, Nebraska; from 1911 taught in Los Angeles. He published some songs and character pieces for piano.

Spendiarov, Alexander, Russian-Armenian composer; b. Kakhovka, Crimea, Nov. 1, 1871; d. Erivan, May 7, 1928. He studied violin as a child; in 1896 went to St. Petersburg and took private lessons with Rimsky-Korsakov. In his works he cultivated a type of Russian orientalism in which the elements of folksongs of the peripheral regions of the old Russian Empire are adroitly arranged in the colorful harmonies of the Russian National School. His best work in this manner was an opera *Almast,* the composition of which he undertook shortly before his death. It was completed and orchestrated by Maximilian Steinberg, and performed posthumously in Moscow on June 23, 1930. Other works are *The Three Palm Trees,* a symph. tableau (1905); *Crimean Sketches* for orch. (1903–12); *2 Songs of the Crimean Tatars* for voice and orch. (1915; Moscow, Dec. 25, 1927); *Études d'Eriwan,* on Armenian melodies (1925).

BIBLIOGRAPHY: A. Shaverdian, *A. Spendiarov* (Moscow, 1929); G. Tigranov, *A. Spendiarov* (Erivan, 1953); R. Atadjan, *A. Spendiarov* (Erivan, 1971).

Spengel, Julius Heinrich, German composer; b. Hamburg, June 12, 1853; d. there, April 17, 1936. He studied at the Cologne Cons.; later at the Berlin Hochschule für Musik with Rudorff, Joachim, Kiel, and A. Schulze; settled as a teacher in Hamburg. In 1878 he was conductor of the Cäcilienverein there; organist of the Gertrudenkirche (1886); made Royal Prof. in 1906.

WORKS: Piano Quintet; *Psalm 39* for 6-part chorus and wind instruments; *Zwiegesang in der Sommernacht,* for chorus and orch.; *König Alfreds Gesang,* for baritone and orch.; male and female choruses; songs.

Sperontes (real name **Johann Sigismund Scholze**), German composer; b. Lobendau, Silesia, March 20, 1705; d. Leipzig, Sept. 27, 1750. Between 1736 and 1745 he brought out a collection of poems and melodies to words by Johann Christian Günther, *Singende Muse an der Pleisse in zweimal 50 Oden;* this became famous, and its success generated many imitations, by composers in Leipzig, Hamburg, and Vienna. Reprint (ed. by E. Buhle) in the *Denkmäler deutscher Tonkunst* 35 and 36.

BIBLIOGRAPHY: P. Spitta, in the *Vierteljahrsschrift für Musikwissenschaft* 1 (1885); H. von Hase, in the *Zeitschrift der Internationalen Musik-Gesellschaft* XIV/4; A. Schering, "Zwei Singspiele des Sperontes," *Zeitschrift für Musikwissenschaft* VII/4.

Speyer, Wilhelm, German violinist and composer; b. Frankfurt, June 21, 1790; d. there, April 5, 1878. He studied in Offenbach with F. Fränzl (violin) and A. André (composition); later in Paris with Baillot (violin). After extensive travels as a concert violinist, he returned to Frankfurt and embraced a mercantile career, but continued his associations with eminent musicians (Spohr, Mendelssohn, etc) and began to compose. He wrote a great deal of chamber music; his violin pieces were often played, but he achieved lasting popularity with his ballads written in a characteristically Romantic style; of these *Der Trompeter* and *Die drei Liebchen* were particularly famous. His son **Edward Speyer** (b. Frankfurt, May 14, 1839; d. Shenley, Hertfordshire, Jan. 8, 1934), lived most of his life in London, where he organized the Classical Concerts Society; he published a monograph on his father, *Wilhelm Speyer, der Liederkomponist* (Munich, 1925), and a book of reminiscences, *My Life and Friends* (posthumous, London, 1937).

Spialek, Hans, Austrian-American composer and arranger; b. Vienna, April 17, 1894. He studied at the Cons. of Vienna; settled in the U.S. in 1924, and became an orchestrator of musical comedies in N.Y. He wrote a number of descriptive pieces for salon orch. and for various ensembles (*Cloister Meditations, Vision, The Tall City, Manhattan Watercolors, The Danube,* etc.); also a *Sinfonietta* (N.Y., Nov. 15, 1936).

Spicker, Max, German-American conductor, composer, and music editor; b. Königsberg, Aug. 16, 1858; d. New York, Oct. 15, 1912. He studied with Louis Köhler (piano); then at the Leipzig Cons. with Reinecke and Richter. In 1882 he settled in N.Y., where he became reader for G. Schirmer, Inc. He wrote many songs; edited *Aus aller Herren Länder* (a collection of folksongs arranged for male chorus), *Anthology of Sacred Song* (4 vols.), *Operatic Anthology* (5 vols.), *The Synagogical Service* (2 vols.; with W. Sparger); etc.

Spiegel, Laurie, American composer of the avantgarde; b. Chicago, Sept. 20, 1945. She studied the classical guitar with Oscar Ghiglia, Renaissance lute playing with Suzanne Bloch and composition with Jacob Druckman at the Juilliard School of Music, N.Y. She moved in quaquaversal directions in her own creative output until 1970 when she plugged herself into an electronic outlet, and in 1973 reached the Ultima Thule of scientifically regulated composition with the GROOVE hybrid system, using a digital computer to control analog audio synthesis equipment at the Bell Laboratories in Murray Hill, New Jersey; was closely associated with experimental color video in collaboration with Nam June Paik, a pioneer of electronic dislocation of images on television sets. She applied the principles of musical variations to the changes of mandala-shaped visual images; also utilized transcendental meditation technique with a single tone subjected to dynamic amplification or diminution. Among her computer-generated works are *The Expanding Universe* (1975), *Waves* (1975) and *Patchwork* (1976). In several of her compositions she harks back to the polyphonic schools of the Renaissance, applying modal stereophonic hockets.

Spiegelman, Joel, American pianist, harpsichordist, conductor and composer; b. Buffalo, New York, Jan. 23, 1933. He studied at Yale School of Music (1949–50), at the Univ. of Buffalo (1950–53), at the Longy School of Music at Cambridge, Mass. (1953–54), and at Brandeis Univ., where he attended the classes of Harold Shapero, Irving Fine and Arthur Berger; in 1956 he went to Paris where he studied privately with Nadia Boulanger. He returned to the U.S. in 1960 and took courses in musicology at Brandeis Univ. He also studied languages, and became fluent in French and Russian. In 1966 he was appointed teacher of harpsichord and theory at Sarah Lawrence College, where he was also instructor in electronic music. In 1977 he organized in N.Y. the new Russian Chamber Orch., composed entirely of Soviet Jews who had left Russia in the 1970s.

WORKS: *Ouverture de Saison 1958* for 2 harps, 2 flutes, piano and celesta (1958); *Kusochki (Morsels)* for piano 4 hands (1966); *3 Miniatures* for clarinet and piano (1972); *Chamber Music,* for piano quartet and percussion (1973); *2 Fantasies* for string quartet (1963, 1974).

Spielter, Hermann, German composer; b. Bremen, April 26, 1860; d. New York, Nov. 10, 1925. He studied with Reinecke and Jadassohn at the Leipzig Cons.; emigrated to the U.S. in 1894 and settled in N.Y. as a teacher. He wrote an operetta, *Die Rajahsbraut* (N.Y., 1910), numerous choral pieces, chamber music, and a piano sonata.

Spiering, Theodore, American violinist and conductor; b. St. Louis, Sept. 5, 1871; d. Munich, Aug. 11, 1925. He studied with Schradieck at the Cincinnati College of Music and with Joachim at the Hochschule für Musik in Berlin. Returning to America, he organized his own quartet, with which he toured the U.S. and Canada (1893-1905); then traveled in Germany (1906-09). In 1909 he was appointed concertmaster of the N.Y. Philharmonic Orch. (under Mahler); during Mahler's last illness he was called upon to conduct 17 concerts of the N.Y. Philharmonic in the spring of 1911. He publ. *Sechs Künstler-Etüden,* for violin; with Rudolf Ganz he edited a number of classical and modern violin pieces.

Spies, Hermine, eminent German contralto, b. Löhneberger Hütte, near Weilburg, Feb. 25, 1857; d. Wiesbaden, Feb. 26, 1893. She was a pupil of Stockhausen in Frankfurt; in 1883 began to give song recitals in Germany; in 1889 made an appearance in England with excellent success; also sang in Austria, Denmark, and Russia. She excelled as an interpreter of songs by Brahms, who had a high regard for her. Shortly before her death she married Dr. W. A. F. Hardtmuth of Wiesbaden
BIBLIOGRAPHY: Marie Spies, *Hermine Spies. Ein Gedenkbuch für ihre Freunde* (Stuttgart, 1894).

Spiess, Meinrad, German composer and theorist; b. Honsolgen, Aug. 24, 1683; d. Yrsee, June 12, 1761. He was a pupil of Giuseppe Antonio Bernabei in Munich; in 1708 he was ordained priest; from 1712 to 1749 was music director of the monastery of Yrsee, eventually becoming Prior. He published a number of collections of sacred choruses, motets, etc., with instrumental accompaniment: *Antiphonarium Marianum* (1713); *Cithara Davidis* (1713); *Philomela ecclesiastica* (1718); *Cultus latreuticomusicus* (1719), *Laus Dei in Sanctis ejus* (1723); *Hyperdulia musica* (1726); *Tractatus musicus compositorio-practicus* (1746); also composed instrumental works and a number of organ pieces.

Spilka, František, Czech composer; b. Štěken, Nov. 13, 1887; d. Prague, Oct. 20, 1960. He studied at the Prague Cons. with Stecker, Knittl, and Dvořák; in 1918 was appointed administrative director of the Prague Cons. He established the "Prague Teachers' Choral Society" in 1908, with which he remained choirmaster until 1921, and gave concerts with it in France and England; later directed the Prague Singing ensemble "Smetana." Spilka developed, together with Ferdinand Vach, a new approach to choral performance, emphasizing sound color.
WORKS: 2 operas: *Stará práva (Ancient Rights,* 1915; Prague, June 10, 1917), and *Cain or The Birth of Death* (1917); an oratorio, *Jan Hus at the Stake* (1907); a cantata, *Miller's Journeyman* (1947); *Rhapsody* for orch. (1896); *Overture* (1897); *6 Sonnets* for violin and piano (1944); *Rhapsodic Sonata* for cello

and piano (1946); numerous piano pieces, songs and choruses.

Spindler, Fritz, German pianist and composer; b. Wurzbach, Nov. 24, 1817; d. Lössnitz, near Dresden, Dec. 26, 1905. He studied with Fr. Schneider at Dessau; settled in 1841 at Dresden, where he had great success as a teacher. Most of his works (over 400 op. numbers) are salon pieces and characteristic pieces for piano; also publ. instructive sonatinas, opp. 157, 290, 294, and a 4-hand sonatina, op. 136.

Spinelli, Nicola, Italian composer; b. Turin, July 29, 1865; d. Rome, Oct. 17, 1909. He studied at the Naples Cons., under Serrao. In 1889 his 1-act opera *Labilia* took the 2nd prize in the famous competition instituted by the publisher Sonzogno, when Mascagni won the 1st prize with *Cavalleria Rusticana;* Spinelli's opera was produced in Rome on May 7, 1890, with indifferent success. His next opera, *A basso porto,* was more fortunate; after its initial production in Cologne on April 18, 1894 (in a German version), it was staged in Rome, in Italian (March 11, 1895), and then in Budapest, St. Petersburg, etc.; it was also produced in the U.S. (St. Louis, Jan. 8, 1900; N.Y., Jan. 22, 1900).

Spisak, Michal, Polish composer; b. Dabrowa Górnicza, Sept. 14, 1914; d. Paris, Jan. 29, 1965. He studied music in Katowice; then took composition with Sikorski in Warsaw and with Nadia Boulanger in Paris, where he lived from 1937 until his death.
WORKS: an opera, *Marynka* (1955); *Serenade* for orch. (1939); *Concertino* for String Orch. (1942); *Aubade* for small orch. (1943); *Allegro de Voiron* for orch. (1943); *Bassoon Concerto* (1944; International Society for Contemporary Music Festival, Copenhagen, June 2, 1947); *Toccata* for orch. (1944); *Suite* for string orch. (1945); *Piano Concerto* (1947); *2 Symphonies concertante* (1947, 1956); *Etudes* for strings (1948); *Divertimento* for 2 pianos and orch. (1948); *Sonata* for violin and orch. (1950); *Trombone Concertino* (1951); *Divertimento* for orch. (1951); *Andante and Allegro* for violin and orch. (1954); *Concerto Giocoso* for chamber orch. (1957); *Oboe Concerto* (1962); *Violin Concerto* (posthumous; Katowice, Jan. 30, 1976); *Quartet* for oboe, 2 clarinets and bassoon (1938); *Sonatina* for oboe, clarinet and bassoon (1946); *Violin Sonata* (1946); *Wind Quintet* (1948); *Duetto concertante* for viola and bassoon (1949); *String Quartet* (1953); *Suite* for 2 violins (1957); *Improvvisazione* for violin and piano (1962); *Concerto for 2 Solo Pianos* (1942); choruses; piano pieces; songs.

Spitalny, Phil, American conductor of popular music; b. Odessa, Russia, Nov. 7, 1889; d. Miami, Florida, Oct. 11, 1970. He emigrated to the United States in 1905; played clarinet in various bands. In 1934 he conceived the idea of organizing an instrumental ensemble consisting only of girls of nubile age and engaging exterior; in 1935 he inaugurated the radio program "Hour of Charm" with his group. In 1937 he won the award of merit of the Radio Committee of the Women's National Exposition of Arts and Industries. With the advent of television, Spitalny's radio program fell into terminal desuetude, and he went to Florida. He was also an amateur composer; made arrangements of amorous songs, among them *The Kiss I Can't Forget.*

Spitta, Friedrich, German theologian and writer on music, brother of **Philipp Spitta;** b. Wittingen, Jan. 10, 1852; d. Göttingen, June 8, 1924. From 1887–1918 prof. of theology at Strasbourg Univ. and from 1919 at Göttingen; from 1896 also editor (with J. Smend) of *Monatschrift für Gottesdienst und kirchliche Kunst,* in which (Jan.-March 1913) he publ. important facts concerning Benedictus Ducis. He publ. *Liturgische Andacht zum Luther-Jubiläum* (1883); *H. Schütz,* festival oration (1886); *Die Passionen nach den vier Evangelisten von H. Schütz* (1886); *Über Chorgesang im evangelischen Gottesdienste* (1886); *"Ein' feste Burg ist unser Gott." Die Lieder Luthers* (1905); *Studien zu Luthers Liedern* (1907); *Das Deutsche Kirchenlied in seinen charakteristischen Erscheinungen* (vol. I: *Mittelalter und Reformationszeit,* 1912); *H. Schütz* (1925); also a new ed. of Mergner's *Paul Gerhardt Lieder* (1918).

Spitta, (Johann August) Philipp, eminent German musicologist; b. Wechold, Hannover, Dec. 27, 1841; d. Berlin, April 13, 1894. Student of philology at Göttingen; teacher at the Ritter und Domschule, Reval, 1864–66; at Sondershausen Gymnasium till 1874; and one year at the Nikolai-Gymnasium, Leipzig, where he was co-founder of the Bach-Verein (1874); in 1875, prof. of music history at Berlin Univ., life-secretary to the Royal Academy of Arts, and teacher at, and vice-director of, the Hochschule für Musik. As a teacher he had extraordinary success; among his pupils were O. Fleischer, A. Sandberger, M. Freidlaender, R. Schwartz, M. Seiffert, E. Vogel, K. Krebs, and J. Combarieu. He was one of the leading spirits in organizing the publication of the *Denkmäler deutscher Tonkunst.*

WRITINGS: *J. S. Bach* (2 vols., 1873, 1880), a comprehensive biography carefully and learnedly written, with valuable discussions of principal works (in English, London, 1884–85; condensed ed., Leipzig, 1935); also a short sketch of Bach in Waldersee's *Vorträge* (1880); a short biography of Schumann for *Grove's Dictionary,* afterwards published separately in German (*Vorträge,* 1882); *Händel und Bach,* 2 festival orations (1885); *Zur Ausgabe der Kompositionen Friedrichs des Grossen* (1890); 2 collections of articles, *Zur Musik* (1892; 16 essays), and *Musikgeschichtliche Aufsätze* (Berlin, 1894); an essay, *Die Passionsmusiken von Sebastian Bach und Heinrich Schütz* (Hamburg, 1893); many papers in the *Allgemeine musikalische Zeitung,* the *Monatshefte für Musikgeschichte,* and more particularly in his own periodical, the *Vierteljahrsschrift für Musikwissenschaft,* founded in 1884 with Chrysander and G. Adler. Spitta also edited a critical ed. of Buxtehude's organ works (2 volumes, 1875, 1876), with valuable historical notes; the complete ed. of Schütz's works (16 vols.); and vol. I of the *Denkmäler deutscher Tonkunst* (1892; contains Scheidt's *Tabulatura nova* of 1624). He left in MS an almost completed *Geschichte der romantischen Oper in Deutschland.* Spitta's correspondence with Brahms was published by *Brahmsgesellschaft* (vol. 15).

Spitzmueller, Alexander, Austrian composer; b. Vienna, Feb. 22, 1894; d. Paris, Nov. 12, 1962. He studied jurisprudence; then took composition lessons with Alban Berg and Hans Apostel. In 1928 he went to Paris, where he became active in radio broadcasting. His early works are in the neo-Classical vein; eventually he followed the method of composition with 12 tones, following its usage by Berg and Webern.

WORKS: *Sinfonietta ritmica* (1934); Symphony for strings (1955); 2 piano concertos (1938, 1954); *May 40,* satirical suite for orch. (Amsterdam, Festival of the International Society for Contemporary Music, June 12, 1948); *Trois Hymnes à la Paix* for orch. (1947); opera, *Der Diener zweier Herren* (1958); ballets, *Le Premier Amour de Don Juan* (1954); *Die Sackgasse* (1957) and *Construction humaine* (1959); Violin Sonata; Cello Sonata; *Variations* for viola and guitar; String Quartet; Saxophone Quartet; a number of sacred and secular choruses.

Spivacke, Harold, eminent American musicologist and librarian; b. New York, July 18, 1904; d. Washington, D.C., May 9, 1977. He studied at N.Y. Univ. (M.A., 1925) and at the Univ. of Berlin, where he received his Dr. phil. in 1933, *magna cum laude* for his dissertation *Über die objektive und subjektive Tonintensität;* while in Berlin he took private lessons with Eugen d'Albert and Hugo Leichtentritt as American-German Students Exchange Fellow and as Alexander von Humboldt Stiftung Fellow. Returning to the U.S., he joined the staff of the music division of the Library of Congress, Washington, D.C., first as assistant chief (1934–37) then as chief, in which capacity he served for 35 years (1937–72). He also held numerous advisory positions with the Department of State, UNESCO, etc. As chief of the music division of the Library of Congress, he was responsible in the acquisition of many important manuscripts by contemporary composers, including a large collection of Schoenberg's original manuscripts. He also commissioned works for the Coolidge Foundation at the Library of Congress, from contemporary composers. He published some valuable bibliographical papers, among them *Paganiniana* (Washington, 1945). In 1939 he was Chairman of the Organizing Committee of the National Music Council, and until 1972 was Archivist and a member of the Executive Committee of the Council.

Spivakovsky, Tossy, outstanding Russian-American violinist; b. Odessa, Feb. 4, 1907. He studied with Willy Hess in Berlin; made his concert debut there at the age of 10; toured Europe (1920–33) and Australia (1933–41); then came to the U.S.; appeared with major American orchestras.

BIBLIOGRAPHY: G. Yost, *The Spivakovsky Way of Bowing* (Pittsburgh, 1949).

Spohr, Ludwig (Louis), celebrated German violinist, composer, and conductor; b. Braunschweig, April 5, 1784; d. Kassel, Oct. 22, 1859. The family moved to Seesen in 1786. His father, a physician, was an amateur flute player, and his mother a singer and pianist. In this musical atmosphere Spohr's talent developed very early; at the age of 5 he began taking lessons on the violin with Rector Riemenschneider and Dufour, a French *émigré*. Spohr then returned to Braunschweig, where he was taught by the organist Hartung and the violinist Maucourt. He had already composed various violin pieces; the duke himself became interested in Spohr, admitted him to the orch., and arranged for his further study with the violinist Franz Eck. In 1802 Eck took Spohr with him on a tour to Russia, where he made the acquaintance of Clementi and John Field; he returned to Braunschweig in 1803 and resumed his post in the ducal orch. In 1804 he made his 1st tour as a violinist, giving concerts in Berlin, Leipzig, and Dresden; in 1805 he became concertmaster in the ducal orch. at Gotha; married the harp player **Dorette Scheidler,** and toured with her in Germany in 1807. His reputation as a violin virtuoso was established, and he began to give more attention to composition. He wrote oratorios, operas, violin concertos, symphonies, and chamber music, which obtained excellent success in Germany. In 1812 he gave a series of concerts in Vienna, and was acclaimed both as a composer and violinist; accepted the position of concertmaster in the orch. of the Theater an der Wien, which he held until 1815. He then made a grand tour of Germany and Italy; played a *concertante* of his own with Paganini in Rome. In 1816 Spohr's opera *Faust* was performed by Weber in Prague. After a visit to Holland in 1817, he received the post of opera conductor in Frankfurt, where he produced one of his most popular operas, *Zemire und Azor* (1819). In 1820 he visited England; appeared with his wife at several concerts of the London Philharmonic Society; this was the 1st of his 6 tours of England, where he acquired a lasting reputation as violinist, conductor, and composer; his works continued to be performed in England for many decades after his death. On his way back to Germany he presented several concerts in Paris in 1820, but his reception there failed to match his London successes. He then proceeded to Dresden, and was recommended by Weber for the post of court Kapellmeister in Kassel, originally offered to Weber. Spohr accepted it, and settled there in 1822. It was in Kassel that he produced his masterpiece, the opera *Jessonda* (1823), which held the stage in Europe throughout the 19th century. He conducted its performances in Leipzig and Berlin; also appeared as conductor and composer at various musical festivals (Düsseldorf, 1826; Nordhausen, 1829; Norwich, 1839; Bonn, 1845; etc.). The success of *Jessonda* was followed by the production in Kassel of his oratorio *Die letzten Dinge* (1826) and his symphony *Die Weihe der Töne* (1832), both of which elicited great praise. His wife died in 1834; he married the pianist **Marianne Pfeiffer** in 1836. Spohr made another journey to England in 1847; visited Frankfurt in 1848. Returning to Kassel, he found himself in an increasingly difficult position because of his outspoken radicalism; the Elector of Hesse refused to grant him further leaves of absence, and Spohr decided to ignore the ban, which resulted in litigation with the Kassel Court. In 1853 he made his last tour of England, appearing at the New Philharmonic Concerts in London. He was retired from Kassel in 1857 on a pension; a few months later he broke his left arm, but despite the accident, at an advanced age, he made another appearance (his last) conducting *Jessonda* in Prague (1858).

Spohr's style was characteristic of the transition period between Classicism and Romanticism. He was a master of technical resources; some of his works demonstrate a spirit of bold experimentation (the *Historical Symph.*; Symph. for 2 orchestras; Quartet Concerto; Nonet, etc.); yet in his esthetics he was an intransigent conservative. He admired Beethoven's early works but confessed his total inability to understand Beethoven's last period; he also failed to appreciate Weber. It is remarkable, therefore, that he was an early champion of Wagner; in Kassel he brought out *Der fliegende Holländer* (1843) and *Tannhäuser* (1853), despite strenuous opposition of the court. He was a highly esteemed teacher; among his pupils were Ferdinand David and Moritz Hauptmann. His autobiography was publ. posthumously as *Louis Spohrs Selbstbiographie* (2 vols.; Kassel, 1860–61; in English, London, 1865 and 1878). The Spohr Society was founded in Kassel in 1908, dissolved in 1934, and revived in 1952.

WORKS: Operas: *Die Prüfung* (Gotha, 1806); *Alruna, die Eulen-Königin* (1808); *Der Zweikampf mit der Geliebten* (Hamburg, Nov. 15, 1811); *Faust* (Prague, Sept. 1, 1816); *Zemire und Azor* (Frankfurt, April 4, 1819); *Jessonda* (Kassel, July 28, 1823); *Der Berggeist* (Kassel, March 24, 1825); *Pietro von Albano* (Kassel, Oct. 13, 1827); *Der Alchymist* (Kassel, July 28, 1830); *Die Kreuzfahrer* (Kassel, Jan. 1, 1845). Oratorios: *Das Jüngste Gericht* (Erfurt, Aug. 15, 1812); *Die letzten Dinge* (Kassel, March 25, 1826; in English, as *The Last Judgment*); *Des Heilands letze Stunden* (Kassel, 1835; in English as *Calvary* at the Norwich Festival, 1839); and *Der Fall Babylons* (Norwich Festival, 1842). Other vocal works: *Das befreite Deutschland,* dramatic cantata; a Mass for 5 voices and double chorus; 6 Psalms; hymns, part-songs, etc.; duets; 10 books of German songs; a sonatina for voice and piano, *An sie am Klavier.* 10 symphonies: No. 1 (Leipzig, June 11, 1811); No. 2 (London, April 10, 1820); No. 3 (1828); No. 4 (1832; subtitled *Die Weihe der Töne,* a "characteristic tone painting in the form of a symphony"; No. 5 (1837); No. 6 (1839), subtitled *Historische Symphonie,* in 4 movements traversing 4 styles of music in historic sequence: Bach-Handel Period, 1720; Haydn-Mozart, 1780; Beethoven, 1810; and the *Allerneueste* ("the very newest," i.e. Spohr's own style) of the year 1840; No. 7 (1840), *Irdisches und Göttliches im Menschenleben,* for double orch., in 3 parts portraying the mundane and divine elements in man's life; No. 8 (1847); No. 9 *Die Jahreszeiten,* in 2 parts: 1, *Winter and Spring,* 2, *Summer and Autumn* (1850); No. 10 (1857). Overtures: *Macbeth; Im ernsten Styl;* etc. 15 violin concertos (among the finest being No. 8, "in modo d'una scena cantante," and No. 9), all edited by Ferdinand David; *Quartet Concerto* for 2 violins, viola, and cello with orch.; 2 clarinet concertos. Chamber music: Nonet for violin, viola, cello, double bass, woodwinds, and horn; Octet for violin, 2 violas, cello, double bass, clarinet, and 2 horns; 4 double quartets for strings; Septet for piano, flute, clarinet, horn, bassoon, violin, and cello; String Sextet; 7 string quintets; Quintet for piano, flute, clarinet, horn, and bassoon; Piano Quintet; 34 string quartets; 5 piano trios; 14 *duos concertants* for 2 violins; 3 *duos concertantes* for piano and violin; 3 *sonates concertants* for harp and violin; Piano Sonata; *Rondoletto* for piano; etc. A new edition of his works *(Neue Auswahl der Werke),* ed. by F. Göthel, was begun in 1963 (Kassel, Verlag der Spohr-Gesellschaft).

BIBLIOGRAPHY: W. Neumann, *L. Spohr. Eine Biographie* (Kassel, 1854); A. Malibran, *L. Spohr. Sein Leben und Wirken* (Frankfurt, 1860); L. Stierlin, *L. Spohr* (Zürich, 1862–63); 2 vols.); F. Hiller, *M. Hauptmanns Briefe an L. Spohr und andere* (Leipzig, 1876; in English, London, 1892); H. M. Schletterer, *L. Spohr* (Leipzig, 1881); L. Nohl, *Spohr* (Leipzig, 1882); C. Robert, *L. Spohr* (Berlin, 1883); La Mara, "Aus Spohrs Leben," in *Klassisches und Romantisches aus der Tonwelt* (Leipzig, 1892); R. Wassermann, *L. Spohr als Opernkomponist* (Rostock, 1910); E. Istel, "5 Briefe Spohrs an Marschner," in "Liliencron-Festschrift" (Leipzig, 1910); F. Göthel, *Das Violinspiel L. Spohrs* (dissertation; Berlin, 1934); Edith von Salburg, *L. Spohr* (Leipzig, 1936); P. Heidelbach, "Ludwig Spohrs Prozess gegen den Kurfürst von Hessen," *Allgemeine Musikalische Zeitung* (1936); Dorothy M. Mayer, *The Forgotten Master: The Life and Times of Louis Spohr* (London, 1959). For details of performances of Spohr's operas see A. Loewenberg, *Annals of Opera* (Cambridge, 1943; new ed., Geneva, 1955).

Spontini, Gaspare (Luigi Pacifico), significant Italian opera composer; b. Majolati, Ancona, Nov. 14, 1774; d. there, Jan. 24, 1851. His father, a modest farmer, intended him for the church and gave him in charge of an uncle, a priest at Jesi, who attempted to stifle his musical aspirations. Spontini sought refuge at Monte San Vito with another relative, who not only found a competent music teacher for him, but effected a reconciliation so that, after a year, he was able to return to Jesi. In 1793 he entered the Cons. della Pietà de' Turchini in Naples, where his teachers were Tritto (singing) and Sala (composition). He rapidly mastered the conventional Italian style of his time; some of his church music performed in Naples came to the attention of a director of the Teatro della Pallacorda in Rome, who commissioned him to write an opera. This was *I Puntigli delle donne,* produced with notable success during Carnival, 1796. In his subsequent opera, *L'Eroismo ridicolo* (Naples, 1798), he was helped by Piccinni's practical advice. When the Neapolitan court fled to Palermo before the French invasion, Spontini was engaged as maestro di cappella and wrote 4 operas in quick succession, which were produced at the Palermo court theater in 1800. He left Palermo soon afterwards and proceeded to Rome (1801), Venice (1802), Naples and Paris (1803). In Paris he brought out 2 French operas at the Théâtre-Italien: *La Petite Maison* (May 12, 1804) and *Julie, ou Le Pot de fleurs* (March 12, 1805), in sedulous imitation of the Parisian light opera, but the attempt failed completely. Fortunately for Spontini, he met the poet Etienne de Jouy, a writer of superior accomplishments, who influenced him to change his style. The result was the one-act opera *Milton,* produced at the Théâtre Feydeau on Nov. 27, 1840. Its music showed greater expressiveness and a finer taste than Spontini's preceding works. The next libretto offered by

Etienne de Jouy to Spontini (after it was rejected by Boieldieu and Méhul) was *La Vestale.* Spontini worked on the score for 3 years, repeatedly revising and rewriting in his desire to attain his best, and the final product became his masterpiece. In the meantime, the Empress Josephine had appointed him her "compositeur particulier," and her appreciation of Spontini increased after the production of his patriotic cantata *L'Eccelsa gara,* celebrating the victory of Austerlitz. Her powerful patronage secured a hearing for *La Vestale,* which was brought out at the Académie Impériale (Grand Opéra), despite virulent open and secret opposition on the part of influential musicians, on Dec. 16, 1807, and won triumphant success. Not only did the public receive it with acclamation; by a unanimous verdict of the judges, Méhul, Gossec, and Grétry, the prize offered for the best dramatic work was awarded to Spontini. Shortly after the equal success of his grand opera *Fernand Cortez* (Nov. 28, 1809), Spontini married the daughter of Jean-Baptiste Érard, and in 1810 became director of the Italian Opera, in which capacity he staged Mozart's *Don Giovanni* in its original form for the first time in Paris. He was dismissed in 1812, on charges of financial irregularity, but in 1814 Louis XVIII appointed him court composer, Spontini having refused reinstatement as operatic director in favor of Catalani. He now wrote stage pieces in glorification of the Restoration: *Pélage, ou Le Roi et la paix* (Aug. 23, 1814); *Les Dieux rivaux* (June 21, 1816); this was followed by *Olympie* (Paris Opéra, Dec. 22, 1819). He then accepted the appointment, by King Friedrich Wilhelm III, of court composer and general musical director at Berlin; made his debut there, in the spring of 1820, with his opera *Fernand Cortez,* fairly electrifying his audiences, although, like *Julie, Milton,* and *La Vestale,* it had been heard before in Berlin. Here Spontini's remarkable ability as a conductor had freest scope; besides repeating his earlier works, he wrote for Berlin the festival play *Lalla Rookh* (1821), remodeled into the opera *Nurmahal, oder das Rosenfest von Kaschmir* (Berlin, May 27, 1822), *Alcidor* (Berlin, May 23, 1825), and *Agnes von Hohenstaufen* (Berlin, June 12, 1829); none of these, however, found favor in other German cities. In spite of his success, and the King's continued favor, Spontini's position in Berlin gradually grew untenable; he had been placed on an equality with the intendant of the Royal Theater, and there were frequent misunderstandings and sharp clashes of authority, not mitigated by Spontini's jealousies and dislikes, his overweening self-conceit and despotic temper. Partly through intrigue, partly by reason of his own lack of self-control, he narrowly escaped imprisonment for *lèse-majesté,* and was finally driven out of the theater by the hostile demonstrations of the audience. He retired in 1841, retaining his titles and full pay, but with his prestige and popularity greatly impaired. Thereafter he was inactive as a composer. He returned to Paris, but met with hostility from the director of the Opéra there. In 1844 he conducted a performance (prepared by Wagner) of *La Vestale* at Dresden. Finally, shattered in health, he retired to his native place and devoted his time to public charities. In 1844 the Pope had given him the rank and title of "Conte de Sant' Andrea"; he was a knight of the Prussian "Ordre pour le mérite," member of the Berlin Akademie (1833), and the French Institute (1839), and had received from the Halle Univ. the degree of Dr. phil.

BIBLIOGRAPHY: L. de Loménie, *M. Spontini, par un homme de rien* (Paris, 1841); E. M. Oettinger, *Spontini* (Leipzig, 1843); I. Montanari, *Elogio* (Ancona, 1851); Raoul-Rochette, *Notice historique sur la vie et les ouvrages de M. Spontini* (Paris, 1852); C. Robert, "G. L. P. Spontini" (Berlin, 1883); Ph. Spitta, "Spontini in Berlin," in *Zur Musik* (1892); W. Altmann, "Spontini an der Berliner Oper," *Sammelbände der Internationalen Musik-Gesellschaft* (1903); E. Prout, "Spontini's *La Vestale*," *Monthly Musical Record* 35 (1905); R. Wagner, "Erinnerungen an Spontini," in his *Gesammelte Schriften*, vol. V; A. Pougin, "Les Dernières Années de Spontini," *Rivista Musicale Italiana* XXXIX (1922); C. Radicotti, *Spontini a Berlino* (Ancona, 1925); C. Bouvet, *Spontini* (Paris, 1930); K. Schubert, *Spontinis italienische Schule* (Strasbourg, 1932); A. Ghislanzoni, *G. Spontini* (Rome, 1951); P. Fragapane, *G. Spontini* (Bologna, 1954); *Atti del primo congresso internazionale di studi Spontiniani 1951* (Fabriano, 1954); F. Schlitzer, *Frammenti biografici di G. Spontini* (Siena, 1955); A. Belardinelli, ed., *Documenti spontiniani inediti* (Florence, 1955; 2 vols.); letters of Spontini publ. by Radiciotti and Pfeiffer in *Note d'archivio* (1932).

Sporck, Georges, French composer; b. Paris, April 9, 1870; d. there, Jan. 17, 1943. He studied with Guiraud and Dubois at the Paris Cons., and later with Vincent d'Indy; was officer of Public Instruction; wrote a number of symph. works of a programmatic nature, often with regional color: *Symphonie vivaraise; Islande; Boabdil; Kermesse; Paysages normandes; Esquisses symphoniques; Préludes symphonique; Méditation; Orientale;* etc.; Violin Sonata; piano pieces (*Études symphoniques,* sonatina, etc.); 2 books of songs. He also publ. instructive editions of classical works (Bach, Mozart, Beethoven, Mendelssohn, Schumann, etc.).

Spratlan, Lewis, American composer; b. Miami, Florida, Sept. 5, 1940. He studied composition with Yehudi Wyner, Gunther Schuller and Mel Powell at Yale Univ. (1958–65); taught at Bay Path Junior College (1965–67), Penn State Univ. (1967–70, where he was director of the electronic music studio); in 1970 he became a member of the faculty of Amherst College.

WORKS: an opera, *Dream* (1976–77); *Missa Brevis* for male chorus and instruments (1965); *Flange* for 14 players (1965); *Unsleeping City* for dancers, oboe, trumpet, violin and 3 percussionists (1966); *Structures after Hart Crane* for tenor, piano and tape (1968); *Cantata Domino* for male chorus, winds and tape (1969); *Moonsong* for chorus, flute, piano and 2 percussionists (1969); Wind Quintet (1970); *Serenade* for 6 instruments (1970); *Trope-Fantasy* for oboe, English horn and harpsichord (1970); *Summer Music* for oboe, horn, violin, cello and piano (1971); *Diary Music I* for chamber ensemble (1971); *Dance Suite* for clarinet, violin, guitar and harpsichord (1973); *Night Songs* for soprano, tenor and orch. (1974); *Fantasy* for piano

and chamber ensemble (1974); *3 Ben Jonson Songs* for soprano, flute, violin and cello (1975).

Springer, Hermann, German musicologist; b. Döbeln, May 9, 1872; d. Feb., 1945 (killed during the fighting near Landsberg, in East Germany). He studied philology and music history in Leipzig, Berlin, and Paris; Dr. phil., 1894, with the dissertation *Das altprovenzalische Klagelied* (1895). He entered the Prussian Library Service in 1899, continuing in this position for nearly 40 years; was a member of various learned societies. He publ. *Beethoven und die Musikkritik* (Vienna, 1927); contributed musicographical papers to German and Austrian publications.

Springer, Max, German writer on music and composer; b. Schwendi, Württemberg, Dec. 19, 1877; d. Vienna, Jan. 20, 1954. He attended the Univ. in Prague, and studied music with Klička. In 1910 he was appointed prof. of Gregorian choral singing and organist in the section for church music of the State Academy, Klosterneuburg, near Vienna, and held this post until his retirement shortly before his death. He publ. *Die Kunst der Choralbegleitung* (1907; English translation, 1908) and manuals on liturgical choral singing; *Graduale Romanum* in modern notation (1930); *Kontrapunkt* (Vienna, 1936). He composed 4 symphonies and a great deal of church music, including 8 Masses.

Spross, Charles Gilbert, American organist and composer; b. Poughkeepsie, N.Y., Jan. 6, 1874; d. there, Dec. 23, 1961. He studied piano with X. Scharwenka while the latter was in N.Y.; organ with various teachers; for nearly 40 years was organist at various churches in Poughkeepsie, Paterson, N.J., New York, etc.; was accompanist to celebrated singers (Fremstad, Schumann-Heink, Nordica, Emma Eames, etc.). He published about 250 songs; 5 sacred cantatas; a violin sonata and other chamber music. After his retirement in 1952, he lived in Poughkeepsie.

Spry, Walter, American pianist, pedagogue, and composer; b. Chicago, Feb. 27, 1868; d. Spartanburg, S.C., Sept. 25, 1953. He studied with Leschetizky in Vienna (1889–90), and at the Hochschule für Musik in Berlin (1890–93). In 1905 he established his own music school in Chicago; from 1917 to 1933 taught at the Columbia School of Music there, and from 1933 to his death, at the Converse College School of Music (Spartanburg, S.C.). He wrote mostly for piano; also composed songs.

Squarcialupi, Antonio, renowned Italian organist (called "Antonio degli Organi"); b. Florence, March 27, 1416; d. there, July 6, 1480. He lived in Siena before 1450; a few years later returned to Florence, where he became organist at the church of Santa Maria del Fiore and enjoyed the protection of Lorenzo the Magnificent. He was highly esteemed by Dufay (cf. F. X. Haberl, "Dufay," in the *Vierteljahrsschirft für Musikwissenschaft,* 1885, p. 436). Since none of his works has survived, only oblique reports on their excellence can be adduced, but his name was immortalized by the famous "Squarcialupi Codex," a collection of Florentine polyphonic music of the 14th century, preserved in the Biblioteca Medicea-Laurenziana in Florence (Cod. Pal. 87). The collection was edited by Johannes Wolf and publ. in 1955.

BIBLIOGRAPHY: Bianca Becherini, "Un Canta in panca fiorentino; Antonio di Guido," *Rivista Musicale Italiana* (July-Dec. 1948).

Squire, William Barclay, English musicologist; b. London, Oct. 16, 1855; d. there, Jan. 13, 1927. He received his education in Frankfurt, Germany, and at Pembroke College, Cambridge, (B.A., 1879; M.A., 1902). In 1885 he was placed in charge of the printed music in the British Museum, retiring as Assistant Keeper in 1920; compiled catalogues of music for the British Museum (publ. in 1899 and 1912); also the catalogue of the King's Music Library (3 vols., 1927-29). He edited (with J. A. Fuller-Maitland) *The Fitzwilliam Virginal Book* (2 vols., London, 1899; reprinted N.Y., 1963); edited Byrd's Masses, Purcell's music for harpsichord, and Elizabethan madrigals.

Squire, William Henry, English cellist and composer; b. Ross, Herefordshire, Aug. 8, 1871; d. London, March 17, 1963. His father was an amateur violinist, and he received his primary music education at home; then studied with Hubert Parry at the Royal College of Music; made his debut as a cellist in London on Feb. 12, 1891, and became a popular recitalist in England; wrote a cello concerto and many other cello pieces. He retired in 1941, and lived in London.

Šrámek, Vladimír, Slovak composer; b. Košice, March 10, 1923. He graduated from the Prague Cons.; was active in the music department of the National Museum (1953-63).

WORKS: chamber opera, *Jezdci* (1955); Trio for 2 violins and viola (1957); *3 Serious Compositions* for flute and piano (1958); *Astronauts,* overture, (1959); *Exercises* for flute, oboe, and clarinet (1959); *Tempi* for string quartet (1959); 2 wind quintets (1959, 1960); *Variabilité* for string trio (1960); *Metamorphoses I-VII* for variable ensemble (1961-63); *Metra symmetrica* for wind quintet (1961); *Rondo* for 8 winds (1961); *Smích (Laughter)* for voice, tape, flute, piano, and percussion (1962); *Spectrum I-III,* musical theater (1963-65); *Die Grube,* solo pantomime with bass clarinet, guitar, and percussion (1963); *Kobaltová květina (The Cobalt Flower),* television play for soprano, alto, female chorus, and orch. (1964); *Kaleidoscope* for string trio (1965); *Anticomposizione* for string trio (1966); *Bericht über eine Katastrophe* for chamber ensemble (1966); *Anderer Bericht über eine Katastrophe* for nonet (1969).

Srebotnjak, Alojz, Slovenian composer; b. Postojni, April 27, 1931. He studied composition with Škerjanc at the Ljubljana Music Academy (1953-58); then studied in Siena (1954-57), in Rome (1958-59) and in London (1960-61). He taught at the Pedagogical Academy of Ljubljana (1964-70), and later at the Ljubljana Academy of Music.

WORKS: *Fantasia notturna* for 3 violins, clarinet, and harp (1956); *Music* for strings (1956); *Vojne slike (Army Scenes)* for voice, viola, piano, and percussion (1956); *Pisma (Letters)* for voice and harp (1956); 3 violin sonatinas (1956, 1966, 1967); *Mati (Mother),* cycle for voice and strings (1958); Sinfonietta (1958); *Preludes* for harp (1960); *Invenzione variata* for piano (1961); *Serenata* for flute, clarinet, and bassoon (1961); *Ekstaza smrti (Ecstacy of Death),* cantata (1961); *Monologues* for flute, oboe, horn, timpani, and strings (1962); *6 Pieces* for bassoon and piano (1963); *Kraška suita* for orch. (1964); *Micro-songs* for soprano and 13 instruments (1964); *Antifona* for orch. (1964); *Episodes* for orch. (1965); Harp Concerto (1970); choruses.

Srnka, Jiří, Czech composer; b. Písek, Aug. 19, 1907. He took violin lessons at the Prague Cons. under A. Marák and J. Feld (1922-24); then studied composition there with Otakar Šín (1924-28) and Novák (1928-32); also had instruction in quarter-tone music with Alois Hába. He subsequently devoted himself to film music; produced scores for over 250 films.

WORKS: *Symphonic Fantasy* (1932); Violin Concerto (1957; Olomouc, Sept. 23, 1958); *Historical Pictures from the Písek Region* for amateur string orch. (1961); *Partita* for violin and chamber orch. (1962); Piano Concerto (1968); Concerto for flute, string orch., and piano (1974; Prague, March 8, 1975); 2 string quartets (1928, 1936); Wind Quartet, (1928); a 12-tone *Suite* for violin and piano (1929); String Quintet, with 2 cellos (1930); *Fantasy* for piano (1934); *2 Quarter-tone Pieces* for piano (1936); *3 Pieces* for violin and piano (1961); songs; choruses.

Šrom, Karel, Czech composer; b. Pilsen, Sept. 14, 1904. He studied composition with Jan Zelinka and Karel Hába (1919-25); from 1928 to 1945 wrote music criticism in Prague; then headed the music department of the Czech Radio (1945-50).

WORKS: 2 symphonies (1930, 1951); *Plivník (The Gnome),* scherzo for orch. (1953); *Vzdech na bruslích (A Sigh on Skates),* symph. allegretto (1957); *Hayaya,* orch. suite for adults and children (1961); Piano Concerto (1961); *Etudes* for orch. (1970); Violin Sonata (1920); 3 string quartets (1923, 1941, 1966); *Scherzo Trio* for string trio (1943); *Vynajitka (Fairytale)* for nonet (1952); *Etudes* for nonet (1959); Concertino for 2 flutes, and string quintet or string orch. (1971); *Whiles,* piano trifles (1942); *7 Pieces* for piano (1942); *Black Hour,* cycle for piano (1965). He wrote a biography of Karel Ančerl (Prague, 1968).

Stabile, Mariano, Italian baritone; b. Palermo, May 12, 1888; d. Milan, Jan. 11, 1968. He studied voice at the Santa Cecilia Academy in Rome, and made his debut in Palermo in 1909. For a number of seasons he sang in provincial opera houses in Italy. The turning point in his career came when he was engaged by Toscanini to sing Falstaff in Verdi's opera at La Scala (Dec. 26, 1921). He triumphed and the role became his major success; he sang it more than a thousand times. He was also noted as the interpreter of the part of Rigoletto. He retired from the stage in 1960.

Stäblein, Bruno, German musicologist; b. Munich, May 5, 1895. He studied music theory with Beer-Walbrunn at the Munich Academy of Music and musicology with Adolf Sandberger and Theodor Kroyer at the Univ. of Munich. He then was theater conductor in Coburg and Regensburg, where he was also active as an advisor in musical studies. He was prof. and chairman of the seminars in musicology at the Univ. of Erlangen (1956–63); in 1967 he was appointed Director of the Society for Bavarian Music History; he edited the important collection *Monumenta Monodica Medii Aevi* (Kassel, 1956–70); contributed a number of informative articles on the music of the Middle Ages and the Renaissance; edited reprints of documentary materials pertaining to these epochs. A Festschrift in his honor was issued for his 70th birthday, with a complete list of his publications (Kassel, 1967).

Stachowski, Marek, Polish composer; b. Piekary Ślaşkie, March 21, 1936. He studied piano composition with Penderecki at the State College of Music in Cracow (1963–66); then taught there and at the Jagiellonian Univ. in Cracow. His music is both constructivistically impressionistic and sonoristically coloristic.

WORKS: *Pieć zmysłów i rósa (5 Senses and the Rose)* for voice, flute, horn, trombone and marimbaphone (1964); *Chamber Music* for flute, harp and percussion (1965); 2 string quartets (1965, 1972); *Musica con una battuta del tam-tam (Music with One Stroke of Tam-Tam)* for string orch. and tam-tam (1968); *Lines of Dylan Thomas* for 2 choruses and orch. (1967); *Sequenze concertanti* for orch. (1968); *Neusis II* for 2 choral groups, percussion, cello and double bass (1968); *Chant de l'espoir (Song of Hope),* after Éluard, for narrator, soprano, baritone, mixed chorus, boys' chorus and orch. (1969); *Irisation* for orch. (1969–70; Graz, Austria, Oct. 23, 1970); *Audition* for flute, cello and piano (1970); *Words* for soprano, bass, chorus and orch. (1971); *Solemn Music* for orch. (1973; Warsaw, Sept. 27, 1974); *Extensions,* 3 pieces in sequence for 1, 2 or 3 performers on piano (1971–74); *Thakurian Songs* for chorus and orch. (1974); *Poème sonore* for orch. (1975; Mönchengladbach, Germany, June 24, 1976).

Stade, Friedrich, German organist and writer on music; b. Arnstadt, Jan. 8, 1844; d. Leipzig, June 12, 1928. He studied in Leipzig with Riedel and Richter; served as church organist (1885–95); edited works by Bach; publ. *Vom Musikalisch-Schönen* (1870; 2nd ed., 1904), using the title of the celebrated treatise by Hanslick, but directed against Hanslick's ideas.

Stade, Heinrich Bernhard, German organist and composer; b. Ettischleben, near Arnstadt, May 2, 1816; d. Arnstadt, May 29, 1882. He was organist and town cantor at Arnstadt; restored the organ of St. Bonifaziuskirche, on which Bach had played (1703–07). He publ. *Der wohlvorbereitete Organist, ein Präludien-, Choral- und Postludienbuch,* in 2 parts; other organ music.

Stade, Wilhelm, German organist and composer; b. Halle, Aug. 25, 1817; d. Altenburg, March 24, 1902. He studied with Fr. Schneider in Dessau; was court organist and conductor at Altenburg (1860–91). With Liliencron he ed. *Die Lieder und Sprüche aus der letzten Zeit des Minnesangs* (1854). He composed the celebrated *Vor Jena,* which became a favorite student song; also wrote 2 symphonies, a violin sonata, 7 books of organ pieces, an attractive and unique *Kindersonate* for piano, 4 hands; many sacred and secular choral works.

Staden, Johann, German organist and composer; b. Nuremberg, 1581 (baptized July 2, 1581); d. there, of the plague, 1634 (buried Nov. 15, 1634). He was court organist to the Margrave of Brandenburg from 1604 to 1616, at Kulmbach and Bayreuth; then returned to Nuremburg, where he was church organist until his death. He publ. 4 vols. of *Harmoniae sacrae* (1616, 1621, 1628, 1632); 2 vols., of church music (1625–26; 2nd vol. contains a brief treastise on thoroughbass); 4 vols. of *Haus-Musik* (1623–28; posthumous collected ed. 1648, containing sacred songs with instrumental accompaniment); *Musicalischer Freuden- und Andachtswecker* (1630); *Hertzentrost-Musica* (1630); *Geistlicher Musik-Klang* (1633); 3 books of dance pieces (1618, 1625, and a posthumous ed., 1643); etc. Selected works by Staden were edited by E. Schmitz for the *Denkmäler der Tonkunst in Bayern* 12 and 14 (7.i and 8.i), and by K. Sannwald for Nagel's *Musik-Archiv* (1936).

BIBLIOGRAPHY: *Monatshefte für Musikgeschichte* XV, p. 104ff.

Staden, Sigmund Theophilus, German organist and composer; son of **Johann Staden;** b. Kulmbach (baptized Nov. 6), 1607; d. there, (buried July 30), 1655. As a youth, he studied in Augsburg with the organist Jacob Baumann, and later in Berlin with the resident English player on the viola da gamba, Walter Rowe. Returning to Nuremberg in 1627, he held the position of town piper; in 1634 succeeded his father as organist at the St. Lorenz Church. Staden wrote the earliest extant German opera, *Seelewig,* in an Italian manner; it was produced in Nuremberg in 1644. The text, and separately the music, for voices and thoroughbass, were publ. in Harsdöffer's *Frauenzimmer Gesprächspiele* (vol. IV, 1644); reprinted by Eitner in vol. XIII of *Monatshefte für Musik-Geschichte.* R.Schulz-Dornburg arranged the score for a production at Cologne in 1912. Staden edited Hans Leo Hassler's *Kirchengesänge* (1637), adding 11 songs by his father and 5 songs of his own.

BIBLIOGRAPHY: E. Schmitz, "Zur Bedeutung der Harsdörfferschen *Frauenzimmer-Gesprächspiele,*" in the "Liliencron-Festschrift" (Leipzig, 1910).

Stadler, Anton, famous Austrian clarinet player; b. Bruck an der Leitha, June 28, 1753; d. Vienna, June 15, 1812. He is remembered chiefly for his friendship with Mozart; his name is attached to Mozart's so-called Stadler Quintet (K. 581); he was also helpful to Mozart in the composition of the Clarinet Concerto (K. 622). Stadler himself was a competent composer for clarinet and for the basset horn, on which he was a virtuoso. His brother, **Johann Stadler** (b. Vienna, May 6, 1775; d. there, May 2, 1804) was also a proficient clarinet player.

Stadler, Maximilian, Austrian organist and composer; b. Melk, Aug. 4, 1748; d. Vienna, Nov. 8, 1833. He was ordained priest in the Benedictine Order; was abbot at Lilienfeld (1786–96); held other church positions; settled in Vienna in 1796. He was a friend of Mozart, and took care of Mozart's MS of the Requiem, which he copied at Mozart's death. When the authenticity of the work was called into question by Gottfried Weber and others, Stadler publ. a pamphlet in its defense, *Verteidigung der Echtheit des Mozartschen Requiems* (Vienna, 1825; supplement, 1826). He was also a composer; publ. a cantata, *Die Frühlingsfeier;* much church music; sonatas for organ; songs. His oratorio *Die Befreiung von Jerusalem* (Vienna, 1811) enjoyed considerable success.

BIBLIOGRAPHY: H. Sabel, *Maximilian Stadlers weltliche Werke* (Cologne, 1940); H. Sabel, "Maximilian Stadler und W. A. Mozart," *Neues Mozart-Jahrbuch* 3 (1943).

Stadtfeld, Alexandre, composer; b. Wiesbaden, April 27, 1826; d. Brussels, Nov. 4, 1853. He studied with Fétis at the Brussels Cons., winning the Belgian Prix de Rome in 1849. He composed the operas *Hamlet* (Darmstadt, 1857), *Abu Hassan, L'Illusion,* and *La Pedrina;* 4 symphonies; overtures; 2 concertinos for piano and orch.; string quartet; piano trio; a Mass; a Te Deum; etc.

BIBLIOGRAPHY: M. Weber, *Alexandre Stadtfeld, Leben und Werk* (Bonn, 1969).

Staempfli, Edward, Swiss composer; b. Bern, Feb. 1, 1908. He studied composition with Jarnach in Cologne and Paul Dukas in Paris. He returned to Switzerland at the outbreak of war; in 1954 he went to Berlin. In his music he was influenced chiefly by the French School of composition; later he adopted the Schoenbergian method of composition with 12 tones.

WORKS: the operas, *Ein Traumspiel* (1943), and *Medea* (1954); 3 symphonies (1938, 1942, 1945); 4 concertante symphonies; the ballets, *Choreographisches divertimento* (1945), *Prinzessin und der Schweinehirt* (1944), *Spannungen* (1962); an oratorio, *Der Spiegel der Welt* (1950); cantata, *Nimmermehr (Nevermore)* 1955); 4 piano concertos (1932–63); 3 violin concertos (1936–66); *Ornamente* for 2 flutes, celesta and percussion (1960); 6 string quartets (1926–62); Quartet for clarinet, violin, cello and harp (1965); Duo for clarinet and piano (1970); several choral works.

Stagno, Roberto (real name **Vincenzo Andriolo**), Italian tenor; b. Palermo, Oct. 11, 1840; d. Genoa, April 26, 1897. He studied with Giuseppe Lamperti; sang all over Europe, and was a member of the staff of the Metropolitan Opera Co. in N.Y. during its first season (1883–84). His second wife was the singer **Gemma Bellincioni,** whom he married in 1881; their daughter **Bianca Stagno-Bellincioni** (b. Budapest, Jan. 23, 1888) was also a singer; she was still living in Italy in 1977.

Stahl, Wilhelm, German organist and writer on music; b. Gross Schenkenberg (Lauenburg), April 10, 1872; d. Lübeck, July 5, 1953. He studied with Stiehl in Lübeck; was organist there at St. Matthew's Church (1896–1922) and at the Lübeck Cathedral (1922–39).

WRITINGS: *Die Lübecker Abendmusiken* (Lübeck, 1937); *Franz Tunder und Dietrich Buxtehude* (Leipzig, 1926); *Geschichte der Kirchenmusik in Lübeck* (Lübeck, 1931); *Dietrich Buxtehude* (Kassel, 1937); *Musikgeschichte Lübecks* (with J. Hennings, Kassel, 1951–52).

Stahlbeg, Fritz, German violinist and composer; b. Ketzin, Germany, June 7, 1877; d. Los Angeles, July 23, 1937. He studied in Stuttgart; emigrated to America in 1899, joining the Pittsburgh Symph. Orch. as a violinist; from 1908 was a member of the N.Y. Philharmonic, and in 1912 was also assistant conductor. He went to Hollywood in 1929, and was in charge of the music dept. for Metro-Goldwyn-Mayer Pictures. He wrote 2 symphonies; a symph. suite, *Im Hochland;* violin pieces; songs.

Stählin, Jakob von, German music historian; b. Memmingen, May 10, 1709; d. St. Petersburg, July 6, 1785. He went to Russia in 1735 and remained there until his death. He publ. an important account, *Nachrichten von der Musik in Russland* (Leipzig, 1769–70), which is the prime source of information on Russian music of the 18th century.

Stainer, Jakob, Austrian manufacturer of violins; b. Absam, July 14, 1621; d. there, 1683. The son of poor peasants, he was a shepherd boy; as a youth he began making "Schwegelpfeifen" and other woodwind instruments; then was apprenticed to a lute maker in Innsbruck. He sold his instruments in his native Tyrol, but soon attracted the attention of the Vienna court, and from 1648 was in the service of Archduke Ferdinand Carl. In 1658 he was given the title of violin maker to the court. His fortunes suffered an adverse turn when, in 1669, he was accused of Lutheran leanings, and spent several months in prison; his mind became unbalanced and he died insane. His brother, **Markus Stainer,** made excellent violins and violas. The Stainer violins are highly prized, and differed greatly from Italian models (the oft-repeated assertions that Jakob Stainer worked in Italian shops are not substantiated), and their shape created flute-like tones of great subtlety.

BIBLIOGRAPHY: S. Ruf, *Der Geigenmacher Jacobus Stainer von Absam im Tirol* (Innsbruck, 1872; 2nd ed., 1892); F. Lentner, *Jacob Stainers Lebenslauf im Lichte archivarischer Forschung* (Leipzig, 1898); E. Heron-Allen, "A Pilgrimage to the House of Jacob Stainer," *Musical Times* (Aug. 1900); Princesse A. de la Tour et Taxis, *Le Violon de Jakob Stainer,* (Paris, 1910); W. Senn, *Jakob Stainer, der Geigenmacher zu Absam* (Innsbruck, 1951).

Stainer, Sir John, English organist and composer; b. London, June 6, 1840; d. Verona, March 31, 1901. He was a chorister at St. Paul's Cathedral in London (1847–56); played organ there and in other churches as a youth; studied theory with Charles Steggall; filled various positions as church organist and teacher, and in 1872 was appointed organist of St. Paul's; failing eyesight compelled him to resign in 1888, in which year he was knighted. In 1889 he became prof. at the Univ. of Oxford, retaining this position until his death.

WORKS: the oratorio *Gideon;* the cantatas *The Daughter of Jairus* (Worcester, 1878), *St. Mary Magdalene* (Gloucester, 1882), and *The Crucifixion* (London, 1887); 4 church services; canticles, anthems, songs; publ. a treatise on harmony, another on the organ, *Dictionary of Musical Terms* (with W. A. Barrett; 1876; 4th ed., 1898), etc.; edited (with his daughter, **Cecie Stainer**) *Dufay and His Contemporaries* (1898; 50 selected compositions) and *Early Bodleian Music from about A.D. 1185 to about A.D. 1505* (3 vols.; 1901); *The Music of the Bible* (London, 1879; revised by Fr. W. Galpin, London, 1914; reprint, N.Y., 1970).
BIBLIOGRAPHY: F. G. Edwards, "John Stainer," *Musical Times* (1901).

Stainlein, Comte Louis Charles Georges Corneille de, cellist and composer; b. Hungary, July 3, 1819; d. Angleur-lez-Liège, Belgium, Nov. 22, 1867. A talented cellist, he appeared with success in Germany and France; with Sivori, Ney, and others he gave concerts of chamber music in Paris.
WORKS: Violin Sonata; Piano Trio; 2 string quartets; String Quintet; String Sextet; pieces for cello and piano; male choruses; songs.

Stainov, Petko, Bulgarian composer; b. Kazanluk, Dec. 1, 1896. Despite an almost complete loss of sight in infancy, he played piano by ear; later took music theory lessons with Ernst Münch at Dresden Cons. (1920–24); returned to Bulgaria in 1926 and taught piano at the State Institute for the Blind in Sofia (1927–44). In 1967 he became director of the National Council of Amateur Art and Music.
WORKS: *Thracian Dances* for orch. (1925–26); *Legend,* symph. poem (1927; Sofia, Jan. 1, 1928); *Balkan,* concert overture (1936); 2 symphonies (1945, 1948); *Youth Concert Overture* (1952); a number of choruses.
BIBLIOGRAPHY: V. Krastev, *Petko Stainov* (Sofia, 1957).

Stair, Patty, American organist and composer; b. Cleveland, Nov. 12, 1869; d. there, April 26, 1926. She studied at the Cleveland Cons. (1882–93); filled several positions as organist in Cleveland; from 1902 taught at the Cleveland Cons. She wrote 2 light operas, *The Fair Brigade* and *Sweet Simplicity; Berceuse* for violin and piano; songs.

Stam, Henk, Dutch composer; b. Utrecht, Sept. 26, 1922. He studied instrumentation with Hendrik Andriessen and piano with Jan Wagenaar and André Jurres at the Utrecht Cons.; later studied musicology at the Utrecht Univ. and composition with Fortner in Germany. He taught at the music school in Deventer (1948–54); was director at the Schools of Music in Zeeland (1954–61) and Rotterdam (1962–73).
WORKS: 5 piano sonatinas (1943; 1946; 1946; 1947; 1955); *Rispetti* for baritone and string orch. (1944); 3 string quartets (1947, 1948, 1949); *Histoire de Barbar,* 8 pieces for piano (1948); *Cassation, divertissement satirique* for 2 speakers, chorus, flute, violin, cello, and percussion (1949); Violin Sonata (1950); Sonata for solo violin (1952); *Suite* for violin and piano (1953);

Ouverture Michiel de Ruyter (1957); Sonata for flute, oboe, bassoon, and harpsichord (1959); *Serenade* for solo cello (1959); *5 Bagatelles* for small orch. (1960); Cello Sonata (1966); *Tropic* for flute, oboe and piano (1971); Flute Sonata (1972); *Klachte der Prinsesse van Oranjen* for chorus and 3 trumpets ad lib. (1973); choruses.

Stamaty, Camille-Marie, pianist; b. Rome, March 23, 1811; d. Paris, April 19, 1870. He was of Greek-French origin; his mother, a Frenchwoman, educated him after the death of his father in 1818, and took him to Paris, where he became a pupil of Kalkbrenner; in 1836 he went to Leipzig, where he studied with Mendelssohn. He returned to Paris the next year and remained there as a teacher; among his students were Saint-Saëns and Gottschalk. He publ. a number of didactic works: *Le Rhythme des doigts, Études progressives; Études concertantes; Esquisse; Études pittoresques; 6 Études caractéristiques sur Obéron,* and 12 transcriptions entitled *Souvenir du Conservatoire;* also publ. 3 piano sonatas, a piano trio, a piano concerto, etc.

Stamitz, (Johann) Anton, Bohemian composer; son of **Johann Wenzel Anton Stamitz;** b. Deutsch-Brod (baptized Nov. 27, 1750); place and date of death unknown to any degree of certainty, but probably in Paris, after Oct. 27, 1796. He was a member of the famous musical family of Bohemia; studied violin with his father; with his brother **Carl Stamitz** he went to Strasbourg, and from there to Paris about 1770; made his appearance in Paris playing with his brother at the Concert Spirituel (March 25, 1772). From 1782 to 1789 he was a member of the Royal Chapel Orch. in Versailles. Rodolphe Kreutzer was one of his pupils. He was exceptionally equipped as a composer of instrumental works; he wrote 15 symphonies; 54 quartets, trios and duets for strings; at least 15 violin concertos; several viola concertos, and 5 piano concertos.
BIBLIOGRAPHY: M. Pincherle, *Feuillets d'histoire du violon* (Paris 1927; pp. 110–17).

Stamitz, Carl (Philipp), Bohemian violinist and composer; son and pupil of **Johann Stamitz;** b. Mannheim, 1745 (baptized, May 8, 1745); d. Jena, Nov. 9, 1801. He was trained by his father, and after his death received further instruction with Christian Cannabich, Ignaz Holzbauer, and Fr. X. Richter. In 1762 he was engaged as violinist in the Electoral Orch. at Mannheim; in 1770, in company with his brother **Johann Anton Stamitz,** he went to Strasbourg, and then to Paris; the brothers made their debut at the Concert Spirituel on March 25, 1772; as soon as he arrived in Paris he became concertmaster to the Duc de Noailles; at various times he played in Germany and Austria, and visited Russia. In 1794 he became Kapellmeister at Jena. He left an extraordinary number of works, but a large part of his manuscripts was lost after his death. The putative number of his symphonies is at least 80, among them 26 *Symphonies concertantes,* some 50 concertos for various instruments and chamber music. Hugo Riemann edited 2 symphonies in the *Denkmäler der Tonkunst in Bayern* 15 (8.ii) and chamber music in vols. 27 and 28 (15 and 16) of the same series;

chamber music was edited by Altmann, C. Meyer, Klengel; a "symphonie concertante" by K. Geiringer (Vienna, 1935); the viola concerto was edited by S. Beck (N.Y. Public Library, 1937).

BIBLIOGRAPHY: Fr. C. Kaiser, *Carl Stamitz* (Marburg, 1962; contains a thematic catalog of orchestral works).

Stamitz, Johann Wenzel Anton, Bohemian violinist and one of the creators of the modern style of instrumental music; b. Deutsch-Brod, June 19, 1717; d. Mannheim, March 27, 1757. He went to a Jesuit school in Iglau (1728–34); in 1741 he entered the service of the Margrave of Pfalz, Carl Philipp, and later of his successor, Carl Theodor (from 1743). His playing at the coronation of the Emperor Charles VII on Feb. 12, 1742 created a sensation, and Prince Carl Theodor, who in 1743 became Elector Palatine, engaged him as chamber musician; the court journals reported on his virtuosity in extravagant terms, extolling his ability to perform his own concerto on several different instruments—violin, viola d'amore, violoncello, and contra-violon solo. In 1744 he was named "first court violinist"; in the same year he married Maria Antonia Lüneborn in Mannheim. So widespread was his fame that Baron Grimm published in Paris a satirical pamphlet, *Le Petit Prophète de Boehmisch-Broda,* ridiculing Stamitz's innovations. Stamitz made his mark in Paris, too, when La Poupelinière engaged him in 1754 as leader and composer for his Orchestre de Passy. He appeared at the Concerts Spirituel, in which he produced a symphony with clarinets in the score, a bold innovation at the time. His musical reforms reached in several directions; he conducted the Mannheim Orch., making it the finest in Europe, principally because of the introduction of dynamic nuances, in contrast with the prevailing chiaroscuro of the time; Mozart admired its playing. He had numerous pupils who achieved fame, among them his own sons **Carl** and **Anton,** Cannabich, W. Cramer, and I. Fränzl. As an instrumental composer, he virtually created the Classical sonata form through the introduction of the contrasting elements into a single movement, represented in Classical music by the primary and secondary subjects, and with variety governing the development of the themes. This new type of thematic statement and development became the foundation of musical composition after Bach's time, cultivated by Stamitz's pupils, as well as others, among them Johann Christian Bach, Schobert, Boccherini, Dittersdorf, Eichner, and Gossec. His music was published in Paris, London and Amsterdam still in his lifetime. His works include 74 symphonies; about 12 violin concertos; sonatas for violin solo and for violin with basso continuo. A selection from his symphonies was published by Hugo Riemann in the *Denkmäler der Tonkunst in Bayern* (with an important introduction); in the same series there are found examples of Stamitz's chamber music. Two symphonies were edited by R. Sondheimer (Berlin, 1933); a symphony edited by H. T. David was published by the N.Y. Public Library (1937); 6 duos for violin and cello were brought out by W. Altmann and others.

BIBLIOGRAPHY: The studies of P. Gradenwitz, *Johann Stamitz: das Leben* (Brno, 1936), "The Symphonies of Johann Stamitz," *Music Review* (1940), "The Stamitz Family: Some Errors, Omissions and Falsifications Corrected," *Notes* (Dec. 1949); Paul Nettl, *Der kleine "Prophète von Böhmisch-Broda"* (Esslingen, 1953); E. K. Wolf, *The Symphonies of Johann Stamitz: Authenticity, Chronology and Style* (N.Y. Univ. dissertation, 3 vols., 1972).

Stanford, Sir Charles Villiers, eminent composer and pedagogue; b. Dublin, Sept. 30, 1852; d. London, March 29, 1924. Brought up in an intellectual atmosphere, he was a diligent student in his early youth; took organ lessons in Dublin with Robert Stewart; in 1862 was sent to London, where he studied piano with Ernst Pauer. In 1870 he entered Queen's College, Cambridge, as an organ student; in 1873 became organist at Trinity College there (resigned 1892). For two years (1875–76) he studied composition with Reinecke in Leipzig, and in 1877 with Kiel in Berlin. He received his M.A. degree in Cambridge in 1877; honorary degrees of Mus. Doc. at Oxford (1883) and at Cambridge (1888). In 1883 he was appointed prof. of composition at the Royal College of Music and conductor of the orch. there; in 1887 he also became prof. of music at Cambridge, holding both positions until his death; he was conductor of the Leeds Festivals from 1901 to 1910, and appeared as guest conductor of his own works in Paris, Berlin, Amsterdam, Brussels, etc.; was knighted in 1902. He was an extremely able and industrious composer in a distinctly Romantic style, yet unmistakably national in musical materials both Irish and English. His music, however, remains virtually unknown outside Great Britain.

WORKS: Operas: *The Veiled Prophet of Khorassan* (London, Feb. 6, 1881); *Savonarola* (Hamburg, April 18, 1884); *The Canterbury Pilgrims* (London, April 23, 1884); *Much Ado About Nothing* (London, May 30, 1901); *The Critic, or An Opera Rehearsed* (London, Jan. 14, 1916); *The Traveling Companion* (posthumous; première, Liverpool, April 30, 1925, by an amateur group; 1st professional performance, Bristol, Oct. 25, 1926). For orch.: 7 symphonies: No. 1 (1876), No. 2, *Elegiac* (1882), No. 3, *Irish* (London, May 17, 1887), No. 4 (Berlin, Jan. 14, 1889), No. 5, inspired by *L'Allegro ed il Pensieroso* of Milton (1894), No. 6 (1905), No. 7 (1911); *5 Irish Rhapsodies* (1901–14); 2 sets of Irish Dances; *Overture in the Style of Tragedy; Suite* for violin and orch. (Berlin, Jan. 14, 1889, Joachim soloist); 2 violin concertos; 3 piano concertos; *Irish Concertino* for violin, cello, and orch. Chamber and piano music: 8 string quartets; Piano Quintet; 2 string quintets; 3 piano trios; 2 violin sonatas; 2 cello sonatas; Piano Sonata; 10 *Dances* for piano; 24 Preludes for piano; *Ballade,* for piano. Choral works: *Eden,* oratorio (1891); Mass (1892); 3 sets of Elizabethan pastorals; *6 Irish Folksongs; Songs of the Sea; Songs of the Fleet* (1910); a number of part-songs; *Ode to Discord,* musical caricature of modern composers (London, June 9, 1909); about 200 songs to English words, and 12 songs to texts by Heine, in German. He edited and arranged *Moore's Irish Melodies; Songs of Erin* (3 vols.; 130 folksongs); *Songs of Old Ireland; Irish Songs and Ballads;* for the Irish Literary Society he ed. *The Complete Petrie Collection* (3 vols., 1902–05; 1,582 Irish airs).

WRITINGS: *Studies and Memories* (1908); *Musical Composition* (1911); *Pages from an Unwritten Diary* (1914); *A History of Music* (with Cecil Forsyth; 1916); *Interludes: Records and Reflections* (1922).

BIBLIOGRAPHY: *Musical Times* (Dec. 1898); R. A. Streatfeild, *Musiciens anglais contemporains* (Paris, 1913); J. F. Porte, *Sir Charles V. Stanford* (London, 1921); J. A. Fuller-Maitland, *The Music of Parry and Stanford* (Cambridge, 1934); H. P. Greene, *Charles Villiers Stanford* (London, 1935). A complete list of works is given by Fr. Hudson in *Music Review*, May 1976.

Stange, Hermann, German organist; b. Kiel, Dec. 19, 1835; d. there, June 22, 1914. He studied at the Leipzig Cons.; subsequently served as organist at Rossal College, in England (1860–64); from 1878 was music director, and from 1887 prof., at Kiel Univ., until his retirement in 1911.

Stange, Max, German singing teacher and composer; nephew of **Hermann Stange;** b. Ottensen, May 10, 1856; d. Berlin, Jan. 25, 1932. He was prof. of singing at the Hochschule für Musik, Berlin. He composed *Jauchzet dem Herrn, alle Welt* for baritone solo, chorus, and orch.; *Nachtstück,* for orch.; *An die Heimat,* overture; *Adagio* for cello and orch.; *Serenade* and *Nachtgebet* for string orch.; *Zwei Romanzen,* for string orch.; many male choruses and songs.

Stanley, Albert Augustus, American organist and composer; b. Manville, R.I., May 25, 1851; d. Ann Arbor, Mich., May 19, 1932. He studied at the Leipzig Cons. with Reinecke, Richter, and others; returning to America in 1876, he served as church organist in Providence; in 1888 was appointed Director of the Univ. Musical Society at Ann Arbor, Michigan. He classified the valuable collection of musical instruments given to the Univ. by F. Stearns in 1898, and compiled an extensive catalogue of it (publ. 1918 and 1921). He wrote a cantata, *The City of Freedom* (Boston, 1883); the symph. poems *The Awakening of the Soul* (1896) and *Altis* (1898); anthems; part-songs.

Stanley, John, English organist and composer; b. London, Jan. 17, 1713; d. there, May 19, 1786. Blind from early childhood, he studied organ with Maurice Greene, and soon was able to fill church positions; composed theater music, and publ. a number of instrumental works. In 1779 he succeeded Boyce as Master of the King's Band of Music. He enjoyed the friendship and esteem of Handel, after whose death he conducted the oratorio performances with J. C. Smith.

WORKS: oratorios: *Jephtha* (1757), *Zimri* (Covent Garden, March 12, 1760), *The Fall of Egypt* (Drury Lane, March 23, 1774); dramatic pastoral *Arcadia* (for Goerge III's wedding; 1761); an opera, *Teraminta;* incidental music; songs; etc.; also 8 solos for flute, violin, or harpsichord; 6 concertos for strings; 30 voluntaries for organ; etc.

BIBLIOGRAPHY: G. Finzi, "John Stanley," *Tempo* (Spring 1953); Mollie Sands, "The Problem of *Teraminta*" *Music & Letters* (1952).

Starczewski, Felix, Polish composer; b. Warsaw, May 27, 1868; d. there, Nov. 29, 1945. He studied in Berlin and Paris; returning to Poland, he was engaged in various activities as teacher, composer, and music critic. He wrote an opera in 1 act, *Taniec kwatów* (Warsaw, April 28, 1918); a violin sonata; songs.

Starer, Robert, American composer; b. Vienna, Jan. 8, 1924. He studied music in Vienna; after the *Anschluss* in 1938 went to Jerusalem and studied at the Palestine Cons. there (1938–43). After the end of the war he emigrated to the U.S.; took courses at the Juilliard School of Music, N.Y. (1947–49), and in 1949 became a member of its staff; also taught at N.Y. College of Music (1959–60) and Jewish Theol. Seminary (1962–63); in 1963 he was appointed prof. of music at Brooklyn College.

WORKS: the operas, *The Intruder* (N.Y., Dec. 4, 1956), *Pantagleize* (N.Y., April 7, 1973), *The Last Lover* (Caremoor, N.Y., Aug. 2, 1975); the ballets, *The Dybbuk* (Berlin, 1960), *Samson Agonistes* (N.Y., 1961), *Phaedra* (N.Y., 1962), *The Lady of the House of Sleep* (N.Y., 1968), *Holy Jungle,* ballet for Martha Graham (N.Y., April 2, 1974); 3 symphonies (1950, 1951, 1969); 3 piano concertos (1947, 1953, 1972); *Concerto à tre* for piano, trumpet, trombone and strings (1954); Concerto for viola, strings, and percussion (Geneva, July 3, 1959); Concerto for violin, cello, and orch. (Pittsburgh, Oct. 11, 1968); String Quartet (1947); *5 Miniatures* for woodwinds (1948); Trio for clarinet, cello, and piano (1964); *Variants* for violin and piano (1963); *Profiles in Brass* for brass quartet (N.Y., May 20, 1974); 2 piano sonatas (1949, 1965); *Sketches in Color* for piano (1963); *Fantasia Concertante* for piano 4-hands (1959); *Evanescents* for piano (1975); several cantatas on Biblical subjects; songs. For a list of works see *Composers of the Americas,* vol. 18 (Washington, D.C., 1972).

Stark, Ludwig, German pianist; b. Munich, June 19, 1831; d. Stuttgart, March 22, 1884. He studied with Ignaz and Franz Lachner in Munich; in 1857 was cofounder of the Stuttgart Cons., where he taught singing and theory; with Lebert he edited the *Grosse Klavierschule* (revised by M. Pauer, 1904); brought out a singing method, *Deutsche Liederschule* (1861); also publ. the *Klassischer Hausschatz* (24 transcriptions for piano of movements of classical chamber music works). He wrote a number of sacred and secular choral pieces, piano music, songs, etc.; published *Kunst und Welt* (1844).

Stark, Robert, eminent German clarinetist; b. Klingenthal, Sept. 19, 1847; d. Würzburg, Oct. 29, 1922. He studied at the Dresden Cons.; began his career as an orchestral player at Chemnitz; from 1873 to 1881 played the clarinet in Wiesbaden; then was prof. at the Musikschule in Würzburg. He publ. valuable and practical pieces for his instrument: 3 concertos, *Romanze* for clarinet and orch.; also a *Ballade* for trombone and orch.; *Quintett concertante,* for flute, oboe, clarinet, horn, and bassoon; *Serenade,* for oboe and piano; instructive works: *Die Kunst der Transposition auf der Klarinette, Grosse theoretisch-praktische Kla-*

rinett-Schule, in 2 parts, followed by Part III, *Die hohe Schule des Klarinett-Spieles* (24 virtuoso studies).

Starker, Janos, Hungarian-American cellist; b. Budapest, July 5, 1924. He made his first appearance as a soloist at the age of ten. After graduating from the Budapest Academy of Music, he was first cellist at the Budapest Opera. He left Hungary in 1946; settled in the U.S. in 1948; held the positions of first cellist in the Dallas Symph. Orch., the Metropolitan Opera Orch. and the Chicago Symph. Orch. In 1958 he was appointed prof. at Indiana Univ. in Bloomington. He toured widely in Europe and America in solo recitals.

Starmer, William Wooding, English organist and expert on bells; b. Wellingborough, Nov. 4, 1866; d. Birmingham, Oct. 27, 1927. He studied at the Royal Academy of Music; in 1924 was appointed lecturer on campanology at Birmingham Univ. He publ. several informative papers on the subject of bells in the *Proceedings of the Musical Association.*

Starokadomsky, Mikhail, Russian composer; b. Brest-Litovsk, June 13, 1901; d. Moscow, April 24, 1954. He studied composition with Miaskovsky at the Moscow Cons., graduating in 1928. He remained in Moscow, where he became prof. of orchestration. His works follow the traditional line of Russian nationalism, but several of his early orchestral scores are purely neo-Classical, and in this respect parallel the European developments.
WORKS: opera, *Sot* (1933); operettas, *Three Encounters* (1942), *The Gay Rooster* (1944), and *The Sun Flower* (1947); Concerto for Orch. (Paris Festival of the International Society for Contemporary Music, June 22, 1937); Violin Concerto (Moscow, March 20, 1939); some chamber music; numerous songs for children, by which he is best known in Russia.

Starr, "Ringo" (real name **Richard Starkey**), English drummer, member of the celebrated Liverpudlian vocal quartet The Beatles; b. Liverpool, July 7, 1940 (delivered by forceps on account of his enormous puerperal bulk). His nickname "Ringo" originated from his ostentatious habit of wearing several rings on each of his fingers. As an adolescent he performed menial jobs as a messenger boy for British railways, a barman on a boat, etc. A sickly boy, he spent several years in hospitals to cure an effusion on the lung, but he played drums in ward bands. He spontaneously evolved a rhythmic technique of an overwhelming animal vitality. In 1962 Ringo Starr joined The Beatles; his association with them continued until the dissolution of the group in 1970. His histrionic ability in handling the drums became the most striking visual feature in the beatlophonic ritual, contributing much to mass frenzy that attended their shows wherever The Beatles went.
BIBLIOGRAPHY: Hunter Davies, *The Beatles,* "the authorized biography" (N.Y., 1968); Ned Rorem, "The Beatles," *N.Y. Review of Books* (Jan. 18, 1968); G. Geppert, *Songs der Beatles. Texte und Interpretationen* (2nd ed., Munich, 1968); E. Davies, "The Psychological Characteristics of Beatle Mania," *Journal of the History of Ideas* (April-June 1969); P. McCabe

and R. D. Schonfeld, *Apple to the Core: The Unmaking of the Beatles* (N.Y., 1972); F. Seloron, *Les Beatles* (Paris, 1972); W. Mellers, *Twilight of the Gods: The Music of the Beatles* (N.Y., 1973).

Staryk, Steven, Canadian-American violinist of Ukrainian parentage; b. Toronto, April 28, 1932. He studied with 15 different teachers before and after enrolling in the Royal Cons. of Music in Toronto; at the age of 24 he became concertmaster of the Royal Philharmonic Orch. of London; then concertmaster of the Concertgebouw Orch. of Amsterdam (1960) and of the Chicago Symph. (1963); also taught at the Amsterdam Cons. As a soloist he appeared all over Europe, Canada, the U.S. and in Japan. In 1969 he was appointed prof. at the Oberlin College Cons. in Ohio.

Starzer, Josef, Austrian composer; b. Vienna, 1726; d. there, April 22, 1787. He was a violinist in the court chapel at Vienna; from 1760 to 1770 he was court composer in St. Petersburg, where he produced 2 ballets: *Floras Sieg* and *L'Amore medico.* After his return to Vienna, he became very popular as a composer of ballets, of which he produced about 20; also wrote instrumental music. 2 divertimentos by Starzer are reprinted in the *Denkmäler der Tonkunst in Österreich* 61 (31).
BIBLIOGRAPHY: L. Braun, "Die Balletkomposition von J. Starzer," *Studien zur Musikwissenschaft* 13.

Stasny, Carl Richard, German pianist; b. Mainz, March 16, 1855; d. Boston, April 22, 1920. He studied with Brüll in Vienna, and later was a pupil of Liszt in Weimar (1879–81); while working as piano teacher at Hoch's Cons. in Frankfurt, he made a special study of Schumann's works with Clara Schumann. In 1891 he settled in Boston, where he taught at the New England Cons. He publ. *Finger Training, Scales, Chords and Arpeggios.*

Stasny, Ludwig, popular Bohemian bandmaster; b. Prague, Feb. 26, 1823; d. Frankfurt, Oct. 30, 1883. He studied at the Prague Cons.; was bandmaster in the Austrian Army, and settled in Frankfurt in 1871. He produced 2 operas in Mainz: *Liane* (1851) and *Die beiden Grenadiere* (1879). He was noted for his popular dances (211 opus numbers) and for his potpourris from Wagner's music dramas.

Stasov, Vladimir, famous Russian writer on music; b. St. Petersburg, Jan. 14, 1824; d. there, Oct. 23, 1906. He attended a law school until 1843; in 1845 he became connected with the St. Petersburg Public Library; in 1872 was appointed director of the Dept. of Fine Arts, which post he held until his death. He played a very important role in the emergence of the Russian National School, and was to the end of his days an ardent promoter of Russian music. It was Stasov who first launched the expression "Moguchaya Kuchka" ("mighty little company," in an article publ. on May 24, 1867, in a St. Petersburg newspaper); although he did not specifically name the so-called "Five" (Balakirev, Borodin, Cui, Mussorgsky, Rimsky-Korsakov), these composers became identified with the cause championed by Stasov. When young

Glazunov appeared on the scene, Stasov declared him a natural heir to the Five. His numerous writings, including biographies of Glinka, Mussorgsky, and others, have the value of authenticity. Those publ. between 1847 and 1886 were re-issued in book form in honor of his 70th birthday (3 vols.; St. Petersburg, 1894); a 4th vol., containing essays written between 1886 and 1904, was brought out in 1905; among them, "Russian Music during the Last 25 years" and "Art in the 19th Century" are particularly important. His collected works, including articles on art and other subjects, were publ. in Moscow in 1952. Some of his *Selected Essays on Music* were published in English (London, 1968).

BIBLIOGRAPHY: *To the Memory of Vladimir Stasov* (St. Petersburg, 1910); V. D. Komarova (his niece), *V. V. Stasov* (St. Petersburg, 1927; 2 vols.); T. Livanova, *Stasov and the Russian Classical Opera* (Moscow, 1957); A. Lebedev and A. Solodovnikov, *Vladimir Stasov* (Moscow, 1966).

Statkowski, Roman, Polish composer; b. Szczpiorna, Jan. 5, 1860; d. Warsaw, Nov. 12, 1925. He studied law at the Univ. of Warsaw, graduating in 1886. In 1886 he entered the St. Petersburg Cons. as a student of Soloviev (composition) and Rimsky-Korsakov (orchestration). In 1904 he returned to Warsaw. He wrote the operas *Filenis* (Warsaw, Sept. 14, 1904; won 1st prize at the International Opera Contest in London) and *Maria* (Warsaw, March 1, 1906); *Polonaise* for orch.; *Fantasy* for orch.; 6 string quartets. His style represents a blend of German and Russian influences.

Staudigl, Josef, Jr., baritone, son of **Josef Staudigl, Sr.;** b. Vienna, March 18, 1850; d. Karlsruhe, April, 1916. He studied with Rokitansky at the Vienna Cons.; in 1884–86 was principal baritone at the Metropolitan Opera House, where he created the role of Pogner in the American première of *Die Meistersinger* (Jan. 4, 1886); then sang until his retirement in 1905 at various German theaters (Berlin, Hamburg, Bayreuth, etc.), often together with his wife, the contralto **Gisela Koppmayer,** whom he married in 1885. In the spring of 1898 they sang with the Damrosch-Ellis Opera Co. on an American tour.

Staudigl, Josef, Sr., Austrian bass; b. Wöllersdorf, April 14, 1807; d. insane at Michaelbeuerngrund, near Vienna, March 18, 1861. He gave up the study of medicine to join the chorus at the Vienna court opera, later becoming leading bass; then was at the Theater an der Wien (1845–48); from 1848 till 1854 was again at the court opera.

Stavenhagen, Bernhard, German pianist; b. Greiz, Nov. 24, 1862; d. Geneva, Dec. 25, 1914. He was one of the last pupils of Liszt, with whom he studied in 1885–86. After a tour as pianist in Europe and the U.S., he became court conductor at Weimar in 1895; in 1898 he obtained a similar position in Munich. In 1907 he went to Geneva, where he conducted the municipal orch. He wrote 2 piano concertos and other piano works.

Stearns, Theodore, American composer; b. Berea, Ohio, June 10, 1880; d. Los Angeles, Nov. 1, 1935. He studied in Germany; returning to America he conducted theater performances; in 1932 became a member of the faculty of the Univ. of California, Los Angeles. His opera-ballet, *Snowbird*, to his own libretto, was produced by the Chicago Civic Opera Co. on Jan. 13, 1923; he also wrote a lyric drama, *Atlantis* (1926) and a symph. poem, *Tiberio*.

BIBLIOGRAPHY: E. E. Hipsher, *American Opera and Its Composers* (Philadelphia, 1934, pp. 387–91).

Stebbins, George Waring, American organist and composer; b. Albion, N.Y., June 16, 1869; d. New York, Feb. 21, 1930. He received his early education from his father, the well-known evangelist George C. Stebbins (1846–1945); then studied organ with H. R. Shelley in N.Y. and with Guilmant in Paris. He held various posts as church organist in Brooklyn and N.Y., and published a number of playable pieces for organ (*Wedding Song, A Song of Joy, Scherzando,* etc.), as well as anthems and hymns.

Steber, Eleanor, eminent American soprano; b. Wheeling, West Virginia, July 17, 1916. She studied singing with her mother; then at the New England Cons. of Music in Boston and with Paul Althouse in N.Y. She made her debut as Sophie in *Der Rosenkavalier* with the Metropolitan Opera Co. (Dec. 7, 1940), and remained with the company until 1966; among the parts she sang were Violetta, Marguerite, Pamina, Mimi, Desdemona, Manon, Tosca, and Marie in *Wozzeck*. In 1953 she sang Elsa in *Lohengrin* at the Bayreuth Festival. On Jan. 15, 1958 she created the title role in Samuel Barber's opera *Vanessa* at the Metropolitan Opera.

Stecker, Karel, Czech organist and writer on music; b. Kosmanos, Jan. 22, 1861; d. Mladá Boleslav, March 13, 1918. He studied law and philosophy in Prague; then entered the Organ School of Prague; in 1888 he became lecturer in music history at the Charles Univ., while being employed also as a church organist in Prague. He composed mostly sacred music and organ pieces; also published a history of music in the Czech language (2 vols., 1894, 1903), a treatise on musical form (1905), and an interesting essay on nonthematic improvisation (1903).

BIBLIOGRAPHY: C. Sychra, *Karel Stecker* (Prague, 1948).

Štědroň, Bohumír, Czech musicologist, brother of **Vladimír Štědroň;** b. Vyškov, Dec. 30, 1905. He studied at the Univ. of Brno; then taught courses on music education at the Pedagogical Academy there (1931–39); in 1963 he was appointed prof. at the Univ. of Brno. He published a fundamental monograph on Janáček, *Dílo L. Janáčka*, in Czech and English, (Prague, 1959), and numerous informative articles dealing with various aspects of Czech music. A Festschrift was offered to him on the occasion of his 60th birthday, containing a list of his writings (1965).

Štědroň, Miloš, significant Czech composer; b. Brno, Feb. 9, 1942. He studied composition at the Janáček Academy of Music in Brno (1965–71).

WORKS: chamber opera, *Aparát (The Apparatus)* (after Kafka's *In the Penal Colony,* 1967); a ballet, *Justina* (after de Sade, 1969); *Meditation* for solo bass clarinet (1963); *Via crucis* for flute, bass clarinet, piano, harpsichord, and percussion (1964); *Dyptich* for bass clarinet, piano, strings, and percussion (1967); *Lai* for bass clarinet and timpani (1967); *Utis II* for bass clarinet and tape (1967); *Util II* for bass clarinet, piano, and tape (1968); *Moto Balladico* for orch. (1968); *O, Sancta Caecilia* for double bass and tape (1968); *Musica Ficta* for wind quintet (1968); *Duplum* for bass clarinet and double bass (1968); *Free Landino Jazz* for bass clarinet and piano (1968); *Agrafon* for madrigal choir, Renaissance instruments, and jazz ensemble (1968); *Affeti graziosi* for violin and piano (1969); *Saluti musicali* for bass clarinet and piano (1969); *Four Together (Everyman for Himself),* for bass clarinet, piano, and jazz combo (1969); *Mourning Ceremony,* cantata for chorus, trumpet, oboe, and church bell (1969; Czech Radio, Feb. 21, 1969); *Quiet Platform* for orch. (1969); vocal symph. for soprano, bass-baritone, and orch. (1969); *Verba,* cantata for chorus and 2 trumpets (1969); String Quartet (1970); Concerto for Double Bass and Strings (1971); *Jazz Moments* for piano (1971); *To the Memory of Gershwin* for piano and jazz orch. (1971); *Diagram* for piano and jazz orch. (1971); *Affetti banalissimi* for piano (1971); *Music for Ballet* for chamber orch. (1972); *Kolo (Wheel),* symph. in memory of Yugoslav partisans of World War II (1971–72); *Jazz trium vocum,* free jazz for chorus and jazz ensemble (1972).

Štědroň, Vladimír, Czech composer (brother of **Bohumír Štědroň**); b. Vyškov, March 30, 1900. He studied law in Prague; simultaneously took lessons in composition with Foerster, Novák and Suk at the Prague Cons. (1919–23). He served for many years as a judge, but found time to compose. His music is couched in an unassuming style inspired by native folksongs.

WORKS: *Fidlovačka,* overture (1916); *Fantastic Scherzo* for orch. (1920); 2 string quartets (1920, 1940–45); *Variation Fantasy* for string quartet (1923); *Illusions,* symph. poem (1936); *Little Domestic Suite* for 2 violins and viola (1937); *Janka,* polka for orch. (1962); *Moto baladico* for orch. (1967); *Monologe* for solo flute (1967); *Monologe* for solo horn (1969).

Stefan, Paul (full name **Paul Stefan Grünfeldt**), Czech writer on music; b. Brno, Nov. 25, 1879; d. New York, Nov. 12, 1943. He was educated at the Univ. of Vienna, where he studied music theory with Hermann Grädener. He was employed as a municipal functionary, and at the same time became associated with the modern group of musicians in Vienna; edited the progressive music periodical *Musikblätter des Anbruch,* and was a co-founder of the International Society for Contemporary Music in 1922. After the *Anschluss* he went to Switzerland, and later to Lisbon, eventually emigrating to the U.S. in 1941.

WRITINGS: *Gustav Mahler* (Munich, 1910; 7th ed., 1921; in English, N.Y., 1913); *Die Feindschaft gegen Wagner* (Regensburg, 1918); *Das neue Haus,* a history of the Vienna Opera (Vienna, 1919); *Neue Musik und Wien* (Vienna, 1921; also in English); *Arnold Schönberg* (Vienna, 1924); *Franz Schubert* (Berlin, 1928); *Geschichte der Wiener Oper* (Vienna, 1932); *Arturo Toscanini* (Vienna, 1936; in English, N.Y., 1936; in Italian, Milan, 1937); *Bruno Walter* (Vienna, 1936). He brought out an abridged German translation of Šourek's biography of Dvořák (Vienna, 1935; in English, N.Y., 1941); also various essays on specific works by composers.

Stefani, Jan, Bohemian-Polish composer and conductor; b. Prague, c.1746; d. Warsaw, Feb. 24, 1829. He was Kapellmeister to Count Kinsky and violinist in the orch. of the Vienna Opera. In 1771 he entered the service of Stanislaus Poniatowski in Warsaw Opera. He wrote several Polish operas, of which *Krakowiacy i Górale (The Cracovites and the Mountaineers),* produced in Warsaw on March 1, 1794, was very successful, and remained in the repertory for 65 years. Other operas (all produced in Warsaw) are *Król w kraju rozkoszy* (Feb. 3, 1787); *Wdzieczni paddani panu* (July 24, 1796); *Frozyna* (Feb. 21, 1806); *Rotmistrz Gorecki* (April 3, 1807). He also wrote a great number of polonaises.

Stefani, Józef, Polish composer and conductor, son of **Jan Stefani**; b. Warsaw, April 16, 1800; d. there, March 19, 1867. He was a pupil of his father and of Chopin's teacher, Elsner; conducted ballet at Warsaw Opera, and wrote a number of light operas, which enjoyed a modicum of success during his lifetime: *Dawne czasy* (April 26, 1826); *Lekcja botaniki* (March 15, 1829); *Figle panien* (Aug. 6, 1832); *Talizman* (Dec. 7, 1849); *Zyd wieczny tulacz* (Jan. 1, 1850); *Piorun* (May 21, 1856); *Trwoga wieczorna* (posthumous, July 25, 1872). He also wrote church music, which was often performed in religious services in Poland.

Stefánsson, Fjölnir, Icelandic composer; b. Reykjavik, Oct. 9, 1930. He studied cello and took theory lessons with Jón Thórarinsson at the Reykjavík Music School, graduating in 1954; then went to England, where he studied composition with Mátyás Seiber (1954–58). Returning to Iceland, he taught at his alma mater (1958–68); in 1968 was appointed a member of the board of the Icelandic Music Information Center. He composed Trio for flute, clarinet and bassoon (1951); Violin Sonata (1954); Duo for oboe and clarinet (1974); numerous arrangements of Icelandic folksongs for chorus.

Steffan , Joseph Anton, Austrian composer; b. Kopidlno, Bohemia, March 14, 1726; d. Vienna, April 12, 1797. A pupil of Wagenseil, he settled in Vienna, where he was a renowned teacher; among his pupils were the princesses Marie Antoinette (later Queen of France) and Caroline (later Queen of Naples). He wrote some church music and numerous works for piano (divertimentos, concertos, and sonatas). Steffan is historically important for his songs, *Sammlung deutscher Lieder* (4 books), which are among the best of that time. Specimens were publ. by M. Friedlander in *Das deutsche Lied im 18. Jahrhundert* (1902); see also *Denkmäler der Tonkunst in Österreich* 79 (42.ii).

Steffani, Abbate Agostino, Italian composer; b. Castelfranco Veneto, July 25, 1654; d. Frankfurt, Feb. 12, 1728. He began his musical career as a choirboy at Padua, where his beautiful soprano voice so charmed Count Tattenbach that the latter obtained permission to take him to the Electoral Court at Munich, where he was trained by Kerll from 1668-71; from 1672-74 he studied at Rome with E. Bernabei at the Elector's expense, and in 1675 was appointed court organist at Munich. In 1678-79 he visited Paris, where he made an advantageous study of Lully's music. He took holy orders in 1680 and was made titular Abbot of Lepsing in 1682. In 1681 he became director of the Elector's chamber music (together with G. A. Bernabei, his former teacher's son); in 1688 he became court Kapellmeister at Hannover. His services as a diplomat were also in demand; in 1696 he brought to a triumphant conclusion the delicate negotiations for the creation of a ninth Elector of Braunschweig, and was rewarded by the appointment of Bishop of Spiga *(in partibus);* from 1698 he was privy councillor and papal protonotary at Düsseldorf, though still holding his position as Kapellmeister at Hannover till 1711, when he joyfully relinquished it to Handel. Some works of the later epoch were produced under the name of his copyist, **Gregorio Piva.**
   WORKS: operas (performed in Munich): *Marco Aurelio* (1680); *Solone* (1685); *Audacia e rispetto* (1685); *Servio Tullio* (1686); *Alarico* (1687); *Niobe* (1688); at Hannover: *Enrico detto il Leone* (Jan. 30, 1689); *La Lotta d'Ercole con Acheloo* (1689); *La Superbia d'Alessandro* (1690; revised in 1691 as *Il Zelo di Leonato*); *Orlando generoso* (1691); *Le Rivali concordi, or Atlanta* (1693); *La Libertà contenta* (1693); *I Baccanali* (1695); *Il Trionfo del fato, o Le Glorie d' Enea* (1695; given at Braunschweig in 1716 as *Enea in Italia, o Didone*); *Briseide* (1696); for Düsseldorf: *Arminio* (1707); *Tassilone* (1709); and *Amor vien dal destino ossia Il Turno Aricino* (1709). Other works: *Psalmodia vespertina a 8* (1674); *Sacer Janus Quadrifrons* (1685; motets *a* 5, with continuo; any voice may be omitted at pleasure); *Sonate da camera a 2 violini, alto e continuo* (1679); *Duetti da camera a soprano e contralto con il basso continuo* (1683; historically important and intrinsically valuable); and the pamphlet *Quanta certezza habbia da' suoi principii la musica* (Amsterdam, 1695; German by Werckmeister, 1699, and Albrecht, 1760). In MS he left 85 chamber duets with continuo (16 of these, with 2 scherzi for 1 voice with instruments and 2 church cantatas, were publ. by A. Einstein and A. Sandberger in *Denkmäler der Tonkunst in Bayern* 11 (6.ii); a chamber cantata for soprano and continuo (publ. by T. W. Werner in *Zeitschrift für Musikwissenschaft* I/8); a famous Stabat Mater for 6 voices and 2 violins, 3 violas, cello, and continuo (organ); also 4 vols. of chamber cantatas and arias. H. Riemann publ. *Alarico* (complete score; also full bibliography of all Steffani's operas) in *Denkmäler der Tonkunst in Bayern* 21 (11.ii); selections from other operas in vol. 23 (12.ii).
   BIBLIOGRAPHY: *Memoirs of the Life of A. S.* (authorship attributed to John Hawkins; London, 18th century); F. M. Rudhart, *Geschichte der Oper am Hofe zu München* (Freising, 1865); G. Fischer, *Musik in Hannover* (2nd ed., Hannover, 1902); A. Neisser, *Servio Tullio von A. S.* (dissertation, Leipzig, 1902); A. Untersteiner, "A. S.," *Rivista Musicale Italiana* 14 (1907); P. Hiltebrandt, *Preussen und die römische Kurie* (Berlin, 1910; vol. I contains material concerning S.); H. Riemann, "A. S. als Opernkomponist," in *Denkmäler der Tonkunst in Bayern* 23 (12.ii; 1912); R. de Rensis, "A. S." *Musica d'Oggi* (1921); T. W. Werner, "A. S.s Operntheater in Hannover," *Archive für Musikforschung* (1938); A. Einstein, in *Kirchenmusikalisches Jahrbuch* 23 (1910), *Neue Musik-Zeitung* (1928), and in *Zeitschrift der Internationalen Musik-Gesellschaft* X/6; J. Loschelder, "Aus Düsseldorfs italienischer Zeit," in K. G. Fellerer, ed., *Beiträge zur Musikgeschichte der Stadt Düsseldorf* (Cologne, 1952); P. Keppler, "Agostino Steffani's Hannover Operas and a Rediscovered Catalogue," in H. S. Powers, *Studies in Music History* (Princeton, N.J., 1968).

Steffen, Wolfgang, German composer; b. Neuhaldensleben, April 28, 1923. He studied at the Cons. in Berlin (1946-49) and with Tiessen at the Musikhochschule there (1949-53); after graduation, he devoted himself principally to the promotion of new music.
   WORKS: *Serenade* for flute and string orch. (1948); Sinfonietta for string orch. (1949); *Dance Impressions I* for piano and orch. (1950) and *II* for piano, percussion, and string orch. (1970); *Intrada seria* for orch. (1953); *Méditations de la nuit* for small orch. (1954); a ballet, *Der göttliche Tänzer* (1954); *Aus dem Lebensbuch eines Tänzers,* ballet suite (1954); Piano Concerto (1955); Violin Concerto (1966); Harpsichord Concerto (1969); *Polychromie* for piano and 10 instruments (1970); *Klangsegmente* for cymbal, harp, harpsichord, and orch. (1973-74); *Sinfonia da camera* (1976); *Nachtwachen,* cantata for chorus, flute, oboe, clarinet, and string quintet (1954); *3 Lieder* for soprano and orch. (1955); *Hermann-Hesse-Zyklus* for chorus, viola, percussion, piano, and organ (1973); *Botschaft,* oratorio (1975-76); Trio for oboe, clarinet, and bassoon (1947); *Theme with 8 Variations* for string quartet (1948); Trio for clarinet, cello, and piano (1959); *Diagram* for viola (or cello) and piano (1965); Wind Quintet (1966); *Jeu* for violin and piano (1967); Trio for flute, cello, and piano (1971); *Triplum 72* for flute, piano, and percussion (1972); *Tetraphonie* for flute ensemble (1974); *Trilogie 75* for bandoneon, flute, and percussion (1975); *Music* for piano and 7 players (1975); for piano: *Fantasy* (1947); Sonata (1955); *Reihenproportionen* (1961); *Notturno* for 4 hands (1968); *Les Spirales* (1969); choruses; songs.

Steggall, Charles, English organist and composer; b. London, June 3, 1826; d. there, June 7, 1905. He was a pupil of Sterndale Bennett at the Royal Academy of Music; became prof. there in 1851. After 52 years of continued service, he resigned his professorship in 1903. He wrote anthems and other religious music; edited *Church Psalmody* (1848), *Hymns Ancient and Modern* (1889), etc. His son **Reginald Steggall** (b. London, April 17, 1867; d. there, Nov. 16, 1938) was also a pupil at the Royal Academy of Music, where he taught organ playing from 1895. He wrote a number of organ pieces; a Mass; a symphony; orchestral variations and overtures.

Steglich, Rudolf, German musicologist; b. Rats-Damnitz, Feb. 18, 1886; d. Scheinfeld, July 8, 1976. Studied musicology with Hugo Riemann in Leipzig (Dr. phil., 1911). He was in the German Army during World War I; then was active as music critic of the Hannover *Anzeiger* (1919–29); in 1929, appointed to the faculty of the Univ. of Erlangen. He was editor of the *Händel-Jahrbuch* (1928–33) and of the *Archiv für Musikforschung* (1936–40); edited works by Bach's sons, old German song collections, etc.

WRITINGS: *Die "Quaestiones in musica": ein Choraltraktat des zentralen Mittelaters* (Leipzig, 1911); *Die elementare Dynamik des musikalischen Rhythmus* (Leipzig, 1930); *J. S. Bach* (Potsdam, 1935); *G. F. Händel: Leben und Werk* (Leipzig, 1939); *Wege zu Bach* (Regensburg, 1949); numerous essays.

Stegmayer, Ferdinand, Austrian conductor and composer; b. Vienna, Aug. 25, 1803; d. there, May 6, 1863. He was the son of **Matthaeus Stegmayer;** studied music with Seyfried; was chorusmaster at Linz and Vienna; then conductor of a German opera troupe in Paris (1829–30). After filling various engagements as theater conductor in Leipzig, Bremen, and Prague, he settled in Vienna in 1848; was teacher of singing at the Vienna Cons.; co-founder, with August Schmidt, of the Vienna Singakademie (1858). He wrote church music, piano pieces, and songs.

Stegmayer, Matthaeus, Austrian singer and composer; b. Vienna, April 29, 1771; d. there, May 10, 1820. He was a chorister in the Dominican church, Vienna; then sang in small provincial theatrical companies, returning to Vienna in 1793; made his debut as a singer at Schikaneder's theater Auf der Wieden in 1796; in 1804 became chorusmaster at the new Theater an der Wien. He was the first to use the term "quodlibet" for theatrical light pieces; arranged Mozart's *Schauspieldirektor* (1814); composed an operetta, *Der Salzburger Hans und sein Sohn, der Hansl* (Vienna, Nov. 14, 1800), and contributed separate numbers to many others (mainly with Ignaz von Seyfried). He wrote the text for the quodlibet *Rochus Pumpernickel,* produced at the Theater an der Wien on Jan. 28, 1809, with music assembled by Seyfried from various works, including pieces by Haydn and Mozart. It was so successful that he followed it with a sequel, *Die Familie Pumpernickel* (Feb. 13, 1810). A complete list of his works as composer, joint composer, and librettist is found in Anton Bauer, *Opern und Operetten in Wien* (Vienna, 1955).

Stehle, J. Gustav Eduard, German organist and composer; b. Steinhausen, Germany, Feb. 17, 1839; d. St. Gall, Switzerland, June 21, 1915. He was organist in Rorschach (1869–74); in 1874 he settled in Switzerland as music director at the St. Gall Cathedral. His cathedral choir of 140 voices was regarded as one of the finest in Europe. For 25 years he also was editor of the *Chorwächter.* He wrote a great deal of religious music: an oratorio, *Legende von der heiligen Cäcilia;* a cantata, *Lumen de Coelo* (to words by Pope Leo

XIII); *Die Nonnen von Compiègne,* for double chorus; *Frithjofs Heimkehr,* for solo, male quartet, and mixed chorus; *Die Heinzelmännchen,* humorous choral ballad for double chorus a cappella; a symph. poem for organ, *Saul;* 438 preludes in the church modes, etc.

BIBLIOGRAPHY: A. Locher, *J.-G.-E. Stehlé* (Strasbourg, 1928).

Stehle, Sophie, German soprano; b. Hohenzollern-Sigmaringern, May 15, 1838; d. Schloss Harterode, near Hannover, Oct. 4, 1921. She was a prominent member of the Munich Opera, where she created the roles of Fricka in *Das Rheingold* (Sept. 22, 1869) and Brünnhilde in *Die Walküre* (June 26, 1870). She also distinguished herself in other Wagnerian parts (Elisabeth, Elsa, Eva).

Stehman, Jacques, Belgian composer; b. Brussels, July 8, 1912; d. Heist-aan-Zee, May 20, 1975. He studied piano with Del Pueyo, composition with Jean Absil, and orchestration with Paul Gilson at the Brussels Cons.; then taught harmony there. His music is cautiously modernistic, with engaging touches of obsolescent jazz.

WORKS: *Symphonie de poche* (1950); *Musique de mai* for strings (1961); *Dialogues* for harp and small orch. (1964); *Melos* for mezzo-soprano, flute and strings (1968); *Escapades* for piano and string orch. (1968); Piano Concerto (1965–72); *Lamento* for cello and piano (1947); *Burlesques en 6 formes* for piano (1934); *Colloque* for 2 pianos (1943); *3 Rythmes* for 2 pianos (1955); *Montmartre* for 2 pianos (1975); songs.

Steibelt, Daniel, renowned German pianist and composer; b. Berlin, Oct. 22, 1765; d. St. Petersburg, Oct. 2, 1823. He studied with Kirnberger (piano and theory); published sonatas for piano and violin, as opp. 1 and 2 (Munich, 1788); then gave concerts in Germany, proceeding to Paris in 1790. There he found himself in strong competition with Ignaz Pleyel, but won out, and became a favorite piano teacher in Paris. His opera *Roméo et Juliette* was produced as the Théâtre Feydeau on Sept. 10, 1793 and, despite the revolutionary turmoil of the time, achieved excellent success. He left Paris in 1796, going to Holland, and then to London; became a soloist at Salomon's Concerts; played the solo part of his 3rd Piano Concerto (March 19, 1798), with its rousing finale *L'Orage, précédé d'un rondeau pastoral,* which as a piano solo became as popular as Koczwara's *Battle of Prague.* In London he produced an opera, *Albert and Adelaide* (Covent Garden, Dec. 11, 1798); returned to Germany in 1799; then proceeded to Vienna, where he challenged Beethoven to a contest of skill, but was easily bested. His next destination was Paris, where he produced Haydn's *Creation* (Dec. 24, 1800), with an orchestra of 156 players, in an arrangement by Steibelt himself; Napoleon was present at that performance. A ballet by Steibelt, *Le Retour de Zéphire,* was produced at the Paris Opéra on March 3, 1802; he then went to London, where he staged 2 ballets, *Le Jugement du berger Paris* (May 24, 1804) and *La Belle Laitère* (Jan. 26, 1805). Returning once more to Paris, he wrote a festive intermezzo, *La Fête de Mars,* to celebrate Napoleon's victory at Austerlitz; it was produced at the Opéra on March 4, 1806. In the autumn of 1808 he gave concerts in Frankfurt and Dresden; in the spring of 1809 he went to Russia by way of Warsaw, Vilna, and Riga. In St. Petersburg he produced a new opera, *Cendrillon*, to a French libretto (Oct. 26, 1810), and 2 ballets. Although he held the position of chapelmaster at the court of Czar Alexander I, he did not prosper, and at his death a public subscription was undertaken to help his family. He publ. 5 piano concertos, 37 sonatas with violin, 29 sonatas and sonatinas for piano solo, 15 rondos, 18 fantasias, etc. His *Méthode de Piano* had considerable vogue.

BIBLIOGRAPHY: G. Müller, *Daniel Steibelt, sein Leben und seine Klavierwerke* (Strasbourg, 1933).

Steigleder, Johann Ulrich, German organist and composer; b. Schwäbisch-Hall, March 21, 1593; d. Stuttgart, Oct. 10, 1635. He was organist at Lindau and then at Stuttgart (1617), serving also as musician to the court of Württemberg. Two of his publications survive: *Ricercar Tabulatura, organis et organoedis* (1624) and *Tabulatur-Buch*, containing 40 variations for organ and other instruments, upon the Lord's Prayer (Strasbourg, 1627). Two variations are to be found in Ritter's *Geschichte des Orgelspiels im 14.-18. Jahrhundert* (1884; new ed. by Frotscher, 1933).

BIBLIOGRAPHY: E. Emsheimer, *J. U. Steigleder* (dissertation, Kassel, 1928).

Stein, Erwin, Austrian conductor and editor; b. Vienna, Nov. 7, 1885; d. London, July 19, 1958. He studied composition with Schoenberg in Vienna (1905–10) and became Schoenberg's early champion. From 1910 to 1914 he conducted various theater orchestras in Austria and Germany; returning to Vienna he was a member, with Schoenberg, Berg and Anton von Webern, of the famous Society for Musical Private Performances, which excluded music critics from attendance (1920–23). He then became an editor for Univeral Edition, Vienna, where he was instrumental in bringing out works by the composers of the modern Vienna School. He also conducted a tour with a Vienna group named Pierrot Lunaire Ensemble. After the *Anschluss* in 1938 he went to London and joined the music publishing firm of Boosey & Hawkes. He contributed a fundamental paper on Schoenberg's method of composition with 12 tones, "Neue Formprinzipien," published in *Anbruch* (1924). He published a selective collection of Schoenberg's letters (Mainz, 1958; in English, London, 1964); a collection of essays, *Orpheus in New Guises* (London, 1953); his theoretical monograph, *Musik, Form und Darstellung* was published posthumously, first in English as *Form and Performance* (London, 1962) and later in German (Munich, 1964).

Stein, Fritz, eminent German musicologist; b. Gerlachsheim, Baden, Dec. 17, 1879; d. Berlin, Nov. 14, 1961. He studied theology in Karlsruhe, then took courses in musicology with Ph. Wolfrum in Heidelberg; subsequently went to Leipzig, where he studied organ with Straube; also attended Riemann's lectures at the Univ. of Leipzig; Dr. phil. (Heidelberg, 1910) with the dissertation *Zur Geschichte der Musik in Heidelberg* (publ. 1912; new ed. 1921, as *Geschichte*

des Musikwesens in Heidelberg bis zum Ende des 18. Jahrhunderts). In 1913 he was appointed prof. of musicology at the Univ. of Jena; was in the German Army during World War I and directed a male chorus for the troops at the front. He was prof. at the Kiel Univ. from 1918 to 1925; in 1933 he became director of the Hochschule für Musik in Berlin, holding this position to the end of the war in 1945. He achieved notoriety when he discovered in the library of the Univ. of Jena the parts of a symphony, marked by an unknown copyist as a work by Beethoven. The symphony became famous as the "Jena Symphony" and was hailed by many as a genuine discovery; the score was publ. by Breitkopf & Härtel in 1911, and performances followed all over the world; Stein publ. his own exegesis of it as "Eine unbekannte Jugendsymphonie Beethovens?" in the *Sammelbände der Internationalen Musik-Gesellschaft* (1911). Doubts of its authenticity were raised, but it was not until 1957 that the American musicologist H. C. Robbins Landon succeeded in locating the original manuscript, proving that the "Jena Symphony" was in reality the work of Friedrich Witt (1770–1837). Stein publ. a monograph on Max Reger (Potsdam, 1939) and *Max Reger: sein Leben in Bildern* (a pictorial biography; Leipzig, 1941; 2nd ed., 1956); brought out a thematic catalogue of Reger's works (Leipzig, 1934; definitive ed., 1953); edited works by Johann Christian Bach, Telemann, Handel, Beethoven, etc.; contributed essays to numerous learned publications. A Festschrift was publ. for him on his 60th birthday (1939).

Stein, Horst, German conductor; b. Elberfeld, May 2, 1928. He studied at the Hochschule für Musik in Cologne, and at the age 23 was engaged as a conductor at the Hamburg State Opera (1951–55); then was on the staff of the State Opera in Berlin (1955–61) and again at the Hamburg Opera (1961–63). From 1963 to 1970 he was music director and conductor at the National Theater in Mannheim; from 1970 to 1973 he was music director at the Hamburg State Opera. He also conducted at the Bayreuth Festival, and appeared as guest conductor at the major European opera houses, in South America and in the U.S. He is regarded as one of the most efficient and competent opera conductors of his generation.

Stein, Johann Andreas, German inventor of the "German" (Viennese) piano action; b. Heidelsheim, Palatinate, May 6, 1728; d. Augsburg, Feb. 29, 1792. He was trained in the Strasbourg workshop of J. A. Silbermann (1748–49). In 1751 he settled in Augsburg, where he built the organ of the Barfüsserkirche; was appointed organist there in 1757. He spent a few months in Paris in 1758 before returning to Augsburg. He experimented with various types of keyboard instruments; invented a "polytoni-clavichordium" (1769), a "melodika" (1772), a "vis-à-vis," and a "Saitenharmonika" (1789). The business was carried on by his son, **Andreas Stein,** and his daughter, **Nanette Stein Streicher** (wife of the Austrian piano maker, J. B. Streicher), who moved it to Vienna in 1802.

BIBLIOGRAPHY: F. Luib, *Biographische Skizze des J. A. Stein* (1886); T. Bolte, *Die Musikerfamilien Stein und Streicher* (Vienna, 1917); K. A. Fischer, *J. A. Stein*

(Augsburg, 1932); Eva Hertz, *J. A. Stein: ein Beitrag zur Geschichte des Klavierbaues* (Würzburg, 1937); Donald Boalch, *Makers of the Harpsichord and Clavichord, 1440 to 1840* (London, 1956; pp. 117-18).

Stein, Leon, American composer and conductor; b. Chicago, Sept. 18, 1910. He studied violin at the American Cons. in Chicago (1922-27), and theory at Crane Junior College in Chicago (1927-29); took private lessons in composition with Leo Sowerby, in orchestration with Eric DeLamarter, and in conducting under Frederick Stock and Hans Lange (1937-40); received his M.M. in 1935 and a Ph.D. in 1949 from De Paul School of Music. In 1931 he was appointed to the faculty of the De Paul School, and taught there for 45 years; served as director of its graduate division and Chairman of the Department of Theory and Composition (1948-66), and Dean of the School of Music (1966-76); was head of the Institute of Music of the College of Jewish Studies in Chicago (1952-57); also conducted the De Paul Univ. Community Orch. His music is academic, but not devoid of occasional modernities.

WORKS: 2 operas: *The Fisherman's Wife* (1954; St. Joseph, Mich., Jan. 10, 1955) and *Deirdre,* after Yeats (1956; performed with a piano reduction, Chicago, May 18, 1957); 2 ballets for piano: *Exodus* (1939; Chicago, Jan. 29, 1939) and *Doubt* (1940; Chicago, Jan. 21, 1940); *Prelude and Fugue* for orch. (1935); *Passacaglia* for orch. (1936); *Sinfonietta* for string orch. (1938); Violin Concerto (1938-39; Chicago, Dec. 3, 1948); 4 symphonies: No. 1 (1940), No. 2 (1942), No. 3 (1950-51), No. 4 (1974); *3 Hassidic Dances* for orch. (1940-41; Chicago, April 13, 1942); *Triptych on 3 Poems of Walt Whitman* for orch. (1943; Chicago, March 29, 1949); *Great Lakes Suite* for small orch. (1943-44); *Rhapsody* for solo flute, harp, and string orch. (1954; Chicago, Nov. 8, 1955); *Adagio and Rondo Ebraico* for orch. (1957); *Then Shall the Dust Return* for orch. (1971); *Adagio and Dance* for piano trio (1931); Sonatina for 2 violins (1931); Violin Sonata (1932); 5 string quartets (1933, 1962, 1964, 1965, 1967); *Adagio and Hassidic Dance* for solo flute (1935); Wind Quintet (1936); *12 Preludes* for violin and piano (1942-49); Trio for 3 trumpets (1953); Quintet for saxophone and string quartet (1957); Sextet for saxophone and wind quintet (1958); Quartet for trombones (1960); 12 solo sonatas: for violin (1960), for flute (1968), and for oboe, clarinet, bassoon, horn, trumpet, trombone, tuba, viola, cello and double bass (1969-70); Trio for violin, saxophone or viola, and piano (1961); *Suite* for saxophone quartet (1962); Saxophone Sonata (1967); Trio for clarinet, saxophone and piano (1969); *Phantasy* for solo saxophone (1970); *Suite* for wind quintet (1970); Brass Quintet (1975); Quintet for harp and string quartet (1976-77). He published *Structure and Style* (Evanston, 1962) and *Anthology of Musical Forms* (Evanston, 1962).

Stein, Leonard, eminent American music scholar; b. Los Angeles, Dec. 1, 1916. He attended Los Angeles City College (1933-36) and studied piano privately with Richard Buhlig (1936-39); enrolled in the class of composition and musical analysis with Arnold Schoenberg at the Univ. of Southern California (1935-36) and at the Univ. of California at Los Angeles (1936-42); in 1939-42 was Schoenberg's teaching assistant; received the degrees of Bachelor of Arts (1939) and a Master of Music (1941) from the University of California at Los Angeles, and the degree of Doctor of Musical Arts from the Univ. of Southern California (1965); was the recipient of a Guggenheim Fellowhip (1965-66). He held several teaching positions: at Occidental College (1946-48); Los Angeles City College (1948-60); Pomona College (1961-62); Univ. of California at Los Angeles (1962-64); the Claremont Graduate School (1963-67); Univ. of California at San Diego (1966); California State College at Dominguez Hills (1967-70); in 1970 was appointed member of the music faculty of the California Institute of the Arts; in 1975 became adjunct prof. in the School of Music at the Univ. of Southern California. In 1975 he was elected Director of the Arnold Schoenberg Institute of Southern California, Los Angeles, and Editorial Director of the *Journal of the Arnold Schoenberg Institute* I/1 (Oct. 1976). He contributed a number of articles on the proper performance of piano works by Schoenberg; member of the editorial board, *Sämtliche Werke* (Mainz and Vienna, vol. 1, 1966); edited Schoenberg's *Nachtwandler* (1969), Piano Concerto (1972); *Ode to Napoleon Bonaparte* (1973); *Brettl-Lieder* (1974); edited and completed Schoenberg's pedagogical works: *Preliminary Exercises in Counterpoint* (1963); *Models for Beginners in Composition* (revision of the text, 1972), *Structural Functions of Harmony* (revision, 1969); *Style and Idea. Selected Writings of Arnold Schoenberg* (London, 1975; received the 1976 ASCAP award).

Stein, Richard Heinrich, German music theorist and composer; b. Halle, Feb. 28, 1882; d. Santa Brigida, Canary Islands, Aug. 11, 1942. He studied law and music; Dr. phil. (Erlangen, 1911) with the thesis, *Die psychologischen Grundlagen der Ethik.* From 1914 to 1919 he lived in Spain; from 1920 to 1932 taught musical subjects in Berlin. In 1933 he left Germany and went to the Canary Islands, where he remained until his death. He was a composer of experimental tendencies; his *Zwei Konzertstücke* for cello and piano, op. 26 (1906), was the first composition containing quarter-tones to be published. In 1909 he wrote a brochure giving a detailed exposition of his quarter-tone system, and in 1914 he built a quarter-tone clarinet. He composed about 100 piano pieces and about 50 songs; *Scherzo fantastico* for orch.; publ. the books *La Música moderna* (Barcelona, 1918; in Spanish and German), *Grieg* (1921), *Tschaikowsky* (1927).

Steinbach, Fritz, German conductor; b. Grünsfeld, June 17, 1855; d. Munich, Aug. 13, 1916. He studied in Leipzig, Vienna, and Karlsruhe. In 1880 he was appointed 2nd Kapellmeister in Mainz, where his interpretations of Beethoven and Brahms won praise; Brahms recommended him as successor to Hans von Bülow at Meiningen (1886); in 1902 he went to Cologne as director of the cons. there; resigned in 1914 and settled in Munich.

Steinbauer, Othmar, Austrian violinist and composer; b. Vienna, Nov. 6, 1895; d. Altenburg, Sept. 5,

1962. He studied violin at the Vienna Music Academy; founded the Chamber Concert Society of Vienna, playing and conducting works of the modern Viennese school. He publ. a theoretical treatise, *Das Wesen der Tonalität* (Munich, 1928). In 1938 he founded the Musikschule der Stadt Wien. After 1945 he devoted himself mainly to manufacturing new instruments; constructed a violin specially adapted for easy performance by amateurs. His own music is quite conservative.

Steinberg, Maximilian, significant Russian composer and pedagogue; b. Vilna, July 4, 1883; d. Leningrad, Dec. 6, 1946. He studied at the St. Petersburg Cons. with Glazunov and Rimsky-Korsakov (whose daughter he married on June 17, 1908). In 1908 he was appointed teacher of theory and composition there. His early compositions reflected the influence of his teachers, but gradually he evolved a more personal style distinguished by rhapsodic eloquence and somewhat touched with procedures of French Impressionism. In 1934 he was appointed director of the Leningrad Cons., and maintained the high standards established before him by Rimsky-Korsakov and Glazunov. Among his pupils were Shostakovich, Shaporin, and other prominent composers of the Soviet period.
WORKS: Symph. No. 1 (1907); Symph. No. 2 (St. Petersburg, Nov. 27, 1909); *Metamorphoses,* ballet (2nd part performed by Diaghilev, Paris, June 2, 1914); *La Princesse Maleine,* after Maeterlinck, for orch. and women's chorus (1916); *Heaven and Earth,* dramatic poem for 6 soloists and orch. (1918); Symph. No. 3 (Leningrad, March 3, 1929, composer conducting); Symph. No. 4 subtitled *Turksib,* to celebrate the opening of the Turkestan-Siberian railroad (Leningrad, Dec. 2, 1933); *In Armenia,* symph. picture (Leningrad, Dec. 24, 1940); Violin Concerto (1946); 2 string quartets, etc. He also wrote a number of lyric songs and piano pieces; made several arrangements of Turkmenian songs for voice and orch.; also arranged for orch. a concerto in D by C. P. E. Bach (1911) and a cello sonata by Gaillard (1924); edited Rimsky-Korsakov's *Foundations of Orchestration* (St. Petersburg, 1913; 2 vols.).
BIBLIOGRAPHY: A. N. Rimsky-Korsakov, *Maximilian Steinberg* (Moscow, 1928; in Russian and German).

Steinberg, Michael, American music critic; b. Breslau, Oct. 4, 1928. He went to England in 1939 and to the U.S. in 1943; studied music at Princeton Univ. (A.B., 1949; M.F.A., 1951); then was in Italy (1952–54). Returning to America, he taught music courses at Princeton Univ., Hunter College, Manhattan School of Music, Univ. of Saskatchewan, Smith College, Brandeis Univ., Boston Univ. and (from 1968) at the New England Cons. of Music. In 1964 he was appointed music critic of the Boston *Globe.* His criticisms, utterly disrespectful of the most sacrosanct musical personalities, aroused periodical outbursts of indignation among outraged artists, aggrieved managers and chagrined promoters. In 1969 several Boston Symph. Orch. players petitioned the management to banish him from their concerts. Then, in a spectacular peri-

peteia, he left the Boston *Globe* in 1976 and was appointed Director of Publications for the Boston Symphony Orchestra.

Steinberg, William (Hans Wilhelm), eminent German-American conductor; b. Cologne, Aug. 1, 1899; d. New York, May 16, 1978. He studied piano and violin at home; conducted his own setting for chorus and orch. of a poem from Ovid's *Metamorphoses* in school at the age of 13; then took lessons in conducting with Hermann Abendroth, and studied piano with Lazzaro Uzielli and music theory with Franz Bölsche at the Cons. of Cologne, graduating in 1920, with the Wüllner Prize for conducting; subsequently became assistant to Otto Klemperer at the Cologne Opera, and in 1924 became its principal conductor. In 1925 he was engaged as conductor of the German Theater in Prague; in 1929 he was appointed general music director at the Frankfurt Opera, where he brought out several modern operas, including Alban Berg's *Wozzeck.* With the advent of the Nazi regime in 1933, he was removed from his position and became orchestral conductor for the Jewish Culture League, restricted to Jewish audiences. In 1936 he left Germany and became one of the conductors of the Palestine Orch., which he rehearsed and prepared for Toscanini, who subsequently engaged him as an assistant conductor of the NBC Symph., N.Y., in 1938. His career as an orchestral conductor was then connected with major American orchestras. He became an American citizen in 1944. He was conductor and music director of the Buffalo Philharmonic (1945–52); in 1952 he was appointed principal conductor of the Pittsburgh Symph. Orch.; concurrently, he served as music director (for 2 seasons) of the London Philharmonic (1958–60); then was music director and conductor of the Boston Symph. (1969–72), while continuing at his post with the Pittsburgh Symph. Orch., retiring in 1976. Also conducted numerous guest appearances with major American and European orchestras, acquiring the reputation of one of the most competent modern conductors; his performances were marked by impeccable taste and fidelity to the music; in this respect he was a follower of the Toscanini tradition.
BIBLIOGRAPHY: Hope Stoddard, *Symphony Conductors of the U.S.A.* (N.Y., 1957; pp. 207–14).

Steinberg, Zeev, German-born Israeli violinist and composer; b. Düsseldorf, Nov. 27, 1918. He emigrated to Palestine in 1934, where he studied viola and composition with Partos. In 1942 he joined the viola section of the Israel Philharmonic in Tel Aviv; in 1957 became the violinist in the New Israeli String Quartet; in 1970 was appointed lecturer at the Tel Aviv Academy of Music. His own compositions present an agreeable blend of Oriental melos, asymmetrical rhythms, and sharp atonal progressions in dissonant counterpoint.
WORKS: Sonata for 2 violas (1955–56); 2 string quartets (1959, 1969); *6 Miniatures* for cello and piano (1961); *4 Bagatelles* for 2 recorders (1962); 2 *concertos da camera:* No. 1, for viola and string orch. (1962); No. 2 for violin and 8 instruments (1966); *Purim Variations* on a nursery song for horn and string trio (1963); *The Story of Rahab and the Spies,* biblical can-

tata (1969); *Festive Prologue* for flute, oboe, and string trio (1969); *2 Songs Without Words* for viola, string quartet, and string orch. (1970); *a little suite for a big flute* for solo bass flute in C (1972); arrangements of works by Vivaldi, Bach, Schubert and others.

Steiner, Emma, American composer and conductor; b. 1850; d. New York, Feb. 27, 1928. Her grandfather led the Maryland 16th Brigade, which won the battle of North Point (near Fort McHenry, Baltimore) on Sept. 13, 1814, enabling Francis Scott Key to finish the last stanza of *The Star-Spangled Banner.* She was a prolific composer, having written 7 light operas, ballets, overtures and songs; purportedly she was also the first woman ever to receive payment for conducting. Conried, the manager of the Metropolitan Opera House, is said to have declared that he would have let her conduct a performance at the Met had he dared to put a woman armed with a baton in front of a totally male orchestra. According to unverifiable accounts, she conducted 6,000 performances of 50 different operas. She also organized an Emma R. Steiner Home for the Aged and Infirm Musicians at Bay Shore, Long Island. On Feb. 28, 1925 she conducted a concert at the Metropolitan Opera to commemorate the 50th anniversary of her first appearance as conductor. Her works, of different genres and light consistence, aggregate more than 200 opus numbers, most of them published by an *ad hoc* firm, MacDonald-Steiner.

Steiner, Max (Maximilian Raoul), American composer of film music; b. Vienna, May 10, 1888; d. Hollywood, Dec. 28, 1971. He studied at the Vienna Cons. with Fuchs and Grädener, and also had some advice from Mahler. At the age of 14 he wrote an operetta. In 1904 he went to England; in 1911 proceeded to Paris. In 1914 he settled in the U.S. After conducting musical shows in N.Y. he moved in 1929 to Hollywood, where he became one of the most successful film composers. His music offers a fulsome blend of lush harmonies artfully derived from both Tchaikovsky and Wagner, arranged in a manner marvelously suitable for the portrayal of psychological drama on the screen. Among his film scores, of which he wrote more than 150, are *King Kong* (1933), *The Charge of the Light Brigade* (1936), *Gone with the Wind* (1939) and *Treasure of Sierra Madre* (1948).

Steinert, Alexander Lang, American composer, conductor, and arranger; b. Boston, Sept. 21, 1900. He was the son of a piano manufacturer; studied at Harvard Univ., graduating in 1922; then took private lessons in composition with Loeffler in Boston, and with Koechlin and Vincent d'Indy in Paris. He lived much of his time in Europe; he was active as a conductor and arranger in Hollywood; for several years he was pianist with the Boston Symph. Orch. His music bears the imprint of the French modern school. WORKS: for orch.: *Nuit méridionale* (Boston, Oct. 15, 1926); *Leggenda sinfonica* (Rome, 1930); *Concerto sinfonico* for piano and orch. (Boston, Feb. 8, 1935, composer soloist); *Rhapsody* for clarinet and orch. (1945); *The Nightingale and the Rose,* after Oscar Wilde, for speaker and orch. (Philadelphia, March 31, 1950); Violin Sonata; Piano Trio; piano pieces; songs.

Steingräber, Johann Georg, German piano maker; son of **Theodor Steingräber;** b. Berlin, Jan. 1, 1858; d. there, March 16, 1932. For several years he was in the U.S. and worked for Steinway & Sons in N.Y.; in 1907 he returned to Berlin. He made excellent harpsichords as well as pianos.

Steingräber, Theodor, German music publisher; b. Neustadt-on-the-Orla, Jan. 25, 1830; d. Leipzig, April 5, 1904. He was the son of a piano manufacturer, and founded a music publishing firm bearing his name in Hannover in 1878; in 1890 it was moved to Leipzig. Under the pseudonym **Gustav Damm,** Steingräber published a piano method (1868). From 1903 to 1916 the firm was managed by Walter Friedel, and from 1916 to 1926 by Friedel's son-in-law Georg Heinrich. The firm was moved to Frankfurt in 1953, and to Offenbach in 1956.

Steingruber, Ilona, Austrian soprano; b. Vienna, Feb. 8, 1912; d. there, Dec. 10, 1962. She studied piano and voice; was on the staff of the Vienna Opera from 1948 to 1951. In 1946 she married the composer **Friedrich Wildgans.**

Steinhard, Erich, German-Bohemian musicologist; b. Prague, May 26, 1886; d. in a concentration camp in Lódź, Poland, c.1942 (was transported there on Oct. 26, 1941). He was a pupil of Knittl and Novák; studied musicology with J. Wolf, H. Kretzschmar, and M. Friedlaender in Berlin; Dr. phil. Prague, 1911 (with a thesis on organum). He became librarian of the Univ. of Prague; from 1921, editor of *Der Auftakt,* and from 1929 music critic for the *Prager Tageblatt.* WRITINGS: *Andreas Hammerschmidt* (Prague, 1914); *Zur deutschen Musik in der Tschechoslowakischen Republik* (2nd part of V. Helfert's *Geschichte der Musik in der Tschechoslowakischen Republik;* Prague, 1936); *Musikgeschichte von der Urzeit zur Gegenwart* (with G. Černušák; Prague, 1936).

Steinhardt, Milton, American musicologist; b. Miami, Oklahoma, Nov. 13, 1909. After preliminary study at the Univ. of Kansas he went to Europe, where he took courses at the Akademie der Tonkunst in Munich, and had violin lessons with Maurice Hewitt in Paris. Returning to the U.S., he enrolled in the Eastman School of Music, Rochester, N.Y. (B.M., 1936; M.M., 1937); then attended courses of Otto Kinkeldey at Cornell Univ. and Curt Sachs and Gustave Reese at N.Y. Univ. (Ph.D., 1950). He was lecturer at Michigan State Univ. (1948–50) and at Ohio Univ. (1950–51), and from 1951 at the Univ. of Kansas. He edited the works of Jacobus Vaet for *Denkmäler der Tonkunst in Österreich* (vols. 98, 100, 103/104, 108/109, 113/114, 116); also published the dissertation *Jacobus Vaet and His Motets* (East Lansing, Michigan, 1951).

Steinitzer, Max, German writer on music; b. Innsbruck, Jan. 20, 1864; d. Leipzig, June 21, 1936. Pupil of A. Kirchner (piano) and J. Hüttner (theory) in Munich; Dr. phil. (Munich, 1885) with the dissertation *Über die psychologischen Wirkungen der musikalischen Formen.* He subsequently conducted theater orchestras in Germany; 1903–11, prof. at the Cons. in Freiburg,

Breisgau; 1911–30, music critic of the *Leipziger Neueste Nachrichten*. An intimate friend of Richard Strauss from boyhood, he wrote a comprehensive and authoritative biography of him.

WRITINGS: *Die menschlichen und tierischen Gemütsbewegungen* (Munich, 1889); *Musikalische Strafpredigten* (Berlin, 1901; 12th ed., 1926); *Musikgeschichtlicher Atlas. Eine Beispielsammlung zu jeder Musikgeschichte* (1908); *Merkbüchlein für Mitglieder von Männerchoren* (1908); *Richard Strauss* (Berlin, 1911; 2nd ed., 1914; 3rd revised ed., 1927); *Richard Strauss in seiner Zeit* (Leipzig, 1914; 2nd ed., 1922); *Zur Entwicklungsgeschichte des Melodrams und Mimodrams* (Leipzig, 1919); *Meister des Gesanges* (Berlin, 1920); *Das Leipziger Gewandhaus im neuen Heim unter Carl Reinecke* (Leipzig, 1924); *Tschaikowsky* (Leipzig, 1925); *Beethoven* (Leipzig, 1927); *Pädagogik der Musik* (Leipzig, 1929).

Steinway & Sons, piano manufacturers of New York and Hamburg. The founder of the firm was **Heinrich Engelhard Steinweg** (b. Wolfshagen, Germany, Feb. 15, 1797; d. New York, Feb. 7, 1871). He learned cabinet making and organ building at Goslar, and in 1818 entered the shop of an organ maker in Seesen, also becoming church organist there. From about 1820 he became interested in piano making and worked hard to establish a business of his own. He married in 1825 and his first piano was probably finished at that time. In 1839 he exhibited 1 grand and 2 square pianos at the Brunswick State Fair, winning the gold medal. The Revolution of 1848 caused him to emigrate to America with his wife, 2 daughters, and 4 of his 5 sons: **Charles (Christian Karl Gottlieb;** b. Seesen, Jan. 4, 1829; d. there, March 31, 1865); **Henry (Johann Heinrich Engelhard;** b. Seesen, Oct. 29, 1830; d. N.Y., March 11, 1865); **William (Johann Heinrich Wilhelm;** b. Seesen, March 5, 1835; d. N.Y., Nov. 30, 1896), and **(Georg August) Albert** (b. Seesen, June 10, 1840; d. N.Y., May 14, 1877), leaving the management of the German business at Seesen in charge of the eldest son, **(Christian Friedrich) Theodore** (b. Seesen, Nov. 6, 1825; d. Brunswick, March 26, 1889). The family arrived in N.Y. on June 29, 1850, and for about 2 years father and sons worked in various piano factories there. On March 5, 1853, they established a factory of their own under the above firm name, with premises in Varick St. In 1854 they won a gold medal for a square piano at the Metropolitan Fair in Washington, D.C. Their remarkable prosperity dates from 1855, when they took 1st prize for a square over-strung piano with cast-iron frame (an innovation then) at the N.Y. Industrial Exhibition. In 1856 they made their first grand, and in 1862 their first upright. Among the numerous honors subsequently received may be mentioned 1st prize at London, 1862; 1st grand gold medal of honor for all styles at Paris, 1867 (by unanimous verdict); diplomas for "highest degree of excellence in all styles" at Philadelphia, 1876. In 1854 the family name (Steinweg) was legally changed to Steinway. In 1865, upon the death of his brothers Charles and Henry, Theodore S. gave up the Brunswick business and became a full partner in the N.Y. firm; he built Steinway Hall on 14th St., which, in addition to the offices and retail warerooms, housed a concert hall that be-

came a leading center of N.Y. musical life. In 1925 headquarters were established in the Steinway Building on 57th St. Theodore S. was especially interested in the scientific aspects of piano construction and made a study of the acoustical theories of Helmholtz and Tyndall, which enabled him to introduce important improvements. He returned to Germany in 1870. On May 17, 1876, the firm was incorporated and William S. was elected president; he opened a London branch in 1876, and established a European factory at Hamburg in 1880. In the latter year he also bought 400 acres of land on Long Island Sound and established there the village of Steinway (now part of L.I. City), where since 1910 the entire manufacturing plant has been located. William S. was for 14 years president of the N.Y. Deutsche Liedertafel. Control and active management of the business, now the largest of its kind in the world, has remained in the hands of the founder's descendants. **Theodore E. Steinway** (d. N.Y., April 8, 1957), grandson of Henry E. Steinway, was president from 1927; in 1955 he was succeeded by his son, **Henry Steinway.**

BIBLIOGRAPHY: O. Floersheim, *W. S.* (Breslau, 1894); E. Hubbard, *The Story of the Steinways* (East Aurora, N.Y., 1911); A. Dolge, *Pianos and Their Makers,* vol. I (1911); Theodore E. Steinway, *People and Pianos* (N.Y., 1953).

Steinweg. Original name of the Steinway family. **Christian Friedrich Theodore Steinway** continued the piano making business established by his father at Seesen until 1852, when he transferred it to Wolfenbüttel; in 1859 he moved it to Brunswick, carrying it on there until 1865, when he left for America. The business was then taken over by his partners, Grotrian, Helfferich, and Schulz ("Theodore Steinweg Nachfolger"). In 1886 Grotrian became sole owner, and the business was carried on by his sons Willi and Kurt, the firm name being "Grotrian-Steinweg."

Stekke, Léon, Belgian composer; b. Soignies, Oct. 12, 1904; d. Anderlecht, near Brussels, Jan. 24, 1970. He studied with Joseph Jongen and Paul Gilson in Brussels; from 1942 till his death he taught at the Royal Cons. in Brussels.

WORKS: an opera, *Les Cornes du Croissant* (Brussels, 1952); 2 cantatas: *Héro et Léandre* (1931) and *La Légende de St.-Hubert* (1933); *Fantaisie-rapsodie* for orch.; *Burlesco* for oboe and orch.; Trumpet Concerto (Brussels, 1948); *Fantaisie élégiaque* for English horn and orch.; *Poème sylvestre* for French horn and orch.; *Impression de cinéma* for bassoon and orch.; *Variations* for trombone and orch.; songs; piano pieces.

Stellfeld, Jean-Auguste, Belgian musicologist; b. Antwerp, Feb. 17, 1881; d. there, Sept. 16, 1952. He was a practicing lawyer, and a judge; at the same time he became associated with various musical organizations in Belgium; accumulated an enormously rich library of music, from the 16th, 17th, and 18th centuries. After his death, the library was purchased by the Univ. of Michigan, Ann Arbor (cf. the article by L. E. Cuyler, G. A. Sutherland, and H. T. David in *Notes,* Dec. 1954). He publ. *Bronnen tot de geschiedenis der antwerpsche clavecimbel- en orgelbouwers in de XVIe* *en XVIIe eeuwen* (Antwerp, 1942); *Andries Pevernage* (Louvain, 1943); *Bibliographie des éditions musicales plantiniennes* (Brussels, 1949).

Stenberg, Jordan, American avant-garde composer of Swedish and Spanish extraction; b. Fresno, Cal., May 31, 1947. He studied music theory with Robert Moran at the San Francisco Cons. and worked on electronic problems with Robert Ashley at Mills College. In his compositions he aims at creating an organic expression of cosmic philosophy as formalized by his deep reading of Russian theosophists and Indian psychologists. His zodiacal parameters are Sun in Gemini, moon in Scorpio, with Libra rising.

WORKS: *88 Fog-Horn Seconds,* a recording of actual fog-horns on electronic tape (1967); *A Snail's Progress in a Goldfish Bowl* for strings glissandi within a definite integral of white noise (1968); *Music for 4 Horse-Drawn Carriages,* a literal equestrian exercise (1968); *Mind Over Matter,* film opera for voices and instruments (1969); *Extension Chords,* to be performed by nomadic bands on the desert floor during a lunar eclipse or at the winter solstice (1970); *A Stitch in Time* for 11 acoustical sources (1970); *The Clock Struck One,* opera-play for voices, instruments and dervish dancers (1970); *Circles, Lines, Planes,* a choreographed acoustical dance notated in the form of an enneagram, to be produced in a canyon by 9 bagpipers and 9 × 9 buglers (1970). He has also written music for flower conservatories to stimulate the growth of timid plants.

Stenborg, Carl, Swedish composer; b. Stockholm, Sept. 25, 1752; d. Djurgarden, Aug. 1, 1813. He studied at the Univ. of Uppsala; from 1773 to 1806 was a singer at the Swedish Opera in Stockholm. His opera *Konung Gustaf Adolphs Jagt* (Stockholm, June 25, 1777) is of significance as the first opera based on a Swedish historical subject.

Stendhal, famous French writer (real name **Marie-Henri Beyle**); b. Grenoble, Jan. 23, 1783; d. Paris, March 23, 1842. He was a military official under Napoleon, taking part in the German and Russian campaigns; from 1815 he lived in Milan, Paris, and Rome; in 1830 became French consul at Trieste, and from 1831 in Civitavecchia. He is best known as a novelist (*Le Rouge et le noir, La Chartreuse de Parme,* etc.), but also wrote on music; under the pseudonym of **Louis Alexandre Bombet** he publ. *Lettres écrites de Vienne, en Autriche, sur le célèbre compositeur Joseph Haydn, suivies d'une vie de Mozart, et de considérations sur Métastase et l'état présent de la musique en France et en Italie* (Paris, 1814; English, London, 1817; new ed. in 1817 as *Vies de Haydn, Mozart et Métastase,* by Stendhal; republ. in 1914 with introduction by R. Rolland: *Stendhal et la musique;* German transl., Vienna, 1921). The life of Haydn is in part translated from Carpani's *Le Haydine;* the first 4 chapters of the life of Mozart are taken from Schlichtegroll's Necrology (1791), the last 3 from Cramer's *Anecdotes sur Mozart.* In Jan., 1824, Stendhal's life of Rossini was publ. in London as *Memoirs of Rossini,* in a transl. made from the original manuscript. The French version, considerably expanded, was publ. in

Paris later the same year (2 vols.; German transl., Leipzig, 1824; republ. in complete ed. of Stendhal's works, Paris, 1922, with introduction by Henry Prunières: "Stendhal et Rossini," which was also publ. in the *Musical Quarterly,* Jan. 1921). The oft-repeated assertion that this work was plagiarized from Carpani's *Le Rossiniane* is without foundation. *The Life of Rossini* was republ. in English, London, 1956.

BIBLIOGRAPHY: A. Paupe, *Histoire des œuvres de Stendhal* (Paris, 1903); H. Prunières, "Stendhal et la musique," *Revue Hebdomadaire* (1921); A. E. A. Beau, *Das Verhältnis Stendhals zur Musik* (dissertation, Hamburg, 1930); D. Maurice, *Stendhal* (Paris, 1931); P. Jourda, *Stendhal, l'homme et l'œuvre* (Paris, 1934); F. C. Green, *Stendhal* (Cambridge, England, 1939); H. Imbert, "Stendhal critique musical," in *Symphonie,* pp. 87–124 (Paris, 1891); J. W. Klein, "Stendhal as a Music Critic," *Musical Quarterly* (Jan. 1943).

Stenhammar, Per Ulrik, Swedish composer; b. Törnvalla, Feb. 20, 1828; d. Stockholm, Feb. 8, 1875. He received his primary musical education from A. F. Lindblad; became interested in sacred music, and wrote choral works in Mendelssohn's style; many solo songs. His oratorio, *Saul och David* (1869), was orchestrated by his son, **Wilhelm Stenhammar.**

Stenhammar, Wilhelm, significant Swedish composer, conductor and pianist, son of **Per Ulrik Stenhammar;** b. Stockholm, Feb. 7, 1871; d. there, Nov. 20, 1927. He studied piano, organ, and theory at the Stockholm Cons., graduating in 1890; then went to Berlin for further piano study with Karl Heinrich Barth; toured Scandinavia and Germany as a concert pianist. In his own music he followed Wagnerian formulas, but his merit as a national composer resides in his ability to absorb and transmute authentic folk melodies. His hymnal tune *Sverige (Sweden),* which is the second song in his cycle of 5 songs for baritone, chorus, and orch., entitled *Ett Folk (The People),* enjoys the status of an unofficial national anthem of Sweden. His first large work for solo voices, chorus, and orch., *I Rosengård (In a Rose Garden;* 1888–89, after K. A. Melin's collection of fairy tales, *Prinsessan och svennen*), was performed in Stockholm on Feb. 16, 1892, attracting considerable attention; on Dec. 9, 1898, he brought out his music drama, *Tirfing* (1897–98), at the Stockholm Opera; this was followed by a German opera, written earlier, *Das Fest auf Solhaug (The Feast at Solhaug,* 1892–93), after Ibsen, which was first heard at Stuttgart on April 12, 1899, and 3 years later in Swedish (Swedish title, *Gildet på Solhaug*), in Stockholm on Oct. 31, 1902. These works are music dramas of a Wagnerian type, but their redeeming value lies in an ingratiating use of folksong materials. From 1897 to 1900 Stenhammar was conductor of the Philharmonic Society in Stockholm; later also led orchestral and choral groups in Göteborg (1917–23); the Univ. of Göteborg made him Mus. Doc. in 1916, in appreciation of his services to the city. His other works are *Snöfrid (Snow Peace,* 1891) and *Midvinter* (1907) for chorus and orch.; the cantata, *Sången (The Song,* 1921); 2 symphonies (1902–03, 1911–15); 2 piano concertos: No. 1 (1893; rescored by Kurt Atterberg, 1945–46), No. 2 (1904–07); the over-

ture, *Excelsior* (1896); *2 Sentimental Romances* for violin and orch. (1910); *Serenade* for orch. (1911-13, revised 1919); incidental music to Strindberg's drama *Drömspelet* (*A Dreamplay*, 1916; rescored for concert performance by Hilding Rosenberg, 1968-69); 6 string quartets (1894; 1896; 1897-1900; 1904-09; *Serenade,* 1910; 1916); Violin Sonata (1899-1900); 2 piano sonatas (1890, 1895); *3 Fantasies* for piano (1895); *Nights of Late Summer,* 5 piano pieces (1914); a cappella choral works; solo songs.
BIBLIOGRAPHY: Sten Broman, "Wilhelm Stenhammar: A Survey," *Music Review* (May 1947).

Štěpán, Václav, Czech pianist and writer on music; b. Pečky, near Kolín, Dec. 12, 1889; d. Prague, Nov. 24, 1944. He studied musicology at the Univ. of Prague (Dr. phil., 1913); from 1919 he was prof. of esthetics at the Prague Cons.; appeared as pianist in Czechoslovakia and in France; contributed valuable articles on Czech musicians to foreign encyclopedias and music dictionaries; publ. 2 vols. of Bohemian folksongs (1917) and 2 vols. of Slovak folksongs (1925); also *Das Symbol in der Programm-Musik* (1914). He wrote some chamber music and other works, but did not pursue a composer's career.

Stepanian, Aro, Armenian composer; b. Elisabethopol, April 24, 1897; d. Erevan, Jan. 9, 1966. He studied at the Leningrad Cons. with Vladimir Shcherbachev. He moved to Erevan, capital of Soviet Armenia, in 1930 and remained there for the rest of his life. He wrote 5 operas on Armenian subjects: *Brave Nazar* (Erevan, Nov. 29, 1935), *David of Sasun* (1937), *Lusabatsin* (*At the Dawn,* 1938), *Nune* (1947), and *Heroine* (1950); he further wrote 3 symphonies (1943, 1945, 1953); 2 piano concertos (1947, 1955); Viola Concerto (1955); *Rhapsody* for piano and orch. (1962); 4 string quartets; 2 violin sonatas; Cello Sonata; numerous choruses and songs.
BIBLIOGRAPHY: M. Kazakhian, *Aro Stepanian* (Erevan, 1962).

Stepanov, Lev, Russian composer; b. Tomsk, Siberia, Dec. 26, 1908. He studied with Miaskovsky at the Moscow Cons., graduating in 1938. He wrote several operas on Russian subjects, among them *Dunia's Happiness* (1937), *The Guards* (Tashkent, Nov. 8, 1947), *Ivan Bolotnikov* (Perm, Dec. 17, 1950); a ballet, *The Native Shore* (1941); 2 piano concertos (1947, 1955); Viola Concerto (1955); chamber music; choruses; many songs.

Stephan, Rudi, German composer; b. Worms, July 29, 1887; d. near Tarnopol, Galicia, Sept. 29, 1915. He studied with Sekles in Frankfurt and with R. Louis in Munich; developed a fine talent for lyric songs, combining German Romantic traits with Impressionism in instrumental coloring. His death in battle was lamented by German musicians.
WORKS: *Music für 7 Saiteninstrumente,* for string quintet, piano, and harp (1912); *Music für Orchester* (1913); *Music für Violine und Orchester* (1914); a ballad, *Liebeszauber,* for baritone and orch.; piano pieces. His opera, *Die ersten Menschen,* was produced posthumously in Frankfurt on July 1, 1920.

BIBLIOGRAPHY: K. Holl, *Rudi Stephan* (1920); A. Machner, *Rudi Stephans Werk* (dissertation, Breslau, 1942).

Stephanescu, George, Rumanian composer; b. Bucharest, Dec. 13, 1843; d. there, April 24, 1925. He studied in Bucharest, and at Paris Cons. with Ambroise Thomas and Auber (1867-71). From 1872 to 1909 he taught voice at the Bucharest Cons. Stephanescu was the composer of the first Rumanian symph. work based on national themes, *Uvertura nationala* (1876), and of the first symph. written by a Rumanian (1869). He also wrote many choruses and solo songs to Rumanian texts.

Stephani, Hermann, German musicologist and composer; b. Grimma, June 23, 1877; d. Marburg, Dec. 3, 1960. He studied at the Leipzig Cons. with Jadassohn and Reinecke, and at the Univ. of Munich with Lipps and Sandberger; Dr. phil., 1902, with the dissertation, *Das Erhabene, insonderheit in der Tonkunst, und das Problem der Form* (Leipzig, 1903; 2nd ed., 1907). In 1921 was appointed to the faculty of the Univ. of Marburg; taught musicology there until 1946. His scholarly publications include: *Der Charakter der Tonarten* (Regensburg, 1923); *Grundfragen des Musikhörens* (Leipzig, 1925); *Das Vierteltonproblem* (Leipzig, 1925); *Polare Harmonik bei Beethoven* (Leipzig, 1927); *Das Problem des Orgelstils* (Essen, 1942). He advocated a reform in score notation through the exclusive use of the G clef with octave indications ("Einheitspartitur") and edited Schumann's *Manfred* Overture using this system (1905). He was a prolific composer; wrote about 100 opus numbers, mostly vocal works; also contrapuntal pieces for various combinations of instruments; edited works by Handel, Weber, etc. A Festschrift was presented to him on his 70th birthday (Regensburg, 1947).

Stephens, Charles Edward, English organist and teacher; b. London, March 18, 1821; d. there, July 13, 1892. He studied piano with Cipriani Potter; in 1843 he was appointed to his first church position as organist, and was active in that capacity in various churches in London until 1875. From 1850 he was associated with the Philharmonic Society, as treasurer and director. He composed a piano trio, several orchestral overtures, a string quartet, and a symphony; all these works were performed in London.

Sterkel, Abbé Johann Franz Xaver, German ecclesiastic and composer; b. Würzburg, Dec. 3, 1750; d. there, Oct. 12, 1817. He studied theology and became a priest; was self-taught in music, but acquired sufficient proficiency as organist to occupy various positions as music director. In 1778 he became chaplain and organist in the Elector's court at Mainz; in 1782 he was in Italy, where he produced his opera *Farnace* (Naples, Jan. 12, 1782). Beethoven heard Sterkel play in 1791, in Aschaffenburg, and was greatly impressed by his style as both composer and pianist. When the French expelled the Elector in 1794, Sterkel left Mainz and returned to his native city. From 1810 he was again court musician to the Elector of Mainz, until 1814, when the military campaign forced him to go back to Würzburg once more. He was a prolific composer; publ. 10 symphonies, 2 overtures, a piano quartet, a string quartet, 6 string trios, 6 piano concertos, a considerable amount of piano music. His *Rondo comique* for piano was very popular.

BIBLIOGRAPHY: A. Scharnagl, *J. F. X. Sterkel: ein Beitrag zur Musikgeschichte Mainfrankens* (Würzburg, 1943).

Sterling, Antoinette, American contralto; b. Sterlingville, N.Y., Jan. 23, 1850; d. London, Jan. 9, 1904. She studied with Abella in N.Y., Mathilde Marchesi in Cologne, and with Pauline Viardot-Garcia in Baden; also took lessons with Manuel García in London. Returning to America, she sang in Henry Ward Beecher's church in Brooklyn; then went to London, where she made her debut at a Covent Garden Promenade Concert (Nov. 5, 1873). She introduced many favorite songs (most of which were especially composed for her), such as Arthur Sullivan's *Lost Chord* (Jan. 31, 1877), Barnby's *When the Tide Comes In,* etc. In 1875 she toured the U.S.; her permanent home was in London.

BIBLIOGRAPHY: Malcolm S. MacKinlay (her son), *Antoinette Sterling and other Celebrities* (London, 1906).

Sterling, Winthrop Smith, American organist and teacher; b. Cincinnati, Nov. 28, 1859; d. there, Nov. 16, 1943. He studied in Leipzig, and later in London, where he remained for several years as organist. From 1887 to 1903 he was head of the organ dept. and teacher of singing at the Cincinnati College of Music; later taught the organ at the Univ. of Miami, Florida. He composed a number of organ pieces and songs.

Stern, Adolf, German writer on music; b. Leipzig, June 14, 1835; d. Dresden, April 15, 1907. He publ. several books dealing with music: *Wanderbuch* (1877; about the Bayreuth Festivals); *Die Musik in der deutschen Dichtung* (1888); *Gluck in Versailles* (1904); edited the poems of Peter Cornelius (1890); and *Liszts Briefe an K. Gille* (1903). He married (1881) the pianist **Margarete Herr** (b. Dresden, Nov. 25, 1857; d. there, Oct. 4, 1899), who was a pupil of Liszt, and after her death he publ. her biography (Leipzig, 1901).

Stern, Isaac, outstanding American violinist; b. Kremenetz, Russia, July 21, 1920. He was taken to the U.S. as an infant and was trained in music by his mother who was a professional singer. He studied the violin with Naoum Blinder and Louis Persinger; made his professional debut with the San Francisco Symph. Orch. at the age of 11, and played in N.Y. on Oct. 11, 1937, eliciting praise from the critics. In 1947 he toured Australia; subsequently appeared regularly in American and European orchestras; in 1956 he made a spectacularly successful tour of Russia. In 1961 he organized a trio with the pianist Istomin and the cellist Leonard Rose. Isaac Stern belongs to the galaxy of virtuoso performers to whom fame is a natural adjunct to talent and industry; he is also active in general cultural undertakings, and is an energetic worker for the cause of human rights.

Stern, Julius, eminent German music pedagogue; b. Breslau, Aug. 8, 1820; d. Berlin, Feb. 27, 1883. He studied violin with Lüstner, and later took courses with Rungenhagen in Berlin; in 1847 he founded the famous Sternscher Gesangverein in Berlin, conducting it until 1874. In 1850 he founded the Stern Cons. in Berlin (with Kullak and Marx); Kullak withdrew in 1855, and Marx in 1857; thenceforth Stern became the sole head of the institution; it prospered and acquired the reputation of one of the greatest music schools in Europe. Stern conducted the Berlin Sinfonie-Kapelle from 1869 to 1871, and later led the "Reichshalle" concerts (1873–75). He was also a composer, and received commendation from Mendelssohn for his songs; publ. *Barcarolle* for voice, cello, and piano; *Les Adieux,* for violin and piano; male choruses; songs. His opera, *Ismene,* was not produced.

BIBLIOGRAPHY: Richard Stern, *Erinnerungsblätter an Julius Stern* (Berlin, 1886).

Stern, Leo, English cellist; b. Brighton, April 5, 1862; d. London, Sept. 10, 1904. He studied cello at the Royal Academy of Music in London with Piatti, and later with Julius Klengel in Leipzig. He was an assistant artist on Adelina Patti's concert tour in 1888; made a tour in America in 1897–98. He composed pieces for cello and songs. His second wife was **Suzanne Adams,** the opera singer.

Sternberg, Constantin, Russian-American pianist and composer; b. St. Petersburg, July 9, 1852; d. Philadelphia, March 31, 1924. He studied piano with Moscheles at the Leipzig Cons., and later had lessons with Th. Kullak; also visited Liszt at Weimar. He toured Russia as a concert pianist; in 1880 emigrated to the U.S. In 1890 he established the Sternberg School of Music in Philadelphia, and was its director until his death. He was greatly esteemed as a piano teacher. He wrote some 200 salon pieces for piano, and *Danses Cosaques* for violin; published *Ethics and Esthetics of Piano Playing* (N.Y., 1917) and *Tempo Rubato and Other Essays* (N.Y., 1920).

Sternberg, Erich Walter, German-born Israeli composer; b. Berlin, May 31, 1891; d. Tel Aviv, Dec. 15, 1974. He studied composition with Hugo Leichtentritt in Berlin; emigrated to Palestine, and taught at the Tel Aviv Cons. He was co-founder of the Israel Philharmonic. As a composer, he was inspired by biblical subjects.

WORKS: a children's opera *Dr. Dolittle* (Jerusalem, 1939); opera "for children and others" *Pacifica, the Friendly Island* (1972–74); 2 string quartets (1924; 1926); *The Story of David and Goliath* for baritone and orch. (1927); *Joseph and His Brothers,* suite for string orch. (1938); *Twelve Tribes of Israel,* variations for orch. (1941; Tel Aviv, May 3, 1942); *My People,* 5 songs for soprano or tenor, and orch. (1945); *Amcha-Suite* for orch. from incidental music to a play; *Höre Israel* for orch. (1948); *Toccata* for piano (1950); *The Raven,* after Poe, for baritone and orch. (1953); Violin Sonata (1955); *Contrapuntal Study* for orch. (1955); *Sichot Haruach (Conversations with the Wind)* for contralto and orch. (1956); *The Distant Flute,* 3 songs for voice and flute (1958); the oratorio *Techiat Israel*

(*The Resurrection of Israel*, 1959); *Tewat Noah (Noah's Ark)*, 4 movements for orch. in the form of a symphony (1960); *Tefilot (Prayers of Humility)* for contralto and chamber orch. (1962); *The Sacrifice of Isaac* for soprano and orch. (1965); *Love Songs* for chorus and orch. (1968); *The Wretched* for baritone and string orch. (1969); *My Brother Jonathan* for chorus and string orch. (1969); Piano Trio; Wind Quintet; songs.

Sternefeld, Daniel, Belgian conductor and composer; b. Antwerp, Nov. 27, 1905. He studied composition with Paul Gilson; took lessons in conducting from Paumgartner, Krauss and Karajan at the Mozarteum in Salzburg. In 1935 he was appointed conductor of the Royal Flemish Opera in Antwerp; was principal conductor of the Belgian Radio and Television Orch. (1948–72); also appeared as guest conductor in Europe and South America. He taught conducting at the Antwerp Cons. (1949–71). His few compositions include an opera influenced by Strauss, *Mater Dolorosa* (1934; Antwerp, 1935); a ballet, *Pierlala* (1938); *Variations Symphoniques* (1928); *Élégie* for orch. (1931); *Suite de vieilles chansons flamandes et wallonnes* for chamber orch. (1934); Symphony (1943); *Frère Jacques*, variations for brass and percussion (1955).

Sternfeld, Frederick William, Austrian-American musicologist; b. Vienna, Sept. 25, 1914. He studied at the Univ. of Vienna (1933–37); then went to the U.S., and enrolled at Yale Univ. (1940–43), obtaining his Ph.D. there. He taught at Wesleyan Univ., Conn. (1940–46); at Dartmouth College (1946–56); since 1956, lecturer at Oxford Univ. He was editor of *Renaissance News* (1946–54); published a number of informative studies in the *Musical Quarterly* and other American and British publications; also a bibliography, *Goethe and Music* (N.Y., 1954).

Sternfeld, Richard, German writer on music; b. Königsberg, Oct. 15, 1858; d. Berlin, June 21, 1926. A thoroughly trained musician, he published valuable books concerning music.

WRITINGS: *Beethoven und Wagner* (1885); *Hans von Bülow* (1898); *Beethovens Missa Solemnis* (1900); *Albert Niemann* (1904); *Schiller und Wagner* (1905); *Richard Wagner und die Bayreuther Bühnenfestspiele* (2 vols., 1906); *Aus Richard Wagners Pariser Zeit* (1906); *Musikalische Skizzen und Humoresken* (1919); *Berühmte Musiker und ihre Werke* (1922).

Steuerlein, Johann, German composer; b. Schmalkalden, July 5, 1546; d. Meiningen, May 5, 1613. He studied in Magdeburg; occupied various positions as a clerk; became a notary public in Meiningen in 1589; in 1604 he was given the rank of poet laureate by the Emperor. At the same time he was active as a song composer, and brought out *21 Geistliche Lieder* for 4 voices (1575), *24 Weltliche Gesänge* (1575); *23 Geistliche Gesänge*, for 4-6 voices (1576), *27 Geistliche Gesänge*, for 4 voices (1588), *8 Geistliche Gesänge*, for 5 voices (1589). He was the composer of the celebrated New Year song, *Das alte Jahr vergangen ist.*

BIBLIOGRAPHY: G. Kraft, "Johann Steuerlein," *Zeitschrift für Musikwissenschaft* (May 1931).

Steuermann, Eduard, eminent Polish-American pianist and composer; b. Sambor, near Lwow, June 18, 1892; d. New York, Nov. 11, 1964. He studied piano with Ferruccio Busoni in Berlin (1911–12), and theory with Schoenberg (1912–14); also took some composition lessons with Engelbert Humperdinck. Returning to Poland, he taught at the Paderewski School in Lwow, and concurrently at the Jewish Cons. in Cracow (1932–36). In 1936 he emigrated to the U.S.; taught piano at Juilliard School of Music, N.Y. (1952–64); also was on the faculty of Philadelphia Cons. (1948–63); gave summer classes at the Mozarteum in Salzburg (1953–63) and Darmstadt (1954, 1957, 1958, 1960); conducted a chamber music seminar in Israel in the summer of 1958. As a concert pianist and soloist with major orchestras, Steuermann was an ardent champion of new music, particularly of Schoenberg; gave the first performance of Schoenberg's Piano Concerto (1944); made excellent arrangements for piano of Schoenberg's operatic and symphonic works, among them *Erwartung, Die glückliche Hand, Kammersymphonie* No. 1 and Piano Concerto; in 1952 he received the Schoenberg Medal from the International Society for Contemporary Music (1952); recorded the complete piano works of Schoenberg. Steuermann was also a composer; although he did not follow Schoenberg's method of composition with 12 tones with any degree of consistency, his music possesses an Expressionistic tension that is characteristic of the modern Vienna School.

WORKS: *Variations* for orch. (1958); *Music for Instruments* (1959–60); *Suite* for Chamber Orch. (1964); *7 Waltzes* for string quartet (1946); Piano Trio (1954); *Improvisation and Allegro* for violin and piano (1955); String Quartet, subtitled *Diary* (1960–61); *Dialogues* for unaccompanied violin (1963); Piano Sonata (1926); *Piano Suite* (1952); *3 Choirs* (1956); *Cantata*, after Franz Kafka, for chorus and orch. (1964); *Brecht-Lieder* for contralto (1945); a number of other songs to Polish and German texts.

Stevens, Bernard, English composer; b. London, March 2, 1916. He studied at Cambridge Univ. and at the Royal College of Music in London; was appointed to its faculty in 1948. He wrote a number of works for various instrumental combinations; his music adheres to traditional concepts of harmony, while the programmatic content is often colored by his radical political beliefs.

WORKS: *Symphony of Liberation* (1946); Violin Concerto (1946); Cello Concerto (1952); Piano Concerto (1955); cantata, *The Harvest of Peace* (1952); cantata, *The Pilgrims of Hope* (1956); Symph. No. 2 (1964); Trio for violin, horn, and piano (1966); *Choriamb* for orch. (1968); *The Turning World* for baritone, chorus and orch. (1971); *The Bramble Briar* for guitar (1974).

Stevens, Denis (William), English musicologist, violinist, and conductor; b. High Wycombe, Buckinghamshire, March 2, 1922. He studied music at Oxford Univ. with R. O. Morris and Egon Wellesz (M.A., 1947); was violinist in the Philharmonia Orch. in London, and in 1949 joined the staff of the British Broadcasting Corporation. He then went to the U.S., where he lectured at the University of California, Berkeley (1962), Pennsylvania State Univ. (1963–64), and at Columbia Univ. (since 1964). He also organized and conducted a choral group, the Ambrosian Singers, with which he toured in Europe and the U.S. His specialty is English music of the Elizabethan Period. He published *Tudor Church Music* (N.Y., 1955); a monograph on Thomas Tomkins (London, 1957); edited the *Mulliner Book* (vol. I of *Musica Britannica*, London, 1951); *A History of Song* (London, 1960); and *The Pelican History of Music* (3 vols.; London, 1960–68).

Stevens, Halsey, significant American composer, educator and writer on music; b. Scott, N.Y., Dec. 3, 1908. He studied with William Berwald at Syracuse Univ. and with Ernest Bloch in California. He held teaching positions at Dakota Wesleyan Univ. (1937–41), Bradley Univ. (1941–46); in 1946 appointed to the faculty of the Univ. of Southern California, Los Angeles. He traveled in Europe; collected materials for a biography of Béla Bartók, in preparation for which he mastered the Hungarian language; published *The Life and Music of Béla Bartók* (N.Y., 1953; revised ed. 1964).
WORKS: Symph. No. 1 (San Francisco, March 7, 1946, composer conducting; revised version, Los Angeles, March 3, 1950); Symph. No. 2 (1945; N.Y., May 17, 1947); *A Green Mountain Overture* (Burlington, Aug. 7, 1948); *Triskelion* for orch. (Louisville, Feb. 27, 1954); *Sinfonia Breve* (Louisville, Nov. 20, 1957); *Symphonic Dances* (1958); Cello Concerto (1964); Septet for clarinet, bassoon, horn, 2 violas and 2 cellos (1957); Quintet for flute, violin, viola, cello and piano (1945); 3 string quartets; 3 piano trios; Violin Sonata; Viola Sonata; Bassoon Sonata; Horn Sonata; several piano sonatas; songs; choruses.
BIBLIOGRAPHY: Paul Pisk, "Halsey Stevens," *Bulletin of the American Composers Alliance* IV/2 (1954).

Stevens, Richard John Samuel, English composer of glees; b. London, March 27, 1757; d. there, Sept. 23, 1837. He was a chorister at St. Paul's Cathedral in London, and served as organist at the Inner Temple (from 1786 to 1810); from 1801 was prof. of music at Gresham College. He received numerous prizes for his glees, of which the most famous were *Sigh no more, Ladies; Ye spotted snakes; The cloud-pact towers; Crabbed Age and Youth,* and *From Oberon in Airy Land;* 3 sets were publ.; he also brought out 3 sonatas for harpsichord, and edited a 3-vol. collection of vocal music by Italian and English composers.
BIBLIOGRAPHY: J. B. Trend, "R. J. S. Stevens," *Music & Letters* 14.

Stevens, Risë, American mezzo-soprano; b. New York, June 11, 1913. She studied voice with Anna Schoen-René at the Juilliard School of Music, N.Y.; later took a course with George Schick in Prague. She made her debut as Mignon in Prague (1938); appeared as Octavian in *Der Rosenkavalier* at the Metropolitan Opera, in Philadelphia, on Nov. 22, 1938; subsequently sang on the radio, and also in motion pictures and on television. In 1939 she married the Czech actor Walter Surovy; they settled in New York. In 1975–78 she

served as president of the Mannes College of Music in New York.

Stevenson, Robert, eminent American musicologist; b. Melrose, New Mexico, July 3, 1916. He studied at the Univ. of Oxford (B. Litt.), Yale Univ. (M. Mus.), Harvard Univ. (S.T.B.), Princeton Theological Seminary (Th.M.) and the Univ. of Rochester, N.Y. (Ph.D.). He studied piano with Artur Schnabel and composition with Howard Hanson; took courses in musicology with Schrade and Westrup. His teaching posts included the Univ. of Texas at El Paso (1946), Westminster Choir College (1946–49), and since 1950, Univ. of California, Los Angeles. An exceptionally erudite scholar, Stevenson possesses a rare (in his profession) felicity of literary expression; he is a brilliant pianist and an occasional composer; he wrote *Nocturne in Ebony* (1945) and *Texas Suite* for orch. (1950). A master of European languages, his investigative specialty is the music of Spain, Portugal and Latin America. He contributed numerous articles on the composers of the Baroque period and on American composers to *Die Musik in Geschichte und Gegenwart* and about 400 articles to the *New Grove Dictionary of Music and Musicians* (announced for London, 1979).
WRITINGS: *Music in Mexico. A Historical Survey* (N.Y., 1952); *Patterns of Protestant Church Music* (Durham, N.C., 1953); *La Música en la catedral de Sevilla, 1478–1606; Documentos para su estudio* (Los Angeles, 1954); *Music before the Classic Era* (London, 1955; 2nd ed., 1958; reprint, Westport, Conn., 1973); *Cathedral Music in Colonial Peru* (Lima, 1959); *The Music of Peru: Aboriginal and Viceroyal Epochs* (Washington, 1960); *Juan Bermudo* (The Hague, 1960); *Spanish Music in the Age of Columbus* (The Hague, 1960); *Music Instruction in Inca Land* (Baltimore, 1960); *Spanish Cathedral Music in the Golden Age* (Berkeley, Calif., 1961); *Mexico City Cathedral Music, 1600–1750* (Washington, 1964); *La Música Colonial en Colombia* (Cali, 1964); *Protestant Church Music in America* (N.Y., 1966); *Music in Aztec and Inca Territory* (Berkeley, Calif., 1968); *Renaissance and Baroque Musical Sources in the Americas* (Washington, 1970); *Foundations of New World Opera, with a Transcription of the Earliest Extant American Opera, 1701* (Lima, 1973). He edited, transcribed and annotated *Vilancicos Portugueses* for *Portugaliae Musica XXIX* (Lisbon, 1976); contributed informative articles dealing with early American composers, South American operas, sources of Indian music and studies on Latin American composers to *The Musical Quarterly, Revista Musical Chilena, Journal of the American Musicological Society, Ethnomusicology, Inter-American Music Bulletin,* etc.

Stevenson, Ronald, Brythonic composer; b. Blackburn, Lancashire, March 6, 1928, of Scottish and Welsh ancestry. He studied piano as a child; began to compose at 14; took courses in composition at the Royal Manchester College at 17. In 1955 he went to Italy on a scholarship granted by the Italian government; studied at the Santa Cecilia Academy in Rome. Returning to England, he was appointed lecturer at Edinburgh Univ. (in the Extra-Mural Dept.) in 1962; was on the music staff at the Univ. of Cape Town,

South Africa, in 1963–65. A fervent intellectual, he contributed cultured articles to *The Listener* and other publications; engaged in a thoroughgoing bio-musical tome on Busoni, with whose art he felt a particular kinship; publ. a book, *Western Music: An Introduction* (London, 1971).

WORKS: He adheres to neo-Baroque polyphony; a formidable exemplar is his *Passacaglia on DSCH* for piano, a brobdingnagian set of variations in 3 parts, 80 minutes long, derived from the initial D and the first three letters of the name of Dmitri Shostakovitch, in German notation (D; S = Es = E-flat; C; H = B), first performed by Stevenson himself in Cape Town, Dec. 10, 1963. Other works include: *Anger Dance* for guitar (1965); *Triptych* on themes from Busoni's opera *Doktor Faust,* for piano and orch. (Piano Concerto No. 1; Edinburgh, Jan. 6, 1966, composer soloist); *Scots Dance Toccata* for orch. (Glasgow, July 4, 1970), *Peter Grimes Fantasy* for piano, on themes from Britten's opera (1971); *Duo-Sonata* for harp and piano (1971); *Piano Concerto No. 2* (1972); numerous settings for voice and piano and for chorus of Scottish folk songs; transcriptions of works of Purcell, Bach, Chopin, Berlioz, Busoni, Paderewski, Delius, Britten, Alban Berg, Pizzetti, Percy Grainger, and many others.

Stewart, Humphrey John, organist and composer; b. London, May 22, 1856; d. San Diego, Calif., Dec. 28, 1932. He studied privately in England; in 1886 emigrated to the U.S. and settled in San Francisco as church organist; he was one of the founders of the American Guild of Organists. His 3 operas were produced in San Francisco: *His Majesty* (1890), *The Conspirators* (1900), and *King Hal* (1911); the scores of the first two were lost in the San Francisco earthquake and fire of 1906. His most successful work was the sacred music drama *The Hound of Heaven* (San Francisco, April 24, 1924); he further wrote the orchestral suites *Montezuma* and *Scenes in California;* a Mass; organ pieces; songs.
BIBLIOGRAPHY: E. E. Hipsher, *American Opera and Its Composers* (Philadelphia, 1934, pp. 391–94).

Stewart, Reginald, Scottish-American conductor and pianist; b. Edinburgh, April 20, 1900. He studied piano with Mark Hambourg in London and Isidor Philipp in Paris; took composition lessons with Nadia Boulanger. In 1933 he went to Canada, and was a founder of the Toronto Philharmonic Orch. (1934). He was then conductor of the Baltimore Symph. (1942–52); from 1941 to 1958 he was director of the Peabody Cons., Baltimore. In 1962 he was named head of the piano department and artist-in-residence at the Music Academy of the West in Santa Barbara, California.

Stewart, Sir Robert Prescott, Irish organist and composer; b. Dublin, Dec. 16, 1825; d. there, March 24, 1894. He was a chorister of Christ Church Cathedral, Dublin, and at the age of 18 was appointed organist there. In 1852 he became vicar-choral at St. Patrick's Cathedral, Dublin; in 1861 he was appointed to the faculty of Dublin Univ., as teacher of harmony. He was engaged as conductor of the Dublin Philharmonic in 1873. He gave concerts as organist in England; wrote

several cantatas and odes for various occasions; also anthems, glees, and miscellaneous songs.
BIBLIOGRAPHY: O. Vignoles, *Memoir of Sir Robert P. Stewart* (London, 1899); J. C. Culwick, *The Works of Sir Robert Stewart* (Dublin, 1902).

Stewart, Thomas, American baritone; b. San Saba, Texas, Aug. 29, 1928. He studied electrical engineering in Waco; later went to New York, where he became a student of Mack Harrell at the Juilliard School of Music. He sang at the N.Y. City Opera and in Chicago; in 1967 went to Germany on a Fulbright grant and was engaged by the Deutsche Staatsoper in Berlin; in the interim he made appearances at Covent Garden, London. He sang at the Wagner Festival in Bayreuth in 1960, and at the Salzburg Festival in 1967. He made his Metropolitan Opera debut in N.Y., on March 9, 1966 as Ford in *Falstaff.* He also sang the roles of Don Giovanni, Escamillo and Iago. He is married to the American soprano **Evelyn Lear.**

Stibilj, Milan, Slovenian composer; b. Ljubljana, Nov. 2, 1929. He studied composition with Karol Pahor at the Ljubljana Academy of Music (1956–61) and with Kelemen at the Zagreb Academy of Music (1962–64); took courses in electronic music at the Univ. of Utrecht (1966–67). He composes in an advanced idiom, exploring the techniques of integral serial organization of musical parameters.
WORKS: *Anekdote* for piano (1957); *Koncertantna glasba (Concertante Music)* for horn and orch. (1959); *Skladbe (Composition)* for horn and strings (1959); *Sarabanda* for 4 clarinets (1960); *Slavček v vrtnica (The Nightingale and the Rose),* symph. poem (1961); *Skladja (Congruences)* for piano and orch. (1963); *Impressions* for flute, harp, and string quintet or string orch. (1963); *Épervier de ta faiblesse, Domine* for narrator and 5 percussionists (1964); *Verz* for orch. (1964); *Assimilation* for solo violin (1965); *Contemplation* for oboe and string quintet (1966); *Apokatastasis,* Slovenian Requiem for tenor, chorus, and orch. (1967); *Condensation* for trombone, 2 pianos, and percussion (1967); *Zoom* for clarinet and bongos (1970); *Indian Summer* for chamber orch. (1974).

Stich, Jan Václav (Johann Wenzel; he Italianized his German name, Johann Stich, as **Giovanni Punto),** famous Czech horn player; b. Žehušice, near Čáslav, Sept. 28, 1746; d. Prague, Feb. 16, 1803. He studied in Prague, Munich, and Dresden; traveled in Germany and Hungary; visited England; then entered the service of the Elector at Mainz (1769–74); subsequently served at the court of the Prince-Bishop of Würzburg, and in 1782 became chamber musician to the Comte d'Artois (later Charles X) in Paris; in Paris he met Mozart, who wrote the *Symphonie concertante* (K. Anhang 9) for him, the flutist Wendling, the oboist Ramm, and the bassoonist Ritter. During the French revolution (1789–99) Stich was in charge of the music at the Théâtre des Variétés Amusantes; returned to Germany in 1799; proceeded to Vienna in 1800; made the acquaintance of Beethoven, who was enchanted by his playing and wrote for him a sonata for horn and piano (op. 17), and played it with him at a concert on April 18, 1800. He went to Prague in 1801. His works comprise 14 horn concertos, much chamber music with horn, a method for horn (1798; a revision of one by his Dresden teacher Hampel); publ. a book of exercises for the horn (Paris, 1795).

BIBLIOGRAPHY: H. A. Fitzpatrick, *The Horn & Horn-Playing and the Austro-Bohemian Tradition 1680-1830* (London, 1970); R. Morley-Pegge, *The French Horn* (2nd ed., London, 1973).

Stiedry, Fritz, eminent Austrian conductor; b. Vienna, Oct. 11, 1883; d. Zürich, Aug. 9, 1968. He studied jurisprudence in Vienna and took a course in composition with Eusebius Mandyczewski. Mahler recommended him to Ernst von Schuch in Dresden, and he became his assistant conductor (1907-08); he subsequently was active as theater conductor in the German provinces, and in Prague. He conducted at the Berlin Opera (1916-23); then led the Vienna Volksoper (1923-25). After traveling as guest conductor in Italy, Spain, and Scandinavia (1925-28), he returned to Berlin and was music director of the Berlin Municipal Opera (1929-33). With the advent of the Nazi regime in 1933, he went to Russia, where he conducted the Leningrad Philharmonic (1933-37). In 1938 he emigrated to the U.S.; conducted the New Friends of Music Orch. in N.Y. In 1946 he joined the staff of the Metropolitan Opera. As a conductor he championed the modern Viennese school of composition. He was a close friend of Schoenberg; conducted first performances of his opera *Die glückliche Hand* in Vienna (1924) and his 2nd Chamber Symph. in N.Y. (1940). But he also gave fine performances of the operas of Wagner and Verdi. In 1958 he left the U.S. and lived mostly in Zürich.

Stiehl, Carl Johann Christian, German organist and music historian; b. Lübeck, July 12, 1826; d. there, Dec. 2, 1911. He was a pupil of his father, **Johann Dietrich Stiehl;** served as church organist in Jever (1848-58) and at Eutin (1858-77); in 1878 returned to Lübeck, where he conducted the Musikverein and Singakademie (until 1897); also wrote music criticism, and was in charge of the music section in the Lübeck Library.

WRITINGS: *Zur Geschichte der Instrumentalmusik in Lübeck* (1885); *Lübeckisches Tonkünstler-Lexikon* (1887); *Musikgeschichte der Stadt Lübeck* (1891); *Geschichte des Theaters in Lübeck* (1902); ed. Buxtehude's sonatas *a* 3 and 4 (vol. 11 of the *Denkmäler deutscher Tonkunst*).

Stiehl, Heinrich (Franz Daniel), German organist, choral conductor, and composer; son of **Johann Dietrich Stiehl;** b. Lübeck, Aug. 5, 1829; d. Reval, May 1, 1886. He studied with Moscheles, Gade, and Hauptmann at the Leipzig Cons.; in 1853 he went to St. Petersburg, where he remained for 13 years as organist at the Lutheran Church and conductor of a German choral society. He was subsequently active in Vienna (1867-69), in Italy (1869-72), London (1872-73), and Belfast (1874-77). In 1880 he was engaged as organist and conductor in Reval, Estonia, where he remained to the end of his life, with occasional appearances in St. Petersburg. He wrote in all 172 op. numbers, including 2 light operas, *Der Schatzgräber* and *Jery und*

Bätely; Die Vision for orch.; 2 piano quartets; 3 piano trios; a violin sonata; a cello sonata; numerous piano pieces of programmatic content, such as *Spaziergänge im Schwarzwald, Italienische Reisebilder, Hexentanz, Musikalische Portraits,* etc.

Stiehl, Johann Dietrich, German organist; b. Lübeck, July 9, 1800; d. there, June 27, 1873. He lived virtually all his life in Lübeck, where he was organist at St. Jacobi; his sons, **Heinrich** and **Carl Johann Christian,** were also organists.

Stierlin, Adolf, German composer, singer, and pedagogue; b. Adenau, Oct. 14, 1859; d. Münster, April 26, 1930. He studied singing and was engaged as bass at various theaters in Germany; in 1897 he opened his own music school in Münster. He wrote the operas *Scapina* (Münster, 1887) and *Zamora* (Halle, 1893); a ballet, *Die sieben Todsünden;* choruses.

Stigelli, Giorgio (real name **Georg Stiegele**), celebrated German tenor; b. 1815; d. in his villa Boschetti, near Monza, Italy, July 3, 1868. He made extensive concert tours in Europe, and appeared in America in 1864-65. He was the composer of many songs, among them the popular *Die schönsten Augen.*

Still, Robert, English composer; b. London, June 10, 1910; d. Bucklebury, Reading, Jan. 13, 1971. He was educated at Eton College (1923-28) and Oxford Univ. (1929-32); later took courses in musicology at the Royal College of Music in London (1932-33). He served with the Royal Artillery during World War II; began to compose in earnest only after the war. He was also interested in psychoanalysis and publ. an essay on Mahler from the Freudian point of view. His works include 4 symphonies (1954, 1956, 1960, 1964); Violin Concerto (1969); Piano Concerto (1970) and 5 string quartets, as well as minor pieces.

Still, William Grant, eminent American composer, "The Dean of Afro-American Composers"; b. Woodville, Miss., May 11, 1895. His father was a musician, cornetist and leader of a local band, but he died when Still was in infancy. His mother, a graduate of Atlanta Univ., moved the family to Little Rock, Arkansas, where she became a high school teacher. He grew up in a home with cultured, middle-class values, and his stepfather encouraged his interest in music by taking him to see operettas and buying him operatic recordings. He attended Wilberforce Univ. as a science student, but became active in musical activities on campus and abandoned science. After leaving the university he worked with various dance bands and wrote arrangements for W. C. Handy; he then attended Oberlin Conservatory. During WWI he played violin in the U.S. Army; afterwards returned to work with Handy, and became oboist in the *Shuffle Along* orchestra (1921); then studied composition with Varèse, and at New England Conservatory with Chadwick; held a Guggenheim Fellowship in 1934-35; was awarded honorary doctorates by Howard Univ. (1941), Oberlin College (1947), and Bates College (1954). Determined to develop a symphonic type of Negro music, he wrote an *Afro-American Symphony*

(1931). In his music he occasionally makes use of actual Negro folksongs, but mostly he invents his thematic materials. He married the writer Verna Arvey, who collaborated with him as librettist in his stage works.

WORKS: FOR ORCH.: *From the Black Belt* (1926); *Darker America* (Rochester, Nov. 21, 1927); *From the Journal of a Wanderer* (Rochester, May 8, 1929); *Africa*, symph. poem (1930); *Afro-American Symphony* (Rochester, Oct. 29, 1931); *Three Dances*, from the ballet *La Guiablesse* (Rochester, May 5, 1933); *Kaintuck (Kentucky)*, for piano and orch. (Rochester, Jan. 16, 1936); *Dismal Swamp* (Rochester, Oct. 30, 1936); *Ebon Chronicle* (Fort Worth, Nov. 3, 1936); Symph. in G minor (1937); *And They Lynched Him on a Tree*, for narrator, contralto, chorus, and orch. (N.Y., June 25, 1940); *Plain Chant for Americans* for baritone and orch. (N.Y., Oct. 23, 1941); *Old California* (1941); *Pages from Negro History* (1943); *In Memoriam: The Colored Soldiers Who Died for Democracy* (N.Y., Jan. 5, 1944); *Poem* (Cleveland, Dec. 7, 1944); *Festive Overture* (Cincinnati, Jan. 19, 1945); 3rd Symphony (1945); *Archaic Ritual* (1946); *Wood Notes* (Chicago, April 22, 1948); 4th Symphony (1949).

FOR SYMPH. BAND: *From the Delta* (1945), *To You, America* (1952), etc. VOCAL WORKS: *Caribbean Melodies*, for chorus, piano, and percussion (1941), *Wailing Woman*, for soprano and chorus (1946), etc.; *Pastorela* for violin and piano (1946).

STAGE WORKS: *La Guiablesse*, ballet (1927); *Sahdji*, ballet (1930); *Blue Steel*, opera in 3 acts (1935); *Lenox Avenue*, ballet (1937); *Troubled Island*, opera in 4 acts (1938); *A Bayou Legend*, opera in 3 acts (1940); *Miss Sally's Party* (1940); *A Southern Interlude*, opera in 2 acts (1942); *Costaso*, opera in 3 acts (1949); *Highway No. 1, U.S.A.*, one-act opera (Miami, May 13, 1963).

BIBLIOGRAPHY: M. Cuney-Hare, *Negro Musicians and Their Music* (Washington, D.C., 1936); A. Locke, *The Negro and His Music* (Washington, D.C., 1936); Verna Arvey, *William Grant Still* (N.Y., 1939); R. B. Haas, editor, *William Grant Still and the Fusion of Cultures in American Music* (Los Angeles, 1972); F. H. Douglass, "A Tribute to William Grant Still," *Black Perspective in Music* (Spring 1974); "A Birthday Offering to William Grant Still Upon the Occasion of His 80th Anniversary," special issue of *Black Perspective in Music* (May 1975). See also *Modern Music . . . Analytic Index* compiled by Wayne Shirley, edited by Wm. and C. Lichtenwanger (N.Y., 1976; pp. 207–8).

Stillman, Mitya, Russian-American viola player and composer; b. Ilyintza, near Kiev, Jan. 27, 1892; d. New York, April 12, 1936. He studied violin; then was a pupil of Glière in composition at the Kiev Cons.; after the Russian Revolution he emigrated to the U.S.; played the viola in the Detroit Symph. Orch. and in the CBS Radio Orch. As a composer, Stillman developed a strong individual style in a peculiarly compact contrapuntal technique. He wrote 8 string quartets, of which No. 7 received a posthumous 1st prize award from the NBC Guild as the best chamber music work for 1936. He also wrote some programmatic orchestral pieces, among them *Dnieprostroy* (1933), *Yalta Suite* for string trio; *Cyprus* for strings, woodwinds and percussion, etc.

Stillman-Kelley, Edgar. See **Kelley, Edgar Stillman.**

Stirling, Elizabeth, English organist and composer; b. Greenwich, Feb. 26, 1819; d. London, March 25, 1895. She studied organ and piano with Edward Holmes, and harmony with G. A. Macfarren. She was appointed organist of All Saints', Poplar, at the age of 20, and retained this position for nearly 20 years, when she competed for one at St. Andrew's, Undershaft. She won the contest, and was organist there until 1880. In 1856 she passed the examination for the degree of Mus. Bac. at Oxford (her work was *Psalm 130* for 5 voices with orch.), but, ironically, her earned degree could not be granted to a woman. In 1863 she married F. A. Bridge. She made many organ transcriptions from classical works; publ. *6 Pedal-Fugues* and other organ pieces; also part-songs, of which *All Among the Barley* won great popularity.

Stobaeus, Johann, German composer; b. Graudenz, July 6, 1580; d. Königsberg, Sept. 11, 1646. In 1595 he went to Königsberg, where, from 1599–1608, he was a pupil of J. Eccard; in 1601 he entered the Electoral chapel as bass and in 1602 was cantor at the Cathedral. He succeeded Krocker as Kapellmeister to the Elector of Brandenburg in 1626. He publ. *Cantiones sacrae 5-6, 7, 8 et 10 vocibus item aliquot Magnificat 5 et 6 vocibus adornatae* (Frankfurt, 1624); a new ed. of *Geistliche Lieder auf . . . Kirchen-Melodeyen* for 5 voices, with some additional songs of his own (1634); Eccard's *Preussiche Festlieder* (2 vols.; 1642, 1644; modern edition by Teschner, 1858).

BIBLIOGRAPHY: R. Eitner, *Monatshefte für Musikgeschichte* (1883); A. Mayer-Reinach, "Zur Geschichte der Königsberger Hofkapelle," *Sammelbände der Internationalen Musik-Gesellschaft* VI/1 (1904); L. Kamieński, *Johann Stobaeus z Grudziadz* (Posen, 1928).

Stock, David F., American composer, b. Pittsburgh, June 3, 1939. He studied trumpet; then enrolled at the Carnegie Institute of Technology in Pittsburgh, where he took courses in composition with Nikolai Lopatnikoff and musicology with Frederick Dorian. He subsequently obtained his M.F.A. (1963) at Brandeis Univ., studying advanced composition with Arthur Berger and Harold Shapero; played trumpet in various orchestras. His works include *Divertimento* for orch. (1957); *Capriccio* for small orch. (1963); *Symphony in One Movement* (1963); Quintet for clarinet and strings (1966); *Flashback* for chamber ensemble (1968).

Stock, Frederick A., German-American conductor; b. Jülich, Nov. 11, 1872; d. Chicago, Oct. 20, 1942. He was trained in music by his father, a bandmaster; then studied violin with G. Japha and composition with Wüllner, Zöllner, and Humperdinck at the Cologne Cons. (1886–91); subsequently played the violin in the Municipal Orch. in Cologne (1891–95). In 1895 he was engaged by Theodore Thomas as first viola in the newly organized Thomas Symph. Orch., Chicago (the future Chicago Symph. Orch.); he was then delegated to conduct the Thomas Orch. at concerts outside of Chicago proper; after Thomas died in 1905, he inherited the Theo. Thomas Orch. He became a naturalized

U.S. citizen in 1919. As a conductor Stock was extremely competent, even though he totally lacked that ineffable quality of making orchestral music a vivid experience in sound; but he had the merit of giving adequate performances of the classics, of Wagner, and of the German Romantic school. He also programmed several American works, as long as they followed the Germanic tradition. The flowering of the Chicago Symph. Orch. was to be accomplished by his successors Fritz Reiner and Georg Solti. Stock was also a composer; his Violin Concerto was performed under his direction by Efrem Zimbalist at the Norfolk Festival on June 3, 1915.

BIBLIOGRAPHY: P. A. Otis, *The Chicago Symphony Orchestra* (Chicago, 1925).

Stockhausen, Franz, Jr., German conductor and educator; son of **Franz Stockhausen, Sr.;** brother of **Julius Stockhausen;** b. Gebweiler, Alsace, Jan. 30, 1839; d. Strasbourg, Jan. 4, 1926. He received his early training from his father; then was a student of Alkan in Paris; subsequently studied at the Leipzig Cons., where his teachers were Moscheles, Richter, and Hauptmann (1860–62). He subsequently occupied various posts as a choral conductor and educator. In 1871 he was appointed director of the Strasbourg Cons.; retired in 1907.

Stockhausen, Franz, Sr., German singer and harpist; b. Cologne, Sept. 1, 1789; d. Colmar, Sept. 10, 1868. In 1822 he organized in Paris the Académie de Chant, and gave concerts as a harpist.

Stockhausen, Julius, German baritone and teacher; son of the harpist and composer **Franz Stockhausen;** b. Paris, July 22, 1826; d. Frankfurt, Sept. 22, 1906. He studied at the Paris Cons. and in London, where he was a pupil of Manuel García. He began his career as a concert singer and a choral conductor; led the Singakademie in Stuttgart (1862–67) and the Sternscher Gesangverein in Berlin (1874–78). Subsequently he was engaged as a singing teacher in Frankfurt. He was a personal friend of Brahms and was regarded as one of the finest interpreters of his lieder. He published *Gesangsmethode,* a standard work on singing (2 vols., 1886, 1887; also in English).

BIBLIOGRAPHY: Julia Wirth-Stockhausen, *Julius Stockhausen der Sänger des deutschen Liedes* (Frankfurt, 1927) and *Unverlierbare Kindheit* (Stuttgart, 1949); A. H. Fox Strangways, "Julius Stockhausen," *Monthly Musical Record* (March-April 1949).

Stockhausen, Karlheinz, German composer, leader of the cosmopolitan avant-garde; b. Mödrath, near Cologne, Aug. 22, 1928. He studied piano at the Musikhochschule in Cologne (1947–50) and took a course in composition with Frank Martin during the latter's residence there (1950–51); then went to Paris, where he studied privately with Olivier Messiaen and Darius Milhaud (1951–53); also investigated the potentialities of *musique concrète* and partly incorporated its techniques into his own empiric method of composition, which from the very first included highly complex contrapuntal conglomerates with uninhibited applications of non-euphonious dissonance as well as re-

course to the primal procedures of obdurate iteration of single tones; all this set in the freest of rhythmic patterns and diversified by constantly changing instrumental colors with obsessive percussive effects. He further perfected a system of constructivist composition, in which the subjective choice of the performer determines the succession of given thematic ingredients and their polyphonic simultaneities, ultimately leading to a totality of aleatory procedures, in which the ostensible application of a composer's commanding function is paradoxically reasserted by the inclusion of prerecorded materials and recombinant uses of electronically altered thematic ingredients. He further evolved energetic missionary activities in behalf of new music as a lecturer and master of ceremonies at avant-garde meetings all over the world; conducted summer seminars for the Ferienkurse für Musik in Darmstadt, which attracted auditors and musical cultists from the 5 continents of the globe; having mastered the intricacies of the English language, he made a lecture tour of Canadian and American universities in 1958; was visiting prof. at the Univ. of California, Davis, in 1966–67; gave highly successful public lectures in England in 1969, which were attended by hordes of musical and unmusical novitiates; published numerous misleading guidelines for the benefit of a growing contingent of his apostles, disciples and acolytes. Stockhausen is a pioneer of "time-space" music, marked by a controlled improvisation, and adding the vectorial (i.e., directional) parameter to the four traditional aspects of serial music (pitch, duration, timbre, and dynamics), with performers and electronic apparatuses placed in different parts of the concert hall; such performances, directed by himself, are often accompanied by screen projections and audience participation; he also specifies the architectural aspects of the auditoriums in which he gives his demonstrations; thus at the world's fair in Osaka, Japan, in 1970, he supervised the construction of a circular auditorium in the German pavilion; these demonstrations continued for 183 days with 20 soloists and 5 lantern projections in live performances of his own works, each session lasting 5 1/2 hours; the estimated live, radio, and television audience was 1,000,000 listeners. In 1963 he inaugurated courses of new music in Cologne; in 1971 he was appointed prof. of composition at the Musikhochschule there.

WORKS: *Kreuzspiel* for orch. (1952); *Kontra-Punkte* for 10 instruments (Cologne, May 26, 1953); *Klavierstück XI* (one of a series of constructivist pieces); *Zeitmasse,* for oboe, flute, English horn, clarinet, and bassoon (1956); *Der Gesang der Jünglinge,* to a text composed of disjected verbal particles from the *Book of Daniel,* dealing with the ordeal of 3 monotheistic Hebrew youths in the Babylonian fiery furnace, scored for 5 groups of loudspeakers surrounding the audience (first performed at the Radio Studio in Cologne, May 30, 1956); *Gruppen,* spatial work for 3 chamber orchestras and 3 conductors beating 3 different tempi (Cologne, March 24, 1959); *Kontakte* for electronic instruments, piano, and percussion (Cologne, June 11, 1960); *Carré* for 4 orchestras, 4 choruses, and 4 conductors (Hamburg, Oct. 28, 1960); *Zyklus* for one percussionist (1961); *Momente* for soprano, 4 choruses (singing, speaking, whispering, screaming, laughing, stamping, clapping, etc.), 13 instrumentalists, and percussion (Cologne, May 21, 1962; extended and revised, 1965); *Mikrophonie I* and *II* for flexible ensembles (1964, 1965); *Stimmung* for 6 singers (1967); *X,* for dancers (1967), autogenetically producing sounds by activating eggshells placed on the floor or piano wires strung across the stage; *Hymnen,* electronic piece (Cologne, Nov. 30, 1967); *Aus den Sieben Tagen,* for optional instruments (1968), written out in graphic notation with verbal instructions, such as "play a tone in the certainty that you have plenty of time and space"; *Telemusik* for an instrumental ensemble and electronic instruments (Warsaw, Sept. 23, 1968); *Plus-Minus* for clarinet, trombone, cello, and 3 pianos (Warsaw, Sept. 25, 1968); *Kurzwellen* for 5 performers (1969); *Prozession* for tamtam, viola, electronium, piano, and microphone (1969); *Für kommende Zeiten* for "17 texts of intuitive music" (1968–70); *Beethausen, opus 1970, von Stockhoven,* bicentennial homage to Beethoven for multimedia, using fragments from Beethoven's works, and including a reading of the Heiligenstadt Testament (1970); *Mantra* for 2 pianos (Donaueschingen, Oct. 18, 1970); *Sternklang,* "park music" for 5 groups (1971); *Musik im Bauch (Music in the Belly)* for percussion and musical clocks (1975); *Sirius,* multimedia work for vocalists, trumpet, bass clarinet, and electronic sound, dedicated to American pioneers on earth and in space (first demonsrated at the National Air and Space Museum at the Smithsonian Institution, Washington, D.C., July 18, 1976).

BIBLIOGRAPHY: Karl H. Wörner, *Karlheinz Stockhausen, Werk und Wollen* (1950–62; in English, London, 1973); J. Cott, *Stockhausen: Conversations with the Composer* (London, 1973); Cornelius Cardew, *Stockhausen Serves Imperialism,* a rambling diatribe by a disenchanted follower who became a militant Maoist (London, 1974); J. Harvey, *The Music of Stockhausen: An Introduction* (London, 1975); Robin Maconie, *Stockhausen* (London, 1976). His annotations to his own works were published in 3 volumes under the title *Texte zur elektronischen und instrumentalen Musik* (Cologne, 1963, 1964, 1966).

Stockhoff, Walter William, American composer; b. St. Louis, Nov. 12, 1876, of German parentage; d. there, April 1, 1968. He was largely autodidact, and began to compose early in life. In his music he was influenced mainly by German Romantic composers, but his thematic material is distinctly American. In some of his early piano music he made use of modernistic devices, such as the whole-tone scale, cadential triads with the added sixth, etc. Busoni wrote an enthusiastic article about Stockhoff (1915) in which he described him as one of the most original composers of America. The orchestral version of Stockhoff's piano suite *To the Mountains* was performed for the first time, under the title *American Symphonic Suite,* in Frankfurt, Germany, on Dec. 10, 1924. Several of his piano works and some chamber music were publ. by Breitkopf & Härtel. Other works include *5 Dramatic Poems* for orch. (1943); Piano Sonata; *Metamorphoses* for piano, etc.

Stoeckel, Carl, American patron of music; son of **Gustav Jakob Stoeckel;** b. New Haven, Connecticut, Dec. 7, 1858; d. Norfolk, Conn., Nov. 1, 1925. His contribution to American music culture was the establishment of the summer festivals on his estate in 1902 in Norfolk, Conn. He offered cash prizes to composers who appeared at the festival in performances of their own works. Sibelius composed his tone-poem *Aallottaret* especially for the Norfolk Festival, and conducted its world première there in 1914. Among other composers represented were J. A. Carpenter, G. W. Chadwick, S. Coleridge-Taylor, H. F. Gilbert, P. Grainger, H. K. Hadley, E. S. Kelly, C. M. Loeffler, H. Parker, D. S. Smith, C. V. Stanford, and Deems Taylor.

Stoeckel, Gustav Jakob, German-American musician; b. Maikammer, Bavarian Palatinate, Nov. 9, 1819; d. Norfolk, Connecticut, May 14, 1907. He emigrated to America in 1847; served as chapel organist at Yale Univ. and was prof. of music there until 1896. He composed some vocal and instrumental pieces, arranged college songs, and assisted in editing the *College Hymn Book* for men's voices.

BIBLIOGRAPHY: D. S. Smith, *G. J. Stoeckel, Yale Pioneer in Music* (New Haven, 1939).

Stoessel, Albert, American conductor and composer; b. St. Louis, Oct. 11, 1894; d. New York, May 12, 1943. He went to Germany as a youth; studied violin with Willy Hess and theory with Kretzschmar in Berlin, and appeared as violin soloist there in 1914. Returning to the U.S., he turned to conducting; succeeded Walter Damrosch as conductor of the N.Y. Oratorio Society; in 1930 was appointed director of the opera dept. of the Juilliard Graduate School of Music, N.Y. He was stricken fatally while conducting the first performance of the symph. sketch *Dunkirk,* by Walter Damorsch. His *Suite Antique,* for 2 violins and piano (1922) enjoyed a few performances. His opera *Garrick* was produced under his direction at the Juilliard School on Feb. 24, 1937. He published *The Technic of the Baton* (N.Y., 1920; new ed., 1928).

Stoeving, (Carl Heinrich) Paul, German-American violinist and composer; b. Leipzig, May 7, 1861; d. New York, Dec. 24, 1948. He studied violin in Leipzig and in Paris; toured as a soloist in Russia and Scandinavia; in 1896 went to London, where he taught at the Guildhall School of Music. At the outbreak of World War I he emigrated to the U.S. and was employed as violin teacher in New Haven and N.Y. He wrote the "song-play" *Gaston and Jolivette* and some violin music of considerable insignificance, but his publications on violin technique have a certin pragmatic value; among them are *The Art of Violin Bowing* (London, 1902); *The Story of the Violin* (London, 1904); *The Mastery of the Bow and Bowing Subtleties* (N.Y., 1920); *The Violin, Cello and String Quartet* (N.Y., 1927); *The Violin: Its Famous Makers and Players* (Boston, 1928).

Stöhr, Richard, Austrian music theorist and composer; b. Vienna, June 11, 1874; d. Montpelier, Vermont, Dec. 11, 1967. He studied medicine (M.D.,

1898), but then turned to music and studied with Robert Fuchs and others at the Vienna Cons. In 1904 he was appointed instructor in theory there, and during his long tenure he had many pupils who later became celebrated (Artur Rodzinski, Erich Leinsdorf, etc.).In 1938 he was compelled to leave Vienna; settled in the U.S., where he taught at the Curtis Institute of Music, Philadelphia (1939–41); then taught music and German at St. Michael's College, Winooski, Vermont. A concert of his works was given by the Vermont State Symph. Orch. on Oct. 31, 1954, including the world première of his *Vermont Suite,* an early symphony, and songs accompanied by the composer. He further wrote 4 symphonies; much chamber music; piano pieces. He publ. a popular manual *Praktischer Leitfaden der Harmonielehre* (Vienna, 1909; 14th ed., 1928); also *Praktischer Leitfaden des Kontrapunkts* (Hamburg, 1911); *Modulationslehre* (1932).

BIBLIOGRAPHY: R. Felber, "Richard Stöhr," in *Cobbett's Cyclopedic Survey of Chamber Music* (London, 1930; vol. 2); H. Sittner, *Richard Stöhr, Mensch, Musiker, Lehrer* (Vienna, 1964).

Stojanovits, Peter Lazar, violinist and composer; b. Budapest, Sept. 6, 1877; d. Belgrade, Sept. 12, 1957. He studied violin with Hubay at the Budapest Cons. and with J. Grün at the Vienna Cons.; in 1913 established his own school for advanced violin playing in Vienna. In 1925 he settled in Belgrade and became director of the Belgrade Cons. His works include the operas *A Tigris* (The Tiger; Budapest, Nov. 14, 1905), *Das Liebchen am Dache* (Vienna, May 19, 1917), *Der Herzog von Reichsstadt* (Vienna, Feb. 11, 1921); an operetta, *Orlić;* 2 ballets; a symph. poem, *Heldentod;* 7 violin concertos, 2 viola concertos, a flute concerto, a horn concerto; several pieces of chamber music, including a piano trio, a piano quartet, and a piano quintet. He publ. *Schule der Skalentechnik* for violin.

Stojowski, Sigismund, Polish pianist; b. Strzelce, May 14, 1869; d. New York, Nov. 5, 1946. He was a pupil of Zelenski at Cracow and of Diémer (piano) and Delibes (composition) at the Paris Cons. (1887–89), winning 1st prize for piano playing and composition; later he took a course with Paderewski. At an orchestral concert of his own works, given in Paris in 1891, he played his Piano Concerto; he remained in Paris until 1906, when he emigrated to the U.S. as head of the piano dept. at the Institute of Musical Art in N.Y.; later held a similar position at the Von Ende School of Music, N.Y.; taught at the Juilliard Summer School for several years. He became a naturalized American citizen in 1938. In his prime he was extremely successful as concert pianist, and in his later years was greatly esteemed as a pedagogue. His works include, besides his Piano Concerto, *Prologue, Scherzo and Variations,* for piano and orch., performed by him (as Piano Concerto No. 2) in London, June 23, 1913, under the direction of Nikisch; many solo piano pieces; *Prayer for Poland,* for chorus and orch. (1915); 2 violin sonatas; a cello sonata.

Stoker, Richard, English composer; b. Castleford, Yorkshire, 1938. He studied composition with Eric Fenby and later with Lennox Berkeley at the Royal Academy of Music in London, and with Nadia Boulanger in Paris. In his music he cultivates the 12-tone technique, but derives it tonally from the quintal cycle of scales. As a believer in the universality of the arts, he writes utilitarian music for dilettantes, amateurs, musicasters, and children.

WORKS: Trio for flute, oboe, and clarinet (1960); *Festival Suite* for trumpet and piano (1961); Clarinet Sonata (1961); Wind Quintet (1962); *Miniature Spring Trio* (1963); Sextet for wind and strings (1963); Violin Sonata (1964); Piano Trio (1965); *Three Miniature Quartets* (1966); an opera, *Johnson Preserv'd* (London, July 4, 1967).

Stokowski, Leopold, celebrated, spectacularly endowed and magically communicative English-American conductor; b. (of Polish father and Irish mother) London, April 18, 1882; d. Nether Wallop, Hampshire, Sept. 13, 1977. He attended Queen's College, Oxford, and the Royal College of Music in London, where he studied organ with Stevenson Hoyte, music theory with Walford Davies and composition with Sir Charles Stanford. At the age of 18 he obtained the position of organist at St. James, Piccadilly. In 1905 he went to America and served as organist and choirmaster at St. Bartholomew's in N.Y.; became a U.S. citizen in 1915. In 1909 he was engaged to conduct the Cincinnati Symph. Orch.; although his contract was for 5 years, he obtained a release after 3 years of tenure in order to accept an offer from the Philadelphia Orch. This was the beginning of a long and spectacular career as symphonic conductor; he led the Philadelphia Orch. for 23 years, bringing it to a degree of brilliance that rivaled the greatest orchestras in the world. In 1931 he was officially designated by the Board of Directors of the Philadelphia Orch. as musical director, which gave him control over the choice of guest conductors and soloists. He conducted most of the repertory by heart, an impressive accomplishment at the time; he changed the seating of the orchestra, placing violins to the left and cellos on the right. After some years of leading the orchestra with a baton, he finally dispensed with it and shaped the music with the 10 fingers of his hands. He emphasized the colorful elements in the music; he was the creator of the famous "Philadelphia sound" in the strings, achieving a well-nigh *bel canto* quality. Tall and slender, with an aureole of blond hair, his figure presented a striking contrast with his stocky mustachioed German predecessors; he was the first conductor to attain the status of a star comparable to that of a motion picture actor. Abandoning the proverbial ivory tower in which most conductors dwelt, he actually made an appearance as a movie actor in the film *One Hundred Men and a Girl.* In 1940 he agreed to participate in the production of Walt Disney's celebrated film *Fantasia,* which featured both live performers and animated characters; Stokowski conducted the music and in one sequence engaged in a bantering colloquy with Mickey Mouse. He was lionized by the Philadelphians; in 1922 he received the Edward Bok Award of $10,000 as "the person who has done the most for Philadelphia." He was praised in superlative terms in the press, but not all music critics approved of his cavalier treatment of sacrosanct masterpieces, for he allowed himself to alter the orchestration; he doubled some solo passages in the brass, and occasionally introduced percussion instruments not provided in the score; he even cut out individual bars that seemed to him devoid of musical action. Furthermore, Stokowski's own orchestral arrangements of Bach raised the pedantic eyebrows of professional musicologists; yet there is no denying the effectiveness of the sonority and the subtlety of color that he succeeded in creating by such means. Many great musicians hailed Stokowski's new orchestral sound; Rachmaninoff regarded the Philadelphia Orch. under Stokowski, and later under Ormandy, as the greatest with which he had performed. Stokowski boldly risked his popularity with the Philadelphia audiences by introducing modern works. He conducted Schoenberg's music, culminating in the introduction of his formidable score *Gurrelieder* on April 8, 1932. Even a greater gesture of defiance of popular tastes was his world premiere of *Amériques* by Varèse on April 9, 1926, a score that opens with a siren and thrives on dissonance. Stokowski made history by joining the forces of the Philadelphia Orch. with the Philadelphia Grand Opera Co. in the first American performance of Alban Berg's modern masterpiece *Wozzeck* (March 31, 1931). The opposition of some listeners was now vocal; when the audible commotion in the audience erupted during Stokowski's performance of Anton von Webern's Symphony, he abruptly stopped conducting, walked off the stage, then returned only to begin the work all over again. From his earliest years with the Philadelphia Orch., Stokowski adopted the habit of addressing the audience, to caution them to keep their peace during the performance of a modernistic score, or reprimanding them for their lack of progressive views; once he even took to task the prim Philadelphia ladies for bringing their knitting to the concert. In 1933 the Board of Directors took an unusual step in announcing that there would be no more "debatable music" performed by the orchestra. Stokowski refused to heed this proclamation; another eruption of discontent ensued when Stokowski programmed some Soviet music at a youth concert and trained the children to sing the Internationale. Stokowski was always interested in new electronic sound; he was the first to make use of the Theremin in the orchestra in order to enhance the sonorities of the bass section. He was instrumental in introducing electrical recordings. In 1936 he resigned as musical director of the Philadelphia Orch.; he was succeeded by Eugene Ormandy but continued to conduct occasional concerts as coconductor of the Philadelphia Orch. In 1940–42 he took a newly organized All-American Youth Orch. on a tour in the U.S. and in South America. During the season 1942–43 he was associate conductor with Toscanini at the NBC Symph. Orch.; he shared the season of 1949–50 with Mitropoulos as conductor of the N.Y. Philharmonic; from 1955 to 1962 he conducted the Houston, Texas, Symph. In 1962 he organized in N.Y. the American Symph. Orch. and led it until 1973. On April 26, 1965, at the age of 83, he conducted the American Symph. Orch. in the first complete performance of the 4th Symphony of Charles Ives. In 1973 he went to London, where he continued to make recordings and conduct occasional concerts; he also appeared in television interviews. He died in his sleep at the age of 95; the rumor had it that he had a contract signed for a gala performance on his 100th birthday in 1982. Stokowski was married 3 times: his first wife was the pianist **Olga Samaroff,** whom he married in 1911; they were divorced in 1923; his second wife was Evangeline Brewster Johnson, heiress to the Johnson and Johnson drug fortune; they were married in 1926 and divorced in 1937; his third marriage, to Gloria Vanderbilt, produced a ripple of prurient newspaper publicity because of the disparity in their ages; he was 63, she was 21; they were married in 1945 and divorced in 1955. Stokowski published a popular book *Music for All of Us* (N.Y., 1943), which was translated into the Russian, Italian and Czech languages.

BIBLIOGRAPHY: Hope Stoddard, *Symphony Conductors of the U.S.A.* (N.Y., 1957; pp. 215–27); Harold Schonberg, *The Great Conductors* (N.Y., 1967); Herbert Kupferberg, *Those Fabulous Philadelphians* (N.Y., 1969; pp. 30–111); E. Johnson, editor, *Stokowski: Essays in Analysis of His Art* (London, 1973); Abram Chasins, *Stoki, the Ageless Apollo* (N.Y., 1979).

Stoltz, Rosine (real name **Victoire Noël**), French mezzo-soprano; b. Paris, Feb. 13, 1815; d. there, July 28, 1903. She was the daughter of a janitor; was sent by Duchess de Berri to a convent, and in 1826 to the Choron School, which she entered under the name of Rosa Nina. She first appeared in public under the assumed name of **Mlle. Ternaux;** later as **Mlle. Héloise Stoltz** (the latter being derived from her mother's maiden name Stoll). Her first important engagement was in Brussels on June 3, 1836, when she sang Rachel in Halévy's *La Juive*, with Adolphe Nourrit, who recommended her to the administration of the Paris Opéra; made her debut there as Rachel on Aug. 25, 1837. She became intimate with Leon Pillet, manager of the Opéra from 1844, and through him wielded considerable influence on appointments of new singers; after a series of attacks in the press, accusing her of unworthy intrigues, she resigned in March, 1847; fought for vindication through 3 obviously inspired pamphlets (C. Cantinjou, *Les Adieux de Madame Stoltz;* E. Pérignon, *Rosine Stoltz*, and J. Lemer, *Madame Rosine Stoltz*), all published in 1847. At the invitation of the Brazilian Emperor Don Pedro (who was romantically attached to her) she made 4 tours of Brazil between 1850 and 1859, at a salary of 400,000 francs a season. She was married to A. Lescuyer (March 2, 1837, legitimizing a son born Sept. 21, 1836); was subsequently married to the Duke Carlo Lesignano (May 18, 1872); assumed the title of Baroness von Ketschendorf, from the castle given her by Ernest Ketschendorf, Duke of Saxe-Cobourg-Gotha. She publ. 6 songs (not composed by her in all probability), and her name (as Princesse de Lesignano) was used as author of a learned volume, *Les Constitutions de tous les pays civilisés* (1880), which was written in her behalf. The mystifying aspects of her private life and public career are recounted by G. Bord in *Rosine Stoltz* (Paris, 1909) and by A. Pougin in "La Vérité sur Madame Stoltz," *Le Ménestrel* (Aug. 28, 1909 *et seq.*).

Stoltzer, Thomas, German composer of sacred music; b. Schweidnitz, Silesia, c.1475; d. as chaplain of the Hungarian King Louis in the battle of Mohács, Aug. 29, 1526. He entered the service of Hungary in 1522. His Latin psalms were publ. in 1538, 1545, and 1569; German songs were included in collections of 1536, 1539, and 1544. His *Octo tonorum melodiae,* containing instrumental fantasies for 5 voices, is a collection of pieces in all 8 church modes. Modern reprints are in the *Denkmäler deutscher Tonkuest* 34 and 65, *Das Chorwerk* 6, and *Das Erbe deutscher Musik* 22 and 66.

BIBLIOGRAPHY: K. L. Hampe, *Die deutschen Psalmen des Thomas Stoltzer* (Halle, 1943); G. Reese, *Music in the Renaissance* (N.Y., 1954).

Stolz, Robert, Austrian operetta composer; b. Graz, Aug. 25, 1880; d. West Berlin, June 27, 1975. He studied music with his father; then took lessons with Robert Fuchs in Vienna and with Humperdinck in Berlin. He conducted performances at the Theater an der Wien for 12 years, and also filled guest engagements in Europe. In 1938 he went to Paris, and in 1940 proceeded to the U.S.; he returned to Vienna in 1946. He possessed an extraordinary facility for stage music and composed 27 operettas in a typical Viennese manner; of these the most famous is *Zwei Herzen im 3/4 Takt* (Zürich, Sept. 30, 1933). Other operettas are: *Die lustigen Weiber von Wien* (Munich, 1909), *Das Glücksmädel* (1910); *Das Lumperl* (Graz, 1915); *Lang, lang, ist's her* (Vienna, March 28, 1917); *Der Tanz ins Glück* (Vienna, Oct. 18, 1921); *Die Tanzgräfin* (Vienna, May 13, 1921); *Mädi* (Vienna, Oct. 5, 1923); *Ein Ballroman oder der Kavalier von zehn bis vier* (Vienna, Feb. 29, 1924); *Eine einzige Nacht* (Vienna, Dec. 23, 1927); *Peppina* (1931); *Wild Violets* (1932); *Venus in Seide* (1932); *Frühling im Prater* (Vienna, Dec. 22, 1949); *Karneval in Wien* (1950); *Trauminsel* (Bregenz, July 21, 1962); *Frühjahrs-Parade* (Vienna, March 25, 1964). He wrote a number of film scores and nearly 2000 lieder. After he was forced to leave Austria he composed a funeral march for Hitler (at a time when Hitler was, unfortunately, very much alive).

BIBLIOGRAPHY: G. Holm, *Im 3/4 Takt durch die Welt,* a biography (Linz, 1948); W.-D. Brümmel and Fr. van Booth, *Robert Stolz, Melodie eines Lebens* (Hamburg, 1967; contains a chronology of his productions).

Stolz, Teresa (Teresina), soprano; b. Kosteletz, Bohemia, June 2, 1834; d. Milan, Aug. 23, 1902. She studied at the Cons. of Prague, and later with Luigi Ricci in Trieste; began her operatic career in Russia; from 1865 until 1879 she appeared with brilliant success at the principal Italian opera houses. She was greatly admired by Verdi, and was famous in the roles of Aida, and of Leonora in *La Forza del destino.* Her farewell appearance was in Verdi's *Requiem* at La Scala, Milan, on June 30, 1879.

BIBLIOGRAPHY: U. Zoppi, *Mariani, Verdi e Stolz* (Milan, 1947).

Stölzel (Stölz), Gottfried Heinrich, German composer; b. Grünstädtl, Jan. 13, 1690; d. Gotha, Nov. 27, 1749. He studied with the cantor Umlauf at Schnee-

berg, and with Melchior Hofmann at Leipzig; became a music teacher in Breslau (1710–12), where his opera *Narcissus* was performed in 1711; this was followed by productions of his operas *Valeria, Artemisia,* and *Orion* (all in 1712). After a journey to Italy, he was in Prague, where he brought out the operas *Venus und Adonis* (1714), *Acis und Galathea* (1715), and *Das durch die Liebe besiegte Glück* (1716). He subsequently went to Bayreuth, where he produced the opera *Diomedes* (1717), to Gera, and to Gotha, where he produced *Der Musenberg* (1723). Altogether he wrote 22 operas, the pastoral *Rosen und Dornen,* 14 oratorios, 8 double sets of cantatas and motets for the church year, other religious works, symphonies, serenades, concertos, etc.; a concerto grosso ed. by Schering is found in the *Denkmäler deutscher Tonkunst* 29–30; a solo cantata for contralto was ed. by J. Bachmair (1926). His autobiography was reprinted in *Selbstbiographien deutscher Musiker,* ed. by Willi Kahl (Cologne, 1948).

BIBLIOGRAPHY: W. Schmidt-Weiss, *G. H. Stölzel als Instrumentalkomponist* (Würzburg, 1939).

Stone, Kurt, German-American musicologist; b. Hamburg, Germany, Nov. 14, 1911. He studied music in Hamburg and Copenhagen; came to New York in 1938 and entered the field of music publishing; held editorial positions with the Associated Music Publishers and G. Schirmer, Inc.; contributed knowledgeable articles on modern music and composers to various periodicals. He also edited reprints of old music, among them *Parthenia* (N.Y., 1951); translated from the German (with his wife Else Stone) the *Handbook of Percussion Instruments* by Karl Peinkofer and Fritz Tannigel (N.Y., 1977); also with his wife ed. and annotated *The Writings of Elliott Carter* (Bloomington, Indiana, 1977).

Stöpel, Franz (David Christoph), German writer on music; b. Oberheldrungen, Nov. 14, 1794; d. Paris, Dec. 19, 1836. He introduced Logier's method of piano teaching in Berlin in 1822; later taught it in other cities, finally in Paris; nowhere with striking success.

WRITINGS: *Grundzüge der Geschichte der modernen Musik* (1821); *Beiträge zur Würdigung der neuen Methode des gleichzeitigen Unterrichts einer Mehrzahl Schüler im Pianofortespiel und der Theorie der Harmonie* (1823); *System der Harmonielehre* (after Logier; 1825); *Über J. B. Logiers System der Musikwissenschaft* (1827); etc.

Stör, Carl, German violinist and composer; b. Stolberg, June 29, 1814; d. Weimar, Jan. 17, 1889. He was a pupil of Götze and Lobe at Weimar; appointed court conductor in 1857, but in a few years failing eyesight compelled his resignation. He composed the opera *Die Flucht* (Weimar, 1843); *Tonbilder zu Schillers "Lied von der Glocke"* for orch.; Violin Concerto; several ballets; a *Ständchen* for cello with orch.; songs.

Storace, (Anna Selina) Nancy, celebrated English soprano; b. London, Oct. 27, 1765; d. there, Aug. 24, 1817. She was of Italian origin; her father **Stefano Storace** was a player on the double bass; her brother **Stephen Storace** was a composer. She was a pupil of

Rauzzini and of Sacchini in Venice; sang in Florence, Milan, and Parma; then went to Vienna in 1784, where she was engaged at the court opera. She created the role of Susanna in Mozart's *Nozze di Figaro* (May 1, 1786). Returning to England in 1787, she became popular as a singer in comic operas.

BIBLIOGRAPHY: M. K. Ward, "Nancy Storace," *Musical Times* (Nov. 1949); B. Matthews, "The Childhood of Nancy Storace," *Musical Times* (1969).

Storace, Stephen, English composer; b. London, Jan. 4, 1763; d. there, March 19, 1796. He was a brother of **Nancy Storace,** and son of **Stefano Storace,** an excellent double-bass player of Italian descent; the original family name was Sorace, but upon moving to England it was found that the pronunciation sore-ass was offensive. He studied violin at the Cons. di S. Onofrio in Naples; then followed his sister to Vienna, and became acquainted with Mozart there. Two of his operas to Italian libretti was produced in Vienna with satisfying success: *Gli Sposi malcontenti* (June 1, 1785) and *Gli Equivoci* (Dec. 27, 1786). Back in London he produced another Italian opera, *La Cameriera astuta* (March 4, 1788) and a number of English operas, among which *The Haunted Tower,* produced on Nov. 24, 1789, became extremely successful, and was revived in performance in London as late as 1922. His other operas were *No Song, No Supper* (April 16, 1790); *The Siege of Belgrade* (Jan. 1, 1791); *The Pirates* (Nov. 21, 1792); *The Prize* (March 11, 1793); *My Grandmother* (Dec. 16, 1793); *The Cherokee* (Dec. 20, 1794); *The Three and the Deuce* (Sept. 2, 1795). A grand opera, *Mahmoud, or The Prince of Persia,* left unfinished at his death, was completed by Michael Kelly and performed posthumously on April 30, 1796. Storace wrote several other pieces for the theater, some of them adaptations, admitted or concealed, of operas by other composers, e.g. Dittersdorf's *Doktor und Apotheker* and Salieri's *Grotta di Trofonio.*

BIBLIOGRAPHY: R. Graves, "The Comic Operas of Stephen Storace," *Musical Times* (Oct. 1954).

Storch, M. Anton, Austrian conductor and composer; b. Vienna, Dec. 22, 1813; d. there, Dec. 31, 1888. He was conductor at the Carl and Josephstadt Theaters in Vienna, and produced several of his operettas and opera-burlesques there: *Romeo und Julie* (Oct. 31, 1863); *Das Festkleid* (April 1, 1865), *Löwen im Dorfe* (Sept. 27, 1866), *Wiener Zugstücke* (April 26, 1868), *Prinz Taugenichts* (March 8, 1870; successful); wrote many favorite male quartets (*Letzte Treue, Grün,* etc.).

Storchio, Rosina, Italian soprano; b. Venice, May 19, 1876; d. Milan, July 24, 1945. She studied in Mantua and made her debut at 16. On Feb. 17, 1904, she created the title role in the world première of *Madama Butterfly* at La Scala in Milan. After a series of tours in South America and in Europe, she was briefly engaged at the Chicago Opera (1920–21); then retired from the stage. She was paralyzed during the last years of her life as a result of an apoplectic stroke.

Storck, Karl, Alsatian writer on music; b. Dürmenach, April 23, 1873; d. Olsberg, May 9, 1920. He stud-

ied at the Universities of Strasbourg and Berlin (Dr. phil. 1897); wrote music criticism for the *Deutsche Zeitung* (Berlin). He publ. a unique edition, *Musik und Musiker in Karikatur und Satire* (Oldenburg, 1911), richly illustrated by numerous reproductions of caricatures on musical subjects; other publications include: *Der Tanz* (1903); *Geschichte der Musik* (1904); *Das Opernbuch* (1905; 44th printing, 1946); *Die Kulturelle Bedeutung der Musik* (1907); *Mozart* (1908; 2nd ed., 1923); *Musik-Politik* (1911); *Emil Jaques-Dalcroze* (1912). He edited selections from the letters of Beethoven (1905; 3rd ed., 1922), Mozart (1906), and Schumann (1906).

Storer, John, English organist and composer; b. Hulland, near Derby, May 18, 1858; d. Berwick-on-Tweed, May 1, 1930. He was a chorister at various churches before entering Oxford Univ. (Mus. Bac., 1878). In 1891 he became music director of the old Globe Theatre in London, and later filled similar positions in London; settled in Waterford, Ireland, as organist of the Roman Catholic Cathedral, and prof. of plainchant at St. John's Ecclesiastical College; left Waterford in 1916 and lived in Sheffield and Reading, England. He composed the operas *The Punchbowl* (London, 1887) and *Gretna Green* (London, 1889); an oratorio, *Deborah and Barak* (1881); 2 symphonies: *The Holiday* (1909) and *Vita* (1914); several Masses; church services; songs; organ pieces.

Stout, Alan, significant American composer; b. Baltimore, Nov. 26, 1932. He studied composition with Henry Cowell at the Peabody Cons. in Baltimore; sporadically had composition lessons with Riegger in N.Y. (1951–56); then went to Denmark and took a course with Holmboe (1954–55); returning to the U.S. he had lessons with John Verrall at the Univ. of Washington (1958–59), acquiring an M.A. in music and in Swedish language; from 1959 to 1962 was employed in the music department of the Seattle Public Library; in 1963 he was appointed to the music faculty of Northwestern Univ.; in 1973 was visiting lecturer at the State College of Music in Stockholm. Besides his primary activities as composer and teacher, he also performed valuable service in editing (with some conjectural reconstruction) fragmentary pieces by Ives, to prepare them for practical performance.

WORKS: FOR ORCH.: 4 symphonies: No. 1 (1959), No. 2 (1951–66; Ravinia Festival, Chicago Symph., Aug. 4, 1968); No. 3 for soprano, male chorus and orch. (1959–62); No. 4 (1962–71; Chicago April 15, 1971); *3 Hymns* for orch. (1953–54); *Intermezzo* for English horn, percussion, and strings (1954); *Pietà* for string or brass orch. (1957); *Serenity* for solo cello or bassoon, percussion, and strings (1959); *Ricercare and Aria* for strings (1959); *Movements* for violin and orch. (1962; Fish Creek, Wisconsin, Aug. 17, 1966); *Movements* for clarinet and string orch. (1969); *Fanfare for Charles Seeger* for orch. (1972); *Pulsar* for 3 brass choirs and timpani (1972). VOCAL WORKS: *2 Hymns* for tenor and orch. (1953); *Die Engel* for soprano, flute, piano, percussion, and brass (1957); *2 Ariel Songs* for soprano and chamber ensemble (1957); *Laudi* for soprano, baritone, and small orch. (1961); *Elegiac Suite* for soprano and strings

(1959-61); *Canticum Canticorum* for soprano and chamber ensemble (1962); *George Lieder* for high baritone and orch. (1962; revised 1965 and 1970; Chicago, Dec. 14, 1972); *Christmas Poem* for soprano and chamber ensemble (1962); *Prologue,* oratorio (1963-64); *Nattstycken (Nocturnes)* for narrator, contralto, and chamber ensemble (1969-70; Chicago, Nov. 10, 1970); *Dialogo per la Pascua* for soloists, chorus, and 8 instruments (1973); *O Altitudo* for soprano, women's chorus, solo flute, and instrumental ensemble (1974); *Passion,* oratorio (1953-75; Chicago, April 15, 1976); choruses, including *The Great Day of the Lord* (with organ, 1956). CHAMBER MUSIC: 10 string quartets (1952-53, 1952, 1954, 1954, 1957, 1959, 1960, 1960, 1962, 1962); *Solemn Prelude* for trombone and organ (1953); Quintet for clarinet and string quartet (1958); *Triptych* for horn and organ (1961); *Suite* for flute and percussion (1962); *Toccata* for saxophone and percussion (1965); Cello Sonata (1966); *Music* for oboe and piano (1966); *Music* for flute and harpsichord (1967); *2 Movements* for clarinet and string quartet (1968); *Recitative, Capriccio and Aria* for oboe, harp, and percussion (1970); *Suite* for saxophone and organ (1973). FOR PIANO: *Varianti* (1962), *Fantasia* (1962), *Suite* (1964-67), 2-Piano Sonata (1975), *Waltz* (1977). FOR ORGAN: a set of 8 *Chorale Preludes* (1960), a set of 3 *Chorale Preludes* (1967), *Study in Densities and Durations* (1966-67) and *Study in Timbres and Interferences* (1977).

Stöwe, Gustav, German pianist and pedagogue; b. Potsdam, July 4, 1835; d. there, April 13, 1891. He studied at the Stern Cons. in Berlin; in 1875 founded the Potsdam Musikschule, and was its director until he died. He publ. *Die Klaviertechnik, dargestellt als musikalisch-physiologische Bewegungslehre* (1886; thorough analysis of the elements of piano touch); wrote piano pieces.

Stoyanov, Pancho, Bulgarian composer, son of **Veselin Stoyanov;** b. Sofia, Feb. 9, 1931. He studied composition with Vladigerov at the Bulgarian State Cons. in Sofia, graduating in 1954, then took courses at the Moscow Cons.; returning to Bulgaria, he taught at the Cons. of Sofia.
WORKS: 4 symphonies (1958, 1971, 1971, 1975); *Divertimento* for string orch. (1959); 2 violin concertinos (1961, 1965); 2 *Rhapsodies* for orch. (1963, 1969); 2 violin sonatas (1953, 1970); 3 string quartets (1953, 1959, 1977); Concertino for flute, clarinet, and bassoon (1969); Piano Quintet (1975); Piano Sonata (1965). He has publ. 9 theoretical texts, including *Interaction Between the Musical Forms* (Sofia, 1975).

Stoyanov, Veselin, Bulgarian composer, b. Shumen, April 20, 1902; d. Sofia, June 29, 1969. He studied piano with his brother **Andrei Stoyanov** at the Bulgarian State Cons. in Sofia, graduating in 1926; then went to Vienna where he studied with Josef Marx and Franz Schmidt. In 1937 he was appointed prof. of musical subjects at the Bulgarian Cons. in Sofia.
WORKS: 3 operas: *Zhensko tsarstvo (Kingdom of Women;* Sofia, April 5, 1935), *Salambo* (Sofia, May 22, 1940) and *Hitar Petar (The Wise Peter,* 1952; Sofia, 1958); a ballet, *Popess Joan* (1966; Sofia, Oct. 22,

1968); a cantata, *Da bade den (Let There Be Day,* 1952); *Capriccio* for orch. (1934); *Bai Ganyu (Uncle Ganyu),* grotesque suite for orch. (1941); 2 piano concertos (1942, 1953); *Kravava pesen (Song of the Blood),* symph. poem (1947); Violin Concerto (1948); Cello Concerto (1960); 2 symphonies (1962, 1968); 3 string quartets (1933, 1934, 1935); Violin Sonata (1934); Piano Sonata (1930); *Suite* for piano (1931); *3 Pieces* for piano (1956).

Stradal, August, Bohemian pianist; b. Teplitz, May 17, 1860; d. Schönlinde, Germany, March 13, 1930. He studied composition with Bruckner at the Vienna Cons. and piano with Door; was a pupil of Liszt in 1884 and became an ardent propagandist for Liszt's piano music; gave concerts in Germany, Austria, France, and England; made arrangements of Liszt's orchestral works; also of works by Bach, Frescobaldi, etc. His original compositions consist of piano pieces (*Ungarische Rhapsodie,* etc.) and songs. He wrote *Erinnerungen an Franz Liszt* (Bern, 1929).
BIBLIOGRAPHY: Hildegard Stradal, *August Stradals Lebensbild* (Bern, 1934).

Stradella, Alessandro, Italian composer; b. Montefestino, Oct. 8, 1644; murdered in Genoa, Feb. 25, 1682. According to a story narrated in Bonnet-Bourdelot's *Histoire de la musique et de ses effets* (Paris, 1715), Stradella was engaged to compose an opera for Venice, but there met the mistress of a Venetian nobleman and ran off with her before his work was produced; the enraged nobleman thereupon engineered an attempt on Stradella's life, but he was merely wounded; it was a later assault on him, in 1682, that finally succeeded. He is the hero of Flotow's opera *Alessandro Stradella* (Hamburg, 1844), and operas by Niedermeyer (Paris, 1837) and Sinico (Lugo, 1863). As a composer, Stradella developed the structural form and expressive power of the aria, and was one of the first to make use of the instrumental crescendo.
WORKS: 148 manuscripts of Stradella are in the Modena Library, including 8 oratorios and 11 dramas; cantatas in Naples Cons. Library; 21 cantatas in the library of San Marco, Venice (10 publ. by L. Escudier, with piano accompaniment by Halévy); others in the Paris National Library, and at the Cons.; 1 motet and 8 cantatas at Christchurch Library, Oxford; a number of cantatas, madrigals, arias, duets, etc., in the British Museum; etc. Among his extant works are the oratorios *S. Giovanni Battista, Esther, S. Pelagia, S. Giovanni Crisostomo, Susanna,* and *S. Edita vergine;* the operas *Il Corispeo, Orazio Cocle sul ponte, Trespolo tutore, La Forza del amore paterno* (1678; new ed. by A. Gentili, Rome, 1931); the cantata *Il Barcheggio* (dated June 16, 1681). The church aria *Pietà, Signore* and the arias *O del mio dolce ardor* and *Se i miei sospiri* have been wrongly attributed to Stradella. An edition of the oratorios was begun in 1969, under the editorship of L. Bianchi.
BIBLIOGRAPHY: A. Catelani, *Delle Opere di A. S. esistenti nell'archivio musicale della R. Biblioteca Palatina di Modena* (Modena, 1866); P. Richard, *A. S.* (Paris, 1866); H. Hess, *Die Opern A.S.s,* in *Publikationen der Internationalen Musik-Gesellschaft,* Supplement II/3 (1906); F. M. Crawford, *S.* (London,

1911); A. Einstein, "Ein Bericht über den Turiner Mordanfall auf A. S.," in "Sandberger-Festschrift" (1918); E. M. Dufflocq. "A. S.," *Bollettino Bibliografico Musicale* (1929); A. Della Corte, in *Musica d'oggi* (1931); A. Gentili, *A. S.* (Turin, 1936); G. Roncaglia, "Le Composizioni strumentali di A. S.," *Rivista Musicale Italiana* (1940–42; also separately, 1942); R. Giazotto, *Vita di Alessandro Stradella* (2 vols., Milan, 1962).

Stradivari (Stradivarius), Antonio, the most celebrated of all violin makers; b. Cremona, 1644 (according to Bacchetta, end of 1648 or beginning of 1649); d. there, Dec. 18, 1737. He was a pupil of Niccolò Amati and worked for him from about 1667–79. He purchased the house in which, for half a century, his workshop was situated, in 1680. His finest instruments were made in the period from 1700 to 1725, but he still worked up to the year of his death; his last instrument was made by him at the age of 92. His label reads: "Antonius Stradivarius Cremonensis. Fecit Anno . . . (A ✗ S)." His cellos command even higher prices than the violins, and violas the highest of all, for he made very few of them. Stradivari had 11 children; of them **Francesco** (b. Feb. 1, 1671; d. May 11, 1743) and **Omobono** (b. Nov. 14, 1679; d. July 8, 1742) were his co-workers. Stradivari also made viols of early types, guitars, lutes, mandolins, etc.

BIBLIOGRAPHY: F. J. Fétis, *A. S., luthier célèbre* (Paris, 1856; English transl., London, 1864); P. Lombardini, *Cenni sulla celebre scuola Cremonense degli stromenti ad arco e sulla famiglia del sommo Antonio Stradivari* (Cremona, 1872; with genealogical table from the 13th century to date of publication); A. Reichers, *The Violin and the Art of Its Construction; A Treatise on S.* (1895); H. Petherick, *A. S.* (London, 1900); W. H., A. F., and A. E. Hill, *A. S. His Life and Work* (London, 1902; the standard work); A. Mandelli, *Nuove indagini su A. S.* (Milan, 1903); H. Herrmann, *Geschichte und Beschreibung von zwei Meisterwerken des A. S.* (N.Y., 1929); R. Bacchetta, *S.* (1937); G. Hoffmann, *S. l'enchanteur* (Paris, 1938); W. D. Orcutt, *The S. Memorial at Washington, D.C.* (Washington, 1938); M. Boger, *Das Geheimnis des Stradivari* (Berlin, 1944); D. J. Balfoort, *A. S.* (Amsterdam, 1945; also in English); E. N. Doring, *How Many Strads? . . . A tabulation of works believed to survive, produced in Cremona by A. S. between 1666 and 1737* (Chicago, 1945); G. Ottani, *S.* (Milan, 1945); H. Goodkind, *Violin Iconography of Antonio Stradivari* (Larchmont, N.Y., 1972); S. Sacconi, *I "segreti" di Stradivari* (Cremona, 1972).

Straesser, Joep, Dutch composer; b. Amsterdam, March 11, 1934. He studied at the Municipal Univ. of Amsterdam (1952–55); then took organ lessons with Van der Horst (1956–59) and composition with Ton de Leeuw (1960–65) at the Amsterdam Cons.; was a church organist (1953–61); in 1962 was appointed to the faculty of the Utrecht Cons.

WORKS: *5 Close-ups* for piano (1960–61, revised 1973); *Music* for oboe quartet (1962); *Psalmus* for male chorus, winds and percussion (1963); *22 Pages,* after a text of John Cage essays, for wind orch., percussion and 3 male voices (Hilversum, Sept. 14, 1965); String Quartet No. 2 (1966); *Chorai* for 48 string instruments and percussion (1966; Hilversum, Sept. 14, 1967; re-composed in 1974 for full orch. and retitled *Chorai Revisited*); *Duet* for 2 cellos (1967); *Seismograms* for 2 percussionists (1967); *Adastra,* music for ballet (1967); *Summer Concerto* for oboe and chamber orch. (1967; Styrian Autumn Festival, Graz, Austria, Oct. 24, 1969); *Ramasasiri (Traveling Song),* on texts in the Papuan language, for soprano, flute, vibraphone, piano, and 2 percussionists (1967–68); *Musique pour l'homme* for soprano, alto, tenor, bass and orch. (1968; Amsterdam, Dec. 9, 1968); *Missa* for chorus and wind instruments (1969); *Intersections I* for wind quintet and 5 instrumental groups spatially positioned (1969); *II* for a hundred or more musicians (1970; Amsterdam, April 3, 1971; except for percussionists, all orch. members improvise freely), *III* for piano (1971), *IV* for oboe, violin, viola, and cello (1972), *V (A Saxophone's World)* for 4 saxophones (1974) and *V-2* for bass clarinet and piano (1975); *Sight-Seeing I, II, III* for flute and prepared piano (1969); *IV* for solo double bass (1970) and *V (Spring Quartet)* for string quartet (1971); *Emergency Case* for flute, piano, and percussion (1970); *Enclosures* for winds and percussion (1970; perf. as a ballet, Rotterdam, Oct. 3, 1971); *Eichenstadt und Abendstern,* 6 songs for soprano and piano (1972); *Encounters* for bass clarinet and 6 percussionists (1973); *Intervals* for chamber chorus, flute, cello, and harp (1975–76); *3 Psalms* for chorus and organ (1976).

Straeten, Edmund. See **Van der Straeten.**

Strakosch, Maurice, Bohemian impresario; b. Gross-Seelowitz, 1825; d. Paris, Oct. 9, 1887. He studied with Sechter at the Vienna Cons.; traveled as a pianist in Europe; came to America in 1848, settling in N.Y. as a teacher; from 1856 he was active mainly as an impresario. He was the brother-in-law of Adelina Patti, and managed her concerts. He gave his first season of Italian opera in N.Y. in 1857, and in 1859 took his company to Chicago; then went to Europe. His opera *Giovanna di Napoli* was brought out in N.Y.; he also wrote salon pieces for piano; publ. *Ten Commandments of Music for the Perfection of the Voice* (posthumous; 1896) and *Souvenirs d'un Impresario* (Paris, 2nd ed., 1887). After his departure from America, his brother, Max Strakosch (1834–92), carried on the management of his enterprises.

Strang, Gerald, American composer; b. Claresholm, Canada, Feb. 13, 1908. He studied at Stanford Univ., at the Univ. of California in Los Angeles, and at the Univ. of Southern California. He joined the ranks of the early Californian modernists headed by Henry Cowell; was assistant to Schoenberg at the Univ. of California, Los Angeles (1936–38). He was on the faculty of Long Beach City College, California (1938–58); then prof. of music at San Fernando Valley State College (1958–65) and at California State College in Long Beach (1965–69); during the academic season 1969–70 he was lecturer on electronic music at the Univ. of California, L.A. His music is strongly formal, with a unifying technical idea determining the content.

WORKS: 2 symphonies (1942, 1947); *Overland Trail* for orch. (1943); Violin Concerto (1951); Sonata for flute solo (1953); *Percussion Music* for 3 players; and *Mirrorrorrim* ("mirror" in mirror spelling) for piano; also a group of 7 pieces under the generic title *Compusition,* generated by a computer (1963–69).

Stransky, Josef, Bohemian conductor; b. Humpoletz, near Deutschbrod, Bohemia, Sept. 9, 1872; d. New York, March 6, 1936. While studying medicine (M.D., Prague, 1896), he also studied music, at Leipzig with Jadassohn and in Vienna with R. Fuchs, Bruckner, and Dvořák. In 1898 he was engaged by A. Neumann as 1st Kapellmeister at the Landestheater in Prague; in 1903 he went in a similar capacity to the Stadttheater in Hamburg; in 1910 he resigned from the Hamburg opera to devote himself to concert work; in the autumn of 1911 became Mahler's successor as conductor of the N.Y. Philharmonic Society, a position he held until 1923. A bequest of one million dollars to the society (by Joseph Pulitzer, 1912) enabled Stransky to carry out successfully the sweeping reforms instituted by his illustrious predecessor (chief of which was a system of daily rehearsals during the season of 23 weeks). He wrote an operetta, *Der General,* which was produced in Hamburg.
    BIBLIOGRAPHY: Howard Shanet, *Philharmonic. A History of New York's Orchestra* (Garden City, N.Y., 1975).

Straram, Walther, French conductor; b. London (of French parents), July 9, 1876; d. Paris, Nov. 24, 1933. He was educated in Paris; played violin in Paris orchestras; then was choirmaster at the Opéra-Comique; later traveled to America as assistant to André Caplet at the Boston Opera Co. Returning to Paris, he established the Concerts Straram, which enjoyed a fine reputation. He conducted the 1st performance of Ravel's *Boléro* for Ida Rubinstein (dance recital, Nov. 22, 1928).

Strassburg, Robert, American music educator and composer; b. New York, Aug. 30, 1915. He studied composition with Marion Bauer at N.Y. Univ.; then enrolled in Harvard Univ. (M.A., 1950). He subsequently lived in Miami; was conductor and founder of the All-Miami Youth Symph. (1957–60). In 1961 he joined the faculty of the Univ. of Judaism in Los Angeles; from 1966 he was on the faculty of California State College. His works include *Four Biblical Statements* for string orch. (1946); *Fantasy and Allegro* for violin and orch. (1947); *Torah Sonata* for piano (1950); folk opera, *Chelm* (1956); *Tropal Suite* for string orch. (1967). He is the author of a monograph, *Ernest Bloch, Voice in the Wilderness* (Los Angeles, 1977).

Strässer, Ewald, German composer; b. Burscheid, June 27, 1867; d. Stuttgart, April 4, 1933. He studied with Wüllner at the Cologne Cons.; taught theory there until 1921; from 1922 to his death was prof. at the Stuttgart Musikhochschule. He wrote 6 symphonies, 5 string quartets, piano pieces, and songs.
    BIBLIOGRAPHY: A. Strässer, *Ewald Strässer* (Stuttgart, 1936).

Stratas, Teresa (real name **Anastasia Strataki**), Canadian soprano of Greek extraction; b. Toronto,

May 26, 1938. She studied at the Cons. of Toronto; made her debut with the Toronto Opera as Mimi in *La Bohème* on Oct. 16, 1958; won the Metropolitan Opera Auditions and appeared with the Metropolitan, N.Y., on Oct. 28, 1959. She also gives solo recitals.

Strategier, Herman, Dutch composer; b. Arnhem, Aug. 10, 1912. He studied music with his father, a church organist, and with H. Andriessen; succeeded his father at St. Walpurgis at Arnhem in 1935, but the church was destroyed in war action in 1944. He taught at the Institute for Catholic Church Music in Utrecht (1939–63); then was appointed to the faculty of Music Science at the Utrecht Univ. He is notable mainly as composer of liturgical music of the Roman Catholic Rite.
    WORKS: FOR VOICES: *Stabat Mater* for chorus and small orch. (1939); *Septem cantica* for mezzo-soprano and piano (1941); *4 Drinkleideren* for baritone and orch. (1945); *Van der mollenfeeste,* an old ballad for chorus and small orch. (1947–48); *Henric van Veldeke* for narrator, baritone, and orch. (1952); *5 Minneliederen* for middle voice, flute, and small string orch. (1952); *Koning Swentibold,* oratorio (1955); *Arnhemsche psalm* for narrator, soloists, chorus, and orch. (1955); *Rembrandt Cantata* (1956); *Requiem* for chorus, wind quintet, and strings (1961); *Ballade van de Maagd van Wognum* for chorus and orch. (1965); *Plaisanterie* for chorus and orch. (1966); *Te Deum* for soprano, alto, chorus, and orch (1967); *Colloquia familiaria* for soprano, chorus, and string orch. (1969); *Zoo, Buddingh'zoo* for baritone, chorus, and small orch. (1970); *Ligeia or the Shadow Out of Time* for chorus, flute, 6 percussionists, organ, and harp (1973). FOR ORCH.: *Divertimento* for string orch. and 4 winds (1937); Flute Concerto (1943); *Haarlem-suite* (1945–47); *Ramiro-suite* (1946); Piano Concerto (1947–48); Symph. No. 1 (1949); Clarinet Concertino (1950); *Musique pour faire plaisir* for strings (1950); *Intrada Sinfonica* (1954); *Rondo Giocoso* (1955); *Rapsodia elegiaca* (1956); *Turandot-suite* (1956); *Kadullen Varieties* for flute, bassoon, and strings (1958); *Triptych* for piano and wind orch. (1960); Accordion Concerto (1969); *Concertante Speelmuziek* for flute, bassoon, and orch. (1970). CHAMBER MUSIC: 3 string quartets (1935, 1936, 1937); *3 Pièces* for oboe and string quartet (1937); Sextet for piano and wind quintet (1951); *Suite* for solo harp (1961); Quartet for flute, violin, viola and cello (1968); *Curven* for accordion and string quartet (1970); *Divertissement* for oboe, clarinet and bassoon (1970); Piano Trio (1974). FOR PIANO: *Suite* for 4 hands (1945); Sonata (1948); Sonatina (1951); *Tema con variazioni* for 4 hands (1952); *Élégie* (1954); *4 Pièces brèves* for 4 hands (1973); *Suite* for piano and harpsichord (1973); *3 Speelmuziekjes* (1974); *6 Etudes* (1974). FOR ORGAN: *Preludium, Intermezzo and Theme with Variations* (1939); *Ritornello capriccioso* (1944); *Toccatina* (1951); *Chaconne* (1955); *Voluntary* (1975). Songs and choruses.

Stratton, George (Robert), English violinist and pedagogue; b. London, July 18, 1897; d. there, Sept. 4, 1954. He studied in London; was concertmaster of the London Symph. Orch. (1933–52); also organized the Stratton String Quartet (1925–42). He publ. (in collaboration with Alan Frank) a practical book, *The Playing of Chamber Music* (London, 1935; reprinted, 1951).

Stratton, Stephen Samuel, English organist; b. London, Dec. 19, 1840; d. Birmingham, June 25, 1906. Pupil of C. Gardner (organ) and C. Lucas (composition); settled in 1866 in Birmingham, where he held various posts as organist, the last being at the Church of the Saviour (1878–82). He was the author (with J. D. Brown) of a valuable work, *British Musical Biography* (1897); also publ. *Mendelssohn* (1901; revised ed., 1934) and *Nicolo Paganini: His Life and Work* (1907). His compositions include chamber music, piano pieces, part songs and songs.

Straube, Karl, prominent German organist; b. Berlin, Jan. 6, 1873; d. Leipzig, April 27, 1950. He was a scion of an ancient ecclesiastical family; his father was an organist and instrument maker in Berlin; his mother was an Englishwoman who was a piano student of Sir Julius Benedict. He studied organ with Dienel; then took organ lessons with Reimann in Berlin. From 1897 to 1902 he was organist at the Cathedral of Wesel; in 1902 he became organist at the famous Thomaskirche in Leipzig; in 1903 he was appointed conductor of the Bachverein there, and in 1907 became prof. at the Leipzig Cons. and organist *ex officio* at Gewandhaus. In 1918 he became cantor at the Thomaskirche. At his suggestion the Gewandhaus Chorus and the Bachverein were united in 1919, and he conducted the combined choir. He conducted the Handel Festival in 1925, leading to the formation of the Handel Society. In his teaching he followed the great tradition of Leipzig organists, traceable to Bach. A Festschrift was published for him on his 70th birthday (Leipzig, 1943). Among Straube's numerous collections of organ and choral pieces are *Alte Orgelmeister* (1904); *45 Choralvorspiele alter Meister* (1907); *Alte Meister des Orgelspiels* (2 vols.; 1929); *Ausgewählte Gesänge des Thomanerchors* (1930); he brought out editions of several works of Bach, Handel and Liszt. His *Briefe eines Thomaskantors* were published posthumously (Stuttgart, 1952).

Straus, Oscar, Austrian operetta composer; b. Vienna, March 6, 1870; d. Ischl, Jan. 11, 1954. (His name was spelled "Strauss" on his birth certificate; he cut off the second "s" to segregate himself from the multitudinous musical Strausses). He studied privately in Vienna with A. Prosnitz and H. Grädener, and with Max Bruch in Berlin. From 1895 to 1900 he conducted at various theaters in Austria and Germany; in 1901 he became conductor of the artistic cabaret "Überbrettl," managed by Ernst von Wolzogen in Berlin, and wrote a number of musical farces for it. He remained in Berlin until 1927; then lived in Vienna and Paris; on Sept. 3, 1939, he became a French citizen. In 1940 he went to America; lived in New York and Hollywood until 1948, when he returned to Europe. He was one of the most successful composers of Viennese operettas.

WORKS: His most celebrated production was *Der tapfere Soldat,* based on G. B. Shaw's play, *Arms and the Man* (Vienna, Nov. 14, 1908; in N.Y. as *The Chocolate Soldier,* Nov. 13, 1909; London, Sept. 10, 1910; numerous performances all over the world). Other operettas are: *Die lustigen Nibelungen* (Vienna, Nov. 12, 1904); *Hugdietrichs Brautfahrt* (Vienna, March 10, 1906); *EinWalzertraum* (Vienna, March 2, 1907; revised 1951); *Didi* (Vienna, Oct. 23, 1909); *Das Tal der Liebe* (Berlin and Vienna, simultaneously, Dec. 23, 1909); *Mein junger Herr* (Vienna, Dec. 23, 1910); *Die kleine Freundin* (Vienna, Oct. 20, 1911); *Love and Laughter* (London, 1913); *Rund um die Liebe* (Vienna, Nov. 9, 1914; in N.Y. as *All Around Love,* 1917); *Die himmelblaue Zeit* (Vienna, Feb. 21, 1914); *Die schöne Unbekannte* (Vienna, Jan. 15, 1915; in N.Y. as *My Lady's Glove,* 1917); *Drei Walzer* (Zürich, Oct. 5, 1935); *Ihr erster Walzer* (Munich, May 16, 1952). He further wrote a *Serenade* for string orch.; *Alt-Wiener Reigen,* for string orch.; *Suite in Tanzform* for violin, cello, and piano; *Der Traum ein Leben,* overture; many piano pieces; an album, *Bilderbuch ohne Bilder* for 4 hands.

BIBLIOGRAPHY: B. Grun, *Prince of Vienna: The Life, the Times, and the Melodies of Oscar Straus* (London, 1955; N.Y., 1957).

Strauss, Eduard, brother of **Johann Strauss, Jr.;** b. Vienna, March 15, 1835; d. there, Dec. 28, 1916. A pupil of G. Preyer in composition, he made a successful debut with his own orch. at the Dianasaal in 1862; acted as Johann's substitute during the latter's tour of Russia (1865); succeeded him in 1870 as conductor of the court balls. For many years he gave concerts in the Volksgarten (summer) and in the hall of the Musikverein (winter); also made extended tours, visiting the U.S. in 1892 and 1901–02. He then dissolved his orch. (founded by his father in 1826), which after three-quarters of a century of uninterrupted success, had become almost a historical institution. His published dances comprise 318 opus numbers, but could not rival his brother's in popularity. In 1906 he published *Erinnerungen.*

Strauss, Franz, German horn virtuoso, father of **Richard Strauss;** b. Parkstein, Feb. 26, 1822; d. Munich, May 31, 1905. Until his retirement in 1889 he was solo hornist at the Hofoper in Munich; although a violent opponent of Wagner, the master valued him highly, and entrusted to him at the premières of *Tristan, Meistersinger,* and *Parsifal* the important solo passages; until 1896 he was prof. of his instrument at the Akademie der Tonkunst, and from 1875–96 conducted an excellent amateur orch., the "Wilde Gungl," in Munich. He wrote a Horn Concerto in C minor (op. 8); *Nocturne* (op. 7) and *Empfindungen am Meere* (op. 12) for horn and piano; 17 *Konzertetüden* and *Übungen für Naturhorn* (2 books).

BIBLIOGRAPHY: F. Trenner, "Der Vater: Franz Strauss," *Zeitschrift für Musik* (June 1955).

Strauss, Johann, Jr., greatly celebrated Austrian composer of light music, "The Waltz King"; b. Vienna, Oct. 25, 1825; d. there, June 3, 1899. His father intended all three of his sons for business; but the mother privately procured instruction on the violin (from Kohlmann) and in composition (Hofmann and Drexler) for Johann, who threw off paternal control, tender though it was, and appeared as conductor of his own ensemble of 15 players at Dommayer's Restaurant in Hietzing (Oct. 15, 1844). His success was instantaneous and his new waltzes won wide popularity. Despite his father's objections to this rivanly in the family, Johann Strauss continued his concerts with increasing success; after his father's death in 1849 he united his father's band with his own; made a tour through Austria, Germany, Poland, and Russia. From 1863 to 1870 he was conductor of the court balls in Vienna, resigning in favor of his brother **Eduard** to obtain more leisure for composition. Turning from dance music, in which he had won supreme artistic and popular success, he then concentrated on operetta. In 1872 he accepted an invitation to visit the U.S., and directed 14 "monster-concerts" in Boston and 4 in N.Y. He contracted 3 marriages: to the singer Henriette Treffz, the actress Angelica Dietrich, and Adele Deutsch. He wrote almost 500 pieces of dance music (498 op. numbers); of his waltzes the greatest popularity was achieved by *An der schönen blauen Donau* (*The Blue Danube Waltz*, op. 314, 1867), whose main tune became one of the best-known in all music. Brahms wrote on a lady's fan the opening measures of it, and underneath: "Leider nicht von Brahms" (Alas, not by Brahms); Wagner, too, voiced his appreciation of the music of Strauss. Other well-known waltzes are *Geschichten aus dem Wiener Wald* (1868), *Wein, Weib, Gesang* (1869), *Wiener Blut* (1870), *Rosen aus dem Süden* (1878); *Frühlingsstimmen* (1881), *Tausend und eine Nacht, Künstlerleben,* etc.; also numerous quadrilles, polkas, polka-mazurkas, marches, galops, etc. His finest operetta is *Die Fledermaus,* an epitome of the Viennese spirit that continues to hold the stage as one of the masterpieces of its genre. It was first staged at the Theater an der Wien on April 5, 1874, and was given within a few months in N.Y. (Dec. 29, 1874); productions followed all over the world. It was performed in Paris with a new libretto as *La Tzigane* (Oct. 30, 1877); the original version was presented there as *La Chauve-souris* on April 22, 1904. Also very successful was the operetta *Der Zigeunerbaron* (Vienna, Oct. 24, 1885). All his operettas were first produced in Vienna, with the exception of *Eine Nacht in Venedig* (Berlin, Oct. 3, 1883). A complete list of Vienna productions includes: *Indigo und die vierzig Räuber* (Feb. 10, 1871); *Der Karneval in Rom* (March 1, 1873); *Cagliostro in Wien* (Feb. 27, 1875); *Prinz Methusalem* (Jan. 3, 1877); *Blindekuh* (Dec. 18, 1878); *Das Spitzentuch der Königin* (Oct. 1, 1880); *Der lustige Krieg* (Nov. 25, 1881); *Simplizius* (Dec. 17, 1887); *Ritter Pázmán* (Jan. 1, 1892); *Fürstin Ninetta* (Jan. 10, 1893); *Jabuka, oder Das Apfelfest* (Oct. 12, 1894); *Waldmeister* (Dec. 4, 1895); *Die Göttin der Vernunft* (March 13, 1897). An edition of his complete works was begun in 1967 by the Johann-Strauss-Gesellschaft, under the direction of F. Racek.

BIBLIOGRAPHY: L. Eisenberg, *J. S.* (Leipzig, 1894); R. von Procházka, *J. S.* (Berlin, 1900); R. Specht, *J. S.* (Berlin, 1909); F. Lange, *J. S.* (Leipzig, 1912); J. Schnitzer, *Meister Johann* (2 vols.; Vienna, 1920); E. Decsey, *J. S.* (Berlin, 1922; reprinted Vienna, 1948); K. Kobald, *J. S.* (Vienna, 1925); S. Loewy, *Rund um J. S.* (Vienna, 1925); H. Sündermann, *J. S., ein Vollender* (Brixlegg, 1937); Ada B. Teetgen, *The Waltz Kings of Old Vienna* (London, 1939); A. Witeschnik, *Die Dynastie Strauss* (Vienna, 1939); H. E. Jacob, *J. S. und das 19. Jahrhundert . . .* (Amsterdam, 1937; English transl. as *J. S., Father and Son, A Century of Light Music* (N.Y., 1940); W. Jaspert, *J. S.* (Berlin, 1939); Erich Schenk, *J. S.* (Potsdam, 1940); David Ewen, *Tales from the Vienna Woods: The Story of J. S.* (N.Y., 1944); J. Andriessen, *J. S., de koning van de wals* (Amsterdam, 1950); J. Pastene, *Three-Quarter Time: The Life and Music of the Strauss Family* (N.Y., 1951); P. Kuringer, *J. S.* (Haarlem, 1952). See also *J. S. schreibt Briefe,* ed. by his third wife, Adele Strauss (Vienna, 1926). A complete catalogue of works is found in C. Flamme, ed., *Verzeichnis der sämtlichen im Drucke erschienenen Kompositionen von Johann Strauss (Vater), Johann Strauss (Sohn), Josef Strauss, und Eduard Strauss* (Leipzig, 1898) and in A. Weinmann, *Verzeichnis sämtlicher Werke von Johann Strauss, Vater und Sohn* (Vienna, 1956); J. Wechsberg, *The Waltz Emperors* (1973); Egon Gartenberg, *Johann Strauss: The End of an Era* (1974). An edition of collected works of Johann Strauss, Jr., was begun in 1967 by the Johann Strauss Gesellschaft in Vienna.

Strauss, Johann, Sr., "The Father of the Waltz"; b. Vienna, March 14, 1804; d. there, Sept. 25, 1849. His father, who kept a beer house and dance hall, apprenticed him to a bookbinder; after Strauss had run away, his parents consented to his becoming a musician. He studied the violin under Polyschansky, and harmony under Seyfried; at 15 joined Pamer's orch. in the Sperl dance hall, and the Lanner Quartet in 1823, later acting as deputy conductor of Lanner's orch.; organized an independent orch. of 14 in 1826, playing at various resorts, and producing his first waltzes (op. 1 is the *Täuberl-Walzer,* for the garden concerts at the Zwei Tauben). His renown spread, and his orch. increased rapidly in size and efficiency; from 1833 he undertook concert tours in Austria, and in 1834 was appointed bandmaster of the 1st Vienna militia regiment. His tours extended to Berlin in 1834, and to Holland and Belgium in 1836; in 1837–38 he invaded Paris with a picked corps of 28, and had immense success both there and in London. In 1845 he was made conductor of the court balls at Vienna.

WORKS: Among 152 published waltzes, the *Lorelei-, Gabrielen-, Taglioni-, Cäcilien-, Victoria-,* and *Bajaderen-Walzer,* the *Elektrische Funken, Mephistos Höllenrufe,* and the *Donau-Lieder* are prime favorites; he also wrote 24 galops, 13 polkas, 32 quadrilles, 6 cotillons and contredances, 18 marches, and 6 potpourris. Both as composer and conductor he distinctly raised the level of dance music. His complete works (251 op. numbers), edited by his son **Johann,** were publ. by Breitkopf & Härtel in 1889; Vols. I-V, Waltzes; vol. VI, Polkas, Galops, Marches; vol. VII, Quadrilles (piano scores only; full scores in *Denkmäler der Tonkunst in Österreich* 63, 68, and 74 (32.ii, 35.ii, and 38.ii).

BIBLIOGRAPHY: L. Scheyrer, *J.S.s musikalische Wanderung durch das Leben* (Vienna, 1851); R. Kleinecke, *J. S.* (Leipzig, 1894); F. Lange, *Josef Lanner und J. S.* (Vienna, 1904; 2nd ed., 1919); M. Farga, *Lanner und S.* (Vienna 1948); M. Schönherr and K. Reinöhl, *J. S. Vater* (Vienna, 1953); H. Jacob, *Johann*

Strauss, Vater und Sohn: Die Geschichte einer musikalischen Weltherrschaft (Bremen, 1960).

Strauss, Josef, Austrian composer of waltzes; brother of **Johann Strauss, Jr.,** b. Vienna, Aug. 22, 1827; d. there, July 21, 1870. He was versatile and gifted, and at various times wrote poetry, painted, and patented inventions. He first appeared in public conducting in Vienna a set of his waltzes (July 23, 1853); was often asked by his brother to replace him as conductor, and accompanied him on tours to Germany, Russia, etc. He wrote 283 op. numbers, of which some are well worthy of his family's renown. His op. 173, *Dynamiden,* was used by Richard Strauss for a theme in *Der Rosenkavalier.*

BIBLIOGRAPHY: A. Witeschnik, *Die Dynastie Strauss* (Vienna, 1939).

Strauss, Richard, great German composer; b. Munich, June 11, 1864; d. Garmisch-Partenkirchen, Sept. 8, 1949. His father, the well-known horn player **Franz Strauss,** supervised his son's education. At the age of 4, he received regular instruction from A. Tombo, the harpist of the court orch.; in his 8th year he began to study the violin with Benno Walter, the concertmaster of the court orch.; from 1875 to 1880 he studied composition with the court conductor, F. W. Meyer. His first attempt at writing music (a Polka in C) dates from the year 1870, when he was 6, and he wrote piano pieces, songs, and even orchestral overtures as a child; his op. 1, a *Festmarsch* for orch., written at the age of 12, was publ. in 1880. In the meantime he had completed an academic course of study at the Gymnasium, graduating in 1882; then attended lectures on philosophy at the Munich Univ. (1882–83). On March 30, 1881, the first major work of Richard Strauss, the Symphony in D minor, was performed in Munich by Hermann Levi; Benno Walter, Strauss's teacher, played his Violin Concerto (Munich, Feb. 8, 1883). These works, written in the forms of the classic masters, revealed an astonishing degree of technical mastery and won for Strauss immediate recognition; he was only 20 when he could boast the distinction of an American première, for on Dec. 13, 1884, Theodore Thomas, then conductor of the N.Y. Philharmonic, gave the first U.S. performance of the Symphony in F minor. Strauss spent the winter of 1883–84 in Berlin, where Hans von Bülow became interested in him and engaged him as assistant conductor with Bülow's orchestra in Meiningen. When Bülow left Meiningen in 1885, Strauss became his successor. Although he remained in Meiningen for only one season (1885–86), this sojourn proved to be a turning point in his career, for in that short time he became intimately associated with the poet and musician Alexander Ritter, who revealed to Strauss the meaning of the revolution in esthetics produced by Wagner and Liszt. Ritter urged on Strauss the concept of "music as expression," and thenceforward Strauss became convinced of the artistic importance of music with a literary or philosophical outline. After a journey to Italy in the spring of 1886, he became one of the conductors of the Court Opera in Munich (1886–89); his duties were not onerous, and he had ample time for composition; in Munich he wrote the symph. fantasy *Aus Italien,* and his first significant works in the new style, the tone poems *Don Juan* and *Tod und Verklärung.* In the autumn of 1889 he was appointed 1st conductor of the Weimar court orch.; there he remained until spring, 1894. In Weimar he brought out *Don Juan* on Nov. 11, 1889, and another tone poem, *Macbeth,* on Oct. 13, 1890; on June 21, 1890, he conducted the 1st performance of *Tod und Verklärung,* at the meeting of the Allgemeiner Deutscher Musik-Verein in Eisenach. These works were revelations of a talent of striking originality and boldness, and made Strauss one of the greatest figures of the nascent era of musical modernism; he was praised extravagantly by admirers, and damned violently by traditionalists. Hans von Bülow called him "Richard the Second," as a legitimate heir to Wagner's mantle. Indeed, Strauss extended Wagner's system of leading motifs to the domain of symphonic music; his tone poems are interwoven with motifs, each representing some relevant programmatic element. Analytical brochures, compiled especially by German commentators, illustrate the complex involvements of thematic allusions in these works. Strauss spent the winter of 1892 in Greece, Egypt, and Sicily, writing the text and music of his first stage work, the opera *Guntram,* which he conducted in Weimar on May 12, 1894. **Pauline de Ahna** sang the leading part; she married Strauss on Sept. 10, 1894, and remained with him throughout his life, dying a few months after he did. Strauss was appointed successor to Bülow as conductor of the Berlin Philharmonic in the autumn of 1894, and led it during the season of 1894–95. In 1896 he conducted his own works in Brussels, Liège, and Moscow, and also in many German cities; in 1897 he visited Amsterdam, Paris, London, and Barcelona. In the meantime, he continued unremittingly to write music; in quick succession, he brought out his masterpieces of musical characterization, *Till Eulenspiegels lustige Streiche* (Cologne, Nov. 5, 1895, Wüllner conducting), the philosophical poem after Nietzsche, *Also sprach Zarathustra* (Frankfurt, Nov. 27, 1896, composer conducting), and *Don Quixote,* variations with a cello solo, after Cervantes (Cologne, March 8, 1898, Wüllner conducting). The series of his great tone poems was concluded with the autobiographical work *Ein Heldenleben* (Frankfurt, March 3, 1899, composer conducting). For his first visit to America in the early months of 1904, Strauss wrote a new work of considerable dimensions, *Symphonia domestica,* which he conducted at Carnegie Hall, N.Y., on March 21, 1904. The score was so naturalistic, and so frankly autobiographical, that it amused and shocked the public, but the music itself fell distinctly below the poetically charged inspiration of the preceding tone poems. Even more literal was his large symphonic work, *Eine Alpensinfonie,* which calls for a wind machine and a thunder machine to portray a storm in the Alps; it was first performed by the composer himself in Berlin, on Oct. 28, 1915. But while his symphonic production lagged, he turned vigorously to the field of the opera, producing works of exceptional merit. After *Guntram,* he wrote *Feuersnot* (Dresden, Nov. 21, 1901), which attracted little attention. Then on Dec. 9, 1905, the Dresden Opera staged the opera *Salome,* after Oscar Wilde's French play, translated into German. In this score he went far beyond the limits of Wagnerian music drama, and created a psychological tragedy of shattering impact; the erotic subject was illustrated by sensuous music. The opera made the rounds of European theaters in quick succession, but when the Metropolitan Opera Co. produced *Salome* in N.Y. (Jan. 22, 1907) there were violent protests, and it was taken out of the repertory, not to be revived until many years later. Scarcely less forceful was the impression produced by the next opera, *Elektra* (Dresden, Jan. 25, 1909), in which the horrors of matricide were pictured with extraordinary strength. Then, as if to make a graceful concession to public taste, Strauss produced *Der Rosenkavalier* (Dresden, Jan. 26, 1911), a charming comedy, which quickly became famous. With *Elektra* and *Der Rosenkavalier*, Strauss established his fruitful collaboration with the poet Hugo von Hofmannsthal, who wrote the librettos for these works, and also for the subsequent operas: *Ariadne auf Naxos* (Stuttgart, Oct. 25, 1912), *Die Frau ohne Schatten* (Vienna, Oct. 10, 1919), *Die ägyptische Helena* (Dresden, June 6, 1928), and *Arabella* (Dresden, July 1, 1933). After Hofmannsthal's death in 1929, Strauss turned to Stefan Zweig for the libretto of *Die schweigsame Frau* (Dresden, June 24, 1935), and to Josef Gregor for *Friedenstag* (Munich, July 24, 1938), *Daphne* (Dresden, Oct. 15, 1938), and *Die Liebe der Danae* (written in 1938–40; produced posthumously, Salzburg, Aug. 14, 1952). The last opera by Strauss was *Capriccio*, to a libretto by the conductor Clemens Krauss (Munich, Oct. 28, 1942). The operas after *Der Rosenkavalier* were received with deference and interest, but were not retained in the permanent repertory. It may be said, therefore, that the great creative period of Strauss ended for his stage works in 1911, with *Der Rosenkavalier,* and for his symphonic compositions in 1899, with *Ein Heldenleben.* From 1898 to 1918 Strauss was on the staff of the Berlin Opera; in 1919 he became co-director (with Franz Schalk) of the Vienna State Opera, holding this position until 1924, not on a permanent basis, however, so that he had time for extended tours, one of which took him again to America in 1921. He also spent much time at his villa in Garmisch, Bavaria. On Nov. 15, 1933, Strauss was appointed president of the Reichsmusikkammer under the Nazi regime, but resigned in June, 1935. He visited London as conductor of his own works in 1937, and received there the gold medal of the Philharmonic Society. He was the recipient of numerous other honors and decorations. In 1902 the Univ. of Heidelberg made him Dr. phil., *honoris causa.* He remained in his home at Garmisch during World War II, and wrote the mournful *Metamorphosen* (with a symbolic quotation from Beethoven's funeral march from the *Eroica*) in the last months of the war; then lived for some time in Switzerland. He was strong enough to travel to England for a series of concerts in 1947; returning to Germany, he had to face the special court at Munich, investigating collaborators with the Nazis, but was officially exonerated (June 8, 1948).

WORKS: OPERAS: *Guntram* (Weimar, May 10, 1894; new version, Weimar, Oct. 22, 1940); *Feuersnot* (Dresden, Nov. 21, 1901); *Salome* (Dresden, Dec. 9, 1905); *Elektra* (Dresden, Jan. 25, 1909); *Der Rosenkavalier* (Dresden, Jan. 26, 1911); *Ariadne auf Naxos*

(Stuttgart, Oct. 25, 1912); *Die Frau ohne Schatten* (Vienna, Oct. 10, 1919); *Intermezzo* (Dresden, Nov. 4, 1924); *Die ägyptische Helena* (Dresden, June 6, 1928); *Arabella* (Dresden, July 1, 1933); *Die schweigsame Frau* (Dresden, June 24, 1935); *Friedenstag* (Munich, July 24, 1938); *Daphne* (Dresden, Oct. 15, 1938); *Die Liebe der Danae* (1938–40; Salzburg, Aug. 14, 1952); *Capriccio* (Munich, Oct. 28, 1942).

BALLETS: *Josephslegende* (Paris, May 14, 1914); *Schlagobers* (Vienna, May 9, 1924).

FOR ORCH.: *Festmarsch* (1876); Symphony in D minor (Munich, March 30, 1881); Violin Concerto (Munich, Feb. 8, 1883); Symph. in F minor (N.Y., Dec. 13, 1884); Horn Concerto No. 1 (Meiningen, March 4, 1885); *Aus Italien,* symph. fantasy (Munich, March 2, 1887); *Don Juan,* tone poem, after Lenau (Weimar, Nov. 11, 1889); *Tod und Verklärung,* tone poem (Eisenach, June 21, 1890); *Burleske* for piano and orch. (Eisenach, June 21, 1890, composer conducting, Eugen d'Albert soloist); *Macbeth,* after Shakespeare (Weimar, Oct. 13, 1890); *Till Eulenspiegels lustige Streiche,* tone poem (Cologne, Nov. 5, 1895); *Also sprach Zarathustra,* tone poem, after Nietzsche (Frankfurt, Nov. 27, 1896); *Don Quixote,* variations based on Cervantes (Cologne, March 8, 1898); *Ein Heldenleben,* tone poem (Frankfurt, March 3, 1899); *Symphonia domestica* (N.Y., March 21, 1904); *Festliches Praeludium* (Vienna, Oct. 19, 1913); *Eine Alpensinfonie* (Berlin, Oct. 28, 1915); *Parergon zur Symphonia domestica,* for piano (left hand) and orch. (Dresden, Oct. 16, 1925, Paul Wittgenstein, soloist); *München Walzer* (originally written for film, 1939; new version, 1945; performed posthumously, Vienna, March 31, 1951), *Festmusik* on the 2600th anniversary of the Japanese Empire (Tokyo, Oct. 27, 1940); *Divertimento* on pieces by Couperin (Vienna, Jan. 31, 1943); Horn Concerto No. 2 (Salzburg, Aug. 11, 1943); *Metamorphosen,* for 23 string instruments (Zürich, Jan. 25, 1946); Oboe Concerto (Zürich, Feb. 26, 1946); Duet Concertino, for clarinet, bassoon, strings, and harp (Radio Svizzera Italiana, April 5, 1948).

CHAMBER MUSIC: String Quartet (1879–80); Cello Sonata (1882–83); *Serenade,* for 13 wind instruments (1881); Piano Quartet (1884); Violin Sonata (1887); Sonatina No. 1, for 16 wind instruments (1943); Sonatina No. 2, for 16 wind instruments (1944–45).

CHORAL WORKS: chorus for *Electra* of Sophocles (1880); *Wanderers Sturmlied,* for chorus and orch. (1884); *Eine deutsche Motette,* for solo voices and 16-part chorus (1923); *Die Tageszeiten,* cycle for men's chorus and orch. (1928); many unpubl. choral pieces.

FOR VOICE AND ORCH.: 4 songs (1896–97); 4 Hymns for soprano (1921); *Drei Gesänge,* for high voice (1948); *Im Abendrot,* for high voice (1948).

FOR VOICE AND PIANO: 26 albums to words in German; of these songs the earliest are the most famous: *Zueignung* (1882); *Die Nacht* (1882); *Allerseelen* (1883); *Ständchen* (1885); *Barcarole* (1886); *Breit über mein Haupt* (1886); *Cäcilie, Heimliche Aufforderung,* and *Morgen* (1893–94); *Traum durch die Dämmerung* (1894); *Ich trage meine Minne* (1896).

FOR RECITATION AND PIANO: *Enoch Arden,* after Tennyson (1890) and *Das Schloss am Meer,* after Uhland (1899). A collected edition of the songs, in 4 vols., was edited by F. Trenner and publ. in 1964–65.

FOR PIANO: 5 pieces (1881); Sonata (1881); *4 Stimmungsbilder* (1883).

ARRANGEMENTS AND EDITIONS: Strauss arranged Gluck's *Iphigénie en Tauride* for production at Weimar; his version was used for the American première at the Metropolitan Opera House, N.Y., Nov. 25, 1916; translated, revised, and enlarged the *Traité d'Instrumentation* of Berlioz (1905); made a new arrangement of Beethoven's *The Ruins of Athens* (Vienna, 1927); edited Mozart's *Idomeneo* (1930); harmonized a number of folksongs for Peters' *Volksliederbuch für Männerchor;* edited and published his father's posthumous works for horn. He publ. his memoirs, *Betrachtungen und Erinnerungen* (Zürich, 1949; edited by W. Schuh; in English, N.Y., 1953).

THEMATIC CATALOGUES: R. Specht, *Vollständiges Verzeichnis der im Druck erschienenen Werke von R. S.* (Vienna, 1910; also contains valuable biographical data); Erich Hermann Mueller von Asow, *R. S., thematisches Verzeichnis* (3 vols., 1955-74).

BIBLIOGRAPHY: BIOGRAPHY: A. Seidl and W. Klatte, *R. S. Eine Charakterskizze* (Prague, 1896); G. Brecher, *R. S. Eine monographische Skizze* (Leipzig, 1900); E. Urban, *R. S.* (Berlin, 1901); Ernest Newman, *R. S.* (London, 1908); M. Steinitzer, *R. S.* (Berlin, 1911; 17th ed., 1928); H. T. Finck, *R. S. The Man and His Works* (Boston, 1917); R. Specht, *R. S. und sein Werk* (2 vols.; Leipzig, 1921); H. W. von Waltershausen, *R. S.* (Munich, 1921); R. C. Muschler, *R. S.* (Hildesheim, 1924); W. Hutschenruyter, *R. S.* (in Dutch; The Hague, 1929); E. Gehring, ed., *R. S. und seine Vaterstadt* (Munich, 1934); F. Gysi, *R. S.* (Potsdam, 1934); R. Tenschert, *Anekdoten um R. S.* (Vienna, 1945); R. Tenschert, *R. S. und Wien* (Vienna, 1949); W. Brandl, *R. S., Leben und Werk* (Wiesbaden, 1949); K. Pfister, *R. S., Weg, Gestalt, Denkmal* (Vienna, 1949); C. Rostand, *R. S.* (Paris, 1949); O. Erhardt, *R. S. Leben, Wirken, Schaffen* (Olten, 1953); F. Trenner, *R. S. Dokumente seines Lebens und Schaffens* (Munich, 1954); E. Krause, *R. S., Gestalt und Werk* (Leipzig, 1955); I. Fabian, *Richard Strauss* (Budapest, 1962); G. Marek, *Richard Strauss: The Life of a Non-Hero* (N.Y., 1967); Han Jefferson, *The Life of Richard Strauss* (London, 1973); A. Kennedy, *Richard Strauss* (London, 1976).

CRITICISM, APPRECIATION: Analyses of the instrumental works are found in H. Kretzschmar's *Führer durch den Konzertsaal* (Leipzig, 1887; 4th ed., 1913) and in Schlesinger's *Musikführer* and *Meisterführer* (Berlin); guides to the dramatic works in Schlesinger's *Opernführer* (Berlin), Wossidlo's *Opernbibliothek* (Leipzig), and the numerous handbooks of Kufferath, Taubmann, Chop, Roese, Gilman, Schanzer, etc. G. Jorisienne, *R. S. Essai critique et biologique* (Brussels, 1898); J. Huneker, *Mezzotints in Modern Music* (N.Y., 1899); E. Urban, *S. contra Wagner* (Berlin, 1902); J. Huneker, *Overtones* (N.Y., 1904); L. Gilman, *Phases of Modern Music* (N.Y., 1904); E. Newman, "R. S. and the Music of the Future," in *Musical Studies* (London, 1905); O. Bie, *Die Moderne Musik und R. S.* (Berlin, 1906); P. Draeseke, *Die Konfusion in der Musik* (Stuttgart, 1906); F. Niecks, *Program Musik in the Last Four Centuries* (London, 1907); E. Schmitz, *R. S. als Musikdramatiker* (Munich, 1907); E. Zeigler, *R.S. in seinen dramatischen Dichtungen* (Munich, 1907); J. C. Manifarges, *R.S. als Dirigent* (Amsterdam, 1907);

R. Rolland, *Musiciens d'aujourd'hui* (Paris, 1908; in English, 1914); L. Gilman, *Aspects of Modern Opera* (N.Y., 1908); L. A. Coerne, *The Evolution of Modern Orchestration* (N.Y., 1908); P. Bekker, *Das Musikdrama der Gegenwart* (Stuttgart, 1909); R. Louis, *Die deutsche Musik der Gegenwart* (Munich, 1909); L. Schmidt, *Aus dem Musikleben der Gegenwart* (Berlin, 1909; with preface by Strauss); F. Santoliquido, *Il Dopo-Wagner: C. Debussy e R. S.* (Rome, 1909); G. Tebaldini, *Telepatia musicale e proposito dell'Elektra di R. S.* (Turin, 1909); M. Steinitzer, *Straussiana und Anderes* (Stuttgart, 1910); O. Hübner, *R. S. und das Musikdrama* (Leipzig, 1910); R. Mayrhofer, *Zur Theorie des Schönen* (Leipzig, 1911); H. Rutters, *R. S. en de S.-feesten* (Amsterdam, 1911); *Modern Music and Drama* (2 vols.; Boston, 1911, 1915; gives list of several hundred titles of articles publ. about Strauss in English and American journals); H. Daffner, *Salome: Ihre Gestalt in Geschichte und Kunst* (Munich, 1912); A. Seidl, *Straussiana* (Regensburg, 1913); M. Steinitzer, *R. S. in seiner Zeit* (Leipzig, 1914; 2nd ed., 1922); P. Rosenfeld, *Musical Portraits* (N.Y., 1920); W. Schrenk, *R. S. und die neue Musik* (Berlin, 1924); J. Subirá, *R. S., su hispanismo* (in Spanish; 1925); C. Gray, *Survey of Contemporary Music* (London, 1927); E. Blom, *The Rose Cavalier* (London, 1930); T. Armstrong, *S.'s Tone-poems* (London, 1931); K. J. Krüger, *Hugo von Hofmannsthal und R. S.* (Berlin, 1935); H. Rüttger, *Das Formproblem bei R. S.* (Berlin, 1937); J. Gregor, *R. S. Der Meister der Oper* (Munich, 1939); R. Tenschert, *3 x 7 Variationen über das Thema R. S.* (Vienna, 1944); W. Schuh, *Über Opern von R. S.* (Zürich, 1947); F. von Schuch, *R. S., Ernst von Schuch und Dresdens Oper* (2nd ed., Leipzig, 1953); G. Hausswald, *R. S., ein Beitrag zur Dresdner Operngeschichte seit 1945* (Dresden, 1953); Strauss issues of the *Allgemeine Musikzeitung* (1939) and *Die Musik* IV/8 and XIII/17; N. Del Mar, *Richard Strauss: A Critical Commentary on His Life and Works* (2 vols.; I, London, 1962; II, Philadelphia, 1969); A. Jefferson, *The Operas of Richard Strauss in Britain, 1910-1963* (London, 1963); W. Mann, *Richard Strauss: A Critical Study of the Operas* (London, 1964); Lotte Lehmann, *Five Operas and Richard Strauss* (N.Y., 1964); W. Schuh, *Der Rosenkavalier* (Frankfurt, 1971).

CORRESPONDENCE: *R. S. Briefwechsel mit Hugo von Hofmannsthal,* ed. by Franz Strauss (S.'s son; Vienna, 1926; in English, N.Y., 1927); *R. S. und Hugo von Hofmannsthal: Briefwechsel* (complete ed., by Franz and Alice Strauss; Zürich, 1952; published in English under the title *A Working Friendship: The Correspondence between Richard Strauss and Hugo von Hofmannsthal,* London, 1961); *R. S. et Romain Rolland; correspondance* (Paris, 1951); *Briefe an die Eltern: 1882-1906* (Zürich, 1954); *Correspondence: Hans von Bülow and R. S.* (London, 1955); *R. S. und Josef Gregor: Briefwechsel, 1934-1949* (Salzburg, 1955); *Briefwechsel zwischen R. S. und Stefan Zweig* (Frankfurt, 1957); *R. S. und Ludwig Thuille, Briefe der Freundschaft 1877-1907* (Munich, 1969).

Stravinsky, Feodor, distinguished Russian bass; father of **Igor Stravinsky;** b. near Rechitza, in the district of Minsk, June 20, 1843; d. St. Petersburg, Dec. 4, 1902. He became a member of the Russian Imperial

Opera at St. Petersburg in 1876 and established himself as one of the greatest Russian basses before Chaliapin; his interpretation of heroic and comical characters in Russian operas evoked unbounded praise from the critics. He was famous as Méphistophélès in Gounod's *Faust,* and was distinguished not only for the power of his voice, but also for his dramatic talent on the stage. Altogether, he made 1,235 appearances in 64 operatic roles.

Stravinsky, Igor, one of the greatest masters of modern music; b. Oranienbaum, near St. Petersburg, June 17, 1882; d. New York, April 6, 1971. His body was flown to Venice and buried in the Russian corner of the cemetery island of San Michele, according to the Greek Orthodox ritual; his *Requiem Canticles* was performed at the grave. He was the son of a famous bass at the Imperial Opera, **Feodor Stravinsky,** and was brought up in an artistic atmosphere. He studied law, and it was not until he reached the age of 19 that a meeting with Rimsky-Korsakov in Heidelberg encouraged him to undertake a serious study of composition. Upon Rimsky-Korsakov's advice, he studied theory with Kalafati. In 1907 Stravinsky began to take regular private lessons with Rimsky-Korsakov in St. Petersburg. On Feb. 5, 1908, his 1st Symph., already showing a mastery of technique, was performed in St. Petersburg. For Maximilian Steinberg's marriage to Rimsky-Korsakov's daughter (June 17, 1908), Stravinsky wrote an orchestral fantasy *Feu d'artifice.* Rimsky-Korsakov died a few days later, and Stravinsky wrote a threnody to pay tribute to his master. On Feb. 6, 1909, Stravinsky's next orchestral work, *Scherzo fantastique,* was performed in St. Petersburg. The famous impresario, Diaghilev, heard it and became interested in the new talent. Diaghilev had just asked Liadov for a ballet to be presented at the Paris season of the Ballet Russe, but Liadov declined; Diaghilev then commissioned Stravinsky to write a suitable work on a Russian subject. The result was the production of the first of Stravinsky's ballet masterpieces, *The Firebird,* produced by Diaghilev's Ballet Russe in Paris on June 25, 1910. Here Stravinsky wrote a score of coruscating brilliance, steeped in Russian folklore, and marking a natural continuation of Rimsky-Korsakov's series of musical fairy tales. There are numerous striking effects in orchestral treatment, such as a glissando of harmonics in the string instruments, and the rhythmic elements are exhilarating; 2 orchestral suites were extracted from the work, the more famous of which was reorchestrated by Stravinsky in 1919, to conform to his new ideas of musical economy, with a general reduction of the orchestral apparatus; but the original scoring remained a favorite with conductors and orchestras. Stravinsky's association with Diaghilev shifted his activities to Paris, where he made his home from 1911, with sojourns in Switzerland. His 2nd ballet for Diaghilev, *Petrouchka* (Paris, June 13, 1911), was highly successful; not only was it remarkably effective on the stage, but the music, arranged in 2 orchestral suites, was so new and original that it marked a turning point in 20th-century modernism; the spasmodically explosive rhythms, the novel instrumental sonorities, with the use of the piano as an integral part of the orchestra, and the bold

innovation in employing 2 different keys sounded simultaneously (C major and F-sharp major, the "Petrouchka Chord") exercised a highly potent influence upon contemporary composers. Two years later Stravinsky brought out a work of even greater revolutionary import, the ballet, *Le Sacre du printemps (Rite of Spring;* Russian title, *Vesna Sviashchennaya,* literally *Spring the Sacred),* produced by Diaghilev and his Ballet Russe in Paris on May 29, 1913; the score still stands out as one of the most daring creations of the modern musical mind. Its impact was tremendous; to some in the audience Stravinsky's "barbaric" asymmetric rhythms and the agglomeration of polytonal discords proved beyond endurance, and there were loud protests; most Paris critics exercised their verbal ingenuity by indignant vituperation, but progressive musicians accepted the work as the beginning of a new era in composition. Shortly before the outbreak of World War I, Diaghilev produced Stravinsky's lyric fairy tale, *Le Rossignol,* after Hans Christian Andersen (Paris, May 26, 1914). The war disrupted musical activities in Europe; Stravinsky spent the years 1914–18 mostly in Switzerland, where he continued to compose; Russian subjects still dominated his creative imagination. He worked on his ballet *Les Noces* (Russian title, *Svadebka,* literally, *Little Wedding),* scored for an unusual ensemble of chorus, soloists, 4 pianos, and 17 percussion instruments. During the last months of the war Stravinsky formulated his idea that economy in musical settings became imperative in an impoverished world. To indicate the way, he wrote the musical stage play *Histoire du Soldat,* scored for only 7 players; the work includes several stylized modern dances. At the same time he wrote a work for 11 instruments entitled *Ragtime,* rhythmically inspired by new American dance music. He resumed his association with Diaghilev and wrote for him the ballet *Pulcinella* (on themes mistakenly attributed to Pergolesi). He also wrote for Diaghilev two 1-act operas, *Mavra,* after Pushkin, and *Renard,* to stories from Russian folk literature (both produced by Diaghilev, Paris, May 18, 1922). These two works were the last in which Stravinsky used Russian subjects. In his next significant composition, the Piano Concerto, commissioned by Koussevitzky, Stravinsky made the clearest statement of his neo-classical period of composition, presaged by Octet and *Pulcinella,* abandoning his erstwhile luxuriance of instrumental color and affective dissonance; however, his reversion to old forms was not an act of ascetic renunciation, but rather a grand experiment in reviving Baroque practices which had fallen into desuetude. He performed it with the Boston Symph. Orch. under Koussevitzky on Jan. 23, 1925, on the occasion of his 1st American tour. The Elizabeth Sprague Coolidge Foundation commissioned him to write a pantomime for string orch.; the result was *Apollon Musagète,* given at the Library of Congress in Washington, on April 27, 1928. This score, serene and emotionally restrained, evokes the court ballets of Lully in its spirit. He continued to explore the possibilities of neo-Classical writing in the *Capriccio* for piano and orch. (Paris, Dec. 6, 1929), but in this score he produced a work of hedonistic entertainment quite modern in its impact, the rhythmic element being exploited to the utmost. A desire for tragic expression became manifest in his opera-oratorio *Oedipus Rex,* to a Latin text (Paris, May 30, 1927). A religious feeling found utterance in the *Symphony of Psalms,* written for the 50th anniversary of the Boston Symph. and dedicated "to the glory of God." It is scored for chorus and orch., omitting the violins and violas, thus emphasizing the lower registers and creating an austere sonority suitable to its solemn subject. Owing to a delay of the Boston performance, the world première of the *Symphony of Psalms* took place in Brussels (Dec. 13, 1930). In 1931 Stravinsky composed a Concerto for Violin and Orch., commissioned by the violinist Samuel Dushkin, and performed by him in Berlin on Oct. 23. On a commission from Ida Rubinstein, Stravinsky wrote a ballet, to a text by André Gide, entitled *Perséphone,* which he conducted at the Paris Opéra on April 30, 1934. For his American tour in 1937 he wrote *Jeu de Cartes,* a "ballet in three deals," to his own scenario derived from an imaginary poker game, and conducted it at the Metropolitan Opera House, N.Y., on April 27, 1937. His concerto for 16 instruments, entitled *Dumbarton Oaks* (after the Washington estate of Mr. and Mrs. Robert Woods Bliss) and performed in Washington, D.C., on May 8, 1938, continued the deliberate practice of neo-Baroque composition (in Paris the work was played under the simple title *Concerto,* without the reference to Dumbarton Oaks). Stravinsky was named Charles Eliot Norton lecturer at Harvard Univ. for 1939–40. He became a French citizen on June 10, 1934, but in 1939 he left France and settled in the U.S., making his home in Hollywood; he became an American citizen on Dec. 28, 1945. He continued to conduct his works in America and in Europe; his creative energy did not abate with the advancing years. He wrote music in variegated styles and for widely different purposes: a *Circus Polka* "composed for a young elephant" commissioned by the Ringling Bros. Circus (1942); *Ebony Concerto,* for clarinet and swing band, performed by Woody Herman in Carnegie Hall, N.Y. (March 25, 1946); a Mass for men's and boys' voices and 10 instruments (Milan, Oct. 27, 1948); as a temporary return to his Russian antecedents, he wrote an orchestral *Scherzo à la russe* (1944). At the time of his application for American citizenship, he publ. an arrangement of the *Star-Spangled Banner* and conducted it with the Boston Symph. (Jan. 14, 1944), but because of complaints on the part of some of the audience about the unorthodox harmonization, and on account of legal injunctions existing in the state of Massachusetts against intentional mutilation of the national anthem, Stravinsky had to cease and desist from repeating it at the second of the pair of concerts that he conducted, and the standard version was played instead. In 1951 Stravinsky completed his opera *The Rake's Progress,* after Hogarth's famous series of engravings, to a libretto by W. H. Auden and C. Kallman, and conducted its world première in Venice on Sept. 11, as part of the International Festival of Contemporary Music there. The opera had tremendous repercussions in the musical world, as still another illustration of Stravinsky's capacity of changing his course towards unexpected destinations; here, the style was a conglomeration of elements of 19th-century Italian opera, early English stage plays, and French opéra comique. In his latest works he applied a method of serial composition, modelled after the creations of Anton von Webern, rather than those of Schoenberg; in this manner he wrote his *Canticum sacrum ad honorem Sancti Marci nominis,* for tenor, baritone, chorus, and orch., which he conducted at St. Mark's Cathedral in Venice on Sept. 11, 1956. In 1957 he wrote *Agon,* a ballet for 12 dancers, containing serial elements in 12-tone motives in some variations; it was presented in Los Angeles on the occasion of his 75th birthday, June 17, 1957. Igor Stravinsky's influence on contemporary music has been profound. Inasmuch as his early masterpieces were produced in Paris, the impact was strongest upon French composers of the generations that grew up in the 1st quarter of the 20th century. Several American composers who studied in France experienced Stravinsky's influence to a considerable degree, as did many from Spain and South America.

Ironically, it was in Stravinsky's own country that his music had the least impact, partly because of his long absence from Russia, partly because of the opposition of the Soviet ideology to modern music in general, and particularly due to Stravinsky's highly dissonant type of composition. Some Soviet critics accused him of selling out his national heritage to provide easy titillation to decadent Parisians. As a result, Stravinsky's music was rarely performed in Soviet Russia and his name was a constant target of attacks in the Soviet musical press as a purveyor of obscurantism. But in 1962 Stravinsky returned to Russia for a visit, and was welcomed as a prodigal son; as if by magic, his works began to appear on Russian concert programs, and Soviet music critics issued a number of analytic studies of his music.

WORKS: FOR THE STAGE: *The Firebird,* ballet (Paris, June 25, 1910); *Petrouchka,* ballet (Paris, June 13, 1911); *Le Sacre du printemps,* ballet, "scenes of pagan Russia" (Paris, May 29, 1913); *Rossignol,* "lyric tale" in 3 acts, after Andersen (Paris, May 26, 1914; also performed as a ballet, Paris, Feb. 2, 1920); *Renard,* burlesque chamber opera (Paris, May 18, 1922); *Mavra,* comic opera, after Pushkin (Paris, June 3, 1922); *Les Noces,* "choreographic Russian scenes" (Paris, June 13, 1923); *Histoire du soldat,* for narrator and 7 instruments (Lausanne, Sept. 28, 1918); *Pulcinella,* ballet "after Pergolesi" (Paris, May 15, 1920); *Oedipus Rex,* opera-oratorio, after Sophocles (concert performance, Paris, May 30, 1927; stage performance, Berlin, Feb. 25, 1928); *Apollon Musagète,* classic ballet (Washington, D.C., April 27, 1928); *Le Baiser de la fée,* ballet on themes by Tchaikovsky (Paris, Nov. 27, 1928); *Perséphone,* ballet with recitation and chorus, to text by André Gide (Paris, April 30, 1934); *Jeu de cartes (Card Game),* "ballet in 3 deals," (N.Y., April 27, 1937); *Orpheus,* ballet (N.Y., April 28, 1948); *The Rake's Progress,* opera, after Hogarth's engravings; libretto by W. H. Auden and C. Kallman (Venice, Sept. 11, 1951, Stravinsky conducting); *Agon,* ballet for 12 dancers (Los Angeles, June 17, 1957); *Noah and the Flood,* biblical spectacle narrated, mimed, sung and danced (NBC television broadcast, N.Y., June 14, 1962).

FOR ORCH.: Symph. in E-flat major, op. 1 (1905–07;

St. Petersburg, Feb. 5, 1908); *Le Faune et la bergère,* for mezzo-soprano and orch., op. 2 (St. Petersburg, Feb. 5, 1908); *Scherzo fantastique,* op. 3 (St. Petersburg, Feb. 6, 1909); *Fireworks,* op. 4 (St. Petersburg, June 17, 1908); *Funeral Chant on the Death of Rimsky-Korsakov,* for chorus and orch. (1908); *The Firebird,* 2 orchestral suites from the ballet (1910; the 2nd reorchestrated in 1919); *Petrouchka,* orchestral suite from the ballet (1910-11); *Le Roi des étoiles,* cantata for voice and orch. (1911); *Le Sacre du printemps,* orchestral suite from the ballet (Paris, April 5, 1914); *Chant du rossignol,* suite in 3 parts from the opera (Geneva, Dec. 6, 1919; 1st performance as a ballet, Paris, Feb. 2, 1920); *Ragtime,* for 11 instruments (composed Nov. 11, 1918); *Pulcinella,* suite from the ballet (1920); *Symphonies of Wind Instruments,* in memory of Debussy (1920; London, June 10, 1921); *Suite No. 1* for small orch. (1917-25; orchestral arrangement of four of the *5 Pièces faciles* for piano, 4 hands: *Andante, Napolitana, Española, Balalaïka*); *Suite No. 2* for small orch. (1921; *March, Waltz, Polka, Galop*); Concerto for Piano and Wind Instruments (Paris, May 22, 1924); *Capriccio* for piano and orch. (Paris, Dec. 6, 1929); *4 Études* for orch.: *Danse, Excentrique, Cantique, Madrid* (Berlin, Nov. 7, 1930); *Symphony of Psalms,* for chorus and orch. (Brussels, Dec. 13, 1930; Boston, Dec. 19, 1930); Violin Concerto (Berlin, Oct. 23, 1931); Concerto *Dumbarton Oaks* (Washington, D.C., May 8, 1938); Symphony in C (Chicago, Nov. 7, 1940); *Tango,* arrangement of the violin piece (Philadelphia, July 10, 1941); *Danses concertantes* (Los Angeles, Feb. 8, 1942); *Circus Polka* (1942; Boston, Jan. 13, 1944); *Ode,* in 3 parts (Boston, Oct. 8, 1943); *Norwegian Moods,* 4 episodes (Boston, Jan. 13, 1944); *Scènes de ballet* (N.Y., Feb. 3, 1945); *Scherzo à la russe* (1944; San Francisco, March 22, 1946, composer conducting); Symphony in 3 Movements (N.Y., Jan. 24, 1946); *Ebony Concerto,* for clarinet and swing band (N.Y., March 25, 1946); Concerto in D for string orch. (Basel, Jan. 21, 1947); *Movements* for piano and orchestra (N.Y., Jan. 10, 1960); *Variations: Aldous Huxley, In Memoriam* (Chicago, April 17, 1965).

CHAMBER MUSIC: *3 Pieces* for string quartet (1914); *3 Pieces* for clarinet solo (1919); Concertino for string quartet (1920); Octet for wind instruments (Paris, Oct. 18, 1923); *Duo concertant,* for violin and piano (Berlin, Oct. 28, 1932); *Suite italienne,* for cello and piano, from *Pulcinella* (1934); *Tango,* for violin and piano (1941); *Élégie,* for unaccompanied violin or viola (1944); Septet for piano and string and wind instruments (1952; Washington, D.C., Jan. 23, 1954); *Epitaphium for Prince Max of Fürstenberg* for flute, clarinet and harp (Donaueschingen, Oct. 17, 1959); *Monumentum pro Gesualdo di Venosa ad CD Annum,* an instrumental surrealization of 3 madrigals by Gesualdo (Venice, Sept. 27, 1960).

VOCAL WORKS: *3 Poems from the Japanese,* for soprano, 2 flutes, 2 clarinets, piano, and string quartet (1912-13); *Pribautki,* songs for voice with 8 instruments (1914); *The Saucer,* 4 Russian songs for women's voices (1914-17); *Berceuses du chat,* suite of 4 songs for female voice and 3 clarinets (1915-16); *Paternoster,* for mixed chorus, a cappella (1926); *Credo* for mixed chorus, a cappella (1932); *Ave Maria,* for mixed chorus, a cappella (1934); Mass for men's and boys' voices and 10 instruments (Milan, Oct. 27, 1948); *Cantata* on 4 poems by anonymous English poets of the 15th and 16th centuries (Los Angeles, Nov. 11, 1952); *3 Songs from William Shakespeare,* for mezzo-soprano, flute, clarinet, and viola (Los Angeles, March 8, 1954); *In Memoriam Dylan Thomas,* for tenor, string quartet, and 4 trombones (Hollywood, Sept. 20, 1954); *4 Russian Songs* for soprano, flute, guitar, and harp (1954); *Canticum sacrum ad honorem Sancti Marci nominis,* for tenor, baritone, chorus, and orch. (Venice, Sept. 13, 1956, composer conducting); arrangement for chorus and orch. of J. S. Bach's *Choral-Variationen über das Weihnachtslied "Vom Himmel hoch da komm' ich her"* (1956); *Threni,* on Lamentations of Jeremiah from the Vulgate, for solo voices, chorus, and orch. (International Festival of Contemporary Music, Venice, Sept. 23, 1958); *Elegy for J.F.K.* for baritone, 2 clarinets and corno di bassetto (Los Angeles, April 6, 1964); *Abraham and Isaac,* sacred ballad for baritone and chamber orch. to Hebrew texts (Jerusalem, Aug. 23, 1964); *Introitus (T.S. Eliot in Memoriam)* for male chorus, harp, piano, timpani, tam-tams, solo viola, and double bass (Chicago, April 17, 1965); *Requiem Canticles* for vocal quartet, chorus, and orch. (Princeton, Oct. 8, 1966).

PIANO MUSIC: 2 sonatas (1904; 1922); *4 Études* (1908); *3 Pièces faciles,* for piano 4 hands (1915); *5 Pièces faciles,* for piano 4 hands (1917); *Étude* for pianola (1917); *Piano Rag-Music* (1920); *Les Cinq Doigts* (1921); *Serenade* in A (1925); Concerto for 2 solo pianos (1931-35); Sonata for 2 pianos (1944).

WRITINGS: *Chroniques de ma vie,* autobiography (Paris, 1935; 2 vols.; in English as *Chronicles of My Life,* London, 1936); *Poétique musicale,* the Charles Eliot Norton Lectures at Harvard Univ. (Paris, 1946; in English as *Poetics of Music,* Cambridge, Mass., 1948); with Robert Craft, Stravinsky brought out 6 vols. of revelatory autobiographical publications: *Conversations with Igor Stravinsky* (N.Y., 1958); *Memories and Commentaries* (N.Y., 1959); *Expositions and Developments* (N.Y., 1962); *Dialogues and a Diary* (N.Y., 1963); *Themes and Episodes* (N.Y., 1967); and *Retrospections and Conclusions* (N.Y., 1969); also *Themes and Conclusions,* amalgamated and edited from *Themes and Episodes* and *Retrospections and Conclusions* (1972).

BIBLIOGRAPHY: C. Van Vechten, in *Music After the Great War* (N.Y., 1915); C. S. Wise, "Impressions of I. S.," *Musical Quartetly* (April 1916); M. Montagu-Nathan, *Contemporary Russian Composers* (N.Y., 1917); R. D. Chennevière, "The Two Trends of Modern Music in S.'s Works," *Musical Quarterly* (April 1919); B. de Schloezer, *I. S.* (Paris, 1926); A. Casella, *S.* (Rome, 1926); J. Vainkop, *I. S.* (in Russian; Leningrad, 1927); V. Belaiev, *I. S.'s Les Noces: An Outline* (London, 1928; also in Russian); Igor Glebov, *S.* (Leningrad, 1929); C. F. Ramuz, *Souvenirs sur I. S.* (Paris, 1929; new ed., Lausanne, 1946); P. Collaer, *S.* (Brussels, 1930); E. W. White, *S.'s Sacrifice to Apollo* (London, 1930); H. Fleischer, *S.* (Berlin, 1931); A. Schaeffner, *I. S.* (Paris, 1931); J. Handschin, *I. S.* (Zürich, 1933); E. Evans, *The Firebird and Petrouchka* (London, 1933); D. de Paoli, *I. S.* (Turin, 1934); M. Blitzstein, "The Phenomenon of S.," *Musical Quarterly*

(July 1935); M. Armitage (ed.), *S.*, a compendium of articles (N.Y., 1936); special S. issue of the *Revue Musicale* (May-June, 1939); A. Kall, "S. in the Chair of Poetry," *Musical Quarterly* (July 1940); S. Babitz, "S.'s Symphony in C," *Musical Quarterly* (Jan. 1941); M. D. Fardel, *S. et les ballets russes* (Nice, 1941); G. F. Malipiero, *S.* (Venice, 1945); A. Casella, *S.* (Brescia, 1947; a different work from his book publ. in 1926); E. W. White, *S.*, *A Critical Survey* (London, 1947; N.Y., 1948); A. Tansman, *I. S.* (Paris, 1948; in English, N.Y., 1949); Theodore Stravinsky, *Le Message d'I. S.* (Lausanne, 1948; in English as *The Message of I. S.*, London, 1953); M. Lederman, ed., *S. in the Theatre* (N.Y., 1949); E. Corle, ed., *I. S.* (N.Y., 1949; a compendium of articles, including some reprinted from M. Armitage's collection of 1936); F. Onnen, *S.* (Stockholm, 1949; in English); J. E. Cirlot, *I. S.* (Barcelona, 1949); R. H. Myers, *Introduction to the Music of S.* (London, 1950); W. H. Auden *et al.*, *I. S.* (Bonn, 1952); L. Oleggini, *Connaissance de S.* (Lausanne, 1952); H. Strobel, *I. S.* (Zürich, 1956; English version as *S.: Classic Humanist*, N.Y., 1955); *The Score* (1957), special number for Stravinsky's 75th birthday; *I. S.: A Complete Catalogue of His Publ. Works* (London, 1957); *Musik der Zeit* (Bonn; 1st Series, vols. 1, 12; New Series, vol. 1); H. Kirchmeyer, *I. S. Zeitgeschichte im Persönlichkeitsbild* (Regensburg, 1958); Roman Vlad, *Stravinsky* (Rome, 1958; in English, London, 1960); Robert Siohan, *Stravinsky* (Paris, 1959; in English, London, 1966); Friedrich Herzfeld, *Igor Stravinsky* (Berlin, 1961); "Special Issue for Igor Stravinsky on His 80th Anniversary," *Musical Quarterly* (July 1962); *Stravinsky and the Dance. A Survey of Ballet Productions. 1910-1962* (N.Y. Public Library, 1962); E. Berlin, *Tonality and Tonal References in the Serial Music of Igor Stravinsky* (Hunter College, N.Y., 1965); E. W. White, *Stravinsky. The Composer and His Works* (Berkeley, Cal., 1966; includes a 381-page "Register of Works," listing all compositions, arrangements, reprints, manuscripts, etc.); W. W. Austin, *Music in the 20th Century* (N.Y., 1966); Paul Henry Lang, ed., *Stravinsky: The Composer and His Works* (London, 1966; 2nd enlarged printing, 1969); special Stravinsky issue of *Tempo* (Summer 1967); C. Hamm, ed., Norton Critical Score ed. of *Petrouchka* (includes backgrounds, analyses, etc.; N.Y., 1967); A. Boucourechliev, ed., *Stravinsky* (Paris, 1968); *The Rite of Spring: Sketches, 1911-1913* (London, 1969); Arnold Dobrin, *Igor Stravinsky: His Life and Time* (London, 1970); B. Boretz and E. T. Cone, eds. *Perspectives on Schoenberg and Stravinsky* (N.Y., 1972); P. Horgan, *Encounters with Stravinsky* (N.Y., 1972); L. Libman, *And Music at the Close. Stravinsky's Last Years, A Personal Memoir* (N.Y., 1972); L. Kutateladge, ed., *Articles, Letters, Reminiscences* (Moscow, 1972); D.-R. De Lerma, *I. F. Stravinsky, 1882-1971: A Practical Guide to Publications of His Music* (N.Y., 1974); Th. Stravinsky, *Catherine and Igor Stravinsky: A Family Album* (iconography and introduction; N.Y., 1973); Vera Stravinsky and Robert Craft, *Stravinsky* (N.Y., 1975).

Stravinsky, Soulima, pianist, son of **Igor Stravinsky;** b. Lausanne, Sept. 23, 1910. He studied in Paris with Isidor Philipp and Nadia Boulanger; then gave piano recitals in Europe and America; appeared frequently with his father, playing his works for 2 pianos.

Strayhorn, William (Billy), black American jazz pianist and composer; b. Dayton, Ohio, Nov. 29, 1915; d. New York, May 30, 1967. He studied music in Pittsburgh; joined Duke Ellington's band as lyricist and arranger in 1939. Many songs credited to Ellington (*Chelsea Bridge, Perfume Suite, Such Sweet Thunder, A Drum Is a Woman,* etc.) are in fact products of a mutually beneficial musical symbiosis, with Ellington suggesting the initial idea, mood and character and Strayhorn doing the actual writing, often using Ellington's quasi-Impressionistic techniques (e.g., modal harmonies, whole-tone scales, etc.). Strayhorn's own acknowledged songs, *Lush Life, Take the 'A' Train* and others, are jazz standards.

Streatfeild, Richard Alexander, English writer on music; b. Edenbridge, June 22, 1866; d. London, Feb. 6, 1919. He studied at Pembroke College, Cambridge; in 1889 he became assistant in the Dept. of Printed Books in the British Museum; was music critic of the *Daily Graphic* (1898-1912). He publ. the following books: *Masters of Italian Music* (1895); *The Opera* (1897; 5th ed., enlarged, 1925); *Modern Music and Musicians* (1906); *Handel* (1909); *Life Stories of Great Composers* (Philadelphia, 1910); *Musiciens anglais contemporains* (French transl., 1913; English original not published); *Handel, Canons and the Duke of Chandos* (London, 1916); contributed many articles to English publications.

Street, Tison, American composer; b. Boston, May 20, 1943. He studied composition with Kirchner and Del Tredici at Harvard Univ.; received his B.A. (1965) and M.A. (1971) there; studied violin with Einar Hansen of the Boston Symph. (1951–59); was a composer-in-residence at the Marlboro Music Festival during 4 summers (1964, 1965, 1966, 1972) and a visiting lecturer at the Univ. of California at Berkeley (1971–72). He was the recipient of awards from the National Institute of the American Academy of Arts and Letters (1973), Rome Prize Fellowship (1973), and Massachusetts Arts and Humanities Foundation (1977).

WORKS: String Trio (1963); *Variations* for flute, guitar and cello (1964); *6 Odds and Ends from "So Much Depends"* for voices and diverse instruments (1964–73); String Quartet (1972); String Quintet (1974, revised 1976); *Piano Phantasy* (1975); *3 Pieces* for consort of viols and harpsichord (1977); *John Major's Medley* for solo guitar (1977); *Adagio in E-flat* for oboe and strings (1977).

Streicher, Johann Andreas, German piano maker; b. Stuttgart, Dec. 13, 1761; d. Vienna, May 25, 1833. During a stay at Augsburg in 1793 he married Nanette Stein (b. Augsburg, Jan. 2, 1769; d. Vienna, Jan. 16, 1835), daughter of the piano manufacturer Johann Andreas Stein; in 1802 succeeded Stein in the business and moved it to Vienna. He invented the piano action in which the hammer strikes from above. He was on friendly terms with Beethoven.

BIBLIOGRAPHY: T. Bolte, *Die Musiker-Familien*

Stein und Streicher (Vienna, 1917); T. von Frimmel, "Beethoven und das Ehepaar Streicher," *Alt-Wiener Kalender* (1925); W. Lütge, "Andreas und Annette Streicher," *Der Bär* (1927).

Streicher, Theodor, Austrian song composer, great-grandson of **Johann Andreas Streicher;** b. Vienna, June 7, 1874; d. Wetzelsdorf, near Graz, May 28, 1940. He studied singing with F. Jäger in Vienna and J. Kniese in Bayreuth; piano with F. Löwe in Vienna; composition with H. Schulz-Beuthen in Dresden. He lived most of his life in Vienna; wrote numerous songs in a Romantic manner, reminiscent of Hugo Wolf. He set to music 36 poems from *Des Knaben Wunderhorn;* wrote *Wanderers Nachtlied,* after Goethe, for chorus a cappella; a sextet for strings; etc. He also orchestrated the accompaniments of Carl Loewe's ballades. In 1934 a "Theodor Streicher Gemeinde" was founded in Vienna to propagate his music.

Strelezki, Anton, English pianist and composer; b. Croydon, England, Dec. 5, 1859; d. 1907. According to some sources, his real name was **Burnand.** He studied with Clara Schumann; settled in London, where he was very popular; place and date of his death are unknown. He publ. a great deal of piano music (more than 225 op. numbers), some of which was widely used: *Valse-Souvenir; Jagdstück; Valsette; Sérénade espagnole; Menuet à l'antique; Barcarolle;* also songs; publ. *Personal Recollections of Chats with Liszt* (1895).

Strelnikov, Nicolai, Russian composer; b. St. Petersburg, May 14, 1888; d. there (Leningrad), April 12, 1939. He studied composition with Liadov in St. Petersburg; in 1922 he became music director of the Young People's Theater in Leningrad. He wrote 2 operas: *A Fugitive* (Leningrad, May 26, 1933) and *Count Nulin,* after Pushkin (1935), but he is chiefly remembered for his operettas: *The Black Amulet* (Leningrad, 1927); *Luna-Park* (Moscow, 1928); *The Heart of a Poet* (Leningrad, 1934); *Presidents and Bananas* (1939). Other works include a piano concerto, choruses and chamber music. He also published monographs on several Russian composers.

Strens, Jules, Belgian composer; b. Ixelles, near Brussels, Dec. 5, 1892; d. there, March 19, 1971. He studied with Paul Gilson; in 1925 was one of eight founders of the "Group des Synthétistes" (all Gilson pupils), endeavoring to establish a modern style of composition within the formal categories of old music. Professionally, he was active mainly as an organist.

WORKS: 2 operas: *Le Chanteur de Naples* (1937) and *La Tragédie d'Agamemnon* (1941); for orch.: *Gil Blas,* symph. variations (1921); symph. poem, *Les Elfes* (1923); *Danse funambulesque* for orch. (1925); *Rapsodie tzigane* for orch. (1927); *Fantaisie concertante* for piano and orch. (1938); *Symphonie Sylvestre* for soli, chorus and orch. (1939); Violin Concerto (1951); Concerto for Organ and String Orch. (1958); chamber music: Piano Trio (1920); 4 string quartets (1925, 1929, 1933, 1935); Cello Sonata (1926); String Sextet (1935); Wind Quintet (1943); Quartet for 4

horns (1950); *Suite* for 4 horns (1951); Viola Sonata (1954); Trio for oboe, clarinet, and bassoon (1954); Piano Quartet (1955); piano pieces; organ pieces; songs.

Strepponi, Giuseppina, Italian soprano, wife of **Giuseppe Verdi;** b. Lodi, Sept. 8, 1815; d. Busseto, Nov. 14, 1897. She was the daughter of the opera conductor in Trieste, **Felice Strepponi;** having completed her studies at the Milan Cons. (1830–35), she made a successful debut in Trieste, and was engaged at the Italian Opera in Vienna. Her appearances in Rome, Florence, Venice, and other Italian cities established her reputation as a foremost interpreter of dramatic roles. She created a sensation by her performance of Abigaile in Verdi's *Nabucco* (Milan, March 9, 1842). Verdi admired her greatly, and after many years of intimacy they were married (1859).

Strickland, Lily Teresa, American composer; b. Anderson, S. C., Jan. 28, 1887; d. Hendersonville, N.C., June 6, 1958. She studied at Converse College, Spartanburg, S.C., later in N.Y. with A. J. Goodrich and W. H. Humiston. She married J. Courtney Anderson of N.Y. in 1912. She traveled in the Orient between 1920 and 1930, and spent several years in India; then returned to the U.S. She publ. a number of successful songs, such as *Mah Lindy Lou, Dreamin' Time, Songs of India, Song from High Hills;* piano suites (*Moroccan Mosaics, Egyptian Scenes, Himalayan Idylls,* etc.); also wrote *Oasis* for orch. (1942), and compiled (with Helen Frost) *Oriental and Character Dances* (N.Y., 1930).

Strickland, William, American conductor; b. Defiance, Ohio, Jan. 25, 1914. He studied organ and singing; then devoted himself to conducting; entered the U.S. Army in 1941; appointed Warrant Officer and Instructor at Army Music School at Fort Myer, Virginia, in 1942; organized the Army Music School Choir, which he conducted in Washington, including a performance at the White House. After discharge from the Army, he founded the Nashville Symph. Orch. and led it from 1946 to 1951. In 1953 he conducted in Austria; returning to the U.S. he was musical director of the Oratorio Society of N.Y. (1955–59); also made guest appearances as radio conductor. In 1958 he went on a tour of Asia; conducted in Manila, Tokyo, and Seoul; in 1962 he went on a European trip; conducted guest engagements in Scandinavia, in Poland, and in Germany (until 1969). He received numerous awards from educational institutes for his service to American music.

Striegler, Kurt, German composer and conductor; b. Dresden, Jan. 7, 1886; d. Wildthurn, near Landau, Aug. 4, 1958. He studied with Draeseke at the Dresden Cons. From 1912 to 1945 he was conductor at the Dresden Opera, and for 40 years (1905–45) he taught at the Musik Hochschule there. In 1945 he became director of the Cons. of Coburg. He wrote 4 symphonies; Violin Concerto; Cello Concerto; *Scherzo* for 7 kettledrums with orch.; much chamber music; numerous choruses; songs and piano pieces; also the operas *Der Thomaskantor* and *Hand und Herz* (Dresden, 1924).

Striggio, Alessandro, Italian lutenist, organist, and composer; b. Mantua, c.1535; d. there, c.1595. He lived at the court of Cosimo de' Medici in Florence, and later in Mantua as court conductor. In 1567 he was in Paris and London, and in 1574 at the court of the Emperor Maximilian. He composed 3 musical intermezzi for *Psiche ed Amore* and other festival music. He published several books of madrigals and *Il Cicalamento delle donne* (1567; descriptive songs in the manner of Janequin); many compositions by Striggio are found in collections of the period (1559–1634); 5 madrigals were reprinted by Torchi in L'Arte *Musicale in Italia* I. His son, **Alessandro** (called **Alessandrino**), was a poet, and a notable player of the violin and lyra. He was active at the court of Mantua (still there in 1628) and in 1607 wrote the libretto of Monteverdi's *La Favola d'Orfeo.* In 1596–97 he publ. 3 books of his father's madrigals for 5 voices.
BIBLIOGRAPHY: Letters of Striggio (the father) were publ. by Gandolfi in *Rivista Musicale Italiana* XX, p. 527ff.; see also A. Solerti, *Gli Albori del melodramma* (Milan, 1904); O. G. Sonneck, "A Description of A. S. and F. Corteccia's Intermedi *Psyche and Amor,* 1565," in *Miscellaneous Studies in the History of Music* (N.Y., 1921).

Strimer, Joseph, Russian-American pianist and composer; b. Rostov-on-the-Don, Oct. 21, 1881; d. New York, Jan. 1962. He studied with Rimsky-Korsakov, Liadov, Steinberg, Tcherepnin, and Glazunov at the St. Petersburg Cons.; after graduation, went to Germany, where he studied conducting with Arthur Nikisch. He lived mostly in Paris after 1920; came to N.Y. in 1941 and established himself as a teacher of piano and composition. He publ. a number of piano pieces; paraphrases of works by Rimsky-Korsakov, Borodin, Liadov, etc.; arrangements of folksongs.

Stringfield, Lamar, American composer and conductor; b. Raleigh, North Carolina, Oct. 10, 1897; d. Asheville, North Carolina, Jan. 21, 1959. He served in the Army of the United States during the World War I; after Armistice he studied music theory with Goetschius and flute with Georges Barrère at the Institute of Musical Art in N.Y.; also took lessons in conducting with Chalmers Clifton. In 1930 he organized the Insitute of Folk Music at the Univ. of North Carolina, and conducted its orch.; then for a season was conductor of the Knoxville Symph. Orch. (1946–47) and of the Charlotte Symph. Orch. (1948–49). The source material of his own compositions is largely derived from the folksongs of the U.S. south. He learned the trade of printing and was able to publish his own works.
WORKS: a musical folk-drama, *Carolina Charcoal* (1952); for orch.: *Indian Legend* (1923), suite *From the Southern Mountains* (1928; contains his best known piece, *Cripple Creek*), *A Negro Parade* (1931); *Moods of a Moonshiner* (1934), *Mountain Dawn* (1945), *About Dixie* (1950); chamber music: *Chipmunks* for flute, clarinet, and bassoon; *From a Negro Melody,* for 12 instruments; *Indian Sketches* for flute and string quartet; *Virginia Dare Dance* for wind quintet; sacred cantata, *Peace,* for chorus a cappella; etc. He published *America and Her Music* (Univ. of North Carolina Press, 1931).

Stringham, Edwin John, American music educator and composer; b. Kenosha, Wisconsin, July 11, 1890; d. Chapel Hill, North Carolina, July 1, 1974. He studied at Northwestern Univ. and at the Cincinnati Cons.; in 1929 went to Italy where he took lessons in composition with Respighi. Returning to the U.S. he occupied teaching posts at the Denver College of Music (1920–29), Teachers College of Columbia Univ. (1930–38), the Juilliard School of Music, N.Y. (1930–45), and at Queens College of the City of N.Y. (1938–46). In 1948 he settled in Chapel Hill, N.C.
WORKS: for orch.: *Visions,* symph. poem (1924); *The Ancient Mariner,* after Coleridge (Denver, March 16, 1928); Symph. No. 1 (Minneapolis, Nov. 15, 1929); *Fantasy on American Folk Tunes* for violin and orch. (1942); chamber music; songs. He published the books *Listening to Music Creatively* (N.Y., 1943; revised ed., 1959); *Creative Harmony and Musicianship* (with H. A. Murphy, N.Y., 1951).

Strobel, Heinrich, eminent German musicologist; b. Regensburg, May 31, 1898; d. Baden-Baden, Aug. 18, 1970. He studied musicology with Sandberger and Kroyer in Munich, obtaining his degree of Dr. phil. in 1922. He was music critic of the *Börsenkurier* in Berlin from 1927 to 1933; in 1939 he went to Paris; after the end of the war he settled in Baden-Baden, where he was active as music critic and music director at the radio station; was editor of the progressive magazine *Melos* until his death. He devoted himself energetically to the cause of modern music; wrote numerous articles on the subject; promoted programs of avant-garde composers on the radio and at the various festivals in Germany. He was the author of a basic biography of Hindemith (Mainz, 1928; new enlarged ed., 1948) and of a monograph on Debussy (Zürich, 1940; 5th German ed., 1961; French edition, Paris, 1942; Spanish edition Madrid, 1966); also published *Igor Stravinsky* (Zürich, 1956; English version as *Stravinsky: Classic Humanist,* N.Y., 1955).

Strobel, Otto, German musicologist; b. Munich, Aug. 20, 1895; d. Bayreuth, Feb. 23, 1953. He studied at the Univ. of Munich (Dr. phil., 1924). After working as an archivist at Bayreuth, he was appointed in 1938 director of the newly created Richard Wagner Institute there. He publ. *Genie am Werk: Richard Wagners Schaffen und Wirken im Spiegel eigenhandschriftlicher Urkunden* (Bayreuth, 1934); *Richard Wagner* (Bayreuth, 1952); edited *König Ludwig II. und Richard Wagner: Briefwechsel,* 4 vols. (Karlsruhe, 1936–37), and a supplement to this, *Neue Urkunden zur Lebensgeschichte Richard Wagners* (Karlsruhe, 1939); *Neue Wagner-Forschungen,* vol. 1 (Karlsruhe, 1943).

Stroe, Aurel, Rumanian composer; b. Bucharest, May 5, 1932. He studied composition with Negrea, Rogalski, I. Dumitrescu, and Chirescu at the Bucharest Cons. (1951–56); had a course in electronic music in Munich (1966) and attended the annual summer courses in new music given in Darmstadt (1966–69) by Kagel, Ligeti, and Stockhausen; in 1962 he joined the faculty of the Bucharest Cons.; then worked at the Bucharest Computing Center (1966–69). His early music is rooted in folklore, but in his later period he experimented with sonoristic constructions, some of which were put together by computerized calculations.

WORKS: 3 operas: *Nu va Primi premiul Nobel (Ça n'aura pas le Prix Nobel,* 1965–69; Kassel, Nov. 28, 1971), *De Ptolemaeo,* mini-opera for tape (1970), and *La Paix,* after Aristophanes (1973), Concerto for String Orch. (1950); Trio for oboe, clarinet, and bassoon (1953); *Pastorale* for orch. (1959); Piano Sonata (1955); *Chipul păcii,* chamber cantata, after Éluard, for mezzo-soprano, chorus and chamber orch. (1959); *Monumentum* for male chorus and orch. (1961); *Uvertura Burlesque* (1961); *Arcade* for 11 instrumental groups (1962); incidental music to *Oedipus in Colonne,* after Sophocles, for mezzo-soprano, male chorus, and orch. (1963; Bucharest, June 16, 1964); *Signum* for winds (1963); *Muzica da concert* for piano, brasses, and percussion (1964; Cluj, April 2, 1966); *Numai prin timp poate fi timpul cucerit (Only Through Time, Time Is Conquered),* after T. S. Eliot, for baritone, organ and 4 gongs (1965); *Laudes I* for 28 strings (1966); *Laudes II* for 12 instrumental formations, including 2 Ondes Martenots (1968); *Canto I* and *II* for 12 instrumental formations (1967, 1971); *Son et echo* for tape (1969); *Rêver c'est desengrener les temps superposés* for clarinet, cello, and harpsichord (1970); String Quartet (1972); *De profundis* for harpsichord, piano, organ, and tape (1973); *Il giardino delle Strutture + Rime de Michelangelo* for baritone, trombone, violin, viola, cello, harpsichord, and tape (1975); songs.

Strong, George Templeton, American composer; b. New York, May 26, 1856; d. Geneva, Switzerland, June 27, 1948. He was the son of the New York lawyer, G. T. Strong, who was also a music lover, and whose diary, expressing his dislike of Liszt and Wagner, was publ. in 1952. From him, and from his mother, who was an amateur pianist, Strong received his first training. In 1879 he went to Leipzig, where he studied with Jadassohn. He entered the Liszt circle at Weimar, and became an adherent of program music; from 1886 to 1889 he lived in Wiesbaden, where he became friendly with MacDowell; he returned briefly to America, and taught theory at the New England Cons., Boston (1891–92); then went back to Europe and settled in Switzerland. He expressed his indignation at the lack of recognition of American composers in their own country; most performances of his works took place in Switzerland. In 1930 he donated many of his original manuscripts to the Library of Congress in Washington. Toscanini performed his orch. suite *Die Nacht* with the NBC Symph. Orch., N.Y., on Oct. 21, 1939; his symph. poem, *Une Vie d'artiste* for violin and orch., was presented at the 20th festival of the Association des Musiciens Suisses at Zürich in June, 1920; he also wrote 3 symphonies and the symph. poems *Undine* and *Le Roi Arthur.*

Strozzi, Pietro, Florentine composer; flourished in the last quarter of the 16th century; was a member of the Bardi circle in Florence, and one of the creators of the "stile rappresentativo," leading to the development of opera. With Caccini, Merulo, and Striggio he wrote the festival music for the wedding of Francesco de' Medici in 1579; in 1595 he set to music Rinuccini's libretto *La Mascherata degli accecati;* 2 madrigals by Strozzi are in Luca Bati's *Secondo Libro di Madrigali* (Venice, 1598).

Strube, Gustav, German-American composer and music educator; b. Ballenstedt, March 3, 1867; d. Baltimore, Feb. 2, 1953. He was taught the violin by his father and later by Brodsky at the Leipzig Cons.; was a member of the Gewandhaus Orch. there until 1891, when he emigrated to America; was a violinist in the Boston Symph. from 1891 to 1913; then he became head of the theory department in the Peabody Cons. at Baltimore. In 1916 he was appointed conductor of the newly organized Baltimore Symph. Orch., which he led until 1930; director of the Peabody Cons. (1916–46). He publ. a useful manual, *The Theory and Use of Chords: A Textbook of Harmony* (Boston, 1928).

WORKS: Symphony, subtitled "Lanier" (after Sidney Lanier, poet and musician; Washington, D.C., March 17, 1925, composer conducting); *Sinfonietta* (1922); *Symphonic Prologue* (Baltimore, April 24, 1927, composer conducting); 2 violin concertos (1924; 1930); *Americana,* for orch. (1930); *Harz Mountains,* symph. poem (1940); *Peace Overture* (1945); 2 string quartets (1923; 1936); 2 violin sonatas (1923); Viola Sonata (1924); Cello Sonata (1925); Piano Trio (1925); Quintet for wind instruments (1930); also an opera, *Ramona* (1916).

BIBLIOGRAPHY: G. Klemm, "Gustav Strube: The Man and the Musician," *Musical Quarterly* (July 1942).

Strungk, Nicolaus Adam, German violinist, organist, and composer; b. Brunswick (baptized Nov. 15), 1640, d. Dresden, Sept. 23, 1700. He studied with his father, Delphin Strungk (1601–94), whose assistant he became at the age of 12; was then organist at the Church of St. Magnus at Brunswick; studied violin at Lübeck under Schnittelbach while attending Helmstadt Univ. At 20 he became 1st violinist in the Brunswick orch., later holding similar positions at Celle and Hannover. In 1678 Strungk became music director at Hamburg; wrote and produced operas in German (in keeping with the nationalist trend of the time), among them *Der glückselig-steigende Sejanus,* and its sequel *Der unglücklich-fallende Sejanus* (1678), with German librettos by Christoph Richter adapted from the Italian; *Die Liebreiche, durch Tugend und Schönheit erhöhete Esther;* and *Doris* (both in 1680); *Theseus; Semiramis;* and *Floreeto* (all in 1683), etc. (The opera *Die drey Töchter Cecrops',* formerly attributed to Strungk, was written by Johann Wolfgang Franck.) Strungk was subsequently chamber organist to the Elector Ernst August of Hannover, where he won the admiration of Corelli. On Jan. 26, 1688, Strungk was appointed vice Kapellmeister in Dresden, succeeding Carlo Pallavicino, whose unfinished opera *Antiope* Strungk completed. In this post he was beset with difficulties arising from friction with Italian musicans, and only managed to maintain his authority through the intervention of his patron, the Elector Johann Georg III; when Bernhard, Kapellmeister in Dresden, died in

1692, Strungk was appointed to succeed him. In 1693 he organized an opera company in Leipzig; between 1693 and 1700 he wrote 16 operas for it, among them *Alceste* (performed at the inauguration of the Leipzig opera house, May 18, 1693), *Agrippina* (1699), etc. Financially, the enterprise was a failure, but Strungk continued to receive his salary from Dresden until his retirement on a pension in 1697. He publ. the important manual *Musicalische Übung auf der Violine oder Viola da Gamba in etlichen Sonaten über die Festgesänge, ingleichen etlichen Ciaconen mit 2 Violinen bestehend* (1691). A selection of airs from his operas was publ. in Hamburg under the title *Ein hundert auserlesenen Arien zweyer Hamburgischen Operen, Semiramis und Esther. Mit beigefügten Ritornellen* (1684). Among his instrumental works, a sonata for 2 violins and viola da gamba, and several other sonatas are extant; MS No. 5056 of the Yale Univ. Music Library (Lowell Mason Collection) contains capriccios and ricercars by Strungk, among them the *Ricercar sopra la Morte della mia carissima Madre Catherina Maria Stubenrauen* (Venice, 1685). Six capriccios and a ricercar by Strungk, included in the *Denkmäler der Tonkunst in Österreich* 17 (13.ii), are wrongly ascribed to Georg Reutter (Senior).

BIBLIOGRAPHY: F. Zelle, *J. Theile und N. A. Strungk* (Berlin, 1891); F. Berend, *Nicolaus Adam Strungk: sein Leben und seine Werke* (Hannover, 1915); G. Frotscher, *Geschichte des Orgelspiels* (Berlin, 1934–35, vol. I).

Strunk, (William) Oliver, distinguished American musicologist; b. Ithaca, N.Y., March 22, 1901. He studied at Cornell Univ. (1917–19); in 1927 took a course in musicology with Otto Kinkeldey there; then entered the Univ. of Berlin (1927–28), where he studied musicology with J. Wolf. From 1928 to 1937 he was on the staff of the music division of the Library of Congress, Washington, D.C.; also taught at the Catholic Univ. there. From 1937 to 1966 he was on the faculty of Princeton Univ. A Festschrift in his honor was published at Princeton under the title *Studies in Music History. Essays for Oliver Strunk* (1968). He published *State and Resources of Musicology in the U.S.* (Washington, 1932) and the extremely valuable compilation, *Source Readings in Music History* (N.Y., 1950), containing English translations of important documents on music from the earliest times. He was in charge of the *Monumenta musicae Byzantinae* (Copenhagen, 1961–71); contributed numerous informative articles on obscure points of music history to various learned publications in several languages. After 1966 he lived mostly in Italy.

Stuart, Leslie (real name **Thomas A. Barrett**), English operetta composer; b. Southport, March 15, 1866; d. Richmond, Surrey, March 26, 1928. He was church organist in various provincial towns in England; settled in London in 1895, where he soon became known as a composer of popular songs. He achieved enormous success with his operetta, *Floradora*, produced in London on Nov. 11, 1899, and subsequently performed in England and America for many seasons, but failed to duplicate this success in any of his later works, which included *The Silver Slipper* (1901), The

School Girl (1903), *The Belle of Mayfair* (1906), *Havana* (1908), *Captain Kidd* and *The Slim Princess* (1910), and *Peggy* (1911).

Stuck, Jean Baptiste, French-Italian composer of operas; b. Livorno, c.1680; d. Paris, Dec. 8, 1755. He played the cello in theater orchestras in Italy and in Paris, and also wrote incidental music for various plays; lived most of his life in Paris, except for a brief sojourn in Bavaria (1714). He wrote 3 operas to French texts: *Méléagre* (1709), *Manto la fée* (1709), *Polidore* (Feb. 15, 1720), and ballets for the Versailles Court; publ. 4 books of cantatas (1706, 1708, 1711, 1714); a collection of airs (1709).

Stucken, Van Der, Frank. See **Van Der Stucken, Frank.**

Stuckenschmidt, Hans Heinz, eminent German music critic and writer; b. Strasbourg, Nov. 1, 1901. He studied piano and composition; from 1929 till 1933 he was music critic of the Berlin daily *B. Z. am Mittag,* and was active as a lecturer and writer on modern music. In 1934 he was forbidden to continue journalism in Germany, and went to Prague, where he wrote music criticism until 1941, when his activities were stopped once more by the occupation authorities; was drafted into the Germany Army; after the war became director of the department for new music of the radio station RIAS in Berlin; also was lecturer at the Technical Univ. there (1948). He publ. *Arnold Schönberg* (Zürich, 1951); *Neue Musik* (as vol. 2 of the series *Zwischen den beiden Kriegen,* Berlin, 1951; in French, Paris, 1956); *Schöpfer der neuen Musik: Portraits und Studien* (Frankfurt, 1958); *J. N. David* (Wiesbaden, 1965); *Maurice Ravel: Variationen über Person und Werk* (Frankfurt, 1966); *Ferruccio Busoni. Zeittafel eines Europäers* (Zürich, 1967; in English, *Ferruccio Busoni. Chronicle of a European,* London, 1970); *Twentieth Century Music,* in English (N.Y., 1969); *Germany and Central Europe,* as part of the series *Twentieth Century Composers* (London, 1970); *Arnold Schönberg, Leben, Umwelt, Werk* (Zürich, 1975; in English as *Schoenberg: His Life, World and Work,* N.Y., 1978). Along with Josef Rufer he founded and edited the monthly music magazine *Stimmen* (Berlin, 1947–49). The Festschrift *Aspekte der neuen Musik* was presented to him on his 65th birthday (Kassel, 1968).

Stückgold, Grete (*née* **Schneidt**), soprano; b. London, June 6, 1895; d. Falls Village, Conn., Sept. 13, 1977. Her mother was English, her father German. She studied voice with **Jacques Stückgold,** whom she married (divorced in 1928). She was a member of the Berlin State Opera before coming to America in 1927. On Nov. 2, 1927 she made her debut at the Metropolitan Opera as Eva in *Die Meistersinger,* and remained on its roster until 1939. In 1953 she opened an opera school in N.Y. Her second husband was the baritone **Gustav Schützendorf.**

Stückgold, Jacques, singing teacher and writer; b. Warsaw, Jan. 29, 1877; d. New York, May 4, 1953. He studied in Venice; in 1899 settled in Germany as singing teacher; in 1933 came to the U.S., and lived in N.Y. He publ. *Der Bankrott der deutschen Gesangskunst* and *Über Stimmbildungskunst.*

Stumpf, Carl, eminent German musicologist; b. Wiesentheid, Lower Franconia, April 21, 1848; d. Berlin, Dec. 29, 1936. He studied philosophy, theology, and the natural sciences at Würzburg and Göttingen (Dr. phil., 1870), and in 1873 became full prof. at Würzburg; from 1879 at Prague, from 1884 at Halle, from 1889 at Munich, and from 1893 at Berlin; retired in 1928. A profound student of music, he wrote valuable works dealing with the physiological and psychological aspects of that subject; edited *Beiträge zur Akustik und Musikwissenschaft* (1898–1924) and, with Hornbostel, the *Sammelbände für vergleichende Musikwissenschaft* (3 vols.; 1922–23). WRITINGS: *Tonpsychologie* (2 vols., 1883, 1890; reprint, Hilversum, 1965), his most important publication; *Die pseudo-aristotelischen Probleme über Musik* (1897); *Geschichte des Konsonanzbegriffs* (1897); *Die Anfänge der Musik* (1911); *Die Sprachlaute. Experimentellphonetische Untersuchungen nebst einem Anhang über Instrumentalklänge* (1926); "Lieder der Bellakula-Indianer," *Vierteljahrsschrift für Musikwissenschaft* II(1886); etc. BIBLIOGRAPHY: E. Schumann, "Die Förderung der Musikwissenschaft durch die akustischpsychologische Forschung C. Stumpfs," *Archiv für Musikwissenschaft* (1923); C. Sachs, "Zu Carl Stumpfs achtzigstem Geburtstag," *Zeitschrift für Musikwissenschaft* 10.

Stuntz, Joseph Hartmann, German conductor and composer; b. Arlesheim, near Basel, July 23, 1793; d. Munich, June 18, 1859. He studied in Munich with Peter Winter; succeeded him as conductor in 1826; wrote several operas produced at Munich; publ. 2 overtures; a string quartet; men's choruses.

Sturgeon, Nicholas, English divine and composer; date and place of birth unknown; d. London, May 31, 1454. In 1442 he became precentor of St. Paul's Cathedral, London. He was the owner, and possibly the scribe, of the MSS found in Old Hall, near Ware; 7 works by Sturgeon (2 not complete) are part of the Old Hall MS collection, including a curious isorhythmic motet, *Salve mater Domini,* for 3 voices, which was probably written for the journey of Henry V to France (1416), on which Sturgeon accompanied him.

Stürmer, Bruno, German composer; b. Freiburg-im-Breisgau, Sept. 9, 1892; d. Bad Homburg, May 19, 1958; studied piano at the Cons. of Karlsruhe; then organ and composition with Philipp Wolfrum at the Univ. of Heidelberg; musicology with Sandberger and Kroyer at the Univ. of Munich. After service in the German Army during World War I, he taught piano in Karlsruhe (1917–22); was theater conductor in Remscheid, Essen, and Duisburg (1922–27); in 1927 founded a music school in Homburg; then was conductor of choral societies in Kassel and elsewhere (until 1945); after 1945, lived in Darmstadt and Frankfurt. He was a prolific composer (about 150 op. num-

bers) in a distinctly modern manner; was particularly adept in choral writing.
WORKS: *Die Messe des Maschinenmenschen,* for baritone, male chorus, and orch. (1932); dance drama, *Die Maske der Katze;* cantatas with orch.: *Von der Vergänglichkeit, Vom Tod zum Leben, Aus Liebe, Gott in der Natur;* for voice with chamber groups: *Erlösungen, Marienlieder, Lieder der Geischa, Lieder aus den Lüften, Musikantenleben, Das Lied vom Kinde,* etc.; *Der Zug des Todes,* for 8-part chorus and percussion; *Der Rattenfänger von Hamelin,* for baritone, children's chorus, and chamber orch.; a Requiem; many choruses a cappella; several instrumental concertos; much chamber music.

Sturzenegger, (Hans) Richard, Swiss composer and cellist; b. Zürich, Dec. 18, 1905; d. Bern, Oct. 24, 1976. He studied cello with F. Reitz at the Zürich Cons. and later had lessons with Pablo Casals; took a course in composition with Nadia Boulanger at the École Normale de Musique in Paris (1924–27); then went to Germany and studied cello with Emanuel Feuermann and composition with Ernst Toch in Berlin (1929–33); returning to Switzerland, he was a member of the Bern String Quartet (1935–49), taught cello at the Bern Cons. (1935–63), and chamber music at the Zürich Cons. (1954–63). In 1963 he became director of the Bern Cons.
WORKS: an opera, *Atalante* (1963–68); 4 cello concertos (1933, 1937, 1947, 1974); *Triptychon* for orch. (1951); *Drei Gesänge Davids* for violin and orch. (1963); *Fresco* for string orch. (1965); *Chorale Fantasy* for contralto, strings, trumpet, and drums (1941); *Cantico di San Francesco* for chorus, strings, and harp (1945); *Richardis,* festival music for chorus, wind orch., and organ (1949); Sonata for solo cello (1934); String Trio (1937); 2 string quartets (1940, 1974); Cello Sonata (1950); *Elegie* for cello, oboe, harp, viola, cello, and double bass (1950); Piano Trio (1964).
BIBLIOGRAPHY: *Richard Sturzenegger, Werkverzeichnis* (Zürich, 1970).

Stutschewsky, Joachim, Ukrainian-born Israeli cellist and composer; b. Romny, Feb. 7, 1891. He began to play the violin and the cello in early childhood; was sent to Germany to take cello lessons with Julius Klengel at the Leipzig Cons. (1909–12); then lived in Zürich (1914–24) where he prepared for publication his multivolume method *Studien zu einer neuen Spieltechnik auf dem Violoncell* (3 vols., Mainz, 1927); *Das Violoncellspiel* (4 vols., Mainz, 1932); *Etudes* (4 vol., Mainz, 1931), and transcriptions for cello. He moved to Vienna in 1924, where he entered into a close association with Schoenberg, Berg, and Webern; together with violinist Rudolph Kolish, founded the Wiener Streichquartet (also known as the Kolish String Quartet). He left Vienna after the *Anschluss* in 1938, and settled in Palestine (Israel). He received many prizes: the Engle Prize (1951, 1959, 1965), the Piatigorsky Prize (1963), and the Israel Philharmonic Prize (1973). In 1977 he was chosen "Distinguished Citizen of Tel Aviv." His compositions are imbued with Jewish motives; in his later music he adopted some modern techniques.
WORKS: *Dveykut* for cello and piano (1924); *Pales-*

tinian *Sketches* for piano (1931); Duo for violin and cello (1940); *Israeli Suite* for cello and piano (1942); *Hassidic Suite* for cello and piano (1946); *Israeli Landscapes* for piano (1949); *Legend* for cello and piano (1952); *Israeli Dances* for flute, cello, and piano (1953); *Verschollene Klänge* for flute, string quartet, and percussion (1955); *Hassidic Fantasy* for clarinet, cello, and piano (1956); *Youth Trio* for piano, violin, and cello (1956); *5 Pieces* for solo flute (1956); String Quartet (1956); a cantata *Songs of Radiant Sadness* for soloists, mixed chorus, speaking chorus, and orch. (1958); Concertino for clarinet and strings (1958); *Terzetto* for oboe, clarinet and bassoon (1959); *Fantasy* for oboe, harp, and strings (1959); String Trio (1960); Wind Sextet (1960); symph. poem *Safed* (1960); chamber cantata *Jemama baschimscha (24 Hours in the Looking Glass)* for narrator, 2 sopranos and 6 instruments (1960); *Israeli Suite* for cello and piano (1962); *Monologue* for solo clarinet (1962); *Concertante Music* for flute and strings (1963); *3 Pieces* for solo bassoon (1963); *Moods* for solo oboe (1963); *Impressions* for clarinet and bassoon (1963); *Soliloquy* for solo viola (1964); *3 Minatures* for 2 flutes (1964); a symph. suite *Israel* (1964; Tel Aviv, May 7, 1973); *Kol kore (Calling Voice)* for solo horn (1965); *Fragments* for 2 clarinets (1966); *4 Movements* for wind quintet (1967); *Three for Three*, 3 pieces for 3 cellos (1967); *4 Inattendus* for piano (1967); Brass Quintet (1967); *Visions* for solo flute (1968); *Thoughts and Feelings* for solo violin (1969); *Prelude and Fugue* for 2 trumpets and 2 trombones (1969); *Composition 1970* for solo cello; *Monologue II* for solo trombone (1970); *Dialogues variés* for 2 trumpets (1970); *Imaginations* for flute, violin, cello, and piano (1971); *Kol Nidrei* for cello and piano (1972); *The Rabbi's Nigun* for cello and piano (1974); *Sine Nomine* for solo cello (1975); *Splinters* for piano (1975); *2 Pieces* for solo double bass (1975); songs; arrangements for cello of works by Mozart, Tartini, and Boccherini.

Styne, Jule (real name **Jules Stein**), American composer of popular music; b. London, England, Dec. 31, 1905. He was taught piano by his parents; taken to the U.S. at the age of 8; appeared with the Chicago Symph. Orch. as a child pianist, but did not pursue a concert career; in 1942 he went to Hollywood and rapidly established himself as a successful composer of musical comedies; wrote the scores of *High Button Shoes* (1947); *Gentlemen Prefer Blondes* (1949); *Bells Are Ringing* (1956); *Gypsy*, to the life story of the striptease artist Gypsy Rose Lee (1959); and *Funny Girl*, a musical biography of the singer Fanny Brice (1965); He also wrote music for the films.

Subirá (Puig), José, eminent Spanish musicologist; b. Barcelona, Aug. 20, 1882. He studied at the Madrid Cons., winning 1st prizes for piano (1900) and composition (1904). He also qualified for the practice of law in 1904 (*Dr. jur.*, 1923). From 1908-10 he studied music history and esthetics at Antwerp. He specialized in the study of old Spanish theater music, and his work in this field is extremely valuable: *La Tonadilla escénica*, 3 vols. (Madrid, 1928-30); *La Participación musical en el antiguo teatro español* (Barcelona, 1930); *Tonadillas teatrales inéditas* (Madrid, 1932); *Celos*

aun del aire matan, Opera del siglo XVII (Barcelona, 1933); *La Opera en los teatros de Barcelona* (2 vols.; Barcelona, 1946); *Historia de la música teatral en España* (Barcelona, 1945); *Historia y ancedotario del Teatro Real* (Madrid, 1949); *El Compositor Iriarte y el cultivo español del melólogo* (2 vols.; Barcelona, 1949-50); *El Teatro del Real Palacio* (Madrid, 1950). Other publications: *Enrique Granados* (Madrid, 1926); *La Música en la Casa de Alba* (Madrid, 1927); *Manuscritos de Barbieri existentes en la Biblioteca Nacional* (Madrid, 1936); *Historia de la música* (2 vols.; Madrid, 1947; revised ed., 1951); *La Música, etapas y aspectos* (Barcelona, 1949); *Historia de la música española y hispano-americana* (Barcelona, 1953); *Sinfonismos madrileños del siglo XIX* (Madrid, 1954); *Temario de crítica musical* (Madrid, 1955). With H. Anglés he publ. *Catálogo musical de la Biblioteca nacional de Madrid* (vol. 1, Barcelona, 1946). In 1953 he was elected member of the Royal Academy of Fine Arts in Madrid. Apart from his musicological works, he publ. a novel, *Su virginal pureza* (1916), and a historic account, *Los Españoles en la guerra de 1914-1918* (4 vols.).

Subotnick, Morton, American avant-garde composer; b. Los Angeles, April 14, 1933. He studied music at the Univ. of Denver; then at Mills College with Darius Milhaud. He subsequently taught at Mills College; was in charge of the Intermedia Program at the School of Arts at N.Y. Univ.; also directed exhibits at the Electric Circus in Greenwich Village in New York. In 1969 he was appointed Associate Dean and Director of Electronic Music at the School of Music at the California Institute of the Arts in Los Angeles. He is at his best in multimedia theatrical presentations, with emphasis on electronic devices. His works include four pieces for mixed media under the all-embracing title *Play!; The Tarot* for 10 instruments and tape; *Concert* for woodwind quintet, 2 film projectors, electronic sounds, and 12 spotlights; *Music for 12 Elevators; Lamination* for orch. and electronic sounds; *The Wild Bull* for electronic music synthesizer; *Before the Butterfly* for orch. (Los Angeles, Feb. 26, 1976); incidental music for the plays *Galileo, The Balcony,* and *The Caucasian Chalk Circle.*

Such, Percy Frederick, English-American cellist; b. London, June 27, 1878; d. New York, Feb. 16, 1959. He studied cello in Germany (1892-98); went to the U.S. in 1928; became prof. of cello at Rutgers Univ.; subsequently was on the faculty of the N.Y. College of Music (1938-49). With Sir Donald Tovey he edited the cello sonatas of Beethoven; published cello arrangements of classical works, and editions of old cello music.

Sucher, Joseph, Hungarian conductor; b. Döbör, Nov. 23, 1843; d. Berlin, April 4, 1908. He studied in Vienna with Sechter; in 1876 was conductor of the Leipzig City Theater; in 1877 he married the soprano **Rosa Hasselbeck;** they were at the Hamburg Stadttheater from 1878 to 1888; Sucher then became conductor of the Berlin Opera, his wife being engaged there as prima donna. He was especially distinguished as an interpreter of the Wagner repertory. He composed several vocal works: *Aus alten Märchen,* for women's voices with orch.; *Waldfräulein,* for soprano solo, mixed chorus, and orch.; *Seeschlacht bei Lepanto* for male chorus and orch; songs.

Sucher, Rosa (née **Hasselbeck**), German operatic soprano; wife of **Joseph Sucher;** b. Velburg, Feb. 23, 1849; d. Eschweiler, April 16, 1927. She received her early musical training from her father, a chorusmaster; sang in provincial operas; then in Leipzig where she married the conductor Joseph Sucher in 1877; they were both engaged by the Hamburg Opera (1878–88). She became noted for her performances of Wagner's roles; she sang at the Bayreuth Festivals (1886–99); on Feb. 25, 1895 she made her American debut as Isolde at the Metropolitan Opera, N.Y. She published her memoirs, *Aus meinem Leben* (Leipzig, 1914).

Suchoň, Eugen, significant Slovak composer; b. Pezinok, Sept. 25, 1908. He studied piano and composition with Kafenda at the Bratislava School of Music (1920–28); then took a course in advanced composition with Vítězslav Novák at the Master School of the Prague Cons. (1931–33). Subsequently he taught composition at the Bratislava Academy (1933–48) and music education at the Pedagogical Faculty of the Bratislava Univ. (1949–60); was named in 1958 National Artist of the Republic of Czechoslovakia. In 1971 he was appointed prof. at the College of Music and Dramatic Art in Bratislava. He is one of the creators of the modern Slovak style of composition, based on authentic folk motives and couched in appropriately congenial harmonies.

WORKS: *Krútňava* (The Whirlpool, 1941–49; Bratislava, Dec. 10, 1949; the most important national Slovak opera of the modern times); opera, *Svätopluk* (1952–59; Bratislava, March 10, 1960); *Fantasy and Burlesque* for violin and orch. (originally a *Burlesque,* 1933; the *Fantasy* was added in 1948); *Balladic Suite* for orch. or piano (1935); *Metamorphoses,* symph. variations (1951–52); *Sinfonietta Rustica* (1956); *6 Pieces* for string ensemble or string quartet (1955–63); *Rhapsodic Suite* for piano and orch. (1965); *Kaleidoscope,* 6 cycles for string orch., percussion, and piano (1967–68); *Symphonic Fantasy on B-A-C-H* for organ, strings, and percussion (1971); Clarinet Concertino (1975); *Prielom Symphony* (1976); *Nox et Solitudo* for soprano, and small orch. or piano (1933); *Carpathian Psalm,* cantata (1937–38); *Ad astra,* 5 songs for soprano and small orch. (1961); *Contemplations* for narrator and piano (1964); Violin Sonata (1930); String Quartet (1931, revised 1939); *Serenade* for wind quintet (1931); Piano Quartet (1932–33); Violin Sonatina (1937); *Poème macabre* for violin and piano (1963); piano pieces, including a *Toccata* (1973).

Suckling, Norman, English composer and writer on music; b. London, Oct. 24, 1904. He received his academic education at Queen's College, Oxford, specializing in French literature; was assistant master at Liverpool Collegiate School (1925–43); then was lecturer in French language and literature at King's College, Newcastle-upon-Tyne in the Federal Univ. of Durham (1943–70). While thus occupied, he developed suffi-

cient mastery of the piano to give concerts, at which he presented programs of modern French music. He published a monograph on Gabriel Fauré (London, 1946) and several books on French literature; also contributed articles on English and French composers to *The Listener* and other literary publications. His compositions are mostly in small forms; his songs are particularly fine.

Introduction and Scherzo for string quartet (1923); *Ode* for violin and piano (1925); *A Vision of Avalon,* chamber opera (1928); *A Cycle of Shakespeare Sonnets* for tenor, violin, and piano (1928); Violin Sonata (1928); *Man in the Beginning,* ballet (1934); *Berceuse élégiaque* for clarinet and piano, to commemorate a pet kitten, and written for the composer's first wife (1943); *Pastorale saugrenue* for flute and bassoon (1944); *Variations on a Theme of Rameau* for flute and piano (1947); many songs to words by English poets.

Suda, Stanislav, blind Czech flutist and composer; b. Starý Plzenec, April 30, 1865; d. Plzen, Sept. 2, 1931. He was brought up at the Prague Institute for the Blind, and developed his innate musical abilities to the point where he could give concerts and compose operas, 3 of which were produced at Plzen: *U Božich Muk* (March 22, 1897); *Lešetínsky Kovář* (April 4, 1903); and *Il divino Boemo* (Dec. 30, 1927). He also wrote an autobiographical symph. poem, *Život ve tmách* (The Life in Darkness).

Sudds, William, English-American composer; b. London, March 5, 1843; d. Gouverneur, New York, Sept. 25, 1920. He was taken to America as a child; was a bandmaster during the Civil War; studied violin with Eichberg in Boston; wrote over 100 piano pieces and about 75 pieces of church music; many songs, etc. He publ. 2 albums of organ music, *Organ Gems* and *50 Organ Voluntaries;* also guides to violin playing.

Suesse, Dana, American composer of popular music; b. Kansas City, Dec. 3, 1911. He took piano lessons with Siloti and composition with Rubin Goldmark in N.Y.; traveled to Paris for lessons with Nadia Boulanger. A precocious musician, he won 2 prizes as composer from the National Federation of Music, at the ages of 9 and 10; played in Paul Whiteman's band; wrote *Symphonic Waltzes* and *Jazz Concerto* for him. His most famous popular song was *You Oughta Be in Pictures.*

Sugár, Rezsö, Hungarian composer; b. Budapest, Oct. 9, 1919. He was a pupil of Kodály at the Budapest Academy of Music (1937–42); taught in Budapest at the Béla Bartók Cons. (1949–68) and since 1968 at the Academy.

WORKS: a ballet *Ácisz és Galatea* (Acis and Galatea, 1957), revised in 1961 as *A tenger lánya* (The Daughter of the Sea); a patriotic oratorio *Hunyadi-Hősi ének* (Heroic Song, 1951); a cantata *Kömüves Kelemen* (Kelemen, the Mason, 1958); *Divertimento* for string orch. (1948); *Rondo* for piano and string orch. (1952); *Concerto in Memoriam Béla Bartók* for orch. (1962); *Metamorfosi* for orch. (1966); *Partita* for string orch. (1967); *Variation Symphony* (1970); *Ser-*

enade for 2 violins and viola (1943); Violin Sonata (1946); 3 string quartets (1947, 1950, 1969); *Frammenti musicali,* sextet for piano and wind quintet (1958); *Rhapsody* for cello and piano (1959); *Baroque Sonatina* for piano (1943-46); songs.

Suggia, Guilhermina, Portuguese cellist; b. Oporto, June 27, 1888; d. there, July 31, 1950. She was a child prodigy and played 1st cello in the Oporto Orch. at the age of 12. Under the patronage of the Queen of Portugal she was sent to Leipzig in 1904 to study with Julius Klengel; made her debut with the Gewandhaus Orch. under Nikisch at the age of 17. In 1906 she married **Pablo Casals** (divorced 1912). Shortly afterwards she settled in London, where she continued to appear in concerts until 1949, when she went back to Portugal. She was greatly appreciated for her fine musicianship as well as virtuosity. In 1923 Augustus John painted her portrait, which became famous.

Suk, Josef, Czech violinist and composer; b. Křečovice, Jan. 4, 1874; d. Benešov, near Prague, May 29, 1935. He studied with his father, a chorusmaster, and at the Prague Cons., after graduation he took a course in composition with Dvořák, whose daughter Otilie he married in 1898. In 1892 he became 2nd violinist in the celebrated Bohemian String Quartet, continuing until 1922, when he became a prof. at the Prague Cons. He was a devoted follower of Dvořák in his style of composition; his works are cast in a characteristically Romantic vein, with the rhythmic elements drawn from Bohemian folk music. When his wife died in 1905, he was disconsolate; he expressed his sorrow in his 2nd symph., *Asrael,* dedicated to her memory and to the memory of Dvořák. He continued to compose, developing an individual manner marked by deep expressiveness and religious feeling.
WORKS: operatic fairy tale, *Radúz and Mahulena* (Prague, April 6, 1898); dramatic legend, *Pod jabloní* (*Under the Apple Trees;* 1902; Prague, Jan. 31, 1934); for orch.: *Dramatic Overture* (Prague, July 9, 1892); Symphony in E major (Prague, Nov. 25, 1899); *Prague,* symph. poem (1904); *Scherzo fantastique* (Prague, April 18, 1905); *Asrael,* 2nd Symph. (Prague, Feb. 3, 1907); *Pohádka léta* (*A Summer Fairy Tale;* Prague, Jan. 26, 1909); *Zrání,* symph. poem (Prague, Oct. 30, 1918); *Meditation on the Chorale "St. Venceslas"* (1914); *Epilogue,* for solo voices, chorus, and orch. (1920-32); *Fantasy,* for violin and orch. (Prague, Jan. 9, 1904); 2 string quartets; Piano Quartet; Piano Trio; Piano Quintet; *Allegro giocoso,* for string quartet; other chamber music; several sets of choruses; a number of piano pieces.
BIBLIOGRAPHY: *Josef Suk,* a collection of articles, ed. by J. M. Květ (Prague, 1935); V. Štěpán, *Novák a Suk* (Prague, 1945); J. Berkovec, *Josef Suk* (Prague, 1956); Jan. M. Květ, *Josef Suk v obrazech* (Prague, 1964); Ratibor Budis, ed., *Josef Suk* (Prague, 1965); Jiři Berkovec, *Josef Suk* (Prague, 1968).

Suk, Josef, Czech violinist, grandson of the composer **Josef Suk** and great-grandson of **Dvořák;** b. Prague, Aug. 8, 1929. He studied at the Prague Cons. (1944-50) with Jaroslav Kocian; after graduation he embarked on a highly successful·concert career in all parts of the world; made his American debut as soloist with the Cleveland Orch., Jan. 23, 1964. From 1951 till 1968 he was violinist in the Suk Trio; then played in the Suk Duo with the pianist Katchen (until 1965).

Suk, Váša, Czech conductor and composer; b. Kladno, Nov. 16, 1861; d. Moscow, Jan. 12, 1933. He studied with Fibich at the Prague Cons.; then played the violin in the Warsaw Symph. (1879-81); conducted opera in Kiev and Moscow (1881-84); in 1906 joined the staff of the Moscow Opera. He was appreciated in Russia for his thoroughness in drilling the singers and the orch.; achieved a fine reputation as an operatic conductor. He wrote an opera, *The Forest King,* which he conducted at Kharkov on Feb. 16, 1900; a symph. poem, *Jan Huss;* a serenade for string orch.; a number of piano pieces and songs.
BIBLIOGRAPHY: I. Remezov, *V. Suk* (Moscow, 1933).

Sukegawa, Toshiya, Japanese composer; b. Sapporo, July 15, 1930. He studied with Ikenouchi from 1951; graduated in composition from the Univ. of Arts in Tokyo in 1957.
WORKS: television opera, *Pôra no Hiroba* (1959); *Passacaglia* for orch. (1954); String Quartet (1956); *Music* for flute, clarinet, violin, cello, percussion, and piano (1958); Piano Sonata (1958); *Divertimento* for 2 pianos (1958); *Partita* for orch. (1960); Wind Quintet (1962); *Legend* for orch. (1965); *5 Metamorphoses* for viola and piano (1966); *3 Parts for 5 Flute Players* (1967); *Tapestry* for piano (1966-68); *3 Scenes* for jushichigen, 3 violins and viola (1969); *A Projection* for solo marimba, piccolo, trombone, piano, and percussion (1969); *The White World* for chorus and piano (1971); *Eika* for chorus and Japanese percussion (1972); *5 Symbolic Pictures* for piano (1972); *5 Pieces after Paul Klee* for solo marimba (1973).

Šulek, Stjepan, Croatian violinist and composer; b. Zagreb, Aug. 5, 1914. He studied violin with Huml, and was largely self-taught in composition; yet he succeeded in becoming a composer of considerable merit. In 1954 he was appointed prof. of composition at the Music Academy in Zagreb.
WORKS: the operas, *Coriolan,* after Shakespeare (Zagreb, Oct. 12, 1958); *Oluja* (*The Tempest;* after Shakespeare, Zagreb, 1969); 6 symphonies (1944, 1946, 1948, 1954, 1963, 1966); festive prologue, *Scientiae et arti* for orch. (1966); 4 piano concertos (1949, 1951, 1963, 1970); Cello Concerto (1950); Violin Concerto (1951); Bassoon Concerto (1958); Violin Concerto (1959); Clarinet Concerto (1967); cantata, *Zadnji Adam* (*The Last Adam,* 1964); other vocal works; piano pieces; songs.
BIBLIOGRAPHY: K. Kovačević, *Hrvatski Kompozitori i Njihova Djela* (Zagreb, 1960); K. Šipuš, *Stjepan Šulek* (Zagreb, 1961).

Sullivan, Sir Arthur Seymour, famous English composer; b. London, May 13, 1842; d. there, Nov. 22, 1900. In 1854 he entered the Chapel Royal as a chorister, under Helmore; publ. an anthem in 1855; was elected (the first) Mendelssohn Scholar in 1856, studing at the Royal Academy of Music from 1857 under

Bennett, Goss, and O'Leary, and at the Leipzig Cons. 1858–61 under Moscheles, Hauptmann, Richter, Plaidy, etc., conducting a performance of his overture to *Lalla Rookh* in 1860, and writing string quartets and music to *The Tempest* (Crystal Palace, April 5, 1862). His cantata *Kenilworth* (Birmingham Festival, Sept. 8, 1864) stamped him as a composer of high rank. In 1864 he visited Ireland and there composed his "Irish Symphony." In 1866 he was appointed prof. of composition at the Royal Academy of Music. About this time he formed a life-long friendship with Sir George Grove, whom he accompanied in 1867 on a memorable journey to Vienna in search of Schubert manuscripts, leading to the discovery of the score of *Rosamunde*. The year 1867 was also notable for the production of the first of those comic operas upon which Sullivan's fame chiefly rests. This was *Cox and Box* (libretto by F. C. Burnand), composed in 2 weeks and performed on April 27 at the home of Arthur Lewis; later it had a long public run. Less successful were *The Contrabandista* (London, Dec. 18, 1867) and *Thespis* (London, Dec. 23, 1871); but the latter is significant as inaugurating Sullivan's collaboration with Sir W. S. Gilbert, the celebrated humorist, who became the librettist of all his most successful comic operas, beginning with *Trial by Jury* (March 25, 1875). This was produced by Richard D'Oyly Carte, who in 1876 formed a company expressly for the production of the "Gilbert and Sullivan" operas. The first big success obtained by the famous team was with *H.M.S. Pinafore* (May 25, 1878), which had 700 consecutive performances in London, and enjoyed an enormous vogue in "pirated" productions throughout the U.S. In an endeavor to protect their interests, Gilbert and Sullivan went to N.Y. in 1879 to give an authorized performance of *Pinafore*, and while there they also produced *The Pirates of Penzance* (Dec. 31, 1879). On April 25, 1881, came *Patience*, a satire on exaggerated esthetic poses exemplified by Oscar Wilde, whose American lecture-tour was conceived as a "publicity stunt" for this work. On Nov. 25, 1882, *Iolanthe, or The Peer and the Peri*, began a run that lasted more than a year. This was followed by the comparatively unsuccessful *Princess Ida* (Jan. 5, 1884), but then came the universal favorite of all the Gilbert and Sullivan operas, *The Mikado* (March 14, 1885). The list of these popular works is completed by *Ruddigore* (Jan. 22, 1887), *The Yeomen of the Guard* (Oct. 3, 1888), and *The Gondoliers* (Dec. 7, 1889). After a quarrel and a reconciliation, the two collaborated in 2 further works, of less popularity, *Utopia Limited* (Oct. 7, 1893) and *The Grand Duke* (March 7, 1896). Sullivan's melodic inspiration and technical resourcefulness, united to the delicious humor of Gilbert's verses, raised the light opera to a new height of artistic achievement, and his works in this field continue to delight countless hearers. Sullivan was also active in other branches of musical life. He conducted numerous series of concerts, more especially those of the London Philh. Society (1885–87) and the Leeds Festivals (1880–98). He was principal of, and prof. of composition at, the National Training School for Music from 1876 to his resignation in 1881. Received the degree of Mus. Doc. *honoris causa* from Cambridge (1876) and Oxford (1879); Chevalier of the Legion of Honor (1878); grand organist to the Freemasons (1887); etc. He was knighted by Queen Victoria in 1883. Parallel with his comic creations, he composed many "serious" works, including the grand opera *Ivanhoe* (Jan. 31, 1891), which enjoyed a momentary vogue. Among his cantatas the most successful was *The Golden Legend*, after Longfellow (Leeds Festival, Oct. 16, 1886). His songs were highly popular in their day and *The Lost Chord* is still a favorite. Among his oratorios, *The Light of the World* (1873) may be mentioned. Other stage works: *The Zoo* (1875); *The Sorcerer* (1877); *Haddon Hall* (1892); *The Chieftain* (revision of *The Contrabandista;* 1894); *The Martyr of Antioch* (Edinburgh, 1898; a stage arrangement of the cantata); *The Beauty-Stone* (with Pinero; May 28, 1898); the romantic opera *The Rose of Persia* (1900); *The Emerald Isle* (completed by E. German, 1901); 2 ballets. *L'Ile enchanté* (1864) and *Victoria and Merrie England* (1897).

BIBLIOGRAPHY: A. Lawrence, *Sir A. S.: Life-Story, Letters and Reminiscences* (with complete list of works; Chicago, 1900); W. J. Wells, *Souvenir of Sir A. S.* (London, 1901) B. W. Findon, *Sir A. S.: His Life and Music* (London, 1904); B. W. Findon, *Sir A. S. and His Operas* (London, 1908); F. Cellier and C. Bridgeman, *Gilbert, S., and D'Oyly Carte* (London, 1914); H. M. Walbrook, *Gilbert and S.: A History and a Comment* (1922); S. J. A. Fitz-Gerald, *The Story of the Savoy Opera* (London, 1924); A. H. Godwin, *Gilbert and S.* (1926); H. Saxe Wyndham, *A. S.* (1926); N. Flower and H. Sullivan, *A. S.* (1927); T. F. Dunhill, *S.'s Comic Operas* (1928); L. Bradstock, *S.* (1928); I. Goldberg, *The Story of Gilbert and S.* (1928); F. J. Halton, *The Gilbert and S. Operas: A Concordance* (N.Y., 1935); H. Pearson, *Gilbert and S.* (N.Y., 1935); G. E. Dunn, *A Gilbert and S. Dictionary* (N.Y., 1936); C. L. Purdy, *Gilbert and S.: Masters of Mirth and Melody* (N.Y., 1947); W. A. Darlington, *The World of Gilbert and S.* (N.Y., 1950); A. Jacobs, *Gilbert and S.* (London, 1951); L. Bailey, *The Gilbert and S. Book* (N.Y., 1952; new ed., 1957); A. Williamson, *Gilbert and S. Operas: A New Assessment* (N.Y., 1953); A. Powers-Waters, *The Melody Maker. The Life of Sir Arthur Sullivan* (N.Y., 1959); M. Green, *Treasury of Gilbert and Sullivan* (London, 1961); R. Mander and J. Mitcheson, *A Picture History of Gilbert and Sullivan* (London, 1962); N. G. Wymer, *Gilbert and Sullivan* (London, 1962); Cl. R. Bulla, *Stories of Gilbert and Sullivan Operas* (N.Y., 1968); J. Helyar, *Gilbert & Sullivan. Papers Presented at the International Conference . . . , 1970* (Univ. of Kansas, 1971); P. M. Young, *Sir Arthur Sullivan* (London, 1971); P. Kline, *Gilbert and Sullivan Production* (N.Y., 1972); L. Ayre, *The Gilbert and Sullivan Companion* (N.Y., 1972); J. M. D. Hardwick, *The Drake Guide to Gilbert and Sullivan* (N.Y., 1973); L. W. A. Baily, *Gilbert and Sullivan and Their World* (London, 1973); Reginald Allen, *Sir Arthur Sullivan: Composer & Personage* (N.Y., 1975).

Sulzer, Julius Salomon, Austrian violinist; son of **Salomon Sulzer;** b. Vienna, 1834; d. there, Feb. 13, 1891. He was a professional violinist and conductor; served as music director of the Hofburgtheater in Vienna from 1875.

Sulzer, Salomon, important Austrian-Jewish composer, reformer of synagogal songs; b. Hohenems, Vorarlberg, March 30, 1804; d. Vienna, Jan. 17, 1890. He was only 16 when he was appointed cantor at the chief synagogue in his hometown. He studied music with Seyfried in Vienna; from 1825 to 1881 was cantor of the new Vienna synagogue. He undertook a bold reform of liturgical music by the introduction of musical form and actual compositions from the classical period, setting Schubert's songs as a model. By so doing he succeeded in bringing traditional Jewish cantillation together with western modes. He brought out an anthology *Schir Zion (The Heart of Zion;* published in 1839–65) and *Denkschrift an die Weiner israelitische Cultus-Gemeinde* (Vienna, 1876).

BIBLIOGRAPHY: M. Steiner, *Salomon Sulzer* (Vienna, 1904); P. Minkowski, *Der Sulzerismus* (Vienna, 1905).

Sumac, Yma (real name **Emperatriz Chavarri**), Peruvian singer; b. Ichocan, Sept. 10, 1927, of Indian-Spanish ancestry. She spent her childhood in the highlands (altitude of 12,000 feet), and instinctively acquired an enormously powerful voice, ranging from the low baritone to high soprano; this phenomenal compass created a sensation when she first appeared in the U.S.; she gave recitals and sang on the radio; also took part in motion pictures. She became a U.S. citizen in 1955.

Sundelius, Marie, Swedish-American singer and vocal teacher; b. Karlsbad, Feb. 4, 1884; d. Boston, June 26, 1958. She was taken to America at the age of 8, and studied singing in Boston; made her debut as an opera singer with the Metropolitan Opera, N.Y., on Nov. 25, 1916; made a tour of Sweden in 1924; then returned to Boston.

Sundgrén-Schnéevoigt, Sigrid Ingeborg, Finnish pianist; b. Helsingfors, June 17, 1878; d. Stockholm, Sept. 14, 1953. She studied at the Cons. of Helsingfors, and then with Busoni in Berlin (1894–97). In 1907 she married the conductor **Georg Schnéevoigt,** with whom she made several tours of Scandinavia and Germany; from 1910 was for many years piano teacher at the Helsingfors Cons.; later lived in Paris.

Suñol y Baulenas, Dom Gregorio María, learned Spanish ecclesiastic; authority on Gregorian chant; b. Barcelona, Sept. 7, 1879; d. Rome, Oct. 26, 1946. He studied at Montserrat and at the Abbey of Solesmes; became prior of the Monastery of Montserrat and president of the Asociación Gregoriana of Barcelona. During his last years he was president of the Pontificio Instituto di Musica Sacra in Rome. He publ. the valuable editions *Método completo de Canto gregoriano* (6 Spanish eds.; also in English, French, and German); *Introducció a la paleografía musical gregoriana* (Montserrat, 1925; also in French, 1935); "Els Cants dels Romeus," in *Analecta Montserratensia* (with examples of folk music from the 14th century); brought out by *Antiphonale missarum juxta ritum sanctae ecclesiae medilolanensis* (1935).

Suolahti, Heikki, Finnish composer; b. Helsinki, Feb. 2, 1920; d. there, Dec. 27, 1936. He studied at the Helsinki Cons. and conducted children's orchestras in festivals. His tragically premature death at 16 moved Sibelius to say that "Finland lost one of her greatest musical talents." Suolahti composed a few fine pieces of music, among them a Violin Concerto, written at the age of 14, and a *Sinfonia piccola* which he composed at 15, and which was performed in Helsinki after his death; he also left some songs.

Supervia, Conchita, Spanish mezzo-soprano; b. Barcelona, Dec. 8, 1895; d. London, March 30, 1936. She sang at La Scala, Milan, at the Paris Opéra, and at the Opéra-Comique; toured in the U.S.; in 1931 she settled in London, and appeared several times at Covent Garden.

Suppé, Franz von, famous operetta composer; b. Spalato, Dalmatia, April 18, 1819; d. Vienna, May 21, 1895. He was of Belgian descent, and his real name was **Francesco Ezechiele Ermenegildo Cavaliere Suppe-Demelli.** At the age of 11 he played the flute, and at 15 wrote a Mass. He was then sent by his father to study philosophy at Padua, where he also took music courses with Cigala and Ferrari; on his father's death he went with his mother to Vienna, where he continued serious study at the Vienna Cons. with Sechter and Seyfried. He became a conductor in the theaters of Pressburg and Baden, and then was on the staff at the Theater an der Wien (until 1862), at the Carl Theater (until 1865) and subsequently at the Leopoldstadt Theater. All the while, he wrote light operas and other theater music of all degrees of levity, obtaining increasing success rivaling that of Offenbach. His music possesses the charm and gaiety of the Viennese genre, but also contains elements of more vigorous, popular rhythms.

WORKS: His most celebrated single work is the overture to *Dichter und Bauer (Poet and Peasant),* which still retains a firm place in the light repertory. His total output comprises about 30 comic operas and operettas and 180 other stage pieces, most of which were brought out in Vienna; of these the following obtained considerable success: *Dichter und Bauer* (Aug. 24, 1846); *Das Mädchen vom Lande* (Aug. 7, 1847); *Der Bandit* (1848; in Italy as *Cartouche); Paragraph 3* (Jan. 8, 1858); *Das Pensionat* (Nov. 24, 1860); *Die Kartenaufschlägerin* (April, 26, 1862); *Zehn Mädchen und kein Mann* (Oct. 25, 1862); *Flotte Bursche* (April 18, 1863); *Franz Schubert* (Sept. 10, 1864); *Die schöne Galatea* (Sept. 9, 1865); *Leichte Cavallerie* (March 24, 1866; enormously popular); *Freigeister* (Oct. 23, 1866); *Banditenstreiche* (April, 27, 1867); *Die Frau Meisterin* (Jan. 20, 1868); *Tantalusqualen* (Oct. 3, 1868); *Isabella* (Nov. 5, 1869); *Cannebas* (Nov. 2, 1872); *Fatinitza* (Jan. 5, 1876; extremely popular); *Der Teufel auf Erden* (Jan. 5, 1878); *Boccaccio* (Feb. 1, 1879; very popular); *Donna Juanita* (Feb. 21, 1880); *Der Gascogner* (March 22, 1881); *Herzblättchen* (Feb. 4, 1882); *Die Afrikareise* (March 17, 1883); *Bellmann* (Feb. 26, 1887); *Die Jagd nach dem Glücke* (Oct. 27, 1888); *Das Modell* (posthumous; Oct. 4, 1895); *Die Pariserin* (posthumous; Jan. 26, 1898); several other operettas were produced in Prague, Berlin, and Hamburg. In addition to his theater works, he wrote a symphony; several string quartets; songs; also a *Missa dalmatica* (1867).

BIBLIOGRAPHY: G. Sabalich, *F. Suppé e l'operetta* (Zara, 1888); O. Keller, *Franz von Suppé, der Schöpfer der deutschen Operette* (Leipzig, 1905); E. Rieger, *Offenbach und seine Wiener Schule* (Vienna, 1920).

Surdin, Morris, Canadian composer; b. Toronto, May 8, 1914. He learned to play piano, violin, cello, horn, and trombone; studied composition with Gesensway in Philadelphia (1937) and with Henry Brant in N.Y. (1950); worked as a music arranger for the Canadian Broadcasting Corporation (1939–41) and with the Columbia Broadcasting System in N.Y. (1949–54); returning to Canada, he became engaged primarily in composition for films and television.

WORKS: an opera-musical, *Wild Rose* (1967); a musical comedy, *Look Ahead* (1962), a ballet, *The Remarkable Rocket,* after Oscar Wilde (1960–61); *4 X Strings* for strings (1947); *Credo* for orch. (1950); *Inheritance* for wind quartet and strings (1951); *Concert Ballet* (1955); *A Spanish Tragedy* for soprano and orch. (1955); *Incident I* for strings (1961); Concerto for Mandolin and Strings (1961–66); *5 Shades of Brass* for trumpet and orch. (1961); Concerto for Accordion and Strings (1966; Toronto, Jan. 29, 1967); *2 Solitudes* for horn or English horn, and strings (1967); *Formula I* and *II* for concert band (1968–69); *Horizon* for string orch. (1968); *Short!* (No. 1) for piano and strings (1969) and *Short!* (No. 2) for piano, wind quartet, and strings (1969); *Alteration I* for piccolo and strings (1970); *Alteration II* for string orch. (1970); *Suite Canadienne* for chorus and orch. (1970); *Feast of Thunder* for soloists, male chorus, and orch (1972); *Terminus* for oboe, bassoon, and strings (1972); *B'rasheet (In the Beginning)* for solo mandolin, solo clarinet, and string orch. (1974; Toronto, June 15, 1974); *Suite* for viola and piano (1954); *Carol Fantasia* for brass (1955); *Incident II* for woodwinds, horns, and harp (1961); *Elements* for 2 violins, double bass, and harpsichord (1965); *Matin* for wind quartet (1965); *Arioso* for 4 cellos (1966); String Quartet (1966); Trio for saxophones (1968); *Piece* for wind quintet (1969); *Serious I–XVI* for solo accordion (1969–73); *Trinitas in Morte* for 3 oboes, bassoon, 3 horns, timpani, 8 cellos, and 2 double basses (1973); For piano: *Naiveté,* 6 pieces (1962); *Poco Giocoso Variations* (1966); *In Search of Form I* and *II* (1970); and *Fragmentations I–III* (1972); choruses; songs.

Surette, Thomas Whitney, eminent American music educator; b. Concord, Massachusetts, Sept. 7, 1861; d. there, May 19, 1941. He studied piano with Arthur Foote and composition with J. K. Paine at Harvard Univ., graduating in 1891; then was active mainly as church organist. Deeply interested in making musical education accessible and effective in the U.S., he founded in 1914 the Concord Summer School of Music; with A. T. Davison he edited *The Concord Series* of educational music, which found a tremendously favorable acceptance on the part of many schools, particularly in New England; the series provided an excellent selection of good music which could be understood by most music teachers and performed by

pupils. Surette was also largely responsible for the vogue of music appreciation courses that swept the country and spilled over into the British Isles. He published *The Appreciation of Music* (with D. G. Mason; 5 vols., of which vols. 2 and 5 were by Mason alone; N.Y., 1907; innumerable subsequent printings), and, on a more elevated plane, *Course of Study on the Development of Symphonic Music* (Chicago, 1915), and *Music and Life* (Boston, 1917); he also published popular articles on music and musicians, notable for their lack of discrimination and absence of verification of data. He was also a composer, of sorts; wrote a light opera, *Priscilla, or The Pilgrim's Proxy,* after Longfellow (Concord, Mass., March 6, 1889; had more than 1,000 subsequent performances in the U.S.) and a romantic opera *Cascabel, or The Broken Tryst* (Pittsburgh, May 15, 1899).

Suriano (or **Soriano**), **Francesco,** a composer of the Roman school; b. Soriano, 1549; d. there, July 19, 1621. Was a chorister at St. John Lateran; later a pupil of Nanino and Palestrina. In 1580, choirmaster at S. Ludivico de' Francesi; from 1581–86, in Mantua; in 1587, at S. Maria Maggiore; 1588, again at S. Ludovico, returning to S. Maria Maggiore in 1595; in 1599, at St. John Lateran, and from 1600 once more at S. Maria Maggiore (pensioned June 23, 1620). He collaborated with F. Anerio in the revision of the *Editio Medicaea* of the Gradual (cf. Palestrina). Publ. 2 books of madrigals *a* 5 (1581, 1592); 1 book of madrigals *a* 4 (1601); motets *a* 8 (1597); Masses *a* 4–8 (1609; includes an arrangement of Palestrina's *Missa Papae Marcelli* for 8 voices); *Canoni . . . sopra l'Ave Maris Stella a 3–8 voci* (1610); 2 books of psalms and motets (1614, 1616); *Villanelle a 3* (1617); a Passion and several Magnificats (1619).

BIBLIOGRAPHY: F. X. Haberl, in *Kirchenmusikalisches Jahrbuch* (1895); R. Molitor, *Die nachtridentiniche Choralreform* (1901–02); S. P. Kniseley, *The Masses of Francesco Suriano* (Gainesville, Florida, 1967).

Surinach, Carlos, Spanish-American composer and conductor; b. Barcelona, March 4, 1915. He studied in Barcelona with Morera (1936–39) and later with Max Trapp in Berlin (1939–43). Returning to Spain in 1943 he was active mainly as conductor. In 1951 he went to the U.S.; became an American citizen in 1959; was visiting prof. of music at Carnegie-Mellon Institute in Pittsburgh in 1966–67.

WORKS: *El Mozo que casó con mujer brava,* 1-act opera (Barcelona, Jan. 10, 1948); ballet, *Monte Carlo* (Barcelona, May 2, 1945); 3 symphonies: No. 1, *Passacaglia-Symphony* (Barcelona, April 8, 1945, composer conducting), No. 2 (Paris Radio, Jan. 26, 1950, composer conducting), and No. 3, *Sinfonía chica* (1957); also a *Sinfonietta flamenca* (Louisville, Jan. 9, 1954); *Feria mágica,* overture (Louisville, March 14, 1956); *Tres Cantos Berberes,* for flute, oboe, clarinet, viola, cello, and harp (1952); *Flamenquerías* for 2 pianos (1952); *Ritmo Jondo,* for clarinet, trumpet, xylophone, and percussion (N.Y., May 5, 1952; extended version in ballet form, *Deep Rhythm,* was performed in N.Y., April 15, 1953); *Tientos,* for English horn, harpsichord, and timpani (1953); *A Place in the Desert* (1960); *Sym-*

phonic Variations (1963); *Drama Jondo,* overture (1964); *Melorhythmic Dramas* for orch. (1966); *The Missions of San Antonio,* symph. canticles (1968); chamber music of various descriptions; songs.

Surzyński, Józef, Polish music scholar; b. Szrem, near Poznan, March 15, 1851; d. Koscian, March 5, 1919. He studied at Regensburg and Leipzig, then theology in Rome. In 1882 he returned to Poznan, dedicating himself to the codification of Polish sacred music; also was conductor of the cathedral chorus there. Beginning in 1885, he brought out the valuable series *Monumenta Musices Sacrae in Polonia,* containing works by Polish composers of the 16th and 17th centuries; also publ. several manuals for use in Polish churches; wrote many choral compositions, using Gregorian modes. His two brothers, **Stefan** and **Mieczyslaw,** were also musicians.

Susa, Conrad, American composer; b. Springdale, Pennsylvania, April 26, 1935. He studied piano, organ, flute, oboe, clarinet, and French horn. Upon receiving a scholarship from Carnegie-Mellon Univ. in Pittsburgh, he took composition courses with Nikolai Lopatnikoff; after graduation he entered the Juilliard School of Music, N.Y., where his composition teachers were William Bergsma and Vincent Persichetti. He subsequently engaged in theater conducting. He excels in choral writing. Among his works are 5 serenades for various groups of voices and instruments, a *Pastorale* for strings and numerous accompanied and unaccompanied choruses. He has achieved his greatest acclaim with his opera *Transformations,* to the texts from the poems by Anne Sexton, produced by the Minnesota Opera Co. in Minneapolis on May 5, 1973; another opera, *Black River,* was produced in Minneapolis on Nov. 1, 1975.

Susato, Johannes (real name **Johannes Steinwert von Soest**), German composer and singing master; b. Unna, 1448; d. Frankfurt, May 2, 1506. He was a chorister at Soest, then was in Cleve and Bruges, where he studied with English musicians; was subsequently active as singing master in Cologne, Kassel, and from 1472, Heidelberg; Virdung was one of his pupils there. He was also a physician, and about 1500 went to Frankfurt as a municipal doctor.

Susato, Tielman, German publisher and composer; son of **Johannes Susato;** b. probably in Cologne, c.1500; d. possibly Antwerp, c.1561. In 1529 he moved from Cologne to Antwerp, where he was a town trumpeter; then established a music printing shop (1543) and issued 13 books of chansons, 4 vols. of Masses, 4 vols. of motets, 4 books of various songs, etc.; several of these miscellaneous works were of his own composition.
BIBLIOGRAPHY: P. Bergmans, "Un Imprimeur musicien: Tilman Susato," *Bulletin de la Société Bibliophile Anversoise* (Antwerp, 1923); A. Goovaerts, *Histoire et bibliographie de la typographie musicale dans les Pays-Bas* (Antwerp, 1881); Ute Meissner, *Der Antwerpener Notendrucker Tylman Susato* (Berlin, 1967); L. Bernstein, "The Cantus-Firmus Chansons of

Tylman Susato," *Journal of the American Musicological Society* (Summer 1969).

Susskind, Walter, Czech-born American conductor; b. Prague, May 1, 1913. He studied theory with Josef Suk, and advanced composition with Alois Hába at the Prague Cons.; also took conducting lessons with George Szell. He made his debut as conductor at the German Opera House in Prague in 1939; then went to England, where he conducted the Carl Rosa Opera Co. (1942–45); he was subsequently conductor of the Scottish National Orch. in Glasgow (1946–52); then conducted the Victoria Symph. Orch. in Melbourne; from 1956 to 1965 he was conductor of the Toronto Symph. Orch.; from 1968 to 1975 was music director of the St. Louis Symph. Orch.; in 1978, appointed music advisor and principal guest conductor of the Cincinnati Symph. Orch.
BIBLIOGRAPHY: Donald Brook, *International Gallery of Conductors* (Bristol, 1951; pp. 200–06).

Süssmayr, Franz Xaver, Austrian composer; b. Schwanenstadt, 1766; d. Vienna, Sept. 17, 1803. He was a pupil of Salieri, and also of Mozart, of whom he became an intimate friend; after Mozart's death his widow entrusted the completion of his Requiem to Süssmayr; he was clever in emulating Mozart's style of composition, and his handwriting was so much like Mozart's that it is difficult to distinguish between them. He was conductor at the National Theater in Vienna fron 1792, and 2nd conductor at the Court Opera from 1794.
WORKS: wrote a number of operas and operettas, which he produced in Vienna, among them: *Moses* (May 4, 1792); *L'Incanto superato* (July 8, 1793); *Der Spiegel von Arkadien* (Nov. 14, 1794); *Idris und Zenide* (May 9, 1795); *Die edle Rache* (Aug. 27, 1795); *Die Freiwilligen* (Sept. 27, 1796); *Der Wildfang* (Oct. 4, 1797); *Der Marktschreier* (July 6, 1799); *Soliman der Zweite, oder Die drei Sultaninnen* (Oct. 1, 1799); *Gülnare* (*Gonora;* July 5, 1800); *Phasma* (July 25, 1801). He wrote *secco* recitatives for Mozart's opera *La Clemenza di Tito* (Prague, Sept. 6, 1791); composed several numbers for the Vienna production of Grétry's *La Double Épreuve,* given there under the title *Die doppelte Erkenntlichkeit* (Feb. 28, 1796). Other works include a clarinet concerto and pieces for the English horn, for guitar, and other instruments. Most of his works are in manuscript.
BIBLIOGRAPHY: G. L. P. Sievers, *Mozart und Süssmayr* (1829); W. Pole, *Mozart's Requiem* (1879); W. Lehner, "F. X. Süssmayr als Opernkomponist," *Studien zur Musikwissenschaft* 18 (1931); H. H. Hausner, *Franz Xaver Süssmayr* (Vienna, 1964); F. Beyer, "Mozarts Komposition zum Requiem. Zur Frage der Ergänzung," *Acta Mozartiana* XVIII/2 (1971).

Suter, Hermann, Swiss composer and conductor; b. Kaiserstuhl, April 28, 1870; d. Basel, June 22, 1926. He was a pupil of his father, an organist and cantor; then studied with Hans Huber in Basel; also took courses in Stuttgart with Faisst and in Leipzig with Reinecke (1888–91). From 1892 to 1902 he conducted choral societies in various Swiss communities; in 1896 was appointed to the faculty of the Zürich Cons.; in 1902, settled in Basel, where he was active as conductor and teacher; was director of the Basel Cons. from 1918 to 1921. His best-known work is the oratorio *Le Laudi di S. Francesco d'Assisi* (1924); he also wrote a number of other vocal works, a symph., a violin concerto, 3 string quartets, a string sextet, and 3 song cycles.

BIBLIOGRAPHY: W. Merian, *Hermann Suter* (Basel, 1936).

Suter, Robert, Swiss composer; b. St. Gallen, Jan. 30, 1919. He studied theory, piano, and composition with W. Geiser at the Basel Cons. (1937–43), and privately with Wladimir Vogel in 1956; then devoted himself primarily to educational work; taught at the Musik-Akademie in Basel; in 1968 was appointed to the editorial board of the Basel Radio.

WORKS: *Lyrical Suite* for chamber orch. (1959); *Fantasia* for clarinet, harp, and string orch. (1964–65); *Sonata* for orch. (1967; Basel, Feb. 22, 1968); *Epitaffio* for winds, strings, and percussion (1968; Lucerne, Aug. 7, 1968); *3 Nocturnes* for viola and orch. (1968–69; Basel, March 19, 1970); *Airs et Ritournelles* for percussion and instrumental group (1973); *Musik* for orch. (1975–76; Basel, May 25, 1977); *Musikalisches Tagebuch Nr. 1* and *Nr. 2* for voice and 7 instruments (1946; 1950); *Die Ballade von des Cortez Leuten* for narrator, chorus, speaking chorus and orch. (1960); *Heilige Leier, sprich, sei meine Stimme* for soprano, flute, and guitar (1960); *...aber auch lobet den Himmel,* after Brecht, for solo voices, male chorus, boy's speaking chorus, and instrumental ensemble (1976; Basel, June 3, 1977); *String Quartet* (1952); *Divertimento* for flute, oboe, and bassoon (1955); *Estampida* for 7 instruments and percussion (1960); *4 Movements* for string trio (1961); *4 Etudes* for wind quintet (1962); *Serenata* for 7 instruments (1963–64); *Fanfares et Pastorales* for 2 horns, trumpet, and trombone (1965); *Duetti* for flute and oboe (1967); *Élégie* for solo cello (1969); *Pastorales d'hiver* for horn, violin, viola, cello, and piano (1972); *Jeux à quatre* for 4 saxophones (1976); *Contrapunti,* etudes for violin and piano (1977); *Piano Sonata* (1966–67).

Sutermeister, Heinrich, important Swiss composer; b. Feuerthalen, Aug. 12, 1910. He studied philology at the Sorbonne Univ. in Paris (1930–31) and composition with Carl Orff and Walter Courvoisier at the Munich Academy of Music (1931–34). Subsequently he devoted himself mainly to composition, until 1963, when he was appointed to the faculty of the Musikhochschule in Hannover, Germany. His main endeavor is to create a type of modern opera that is dramatically effective and melodically pleasing; in his musical philosophy he follows the organic line of thought, with the natural impulses of the human body determining the rhythmic course of a composition; discordant combinations of sounds are legitimate parts of modern harmony in Sutermeister's works, but he rejects artificial doctrines such as orthodox dodecaphony.

WORKS: for the stage: the operas *Die schwarze Spinne* (radio opera, 1935; Bern radio, Oct. 15, 1936; revised for the stage and produced in St. Gall, March 2, 1949), *Romeo und Julia* (after Shakespeare, 1938–40; Dresden, April 13, 1940; his first and greatest

success), *Die Zauberinsel* (after Shakespeare's *The Tempest,* 1941–42; Dresden, Oct. 31, 1942), *Niobe* (1943–45; Zürich, June 22, 1946), *Raskolnikoff* (after Dostoyevsky's *Crime and Punishment,* 1946–48; Stockholm, Oct. 14, 1948), *Der rote Stiefel* (1949–51; Stockholm, Nov. 22, 1951), *Titus Feuerfuchs* (burlesque opera, 1956–58; Basel, April 14, 1958), *Seraphine* (opera-buffa after Rabelais; Zürich radio, June 10, 1959; stage premiere, Munich, Feb. 25, 1960), *Das Gespenst von Canterville* (television opera after Oscar Wilde, 1962–63; German television, Sept. 6, 1964), *Madame Bovary* (after Flaubert, 1967; Zürich, May 26, 1967), *La Croisade des Enfants* (television opera, 1969), and *Der Flaschenteufel (The Bottle Imp,* television opera after R. L. Stevenson, 1969–70; German television, 1971); a radio ballad, *Füsse im Feuer,* was also arranged for an operatic production and staged at the Berlin City Opera (Feb. 12, 1950) and a radio melodrama, *Fingerhütchen* (produced in operatic form at St. Gallen on April 26, 1950); 2 ballets: *Das Dorf unter dem Gletscher* (1936; Karlsruhe, May 2, 1937) and *Max und Moritz* (1951; first stage performance, St. Gall, 1963); 8 numbered cantatas: No. 1, *Andreas Gryphius,* for chorus a cappella (1935–36), No. 2 for contralto, chorus and 2 pianos (1943–44), No. 3, *Dem Allgegenwärtigen,* for soloists, chorus and orch. (1957–58), No. 4, *Das Hohelied,* for soloists, chorus and orch. (1960), No. 5, *Der Papagei aus Kuba,* for chorus and chamber orch. (1961), No. 6, *Erkennen und Schaffen* (in French, *Croire et créer*), for soloists, chorus and orch. (1963), No. 7, *Sonnenhymne des Echnaton,* for male chorus, 2 horns, 3 trumpets, 2 trombones, tuba, piano, and percussion (1965), and No. 8, *Omnia ad Unum,* for baritone, chorus, and orch. (1965–66); *Missa da Requiem* for soloists, chorus and orch. (1952; Basel, June 11, 1954); *Ecclesia* for soloists, chorus and orch. (1972–73; Lausanne, Oct. 18, 1975); *Te Deum* for soprano, chorus and orch. (1974); *Divertimento No. 1* for string orch. (1936) and *No. 2* for orch. (1959–60); 3 piano concertos (1943, 1953, 1961–62); 2 cellos concertos (1954–55, 1971); *Sérénade pour Montreux* for 2 oboes, 2 horns, and string orch. (1970); *Clarinet Concerto* (1974); chamber pieces.

Sutherland, Joan, celebrated Australian soprano; b. Sydney, Nov. 7, 1926. She received her early vocal training in Australia; in 1951 she went to London, where she studied voice with Clive Carey at the Royal College of Music. She was then engaged at Covent Garden, obtaining a signal success as Lucia on Feb. 17, 1959; she appeared in the same role at the Metropolitan Opera House, N.Y., Nov. 26, 1961, with a similar acclaim. She excels in the Italian bel canto repertory, but the extraordinary flexibility of her voice makes her interpretations of dramatic parts equally fine. She is married to the Australian conductor **Richard Bonynge**.

BIBLIOGRAPHY: R. Braddon, *Joan Sutherland* (London, 1962).

Sutherland, Margaret, Australian composer; b. Adelaide, Nov. 20, 1897. She studied piano with Edward Goll and composition with Fritz Hall at the Marshall Hall Cons. (1914); then taught at the Melbourne Cons.

In 1923-25 she traveled in Europe. In 1970 she was awarded an Order of the British Empire for her services to Australian music. Her own compositions are marked by classical restraint; most of them follow Baroque forms.

WORKS: Violin Sonata (1925); Trio for clarinet, viola, and piano (1934); *Suite on a Theme of Purcell* for orch. (1935); *House Quartet* for clarinet or violin, viola, horn or cello, and piano (1936); *Pavane* for orch. (1938); *The Soldier* for chorus and strings (1938); 2 string quartets (1939, 1967); *Prelude and Jig* for strings (1939); a ballet, *Dithyramb* (1941); Sonata for clarinet and piano (1944); Concerto for strings (1945); *Adagio* for 2 solo violins and orch. (1946); Trio for oboe and 2 violins (1951); *Contrasts* for 2 violins (1953); a tone poem, *Haunted Hills* (1953); Violin Concerto (1954); *4 Symphonic Studies* (1954); Concerto Grosso for orch. (1955); Quartet for English horn and string trio (1955); *6 Bagatelles* for violin and viola (1956); Piano Sonatina (1958); *Divertimento* for string trio (1958); Sonatina for oboe and piano (1958); *3 Temperaments* for orch. (1958); *Fantasy* for violin and orch. (1960); *Concertante* for oboe, percussion, and string orch. (1962); a 1-act chamber opera, *The Young Kabbarli* (1964); Quartet for clarinet and strings (1967); *Extension* for piano (1967); *Chiaroscuro 1* and *2* for piano (1968); *Voices 1* and *2* for piano (1968).

Sutro, Florence Edith (*née* **Clinton**), American music educator; b. New York, May 1, 1865; d. there, April 29, 1906. A graduate of the N.Y. Cons. of Music, she was the first woman in the U.S. to receive a degree of Mus. Doc. In 1898 she organized the National Federation of Musical Clubs, and was its first president; for her efforts in behalf of women composers and executants she was awarded a gold medal at the Atlanta Exposition in 1895. On Oct. 1, 1884, she married Theodore Sutro, a prominent lawyer of New York. She wrote *Women in Music and Law* (N.Y., 1895).

Sutro, Rose Laura, (b. Baltimore, Sept. 15, 1870; d. there, Jan. 11, 1957) and **Ottilie** (b. Baltimore, Jan. 4, 1872; d. there, Sept. 12, 1970), American duo-pianists; daughters of Otto Sutro, a patron of art and founder of the Baltimore Oratorio Society. Both began piano lessons with their mother, and in 1889 were sent to Berlin, where they continued their studies. They made a spectacular debut in London on July 13, 1894; first American appearance, Brooklyn, Nov. 13, 1894, followed by a tour of the U.S. Returning to Europe, they won fresh laurels, and were invited to play before Queen Victoria. Max Bruch wrote his Concerto for 2 Pianos and Orch. expressly for them, and they gave its première with the Philadelphia Orch. on Dec. 29, 1916. In 1953 the sisters established the Sutro Club Room at the Maryland Historical Society in memory of their father.

Svanholm, Set, Swedish tenor; b. Västeras, Sept. 2, 1904; d. Saltsjoe-Duvnaes, Oct. 4, 1964. He studied in Stockholm, and was church organist before studying voice; made his debut in 1930 as a baritone, but beginning in 1936 sang tenor parts. He was equally successful in the Italian repertory as in Wagnerian roles; sang in all major European opera houses; in 1946 he ap-

peared as Tristan in Rio de Janeiro; he made his American debut with the Metropolitan Opera on Nov. 15, 1946 as Siegfried, and continued on its staff until 1955. His other successful roles were Rhadames, Lohengrin, Parsifal, Tännhauser, and Otello.

Svečenski, Louis, Croatian-American violinist; b. Osijek, Nov. 6, 1862; d. New York, June 18, 1926. He studied violin with J. Grün and J. Hellmesberger at the Vienna Cons.; emigrated to America in 1885 and became a member of the Boston Symph. Orchestra (1885–1903); he was also the violist throughout the entire career of the Kneisel Quartet (1885–1917); in 1917 went to live in N.Y.. He publ. *25 Technical Exercises for Viola.*

Sveinsson, Atli Heimir, Icelandic composer; b. Reykjavik, Sept. 21, 1938. He studied at the Reykjavik School of Music; then in Cologne with Raphael, B. A. Zimmermann, and Petzold at the Hochschule für Musik (1959–62), and with Stockhausen and Pousseur at the School for New Music (1963); attended seminars in electronic music with Koenig in Bilthoven, Holland (1964). Returning to Iceland, he devoted himself to teaching.

WORKS: *Hlými (Sonant)* for chamber orch. (1963); *Fönsun I-III* for singers, actors, tape and chamber ensemble; *Klif (Tautology)* for flute, cello, and piano (1968); *Seimur (Soundings)* for 1 or 2 pianos, and any number of instruments (1968); *Spectacles* for percussion and tape (1969); *Tengsl (Connections)* for orch. (1970); *Bizzarreries I* for flute, piano, and tape (1970); *Könnun,* viola concerto (1971); Flute Concerto (1973); *Flower Shower* for orch. (1974); *I Call It* for contralto, piano, cello, and 2 percussionists (1974); incidental music.

Svendsen, Johan (Severin), eminent Norwegian composer; b. Christiania, Sept. 30, 1840; d. Copenhagen, June 14, 1911. He acquired practical experience in music from his father, a bandmaster, and played several instruments; then conducted a band himself. It was not before he was 23 that he began serious study at the Leipzig Cons. with F. David, Reinecke, and others; then played violin in theater orchestras in Paris; wrote incidental music for Coppée's play *Le Passant* (Paris, Jan. 14, 1869), a violin concerto, and other violin works. In 1870 he went back to Leipzig; then traveled to America, and married an American lady, Sarah Levett. Returning to Norway, he became conductor of the Christiania Musical Association (1872–77 and again in 1880–83). In 1883 was appointed court conductor in Copenhagen; from 1896 also conducted at the Royal Theater there. His most popular works are the *4 Norwegian Rhapsodies* for orch. and the *Carnaval des artistes norvégiens* (also for orch.), based on genuine folk melodies; he further wrote 2 symphonies; a string quartet; a string quintet; a string octet; a cello concerto; 2 albums of songs to German, French, and Norwegian words; a *Romance* for violin and orch. (very popular); arrangements of Scandinavian melodies for string quartet; etc.

BIBLIOGRAPHY: A. Grönwold, *Norske musikere* (1883); G. Schjelderup, in *Norges Musikhistorie.* Letters of Svendsen were publ. by G. Hauch in *Tilsku-*

eren (Copenhagen, 1913); Bjarne Kortsen, *Chamber Music Works by Johan Svendsen* (Bergen, 1971).

Svetlanov, Evgeny, Russian conductor and composer; b. Moscow, Sept. 6, 1928. He studied composition with Gnessin and Shaporin, and conducting with Gauck. After graduation in 1955 he joined the staff of the Bolshoi Theater in Moscow; was its principal conductor from 1962 to 1964. In 1965 he was appointed music director of the State Orchestra of the U.S.S.R. He wrote a Symphony (1956); *Siberian Fantasy* for orch. (1953); Piano Concerto (1951); incidental music for plays; film scores.

Sviridov, Georgy, significant Soviet Russian composer; b. Fatezh, near Kursk, Dec. 16, 1915. He studied at the Leningrad Cons. with Shostakovich. In his music, Sviridov adheres to the ideals of Socialist Realism, seeking inspiration in Russian folk songs; the texts of his vocal works are usually taken from Russian literature. His *Oratorio Pathétique* (1959), to words by Mayakovsky, composed in a grandly songful "optimistic" style, became one of the most successful scores by a Soviet composer.
WORKS: for the theater: music for Shakespeare's *Othello* (1944); *Twinkling Lights,* operetta (1951); music for the film *Blizzard* (1964); music for the film *Time Forge Ahead!* (1966); Symphony for string orch. (1940); *Little Triptych* (1964); chamber music: Piano Quintet (1945); Piano Trio (1945); String Quartet (1945); *Music for Chamber Orchestra* (1964); choral works: *The Decembrists,* oratorio (1955); *Poem to the Memory of Sergei Essenin* (1956); *Poem about Lenin,* for bass, chorus, and orch. (1960); *5 Songs about Our Fatherland* for voices, chorus and orch. (1967); numerous piano pieces and songs.
BIBLIOGRAPHY: D. Frishman, ed., *Georgy Sviridov* (a collection of articles; Moscow, 1971).

Svoboda, Tomáš, Czech composer; b. Paris, Dec. 6, 1939, of Czech parents (his father was a renowned mathematician, Antonín Svoboda). The family went to Prague in 1946; he studied piano privately and composition with Hlobil, Kabeláč and Dobiáš at the Prague Cons., graduating in 1959. In 1964 he left Czechoslovakia and settled in the U.S. In 1970, appointed member of the faculty at Portland State Univ., Oregon. His music is marked by broad melodic lines in economically disposed harmonies; there are elements of serialism in chromatic episodes.
WORKS: Symph. No. 1 (Prague, Sept. 7, 1957); Symph. No. 2 (1964–65); Symph. No. 3 (1965); Trio for piano, oboe and bassoon (1962); *Řezanička,* dance for string orch. (1962); *Classical Sonatina* for oboe and piano (1962); *Etude* for chamber orch. (1963); *Ballade* for bassoon and piano (1963); Viola Sonata (1963); Suite for bassoon, strings, and harpsichord (1963); *Ballet Etudes* for 7 instruments (1963); *Chamber Concertino* for harp and chamber orch. (1964); *Suite* for mezzo-soprano and orch. (1964); *Parabola* for clarinet, piano, violin, viola, and cello (1971); 2 string quartets (1960, 1967); *Child's Dream* for children's chorus and orch. (1973); Duo for flute and oboe (1974).

Swan, Alfred (Julius), Russian-born English-American musicologist and educator; b. St. Petersburg (of English parents), Oct. 9, 1890; d. Haverford, Pennsylvania, Oct. 2, 1970. After attending a German-language school in St. Petersburg, he studied at Oxford Univ., receiving the degrees of B.A. and M.A. Returning to Russia in 1911 he took courses in composition at the St. Petersburg Cons. During the Civil War in Russia, he served with the American Red Cross in Siberia (1918–19); then emigrated to the U.S.; taught at the Univ. of Virginia (1921–23); in 1926 he was appointed head of the music dept. at Swarthmore College and Haverford College, Pennsylvania, retiring from these posts in 1958. His specialty was Russian music.
WRITINGS: *Scriabin* (London, 1923; reprint, N.Y., 1969); *Music 1900–1930* (N.Y., 1930); "Znamenny Chant of the Russian Church," *Musical Quarterly* (April, July, Oct. 1940); many other articles on Russian music and Russian composers in various publications. He also brought out a useful brochure *The Music Director's Guide to Musical Literature* (N.Y., 1941). His *Russian Music and Its Sources in Chant and Folksong* was published posthumously (N.Y., 1973). He was also a composer; he wrote a trio for flute, clarinet and piano (1932); 2 violin sonatas (1913, 1948); 4 piano sonatas (1932–46); several albums of songs. He edited *Songs from Many Lands* (1923) and *Recueil de chansons russes* (1936).

Swan, Timothy, American hymn-tune writer; b. Worcester, Mass., July 23, 1758; d. Northfield, July 23, 1842. His only musical training consisted of 3 weeks at a singing school, and while serving in the Continental Army he also learned to play the flute. From 1783 he lived in Suffield, Conn., and in 1807 moved to Northfield, Mass. Composed the hymn tunes *Poland, China, Ocean,* and *Pownal.* Publ. *The Songster's Assistant* (c.1800); *New England Harmony* (1801); and also probably was the author of *The Songsters' Museum* (1803).
BIBLIOGRAPHY: F. J. Metcalf, *American Writers and Compilers of Sacred Music* (N.Y., 1925, p. 103ff.); G. B. Webb, *Timothy Swan: Yankee Tunesmith* (Univ. of Illinois at Urbana-Champaign, 1972).

Swanson, Howard, black American composer; b. Atlanta, Aug. 18, 1907. The family moved to Cleveland in 1917. As a youth he earned a living by manual labor on the railroad and as a postal clerk. He then entered the Cleveland Institute of Music, where he took evening courses with Herbert Elwell; obtained a stipend to go to Paris, where he studied composition with Nadia Boulanger (1938–40). He then returned to the U.S., and obtained a job with the Internal Revenue Service (1941–45). His songs attracted the attention of Marian Anderson, who performed them in N.Y. His first signal success came with *Short Symphony* (Symph. No. 2, 1948), a work of simple melodic inspiration, which received considerable acclaim at its first performance by the N.Y. Philharmonic conducted by Mitropoulos (Nov. 23, 1950). In 1952 it was the choice of the Music Critics' Circle. His other works include Symph. No. 1 (1945); Symph. No. 3 (N.Y. March 1, 1970); *Songs for Patricia* for voice and piano (1951); Trio for flute, oboe and piano (1976); Songs: *Pierrot, Night Song, Rain, Ghosts in Love, Junk Man*, etc.

BIBLIOGRAPHY: M. Yestadt, "Song Literature for the 70's: A Socio-Musical Approach," *NATS Bulletin* (May-June 1973).

Swarowsky, Hans, Austrian conductor; b. Budapest, Sept. 16, 1899; d. Salzburg, Sept. 10, 1975. He studied in Vienna with Schoenberg and Anton von Webern, with whom he formed a friendly association; he also was in close relationship with Richard Strauss. He devoted himself mainly to conducting; occupied posts as opera conductor in Hamburg (1932) and in Berlin (1934). From 1937 to 1940 he was conductor of the Zürich Opera; from 1940 to 1944 he directed the Salzburg Festival; during the season 1944-45 led the Polish Philharmonic in Cracow. After the end of the war he was principal conductor of the Vienna Symph. (1945-47) and of the Graz Opera (1947-50); in 1957-59 he was conductor of the Scottish National Orch. in Glasgow; in 1959 was appointed principal conductor of the Vienna State Opera. In his programs he gave prominent place to the works of the Vienna School; his performances of Mahler were particulary fine. Swarowsky was an excellent instructor in conducting; he led a special seminar at the Vienna Music Academy; among his students were Claudio Abbado and Zubin Mehta. He was a highly competent editor of music by various composers; also translated a number of Italian libretti into German.

Swarthout, Gladys, American mezzo-soprano; b. Deepwater, Mo., Dec. 25, 1900; d. Florence, July 7, 1969. She studied at the Bush Cons. in Chicago, also opera with L. Mugnone; made her debut in a minor part with the Chicago Civic Opera in 1924; and then made regular appearances with the Ravinia Opera Co. in Chicago. On Nov. 15, 1929, she sang the part of La Cieca in *La Gioconda* at the Metropolitan Opera; she remained on its roster until 1945. She married the singer **Frank Chapman** in 1932. Publ. an autobiography, *Come Soon, Tomorrow* (N.Y., 1945).

Sweelinck, Jan Pieterszoon, great Dutch organist and composer; b. Deventer (or Amsterdam), May 1562; d. Amsterdam, Oct. 16, 1621. Contrary to repeated assertions that Sweelinck was a pupil of Zarlino in Venice, documentary evidence proves that he remained in Amsterdam virtually all his life; this also refutes the theory that Sweelinck was the carrier of Venetian ideas and techniques in Northern Europe. About 1580 he became organist of the Old Church in Amsterdam, a position previously held by his father, Pieter Sweelinck (d. 1573). As a player and teacher he was celebrated far and wide; most of the leading organists in Northern Germany, of the next generation, were his pupils. During his life-time only some of his vocal music was publ.; but his organ music is more remarkable and important: Sweelinck was the first to employ the pedal in a real fugal part, and originated the organ fugue built up on one theme with the gradual addition of counterthemes leading up to a highly involved and ingenious finale—a form perfected by Bach. In rhythmic and melodic freedom, his vocal compositions show an advance over the earlier polyphonic style,

though replete with intricate contrapuntal devices. A complete ed. of Sweelinck's works, in 12 vols., edited by Max Seiffert for the *Vereeniging voor Nederlandsche Muziekgeschiedenis*, was publ. by Breitkopf & Härtel (1895-1903); vol. I, works for organ and clavier; vol. II, 1st half of the First Book of Psalms (1604); vol. III, 2nd half of the same; vol. IV, 1st half of the Second Book of Psalms (1613); vol. V, 2nd half of the same; vol. VI, Third Book of Psalms (1614); vol. VII, Fourth Book of Psalms (1621); vol. VIII, *Cantiones sacrae a* 5; vol. IX, *Chansons a* 5; vol. X, *Rimes françaises et italiennes a* 2-4; vol. XI, processional compositions; vol. XII, Rules for composition, ed. by H. Gehrmann. Vols. II-VII comprise the 150 Psalms of David in the rhymed French version by Marot and Beza. A new *Opera Omnia* was begun by the same series in 1966.

BIBLIOGRAPHY: F. H. J. Tiedeman: *J. P. S., een bio-bibliografische Schets* (Amsterdam, 1876; 2nd ed., 1892); M. Seiffert, "J. P. S. und seine direkten deutschen Schüler," *Vierteljahrsschrift für Musikwissenschaft* (1891); M. Seiffert, "J. P. S.," *Tijdschrift van de Vereeniging voor Nederlandsche Muziekgeschiedenis* (1900); D. F. Scheurleer, "Sweelinckiana," in the same (1914); C. Van den Borren, *Les Origines de la musique de clavier dans les Pays-Bas jusque vers 1630* (Brussels, 1914); O. Gombosi, "S.," *Tijdschrift* (as above) (1932); E. R. Sollitt, *From Dufay to S.* (N.Y., 1933); B. van den Sigtenhorst Meyer, *J. P. S. en zijn instrumentale muziek* (The Hague, 1934; 2nd ed., 1946); B. van den Sigtenhorst Meyer, *De vocale Muziek van J. P. S.* (The Hague, 1948); R. L. Tusler, *The Organ Music of J. P. S.* (2 vols.; Bilthoven, 1958; in English); R. H. Tollefsen, "J. P. Sweelinck. A Bio-Bibliography, 1604-1842," *Tijdschrift* XXII/2 (1971).

Swert, Jules de. See **Deswert, Jules.**

Swift, Richard, American composer; b. Middlepoint, Ohio, Sept. 24, 1927. He studied at the Univ. of Chicago (M.A. 1956); then became a member of the faculty of the Univ. of California at Davis; was appointed chairman of the music dept. there in 1963. In his compositions he applies a variety of functional serial techniques, including electronic and aleatory devices, while preserving the external forms of Baroque music.

WORKS: *A Coronal* for orch. (Louisville, April 14, 1956); *Serenade Concertante* for piano and wind quintet (1956); Sonata for clarinet and piano (1957); Trio for clarinet, cello and piano (1957); Concerto for piano and chamber ensemble (1961); *Extravaganza* for orch. (1962); *The Trial of Tender O'Shea*, one-act opera (Univ. of Calif., Davis, Aug. 12, 1964); *Thrones* for alto flute, and double bass (1966); *Tristia* for orch. (Oakland, Calif., April 20, 1968); Violin Concerto (Oakland, Calif., May 28, 1968); Symphony (1970); 3 string quartets (1955, 1958, and 1964); 2 works for 3 instruments entitled *Music for a While*; 8 works for different instrumental groups, or solos, entitled *Stravaganza*, and 3 works under the generic title *Domains* for voice, instruments and percussion; 25 sets of incidental music for the theater, including *musique concrète* and electronic sounds.

Swoboda, Adalbert (Viktor), Czech-German writer on music; b. Prague, Jan. 26, 1828; d. Munich, May 19, 1902. He founded (1880) and edited till his death the *Neue Musikzeitung* in Stuttgart; author of *Illustrierte Musikgeschichte* (2 vols., 1893).

Swoboda, Henry, Czech-American conductor; b. Prague, Oct. 29, 1897; studied music with Zemlinsky and Talich; received his Ph.D. at the German Univ. of Prague. From 1931 to 1938 he was conductor with the Prague Radio. In 1938 he settled in the U.S.; conducted occasional concerts in the U.S. and in Europe; served as music director of recording companies; wrote articles on American music. In 1964 he was appointed conductor of the Univ. Orch. and director of the Opera Workshop at the Univ. of Texas, Austin.

Sychra, Antonín, Czech musicologist; b. Boskovice, June 9, 1918; d. Prague, Oct. 20, 1969. He studied music in Brno and Prague; settling in Prague, he publ. a number of scholarly monographs on esthetics; also taught music history at the Charles Univ. in Prague. Published *Estetika Dvořákovy symfonické tvorby* (Prague, 1959); *Leoš Janáček* (Prague, 1956); "The Method of Psychoacoustic Transformation Applied to the Investigation of Expression in Speech and Music" (in English; publ. in *Kybernetica*, 1969); several other papers on the application of cybernetics to musical analysis.

Sydeman, William, American composer; b. New York, May 8, 1928. He studied at Mannes College with Felix Salzer; later had a session with Sessions at Tanglewood. In 1959 he joined the faculty of Mannes College, N.Y. His style of composition stems primarily from Mahler and Berg, and tends towards atonal expressionism invigorated by spasmodic percussive rhythms in asymmetrically arranged meters. WORKS: *Orchestral Abstractions* (1958; N.Y., Jan. 10, 1962); *Study for Orchestra* (1959); Concertino for oboe, piano, and string orch. (1956); Divertimento for 8 instruments (1957); *Concerto da Camera No. 1* for violin and chamber orch. (1959); *Concerto da Camera No. 2* for violin and chamber orch. (1960); *Chamber Concerto* for piano, 2 flutes, and string quartet (1961); *7 Movements* for septet (1960); 2 woodwind quintets (1955, 1959); Westbrook Quintet for clarinet, horn, double bass, piano, and percussion (1959); String Quartet (1955); Quartet for clarinet, violin, trumpet, and double bass (1955); Quartet for oboe and strings (1961); *The Affections,* suite for trumpet and piano (1965); *Malediction,* for tenor, a speaking actor, string quartet, and electronic tape, to words from Laurence Sterne's *Tristram Shandy* (N.Y., Feb. 5, 1971); numerous other works for various instrumental ensembles.

Sygiètynski, Tadeusz, Polish conductor and arranger; b. Warsaw, Sept. 24, 1896; d. there, May 19, 1955. He studied music in Lwow with Roman Statkowski and Henryk Melcer; later took courses with Max Reger in Leipzig and with Schoenberg in Vienna. In 1949 he organized in Poland the Mazowsze State Song and Dance Ensemble for the purpose of popularizing Polish folk music; toured with it in the Far East and in Western Europe with considerable acclaim. He made numerous arrangements of Polish folksongs for this group; in 1951 he received a State prize, and later was awarded the Banner of Labor by the State Council of Poland.

Sykes, James Andrews, American pianist; b. Atlantic City, N.J., July 10, 1908. He studied at Princeton (A.B., 1930) and at the Univ. of Rochester (A.M., 1933); subsequently held teaching positions at Colorado College (1935–46) and Colgate Univ. (1947–53); 1953, appointed prof. at Dartmouth College. He toured West Germany (1954); South America (1960); Greece, Turkey, Malaysia, Vietnam, Pakistan, Iran, Lebanon, and Japan, as an American Specialist for the State Dept. (1965). He specializes in modern American piano music.

Sykora, Bogumil, Russian cellist; b. Glinsk, Jan. 15, 1890; d. New York, Jan. 19, 1953. He studied with Julius Klengel at the Leipzig Cons. (1909) and made his professional debut there on Jan. 20, 1911; toured Russia (1913–1915); then came to America; gave his 1st recital in N.Y. on Dec. 12, 1916. He composed a concerto and a number of pieces for cello.

Symonds, Norman, Canadian composer; b. Nelson, British Columbia, Dec. 23, 1920. He studied clarinet and piano at the Royal Cons. in Toronto (1945–47); took lessons in composition privately with Gordon Delamont in Toronto (1947–50). In 1953 he organized his own jazz octet, which continued in action until 1957. Most of his compositions are in the "third stream" idiom that combines jazz and symphonic styles.
BIBLIOGRAPHY: a 1-act opera, *The Spirit of Fundy* (1972); a jazz opera, *Opera for 6 Voices* (1961); a television ballet, *Tensions,* with jazz quintet and orch. (1962); *Concerto Grosso* for jazz quintet and orch. (1957); *Autumn Nocturne* for tenor saxophone and strings (1960); *Pastel* for string orch. (1963); *The Nameless Hour* for improvising soloist and string ensemble (1966); *The Democratic Concerto* for jazz quintet and orch. (Winnipeg, Dec. 14, 1967); *Impulse* for orch. (Toronto, March 18, 1969); *3 Atmospheres* for orch. (1970); *The Story of the Wind* for narrator, singer, and jazz ensemble (1970); *Concerto for Flute and Others* (1971); *The Land* for narrator, singer and jazz ensemble (1972–73); *Maya* for small orch. (1973); *Circles* for saxophone and 4 synthesizers (1977); 2 concertos for jazz octet (1955, 1956); *Forest and Sky* for orch. (1977); electronic pieces.

Szabados, Béla Antal, Hungarian composer; b. Budapest, June 3, 1867; d. there, Sept.15, 1936. He studied with Erkel and Volkmann at the Budapest Academy of Music; later joined its staff as piano teacher and vocal coach. He wrote 2 operas, *Maria* (Budapest, Feb. 28, 1905; in collaboration with Arpád Szendy), and *Fanny* (Budapest, Feb. 16, 1927); 11 musical comedies; 4 string quartets; a psalm, and several song cycles; also publ. several vocal manuals.

Szabelski, Boleslaw, Polish organist and composer; b. Radoryż, near Lublin; Dec. 3, 1896. He was an organist; studied composition with Szymanowski and Statkowski at the Warsaw Cons.; then became a teacher of organ and composition at the State College of Music in Katowice (1929–39, 1945–74).

WORKS: 5 symphonies: (1926, 1934, 1951, 1955, 1968); *Suite* for orch. (1938); Organ Sonata (1943); Sinfonietta for string orch. and percussion (1946); *Poemat bohaterski (Heroic Poem)* for chorus and orch. (1952); *Solemn Overture* (1953); *Concerto Grosso* for orch. (1954); Piano Concertino (1955); 2 string quartets (1935, 1956); *3 Sonnets* for orch. (1958); *Improvisations* for chorus and chamber orch. (1959); *Wiersze (Verses)* for piano and orch. (1961); *Aphorism "9"* for chamber ensemble (1962); Flute Concerto (1964); *Nicolaus Copernicus*, oratorio (1976; Poznań, April 2, 1976); *The Wola Redoubt* for 3 vocal soloists and orch. (1976; Warsaw, Nov. 5, 1976).

Szabó, Ferenc, distinguished Hungarian composer; b. Budapest, Dec. 27, 1902; d. there, Nov. 4, 1969. He studied with Kodály, Siklós, and Leo Weiner at the Budapest Academy of Music (1922–26); in 1926 he became aligned with the labor movement in Hungary; in 1932 went to Russia, where he became closely associated with the ideological work of the Union of Soviet Composers. In 1945 he returned to Hungary and was appointed prof. at the Budapest Academy; served as its director in 1958–67. He was awarded the Kossuth Prize in 1951 and 1954. His music initially followed the trends of Central European modernism, with strong undertones of Hungarian melorhythms, but later he wrote music in the manner of Socialist Realism; his choruses are permeated with the militant spirit of the revolutionary movement.

WORKS: a 3-act opera *Légy jó mindhalálig (Be Faithful Until Death*, 1968–69; posthumous, Budapest, Dec. 5, 1975; score completed by his pupil András Borgulya); ballet *Lúdas Matyi* (1960; Budapest, May 16, 1960); an oratorio *Föltámadott a tenger (In Fury Rose the Ocean*, 1955; Budapest, June 15, 1955); a cantata *Meghalt Lenin (Lenin Is Dead*, 1933); *Suite* for chamber orch. (1926; revised as *Sérénade Oubliée*, 1964); *Class Struggle*, symph. poem (Moscow, April 27, 1933); *Sinfonietta* for an ensemble of Russian national instruments (1935); *Lyrical Suite* for string orch. (1936); *Moldovan Rhapsody* for orch. (1940); Concerto for Orch., subtitled *Hazatérés (Homecoming*, 1948); *Számadás (Summary)*, symph. poem (1949); *Emlékeztető (Memento)*, a symph. (1952); 2 string quartets (1926, 1962); Trio for 2 violins and viola (1927); Sonata for solo cello (1929); 2 sonatas for solo violin (1930); *Sonata alla rapsodia* for clarinet and piano (1964); *Toccata* for piano (1928); *8 Easy Piano Pieces* (1933); 3 piano sonatas (1940, 1947, 1957–61); *Felszabadult melódiák (Melodies of Liberation)* cycle of piano pieces (1949); a cappella choruses: *Song of the Wolves* (1929); *Work and Bread* (1930); *Liberty Be the Watchword* (1932), *November 7th* (1932), and *Song at Dawn* (1953); *Vallomás (Declaration)* for chorus, brass, and percussion (1967).

Szabolcsi, Bence, eminent Hungarian music scholar; b. Budapest, Aug. 2, 1899; d. there, Jan. 21, 1973. He studied jurisprudence at the Univ. of Budapest; concurrently took courses in music with Kodály at the Budapest Academy and with Abert at the Univ. of Leipzig. He was editor of the Hungarian music periodical *Zenei Szemle* (with Bartha) from 1926 on (except for the war years, when it suspended publication). With Aladár Tóth he brought out a music dictionary in the Hungarian language (1930–31); published a history of music (Budapest, 1940), a monograph on Beethoven (Budapest, 1948), and a number of valuable papers in various European magazines. But his most abiding concern was the publication of documents on Béla Bartók. On his 70th birthday he was presented a Festschrift, edited by Bartha, *Bence Szabolcsi Septuagenario* (Budapest, 1969). Among his writings on Bartók, the most important are *Bartók—Sa vie et son œuvre* (Budapest, 1956; 2nd ed., 1968); *Béla Bartók* (Leipzig, 1968); *Béla Bartók, Musiksprachen* (Leipzig, 1972). Two of his books were published in English: *The Twilight of Ferenc Liszt* (Budapest, 1959) and *A Concise History of Hungarian Music* (Budapest, 1964).

Szalonek, Witold, Polish composer; b. Katowice, March 2, 1927. He studied composition with Woytowicz at the State College of Music in Katowice (1949–56); attended summer courses in new music at Darmstadt (1960) and had a course in musical analysis with Nadia Boulanger in Paris (1962–63). Returning to Poland, he taught at the Katowice State College, and became its director in 1972.

WORKS: *Pastorale* for oboe, and orch. or piano (1952); Trio for flute, clarinet and bassoon (1952); *Toccata polyphonica* for string orch. (1954); *Suite kurpienne* for solo contralto and 9 instruments (1955); *Symphonic Satire* (1956); Cello Sonata (1958); *Wyznania (Confessions)*, triptych for narrator, chorus, and chamber orch. (1959); Flute Concertino (1962); *Arabesques* for violin and piano (1964); *Les sons* for orch. without violins and cellos (1965); *4 Monologues* for solo oboe (1966); *Mutations* for chamber orch. (1966); *Proporzioni* for flute, viola, and harp (1967); *Improvisations sonoristiques* for clarinet, trombone, cello, and piano (1968); *Mutanza* for piano (1968); *1+1+1+1* for 1, 2, 3, or 4 string instruments (1969); a cantata, *Ziemio mila (O, Pleasant Earth)* for voice and orch. (1969); *Proporzioni II* for flute, cello, and piano or harp (1967–70); *Aarhus Music* for wind quintet (1970; Aarhus is a city in Denmark where Szalonek lectured in 1970); *3 Sketches* for harp (1972); *Connections* for wind quintet, 4 strings, and piano (1972).

Szalowski, Antoni, Polish composer; b. Warsaw, April 21, 1907; d. Paris, March 21, 1973. He studied composition with Sikorski at the Warsaw Cons., graduating in 1930; in 1936 took lessons with Nadia Boulanger in Paris, and remained there until his death. His music follows the Parisian manner of modern Baroque.

WORKS: 4 string quartets (1928, 1934, 1936, 1956); *Symphonic Variations* (1928); Piano Concerto (1930); *Overture* (1936); symph. (1939); Sinfonietta (1940); *Partita* for orch. (1942); Concertino for strings (1942); Oboe Sonatina (1946); *Triptych* for orch. (1950); Concertino for flute and string orch. (1951); Wind Quintet (1954); Violin Concerto (1954); *Divertimento* for oboe, clarinet and bassoon (1955); *La Danse* for orch. (1957); *Moto perpetuo* for orch. (1958); *Intermezza* for orch. (1961); *Kolysanka* for orch. (1964); numerous piano pieces and songs.

Szántó, Theodor, Hungarian pianist and composer; b. Vienna, June 3, 1877; d. Budapest, Jan. 7, 1934. He studied with Dachs (piano) and Fuchs (composition) at the Vienna Cons., and later with Busoni in Berlin (1898-1901). In 1905 he settled in Paris; from 1914 to 1921 lived in Switzerland; then divided his time between Paris and Budapest. His opera on a Japanese story, *Typhoon,* was produced in Mannheim, on Nov. 29, 1924, and there were a few subsequent performances in other cities. He also wrote a *Japanese Suite* for orch. (1926); several symph. works based on Hungarian folksongs; chamber music; many piano pieces (of which *Variations on a Hungarian Folksong* became fairly well known.

Székely, Endre, Hungarian composer; b. Budapest, April 6, 1912. He studied with Siklós at the Budapest Academy of Music (1933-37). After the end of the war in 1945 he became active as conductor of workers' choral groups; edited the periodicals, *Éneklö munkás (The Singing Worker)* and *Éneklö nép (The People Sing).* In 1960 he was appointed to the faculty of the Budapest Training College for Teachers.

WORKS: opera, *Vizirózsa (Water Rose;* 1959; Budapest Radio, 1962); operetta, *Aranycsillag (The Golden Star;* Budapest, 1951); *Meditations* for tenor and orch. (1961-62); *Maqamat* for soprano and chamber ensemble (1970); 3 Suites: No. 1 for small orch. (1947), No. 2 for string orch. (1961); and No. 3 for full orch. (1965); Symphony (1956); *Rhapsody* for violin and orch. (1956); *Partita* for strings (1957); Concerto for piano, percussion and strings (1958); *Sinfonia concertante* for violin, piano and chamber orch. (1960-61); Concerto for 8 solo instruments and orch. (1964); *Partita* for orch. (1965); *Fantasma* for orch. (1969); Trumpet Concerto (1971); *Riflessioni,* concerto for cello and orch. (1973); *Humanisation* for chamber ensemble and tape (1974); String Trio (1943); 3 wind quintets (1952, 1961, 1966); 4 string quartets (1953; 1958, 1962, 1972); *Rhapsody* for viola and piano (1956); 2 wind trios (1958, 1959); *Capriccio* for flute and piano (1961); *Chamber Music for 8* (1963); Chamber Music for 3 (1965); *Musica notturna* for piano, wind quintet, and string quintet (1967); *Trio* for percussion, piano, and cello (1968-69); 3 piano sonatas (1952, 1962, 1972); choruses; songs.

Szelényi, István, Hungarian composer; b. Zólyom, Aug. 8, 1904; d. Budapest, Jan. 31, 1972. He studied at the Budapest Academy of Music with Kodály; toured as a concert pianist (1928-30); was prof. at the State Music High School in Budapest (1945-49), at the Bartók Cons. (1950-66) and at the Liszt Academy (1966-72). In 1951-56 he edited the periodical *Új Zenei Szemle (New Music Review).*

WORKS: 2 pantomines, *A tékozló fiú (The Prodigal Son;* 1931); and *Babiloni vásár (The Fair at Babylon;* 1931); an operetta *Hidavatás* (1936); oratorios, including *Virata* (1935), *Spartacus* (1960), *Ten Days that Shook the World* (1964) and *Pro Pace* (1968); Symph. No. 1 (1926); Violin Concerto (1930); *Ouverture activiste* (1931); Triple Concerto for violin, cello, piano,

and wind orch. (1933); *Géptánc—Munkatánc (Machine Dance—Work Dance)* for orch. (1942); *Az ösök nyomában (In the Footsteps of the Ancestors),* symph. for string orch. (1946); *Egy gyár szimfóniája (Symphony for a Factory,* 1946-47); *Hommage à Bartók* for orch. (1947); Violin Concertino (1947-48); *Suite* for string orch. (1952); *Summa vitae* for piano and orch. (1956); *Concerto da Camera* for orch. (1963); *Dance Suite* for string orch. (1964); Piano Concertino (1964); *Variations Concertants* for piano and orch. (1965); Piano Concerto (1969); 2 solo violin sonatas (1925, 1934); Flute Sonata (1926); 4 string quartets (1927, 1928, 1929, 1964); 2 piano trios (1934, 1962); Sonata for 4 violins (1946); 2-Violin Sonatina (1963); *Sinfonietta a tre* for 3 violins (1964); *3 Dialogues* for violin and cello (1965); *Chamber Music* for 2 trumpets, 2 horns, and 2 trombones (1966); 7 piano sonatas (1924-69); Piano Sonatina (1960); *Toccata* for piano (1964); *Musical Picture Book* for piano (1967); choral works; songs. He also published books on music history, on Hungarian music, and on principles of folksong harmonization.

Szeligowski, Tadeusz, notable Polish composer and pedagogue; b. Lwów, Sept. 12, 1896; d. Poznań, Jan. 10, 1963. He studied composition with Jachimecki in Cracow (1918-23) and with Nadia Boulanger in Paris (1929-31); returning to Poland, he taught classes in Poznań (1932-39 and 1947-62) and in Warsaw (1951-62).

WORKS: 3 operas: *Bunt Żaków (Rebellion of Clerks,* 1951; Wroclaw, July 14, 1951), *Krakatuk,* after E. T. A. Hoffmann (1955; Gdańsk, Dec. 30, 1956), and *Theodor gentleman* (1960; Wroclaw, 1963); 2 ballets: *Paw i dziewczyna (The Peacock and the Maiden,* 1948; Wroclaw, Aug. 2, 1949) and *Mazeppa* (1957; Warsaw, 1959); *Kaziuki,* suite for orch. (1928); Concero for Orch. (1932); Clarinet Concerto (1932); *Epitaph for Karol Szymanowski* for string orch. (1937); Piano Concerto (1941; Cracow, May 17, 1946); *Suita lubelska* for small orch. (1945); *Nocturne* for orch. (1947); *Burlesque Overture* (1952); *Triptych* for soprano and orch. (1946); *Kantata o sporcie* for voice, chorus and orch. (1947); *Wesele lubelskie (Lublin Wedding),* suite for soprano, chorus and small orch. (1948); *Rapsod* for soprano and orch. (1949); *Panicz i dziewczyna (The Young Squire and the Country Girl),* musical dialogue for soprano, baritone, chorus, and orch. (1949); a cantata, *Karta serc (The Charter of Hearts,* 1952); *Renegade,* ballad for bass and orch. (1953); songs; 2 string quartets (1929, 1934); *Nocturne* for cello and piano (1945); *Orientale* for cello and piano (1945); Wind Quintet (1950); Flute Sonata (1953); *Air grave et air gai* for English horn and piano (1954); Piano Trio (1956); Piano Sonatina (1940); Piano Sonata (1949).

Szell, George, greatly distinguished Hungarian-American conductor; b. Budapest, June 7, 1897; d. Cleveland, July 30, 1970. His family moved to Vienna when he was a small child. He studied piano with Richard Robert and composition with Mandyczewski; also in Prague with J. B. Foerster. He played a Mozart piano concerto with the Vienna Symph. Orch. when he was 10 years old, and the orchestra also performed an overture of his composition. At the age of 17 he led the Berlin Philharmonic in an ambitious program, which included a symphonic work of his own. In 1915 he was engaged as an assistant conductor at the Royal Opera of Berlin; in 1917 he was conductor of the Strasbourg Municipal Theater. His next appointments as opera conductor were in Prague (1919), Düsseldorf (1922–24), and the State Opera House in Berlin (1924–29). From 1929 to 1937 he filled conducting engagements in Prague and Vienna. He made his U.S. debut as guest conductor of the St. Louis Symph. Orch. in 1931. In 1937 he was appointed conductor of the Scottish Orchestra in Glasgow; he was also a regular conductor with the Residentie Orkest in The Hague (1937–39). He then conducted in Australia. At the outbreak of war in Europe in 1939 he was in America, which was to become his adoptive country. His American conducting engagements included appearances with the Los Angeles Philharmonic. the National Broadcasting Symph. Orch., Chicago Symph., Detroit Symph. and the Boston Symph. In 1944 he was appointed conductor of the Metropolitan Opera House in New York, where he received the highest praise for his interpretation of Wagner's music dramas. He also conducted performances with the New York Philharmonic in 1944–45. In 1946 he was appointed conductor of the Cleveland Orchestra, a post which he held for 24 years. He was a stern disciplinarian, demanding the utmost exertions from his musicians to achieve tonal perfection, but he was also willing to labor tirelessly at his task. Under his guidance, the Cleveland Orchestra rose to the heights of symphonic excellence, taking its place in the foremost rank of American orchestras.

Szendrei, Aladár (in the U.S. he changed his name to **Alfred Sendrey**), Hungarian-American conductor and composer; b. Budapest, Feb. 29, 1884; d. Los Angeles, March 3, 1976. He studied with Hans Koessler at the Budapest Academy of Music (1901–1905); after serving as theater conductor in Germany he went to the U.S., where he conducted opera in Chicago (1911–12) and N.Y. (1913–14). He returned to Europe in 1914; served in the Austrian Army during World War I; after Armistice conducted opera in Leipzig (1918–24) and also symphony concerts there (1924–32). In 1933 he left Germany and went to Paris, where he conducted at the Radiodiffusion Française; he also taught conducting; Charles Munch took private lessons in conducting with him in Paris (1933–40); after the fall of Paris he emigrated to the U.S. and settled in Los Angeles. He was prof. of Jewish music at the Univ. of Judaism, Los Angeles (1962–73).
WORKS: *Der türkisenblaue Garten,* 1-act opera (Leipzig, Feb. 7, 1920); *Danse d'odalisque,* a ballet; several orchestral overtures and various pieces of chamber music.
WRITINGS: *Rundfunk und Musikpflege* (Leipzig, 1931); *Dirigierkunde* (Leipzig, 1932; 2nd ed., 1952); *Bibliography of Jewish Music* (N.Y., 1951); and in English, under the naturalized American name Sendrey, *David's Harp: A Popular History of the Music in Biblical Times* (N.Y., 1964); *Music in Ancient Israel* (1969); *The Music of the Jews in the Diaspora* (1969);

Music in the Social and Religious Life of Antiquity (1974).

Szendy, Arpád, Hungarian pianist and composer; b. Szarvas, Aug. 11, 1863; d. Budapest, Sept. 10, 1922. He studied at the Budapest Cons. and at the Academy of Music there; then became a student of Liszt (1881). In 1890 he was appointed to the faculty of the Academy of Music; enjoyed great esteem in Hungary as a piano teacher. He publ. numerous editions of piano classics; wrote an opera, *Mária* (with Béla Szabados; Budapest, Feb. 28, 1905); a string quartet; much piano music; songs.

Szenkar, Eugen, Hungarian conductor; b. Budapest, April 9, 1891; d. Düsseldorf, March 28, 1977. He studied music with his father, a prominent organist; later attended classes at the Academy of Music in Budapest. He began his career as an assistant choral conductor at the Budapest Opera; then was successively conductor of the German Opera in Prague (1911–13), the Popular Opera in Budapest (1913–15), the Mozarteum at Salzburg (1915–16), at Altenburg (1916–20), at the Frankfurt Opera (1920–23), at the Volksoper in Berlin (1923–24) and at the Cologne Opera (1924–33). With the advent of the Nazi regime, as a Jew he was forced to interrupt his activities, and went to Moscow where he remained from 1933 to 1937. In 1939 he went to Brazil and was conductor of the Brazilian Symph. Orch. in Rio de Janeiro; in 1941, in response to Brazilian social and governmental conventions, he accepted Brazilian citizenship. In 1950 he went back to Germany; from 1952 to 1960 was music director of the Düsseldorf Opera and of the Düsseldorf Symph. Orch.; also filled in guest engagements in Germany.

Szervánszky, Endre, Hungarian composer; b. Kistétény, Dec. 27, 1911; d. Budapest, June 25, 1977. Of a musical family, he learned to play the clarinet as a child; studied composition with Siklós and clarinet with F. Förster at the Liszt Academy of Music in Budapest (1923–28, 1931–36); taught at the National Cons. (1942–48) and after 1948 at the Liszt Academy. His music follows the modern Hungarian school of composition of Kodály and Bartók; he was the recipient of the Kossuth Prize in 1951 and 1955 and of the Erkel Prize in 1953 and 1954; in 1972 was awarded the title "Merited Artist of the Hungarian People's Republic."
WORKS: *Napkeleti mese (Oriental Tale),* dance play (1948–49); the cantatas *Három köröszteny játék (3 Christian Plays,* 1940), *Honvéd Cantata (Home Guard Cantata,* 1949), and *Tavasi szél (Spring Breeze,* 1950); a requiem *Sötét mennyország (Dark Heaven,* 1963); *Divertimento I* for strings (1939), *II* for small orch. (1942) and *III* for strings (1942–43); 2 suites for orch. (1944–45, 1946); Symph. No. 1 (1946–48); *Serenade* for strings (1947–48); *Rhapsody* for orch. (1950); *Serenade* for clarinet and orch. (1950–51); Flute Concerto (1953); *Variations* for orch. (1964); Clarinet Concerto (1965); 2 string quartets (1936–37, 1956–57); *20 Little Duets* for 2 violins (1942); Violin Sonata (1945); *25 Duos* for 2 violins (1946); Clarinet Quintet (1948); Trio for oboe, clarinet, and bassoon (1950); Trio for flute, violin, and viola (1951); Flute

Sonatina (1951); 2 wind quintets (1953, 1957); *5 Concert Etudes* for solo flute (1956); *Suite* for 2 flutes (1956); *2 Duos* for 2 flutes (1972); Piano Sonatina (1940); Sonatina for piano duet (1950); songs; choruses; incidental music to films and plays.

Szeryng, Henryk, distinguished Polish violinist; b. Zelazowa Wola, Sept. 22, 1918. He studied with Willy Hess and Carl Flesch in Berlin, and with Jacques Thibaud in Paris. In 1933 he went to America; in 1948 he was engaged as prof. at the Cons. of Mexico City, while continuing his career as a concert violinist in Europe amd America.

Szigeti, Joseph, great Hungarian violinist; b. Budapest, Sept. 5, 1892; d. Lucerne, Feb. 19, 1973. He studied violin with Hubay in Budapest; from 1906 to 1913 he lived in England; from 1917 to 1925 he gave master courses in violin at the Geneva Cons.; subsequently devoted himself mainly to concert appearances. In 1940 he went to the U.S., becoming an American citizen in 1951; eventually returned to Europe. Szigeti was particularly noted as an intellectual violinist; he may have lacked flashy virtuosity, but he was greatly admired by musicians. He was a champion of 20th-century music; played works of Stravinsky, Prokofiev, Béla Bartók, and Ernest Bloch. He published several semi-autobiographical books: *With Strings Attached* (N.Y., 1947); *A Violinist's Notebook* (London, 1965); *Szigeti on the Violin: Improvisations on a Violinist's Themes* (N.Y., 1969). He also annotated new editions of Beethoven's Violin Concerto and the Violin Concerto of Brahms.

BIBLIOGRAPHY: R. Gelatt, *Music Makers* (N.Y., 1953; pp. 135–48); Y. L. Soroker, *Joseph Szigeti* (Moscow, 1968).

Szokolay, Sándor, Hungarian composer; b. Kunágota, March 30, 1931. He studied at the Budapest Academy of Music with Szabó and Farkas (1950–57); worked in the music department of the Hungarian Radio (1957–61); in 1966 was appointed to the faculty of the Budapest Academy of Music. He was awarded the Erkel Prize in 1960 and 1965 and the Kossuth Prize in 1966.

WORKS: 3 operas: *Vérnász*, after García Lorca (*Blood Wedding*, 1962–64; Budapest, Oct. 30, 1964); *Hamlet*, after Shakespeare (1966–68; Budapest, Oct. 19, 1968); *Sámson* (1973; Budapest, Oct. 23, 1973); 3 ballets: *Orbán és az ördög* (*Urban and the Devil*, 1958), *Az iszonyat balladája* (*The Ballad of Horror*, 1960) and *Tetemrehívás* (*Ordeal of the Bier*, 1961–62; Pécs, 1962); the oratorios *A tüz marciusa* (*The Fire of March*, 1958) and *Isthar's Descent to Hell* (1960); *Cantata Nigra* (*Negro Cantata*, 1962); *Déploration*, requiem in memory of Poulenc (1964); *A zene hatalma* (*The Power of Music*), choral fantasy with orch. (1969); *Musza Dag*, oratorical incidental music for chorus and orch. (1969); *Concert Rondo* for piano and string orch. (1955); Violin Concerto (1956); Piano Concerto (1958); Trumpet Concerto (1969); Sonata for solo violin (1956); String Quartet (1973); Piano Sonatina (1955); songs.

Szöllösy, András, Hungarian composer; b. Szászváros, Transylvania, Feb. 27, 1921. He studied with Kodály and Viski at the Budapest Music Academy (1939–44); then took a course in composition with Goffredo Petrassi at the Accademia di Santa Cecilia in Rome (1947–48). In 1950 he was appointed to the faculty of his alma mater. His music draws upon all modern resources, often building up massive sound blocks.

WORKS: 2 ballets, *Oly korban éltem* (*Improvisations on the Fear*, 1963) and *Pantomime* (1965); *Nyugtalan ösz* (*Restless Autumn*), cantata for baritone and piano (1955); *Kolzsvári éjjel* (*Night at Kolozsvár*), elegy for voice and wind quintet (1955); Concerto for strings, brass, piano, and percussion (1957); *3 Pezzi* for flute and piano (1964); Concerto for 16 strings (1968); Concerto for chamber orch. (1970); *Transfigurazioni* for orch. (1972; Budapest, June 1, 1973); *Musica per orchestra* (1972; Vienna, Sept. 26, 1973); *Musica concertante* for small orch. (1972–73); *Preludio, Adagio e Fuga* for orch. (1973); songs; choruses. He published the books and collections; *Kodály's Art* (1943); *Selected Musical Writings of Béla Bartók* (1948); *Arthur Honegger* (1960); and *Collected Writings of Bartók*, I (1967).

Szönyi, Erzsébet (Elisabeth), Hungarian composer; b. Budapest, April 25, 1924. She studied piano and composition at the Budapest Academy of Music, graduating in 1947; then went to Paris, where she took courses at the Paris Cons. with Tony Aubin and Messiaen; also took private lessons in composition with Nadia Boulanger. Returning to Budapest, she joined the faculty of the Academy of Music. In 1959 she was awarded the Erkel Prize.

WORKS: 3 operas: *Dalma* (1952); a children's opera, *The Stubborn Princess* (1955); *Florentine Tragedy*, after Oscar Wilde (1957); 2 musical comedies: *The Hypochondriac* (1961) and *The Small Ragged One* (1962); 2 *Divertimentos* for orch. (1948, 1951); Organ Concerto (1958); *Musica Festiva* for orch. (1964); 2 piano sonatinas (1944, 1946); Piano Sonata (1953); choral works. She published *Methods of Musical Reading and Writing I, II & III* (Budapest, 1953; English edition, 1972) and *Kodály's Principles in Practice* (Budapest, 1973).

Szulc, Jósef Zygmunt, Polish operetta composer; b. Warsaw, April 4, 1875; d. Paris, April 10, 1956. He studied at the Warsaw Cons. with Noskowski; then took piano lessons in Paris with Moszkowski. He remained in Paris as a piano teacher; then turned to composition of light operas. His first work in this genre, *Flup* (Brussels, Dec. 19, 1913), was surprisingly successful and had numerous performances in Europe; he continued to produce operettas at regular intervals; the last one was *Pantoufle* (Paris, Feb. 24, 1945). He also wrote a ballet, *Une Nuit d'Ispahan* (Brussels, Nov. 19, 1909).

Szumowska, Antoinette, Polish pianist and teacher; b. Lublin, Feb. 22, 1868; d. Rumson, N.J., Aug. 18, 1938. She studied at the Warsaw Cons. with Michalowski, and later took lessons with Paderewski in Paris (1890–95). In 1895 she emigrated to the U.S., settling in Boston, where she taught at the New England Cons. for many years. In 1896 she married the cellist **Josef Adamowski,** and with him and his brother Timothée, violinist, formed the "Adamowski Trio," which presented numerous concerts in New England.

Szymanowska, Maria (*née* **Wolowska**), Polish pianist and composer; b. Warsaw, Dec. 14, 1789; d. St. Petersburg, July 24, 1831. She studied piano with local teachers in Warsaw, and began to play in public as a child. In 1810 she married a Polish landower, Theophilus Joseph Szymanowski (divorced in 1820). In 1822 she toured in Russia, and was appointed court pianist; in 1823, played in Germany; in 1824, in France; then in England, Holland, and Italy (1824–25), returning to Warsaw in 1826. In 1828 she settled in St. Petersburg as pianist and teacher, and remained there until her death (of cholera). She was admired by Goethe, whom she met in Germany; his poem *Aussöhnung (Trilogie der Leidenschaft)* alludes to her (cf. Goethe's correspondence with Zelter). She publ. 24 mazurkas and several character pieces for piano, of which *Le Murmure* became popular. Her piano studies were commended by Schumann.

BIBLIOGRAPHY: I. Boelza, *Maria Szymanowska* (Moscow, 1956).

Szymanowski, Karol, pre-eminent Polish composer; b. Timoshovka, Ukraine, Oct. 6, 1882; d. Lausanne, March 28, 1937. The son of a cultured landowner, he grew up in a musical environment. He began to play the piano and compose very early in life. His first teacher was Gustav Neuhaus in Elisavetgrad; in 1901 he went to Warsaw, where he studied with Noskowski. His first work, *9 Preludes* for piano, op. 1, was publ. in 1906 in Berlin by the Association of Young Polish Composers (later known as "Young Poland in Music"). Szymanowski lived in Berlin from 1906 to 1908, writing symphonic and other music, much influenced by Richard Strauss. He returned to Warsaw in 1909, and his 1st Symph. was performed there on March 26, 1909; however, he was dissatisfied with the score, and withdrew it from further performance. In 1911 he completed his 2nd Symph., which demonstrated a stylistic change from German dominance to Russian influences, paralleling the harmonic evolution of Scriabin; it was played for the first time in Warsaw, on April 7, 1911. From 1912 to 1914 Szymanowski lived in Vienna, where he wrote his 1-act opera, *Hagith;* the years of World War I (1914–18) he spent in Timoshovka, where he wrote his 3rd Symph.; appeared in concert with the violinist Paul Kochanski in Moscow and St. Petersburg, giving 1st performances of his violin works; it was for Kochanski that he composed his violin triptych, *Mythes (La Fontaine d'Aréthuse* in this cycle is one of his best-known compositions). About this time, his music underwent a new change in style, veering towards French Impressionism. During the Russian Revolution of 1917 the family estate at Timoshovka was ruined, and Szymanowski lost most of his possessions. He lived in Elisavetgrad from 1917 to 1919, where he continued to compose industriously, despite the turmoil of the civil war. Early in 1920 he settled in Warsaw; traveled to other Polish cities, and soon established his reputation as the most important modern composer of Poland. His in-

ternational renown also was considerable; his works were often performed in Europe, and figured at festivals of the International Society for Contemporary Music. He visited Paris, London, and New York (1921). In 1926 he was appointed director of the Warsaw Cons. and reorganized the system of teaching along more liberal lines. His *Stabat Mater* produced a profound impression (1928), and his ballet *Harnasie,* composed in 1926, and based on the life and music of the Tatra mountain dwellers, demonstrated his ability to treat national subjects in an original and highly effective manner. In 1932 he appeared as soloist in the first performance of his *Symphonie Concertante* for piano and orch. at Poznań, and repeated his performances in Paris, London, and Brussels. In April, 1936, greatly weakened in health by chronic tuberculosis, he attended the première of his ballet *Harnasie* at the Paris Opéra. Through successive influences, Szymanowski developed into a national composer whose music acquired universal significance. Of particular interest is his treatment of the mazurka; though he was a lifelong admirer of Chopin, he found a way to treat this dance form in a new and personal manner.

WORKS: *Hagith*, opera, (Warsaw, May 13, 1922); *Król Roger,* opera in 3 acts (1920–24; Warsaw, June 19, 1926); *Mandragora,* pantomime (Warsaw, June 15, 1920); ballet, *Harnasie* (1926; Prague, May 11, 1935). For orch.: *Concert Overture* (Warsaw, Feb. 6, 1906); 3 symphonies: No. 1 (Warsaw, March 26, 1909), No. 2 (Warsaw, April 7, 1911), No. 3, in one movement, subtitled *Song of the Night* for tenor, mixed chorus and orch. (London, Oct. 24, 1921, Albert Coates conducting); 1st Violin Concerto (Warsaw, 1922); 2nd Violin Concerto (Warsaw, 1922); 2nd Violin Concerto (Warsaw, Oct. 6, 1933); *Symphonie Concertante* for piano and orch. (Poznań, Oct. 9, 1932, composer soloist). Vocal works with orch.: *Stabat Mater* (1926; Warsaw, Jan. 11, 1929); *Veni Creator* (1929); *Litania* (1933). Chamber music: 2 string quartets (1917; 1927); Violin Sonata (1904); *Notturno e tarantella,* for violin and piano (1914); *Mythes,* 3 poems for violin and piano: *La Fontaine d'Aréthuse, Narcisse, Dryades et Pan* (1915). For piano: 3 piano sonatas; *Fantasy* (1905); *Métopes,* 3 poems: *L'Ile des sirènes, Calypso, Nausicaa* (1915); 12 études (1917); *Masques,* 3 poems: *Shéhérazade, Tantris le bouffon, Sérénade de Don Juan* (1917); 4 Polish dances (1926); 20 mazurkas (1924–26); etc. About 100 songs, including a set of 5 to words by James Joyce (1926), 8 Love Songs of Hafiz (also with orch.), 12 Kurpian Songs (1932). A complete edition of Szymanowski's works in 26 vols. was begun in Cracow in 1965 (vols. 1, 3, 5, 6, 7, 8, 9, 14, 15 and 23 appeared by 1973).

BIBLIOGRAPHY: Z. Jachimecki, "Karol Szymanowski," *Musical Quarterly* (Jan. 1922); A. Tansman, "Karol Szymanowski," *Revue Musicale* (May 1922); G. Pannain in *Modern Composers* (transl. from the Italian, N.Y., 1932); Z. Jachimecki, "Karol Szymanowski," *Slavonic and East European Review* (July 1938); Szymanowski issue of *Muzyka Polska* (Warsaw, 1937); S. Lobaczewska, *Karol Szymanowski* (Cracow, 1950; exhaustive biography and musical analysis); S. Golachowski, *Karol Szymanowski* (Cracow, 1956); J. M. Chomiński, *Studia nad twórczościa Karola Szymanowskiego* (Cracow, 1969).

T

Tabachnik, Michel, Swiss conductor and composer of Russian extraction; b. Geneva, Nov. 10, 1942. He studied at the Geneva Cons.; attended courses in modern music of Boulez, Pousseur and Stockhausen and the Darmstadt summer series. In 1972 he became principal conductor for the Gulbenkian Foundation in Lisbon; also conducted guest engagements in Europe. He composed *Mondes* for orch. (1972); *Movimenti,* electronic score (1973); *Les Imaginaires* for orch. (1974).

Tabourot, Jehan. See **Arbeau, Thoinot.**

Tacchinardi, Nicola, Italian tenor; b. Leghorn, Sept. 3, 1772; d. Florence, March 14, 1859. After singing on Italian stages (La Scala, Milan, 1805), he was engaged at the Théâtre des Italiens, Paris, 1811–14, with Crivelli; from 1822–31, "primo cantante" in the Grand Ducal chapel at Florence, also appearing repeatedly on the stage; then lived in Florence as a teacher, one of his pupils being his daughter, **Fanny Tacchinardi-Persiani.** He publ. vocalises and exercises; also *Dell'opera in musica sul teatro italiano e de' suoi difetti.* His son, **Guido Tacchinardi** (b. Florence, March 10, 1840; d. there, Dec. 6, 1917), was a composer and theorist; from 1891 director of the Istituto Musicale at Florence.

Tadolini, Giovanni, Italian composer; b. Bologna, 1785; d. there, Nov. 29, 1872. He studied composition with Mattei and singing with Babini; from 1811 to 1814 he was on the staff of the Théâtre des Italiens in Paris; then went to Italy, where he produced a succession of operas: *Le Bestie in uomini* (Venice, 1815); *La Principessa di Navarra* (Bologna, 1816); *Il Credulo deluso* (Rome, 1817); *Tamerlano* (Bologna, 1818); *Moctar* (Milan, 1824); *Mitridate* (Venice, 1826); *Almansor* (Trieste, 1827); from 1830 to 1839 he was again at his post at the Théâtre des Italiens. He also wrote many canzonets and romances; one of them, *Eco di Scozia,* was popular in his time.

Taffanel, (Claude-) Paul, French flutist and conductor; b. Bordeaux, Sept. 16, 1844; d. Paris, Nov. 22, 1908. He was a pupil of Dorus (flute) and Reber (composition). From 1864 to 1890 he was flutist in the Paris Opéra orch.; 1867–90, flutist of the Cons. concerts, which he conducted 1890–1903; from 1892 till his death he was one of the "chefs d'orchestre" at the Opéra; in 1893 succeeded Altès as prof. of flute-playing at the Cons. In 1879 he founded the "Société des quintettes pour instruments à vent." With Gaubert he wrote *Méthode complète de flûte.*

Tag, Christian Gotthilf, German composer; b. Bayerfeld, Saxony, April 2, 1735; d. Niederzwonitz, near Zwickau, June 19, 1811. From 1749 to 1755 he studied at the Kreuzschule in Dresden; in 1755–1808 was cantor at Hohenstein.
WORKS: 6 Chorale Preludes (1783); 12 Preludes and a Symphony for organ (1795); songs (1783, 1785, 1793, 1798); 70 variations for piano on an Andantino (1785); *Der Glaube,* melody with organ (1793); *Urians Reise um die Welt* and *Urians Nachricht von der Auf-*

klärung (1797); *Naumann, ein Todtenopfer* (1803; voice with piano); *Melodie zum Vaterunser und den Einsetzungsworten* (1803; with organ); *Wörlitz,* an ode (1803; voice with piano); many sacred and instrumental works are in manuscript.
BIBLIOGRAPHY: J. F. Rochlitz, *Für Freunde der Tonkunst,* vol. III (1830); H. J. Vieweg, *Christian Gotthilf Tag* (Leipzig, 1933).

Tagliapietra, Gino, Italian pianist and composer; b. (of Italian parentage) Ljubljana, May 30, 1887; d. Venice, Aug. 8, 1954. He studied piano with Julius Epstein in Vienna and with Busoni in Berlin; in 1906 was appointed to the faculty of the Liceo Benedetto Marcello in Venice. His compositions include a ballet, *La Bella dormente nel bosco* (Venice, March 11, 1926); a piano concerto; numerous studies for piano. He edited for Ricordi an important anthology of keyboard music from Willaert to modern times. *Antologia di musica antica e moderna* (1931–32; 18 vols., containing 519 works by 157 composers).

Tagliapietra, Giovanni, Italian baritone; b. Venice, Dec. 24, 1846; d. New York, April 11, 1921. He studied naval architecture and was a graduate from the Univ. of Padua. After a study of singing with Giovanni Corsi, he appeared in various Italian opera houses; made a tour of South America; in 1874 was engaged as member of Max Strakosch's company and sang in the U.S. In 1876 he married the famous pianist **Teresa Carreño,** but was divorced; his brother Arturo was married to her in 1902.

Tagliavini, Ferruccio, prominent Italian tenor; b. Reggio, Aug. 14, 1913. After studying at the Cons. of Parma, he won 1st prize for singing at the May Festival in Florence (1938); made his opera debut there as Rodolfo in *La Bohème* (1939); later sang at La Scala, Milan, and other opera houses in Italy; in 1946 toured South America; on Jan. 10, 1947, made a very successful 1st appearance, as Rodolfo, at the Metropolitan Opera, N.Y.; has also given recitals in the major American cities; subsequently traveled widely in both hemispheres. In 1941 he married the soprano **Pia Tassinari.**
BIBLIOGRAPHY: C. Tedeschi, *Ferruccio Tagliavini* (Rome, 1942).

Tagore, Sir Surindro Mohun (Rajah Saurindramohana Thakura), Hindu musicologist; b. Calcutta, 1840; d. there, June 28, 1914. At the age of 17 he began to study Hindu music under Luchmi Prasad and Kshetra Mohun Gosvami, and European music under a German teacher in Calcutta; founded and endowed from his personal fortune the Bengal Music Soc. (1871) and the Bengal Academy of Music (1881), continuing to preside over both until his death. A connoisseur of Eastern instrumentation, he was at various times commissioned by the principal museums of Europe to procure for them instruments of Asiatic nations; perhaps the finest collection is that in the Metropolitan Museum of Art in N.Y. He wrote nearly 60 books on an amazing variety of subjects; those concerning music (publ. in Calcutta, in the Bengali language, and some in English) include the following: *Yantra Kosha, or A Treasury of the Musical Instruments of Ancient and Modern India* (1875); *Hindu Music, from Various Authors* (1875; 2nd ed., in 2 vols., 1882); *Short Notices of Hindu Musical Instruments* (1877); *6 Principal Ragas* (1877); *The 8 Principal Ragas of the Hindus* (1880); *The Five Principal Musicians of the Hindus, or A Brief Exposition of the Essential Elements of Hindu Music* (1881); *The Musical Scales of the Hindus with Remarks on the Applicability of Harmony to Hindu Music* (1884); *The 22 Musical Srutis of the Hindus* (1886); *Universal History of Music* (1896).

BIBLIOGRAPHY: F. Chrysander, "Über Tagores Hindu Music," *Allgemeine musikalische Zeitung* (1879; p. 540ff.); F. Chrysander, "Über altindische Opfermusik," *Vierteljahrsschrift für Musikwissenschaft* (1885; p. 21ff.).

Tailleferre, Germaine, French composer; b. Pau-St.-Maur, near Paris, April 19, 1892. She studied at the Paris Cons., and later took lessons with Ravel; associated herself with the vanguard of modern musicians. She obtained wide recognition as the only feminine member of the group known as "Les Six" (Honegger, Milhaud, Poulenc, Auric, and Durey being the other members). Her style of composition is simple and unaffected; some of her songs and piano pieces possess a certain poetic charm.

WORKS: *Image,* for piano, flute, clarinet, string quartet, and celesta (1918); String Quartet (1919); 2 violin sonatas (1921; 1951); *Jeux de plein air,* for 2 pianos (1922; also for orch.); Piano Concerto (1924); Concertino for harp and orch. (Boston Symph. Orch., Cambridge, Mass., March 3, 1927); ballet, *Le Marchand d'oiseaux* (Paris, May 25, 1923); *Chansons françaises,* for voice and instruments (Liège Festival of the International Society for Contemporary Music, Sept. 2, 1930); *Ouverture,* for orch. (Paris, Dec. 25, 1932); Concerto for 2 pianos, voice, and orch. (Paris, May 3, 1934); *Pastorale,* for flute and piano (1942); ballet, *Paris-Magie* (Paris, June 3, 1949); opera, *Il était un petit navire* (Paris, March 9, 1951); songs; piano pieces.

Tajčević, Marko, Serbian composer; b. Osijek, Jan. 29, 1900. He studied in Zagreb, Prague and Vienna; in 1945 was appointed prof. at the Belgrade Music Academy. He is primarily a folklore composer and is at his best in choral works derived from regional folksongs. His *7 Balkan Dances* for piano are brilliant stylizations of Serbian melorhythms.

Takács, Jenö, Hungarian composer; b. Siegendorf, Sept. 25, 1902. He studied composition with Joseph Marx and Hans Gál at the Vienna Cons.; in 1927 he was engaged as teacher at the Cons. of Cairo, Egypt; then traveled to Manila, Philippine Islands, returning to Cairo in 1935. During his travels, he collected much material on Oriental music; his research in this field is reflected in some of his own works. From 1940 to 1942 he taught at the Music School at Szombathely, Hungary; then was director of the Cons. of Pécs, Hungary (1942–47) and later at the Cons. of Lausanne and Geneva (1949–51); in 1952 he was engaged as prof. of

piano at the Cincinnati Cons.; retired in 1971 and went back to his birthplace, Siegendorf. In 1962 he was awarded the State Prize of Austria. Reflecting his background of travel and residence in many different countries, his music contains elements of Hungarian, Oriental, American and cosmopolitan idioms.

WORKS: the ballet *The Nile Legend* (Budapest, May 8, 1940); *Philippine Suite,* for orch. (1934); *Antiqua Hungarica,* for orch. (1941); 2 piano concertos (1932; 1937); *Partita* for guitar and orch. (1950); *Gumbry,* Oriental rhapsody for violin and piano (1930); Sonata for trombone and piano (1957); *Homage to Pan* for 4 pianos (1968); *Essays in Sound* for clarinet (1968); *2 Fantastics* for alto saxophone (1969); *Musica reservata* for double bass (1970); *Tagebuch-Fragmente* for 2 pianos (1973). He published several short essays on the music of the countries in which he lived, among them *Music of the Philippines* (Manila, 1933), *Tune and Chant in Egypt* (Johannesburg, South Africa, 1935).

Takagi, Tôroku, Japanese composer and pianist; b. Okayama, July 7, 1904. He graduated from the Tokyo Academy of Music in 1928; later studied in Paris. His opera *Shunko-Den* was produced in Tokyo, Nov. 20, 1948. His other works include a ballet, *Crane* (1939); *Korean Dance,* suite for orch. (1940); 2 piano concertos (1942, 1944); Cello Concerto (1943); *Japanese Dance Music* for 2 pianos (1941, 1943); songs.

Takahashi, Yuji, Japanese composer and pianist; b. Tokyo, Sept. 21, 1938. He studied composition with Shibata and Ogura at the Toho School of Music in Tokyo (1954–58); then went to Berlin and was trained in electronics as a student of Xenakis; also studied computer music in N.Y. (1966–68) and was a member of the Center for Creative and Performing Arts at the State Univ. of N.Y. in Buffalo (1968–69). In his own music he follows the stochastic procedures as practiced by Xenakis. He also has acquired a considerable renown as pianist in programs of avant-garde music.

WORKS: *Phonogène* for 2 instruments and tape (1962); *Chromamorphe I* for violin, double bass, flute, trumpet, horn, trombone, and vibraphone (1963); *Chromamorphe II* for piano (1964); *Six Stoicheia (Elements in Succession)* for 4 violins (1965); *Bridges I* for electric harpsichord or piano, amplified cello, bass drum, and castenets (1967); *Bridges II* for 2 oboes, 2 clarinets, 2 trumpets, and 3 violas (1968); *Rosace I* for amplified violin (1967); *Rosace II* for piano (1967); *Operation Euler* for 2 or 3 oboes (1967); *Metathèse* for piano (1968); *Prajna Paramita* for 4 voices, each in one of four instrumental ensembles (1969); *Orphika* for orch. (Tokyo, May 28, 1969); *Yé Guèn* for tape (1969); *Nikité* for oboe, clarinet, trumpet, trombone, cello, and double bass (1971); *Kagahi* for piano and 30 instruments (Ojai, California, May 30, 1971); *Michi-Yuki* for chorus, 2 percussionists and electric cello (1971); *Corona Borealis* for piccolo, oboe, clarinet, bassoon, and horn (1971); *Tadori* for tape (1972).

Takata, Saburô, Japanese composer; b. Nagoya, Dec. 18, 1913. He studied composition with Klaus Pringsheim at the Tokyo Academy of Music; in 1953 was appointed prof. at the Kunitachi Music College in Tokyo.

WORKS: opera, *The Dark-Blue Wolf* (1970–72; Tokyo, Oct. 15, 1972); a cantata, *Wordless Tears*, for narrator, soprano, baritone, chorus, and orch. (Tokyo, March 27, 1964); *Ballade Based on a Folk Song from Yamagata (Fantasy and Fugue)* for orch. (Tokyo, Nov. 15, 1941; revised 1965); *Seasons*, suite for orch. (1942); *Ballade* for violin and orch. (1943; Tokyo, Jan. 13, 1945); *The New Earth and Man* for orch. (1944); 2 *Rhapsodies* for orch. (both 1945); Octet for clarinet, bassoon, horn, trumpet, and string quartet (1939); *Prelude and Fugue* for string quartet (1940); Violin Sonata (1948–49); Cello Sonatina (1949–50); *Suite* for flute, oboe, 2 clarinets and bassoon (1951); *Marionette*, suite for string quartet (1954); *Fantasy* for string quartet (1968); 2 piano sonatas (1935, 1941); 5 *Preludes* for piano (1947); organ pieces; choruses; songs.

Takata, Shin-ichi, Japanese composer; b. Tokyo, Jan. 24, 1920. He studied at the Tokyo Academy of Music; has written a symph. poem, *In Praise of Peace* (Tokyo, Nov. 25, 1948), of which a full score has been published. The style of this work reveals the influence of Richard Strauss.

Takemitsu, Toru, prominent Japanese composer; b. Tokyo, Oct. 8, 1930. He studied composition privately with Yasuji Kiyose. In 1951, jointly with Yuasa and others, he organized in Tokyo the avant-garde group "Experimental Laboratory," with the aim of creating new music that would combine traditional Japanese modalities with modernistic procedures. His own music exemplifies with uncanny penetration this declaration of intent; his orchestral and other compositions enjoy frequent performances in Japan, the U.S. and in Europe.

WORKS: *Requiem* for string orch. (1957; Tokyo, June 20, 1958); *Tableau noir* for narrator and orch. (1958); *Solitude Sonore* for orch. (1958); *Ki No Kyoku (Music for Trees)* for orch. (1961); *Coral Island* for soprano and orch. (1962); *Arc*, Part I (1963, in 3 movements) and Part II (1964–66, in 3 movements) for piano and orch.; *Arc* for strings (1963; from the third movement of *Arc*, Part I); *Textures* for piano and orch. (1964; the first movement of *Arc*, Part II); *The Dorian Horizon* for 17 string instruments (1966); *November Steps* for biwa, shakuhachi and orch. (N.Y. Philharmonic, Nov. 9, 1967); *Green (November Steps II)* for orch. (1967; Tokyo, Nov. 3, 1967); *Asterism* for piano and orch. (1968; Toronto, Jan. 14, 1969); *Crossing* for 12 female voices, guitar, harp, piano, vibraphone, and 2 orch. (1969); *Eucalypts I* for flute, oboe, harp, and strings (Tokyo, Nov. 16, 1970); *Winter* for orch. (Paris, Oct. 29, 1971); *Corona* for 22 strings (1971); *Gemeaux* for oboe, trombone and 2 orch. with separate conductors (1971–72); *Autumn* for biwa, shakuhachi, and orch. (1973); *Gitimalay (Bouquet of Songs)* for marimba and orch. (1975); *Quatrain* for violin, cello, clarinet, piano, and orch. (1975; Tokyo, Sept. 1, 1975); *A Flock Descends into the Pentagonal Garden* for orch. (San Francisco, Nov. 30, 1977); *Son Calligraphie I-III* for double string quartet (1958, 1958, 1963); *Mask* for 2 flutes (1959); *Landscape* for string

quartet (1960); *Ring* for flute, terz-guitar, and lute (1961); *Sacrifice* for flute, lute, and vibraphone (1962); *Valeria* for violin, cello, guitar, electric organ, and 2 obbligato piccolos (1962); *Corona* for strings (1962); *Cross Talk* for 2 bandoneons and tape (1968); *Stanza I* for piano, guitar, harp, vibraphone, and female voice (1968), *II* for solo harp (1971) and *III* for solo oboe, or oboe and shō (1971); *Eucalypts II* for flute, oboe, and harp (1970); *Seasons* in versions for 1 or 4 percussionists (1970); *Voice* for solo flute (1971); *Munari by Munari* for percussion (1972); *Distance* for solo oboe, or oboe and shō (1972); *Voyage* for 3 biwas (1973); *Folios* for solo guitar (1974); *Garden Rain* for 4 trumpets, 3 trombones, bass trombone, tuba, and bassoon, separated into 2 groups (1974); *Waves* for solo clarinet, horn, 2 trumpets, and percussion (1976); *Bryce* for flute, 2 harps, marimba, and percussion (1976); the piano works, 2 *Lentos* (1950), *Undisturbed Rests* (1952–59), *Piano Distance* (1961), *Corona* for pianist(s) (1962), and *For Away* (1973); the tape pieces, *Static Relief* (1955), *Vocalism A-1* (1956), *Water Music* (1960), and *Toward* (1970); several notable film scores, including those for *Hara-Kiri* (1962), *Woman of the Dunes* (1964), and *Kwaidan* (1964).

Taktakishvili, Otar, Soviet Georgian composer; b. Tiflis, July 27, 1924. He studied at the Tiflis Cons., graduating in 1947; in 1949 was appointed prof. of composition theory. His music is imbued with the characteristic melorhythms of the Caucasus; he has a natural knack for instrumental color.

WORKS: opera, *Mindia* (Tbilisi, July 23, 1961); 2 symphonies (1949, 1953); 3 Overtures (1950; 1951; 1955); symph. poems *Samgori* (1950) and *Mtsyri* (1956); Cello Concerto (1947); Piano Concerto (his most successful work, written in a virtuoso manner; Tbilisi, Nov. 15, 1951); Trumpet Concerto (1954); Piano Trio (1947); several cantatas and choruses; solo songs; many piano pieces.

BIBLIOGRAPHY: L. Poliakova, *Otar Taktakishvili* (Moscow, 1956).

Taktakishvili, Shalva, Soviet Georgian composer; b. Kvemo-Khviti, Aug. 27, 1900; d. Tbilisi, July 18, 1965. He studied at the Cons. of Tbilisi; then taught music theory at the Batum Music School, of which he was a co-founder; then served as conductor at the Tbilisi Radio, and from 1952 to the time of his death, conducted the Georgian State Orch.

WORKS: the operas *Sunrise* (Tbilisi, 1926) and *The Delegate* (Tbilisi, 1939); 2 Overtures (1944, 1949); a symph. poem *The Year 1905* (1931); Cello Concerto (1932); 2 string quartets (1930, 1933), Violin Sonata (1952); numerous piano pieces, choruses and songs.

BIBLIOGRAPHY: P. V. Hukua, *Shalva Taktakishvili* (Tbilisi, 1962).

Taku, Koji, Japanese composer; b. Sakai-City (Osaka), March 10, 1904. He studied piano with Alfred Cortot and composition with Nadia Boulanger at the École Normale de Musique in Paris; upon return to Japan he taught at the Tokyo Music Academy. He composed 2 ballets, *White Flower* (1942) and *Journey* (1954); String Quartet (1933); Piano Sonata (1942); *Variations on a Theme of Poulenc* for piano (1952);

Suite for harpsichord and chamber ensemble (1953); several albums of piano pieces for children.

Tal (real name **Gruenthal**), **Joseph,** eminent Israeli composer; b. Pinne, near Posen, German Poland, Sept. 18, 1910. He studied composition in Berlin with Max Trapp and Heinz Tiessen; after the advent of the Nazi regime, he emigrated to Palestine; in 1937 became prof. of piano and composition at the Academy of Music in Jerusalem, and was its director until 1953. In 1965 he was appointed director of the Institute for Electronic Music at the Hebrew Univ. of Jerusalem. In 1969 he was named member of the Academy of the Arts in West Berlin. His early works follow the European tradition of enlightened modernism, with some application of serial procedures; then he became interested in the enhancement of instrumental resources by electronics.

WORKS: the operas *Amnon and Tamar* (1961) and *Ashmedai* (Hamburg, Nov. 13, 1971; his most important work); the ballets with electronic sound, *Ranges of Energy* (Breukelen, near Utrecht, 1963), *From the Depth of the Soul* (1964), and *Variations* (1970); 2 symphonies (1953, 1960); *Festive Vision* for orch. (1959); 3 pianos concertos (1944, 1953, 1956); Viola Concerto (1954); 3 concertos for piano and electronic instruments (1962, 1964, 1970); Concerto for harpsichord and orch. (1964); Concerto for harp and orch. (1971); Concerto for cello and string orch. (1961); Double Concerto for violin cello and string orch. (1970); Woodwind Quintet (1966); 2 string quartets (1959, 1964); pieces for violin, oboe, and viola with piano; electronic music: *I Called Upon the Lord in Distress* (1971); *The Death of Moses* for soloists, chorus, orch. and electronic instruments (1967); choreographic poem *Exodus* for baritone and orch. (1946); *Succoth Cantata* for solo voice, chorus and orch. (1955).

Talbot, Howard (real name **Munkittrick**), English operetta composer; b. Yonkers, N.Y., March 9, 1865; d. London, Sept. 12, 1928. He was taken to England at the age of 4, and studied music at the Royal College of Music under Parry, Bridge, and Gladstone; from 1900, was active as conductor in various London theaters. He was a prolific composer of light operas, all produced in London; his greatest success was *A Chinese Honeymoon* (1899); his last work was *The Daughter of the Gods* (posthumous, 1929). Other operettas: *Monte Carlo* (1896); *Three Little Maids* (1902); *The Blue Moon* (1905); *The White Chrysanthemum* (1905); *The Girl Behind the Counter* (1906); *The Three Kisses* (1907); *The Belle of Brittany* (1908); *The Arcadians* (1909); *The Pearl Girl* (1913); *A Narrow Squeak* (1913); *A Mixed Grill* (1914); *A Lucky Miss* (1914); *The Light Blues* (1915); etc.

Talich, Václav, Czech conductor; b. Kroměříž, May 28, 1883; d. Beroun, March 16, 1961. He received his early musical training from his father Jan Talich; then studied violin with Ševčík at the Prague Cons. (1897–1903). He was concertmaster of the Odessa Orch. in Russia, and then taught violin in Tiflis. He returned to Prague in 1907; conducted the Philharmonic Orch. of Ljubljana; in 1910 went to Leipzig where he took lessons in composition with Max Reger and Hans Sitt and in conducting with Arthur Nikisch. He was then opera conductor at Pilsen (1912–15) and principal conductor of the Prague Philharmonic (1919–35), which he brought to a high degree of excellence; toured with it in Italy, Germany, France and England; subsequently was conductor of the National Opera in Prague (1935–45); then moved to Bratislava, where he conducted the Slovak Philharmonic Orch. (1949–52); conducted the Prague Philharmonic again (1952–54); then retired from concert appearances. He also taught conducting in Prague and Bratislava; among his pupils were Ančerl, I. Krejčí and others.

Talley, Marion, American soprano; b. Nevada, Missouri, Dec. 20, 1907. She was educated in Kansas City; sang in church there, and at the age of 15 appeared in a local performance of *Mignon,* producing such a favorable impression that the community raised funds to send her to Italy for serious study. Returning to the U.S., she made her debut at the Metropolitan Opera, N.Y. on Feb. 17, 1926 as Gilda in *Rigoletto,* when she was barely 18; since an appearance of a young American singer at the Metropolitan Opera was at the time a rarity, the occasion generated sensational publicity. But she remained at the Metropolitan Opera for only a year, so that the extravagant hopes held for her as a native talent were not fulfilled. She subsequently had a brief career as a singer on the radio; then went to California and settled in Beverly Hills.

Tallis (or **Tallys, Talys**), **Thomas,** English organist and composer; b. c.1505; d. Greenwich, Nov. 23, 1585. He was "joculator organorum" at the Dover Priory (1532), at St. Mary-at-Hill in London (1537) and at the Augustine Abbey Holy Cross in Waltham, Essex (until 1540); served as Gentleman of the Chapel Royal during the reigns of Henry VIII, Edward VI, Mary, and Elizabeth, and joint organist with Byrd. With the latter, he obtained in 1575 letters patent for the exclusive privilege of printing music and ruled music paper, the first work issued by them being 34 *Cantiones quae ab argumento sacrae vocantur, 5 et 6 partium,* in 1575 (16 motets by Tallis and 18 by Byrd). Tallis's most famous work is *Spem in alium non habui,* a "song of 40 parts" for eight 5-part choirs (specimen page in first ed. of *Grove's Dictionary,* vol. III, p. 274). A composer of great contrapuntal skill, he was among the first to set English words to music for the rites of the Church of England. Surviving are 2 Masses, 2 Magnificats, 2 Lamentations, 52 motets and other pieces with Latin text, 18 English anthems, 3 sets of Psalms, etc., as well as some keyboard music. In Barnard's *First Book of Selected Church Music* (1641) is a First Service, and a Short Service (*a* 4), Preces, Responses, etc., often republished (by Rimbault, Novello, Jebb, Davison & Apel, etc.); J. Day's *Morning and Evening Prayer* (1560), Boyce's *Cathedral Music,* and the histories by Hawkins and Burney contain specimens of his music. Rimbault republ. the *Order of Daily Service, with the Musical Notation.* R. Terry ed. a Mass *a* 4 in 1908 (Breitkopf & Härtel), and most of Tallis's church music is in vol. VI of *Tudor Church Music* (1928). There are many works in MS at Oxford, Cambridge, and in the British Library.

BIBLIOGRAPHY: H. B. Collins, "T. T.," *Music & Letters* (1929); B. Schofield, "The Manuscripts of T.'s Forty-Part Motet," *Musical Quarterly* (April 1951); D. Stevens, "The Keyboard Music of T. T.," *Musical Times* (July 1952); R. Illing, *T.'s Psalm Tunes* (Adelaide, 1968); P. Doe, *Tallis* (2nd ed., London, 1976).

Talma, Louise, American composer; b. Arcachon, France, Oct. 31, 1906. She studied at N.Y. Univ. (B.M.) and at Columbia Univ. (M.A.); took piano lessons with Isidor Philipp and composition with Nadia Boulanger at the Fontainebleau School of Music, France. In 1946 she received a Guggenheim Fellowship; joined the faculty at Hunter College, N.Y. In her music she adopts a strongly contrapuntal neo-Baroque style.

WORKS: *Toccata,* for orch. (1944); *Introduction and Rondo Giocoso* (1946); *Three Madrigals* for women's voices and string quartet (1929); *La Belle Dame Sans Merci,* for baritone solo (1929); *Terre de France,* a song cycle (1925); *Five Sonnets from the Portuguese,* song cycle (1934); *Piano Sonata* (1943); *The Divine Flame,* oratorio (1948); *Let's Touch the Sky,* cycle of poems, after e. e. cummings, for chorus and woodwind instruments (1952); *The Alcestiad,* opera (Frankfurt, Germany, March 1, 1962); *All the Days of My Life* for tenor, clarinet, cello, piano, and percussion (1965); *Voices of Peace* for chorus and strings (1973); *Summer Sounds* for clarinet and string quartet (1973); *Textures* for piano (1978); other piano pieces.

BIBLIOGRAPHY: Madeleine Goss, *Modern Music-Makers* (N.Y., 1952).

Taltabull, Cristòfor, Catalan composer and pedagogue; b. Barcelona, July 28, 1888; d. there May 1, 1964. He studied piano with Granados and composition with Felipe Pedrell. In 1908 he went to Germany, where he took lessons with Max Reger. In 1912 he went to Paris, where he engaged in various occupations, as an accompanist to singers, as proofreader for the publisher Durand, as a music copyist; he also composed popular songs for the vaudeville and wrote film music. After the outbreak of the Second World War in 1939, he returned to Barcelona, where he became a teacher of composition. Many important Spanish composers of the younger generation were his pupils. As a composer, he was particularly successful in songs to French and Catalan texts. His style of composition is Impressionistic, mainly derived from Debussy, and he had a delicate sense of color and rhythm; thematically, most of his music retains Spanish, or Catalan, melorhythmic characteristics.

Tamagno, Francesco, famous Italian tenor; b. Turin, Dec. 28, 1850; d. Varese, near Turin, Aug. 31, 1905. He was at first apprenticed to a baker, and later to a locksmith; entered the Turin Cons. as a pupil of Pedrotti, and in 1873 made his debut as 2nd tenor at the Teatro Regio there, his powerful voice immediately attracting attention. Following his appearance in *Un Ballo in maschera* at Palermo on Jan. 17, 1874, his success was rapid. In 1876–77 he sang at the Liceo of Barcelona, and from 1877 at La Scala, Milan, where in 1887 he created the role of Otello in Verdi's opera. He sang at the Metropolitan Opera House, N.Y., during the season 1894–95 (debut, Nov. 21, 1894, as Arnold in Rossini's *Guillaume Tell*). Other engagements included South America, Lisbon, Madrid, Paris, and London. In 1902, having made a fortune, he retired from the stage.

BIBLIOGRAPHY: E. de Amicis, *Francesco Tamagno* (Palermo, 1902); M. Corsi, *Tamagno* (Milan, 1937); E. Gara, "Francesco Tamagno," *La Scala* (Jan. 1954).

Tamberg, Eino, Estonian composer; b. Tallinn, May 27, 1930. He studied composition with E. Kapp at the Cons. in Tallinn (1950–53); served as a sound engineer at the Estonian Radio; in 1967 joined the staff of the Cons. of Tallinn.

WORKS: operas, *Raudne kodu* (*The House of Iron,* Tallinn, July 15, 1965), glorifying the revolutionary spirit of Estonian proletarian patriots; *Cyrano de Bergerac* (1974); 2 ballets: *Poiss ja liblik* (*The Boy and the Butterfly,* 1963) and *Joanna tentata* (1970); 2 oratorios: *Rahva vabaduse eest* (*For the Freedom of the People,* 1953) and *Kuupaiste-oratorium* (*Moonlight Oratorio,* 1962); *Symphonic Suite* (1955); *Concerto Grosso* for orch. (1956); *Symphonic Dances* (1957); *Ballet-Symphony* (1959); *Oedipus Rex,* suite for chorus and orch. (1959); *Toccata* for orch. (1967); *Trumpet Concerto* (1972); a cantata, *Fanfare des Sièges* (1975); *String Quartet* (1958); *Rondo* for violin and piano (1961); *Song for Africa* for male chorus and percussion (1961); *Music* for solo oboe (1970); *Wind Quintet* (1976); choruses; songs.

Tamberlik, Enrico, celebrated Italian tenor; b. Rome, March 16, 1820; d. Paris, March 13, 1889. He studied singing with Zirilli in Rome and with Guglielmi in Naples, where he made his stage debut in 1840. On April 4, 1850, he made his 1st London appearance, as Masaniello in Auber's *La Muette de Portici,* at the Royal Italian Opera, Covent Garden, and sang annually in London until 1864, with the exception of 1857, when he undertook an extensive European tour, including Spain and Russia. In 1860 he settled in Paris, and lived there most of his life. Verdi admired him, and wrote the part of Don Alvaro in *La Forza del destino* for him; Tamberlik sang in its world première at St. Petersburg, Russia, on Oct. 30, 1862, and this role became one of his most famous interpretations. He appeared at the Academy of Music, N.Y., on Sept. 18, 1873, but his American season was a brief one. He was famous for his rich high notes, and his ability to sustain the high C was legendary.

BIBLIOGRAPHY: H. Brody, "La Carrière d'un ténor italien," *Revue Musicale* (April 15, 1904, *et seq.*).

Tamburini, Antonio, Italian baritone; b. Faenza, March 28, 1800; d. Nice, Nov. 9, 1876. First learned to play the horn as a pupil of his father; then studied singing with A. Rossi and B. Asioli; debut at Cento in 1818; thereafter sang on the chief stages of Italy, being engaged by Barbaja from 1824–32. During 1832–41 he sang at the Théâtre Italien, Paris, as part of a brilliant company that included Grisi, Persiani, Viardot, Rubini, and Lablache, appearing in London in the alternate seasons; after a short stay in Italy, he remained for ten years in Russia. In 1855 he retired to his estate at Sèvres, near Paris. His greatest triumph was in Bellini's *La Straniera,* in which he created a frenzy of enthusiasm by his singing of the aria *Meco tu vieni, o misera.* In 1822 he married the singer **Marietta Goja.**

BIBLIOGRAPHY: J. de Biez, *Tamburini et la musique italienne* (Paris, 1877); H. Gelli-Ferraris, *Antonio Tamburini nel ricordo d'una nipote* (Livorno, 1934).

Tamkin, David, American composer; b. Chernigov, Russia, Aug. 28, 1906; d. Los Angeles, June 21, 1975. He was taken to the U.S. as an infant; the family settled in Portland, Oregon, where he studied violin with Henry Bettman, a pupil of Ysaÿe; took lessons in composition with Ernest Bloch. In 1937 he settled in Los Angeles; from 1945 to 1966 he was principal composer at Universal Pictures in Hollywood. His music is deeply permeated with the melodic and rhythmic elements of the Hassidic Jewish cantillation. His magnum opus is the opera *The Dybbuk* to a libretto by his brother Alex Tamkin from S. Ansky's Jewish classic of that title; he composed the work in 1928–31 but it was not produced until Oct. 4, 1951, by the N.Y. City Opera. In 1962 he wrote another opera, *The Blue Plum Tree of Esau* (also to his brother's libretto); among his other works are 2 string quartets, a woodwind sextet, and several choruses.

Tanaka, Toshimitsu, Japanese composer; b. Aomori, July 17, 1930. He studied music at the Kunitani Music College in Tokyo; after graduation in 1951, he joined its staff. His music is based on the melorhythmic patterns of Japanese folksongs.

WORKS: 2 dance suites: *Tamanna* for 2 pianos and percussion (1967) and *Magic Festival in the Mountain Crease* for chorus, ryūteki and various types of wadaiko (1968); *Epic "Wolf Boy" for Shamisen* for solo soprano, shamisen, shakuhachi, wadaiko, and strings (Tokyo, Nov. 27, 1968); a requiem, *The Grave,* for chorus and orch. (Radio Tokyo, Nov. 5, 1972); Violin Sonata (1957); String Quartet (1962); *Suite* for marimba, 7 strings and 2 percussionists (1971); choruses; songs.

Tanev, Alexander, Hungarian-born Bulgarian composer; b. Budapest, Oct. 23, 1928. He studied composition with Veselin Stoyanov at the Bulgarian State Cons. in Sofia, graduating in 1957. His works include *Sinfonietta* (1959); *Youth Concerto* for violin and string orch. (1969); *Rondo Scherzando* for trombone and orch. (1971); Concerto for winds and percussion (1972); *Builder's Music* for 2 pianos and percussion, or orch. (1974); choruses; songs.

Taneyev, Alexander, Russian composer, b. St. Petersburg, Jan. 17, 1850; d. there, Feb. 7, 1918; a distant relative of **Sergei Taneyev.** He studied composition with F. Reichel in Dresden; upon his return to St. Petersburg, he took lessons with Rimsky-Korsakov. Music was his avocation; he followed a government career, advancing to the post of head of the Imperial Chancellery. The style of his music is Romantic, lapsing into sentimentalism; the main influence is that of Tchaikovsky.

WORKS: operas, *Cupid's Revenge* (concert performance, St. Petersburg, May 19, 1899) and *Buran (The Snow Storm); Festival March* for orch.; 3 symphonies (1890; 1903; 1908); 2 orchestral mazurkas; *Hamlet Overture;* 2 suites for orch.; *Ballade* after a poem *(Alyosha Popovich)* by Alexei Tolstoy, for orch.; 3 string quartets; *Arabesque* for clarinet and piano; piano pieces; songs.

Taneyev, Sergei, greatly significant Russian composer and pedagogue; b. district of Vladimir, Nov. 25, 1856; d. Dyudkovo, Zvenigorodsk District, June 19, 1915. He began taking piano lessons at the age of 10 at the Moscow Cons.; after attending academic school for a year, he re-entered the Cons. and studied piano with Nicholas Rubinstein and composition with Tchaikovsky, forming a lifelong friendship with the latter. He made a very successful debut in Moscow as a pianist, playing the D minor Concerto of Brahms (Jan. 31, 1875); after a tour of Russia with Leopold Auer, he visited Turkey, Greece, and Italy; spent the winter of 1877–78 in Paris; in the autumn of 1878 he succeeded Tchaikovsky as prof. of harmony and orchestration at the Moscow Cons.; after the death of Nicholas Rubinstein in 1881, he took over the latter's piano classes there; from 1885 to 1889 he was director; from 1889 to 1906 he taught composition. Taneyev was a first-class pianist; Tchaikovsky regarded him as one of the finest interpreters of his music; but Taneyev was not interested in a virtuoso career, and gradually confined himself to composition and pedagogy. His position as a composer is anomalous: he is one of the most respected figures of Russian music history, and there is a growing literature about him; his correspondence and all documents, however trivial, concerning his life, are treasured as part of the Russian cultural heritage; yet outside Russia his works are rarely heard. He wrote a treatise on counterpoint, *Podvizhnoi kontrapunkt strogavo pisma* (1909; in English as *Convertible Counterpoint in the Strict Style;* Boston, 1962). The style of his compositions presents a compromise between Russian melos and Germanic contrapuntal writing; the mastery revealed in his symphonies and quartets is unquestionable. His most ambitious work was the trilogy *Oresteia* after Aeschylus, in 3 divisions, *Agamemnon, Choëphorai,* and *Eumenides,* first performed in St. Petersburg on Oct. 29, 1895. Other works are *John of Damascus,* cantata, after Alexei Tolstoy (1884); *At the Reading of the Psalm,* cantata (1914); Symph. in C minor (1896–97; first performed under the direction of Glazunov, St. Petersburg, April 2, 1898); 2 string quintets; 6 string quartets; 1 piano quartet; 2 string trios; 1 piano trio; about 50 songs, most of them of a very high quality. After his death an almost completed *Treatise on Canon and Fugue* was found among his papers and published in 1929.

BIBLIOGRAPHY: K. A. Kuznetzov, ed., *Memorial and Bibliography of S. I. Taneyev* (Moscow, 1925); V. Yakovlev, *S. I. Taneyev: His Musical Life* (Moscow, 1927); V. Karatygin, "To the Memory of S. I. Taneyev," *Musical Quarterly* (Oct. 1927); V. Protopopov, ed., *Memorial of S. Taneyev* (Moscow, 1947); G. Bernandt, *S. Taneyev* (Moscow, 1950); a symposium, *S. Taneyev; Materials and Documents* (vol. I, 1952); Jacob Weinberg, "S. Taneyev," *Musical Quarterly* (Jan. 1958); T. Khoprova, *S. I. Taneyev* (Leningrad, 1968); F. G. Arzamanov, *S. I. Taneyev* (Moscow, 1963); N. D.

Bazhanov, *Taneyev* (Moscow, 1971); L. Z. Korabelnikova, *S. I. Taneyev at the Moscow Conservatory* (Moscow, 1974).

Tango, Egisto, Italian conductor; b. Rome, Nov. 13, 1873; d. Copenhagen, Oct. 5, 1951. He first studied engineering; then entered the Naples Cons.; made his debut as opera conductor in Venice (1893); conducted at La Scala, Milan (1895); then at Berlin (1903–08). He conducted at the Metropolitan Opera, N.Y., in 1909–10; in Italy (1911–12); and in Budapest (1913–19), where he gave the earliest performances of stage works by Béla Bartók. From 1920 to 1926 he was active in Germany and Austria. In 1927 he settled in Copenhagen. He was distinguished for the technical precision and interpretative clarity of his performances.

Tannenberg, David, German-American organ builder; b. Berthelsdorf, Upper Lusatia, March 21, 1728; d. York, Pa., May 19, 1804. Tannenberg came to America in 1749 and became a member of the Moravian Church settlement at Bethlehem, Pa. Following the death of his teacher and colleague Johann Gottlob Clemm, he established himself in Lititz, Pa.; made 32 organs for churches in Pennsylvania, New York, Maryland, Virginia, and North Carolina; he also made a few pianos.
BIBLIOGRAPHY: P. E. Beck, "David Tannenberger, Organ Builder," *Papers Read Before the Lancaster, Pa. Historical Society* (Jan. 1926); D. M. McCorkle, "The Moravian Contribution to American Music," *Notes* (Sept. 1956; reprinted as Moravian Music Foundation Publication No. 1, Winston-Salem, N.C., 1956); D. M. McCorkle, "Musical Instruments of the Moravians of North Carolina," *American German Review* (Feb.-March 1955).

Tannhäuser, lyric poet and Minnesinger; b. c.1200 probably in Oberpfalz; d. after 1266. He led a wandering life typical of his calling; for a time was at the court of Friedrich II, Duke of Austria; then with Otto II of Bavaria. His name became legendary through the tale of the Venusberg, pagan intimacy with Venus, penitence, pilgrimage to Rome, and the miracle of the flowering of his pilgrim's staff. Wagner's *Tannhäuser* is based on this legend, unconnected with the life of the real Tannhäuser.
BIBLIOGRAPHY: F. Zander, *Die Tannhäusersage und der Minnesinger Tannhäuser* (1858); J. Siebert, *Tannhäuser* (1894).

Tansman, Alexandre, Polish composer; b. Lodz, June 12, 1897. He studied with Piotr Rytel in Warsaw, and piano with Lütschg. After a brief service in the Polish Army, he went to Paris, which became his permanent home. He first appeared in public, playing his piano works, in Paris on Feb. 17, 1920; performances of his symph. and chamber music followed in rapid succession; his *Danse de la sorcière* for chamber orch. was presented at the Zürich Festival of the International Society for Contemporary Music (June 22, 1926). He made an extensive tour of the U.S. in 1927–28 as pianist in his own works. In 1933 he toured the Far East. After the occupation of Paris by the Germans in 1940,

he made his way to the U.S.; lived in Hollywood, where he wrote music for films; returned to Paris in 1946. His music is distinguished by a considerable melodic gift and a vivacious rhythm; his harmony is often bitonal; there are some Impressionistic traits that reflect his Parisian tastes.
WORKS: OPERAS: *La Nuit kurde* (1925–27; Paris Radio, 1927); *Le Serment* (Brussels, March 11, 1955); *Sabbatat Lévi, le faux Messie,* lyric fresco (Paris, 1961); *Le Rossignol de Boboli* (Nice, 1965); ballets: *Sextuor* (Paris, May 17, 1924; also in Chicago, as *The Tragedy of the Cello,* Dec. 26, 1926); *La Grande Ville* (1932); *Bric-à-Brac* (1937); *Train de nuit* for 2 pianos (London, 1950); *Les Habits neufs du roi,* after H. C. Andersen (Venice, 1959); *Resurrection,* after Tolstoy (Nice, 1962); FOR ORCH.: 7 symphonies: No. 1 (1925; Boston, March 18, 1927), No. 2 (1926), No. 3, *Symphonie concertante* (1931), No. 4 (1939), No. 5 (1942; Baltimore, Feb. 2, 1943), No. 6, *In Memoriam* (1943), No. 7 (1944; St. Louis, Oct. 24, 1947); *Danse de la sorcière* (Brussels, May 5, 1924); *Sinfonietta* (Paris, March 23, 1925); *Ouverture symphonique* (Paris, Feb. 3, 1927); Piano Concerto No. 1 (Paris, May 27, 1926, Tansman soloist); Piano Concerto No. 2 (Boston, Dec. 28, 1927, Tansman soloist); *Suite* for 2 pianos and orch. (Paris, Nov. 16, 1930); Viola Concerto (1936); *Fantaisie* for violin and orch. (1937); *Fantaisie* for cello and orch. (1937); *Rapsodie polonaise* (St. Louis, Nov. 14, 1941); *Études symphoniques* (1943); Concertino for guitar and orch. (1945); *Ricercari* (St. Louis, Dec. 22, 1949); *Capriccio* (Louisville, March 6, 1955); CHAMBER MUSIC: 8 string quartets (1917–56); *Suite baroque* (1958); *Symphonie de chambre* (1960); *Stèle: In memoriam Igor Stravinsky* (1972); *Dyptique* for chamber orch. (1969); Cello Concerto (1962); Flute Concerto (1968); *Danse de la sorcière,* for woodwind quintet and piano (a version of the ballet; 1925); String Sextet (1940); *Divertimento,* for oboe, clarinet, trumpet, cello, and piano (1944); Violin Sonata (1919); Flute Sonata (1925); Cello Sonata (1930); etc.; FOR PIANO: *20 pièces faciles polonaises* (1924); 5 sonatas; mazurkas, and other Polish dances; *Sonatine transatlantique* (1930; very popular; contains imitations of jazz; also for orch., Paris, Feb. 28, 1931; used by Kurt Jooss for his ballet *Impressions of a Big City,* Cologne, Nov. 21, 1932); *Pour les enfants,* 4 albums for piano. He publ. a monograph on Stravinsky (Paris, 1948; in English, *Igor Stravinsky: The Man and His Music,* N.Y., 1949).
BIBLIOGRAPHY: Irving Schwerké, *Alexandre Tansman, Compositeur polonais* (Paris, 1931); R. Petit, "Alexandre Tansman," *Revue Musicale* (Feb. 1929).

Tans'ur (real name **Tanzer**), **William,** English organist, composer, and lexicographer; b. Dunchurch (baptized, Nov. 6), 1706; d. St. Neots, Oct. 7, 1783. He was a church organist and taught music in various provincial towns in England. His publications include: *The Royal Melody Compleat, or the New Harmony of Sion* (2nd ed., 1760; 3rd ed., in 3 parts, 1764, 1765, 1766; at least 11 American eds. are known, publ. as *The American Harmony, or Royal Melody Complete,* or under similar, slightly varying titles); *Heaven on Earth, or the Beauty of Holiness* (1738); *Sacred Mirth,* or the *Pious Soul's Daily Delight* (1739); *The Universal Harmony* (1743, etc.); *The Psalm-Singer's Jewel* (1760, etc.); *Melodia sacra* (1771, 1772); *New Musical Grammar* (1746; 7th ed., 1829); an epitome of this last, *The Elements of Musick Displayed* (1772). For details on various eds. see I. Lowens and Allen P. Britton, in *Papers of the Bibliographical Society of America* 4 (1955; pp. 340-54).

Tapper, Thomas, American music educator; b. Canton, Mass., Jan. 28, 1864; d. White Plains, N.Y., Feb. 24, 1958. He studied music in Europe; from 1897 to 1905 was editor of the *Musician;* then taught at N.Y. Univ. (1908-12); was lecturer at the Institute of Musical Art (1905-24); also filled other editorial and educational positions. Publications: *The Music Life* (1891); *The Education of the Music Teacher* (1914); *Essentials in Music History* (1914; with Percy Goetschius); *The Melodic Music Course,* 28 vols. (with F. H. Ripley); *Harmonic Music Course,* 7 vols.; *The Modern Graded Piano Course,* 19 vols.; *Music Theory and Composition,* 6 vols.; *From Palestrina to Grieg* (Boston, 1929; 2nd ed., 1946). His wife, **Bertha Feiring Tapper** (b. Christiania, Norway, Jan. 25, 1859; d. New York, Sept. 2, 1915), was a good pianist; studied with Agathe Backer-Gröndahl in Norway and with Leschetizky in Vienna; came to America in 1881; taught piano at the New England Cons., Boston (1889-97) and at the Institute of Musical Art, N.Y. (1905-10); edited 2 vols. of Grieg's piano works; publ. piano pieces and songs. She married Thomas Tapper on Sept. 22, 1895.

Tappert, Wilhelm, German music scholar and writer; b. Ober-Thomaswaldau, Silesia, Feb. 19, 1830; d. Berlin, Oct. 27, 1907. He was trained as a schoolmaster till 1856, when he entered Kullak's Academy of Music in Berlin; studied theory privately with Dehn; settled in Berlin. He was editor of the *Allgemeine deutsche Musikzeitung* (1876-80); collected a large assemblage of old tablatures, including unique specimens; after his death this collection and his entire valuable library was acquired by the Royal Library of Berlin. An ardent admirer of Wagner, he publ. a curious volume, *Ein Wagner-Lexikon: Wörterbuch der Unhöflichkeit, enthaltend grobe, höhnende, gehässige und verläumderische Ausdrücke welche gegen den Meister Richard Wagner, seine Werke und seine Anhänger von den Feinden und Spöttern gebraucht worden sind. Zur Gemütsergötzung in müssigen Stunden gesammelt,* a collection of anti-Wagner reviews (Leipzig, 1877); a 2nd, enlarged edition was published under the title *Richard Wagner im Spiegel der Kritik* (Leipzig, 1903). Other publications: *Musik und musikalische Erziehung* (1867); *Musikalische Studien* (1868); *Das Verbot der Quintenparallelen* (1869); *Wandernde Melodien* (2nd ed., 1889); *54 Erlkönig-Kompositionen* (1898; 2nd ed., 1906); *Sang und Klang aus alter Zeit* (1906); also arrangements of old German songs. He composed 50 left-hand studies for piano; other piano pieces.

Tappolet, Willy, Swiss writer on music; b. Lindau, near Zürich, Aug. 6, 1890. He studied philology and music in Berlin, Zürich, and Geneva; in 1950 he was appointed to the faculty of Geneva Univ. He is the author of monographs on Honegger (Zürich, 1933; in French, Neuchâtel, 1939; enlarged German ed., Zürich, 1954); and Ravel (Olten, 1950); also wrote *La Notation musicale et son influence sur la pratique de la musique du moyen-âge à nos jours* (Neuchâtel, 1947), and articles for various publications.

Tăranu, Cornel, Rumanian composer; b. Cluj, June 20, 1934. He studied with Toduţă and Muresianu at the Cons. in Cluj (1951-57); traveled to Paris and took lessons with Nadia Boulanger and Messiaen (1966-67); attended the seminars of Ligeti and Maderna at Darmstadt (1968-70); then returned to Cluj and was appointed prof. of the Cluj Cons. His music is austerely formal, with atonal sound structures related through continuous variation, with permissible aleatory interludes from performers.

WORKS: opera, *Secretul lui Don Giovanni (The Secret of Don Juan;* 1969-70); the cantatas *Cîntare unui ev aprins (Hymn for a Fiery Age,* 1962); and *Stejarul lui Horia (The Oak of Horia,* 1963); symph. for string orch. (1957); *Secvenţe (Sequences)* for string orch. (1960); *Sinfonia brevia* (1962); *Simetrii (Symetries)* for orch. (1964; Cluj, May 14, 1965); *Incantaţii (Incantations)* for orch. (1965; Cluj, Jan. 15, 1966); Piano Concerto (1966; Cluj, May 29, 1967); *Intercalări (Intercalations)* for piano and orch. (1967-69; Cluj, Dec. 13, 1969); *Sinfonietta giocosa* for string orch. (1968); *Alternanţe (Alternations)* for orch. (1968; Bucharest, May 29, 1969); *Racorduri (Transitions)* for chamber orch. (1971); String Trio (1952); *Poem-Sonata* for clarinet and piano (1954); Cello Sonata (1960); Flute Sonata (1961); Oboe Sonata (1963); *3 Pieces* for clarinet and piano (1964); *Dialogues for 6* for flute, clarinet, trumpet, vibraphone, percussion, and piano (1966); *Ébauche* for voice, clarinet, violin, viola, cello, and piano (1966-68); *Le Lit de Procruste (The Bed of Procrustes)* for baritone, clarinet viola and piano (1968-70); *Odă în Metru Antic (Ode in Ancient Meter),* cantata for baritone, clarinet, piano and percussion (1975); piano pieces; songs.

Tarchi, Angelo, Italian composer; b. Naples, about 1755; d. Paris, Aug. 19, 1814. He studied at the Cons. dei Turchini in Naples with Fago and Sala; in 1786 was in London; in 1797 settled in Paris. He wrote about 45 operas in Italian, and 6 in French; of these the following were produced at La Scala in Milan: *Ademira* (Dec. 27, 1783); *Ariarte* (Jan., 1786); *Il Conte di Saldagna* (June 10, 1787); *Adrasto* (Feb. 8, 1792); *Le Danaidi* (Dec. 26, 1794); and *L'Impostura poco dura* (Oct. 10, 1795). In Paris he produced the French version of *Il Conte di Saldagna* as *Bouffons de la foire St. Germain* (1790), *D'Auberge en auberge* (Opéra-Comique, April 26, 1800), etc. He acquired a certain notoriety by his attempt to rewrite the 3rd and 4th acts of Mozart's *Le Nozze di Figaro* (1787); regarding this episode, see A. Einstein, "Mozart e Tarchi," *Rassegna Musicale* (July 1935); see also C. Sartori, "Lo Zeffiretto di Angelo Tarchi," *Rivista Musicale Italiana* (July 1954).

Tarditi, Giovanni, Italian bandleader and composer; b. Acqui, March 10, 1857; d. Rome, Sept. 19, 1935. He traveled as bandleader in Europe and America; publ.

manuals for band playing, such as *Segnalofono* for trumpet calls; wrote the operettas *Monte Carlo* (Genoa, March 1, 1897) and *L'Isola degli antropofagi* (Rome, June 1, 1925), military marches, etc.

Tardos, Béla, Hungarian composer; b. Budapest, June 21, 1910; d. there, Nov. 18, 1966. He studied with Kodály at the Budapest Academy of Music (1934–36); upon graduation was active as a concert manager and music publisher. He composed much choral music for mass singing employing the modalities of Hungarian folksongs.

WORKS: a comic opera, *Laura* (1958, revised 1964; posthumous, Debrecen, Dec. 11, 1966); 3 cantatas: *May Cantata* (1950); *A város peremén* (*Upon the City's Outskirts,* 1958) and *Az új Isten* (*The New Gold,* 1966); *Overture* (1949); *Suite* for orch. (1950); Piano Concerto (1954); *Overture to a Fairy Tale* (1955); Symphony, in memory of the victims of Fascism (1960); *Fantasy* for piano and orch. (1961); Violin Concerto (1962); *Evocatio* for orch. (1964); Wind Octet (1935); Piano Quartet (1941); 3 string quartets (1947, 1949, 1963); *Improvisations* for clarinet and piano (1960); *Prelude and Rondo* for flute and piano (1962); *Quartettino-Divertimento* for 4 wind instruments (1963); *Cassazione* for harp trio (1963); Violin Sonata (1965); *5 Bagatelles* for piano (1955); *6 Small Studies* for piano (1963); songs.

Tarisio, Luigi, Italian violin maker and trader; b. Fontanetto, near Milan, c.1795; d. Milan, Oct., 1854. He began life as a carpenter, and in his spare hours acquired sufficient skill on the violin to play dance music at country fairs, etc. His trade brought him into many humble homes, where he found old violins, the value of which was not suspected by their owners. Gifted with extraordinary powers of observation, he soon recognized the value of those neglected instruments, and, whenever possible, acquired them. After some time he began to imitate the models thus collected; then in the capacity of repairer, he obtained access to Italian chapels and monasteries, where he discovered many valuable instruments. In 1827 he paid his first visit to Paris, disposing of a number of Italian violins to celebrated dealers. Soon he was acknowledged as the foremost connoisseur, so that his regular visits to Paris were eagerly looked for. In 1851 he made his first trip to London. Tarisio was the first to recognize the value of the now famous Italian violins; it was he who created a market for them. He left a collection of over 200 violins, which was acquired by Vuillaume of Paris.

BIBLIOGRAPHY: G. Hart, *The Violin: Famous Makers and Their Imitators* (London, 1875; 4th ed., 1887); H. R. Haweis, *Old Violins* (London, 1898); Hill, A. E. et al., *Antonio Stradivari* (London, 1902); W. A. Silverman, *The Violin Hunter* (N.Y., 1957; mostly anecdotal).

Tarp, Svend Erik, Danish composer; b. Thisted, Jutland, Aug. 6, 1908. He studied theory with Knud Jeppesen and piano with Rudolf Simonsen at the Copenhagen Cons. (1929–31); then was appointed to its faculty (1934–42); concurrently lectured at the Univ. of Copenhagen (1935–42) and Royal Opera Academy (1935–40); occupied various administrative and editorial posts in music organizations in Denmark; was chairman of the board of directors of the Society for Publishing of Danish Music (1935–58 and again after 1976); was editor of *Edition Dania* (1941–60).

WORKS: 2 operas: *Princessen i det Fjerne* (*The Princess at a Distance,* 1952; Copenhagen, May 18, 1953) and *9,90,* a burlesque television opera (Copenhagen, Aug. 12, 1962); 2 ballets: *Skyggen* (*The Shadow,* after Hans Christian Andersen, 1941–44; Copenhagen, April 1, 1960) and *Den detroniserede Dyretoemmer* (*The Dethroned Tamer,* 1943–44; Copenhagen, Feb. 5, 1944); Sinfonietta for chamber orch. (1931); Violin Concertino (1931); Flute Concertino (1937); *Orania,* suite for orch. (1937); *Mosaïque,* miniature suite for orch. (1937); *Comedy Overture No. 1* (1939); *Comedy Overture No. 2* (1950); Piano Concerto (1943); 7 symphonies: No. 1, *Sinfonia devertente* (1945), No. 2 (1948), No. 3, *Sinfonia quasi una fantasia* (1958), No. 4 (1975), No. 5 (1975), No. 6 (1976), No. 7 (1977); *Pro defunctis,* overture (1945); *Partita* for orch. (1947); *The Battle of Jericho,* symph. poem (1949); *Preludio patetico* for orch. (1952); *Divertimento* for orch. (1954); *Scandinavian Design* for orch. (1955); *Lyrical Suite* for orch. (1956); *Little Dance Suite* for orch. (1964); *Little Festival Overture* (1969); *Te Deum* for chorus and orch. (1938); *Christmas Cantata* for narrator, baritone, chorus, organ, and orch. (1946); *Serenade* for flute, clarinet, and string trio (1930); *Serenade* for flute and string trio (1936); Duet for flute and viola (1941); String Quartet (1973); Piano Sonata (1950); other piano pieces; music for about 40 films and 15 radio and television dramas; songs.

Tárrega, Francisco, Spanish guitar virtuoso; b. Villarreal, Castellón, Nov. 21, 1852; d. Barcelona, Dec. 15, 1909. He studied at the Madrid Cons.; composed many pieces for his instrument, also made many transcriptions of classical and modern works.

BIBLIOGRAPHY: E. Pujor, *Tárrega, ensayo biográfico* (1960).

Tartini, Giuseppe, Italian violinist, composer, and theorist; b. Pirano, Istria, April 8, 1692; d. Padua, Feb. 26, 1770. While studying, at his parents' desire, for the priesthood, he took violin lessons that strengthened his ardent longings for a secular career; his father finally allowed him to study law at Padua (1710), but music, especially the violin, and fencing were his passion. A charge of abduction, following on his secret marriage to a protegée of Cardinal Cornaro, obliged him to take refuge in the Franciscan monastery at Assisi; for two years he studied the violin and composition (under the organist Czernohorsky, called "il Padre Boemo") and then returned to Padua, a reconciliation having been effected with the Cardinal. Shortly afterward he heard the violinist Veracini at Venice, and was stimulated to more arduous endeavor; he retired to Ancona for further study of the violin. About this time (1714) he discovered the combination tones, and utilized them in perfecting purity of intonation. His fame then increasing, in 1721 he was appointed solo violinist and conductor of the orch. at St. Antonio in Padua. He spent the years 1723-25 as chamber musician to Count Kinsky in

Prague, having been invited there to perform at the coronation of Carl VI; he then resumed his duties at Padua, and in 1728 founded a violin school there, in which were trained many distinguished violinists (Nardini, Pasqualino, Lahoussaye, etc.). Although repeatedly invited to visit Paris and London, he refused to leave Italy after his return to Padua; in 1740 he visited Rome, and on his way home made a triumphal tour of the principal Italian cities. Tartini was one of the great masters of the violin; his style of bowing still serves as a model, and his compositions are regarded as classics. As a theorist he follows Rameau, and derives the minor chord from an undertone series opposed to the overtone series; like Zarlino, he regards the minor chord as the opposite of the major.

WORKS: about 150 concertos and 100 violin sonatas as well as some choral pieces, of which a *Salve Regina* was his last composition. Publ. works: op. 1, 6 concertos (1734; 3 republ. in Paris; 3 others republ. there with 2 viola parts added by Blainville, as *Concerti grossi*); also as op. 1, 12 violin sonatas with cello and cembalo; op. 2, 6 sonatas for same; op. 3, 12 sonatas (incl. op. 2) for violin and bass; op. 4, *Sei concerti a violino solo, 2 violini, viola e violoncello o cembalo di concerto;* also as op. 4, 6 sonatas for violin with continuo; op. 5, 6, and 7 each comprise 6 sonatas for violin and continuo; op. 8, *Sei sonate a 3, due violini col basso;* op. 9, 6 sonatas a 3; and *L'Arte dell'arco* (reprinted in French by Choron in *Principes de composition,* and separately by André); the famous *Trillo del diavolo* was a posthumous work (it was discovered by Baillot and first publ. in Cartier's *L'Art du violon*); the concertos have been republ. in various editions and in varying combinations; sonatas have been republished by Alard, David, and others.

THEORETICAL WORKS: *Trattato di musica secondo la vera scienza dell'armonia* (1754); *Risposta alla critica del di lui Trattato di musica di Msgr. Le Serre di Ginevra* (1767); *De' principj dell'armonia musicale contenuta nel diatonico genere* (1767); *Lettera alla signora Maddalena Lombardini inserviente ad una importante lezione per i suonatori di violino* (1770; English transl. by Burney, London, 1771); *Traité des agréments de la musique* (1782; English translation by Sol Babitz in *Journal of Research in Music Education,* Fall 1956).

BIBLIOGRAPHY: Fanzago, *Orazione delle lodi di G. T.* (Padua, 1770); J. A. Hiller, *Lebensbeschreibungen berühmter Musikgelehrten und Tonkünstler* (Leipzig, 1784); F. Fanzago, *Elogi* (Padua, 1792); C. Ugoni (1802; in *Della letteratura italiana,* vol. I, pp. 1–28); F. Fayolle, *Notices sur Corelli, Tartini, etc.* (Paris, 1810); G. Benedetti, *Brevi cenni su G. T.* (Trieste, 1897); M. Tamaro, *G. T.* (Parenzo, 1897; in *Atti e memorie della Società istriana,* vol. XII); A. Bachmann, *Les Grands Violinistes du passé* (Paris, 1913); C. Bouvert, *Une Leçon de T.* (Paris, 1918); M. Dounias, *Die Violinkonzerte G. T.s* (Munich, 1935); H. P. Schökel, *G. T.* (Berlin, 1936); A. Capri, *G. T.* (Milan, 1945; includes a thematic index of the Tartini MSS at Padua); A. Spalding, *A Fiddle, a Sword, and a Lady* (N.Y., 1953; a fictionalized account of Tartini's life). A thematic index of Tartini's concertos was publ. by G. Tebaldini, in *L'Archivio mus.* (Padua, 1895).

Taskin, (Émile-) Alexandre, French baritone, grandson of **Henri-Joseph Taskin;** b. Paris, March 8, 1853; d. there, Oct. 5, 1897. He was a pupil of Ponchard and Bussine at the Paris Cons.; debut at Amiens, 1875. Sang in Lille and Geneva; returned to Paris in 1878; engaged at the Opéra-Comique in 1879, and created important parts in many new operas. He retired in 1894, and from then until his death he was prof. of lyrical declamation at the Cons. On the night of the terrible catastrophe of the burning of the Opéra-Comique (May 25, 1887) he was singing in *Mignon;* through his calmness and bravery many lives were saved, and the government decorated him with a medal.

Taskin, Pascal, French manufacturer of keyboard instruments; b. Theux, near Liège, 1723; d. Paris, Feb. 1793. He went to Paris at an early age and entered Blanchet's atelier, later succeeding to the business and becoming highly celebrated as an instrument maker. He invented the leather plectra for the harpsichord (1768), replacing the crow quills previously in use. He built his first piano in 1776. His nephew **Pascal-Joseph Taskin** (b. Theux, Nov. 20, 1750; d. Versailles, Feb. 5, 1829) was Keeper of the King's Instruments from 1772 until the Revolution; his son **Henri-Joseph Taskin** (b. Versailles, Aug. 24, 1779; d. Paris, May 4, 1852) was an organist and composer.

BIBLIOGRAPHY: H. Boalch, *Makers of the Harpsichord* (London, 1956).

Tate, Phyllis (Margaret Duncan), English composer; b. Gerrards Cross, Bucks, April 6, 1911. She studied composition with Harry Farjeon at the Royal Academy of Music, London; composed a symph., a cello concerto, and several other works, but withdrew them as immature. In her music she follows the *Zeitgeist* of the modern era; her music bristles with abrasive dissonance and asymmetrical rhythms, while the form retains its classical purity. She married the musical scholar and publishing official **Alan Frank** in 1935.

WORKS: Cello Concerto (1933) *Valse lointaine* for small orch. (1941); *Prelude, Interlude and Postlude,* for chamber orch. (1942); Saxophone Concerto (1944); Sonata for clarinet and cello (1947; performed at the Salzburg Festival of the International Society for Contemporary Music, June 23, 1951); String Quartet (1952); *Occasional Overture* (1955); *The Lady of Shalott,* after Tennyson, cantata for tenor, viola, percussion, 2 pianos and celesta (1956); *The Lodger,* opera (London, July 14, 1960); television opera, *Dark Pilgrimage* (1963); *A Victorian Garland,* after Matthew Arnold, for soprano, contralto, horn, and piano (1965); *Secular Requiem* for chorus and orch. (1967); *Christmas Ale* for soloists, chorus, and orch. (1967); *Apparitions,* a ballad sequence for tenor, harmonica, string quartet, and piano (1968); *Illustrations* for brass band (1969); *Variegations* for solo viola (1971); music for schools and amateur musicians; *Twice in a Blue Moon,* fantasy operetta (1968); *Serenade to Christmas* for mezzo-soprano, chorus and orch. (1972); *Lyric Suite* for 2 pianos (1973); *The Rainbow and The Cuckoo* for oboe, violin, viola, and cello (1974); *Sonatina Pastorale* for harmonica and harpsichord (1974); *St. Martha and the Dragon* for narrator, soloists, chorus and orch. (1976); *Seasonal Sequence* for viola and piano (1977); *Panorama* for strings (1977); *All the World's a Stage* for chorus and orch. (1977).

BIBLIOGRAPHY: M. Carner, "The Music of Phyllis Tate," *Music & Letters* (April 1954); H. Searle, "Phyllis Tate," *Musical Times* (May 1955).

Tatum, Art (Arthur), black American jazz pianist; b. Toledo, Ohio, Oct. 13, 1909; d. Los Angeles, Nov. 5, 1956. He was blind in one eye and had limited vision in the other; he attended a school for the blind in Columbus, Ohio, and learned to read Braille music notation; at the age of 16 began to play in night clubs. In 1932 he went to N.Y. and became successful on the radio. In 1938 he made a spectacular tour of England; then was again in N.Y. for many years; eventually went to California, where he died of uremia. He brought "stride" piano playing to a point of perfection, scorning such academic niceties as proper fingering, but achieving small miracles with ornamental figurations in the melody, while throwing effortless cascades of notes across the keyboard; he also had a knack of improvising variations on popular pieces by defenseless deceased classical composers; his audiences adored Art's art, while professional musicians knitted their brows in wild surmise.

Tauber, Richard (real name **Ernst Seiffert**), eminent Austrian tenor; b. Linz, May 16, 1892; d. London, Jan. 8, 1948. He studied music at Hoch's Cons. in Frankfurt; made his debut at Chemnitz as Tamino in *Die Zauberflöte* (March 2, 1913) with such success that he was engaged in the same year at the Dresden Opera; in 1915 he appeared with the Berlin Royal Opera at Salzburg. Later he abandoned serious opera and sang mostly in light opera; was particularly successful in the leading parts of Lehár's operettas. He made his American debut on Oct. 28, 1931, in a N.Y. recital. In 1938 he went to England; became a British subject in 1940. In London he wrote an operetta *Old Chelsea,* and took the leading role at its production there (Feb. 17, 1943). He made his last American appearance at Carnegie Hall, N.Y., on March 30, 1947.

BIBLIOGRAPHY: H. Ludwigg, ed., *Richard Tauber* (Berlin, 1938); Diana Napier Tauber (his second wife), *Richard Tauber* (Glasgow, 1949).

Taubert, Ernst Eduard, German composer and music critic; b. Regenwalde, Sept. 25, 1838; d. Berlin, July 14, 1934. He studied theology in Bonn, and music there with Albert Dietrich; later with Friedrich Kiel in Berlin, where he became teacher at the Stern Cons. and music critic for the *Berliner Post;* also contributed to various German music magazines. His works include a piano quintet; a wind quintet; a piano quartet; 5 string quartets; a piano trio; a *Ballade* for orch.; piano pieces for 2 and 4 hands; songs.

Taubert, (Carl Gottfried) Wilhelm, German composer; b. Berlin, March 23, 1811; d. there, Jan. 7, 1891. Piano pupil of Neithardt, later of L. Berger, and for composition of Bernhard Klein. Appeared early as a concert player; taught music in Berlin, became assistant conductor of the court orch. in 1831; court Kapellmeister from 1845 to 1870. He conducted his 1st Symph. in Berlin at the age of 20 (March 31, 1831).

His operas (all produced in Berlin) include: *Die Kirmes* (Jan. 23, 1832); *Marquis und Dieb* (Feb. 1, 1842); *Der Zigeuner* (Sept. 19, 1834); *Joggeli* (Oct. 9, 1853); *Macbeth* (Nov. 16, 1857); *Cesario,* after Shakespeare's *Twelfth Night* (Nov. 13, 1874). He composed much instrumental music, but is best remembered for his *Kinderlieder* (op. 145, 160), the favorites among his 300 songs.

BIBLIOGRAPHY: W. Neumann, *Wilhelm Taubert und Ferdinand Hiller* (Kassel, 1857).

Taubman, Howard, American music critic; b. New York, July 4, 1907. He studied at Cornell Univ.; joined the staff of the *N.Y. Times* in 1930; in 1955 succeeded Olin Downes as chief music critic there, and in 1960 succeeded Brooks Atkinson as drama critic of the *New York Times;* retired in 1972 and was succeeded as chief music critic by Harold C. Schonberg; then became music adviser for television productions sponsored by the Exxon Co.

WRITINGS: *Opera: Front and Back* (N.Y., 1938); *Music as a Profession* (N.Y., 1939); *Music on My Beat* (N.Y., 1943); *The Maestro: The Life of Arturo Toscanini* (N.Y., 1951); *How to Build a Record Library* (N.Y., 1953; new ed., 1955); *How to Bring Up Your Child to Enjoy Music* (Garden City, N.Y., 1958).

Taubmann, Otto, German conductor and composer; b. Hamburg, March 8, 1859; d. Berlin, July 5, 1929. After graduation from school he followed a commercial career for 3 years; then studied music under Wüllner, Rischbieter, Nicodé, and Blassmann at the Dresden Cons.; traveled a year for further study, and began his career as theater conductor; 1886–89, director of the Wiesbaden Cons.; 1891–92, theater conductor in St. Petersburg; 1892–95, conductor of the Cäcilienverein in Ludwigshafen; then settled in Berlin, where from 1898 he was music critic of the *Börsen-Courier.* He composed chiefly choral works, of which the most successful was *Eine Deutsche Messe* for soli, double chorus, organ, and orch. (1896).

Taudou, Antoine (-Antonin-Barthélemy), French violinist and composer; b. Perpignan, Aug. 24, 1846; d. St.-Germain-en-Laye, July 6, 1925. He studied at the Paris Cons., winning the Grand Prix de Rome in 1869 with the cantata *Francesca da Rimini;* 1883, prof. of harmony at the Cons. He published *Marche-Ballet, Chant d'automne,* and *Marche nocturne,* for orch.; Violin Concerto; String Quartet; Piano Trio; Trio for flute, viola, and cello; etc.

Tauriello, Antonio, Argentinian composer; b. Buenos Aires, March 20, 1931. He studied piano with Walter Gieseking and composition with Alberto Ginastera; still a youth, he was engaged to conduct opera and ballet at the Teatro Colón, Buenos Aires. His music is neo-Classical in its general mold.

WORKS: *Serenade* for orch. (1957); *Ricercare* for orch. (1063); *Transparencies* for 6 instrumental groups (Washington, D.C., 3rd Inter-American Music Festival, May 12, 1965); Piano Concerto (Washington, D.C., 4th Inter-American Music Festival, June 29, 1968; Hilde Somer, soloist); *Mansión de Tlaloc* for piano, percussion, and strings (1969); *Signos de los tiempos* for flute, clarinet, violin, cello, and piano (1969).

Tausch, Franz, celebrated German clarinetist; b. Heidelberg, Dec. 26, 1762; d. Berlin, Feb. 9, 1817. At the age of 8 he played in the Electoral orch. at Mannheim; was engaged at Munich (1777–89), and then in the court orch. at Berlin, where he founded a school for wind instruments in 1805; Heinrich Bärmann was his pupil. He published 2 clarinet concertos, 3 concertantes for 2 clarinets, Andante and Polonaise for clarinet, clarinet duos, trios for 2 clarinets with bassoon, 6 quartets for 2 basset horns and 2 bassoons (with 2 horns *ad. lib.*), 6 military marches, *a* 10, etc.

Tausch, Julius, German conductor and composer; b. Dessau, April 15, 1827; d. Bonn, Nov. 11, 1895. He studied with Fr. Schneider, and at the Leipzig Cons. (1844–46); then settled in Düsseldorf; there he became conductor of the Künstlerliedertafel; was Schumann's deputy from 1853, and in 1855 his successor as conductor of the Music Society and Subscription Concerts in Düsseldorf, retiring in 1890. He composed the cantatas, *Der Blumen Klage auf den Tod des Sängers; Dein Leben schied, dein Ruhm begann; Germanenzug; Rheinfahrt;* piano pieces; male choruses.

Tausig, Carl, celebrated piano virtuoso; b. Warsaw, Nov. 4, 1841; d. Leipzig, July 17, 1871. He was trained by his father, **Aloys Tausig** (1820–85), who was a pupil of Thalberg and wrote brilliant piano music. Carl Tausig studied with Liszt, and emulated his bravura style; made his debut in 1858, at an orchestral concert conducted by Hans von Bülow at Berlin. During the next two years he gave concerts in German cities, making Dresden his headquarters; then went to Vienna in 1862, giving orch. concerts with "advanced" programs similar to Bülow's at Berlin. He settled in Berlin in 1865, and opened a Schule des höheren Klavierspiels. He gave concerts in the principal towns of Germany, and at St. Petersburg and other Russian centers. He died of typhoid fever at the age of 29.
WORKS: (for piano); 2 études de concert; *Ungarische Zigeunerweisen; Nouvelles soirées de Vienna; Valses-Caprices* on themes from Strauss; *Tägliche Studien* (transposing chromatc exercises; ed. by Ehrlich); also transcriptions and arrangements.
BIBLIOGRAPHY: K. F. Weitzmann, *Der Letzte der Virtuosen* (Leipzig, 1868); W. von Lenz, *Die grossen Pianoforte-Virtuosen unserer Zeit* (Berlin, 1872; in English, N.Y., 1899).

Tausinger, Jan, Rumanian-born Czech composer; b. Piatra Neamt, Nov. 1, 1921. He studied composition with Cuclin, Jora, and Mendelsohn at the Budapest Cons., graduating in 1947; had lessons in conducting with Ančerl; took courses in advanced harmony with Alois Hába and Bořkovec at the Prague Academy (1948–52); from 1952 to 1958 was director of the State Cons. in Ostrava; subsequently occupied other posts in the musical organizations of the area. His music is greatly diversified in style, idiom and technique, ranging from neo-Classical modalities to integral dodecaphony; he makes use of optical representational nota-

tion when justified by the structure of a particular piece.
WORKS: opera, *Ugly Nature* (1971); ballet, *Dlouhá noc (The Long Night,* 1966); Symph. No. 1, *Liberation* (1952); Violin Sonata (1954); *Partita* for viola and piano (1958); String Trio (1960); 4 string quartets (1961, 1966, 1967, 1968); Violin Concerto (1963); *Colloquium* for 4 wind instruments (1964); *Confrontazione I* and *II* for orch. (1964); *Concertino Meditazione* for viola and chamber ensemble (1965); Trio for violin, viola, and guitar (1965); *Le Avventure* for flute and harp (1965); *Canto di speranza* for piano quartet (1965); *Happening* for piano trio (1966); *De rebus musicalibus* for flute, bass clarinet, vibraphone, piano, and percussion (1967); *Noc (The Night),* musical collage to a poem by Pushkin (1967); *Správná věc (The Right Thing),* symph. tableau, to works by Vladimir Mayakovsky, for tenor, baritone, chorus, and orch. (1967); *Čmáranice po nebi (Scrawling in the Sky),* to a poem by an early Russian futurist Khlebnikov, a song cycle for soprano, flute, bass clarinet, piano, and percussion (1967); *Musica Evolutiva* for chamber orch. (1967; Zagreb, Nov. 24, 1971); *Sonatina emancipata* for trumpet and piano (1968); *7 Microchromophones* for piano, viola and clarinet (1973); String Trio (1973); *On revient toujours,* suite for violin and piano (1974); *Hukvaldy,* nonet (1974); *Sinfonica Bohemica* for bass, male chorus, trumpet, harpsichord, and orch. (1973–75); several piano pieces, choruses and songs.

Tauwitz, Eduard, German conductor and composer; b. Glatz, Silesia, Jan. 21, 1812; d. Prague, July 25, 1894. He was Kapellmeister at theaters in Vilna (1837), Riga (1840), Breslau (1843), and Prague (1846; pensioned in 1863). He wrote more than 1,000 compositions, including 3 operas: *Trilby* (Vilna, 1836), *Bradamante* (Riga, 1844), and *Schmolke und Bakel* (Breslau, 1846), church music, songs, and part-songs.

Tavener, John, British composer; b. London, Jan. 28, 1944. He studied with Lennox Berkeley at the Royal Academy of Music; also took a course with the Australian composer David Lumsdaine. Among the formative influences of his creative evolution were medieval hymnology and Indian transcendentalism; his technical equipment is, by contrast, ultramodern, including combinatorial serialism and electronic generation of sound.
WORKS: (all first performed in London): *The Cappemakers,* a dramatic cantata for two narrators, 10 soloists, male chorus and chamber orch. (Jan. 14, 1964); *3 Holy Sonnets* for baritone and chamber orch., to texts from John Donne (1964); *Cain and Abel,* dramatic cantata for soloists and chamber orch. (Oct. 22, 1966); *The Whale,* dramatic cantata for narrator, soloists, chorus, and orch. (Jan. 24, 1968); *Grandma's Footsteps* for chamber orch. (March 14, 1968); *Introit for March 27th* for soprano, contralto, chorus, and orch. (March 27, 1968); *Chamber Concerto* for chamber orch. (June 12, 1968); *3 Surrealist Songs* for mezzo-soprano, tape, piano, and percussion (1968); *In Alium* for soprano, orch., and tape (Aug. 12, 1968); *A Celtic Requiem,* dramatic cantata for soloists, children's choir, chorus, and orch. (July 16, 1969); *Coplas* for chorus, soloists and tape (July 9, 1970); *Nomine Jesu* for 5 male speaking voices, mezzo-soprano, cho-

rus, two alto flutes, organ, and harpsichord (Aug. 14, 1970); *Requiem for Father Malachy* (1973); Concerto for piano and chamber orch. (London, Oct. 1, 1975).

Taverner, John, English composer; b. c.1490; d. Boston, Lincolnshire, Oct. 18, 1545. He was probably a native of Tattershall, where he was a lay clerk until his appointment as master of the choristers and organist at Cardinals' College, Oxford, in 1526. In 1528 he was imprisoned for heresy, but soon released; he left Oxford in 1530, and also gave up music, spending the rest of his life in promoting religious persecution as a paid agent of Thomas Cromwell. In 1537 he was elected a member of the Guild of Corpus Christi in Boston, England, becoming a steward in 1543. He was one of the greatest of the early English church composers. His church music, printed in vols. I and III of *Tudor Church Music* (1923–24), includes 8 Masses, several sections of Masses, 3 Magnificats, a Te Deum, and 28 motets. He also wrote 3 secular vocal compositions for W. de Worde's *Song-book* (1530).
BIBLIOGRAPHY: H. B. Collins, "John Taverner's Masses," *Music & Letters* (1924).

Taylor, Clifford, American composer; b. Avalon, Pennsylvania, Oct. 20, 1923. He studied composition with Lopatnikoff at the Carnegie-Mellon Univ. in Pittsburgh, and with Irving Fine, Hindemith, Piston, and Thompson at Harvard Univ. (M.A., 1950). He taught at Chatham College in Pittsburgh (1950–63); in 1963 joined the faculty of Temple Univ., in Philadelphia.
WORKS: opera, *The Freak Show* (1975); *Theme and Variations* for orch. (1951); *Concerto Grosso* for string orch. (1957); 2 symphonies: No. 1 (1958) and No. 2 (1965; Philadelphia Orch., Dec. 16, 1970); Concerto for organ and chamber orch. (1963); *Sinfonia Seria* for concert band, flute, and baritone horn (1965); Piano Conerto (1974); Violin Sonata (1952); String Quartet for amateurs (1959); Trio for clarinet, cello, and piano (1959–60); String Quartet No. 1 (1960); *Concert Duo* for violin and cello (1961); Duo for saxophone and trombone (1965) *Serenade* for percussion ensemble (1967); *Movement for Three* for violin, cello and piano (1967); *5 Poems* for oboe and 5 brasses (1971); *Fantasia and Fugue* for piano (1959); *30 Ideas* for piano (1972); *36 More Ideas* for piano (1976); numerous a cappella choruses, including choral settings of Western Pennsylvania folksongs (1958), and *A Pageant of Characters from William Shakespeare* for chorus and soloists (1964); songs.

Taylor, David Clark, American singing teacher; b. New York, Nov. 11, 1871; d. there, Dec. 6, 1918. A graduate of the College of the City of N.Y. (B.A., 1890), he studied piano with O. W. Wilkinson (1888–94), theory with A. Remy (1893–97), and singing (1890–96) with several teachers in N.Y. He was long connected with the Macmillan Co. He wrote the books *The Psychology of Singing* (N.Y., 1908); *Self Help for Singers* (N.Y., 1914); *New Light on the Old Italian Method* (N.Y., 1916); *The Melodic Method in School Music* (N.Y., 1918).

Taylor, (Joseph) Deems, greatly popular American composer and writer; b. New York, Dec. 22, 1885; d.

New York, July 3, 1966. He graduated from N.Y. Univ. (B.A., 1906); studied theory with O. Coon (1912–13). Afer doing editorial work for various publications and serving as war correspondent for the *N.Y. Tribune* in France (1916–17), he became music critic for the *N.Y. World* (1921–25), editor of *Musical America* (1927–29), and critic for the *N.Y. American* (1931–32). Member of the National Insitute of Arts and Letters; Mus. Doc. *(honoris causa),* N.Y. Univ., 1927; Litt. D., Juniata College, 1931. Following the success of his orchestral suite *Through the Looking-Glass,* after Lewis Carroll's tale (1923), he was commissioned by Walter Damrosch to compose a symph. poem, *Jurgen* (1925). Meanwhile, 2 widely performed cantatas, *The Chambered Nautilus* and *The Highwayman,* had added to his growing reputation, which received a strong impetus when his opera *The King's Henchman* (libretto by Edna St. Vincent Millay), commissioned by the Metropolitan Opera, was produced in that house on Feb. 17, 1927. Receiving 14 performances in 3 seasons, it established a record for American opera at the Metropolitan Opera House, but it was surpassed by Taylor's next opera, *Peter Ibbetson* (Feb. 7, 1931); this attained 16 performances in 4 seasons. These successes, however, proved ephemeral, and the operas were allowed to lapse into unmerited desuetude. From 1942 to 1948 he was president of the American Society for Composers, Authors and Publishers.
WORKS: *The Echo,* musical comedy (N.Y., 1909); *The King's Henchman,* opera (N.Y., Feb. 17, 1926); *Peter Ibbetson,* opera (N.Y., Feb. 7, 1931); *Ramuntcho,* opera (Philadelphia, Feb. 10, 1942); *The Drago,* opera (N.Y. Univ., Feb. 6, 1958); *The Siren Songs,* symph. poem (1912; N.Y., July 18, 1922); *Through the Looking-Glass,* suite for chamber orch. (1917–19; N.Y., Feb. 18, 1919; rescored for full orch., 1921–22; N.Y., March 10, 1923); *The Portrait of a Lady,* for 11 instruments (1918); *Jurgen,* symph. poem (N.Y., Nov. 19, 1925); *Circus Day,* suite for jazz orch. (1925; for symph. orch., 1933); ballet music from *Casanova* for orch. (N.Y., April 18, 1937); *Marco Takes a Walk,* variations for orch. (N.Y., Nov. 14, 1942); *A Christmas Overture* (N.Y., Dec. 23, 1943, composer conducting); *Élégie,* for orch. (Los Angeles, Jan. 4, 1945); *Restoration Suite,* for orch. (Indianapolis, Nov. 18, 1950); *The Chambered Nautilus,* cantata for mixed voices and orch. (1914); *The Highwayman,* cantata for baritone, women's voices, and orch. (1914); *Lucrece,* suite for string quartet; *A Kiss in Xanadu,* pantomime for piano or 2 pianos; part-songs; songs; piano pieces.
WRITINGS: *Of Men and Music* (N.Y., 1937); *The Well Tempered Listener* (N.Y., 1940); *Walt Disney's Fantasia* (N.Y., 1940); *Music to My Ears* (N.Y., 1949); *Some Enchanted Evenings: The Story of Rodgers and Hammerstein* (N.Y., 1953). With R. Kerr he revised Rupert Hughes' *Biographical Dictionary of Musicians* (N.Y., 1940).
BIBLIOGRAPHY: J. T. Howard, *Deems Taylor* (N.Y., 1927). See also *Modern Music . . . Analytic Index* compiled by Wayne Shirley, ed. by Wm. and C. Lichtenwanger (N.Y., 1976, pp. 219–20).

Taylor, Franklin, English pianist and teacher; b. Birmingham, Feb. 5, 1843; d. London, March 19, 1919.

Pupil of C. Flavell (piano) and T. Bedsmore (organ); also studied 1859–61 at Leipzig Cons. Returning to London, he settled there as a highly successful concert pianist and teacher; 1876–82, prof. at the National Training School, and from 1883 at the Royal College of Music. He publ. *Primer of Pianoforte Playing* (1877); *Pianoforte Tutor; Technique and Expression in Pianoforte Playing* (1897).

Taylor, Raynor, English-American composer; b. in England, c.1747; d. Philadelphia, Aug. 17, 1825. He received his early training as a chorister in the Chapel Royal, and in 1765 became organist of a church in Chelmsford; that same year he was also appointed music director at Sadler's Wells Theatre, London. In 1792 he emigrated to the U.S., going first to Baltimore and then to Annapolis, where he was organist of St. Anne's Church. Moving to Philadelphia in 1793, he became organist of St. Peter's there, and in 1820 was one of the founders of the Musical Fund Society. A gifted singer, he gave humorous musical entertainments which he called "olios," and in 1796 conducted an orchestral concert that included several of his own compositions. In collaboration with A. Reinagle, who had been his pupil in London, he composed a "Monody" on the death of Washington (1799), and a ballad opera, *Pizarro, or the Spaniards in Peru* (1800); some of his song manuscripts are in the N.Y. Public Library.
  BIBLIOGRAPHY: L. C. Madeira, *Annals of Music in Philadelphia* (1896); O. G. Sonneck, *Early Concert-Life in America* (1905); J. T. Howard, *A Program of Early American Piano Music* (1931).

Tchaikovsky, Boris, Russian composer; b. Moscow, Sept. 10, 1925. He studied at the Moscow Cons. with Shostakovitch, Shebalin, and Miaskovsky. He publ. his earliest piano works at the age of 13; wrote an opera, *The Star* (1949); Symph. No. 1 (1947); *Fantasy on Russian Themes* for orch. (1950); *Slavic Rhapsody* for orch. (1951); *Symphonietta* (1953); Symph. No. 2 (1967); Piano Concerto (1969); Violin Concerto (1970); 4 string quartets; Piano Trio; Violin Sonata; piano pieces. He is not related to Piotr Ilyich Tchaikovsky.

Tchaikovsky, Modest, Russian playwright and librettist; brother of **Piotr Ilyich Tchaikovsky;** b. Alapaevsk, Perm district, May 13, 1850; d. Moscow, Jan. 15, 1916. He was the closest intimate of Tchaikovsky, and the author of the basic biography. His plays had only a passing success, but he was an excellent librettist; he wrote the librettos of Tchaikovsky's last 2 operas, *The Queen of Spades* and *Iolanthe.*

Tchaikovsky, Piotr Ilyich, famous Russian composer; b. Votkinsk, district of Viatka, May 7, 1840; d. St. Petersburg, Nov. 6, 1893. The son of a mining inspector at a plant in the Urals, he was given a good education; had a French governess and a music teacher. When he was 10, the family moved to St. Petersburg, and he was sent to a school of jurisprudence, from which he graduated at 19 and became a government clerk; while at school he studied music with Lomakin, but did not display conspicuous talent as either pianist or composer. At the age of 21 he was accepted in a musical institution, newly established by Anton Rubinstein, which was to become the St. Petersburg Conservatory. He studied with Zaremba (harmony and counterpoint) and Rubinstein (composition); graduated in 1865, winning a silver medal for his cantata to Schiller's *Hymn To Joy.* In 1866 he became prof. of harmony at the Moscow Cons. under the directorship of Nicholas Rubinstein. As if to compensate for a late beginning in his profession, he began to compose with great application. His early works (a programmatic symphony, subtitled *Winter Dreams,* some overtures and small pieces for string quartet) reveal little individuality. With his symph. poem *Fatum* (1869) came the first formulation of his style, highly subjective, preferring minor modes, permeated with nostalgic longing and alive with keen rhythms. In 1869 he undertook the composition of his overture-fantasy *Romeo and Juliet;* not content with what he had written, he profited by the advice of Balakirev, whom he met in St. Petersburg, and revised the work in 1870; but this version proved equally unsatisfactory; Tchaikovsky laid the composition aside, and did not complete it until 1879; in its final form it became one of his most successful works. A Belgian soprano, Désirée Artôt, a member of an opera troupe visiting St. Petersburg in 1868, took great interest in Tchaikovsky, and he was moved by her attentions; for a few months he seriously contemplated marriage, and so notified his father (his mother had died of cholera when he was 14 years old). But this proved to be a passing infatuation on her part, for soon she married the Spanish singer Padilla; Tchaikovsky reacted to this event with a casual philosophical remark about the inconstancy of human attachments. Throughout his career Tchaikovsky never allowed his psychological turmoil to interfere with his work. Besides teaching and composing, he contributed music criticism to Moscow newspapers for several years (1868–74), traveled often abroad, and visited the first Bayreuth Festival in 1876, reporting his impressions for the Moscow daily *Russkyie Vedomosti.* His closest friends were members of his own family, his brothers (particularly Modest, his future biographer) and his married sister Alexandra Davidov, at whose estate, Kamenka, he spent most of his summers. The correspondence with them, all of which was preserved and eventually published, throws a true light on Tchaikovsky's character and his life. His other intimate friends were his publisher Jurgenson, Nicholas Rubinstein, and several other musicians. The most extraordinary of his friendships was the epistolary intimacy with Nadezhda von Meck, a wealthy widow, whom he never met, but who was to play an important role in his life. Through the violinist Kotek she learned about Tchaikovsky's financial difficulties, and commissioned him to write some compositions, at large fees; then arranged to pay him an annuity of 6,000 rubles. For more than 13 years they corresponded voluminously, even when they lived in the same city (Moscow, Florence); on several occasions Madame von Meck hinted that she would not be averse to a personal meeting, but Tchaikovsky invariably declined such a suggestion, under the pretext that one should not see one's guardian angel in the flesh. On Tchaikovsky's part, this correspondence had to remain within the circumscribed domain of art, personal philosophy, and reporting of daily events, without touching on the basic problems of his existence. On July 18,

1877, Tchaikovsky contracted marriage with a conservatory student named Antonina Milyukova, who had declared her love for him. This was an act of defiance of his own nature; Tchaikovsky was a deviate, and made no secret of it in the correspondence with his brother Modest (who was also abnormal in this respect). He thought that by flaunting a wife he could prevent the already rife rumors about his abnormality from spreading further. The result was disastrous, and Tchaikovsky fled from his wife in horror. He attempted suicide by walking into the Moskva River in order to catch pneumonia, but suffered nothing more severe than simple discomfort. He then went to St. Petersburg to seek the advice of his brother Anatol, a lawyer, who made suitable arrangements with Tchaikovsky's wife for a separation. (They were never divorced; she died in an insane asylum in 1917.) Madame von Meck, to whom Tchaikovsky wrote candidly of the hopeless failure of his marriage (without revealing the true cause of that failure), made at once an offer of further financial assistance, which Tchaikovsky gratefully accepted. He spent several months during 1877–78 in Italy, in Switzerland, in Paris, and in Vienna. During these months he completed one of his greatest works, the 4th Symphony, dedicated to Mme. von Meck. It was performed for the 1st time in Moscow on March 4, 1878, but Tchaikovsky did not cut short his sojourn abroad to attend the performance. He resigned from the Moscow Cons. in the autumn of 1878, and from that time dedicated himself entirely to composition. The continued subsidy from Mme. von Meck allowed him to forget money matters. Early in 1879 he completed his most successful opera, *Eugene Onegin* ("lyric scenes," after Pushkin); it was first produced in Moscow by a conservatory ensemble, on March 29, 1879, and gained success only gradually; the 1st performance at the Imperial Opera in St. Petersburg did not take place until 5 years later (Oct. 31, 1884). A morbid depression was still Tchaikovsky's natural state of mind, but every new work sustained his faith in his destiny as a composer, despite many disheartening reversals. His Piano Concerto No. 1, rejected by Nicholas Rubinstein as unplayable, was given its world première (somewhat incongruously) in Boston, on Oct. 25, 1875, played by Hans von Bülow, and afterwards was performed all over the world by famous pianists, including Nicholas Rubinstein himself. His Violin Concerto, criticized by Leopold Auer (to whom the score was originally dedicated) and attacked by Hanslick with sarcasm and virulence at its world première by Brodsky in Vienna (1881), survived all its detractors, to become one of the most celebrated pieces in the violin repertory. The 5th Symphony (1888) was successful from the very first. Early in 1890 Tchaikovsky wrote his 2nd important opera, *The Queen of Spades*, which was produced at the Imperial Opera in St. Petersburg in that year. His ballets *Swan Lake* (1876) and *The Sleeping Beauty* (1889) became famous on Russian stages. But at the peak of his career, Tchaikovsky suffered a severe psychological blow; Mme. von Meck notified him of the discontinuance of her subsidy, and with this announcement she abruptly terminated their correspondence. Tchaikovsky could now well afford the loss of the money, but his pride was deeply hurt by the manner in which Mme. von Meck had acted. It is indicative of Tchaikovsky's inner strength that even this desertion of one whom he regarded as his staunchest friend did not affect his ability to work. In 1891 he undertook his first and only voyage to America. He was received with honors as a celebrated composer; he led 4 concerts of his works in N.Y. and one each in Baltimore and Philadelphia. He did not linger in the U.S., however, and returned to St. Petersburg in a few weeks. Early in 1892 he made a concert tour as conductor in Russia, and then proceeded to Warsaw and Germany. In the meantime he had purchased a house in the town of Klin, not far from Moscow, where he wrote his last symphony, the *Pathétique*. Despite the perfection of his technique, he did not arrive at the desired form and substance of this work at once, and discarded his original sketch. The title *Pathétique* was suggested to him by his brother Modest; the score was dedicated to his nephew, Vladimir Davidov. Its music is the final testament of Tchaikovsky's life, and an epitome of his philosophy of fatalism. In the 1st movement, the trombones are given the theme of the Russian service for the dead. Remarkably, the score of one of his gayest works, the ballet *The Nutcracker*, was composed simultaneously with the early sketches for the *Pathétique*. Tchaikovsky was in good spirits when he went to St. Petersburg to conduct the première of the *Pathétique*, on Oct. 28, 1893 (which was but moderately successful). A cholera epidemic was then raging in St. Petersburg, and the population was specifically warned against drinking unboiled water, but apparently Tchaikovsky carelessly did exactly that. He showed the symptoms of cholera soon afterwards, and nothing could be done to save him. The melodramatic hypothesis that the fatal drink of water was a defiance of death, in perfect knowledge of the danger, since he must have remembered his mother's death of the same dread infection, is untenable in the light of published private letters between the attendant physician and Modest Tchaikovsky at the time. Tchaikovsky's fatalism alone would amply account for his lack of precaution.

As a composer, Tchaikovsky stands apart from the militant national movement of the "Mighty Five." The Russian element is, of course, very strong in Tchaikovsky's music, and upon occasion he made use of Russian folksongs in his works, but this national spirit is instinctive rather than consciously cultivated. His personal relationship with the St. Petersburg group of nationalists was friendly without being intimate; his correspondence with Rimsky-Korsakov, Balakirev, and others was mostly concerned with professional matters. Tchaikovsky's music was frankly sentimental; his supreme gift of melody, which none of his Russian contemporaries could match, secured for him a lasting popularity among performers and audiences. His influence was profound on the Moscow group of musicians, of whom Arensky and Rachmaninoff were the most talented. He wrote in every genre, and was successful in each; besides his stage works, symphonies, chamber music, and piano compositions, he composed a great number of lyric songs that are the most poignant creations of his genius. By a historical paradox, Tchaikovsky became the most popular Russian composer under the Soviet regime. His subjectivism, his fatalism, his emphasis on melancholy moods, even his reactionary political views (which included a brand of amateurish anti-Semitism), failed to detract from his stature in the new society. In fact, official spokesmen of Soviet Russia repeatedly urged Soviet composers to follow in the path of Tchaikovsky's esthetics. Tchaikovsky's popularity is also very strong in Anglo-Saxon countries, particularly in America; much less so in France and Italy; in Germany his influence is insignificant.

WORKS: OPERAS: *The Voyevode* (1867–68; Moscow, Feb. 11, 1869); *Undine* (1869); *The Oprichnik* (1870–72; St. Petersburg, April 24, 1874); *Vakula the Smith* (1874; St. Petersburg, Dec. 6, 1876); *Eugene Onegin* (1877–78; Moscow, March, 29, 1879); *The Maid of Orleans* (1878–79; St. Petersburg, Feb. 25, 1881); *Mazeppa* (1881–83; Moscow, Feb. 15, 1884); *Tcherevichki* (*The Little Shoes;* revised version of *Vakula the Smith;* 1885; Moscow, Jan. 31, 1887); *The Sorceress* (1888–87; St. Petersburg, Nov. 1, 1887); *The Queen of Spades* (1890; St. Petersburg, Dec. 19, 1890); *Iolanthe* (1891; St. Petersburg, Dec. 18, 1892).

BALLETS: *Swan Lake* (1875–76; Moscow, March 4, 1877); *The Sleeping Beauty* (1888–89; St. Petersburg, Jan. 15, 1890), *The Nutcracker* (1891–92; St. Petersburg, Dec. 18, 1892).

FOR ORCH.: 6 symphonies: No. 1 (*Winter Dreams;* 1868; revised 1874; Moscow, Feb. 15, 1868); No. 2, the *Little Russian* or *Ukrainian Symph.* (Moscow, Feb. 7, 1873); No. 3 (1875; Moscow, Nov. 19, 1875); No. 4 (1877; Moscow, March 4, 1878); No. 5 (1888; St. Petersburg, Nov. 17, 1888); No. 6 (*Pathétique;* 1893; St. Petersburg, Oct. 28, 1893); overture to Ostrovsky's play *The Storm* (1864); symph. poem *Fatum* (1868; Moscow, Feb. 27, 1869); overture *Romeo and Juliet* (1869; Moscow, March 16, 1870; final version 1880); symph. fantasy *The Tempest,* after Shakespeare (1873; Moscow, Dec. 19, 1873); 1st Piano Concerto (1874–75; Boston Oct. 25, 1875); *Sérénade mélancolique,* for violin with orch. (1875; Moscow, Jan. 28, 1876); *Slavonic March* (1876; Moscow, Nov. 17, 1876); symph. fantasy *Francesca da Rimini,* after Dante (1876; Moscow, March 9, 1877); suite from the ballet *Swan Lake* (1876); *Variations on a Rococo Theme,* for cello and orch. (1876); Moscow, Nov. 30, 1877); *Valse-Scherzo,* for violin with orch. (1877; Paris, Oct. 21, 1878); *Suite* No. 1 (1878–79; Moscow, Nov. 23, 1879); Violin Concerto (1878; Vienna, Dec. 4, 1881); Piano Concerto No. 2 (1879–80; Moscow, May 30, 1882); *Italian Capriccio* (1880; Moscow, Dec. 18, 1880); *1812 Overture* (1880; Moscow, Aug. 20, 1882); *Serenade* for string orch. (1880; Moscow, Jan. 28, 1882); *Suite* No. 2 (1883; Moscow, Feb. 16, 1884); *Suite* No. 3 (1884; St. Petersburg, Jan. 28, 1885); *Concert Fantasy* for piano with orch. (1884; Moscow, March 6, 1885); symphony *Manfred,* after Byron (1885; Moscow, March 23, 1886); *Suite* No. 4, *Mozartiana* (1887; Moscow, Nov. 26, 1887); overture-fantasy, *Hamlet* (1888; St. Petersburg, Nov. 24, 1888); *Pezzo capriccioso,* for cello with orch. (1887; Moscow, Dec. 7, 1889); suite from the ballet *The Sleeping Beauty* (1889); symph. ballad, *The Voyevode,* after Pushkin's translation of Mickiewicz's ballad (1890–91; Moscow, Nov. 18, 1891); suite from the ballet *Nutcracker* (1892; St. Petersburg, March 19,

1892); 3rd Piano Concerto (one movement only; posthumous; St. Petersburg, Jan. 19, 1895); *Andante and Finale* for piano with orch. (1893; actually 2nd and 3rd movements of the 3rd Piano Concerto; posthumous; St. Petersburg, Feb. 20, 1896).

CHAMBER MUSIC: 3 string quartets (1871; 1874; 1876); Piano Trio, in memory of Nicholas Rubinstein (Moscow, Oct. 30, 1882); *Souvenir de Florence,* for string sextet (1887; St. Petersburg, Dec. 7, 1892); also *Souvenir d'un lieu cher,* for violin and piano (1878); several fragments of early works.

FOR PIANO: *Scherzo à la russe* (1867); *Souvenir de Hapsal,* 3 pieces (No. 3 is the famous *Chant sans paroles;* 1867); *Valse-Caprice* (1868); *Romance* in F minor (1868); *Valse-Scherzo* (1870); *Capriccio* (1870); *2 morceaux: Rêverie, Polka de Salon, Mazurka de Salon* (1870); *2 morceaux: Nocturne* and *Humoresque* (1871); *6 morceaux: Rêverie du Soir, Scherzo humoristique, Feuillet d'album, Nocturne, Capriccioso, Thème original et variations* (1872); *6 morceaux sur un seul thème: Prelude, Fugue, Impromptu, Marche funèbre, Mazurka, Scherzo* (1973); *Grande sonate,* in G major (1879); *Les Quatre Saisons,* 12 characteristic pieces for each month of the year (1875–76; of these the most famous are No. 6, *Barcarole;* No. 10, *Chant d'automne;* No. 11, *En Traineau;* No. 12, *Noël*); *12 morceaux* (1876–78; among them *Chanson triste* and *Danse russe*); *Album pour enfants,* 24 pieces (1878); *6 pièces* (1882); *Dumka* (1886); *18 morceaux* (1893); Sonata in C-sharp minor (1865; posthumous).

VOCAL WORKS: cantata, *An die Freude* (Schiller), for chorus and orch. (1865); *Liturgy of St. John Chrysostom,* for mixed chorus in 4 parts (1878); Vesper Service, for mixed chorus (1882); *Moskva,* coronation cantata for solo voices, chorus, and orch. (1883); 3 Cherubic Hymns, for mixed chorus (1884); 6 Church Songs (1885); other sacred and secular vocal pieces; about 100 songs among them such favorites as *Nur wer die Sehnsucht kennt* (after Goethe), *Berceuse,* etc.; 6 duets.

He publ. a *Manual of Harmony* (Moscow, 1870; many eds. English transl. as *Guide to the Practical Study of Harmony,* 1900). The collected criticisms and reminiscences were publ. in 1898; new ed., revised and enlarged, Moscow, 1953; diaries, comprising 11 separate fragments, covering the years between 1873 and 1891, were publ. in Moscow in 1923 (English transl., N.Y., 1945). A centennial edition of the complete works, in as many as 120 vols., was begun in 1940, interrupted during the war years, and resumed in 1946. Most of the manuscripts, correspondence, etc. are preserved in Tchaikovsky's house in Klin (now the Tchaikovsky Museum). A thematic catalogue was issued by B. Jurgenson (Moscow, 1897; reprinted N.Y., 1941). More recently the Tschaikowsky-Studio Institute International issued the *Systematisches Verzeichnis der Werke von P. I. Tschaikowsky* (Hamberg, 1973).

BIBLIOGRAPHY: The basic source is the 3-vol. biography by Modest Tchaikovsky, *The Life of P. I. T.* (Moscow, 1900–02), but in it the author was compelled to withhold essential facts of Tchaikovsky's life; translations were made, into German by Paul Juon (2 vols.; Leipzig, 1900, 1902) and into English by Ross Newmarch (abridged) as *The Life and Letters of*

P. I. T. (London, 1906). Chapters on Tchaikovsky are included in all music histories and books dealing specifically with Russian music. Books and articles in various languages that should be noted include: V. Tcheshikhin, *P. T. Attempt at a Characterization* (Riga, 1893); H. Laroche and N. Kashkin, *In Memory of T.* (Moscow, 1894); N. Kashkin, *Reminiscenses of T.* (Moscow, 1897); E. Markham Lee, *T.* (Music of the Masters series; N.Y., 1904); Edwin Evans, Sr., *T.* (London, 1906; revised ed., 1935); *P. I. T.,* a symposium, in the series "The Past of Russian Music" (Petrograd, 1920), containing documents relating mainly to the Tchaikovsky Museum in Klin; Igor Glebov, *T.: An Essay of Characterization* (Petrograd, 1922); Igor Glebov, *P. I. T.: His Life and Works* (Petrograd, 1922; a different book from the preceding); H. Laroche, *Collected Musico-Critical Articles,* vol. 2 (Moscow, 1922); M. Steinitzer, *T.* (Leipzig, 1925); R. H. Stein, *T.* (Stuttgart, 1927); Eric Blom, *T.; Orchestral Works* (Musical Pilgrim series; London, 1927); M. D. Calvocoressi and Gerald Abraham, *Masters of Russian Music* (London, 1936; pp. 249–334; this essay publ. separately, 1949); Nikolai von Pals, *P. T.* (Potsdam, 1939); H. Weinstock, *T.* (N.Y., 1943); Gerald Abraham, *T.: A Short Biography* (London, 1944); H. Célis and W.-P. Right, *T.* (Brussels, 1945); Gerald Abraham, *T.: A Symposium* (London, 1945; in the U.S. as *The Music of T.,* (N.Y., 1946); D. Brook, *6 Great Russian Composers* (London, 1946); D. Shostakovich and others, *Russian Symphony; Thoughts about T.* (N.Y., 1947); R. Hofmann, *T.* (Paris, 1947); A. Alshvang, *Analytic Essay on T.'s Creative Work* (Moscow, 1951); J. A. Kremlev, *Symphonies of P. I. Tchaikovsky* (Moscow, 1955); G. Dombayev, *Creative Work of T.* (Moscow, 1958); B. I. Rabinovich, *P. I. Tchaikovsky and Songs of the People* (Moscow, 1963); *House-Museum of P. I. Tchaikovsky in Klin,* a guide (2nd revised edition, Moscow, 1967); A. A. Alshvang, *P. I. Tchaikovsky* (Moscow, 1970); B. V. Asafiev, *On the Music of Tchaikovsky: Selections* (Leningrad, 1972); J. Warrack, *Tchaikovsky* (1973); L. M. Konisskaya, *Tchaikovsky in St. Petersburg* (Leningrad, 1974). Numerous pamphlets dealing with Tchaikovsky's operas, ballets, orchestral works, etc. have been issued in Russia; of these, the most valuable are: N. Findeisen, *T.'s Chamber Music* (Moscow, 1930), A. Budiakovsky, *P. I. T., Symphonic Music* (Leningrad, 1935), V. Bogdanov-Berezovsky, *Operatic and Choreographic Works of T.* (Moscow, 1940), B. M. Yarustovsky, *Operatic Dramaturgy of T.* (Moscow, 1947), and N. Nikolayeva, *Symphonies of T.* (Moscow, 1958). V. Yakovlev compiled a most detailed chronology (often day by day) of Tchaikovsky's life, *Days and Years of T.* (Moscow, 1940). Of the greatest importance is the publication of the complete extant correspondence between Tchaikovsky and Mme. von Meck, in 3 vols. (Moscow, 1933; 1934; 1936). Other correspondence include *Letters to Relatives* (vol. 1, Moscow, 1940); *Correspondence with P. I. Jurgenson* (2 vols., Moscow, 1939, 1952); letters to and from S. Taneyev (Moscow, 1951); selected letters to intimates (Moscow, 1955). Magazine articles on Tchaikovsky include the following, publ. in the *Musical Quarterly:* Olga Bennigsen, "A Bizarre Friendship: T. and Mme. von Meck" (Oct. 1936); N. Slonimsky, "Further Light on T." (April 1938); S. Ber-

tenson, "The T. Museum at Klin" (July 1944). There are several fictional biographies of Tchaikovsky; among them one written by Catherine D. Bowen and Barbara von Meck, *Beloved Friend* (N.Y., 1937); Klaus Mann, *Symphonie pathétique* (Amsterdam, 1938, in German; in English, N.Y., 1948).

Tchakarov, Emil, Bulgarian conductor; b. Burgas, June 29, 1948. He studied at the State Cons. in Sofia, where he conducted the youth orch. (1965–72); then directed the Bulgarian Television Chamber Orch. (1968–70). In 1971 he won first prize at the International Conductors' Competition of the Herbert von Karajan Foundation; in 1972 he studied conducting with Franco Ferrara and in 1974 with Eugen Jochum. Still in his 20s he filled engagements as guest conductor all over the world: with the Berlin Philharmonic, with the Vienna Radio Orch., San Francisco Symph. Orch., the Holland Radio Orch., and various symphonic groups in France, England, Canada, Australia, Japan, and Russia. In 1974 he was appointed permanent conductor of the State Philharmonic in Plovdiv, Bulgaria.

Tcherepnin, Alexander, greatly significant Russian composer and pianist; son of **Nicolas Tcherepnin;** b. St. Petersburg, Jan. 20, 1899; d. Paris, Sept. 29, 1977. (The name is pronounced with the stress on the last syllable). He studied piano as a child with his mother; was encouraged by his father in his first steps in composition, but did not take formal lessons with him. He began to compose in his early youth; wrote a short comic opera at the age of 12, and a ballet when he was 13; then produced a number of piano works; composed 14 piano sonatas before he was 19 years old. In 1917 he entered the Petrograd Cons., where he studied music theory with Sokolov, and piano with Kobiliansky, but remained there only one school year; then joined his parents in a difficult journey to Tiflis, in the Caucasus, during a gradually expanding civil war; in Tiflis, he took lessons in composition with Thomas de Hartmann. In 1921 the family went to Paris, where he continued his studies, taking piano lessons with Isidor Philipp and composition with Paul Vidal. In 1922 he played a concert of his own music in London; in 1923 he was commissioned by Anna Pavlova to write a ballet, *Ajanta's Frescoes,* which she produced in London with her troupe. Tcherepnin progressed rapidly in his career as a pianist and a composer; he played in Germany and in Austria; made his first American tour in 1926. Between 1934 and 1937 he made two journeys to the Far East; gave concerts in China and Japan; numerous Chinese and Japanese composers studied with him; he organized a publishing enterprise in Tokyo for the publication of serious works by young Japanese and Chinese composers. He married a Chinese pianist, **Lee Hsien-Ming.** Despite his wide travels, he maintained his principal residence in Paris, and remained there during the war. He resumed his international career in 1947; gave concerts in Scandinavia and elsewhere in Europe. In 1949 he and his wife joined the faculty of De Paul Univ. in Chicago, and taught there for 15 years. In the meantime his music began to be well known; he had 34 publishers; his symphonic works were conducted by Koussevitzky,

Stokowski, Monteux, Munch, Mitropoulos, Fritz Reiner, Kubelik, William Steinberg, Skrowaczewski, and other famous conductors; he was also a frequent soloist in his piano concertos, which he performed with the major symphony orchestras in America and Europe. He became an American citizen in 1958. In May, 1967 Tcherepnin made his first visit to Russia after nearly half a century abroad. In his early works he followed the traditions of Russian Romantic music; characteristically, his Piano Sonata No. 13, which he wrote as a youth, is entitled *Sonatine romantique.* But as he progressed in his career, he evolved a musical language all of his own; he derived his melodic patterns from a symmetrically formed scale of 9 degrees, subdivided into three equal sections (e.g. C, D, E-flat, E, F-sharp, G, G-sharp, A-sharp, B, C); the harmonic idiom follows a similar intertonal formation; Tcherepnin's consistent use of such thematic groupings anticipated the serial method of composition. Furthermore, he developed a type of rhythmic polyphony, based on thematic rhythmic units, which he termed "interpunctus." However, he did not limit himself to these melodic and rhythmic constructions; he also explored the latent resources of folk music, both Oriental and European; he was particularly sensitive to the melorhythms of Russian national songs. A composer of remarkable inventive power, he understood the necessity of creating a communicative musical language, and was primarily concerned with enhancing the lyric and dramatic qualities of his music. At the same time he showed great interest in new musical resources, including electronic sound. His sons **Serge** and **Ivan** are both engaged in experimental musical production.

WORKS: OPERAS: *Ol-Ol,* after Leonid Andreyev (Weimar, Jan. 31, 1928); *Die Hochzeit der Sobeide,* after Hugo von Hofmannsthal (Vienna, March 17, 1933); *The Farmer and the Fairy* (Aspen Festival, Colorado, Aug. 13, 1952); completed Mussorgsky's opera *The Marriage* (Essen, Sept. 14, 1937). BALLETS: *Ajanta's Frescos* (Anna Pavlova's production, London, Sept. 10, 1923); *Training* (Vienna, June 19, 1935); *Der fahrend Schüler mit dem Teufelsbannen* (1937; score lost during the war; reconstructed, 1965); *Trepak* (Mordkin's Russian Ballet, Richmond, Virginia. Oct. 10, 1938); *La Légende de Razin* (1941); *Déjeuner sur l'herbe* (Paris, Oct. 14, 1945); *L'Homme à la Peau de Léopard* (with Arthur Honegger and Tibor Harsányi; Monte Carlo, May 5, 1946); *La Colline des fantômes* (1946); *Jardin persan* (1946); *Nuit kurde* (Paris, 1946); *La Femme et son ombre,* after Paul Claudel (Paris, June 14, 1948); *Aux temps des tartares* (Buenos Aires, 1949). CANTATAS: *Vivre d'amour* (1942); *Pan Kéou* (Paris, Oct. 9, 1945); *Le Jeu de la Nativité* (Paris, Dec. 30, 1945); *Les Douze,* poem by Alexander Block for narrator, strings, harp and percussion (Paris, Nov. 9, 1947); *Vom Spass und Ernst,* folksong cantata for voice and strings (1964); *The Story of Ivan the Fool,* cantata with a narrator (London, Dec. 24, 1968). FOR ORCH.: *Overture* (1921); *Symph. No. 1* (Paris, Oct. 29, 1927); *Symph No. 2* (Chicago, March 20, 1952); *Symph. No. 3* (Indianapolis, Jan. 15, 1955); *Symph No. 4* (Boston, Dec. 5, 1958); *Symphony-Prayer* (Chicago, Aug. 19, 1960). *Magna Mater* (Munich, Oct. 30, 1930); *Russian Dances* (Omaha, Feb. 15,

1934); *Mystère* for cello and chamber orch. (Monte Carlo, Dec. 8, 1926); *Concerto da camera* for flute, violin, and chamber orch. (1924); *Concertino* for violin, cello, piano, and strings (1931); *Suite georgienne* (Paris, April 17, 1940); 6 piano concertos: No. 1 (Monte Carlo, 1923); No. 2 (Paris, Jan. 26, 1924, composer soloist); No. 3 (Paris, Feb. 5, 1933, composer soloist); No. 4 (retitled *Fantasia;* 1947); No. 5 (West Berlin, Oct. 13, 1963, composer soloist); No. 6 (Lucerne, Sept. 5, 1972); *Serenade* for string orch. (1964); *Musica sacra* for string orch. (Lourdes, April 28, 1973). *Évocation* (1948); *Suite* (Louisville, May 1, 1954); Concerto for harmonica and orch. (Venice, Sept. 11, 1956); *Divertimento* (Chicago, Nov. 14, 1957). CHAMBER MUSIC: Piano Trio (1925); 2 string quartets (1922, 1926); Piano Quintet (1927); *Ode* for cello and piano (1919); 3 cello sonatas (1924, 1925, 1926); Violin Sonata (1922); *Elegy* for violin and piano (1927); *Le Violoncelle bien temperé,* 12 preludes for cello with piano, 2 of them with a drum (Berlin, March 23, 1927); *Suite* for cello solo (1946); *Mouvement perpétuel* for violin and piano (1935); Sonatina for kettledrums and piano (1939); *Sonatine sportive,* for bassoon or saxophone and piano (1939); *Andante* for tuba and piano (1939): Trio for flutes (1939); Quartet for flutes (1939); *Marche* for 3 trumpets (1939); *Sonata da Chiesa* for viola da gamba and organ (1966). FOR PIANO: *Scherzo* (1917); *10 Bagatelles* (1913–18); *Sonatine romantique* (1918); 2 sonatas (1918, 1961); *Toccata* (1921); *Feuilles libres* (1920–24); *5 Arabesques* (1921); *9 Inventions* (1921); *2 Novelettes* (1922); *4 Préludes nostalgiques* (1922); *6 Études de travail* (1923); *Message* (1926); *Entretiens* (1930); *Études de piano sur la gamme pentatonique* (1935); *Autour des montagnes russes* (1937); *Badinage* (1942); *Le Monde en Vitrine* (1946); *12 Preludes* (1952); *8 Piano Pieces* (1954); *Suite* for harpsichord (1966). VOCAL WORKS: *Lost Flute,* 7 songs on poems translated from the Chinese, for narrator and piano (1954); several albums of songs to poems in Russian, French, and Chinese. He compiled an *Anthology of Russian Music* (with English and German texts, Bonn, 1966).

BIBLIOGRAPHY: Willi Reich, *Alexander Tcherepnin* (Bonn, 1961, in German; French translation, Paris, 1962); N. Slonimsky, "Alexander Tcherepnin, Septuagenarian," *Tempo* (Jan. 1969).

Tcherepnin, Ivan, American composer, son of **Alexander Tcherepnin;** b. Paris, Feb. 5, 1943. He received his early musical training at home in Paris; then followed his father to the U.S., where he entered Harvard Univ., graduating in 1964; also attended courses with Karlheinz Stockhausen and Henri Pousseur in Cologne, and with Pierre Boulez in Darmstadt; studied electronic techniques in Toronto in 1966; returned to Harvard for graduate studies as a pupil of Randall Thompson and Leon Kirchner, obtaining his M.A. degree in 1969. He was instructor at the San Francisco Cons. of Music (1969–72); in 1972 was appointed to the faculty of Harvard Univ. to teach courses in electronic composition.

WORKS: *Suite progressive pentatonique* for flute, cello, and timpani (1959); *Deux entourages sur un thème Russe* for Ondes Martenot, percussion, and piano (1961); *Mozartean Suite* for flute, clarinet and bassoon (1962); *Reciprocals* for flute, clarinet, and bassoon (1962); *Work Music* for electric guitar, French horn, clarinet, and cello (1965); *Sombres Lumières* for flute, guitar, and cello (1965); *Wheelwinds* for 9 wind instruments (1966); *Rings* for string quartet and ring modulators (1968); *Summer Music* for brass sextet (1970); *Light Music with Water* for 4 instrumental groups, 4 sound-activated strobe lights, electronic accessories, and prepared tape (1970); electronic music for films; an electronic score, *Set, Hold, Clear, and Squelch,* composed for Merce Cunningham's Dance Co. (N.Y., Feb. 21, 1976).

Tcherepnin, Nicolas, noted Russian composer, conductor and eminent pedagogue; b. St. Petersburg, May 14, 1873; d. Issy-les-Moulineaux, near Paris, June 26, 1945. He was a student of Rimsky-Korsakov at the St. Petersburg Cons. (1895–98); in 1905 was appointed to its faculty; taught orchestration and conducting; Prokofiev was among his many students. He conducted at the festival of Russian music in Paris in 1908; until 1912 toured with the Diaghilev Ballet Russe in Europe. He then returned to Russia; after the Revolution of 1917, he proceeded to the Caucasus, and was director of the Tiflis Cons. (1918–21); then went to Paris, accompanied by his son **Alexander,** and remained there until his death; served as director of the Russian Cons. in Paris (1925–29 and 1938–45). His music embodies the best elements of the Russian National School; it is melodious and harmonious; lyrical and gently dynamic; in some of his works there is a coloristic quality suggesting French Impressionistic influence.

WORKS: OPERAS: *Vanka* (Belgrade, 1935); *Svat,* after Ostrovsky. Ballets, *Pavillion d'Armide* (St. Petersburg, Nov. 25, 1907); *Narcisse et Echo* (Monte Carlo, April 26, 1911, composer conducting); *Masque de la Mort Rouge,* after Poe (Petrograd, Jan. 29, 1916, composer conducting); realization and completion of Mussorgsky's opera *The Fair at Sorochinsk* (Monte Carlo, March 17, 1923; Metropolitan Opera, N.Y., Nov. 29, 1930). FOR ORCH.: *Prelude* to Rostand's play *La Princesse lointaine* (1897); *Fantaisie dramatique* (1903); *Le Royaume enchanté,* symph. tableau (1904); Piano Concerto (1907). CHAMBER MUSIC: *Poème lyrique; Cadence fantastique; Un Air ancien* for flute and piano; *Pièce calme* for oboe and piano; *Pièce insouciante* for clarinet and piano; *Variations simples* for bassoon and piano; *Fanfare* for trumpet and piano; String Quartet; Quartet for horns; *Divertissement* for flute, oboe and bassoon. FOR PIANO: *14 Esquisses sur les images d'un alphabet russe* (an orchestral version of 8 of these was performed by the Boston Symph. Orch., Nov. 27, 1931); *Primitifs; Pièces de bonne humeur; Pièces sentimentals.* VOCAL WORKS: liturgical music of the Russian Orthodox rite, including Masses a cappella; *Pilgrimage and Passions of Virgin Mary* (Paris, Feb. 12, 1938); over 200 songs, some of them perennial favorites in Russia.

Tcherepnin, Serge, American composer; son of **Alexander Tcherepnin;** b. Paris, Feb. 2, 1941. He studied violin as a child; was taken to the U.S. in 1949; received his training in theory with his father; then took courses with Karlheinz Stockhausen and Pierre Boul-

ez in Darmstadt. He pursued his regular academic education at Harvard Univ. where he studied with Walter Piston, Leon Kirchner and Billy Jim Layton, obtaining his B.A. in 1964. In 1966 he went to Milan to study electronic techniques. He then worked at the electronic studios at N.Y. Univ. (1968–70); in 1970 became instructor in electronic music at the School of Music in Valencia, Calif. He is the inventor of a portable music synthesizer, patented as the Serge Modular Music System.

WORKS: String Trio (1960); String Quartet (1961); *Kaddish* for speaker, clarinet, violin, oboe, flute, piano, and percussion, to a poem by Allan Ginsberg (1962); *Figures—Ground* for an optional ensemble of 7 to 77 instruments (1964); several multi-media pieces for Theater and films.

Tchesnokov, Pavel, Russian composer; b. near Voskresensk, Oct. 24, 1877; d. Moscow, March 14, 1944. He studied at the Moscow Cons. with Vassilenko, graduating in 1917; also took courses with Sergei Taneyev and Ippolitov-Ivanov. He devoted himself exclusively to choral composition, both secular and sacred; was from 1920 prof. of choral conducting at the Moscow Cons. He published a manual for choral singing (Moscow, 1940).

Tebaldi, Renata, celebrated Italian soprano; b. Langhirano, Parma, Feb. 1, 1922. She received her musical training at home with her mother, a singer, and her father, a cello player; went to Parma, where she studied with Passani; then to Milan, where she took a course with Carmen Melis (1939–42). She made her opera debut in Rovigo in the role of Elena in Boito's opera *Mefistofele.* She undertook a wide European tour as a guest singer at Covent Garden, London, at the Vienna State Opera, and at the Paris Opéra. She made her American debut in San Francisco in 1951; on Jan. 31, 1955 she appeared with the Metropolitan Opera, N.Y., as Desdemona in Verdi's *Otello;* she remained on the staff of the Metropolitan until 1970; but continued her tours in Europe; also sang in South America. Her voice represents the finest achievement of the modern Italian bel canto; she excels both in lyric and dramatic parts. Her repertory includes Tosca, Mimi, Madama Butterfly, Manon, Marguerite, Violetta and Aida.

BIBLIOGRAPHY: Kenn Harris, *Renata Tebaldi* (N.Y., 1974).

Tebaldini, Giovanni, Italian music scholar; b. Brescia, Sept. 7, 1864; d. San Benedetto del Tronto, May 11, 1952. He studied with Ponchielli and Amelli at the Cons. of Milan; served as maestro di cappella at San Marco in Venice (1889–94), at the Padua Cathedral (1894–97), and at the Cathedral of Loreto (1902–24); was director of the Cons. of Parma (1897–1902) and at the Cons. di San Pietro in Naples (1924–30); then went to Genoa, where he was appointed director of the Ateneo Musicale. His specialty was Italian sacred music, but his name suddenly sprang into sensational prominence when he published an article provocatively entitled "Telepatia musicale" (*Rivista Musicale Italiana,* March 1909), in which he cited thematic similarities between the opera *Cassandra,* by the relatively obscure Italian composer Vittorio Gnecchi, which was produced in 1905, and *Elektra* by Richard Strauss, written considerably later, implying a "telepathic" plagiarism on the part of Strauss. However, the juxtaposition of musical examples from both operas proved specious and failed to support Tebaldini's contention.

WRITINGS: *La Musica sacra in Italia* (Milan, 1894); *Gasparo Spontini* (Recanati, 1924); *Ildebrando Pizzetti* (Parma, 1931); also *Metodo teorico pratico per organo* (with Enrico Bossi; Milan 1897).

Tedesco, Ignaz (Amadeus), Bohemian pianist, called the "Hannibal of octaves"; b. Prague, 1817; d. Odessa, Nov. 13, 1882. He studied with Triebensee and Tomaschek; made successful concert tours, especially in Southern Russia; settled in Odessa. He composed for piano in a salon style; made transcriptions.

Teed, Roy, English pianist and composer; b. Herne Bay, Kent, May 18, 1928. He studied composition with Lennox Berkeley at the Royal Academy in London; also obtained a diploma in piano. He composed Piano Concerto (1952); *Festival Suite* for cello and string orch. (1958); *Introduction and Scherzo* for flute, oboe, and piano (1960); *So Blest a Day,* a Christmas cantata (1960); *The Pied Piper* for soloists, chorus, and orch. (1961); Quartet for flute and strings (1961); *Around the Town,* a comedy march (1962); *The Jackdaw of Rheims,* a narrative cantata (1964); numerous choruses and carols.

Teichmüller, Robert, German pianist and teacher; b. Brunswick, May 4, 1863; d. Leipzig, May 6, 1939. He studied piano with his father and with Reinecke at the Leipzig Cons., where from 1897 until his death he taught piano; made prof. in 1908. With K. Hermann he publ. a valuable guide, *Internationale moderne Klaviermusik* (Leipzig, 1927).

BIBLIOGRAPHY: A. Baresel, *R. T. als Mensch und Künstler* (Leipzig, 1922); A. Baresel, *R. T. und die Leipziger Klaviertradition* (Leipzig, 1934).

Teike, Carl (Albert Hermann), German composer of band music; b. Altdamm, Feb. 5, 1864; d. Landsberg, May 22, 1922. He studied French horn in his early youth; at 19 joined the band of the 123rd König Karl Regiment stationed at Ulm on the Danube. He soon began writing marches that were to become perennial favorites with German bands; at 25 he composed *Alte Kameraden (Old Comrades),* one of the best-known of German military marches, marked by a typically stolid square rhythm, with heavily accented downbeats. Teike resigned from the regiment as a result of disagreement with the bandmaster and joined the Royal German Police at Potsdam (1895–1908); then served with the postal service at Landsberg; he continued, however, to compose marches; during World War I he wrote the march *Graf Zeppelin* (known in English editions as *Conqueror*) which, despite its narrow militaristic nature, enjoyed international fame.

Tekeliev, Alexander, Bulgarian composer; b. Svilengrad, June 3, 1942. He studied composition with Veselin Stoyanov at the Bulgarian State Cons. in Sofia,

graduating in 1968; then became head of the music department of the Committee for Television and Radio in Sofia; also assumed music teaching duties at the Institute for Musical and Choreographical Training.

WORKS: an oratorio-requiem *The Year 1923* (1971); Clarinet Concerto (1968); *Ode to the USSR* for narrator, chorus and orch. (1970): *Adagio and Scherzo* for string orch. (1972); *Poem* for viola and orch. (1973); 2 chamber symphonies (1974, 1976); choral music and songs.

Telemann, Georg Michael, German theorist and composer; grandson of **Georg Philipp Telemann;** b. Plön, Holstein, April 20, 1748; d. Riga, March 4, 1831. In 1773 he went to Riga and became cantor there (pensioned in 1828). He publ. *Unterricht im Generalbass-Spielen, auf der Orgel oder sonst einem Clavier-Instrumente* (1773); *Beytrag zur Kirchenmusik* (1785; organ pieces); *Sammlung alter und neuer Kirchenmelodien* (1812); *Über die Wahl der Melodie eines Kirchenliedes* (1821); composed a book of trio sonatas, 6 violin sonatas, organ works.

Telemann, Georg Philipp, highly significant German composer; b. Magdeburg, March 14, 1681; d. Hamburg, June 25, 1767. He had only an ordinary school training in the musical rudiments, and owed his later eminence to self-instruction. At 12 he wrote an opera *à la Lully;* at 14 he conducted the music for a church at Hildesheim; in 1701 he entered Leipzig Univ. as a student of law and modern languages, and in 1704 became organist at the Neukirche, enlarging his choir by a students' singing society ("Collegium musicum") organized by himself. From 1704 to 1708 he was Kapellmeister to Count Promnitz at Sorau; then Konzertmeister at the court of Eisenach, where he succeeded Hebenstreit in 1709 as court conductor, retaining title and emoluments when called to Frankfurt in 1712 as Kapellmeister at the churches of the "Barefooted Friars" and St. Catherine. From 1721 till his death he was town musical director at Hamburg, declining, on Kuhnau's death in 1722, the proffered position of cantor of the Thomasschule at Leipzig. An astonishingly productive composer, he wrote with ease and fluency in any desired style; he was far better known in his time than Bach, though subsequently his fame suffered an eclipse. After Handel and Keiser he was the most notable of the early German dramatic composers.

WORKS: about 40 operas; of these the following were produced in Hamburg: *Der geduldige Socrates* (Jan. 28, 1721); *Der neu-modische Liebhaber Damon* (June, 1724); *Die ungleiche Heirat* (Sept. 27, 1725); *Miriways* (May 26, 1728); *Flavius Bertaridus König der Longobarden* (Nov. 23, 1729); 21 operas were written for Leipzig, and 4 for Weissenfels. Other works: 12 series of cantatas and motets for the church year (about 3,000 numbers with orch. or organ); 44 Passions; 32 installation numbers for preachers; 33 *Hamburger Capitänsmusiken* (each being a cantata with instrumental introduction); 20 pieces for jubilees, consecrations, or coronations; 12 funeral services; 14 numbers of wedding music; over 600 overtures; many serenades and marches; trio sonatas and other chamber music; also cantatas, odes, and oratorios. Most of his publ. works were engraved by Telemann himself. The following are among those that have been reprinted: the opera *Pimpinone*, in the *Erbe deutscher Musik* 6 (1936); oratorio *Der Tag des Gerichts* and the "monodrama" *Ino* (solo cantata for soprano with orch.), in the *Denkmäler deutscher Tonkunst* 28; a violin concerto (vol. 29); trio sonata in Riemann's *Collegium Musicum;* a "symphony" in Schering's *Perlen alter Kammermusik;* a concerto for 4 violins ed. by H. von Dameck; concerto ed. by H. Engel; an oboe concerto ed. by F. Stein; a flute quartet ed. by Ermeler; *Sing-, Spiel- und Generalbassübungen,* ed. by M. Seiffert (1914); clavier fantasias ed. by Seiffert (Frankfurt, 1923); *Musique de Table* (instrumental suites), ed. by Seiffert, in the *Denkmäler deutscher Tonkunst* 61-62; 24 Odes (vol. 57); also several cantatas, etc. An edition of his works, issued by the Auftrag der Gesellschaft für Musikforschung, was begun in 1950 and reached 24 vols. by 1977.

BIBLIOGRAPHY: Telemann's autobiography in J. Mattheson's *Grundlage einer Ehrenpforte* (Hamburg, 1740; reprinted by M. Schneider, Berlin, 1910); a brief *curriculum vitae* and a letter in J. Mattheson, *Grosse General-Bass-Schule, oder der exemplarischen Organisten Probe* (2nd ed., Hamburg, 1731), reproduced in Willi Kahl, *Selbstbiographien deutscher Musiker* (Cologne, 1948); K. Ottzenn, *Telemann als Opernkomponist* (Berlin, 1902); R. Rolland, *Voyage musical au pays du passé* (1919; English transl., 1922); M. Seiffert, "Telemanns *Musique de Table* als Quelle für Händel," *Bulletin de la Société Union Musicologique* (1924); H. Gräser, *Telemanns Instrumental-Kammermusik* (Frankfurt, 1925); R. Meissner, *G. P. Telemanns Frankfurter Kirchen-Kantaten* (Frankfurt, 1924); E. Valentin, *G. P. Telemann* (Burg, 1931; revised ed., 1952); H. Büttner, *Das Konzert in den Orch.-Suiten Telemanns* (Leipzig, 1931); L. de La Laurencie, "Telemann à Paris," *Revue Musicale* (1932); H. Hörner, *Telemanns Passionsmusiken* (Leipzig, 1933); K. Schäfer-Schmuck, *Telemann als Klavierkomponist* (Leipzig, 1934); W. Menke, *Das Vokalwerk G. P. Telemanns* (Kassel, 1942). A series of studies on the life and works of Telemann was begun in 1966; Vol. I, *Telemann und seine Zeitgenossen;* Vol. II: *Telemanns Liedschaffen und seine Bedeutung für die Entwicklung der deutschen Liedes in der ersten Hälfte des 18. Jahrhundert;* Vol. III *G. Ph. Telemann und J. J. Quantz;* Vol. IV: *Telemann Renaissance; Werk und Wiedergabe.*

Tellefsen, Thomas Dyke, Norwegian pianist and composer; b. Trondheim, Nov. 26, 1823; d. Paris, Oct. 6, 1874. In 1842 he went to Paris, where he studied with Kalkbrenner; in 1844 he became a pupil of Chopin, and accompanied him to England and Scotland in 1848. He publ. an edition of Chopin's works, and played Chopin's music at recitals in Paris and in Scandinavia. His own compositions were imitative of Chopin; he wrote nocturnes, waltzes, and mazurkas, but he also made use of Norwegian folksongs in many of his works, and thus became an early proponent of national music in Norway.

Telmányi, Emil, Hungarian violinist; b. Arad, June 22, 1892. He studied with Hubay at the Academy of Music in Budapest. In 1911 he began an active career as concert player; in 1918 he married a daughter of Carl Nielsen; his 2nd wife, whom he married in 1936, is the pianist **Annette Schiöler.** In 1940 he settled in Denmark and taught at the Cons. of Aarhus, retiring in 1969; then lived in Holte, near Copenhagen. He toured the U.S. in 1950. He made a number of arrangements for violin of works by Chopin, Schumann, Brahms, and others; supervised the devising of a curved bow for the playing of Bach's unaccompanied sonatas and partitas.

Telva, Marian, American contralto; b. St. Louis, December 26, 1897; d. Norwalk, Connecticut, Oct. 23, 1962. Her real name was **Marian Toucke,** but she changed it to Telva for the sake of euphony. She sang in church in her home town; then went to New York for further study, and soon was engaged at the Metropolitan Opera where she sang minor roles between 1920 and 1933. In the meantime she married a wealthy banker and afterwards made only sporadic appearances as a concert singer.

Temianka, Henri, American violinist and conductor; b. Greenock, Scotland, Nov. 19, 1906, of Polish-Jewish parentage. He was taken to Holland as a child; took violin lessons with Willy Hess in Berlin and Jules Boucherit in Paris. In 1926 he emigrated to America and studied at the Curtis Institute of Music in Philadelphia with Carl Flesch (violin) and Artur Rodzinski (conducting). He was the founder and leader of the Paganini Quartet; appeared as soloist with major orchestras in Europe and America. He settled in Los Angeles, where he organized the California Chamber Symphony, with which he toured in the U.S. and Canada. He published a book of reminiscences, *Facing the Music* (N.Y., 1971).

Templeton, Alec, blind pianist and composer; b. Cardiff, Wales, July 4, 1909; d. Greenwich, Conn., March 28, 1963. He studied at the Royal College of Music in London until 1923 and at the Royal Academy of Music until 1931. He settled in the U.S. in 1935, becoming a citizen in 1941; was extremely successful as a radio pianist, especially with his humorous musical sketches, parodies, etc., such as *Bach Goes to Town, Mozart Matriculates,* etc. He also wrote some more ambitious works, including *Concertino lirico* (1942) and *Gothic Concerto* for piano and orch (N.Y., Dec. 19, 1954, composer soloist).

BIBLIOGRAPHY: *Alec Templeton's Music Boxes, as told to R. B. Baumel* (N.Y., 1958).

Templeton, John, Scottish tenor; b. Riccarton, near Kilmarnock, July 30, 1802; d. New Hampton, July 2, 1886. He sang in various churches in Edinburgh; then went to London, where he took lessons in singing with Tom Cooke; also studied theory with Blewitt. On Oct. 13, 1831 he made his debut in a London theater; subsequently became a regular member of Drury Lane. Maria Malibran selected him as tenor for her operatic appearances in London (1833-35). In 1842 he was in Paris; during the season of 1845-46 he made an

American tour announced as "Templeton Entertainment," singing folksongs of Great Britain; his commentaries and reminiscences were publ. as *A Musical Entertainment* (Boston, 1845). He retired in 1852.

BIBLIOGRAPHY: W. H. Husk, ed., *Templeton and Malibran. Reminiscences* (London, 1880).

Tenducci, Giusto Ferdinando, celebrated Italian castrato; b. Siena, c.1736; d. Genoa, Jan. 25, 1790. He went to England in 1758 and was received with enthusiasm; led the Handel Festivals from 1784 until his departure for Italy in 1789. He was nicknamed "Triorchis" (triple-testicled), on account of the singular plurality of his reproductive organs that enabled him to marry; indeed, he eloped in 1767 with one of his pupils, 16-year old Dorothy Maunsell, but the marriage was annulled in 1775. She published an account of the affair under the title *A True and Genuine Narrative of Mr. and Mrs. Tenducci* (London, 1785). He wrote a treatise on singing, *Instruction of Mr. Tenducci to his Scholars* (London, 1785); also composed music for a comic opera *The Campaign*, produced in London in 1784, and a group of *Ranelagh Songs*.

BIBLIOGRAPHY: A. Heriot, *The Castrati in Opera* (London, 1956; pp. 185–89; provides an account of Tenducci's extraordinary marriage).

Tennstedt, Klaus, brilliant German conductor; b. Merseburg, June 6, 1926. He studied piano and violin at the Leipzig Cons.; in 1948 was appointed concertmaster at the municipal theater in Halle, and in 1952 became principal conductor there. He subsequently occupied conducting posts at the Dresden Opera (1958–62) and at the State Theater in Schwerin (1962–71); also conducted concerts with the Gewandhaus orch. in Leipzig, and filled conducting engagements in Czechoslovakia and in Russia. In 1971 he went to Sweden, where he conducted at the State Theater in Göteborg and lead the Swedish Radio Symphony in Stockholm. He subsequently was engaged as opera conductor in Kiel, Germany; in 1974 he was invited to conduct the Toronto Symph. Orch.; this was followed by a highly successful debut with the Boston Symph. Orch.; Feb. 24, 1977 he began a 2-week engagement with the N.Y. Philharmonic. His concerts in Western Europe and in America were received with exceptional acclaim; even his idiosyncrasies (such as bending the knees in anticipation of a powerful crescendo, and other graphic body motions, which caused one critic to liken him to "a demented stork"), did not seem to lessen the enthusiasm of both the players and the audiences.

Tenschert, Roland, Austrian musicologist; b. Podersam, Bohemia, April 5, 1894; d. Vienna, April 3, 1970. He studied at the Leipzig Cons. and in Vienna (Dr. phil., 1921); from 1926 to 1931 he was librarian and teacher at the Mozarteum in Salzburg; in 1945, became prof. of music history at the Vienna Academy of Music.

WRITINGS: *Mozart: ein Künstlerleben in Bildern und Dokumenten* (Leipzig, 1931); *Mozart* (Leipzig, 1931); *J. Haydn* (Berlin, 1932); *Vater Hellmesberger: ein Kapitel Wiener Musikerhumor* (Vienna, 1947); *Musikerbrevier* (Vienna, 1940); *Mozart: ein Leben für die Oper* (Vienna, 1941); *Dreimal sieben Variationen über das Thema Richard Strauss* (Vienna, 2nd ed., 1945); *Frauen um Haydn* (Vienna, 1946); *Salzburg und seine Festspiele* (Vienna, 1947); *Richard Strauss und Wien, eine Wahlverwandtschaft* (Vienna, 1949); *C. W. Gluck* (Olten, 1951); *W. A. Mozart* (Salzburg, 1951; in English, 1952).

BIBLIOGRAPHY: E. Tenschert, *Musik als Lebensinhalt* (Vienna, 1971; contains a list of writings).

Teodorini, Helena, Rumanian soprano; b. Craiova, March 25, 1857; d. Bucharest, Feb. 27, 1926. She studied piano with Fumagalli and singing with Sangiovanni at the Cons. Verdi in Milan; made her debut as a contralto at the Teatro Municipale in Cuneo in 1879; gradually her voice changed to a mezzo-soprano of wide range. She made her first appearance in La Scala, Milan, on March 20, 1880; then sang in Warsaw (1881), and in Madrid (1884–86); subsequently she toured in South America. In 1905 she established herself as a vocal teacher in Paris; eventually returned to Rumania. In 1964 the Rumanian government issued a postage stamp in her honor bearing her stage portrait.

BIBLIOGRAPHY: Viorel Cosma, *Elena Teodorini* (Bucharest, 1962).

Terényi, Eduard, Rumanian composer; b. Tîrgu-Mures, March 12, 1935. He studied with Jodál and Demian at the Cons. of Cluj (1952–58); in 1960 became an instructor on its faculty. In his own compositions he applies a variety of modernistic resources.

WORKS: *Pasărea măiastră (The Wonderful Bird)*, variations for orch., dedicated to the Rumanian sculptor Brancusi (1965); Piano Concerto (1969); Violin Sonatina (1955, revised 1965); *3 Pieces* for prepared piano (1968); *Prelude, Toccata, Fantasy* and *Fugue* for organ (1968); *Cantată lirică*, cycle for voice and flute (1966); other songs.

Terhune, Anice (*née* Potter), American pianist and composer; b. Hampden, Mass., Oct. 27, 1873; d. Pompton Lakes, New Jersey, Nov. 9, 1964. She studied in Cleveland, in Rotterdam (with Louis Coenen), and in N.Y. (with E. M. Bowman). In 1901 she married Albert Payson Terhune, the author. She publ. several books of songs for children (*Dutch Ditties, Chinese Child's Day, Colonial Carols, Our Very Own Book*, etc.) and a number of separate songs; also many piano pieces for children; the operas *Hero Nero* (1904) and *The Woodland Princess* (1911); a book, *Music-Study for Children* (1922), and an autobiography, *Across the Line* (N.Y., 1945).

Ternina, Milka, Croatian soprano; b. Vezisče, near Zagreb, Dec. 19, 1863; d. Zagreb, May 18, 1941. She studied voice at the Vienna Cons. with Gänsbacher; made her operatic debut in Zagreb (1882); then sang in Leipzig (1883–84) and Graz (1884–86). She subsequently was a member of the Bremen Opera (1886–89), and of the Munich Opera (1890–99), where she distinguished herself as a Wagnerian singer. She was engaged by Walter Damrosch for his German Opera Co. in N.Y., and made her American debut as Elsa in *Lohengrin* on March 4, 1896; also appeared at Covent Garden, London, as Isolde (June 3, 1898); after a series of successes at the Bayreuth Festivals, she was engaged by the Metropolitan Opera Co., singing there every season from 1899 until 1904; sang Tosca at the American première (Feb. 4, 1901) and Kundry in *Parsifal* (Dec. 24, 1903). She retired from the stage in 1906 and settled in Zagreb, where she remained until her death.

Terrabugio, Giuseppe, Italian composer; b. Fiera di Primiero, May 13, 1842; d. there, Jan. 8, 1933. He studied in Padua, and then in Munich under Rheinberger. In 1883 he settled in Milan, where, as editor of *Musica Sacra,* he exerted a strong influence in reforming Italian church music. His publ. works (about 100 opus numbers) are almost exclusively for the church (12 Masses, a Requiem, litanies, motets, etc.); he also publ. *L'Organista pratico* (3 vols.).

Terradellas, Domingo (Italianized as **Domenico Terradeglias**), Spanish composer; b. Barcelona, 1713 (baptized Feb. 13); d. Rome, May 20, 1751. He studied with Durante at the Cons. dei Poveri di Gesù Cristo in Naples (1732–36); began his career as composer with the opera *Astarto* (Rome, Jan. 3, 1739); from 1743 to 1745, he was at S. Giacomo degli Spagnuoli, Rome; in 1746 he went to London, where he produced his operas *Mitridate* (Dec. 2, 1746) and *Bellerofonte* (April 4, 1747); returned to Italy in 1750, after traveling through Belgium and France (1748–49). There is no foundation for the story that he drowned himself in the Tiber owing to the failure of his opera *Sesostri* (Rome, 1751). 12 arias and 2 duets were publ. in 1747 by J. Walsh of London, who also publ. "the favourite songs" from the operas *Mitridate* and *Bellerofonte.*
    BIBLIOGRAPHY: J. R. Carreras y Bulbena, *Domingo Terradellas* (Barcelona, 1908); H. Volkmann, "Domingo Terradellas," *Zeitschrift der Internationalen Musik-Gesellschaft* XIII (p. 306).

Terrasse, Claude, French composer; b. Grand-Lemps, near Grenoble, Jan. 27, 1867; d. Paris, June 30, 1923. He studied at the Lyons Cons. and at the École Niedermeyer in Paris; from 1888 to 1895, church organist in Arcachon, then in Paris until 1899, when he began to write for the stage, producing a series of successful operettas; the best-known are *Les Travaux d'Hercule* (March 7, 1901); *Le Sire de Vergy* (April 16, 1903); *Monsieur de la Palisse* (Nov. 2, 1904); *La Marquise et le marmiton* (Dec. 11, 1907); *Le Coq d'Inde* (April 6, 1909); *Le Mariage de Télémaque* (May 4, 1910); *Les Transatlantiques* (May 20, 1911); *Cartouche* (March 9, 1912).

Terry, Charles Sanford, eminent English music scholar; b. Newport Pagnell, Buckinghamshire, Oct. 24, 1864; d. Westerton of Pitfodels, near Aberdeen, Nov. 5, 1936. He became prof. of history at the Univ. of Aberdeen in 1903, and occupied himself with historical research; at the same time he devoted much of his energy to the study of Bach and his period. His biography of Bach (1928; revised ed., 1933; German transl., Leipzig, 1934) places Bach's life within the historical perspective with a fine discernment; it has become a standard in the literature on Bach in English. Other books and editions dealing with Bach include:

Bach's Chorals (3 vols., 1915–21); *J. S. Bach's Original Hymn-Tunes for Congregational Use* (1922); *J. S. Bach, Cantata Texts, Sacred and Secular* (1926); *The Four-Part Chorals of J. S. Bach* (5 vols., 1929); *The Origin of the Family of Bach Musicians* (1929); *Bach: The Historical Approach* (1930); *Bach's Orchestra* (1932); *The Music of Bach: An Introduction* (1933). To the Musical Pilgrim series he contributed analyses of the B minor Mass (1924), the cantatas and oratorios (1925), the Passions (1926), and the Magnificat, Lutheran Masses, and motets (1929). He arranged and publ. a stage version of the "Coffee Cantata" as *Coffee and Cupid* (1924); also translated into English Forkel's life of J. S. Bach (1920), and wrote a biography of Johann Christian Bach (1929).

Terry, Sir Richard Runciman, English music editor; b. Ellington, Northumberland, Jan. 3, 1865; d. London, April 18, 1938. In 1890 appointed organist and music master at Elstow School; 1892–96, organist and choirmaster at St. John's Cathedral, Antigua, West Indies; 1896–1901, at Downside Abbey. There he attracted attention by the revival of the Catholic church music of early English masters (Byrd, Tallis, Tye, Morley, Mundy, White, Fayrfax, etc.); 1901–24, organist and director of music at Westminster Cathedral. He was chairman of the committee appointed to prepare the English supplement of the Vatican Antiphonary, and music editor of the *Westminster Hymnal,* the official Roman Catholic hymnal for England. He was knighted in 1922. Besides Masses, motets, and other church music, he composed 48 *Old Rhymes with New Tunes* (1934). Edited *The Shanty Book* (2 vols.; 1921; 1926); *Old Christmas Carols* (1923); *Hymns of Western Europe* (with Davies and Hadow; 1927); *Salt Sea Ballads* (1931); *A Medieval Carol Book* (1932); *200 Folk Carols* (1933); *Calvin's First Psalter,* 1539, harmonized (1932); also the collections of 16th-century music *Downside Masses* and *Downside Motets, Motets Ancient and Modern,* and many separate works by early English composers. He wrote the books, *Catholic Church Music* (1907), *On Music's Borders* (1927), *A Forgotten Psalter and Other Essays* (1929), *The Music of the Roman Rite* (1931), *Voodooism in Music and Other Essays* (1934).
    BIBLIOGRAPHY: H. Andrews, *Westminster Retrospect: A Memoir of Sir Richard Terry* (London, 1948).

Terschak, Adolf, Hungarian flutist and composer; b. Hermannstadt, Transylvania, April 6, 1832; d. Breslau, Oct. 3, 1901. He studied at the Vienna Cons.; made long tours, as far west as London, and as far east as Siberia. He wrote numerous pieces for the flute with orch. or piano; also character pieces for orch.; published *École de mécanisme* for the flute.

Tertis, Lionel, eminent English viola player; b. West Hartlepool, Dec. 29, 1876; d. London, Feb. 22, 1975. He studied violin at the Leipzig Cons. and at the Royal Academy of Music in London; played the viola in various quartets, and decided to make it his chief instrument. He eventually became one of the most renowned viola players in Europe; traveled also in America. He was named in 1950 Commander of the British Empire. He wrote *Beauty of Tone in String*

Playing (London, 1938); a 2-volume autobiography, *Cinderella No More* (1953) and *My Viola and I: A Complete Autobiography* (1974). He designed and published specifications of a very large viola; for that, see *Music & Letters,* July 1947).

Terzakis, Dimitris, Greek composer; b. Athens, March 12, 1938. He studied composition with Y. Papaioannou at the Athens Cons. (1960–65); went to Germany and took courses with B. A. Zimmermann and Herbert Eimert at the Hochschule für Musik in Cologne (1965–67); attended summer courses of new music at Darmstadt; subsequently was on the staff of the Hochschule für Musik in Düsseldorf. In his music he steers a resolute course of the cosmopolitan avant-garde, leaving no tonal stone unturned; yet ancestral Grecian ethos is present both in the titles and in the modalities of his output.

WORKS: *8 Aphorisms* for piano (1964); Septet for 7 flutes (1965); *Medea* for voice, percussion and cello (1965–66); *Echochronos I* for tape (1967), *II* for 8 instruments and percussion (1968, revised 1973) and *III* for 7 amplified instruments and tape (1969–70); *Oceanids* for women's voices and orch. (1967); Trio for cello, guitar, and percussion (1967); *Chronika* for flute and guitar (1968); *Oikos* for 8-part a cappella chorus (1969); String Quartet (1969); *Stixis* for solo oboe (1969–70); *Chroai* for orch. (1970); *Achos* for guitar, voice and percussion (1970); *Nuances* for mezzo-soprano, viola, percussion, and tape (1970); *Hommage à Morse* for strings and wind octet (1970); *Transcriptions télégraphiques* for orch. (1971; Baden-Baden, June 12, 1974); *X* for chorus, instrumental ensemble, and tape (1971); *Katavasia (Retreat),* cantata for 6 solo voices (1971–72); *3 Pieces* for solo violin (1972); *Ethos A* for oboe, cello, and tape (1972) and *B* for mezzo-soprano, flute, and cello (1972); *Sticheron* for chorus and 6 instruments (1972); Duo for cello and percussion (1973); *To Allithoro Psari (The Squinty Fish)* for tape (1973); *Kosmogramm* for orch. (1974; Kassel, Germany, Nov. 1, 1974).

Terziani, Eugenio, Italian composer; b. Rome, July 29, 1824; d. there, June 30, 1889. He studied with Mercadante at the Naples Cons.; at the age of 19 produced an oratorio, *La Caduta di Gerico* (Rome, March 31, 1844), followed by the operas *Giovanna regina di Napoli* (Rome, June 1, 1845) and *Alfredo* (Rome, Feb. 21, 1852); was conductor in Rome at the Teatro Apollo from 1850; then at La Scala, Milan (1867–71), and finally (from 1877) prof. of composition at the Accademia di Santa Cecilia in Rome. His last opera, *L'Assedio di Firenze,* was produced in Rome, Feb. 24, 1883. He was also the composer of a ballet, *Una Silfide a Pechino* (Rome, Dec. 26, 1859), and of much sacred music.

Teschner, Gustav Wilhelm, German music editor and teacher of singing; b. Magdeburg, Dec. 26, 1800; d. Dresden, May 7, 1883. He was a pupil of Zelter in Berlin and of Crescentini in Italy; mastered Italian teaching methods thoroughly, specializing in the Italian repertory. He publ. elementary vocal exercises of his own, and edited many works by Italian masters (Clari, 8 books; Crescentini, 5 books; Zingarelli, 10 books; etc.); also brought out early choral church music.

Tesi (Tesi-Tramontini), Vittoria, famous Italian contralto; b. Florence, Feb. 13, 1700; d. Vienna, May 9, 1775. She received her instruction in Florence and Bologna; appeared on the stage at the age of 16 in Parma; then was engaged in Venice (1718) and Dresden (1719). She sang in Italy every year, and also appeared in Madrid (1739) and Vienna (1747–48). She was married to one Tramontini, a barber by trade, and adopted the professional name Tesi-Tramontini. She was remarkably free in her morals, and many stories, in which it is impossible to separate truth from invention, were circulated about her life. Her letters to a priest were publ. by Benedetto Croce in his book *Un Prelato e una cantante del secolo XVIII* (Bari, 1946).

Tessarini, Carlo, Italian violinist and composer; b. Rimini, c.1690; d. after 1766. He was a follower, if not actually a pupil, of Corelli; in 1729 he was violinist at the San Marco in Venice and later served at the Cathedral of Urbino; he then went to Rome and to Fano (1742), and finally entered the service of Cardinal Hannibal in Brünn, Moravia. His violin sonatas, generally in 3 movements, contributed to the establishment of a 3-movement sonata as a norm. He publ. several trio sonatas, duets, concertinos, concerti grossi, and a violin method, *Grammatica di musica* (Rome, 1741; also in French and English transl.).

BIBLIOGRAPHY: A. Schering, *Geschichte des Instrumentalkonzerts* (Leipzig, 1905; p. 107ff.).

Tessier, André, French musicologist; b. Paris, March 8, 1886; d. there, July 2, 1931. He studied law, history of art and other subjects; then devoted himself to musicology; was archivist in the Ministry of Fine Arts; also editor of the *Revue de Musicologie,* in which his catalogue of the Versailles Library was publ. (nos. 38–39). He edited the complete works of Chambonnières (with P. Brunold; 1925), and Denis Gaultier's *Rhétorique des Dieux* (facsimile, 1932; transcription, 1933). He was the author of a book on Couperin (Paris, 1926); prepared materials for the complete edition of Couperin's works, but died before his work was finished. A complete list of his writings was publ. by A. Schaeffner in the *Revue de Musicologie* (Dec. 1953).

BIBLIOGRAPHY: P. Brunold, "Quelques souvenirs sur André Tessier," *Revue de Musicologie* (Aug. 1931).

Tessier, Charles, French lutenist and composer; b. Pézanas (Hérault), c.1550; date and place of death unknown. He was chamber musician to Henri IV; traveled in England; his book, *Chansons et airs de cour* for 4 and 5 voices, was publ. in London (1597), dedicated to Lady Penelope Riche (Sir Philip Sidney's "Stella"); his *Airs et villanelles,* for 3, 4, and 5 voices, were publ. in Paris (1604).

BIBLIOGRAPHY: *Musical Antiquary* 1 (1901; p. 53).

Tessier, Roger, French composer; b. Nantes, Jan. 14, 1939. He received his education in Nantes and Paris. His works, mostly for small instrumental groups, include a string trio (1964), *Concerto da camera* (1965), *5 Etudes* for wind instruments, piano, percussion, and harp (1965), and *Suite concertante* for flute, piano and strings (1969).

Tessmer, Hans, German writer on music; b. Berlin, Jan. 19, 1895; d. there (killed in an air raid), March 1, 1943. He studied music in Berlin, becoming music critic of the *Tägliche Rundschau* in 1921; also was engaged as stage director at the opera houses in Dresden (1923-27), Berlin (1928-30), Stuttgart (1934-35), and Görlitz (from 1935).

WRITINGS: *Profile und Fantasien* (1921); *Anton Bruckner* (1922); *Richard Wagner* (1930); *Robert Schumann* (1930); also a fictionalized story of Schumann, *Der klingende Weg* (1923). He revised Cherubini's opera, *Lo Sposo di tre, marito di nessuna,* and produced it under the title *Don Pistacchio, der dreifach Verlobte* (Dresden, Nov. 27, 1926).

Testore, Carlo Giuseppe, Italian instrument maker; b. Novara, c.1660; d. c.1720. He was a pupil of Grancino and worked in Milan (1690-1715); made mostly cellos and double basses, and only a few violins. His son, **Paolo Antonio** (1690-1760), made violins on the model of Guarneri.

BIBLIOGRAPHY: O. A. Mansfield, "Carlo Giuseppe Testore," *British Musician* (1927; p. 38).

Testori, Carlo Giovanni, Italian theorist; b. Vercelli, March 24, 1714; d. there, May 20, 1782. He publ. *La Musica raggionata* (Vercelli, 1767), a theoretical treatise based on the system of Rameau; it was followed by 3 supplements (1771, 1773, 1782).

BIBLIOGRAPHY: C. Negri, *Brevi considerazioni sull'evoluzione storica ed estetica della musica: Biografie di musicisti vercellesi* (Vercelli, 1909); R. Allorto, "La Musica raggionata di Carlo Giovanni Testori," *Rivista Musicale Italiana* (July–Sept. 1951).

Tetrazzini, Eva, Italian soprano; sister of **Luisa Tetrazzini;** b. Milan, March, 1862; d. Salsomaggiore, Oct. 27, 1938. She studied with Ceccherini in Florence, and made her debut there in 1882, as Marguerite in *Faust.* She sang Desdemona in Verdi's *Otello* at its first American production (N.Y., April 16, 1888). On May 15, 1887 she married the conductor **Cleofonte Campanini.** She sang with the Manhattan Opera, N.Y. in 1908; then returned to Italy.

Tetrazzini, Luisa (real Christian name **Luigia**), celebrated Italian coloratura soprano; b. Florence, June 28, 1871; d. Milan, April 28, 1940. She learned the words and music of several operas by listening to her elder sister **Eva;** then studied at the Liceo Musicale in Florence with Ceccherini, who was also her sister's teacher. She made her opera debut as Inez in *L'Africaine* in Florence (1890); then traveled with various opera companies to South America. In 1904 she reached the U.S. and made her American debut at the Tivoli Opera House in San Francisco. She made her London debut at Covent Garden as Violetta on Nov. 2, 1907. She was then engaged by Hammerstein to sing with his Manhattan Opera House in N.Y., where she sang Violetta on Jan. 15, 1908; she remained with the

Manhattan Opera until its closing in 1910; subsequently appeared for a single season at the Metropolitan Opera (1911-12). She made the first broadcast on the British radio in 1925; her last American appearance was in N.Y. in 1931. She then returned to Italy and taught singing in Milan. Her fame was worldwide, and her name became a household word, glorified even in food, as in Turkey Tetrazzini. She published *My Life of Song* (London, 1921) and *How to Sing* (N.Y., 1923).

Teyber, Anton, Austrian composer; b. Vienna, Sept. 8, 1754; d. there, Nov. 18, 1822. He studied with Padre Martini at Bologna; from 1792 was cembalist at the Imperial Opera in Vienna, and assistant of Salieri; from 1793, court composer and music master to the Imperial children. He wrote an opera, 2 oratorios, a Passion, a melodrama, many Masses, symphonies, string quartets, minuets, etc. Some of his songs are printed in *Denkmäler der Tonkunst in Österreich* 79 (42.ii).

Teyber, Franz, Austrian composer; brother of **Anton Teyber;** b. Vienna, Nov. 15, 1756; d. there, Oct. 22, 1810. He studied with Wagenseil; after a concert tour in Southern Germany and Switzerland, he conducted Schikaneder's itinerant opera troupe; was then Konzertmeister at Karlsruhe and Bern, and from 1799 to 1810 composer to Schikaneder's Theater an der Wien. He produced a number of operas and Singspiele there and in other theaters in Vienna: *Die Dorfdeputierten* (Dec. 18, 1785); *Fernando und Jariko, oder Die Indianer* (Sept. 5, 1789); *Alexander* (June 13, 1801); *Der Schlaftrunk* (Nov. 12, 1801); *Die Neuigkeitskrämer* May 12, 1802); *Pfändung und Personalarrest* (Dec. 7, 1803); *Scheredin und Almanzor* (Aug. 9, 1804); *Der Zerstreute* (Jan. 29, 1805); *Ruthards Abentheuer* (July 26, 1808); *Pumphia und Kulikan* (Oct. 8, 1808); *Das Spinner-Kreutz am Wienerberge* (posthumous; Aug. 24, 1811).

Teyte (real name **Tate**), **Maggie,** English soprano; b. Wolverhampton, April 17, 1888; d. London, May 26, 1976. She studied in London; then was a pupil of Jean de Reszke in Paris (1903-07). In order to insure correct pronunciation of her name in France, she changed the original spelling Tate to Teyte. She made her operatic debut as Zerlina at Monte Carlo (1907); was very successful as a concert singer in Paris, and appeared with Debussy at the piano; Debussy also selected her as successor to Mary Garden in the role of Mélisande (1908). She sang at the Opéra-Comique (1908-10), with Beecham's Opera Co. in London (1910-11), with the Chicago Opera Co. (1911-14), and the Boston Grand Opera Co. (1915-17). She continued her recitals of French music in London during World War II. In 1958 she was named Dame of the British Empire. She publ. a book of memoirs, *Star on the Door* (London, 1958).

BIBLIOGRAPHY: C. Wallis, "Maggie Teyte," *Opera* (London, April 1952).

Thadewaldt, Hermann, German conductor and composer; b. Bodenhagen, April 8, 1827; d. Berlin, Feb. 11, 1909. He was bandmaster at Düsseldorf (1850-51) and

Dieppe (1853–55); from 1857 to 1869, conductor of his own orch. in Berlin, and in 1871 of the concerts at the Zoölogical Gardens there. In 1872 he founded the Allgemeiner deutscher Musikerverband, of which he was the first president, and to whose interests he devoted his entire time until his death. He published a symph. poem, *Das Rätsel der Sphinx; Im Walde* for orch.; *Meermusik* for string orch.; *Herbstlied* for string quintet; etc.

Thalberg, Sigismond, celebrated piano virtuoso and composer; b. Geneva, Jan. 8, 1812; d. Posillipo, near Naples, April 27, 1871. His parents were Joseph Thalberg of Frankfurt and Fortunée Stein, also of Frankfurt, but resident in Geneva. Thalberg, however, pretended to be the natural son of Prince Moritz Dietrichstein, who took charge of his education. His first instructor was Mittag, the bassoonist of the Vienna Court Opera; he subsequently studied piano with Hummel and composition with Sechter. He played as a precocious pianist in the aristocratic salons of Vienna, and began to compose piano music. In 1830 he made a successful concert tour through Germany; in 1834 he was appointed court pianist in Vienna; in 1835 he went to Paris, where he perfected his playing under Kalkbrenner; from that time he became one of the most admired piano virtuosos of Paris, and soon extended his triumphs through most of Europe, including Russia. In 1843 he married the widow of the painter Boucher. In 1855 he set out on a concert tour through Brazil and the U.S. (1856); made a 2nd Brazilian tour in 1863, and in 1864 retired to Naples. Thalberg was unexcelled as a performer of fashionable salon music and virtuoso studies. He possessed a wonderful legato, eliciting from Liszt the remark, "Thalberg is the only artist who can play the violin on the keyboard." His technical specialty was to play a central melody with the thumb of either hand, surrounding it with brilliant arpeggios and arabesques. To present this technique graphically in notation, he made use of the method initiated by Francesco Pollini of writing piano music on 3 staves. He wrote 2 operas, *Florinda* (London, July 3, 1851) and *Cristina di Suezia* (Vienna, June 3, 1855), which were not successful; but his brilliant piano pieces were the rage of his day, easily eclipsing, in popular favor, those of Chopin, his close contemporary. Among them are a group of nocturnes, several *Caprices*, *2 Romances sans paroles*; *Grandes valses brillantes*; *Le Départ, varié en forme d'étude; Marche funèbre variée; Barcarole; Valse mélodique; Les Capricieuses; Tarentelle; Souvenir de Pest; La Cadence* (very popular); *Les Soirées de Pausilippe* (6 albums); *Célèbre Ballade; La Napolitaine*; several sonatas, many pianistic studies; fantasies on operas by Rossini, Bellini, Meyerbeer, Weber, Verdi, and others.
BIBLIOGRAPHY: H. C. Schonberg, *The Great Pianists* (N.Y., 1963); G. Puchelt, *Verlorene Klänge. Studien zur deutschen Klaviermusik 1830–1880* (Berlin, 1969); V. Vitale, "Sigismond Thalberg a Posillipo," *Nuova Rivista Musicale Italiana* (Oct.-Dec. 1972).

Thallon, Robert, organist and composer; b. Liverpool, March 18, 1852; d. Brooklyn, March 13, 1910. He was taken to N.Y. as a small child; studied in Germany, in Paris and Florence (1864–76); upon his return to the U.S., he settled in Brooklyn as organist and music teacher; publ. a number of songs and piano pieces, and some orchestral arrangements.

Thayer, Alexander Wheelock, American writer; authority on Beethoven; b. South Natick, Mass., Oct. 22, 1817; d. Trieste, July 15, 1897. After graduation at Harvard Univ. in 1843, he became assistant librarian there; during 6 years' work in the library, he matured a plan for writing a detailed and trustworthy biography of Beethoven. For preliminary study, and to collect material, he first spent 2 years (1849–51) in Germany, also writing letters for newspapers; in 1852 he joined the staff of the *New York Tribune*, and returned to Europe in 1854, where, excepting 2 years (1856–58) spent in Boston, he remained. Dr. Lowell Mason and Mrs. Mehetable Adams (of Cambridge, Mass.) gave generous and disinterested aid at this juncture. In 1862 Thayer was attached to the American embassy at Vienna; in 1865 Abraham Lincoln appointed him consul at Trieste, a post held for life. He then publ. a *Chronologisches Verzeichniss der Werke Ludwig van Beethoven* (Berlin, 1865); in 1866 vol. I of his life-work, *Ludwig van Beethovens Leben*, appeared in German, translated from the English MS by Deiters; vol. II was publ. in 1872; vol. III, in 1879. In 1877 he publ. *Ein kritischer Beitrag zur Beethoven-Litteratur*. Unhappily, his wonderful capacity for work was overtaxed, and vol. IV of his nobly conceived work, executed with a painstaking thoroughness and scrupulous fidelity beyond praise, was left unfinished. Though he lived for years in straitened circumstances, he resolutely refused offers from firms like Novello & Co. and G. Schirmer, hoping to recast entirely the English version of his *Beethoven*, which was publ. in 3 vols. by Krehbiel in 1921. A redaction of his *Life of Beethoven*, prepared by Elliot Forbes, was publ. in 1963.
BIBLIOGRAPHY: H. E. Krehbiel, "A. W. Thayer and His *Life of Beethoven*," *Musical Quarterly* (Oct. 1917); Christopher Hatch, "The Education of A. W. Thayer," *Musical Quarterly* (July 1956).

Thayer, Arthur Wilder, American music educator and choral conductor; d. Dedham, Mass., Aug. 26, 1857; d. there, Nov. 17, 1934. He first studied singing; then took lessons in music theory with Chadwick and in conducting with Zerrahn. He led various choral societies in New England and was music director of schools around Boston. He published a number of songs and some pieces of sacred choral music.

Thayer, (Whitney) Eugene, American organist; b. Mendon, Mass., Dec. 11, 1838; d. Burlington, Vt., June 27, 1889. He began to study the organ at 14; in 1862 assisted at the opening of the great organ in the Music Hall, Boston, where he became regular organist after study (1865–66) under Haupt, Wieprecht, etc., in Germany; also conductor of the Boston Choral Union, etc. For a Festival Cantata he received the degree of Mus. Doc. from Oxford Univ. He publ. a Mass; 4 organ sonatas; part-songs; also *The Art of Organ Playing* (5 parts).

Thayer, William Armour, American organist and song composer; b. Brooklyn, N.Y., Oct. 5, 1874; d. there, Dec. 9, 1933. Pupil of J. H. Brewer (organ), D. Buck (theory), and J. D. Mehan (voice); 1893–1914, organist of St. James' Protestant Episcopal Church, Brooklyn; from 1914, of St. Mark's Methodist Episcopal Church; from 1907 also prof. of music at Adelphi College, Brooklyn. He publ. many songs, of which the best known is *My Laddie.*

Thebom, Blanche, American mezzo-soprano; b. Monessen, Pa., Sept. 19, 1918, of Swedish parents. She studied singing with Margaret Matzenauer and Edyth Walker; made her concert debut in N.Y. on Jan. 12, 1944, and her operatic debut at the Metropolitan Opera, N.Y., as Fricka, Dec. 14, 1944. She then sang in various opera houses, in America and Europe, with increasing success. In 1958 she appeared as a guest artist in Russia. In 1968 she was appointed head of the Southern Regional Opera Co. in Atlanta. Among her best roles are Ortrud in *Lohengrin,* Azucena in *Il Trovatore,* Amneris in *Aida,* Laura in *La Gioconda,* and Carmen.

Theile, Johann, German composer; b. Naumburg, July 29, 1646; d. there (buried June 24), 1724. Pupil of H. Schütz at Weissenfels; in 1673, Kapellmeister to the Duke of Holstein at Gottorp; went to Hamburg and wrote (for the opening of the Hamburg Opera House in 1678) the Singspiele *Adam und Eva* (Jan. 12, 1678) and *Orontos;* he also produced a Christmas Oratorio in 1681. In 1685, Kapellmeister to the Brunswick court at Wolfenbüttel; then Kapellmeister at Merseburg. He was called by contemporaries "the father of counterpoint." Among his numerous pupils were Buxtehude and Zachau.
    WORKS: a German Passion (publ. Lübeck, 1675, reprinted by Zelle in *Denkmäler deutscher Tonkunst* 17); *Noviter inventum opus musicalis compositionis 4 et 5 vocum, pro pleno choro* (20 Masses), and *Opus secundum, novae sonatae rarissimae artis et suavitatis musicae* (a collection of instrumental sonatas, preludes, courantes, airs, and sarabands *a* 2–5, in single, double, triple, and quadruple counterpoint).
    BIBLIOGRAPHY: F. Zelle, *Johann Theile und N. A. Strungk* (Berlin, 1891); W. Maxton, *Johann Theile* (dissertation, Tübingen, 1926).

Theodorakis, Mikis (Michael George), Greek composer; b. Chios, July 29, 1925. He studied at the Athens Cons.; composed melodies in the authentic spirit of modern Greek folksongs; wrote music for productions of ancient Greek tragedies, among them *Œdipus Tyrannos.* He achieved international success with the musical score for the film *Zorba the Greek.* At the same time he was actively engaged in politics. In 1963 he was chosen chairman of the Greek United Democratic Left Party; in 1964 he was elected a member of the Greek Parliament and joined the Communist Party. After the military coup of 1967 he was arrested and held on a farm near Corinth; later was sent to Zatouna, in the central Peloponnesus; there he wrote the music for the film *Z,* dealing with the police murder of the Socialist politician Gregory Lambrakis in Salonika in 1963. The film and the music were greatly acclaimed in Europe and America, and the fate of Theodorakis became a cause célèbre. Yielding to pressure from the international public opinion, the military Greek government freed Theodorakis in 1970, and he went to Paris; in July 1970 he was a participant in the Congress at the United Nations World Youth Assembly in New York.
    WORKS: Piano Trio (1945); 2 violin sonatinas (1945, 1958); *Œdipus Tyrannus* for orch. (1946; version for strings, 1955); *Preludio-Penia-Choros* for percussion, celesta and strings (1948); Symph. No. 1 (1948–52; Athens, 1954); Suite No. 1 for piano and orch. (1954; Athens, Feb. 24, 1957); Suite No. 2 for chorus and orch. (Paris, 1956); Suite No. 3, *The Insane Mother* for soprano, chorus and orch. (1956); *Antigone,* ballet (1958-59); *Axion Esti,* a pop oratorio (1960); *Epiphania Averoff,* oratorio (performed at the Averoff prison, 1968); *Raven,* cantata (1970).
    BIBLIOGRAPHY: J. Coubard, *Mikis Theodorakis* (Paris, 1969).

Theremin, Leon (real name **Termen;** pronounced in Russian with the accent on the last syllable; gallicized as Thérémin; anglicized as Theremin, with the accent on the first syllable), Russian inventor of the space-controlled electronic instrument that bears his name; b. St. Petersburg, Aug. 15, 1896. He studied physics and astronomy at the Univ. there; also cello and theory. He continued his studies in physics at the Leningrad Physico-Technical Institute, where in 1919 he became director of the Laboratory of Electrical Oscillators. On Aug. 5, 1920 he gave a demonstration at the Physico-Technical Institute in Petrograd of his Aetherophone, which was the prototype of the Thereminovox, later known simply as Theremin. He also gave a special demonstration of it for Lenin, who was interested in artistic uses of electricity. In 1927 he demonstrated his new instruments in Germany, France, and the U.S., where on Feb. 28, 1928, he obtained a patent for the Thereminovox. On April 29, 1930, at Carnegie Hall, he presented a concert with an ensemble of 10 of his instruments, also introducing a space-controlled synthesis of color and music. On April 1, 1932, in the same hall, he introduced the first electrical symph. orch., conducted by Stoessel, including Theremin fingerboard and keyboard instruments. He also invented the Rhythmicon, for playing different rhythms simultaneously or separately (introduced by Henry Cowell), and an automatic musical instrument for playing directly from specially written musical scores (constructed for Percy Grainger). Until 1938 Theremin was director of his own research laboratory in N.Y.; then returned to Russia. In 1964 he was appointed prof. of acoustics at the Moscow Univ.; was still active in 1977.

Thibaud, Jacques, celebrated French violinist; b. Bordeaux, Sept. 27, 1880; d. in an airplane crash near Mt. Cemet in the French Alps, Sept. 1, 1953, en route to French Indo-China. He was taught by his father, and then entered the class of Martin Marsick at the Paris Cons., winning 1st prize in 1896. Obliged to earn his living, he played the violin at the Café Rouge, where he was heard by the conductor Colonne, who offered him a position in his orch.; in 1898 he made his debut as soloist (with Colonne) with such success that he was engaged for 54 concerts in Paris in the same season. Subsequently he appeared in all the musical centers of Europe, and from 1903 visited America numerous times. With his 2 brothers, a pianist and a cellist, he formed a trio, which had some success; but this was discontinued when he joined Alfred Cortot and Pablo Casals in a famous trio. His playing was notable for its warmth of expressive tone and fine dynamics; his interpretations of Beethoven ranked very high, but he was particularly authoritative in French music.

BIBLIOGRAPHY: J.-P. Dorian, ed., *Un Violon parle; souvenirs de Jacques Thibaud* (Paris, 1947).

Thibault, Geneviève (Comtesse de Chambure), French musicologist; b. Neuilly-sur-Seine, May 20, 1902; d. Strasbourg, Aug. 31, 1975. She studied at the Sorbonne, Paris, under André Pirro; then became engaged in business, but continued her great interest in musical research; assembled a fine private library, containing rare editions of Renaissance music, which she opened to research scholars; initiated the Société de Musique d'Autrefois, for the purpose of presenting concerts of old music performed on old instruments; from 1955, lectured at the Sorbonne. Her own contributions to musicology (usually in collaboration with other scholars) include: *Poètes et musiciens du XVe siècle* (Paris, 1924; with E. Droz); *Trois chansonniers français du XVe siècle* (Paris, 1927; with A. Pirro, E. Droz, and Y. Rokseth); *Bibliographie des poésies de P. de Ronsard mises en musique au XVIe siècle* (Paris, 1941; with L. Perceau); *Bibliographie des éditions d'Adrien Le Roy et Robert Ballard* (Paris, 1955; with F. Lesure); *Eighteenth-Century Musical Instruments in France and Britain* (London, 1973). She also compiled an inventory of musical instrument collections, completed after her death by Jean Jenkins (Amsterdam, 1978).

Thibaut, Anton Friedrich Justus, German music scholar and learned collector; b. Hameln, Jan. 4, 1772; d. Heidelberg, March 28, 1840. He studied law, and from 1806 was prof. of jurisprudence in Heidelberg; also director of a singing club there; wrote *Über Reinheit der Tonkunst* (1825; often republ.; new ed., with biography of Thibaut by R. Heuler, 1907; in English as *On Purity in Musical Art*, 1877). His valuable music library (catalogue publ. in 1842) was acquired by the Hofbibliothek in Munich.

BIBLIOGRAPHY: E. Baumstark, *A. F. J. Thibaut* (Leipzig, 1841).

Thibaut IV, King of Navarre and **Count of Champagne,** one of the most notable of the trouvères; b. Troyes, May 30, 1201; d. Pamplona, July 7, 1253. 63 of his songs were publ. by Bishop La Ravallière in 1742 as *Poésies du Roi de Navarre;* the transcription of the melodies is very faulty. In Pierre Aubry's ed. of the *Chansonnier de l'Arsenal* (Paris, 1909) there are 59 melodies by Thibaut transcribed in modern notation; see also the examples in J. Beck's transcription of the *Chansonnier Cangé* (*Les Chansonniers des troubadours et des trouvères*), 4 vols. (Philadelphia, 1927–38), and A. Schering, *Geschichte der Musik in Beispielen* (1931), p. 7.

BIBLIOGRAPHY: P. Aubry, *Trouvères and Troubadours* (English transl., N.Y., 1914, p. 122).

Thiel, Carl, German editor and pedagogue; b. Klein-Öls, Silesia, July 9, 1862; b. Bad Wildungen, July 23, 1939. Pupil of the Königliche Institut für Kirchenmusik and of Bargiel's master class at the Akademie der Künste. On a government stipend he traveled in Italy; won the Mendelssohn Prize in 1894, and became organist at the Sebastiankirche in Berlin; later teacher at the Institut für Kirchenmusik. In 1930 he became director of the Kirchenmusikschule in Regensburg. He ed. old a cappella music; composed Masses, motets, cantatas.

BIBLIOGRAPHY: C. A. Preising, *Carl Thiel* (Regensburg, 1951).

Thiele, (Johann Friedrich) Louis, German organist; b. Quedlinburg, Nov. 18, 1816; d. Berlin, Sept. 17, 1848. He studied with A. W. Bach at the Royal Institute for Church Music at Berlin; from 1839 was organist of the Parochialkirche. He published concert pieces, variations, preludes, etc., for organ.

Thiemé, Frédéric, French music pedagogue; b. Reims, June 3, 1750; d. Bonn, March 29, 1802. He taught general music courses in Paris from 1780 until 1792; in the wake of the French Revolution he went to Germany and settled in Bonn, where he was known under the German name Friedrich Thieme. He published *Eléments de musique pratique* (Paris, 1783); *Principes abrégés de musique;* several books of violin duos; papers on acoustics.

Thienen, Marcel van, French composer; b. Paris, Oct. 3, 1922. He studied at the Paris Cons., graduating as a violinist in 1941. In 1953 he went to Haiti, where he organized the Conservatoire National de Musique. In 1956 he returned to Paris and established a studio for electronic music. His music aims to achieve an immediate effect by using topical subjects, much in the manner of Erik Satie.

WORKS: opera-farce, *Le Ferroviaire* (1951); *Petite symphonie sur le temps* (1944); *Petite suite digestive* (1951); several pieces for various instruments under the generic title *Amusette; Le Damné* for soprano, baritone, men's chorus, electronic music, and orch. (1964); songs with orchestral accompaniment.

Thierfelder, Albert (Wilhelm), German composer and writer on music; b. Mülhausen, Thuringia, April 30, 1846; d. Rostock, Jan. 6, 1924. He studied at Leipzig Univ. 1865–69, and at the same time with Hauptmann, Richter, and Paul. 1870–87, singing teacher and cantor at Brandenburg; from 1887, music director and prof. at Rostock Univ., succeeding Kretzschmar; received title of "Professor" in 1898. He publ. *Altgriechische Musik: Sammlung von Gesängen aus dem klassischen Alterthume vom 5. bis 1. Jahrhundert vor Christus nach den überlieferten Melodien mit Altgriechischem und deutschem Texte nebst einleitenden Vorbemerkungen herausgegeben und für den Konzertvortrag eingerichtet* (3 vols.; Leipzig, 1899, 1900, 1919), being a collection of the remains of ancient

Greek musik; also *System der altgriechischen Instrumentalnotenschrift* (1897).

Thiman, Eric Harding, English music educator, organist, and composer; b. Ashford, Kent, Sept. 12, 1900; d. London, Feb. 13, 1975. He studied at the Royal Academy of Music; was prof. there from 1930 (having obtained the degree of Doctor of Music in 1927). He published *A Guide to Elementary Harmony* (London, 1941); *Practical Free Counterpoint* (London, 1947); *Musical Form for Examination Students* (1951); wrote a number of organ and choral works and some light orch. music (*Dance for a Children's Party, Stirling Castle March,* etc.).

Thimus, Albert, Freiherr von, German writer on music; b. Aachen, May 21, 1806; d. Cologne, Nov. 6, 1878. He publ. *Die harmonikale Symbolik des Altertums* (2 vols., 1868–76). As an introduction to this work, R. Hasenclever wrote *Die Grundzüge der esoterischen Harmonik des Altertums* (1870).
BIBLIOGRAPHY: R. Haase, "Der Aachener Albert von Thimus," in C. M. Brand, ed., *Beiträge zur Musikgeschichte der Stadt Aachen* (Cologne, 1954).

Thiriet, Maurice, French composer; b. Meulan, May 2, 1906; d. Puys, near Dieppe, Sept. 28, 1972. He studied with Charles Koechlin and Roland-Manuel; then became engaged in radio work in Paris. His music reflects his preoccupation with the theater.
WORKS: opera-bouffe, *Le Bourgeois de Falaise* (Paris, June 21, 1937); *La Nuit vénitienne,* ballet (Paris Opéra, March 17, 1938); *La Précaution inutile,* ballet on themes by Rossini (1946); *Rapsodie sur des thèmes incas,* for orch. (Lyons, Jan. 20, 1936); *Afriques,* for orch. (1949); ballet, *Bonaparte à Nice* (Nice, 1960); ballet, *Le More de Venise* (Monte Carlo, 1960); ballet, *Les Amants de Mayerling* (Nice, 1961); ballet, *La Chambre noire* (Toulouse 1969); *Blues de l'horloge,* for violin and piano; songs; piano pieces.
BIBLIOGRAPHY: Jean Solar, *Maurice Thiriet* (Paris, 1958).

Thoinan, Ernest, French writer on music (pen name of **Antoine-Ernest Roquet**); b. Nantes, Jan. 23, 1827; d. Paris, May 26, 1894. He was a merchant by trade, but also an ardent student of music; during his extensive travels in Italy, England and Russia, he collected a fine music library.
WRITINGS: *La Musique à Paris en 1862* (1863); *L'Opéra "Les Troyens" au "Père Lachaise"* (1863; a satire); *Les Origines de la chapelle-musique des souverains de France* (1864); *Les Origines de l'opéra français* (1886; with Ch. Nuitter); *Déploration de Guillaume Crétin sur le trépas de Jean Ockeghem* (1864); *Maugars, célèbre joueur de viole* (1865); *Antoine de Cousu et les singulières destinées de son livre rarissime "La Musique universelle"* (1866); *Curiosités musicales et autres trouvées dans les œuvres de Michel Coyssard* (1866); *Un Bisaïeul de Molière; recherches sur les Mazuel, musiciens des XVIe et XVIIe siècles* (1878); *Louis Constantin, roi des violons* (1878); *Notes bibliographiques sur la guerre musicale des Gluckistes et Piccinistes* (1878); *Les Hotteterre et les Chéde-*

ville (1894); also an annotated ed. of the *Entretien des Musiciens* [1643] by Annibal Gantez (1878).

Thomán, István, Hungarian pianist and pedagogue; b. Homonna, Nov. 4, 1862; d. Budapest, Sept. 22, 1940. He studied with Erkel and Volkmann, and was a piano student of Liszt. In 1888 he was appointed professor at the Royal Music Academy in Budapest; he was greatly esteemed as a teacher; among his students were Dohnányi and Béla Bartók. He published a collection of technical piano studies in 6 volumes, and also composed songs and piano pieces. His wife, **Valerie Thomán** (b. Budapest, Aug. 16, 1878; d. there, Sept. 8, 1948) was a renowned concert singer, who gave early performances of works by Kodály and Bartók; their daughter **Maria Thomán** (b. Budapest, July 12, 1909; d. there, July 18, 1948) was an excellent violinist.

Thomas, Ambroise, French composer; one of the finest representatives of Romantic French opera; b. Metz, Aug. 5, 1811; d. Paris, Feb. 12, 1896. He entered the Paris Cons. in 1828; his teachers there were Zimmermann and Kalkbrenner (piano) and Lesueur (composition); in 1829 he won the 1st prize for piano playing, in 1830 for harmony, and in 1832 the Grand Prix de Rome with the dramatic cantata *Hermann et Ketty.* After 3 years in Italy, and a visit to Vienna in 1836, he returned to Paris and applied himself with great energy to the composition of operas. In 1851 he was elected to the Académie. In 1871 he became director of the Paris Cons., as successor to Auber (disregarding the brief incumbency of Salvador Daniel, adherent of the Paris Commune, who was killed in battle on May 23, 1871). As composer of melodious operas in the French style, he was second only to Gounod; his masterpiece was *Mignon,* based on Goethe's *Wilhelm Meister* (Opéra-Comique, Nov. 17, 1866); this opera became a mainstay of the repertory all over the world; it had nearly 2,000 performances in less then 100 years at the Opéra-Comique alone. Equally successful was his Shakespearean opera *Hamlet,* produced shortly after *Mignon* (Paris Opéra, March 9, 1868).
WORKS: The complete list of his operas (all produced in Paris) includes: *La Double Échelle* (Aug. 23, 1837); *Le Perruquier de la régence* (March 30, 1838); *Le Panier fleuri* (May 6, 1839); *Carline* (Feb. 24, 1840); *Le Comte de Carmagnola* (April 19, 1841); *Le Guerillero* (June 22, 1842); *Angélique et Médor* (May 10, 1843); *Mina, ou Le Ménage à trois* (Oct. 10, 1843); *Le Caïd* (Jan. 3, 1849); *Le Songe d'une nuit d'été* (April 20, 1850); *Raymond, ou Le Secret de la reine* (June 5, 1851); *La Tonelli* (March 30, 1853); *La Cour de Célimène* (April 11, 1855); *Psyché* (Jan. 26, 1857); *Le Carnaval de Venise* (Dec. 9, 1857); *Le Roman d'Elvire* (Feb. 4, 1860); *Mignon* (Nov. 17, 1866); *Hamlet* (March 9, 1868); *Gille et Gillotin* (April 22, 1874); *Françoise de Rimini* (April 14, 1882). He contributed an act to a ballet, *La Gipsy* (Opéra, Jan. 28, 1839), and wrote the ballets *Betty* (Opéra, July 10, 1846) and *La Tempête* (Opéra, June 26, 1889); *Messe solennelle* (1857); other sacred works; some chamber music; songs.
BIBLIOGRAPHY: A. Hervey, *Masters of French Music* (London, 1894); J. Simon, "Ambroise Thomas,"

Revue de Paris (March-April 1896); H. Delaborde, *Notice sur la vie et les œuvres d'Ambroise Thomas* (Paris, 1896); C. Bellaigue, *Études musicales et nouvelles silhouettes des musiciens* (Paris, 1898; in English, 1899); E. Destranges, "Ambroise Thomas," *Revue Musicale de Lyon* (1911, p. 97); H. de Curzon, *Ambroise Thomas* (Paris, 1921).

Thomas Aquinas (Saint), b. Roccasecca, near Aquino, Italy, 1227; d. Fossa Nuova, near Terracina, March 7, 1274. This famed theologian and scholastic philosopher entered the Dominican order in 1245. In 1263 Pope Urban IV commissioned him to compose a communion service, which contains the memorable numbers *Lauda Sion* (Corpus Christi sequence) and *Pange lingua, Sacra solemnis, Verbum supernum,* and *Adoro te* (hymns). An extended chapter on music is contained in his *Summa Theologica* (II, quaestio XLI).
BIBLIOGRAPHY: *D. Thomas Aquinatis de arte musica nunc primum ex codice bibl. univ. Ticinensis ed. illustr. Sac. Guarinus Amelli* (1880); G. Amelli, *S. Tomaso e la musica* (1876); C. F. Bellet, *St. Th. d'Aquin* (Paris, 1902); J. L. Callahan, *A Theory of Esthetics According to the Principles of St. Th. Aquinas* (dissertation, Catholic Univ., Washington, D.C., 1927).

Thomas, Arthur Goring, English composer; b. Ratton Park, Sussex, Nov. 20, 1850; d. London, March 20, 1892. He was a pupil of Émile Durand in Paris (1874-77), and of Arthur Sullivan and Ebenezer Prout at the Royal Academy of Music in London; later studied orchestration in Berlin with Max Bruch. He was mainly interested in creating English operas in the best German tradition; his operas were performed in England and Germany, and he had many important supporters for his art in England, but his music totally lacked vitality, and became of only antiquarian interest after his death. In the last year of his life he suffered from a mental illness.
WORKS: operas: *The Light of the Harem* (partial performance, London, Nov. 7, 1879); *Esmeralda* (London, March 26, 1883; also in German, produced in Berlin, Hamburg, and Cologne); *Nadeshda* (London, April 16, 1885); *The Golden Web* (posthumous; Liverpool, Feb. 15, 1893); he further wrote a choral ode, *The Sun Worshippers* (Norwich Festival, 1881); the cantata *The Swan and the Skylark* (posthumous; Birmingham Festival, 1894; orchestrated by C. V. Stanford); a vocal scene, *Hero and Leander* (1880); *Out of the Deep,* anthem for soprano solo, chorus, and orch. (1878); some chamber music; songs.

Thomas, Christian Gottfried, German composer and writer on music; b. Wehrsdorf, near Bautzen, Feb. 2, 1748; d. Leipzig, Sept. 12, 1806. He published *Praktische Beiträge zur Geschichte der Musik* (1778); chiefly for the music trade); *Unparteiische Kritik der vorzüglichsten seit 3 Jahren in Leipzig aufgeführten Kirchenmusiken, Concerte und Opern* (1798, 1799); and *Musikalische kritische Zeitschrift* (1805; 2 vols.). His compositions include a *Gloria* for 3 choirs, with instruments; a cantata; quartets.

Thomas, Eugen, Dutch conductor; b. Surabaya, Java, Jan. 30, 1863; d. Schloss Orth, near Gmunden, Aug.,

1922. In 1878 he went to Delft, Holland, where he studied engineering, and at the same time music; he completed his music studies at the Vienna Cons.; was founder (1902) and conductor of the *Wiener a cappella Chor.* He published *Die Instrumentation der "Meistersinger" von R. Wagner* (2 vols., 1899; 2nd ed., 1907); and the *Wiener Chorschule* (1907).

Thomas, Gustav Adolf, German organist and composer; b. Reichenau, near Zittau, Oct. 13, 1842; d. St. Petersburg, May 27, 1870. He studied at the Leipzig Cons.; was organist at the Reformed Church in Leipzig; then succeeded H. Stiehl as organist at St. Peter's in St. Petersburg. He wrote excellent works for organ: *Konzert-Fantasie; Sechs Trios über bekannte Choralmelodien; Fuga eroica; études;* piano pieces; ed. Bach's *Kunst der Fuge* and Handel's organ concertos.

Thomas, John, celebrated Welsh harpist; b. Bridgend, Glamorganshire, March 1, 1826; d. London, March 19, 1913. He also used the name **Aptommas** (or **Apthomas;** i.e. son of Thomas) and **Pencerdd Gwalia** (Chief of Minstrels, bardic name bestowed on him at the Aberdare Eisteddfod in 1861). He entered the Royal Academy at 14; studied harp with Chatterton, and upon the latter's death in 1872, succeeded him as Harpist to the Queen. He gave in London a series of annual concerts of Welsh music; the first took place at St. James's Hall, July 4, 1862, with a chorus of 400, and 20 harps. He was also a leader of the Eisteddfod festivals. He wrote 2 harp concertos; the dramatic cantata *Llewelyn* (1863) and *The Bride of Neath Valley,* a Welsh scene (1866); published a collection of Welsh melodies (1862) and a *History of the Harp* (London, 1859); made transcriptions for harp of many classical pieces. His brother, **Thomas Thomas** (1829-1913), also a harpist, went to America in 1895, eventually settling in Ottawa.

Thomas, John Charles, American baritone; b. Meyersdale, Pa., Sept. 6, 1891; d. Apple Valley, California, Dec. 13, 1960. He studied at the Peabody Cons. in Baltimore; from 1913 sang in musical comedy in N.Y.; then entered the concert field, in which he achieved outstanding success. He also sang in opera; was a member of the Théâtre de La Monnaie in Brussels (1925-28); later at Covent Garden, London (debut as Valentin in *Faust*). In 1930 he appeared with the Chicago Opera Co.; on Feb. 2, 1934, he sang the role of the elder Germont in *La Traviata,* at his first appearance with the Metropolitan Opera; he continued to be on its roster until 1943; then settled in California.

Thomas, John Rogers, American baritone and composers of songs; b. Newport, Wales, March 26, 1829; d. New York, April 5, 1896. He was a lawyer's clerk in London; came to America in 1849, and acquired considerable success as an oratorio singer. A number of his songs enjoyed tremendous popularity in their day (*The Mother's Prayer, The Cottage by the Sea, Beautiful Isle of the Sea, Must we then meet as strangers,* etc.). He published an operetta, *Diamond Cut Diamond;* a children's cantata, *The Picnic;* and much sacred music.

Thomas, Kurt, German choral conductor; b. Tönning, Schleswig-Holstein, May 25, 1904; d. Bad Oeynhausen, West Germany, March 31, 1973. He studied organ with Karl Straube, piano with Teichmüller, and composition with Grabner at the Leipzig Cons.; then taught music theory there (1925–34); from 1934 to 1939 he was prof. at the Berlin Hochschule für Musik; held various teaching appointments in Frankfurt, Detmold, and Leipzig. He was subsequently conductor of choral concerts of the Bach-Verein in Cologne (1960–65); in 1969 was appointed instructor in choral conducting at the Music Academy in Lübeck. On the occasion of his 65th birthday he was honored with a Festschrift, *Chorerziehung und Neue Musik* (Wiesbaden, 1969). He published a useful manual *Lehrbuch der Chorleitung* in 3 vols. (Leipzig, 1935; many reprints; also in English as *The Choral Conductor*, N.Y. 1971).

Thomas, Michael Tilson, greatly talented American conductor; b. Hollywood, Dec. 21, 1944. A grandson of Boris and Bessie Thomashefsky, founders of the Yiddish Theater in New York, he was brought up in a cultural atmosphere; studied composition with Ingolf Dahl at the Univ. of Southern California; concurrently took courses in chemistry. His conducting career began when he led concerts at the Ojai Music Festival (1967–69); was also assistant to Pierre Boulez at the Bayreuth Opera. In 1969 he was appointed associate conductor of the Boston Symph. Orch., the youngest ever to receive such a distinction. He was catapulted into public notice spectacularly on Oct. 22, 1969, when he was called upon to conduct the second part of the New York concert of the Boston Symph. Orch., substituting for the regular conductor, William Steinberg, who was taken suddenly ill. In 1971 he was engaged as conductor and music director of the Buffalo Philharmonic.

Thomas, Theodore, renowned German-American conductor; b. Esens, East Friesland, Oct. 11, 1835; d. Chicago, Jan. 4, 1905. Taught by his father, a violinist, he played in public at 6. In 1845 the family went to New York, where Thomas soon began to play for dances, weddings, and in theaters, helping to support the family; in 1851 he made a concert tour as soloist, and in 1853 he joined Jullien's orch. on the latter's visit to N.Y., later touring the country with Jenny Lind, Grisi, Sontag, Mario, etc. He became a member of the N.Y. Philharmonic Society in 1854. In 1862 he organized an orch. for "Symphony Soirées" at Irving Hall, New York, which were continued until 1878 (after 1872 in Steinway Hall); in 1866 he started summer concerts in Terrace Garden, removing in 1868 to Central Park Garden. The influence of these enterprises on musical culture in New York was enormous; Thomas' programs attained European celebrity. The first concert tour with the orch. was made in 1869, with 54 players, and for nine consecutive years he made annual tours of the East and Middle West. In 1873 he established the famous Cincinnati Biennial Festival, which he conducted till his death. He also founded the Cincinnati College of Music, of which he was president and director from 1878–80, having given up his own orch. in New York and the conductor-

ship of the N.Y. Philh. Society (1877–78) to accept this post. After his resignation he returned to New York, where he immediately reorganized his own orch. and was reelected conductor of the Philh. Society and the Brooklyn Philh. Orch. (having been conductor of the latter in 1862–63, 1866–68, and 1873–78). Besides conducting these orchestral bodies, he was at different times director of several choruses; from 1885–87 he was conductor and artistic director of the American Opera Co. In 1891 he settled permanently in Chicago as conductor of the Chicago Orchestra. In recognition of Thomas' distinguished services a permanent home, Orchestra Hall, was built by popular subscription, and formally opened in Dec., 1904, with a series of festival concerts, which were the last directed by him. After his death the name of the orch. was changed to the "Theodore Thomas Orch."; in 1912 the final title, Chicago Symph. Orch. was officially reinstated.

The influence of Thomas upon the musical development of the U.S. has been strong and lasting. An ardent apostle of Wagner, Liszt, and Brahms, he also played for the first time in America works of Tchaikovsky, Dvořák, Rubinstein, Bruckner, Goldmark, Saint-Saëns, Cowen, Stanford, Raff, and Richard Strauss.

BIBLIOGRAPHY: *T. T. A Musical Autobiography,* ed. by G. P. Upton (2 vols.; Chicago, 1905); R. F. Thomas (his wife), *Memoirs of T. T.* (N.Y., 1911); P. A. Otis, *The Chicago Symphony Orchestra* (Chicago, 1925); C. E. Russell, *The American Orchestra and T. T.* (N.Y., 1927); T. T. and F. A. Stock, *Talks About Beethoven's Symphonies* (N.Y., 1930); E. T. Rice, "T. and Central Park Garden," *Musical Quarterly* (April 1940); A. Loft, "Richard Wagner, T. T., and the American Centennial," *Musical Quarterly* (April 1951); T. Russell, *Theodore Thomas: His Role in the Development of Musical Culture in the U.S.* (Univ. of Minnesota, 1969).

Thomas (Thomas-San-Galli), Wolfgang Alexander, German writer on music; b. Badenweiler, Sept. 18, 1874; d. Baden-Baden, June 14, 1918. Studied philosophy, history, and law in Freiburg, Bonn, Munich, and Marburg (Dr. jur., 1898); 1899–1908, viola player of the Süddeutsches Streich-Quartett in Freiburg; 1908–11, ed. of the *Rheinische Musik- und Theaterzeitung* in Cologne; then in Berlin as writer. In 1898 he married the pianist **Helene San Galli.**

WRITINGS: *Sein oder Nichtsein? Aphorismen über Ethisches und Ästhetisches* (1905); *Joh. Brahms. Eine musikpsychologische Studie* (1905); *Musik und Kultur* (1908); *Musikalische Essays* (1908); *Die "unsterbliche Geliebte" Beethovens, Amalie Sebald* (1909; attempt to prove that the famous letter was addressed to Amalie Sebald); *Beethoven und die unsterbliche Geliebte. Amalie Sebald, Goethe, Therese Brunswick, und Anderes* (1910); *Mozart-Schatzkästlein* (1911); *Joh. Brahms* (1912; biography); *L. van Beethoven* (1913; biography). Edited *Beethovens Briefe* (1910; selection with commentary) and *Beethovens Briefe an geliebte Frauen* (1913).

Thomé, Francis (baptismal names **Joseph-François-Luc**), French composer; b. Port Louis, Island of Mauritis, Oct. 18, 1850; d. Paris, Nov. 16, 1909. He went to Paris as a youth, and studied at the Cons. with Marmontel (piano) and Duprato (theory). He became a successful teacher; wrote the operas, *Le Caprice de la Reine* (Cannes, 1892) and *Le Château de Königsberg* (Paris, 1896); the ballets, *Djemmah* (1886), *La Folie parisienne* (1900), etc.; the religious mystery play *L'Enfant Jésus* (1891); 2 symphonic odes, *Hymne à la nuit* and *Vénus et Adonis;* etc. But he is remembered chiefly for his piano pieces, of which *Simple aveu* and *Les Lutins* became very popular.

Thompson, John Sylvanus, American pianist and teacher; b. Williamstown, Pa., March 8, 1889; d. Tucson, Arizona, March 1, 1963. He was educated at the Leefson-Hille Cons., Philadelphia, and the Univ. of Pennsylvania. He traveled through the U.S. as a concert pianist; also appeared in London and Berlin. In 1917 he settled in Kansas City. He publ. much teaching material, including the very successful *Modern Course for Piano (Something New Every Lesson)* (Cincinnati, 1936; 6 vols.); *The Adult Preparatory Piano Book* (Cincinnati, 1943); *Melody All the Way* (Cincinnati, 1949–51; 7 vols.; last 2 vols. are subtitled *Supplementary Piano Course).*

Thompson, John Winter, American organist and composer; b. Leland, Mich., Dec. 21, 1867; d. St. Charles, Ill., March 8, 1951. After graduating from Oberlin Cons. (1890) he went to Germany, where he studied at the Leipzig Cons. with Schreck. Returning to the U.S., he became teacher of organ at Knox College, Galesburg, Ill. He published organ works, motets, and anthems; also *A Course in Harmony* (Boston, 1923).

Thompson, Oscar, American music critic and editor; b. Crawfordsville, Ind., Oct. 10, 1887; d. New York, July 3, 1945. He was educated at the Univ. of Washington, Seattle; studied music with G. Campanari and others; took up journalism and in 1919 joined the staff of *Musical America,* later becoming associate ed., and finally editor (1936–43). He was music critic for the *N.Y. Evening Post* (1928–34); from 1937 to his death was music critic for the *N.Y. Sun* (succeeding W. J. Henderson). In 1928 he established the first class in music criticism in the U.S., at the Curtis Institute, Philadelphia; also gave courses at the N.Y. College of Music. In 1939 he brought out *The International Cyclopedia of Music and Musicians* in one vol. of more than 2,000 pages, with feature articles by eminent authorities; it went through 10 editions and reprints. He wrote the books *Practical Musical Criticism* (1934); *How to Understand Music* (1935); *Tabulated Biographical History of Music* (1936); *The American Singer* (1937); *Debussy, Man and Artist* (1937); ed. *Plots of the Operas* (1940) and *Great Modern Composers* (1941), both vols. being extracts from the *Cyclopedia.* See I. Lowens in *Dictionary of American Biography,* Supplement III.

Thompson, Randall, eminent American composer; b. New York, April 21, 1899. He was educated at Harvard Univ. (B.A., 1920; M.A., 1922); his teachers there were Walter Spalding, E. B. Hill, and A. T. Davison; he also studied with Ernest Bloch. From 1922 to 1925 he

held a fellowship at the American Academy in Rome; won a Guggenheim Fellowship twice (1929, 1930). From 1927 to 1929, and again in 1936–37, he was assistant prof. of music at Wellesley College; from 1937 to 1939, prof. of music at the Univ. of California, Berkeley; from 1939 to 1941, he was director of the Curtis Institute of Music, Philadelphia; then was head of the music division of the School of Fine Arts of the Univ. of Virginia (1941–46); from 1946 to 1948, prof. of music at Princeton Univ.; from 1948 to 1965 he was on the faculty of Harvard Univ. He excels in vocal composition; his *Alleluia* for chorus a cappella and *The Testament of Freedom,* to words by Thomas Jefferson, scored for men's voices with piano or orch., have attained exceptional success; of his works for orch., the most popular is the 2nd Symph. In another genre are the humorous choral pieces *Americana,* to texts culled from the American press, and originally published in the *American Mercury.*

WORKS: opera *Solomon and Balkis* (radio performance, N.Y., March 29, 1942; 1st stage production, Cambridge, Mass., April 14, 1942); incidental music to *The Grand Street Follies* (N.Y., June 25, 1926); incidental music to *The Straw Hat* (N.Y., Oct. 14, 1926); for orch.: *Pierrot and Cothurnus* (Rome, May 17, 1923, composer conducting); *The Piper at the Gates of Dawn,* symph. prelude (Rome, May 27, 1924, composer conducting); Symph. No. 1 (Rochester, N.Y., Feb. 20, 1930); Symph. No. 2 (Rochester, March 24, 1932); Symph. No. 3 (N.Y., May 15, 1949); *A Trip to Nahant,* fantasy for orch. (Philadelphia, March 18, 1955); *Jazz Poem,* for piano and orch. (Rochester, Nov. 27, 1928, composer at the piano); for chorus: *5 Odes of Horace* (1924); *Pueri Hebraeorum,* for women's voices a cappella (1928); *Rosemary,* for women's voices a cappella (1929); *Americana,* for chorus and piano or orch. (1932); *The Peaceable Kingdom,* for chorus a cappella (1936); *Tarantella,* for men's voices and piano (1937); *The Lark in the Morn,* for chorus a cappella (1938); *Alleluia,* for chorus a cappella (1940); *The Testament of Freedom,* for men's voices and piano or orch. (Univ. of Virginia, April 13, 1943; numerous subsequent performances by major choral organizations and orchestras); *Ode to the Virginian Voyage,* for chorus and orch. (Jamestown, Va., April 1, 1957); *Requiem* for double chorus a cappella (Berkeley, Calif., May 22, 1958); *The Passion According to Saint Luke,* oratorio (Boston, March 28, 1965); *The Wind in the Willows,* for string quartet (1924); *Suite* for oboe, clarinet, and viola (1940); String Quartet (1941). He published a book, *College Music* (N.Y., 1935).

BIBLIOGRAPHY: Quincy Porter, "Randall Thompson," *Modern Music* 19 (1942); Elliot Forbes, "The Music of Randall Thompson," *Musical Quarterly* (Jan. 1949).

Thompson, Will Lamartine, American hymn tune writer; b. East Liverpool, Ohio, Nov. 7, 1847; d. there, Sept. 20, 1909. He studied music at the Boston Cons.; wrote a number of religious and patriotic songs. His best known hymn is *Softly and Tenderly Jesus Is Calling.*

BIBLIOGRAPHY: R. G. McCutchan, *Our Hymnody* (N.Y., 1937).

Thomson, César, eminent Belgian violinist; b. Liège, March 17, 1857; d. Lugano, Aug. 21, 1931. He entered the Liège Cons. at the age of 7, winning the Gold Medal at 11; he subsequently studied with Vieuxtemps, Léonard, Wieniawski, and Massart. For several years he was household musician to a wealthy Russian patron of arts, Baron Paul von Derwies, at Lugano; in 1879 he became concertmaster of Bilse's orch. in Berlin; in 1882 he became prof. of violin at the Liège Cons.; he left Liège for Brussels in 1898, when he succeeded Ysaÿe as prof. of violin at the Brussels Cons.; there he founded a celebrated string quartet (with Lamoureux, Vanhout, and Jacobs). In 1914 he settled in Paris as prof. at the Cons. In 1924 he visited America; taught at the Cons. of Ithaca, N.Y., and at the Juilliard School of Music, N.Y., returning to Europe in 1927. He was a famous violin teacher, emphasizing the perfection of technical and expressive performance, rather than bravura. He made arrangements for the violin of various works by early Italian composers.

Thomson, George, Scottish collector of folksongs; b. Limekilns, Dunfermline, March 4, 1757; d. Leith, Feb. 18, 1851. For 59 years (1780–1839) he was secretary to the Board of Trustees for the Encouragement of Arts and Manufactures in Scotland. An ardent collector of Scotch, Welsh, and Irish melodies, he issued a series of vols. containing authentic melodies, with piano accompaniments and instrumental arrangements by the most celebrated musicians of his time, including Beethoven, Haydn, Pleyel, and Koželuh. Each song had, in accordance with his plan, a prelude, coda, and *ad libitum* parts throughout (for violin, or flute, or cello). The collections are: *A Select Collection of Original Scottish Airs* (London, 6 vols.; vol. I, 1793; vol. II, 1798; vol. III, 1799; vol. IV, 1802; vol. V, 1818–26; vol. VI, 1841); *Collection of the Songs of R. Burns, Sir W. Scott, etc.* (London, 1822; 6 vols.); *Select Collection of Original Welsh Airs* (London, 1809; 3 vols.); *Select Collection of Original Irish Airs* (London, 1814–16; 2 vols.); *20 Scottish Melodies* (Edinburgh, 1839).
BIBLIOGRAPHY: J. C. Hadden, *George Thomson, the Friend of Burns. His Life and Correspondence* (London, 1898; contains full and interesting details, notably Beethoven's letters); R. Aldrich, "Beethoven and George Thomson," *Music & Letters* (April 1927); Karl Geiringer, "Haydn and the Folksong of the British Isles," *Musical Quarterly* (April 1949); C. B. Oldman, "Beethoven's Variations on National Themes," *Music Review* (Feb. 1951); Cecil Hopkinson and C. B. Oldman, *Thomson's Collections of National Song* (Edinburgh Bibliographical Society Transactions, 1940 and 1954).

Thomson, John, Scottish composer and writer on music; b. Sprouston, Roxburgh, Oct. 28, 1805; d. Edinburgh, May 6, 1841. He studied in Leipzig with Schnyder von Wartensee, and became an intimate of Mendelssohn, Schumann, and Moscheles. In 1839 he was appointed the first Reid prof. of music at Edinburgh Univ. At the 3rd concert given by the Edinburgh Professional Society (Feb., 1837), an analytical program was issued by Thomson, then conductor; this is the first recorded instance of the use of such programs. He composed 2 operas, *Hermann, or The Bro-*

ken Spear (London, Oct. 27, 1834) and *The Shadow on the Wall* (London, April 20, 1835); also wrote incidental music to Walter Scott's *The House of Aspen* (Edinburgh, Dec. 19, 1829).

Thomson, Virgil, many-faceted American composer of great originality and a music critic of singular brilliance; b. Kansas City, Missouri, Nov. 25, 1896. He studied at Harvard Univ.; took piano lessons with Heinrich Gebhard and organ with Wallace Goodrich in Boston; then went to Paris, where he had a course with Nadia Boulanger (1921–22); returning to America, he studied composition with Rosario Scalero in N.Y. He then was organist at King's Chapel in Boston (1923–24). In 1925 he went to Paris for a prolonged stay; there he established friendly contacts with the cosmopolitan groups of musicians, writers, and painters; his association with Gertrude Stein was particularly significant in the development of his esthetic ideas. In his music he refused to follow any set of modernistic doctrines; rather he embraced the notion of popular universality, which allowed him to use the techniques of all ages and all degrees of simplicity or complexity, from simple triadic harmonies to dodecaphonic intricacies; in so doing he achieved an eclectic illumination of astonishing power of direct communication, expressed in his dictum "jamais de banalité, toujours le lieu commun." Beneath the characteristic Parisian persiflage in some of his music there is a profoundly earnest intent. His most famous composition is the opera *Four Saints in Three Acts,* to the libretto by Gertrude Stein, in which the deliberate confusion wrought by the author of the play (there are actually 4 acts and more than a dozen saints, some of them in duplicate) and the composer's almost solemn, hymnlike treatment, create a hilarious modern opera-buffa. It was first introduced at Hartford, Conn., on Feb. 8, 1934, characteristically announced as being under the auspices of the "Society of Friends and Enemies of Modern Music," of which Thomson was director (1934–37); the. work became an American classic, with constant revivals staged in America and Europe. In 1940 Thomson was appointed music critic of the *New York Herald Tribune.* Far from being routine journalism, Thomson's music reviews are minor masterpieces of literary brilliance and critical acumen. He resigned in 1954 to devote himself to composition and conducting.
WORKS: OPERAS, *Four Saints in Three Acts* (Hartford, Conn., Feb. 8, 1934); *The Mother of Us All,* libretto by Gertrude Stein on the life of the American suffragist Susan B. Anthony (N.Y., May 7, 1947); *Byron* (N.Y., April 13, 1972); FOR ORCH.: *Symphony on a Hymn Tune* (1928; N.Y., Feb. 22, 1945, composer conducting); Symph. No. 2 (Seattle, Nov. 17, 1941); *The Seine at Night* (Kansas City, Feb. 24, 1948); *Wheatfield at Noon* (Louisville, Dec. 7, 1948); Cello Concerto (Philadelphia, March 24, 1950); *5 Songs* for voice and orch., after William Blake (Louisville, Feb. 6, 1952); *Sea Piece with Birds* (Dallas, Dec. 10, 1952; grouped with *The Seine at Night* and *Wheatfield at Noon* as *Three Pictures for Orchestra*); Concerto for flute, strings, and percussion (Venice, Sept. 18, 1954); *A Solemn Music,* for band (1949); *Missa pro Defunctis* for chorus and orch. (State Univ. College of Educa-

tion, Potsdam, N.Y., May 14, 1960); *The Feast of Love* for baritone and orch. (Washington, Nov. 1, 1964); CHAMBER MUSIC: *Sonata da chiesa* for 5 instruments (1926); Violin Sonata (1930); String Quartet No. 1 (1932); String Quartet No. 2 (1932); 4 piano sonatas; 2 sets of études for piano; organ pieces; sacred choral works; *Hymns from the Old South,* for mixed chorus a cappella; songs to French and English texts; Mass for solo voice (unison chorus, 1960); a number of *Portraits* for various instruments, among them more than 50 for piano, 8 for violin solo, 5 for 4 clarinets, 4 for violin and piano, etc., each "portrait" being a musical characterization of a definite person. FILM MUSIC: *The Plough that Broke the Plains* (1936; an orch. suite was drawn from it); *Louisiana Story* (1948; 2 orch. suites from it, including *Acadian Songs and Dances*); *The Goddess* (1957); *Power among Men* (1958); *Journey to America* for the American Pavilion at the N.Y. World's Fair (1964).

WRITINGS: *The State Of Music* (N.Y. 1939); *The Musical Scene* (N.Y. 1945); *The Art of Judging Music* (N.Y. 1948); *Music, Right and Left* (N.Y., 1951); an autobiography, disarmingly titled *Virgil Thomson* (N.Y. (1966); *Music Reviewed 1940–54,* a collection of criticisms (N.Y. 1967); *American Music Since 1910* (N.Y., 1971).

BIBLIOGRAPHY: K. O. Hoover and John Cage, *Virgil Thomson: His Life and Music* (N.Y., 1959). See also *Modern Music . . . Analytic Index* compiled by W. Shirley, and edited by W. and C. Lichtenwanger (N.Y., 1976; pp. 222–24).

Thooft, Willem Frans, Dutch composer; b. Amsterdam, July 10, 1829; d. Rotterdam, Aug. 27, 1900. He studied with A. Dupont in Brussels and with Hauptmann at the Leipzig Cons.; then went to Rotterdam, where he organized the German Opera.

WORKS: an opera, *Aleida von Holland* (Rotterdam, 1866); *Gevonden,* for baritone solo, male chorus, and orch.; 3 symphonies (including one with chorus, surnamed *Kaiser Karl V*); *In Leid und Freud,* fantasy for orch.; *Die Jungfrau von Orleans,* overture; psalms; piano pieces; songs.

Thórarinsson, Leifur, Icelandic composer; b. Reykjavik, Aug. 13, 1934. He studied with Jón Thórarinsson at the Reykjavik School of Music; then in Vienna with Hanns Jelinek (1954) and with both Wallingford Riegger and Gunther Schuller in N.Y. Returning to Iceland, he became a music critic and member of the modern group "Musica Nova;" later moved to Denmark.

WORKS: *Child's Play* for piano (1954); Piano Sonata (1957); *Mosaic* for violin and piano (1960); Piano Trio (1961); *Epitaph (Wallingford Riegger in Memoriam)* for orch. (1961); *Kadensar* for harp, oboe, clarinet, bass clarinet and bassoon (1962); Symph. No. 1 (1963); a musical comedy, *Hornakórallinn* (1966); String Quartet (1969); Violin Concerto (1970, revised 1976); *Óró* for 7 instruments; *Variations* for clarinet, cello and piano.

Thorborg, Kerstin, Swedish contralto; b. Venjan, May 19, 1896; d. Hedemora, Sweden, April 12, 1970. She studied at the Stockholm Opera School; was en-

gaged as a regular member of the Stockholm Opera (1925–30); then sang in Berlin and Vienna. On Dec. 21, 1936, she made her American debut as Fricka at the Metropolitan Opera House, N.Y.; remained with the Metropolitan Opera until 1950; gave concerts throughout the U.S. and Canada; then returned to Sweden and became a voice teacher in Stockholm.

Thorne, Edward Henry, English organist and composer; b. Cranbourne, Dorset, May 9, 1834; d. London, Dec. 26, 1916. He was a chorister at St. George's Chapel; served as church organist in London; gave organ and piano recitals in London and elsewhere; was especially noted for his Bach programs. He was made Mus. Doc. by the Archbishop of Canterbury in 1913. He wrote a number of sacred choral works; an overture, *Peveril of the Peak* (after Walter Scott); 2 piano trios; violin sonatas; cello sonatas; published 7 books of organ pieces.

Thorne, Francis, American composer; b. Bay Shore, Long Island, N.Y., June 23, 1922. Of a cultural heritage (his maternal grandfather was the opera expert **Gustave Kobbé**), he absorbed musical impressions crouching under the grand piano while his father, a banker, played ragtime; at puberty, sang in a school chorus; entering Yale Univ., he was a member of the varsity rowing team, as a prelude to service in the U.S. Navy during World War II. Returning from the wars, he joined the stock-brokerage firm of Harris, Upham & Co. as a customers' man, but soon defected and joined various N.Y. jazz groups as pianist; then went to Italy; took lessons in advanced composition with David Diamond in Florence. Impressed, depressed and distressed by the inhumanly impecunious condition of middle-aged atonal composers, he established an eleemosynary Thorne Music Fund, drawing on the hereditary wealth of his family, and disbursed munificent grants to those who qualify, among them Stefan Wolpe, Ben Weber, Lou Harrison, Lester Trimble, John Cage and David Diamond. Thorne's own music shares with that of his beneficiaries the venturesome spirit of the cosmopolitan avant-garde, with a prudently dissonant technique serving the conceptual abstractions and titular paronomasia of many modern compositions.

WORKS: Symph. No. 1 (1961); *Elegy* for orch. (1963); *Burlesque Overture* (1964); Symph. No. 2 (1964); *Rhapsodic Variations* for piano and orch. (1965); Piano Concerto No. 1 (1966); *Gemini Variations* for viola, double bass, and orch. (1968); *Sonar Plexus* for electric guitar and orch. (1968); *Chamber Deviation I* for clarinet, double bass, and percussion (1968); Symph. No. 3 for percussion and strings (1969); *Liebesrock* for 3 electric guitars and orch. (1969); *Contra Band Music* for band (1970); *Antiphonies* for wind instruments and percussion (1970); *Chamber Deviation II* for brass quintet, guitar, and percussion (1971); Piano Sonata (1972); *Fanfare, Fugue and Funk* for orch. (1972); Piano Concerto No. 2 (1973); *Cantata Sauce* (1973); Cello Concerto (1974); Violin Concerto (1976); Symph. No. 4 (1977); 3 string quartets.

Thornhill, Claude, American pianist and bandleader; b. Terre Haute, Indiana, Aug. 10, 1909; d. Caldwell, N.J., July 1, 1965. He received regular academic training at the Cincinnati Cons. and at the Curtis Institute of Music in Philadelphia; was arranger for Benny Goodman and others; in 1940 organized a band of his own. Because of his uncommon musical literacy, he was able to make use of plausible novelties in his arrangements.

Thouret, Georg, German writer on music; b. Berlin, Aug. 25, 1855; d. there, Jan. 17, 1924. He studied philology and history in Tübingen, Berlin, and Leipzig. The discovery of forgotten military music in the castles of Berlin, Charlottenburg, and Potsdam led him to make a special study of the subject; for the Vienna Exposition (1892) he arranged an exhibition of German military music; published the collections *Altpreussische Militärmärsche* and *Musik am preussischen Hofe.*
WRITINGS: *Führer durch die Fachausstellung der deutschen Militärmusik* (1892; official catalogue of the Vienna Exposition); *Katalog der Musiksammlung auf der königlichen Hausbibliothek im Schlosse zu Berlin* (1895); *Friedrich der Grosse als Musikfreund und Musiker* (1898).

Thrane, Waldemar, Norwegian composer; b. Christiania, Oct. 8, 1790; d. there, Dec. 30, 1828. He studied violin with K. Schall in Copenhagen; then went to Paris, where he was a pupil of Baillot (violin), Reicha and Habeneck (composition). Returning to Christiania, he conducted theater music; and also directed a music school. He is historically important as the composer of the first Norwegian opera, *Fjeldeventyret (A Mountain Adventure);* the score was published in 1824; the first concert performance took place in Christiania in 1827; the first stage production was given posthumously (Christiania, April 9, 1850).
BIBLIOGRAPHY: J. G. Conradi, *Musikkens Udvikling i Norge* (Christiania, 1878).

Thuille, Ludwig (Wilhelm Andreas Maria), renowned German composer and pedagogue; b. Bozen, Tyrol, Nov. 30, 1861; d. Munich, Feb. 5, 1907. He studied with Pembaur at Innsbruck (piano and theory); then went to Munich, where he was a pupil of Karl Bärmann (piano) and Rheinberger (composition) at the Music School there; in 1883 he became prof. there. Encouraged by Alexander Ritter, he began to compose music in the grand Wagnerian manner; wrote 3 operas, chamber music, song cycles, and choral works. But he made his mark chiefly as a fine pedagogue; with Rudolf Louis he publ. the well-known manual, *Harmonielehre* (1907; abridged ed. as *Grundriss der Harmonielehre*, 1908; new revised ed., by Courvoisier and others, 1933).
WORKS: operas: *Theuerdank* (Munich, March 12, 1897), *Lobetanz* (Karlsruhe, Feb. 6, 1898), *Gugeline* (Bremen, March 4, 1901); *Romantische Ouvertüre* (introduction to the opera *Theuerdank*); Symph. (1886); Sextet for piano and wind instruments; Piano Quintet; Cello Sonata.
BIBLIOGRAPHY: F. Munter, *Ludwig Thuille* (Mu-

nich, 1923); E. Istel, "Ludwig Thuille," *Musical Quarterly* (July 1932).

Thuren, Hjalmar Lauritz, Danish musical folklorist; b. Copenhagen, Sept. 10, 1873; d. there, Jan. 13, 1912. From 1899 to 1907 he taught at the Fredericksberg Folk-School and was secretary of the Danish Folklore Society. He made valuable studies of folk music in Denmark, in the Faroe Islands, and among the Eskimos.
WRITINGS: *Dans og Kvaddigtning paa Färöerne* (1901), *Folkesangen paa Färöerne* (1908); *The Eskimo Music* (with W. Thalbitzer; Copenhagen, 1911; in French as *La Musique chez les Eskimos*, "Publications de la revue S. I. M.," 1912); *Melodies From East Greenland* (1914).

Thürlings, Adolf, German writer on music; b. Kaldenkirchen, July 1, 1844; d. Bern, Feb. 15, 1915. He took the Dr. phil. degree in Munich with the dissertation *Die beiden Tongeschlechter und die neuere musikalische Theorie* (Berlin, 1877); published *Die schweizerischen Tonmeister im Zeitalter der Reformation* (1903); also ed. works by Senfl in *Denkmäler der Tonkunst in Bayern* 5 (3.ii).

Thurner, Frédéric Eugène de, French oboe virtuoso; b. Montbéliard, Dec. 9, 1785; d. Amsterdam, March 21, 1827. He wrote 3 symphonies, an overture, 4 oboe concertos, 4 quartets for oboe and strings, rondos and divertissements for oboe with string quartet, trio for oboe with 2 horns, duos for oboe and piano, piano music, etc.

Thursby, Emma, American soprano; b. Brooklyn, Feb. 21, 1845; d. New York, July 4, 1931. She studied with Achille Errani in N.Y.; in 1873 went to Italy, where she studied with Lamperti and San Giovanni in Milan. Upon her return to America in 1875 she was engaged by the bandleader Gilmore for his summer concerts, and toured the country with him; subsequently appeared in the European music centers; in 1903 she sang in China and Japan; then returned to the U.S., living in retirement in N.Y.
BIBLIOGRAPHY: R. McC. Gipson, *The Life of Emma Thursby, 1845–1931* (N.Y., 1940). See also V. L. Scott in *Notable American Women* (Cambridge, Mass., 1971) III.

Thybo, Leif, Danish composer and organist; b. Holstebro, June 12, 1922. He studied at the Cons. in Copenhagen, graduating in 1947; then was active as a church organist; in 1952 was appointed prof. of music at the Cons. of Copenhagen.
WORKS: chamber opera, *Den odödliga berättelsen (The Immortal Story;* Vadstena, Sweden, July 8, 1971); Concerto for chamber orch. (1947); 2 organ concertos (1954, 1956); Concerto for strings (1957); *Philharmonic Variations* for orch. (1958); Concertino for organ, chamber orch., and mezzo-soprano (Copenhagen, Oct. 19, 1960); Cello Concerto (1961); Piano Concerto (1961–63); Concerto for flute and chamber orch. (1966); Violin Concerto (1969); Viola Concerto (1972); *Markus-passionen (Passion According to St. Mark)* for soloists, chorus and orch. (Copenhagen,

March 19, 1964); *Te Deum* for chorus and winds (Copenhagen, Nov. 18, 1965); *Prophetia* for soprano, bass, chorus, and orch. (Copenhagen, Feb. 28, 1965); *In dieser Zeit* for solo voice, vocal quartet, and instruments (1967); *Dialogue* for soloists, chorus, and instruments (Copenhagen, May 27, 1968); *The Ecstacy* for soprano, narrator, recorder, oboe, viola da gamba, and spinet (1972); Cello Sonata (1950); 2 violin sonatas (1953, 1960); Sonata for violin and organ (1955); Trio for clarinet, cello, and piano (1963); String Quartet (1963); Flute Quintet (1965); *Concerto breve* for piano, flute, violin, viola, and cello (1966); *Hommage à Benjamin Britten* for flute quartet (1968); Trio for oboe, horn, and bassoon (1970); 2 piano sonatas (1947, 1956); other piano works; organ pieces; songs.

Tibaldi Chiesa, Maria, Italian writer on music; b. Milan, April 28, 1896. She studied at the Univ. of Rome; wrote opera librettos, and published books of verse. Her musical publications include: *Schubert* (1932; 2nd ed., 1933); *Ernest Bloch* (1933); *Mussorgsky* (1935); *Vita romantica di Liszt* (1937); *Cimarosa e il suo tempo* (1939); *Paganini* (3rd ed., 1944); *Ciaikovsky* (1943).

Tibbett, Lawrence, American baritone; b. Bakersfield, Calif., Nov. 16, 1896; d. New York, July 15, 1960. His real name was **Tibbet,** but it was accidentally misspelled when he appeared in opera, and the final extra letter was retained. His early ambition was to be an actor, and he made a few appearances in various plays in Los Angeles as a young man. He took vocal lessons with Basil Ruysdael in Los Angeles, sang in light operas; then went to N.Y., where his teacher was Frank La Forge. He made his operatic debut in N.Y. with the Metropolitan Opera on Nov. 24, 1923, in a minor role; then sang Valentin in *Faust* (Nov. 30, 1923); achieved a striking success as Ford in the revival of Verdi's *Falstaff* (Jan. 2, 1925); from then on he became one of the most successful singers at the Metropolitan Opera, where he remained until 1950; he made his last appearance with the Metropolitan Opera on March 24, 1950, as Ivan in *Khovanshchina*.

Tiby, Ottavio, Italian musicologist; b. Palermo, May 19, 1891; d. there, April 12, 1955. He studied at the Cons. of Palermo, graduating in composition in 1921; later studied in Rome. Returning to Palermo, he devoted himself to collecting Sicilian songs; was also an authority on Byzantine music.
WRITINGS: *Acustica musicale e organologia degli strumenti musicali* (Palermo, 1933); *La Musica bizantina: teoria e storia* (Milan, 1938); *La Musica in Grecia e a Roma* (Florence, 1942); edited *Antichi musicisti italiani* (1934).

Tichatschek, Joseph Aloys, Bohemian tenor; b. Ober-Weckelsdorf, July 11, 1807; d. Dresden, Jan. 18, 1886. He was the son of a poor weaver; in 1827 went to Vienna as a medical student, but then joined the chorus at the Kärnthnerthor Theater, and had vocal instruction from Ciccimara; was soon engaged at Graz for 2 years; then sang in Vienna. His career received a new impetus after his highly successful appearance at the Dresden Opera (Aug. 11, 1837); he remained there for 33 years, retiring in 1870. He created the roles of Rienzi (Oct. 20, 1842) and Tannhäuser (Oct. 19, 1845) in Wagner's operas. Wagner mentions him often and with great praise in his autobiography.

Tieffenbrucker. See **Duiffopruggar.**

Tiehsen, Otto, German composer; b. Danzig, Oct. 13, 1817; d. Berlin, May 15, 1849. He studied at the Royal Academy in Berlin, where he settled as a teacher. He wrote the comic opera *Annette* (Berlin, 1847); *Christmas Cantata; Kyrie* and *Gloria a 6*; songs of high merit.

Tiensuu, Jukka, Finnish composer; Helsinki, Aug. 30, 1948. He studied piano and composition under Paavo Heininen at the Sibelius Academy in Helsinki; later traveled in America. He composed *Preludio and Fuga* for string quartet (1970); *Largo* for string orch. (1971); *Concerto da camera* for flute, English horn, clarinet, bassoon, and cello (1972); *Overture* for flute and harpsichord (1972); *Fiato* for wind orch. (1974); *Threnos* for orch. (Helsinki, Feb. 26, 1975).

Tierney, Harry, American composer of popular music; b. Perth Amboy, N.J., May 21, 1890; d. New York, March 22, 1965. He studied piano and planned a concert career; then turned to composition of popular songs; wrote many numbers for the Ziegfeld Follies. His musical shows *Irene* (N.Y., Nov. 18, 1919), *Up She Goes* (N.Y., Nov. 6, 1922) and *Kid Boots* (N.Y., Dec. 31, 1923) were quite successful, but they were eclipsed by the fame of his *Rio Rita* (N.Y., Feb. 2, 1927). His early song *M-i-s-s-i-s-s-i-p-p-i* (1916) flooded the nation.

Tiersch, Otto, German music theorist; b. Kalbsrieth, Sept. 1, 1838; d. Berlin, Nov. 1, 1892. He studied with J. G. Töpfer at Weimar and with Bellermann at Berlin; taught singing at the Stern Cons. in Berlin. As a theorist he was a disciple of Hauptmann.
WRITINGS: *System und Methode der Harmonielehre* (1868); *Elementarbuch der musikalischen Harmonie- und Modulationslehre* (1874); *Kurze praktische Generalbass-, Harmonie- und Modulationslehre* (1876); *Kurzes praktisches Lehrbuch für Contrapunkt und Nachahmung* (1879); *Kurzes praktisches Lehrbuch für Klaviersatz und Accompagnement* (1881); *Notenfibel* (1882); *Die Unzulänglichkeit des heutigen Musikstudiums an Conservatorien, etc.* (1883); *Allgemeine Musiklehre* (1885; with Erk); *Rhythmik, Dynamik und Phrasierungslehre der homophonischen Musik* (1886).

Tiersot, (Jean-Baptiste-Élisée-) Julien, French musicologist; b. Bourg-en-Bresse, July 5, 1857; d. Paris, Aug. 10, 1936. He was a pupil of Savard, Massenet, and César Franck at the Paris Cons.; in 1883 was appointed assistant librarian at the Cons., and in 1910, chief librarian, retiring in 1920. He dedicated himself to musical ethnography, and contributed greatly to the documentation on French folk music. He was prof. at the École des Hautes Études Sociales and president of the Société Française de Musicologie. His compositions include a Mass on the tercentenary of the death of Roland de Lassus (1894); *Danses populaires françaises* for orch. (1900); *Hellas* (after Shelley) for chorus and orch.; etc.

WRITINGS: *Histoire de la chanson populaire en France* (1889); *Musiques pittoresques* (1889); *Rouget de Lisle, son œuvre, sa vie* (1892); *Les Types mélodiques dans la chanson populaire française* (1894); *Étude sur les Maîtres-Chanteurs de Richard Wagner* (1899); *Ronsard et la musique de son temps* (1903); *Index musical pour le Romancero populaire de la France par G. Doncieux* (1904); *Hector Berlioz et la société de son temps* (1904); *Notes d'ethnographie musicale* (Part I, 1905; Part II is *La Musique chez les peuples indigènes de l'Amérique du Nord,* 1910); *Les Fêtes et les chants de la Révolution française* (1908); *Gluck* (1910); *Beethoven, musicien de la Révolution* (1910); *J.-J. Rousseau* (1912); *Histoire de la Marseillaise* (1915); *Un Demi-siècle de musique française 1870-1917* (1918; 2nd ed., 1924); *La Musique dans la comédie de Molière* (1921); *La Damnation de Faust de Berlioz* (1924); *Lettres de musiciens écrites en français du XVe au XXe siècle* (2 vols.; 1924, 1936); *Smetana* (1926); *Les Couperin* (1926); *La Musique aux temps romantiques* (1930); *La Chanson populaire et les écrivains romantiques* (1931); *Don Juan de Mozart* (1933); *J.-S. Bach* (1934). Collections of music: *Chansons populaires recueillies dans les Alpes françaises* (1903); *Noëls français* (1901); *Chants populaires, pour les écoles* (3 vols., 1907-29); *44 French Folksongs and Variants from Canada, Normandy, and Brittany* (N.Y., 1910); *60 Folksongs of France* (Boston, 1915); *Chansons de Ronsard* (1924); *Chansons populaires françaises* (1921); *Mélodies populaires des provinces de France* 1928); *Chansons nègres* (1933).

BIBLIOGRAPHY: L. de La Laurencie, *Un Musicien bressan: J. Tiersot* (Bourg, 1932).

Tiessen, Heinz, German composer and conductor; b. Königsberg, April 10, 1887; d. Berlin, Nov. 29, 1971. He studied music with Rüfer and Klatte in Berlin; was music critic of the *Allgemeine Musikzeitung* (1912-17); led "Der junge Chor" for children of workers (1924-32). In 1925 he was appointed to the faculty of the Hochschule für Musik in Berlin; from 1946 to 1949 was director of the Municipal Cons. of Berlin, returning in 1949 to the Hochschule. His style of composition is influenced by Richard Strauss, with whom he was friendly; he published a guide to Strauss' *Josephslegende* (1914); *Zur Geschichte der jüngsten Musik, 1913-28* (Mainz, 1928); and *Musik der Natur,* a study of bird songs (1953). His compositions include 2 symphonies; Piano Concerto; *Naturtrilogie* for piano solo; Septet for flute, clarinet, horn, and string quartet; String Quintet; about 60 songs; incidental music to plays. See his autobiography, "Selbstzeugnis des Künstlers," in *Musica* (Kassel, April 1948).

Tietjens, Therese Johanne Alexandra, famous German soprano; b. Hamburg, July 17, 1831; d. London, Oct. 3, 1877. She was trained in Hamburg and made a successful debut there in 1849; sang at Frankfurt, and was engaged for the Vienna Court Opera in 1856; went to London in 1858, and remained there until her death, for long years the reigning favorite, singing at Her Majesty's Theatre, Drury Lane, Covent Garden and the Haymarket. She visited Paris in 1863, and America in 1874 and 1876, appearing at the Academy of Music in N.Y. under Strakosch's management.

Tigranian, Armen, Armenian composer; b. Alexandropol, Dec. 26, 1879; d. Tbilisi, Feb. 10, 1950. He studied flute and theory in Tbilisi; returned to Alexandropol in 1902 and organized a choral society, specializing in Armenian music; in 1913 settled in Tbilisi, where he became an esteemed music pedagogue; received the order of Lenin in 1939. He composed the operas *Anush* (Alexandropol, Aug. 17, 1912) and *David-bek* (Erivan, Dec. 3, 1950); *Dance Suite* for orch. (1946); cantata, *The Bloody Night (1936); Suite of Armenian Dances* for piano; numerous other piano pieces; songs; theater music.

BIBLIOGRAPHY: K. Melik-Wrtanessian, *Armen Tigranian* (Moscow, 1939); R. Atanian and M. Muradian, *Armen Tigranian* (Moscow, 1966).

Tijardović, Ivo, Croatian composer; b. Split, Sept. 18, 1895. He studied in Zagreb; began his professional career by conducting theater orchestras; wrote operettas of the Viennese type; of these, *Little Floramy* (1924) became successful in Yugoslavia. His opera *Dimnjiaci Uz Jadran (The Chimneys of the Adriatic Coast),* produced in Zagreb on Jan. 20, 1951, depicts the patriotic uprising of Yugoslav partisans during World War II; *Marco Polo,* opera (Zagreb, Dec. 3, 1960).

BIBLIOGRAPHY: I. Plamenac, *Ivo Tijardović* (Split, 1954).

Tikka, Kari, Finnish conductor and composer; b. Siilinjärvi, April 13, 1946. He studied composition with Joonas Kokkonen and oboe at the Sibelius Academy in Helsinki and later in Berlin. He learned the practical side of the art in conducting at the Finnish National Opera. In 1975 he was appointed conductor of the Royal Swedish Opera in Stockholm.

WORKS: *3 Fantasiestücke* for flute, clarinet, bassoon, trumpet, horn, viola, and cello (1969); *Two Days à la Vam* for orch. (1970); *Two Aphorisms* for 2 violas and cello (1971); *2 Pezzi* for flute, clarinet, bassoon, piano, and 4 percussionists (1973).

Tikotsky, Evgeny, Russian composer; b. St. Petersburg, Dec. 25, 1893; d. Minsk, Nov. 24, 1970. He studied composition with Deshevov; in 1944 became musical director of the Philharmonic Concerts in Minsk.

WORKS: the operas *Mihas Podhorny* (Minsk, March 10, 1939) and *Alesya* (Minsk, Dec. 24, 1944); 6 symphonies (1927, 1940, 1949, 1955, 1958, 1963); *Stormy Petrel,* after Maxim Gorky, for bass, chorus, and orch. (1944); Trombone Concerto (1944); Piano Concerto (1953); piano pieces; songs.

Till, Johann Christian, American Moravian teacher, organist, and composer; b. Gnadenthal, near Nazareth, Pa., May 18, 1762; d. Bethlehem, Pa., Nov. 19, 1844. From 1793 till 1808 he was teacher and organist at Hope, N.J.; from 1813 to 1844 was organist of the Bethlehem congregation. In his later years he also made pianos. His compositions are listed in A. G. Rau and H. T. David, *A Catalogue of Music by American Moravians* (Bethlehem, 1938).

Tillyard, Henry Julius Wetenhall, English musicologist; b. Cambridge, Nov. 18, 1881; d. Cambridge, England, Jan. 2, 1968. He studied at Cambridge Univ. (1900–04) and at the English schools in Rome and Athens (1904–07); specializing in ancient and medieval music; studied Greek church music with J. T. Sakellarides in Athens. Until 1918 he was lecturer at the Univ. of Edinburgh; in 1919 he became prof. at the Univ. of Johannesburg, South Africa; in 1922 was at Birmingham Univ.; and in 1926 at the Univ. of Cardiff. He published *Byzantine Music and Hymnology* (London, 1923) and *Handbook of the Middle Byzantine Musical Notation* (Copenhagen, 1935; vol. 1 of *Monumenta musicae byzantinae. Subsidia*).

Tilman, Alfred, Belgian composer; b. Brussels, Feb. 3, 1848; d. Schaerbeck, near Brussels, Feb. 20, 1895. He studied at the Brussels Cons. (1866–71); wrote the cantata *La Sirène;* 24 vocal fugues for 2 and 3 voices.

Tilmant, Théophile, French conductor; b. Valenciennes, July 8, 1799; d. Asnières, May 7, 1878. From 1838 to 1849 he served as 2nd maître de chapelle at the Théâtre Italien; then 1st maître de chapelle at the Opéra-Comique, until his retirement in 1868; was also conductor of the Cons. Concerts from 1860 to 1863.

Timm, Henry Christian, German-American pianist, organist, and composer; b. Hamburg, July 11, 1811; d. New York, Sept. 4, 1892. After study in Germany, he settled in the U.S. in 1835; was employed as church organist in N.Y., Boston, etc. He was president of the N.Y. Philharmonic from 1847 to 1863. He wrote choral works, organ pieces, and some piano music; made numerous transcriptions for 2 pianos of various classical works.

Timmermans, Ferdinand, Dutch organist and carillonneur; b. Rotterdam, Sept. 1, 1891. He studied organ with J. H. Besselaar and H. de Vries. In 1924 he became the municipal carillonneur at Rotterdam and in 1926 at Schiedam. He subsequently gave exhibitions in Belgium, France, and England; soon he won the reputation of being one of the world's greatest carillonneurs. On May 5, 1954 he gave a concert in Washington playing on the 50-bell carillon presented to the U.S. by the people of Holland. He published *Luidklokken en beiaarden in Nederland* (Amsterdam, 1944).

Tinayre, Yves (Jean), French singer and music scholar; b. Paris, April 25, 1891; d. New York, July 12, 1972. He studied voice in London and Milan; gave recitals in France, England, Austria, etc., specializing in old songs; also revived some medieval French, German, and Italian sacred songs.

Tinctoris, Johannes (called **John Tinctor**), renowned Belgian music theorist and an early musical lexicographer; b. probably Nivelles, 1435; d. there, before Oct. 12, 1511. About 1475, he was maestro to Ferdinand of Aragon at Naples, who dispatched him in 1487 to France and other countries in quest of singers for his

chapel; but Tinctoris never went back, and became a canon at Nivelles. He was one of the most eminent theorists of his time, and the author of the earliest dictionary of musical terms, *Terminorum musicae diffinitorium* (Naples, 1473; reprint in Coussemaker's *Scriptores* IV, and, with a German transl. by H. Bellermann, in Chrysander's *Jahrbuch,* 1863; in English, London, 1849; with a French transl., Paris, 1951). The only other work known to have been printed during his life is *De inventione et usu musicae* (after 1487); a number of treatises preserved in manuscript were published for the first time in Coussemaker's edition of the complete works of Tinctoris (1875) and reprinted in vol. IV of the *Scriptores.* Extant compositions are a *Missa l'homme armé* (ed. by L. Feininger in *Monumenta polyphoniae liturgicae Sanctae Ecclesiae romanae,* Series I, I–9) and some chansons in manuscript; other chansons and a Lamentation in Petrucci's *Odhecaton A;* a *Missa,* edited by F. Feldmann, constitutes Vol. I of *Opera Omnia,* published by the American Institute of Musicology in 1960.

BIBLIOGRAPHY: G. Pannain, *La Teoria musicale di G. Tinctoris* (Naples, 1913); K. Weinmann, *Johannes Tinctoris und sein unbekannter Traktat "De inventione et usu musicae"* (Regensburg, 1917); Ch. Van den Borren, *J. Tinctoris* (Brussels, 1931); Lucie Balmer, *Tonsystem und Kirchentöne bei J. Tinctoris* (dissertation, Bern, 1935); G. Reese, *Music in the Renaissance* (N.Y., 1954); René Vannes, ed., *Dictionnaire des Musiciens* (Brussels, 1947).

Tinel, Edgar, Belgian composer; b. Sinay, March 27, 1854; d. Brussels, Oct. 28, 1912. He was taught at first by his father, a schoolmaster and organist; entered the Brussels Cons. on 1863 as a pupil of Brassin, Dupont, Gevaert, Kufferath, and Mailly; in 1873 took 1st prize for piano playing; won the Belgian Prix de Rome in 1877 with the cantata *De Klokke Roeland.* In 1882 he became director of the Institute for Sacred Music at Mechlin; was appointed to the staff of the Brussels Cons. in 1896, and in 1909 (after Gevaert's death) became the director.

WORKS: *Franciscus,* oratorio (Mechlin, 1888; N.Y., 1893); *Godoleva,* music drama (Brussels, July 22, 1897); *Katharina,* sacred opera (Brussels, Feb. 27, 1909); many German and Flemish songs; *Te Deum* for mixed chorus and organ; *Missa in honorem beatae Mariae Virginis de Lourdes* for 5-part chorus a cappella; psalms; motets; sacred songs. He published *Le Chant grégorien, théorie sommaire de son exécution* (1890).

BIBLIOGRAPHY: A. van der Elst, *Edgar Tinel* (Ghent, 1901); Paul Tinel (his son), *Edgar Tinel: le récit de sa vie et l'exégèse de son œuvre de 1854 à 1886* (Brussels, 1922); Paul Tinel, *Edgar Tinel* (Brussels, 1946).

Tiomkin, Dmitri, Russian-American composer of film music; b. St. Petersburg, May 10, 1894; studied piano at the St. Petersburg Cons. with Isabelle Vengerova; left Russia in 1921; lived in Berlin. He began his career as a concert pianist in Europe; came to America in 1925; after a few years in New York, settled in Hollywood, where he became a highly successful composer of film music. He received an Academy Award for best score and best theme song of *High Noon* (1952); was also the recipient of awards of merit, scrolls of appreciation, plaques of recognition, golden globes, etc. He published a dictated autobiography under the title *Please Don't Hate Me* (N.Y., 1959).

Tippett, Sir Michael, renowned English composer; b. London, Jan. 2, 1905. He studied composition with R. O. Morris and conducting with Sir Adrian Boult and Sir Malcolm Sargent at the Royal College of Music in London; then held miscellaneous jobs as school teacher and choir conductor. His early music followed the neo-Romantic direction, but soon he evolved a style and a technique all of his own, marked by a rhapsodic eloquence and strengthened by a solid polyphonic texture; he is equally adept in lyric sentiment and in dramatic expression; often he couches individual sections in dance forms. He excels in large vocal and instrumental forms; he is a master of the modern idiom, attaining heights of dissonant counterpoint without losing the teleological sense of inherent tonality. A man of great general culture, he has a fine literary gift; he writes his own libretti for his operas and other vocal works. In 1959 he was named Commander of the British Empire (C.B.E.) and in 1966 he received his knighthood.
WORKS: operas: *The Midsummer Marriage* (London, Jan. 27, 1955); *King Priam* (Conventry, May 29, 1962); *The Knot Garden* (London, Dec. 2, 1970); *The Ice Break* (London, July 6, 1977); vocal works: *A Child of Our Time* (London, March 19, 1944); *Crown of the Year* for women's voices and instruments (1958); *Music for Words Perhaps*, to text by William Yeats (1960); *Music* for unison chorus, strings, and piano, after Shelley (1960); *The Vision of St. Augustine* to a Latin text for baritone, chorus, and orch. (London, Jan. 19, 1966); *The Shires Suite* for chorus and orch. (London, July 8, 1970); for orch: Symph. No. 1 (1945); Symph. No. 2 (London, Feb. 5, 1958); Symph. No. 3 (1972); Symph. No. 4 (Chicago, Oct. 6, 1977); Concerto for Double String Orch. (1939); *Fantasia on a theme by Handel* for piano and orch. (London, March 7, 1942); *Suite in D* for orch. (1948); *Little Music* for string orch. (1952); *Fantasia concertante on a theme by Corelli* for string orch. (1953); Piano Concerto (1955); 3 string quartets (1935, 1942, 1946); *Inventions* for 2 recorders (1954); Sonata for 4 horns (1955); 3 piano sonatas (1937, 1962, 1973); a number of song cycles; hymns; anthems.
BIBLIOGRAPHY: A. Milner, "The Music of Michael Tippett," *Musical Quarterly* (Oct. 1974); Ian Kemp, editor, *Michael Tippett: A Symposium on His 60th Birthday* (London, 1965).

Tirabassi, Antonio, musicologist; b. Amalfi, Italy, July 10, 1882; d. Brussels, Feb. 5, 1947. He began his career as a church organist; in 1910 went to Belgium, where he founded the Institut Belge de Musicologie (1920); brought out editions of works by Monteverdi, Corelli, and other composers. He wrote the books *École flamande (1450 à 1600). La mesure dans la notation proportionelle et sa transcription moderne* (Brussels, 1927); *Grammaire de la notation proportionnelle et sa transcription moderne* (Brussels, 1930).

BIBLIOGRAPHY: M. Schiavo, *Antonio Tirabassi* (Salerno, 1970).

Tircuit, Heuwell (Andrew), American composer, percussion player and music critic; b. Plaquemine, Louisiana, Oct. 18, 1931. He played drums at the age of 9; served in U.S. Army Bands (1954–56). In 1956 he went to Japan; played percussion in Japanese orchestras and wrote music criticism for the *Japan Times*; returned to the U.S. in 1963; was music critic of the *San Francisco Chronicle*. In his compositions, he cultivates a disestablishmentarian latitudinarianism uncircumscribed by doctrinaire precepts; as a professional drummer he makes liberal use in his music of a broad variety of percussionable objects.
WORKS: 2 string quartets (1953, 1957); Trumpet Sonata (1954); Cello Concerto (1960); Violin Sonata (1960); Viola Sonata (1961); *Knell* for 27 flutes and percussion (1962); *Symphony Concertante* (1976).

Tirindelli, Pier Adolfo, Italian violinist and composer; b. Conegliano, May 5, 1858; d. Rome, Feb. 6, 1937. He studied violin at the Milan Cons., then in Vienna with Grün and in Paris with Massart. From 1885 to 1895 he taught violin at the Liceo Benedetto Marcello in Venice. He then went to the U.S.; taught violin at the Cincinnati Cons. (1896–1920). He wrote an Italian opera, *Atenaide* (Venice, Nov. 19, 1892) and a French opera, *Blanc et noir* (Cincinnati, Dec. 15, 1897); also composed some attractive songs to Italian and French words, among them *Mistica, Vaticinio, Je ne t'aime plus, Une Existence,* etc.
BIBLIOGRAPHY: E. Montanaro, *P. A. Tirindelli e la sua musica* (Rome, 1933).

Tischer, Gerhard, German music publisher; b. Lübnitz, Nov. 10, 1877; d. Starnberg, Dec. 1, 1959. He studied music theory in Berlin; obtained his Dr. phil. with the dissertation *De aristotelischen Musikprobleme* (1903); lectured on music theory at the Handelhochschule in Cologne (1904–19) and at the Univ. of Cologne (1919–21). In 1910 he founded in Cologne the music publishing firm of "Tischer & Jagenberg," and in 1923 bought the "Wunderhorn Verlag" of Munich. In 1943 the firm moved to Starnberg; it was liquidated in 1969.

Tischhauser, Franz, Swiss composer; b. Bern, March 28, 1921. He studied at the Zürich Cons.; in 1951 joined the staff of the Zürich Radio and in 1971 was appointed director of its music department.
WORKS: ballet, *Birthday of the Infanta* (1941); Concertino for piano and small orch. (1945); *Divertimento* for 2 horns and string orch. (1948); *Punctus contra punctum* for tenor, baritone, and small orch. (1962); *Omaggi a Mälzel* for 12 stringed instruments (1963); *Mattinata* for 23 wind instruments (1965); *Antiphonarium profanum* for 2 men's choruses a capella (1967); *Kontertänze* for 2 orchestras (1968); *Eve's Meditation on Love,* for soprano, tuba, and string orch. (1972); *the Beggar's Concerto* for clarinet and string orch. (1975–76).

Tischler, Hans, Austrian-American musicologist; b. Vienna, Jan. 18, 1915. He studied piano with Paul

Wittgenstein; composition with Richard Stöhr and Franz Schmidt; musicology with Robert Lach, Egon Wellesz and Robert Haas at Vienna Univ. He left Austria in 1938, settling in the U.S.; continued his musicological studies with Leo Schrade at Yale Univ. (Ph.D., 1942). He taught music theory at West Virginia Wesleyan College (1945–47) and at Roosevelt Univ. in Chicago (1947–65). In 1965 he was appointed prof. of music at Indiana Univ., Bloomington. He published *The Perceptive Music Listener* (N.Y., 1955); *Practical Harmony* (Boston, 1964); edited *A Complete Edition of the Earliest Motets* (Rome, 1966); *A Complete Edition of the Parisian Two-Part Organa* (Rome, 1966).

Tishchenko, Boris, Soviet composer; b. Leningrad, March 23, 1939. He studied composition at the Leningrad Cons. with Salmanov, Voloshinov, and Evlakhov, graduating in 1962; later took lessons with Shostakovich. In his works he demonstrates a strong rhythmic power and polyphonic mastery; his musical idiom is greatly advanced without overstepping the bounds of tonality.
WORKS: 1-act opera, *The Stolen Sun* (1968); ballets: *The Twelve,* after the poem of Alexander Blok (Leningrad, Dec. 31, 1964); *Yaroslavna* (1974); *Lenin Lives,* cantata (1959); 5 symphonies (1960, 1964, 1966, 1970, 1974); Violin Concerto (1958); 2 cello concertos (1963, 1969); Piano Concerto (1962); Flute Concerto (1972); *Palekh,* homage to Russian folk painters, for chamber orch. (1965); 3 string quartets (1957, 1959, 1969); 2 Sonatas for solo violin (1957); Sonata for solo cello (1960); *Capriccio* for Violin and Piano (1965); 6 piano sonatas (1957, 1960, 1965, 1972, 1973, 1975); *Sad Songs* for soprano and piano (1962); *Suzdal,* folk texts from the Suzdal region, for soprano, tenor, and chamber orch. (1964); *Hard Frost,* aria for mezzo-soprano and orch. (1975).

Tisne, Antoine, French composer; b. Lourdes, Nov. 29, 1932. He studied with Darius Milhaud and Jean Rivier at the Paris Cons., obtaining Premier Second Grand Prix de Rome in 1962.
WORKS: Symph. No. 1 (1960); 3 piano concertos (1958, 1961, 1963); *À une ombre* for 22 players (1963); Violon Sonata (1963); String Quartet (1963); Cello Sonata (1964); *Visions des temps immémoriaux* for Ondes Martenot, piano, and percussion (1965); *Caractères* for 10 wind instruments (1965); Flute Concerto (1965); Cello Concerto (1965); Symph. No. 2 (1966); *Cosmogonies* for 3 orchestras (Paris, Dec. 10, 1968); *Disparates* for wind quintet (1968); *Elégie* for double bass and piano (1969); *Séquences pour un rituel* for string orch. (1969); *Hommage à Calder* for clavecin (1969).

Titelouze, Jean, the founder of the French school of organ playing; b. St.-Omer, 1563; d. Rouen, Oct. 24, 1633. He was appointed organist in 1585 at St.-Jean in Rouen; from 1588 till his death he was organist at the Cathedral there. His complete organ works are published in Guilmant's *Archives des Maîtres de l'orgue.*
BIBLIOGRAPHY: A. G. Ritter, *Zur Geschichte des Orgelspiels im 14.-18. Jahrhundert* (Leipzig, 1884); A Pirro, *J. Titelouze* (Paris, 1898); E. von Werra, "J. Titelouze," *Kirchenmusikalisches Jahrbuch* (1910).

Titl, Anton Emil, Bohemian conductor and composer; b. Pernstein, Oct. 2, 1809; d. Vienna, Jan. 21, 1882. In 1850 he became conductor at the Burgtheater in Vienna; wrote two operas: *Die Burgfrau* (Brünn, 1832) and *Das Wolkenkind* (Vienna, March 14, 1845); a Mass for 8 voices; overtures; violin pieces. His *Serenade* for violin was very popular in numerous arrangements.

Titov, Alexei, Russian composer; b. St. Petersburg, June 24, 1769; d. there, Nov. 20, 1827. He served in the cavalry, reaching the rank of major general at his retirement; was an amateur violinist, and wrote operas in the traditional Italian style; of these, the following were produced in St. Petersburg: *Andromeda and Perseus* (1802); *The Judgment of Solomon* (1803); *Nurzadakh* (June 7, 1807); *The Wedding of Filatka* (April 25, 1808); *Errant Moment* (July 10, 1812); *Emmerich Tekkely* (Dec. 13, 1812); *Intrigue in the Basket* (May 12, 1817); *Valor of the People of Kiev, or These Are the Russians* (May 12, 1817); *The Feast of the Mogul* (Sept. 15, 1823); *The Brewer, or The Hidden Ghost of Evil* (Moscow, 1788); a ballet-pantomime, *Le Nouveau Werther,* was first given in St. Petersburg, on Jan. 30, 1799. His brother **Sergei Titov** (1770–1827) was a cellist who wrote the operas (all produced in St. Petersburg), *The Forced Wedding* (Sept. 4, 1789), *Credulous Folk* (July 10, 1812), and *Old-Fashioned Christmas* (Jan. 25, 1813).

Titov, Nicolai, Russian song writer, son and pupil of **Alexei Titov;** b. St. Petersburg, May 10, 1800; d. there, Dec. 22, 1875. He received a military upbringing; like his father, he reached the rank of major general. He had no formal musical education; took some singing lessons, and studied a manual of thoroughbass; he was a typical dilettante, but possessed a gift of melodic invention; he knew Glinka and Dargomyzhsky, who helped him to develop his ability. He wrote about 60 songs, which were extremely popular in his time; his early song, *The Pine Tree,* published in 1820, is erroneously believed to be the first Russian art song, but it had precursors; other of his songs that were popular include *Perfidious Friend, The Blue Scarf,* and *A Tree Branch.* He wrote a curious *Quadrille* for piano 3 hands, the treble part to be played by a beginner; another interesting project was a "musical romance in 12 waltzes" (under the general title *When I Was Young*), which remained incomplete. A waltz, entitled *Past Happiness,* the *Quadrille,* and 4 songs were reproduced in *History of Russian Music in Examples,* edited by S. Ginsburg (Moscow, 1942; vol. 2, pp. 381–93).

Titta Ruffo. See **Ruffo, Titta.**

Tobani, Theodore Moses, German-American composer and arranger of a multitude of marches, gavottes, waltzes, and other popular forms; b. Hamburg, May 2, 1855; d. Queens, N.Y., Dec. 12, 1933. His family emigrated to the U.S. about 1870; Tobani earned his living as a youth playing violin at theaters and drinking emporia; then became associated with the music publishing firm of Carl Fischer in N.Y.; he is said to have composed or arranged over 5,000 pieces for piano or organ that enjoyed gratifying commercial success; the best known of these works, and one epitomizing the sentimental popular tastes of the time, was *Hearts and Flowers* (op. 245), which Tobani claimed to have tossed off in an hour in the late summer of 1893. Since he published so much music, he used a number of pseudonyms, among which **Florence Reed** and **Andrew Herman** were his favorites.

Tocchi, Gian-Luca, Italian composer; b. Perugia, Jan. 10, 1901. He studied in Rome with Respighi; his early works were written in a Romantic and Impressionist manner: a symph. poem *Il Destino*, after Maeterlinck; a *Rapsodia romantica* (1929), *Tre canzoni alla maniera popolare italiana* (1931); he then changed to contemporary subjects, exemplified by such works as *Record* (1933), *Film* (1936), and a Concerto for jazz band.

Toch, Ernst, eminent Austrian-American composer; b. Vienna, Dec. 7, 1887; d. Los Angeles, Oct. 1, 1964. His father was a Jewish dealer in unprocessed leather, and there was no musical strain in the family; Toch began playing piano without a teacher in his grandmother's pawnshop; he learned musical notation from a local violinist, and then copied Mozart's string quartets for practice; using them as a model, he began to compose string quartets and other pieces of chamber music; at the age of 17 he had one of them performed by the famous Rosé Quartet in Vienna. From 1906 to 1909 he attended musical courses at the Univ. of Vienna. In 1909 he won the prestigious Mozart Prize and a scholarship to study at the Frankfurt Cons., where he studied piano with Willy Rehberg and composition with Iwan Knorr. In 1910 he was awarded the Mendelssohn Prize; also won 4 times in succession the Austrian State Prize. In 1913 he was appointed instructor in piano at Zuschneid's Hochschule für Musik in Mannheim. In 1914–18 he served in the Austrian Army; during a furlough in Vienna in 1916 he married Lilly Zwack. After the Armistice he returned to Mannheim, resumed his musical career, and became active in the modern movement, soon attaining, along with Hindemith, Krenek and others a prominent position in the new German school of composition. In the meantime he continued his academic studies; earned his Dr. phil. degree in 1921 with the dissertation *Beiträge zur Stilkunde der Melodie* (published in Berlin under the title *Melodielehre*). In 1929 he went to live in Berlin where he established himself as a piano teacher. In 1932 he made an American tour as pianist playing his own works; returned to Berlin, but with the advent of the Nazi regime, was forced to leave Germany; he went to Paris, then to London, and in 1935 emigrated to the U.S.; gave lectures on music at the New School for Social Research in N.Y.; in 1937 moved to Hollywood, where he wrote music for films. He became an American citizen on July 26, 1940; in 1940–41 he taught composition at the Univ. of Southern Calif., Los Angeles; subsequently taught privately; among his students were many who, like André Previn, became well-known composers in their own right. Between 1950 and 1958 he lived in Vienna and Switzerland. Toch's music was rooted in the tradition of German and Austrian Romantic movement of the

19th century, but his study of the classics made him aware of the paramount importance of formal logic in the development of thematic ideas. His early works were mostly for chamber music, and piano solo; following the *Zeitgeist* during his German period he wrote several pieces for the stage in the light manner of sophisticated entertainment; also composed effective piano works of a virtuoso quality, which enjoyed considerable popularity among pianists of the time. Toch possessed a fine wit and a sense of exploration; his *Geographical Fugue* for speaking chorus articulating in syllabic counterpoint the names of exotic places on earth became a classic of its genre. It was not before 1950 that he wrote his first full-fledged symphony, but from that time on until his death of stomach cancer he composed fully 7 symphonies, and in addition a sinfonietta for string orch. He was greatly interested in new techniques; the theme of his last string quartet (No. 13; 1953) is based on a 12-tone row. In the score of his 3rd Symph. he introduced an optional instrument, the Hisser, a tank of carbon dioxide that produced a hissing sound through a valve. Among the several honors he received was the Pulitzer Prize for his 3rd Symph. (1956), membership in the National Institute of Arts and Letters (1957), and the Cross of Honor for Sciences and Art from the Austrian government (1963). An Ernst Toch Archive was founded at the Univ. of California, Los Angeles, in 1974, serving as depository for his manuscripts, published and unpublished.

WORKS: FOR THE STAGE: *Wegwende* (1925), *Die Prinzessin auf der Erbse* (Baden-Baden, July 17, 1927), *Egon und Emilie* (Mannheim, 1928), *Der Fächer* (Königsberg, June 8, 1930); *The Last Tale* (1964); oratorio, *Das Wasser* (Berlin, June 18, 1930). FOR ORCH.: *An mein Vaterland*, with soli, chorus, and organ (1915); *Fantastische Nachtmusik* (Mannheim, March 22, 1921); *Die Chinesische Flöte*, for soprano and chamber mus. (Frankfurt, June 24, 1923); *Tanz-Suite*, for small orch. (Mannheim, Nov. 19, 1923); *5 Pieces* for chamber orch. (1924); Cello Concerto (Kiel, June 17, 1925); Piano Concerto (Düsseldorf, Oct. 8, 1926, Gieseking soloist); *Spiel*, for band (Donaueschingen, July 24, 1926); *Komödie für Orchester* (Berlin, Nov. 13, 1927); *Bunte Suite* (Frankfurt, Feb. 22, 1929); *Fuge aus der Geographie* for spoken chorus (Berlin Festival of New Music, June 17, 1930); *Kleine Theater-Suite* (Berlin, Feb. 9, 1931); Symph. for piano and orch. (Piano Concerto No. 2; 1932; London, Aug. 20, 1934); *Big Ben*, variations on the Westminster chimes (Boston Symph., Cambridge, Mass., Dec. 20, 1934); *Pinocchio*, "a merry overture" (Los Angeles, Dec. 10, 1936; very successful); *Hyperion*, dramatic prelude after Keats (Cleveland, Jan. 8, 1948); 7 symphonies: No. 1 (Vienna, Dec. 20, 1950); No. 2, dedicated to Albert Schweitzer (Vienna, Jan. 11, 1952); No. 3 (Pittsburgh, Dec. 2, 1955; won the Pulitzer Prize); No. 4 (Minneapolis, Nov. 22, 1957); No. 5, named *Jephta, Rhapsodic Poem* (Boston, March 13, 1964); No. 6 (1963); No. 7 (1964); Sinfonietta for string orch. (1964); Sinfonietta for wind orch. (1964); *3 Pantomimes* for orch. (1963–64); *Notturno* (Louisville, Jan. 2, 1954); *Peter Pan*, fairy tale (Seattle, Feb. 13, 1956). CHAMBER MUSIC: 13 string quartets (1902–1953); Violin Sonata (1928); Cello Sonata

(1929); Piano Quintet (1938); Duos for 2 Violins (1909, for open string only in the pupil's part); Serenade for 3 violins (1912); Serenade for 2 violins and viola (1917); *2 Divertimenti* for string duos (1926); *2 Etudes* for cello solo (1930; String Trio (1936); *3 Impromptus* for violin solo, viola solo, and cello solo (1963); *5 Pieces* for flute, oboe, clarinet, bassoon, 2 horns, and percussion (1959); *Sonatinetta* for flute, clarinet, and bassoon (1959); Quartet for oboe, clarinet, bassoon, and viola (1964). FOR PIANO: *Burlesken Suite* (1923; includes the popular *Der Jongleur*), *3 Klavierstücke* (1925); *5 Capriccetti* (1925); *Tanz und Spielstücke* (1927); Sonata (1928); *Kleinstadtbilder*, 14 easy pieces (1929); *Fünfmal Zehn Etüden* (50 etudes; 1931); *Profiles* (1946); *Ideas* (1946); *Divisions* (1956); *Sonatinetta* (1956); *3 Little Dances* (1961); *Reflections*, 5 pieces (1961); Sonata for piano 4 hands (1962). VOCAL WORKS: *Cantata of the Bitter Herbs* for solo voices, narrator, chorus, and orch., a text from the Bible (1938); *The Inner Circle*, 6 choruses a cappella (1953); *Valse* for speaking chorus and percussion (1961); *9 Lieder* for soprano and piano (1926); *There Is a Season for Everything* for mezzo-soprano, flute, clarinet, violin, and cello, to words from *Ecclesiastes* (1953); *Vanity of Vanities* for soprano, tenor, flute, clarinet, violin, viola, and cello, to words from *Ecclesiastes* (1954); *Phantoms* for narrator, women's speaking chorus, and chamber orch. (1957). FILM SCORES: *Peter Ibbetson* (1935); *Outcast* (1937); *The Cat and the Canary* (1939); *Dr. Cyclops* (1940); *The Ghost Breakers* (1940); *None Shall Escape* (1944); *Address Unknown* (1944); *The Unseen* (1945). BOOKS: *Die Melodielehre* (Berlin, 1923); *The Shaping Forces in Music* (N.Y., 1948; new edition, with a valuable introduction by Toch's grandson Lawrence Weschler, and a complete list of works; N.Y., 1977).

BIBLIOGRAPHY: E. Beninger, "Pianistische Probleme, im Anschluss an die Klavierwerke von Ernst Toch," *Melos* (1928); Paul Pisk, "Ernst Toch," *Musical Quarterly* (Oct. 1938); Lawrence Weschler, *Ernst Toch, 1887–1964: A Biographical Essay Ten Years after His Passing*, a publication of the Ernst Toch Archive of The Music Library of the Univ. of California Los Angeles (1974).

Toda, Kunio, Japanese composer; b. Tokyo, Aug. 11, 1915. He studied law at Tokyo Univ., graduating in 1938; concurrently studied music; then entered Japanese diplomatic service; served as cultural attaché in the Japanese embassies in Germany and Russia; at the outbreak of the war he returned to Japan, where he resumed his musical studies with Saburo Moroi; in 1955 he was appointed a lecturer at the Toho Junior College of Music; taught also at the Toho Gakuen School of Music.

WORKS: 2 operas: *Akemi* (1956; Tokyo, 1956) and *Kyara Monogatari* (*The Story of Kyara City*; Tokyo, 1973); 5 ballets: *Salome in Studio* (Tokyo, Nov. 23, 1951), *Le Cirque rouge* (Tokyo, Nov. 4, 1953), *The Cave* (Tokyo, Nov. 7, 1954), *Dance of the Red Death*, after Edgar Allan Poe (Osaka, 1956) and *Miranda* (Tokyo, Oct. 26, 1968); a scenic oratorio-mystery, *Santo Paulo* for 4 soloists, chorus and orch. (1961–64; concert version, Tokyo, Feb. 15, 1973); *Symphonic Overture* (1943); *Légende*, symph. fantasy (1944); 2 piano

concertos (1944, 1955); *Passacaglia and Fugue* for orch. (1949); *Overtura Buffa* (1950); Symph. in G (1956); *Concerto Grosso* for 6 solo instruments and orch. (Tokyo, Jan. 25, 1968); Piano Trio (1948); *Amoroso* for violin and piano (1951); Violin Sonata (1957); *Message* for soprano, clarinet, and harp (1961); *Bassoon Sonata* (1966); *Triptychon* for solo baritone, recorder, and guitar (1967, revised 1972); *3 Intermezzi* for piano (1942); *Fantaisie sur les sons de koto* for piano (1961); Piano Sonatina (1966); *Quattro pezzi deformati* for piano (1968); choruses; songs.

Todi, Luiza Rosa de Aguilar, Portuguese mezzo-soprano; b. Setubal, Jan. 9, 1753; d. Lisbon, Oct. 1, 1833. She appeared on the stage at 15; married the violinist **Francisco Todi** at 16; studied singing with David Perez. After appearances in London (1772 and 1777) she sang in Madrid (1777), Paris (1778–79 and 1781–82), and Berlin (1782). In 1783 her rivalry with Elisabeth Mara became a sensation in musical Paris, two hostile factions being formed, the Todistes and Maratistes. In 1784 she went to Russia, where she obtained considerable success at the court of Catherine the Great; in 1787 Friedrich Wilhelm II engaged her at a high salary in Berlin; in 1789 she sang again in Paris; in 1793 she returned to Portugal; during the last years of her life she was completely blind.

BIBLIOGRAPHY: J. Vasconcellos, *Luiza Todi* (Oporto, 1873); R.-Aloys Mooser, *Annales de la Musique et des Musiciens en Russie au XVIIIᵐᵉ siècle* (Geneva, 1948–51; vol. 2, pp. 509–13).

Toduţă, Sigismund, Rumanian composer; b. Simeria, May 30, 1908. He studied with Negrea at the Cons. in Cluj (1931–33) and later at the Santa Cecilia Academy in Rome (1936–38) with Pizzetti (composition) and Casella (piano). In 1946 he was appointed to the faculty of the Cluj Cons. (director, 1962–64); in 1971 became conductor of the Cluj State Philharmonic. His music is distinguished by a flowing romantic melody in large rhapsodic sonorities.

WORKS: opera, *Mesterul Manole* (1943–47); oratorio, *Miorita* (1958); *Balada Steagului* for soprano, chorus, and orch. (1961); *Eglogă* for orch. (1933); *Symphonic Variations* (1940); Piano Concerto (1943); 3 concertos for string orch. (1951, 1971, 1973); *Divertissement* for string orch. (1951); 5 symphonies: No. 1 (1954); No. 2, in memory of Enesco, with organ (1956); No. 3, *Ovidiu* (1957); No. 4 for strings (1961); No. 5 (1963); *Uvertură festivă* (1959); Sinfonietta (1971); Concerto for winds and percussion (1976); Cello Sonata (1952); Flute Sonata (1952); Violin Sonata (1953); *Adagio* for cello and piano (1954); Oboe Sonata (1956); *Passacaglia* for piano (1943); Piano Sonatina (1950); *Prelude, Chorale and Toccata* for piano (1975); choruses; songs.

Toebosch, Louis, Dutch composer and organist; b. Maastricht, March 18, 1916. He studied at the School of Church Music in Utrecht, the Music Lyceum in Maastricht, and then the Royal Cons. in Liège, Belgium (1934–39); was active as a church organist in Breda (1940–65); conducted the Tilburg Symph. Orch. (1944–50); taught at the Conservatories of Tilburg and Maastricht (1944–65); was director of the Brabant

Cons. (1965–74). His music combines the polyphonic style of the Renaissance with modern techniques; he applies the 12-tone method of compostion in both secular and sacred music.

WORKS: 2 suites for orch. (1939, 1948); *Allegro* for organ and orch. (1941); *Tema con variazioni* for orch. (1945); *Breda Suite* for orch. (1948); *Het Lied van Hertog Jan* for orch. (1949); oratorio, *St. Vincentius* (1954); *Carnavalsige Ouverture* (1955); *Concertante Ouverture* (1956); *Variations* for orch. (1957); Sinfonietta No. 1 for male chorus and orch. (1957); Sinfonietta No. 2 for orch. (1961); *Kerstcantate (Christmas Cantata)* for soprano, male chorus, and orch. (1959); *Feestelijke Ouverture* (1960); *Philippica Moderata*, written for the 50th anniversary of scientific research of Philips Co., for contralto, baritone, chorus, and orch. (1963; winner of the 1966 Sem Dresden Prize); *Agena*, divertimento for small orch. (1966); *Changements* for organ and orch. (Rotterdam, March 28, 1968); Piano Sonata (1947); the organ pieces *Praeludium et Fuga super Te Deum laudamus* (1954), *Toccana* (1973) and *Orgelspiegel (Organ Mirror*, 1975); *Sarabande and Allegro* for wind quintet (1959); *Suite polyphonica* for 2 pianos (1962); *The King's Quartet* for string quartet (1968); *Aria and Finale* for solo viola (1969); *Pasticcio di Rofena* for piano, 4 hands (1973).

Toëschi, Carlo Giuseppe (Toesca della Castella-Monte), Italian violinist and composer; b. Ludwigsburg, 1731 (baptized, Nov. 11, 1731); d. Munich, April 12, 1788. He was the son of **Alessandro Toëschi,** a member of the Mannheim Orch., who had moved to Germany. He studied with Johann Stamitz in Mannheim and entered its orch. in 1752 as a violinist; in 1759 he became concertmaster of the Mannheim Orch. He followed the court of Munich in 1778, and was appointed court musician in 1780. A highly productive composer, he wrote about 25 ballet scores, and at least 66 known symphonies; 19 flute concertos and 11 violin concertos; also a number of quartets, quintets, sextets, trio sonatas, violin sonatas and other pieces of chamber music. Riemann published his symph. *a* 8 in the *Denkmäler der Tonkunst in Bayern* 13 (7.ii); in the same series are reprinted a flute quartet and flute quintet (vol. 27 [15]) and a trio (vol. 28 [16], which also contains a thematic catalogue, listing 60 chamber works). A symph. in D was arranged by A. Carse, and publ. in London (1936).

BIBLIOGRAPHY: R. Münster, *Die Sinfonien Toeschis* (dissertation; Munich, 1956).

Toëschi, Johann Baptist (Giovanni Battista), Italian-German violinist and composer; brother of **Carlo Giuseppe Toëschi;** b. Stuttgart, 1735 (baptized Oct. 1, 1735); d. Munich, 1800 (buried April 3, 1800). Like his brother, he was a violinist in the Mannheim Orch. (from 1755); followed the court to Munich in 1778, and became music director in Munich in 1793. He produced a ballet, *Arlechin, Kaiser in China,* (Mannheim, April 26, 1778); composed a great number of chamber music pieces. A thematic catalogue of his works appears in the *Denkmäler der Tonkunst in Bayern* 28 (16).

Tofft, Alfred, Danish composer; b. Copenhagen, Jan. 2, 1865; d. there, Jan. 30, 1931. Abandoning a commercial career, he studied music with J. Nebelong (organ) and G. Bohlmann (theory): was music critic for *Berlinske Tidende* in Copenhagen, and president of the Danish Composers Society. He was a fine organist and a talented composer of songs (op. 2, *Heine-Album;* op. 4, *Jacobsen-Album;* etc.). Two operas were produced in Copenhagen: *Vifandaka* (Jan. 1, 1898) and *Anathema* (May 10, 1928).

Togni, Camillo, Italian composer; b. Gussago, Oct. 18, 1922. He studied with Alfredo Casella in Rome (1939–43); took courses in philosophy at the Univ. of Pavia; then devoted himself entirely to music. His early works follow the neo-Classical style of the Italian Baroque; later he adopted the 12-tone method of composition.

WORKS: *Variations* for piano and orch. (1946); *Psalmus CXXVII* for solo voices, violin, viola, and cello (Brussels Festival of the International Society for Contemporary Music, June 24, 1950); *Ricercar* for baritone and 5 instruments, to the text from *La nausée* by Sartre (1953); *Fantasia Concertante*, for flute and string orch. (Cologne, March 25, 1958); *Recitativo* for electronic sound (1961); *Gesang zur Nacht* for contralto and chamber orch. (1962); *3 Rondeaux per dieci* for soprano and 9 instruments (1964); *Aubade* for 6 instruments (1965); 4 capriccios for piano (1954, 1956, 1957, 1969); *3 Pieces* for chorus and orch. (Venice, Sept. 17, 1972).

Tokatyan, Armand, Bulgarian operatic tenor of Armenian descent; b. Plovdiv, Feb. 12, 1896; d. Pasadena, Calif., June 12, 1960. He was educated in Alexandria, Egypt; then studied voice with Cairone in Milan and Wolf in Vienna. He made his operatic debut in Milan, in 1921; then went to the U.S. where he toured with the Scotti Opera Co. He made his debut at the Metropolitan Opera House, N.Y., on Nov. 19, 1922, as Turiddu in a concert performance of *Cavalleria Rusticana*, and remained a member of the staff of the Metropolitan Opera until 1946. He also made appearances in London, Berlin, and Vienna.

Tolbecque, Auguste, French cellist; b. Paris, March 30, 1830; d. Niort, March 8, 1919. He won 1st prize for cello at the Paris Cons. in 1849; taught at the Marseilles Cons. (1865–71); later was cellist at the Paris Cons. concerts. He published *La Gymnastique du violoncelle* (op. 14; excellent exercises and mechanical studies), a *Konzertstück* for cello and orch., and pieces for cello and piano; produced a 1-act comic opera, *Après la valse* (Niort, 1894). Also wrote *Souvenirs d'un musicien en province* (1896), *Notice historique sur les instruments à cordes et à archet* (1898), and *L'Art du luthier* (1903).

Tolbecque, Jean-Baptiste-Joseph, Belgian violinist; b. Hanzinne, April 17, 1797; d. Paris, Oct. 23, 1869. He was a pupil of Kreutzer and Reicha at the Paris Cons.; played violin at the Théâtre Italien and then became a successful conductor at court balls, for which he wrote waltzes, galops, quadrilles, and other fashionable dances which enjoyed tremendous success. In

1851 he staged his ballet, *Vert-Vert* (in collaboration with Deldevez), at the Paris Opéra. His 3 brothers, **Isidore-Joseph** (1794–1871), **Auguste-Joseph** (1801–69), and **Charles-Joseph** (1806–35), were professional violinists and theater conductors.

Toldrá, Eduardo, Catalan conductor; b. Villanueva y Geltrú, Catalonia, April 7, 1895; d. Barcelona, May 31, 1962. He studied the violin, and was a member of a string quartet, with which he toured in Europe. In 1921 he became prof. of violin at the Barcelona Municipal School of Music; in 1943, was appointed conductor of the Municipal Orch. He published an album of pieces in the form of Catalan folk dances.
BIBLIOGRAPHY: M. Capdevila Massana, *Eduardo Toldrá* (Barcelona, 1964; new augmented edition, 1972).

Tollefsen, Carl H., American violinist; b. Hull, England, Aug. 15, 1882; d. Brooklyn, N.Y., Dec. 10, 1963. He emigrated to America as a youth, and studied at the National Cons., N.Y. (1898–1902) and later at the Institute of Musical Art (1906–08), where his teachers were Franz Kneisel (violin), Goetschius and Rubin Goldmark (composition); was a violinist in various orchestras in N.Y. On Aug. 7, 1907 he married the pianist **Augusta Schnabel** (b. Boise, Idaho, Jan. 5, 1885; d. Brooklyn, April 9, 1955), and formed the Tollefsen Trio with her and with Paul Kéfer; this trio toured the U.S. for more than 30 years (succeeding cellists were M. Penha, P. Gruppe, R. Thrane, and W. Durieux). In 1939 he founded the Brooklyn Chamber Music Society. He formed a large collection of autographs of famous musicians and manuscript biographies (including the biographical archives gathered by Alfred Rémy, editor of the 3rd ed. of *Baker's Biographical Dictionary of Musicians*). In 1947 the cellist Youry Bilstin bequeathed to him a collection of old instruments. After Tollefsen's death his entire collection was turned over to the South Illinois Univ. Lovejoy Library at Edwardsville.

Tolonen, Jouko, Finnish composer; b. Porvoo, Nov. 2, 1912. He studied piano with Linko and composition with Krohn, Madetoja, and Fougestedt at the Univ. of Helsinki; was executive director of the Finnish National Opera from 1956–60; taught at the Univ. of Turku (Åbo) after 1972. He composed *Andante and Rondo alla burla* for orch. (1948); *Andante* for piano and strings (1950); Symphony (1952); *3 Arabesques* for orch. (1953); *Les Fanfares* for brass (1970).

Tolstoy, Dmitri, Soviet composer, son of the writer Alexei Tolstoy; b. Berlin, Jan. 20, 1923. He went to Russia with his father after temporary emigration; studied at the Leningrad Cons., graduating in 1947; took courses in composition with Shebalin in Moscow and Shostakovich in Leningrad.
WORKS: *Poem about Leningrad* for orch. (1953); *Spring Victory*, cantata (1946); *Masquerade*, opera (Moscow, Jan. 17, 1956); *Mariuta*, opera (Perm, Dec. 30, 1960); 3 piano sonatas; 12 preludes for piano; many songs.

Tomaschek, Johann Wenzel (Bohemian spelling, **Jan Václav Tomášek**), composer and teacher; born Skutsch, Bohemia, April 17, 1774; d, Prague, April 3, 1850. He learned the rudiments of singing and violin playing from Wolf, *regens chori* at Chrudim; studied as a chorister at the Minorite monastery, Iglau; took the law course at Prague Univ., 1790–93, supporting himself by giving lessons, and also studying the chief German theoretical works. Finally he applied himself wholly to music; found a patron in Count Bucquoy de Longeval; and became the most noted teacher in Prague (Dreyschock, Schulhoff, v. Bocklet, Kittl, Kuhe, Dessauer, Tedesco, Sig. Goldschmidt, Hanslick, etc., were his pupils). He was an admirable pianist and organist, and a composer of high merit.
WORKS: Among 110 works with opus numbers are a Requiem in C minor (op. 70); a *Krönungsmesse* in E-flat (op. 81); cantatas; hymns; Bohemian and German songs; Symphony in E-flat (op. 19); Piano Concerto (op. 18); Piano Quartet in E-flat (op. 22); Piano Trio (op. 7); several piano compositions (sonatas, opp. 14, 15, 21, 48, and a fifth in B; 6 sets of Eclogues, each having 6 numbers, opp. 35, 47, 51, 63, 66, 83, 2 sets of 6 Rhapsodies, opp. 40, 41; 3 *Ditirambi*, op. 65; 6 *Allegri capricciosi di bravura*, op. 52 and op. 84). His opera *Seraphine, oder Grossmut und Liebe* (Prague, Dec. 15, 1811) was well received.
BIBLIOGRAPHY: Autobiography in vol. IV of *Libussa* (Prague, 1845); E. Hanslick, *Aus meinem Leben* (Berlin, 1894; vol. I, p. 25 ff.); R. v. Procházka, *Arpeggien* (Dresden, 1897; p. 44 ff.); W. Kahl, "Aus der Frühzeit des lyrischen Klavierstücks," *Zeitschrift für Musik* 89, no. 8 (1922); K. Emingerova, "T.," in *Národní Kultura* (1924); M. Tarantova, *V. J. T.* (Prague, 1946); P. Nettl, *Forgotten Musicians* (N.Y., 1951, pp. 91–109); excerpts from his memoirs were published in the *Musical Quarterly* (April 1946).

Tomášek, Jaroslav, Czech composer; b. Koryčany, Moravia, April 10, 1896; d. Prague, Nov. 26, 1970. He studied music with Vítězslav Novák; also attended a course in musicology at the Univ. of Prague. He composed mostly in small forms: 2 song cycles: *To Woman* for high voice (1919–20; with orchestra, 1944–46) and *Grief* for tenor, soprano, bass, and orch. (1958–59); *Rondo* for piano left hand (1924); Piano Sonata for left hand (1925); 2 string quartets; *Symphonic Rondo* for piano and orch. (1962); songs. His wife, **Jaromíra Tomášková-Nováková** (b. Jaroměř, May 23, 1892; d. Prague, April 25, 1957) was a concert soprano; she taught singing at the Prague Cons. from 1920 on.

Tomasi, Henri, French composer; b. Marseilles, Aug. 17, 1901; d. Paris Jan. 13, 1971. He studied with Paul Vidal at the Paris Cons.; won the 2nd Grand Prix de Rome for his cantata *Coriolan* (1927). He served in the French Army (1939–40); in 1952 was awarded the Grand Prix de Musique Française in 1952. His music is marked by Impressionistic colors; he was particularly attracted to exotic subjects, depicting in fine instrumental colors the scenes in Corsica, Cambodia, Laos, Sahara, Tahiti, etc. He also wrote music inspired by the Gregorian Chant and medieval religious songs. During his last period he was motivated in his music by political events, and wrote pieces in homage to the "Third World," and Vietnam.

WORKS: OPERAS: *Don Juan de Mañara* (Munich, March 29, 1956); *Altantide* (Mulhouse, Feb. 26, 1954); *Sampiero Corso* (Bordeaux, May, 1956); *Il poverello* (1957); opera-bouffe *Princesse Pauline* (1960); chamber opera-bouffe *L'élixir du R.P. Gaucher,* after *Les Lettres de mon moulin* by Alphonse Daudet (1962); *Le Triomphe de Jeanne* (Rouen, 1956). BALLETS: *La Grisi* (Paris, Oct. 7, 1935); *La Rosière de village* (Paris, May 26, 1936); *Les Santons* (Paris, Nov. 18, 1938); *La Féerie cambodgienne* (Marseilles, Jan. 31, 1952); *Les Folies mazarguaises* (Marseilles, Oct. 5, 1953); *Noces de Cendre* (Strasbourg, Jan. 19, 1954); choreographic poem, *Dassine, sultane du Hoggar* for 2 speakers, chorus, and orch. (1959); *Les Barbaresques* (Nice, 1960); *Nana,* after Émile Zola (1962). FOR ORCH.: *Chants de Cyrnos,* symph. poem (Paris, Nov. 30, 1929); *Mélodies corses* (1931); *Vocero,* symph. poem (Paris, Feb. 5, 1933); *Scènes municipales* (1933); *Tam-Tam,* symph. poem (Paris, June 13, 1933); *Chants laotiens* (1934); *Deux danses cambodgiennes* (1934); *Chant des geishas* (1936); *Impressions sahariennes* (1938); Symph. (Paris, May 4, 1943); *Concert asiatique* for percussion and orch. (1939); Flute Concerto (1947); Trumpet Concerto (1949); Viola Concerto (1951); Saxophone Concerto (1951); Horn Concerto (1955); Clarinet Concerto (1956); Trombone Concerto (1956); Bassoon Concerto (1958); Oboe Concerto (1958); Violin Concerto (1962); Cello Concerto (1970); *Jabadao,* symph. poem (Paris, Jan. 10, 1960); *Taïtienne de Gauguin* (1963); *Symphonie du tiers monde* (Paris, Feb. 18, 1968); *Chant pour le Vietnam,* symph. poem for wind band and percussion (Paris, Dec. 7, 1969). CHAMBER MUSIC: *Concerto champêtre* for oboe, clarinet, and bassoon (1939); String Trio (1943); *Divertimento Corsica,* for woodwind trio (1952); Wind Quintet (1952); *Concerto de printemps* for flute, strings, and percussion (1965); *La Moresca* for 8 wind instruments (1965); *Danseuses de Degas* for harp and string quartet (1964); *Sonatine attique* for clarinet (1966); many piano pieces; song cycles.

Tomasini, Luigi (Aloysius), Italian violinist and composer; b. Pesaro, June 22, 1741; d. Esterház, April 25, 1808. From 1756 he was a violinist at Prince Paul Anton Esterházy's residence in Eisenstadt, and was a friend of Haydn there; in 1761 became concertmaster in Haydn's orch.; remained in the Household of Prince Nicholas, successor to Paul Anton Esterházy, and was pensioned in 1790. Several of Haydn's concertos were dedicated to Tomasini, who was a composer of considerable merit himself; wrote 24 divertimentos for baryton, viola, and cello, string quartets, etc. His son, **Anton Tomasini** (b. Eisenstadt, 1775; d. there, June 12, 1824), was a viola player; another son, **Luigi Tomasini,** was an excellent violinist in Haydn's orchestra, highly commended by Haydn; he went to Vienna in 1796 and to Berlin in 1808.

Tómasson, Jónas, Icelandic composer; b. Isafjordur, Nov. 21, 1946. He studied composition with Sigurbjörnsson in Reykjavik and with Ton de Leeuw in Amsterdam; then taught at the Isafjordur Music School.

WORKS: Wind Quintet (1970); *1,41* for orch. (1970); 13 compositions entitled Sonatas, among them one for flute, oboe, clarinet, and bassoon; one for organ and cello; and one for string quartet (1975); Viola Concerto (1971); *4 Quartets* for flute, clarinet, bass clarinet, and horn; *Invention and Coda* for chamber ensemble; *Cantata I* for 5 voices and chamber ensemble; *Cantata II* for soprano, flute, bassoon, clarinet, horn, and cello (1973); *Play, Play* for orch.; *Eleven Thoughts about the Settlement* for orch. (1974); *Orgia* for orch. (1977).

Tombelle, Fernand de la. See **La Tombelle, Fernand de.**

Tomilin, Victor, Russian composer; b. Berdichev, May 15, 1908; killed in combat near Leningrad, Dec. 9, 1941. He was a pupil of Vladimir Shcherbachev at the Leningrad Cons., graduating in 1932. He wrote 2 symph. suites, *Episodes of Civil War* (1936) and *Crimean Suite* (1939); a number of songs and piano pieces.

Tomkins, Thomas, English organist and composer; b. St. David's, 1572; d. Martin Hussingtree, near Worcester, June (buried June 9), 1656. He came from a family of musicians, of whom many members flourished in the 16th and 17th centuries. He was a pupil of William Byrd; was appointed organist of the Worcester Cathedral about 1596, holding this position for half a century, until 1646. In 1607 he received the degree of Mus. B. at Oxford, and in 1621 was appointed one of the organists of the Chapel Royal. He was one of the most inspired of the English madrigalists; his ballets, his keyboard pieces, and his sacred works are also of a high quality. His published works include *Songs of 3, 4, 5 and 6 parts* (reprinted in the *English Madrigal School,* vol. 18), and *Musica Deo Sacra* (posthumous, 1668), containing 5 services and 95 anthems (services reprinted in *Tudor Church Music* vol. 7). Other church music is in manuscript. His keyboard music was published by Stephen D. Tuttle in *Musica Britannica* vol. 5; 2 pieces are in Davison and Apel, *Historical Anthology of Music,* vol. 1 (Cambridge, Mass., 1946).

BIBLIOGRAPHY: S. de B. Taylor, *Thomas Tomkins* (London, 1933); G. Reese, *Music in the Renaissance* (N.Y., 1954); Denis Stevens, *Thomas Tomkins* (London, 1957).

Tomlins, William Lawrence, British-American music educator and choral leader; b. London, Feb. 4, 1844; d. Delafield, Wis., Sept. 26, 1930. He was a pupil of G. A. Macfarren and E. Silas; in 1869 emigrated to the U.S.; 1875–98 conducted the Apollo Glee Club, Chicago; having made a specially of training children's choruses and teachers, he established in 1903 the National Training School for Music Teachers, in Chicago. He published *Children's Songs, and How to Sing Them* (1885).

Tommasini, Vincenzo, Italian composer; b. Rome, Sept. 17, 1878; d. there, Dec. 23, 1950. He studied violin with Pinelli; theory with Falchi at Santa Cecilia in Rome; then went to Berlin, where he took lessons with Max Bruch; after sojourns in Paris, London, and N.Y. he returned to Rome. He wrote music in the poetic tradition of Italian Romanticism; his operas, symph. works, and chamber music obtained immediate performances and favorable reception; however, his most successful piece, *Le Donne di buon umore (The Good-humored Ladies),* was not an original work, but a comedy-ballet written on music from sonatas by Domenico Scarlatti, arranged in a series of tableaux and brilliantly orchestrated; this was a commission for the Ballet Russe of Diaghilev, who staged it at Rome in April, 1917, and kept it in the repertory during his tours all over the world. Other works by Tommasini include the operas *Medea,* to the composer's own libretto (Trieste, April 8, 1906) and *Uguale fortuna* (Rome, 1913); for orch.: *La Vita è un sogno* (1901); *Poema erotico* (1909); *Inno alla beltà* (1911); *Ciari di luna* (Rome, 1916); *Il beato regno* (Rome, 1922); *Paesaggi toscani* (Rome, 1923); *Il Carnevale di Venezia* (N.Y., Oct. 10, 1929, Toscanini conducting); *Nápule (Naples),* a fantasy (Freiburg, Dec. 7, 1931); Violin Concerto (1932); *Quattro pezzi* (1934); *Le Diable s'amuse,* ballet suite on themes by Paganini (1936); Concerto for string quartet and orch. (1939); *La Tempesta* (1941); *Tiepolesco,* ballet suite (1945); *Duo concertante,* for piano and orch. (1948); 3 string quartets; Violin Sonata; Harp Sonata; *Due Macchiette* for cello and piano (1940); piano pieces; published *La Luce invisible* (1929) and *Saggio di estetica sperimentale* (1942).

BIBLIOGRAPHY: G. Gatti, "Some Italian Composers of Today: Tommasini," *Musical Times* (Nov. 1921); M. Zanotti-Bianco, "Vincenzo Tommasini," *Chesterian* (Feb. 1923); A. Casella, "Vincenzo Tommasini," *Revue Musicale* (1927); M. Rinaldi, "Vincenzo Tommasini," *Rivista Musicale Italiana* (Oct-Dec. 1951).

Toni, Alceo, Italian musicologist and composer; b. Lugo, May 22, 1884; d. Milan, Dec. 4, 1969. He was a pupil of L. Torchi and E. Bossi in Bologna; then lived in Milan. He edited numerous works by Corelli, Locatelli, Torelli, Monteverdi, Carissimi, and other old Italian composers. His own compositions include a Requiem Mass, chamber music, and songs. Some of his many articles were collected in a book, *Studi critici di interpretazione* (Milan, 1923). With Tulio Serafin, he compiled a 2-vol. edition, *Stile, tradizioni e convenzioni del melodramma italaiano del Settecento e dell'Ottocento* (Milan, 1958-65).

Tonning, Gerard, American choral conductor and composer; b. Stavanger, Norway, May 25, 1860; d. New York, June 10, 1940. He studied in Munich with Rheinberger and others; in 1887 he emigrated to America, settling in Duluth, Minn., where he organized several choral societies; in 1905 he moved to Seattle, where he remained until 1917; then went to New York.

WORKS: a historical opera, to a Norwegian libretto, *Leif Erikson* (Seattle, Dec. 10, 1910; Brooklyn Academy of Music, Oct. 4, 1924; both performances in the Norwegian language); a 1-act romantic opera, *All in a Garden Fair* (Seattle, Nov. 1, 1913); a pantomime, *Woman's Wiles, or Love Triumphant;* Piano Trio;

Suite moderne for violin and piano; *Rapsodie norvégienne* for violin and piano; piano pieces (*Norwegian Dances,* 3 nocturnes, etc.); songs (*Arabian Love Songs* for 4 solo voices); etc.

BIBLIOGRAPHY: E. E. Hipsher, *American Opera and Its Composers* (Philadelphia, 1934, pp. 404-07).

Töpfer, Johann Gottlob, famous German organist and writer on organ building; b. Niederrossla, Dec. 4, 1791; d. Weimar, June 8, 1870. He studied with the cantor Schlömilch; then at Weimar with Destouches and A. E. Müller; also attended the Weimar Seminary, where he became teacher of music in 1817; from 1830 was town organist of Weimar. An expert on organ construction, he wrote *Die Orgelbaukunst* (1833); *Die Scheibler'sche Stimm-Methode* (1842); *Die Orgel; Zweck und Beschaffenheit ihrer Theile* (1843); *Lehrbuch der Orgelbaukunst* (a fundamental work, 1855; 4 vols.; 2nd ed. by M. Allihn, 1888; 3rd ed. by P. Smets, 1934-39); *Theoretisch-praktische Organistenschule* (1845); *Allgemeines und vollständiges Choralbuch* (a 4, with organ interludes); a cantata, *Die Orgelweihe; Konzertstück* for organ; sonatas, fantasias preludes, fugues, etc., for organ; piano pieces.

BIBLIOGRAPHY: A. W. Gottschalg, *Johann Gottlob Töpfer* (Berlin, 1870).

Toradze, David, Soviet Georgian composer; b. Tiflis, April 14, 1922; studied at the Tiflis Cons.; then at the Moscow Cons. with Glière; in 1954, became prof. at the Tiflis Cons. He wrote the operas *The Call of the Mountains* (Tiflis, Nov. 20, 1947) and *The Bride of the North* (1958); a ballet, *For Peace* (Tiflis, June 17, 1953); a symph. (1946); chamber music; choruses; songs.

Torchi, Luigi, eminent Italian musicologist; b. Mondano, near Bologna, Nov. 7, 1858; d. Bologna, Sept. 18, 1920. He studied at the Liceo Musicale of Bologna, the Naples Cons. (composition with Serrao), and the Leipzig Cons. (Jadassohn and Reinecke); from 1885-91, prof. of music history and esthetics, also librarian, at the Liceo Musicale Rossini in Pesaro; from 1895 to 1916 he held similar positions at Bologna Cons., also teaching composition there. From its foundation (1894) until 1904 he was editor of the *Rivista Musicale Italiana,* for which he wrote many valuable essays. In 1890 he published *R. Wagner: Studio critico* (1890; 2nd ed., 1913). Besides a collection of *Eleganti canzoni ed arie italiane* of the 17th century (Milan, 1894) and *A Collection of Pieces for the Violin Composed by Italian Masters of the 17th and 18th Centuries* (London; both with piano accompaniment by Torchi), in 1897 he began publishing the important anthology *L'Arte Musicale in Italia.*

BIBLIOGRAPHY: F. Vatielli, "Necrologia di Luigi Torchi," *Rivista Musicale Italiana* (1920).

Torelli (Torrelli), Gasparo, Italian composer; b. Borgo San Sepolcro, near Lucca; d. some time after 1613. He published *Brevi concetti d'amore* (madrigals *a* 5; 1598); 4 books of *Canzonette a 3* (1593-1608); and *I fidi amanti,* "favola pastorale" (in madrigal style, 4 voices; 1600; reprinted in Torchi's *L'Arte Musicale in Italia* vol. 4).

Torelli, Giuseppe, Italian violinist and composer, probable originator of the solo concerto for violin; b. Verona, April 22, 1658; d. Bologna, Feb. 8, 1709. He studied in Bologna, where he was a member of the Accademia Filarmonica and viola player at the church of S. Petronio (1686–95). Made a concert tour in Germany in 1695, and became Kapellmeister to the Margrave of Brandenburg at Ansbach (1697–99). From 1699 he was in Vienna, where he produced an oratorio; returned to Bologna in 1701. He had generally been regarded as the originator of the "concerto grosso" until Arnold Schering, in 1903, showed that Stradella, who died in 1682, had written such works. But Torelli's *Concerti grossi,* op. 8 (1709), were the first to be published (Corelli's op. 6 was not published until 1712, though composed earlier).

WORKS: op. 1, *Balletti da camera a 3 violini e basso continuo;* op. 2, *Concerto da camera a 2 violini e basso* (1686); op. 3, *Sinfonie a 2-4 stromenti* (1687); op. 4, *Concertino per camera a violino e violoncello;* op. 5, *6 sinfonie a 3, e 6 concerti a 4* (1692); op. 6, *Concerti musicali a 4* (with organ); op. 7, *capricci musicali per camera a violino e viola ovvero arciliuto;* op. 8, *Concerti grossi con una pastorale per il Santissimo Natale* (1709), written for 2 violini concertanti, 2 violini di ripieno, viola, and continuo. The so-called "Christmas Eve Concerto" (op. 8, no. 6) and other works from op. 8 and op. 6 have been reprinted in modern editions.

BIBLIOGRAPHY: A. Schering, *Geschichte des Instrumentalkonzerts* (1903); F. Vatielli, *Arte e vita musicale a Bologna* (Bologna, 1927); R. Brenzoni, "Giuseppe Torelli, musicista veronese," *Note d'Archivio per la storia musicale* (1936); F. Giegling, *Giuseppe Torelli, Ein Beitrag zur Entwicklungsgeschichte des italienischen Konzerts* (Kassel, 1949).

Torjussen, Trygve, Norwegian composer and music teacher; b. Drammen, Nov. 14, 1885; d. Oslo, Feb. 12, 1977. He studied in Oslo, Rome and Stuttgart; was on the staff at the Oslo Cons. (1911–17) and of the Barratt-Due Music Institute (1931–41). Among his works are various suites for small orch.; *Kark* for tenor, bass, female chorus, and orch. (Oslo, 1939); *A Musical Bridge-Evening* for string quartet (Oslo, 1935); over 70 piano pieces, including a sonata; 30 songs.

Torkanowsky, Werner, German-American conductor, b. Berlin, March 30, 1926. He studied music with his mother; went to Palestine after 1933; emigrated to the U.S. in 1948. He began his musical career as a violinist; was a member of the Pittsburgh Symph. Orch. In 1955 he joined the master class of Pierre Monteux in Maine; subsequently conducted at the Spoleto Festivals. From 1963 to 1977 he was conductor of the New Orleans Philharmonic Symphony Orchestra.

Törne, Bengt von, Finnish composer; b. Helsinki, Nov. 22, 1891; d. Turku, May 4, 1967. He studied composition with Furuhjelm at the Helsinki Institute of Music, and, during the winter of 1916–17, took a course in orchestration with Sibelius. He wrote 6 symphonies (1935, 1939, 1948, 1954, 1964, 1966); 3 sinfoni-

ettas; *Sinfonia da camera* for strings (1951); Piano Concerto; Piano Quintet; 2 string quartets; 2 violin sonatas; a piano trio; published a monograph on Sibelius (London, 1937; in Italian, Florence, 1943; in Finnish, Helsinki, 1945; in Swedish, Stockholm, 1945).

Torner, Eduado Martínez, Spanish folklore specialists; b. Oviedo, April 8, 1888; d. London, Feb. 17, 1955. He was a pupil of Vincent d'Indy at the Schola Cantorum in Paris; returned to Spain in 1914 and settled in Madrid. He published the folksong collections *Cancionero musical de la lírica popular asturiana* (Madrid, 1920); *40 Canciones españolas* (1924), and *Cancionero musical* (1928); also the essay, *Temas folklóricos; música y poesía* (1935); edited and arranged for piano selected pieces from tablature books of the 16th century, and published them under the title *Colección de vihuelistas españoles del siglo XVI* (Madrid, 1923).

BIBLIOGRAPHY: A. Muñiz Toca, *Vida y obra de E. M. Torner* (Oviedo, 1961).

Torrance, Rev. George William, Irish clergyman and composer; b. Rathmines, near Dublin, 1835; d. Kilkenny, Aug. 20, 1907. Chorister at Christ Church Cathedral, Dublin; organist at St. Andrew's and St. Anne's; studied music at Leipzig, 1856; ordained as a priest, 1866; in 1869 he emigrated to Melbourne, Australia, where he remained till 1897; he was appointed chaplain to the bishop of Ossory in 1897; in 1900 was made Prebendary of Killamery, canon of St. Canice's Cathedral and librarian of St. Canice's Library, Kilkenny. Torrance's madrigal *Dry be that tear* won the medal of the Madrigal Society in 1903.

Torrefranca, Fausto, eminent Italian musicologist; b. Monteleone Calabro, Feb. 1, 1883; d. Rome, Nov. 26, 1955. Trained as an engineer, he took up music under E. Lena in Turin (harmony and counterpoint) and also studied by himself. It was through his initiative that the first chair of musicology was established in Italy; in 1913, lecturer at the Univ. of Rome; from 1914–24, prof. of music history at the Cons. di S. Pietro in Naples, and from 1915 also librarian there; from 1924 librarian of the Milan Cons. From 1907 he was editor for several years of the *Rivista Musicale Italiana.* In 1941 he was appointed prof. of music history at the Univ. of Florence.

WRITINGS: *La Vita musicale dello spirito* (Turin, 1910); *L'Intuizione musicale quale sintesi a priori estetica* (1911); *Giacomo Puccini e l'opera internazionale* (1912); *Le Sinfonie dell'Imbrattacarte, G. B. Sanmartini* (1915); *Le Origine italiane del romanticismo musicale* (1930); *Il Segreto del quattrocento* (1939).

Torri, Pietro, Italian composer; b. Peschiera, c.1650; d. Munich, July 6, 1737. He served as court organist and later Kapellmeister at the court in Bayreuth (until 1684); in 1689 he became organist at Munich; in 1696 he was conductor for the carnival season at Hannover; in 1703 he was appointed chamber music director at Munich, following the Elector to Brussels upon the latter's exile. In Brussels he produced the oratorio *Les Vanités du monde* (1706); from 1715 was again in Munich, where he was named Kapellmeister in 1732. He composed 26 operas; he produced at the Munich Court the operas *Lucio Vero* (Oct. 12, 1720) and *Griselda* (Oct. 12, 1723); also some chamber duets. Selections from the operas were published in *Denkmäler der Tonkunst in Bayern* 31 (19/20).

BIBLIOGRAPHY: H. Junker, "Zwei Griselda Opern," in the *Sandberger-Festschrift* (1928); K. Kremer, *Pietro Torri und seine Kammermusikwerke* (dissertation; Munich, 1956).

Torrington, Frederick Herbert, English organist; b. Dudley, Worcestershire, England, Oct. 20, 1837; d. Toronto, Canada, Nov. 19, 1917. He went to Canada in 1856; served as a church organist in Montreal (1856–68); then was music director at King's Chapel, Boston; in 1873 was appointed organist at the Metropolitan Church, Toronto, and conductor of the Toronto Philharmonic Society. He composed organ music and hymn tunes.

Tort, César, Mexican composer; b. Puebla, Sept. 4, 1929. He studied piano with Ramón Serratos in 1946; composition with Conrado del Campo at the Cons. in Madrid (1950–53). Returning to Mexico, he dedicated himself to a reform of musical education of children. He wrote mostly for piano: *Impresiones* (1954), *El Orador* (1955), *El Piano Mágico* (1972), etc.; also a symph. poem *Estirpes* (1958) and a cantata *La Espada* (1966).

Tortelier, Paul, French cellist; b. Paris, March 21, 1914. He entered the Paris Cons., and won 1st prize for cello at the age of 16; was engaged as 1st cellist by the Boston Symph. Orch. in 1935, but went back to France in 1939; in 1955 he settled in Israel; continued to give concerts in Europe. Among his works are a cello concerto and 3 violin concertos. He published a teaching manual, *How I Play, How I Teach* (St. Louis, 1975).

Tosar, Héctor, Uruguayan composer; b. Montevideo, July 18, 1923. He studied piano and composition in his native city; taught at the Montevideo Cons. (1951–54). His music is neo-Classical in facture, with a considerable influx of Latin American melorhythms.

WORKS: 3 symphonies (1945, 1950, 1973); Concertino for piano and orch. (1941); *Sinfonia Concertante* for piano and orch. (1957); Violin Sonata (1947); Clarinet Sonata (1957); *Oda a amigas* for speaker and orch. (1951); *Naves Errantes* for baritone and 11 instruments (1964); madrigals; sacred choruses; songs; many piano pieces; *Stray Birds*, triptych for baritone and 11 instruments to the text by Rabindranath Tagore (Washington, May 11, 1965).

Tosatti, Vieri, Italian composer; b. Rome, Nov. 2, 1920. He studied piano and composition with Pizzetti in Rome. In his compositions he often exploits sensational or morbid subjects, setting them to pungent music, with a liberal application of special effects.

WORKS: *Il Concerto della demenza,* for narrator, 2 pianos, and chamber orch. (1946); music drama, *Dionisio* (1947); "paradoxical drama" *Il Sistema della dolcezza* (1949); "boxing opera" *La Partita a pugni* (*Fist Fight;* Venice Festival of Contemporary Music,

Sept. 8, 1953); operas: *Il giudizio universale* (Milan, 1955), *L'isola del tesoro* (Bologna, 1958), and *La Fiera della Meraviglie* (Rome, 1963); Piano Concerto (1945); Viola Concerto (1966); *Concerto iperciclico* for clarinet and orch. (1970); Concerto for wind quintet and piano (1945); *Introduzione fiabesca* for piano trio (1943); *Piccola sonata* for violin and piano (1945); *Sinfonia corale* for chorus and orch. (1944); *Requiem* (1963); *2 coretti* for 3 women's voices (1970); songs; a variety of whimsical piano pieces.

Toscanini, Arturo, one of the greatest conductors of modern times; b. Parma, Italy, March 25, 1867; d. New York, Jan. 16, 1957. He entered the Parma Cons. at the age of 9, studying the cello with Carini and composition with Dacci; graduated in 1885 as winner of the 1st prize for cello. In 1886 he was engaged as cellist for the Italian opera in Rio de Janeiro; on the 2nd night of the spring season (June 25, 1886) he was unexpectedly called upon to substitute for the regular conductor, when the latter left the podium at the end of the introduction after the public hissed him; the opera was *Aida,* and Toscanini led it without difficulty; he was rewarded by an ovation and was engaged to lead the rest of the season. Returning to Italy, he was engaged to conduct the opera at the Teatro Cavignano in Turin, and later conducted the Municipal Orch. there. Although still very young, he quickly established a fine reputation. For 10 seasons, between 1887 and 1898, he conducted opera and symph. orchestras in major Italian cities. On May 21, 1892 he led the world première of *Pagliacci* in Milan, and on Feb. 1, 1896, the première of Puccini's *La Bohème* in Turin. He also conducted the Italian premières of *Götterdämmerung* (Turin, 1895) and *Siegfried* (Milan, 1899). In 1898 the impresario Gatti-Casazza engaged him as chief conductor for La Scala, Milan, where he remained until 1903, and again from 1906 to 1908. In the interim, he conducted opera in Buenos Aires (1903–04 and 1906). When Gatti-Casazza became general manager of the Metropolitan Opera Company (1908), he invited Toscanini as principal conductor; Toscanini's debut in N.Y. was in *Aida* (Nov. 16, 1908). While at the Metropolitan Opera, Toscanini conducted 2 world premières, Puccini's *The Girl of the Golden West* (Dec. 10, 1910) and Giordano's *Madame Sans-Gêne* (Jan. 25, 1915); he also brought out for the first time in America Gluck's *Armide* (Nov. 14, 1910), Wolf-Ferrari's *Le Donne curiose* (Jan. 13, 1912), and Mussorgsky's *Boris Godunov* (March 19, 1913). On April 13, 1913 he gave his first concert in N.Y. as a symph. conductor, leading Beethoven's 9th Symph. In 1915 he returned to Italy; during the season of 1920–21 he brought the Scala Orch. on a tour of the U.S. and Canada. From 1921 to 1929 he was artistic director of La Scala; there, he conducted the posthumous première of Boito's opera *Nerone,* which he himself completed for performance (May 1, 1924). In 1926–27 he was guest conductor of the N.Y. Philharmonic Orch., returning in the following season as associate conductor with Mengelberg. After the fusion of the N.Y. Philharmonic and the N.Y. Symph. in 1928, Toscanini was engaged as permanent condutor of the newly organized ensemble; in the spring of 1930 he took the orchestra on a tour of

Europe; he resigned this position in 1936. Deeply touched by the plight of the Jews in Germany, he acceded to the request of the violinist Hubermann, founder of the Palestine Symph. Orch., to conduct the inaugural concert of that orch. at Tel Aviv (Dec. 26, 1936). In the meantime he had filled summer engagements at the Salzburg Festivals (1933, 1935, 1936, 1937). Returning to the U.S., he became musical director of the NBC Symph. Orch., a radio orch. that had been organized especially for him, giving his opening concert on Dec. 25, 1937; in 1940 he took it on a tour of South America. He continued to lead the NBC Symphony until the end of his active career; he conducted his last concert from Carnegie Hall, N.Y., on April 4, 1954 (10 days after his 87th birthday), and then sent a doleful letter of resignation to the NBC, explaining the impossibility of further appearances. He died in his sleep, a few weeks before his 90th birthday.

Toscanini was a unique figure among conductors; undemonstrative in his handling of the orchestra, he possessed an amazing energy and power of command. He demanded absolute perfection, and he erupted in violence when he could not obtain from the orchestra what he wanted (a lawsuit was brought against him in Milan, when he accidentally injured the concertmaster with a broken violin bow). Despite the vituperation he at times poured on his musicians, he was affectionately known to them as "The Maestro" who could do no wrong. His ability to communicate his desires to singers and players was extraordinary, and even the most celebrated opera stars or instrumental soloists never dared to question his authority. Owing to extreme nearsightedness, Toscanini committed all scores to memory; his repertory embraced virtually the entire field of Classical and Romantic music; his performances of Italian operas, of Wagner's music dramas, of Beethoven's symphonies, and of modern Italian works were especially inspiring. Among the moderns, he conducted works by Richard Strauss, Debussy, Ravel, Prokofiev, Stravinsky, and among Americans, Samuel Barber, whose *Adagio for Strings* he made famous; he also had his favorite Italian composers (Catalani, Martucci) whose music he fondly fostered. In his social philosophy, he was intransigently democratic; he refused to conduct in Germany under the Nazi regime. He militantly opposed Fascism in Italy, but he never abandoned his Italian citizenship, despite his long years of residence in America.

BIBLIOGRAPHY: G. M. Ciampelli, *Arturo Toscanini* (Milan, 1923); E. Cozzani, *Arturo Toscanini* (Milan, 1927); T. Nicotra, *Arturo Toscanini* (transl. from the Italian, N.Y., 1929); D. Bonardi, *Toscanini* (Milan, 1929); Paul Stefan, *Arturo Toscanini* (Vienna, 1936; in English, N.Y., 1936); L. Gilman, *Toscanini and Great Music* (N.Y., 1938); S. W. Hoeller, *Arturo Toscanini* (pictorial biography; N.Y., 1943); A. Della Corte, *Toscanini* (Vicenza, 1946); G. M. Ciampelli, *Toscanini* (Milan, 1946); D. Nives, *Arturo Toscanini* (Milan, 1946); A. Segre, "Toscanini: The First Forty Years," and H. Taubman, "Toscanini in America," *Musical Quarterly* (April 1947); F. Sacchi, *Toscanini* (Milan, 1951; publ. in English under the title *The Magic Baton: Toscanini's Life for Music*, N.Y., 1957, with supple-

mentary data); David Ewen, *The Story of Arturo Toscanini* (N.Y., 1951); H. Taubman, *The Maestro: The Life of Arturo Toscanini* (N.Y., 1951); S. Chotzinoff, *Toscanini: An Intimate Portrait* (N.Y., 1956); R. C. Marsh, *Toscanini and the Art of Orchestral Performance* (Philadelphia, 1956); Patrick Cairns (Spike) Hughes, *The Toscanini Legacy: A Critical Study of Arturo Toscanini's Performances of Beethoven, Verdi, and Other Composers* (London, 1959); Luciana Frassati, *Il Maestro Arturo Toscanini e il suo mondo* (Turin, 1967); Arturo F. Armani, ed., *Toscanini e La Scala* (Milan, 1972); G. Marek, *Toscanini* (N.Y., 1975).

Toselli, Enrico, Italian pianist and composer; b. Florence, March 13, 1883; d. there, Jan. 15, 1926. He studied with Sgambati and Martucci; gave concerts in Italy as pianist, and composed a number of songs; of these, *Serenata* because enormously popular; also wrote the symph. poem *Fuoco* (after d'Annunzio) and an opera, *La Principessa bizzarra* (Milan, 1913). In 1907 he married the former Crown Princess Luise of Saxony, creating an international furor; wrote an account of this affair, *Il mio matrimonio con Luisa di Sassonia* (Milan, 1918).

Tosi, Pier Francesco, Italian contralto (castrato) and singing teacher; b. Bologna, 1654; d. Faenza, April 1732. He studied with his father, Giuseppe Felice Tosi; sang successfully in Italy; in 1692 settled in London, where he gave regular concerts, and was highly esteemed as a vocal teacher. He served as chapel master at the Austrian court in Vienna from 1705 to 1711; was again in London (1727); in 1730 went to Bologna and was ordained a priest. He owes his fame chiefly to the work *Opinioni de' cantori antichi e moderni o sieno osservazioni sopra il canto figurato* (Bologna, 1723; in English, 1742, as *Observations on the Florid Song*; in German as *Anleitung zur Singkunst*, 1757, in French as *L'Art du Chant*, 1774. The English edition was republished in London in 1967.

Tosti, Sir Francesco Paolo, Italian singing master and vocal composer; b. Ortona, Abruzzi, April 9, 1846; d. Rome, Dec. 2, 1916. He was a pupil, from 1858, of the Collegio di S. Pietro a Majella, Naples, and was appointed sub-teacher (maestrino) by Mercadante. He visited London in 1875; had great success in concerts and settled there as a teacher, becoming singing master to the Royal Family in 1880, and prof. of singing at the Royal Academy of Music in 1894; was knighted in 1908. In 1913 he returned to Italy, taking up his residence in Rome. Besides many original songs, both English and Italian, he published a collection of *Canti popolari abruzzesi*. His songs were highly popular; some of the best-known are *Goodbye Forever and Forever, Mattinata,* and *Vorrei morire.*

BIBLIOGRAPHY: E. A. Mario, *Francesco Paolo Tosti* (Siena, 1947); A. Piovano, *Ommagio a F. P. Tosti* (Ortona, 1972).

Totenberg, Roman, Polish violinist; b. Lódź, Jan. 1, 1913. He studied violin with Michalowicz in Warsaw, Carl Flesch in Berlin, and Georges Enesco in Paris. In 1932 he won the Mendelssohn Prize in Berlin. In 1935–36 he toured Europe with Karol Szymanowski, giving violin-piano recitals; then emigrated to the U.S.; became an American citizen in 1943. From 1950 to 1960 he was in charge of the violin dept. at the Aspen, Colorado, Institute; in 1961 was appointed prof. of music and head of the string dept. at Boston Univ., and settled in Belmont, Massachusetts.

Tottmann, Albert (Karl), German violinist and writer on music; b. Zittau, July 31, 1837; d. Leipzig, Feb. 26, 1917. He studied in Dresden and Leipzig; was a violinist in Gewandhaus Orch.
WRITINGS: *Kritisches Repertorium der gesammten Violin- und Bratschen-Litteratur* (1873; 3rd ed., 1900, as *Führer durch die Violin-Literatur;* a compendious and valuable work); *Abriss der Musikgeschichte* (1883); *Der Schulgesang und seine Bedeutung für die Verstandes und Herzensbildung der Jungend* (1887; 2nd ed., 1904); *Das Büchlein von der Geige* (1890; 2nd, augmented ed., 1904); *Mozarts Zauberflöte* (1908). He composed a melodrama, *Dornröschen;* sacred and secular choruses; songs.

Toulmouche, Frédéric (Michel), French composer; b. Nantes, Aug. 3, 1850; d. Paris, Feb. 20, 1909. He studied with Victor Massé in Paris; in 1894 became director of the theater "Menus-Plaisirs." He composed several opéras-comiques: *Le Moûtier de St.-Guignolet* (Brussels, 1885), *La Veillée des noces* (Paris, 1888; in London, 1892, as *The Wedding Eve*), *L'Âme de la patrie* (St. Brieuc, 1892), *La Perle du Cantal* (Paris, 1895), *La St.-Valentin* (Paris, 1895); about a dozen operettas and some ballets.

Tourel, Jennie (real name **Jennie Davidson**), American mezzo-soprano of Russian-Jewish parentage; b. St. Petersburg, June 22, 1900; d. New York, Nov. 23, 1973. She played flute; then studied piano. After the Revolution, her family left Russia and settled temporarily near Danzig; later moved to Paris where Jennie Tourel continued to study piano and contemplated a concert career; then began to take voice lessons with Anna El-Tour, and decided to devote herself to professional singing; she changed her last name to Tourel by transposing the syllables of her teacher's name. She made her opera debut at the Paris Opéra-Comique in 1933 in the role of Carmen. In 1940, just before the occupation of Paris by the Nazi troops, she went to Lisbon, Portugal, and eventually emigrated to the U.S.; became a naturalized citizen in 1946. She continued to appear in concert and occasionally in opera; also taught singing in New York.

Tourjée, Eben, American music educator; b. Warwick, R.I., June 1, 1834; d. Boston, April 12, 1891. While working in a cotton factory in Harrisville, R.I., he played the organ in church; then went to Germany and studied with Carl August Haupt in Berlin. Returning to America he settled in Boston, and in 1867 founded there (with R. Goldbeck) the New England Cons. of Music, which he directed till his death. He assisted Patrick S. Gilmore in organizing the 2 great "peace jubilees" in Boston (1869, 1872); was the first president of the Music Teachers National Association (1876), and dean of the College of Music of Boston Univ.

BIBLIOGRAPHY: *Dictionary of American Biography* 18.

Tournemire, Charles, French organist and composer; b. Bordeaux, Jan. 22, 1870; d. Arcachon, Nov. 3, 1939. He was a pupil of César Franck at the Paris Cons., winning the 1st prize for organ in 1891; also studied composition with d'Indy at the Scola Cantorum. In 1898 he succeeded Pierné as organist at Ste. Clotilde. His dramatic cantata, *Le Sang de la sirène,* won the Prize of the City of Paris (performed Nov. 17, 1904). As an organ virtuoso he toured throughout Europe. He was prof. of ensemble playing at the Paris Cons. Other works: opera, *Les Dieux sont morts* (Paris Opéra, March 19, 1924); 8 symphonies (No. 5 is the "Mountain Symph."); *Psalm 57* for mixed chorus a cappella; Sextet for piano and winds; Piano Quartet; for organ: 51 *Offices de l'année liturgique (L'Orgue mystique); 4 Pièces symphoniques;* etc. Also a monograph, *César Franck* (Paris, 1931).
BIBLIOGRAPHY: F. Peeters, "L'Œuvre d'orgue de Charles Tournemire," *Musica Sacra* (Bruges, 1940).

Tours, Berthold, Belgian violinist, composer, and music editor; b. Rotterdam, Dec. 17, 1838; d. London, March 11, 1897. He received his musical training from his father Barthélemy Tours (1797–1864); went to London in 1861; in 1878 became musical adviser to Novello & Co., and editor of their publications. He published a *Primer of the Violin* and wrote many anthems for Anglican services.

Tours, Frank E., English-American composer, son of **Berthold Tours;** b. London, Sept. 1, 1877; d. Santa Monica, Calif. Feb. 2, 1963. He studied with Stanford, Parratt, and Bridge at the Royal College of Music; came to N.Y. in 1904 and conducted light opera productions. Later he entered the motion picture field. He wrote many successful songs, among them *Mother o' Mine, Beyond the Sunset, Red Rose,* and *In Flanders Fields.*

Tourte, François, French violin bow maker; b. Paris, 1747; d. there 1835. He was the creator of the modern bow; the shape of the wood and inward curve of the stick, the selection and preparation of the wood (Pernambuco), the length of the bow and all its modern appurtenances are the product of his skill.

Tovey, Sir Donald Francis, eminent English musical scholar; b. Eton, July 17, 1875; d. Edinburgh, July 10, 1940. He studied privately with Sophie Weisse (piano), Sir W. Parratt (counterpoint), James Higgs (composition) until 1894, when he won the Nettleship scholarship at Balliol College, Oxford; graduated with Classical Honors (B.A., 1898). In 1900–01 he gave a series of chamber music concerts in London, at which he performed several of his own works; in 1901–02 he gave similar concerts in Berlin and Vienna; played his piano concerto in 1903 under Henry Wood and in 1906 under Hans Richter; from 1906 to 1912 he gave in London regular series of chamber music concerts, known as "The Chelsea Concerts." In 1914 he succeeded Niecks as Reid Prof. of music at Edinburgh Univ. (named after John Reid); there he established the "Reid Symph. Concerts," for which he organized in 1917 the "Reid Symph. Orch." of 50 musicians. He made his American debut as pianist in 1925, and in 1927–28 made a tour of the U.S. He was knighted in 1935. Though highly esteemed as a composer, he was most widely known as a writer and lecturer on music, his analytical essays being models of their kind. Besides much chamber music and several piano pieces (a sonata, *Balliol Dances* for 4 hands, etc.), he composed an opera, *The Bride of Dionysus* (Edinburgh, April 25, 1932); a symph. (1913); a cello concerto (première by Pablo Casals, Tovey conducting, Edinburgh, Nov. 22, 1934); etc. He published a collection of 16th-century church music, *Laudate Pueri* (Part I of *Northlands Singing Book*), and edited Bach's *Kunst der Fuge.* He wrote many of the music articles for the *Encylopaedia Britannica* (from the 11th ed.).

WRITINGS: *A Companion to Bach's Art of Fugue* (1931); *A Companion to Beethoven's Pianoforte Sonatas* (1931); *Musical Form and Matter* (1934); *Normality and Freedom in Music* (1936); *Essays in Musical Analysis*, 6 vols. (1935–39); I and II, orchestral works; III, concertos; IV, polyphony and illustrative music; V, vocal music; VI, supplement, index, and glossary. Posthumous publications: *Walter Parratt: the Master of Music* (with G. Parratt; London, 1941); *A Musician Talks* (London, 1941); *Musical Articles from the Enyclopaedia Britannica* (London, 1944); *Beethoven* (London, 1944); *Essays in Musical Analysis: Chamber Music* (London, 1944); *Essays and Lectures on Music* (London, 1949; U.S. ed. as *The Main Stream of Music*).

BIBLIOGRAPHY: M. Grierson, *Donald Francis Tovey* (London, 1952).

Townsend, Douglas, American composer and musicologist; b. New York, Nov. 8, 1921. He studied composition with Tibor Serly, Stefan Wolpe, Felix Greissle, and Otto Luening; became active in N.Y. as music editor; arranged for performance and publication works by Pergolesi, Süssmayr, Danzi, Tommaso Giordani, Rosetti, etc. Writes for and is an official of the Musical Heritage Society (recordings).

WORKS: Septet for brass (1947); *Sinfonietta* (1949); *Fantasy* for chamber orch. (1951); *The Infinite,* ballet (N.Y., Feb. 13, 1952); *Canzona* for flute, viola, and bassoon (1954); *Lima Beans,* chamber opera (N.Y., Jan. 7, 1956); *Ballet Suite* for 3 clarinets (1956); Duo for violas (1957); *Tower Music* for brass quintet (1957); *4 Fantasies on American Songs,* for orch. (1957); Symph. for string (N.Y., Nov. 29, 1958); 3 chamber concertos: No. 1 for violin and strings; No. 2 for trombone and strings; No. 3 for piano, horn, and flute, with strings.

Toyama, Yuzo, Japanese composer; b. Tokyo, May 10, 1931. He graduated from the Tokyo Music Academy in 1952; studied in Vienna (1958–60); in 1953, organized (with Mamiya and Hayashi) the group "Yagi no Kai" with the purpose of promoting Japanese music.

WORKS: chamber opera, *Such a Long Absence* (Osaka, April 3, 1972); a musical, *Gion Festival,* for soloists, chorus and orch. (1966); a ballet, *Yugen* (1965); *Little Symphony* (1953); *Rhapsody* for orch.

(1960); *Divertimento* for orch. (1961; Prague, Jan. 2, 1962); 2 piano concertos (1962, 1963); 2 violin concertos (1963, 1966); *Fantasy* for clarinet and string orch. (1963); *Rhapsody* on an Okinawan Melody for orch. (1961); *Toki (War Cry) No. 1* and *Toki No. 2* for orch. (1965, 1966); symph. *Homeward* (1966); Cello Concerto (1967); *Kaleidoscope* for orch. (1968); *Ofukuro* for chorus and strings (1968); *Response,* suite for chorus and string orch. (1968–69); symph., *Song of Flame* for chorus and orch. (1970); cantata, *Kyoto,* for soprano, chorus, harp, and orch. (1970); Trio for flute, cello, and piano (1958); *Chamber Concerto* for wind quintet, piano, double bass, vibraphone, and percussion (1958); Violin Sonata (1964); *Divertimento* for string ensemble (1965); *Guzai* for string quartet (1965); *Meditation* for violin and piano (1970); choruses.

Toye, (John) Francis, English music critic; b. Winchester, Jan. 27, 1883; d. Florence, Oct. 31, 1964. He was a pupil of S. P. Waddington and E. J. Dent; became a critic for various papers in London; in 1923 he lectured on modern music in the U.S.; in 1939–46 lived in Rio de Janeiro; from 1946, in Florence. He wrote the books *The Well-Tempered Musician* (1925); *Giuseppe Verdi: His Life and Works* (1931; new edition, London, 1962); *Rossini: A Study in Tragi-comedy* (1934); *For What We Have Received* (autobiography; N.Y., 1948); *Italian Opera* (London, 1952); *Truly Thankful?* (autobiographical; London, 1957).

Toye, Geoffrey, English conductor and composer; brother of **Francis Toye;** b. Winchester, Feb. 17, 1889; d. London, June 11, 1942. He studied at the Royal College of Music in London; became a conductor at various theaters there; was manager of opera productions at Sadler's Wells. He wrote an opera, *The Red Pen* (broadcast from London, Feb. 7, 1927); a ballet; and some other works.

Tozzi, Giorgio, American bass of Italian descent; b. Chicago, Jan. 8, 1923. He studied in Italy, and after touring as a concert singer, sang at La Scala in Milan. In 1955 he was engaged at the Metropolitan Opera in New York; made a fine impression as Figaro in *Le Nozze di Figaro* and Don Basilio in *Il Barbiere di Siviglia.* He achieved spectacular success in the role of Hans Sachs in the film of *Die Meistersinger,* produced for German television by the Hamburg State Opera in 1969.

Trabaci, Giovanni Maria, Italian composer; b. Montepeloso, c.1575; d. Naples, Dec. 31, 1647. He studied with Giovanni Macque; became organist at the Viceregal Chapel in Naples in 1601; after Macque's death (1614) he succeeded him as choir director there. During the rebellion of the Neapolitan populace against the fruit tax of 1647, Trabaci fled to the monastery of the Trinità degli Spagnuoli, where he died. The bulk of his music consists of psalms, Masses, motets, and madrigals. Two keyboard publications are extant: *Ricercare, canzone francese, capricci, canti fermi, gagliarde, partite diverse, etc., Libro primo* (Naples, 1603) and *II secondo libro di ricercare ed altri varii capricci* (Naples, 1615). Some of his vocal works were published by Pannain in *Istituzioni e monumenti dell'arte musicale italiana* (vol. 5); these include 12 motets *a* 5, 4 *a* 6, and 4 *a* 8; also two Masses for double chorus. Keyboard works are reprinted in L. Torchi, *L'Arte Musicale in Italia* (vol. 3), in Tagliapietra, *Antologia di musica antica e moderna* (vol. 5), and in Davison and Apel, *Historical Anthology of Music.* Trabaci's canzonas include examples of rhythmic variants of a single theme ("variation canzonas"), anticipating Frescobaldi in this respect.

BIBLIOGRAPHY: W. Apel, "Neapolitan Links between Cabezón and Frescobaldi," *Musical Quarterly* (Oct. 1938).

Traetta, Filippo, Italian musician; son of **Tommaso Traetta;** b. Venice Jan. 8, 1777; d. Philadelphia, Jan. 9, 1854. He was a pupil of Fenaroli and Perillo at Venice, later of Piccinni at Naples. Becoming a soldier in the patriot ranks, he was captured and cast into prison; escaped 6 months afterward, and sailed to Boston, arriving there in 1799. There he wrote his *Vocal Exercises,* and *Washington's Dead March.* Proceeding to New York, he wrote the cantatas *The Christian's Joy and Prophecy;* also an opera, *The Venetian Masker.* He managed a traveling theatrical troupe; lived in Virginia for some years, and settled in Philadelphia, c.1828, founding the "American Conservatorio" with his pupil U. K. Hill. He produced 2 oratorios, *Jerusalem in Affliction* (1828) and *Daughter of Zion* (1829); later 2 cantatas, *The Nativity* and *The Day of Rest;* also instrumental and vocal quartets, trios and duets; songs; etc.; published *Rudiments of the Art of Singing* (2 vols.; 1841–43) and *An Introduction to the Art and Science of Music* (1829) for his Cons. He was active as a singing teacher until his death.

BIBLIOGRAPHY: F. L. Ritter, *Music in America* (1883); *Dictionary of American Biography* 18 (1936).

Traetta, Tommaso (Michele Francesco Saverio), Italian composer; b. Bitonto, Naples, March 30, 1727; d. Venice, April 6, 1779. He entered the Cons. di Loreto in Naples at the age of 11, and was there a pupil of Durante. His first opera, *Il Farnace,* was produced at the Teatro San Carlo with fine success, on Nov. 4, 1751; there followed several more operas in Naples, and later in other Italian cities: *Buovo d'Antona* (Venice, Dec. 27, 1758), *Ippolito ed Aricia* (Parma, May 9, 1759), etc. In 1758 he was appointed maestro to the Duke of Parma, and singing master to the princesses; his *Armida* was staged in Vienna (Jan. 3, 1761) with excellent success, and he was commissioned to write another opera for Vienna, *Ifigenia in Tauride,* which was produced there on Oct. 4, 1763. He settled in Venice in 1765, and was director of the Cons. dell'Ospedaletto S. Giovanni there for 3 years. In 1768 he was engaged for the court of Catherine the Great as successor to Galuppi, and arrived in St. Petersburg in the autumn of that year. He staged several of his operas there (mostly versions of works previously performed in Italy); also arranged music for various occasions (anniversary of the coronation of Catherine the Great, celebration of a victory over the Turkish fleet, etc.). He left Russia in 1775, and went to London, where he produced the operas *Germondo, Telemacco,* and *I Capricci del Sesso* (all in 1777) without much success;

returned to Italy, and produced 3 more operas in Venice; he wrote 48 operas in all. In many respects, he was an admirable composer, possessing a sense of drama and a fine melodic gift. In musical realism, he adopted certain procedures that Gluck was to employ successfully later on; he was highly regarded by his contemporaries. Besides operas, he wrote an oratorio, *Salomone* (1768), a Stabat Mater, and other church music. Excerpts from Traetta's operas, edited by H. Goldschmidt, are in the *Denkmäler der Tonkunst in Bayern* 25 and 29 (14.i and 17).

BIBLIOGRAPHY: V. Capruzzi, *Traetta e la musica* (Naples, 1878); C. H. Bitter, *Die Reform der Oper durch Gluck und Wagner* (Brunswick, 1884); H. Kretzschmar, *Geschichte der Oper* (1919); A. Nuovo, *Tommaso Traetta* (Rome, 1922); A. Damerini, "Un Precursore italiano di Gluck: Tommaso Traetta," *Il Pianoforte* (July 1927) and "Tommaso Traetta," *Bollettino Bibliografico Musicale* (July 1927); V. Raeli, "Tommaso Traetta," *Rivista Nazionale di Musica* (March 1927); A. Bonaventura, "Tommaso Traetta," *Pensiero Musicale* (April-May 1927); V. Raeli, "The Bicentenary of Tommaso Traetta," *Chesterian* (1927); A. Mooser, *Annales de la musique et des musiciens en Russie au XVIIIᵉ siècle* (Geneva, 1949–51; vol. II, pp. 87–132); F. Schlitzer, ed., *Tommaso Traetta, Leonardo Leo, Vincenzo Bellini: Notizie e documenti* (Siena, 1952); E. Saracino, *Tommaso Traetta* (Bitonto, 1954); F. Casavola, *Tommaso Traetta di Bitonto* (Bari, 1957); D. Binetti, *Tommaso Traetta nella vita e nell'arte* (1972).

Tragó, José, Spanish pianist and pedagogue; b. Madrid, Sept. 25, 1856; d. there, Jan. 3, 1934. He studied at the Conservatories of Madrid and Paris, winning 1st prizes for piano at both; was for many years prof. at the Madrid Cons. He was the teacher of Manuel del Falla and Joaquín Turina.

Trambitsky, Victor, Russian composer; b. Brest-Litovsk, Feb. 12, 1895; d. Leningrad, Aug. 13, 1970. He studied with Kalafati at the St. Petersburg Cons. In 1930 he moved to Sverdlovsk, as prof. at the Cons. there. He composed the operas *Gadfly* (Sverdlovsk, 1929), *Orlena* (Sverdlovsk, 1935), *Storm* (Sverdlovsk, 1942), *The Laceworker Nastia* (Leningrad, 1963); a Symph. (1945); *Symphonic Pictures* (1955); Violin Concerto (1921); arrangements of Russian folksongs.

Trampler, Walter, German-American violinist and violist; b. Munich, Aug. 25, 1915. He studied violin in Munich, and was employed in the German Radio Orch. (1935–38). In 1939 he emigrated to America; was a violinist in the Boston Symph. Orch. (1942–44); in 1947 he founded and played viola in The New Music String Quartet, which was active until 1956. From 1962 to 1972 he taught viola and chamber music at the Juilliard School of Music, N.Y. In 1972 he joined the staff of Boston University.

Tranchell, Peter (Andrew), British composer; b. Cuddalore, British India, July 14, 1922. He studied at Kings College, Cambridge; Mus. Bac. (1949). Most of his works are evocative of old English balladry; yet he has also experimented with modern techniques, as in his 6 piano pieces entitled *Dodecafonia*. His opera *The Mayor of Casterbridge* was produced in Cambridge, on July 30, 1951. Other works include the ballets, *Falstaff* (1950); *Fate's Revenge* (1951); *Euridice* (1952); *Spring Legend* (1957); *Images of Love* (1964); *Scherzetto* for orch. 1960); *Festive Overture* (1966); Concerto grosso (1972); Trio for violin, horn, and piano; *Triolet* for flute, clarinet, and piano; songs from Chinese poets with instrumental accompaniment; organ pieces; piano pieces; solo songs.

Trapp, Max, German composer; b. Berlin, Nov. 1, 1887; d. there, May 31, 1971. He studied piano with Ernst von Dohnányi and composition with Paul Juon; then taught at the Berlin Hochschule für Musik and also at the Cons. of Dortmund; in 1929, became a member of the Berlin Academy of Arts, where he taught a master class in composition (1934–45); from 1951 to 1953 he was on the staff of the Municipal Cons. in Berlin. His style is neo-Classical with a strong polyphonic texture, in the tradition of Max Reger. He was also active as a landscape painter.
WORKS: 6 symphonies: No. 1, *Sinfonia giocosa* (1915), No. 2 (1918), No. 3 (1924), No. 4 (1931), No. 5 (1936), No. 6 (1946); 3 concertos for orch. (1934; 1940; 1946); Violin Concerto (1922); Piano Concerto (1930); Cello Concerto (1935); Piano Quintet (1910); 3 piano quartets; 2 string quartets; piano pieces; songs; a cantata, *Vom ewigen Licht* (1942).
BIBLIOGRAPHY: W. Matthes, "Max Trapp," *Zeitschrift für Musik* (Oct. 1937).

Traubel, Helen, American soprano; b. St. Louis, June 20, 1899; d. Santa Monica, California, July 28, 1972. She made her concert debut at St. Louis in 1925, and appeared for the first time during the regular Metropolitan Opera season, in N.Y., as Sieglinde on Dec. 28, 1939. She made several transcontinental tours; sang in Buenos Aires in 1943; also gave numerous concerts in Europe. She was married to Louis Carpenter in 1922; they were divorced the same year, and in 1938 she married William L. Bass. In 1953 she made appearances in N.Y. night clubs; this prompted objections of the Metropolitan Opera management, and as a result she resigned from the Metropolitan. She published the mystery novels *The Ptomaine Canary* and *The Metropolitan Opera Murders* (N.Y., 1951), and an autobiography, *St. Louis Woman* (N.Y., 1959).

Trautwein, Friedrich, German electrical engineer; b. Würzburg, Aug. 11, 1888; d. Düsseldorf, Dec. 21, 1956. He was trained in engineering; was an instructor in musical acoustics at the Berlin Musikhochschule. In 1930 he constructed an electronic musical instrument which became known, after the first syllable of his name, as the Trautonium. Hindemith wrote a concerto for it. Trautwein contributed numerous articles on electronic music to German periodicals.

Trautwein, Traugott, founder (1820) of the music publishing business "Trautwein'sche Buch- und Musikalien-Handlung," in Berlin. The firm was transferred in 1840 to J. Guttentag, and then in 1858 to Martin Bahn, under whose management it became famous for new editions of early music. After Bahn's death

(May 21, 1902) the firm was consolidated with A. Heinrichshofen of Magdeburg.

Travers, John, English organist and composer; b. c.1703; d. June, 1758. Chorister of St. George's Chapel, Windsor; pupil of M. Greene and Dr. Pepusch; from 1737 organist of the Chapel Royal. He published *The Whole Book of Psalms for 1, 2, 3, 4, and 5 voices, with a thorough bass for the harpsichord* (2 vols., 1750) and *18 Canzonets for 2 and 3 voices, the words chiefly by Matthew Prior* (1745); 12 voluntaries for organ or harpsichord were published posthumously.

Trebelli, Zelia (real name **Zelia Gilbert**), French mezzo-soprano; b. Paris, 1838; d. Etretat, Aug. 18, 1892. She studied with Wartel; made her debut in 1859 as Rosina in *Il Barbiere di Siviglia,* followed by appearances in England (1862). She was long a favorite in London; also toured in the U.S. (1878 and 1884).
BIBLIOGRAPHY: M. de Mensiaux, *Trebelli: A Biographical Sketch* (London, 1890).

Tregian, Francis, English musician; b. 1574; d. London, 1619. He was a recusant, and fled England to escape persecution; was attached to Catholic dignitaries in Douai and in Rome. Returning to England to settle his father's estate, he was convicted in 1609, remaining in prison until his death. His significance for English music lies in the fact that he was the scribe of the *Fitzwilliam Virginal Book* and of 2 manuscripts containing more than 2000 motets, madrigals, etc., some of them possibly of his own composition.
BIBLIOGRAPHY: Elizabeth Cole, "In Search of Francis Tregian," *Music & Letters* (Jan. 1952).

Treharne, Bryceson, English-American music editor and composer; b. Merthyr Tydfil, Wales, May 30, 1879; d. New York, Feb. 4, 1948. He studied at the Royal College of Music in London, under Parry, Stanford, and Davies. In 1901 he went to Australia; was prof. at the Univ. of Adelaide; returning to Europe in 1911, he lived in Paris, Milan, Vienna, and Munich; at the outbreak of World War I, he was interned in Germany, at Ruhleben. There he wrote nearly 200 songs and other works; an exchange of prisoners of war enabled him to return to England. In 1917 he settled in America; was music editor for the Boston Music Co. and Willis Music Co. (1928–47). Among his songs are *Ozymandias, The Fair Circassian, A Lover's Prayer, The Night, Dreams, Love's Tribute and Renunciation*.

Treigle, Norman, American operatic baritone; b. New Orleans, March 6, 1927; d. there, Feb. 16, 1975. He made his debut at the New Orleans Opera at the age of 20; in 1953 was engaged by the N.Y. City Opera. He won immediate acclaim for his finely modulated dramatic voice and his stage presence; he distinguished himself as Figaro in Mozart's *Le nozze di Figaro* and as Boris Godunov; he also sang in modern operas. His sudden death of a heart attack deprived the American musical theater of one of its finest singing artists.

Tremblay, George, Canadian-American composer; b. Ottawa, Jan. 14, 1911. He studied music with his father, a church organist; in 1919 was taken to the U.S., eventually settled in Los Angeles; there he attended classes with Schoenberg (1936), and adopted an integral method of composition with 12 tones.

WORKS: 3 symphonies (1949, 1952, 1970); Wind Sextet (1968); 2 wind quintets (1940; 1950); 4 string quartets (1936–63); Piano Quartet (1958); Quartet for oboe, clarinet, bassoon, and viola (1964); Piano Trio (1959); String Trio (1964); Duo for viola and piano (1966); Double-bass Sonata (1967); 3 piano sonatas and other piano works.

Tremblay, Gilles, Canadian composer; b. Arvida, Quebec, Sept. 6, 1932. He had private lessons with Papineau-Couture; studied piano with Germaine Malépart and composition with Claude Champagne at the Montreal Cons. (1949–54). In 1954 he went to Paris where he took courses with Messiaen (analysis), Yvonne Loriod (piano), Andrée Vaurabourg-Honegger (counterpoint), and Maurice Martenot (Ondes Martenot); subsequently worked with the Groupe de Recherches Musicales at the Paris Radio (1960–61). He returned to Canada in 1961; in 1962 was appointed prof. at the Montreal Cons. He follows the modern French method of composition and uses optical notation in his scores.

WORKS: *Scherzo* for piano (1950); *Double Quintet* for winds (1950); *Mouvement* for 2 pianos (1954); *2 Pièces (Phases and Réseaux)* for piano (1956–58); *Cantiques de durées* for orch. (1960; Paris, March 24, 1963); *Mobile* for violin and piano (1962); *Champs I* for piano and 2 percussionists (1965); *Sonorisation du Pavillon de Québec* at Expo '67 in Montreal, for an icositetrastereophonic electro-acoustical system of 24 channels (1967); *Souffles (Champs II)* for 2 flutes, oboe, clarinet, horn, 2 trumpets, 2 trombones, 2 percussionists, double bass, and piano (1968; Montreal, March 21, 1968); *Vers (Champs III)* for 2 flutes, clarinet, trumpet, horn, 3 violins, double bass, and 3 percussionists (Stratford Festival, Ontario, Aug. 2, 1969); *Solstices (où Les Jours et les saisons tournent)* for flute, clarinet, horn, double bass, and 2 percussionists (Montreal, May 17, 1972); *Jeux de Solstices* for 4 instrumental soloists (violin, flute, clarinet, and trumpet) and small orch. (Ottawa, April 23, 1974); *Oralléluiante* for soprano, bass clarinet, horn, 3 double basses, and 2 percussionists (1975); *Fleuves* for orch. (1975–76; Montreal, May 3, 1977).

Trend, John Brande, English music scholar; b. Southampton, Dec. 17, 1887; d. Cambridge, April 20, 1958. He received his education at Cambridge Univ.; spent several years in Spain; in 1933 was appointed prof. of Spanish at Cambridge Univ. He wrote the books *A Picture of Modern Spain: Men and Music* (London, 1921); *Luis Milán and the Vihuelistas* (London, 1925); *The Music of Spanish History to 1600* (London, 1926); *Manuel de Falla and Spanish Music* (N.Y., 1929).

Trento, Vittorio, Italian composer; b. Venice, 1761; d. Lisbon, 1833. He was a pupil of Bertoni; produced several ballets at Venice, followed by a number of cantatas, farces, and comic operas. He was cembalist at the Teatro S. Samuele, Venice, and then at La Fenice; music director of the Italian opera at Amsterdam (1806),

and some years later at Lisbon. His most popular stage work was the opera buffa *Quanti casi in un sol giorno, ossia Gli assassini* (Venice, Dec., 1801), which was also given in London, as *Roberto l'Assassino* (Feb. 3, 1807). Other operas are: *Teresa vedova* (Venice, Jan. 13, 1802), *Ines de Castro* (Leghorn, Nov. 9, 1803), *Ifigenia in Aulide* (Naples, Nov. 4, 1804), *Andromeda* (Naples, May 30, 1805), and *Le Gelosie villane* (Florence, Nov. 2, 1825).

Treu (Italianized as **Fedele**), **Daniel Gottlieb,** German composer; b. Stuttgart, 1695; d. Breslau, Aug. 7, 1749. He studied violin with Kusser, and with Vivaldi at Venice. After bringing out 12 operas at Venice, he took an Italian opera troupe to Breslau, where he produced his operas *Astarte, Coriolano, Ulisse e Telemacco,* and *Don Chisciotte* with much success. In 1727 he became Kapellmeister at Prague; then was again in Breslau.

Tréville, Yvonne de (real name **Edyth La Gierse**), American coloratura soprano; b. (of French father and American mother) Galveston, Texas, Aug. 25, 1881; d. New York, Jan. 25, 1954. She made her debut in N.Y. as Marguérite (1898); then went to Paris, where she studied with Madame Marchesi; appeared at the Opéra-Comique as Lakmé (June 20, 1902); sang in Madrid, Brussels, Vienna, Budapest, Cairo, and in Russia; from 1913, gave concert tours in the U.S. and sang in light operas. Her voice had a compass of 3 full octaves, reaching high G.

Trial, Jean-Claude, French composer; b. Avignon, Dec. 13, 1732; d. Paris, June 23, 1771. He studied violin in his native city, then went to Paris, where he became associated with Rameau; was conductor at the Paris Opéra. He wrote several operas: *Silvie* (Fontainebleau, Oct. 17, 1765), *Théonis ou Le Toucher* (Paris, Oct. 11, 1767), *La Fête de Flore* (Paris, June 18, 1770); also instrumental pieces.

Trifunović, Vitomir, Serbian composer; b. Bukovica, Nov. 4, 1916. He studied composition with Slavenski and Živković at the Belgrade Academy of Music; became an editor for new music at Radio Belgrade in 1959. His early music is Romantic, but later he acquired a thoroughly modern sound.

WORKS: Piano Sonatina (1956); Violin Sonata (1958); 2 string quartets (1959, 1973); *Šumadija,* suite for chamber orch. (1960); *Lamentoso* for string orch. (1961); *Heroic Overture* (1962); *Toccata* for orch. (1963); *Simfonijska slika (Symphonic Picture,* 1964); *Folklorni triptih (Folklore Triptychon)* for orch. (1961); *Symphonic Dance* (1968); *Synthesen 4* for orch. (1969); a cantata, *Vidici (The Horizons,* 1971); *Antinomije* for orch. (1972); *Asocijacije (Associations)* for orch. (1973); arrangements of folk music.

Trimble, Lester, American composer; b. Bangor, Wisconsin, Aug. 29, 1920. He studied composition with Nikolai Lopatnikoff at the Carnegie Institute of Technology in Pittsburgh and later took private lessons in Paris with Darius Milhaud and Arthur Honegger; subsequently taught at the Juilliard School of Music.

WORKS: 2 string quartets (1950, 1955); Symph.

No. 1 (1951); Sextet for woodwinds, horn, and piano (1952); Violin Concerto (1955); *Closing Piece* for orch. (1957); *5 Episodes* for orch. (1961); *Kennedy Concerto* for chamber orch. (1964); *In Praise of Diplomacy and Common Sense* for baritone, percussion, male speaking chorus, and 2 speaking soloists (1965); Symph. No. 2 (1968); *Solo for a Virtuoso* for solo violin (1971); *Panels I* for chamber ensemble (Tanglewood Festival, Berkshire, Mass. Aug. 6, 1973); several other pieces entitled *Panels.*

Tritto, Giacomo, Italian composer; b. Altamura, April 2, 1733; d. Naples, Sept. 16, 1824. He studied with Cafaro at the Cons. della Pietà de' Turchini; became subteacher (primo maestrino) and Cafaro's assistant in teaching harmony, also succeeded him as concertmaster at the Teatro San Carlo. From 1799 to 1807 he was principal teacher (primo maestro) at the Cons.; followed Paisiello in 1816 as maestro of the Royal Chapel. Bellini, Spontini, Mercadante, Meyerbeer, and Conti were his pupils. His first opera, *La Fedeltà in amore,* was performed at Naples in 1764; some 50 others were produced subsequently in Naples, Rome, Venice, Milan, etc.; of these *Le Vicende amorose* (Rome, 1788) and *Gli Americani* (Naples, Nov. 4, 1802) were fairly successful. Other works included 3 cantatas, a Mass for double chorus with 2 orchestras, 7 other Masses (3 of them with orch.); 2 Passions with orch., a Te Deum, motets, etc. (none printed). He published *Partimenti e regole generali per conoscere qual numerica dar si deve ai vari movimenti del basso* (1821), and *Scuola di contrappunto, ossia Teoria musicale* (1823).
BIBLIOGRAPHY: F. Florimo, *La Scuola musicale di Napoli,* vol. III (Naples, 1880); J. A. de la Fage, in *Miscellanées musicales* (Paris, 1844); G. de Napoli, "Giacomo Tritto," *La Lettura* (Oct. 1924) and *La Triade melodrammatica altamurana: G. Tritto, V. Lavigna, S. Mercandante* (Milan, 1931).

Trneček, Hanuš, Czech harpist and composer; b. Prague, May 16, 1858; d. there, March 28, 1914. He studied at the Prague Cons.; was harpist at the Hoftheater in Schwerin (1882–88); then taught harp and piano at the Prague Cons.
WORKS: the operas *Der Geiger von Cremona* (Schwerin, 1886), *Amaranta* (Prague, Nov. 16, 1890; in Czech), *Andrea Crini* (Prague, Feb. 2, 1900); Symphony; Piano Concerto; Violin Concerto; piano pieces.

Trojan, Václav, Czech composer; b. Pilsen, April 24, 1907. He studied composition with Křička and Alois Hába, conducting with Ostrčil and Dědeček, and organ at the Prague Cons., graduating in 1928. He is mainly known as a composer of music for children.
WORKS: a six-act children's opera, *Kolotoč (The Merry-go-round;* 1936–40; Ostrava, 1960); a "stage poem" with dance, *The Golden Gate* (1973; Prague, Feb. 17, 1974); *Pohádky (Fairy tales)* for accordion and orch. (1959); *Sinfonietta armoniosa* for chamber orch. (1971); *Capricious Variations* for trombone, saxophone, and orch. (1971); music scores for films, including *Spaliček* (1947) and *Císařův slavík (The Emperor's Nightingale,* 1948); 2 string quintets (1928, 1929); Wind Quintet on folk themes (1935).

Tromlitz, Johann Georg, German flutist and flute maker; b. Reinsdorf über Artern (Halle), Nov. 8, 1725; d. Leipzig, Feb. 4, 1805. He published *Kurze Abhandlung von Flötenspielen* (1786); *Ausführlicher und gründlicher Unterricht die Flöte zu spielen* (1791); *Über di Flöte mit mehreren Klappen* (1800); and articles in the *Allgemeine Musik-Zeitung* (1799); also 3 concertos for flute and strings; 2 books of sonatas for piano and flute; 6 *Partien* for flute; songs.

Trotère, Henry (real name **Trotter**), English song composer; b. London, Dec. 14, 1855; d. there, April 10, 1912. Some of his songs that enjoyed success were *Once for All, Léonore, Ever dear, Asthore, The Deathless Army, Love can wait.*

Trotter, Thomas Henry Yorke, English musical educator; b. London, Nov. 6, 1854; d. there, March 11, 1934. He studied at New College, Oxford (M.A., 1887; Mus. Doc. 1892); also took music lessons with Frank Bridge; was principal of the London Academy of Music from 1915, developing there a new system for teaching music, based on ear-training and cultivation of the rhythmic sense; he came to the U.S. and introduced his system at the Eastman School of Music in Rochester, N.Y. He wrote the books *Constructive Harmony* (1911); *Rhythmic Gradus; Ear-training and Sight-reading Gradus; The Making of Musicians* (1914); *Music and Mind* (1924).

Troutbeck, Rev. John, English compiler of hymnals; b. Blencowe, Cumberland, Nov. 12, 1832; d. London, Oct. 11, 1899 He studied at Oxford (B.A., 1856; M.A., 1858); 1865–69, served as precentor of Manchester Cathedral; in 1869, canon of Westminster. He published *The Manchester Psalter* (1868); *Manchester Chant Book* (1871); *Cathedral Paragraph Psalter; Hymn Book for Use in Westminster Abbey; Music Primer for Schools,* with R. F. Dale (1873; often reprinted); *Church Choir Training* (1879). He made translations of German, French, and Italian opera librettos published by Novello.

Trudić, Božidar, Serbian composer; b. Smederevska Palanka, March 24, 1911. He studied with Slavenski; became a teacher in Sarajevo. His music is inspired by Serbian folksongs, but the harmonic treatment is often modernistic. Among his works are a cantata *1804* (Sarajevo, Dec. 26, 1956); Violin Concerto (1951); Cello Concerto (1952); 2 symphonies (1946, 1957); choruses and songs.

Truhn, Friedrich Hieronymus, German composer and writer on music; b. Elbing, Nov. 14, 1811; d. Berlin, April 30, 1886. He studied with Dehn, Klein, and Mendelssohn; wrote for the Leipzig *Neue Zeitschrift für Musik* during Schumann's editorship; lived chiefly at Berlin, where he founded and conducted the Neue Liedertafel; made a concert tour with Hans von Bülow in 1854.
WORKS: marionette opera, *Der baierische Hiesel* (Berlin, 1832); operetta, *Der vierjährige Posten* (1833);

comic opera, *Trilby* (Berlin, May 22, 1835); melodrama, *Kleopatra* (Berlin, 1853); also wrote *Über Gesangskunst* (1885).

Truinet. See **Nuitter.**

Trunk, Richard, German critic and conductor; b. Tauberbischofsheim, Baden, Feb. 10, 1879; d. Herrsching-am-Ammersee, June 2, 1968. He studied with Iwan Knorr at Hoch's Cons. in Frankfurt (1894–95); 1896–99 at the Royal Academy in Munich. In 1906 he was appointed teacher of singing at the Theresien-Gymnasium; 1907–12, music critic of the *Münchner Post;* 1912–14, conductor of the *Arion* in New York and of the *Arion* in Newark. He then returned to Munich; from 1916 to 1922, was critic of the Bayreuth *Staatszeitung;* from 1925 to 1934, co-director of the Rheinische Musikschule in Cologne, head of the choral class at the Hochschule, and conductor of the Cologne Männerchorverein; in 1934 succeeded Hausegger as director of the Akademie der Tonkunst in Munich. After 1945 he went to live in Riederau-am-Ammersee. He wrote over 100 songs; also choruses, chamber music, etc.

Trutovsky, Vasily, Russian composer and collector of folksongs; b. Ivanovskaya Sloboda, c. 1740; d. St. Petersburg, 1810. He was the son of an orthodox priest; was a court singer and player on the gusli during the reigns of Empress Elizabeth, Peter III, and Catherine II. His historic achievement was the compilation of the first comprehensive collection of Russian folksongs, in 4 issues (1776, 1778, 1779, 1795). He also was the first in Russia to publish piano pieces; the earlier publications of Russian piano music were anonymous. His *Chanson russe variée* for harpsichord or piano (St. Petersburg, 1780) was republished in *Old Russian Piano Music,* ed. by A. Drozdov and T. Trofimov (Moscow, 1946).

Tschaikowsky. See **Tchaikovsky.**

Tschirch, (Friedrich) Wilhelm, German choral conductor and composer; b. Lichtenau, June 8, 1818; d. Gera, Jan. 6, 1892; He was a pupil of the Royal Institute for Church Music, Berlin; music director at Liegnitz 1843–52; then court conductor at Gera. By invitation of the German-American choral societies he visited the U.S. in 1869, and produced many of his celebrated men's choruses at N.Y., Philadelphia, Baltimore, Washington, and Chicago. He published salon pieces for piano under the pseudonym **Alexander Czersky.**

Tschudi. See **Broadwood.**

Tsfasman, Alexander, foremost Russian conductor of jazz; b. Alexandrovsk, Ukraine, Dec. 14, 1906; d. Leningrad, Jan. 25, 1971. He studied piano with Felix Blumenfeld at the Moscow Cons. In 1926 he organized a jazz band in Moscow, and from 1939 to 1946 was music director of the All-Union Radio Jazz Band; toured with it all over Russia. He also composed a concerto for piano and jazz band, and numerous popular songs.

Tsintsadze, Sulkhan, Soviet Georgian cellist and composer; b. Gori, Aug. 23, 1925. He studied cello in Tiflis, and later at the Moscow Cons., graduating in 1950; also studied composition there.

WORKS: opera, *The Golden Fleece* (1953); Symph. (1954); Piano Concerto on native Georgian themes (1954); Violin Concerto (1947); Cello Concerto (1947); 4 string quartets; 3 suites for string quartet, on songs of the nations of the Soviet Union; pieces for cello and piano; film music.

Tsouyopoulos, Georges, Greek composer; b. Athens, Oct. 11, 1930. He received his early training in Athens and Milan; then went to Zürich to study with Hindemith. In 1962 he settled in Munich. His early compositions are neo-Classical in style; later he adopted serial methods, determinedly pursuing the goal of structural indeterminacy.

WORKS: *Sinfonietta da Camera* for 8 instruments (1955); *Serenata* for soprano, flute, guitar and viola (1957); *Due Madrigali* for soprano and orch. (1957); *Tre Frammenti* for chorus and orch. (1958); 3 Toccatas for piano (1958, 1959, 1965); *Music for Percussion* (1959); 2 string quartets; vocal pieces.

Tsukatani, Akihirô, Japanese composer; b. Tokyo, March 16, 1919. He graduated in law from the Tokyo Univ. in 1941 and became a prof. in the history of economics there; concurrently he took lessons in music theory from Saburo Moroi. In 1949, with Yoritsuné Matsudaira, he organized the Shin Sakkyokuka Kyokai (New Composers' Association); taught music at Tokyo Univ.

WORKS: 3 operas: *Pongo,* based on a Japanese Noh drama (1965); *Ajatasatru* (1966); *Kakitsubata* (Tokyo, May 24, 1967); a musical, *Fairy's Cap,* for chorus, piano, and percussion (Tokyo, Dec. 9, 1968); *Saiten (Festival),* symph. suite (1950); *Mythology of Today,* ballet suite (1956); *Suite* for percussion and string orch. (1960); Piano Concerto (1961); *Japan Festival Dance Music* for chamber orch. (1969); Sonata for flute, cello, and piano (1949); Clarinet Sonata (1952); *Suite* for horn, trumpet, trombone, and timpani (1959); *Fu 1* and *Fu 2* for solo flute (1970); *3 Worlds* for solo flute (1971–72); *2 Movements* for solo cello (1972); *Fantasia* for violin, piano, and tam-tam (1973); choruses; songs.

Tua, Teresina (real name **Maria Felicità**), Italian violinist; b. Turin, May 22, 1867; d. Rome, Oct. 29, 1955. She studied with Massart at the Paris Cons., where she took the 1st prize in 1880; toured the Continent with brilliant success; made her English debut at the Crystal Palace, London, May 5, 1883; also appeared in America (1887). In 1889 she married Count Franchi-Verney della Valetta, and withdrew from the concert stage till the autumn of 1895, when she set out on a successful European tour, including Russia, where her accompanist and joint artist was Rachmaninoff. Franchi died in 1911; in 1913 she married Emilio Quadrio. She taught at the Milan Cons. from 1915 to 1924, and then at the Santa Cecilia in Rome; subsequently abandoned her career, and entered the convent dell'Adorazione in Rome as Sister Maria di Gesù.

Tubb, Carrie (Caroline Elizabeth), English soprano; b. London, May 17, 1876; d. there, Sept. 20, 1976, at the age of 100. She studied at the Guildhall School of Music; started her career singing minor roles in productions by the Beecham Opera Co.; then abandoned the stage and devoted herself to the oratorio and solo recitals. She excelled both in Mozart arias and in concert excerpts from Wagner and Verdi. At the zenith of her career her singing was described in glowing superlatives by such otherwise sober auditors as Eric Blom. As her voice betrayed the inexorable signs of senescence, she applied herself to teaching, following G. B. Shaw's dictum, "Who can, do; who cannot, teach."

Tubin, Eduard, Estonian-born Swedish composer; b. Kallaste, near Tartu (Dorpat), June 18, 1905. He studied with A. Kapp at the Cons. in Tartu and with Kodály in Budapest. In 1931 he became conductor of the Tartu Symphony Orch. In 1944 he moved to Sweden.
WORKS: operas: *Barbara von Tisenhusen* (Tallin, Estonia, Dec. 4, 1969) and *Prosten från Reigi* (*The Priest from Reigi,* 1971); the ballet, *Skratten* (*The Laugh,* 1939–41; ballet suite, 1961); 10 symphonies: No. 1 (1931–34); No. 2 (1937); No. 3 (1942); No. 4 (1943); No. 5 (1946); No. 6 (1952–54); No. 7 (1958); No. 8 (1966); No. 9, *Sinfonia semplice* (1969); No. 10 (1973); *Estonian Dance Suite* for orch. (1938); 2 violin concertos (1942, 1945); Concertino for piano and orch. (1944–46); Double Bass Concerto (1948); Balalaika Concerto (1964); 2 violin sonatas (1934–36; 1949); Saxophone Sonata (1951); Solo Violin Sonata (1962); Viola Sonata (1965); *Capriccio* for violin and piano (1971); *5 Hasjasoidu laulud* for baritone and orch. (1975); songs, piano pieces.

Tucci, Gabriela, Italian soprano; b. Rome, Aug. 4, 1929. She won the international singing competition in Spoleto, and sang Leonora in *La Forza del Destino* there in 1951. She rapidly gained recognition and was engaged at La Scala, Milan, and at the Rome Opera. She made her American debut at the San Francisco Opera in 1959, and sang at the Metropolitan Opera in New York from 1960 to 1971. In 1964 she sang at the Bolshoi Theater in Moscow. She possesses a dependable and well-modulated operatic voice; she is equally effective as Mimi in *La Bohème* and Violetta in *La Traviata,* as Aida and as Tosca.

Tucher, Gottlieb, Freiherr von, German writer on music; b. Nuremberg, May 14, 1798; d. Munich, Feb. 17, 1877. He was in the judicial service in Bavaria; from 1856 to 1868 was judge of the Supreme Court of Munich. His musical publications include *Kirchengesänge der berühmesten älteren italienischen Meister* (1827; dedicated to Beethoven), and *Schatz des evangelischen Kirchengesangs* (1848; 2 vols.); he also wrote *Über den Gemeindegesang der evangelischen Kirche* (1867).

Tucker, Richard (real name **Reuben Ticker**), brilliant American tenor; b. Brooklyn, Aug. 28, 1913; d. Kalamazoo, Michigan, Jan. 8, 1975. He sang in a synagogue choir in N.Y. as a child; then began taking voice lessons with Paul Althouse. On Jan. 25, 1945 he made his debut at the Metropolitan Opera House, N.Y., in *La Gioconda;* later sang leading parts as a lyric tenor. He subsequently appeared with great success in Milan, London, and Vienna, both in opera and in recital.

Tuckerman, Samuel Parkman, American organist and composer; b. Boston, Feb. 11, 1819; d. Newport, R.I., June 30, 1890. He was a pupil of Carl Zeuner in Boston; from 1856 to 1864 he lived in England. He wrote much church music; edited *The Episcopal Harp* (Boston, 1844), *The National Lyre* (Boston, 1848) *Cathedral Chants* (1858), and *Trinity Collection of Church Music* (Boston, 1864).

Tuckey, William, English singing master; b. Somersetshire, 1708; d. Philadelphia, Sept. 14, 1781. He claimed to have been a vicar-choral at Bristol Cathedral before going to America, where he was active from 1754; established himself as a singing teacher in New York. On Jan. 16, 1770, he conducted what was probably the 1st performance in America of Handel's *Messiah* (overture and 16 numbers). He composed a *"Thanksgiving Anthem"* (1760), a setting of the 97th Psalm.
BIBLIOGRAPHY: O. G. Sonneck, *Early Concert-Life in America* (1907).

Tuckwell, Barry, Australian virtuoso horn player; b. Melbourne, March 5, 1931, in a musical family. He was taught piano by his father and violin by his older brother; was a chorister at St. Andrew's Cathedral in Sydney, and also acted as an organist there. At 13 he began studying the French horn with Alan Mann at the Cons. of Sydney; making rapid progress, he joined the Sydney Symphony, then conducted by Eugene Goossens (1947–50). In 1950 he went to England where he met Dennis Brain, the virtuoso horn player, who gave him valuable suggestions on the horn technique; he also gathered some ideas about the horn sound from listening to recordings by Tommy Dorsey. He filled positions as assistant first horn with the Hallé Orch. in Manchester (1951–53), with the Scottish National Orch. (1953–54) and, as the first horn, with the Bournemouth Symph. Orch. (1954–55); then served for 13 years (1955–68) as the first horn player with the London Symph. Orch. After leaving the London Symph. Orch. he launched a career as soloist, achieving recognition as one of the foremost virtuosos on the instrument. In the academic field, he compiled a horn method and edited horn literature. Several modern composers wrote special works for him: Thea Musgrave (a Concerto that requires the horn to play quarter-tones); Richard Rodney Bennett (*Actaeon* for horn and orch.); Iain Hamilton (*Voyage* for horn and orch.); Alun Hoddinott (Concerto); and Don Banks (Concerto). In 1978 he made his first appearance as conductor in the U.S., in a program of Baroque music.
BIBLIOGRAPHY: Winthrop Sargeant, "Profiles: Something I Could Do," *The New Yorker* (March 14, 1977).

Tudor, David, American avant-garde pianist and aleatory composer; b. Philadelphia, Jan. 20, 1926. He studied organ with William Hawke, piano with Irma Wolpe, and composition with Stefan Wolpe. He played the organ in St. Mark's Church in Philadelphia (1938–43) and at Swarthmore College (1944–48); these ecclesiastical services to the contrary notwithstanding, he simultaneously plunged into uninhibited experimentation; developed a hyper-modern virtuoso technique as a quaquaversal hyperdactyl pianist; earned an awesome reputation by performing the insurmountable, impregnable, and inscrutable 2nd Piano Sonata of Pierre Boulez (N.Y., Dec. 17, 1950) from memory. He became the unique collaborator, animator, and divinator of the recondite practices of John Cage, and was the first to unplay John Cage's monumental tacit piece *4'33"* (Woodstock, N.Y., Aug. 29, 1952); was also unheard in it in Cologne, Germany, and elsewhere, obtaining vociferous acclaim. In audible performance he often applies special piano techniques; in playing *Five Piano Pieces for David Tudor* by Sylvano Bussotti, he is apt to put on thick leather gloves for tone-clusters. As a composer, he has the following works to his credit: *Fluorescent Sound* (Stockholm, Sept. 13, 1964); *Bandoneon—!* (factorial bandoneon, idempotentially multiplied ad infinitum); *Reunion* (in collaboration with the painter Marcel Duchamp and others); *Rainforest,* for dancers; and, in collaboration with John Cage, *Talk I* (Ann Arbor, Mich., Sept. 19, 1965) and *Fontana Mix* for bass drum and electronic circuits (Brandeis Univ., Waltham, Mass., April Fools' Day, 1967). Some of his biographers claim for him a direct descent, through a morganatic line, from Henry Tudor (Henry VII), and/or from one of the decapitated lovers of the beheaded Queen Anne Boleyn. Since Henry VIII himself dabbled in "aleatorick musick," David Tudor's own preoccupation with tonal indeterminacy may be a recessive royal trait.

Tudway, Thomas, English composer; b. 1650; d. Cambridge, Nov. 23, 1726. From 1660 chorister in the Chapel Royal, under Dr. Blow; lay-vicar at St. George's Chapel, Windsor, 1664; organist of King's College, Cambridge, 1670; teacher of choristers there, 1679; prof. of music, Cambridge Univ., 1704; suspended 1706–07, retired 1726. Mus. Bac., Cantab., 1681; Mus. Doc., 1705. He composed services, motets, and anthems; his *Collection of Services and Anthems used in the Church of England from the Reformation to the Restoration of King Charles II,* in 6 manuscript vols., is in the British Library.

Tufts, John, American minister and pioneer compiler of church music; b. Medford, Mass., Feb. 26, 1689; d. Amesbury, Mass., Aug. 17, 1750. He graduated from Harvard Univ. in 1708; was ordained minister at Newbury, Mass., in 1714; upon retirement in 1738 he moved to Amesbury, Mass., where he settled as a shopkeeper. About 1721 he published *A Very Plain and Easy Introduction to the Art of Singing Psalm Tunes* (no copy previous to the 1721 ed. is known to exist); in this book, letters instead of notes were used on the staff; it was very popular (at least 11 eds. publ. up to 1774; reprint, Philadelphia, 1954).
BIBLIOGRAPHY: N. D. Gould, *Church Music in America* (1853); F. J. Metcalf, *American Writers and Compilers of Sacred Music* (1925); E. H. Pierce, "The Rise and Fall of the 'Fugue-Tune' in America," *Musi-*

cal Quarterly (April 1930); *Dictionary of American Biography* 19 (1936); C. K. Shipton, *Sibley's Harvard Graduates* (Boston, 1937; pp. 457–61); I. Lowens, "John Tufts' Introduction to the Singing of Psalm-Tunes (1721–1744): The First American Music Textbook," *Journal of Research in Music Education* 2 (1954).

Tufts, John Wheeler, American organist and teacher; b. Dover, N.H., May 12, 1825; d. Camden, Maine, March 18, 1908. He went to Germany in 1846; studied in Leipzig, where his teachers were Moscheles in piano and Hauptmann in theory. He returned to America in 1848 and organized in Bangor, Maine, a choral society which he conducted for several years; he then served as church organist in Portland, Maine and in Boston. He wrote many songs and hymn tunes, and brought out a series of school-music works, notably the *Normal Music Course* and the *Cecilian Series of Study and Song.*

Tulindberg, Erik, Finnish composer; b. in Lillkyro, Feb. 22, 1761; d. Abo (Turku), Sept. 1, 1814. He studied academic disciplines at the Abo Academy, obtaining the degree of Magister Philosophiae in 1782; was subsequently a municipal functionary. Music was his avocation; he learned to play the violin; owned a large library, including works of Mozart, Haydn, and Boccherini; in 1797 he was elected member of the Swedish Academy of Music. He wrote a violin concerto and 6 string quartets in the traditional style of the Viennese School.

Tulou, Jean-Louis, French flutist; b. Paris, Sept. 12, 1786; d. Nantes, July 23, 1865. He was a pupil of Wunderlich at the Paris Cons.; in 1813 succeeded Wunderlich at the Paris Opéra, resigning in 1822, but resuming the position in 1826 (with the title of "première flûte solo"); in 1829 was appointed flute prof. at the Cons.; retired from both positions in 1856. He performed on the old-fashioned flute, and obstinately opposed the introduction of Böhm's improved instrument into the Paris Conservatoire. He wrote 5 flute concertos; *airs variés* for flute with orch.; a trio for 3 flutes; flute duos; many solo pieces for flute.

Tuma, Franz, Bohemian virtuoso on the viola da gamba and composer; b. Kostelecz, Oct. 2, 1704; d. Vienna, Feb. 4, 1774. He was a pupil of Czernohorsky at Prague and Fux at Vienna; from 1741, chamber composer to the dowager Empress Elisabeth. He composed 30 Masses, a Miserere, responses, etc.; also instrumental pieces. A selection of Tuma's works was published by O. Schmid (choruses, Passion music, piano pieces); a symphony was ed. by Paul Pisk.
BIBLIOGRAPHY: O. Schmid, in *Sammelbände der Internationalen Musik-Gesellschaft* II.

Tunder, Franz, celebrated German organist and composer; b. Burg auf Fehmarn, 1614; d. Lübeck, Nov. 5, 1667. From 1632–41, court organist at Gottorp, where he studied with J. Heckslauer, a pupil of Frescobaldi; 1641, organist of the Marienkirche in Lübeck, being succeeded at his death by his son-in-law, **Dietrich Buxtehude.** 7 chorale fantasias for organ by Tunder were discovered in 1903 in the Lüneburg tablature books (1 published by Straube, in *Alte Meister des Orgelspiels*, new series); solo and choral cantatas ed. by M. Seiffert in *Denkmäler deutscher Tonkunst* 3; 2 preludes and fugues for organ ed. by R. Buchmayer (1927); 4 organ preludes etc. in *Organum*. A complete ed. of Tunder's organ chorale arrangements was begun in 1958, edited by Rudolf Walter. *Collected Organ Works*, ed. by Klaus Beckmann (Wiesbaden, 1974). Two works by Tunder from the Pelplin manuscript in Poland were publ. in Vol. X, Part 2 of *Corpus of Early Keyboard Music*, under the auspices of the American Institute of Musicology (1967).

BIBLIOGRAPHY: W. Stahl, *F. T. und D. Buxtehude* (Leipzig, 1926) and "F. T.," *Archiv für Musikwissenschaft* 8; J. Hennings, "Tunderiana," *Lübeckische Blätter*, Jahrg. 75, Nr. 53 (1934).

Tupkov, Dimiter, Bulgarian composer; b. Sofia, July 12, 1929. He studied with Goleminov at the Bulgarian State Cons. in Sofia, graduating in 1956; then joined its faculty.

WORKS: Flute Concerto (1955); *The Story of Belassitsa Mountain*, overture (1956); 3 *Children's Sinfoniettas* (1961, 1968, 1975); *Concerto for Orch.* (1969); *Rhapsodic Divertimento* for orch. (1970); Harp Concerto (1971); *6 Bagatelles* for orch. (1972); *September Overture* (1974); *Peace Cantata* (1975); 2 string quartets (1956, 1958); choral songs; folk-song arrangements.

Turchaninov, Piotr, Russian composer of sacred music; b. Kiev, Nov. 20, 1779; d. St. Petersburg, March 16, 1856. He studied music with Sarti when the latter was at the St. Petersburg court; was ordained priest in 1803; taught singing at the imperial court chapel; from 1831 to 1841 was high priest at various churches. His masterly arrangements and harmonizations of old liturgical melodies of the Russian church were published in 5 vols., edited by Kastalsky (Moscow, 1906). His autobiography was published in St.Petersburg in 1863.

BIBLIOGRAPHY: A. Preobrazhensky, *The High Priest P. I. Turchaninov* (St. Petersburg, 1910); V. Lebedev, *P. I. Turchaninov* (Tambov, 1910).

Turchi, Guido, Italian composer; b. Rome, Nov. 10, 1916. He studied composition with Ildebrando Pizzetti, and in his early music followed Pizzetti's style of Italian Baroque, with Romantic and Impressionistic extensions; he then changed his idiom towards a more robust and accentuated type of music making, influenced mainly by a study of the works of Béla Bartók. Turchi's Concerto for string orch. is dedicated to Bartók's memory. From 1960 to 1967 he taught at the Cons. of Rome; in 1967 was appointed director of the Cons. of Parma.

WORKS: Trio for flute, clarinet, and viola (1945); *Invettiva* for small chorus and 2 pianos (1946); Concerto for string orch. (Venice, Sept. 8, 1948); *Piccolo concerto notturno* for orch. (1950); opera, *Il buon soldato Svaik* (Milan, April 6, 1962); *Tre Metamorfosi* for orch. (1970).

BIBLIOGRAPHY: F. d'Amico, "Guido Turchi," *Tempo* (Autumn 1951).

Tureck, Rosalyn, remarkable American pianist and player on the harpsichord and clavichord; b. Chicago, Dec. 14, 1914, in a musical family of Russian and Turkish background. She studied piano in Chicago with Sophia Brilliant-Liven (1925–29), Jan Chiapusso (1929–31), and Gavin Williamson (1931–32); then went to New York and took a course with Olga Samaroff at the Juilliard School of Music, graduating *cum laude* in 1935. She played her first piano recital in 1923, at the age of 9. She was soloist with the Philadelphia Orch. in 1935 playing the B-flat Concerto of Brahms; later appeared also with the N.Y. Philharmonic in Beethoven's "Emperor" Concerto. Her lifelong dedication to Bach came about in an extraordinary way. As she reports it in a newspaper interview, she was practicing the A minor fugue from Book I of the *Well-Tempered Clavier* on Wednesday, Dec. 9, 1931, a few days before her 17th birthday, when she suddenly lost consciousness. When she came to, she experienced a veritable epiphany and had an immediate and intuitive understanding of the inner meaning of Bach's music. On Nov. 8, 1937, she gave the first concert of a series of 6 all-Bach recitals in N.Y., an unprecedented venture. She repeated this series in Carnegie Hall, N.Y., 40 years later; in most of these concerts she allowed a dinner intermission for the audience. One of the most remarkable features on the program was her performance of Bach's *Goldberg Variations* on the piano and harpsichord at the same concert, making use of all repeats in the score. In 1947 she made her first European tour; subsequently played in South America, South Africa and Israel. In 1958 she performed two Bach concertos, conducting the N.Y. Philharmonic from the keyboard; she gave similar performances with other American orchestras, in London, and Madrid. In 1971 she made a world tour, which included India and the Far East. Her teaching engagements included the Philadelphia Cons. of Music (1935–42), Mannes School of Music in N.Y. (1940–43), Juilliard School of Music, N.Y. (1943–55), and Univ. of California, San Diego (1966–72). She holds the honorary degrees of Mus. D. from Roosevelt Univ. (1968) and Oxford Univ. (1977). She published *An Introduction to the Performance of Bach* (London, 1959–60, in 3 vols.), which appeared also in Japanese (1966) and Spanish (1972); edited for publication works by Bach, Paganini, Alessandro Scarlatti, etc. In 1966 she founded the International Bach Society, for the purpose of promoting the knowledge of Bach's music. Both as a performer and a scholar she enjoys a reputation in the field of Baroque music comparable only to that of Wanda Landowska. She has been described in the press as "High Priestess of Bach." However, her service to Bach is not limited to tradition; she has performed Bach on the electronic keyboard instrument, the Thereminovox, under the guidance of its Russian inventor Leon Theremin during his stay in N.Y. in 1932. In 1969 she played Bach on the Moog Synthesizer; in 1971 she extended the contemporary view of Bach to give an evening of "Bach and Rock." In order to demonstrate the universality of Bach's ornamentation, she has presented concerts of works by Bach in juxtaposition with Chinese and Indian music.

Turina, Joaquín, prominent Spanish composer; b. Seville, Dec. 9, 1882; d. Madrid, Jan. 14, 1949. He studied with local teachers; then entered the Madrid Cons. as a pupil of Tragó (piano). In 1905 he went to Paris, where he studied composition with Vincent d'Indy at the Schola Cantorum, and piano with Moszkowski. In Paris a meeting with Albéniz and Manuel de Falla proved a turning point in his career; he determined to write national Spanish music; returning to Madrid in 1913, he produced 2 symph. works in a characteristic Spanish style: *La Procesión del rocío* and *Sinfonía sevillana,* combining Romantic and Impressionist elements in an individual manner; the same effective combination is found in his chamber music of Spanish inspiration (*Escena andaluza, La Oración del torero,* etc.) and his piano music (*Sonata romántica, Mujeres españolas,* etc.); he also wrote operas and incidental music for the theater. In 1931 he was appointed prof. of music at the Cons. of Madrid.

WORKS: OPERAS: *Margot* (Madrid, Oct. 10, 1914) and *Jardín de oriente* (Madrid, March 6, 1923). INCIDENTAL MUSIC: *Navidad* (Madrid, 1916), *La Adúltera penitente* (Barcelona, 1917), *La Anunciación* (Madrid, 1924). ORCH. MUSIC *La Procesión del rocío,* symph. poem (Madrid, March 30, 1913), *Evangelio,* symph. poem (Madrid, April 8, 1915), 3 *Danzas fantásticas* (1920), *Sinfonía sevillana* (San Sebastian, Sept. 11, 1920), *Rítmos,* choreographic fantasy (Barcelona, Oct. 25, 1928), *Rapsodia sinfónica,* for piano and string orch. (Madrid, March 11, 1933). CHAMBER MUSIC: Piano Quintet (1907), String Quartet (1911), *Escena andaluza,* for viola, string quartet, and piano (1912), *La Oración del torero,* for string quartet (1925), 2 piano trios (1926; 1933), 2 violin sonatas (1929; 1934), Piano Quartet (1931), *Serenata* for string quartet (1935), *Círculo,* for violin, cello, and piano (1936), *Las nueve musas* (9 pieces for various instruments; 1945). PIANO MUSIC: *Sevilla,* suite pintoresca (1909), *Sonata romántica* (1909), *Coins de Séville,* suite (1911), *Tres danzas andaluzas* (1912), *Album de viaje* (1916), *Mujeres españolas* (2 sets, 1917, 1932), *Cuentos de España,* 2 sets of 7 pieces each (1918; 1928), *Niñerías,* 2 sets of children's pieces (1919; 1931), *Sanlúcar de Barrameda* (1922), *El Cristo de la Calavera* (1924), *Jardines de Andalucía,* suite (1924), *La Venta de los gatos* (1925), *El Barrio de Santa Cruz* (1925), *La Leyenda de la Giralda,* suite (1927), *Dos danzas sobre temas populares españoles* (1927), *Verbena madrileña,* 5 pieces (1927), *Mallorca,* suite (1928), *Evocaciones,* 3 pieces (1929), *Recuerdos de la antigua España,* 4 pieces (1929), *Viaje marítimo,* suite (1930), *Ciclo pianístico: Tocata y fuga, Partita, Pieza romántica, El Castillo de Almodóvar* (1930–31), *Miniaturas,* 8 pieces (1930), *Danzas gitanas,* 2 sets of 5 pieces each (1930; 1934), *Tarjetas postales* (1931), *Sonata fantasía* (1930), *Radio Madrid,* suite (1931), *Jardín de niños,* 8 pieces (1931), *El Circo,* 6 pieces (1932), *Silhuetas,* 5 pieces (1932), *En la zapateria,* 7 pieces (1933), *Fantasia italiana* (1933), *Trilogia: El poema infinito* (1933), *Ofrenda* (1934), *Hipócrates* (1934), *Rincones de Sanlúcar* (1933), *Bailete, suite de danzas del siglo XIX* (1933), *Preludios* (1933), *Fantasía sobre cinco notas* (1934), *Concierto sin orquesta* (1935), *En el cortijo,* 4 pieces (1936–40); *Prelude,* for organ (1914); *Musette,* for organ (1915). GUITAR MUSIC: *Se-*
villana (1923), *Fandanguillo* (1926), *Ráfaga* (1930), *Sonata* (1932), *Homenaje a Tárrega,* 2 pieces (1935). SONGS *Rima* (1911), *Poema en forma de canciones* (1918), 3 arias (1923), *Canto a Sevilla,* cycle (1927), *2 Canciones* (1927), *Corazón de mujer* (1927), *Tríptico* (1929), *3 Sonetos* (1930), *3 Poemas* (1933), *Homenaje a Lope de Vega* (1935). BOOK: *Enciclopedia abreviada de la música* (Madrid, 1917).

BIBLIOGRAPHY: C. Bosch, *Impresiones estéticas* (Madrid, 1918); H. Collet, *L'Essor de la musique espagnole au XXe siècle* (Paris, 1929); A. Salazar, *La Música contemporánea en España* (Madrid, 1930); F. Sopeña, *Joaquín Turina* (Madrid, 1943); W. Dean, "Joaquín Turina," *Chesterian* (April 1949).

Türk, Daniel Gottlob, German organist and teacher; b. Clausnitz, Saxony, Aug. 10, 1756; d. Halle, Aug. 26, 1813. He was a pupil in harmony and counterpoint of Homilius while studying at the Kreuzschule, Dresden; he had learned to play the violin at home and after he entered Leipzig Univ. J. A. Hiller continued his instruction, and engaged him as violinist at the theater and the "Grosses Concert." In 1776 he was cantor of the Ulrichskirche, Halle, and music teacher at the Gymnasium; 1779, music director of the Univ.; on becoming organist at the Liebfrauenkirche in 1787, he resigned his positions as cantor and teacher. He published an important clavier method (1789; 2nd ed., 1802) and instructive pieces for piano; 18 sonatas and sonatinas for piano; songs; theoretical works. An opera, church music, symphonies, organ pieces, are in manuscript. Some piano pieces for 4 hands were edited by Doflein (1933).

BIBLIOGRAPHY: H. Glenewinkel, *D. G. T.* (dissertation, Halle, 1909); G. E. Hedler, *D. G. T.* (dissertation, Leipzig, 1936); *Daniel Gottlob Türk,* Festschrift published on the 125th anniversary of his death (Halle, 1938).

Turle, James, English organist and composer; b. Somerton, Somerset, March 5, 1802; d. London, June 28, 1882. He was assistant organist to Greatorex at Westminster Abbey till 1831; then succeeded him as organist and master of the choristers, resigning in 1875. He conducted the "Antient Concerts," 1840–43; was music master at the School for the Indigent Blind 1829–56. He composed services, anthems, chants, and hymn tunes; edited several collections of church music (e.g., *The Westminster Abbey Chant Book,* with Dr. Bridge).

Turner, Alfred Dudley, American pianist and teacher; b. St. Albans, Maine, Aug. 24, 1854; d. there, May 7, 1888. He studied at the New England Cons. of Music and the Boston College of Music, and later taught at these schools. He composed 3 *Morceaux,* for piano and cello; *Suite* for piano and cello; *Sonate dramatique* for piano; 2 violin sonatas; sonatas; piano pieces.

Turner, Charles, American composer; b. Baltimore, Nov. 25, 1921. He studied composition with Samuel Barber; later took courses with Nadia Boulanger. He served as a naval officer during World War II; played concerts in Europe; in 1954 received a fellowship awarded by the Italian government, and took up residence in Rome. Among his works are the ballet *Pastorale* (N.Y., Jan. 14, 1957); *The Marriage of Orpheus* for orch. (1965); chamber music.

Turner, Godfrey, English composer; b. Manchester, March 27, 1913; d. (suicide) N.Y., Dec. 7, 1948. He studied with E. J. Dent at Cambridge Univ. (musicology) and with Nadia Boulanger in Paris. He came to the U.S. in 1936; taught at the San Francisco Cons. (1938–43); was music editor for Boosey & Hawkes, N.Y. (1944–46); then secretary of the American Music Center, N.Y. (1946–48).

WORKS: *Trinity Concerto,* for chamber orch.; Viola Concerto; *Sonata concertante,* for piano and string orch.; *Fanfare, Chorale and Finale* for brass; *Saraband and Tango; Gregorian Overture* (Columbus, Ohio, Dec. 2, 1947; winner of the Broadcast Music, Inc., Contest).

Turner, Robert Comrie, Canadian composer; b. Montreal, June 6, 1920. He studied with Champagne at McGill Univ. in Montreal, graduating in 1943; with Herbert Howells and Gordon Jacob at the Royal College of Music in London (1947–48), with Messiaen at the Berkshire Music Center in Tanglewood, Massachusetts (summer, 1949), and with Roy Harris at Nashville (1949–50); received his Mus. Doc. degree from McGill Univ. in 1953. From 1952 to 1967 he was a music producer for the Canadian Broadcasting Corporation in Vancouver; taught at the Univ. of British Columbia (1955–57) and at the Acadia Univ. in Wolfville, Nova Scotia (1968–69); in 1969 was appointed to the music faculty of the Univ. of Manitoba.

WORKS: opera *The Brideship* (Vancouver, Dec. 12, 1967); *Canzona* for orch. (1950); Concerto for chamber orch. (1950); *Sinfonia* for small orch. (1953); *Opening Night,* overture (1955); *Lyric Interlude* for orch. (1956); *A Children's Overture* (1958); *The Pemberton Valley,* suite for orch. from a film score (1958); Symphony for string orch. (Montreal, March 27, 1961); *3 Episodes* for orch. (Toronto, Feb. 27, 1966); 2-Piano Concerto (1971); *Eidolons,* 12 images for chamber orch. (Vancouver, Sept. 12, 1972); Chamber Concerto for bassoon and 17 instruments (1973); *Capriccio Concertante* for cello, piano, and orch. (1975); *From a Different Country (Homage to Gabrielli)* for solo brass quintet and chamber orch. (1976); 3 string quartets (1949, 1954, 1975); Oboe Sonatina (1956); *Robbins Round,* concertino for jazz band (1959); *Variations and Toccata* for wind and string quintets (1959); *Mobile* for chorus and 7 percussionists (1960); *Serenade* for wind quintet (1960); *4 Fragments* for brass quintet (1961); *Fantasia* for organ, brass quintet and timpani (1962); *The Phoenix and the Turtle* for mezzo-soprano and 8 instruments (Vancouver, Aug. 23, 1964); *Suite in Homage to Melville* for soprano, alto, and piano (1966); *Diversities* for violin, bassoon, and piano (1967); Piano Trio (1969); *Nostalgia* for saxophone and piano (1972); *Sonata Lyrica* for piano (1955, revised 1963); *Nocturne* for piano (1956; orchestrated 1965); *6 Voluntaries* for organ (1959).

Turner, Walter James, English poet and writer on music; b. Shanghai, China, Oct. 13, 1889; d. London,

Nov. 18, 1946. He studied with his father (organist of St. Paul's Cathedral, Melbourne, Australia), and privately in Dresden, Munich, and Vienna. He settled in London, where he became music critic for *The New Statesman.*

WRITINGS: *Music and Life* (1922); *Variations on the Theme of Music* (1924); *Orpheus, or the Music of the Future* (1926); *Beethoven: The Search for Reality* (1927; new ed., 1933); *Musical Meanderings* (1928); *Music: A Short History* (1932; 2nd ed., 1949); *Facing the Music* (1933); *Wagner* (1933); *Berlioz: The Man and His Work* (1934); *Music: An Introduction to Its Nature and Appreciation* (1936); *Mozart, the Man and his Work* (1938); *English Music* (1941); *English Ballet* (1944).

Turner, William, English composer; b. Oxford, 1651; d. London, Jan. 13, 1740. He was a chorister at Christ Church, Oxford, under E. Lowe, and later at the Chapel Royal under H. Cooke; in 1669 he was made a Gentleman of the Chapel Royal; received the degree of Mus. Doc. from Cambridge Univ. in 1696. He composed church music, anthems, songs, catches.

Turnhout, Gérard de (real name **Gheert Jacques**), Netherlands composer; b. Turnhout, c.1520; d. Madrid, Sept. 15, 1580. In 1545, he was choir singer at Antwerp Cathedral; was appointed Kapellmeister there in 1563; in 1572 Philip II of Spain called him to Madrid as maestro of the Royal Chapel. He published a book of motets *a* 4-5 (1568), a book of motets and chansons *a* 4-6 (1569), and a Mass in *Praestantissimorum divinae musices auctorum Missae X* (1570). His son **Jean de Turnhout** was Kapellmeister to the Archduke Alexander Farnese, governor of the Netherlands, at Brussels from 1586; from 1611, served as Kapellmeister of the Royal Chapel there. He published 2 books of madrigals and one of motets.

Turok, Paul, American composer; b. New York, Dec. 3, 1929. He studied composition at Queens College with Karol Rathaus (B.A., 1950); then at the Univ. of California, Berkeley, with Roger Sessions (M.A., 1951) and at the Juilliard School of Music with Bernard Wagenaar (1951-53). He subsequently held several teaching posts, among them at the City College of N.Y. (1959-63) and at Williams College (1963-64). As a composer, he follows the principle of stylistic freedom and technical precision, without doctrinaire adherence to any circumscribed modernistic modus operandi.

WORKS: *Richard III,* opera (1975); *Scene: Domestic,* chamber opera (Aspen, Aug. 2, 1973); *Youngest Brother,* ballet (N.Y., Jan. 23, 1953); for orch.: Violin Concerto (1953); *Symphony in Two Movements* (1955); *Lyric Variations* for oboe and strings (Louisville, Mar. 9, 1973); *Scott Joplin Overture* (Cleveland, June 19, 1973); *Sousa Overture* (Philadelphia, May 13, 1976); *Ragtime Caprice* for piano and orchestra (1976); chamber music: *Variations on a Theme by Schoenberg* for string quartet (1952); 3 string quartets (1956-70); String Trio (1974); Wind Quintet (1960); Brass Quintet (1971); Clarinet Trio (1974); sonatas for unaccompanied viola (1975); solo pieces for cello, oboe, bassoon, horn, trumpet trombone; music for 9 horns, music for 5 horns; a piece for violin and percussion; vocal works; 3 songs for soprano and flute; *Chorus of the Frogs; Transcendental Etudes,* and other works for piano.

Turpin, Edmund Hart, English organist and composer; b. Nottingham, May 4, 1835; d. London, Oct. 25, 1907. He was a pupil of Hullah and Pauer in London, where he settled in 1857; served as organist of various churches; published a collection for organ, *Student's Edition of Classical Authors;* wrote the oratorios *St. John the Baptist* and *Hezekiah;* hymn tunes; many works for organ. He was editor of *The Musical Standard* (from 1880) and for a time also of *The Musical World.*
BIBLIOGRAPHY: C. W. Pearce, *A Biographical Sketch of E. H. Turpin* (London, 1911).

Turski, Zbigniew, Polish composer; b. Konstancin, near Warsaw, July 28, 1908. He studied composition with Rytel at the State Cons. in Warsaw; was music director of the Polish Radio (1936–39); after World War II he conducted the Baltic Philharmonic in Gdańsk (1945–46); in 1957 established himself in Warsaw. He writes in an advanced harmonic idiom, influenced by French modernism. All of his early music manuscripts were lost during W.W. II.
WORKS: a micro-opera, *Causettes* (*Chats,* 1966; Warsaw, 1967); a ballet, *Medalion Gdański* (1964); *Sinfonia da camera* (1947); Symph. No. 2, *Sinfonia Olimpica,* (1948; awarded a prize by the music jury of the 14th Olympiad, London); 2 violin concertos (1951, 1959); Symph. No. 3 (1953); *Little Overture* (1955); 2 cantatas, *Ziemia* (1952) and *Vistula River* (1953); *L'Ombre (Shade),* nocturne for tenor, chorus, and percussion (1967); *Canti de Nativitate Patriae* for tenor, bass, chorus, and orch. (1969); *Regno Ejukori,* triptych for bass and orch. (Wroclaw, Sept. 2, 1974); String Quartet No. 2 (1951); miscellaneous piano pieces; songs; music for the theater, films, and radio.

Tusler, Robert Leon, American musicologist; b. Stoughton, Wisconsin, April 1, 1920; studied piano and organ at Friends' Univ., Wichita, Kansas (B.M., 1947); musicology at the Univ. of Calif., Los Angeles (M.A., 1952); then at the Univ. of Utrecht, Holland (1956–58). In 1958 he joined the music faculty of the Univ. of Calif., Los Angeles. He wrote the books *The Style of J. S. Bach's Chorale Preludes* (Berkeley, Calif., 1956); *The Organ Music of Jan Pieterszoon Sweelinck* (Bilthoven, 1958).

Tuthill, Burnet Corwin, American composer, conductor and pedagogue; b. New York, Nov. 16, 1888. He played clarinet in a school band; then enrolled in the music dept. of Columbia Univ. (M.A., 1910); conducted the Columbia Univ. orch. from 1909 to 1913; then led the People's Choral Union. In 1919 he founded the Society for the Publication of American Music, which continued to function for some 50 years, during which it published about 85 works by American composers. In 1922 he became General Manager of the Cincinnati Cons. of Music; in 1924 he expanded this post into the important National Association of Schools of Music to establish accreditation of music

schools in the U.S.; from its foundation to 1959 he was its Executive Secretary. In 1935 he received the degree of Mus. M. from the Cincinnati College of Music; from 1935 to 1959 he was Director of Music at Southwestern College in Memphis. He began to compose rather late in life but compensated for this by continuous productivity until he reached his 90th year of life. Since retiring, he has lived in Knoxville, Tenn.
WORKS: *Bethlehem,* pastorale for orch. (Interlochen, Michigan, July 22, 1934); *Laurentia,* symph. poem (Rochester, N.Y., Oct. 30, 1936); *Come Seven,* rhapsody for orch. (1935; St. Louis, Feb. 19, 1944); Symphony in C (1940); Clarinet Concerto (1949); Concerto for double bass and wind orch. (1962); *Trombone Trouble* for 3 trombones and orch., or band (1962); Concerto for tenor saxophone (1965); Concerto for tenor trombone (1967); Tuba Concerto (1975); many pieces for clarinet: 3 clarinet trios; *Fantasy Sonata* for clarinet and piano; Sonatina in a canon for flute and clarinet; Fugue for 4 clarinets; Clarinet Quintet; Duo for clarinet and bassoon; Rhapsody for clarinet and piano; Quintet for piano and 4 clarinets; *Rondo Concertante* for 2 clarinets and band; *Two Snacks for a Lonesome Clarinet;* Violin Sonata; Viola Sonata; *Nocturne* for flute and string quartet; Piano Trio; *When Johnnie Comes Marching Home,* variations for wind quintet and piano; Oboe Sonata; Trumpet Sonata; Flute Sonata; Quartet for 4 saxophones; Saxophone Sonata; organ pieces; sacred choruses; songs.

Tuukkanen, Kalervo, Finnish conductor and composer; b. Mikkeli, Oct. 14, 1909. He studied composition with Leevi Madetoja and theory with Krohn in Helsinki; subsequently conducted local orchestras and choirs: in 1967–69 was visiting professor of music at the Chinese Univ. of Hong Kong. He is the author of a monograph on his teacher, *Leevi Madetoja* (Helsinki, 1947). He has written 5 symphonies (1944, 1949, 1952, 1958, 1961); 2 violin concertos (1943, 1956); Cello Concerto (1946); *Sinfonietta* (1948); *Man and the Elements* for soprano, chorus, and orch. (1949); an opera, *Indumati,* (1962); *Youth Cantata* (1963).

Tuxen, Erik, German-Danish conductor; b. Mannheim (of Danish parents) July 4, 1902; d. Copenhagen, Aug. 28, 1957. In 1916 he moved to Denmark; studied architecture and music in Copenhagen; conducted the Danish State Radio Orch. (1936–41); made guest appearances in the U.S. (1950–51), presenting a concert of Scandinavian music at Carnegie Hall (April 2, 1951); in the summer of 1954 he conducted in South America.

Tveitt, Geirr, Norwegian composer and pianist; b. Hardanger, Oct. 19, 1908. He took piano lessons; then studied successively in Leipzig, Vienna and Paris, with Florent Schmitt and Honegger, among others; made concert tours of Europe as a pianist. Returning to Norway he became a recipient of the Norwegian State Salary of Art, a life pension given by the government to eminent artists. His music reflects folkways of his native region.
WORKS: 5 operas: *Nordvest—Sud—Nordaust—Nord* (1939); *Dragaredokko* (1940); *Roald Amundsen;*

Stevleik, chamber opera; *Jeppe* (1964; Bergen, June 10, 1966; revised 1968); 3 ballets: *Baldurs draumar* (*Dreams of Baldur*; Berlin, 1935), *Birgingu* (Oslo, 1939) and *Husguden* (*The Household Deity*; Bergen, 1956); 6 piano concertos: No. 1 (Germany, 1930); No. 2 (Vienna, 1933); No. 3, *Hommage à Brahms* (Bergen, 1947); No. 4, *Northern Lights* (Paris, 1947); No. 5 (Paris, 1954); No. 6 (1960); Concerto for string quartet and orch. (Oslo, 1933); Variations for 2 pianos and orch. (Oslo, 1937); *8 Dances* for orch. (Paris, 1939); Violin Concerto (Oslo, 1939); 2 harp concertos; 2 concertos for the hardanger fiddle (Bergen, 1956; Brussels, 1965; the only concertos written for this, the Norwegian national instrument); *100 Folk Tunes from Hardanger*, originally for piano, then arranged in 5 orch. suites; 4 symphonies: No. 1 (Bergen, 1958); *Skaldaspillirs kvad: Håkonarmdl* for soloists, chorus and orch. (Bergen, 1962); incidental music to the play *Jonsoknatt* for small orch. (Oslo, 1936); Quartet for 4 violins (Oslo, 1935); 2 string quartets; 3 string sextets (No. 3, Oslo, 1934); *8 Arabian Melodies* for flute, celesta and percussion (Oslo, 1962); fully 29 piano sonatas. He publ. *Tonalitätstheorie des parallelen Leittonsystems* (Oslo, 1937; traces the origin of church modes back to old Norwegian scale forms).

Twardowski, Romuald, Polish composer; b. Vilna, June 17, 1930. He studied composition and piano in Vilna (1952–57), and with Woytowicz at the State College of Music in Warsaw (1957–60); studied medieval polyphony with Nadia Boulanger in Paris (1963).

WORKS: 3 operas: *Cyrano de Bergerac* (1962; Bytom, 1963); a "morality," *Tragedyja albo rzecz o Janie i Herodzie* (*Tragedy, or Story of John and Herod*, 1965; Łódź, 1969) and *Lord Jim*, after Joseph Conrad (1972–73); a radio opera, *Upadek ojca Suryna* (*The Fall of Father Surin*, 1968; scenic version, Cracow, 1969); 2 ballets: *The Naked Prince* (1960; Warsaw, 1964) and *The Magician's Statues* (1963; Wroclaw, 1971); *3 Sketches* for strings (1955); Piano Concerto (1956); Concerto for Orch. (1957); *Suita w dawnym stylu* (*Suite in Old Style*) for orch. (1957); *Mala symfonia konzertujqca* (*Little Symphony Concertante*) for piano, strings, and percussion (1958); *Antifone* for 3 orch. groups (1961); *Nomopedia*, 5 movements for orch. (1962); *Ode 64* for orch. (1964); *The St. Mary Triptych*, 3 scenes and dances for string orch. (1973); *Prelude, Toccata and Chorale* for orch. (1973); *Study in A* for orch. (1974; Warsaw, Sept. 21, 1976); *2 Landscapes* for orch. (1975); a cantata, *Pieśń o Bialym Domu* (*Song about the White House*) for tenor, chorus, 2 pianos and percussion (1959); *Cantus antiqui* for soprano, harpsichord, piano, and percussion (1962); *Trittico fiorentino: I, Tre studi secondo Giotto* for chamber orch. (1966), *II, Sonetti di Petrarca* for tenor solo and 2 choruses a cappella (1965) and *III, Impressioni fiorentini* for 4 instrumental choruses (1967); *Mala liturgia prawoslawna* (*Little Orthodox Liturgy*) for vocal ensemble and 3 instrumental groups (1969); *Oda do mlodości* (*Ode to Youth*) for narrator, chorus, and orch. (1969); *3 sonnets d'adieux* for bass-baritone, piano, strings, and percussion (1971); *Polish Landscape*, 3 songs for bass-baritone and orch. (1975); *Little Sonata* for piano (1958); *Toc-* cata for 2 pianos (1974); *Improvisations and Toccata* for 2 pianos (1974).

Tweedy, Donald, American composer; b. Danbury, Conn., April 23, 1890; d. there, July 21, 1948. He was educated at Harvard Univ. (B.A., 1912; M.A., 1917), where his teachers were Walter Spalding and E. B. Hill. He taught at Vassar College (1914–16), the Eastman School of Music (1923–27), Hamilton College (1937–38), and Texas Christian Univ. (1945–46). He published a *Manual of Harmonic Technic Based on the Practice of J. S. Bach* (1928).

WORKS: ballet, *Alice in Wonderland* (1935); *L'Allegro*, symph. study (Rochester, May 1, 1925); *3 Dances* for orch. (1925); *Williamsburg*, suite for orch. (1941); Viola Sonata (1916); Violin Sonata (1920); Cello Sonata (1930); piano pieces.

Tye, Christopher, English organist and composer; b. c.1500; d. c.1572. In 1537 he received his Mus. B. from Cambridge; on Sept. 10, 1541, he was appointed organist of Ely Cathedral (resigned in 1561); Mus. Doc. at Cambridge in 1545; was ordained a priest in 1560 at Doddington. He described himself as a gentleman of the King's Chapel on the title page of his only published work, *The Actes of the Apostles, translated into Englyshe metre to synge and also to play upon the Lute* (London, 1553; it includes the first 14 chapters of Acts). The hymn tunes *Windsor* and *Winchester Old* are adaptations from this collection. Tye was an important composer of English church music; he left Masses, services, motets, and anthems. The *Euge Bone Mass* was ed. by Arkwright in *The Old English Edition* (no. 10); other examples are found in *The Oxford History of Music* (vol. II) and in Walker's *History of Music in England*.

BIBLIOGRAPHY: G. Reese, *Music in the Renaissance* (N.Y., 1954).

Tyes, John, English organist and composer who flourished early in the 15th century. A Gloria for 2 voices and one instrument and a Sanctus for 4 voices are among the works included in the *Old Hall Manuscript*.

Tyndall, John, eminent physicist and acoustician; b. Leighlin Bridge, Ireland, Aug. 2, 1820; d. Hindhead, Surrey, England, Dec. 4, 1893. His 2 works in the domain of acoustics are *Sound* (1867, and many subsequent eds.), a lucid and scholarly explanation of acoustical phenomena, and *On the Transmission of Sound by the Atmosphere* (1874). He was prof. of natural philosophy at the Royal Institute from 1853.

BIBLIOGRAPHY: *Dictionary of National Biography* (vol. 19, pp. 1358–63).

Typp, W., English singer and composer who was active in the early decades of the 15th century. An Agnus Dei, 2 Credos, and 4 Sanctus settings by him are found among the *Old Hall Manuscripts*.

Tyrwhitt, Gerald. See **Berners, Lord.**

Tzarth (Czarth, Zarth), Georg, Bohemian violinist; b. April 8, 1708; d. probably in Mannheim, 1778. He was a friend of Franz Benda, whom he accompanied to Warsaw; in 1734 he entered the chapel of Crown Prince Frederick at Rheinsberg; in 1758 joined the court orch. at Mannheim. He wrote symphonies, concertos, string trios, violin sonatas, etc. in the "Mannheim School" style; examples of his works, edited by Riemann, are in the *Denkmäler der Tonkunst in Bayern* 27/28 (15/16).

Tzvetanov, Tzvetan, Bulgarian composer; b. Sofia, Nov. 6, 1931. He studied composition with Khadjiev and Vladigerov at the Bulgarian State Cons. in Sofia, graduating in 1956; then joined its faculty. His works include Sinfonietta (1956); a ballet, *Orpheus and Rhodopa* (1960); *The Great Beginning,* symph. poem (1962); 4 symphonies: No. 1 (1964); No. 2 for strings, piano, harp, xylophone, vibraphone, kettledrums, and triangle (1968); No. 3, *1923* (1972; Sofia, Feb. 27, 1973); No. 4 (1975); *The Ladder,* ballad for solo alto, male chorus, and orch. (1965); Concertino for piano and chamber orch. (1971); *Festive Concerto* (1974); Violin Sonata (1954); *Variations* for string quartet.

Tzybin, Vladimir, Russian flutist and composer; b. Ivanovo-Voznesensk, 1877; d. Moscow, May 31, 1949. He played flute in the orch. of the Bolshoi Theater in Moscow from 1896 to 1907 and from 1921 to 1929. From 1907 to 1920 he was first flutist at the Imperial Opera of St. Petersburg. He composed 2 operas: *Flengo* (1918) and *Tale of the Dead Princess and Seven Heroes* (1947); publ. several collections of flute pieces. He was esteemed as a pedagogue.

U

Uber, Christian Friedrich Hermann, German composer; b. Breslau, April 22, 1781; d. Dresden, March 2, 1822. He was a law student at Halle, but also studied music under Türk, and became chamber musician to Prince Louis Ferdinand of Prussia. After holding various positions as violinist and conductor, he settled in Dresden. He wrote the operas *Der falsche Werber* (Kassel, 1808) and *Der frohe Tag* (Mainz, 1815); incidental music to various plays; some violin works; songs to texts in German and French.

Uberti (Hubert), Antonio, male soprano; b. (of German parents) Verona, 1697; d. Berlin, Jan. 20, 1783. He was one of the most brilliant pupils of Porpora, and was known as "il Porporino" (little Porpora). In 1741 he entered the service of Frederick the Great in Berlin. He was greatly renowned in Germany for his singing of Italian operas.

Uccellini, Marco, Italian composer; b. Folimpopoli, c.1603; d. there Sept. 10, 1680. He was maestro di cappella at the ducal court of Modena from 1645, and at the Modena Cathedral from 1654. From 1639 to 1667 he publ. a variety of chamber music (sonatas, arias, canzonas, etc.); his advanced violin technique calls for use of the 6th position. He also wrote an opera, *Li Eventi di Filandro ed Edessa,* which was presented in Parma in 1675 (the music is not extant); 2 ballet pieces: *Le Navi d'Enea* (1673) and *Il Giove d'Elide fulminato* (1677). Riemann publ. a sonata by Uccellini in *Alte Kammermusik;* some pieces were publ. by Wasielewski; others by Torchi in *L'Arte Musicale in Italia* (vol. VII).

Udbye, Martin Andreas, Norwegian composer; b. Trondheim, June 18, 1820; d. there, Jan. 10, 1889. He studied in Leipzig with Hauptmann; returning to Trondheim, he was organist at various churches. He wrote 2 operettas, *Hjemve* (Oslo, April 8, 1864) and *Junkeren og Flubergrosen* (Oslo, Jan. 7, 1870); several cantatas; 3 string quartets; military marches; organ pieces; piano works; songs.

d'Udine, Jean (real name **Albert Cozanet**), French writer on music; b. Landivisiau, Finistère, July 1, 1870; d. Paris, May 9, 1938. He was a practicing lawyer, but also wrote music criticism. In 1909 he founded in Paris the École Française de Gymnastique Rythmique for teaching the methods of Jaques-Dalcroze.
WRITINGS: *La Corrélation des sons et des couleurs en art* (1897); *Lettres paradoxales sur la musique* (Paris, 1900); *L'Orchestration des couleurs* (1903); *Paraphrases musicales* (Paris, 1904); *Gluck* (1906); *L'Art et le geste* (1912); *Les Transmutations rythmiques* (1921); *Qu'est-ce que la musique?* (1925); *Traité de géométrie rythmique* (1926). Also wrote songs: *Les Chants de la jungle* (1905), *Rondels pour après* (1924), etc.

Ugalde, Delphine (née **Beaucé**), French soprano; b. Paris, Dec. 3, 1829; d. there, July 19, 1910. She received her first instruction in singing from her mother, an actress; subsequently studied with Moreau-Sainti; made her debut in Paris in 1848 as Angèle in Auber's *Domino noir;* in 1866 assumed the management of the Bouffes-Parisiens, taking leading roles in Offenbach's operettas; in 1867 she appeared in her own operetta, *La Halte au moulin.* She retired in 1871, and settled down as a successful vocal teacher.

Ugarte, Floro M., Argentine composer; b. Buenos Aires, Sept. 15, 1884; d. there, June 11, 1975. He studied in Buenos Aires, and at the Paris Cons. under Fourdrain, with whom he collaborated in writing the ballet *Sigolene.* He returned to Argentina in 1913; in 1924 became prof. of the National Cons. there; was also for several years musical director of the Teatro Colón; in that capacity he visited N.Y. in 1940, to engage singers.
WORKS: operatic fairy tale, *Saika* (Buenos Aires, July 21, 1920); *Entre las montañas,* symph. suite (conducted in Buenos Aires by Richard Strauss in 1923 during his guest appearances there); *La Rebelión del agua,* symph. poem (Buenos Aires, Oct. 16, 1935); *De mi tierra,* symph. suite (1927); *Piri,* choreographic poem (1944); Symph. in A (1946; Buenos Aires, May 13, 1952); *Tango,* for orch. (Buenos Aires, Sept. 5, 1951); Violin Concerto (1963); chamber music; songs; piano pieces.

Ugolini, Vincenzo, Italian composer; b. Perugia, c.1570; d. Rome, May 6, 1638. Pupil of B. Nanini in Rome, where from 1592 to 1603 he was choirmaster at the Church of S. Maria Maggiore; from 1609 to 1615, at the Cathedral of Benevento; then returned to Rome, and in 1616 became choirmaster of S. Luigi dei Francesi; in 1620 he succeeded Suriano as maestro of the Cappella Giulia of St. Peter's (until 1626); in 1631 he resumed his former post at S. Luigi dei Francesi, retaining it till death. He was the teacher of Benevoli. A notable representative of Palestrina's school, he publ. 4 books of motets for 1, 2, 3, and 4 voices with continuo (1616–19); 2 books of Psalms for 8 voices (1620); 2 books of Masses and motets for 8 and 12 voices (1623); 1 book of songs and motets *a* 12 (1624); 2 books of madrigals *a* 5 (1615).

Ugolino de Orvieto, Italian musical theorist; b. Forli, c.1380; d. Ferrara, c.1457. He was archpriest at the Cathedral of Ferrara from about 1440; his treatise, *De musica mensurata* (MS) is in the Biblioteca Casanatense in Rome. Publication of his *Declaratio Musicae Disciplinae* was undertaken by A. Seay in the *Corpus Scriptorum Musicae* (Rome, American Institute of Musicology), the first vol. appearing in 1959.
BIBLIOGRAPHY: U. Kornmüller, "Die Musiklehre des Ugolino de Orvieto," *Kirchenmusikalisches Jahrbuch* (1895).

Uhl, Alfred, Austrian composer; b. Vienna, June 5, 1909. He was a pupil of Franz Schmidt; was in the Austrian Army (1940–43), and was severely wounded. In 1945 he was appointed teacher of composition at the Vienna Academy of Music. His music is patterned after Classical forms, with particular emphasis on contrapuntal clarity.

WORKS: *Kleines Konzert* for viola, clarinet, and piano (1936; version for piano trio, 1972); *Eine vergnügliche Musik* for 8 wind instruments (1943); *4 Capriccios* for orch. (1944); *Konzertante Sinfonie* for clarinet and orch. (1944); String Quartet (1945–46); *Sonata graziosa* for orch. (1947); Concertino for violin and 22 wind instruments (1950); *Gilgamesch*, oratorio (1954–56; revised, 1968–69); *Wer einsam ist der hat es gut*, cantata (1960); *Jubiläumsquartett* for strings (1961); opera, *Der mysteriöse Herr X* (1962–65; Vienna, 1966); *Concerto a ballo* for orch. (1967); *Festlicher Auftakt* for chorus, organ, and orch. (1970).

Uhlig, Theodor, German violinist and writer on music; b. Wurzen, near Leipzig, Feb. 15, 1822; d. Dresden, Jan. 3, 1853. He studied violin with Schneider in Dessau, and in 1841 became a violinist in the Dresden Orch. He was one of the most devoted friends and admirers of Wagner; made the vocal score of *Lohengrin;* Wagner's letters to him were publ. in 1888 (English transl., 1890). His death at the age of 30 was lamented. Of his 84 works (symphonies, chamber music, theater pieces, etc.) only a violin concerto and some piano pieces and songs were published. His articles are of some importance; they were publ. as *Musikalische Schriften* by L. Frankenstein (Regensburg, 1913).

BIBLIOGRAPHY: M. Ahrend, *Theodor Uhlig, der früh verstorbene Wagnerianer* (Bayreuth, 1904).

Ujj, Béla, Hungarian composer of operettas; b. Vienna, July 2, 1873; d. there, Feb. 1, 1942. He lost his sight in childhood, but studied music and composed a number of successful operettas which were produced in Vienna. They include the following: *Der Herr Professor* (Dec. 4, 1903); *Kaisermanöver* (March 4, 1905); *Die kleine Prinzessin* (May 5, 1907); *Drei Stunden Leben* (Nov. 1, 1909); *Chanteclee* (Oct. 25, 1910); *Der Türmer von St. Stephan* (Sept. 13, 1912); *Teresita* (June 27, 1914); *Der Müller und sein Kind* (Oct. 30, 1917).

Ulbrich, Maximilian, Austrian composer; b. Vienna, c.1752; d. there, Sept. 14, 1814. He studied with Wagenseil; was a government clerk and pursued music as an avocation. His Singspiel *Der blaue Schmetterling* was produced in Vienna on April 2, 1782; he also wrote an oratorio; several symphonies; church music.

Ulfrstad, Marius Moaritz, Norwegian composer; b. Borgund, Sept. 11, 1890; d. Oslo, Oct. 29, 1968. He played organ as a youth; graduated in organ and music theory from the Cons. in Oslo (1910); then studied in Berlin with Humperdinck and others, and with Pizzetti in Florence; also had some informal sessions with Ravel in Paris. Returning to Oslo, he founded his own music school there (1921); was music critic of the *Morgenposten* (1922–40).

WORKS: cantatas, *Arnljot Gjelline* (Oslo, 1932), *Eternal Spring* (Oslo, 1932), *Saint Olav* (Oslo, 1933), *The Spark* (Trondheim, 1935); 5 symphonies (1921–44); 2 violin concertos (1923, 1935); Piano Concerto (1935); several suites for orch., most of them inspired by geography of Norway, Iceland, and Greenland (*Stavern og Sörlands, Islandia, Arctic, Norvegia, Grönlandia, Svalbardia, Möre og Romsdal, Oslo, Norwegian Middleage,* etc.); some chamber music; incidental music; about 250 choral pieces; nearly 1,000 songs, including arrangements of folksongs.

Ullmann, Viktor, Austrian composer; b. Teschen, Jan. 1, 1898; d. in Auschwitz in all probability, Oct. 1944. He studied composition with Schoenberg; then went to Prague. He wrote music in the Expressionistic manner, without renouncing latent tonality. His works include the operas *Peer Gynt* and *Der Sturz des Antichrist.* As an homage to Schoenberg, he wrote an orchestral work, *5 Variations and Double Fugue* based on the themes of a Schoenberg *Klavierstück.* After the seizure of Czechoslovakia by the Nazis, he was sent to the concentration camp in Theresienstadt; there he composed a one-act opera *Der Kaiser von Atlantis,* depicting a tyrannical monarch who outlaws death, but later begs for its return to relieve humanity from the horrors of life. The manuscript was preserved, and the work was performed for the first time in Amsterdam on Dec. 16, 1975.

Ulrich, Homer, American musicologist; b. Chicago, March 27, 1906. He studied bassoon and cello at the Chicago Musical College, and played these instruments in various orchestras; was bassoonist with the Chicago Symph. Orch. (1929–35); received his M.A. at the Univ. of Chicago with the thesis *The Penitential Psalms of Lasso* (1939). He was head of the music dept. of Monticello College (1935–38); then taught at the Univ. of Texas (associate prof., 1939; prof., 1951); also played bassoon with the San Antonio Symph. In 1953 he was appointed head of the music dept. of the Univ. of Maryland; retired in 1972. He published *Chamber Music* (a valuable survey; N.Y., 1948); *Education of a Concert-Goer* (N.Y., 1949); *Symphonic Music* (N.Y., 1952); *Famous Women Singers* (N.Y., 1953); *Music; A Design for Listening* (N.Y., 1957); *A History of Music and Musical Style* (with Paul Pisk; N.Y., 1963); *A Survey of Choral Music* (N.Y. 1973).

Ulrich, Hugo, German composer; b. Oppeln, Silesia, Nov. 26, 1827; d. Berlin, May 23, 1872. After studying in Breslau, he went to Berlin in 1846 and took lessons from Dehn. For a few years he taught at the Stern Cons. (1859–63); otherwise earned his living by working for publishers. He wrote 3 symphonies, of which the 2nd, entitled *Symphonie triomphale,* won a prize of 1500 francs offered by the Brussels Academy in 1853. Other works include a piano trio, a cello sonata, a string quartet, piano pieces, and songs. He made excellent arrangements of Beethoven's symphonies for piano, 4 hands.

Ulybyshev, Alexander. See **Oulibishev, Alexander.**

Umlauf, Ignaz, Austrian composer; b. Vienna, 1746; d. Meidling. June 8, 1796. In 1772 he became violinist in the court theater, and in 1778, conductor of the German Opera in Vienna; in 1789 was appointed subconductor (under Salieri) of the Imperial Chapel in

Vienna. He was a highly popular composer of Singspiele; inaugurated the season of the German Singspiele at the Burg Theater (Feb. 17, 1778) with his piece *Bergknappen;* there followed a number of others: *Die Apotheke* (June 20, 1778); *Die pucefarbenen Schuhe, oder Die schöne Schusterin* (June 22, 1779); *Das Irrlicht, oder Endlich fand er sie* (Jan. 17, 1782); *Der Oberamtmann und die Soldaten* (1782); *Der Ring der Liebe* (Dec. 3, 1786). *Zu Steffan sprach im Traume,* an aria from *Das Irrlicht,* enjoyed great popularity; Eberl wrote a set of variations on it, which was misattributed to Mozart. The score of Umlauf's 1st Singspiel, *Die Bergknappen,* was edited by R. Haas in the *Denkmäler der Tonkunst in Österreich* 36 (18.i).

Umlauf, Michael, Austrian violinist and composer, son of **Ignaz Umlauf;** b. Vienna, Aug. 9, 1781; d. Baden, near Vienna, June 20, 1842. He played the violin at the Vienna Opera; conducted at court theaters; wrote piano music; brought out a Singspiel, *Der Grenadier* (Vienna, July 8, 1812). He assisted Beethoven in conducting the 9th Symphony and other works (actually led the performances, with Beethoven indicating the initial tempos).

Unger (Ungher), Caroline, famous Hungarian contralto; b. Stuhlweissenburg, Oct. 28, 1803; d. at her villa near Florence, March 23, 1877. She studied voice in Milan with D. Ronconi, and in Vienna with Aloysia Lange (Mozart's sister-in-law) and with Johann Michael Vogl. Beethoven chose her to sing the contralto parts in the first performances of his *Missa Solemnis* and 9th Symph. (May 7, 1824); long afterwards she recounted that she turned Beethoven's head around that he might see the applause, which he could no longer hear. She went to Italy, where she changed the spelling of her name to Ungher, to secure proper pronunciation in Italian. Several Italian composers (Donizetti, Bellini, Mercadante) wrote operas especially for her. In 1833 she appeared in Paris. In 1839 she was engaged to be married to the poet Lenau, but the engagement soon was broken; in 1841 she married the French writer François Sabatier (1818–91) and retired from the stage. She publ. an album of 46 songs, under the title *Lieder, Mélodies et Stornelli.*
BIBLIOGRAPHY: O. Hartwig, "Fr. Sabatier und Karoline Sabatier-Unger," *Deutsche Rundschau* (May 1897); F. Margit Polgár, *Unger-Sabatier* (Budapest, 1941).

Unger, Georg, German tenor; b. Leipzig, March 6, 1837; d. there, Feb. 2, 1887. He was originally a student of theology; made his operatic debut in Leipzig at the age of 30. Hans Richter heard him in Mannheim and recommended him to Wagner for the role of Siegfried. He studied the part with Hey, and his interpretation of it made him famous.

Unger, Heinz, German-Canadian conductor; b. Berlin, Dec. 14, 1895; d. Toronto, Feb. 25, 1965. He studied in Berlin and Munich; was active as a choral conductor in Berlin until the advent of the Nazi regime in 1933. He then went to Russia; was conductor of the Leningrad Radio Orch. (1934–36). After a sojourn in England, he settled in Canada in 1948 and acquired a great renown as conductor of the Toronto Symph. Orch. He publ. an account of his conducting experiences in Russia under the title *Hammer, Sickle and Baton* (London, 1939).

Unger, Hermann, German composer and writer on music; b. Kamenz, Oct. 26, 1886; d. Cologne, Dec. 31, 1958. He studied philology in Leipzig and Munich; received his Dr. phil. in 1910 with a dissertation on Greek poetry; then took a course in musicology in Munich with Edgar Istel and Joseph Haas; subsequently went to Meiningen, where he took lessons with Max Reger (1910–13). He served in the German Army in World War I; then was lecturer at the Cons. of Cologne (1919–25) and at the Cologne Hochschule für Musik (1925–46).
WORKS: operas: *Der Zauberhandschuh* (1927) and *Richmodis von Aducht* (1928); a Christmas fairy tale, *Die Geschichten vom Weihnachtsbaum* (1943); 2 symphonies; several symph. poems; much chamber music; choral works; song cycles; piano suites.
WRITINGS: *Musikalisches Laienbrevier* (Munich, 1921); *Max Reger* (Munich, 1921); *Musiktheoretische Laienfibel* (Stuttgart, 1922); *Musikgeschichte in Selbstzeugnissen* (Munich, 1928); *Musikanten gestern und heute* (Siegen, 1935); *Anton Bruckner und seine 7. Sinfonie* (Bonn, 1944); *Harmonielehre* (Frankfurt, 1946); *Die musikalische Widmung* (Munich, 1958).

Unger, Max, German musicologist; b. Taura, May 28, 1883; d. Zürich, Dec. 1, 1959. He studied at the Leipzig Cons., and also attended Riemann's lectures at the Univ. of Leipzig; obtained his Dr. phil. in 1911 with the dissertation *Muzio Clementis Leben* (publ. Langensalza, 1914). He was active as a music critic, but was compelled to leave Germany in 1933 after the advent of the Nazi regime; lived mostly in Zürich. He devoted his research mainly to Beethoven; published about 150 papers dealing with various aspects of Beethoven's life and works; of these the most important are *Auf Spuren von Beethovens unsterblicher Geliebten* (Langensalza, 1911), *Ludwig van Beethoven und seine Verleger S. A. Steiner und Tobias Haslinger in Wien, A. M. Schlesinger in Berlin* (Berlin, 1921), *Beethovens Handschrift* (Bonn, 1926), *Ein Faustopernplan Beethovens und Goethes* (Regensburg, 1952); edited the catalogue of the Bodmer Beethoven collection in Zürich, under the title *Eine schweizer Beethovensammlung: Katalog* (Zurich, 1939).

Uninsky, Alexander, Russian-American pianist; b. Kiev, Feb. 2, 1910; d. Dallas, Texas, Dec. 19, 1972. He studied at the Kiev Cons.; in 1932 he won the first prize at the International Chopin Contest in Warsaw; after a concert tour in Europe, he went to the U.S. in 1943, and gave recitals; he excelled as a performer of Chopin's music. In 1955 he was appointed prof. of piano at the Cons. of Toronto, Canada; then held a similar position at the Southern Methodist Univ. in Dallas.

Untersteiner, Alfredo, Italian musicologist; b. Rovereto, April 28, 1859; d. Merano, Jan., 1918. He studied with Pembaur in Innsbruck; lived in Merano; was interned there as an enemy alien by the Austrians during World War I, and died in a concentration camp. He publ. *Storia della musica* (2 vols.; 1900; many reprints; in English as *A Short History of Music*, N.Y., 1902) and *Storia del violino, dei violinisti e della musica per violino* (1904).

Upton, George Putnam, American writer on music; b. Boston, Oct. 25, 1834; d. Chicago, May 19, 1919. He studied at Brown Univ., graduating in 1854; then went to Chicago, where he joined the editorial staff of the *Chicago Tribune* and wrote music criticism. He published a number of worthwhile books of reference of which *The Standard Operas* was the most successful. WRITINGS: *Letters of Peregrine Pickle* (1870); *Woman in Music* (1880); *The Standard Operas* (1886; new ed., 1928; enlarged by Felix Borowski, 1936; reprint, 1947); *The Standard Oratorios* (1887; 12th ed., 1909); *The Standard Cantatas* (1888; 7th ed., 1899); *The Standard Symphonies* (1889); *Musical Pastels* (1902); *The Standard Light Operas* (1902); edited autobiography of Theodore Thomas (1905); *E. Reményi. Musician, Littérateur and Man* (with G. D. Kelley; 1906); *Musical Memories, The Standard Concert Guide* (1908; new eds., 1930, 1947); *Standard Concert Repertory* (1909); *Standard Musical Biographies* (1910); *The Song* (1915); *In Music's Land* (1920).

Upton, William Treat, American musicologist; b. Tallmadge, Ohio, Dec. 17, 1870; d. Adelphi, Maryland, Jan. 19, 1961. He was educated at Oberlin College and Cons. of Music; later studied piano with Leschetizky in Vienna (1896–98) and Joseph Lhèvinne in Berlin (1913–14). From 1898 he taught piano at Oberlin Cons.; also was church organist in Cleveland (until 1918). WRITINGS: *Art-Song in America* (Boston, 1930; supplement, 1938); *Anthony Philip Heinrich: A 19th-Century Composer in America* (N.Y., 1939); *William Henry Fry, American Journalist and Composer-Critic* (N.Y., 1954); a new edition of O. G. Sonneck's *Bibliography of Early Secular American Music* (Washington, 1945), greatly augmented.

Urbach, Otto, German pianist and composer; b. Eisenach, Feb. 6, 1871; d. Dresden, Dec. 14, 1927. He studied with Iwan Knorr and Humperdinck in Frankfurt, with Draeseke in Dresden, and with Klindworth in Berlin. In 1898 he was appointed prof. of piano at the Dresden Cons. He wrote an opera, *Der Müller von Sans-Souci* (Frankfurt, 1896); an overture, *Bergfahrt;* String Quartet; Septet for wind instruments; piano pieces; many songs.

Urban, Friedrich Julius, German singing teacher and composer; brother of **Heinrich Urban;** b. Berlin, Dec. 23, 1838; d. there, July 17, 1918. He studied with Ries (violin) and Elsler (singing); was a successful singing teacher in Berlin; publ. a manual, *Die Kunst des Gesangs,* and some songs and choruses.

Urban, Heinrich, noted German music pedagogue; brother of **Friedrich Julius Urban;** b. Berlin, Aug. 27, 1837; d. there, Nov. 24, 1901. He studied with Ries (violin) Laub, and others in Berlin; was a professional violinist; wrote much symphonic and chamber music;

in 1881 he became prof. at Kullak's Academy in Berlin; acquired fame as a theory teacher; among his pupils was Paderewski. His works include a concert overture, *Scheherazade;* a symph., *Frühling;* a violin concerto; many violin pieces; songs.

Urbánek, Mojmir, Czech music publisher; b. Prague, May 6, 1873; d. there, Sept. 29, 1919. He was a son of the music publisher **Franz Urbánek** (1842–1919); left his father's firm and founded his own business in 1901, developing it into the largest of its kind in Czechoslovakia; included a music shop, printing plant, concert agency, and concert hall ("Mozarteum"); published works by Suk, Novák, Foerster, and other Czechoslovak composers, and the musical monthly *Dalibor.*

Urbanner, Erich, Austrian composer; b. Innsbruck, March 26, 1936. He studied composition with Karl Schiske and Hanns Jelinek at the Vienna Academy of Music (1955–61); then engaged in teaching score reading and composition. WORKS: *Intrada* for orch. (1957); Piano Concerto (1958); Symphony (1963); *Serenade* for string orch. (1964); *Dialogue* for piano and orch. (1965); *Theme, 19 Variations and Night Piece* for orch. (1968); *Kontraste* for orch. (1970); Violin Concerto (1971); Concerto *"Wolfgang Amadeus"* for 2 orch., 3 trombones, and celeste (1972; Salzburg, Jan. 1, 1973); Double Bass Concerto (1973); 3 string quartets (1956, 1957, 1972); *8 Pieces* for flute and piano (1957); *8 Aphorisms* for flute, clarinet and bassoon (1966); *Improvisation III* for chamber ensemble, and *IV* for wind quintet (both 1969); *Solo* for violin (1971); *Lyrica* for chamber ensemble (1971); *Kammermusik* for flute, oboe, bassoon, violin, cello, and harpsichord (1972); 2 piano sonatinas (1956, 1957); *Improvisation II* for 2 pianos (1966).

Urfey, Thomas d' (known as **Tom Durfey**), English playwright and poet; b. Exeter, 1653; d. London, Feb. 26, 1723. He produced about 30 plays, the songs in some of which were set to music by Purcell (e.g., *The Comical History of Don Quixote,* in 3 parts, 1694–96). He ingratiated himself into the intimate circle of Charles II by his talent for singing his poems, adapted to popular airs of his time. Between 1683 and 1710 he publ. several collections of airs with music, and in 1719 he ed. *Songs Compleat, Pleasant and Divertive* (5 vols., his own songs assembled in vols. 1 and 2); this was reissued the same year under the better-known title, *Wit and Mirth: or Pills to Purge Melancholy* (a 6th vol. was added in 1720), and the whole was reprinted and edited by C. L. Day (N.Y., 1959). BIBLIOGRAPHY: C. L. Day, *The Songs of Thomas D'Urfey* (Cambridge, Mass., 1933).

Urhan, Chrétien, French violinist, b. Montjoie, near Aix-la-Chapelle, Feb. 16, 1790; d. Paris, Nov. 2, 1845. He was a pupil of Le Sueur in composition; revived the viole d'amour, playing in Baillot's Quartet; from 1816 he was violinist (later soloist) in the Opéra orch. In the Cons. Concerts he employed a 5-stringed violin (*violon-alto,* with the tuning c-g-d^1-a^1-e^2), producing charming effects. He composed some chamber music.

BIBLIOGRAPHY: P. D. Förster, *Chrétien Urhan* (Raigern, 1907); P. Garnault, "Chrétien Urhan," *Revue de Musicologie* (1930).

Uriarte, Father Eustaquio de, Spanish musicologist; b. Durango, Nov. 2, 1863; d. Motrico, Sept. 17, 1900. In 1878 he entered the Augustinian Order at Valladolid and in 1888 went to the monastery of Silos, near Burgos, devoting himself to the study and restoration of Gregorian chant; was a promoter of the Asociación Isidoriana, for the reform of religious music in Spain. His fundamental work was the *Tratado teórico-prático de canto gregoriano, según la verdadera tradición* (Madrid, 1891). His shorter studies were publ., with a biographical sketch, by L. Villalba: *Estética y crítica musical del padre Uriarte* (Barcelona, 1904).

Uribe-Holguín, Guillermo, foremost composer of Colombia; b. Bogotá, March 17, 1880; d. there, June 26, 1971. He studied violin with Narciso Garay; in 1907 went to Paris, where he studied with Vincent d'Indy at the Schola Cantorum; then took violin lessons with César Thomson and Émile Chaumont in Brussels. He returned to Colombia in 1910 and became director of the newly reorganized National Cons. in Bogotá; resigned in 1935 and devoted his time to the family coffee plantation; however, he continued to compose and conduct. In 1910 he married the pianist **Lucía Gutiérrez.** His music bears the imprint of the modern French style, but his thematic material is related to native musical resources; particularly remarkable are his *Trozos en el sentimiento popular* for piano, of which he wrote about 350; they are stylizations of Colombian melorhythms in a brilliant pianistic setting. He publ. an autobiography, *Vida de un músico colombiano* (Bogotá, 1941).
WORKS: for orch. (all performed by the composer in Bogotá): *Sinfonia del terruño* (Oct. 20, 1924); *Tres danzas* (May 27, 1927); *Marcha festiva* (Aug. 20, 1928); *Serenata* (Oct. 29, 1928); *Carnavalesca* (July 8, 1929); *Cantares* (Sept. 2, 1929); *Villanesca* (Sept. 1, 1930); *Bajo su ventana* (Oct. 20, 1930); *Suite típica* (Nov. 21, 1932); *Concierto a la manera antigua*, for piano and orch. (Oct. 15, 1939); *Bochica* (April 12, 1940); 11 symphonies (1910–1950); *Conquistadores* (Bogotá, April 3, 1959); 2 violin concertos; Viola Concerto; 10 string quartets; 2 piano trios; 7 violin sonatas; Cello Sonata; Viola Sonata; Piano Quartet; 2 piano quintets; choruses; sacred works; numerous song cycles.
BIBLIOGRAPHY: F. C. Lange, "Guillermo Uribe-Holguín," *Boletín Latino-Americano de Musica* (Bogotá, 1938).

Urich, Jean, composer and publisher; b. on island of Trinidad, Sept. 9, 1849; d. London, Dec. 14, 1939. He studied in Paris with Lenepveu (1868), and in London with Gounod during the latter's sojourn there (1871–74). In 1890 he founded the *Édition Paul Dupont* in Paris, and edited *Le Figaro Musical.*
WORKS: operas *L'Orage* (Brussels, 1879); *Flora Macdonald* (Bologna, 1885); *Le Pilote* (Monte Carlo, 1890); *Le Carillon* (Aix-les-Bains, 1895); *Hermann und Dorothea* (Berlin, 1899); *La Cigale et la fourmi*

(as *The Cicada,* London, 1912); *Tsing-Tau* (London, 1914).

Urio, Francesco Antonio, Italian church composer; b. Milan, c.1660; d. there after 1700. He became a Franciscan monk; in 1690 was maestro at the Church of the 12 Apostles in Rome. Publ. *Motetti di concerto a 2, 3, e 4 voci con violini e senza*, op. 1 (Rome, 1690); *Salmi concertati a 3 voci con violini,* op. 2 (Bologna, 1697); also composed a *Te Deum,* from which Handel "borrowed" numerous themes, chiefly for his *Dettingen Te Deum,* and also for his *Saul* and *Israel in Egypt.* Urio's *Te Deum* was publ. by Chrysander in vol. 5 of his collection, *Denkmäler der Tonkunst* (later publ. as Supplement 2 of Handel's complete works).
BIBLIOGRAPHY: E. Prout, "Urio's Te Deum and Handel's Use Thereof," *Monthly Musical Record* (Nov. 1871); S. Taylor, *The Indebtedness of Handel to Works by Other Composers* (Cambridge, 1906); P. Robinson, *Handel and His Orbit* (London, 1908).

Urlus, Jacques, noted German tenor; b. Hergenrath, near Aachen, Jan. 9, 1867; d. Noordwijk, June 6, 1935. When he was 10, his parents moved to Tilburg, Holland, and there he received his first instruction from an uncle, who was a choral conductor; then he studied engineering in Utrecht; subsequently studied singing with Cornelia van Zanten. He made his operatic debut as Beppo in *Pagliacci* at Amsterdam (Sept. 20, 1894); then was engaged at the Stadttheater in Leipzig (1900–15). He made his American debut in Boston as Tristan (Feb. 12, 1912); sang this role at his first appearance with the Metropolitan Opera (Feb. 8, 1913); was on its staff until 1917.
BIBLIOGRAPHY: Otto Spengler, *Jacques Urlus* (N.Y., 1917; in German and English).

Urreta, Alicia, Mexican pianist and composer; b. Veracruz, Oct. 12, 1935. She studied piano with Joaquín Amparán and harmony with Rodolfo Halffter in Mexico City (1948–54); then engaged in teaching. Among her works are a radio opera, *Romance de Doña Balada* (Mexico City, 1972); *De natura mortis* for voice, instruments, and tape (1972); several scores of *musique concrète.*

Urrutia-Blondel, Jorge, Chilean composer; b. La Serena, Sept. 17, 1905. He studied with Humberto Allende and Domingo Santa Cruz; in 1928 he traveled to Europe, where he took lessons with Charles Koechlin, Paul Dukas, and Nadia Boulanger in Paris, and with Hindemith and Hans Mersmann in Berlin. Returning to Chile, he was appointed prof. of harmony at the Cons. in Santiago. His major work is the ballet *La Guitarra del diablo* (1942) based on Chilean folksongs (Santiago, Nov. 27, 1942), from which he extracted 2 symph. suites. Other works: *Música para un Cuento de Antaño* for orch (1948); Piano Concerto (1950); Piano Trio (1933); Concertino for harp and guitar (1943); String Quartet (1944); Violin Sonata (1954); several choruses; song cycles on Chilean motives; piano pieces.
BIBLIOGRAPHY: Vincente Salas Viú, *La Creación musical en Chile 1900-1951* (Santiago, 1952; pp. 459–67).

Urso, Camilla, French-American violinist; b. Nantes, June 13, 1842; d. New York, Jan. 20, 1902. Her father was an Italian musician, and her mother a Portuguese singer. Her father took her on an American tour when she was 10 years old; she appeared as a child wonder with various enterprises including P. S. Gilmore's band; also toured Australia and South Africa; eventually ceased public appearances and earned a living as a violin teacher.

BIBLIOGRAPHY: C. Barnard, *Camilla: A Tale of a Violin, Being the Artist Life of Camilla Urso* (Boston, 1874); A. R. Coolidge in *Notable American Women* (Cambridge, Mass., 1971), III.

Urspruch, Anton, German pianist and composer; b. Frankfurt, Feb. 17, 1850; d. there, Jan. 11, 1907. He had lessons with Raff and Liszt; subsequently taught at the Raff Cons. in Frankfurt. He wrote a comic opera *Das Unmöglichste von Allem,* after Lope de Vega's comedy *El mayor imposible* (Karlsruhe, Nov. 5, 1897). Other works: Symph., Piano Concerto, Piano Quintet, Piano Trio, Violin Sonata, Cello Sonata; many piano pieces.

Ursprung, Otto, German musicologist; b. Günzlhofen, Jan. 16, 1879; d. Schöndorf-am-Ammersee, Sept. 14, 1960. He studied philosophy and theology at the Univ. of Munich (1899–1904) and was ordained as a Catholic priest. From 1932 to 1949 he taught at the Univ. of Munich. He wrote the books *Restauration und Palestrina-Renaissance in der katholischen Kirchenmusik* (Augsburg, 1924); *Münchens musikalische Vergangenheit* (Munich, 1927); *Die katholische Kirchenmusik* (Potsdam, 1931).

Ursuleac, Viorica, Rumanian soprano, b. Cernauti, March 26, 1899. She studied at the State Academy in Vienna; joined the Berlin Opera in 1933; was also connected with the Vienna Opera from 1934; created the role of Maria in Richard Strauss's opera *Der Friedenstag* (1938). She was the wife of the conductor **Clemens Krauss.**

Usandizaga, José María, Basque composer; b. San Sebastián, March 31, 1887; d. Yanti Oct. 5, 1915. He studied piano with Planté and composition with Vincent d'Indy at the Schola Cantorum in Paris; upon return to Spain he associated himself with the Basque musical movement, to which he gave a great impetus with the production of his opera *Mendy-Mendiyan* (Bilbao, 1910); his second opera *Las Golondrinas (The Swallows),* obtained excellent success at its production in Madrid on Feb. 5, 1914. His last opera, *La Llama (The Flame),* was produced in Madrid in 1915. He also wrote several symphonic overtures; 2 string quartets; many piano pieces on Basque themes. His death of tuberculosis at the age of 28 was deeply lamented by Spanish musicians.

BIBLIOGRAPHY: L. Villalba, *J. M. Usandizaga* (Madrid, 1918); J. M. de Arozamena, *José María Usandizaga y la bella época donostiarra* (San Sebastian, 1969).

Usiglio, Emilio, Italian conductor and composer; b. Parma, Jan. 8, 1841; d. Milan, July 7, 1910. He studied with Mabellini; was a successful opera conductor; gave the first Italian performance of *Carmen.* He was married to the singer **Clementina Brusa.**

WORKS: operas: *La Locandiera* (Turin, Sept. 5, 1861); *L'Eredità in Corsica* (Milan, June 17, 1864); *Le Educande di Sorrento* (Florence, May 1, 1868); *La Scommessa* (Florence, July 6, 1870); *Le Donne curiose* (Madrid, Feb. 11, 1879); *Le Nozze in prigione* (Milan, March 23, 1881); several ballets.

Usmanbaş, Ilhan, Turkish composer; b. Istanbul, Sept. 28, 1921. He studied cello as a child; then studied harmony and counterpoint with Saygun at the Ankara Cons.; in 1948 he was appointed to its faculty. In 1952 he traveled in the U.S. His early compositions followed the ethnic patterns of Turkish folksongs, but after his travels in the U.S. he gradually adopted serial techniques, with occasional aleatory episodes.

WORKS: Violin Concerto (1946); Symph. (Ankara, April 20, 1950); *Music* for string orch., percussion, piano, and narrator (1950); *Mortuary,* for narrator, chorus, and orch. (1952–53); Clarinet Quintet (1949); Oboe Sonata (1949); Trumpet Sonata (1949); *3 Pictures of Salvador Dali* for strings (1953); *Un Coup de dés* for chorus and orch. (1959); *Shadows* for orch. (1964); *Immortal Sea Stones* for piano (1965); *Questionnaire* for piano (1965); *A Jump into Space* for violin and 4 instruments (1966); *Bursting Sinfonietta* for orch. (1968); *Open Forms* for different groups (1968); *Music for a Ballet* for orch. (1969); *String Quartet '70* (1970); *Senilikname* for voice, percussion, harp and women's chorus (1970).

Uspensky, Victor, Russian composer; b. Kaluga, Aug. 31, 1879; d. Tashkent, Oct. 9, 1949. He was brought up in Central Asia, where his father held a government post; attended composition classes of Liadov at the St. Petersburg Cons.; graduated in 1913. In 1918 he went to Tashkent; from 1932 to 1948 was in charge of the Musical Folklore Division of Uzbekistan, and did valuable research work in native folklore; also worked on the restoration of Uzbek musical instruments; from these authentic materials he fashioned an Uzbek opera, *Farhad and Shirin,* produced in Tashkent on Feb. 26, 1936. Other works include *Turkmenian Capriccio* for orch. (1945); *Uzbek Rhapsody* for orch. (1946); several choral works; piano pieces; songs. He collaborated with Victor Belaiev in a scholarly treatise, *Turkmenian Music* (Moscow, 1928).

Ussachevsky, Vladimir, Russian-American composer and expert in electronic music; b. Hailar, Manchuria (of Russian parents), Nov. 3, 1911. He came to America in 1930; studied at Pomona College, Calif., graduating in 1935; then enrolled in the Eastman School of Music, Rochester, and took courses in composition with Howard Hanson and Bernard Rogers; received his Ph.D. there in 1939. In 1947 he was appointed to the faculty of Columbia Univ. He became interested in electronic music; perfected an instrument capable of transforming recorded music in various ways, automatically producing repeated notes and other effects; he was one of the first composers to make use of electronic sound on tape recorders as part of a musical work; he also arranged electronic scores for films, particularly those of science fiction.

WORKS: *Jubilee Cantata* for chorus and orch. (1938); *Theme and Variations,* for orch. (1935); *Miniatures for a Curious Child,* for orch. (1950); Piano Concerto (1951); Piano Sonata (1952); *Sonic Contours,* for tape recorder with instruments (Museum of Modern Art, N.Y., Oct. 28, 1951); *Poem of Cycles and Bels,* for tape recorder and orch. (with Otto Luening; Los Angeles, Nov. 18, 1954); *Linear Contrasts,* for electronic sound (1958); *Wireless Fantasy,* for electronics (1960); *Creation,* for 4 choruses and tape (1961); *Of Wood and Brass,* for tape (1965); *Suicide Music,* for Marvin Levy's opera *Mourning Becomes Electra* (1967); *Suite from Music for Films,* for tape (1967); *Computer Piece* (1968); *4 Miniatures,* suite for electronic music (1968).

Ustvolskaya, Galina, Soviet composer; b. Petrograd, July 17, 1919. She was a student of Shostakovich at the Leningrad Cons., graduating in 1947. Her early music was marked by a romantic Russian manner; later she progressed toward greater melodic diversity and harmonic complexity; in some of her chamber music she boldly applies serial procedures.

WORKS: *Stepan Razin's Dream,* for bass and orch. (Leningrad, Feb. 10, 1949); *A Man from the Tall Mountain,* for voices and orch. (Leningrad, May 22, 1952); Sinfonietta (1951); 2 symphonies: No. 1 for 2 boy sopranos and orch. (1955); No. 2 for voice, wind instruments, and piano (1964); symph. poems, *Heroic Deed* (1957); *Fire in the Steppes* (1958); Piano Concerto (1947); Octet for 4 violins, 2 oboes, piano, and kettledrums (1951); *Composition* for piccolo, tuba, and piano (1970); *Composition* for double bass and piano (1971); Violin Sonata; Cello Sonata; 3 piano sonatas (1948, 1951, 1952).

Utendal, Alexander, Flemish composer; b. Netherlands, c.1530; d. Innsbruck, May 7, 1581. He was court musician to the Archduke Ferdinand of Austria at Innsbruck. Publ. *7 Penitential Psalms* (1570); 3 books of motets (1570–77); Masses and Magnificats (1573); *Fröliche neue teutsche und französische Lieder* for 4–8 voices (1574).

Uttini, Francesco Antonio Baltassare, Italian composer; b. Bologna, 1723; d. Stockholm, Oct. 25, 1795. He studied with Perti; in 1743 he became a member of the Accademia dei Filarmonici in Bologna. He first appeared as a singer; in 1755 he went to Stockholm as conductor of an Italian opera company, and remained there until his death, except for a visit to London in 1768. He was court conductor at the Stockholm Opera from 1767 to 1787, and wrote 7 Italian and 5 French operas. Historically he is important as the composer of the earliest operas on Swedish texts; the first, *Thetis och Pelée,* was written for the inauguration of the new opera house (Jan. 18, 1773); another opera to a Swedish libretto, translated from the French, was *Aline Drotning uti Golconda (Aline Queen of Golconda)* produced at the Stockholm Opera on Jan. 11, 1776. Of Uttini's Italian operas the best is *Il Re pastore* (Stockholm, July 24, 1755). A great admirer of Gluck, he brought out many of that composer's works in Stockholm. He also wrote 2 oratorios, 3 symphonies (for, 4, 6, and 8 instruments), 12 sonatas, 9 trios for 2 violins with continuo; 6 of his sonatas were publ. at London in 1768.

BIBLIOGRAPHY: E. Sundström, "F. A. Uttini och Adolf Fredriks italienska operatrupp," *Svensk Tidskrift för Musikforskning* 13 (1931).

V

Vaccai, Nicola, Italian composer and singing teacher; b. Tolentino, March 15, 1790; d. Pesaro, Aug. 5, 1848. He went to Rome as a youth and took lessons in counterpoint with Jannaconi; then studied with Paisiello in Naples (from 1812). He became a singing teacher in Venice (1818–21), Trieste (1821–23), Vienna (1823), Paris (1829–31), and London (1832), with an ever-growing reputation; was prof. of composition at the Milan Cons. (1838–44); in 1844 he retired to Pesaro, where he remained until his death.

WORKS: operas: *Pietro il Grande* (Parma, Jan. 17, 1824); *La Pastorella feudataria* (Turin, Sept. 18, 1824); *Giulietta e Romeo,* after Shakespeare (Milan, Oct. 31, 1825; the last scene was often used in performances of Bellini's *I Capuletti e i Montecchi*); his subsequent 9 operas were failures. He publ. *Metodo pratico di canto italiano per camera;* and *12 ariette per camera, per l'insegnamento del belcanto italiano.*

BIBLIOGRAPHY: G. Vaccai, *Vita di N. Vaccai* (Bologna, 1882).

Vacek, Miloš, Czech composer; b. Horní Roveň, June 20, 1928. He studied organ at the Prague Cons. (1943–47); then took a course in composition with Řídký and Pícha at the Prague Academy of Arts and Music (1947–51); wrote music scores for the Prague Puppet Theater which became popular.

WORKS: an opera, *Jan Želivský* (1953–56, revised 1974); 6 ballets, *The Comedian's Fairytale* (1957), *Wind in the Hair* (1960–61), *The Last Dandelion* (1964), *Meteor* (1966), *The Mistress of Seven Robbers* (1966) and *Lucky Sevens* (1966); a blues drama, *The Night Is My Day,* inspired by the life of Bessie Smith, American blues singer (Frankfurt, March 15, 1964); the musicals, *The Emperor's New Clothes* (1962), *Madame Sans-Gêne* (1968), and *Wind from Alabama* (1970); Sinfonietta (1951); *The Brigand's Rhapsody* for orch. (1952); *Spring Suite* for flute, horn or English horn, clarinet, and string orch. (1963); *Serenade* for strings (1965); *Fairytale Suite* for orch. (1966); *Festive Day,* symph. march (1971); *Amoroso of My Country* for orch. (1973); *Majova (May),* a sinfonia (1974); *Poema, o padlých hrdinech (Poem of Fallen Heroes)* for orch. and vocalizing soprano (1974); *The Olympic Flame,* symph. poem (1975); a cantata, *The Landscape of My Youth* (1976); *Sonnets of Early Spring,* lyrical cycle for soprano and orch. (1972–73); *Suite* for cello and piano (1947); Violin Sonatina (1949); String Quartet (1949); *Divertimento* for violin, cello, guitar, and bass clarinet (1965); *Sumava Metamorphoses* for flute, oboe, violin, viola, and cello (1971); *Hunting Suite* for 4 horns (1973); *Sonata Drammatica* for piano (1972); *Dramatic Prelude* for organ (1958); *Organum Pragense* for organ (1966).

Vach, Ferdinand, Moravian choral leader; b. Jažlovice, Feb. 25, 1860; d. Brno, Feb. 16, 1939. He studied at the Organ School in Prague; 1886, appointed conductor of the "Moravian" choir at Kroměříž; also taught singing at the Pedagogium there, and from among his pupils formed the Moravian Teachers' Choir in 1903, with which he toured in Germany, Russia, and England (1919). In 1905 he became prof. at the Teachers' School in Brno; composed choruses and cantatas; church music.

Vachon, Pierre, violinist and composer; b. Arles, 1731; d. Berlin, 1802. Pupil of Chabran in Paris from 1751; played at the Concert Spirituel in 1758; from 1761, solo violinist to the Prince de Conti; from 1784, at the Royal Chapel in Berlin; pensioned in 1798. Besides stage works, he composed violin concertos, string quartets, trios, sonatas, etc. (publ. in Paris, London, and Berlin). A quartet for strings and continuo (op. 5, no. 3) was ed. by Sidney Beck for the N.Y. Public Library (1937).

Vačkář, Dalibor, Czech composer and writer; b. Korčula, Yugoslavia, Sept. 19, 1906. He is the son of **Václav Vačkář** (1881–1954), Czech composer of popular music. He studied violin with Reissiga and composition with O. Šín at the Prague Cons. (1923–29), completing studies there at the Master Class with K. Hoffmann and J. Suk (1929–31); played violin in the Prague Radio Orch. (1934–45); produced music for over 30 films under various pseudonyms. Under the pen name **Dalibor C. Faltis** he published 4 books of poems, a book of short stories, 12 plays, and 3 opera libretti.

WORKS: 2 ballets: *Švanda dudák (Svanda the Bagpiper,* 1950; Prague Radio, April 7, 1954) and *Sen noci svatojanské,* after Shakespeare (*A Midsummer's Night Dream,* 1955–57); *Overture* (1929); 2 violin concertos (1931, 1958); 4 symphonies: No. 1, *Optimistická (Optimistic,* 1941); No. 2, *Země vyvolená (The Chosen Land)* with contralto and chorus (1947); No. 3, *Smoking Symphony* (1947–48; the curious subtitle, meaning smoking attire, i.e., tuxedo, is in English only); No. 4, *Míru (Peace,* 1949–50); *Symphonic Scherzo* (1945); Sinfonietta for strings, horn, timpani, and piano (1947); Piano Concerto (1953); *Prelude and Metamorphoses* for orch. or piano (1956); *Furiant-fantasie* for chamber orch. (1960); *Concerto da camera* for bassoon and chamber string orch. (1962); *Charakteristikon,* concerto for trombone and orch. (1965); *Legenda o člověku (Legend of Men),* concerto for harpsichord, winds, and percussion (1966); Clarinet Concerto (1966); *Prelude* for chamber string orch. (1966); *Concerto Grosso* for saxophone, accordion, guitar, and orch. (1967); *Musica Concertante* for orch. (1974); *Trio giocoso* for piano trio (1929); Violin Sonata (1930); String Quartet (1931–32); *Jaro 38,* piano trio (1938); *Monolog* for solo violin (1940); Quartet for piano, oboe, clarinet, and bassoon (1948); *Quintetto giocoso* for winds (1950; music from the ballet *Švanda dudák*); *Dedication* for violin and piano (1960); Concerto for string quartet (1960); *Suita giocosa* for piano trio (1960); *Dialogue* for solo violin (1961); *3 Studies* for harpsichord (1961); *Pianoforte cantante,* 5 reminiscences for piano, percussion and double bass (1968); *Partita* for solo trumpet (1968); *Smoking Sonata* for piano (1936); *Extempore,* 6 pieces for piano (1937); *Piano Fantasy,* on a theme from Schubert's *The Arch* (1962); *Perspektivy* for piano (1971); choruses; songs. Together with his father, he wrote *In-*

strumentation for Symphonic Orchestra and Brass Band (Prague, 1954).

Vačkář, Tomáš, Czech composer, son of **Dalibor Vačkář;** b. Prague, July 31, 1945; d. (suicide) there, May 2, 1963. He came from a well-known Czech family of musicians; his grandfather, **Václav Vačkář** was a composer of light music, and his father, **Dalibor Vačkář,** an eminent composer, dramatist, and poet. Young Tomáš was a gifted composer, but chose to end his life shortly after his graduation from the Prague Cons. at the age of 18. His works, all written between July, 1960, and April, 1963, include *Sonatina furore* for piano; *Concerto Recitativo* for flute, string orch., and piano; *Tři Dopisy divkam (3 Letters to a Girl),* after a poem by an anonymous Czech student, for voice, and piano or winds and percussion; *Teenagers,* piano sonata; *Metamorfózy na tema japonske ukolebavky (Metamorphoses on the Theme of a Japanese Lullaby)* for orch.; *Scherzo melancolico* for orch.; *Skicář Tomáše Vačkáře (Tomáš Vačkář's Sketchbook),* 10 pieces for piano; a *Requiem* remained unfinished.

Vaet, Jacobus, Flemish composer; b. 1529; birthplace is not certain; it may be Courtrai or Harlebeke; d. Vienna, Jan. 8, 1567. He was a choirboy in the Church of Notre Dame at Courtrai (1543–46); after his voice changed, he received a subsidy for 2 years of further study; in 1550 he was a tenor in the Flemish Chapel of Charles V; on Jan. 1, 1554, he was listed as Kapellmeister of the chapel of Maximilian, then the nominal King of Bohemia. His position was enhanced when his patron became Emperor Maximilian II. Vaet's music exhibits a great variety of techniques, ranging in style from those of Josquin des Prez to those of Lassus. The formative influence, however, is mainly that of Nicolas Gombert, with a characteristic florid imitation in contrapuntal parts. The extant works of Vaet comprise 82 motets and hymns, 10 Masses, 8 Magnificats, and 3 chansons; a relatively large number of his motets (at least 11) are ceremonial, written to celebrate state or court occasions. 2 vols. of his motets, *Modulationes 5 vocum* and *Modulationes 5 et 6 vocum,* were publ. in 1562 by Gardano in Venice; a 6-voice motet, *Qui operatus est Petro,* was printed in luxurious format on a large single parchment sheet by Hofhalter of Vienna in 1560 (facsimile in Haas, *Aufführungspraxis der Musik,* Potsdam, 1931, p. 129). Zacconi printed a hymn in his *Prattica di musica,* Libro I, folio 50. Vaet is represented also in the publications of Berg and Neuber (30 motets), Giovanelli (24 motets), Susato (7 motets), Gerlach (3 motets), Phalèse (3 motets, 2 chansons), Stephani (2 motets, 1 chanson), Waelrant and Laet (1 chanson), Nicolas du Chemin (1 chanson), and Rühling (1 motet in organ tablature). Reprints appear in Commer's *Collectio operum musicorum Batavorum* (20 motets) and his *Musica sacra* (1 Mass), and in Maldeghem, *Trésor musical* (1 motet). E. H. Meyer edited *Jacobus Vaet, Sechs Motetten* as vol. 2 of *Das Chorwerk* (1929), and Milton Steinhardt edited *Jacobus Vaet, Zwei Hymnen* as vol. 8 of *Musik alter Meister* (1958). A complete edition of his work was undertaken by M. Steinhardt

in *Denkmäler der Tonkunst in Österreich,* vols. 98, 100, 103/104, 108/109, 113/114, 116.

BIBLIOGRAPHY: Milton Steinhardt, *Jacobus Vaet and His Motets* (Michigan State College Press, 1951; thematic index and 3 complete works included); Milton Steinhardt, "The Hymns of Jacobus Vaet," *Journal of the American Musicological Society* (Fall 1956); G. Reese, *Music in the Renaissance* (N.Y., 1954); M. Steinhardt, "Addenda to the Biography of Jacobus Vaet," in *The Commonwealth of Music* (N.Y., 1964), and "The *Missa Di me tenes:* A Problem of Authorship" in *Aspects of Medieval and Renaissance Music* (N.Y., 1965).

Vainberg, Moisei, Soviet composer; b. Warsaw, Dec. 8, 1919. He studied piano with Turczynski at the Warsaw Cons., graduating in 1939; then went to Minsk, where he studied composition with Zolotarev at the Minsk Cons.; in 1943 settled in Moscow. In his music he follows the precepts of Socialist Realism in its ethnic aspects; according to the subject, he makes use of Jewish, Polish, Moldavian, or Armenian folk melos, in tasteful harmonic arrangements devoid of abrasive dissonances.

WORKS: operas: *The Sword of Uzbekistan* (1942); *The Woman Passenger* (1968); *Love of D'Artagnan,* after Alexandre Dumas (1972); ballets: *Battle for Fatherland* (1942); *The Golden Key* (1955); *The White Chrysanthemum* (1958); *Requiem* (1967); cantatas: *On This Day Was Born Lenin* for chorus and orch. (1970); *Hiroshima Haikus* (1966); *The Diary of Love* (1965); for orch.: 11 symphonies: No. 1, (1942); No. 2, for string orch. (1946); No. 3 (1949); No. 4 (1957); No. 5 (1962); No. 6, with boys' chorus (1963); No. 7 for strings and harpsichord (1964); No. 8, subtitled *The Flowers of Poland,* for tenor, chorus, and orch. (1964); No. 9, subtitled *Surviving Pages,* for reader, chorus, and orch. (1967); No. 10, for string orch. (1968); No. 11, *Triumphant Symphony* for chorus and orch., dedicated to Lenin's centennial (1970); 2 sinfoniettas (1948, 1960); *Moldavian Rhapsody* for orch. (Moscow, Nov. 30, 1949); *Slavic Rhapsody* for orch. (1950); Cello Concerto (1956); Violin Concerto (1960); Flute Concerto (1961); Trumpet Concerto (1967); Clarinet Concerto (1970); 12 string quartets (1937–70); Piano Quintet (1944); Piano Trio (1945); String Trio (1951); 20 sonatas and 2 sonatinas for various instruments with piano; 24 preludes for cello solo; 23 preludes for piano; songs.

Valabrega, Cesare, Italian pianist and writer on music; b. Novara, Dec. 27, 1898. He studied piano at the Cons. of Pesaro and literature at the Univ. of Bologna; taught music history in Naples and Perugia; then settled in Rome as lecturer and critic. He wrote the books *Schumann: arte e natura; arte e vita; arte e fede* (1934; 3rd ed., 1956); *Domenico Scarlatti: il suo secolo, la sua opera* (1937; 2nd ed., 1955); *Il piccolo dizionario musicale per tutti* (1929; 2nd ed., 1952); *Johann Sebastian Bach* (1950); *La Lirica di camera di Vincenzo Davico* (1953).

Valcárcel, Edgar, Peruvian composer and pianist, nephew of **Teodoro Valcárcel;** b. Puno, Dec. 4, 1932. He studied composition with Andrés Sas at the Lima

Cons.; then went to N.Y., where he studied with Donald Lybbert at Hunter College; subsequently traveled to Buenos Aires where he took composition lessons with Alberto Ginastera; also had sessions with Olivier Messiaen in Paris, and with Riccardo Malipiero, Bruno Maderna, and Luigi Dallapiccola in Italy; furthermore, he joined the Electronic Music Center of Columbia-Princeton Univs. and worked with Vladimir Ussachevsky; he held two Guggenheim Foundation grants (1966 and 1968). In Peru he became a teacher of piano and harmony at the Cons. of Lima. In his compositions he adopted an extremely advanced idiom that combined serial and aleatory principles, leaving to the performer the choice to use or not to use given thematic materials.

WORKS: FOR ORCH.: Concerto for clarinet and strings (Lima, March 6, 1966); *Quenua* (Lima, Aug. 18, 1965); *Aleaciones* (Lima, May 5, 1967); Piano Concerto (Lima, Aug. 8, 1968); *Checán II* (Lima, June 5, 1970); *Ma'karabotasaq hachana (1971); Sajra* (1974); CHAMBER MUSIC: 2 string quartets (1962, 1963); *Espectros I* for flute, viola and piano (1964); *Espectros II* for French horn, violoncello, and piano (1968); *Dicotomías III* for 12 instruments (Mexico, Nov. 20, 1966); *Fisiones* for 10 instruments (1967); *Hiwana uru* for 11 instruments (1967); Trio for amplified violin, trombone, and clarinet (1968); *Poema,* for amplified violin, voice, piano, and percussion (1969); *Chacán I* for 6 instruments (1969); *Checán III* for 19 instruments (1971); *Montage 59* for string quartet, clarinet, piano, and lights (1971); *Espectros III* for oboe, violin, and piano (1974); *Checán V* for strings (1974); FOR PIANO: *Dicotomías I* and *II* (1966); 2 sonatas (1963, 1972); ELECTRONIC WORKS: *Antaras* for flute, percussion, and electronic sounds (1968); various multimedia pieces with chorus, electronic sounds, and lights; several choruses a cappella.

Valcárcel, Teodoro, Peruvian composer; b. Puno, Oct. 17, 1900; d. Lima, March 20, 1942. He studied at the Cons. of Milan and with Felipe Pedrell in Barcelona. Returning to Peru in 1920, he settled in Lima; in 1928 he won the National Prize for Peruvian composers, and was awarded a gold medal from the municipality of Lima for his studies in Peruvian folk music. In 1929 he went to Europe once more; presented a concert of his works in Paris (April 12, 1930). He was of pure Indian origin; as a native of the highlands, he was able to collect Indian songs unpolluted by urban influences. He publ. *30 Cantos de alma vernacular; 4 Canciones incaicas; 25 Romances de costa y sierra pervana; 180 Melodias del folklore.* Among his original works are the ballets (with singing) *Suray-Surita* and *Ckori Kancha;* a symph. poem, *En las ruinas del Templo del Sol* (1940); a violin concerto, entitled *Concierto indio* (1939); *3 Ensayos* for an ensemble of native instruments; *Fiestas andinas* for piano; *Suite autóctona* for violin and piano; songs. A catalogue of his works was publ. by R. Holzmann in *Boletín Bibliográfico* (Lima, Dec. 1942).

Valderábano, Enrique Enriquez de. See **Enriquez de Valderrábano, Enrique.**

Valderrama, Carlos, Peruvian composer; b. Trujillo, Sept. 4, 1887; d. Lima, Aug. 1, 1950. He studied engineering at Cornell Univ., then decided to devote himself to music; made his debut as a pianist at Carnegie Hall, N.Y. (Feb. 22, 1920). He wrote many piano pieces on old Inca themes, in a salon style (several of them published), and some ballet music.

Valdrighi, Luigi Francesco, Italian music scholar; b. Modena, July 30, 1827; d. there, April 20, 1899. He was notable for his excellent collection of early musical instruments, which he bequeathed to the Museum of Modena. He published numerous valuable monographs on the music and musicians of Modena; among his theoretical writings, the most important was *Nomocheliurgografia antica e moderna* (1884; with 2 supplements, 1888 and 1894). With G. Ferrari-Moreni he completed a chronicle of the theater life in Modena, *Cronistoria dei teatri di Modena* (1873).

BIBLIOGRAPHY: E. Zoccoli, *Il Conte Luigi Francesco Valdrighi* (Modena, 1899).

Válek, Jiří, remarkable Czech composer; b. Prague, May 28, 1923. He studied composition at the Prague Cons. and the Master's School with Řídký (1946–48); received a doctorate of philosophy from Charles Univ. (1951). He was secretary of the Guild of Czech Composers (1949–51) and editor-in-chief of children's musical programming of the Czech Radio in Prague (1951–53), of the editorial division of the Central House of the Czech Army (1953–58), and of Panton, the publishing house of the Guild (1959–63); then was engaged as an instructor in music theory at the Prague Cons.

WORKS: 12 programmatic symphonies: No. 1, *Rok 1948 (The Year 1948)* for trumpet, piano, and orch. (1948); No. 2, *Klasická (Classic)* for 2 flutes, 2 clarinets, chamber string orch., and piano (1957); No. 3, *Romantická,* for soprano saxophone, tenor saxophone, and orch. (1962); No. 4, *Dialogy s vnitřním hlasem (Dialogues with an Inner Voice),* to Shakespearean texts, for contralto, baritone, large wind orch., percussion, and piano (1967); No. 5, *Guernica,* after the Picasso painting (1968); No. 6, *Ekpyrosis,* reflecting philosophical ideals of Heraclitus, for flute, string orch., percussion, and piano (1968–69); No. 7, *Pompejské fresky (Pompeiian Frescoes)* for chamber orch., piano, and percussion (1969–70); No. 8, *Hic sunt homines!* on the theme of a novella by Stefan Zweig, for soprano and orch. (1970–71); No. 9, *Renesanční (Renaissance),* triple concerto for violin, viola, cello, and string orch. (1971); No. 10, *Barokní (Baroque),* to commemorate the 300th anniversary of the death of Czech Baroque painter Karel Škréta and the 150th anniversary of the birth of Smetana, a double concerto for violin, piano, and orch. (1973); No. 11, *Revoluční (Revolutionary),* to the 30th anniversary of Czech liberation, for piano trio, wind quintet, and orch. (1974); and No. 12, *Shakespearean,* a double concerto for violin, viola, and chamber string orch. (1976); Sinfonietta (1944); *The Dam,* symph. poem (1959); *Reflections on a Summer Lake,* dance suite for orch. (1972); *Beyond the Bounds of Tomorrow,* ceremonial march for orch. (1972); *La Portenza della Primavera,* 5 dithyrambs for soprano and orch. (1972); *Hymnus slunce (Hymn to the Sun),* a violin concerto (1975); 4 string quartets (1943; 1945; *The Rumburk Uprising,* 1960; *Quattrocento,* 1972–73); 2 violin sonatas (1944, 1960); 2 viola sonatas (1948, 1961); *Serenade* for 9 winds and piano (1959); *Eroica,* sonata for trumpet or clarinet, and piano (1960); *Suite dramatica* for double bass and piano (1967); *Concerto-notturno* for violin, viola, and cello (1967); *Shakespeare Variations* for nonet (1967); Flute Sonata (1969); *Nenie* for solo violin or cello (1969); Concerto for flute, oboe, violin, viola, cello, and harpsichord (1970); *Villa dei Misteri,* 11 fresques for violin and piano (1971); *Aesop* for children's choir, narrator, ballet, flute, 2 clarinets, bassoon, and percussion (1972); 3 piano sonatas (*The Year 1942,* 1942; 1961; 1970); songs.

Valen, Fartein, Norwegian composer noted for his originality both in thematic invention and use of audacious modern techniques; b. Stavanger, Aug. 25, 1887; d. Haugesund, Dec. 14, 1952. His father was a missionary in Madagascar, and Valen spent his childhood there. Upon returning to Norway, he studied philology at the Univ. of Oslo (1906–09), and music theory and organ with Elling at the Oslo Cons.; subsequently went to Berlin and enrolled in the Hochschule für Musik in the class of composition of Max Bruch (1909–13). From 1913 to 1923 he stayed on his family's farm in Valevåg; from 1924 to 1939 he was in Oslo; then retired on the family farm. In 1935 he received the Norwegian State Salary of Art (a government life pension). His early music reflects the influence of Brahms, but later he developed a *sui generis* method of composition which he termed "atonal polyphony," completely free from traditional tonal relationships, but strongly cohesive in contrapuntal fabric and greatly varied in rhythm; his first work in which he made use of this technique was a piano trio written in 1924. He never adopted an explicit 12-tone method of composition, but a parallelism with Schoenberg's music is observable. Valen stood apart from all nationalist developments in Oslo, yet his music attracted attention in modern circles, and a Valen Society was formed in Norway in 1949, and in England in 1952, shortly before his death. WORKS: FOR ORCH: 5 symphonies: No. 1 (1937–39; Bergen, March 16, 1956), No. 2 (1941–44; Oslo, March 28, 1957), No. 3 (1944–46; Oslo, April 13, 1951), No. 4 (1947–49; Malmö, Sweden, Oct. 16, 1956), No. 5 (1951–52, unfinished); *Pastorale* (1929–30); *Sonetto di Michelangelo* (1932); *Nenia* (1932); *Cantico di ringraziamento* (*Song of Thanksgiving,* 1932–33); *An die Hoffnung* (*To Hope,* after Keats' poem; 1933); *Epithalamion* (1933); *Le cimetière marin* (*Graveyard By the Sea,* 1933–34); *La Isla de las Calmas* (*The Silent Island,* 1934); *Ode til Ensomheten* (*Ode to Solitude,* 1939); Violin Concerto (1940; Oslo, Oct. 24, 1947; also performed at the Amsterdam Festival, June 12, 1948); Concerto for piano and chamber orch. (1949–51; Oslo, Jan. 15, 1953); FOR SOPRANO AND ORCH.: *Ave Maria* (1917–21); *3 Gedichte von Goethe* (1925–27); *Mignon,* 2 songs after Goethe (1920–27); *2 Chinesische Gedichte* (1925–27); *Dearest Thou Now, O Soul,* after Whitman (1920–28); *La Noche oscura del Alma* (*The Dark Night of the Soul),* after St. John of the Cross (1939); CHAMBER MUSIC: Violin Sonata (1916); Piano Trio (1917–24); 2 string quartets (1928–29, 1930–31); *Serenade* for wind quintet (1946–47); FOR PIANO: *Legend* (1907); 2 sonatas: No. 1 (1912) and No. 2, *The Hound of Heaven,* after the poem by Francis Thompson (1940–41); *4 Pieces* (1934–35); *Variations* (1935–36); *Gavotte and Musette* (1936); *Prelude and Fugue* (1937); *2 Preludes* (1937); *Intermezzo* (1939–40); FOR ORGAN: *Prelude and Fugue* (1939) and *Pastoral* (1939); songs; motets.

BIBLIOGRAPHY: O. Gurvin, *Fartein Valen, En banebryter i nyere norsk musikk* (*Fartein Valen, a Pioneer in Norwegian Music,* Oslo, 1962); B. Kortsen, *Studies of Form in Fartein Valen's Music* (Oslo, 1962); B. Kortsen, *Melodic Structure and Thematic Unity in Fartein Valen's Music* (2 vols., Glasgow, 1963); B. Kortsen, *Fartein Valen, Life and Music* (3 vols., Oslo, 1965).

Valencia, Antonio María, Colombian pianist and composer; b. Cali, Nov. 10, 1902; d. there, July 22, 1952. He studied at the Schola Cantorum in Paris (from 1923) with Vincent d'Indy and Paul Le Flem; returning to Colombia in 1930, he founded the Cali Cons., and was its director until his death. WORKS: *Chirimía y bambuco sotareño* for orch. (1942); *Egloga incaica* for flute, oboe, clarinet, and bassoon (1935); *Emociones caucanas,* for piano, violin, and cello (1938); numerous pieces for piano solo, inspired by native melorhythms (*8 Ritmos y cantos suramericanos, Sonatina boyacense,* etc.); Requiem (1943); other church music; choruses and songs.

Valente, Antonio (known as "il Cieco," i.e. the blind man), Italian organist and composer; b. Naples, about 1520. Blind from infancy, he played the organ; was organist at Sant'Angelo a Nido in Naples. His first publication, *Intavolatura de cimbalo: Recercate, fantasie et canzoni francese desminuite con alcuni tenori balli et varie sorti di contraponti . . .* (Naples, 1575, is in Spanish keyboard tablature and contains early keyboard fantasias, written out in detail; his 2nd book, *Versi spirituali sopra tutte le note, con diversi canoni spartiti per suonar negli organi, messe, vespere et altri offici divini* (Naples, 1580), represents an early type of keyboard partitura; 3 numbers were reprinted by L. Torchi in *L'Arte Musicale in Italia* 3.

BIBLIOGRAPHY: N. Caravaglios, "Una nuova *Intavolatura de Cimbalo* di Antonio Valente Cieco," *Rivista Musicale Italiana* 23 (p. 491); Willi Apel, "Neapolitan Links between Cabezón and Frescobaldi," *Musical Quarterly* (Oct. 1938).

Valente, Giorgio. See **Vitalis, George.**

Valente, Vincenzo, Italian operetta composer; b. Corigliano Calabro, Feb. 21, 1855; d. Naples, Sept. 6, 1921. At the age of 15 he wrote a song, *Ntuniella,* which became popular; continued writing Neapolitan songs of great appeal (*Basta ca po', Comme te voglio amá!, Canzone Cafona, Mugliera comme fa, Ninuccia, Tiempe felice, L'Acqua,* etc.), about 400 songs in all. He also brought out numerous operettas: *I Granatieri* (Turin, Oct. 26, 1889), *La Sposa di Charolles* (Rome, March 3, 1894), *Rolandino* (Turin, Oct. 15, 1897), *L'Usignuolo* (Naples, May 10, 1899), *Lena* (Foggia, Jan. 1, 1918), *L'Avvocato Trafichetti* (Naples, May 24, 1919), *Nèmesi* (posthumous, Naples, July 23, 1923). His son, **Nicola Valente** (b. Naples, Aug. 28, 1881), was also a composer of Neapolitan songs and light operas.

Valentin, Erich, German musicologist; b. Strasbourg, Nov. 27, 1906. He studied with Otto Volkmann in Magdeburg, and with Sandberger in Munich (Ph.D., 1928); held several posts as lecturer on music and librarian. From 1957, co-editor of *Neue Zeitschrift für Musik.* From 1964 to 1972 he was director of the State Hochschule für Musik in Munich.
WRITINGS: *Die Entwicklung der Tokkata im 17. und 18. Jahrhundert* (dissertation; Münster, 1930); *Georg Philipp Telemann: eine Biographie* (Burg, 1931; 2nd ed., Hamelin, 1947); *Richard Wagner* (Regensburg, 1937); *Dichtung und Oper: eine Untersuchung zum Stilproblem der Oper* (Leipzig, 1938); *Hans Pfitzner* (Regensburg, 1939); *Wege zu Mozart* (Regensburg, 1941; 4th ed., 1950); *Beethoven* (Salzburg, 1942; English transl., N.Y., 1958); *W. A. Mozart: Wesen und Wandlung* (Hamelin, 1948); *Handbuch der Chormusik* (Regensburg, 1953); *Handbuch der Instrumentenkunde* (Regensburg, 1954); contributed articles to various musical magazines; brought out editions of works by Mozart, Telemann, etc. A Festschrift in his honor, *Erich Valentin zum 70 Geburtstag,* with dedicatory articles by his friends and students, edited by Günther Weiss, was published in Regensburg in 1976.

Valentini, Giovanni, Italian composer; b. Venice, 1582; d. Vienna, April, 1649. He was a pupil of Giovanni Gabrieli; from 1614, organist to the Archduke Ferdinand at Graz, becoming court organist at Vienna when Ferdinand ascended the throne in 1619; in 1629 succeeded Prioli as Imperial Kapellmeister. He was a renowned teacher of organ. Published *Motetti a 6 voci* (1611); 5 books of madrigals for 3 to 11 voices with instruments; *Musiche a 2 voci* with bass for organ (1622); *Canzoni per sonar,* 4–8 voices; in MS, Masses, Magnificats, a Stabat Mater, and sonatas; Riemann published an "Enharmonische Sonate" in *Alte Kammermusik* but its authenticity is disputed.

Valentini, Giuseppe, Italian violinist and composer; b. Florence, c.1680; d. there, c.1746. He was at Rome in 1700; from 1710 at Bologna in the service of the Prince di Caserta, and from 1735 at the grand-ducal court of Florence. His violin technique was highly developed (some compositions call for the 6th position). Published 12 *Sinfonie* for 2 violins and continuo (organ); 7 *Bizarrerie* for 2 violins and cello; 12 *Fantasie* for 2 violins and continuo; 12 *Sonate* for the same; *Idee per camera* for violin solo and cello (or cembalo); 12 *Concerti grossi* for strings and continuo; 12 *Sonate o Alletamenti* for violin and continuo.

Valentini, Pier Francesco, Italian theorist and composer of the Roman School; b. Rome, c.1570; d. there, 1654. He was a pupil of G. M. Nanini.
WORKS: *Canone sopra le parole del Salve Regina, "Illos tuos misericordes oculos ad nos converte,"* con le resolutioni a 2, 3, 4 e 5 voci (1629; a canon with over 2000 possible resolutions; the theme is in Kircher's *Musurgia,* I, p. 402); *Canone nel nodo di Salomone a 96 voci* (1631; also in *Musurgia,* I, p. 104); *Canone a 6, 10, 20 voci* (1645); 2 books of madrigals *a 5* with continuo ad lib. and 2 books of motets with instruments (1654); 6 books of *Canzonetti spirituali* for 1 to 4 voices (1655–56); 2 books of *Musiche spirituali* for 1 and 2 voices, *Canzoni, sonetti ed arie a voce sola,* 4 books of *Canzonette ed arie a 1, 2 voci* (all 1657); 2 books of litanies and motets for 2 to 4 voices. Also 2 stage works *(favole),* La Mitra and La Trasformazione di Dafne (both 1654), and several theoretical works (in MS).
BIBLIOGRAPHY: L. Kurz, *Die Tonartenlehre des römischen Theoretikers und Komponisten P. F. Valentini* (dissertation; Kassel, 1937).

Valentino, Henri-Justin-Armand-Joseph, French conductor; b. Lille, Oct. 14, 1785; d. Versailles, Jan. 20, 1865. In 1820 he was 2nd conductor, and in 1824 became 1st conductor, at the Opéra in Paris; from 1831 to 1837 was conductor at the Opéra-Comique; then founded a society of popular concerts of classical music, as a rival enterprise to the Conservatory Concerts, at the Salle St.- Honoré (since called the "Salle Valentino"), but discontinued them in 1841.

Valerius, Adrianus (Adriaan), Dutch musician; b. Middelburg, 1575; d. Veer, Jan. 27, 1625. From 1606 lived in Veer as a notary; published an important lute tablature book, *Nederlandtsche Gedenckclanck* (Haarlem, 1626; reprinted in part in the publ. of the *Vereeniging voor Nederlandsche Muziekgeschiedenis* II [1871]; 2nd ed., The Hague, 1893; 3rd ed., Utrecht, 1931; new ed., Amsterdam, 1942); see also *Six Ancient Songs of the Netherlands, from A. V.* (ed. by E. Kremser; English text by Th. Baker; N.Y., 1894).
BIBLIOGRAPHY: J. W. Enschedé, "De Wilhelmusmelodie in de Gedenckclanck van Valerius," *Tijdschrift van de Vereeniging voor Nederlandsche Muziekgeschiedenis* 5 (1897).

Valkare, Gunnar, Swedish composer of the extreme avant-garde; b. Norrköping, April 25, 1943. He studied composition with Lidholm at the Royal Cons. of Stockholm (1963–70). His music is militantly aggressive in its tonal, atonal, and polytonal assault on the most cherished notions of harmonious sweetness.
WORKS: *4 Cardiograms* for solo singers, chorus, and instruments in varying combinations (1965–66); *A Study in the Story of Human Stupidity* for orch. (Aarhus, Denmark, Feb. 5, 1968); *Nomo* for 7 narrators, 6 winds, and tape (1967); a church drama, *Eld för ett altare (Fire from an Altar,* 1968); *Kanske en pastoral om det får tina upp (Perhaps a Pastorale if It Will Thaw)* for percussion, piano, and strings (1968); a musical-dramatic dance, *A Play about the Medieval Värend and the Dacke Feud,* for winds, violin, nickelharp, and xylophone (1971); *Från mitt rosa badkar (From My Rosy Bathtub)* for orch., pop-group, and chorus (1971); *Det ringer i mitt öra (There Is a Ringing in My Ears)* for voices and instruments (1972); *Tahuantisuyos ekonomi* for chorus, winds and strings (1974); *Mellan berg och hav, mellan himmel och jard (Between the Mountains and the Ocean, Between the*

Sky and the Earth), a play on Chinese history, for singer, actor, and instrumental ensemble (1975).

Vallas, Léon, French writer on music; b. Roanne (Loire), May 17, 1879; d. Lyons, May 9, 1956. After studying medicine in Lyons, he took up music; in 1903 founded the *Revue Musicale de Lyon* (from 1912 to 1914 this was known as the *Revue de Musique Française*, and from 1920 to 1929, as *Nouvelle Revue Musicale);* in 1908 he was engaged as lecturer on music history at the Univ. of Lyons.
WRITINGS: *La Musique à l'Académie de Lyon au XVIIIe siècle* (part of his doctoral thesis, Lyons, 1908; the complete work was publ. as *Un Siècle de musique et de théâtre à Lyon, 1688-1789,* Lyons, 1932); *Le Théâtre et la ville, 1694-1712* (1919); *Les Idées de Claude Debussy, musicien français* (Paris, 1927; English transl. as *The Theories of Claude Debussy,* London, 1929); *Georges Migot* (Paris, n.d.); *Claude Debussy et son temps* (Paris, 1932; English transl. as *Claude Debussy, His Life and Works,* London, 1933); *Achille-Claude Debussy,* a brief biography (Paris, 1944); a 2-vol. biography of Vincent d'Indy: vol. 1, *La Jeunesse (1851-1886);* vol. 2, *La Maturité, la vieillesse (1886-1931),* publ. in Paris (1946; 1950); *La Véritable Historie de César Franck* (Paris, 1955; reprint 1972; an English edition appeared in 1951, earlier than the Paris printing; reprint, Westport, Conn., 1973).

Valle de Paz. See **Del Valle de Paz.**

Vallerand, Jean, Canadian composer; b. Montreal, Dec. 24, 1915. He studied violin at an early age; then took lessons in composition from Champagne (1935-42); served as director of music programs for the French Radio Network of the Canadian Broadcasting Corporation (1960-66). As a composer, he wrote music in a neo-Romantic manner; in his later compositions he experimented with serial techniques.
WORKS: *Le Magicien,* a chamber opera; *De Diable dans le beffroi* for orch. (1939); Violin Sonata (1950; orchestrated as a violin concerto, 1951); String Quartet (1958); *Réverbérations contractoires* for orch. (Montreal, March 6, 1961); *Cordes en mouvements (Strings in Motion)* for string orch. (1961; Montreal, March 27, 1961); *Étude Concertate* for violin and orch. (1969).

Valleria (real name **Schoening), Alwina,** American soprano; b. Baltimore, Oct. 12, 1848; d. Nice, Feb. 17, 1925. She studied singing in London with Luigi Arditi; made her first appearance in London (June 2, 1871); was engaged to sing Italian opera at St. Petersburg; returning to England, she became very successful in opera, including the Wagnerian repertory. She made her American debut as Marguérite (N.Y., Oct. 22, 1879); sang Leonora in *Il Trovatore* at the Metropolitan Opera House (Oct. 26, 1883); but retired from the stage after that season.

Valle-Riestra, José María, Peruvian composer; b. Lima, Nov. 9, 1859; d. there, Jan. 25, 1925. He studied as a child in London; after his return to Lima, he continued his musical education without a teacher; as a mature musician, he went to Paris for further studies with André Gédalge (1895-97). When the Academia

Nacional de Música was organized in Lima, he was appointed prof. there. In his compositions, it was his aim to contribute towards the establishment of a national school by the employment of old Inca melodies. His opera *Ollanta* (Lima, Dec. 26, 1900) was a successful dramatization of an Inca subject. His other two operas on Inca themes were *Las Rosas de Jamaica* (1 act), and *Atahualpa* (3 acts). He also wrote *Misa de Requiem* for chorus and orch.; *En Oriente* for orch.; *Elegía* for string orch.; choruses a cappella; songs.

Vallet, Nicolas, French lutenist; b. Corbéni, 1583; d. Amsterdam, c.1626. In 1615 he publ. at Amsterdam a book of French, German, and English songs, also preludes, fantasias, etc., in lute tablature: *Secretum Musarum* (2nd ed., 1618, with the title *Paradisus musicus testudinis);* also publ. *Le second livre de tabulature de luth* (1618), and *21 Psaumes de David* (in lute tablature; 1619).

Vallotti, Francesco Antonio, Italian theorist and composer; b. Vercelli, June 11, 1697; d. Padua, Jan. 19, 1780. A Franciscan monk, he was a pupil of Calegari at Padua; from 1728, maestro at the church of S. Antonio. He was one of the foremost organists of his time.
WRITINGS: *Responsoria in parasceve, Resp. in Sabbato Sancto,* and *Resp. in Coena Domini,* all *a 4* (Masses, motets, etc., in MS at Padua); *Della scienza teorica e pratica della moderna musica,* Book 1 (Padua, 1779; republ. by Bernandino Rizzi, Padua, 1950; other 3 books unpubl.), a learned work agreeing in the main principles with Rameau and Tartini, and correcting some of their errors; Vallotti's system is explained in *La vera idea delle musicali numeriche signature,* by L. A. Sabbatini, who, like Abbé Vogler, was Vallotti's pupil.
BIBLIOGRAPHY: L. A. Sabbatini, *Notizie sopra la vita e le opere di F. A. Vallotti* (Padua, 1780).

Valvasensi, Lazaro, Italian organist and composer; b. Valvasone (Udine), c.1600; date of death unknown. In 1622 he was organist at Murano (Venice); in 1626, choirmaster at Tolmezzo (Udine); from 1634-40, organist at Valvasone. Publ. *Letanie della B. V. a 5 voci, con un Mottetto nell'ultimo concertato per sonar nell'Organo* (Venice, 1622); *Compieta concertata a 4 voci* with continuo (Venice, 1626); *Secondo giardino d'amorosi fiori* (23 solo airs and 1 duet, with instrumental accompaniment; Venice, 1634; unique copy at Christ Church, Oxford).

Valverde, Joaquín, Spanish composer of light opera; b. Badajoz, Feb. 27, 1846; d. Madrid, March 17, 1910. He played the flute in bands from the age of 13; then studied at the Cons. of Madrid; received a prize for his orchestral work, *Batylo* (1871). From 1871 to 1889 he conducted theater orchestras in Madrid; taught flute at the Madrid Cons., and wrote melodic studies for his instrument. In collaboration with Chueca he wrote a number of zarzuelas, of which the most celebrated was *La gran vía* (Madrid, July 2, 1886; produced in London on April 18, 1906 as *Castles in Spain);* it contains the march *Cádiz,* which became immensely popular.

His son, **Joaquín Valverde y San Juan,** known under his diminutive given name **Quinito** (b. Madrid, Jan. 2, 1875; d. Mexico City, Nov. 4, 1918), was also a composer; wrote some 250 light pieces for the theater; his zarzuela *El gran capitán* was especially successful. He died during an American tour which he undertook as conductor of a light opera company.

Van Aerde, Raymond (Joseph Justin), Belgian musicologist; b. Mechlin, June 4, 1876; d. there, March 16, 1944. He was a librarian and a lecturer on music history at the Cons. of Mechlin. He wrote a life of Cipriano de Rore (Mechlin, 1909); *Les Tuerlinckx, luthiers à Malines* (Mechlin, 1914); *Ménestrels communaux et instrumentistes à Malines de 1311 à 1790* (Mechlin, 1911); *Musicalia; documents pour servir à l'histoire de la musique à Malines* (2 vols.; Mechlin, 1925–30); *Les Ancêtres flamands de Beethoven* (Mechlin, 1928).

Van Beinum, Eduard. See **Beinum, Eduard van.**

Van Bree, Joannes. See **Bree, Jean Bernard van.**

Vancea, Zeno, outstanding Rumanian composer and musicologist; b. Bosca-Vasiovei (Banat), Oct. 21, 1900. He studied at the Cluj Cons. (1919–21); then took lessons in composition with Ernst Kanitz in Vienna. Returning to Rumania, he taught at Conservatories in Tîrgu-Mures (1929–40); director, 1945–48), Timisoara (1940–45), and Bucharest (1949–68). He was the editor of the important Rumanian monthly *Muzica* (1953–64). Vancea belongs to the national school of Rumanian composers; in his music he makes use of folksong patterns without direct quotations. Harmonically, he adopts many procedures of cosmopolitan modern music, while cautiously avoiding abrasive sonorities. WORKS: ballet *Priculiciul (The Werewolf,* 1932–33; Bucharest, 1942; revised 1957); *Requiem* (1941); a cantata *Cîntecul pǎcii (Song of Peace,* 1961); *2 Rapsodia bǎnǎteana* for orch. (1926, 1950); *Scoarte,* suite for chamber orch. (1928); *2 Grotesque Dances* for orch. (1937); 2 sinfoniettas (1948, 1967); *O zi de varǎ (On a Summer Day),* suite for orch. (1951); *Symphonic Triptych* (1958; also known as *Preambule, Intermezzo and March*); *Burlesca* for orch. (1959); Concerto for small orch. (1960); *5 Pieces* for string orch. (1964); *Symphonic Prologue* (1973); *Cvartet bizantin,* string quartet in the Byzantine style (1931); 6 string quartets (1934, 1953, 1957, 1965, 1969–70, 1975); choruses; solo songs. He published a valuable book on Rumanian music of the 19th and 20th centuries, *Creatia muzicalǎ româneascǎ Sec. XIX-XX* (Bucharest, 1968).

Van Cleve, John Smith, American pianist and composer; b. Maysville, Ky., Oct. 30, 1851; d. New York, Dec. 28, 1917. He became totally blind at the age of 9; studied with Apthorp in Boston; was active in Cincinnati as a piano teacher and music critic (1879–97); then lived in Chicago; in 1913 moved to N.Y. He publ. a *Gavotte humoresque* for piano, and some other pieces.

BIBLIOGRAPHY: L. C. Elson, *The History of American Music* (N.Y., 1904; p. 331).

Van Delden, Lex. See **Delden, Lex van.**

Van de Moortel, Arie, Belgian composer and violist; b. Laeken, July 17, 1918; d. Brussels, May 1, 1976. He studied at the Royal Cons. in Brussels and in Ghent; made his debut as a violist in 1938 in the "Trio of the Court of Belgium"; taught chamber music at the Brussels Cons. (1946–76) and was director of the music academy at Anderlecht (1957–76). WORKS: *Silly Symphony;* trio for oboe, clarinet, and bassoon (1939, revised 1954); Concerto for Orch.; *Toccata* for piano; Viola Sonata; *Nocturne* for clarinet, saxophone, cello, and piano; Sonata for solo harp (1955); *Capriccio* for carillon (1957); *Danse d'Espagne* for solo harp; *Improvisation on a Choral Theme* for flute and piano (1967); Sonata for flute solo (1968); Violin Sonatina (1969); *Rondo-pastorale,* in memoriam E. Ysaÿe, for violin and piano (1970); *Sonata ostinato* for violin and organ (1974).

Van den Boorn-Coclet, Henriette, Belgian composer; b. Liège, Jan. 15, 1866; d. there, March 6, 1945. She studied with Radoux and Dupuis at the Liège Cons., and subsequently taught harmony there. Her compositions attracted considerable attention. She wrote a symph.; a symph. poem, *Le Renouveau; Sérénade,* for cello and piano; various piano pieces (*Mazurka, Caprice,* etc.); songs.

Van den Borren, Charles (-Jean-Eugène), eminent Belgian musicologist; b. Ixelles, near Brussels, Nov. 17, 1874; d. Brussels, Jan. 14, 1966. He studied theory with E. Closson; after receiving the degree of *Dr. juris,* he practiced law until 1905; then devoted himself to historical research in music; became one of the greatest authorities on the music of the Renaissance; was lecturer at the Univ. of Liège (1927–44); from 1926, prof. of music history at the Université Libre de Brussels; held many positions in learned societies. WRITINGS: *L'Œuvre dramatique de César Franck* (1907); *Les Origines de la musique de clavecin en Angleterre* (1912; English transl. as *The Sources of Keyboard Music in England,* 1914); *Les Musiciens belges en Angleterre à l'époque de la Renaissance* (1913); *Les Origines de la musique de clavecin dans les Pays-Bas (Nord et Sud) jusque vers 1630* (1914); *Les Débuts de la musique à Venise* (1914); *Orlande de Lassus* (1920); *Le Manuscrit musical M.222 C.22 de la Bibliothèque de Strasbourg* (Antwerp, 1924); *Guillaume Dufay* (1926); *Études sur le quinzième siècle musical* (Antwerp, 1941); *Peter Benoit* (Brussels, 1942); *Roland de Lassus* (Brussels, 1944); *Geschiedenis van de muziek in de Nederlanden* (2 vols.; Antwerp, 1948–51); etc. He edited *Polyphonia sacra* (15th-century pieces; publ. London, 1932); *Pièces polyphoniques profanes de provenance liégeoise (XVe siècle)* (Brussels, 1950); co-editor of the collected works of Philippe de Monte (1927–39). BIBLIOGRAPHY: A compendium, *Hommage à Charles Van den Borren* (Antwerp, 1945), with a list of his works; another Hommage was published to honor his 80th birthday (Brussels, 1954), and another to commemorate the centenary of his birth (Brussels, 1974).

Van den Eeden, Jean-Baptiste. See **Eeden, Jean-Baptiste van den.**

Van der Horst, Anthon. See **Horst, Anthon van der.**

Van der Linden, Cornelis, Dutch conductor and composer; b. Dordrecht, Aug. 24, 1839; d. Amsterdam, May 29, 1918. He studied with Kwast (piano) and F. Böhme (theory); after sojourns in Belgium, Paris, and Germany, he conducted various choral organizations; from 1875, also led symphony concerts; he was conductor of the newly established Neederlandsche Oper in Amsterdam (1888–94); produced 2 of his own operas there: *Catharina en Lambert* (Nov. 24, 1888) and *Leiden Ontzet (The Relief of Leiden;* April 1, 1893); he also wrote 7 overtures and many choral works.

Vandermaesbrugge, Max, Belgian composer; b. Couillet, June 14, 1933. He studied with Moulaert, Souris, Stehman, Louel and Absil at the Royal Cons. in Brussels (1951–60); taught piano and solfeggio at the Music Academy in Anderlecht (1955–62), Josseten-Noode (1958–62), de Forest (1959–62), and at Etterbeck (1963–66). In 1966 he was appointed to the faculty of the Brussels Cons.; in 1972 succeeded Defossez as inspector of Belgian music schools.
WORKS: *Drum follies,* variations for 10 percussionists (1961); *Caprice* for violin and piano (1961); *4 Fables de Florian* for soprano, contralto and baritone (1961); *Miniature Variations* for guitar solo (1962); Duo for flute and viola (1962); *En petits caractères* for 2 trumpets and piano obbligato (1963); Quartet for 4 clarinets (1965); *Tema e Variazioni* for carillon (1967); *Divertimento* for flute and strings (1969); *Hiver,* symph. poem (1970); *4 Instantanés* for flute and guitar (1972); *Sinfonia* for strings (1972); *Saxofolies* for saxophone septet (1974).

Van der Straeten, Edmond, Belgian music historian; b. Audenarde, Dec. 3, 1826; d. there, Nov. 26, 1895. He studied philosophy in Ghent; went to Brussels in 1857 as secretary to Fétis, with whom he studied counterpoint. He held a lifelong position at the Royal Library, and rarely left Belgium; was active as music critic (1859–72); wrote an opera, *Le Proscrit.* His reputation rests upon his scholarly publications, dealing with music in the Low Countries.
WRITINGS: He publ. a monumental work of reference, *La Musique au Pays-Bas avant le XIXe siècle* (1867–88; 8 vols.); other writings are: *Coup d'œil sur la musique actuelle à Audenarde* (1851); *Notice sur Charles-Félix de Hollande* (1854); *Notice sur les carillons d'Audenarde* (1855); *Recherches sur la musique à Audenarde avant le XIXe siècle* (1856); *Examen des chants populaires des Flamands de France, publiés par E. de Coussemaker* (1858); *J.-F.-J. Janssens* (1866); *Wagner; Verslag aan den heer minister van binnenlandsche Zaaken* (1871); *Le Théâtre villageois en Flandre* (2 vols.; 1874, 1880); *Les Musiciens belges en Italie* (1875); *Voltaire musicien* (1878); *Les Ballets des rois en Flandre; xylographie, musique, coutumes,* etc. (1892); *Charles V musicien* (1894); *Les Willems, luthiers gantois du XVIIe siècle* (1896; with C. Snoeck).

Van der Straeten, Edmund Sebastian Joseph, German cellist; b. Düsseldorf, April 29, 1855; d. London, Sept. 17, 1934. He studied cello in Cologne and London; also played the viola da gamba, and organized a trio with his son Ludwig and N. Greiffenhagen which gave performances of music for viols by composers of the Baroque. He wrote *The Technics of Violoncello Playing* (1898; 2nd ed. 1905); *The Romance of the Fiddle* (1911); *History of the Violoncello, the Viol da Gamba, Their Precursors and Collateral Instruments* (1915); *The History of the Violin* (2 vols.; 1933).

Van der Stucken, Frank (Valentin), American conductor; b. Fredericksburg, Texas, Oct. 15, 1858; d. Hamburg, Aug. 16, 1929. He was taken by his parents to Antwerp as a child, and studied music with Peter Benoit; then became associated with Reinecke in Leipzig; he also met Liszt. In 1884 he returned to the U.S., and became a choral conductor. He was the first to conduct a concert of American music in Europe, when at the Paris Exposition (July 12, 1889) he gave the first European performances of works by MacDowell, Foote, Chadwick, and Huss; also gave similar programs in Germany. From 1895 to 1903 he was director of the Cincinnati College of Music; concurrently, he conducted concerts of the Cincinnati Symph. Orch. (1895–1907). In 1898 he was called upon to lead the remaining concerts of the season of the N.Y. Philharmonic, following the death of Anton Seidl. In 1907 he went to Germany and remained there for the rest of his life. He composed a few orchestral pieces and choruses.

Van der Velden, Renier, Belgian composer; b. Antwerp, Jan. 14, 1910. He studied in Brussels with Jan Broeckx, Karel Candael and Joseph Jongen; in 1945 was appointed program director of the French services of the Belgian Radio in Antwerp. In 1970 he became a member of the Royal Flemish Academy of Arts, Letters and Sciences.
WORKS: 12 ballets: *Indruk aan Zee* for small orch. (1930); *Provinciestad 1900* (1937); *L'Enlèvement de Proserpine* (1947); *Les Amours de torero* (1948); *De zakdoekjes* (1947); *Dulle Griet* (1949; revised 1967); *Les Ancêtres* (1949); *Arlequinade* (1950); *Judith,* for 2 pianos and percussion (1951; orch. version, 1953); *De Triomf van de dood* (1963); *Oostendse maskers* (1965) and *Ballet Music* for 20 winds and piano (1972); *Impression maritime* for small orch. (1930); *Divertimento* for string orch. (1938); *Hommage à Ravel,* symph. suite (1938; the second part, *Habanera,* is often played separately); Trumpet Concerto (1940); Oboe Concerto (1941); Sinfonietta for string orch. (1942); 2 suites for orch. (1945, 1955); Concertino for clarinet, bassoon, piano, and string orch. (1949); *Kammermuziek* for viola and chamber ensemble (1956); Violin Concerto (1958); Concertino for viola and chamber orch. (1964); Concertino for flute and strings (1965); *Beweging (Movement)* for orch. (1968); *Etude* for 11 instruments (1969); Sinfonietta (1969); Concertino for piano and strings (1971); *Hulde aan Janáček*

(Homage to Janáček), 3 short pieces for flute, oboe, and string orch. (1973); 2 concertos for wind quintet (1939, 1955); *Adagio and Finale* for string trio (1940); Trio for oboe, clarinet, and bassoon (1943); Sextet for wind quintet and piano (1948); *Divertimento* for oboe, clarinet, and bassoon (1957); Concertino for brass quintet and 2 pianos (1965); *Fantaisie* for 4 clarinets (1967); *2 Dialogues* for clarinet and piano (1971); 2 suites for piano (1937, 1944); *Bewegung* for 2 pianos (1965); songs, among them *8 Poèmes de Karel van de Woestijne* for high voice and piano (1946; orchestrated 1951).

Van de Woestijne, David, Belgian composer; b. Llanidloes, Wales, Feb. 18, 1915. He is the son of painter Gustave van de Woestijne and the nephew of the Flemish poet Karel van de Woestijne; studied at the Cons. in Malines with Defauw and Gilson; also took lessons with the Spanish composer Oscar Esplá during the latter's stay in Belgium. His music reflects the trends of cosmopolitan modernism gravitating towards neo-Baroque techniques.

WORKS: opera, *Graal 68 ou L'Impromptu de Gand* (Ghent, 1968); an opera-ballet *Le Débat de la folie et de l'amour* (1959); television opera, *De zoemende muzikant* (1967); Double Concerto for piano, cello, and orch. (1935); *Fantasia* for oboe and orch. (1936); Piano Concerto (1938); *Ballade* for piano and orch. (1940); Concerto for violin and 12 solo instruments (1945); *Sérénades* for piano, 12 wind instruments, double bass and percussion (1946; International Society for Contemporary Music Festival, Copenhagen, June 2, 1947); Concerto for Orch. (1946); 2 cantatas: *La Belle Cordière* for soprano and orch. (1954) and *Les Aéronauts* for soli, chorus, speaking chorus and orch. (1963); Symphony (1958); Symphony in One Movement (1965); *Concertino da camera* for flute, oboe, and strings (1967); *Aswoensdag (Ash Wednesday)* for narrator, soli, chorus, and orch. (1971); 2-Piano Concerto (1972); *Divertimento* for oboe, clarinet and bassoon (1942); Quintet for flute, oboe, violin, viola, and cello (1953); Violin Sonata (1956); *Variations* for 7 instruments (1965); *Sarabande* for 2 guitars (1965); String Quartet (1970); *Devant une sculpture* for 12 instruments (1972); *Toccata* for piano (1935); Piano Sonatina (1945); 2-Piano Sonata (1955); songs.

Van Dieren, Bernard. See **Dieren, Bernard van.**

Van Doorslaer, Georges, Belgian musicologist; b. Mechlin, Sept. 27, 1864; d. there, Jan. 16, 1940. He was a physician by profession, but studied music as an avocation; wrote several valuable treatises dealing with Belgian musicians: *Herry Bredemers, 1472–1522* (Antwerp, 1915); *De Toonkunstenaars der familie Vredeman* (Antwerp, 1920); *La Vie et les œuvres de Philippe de Monte* (Brussels, 1921); *Rinaldo del Mel* (Antwerp, 1922). Also edited 8 vols. in the collected ed. of works by Philippe de Monte.

Van Dresser, Marcia, American soprano; b. Memphis, Tenn., Dec. 4, 1877; d. London, July 11, 1937. She studied in Chicago and N.Y.; sang minor parts at the Metropolitan Opera (1903–04); then after further study in Germany, she made her European debut in

Dresden (1907); was a member of the Dessau Opera (1908–10) and of the Frankfurt Opera (1911–14). Returning to the U.S. in 1915, she gave a recital in N.Y. (March 22, 1915), and joined the Chicago Opera (1915–17).

Van Durme, Jef, Belgian composer; b. Kemzeke-Waas, May 7, 1907; d. Brussels, Jan. 28, 1965. He studied at the Royal Flemish Cons. in Antwerp with Flor Alpaerts; in 1931 he went to Vienna, where he took lessons in advanced composition with Alban Berg.

WORKS: 5 operas: *Remous,* after Weterings (Brussels, 1936); *The Death of a Salesman,* after Arthur Miller (1954–55); *King Lear* (1955–57), *Anthony and Cleopatra* (1957–59) and *Richard III* (1960–61), all after Shakespeare; 2 ballets, *De dageraad* (1932–33; Antwerp, 1934) and *Orestes* (1934–35; suite for orch., 1936–40); 2 symph. poems, *Hamlet* (1929) and *Beatrice* (1930); an oratorio, *De 14 stonden* (1931); 6 symphonies: No. 1 (1934); No. 2 (1938–39); No. 3 (1945–46); No. 4 (1950–51); No. 5 (1952); No. 6 (1953); 2 *Elegies* for orch. (1933, 1938); *Poème heroïque* (1935); *Breughel Symphony* (1935–42); 2 *Sinfonia da Cameras* (1937, 1949); 3 *Ballads* for orch.: No. 1, *In memoriam Alban Berg* (1938); No. 2 (1947–48); No. 3 (1961); 2 piano concertos (1943, 1946); *Symphonic Prologue* (1944–45); Violin Concerto (1946–47); 3 suites for orch. (1947, 1948–60, 1962); *Van Gogh Suite* for orch. (1954); Sinfonietta for strings (1962); 3 violin sonatas (1928, 1938, 1947); Sextet for piano and wind quintet (1930); 5 string quartets (1932–33, 1937, 1945–48, 1948–53, 1953); Piano Quartet (1934); 2 piano sonatas (1946, 1952–53); 4 piano trios (1928, 1929, 1942, 1949); Cello Sonata (1952); Wind Quintet (1951–52); piano pieces; 21 songs, 2 with orch.

Van Duyze, Florimond, Belgian music scholar and composer; b. Ghent, Aug. 4, 1843; d. there, May 18, 1910. He studied at the Ghent Cons.; published some valuable collections of old Netherland vocal music, among them *Het oude nederlandsche Lied* (4 vols.; 1903–08).

BIBLIOGRAPHY: P. Bergmans, "Florimond van Duyze" *Annuaire de l'Académie royale des sciences* (Brussels, 1919).

Van Dyck, Ernest (Marie Hubert), Belgian tenor; b. Antwerp, April 2, 1861; d. Berlaer-lez-Lierre, Aug. 31, 1923. He studied law; was a journalist in Paris; sang in the Ninth Symph. of Beethoven at a Lamoureux concert (Dec. 2, 1883); made his operatic debut as Lohengrin in the memorable French première, on May 3, 1887; from 1888 to 1898 he was a member of the Vienna Opera; from 1898 to 1902 he sang Wagnerian roles at the Metropolitan Opera (debut as Tannhäuser, Nov. 29, 1898). After his return to Europe he continued to appear as a Wagnerian tenor until 1906, when he settled down as a singing teacher in Brussels and Antwerp. In 1886 he married Augusta Servais, a sister of the famous cellist.

Van Gilse, Jan. See **Gilse, Jan van.**

Van Hagen, Peter Albrecht, Dutch musician active in America; b. Holland, 1750; d. Boston, 1803. After his arrival in America from Holland in 1774, he settled in Charleston, S.C., as a music teacher; from 1789 to 1796 was in N.Y., giving concerts with his wife and son; in 1796 the family moved to Boston. He composed a *Federal Overture* (1797; not to be confused with *The Federal Overture* by B. Carr); *Funeral Dirge for George Washington* (1800); much theater music. His son, **Peter Albrecht, Jr.** (1781–1837), born in Charleston, was also a musician; he wrote songs and composed an overture.

BIBLIOGRAPHY: O. G. Sonneck and W. T. Upton, *Early Concert-Life in America* (1907; revised, 1945).

Van Hal, Johann Baptist. See **Wanhal, Johann Baptist.**

Van Hoogstraten, Willem. See **Hoogstraten, Willem van.**

Van Hoose, Ellison, American tenor; b. Murfreesboro, Tenn., Aug. 18, 1868; d. Houston, Texas, March 24, 1936. He studied with Luckstone in N.Y., Jean de Reszke in Paris, and also in Rome and London. He made his operatic debut with the Damrosch Opera Co. in Philadelphia as Tannhäuser (Dec. 11, 1897); toured with Mme. Melba in the U.S. (1903–05) and Mme. Sembrich (1906–07); toured in Europe (1908–10); was a member of the Chicago Opera Co. (1911–12); then devoted himself mainly to oratorio singing.

Van Katwijk, Paul. See **Katwijk, Paul van.**

Van Lier, Bertus, Dutch composer; b. Utrecht, Sept. 10, 1906; d. Roden, Feb. 14, 1972. He studied composition with Willem Pijper in Amsterdam and conducting with Scherchen in Strasbourg; settled in Utrecht as conductor, composer and music critic. He taught at the Rotterdam Cons. (1945–60) and thereafter worked in the department of art history at the Univ. of Groningen. His early compositions are modeled on Pijper's "germ-cell" theory, to which he imparted a literary symbolism.

WORKS: ballet *Katharsis* (1945; concert version, Utrecht, Nov. 29, 1950); 3 symphonies (1928; 1930–31, revised 1946; 1938–39); Concertino for cello and chamber orch. (1933); *De Dijk (The Dike)* for narrator and chamber orch. (1937); *Canticum* for female chorus, 2 flutes, piano 4-hands, and strings (1939); *O. Netherlands, Pay Attention,* cantata for chorus, tympani, and strings (1945); *Het Hooglied (The Song of Songs)* for soloists, chorus, and small orch. (1949; composed in Dutch and English); Bassoon Concerto (1950); *Symfonia* for 2 string orchestras, double wind quintet, and timpani (1954); *Cantate voor Kerstmis (Christmas Cantata)* for chorus and orch. (1955); *Divertimento facile* for orch. (1957); *Concertante Music* for violin, oboe, and orch. (1959); *5 Mei: Zij (Fifth of May: They),* oratorio (Radio Hilversum, May 5, 1963, 18th anniversary of the liberation of Holland); *Intrada Reale e Sinfonia Festiva* for orch. (1964); *Variaties en thema* for orch. (1967; Bergen, Norway, Jan. 17, 1968); String Quartet (1929); Solo Violin Sonata (1931); *Small Suite* for violin and piano (1935); *3 Old Persian Quatrains* for soprano, bass flute, oboe d'amore, and

piano (1956); incidental music for Sophocles' *Ajax* (1932) and *Antigone* (1952); piano pieces; choruses. He published a number of essays on music under the title *Buiten de Maastreep (Beyond the Bar Line,* Amsterdam, 1948) and *Rhythme en metrum* (Groningen, 1967).

Van Lier, Jacques, Dutch cellist; b. The Hague, April 24, 1875; d. Worthing, England, Feb. 25, 1951. He studied cello with Hartog at The Hague and with Eberle in Rotterdam; joined the Berlin Philharmonic in 1897; from 1899 to 1915 was instructor of cello at the Klindworth-Scharwenka Cons. in Berlin. He was cellist in the Holländisches Trio, with J. van Veen (violin) and Coenraad Bos (piano), which enjoyed a European reputation (1900–07); in 1915 settled in The Hague; after 1939 went to England. He publ. *Violoncellbogentechnik* and *Moderne Violoncelltechnik der linken und der rechten Hand;* also edited about 400 classical pieces for cello.

BIBLIOGRAPHY: *Musical Opinion* (Oct. 1931).

Van Maldeghem, Robert Julien. See **Maldeghem, Robert Julien van.**

Van Maldere, Pierre. See **Maldere, Pierre van.**

Vanni-Marcoux. See **Marcoux, Vanni.**

Vannuccini, Luigi, noted Italian singing master; b. Fojano, Dec. 4, 1828; d. Montecatini, Aug. 14, 1911. He studied at the Cons. in Florence, where he became an opera conductor (1848); then turned to the study of the piano, and appeared as a concert pianist with excellent success; finally settled in Florence, devoted himself exclusively to vocal training, and acquired fame as a singing master. He publ. some songs and piano pieces.

BIBLIOGRAPHY: L. Neretti, "Luigi Vannuccini," *Musica d'Oggi* (1931).

Van Otterloo, Willem. See **Otterloo, Willem van.**

Van Raalte, Albert. See **Raalte, Albert van.**

Van Rooy, Anton (Antonius Maria Josephus), Dutch baritone; b. Rotterdam, Jan. 1, 1870; d. Munich, Nov. 28, 1932. He was a chorister in a church; studied voice with Stockhausen at Frankfurt. In 1897 he was engaged to sing at Bayreuth, and performed there the 3 Wotans with excellent success. On Dec. 14, 1898 he made his American debut as Wotan in *Die Walküre* at the Metropolitan Opera, where he appeared each season until 1908, singing in the summers at Covent Garden, London, and Bayreuth. In 1908 he was engaged as a regular member of the Frankfurt Opera. He was particularly distinguished in Wagnerian roles, but also was noted for his interpretations of Escamillo in *Carmen* and Valentin in *Faust.*

Van Rossum, Frédéric, Belgian composer; b. Ixelles, near Brussels, Dec. 5, 1939. He studied with Marcel Quinet at the Brussels Cons. (1956–62); then taught piano there (1965–68); later was instructor in music analysis. He won a Premier Grand Prix de Rome in 1965 for his *Cantate de la Haute Mer.*

WORKS: *Petite Piece* for clarinet and piano (1961); Piano Sonata (1963); *Capriccio* for wind quintet (1963); *Sinfonietta* (1964); *Cantata sacrée* for chorus, strings, and harpsichord (1966); *12 Miniatures* for piano or orch. (1967); String Quartet (1967); *Divertimento* for string orch. (1967); *Sinfonie Concertante* for horn, piano, percussion, and orch. (1968); *Graffiti* for violin and piano (1968); *Duetto* for cello and piano (1968); *Pyrogravures* for wind quintet (1968); *Threni* for mezzo-soprano and orch. (1969); *Der Blaue Reiter,* in homage to German expressionistic painters, for orch. (1971); *Epitaph* for string orch. (1972); Piano Quintet (1972); *Rétrospection* for soprano, contralto, chorus, 2 pianos, and percussion (1973); *Réquisitoire* for brass and percussion (1973); Piano Concerto (1975).

Van Slyck, Nicholas, American pianist and composer; b. Philadelphia, Oct. 25, 1922. He studied composition with Walter Piston at Harvard Univ.; subsequently became professor at the Longy School of Music in Cambridge, Mass., and eventually its director. Among his works are 3 piano concertos, 6 piano sonatas, and much chamber music.

Van Vactor, David, American composer and conductor; b. Plymouth, Ind., May 8, 1906. He studied at Northwestern Univ. with Arthur Kitti (flute) and Arne Oldberg, Felix Borowski and Albert Noelte (composition). After a year in Vienna (1928) he returned to Chicago, where he became a flutist in the Chicago Symph. Orch. (1931–43). He organized a woodwind quintet, and toured Latin America; went to South America as conductor in 1946. From 1943 to 1945 he was flutist and assistant conductor of the Kansas City Philharmonic; in 1947 he was appointed conductor of the Knoxville Symph. Orch. The idiom of his music is medium modern, set in sophisticatedly enhanced tonalities and sparked with ingenious atonalities.

WORKS: *Chaconne* for string orch. (Rochester, May 17, 1928); *5 Little Pieces for Big Orchestra* (Ravinia Park, Ill., July 5, 1931); *The Masque of the Red Death,* after Poe (1932); Flute Concerto (Chicago, Feb. 26, 1933); *Passacaglia and Fugue* (Chicago, Jan. 28, 1934); *Concerto grosso* for 3 flutes, harp, and orch. (Chicago, April 4, 1935); *Overture to a Comedy,* No. 1 (Chicago, June 20, 1937); *Symphonic Suite* (Ravinia Park, Ill., July 21, 1938); Symphony in D (1936–37; N.Y., Jan. 19, 1939, composer conducting; awarded prize of $1,000 in the American Composers Contest sponsored by the N.Y. Philharmonic); *Divertimento,* for small orch. (Ravinia Park, Ill., July 8, 1939); *Overture to a Comedy,* No. 2 (Indianapolis, March 14, 1941); *Variazioni Solenne* (performed under the title *Gothic Impressions* by the Chicago Symph. Orch., Feb. 26, 1942); *Music for the Marines* (Indianapolis, March 27, 1943); *5 Bagatelles,* for strings (Chicago, Feb. 7, 1938); Viola Concerto (Ravinia Park, Ill., July 13, 1940); Flute Quintet (1932); *Suite* for 2 flutes (1933); String Quartet (1940); String Trio (1942); Flute Sonata (1945); *Pastorale and Dance* for flute and strings (1947); Violin Concerto (Knoxville, April 10, 1951); Symph. No. 2 (Pittsburgh, April 3, 1959);

Woodwind Quintet (1959); Octet for brass (1963); *Suite on Chilean Folk Themes* for orch. (1963); *Sinfonia breve* (Indianapolis, Oct. 30, 1966); *Economy Band No. 2* for horn, tuba, and percussion (1969); Symph. No. 4, *Walden* for chorus and orch. to texts from Thoreau's *Walden* (Knoxville, March 1, 1970); Symph. No. 5 (Knoxville, March 4, 1976); *Crucifixus,* Easter cantata (1976); *Episodes Jesus Christ* for chorus and orch. (1977).

Van Vechten, Carl, American novelist and writer on music; b. Cedar Rapids, Iowa, June 17, 1880; d. New York, Dec. 21, 1964. He graduated from the Univ. of Chicago (1903); was music critic of the *N.Y. Times* (1906–07 and 1910–13); was its Paris correspondent in 1908–09. In 1931 he occupied himself with photography, and took a great number of pictures of musicians; his collection of photographs is at Fiske Univ. in Nashville. He publ. *5 Old English Ditties* (1904). His books on music: *Music After the Great War* (1915); *Music and Bad Manners* (1916); *Interpreters and Interpretations* (1917); *The Music of Spain* (1918); *Red: Papers on Musical Subjects* (1925).

BIBLIOGRAPHY: E. G. Lueders, *Carl Van Vechten and the Twenties* (Albuquerque, 1955).

Van Vleck, Jacob, a Moravian minister, violinist, and organist; b. New York, 1751; d. Bethlehem, Pa., July 3, 1831. He was director of the Young Ladies' Seminary at Bethlehem from 1790–1800; consecrated a bishop in 1815. Among the Moravians who were active as composers, he was the first American-born.

BIBLIOGRAPHY: A. G. Rau and H. T. David, *A Catalogue of Music by American Moravians* (Bethlehem, 1938); H. T. David, "Background for Bethlehem: Moravian Music in Pennsylvania," *Magazine of Art* (April 1939); H. T. David, "Musical Life in the Pennsylvania Settlements of the *Unitas Fratrum,*" *Transactions of the Moravian Historical Society* (1942; reprinted as Moravian Music Foundation Publication No. 6, Winston-Salem, N.C., 1959); J. O. Falconer, "The Second Berlin Song School in America," *Musical Quarterly* (July 1973).

Van Vliet, Cornelius, Dutch cellist; b. Rotterdam, Sept. 1, 1886; d. Morelia, Mexico, Jan. 1973. He began to study cello at 9; in 1903 went to Leipzig, where he appeared as soloist; then joined the Prague Philharmonic and traveled with it in Poland and Russia; in 1908 was engaged by Mahler as 1st cellist with the Vienna Philharmonic; in 1911 settled in the U.S. He was 1st cellist of the Minneapolis Symph. Orch. (1912–19); 1st cellist of the N.Y. Philharmonic (1919–29); 1st cellist of the Pittsburgh Symph. Orch. (1938–41); prof. of cello at the Univ. of Colorado (1948–53). In 1954 he went to Mexico.

Van Westerhout, Niccolò, Italian composer; b. (of Dutch parentage) Mola di Bari, Dec. 17, 1857; d. Naples, Aug. 21, 1898. He was a pupil of Nicola d'Arienzo at the Naples Cons.; then became a prof. of harmony there. He wrote 3 operas: *Cimbelino* (Rome, April 7, 1892), *Fortunio* (Milan, May 16, 1895), and *Dona Flor* (Mola di Bari, April 18, 1896, on the opening of the Teatro Van Westerhout, named after him); another opera, *Colomba,* was produced posthumously

(Naples, March 27, 1923); also 2 symphonies, a violin concerto; publ. many piano pieces of considerable merit, and songs.

Van Wyk, Arnold. See **Wyk, Arnold van.**

Van Zandt, Marie, American coloratura soprano; b. N.Y., Oct. 8, 1861; d. Cannes, Dec. 31, 1919. She studied with her mother, the well-known American soprano, **Jennie van Zandt;** made her debut in Turin (1879); was engaged at the Opéra-Comique, Paris (1880–85); sang at the Metropolitan Opera, N.Y. during the season of 1891–92; in 1896 she rejoined the Opéra-Comique. Delibes wrote the role of Lakmé for her, and she created it at the Opéra-Comique on April 14, 1883.

Van Zanten, Cornelia, famous Dutch soprano and pedagogue; b. Dordrecht, Aug. 2, 1855; d. The Hague, Jan. 10, 1946. She studied with K. Schneider at the Cologne Cons., and in Milan with Lamperti, who developed her original contralto into a coloratura soprano voice. She made her debut in Turin; then sang in Germany; toured in America in 1886–87 as a member of the National Opera Co. under the directorship of Theodore Thomas; then returned to Europe; appeared in special performances of *Der Ring des Nibelungen* in Russia; finally became a member of the Nederlandsche Oper in Amsterdam; also taught at the Amsterdam Cons. (1895–1903); subsequently lived in Berlin, highly esteemed as a singing teacher; eventually settled in The Hague. She publ. songs to German and Dutch texts; with C. E. Poser, brought out *Leitfaden zum Kunstgesang* (Berlin, 1903).
BIBLIOGRAPHY: J. W. Hofstra, "C. van Zanten," *Mens en Melodie* 1 (1946).

Varèse, Edgar, one of the most remarkable composers of his century who introduced a totally original principle of organizing the materials and forms of sound, profoundly influencing the direction of new music; b. Paris, Dec. 22, 1883; d. New York, Nov. 6, 1965. He was of French and Italian parentage; the original spelling of his first Christian name was Edgard, but most of his works were published under the name Edgar; about 1940 he chose to return to the legal spelling, Edgard. He spent his early childhood in Bourgogne; began to compose at an early age. At 12, he wrote an opera, *Martin Paz*, after a novel of Jules Verne. In 1903 he returned to Paris; in 1904 he entered the Schola Cantorum in Paris, where he studied with Vincent d'Indy, Albert Roussel, and Charles Bordes; in 1906 he attended the classes of Widor at the Paris Cons. In 1907 he received the "bourse artistique" (a stipend) offered by the City of Paris; founded and conducted the chorus of the Université Populaire and organized the concerts of the Château du Peuple. In 1908 he went to Berlin where he organized and conducted the Symphonischer Chor; composed his first large work, a symphonic poem *Bourgogne* (1910), which was performed in Berlin. He was encouraged in his composition by Debussy, from whom he received a friendly letter, urging him to ignore hostile criticism. In Paris he met many artists and writers in the cultural French milieu. As early as 1913 he began an ear-

nest quest for new musical resources, and worked on related problems with the acoustician René Bertrand; he was also on friendly terms with the Italian musical futurist Luigi Russolo, although he disapproved of the attempt to find a way to new music through the medium of pitchless noise. In 1915 he went to America, and settled in New York; there he organized the New Symph. Orch. for performances of modern music, which presented its first concert on April 11, 1919; in 1922 he founded, with Carlos Salzedo, the International Composers' Guild, which gave an inaugural concert in N.Y. on Dec. 17, 1922. In 1926 he founded, with a few progressive musicians, the Pan American Society, dedicated to the promotion of music of the Americas. He intensified his study of the nature of sound, working with the acoustician Harvey Fletcher (1926–36) and with the Russian electronic engineer Leo Theremin. These studies led him to the formulation of the concept of "organized sound" in which the sonorous elements in themselves determine the progress of the music; although the principle of the thematic development was thus eliminated, the cohesion of musical ideas was, paradoxically, made all the more solid; the distinction between consonances and dissonances became no longer valid in Varèse's method of composition. The resulting product was unique in modern music; characteristically, Varèse attached to his works titles from the field of mathematics or physics, such as *Intégrales, Hyperprism* (a projection of a prism into the 4th dimension), *Ionisation* (atomic fission), *Density 21.5* (specific weight of platinum), etc. In view of the totally unfamilar idiom of Varèse's music and the tremendous difficulty in performing it, there were but few conductors who ventured to present his works to the public; in smaller forms Varèse wrote only a few songs, which he soon disavowed. Among conductors of major symphony orchestras only Stokowski was bold enough to put Varèse's formidable scores *Amériques* and *Arcana* on his programs with the Philadelphia Orch.; they evoked yelps of derision and indignation from the public and the press. But an extraordinary reversal of attitude towards Varèse's music, owing perhaps to the general advance of musical intelligence and the emergence of younger music critics, took place some years later, resulting in a spectacular increase in the number of performances; also musicians themselves learned to overcome the rhythmic difficulties presented in Varèse's scores. Fortunately Varèse lived to witness this long delayed recognition of his music as a major stimulus in the art; his name joined those of Stravinsky, Ives, Schoenberg, and Anton von Webern among great masters of 20th-century music.

WORKS: unfinished opera, *Oedipus und die Sphinx*, after Hofmannsthal (1908–14); for orch.: *La Chanson des jeunes hommes* (1905); *Le Prélude à la fin d'un jour* (1905); *Rapsodie romaine* (1906); *Bourgogne* (1907; Berlin, Dec. 15, 1910); *Gargantua* (1909; unfinished); *Mehr Licht* (1911); *Les Cycles du Nord* (1915); *Amériques* (Philadelphia, April 9, 1926, Stokowski conducting); *Arcana* (1925–27; Philadelphia, April 8, 1927, Stokowski conducting); for small ensembles: *Offrandes* for voice and small orch. (N.Y., April 23, 1922, Carlos Salzedo conducting); *Hyperprism,* for 9 wind instruments and 18 percussion devices (N.Y., March 4, 1923); *Octandre* for flute, oboe, clarinet, bassoon, horn, trumpet, trombone, and double bass (N.Y., Jan. 13, 1924); *Intégrales* (N.Y., March 1, 1925); *Ionisation*, for 40 percussion instruments of indefinite pitch, piano, and 2 sirens (1931; N.Y., March 6, 1933, Nicolas Slonimsky conducting); *Ecuatorial* for bass, instruments, and thereminovox (N.Y., April 15, 1934); *Density 21.5* for unaccompanied flute (N.Y., Feb. 16, 1936, Georges Barrère soloist on his platinum flute of specific gravity 21.5; hence the title); *Étude pour espace*, for mixed chorus, 2 pianos, and percussion; (N.Y., Feb. 23, 1947); *Déserts* for wind instruments, percussion, and 3 interpolations of electronic sound (Paris, Dec. 2, 1954); *Poeme électronique* (Philips Pavilion at the Brussels World Exposition, spatially distributed over 400 loudspeakers, 1958); *Nocturnal* for soprano and bass, 12 wind instruments, strings, piano, percussion, from the text from *House of Incest* by Anaïs Nin (unfinished; completed by Chou Wen-chung from sketches). Varèse published several seminal papers, among them "Les Instruments de musique et la machine électronique," in *L'âge nouveau* (1955) and "The Liberation of Sound," in *Perspectives of New Music* (Fall–Winter 1966).

BIBLIOGRAPHY: Henry Cowell, "The Music of Edgar Varèse" in *American Composers on American Music* (Stanford, 1933); Henry Cowell, "The Music of Edgar Varèse," *Modern Music* (Jan.–Feb. 1928); J. H. Klarón, *Edgar Varèse* (Boston, 1929); Paul Rosenfeld, *An Hour with American Music* (Philadelphia, 1929; pp. 160–79); F. Waldman, "Edgar Varèse," *Juilliard Review* (Fall 1954); O. Vivier, "Innovations instrumentales d'Edgar Varèse," *La Revue Musicale* (Jan. 1956); M. Wilkinson, "An Introduction to the Music of Edgar Varèse," *Score* (March 1957); several articles, in memoriam, *Perspectives of New Music* (Spring–Summer 1966); Chou Wen-chung, "Open Rather Than Unbounded," *Perspectives of New Music* (Fall–Winter 1966); Fernand Ouellette, *Edgard Varèse* (Paris, 1966); Georges Charbonnier, *Entretiens avec Edgar Varèse* (Paris, 1970); Louise Varèse, *A Looking Glass Diary*, vol. I: 1883–1928 (N.Y., 1972); Odile Vivier, *Varèse*, (Paris, 1973); Hilda Jolivet, *Varèse* (Paris, 1973); Grete Wehmeyer, *Edgard Varèse* (Regensburg, 1977).

Varga, Ovidiu, Rumanian composer; b. Pascani, Oct. 5, 1913. He studied violin and composition in Jassy; subsequently became prof. at the Bucharest Cons. He excels in vocal music; has written several cantatas on patriotic subjects; a concerto for string orch. and percussion (1957); many mass songs and instrumental pieces.

Varga, Tibor, Hungarian violinist; b. Györ, July 4, 1921. He studied violin with Hubay at the Budapest Music Academy; subsequently took lessons with Carl Flesch in Berlin; gave concerts as a child; then went to London, where he became active mainly as a teacher. In 1964 he organized a series of summer concerts in Sion, Wallis, where he took up residence, and also conducted classes in interpretation; both as a performer and instructor, he devoted his efforts mainly to the promotion of modern music.

Varlamov, Alexander, Russian composer of songs; b. Moscow, Nov. 27, 1801; d. St. Petersburg, Oct. 27, 1848. At the age of 10 he entered the Imperial Chapel at St. Petersburg, where his fine voice attracted the attention of Bortniansky, the director, who then became his teacher. As a young man he was attached to the Russian Embassy at The Hague as leader of the Russian church choir there (1819–23); then returned to Moscow, where he taught singing and violin (1823–29); later went to St. Petersburg as a singing teacher. He wrote 223 songs (publ. in 12 vols. by Stellovsky) in the Russian folk style; one of them, *Krasny Sarafan (The Red Dress),* achieved tremendous popularity; Wieniawski made use of it in his violin piece, *Souvenir de Moscou.* He was the author of the first Russian singing method, *Shkola Penya* (Moscow, 1840).

BIBLIOGRAPHY: Natalya Listova, *Alexander Varlamov* (Moscow, 1968).

Varnay, Astrid, soprano; b. Stockholm, April 25, 1918, of Hungarian parents, both professional singers. She was taken to America as a child, and studied first with her mother, then with Hermann Weigert (1890–1955), whom she married in 1944. She made her debut as Sieglinde at the Metropolitan Opera (Dec. 6, 1941), substituting for Lotte Lehmann without rehearsal; appeared at the Metropolitan Opera for the last time in 1974; lived mostly in Munich.

Varney, Louis, French composer; b. New Orleans, La., May 30, 1844; d. Cauterets, France, Aug. 20, 1908. His father, **Pierre Joseph Alphonse Varney,** was director of a French opera company in New Orleans (1840–50). Louis Varney was taken to Paris at the age of 7 and remained there for the rest of his life. From 1876 he produced about 40 light theater works, including the comic opera *Les Mousquetaires au couvent* (Paris, March 16, 1880), which remained a standard item in the French light opera repertory.

Varney, Pierre Joseph Alphonse, French composer; b. Paris, Dec. 1, 1811; d. there, Feb. 7, 1879. He studied with Reicha at the Paris Cons.; was active as theater conductor in Belgium, Holland, and France. From 1840 to 1850 he was director of the French Opera Company in New Orleans, where he married Jeanne Aimée Andry; their son **Louis Varney** was born there. The family returned to Paris in 1851. Varney set to music a poem by Rouget de Lisle, *Mourir pour la patrie,* which became popular during the Paris Revolution of 1848.

Varro, Marie-Aimée, French pianist; b. Brunoy, Feb. 18, 1915; d. Neuchâtel, Sept. 14, 1971. She studied piano at the Paris Cons., obtaining the Premier Prix; she subsequently worked with Robert Casadesus and Alfred Cortot; completed her advanced studies with Emil von Sauer in Vienna, who gave her indications for authentic interpretation of Liszt's piano works, which he had received from Liszt himself. In her own career, she specialized in the works of the great Romantic composers, particularly Schumann, Chopin, Liszt, and Brahms. She gave recitals in Europe and America; also appeared as soloist with major orchestras.

Varviso, Silvio, Swiss conductor; b. Zürich, Feb. 26, 1924. He studied piano and conducting at the Zürich Cons.; was conductor at St. Gallen (1946-50); at the Basel Stadttheater (1950-58); guest conductor at the Berlin Opera (1958-61); then with the San Francisco Opera (1959-61); made his Metropolitan Opera debut in N.Y. in 1961. He was conductor of the Stockholm Opera from 1965-72; in 1972, appointed musical director of the Stuttgart Opera.

Varvoglis, Mario, Greek composer; b. Athens, Dec. 22, 1885; d. there, July 30, 1967. He studied at the Paris Cons. with Leroux, and later at the Schola Cantorum with Vincent d'Indy. Returning to Greece in 1922, he was appointed prof. of music history at the Athens Cons. His early music was influenced by Massenet; later he evolved a more independent style, using some Greek melodic patterns. His symph. prelude *Sainte-Barbara* (1912) was publ. by the French Institute of Athens in 1948. He also wrote the 1-act opera *An Afternoon of Love* (1935); incidental music to the classical Greek tragedies *Agamemnon* (1932) and *Medea* (1942); *Suite pastorale* for strings (1910); *Caprice grec* for cello solo and orch. (1914); symph. poem *Behind the Wire Fence* (1945); and a "study in symph. contrasts" *Lauriers et cyprès* (1950). In 1937 he received the Grand Prize for Music of the Athens Academy of Arts.

Vasconcellos, Joaquim de, Portuguese lexicographer; b. Oporto, Feb. 10, 1849; d. there, March 2, 1936. From 1865 to 1869 he studied at the Univ. of Coïmbra; 1871-75, traveled in Germany, France, England, and Spain; from 1883 prof. of German at the Lyceum of Oporto, and from 1884 also director of the Museum for Industries and Commerce. He publ. the biographical dictionary *Os Musicos portuguezes* (1870), containing much new matter, and many emendations of old; a monograph on *Luiza Todi* (1873; 2nd ed., 1929); *Ensajo critico sobre o catalogo del rey Don João IV* (1873); publ. a facsimile ed. of the catalogue of the Royal Library of Lisbon, destroyed by the earthquake of 1755 (1874-76; with index and commentary, 1905); also contributed to Pougin's supplement to Fétis' *Biographie universelle.*

Vasconcelos, Jorge Croner de, Portuguese composer; b. Lisbon, April 11, 1910. He took piano lessons with Aroldo Silva in Lisbon (1927-31); studied composition with Luís de Freitas Branco at the National Cons. there (1927-34); then went to Paris and had courses with Paul Dukas, Nadia Boulanger, and Roger-Ducasse (1934-37). Returning to Portugal in 1939, he taught composition at the Lisbon Cons.
WORKS: ballets, *A Faina do Mar* (1940) and *Coimbra* (1959); *Melodias sobre antigos textos portugueses* for voice, flute, and string quartet (1937); Piano Quartet (1938); *Partita* for piano (1961); *A vela vermelha* for orch. (1962); *Vilancico para a Festa de Santa Cecilia* for chorus and orch. (1967).

Vásquez, Juan, Spanish composer; b. Badajoz, c.1550; d. 1604. He composed many excellent villancicos, for 3, 4, and 5 voices, often using folksongs for the chief melodic part. Many of these are found in Spanish tablature books of the period (e.g., those of Milán, Fuenllana, Enriquez de Valderrábano, Pisador, and Daza, from 1535 to 1576), arranged as solo songs with instrumental accompaniment. He publ. *Villancicos y canciones a 3 y a 4* (Osuna, 1551); *Recopilación de sonetos y villancicos a 4 y a 5* (Seville, 1560); modern ed. by H. Anglès in *Monumentos de la Música Española*, Barcelona, 1946).

Vasseur, Léon (-Félix-Augustin-Joseph), French composer; b. Bapaume, Pas-de-Calais, May 28, 1844; d. Paris, July 25, 1917. He studied at the École Niedermeyer in Paris; in 1870 became organist of the Versailles Cathedral; after a few years he turned to composing light music; also conducted theater orchestras. He wrote about 30 operettas, but his most successful one was his first production, *La Timbale d'argent* (Paris, April 9, 1872). He also publ. sacred music: *L'Office divin* (a collection of Masses, offertories, antiphons, etc.); *20 motets des grands maîtres;* a method for organ or harmonium; transcriptions for harmonium and piano.

Vassilenko, Sergei, noted Russian composer; b. Moscow, March 30, 1872; d. there, March 11, 1956. He studied jurisprudence at the Moscow Univ., graduating in 1895; concurrently took private music lessons with Gretchaninov and G. Conus; in 1895 entered the Moscow Cons. in the classes of Taneyev, Ippolitov-Ivanov, and Safonov, graduating in 1901; while still a student, he served as assistant in Safonov's opera class. He also studied ancient Russian chants under the direction of Smolensky. In 1906 he joined the faculty of the Moscow Cons.; subsequently was prof. of orchestration there (1932-41 and 1943-56). From 1907 to 1917 he conducted in Moscow a series of popular symphonic concerts in programs of music arranged in a historical sequence; in 1909 and 1912 he conducted concerts in Berlin. In 1938 he went to Tashkent, Uzbekistan, to help native musicians develop a national school of composition. His music is inspired primarily by the pattern of Russian folksong, but he was also attracted by exotic subjects, particularly those of the East; in his harmonic settings there is a distinct influence of French Impressionism.
WORKS: OPERAS: *The Legend of the Great City of Kitezh and the Calm Lake Svetoyar,* dramatic cantata (Moscow, March 1, 1902; operatic version, Moscow, March 3, 1903; composed several years before Rimsky-Korsakov's famous opera on the same subject); *Son of the Sun* (Moscow, May 23, 1929; deals with the Boxer Rebellion in China); *Christopher Columbus* (1933); *Buran* (Tashkent, June 12, 1939); *The Grand Canal* (Tashkent, Jan. 12, 1941); *Suvorov* (Moscow, Feb. 23, 1942). BALLETS, etc.: *Noya* (1923); *Joseph the Handsome* (Moscow, March 3, 1925); *Lola* (1926; revised, and produced Moscow, June 25, 1943); *The Gypsies,* after Pushkin (Leningrad, Nov. 18, 1937); *Akbilyak* (Tashkent, Nov. 7, 1943); *Mirandolina* (Moscow, Jan. 16, 1949). FOR ORCH.: 5 symphonies: No. 1 (Moscow, Feb. 17, 1907), No. 2 (Moscow, Jan. 7,

1913), No. 3, *Italian,* for wind instruments and Russian folk instruments (1925), No. 4, *Arctic* (Moscow, April 5, 1933), No. 5 (1938); *Vir,* for bass and orch. (Kislovodsk, July 6, 1896); *Three Combats,* symph. poem (1900); *Poème épique,* symph. poem (Moscow, March 14, 1903); *The Garden of Death,* symph. poem after Oscar Wilde (Moscow, May 4, 1908); *Hircus Nocturnus* (Moscow, Feb. 3, 1909; his most popular work; frequently performed abroad; N.Y., Nov. 20, 1918, by the Russian Symph. Orch.); *Incantation* for voice and orch. (1910); Violin Concerto (1910–13); *Au Soleil,* suite for orch. (Moscow, 1911); *Valse Fantastique* (Moscow, Jan. 16, 1915); *Zodiac,* suite on old French melodies (1914); *Exotic Suite* for tenor and 12 instruments (1916); *Chinese Suite* (Leningrad, Oct. 30, 1927); *Hindu Suite* (Moscow, 1927); *Turkmenian Suite* (Moscow, 1931); *Soviet East* (1932); *Uzbek Suite* (1942); Cello Concerto (1944); *Ukraine* (1945); Trumpet Concerto (1945); several works for folk instruments; Concerto for balalaika and orch. (1931). CHAMBER MUSIC: 3 string quartets; Piano Trio; Viola Sonata; *Serenade* for cello and piano; *Oriental Dance,* for clarinet and piano (1923); *Japanese Suite,* for wind instruments, xylophone, and piano (1938); *Chinese Sketches,* for woodwind instruments (1938); Woodwind Quartet on American themes (1938); Suite for balalaika and accordion (1945). SONGS: a number of songs, of which *A Maiden Sang in a Church Choir* (1908) is the best; *10 Russian Folksongs,* for voice, oboe, balalaika, accordion, and piano (1929). Vassilenko publ. a book of memoirs, *Pages of Reminiscences* (Moscow, 1948) and vol. I of a manual of orchestration (1952).

BIBLIOGRAPHY: Victor Belaiev, *S. N. Vassilenko* (Moscow, 1927; in Russian and German); G. Polianovsky, *Sergei Vassilenko* (Moscow, 1964).

Vassiliev-Buglay, Dmitri, Soviet composer of popular songs; b. Moscow, Aug. 9, 1888; d. there, Oct. 15, 1956. He studied with Kastalsky at the Moscow Synod Seminary (1898–1906); after the Revolution he became an active member of RAPM (Russian Association of Proletarian Musicians), postulating the necessity of creating music for the needs of the class-conscious, socialist proletariat, and also joined the Union of Revolutionary Composers and Musical Workers. He was one of the pioneers of mass Soviet songs; wrote patriotic ballads and many choruses to revolutionary texts. He also composed the opera *Fatherland's Call,* to promote self-discipline on collective farms.

BIBLIOGRAPHY: D. Lokshin, *Dmitri Vassiliev-Buglay* (Moscow, 1958).

Vatielli, Francesco, Italian musicologist; b. Pesaro, Jan. 1, 1877; d. Portogruaro, Dec. 12, 1946. He studied philology in Bologna and Florence; music at the Liceo Musicale Rossini in Pesaro; in 1905 he was appointed instructor of music history at the Liceo Musicale in Bologna; was co-founder of the Associazione dei Musicologisti Italiani; also edited various music journals. He wrote incidental music for several plays, piano pieces, and songs; publ. a number of important papers dealing mainly with music in Bologna: *Vita ed arte musicale a Bologna* (1922; reprinted in 1927 as *Arte e vita musicale a Bologna;* 2 vols.); also books on other subjects: *La "Lyra Barberina" di G. B. Doni* (1908); *Primordi dell'arte del violoncello* (1918); *Materia e forme della musica* (1922; 2nd ed., 1928); *Il Principe di Venosa e Leonore d'Este* (on Gesualdo; Milan, 1941); edited a collection of 17th-century airs, *Antiche cantate d'amore* (3 vols.; 1916–20); also *Antiche cantate spirituali, Antichi maestri bolognesi,* etc.

BIBLIOGRAPHY: A. Della Corte, "Francesco Vatielli," *Rivista Musicale Italiana* (April–Sept. 1947).

Vaucorbeil, Auguste-Emmanuel, French composer; b. Rouen, Dec. 15, 1821; d. Paris, Nov. 2, 1884. He studied with Marmontel and Cherubini at the Paris Cons.; produced a comic opera, *La Bataille d'amour* (Paris, April 13, 1863); another opera, *Mahomet,* remained unperformed. His lyric scene, *La Mort de Diane,* for solo, chorus, and orch., had some success. In 1872 he became government commissioner for the Paris theaters; from 1879, director of the Opéra.

Vaughan, Denis, Australian conductor; b. Melbourne, June 6, 1926. He studied organ in London with George Thalben Ball and in Paris with André Marchal; also took double bass lessons in London and Vienna. He served in the multiple, but apparently not mutually exclusive, capacities of bass player, organist, harpsichordist and pianist, with the Royal Philharmonic Orch. of London, beginning with its American tour in 1950. In 1953 he became assistant conductor to Sir Thomas Beecham; then was assistant to Vittorio Gui at Glyndebourne (1951) and to Hans Knappertsbusch in Bayreuth (1957). While thus engaged, he discovered myriad discrepancies in the printed scores of operas by Verdi and Puccini, and proceeded to agitate for publishing corrected editions of these works. Expanding his multifarious activities, he served as consultant for the design of the organ in Alice Tully Hall at Lincoln Center, N.Y. He also gave organ recitals. His main endeavor, however, remained conducting. He formed an orchestra in Naples, with which he toured in Europe. In 1972 he joined the permanent staff of the Munich Opera; in 1977 he made a tour of Australia with the Australian symph. orchestras, conducting in Sydney, Melbourne, Brisbane, etc. The press everywhere sang his praises, deservedly so.

Vaughan Williams, Ralph (real last name **Williams**), foremost English composer; b. Down Ampney, Gloucestershire, Oct. 12, 1872; d. London, Aug. 26, 1958. He was the son of a clergyman, and received his education at the Charterhouse School, London (1887–90) and at Trinity College, Cambridge (1892–95); obtained his B. Mus. in 1894, and B.A. in 1895; took the degree of Mus. Doc. at Cambridge in 1901. In 1890–92 and again in 1895–96 he studied at the Royal College of Music, London, where his teachers were Parratt (organ), Parry and Stanford (composition); in 1897–98 he studied with Max Bruch in Berlin. In 1909, when he was already a mature composer, he went to Paris to seek advice from Ravel, and had several sessions with him to advance his technique of composition still further. In 1904 he joined the English Folk Song Society, and became profoundly interested in the native materials of English music. His *3 Norfolk*

Rhapsodies for orch. (he discarded Nos. 2 and 3), written in 1906, demonstrate this national trend in his work; the opera *Hugh the Drover* (1911–14) is strongly impregnated with English folk music. His *Fantasia on a Theme by Tallis* for strings (1910) indicates a widening of his concept of the English idiom by embracing music of the Tudor period, both sacred and secular; modal counterpoint in particular claimed his attention. Outstanding among his works is the *London Symphony* (1914; revised 1920), revealing the esthetic attitude of the modern period, but rooted in the Elizabethan tradition. In his later works, Vaughan Williams adopted an advanced technique of harmonic writing, with massive agglomerations of chordal sonorities; parallel progressions of triads are especially favored, but there is no intention of adhering to any uniform method of composition; rather, there is a great variety of procedures integrated into a distinctively personal and thoroughly English style. A parallel with Sibelius (for whom Vaughan Williams always professed admiration and to whom he dedicated his 5 Symphony) may plausibly be drawn; both are proponents of nationalism without isolationism, and stylistic freedom without eclecticism. During World War I Vaughan Williams served with the British Army in Macedonia and France, becoming an officer in the artillery; after the Armistice he became prof. of composition at the Royal College of Music, London; also conducted the London Bach Choir (1920–28). In 1922 he visited the U.S. to conduct his *Pastoral Symphony* at the Norfolk, Conn., Festival (June 7); in 1932, made another U.S. visit, as a lecturer at Bryn Mawr College. In 1935 he received the Order of Merit from King George V. After the death of his first wife in 1951, he married his secretary, Mrs. Ursula Wood (Feb. 7, 1953). In 1954 he made his third tour in the U.S.; lectured at Cornell and Yale. He continued to compose vigorously; completed his 9th Symphony at the age of 85.

WORKS: OPERAS: *The Shepherds of the Delectable Mountains,* a "pastoral episode" after Bunyan's *The Prilgrim's Progress* (London, July 11, 1922); *Hugh the Drover,* a ballad opera (1911–14; London, July 14, 1924); *Sir John in Love,* after Shakespeare's *Merry Wives of Windsor* (London, March 21, 1929); *The Poisoned Kiss,* a "romantic extravaganza" (Cambridge, May 12, 1936); *Riders to the Sea* (London, Nov. 30, 1937); *The Pilgrim's Progress,* a "morality" (1949; Covent Garden, London, April 26, 1951; includes material from the earlier opera *The Shepherds of the Delectable Mountains).*

BALLETS: *Old King Cole* (Cambridge, 1923); *On Christmas Night* (Chicago, 1926); *Job,* a masque for dancing (London, July 5, 1931).

INCIDENTAL MUSIC: to Ben Jonson's *Pan's Anniversary* (1905), *The Wasps* by Aristophanes (1909), *The Mayor of Casterbridge,* by Thomas Hardy (1953); film music: *Coastal Command* (1942); *The People's Land* (1943); *The Story of a Flemish Farm* (1943; suite for orch. from it, London, July 31, 1945); *Stricken Peninsula* (1945); *The Loves of Joanna Godden* (1947); *Scott of the Antarctic* (1949; material taken from it incorporated in *Sinfonia antartica).*

VOCAL WORKS: *Willow Wood,* for baritone, women's chorus, and orch., after Dante Gabriel Rosetti (1903; Liverpool Festival, 1909); *Towards the Unknown Region,* for chorus and orch., after Walt Whitman (1905; revised 1918); *A Sea Symphony* (Symph. No. 1), for soprano, baritone, chorus, and orch., after Walt Whitman (Leeds Festival, 1910); *5 Mystical Songs,* for baritone, chorus, and orch. (Worcester Festival, 1911); *Fantasia on Christmas Carols* (Hereford Festival, 1912); *2 motets for double chorus* (1913); *Mass in G minor* (1923); *Sancta Civitas,* oratorio (Oxford, May 7, 1926); *Te Deum,* for mixed chorus and organ (1928); *Benedicite,* for soprano, chorus, and orch. (1929); *Magnificat,* for contralto, women's chorus, and orch. (1932); *Dona nobis pacem,* for soprano, baritone, chorus, and orch. (Huddersfield, Oct. 2, 1936); *5 Tudor Portraits,* for contralto, baritone, chorus, and orch. (Norwich Festival, 1936); *Flourish for a Coronation* (London, 1937); *Thanksgiving for Victory,* for soprano solo, speaker, chorus, and orch. (London, May 8, 1945); *The Sons of Light* (London Philharmonic with a chorus of 1,000 school children; May 6, 1951); *Epithalamion,* cantata (1953); *This Day,* cantata (Worcester Festival, Sept. 8, 1954); *A Vision of Aeroplanes,* motet for chorus and organ (St. Michael's Cornhill, London, June 4, 1956); numerous songs to words by English poets; arrangements of English folksongs; hymn tunes; carols.

FOR ORCH.: *Serenade* for small orch. (1901); *Bucolic Suite* (1902); *2 Impressions: Harnham Down* and *Boldrewood* (1902); *3 Norfolk Rhapsodies:* No. 1, in E minor (London, Aug. 23, 1906); Nos. 2 and 3 (Cardiff Festival, Sept. 27, 1907; withdrawn by the composer); *Fantasia on a Theme by Tallis,* for strings (Gloucester Festival, Sept. 6, 1910, composer conducting); Symph. No. 2, *A London Symphony* (1914; revised version, London, May 4, 1920); *The Lark Ascending,* romance for violin and orch. (1914; London, June 14, 1921); Symph. No. 3, *Pastoral Symphony* (London, Jan. 26, 1922); *Flos Campi,* suite for viola, small chorus, and small orch. (London, Oct. 19, 1925); *Concerto accademico,* for violin and orch. (London, Nov. 6, 1925); *Fantasy on Sussex Folk-Tunes,* for cello and orch. (1930); Piano Concerto (London, Feb. 1, 1933; also arranged for 2 pianos with orch.); *Suite* for viola and orch. (London, Nov. 12, 1934); Symph. No. 4, in F minor (London, April 10, 1935); *5 Variants of "Dives and Lazarus,"* for string orch. and harp, commissioned by the British Council for the N.Y. World's Fair (N.Y. Philharmonic, June 10, 1939); Symph. No. 5, in D major (London, June 24, 1943); Concerto for oboe and strings (Liverpool, Sept. 30, 1944); Symph. No. 6, in E minor (London, April 21, 1948); *Romance,* for harmonica and orch. (N.Y., May 3, 1952); Symph. No. 7, *Sinfonia antartica* (1951–52; Manchester, Jan. 14, 1953); Concerto for bass tuba and orch. (London, June 13, 1954); Symph. No. 8 (Manchester, May 2, 1956); Symph. No. 9 (London, April 2, 1958).

CHAMBER MUSIC: String Quartet No. 1 (1908; revised 1921); *Fantasy Quintet,* for 2 violins, 2 violas, and cello (1910); *On Wenlock Edge,* for tenor, string quartet, and piano (1909); *6 Studies in English Folksong,* for cello and piano (1927); String Quartet No. 2 (1945); some short piano pieces; Introduction and Fugue, for 2 pianos (1946); organ pieces.

PUBLICATIONS: *English Folksongs* (a lecture presented at the English Folk Dance and Song Society,

London, 1912); *National Music* (London, 1934; embodies lectures at Bryn Mawr College); *Some Thoughts on Beethoven's Choral Symphony, with Writings on Other Musical Subjects* (London, 1953; contains reprints of several of his earlier articles); *The Making of Music* (Ithaca, N.Y., 1955; lectures delivered at Cornell Univ. and Yale Univ. in 1954). Editions: "15 Folk-Songs from the Eastern Counties" for voice and piano, in the *Journal of the Folk-Song Society* I/8; Purcell's *Welcome Odes* (vols. XV and XVIII of the Purcell Society ed.); *The English Hymnal* (1906); *The Oxford Carol Book* (with Percy Dearmer and Martin Shaw; 1928).

BIBLIOGRAPHY: Monographs in the Musical Pilgrim series (London): A. E. F. Dickinson, *An Introduction to the Music of R. V. W.* (1928), Frank Howes, *The Dramatic Works of R. V. W.* (1937), Frank Howes, *The Later Works of R. V. W.* (1937). Other books: Hubert Foss, *R. V. W. : A Study* (London, 1950); Percy M. Young, *V. W.* (in Contemporary Composers series; London, 1953); Frank Howes, *The Music of R. V. W.* (London, 1954); S. Pakenham, *R. V. W.; A Discovery of His Music* (London, 1957); J. Day, *Vaughan Williams* (London, 1961); A. E. Dickinson, *Vaughan Williams* (London, 1963); M. Kennedy, *The Works of Ralph Vaughan Williams* (London, 1964); Ursula Vaughan Williams, *R. V. W. : A Biography of Ralph Vaughan Williams* (London, 1964); M. Hurd, *Vaughan Williams* (London, 1970); J. E. Lunn and U. Vaughan Williams, *Ralph Vaughan Williams: A Pictorial Biography* (1971). Magazine articles: in *Music & Letters:* A. H. Fox Strangways, "R. V. W. " (1920), H. Howells, "V. W.'s 'Pastoral' Symphony" (1922); E. Rubbra, "The Later V. W. " (Jan. 1937), W. Kimmel, "V. W.'s Choice of Words" (1938), H. Murrill, "V. W.'s *Pilgrim*" (1951); in the *Music Review:* "V. W.'s Fifth Symph." (Jan. 1945), R. Hawthorne, "A Note on the Music of V. W." (1948), A. E. F. Dickinson, "Toward the Unknown Region" (1948), Elsie Payne, "V. W. and Folksong" (1954); in the *Musical Quarterly:* W. Kimmel, "V. W.'s Melodic Style" (Oct. 1941). Other magazine articles: H. C. Colles, "The Music of V. W.," *Chesterian* (1922); A. E. F. Dickinson, "A Bibliography of Works by R. V. W.," *Gamut* (July 1928); H. Howells, "V. W.," *Score* (Dec. 1952); chapters in books: G. Pannain, "R. V. W.," in *Modern Composers* (English transl. from Italian, London, 1932), D. F. Tovey, *Essays in Musical Analysis*, vols. II and IV (London, 1935–39), E. Blom, "R. V. W.," in *The Book of Modern Composers*, ed. by David Ewen (N.Y., 1942).

Vautor, Thomas, English composer; b. c.1590; date and place of death unknown. In 1616 he recieved the degree of B. Mus. at Lincoln College, and in 1619 publ. a collection of madrigals, *The First Set: Beeing Songs of divers Ayres and Natures, of 5 and 6 parts* (reprinted by Fellowes in *The English Madrigal School* 34. Another work by Vautor is *An Elegie in the Death of his right worshipful Master, Sir Thomas Beaumont* (1614).

BIBLIOGRAPHY: E. H. Fellowes, *The English Madrigal Composers* (1921).

Veazie, George Augustus, American music educator; b. Boston, Dec. 18, 1835; d. Chelsea, Mass., Nov. 20, 1915. From 1869 to 1903 he was supervisor of music in the public schools of Chelsea; during many years of cooperation with Luther W. Mason he brought about important reforms and improvements in the system of primary instruction. He composed several light operas and numerous part-songs, and edited collections of school songs.

Vecchi, Orazio (Horatio), Italian composer; b. Modena, 1550 (baptized Dec. 6); d. there, Feb. 19, 1605. He was a pupil of Salvatore Essenga in Modena; he was maestro di cappella in Salò (1581–84), and at the Cathedral of Modena (1584–86); in 1586 took Holy Orders; then went to Correggio, where he obtained a canonry. In 1596 he reutrned to Modena and was appointed maestro at the Cathedral (Oct. 26); 2 years later he was also maestro at the ducal court there, and music master to the young princes. On Oct. 7, 1604, he was deprived of his post as choirmaster at the Cathedral, probably through the intrigues of a former pupil, Geminiano Capilupi; this circumstance is believed to have hastened his death. Vecchi was highly regarded as a composer in his day; his works (Masses, motets, madrigals, canzonette, etc.) were chiefly printed in Venice, but editions also appeared in Germany and elsewhere. He was invited to the court of the Emperor Rudolf II at Vienna, and in 1600 went to Rome in the suite of Cardinal Alessandro d'Este. His lasting fame is due above all to his "commedia harmonica" *L'Amfiparnasso*, performed at Modena in 1594 and printed at Venice in 1597; this is a kind of musical farce written not in the monodic style of Peri's *Dafne*, but in madrigal style, with all the text sung by several voices (i.e., a chorus *a* 4–5); it has been called a "madrigal opera," but it was not intended for the theater and it stood entirely apart from the path that opera was to take. Modern editions of *L'Amfiparnasso* have been publ. by Eitner, vol. 26 of the *Publikationen der Gesellschaft der Musikforschung* and Torchi, *L'Arte Musicale in Italia* 4. Of special interest among Vecchi's other compositions is the *Veglie di Siena ovvero i varii humori della musica moderna a 3–6 voci* (1604; also Nuremburg, 1605, as *Noctes ludicrae;* modern ed. by B. Somma), which uses colorful devices to express a wide variety of moods and feelings. Examples of Vecchi's music are in Schering's *Beispielen* (no. 164); Chilesotti's *Biblioteca di rarità musicali,* vol. 5; Torchi's *L'Arte Musicale in Italia* 2; Einstein's *Golden Age of the Madrigal,* etc.

BIBLIOGRAPHY: A. Catellani, *Della vita e delle opere di O. V.* (Milan, 1858); E. J. Dent, "The *Amfiparnasso* of O. V.," *Monthly Musical Record* 423–24 (1906); E. J. Dent, "Notes on the *Amfiparnasso* of O. V.," *Sammelbände der Internationalen Musik-Gesellschaft* (1910–11); L. Frati, "Un Capitolo autobiografico di O. V.," *Rivista Musicale Italiana* (1915); J. C. Hol. *H. V. als weltlicher Komponist* (diss., Basel, 1917), "H. V. et l'évolution créatrice," in "Scheurleer-Festschrift" (1925); "H. V.," *Rivista Musicale Italiana* (1930), and *H. V.s weltliche Werke* (Strasbourg, 1934); G. Roncalgia, "Il Luogo e la data di nascita di O. V.," *Rassegna Musicale* (April 1929); C. Perinello, "L'Amfiparnasso, commedia harmonica d'H. V.," *Rivista*

Musicale Italiana (1937); G. Roncaglia, "O. V.," *Rivista Musicale Italiana* (1949); *O. V., Precursore del melodramma*, a symposium on the 400th anniversary of Vecchi's birth (Modena, 1950); A. Lualdi, "O. V.," *Rivista Musicale Italiana* (1950); G. Camillucci, "*L'Amfiparnasso*, commedia harmonica," *Rivista Musicale Italiana* (1951); G. Roncaglia, "Gli Elementi precursori del melodramma nell'opera di O. V.," *Rivista Musicale Italiana* (1953); L. Ronga, "Lettura storica dell' *Amfiparnasso* di O. V.," *Rassenga Musicale* (1953).

Vecchi, Orfeo, Italian composer of sacred music; b. Milan, 1550; d. there, 1604. He was maestro di cappella at Santa Maria della Scala in Milan; most of his manuscripts are preserved there. His extant published works include 3 collections of Masses for 5 voices (1588; 1598; 1602); 2 Magnificats; 7 Penitential Psalms for 6 voices (1601); *Cantiones sacrae*, for 6 voices (1603) and for 5 (1608), etc.
BIBLIOGRAPHY: F. X. Haberl, "Orfeo Vecchi," *Kirchenmusikalisches Jahrbuch* (1907); A. Einstein, "Un Libro di canzoni spirituali di Orfeo Vecchi," *Bibliofilia* (Florence, 1938).

Vecsei, Desider Josef, Hungarian pianist; b. Budapest, Sept. 25, 1882; d. Hollywood, March 1, 1966. He studied in Budapest, and then with Emil Sauer at the Vienna Cons. He made concert appearances as a child; toured in Europe until 1915; then went to the U.S., and settled in Hollywood as a piano teacher. He wrote songs and piano pieces.

Vecsey, Franz von, Hungarian violinist; b. Budapest, March 23, 1893; d. Rome, April 6, 1935. He received his first instruction from his father, Ludwig Vecsey, a good violinist; at the age of 8 he became a pupil of Hubay, and made such rapid progress that his parents decided to send him on a European tour as a child prodigy; he appeared in Berlin (Oct. 17, 1903), London (May 2, 1904), and N.Y. (Jan. 10, 1905); toured Italy, Scandinavia, and Russia; then lived in Germany and Italy. He composed some violin pieces.

Vécsey, Jenö, Hungarian musicologist and composer; b. Felsöcéce, July 19, 1909; d. Budapest, Sept. 19, 1966. He studied at the Univ. of Sciences and took a course in composition with Kodály at the Budapest Academy of Music (1930–35). He joined the staff of the National Széchényi Library in 1942; was appointed to the Music Department and made valuable contributions to the historical and bibliographical music literature preserved there. He initiated and directed editorial work on the *Musica Rinata* series (1963–66); did preparatory work on the new Haydn Collected Edition.
WORKS: a ballet, *Scholar Kele* (1943); *Divertimento* for orch. (1939–40); *Intermezzi* for strings (1942); *Rhapsody* for orch. (1940–41); *2 Symphonic Dances* (1945); symph. poem *Castle Boldogkö* (1951; revised and retitled *Prelude, Notturno and Scherzo*, 1958); Piano Concertino (1953–56); Double Bass Concertino (1954); *Rhapsody* for harp and orch. (1954); String Quartet (1942); String Sextet (1956); *Bagatelles* for 2 pianos (1962); songs.

Veerhoff, Carlos, Argentinian-German composer; b. Buenos Aires, June 3, 1926. He studied in Berlin with Grabner (1943–44); returned to Argentina and taught in Tucumán. He moved permanently to Germany in 1951; was an assistant to Fricsay in Berlin (1951–52) and studied with Boris Blacher at the Hochschule für Musik there (1952); then settled in Munich.
WORKS: 2 operas, *Targusis* (1958) and *Die goldene Maske* (1968); a chamber opera, *Der Grune* (1972); a mini-opera, *Es gibt doch Zebrastreifen* (Ulm, West Germany, Jan. 20, 1972); 2 ballets, *Pavane royale* (1953) and *El porquerizo del ray* (Buenos Aires, Teatro Colón, 1963); *Prólogo sinfónico* (1951); *Symphonic Movement* (1952); 4 symphonies: No. 1, *Panta rhei (Everything Flows;* the philosophic apothegm of Heraclitus; 1953), No. 2, in one movement (1956), No, 3, *Spirales* (1966, revised 1969), No. 4 (1974); *Mirages* for orch. (1961); *Akróasis* for 24 winds and percussion (1966); *Textur* for string orch. (1969, revised 1971); *Torso* for orch. (Lübeck, Jan. 14, 1974); *Sinotrauc* for orch. (Munich, Jan. 19, 1973); *Gesänge auf dem Wege* for baritone and orch. (1964); *Ut omnes unum sint*, chamber cantata (1967); 2 string quartets (1951, 1974); 2 wind quintets (1958, 1969); Solo Violin Sonata (1954); *Dialogues* for saxophone and piano (1967).

Vega, Aurelio de la, Cuban-American composer; b. Havana, Nov. 28, 1925. He studied law at the Univ. of Havana (1945–47) and music with Frederick Kramer (1942–46). In 1947 he went to the U.S. and served as cultural attaché at the Cuban Consulate in Los Angeles; there he took composition lessons with Ernst Toch. Returning to Cuba, he was Dean of the Music School at the Univ. of Oriente in Santiago de Cuba (1953–59); in 1959 settled in California, and taught at the San Fernando Valley State College (California State Univ., Northbridge). In his early works he cultivated Cuban melorhythms, but later adopted increasingly radical modernistic methods of composition with fantastically reticulated, circumvoluted, and in some instances palindromic, contrapuntal schemes, graphically notated in optically proportioned note values, so that the linear extant of a bar is invariant in relation to the aggregate of rhythmic units contained therein, reaching its heroic ultima ratio in a work entitled *Olep ed Arudamot* (backward reading of a Spanish idiom meaning "pulling your leg"); the visual impression of the score itself is that of an abstract expressionist painting. Sonorifically, he avails himself of a great variety of acoustical materials, electronic and humanoid, including the whirring sound of shuffling feet by string players.
WORKS: Piano Trio (1949); *Soliloquio* for viola and piano (1950); *Obertura a una Farsa Seria* (Havana, April 28, 1951); *Leyenda del Ariel Criollo* for cello and piano (1953); *Elegía* for strings (London, Nov. 16, 1954); String Quartet (1957); Wind Quintet (1959); Trio for flute, oboe, and clarinet (1960); *Sinfonía en cuatro partes* (Inter-american Music Festival, Washington, D.C., April 30, 1961); *Structures* for piano and string quartet (1962); *Coordinates* for magnetic tape (1963); *Analigus* for orch. (1966); *Intrata* for Orchestra (Los Angeles, May 12, 1972); *Olep ed Arudamot* (available in several versions; 1974); *Septi-*

cilium, for solo clarinet and instrumental ensemble (1975); *Inflorescence,* for soprano, bass clarinet, and tape, to the text by the composer (Los Angeles, Oct. 25, 1976); *The Infinite Square,* for any combination of any instruments and/or voices (Los Angeles, Sept. 24, 1977); *Adiós* for orch., to bid farewell to the departing conductor of the Los Angeles Philharmonic Zubin Mehta (conducted by Mehta, Los Angeles, April 20, 1978); piano music; songs.

Vega, Carlos, Argentine writer on music; b. Canuelas, near Buenos Aires, April 14, 1898; d. Buenos Aires, Feb. 10, 1966. He studied at the Univ. of Buenos Aires (philosophy and literature); subsequently devoted himself mainly to folklore research in music. In 1933 he was placed in charge of the folklore division of the literature faculty at the Univ. of Buenos Aires. He traveled throughout the rural regions of Argentina and other South American countries to collect materials on folksongs and folk dances, using the phonograph for recording them; devised a special choreographic notation. His many books are basic sources for the study of Argentine folk music.

WRITINGS: *Danzas y canciones argentinas* (Buenos Aires, 1936); *La Música popular argentina: Canciones y danzas criollas* (1941); *Panorama de la música popular argentina* (Buenos Aires, 1944); a series of monographs on Argentinian dances (with choreographic ideograms): *La Chacarera, El Cuando, El Gato, El Triunfo, El Carnavalito, La Condición* (Buenos Aires, 1944–45); *Los Instrumentos musicales de la Argentina* (Buenos Aires, 1946).

Veinus, Abraham, American musicologist; b. New York, Fed. 12, 1916. He studied at the City College of N.Y., Cornell Univ. (M.A., 1937), and Columbia Univ. (1946–48). In 1948 he joined the faculty of the Dept. of Fine Arts at Syracuse Univ. He wrote the books *The Concerto* (1944), *Victor Book of Concertos* (1948), *Pocket Book of Great Operas* (with Henry Simon, 1949), *Understanding Music* (with W. Fleming, N.Y., 1958).

Veit, Wenzel Heinrich, Bohemian composer; b. Leitmeritz, Jan. 19, 1806; d. there, Feb. 16, 1864. He was a member of the judiciary, but applied himself earnestly to the study of music; was music director at Aachen. He wrote a number of works in various genres; he is remembered chiefly for his effective choruses and solo songs.

WORKS: *Festmesse* in D, for soli, chorus, and orch.; overtures; a symph.; 5 string quintets; 4 string quartets; a piano trio; male choruses in Czech and German; songs.

BIBLIOGRAPHY: A. John, *W. H. Veit. Lebensbild eines deutschen Tondichters* (Eger, 1903); H. Ankert, *W. H. Veit als Musikdirektor in Aachen* (Leitmeritz, 1906); K. Fiala, *W. H. Veit* (Liberec, 1964).

Velasco-Llanos, Santiago, Colombian composer; b. Cali, Jan. 28, 1915. He studied in Cali with Antonio María Valencia, and later with Domingo Santa Cruz and Pedro Humberto Allende in Santiago, Chile. Returning to Colombia, he was appointed Director of the Cali Cons.

WORKS: *Sinfonia breve* (1947); *Sinfonietta* (1966); *Bambuco jocoso* for orch. (1967); 2 string quartets; piano pieces; choruses; songs.

Velasco Maidana, José María, Bolivian composer and conductor; b. Sucre, July 4, 1899. He studied violin in Buenos Aires; subsequently taught music history at the National Cons. of La Paz. In 1937 he conducted some of his works in Buenos Aires, and in 1938 in Berlin; in 1943, toured in South America and Mexico. His ballet *Amerindia,* on a subject from pre-Columbian history, was produced in Berlin (Dec. 6, 1938), and later in La Paz (May 27, 1940). He conducted the 1st performance of his symph. works with the La Paz Symph. Orch., of which he was regular conductor: *Cory Wara* (Oct. 6, 1941); *Los Hijos del Sol* (Feb. 6, 1942); *Vida de Cóndores* (March 14, 1942); *Los Huacos* (April 22, 1942); *Los Khusillos* and *Cuento Brujo* (April 11, 1943).

Velázquez, Higinio, Mexican composer; b. Guadalajara, Jan. 11, 1926. He studied composition with Bernal Jiménez and Rodolfo Halffter; was a violinist in the National Symph. Orch.; in 1969 became violinist in the string quartet of the National Institute of Fine Arts.

WORKS: *Vivencias* for orch. (1958); *Cacique,* overture (1958); "sinfonia breve," *Juárez* (1961); *Revolución,* symph. poem (1963); *Elegía* for oboe and piano (1969); *Estructuas* for piano (1969); Sonatina for cello solo (1970); String Quartet (1970); *Andante atonal* for strings (1971).

Velimirović, Miloš, eminent Serbian-American music scholar; b. Belgrade, Dec. 10, 1922. He studied violin and piano at the Music Academy in Belgrade with Petar Stojanovic; in 1943 was sent to a forced labor camp by the German occupation authorities; after the end of the war he studied Byzantine Art at the Univ. of Belgrade, graduating in 1951; simultaneously took composition lessons with Mihovil Logar at the Belgrade Music Academy; in 1952 he emigrated to the U.S.; studied at Harvard Univ., obtaining his M.A. in 1953 and his Ph.D. in 1957; also took a course in Byzantine music with Egon Wellesz at Dumbarton Oaks (1954). He subsequently devoted himself to teaching; was on the faculty of Yale Univ. (1957–69), and at the Univ. of Wisconsin (1969–73); in 1973 was appointed prof. of Music at the Univ. of Virginia in Charlottesville; served as Chairman of the Dept. of Music there (1974–77). A linguist, he has contributed a number of scholarly articles to various publications, mainly on the subjects connected with liturgical music in Byzantine and in the Slavic countries. He published *Byzantine Elements in Early Slavic Chant* (2 vols. Copenhagen, 1960); Associate Editor (jointly with Egon Wellesz), *Studies in Eastern Chant* (4 vols.; London, 1966–78), "Liturgical Drama in Byzantium and Russia," *Dumbarton Oaks Papers* (1962); articles on Russian and Slavic church music for the 6th edition of *Grove's Dictionary* (1979).

Venatorini. See **Mysliveczek, Joseph.**

Venegas de Henestrosa, Luis, Spanish organist and composer; b. Henestrosa, Burgon, c.1500; d. Toledo, after 1557. He was in the service of Cardinal Juan Tavera in Toledo; publ. the oldest known Spanish book of organ music, *Libro de cifra nueva para tecla, harpa y vihuela* (Alcalà de Henares, 1557; modern ed. by H. Anglès, Barcelona, 1944); this contains organ pieces by Palero, P. Vila, Soto, Venegas himself, etc.; also pieces for vihuela, transcriptions of sacred works by Morales, Josquin, Soto, etc., and solo songs with instrumental accompaniment. The book is written in Spanish organ tablature.

BIBLIOGRAPHY: G. Morphy, *Les Luthistes espagnols du XVIᵉ siècle* (Leipzig, 1902); J. B. Trend, *Luis Milan and the Vihuelistas* (London, 1925); H. Anglès, "Orgelmusik der Schola Hispanica vom XV.-XVII. Jahrhundert," in "Peter Wagner-Festschrift" (Leipzig, 1926); J. Ward, "The Editorial Methods of Venegas de Henestrosa," *Musica Disciplina* (1952).

Vengerova, Isabelle, distinguished piano pedagogue; b. Minsk, Russia, March 1, 1877; d. New York, Feb. 7, 1956. She studied at the Vienna Cons. with Joseph Dachs, and privately with Leschetizky; then with Anna Essipoff in St. Petersburg. In 1906 she was appointed instructor at the St. Petersburg Cons.; in 1910, prof. there. She toured Russia as pianist; in 1923 came to the U.S.; American debut with the Detroit Symph. Orch. (Feb. 8, 1925) in Schumann's piano concerto. She became prof. at the Curtis Institute of Music in Philadelphia when it was founded in 1924; in 1950, received an honorary doctor's degree there. Among her piano pupils at the Curtis Institute were Leonard Bernstein, Samuel Barber, and Lukas Foss. She also taught privately in New York.

Vennard, William D., American voice teacher; b. Bloomington, Illinois, Jan. 31, 1909; d. Los Angeles, Jan. 10, 1971. He was a graduate of Northwestern Univ. and the American Cons. of Music in Chicago. In 1946 he joined the faculty of the Univ. of Southern Calif. in Los Angeles. He was a prolific writer of articles for professional journals, including *American Music Teacher, Journal of Speech and Hearing* and *Folia Phoniatrica.* He publ. the manuals *Singing: The Mechanism and the Technique* and *Developing Voices;* he also appeared as a singer at various functions in California.

Venth, Carl, German-American violinist, conductor, and composer; b. Cologne, Feb. 16, 1860; d. San Antonio, Texas, Jan. 29, 1938. His father was a German, his mother Croatian. He studied violin with his father, and composition with Ferdinand Hiller at the Cologne Cons. In 1880 he emigrated to the U.S.; was concertmaster of the Metropolitan Opera Orchestra (1884–88) and of the St. Paul Symph. Orch. (1907–12); conducted the Brooklyn Symph. Orch. (1889–02); and of the Dallas Symph. Orch. (1911–13). In 1913 he organized the Fort Worth Symph. Orch., which he conducted for several years. In 1932 he joined the faculty of San Antonio Univ., remaining there until his death. In his own compositions he cultivated exotic subjects for the theater.

WORKS: *Pan in America,* a "lyric dance drama" (won the prize of the National Federation of Music Clubs; produced at its Biennial Convention, Asheville, N. C., June 13, 1923); *The Rebel,* a fairy opera with dance (Fort Worth, May 29, 1926); *La Vida de la Misión* (San Antonio, Oct. 28, 1958); also *Lima Beans,* short opera; *Alexander's Horse,* a musical play; *The Juggler,* for voices and instruments; *Dolls,* a "musical extravaganza"; *The Sun God,* an "oriental" opera; *Cathal,* a short music drama; *Jack,* music drama; several symph. works (*Forest Scenes, Norse Dance, Indian Prologue,* etc.); a Mass in D; 2 string quartets; a piano trio; numerous piano compositions (*Sonata appassionata,* 2 rhapsodies, etc.); songs. His autobiography, *My Memories,* was published posthumously (1939).

BIBLIOGRAPHY: E. E. Hipsher, *American Opera and Its Composers* (Philadelphia, 1934; pp. 416–18).

Venzano, Luigi, Italian composer; b. Genoa, 1814; d. there, Jan. 26, 1878. He played cello at the Carlo Felice Theater in Genoa, and taught at the Cons. there; publ. many songs, including *Valzer cantabile,* which is often sung in the lesson scene of *The Barber of Seville;* also composed an operetta, *La Notte dei schiaffi* (Genoa, April 25, 1873) and a ballet, *Benvenuto Cellini* (Milan, Aug. 24, 1861); publ. piano pieces and singing exercises.

Veprik, Alexandr, Soviet composer; b. Balta, near Odessa, June 23, 1899; d. Moscow, Oct. 13, 1958. While still a young boy he went to Leipzig, where he took piano lessons with Karl Wendling; returning to Russia, he entered the Moscow Cons., where he took a course in composition with Miaskovsky (1921–23); from 1923 to 1943 he taught orchestration there. He was associated with the Jewish cultural movement in Russia, and composed several works in the traditional ethnic manner of Jewish cantillations. In his harmonic and formal treatment he followed the "orientalistic" tradition of the Russian National School.

WORKS: the opera *Toktogul,* on Kirghiz motives (Frunze, Kirghizia, 1940); for chorus and orch.: *Fascism be Cursed!* (1944); *The People Hero* (1955); for orch.: 2 symphonies (1931, 1938); *Dances and Songs of the Ghetto* (1927); *Kaddish* for voice with instruments (1925); *The Song of Jubilation* (Moscow, March 17, 1937); *Pastorale* (1946); chamber music: *Rhapsody* for viola and piano (1926); 3 piano sonatas (1922, 1924, 1928); film music; also *Jewish Communist Youth Song* (1926).

WRITINGS: *The Problem of Class Aspects of Orchestration* (Moscow, 1931); *Treatment of Orchestral Instruments* (posthumous, Moscow, 1961).

BIBLIOGRAPHY: A. Bogdanov-Berezovsky, *Alexandr Veprik* (Moscow, 1964).

Veracini, Francesco Maria, Italian violinist and composer; b. Florence, Feb. 1, 1690; d. Florence, Oct. 31, 1768. Pupil of his uncle, Antonio Veracini, of Casini, and of Gasparini; an eminent virtuoso, he toured widely, and in 1714 was heard in Venice by Tartini, greatly influencing the letter's style; 1715–17, soloist at the Italian Opera in London; 1717–22, chamber virtuoso at the court of Dresden; 1735–45, in London again, producing several operas there; being eclipsed by Geminiani, he retired to Pisa about 1746, dying in extreme poverty. Publ. 24 violin sonatas with continuo (1721, 1744); modern reprints by L. Torchi and others.

BIBLIOGRAPHY: L. Torchi, in *Rivista Musicale Italiana* (1889; p. 69); M. Pincherle, *Les Violinistes* (Paris, 1924); A Damerini, "Elogio dell'asino e monte di Stradella in un trattato di F. M. Veracini," *La Scala* (March 1956).

Verbesselt, August, Belgian flutist and composer; b. Klein-Willebroek, Oct. 22, 1919. He studied at the Antwerp Cons.; was since 1942 flute soloist at the Antwerp Opera. His works include a Flute Concerto (1952); *Hexatone-Synthèse* for flute, oboe, clarinet, cello and harp (1964); *Diagrams* for chamber orch. (1972); and *Universum* for 2 orchestras and tape (1975). He also wrote ballet music.

Verbrugghen, Henri, Belgian violinist and conductor; b. Brussels, Aug. 1, 1873; d. Northfield, Minn., Nov. 12, 1934. He studied with Hubay and Ysaÿe at the Brussels Cons.; in 1893 was engaged as violinist in the Scottish Orch. in Glasgow; then was concertmaster in various orchestras in Wales; also conducted summer concerts there, while retaining his position in Glasgow. In 1915 he went to Australia, and established the National Cons. in Sidney. In 1922-23 he was guest conductor of the Minneapolis Symph. Orch.; then became its regular conductor (until 1932).

Verdelot, Philippe, noted Flemish composer; b. Carderousse, near Orange; d. probably in Florence, before 1552. He settled in Italy while young, and became a singer at San Marco in Venice about 1525; from about 1530 he was choirmaster at San Giovanni in Florence. His works were widely printed, both in Italy and France; he was one of the earliest composers of madrigals; most of his approximately 100 works of that type appeared in collections along with those by other composers. Willaert arranged 22 of Verdelot's madrigals as solo songs with lute accompaniment, in tablature: *Intavolatura degli Madrigali di Verdelotto de cantare e sonare nel lauto* (Venice, 1536). Verdelot's last publication was a book of motets, *Electiones diversorum Motetorum distinctae* (1549). Only a single Mass by him is known, entitled *Philomenia*, included in Scotto's *Liber V missarum* (1544). Verdelot added a 5th part to Janequin's *Bataille*, first publ. in Susato's 10th book of *Chansons* (Antwerp, 1545; modern reprint by Commer). Reprints of madrigals by Verdelot are in Maldehem's *Trésor musical.*

BIBLIOGRAPHY: A. Einstein, "Claudio Merulos Ausgabe der Madrigale des Verdelot," *Sammelbände der Internationalen Musik-Gesellschaft*, vol. 8; pp. 220-254, 516; A. Einstein, *The Italian Madrigal* (Princeton, 1949; vol. 1, pp. 154-57; vol. 3, pp. 21-32); G. Reese, *Music in the Renaissance* (N.Y., 1954); N. Böker-Heil, *Die Motetten von Philippe Verdelot* (Cologne, 1967).

Verdi, (Fortunino) Giuseppe (Francesco), illustrious Italian composer of operas; b. Le Roncole, near Busseto, Duchy of Parma, Oct. 10, 1813; d. Milan, Jan. 27, 1901. His father was an innkeeper; the son's precocious talent was trained by the village organist, Baistrocchi; his progress was so extraordinary that he often substituted for his teacher at the church organ, and as a mere boy, succeeded him at the post, receiving a regular, though modest, payment for his services. He studied with Ferdinando Provesi at Busseto for 4 years, until the age of 16, and began to compose music, which he played at a local church; an overture by him was performed at the municipal theater in 1828. A Busseto merchant named Antonio Barezzi enabled Verdi to continue his musical education in Milan. Verdi applied for admission to the Milan Cons.; being older than the average age for entrance, he had to take a special examination, which, however, he failed to pass; the registrar, Francesco Basili, reported that his piano playing was inadequate, and his hand position wrong; as to Verdi's ability in composition, the report found the presence of talent, but insufficient technical knowledge. In all probability, this judgement reflected the actual state of Verdi's musical education at that time, but the examiners showed a lack of imagination in not waiving the rigid rules in an exceptional case. Verdi then turned to private instruction with Vincenzo Lavigna, the maestro al cembalo at La Scala. Verdi labored industriously over counterpoint, canon, and fugue, and assiduously frequented the opera, absorbing the art of dramatic composition. In the summer of 1834 he was engaged as municipal maestro at Busseto, but held this post for only 6 months, going to Milan for another period of study with Lavigna. From July 1835 to Sept. 1838 he was again in Busseto, holding the posts of director of the local music school and of the Philharmonic Society, returning to Milan in 1838. On May 4, 1836, he married Barezzi's daughter, Margherita; they had 2 children, who died in infancy; Margherita herself died in Milan on June 18, 1840. In Busseto Verdi wrote his 1st opera, *Oberto, conte di San Bonifacio,* which was accepted by La Scala, Milan, and performed there with success on Nov. 17, 1839. His next opera, *Un Giorno di regno* (1840), was a failure. He then set to work on a new opera, *Nabucco,* which was given at La Scala (1842) with tremendous success, Signorina Giuseppina Strepponi taking the leading feminine role of Abigaile; this was followed by another successful opera, *I Lombardi alla prima Crociata* (La Scala, 1843); the subject, derived from events in the First Crusade, appealed to the Milan public, arousing their national aspirations for freedom. From that time, Verdi's standing with the management of La Scala was assured, and other opera houses in Italy were open to his productions. After his domestic tragedy, he was greatly consoled by the friendship and constant companionship of **Giuseppina Strepponi,** whom he eventually married on Aug. 29, 1859. His opera *Ernani* (1844), after Victor Hugo's romantic play, *Hernani,* written for the Teatro La Fenice in Venice, was acclaimed and produced on 15 different stages within a year. Then followed a series of works that added little to Verdi's fame: *I due Foscari* (1844); *Giovanna d'Arco* (1845); *Alzira* (1845); *Attila* (1846); *Macbeth* (1847); *I Masnadieri* (1847); *Il Corsaro* (1848); and *La Battaglia di Legnano* (1849). *Luisa Miller* obtained some success in Naples (1849), but *Stiffelio,* produced at Trieste in 1850, was a complete failure. Despite the unevenness of these productions, Verdi's financial prosperity grew, and he showed considerable business acumen in dealing with publishers and impresarios. He traveled to London in 1847; spent some time in Paris in 1848; then returned to Italy. Early in 1851 he completed his first real masterpiece, *Rigoletto*, which was brought out at La Fenice in Venice; it was followed by *Il Trovatore*, produced in Rome (1853) and *La Traviata*, staged at La Fenice (1853). These 3 operas firmly established Verdi's reputation. His 1st French opera, *Les Vêpres siciliennes*, was produced at the Paris Opéra (1855) with moderate success; there followed *Simone Boccanegra*, written for Venice (1857), *Un Ballo in maschera* (Rome, 1859), *La Forza del destino*, brought out in St. Petersburg (1862), and Verdi's 2nd and last French opera, *Don Carlos* (Paris Opéra, 1867). In the meantime, Verdi became involved in the Italian struggle for independence. He was not a politician, and never participated in revolutionary agitation, beyond expressing his patriotic views. But his choice of subject for his grand opera, *Un Ballo in maschera* (originally entitled *La Vendetta in Domino*), based on the play by Scribe describing the assassination of the Swedish King Gustav III in 1792, was ill-timed because of the recent attempted assassination of Napoleon III. Verdi was compelled to transfer the scene of action in his opera from Sweden to Massachusetts, with Gustav III becoming Governor Riccardo of Boston; this episode stirred Verdi's admirers, who linked his name with that of Victor Emmanuel, the future King of Italy. The cry "Viva Verdi" became, by using the 5 letters of his name as initials, a politician slogan: "Viva Vittorio Emmanuelu Re D'Italia." In 1869 Verdi received an offer to write an opera on an Egyptian subject for the new theater in Cairo to celebrate the opening of the Suez Canal. The financial terms were extremely advantageous; the scenario was in French; Antonio Ghislanzoni wrote the Italian libretto, entitled *Aida*. The opera was produced in Cairo on Christmas Eve in 1871, attended by a multitude of notables and newspaper correspondents; characteristically, Verdi refused to make the journey to Cairo and hear the première, explaining that it was his art and not he personally that was important. The style of *Aida* showed a remarkable advance from his earlier masterpieces. Verdi injected here a new element of tone painting; the orchestra ceased to be a mere accompaniment and became a vital element in the drama. *Aida's* popular success fully justified the praise bestowed upon it; productions followed in Italy, all over Europe, and in America. Verdi's next work was not an opera, but the *Messa da Requiem*, written in memory of Alessandro Manzoni, and performed for the 1st time at the Milan Cathedral on the 1st anniversary of Manzoni's death (1874). After Rossini's death (1868), Verdi conceived the idea of honoring his memory by a requiem to which 13 Italian composers were to contribute one number each, Verdi reserving himself for last, the *Libera me*. The plan did not succeed, and Verdi incorporated his number in the "Manzoni Requiem." 15 years elapsed after *Aida* until the production of a new Verdi opera, *Otello* (La Scala, 1887); the libretto, after Shakespeare, was by Arrigo Boito, and it possessed a poetic value of its own; Verdi, at the age of 73, suc-

ceeded in creating for it a score of great dramatic intensity and lyric beauty. Yet he never departed from the basic Italian operatic style, which he cultivated all his life; no concession was made to the growing fashion of music drama, in the Wagner manner; clear separation of aria, recitative, and chorus was still the rule. *Otello* surprised the musical world by its power in the delineation of character. Still greater was the astonishment generated by the appearance of Verdi's last opera, *Falstaff*, also to a libretto by Boito, after Shakespeare's *The Merry Wives of Windsor*, which Verdi completed in his 80th year. The score reveals a genius for subtle comedy; in this work of Verdi's old age, he, for the first time, applied a highly developed art of counterpoint; the orchestra here has more of a symphonic character than in any of Verdi's preceding operas. Verdi's last work was a group of sacred choruses, *4 Pezzi sacri;* in one of them, *Ave Maria*, Verdi made use of the so-called "scala enigmatica" (c, d-flat, e, f-sharp, g-sharp, a-sharp, b, c,).

Innumerable honors were showered upon Verdi by royalty and society. In 1860 he was elected to the 1st National Parliament of Italy (resigned in 1865); in 1875 he was nominated a senator. After the première of *Falstaff*, the King of Italy wished to create him "Marchese di Busseto," but Verdi declined the honor. In 1899 he founded in Milan the "Casa di Ropaso per Musicisti" in memory of his second wife (d. 1897); for its maintenance he set aside 2,500,000 lire, and after his death the income from his works, payable for 30 years. The full extent of the provision may be estimated from the fact that during his life Verdi received in royalties from *Aida* alone the sum of 4,000,000 lire. Verdi was unquestionably the greatest figure in Italian opera. He instinctively understood the purpose and function of music in the theater, and developed a superb craft of dramatic and lyric writing. His melodic gift was of the greatest inventiveness; in his best operas he created arias and ensembles of extraordinary affective appeal. As musical tastes changed under the impact of Wagner, Liszt, and their followers, Verdi's music lost stature; in the view of some critics, it was lowered to the level of "barrel-organ" repertory. A movement "back to Verdi" developed in the 2nd quarter of the 20th century, as Wagnerianism began to recede. The frequency of performances of Verdi's operas rose sharply, not only in Italy, but also in Germany and Austria, France and England, and in America, and modern composers became interested in Verdi's music as a product of pure art, unobscured by artifice. The 50th anniversary of Verdi's death was widely observed in 1951; special performances and festivals were given; Toscanini conducted a concert of Verdi's works, including the "Manzoni Requiem," in Carnegie Hall, N.Y., on Jan. 27, 1951. Excerpts from Verdi's operas were presented in the Roman Colosseum in Oct. 7, 1951.

WORKS: OPERAS: *Oberto, Conte di San Bonifacio* (Milan, Nov. 17, 1839); *Un Giorno di regno* (also as *Il finto Stanislao;* Milan, Sept. 5, 1840); *Nabucco* (Milan, March 9, 1842; N.Y., April 4, 1848); *I Lombardi alla prima Crociata* (Milan, Feb. 11, 1843; N.Y., March 3, 1847; Paris, Nov. 26, 1847, as *Jérusalem*, with a new libretto and a ballet); *Ernani* (after Victor Hugo's *Hernani;* Venice, March 9, 1844; London, March 8, 1845;

N.Y., Park Theater, April 15, 1847; Metropolitan Opera, Jan. 28, 1902); *I due Foscari* (Rome, Nov. 3, 1844; N.Y., June 6, 1847); *Giovanna d'Arco* (Milan, Feb. 15, 1845); *Alzira* (Naples, Aug. 12, 1845); *Attila* (Venice, March 17, 1846; N.Y., March 15, 1850); *Macbeth* (Florence, March 14, 1847; N.Y., Niblo's Garden, April 24, 1850; St. Petersburg, 1854, as *Sivardo, il Sassone;* revised version, Paris, April 21, 1865); *I Masnadieri* (after Schiller's *Die Räuber;* London, July 22, 1847; Milan, Sept. 20, 1853; N.Y., June 2, 1860); *Il Corsaro* (Trieste, Oct. 25, 1848); *La Battaglia di Legnano* (Rome, Jan. 27, 1849; later as *L'Assedio d'Arlem); Luisa Miller* (Naples, Dec. 8, 1849; N.Y., Castle Garden, July 20, 1854; London, June 3, 1858; Metropolitan Opera, Dec. 21, 1929); *Stiffelio* (Treiste, Nov. 16, 1850); *Rigoletto* (after Hugo's *Le Roi s'amuse;* Venice, March 11, 1851; London, May 14, 1853; N.Y., Academy of Music, Feb. 19, 1855; Metropolitan Opera, Nov. 16, 1883); *Il Travatore* (Rome, Jan. 19, 1853; N.Y. Academy of Music, May 2, 1855; Metropolitan Opera, Oct. 26, 1883); *La Traviata* (also given as *Violetta;* Venice, March 6, 1853; N.Y., Academy of Music, Dec. 3, 1856; Metropolitan Opera, Nov. 6, 1883); *Les Vépres siciliennes* (libretto by Scribe; Paris, June 13, 1855; N.Y., Academy of Music, Nov. 7, 1859; Milan, Feb. 4, 1856, as *Giovanna di Guzman); Simone Boccanegra* (Venice, March 12, 1857; revised, Milan, March 24, 1881; Metropolitan Opera, Jan. 28, 1932); *Aroldo* (a revision of *Stiffelio;* Rimini, Aug. 16, 1857); *Un Balla in maschera* (Rome, Feb. 17, 1859; N.Y. Academy of Music, Feb. 11, 1861; Metropolitan Opera, Dec. 11, 1889); *La Forza del destino* (St. Petersburg, Nov. 10, 1862; N.Y., Academy of Music, Feb. 24, 1865; Metropolitan Opera, Nov. 15, 1918); *Don Carlos* (Paris, March 11, 1867; N.Y., Academy of Music, April 12, 1877; Metropolitan Opera, Dec. 23, 1920); *Aida* (Cairo, Dec. 24, 1871; Milan, Feb. 8, 1872; N.Y., Academy of Music, Nov. 25, 1873; Metropolitan Opera, in German, Nov. 12, 1886); *Otello* (Milan, Feb. 5, 1887; N.Y., Academy of Music, April 16, 1888; Metropolitan Opera, March 24, 1891); *Falstaff* (Milan, Feb. 9, 1893; Metropolitan Opera, Feb. 4, 1895).

OTHER WORKS: Requiem Mass ("Manzoni Requiem"; Milan, May 22, 1874); *4 Pezzi sacri* (1886–97): *Ave Maria* for chorus a cappella, *Stabat Mater* for chorus and orch., *Laudi alla Vergine Maria* for female chorus a cappella, and a *Te Deum* for solo soprano, double mixed chorus and orch.; *Inno delle Nazioni* (for the London Exhibition of 1862); String Quartet in E minor (1873); *Ave Maria* for soprano and strings (1880); *Pater noster* for 5-part chorus a cappella (1880); *6 Romanze (Non t'accostare all'urna; More, Elisa; In solitaria stanza; Nell'orror di notte oscura; Perduta ho la pace; Deh pietosa);* 2 songs for bass, *L'Esule* ans *La Seduzione; Guarda che bianca luna,* nocturne for soprano, tenor, and bass with flute obbligato; *Album di sei romanze (Il Tramonto; La Zingara; Ad una stella; Lo Spazzacamino; Il Mistero; Brindisi); Il Povertto,* romanza; *Tu dici che non m'ami,* stornello.

BIBLIOGRAPHY: BIOGRAPHY: A. Pougin, *V.: Histoire anecdotique de sa vie et de ses œuvres* (Paris, 1886; in English, N.Y., 1887); E. Hanslick, *G. V. Zur Geschichte seines Lebens, inbesondere seiner Jugendzeit,* in *Suite* (Vienna, 1885); Prince de Valori, *V. et son œuvre* (Paris, 1895); L. Parodi, *G. V.* (Genoa, 1895); F. Crowest, *V.: Man and Musician* (London, 1897); G. Monaldi, *V.* (Turin, 1899; 3rd ed., Milan, 1943; German transl. as *G. V. und seine Werke,* Stuttgart, 1898, publ. before the Italian original); G. Cavarretta, *V.: Il Genio, la vita, le opere* (Palmero, 1899); C. Perinello, *G. V.* (Berlin, 1900); M. Basso, *G. V.: La sua vita, le sue opere, la sua morte* (Milan, 1901); N. Marini, *G. V.* (Rome, 1901); E. Checchi, *G. V.* (Florence, 1901); O. Boni, *V.: L'Uomo, le opere, l'artista* (Parma, 1901; 2nd ed., 1913); E. Colonna, *G. V. nella vita e nelle opere* (Palmero, 1902); L. Sorge, *G. V.: Uomo, artista, patriota* (Lanciano, 1904); P. Voss, *G. V. Ein Lebensbild* (Diessen, 1904); F. Garibaldi, *G. V. nella vita e nell'arte* (Florence, 1904); A. Visetti, *V.* (London, 1905); G. Bragagnolo and E. Bettazzi, *La Vita di G. V. narrata al popolo* (Milan, 1905); A. d'Angeli, *G. V.* (Bologna, 1910; 2nd ed., 1912); C. Bellaigue, *V. Biographie critique* (Paris, 1912; Italian transl., Milan, 1913); G. Mondali, *Il Maestro della rivoluzione italiana* (Milan, 1913); M. Lottici, *Bio-bibliografia di G. V.* (Parma, 1913); A. Righetti, *G. V.: Vita aneddotica* (Rome, 1913); Sir A. Mackenzie, *V.* (N.Y., 1913); M. Chop, *V.* (Leipzig, 1913); G. Roncaglia, *G. V.* (Naples, 1914); A. Neisser, *G. V.* (Leipzig, 1914); A. Weissmann, *V.* (Berlin, 1922); A. Bonaventura, *G. V.* (Paris, 1923); F. Werfel, *V.* (a biographical novel: Berlin, 1924; English translation, N.Y., 1925); G. Monaldi, *V. anedottico* (Turin, 1926); F. Ridella, *V.* (Genoa, 1928); E. Gascó Contell, *V., su vida y sus obras* (Paris, 1927); F. Bonavia, *V.* (London, 1930; 2nd ed., 1947); L. A. Garibaldi, ed., *G. V. nelle lettere di E. Muzio ad A. Barezzi* (Milan, 1931); C. Gatti, *V.* (Milan, 1931; 2nd ed., 1951; English transl., N.Y., 1955); F. Toye, *G. V.* (London, 1931); A. Baresel, *Was weisst du von V.* (1931); H. Gerigk, *G. V.* (Potsdam, 1932); R. de Rensis, *Franco Faccio e V.* (Milan, 1934); R. Manganella, *V.* (Milan, 1936); L. d'Ambra, *G. V.* (Milan, 1937); D. Hussey, *V.* (London, 1940); *Verdi, studi e memorie,* ed. by G. Mulè and G. Nataletti (Rome, 1941; contains precise documentation of ascertainable facts of Verdi's life; very valuable); G. Roncaglia, *G. V.* (Florence, 1941); F. Botti, *G. V.* (Rome, 1941); K. Holl, *V.* (Vienna, 1942); U. Zoppi, *Angelo Mariani, G. V. e Teresa Stolz* (Milan, 1947); F. H. Törnblom, *V.* (Stockholm, 1948); D. Humphreys, *V., Force of Destiny* (N.Y., 1948); A. Oberdorfer, *G. V.* (Verona, 1949); A. E. A. Cherbuliez, *G. V.* (Zürich, 1949); G. Cenzato, *Itinerari verdiani* (Parma, 1949; 2nd ed., Milan, 1955); L. Orsini, *G. V.* (Turin, 1949); L. Gianoli, *V.* (Brescia, 1951); F. Abbiati, ed., *G. V.* (Milan, 1951); *G. V.* (collection of articles; Siena, 1951); G. Monaldi, *V., la vita, le opere* (Milan, 1951); E. Radius, *V. vivo* (Milan, 1951); G. Stefani, *V. e Trieste* (Trieste, 1951); G. Mondini, *Nel cinquantennio della morte di G. V.* (Cremona, 1952); F. Botti, *V. e l'ospedale di Villanova d'Arda* (Parma, 1952); T. R. Ybarra, *V., Miracle Man of Opera* (N.Y., 1955); V. Sheean, *Orpheus at Eighty* (N.Y., 1958); P. Petit, *Verdi* (Paris, 1958); Franco Abbiate, *Guiseppe Verdi* (Milan, 1959); Frank Walker, *The Man Verdi* (N.Y., 1962); G. Martin, *V., Verdi, His Music, Life and Times* (N.Y., 1963); J. Wechsberg, *Verdi* (1974); William Weaver, compiler, *Verdi. A Documentary Study* (N.Y., 1977).

CRITICISM, APPRECIATION: A. Basevi, *Studio sulle opere di G. V.* (Florence, 1859); G. Bertrand, *Les Nationalités musicales étudiées dans le drame lyrique. Verdisme et Wagnérisme* (Paris, 1872); E. Hanslick, *V.,* in *Die moderne Oper* (Berlin, 1875; 8th ed., 1885); B. Roosevelt, *V., Milan and Otello* (Milan, 1887); V. Maurel, *À propos de la mise-en-scène du drame lyrique "Otello"* (Rome, 1888); E. Destranges, *L'Évolution musicale chez V.: Aïda, Otello, Falstaff* (Paris, 1895); C. Abate, *Wagner e V. Studio critico-musicale* (Mistretta, 1896); I. Pizzi, *Ricordi verdiani inediti* (Turin, 1901; contains 11 letters); special Verdi issue of *Rivista Musicale Italiana* (1901); A. Soffredini, *Le Opere di G. V.: Studio critico-analitico* (Milan, 1901); G. Tebaldini, *Da Rossini a V.* (Naples, 1901); P. Bellezza, *Manzoni e V., i due grandi* (Rome, 1901); J. G. Huneker, *Overtones* (N.Y., 1904); F. Flamini, *Pagine di critica e d'arte* (Leghorn, 1905; contains a study on the operas of Verdi); J. C. Hadden, *The Operas of V.* (London, 1910); K. Regensbuger, *Über den "Trovador" des García Gutiérrez, die Quelle von Verdis "Il Trovatore"* (Berlin, 1911); C. Vanbianchi, *Saggio di bibliografia verdiana* (Milan, 1913); A. St. John-Brennon, "G. V.," *Musical Quarterly* (Jan. 1916); E. Istel, "The 'Othello' of V. and Shakespeare," *Musical Quarterly* (July 1916) and "A Genetic Study of the Aïda Libretto," *Musical Quarterly* (Jan. 1917); L. Unterholzner, *G. V.s Operntypus* (Hannover, 1933); P. Berl, *Die Opern V.s in ihrer Instrumentation* (diss., Vienna, 1931); A. Maecklenburg, "V. and Manzoni," *Musical Quarterly* (April 1931); G. Menghini, *G. V. e il melodramma italiano* (Rimini, 1931); M. Mila, *Il Melodramma di V.* (Bari, 1933); A. Parente, *Il Problema della critica verdiana* (Turin, 1933); R. Gallusser, *V.s Frauengestalten* (diss., Zürich, 1936); J. Loschelder, *Das Todesproblem in V.s Opernschaffen* (Cologne, 1938); G. Engler, *V.s Anschauung vom Wesen der Oper* (diss.; Breslau, 1938); G. Roncaglia, *L'Ascensione creatrice di G. V.* (Florence, 1940); M. Rinaldi, *V. critico* (Rome, 1951); C. Gatti, *Revisioni e rivalutazioni verdiane* (Turin, 1952); M. Mila, *Il melodramma di V.* (Milan, 1960); C. Osborne, *The Complete Operas of V.* (N.Y., 1970); Julian Budden, *The Operas of V.,* vol. I (N.Y., 1973).

CORRESPONDENCE, ICONOGRAPHY: G. Cesari and A. Luzio, *G. V. I copialettere pubblicati e illustrati* (Leipzig, 1913); G. Monaldi, *Saggio di iconografia verdiana* (Bergamo, 1913); T. Costantini, *Sei lettere inedite* (relating to the production of *Aida* in Cairo; Trieste, 1908); J. G. Prod'homme, "Unpublished Letters from V. to Camille Du Locle (1866–76)," *Musical Quarterly* (Jan. 1921); A. Martinelli, *G. V. Raggi e Penombre. Le ultime lettere* (Trieste, 1926); *Briefe* (transl. into German by P. Stefan, Vienna, 1926); G. Morazzoni, *Lettere inedite di G. V.* (Milan 1929); A. Alberti, *V. intimo: carteggio di G. V. con il conte O. Arrivabene* (Verona, 1931); *Sei lettere inedite a G. Bottesini* (Trieste, 1934); A. Luzio, *Il Pensiero artistico e politico di G. V. nelle sue lettere inedite al conte O. Arrivabene* (Milan); C. Gatti, *V. nelle immagini* (Milan, 1941); C. Graziani, *G. V.: Autobiografia dalle lettere* (Milan, 1941; new ed., 1951, under Graziani's real name, Aldo Oberdorfer); F. Werfel and P. Stefan, eds., *V., The Man in His Letters* (N.Y., 1942).

Vere, Clémentine Duchene de (real name **Wood de Vere**), French soprano; b. Paris, Dec. 12, 1864; d. Mount Vernon, N.Y., Jan. 19, 1954. Her father was a Belgian nobleman; her mother, an English lady. Her musical education was completed under the instruction of Mme. Albertini-Baucardé in Florence, where she made her début at the age of 16 as Marguerite de Valois in *Les Huguenots.* On Feb. 2, 1896 she made her American debut at the Metropolitan Opera, N.Y.; her roles with it were Violetta, Gilda, Marguerite in Gounod's *Faust,* and Lucia. In 1892 she married the conductor **Romualdo Sapio;** after 1914 she lived mostly in N.Y., as a private teacher. Her voice was a brillant high soprano; she excelled in coloratura.

Veremans, Renaat, Belgian composer; Lierre, March 2, 1894; d. Antwerp, June 5, 1969. He studied at the Lemmens Institute in Mechlin and at the Antwerp Cons. with Auguste De Boeck; awarded the Premier Prix in organ and piano in 1914; from 1921 to 1944 he served as director of the Flemish Opera in Antwerp; for 31 years taught at the Antwerp Cons. In his music he follows the Romantic tradition of the Belgian-Flemish School of composition.
WORKS: 4 operas: *Beatrijs* (1928), *Anna-Marie* (Antwerp, Feb. 22, 1938), *Bietje* (1954), and *Lanceloot en Sanderien* (Antwerp, Sept. 13, 1968); 2 operettas: *The Strange Adventure* and *The Mill of Sans Souci;* 2 oratorios: *The XIV Stations of the Cross* and *The 5 Joyful Mysteries; Groenendal Cantata;* 3 symphonies (1959, 1961, 1968); Trumpet Concerto (1960); Concerto for flute and chamber orch. (1962); Concerto for oboe and small orch. (1964); Horn Concerto (1965); symph. poems: *Morgendeschemer (Dawn), Night and the Awakening of Day beside the River Nete* and *Sylan Scenes;* chamber music; choruses; many songs.

Veress, Sándor, Hungarian-Swiss composer; b. Kolozsvár, Feb. 1, 1907. He studied piano with his mother, and later with Béla Bartók; composition with Zoltán Kodály at the Royal Academy of Music in Budapest (1924–30); then took lessons with László Lajtha at the Hungarian Ethnographical Museum (1928–35). He worked with Bartók on the folklore collection at the Academy of Sciences in Budapest (1936–41); subsequently taught courses at the State Academy of Music in Budapest (1943–48). In 1950 he went to Switzerland, where he received an appointment as a prof. of composition at the Bern Univ. In 1965–67 he was visiting prof. at the Peabody Cons. in Baltimore; then was a lecturer at the Univ. of Adelaide, Australia (1967), and at the Univ. of Oregon in Portland (1972); then returned to Switzerland and resumed his teaching position at the Univ. of Bern.
WORKS: 2 ballets: *Die Wunderschalmei* (1937) and *Térszili Katicza* (1942–43; Stockholm, Feb. 16, 1949); *Divertimento* for orch. (1935); *Partita* for orch. (1936); Violin Concerto (1937–39; Zürich, Jan. 9, 1951); 2 symphonies: No. 1 (1940) and No. 2, *Sinfonia Minneapolitana* (1953; Minneapolis, March 12, 1954); *4 Transylvanian Dances* for string orch. (1944–49); *Threnos, in memoriam Béla Bartók* for orch. (1945); *Hommage à Paul Klee,* fantasia for 2 pianos and string orch. (1951; Bern, Jan. 22, 1952); Concerto for piano, strings, and percussion (1952; Baden-Baden,

Jan. 19, 1954; composer soloist); Sonata for orch. (1952; Brussels, July 8, 1952); Concerto for string quartet and orch. (1960-61; Basel, Jan. 25, 1962); *Passacaglia concertante* for oboe and strings (1961; Lucerne, Aug. 31, 1961); *Variations on a Theme of Kodály* for orch. (1962); *Elegie* for baritone, string orch., and harp (1964); *Expovare* for flute, oboe, and strings (1964); *Musica concertante* for strings (1965-66); Sonatina for oboe, clarinet, and bassoon (1931); 2 string quartets (1931, 1936-37); Violin Sonatina (1932); Cello Sonatina (1933); Sonata for solo violin (1935); Sonata No. 2 for violin and piano (1939); String Trio (1954); Piano Trio (1962); Sonata for solo cello (1967); Trio for clarinet, violin, and cello (1972); piano pieces, including a Sonatina (1932); songs.

Veretti, Antonio, Italian composer; b. Verona, Feb. 20, 1900. He studied composition with Alfano at the Liceo Musicale of Bologna, graduating in 1921. He taught at the Cons. of Rome (until 1943); was director of the Conservatorio G. Rossini in Pesaro (1950-52) and director of the Cons. of Cagliari, Sardinia (1953-55); in 1956 he became director of the L. Cherubini Cons. His music follows the traditional lines of Italian modernism, but in some of his later works he experimented with serial techniques.

WORKS: 2 operas: *Il Medico volante* (*The Willing Doctor*, 1928; won a prize of the newspaper *Il Secolo*, but was never performed) and *Il Favorito del re* (*The King's Favorite*; La Scala, Milan, March 17, 1932; a condensed version, titled *Burlesca*, was performed in Rome, Jan. 29, 1955); 2 ballets: *Il galante tiratore* (*The Gallant Killer*; San Remo, Feb. 11, 1933) and *Una Favola di Andersen* (*A Fable by Andersen*; Venice, Sept. 15, 1934); a choreographic musical mystery, *I Sette Peccati* (*The 7 Deadly Sins*; La Scala, April 24, 1956); 2 oratorios: *Il Cantico dei Cantici* (Bologna, 1922) and *Il Figliuol prodigo* (Rome, Nov. 21, 1942); *Sinfonia Italiana* (1929; Liège Fest. of the International Society for Contemporary Music, Sept. 4, 1930); *Suite* for orch. (1934); *Morte e deificazione di Dafni* for voice and 11 instruments (Venice Festival, Sept. 8, 1937); *Sinfonia Epica* (1938); *Divertimento* for harpsichord and 6 instruments (1939); *Sinfonia sacra* for male voices and orch. (1946; Rome, April, 1947); Piano Concerto (1949; Venice International Fest., Sept. 9, 1950); *Quattro Poesie di Giorgio Vigolo* for voice, and orch. or piano (1950; orch. version, Torino, Feb. 17, 1956); *Ouverture della Campana* (1951; RAI radio, Nov. 10, 1951); *Fantasie* for clarinet, and orch. or piano (1959); Concertino for flute, and chamber orch. or piano (1959); *Prière pour demander une étoile* for a cappella chorus (1966; version with orch., 1967); *Duo strumentale* for violin and piano (1925); Cello Sonata (1926); Piano Trio (1927); Violin Sonata (1952); *Elegie in Friulano* for voice, violin, clarinet, and guitar (1963); music for films.

BIBLIOGRAPHY: N. Costarelli, "Antonio Veretti," *Rassegna Musicale* (Jan.-March 1955).

Verevka, Grigory, Ukrainian composer; b. Bereznia, Tchernigov district, Dec. 25, 1895; d. Kiev, Oct. 21, 1964. He was a boy chorister in Tchernigov; then studied at the Kiev Institute of Music and Drama; became engaged in choral conducting. He wrote a number of choruses which entered general repertory; made choral arrangements of nearly 100 Revolutionary songs.

Verheyden, Edward, Belgian composer; b. Antwerp, Oct. 8, 1878; d. there, April 10, 1959. He studied violin in Antwerp and Brussels; then turned to composition. He wrote the operas *Heibieke* (1908) and *De Geest* (1924); symphonic works; lieder and choruses.

Verhulst, Johannes (Josephus Herman), Dutch conductor and composer; b. The Hague, March 19, 1816; d. there, Jan. 17, 1891. He studied violin at The Hague and Cologne; in 1838 went to Leipzig, where he became friendly with Mendelssohn; was engaged as conductor of the "Euterpe" concerts (until 1842); then returned to The Hague. He was conductor of the renowned "Diligentia" concerts at The Hague from 1860 until 1886; also conducted in Amsterdam and Rotterdam. He wrote a number of symph. works; chamber music, sacred songs, choruses to Dutch words.

Vermeulen, Matthijs, remarkable Dutch composer and music critic; b. Helmond, Feb. 8, 1888; d. Laren, July 26, 1967. Principally self-taught, he traveled to Amsterdam in 1905, where he received musical guidance from Daniël le Lange and Alphons Diepenbrock; in 1908 he began to write music criticism for Dutch and French publications, and continued his journalistic activities until 1956. In 1921 he went to France; returned to Holland in 1947, when he became music editor of *De Groene Amsterdammer*. He entertained a strong belief in the mystical powers of music; in order to enhance the universality of melodic, rhythmic, and contrapuntal elements, he introduced in his compositions a unifying set of *cantus firmi* against a diversified network of interdependent melodies of an atonal character. He was outside the common current of musical fashions, and his works were not performed for many years after their composition.

WORKS: 7 symphonies: No. 1, *Symphonia Carminum* (1912-14; Amsterdam, May 5, 1964); No. 2, *Prélude à la nouvelle journée* (1919-20; Amsterdam, July 5, 1956; had been a prize-winning work at the Queen Elisabeth Composition Competition in Brussels in 1953); No. 3, *Thrène et Péan* (1921-22; Amsterdam, May 24, 1939); No. 4, *Les Victoires* (1940-41; Rotterdam, Sept. 30, 1949); No. 5, *Les Lendemains chantants* (1944-45; Amsterdam, Oct. 13, 1949); No. 6, *Les Minutes heureuses* (1956-58; Utrecht, Nov. 25, 1959); No. 7, *Dithyrambes, pour les temps à venir* (1963-65; Amsterdam, April 2, 1967); the songs *The Soldier* (1916), *On ne passe pas* (1917), *Les Filles du Roi d'Espagne* (1917), *La Veille* (1917; orchestrated 1929), *3 Salutations à Notre Dame* (1942), *Le Balcon* (1943) and *3 Chants d'amour* (1962); 2 cello sonatas (1918, 1938); String Trio (1924); Violin Sonata (1925); *Passacaille et Cortège* for orch. (1930; concert fragments from his music for the open-air play *The Flying Dutchman*); *Symphonic Prolog* (1930); String Quartet (1960-61).

WRITINGS: *De twee muzieken* (*The Two Musics*, 2 vols., Leyden, 1918), *Klankbord* (*Sound Board*, Amsterdam, 1928) and *De eene Grondtoon* (*The One Key Note*, Amsterdam, 1929); *Het avontuur van de geest* (*The Adventure of the Spirit*, Amsterdam, 1947); *Prin-*

ciepen der Europese muziek (*Principles of European Music,* Amsterdam, 1948); and *De Myziek dat Wonder* (*Music, A Miracle,* Amsterdam, 1958).

BIBLIOGRAPHY: W. Paap, "De Componist Matthijs Vermeulen," *Mens en Melodie* (Nov. 1949); "Matthijs Vermeulen," *Sonorum Speculum* 28 (1966); Reinbert de Leeuw, "Matthijs Vermeulen," *Sonorum Speculum* 52 (1973).

Verne, Mathilde, Alice, and **Adela,** English pianists, sisters of **Marie Wurm.** Their real name was Wurm, but they adopted the name Verne in 1893. **Mathilde Verne** (b. Southampton, May 25, 1865; d. London, June 4, 1936) studied with her parents, and then became a pupil of Clara Schumann in Frankfurt; was very successful in England; from 1907 to 1936 gave concerts of chamber music in London; was a renowed teacher. **Alice Verne Bredt** (b. Southampton, Aug. 9, 1868; d. London, April 12, 1958) was best known as a piano teacher; also composed pedagogical works. **Adela Verne** (b. Southampton, Feb. 27, 1877; d. London, Feb. 5, 1952) studied with her sisters, and later took lessons from Paderewski in Switzerland; returning to London, she developed a successful career, and became extremely popular as a concert player in England; also made tours in the U.S.A.

BIBLIOGRAPHY: Mathilde Verne, *Chords of Remembrance* (London, 1936).

Verneuil, Raoul de, Peruvian composer; b. Lima, April 9, 1899. He studied in Paris with André Bloch, and lived there for many years; returned to Lima in 1940, after a brief sojourn in N.Y. On Nov. 21, 1940, he gave a concert of his chamber music in Lima. His works include *Danza Peruana* for orch.; *Inca Legend* for voice and 8 instruments; *Ritmos del Sol* for 12-part chorus; piano pieces.

Verrall, John, American composer; b. Britt, Iowa, June 17, 1908. He studied piano and composition with Donald Ferguson; then went to Europe, where he attended classes at the Royal College of Music in London and took lessons with Kodály in Budapest. Returning to the U.S., he entered the Univ. of Minnesota (B.A. 1934). He held teaching positions at Hamline Univ. (1934–42), at Mount Holyoke College (1942–46), and at the Univ. of Washington, Seattle (1948–73).

WORKS: operas: *The Cowherd and the Sky Maiden,* after a Chinese legend (Seattle, Jan. 17, 1952), *The Wedding Knell,* after Hawthorne (Seattle, Dec. 5, 1952), *Three Blind Mice* (Seattle, May 22, 1955); for orch: Symph. No. 1 (Minneapolis, Jan. 16, 1940); Symph. No. 2 (1943); Violin Concerto (1946); *Symphony for Young Orchestras* (1948); *The Dark Night of St. Joan,* for chamber orch. (1949); *Sinfonia Festiva* for band (1954); Piano Concerto (1960); Chamber Symph. (1967); Viola Concerto (1968); *Nonet* for string quartet and wind quartet (1970); *Appalachian Folk Song,* for cello and piano (1953); *Suite* for 3 clarinets (1957); *Nocturne* for bass clarinet and piano (1958); String Quartets (1940, 1943, 1948, 1949, 1952, 1956, 1961); Horn Sonata (1942); 2 Viola Sonatas (1942, 1964); Flute Sonata (1972); numerous piano works and choruses. He published the teaching manuals *Elements of Harmony* (1937), *Form and Meaning in the Arts* (1958), *Fugue and Invention in Theory and Practice* (1966), *Basic Theory of Music* (1970).

Verstovsky, Alexei, important Russian opera composer; b. on the family estate in the district of Tambov, March 1, 1799; d. Moscow, Nov. 17, 1862. He was taken as a child to the town of Ufa in the Urals; at the age of 17 was sent to St. Petersburg, where he entered the Institute of Transport Engineers; at the same time he studied music privately with several excellent European teachers, resident in Russia; took piano lessons with Johann Heinrich Miller, Daniel Steibelt and the famous pianist and composer John Field; studied violin with Ludwig Maurer and voice with Tarquini. He became a member of the flourishing literary and artistic milieu in St. Petersburg; among his friends was Pushkin. In 1823 he went to Moscow. Almost all of his compositions for the stage followed the French model, with long scenes of speech accompanied on the keyboard; his first production was a vaudeville, *The Sentimental Landlord in the Country* (1817); he also composed popular songs and couplets for various plays. He contributed a great deal to the progress of operatic art in Russia, but his music lacked distinction and inventive power; with the advent of Glinka and Dargomyzhsky on the Russian operatic scene, Verstovsky's productions receded into insignificance.

WORKS: light operas (all produced in St. Petersburg): *Grandmother's Parrot* (Aug. 10, 1819); *Quarantine* (Aug. 7, 1820); *New Mischief* (Feb. 24, 1822); *The Madhouse* (Oct. 28, 1822); *A Charade in Action* (Jan. 15, 1823); with Maurer; a long series of vaudevilles (all produced in Moscow): *Who Is Brother, Who Is Sister?* (Feb. 5, 1824); *Teacher and Pupil* (May 6, 1824); *The Petitioner* (June 10, 1824); *30,000 Men* (Feb. 10, 1825); *The Caliph's Amusements* (April 21, 1825); *The Miraculous Nose* (Oct. 20, 1825); *Itinerant Doctors* (Feb. 16, 1827); *5 Years in 2 Hours* (Feb. 1, 1828); *15 Years in Paris* (Feb. 8, 1828); *Man and Wife* (June 4, 1830); *The Old Hussar* (June 17, 1831); serious operas (all produced in Moscow): *Pan Tvardovsky* (June 5, 1828); *Vadim, or 12 Sleeping Maidens* (Dec. 7, 1832); *Askold's Grave* (Sept. 27, 1835; his most important work; still in the repertory of Russian opera houses); *Homesickness* (Sept. 2, 1839); *Gromoboy* (Feb. 5, 1858). A modern edition of Verstovsky's songs and couplets from his music to theatrical plays was brought out in Moscow, 1971.

BIBLIOGRAPHY: V. Cheshikhin, *History of Russian Opera* (St. Petersburg, 1905, pp. 98–108); B. Dobrohotov, *Verstovsky* (Moscow, 1949).

Vesque von Püttlingen, Johann, Austrian composer; b. Opole, Poland, July 23, 1803; d. Vienna, Oct. 29, 1883. He studied law in Vienna and became a councillor of state; at the same time he studied music with Moscheles (piano) and Sechter (theory), and made his mark as a composer of operas, under the pseudonym **J. Hoyen.** The following operas by him were produced in Vienna: *Turandot* (Oct. 3, 1838), *Johanna d'Arc* (Dec. 30, 1840), and *Abenteuer Carls des Zweiten* (Jan. 12, 1850). His opera *Der lustige Rat* was produced in Weimar on April 12, 1852. He published a useful book, *Das musikalische Autorrecht* (1865).

BIBLIOGRAPHY: E. Hanslick, "Vesque von Püttlingen," *Musikalisches Skizzenbuch* (Berlin, 1888); H. Schultz, *Johann Vesque von Püttlingen* (Regensburg, 1930).

Vetter, Walther, German musicologist; b. Berlin, May 10, 1891; d. Berlin, April 1, 1967. He was a student of Hermann Abert in Halle; occupied various teaching posts: in Danzig (1921–27), Breslau (1934–36), Greifswald (1936–41), Poznań (Posen) during German occupation (1941–43); then was prof. of musicology at Humboldt Univ., Berlin (1946–58).
WRITINGS: *Das frühdeutsche Lied* (2 vols., Münster, 1928); *Franz Schubert* (Potsdam, 1934); *Antike Musik* (Munich, 1935); *J. S. Bach* (Leipzig, 1938); *Beethoven und die militärisch-politischen Ereignisse seiner Zeit* (Poznan, 1943); *Der Kapellmeister Bach* (Potsdam, 1950); *Der Klassiker Schubert* (2 vols., Leipzig, 1953); *Mythos-Melos-Musica,* collection of articles, in 2 vols. (Leipzig, 1957, 1961).

Viadana, Lodovico da, Italian composer; b. Viadana, near Mantua, 1560; d. Gualtieri, May 2, 1627. His family name was **Grossi,** but he is generally known by the name of his birthplace. In 1596 he became a Franciscan monk; from 1594 till 1609, was maestro di cappella at the Mantua Cathedral; from 1610 to 1612, chorusmaster at Fano (Papal States), then in Venice, and finally in Mantua again. He was formerly accredited with the invention of the basso continuo (thoroughbass), but Peri's *Euridice* (publ. 1600) has a figured bass in certain numbers, as does Banchieri's *Concerti ecclesiastici* (publ. 1595), whereas Viadana's *Cento concerti con il basso continuo* did not appear till 1602 (Venice). However, he was the first to write church concertos with so few parts that the organ continuo was employed as a necessary harmonic support. A very prolific composer, he publ. numerous Masses, psalms, Magnificats, Lamentations, motets, etc.
BIBLIOGRAPHY: A. Parazzi, *Della Vita e delle opere musicali di L. Grossi-Viadana* (Milan, 1876); F. X. Haberl, in *Kirchenmusikalisches Jahrbuch* (1881) and *Musica Sacra* (1897); M. Schneider, *Die Anfänge des Basso Continuo* (with 11 numbers from the *Cento concerti* of 1602; 1918); F. T. Arnold, *The Art of Accompaniment from a Thorough-Bass* (London, 1931); F. B. Pratella, "Viadana e la sinfonia," *Il Pensiero Musicale* (Sept.-Nov. 1922); G. Reese, *Music in the Renaissance* (N.Y., 1965).

Vianesi, Auguste-Charles-Léonard-François, conductor; Italian conductor; b. Livorno, Nov. 2, 1837; d. New York, Nov. 4, 1908. After studying in Italy, he went to Paris in 1857; in 1859 he became conductor at Drury Lane, London; later conducted Italian Opera at Covent Garden; in 1887 became principal conductor at the Grand Opéra, Paris. He conducted the performance of *Faust* at the opening night of the Metropolitan Opera House (N.Y., Oct. 22, 1883), and was on its staff throughout its first season; also conducted during the season of 1891–92; then remained in N.Y. as a vocal teacher.

Vianna, Fructuoso, Brazilian composer; b. Itajubá, Oct. 6, 1896. He studied in Rio de Janeiro with Henri-

que Oswald, and later in Paris (1923). Upon his return to Brazil, he was appointed to the faculty of the Cons. of S. Paulo. He wrote a number of piano pieces based on Brazilian melodic and rhythmic modes: *Dança de Negros, Tamborzinho, Tanguinho, Corta-Jaca,* 7 *Miniaturas sobre temas brasileiros, Seresta,* 5 "valsas," 6 "toadas," etc.; several choral works and songs; a few violin pieces.

Vianna da Motta, José. See **Da Motta, José Vianna.**

Viardot-García, Pauline, celebrated singer; daughter of **Manuel del Popolo García;** b. Paris, July 18, 1821; d. there, May 18, 1910. She was taken by her parents to England and America; on returning to Paris in 1828 she had piano lessons with Liszt. Her father and mother both gave her vocal instruction; Reicha was her teacher in harmony. Her concert debut was at Brussels in 1837; later she was engaged by Viardot, the director of the Théâtre Italien, Paris; she sang there until her marriage to Viardot in 1841; he then accompanied her on long tours throughout Europe. She created the role of Fides in Meyerbeer's *Le Prophète* at the Paris Opéra in 1849, and that of Sapho in Gounod's opera, 1851; after another succession of tours, she took the role of Orphée in Berlioz's revival of Gluck's opera at the Théâtre Lyrique (1859), singing the part 150 nights to crowded houses. She retired in 1863. Her voice was a mezzo-soprano of extraordinary compass. For some years she taught at the Paris Cons.; among her pupils were Désirée Artôt and Antoinette Sterling. A thoroughly trained musician, she also composed operas, one of which, *La Dernière Sorcière,* was performed (in a German version) at Weimar (April 8, 1869). In Paris she maintained a long Platonic friendship with the Russian novelist Turgenev. She owned the holograph of Mozart's *Don Giovanni,* which she left to the Library of the Cons. in Paris.
BIBLIOGRAPHY: La Mara, *P. Viardot-Garcia* (Leipzig, 1882); L. H. Torrigi, *P. Viardot-Garcia. Sa biographie, ses compositions, son enseignement* (Geneva, 1901); C. H. Kaminski, *Lettres à Mlle. Viardot d'Ivan Tourgéneff* (Paris, 1907); the memoirs of her daughter, Louise Héritte-Viardot, *Memories and Adventures* (London, 1913; transl. from original German MS; also in French, Paris, 1923); "P. Viardot-Garcia to J. Rietz. Letters of Friendship," *Musical Quarterly* (July 1915-Jan. 1916); T. Marix-Spire, "Gounod and His Interpreter, Pauline Viardot," *Musical Quarterly* (April, July 1945); A. Rachmanowa (pseud.), *Die Liebe eines Lebens: Iwan Turgenjew und Pauline Viardot* (Frauenfeld, 1952); April FitzLyon, *The Price of Genius: A Life of Pauline Viardot* (London, 1964).

Vicentino, Nicola, Italian music theorist; b. Vicenza, 1511; d. Rome, 1572. Pupil of Willaert at Venice; then became maestro and music master to Cardinal Ippolito d'Este in Ferrara and in Rome. There his book of madrigals for 5 voices, an attempt to revive the chromatic and enharmonic genera of the Greeks, led to an academic controversy with the learned Portuguese musician Lusitano; defeated, Vicentino publ. a theoretical treatise, *L'antica musica ridotta alla moderna prattica* (1555), which contains a description of his invention, an instrument called the archicembalo (having 6 keyboards, with separate strings and keys for distinguishing the ancient genera—diatonic, chromatic, and enharmonic). He also invented and described (1561) an "archiorgano." In chromatic composition he was followed by Cipriano de Rore and Gesualdo. His work paved the way for the monodic style, and the eventual disuse of the church modes.

BIBLIOGRAPHY: H. Riemann, *Geschichte der Musiktheorie* (Leipzig, 1898); Th. Kroyer, "Die Anfänge der Chromatik im italienischen Madrigal des XVI. Jahrhunderts," *Beihefte der Internationalen Musik-Gesellschaft;* G. Reese, *Music in the Renaissance* (N.Y., 1954).

Vickers, Jon, Canadian tenor; b. Prince Albert, Saskatchewan, Oct. 29, 1926. He studied at the Toronto Cons.; went to London, where he sang at Covent Garden; in the summer of 1958 appeared as Siegmund in *Die Walküre* at the Wagner Festival in Bayreuth, creating a fine impression; in 1959 was with the Vienna State Opera; made his debut at the Metropolitan Opera as Canio in *Pagliacci* on Jan. 17, 1960; from then on advanced rapidly to the front ranks as a Wagnerian Heldentenor.

Victoria, Tomás Luis de (Italianized form, **Tommaso Luigi da Vittoria**), one of the greatest of Spanish Renaissance composers; b. Avila, c.1549; d. Madrid, Aug. 27, 1611. There is no record of Victoria's early years in Avila, but in all probability he received his first musical training as a choirboy at the Cathedral there. In 1565 he went to Rome, and to prepare himself for the priesthood entered the Collegium Germanicum, a seminary founded by St. Ignatius Loyola in 1552. In Rome his teacher may have been Palestrina, who from 1566 to 1571 was music master at the Roman Seminary, at this time amalgamated with the Collegium Germanicum. Victoria was about the same age as Palestrina's two sons, Rodolfo and Angelo, who were students at the Roman Seminary; the Italian master is known to have befriended his young Spanish colleague, and when Palestrina left the Roman Seminary in 1571, it was Victoria who succeeded him as maestro there. In 1569 Victoria had left the Collegium Germanicum to become choirmaster and organist in the Church of Sta. Maria di Montserrato; from this time on he also officiated frequently at musical ceremonies in the Church of S. Giaccomo degli Spagnuoli. In June, 1573, he returned to the Collegium Germanicum as maestro di cappella; 2 years later the Collegium moved to new quarters in the Palazzo S. Apollinare, and Victoria thereby became choirmaster of the adjoining Church of S. Apollinare. In Aug., 1575, he was ordained a priest; in Jan. of that year he had received a benefice at León from the Pope, and in 1579 he was granted another benefice at Zamora, neither requiring residence. In 1587 he resigned his post at the Collegium Germanicum and was admitted as a priest to the Church of S. Girolamo della Carità, where he lived until 1585; this was the church where St. Philip Neri held his famous religious meetings, which led to the founding of the Congregation of the Oratory in 1575. Though Victoria was not a member of the Oratory, he must have taken some part in its important musical activities, living as he did for 5 years under the same roof with its founder (St. Philip left S. Girolamo in 1583); he is known to have been on terms of the closest friendship with Juvenal Ancina, a priest of the Oratory who wrote texts for many of the "Laudi spirituali" sung at the meetings of the Congregation. In 1583, dedicating a volume of Masses to Philip II, Victoria expressed a desire to return to his native land, but this wish does not appear to have been fulfilled until some 12 years later. He probably returned to Spain in 1594; in the dedication of his 2nd book of Masses (1592) he mentions for the first time his appointment as chaplain to the widowed Empress-Mother Maria, sister of Philip II, who in 1582 had taken up her residence in the Convent of the Descalzas Reales in Madrid. After his return to Spain, Victoria became organist and choirmaster at this convent, and when the Empress Maria died in 1603, he continued to act as chaplain to her daughter, the Princess Margaret, who was a nun in the Descalzas Reales. His last work, a Requiem Mass for the Empress Maria, regarded as his masterpiece, was publ. in 1605.

Beginning with a vol. of motets in 1572, dedicated to his chief patron, Cardinal Otto Truchsess, Bishop of Augsburg, most of Victoria's works were printed in Italy, in sumptuous editions, showing that he had the backing of wealthy patrons. A vol. of Masses, Magnificats, motets, and other church music publ. at Madrid in 1600 is of special interest because it makes provision for an organ accompaniment.

A man of deep religious sentiment, Victoria expresses in his music all the ardor and exaltation of Spanish mysticism. He is generally regarded as a leading representative of the Roman School, but it should be remembered that, before the appearance of Palestrina, this school was already profoundly marked by Hispanic influences through the work of Morales, Guerrero, Escobedo, and other Spanish composers resident in Rome. Thus Victoria inherited at least as much from his own countrymen as from Palestrina, and in its dramatic intensity, its rhythmic variety, its tragic grandeur and spiritual fervor, his music is thoroughly personal and thoroughly Spanish.

WORKS: motets for 4, 5, 6, and 8 voices (Venice, 1572; contains the well-known motets *O quam gloriosum* and *O vos omnes); Liber primus qui Missas, Psalmos, Magnificat, ad Virginem Dei Matrem Salutationes, aliaque complectitur* (Venice, 1576); *Cantica B. Virginis per annum* (Rome, 1581); *Hymni totius anni* (Rome, 1581; new ed., Venice, 1600); motets for 4, 5, 6, 8, and 12 voices (Rome, 1583); *Missarum libri duo,* 4-6 voices (Rome, 1583); *Officium Hebdomadae Sanctae* (Rome, 1585); *Motecta Festorum totius anni,* 4, 5, 6, and 8 voices (Rome, 1585; new eds. printed at Milan and Dillingen in 1589); *Missae Liber secundus,* 4-8 voices (Rome, 1592); *Missae, Magnificat, Motecta, Psalmi* for 8, 9, and 12 voices (Madrid, 1600; contains both old and new works); *Officium Defunctorum,* 6 voices (Madrid, 1605) Pedrell brought out a complete modern ed. of Victoria's works in 8 vols. (Breitkopf & Härtel, 1902-13), a corrected edition edited by H. Anglès was published 1965-68.

BIBLIOGRAPHY: L. Cellar, *La Semaine Sainte au Vatican* (Paris, 1867); H. Collet, *Le Mysticisme musical espagnol au XVIe siècle* (Paris, 1913) and *T. L. de*

Victoria (Paris, 1914); F. Pedrell, *T. L. de Victoria* (Valencia, 1918); R. Mitjana, *Estudios sobre algunos músicos españoles del siglo XVI* (Madrid, 1918); R. Casimiri, *"Il Vittoria"* (Rome, 1934); Hans von May, *Die Kompositionstechnik T. L. de Victorias* (Bern, 1943); P. Wagner, *Geschichte der Messe* I, p. 421 ff., Hugo Leichtentritt, *Geschichte der Motett*, p. 373 ff; G. Reese, *Music in the Renaissance* (N.Y., 1954); T. N. Rive, "Victoria's *Lamentationes Geremiae*," *Anuario Musical* (1967); H. Anglès, "Problemas que presenta la nueva edición de las obras de Morales y de Victoria," in J. Robijns *et al.*, *Renaissance-muziek* (Leuven, 1969).

Victory, Gerard, Irish composer; b. Dublin, Dec. 24, 1921. He studied modern languages at Univ. College in Dublin and music at Trinity College; in 1967 was appointed music director of the Dublin Radio. His compositions are imbued with the broad pentatonic melos of Irish folk music; but in some of his instrumental works of a later period he began to apply serial structures.
WORKS: *An Fear a Phós Balbhin (The Silent Wife)* opera to a libretto in Gaelic (Dublin, April 6, 1953); *Music Hath Mischief* (Dublin, Dec. 2, 1968); *Chatterton* (1967); the operettas *Nita* (1944) and *Once Upon a Moon* (1949); a ballet, *The Enchanted Garden* (1950); for orch.; *The Midnight Court* (1959); *Short Symphony* (1961); *5 Mantras* (1963); Piano Concerto (1954); Wind Quintet (1957); *Rodomontade* for 5 woodwind instruments (1964); String Quartet (1963); *Voyelles* for soprano, flute, percussion, and string orchestra, to the text of Arthur Rimbaud (1966); Harp Concerto (London, Oct. 1, 1975); film music.

Vidal, Louis-Antoine, French writer on music; b. Rouen, July 10, 1820; d. Paris, Jan. 7, 1891. He studied cello with Franchomme; made a speciality of string-instrument research; publ. a valuable survey, *Les Instruments à archet, les faiseurs, les joueurs d'instruments, leur histoire sur le continent européen, suivie d'un catalogue général de la musique de chambre* (3 vols.; Paris, 1876–78; with 120 illustrative plates); sections of this work were publ. separately as *Les Vieilles Corporations de Paris* (1878) and *La Lutherie et les luthiers* (1889).

Vidal, Paul, noted French composer and pegagogue; b. Toulouse, June 16, 1863; d. Paris, April 9, 1931. He studied at the Paris Cons. and in 1883 won the Prix de Rome with his cantata *Le Gladiateur*; in 1889 he joined the staff of the Paris Opéra as choral director; later became conductor there (until 1906). He taught elementary courses at the Paris Cons. from 1894 until 1910, when he was appointed prof. of composition.
WORKS: ballet, *La Maladetta* (Paris Opéra, Feb. 24, 1893); opera, *Guernica* (Opéra-Comique, June 7, 1895); a mystery play, *Noël, ou Le Mystère de la Nativité* (Galerie Vivienne, Paris, Nov. 25, 1890); operetta, *Éros* (Bouffes-Parisiens, April 22, 1892); several instructive manuals, much used in France: *Manuel pratique d'harmonie; Notes et observations sur la compositions et exécution;* compiled *52 Leçons d'harmonie de Luigi Cherubini* (3 vols.); *Solfège* (2 vols., Paris, 1922).

Vidu, Ion, Rumanian composer; b. Minerau (Banat), Dec. 14, 1863; d. Lugoj (Banat), Feb. 7, 1931. He studied in Jassy; became choral conductor in Lugoj. He wrote a great number of choruses in a distinct native style, but harmonized his melodies according to German models; many of his arrangements have become repertory pieces in Rumania.

Vieira, Ernesto, Portuguese music historian; b. Lisbon, May 24, 1848; d. there, April 26, 1915. His main achievement was the publication of the *Diccionario biografico de musicos protuguezes* (Lisbon, 1900), which supplemented the earlier dictionary by Vasconcellos (1870).

Vierdanck, Johann, German organist and composer; b. 1605; d. c.1646. He was a chorister in Dresden, where he was a pupil of Schütz; was sent to Vienna in 1628 for further study; was church organist at the Marienkirche, Stralsund (1641–56). He publ. *Ballette und Corrente* for violin with continuo (1637; 1641); spiritual "concertos" for 2–9 voices; of these, several were brought out in modern eds. by Hans Engel (Kassel, 1932 and 1934) and Hans Erdmann (Kassel, 1950).

Vierling, Georg, German organist and composer; b. Frankenthal, Bavaria, Sept. 5, 1820; d. Wiesbaden, May 1, 1901. He was a pupil of his father, the organist **Jacob Vierling** (1796–1867); then studied composition with A. B. Marx in Berlin. He occupied various posts as organist and choral conductor in the German provinces; settled in Berlin, where he founded and conducted the Bach-Verein. A catalogue of his works was issued in 1897; they include the secular cantatas *Der Raub der Sabinerinne, Alarichs Tod,* and *Constantin;* the choral works (with orch.) *Hero und Leander* and *Zur Weinlese;* a symph.; several overtures (*Maria Stuart, Die Hexe, Im Frühling,* etc.); *Capriccio* for piano and orch.; *Phantasiestück* for cello and piano; 2 string quartets; a piano trio; a number of piano pieces (*Valse-Caprice,* 2 Impromptus, etc.); songs.

Vierling, Johann Gottfried, German organist and composer; b. Metzels, near Meiningen, Jan. 25, 1750; d. Schmalkalden, Nov. 22, 1813. His teachers were C. P. E. Bach in Hamburg and Kirnberger in Berlin, from whom he acquired contrapuntal skill in composition in the Baroque style. He publ. several collections or organ pieces; a piano quartet; 2 piano trios; 8 piano sonatas; brought out the theoretical manuals, *Versuch einer Anleitung zum Präludieren* (1794) and *Allgemein fasslicher Unterricht im Generalbass* (1805).
BIBLIOGRAPHY: K. Paulke, "J. G. Vierling," *Archiv für Musikwissenschaft* (1922).

Vierne, Louis, blind French organist and composer; b. Poitiers, Oct. 8, 1870; d. Paris, June 2, 1937. He was a pupil of César Franck and Widor at the Paris Cons., winning 1st prize for organ playing; in 1892 he became Widor's assistant at St. Sulpice, and in 1900 was appointed organist at Notre Dame, holding this position until his death (he died suddenly while playing the organ at a service there). From 1912 he taught organ at the Schola Cantorum; gave many concerts in Europe; in 1927 played in the U.S. His organ works include 5 "symphonies" and many smaller pieces. Among his pupils were Nadia Boulanger, Marcel Dupré, and Joseph Bonnet.

BIBLIOGRAPHY: *In Memoriam Louis Vierne* (Paris, 1939); B. Gavoty, *Louis Vierne, la vie et l'œuvre* (Paris, 1943).

Vieru, Anatol, outstanding Rumanian composer; b. Iasi (Jassy), June 8, 1926. He studied harmony with Paul Constantinescu, orchestration with Theodore Rogalski, and conducting with Constantin Silvestri at the Bucharest Cons.; in 1951 went to Russia, where he studied composition at the Moscow Cons. with Khachaturian (1951–54). In 1954 he was appointed to the faculty of the Bucharest Cons. From his earliest years he began to compose in a relatively advanced idiom, without losing contact with the characteristic melorhythmic patterns of Rumanian folksongs. Interesting in this respect is his oratorio *Miorița* (1957; Bucharest, Feb. 27, 1958), after a Rumanian folk tale, in which he applies serial procedures to folklore materials. His Concerto for cello and orch. (1962; Geneva, March 27, 1963), written in an original manner combining neo-Baroque and Impressionistic traits, brought him international acclaim when it received first prize in a 1962 Geneva competition. Other works: *Cantata anilor-lumină* (*Cantata of Luminous Years*; Bucharest, June 18, 1960); *Suite in the Old Style* for string orch. (1946); *Symphonic Dances* for orch. (1952); 2 concertos for orch.: No. 1 (1954) and No. 2 (1958; transcription of his string quartet No. 1); Flute Concerto (1958); *Chamber Symphony* for 15 instruments and mezzo-soprano (1962); *Jocuri* (*Games*) for piano and orch. (1963); Violin Concerto (1964); *Odă Tăcerii* (*Ode to Silence*), a symphony (1966–67); *Muzeu muzical* (*Museum Music*) for 12 string instruments and (electronic) harpsichord (1968); *Clepsidra* (*Water Clock*) *I* for orch. and trumpet obbligato (1968–69); *Clepsidra II* for chorus, orch., panpipes and cimbalom (1971); *Birth of a Language* for piano 4-hands (1973; the pianists also have speaking parts); Symph. No. 2 (1973; West Berlin, March 21, 1974); *2 Pieces* for trumpet and piano (1953); 2 string quartets (1955, 1956); Clarinet Quintet (1957); *Muzica pentru Bacovia si Labis* for various combinations of tenor, mezzo-soprano, clarinet, violin, flute, and piano (1959–63; consists of the separate works: *Lupta cu inerția, Nocturne și Rezonanțe Bacovia,* and *Destinderi*); *Sita lui Eratostene* (*Crible*) for violin, viola, clarinet, cello, and piano (1968); Solo Cello Sonata (1963); *Trepte ale tăcerii* (*Steps of Silence*) for string quartet and 6 percussion instruments (1966; Library of Congress, Washington, Jan. 12, 1968; as a ballet, N.Y., Nov. 13, 1968); *Din lumea copiilor,* 20 miniatures for piano (1958); *Nautilos,* piece for piano and tape (1968); *Steinland* for organ and tape (1973); *Scène nocturne,* suite of 7 pieces, after 8 Garcia Lorca poems, for double chorus a cappella (1964); other choral music; songs; film music; an electronic piece, *Pays de Pierre* (1972).

Vietinghoff-Scheel, Boris, Baron, Russian composer; b. in Latvia, 1829; d. St. Petersburg, Sept. 25, 1901. He was a student of Henselt and Dargomyzhsky in St. Petersburg. Three of his operas were produced in St.

Petersburg: *Mazeppa* (May 17, 1859), *Tamara* (May 2 1886), and *Don Juan de Tenorio* (Nov. 2, 1888); 2 other operas, *Mary Stuart* and *Heliodora,* were not produced. He also wrote a *Fantastic Overture* (1859; Liszt commented with interest on the use of the whole-tone scale in the finale; see *Letters of Franz Liszt,* London, 1894; vol. 1). Vietinghoff published a book of memoirs, *World Celebrities* (St. Petersburg, 1899).

Vieuille, Felix, French bass; b. Saugeon, Oct. 15, 1872; d. there, Feb. 28, 1953. He was a member of the Opéra-Comique from 1898; created the role of Arkel at the première of Debussy's *Pelléas et Mélisande* (1902).

Vieuxtemps, Henri, celebrated Belgian violinist and composer; b. Verviers, Feb. 17, 1820; d. Mustapha, Algiers, June 6, 1881. His first teacher was his father, a piano tuner, who soon turned him over to Lecloux, with whom he made a concert tour at the age of 8. He then continued his studies with Bériot in Brussels (1829–30); took harmony lessons from Sechter in Vienna (1833) and Reicha in Paris (1835). In 1834 he visited London, where he appeared with the Philharmonic (June 2, 1834). In 1837 he revisited Vienna; in 1838–39 gave concerts in Russia. During his constant travels, he composed violin concertos and other violin works which became part of the standard repertory, and which he performed in Europe to the greatest acclaim. He made his first American tour in 1844–45. In 1846 he was engaged as prof. at the St. Petersburg Cons., and remained in Russia for 5 seasons; his influence on Russian concert life and violin composition was considerable. In 1853 he recommended his concert tours in Europe; paid 2 more visits to America, in 1857 (with Thalberg) and in 1870 (with Christine Nilsson). He was prof. of violin playing at the Brussels Cons. (1871–73); a stroke of paralysis, affecting his left side, forced him to end all concert activities, but he continued to teach privately. He went to Algiers for rest, and died there; one of his most prominent pupils, Jenö Hubay, was with him at his death. In 1844, Vieuxtemps married the pianist **Josephine Eder** (b. Vienna, Dec. 15, 1815; d. Celle-St. Cloud, June 29, 1868). With Bériot, Vieuxtemps stood at the head of the modern French school of violin playing; contemporary accounts speak of the extraordinary precision of his technique and of his perfect ability to sustain a flowing melody; the expression "le roi de violon" was often applied to him in the press. Besides his 7 violin concertos (the last one being posthumous), he wrote for violin and orch.: *Fantaisie-Caprice; Souvenirs de Russie; Fantasia appassionata; Ballade et polonaise;* and *Old England,* a caprice on English airs of the 16th and 17th centuries. For violin and piano he composed *Hommage à Paganini; Grosse Fantasie über slavische Volksmelodien; Andante und Rondo; Suite* in B minor; *Marche funèbre; Danse Négro-Créole* (1844); etc.; numerous brilliant transcriptions of operatic airs.

BIBLIOGRAPHY: L. Escudier, *Mes Souvenirs: Les Virtuoses* (Paris, 1868); M. Kufferath, *Henri Vieuxtemps* (Brussels, 1882); J. T. Radoux, *Vieuxtemps, sa vie, ses œuvres* (Liège, 1891); P. Bergmans, *Henri Vieuxtemps* (Turnhout, 1920).

Viganò, Salvatore, Italian composer and choreographer; b. Naples, March 25, 1769; d. Milan, Aug. 10, 1821. He was the son and pupil of a dancer; studied music with **Luigi Boccherini,** who was his uncle; began his career as dancer at Rome in 1786 and also produced there an opera buffa, *La Vedova scoperta;* then went to Madrid, where he married the celebrated ballerina María Medina; in 1790 returned to Italy; in 1793 was at Vienna; then made a tour of the principal European cities. He is remembered chiefly because Beethoven wrote the music for Viganò's "heroic ballet" *Die Geschöpfe des Prometheus* (Vienna, March 28, 1801), in which Viganò danced the leading male role.

BIBLIOGRAPHY: C. Ritorni, *Commentarii della vita e delle opere coreodrammatiche di Salvatore Viganò* (Milan, 1838); H. Prunières, "Salvatore Viganò," *Revue Musicale* (1921); Thayer's *Life of Beethoven.*

Vila, Pedro Alberto, Spanish composer; b. 1517; d. Barcelona, Nov. 16, 1582. He was organist and canon of the Cathedral at Barcelona; was one of the few Spanish composers who cultivated the madrigal; publ. *Odarum quas vulgo Madrigales appellamus* (Barcelona, 1561) with texts in Spanish, Catalan, Italian, and French; some of his organ works are found in the tablature book of Venegas de Henestrosa. His nephew **Luis Ferrán Vila** succeeded him as organist at the Barcelona Cathedral.

BIBLIOGRAPHY: F. Pedrell, *Catàlech de la Biblioteca Musical de la Diputació de Barcelona* (1908–09); S. Kastner, *Contribución al estudio de la música española y portuguesa* (Lisbon, 1941).

Vilback, Renaud de, French organist and composer; b. Montpellier, June 3, 1829; d. Paris, March 19, 1884. He studied piano, organ, and composition at the Paris Cons. under Lemoine and Halévy, winning the Grand Prix de Rome at the age of 15. In 1856, became organist at St.-Eugène, Paris. He wrote 2 operas, *Au clair de lune* (1857) and *Almanzor* (1858); publ. a method for piano (*3 Morceaux de salon, Les Amazones,* etc.) and transcriptions from operas.

Vilboa (Villebois), Konstantin, Russian composer of French origin; b. St. Petersburg, May 29, 1817; d. Warsaw, July 16, 1882. He studied in a military school, and was sent by the government to collect folksongs in the country; also directed various choirs in military establishments. In 1876 he went to Warsaw as a functionary in the ministry of war, and remained there until his death. His opera *Natasha, or the Volga Brigands* was produced in Moscow on Nov. 12, 1861, and in St. Petersburg in 1863. Two other operas, *Taras Bulba* (after Gogol) and *Tziganka (The Gypsy),* remain unperformed.

Vilhar, Franz, Croatian composer; b. Senožeče, Jan. 5, 1852; d. Zagreb, March 4, 1928. He studied music with Skuherský in Prague; after serving as organist in various churches, he settled in Zagreb, in 1891, as choirmaster at St. Mark's. He composed a Croatian opera, *Smiljana* (Zagreb, Jan. 31, 1897), *Croatian Dances,* for orch., and a number of choruses that were popular for a time.

Villa, Ricardo, Spanish composer and conductor; b. Madrid, Oct. 23, 1873; d. there, April 10, 1935. He studied at the Cons. of Madrid, and conducted the municipal band there, which he organized in 1909; wrote the operas *El Cristo de la Vega* and *Raimundo Lulio;* and a number of pieces for band in the Spanish vein: *La Visión de Fray Martín, Impresiones sinfónicas, Cantos regionales asturianos; Rapsodía asturiana,* for violin and orch. (played by Sarasate); *Fantasía española* for piano and orch.; also light music.

Villalba Muñoz, Padre Luis, Spanish musiciologist and composer; b. Valladolid, Sept. 22, 1873; d, Madrid, Jan. 9, 1921. He entered the Augustinian Order at the age of 14; was chorusmaster at the monastery of the Escorial (1898–1917); also taught history and other subjects; later lived in Madrid; edited the review *La Ciudad de Dios,* to which he contributed valuable essays on Spanish music; also edited the *Biblioteca Sacro-Musical.* He publ. the valuable *Antología de organistas clásicos españoles,* 10 *Canciones españolas de los siglos XV y XVI;* wrote monographs on Pedrell, Granados, and Usandizaga, and *Ultimos músicos españoles del siglo XIX* (Madrid, 1914); composed organ works; sacred choruses; chamber music.

Villa-Lobos, Heitor, remarkable Brazilian composer of great originality and unique ability to recreate native melodic and rhythmic elements in large instrumental and choral forms; b. Rio de Janeiro, March 5, 1887; d, there, Nov. 17, 1959. He studied music with his father, a writer and amateur cello player; after his father's death in 1899, Villa-Lobos earned a living by playing the cello in cafés and restaurants. In 1905 he traveled to the northern states of Brazil in order to collect authentic folk songs. In 1907 he entered the National Institute of Music in Rio de Janeiro where he studied with Frederico Nascimento, Angelo França, and Francisco Braga. In 1912 he undertook an expedition into the interior of Brazil where he gathered a rich collection of Indian songs. On Nov. 13, 1915, he presented in Rio de Janeiro a concert of his compositions, creating a sensation by the exuberance of his music and the radical character of his technical idiom. He met the pianist Artur Rubinstein, who became his ardent admirer; for him Villa-Lobos composed a transcendentally difficult *Rudepoema.* In 1923 Villa-Lobos went to Paris on a Brazilian government grant; upon return to Brazil in 1930, he was appointed director of music education in Rio de Janeiro. He introduced bold innovations into the national program of music education, with an emphasis on the cultural resources of Brazil; compiled a *Guia pratico,* containing choral arrangements of folksongs of Brazil and other nations; organized the "orpheonic concentrations" of school children, whom he trained to sing according to his own chironomic method of solfeggio. In 1944 he made his first tour of the U.S., and conducted his works in Los Angeles, Boston, and New York. In 1945 he established in Rio de Janeiro the Brazilian Academy of Music; in 1947 he made his second visit to the U.S.; in 1949 he was in Europe, but retained his permanent home in Rio de Janeiro. Villa-Lobos was one of the most original composers of the 20th century. He lacked formal academic training, but far from hampering development, this deficiency liberated him from pedantic restrictions so that he evolved an idiosyncratic technique of composition, curiously eclectic, but all the better suited to his musical esthetics. An ardent Brazilian nationalist, he resolved from his earliest attempts in composition to use authentic Brazilian song materials as the source of his inspiration; yet he avoided using actual quotations from popular songs; rather he wrote melodies which are authentic in their melodic and rhythmic contents. In his desire to relate Brazilian folk resources to universal values, he wrote a series of extraordinary works, *Bachianas Brasileiras,* in which Brazilian melorhythms are treated in Bachian counterpoint. He also composed a number of works under the generic title *Chôros,* a popular Brazilian dance form, marked by incisive rhythm and a ballad-like melody. An experimenter by nature, Villa-Lobos devised a graphic method of composition, using geometrical contours of drawings and photographs as outlines for the melody; in this manner he wrote *The New York Skyline,* using a photograph for guidance. Villa-Lobos wrote operas, ballets, symphonies, chamber music, choruses, piano pieces, songs; the total number of his compositions is in excess of 2,000.

WORKS: OPERAS: *Izaht* (1914; revised, 1932; 1st performance, in concert form, Rio de Janeiro, April 6, 1940), *Magdalena,* light opera (Los Angeles, July 26, 1948); *Yerma,* after Federico García Lorca (1955; produced posthumously, in Spanish, at Santa Fe, Aug. 12, 1971).

BALLETS: *Uirapurú* (Buenos Aires, May 25, 1935); *Dança da terra* (Rio de Janeiro, Sept. 7, 1943).

FOR ORCH.: 12 symphonies: No. 1, *Imprevisto* (Rio de Janeiro, Aug. 30, 1920), No. 2, *Ascenção* (1917), No. 3, *Guerra* (Rio de Janeiro, July 30, 1919), No. 4, *Vitória* (1920), No. 5, *Paz* (1921), No. 6, *Montanhas do Brasil* (1944), No. 7, *America* (1945), No. 8 (1950; Philadelphia, Jan.14, 1955), No. 9 (1952), No. 10, with chorus (1954), No. 11 (Boston, March 2, 1956, composer conducting), No. 12 (Inter-American Music Festival, Washington, D.C., April 20, 1958). CHOROS: No. 1, for guitar (1920), No. 2, for flute and clarinet (1921), No. 3, for male chorus and 7 wind instruments (1925), No. 4, for 3 horns and trombone (1926), No. 5, *Alma Brasileira,* for piano solo (1926), No. 6, for orch. (1926; Rio de Janeiro, July 15, 1942), No. 7, for flute, oboe, clarinet, saxophone, bassoon, violin, and cello (1924), No. 8, for large orch., and 2 pianos (Paris, Oct. 24, 1927), No. 9, for orch. (1929; Rio de Janeiro, July 15, 1942, composer conducting), No. 10, *Rasga o Coração,* for chorus and orch. (Rio de Janeiro, Dec. 15, 1926), No. 11, for piano and orch. (Rio de Janeiro, July 15, 1942), No. 12 for orch. (Cambridge, Mass., Feb. 21, 1945, Villa-Lobos conducting the Boston Symph. Orch.), No. 13, for 2 orchestras and band (1929), No. 14, for orch., band, and chorus (1928); also a supernumerary *Chôros bis* for violin and cello (1928). BACHIANAS BRASILEIRAS: No.1, for 8 cellos (Rio de Janeiro, Sept. 12, 1932); No. 2 for chamber orch. (1933), No. 3, for piano and orch. (1934), No. 4, for orch. (N.Y., June 6, 1942), No. 5, for voice and 8 cellos (Rio de Janeiro, March 25, 1939), No. 6, for flute and bassoon (1938), No. 7, for orch. (Rio de Janeiro, March 13, 1944), No. 8, for orch. (Rome, Aug. 6, 1947). OTHER ORCHESTRAL

WORKS: *Dansas Africanas* (1914; Paris, April 5, 1928), *Amazona* (1917; Paris, May 30, 1929), *Fantasy of Mixed Movements,* for violin and orch. (Rio de Janeiro, Dec. 15, 1922), *Suite Suggestiva* for orch. and voice (1929), *Momo Precoce* (Paris, Feb. 23, 1930), *Caixinha de Boãs Festas* (Rio de Janeiro, Dec. 8, 1932), *Descobrimento do Brasil* (4 suites; 1937), *The New York Skyline* (1940), *Rudepoema* (orchestral version of the piano work of that name; Rio de Janeiro, July 15, 1942, composer conducting), *Madonna,* tone poem (Rio de Janeiro, Oct. 8, 1946, composer conducting), Piano Concerto (Rio de Janeiro, Oct. 11, 1946), *Mandú-Carará,* symph. poem with chorus (N.Y., Jan. 23, 1948), Guitar Concerto (1952), *Odyssey of a Race,* symph. poem written for Israel (Mount Carmel Festival of the International Society for Contemporary Music, Haifa, May 30, 1954), Harmonica Concerto (1955), *Erosion, or The Origin of the Amazon River* (Louisville, Nov. 7, 1951), *Dawn in a Tropical Forest* (Louisville, Jan. 23, 1954), Harp Concerto (Philadelphia, Jan. 14, 1955), *Grand Concerto,* for cello and orch. (1915), Cello Concerto No. 2 (N.Y., Feb. 5, 1955).

CHAMBER MUSIC: 17 string quartets (1915, 1915, 1916, 1917, 1931, 1938, 1942, 1944, 1945, 1946, 1948, 1950, 1952, 1953, 1954, 1955, 1958), Quartet for harp, celesta, flute, and saxophone, with female voices (1921), Piano Quartet (1912), Piano Quintet (1916), Woodwind Quintet (1928), *Mystic Sextet,* for flute, clarinet, saxophone, celesta, harp, and guitar (1917), Nonet (1923), 3 piano trios (1911, 1916, 1918), Trio for oboe, clarinet, and bassoon (1921), Trio for violin, viola, and cello (1945), 4 Sonatas-Fantasia for violin and piano (1912, 1914, 1915, 1918), 2 cello sonatas (1915, 1916).

VOCAL MUSIC: For chorus: *Crianças* (1908), *Na Bah a tem* (1925), *Canção da Terra* (1925), *As Costureiras* (1932), oratorio, *Vidapura* (Rio de Janeiro, Nov. 28, 1934), etc. Songs: *Confidencia* (1908), *Noite de Luar* (1912), *Mal Secreto* (1913), *Fleur fanée* (1913), *Il Nome di Maria* (1915), *Sertão no Estio* (1919), *Canções tipicas brasileiras* (10 numbers; 1919), *Historiettes* (6 numbers; 1920), *Epigrammes ironiques et sentimentales* (8 numbers; 1921), *Suite* for voice and violin (1923), *Poème de l'Enfant et de sa Mère,* for voice, flute, clarinet, and cello (1923), *Serestas* (suite of 14 numbers; one of his best song cycles; 1925), *3 Poemas indigenas* (1926), *Modinhas e Canções* (2 albums, 1933, 1943).

FOR PIANO: *Valsa Romantica* (1908), *Brinquedo de Roda* (6 pieces; 1912), *Primeira Suite Infantil* (1912), *Segunda Suite Infatil* (1913), *Danças Africanas* (1915), *Prole do Bebé,* suite No. 1 (8 pieces, including the popular *Polichinello;* 1918), *Fábulas Características* (3 pieces; 1914–18), *Historia da Carochinha* (4 pieces; 1919), *Carnaval das Crianças Brasileiras* (8 pieces; 1919), *Lenda do Caboclo* (1920), *Dança Infernal* (1920), *Prole do Bebê,* Suite No. 2 (9 pieces; 1921), *Sul América* (1925), *Cirandinhas* (12 pieces; 1925), *Rudepoema* (1921–26), *Cirandas* (16 pieces; 1926), *Alma Brasileira* (*Chôros No. 5;* 1926), *Prole do Bebé,* Suite No. 3 (9 pieces; 1929), *Lembrança do Sertão* (1930), *Caixinha de Música Quebrada* (1931), *Ciclo Brasileiro* (4 pieces; 1936), *As Três Marias* (1939; very popular), *Poema Singelo* (1942).

BIBLIOGRAPHY: F. C. Lange, "Villa-Lobos, Pedagogo Criador," *Boletín Latino-Americano de Música* (Montevideo, 1935; p. 189ff.); Burle Marx, "Brazilian Portrait," *Modern Music* (Oct.-Nov. 1939); special issue of *Musica Viva* (Rio de Janeiro, 1941); N. Slonimsky, *Music of Latin America* (N.Y., 1945; pp. 142-50); O. L. Fernandez, "A Contribuição Harmonica de Villa-Lobos para a Música Brasileira," *Boletín Latino-Americano de Música* (Rio de Janeiro, 1946, pp. 183-300); O. Meyer-Serra, *Música y Músicos de Latino-América* (Mexico, 1947; vol. 2, pp. 1059-85); L. M. Peppercorn, "The History of Villa-Lobos' Birth-Date," *Monthly Musical Record* (July-Aug. 1948); Vasco Mariz, *Heitor Villa-Lobos, Compositor brasileiro* (Rio de Janeiro, 1948; 5th edition, revised and augmented, 1977); C. M. de Paula Barros, *O Romance de Villa-Lobos* (Rio de Janeiro, 1951); C. Maul, *A gloria escandaloso de Heiter Villa-Lobos,* (Rio de Janeiro, 1960; a scurrilous "exposé," unconvincingly accusing Villa-Lobos of plagiarism); M. Beaufils, *Villa-Lobos, Musicien et poète du Brésil* (Rio de Janeiro, 1967); L. Guimares, *Villa-Lobos* (Rio de Janeiro, 1972); F. Pereira da Silva, *Villa-Lobos* (Rio de Janeiro, 1974).

Villanis, Luigi Alberto, Italian writer on music; b. San Mauro, near Turin, June 20, 1863; d. Pesaro, Sept. 27, 1906. He studied law; later devoted himself to musical journalism; published numerous pamphlets dealing with musical esthetics. He published *Il Leitmotiv nella musica moderna* (1891); *Estetica del libretto nella musica* (1892); *Lo Spirito moderno nella musica* (1902); *Saggio di psicologia musicale* (1904); *Piccola guida alla bibliografia musicale* (1906); *L'Arte del pianoforte in Italia* (1907).

Villar, Rogelio, Spanish composer and music critic; b. León, Nov. 13, 1875; d. Madrid, Nov. 4, 1937. He studied at the Madrid Cons., and later taught ensemble there; was editor of the *Revista Musical Hispano-Americana* (ceased publ. in 1917). He composed some symph. pieces, 2 string quartets, violin sonatas, piano published works; *Músicos españoles,* 2 series (biographical sketches of contemporary Spanish musicians); *La Armonía en la música contemporánea* (Madrid, 1927); *Soliloquios de un músico español* (Madrid, 1928), etc.

Villoing, Alexander, notable Russian pianist; b. Moscow, March 12, 1804; d. there, Sept. 2, 1878. He was born of a French émigré family; studied piano with the famous Irish pianist and composer John Field, who was then resident in Moscow. Villoing established himself in Moscow as a piano teacher (1830-62); enjoyed the reputation as one of the best pedagogues in Russia. Anton and Nicholas Rubinstein were among his pupils; he traveled with them in Europe. His *École pratique du piano* (St. Petersburg, 1863) was accepted by the St. Petersburg Cons. as a teaching guide. He published a book of piano exercises which he called *Exercises for the Rubinstein Brothers.*

Villoing, Vassily, Russian violinst, pianist, composer, conductor and music teacher; b. Moscow, Oct. 28, 1850; d. Nizhny-Novgorod, Sept. 15, 1922. He studied piano with his uncle, the Russian pianist **Alexander Villoing,** and violin with Ferdinand Laub at the Moscow Cons. He then moved to the city of Nizhny-Novgorod where he organized a music school and conducted a local orch. founded by him. Among his piano students were Dobrowen and Liapunov. He composed 3 operas, 4 string quartets and a number of piano pieces and songs.

Villoteau, Guillaume-André, French music scholar; b. Bellême, Orne, Sept. 19, 1759; d. Tours, April 27, 1839. He was a chorister at the Cathedral of Le Mans, and later at Notre-Dame in Paris. Having studied philosophy at the Sorbonne, he was qualified for election as a member of the scientific commission that accompanied Napoleon to Egypt, and made a special study of Oriental music. He contributed 4 essays to the 20-vol. edition, *La Description de l'Égypte* (Paris, 1809-26), entitled "Mémoire sur la musique de l'antique Égypte"; "Dissertation sur les diverses espèces d'instruments de musique que l'on remarque parmi les sculptures qui décorent les antiques monuments de l'Égypte"; "De l'état actuel de l'art musical en Égypte"; and "Description historique, technique et littéraire des instruments de musique des Orientaux"; also publ. *Mémoire sur la possibilité et l'utilité d'une théorie exacte des principes naturels de la musique* (1807), being an introduction to his *Recherches sur l'analogie de la musique avec les arts qui ont pour object l'imitation du langage* (1807; 2 vols.).

Viña (Manteola), Facundo de la, Spanish composer; b. Gijon, Feb. 21, 1876; d. Madrid, Nov. 19, 1952. He studied at the Madrid Cons. and later in Paris; his music reflects the character of Asturian regional folklore. He composed the operas *Almas muertas, La Princesa flor de roble, La Espigadora* (Barcelona, 1927); symph. poems: *Canto de trilla, Sierra de Gredos, Covadonga, Por tierras de Castilla.*

Vincent, Alexandre-Joseph Hydulphe, French music theorist; b. Hesdin, Pas-de-Calais, Nov. 20, 1797; d. Paris, Nov. 26, 1868. An investigator of ancient Greek and Latin music, he advanced the idea that the Greeks used chorus (harmony); he likewise sought to revive the employment of the intervals smaller than a halftone that were described in Greek theory. On these subjects he published a great number of essays, some of which were reprinted in pamphlet form. Especially important is his *Notice sur divers manuscrits grecs relatifs à la musique* (1847).

Vincent, Charles John, English organist; b. Houghton-le-Spring, Durham, Sept. 19, 1852; d. Monte Carlo, Feb. 28, 1934. He was a chorister at the Cathedral of Durham; studied at the Leipzig Cons. (1876-78); then was church organist in England; Mus. Bac., Oxford, 1878; Mus. Doc., 1885. He published a number of useful textbooks: *A Year's Study at the Piano, First Principles of Music, Choral Instructor for Treble Voices,* etc.; composed an oratorio, *Ruth;* several church cantatas; operettas; vocal duets; more than 100 songs.

Vincent, Heinrich Joseph (real name **Winzenhörlein**), German singer, composer, and theorist; b. Teilheim, near Würzburg, Feb. 23, 1819; d. Vienna, May 19,

1901. He studied law, and also sang tenor parts in theaters in Vienna (1847), Halle, and Würzburg; eventually settled in Vienna as a singing teacher. He composed 2 operas, *Die Bettlerin* (Halle, 1864) and *König Murat* (Würzburg, 1870); also operettas and popular songs. He followed the tenets of the Chroma Society in championing the harmonic system based on the functional equality of the 12 notes of the chromatic scale; published the studies *Kein Generalbass mehr* (1860), *Die Einheit in der Tonwelt* (1862), *Die Neuklaviatur* (1874), *Die Zwölfzahl in der Tonwelt* (1885), *Eine neue Tonschrift* (1900), and articles on the chromatic keyboard and notation.

Vincent, Henry Bethuel, American organist and composer; b. Denver, Dec. 28, 1872; d. Erie, Penn., Jan. 7, 1941. He studied organ with W. H. Sherwood in Oberlin and Widor in Paris; settled in Erie as organist and choirmaster. He wrote an oratorio, *The Prodigal Son* (Erie, 1901), an opera, *Esperanza* (Washington, 1906), an operetta, *Indian Days;* anthems; organ pieces; songs including a cycle, *The Garden of Kama.*

Vincent, John, American composer and teacher; b. Birmingham, Alabama, May 17, 1902; d. Santa Monica, California, Jan. 21, 1977. He studied flute with Georges Laurent at the New England Cons., Boston (1922–26), and composition there with Converse and Chadwick (1926–27); then took courses at the George Peabody College in Nashville (M.A. 1933) and at Harvard Univ., where his principal teacher was Walter Piston (1933–35); went to Paris, where he studied at the École Normale de Musique (1935–37) and took private lessons with Nadia Boulanger. He received his Ph.D. from Cornell Univ. in 1942. He subsequently occupied various teaching positions: was in charge of El Paso, Texas, public schools (1927–30); then taught at George Peabody College in Nashville (1930–33), at Western Kentucky Teachers College (1937–46), and at the Univ. of California, Los Angeles (1946–69). In his music he evolved a tonal idiom which he termed "paratonality"; fugal elements are particularly strong in his instrumental compositions.
WORKS: opera, *Primeval Void,* to his own libretto (1969); ballet: *Three Jacks* (1942); for orch.: Symph. in D (Louisville, Feb. 5, 1952; revised version, Philadelphia, April 12, 1957); *Consort,* for piano and strings (Seattle, April 9, 1962; later amplified for full string orch., and renamed Symph. No. 2); *Symphonic Poem after Descartes* (Philadelphia, March 20, 1959; his most significant work, with the motto of Descartes, "Cogito ergo sum," suggested by the thematic rhythm on the kettledrums); *La Jolla Concerto* for chamber orch. (La Jolla, Calif., July 19, 1959); *Benjamin Franklin Suite* for orch. and glass harmonica (based on the string quartet attributed to Benjamin Franklin; Philadelphia, March 24, 1963); *Rondo-Rhapsody* (Washington, May 9, 1965); *The Phoenix, Fabulous Bird,* symph. poem (Phoenix, Arizona, Feb. 21, 1966); 2 string quartets (1936; 1967); *Nude Descending the Staircase,* for string orch., after Marcel Duchamp's painting (1948); *Stabat Mater,* for male chorus and soprano solo (1969); *Mary at Calvary,* for chorus and organ (1972); *Percussion Suite* (1973); *Nacre,* a tone poem for band (1973); choruses (*O God, Our Help in*

Ages Past; Cindy Gal; Glory to God; Behold the Star; etc.); *Baroque Album,* 16 Baroque works transcribed for string orch. with piano (1972). He published the books *Music for Sight Reading,* (N.Y., 1940); *More Music for Sight Reading* (N.Y., 1941); *The Diatonic Modes in Modern Music* (N.Y., 1951; completely revised, Hollywood, 1974).

Vinci, Leonardo, Italian composer; b. Strongoli, 1690; d. Naples, May 27, 1730. He studied at the Cons. dei Poveri de Gesù Cristo in Naples, where he was a pupil of Gaetano Greco. In 1725 he received the post of vice-maestro at the Royal Chapel in Naples, and remained there until his death 5 years later. He produced about 40 operas for various Italian cities (25 for Naples, 11 for Rome), of which the most important are: *Silla Dittatore* (Naples, Oct. 1, 1723); *Astianatte* (Naples, Dec. 2, 1725); *La Caduta dei Decemviri* (Naples, Oct. 1, 1727); *Artaserse* (libretto by Metastasio; Rome, Feb. 4, 1730).
BIBLIOGRAPHY: E. J. Dent, "Notes on Leonardo Vinci," *Musical Antiquary* (July 1913); A. Della Corte, *L'Opera comica italiana nel 1700,* vol. I (Bari, 1923); A. Cametti, "Leonardo Vinci e i suoi drammi in musica al Teatro delle Dame," *Musica d'Oggi* (Oct. 1924); U. Prota-Giurleo, *Nicola Logroscino* (Naples, 1927; appendix, "La Morte di Vinci," pp. 61–63); K. Geiringer, "Ein Geburtstagkantate von P. Metastasio und L. Vinci," *Archiv für Musikwissenschaft* 9 (1926); G. Silvestri Silva, *Illustri musici calabresi: Leonardo Vinci* (Genoa, 1935).

Vinci, Pietro, Italian composer; b. Nicosia, Sicily, 1540; d. there, 1584. He was maestro di cappella at Santa Maria Maggiore, Bergamo (1568–80); returned to Nicosia in 1580. He publ. 10 books of madrigals, motets, *Sonetti spirituali,* etc.
BIBLIOGRAPHY: F. Mompellio, *Pietro Vinci, madrigalista siciliano* (Milan, 1937).

Vincze, Imre, Hungarian composer; b. Kocs, Sept. 26, 1926; d. Budapest, May 3, 1969. He studied with Szabó at the Budapest Academy of Music; later taught there; won the Erkel Prize in 1952 and 1956. He wrote 3 symphonies (1951, 1953, 1963); *Felicitation,* overture (1954); *Movimento Sinfonico* (1957); *Aforismo* for orch. (1959); Concertino for orch. (1961); *Rapsodia concertante* for piano and orch. (1966); 4 string quartets (1954, 1958, 1961, 1965); Violin Sonata (1956); *Divertimento* for wind quintet (1962); Bassoon Sonata (1964); *Fantasy and Fugue* for organ (1960); choral works; film music.

Viñes, Ricardo, Spanish pianist; b. Lérida, Feb. 5, 1875; d. Barcelona, April 29, 1943. He studied in Barcelona with Juan Pujol, and with Godard at the Paris Cons., winning the 1st prize for piano in 1894. In 1895 he gave his first concert in Paris, and established himself in later years as an ardent propagandist of new French and Spanish music; he possessed particular affinity with the composers of the modern French School and performed their works in a colorful and imaginative manner. He gave concerts in London, Berlin, and other musical centers, but lived most of his life in Paris; contributed articles on Spanish music to publications in France and Spain.

Vinogradsky, Alexander, Russian conductor; b. Kiev, Aug. 5, 1855; d. there, Oct. 17, 1912. He studied at the St. Petersburg Cons.; in 1888 became conductor of the symph. concerts of the Imperial Russian Music Society in Kiev; also conducted in Paris, Vienna, and Berlin. He wrote 2 symphonies; a symph. fantasy, *En Bourgogne;* a symph. poem, *La Nonne;* a number of minor pieces.

Viola, Alfonso della, Italian composer; b. Ferrara, 1508; d. there, 1570; was maestro di cappella to Duke Ercole II d'Este at Ferrara. He is noteworthy as an early composer of pastorals and incidental music for the court of Ferrara: *L'Orbecche* (1541), *Il Sacrifizio* (1554), *Lo Sfortunato* (1557), and *Aretusa* (1563), all in madrigal style, the dialogue sung by a chorus. Publ. 2 books of madrigals *a* 4 (1539, 1540).

Viola, Francesco, Italian 16th-century madrigalist, pupil of Adrian Willaert; was for some time in the service of Alfonso d'Este, Duke of Ferrara, whom he accompanied to Venice in 1562; publ. a book of madrigals *a* 4 at Venice in 1550; other madrigals in various collections; also edited the collection *Musica nova,* containing motets and madrigals by Willaert.

Viola, P. Anselm, Catalan composer, b. Teruel, July, 1738; d. Montserrat, Jan. 25, 1798. He was a monk at Montserrat; wrote much instrumental music of surprising excellence in a fine Baroque style. His Concerto for 2 oboes, 2 horns, violins and cellos obbligato is included in vol. II of *Música Instrumental,* publ. by the Monastery of Montserrat in 1936, edited by Dom David Pujol.

Viole, Rudolf, German pianist and composer; b. Schochwitz, Mansfeld, May 10, 1825; d. Berlin, Dec. 7, 1867. He was a pupil of Liszt, who recommended his compositions and edited his 100 études; Viole wrote mostly for piano, including 11 sonatas, a *Caprice heroïque,* a ballade, a polonaise, etc.

Viotta, Henri (Henricus Anastasius), Dutch conductor and music scholar; son of **Johannes Josephus Viotta;** b. Amsterdam, July 16, 1848; d. Montreux, Feb. 17, 1933. He studied with his father and with R. Hol in Amsterdam; was a student of jurisprudence at the Univ. of Leyden; *Dr. juris* (1877) with the dissertation *Het Auteursrecht van den Componist,* but gave up legal practice; became conductor of various musical groups in Amsterdam, including the Wagner Society. In 1896 he was appointed director of the Cons. at The Hague, retaining this position until 1917; founded the Residentie Orch. there (1903), and conducted it for a number of seasons, retiring in 1917. He publ. a valuable *Lexicon der Toonkunst* (3 vols., 18881–85); and *Handboek der Muziekgeschiedenis* (1916). In 1920 he went to live in Switzerland.

Viotta, Johannes Josephus, Dutch composer; b. Amsterdam, Jan. 14, 1814; d. there, Feb. 6, 1859. He was of Italian descent; studied medicine; music was his avocation. He wrote mainly for the voice, and some of his songs in the popular vein (*De zilveren vloot, Een scheepje in de haven lag,* etc.) became exceedingly well known. In Holland he played a very important role, especially in spreading the cult of Mendelssohn and other German composers.

Viotti, Giovanni Battista, famous Italian violinist and composer; b. Fontanetto da Po, May 12, 1755; d. London, March 3, 1824. His father, a blacksmith, was an amateur musician; taught him music, and bought a small violin for him to practice on. At the age of 13 he was sent to Turin, where he gained the favor of Alfonso del Pozzo, Prince della Cisterna, who paid for his lessons with Pugnani. Viotti soon acquired a virtuoso technique, and also began to compose violin music. In 1780 he made a grand tour of Germany, Poland, and Russia with Pugnani, and was welcomed at the court of Catherine the Great. On March 15, 1782, he made his first appearance in Paris at the Concert Spirituel. He became a court musician to Marie Antoinette, and in 1788 was appointed manager of the Théâtre de Monsieur, jointly with the Queen's hair dresser Léonard; he reorganized the enterprise, and invited famous singers to participate in operatic productions. He was also successful as a teacher; among his pupils were Baillot and Rode. He was intimate with Cherubini, and lodged with him in 1785; often played in private, but shunned public appearances, being satisfied with the generous emolument from the court. He remained in Paris for 3 years after the revolution, but in 1792, when the situation became extremely dangerous for friends of the Queen, he went to London, where he was employed as conductor of Italian operas; also was soloist in his own concertos at the celebrated Salomon concerts (1794–95). In 1798 he was obliged to leave England on suspicion of political intrigue; lived for some years at Schönfeld, near Hamburg, devoting himself to composition. In 1801 he returned to London and engaged in a wine business, but sustained financial losses. After the restoration of the French monarchy, he returned to Paris; was appointed director of the Italian Opera (1819–22), but suffered repeated reverses, and in 1822 returned to London, broken in spirit and health, and heavily in debt. He died 2 years later.

Viotti's role in the history of instrumental music, both in performance and composition, was very important. He elevated performing standards from mere entertainment to artistic presentation, and may be regarded as one of the chief creators of modern violin playing. He was the first to write violin concertos in a consciously formulated sonata form, with the solo part and the orchestral accompaniment utilizing the full resources of instrumental sonority more abundantly than ever before in violin concertos. He publ. 29 violin concertos (of which No. 22, in A minor, is a great favorite); 10 piano concertos (some of which are transcriptions of violin concertos); 2 *Symphonies concertantes,* for 2 violins, strings, oboes, and horns; 21 string quartets; 36 string trios; 54 duets for 2 violins; 6 serenades for 2 violins; several duos for 2 cellos; 3 divertissements for violin unaccompanied; 12 sonatas for violin and piano; 9 piano sonatas. His song known as "La Polacca de Viotti" (used in Paisiello's *La Serva padrona*, 1794) acquired great popularity. For the rectification of Viotti's birth date (heretofore given as May 23, 1753), see *Stampa di Torino* of Sept. 29, 1935, which publ. for the first time the text of his birth certificate; an infant brother of Viotti was born in 1753; their Christian names were identical (the brother having died before the birth of the future musician) which led to confusion; the bicentennial of Viotti was widely celebrated in the wrong year (1953).

BIBLIOGRAPHY: A. M. d'Eymar, *Anecdotes sur Viotti, précédées de quelques réflexions sur l'expression en musique* (Paris, 1972); F. Fayolle, *Notices sur Corelli et Viotti* (Paris, 1810); P. M. Baillot, *Notice sur J. B. Viotti* (Paris, 1825); E. F. Miel, *Notice historique sur J. B. Viotti* (Paris, 1827); A. Pougin, *Viotti et l'école moderne de violin* (Paris, 1888); H. de Curzon, "Quelques souvenirs de Viotti," *Ménestrel* (April 1924); L. de La Laurencie, "Les Débuts de Viotti comme directeur de l'Opéra en 1819," *Revue de Musicologie* (Aug. 1924); L. de La Laurencie, *L'École française de violon de Lully à Viotti* (Paris, 1922–25); M. Pincherle, *Les Violinistes compositeurs et virtuoses* (Paris, 1922); W. H. Riehl, *Viotti und das Geigenduett*, in *Musikalische Charakterköpfe* (vol. II); A. Moser, *Geschichte des Violinspiels* (Berlin, 1923); A. Della Corte, *L'Interpretazione musicale e gli interpreti* (Turin, 1951); R. Giazotto, *G. B. Viotti* (Milan, 1956).

Virdung, Sebastian, German theorist; b. Amberg, 1465; was at first a priest in Eichstätt, and from 1500 a member of the court chapel in Heidelberg; wrote a work of importance for the history of musical instruments: *Musica getutscht und auszgezogen durch Sebastianum Virdung, Priesters von Amberg, und alles Gesang ausz den Noten in die Tabulaturen diser benannten dryer Instrumenten, der Orgeln, der Lauten und der Flöten transferieren zu lernen kurtzlich gemacht* (Basel, 1511; facsimile reprint in Eitner's *Publikationen älterer praktischer und theoretischer Musikwerke*, vol. 11, 1882; also by L. Schrade, Kassel, 1931, and by K. W. Niemöller, Kassel, 1970). Virdung's method was violently attacked by Arnolt Schlick in his *Tabulatur etlicher Lobgesänge* (1512). Four of Virdung's songs are in Schöffer's *Teutsche Lieder mit 4 Stimmen* (1513).

BIBLIOGRAPHY: B. A. Wallner, "Sebastian Virdung von Amberg," *Kirchenmusikalisches Jahrbuch* (1911); H. H. Lenneberg, "The Critic Criticized: Sebastian Virdung and His Controversy with Arnold Schlick," *Journal of the American Musicological Society* (Spring 1957).

Viscarra Monje, Humberto, Bolivian composer; b. Sorata, March 30, 1898; d. La Paz, Sept. 2, 1971. He studied at the National Cons. of Bolivia in La Paz; then went to Europe, and studied piano and composition in Italy and France. Returning to Bolivia he served as director of the Cons. of La Paz (1930–32 and 1950–68). He composed some attractive piano pieces based on Bolivian motives.

Visée, Robert de, French guitar player, lutenist, and composer; b. c.1650; d. c.1725. He was court musician from about 1686 to 1721; publ. 2 books of guitar pieces (1682; 1686) and *Pièces de théorbe et de luth, mises en partition* (1716).

Visetti, Alberto Antonio, Italian singing teacher; b. Salona, May 13, 1846; d. London, July 10, 1928. He studied at the Milan Cons.; first appeared as pianist; went to Paris, where he was appointed chamber musician to Empress Eugénie. After the fall of the Empire in France, he settled in London, where he taught singing; also conducted the Bath Philharmonic Society (1878–90). He publ. a *History of the Art of Singing* and *Verdi* (1905); the score of his opera *Les Trios Mousquetaries* was lost during the siege of Paris (1871). He also wrote a cantata, *The Desert and the Praise of Song;* and a waltz-song for Adelina Patti, *La Diva.*

Vishnevskaya, Galina, Russian soprano; b. Leningrad, Oct. 25, 1926. After vocal studies in Leningrad she sang in operetta; in 1952 she joined the operatic staff of the Bolshoi Theater in Moscow; there her roles were Violetta, Tosca, Madama Butterfly and an entire repertoire of soprano parts in Russian operas. She is married to the famous cellist **Mstislav Rostropovich.** Owing to the recurrent differences that developed between Rostropovich and the cultural authorites of the Soviet Union (Rostropovich had sheltered the dissident writer Solzhenitsyn in his summer house), they left Russia in 1974; eventually settled in the U.S., when Rostropovich was appointed conductor of the National Symph. Orch. in Washington. In March, 1978, both he and Vishnevskaya, as "ideological renegades," were stripped of their Soviet citizenship by a decree of the Soviet government.

Viski, János, Hungarian composer; b. Kolozsvár, June 10, 1906; d. Budapest, Jan. 16, 1961. He studied violin at an early age; then took lessons in composition from Kodály at the Budapest Academy of Music (1927–32). From 1942 until his death he was prof. of composition at the Budapest Academy of Music; won the Erkel Prize in 1954 and the Kossuth Prize in 1956. Most of his music is permeated with Hungarian melorhythms, and is set in classical forms.

WORKS: *Symphonic Suite* (1935); *2 Hungarian Dances* for orch. (1938); *Enigma,* symph. poem (1939–40); Violin Concerto (1947); Piano Concerto (1953); Cello Concerto (1955); *Az irisórai szarvas (The Deer of Irisóra)* for baritone and orch. (1958); String Trio (1930, lost); *Epitaph for Anton Webern* for piano (1960); choral works; songs.

Vitali, Filippo, Italian composer; b. Florence, c.1590; d. 1653. In 1631 he became a singer in the Pontifical Choir in Rome; also chamber virtuoso to Cardinal Barberini; in 1642 returned to Florence and succeeded Gagliano as maestro of the ducal chapel and of the Cathedral of S. Lorenzo; in 1648–49, maestro at Sta. Maria Maggiore in Bergamo. His "favola in musica" *L'Aretusa,* performed on Feb. 8, 1620, at the home of Monsignor Corsini, is regarded as the first attempt at opera in Rome (publ. there in 1620). In 1622 he composed 6 intermedi for the comedy *La Finta Mora* by J. Cicognini, performed at the palace of Cardinal de' Medici in Florence (publ. there, 1623). Also publ. several books of madrigals, arias with instrumental accompaniment, psalms, motets, and hymns. Vitali was outstanding among composers in the monodic style.

Vitali, Giovanni Battista, Italian composer; b. Bologna, Feb. 18, 1632; d. Modena, Oct. 12, 1692. Pupil of M. Cazzati in Bologna; from about 1667 he played the viola da braccio in the Church of S. Petronio there; from 1674 he was 2nd, and from 1684 1st, maestro di cappella at the ducal court of Modena.
WORKS: *Correnti e Balletti da camera* for 2 violins and continuo (1666 and other eds.); *Sonate a 2 violini col basso cont. per l'organo* (1667, etc.); *Balletti, Correnti e Sinfonie da camera a 4 stromenti* (1667, etc.); *Balletti, Correnti, etc., a violino e violone o spinetta, con il secondo violino a beneplacito* (1668, etc.); *Sonate da chiesa a 2, 3, 4 e 5 stromenti* (1669); *Salmi concertati da 2 a 5 voci con stromenti* (1677); *Sonate a 2 violini e basso cont.; Varie sonate alla francese ed all'italiana a 6 stromenti* (1684); *Balli in stile francese a 5 stromenti* (1690); *Sonate da camera a 3 stromenti* (1692); etc. 18 pieces are in Torchi's *L'Arte Musicale in Italia* (vol. 7), and his *Artifici Musicali* of 1689 was publ. as vol. 14 of the Smith College Music Archives (1959), ed. by L. Rood and G. P. Smith.

Vitalini, Alberico, Italian composer; b. Rome, July 18, 1921. He studied at the Cons. of Santa Cecilia in Rome, obtaining the diplomas in violin (1940), viola (1942), composition (1944), and conducting (1945). He subsequently became active mainly as a conductor; in 1950 was appointed director of musical programs of the Radio Vaticana; in 1973 was nominated a member of the Accademia Internazionale de Propaganda Culturale. He specializes in sacred choral music.
WORKS: *Fantasia* for piano and orch. (1949; Rome, 1969), *Assisi,* for chorus and orch. (1949; Rome, 1967), *Le Sette Parole di Cristo* for baritone and string orch. (Rome 1952); *Magnificat* for soprano, chorus, and orch. (1954; Rome 1957), *Tiberiade,* for small orch. (1955), *Canti in Italiano,* for new liturgy in Italian language (1965–71).

Vitalis, George, Greek composer and conductor; b. Athens, Jan. 9, 1895; d. there, April 27, 1959. He studied with Armani in Milan; conducted light opera in Athens (1923–36); came to the U.S. in 1945; settled in N.Y. He composed the operas *Perseus and Andromeda, The Return of the Gods,* and *Golfo* (N.Y., Jan. 1, 1949, in concert form, composer conducting); *Greek Fantasy,* for orch. (Athens, Nov. 11, 1945); light orchestra pieces under the pseudonym **Giorgio Valente.**

Vitry, Philippe de (Philippus de Vitriaco), famous churchman and musician; b. Vitry, Champagne, Oct. 31, 1291; d. Meaux, June 9, 1361. There are 6 towns in Champagne named Vitry, and it is not known in which of these Vitry was born; he was ordained a deacon early in life and from 1323 held several benefices; he was canon of Soissons and archbishop of Brie. He became a clerk of the royal household in Paris, and about 1346 was made counselor of the court of requests ("maître des requêtes"); from 1346–50 he was also in the service of Duke Jean of Normandy (heir to the throne), with whom he took part in the siege of

Aiguillon (1346); when Duke Jean became king in 1350, he sent Vitry to Avignon on a mission to Pope Clement VI, who on Jan. 3, 1351 appointed him bishop of Meaux. Vitry was known as a poet and a composer, but his enduring fame rests on his *Ars nova,* a treatise expounding a new theory of mensural notation, particulary important for its development of the principle of binary rhythm; it also gives the most complete account of the various uses to which colored notes were put. Of the 4 treatises attributed to Vitry in Coussemaker's *Scriptores,* III, only the *Ars nova* (also publ., with corrections, in *Musica Disciplina,* 1956), is now considered authentic. Most of Vitry's works are lost; the extant pieces were publ. by L. Schrade in vol. I of his *Polyphonic Music of the 14th Century* (Monaco, 1956). Separate pieces were brought out in *Denkmäler der Tonkunst in Österreich* 76 (40).
BIBLIOGRAPHY: Hugo Riemann, *Geschichte der Musiktheorie im 9.-19. Jahrhundert* (1898); Joh. Wolf, *Geschichte der Mensuralnotation* (1904); J. Combarieu, *Histoire de la musique,* vol. I (1913); A. Coville, "Philippe de Vitry, Notes biographiques," *Romania* (Oct. 1933); G. Reese, *Music in the Middle Ages* (N.Y., 1940); L. Schrade, "Philippe de Vitry: Some New Discoveries," *Musical Quarterly* (July 1956).

Vittadini, Franco, Italian composer; b. Pavia, April 9, 1884; d. there, Nov. 30, 1948. He studied at the Milan Cons.; settled in Pavia, where he headed a music school.
WORKS: the operas *Anima allegra* (Rome, April 15, 1921; Metropolitan Opera, N.Y., Feb. 14, 1923), *Nazareth* (Pavia, May 28, 1925), *La Sagredo* (Milan, La Scala, April 26, 1930), *Caracciolo* (Rome, Feb. 7, 1938); a pastoral triptych" *Il Natale di Gesù* (Bari, Dec. 20, 1933); *Fiordisole,* ballet (Milan, Feb. 14, 1935); *Le sette parole di Cristo,* oratorio; 10 Masses; symph. poem, *Armonie della notte* (1925); organ pieces.
BIBLIOGRAPHY: A. Baratti, *Vita del musicista F. Vittadini* (Milan, 1955).

Vittoria, Tommaso Luigi da, See **Victoria, Tomás Luis de.**

Vivaldi, Antonio, greatly renowned Italian composer; b. Venice, March 4, 1678; d. Vienna, July (buried July 28), 1741. He was the son of **Giovanni Battista Vivaldi,** a violinist at San Marco in Venice, and he studied violin with him; also took theory lessons with Giovanni Legrenzi. He entered the priesthood, taking the tonsure in 1693, and holy orders ten years later. Because of his red hair he was called "il prete rosso" (the Red Priest). In 1703 he became violin teacher at the Ospedale della Pietà in Venice; in 1718 he became music director at the court of Prince Philip, Landgrave of Hesse Darmstadt at Mantua; in 1725 he traveled to Amsterdam, where he arranged for publication of several of his works; among them was a collection of 12 violin concertos under the title *La cetra* (1727), which he dedicated to Emperor Charles VI, who then invited him to come to his court in Vienna. Vivaldi accepted the offer, and remained in Vienna to the end of his life, except for visits to Prague and

Dresden. Vivaldi devoted the early years of his career as a composer mainly to operatic productions, which were successfully staged in Florence, Milan, Rome, Verona and other Italian cities, as well as in Vienna; however, Vivaldi's greatness lies mainly in his superb instrumental works, particularly concerti grossi and solo concertos. Despite the difference in treatment and function between his operas and instrumental music, Vivaldi often used material from his operas in his concerti, and vice versa; thus, some of his operatic arias are constructed in the form of a Baroque air in a suite, while the slow movements of instrumental works often find their analogous structures in the operatic "laments." The importance of Vivaldi was enhanced in music history through Bach's use of Vivaldi's concertos as models for his own keyboard concertos; however, of the 16 "Concertos after Vivaldi" for clavier publ. in the *Bach Gesellschaft* edition, only 6 are transcriptions of Vivaldi. Until about the middle of the 20th century Vivaldi was regarded by most music historians as merely an estimable composer who dwelt in the shadow of Bach; not even the basic biographical data (exact date of birth, place and date of death) were established with accuracy until the middle of the 20th century. But comparisons with Bach are misguided. Vivaldi's music possesses neither the surpassing genius nor the conceptual grandeur of Bach's works; his contrapuntal skill was minimal compared to Bach's epic achievements in fugal writing. Furthermore, the uniformity of Vivaldi's structures and the extraordinary repetitiousness of thematic statements in his instrumental works tend to blur the individuality of each particular piece; it has been said that Vivaldi did not write 400 concertos known under his name, but only one concerto which he copied 399 times. Proper taxonomy of Vivaldi's works is further complicated by the profuse cross-pollination of his operatic and instrumental fragments and even of complete sections of various compositions, as well as the abundance of arrangements of pieces by other composers. Under such circumstances, duplication of individual items becomes a rule rather than an exception. Vivaldi's catalogue of works must therefore be subject to periodic verifications and rectifications. 770 works can be assumed to exist, among them 46 operas, of which 21 are extant (Vivaldi himself listed in 1739 the number of his operas, as 94, but he included in it numerous separate arias and instrumental intermezzi); 344 solo concertos; 81 concertos for 2 or more solo instruments; 61 sinfonias; 23 chamber concertos; 93 sonatas and trios; 3 oratorios, 8 serenades; 38 secular solo cantatas, 12 motets, 37 liturgical works; many of these exist in several versions.

WORKS: 21 extant operas: *Ottone in villa* (Vicenza, 1713); *Orlando finto pazzo* (Venice, 1714); *L'Incoronazione di Dario* (Venice, 1716); *Arsilda regina di Ponto* (Venice, 1716); *Armida al campo D'Egitto* (Venice, 1718); *Il teuzzone* (Mantua, 1719); *Tito Manlio* (Mantua, 1719); *La verità in cimento* (Venice, 1720); *Ercole sul Termodonte* (Rome, 1723); *Giustino* (Rome, 1724); *Dorilla in Tempo* (Venice, 1726); *Farnace* (Venice, 1727); *Orlando furioso* (Venice, 1727); *L'Atenaide* (Florence, 1729); *La fida ninfa* (Verona, 1732); *L'Olimpiade* (Venice, 1734); *Griselda* (Venice,

1735); *Catone in Utica* (Verona, 1737); the following are probably by Vivaldi, but only the libretti are extant: *Scanderbeg* (Florence, 1711); *Ipermestra* (Florence, 1727); *Semiramide* (Mantua, 1732); *Montezuma* (Venice, 1733); and *Feraspe* (1739); 2 oratorios, *Moyses Deus Pharaonis* (Venice, 1714); and *Juditha triumphans devicta Holofernis barbarie* (Venice, 1716), 38 solo secular cantatas, 12 motets, 37 liturgical works. Instrumental works: *12 Sonate da camera* for 2 violins and continuo, op. 1; 18 violin sonatas with continuo, op. 2 and 5; *L'Estro armonico*, 12 concertos for 1, 2, or 4 solo violins, solo cello, strings, and continuo, op. 3; *La Stravaganza*, 12 concertos for solo violin, strings, and continuo, op. 4; 18 concertos for 3 violins, viola, and continuo, op. 6 and 7; *Il Cimento dell'Armonia e dell'Invenzione,* including *Le quattro stagione (The Four Seasons),* 12 concertos for solo violin, strings, and continuo, op. 8; *La Cetra,* 12 concertos for solo violin, strings and continuo, op. 9; 6 concertos for flute, strings, and organ, op. 10; 12 concertos for solo violin, strings, and organ, op. 11 and 12. A complete edition of Vivaldi's instrumental works, under the general editorship of Gian Francesco Malipiero, was brought out in 1947–72, in 16 series comprising 530 compositions; numerous individual works were published separately. An all-encompassing catalogue is by Peter Ryom, *Les Manuscrits de Vivaldi* (Paris, 1977); other catalogues are: M. Rinaldi, *Catalogo numerico tematico delle composizioni di Antonio Vivaldi* (Rome, 1945); A. Fanna, *Antonio Vivaldi, Catalogo numerico-tematico delle opere strumentali* (Milan, 1968); L. Coral, *A Concordance of the Thematic Indexes to the Instrumental Works of Antonio Vivaldi* (2nd ed., Ann Arbor, Mich., 1972); Peter Ryom, *Antonio Vivaldi, Table de concordances des œuvres* (Copenhagen, 1973); P. Damilano, *Inventario delle composizioni musicali manuscripti di Antonio Vivaldi* (Turin, 1968).

BIBLIOGRAPHY: A. Schering, *Geschichte des Instrumental-Konzerts* (Leipzig, 1905; reprint, Wiesbaden, 1972); Alfredo Casella, et al., *Antonio Vivaldi: note e documenti* (Siena, 1939); M. Rinaldi, *Antonio Vivaldi* (Vilan, 1943); S. A. Luciani, *Vivaldi: Concerti e Sonate* (Milan, 1946); M. Pincherle, *Antonio Vivaldi et la musique instrumentale* (2 vols. Paris, 1948); G. Guerrini, *Antonio Vivaldi: la vita e l'opera* (Florence, 1951); M. Pincherle, *Vivaldi* (Paris, 1955; in English, *Vivaldi, Genius of the Baroque;* N.Y., 1962); Walter Kolneder, *Antonio Vivaldi: Leben und Werk* (Wiesbaden, 1964; also in English, London, 1970); W. Kolneder, "Die Vivaldi-Forschung: Geschichte, Probleme, Aufgaben," *Österreichische Musikzeitschrift* (June 1967).

Vivell, Cölestin, German ecclesiastic; writer on Gregorian Chant; b. Wolfach, Oct. 21, 1846; d. Seckau, March 10, 1923. Having completed his university studies, he joined the order of Benedictines at Beuron; from 1883 lived in the monastery at Seckau, Styria.

WRITINGS: *Der gregorianische Gesang. Eine Studie über die Echtheit seiner Tradition* (Graz, 1904); *Die liturgisch gesangliche Reform Gregors des Grossen* (Seckau, 1904); *Erklärung der vatikanischen Choralschrift* (Graz, 1906); *Vom Musiktraktate Gregors des Grossen* (Leipzig, 1911); *Initia Tractatuum musi-*

ces ex codicibus (Graz, 1912; alphabetical list of beginnings of treatises in Gerbert's and Coussemaker's *Scriptores*); *Fritolfi Breviarum de musica* (Vienna, 1919).

Vives, Amadeo, Spanish composer; b. Collbató, near Barcelona, Nov. 18, 1871; d. Madrid, Dec. 1, 1932. He was a pupil of Felipe Pedrell in Barcelona; with L. Millet, founded the famous choral society Orfeó Catalá (1891). In his first opera, *Artus* (Barcelona, 1895), he made use of Catalonian folksongs. Subsequently he moved to Madrid, where he produced his comic opera *Don Lucas del Cigarral* (Feb. 18, 1899); his opera *Euda d'Uriach*, originally to a Catalan libretto, was brought out in Italian at Barcelona (Oct. 24, 1900). Then followed his most popular opera, *Maruxa* (Madrid, May 28, 1914); other operas are *Balada de Carnaval* (Madrid, July 5, 1919) and *Doña Francisquita* (Madrid, Oct. 17, 1923). The style of his stage productions shared qualities of the French light opera and the Spanish zarzuela; he wrote nearly 100 of these; also composed songs and piano pieces; publ. a book of essays, *Sofia* (Madrid, 1923).

Vivier, Albert-Joseph, Belgian music theorist; b. Huy, Dec. 15, 1816; d. Brussels, Jan. 3, 1903. He studied with Fétis at the Brussels Cons.; wrote an interesting *Traité complet d'harmonie* (1862, and many later eds.) in which he explained secondary chords as accidental formations through incorporation of auxiliary notes; also wrote essays on acoustics (*Des vrais rapports des sons musicaux, Éléments d'acoustique musicale,* etc.). His opera *Spadillo le tavernier* was produced in Brussels on May 22, 1857.

Vivier, Claude, Canadian composer; b. Montreal, April 14, 1948. He studied composition with Tremblay at the Montreal Cons. (1967–70); then went to Holland, and worked in electronic music with Koening at the Institute of Sonology in Utrecht; then attended Stockhausen's classes in electronic music in Cologne (1972–74). In 1976 he embarked on a tour of the Orient to study non-Western musical cultures.
WORKS: String Quartet (1968); *Prolifération* for Ondes Martenot, piano and percussion (1968–69); *Hiérophanie* for chamber ensemble (1970); *Deva et Asura* for chamber ensemble (1972); *Désintégration* for unspecified instruments (1972); *O! Kosmos* for chorus a cappella (1973).

Vivier, Eugène-Léon, French horn virtuoso; b. Brioude, Haute-Loire, Dec. 4, 1817; d. Nice, Feb. 24, 1900. He learned to play violin, then took up the French horn. He moved to Paris, where he became successful through his connections at the French court. An eccentric, he prided himself on his ability to play 2 notes simultaneously on his instrument, through clever overblowing. He publ. a number of pamphlets on music and the theater, and also an autobiography (largely fictitious), *La Vie et les aventures d'un corniste* (Paris, 1900).

Vix, Geneviève, French soprano; b. Nantes, Dec. 31, 1879; d. Paris, Aug. 25, 1939. She studied at the Paris Cons.; won 1st prize for opera (1908); sang at the Paris Opéra, in Madrid, and in Buenos Aires; made her American debut with the Chicago Opera Co. as Manon in Massenet's opera (Dec. 1, 1917); married Prince Cyril Naryshkin in N.Y. (Feb. 9, 1918). She possessed a fine lyric voice and was also adept as an actress.

Vlad, Roman, Italian composer and writer on music; b. Cernauti, Rumania, Dec. 29, 1919. He was a pupil at the Cernauti Cons.; in 1938 went to Rome, where he studied piano and composition with Casella; in 1943 he adopted the 12-tone method of composition.
WORKS: *La Strada sul caffé,* ballet (Rome, June 9, 1945); *La Dama delle camelie,* ballet in form of 5 waltzes (Rome, Nov. 20, 1945); *Sinfonia* (Venice Festival, Sept. 8, 1948); *Divertimento* for 11 instruments (Capri, Sept. 15, 1948); *De Profundis,* for soprano, mixed chorus, and orch. (Paris, June 2, 1949); *Storia d'una mamma,* musical fable (Venice Festival, Oct. 5, 1951); 5 Elegies for voice and string orch. (1952); *Le Ciel est vide,* for chorus and orch. (Turin, Oct. 29, 1954); *Variazioni concertanti* for piano and orch. based on a series of 12 notes in Mozart's *Don Giovanni* (Venice Festival, Sept. 18, 1955); *Studi dodecafonici* for piano (1943–57); *Colinde transilvane* for chorus (1957); *Musica concertata* for harp and orch. (Turin, April 24, 1958); *Tre Invocazioni* for voice and orch. (Rome, June 6, 1958); *Masques Ostendais,* ballet (Spoleto Festival, June 12, 1959); *Il Dottore di vetro,* radiophonic opera (Rome, Feb. 26, 1960); *Il Ritorno,* ballet (Cologne, 1962); *Ode Super "Chrysea Phorminx"* for guitar and orch. (1964); *La Fontana,* television opera (1967); *Divertimento sinfonieo* for orch. (1968); *Il magico flauto di Severino* for flute and piano (1971); publ. the books *Modernità e tradizione nella musica contemporanea* (Turin, 1955), *Storia della dodecafonia* (Milan, 1958), and a monograph on Stravinsky (Turin, 1958; in English, London, 1960; 2nd revised ed., 1967).

Vladigerov, Alexander, Bulgarian conductor and composer; son of **Pantcho Vladigerov;** b. Sofia, Aug. 4, 1933. He studied composition with his father and conducting with Simeonov at the Bulgarian State Cons. in Sofia, graduating in 1956; also took conducting courses in Kiev with Rakhlin. He was conductor of the orch. in Ruse; then was engaged as conductor for the Bulgarian Radio and Television.
WORKS: a children's operetta, *Little Red Riding Hood* (1969); 2 musicals, *The Jolly Town Musicians* (1971), and *The Wolf and the Seven Kids* (1973); *Youth March* for orch. (1948); *Rondo Concertante* for violin and orch. (1955); *Rumanian Dance* for orch. (1960); piano pieces.

Vladigerov, Pantcho, prominent Bulgarian composer; b. Zürich, March 13, 1899, in a geminal parturition. Distrustful of Bulgarian puerperal skill, his mother sped from Shumen to Zürich when she learned that she was going to have a plural birth. Pantcho's nonidentical twin brother **Luben,** a violinist, was born 16 hours earlier than Pantcho, on the previous day, March 12, 1899. Vladigerov studied piano and theory with local teachers in Sofia; then went to Berlin where he took lessons in composition with Paul Juon and

Georg Schumann, and piano with Leonid Kreutzer at the Akademie der Künste in Berlin. He remained in Berlin where he served as conductor and composer of the Max Reinhardt Theater. In 1932 he returned to Bulgaria, and was appointed prof. of the Music Academy in Sofia. His music is rooted in Bulgarian folksong; he artfully combines the peculiar melodic and rhythmic patterns of native material with stark modern harmonies; the method is similar to that of Béla Bartók.

WORKS: an opera *Tsar Kaloyan* (1935-36; Sofia, April 20, 1936); a ballet *Legenda za ezeroto* (*Legend of the Lake*, 1946; Sofia, Nov. 11, 1962; 2 orch. suites were drawn in 1947 and 1953); 5 piano concertos (1918, 1930, 1937, 1953, 1963); *Legend* for orch. (1919); *3 Impressions* for orch. (1920; orchestration of 3 of his *10 Impressions* for piano); 2 violin concertos (1921, 1968); *Burlesk Suite* for violin and orch. (1922); *Scandinavian Suite* for orch. (1924); *Bulgarian Suite* for orch. (1927); *Vardar*, Bulgarian rhapsody for orch. (1927; orchestration of his earlier violin and piano piece); 7 *Bulgarian Symphonic Dances* (1931); 2 overtures: *Zemja* (1933); and *The Ninth of September* (1949); 2 symphonies: No. 1 (1939) and No. 2, *Majska* (*May*) for string orch. (1949); *Concert Fantasy* for cello and orch. (1941); 4 *Rumanian Symphonic Dances* (1942); *Improvisation and Toccata* for orch. (1942; orchestration of the final 2 pieces of his piano cycle *Episodes*); 2 *Rumanian Symphonic Sketches* (1943); *Prelude and Balkan Dance* for orch. (1950); *Evreyska poema (Jewish Poem)* for orch. (1951); *Song of Peace*, dramatic poem for orch. (1956); 7 *Pieces* for string orch. (1969-70; orchestration of pieces taken from 3 different piano cycles); Violin Sonata (1914); Piano Trio (1916); works for violin and piano: 2 *Improvisations* (1919), 4 *Pieces* (1920), *Vardar* (1922), 2 *Bulgarian Paraphrases* (1925) and 2 *Pieces* (1926); String Quartet (1940); several piano cycles, many of which are also scored for chamber orch.: 4 *Pieces* (1915); 11 *Variations* (1916); 10 *Impressions* (1920); 4 *Pieces* (1920); 3 *Pieces* (1922); 6 *Exotic Preludes* (1924); *Classical and Romantic*, 7 pieces (1931); *Bulgarian Songs and Dances* (1932); *Sonatina Concertante* (1934); *Shumen*, 6 miniatures (1934); 5 *Episodes* (1941); *Aquarelles* (1942); 3 *Pictures* (1950); *Suite*, 5 pieces (1954); 3 *Pieces* (1957); 3 *Concert Pieces* (1959); 5 *Novelettes* (1965); 5 *Pieces* (1965); orchestration of Dinicu's *Hora Staccato*.

BIBLIOGRAPHY: E. Pavlov, *Pantcho Vladigerov: A Monograph* (Sofia, 1961).

Vlasov, Vladimir, Russian composer and ethnomusicologist; b. Moscow, Jan. 7, 1903. He studied violin at the Moscow Cons.; was active as a teacher. In 1936 he traveled to Frunze, Kirghizi, where he diligently went about collecting authentic songs of the natives. In collaboration with Vladimir Fere, similarly intentioned, he wrote a number of operas based on Kirghiz national melorhythms supplied by local musicians. These operas were subsequently produced in Frunze and at the ethnic festivals in Moscow. They include: *Golden Girl* (Frunze, May 1, 1937); *Moon Beauty* (Frunze, April 15, 1939); *For People's Happiness* (Frunze, May 1, 1941); *Patriots* (Frunze, Nov. 6, 1941); *Son of the People* (Frunze, Nov. 8, 1947); *On the*

Shores of Issyk-Kul (Frunze, Feb. 1, 1951); *The Witch*, radio opera (1961); *The Golden Maiden* (1972). He also wrote a cello concerto (1963); 3 string quartets and a variety of minor pieces and songs.

Vlijmen, Jan van, Dutch composer; b. Rotterdam, Oct. 11, 1935. He studied composition with Kees van Baaren. Upon completion of his musical education at the Utrecht Cons., he was director of the Amersfoort Music School (1961-65); taught theoretical subjects at the Utrecht Cons. (1965-68); became deputy director of The Hague Cons. in 1967, and upon Baaren's death, became its director in 1971.

WORKS: 2 operas, in collaboration with fellow Dutch composers: *Reconstructie*, an anti-U.S. opera, composed with Louis Andriessen, Misha Mengelberg, Reinbert de Leeuw and Peter Schat (1968-69; Holland Festival, June 29, 1969) and *Axel*, with Reinbert de Leeuw (1975-77; Holland Festival, Scheveningen, June 10, 1977); string quartet (1955); *Morgensternlieder* for mezzo-soprano and piano (1958); 2 wind quintets (1958, 1972); *Construzione* for 2 pianos (1959); *Serie* for 6 instruments (1960); *Gruppi* for 20 instruments in 4 groups, and percussion (1961-62); *Mythos* for mezzo-soprano and 9 instruments (1962); *Spostamenti* for orch. (1963); *Serenata I* for 12 instruments and percussion (1963-64, revised 1967); *Serenata II* for flute and 4 instrumental groups (Amsterdam, Sept. 10, 1965); *Sonata* for piano and 3 instrumental groups (1966); *Dialogue* for clarinet and piano (1966); *Per diciasette* for 17 winds (1967); *Interpolations* for orch. and electronic sound (Rotterdam, Nov. 24, 1968); *Ommagio a Gesualdo* for violin and 6 instrumental groups (Amsterdam, April 9, 1971); 4 *Songs* for mezzo-soprano and orch. (1975).

Vockerodt, Gottfried, German writer; b. Mühlhausen, Thuringia, Sept. 24, 1665; d. Gotha, Oct. 10, 1727. It was his opinion that excessive enjoyment of music injures the intellect, and that Nero and Caligula became totally depraved through their passion for music. He advocated these ideas in *Consultatio de cavenda falsa mentium intemperatarum medicina* (1696); *Missbrauch der freien Künste, insonderheit der Musik* (1697); and *Wiederholtes Zeugnis der Wahrheit gegen die verderbte Musik und Schauspiele, Opern, etc.* (1698).

Vockner, Josef, Austrian organist, composer, and teacher; b. Ebensee, March 18, 1842; d. Vienna, Sept. 11, 1906. He was a pupil of Bruckner; became prof. of organ at the Vienna Cons. Composed an oratorio, *Das jüngste Gericht;* a cello sonata; a piano quartet; fugues and other pieces for organ; songs.

Vogel, Adolf, German bass-baritone; b. Munich, Aug. 18, 1897; d. Vienna, Dec. 20, 1969. He studied voice with Anna Bahr-Mildenburg and J. Kiechle; was a member of the Munich Opera from 1933 to 1937; made his American debut at the Metropolitan Opera as Alberich (Dec. 3, 1937); remained on its roster for 2 seasons.

Vogel, Charles Louis Adolphe, French violinist and composer; b. Lille, May 17, 1808; d. Paris, Sept. 11,

1892. He was a grandson of **Johann Christoph Vogel;** studied at the Paris Cons. with A. Kreutzer (violin) and Reicha (theory). After winning popularity with his song *Les Trois Couleurs* during the July Revolution (1830), he brought out a series of successful operas: *Le Podestat* (Paris, 1831), *Le Siège de Leyde* (The Hague, March 14, 1847), *La Moissonneuse* (Paris, 1853), *Rompons* (Paris, 1857), *Le Nid de Cigognes* (Baden-Baden, 1858), *Gredin de Pigoche* (Paris, 1866), and *La Filleule du roi* (Brussels, 1875). He also wrote symphonies, chamber music, sacred works, songs, piano pieces.

Vogel, Emil, German musicologist; b. Wriezen-on-Oder, Jan. 21, 1859; d. Nikolassee, near Berlin, June 18, 1908. He studied at Greifswald and Berlin; in 1893 he organized the Peters Music Library in Leipzig and was librarian till 1901; at the same time he also ed. the *Peters Jahrbuch.* He published the catalogue *Die Handschriften nebst den älteren Druckwerken der Musikabteilung der herzoglichen Bibliothek zu Wolfenbüttel* (1890), and *Bibliothek der gedruckten weltlichen Vokalmusik Italiens aus den Jahren 1500–1700* (1892; new ed., completely revised by Alfred Einstein, publ. in *Notes* (June 1945–Sept. 1948).

Vogel, Friedrich Wilhelm Ferdinand, German organist and composer; b. Havelberg, Prussia, Sept. 9, 1807; d. Bergen, Norway, July 20, 1892. He studied with Birnbach in Berlin; made tours as organ virtuoso; taught at Hamburg (1838–41) and Copenhagen (1845–52); then settled in Bergen, where he founded an organ school. He publ. a number of works for organ, including 60 chorale-preludes, 10 postludes, and 2 preludes and fugues; also chamber music; overtures; choruses.

Vogel, Johann Christoph, German composer; b. Nuremberg, 1758 (baptized March 18); d. Paris, June 27, 1788. He was a pupil of Riepel at Regensburg; went to Paris in 1776, and wrote 2 operas in Gluck's style: *La Toison d'or* (Paris, Sept. 5, 1786) and *Démophon,* which he completed shortly before his untimely death at the age of 32, and which was produced posthumously (Paris, Sept. 22, 1789). He also composed a great deal of instrumental music: 3 symphonies; a bassoon concerto; 3 clarinet concertos; 6 string quartets; 6 quartets for horn and strings; 3 quartets for bassoon and strings; 6 trios for 2 violins and bass; 6 duos for 2 clarinets; 6 duos for 2 bassoons; etc.

Vogel, Wilhelm Moritz, German pianist and composer; b. Sorgau, Silesia, July 9, 1846; d. Leipzig, Oct. 30, 1922. He studied in Leipzig, and settled there as a teacher; also conducted choral societies and wrote music criticism. He published series of instructive piano pieces, and a method (in 12 parts); also songs and organ works; edited *Deutsches Schulliederbuch* (a collection of 200 part-songs); brought out a *Geschichte der Musik* (1900) and several didactic books.

Vogel, Wladimir, Russian-born Swiss composer; b. Moscow, Feb. 29, 1896, of a German father and Russian mother; was interned in Russia during World War I as a German subject; in 1918 he went to Berlin,

where he studied with Tiessen and Busoni (1920–24); left Berlin in 1933, and after a brief stay in France, went to Switzerland; became a Swiss citizen in 1954; in 1964 settled in Zürich. Profoundly preoccupied with philosophical and mystical aspects of music, he at first followed the congenial ideas and tonal esthetics of Scriabin; later experimented with composition according to Schoenberg's method of 12-tone music.
WORKS: oratorio *Thyl Claes (Till Eulenspiegel)* in 2 parts: *Oppression* (1938; Geneva, 1943) and *Liberation* (1943–45; Geneva, 1947; an orch. suite from the oratorio was given at the Palermo Festival of the International Society for Contemporary Music, April 26, 1949); *Wagadus Untergang durch die Eitelkeit,* cantata for 3 soloists, mixed chorus, speaking chorus, and 5 saxophones (1930); *Sinfonia fugata* for orch. (1930–32); *2 Studies* for orch. (London Festival, July 28, 1931); *Tripartita* for orch. (1934; Geneva, Nov. 21, 1935); Violin Concerto (1937); *Passacaglia* for chamber orch. (1946); *Sept Aspects d'une série de douze sons* for orch. (1949–50; Venice International Festival, Sept., 1950); *Spiegelungen* for orch. (1952; Frankfurt, June 26, 1953); Cello Concerto (1954; Zürich, Nov. 27, 1956); *An die Jugend der Welt* for chorus and small orch. (1954); *Goethe-Aphorismen* for soprano and strings (Venice Inter. Festival, Sept., 1955); *Eine Gotthardkantate* for baritone and string (1956); *Jona ging doch nach Ninive* for baritone, speaking soloists and chorus, mixed chorus, and orch. (1958); *Meditazione su Amadeo Modigliani* for 4 soloists, narrator, chorus, and orch. (1960; Lugano, March 31, 1962); *Die Flucht,* dramatic oratorio (1963–64; Zürich, Nov. 8, 1966); *Hörformen I/II ("Listening Forms")* for orch. (1967–69); *Schritte* for alto and orch. (1968); *Cantique en forme d'un canon à quatre voix* for orch. (1969); *Gli Spaziali* for speakers, vocalists and orch., to words from the writings of Leonardo da Vinci, *Autour de la Lune* by Jules Verne and utterances of the American astronauts (1969–71); *Aus der Einheit—die Vielfalt, in der Vielfalt—die Einheit,* "Hörformen" for piano and string orch. (1973); *Abschied* for string orch. (1973); *Meloformen* for string orch. (1974); *Hommage* for strings (1974); *Musik* for wind quartet and strings (1975); *Composition* for chamber orch. (1976); chamber music: *La Ticinella* for flute, oboe, clarinet, saxophone, and bassoon (1941); *12 Variétudes* for flute, clarinet, violin, and cello (1942); *Inspiré par Jean Arp* for violin, flute, clarinet, and cello (1965); *Analogien,* "Hörformen" for string quartet (1973); *Monophonie* for solo violin (1974); *Für Flöte, Oboe, Klarinette und Fagott* (1974); *Poème* for solo cello (1974); *Terzett* for flute, clarinet, and bassoon (1975); for piano: *Nature vivante,* 6 expressionistic pieces (1917–21); *Einsames Getröpfel und Gewuschel* (1921, revised 1968); *Dai tempi più remoti,* 3 pieces (1922–31, revised 1968); *Etude-Toccata* (1926); *Epitaffio per Alban Berg* (1936); *Klaviereigene Interpretationsstudie einer variierten zwölftonfolge* (1972); *4 Versionen einer Zwölftonfolge* (1972).
BIBLIOGRAPHY: Hans Oesch, *Wladimir Vogel; sein Weg zu einer neuen musikalischen Wirklichkeit* (Bern, 1967).

Vogeleis, Martin, Alsatian music scholar; b. Erstein, June 5, 1861; d. Sélestat, Aug. 11, 1930. He studied for the priesthood, and was ordained in 1885; taught music at the Episcopalian Seminary in Zillesheim (1886–91); then was chaplain and choirmaster in Grafenstaden (1891–96); pastor in Behlenheim (1896–1906); from 1908 was pastor in Schlettstadt (Sélestat). He made a special study of music in Alsace; publ. *Quellen und Bausteine zu einer Geschichte der Musik und des Theaters im Elsass 500–1800* (1911).

Vogelweide, Walther von der, famous German Minnesinger and lyric poet; b. probably in Tyrol, c.1170; d. Würzburg, c.1230. In Wagner's *Tannhäuser* he appears as one of the rival singers at the Wartburg. He led a wandering life; was in Worms in 1198; in Frankfurt in 1212; then in Würzburg. Very few of his melodies are extant; 3 of these were found in the Münster "Bruchstücke" (MS collection of musical fragments from the Middle Ages), including the so-called "Palestine Song" (1228); 5 others are contained in the Colmar Codex and in the "Singebuch" of Adam Puschmann.

BIBLIOGRAPHY: R. Kralik, in the supplement to Mantuani's *Geschichte der Musik in Wein,* vol. 1 (1904); R. Wustmann, "Die Hofweise Walthers von der Vogelweide," in the "Liliencron-Festschrift" (1910); R. Wustmann, *Walther von der Vogelweide* (1912); R. Molitor, "Die Lieder des Münsterischen Fragmentes," *Sammelbände der Internationalen Musik-Gesellschaft* 12 (with fascimiles); R. Wustmann, "Walthers Palästinalied," *Sammelbände der Internationalen Musik-Gesellschaft* 13; F. Ludwig, in Adler's *Handbuch der Musikgeschichte* (Frankfurt, 1924); F. Gennrich, "7 Melodien zu mittelhochdeutschen Minneliedern," *Zeitschrift für Musikwissenschaft* (1924–25); H. J. Moser, *Geschichte der deutschen Musik,* vol. 1 (5th ed., 1928); H. J. Moser, *Gedenkblatt auf Walther von der Vogelweide* (1929); H. Rietsch, in the *Denkmäler der Tonkunst in Österreich* 41 (20.ii); C. Bützler, *Untersuchungen zu den Melodien Walthers von der Vogelweide* (Jena, 1940); H. Böhm, *Walther von der Vogelweide* (Stuttgart, 1949); J. A. Huisman, *Neue Wege zur dichterischen und musikalischen Technik Walthers von der Vogelweide* (dissertation; Utrecht, 1950); K. K. Klein, *Zur Spruchdichtung und Heimatfrage Walthers von der Vogelweide* (Innsbruck, 1952); D. Kralik, *Die Elegie Walthers von der Vogelweide* (Vienna, 1952); F. Maurer, ed., *Die Lieder Walthers von der Vogelweide unter Beifügung erhaltener und erschlossener Melodien,* vol. 1 (Tübingen, 1955).

Vogl, Heinrich, famous German tenor; b. Au, suburb of Munich, Jan. 15, 1845; d. Munich, April 21, 1900. He studied music with Fr. Lachner; made a successful debut as Max in *Der Freischütz* at the Munich Court Opera (Nov. 5, 1865) and remained on its roster until his death. He succeeded Schnorr von Carolsfeld as the model Tristan in Wagner's opera and was for years considered the greatest interpreter of that role. He frequently sang at Bayreuth; created the role of Loge in *Das Rheingold* (1869) and of Siegmund in *Die Walküre* (1870). He was also a composer; wrote an opera, *Der Fremdling,* in which he sang the leading role (Munich, May 7, 1899). In 1868 he married the German

soprano **Therese Thoma** (b. Tutzing, Nov. 12, 1845; d. Munich, Sept. 29, 1921), who sang the part of Isolde with him.

BIBLIOGRAPHY: H. von der Pfordten, *Heinrich Vogl. Zur Erinnerung und zum Vermächtnis* (Munich, 1900); K. Pottgiesser, "Heinrich Vogl," *Allgemeine Musikzeitung* (May 4, 1900).

Vogl, Johann Michael, Austrian baritone; b. Steyr, Aug. 10, 1768; d. Vienna, Nov. 20, 1840. He studied law in Vienna; Süssmayr, then conductor of the Vienna Court Theater, discovered his voice, and persuaded him to join his opera company; Vogl remained on its roster from 1794 until 1822. He was the first professional singer to perform Schubert's songs at concerts.

BIBLIOGRAPHY: A. Liess, *J. M. Vogl, Hofoperist und Schubertsänger* (Graz, 1954).

Vogler, Georg Joseph, Abbé or **Abt,** noted German composer and theorist; b. Würzburg, June 15, 1749; d. Darmstadt, May 6, 1814. The son of a violin maker, he mastered the organ at an early age; studied theology and law at Würzburg and Bamberg. In 1771 he went to Mannheim; there he wrote music for a ballet and gained the favor of the Elector, who provided him with funds for study in Italy. After a brief course in Bologna with Padre Martini, he proceeded to Padua, where he studied composition with Vallotti; but soon left for Rome, and took holy orders in 1773; was made Apostolic Protonotary, Chamberlain to the Pope, Knight of the Golden Spur; also joined the Academy of the Arcadians. In 1775 he returned to Mannheim as court chaplain and 2nd Kapellmeister, and founded there the Mannheimer Tonschule for teaching his own method of composition. In 1780 he followed the Electoral Court to Munich. In 1781 he was in Paris, where he submitted a paper to the Académie Royale des Sciences, *Essai de diriger le goût des amateurs de musique,* an explanation of his system of teaching (publ. Paris, 1782); in Paris he also produced his opera, *La Kermesse* (1783), which was a fiasco. From France he traveled to Spain, Portugal, England, and Denmark. In 1786 he was engaged as court conductor in Stockholm, where he founded a music school; in 1788 he spent some time in St. Petersburg; in 1790 he was in London as organist; after traveling in Poland and Germany, he returned to Stockholm in 1791. In 1794 he went to Paris, and subsequently traveled to Greece and the Near East. From 1796 to 1799 he was again in Sweden, and afterwards visited Copenhagen. In 1800 he went to Berlin; was then in Vienna and Prague. Wherever he went, he solicited interest for his system of organ construction, and exhibited a portable organ called "orchestrion," but was unsuccessful. After spending 2 years in Vienna, where he produced his opera *Samori* (1804), and brief sojourns in various German towns, he finally settled in Darmstadt; established a "Tonschule"; Carl Maria von Weber and Meyerbeer became his pupils there. In teaching, Vogler found his most congenial work; his pedagogical and acoustic writings were also of importance.

WORKS: OPERAS: *Der Kaufmann von Smyrna* (Mannheim, 1771); *Albert III von Bayern* (Munich, 1781), *Erwin und Elmire,* after Goethe (Darmstadt,

1781), *La Kermesse* (Paris, Nov. 15, 1783), *Castore e Polluce* (Munich, Jan. 12, 1787), *Gustav Adolph och Ebba Brahe* (Stockholm, Jan. 24, 1788), *Samori* (Vienna, May 17, 1804). BALLETS: *Rendez-vous de chasse* (Darmstadt, 1772) and *Le Forgeron villageois;* other stage music. SACRED WORKS: many including Masses and a Requiem (his masterpiece); 3 Misereres, motets, Te Deum, Stabat Mater (with orch.), about 50 hymns. INSTRUMENTAL MUSIC: 6 trios for piano, violin, and bass, op. 1; 6 easy sonatas for piano, op. 2; 6 easy sonatas for violin and piano, op. 3; 6 sonatas for 2, 3, and 4 instruments, op. 4; 6 concertos for piano, op. 5; 6 piano trios, op. 6; 6 piano trios, op. 7; 12 divertissements for piano, op. 8; a piano concerto; Nocturne for piano and strings; *Quatuor concertante* for piano, violin, viola, and bass; 6 sonatas for 2 pianos; sonata for piano 4 hands; sonata for piano and strings, called *Der eheliche Zwist; Polymelos, ou caractères de musique des différentes nations,* for piano and strings; other variations on national airs; a set of variations on *Ah que vous dirai-je Maman* for piano with orch.; several symphonies and overtures; 32 preludes for organ in every key (a didactic work).
WRITINGS: *Tonwissenschaft und Tonsetzkunst* (Mannheim, 1776); *Stimmbildungskunst* (Mannheim, 1776); *Churpfälzische Tonschule* (Mannheim, 1778), all 3 republished together as *Mannheimer Tonschule;* a monthly paper, *Betrachtungen der Mannheimer Tonschule* (1778–81); *Inledning til harmoniens kännedom* (Introduction to the Theory of Harmony; Stockholm, 1795); Swedish methods for piano, organ, and thorough bass (Stckholm, 1797); *Choralsystem* (Copenhagen, 1800); *Data zur Akustik* (Offenbach, 1801); *Gründliche Anleitung zum Clavierstimmen* (Stuttgart, 1807); *System für den Fugenbau* (Offenbach, 1811); *Über Choral und Kirchengesänge* (Munich, 1814).
BIBLIOGRAPHY: J. Fröhlich, *Biographie des grossen Tonkünstlers Abt Vogler* (Würzburg, 1845); H. Künzel, *Abt Vogler* (Darmstadt, 1867); E. Pasqué, *Abt Vogler als Tonkünstler, Lehrer und Priester* (Darmstadt, 1884); K. E. von Schafhäutl, *Abt G. J. Vogler, Sein Leben, sein Charakter und musikalisches System* (Augsburg, 1888; with a list of works); M. Brenet, "L'Abbé Vogler à Paris," *Archives historiques artisitques et littéraires* (Feb. 1891); J. Simon, *Abt Voglers kompositorisches Wirken* (Berlin, 1904); E. Rupp, *Abbé Vogler als Mensch, Musiker, und Orgelbautheoretiker* (Ludwigsburg, 1922); P. Vretblad, *Abbé Vogler in Stockholm* (Würzburg, 1924); P. Vretblad, *Abbé Vogler* (1933); H. Kelletat, *Zur Geschichte der deutschen Orgelmusik in der Frühklassik* (Kassel, 1933); H. Schweiger, *Abbé G. J. Voglers Orgellehre* (dissertation; Vienna, 1938); H. Schweiger, "Abt Vogler," *Musical Quarterly* (April 1939).

Vogrich, Max (Wilhelm Karl), pianist and composer; b. Szeben (Hermannstadt), Transylvania, Jan. 24, 1852; d. New York, June 10, 1916. He gave a piano concert at the age of 7; then studied at the Leipzig Cons. with Reinecke and Moscheles; traveled as pianist in Europe, South America, and the U.S.; also toured Australia. In 1886 he settled in N.Y.; then lived in Weimar (1902–08), and in London until 1914, returning to N.Y. at the outbreak of World War I. He wrote several operas to his own librettos; *Vanda* (Florence, 1875), *King Arthur* (Leipzig, Nov. 26, 1893), *Der Buddha* (Weimar, 1904), etc.; an oratorio, *The Captivity* (1884); 2 symphonies; Piano Concerto; several pieces for violin, including a violin concerto subtitled *E pur si muove* (1913); 12 concert studies for piano; *Album of Ancient and Modern Dances* for piano (20 dances, 2 books); anthems; songs. He edited the complete piano works of Schumann, Clementi's *Gradus ad Parnassum* (in progressive order), and other collections.

Vogt, Augustus Stephen, Canadian choral conductor; b. Elmira, Ontario, Aug. 14, 1861; d, Toronto, Sept. 17, 1926. He studied at the New England Cons., and then at the Leipzig Cons. In 1888 settled in Toronto; founded and conducted the Mendelssohn Choir there (1894–97 and 1900–17); toured with it in the U.S.; principal of the Toronto Cons. (1913–26). He was an important figure in music education in Canada; published choral works: *The Sea, Crossing the Bar, An Indian Lullaby, The Lord's Prayer,* etc.; *Standard Anthem Book* (1894) and *Modern Pianoforte Technique* (1900).
BIBLIOGRAPHY: A. Bridle, "Vogt, a Great Chorus Master," *Year Book of Canadian Art* (1913).

Vogt, Gustav, French oboe player and composer; b. Strasbourg, March 18, 1781; d. Paris, May 30, 1870. He studied at the Paris Cons.; was 1st oboist at the Opéra-Comique, and then at the Opéra (1814–34). He taught at the Paris Cons.; wrote 4 oboe concertos; duos for 2 oboes; potpourris and marches for military band.

Vogt, Johann (Jean), German pianist and composer; b. Gross-Tinz, near Liegntiz, Jan. 17, 1823; d. Eberswalde, July 31, 1888. He studied in Berlin and Breslau; taught piano playing in St. Petersburg (1850–55); subsequently lived in Dresden and in Berlin; visited N.Y. (1871–73). He wrote a piano trio, a string quintet, many salon pieces for piano (in all, over 150 opus numbers).

Voigt, Henriette (*née* Kunze), German pianist; b. Leipzig, Nov. 24, 1808; d. there, Oct. 15, 1839. She studied with Ludwig Berger; married the merchant Karl Voigt, whose house was the rendezvous of the most eminent musicians of the time. Schumann dedicated to her his piano sonata in G minor (op. 22).
BIBLIOGRAPHY: "Acht Briefe und ein Faksimile von F. Mendelssohn-Bartholdy" (Leipzig, 1871, English translation in *Macmillan's Magazine,* June 1871); J. Gensel, *Schumanns Briefwechsel mit Henriette Voigt* (Leipzig, 1892); J. Gensel, *Aus Rochlitzens Briefen an Henriette Voigt* (Leipzig, 1906).

Voigt, Johann Georg Hermann, German organist and composer; b. Osterwieck, May 14, 1769; d. Leipzig, Feb. 24, 1811. He served for many years as organist at the Thomaskirche, Leipzig; publ. chamber music and piano pieces.

Volbach, Fritz, German choral conductor and composer; b. Wipperfürth, near Cologne, Dec. 17, 1861; d.

Wiesbaden, Nov. 30, 1940. He studied at the Cologne Cons., with Hiller, Jensen, and Seiss, and in Berlin with Taubert and Löschhorn. In 1891 he was appointed conductor of the Liedertafel and the Damengesangverein in Mainz; brought out many choral works by modern German composers; Dr. phil., Bonn Univ., for the dissertation *Die Praxis der Händel-Aufführung* (publ. 1900). A versatile musician, he had command of almost every orchestral instrument.

WORKS: the symph. poems *Ostern* and *Es waren zwei Königskinder;* Symphony; Piano Quintet; numerous choral works, among them a *Festkantate* for the 5th centenary of the birth of Gutenberg (1900); publ. valuable books: *Lehrbuch der Begleitung des gregorianischen Gesangs* (1888); *Händel* (1898; in Reimann's *Berühmte Musiker*); *Die Zeit des Klassizismus: Beethoven* (1905; 2nd ed., 1929); *Die deutsche Musik im 19. Jahrhundert* (1909); *Das moderne Orchester in seiner Entwickelung* (1910; 2nd ed., 1919); *Die Instrumente des Orchesters* (1913; 2nd ed., 1921); *Handbuch der Musikwissenschaften*, 2 vols. (1926, 1930); *Die Kunst der Sprache* (1929); *Der Chormeister* (1931). A volume of memoirs, *Erlebtes und Erstrebtes*, was publ. posthumously (Mainz, 1956).

BIBLIOGRAPHY: J. Hagemann, "Fritz Volbach," in *Monographien moderner Musiker* (Leipzig, 1909); G. Schwake, *Fritz Volbachs Werke* (Münster, 1921).

Volckmar, Wilhelm Valentin, German organist and composer; b. Hersfeld, Dec. 26, 1812; d. Homberg, near Kassel, Aug. 27, 1887. In 1835 he settled at Homberg, where he taught music and played organ. He wrote several organ concertos, 20 organ sonatas, an organ symphony; publ. *Orgelschule, Schule der Geläufigkeit* for organ, pieces for piano and for violin, hymns, songs.

Volkert, Franz, organist and composer, b. Heimersdorf, Bohemia, Feb. 2, 1767; d. Vienna, March 22, 1845. He was active as organist; was (from 1821) conductor at the Leopoldstadt Theater (Vienna); produced over 100 comic operas, Singspiele, melodramas, farces, etc., many of which were popular; also church music, chamber music, and organ pieces.

Volkmann, Hans, German musicologist; grandnephew of **Robert Volkmann;** b. Bischofswerda, April 29, 1875; d. Dresden, Dec. 26, 1946. He studied German philology and music in Munich and Berlin; undertook research in Italy and France; in 1921 settled in Dresden, where he taught music history; in 1946 became prof. at the Dresden Cons.

WRITINGS: *Neues über Beethoven* (1904); *Emanuel d'Astorga* (2 vols.; 1911; 1919; fundamental and important biography; establishes the verifiable facts of d'Astorga's life); *Beethoven in seinen Beziehungen zu Dresden* (Dresden, 1942). He publ. the standard biography of Robert Volkmann (Leipzig, 1903; abridged ed., 1915); ed. *Briefe von Robert Volkmann* (1917), and compiled a *Thematisches Verzeichnis der Werke von Robert Volkmann* (Dresden, 1937).

Volkmann, Robert (complete name **Friedrich Robert Volkmann**), significant German composer; b. Lommatzsch, April 6, 1815; d. Budapest, Oct. 29, 1883. He studied with his father, a cantor (organ and piano); with Friebel (violin and cello) and Anacker (composition); then in Leipzig with K. F. Becker; was greatly encouraged by Schumann. After teaching music in Prague (1839–42), he settled in Budapest, where he spent the rest of his life, except 4 years (1854–58) in Vienna. In 1875 he was appointed prof. at the National Academy of Music in Budapest. His music was regarded very highly in his lifetime, but after his death it faded into oblivion; however, several publications dealing with his works, including a thematic index, were brought out by his grand-nephew, **Hans Volkmann.**

WORKS: 2 symphonies; 3 serenades for strings; 2 overtures; Cello Concerto; 6 string quartets; 2 piano trios; *Konzertstück* for piano and orch.; *Chant du Troubadour* for violin and piano; *Allegretto capriccioso* for violin and piano; 2 violin sonatinas; *Konzertstück* for piano and orch.; *Romanze* for cello and piano; *Capriccio* for cello and piano; *Schlummerlied* for harp, clarinet, and horn (also arranged for piano, viola and cello; his last completed work). For piano solo: *Phantasiebilder, Dithyrambe und Toccate, Souvenir de Maróth, Nocturne,* Sonata in C minor, *Buch der Lieder, Deutsche Tanzweisen, Cavatine und Barcarole, Visegrád,* 4 marches, *Wanderskizzen, Fantasie, Intermezzo, Variations* on a theme of Handel, *Lieder der Grossmutter,* 3 *Improvisations, Am Grab des Grafen Széchenyi, Ballade und Scherzetto,* transcriptions of songs by Mozart and Schubert, etc. For piano 4 hands: *Musikalisches Bilderbuch, Ungarische Skizzen, Die Tageszeiten,* 3 marches, *Rondino und Marsch-Caprice;* transcriptions of his other works. Vocal works: 2 Masses for male chorus, 5 sacred songs for mixed chorus; offertories; Christmas carol of the 12th century; old German hymn for double male chorus; 6 duets on old German poems; alto solo with orch., *An die Nacht;* dramatic scene for soprano and orch., *Sappho; Kirchenarie,* for bass, flute, and strings; *Weihnacht,* for female chorus; *Im Wiesengrün,* for mixed chorus; etc.

BIBLIOGRAPHY: B. Vogel, *Robert Volkmann* (Leipzig, 1875); H. Volkmann, *Robert Volkmann. Sein Leben und seine Werke* (Leipzig, 1903; standard biography; abridged ed., 1915); C. Preiss, *Robert Volkmann. Kritische Beiträge zu seinem Schaffen* (Graz, 1912); V. von Herzfeld, "Robert Volkmann," *Musical Quarterly* (July 1915).

Volkonsky, Andrei, Russian composer; b. Geneva, of Russian parents of princely nobility, Feb. 14, 1933. He studied piano with Dinu Lipatti in Geneva and composition with Nadia Boulanger in Paris. In 1947 he went to Russia, where he studied music theory with Shaporin at the Moscow Cons. (1950–54). In 1955 he was a co-founder with Barshai of the Moscow Chamber Orch.; then devoted himself to harpsichord playing; in 1964 he organized in Moscow a concert group "Madrigal," with which he gave annual series of highly successful concerts in the Soviet Union, East Germany, and Czechoslovakia. His early works were set in evocative Impressionistic colors, in the manner of the French modern school, but soon he deployed a serial technique of composition, analogous to Schoenberg's method of composition with 12 tones outside traditional tonality. He was outspoken in his criticism of the direction that Soviet music was taking and he entirely rejected the official tenets of Socialist Realism. This attitude and the nature of his own music resulted in the cancellation of performances of his works; he was expelled from the Union of Soviet Composers, and could no longer give concerts. In 1973 he left Russia, and returned to Switzerland.

WORKS: the cantatas *Rus* (Russia), after Gogol (1952) and *The Image of the World* (Moscow, May 8, 1953); Concerto for Orchestra (Moscow, June 10, 1954); *Capriccio* for orch.; Piano Quintet (1954); String Quartet (1955); Piano Sonata (1956); *Musica stricta* for piano (1956); *2 Japanese Songs* for chorus, electronic sound, and percussion (1957); *Music* for 12 instruments (1957); *Serenade to an Insect* for chamber orch. (1959); *Suite des miroirs* for soprano, organ, guitar, violin, flute, and percussion (1960); Viola Sonata (1960); *The Lament of Shaza* for soprano and small orch. (1961; Moscow, May 12, 1965); *Jeux à 3* for flute, violin, and harpsichord (1962); *Concerto itinérant* for soprano, violin, percussion, and 26 instruments (1967); *Réplique* for small orch. (1969); *Les Mailles du temps* for 3 instrumental groups (1969); some music for plays.

Volkov, Feodor, Russian musician; b. Kostroma, Feb. 19, 1729; d. St. Petersburg, April 14, 1763. He was educated in Yaroslavl, where he organized a theatrical group, which presented performances of plays with music. In 1754 he entered a military school in St. Petersburg; in 1759 he was sent to Moscow, where he was in charge of the spectacles accompanying the coronation of Catherine II (1763). Volkov was an able practical musician, even though he totally lacked professional training. His supposed authorship of the comic opera *Taniusha, or A Happy Encounter* (1756) is extremely doubtful; in fact, the existence of such an opera has never been proved. Volkov's role in the early history of the Russian musical stage is confined to his activities as an organizer,.

BIBLIOGRAPHY: V. Tcheshikhin, *History of Russian Opera from 1674 to 1903* (St. Petersburg, 1905; pp. 57-60).

Vollerthun, Georg, German composer and conductor; b. Fürstenau, Sept. 29, 1876; d. Strausberg (near Berlin), Sept. 15, 1945. He studied with Tappert, Radecke, and Gernsheim; was theater conductor in Prague, Berlin, Barmen, and Mainz (1899-1905); spent 3 years in Paris (1908-10); then settled in Berlin as music critic and teacher; from 1922 lived mostly in Strausberg.

WORKS: the operas *Veeda* (Kassel, 1916), *Island-Saga* (Munich, Jan. 17, 1925), *Der Freikorporal* (Hannover, Nov. 10, 1931; his most successful opera; also given in Berlin, June 10, 1933); and *Das königliche Opfer* (Hannover, 1942); *Alt-Danzig Suite* for orch. (1938); cantatas and other vocal works; many German songs.

BIBLIOGRAPHY: E. Krieger, *Georg Vollerthun* (Berlin, 1942).

Voloshinov, Victor, Soviet composer; b. Kiev, Oct. 17, 1905; d. Leningrad, Oct. 22, 1960. He studied composition with Stcherbatchev at the Leningrad Cons.;

later became a prof. there. He wrote the operas *Glory* (1939) and *Stronger Than Death* (1942); several symph. suites on Central Asian themes; chamber music; songs; incidental music for the theater. He enjoyed great renown as a pedagogue; many Soviet composers were his students.

Volpe, Arnold, Russian-American conductor; b. Kovno, Lithuania, July 9, 1869; d. Miami, Florida, Feb. 2, 1940. He studied with Leopold Auer at the St. Petersburg Cons. (1887-91), and composition there with Soloviev (1893-97). In 1898 he emigrated to America, settling in N.Y.; in 1902 founded the Young Men's Symph. Orch. of N.Y., which he conducted until 1919; also conducted a group called the Volpe Symph. Orch. (1904-14). In 1918 he organized the summer concerts at the Lewisohn Stadium in N.Y., and conducted for a few seasons there; then moved to Washington, D.C., where he was musical director of the Washington, D.C., Opera Co. (1919-22); subsequently was director of the Kansas City Cons. (1922-25); in 1926 he went to Florida where he organized the Univ. of Miami Symph. Orch. He composed some chamber music and many songs to English words.

BIBLIOGRAPHY: Marie Volpe (his widow), *Arnold Volpe. Bridge between Two Musical Worlds* (Coral Gables, Florida, 1950).

Vomáčka, Boleslav, Czech composer; b. Mladá Boleslav, June 28, 1887; d. Prague, March 1, 1965. He studied law at the Charles Univ. in Prague (LL.D., 1913); took music courses with Vítězslav Novák (1909-10); was in the service of the Labor Ministry in Prague (1919-50); wrote music criticism in several newspapers there; was editor of *Listy Hudební Matice* (1922-35). He began to compose early in life; developed a strong national style of composition.

WORKS: operas, *Vodník (The Water Spirit,* 1934-37; Prague, Dec. 17, 1937), *Boleslav I* (1955; Prague, March 8, 1957), and *Čekanky (Waiting for a Husband,* 1956); an oratorio, *Živi Mrtvým (The Living to the Dead,* 1927-28; Prague, Feb. 24, 1929); the cantatas, *Romance Svatojirská (Romance of St. George,* 1922-43), *Strážce majáku (The Keeper of the Lighthouse,* 1931-33), *The Partisan Bojka* (1952), and *Under the Banner of Communism* (1959); *Vlastenecké zpěvy (Patriotic Hymns)* for chorus and orch. (1939); *1914,* cycle of 5 songs with orch. (1919-20); *Cesta z bojiště (The Return from the Battlefield),* cycle of 5 songs with orch. (1922-28); *Mladi (Youth),* symph. poem with chorus (1914-16); *Czech Eroica,* a symphony (1944-46); *Dukla,* overture (1948); *Fanfáry míru (Fanfares of Peace),* 3 pieces for trumpet and orch. (1960); Violin Sonata (1912); *Quartettino* for strings (1941); Nonet for wind instruments (1957); String Quartet (1959); 2 piano sonatas (1917; *Sonata quasi fantasia,* 1942); piano pieces; *S.O.S.* for male chorus (1927); *Balada o snu (Ballad of a dream)* for mixed chorus (1933); many part-songs.

BIBLIOGRAPHY: H. Doležil, *Boleslav Vomáčka* Prague, 1941).

Von Blon, Franz, German composer and conductor; b. Berlin, July 16, 1861; d. there, Oct. 21, 1945. He studied in Berlin at the Stern Cons.; was active as conductor in Warsaw and Berlin; wrote several operettas (*Sub rosa, Die Amazone, Die tolle Prinzess,* etc.) and much light music for piano; also a number of military marches, of which one, *Unter dem Siegesbanner,* became extremely popular.

Von der Hoya, Amadeo, American violinist; b. New York, March 13, 1874; d. Linz, Austria, April 4, 1922. He studied violin in Berlin; concertmaster of the Vienna Opera (1894–96); in 1901 appointed concertmaster of the Musikverein in Linz. He publ. *Grundlagen der Violintechnik,* a valuable method; also *Moderne Lagenstudien für Violine* and *Studienbrevier.*

Voormolen, Alexander Nicolas, Dutch composer; b. Rotterdam, March 3, 1895. He studied with Johan Wagenaar at the Utrecht School of Music; went to Paris in 1916, where he took lessons with Albert Roussel; returned to Holland in 1923 and was active as a music critic; served as librarian of the Royal Cons. of The Hague (1938–55).
WORKS: 4 ballets: *Le Roi Grenouille* (1916; withdrawn), *Baron Hop* in 2 suites (1923–24, 1931), *Diana* (1935–36) and *Spiegel-Suite* for small orch. to Langendijk's play (1943); *De drie Ruitertjes (The 3 Little Horsemen),* variations on a Dutch song, for orch. (1927); *Een Zomerlied* for orch. (1928); Oboe Concerto (1938); *Sinfonia* (1939); *Kleine Haagsche Suite* for small orch. (1939); *Pastorale* for oboe and string orch. (1940); Cello Concerto (1941); *Arethuza,* symph. myth after Dutch novelist L. Couperus (1947); *La Sirène* for solo saxophone and orch. (1949); Concerto for 2 harpsichords or pianos, and orch. (1950); *Sinfonia concertante* for clarinet, horn, and string orch. (1951); *Eline,* nocturne for orch. (1957; orchestrated and enlarged version of the 1951 piano piece); *Chaconne en Fuga* for orch. (1958); 2 violin sonatas (1917, 1934); *Suite* for cello and piano (1917); Piano Trio (1918); *Suite* for harpsichord (1921); *Divertissement* for cello and piano (1922); 2 string quartets (1939, 1942); Viola Sonata (1935); for piano: *Valse triste* (1914); *Suite* No. 1 (1914–16); *Falbalas* (1915); *Eléphants* (1919); *Tableaux des Pays Bas,* in 2 series (1919–20; 1924); *Scène et danse érotique* (1920); *Le Souper clandestin* (1921); *Sonnet* (1922); *Livre des enfants,* in 2 series (1923, 1925); *Berceuse* (1924); Sonata (1944); *Eline,* nocturne (1951); for voice: *Beatrijs,* melodrama for narrator and piano (1921); *Drie Gedichten* for voice and orch. (1932); *Een nieuwe Lente op Holland's erf* for voice and orch. (1936); *Herinneringen aan Holland (Memories of Holland)* for baritone, bass clarinet, and strings (1966); *Stanzas of Charles II* for baritone, flute, English horn, celesta, percussion, and strings (1966); cantata *Amsterdam* (1967); *From: The Recollection* for medium voice, string orch., and celesta (1970); *Ex minimis patet ipse Deus,* hymn for middle voice, strings, and celesta (1971; exists in many alternate versions); *Ave Maria* for chorus, harp, and string orch. (1973; exists in many alternate versions); songs and choruses to Dutch, German and French texts.
BIBLIOGRAPHY: Cor Backers, *Nederlandse Componisten van 1400 tot op onze Tijd* (The Hague, 1949); pp. 141–47); Eduard Reeser, "Alexander Voormolen," *Sonorum Speculum* 22-23 (1965).

Voorn, Joop (Josephus Hermanus Maria), Dutch composer; b. The Hague, Oct. 16, 1932. He studied at the Brabant Cons. and since 1969 has taught there. He composed *Cyclus* for organ (1967); *Psalm CXIV—In Exitu* for soprano, children's chorus, and orch. (1968); *Ludi ed Interludi* for piano (1969); 2 string quartets (No. 2, 1970); *Nakupenda,* trio for flute, violin, and viola (1971); *Soft Music for Angela* for solo flute (1973); *Immobile: Music for Tutankhamun* for orch. (Brabant, Dec. 2, 1975); *Sucevita chorals* for 2 oboes, 2 clarinets, bass clarinet, and bassoon (1974); Trio for oboe, clarinet, and bassoon (1974); *Petit concert de printemps* for flute and strings (1975; Brabant, April 25, 1976); *Prelude and Fugue,* quintet for piano, oboe, clarinet, horn, and bassoon (1975–76).

Vopelius, Gottfried, German composer; b. Herwigsdorf, near Zittau, Jan. 28, 1635; d. Leipzig, Feb. 3, 1715. He was cantor of St. Nicholas at Leipzig from 1675; harmonized old German hymns and publ. a *Neu Leipziger Gesangbuch* (1682), containing 100 hymns originally brought out in Schein's *Cantional oder Gesangbuch* (1627).

Voříšek, Jan Hugo. See **Worzischek, Johann Hugo.**

Vorlová, Sláva, Czech composer; b. Náchod, March 15, 1894; d. Prague, Aug. 24, 1973. She studied piano with her mother and composition with Vítězslav Novák in Prague. The war interrupted her musical studied; resumed her composition after the end of the Nazi occupation of Czechoslovakia. She became interested in writing music for instruments rarely used for solo performances; she wrote one of the few concertos for bass clarinet. Her music is tinted with impressionistic colors.
WORKS: 4 operas: *Zlaté ptáče (The Golden Bird;* 1949–50), *Rozmarýnka (Rosemary,* 1952; Kladno, 1955), *Náchodská Kasace (The Náchod Cassation,* 1955) and *Dva světy (Two Worlds,* 1958); *Fantasy* for cello and orch. (1940); *Symphony JM,* dedicated to Jan Masaryk (1947–48); *Songs of Gondwana,* symph. epos with soloists and chorus (1948–49); *Božena Němcová,* suite in 8 parts (1950–51); Oboe Concerto (1952); Trumpet Concerto (1953); Viola Concerto (1954); Clarinet Concerto (1957); Flute Concerto (1959); Concerto for bass clarinet and strings (1961); Concerto for oboe and harp (1963); Concerto for double bass and strings (1968); *3 Bohemian Dances* for orch. (1952–53); *The Gamekeeper's Wife,* melodramatic triptych (1960); *Memento* for orch. (1957); *Thuringian Dances* for orch. (1957); *Kybernetic Studies* for orch. (1962); *Dedications* for orch. (1965); *Bhukhar (Fever Birds)* for orch. (1965); *Model Kinetic,* ballet music (1966); *Correlations* for bass clarinet, piano, and strings (1968); *Polarization* for harp, wind orch., and percussion (1970); *Emergence* for violin and orch. (1973; posthumous, Prague, March 24, 1974); String Quartet (1939); Nonet (1944); *Melodious Variations* for string quartet (1950); *Puzzles* for 2 pianos (1953); *Miniatures* for bass clarinet and piano (1962); *Dessins Tetraharpes* for 4 harps (1963); *2 African Fables* for narrator, alto flute, and percussion (1964); *Variations on a Theme by Handel* for bass clarinet and piano (1965); *6 pro 5* for brass quintet (1967); *Immanence*

for bass clarinet, piano, and percussion (1970); *Brief Considerations* for soprano, alto, and piano (1971); songs.

Voss, Charles, German pianist; b. Schmarsow, Sept. 20, 1815; d. Verona, Aug. 29, 1882. He studied in Berlin, but made his career in Paris, where he went in 1846; enjoyed great success in Paris society as pianist and composer; publ. a great number of salon pieces, transcriptions, paraphrases, etc.; also wrote piano concertos and études. His First Piano Concerto, in F minor, was praised by Mendelssohn.

Voss (Vossius), Isaac, music theorist; b. Leyden, Holland, 1618; d. Windsor, England, Feb. 21, 1689. He was the son of the German scholar Gerhard Johann Voss (1577–1649), who lived in Holland. After his father's death, he went to Stockholm, where he was at the court of Queen Christina (1649–52); subsequently went to England, where he remained till his death. He published an important treatise in Latin, *De poematum cantu et viribus rythmi* (1673).

Vostřák, Zbynek, Czech composer and conductor; b. Prague, June 10, 1920. He studied composition privately with Rudolf Karel (1938–43); attended the conducting classes of Pavel Dědeček at the Prague Cons. In 1963 he became conductor of the Prague chamber ensemble, Musica Viva Pragensis; worked in an electronic music studio in Prague. His music evolved from the Central European type of modernism; later he annexed serial techniques, electronic sound, and aleatory practices.
WORKS: operas, *Rohovín Čtverrohý (The 4-Horned Rohovin,* 1947–48; Olomouc, 1949); *Kutnohorští havíři (The King's Master of the Mint,* 1951–53; Prague, 1955); *Pražské nokturno (A Prague Nocturne,* 1957–58; Ústí-on-the-Elbe, 1960); *Rozbitý džbán (The Broken Jug)* (1960–61; Prague, 1963); 4 ballets: *The Primrose* (1944–45), *Filosofská historie (A Story of Students of Philosophy,* 1949), *Viktorka (Little Victoria,* 1950) and *Sněhurka (Snow White,* 1955); *Serenade* for small orch. (1940); *Prague Overture* (1941); *Zrození měsíce (The Birth of the Moon)* for chamber orch. (Prague, March 8, 1967); *Kyvadlo času (The Pendulum of Time)* for cello, 4 instrumental groups, and electric organ (1966–67; Donaueschingen, Oct. 19, 1968); *Metahudba (Metamusic)* for orch. (1968; Prague, March 2, 1970); *Tajemství elipsy (The Secret of Ellipsis)* for orch. (1970; Prague, March 5, 1971); *3 Sonnets after Shakespeare* for bass and chamber orch. (1963); *Cantata,* to words by Kafka, for chorus, winds, and percussion (1964); *Burlesque* for clarinet and piano (1945); *Contrasts* for string quartet (1961); *Crystallizations* for 12 winds (1962); *Recollection* for solo violin (1962); *Affects* for 7 instruments (1963); *Elements* for string quartet (1964); *Synchronia* for 6 instruments (1965); *Trigonum* for violin, oboe, and piano (1965); *Tao,* cards for 9 players (1967); *Kosmogonia* for string quartet (1968); *Sextant* for wind quintet (1969); *Concomitances* for percussionist and tape (1971); *3 Essays* for piano (1962); the tape pieces, *2 Foci* (1969), *Telepathy* (1969); *7 Thresholds* (1970) and *The Net of Silence* (1971).

Votapek, Ralph, American pianist; b. Milwaukee, March 20, 1939. He studied at the Wisconsin Cons. in his hometown; then took piano lessons at the Manhattan School of Music and the Juilliard School of Music, N.Y., where his principal teachers were Rosina Lhévinne and Robert Goldsand. He won the Van Cliburn International Competition for pianists in 1962, and then embarked on a successful career as a soloist, in recital, and with orchestras; played in major cities of the U.S.; made 7 tours of South America; in 1975 played engagements in Russia. He settled in East Lansing, Michigan, as artist-in-residence at Michigan State Univ., and continued his concert career.

Vranken, Jaap, Dutch organist and composer; b. Utrecht, April 16, 1897; d. The Hague, April 20, 1956. He was the son of the organist **Joseph Vranken** (1870–1948), with whom he studied organ and theory. In 1916–18 he was in the U.S., studying with Percy Goetschius. He returned to Holland in 1920, and was appointed organist at the church of St. Anthonius in The Hague; acquired a fine reputation as a teacher. He composed mostly sacred music; also instrumental music in classical style; publ. a manual on counterpoint (1948). His last work was a *Missa Polyphonica* (1953).

Vredenburg, Max, Belgian-born Dutch composer; b. Brussels, Jan. 16, 1904, of Dutch parents; d. Laren, Holland, Aug. 9, 1976. He was taken to Holland as a child and received elementary musical education there; in 1926 went to Paris and studied at the École Normale with Paul Dukas; was a music correspondent for a Rotterdam newspaper; at the outbreak of World War II, he was sent by the Dutch government to Java, where he was interned by the Japanese (1942–45); but he was allowed to organize concerts in Indonesia with a fellow internee, the violinist Szymon Goldberg; returned to Holland after the end of the war and settled in Amsterdam; in 1953 succeeded Sem Dresden as director of the Dutch section of Jeunesses Musicales. In 1957 he established the National Youth Orchestra, which he led until his death.
WORKS: *Au Pays des Vendanges,* wind quintet (1951); *Oboe Concerto* (1951); *Akiba* for mezzo-soprano and chamber orch. (1951); *Du Printemps* for mezzo-soprano and chamber orch. (1952); *Lamento* for viola and piano (1953); *Suite dansante* for youth orch. (1956); *Horizons hollandaises* for orch. (1959); Trio for oboe, clarinet, and bassoon (1965). He published a book, *Langs de vijf Lijnen* (1947).

Vretblad, Viktor Patrik, Swedish organist and musicologist; b. Svartnäs, April 5, 1876; d. Stockholm, Jan. 15, 1953. He studied at the Stockholm Cons. (1895–1900) and later in Berlin; wrote music criticism; acted as church organist; was an official of the Ministry of the Postal Services for 40 years (1900–40). He devoted his research mainly to early Swedish music; publ. basic biographies of J. H. Roman (Stockholm, 1914 and 1945); *Konsertlivet i Stockholm under 1700-talet* (1918); *A. Hallén* (1918); *Abbé Vogler* (1933).

Vreuls, Victor, Belgian composer; b. Verviers, Feb. 4, 1876; d. Brussels, July 27, 1944. He studied at the Cons. in Verviers; later took harmony lessons with Sylvain Dupuis and counterpoint with J. T. Radoux at the Cons. in Liège. He then went to Paris, where he took a course with d'Indy at the Schola Cantorum; from 1906 to 1926 held the post of director of the Luxembourg Cons.

WORKS: 2 operas: *Olivier le simple* (1909-11; Brussels, March 9, 1922) and *Un Songe d'une nuit d'été,* after Shakespeare (1923-24; Brussels, Dec. 17, 1925); a ballet, *Le Loup-garou (The Werewolf,* 1935; Ghent, 1937); 3 symph. poems: *Cortège heroïque* (1894), *Jour de fête* (1904) and *Werther* (1907); Symphony with solo violin (1899); 2 *Poèmes* for cello and orch. (1900, 1930); *Élégie* for flute and chamber orch. (1917); *Morceau de concert* for trumpet and orch. (1917); *Fantaisie* for horn and orch. (1918); *Romance* and *Caprice* for violin and chamber orch. (both 1924); *Suite de danses* for orch. (1939); *Ouverture pour un drame* (1940); Piano Quartet (1894); Piano Trio (1896); 2 violin sonatas (1899, 1919); String Quartet (1918); Cello Sonata (1922); choruses; songs.

Vriend, Jan, Dutch composer; b. Sijbekarspel, Nov. 10, 1938. He studied piano and music theory with Ton de Leeuw at the Amsterdam Cons.; attended a course in electronic music given by G. M. Koenig at the Institute of Sonology at the Utrecht Univ. (1966-67) and a series of lectures on "formalization in music" given by Xenakis at the Schola Cantorum in Paris (1968). He taught theory and conducted ensembles for contemporary music at the Utrecht Cons. (1968-69). He builds his musical thematics on the theories of Xenakis, involving probabilities and stochastic teleologies.

WORKS: *Four 12-Tone Studies* for piano (1960); *Pour le flûte* for solo flute (1961); String Quartet (1962-63); *Paroesie for* 10 instruments (1963); *Mater-Muziek* for 65 performers and electronic sound (1966); *Diamant,* subtitled "a symphony for the Earth," for orch. (1964-67); *Transformation (on the way to Halleluja)* for chorus and orch. (1965-67); *Huantan* for organ and 28 wind instruments in 4 groups (1967-68); *Introitus (Hommage to Ton de Leeuw)* for chorus, 6 clarinets, 2 bass clarinets and 4 trombones (1969); *Bau* for small orch. (1970); *Elements of Logic* for wind orch. (in collaboration with Jos Kunst, 1972; Scheveningen, Feb. 25, 1973); *Kri* for chorus and chamber ensemble (1975).

Vrieslander, Otto, German composer and writer on music; b. Münster, July 18, 1880; d. Tegna, Switzerland, Dec. 16, 1950. After attending the Cologne Cons. he went to Munich in 1904; in 1911-12, he was in Vienna, where he studied with Heinrich Schenker, becoming one of his disciples. From 1912 he lived in Ebertsberg, near Munich; in 1929 settled in Switzerland. He wrote some highly expressive song cycles (*Lieder aus des Knaben Wunderhorn, Pierrot lunaire,* etc.); edited works by C. P. E. Bach, six of whose symphonies he arranged for piano 4 hands; publ. various studies on him: *Ph. E. Bachs Klavierstücke für Anfänger mit kompositionstechnischer Analyse* (1914); *Lieder und Gesänge von Ph. E. Bach nebst Einleitung* (1922); "Ph. E. Bach als Klavierkomponist," in *Gany-*

med (Dresden, 1922); *Ph. E. Bach* (1923); "Ph. E. Bach als Theoretiker," in *Von neuer Musik* (1925).

Vrionides, Christos, conductor; b. Khania, Crete, Jan. 12, 1894; d. Yaphank, Long Island, N.Y., Dec. 31, 1961. He studied in Athens at the Odeon, and taught theory and double bass there (1920-22); then came to the U.S.; studied at the Institute of Musical Art, N.Y. (graduated 1929); conducted the Vrionides Sinfonietta in N.Y. (1929-35); also led the Byzantine Vocal Ensemble (1924-38); taught Greek liturgy in N.Y. and Boston. His musical settings of the liturgy of the Greek Orthodox Church have been accepted in Greek churches in the U.S. and South America.

Vronsky, Vitya (real name **Victoria Vronsky**), pianist; b. Evpatoria, Crimea, Aug. 22, 1909; studied at the Kiev Cons.; then with Petri and Schnabel in Berlin, and with Cortot in Paris. She married the pianist **Victor Babin** on Aug. 31, 1933; came to America in 1937; toured widely with Babin in 2-piano recitals.

Vroye, Théodore-Joseph de, Belgian music scholar; b. Villers-la-Ville, Aug. 19, 1804; d. Liège, July 19, 1873. He entered the priesthood in 1828, and in 1835 became canon of the Liège Cathedral. He made a profound study of Gregorian Chant; publ. *Vesperal* (1829); *Graduel* (1831); *Traité du plain-chant à l'usage des séminaires* (1839); *Manuale cantorum* (1849); *Processionale* (1849); *Rituale Romanum* (1862); *De la musique religieuse* (1866; with Elewyck).

Vuataz, Roger, Swiss composer and organist; b. Geneva, Jan. 4, 1898. He studied with Otto Barblan and Jaques-Dalcroze at the Geneva Cons.; was a church organist for over fifty years in Geneva (1917-73); and a music critic there (1940-60); was director of musical programming at Radio Geneva (1961-71); taught at the Geneva Cons. (1962-69); conducted choruses.

WORKS: an opera-buffa, *Monsieur Jabot* (Geneva, Nov. 28, 1958); 3 ballets: *Le Rhône* for chorus and orch. (1929), *Poème méditerranéen pour un ballet* for orch. (1938-50) and *Solitude* for orch. (1962); radiophonic pieces; *Genève ouverte au ciel,* "évocation lyrique" in 5 pictures for tenor, narrator, 3 choruses, orch. and organ (1941); 2 oratorios: *Abraham* (1927, revised 1936) and *Jésus* (1949); *Suite symphonique* (1925); *8 Poèmes d'Orient* for soprano and orch. (1925); *Petit concert* for orch. (1932); *Triptych* for orch. (1929-42); *Images de Grèce,* symphony (1938-39); *Nocturne and Dance* for trumpet and orch. (1940); *4 Rondeaux de Charles d'Orléans* for soprano and orch. (1946-61); Violin Concerto (1948); *Epopée antique,* 2 suites for orch. (1947-51); *Estampes genevoises,* suite for orch. (1959); Piano Concerto (1964); *Fantaisies I-III,* concerto for harp and orch. (1973); *Images poétiques et pathétiques,* for cello and orch. (1977); Cello Sonata (1928); 2 suites for solo Ondes Martenot (1930); Violin Sonatina (1933-34); *Musique* for wind quintet (1937-61); *Frivolités,* suite for sextet (1952); *Destin,* "symphonie à trois" for saxophone, harp and percussion (1954); Flute Sonata (1948-54); *Thrène* for horn and piano (1960); String Quartet (1970); *Nocturnes,* for solo cello (1974); piano pieces.

Vučković, Vojislav, Serbian composer; b. Pirot, Oct. 18, 1910; d. Belgrade (killed by German police), Dec. 25, 1942. He studied in Prague with J. Suk and Zdeněk Nejedlý. Returning to Belgrade in 1934, he displayed energetic activity as composer, conductor, publicist and writer on economic subjects; publ. pamphlets on materialistic interpretation of music in the light of Marxist dialectics. He was in the resistance movement during the German occupation, and was killed by the Nazis in the street.

WORKS: 2 symphonies; a symph. poem, *Burevesnik (Stormy Petrel;* 1942; Belgrade, Dec. 25, 1944); *Heroic Oratorio* (1942; Cetinje, Spet. 5, 1951); chamber music; choruses. After a period of composition in the Expressionistic manner (including the application of quarter-tones) he abruptly changed his style out of ideological considerations to programmatic realism.

BIBLIOGRAPHY: V. Peričić, ed., *Vojislav Vučković, Umetnik i borac* (2 vols., Belgrade, 1968).

Vuillaume, Jean-Baptiste, celebrated French violin maker; b. Mirecourt, Oct. 7, 1798; d. Paris, Feb. 19, 1875. He came of a family of violin makers, and learned the trade from his father, **Claude Vuillaume** (1772–1834). At 19 he went to Paris and worked with Chanot till 1821, and from 1821–25 for Lété, with whom he then entered into partnership. After Lété's retirement in 1828, Vuillaume worked alone, and put his own name on several instruments which he had constructed with the greatest care and fine craftsmanship; but he was unable to overcome the general distrust of the native product, and began manufacturing imitations of Italian instruments. After long and patient labor he placed a "Stradivarius" violin on the market for 300 francs, bearing the master's label, and possessing a full, sonorous tone; also built a cello priced at 500 francs. The sight of a Duiffoprugcar viola da gamba inspired him with the idea of further imitations; hence the hundreds of "Duiffoprugcar" violins and cellos with their quaint shape, carved scrolls, inlays, and the motto "viva fui in sylvis, etc." By dint of indefatigable researches and experiments, Vuillaume carried the construction of these various instruments to the highest perfection. His own inventions were numerous: in 1849 the huge "Octobasse," a double bass 4 meters in length, 3-stringed (CC–GG–C), with a special lever-mechanism to aid the left hand (an "octobasse" is in the Museum of the Paris Cons.); in 1855 a viola, which he called the "contre-alto," with greater strength of tone, but clumsy to play; in 1867 a kind of mute, the "pédale sourdine"; also a machine for manufacturing gut strings of perfectly equal thickness. He likewise formulated the laws governing the tapering of the stick of the Tourte bow.

BIBLIOGRAPHY: R. Millant, *Jean-Baptiste Vuillaume, sa vie et son œuvre* (London, 1972; in French, English, and German).

Vuillermoz, Émile, French music critic; b. Lyons, May 23, 1878; d. Paris, March 2, 1960. He studied organ and piano in Lyons, and composition at the Paris Cons. with Fauré. He was one of the organizers of the Société Musicale Indépendante (1911) and edited the *Revue Musicale S. I. M.;* eventually became music critic of the daily *L'Excelsior* and also contributed articles to *Le Temps.* He publ. *Musiques d'aujourd'hui* (1923), *La Vie amoureuse de Chopin* (1927), and *Histoire de la musique* (Paris, 1949; revised and completed by Jacques Lonchampt, 1973); *Gabriel Fauré* (Paris, 1960; in English, Philadelphia, 1969); *Claude Debussy* (Geneva, 1967).

Vuillermoz, Jean, French composer; b. Monte Carlo, Dec. 29, 1906; d. Lobsonn, Alsace, June 21, 1940 (killed while on patrol duty in the last hours before Franco-German armistice). He studied with Busser and Rabaud at the Paris Cons.; received 2nd Prix de Rome for his cantata *Le Pardon* (1932).

WORKS: *Triptique* for orch. (Paris, May 31, 1932); Concerto for French horn and orch. (Paris, March 11, 1934); a ballet, *Veglione* (1937); Cello Concerto; *Promenade zoologique* for chamber orch.; Piano Trio; String Trio.

Vukdragović, Mihailo, Serbian composer; b. Okučani, Nov. 8, 1900. He studied in Prague; in 1927 returned to Belgrade and was active as conductor and pedagogue. He wrote several works in Impressionistic style before embracing the esthetics of socialist realism.

WORKS: symph. poem *Put u pobedu (Road to Victory;* Belgrade, Oct. 19, 1945); cantata *Vezilja slobode (Champion of Freedom;* Belgrade, Jan. 5, 1948); cantata for bass, speaker, chorus and orch., *Srbija (Serbia;* Niš, July 6, 1961); 2 String Quartets (1925, 1944).

BIBLIOGRAPHY: V. Peričić, *Muzički Stvaraoci u Srbiji* (Belgrade, 1969; pp. 582–90).

Vulpius (Latinized form of real name, **Fuchs**), **Melchior,** German composer; b. Wasungen, c.1570; d. Weimar, 1615 (buried Aug. 7). From 1596 to his death, he was cantor in Weimar.

WORKS: 2 books of *Cantiones sacrae* (1602, 2nd ed., 1603; and 1604, 2nd ed., 1611); *Kirchengesänge und geistliche Lieder* for 4 and 5 voices (1604); *Canticum beatissimae Virginis Mariae,* for 4–8 voices (1605); *Lateinische Hochzeitstücke* (1608); *Opusculum cantionum sacrarum,* for 4–6 voices (1610); *Das Leiden und Sterben unseres Herrn* (Passion after Matthew; 1613); 3 books of *Sonntägliche Evangelische Sprüche* for 4 voices (1619, 1620, 1621); also a new ed. of Heinrich Faber's *Compendiolum musicae* (1610) with a German translation and a supplementary chapter. Modern editions are: the Matthew-Passion by Ziebler (1934); hymns by Heyden (1932); Christmas choruses by Twittenhoff and Heyden (1932).

BIBLIOGRAPHY: C. von Winterfeld, *Zur Geschichte heiliger Tonkunst,* I (1850); H. H. Eggebrecht, "Melchior Vulpius," in *Max Schneider Festschrift* (1955).

Vycpálek, Ladislav, Czech composer; b. Prague, Feb. 23, 1882; d. there, Jan. 9, 1969. He studied philosophy at the Charles Univ. in Prague, obtaining his doctorate in 1906; then took private lessons in composition with Vítězslav Novák (1908–12). From 1907 to 1942 he worked as music librarian.

WORKS: 3 cantatas: *Kantáta o posledních věcech člověka (Cantata on the Last Things of Man,*

1920–22), *Blahoslavený ten člověk* (*Blessed Is the Man*, 1933) and *České requiem/Smrt a spasení* (*Czech Requiem/Death and Salvation*, 1940); String Quartet (1909); *Cestou (The Way)*, 6 pieces for piano (1901–14); *Chvála houslí (In Praise of the Violin)*, sonata for violin, piano and mezzo-soprano, to the poem by S. Hanuš "The Violin of an Old German Master" (1927–28); Duo for violin and viola (1929); *Suite* for solo viola (1929); *Suite* for solo violin (1930); *Vzhůru srdce (Courage, My Heart!)*, 2 variation fantasies to songs from the Huss period, for orch. (1950); *Doma (At Home)*, suite for piano (1959); choruses; many songs.

BIBLIOGRAPHY: J. Smolka, *Ladislav Vycpálek* (Prague, 1960).

Vyshnegradsky, Ivan. See **Wyschnegradsky, Ivan.**

W

Waack, Karl, German conductor; b. Lübeck, March 6, 1861; d. Neumünster, March 7, 1922. He was a pupil of the grand-ducal Musikschule in Weimar; settled in Riga as teacher and conductor of the Wagnerverein. After the outbreak of the war in 1914, he went to Lübeck, where he conducted the Verein der Musikfreunde. He edited *Tristan und Isolde* (1904) and *Lohengrin* (1907) for Breitkopf & Härtel's *Textbibliothek* (with leading motifs in notation, and references to the full and piano scores); also wrote historical introductions and prepared tables of motifs for all the Wagner operas in the new editions brought out by Breitkopf & Härtel (1913). He published *Richard Wagner, ein Erfüller und Vollender deutscher Kunst* (1918).

Waart, Edo de, Dutch conductor; b. Amsterdam, June 1, 1941. He was a member of a musical family; his father was in the chorus at the Netherlands Opera. He studied oboe at the Muzieklyceum in Amsterdam and was oboist in the Concertgebouw Orch. (1963–65); also took courses in conducting with Franco Ferrara at the Holland Radio Philharmonic. In 1964 he was the 1st prize winner in the Mitropoulos Competition for young conductors in N.Y.; in 1965 became assistant to Leonard Bernstein at the N.Y. Philharmonic. Returning to Holland, he served as assistant conductor at the Concertgebouw (1966–67); in 1967 was appointed conductor of the Rotterdam Orch., becoming its music director in 1973. In 1975 he was engaged as principal guest conductor of the San Francisco Symph. Orch.; in 1977 was appointed its principal conductor and music director.

Waart, Hendrikus Aloysius Petrus de, Dutch composer and organist; b. Amsterdam, June 28, 1863; d. Voorburg, near The Hague, April 2, 1931. He studied in The Hague; then taught piano and organ at the Cons. there; wrote 3 symphonies, numerous choral works, a string trio, piano works, songs.

Wachs, Paul Étienne Victor, French pianist and composer; b. Paris, Sept. 19, 1851; d. St. Mandé, July 6, 1915. He studied with César Franck and Victor Massé at the Paris Cons., and won 1st prize for organ playing; subsequently was engaged as church organist in Paris. He wrote works for organ, chamber music, etc., but achieved his most signal success as composer of attractive salon pieces for piano (*Pluie d'étoiles, Le Collier de perles, Les Doigts,* etc.); also well known are his *Pastorale* and *Hosanna* for organ.

Wachtel, Theodor, German tenor; b. Hamburg, March 10, 1823; d. Frankfurt, Nov. 14, 1893. The son of a livery-stable keeper, he carried on the business from the age of 17, after his father's death. When his voice was discovered, he was sent to Hamburg for study, and soon appeared in opera. After further study in Vienna, he sang at the Berlin Opera (1865–68); in 1869 he appeared in Paris; made 2 American tours (1871 and 1875); accumulated a considerable fortune. His voice was a powerful and brilliant lyric tenor; the role in which he made himself famous was that of the postillion in Adam's *Postillon de Longjumeau,* which he sang more than 1,000 times; also was successful as Raoul in *Les Huguenots.* His sole attempt as a Wagner singer, in *Lohengrin* (Leipzig, 1876), was a dismal failure.

Wachtmeister, Axel Raoul, Count, composer; b. London (son of the Swedish ambassador there), April 2, 1865; d. Paris, Dec. 12, 1947. He studied music with Gédalge and Vincent d'Indy. He lived mostly in Paris, going to Sweden in the summers; spent some time in the U.S.; his cantata *Sappho* was performed in N.Y. in 1917. He also wrote 2 symphonies; a symph. poem, *Le Récit de l'horloge; Hymne à la lune,* for baritone, chorus, and orch. (Cincinnati, 1933); *Suite romantique* for piano; songs.

Wackernagel, Philipp, German music historian; b. Berlin, June 28, 1800; d. Dresden, June 20, 1877. He publ. several books dealing with music: *Das deutsche Kirchenlied, von Luther bis auf N. Hermann* (1841; 2 vols.); *Bibliographie zur Geschichte des deutschen Kirchenliedes im 16. Jahrhundert* (1855); and *Das deutsche Kirchenlied von der ältesten Zeit bis zum Anfang des 17. Jahrhunderts* (5 vols., 1864–77).

Waddington, Sidney Peine, English composer and pedagogue; b. Lincoln, July 23, 1869; d. Uplyme, Devon, June 2, 1953. He studied in London, Frankfurt, and Vienna; returning to England, he was engaged as chorusmaster at St. Mary of the Angels, Bayswater, London (1894–1905); in 1905 joined the staff of the Royal College of Music as harmony teacher. He wrote an operetta for children, *Whimland; Ode to Music* for soli, chorus, and orch.; Piano Concerto; Piano Quintet; String Quartet; String Trio; *Suite de Pièces* for piano 4 hands; Violin Sonata; Cello Sonata; etc.

Wade, Joseph Augustine, Irish composer; b. Dublin, 1796; d. London, July 15, 1845. He went to London in 1821, and established himself as a highly successful composer of popular ballads; his song *Meet me by moonlight alone* (1826) enjoyed great vogue, as did his vocal duet *I've wandered in dreams.* He also wrote an opera, *The Two Houses of Granada* (London, Oct. 31, 1826), and an operetta, *The Pupil of Da Vinci* (London, Nov. 30, 1839).

Waefelghem, Louis van, Belgian violinist and composer; b. Bruges, Jan. 13, 1840; d. Paris, June 19, 1908. He studied violin at the Brussels Cons. with Meerts; went to Germany in 1860; played violin in the orch. of the Budapest Opera; settled in Paris in 1863; often visited London as chamber music player. With Grillet, Diémer, and Delsart, he founded the Société des Instruments Anciens in Paris (1895), where he played the viola d'amore; composed and arranged a number of pieces for that instrument.

Waelput, Hendrik, Flemish composer; b. Ghent, Oct. 26, 1845; d. there, July 8, 1885. He studied at the Brussels Cons.; won the Prix de Rome for his cantata *Het Woud (The Forest).* He was director of the Bruges Cons. (1869–71); conducted theater orchestras at The

Hague, Dijon, Douai, Fécamp, and Lille (1872–76). From 1876 to 1879 he was active in Ghent; in 1879 appointed prof. of harmony at Antwerp Cons.; returned to Ghent in 1884. He wrote two operas: *La Ferme du diable* (Ghent, 1865) and *Stella* (in Flemish; Brussels, March 14, 1881); 5 symphonies, cantatas, and other works.

BIBLIOGRAPHY: E. Callaert, *Levensschets van Hendrik Waelput* (1886); P. Bergmans, *Notice biographique sur Henry Waelput* (1886); E. de Vynck, *Henry Waelput* (Brussels, 1935).

Waelrant, Hubert, Flemish composer and theorist; b. Tongerloo, Brabant, c.1517; d. Antwerp, Nov. 19, 1595. He matriculated at the Univ. of Louvain in 1534; in 1544 became a tenor at Notre Dame in Antwerp, where he founded a music school in 1547. In 1554 he established a music publishing business in partnership with Jean Laet, retiring in 1558. As a teacher he abandoned the old system of solmization by hexachords and introduced a new system of the 7 tonenames, *bo ce di ga lo ma ni* (hence called "Bocedization"; also "Voces belgicae"). His compositions include a book of chansons, publ. by Phalèse in Louvain (1553–54), and a book of madrigals for 5 voices (Antwerp, 1558); as a publisher he brought out several sacred works by various composers; edited a collection, *Symphonia angelica*, containing madrigals of his own (1585).

BIBLIOGRAPHY: G. Becker, *Hubert Waelrant et ses psaumes. Notice biographique et bibliographique* (Paris, 1881); G. Reese, *Music in the Renaissance* (N.Y., 1954).

Waesberghe, Joseph Smits van, Dutch musicologist; b. Breda, April 18, 1901. He studied philosophy; joined the Jesuit Order; then took courses in music with C. Huygens (church music) and Marius Monnikendam (theory); taught at the Cons. of Rotterdam (1928–43) and in 1943 was appointed to the staff of the Amsterdam Cons.

WRITINGS: *Muziekgeschiedenis der Middeleeuwen,* a voluminous survey of medieval music history in 2 parts (Tilburg, 1935–39 and 1939–47); *Klokken en Klokkegieten in de Middeleeuwen* (1937); *Muziek en Drama in de Middeleeuwen* (Amsterdam, 1942; in English, as *Music and Drama in the Middle Ages,* Stockholm 1947); *De Gregoriaansche Zang* (Amsterdam, 1943; in English, as *Gregorian Chant and Its Place in the Catholic Liturgy,* Stockholm, 1947); *School en Muziek in de Middeleeuwen* (Amsterdam, 1949); *Melodieleer* (Amsterdam, 1950; in English as *A Textbook of Melody,* Dallas, American Institute of Musicology, 1955). A Festschrift *Organicae Voces,* was presented him on his 60th birthday (Amsterdam, 1963).

Wagemans, Peter Jan, Dutch composer; b. The Hague, Sept. 7, 1952. He studied organ, composition (with Vlijmen) and music theory; often performs 2-piano pieces on radio. He composed Symphony (1972); *Overture* (1972); Wind Quintet (1973); Saxophone Quartet (1975); *Music I* for winds and timpani (1975); *Music II* for strings, 3 trumpets, 3 trombones, and percussion (1976); *From "De zangen van Maldor-*or" for orch. (1976); *Alla marcia* for tuba and 12 instrumentalists (1977).

Wagenaar, Bernard, American composer and teacher; son of **Johan Wagenaar;** b. Arnhem, Holland, July 18, 1894. d. York, Maine, May 19, 1971. He studied music with his father; violin with Gerard Veerman in Utrecht. In 1920 he came to the U.S.; was a violinist in the N.Y. Philharmonic (1921–23). In 1927 he became instructor of composition and orchestration at the Juilliard Graduate School of Music, N.Y.

WORKS: *Pieces of Eight,* operatic comedy (1943; N.Y., 1944); Symph. No. 1 (N.Y., Oct. 7, 1928); *Divertimento* (Detroit, Nov. 28, 1929); *Sinfonietta* (N.Y., Jan. 16, 1930); Symph. No. 2 (N.Y., Nov. 10, 1932, Toscanini conducting); Symph. No. 3 (N.Y., Jan. 23, 1937, composer conducting); Violin Concerto (1940); Triple Concerto for flute, harp, cello, and orch. (N.Y., May 20, 1941, composer conducting); Symph. No. 4 (Boston, Dec. 16, 1949); *5 Tableaux* for cello and orch. (Amsterdam, Jan. 9, 1955); *3 Songs from the Chinese* (1921); Violin Sonata (1925); 3 string quartets; Piano Sonata; Sonatina for cello and piano; Concertino for 8 instruments.

BIBLIOGRAPHY: D. Fuller, "Bernard Wagenaar," *Modern Music* (May 1944); *Modern Music . . . Analytic Index,* compiled by Wayne Shirley, edited by Wm. and C. Lichtenwanger (N.Y., 1976), p. 223.

Wagenaar, Johan, Dutch organist and composer; b. Utrecht, Nov. 1, 1862; d. The Hague, June 17, 1941. He studied with Richard Hol in Utrecht (1875–85) and with H. von Herzogenberg in Berlin (1889); established himself as an organist at the Utrecht Cathedral; in 1904 he became director of the Utrecht Music School; from 1919 to 1937, director of the Royal Cons. at The Hague.

WORKS: the operas *De Doge van Venetie* (Utrecht, 1904) and *De Cid* (Utrecht, 1916); also the burlesque opera *Jupiter Amans* (Scheveningen, 1925); the symph. poems *Levenszomer* (1901) *Saul and David* (1906) and *Elverhöt* (1940); the overtures *Koning Jan* (1889), *Cyrano de Bergerac* (1905), *De getemde feeks* (1906), *Driekoningenavond* (1927), and *De philosofische prinses* (1931); numerous choral works; songs; organ pieces.

BIBLIOGRAPHY: C. Backers, *Nederlandse Componisten van 1400 tot op onze Tijd* (The Hague, 1941; pp. 96–99).

Wagenmann, Josef Hermann, German singing teacher and writer; b. Engingen, May 11, 1876; d. Berlin, July 30, 1940. He studied jurisprudence in Heidelberg and Leipzig; then studied singing with various teachers in Italy; became a renowned singing teacher in Berlin; in 1934 was appointed prof. at the Academy for Church- and School-Music there. He publ. *Neue Ära der Stimmbildung für Singen und Sprechen* (1903); *Umsturz in der Stimmbildung* (1904; 2nd ed., 1922); *Lilli Lehmanns Geheimnis der Stimmbänder* (1905; 2nd ed., 1926); *Ein automatischer Stimmbildner* (1906); *Enrico Caruso und das Problem der Stimmbildung* (1911; 3rd ed., 1924); *Heinrich Knote* (1931).

Wagenseil, Georg Christoph, Austrian composer and theorist; b. Vienna, Jan. 29, 1715; d. there, March 1, 1777. He studied with J. J. Fux; was music teacher of the Empress Maria Theresa and her children; in 1739 was appointed court composer; remained in the Imperial services until his death. He wrote many operas in Italian.
WORKS: produced in Vienna: *La Generosità trionfante* (1745); *Ariodante* (May 14, 1746); *La Clemenza di Tito* (1746); *Alexander der Grosse in Indien* (July 7, 1748); *Il Siroe* (1748); *L'Olimpiade* (May 13, 1749); *Andromeda* (1749); *Antigone* (May 13, 1750); *Armida placato* (1750); *Euridice* (1750); *Le Cacciatrici amanti* (1755); *Demetrio* (1760); 3 oratorios; 30 symphonies; 27 harpsichord concertos; organ works. Two symphonies and a trio sonata are in the *Denkmäler der Tonkunst in Österreich* 31 (15.ii); a divertimento was ed. by Blume. Wagenseil publ. the following: *Suavis, artificiose elaboratus concentus musicus, continens: 6 selectas parthias ad clavicembalum compositas* (1740); *18 Divertimenti di cembalo,* opp. 1–3; a divertimento for 2 harpsichords; 2 divertimentos for harpsichord, 2 violins, and cello, op. 5; 10 symphonies for harpsichord, 2 violins, and cello, op. 4, 7, 8; 6 violin sonatas with harpsichord, op. 6.
BIBLIOGRAPHY: K. Horwitz, *Wagenseil als Symphoniker* (dissertation, Vienna, 1906); W. Vetter, "G. C. Wagenseil, ein Vorläufer Glucks," *Zeitschrift für Musikwissenschaft* 8 (1926); W. Vetter, "Der Opernkomponist G. C. Wagenseil und sein Verhältnis zu Mozart und Gluck," in the "Hermann Abert-Gedenkschrift" (Halle, 1928); J. Pelikant, *Die Klavier-Werke Wagenseils* (Vienna, 1926); G. Hausswald, "Der Divertimento-Begriff bei G. C. Wagenseil," *Archiv für Musikwissenschaft* (1952).

Wagenseil, Johann Christoph, German historian and librarian; b. Nuremberg, Nov. 26, 1633; d. Altdorf, Oct. 9, 1708. He published an important book, *De Sacri Rom. Imperii Libera Civitate Noribergensi Commentatio* (Altdorf, 1697), with a 140-page supplement (in German), *Buch von der Meister-Singer holdseligen Kunst: Anfang, Fortübung, Nutzbarkeiten und Lehr-Sätz,* containing poems and melodies by Frauenlob, Mügling, Marner, and Regenbogen; this section was the main literary source that Wagner used in *Die Meistersinger von Nürnberg.*
BIBLIOGRAPHY: K. Mey, *Der Meistergesang in Geschichte und Kunst* (2nd ed., 1901); H. Thompson, *Wagner & Wagenseil. A Source of Wagner's Opera "Die Meistersinger"* (London, 1927).

Waghalter, Ignatz, conductor and composer, b. Warsaw, March 15, 1882; d. New York, April 7, 1949. He studied in Berlin, where he became conductor of the Komische Oper (1907–11); then conducted in Essen (1911–12), and at the Deutsches Opernhaus in Berlin-Charlottenburg. In 1925 he succeeded Stransky as conductor of the State Symph. Orch. in N.Y. (for one season only); then returned to Berlin; in 1933 he went to Prague, and in 1934 to Vienna. He then went to America, settling in N.Y. in 1938.
WORKS: the operas *Der Teufelsweg* (Berlin, 1911), *Mandragola* (Berlin, Jan. 23, 1914; N.Y., March 4, 1925), *Jugend* (Berlin, 1917), *Der späte Gast* (Berlin,

1922), and *Sataniel* (Berlin, 1923); also operettas (*Der Weiberkrieg* and *Wem gehört Helena?*); Violin Concerto; Violin Sonata; String Quartet; piano pieces.
BIBLIOGRAPHY: Hugo Leichtentritt, *Ignatz Waghalter* (N.Y., 1924).

Wagner, Cosima, wife of **Richard Wagner,** daughter of **Franz Liszt** and the Countess Marie d'Agoult; b. Bellaggio, on Lake Como, Dec. 24, 1837; d. Bayreuth, April 1, 1930. She received an excellent education in Paris; married **Hans von Bülow** on Aug. 18, 1857; there were two daughters of this marriage, Blandine and Daniela; the third daughter, Isolde, was Wagner's child, as was the fourth, Eva, and the son, Siegfried. A divorce followed on July 18, 1870; the marriage to Wagner took place in a few weeks, on Aug. 25, 1870. A woman of high intelligence, practical sense, and imperious character, Cosima Wagner emerged after Wagner's death as a powerful personage in all affairs regarding the continuance of the Bayreuth Festivals as well as the complex matters pertaining to the rights of performance of Wagner's works all over the world. She publ. her reminiscences of Liszt: *Franz Liszt, Ein Gedenkblatt von seiner Tochter* (Munich, 2nd ed., 1911).
BIBLIOGRAPHY: M. Strauss, *Wie ich Frau Cosima Wagner sehe* (Magdeburg, 1912); E. Schuré, *Femmes inspiratrices* (Paris, 1930); W. Siegfried, *Frau Cosima Wagner* (Stuttgart, 1930); F. Blei, *Gefährtinnen* (Berlin, 1931); R. Du Moulin-Eckart, *Cosima Wagner* (Munich, 1929); English translation, in 2 vols., N.Y., 1930); M. von Waldberg, *Cosima Wagners Briefe an ihre Tochter Daniela von Bülow, 1866–85* (Stuttgart, 1933); L. Scalero, *Cosima Wagner* (Zürich, 1934); P. Pretzsch, *Cosima Wagner und H. S. Chamberlain im Briefwechsel, 1888–1908* (Leipzig, 1934); *Briefwechsel zwischen Cosima Wagner und Fürst Ernst zu Hohenlohe-Langenburg* (Stuttgart, 1937); M. von Millenkovich (M. Morold), *Cosima Wagner, ein Lebensbild* (Leipzig, 1937); E. Thierbach, ed., *Die Briefe Cosima Wagners an Friedrich Nietzsche* (Weimar, 1938–40); Alice Hunt Sokoloff, *Cosima Wagner, Extraordinary Daughter of Franz Liszt* (N.Y., 1969).

Wagner, Georg Gottfried, German violinist; b. Mühlberg, April 5, 1698; d. Plauen, March 23, 1756. He studied with Kuhnau at the Thomasschule in Leipzig (1712–19); was a violinist in Bach's orch., and was recommended by Bach for the post of cantor at Plauen, which he held from 1726 to his death. He wrote numerous sacred works and instrumental compositions; his motet *Lob und Ehre* was misattributed to Bach by Breitkopf & Härtel (publ. 1819).
BIBLIOGRAPHY: B. Hammerschmidt, *G. G. Wagner* (Chemnitz, 1912).

Wagner, Gerrit Anthonie Alexander, Dutch conductor and composer; b. Amsterdam, March 8, 1862; d. Antwerp, Nov. 24, 1892. He studied with Brandts-Buys in Amsterdam and with Benoit and Blockx in Antwerp; became a choral conductor there. He wrote an oratorio, *Babylonische Gevangenschap;* a symph. poem, *Zusterengelen;* much choral music; his promising career was terminated by an early death.

Wagner, Johanna, German soprano; b. Lohnde, near Hannover, Oct. 13, 1826; d. Würzburg, Oct. 16, 1894. She was a natural daughter of Lieutenant Bock von Wülfingen of Hannover, and was adopted by Richard Wagner's brother, Albert; was thus regarded as Wagner's niece. Of a precocious talent, she acted on the stage as a small child; through Wagner she obtained a position at the Dresden Opera when she was 17; produced an excellent impression as Agathe in *Der Freischütz,* and was engaged as a regular member. She studied the part of Elisabeth in *Tannhäuser* with Wagner, and sang it in the première of the opera on Oct. 19, 1845, when she was a barely 19 years old. In 1846 she went to Paris for further study, with Mme. Viardot-Garcia (1846–48); then was engaged at the Hamburg Opera (1849) and finally at the Court Opera in Berlin (1850–61). In 1859 she married the district judge Jachmann. After 1862 she acted mainly on the dramatic stage, reappearing in opera at the Bayreuth Festival in 1876 in the parts of Schwertleite and the First Norn. In 1882 she settled in Munich as a singing teacher.

BIBLIOGRAPHY: J. Kapp and H. Jachmann, *Richard Wagner und seine erste "Elisabeth," Johanna Jachmann-Wagner* (Berlin, 1927; in English as *Wagner and His First Elisabeth,* London, 1944).

Wagner, Josef Franz, Austrian composer of light music; b. Vienna, March 20, 1856; d. there, June, 1908. He was a popular leader of military bands in Vienna; produced the operettas *Der Herzbub* (Vienna, Feb. 7, 1895), which had little success, but achieved fame as the composer of the Austran march *Under the Double Eagle,* which became a semi-official march of the Austro-Hungarian Empire.

Wagner, Joseph Frederick, American composer and conductor; b. Springfield, Mass., Jan. 9, 1900; d. Los Angeles, Oct. 12, 1974. He was educated at the Technical High School in Providence and studied piano and organ privately; then entered the New England Cons., where he studied composition with Frederick Converse; later took lessons in composition with Alfredo Casella in Boston in 1927, with Nadia Boulanger in Paris (1935); studied conducting with Pierre Monteux in Paris and Felix Weingartner in Basel, Switzerland. He was assistant director of music in Boston public schools (1923–44); taught at Boston Univ. (1929–40), Hunter College, N.Y. (1945–56), and Brooklyn College (1945–47). In 1925 he organized the Boston Civic Symph. Orch., which he conducted until 1944; subsequently was conductor of the Duluth Symph. Orch. (1947–50) and of the Orquesta Sinfónica Nacional de Costa Rica in San José (1950–54); was also guest conductor in Helsinki, Stockholm, Washington and Buffalo. In 1960 he settled in Hollywood; in 1961 was appointed prof. at Pepperdine College in Los Angeles. His music is distinguished by excellent craftsmanship; it is set in a fairly advanced idiom, with bitonality as a frequent resource in his later works. Shortly before his death he completed the score of *Tribute to America* (Symph. No. 4) for chorus, soprano solo, narrator, and orch., planned for the bicentennial year 1976, but never performed. Indeed, most performances of Joseph Wagner's orchestral works were conducted by himself. Wistfully, he kept a file of rejection slips from conductors, arranged in alphabetical order, from A to Z (from Abravanel to Zipper). A memorial brochure, *Joseph Wagner: A Retrospective of a Composer-Conductor,* edited by Lance Bowling, with an introductory article, "Joseph Wagner: The Most Undiscovered among American Composers" by Nicolas Slonimsky, was published in Lomita, California, in 1976.

WORKS: opera, *New England Sampler,* (Los Angeles, Feb. 26, 1965); the ballets: *The Birthday of the Infanta,* after Oscar Wilde (1935), *Hudson River Legend* (1941; Boston, March 1, 1944); for orch.; *Miniature Concerto* for piano and orch. (1919; Providence, June 11, 1920; revised as *Concerto in G Minor;* New Brunswick, N.Y., Aug. 3, 1930); *Rhapsody* for piano, clarinet and strings (1925); Symph. No. 1 (Rochester, N.Y., Oct. 19, 1944); Symph. No. 2 (1945; Wilmington, March 1, 1960); Symph. No. 3 (1951); Violin Concerto (1955); Sinfonietta No. 1 (1931); Sinfonietta No. 2 for string orch. (1941); *Pastoral Costarricense* (1958); *Merlin and Sir Boss,* symph. tale for concert band, after Mark Twain's *A Connecticut Yankee* (1963); Concerto for organ, brass, and percussion (1963); Harp Concerto (1964); chamber music: Violin Sonata (1941); *Introduction and Scherzo* for bassoon and piano (1951); *Patterns of Contrast* for wind quartet (1959); *Fantasy Sonata* for harp solo (1963); *Preludes and Toccata* for harp, violin, and cello (1964); *Fantasy and Fugue* for woodwind quartet (1968); *Sonata of Sonnets* for voice and piano (1961); *12 Concert Preludes* for organ (1974); for piano: *Radio City Snapshots* (1945); *Sonata With Differences* (1952); for chorus: *David Jazz* for men's chorus with piano (1934); *Under Freedom's Flag* (1940); *Ballad of Brotherhood* (1947); *Missa Sacra* for chorus, mezzo-soprano, and orch. (1952); *American Ballad* for chorus a cappella (1963). He published two useful books, *Orchestration: A Practical Handbook* (N.Y., 1958) and *Band Scoring* (N.Y., 1960).

Wagner, Karl Jakob, German composer, b. Darmstadt, Feb. 22, 1772; d. there, Nov. 25, 1822. He was a French horn player and conductor in the Darmstadt Orch.; studied theory with Abbé Vogler. He wrote 4 operas, all produced in Darmstadt: *Pygmalion* (1809), *Der Zahnarzt* (1810), *Siaph und Nitetis* (1811), and *Chimene* (1821); 2 symphonies; 4 overtures; trios for violin, flute, and cello; duos for flute and violin; 40 horn duos; 3 violin sonatas; piano pieces.

Wagner, Peter (Joseph), eminent German musicologist; b. Kürenz, near Trier, Aug. 19, 1865; d. Freiburg, Switzerland, Oct. 17, 1931. He studied at the Univ. of Strasbourg; received his degree of Dr. phil. with the dissertation *Palestrina als weltlicher Komponist* (1890); studied further in Berlin under Bellermann and Spitta; in 1893 he was appointed instructor of church music at the Univ. of Freiburg, Switzerland. In 1901 he established at the Univ. the Gregorianische Akademie for theoretical and practical study of plainsong, in which field he was an eminent authority. He was a member of the Papal Commission for the *Editio Vaticana* of the Roman Gradual, and was made a Papal Chamberlain. In the course of numerous visits to

Spain he did valuable research on the Mozarabic liturgical chant.

WRITINGS: *Einführung in die gregorianischen Melodien* (1895); 2nd ed. in 3 parts, I. *Ursprung und Entwicklung der liturgischen Gesangsformen bis zum Ausgang des Mittelalters* (1901; 3rd ed. 1911; English translation, 1907), II, *Neumenkunde* (1905; reprint, 1912) III, *Gregorianische Formenlehre; eine choralische Stilkunde* (1921); *Das Freiburger Dreikönigspiel* (1903); *Über traditionellen Choral und traditionellen Choralvortrag* (1905); *Elemente des gregorianischen Gesanges* (1909; 2nd ed., 1916); *Geschichte der Messe* (vol. I, 1913 [to 1600]); *Einführung in die katholische Kirchenmusik* (1919). A Festschrift for him, ed. by K. Weinmann, was publ. in 1926.

Wagner, (Wilhelm) Richard, illustrious German composer; creator of the music drama; b. Leipzig, May 22, 1813; d. Venice, Feb. 13, 1883. His father, clerk in the city police court, died when Wagner was but six months old; his mother, Johanna Rosina, *née* Paetz (or Beetz), was ostensibly the daughter of a baker, though it is possible she was the natural daughter of Prince Friedrich Ferdinand Constantin of Weimar; about nine months after her husband's death, Johanna married the actor and playwright Ludwig Geyer, who had been an intimate member of the family circle for some time (the possiblity that Geyer was Wagner's real father cannot be excluded; Wagner himself harbored such a suspicion). The family then moved to Dresden, where Wagner entered the Kreuzschule at the age of nine, remaining there until 1827 (his stepfather Geyer died in 1821). He was interested in the study of Greek, and showed strong literary inclinations, writing a grand tragedy, *Leubald und Adelaïde,* in Shakespearian style, at the age of 14. In 1825 he began to take piano lessons from a certain Humann, and with characteristic impatience tried to play the *Freischütz* overture as soon as he had learned some 5-finger exercises; actually he made little progress on the piano; nor did he do better with the violin, which he took up with Robert Sipp. He was already beginning to be fascinated by opera, and with the idea of trying to write music for his "tragedy" he began studying Logier's *System der Musikwissenschaft und der praktischen Komposition.* In 1827 the family settled in Leipzig, and in 1828 Wagner was sent to Nikolaischule there (from 1830 he also attended the Thomasschule for a short time). About this time he had some lessons in theory from the organist C. G. Müller, and soon began to compose, writing a string quartet, a piano sonata, and an overture, which the conductor H. Dorn performed on Christmas Eve, 1830. In 1831, after a brief plunge into the wild student life at Leipzig Univ., he received his first serious training in composition from Theodor Weinlig, cantor of the Thomasschule. The following year his op. 1 (a piano sonata) and op. 2 (4-hand *Polonaise)* were publ. by Breitkopf & Härtel; to this year (1832) also belong the Concert Overture in C (performed in Leipzig, April 30, 1832) and Symphony in C, first performed in the summer in Prague and later in Leipzig (Jan. 10, 1833). These works were the result of Wagner's study of Beethoven's symphonies. In 1832 Wagner wrote his first opera libretto, *Die Hochzeit,* for which he composed an introduction, a septet, and a chorus. In 1833 he began his career as a professional musician, being invited by his brother **Albert,** stage manager and singer at the Würzburg Theater, to take the position of chorusmaster there. He found leisure to compose a romantic opera in 3 acts, *Die Feen,* to a libretto of his own after *La Donna serpente* by Carlo Gozzi. In 1834 he was made conductor of the Magdeburg Theater; he brought out two overtures, to *Die Feen* and *Columbus,* and finished the book and score of a 2-act opera, *Das Liebesverbot* (after Shakespeare's *Measure for Measure),* the performance of which took place on March 29, 1836. He then went to Königsberg, became conductor of the theater, and married (Nov. 24, 1836) the actress Minna Planer. His sole new work here was the overture *Rule Britannia.* Next year he was appointed conductor of the Riga opera; he also conducted orchestral concerts, and completed the libretto of *Rienzi, der Letzte der Tribunen,* a tragic opera in 5 acts, of which he composed the first 2 in Riga. During a stay in Boulogne, he met Meyerbeer, who gave him letters to musicians and publishers in Paris; he arrived there with his wife in September, and remained there until 1842. Unsuccessful in his attempts to get a hearing for *Rienzi,* he found himself in dire straits; his financial situation became desperate; on Oct. 28, 1840 he was put in the debtors' prison, and was not released until Nov. 17 of that year. In the midst of his troubles, he completed the grand *Faust-Ouvertüre,* intended for the first movement of a "Faust Symphony"; the score of the opera *Rienzi* was finished, and sent to the Intendant of the Dresden Court Theater. Sketches for *Der fliegende Holländer* had also been submitted to the Director of the Opéra, who viewed them with approval, but the upshot was that Wagner was obliged to sell his libretto for 500 francs; it was then put into French verse and set to music by Dietsch (produced at the Paris Opéra, Nov. 9, 1842). Nevertheless, Wagner went rapidly ahead with the composition of his own version. In the meantime the Dresden Opera accepted Wagner's opera *Rienzi;* Wagner went to Dresden to supervise rehearsals; *Rienzi* was produced at the Dresden Opera on Oct. 20, 1842, with excellent success. The Dresden Opera also staged Wagner's newly completed score of *Der fliegende Holländer* (Jan. 2, 1843), which led to his appointment as Royal Kapellmeister to the Saxon Court. Secure in his official position, Wagner conducted a rich repertory of the finest operas (*Iphigenie in Aulis, Der Freischütz, Euryanthe, Don Giovanni, Die Zauberflöte, Fidelio,* etc.) in masterly fashion at the Dresden Court Theater; he also conducted the Dresden Liedertafel, for which he composed a "biblical scene," *Das Liebesmahl der Apostel,* for 3 choirs of men's voices, singing at first a cappella, finally with full orch. The 3-act opera *Tannhäuser und der Sängerkrieg auf Wartburg* (originally sketched in 1842 as *Der Venusberg)* was finished in April, 1844, and produced at Dresden on Oct. 19, 1845. Wagner then began work on the 3-act romantic opera *Lohengrin,* which was finished on April 28, 1848, but he was not able to secure its production in Dresden (only the finale to Act I was performed at the 300th anniversary of the court orch. on Sept. 22, 1848); the opera was finally produced by Liszt at Weimar in 1850 (Wagner himself did not hear the work until 1861). In 1848 he wrote the poem of *Siegfried's Death* (3-act drama with prologue). By this time Wagner had joined a radical political organization, the Vaterlandsverein, and soon allowed himself to be drawn into active participation in the revolutionary movement that came to a head with the May uprising of 1849. He was obliged to flee in order to escape arrest, going first to Weimar, where he was given a most friendly reception by Liszt, then to Jena, and finally to Zürich, where he was joined by his wife Minna. He now embarked upon a period of intense literary activity; wrote important essays explaining his philosophy of art: *Die Kunst und die Revolution* (1849), *Das Kunstwerk der Zukunft* (1850), *Kunst und Klima* (1850), and *Oper und Drama* (1851). The ideas advanced in *Das Kunstwerk der Zukunft (Art-Work of the Future)* gave rise to the description of Wagner's music as "Zukunftsmusik" in derision by opponents, but accepted by Wagner, Liszt, and their disciples as honorable. In 1852 Wagner completed the poems of the Nibelung trilogy (privately printed 1853). In Jan., 1850, he made another trip to Paris with the vain hope of having an opera produced there; he became involved in a love affair with a married woman named Jennie Laussot, but the affair came to nothing and Wagner returned to Minna in Zürich; there he met a wealthy merchant, Otto Wesendonck, with whose wife, Mathilde, he fell deeply in love. In 1857 Wagner and Minna took up their abode on Wesendonck's estate. Meanwhile Wagner had completed the full score of *Das Rheingold* (1854) and that of *Die Walküre* (1856), and in 1854, while under the influence of Schopenhauer's philosophy, he had conceived the idea of *Tristan und Isolde;* in 1856–57 he was at work both on *Tristan* and on *Siegfried,* always under the spell of his love for Mathilde Wesendonck, five of whose poems he set to music about this time. This situation led to a domestic crisis; Minna left Wagner and returned to Germany, while Wagner went to Venice, where he completed the 2nd act of *Tristan* in March, 1859 (the 3rd act was finished at Lucerne in Aug. of that year). Meanwhile, in the spring of 1855, Wagner had added to his reputation as a conductor by leading 8 concerts of the London Philharmonic Society. In Paris, where he was in 1859, he conducted concerts of his own music, making many friends, but also stirring up active opposition, and incurring heavy debts. However, powerful interests in Paris were enlisted in his favor; the Emperor Napoleon III ordered that *Tannhäuser* (with the Venusberg scene revised) should be put in rehearsal at the Opéra, and it was given on March 13, 1861, though in the face of such tumultuous opposition by a hostile clique that it was withdrawn after the 3rd performance. But Wagner's general prospects were now improved owing to the fact that he had received an amnesty in the summer of 1860, allowing him to return to Germany (except Saxony, to which the amnesty was not extended until March, 1862). In 1859 Minna had rejoined him in Paris; but in the summer of 1861 she separated from him permanently (she died at Dresden in 1866). In 1861 he went to Vienna in the hopes of having *Tristan* produced, and while there heard *Lohengrin* for the first time (May 31, 1861). Back in Paris he worked on the libretto of his comic opera *Die Meistersinger von Nürnberg* (finished Jan.,

1862), which he had sketched as far back as 1845. After completing the text he went to Biebrich-am-Rhine and began to compose the music, though the score was not finished until 1867. He made another visit to Vienna, where *Tristan* was finally accepted for production at the Court Opera, but after 77 rehearsals it was given up as "impracticable." In 1863 he gave some successful concerts in Moscow and St. Petersburg. But he had been harassed by debts, due largely to his extravagance, aggravated by his unstable position; help from various friends provided only temporary relief; in March, 1864, he was forced to flee from his creditors, going to Stuttgart by way of Mariafeld. At this crisis King Ludwig II of Bavaria, who had just ascended the throne, invited Wagner to Munich with the promise of the amplest aid in carrying out his projects. It was at this time that Wagner also reached a crisis in his emotional life. He became intimate with Liszt's daughter, Cosima, who was married to the conductor Hans von Bülow; the passion was reciprocated and received a further impetus after the arrival in Munich of Cosima and her husband, the latter chosen to conduct Wagner's works there (he gave the 1st performance of *Tristan* on June 10, 1865). On April 10, 1865, Isolde, the daughter of Cosima and Wagner, was born. During the summer of 1865 Wagner worked on a sketch of *Parsifal* (the idea was first conceived in 1845) and began to dictate his autobiography, *Mein Leben,* to Cosima. But court cabals, and the persistent opposition of his numerous enemies, united to the circumstances of his private life, rendered Wagner's position in Munich untenable, and in Dec., 1865, he left the city at King Ludwig's request, going to Switzerland. The following April he settled in the village of Triebschen, on Lake Lucerne, where he was soon joined by Cosima (their son Siegfried was born there on June 6, 1869). In 1867 he finished *Die Meistersinger,* which was produced in Munich on June 21, 1868; this was followed by the première of *Das Rheingold,* also in Munich, on Sept. 22, 1869; in the latter year Wagner completed the score of *Siegfried* and began *Götterdämmerung* (finished in 1874). In July, 1870, Cosima was divorced by Bülow, and on Aug. 25, 1870 she and Wagner were married. A significant episode of this period was the meeting with Nietzsche (1868), who was at first an ardent admirer of Wagner but later became a bitter opponent. In 1871 Wagner began the publication of his collected writings, and in that year the first Wagner Society was founded at Mannheim by Emil Heckel. For many years Wagner had cherished the ambition of building his own theater for the production of his operas in a way that would meet his artistic ideals. He received the offer of a site for his theater from the city of Bayreuth in 1872, and at once seized the opportunity. In April, 1872 he moved to Bayreuth; on May 22 the cornerstone of the Festspielhaus was laid, the ceremony commemorated by a performance of Beethoven's 9th Symphony (this was Wagner's 59th birthday). On his 60th birthday (May 22, 1873), Wagner began to build his own home in Bayreuth, "Wahnfried," which was ready for occupancy in the spring of 1874. The fund required for erecting the new theater, which was built according to Wagner's original plans, was raised by private subscription, by the contributions of Wagner Societies and by a series of concerts arranged by Wagner in various German cities. At length, in August, 1876, the dream of his life was realized; three complete performances of *Der Ring des Nibelungen* were presented at the Bayreuth theater, attended by musical notables and honored by the presence of Emperor William I and King Ludwig. Hans Richter conducted the orchestra, in which Wilhelmj led the violins. Musically a grand success, the undertaking left Wagner again heavily involved in debt; concerts given at the Albert Hall, London, in 1877, gave meager pecuniary returns; but he was finally relieved by the setting aside of the royalties derived from performances of the *Ring* at Munich. The next few years were occupied with literary work, and with the completion of his last dramatic composition, *Parsifal*, finished in 1882, and produced for the first time in Munich on July 26 of that year, other performances following through July and August, all under Wagner's personal supervision. He also made arrangements for the performances of 1883; in the autumn of 1882 ill health compelled him to seek relief in Venice, where he spent the winter; death (from an attack of angina pectoris) overtook him suddenly on Feb. 13, 1883. His remains were interred in the garden of his villa "Wahnfried" at Bayreuth.

In comprehensiveness and grandeur of conception, originality and boldness of execution, vividness of characterization, intensity of expression and sustained power, Wagner towers like a colossus above all other opera composers. From the outset he wrote his own librettos, based on his own poems. His early operas, *Die Feen, Das Liebesverbot,* and *Rienzi,* represent a formative period. With *Der fliegende Holländer* the individual Wagner, the genius, is unveiled, almost abruptly. The mythical tale, a conflict of stormy emotions and the apotheosis of love and self-sacrifice, appealed directly to the heart; the music is as wildly romantic, as tenderly pathetic, and as sternly tragic, as the successive situations demand, and it was written not to exhibit the beauty and agility of the voices, but to follow the drama into its least details without the customary breaks made by set numbers (arias, duets, ensembles). The dramatic and musical unity is secured by the ingenious, and yet logical use of *Leitmotive,* leading motifs that allude to characters, objects, or abstract concepts in the music dramas (the term was popularized by Hans von Wolzogen; Wagner never used it himself). With *Tannhäuser* and *Lohengrin* (1848) Wagner's poetic second period, the romantic, closes. In these two operas he employs substantially the same manner, though with growing variety and refinement. The third period opens six years later, with *Das Rheingold* (1854). With this work Wagner's ideas are carried out to their logical conclusion. He assumes the role of a reformer of the musico-dramatic stage; he unsparingly criticizes and condemns the faulty and illogical plan of Italian opera and French grand opera, and naturally discards these titles, calling his own subsequent works "music dramas." To quote his own words, "the mistake in the art-form of the opera consists in this, that a means of expression (music) was made the end, and the end to be expressed (the drama) was made a means." The choice of subject is of the utmost importance, for not all subjects lend themselves to musical characteriza-

tion. He formulated this conviction as follows: "The subject to be treated by the word-tone poet *[Worttondichter]* is purely human, freed from all convention and from everything historically formal." The new art-work procreated its own artistic form: continuous thematic development of leading-motifs. Wagner's orchestra became an exponent of the dramatic action; the highly individualized and pregnant leading-motifs, now singly, in bold relief, now subtly intertwined and varied, plastically present the ever-changing soul-states of the characters of the drama and form the connecting links for the dramatic situations; the singing of the actors is revolved into a musical declamation, which Wagner himself described as "Sprechsingen."

Wagner's reform was incomparably more far-reaching in aim, import, and effect than Gluck's, whose main purpose was to counteract the arbitrary predominance of the singers; this Wagner tried to accomplish through insistence upon the drama and dramatic truth. When he rejected traditional opera, he did so with the conviction that this artificial form could never serve as a basis for true dramatic expression. In its place he gave the world a new form, the music drama. So revolutionary was Wagner's art, that he was obliged to train singers and conductors in the new style of interpretation demanded by his works. Thus he became the founder of interpretative conducting and of a new school of dramatic singing.

WRITINGS: Wagner spent a large amount of his enormous productive activity in writing. Besides the dramatic works he set to music, he wrote the texts of a 2-act comic opera, *Männerlist grösser als Frauenlist, oder Die glückliche Bärenfamilie* (1837); a 4-act tragic opera, *Die hohe Braut, oder Bianca und Giuseppe* (first sketch, 1836; completed 1842; composed by J. F. Kittl, and produced in Prague, 1848); a 3-act "grosse Heldenoper" *Siegfrieds Tod* (1848; later expanded into *Götterdämmerung*); a 2-act comedy in ancient style, *Eine Kapitulation* (1871); dramatic sketches, *Die Bergwerke zu Falun* (1841), *Die Sarazenin* (1841), *Friedrich der Rothbart* (1846; enlarged 1848), *Jesus von Nazareth* (1848), *Wieland der Schmied* (1856), *Die Sieger* (1856). He expounded his theories on music and the music drama in several works, the more important of which are *Die Kunst und die Revolution* (1849), *Das Kunstwerk der Zukunft* (1850), *Kunst und Klima* (1850), *Oper und Drama* (1851), *Eine Mittheilung an meine Freunde* (1851), *Über das Dirigieren* (1869), *Beethoven* (1870). In his later years he also touched upon a large number of religious, social, and economic subjects. The first edition of Wagner's collected writings, edited by himself, was publ. at Leipzig in 9 vols. (1871–73) as *Gesammelte Schriften und Dichtungen;* it contains the dramatic works from *Rienzi* to *Der Ring des Nibelungen,* the social and esthetic essays, besides numerous others written between 1840 and 1871; the 2nd ed. (1883), with an additional vol. (*Parsifal* and essays), was also prepared by Wagner personally; the 3rd (1887) and 4th (1897) editions are only reprints; English translation by W. A. Ellis, *The Prose Works of Richard Wagner,* was published in 8 vols. in London (1892–1900). Not contained in these editions, and publ. separately, are: *Entwürfe, Gedanken, Fragmente* (ed. by H. von

Wolzogen; Leipzig, 1885); *Jesus von Nazareth* (Leipzig, 1887); *Nachgelassene Schriften und Dichtungen* (Leipzig, 1895; 2nd ed., 1902); *Gedichte* (ed. by K. F. Glasenapp; Berlin, 1905); *Entwürfe zu "Die Meistersinger," "Tristan und Isolde" und "Parsifal"* (ed. by H. von Wolzogen; Leipzig, 1907); essays and criticisms of the first Paris period ed. by R. Sternfeld as *Aus R. W.s Pariser Zeit* (Berlin, 1907); the texts of *Die Feen, Die hohe Braut, Das Liebesmahl der Apostel,* a fragment of *Die Hochzeit,* the sketch to *Die Bergwerke zu Falun,* and early eassys ed. by J. Kapp as *Der junge W.* (Berlin, 1910). All these works were included in the 5th edition, ed. by H. von Wolzogen and R. Sternfeld (12 vols.; Leipzig, 1911). An edition of Wagner's writings (10 vols.) was publ. by Kistner and Siegel, in 1930 (2 supplementary vols. ed. by R. Sternfeld, 2 by W. Altmann, 1933). A detailed autobiography, *Mein Leben,* in 4 sections, was published in several installments: the first 3 sections, bringing the autobiography up to August, 1861, was printed between 1870 and 1875; the 4th part, covering the years 1861–64, was printed in 1881; all were published in a limited edition of a dozen or so copies, to be distributed only among friends; it was eventually brought out in 2 vols. at Munich, 1911 (simultaneously in English, French, and Russia; new critical ed. by W. Altmann, Leipzig, 1933). Very valuable and important is Wagner's voluminous published correspondence (see BIBLIOGRAPHY). See also K. F. Glasenapp and H. von Stein, *W.-Lexikon. Hauptbegriffe der Kunst und Weltanschauung W.s in wörtlichen Ausführungen aus seinen Schriften zusammengestellt* (Stuttgart, 1883) and K. F. Glasenapp, *W.-Enzyklopädie. Haupterscheinungen der Kunst- und Kulturgeschichte im Lichte der Anschauung W.s in wörtlichen Ausführungen aus seinen Schriften dargestellt* (2 vols.; Leipzig, 1891).

WORKS: OPERAS AND MUSIC DRAMAS: *Die Hochzeit* (fragment; composed 1832); *Die Feen* (composed 1833, produced Munich, June 29, 1888); *Das Liebesverbot* (Magdeburg, March 29, 1836, as *Die Novize von Palermo;* revived Munich, March 24, 1923; Berlin, Jan. 20, 1932); *Rienzi, der letzte der Tribunen* (Dresden, Oct. 20, 1842; Paris Théâtre Lyrique, April 6, 1869; N.Y., March 4, 1878; London, Jan. 27, 1879); *Der fliegende Holländer* (Dresden, Jan. 2, 1843; London, July 23, 1870; Philadelphia, Nov. 8, 1876; N.Y., Jan. 26, 1877); *Tannhäuser* (Dresden, Oct. 19, 1845; N.Y., April 4, 1859; London, May 6, 1876; "Paris version" given at the Opéra, March 13, 1861); *Lohengrin* (Weimar, Aug. 28, 1850; N.Y., April 3, 1871; London, May 8, 1875; Paris, May 3, 1887); *Tristan und Isolde* (Munich, June 10, 1865; London, June 20, 1882; N.Y., Dec. 1, 1886); *Die Meistersinger von Nürnberg* (Munich, June 21, 1868; London, May 30, 1882; N.Y., Jan. 4, 1886). *Der Ring des Nibelungen,* "dramatic trilogy" in 3 parts and an introduction, the latter consisting of *Das Rheingold* (Munich, Sept. 22, 1869; London, May 6, 1882; N.Y., Jan. 4, 1889); Part I, *Die Walküre* (Munich, June 26, 1870; N.Y., April 2, 1877; London, May 6, 1882); Part II, *Siegfried* (Bayreuth, Aug. 16, 1876; London, May 8, 1882; N.Y., Nov. 9, 1887); Part III, *Götterdämmerung* (Bayreuth, Aug. 17, 1876; London, May 9, 1882; N.Y., Jan. 25, 188; first complete performance of entire *Ring* cycle, Bayreuth, Aug. 13, 14,

16, 17, 1876; N.Y., Metropolitan Opera House, March 4, 5, 8, and 11, 1889; without cuts, Feb. 20, 22, 27, and March 1, 1900). *Parsifal* (Bayreuth, July 26, 1882; N.Y., Dec. 24, 1903; Paris, Jan. 2, 1914; London, Feb. 2, 1914).

ORCHESTRAL WORKS: Overture in B-flat (composed 1830; score lost); Overture in D minor (1831; Leipzig, Feb. 23, 1832; unpubl.); Overture in C (1831); Overture to Raupach's *König Enzio* (1832; publ. 1908); Symphony in C (1832; publ. 1911); Symphony in E (1834; fragment; unpubl); Overture to Apel's *Columbus* (1835; publ. 1904); Overture *Rule Britannia* (1836; publ. 1904); Overture *Polonia* (begun 1832, finished 1836; publ. 1904); *Eine Faustouvertüre* (1839–40; Dresden, July 22, 1844; rewritten and publ. 1855); *Trauermusik* for wind instruments, after motifs from *Euryanthe* (1844; Dresden, Dec. 14, 1844, on the arrival of Weber's remains from London; publ. 1906); *Huldigungsmarsch,* dedicated to King Ludwig II (1864; originally for military band; orchestral score begun by Wagner, finished by Raff; publ. 1869); *Siegfried-Idyll* (1870; Triebschen, Dec. 25, 1870; publ. 1877); *Kaisermarsch* (1871; Berlin, May 5, 1871; publ. 1871); *Grosser Festmarsch,* for the Philadelphia Centennial Exposition (1876; Philadelphia, May 10, 1876; publ. 1876).

CHORAL WORKS: *Neujahrskantate* for mixed chorus and orch. (1834; Magdeburg, Dec. 31, 1834; publ. 1914, arranged with a new text by Peter Cornelius as *Künstlerweihe,* and produced at Bayreuth on Wagner's 60th birthday); *Volkshymne* for mixed chorus and orch. (1837; Riga, Nov. 21, 1837; publ. 1914); *La Descente de la Courtille* for mixed chorus and orch. (1840; publ. 1914); *Weihegruss* for men's chorus and orch., for unveiling of the statue of King Friedrich August of Saxony (1843; Dresden, June 7, 1843; vocal parts publ. 1906, full score 1914); *Das Liebesmahl der Apostel,* biblical scene for men's chorus and orch. (1843; Dresden, July 6, 1843; publ. 1844); *Gruss seiner Treuen an Friedrich August den Geliebten* for men's chorus a cappella, on the return from England of King Friedrich August of Saxony (1843; Dresden, Aug. 12, 1843; publ. 1914); *An Webers Grabe* for men's chorus a cappella, for the interment of Weber's remains (1844; Dresden, Dec. 15, 1844; publ. 1871).

PIANO WORKS: Sonata in D minor (1829; lost); *Doppelfuge* (composed probably in 1831; 103 bars, with corrections in Weinlig's hand; publ. 1912, in *Die Musik*); Sonata in B-flat (1831; publ. 1832); *Polonaise* in D, 4 hands (1831; publ. 1832); *Fantasie* in F-sharp minor (1831; publ. 1905); Sonata in A (1831; unpubl.); *Albumsonata* in E-flat (for Mathilde Wesendonck; 1853; publ. 1877); *Züricher Vielliebchen,* waltz in E (1853; publ. 1896, in *Musikalische Rundschau*); *Albumblatt* in C (for Countess Metternich; 1861; publ. 1871); *Ankunft bei den schwarzen Schwänen* (*Albumblatt* for Countess Pourtalès; 1861; publ. 1897); *Albumblatt* in E-flat (for Frau Betty Schott; 1875; publ. 1876).

SONGS: *Glockentöne* (1832; unpubl.); *Sieben Kompositionen zu Goethes Faust: 1, Lied der Soldaten. 2, Bauern unter der Linde. 3, Branders Lied. 4, Lied des Mephistopheles (Es war einmal ein König). 5, Lied des Mephistopheles (Was machst du mir). 6, Gesang Gretchens (Meine Ruh ist hin). 7, Melodram Gretchens*

(*Ach neige, du Schmerzensreiche*) (1832; publ. 1914); *Carnevalslied* from *Das Liebesverbot* (1835; publ. 1885); *Der Tannenbaum* (1838; publ. 1871); *Les Deux Grenadiers* (Heine's poem; French transl. by Heine himself; composed and publ. 1839); *Trois Romances: 1, Dors, mon enfant. 2, Attente. 3, Mignonne* (1839-40; publ. as supplement to Lewald's *Europa*, 1841-42); *Les Adieux de Marie Stuart* (1840; publ. 1913); *Tout n'est qu'images fugitives* (1840; publ. 1914); *Fünf Gedichte: 1, Der Engel. 2, Schmerzen. 3, Träume. 4, Stehe still. 5, Im Treibhaus* (Nos. 1-3 composed Dec., 1857; No. 4, Feb., 1858; No. 5, June, 1858; all publ. 1862); *Kraft-Liedchen* (1871; publ. in *Wiener Illustrierte Zeitung*, Oct. 14, 1877).

ARRANGEMENTS: Piano score of Beethoven's Ninth Symphony (1830; unpubl.), of Donizetti's *La Favorita* and *Elisir d'Amore* (both publ. 1840) and of Halévy's *La Reine de Chypre* and *Le Guitarrero* (both publ. 1841); Gluck's *Iphigénie en Aulide*, new translation and new close to overture (1846; Dresden, Feb. 22, 1847; full score of new close, and complete piano score [by von Bülow] publ. 1859); Palestrina's *Stabat Mater*, with indications for performance (1848; Dresden, March 8, 1848; publ. 1877); Mozart's *Don Giovanni*, version of dialogues and recitatives and, in parts, new translation (1850; not produced; unpubl.).

The first complete edition of Wagner's works was publ. by Breitkopf & Härtel (1912-22); a subsequent edition was begun in 1970 by the Bayerischen Akademie der Schönen Künste, Munich, under the direction of C. Dahlhaus.

BIBLIOGRAPHY: The literature on Wagner is virtually inexhaustible; the following is a selective list, divided into 15 categories: biographical; correspondence; personal reminiscences; relations with contemporaries; criticism, appreciation; Wagner's art in relation to esthetics, philosophy, and religion; Wagner's art in relation to theory and technique; Wagner and Bayreuth; Wagner's literary sources; analyses, guides, stories of the operas; characters; Wagner as writer; catalogues, yearbooks, etc.; iconography; miscellaneous.

BIOGRAPHICAL: R. Wagner, *Mein Leben* (see above, WRITINGS); C. Cabrol, *R. W.* (Paris, 1861); A. de Gasperini, *La nouvelle Allemagne musicale: R. W.* (Paris, 1866); F. Filippi, *R. W.* Leipzig, 1876); P. Lindau, *R. W.* (Paris, 1885); K. F. Glasenapp, *R. W.s Leben und Wirken* (2 vols.; Leipzig, 1876-77; 2nd ed., 1882; 3rd ed., in 6 vols., as *Das Leben R. W.s*, Leipzig, 1894-1911); F. Hueffer, *R. W.* (London, 1883; new ed., 1912); A. Jullien, *R. W. Sa vie et ses œuvres* (Paris, 1886; English transl., Boston, 1892, reprinted Philadelphia, 1910); G. Kobbé, *W.'s Life and Works* (2 vols., N.Y., 1890); H. T. Finck, *W. and His Works* (2 vols.; N.Y., 1893; 5th ed., 1898); H. S. Chamberlain, *R. W.* (Munich, 1896; 4th ed., 2 vols., 1912; English transl., London, 1897); W. A. Ellis, *Life of R. W.* (6 vol.; London, 1900-08; vols. I-III based on Glasenapp; reprinted N.Y., 1977, with new introduction by George Buelow); W. J. Henderson, *R. W., His Life and His Dramas* (N.Y., 1901; revised, 1923); Mrs. M. Burrell, *R. W. His Life and Works from 1813 to 1834* (London, 1898; a sumptuous folio richly illustrated; with many facsimiles of original documents, etc.); R. Bürkner, *R. W. Sein Leben und sein Werke* (Jena, 1906; 6th ed.,

1911); M. Koch, *R. W.* (3 vols.; Berlin, 1906, 1912, 1914; with detailed bibliography); J. Kapp, *R. W.* (Berlin, 1910; 32nd printing, 1929); F. Pfohl, *R. W. Sein Leben und Schaffen* (Berlin, 1911; 4th ed., Bielefeld, 1924); E. Newman, *W. As Man and Artist* (London, 1914; 2nd American ed., N.Y., 1924); H. Lichtenberger, *W.* (Paris, 1925); W. Wallace, *W. As He Lived* (London, 1925; new ed., 1933); L. Barthou, *La Vie amoureuse de R. W.* (Paris, 1925; in English as *The Prodigious Lover*, N.Y., 1927); V. d'Indy, *R. W. et son influence sur l'art musical français* (Paris, 1930); H. Reisiger, *Unruhiges Gestirn; die Jugend R. W.s* (Leipzig, 1930; in English as *Restless Star*, N.Y., 1932); Max Morold (penname of Max v. Millenkovitch), *W.s Kampf und Sieg* (Zürich, 1930); G. de Pourtalès, *R. W.* (Paris, 1932; English transl., N.Y., 1932); A. Spring, *R. W.s Weg und Wirken* (Stuttgart, 1933); P. Lalo, *R. W.* (Paris, 1933); W. J. Turner, *W.* (London, 1933); Sir W. H. Hadow, *W.* (London, 1934); M. Fehr, *R. W.s Schweizer Zeit* (2 vols., Aarau, 1934-53); R. L. Jacobs, *W.* (London, 1935); Ernest Newman, *The Life of R. W.* (4 vols.; N.Y., vol. I [1813-48], 1933; vol. II [1848-59], 1937; vol. III [1859-66], 1941; vol. IV [1866-83], 1946; the most thorough and authoritative biography); H. Malherbe, *R. W. Révolutionnaire* (Paris, 1938); E. Kretzschmar, *R. W. Sein Leben in Selbstzeugnissen, Briefen und Berichten* (Berlin, 1939); O. Strobel, *Neue Urkunden zur Lebensgeschichte R. W.s 1864-1882* (Karlsruhe, 1939; a supplement to the 4 vols. of corresspondence between W. and Ludwig II; SEE CORRESPONDENCE); M. von Millenkovitch, *Dreigestirn: W., Liszt, Bülow* (Leipzig, 1941); W. Reich, *R. W., Leben, Fühlen, Schaffen* (Olten, 1948); K. Ipser, *R. W. in Italien* (Salzburg, 1951); T. W. Adorno, *Versuch über Wagner* (Berlin, 1952); P. A. Loos, *R. W., Vollendung und Tragik der deutschen Romantik* (Munich, 1952); O. Strobel, *R. W. Leben und Schaffen* (Bayreuth, 1952); Z. von Kraft, *R. W.: ein dramatisches Leben* (Munich, 1953); R. Dumesnil, *R. W.* (Paris, 1954); C. von Westernhagen, *R. W.: sein Werk, sein Wesen, seine Welt* (Zürich, 1956).

CORRESPONDENCE: *Briefwechsel zwischen W. und Liszt* (2 vols., Leipzig, 1887; 2nd ed., 1900; English transl., London, 1888; 2nd ed., 1897, with index by W. A. Ellis). These two editions contain only the letters from 1841-61, and many passages referring to persons still living at the time of publication were omitted; in the 3rd ed., prepared by E. Kloss (1 vol., 1910), all letters up to Wagner's death are included, and the omitted portions restored. Eliza Wille, *Fünfzehn Briefe des Meisters* [to her], *nebst Erinnerungen und Erläuterungen* (Leipzig, 1887); *W.s Briefe an Dresdener Freunde* (Uhlig, Fischer, Heine; Leipzig, 1888; English transl., London, 1890); La Mara, *R. W.s Briefe an Aug. Röckel* (Leipzig, 1894; 2nd ed., 1903; English transl., London, 1897); H. S. Chamberlain, *R. W.s echte Briefe an Ferd. Praeger* (Bayreuth, 1894; 2nd ed., Berlin, 1908); E. Kastner, *Briefe von R. W. an seine Zeitgenossen (1830-83)* (Berlin, 1897; very incomplete); K. Heckel, *Briefe an Emil Heckel* (Berlin, 1898; 3rd ed., 1911; English transl., London, 1899); W. Golther, *R. W. an Mathilde Wesendonck, Tagebuchblätter und Briefe* (Berlin, 1904; 84th printing, 1922; English transl., London, 1905); W. Altmann, *R. W.s Briefe nach Zeitfolge und Inhalt* (Leipzig, synopses of

3143 letters (Leipzig, 1905); W. Golther, *Briefe R. W.s an Otto Wesendonck* (Berlin, 1905; English transl., London, 1911); D. Spitzer, *R. W.s Briefe an eine Putzmacherin* (Vienna, 1906; in English as *R. W. and the Seamstress,* N.Y., 1941); K. Fr. Glasenapp, ed., *Familienbriefe von R. W.* (Berlin, 1906; English transl., London, 1911); E. Kloss, *R. W. an seine Künstler* (Berlin, 1908); H. von Wolzogen, *R. W. an Minna Wagner* (2 vols., Berlin, 1908; English transl., London, 1909); E. Kloss, *R. W. an Freunde und Zeitgenossen* (Berlin, 1909); T. Apel, Jr., *R. W. an Theodor Apel* (Leipzig, 1910); W. Altmann, *R. W.s Briefwechsel mit seinen Verlegern* (3 vols.; Leipzig, 1911). Almost all the above collections were republ. in 1912 by Breitkopf & Härtel as *R. W.s Briefe* (17 vols.); a number of the letters appear in mutilated form (portions expressing political and religious views being suppressed). An unmutilated edition was begun by J. Kapp and E. Kastner, *R. W.s gesammelte Briefe* [1830–50] (2 vols.; Leipzig, 1914). J.-G. Prod'homme, "W. and the Paris Opéra" (unpubl. letters from Feb. and March 1861), *Musical Quarterly* (April 1915); E. Kloss, *Briefe an Hans von Bülow* (Jena, 1916); S. von Hausegger, *R. W.s Briefe an Frau Julie Ritter* (Munich, 1920); L. Karpath, *Briefe an Hans Richter* (Berlin, 1924); W. Altmann, *R. W.s Briefe, ausgewählt und erläutert* (2 vols., Leipzig, 1925; English translation, London, 1927); R. Sternfeld, *R. W. Aufsätze und Briefe des Meisters aus Paris* (Grossenwörden, 1927); W. Lippert, *R. W.s Verbannung und Rückkehr, 1849–62* (Dresden, 1927; English transl. as *W. in Exile,* London, 1930); H. Scholz, *R. W. an Mathilde Maier* (Leipzig, 1930); E. Lenrow, *The Letters of R. W. to A. Pusinelli* (N.Y., 1932); J. Tiersot, *Lettres françaises de R. W.* (Paris, 1935); W. Schuh, *Die Briefe R. W.s an Judith Gautier* (Zürich, 1936); K. Geiringer, "W. and Brahms" (with unpubl. letters), *Musical Quarterly* (April 1936); O. Strobel, *König Ludwig II und R. W.; Briefwechsel* (5 vols.; Karlsruhe, 1936–39); A. Holde, "Four Unknown Letters of R. W.," *Musical Quarterly* (April 1941); J. N. Burk, ed., *Letters of R. W. The Burrell Collection* (N.Y., 1950; in German, Frankfurt, 1953).

PERSONAL REMINISCENCES: H. von Wolzogen, *Erinnerungen an R. W.* (Leipzig, 1883; English transl., Bayreuth, 1894); A. Schilling, *Aus R. W.s Jugendzeit* (Berlin, 1898; reminiscences of Wagner's step-sister Cäcilie Avenarius); E. Schuré, *Souvenirs sur R. W.* (Paris, 1900; German tranls., Leipzig, 1900); E. von Possart, *Die Separat-Vorstellungen vor König Ludwig II. Erinnerungen* (Munich, 1901); L. Schemann, *Meine Erinnerungen an R. W.* (Stuttgart, 1902); G. A. Kietz, *R. W. in den Jahren 1842–49 und 1873–75* (Dresden, 1905); A. Kohut, *Der Meister von Bayreuth* (Berlin, 1905); E. Michotte, *Souvenirs personnels* (Paris, 1906); A. Gobineau, *Ein Erinnerungsbild aus Wahnfried* (Stuttgart, 1907); A. Neumann, *Erinnerungen an R. W.* (Leipzig, 1907; English transl., N.Y., 1908); H. Schmidt and U. Hartmann, *R. W. in Bayreuth. Erinnerungen* (Leipzig, 1910); Siegfried Wagner, *Erinnerungen* (Stuttgart, 1923; extended ed., privately printed, 1935); Judith Gautier, *Auprès de R. W.; Souvenirs (1861–1883)* (Paris, 1943).

RELATIONS WITH CONTEMPORARIES: J. L. Craemer, *König Ludwig II. und R. W.* (Munich, 1901); F. Gerard, *Romance of King Ludwig II of Bavaria. His Relation*

with *R. W.* (London, 1901); S. Röckel, *Ludwig II. und R. W. in den Jahren 1864–65* (Munich, 1903; 2nd ed., 1913); J. Kapp, *R. W. und Franz Liszt. Eine Freundschaft* (Berlin, 1908); H. Bélart, *Friedr. Nietzsches Freundschaftstragödie mit R. W.* (Dresden, 1912) and *R. W.s Liebestragödie mit Mathilde Wesendonck* (Dresden, 1912); J. Kapp, *R. W. und die Frauen* (Berlin, 1912; new revised ed., 1951; in English as *The Women in W.'s Life,* N.Y., 1931); E. Förster-Nietzsche, *W. und Nietzsche zur Zeit ihrer Freundschaft* (Munich, 1915; English translation as *The Nietzsche-Wagner Correspondence,* N.Y., 1921); C. Sarti, *W. and Nietzsche* (N.Y., 1915); E. Schuré, *Femmes inspiratrices* (Paris, 1930); E. Schuré, *Au banquet des dieux: F. Liszt, R. W. et ses amis* (Paris, 1931); L. Barthou, "R. W. et Judith Gautier," *Revue de Paris* (1932); P. G. Dippel, *Nietzsche und W.* (Berne, 1934); D. Fischer-Dieskau, *Wagner und Nietzsche* (1974).

CRITICISM, APPRECIATION: Liszt's fine essays on *Tannhäuser* (1849), *Lohengrin* (1850), *Der fliegende Holländer* (1854), and *Das Rheingold* (1855) are in vol. III, 2, of his *Gesammelte Schriften* (Leipzig, 1899); F. Hinrichs, *R. W. und die neuere Musik: eine kritische Skizze* (Halle, 1854); F. K. F. Müller, *R. W. und das Musik-Drama* (Leipzig, 1861); L. Nohl, *Gluck und W. Über die Entwickelung des Musikdramas* (Munich, 1870); F. Nietzsche, *Die Geburt der Tragödie aus dem Geiste der Musik* (Leipzig, 1872; in vol. I of *Nietzsches Werke,* 1895; English transl. in O. Levy's ed. of complete works, Edinburgh, 1910–14); E. Dannreuther, *W. His Tendencies and Theories* (London, 1873); F. Hueffer, *R. W. and the Music of the Future* (London, 1874); E. Schuré, *Le Drame musical: I. La Musique et la Poésie dans leur développement historique. II. Wagner. Son Œuvre et son idée* (Paris, 1875; 3rd ed., augmented, 1894); L. Nohl, *Das moderne Musikdrama* (Vienna, 1884); F. Nietzsche, *Der Fall W.* and *N. contra W.* (both Leipzig, 1888; in vol. VIII of *Nietzsches Werke,* 1895; English transl. in vol. XI of complete works; bitter invective in place of former admiration); H. E. Krehbiel, *Studies in the Wagnerian Drama* (N.Y., 1891); M. Kufferath, *Le Théâtre de W. de Tannhäuser à Parsifal. Essais de critique littéraire, esthétique et musicale* (6 vols.; Paris, 1891–98); H. S. Chamberlain, *Das Drama R. W.s Eine Anregung* (Leipzig, 1892; 5th ed., 1913; English transl., London, 1915); G. Servières, *R. W. jugé en France* (Paris, 1897); G. B. Shaw, *The Perfect Wagnerite* (London 1898; also in vol. 17 of complete works, 1932); Arthur Seidl, *Wagneriana* (3 vols.; Berlin, 1901–02; continuation as *Neue Wagneriana,* Bonn, 1914); E. Istel, *Das Kunstwerk R. W.s* (Leipzig, 1910; 2nd ed., 1919); G. Adler, *R. W.* (lectures; Vienna, 1904; 2nd ed., 1922); P. Bekker, *R. W. Das Leben im Werke* (Stuttgart, 1924; English transl., London, 1931); J. Kapp, *W. und die Berliner Oper* (Berlin, 1933); J. Kapp, *Das Liebersverbot, Entstehung und Schicksale des Werkes von R. W.* (Berlin, 1933); A. Bahr-Mildenburg, *Tristan und Isolde* (Leipzig, 1936; vol. I of *Darstellung der Werke R. W.s aus dem Geiste der Dichtung und Musik*); R. C. Schuster, *R. W. und die Welt der Oper* (Munich, 1937); L. Gilman, *W.'s Operas* (N.Y., 1937); T. Mann, *Freud, Goethe, W.* (N.Y., 1937); E. Borrelli, *Estetica wagneriana* (Florence, 1940); J. Barzun, *Darwin, Marx, Wagner* (Boston, 1941); M. Doisy, *L'Œuvre de*

R. W. du Vaisseau fantôme à Parsifal (Brussels, 1945); M. Beaufils, *W. et le wagnérisme* (Paris, 1947); P. W. Jacob, *Taten der Musik; R. W. und sein Werk* (Regensburg, 1952); E. Zuckerman, *The First 100 Years of Wagner's Tristan* (N.Y., 1964); C. White, *An Introduction to the Life and Works of R. W.* (Englewood Cliffs, N.J., 1967).

WAGNER'S ART IN RELATION TO ESTHETICS, PHILOSOPHY AND RELIGION: F. von Hausegger, *R. W. und Schopenhauer* (Leipzig, 1878; 2nd ed., 1897); J. Freson, *Essais de philosophie et de l'art: l'esthétique de R. W.* (2 vols.; Paris, 1893); M. Hébert, *Le Sentiment religieux dans l'œuvre de R. W.* (Paris, 1894); R. Louis, *Die Weltanschauung R. W.s* (Leipzig, 1898); D. Irvine, *Parsifal and W.'s Christianity* (London, 1899); M. Kufferath, *Musiciens et philosophes: Tolstoy, Schopenhauer, Nietzsche, W.* (Paris, 1899); P. Moos, *R. W. als Ästhetiker* (Berlin, 1906); R. Richter, *Kunst und Philosophie bei R. W.* (Leipzig, 1906); H. Bélart, *F. Nietzsche und R. W.: Ihre persönlichen Beziehungen, Kunst- und Weltanschauungen* (Berlin, 1907); G. Robert, *Philosophie et drame. Essai d'une explication des drames wagnériens* (Paris, 1907); O. Schmiedel, *R. W.s religiöse Weltanschauung* (Tübingen, 1907); W. Vollert, *R. W.s Stellung zur christlichen Religion* (Wismar, 1907); L. Dauriac, *Le Musicien-poète R. W. Étude de psychologie musicale* (Paris, 1908); G. Braschowanoff, *Von Olympia nach Bayreuth* (2 vols.; Leipzig, 1911–12); F. Gross, *Die Wiedergeburt des Sehers* (Zürich, 1927); A. Drews, *Ideengehalt von W.s dramatischen Dichtungen* (Leipzig, 1931); G. Wooley, *R. W. et le symbolisme français* (Paris, 1931); F. Gross, *Der Mythos W.s* (Vienna, 1932); G. Frommel, *Der Geist des Antike bei R. W.* (Berlin, 1933); I. Wyzewska, *La Revue wagnérienne; essai sur l'interprétation esthétique de W. en France* (Paris, 1934); K. R. Karzer, *R. W. der Revolutionär gegen das 19. Jahrhundert* (1934); W. Engelsmann, *Erlösung dem Erlöser: R. W.s religiöse Weltgestalt* (Leipzig, 1936); M. Boucher, *Les Idées politiques de R. W.* (Paris, 1948; in English, N.Y., 1950); K. Overhoff, *R. W.s germanisch-christlicher Mythos* (Dinkelsbühl, 1955).

WAGNER'S ART IN RELATION TO THEORY AND TECHNIQUE: C. Kistler, *Harmonielehre* (Heilbronn, 1879; 2nd ed., greatly augmented, 1903; based on Wagner's harmonic innovations); K. Mayrberger, *Die Harmonik R. W.s* (Chemnitz, 1883); S. Jadassohn, *Melodik und Harmonik bei R. W.* (Berlin, 1899); E. Thomas, *Die Instrumentation der "Meistersinger" von R. W.* (2 vols.; Mannheim, 1899; 2nd ed., Leipzig, 1907); G. Capellen, *Ist das System Simon Sechters ein geeigneter Ausgangspunkt für die theoretische Wagnerforschung?* (Leipzig, 1902); É. Poirée, *Le Discours musical, son principe, ses formes expressives, spécialement d'après la partition des "Maîtres-Chanteurs" de R. W.* (Paris, 1902); E. Ergo, *Über R. W.s Harmonik und Melodik* (Leipzig, 1914); E. Kurth, *Romantische Harmonik und ihre Krise in W.s "Tristan"* (Bern and Leipzig, 1920; 2nd ed., Berlin, 1923; valuable); A. Lorenz, *Das Geheimnis der Form bei R. W.* (4 vols.; Berlin: I, *Der Ring*, 1924; II, *Tristan*, 1926; III, *Meistersinger*, 1930; IV, *Parsifal*, 1933; valuable).

WAGNER AND BAYREUTH: F. Nietzsche, *W. in Bayreuth* (Chemnitz, 1876; in vol. I of *Nietzsches Werke*, Leipzig, 1895; new ed., 1931; English transl. in complete works, Edinburgh, 1910–14); H. von Wolzogen, *Grundlage und Aufgabe des Allgem. Patronalvereins zur Pflege und Erhaltung der Bühnenfestspiele in B.* (Chemnitz, 1877); K. Heckel, *Die Bühnenfestspiele in B.* (Leipzig, 1891); H. Porges, *Die Bühnenproben zu den Festspielen des Jahren 1876* (Leipzig, 1896); F. Weingartner, *B., 1876–96* (Berlin, 1896; 2nd ed., 1904); H. S. Chamberlain, *Die ersten 20 Jahre der B. Bühnenfestspiele* (Bayreuth, 1896); E. Kloss, *Zwanzig Jahre B.* (Berlin, 1896; English transl., London, 1896); F. Hofmann, *B. und seine Kunstdenkmale* (Munich, 1902); W. Golther, *B.* (Berlin, 1904); R. Sternfeld, *R. W. und die B. Bühnenfestspiele* (2 vols.; Berlin, 1906; new ed., 1927); M. G. Conrad, *W.s Geist und Kunst in B.* (Munich, 1906); K. F. Glazenapp, *Bayreuther Briefe von R. W.* (Berlin, 1907; abridged English translation, as *The Story of Bayreuth as Told in the Bayreuth Letters of R. W.* Boston, 1912); A. Prüfer, *Das Werk von B.* (Leipzig, 1909); A. Prüfer, *R. W. in B.* (Leipzig, 1910); H. von Wolzogen, *Heinrich von Steins Briefwechsel mit H. von Wolzogen. Ein Beitrag zur Geschichte des Bayreuther Gedankens* (Leipzig, 1910); H. Bahr and A. Bahr-Mildenburg, *Bayreuth und das W.-Theater* (Leipzig, 1910; 2nd ed., 1912; English transl., London, 1921); R. Du Moulin-Eckart, *Wahnfried* (Leipzig, 1925); P. Bülow, *R. W. und sein Werk von Bayreuth* (Frankfurt, 1927); F. Klose, *Bayreuth. Eindrücke und Erlebnisse* (Regensburg, 1929); O. Bie, *R. W. und Bayreuth* (Leipzig, 1931); J. Kneise, *Der Kampf zweier Welten um das Bayreuther Erbe* (Kassel, 1931); L. Reichwein, *Bayreuth* (Bielefeld and Leipzig, 1934); H. B. Brand, *Aus R. W.s Leben in Bayreuth* (Munich, 1935); S. Rützow, *R. W. und Bayreuth* (Munich, 1943); 2nd ed., 1953); J. Bertram, *Der Seher von Bayreuth* (Berlin, 1943); E. Ebermayer, *Magisches Bayreuth, Legende und Wirklichkeit* (Stuttgart, 1951).

WAGNER'S LITERARY SOURCES: F. Schultz, *Das neue Deutschland. Seine alten Heldensagen und R. W.* (Leipzig, 1888); E. Meinck, *Die sagenwissenschaftlichen Grundlagen der Nibelungendichtung W.s* (Berlin, 1892); J. L. Weston, *The Legends of the Wagnerian Drama* (London, 1896; new ed., 1903); A. M. Bowen, *The Sources and Text of W.'s "Die Meistersinger von Nürnberg"* (Munich, 1897); J. Nover, *Die Tannhäusersage und ihre poetische Gestaltung* (Hamburg, 1897); E. Wechsler, *Die Sage vom hl. Gral in ihrer Entwickelung bis auf R. W.s "Parsifal"* (Halle, 1898); J. Nover, *Die Lohengrinsage und ihre poetische Gestaltung* (Hamburg, 1899); Hermann von der Pfordten, *Handlung und Dichtung der Bühnenwerke R. W.s nach ihren Grundlagen in Sage und Geschichte* (Berlin, 1900; 4th ed., 1908); W. Golther, *Die sagengeschichtlichen Grundlagen der Ringdichtung R. W.s* (Berlin, 1902); S. Valot, *Les Héros de R. W. Études sur les origines indoeuropéennes des légendes wagnériennes* (Paris, 1903); W. C. Sawyer, *Teutonic Legends in the Nibelungenlied and the Nibelungen Ring* (Philadelphia, 1904); W. Golther, *Tristan und Isolde in den Dichtungen des Mittelalters und der neuen Zeit* (Leipzig, 1907); R. von Kralik, *Die Gralssage* (Ravensburg, 1907); E. Elster, *Tannhäuser in Geschichte, Sage und Dichtung* (Bromberg, 1908); L. von Schroeder, *Die Wurzeln der Sage vom hl. Gral* (Vienna, 1910); F. Strich, *Die Mythologie in der deutschen Litteratur von Klopstock bis W.* (2 vol.; Halle, 1910); W. Golther,

Zur deutschen Sage und Dichtung (Leipzig, 1911); O. Rank, *Die Lohengrinsage* (Vienna, 1911); W. Golther, *Parsifal und der Gral in deutscher Sage des Mittelalters und der Neuzeit* (Leipzig, 1913); A. Bonilla y San Martín, *Las Leyendas de W. en la literatura española* (Madrid, 1913); G. Brownell, *The Wagnerian Romances* (N.Y., 1925); H. Thompson, *W. and Wagenseil: A Source of W.'s Opera "Die Meistersinger"* (London, 1927); M. Unger, "The Cradle of the Parsifal Legend," *Musical Quarterly* (July 1932); A. Salazar, "Parsifal in Romanic Lands," *Musical Quarterly* (Jan. 1939); R. M. Rayner, *Wagner and "Die Meistersinger"* (Oxford, 1940); H. Hirsch, *R. W. und das deutsche Mittelalter* (Vienna, 1944).

ANALYSES, GUIDES, STORIES OF THE OPERAS: G. Kobbé, *R. W.s "Tristan und Isolde"* (N.Y., 1886); A. Smolian, *The Themes of "Tannhäuser"* (London, 1891); A. Lavignac, *Le Voyage artistique à Bayreuth* (Paris, 1897; 14th printing, 1925; English transl. as *The Music-Dramas of R. W.*, N.Y., 1898; new ed., 1932); J. Tiersot, *Études sur les Maîtres-Chanteurs de Nuremberg, de R. W.* (Paris, 1899); G. Kobbé, *W.'s Music Dramas Analyzed* (N.Y., 1904); G. Kobbé, *How to Understand W.'s Ring* (7th ed., N.Y., 1916); W. Dry, *Erläuterungen zur R. W.s Tondramen* (2 vols., Leipzig, 1906–07); S. H. Hamer, *The Story of "The Ring"* (N.Y., 1907); M. Burckhardt, *Führer durch R. W.s Musikdramen* (Berlin, 1909); L. Windsperger, *Das Buch der Motive und Themen aus sämtlichen Opern und Musikdramen R. W.s* (for piano, with explanatory text; Mainz, 1921); W. Wilmshurst, *Parsifal* (London, 1922; Musical Pilgrim series); A. Cœuroy, *La Walkyrie de R. W.* (Paris, 1924); C. Winn, *The Mastersingers of W.* (London, 1925; Musical Pilgrim series); A. Himonet, *Lohengrin de R. W.* (Paris, 1925); A. E. F. Dickinson, *The Musical Design of "The Ring"* (London, 1926; Musical Pilgrim series); E. Newman, *Stories of the Great Operas* (vol. I, R. W.; N.Y., 1928); A. Buesst, *R. W., The Nibelung's Ring* (London, 1932; 2nd ed., 1952); R. Grisson, *Beiträge zur Auslegung von R. W.'s "Ring des Nibelungen"* (Leipzig, 1934); V. d'Indy, *Introduction à l'étude de Parsifal de W.* (Paris, 1937); E. Hutcheson, *A Musical Guide to R. W.'s Ring of the Nibelung* (N.Y., 1940); S. A. Luciani, *Il Tristano e Isolda di R. W.* (Florence, 1942); G. Gavazzeni, *Il Siegfried di R. W.* (Florence, 1944); K. Overhoff, *R. W.s Tristan Partitur; eine musikalisch-philosophische Deutung* (Bayreuth, 1948); E. Newman, *The Wagner Operas* (N.Y., 1949); K. Overhoff, *R. W.s Parsifal* (Lindau im Bodensee, 1951); R. Donnington, *Wagner's "Ring" and Its Symbols* (London, 1963).

CHARACTERS: C. Maude, *W.'s Heroes* (London, 1896); and *W.'s Heroines* (London, 1896); H. von Wolzogen, *R. W.s Heldengestalten erläutert* (Hannover, 1896); A. Höfler, *Wotan. Eine Studie zum "Ring des Nibelungen"* (Veinna, 1897); H. Bélart, *Taschenbuch der Wagnerkünstlerin. W.s Frauengestalten in gesangdramatischer Beziehung* (Leipzig, 1898); E. Destranges, *Les Femmes dans l'œuvre de R. W.* (Paris, 1899); F. Schwabe, *Die Frauengestalten W.s als Typen des "Ewig-weiblichen"* (Munich, 1902); H. Materna, *R. W.s Frauengestalten* (Leipzig, 1904); W. Broesel, *Evchen Pogner* (Berlin, 1906); H. Güntert, *Kundry* (Heidelberg, 1928).

WAGNER AS WRITER: H. von Wolzogen, *Die Sprache in R. W.s Dichtungen* (Leipzig, 1878); J. Gautier, *R. W. et son œuvre poétique* (Paris, 1882); B. Vogel, *W. als Dichter. Ein Überblick seines poetischen Schaffens* (Leipzig, 1889); A. Ernst, *L'Art de W.: l'œuvre poétique* (Paris, 1893); H. Lichtenberger, *R. W., poète et penseur* (Paris, 1898; new ed., 1931; German transl., Dresden, 1899 [augmented ed. 1913]); O. Lüning, *R. W. als Dichter und Denker* (Zürich, 1900); W. Golther, *R. W. als Dichter* (Berlin, 1904; English transl., London, 1905); R. Weltrich, *R. W.s "Tristan und Isolde" als Dichtung. Nebst einigen allgemeinen Bemerkungen über W.s Kunst* (Berlin, 1904); E. Meinck, *Fr. Hebbels und R. W.s Nibelungen-Trilogien* (Leipzig, 1905); J. Schuler, *The Language of R. W.'s "Ring des Nibelungen"* (Lancaster, Pa., 1910); K. Reichelt, *R. W. und die englische Literatur* (Leipzig, 1912); E. von Schrenck, *R. W. als Dichter* (Munich, 1913); P. Bülow, *Die Jugendschriften R. W.s* (Leipzig, 1917); W. Ramann, *Der dichterische Stil R. W.s* (Leipzig, 1929); O. Strobel, *Skizzen und Entwürfe zur Ring-Dichtung* (Munich, 1930); H. Galli, *W. und die deutsche Klassik* (Berne, 1936).

CATALOGUES, YEARBOOKS, ETC.: E. Kastner, *Chronologisch-systematischer W.-Katalog* (Offenbach, 1878); N. Oesterlein, *Katalog einer W.-Bibliothek* (4 vols.; Leipzig, 1882, 1886, 1891, 1895; describes the treasures of the W.-Museum and contains full bibliography of books and articles publ. about Wagner during his life [10, 181 titles]); E. Kastner, *Verzeichnis der ersten Aufführungen von R. W.s dramatischen Werken* (Vienna, 1896; 2nd ed., Leipzig, 1899); H. Silège, *Bibliographie wagnérienne française [1851-1902]* (Paris, 1902); P. Pabst, *Verzeichnis von R. W.s Werken, Schriften und Dichtungen, deren hauptsächlichsten Bearbeitungen, sowie von besonders interessanter Litteratur, Abbildungen, Büsten und Kunstblättern, den Meister und seine Schöpfungen betreffend* (Leipzig, 1905); L. Frankenstein, *Bibliographie der auf R. W. bezüglichen. Literatur für die Jahre 1907-11* (Berlin, 1912); J. Kürschner, *R. W.-Jahrbuch* (Stuttgart, 1886; only 1 vol. publ.); L. Frankenstein, *R. W.-Jahrbuch* (Berlin, 1906, 1907, 1908, 1912, 1913); M. Burrell, *Catalogue of the Burrell Collection of W. Documents, Letters and Other Biogr. Material* (London, 1929); O. Strobel, *Führer durch die wiederholte Ausstellung einer umfassenden Auswahl von Schätzen aus dem Archiv des Hauses Wahnfried: Genie am Werk, R. W.s Schaffen und Wirken im Spiegel eigenhandschriftlicher Urkunden* (Bayreuth, 1934). The volumes of *Bayreuther Blätter* (founded by Wagner in 1878) are of value; see also the publications of the various Wagner societies: Wagner Society of America, Chicago, Illinois *(Wagner News);* Wagner Society, London *(Wagner);* Schweizerische R. W. Gesellschaft, Baar, Switzerland *(Triebschner Blätter).*

ICONOGRAPHY: J. Grand-Carteret, *R. W. en caricatures* (Paris, 1892); E. Fuchs and E. Kreowski, *R. W. in der Karikatur* (Berlin, 1907; 6th ed., 1913); A. Vanselow, *R. W.s photographische Bildnisse* (Munich, 1908); E. Engel, *R. W.s Leben und Werke im Bilde* (2 vols.; Vienna, 1913; new ed., Leipzig, 1922); J. Kapp, *R. W. sein Leben, sein Werk, seine Welt in 260 Bildern* (Berlin, 1933); P. Bülow, *R. W. sein Leben in Bildern* (Leipzig, 1936); R. Bory, *R. W. sein Leben und sein Werk in Bildern* (Leipzig, 1938).

MISCELLANEOUS: C. Baudelaire, *R. W. et Tannhäuser à Paris* (Paris, 1861); W. Tappert, *Wagner-Lexikon. Wörterbuch der Unhöflichkeit* (Leipzig, 1877; new augmented ed. as *R. W. im Spiegel der Kritik*, 1903; an interesting collection of adverse and abusive comments); *Über Schicksale und Bestimmung des W.-Museums* (Leipzig, 1892); E. Kloss, *Das W.-Museum in Eisenach*, in *Ein W.-Lesebuch* (Leipzig, 1904); K. Grunsky, *R. W. und die Juden* (Munich, 1921); W. Lange, *R. W. und seine Vaterstadt, Leipzig* (Leipzig, 1921); J. Marnold, *Le Cas W.: la musique pendant la guerre* (Paris, 1920); *W. et la France*, special issue of the *Revue Musicale* (Oct. 1923; reprinted N.Y., 1977); P. Stefan, *Die Feindschaft gegen W.* (Regensburg, 1918); E. Newman, *Fact and Fiction about W.* (N.Y., 1931); E. Stemplinger, *W. in Munich* (Munich, 1933); W. Golther, *R. W. Leben und Werke in urkundlichen Zeugnissen, Briefen, Schriften, Berichten* (Ebenhausen, near Munich, 1936); W. Lange, *R. W.s Sippe*, with genealogical table (Leipzig, 1938); L. Weinhold, *Handschriften von R. W.* in Leipzig (Leipzig, 1938); O. Daube, *Humor bei R. W.* (Gütersloh, 1944); L. Stein, *The Racial Thinking of R. W.* (N.Y., 1950); L. Strecker, *R. W. als Verlagsgefährte* (Mainz, 1951).

Wagner, Roger, American choral conductor; b. Le-Puy, France, Jan. 16, 1914. He studied organ with Marcel Dupré; settled in Los Angeles in 1937; studied philosophy and French literature at the Univ. of Calif. and at the Univ. of Southern Calif., Los Angeles; studied orchestration with Lucien Caillet and conducting with Bruno Walter. In 1948 he founded the Roger Wagner Chorale, and toured with it in the U.S., Canada and Latin America. In 1965 he organized the Los Angeles Master Chorale and Sinfonia Orchestra, which opened its inaugural season on Jan. 27, 1965. He took his Master Chorale on a tour of Russia in 1974.

Wagner, Siegfried, son of **Richard** and **Cosima Wagner;** b. Triebschen, June 6, 1869; d. Bayreuth, Aug. 4, 1930. His parents were married on Aug. 25, 1870, and Siegfried was thus legitimatized. Wagner wrote *Siegfried Idyll* for him, and it was performed in Wagner's house in Triebschen on Christmas Day, 1870 (Cosima Wagner's birthday). He attended a polytechnic school, but the lure of music proved overwhelming, and he took up studies under Julius Kniese and Humperdinck; began to compose; also embarked on a conductorial career; appeared as a symph. conductor in Germany, Austria, Italy, and England. In 1894 he was appointed assistant conductor in Bayreuth, and in 1896 became one of the regular conductors. He conducted from memory, and left-handed. In 1909 he succeeded his mother as general supervisor of the Bayreuth Festivals. On Sept. 21, 1915, he married Winifred Williams, an adopted daughter of Karl Klindworth. In 1923-24 he visited the U.S. in order to raise funds for the reopening of the Bayreuth Festspielhaus, which had been closed in the course of World War I. In his career as composer, he was greatly handicapped by the inevitable comparisons with his father. He wrote a symph. poem *Sehnsucht*, after Schiller (1895); *Fahnenschwur* for men's chorus and orch. (1914); a violin concerto (1915); chamber

music and vocal works. But his main interest was in music drama; like his father, he wrote his own librettos.

WORKS: operas: *Der Bärenhäuter* (Munich, Jan. 22, 1899); *Herzog Wildfang* (Munich, March 14, 1901); *Der Kobold* (Hamburg, Jan. 29, 1904); *Bruder Lustig* (Hamburg, Oct. 13, 1905); *Sternengebot* (Hamburg, Jan. 21, 1908); *Banadietrich* (Karlsruhe, Jan. 15, 1910); *An Allem ist Hütchen Schuld* (Stuttgart, Dec. 6, 1917); *Schwarzschwanenreich* (Karlsruhe, Nov. 5, 1918); *Sonnenflammen* (Karlsruhe, 1926); *Der Heidenkönig* (Cologne, Dec. 16, 1933); *Der Schmied von Marienburg* (Rostock, Dec. 16, 1923). His reminiscences, *Erinnerungen*, were publ. at Stuttgart in 1923.

BIBLIOGRAPHY: L. Karpath, *Siegfried Wagner als Mensch und Künstler* (Leipzig, 1902); K. F. Glasenapp, *Siegfried Wagner und seine Kunst* (Leipzig, 1911; 3rd ed., 1919); P. Pretzsch, *Die Kunst Siegfried Wagners* (1919); O. Daube, *Siegfried Wagner und sein Werk* (Bayreuth, 1925); R. Du Moulin-Eckart, *Wahnfried* (Leipzig, 1925); H. Rebois, *Lettres de Siegfried Wagner* (Paris, 1933); O. Daube, *Siegfried Wagner und die Märchenoper* (Leipzig, 1936); Zdenko von Kraft, *Der Sohn: Siegfried Wagners Leben und Umwelt* (1969).

Wagner, Wieland, grandson of **Richard Wagner,** great-grandson of **Franz Liszt;** b. Bayreuth, Jan. 5, 1917; d. Munich, Oct. 16, 1966. He received his general education in Munich, and devoted himself to the problem of modernizing the productions of Wagner's operas. When Bayreuth Festivals were resumed in 1951, after World War II, Wieland Wagner assumed the tasks of its scenic director. Abandoning the luxuriant scenery of 19th century opera, he emphasized the symbolic meaning of Wagner's music dramas, eschewing realistic effects, such as machinery propelling the Rhine maidens through the wavy gauze of the river, or the bright paper flames of the burning Valhalla. He even introduced Freudian sexual overtones, such as in his production of *Tristan und Isolde*, where a phallic pillar was conspicuously placed on the stage.

Wagner-Régeny, Rudolf, Hungarian-German composer, b. Régen, Transylvania, Aug. 28, 1903; d. Berlin, Sept. 18, 1969. He studied piano with Robert Teichmüller at the Leipzig Cons., conducting and theory at the Musikhochschule in Berlin. He occupied various posts as theater and cinema conductor; was in the German Army during World War II; director of the Musikhochschule in Rostock (1947–50); in 1950 was appointed director of the State Cons. in East Berlin.

WORKS: In 1934 he was commissioned (together with J. Weismann) by the Ministry of Culture to write new musical settings for *A Midsummer Night's Dream*, to replace Mendelssohn's score; his music was produced at Düsseldorf, on June 6, 1935. Other works: the operas *Moschopulus* (Gera, 1928), *Der nackte König* (Gera, 1928), *Sganarelle* (Essen, 1929), *Die heilige Courtisane* (1932), *Der Günstling* (Dresden, Feb. 20, 1935), *Die Bürger von Calais* (Berlin, Jan. 28, 1939), *Johanna Balk* (Vienna, April 4, 1941), *Das Opfer* (1942), *Der Darmenwäscher* (1950); *Prometheus* (Kassel, Sept. 12, 1959); *Das Bergwerk zu Falun*

(Salzburg, Aug. 16, 1961); several ballets, among them *Der zerbrochene Krug* (1937); *Mythologische Figurinen* for orch. (Salzburg Festival of the International Society for Contemporary Music, June 21, 1952); *3 Movements* for orch. (1952); *Einleitung und ode* for orch. (1967); String Quartet (1948); *Divertimento* for 3 woodwinds and timpani (1954); various pieces of chamber music.

BIBLIOGRAPHY: A. Burgartz, *Rudolf Wagner-Régeny* (Berlin, 1935); T. Müller-Medek, ed., *Rudolf Wagner-Régeny: Begegnungen, Biographische Aufzeichnungen, Tagebücher und sein Briefwechsel mit Caspar Neher* (Berlin, 1968).

Wahlberg, Rune, Swedish conductor and composer; b. Gävle, March 15, 1910. He studied in Stockholm (1928–35), in Leipzig (1936–37) and Göteborg (1943–51); active as conductor and concert pianist.

WORKS: Piano Concerto (1938); *Meditation* for violin and orch. (1941); 4 symphonies: No. 1 (1941), No. 2 (1945), No. 3 (1951; Toronto, March 6, 1961), No. 4 (1959; Hofors, March 13, 1960); *Nordic Suite* for orch. (1943); *Afrodite*, suite for orch. (1944); *Preludium, Larghetto and Fugue* for orch. (1952); *Nordland* for male chorus and orch. (1957); Violin Concerto (1958); Violin Sonata (1959); *Concerto barocco* for violin and string orch. (1960); Cello Concerto (1961); Bass Clarinet Concerto (1961); *Concert Suite* for strings (1961); *Prisma*, saxophone quartet (1961); Violin Concertino (1963); *Florez och Blanzeflor* for male chorus and orch. (1963); *Concert Fantasy* for piano and orch. (1967); *Havsfyren* for male chorus and orch. (1971); *Helgdagsvisa* for 4 violins (1971); String Quartet (1972); *Concerto fantastico* for percussion (1973); *Lyric Fantasy* for violin and piano (1975); *En Saga,* an opera (1952).

Wailly, (Louis Auguste) Paul (Warnier) de, French composer; b. Amiens, May 16, 1854; d. Paris, June 18, 1933. He was a pupil of César Franck, and in his works showed himself a follower of Franck's precepts. He wrote 3 symphonies; a dramatic oratorio, *L'Apôtre* (1924); *26 Pièces* for harmonium; publ. *La Vie et l'âme de César Franck* (Paris, 1922).

BIBLIOGRAPHY: A. Laurent, *Paul de Wailly: l'artiste, l'œuvre* (Paris, 1933); A. Laurent, *Paul de Wailly: le compositeur, l'artiste* (Eu, 1940).

Waisselius, Matthäus, German composer and lute player; b. c.1540; d., probably in Königsberg, 1602. He was a schoolmaster in the vicinity of Königsberg; publ. several books, in tablature notation, of music for the lute, among them *Cantiones 4, 5, et 6 vocum* (Frankfurt, 1573) and *Lautenbuch,* comprising instruction for the lute and a selection of dance tunes (1592).

Walaciński, Adam, Polish composer; b. Cracow, Sept. 18, 1928. He studied violin with E. Umińska at the State College of Music in Cracow (1947–52); had private composition lessons with S. Kisielewski (1953–55) and with Boguslaw Schäffer; was violinist in the Cracow Radio Orch. (1948–56). In 1972 he was appointed instructor at the Cracow College of Music.

He is a member of the avant-garde "Grupa Krakowska."

WORKS: *Composition "Alfa"* for orch. (1958); String Quartet (1959); *Modifications* for viola and piano (1960); *Rotazioni* for piano (1961); *Intrada* for 7 players (1962); *Canto Tricolore* for flute, violin and vibraphone (1962); *Horizons* for chamber orch. (1962); *Sekwencje* for concertante flute and orch. (1963); *Liryka sprzed zaśniecia (A Lyric Before Falling Asleep)* for soprano, flute, and 2 pianos (1963); *Concerto da camera* for violin and string orch. (1964, revised 1967); *Fogli volanti,* optically notated composition for string trio (1965); *Canzona* for cello, piano, and tape (1966); *Epigrams* for chamber ensemble (1967); *Dichromia* for flute and piano (1967); *Refrains et réflexions* for orch. (1969); *Notturno 70* for 24 strings, 3 flutes, and percussion (1970); *Allaloa,* optically notated composition for electronically transformed piano (1970); *Torso* for orch. (1971; Cracow, Jan. 21, 1972); *On peut écouter* for flute, oboe and bassoon (1971); *Divertimento interrotto* for 13 players (1974); *Mirophonies* for soprano, actor, clarinet, viola, cello, harp, and percussion (1974).

Walcker, Eberhard Friedrich, German organ builder; b. Cannstadt, near Stuttgart, July 3, 1794; d. Ludwigsburg, Oct. 2, 1872. Trained in the workshops of his father, a skilled organ builder, he set up for himself in Ludwigsburg in 1820 and won great renown by his excellent work and numerous inventions. After his death the business passed to his five sons, **Heinrich** (b. Oct. 10, 1828; d. Kirchheim, Nov. 24, 1903), **Friedrich** (b. Sept. 17, 1829; d. Dec. 6, 1895), **Karl** (b. March, 6, 1845; d. Stuttgart, May 19, 1908), **Paul** (b. May 31, 1846; d. 1928), and **Eberhard** (b. April 8, 1850; d. 1927). In 1916 **Oscar Walcker** (son of Friedrich; b. Jan. 1, 1869; d. Nov. 4, 1948) became head of the firm; in 1932 he effected a merger with the firm Ziegler of Steinsfurt (in 1910 a merger with the firm of W. Sauer of Frankfurt had taken place). His reminiscences, *Erinnerungen eines Orgelbauers,* were publ. in Kassel, 1948. The firm has built more than 2,500 organs; some of the largest are those in Ulm Cathedral (1856; 95 speaking stops; rebuilt and enlarged in 1914 to 171), Music Hall, Boston (now removed; 1863; 86 stops); Paulskirche, Frankfurt (1833; 74 stops); St. Peter's, St. Petersburg (1840; 65 stops); Reval Cathedral (1842; 65 stops); Votivkirche, Vienna (1878; 61 stops); Riga Cathedral (1885; 124 stops); St. Stephen's Cathedral, Vienna (1886; 90 stops); St. Michael's, Hamburg (1912; 154 stops, 5 manuals and pedal).

BIBLIOGRAPHY: J. Fischer, *Das Orgelbauergeschlecht Walcker* (Kassel, 1949).

Wald, Max, American composer and teacher; b. Litchfield, Ill., July 14, 1889; d. Dowagiac, Mich., Aug. 14, 1954. After studying in Chicago, he was active as theater conductor; went to Paris in 1922 to study with Vincent d'Indy, and remained in Europe until 1936; then returned to Chicago and became chairman of the theory department of the Chicago Musical College.

WORKS: His symph. poem *The Dancer Dead* won 2nd prize in the National Broadcasting Co. competition in 1932, and was broadcast from N.Y. on May 1, 1932. His other works include *Retrospectives* for orch.

(Chicago, Jan. 15, 1926), *Comedy Overture* (1937); *In Praise of Pageantry,* for orch. (Chicago, Oct. 31, 1946); *October Moonlight,* a song cycle for soprano, string quartet, flute, clarinet, and piano (1937); 2 piano sonatas; other piano music; also an opera, *Mirandolina* (1936), and a light opera, *Gay Little World* (1942).

Waldersee, Paul, Graf von, German music editor; b. Potsdam, Sept. 3, 1831; d. Königsberg, June 14, 1906. He was a Prussian officer (1848–71), but became absorbed in musical studies; was co-editor of Breitkopf & Härtel's collected editions of Mozart and Beethoven; edited the valuable *Sammlung musikalischer Vorträge* (1879–84) and the 2nd edition of Köchel's catalogue of Mozart's works (Leipzig, 1905).

Waldrop, Gid, American composer; b. on a ranch in Haskell County, Texas, Sept. 2, 1919. He studied at the Eastman School of Music in Rochester, N.Y. (Ph.D., 1952). He was editor of the *Musical Courier* (1954–58). In 1961 he was appointed Assistant to the President of the Juilliard School of Music; in 1963 became dean. He wrote a trio for viola, clarinet, and harp (1939); *Lydian Trumpeter* for trumpet and piano (1946); Symph. (1952); choruses.

Waldstein, Ferdinand Ernst Gabriel, Graf von, amateur musician; friend of Beethoven; b. Dux, Bohemia, March 24, 1762; d. Vienna, Aug. 29, 1823. While serving his novitiate in the Deutscher Orden at Bonn (1787–88), he became acquainted with Beethoven, and on several occasions aided him materially, pretending that the sums were extra allowances from the Elector; after Beethoven's departure for Vienna, Waldstein introduced him in the circles of the aristocracy there; in later life their friendship seems to have cooled. Beethoven wrote a set of variations in C for piano 4 hands on a theme of Waldstein's (publ. 1794), and later (1805) dedicated to him the great Sonata in C, op. 53. Waldstein also planned the *Ritter-Ballet* (1791), to which Beethoven wrote the music (score published 1872).
BIBLIOGRAPHY: J. Heer, *Der Graf von Waldstein und sein Verhältnis zu Beethoven* (Bonn, 1933).

Waldteufel, Emil, famous French waltz composer; b. Strasbourg, Dec. 9, 1837; d. Paris, Feb. 12, 1915. He received his first instruction from his father, professor at the Strasbourg Cons.; then went to the Paris Cons., where he studied with Marmontel, leaving before completing his studies to accept a position with the piano manufacturer Scholtus. The success of his first waltzes, *Joies et Peines* and *Manola* (publ. at his own expense), determined him to devote himself entirely to writing dance music; he lived all his life in Paris, making several very successful concert tours to London, Berlin, Vienna, etc., conducting his own music. In 1865 he was appointed chamber musician to the Empress Eugénie and director of the court balls. He publ. 268 dances, mostly for orch.; a selection of the most popular ones appeared in 5 vols.; several waltzes (*Die Schlittschuhläufer* [also known as *The Skaters* and *Les Patineurs*], *Les Sirènes, Mon Rêve, Les Violettes, Estudiantina, Dolores, Toujours ou Jamais,*

etc.) for a time almost rivalled in popularity those of Johann Strauss.

Waley, Simon, English pianist and composer; b. London, Aug. 23, 1827; d. there, Dec. 30, 1875. He studied in London with Moscheles and Bennett (piano); later with Molique (theory); began to compose as a child, and developed rapidly; wrote a piano concerto; 2 piano trios; and many solo pieces; 2 psalms for the synagogue service, which were publ. in vol. 1 of *Musical Services of the West London Synagogue.* Eventually he abandoned composition, and turned to a mercantile career; became a member of the London Stock Exchange.

Walker, Edyth, American mezzo-soprano, b. Hopewell, N.Y., March 27, 1867; d. New York, Feb. 19, 1950. She studied singing with Aglaja Orgeni at the Dresden Cons.; made her debut as Fides in *Le Prophète* at the Berlin Opera on Nov. 11, 1894. She then became a member of the Vienna Court Opera, where she was engaged until 1903. She made her American operatic debut with the Metropolitan Opera as Amneris (N.Y., Nov. 30, 1903); remained with the company until 1906; then sang in Germany, particularly excelling in Wagnerian roles. In 1936 she returned to N.Y.
BIBLIOGRAPHY: F. D. Perkins, in *Notable American Women* III (Cambridge, Mass., 1971).

Walker, Ernest, English writer on music; b. Bombay, India, July 15, 1870; d. Oxford, Feb. 21, 1949. He was educated at Balliol College, Oxford; D. Mus., 1898; became director of music there (1901–25); also examiner and member of the Board of Studies for music at Oxford Univ. He publ. the valuable compendium, *A History of Music in England* (Oxford, 1907; 2nd ed., 1924; 3rd ed., revised by J. A. Westrup, 1952); a monograph on Beethoven in the Music of the Masters series (1905). His collections of essays, *Free Thought and the Musician,* was publ. in 1946. He was also a composer; wrote a number of choral works; 2 piano quartets; a piano quintet; a horn quintet; a cello sonata; piano pieces; songs to German and English words.
BIBLIOGRAPHY: M. Deneke, *Ernest Walker* (London, 1951).

Walker, Frank, English musicologist; b. Gosport, Hampshire, June 10, 1907; d. (committed suicide), Tring, England, March 4, 1962. He studied telegraphy; in 1926 went to Rio de Janeiro as a representative of the Western Telegraph Co. From 1931 to 1943 he was in London; in 1944–45 he was in Naples, and later in Vienna, before returning to London. He contributed valuable articles on the composers of the Neapolitan School; wrote the books *Hugo Wolf* (London, 1951) and *The Man Verdi* (London, 1962).

Walker, George, American composer; b. Washington, June 27, 1922. He graduated from Oberlin College in 1941; studied piano with Rudolf Serkin, composition with Rosario Scalero and Gian Carlo Menotti, and chamber music with Piatigorsky and Primrose at the Curtis Institute of Music in Philadelphia, receiving an Artist Diploma in 1945; then took lessons with Nadia Boulanger at the American Cons. in Fontainebleau, France (1947). He subsequently held a number of teaching positions: at Dillard Univ. in New Orleans (1953), New School for Social Research and the Dalcroze School of Music in New York (1960), Smith College (1961–68), Univ. of Boulder (1968–69); in 1969 he was appointed instructor in piano and music theory at Rutgers Univ., and in 1974 joined the faculty of the Peabody Cons. in Baltimore. In 1960 he received a Guggenheim Fellowship award; also held two Rockefeller Fellowships (1971 and 1975).

WORKS: Trombone Concerto (1957); *Address* for orch. (1959; first performance, Mons, Belgium, Oct. 22, 1971); Symphony (1961); *Antiphonies* for chamber orch. (1968); *Variations* for orch. (1971); *Spirituals* for orch. (1974); Piano Concerto (1975); *Dialogues* for cello and orch. (1975–76); *Mass* for soloists, chorus and orch. (1976); 2 string quartets (1946; 1967); Cello Sonata (1957); Violin Sonata (1958); *Perimeters* for clarinet and piano (1966); *Music for Three* for violin, cello, and piano (1970); *5 Fancies* for clarinet and piano 4 hands (1974); *Music (Sacred and Profane)* for brass (1975); 3 piano sonatas (1953; 1957; 1975); numerous vocal works, including *3 Lyrics* for chorus (1958 and *3 Spirituals* for medium voice and piano (1975).

Walker, John, English voice teacher; b. Colney Hatch, Middlesex, March 18, 1732; d. London, Aug. 1, 1807. He wrote *The Melody of Speaking Delineated* (1787; often republished) with an original notation for representing the musical inflections of the speaking voice.

Walker, Joseph Cooper, Irish writer; b. Dublin, Nov., 1760; d. St.-Valéry, France, April 12, 1810. He publ. the valuable books *Historical Memoirs on the Irish Bards,* with notes on Irish music (London, 1786), and *An Historical Account and Critical Essay on the Opera* (1805).

Wallace, William, Scottish composer and music educator; b. Greenock, July 3, 1860; d. Malmesburg, Wiltshire, Dec. 16, 1940. The son of a surgeon, he studied medicine at Glasgow Univ. (M.D., 1888); specialized in ophthalmology in Vienna, and was employed in the Royal Army Medical Corps during World War I. He was self-taught in music; devoted much of his energy to the protection of the rights of British composers; served on the Composers' Copyright Committee of the Society of British Authors; also taught at the Royal Academy of Music.

WORKS: the symph. poems *The Passing of Beatrice* (1892), *Amboss oder Hammer,* after Goethe (1896), *Sister Helen* (1899), *To the New Century* (1901), *William Wallace* (for the 6th centenary of the death of the national hero of Scotland, and namesake of the composer; 1905), *François Villon* (1909); a symph., *The Creation* (1899); the suites for orch.: *The Lady from the Sea,* after Ibsen (1892) and *Pelléas and Mélisande,* after Maeterlinck (1900); overture, *In Praise of Scottish Poesie* (1894); *The Massacre of the Macpherson,* burlesque cantata; song cycles, *Freebooter Songs* (with orch.; his most famous work), *Lords of the Sea,* and *Jacobite Songs.*

WRITINGS: *The Threshold of Music: An Inquiry into the Development of the Musical Sense* (1908);

The Musical Faculty: Its Origins and Processes (1914); *Richard Wagner as He Lived* (1925); *Liszt, Wagner and the Princess* (1927).

Wallace, William Vincent, Irish composer; b. Waterford, March 11, 1812; d. Château de Bagen (Haute-Garonne), France, Oct. 12, 1865. The son of a bandmaster, Wallace was brought up in a musical atmosphere. He was 15 when the family moved to Dublin, and soon entered a professional career, playing violin in theater orchestras and organ in churches. One of his earliest compositions was *The Harp in the Air,* which later became famous when he incorporated it into his opera *Maritana.* In 1831 he married Isabella Kelly. He applied himself to the study of violin, and subsequently was able to give successful concerts. With his wife he traveled in Australia, South America, Mexico, and the U.S. Returning to Europe in 1844, he toured Germany; in 1845 he was in London, where he produced his opera *Maritana* (Drury Lane, Nov. 15, 1845), which obtained excellent success; it was followed by another opera, *Matilda of Hungary* (Drury Lane, Feb. 2, 1847), which was a failure. In 1850 he resumed his wanderings and revisited the U.S.; he declared his first marriage invalid, and married an American pianist, **Helen Stoepel.** Back in England, he produced several operas, of which *Lurline* (Covent Garden, Feb. 23, 1860) had tremendous acclaim; his other operas were *The Amber Witch* (Haymarket, Feb. 28, 1861), *Love's Triumph* (Covent Garden, Nov. 3, 1862), and *The Desert Flower* (Covent Garden, Oct. 12, 1863); several operas remain unfinished. His piano music enjoyed great vogue during his lifetime; some noted numbers are *La Gondola; 2 Nocturnes; Chant d'amour; Nocturne mélodique; Mélodie irlandaise; Music Murmuring in the Trees; Valse brillante de salon; Tarentelle,* etc.

BIBLIOGRAPHY: A. Pougin, *W. V. Wallace, étude biographique et critique* (Paris, 1866); W. H. G. Flood, *W. V. Wallace: A Memoir* (Waterford, 1912).

Wallaschek, Richard, Austrian theorist; b. Brünn, Nov. 16, 1860; d. Vienna, April 24, 1917. He studied law and philosophy in Vienna, Heidelberg, and Tübingen; from 1890 to 1895 was in London, engaged in research work; in 1896 joined the faculty of the Univ. of Vienna; wrote music criticism. He wrote a number of essays on esthetics, primitive music, and psychology of musical perception. His publications include *Ästhetik der Tonkunst* (1886) and several books publ. in London, in English: *On the Origin of Music* (1891), *Natural Selection and Music* (1892), *On the Difference of Time and Rhythm in Music* (1893), *Primitive Music: An Inquiry into the Origin and Development of Music, Song, Instruments, Dances and Pantomines of Savage Races* (1893; German ed., enlarged, as *Anfänge der Tonkunst,* 1903; reprint, N.Y., 1970); *Das k. k. Hofoperntheater* (Vienna, 1909).

BIBLIOGRAPHY: R. Lach, *Zur Erinnerung an Richard Wallaschek* (Vienna, 1917).

Wallenstein, Alfred, American cellist and conductor; b. Chicago, Oct. 7, 1898 (of German parents). The family moved to Los Angeles when he was a child; after playing the cello in theater orchestras, he went

to Germany in 1920 and took cello lessons with Julius Klengel; returning to the U.S., he was first cellist with the Chicago Symph. Orch. (1922–29), and first cellist of the N.Y. Philharmonic under Toscanini (1929–36). In 1933 he founded in N.Y. the Wallenstein Sinfonietta; from 1943 to 1956 he was conductor of the Los Angeles Philharmonic Orch.; in the spring of 1956 he traveled with it to Japan. In 1961–63 he was conductor of the Symphony of the Air; later was visiting conductor at the Juilliard School of Music.
BIBLIOGRAPHY: Hope Stoddard, *Symphony Conductors of the U. S. A.* (N.Y., 1957; pp. 274–79).

Wallenstein, Martin, German pianist and composer; b. Frankfurt, July 22, 1843; d. there, Nov. 29, 1896. He studied with Dreyschock in Prague, and with Hauptmann and Rietz in Leipzig; made many successful tours as a pianist. His opera, *Das Testament,* was produced at Frankfurt in 1870; he also wrote a piano concerto; many piano studies and characteristic pieces.

Waller, "Fats" (real first name **Thomas**), black American jazz pianist and composer; b. N.Y., May 21, 1904; d. Kansas City, Dec. 15, 1943. As a child he had private piano instruction and studied violin and double bass in school, but his most significant early lessons came from the player piano and nickelodeon pianists whom he studiously imitated; at 14 was playing organ professionally in a Harlem theater; at 16 he resumed formal study with ragtime pianist James P. Johnson; George Gershwin advised him to make a study of classical piano and he took lessons with Leopold Godowsky. Soon Waller began making piano rolls and recordings; he also composed music for Broadway revues; obtained an excellent success with *Hot Chocolates* (1929), which includes the song *Ain't Misbehavin';* in the 1930s he made many radio appearances; also had small roles in Hollywood movie vignettes. As a jazz pianist, he was considered a leading exponent of "stride piano," playing with a delicacy and lightness of touch that belied his considerable bulk of almost 300 lbs. But much of his popularity was due to his skills as an entertainer; he was especially effective in improvising lyrics to deflate the sentimentality of popular songs. A musical tribute to Fats Waller, the revue *Ain't Misbehavin',* was one of the great successes of the N.Y. theater season in 1978.
BIBLIOGRAPHY: J. R. T. Davies, *The Music of Fats Waller* (London, 1953); W. I. Kirkeby, *Ain't Misbehavin'. The Story of Fats Waller* (N.Y., 1966); Morroe Berger, "Fats Waller—The Outsider Insider," *Journal of Jazz Studies* (Oct. 1973); J. Vance, *Fats Waller. His Life and Times* (N.Y., 1977); Maurice Waller (his son) and A. Calabrese, *Fats Waller* (N.Y., 1977).

Wallerstein, Anton, German violinist and composer; b. Dresden, Sept. 28, 1813; d. Geneva, March 26, 1892. He played in public as a child; joined the Dresden court orch. (1829–32) and later was a member of the Hannover Orch. (1832–41). He wrote a number of popular dance compositions, of which about 300 were publ.; also violin pieces and songs.

Wallerstein, Lothar, Bohemian pianist and conductor; b. Prague, Nov. 6, 1882; d. New Orleans, Nov. 13, 1949. He studied art and music in Prague and Munich; also attended the Geneva Cons., where he later taught piano; after a brief engagement as accompanist at the Dresden Opera (1909), he held the posts of conductor and stage director in Poznan (1910–14), in Breslau (1918–22), in Frankfurt (1924–26), at the Vienna State Opera (1927–29), and at La Scala of Milan (1929). He came to the U.S. in 1941, and lived in New Orleans.
BIBLIOGRAPHY: A. Berger, *Über die Spielleitung der Oper. Betrachtungen zur musikalischen Dramaturgie Dr. Lothar Wallensteins* (Graz, 1928).

Wallnöfer, Adolf, Austrian tenor and composer; b. Vienna, April 26, 1854; d. Munich, June 9, 1946. He studied singing with Rokitansky; composition with Krenn and Dessoff. He began his career as a baritone, but developed his voice into a tenor in 1880; joined Neumann's Wagner troupe in 1881; then sang in Bremen and at the German Opera in Prague (1885–95); in 1896–98, appeared in the U.S.; then toured in Russia (1899); in 1906 he was engaged at the Vienna Opera; in 1908 he went to Munich, where he remained until his death. He composed an opera, *Eddystone* (Prague, 1889); several works for solo voice, chorus, and orch. (*Die Grenzen der Menschheit, Gersprenz, Hymne an die Erde,* etc.); piano pieces; numerous songs and ballads, a selection of which was publ. in 5 vols. He published *Resonanztonlehre* (1911).

Walmisley, Thomas (Attwood), English organist and composer; son of **Thomas Forbes Walmisley;** b. London, Jan. 21, 1814; d. Hastings, Jan. 17, 1856. His father placed him under the guidance of Thomas Attwood, his own teacher. He showed remarkable progress, and became organist at Trinity and St. John's Colleges at Cambridge at the age of 19. In 1836 he became a prof. of music; continued to study nonetheless; received his B.A. degree in 1838 and M.A. in 1841. He wrote several odes and anthems for Trinity College. He enjoyed the reputation of being one of the best organists in England of his day. His anthems and church services were brought out by his father, who survived him by 10 years; they were included in the vol. *Cathedral Music* (1857).

Walmisley, Thomas Forbes, English organist and composer; b. London, May 22, 1783; d. there, July 23, 1866. He was a chorister at Westminster Abbey; studied organ with Thomas Attwood; then was organist at the Female Orphan Asylum (1810–14) and at St. Martin-in-the-Fields (1814–54). He was a popular composer of glees; publ. 3 sets containing 6 glees each; also *A Collection of Glees, Trios, Rounds and Canons* (1826); several single glees and songs.

Walsh, John, English music publisher; b. c.1666; d. London, March 13, 1736. From about 1690 he had his business at the sign of the "Golden Harp and Hoboy" in the Strand, London; in 1692 he was appointed "musical instrument maker in ordinary to His Majesty." He developed a flourishing trade, and achieved great renown; in England he was unquestionably the foremost publisher of music in his time. In 1711 he publ.

Handel's *Rinaldo,* and remained Handel's principal publisher. He was succeeded by his son, also named **John Walsh** (b. London, Dec. 23, 1709; d. London, Jan. 15, 1766), who maintained the firm's high standards.

BIBLIOGRAPHY: F. Kidson, "Handel's Publisher, John Walsh, His Successors and Contemporaries," *Musical Quarterly* (July 1920); Wm. C. Smith, "Handel's *Rinaldo;* An Outline of the Early Editions," *Musical Times* (Aug. 1935); W. C. Smith, *A Bibliography of the Musical Works Published by J. Walsh during the Years 1695-1720* (London, 1948); W. C. Smith and C. Humphries, *A Bibliography of the Musical Works Published by the Firm of John Walsh During the Years 1721-1766* (London, 1968).

Walter, Arnold, Moravian-born Canadian composer; b. Hannsdorf, Aug. 30, 1902; d. Toronto, Oct. 6, 1973. He received a doctorate in law from Prague Univ. in 1926; then studied music in Berlin with H. Albert, Joh. Wolf, and Curt Sachs; emigrated to Canada in 1937 and taught at the Upper Canada College in Toronto; was director of the Royal Cons. Senior School (1945-52) and director of the music faculty of the Univ. of Toronto (1952-68); among his numerous honors is the Companion of the Order of Canada (1971). He turned to composition rather late in life; most of his music is Romantic in its sources of inspiration.

WORKS: Cello Sonatina (1940); Violin Sonata (1940); Piano Trio (1940); *Sacred Songs* for soprano and string trio (1941); Symph. in G minor (1942; Toronto, Feb. 1, 1944); *Toccata* for piano (1947); *For the Fallen,* cantata (1949); Piano Sonata (1950); Concerto for Orch. (1958); *Legend* for piano (1962); electronic pieces.

Walter, Bruno (real name **B. W. Schlesinger**), eminent German conductor; b. Berlin, Sept. 15, 1876; d. Beverly Hills, Calif., Feb. 17, 1962. He studied at Stern's Cons., Berlin with H. Ehrlich, L. Bussler, and R. Radecke. At the age of 17 he became opera coach at the Municipal Opera of Cologne; also did occasional conducting there; in the following year he was engaged as assistant conductor at the Hamburg Stadttheater, under Gustav Mahler; this contact was decisive in his career, and he became in subsequent years an ardent champion of Mahler's music; conducted the premières of the posthumous Symph. No. 9 and *Das Lied von der Erde.* During the season 1896-97 Walter was engaged as 2nd conductor at the Stadttheater in Breslau; then became principal conductor in Pressburg, and in 1898 at Riga, where he conducted for two seasons. In 1900 he received the important engagement of conductor at the Berlin Opera under a 5-year contract; however he left this post in 1901 when he received an offer from Mahler to become his assistant at the Vienna Opera. He established himself as an efficient opera conductor; also conducted in England (first appearance, March 3, 1909, with the Royal Philharmonic Society, London). He remained at the Vienna Opera after the death of Mahler; on Jan. 1, 1914, he became court conductor and music director in Munich; under his guidance, the Munich Opera enjoyed brilliant performances, particularly of Mozart's works. Seeking greater freedom for his artistic activities, he left Munich in 1922, and gave

numerous performances as guest conductor with European orchestras; from 1922 he also conducted summer concerts of the Salzburg festival; his performances of Mozart's music there set a standard. He also appeared as pianist in Mozart's chamber works. On Feb. 15, 1923, he made his American debut with the N.Y. Symph. Society, and appeared with it again in 1924 and 1925. From 1925 till 1929 he was conductor of the Städtische Oper in Berlin-Charlottenburg; in 1929 he succeeded Furtwängler as conductor of the Leipzig Gewandhaus Orch., but continued to give special concerts in Berlin. On Feb. 25, 1932, he was guest conductor of the N.Y. Philharmonic, acting also as soloist in a Mozart piano concerto; was reengaged during the next 3 seasons as associate conductor with Toscanini. He was also guest conductor in Philadelphia, Washington, and Baltimore. With the advent of the Nazi regime in Germany his engagement with the Gewandhaus Orch. was cancelled, and he was also prevented from continuing his orchestral concerts in Berlin. He filled several engagements with the Concertgebouw in Amsterdam, and also conducted in Salzburg. In 1936 he was engaged as music director of the Vienna Opera; this was terminated with the annexation of Austria in 1938. Walter with his family then went to France, where he was granted French citizenship. After the outbreak of World War II he sailed for America, establishing his residence in California, and eventually becoming an American citizen. He was guest conductor with the NBC Symph. Orch. (1940); also conducted many performances of the Metropolitan Opera, N.Y. (debut in *Fidelio* on Feb. 14, 1941). From Feb. 1947 to 1949 he was conductor and musical adviser of the N.Y. Philharmonic. Walter achieved the reputation of a perfect Classicist among contemporary conductors; his interpretations of the masterpieces of the Vienna School are particularly notable. He is acknowledged to have been a foremost conductor of Mahler's symphonies. His own compositions include 2 symphonies; *Siegesfahrt* for solo voices, chorus, and orch.; a string quartet; a piano quintet; a piano trio; several albums of songs. He publ. the books *Von den moralischen Kräften der Musik* (Vienna, 1935); *Gustav Mahler* (Vienna, 1936; English transl., London, 1937; new transl. with additions, N.Y., 1958); *Theme and Variations,* an autobiography (N.Y., 1947); and *Von der Musik und vom Musizieren* (Frankfurt, 1959; in English, N.Y., 1961).

BIBLIOGRAPHY: M. Komorn-Rebhan, *Was wir von Bruno Walter lernten* (Vienna, 1913); Paul Stefan, *Bruno Walter* (Vienna, 1936); Thomas Mann, "To Bruno Walter on His 70th Birthday," *Musical Quarterly* (Oct. 1946); Donald Brook, *International Gallery of Conductors* (Bristol, 1951; pp. 207-20); B. Gavoty, *Bruno Walter* (Geneva, 1956); *Briefe 1894-1962,* edited by Lotte Walter-Lindt (1969).

Walter, Fried, German composer; b. Ottendorf-Okrilla, near Dresden, Dec. 19, 1907; studied in Dresden; filled various posts as opera coach and conductor in Germany; in 1949 became a chief of the light music dept. at the Berlin Radio.

WORKS: operas, *Königin Elizabeth* (Stockholm, Nov. 24, 1939), *Andreas Wolfius* (Berlin, Dec. 19, 1940), and *Dorfmusik* (Wiesbaden, Nov. 1, 1943); a dance drama, *Kleopatra* (Prague, 1943); a dance fairy tale, *Der Pfeil* (Berlin, Dec. 22, 1946); a *Kleine Sinfonie* (1942); numerous dramatic ballads; chamber music; songs.

Walter, Friedrich Wilhelm, German writer on music; b. Mannheim, Sept. 3, 1870; d. Heidelberg, Nov. 4, 1956. He studied in Heidelberg; Dr. phil., 1892; lived most of his life in Mannheim, and publ. a number of valuable monographs dealing with musical life there: *Die Entwickelung des Mannheimer Musik- und Theaterlebens* (1897), *Geschichte des Theaters und der Musik am kurpfälzischen Hofe* (1898), and *Archiv und Bibliothek des Grossherzoglichen Hof- und National-Theaters in Mannheim* (2 vols.; 1899).

Walter, Georg A., German composer and teacher; b. Hoboken, N.J., Nov. 13, 1875 (of German parents); d. Berlin, Sept. 13, 1952. He studied singing in Berlin, Milan, and London; composition with Wilhelm Berger in Berlin; made a career as a singer, particularly distinguishing himself in the works of Bach and Handel. He was prof. at the Stuttgart Hochschule (1925–34); then taught in Berlin until 1945. He wrote a number of songs; brought out new editions of works by the sons of Bach, Schütz, etc.

Walter, George William, American organist; b. New York, Dec. 16, 1851; d. Washington, March 11, 1911. At the age of 5 he played the organ at Trinity Chapel; studied with J. K. Paine in Boston and with S. P. Warren in N.Y.; settled in Washington in 1869. He enjoyed a high reputation as an improviser; accumulated a musical library which was one of the finest in America.

Walter (Walther; real name, Blanckenmüller), Johann (Johannes), one of the earliest composers for the Lutheran church; b. Kahler, Thuringia, 1496; d. Torgau, March 25, 1570. In 1517 he entered the chapel of the Elector Friedrich the Wise of Saxony as a bass (the Elector divided his residence between Altenburg and Torgau). In 1524, at Wittenberg, he publ. the *Geystlich Gesangk-Buchlayn* for 3–5 voices, the first Protestant singing book. In 1525 he was summoned to Wittenburg by Luther to assist in the composition and regulation of the German Mass. Shortly after the death of the Elector Friedrich (1525) his chapel was disbanded, and Walter became cantor of the Municipal Latin-School in Torgau and director of the "Stadtkantorei" (community choir) there (1526–48). In 1548 he was called upon by the new Elector, Moritz, of Saxony, to organize the court chapel in Dresden, and remained there as Kapellmeister until 1554, when he retired to Torgau on a pension. He publ. *Cantio septem vocum in laudem Dei omnipotentis et Evangelii ejus* (1544); *Magnificat 8 tonorum* (1557); *Ein newes christliches Lied* (1561); *Ein gar schöner geistlicher und christlicher Bergkreyen* (1561); *Lob und Preis der himmlischen Kunst Musica* (1564); *Das christlich Kinderlied Dr. Martin Luthers, "Erhalt uns Herr bei deinem Wort"* (1566), etc. The *Geystlich Gesangk-Buchleyn* was reprinted in vol. VII of the *Publikationen der Gesellschaft für Musikforschung* (1878); a list of other reprints is found in W. Ehmann's article "Johann Walter, der erste Kantor der protestan-

tischen Kirche," in *Musik und Kirche* 6 (1934). Instrumental works by Walter were discovered in the library of the Thomasschule in Leipzig by B. Engelke in 1912 (examples in A. Schering's *Geschichte der Musik in Beispielen,* nos. 80 and 81). A complete ed. of Walter's works was edited by Otto Schröder and Max Schneider in 6 vols. (Kassel, 1953–70).
BIBLIOGRAPHY: O. Kade, *Johann Walthers Wittenbergisch geistlig Gesangbuch von 1524* (1878); H. Holstein, "Der Lieder- und Tondichter Johann Walther," *Archiv für Literaturgeschichte* (1884); A. Aber, *Die Pflege der Musik unter den Wettinern* (1921); R. Haas, "Zu Walthers Choralpassion nach Matthäus," *Archiv für Musikwissenschraft* 4 (1922); A. Schmitz in "Siebs-Festschrift" (1933); W. Gurlitt, "Johannes Walter und die Musik der Reformationzeit," *Luther-Jahrbuch* (1933); O. Michaelis, *Johann Walther, der Musiker-Dichter in Luthers Gefolgschaft* (Leipzig, 1939); C. Gerhardt, *Die Torgauer Walter-Handschriften; eine Studie zur Quellenkunde der Musikgeschichte der deutschen Reformationzeit* (Kassel, 1949); G. Reese, *Music in the Renaissance* (N.Y., 1954).

Walter, Karl, German organist and campanologist; b. Cransberg, Oct. 27, 1862; d. Montabaur, Dec. 4, 1929. He studied at the Seminary in Montabaur, where he became instructor in 1893; in 1899 was appointed diocesan inspector for the building of organs and bells; in 1903 became instructor of church music at Limburg Seminary. He wrote organ music and sacred works; publ. several manuals on organ building, and on the construction of bells, a field in which he was an authority. His publications are *Kleine Orgelbaulehre* (1904); *Orgelbegleitung zu den Melodien des Gesangbuchs für das Bistum Limburg* (1907; 2nd ed., 1911); *Glockenkunde* (1913); *Kleine Glockenkunde* (1916).

Walter, Thomas, American clergyman and author of singing books; b. Roxbury, Mass., Dec. 13, 1696; d. there, Jan. 10, 1725. He was the son of a clergyman and a nephew of Cotton Mather; educated at Harvard College (M.A., 1713); on Oct. 29, 1718, he was ordained; was assistant pastor to his father at Roxbury. With the aim of correcting what he described as "an horrid medley of confused and disorderly sounds" prevailing in the singing in New England churches, he publ. *The Grounds and Rules of Musick Explained; or, an Introduction to the Art of Singing by Note; Fitted to the meanest capacities* (Boston, 1721; several other eds. up to 1764). It was the 2nd singing book to be publ. in America, following that of John Tufts. He also publ. *The Sweet Psalmist of Israel* (1722).
BIBLIOGRAPHY: F. J. Metcalf, *American Writers and Compilers of Sacred Music* (1925); E. H. Pierce, "The Rise and Fall of the 'Fugue-Tune' in America," *Musical Quarterly* (April 1930); M. B. Jones, "Bibliographical Notes on Thomas Walter's 'Grounds and Rules,' " *Proceedings of the American Antiquarian Society* (Oct. 1932; also reprinted separately, Worcester, Mass., 1933).

Waltershausen, (Hermann) Wolfgang von, German composer and writer on music; b. Göttingen, Oct. 12,

1882; d. Munich, Aug. 13, 1954. He was a pupil of M. J. Erb in Strasbourg and of Ludwig Thuille in Munich, where he settled. In 1917 he established there a seminar for operatic dramaturgy; prof. and assistant director at the Akademie der Tonkunst (1920–23); then director (1923–33). After 1933 he remained in Munich as private teacher; in 1948 established a seminar for all musical subjects in Munich. In his own music he adopted a neo-Romantic style, rather advanced in harmonic treatment.

WORKS: operas: *Oberst Chabert,* to his own libretto after Balzac (Frankfurt, Jan. 18, 1912; also several productions in other German cities; his most successful work); *Else Klapperzehen* (Dresden, May 15, 1909); *Richardis,* a dramatic mystery (Karlsruhe, Nov. 14, 1915); *Die Rauensteiner Hochzeit* (Karlsruhe, 1919); *Die Gräfin von Tolosa* (1934); other works: *Apokalyptische Symphonie* (1924); the symph. poem, *Hero und Leander* (1925); *Krippenmusik* for chamber orch. with harpsichord (1926); an orchestral partita (1928); piano pieces, and songs. Having lost his right arm in a childhood accident, he developed a piano technique for the left hand alone, and publ. studies and transcriptions for left hand which he performed in public. He also publ. a number of valuable writings on music: *Musikalische Stillehre in Einzeldarstellungen* (1920–23); *Richard Strauss* (1921); *Musik, Dramaturgie, Erziehung* (1926); *Dirigenten-Erziehung* (1929); "Der stilistische Dualismus in der Musik des 19. Jahrhunderts," in the "Adler-Festschrift" (Vienna, 1930); *Die Kunst des Dirigierens* (1943; 2nd ed., 1954); also publ. a book of poetry (1952).

Walther, Johann Gottfried, noted German composer and musicographer; b. Erfurt, Sept. 18, 1684; d. Weimar, March 23, 1748. He was a pupil of J. Bernhard Bach at Erfurt, where he was made organist of the Thomaskirche in 1702; in 1707 he was town organist at Weimar, and music master to the children of the ducal family; from 1721, court musician. He stands next to Bach as a master of chorale-variations for organ. His greatest work is the *Musikalisches Lexikon oder Musikalische Bibliothek,* the first music encyclopedia of biography, bibliography, and terms (Leipzig, 1732; facsimile ed., Kassel, 1953 by R. Schaal, with bibliographical notes); he had previously publ. the 64-page *Alte und neue musikalische Bibliothek, oder Musikalisches Lexikon* (1728; only entries under letter A printed, as a preliminary to the main work). His published musical compositions include: *Clavierconcert* (unaccompanied; 1741); Prelude and Fugue (1741); 4 chorale-variations *(Jesu meine Freude, Meinen Jesum lass' ich nicht, Allein Gott in der Höh' sei Ehr', Wie soll ich dich empfangen);* many chorale-variations, preludes, fugues and toccatas, in MS; also 5 collections of "Choralbearbeitungen" by other composers. His organ works were ed. by M. Seiffert in vols. 26 and 27 of *Denkmäler deutscher Tonkunst* (with biographical sketch). His *Praecepta der musikalischen Composition* was publ. at Leipzig, 1955, ed. by Peter Benary.

BIBLIOGRAPHY: H. Gehrmann, "J. G. Walther als Theoretiker," *Vierteljahrsschrift für Musikwissenschaft* (1891); G. Schünemann, "J. G. Walther und H.

Bokemeyer," *Bach-Jahrbuch* (1933); O. Brodde, *J. G. Walther. Leben und Werk* (1937).

Walther, Johann Jakob, notable German violinist and composer; b. Witterda, near Erfurt, 1650; date and place of death unknown. He was concertmaster at the Electoral Court of Saxony in Dresden (from 1674), and Italian secretary, in charge of the correspondence with Rome, to the Elector of Mainz (from 1688); in 1693 he was designated as *Doctor.* He publ. *Scherzi da violino solo* with continuo (1676; reprinted in *Das Erbe deutscher Musik* 17); *Hortulus Chelicus, uni violino, duabus, tribus et quatuor subinde chordis simul sonantibus* (1688; 2nd ed. as *Wohlgepflanzter Violinischer Lustgarten,* 1694).

BIBLIOGRAPHY: J. W. von Wasielewski, *Die Violine und ihre Meister* (7th ed., 1927); G. Beckmann, *Das Violinspiel in Deutschland vor 1700* (1918); A. Moser, *Geschichte des Violinspiels* (1923).

Walther von der Vogelweide. See **Vogelweide.**

Walthew, Richard Henry, English composer and pedagogue; b. London, Nov. 4, 1872; d. East Preston, Sussex, Nov. 14, 1951. He studied with Parry at the Royal College of Musik (1890–94); after a directorship of the Passmore Edwards Settlement Place (1900–04), he was appointed instructor of the opera class at the Guildhall School of Music; in 1907 became prof. of music at Queen's College; also conducted provincial orchestras. His works include two operettas: *The Enchanted Island* (London, May 8, 1900) and *The Gardeners* (London, Feb. 12, 1906); the cantatas: *Ode to a Nightingale* and *The Pied Piper of Hamelin;* Piano Concerto; Piano Quintet; Piano Quartet; two piano trios; Violin Sonata; vocal quartets with piano; songs. Author of *The Development of Chamber Music* (1909).

BIBLIOGRAPHY: *Cobbett's Cyclopedic Survey of Chamber Music* (London, 1930); K. H. Leech, "R. H. Walthew," *Musical Opinion* (Jan. 1952).

Walton, Sir William (Turner), eminent English composer; b. Oldham, Lancashire, March 29, 1902. He received his early education from his father, a music teacher; was sent to the Christ Church Cathedral Choir School at Oxford at the age of 10, and at 16 entered Christ Church College; studied under Sir Hugh Allen at Oxford, and also received advice from E. J. Dent, Busoni, and Ansermet. At the age of 17 he wrote a piano quartet. On June 12, 1923, his amusing and original work, *Façade,* for speaking voice and instruments, to poems by Edith Sitwell, created something of a sensation in London. However, the somewhat impish wit displayed in *Façade* is but one aspect of Walton's creative personality; in his later works there is evident a deep emotional stream, a fine eloquence, and a definitely English melodic style; the sense of tonality is strong in the modern harmonic structure, and the formal design is invariably clear. Walton's temperament lends itself to great versatility; he is successful both in lighter music, as exemplified by his overtures *Portsmouth Point* and *Scapino,* and compositions of an epical character, such as the oratorio *Belshazzar's Feast.* His symphonic works show him as an inheritor of the grand Romantic tradition; his Viola Concerto and his Violin Concerto demonstrate his adroitness in modern instrumental writing. He was knighted in 1951.

WORKS: FOR THE STAGE: opera, *Troilus and Cressida* (London, Dec. 3, 1954); ballet, *The Quest* (1943); *Façade*, an "entertainment" for declamation, flute, clarinet, saxophone, trumpet, cello, and percussion (London, June 12, 1923; revised in 1942, with an augmented orch.); *The Wise Virgins*, a ballet arranged from 6 pieces by Bach (1940); *The Bear*, an extravaganza in one act (Aldeburgh Festival, June 3, 1967). FOR ORCH.: *Portsmouth Point*, overture (Zürich Festival of the International Society for Contemporary Music, June 22, 1926); *Siesta* (1926); *Sinfonia concertante* for piano and orch. (London. Jan. 5, 1928); Viola Concerto (London, Oct. 3, 1929); Symph. No. 1 (London, Nov. 6, 1935); *Crown Imperial*, coronation march for George VI (1937); 2 orchestral suites from *Façade* (also used as ballet scores): No. 1 (Siena Festival of the International Society for Contemporary Music, Sept. 14, 1928); No. 2 (N.Y., March 30, 1938); Violin Concerto (Cleveland, Dec. 7, 1939, Jascha Heifetz soloist); *Spitfire* (*Prelude and Fugue*) for orch. (1942; glorifying the famous British combat plane); *Orb and Sceptre*, coronation march for Elizabeth II (1953); *Johannesburg Festival Overture* (Johannesburg, South Africa, Sept. 25, 1956); Cello Concerto (Boston, Piatigorsky soloist, Jan. 25, 1957); *Partita* (Cleveland, Jan. 30, 1958); *Fanfare* for the Queen's entrance at the NATO Parliamentary Conference (London, June 5, 1959); Symph. No. 2 (Edinburgh, Sept. 2, 1960); *Variations on a Theme by Hindemith* for orch. (London, March 8, 1963); *Capriccio Burlesco* for orch. (N.Y., Dec. 7, 1968); *Improvisations on an Impromptu of Britten* for orch. (San Francisco, Jan. 14, 1970); Sonata for string orch. (1972; orchestration of the 1947 string quartet); *Varii Capricci* for orch. (London, May 4, 1976; orchestration of the *5 Bagatelles* for guitar). VOCAL WORKS: *Belshazzar's Feast*, oratorio for baritone, chorus, and orch. (Leeds Festival, Oct. 10, 1931); *In Honour of the City of London*, for chorus and orch. (Leeds Festival, 1937); *Te Deum* for the coronation of Queen Elizabeth II (London, June 2, 1953); *Gloria* for vocal soloists, mixed chorus, and orch. (Liverpool, Nov. 24, 1961); *A Song for the Lord Mayor's Table* for soprano and piano (London, July 18, 1962); *The Twelve* for chorus and organ (Oxford, May 16, 1965); *Missa Brevis* for double mixed chorus and organ (Coventry, April 10, 1966); *Cantico del Sole* for chorus a cappella (1974). CHAMBER MUSIC: Piano Quartet (1918; revised, 1974); String Quartet (1922; Salzburg Festival of the International Society for Contemporary Music, Aug. 4, 1923); *Toccata* for violin and piano (1923); 2nd String Quartet (1947); Violin Sonata (1949); *5 Bagatelles* for solo guitar (1972). FILM MUSIC: *Escape Me Never* (1934), *As You Like It* (1936), *Stolen Life* (1939), *Major Barbara* (1941), *Henry V* (1944), *Hamlet* (1947), *Richard III* (1954), etc.; several suites have been drawn from these scores.

BIBLIOGRAPHY: H. J. Foss, "William Walton," *Musical Quarterly* (Oct. 1940); F. S. Howes, *The Music of William Walton*, 2 vols. (London, 1942 and 1943; new amplified edition 1965); E. Evans, "William Walton," *Musical Times* (1944); K. Avery, "William

Walton," *Music & Letters* (Jan. 1947); *Modern Music . . . Analytic Index*, compiled by Wayne Shirley and edited by Wm. and C. Lichtenwanger (N.Y., 1976), p. 235.

Waltz, Gustavus, German bass; place and date of birth unknown; d. London about 1753; was in Handel's household in London. He appeared on the London stage in 1732 in Handel's *Acis and Galatea* and subsequently sang in Handel's oratorios. He is chiefly celebrated because of the reported acrid comment of Handel on Gluck: "He knows no more of counterpoint than my cook Waltz."

BIBLIOGRAPHY: W. C. Smith, "Gustavus Waltz: Was He Handel's Cook?" in *Concerning Handel* (London, 1948).

Walzel, Leopold Matthias, Austrian composer; b. Vienna, Nov. 29, 1902; d. there, June 9, 1970. A lawyer by profession, he also studied music at the Univ. of Vienna; composed 5 symphonies, an opera *Salamis*, a piano quartet, an octet, 2 quintets and several song cycles.

Wambach, Emile, Belgian composer; b. Arlon, Luxembourg, Nov. 26, 1854; d. Antwerp, May 6, 1924. He studied with Benoit, Mertens, Callaerts at the Antwerp Cons.; in 1913 became its director. He wrote music in the National Flemish style following the model of Benoit. He wrote the Flemish opera *Nathans Parabel;* 4 oratorios: *Mozes op den Nijl* (1881); *Yolande* (1884), *Blancefloer* (1889), and *Jeanne d'Arc* (1909); choral works; piano pieces; songs.

BIBLIOGRAPHY: L. Vocht, "Levensbericht over Emile Wambach," *Annuaire* of the Académie Royale de Belgique 118 (1952; with a list of works).

Wangemann, Otto, German music scholar; b. Loitzon-the-Peene, Jan. 9, 1848; d. Berlin, Feb. 25, 1914. He studied with F. Kiel in Berlin; in 1886 settled there as church organist and singing teacher. He publ. *Grundriss der Musik-Geschichte* (1878); *Geschichte der Orgel* (1897; 3rd ed., 1887); *Geschichte des Oratoriums* (1880); also singing manuals for schools; *Weihnachtsmusik* for solo voices, chorus, and orch.; school songs; piano pieces.

Wanhal (Vanhall), Johann Baptist, Bohemian composer; b. Nechanicz, Bohemia, May 12, 1739; d. Vienna, Aug. 20, 1813. His musical ability brought him the patronage of Countess Schaffgotsch, who enabled him to study in Vienna with Dittersdorf; another patron, Baron Riesch, sent him to Italy for further study. He settled in Vienna. An extremely prolific composer, he wrote a great number of piano pieces, which enjoyed considerable popularity among amateurs. He also composed an enormous amount of instrumental music (some 100 symphonies and as many string quartets); 26 Masses; 2 Requiems; 36 offertories. Among his published works are 12 symphonies for strings, 2 oboes, and 2 horns; 12 string quartets; 12 trios for 2 violins and cello; quartets (concerti) for piano and strings; quartets for piano, flute, violin, and cello; piano trios; 5 piano sonatas for 4 hands, and 6 for 2 hands; violin duos; 6 violin sonatas with piano;

characteristic sonatas *(Militaire, The Battle of Würzburg, The Battle of Trafalgar);* many piano sonatinas; 70 books of piano variations; fantasias, dances, and other piano pieces, fugues, preludes, etc., for organ; etc.

BIBLIOGRAPHY: M. von Dewitz, *J. B. Vanhall, Leben und Klavierwerke* (dissertation; Munich, 1933); G. Wolters, *J. Wanhal als Sinfoniker* (dissertation; Cologne, 1933); P. R. Bryan, *The Symphonies of Johann Vanhall* (dissertation, 2 vols.; Ann Arbor, 1957).

Wanless, John, English organist and composer; flourished early in the 17th century. He was organist at the Lincoln Cathedral between 1616 and 1625; only a few of church works are extant, among them an anthem *Plead thou my cause.* His son, **Thomas Wanless** (d. 1721), was organist of York Minster from 1691 till 1695. He publ. a psalter, *The Metre Psalm-tunes* in 4 parts (London, 1702); composed a *York Litany.*

Wannenmacher (Latinized as **Vannius**), **Johannes,** German composer; b. Neuenburg on the Rhine; d. Interlaken, 1551. He was cantor at Bern, Switzerland, in 1510, and at Freiburg-im-Breisgau in 1514; because of his inclinations toward Lutheranism, he was obliged to leave Germany; settled in Interlaken in 1531 as town clerk, and remained there until his death. He was greatly esteemed in his time as a fine polyphonist; Glareanus cites a motet for 4 voices in the *Dodecachordon.* Wannenmacher's *An Wasserflüssen Babylon* for 3–6 voices was publ. in Ott's *Liederbuch* (1544); some German songs by him were publ. posthumously.

BIBLIOGRAPHY: A. Geering, *Die Vokalmusik in der Schwiez zur Zeit der Reformation: Leben und Werke von Bartholomäus Frank, Johannes Wannenmacher, Cosmas Alder* (Aarau, 1933).

Warburg, Felix Moritz, patron of music; b. Hamburg, Jan. 14, 1871; d. New York, Oct. 20, 1937. He came to the U.S. in 1894, and became associated with the banking firm of Kuhn, Loeb & Co.; U.S. citizen, 1900. He participated in many musical activities as a sponsor; was a member of the board of the Institute of Musical Art. He owned a quartet of Stradivarius instruments, and sponsored the concerts of the Stradivarius String Quartet.

Ward, Frank Edwin, American organist and composer; b. Wysox, Pa., Oct. 7, 1872; d. Wolfeboro, N.H., Sept. 15, 1953. He studied at the N.Y. College of Music with J. P. Lawrence (organ) and S. A. Pearce (theory); was a student of MacDowell at Columbia Univ. (1898–1903); later became associate prof. of music there (1909–19); for 40 years (1906–46) was organist and choirmaster at the Church of the Holy Trinity, N.Y. His works include a Lenten cantata, *The Saviour of the World;* a Christmas cantata, *The Divine Birth; Ocean Rhapsody* for orch.; services; anthems; organ pieces; part-songs; also 2 string quartets and other chamber music.

Ward, John, English composer; b. Canterbury, 1571 (baptized Sept. 8, 1571); d. c.1638. He was in the service of Sir Henry Fanshawe, to whom he dedicated

The First Set of English Madrigals (London, 1613); wrote services and anthems, and pieces for the virginals. His madrigals were reprinted in vol. XIX of *The English Madrigal School.*

BIBLIOGRAPHY: E. H. Fellowes, *The English Madrigal Composers* (1921).

Ward, John Milton, American musicologist; b. Oakland, Calif., July 6, 1917. He studied at the Univ. of Washington (M.M., 1942); obtained his Ph.D., at N.Y. (1953); then was instructor at the Dept. of Fine Arts, Michigan State Univ. (1947–53); was on the faculty of the Univ. of Illinois (1953–55), and after 1955 at Harvard Univ. He brought out *The Dublin Virginal MS* (Wellesley, Mass., 1954; 2nd revised edition 1964); contributed numerous essays and specialized articles to various scholarly music magazines.

Ward, Robert, American composer; b. Cleveland, Sept. 13, 1917. He studied at the Eastman School of Music, Rochester, N.Y., with Howard Hanson and Bernard Rogers (B. Mus., 1939) and at the Juilliard School of Music, N.Y., with Frederick Jacobi (composition) and Albert Stoessel (conducting); obtained his M.A. in 1946; subsequently he taught at the Juilliard School (1946–56); served as vice-president and managing editor of the Galaxy Music Corporation; then was a prof. of music at the North Carolina School of the Arts. As a composer, he has evolved an effective idiom, modern but not aggresively so; he particularly excels in dramatic and compact stage works on American subjects.

WORKS: operas: *Pantaloon,* after Leonid Andreyev's play, *He Who Gets Slapped* (Juilliard School of Music, N.Y. May 17, 1956); *The Crucible* (N.Y., Oct. 26, 1961; received the Pulitzer Prize); *The Lady From Colorado* (Central City, Colorado, July 3, 1964; received the Pulitzer Prize); *Claudia Legare,* after Ibsen's *Hedda Gabler* (Minneapolis, April 14, 1978); for orch.: Symph. No. 1 (N.Y., May 10, 1941); *Jubilation Overture* (Los Angeles, Nov. 21, 1946); Symph. No. 2 (Washington, Jan. 25, 1948); Symph. No. 3 (Washington, March 31, 1950); Symph. No. 4 (1958); Symph. No. 5, *Canticles for America* (1976); *Jonathon and the Gingery Snare,* for narrator, small orch., and percussion (Young People's Concert, N.Y. Philharmonic, Feb. 4, 1950); *Euphony* for orch. (1954); *Divertimento* (1961); *Festive Ode* (1966); *Antiphony* for wind instruments (1967); Piano Concerto (1968); String Quartet (1965); other chamber music; choruses and songs.

BIBLIOGRAPHY: *Composers of the Americas* Vol. 9 (Washington, D.C. 1963).

Ware, Harriet, American pianist and composer; b. Waupun, Wis., Aug. 26, 1877; d. New York, Feb. 9, 1962. She received her musical instruction from her father, who was a professional musician and choral conductor; she then studied piano with Dr. William Mason in N.Y. and with Sigismund Stojowski in Paris; composition with Hugo Kaun in Berlin; in 1906 she returned to the United States. Her *Women's Triumphal March* was made the national song of the Federation of Women's Clubs in 1927; her symph. poem *The Artisan* was given by the N.Y. Symph. Orch. in 1929. Some of her songs *(Boat Song, Joy of the Morn-*

ing, *The Call of Radha, Stars, Sunlight Waltz Song,* etc.) have achieved considerable popularity. She also wrote the choral cycles, *Trees* and *Undine;* an operetta, *Waltz For Three;* piano pieces *(Mountain Pictures, Midnight Waltz,* etc.).

Wareing, Herbert Walter, English composer; b. Birmingham, April 5, 1857; d. Malvern, March 29, 1918. He studied at the Leipzig Cons. with Reinecke, Jadassohn, and Papperitz; upon his return to England he filled various positions as organist; in 1909 became prof. of piano at Malvern College, where he remained until his death. He wrote several operettas for children: *Princess Snowflake, The Court of Queen Summergold, A Garden of Japan, A Day in Roseland;* cantatas, *The Wreck of the Hesperus, The Angel Reapers, The Nativity, The Good Shepherd, New Year's Eve;* numerous choruses and solo songs; church services; piano pieces.

Warfield, William, American Negro baritone; b. Helena, Arkansas, Jan. 22, 1920. He studied at the Eastman School of Music, Rochester, N.Y., graduating in 1946; sang in opera and musical comedy; gave his first N.Y. song recital in March 19, 1950, with excellent critical acclaim. He subsequently toured Europe in the role of Porgy in the production of Gershwin's *Porgy and Bess.* He married the soprano **Leontyne Price** in 1952 (divorced in 1972). In 1974 was appointed a prof. of music, Univ. of Illinois.

Waring, Fred M., American choral conductor; b. Tyrone, Pa., June 9, 1900. He trained choruses; formed a group called "The Pennsylvanians," which became popular on the radio. He is the chairman of the board of the Waring Manufacturing Co., producing the widely used Waring Blenders.

Warlich, Reinhold von, baritone; b. St. Petersburg, May 24, 1877; d. New York, Nov. 10, 1939. His father, a German musician resident in Russia, was an opera conductor in St. Petersburg, and Warlich received his training at home; then studied at the Hamburg Cons., in Florence, and in Cologne. He toured in Europe as a singer of German lieder, and was especially distinguished as an interpreter of Schubert, whose song cycles he gave in their entirety. He lived for some time in Canada; later was singing teacher in Paris and London; made concert tours in the U.S. from 1909, eventually settling in N.Y.

Warlock, Peter. See **Heseltine, Philip.**

Warnecke, (Johann Heinrich) Friedrich, German double-bass player and pedagogue; b. Bodenteich, Nov. 19, 1856; d. Hamburg, March 1, 1931. He studied with Bontemps in Ülzen and with Walther in Hannover; was a member of various military bands (1874–89); then settled in Hamburg; from 1893 to 1924 he was a member of the Hamburg Philharmonic and prof. at the Hamburg Cons. He publ. *Das Studium des Kontrabass-Spiels* (2 parts; with German and English text); piano pieces and songs. Author of *"Ad infinitum." Der Kontrabass, seine Geschichte und seine Zu-*

kunft. Probleme und deren Lösung zur Hebung des Kontrabass-Spiels (1909) and *Der Kontrabass* (1929).

Warner, Harry Waldo, English viola player and composer; b. Northampton, Jan. 4, 1874; d. London, June 1, 1945. He studied violin with Alfred Gibson and theory with R. Orlando Morgan at the Guildhall School of Music; was engaged as viola player in the London String Quartet (1907–28). In 1921 he received the Elizabeth Sprague Coolidge prize for piano trio, and a Cobbett prize for another piano trio. He also wrote several other attractive pieces for string quartet; one of them, arranged for string orch., was performed in London on Sept. 22, 1928, under the title *Suite in the Olden Style.*

BIBLIOGRAPHY: *Cobbett's Cyclopedic Survey of Chamber Music* (London, 1930).

Warner, Sylvia Townsend, English novelist and writer on music; b. London, Dec. 6, 1893; d. Maiden Newton, Dorset, England, May 1, 1978. Apart from her well-known novels and books of poetry, she published valuable papers in music history, among them, *The Point of Perfection in 16th Century Notation* (1919); was one of the editors of the collection *Tudor Church Music.* She also composed a rhapsody for voice and string quartet, *Memorial;* and a song cycle, *Children of the Earth.*

Warnots, Henri, Belgian tenor and composer; b. Brussels, July 11, 1832; d. Saint-Josse-ten-Noode, Feb, 27, 1893. He studied at the Brussels Cons.; then sang in Paris and Strasbourg. In 1867, he became prof. at the Brussels Cons.; in 1870, established a music school in Saint-Josse-ten-Noode, where he remained until his death. His operetta, *Une Heure de mariage,* was produced in Strasbourg on Jan. 24, 1865.

Warren, Elinor Remick, American pianist and composer of songs; b. Los Angeles, Feb. 23, 1905. She was educated at the Westlake School for Girls, and at Mills College; publ. her first composition while still in high school; later studied in N.Y. with Frank La Forge, Paolo Gallico, and Clarence Dickinson; appeared as pianist.
WORKS: *The Harp Weaver,* for women's chorus, baritone, harp, and orch.; *The Passing of King Arthur* for orch.; *Singing Earth,* song cycle for voice and piano (or orch.); *Abram in Egypt,* cantata (1961); *Good Morning America!* for narrator, chorus, and orch. (California State Univ., Fullerton, Nov. 21, 1976); a symphony (1970); many songs (*White Horses of the Seas, Children of the Moon, My Lady Lo Fu, We Two, Christmas Candle,* etc.).

Warren, George William, American organist and composer of sacred music; b. Albany, N.Y., Aug. 17, 1828; d. New York, March 17, 1902. He was self taught; held positions as church organist in Albany (1846–60), in Brooklyn (1860–70), and at St. Thomas', N.Y. (from 1870 until his death). He publ. *Warren's Hymns and Tunes, as Sung at St. Thomas Church* (1888); also wrote salon piano music; his "Marche di Bravura" *The Andes* was the rage of the salons in 1862–63, especially in a 2-piano arrangement made by

Louis Moreau Gottschalk. He is remembered chiefly for his tune *National Hymn,* to which *God of Our Fathers* is sung.

Warren, Harry, American composer of popular songs; b. Brooklyn, Dec. 24, 1893. He was a drummer in carnival brass bands; earned a living as a stage hand, a vaudeville actor, and a nightclub pianist. Endowed with a God-given gift of fetching melody, he turned out without benefit of academic music training a slew of songs that became perennial favorites, among them *Lullaby of Broadway, Chattanooga Choo-Choo, Topeka and the Santa Fé, You Must Have Been a Beautiful Baby, Jeepers Creepers, I Found a Million Dollar Baby in a 5 & 10 Cent Store, Shuffle Off to Buffalo, We're in the Money,* and *Cheerful Little Earful.* In 1932 he went to Hollywood and wrote music for films.

Warren, Leonard, American baritone; b. New York, April 21, 1911; d. New York City, March 4, 1960, during the performance of *La Forza del destino,* on the stage of The Metropolitan Opera House. The original family name was **Warenoff;** it was Americanized as Warren when his father came from Russia to the U.S. His father was in the fur business in N.Y., and Leonard Warren helped him, while studying at the Greenwich House Music School. He won an audition with the Metropolitan Opera in 1938 and was granted a stipend to study in Milan. Returning to America, he made his debut at the Metropolitan Opera on Jan. 13, 1939 as Paolo in *Simon Boccanegra.* He quickly advanced in the favor of the public; sang baritone roles in Verdi's operas with excellent success; also toured in South America and Canada. He appeared at La Scala, Milan, in 1953 as Rigoletto (one of his best roles). In the spring of 1958 he made a successful tour in Russia.

Warren, Raymond, English composer; b. Weston-Super-Mare, Nov. 7, 1928. He studied with Robin Orr at Cambridge Univ. (1949–52) and later took lessons with Michael Tippett and Lennox Berkeley; received his Mus. B. at Cambridge Univ. (1952); taught at the Univ. of Belfast (1955–72); in 1972 was appointed a prof. of music at Bristol Univ.
    WORKS: *The Lady of Ephesus,* one-act chamber opera (Belfast, Feb. 16, 1959); *Finn and the Black Hag,* children's opera after an Irish folk tale (Belfast, Dec. 11, 1959); *The Passion,* oratorio (Belfast, Feb. 19, 1962); *Graduation Ode,* comic opera (Belfast, Nov. 17, 1963); Symph. No. 1 (1965); Violin Concerto (1966); *Songs of Old Age* for baritone and piano (1968); 2 string quartets (1966; 1975); Symph. No. 2 (1971); *Duo Concertante* for cello and piano (1973); songs.

Warren, Richard Henry, American organist and composer; son of **G. W. Warren;** b. Albany, N.Y. Sept. 17, 1859; d. South Chatham, Mass., Dec. 3, 1933. He was organist and choirmaster in various churches in N.Y.; founded (1886) the Church Choral Society, which he conducted until 1895 and again from 1903 to 1907, producing many important works, including the American premières of choral compositions by Dvořák, Liszt, Gounod, Saint-Saëns, etc. Horatio Parker

wrote his *Hora Novissima* for this society, and Warren brought it out on May 3, 1893. Among Warren's own compositions are the operettas *Igala* (1880), *All on a Summer's Day* (1882), *Magnolia* (1886), *The Rightful Heir* (1899); a "romantic opera," *Phyllis* (N.Y., May 7, 1900); a cantata, *Ticonderoga* (1894); services; anthems; songs.

Warren, Samuel Prowse, American organist; b. Montreal, Feb. 18, 1841; d. New York, Oct. 7, 1915. He studied organ with Haupt in Berlin, piano with Gustav Schumann, and theory with Wieprecht. After filling various positions in N.Y. churches, he inaugurated a series of organ recitals, which were greatly appreciated, and created for him a reputation as one of the foremost concert organists in the U.S. He publ. many organ pieces and songs; also made excellent transcriptions for organ of works by Weber, Beethoven, Schumann, and Wagner.

Wartel, Pierre-François, noted French singer and teacher; b. Versailles, April 3, 1806; d. Paris, Aug. 3, 1882. He studied at the Paris Cons. with Nourrit; was engaged as tenor at the Paris Opéra (1831–46), but became known chiefly as an experienced singing teacher; Christine Nilsson was one of his many famous pupils. He also gave song recitals, in which he performed songs by Schubert for the first time in France. His wife, **Atale Thérèse Annette Wartel** (*née* **Adrien;** b. Paris, July 2, 1814; d. there, Nov. 6, 1865), was a talented pianist; she also composed piano studies and other pieces.

Washburn, Robert, American composer b. Bouckville, New York, July 11, 1928. He attended the State College of Potsdam, N.Y., where he received his M.S. He served in the U.S. Air Force (1950–54) and later studied composition at the Eastman School of Music in Rochester, N.Y., with Bernard Rogers. In 1954 he was appointed prof. of music at the State College of Education at Potsdam, N.Y.
    WORKS: Symph. No. 1 (1959); *Synthesis* for orch. (1960); *St. Lawrence Overture* (1962); Sinfonietta for string orch. (1964); *Serenade* for strings (1966); *Symphonic Essay* (1967); *North Country Overture* (1969); *Blue Lake Overture* (1970); *Excursion* for orch. (1970); *Elegy* for orch. (1974); *Sinfonia* for voices and instruments (1977); chamber music.

Wasielewski, Wilhelm Joseph von, eminent German music scholar; b. Gross-Leesen, near Danzig, June 17, 1822; d. Sondershausen, Dec. 13, 1896. He studied violin as a private pupil of Ferdinand David in Leipzig, and also had lessons with Mendelssohn (1843–45). He joined the Gewandhaus Orch. (until 1850); went to Düsseldorf, where he was concertmaster under Schumann (1950–52); then was choral conductor in Bonn (1852–55); in 1855 he settled in Dresden as a writer, in which capacity he greatly distinguished himself. In 1869 he became town music director in Bonn, remaining in that position until 1884, when he went to Sondershausen.
    WRITINGS: *Robert Schumann* (1858; 4th ed., 1906; English transl., 1871), with important supplementary matter in *Schumanniana* (1883); *Die Violine und ihre*

Meister (1869; 2nd augmented ed., 1883; 7th ed., 1927); *Die Violine im 17. Jahrhundert und die Anfänge ser Instrumentalkomposition* (1874; 2nd ed., 1905); *Geschichte der Instrumentalmusik im 16. Jahrhundert* (1878); *Beethoven* (1888; 2 vols.); *Das Violoncell und seine Geschichte* (1889; 3rd ed, by his son Waldemar, 1925; in English, 1894); *Carl Reinecke, sein Leben, Wirken und Schaffen* (Leipzig, 1892); and *Aus 70 Jahren,* memoirs (Stuttgart, 1897).

Wassermann, Heinrich Joseph, German conductor and composer; b. Schwarzbach, near Fulda, April 3, 1791; d. Riehen, near Basel, Sept. 3, 1838. He was a pupil of Spohr; became an orchestral conductor in Switzerland. He wrote a *Thème original varié* for string quartet; Quartet for flute, violin, viola, and cello; *Air varié* for bassoon and string orch.; *Divertissement* (on the Tyrolian "Alma Lied") for violin and orch.; a number of orchestral dances; pieces for guitar.

Watanabe, Akeo, Japanese conductor; b. Tokyo, June 5, 1919. He studied conducting with Joseph Rosenstock, who was then resident in Japan; in 1950 went to the U.S. and took a course in conducting with Jean Morel at the Juilliard School of Music, N.Y.; returning to Japan, he founded in 1956 the Nippon Philharmonic Orch., which he led until 1968; he also made guest appearances as conductor in the U.S. and in Europe. In 1972 he was appointed music director of the Tokyo Metropolitan Orchestra.

Waters, Edward N. (Neighbor), eminent American musicologist; b. Leavenworth, Kanas, July 23, 1906. He studied piano and theory at the Eastman School of Music (B.M., 1927; M.M. in musicology, 1928). In 1931 he joined the staff of the Music Division, Library of Congress, Washington, D.C.; from 1972 to 1976 served as chief of the Music Division; was president of the Music Library Association (1941–46); was program annotator for the concerts of the National Symph. Orch., Washington (1934–43); editor, *Notes* of the music Library Association (1963–66); author of many articles and book reviews in professional journals. The Cleveland Institute of Music conferred upon him the honorary degree of Doctor of Music (1973). He is the author of a definitive biography of Victor Herbert (N.Y., 1955).

Waters, Ethel, American jazz and blues singer; b. Chester, Pennsylvania, Oct. 31, 1896 (the fruit of a knife-point rape, when her mother was $12\frac{1}{2}$ years old); d. New York, Sept. 1, 1977. After a disastrous marriage when she was 13, she worked as a laundress in Philadelphia. When her ability as a natural singer was discovered, she appeared in vaudeville, singing the *St. Louis Blues* and jazz songs. Later she joined a traveling show. She became the first black singer to be featured by all-white bands in 1929, when she appeared with Benny Goodman and the Dorsey Brothers. Her memoirs, *To Me It's Wonderful,* were published at N.Y. in 1972.
BIBLIOGRAPHY: David Ewen, *All the Years of American Popular Music* (Englewood Cliffs, N.J., 1977; pp. 333–35).

Watson, Henry, English composer; b. Burnley, Lancashire, April 30, 1846; d. Salford, Jan. 8, 1911. He studied with private teachers; then was organist in various churches. In 1867 he founded (with Henry Wilson) the Manchester Vocal Union, becoming its conductor in 1885 (after Wilson's death); also taught the choral class at the Royal College of Music, Manchester. In 1899 he presented his valuable library (some 30,000 vols.) to the Corporation of Manchester. He composed an opera, *Fair Rosine* (Manchester, 1882); *A Shakespearian Cantata; The Deliverance of Israel,* oratorio for solo voices, chorus, and orch.; many part-songs.

Watson, William Michael, English composer and poet; b. Newcastle-on-Tyne, July 31, 1840; d. London, Oct. 3, 1889. He established the West End School of Music in London in 1883; composed a cantata, *Aladdin* (1885), part-songs, piano pieces, etc.

Watts, André, brilliant American pianist; b. in a U.S. Army camp in Nuremberg, June 20, 1946, of a Hungarian mother and a black American soldier. His parents were divorced in 1962. He studied in Philadelphia; attracted national attention at 16 as soloist with Leonard Bernstein's Young People's Concert televised on Jan. 15, 1963; since then played to tumultuous applause in America and in Europe. On Aug. 14, 1971, he gave a highly successful recital in his native Nuremberg. He received an honorary doctorate from Yale Univ. in 1973.

Watts, Wintter, American composer; b. Cincinnati, March 14, 1884; d. Brooklyn, Nov. 1, 1962. He studied at the Institute of Musical Art, N.Y. He received the American Prix de Rome, which enabled him to study at the American Academy in Rome (1923–25). He lived for some time in Europe, returning to N.Y. in 1931. Among his larger works are a *Bridal Overture* (1916) and an orchestral suite, *Etchings* (1921), but he is chiefly known as a composer of fine songs: *Wings of Night, Joy, With the Tide, Wild Tears, Alone;* a cycle of 9 songs to poems by Sara Teasdale, *Vignettes of Italy;* etc.
BIBLIOGRAPHY: W. T. Upton, *Art-Song in America* (N.Y., 1930; pp. 182–97).

Waxman, Franz, German-American composer; b. Königshütte, Germany, Dec. 24, 1906; d. Los Angeles, Feb. 24, 1967. He studied in Dresden and Berlin; went to the U.S. in 1934 and settled in Hollywood, where he took lessons with Arnold Schoenberg; became a successful composer for films; his musical score for *Sunset Boulevard* won the Academy Award for 1950; other works include a Sinfonietta for string orch. and timpani (1955); oratorio *Joshua* (Dallas, May 23, 1959); a fantasy on *Carmen* for violin and orch.; etc.

Wayditch, Gabriel (real name, **Baron Gabriel Wajditsch Verbovac von Dönhoff**), Hungarian-American composer; b. Budapest, Dec. 28, 1888; d. New York, July 28, 1969. He studied piano with Emil Sauer and composition with Hans Koessler at the Budapest Academy of Music. In 1907 he emigrated to the U.S.; lived mostly in New York. He wrote 14 lengthy operas to his own libretti in Hungarian, dealing mostly with oriental or religious subjects; of these only one, *Horus,* was performed in his lifetime, at his own expense (Philadelphia, Jan. 5, 1939). His longest opera, *The Heretics,* takes 8 hours to perform; the shortest, *The Caliph's Magician,* in one act, takes 2 hours. The other operas are: *Opium Dreams, Buddha, Jesus before Herod, Maria Magdalena, Maria Tesztver, Nereida, Sahara, The Catacombs, Anthony of Padua, The Venus Dwellers, Neptune's Daughter.*

Weaver, Powell, American pianist and composer, b. Clearfield, Pa., June 10, 1890; d. Kansas City, Dec. 22, 1951. He studied organ with Pietro Yon in N.Y., and composition with Respighi in Rome. Returning to the U.S., he was engaged as accompanist to prominent singers; also gave organ recitals.
WORKS: for orch.: *Plantation Overture* (1925), *The Little Faun* (1925; Boston Women's Symph. Orch., April 14, 1929), *The Vagabond,* symph. poem (Minneapolis, March 6, 1931), *Dance of the Sand-Dune Cranes,* for piano and orch. (1941); choral works: *Boating, Song, Spirit of God, Moon-Marketing, The Humming-Bird,* also a *Sabbath Evening Service;* chamber music: *An Ode,* for piano and strings, a violin sonata, etc.

Webb, Daniel, English writer on music; b. Taunton, 1735; d. Bath, Aug. 2, 1815. He publ. the important paper, *Observations on the Correspondence between Poetry and Music* (London, 1769; reprinted in his *Miscellanies,* 1803).

Webb, Frank Rush, American organist and bandmaster; b. Covington, Indiana, Oct. 8, 1851; d. Baltimore, Oct. 20, 1934. He studied at the New England Cons. in Boston; then was church organist in Indianapolis and piano teacher in Ohio; from 1883 to 1910, he was director of the School of Music in the Virginia Female Institute, Staunton, Va.; from 1883 to 1892, bandmaster of the Stonewall Brigade Band. He published nearly 200 pieces for the military band; also much salon music for piano, amounting to 108 op. numbers; church music; songs.
BIBLIOGRAPHY: M. M. Brice, *The Stonewall Brigade Band* (Verona, Virginia, 1967).

Webb, George James, American organist and magazine editor; b. Rushmore Lodge, near Salisbury, England, June 24, 1803; d. Orange, N.J., Oct. 7, 1887. He settled in Boston in 1830; served as organist of the Old South Church; was a founder of the Boston Academy of Music in 1836, and president of the Handel and Haydn Society in 1840. In 1870 he settled in Orange, N.J., but continued musical activities in N.Y. as teacher. He edited two periodicals: *The Musical Library* (1835–36), with L. Mason; and *The Musical Cabinet* (1841–42), with T. B. Hayward; also brought out the *Young Ladies' Vocal Class Book* (Boston, 1853); *The Glee Hive* and *The New Odeon* (both with L. Mason); and *Cantica laudis* (N.Y., 1850; also with Mason); publ. *Vocal Technics* and *Voice Culture* (with C. G. Allen). His hymn tune, known simply as *Webb,* became popular.

Webbe, Samuel, Jr., English composer, son of **Samuel Webbe, Sr.;** b. London, 1770; d. there, Nov. 25, 1843. He was a pupil of his father, and also received instruction from Clementi. He wrote many glees and catches, obtaining several prizes from the Catch Club; also produced his musical comedy, *The Speechless Wife* (Covent Garden, May 22, 1794). He lived in Liverpool from 1798 until 1817; returned to London, where he taught at Logier's School of Music and served as organist at the Spanish Embassy. Besides glees, duets, hymn tunes, organ voluntaries, sonatas for harpsichord, etc., he wrote *L'Amico del principiante* (28 short solfeggi) and *Harmony Epitomised, or Elements of the Thorough-bass;* also ed. *Convito Armonico* (4 vols.; a collection of madrigals, glees, catches, canons, etc., by prominent composers).

Webbe, Samuel, Sr., famous English composer of catches and glees; b. London, 1740; d. there, May 25, 1816. He began his career as a copyist for the London publisher Welcker, who enabled him to study music with the organist Barbandt; was appointed organist and choirmaster at the Chapel of the Portuguese Embassy in 1776, and later obtained a similar appointment at the Sardinian Embassy (holding both positions concurrently); from 1794 until his death he was secretary of the Catch Club, also librarian of the Glee Club (from 1787). In 1766 his canon *O that I had wings* won the prize of the Catch Club, and subsequently he carried off 26 other prizes with various catches and glees (reprinted later with 3 additional vols.), *Cecilian Ode* for 6 voices, Concerto for harpsichord, *Divertissement* for wind band, and several collections of Masses and motets. His glee, *Glorious Apollo,* was the opening work sung at every meeting of the Glee Club throughout its history.

Webber, Amherst, English composer; b. Cannes, France, Oct. 25, 1867; d. London, July 25, 1946. He studied in Oxford, Dresden, and Paris. His first professional occupation was that of an opera coach at Covent Garden in London and at the Metropolitan Opera in New York. He wrote a comic opera *Fiorella* (London, June 7, 1905), and many songs to French and English words. His Symphony had several performances in Europe and America.

Weber, Alain, French composer; b. Château-Thierry, Dec. 8, 1930. He studied at the Paris Cons. with Tony Aubin and Messiaen; received the Premier Grand Prix de Rome in 1952. His music is hedonistic in its lucid harmony and kinetic rhythmic dash.
WORKS: ballet, *Le Petit Jeu* (Paris, 1953); chamber opera, *La Voie unique* (1958); *Suite pour une pièce vue* for orch. (1954); *Symphonie* (1957); symph. poem, *Midjaay* (1963); Horn Concerto (1954) Trumpet Concerto (1965); *Strophes* for trumpet, strings and percussion (1966); *Solipsisme* for string quartet, piano, and percussion (1968); Wind Quintet (1954); Woodwind Trio (1959); Sonata for oboe and harp (1960); *Variants* for 2 pianos and percussion (1964); *Strophes* for trumpet and orch. (1966); *Commentaires concertantes* for flute and orch. (1967); *Palindromes* for bassoon and piano (1967); Violin Sonata (1968); *Synecdoque* for oboe solo (1968); *Syllepse* for chamber orch. (1970).

Weber, Ben, American composer; b. St. Louis, July 23, 1916. He studied medicine at the Univ. of Illinois; then entered De Paul Univ. in Chicago, where he studied voice, piano and music theory. In composition he was practically self-taught, but was attracted to the method of composition with 12-tones after meeting Schoenberg; paradoxically, he retained the firm tonal foundation of his melodic and contrapuntal structures. He moved to New York, where he held various positions in the recording industry; also taught composition privately. He received 2 Guggenheim grants (1950, 1953), the Thorne music award (1965) and the Koussevitzky grant (1967).

WORKS: for orch: *Symphony on Poems of William Blake* for baritone and chamber orch. (N.Y., Oct. 28, 1952); Violin Concerto (1954); *Prelude and Passacaglia* (Louisville, Feb. 19, 1955); *Rapsodie Concertante* for viola and orch. (1957); *Chamber Fantasy* for small orch. (1959); Piano Concerto (1961); 2 string quartets (1942, 1952); 2 string trios (1943, 1946); *The Pool of Darkness,* for flute, violin, trumpet, bassoon, cello, and piano (1950); *Aubade* for flute, harp, and cello (1950); Concerto for piano, cello, and woodwind quintet (1950); *Colloquy* for brass septet (1953); *Serenade* for harpsichord, flute, oboe, and cello (1953); Concertino for flute, oboe, clarinet, and string quartet (1955); *Serenade* for string quintet (1955); *Nocturne* for flute, celesta, and cello (1962); *Dolmen: An Elegy* for winds and strings (1964); *Concert Poem* for violin and orch. (1970); *Sinfonia Clarion* for orch. (N.Y., Feb. 26, 1974); *Consort of Winds* for wind quintet (1974); *Capriccio* for cello and piano (1975); 2 violin sonatas; *2 Dances* for cello and piano; songs.

BIBLIOGRAPHY: *Composers of the Americas,* Vol. 9 (Washington, D.C., 1963).

Weber, Bernhard Anselm, German pianist and composer; b. Mannheim, April 18, 1764; d. Berlin, March 23, 1821. He studied with Abbé Vogler and Holzbauer; also took courses in theology and law at the Univ. of Heidelberg; then traveled as performer on the Xänorphica, a keyboard instrument invented by Röllig. In 1787 he became music director of Grossmann's opera troupe; went to Stockholm in 1790; in 1792 was appointed conductor of the Königstadt Theater in Berlin, remaining in this capacity after its union with the Italian Opera. A great admirer of Gluck, he was the first to introduce Gluck's operas in Berlin, and his own works closely followed Gluck's style. He produced in Berlin 2 of his operas: *Mudarra* (March 10, 1800) and *Die Wette* (Jan. 21, 1805). Some of his songs were popular for a time.

BIBLIOGRAPHY: H. Fischer, *B. A. Weber* (dissertation; Berlin, 1923).

Weber, Bernhard Christian, German organist and composer; b. Wolferschwenda, Dec. 1, 1712; d. Tennstedt, Feb. 5, 1758. He settled in Tennstedt as town organist in 1732. Inspired by Bach's example, and at the instigation of Bach's pupil G. H. Noah, Weber composed for organ a work containing 24 preludes and fugues in all keys, and entitled it *Das wohltemperierte Klavier.*

Weber, Carl Maria (Friedrich Ernst), Freiherr von, celebrated German composer; the founder of the German Romantic school; b. Eutin, Oldenburg, Nov. 18, 1786; d. London, June 5, 1826. His father, Franz Anton von Weber (1734–1812), was an army officer and a good musical amateur who played the violin and served as town musician in Eutin. It was his fondest wish to see one of his children become a great musician; Constanze Weber, Mozart's wife, was his niece (so that Carl Maria was Mozart's first cousin by marriage) and Mozart was constantly the family's ideal to follow. Carl Maria's mother was a singer of some ability; she died when he was 12 years old. Franz Anton von Weber led a wandering life as musical director of a traveling theatrical troupe, and he took his family with him. Although this mode of life interfered with Weber's regular education, it gave him practical knowledge of the stage, and stimulated his imagination as a dramatic composer. Weber's first teacher was his stepbrother Fritz, a pupil of Haydn; at Hildburghausen, where he found himself with his father's company in 1796, he received piano instruction from J. P. Heuschkel. The next year he was in Salzburg, where he attracted the attention of Michael Haydn, who taught him counterpoint. As his peregrinations continued, he was taught singing by Valesi (J. B. Wallishauser), and composition by J. N. Kalcher, in Munisch (1798–1800); by that time he had already publ. his first work, 6 fughettas for piano (1798). At the age of 13, he wrote an opera, *Die Macht der Liebe und des Weins;* it was never performed, and the score is lost. Through a meeting with Aloys Senefelder, the inventor of lithography, became greatly interested in engraving; still a mere boy, he acquired considerable skill in the process, and even worked out some improvements; engraved his variations for piano, op. 2, himself, in 1800. His father, too, became interested in the business possibilities of lithography, and set up a workshop with him in Freiberg, Saxony; the venture did not succeed, and Carl Maria turned again to music; wrote a 2-act opera, *Das Waldmädchen,* which was produced in Freiberg 6 days after his 14th birthday, on Nov. 24, 1800; performances followed in Chemnitz (Dec. 5, 1800) and, 4 years later, in Vienna. In 1801 the family was once more in Salzburg, where Weber studied further with Michael Haydn, and wrote another opera, *Peter Schmoll und seine Nachbarn;* after a stay in Hamburg (1802), they proceeded to Augsburg (1803) and finally to Vienna. There, Weber made a serious study of the works of the great masters under the guidance of Abbé Vogler, at whose recommendation he secured the post of conductor of the Breslau City Theater (1804); in 1806 he became Musik-Intendant to Duke Eugen of Württemberg at Schloss Carlsruhe in Silesia; in Sept. 1807 he was engaged as private secretary to Duke Ludwig at Stuttgart, and music master to his children. This employment was abruptly terminated when Weber became innocently involved in a scheme of securing a ducal appointment for a rich man's son in order to exempt him from military service, and accepted a loan of money; as a result of the disclosure of this affair, Weber was arrested and kept in prison for 2 weeks, after which he was expelled from Stuttgart. He went to Darmstadt, where he rejoined his old teacher Abbé

Vogler, for whom he did some editorial and analytic work in publishing an edition of Bach's chorales. On Sept. 16, 1810, Weber's opera *Silvana* was successfully presented in Frankfurt; on June 4, 1811, he brought out in Munich a new opera, *Abu Hassan.* In the meantime, he appeared as pianist, giving concerts in Frankfurt, Würzburg, Nuremberg, Bamberg, Weimar, Gotha, and other German towns. In 1813 he received his first important appointment, that of conductor of the German Opera in Prague; there he presented a distinguished repertory, which included Beethoven's *Fidelio;* traveled to Vienna to engage a company of singers; among them was **Caroline Brandt,** his future wife. His reputation as music director and composer rose considerably, and the King of Saxony called him to Dresden to take charge of the German Opera Theater there. He opened his Dresden season on Jan. 30, 1817; became friendly with Friedrich Kind, a Dresden lawyer and writer, and suggested to him the idea of writing a libretto on a typically German subject. They agreed on *Der Freischütz,* a fairy tale from J. A. Apel's and F. Laun's collection of ghost stories, *Gespensterbuch.* The composition of this work, which was to prove his masterpiece, occupied him fully 3 years; the overture was finished in May 1820; interrupting his work, he wrote (in 3 weeks) several musical numbers to *Preciosa,* a play in 4 acts with spoken dialogue; it was produced in Berlin on March 14, 1821; another stage work, *Die drei Pintos,* which Weber started at about the same time, was left unfinished. Finally, *Der Freischütz* was completed, and accepted for performance at the new Berlin Opera Theater. There existed an undercurrent of rivalry with Spontini, director of the Berlin Opera and an almost absolute master of operatic policy in Berlin; the challenge was that of rising German nationalism against the Italian-French tradition. Weber conducted the première on June 18, 1821; the work's success surpassed all expectations; the cause of new Romantic art was won; *Der Freischütz* was soon staged by all the major opera houses of Europe. In English, it was given first in London, on July 22, 1824; translations into other languages followed. Weber's next opera was *Euryanthe,* produced in Vienna, on Oct. 25, 1823, with only moderate success. Meanwhile, Weber's health was affected by incipient tuberculosis and he was compelled to go to Marienbad for a cure (1824). He recovered sufficiently to begin the composition of *Oberon,* commissioned from him by Covent Garden, London; the English libretto was by J. R. Planché, based on a translation of C. M. Wieland's *Oberon.* Once more, illness interrupted Weber's progress on his work; he spent some time in Ems to recuperate, and then embarked on the voyage to England early in 1826. He rehearsed the opera thoroughly, and conducted the première at Covent Garden on April 12, 1826, obtaining tremendous success with the London audience. Despite his greatly weakened condition, he conducted eleven more performances of *Oberon,* and participated also in various London concerts, playing for the last time a week before his death. He was buried in London; his remains were removed to Dresden on Dec. 15, 1844; on that occasion Richard Wagner delivered an oration and conducted a funeral march on motifs from *Euryanthe,*

as well as a funeral ode for double chorus expressly written for the service.

Weber's role in music history is epoch-making; in his operas, particulary in *Der Freischütz,* he opened the era of musical Romanticism, in decisive opposition to the established Italianate style. The highly dramatic and poetic portrayal of a German fairy tale, with its aura of supernatural mystery, appealed to the public, whose imagination had been stirred by the emergent Romantic literature of the period. Weber's melodic genius and his mastery of the craft of composition made it possible for him to break with tradition and to start on a new path, at a critical time when individualism and nationalism began to emerge as sources of creative artistry. His instrumental works, too, possess a new quality which signalizes the transition from Classical to Romantic music. For piano he wrote pieces of extraordinary brilliance, introducing some novel elements in chord writing and passage work. He was himself an excellent pianist; his large hands gave him an unusual command of the keyboard—he could stretch the interval of a twelfth. Weber's influence on the development of German music was very great. The evolutionary link to Wagner's music drama is evident in the coloring of the orchestral parts in Weber's operas and in the adumbration of the principle of leading motifs.

WORKS: OPERAS: *Das Waldmädchen* (Freiberg, Nov. 24, 1800); *Peter Schmoll und seine Nachbarn* (Augsburg, March, 1803); *Rübezahl* (1805; unfinished); *Silvana* (Frankfurt, Sept. 16, 1810); *Abu Hassan* (Munich, June 4, 1811); *Preciosa* (Berlin, March 14, 1821); *Der Freischütz* (Berlin, June 18, 1821); *Die drei Pintos* (1821; unfinished; completed by Gustav Mahler after Weber's sketches and produced in Leipzig, Jan. 20, 1888); *Euryanthe* (Vienna, Oct. 25, 1823); *Oberon, or The Elf King's Oath* (London, April 12, 1826).

INCIDENTAL MUSIC: to Gozzi's *Turandot* (1809), Moreto's *Donna Diana* (1817), Adolf Müllner's *König Yngurd* (1817), Theodor Hell's *Das Haus Anglade* (1818), Grillparzer's *Sappho* (1818), Gehe's *Heinrich IV* (1818), Rublack's *Leib' um Liebe* (1818), Houwald's *Der Leuchtturm* (1820), Ludwig Robert's *Den Sachsensohn vermählet heute* (1822).

VOCAL WORKS: the cantata *Der erste Ton,* for declamation, chorus, and orch. (1808); op. 36, *In seiner Ordnung schafft der Herr,* for soli, chorus, and orch. (1812); op. 44, *Kampf und Sieg,* cantata on the battle of Waterloo (1815); *L'Accoglianza* for 6 solo voices, chorus, and orch. (1817); op. 58, *Jubel-Kantate* for soli, chorus, and orch. (1818); op. 61, *Natur und Liebe,* cantata for 2 sopranos, 2 tenors, and 2 basses, with piano (1818); other occasional cantatas; 2 Masses (E-flat, G); 2 offertories, for soli, chorus, and orch.; 6 part-songs for men's voices, op. 42 (to Th. Körner's *Leyer und Schwert;* achieved great popularity with students); 5 part-songs for men's chorus, op. 53b; 6 part-songs for men's chorus, op. 68; 5 scenes for soprano with orch. (op. 16, "Il Momento s'avvicina," op. 50, "Misera me," for *Atalia,* 1811; op. 51, "Non paventar, mia vita," for *Indes de Castro,* 1816; op. 52, "Ah, se Edmondo fosse l'uccisor," for Méhul's *Hélène,* 1815; op. 56, "Was sag' ich? Schaudern macht mich der Gedanken," for Cherubini's *Lodoiska*); op. 53, scena for tenor, double chorus, and orch., "Signor, se padre sei," for *Ines de Castro;* scena and aria for tenor, men's chorus, and orch., "Qual altro attendi"; recitative, "Doch welche Töne steigen jetzt hernieder," for Spontini's *Olympie;* many songs (opp. 13, 15, 23, 25, 29, 30, 41, 43, 46, 47, 54, 64, 66, 71, 80); 8 part-songs for mixed voices, with and without accompaniment; 6 canons for 3 and 4 voices; duets (op. 31); 10 Scottish folksongs arranged with accompaniment of flute, violin, cello, and piano.

FOR ORCHESTRA: op. 27, *Der Beherrscher der Geister,* overture (to the unfinished opera, *Rübezahl*); op. 59, *Jubel-Ouvertüre;* 2 symphonies, both in C major; march for wind instruments; waltz for wind instruments; 2 piano concertos (op. 11, C; op. 32, E-flat) and *Konzertstück* in F minor (op. 79); Concertino for clarinet and orch. in E-flat major (op. 26) and 2 clarinet concertos (op. 73, F minor; op. 74, E-flat); *Andante und Rondo* in C minor for bassoon and orch. (op. 35); Concerto in F for bassoon and orch (op. 75); Concertino in E minor for horn and orch. (op. 45); *Romanza siciliana* for flute and orch.; 6 *Variations on a German Folksong* for cello and orch.; *Adante and Variations* in D minor for cello and orch.; *Adagio and Rondo* for "harmonichord" and orchestra.

CHAMBER MUSIC: op. 8, Piano Quartet in B-flat; op. 13, 6 Sonatas for violin and piano (F, G, D minor, E-flat, A, C); op. 22, *Variations on a Norwegian Theme* for violin and piano, in D minor; op. 33, Variations for clarinet and piano in B-flat; op. 34, Clarinet Quintet in B-flat; op. 48, *Duo concertant* in E-flat for clarinet and piano; op. 63, Piano Trio in G minor.

FOR PIANO: 4 sonatas (op. 24, C; op. 39, A-flat; op. 49, D minor; op. 70, E minor); op. 1, *Sechs Fughetten;* op. 2, *Variations* on an original theme; op. 3, *Douze Allemandes;* op. 5, *Variations on an Air de ballet* from Vogler's *Castor et Pollux;* op. 6, *Variations on an Air* from Vogler's *Samori;* op. 7, *Variations* on an original theme; op. 12, *Momento capriccioso;* op. 21, *Grande Polonaise* in E-flat; op. 28, *Variations* on a theme from Méhul's *Joseph;* op. 40, *Variations* on a Russian theme; op. 50, *Polonaise brillante* in E; op. 53, *Caprice and Variations* on a theme from *Preciosa;* op. 55, *Variations* on a Gypsy theme; op. 62, *Rondo brillant* in E-flat major; op. 65, *Aufforderung zum Tanz* (*Invitation to the Dance;* in 2 orchestral versions, by Berlioz and Weingartner, and in innumerable arrangements for various instruments); op. 72, *Polacca brillante* (arranged for piano and orch. by Liszt); op. 81, *Les Adieux,* fantasy; *18 Valses favorites de l'Impératrice de France.* Piano 4 hands: op. 3, *Sechs leichte Stücke;* op. 10, *Six sonates progressives et agréables;* op. 60, *Acht leichte Stücke.* A popular piece publ. under the title *Weber's Last Waltz* (or *Weber's Last Thought*) is a composition of K. G. Reissiger, not Weber.

A complete edition of Weber's works was undertaken in 1926 under the general editorship of H. J. Moser; only the following vols. were published: vols. I–II, early operas, ed. by A. Lorenz and W. Kaehler; vol. III, the Salzburg Mass, ed. by C. Schneider; *Preciosa,* ed. by L. K. Mayer. Previously unpublished works are found in L. Hirschberg's *Reliquienschrein des Meisters C. M. von Weber* (Berlin, 1827). A complete thematic catalogue of Weber's works was publ.

by F. W. Jähns, *C. M. von Weber in seinen Werken* (Berlin, 1871).

WRITINGS: An unfinished novel, criticisms, explanatory remarks on new works produced by him in Dresden, poems, etc., were publ. by Th. Hell as *Hinterlassene Schriften von C. M. von Weber* (3 vols.; Dresden, 1828; 2nd ed., 1850). A more complete and a better ed. is that of G. Kaiser, *Sämtliche Schriften von C. M. von Weber* (Berlin, 1908). R. Kleinecke publ. *Ausgewählte Schriften von K. M. von Weber* (Leipzig, 1892); a more recent collection was publ. by W. Altmann, *Webers Ausgewählte Schriften* (Regensburg, 1928). *Ein Brevier* was ed. by H. Dünnebeil (Berlin, 1949).

BIBLIOGRAPHY: BIOGRAPHY: Weber's "Autobiographische Skizze," in Kaiser's ed. of Weber's *Sämtliche Schriften* (pp. 3–8); W. Neumann, *Weber. Eine Biographie* (Kassel, 1855); Max M. von Weber (son of the composer), *C. M. von Weber. Ein Lebensbild* (3. vols., Leipzig, 1864–66; English adaptation by J. P. Simpson as *Weber: The Life of an Artist,* 2 vols., London, 1865; abridged ed. by R. Pechel, Berlin, 1912; still the standard biography); F. W. Jähns, *Weber. Eine Lebensskizze nach authentischen Quellen* (Leipzig, 1873); J. Benedict, *Weber* (London and N.Y., 1881; 5th ed., 1899; in the series Great Musicians); L. Nohl, *Weber* (Leipzig, 1883); A. Reissmann, *Weber, sein Leben und seine Werke* (Berlin, 1886); H. Gehrmann, *Weber* (Berlin, 1899); G. Servières, *Weber* (Paris, 1906; new ed., 1925; in the series *Musiciens célèbres*); H. von der Pfordten, *Weber* (Leipzig, 1919); A. Cœuroy, *Weber* (Paris, 1925; in the series *Les Maîtres de la musique;* new ed., 1953); J. Kapp, *Weber. Eine Biographie* (Berlin, 1922; 5th revised ed., 1931); E. Kroll, *Weber* (Postdam, 1934); L. P. and R. P. Stebbins, *Enchanted Wanderer: The Life of C. M. von Weber* (N. Y., 1940); W. Saunders, *Weber* (London and N.Y., 1940); H. J. Moser, *C. M. von Weber. Leben und Werk* (Leipzig, 1941; 2nd ed., 1955); P. Raabe, *Wege zu Weber* (Regensburg, 1942); W. Zentner, *C. M. von Weber. Sein Leben und sein Schaffen* (Olten, 1952); H. Schnoor, *Weber: Gestalt und Schöpfung* (Dresden, 1953); H. Dünnebeil, *Webers Leben und Wirken in chronologischen Tafeln* (Berlin, 1953); F. Grüniger, *C. M. von Weber: Leben und Werk* (Freiburg-im-Breisgau, 1954); J. Warrack, *Carl Maria von Weber* (N.Y., 1968).

CRITICISM, APPRECIATION: A. Jullien, *Weber à Paris en 1826* (Paris, 1877); Wagner's articles on Weber are found in vol. VII of his complete works (English translation, London, 1898; also in C. F. Glasenapp's *Wagner-Encyklopädie,* II, pp. 259-80, Leipzig, 1891); G. F. Kaiser, *Beiträge zu einer Charakteristik Webers als Musikschriftsteller* (Leipzig, 1910); G. Servières, *Le "Freischütz" de Weber* (Paris, 1913); W. Georgii, *Weber als Klavierkomponist* (dissertation; Halle, 1914); H. W. von Waltershausen, *Der Freischütz. Ein Versuch über die musikalische Romantik* (Munich, 1920); H. Allekotte, *Webers Messen* (Bonn, 1913); E. J. Dent, "A Weber Centenary," *Music & Letters* (July 1921); F. Hasselberg, *Der Freischütz. Friedrich Kinds Operndichtung und ihre Quellen* (Berlin, 1921); M. Degen, *Die Lieder von Weber* (Basel, 1923); A. Cœuroy, "Le Problème d'Euryanthe," *Le Correspondent* (Oct. 25, 1923); A. Cœuroy, "Weber as Writer," *Musical Quar-*

terly (Jan. 1925); E. Reiter, *Webers künstlerische Persönlichkeit aus seinen Schriften* (Leipzig, 1926); H. Abert, "Weber und sein *Freischütz*," *Jahrbuch der Musikbibliothek Peters* (1927; reprinted in Abert's *Gesammelte Schriften*, Halle, 1929); J. G. Prod'homme, "The Works of Weber in France," *Musical Quarterly* (July 1928); A. Sandt, *Webers Opern in ihrer Instrumentation* (Frankfurt, 1932); G. Kinsky, "Was Mendelssohn Indebted to Weber?" *Musical Quarterly* (April 1933); G. Abraham, "Weber as Novelist and Critic," *Musical Quarterly* (Jan. 1934); P. Listl, *C. M. von Weber als Ouvertürenkomponist* (dissertation; Würzburg, 1936); A. Einstein, "C. M. Weber," *Music & Letters* (Jan. 1937); H. Schnoor, *W. auf dem Welttheater; ein Freischützbuch* (Dresden, 1942); P. R. Kirby, "Weber's Operas in London," *Musical Quarterly* (July 1946).

CORRESPONDENCE: L. Nohl, *Musiker-Briefe* (Leipzig, 1867; 2nd ed., 1873; English transl. by Lady Wallace as *Letters of Distinguished Musicians*, London, 1867); L. Nohl, *Musik für musikalisch-gebildete* (Leipzig, 1882); A. von Weber (grandson of the composer), *Reise-Briefe von Weber an seine Gattin Caroline* (Leipzig, 1886); E. Rudorff, *Briefe von Weber an Heinrich Lichtenstein* (Brunswick, 1900); G. Kaiser, *Webers Briefe an den Grafen Karl von Brühl* (Leipzig, 1911); L. Hirschberg, *77 bisher ungedruckte Briefe Webers* (Hildburghausen, 1926); G. Kinsky, "Ungedruckte Briefe Webers," *Zeitschrift für Musik* (1926).

WEBER AND HIS CONTEMPORARIES: J. C. Lobe, "Gespräche mit Weber," in his *Fliegende Blätter für Musik* (Leipzig, 1853; reprinted in his *Consonanzen und Dissonanzen*, 1869); M. Runze, "Loewe und Weber," in his *Loewe Redivivus* (Berlin, 1888); H. A. Krüger, *Pseudoromantik, Friedrich Kind und der Dresdener Liederkreis* (Leipzig, 1904); H. B. and C. O. E. Cox, *Leaves from the Journal of Sir G. Smart* (London, 1907); K. Huschke, "Webers Beziehungen zu Ludwig von Beethoven und Franz Schubert," *Deutsche Revue* (May-June 1919); E. Kroll, "E. T. A. Hoffmann und Weber," *Neue Musik-Zeitung* (1921); K. Huschke, "Spohr und Weber," *Allgemeine Musik Zeitung* (1934); E. Kroll, "Beethoven and Weber," *Neues Beethoven-Jahrbuch* (Augsburg, 1935); O. Kroll, "Weber und Bärmann," *Neue Zeitschrift für Musik* (1936).

MISCELLANEOUS: R. Haas, "Ein Notizen-Buch C. M. von Webers aus Prag," *Der Merker* (1916); A. Maecklenburg, "Der Fall Spontini-Weber," *Zeitschrift für Musikwissenschaft* (1923-24); O. Hellinghaus, *Weber. Sein Persönlichkeit in seinen Briefen und Tagebüchern und in Aufzeichnungen seiner Zeitgenossen* (Freiburg-im-Breisgau, 1924); E. Kroll, *Weber. Sein Leben in Bildern* (Leipzig, 1936); F. Rapp, *Ein unbekanntes Bildnis Webers* (Stuttgart, 1937); G. Hausswald, ed., *Weber: Eine Gedenkschrift* (Dresden, 1951).

Weber, Franz, German organist and conductor; b. Cologne, Aug. 26, 1805; d. there, Sept. 18, 1876. He studied with Bernhard Klein in Berlin; in 1838 was appointed organist of the Cologne Cathedral. He wrote a *Kriegsgesang der Rheinpreussen* for male chorus and orch.; publ. several song books (*Kommersbuch, Turner-Liederbuch, Des deutschen Soldaten Liederbuch,* etc.).

Weber, Friedrich August, German physician and composer; b. Heilbronn, Jan. 24, 1753; d. there, Jan. 21, 1806. He wrote numerous oratorios and cantatas with orch.; also symphonies, chamber music, piano sonatas for 4 hands; contributed articles on music to various journals.

Weber, Friedrich Dionys, Bohemian composer and writer on music; b. Velichov, Oct. 9, 1766; d. Prague, Dec. 25, 1842. He studied with Abbé Vogler; in 1811 was one of the founders of the Prague Cons., and its first director; among his pupils were Moscheles and Kalliwoda. He wrote several operas, 18 cantatas, a number of military marches, a sextet for 6 trombones, a sextet for 6 cornets, quartets for 4 cornets, variations for violin and cello, numerous popular quadrilles, *Ländler,* etc., for piano; publ. *Das Konservatorium der Musik zu Prag* (1817), *Allgemeine theoretisch-praktische Vorschule der Musik* (1828), *Theoretisch-prakitisches Lehrbuch der Harmonie und des Generalbasses* (1830-41; 4 parts).

Weber, Georg Viktor, German ecclesiastic and choral conductor; b. Ober-Erlenbach, Feb. 25, 1838; d. Mainz, Sept. 24, 1911. He took holy orders in 1863; in 1866 was appointed music director and organist at the Cathedral of Mainz, where he presented fine concerts of a cappella music of the 15th and 16th centuries with his excellent choir. He was also an expert on organ building.

WRITINGS: *Manuale cantus ecclesiastici juxta ritum S. Rom. ecclesiae* (1878; 2nd ed., 1897); *Orgelbuch zum Mainzer Diocesan-Gesangbuch* (1880; 3rd ed., 1896); *Über Oregeldispositionen* (1890); *Die Verbesserung der "Medicaea"* (1901).

Weber, Gottfried, eminent German theorist and composer; b. Freinsheim, near Mannheim, March 1, 1779; d. Kreuznach, Sept. 21, 1839. He studied law at Heidelberg and Göttingen, and filled positions as judge in Mannheim (1802), Mainz (1814), and Darmstadt (1818); was appointed public prosecutor for the state of Hesse in 1832. He was an excellent amateur pianist and also played the flute and the cello; in 1806 founded a musical society called "Conservatorium" in Mannheim; in 1824 began the magazine *Caecilia,* and edited it until his death. He made a thorough study of the theoretical works of Marpurg, Kirnberger, Abbé Vogler, and others, and then brought out his important treatise, *Versuch einer geordneten Theorie der Tonsetzkunst* (3 vols., 1817-21; 2nd ed. in 4 vols., 1824; 3rd ed. in 4 vols., 1830-32), in which he introduced the now widely accepted symbols for designating the major keys with capital letters and minor keys with small letters, Roman figures for degrees of the scale, etc. It was publ. in English in Boston (1846) and London (1851). His other theoretical publications include *Über chronometrische Tempobezeichnung* (1817); *Beschreibung und Tonleiter der G. Weber'schen Doppelposaune* (1817); "Versuch einer praktischen Akustik der Blasinstrumente," in Ersch and Gruber's *Encyclopädie; Allgemeine Musiklehre zum Selbstunterrichte* (1822; 3rd ed., 1831; in English, Boston, 1824); "Über Saiteninstrumente mit Bünden," *Berliner Musikzeitung* (1825); *Die Generalbasslehre* *zum Selbstunterrichte* (1833); many essays for the *Allgemeine musikalische Zeitung* and for his own paper, *Caecilia*. He questioned the authenticity of Mozart's Requiem (in *Caecilia*, 1826). As a composer, he wrote 3 Masses, a Requiem, and a Te Deum (all with orch.); variations for guitar and cello; some chamber music; part-songs.

Weber, Gustav, Swiss composer; b. Münchenbuchsee, Oct. 30, 1845; d. Zürich, June 12, 1887. He studied at the Leipzig Cons. and with Tausig in Berlin; his symphonic poem *Zur Iliade* was presented by Liszt at the Beethoven Centennial Festival in 1870. In 1872 he settled in Zürich as church organist, teacher at the Cons., and choral conductor. He publ. a group of waltzes for piano 4 hands; piano quartet; piano trio; violin sonata; *Prinz Carneval*, an album of children's pieces; many choruses; choral arrangements of old German songs. For several years he was editor of the *Schweizerische Musikzeitung.*
BIBLIOGRAPHY: A. Schneider, *G. Weber* (Zürich, 1888); A. Steiner, *Gustav Weber* (Zürich, 1910).

Weber, Josef Miroslav, Czech violinist and composer; b. Prague, Nov. 9, 1854; d. Munich, Jan. 1, 1906. He was taught by his father, and played violin in public as a child; then studied at the Prague Cons. He subsequently occupied posts as concertmaster in Sondershausen (1873–75), Darmstadt (1875), and Wiesbaden (until 1893); finally became concertmaster of the Court Opera in Munich, where he remained until his death. He wrote the operas *Der selige Herr Vetter* (Wiesbaden, 1894) and *Die neue Mamsell* (Munich, 1896); a ballet, *Die Rheinnixe* (Wiesbaden, 1884); Violin Concerto; Septet for violin, viola, cello, clarinet, bassoon, and 2 horns; String Quintet; etc.

Weber, Ludwig, German composer; b. Nuremberg, Oct. 13, 1891; d. Borken, June 30, 1947. Until 1925 he was a school teacher in Nuremberg, and was self-taught in music, except for some private instruction with Hermann Abendroth and Courvoisier. After occupying some minor posts as music teacher, he became conductor of the municipal chorus in Mülheim; associated himself with the musical youth movement, and wrote a number of choral and other works in the folksong manner.
WORKS: Symph. in B minor; *Hymnen an die Nacht* for chorus and orch.; Quintet for wind instruments; 2 string quartets; *Der Natur* for chorus and orch.; *Heilige Namen* for chorus and orch.; *Fröhlich soll meinem Herze* (4–16 voices unaccompanied); 3 one-act operas: *Midas, Christgeburt,* and *Totentanz.*
BIBLIOGRAPHY: F. W. Herzog, *Ludwig Weber* (Wolfenbüttel, 1929); K. Ziebler, *Ludwig Weber* (1939). A memorial volume, published at Stuttgart in 1950: *25. Jubiläums Aufführung des "Christgeburt."*

Weber, Margrit, Swiss pianist; b. Ebnat-Kappel, Feb. 24, 1924. She studied organ in Zürich; was employed as an organist at the age of 15; then devoted herself chiefly to the piano. She toured Europe in concert recitals presenting many new works; in 1956 and in 1965 she played in the U.S. and Canada. She was the soloist in the first performances of piano concertos by Martinu and Alexander Tcherepnin, and of Stravinsky's *Movements* for piano and orch., which she performed under Stravinsky's own direction in N.Y., on Jan. 10, 1960. See *Modern Music . . . Analytic Index,* compiled by Wayne Shirley, edited by Wm. and C. Lichtenwanger (N.Y., 1976), pp. 236–237.

Weber, Wilhelm, German choral conductor and composer; b. Bruchsal, Nov. 16, 1859; d. Augsburg, Oct. 14, 1918. After studying at the Stuttgart Cons. he went to Augsburg, where he taught at the Musikschule from 1884, becoming its director in 1905. From 1892 he was conductor of the Oratorienverein, notable for its numerous German premières of works by foreign composers; he also conducted at various festivals in Germany. He publ. 2 books of *Landsknechtslieder* and other songs; choruses; piano pieces. Author of *Beethovens Missa solemnis* (1897; 2nd ed., 1903) and *Händels Oratorien, übersetzt und bearbeitet von F. Chrysander* (3 vols.; 1898; 1900; 1902).

Webern, Anton von, remarkable Austrian composer (he removed the nobiliary particle "von" in 1918, and signed his name simply Anton Webern); b. Vienna, Dec. 3, 1883; d. Mittersill, Sept. 15, 1945 (accidentally killed by an American military policeman). He studied musicology with Guido Adler at the Univ. of Vienna (Dr. phil., 1906, with a dissertation on Isaac's *Choralis Constantinus*); studied composition privately with Schoenberg, whose ardent disciple he became. From 1908 till 1914 he conducted theater orchestras in Vienna, in Prague, and in Germany. After the end of World War I he settled in Mödling, near Vienna, where he taught composition; was closely associated with the Society for Private Musical Performances, organized in Vienna by Schoenberg with the intention of promoting modern music without being exposed to reactionary opposition (music critics were not admitted to these performances); Webern supervised the programs during its existence (1918–21); He subsequently conducted the orch. of the workers' concerts and the workers' chorus in Vienna (1922–24); also appeared as guest conductor with the BBC Orch. in London (1929) and in Barcelona (1932). Throughout World War II he remained in Vienna; after his son was killed in an air bombardment of a train in Feb. 1945, Webern and his wife fled from Vienna, and went to live with their married daughter in Mittersill, near Salzburg. He was mortally wounded by a member of the U.S. military police when he stepped out of the house in the evening, unaware of the curfew established by the U.S. occupation troops. Webern left relatively few works, and most of them are of short duration (the 4th of his Five Pieces for Orch., op. 10, scored for clarinet, trumpet, trombone, mandolin, celesta, harp, drum, violin, and viola, takes only 19 seconds to play), but in his music he achieves the utmost subtilization of expressive means. He adopted the 12-tone method of composition almost immediately after its definitive formulation by Schoenberg (1924), and extended the principle of nonrepetition of notes to tone colors, so that in some of his works (e.g., Symph., op. 21) solo instruments are rarely allowed to play 2 successive thematic notes. Dynamic marks are similarly diversified. Typically, each 12-tone row is divided into symmetric sections of 2, 4, or 6 members, which enter mutually into intricate but invariably logical canonic imitations. Inversions and augmentations are inherent features; melodically and harmonically, the intervals of the major 7th and minor 9th are stressed; single motifs are brief, and stand out as individual particles or lyric ejaculations. The impact of these works on the general public and on the critics was usually disconcerting, and upon occasion led to violent demonstrations; however, the extraordinary skill and novelty of technique made this music endure beyond the fashions of the times; performances of Webern's works multiplied after his death, and began to influence increasingly larger groups of modern musicians; Stravinsky acknowledged the use of Webern's methods in his latest works; jazz composers have professed to follow Webern's ideas of tone color; analytical treatises have been publ. in several languages.

WORKS: FOR ORCH.: *Passacaglia*, op. 1 (1908); *6 Orchestral Pieces*, op. 6 (Vienna, March 31, 1913); *5 Orchestral Pieces*, op. 10 (1913; Zürich Festival of the International Society for Contemporary Music, June 23, 1926); Symph. for chamber orch., op. 21 (1928; N.Y., League of Composers, Dec. 18, 1929); *Variations*, op. 30 (1940). CHORAL MUSIC: *Entflieht auf leichten Kähnen*, op. 2, for unaccompanied chorus (1908); *2 Songs*, to words by Goethe, op. 19, for chorus, celesta, guitar, violin, clarinet, and bass clarinet (1926); *Das Augenlicht* for chorus and orch., op. 26 (1935; London Festival, June 17, 1938); 2 cantatas, op. 29 and op. 31 (1940 and 1943). CHAMBER MUSIC: *5 Movements* for string quartet, op. 5 (1909); *6 Bagatelles* for string quartet, op. 9 (1913); Trio for violin, viola, and cello, op. 20 (1927); Quartet for violin, clarinet, saxophone, and piano, op. 22 (1930); Concerto for 9 instruments, op. 24 (Prague Festival, Sept. 4, 1935); String Quartet, op. 28 (1938); *4 Pieces* for violin and piano, op. 7 (1910); *3 Little Pieces* for cello and piano, op. 11 (1914). OTHER MUSIC: *Variations* for piano solo, op. 27 (1936); song cycles with instrumental accompaniment, opp. 8, 13, 14, 15, 16, 17, 18; songs with piano accompaniment, opp. 3, 4, 12, 23, 25; arrangements for orch. of Schubert's *Deutsche Tänze*, of Bach's *Ricercare a 6* from *Das musikalische Opfer*. Published *Der Weg zur Komposition mit 12 Tönen* (Vienna, 1932); *Der Weg zur neuen Musik* (Vienna, 1933; in English as *The Path to the New Music*, 1965); edited a vol. of compositions from Isaac's *Choralis Constantinus* in the *Denkmäler der Tonkunst in Österreich 32* (16.i).

BIBLIOGRAPHY: E. Stein, "Anton von Webern," *Chesterian* (Oct. 1923); W. Reich, "Anton von Webern," *Die Musik* (1930); T. Wiesengrund-Adorno, "Berg and Webern, Schönberg's Heirs," *Modern Music* (1931); a special issue of the Vienna magazine *23* (1934); H. Searle, "Webern's Last Works," *Monthly Musical Record* (Dec. 1946); R. Leibowitz, *Schoenberg et son école* (Paris, 1947; English transl., N.Y., 1949); L. Rognoni, *Espressionismo e dodecafonia* (Turin, 1954); R. Craft, "Anton Webern," *Score* (Sept. 1955); R. Vlad, *Storia della dodecafonia* (Milan, 1958); the compendium, *Anton Webern, Dokumente, Bekenntnisse, Erkenntnisse, Analysen* (Vienna, 1955); Hans Moldenhauer, *The Death of Anton Webern* (N.Y.,

1961); W. Kolneder, *Anton Webern: Einführung in Werk und Stil* (Rodenkirchen, 1961; in English, Berkeley, 1967); Claude Rostand, *Anton Webern: L'Homme et son œuvre* (Paris, 1969); W. M. Stroh, *Anton von Webern; historische Legimation* (Göppingen, 1973). Facsimile reproductions from Webern's sketchbooks were published with a commentary by Ernst Krenek and a foreword by Hans Moldenhauer (N.Y., 1969).

Webster, Beveridge, American pianist; b. Pittsburgh, May 30, 1908. He studied music with his father, who was director of the Pittsburgh Cons. of Music; at the age of 13 he was sent to Paris to study with Isidor Philipp at the Paris Cons.; graduated in 1926, winning the Grand Prix for piano playing. He gave concerts in Europe; returned to the U.S. in 1934, and developed a successful concert career, appearing with major symph. orchestras; also continued to give concerts in Europe. In 1946 he was appointed prof. of piano at the Juilliard School of Music, N.Y.; gave a piano recital at the Juilliard Theater on his 70th birthday in May 1978.

Wecker, Georg Kaspar, German organist and composer; b. Nuremberg, 1632 (baptized April 2); d. there, April 20, 1695. He studied organ with Erasmus Kindermann, and soon obtained a position as church organist in Nuremberg; his last appointment was at the Sebaldkirche there (1686–95). He also was a respected teacher; Johann Krieger and Pachelbel were among his pupils. Several of his sacred songs were publ. in hymn books in Nuremberg; 3 sacred choral works are reproduced in the *Denkmäler der Tonkunst in Bayern 10* (6.i).

Weckerlin, Jean-Baptiste-Théodore, eminent French music scholar and composer; b. Gebweiler, Alsace, Nov. 9, 1821; d. Buhl, May 20, 1910. He was trained for his father's business of cotton-dyeing; but went over to music in 1844, studying under Ponchard (singing) and Halévy (composition) at the Paris Cons., producing a heroic symphony, *Roland*, for soli, chorus, and orch., in 1847; on leaving the Cons. in 1849, he gave music lessons, took part with Seghers in the direction of the Société Sainte-Cécile, which brought out some of his works; and achieved success in 1853 with a 1-act comic opera, *L'Organiste dans l'embarras* (100 performances at the Théâtre-Lyrique). This was followed by 2 comic operas in Alsatian dialect, *Die drifach Hochzitt im Bäsethal* (Colmar, 1863) and *D'r verhäxt' Herbst* (Colmar, 1879), and the 1-act opera *Après Fontenoy* (Théâtre-Lyrique, 1877). Meantime he had become an assistant librarian at the Paris Cons. (1869); in 1876 succeeded Félicien David as librarian, and in 1885 publ. a bibliographical catalogue; was also chosen librarian of the Société des Compositeurs, for whose bulletins he wrote important articles. He retired in 1909. He won distinction as a composer of grand choral works; also wrote choruses a cappella, songs, and a grand *Symphonie de la forêt*, for orch.; but his greatest achievement was the compilation of old French songs. His *Échos du temps passé* (1853–55) and *Souvenirs du temps passé* (1864) are collections of chansons, noëls, madrigals, etc., from the 12th–18th centuries; the *Musiciana* (3 vols.; 1877, 1890, 1899) is a collection from rare and curious works on music, with anecdotes, etc.; other collections are *Les Échos d'Angleterre* (1877; folksongs with piano); *Chansons et rondes populaires* (children's songs with piano); *Les Poètes français mis en musique* (1868); *Chansons populaires des provinces de la France; L'ancienne chanson populaire en France* (1886); *Chansons populaires du Pays de France* (2 vols.; 1903). A catalogue of his private library was publ. at Leipzig in 1910.

Weckmann, Matthias, German organist and composer; b. Niederdorla, near Mühlhausen, Thuringia, 1621; d. Hamburg, Feb. 24, 1674. He was the son of a schoolmaster; was a chorister in the Dresden court chapel, where he was a pupil of Heinrich Schütz. In 1637 he was sent to Hamburg for further study with Reinken, Jakob Praetorius, and H. Scheidemann, by whom he was trained in the organ method of Sweelinck. In 1641 he became organist for the crown prince in Dresden, and in 1642 was appointed to a similar post in Copenhagen; he returned in 1647 to Dresden, where he became a friend of J. J. Froberger; in 1655 he went to Hamburg as organist at the Jacobikirche, and there founded, with Christoph Bernhard, the *Collegium musicum,* a concert society for the performance of new works (it was discontinued after Weckmann's death). Weckmann's solo cantatas and choral works with instrumental accompaniment were publ. by Max Seiffert in the *Denkmäler deutscher Tonkunst* 6; instrumental pieces and songs in the *Erbe deutscher Musik* (series 2, vol. 4); 2 numbers are reproduced in A. Schering's *Geschichte der Musik in Beispielen* (nos. 212 and 213); etc.
BIBLIOGRAPHY: M. Seiffert, "Matthias Weckmann und das Collegium Musicum in Hamburg," *Sammelbände der Internationalen Musik-Gesellschaft* 2 (1900); G. Ilgner, *Matthias Weckmann. Sein Leben und seine Werke* (Wolfenbüttel, 1939).

Wedge, George (Anson), American organist and educator; b. Danbury, Conn., Jan. 15, 1890; d. Barbados, Oct. 31, 1964. He studied organ, piano, and composition at the Institute of Musical Art in N.Y.; subsequently occupied various teaching positions: at N.Y. Univ. (1920–27); at the Curtis Institute of Music, Philadelphia (1924–26); dean of the Institute of Musical Art and of the Juilliard School of Music (1938–46); director of the Juilliard Summer School (1932–47). He publ. *Ear-training and Sight-singing* (1921); *Advanced Ear-training and Sight-singing* (1922); *Keyboard Harmony* (1924); *Rhythm in Music* (1927); *Applied Harmony,* in 2 vols. (1930–31); *The Gist of Music* (1936).

Weelkes, Thomas, English composer; b. c.1575; d. London, Nov. 30, 1623. In 1597 he publ. a book of madrigals for 3–6 voices; in 1598, he publ. *Balletts and Madrigals* for 5 voices, dedicated to Edward Darcey, Groom of the Privy Chamber; in 1600 he brought out two more books, containing madrigals for 5 and 6 voices; served as organist at the College of Winchester (1600–02). He was a friend of Morley, to whose collection *The Triumphes of Oriana* (1601–03) he contributed a fine madrigal for 6 voices, *As Vesta was from Latmos Hill Descending.* In 1602 he was granted the degree of B. Mus. at the New College, Oxford, and was appointed organist of Chichester Cathedral. A subsequent publication was *Ayres; or, Phantasticke Spirits for 3 voices* (1608; reprinted by Arkwright in the *Old English Edition*). Weelkes was one of the greatest English madrigalists, possessing remarkable power in melodic characterization of the text; he occasionally used chromatic progressions in harmony that were well in advance of his time. He wrote a considerable amount of church music (services and anthems); also instrumental works (2 pavanes and other pieces, for 5 viols). His madrigals and other vocal works are reprinted in *The English Madrigal School,* ed. by E. H. Fellowes (vols. 9–13); anthems in the series *Tudor Church Music* and in *Musica Britannica* 23.
BIBLIOGRAPHY: E. H. Fellowes, *The English Madrigal Composers* (London, 1921; 2nd ed., 1948); D. M. Arnold, "Thomas Weelkes and the Madrigal," *Music & Letters* (Jan. 1950); David Brown, *Thomas Weelkes: A Biographical and Critical Study* (1969).

Weerbecke, (Weerbeke, Werbecke), Gaspar van, Flemish composer; b. Audenarde, Flanders, c.1445. Pupil of Ockeghem; in 1472 he was organizer of the ducal court chapel at Milan, his singers including Josquin des Prez; from 1481 to 1489, singer in the papal chapel at Rome, a post he resumed from 1500 to 1509 after sojourns in Milan and Flanders; there is no trace of him after 1514. Masses, motets, and Lamentations by Weerbecke were publ. by Petrucci (1505–09).
BIBLIOGRAPHY: G. Cesari, in the *Rivista Musicale Italiana* (1922); G. Croll, "Gaspar van Weerbeke," *Musica Disciplina* 6 (1952; with a list of works); G. Reese, *Music in the Renaissance* (N.Y., 1954).

Wegeler, Franz Gerhard, German physician and music amateur; b. Bonn, Aug. 22, 1765; Coblenz, May 7, 1848. He was a practicing physician in Bonn and Coblenz, and knew Beethoven as a youth. With Ries, he publ. *Biographische Notizen über Ludwig van Beethoven* (1838; supplement, 1845; reprinted by A. Kalischer, 1906).
BIBLIOGRAPHY: S. Ley, ed., *Beethoven als Freund der Familie Wegeler* (Bonn, 1927).

Wegelius, Martin, eminent Finnish composer and pedagogue; b. Helsinki, Nov. 10, 1846; d. there, March 22, 1906. He studied philosophy, taking his master's degree in 1869; studied music with Rudolph Bibl in Vienna (1870–71), and with Richter and Paul in Leipzig (1871–73); he went to Leipzig for further study in 1877–78. Returning to Finland, he became operatic coach at the Helsinki National Theater. In 1882 he was appointed director of the newly founded Helsinki Cons., holding this post until his death. Under his guidance, the institution became one of the finest schools in Europe, with excellent teachers. Sibelius was one of the pupils of Wegelius; others were Järnefelt, Melartin, and Palmgren. Wegelius emphasized the cultivation of national Finnish music, and thus was mainly responsible for the magnificent development of Finland as a musical nation.
WORKS: overture *Daniel Hjort* (1872); *Divertissement à la hongroise* (1880); *Rondo quasi fantasia* for

piano and orch. (1872); *Mignon,* 6 songs with orch., after Goethe's *Westöstlicher Diwan* (1875); a Christmas cantata (1877); a festival cantata, *The 6th of May* (1878); a violin sonata; piano pieces; songs. He publ. (in Swedish) a number of manuals and books on music history: *Lärobok i allmän musiklära och analys* (2 vols., 1888–89); *Hufvuddragen af den västerländska musikens historia* (3 vols., 1891–93); *Kurs i tonträffning* (3 vols., 1893–95); *Kurs i homofon sats* (2 vols., 1897–1905); etc.

BIBLIOGRAPHY: K. T. Flodin, *Martin Wegelius* (in Swedish, Stockholm, 1916; in Finnish, Helsinki, 1922); *Martin Wegelius* (letters; 2 vols.; Helsinki, 1918–19); Arvi Karvonen, "Martin Wegelius," in *Suomen Säveltäjiä,* ed. by Sulho Ranta (Helsinki, 1945; pp. 169–83).

Wehle, Gerhard Fürchtegott, German musicologist and composer; b. Paramaribo, Dutch Guiana, Oct. 11, 1884; d. Berlin, Oct. 15, 1973. He studied in Germany, and settled in Berlin (1907); he was active primarily as a music critic and pedagogue; taught improvisation and other subjects; published *Die Kunst der Improvisation* (2 vols.; Münster, 1925–26); *Die Orgel-Improvisation* (Leipzig, 1932; both titles reissued 3 vols., Hamburg, 1950–53); *Neue Wege im Kompositions-Unterricht* (2 vols.; Hamburg, 1955); *Die höhere Kompositionstechnik* (2 vols., Hamburg). Among his musical works are 26 symphonic cantatas; 3 symphonies; much chamber music. He was also a successful novelist.

Wehle, Karl, Bohemian pianist; b. Prague, March 17, 1825; d. Paris, June 3, 1883. Trained for a mercantile career, he abandoned it for music; studied piano with Moscheles at Leipzig and Kullak in Berlin; made extended tours to Asia, Africa, America, and Australia, but resided chiefly in Paris. He publ. a number of brilliant compositions for piano, among them a *Sérénade napolitaine, Allegro à la hongroise, 3 Tarentelles, 2 Impromptus, Berceuse javanaise, Marche cosaque, Fête bohémienne, Un Songe à Vaucluse,* etc.

Wehrli, Werner, Swiss composer; b. Aarau, Jan. 8, 1892; d. Lucerne, June 27, 1944. He studied at the Zürich Cons. with Hegar and in Frankfurt with Knorr; wrote a number of "festival operas" in a Romantic vein; cantatas and chamber music. His oratorio *Wallfahrt* (1939) enjoyed a modicum of success. His opera *Das heiss Eisen,* after Hans Sachs, was produced in Bern on Dec. 11, 1918.

BIBLIOGRAPHY: G. H. Leuenberger, "Werner Wehrli," *Schweizerische Musikzeitung* (May 1952).

Weidig, Adolf, American music teacher and composer; b. Hamburg, Nov. 28, 1867; d. Hinsdale, Ill., Sept. 23, 1931. He studied at the Hamburg Cons. with Bargheer (violin) and later with Hugo Riemann (theory); then in Munich with Rheinberger (composition). In 1892 he settled in Chicago; played the violin in the Chicago Orchestra (1892–96); in 1898 he joined the faculty of the American Cons. of Music; conducted his own works in Chicago, Minneapolis, and also in Germany. He was greatly esteemed as a teacher; publ. *Harmonic Material and Its Uses* (1923); composed 2 symphonies; a symph. poem, *Semiramis; Drei Episo-*

den for orch.; a string quintet; 3 string quartets; a piano trio; songs.

BIBLIOGRAPHY: *Dictionary of American Biography.*

Weidt, Lucy, German soprano; b. Troppau, Silesia, 1880; d. Vienna, July 28, 1940. She studied piano and singing with her father, and then with Rosa Papier in Vienna, where she made her debut in 1904. She sang in Germany, appearing at the Wagner festival in 1908–10. On Nov. 18, 1910 she made her first American appearance as Brünnhilde in *Die Walküre,* at the Metropolitan Opera, N.Y.; after a season there, she sang in Italy. In 1909 she married Baron Joseph von Urmenyi. Her voice was of unusual attractiveness and power, enabling her to perform Wagnerian parts with distinction.

Weigel, Eugene, American composer; b. Cleveland, Oct. 11, 1910. He studied violin with Maurice Hewitt and composition with Arthur Shepherd in Cleveland; after holding various teaching positions, he was appointed in 1956 to the music faculty at Montana State Univ. Among his works are an opera, *The Mountain Child* (Missoula, Montana, Univ. of Montana, July 27, 1958); *Prairie Symphony* (1953); Quintet for clarinet and strings (1946); other chamber music; piano pieces; songs.

Weigl, Bruno, Czech writer on music and composer; b. Brno, June 16, 1881; d. there, Sept. 25, 1938. He published several useful teaching manuals in German: *Die Geschichte des Walzers, nebst einem Anhang über die moderne Operette* (Langensalza, 1910), *Handbuch der Violoncell-Literatur* (Vienna, 1911; revised edition 1929); *Harmonielehre* (2 vols.; Mainz, 1925); composed a comic opera, *Mandragola* (Brno, 1912); song cycles; organ works.

Weigl, Joseph, Austrian composer; b. Eisenstadt, March 28, 1766; d. Vienna, Feb. 3, 1846. His father, Joseph Franz Weigl (1740–1820), was a cellist in the service of Prince Esterházy with Haydn; his mother was a singer; he was a godson of Haydn. Brought up in a musical environment, he wrote an operetta, *Die unnützige Vorsicht,* at the age of 16 for a puppet show; Salieri accepted him as a pupil; he also studied with Albrechtsberger. He was assistant conductor to Salieri at the Vienna Court Theater from 1790 till 1823. Altogether, Weigl wrote 14 operas in Italian and 19 in German. The most successful were *La Principessa d'Amalfi* (Vienna, Jan. 12, 1794; Haydn described it as a masterpiece in a letter to Weigl after the performance) and *Die Schweizerfamilie* (Vienna, March 14, 1809; produced in Paris, Feb. 6, 1827 as *Emmeline, ou La Famille suisse;* also staged in opera houses all over Europe until about 1900, when it disappeared from the repertory). The following operas by Weigl were produced in Vienna with varying success: *Il Pazzo per forza* (Nov. 14, 1788), *La Caffettiera bizzarra* (Sept. 15, 1790), *L'Amor marinaro* (Oct. 15, 1797), *Das Dorf im Gebürge* (April 17, 1798), *Die Uniform* (Feb. 15, 1805), *Vestas Feuer* (Aug. 10, 1805), *Kaiser Hadrian* (May 21, 1807), *Adrian von Ostade* (July 3, 1807), *Das Waisenhaus* (Oct. 4, 1808), *Nachtigall und Rabe*

(April 20, 1818), *Margarethe von Anjou* (March 16, 1819), *Baals Sturz* (April 13, 1820), *König Waldemar* (May 11, 1821), *Edmund und Caroline* (Sept. 21, 1821), *Die eiserne Pforte* (Feb. 27, 1823); three operas were produced at La Scala, Milan: *Cleopatra* (Dec. 19, 1807), *Il Rivale di se stesso* (April 18, 1808), and *L'Imboscata* (Nov. 8, 1815). Weigl also wrote 18 ballets; 2 oratorios; 22 cantatas; 11 Masses and other church music.

BIBLIOGRAPHY: W. Neumann, *Joseph Weigl* (Kassel, 1855); A. Eisner-Eisenhof, "Joseph Weigl," *Rivista Musicale Italiana* (1904); W. Bollert, "Joseph Weigl und das deutsche Singspiel," in his *Aufsätze zur Musikgeschichte* (Bottrop, 1938); for details of productions of Weigl's operas, see A. Loewenberg's *Annals of Opera* (Cambridge, 1943; 2nd ed., Geneva, 1955).

Weigl, Karl, Austrian composer; b. Vienna, Feb. 6, 1881; d. New York, Aug. 11, 1949. He studied piano with Door and music theory with Fuchs at the Cons. of the Gesellschaft der Musikfreunde in Vienna; also took composition lessons with Zemlinsky; attended courses in musicology at the Univ. of Vienna (Ph.D. 1903); subsequently was an opera coach under Mahler. In 1918 he was appointed to the faculty of the New Vienna Cons.; from 1930 to 1938 taught music theory at the Univ. of Vienna. After the *Anschluss* in 1938, he emigrated to New York. He was respected both in Austria and in America as a composer, and a concerted effort was made to promote his music, but with little success. His 5th Symphony, subtitled *Apocalyptic*, was performed posthumously by Leopold Stokowski with the American Symphony Orch. (N.Y., Oct. 27, 1968). He wrote 6 symphonies: No. 1 (1908); No. 2 (1912); No. 3 (1931); No. 4 (1936); No. 5 (1945); No. 6 (1947); several overtures; Violin Concerto (1928); 8 string quartets; String Sextet; 2 violin sonatas; numerous choruses; piano pieces; songs.

Weigl, Thaddäus, Austrian composer and publisher; brother of **Joseph Weigl;** b. Vienna, April 8, 1776; d. there Feb. 29, 1844. He wrote the Singspiele *Die Marionettenbude* (Vienna, March 17, 1795) and *Idoli* (Vienna, March 12, 1796); also 13 ballets. In 1801 he established in Vienna a publishing firm, which issued several works by Schubert.

Weil, Hermann, German baritone; b. Karlsruhe, May 29, 1877; d. (of a heart attack, while fishing in Blue Mountain Lake, N.Y.), July 6, 1949. He studied voice with Adolf Dippel in Frankfurt; made his debut as Wolfram in *Tannhäuser* at Freiburg, Baden, on Sept. 6, 1901; then sang in Vienna, Brussels, Amsterdam, Milan, and London; participated in the Bayreuth festivals during the summers of 1909–12. On Nov. 17, 1911 he made a successful American debut as Kurvenal in *Tristan und Isolde*, at the Metropolitan Opera, N.Y., under Toscanini. In 1917 he returned to Germany. The extensive range of his voice, spanning 3 full octaves, enabled him to undertake bass parts as well as those in the baritone compass. He had about 100 roles in his repertory, excelling in Wagnerian operas.

Weill, Kurt, remarkable German composer of modern operas; b. Dessau, March 2, 1900; d. New York, April 3, 1950. He was a pupil of Albert Bing in Dessau; in 1918 studied for one semester at the Berlin Hochschule für Musik under Humperdinck and Krasselt. He was then engaged as opera coach in Dessau, and was also theater conductor at Lüdenscheid. In 1921 he moved to Berlin, and became a student of Busoni. Under the impact of new ideas in the theater, calling for bold portrayal of contemporary themes, and cultivating social satire, he began writing short operas in a modernistic manner: *Der Protagonist* (Dresden, March 27, 1926) and *Royal Palace* (Berlin, March 2, 1927). His next work was a "Songspiel," *Aufstieg und Fall der Stadt Mahagonny*, a satire on life in America, to a libretto by Bert Brecht. Its première was given at the Baden-Baden Festival on July 17, 1927; Weill subsequently remodeled the play, and it was presented in an extended version at Leipzig (March 9, 1930). He then wrote an opera buffa *Der Zar lässt sich photographieren* (Leipzig, Feb. 18, 1928). His first striking success came with a modernistic version of *The Beggar's Opera*, to a pungent libretto by Bert Brecht; it was staged under the title *Die Dreigroschenoper* in Berlin, on Aug. 31, 1928, and soon became the rage all over Germany; also produced in translations in Poland, Holland, Denmark, Hungary, Russia, France, and England; given in N.Y. on April 13, 1933, as *The Threepenny Opera;* Marc Blizstein made a new libretto, versified in a modern American style, and in this form the work was presented for the first time at the Brandeis Univ. Festival, Waltham, Mass., on June 14, 1952. Other stage works by Weill produced in Germany were a school opera *Der Jasager* (1930), *Die Bürgschaft* (Berlin, March 10, 1932), and *Der Silbersee* (1933). After the establishment of the Nazi government, Weill and his wife, the actress and singer **Lotte Lenya,** who appeared in many of his musical plays, were driven out of Germany; he went to Paris, where he wrote an opera, *Marie galante* (1933), and to London, where he produced a satirical musical play, *A Kingdom for a Cow* (1935). In 1935 he settled in America, remaining there until his death. Quickly absorbing the modes and fashions of American popular music, he succeeded, with amazing fidelity, in creating American-flavored musical plays; this stylistic transition was facilitated by the fact that in his European productions he had already injected elements of American popular songs and jazz rhythms. His highly developed assimilative faculty enabled him to combine this Americanized idiom with the advanced techniques of modern music (atonality, polytonality, polyrhythms), and present the product in a pleasing and yet sophisticated and challenging manner. For the American theater he wrote the scores for the operas *Street Scene* (by Elmer Rice; N.Y., Jan. 9, 1947) and *Lost in the Stars* (by Maxwell Anderson; N.Y., Oct. 30, 1949); the musical comedies *Knickerbocker Holiday* (book and lyrics by Maxwell Anderson; Hartford, Conn., Sept. 26, 1938; contains the popular *September Song*); *Lady in the Dark* (by Moss Hart), and *One Touch of Venus* (by S. J. Perelman and Ogden Nash); music for *The Firebrand of Florence* (by E. J. Mayer and Ira Gershwin) and *A Flag Is Born* (by Ben Hecht); also for several films. He achieved a signal success with the production of his "folk opera" *Down in the Valley* (Indiana Univ., Bloomington, July 15, 1948), based on Kentucky mountain songs; many performances were given all over the U.S. Other works include the ballet *Die sieben Todsünden* (1933); the radio cantata *Lindberghflug* (in collaboration with Bert Brecht; commemorating Lindbergh's transatlantic flight, 1927; Berlin, Dec. 5, 1929); *The Ballad of Magna Carta*, modern historical drama with text by Maxwell Anderson (Columbia network broacast, Feb. 4, 1940); *Der neue Orpheus*, cantata; *Vom Tod im Walde*, ballade for bass voice and 10 wind instruments; *Recordare* for chorus a cappella; *Rilke-Lieder*, for voice with orch. For orch.: *Fantasie, Passacaglia und Hymnus* (1923) and *Quodlibet* (1924); *Frauentanz* for soprano, viola, flute, clarient, horn, and bassoon (Salzburg Festival of the International Society for Contemporary Music, Aug. 6, 1924); Concerto for violin and woodwind instruments (Zürich Festival, June 23, 1926); String Quartet, and other chamber music; piano pieces; songs. A *Berliner Symphonie*, written in 1921 and regarded as lost, was rediscovered in 1958.

BIBLIOGRAPHY: Paul Bekker, *Briefe an zeitgenössische Musiker* (1932); V. Thomson, "Most Melodious Tears," *Modern Music* (Nov.-Dec. 1933); H. W. Heinsheimer, "Kurt Weil," *Tomorrow* (March 1948); H. Strobel, "Erinnerung an Kurt Weill," *Melos* (May 1950); D. Drew, "Topicality and the Universal: The Strange Case of Weill's *Die Bürgschaft*," *Music & Letters* (July 1958). For details on performances of Weill's operas see A. Loewenberg, *Annals of Opera* (Cambridge, 1943; 2nd ed., Geneva, 1955).

Weinberg, Jacob, pianist and composer; b. Odessa, July 5, 1879; d. New York, Nov. 2, 1956. He studied at the Moscow Cons. with Igumnov (piano), Taneyev and Ippolitov-Ivanov (composition); was a private pupil of Leschetizky in Vienna (1910–11); taught piano at the Odessa Cons. (1915–21) ; then went to Palestine, where he stayed for 5 years (1921–26). In 1926 he came to the U.S.; taught piano at Hunter College and the N.Y. College of Music. He composed an opera on a modern Hebrew subject, *Hechalutz (The Pioneers);* fragments were performed in Jerusalem, in Hebrew on April 4, 1925; the complete opera was performed in N.Y. on Nov. 25, 1934, under the title *The Pioneers of Israel*, in English; he also wrote the oratorios *Isaiah* (1948) and *The Life of Moses* (1952); *The Gettysburg Address*, ode for chorus and orch. (N.Y., 1936); *Sabbath Liturgy* for baritone, chorus, and organ; Piano Concerto; Piano Trio; String Quartet; Violin Sonata; contributed essays on Russian music to the *Musical Quarterly* and other periodicals.

Weinberger, Jaromir, notable Czech composer; b. Prague, Jan. 8, 1896; d. St. Petersburg, Florida, Aug. 8, 1967 (suicide by overdose of sedative drugs). He studied with Křička and Hofmeister at the Prague Cons., then briefly with Max Reger in Leipzig. In 1922 he visited the U.S., and taught for a semester at the Cons. of Ithaca, N.Y. Returning to Europe, he was active as teacher in Bratislava, Prague, and Vienna; lived mostly in Prague until 1937; in 1939 he settled permanently in the U.S., living in St. Petersburg, Florida. He achieved sudden fame with the production of

his opera in a popular Bohemian style, *Švanda dudák (Schwanda, the Bagpiper)*, at the Czech Opera in Prague, on April 27, 1927. Its success was immediate, and performances followed all over Europe in several languages; it was produced in German (as *Schwanda der Dudelsackpfeifer*) at the Metropolitan Opera, N.Y., on Nov. 7, 1931; the *Polka and Fugue* from this opera has become a popular number in the orchestral repertory. His other operas include *Die geliebte Stimme* (Munich, Feb. 28, 1931); *Lidé z Pokerflatu (The Outcasts of Poker Flat*, after Bret Harte; Brno, Nov. 19, 1932); *A Bed of Roses*, light opera (Prague, 1934); and *Wallenstein*, lyric tragedy after Schiller (Vienna, Nov. 18, 1937); for orch.: *Marionette Overture* (1913); 6 Bohemian songs and dances (1929); *Under the Spreading Chestnut Tree*, variations and fugue (N.Y., Oct. 12, 1939); *Song of the High Seas* (N.Y., Nov. 9, 1940); *Lincoln Symphony* (Cincinnati, Oct. 17, 1941); *Czech Rhapsody* (Washington, D.C., Nov. 5, 1941); *A Bird's Opera* (Detroit, Nov. 13, 1941); *Préludes religieuses et profanes* (1953); *Ecclesiastes*, for soprano, baritone, mixed chorus, and organ (1945); other choral works; violin pieces; piano pieces; etc.

Weiner, Lazar, Russian-American composer and choral conductor; b. Cherkassy, near Kiev, Oct. 27, 1897. He emigrated to the U.S. in 1914, and studied composition with Robert Russell Bennett, Frederick Jacobi, and Joseph Schillinger; became active mainly as a choral conductor; from 1929 to 1964 was in charge of the Choir of Central Synagogue, N.Y.; was also on the faculty of the Hebrew Union College School of Scared Music. His works include the cantatas *Legend of Toil* (1933), *Man in the World* (1939), *Fight for Freedom* (1943), *To Thee, America* (1944), and *The Last Judgment* (1966); also an opera *The Golem* (1958); several sabbath services, and a number of song cycles to Yiddish words. His son, **Yehudi Weiner**, a talented composer, changed his name to **Wyner**, to approximate phonetically the correct pronunciation.

Weiner, Léo, outstanding Hungarian composer; b. Budapest, April 16, 1885; d. there, Sept. 13, 1960. He was a pupil of Hans Koessler at the Budapest Academy of Music (1901–06), winning several prizes for excellence; in 1906 he won the "Franz-Josef-Jubiläumspreis," which enabled him to study further in Austria, Germany, and France. Returning to Budapest, he became a prof. at the Academy (1908); was pensioned in 1949. He won the Coolidge Prize in 1922 for his Second String Quartet, the Kossuth Prize in 1950, and became "Eminent Artist of the Hugarian People's Republic" in 1953. In his works he adopted a characteristic Hungarian style, within the framework of Romantic forms.

WORKS: *Scherzo* for orch. (1905); *Serenade* for orch. (1906; Budapest, Oct. 22, 1906; his most successful work); *Farsang (Carnival-Time)*, humoresque for small orch. (1907); incidental music for Vörösmarty's play *Csongor and Tünde* (1913; also an orch. suite); Piano Concertino (1923); 5 divertimenti: Nos. 1 and 2, on old Hungarian tunes, for strings (1923, 1938) and Nos. 3–5 for orch. (1948, 1951, 1951); *Katonásdi (Playing at Soldiers)* for orch. (1924); *Suite (Hungarian*

Folk Dances) for orch. (1931); *Pastorale, Fantasy and Fugue* for string orch. (1938); *Ballad* for clarinet and orch. (1949); *Romance* for cello, harp, and orch. (1949); *Variations on a Hungarian Folk Song* for orch. (1950); 2 violin concertos (1950, 1957; being transcriptions of violin sonatas of 1911 and 1918); *Prelude, Nocturne et Scherzo Diabolico* for orch. (1950); *Festive Music,* overture (1951); *Toldi,* symph. poem (1952; 2 suites, 1954–55); *Passacaglia* for orch. (1955); 3 string quartets (1906; 1921; *Pastorale, Fantasy and Fugue,* 1938); String Trio (1908); 2 violin sonatas (1911, 1918); *Ballad* for clarinet and piano (1911); *Romance* for cello and piano (1921); *Recruiting Dance from Pereg* for violin or viola or clarinet, and piano (1951); a number of piano pieces; cadenzas for Beethoven's piano concertos Nos. 1–4 (1949); orchestral transcriptions of works by Bach, Beethoven, Liszt, Schubert, and Bartók; didactic volumes on musical form (1911), on harmony (1911 and 1917), on analytical harmony (1943), and on forms of instrumental music (1954).

Weingartner, (Paul) Felix, Edler von Münzberg, illustrious German conductor; b. Zara, Dalmatia, June 2, 1863; d. Winterthur, Switzerland, May 7, 1942. After his father's death in 1867, his mother took him to Graz, where he studied music with W. A. Remy. He published some piano pieces when he was 16 years old; Brahms recommended him for a stipend which enabled him to go to take music courses with Reinecke, Jadassohn, and Paul at the Leipzig Con. (1881–83). He received the Mozart Prize at his graduation; he was introduced to Liszt, who recommended Weingartner's opera *Sakuntala* for production in Weimar (March 23, 1884), a signal honor for a young man not yet 21 years old. While progressing rapidly as a composer, Weingartner launched a brilliant career as conductor, which was to become his prime vocation. He conducted in Königsberg (1884), Danzig (1885–87), Hamburg (1887–89), and Mannheim (1889–91). In 1891 he was engaged as conductor at the Berlin Opera; from 1898 to 1903 he led the Kaim Orch. in Munich; simultaneously he was conductor of the symph. concerts of the Royal Orch. in Berlin. His reputation as a fine musician was enhanced by his appearances as an ensemble player in the Weingartner Trio, with himself as pianist, Rettich as violinist, and Warnke as cellist. In 1908 he succeeded Mahler as music director of the Vienna State Opera, and conducted there until 1910. From 1912 to 1914 he conducted the Municipal Opera in Hamburg; from 1914 to 1919 was in charge of the Darmstadt Orch. He was subsequently music director at the Vienna Volksoper (1919–24), and conducted the Vienna Philharmonic (until 1927), when he was appointed director of the Basel, Switzerland, Cons.; was conductor at the Vienna State Opera during the season 1935–36. In the interim he had great engagements with major European orchestras; made his American debut with the N.Y. Philharmonic on Feb. 10, 1905, and later conducted the N.Y. Symph. Society (Jan.-March, 1906). He appeared as opera conductor with the Boston Opera Co. on Feb. 12, 1912, conducting *Tristan und Isolde;* he and his 3rd wife, the mezzo-soprano **Lucille Marcel,** were engaged for a season with the Boston

Opera Co. in 1913. (His first wife was Marie Juillerat, whom he married in 1891; his second wife was the Baroness Feodora von Dreifus, whom he married in 1903). He eventually settled in Interlaken, Switzerland, where he established a summer conducting school. Weingartner was a competent music editor; he was on the editorial board for the complete works of Berlioz (1899) and of Haydn (1907). Despite the pressure of his activities as a conductor, he found time for composition. After his early opera *Sakuntala,* he produced several others: *Genesius* (Berlin, Nov. 15, 1892); *Orestes,* a trilogy (Leipzig, Feb. 15, 1902); *Kain und Abel* (Darmstadt, May 17, 1914); *Dame Kobold* (Darmstadt, Feb. 23, 1916); *Die Dorfschule* (Vienna, May 13, 1920); *Meister Andrea* (Vienna, May 13, 1920); wrote his own librettos, and conducted the first performances. He also composed 6 symphonies and a great deal of chamber music; made arrangements of Beethoven's "Hammerklavier" Sonata, op. 106, and of Weber's *Aufforderung zum Tanz.* He was an excellent writer on musical subjects. Among his publications are: *Die Lehre von der Wiedergeburt und das musikalische Drama* (1895); *Über das Dirigieren* (1896; 5th ed., 1913; a fundamental essay on conducting); *Bayreuth 1876–1896* (1897; 2nd ed., 1904); *Die Symphonie nach Beethoven* (1897; 4th ed., 1901; in English, 1904; new translation as *The Symphony since Beethoven,* 1926); *Ratschläge für Aufführung der Sinfonien Beethoven* (1906; 3rd ed., 1928; in English, London, 1907); a polemical pamphlet, *Erlebnisse eines kgl. Kapellmeisters in Berlin* (1912; an attack upon the Berlin intendancy; a rebuttal was publ. by A. Wolff, in *Der Fall Weingartner,* 1912); *Ratschläge für Aufführung der Sinfonien Schuberts und Schumanns* (1918); *Ratschläge für Aufführung der Sinfonien Mozarts* (1923); *Musikalische Walpurgisnacht* (1907, a satirical comedy); *Akkorde* (1912; collected essays); *Bo Yin Ra* (1927); *Lebenserinnerungen* (vol. I, 1923; vol. II, 1929; English version as *Buffets and Rewards: A Musician's Reminiscences,* London, 1937); *Unwirkliches und Wirkliches* (1936).

BIBLIOGRAPHY: E. Krause, *Felix Weingartner als schaffender Künstler* (Berlin, 1904); P. Riesenfeld, *Felix Weingartner. Ein kritischer Versuch* (Breslau, 1906); W. Hutschenruyter, *Levensschets en portret van Felix Weingartner* (Haarlem, 1906); Paul Stefan, *Gustav Mahlers Erbe* (Munich, 1908); J. C. Lustig, *Felix Weingartner. Persönlichkeiten* (Berlin, 1908); P. Raabe, "Felix Weingartner," *Die Musik* (Jan. 1908); F. Günther, *Felix Weingartner* (1917); W. Jacob, *Felix Weingartner* (Wiesbaden, 1933); *Festschrift für Dr. Felix Weingartner* (for his 70th birthday; Basel, 1933).

Weinlig, Christian Ehregott, German organist and composer, b. Dresden, Sept. 30, 1743; d. there, March 14, 1813. He studied with Homilius, at the Kreuzschule; in 1767 he was organist at the Evangelical Church, Leipzig; in 1773, at Thorn; in 1780, accompanist at the Italian Opera, Dresden, and organist at the Frauenkirche; in 1785, succeeded his teacher Homilius as cantor of the Kreuzschule. He publ. sonatas for piano with flute and cello; brought out several oratorios; also light theater pieces.

Weinlig, (Christian) Theodor, noted German music theorist and teacher; nephew and pupil of **Christian Ehregott Weinlig;** b. Dresden, July 25, 1780; d. Leipzig, March 7, 1842. After a period of study under his uncle, he became a pupil of Stanislao Mattei in Bologna; returning to Dresden, he was cantor at the Kreuzschule (1814–17); in 1823 he succeeded Schicht as cantor of the Thomasschule, Leipzig. He enjoyed high repute as a teacher of theory and composition; Richard Wagner was his pupil. His own works include a *Deutsches Magnificat* for soli, chorus, and orch.; vocalises; publ. a practical manual, *Theoretisch-praktische Anleitung zur Fuge, für den Selbstunterricht* (1845; 2d ed., 1852).

BIBLIOGRAPHY: A. Kurz, *Geschichte der Familie Weinlig von 1580-1850* (Bonn, 1912); R. Roch, *Theodor Weinlig* (Leipzig, 1917).

Weinmann, Karl, German musicologist, authority on church music; b. Vohenstrauss, Upper Palatinate, Dec. 22, 1873; d. Pielenhofen, near Regensburg, Sept. 26, 1929. He was a pupil of Haberl and Haller at the Kirchenmusikschule in Regensburg; after further study under Peter Wagner in Freiburg, Switzerland, he obtained the degree of Dr. phil. with the dissertation *Das Hymnarium Parisiense* (1905). After his ordination to the priesthood, he became prof. at the Kirchenmusikschule in Regensburg; in 1910 succeeded Haberl as its director; in 1917 he was made Dr. theol. He was editor of the *Kirchenmusikalisches Jahrbuch* (from 1908) of *Musica Sacra* (from 1911), and of the *Cäcilienvereinsorgan* (From 1926). He ed. for Pustet (after the *Editio vaticana*) *Römisches Gradualbuch* (1909; 4th ed., 1928); *Graduale* (1910); *Kyriale* (1911); *Totenoffizium* (1912; 2nd ed., 1928); *Graduale parvum* (1913); *Römisches Vesperbuch mit Psalmenbuch* (1915); *Karwochenbuch* (1924); *Feier der heiligen Karwoche* (1925); *Sonntagsvesper und Komplet* (2nd ed., 1928). Was also ed. of the collection *Kirchenmusik,* for which he wrote *Geschichte der Kirchenmusik* (1906; 4th ed., 1925; English transl., 1910; also transl. into French, Italian, Polish, and Hungarian), and monographs on Leonhard Paminger (1907 and Carl Proske (1909). Other writings include *Palestrinas Geburtsjahr* (Regensburg, 1915); *Stille Nacht, heilige Nacht: die Geschichte des Liedes zu seinem 100. Geburtstag* (1918; 2nd ed., 1920); *Das Konzil von Trient und die Kirchenmusik* (1919).

Weinrich, Carl, eminent American organist; b. Paterson, N.J., July 2, 1904. After graduation from N.Y. Univ. (B.A., 1927), he studied at the Curtis Institute of Music in Philadelphia (1927–30); also studied organ privately with Lynnwood Farnam and Marcel Dupré, and piano with Abram Chasins. In 1930 he became successor of Lynnwood Farnam as organist at the Holy Communion Church, N.Y.; taught organ at the Westminster Choir School, Princeton, N.J. (1934–40) and at Columbia Univ. (1942–52); in 1943, appointed director of music at the Princeton Univ. Chapel.

Weinstock, Herbert, American writer on music; b. Milwaukee, Wis., Nov. 16, 1905; d. New York, Oct. 21, 1971. Educated in his native town; later took courses at the Univ. of Chicago. He publ. the following books: *Tchaikovsky* (1943; also publ. in French, Portuguese, Spanish, and German); *Handel* (1946; also in German); *Chopin: The Man and His Music* (1949; 2nd ed., 1959); *Music as an Art* (1953); co-author, with Wallace Brockway, of *Men of Music* (1939; revised and enlarged, 1950) and *The Opera: A History of Its Creation and Performance* (1941); *Donizetti and the World of Opera in Italy, Paris and Vienna in the First Half of the 19th Century* (N.Y., 1963); *Rossini* (N.Y., 1968); *Vincenzo Bellini: His Life and Operas* (N.Y., 1971). For some years before his death he was music editor for the book publishing firm of Alfred A. Knopf, N.Y.

Weinwurm, Rudolf, Austrian choral conductor; b. Schaidldorf-on-the-Thaja, April 3, 1835; d. Vienna, May 26, 1911. He was trained musically as a chorister in the Imperial Chapel, Vienna; conducted the Vienna Singakademie (from 1864) and the Männergesangverein (from 1866); in 1880 he became musical director of Vienna Univ. He publ. the manuals *Allgemeine Musiklehre* (1870); *Musikalische Lehrmittel* (1873); *Methodik des Gesangunterrichts* (1876); composed a *Deutsches Requiem* for male chorus a cappella, and one for female chorus with organ; also other church music.

Weinzierl, Max, Ritter von, Austrian conductor and composer, b. Bergstadtl, Bohemia, Sept. 16, 1841; d. Mödling, near Vienna, July 10, 1898. He served as conductor at various theaters in Vienna; from 1882 he was chorusmaster of the Männergesangverein. He wrote the operas *Don Quixote* (Vienna, Feb. 15, 1879; with L. Roth), *Die weiblichen Jäger* (Vienna, May 5, 1880), *Moclemos* (Vienna, June 5, 1880), *Fioretta* (Prague, 1886), *Page Fritz* (Prague, 1889), *Der Schwiegerpapa* (Berlin, 1893); the oratorio *Hiob* (Vienna, 1870); the choral works with orch.: *Nachtgruss, Liedesweihe, Gesang der Nixen, Die Sphinx, Der Zigeuner, Donausage, Hubertus,* etc.; many male choruses a cappella.

Weinzweig, John, prominent Canadian composer; b. Toronto, March 11, 1913. He learned to play piano, tuba, and saxophone; then took lessons in orchestration with MacMillan, in counterpoint with Willan, and in harmony with Leo Smith at the Univ. of Toronto (1934–37); continued his study in composition with Bernard Rogers at the Eastman School of Music, Rochester, N.Y. (1937–38). In 1939 he was appointed to the Faculty of the Toronto Cons.; in 1952 joined the music staff at the Univ. of Toronto. On Feb. 3, 1951, he organized the Canadian League of Composers and was its first president.

WORKS: ballet, *Red Ear of Corn* (Toronto, March 2, 1949); *Legend* for orch. (1937); *The Enchanted Hill* for orch. (1938); *Suite* for orch. (1938); *Spectre* for string orch. and timpani (1938); *A Tale of Tamotu* for bassoon and orch. (1939); *Symph.* (1940); *Rhapsody* for orch. (1941); *Interlude in an Artist's Life* for string orch. (1943); *Our Canada* for orch. (1943); *Divertimento No. 1* for flute and string orch. (Vancouver, Dec. 29, 1946); *Divertimento No. 2* for oboe and string orch. (Toronto, April 30, 1948); *Divertimento No. 3* for bassoon and string orch. (Toronto, May 5, 1961); *Di-*

vertimento No. 5 for solo trumpet, trombone, and wind ensemble (Pittsburgh, June 9, 1961; numbered out of chronological order); *Divertimento No. 4* for clarinet, and string orch. or string quintet (Vancouver, Sept. 19, 1968); *Divertimento No. 6* for saxophone and string orch. (Toronto, Aug. 21, 1972); *Edge of the World,* symph. poem (1946); *Round Dance* for small orch. (1950; version for full orch., 1977); Violin Concerto (Toronto, May 30, 1955); *Wine of Peace,* 3 songs for soprano and orch. (1957); *Symphonic Ode* (1958); Piano Concerto (Toronto, Dec. 15, 1966); Concerto for harp and chamber orch. (Toronto, April 30, 1967); *Dummiyah (Silence)* for orch. (Toronto, July 4, 1969); 3 string quartets (1937, 1946, 1962); Violin Sonata (1941); cello sonata, *Israel* (1949); Wind Quintet (1964); Clarinet Quartet (1965); *Around the Stage in Twenty-five Minutes during which a Variety of Instruments Are Struck* for solo percussionist (1970); *Trialogue* for soprano, flute, and piano (1971); *Riffs* for solo flute (1974); *Pieces of Five,* brass quintet (1976); *Contrast* for solo guitar (1976); *Refrains* for double bass and piano (1977); 2 suites for piano (1939, 1950); Piano Sonata (1950); *Impromptus* for piano (1973); *Improvisation on an Indian Tune* for organ (1942); choruses; *Private Collection,* 8 songs for soprano and piano (1975).

Weis, (Carl) Flemming, Danish composer and organist; b. Copenhagen, April 15, 1898. He studied composition with Carl Nielsen and Gustav Helsted at the Royal Danish Cons. in Copenhagen (1917-20); then took lessons in composition with Paul Graener and organ with Karl Straube at the Hochschule für Musik in Leipzig (1921-23). He served as organist of the St. Anna Church in Copenhagen (1929-68); was a member of the board of the Society for Contemporary Music (1926-56; president, 1942-56) and a member of the board of the Danish Society of Composers (president, 1963-75). His music follows the traditions of the Danish School; under the influence of his teacher Carl Nielsen he wrote a number of symphonic pieces imbued with Romantic fervor and gentle humor.
WORKS: *Praeludium og intermezzo* for oboe and strings (1933); Concertino for clarinet and strings (1935); *Symphonic Overture* (1938); *In temporis vernalis* for orch. (1945; Copenhagen Jan. 14, 1948); *Introduction Grave* for piano and orch. (1941); 2 symphonies (1942, 1948); *Det forjoettede Land (The Promised Land)* for chorus and orch. (Copenhagen, Nov. 8, 1949); *Musikantiski Ouverture* (1949); *Sinfonia proverbiorum* for chorus and orch. (Copenhagen, June 21, 1959); Concertino for strings (1960); *Femdelt Form III (Quintuple Form)* for orch. (Randers, Feb. 5, 1963); *Sine nomine* for orch. (Copenhagen, March 18, 1973); *Chaconne* for orch. (1974); 4 string quartets (1922, 1925, 1937, 1977); *Music* for 3 woodwinds (1928); Clarinet Sonata (1931); Violin Sonata (1932-41); *Serenade uden reelle Hensigter (Serenade without Serious Intentions)* for wind quintet (1938); Sonatina for flute, violin, and cello (1942); *Diverterende Musik (Diverting Music)* for flute, violin, viola, and cello (1943); Oboe Sonata (1946); Variations for wind quintet (1946); Flute Sonata (1956); *Fantasia Seria* for string quartet (1956); *5 Epigrams* for string quartet (1960); *Femdelt Form II* for string quintet

(1962); *Rhapsodic Suite* for solo violin (1966); *Static Situations* for string quartet (1970); *Tre søstre (3 Sisters)* for solo cello (1973); *3 Mobiles* for flute, violin, viola, and cello (1974); *3 Aspects* for guitar (1975); *3 Japanese Bird Cries* for soprano, viola, and guitar (1976); *Dialogues* for flute and guitar (1977). For piano: *Suite* in B (1945-46), Sonatina (1949), *12 Monologues* (1958), *Femdelt Form I* (1961), *Limitations I* (1965); *Limitations II* (1968). For organ: Concertino (1957); *Coeli enarrant* for soprano and organ (1955-56); choruses; songs; anthems.

Weis, Karel, Czech conductor and composer; b. Prague, Feb. 13, 1862; d. there, April 4, 1944. He studied violin at the Prague Cons.; also organ with Skuhersky and composition with Fibich at the Organ School in Prague; subsequently filled various posts as organist and conductor in Prague and other towns in Bohemia. He devoted much of his time to collecting Bohemian folksongs, and publ. them in 15 vols. (1928-41).
WORKS: the operas *Viola,* after Shakespeare's *Twelfth Night* (Prague, Jan. 17, 1892), *Der polnische Jude* (Prague, March 3, 1901; very successful; produced in English at the Metropolitan Opera House, March 9, 1921), *Die Dorfmusikanten* (Prague, Jan. 1, 1905), *Der Revisor* (after Gogol; 1907), *Utok na mlýn* (after Zola's *L'Attaque su Moulin;* Prague, March 29, 1912), *Lešetínský kovář (The Blacksmith of Lešetín;* Prague, June 6, 1920); Symph.; String Quartet; piano pieces; songs.
BIBLIOGRAPHY: L. Firkušný, *Karel Weis* (Prague, 1949).

Weisbach, Hans, German conductor; b. Glogau, July 19, 1885; d. Wuppertal, April 23, 1961. He studied at the Hochschule für Musik in Berlin; then became an opera coach in Munich; subsequently conducted in various provincial towns in Germany; held the post of music director and conductor at Düsseldorf (1926-33); then conducted the Leipzig Radio Orch. (1933-39) and the Municipal Orch. of Vienna (1938-45); in 1947 he was appointed music director at Wuppertal. He made several appearances in London; also conducted in Russia.
BIBLIOGRAPHY: C. Heinzen, "Hans Weisbach," *Die Musik* (Feb. 1931).

Weisberg, Arthur, American bassoonist and conductor; b. New York, April 4, 1931. He attended the Juilliard School of Music, N.Y., where he studied bassoon with Simon Kovar and conducting with Jean Morel. He played bassoon with the Houston, Baltimore, and Cleveland orchestras; from 1956 to 1972 was bassoonist with the N.Y. Woodwind Quintet. In 1960 he formed the Contemporary Chamber Ensemble, with which he travels widely in Europe and America. He held teaching posts at the Juilliard School of Music (1962-69), at the State Univ. of N.Y. (from 1965) and at Yale Univ. (from 1974).

Weisgall, Hugo, American composer; b. Ivančice, Moravia, Oct. 13, 1912. His family emigrated to the U.S. in 1920, and settled in Baltimore; he studied music theory with Louis Cheslock at the Peabody Cons.

there; later had private sessions with Sessions in N.Y.; also took composition lessons with Rosario Scalero at the Curtis Institute in Philadelphia. In 1952 he was appointed chairman of the faculty at the Seminary College of Jewish Music in N.Y.; in 1957 joined the staff of the Juilliard School of Music; also taught at Queens College. His music constitutes the paragon of enlighted but inoffensive modernism; he is a master of all musical idioms, and a bungler of none. His intentions in each of his works never fail in the execution; for this reason his music enjoys numerous performances, which are usually accepted with pleasure by the audiences, if not by the majority of important music critics.

WORKS: the operas: *Night* (1932); *Lillith* (1934); *The Tenor* (Baltimore Feb. 11, 1952); *The Stronger*, after Strindberg (Westport, Conn., Aug. 9, 1952); *6 Characters in Search of an Author* (N.Y., April 26, 1959); *Purgatory*, in one act to the text of W. B. Yeats (Library of Congress, Washington, Feb. 17, 1961); *Athaliah*, (N.Y., Feb. 17, 1964); *Nine Rivers from Jordan*, (N.Y., Oct. 9, 1968); *The Hundred Nights* (N.Y., April 22, 1976); the ballets: *Quest* (Baltimore, May 17, 1938); *One Thing Is Certain* (Baltimore, Feb. 25, 1939); *Overture in F* (London, July 29, 1943); *A Garden Eastward*, a cantata for high voice and orch. (Baltimore, Jan. 31, 1953); *Soldier Songs* for baritone and orch. (1946); 2 choral etudes (1937; 1953); a number of songs.

BIBLIOGRAPHY: G. Rochberg, "Hugo Weisgall," *Bulletin of American Composers Alliance* (1958); B. Saylor, "The Music of Hugo Weisgall," *Musical Quarterly* (1973).

Weisgarber, Elliot, American composer; b. Pittsfield, Mass., Dec. 5, 1919. He studied with Bernard Rogers and Howard Hanson at the Eastman School of Music in Rochester, N.Y. (1939–43); then had lessons with Nadia Boulanger in Paris (1952–53) and with Halsey Stevens in Los Angeles (1958–59). From 1966 to 1969 he was in Japan, where he studied koto and other indigenous instruments. Returning to America, he taught at the Women's College of the Univ. of North Carolina (1944–60); in 1960 was appointed instructor in composition and Asian music at the Univ. of British Columbia.

WORKS: Sonata for flute, clarinet, and piano (1953); *Divertimento* for string trio (1956); *Divertimento* for horn, viola, and piano (1959); *Sinfonia Pastorale* (1961); *Sinfonia concertante* for oboe, 2 horns, and string (1962); Flute Sonata (1963); *Suite* for viola and piano (1964); Sonata for solo cello (1965); *Kyōto Landscapes,* lyrical evocations for voice and orch. (1970); *Illahee Chanties* for chamber orch. (1971); Bassoon Sonata (1973); *Epigrams* for flute and piano (1973); *Night* for solo baritone, chorus, and string quartet (1973); *Autumnal Music* for English horn and string orch. (1973); *Musica Serena* for orch. (1974); *Netori: A Fantasia* for saxophone and orch. (1974); *A Pacific Trilogy* for orch. (1974); Violin Concerto (1974); String Quartet (1975); *Fantasia a tre* for horn, violin, and piano (1975); several works for Japanese instruments.

Weismann, Julius, German composer; b. Freiburg-im-Breisgau, Dec. 26, 1879; d. Singen (Bodensee), Dec. 22, 1950. He studied in Munich with Rheinberger and Thuille; devoted himself mainly to the composition of operas, the most important of which was *Leonce und Lena* (Freiburg-im-Breisgau, June 21, 1925). Other operas: *Schwanenweiss*, after Strindberg (Duisburg, Sept. 29, 1923); *Ein Traumspiel* (Duisburg, 1925); *Regina del Lago* (Karlsruhe, 1928); *Die Gespenstersonate*, after Strindberg (Munich, Dec. 19, 1930); *Landsknechte* (Essen, 1936); *Die pfiffige Magd*, after Holberg (Leipzig, Feb. 11, 1939); a symph., *Über einem Grabe*, for chorus and orch.; *Fingerhütchen*, fairy ballad for baritone solo, female chorus, and orch.; *Macht hoch die Tür*, cantata; *Tanzfantasie* for orch.; Piano Concerto; Violin Concerto; much chamber music, including 2 piano trios, 2 violin sonatas, etc.

BIBLIOGRAPHY: W. Thomas-San Galli, "Julius Weismann," in vol. 2 of *Monographien moderner Musiker* (Leipzig, 1907); F. Doldinger, "Julius Weismann," *Neue Musikzeitschrift* (Dec. 1947); H. J. Moser, "Julius Weismann," *Musica* (June 1955).

Weismann, Wilhelm, German composer; b. Alfdorf, Sept. 20, 1900. He studied at the Stuttgart Cons. with Karg-Elert, and in Leipzig with M. Ludwig. In 1948 he was appointed to the faculty of the Hochschule für Musik in Leipzig; severed as editor for the C. F. Peters Publishing firm in Leipzig (until 1965), while continuing his teaching at the Hochschule für Musik. He wrote a number of choral works, both secular and sacred; also composed several collections of madrigals, as well as solo cantatas. He supervised a complete edition of madrigals by Gesualdo.

Weiss, Adolph, American composer and bassoonist; b. Baltimore, Sept. 12, 1891 (of German parents); d. Van Nuys, Calif. Feb. 21, 1971. He studied the piano, violin, and the bassoon; at the age of 16, was engaged as 1st bassoonist of the Russian Symph. Orch. of N.Y.; then played in the N.Y. Philharmonic under Mahler; for many years was with the N.Y. Symph. under Walter Damrosch. In the meantime he studied composition with Cornelius Rybner at Columbia Univ. In 1916 he joined the Chicago Symph. Orch. as bassoonist; studied theory with Adolf Weidig and Theodore Ötterstrom there; then was bassoonist with the Rochester, N.Y., Orch. In 1925 he went to Europe to study with Arnold Schoenberg, whose influence was decisive in the formation of his musical style, which is in the 12-tone idiom. Returning to the U.S., he played in the San Francisco Symph. Orch.; then moved to Hollywood, where he settled.

WORKS: *Fantasie* for piano (1918); *I Segreti* for orch. (1922; Rochester, May 1, 1925); 3 string quartets (1925, 1926, 1932); Chamber Symph. for 10 instruments (1927); *12 Preludes* for piano (1927); *American Life,* "Scherzoso Jazzoso" for large orch. (N.Y., Feb. 21, 1930); *Sonata da Camera* for flute and viola (1929); *7 Songs* for soprano and string quartet (1928); *The Libation Bearers,* choreographic cantata, for soloists, chorus, and orch. (1930); Quintet for flute, oboe, clarinet, bassoon, and horn (1931); Piano Sonata (1932); *Theme and Variations* for large orch. (1933); *Suite* for orch. (1938); *Petite Suite* for flute, clarinet, and bassoon (1939); Violin Sonata (1941); *Passacaglia* for horn and viola (1942); *10 Pieces* for low instrument and orch. (1943); *Ode to the West Wind* for baritone, viola, and piano (1945); *Protest* for 2 pianos (1945); Sextet for flute, oboe, clarinet, bassoon, horn, and piano (1947); Trio for clarinet, viola, and cello (1948); Concerto for bassoon and string quartet (1949); *Pulse of the Sea*, an étude for piano (1950); Concerto for trumpet and orch. (1952); Trio for flute, violin, and piano (1955); *5 Fantasies* for violin and piano (1956); *Tone Poem* for brass and percussion (1957); *Rhapsody* for 4 French horns (1957); *Vade Mecum* for a group of wind instruments (1958).

BIBLIOGRAPHY: W. Riegger, "Adolph Weiss and Colin McPhee," in H. Cowell, ed., *American Composers on American Music* (Stanford Univ., 1933); *Bulletin of American Composers Alliance* (1958, No. 3).

Weiss, Amalie. See **Joachim, Amalie.**

Weiss, Franz, viola player; b. Silesia, Jan. 18, 1778; d. Vienna, Jan. 25, 1830. When Prince Razumovsky formed his string quartet in Vienna (1808), Franz Weiss was engaged as viola player, with Schuppanzigh as 1st violin, Prince Razumovsky as 2nd violin, and Linke as cellist. Weiss composed some chamber music; *Variations brillantes* for violin and orch.; several piano sonatas; a symph. for flute, bassoon, and trumpet; etc.

Weiss, Johann, Austrian hymnologist; b. St. Ruprecht-on-Raab, Styria, Nov. 20, 1850; d. there, Sept. 7, 1919. He studied theology; in 1881 appointed teacher of hymnology at the Graz Seminary; was organist at the Graz Cathedral (1884-91). He published *Die musikalischen Instrumente in den heiligen Schriften des Alten Testaments* (1895).

Weiss, Julius, German violinist; b. Berlin, July 19, 1814; d. there, June 30, 1898. He studied with Henning; wrote music criticism; publ. instructive works for violin; was also active in music publishing.

Weiss, Sylvius Leopold, German lute player and composer; b. Breslau, Oct. 12, 1686; d. Dresden, Oct. 16, 1750. He learned to play the lute from his father; served as lutenist at the court of Düsseldorf (1706); then with Alexander Sobieski, Prince of Poland, in Rome (1708-14); and at Hesse-Kassel (1715-16). In 1717 he went to Dresden, where he remained for the rest of his life, with the exception of a few months in Berlin (1728). He was regarded as one of the greatest lute players of his time; in 1728, publ. a treatise on the lute. 6 of his suites are reprinted in vol. 12 of the *Reichsdenkmale (Das Erbe deutscher Musik)*.

BIBLIOGRAPHY: H. Neemann, "Die Lautenhandschriften von S. L. Weiss in der Bibiliothek Dr. Werner Wolffheim, Berlin," *Zeitschrift für Musikwissenschaft* 10 (1928); H. Neemann, "Die Lautenistenfamilie Weiss," *Archiv für Musikforschung* 4 (1939).

Weissberg, Yulia, Russian composer; b. Orenburg, Dec. 25, 1878; d. Leningrad, March 1, 1942. She studied at the St. Peterburg Cons. with Rimsky-Korsakov, and married his son **Andrei;** in 1907 took a course with Max Reger in Germany; was a co-editor of the periodical *Muzykalny Sovremennik* (1915-17).

WORKS: operas: *Mermaid*, after Andersen (1923), *Gülnara* (1935), *The Dead Princess* (1937); 2 children's operas: *Little Rabbit's House* (1935) and *Geese and Swans* (1937); *The Twelve*, to the poem of Alexander Blok, for chorus and orch. (Leningrad, May 12, 1926); symph. poem, *In the Night* (1929); *Sailor's Dance*, for orch. (1936); several song cycles for voice with instruments; children's choruses; a number of solo songs; transcriptions of folksongs.

Weisse, Hans, Austrian music theorist and composer; b. Vienna, March 31, 1892; d. New York, Feb. 10, 1940. He studied with Schenker and became an exponent of his theory. In 1931 he came to the U.S. and gave courses in theory at the Mannes Music School, in N.Y. He wrote mostly chamber music: 3 string quartets (1920-36); String Sextet (1924); Quintet for clarinet and strings (1928); Octet for strings and winds (1929); Concerto for flute, oboe, and harpsichord (1937); *Choral Partita*, for string and winds (1938).

Weissenbäck, (Franz) Andreas, Austrian choral conductor and composer; b. St. Lorenzen, Styria, Nov. 26, 1880; d. Vienna, March 14, 1960. He studied in Graz; in 1899, entered the monastery at Klosterneuburg, near Vienna; became a Catholic priest in 1904; then took up musicology under Guido Adler at the Univ. of Vienna (Dr. phil., 1912); was for many years choirmaster at Klosterneuburg. He published *Sacra Musica*, a lexicon of Catholic church music (1937); contributed valuable papers to various publications, particulary on Gregorian Chant; also was an expert on church bells. He composed a German Mass for male chorus; publ. many sacred works; also a Mass for mixed chorus and 7 wind instruments, including 2 saxophones.

Weissheimer, Wendelin, conductor and composer; b. Osthofen, Alsace, Feb. 26, 1838; d. Nuremberg, June 16, 1910. He studied at the Leipzig Cons. and later took lessons in composition with Liszt at Weimar. He was opera conductor at Würzburg, at Mainz, and at Strasbourg; then lived in various towns on the Rhine and in Bavaria. As a composer, he followed the Wagnerian vogue; wrote 2 dramas, *Theodor Körner* (Munich, May 28, 1872) and *Meister Martin und seine Gesellen* (Karlsruhe, April 14, 1879); also 18 songs to words by Goethe; *5 Geistliche Sonette* for voice, flute, oboe, clarinet, and harmonium. His book of reminiscences, *Erlebnisse mit Richard Wagner, Franz Liszt und vielen anderen Zeitgenossen, nebst deren Briefen* (Stuttgart, 1898), quotes many letters from Wagner, with whom he maintained an intimate friendship.

Weissmann, Adolf, German writer on music; b. Rosenberg, Silesia, Aug. 15, 1873; d. Saïda, near Haifa, April 23, 1929. He studied in Berlin, Breslau, Florence, etc.; Dr. phil., 1914. He was critic for the *Berliner Tageblatt* (1900-15) and from 1916 for the *Berliner Zeitung am Mittag;* also wrote for German music magazines; went on a lecture tour in Palestine and died there.

WRITINGS: *Berlin als Musikstadt (1740–1911)* (1911); *G. Bizet* (1907; in the collection *Die Musik,* ed. by Richard Strauss); *Chopin* (1912; 3rd ed., 1919); *Der Virtuose* (1918); *Die Primadonna* (1920); *Der klingende Garten. Impressionen über das Erotische in der Musik* (1920); the 3 preceding titles together as *Die Musik der Sinne* (1925); *Giacomo Puccini* (1922); *Die Musik in der Weltkrise* (1922; English transl. as *The Problems of Modern Music,* London, 1925); *Verdi* (1922); *Der Dirigent in 20. Jahrhundert* (1925); *Die Entgötterung der Musik* (1928; English transl., as *Music Come to Earth,* London, 1930).

BIBLIOGRAPHY: E. Preussner, "Adolf Weissmann," *Die Musik* 21 (1929).

Weissmann, John, Hungarian musicologist; b. Budapest, July 10, 1910. He studied at the Budapest Cons.; was opera coach at the Municipal Theater (1932–34); then assistant conductor there (1935–37). In 1937 he settled in London, where he attended classes of conducting at the Royal Academy of Music. Subsequently he devoted his attention mainly to musicology; contributed numerous valuable essays to various periodicals.

Weitzmann, Carl Friedrich, noted German theorist and composer; b. Berlin, Aug. 10, 1808; d. there, Nov. 7, 1880. He studied violin with Henning and theory with Klein; later, at Kassel, was a pupil of Spohr and Hauptmann. He then held the post of concertmaster in Riga (1832–34), Reval (1834–36), and St. Petersburg (1836–46). After sojourns in Paris and London (1846–48), he settled in Berlin as a teacher of composition. He was an ardent disciple and friend of Wagner and Liszt; among his posthumous papers was found the original manuscript of a double fugue for piano by Wagner, with corrections in the handwriting of Weinlig (Wagner's teacher). The piece was publ. by E. Istel in *Die Musik* (July 1912). Weitzmann was an original thinker in his harmonic theories; made an investigation of the modulatory functions of the whole-tone scale, and interested Liszt in its use. He composed a 4th variation to Liszt's *Todtentanz.* A full exposition of his theories is found in a book by his American pupil, E. M. Bowman, *K. F. Weitzmann's Manual of Musical Theory* (N.Y., 1877). Weitzmann's theoretical works in German include *Der übermässige Dreiklang* (1853); *Der verminderte Septimenakkord* (1854); *Geschichte der Septimen-Akkordes* (1854); *Harmoniesystem* (1860); *Die neue Harmonielehre im Streit mit der alten* (1861); *Geschichte des Klavierspiels ind der Klavierlitteratur* (1863, as Part III of the Lebert-Stark piano method; 2nd ed., 1879, printed separately, with an added *Geschichte des Klaviers;* in English, N.Y., 1894, with a biographical sketch by Otto Lessmann; 3rd German ed., Leipzig, 1899, as *Geschichte der Klaviermusik,* edited by Max Seiffert, with a supplement, *Geschichte des Klaviers,* by Otto Fleischer); *Der letzte der Virtuosen* (on Tausig; 1868); many essays in various musical periodicals. As a composer, he followed the fashionable Romantic trends; wrote the operas *Räuberliebe* (1834), *Walpurgisnacht* (1835), and *Lorbeer und Bettelstab* (1836), which he brought out in Reval; 3 books of *Valses nobles* for piano; *Preludes and Modulations* for piano, 2 parts,

"Classic" and "Romantic"; also wrote 2 books of ingenious canonic *Rätsel* for piano 4 hands, and 2 books of *Kontrapunkt-Studien* for piano.

Welch, Roy Dickinson, American pianist and music educator; b. Dansville, N.Y., Jan. 19, 1885; d. Princeton, N.J., Jan. 8, 1951. He studied at the Univ. of Michigan (B.A., 1909); then went to Berlin, where he took piano lessons from Josef Lhévinne (1910–12). From 1914 to 1935 he was chairman of the music dept. of Smith College, Northampton, Mass.; went to Europe on a Guggenheim Fellowship (1930–32); in 1935 was appointed chairman of the music dept. of Princeton Univ. He publ. *The Study of Music in the American College* (Northampton, Mass., 1925) and *The Appreciation of Music* (N.Y., 1927; revised ed., 1945).

Weld, Arthur Cyril Gordon, American conductor; b. Boston, March 4, 1862; d. near West Point, N.Y., Oct. 11, 1914 (of apoplexy, while driving an automoblie). He studied in Dresden, in Berlin, and in Munich. Upon returning to America, he became general director of the H. W. Savage Opera Co., and conducted the first performance of the famous musical comedy *Floradora* (N.Y., 1900). Some of his songs were publ.

Weldon, George, English conductor; b. Chichester, June 5, 1906; d. Cape Town, South Africa, Aug. 17, 1963. He studied at the Royal College of Music with Malcolm Sargent; conducted various provincial orchestras; traveled as guest conductor in North Africa, Turkey, and Yugoslavia. He was conductor of the Birmingham City Orch. from 1943 to 1950.

BIBLIOGRAPHY: Donald Brook, *International Gallery of Conductors* (London, 1951; pp. 221–23).

Weldon, Georgina (*née* **Thomas**), English soprano; b. London, May 24, 1837; d. Brighton, Jan. 11, 1914. She took up singing after her marriage to Capt. Weldon in 1860, and did not appear in public until 1870. She organized an orphan asylum for the purpose of musical education, and also dabbled in music publishing. Special interest attaches to her because of her romantic friendship with Gounod, who during his London sojourn (1870–75) lived at her residence, and whom she assisted in training the "Gounod Choir." She translated his autobiography (which goes only as far as 1859) into English (1875). Their relationship deteriorated, leading to a legal entanglement in connection with her claims regarding the copyright of Gounod's choral works; she wrote acrimonious letters to the press, defending her stand. She also publ. some songs of her own (to French texts) and the didactic manuals *Hints for Pronunciation in Singing* (1872) and *Musical Reform* (1875).

Welin, Karl-Erik, Swedish organist, pianist and composer of the extreme avant-garde; b. Genarp, May 31, 1934. He studied organ with Alf Linden at the Royal College of Music in Stockholm (1956–61); took composition lessons with Gunnar Bucht (1958–60) and Lidholm (1960–64); then attended summer seminars in new music at Darmstadt (1960–62), working with the American pianist David Tudor on avant-garde techniques. In 1958 he joined the experimental group "Fylkingen" in Stockholm. As a composer, he followed in his youthful works the fashionable Impressionistic trends, mostly in miniature forms, in colorful and unusual instrumental groupings. He created a sensation at his piano recital at the Stockholm High School of Music on March 6, 1964, when he exploded a pyrotechnical device lodged in the frame of the piano and then proceeded to saw off the piano legs with an electrically powered handsaw, accidentally cutting himself so seriously that he had to undergo surgery.

WORKS: *4 Chinese Poems* for chorus (1956); *Sermo modulatus* for flute and clarinet (1959); *Renovations* for soprano, flute, violin, mandolin, celesta, and percussion (1960); *Cantata* for children's chorus, violin, flute, and harpsichord (1960); *Manzit* for clarinet, trombone, violin, piano, and percussion (1962); *Esservecchia* for electric guitar, horn, trombone, and piano (1963); *Warum nicht?* for flute, violin, cello, xylophone, vibraphone, and tam-tam (1964); *Pereo* for 36 strings (1964); *Kazimir* for 4 flutes (1965); *Visoka 12* for 2 flutes, 2 violins, and 2 cellos (1965); *Etwas für . . .* for wind quintet (1966); a children's television opera, *Dummerjöns (Tom Fool),* after H. C. Andersen (1966–67); *Eigentlich nicht,* 2nd string quartet (1967); *Copelius,* a ballet of concrete music (1968); *Ondine,* theater music (1968); *Vindarnas grotta (Cave of the Winds),* a television ballet (Stockholm Television, March 30, 1969); *Glazba* for 3 flutes, bassoon, and soprano (1968); *Ben fatto* for a solo instrument or an infinite number of instruments (1968); *Improvisiation* for organ (1969); *PC-132,* for string quartet (1970); *A New Map of Hell,* for chorus (1971); *Recidivans,* a 3rd string quartet (1972); *Aver la forza di . . .* for chorus and string orch. (1972); an opera, *Drottning Jag (Queen Ego,* 1972; Stockholm, Feb. 17, 1973); *Harmonies* for clarinet, trombone, cello, and piano (1972); *Pagabile* for chamber ensemble (1972); *Residuo,* 4th string quartet (1974).

Welitsch, Ljuba (real name **Velitchkova**), Bulgarian soprano; b. Borisovo, near Varna, July 10, 1913. She played the violin as a child; then entered high school; subsequently took courses in philosophy at the Univ. of Sofia; then went to Vienna, where she studied voice with Lierhammer. She made her operatic debut as Nedda in *Pagliacci* at the Graz Opera (1936); from 1941 to 1943 she sang in Hamburg and Berlin; in 1943–46, was in Munich. On June 11, 1944 she made her first appearance as Salome (later to become her most famous role) in Vienna, under the direction of Richard Strauss himself, on his 80th birthday. She made her debut in London with the Vienna State Opera as Donna Anna in *Don Giovanni* on Sept. 20, 1947. Her American debut, at the Metropolitan Opera House, N.Y., in *Salome* (Feb. 4, 1949) was greatly acclaimed. She remained a member of the Metropolitan Opera until 1952.

Welk, Lawrence, popular American conductor of entertainment music; b. Strasburg, North Dakota, March 11, 1903. He received his training in California; in 1955 he began a series of television concerts which became increasingly popular, thanks to his skillful selection of programs containing a varied mixture of semi-classical pieces, western American ballads, and Slavic folk-dance tunes. His use of an accordion section in his arrangements, steadfast rhythmic beat, and sentimentalized tempi impart to his renditions a rudimentary sound quality that makes him a favorite with undiscriminating audiences. He published (with some outside help) an autobiography, *Wunnerful, Wunnerful!* (N.Y., 1971), radiating euphoria, and a sequel: *Ahone, ah-two: Life with My Musical Family* (N.Y., 1974).

Wellek, Albert, Austrian musicologist; b. Vienna, Oct. 16, 1904; d. Mainz, Aug. 27, 1972. He studied philosophy at the universities of Prague, Vienna, and Leipzig; also took music courses at the Prague Cons. In 1929 he became especially interested in the problems of musical psychology; served as assistant to Felix Krueger in his dept. of psychology at the Univ. of Leipzig; in 1943 he was appointed prof. of psychology at Breslau, and subsequently taught at the Univ. of Mainz, where he remained until his death. He wrote *Das absolute Gehör und seine Typen* (Leipzig, 1938); *Typologie der Musikbegabung im deutschen Volke* (Munich, 1939); also numerous articles dealing with the development of new musical resources, including quarter-tones and dodecaphony.

Wellesz, Egon, eminent Austrian composer and musicologist; b. Vienna, Oct. 21, 1885; d. Oxford, Nov. 9, 1974. He studied harmony with Carl Frühling , musicology with Guido Adler, and counterpoint and composition with Schoenberg in Vienna (1904–06); obtained the degree of Dr. phil. in 1908 with a thesis on Giuseppe Bonno, publ. in the *Sammelbände der Internationalen Musik-Gesellschaft* 11 (1910). From 1911 to 1915 he taught music history at the Neues Conservatorium in Vienna; in 1913 he was engaged as lecturer on musicology at the Univ. of Vienna, and was prof. there from 1930 to 1938, when the annexation of Austria by Nazi Germany compelled him to leave. He went to England in 1939; joined the music depart. of Oxford Univ., which in 1932 had conferred upon him the degree of Mus. Doc. *(honoris causa).* In 1940 he became lecturer in the history of music at Oxford Univ.; in 1946 he was appointed to the editorial board of the *New Oxford History of Music,* to which he then contributed, and was Univ. Reader in Byzantine music at Oxford (1948–56); was president of the Oxford Univ. Byzantine Society (1955–66); was awarded the order of the Commander of the British Empire in 1957. In 1956–57 he gave lectures in the U.S. A scholar and a musician of extraordinary capacities, Wellesz distinguished himself as a composer of highly complex musical scores, and as an authority on Byzantine music.

WORKS: OPERAS: *Die Prinzessin Girnara* (1919–20; Hannover, May 15, 1921; revised version, Mannheim, Sept. 2, 1928), *Alkestis* (1922–23; Mannheim, March 20, 1924), *Opferung des Gefangenen* (1924–25; Cologne, April 10, 1926), *Scherz, List und Rache* (1926–27; Stuttgart, March 1, 1928), *Die Bakchantinnen* (1929–30; Vienna, June 20, 1931), and *Incognita* (1951; Oxford, Dec. 5, 1951). BALLETS: *Das Wunder der Diana* (1915; Mannheim, March 20, 1924), *Persisches Ballet* (1920; Donaueschingen,

1924), *Achilles auf Skyros* (1921; Stuttgart, March 4, 1927), and *Die Nächtlichen* (1923; Berlin, Nov. 20, 1924). FOR ORCH.: 9 symphonies: No. 1 in C (1945); No. 2 in E-flat (1948); No. 3 in A (1951), No. 4, *Symphonia Austriaca*, in G (1953), No. 5 (1956), No. 6 (1965; Nuremberg, June 1, 1966), No. 7 (1968), No. 8 (1971), and No. 9 (1971; Vienna, Nov. 22, 1972); *Vorfrühling*, symph. poem (1912); *Suite* for violin and chamber orch. (1924); Piano Concerto (1934); *Prosperos Beschwörungen* after Shakespeare's *The Tempest* (1936–38); Violin Concerto (1961; Vienna, Jan. 19, 1962); *Music* for string orch. (1964); *Divertimento* for chamber orch. (1969) and *Symphonischer Epilog* (1969). FOR VOICE: *Gebete der Mädchen zur Maria* for soprano, chorus, and orch. (1909); *Mitte des Lebens*, cantata (1932); *Amor timido*, cantata for soprano and orch. (1935); *5 Sonnets by Elizabeth Barrett Browning* for soprano and string quartet (1935); *Lied der Welt* for soprano and orch. (1937); *Leben, Traum und Tod* for cantralto and orch. (1937); *Short Mass* for chorus and small orch. (1937); *The Leaden Echo and the Golden Echo*, after Hopkins, for soprano, violin, clarinet, cello, and piano (1944); *4 Songs of Return* for soprano and small orch. (1961); *Duineser Elegie* for soprano, chorus, and chamber ensemble (1963); *Ode to Music* for baritone and chamber orch. (1964); *Vision* for soprano and orch. (1966); *Mirabile Mysterium*, Christmas cantata (1967); *Canticum Sapientiae* for baritone, chorus, and orch. (1968; Graz, Austria, Oct. 25, 1969). CHAMBER MUSIC: 9 string quartets (1912, 1917, 1918, 1920, 1944, 1947, 1948, 1957, 1966); *Geistiges Lied* for piano trio (1918); Sonata for solo cello (1921); *2 Pieces* for clarinet and piano (1922); Sonata for solo violin (1924); *Suite* for violin and piano (1937); *Little Suite* for solo flute (1937); Octet for clarinet, horn, bassoon, and string quintet (1948–49); *Suite* for wind quintet (1954); Clarinet Quintet (1959); 2 string trios (1962, 1969); *5 Miniatures* for violin and piano (1965); *Music* for string quartet (1968); String Quintet (1970). FOR PIANO: *3 Piano Pieces* (1912); *Epigramme* (1913), *5 Dance Pieces* (1927), *Triptych* (1966), and *Studies in Grey* (1969). *Partita* for organ (1966).

WRITINGS: *Arnold Schönberg* (Vienna, 1921; English translation, London, 1924); *Der Beginn des musikalischen Barock und Die Anfänge der Oper in Wien* (Vienna, 1922); *Byzantinische Kirchenmusik* (Breslau, 1927); *Eastern Elements in Western Chant* (Oxford, 1947); *A History of Byzantine Music and Hymnography* (Oxford, 1949); *Essays on Opera* (London, 1950); *The Origin of Schoenberg's Twelve-Tone System* (Washington, 1958); numerous essays on a variety of subjects in German and English periodicals. He edited Fux's *Costanza e Fortezza*, in the *Denkmäler der Tonkunst in Österreich* 34/35 (17); *Trésor de Musique Byzantine*, vol. I (Paris, 1934); *Die Hymnen des Sticherarium für September* (1936; vol. I of the *Monumenta Musicae Byzantinae, Transcripta*); vol. I of the *New Oxford History of Music*, "Ancient and Oriental Music" (1957); and *Die Hymnen der Ostkirche* (Kassel, 1962).

BIBLIOGRAPHY: O. F. Beer, "Egon Wellesz und die Oper," *Die Musik* (Sept. 1931); H. F. Redlich, "Egon Wellesz," *Musical Quarterly* (Jan. 1940); R. Reti, "Egon Wellesz, Musician and Scholar," *Musical Quarterly* (Jan. 1956); R. Schollum, *Egon Wellesz* (Vienna, 1964).

Wels, Charles, American pianist and composer; b. Prague, Aug. 24, 1825; d. New York, May 12, 1906. After studying in Prague, he went to America in 1849 and settled in N.Y.; filled various positions as church organist and teacher; retired in 1901. He composed about 170 op. numbers, including 5 Masses; a piano concerto; fantasias, other pieces, transcriptions, and arrangements for piano, 2 or 4 hands; several male quartets; songs.

Welsh, Thomas, English singer and composer; b. Wells, c.1780; d. Brighton, Jan. 24, 1848. He was a chorister at Wells Cathedral, and a pupil of J. B. Cramer and Baumgarten. He made his opera debut in London at the age of 12; after his voice changed he became a bass, and sang in oratorio. He was particularly distinguished as a vocal teacher; publ. *Vocal Instructor, or the Art of Singing Exemplified in 15 Lessons leading to 40 Progressive Exercises* (1825); piano sonatas; glees, duets, and part-songs; also wrote several musical pieces for the theater. His wife and pupil **Mary Anne,** *née* **Wilson** (1802–67), was a noted soprano who made her debut at Drury Lane, Jan. 18, 1821, in Arne's *Artaxerxes*.

Welte, Michael, German manufacturer of musical instruments; b. Unterkirnach, Black Forest, Sept. 29, 1807; d. Freiburg-im-Breisgau, Jan. 17, 1880. Having served an apprenticeship with Josef Blessing, a maker of musical clocks, he established himself at Voehrenbach (1832); exhibited his first "orchestrion" at Karlsruhe in 1849; later took his sons (**Emil, Berthold,** and **Michael, Jr.**) into partnership. His instruments obtained 1st prizes at London (1862), Paris (1867), Munich (1885), Vienna (1892), Chicago (1893), St. Louis (1904), Leipzig (1909), and Turin (1911); in 1872 the factory was removed to Freiburg-im-Breisgau. His oldest son, **Emil Welte** (b. Voehrenbach, April 20, 1841; d. Norwich, Conn., Oct. 25, 1923), established a branch in N.Y. (1865); he improved the then newly invented paper roll (taking the place of the earlier wooden cylinders), and was the first to use it, in connection with a pneumatic action, in a large orchestrion built for Theiss' Alhambra Court (N.Y.). A son of Berthold Welte, **Edwin** (b. Freiburg, 1875, d. there, Jan. 4, 1958), applied the paper roll to the piano, creating in 1904 the "Welte-Mignon Reproducing Piano," which could control pedaling and gradations of touch, a definite improvement on the ordinary player-piano which could produce only pitches. Josef Hoffmann, Paderewski, and Wanda Landowska made rolls for it. The application of the same principle to the organ resulted in the invention of the "Philharmonic Organ" (1912). The firm ceased to exist in 1954.

Wen-chung, Chou. See **Chou, Wen-chung.**

Wendel, Ernst, German violinist and conductor; b. Breslau, March 26, 1876; d. Jena, May 20, 1938. He studied violin with Joachim in Berlin; theory with Bargiel. In 1896 he went to America and was a member of the Chicago Symph. Orch. for 2 seasons; returning to

Germany, he was conductor of the Musikverein in Königsberg (1898-1909); then conductor in Bremen, Berlin, Frankfurt, and Nuremberg. He composed *Das Grab im Busento* and *Das deutsche Lied,* both for men's chorus with orch.; also men's choruses a cappella and songs.

Wendel, Eugen, Rumanian composer; b. Valea-Rea, Dec. 18, 1934. He studied with Vancea, Olah and Stroe at the Bucharest Cons. (1959-65); worked as a sound engineer with the Rumanian recording firm, Electrecord.

    WORKS: Concerto for Orch. (1964); *Symphonic Meditations* (1965); *Gravitations* for orch. (1968); *Transmutations* for orch. (1969); *Resonances* for orch. (1972); Violin Sonata (1963); String Quartet (1964); *Interferences* for violin, viola, cello, clarinet, and piano (1966); *Fusion* for clarinet, piano, and tape (1968); *Rêve,* music for 8 instrumentalists (1969; also a version for clarinet, violin, viola, cello, and piano); *Genèse* for piano quartet (1972); *Verso* for solo oboe (1973); Piano Sonata (1966); choruses; songs.

Wendland, Waldemar, German composer; b. Liegnitz, May 10, 1873; d. Zeitz, Aug. 15, 1947. He studied for a short time with Humperdinck, while acting as an assistant conductor at the Frankfurt Opera; then settled in Berlin. He wrote the operas *Das kluge Felleisen* (Madgeburg, 1909), *Das vergessene Ich* (Berlin, 1911), *Der Schneider von Malta* (Leipzig, 1818), *Peter Sukoff* (Basel, 1921), *Die vier Temperamente* (Freiburg, 1927), *Koreanisches Märchen* (Altenburg, May 11, 1946); several ballets; orchestral works; chamber music; about 200 songs.

Wendling, Johann Baptist, Alsatian flutist; b. Rappoltsweiler, June 17, 1723; d. Munich, Nov. 27, 1797. He was an excellent flute player; was active in Mannheim; accompanied Mozart on his journey to Paris in 1778; then lived in Mannheim and in Munich. He wrote a number of flute concertos. His wife, **Dorothea Wendling** (1736-1811) was an opera singer; Mozart wrote an aria for her.

Wendling, Karl, German pianist; b. Frankenthal, Nov. 14, 1857; d. Leipzig, June 20, 1918. He studied at the Leipzig Cons.; made a specialty of the Jankó keyboard, on which he became highly proficient; also taught piano at the Leipzig Cons.; publ. *Meisterwerke aus der Etüden-Literatur* (4 books, in progressive order).

Wendt, Ernst Adolf, German pianist and composer; b. Schwiebus, Prussia, Jan. 6, 1806; d. Neuwied, Feb. 5, 1850. He was a pupil of Zelter in Berlin; then became instructor at the Teacher's Seminary there. He publ. variations for piano and orch.; a piano trio; a 4-hand piano sonata; a collection of his organ pieces was publ. by Karl Becker as *Wendt Album.*

Wennerberg, Gunnar, Swedish writer and composer; b. Linköping, Oct. 2, 1817; d. Läckö, Aug. 24, 1901. He studied at the Univ. of Uppsala, and entered the Swedish Parliament. He learned music by himself; began to write songs for male voices, which became

very successful in Sweden; publ. the collections *Frihetssånger* (1847) and *Gluntarne* (1849-51; reprinted, Uppsala, 1949); also composed a Christmas oratorio, and settings of the Psalms of David for solo voices, chorus, and piano. His literary works were publ. in 4 vols. (1881-85).

    BIBLIOGRAPHY: S. Almquist, *Om Gunnar Wennerberg: hans tid och hans gärning* (Stockholm, 1917); C. F. Hennerberg, *Förteckning över G. Wennerbergs Tonverk* (Stockholm, 1918); G. Jeanson, *G. Wennerberg som Musiker* (Stockholm, 1929).

Wenzel, Ernst Ferdinand, German pianist and teacher; b. Walddorf, near Löbau, Jan. 25, 1808; d. Bad Kösen, Aug. 16, 1880. A student of philosophy at Leipzig Univ., he also had private piano lessons with Fr. Wieck, became a friend of his fellow-pupil Schumann, and was a frequent contributor to the *Neue Zeitschrift für Musik* during Schumann's editorship (till 1844). He was also an intimate friend of Mendelssohn; taught piano at Leipzig Cons. from its foundation in 1843 until his death; the majority of English-speaking students there were in his classes, or had private instruction from him.

Wenzel, Leopold, Italian violinist, conductor, and composer; b. Naples, Jan. 23, 1847; d. Asnières, near Paris, Aug. 21, 1925. He studied at the Cons. S. Pietro a Majella, Naples, but left it at the age of 13, traveling as a violinist in Greece, Turkey, and Egypt, eventually going to Paris as theater conductor. From 1889 to 1914 he was in London, conducting at the Empire Theatre and the Gaiety Theatre. He wrote about 20 ballets, the most successful being *Dream of Wealth, Katrina,* and *The Girl I Left Behind Me;* the operettas *Le Chevalier Mignon* (Paris, 1884), *L'Élève du Conservatoire* (Paris, 1894); also many songs.

Wenzinger, August, Swiss cellist and music editor; b. Basel, Nov. 14, 1905. He studied cello in Basel; took a course in composition with Jarnach in Cologne (1927-29); subsequently devoted himself to the viola da gamba, and was a founder of a concert group promoting the revival of old instruments; gave courses in the Schola Cantorum Basiliensis (until 1970). He published *Gambenübung* (2 vols.; 1935, 1938) and *Gambenfibel* (with Marianne Majer; 1943); edited Haydn's Cello Concerto in D major and Bach's unaccompanied suites for cello.

Werba, Erik, eminent Austrian pianist composer and writer on music; b. Baden, near Vienna, May 23, 1918. He studied piano with Oskar Dachs and composition with Joseph Marx at the Academy of Vienna; musicology with Lach, Wellesz, and Schenk; received his Dr. phil., in 1940 at the Univ. of Vienna. In 1948 he was appointed prof. at the Vienna State Academy; from 1964 to 1971 he was also visiting prof. at the Music Academy in Graz. He was engaged mainly as a piano accompanist to famous singers, with whom he traveled in Europe and Japan; returning to Vienna, he devoted himself primarily to musical journalism; in 1953 he became editor of *Österreichische musikalische Zeitung;* published a number of informative and reliable monographs on Austrian composers: Joseph

Marx (Vienna, 1964), Hugo Wolf (Vienna, 1971), and Erich Marckhl (Vienna, 1972). He composed a Singspiel, *Trauben für die Kaiserin* (Vienna, 1949); several song cycles and chamber music pieces, among them, *Sonata notturna* for bassoon and piano (1972).

Werckmeister, Andreas, German organist and theorist; b. Beneckenstein, Nov. 30, 1645; d. Halberstadt, Oct. 26, 1706. He studied organ with his uncles, Christian and Victor; was organist at Hasselfelde (1664–74), at Quedlinburg (1675–96), and finally at Halberstadt, from 1696 to his death. He publ. the important treatise *Orgelprobe* (1681; 2nd ed., 1698; 3rd ed., 1716; 4th ed., 1764; English transl. in *Organ Institute Quarterly* 6, 1956); *Musicae mathematicae Hodegus curiosus, oder richtiger musikalisher Weg-Weiser* (1686; 2nd ed., 1698); *Der edlen Music-Kunst Würde, Gebrauch und Missbrauch* (1691); *Musikalische Temperatur* (1691; the earliest treatise on equal temperament); *Hypomnemata musica, oder musikalisches Memorial* (1697); *Die nothwendigsten Anmerckungen und Regeln wie der Bassus continuus könne tractiret werden* (1698); *Harmonologia musica, oder kurtze Anleitung zur musikalischen Composition* (1702); *Organum Gruningense redivivum, oder kurtze Beschreibung des in der grüningischen Schloss-Kirchen berühmten Orgel-Wercks* (1705); *Musikalische Paradoxal-Discourse* (posthumous; 1707). A facsimile reprint of the *Orgelprobe* (ed. of 1698) was publ. in Kassel in 1927; the *Organum Gruningense* was republ. in Mainz, in 1932.

BIBLIOGRAPHY: W. Serauky, "Andreas Werckmeister als Musiktheoretiker," in the *Max Schneider Festschrift* (Halle, 1935); R. Dammann, "Zur Musiklehre des Andreas Werckmeister," in *Archiv für Musikwissenschaft* 11 (1954).

Werder, Felix, German-born Australian composer; b. Berlin, Feb. 24, 1922. He acquired early music training from his father, a cantor and composer of liturgical music; also learned to play piano, viola, and clarinet. His family emigrated to England in 1934 to escape Nazi persecution; then went to Australia. Werder taught music at high schools in Melbourne and was a music critic for the Melbourne newpaper *The Age* (1960–77). He wrote 500 works, but discarded about 60% of them; his musical idiom was determined by the cross-currents of European modernism, with a gradual increase in the forcefulness of his resources; these include electronics.

WORKS: FOR THE STAGE: 6 operas: *Kisses for a Quid* (1961), *The General* (1966), *Agamemnon* (1967), *The Affair* (1969), *Private* (television opera, 1969), and *The Vicious Square* (1971); a ballet, *En Passant* (1964). FOR ORCH: 5 symphonies: No. 1 (1951; withdrawn), No. 2 (1959), No. 3, *The Laocoon* (1965), No. 4 (1970), and No. 5 (1971); Flute Concerto (1954); Piano Concerto (1955); 2 violin concertos (1956, 1966); *Brand*, symph. poem (1956); *Sinfonia in Italian Style* (1957); *La Primavera*, symph. poem (1957); *Abstraction* (1958); *Hexastrophe* (1961); *Monostrophe* (1961); Clarinet Concerto (1962); Viola Concerto (1963); *Konzert Musik* for 10 solo instruments and orch. (1964); *Dramaturgie* (1966); *Morgen Rot* for violin and chamber orch. (1968); *Strettophone* (1968); *Tower Concerto*

(1968); *After Watteau* for violin and orch. (1968); *Sound Canvas* (1969); *Klang Bilder* (1969); *Triple Measure* (1970); *Don Giovanni Retired*, epilogue (1971); *Prom Gothic* for organ and orch. (1972). FOR VOICE: an oratorio, *Francis Bacon Essays* (1971); an anti-Vietnam War cantata, *Radics Piece* (1967); songs. CHAMBER MUSIC: 9 string quartets (Nos. 1–3, withdrawn; Nos. 4–9: 1955, 1956, 1962, 1965, 1966, 1968); 3 violin sonatas (1947, 1958, 1963); Piano Quartet (1954); *3-Part Fantasias* for string trio (1955); Cello Sonata (1956); 3 piano trios (1958, 1963, 1969); Quintet for clarinet, horn, and string trio (1959); Flute Sonata (1960); Clarinet Sonata (1960); Horn Sonata (1960); Sonata for wind quintet (1961); Septet for flute, clarinet, horn, and strings (1963); Piano Quintet (1963); Solo Violin Sonata (1965); *Apostrophe* for wind quintet (1965); Quintet for clarinet and string quartet (1965); *Satyricon* for 6 horns (1967); Sonata for cello solo (1968); *Strophe* for solo violin (1968); Trio for harp, bass clarinet, and percussion (1969); *Activity* for piano and percussion (1969); *Triphony* for flute, guitar, and bongos (1969); *Faggotiana* for bassoon and string trio (1970); *Tetract* for viola, oboe, and 2 percussionists (1970); *Divertimento* for guitar and string quartet (1970); Wind Quartet (1971); *Percussion Play* for solo percussion (1971); *Banker*, music theater for 2 synthesizers, percussion, guitar, and piano (1973). FOR KEYBOARD: 4 piano sonatas (1942, 1953, 1968, 1970); 2-Piano Sonata (1960); Harpsichord Sonata (1963); *Toccata* for organ (1971).

Werder, Richard, American composer and pianist; b. Williamsburg, Iowa, Dec. 21, 1919. He studied at the Juilliard School of Music, N.Y., and at Columbia Univ.; later taught at the Catholic Univ. in Washington. Among his works, mostly for piano, are *Black on White, The Drum, Procession of the Pachyderms, Resting Time,* and *Down, Up.*

Werle, Lars Johan, Swedish composer; b. Gävle, June 23, 1926. He studied with Sven-Erik Bäck (composition) and Carl-Allan Moberg (musicology) at Uppsala Univ. (1948–51); held positions at the Swedish Broadcasting Corporation and as instructor at the National School of Music Drama in Stockholm. In his music he employs an amiably modern idiom, stimulating to the untutored ear, while retaining the specific gravity of triadic tonal constructions. His three theater operas have been received with smiling approbation.

WORKS: *Drömmen om Thérèse* (The Dream of Thérèse), with electronic sound, after Zola's short story, *Pour une nuit d'amour* (Stockholm, May 26, 1964); *Resan (The Voyage)*, after a novel by J. P. Jersild, containing film-projection (Hamburg, March 2, 1969); *Tintomara*, after C. J. L. Almquist's novel, *The Queen's Jewels* (Stockholm, Jan. 18, 1973); a television opera, *En saga om sinnen* (Swedish television, June 21, 1971); *Pentagram* for string quartet (1959); *Sinfonia da camera* (1960); *Summer Music 1965* for strings and piano (1965); *Attitudes* for piano (1965); *Zodiak*, ballet (Stockholm, Feb. 12, 1967); *Canzona 126 di Francesco Petrarca* for chorus (1967); *Nautical Preludes* for chorus (1970); *Variété* for string quartet (1971); 2 "run-and-sing" stage works: *Fabel* for 5 singers, percussion, and piano (1974) and *Flower Power* for 6 singers and 6 instrumentalists (1974).

Wermann, Friedrich Oskar, German organist and composer; b. Neichen, near Trebsen, April 30, 1840; d. Oberloschwitz, near Dresden, Nov. 22, 1906. He was a pupil of Fr. Wieck (piano); later of Reinecke, Hauptmann, and Richter at the Leipzig Cons. He occupied various positions as organist in Alsace, before settling in Dresden (1868) as teacher and church organist; also conducted the Lehrergesangverein there. He composed a Christmas fairy tale, *Die Wunderglocke;* a symph. poem, *König Witichis;* several overtures; a *Reformationskantate;* a *Passionskantate;* 2 Masses; several psalms for double chorus a cappella; numerous organ works; études for piano; part-songs.

Werner, Arno, German organist and musicologist; b. Prittitz, Weissenfels, Nov. 22, 1865; d. Bitterfeld, Feb. 15, 1955. He studied at the Royal Institute for Church-Music in Berlin (1889–90); in 1890 became municipal organist at Bitterfeld; in 1894 was appointed music teacher at the Gymnasium there, retiring in 1931; continued his activities as musicologist until his death; contributed articles to *Die Musik in Geschichte und Gegenwart* (1953).
WRITINGS: *Samuel und Gottfried Scheidt* (1900); *Geschichte der Kantorei-Gesellschaften im Gebiete des Kurfürstentums Sachsen* (1902); *Die Kantorei zu Bitterfeld* (1903); *Städtidche und fürstliche Musikpflege in Weissenfels* (1911); *Städtische und fürstliche Musikpflege in Zeitz* (1922); *Zur Geschichte der Kantorei in Zörbig* (1927); *Musikpflege in Stadt und Kreis Bitterfeld* (1931); *Vier Jahrhunderte im Dienste der Kirchenmusik. Geschichte der Kantoren, Organisten und Stadtpfeifer seit der Reformation* (1932); *Der deutsche Kantor* (1933); *Freie Musikgemeinschaften im mitteldeutschen Raum* (1940).

Werner, Eric, musicologist; b. Lundenberg, near Vienna, Aug. 1, 1901. He studied composition with Kornauth in Vienna, and with Schrecker and Busoni in Berlin; also took courses at the universities of Graz, Vienna, Prague, Berlin, Göttingen, and Strasbourg; held teaching positions in Saarbrücken (1926–33) and Breslau (1935–38). In 1938 he settled in the U.S. He is an authority on Jewish and early Christian music; published *In the Choir Loft* (N.Y., 1957); *The Sacred Bridge* (London, 1958); *Mendelssohn: A New Image of the Composer and His Age* (N.Y., 1963); composed a *Symphony-Requiem;* chamber music; various other pieces.

Werner, Gregor Joseph, Austrian music scholar and composer; b. Ybbs, Lower Austria, 1693 (baptized Jan. 29, 1693); d. Eisenstadt, March 3, 1766. In 1728 he was appointed Kapellmeister to Prince Esterházy at Eisenstadt; in 1761 Haydn was named Vice-Kapellmeister, and succeeded him after his death. Werner wrote a number or works, including 40 Masses, 18 oratorios, and many instrumental pieces. Haydn had great respect for him, and arranged his fugues for string quartet. Among modern reprints are his *Hirtenkantate, Hirtenmusik, Kleine Hirtenmusik,* etc.,

edited by E. F. Schmid; other pieces appeared in *Das Erbe deutscher Musik* (vol. 31).

Werner, Heinrich, German composer; b. Kirchohmfeld, Oct. 2, 1800; d. Brunswick, May 3, 1833. His song *Haidenröslein* became a perennial favorite in Germany; he also publ. male quartets and light piano music.
BIBLIOGRAPHY: Fr. Mecke, *Heinrich Werner* (dissertation; Bonn, 1913); P. Egert, *Festschrift zur Einweihung des Denkmals für den Komponisten Heinrich Werner in Kirchohmfeld* (1910).

Werner, Johann Gottlob, German organist and teacher; b. Grossenhain, 1777; d. Chemnitz, July 19, 1822. After holding minor positions as organist in provincial towns, he was appointed cathedral organist and music director at Merseburg, but died 3 years later. He publ. organ methods which were much in use: *Orgelschule* (1805; Part II as *Lehrbuch, das Orgelwerk . . . kennen . . . zu lernen,* 1823; both often republ.); *Musikalisches ABC* for beginners on the piano (1806; often republ.); *Choralbuch zum holländischen Psalm- und Gesangbuch* (1814); *Choralbuch zu den neuern sächsischen Gesangbüchern* (Leipzig); *Versuch einer kurzen und deutlichen Darstellung der Harmonielehre* (2 parts, 1818, 1819); many chorale-preludes; 40 organ pieces for beginners; etc.

Werner, Josef, German cellist; b. Würzburg, June 25, 1837; d. Munich, Nov. 14, 1922. He studied at the Würzburg Cons.; became a teacher at the Munich Musikschule; publ. a *Praktische Violoncell-Schule* (with 7 supplements); *Der erste Anfang im Violoncellspiel;* several books of *Übungen für Violoncell;* numerous pieces for cello with piano; a quartet for 4 cellos.

Werner, Theodor Wilhelm, German writer on music; b. Hannover, June 8, 1874; d. Salzburg, Dec. 6, 1957. He studied philology; then music with Draeseke and Noren in Dresden; musicology with Johannes Wolf in Berlin, Sandberger and Kroyer in Munich; Dr. phil., 1917. He became instructor at Hannover; also wrote music criticism; from 1945 lived in Salzburg. He publ. *Musik in Frankreich* (1927); ed. works by G. Benda (*Denkmäler deutscher Tonkunst* 64), Telemann (*Das Erbe deutscher Musik* 6), and others; composed 2 symphonies; 2 string quartets; choruses.

Wernick, Richard, American composer; b. Boston, Jan. 16, 1934. He studied composition with Irving Fine, Harold Shapero, and Arthur Berger at Brandeis Univ. (1952–55); took lessons also with Ernst Toch in Los Angeles and Boris Blacher at Tanglewood, where he also studied conducting with Leonard Bernstein. In his early works he integrated the techniques of all these instructors, but ultimately fashioned an individual style of composition. From 1958 to 1964 he was active as a composer for film, television, and theater in New York; then became engaged in teaching; was on the faculty of the State Univ. of N.Y. at Buffalo (1964–65) and at the Univ. of Chicago (1965–68); in 1969 he joined the music dept. of the Univ. of Pennsylvania. He received the 1977 Pulitzer Prize in music for his *Visions of Terror and Wonder.*

WORKS: *Music* for solo viola d'amore (1963); *Aevia* for orch. (1965); *Stretti* for violin, clarinet, viola, and guitar (1965); *Lyrics from 1 × 1* for female voices, bass, and percussion (1966); *Haifu of Basho* for soprano, 7 players and tape (1967); *Cadenzas and Variations I* for viola and piano (1968); *Cadenzas and Variations II* for unaccompanied violin (1969); *Hexagrams* for orch. (1970); *Kaddish-Requiem* for mezzo-soprano, chamber ensemble, and tape (1969); *Moonsongs from the Japanese* for mezzo-soprano and tape (1969); *A Player for Jerusalem* for female voice and percussion (1970–71); 2 string quartets; *Visions of Terror and Wonder* for mezzo-soprano and orch. to texts from the Bible and the Koran, in Hebrew, Arabic, and Greek (Aspen Music Festival, Colorado, July 19, 1976; won the Pulitzer Prize, 1977).

Werrekoren (Verecoren, Werrecore), Hermann Mathias, 16th-century German composer. He was maestro di cappella in Milan (1538–55); his principal work is a descriptive composition for 4 voices a cappella entitled *Die Schlacht vor Pavia* (The Battle of Pavia), publ. in Schmeltzl's collection *Guter seltzamer . . . teutscher Gesang* (Nuremberg, 1544) and reprinted by Gardano in Venice in 1549 as *La Battaglia Taliana;* also publ. a book of motets for 4 voices (1555); various other motets were publ. in the collections of the period. Werrekoren was mistakenly identified with Matthäus Le Maistre by Fétis and Kade; research by Haberl, Elsa Bienenfeld, and Cecie Stainer demonstrated the fallacy of this assumption.
BIBLIOGRAPHY: Haberl's articles in the *Kirchenmusikalisches Jahrbuch* (1871 and 1873); Elsa Bienenfeld in the *Sammelbände der Internationalen Musik-Gesellschaft* (1904–05).

Werrenrath, Reinald, American baritone; b. Brooklyn, Aug. 7, 1883; d. Plattsburg, N.Y., Sept. 12, 1953. He was a pupil of his father, a tenor; then studied with David Bispham and Herbert Witherspoon. He began his career as a concert singer; also in oratorio; made his operatic debut on Feb. 19, 1919, at the Metropolitan Opera House, N.Y., as Silvio in *I Pagliacci,* and remained with the company until 1921; then devoted himself to teaching and concert singing; appeared in public for the last time at Carnegie Hall, N.Y., on Oct. 23, 1952. He edited *Modern Scandinavian Songs* (2 vols.; Boston, 1925–26). He was married 3 times: to Ada Peterson (1909; divorced, 1927); to Verna True Nidig (1928; divorced, 1941); and to Frances M. Aston (1942).

Wert, Giaches de (Jakob van Wert), Flemish contrapuntist; b. Weert, between May 6 and Aug. 18, 1535; d. Mantua, May 6, 1596. He was a boy chorister in the retinue of Maria di Cardona, Marchesa della Padulla, and followed the household to Italy. At the age of 9 he entered the ducal choir at Novellara; in 1549 he went to Ferrara to study with Cyprian de Rore. In 1558 he was appointed maestro di cappella at the court at Novellara; then joined the court chapel of the Duke of Mantua, who appointed him maestro di cappella in 1565. He held this position until his death, with an interval as vice-maestro at Novellara (1567–74); from 1565 to 1583 was also choirmaster of the Church of Santa Barbara in Mantua. He was greatly esteemed by contemporary musicians; Palestrina praised him, and he was also mentioned favorably by Thomas Morley, Artusi, G. B. Doni, and Monteverdi. His compositions were included in many collections of sacred and secular music, beginning in 1558. He publ. 11 books of madrigals for 5 voices, one for 4 voices, and one for 5 and 6 voices; one book of canzonets, and 3 of motets for 5 and 6 voices. 16 vols. of his collected works were published in Rome between 1961 and 1973.
BIBLIOGRAPHY: A.-M. Bautier-Regnier, "Jacques de Wert," *Revue Belge de Musicologie* (1950); G. Reese, *Music in the Renaissance* (N.Y., 1954); C. MacClintock, "Some Notes on the Secular Music of Giaches de Wert," *Musica Disciplina* 10 (1956).

Wesembeek. See **Burbure de Wesembeek.**

Wesendonck, Mathilde (*née* **Luckemeyer**), German poetess, friend of Wagner; b. Elberfeld, Dec. 23, 1828; d. at her villa Traunblick, near Altmünster on the Traunsee, Austria, Aug. 31, 1902. Her first meeting with Wagner took place in Zürich, early in 1852, and soon developed into a deep friendship. She wrote the famous *Fünf Gedichte (Der Engel, Stehe still, Träume, Schmerzen, Im Treibhaus),* which Wagner set to music as studies for *Tristan und Isolde.* On May 19, 1848, she married **Otto Wesendonck** (b. March 16, 1815; d. Berlin, Nov. 18, 1896); in 1857 he gave Wagner the use of a beautiful house on his estate on Lake Zürich, where the 1st act of *Tristan und Isolde* was written, and the 2nd act sketched.
BIBLIOGRAPHY: A. Heintz, "Meine Erinnerungen" (reminiscences of Mathilde Wesendonck) in the *Allgemeine Musikzeitung* (Feb. 14, 1896); W. Golther, ed., *Richard Wagner an Mathilde Wesendonck. Tagebuchblätter und Briefe* (Berlin, 1904; many subsequent eds., English transl. London, 1905); W. Golther, ed., *Briefe Richard Wagners an Otto Wesendonck* (Berlin, 8th printing, 1905; English, London, 1911); H. Bélart, *Richard Wagners Liebestragödie mit Mathilde Wesendonck* (Dresden, 1912); E. H. Müller von Asow, ed., *Johannes Brahms und Mathilde Wesendonck; ein Briefwechsel* (Vienna, 1943).

Wesley, Charles, English organist and harpsichord player; nephew of **John Wesley;** b. Bristol, Dec. 11, 1757; d. London, May 23, 1834. He was a pupil of Kelway and Boyce in London; then held various positions as church organist; publ. *Six Concertos for the Organ or Harpsichord,* op. 1; anthems, hymns, etc.; 6 string quartets. He was the brother and teacher of **Samuel Wesley.**
BIBLIOGRAPHY: R. Green, *Works of John and Charles Wesley* (London, 1896); R. S. Stevenson, in *Notes* (March 1970, pp. 515–17).

Wesley, John, the founder of the Wesleyan Methodist Church; nephew of **John Wesley;** b. Epworth, June 17, 1703; d. London, March 2, 1791. He was educated at Christ Church, Oxford; in 1735 he came to America with his brother Charles to do missionary work, and 2 years later publ. his 1st *Collection of Psalms and Hymns* (Charlestown, 1737). Returning to England, he spread the doctrine of Methodism and became famous as a preacher and writer. He has been called "the father of Methodist hymnology."

BIBLIOGRAPHY: R. Green, *Works of John and Charles Wesley* (London, 1896); J. T. Lightwood, *Methodist Music in the 18th Century* (London, 1927); J. L. Nuelsen, *John Wesley und das deutsche Kirchenlied* (Bremen, 1938).

Wesley, Samuel, English organist and composer; brother of **Charles Wesley;** nephew of **John Wesley;** b. Bristol, Feb. 24, 1766; d. London, Oct. 11, 1837. He studied with his brother, and began to compose at the age of 8; learned to play the violin as well as the organ. He publ. *Eight Lessons for the Harpsichord* when he was 11 (1777). Subsequently he developed his fine talent as an organist and was generally regarded as the greatest performer and improviser of his time. Although he suffered from a skull injury as a result of a fall, which seriously interfered with his activities, he continued to give public concerts till the year of his death.

WORKS: 11 organ concertos; voluntaries, preludes, and fugues for organ; 4 symphonies; 4 overtures; 2 string quartets; a string quintet; a trio for oboe, violin, and cello; a trio for 2 flutes and piano; much church music, including 4 Masses, motets, several services, anthems, and psalm-tunes; choral pieces; songs; vocal duets; a number of rondos for piano, based on popular songs and on operatic arias; also numerous glees, for 3 and 4 voices.

BIBLIOGRAPHY: W. Winters, *An Account of the Remarkable Musical Talents of Several Members of the Wesley Family* (London, 1874); E. Wesley (his daughter), *Letters of Samuel Wesley to Mr. Jacobs relating to the Introduction into this Country of the Works of Bach* (London, 1875; 2nd ed., 1878); G. J. Stevenson, *Memorials of the Wesley Family* (London, 1876); J. T. Lightwood, *Samuel Wesley, Musician: The Story of His Life* (London, 1937); E. Douthey, *The Musical Wesleys* (London, 1968).

Wesley, Samuel Sebastian, English organist and composer; natural son of **Samuel Wesley;** b. London, Aug. 14, 1810; d. Gloucester, April 19, 1876. He was a boy chorister at the Chapel Royal; from the age of 16 he held appointments as organist in London churches; 1832, organist of Hereford Cathedral; 1835, at Exeter Cathedral; 1842, at Leeds Parish Church; 1849, at Winchester Cathedral; 1865, at Gloucester Cathedral. He received the degrees of B. Mus. and D. Mus. at Oxford (1839). His works include 4 church sevices; 2 psalms; 27 anthems; several glees; an *Ode to Labour* (1864); pieces for organ; and songs. He publ. *A Few Words on Cathedral Music and the Musical System of the Church, with a Plan of Reform* (1849).

BIBLIOGRAPHY: G. J. Stevenson, *Memorials of the Wesley Family* (London, 1876); E. Douthey, *The Musical Wesleys* (London, 1968).

Wessel, Mark, American composer; b. Goldwater, Michigan, March 26, 1894; d. Beverly Hills, Michigan, May 2, 1973. He studied at Northwestern Univ. (M.M., 1918); then went to Europe and had instruction with Schoenberg in Vienna (1922). Returning to America, he was active primarily as a teacher. He wrote a symphony (1932); 2 piano concertos; *Plains and Mountains* for piano and string quartet (1937); Sextet for piano and 5 wind instruments; 2 cello sonatas; piano pieces.

West, John Ebenezer, English organist and composer; b. London, Dec. 7, 1863; d. there, Feb. 28, 1929. He was a nephew of **Ebenezer Prout,** and studied with him at the Royal Academy of Music; was organist and choirmaster at various London churches; in 1884 was appointed to the editorial staff of Novello & Co. He wrote 2 cantatas, *The Healing of the Canaanite's Daughter* (1882) and *Seed-time and Harvest* (1892); several church services and anthems; an orchestral march, *Victoria, Our Queen;* organ music; publ. an important book, *Cathedral Organists* (London, 1899; new ed., 1921).

Westbrook, William Joseph, English organist and composer; b. London, Jan. 1, 1831; d. Sydenham, March 24, 1894. He was organist at several churches in London; in 1851 appointed to St. Bartholomew's, Sydenham, and held this post until his death. In 1862 he founded the periodical *Musical Standard* (with Hammond and Crowdy). He wrote an oratorio, *Jesus;* a cantata, *The Lord Is My Shepherd;* services, anthems, part-songs; sonatas and voluntaries for organ; several textbooks on the organ, etc.

Westergaard, Peter, American composer and pedagogue; b. Champaign, Illinois, May 28, 1931. He studied composition at Harvard Univ. with Walter Piston (A.B., 1953); then had fruitful sessions with Sessions at Princeton Univ. (M.F.A., 1956). In 1956 he went to Germany, where he studied with Fortner in Detmold. Returning to the U.S., he joined the music faculty of Columbia Univ., N.Y.; in 1968 became associate prof. at Princeton Univ.; prof. in 1971; chairman of the music dept., 1974. He published *An Introduction to Tonal Theory* (N.Y., 1975). In his music he explores the possibility of total organization of tones, rhythms, and other elements of composition.

WORKS: chamber operas, *Charivari* (1953) and *Mr. and Mrs. Discobbolos* (N.Y., 1966); *Symphonic Movement* (1954); *Five Movements* for small orch. (1958); *Invention* for flute and piano (1955); Quartet for violin, vibraphone, clarinet, and cello (1961); Trio for flute, cello, and piano (1962); *Variations* for 6 instruments (1964); *Divertimento on Discobolic Fragments* for flute and piano (1967); *Noises, Sounds and Sweet Airs* for flute, clarinet, horn, trumpet, celesta, harpsichord, percussion, and strings (1968); the cantatas: *The Plot Against the Giant,* to words by Wallace Stevens (1956), *A Refusal to Mourn the Death, by Fire, of a Child in London* for bass and 10 instruments, to words by Dylan Thomas (1958), and *Leda and the Swan* for mezzo-soprano, clarinet, viola, vibraphone, and marimba (1961); *Spring and Fall: To a Young Child* for voice and piano (1960); *Moto perpetuo* for 6 wind instruments (1976).

Westergaard, Svend, Danish composer; b. Copenhagen, Oct. 8, 1922. He studied composition with Høffding, Hjelmborg and Jersild at the Royal Danish Cons.

in Copenhagen, graduating in 1947; from 1947 to 1971 taught there.

WORKS: *Elegy* for strings (1949); *Pezzo sinfonico* (1950); Oboe Concerto (1950); 2 symphonies: No. 1, *Sinfonia* (1955) and No. 2, *Sinfonia da camera* (1968); *L'homme armé,* canzona for 16 instruments (1959); *Capriccio* for violin and string orch. (1960); *Variazioni sinfoniche* (Danish radio, June 12, 1960); Cello Concerto (Aarhus, Oct. 22, 1962); *Pezzo concertante* for orch. (Danish radio, Aug. 19, 1965); *Sinfonia da camera* (Copenhagen, March 24, 1969); *Varianti sinfoniche* for winds and percussion (1972); 2 wind quintets (1948, 1949); *Tema con variazioni* for clarinet quintet (1949); String Quartet (1968); Sonata for solo flute (1971).

Westerhout, Niccolò van. See **Van Westerhout, Niccolò.**

Westlake, Frederick, English pianist and composer; b. Romsey, Hampshire, Feb. 25, 1840; d. London, Feb. 12, 1898. He studied at the Royal Academy of Music with W. Macfarren (piano) and G. A. Macfarren (harmony); in 1862 was appointed to the faculty as piano teacher. He wrote several Masses, hymns, piano pieces, and a collection of part-songs, *Lyra Studentium.*

Westmorland, John Fane, Earl of (Lord Burghersh), English composer; b. London, Feb. 3, 1784; d. Apthorpe House, Northants, Oct. 16, 1859. He was in the British Army, fought in the Spanish campaign and in Egypt, attaining the rank of general in 1854; also occupied various diplomatic posts between wars. He studied music in Lisbon with Marcos Portugal (1809–12); was a founder of the Royal Academy of Music in London (1822). He wrote 7 Italian operas; the following were performed at his own palace in Florence (where he served as British Resident): *Fedra* (Nov. 17, 1824); *L'Eroe di Lancastro* (June 13, 1829); *Lo Scompiglio teatrale* (1830). Other works include several church services; some piano music; also a *Sinfonia in D* for orch. A list of his works is found in W. W. Cazelet's *The History of the Royal Academy of Music* (London, 1854).

Westphal, Rudolf (Georg Hermann), notable German music scholar; b. Oberkirchen, July 3, 1826; d. Stadthagen, July 10, 1892. He was a student of classical philology in Marburg; taught at the Univ. of Breslau (1858–62); then went to Moscow as teacher at a lyceum (1875–80); subsequently lived in Leipzig, Bückeburg, and Stadthagen. He wrote numerous learned papers on Greek music, and maintained that the Greeks employed polyphony, a theory that he himself eventually abandoned as untenable.

WRITINGS: *Metrik der griechischen Dramatiker und Lyriker* (with Rossbach; 3 vols., 1854–63; 3rd ed. as *Theorie der musischen Künste der Hellenen,* 1885–89); *Die Fragmente und Lehrsätze der griechischen Rhythmiker* (1861); *System der antiken Rhythmik* (1865); *Geschichte der alten und mittelalterlichen Musik* (1865; unfinished; includes *Plutarch über die Musik,* 1864); *Theorie der neuhochdeutschen Metrik* (1870; 2nd ed., 1877); *Elemente des musikal-*

ischen Rhythmus mit besonderer Rücksicht auf unsre Opernmusik (1872); *Allgemeine Theorie der musikalischen Rhythmik seit J. S. Bach* (1880); *Die Musik des griechischen Altertums* (1883); *Allgemeine Metrik der indo-germanischen und semitischen Völker auf Grundlage der vergleichenden Sprachwissenschaft* (1892; with addendum by R. Kruse, *Der griechische Hexameter in der deutschen Nachdichtung*); and *Metrik und Rhythmik des klassischen Hallenentums,* 2 vols. (1883–93).

Westrup, Sir Jack Allan, English musicologist; b. London, July 26, 1904; d. Headley, Hampshire, April 21, 1975. He received his education at Dulwich College, London, and Balliol College, Oxford (B. Mus., 1926; M.A., 1929; D. Mus., 1944); assistant master at Dulwich College (1928–34); in 1947 he was appointed prof. of music at Oxford Univ., succeeding Sir Hugh Allen. He edited Monteverdi's *Orfeo* (1925) and *L'Incoronazione di Poppea* (1927); was chairman of the editorial board of the *New Oxford History of Music,* to which he has contributed; publ. *Purcell,* in the Master Musicians series (London, 1937); *Handel* (London, 1938), and *Liszt* (London, 1940), in the Novello series; *Sharps and Flats,* essays (London, 1940); *British Music* (London, 1943; new ed., 1949); *An Introduction to Musical History* (London, 1955); with F. L. Harrison, he edited the *Collins Music Encyclopedia* (London, 1959; American ed., *The New College Encyclopedia of Music,* N.Y., 1960). After Blom's death in 1959, he took over the editorship of *Music & Letters.* He was knighted in 1961.

Wettergren (née Palson), Gertrud, Swedish contralto; b. Eslöv, Feb. 17, 1897. She studied at the Stockholm Cons., and later in London; made her operatic debut at the Royal Opera in Stockholm, 1922, and remained on its roster for 10 years. On Dec. 20, 1935, she appeared at the Metropolitan Opera House, as Amneris in *Aida;* also sang with the Chicago City Opera (1936–38); then returned to Sweden. In 1925 she married Erik Wettergren (director of the National Museum of Stockholm).

Wetz, Richard, German composer and teacher; b. Gleiwitz, Feb. 26, 1875; d. Erfurt, Jan. 16, 1935. He studied with R. Hofmann in Leipzig and Thuille in Munich; in 1906 went to Erfurt as choral conductor and teacher; also taught in Weimar.

WORKS: an opera, *Das ewige Feuer* (Düsseldorf, March 19, 1907); *Kleist-Ouvertüre; Traumsommernacht,* for women's chorus and orch.; *Gesang des Lebens,* for male chorus and orch.; *Nicht geboren ist das Beste,* for mixed chorus and orch.; *Hyperion,* for baritone solo, chorus, and orch.; about 100 songs. He publ. monographs on Bruckner (1922), Liszt (1925), and Beethoven (1927; 2nd ed., 1933). A Richard Wetz Society was founded in Gleiwitz in 1943.

BIBLIOGRAPHY: G. Armin, *Die Lieder von Richard Wetz* (Leipzig, 1911); E. L. Schellenberg, *Richard Wetz* (Leipzig, 1911; 2nd ed.; 1914); H. Polack, *Richard Wetz. Sein Werk* (Leipzig, 1935).

Wetzel, Justus Hermann, German composer and musicologist; b. Kyritz, March 11, 1879; d. Überlingen,

(Bodensee), Dec. 6, 1973. He studied natural sciences, philosophy, and history of art (Dr. phil., 1901); then took up music, and was teacher at the Riemann Cons. in Stettin (1905–07); settled in Berlin in 1910; taught at the Academy for Church and School Music (from 1925; prof., 1935). He composed about 400 songs; choral works; chamber music; piano pieces; edited and arranged several collections of German songs.

BIBLIOGRAPHY: F. Welter, *Justus Hermann Wetzel* (Berlin, 1931; with list of works).

Wetzler, Hermann Hans, German-American conductor and composer; b. Frankfurt, Sept. 8, 1870; d. New York, May 29, 1943. He was brought to the U.S. as a child, but in 1882 returned to Germany, where he studied at Hoch's Cons. in Frankfurt with Clara Schumann (piano), Iwan Knorr (counterpoint), and Humperdinck (instrumentation). In 1892 he went to N.Y.; was church organist for several years; in 1903 he established the Wetzler Symph. Concerts, which had considerable success; Richard Strauss conducted a series of 4 concerts of his own works with the Wetzler group (Feb.-March, 1904), including the world première of the *Sinfonia Domestica*. In 1905 Wetzler went to Europe again; conducted opera in various German cities and in Basel. In 1940 he returned to the U.S. He composed an opera, *Die baskische Venus* (Leipzig, Nov. 18, 1928); *Assisi,* legend for orch. written in commemoration of the 700th anniversary of the death of St. Francis of Assisi (1925); *Symphonic Dance in Basque Style* (1927); *Symphonie Concertante,* for violin and orch. (1932); chamber music; choral works; songs.

Weweler, August, German composer; b. Reike, Oct. 20, 1868; d. Detmold, Dec. 8, 1952. He studied at the Leipzig Cons. with Jadassohn and others; in 1898 settled in Detmold as a teacher. He composed the operas *Dornröschen* (Kassel, 1903) and *Der grobe Märker* (Detmold, 1908); the oratorio *Die Sintflut* (Detmold, 1914); a ballet, *Des Malers Traumbild;* male choruses and piano pieces. He published the book *Ave Musica! Das Wesen der Tonkunst und die modernen Bestrebungen* (1913; 2nd ed., 1919).

Weymarn, Pavel, Russian writer on music and composer; b. St. Petersburg, 1857; d. Narva, Sept. 22, 1905. He studied piano and theory at the St. Petersburg Cons.; in 1888–90 edited the music periodical *Bayan;* publ. monographs on Napravnik (1889) and Cui (1897); was music critic for several Russian newspapers. He composed a string quartet and some piano pieces and songs.

Weyrauch, August Heinrich von, German song composer; b. Riga, April 30, 1788; date of death unknown. In 1824 he publ. (under his own name) a song, *Nach Osten* (words by Wetzel). About 1840 an anonymous Paris publisher reprinted it, with Schubert's name on the title page, as *Adieu* (French words by Bélanger); a piano transcription of it, also crediting the authorship to Schubert, was published by Döhler in Germany (1843); Schlesinger of Berlin reprinted the song, with a German transl. of the French text, as Schubert's in 1845; since then it has been reprinted many times as Schubert's by European and American publishers.

BIBLIOGRAPHY: O. E. Deutsch, *Schubert: Thematic Catalogue of All His Works in Chronological Order* (London, 1951, p. 491).

Weyse, Christoph Ernst Friedrich, German-Danish composer; b. Altona, March 5, 1774; d. Copenhagen, Oct. 8, 1842. He was a pupil of his grandfather, a cantor at Altona; in 1789 he went to Copenhagen, where he studied with J. A. P. Schulz. In 1794 he was appointed organist at the Reformed Church; in 1805 became organist at the Fruekirke; in 1819 he was appointed court composer. Through the court conductor Kunzen he became interested in a movement for the establishment of a national school of Danish opera, for which his works (together with those of Kuhlau) effectively prepared the way.

WORKS: operas (all performed in Copenhagen): *Sovedrikken* (*The Sleeping-Potion;* April 21, 1809); *Faruk* (Jan. 30, 1812); *Ludlams Hule* (*Ludlam's Cave;* Jan. 30, 1816); *Floribella* (Jan. 29, 1825); *Eventyr i Rosenborg Have* (*Adventure in Rosenborg Gardens;* May 26, 1827); *Balders Dod* (*The Death of Baldur;* Nov. 23, 1832); *Festen paa Kenilworth* (after Walter Scott; Jan. 6, 1836); about 30 cantatas; *Miserere* for double chorus and orch.; *Te Deum* for chorus and orch.; 4 symphonies; preludes and fugues for organ; piano pieces (including sonatas and études); songs. He collected 100 Danish folksongs, of which he harmonized 59; they were published by his pupil A. P. Berggreen as *100 gamle Kämpevisemelodier* (Old Ballad Melodies).

BIBLIOGRAPHY: A. P. Berggreen, *C. E. F. Weyses Biographie* (Danish; Copenhagen, 1876); R. von Liliencron, "Weyse und die dänische Musik seit dem vorigen Jahrhundert," in Raumer-Riehl, *Historisches Taschenbuch* (Leipzig, 1878); W. Behrend, "Weyse und Kuhlau," *Die Musik* III/22 (1904); J. P. Larsen, *Weyses Romancer og Sange* (Copenhagen, 1944).

Whear, Paul William, American composer; b. Auburn, Indiana, Nov. 13, 1925. He studied with Wayne Barlow at the Eastman School of Music, Rochester, N.Y., and with Gardner Read at Boston Univ. In 1960 he became chairman of the Music Dept. at Doane College, Crete, Nebraska. His principal works include a Violin Concerto (1950); the symphonic poems, *Proemion* (1949) and *St. Joan* (1951); a cantata *The Ten Commandments* (1955); *Renaissance Suite* for orch. (1958); 3 string quartets; choruses.

White, Clarence Cameron, American Negro violinist and composer; b. Clarksville, Tenn., Aug. 10, 1880; d. New York, June 30, 1960. He studied at Howard Univ. and the Oberlin Cons.; in London with Samuel Coleridge-Taylor, and in Paris with Laparra; held various positions as violinist and teacher in Boston, at West Virginia State College, and Hampton Institute. Won the Harmon Foundation Award and the Rosenwald Foundation Fellowship for composition; also the David Bispham Medal, for his opera *Ouanga,* to a libretto by John F. Matheus from a Haitian historic episode (concert performance, Chicago, Nov. 1932; stage performance, South Bend, Indiana, June 10, 1949). His

Elegy for orch. won the 1954 Benjamin Award for "tranquil music" (New Orleans, March 16, 1954); also composed, for violin, *Bandana Sketches* (1920), *Cabin Memories* (1921), *From the Cotton Fields* (1921); for orch.; Symph. in D minor, *Piece for Strings and Timpani,* and *Kutamba;* the ballet *A Night in Sans Souci;* arranged for voice and piano *40 Negro Spirituals* (1927) and *Traditional Negro Spirituals* (1940); exercises for violin.

White, Donald Howard, American composer and pedagogue; b. Narberth, Penn., Feb. 28, 1921. He studied with Bernard Rogers and Howard Hanson at the Eastman School of Music, Rochester, N.Y. After graduation he was appointed to the music faculty of DePauw Univ., Greencastle, Indiana, in 1947; named full prof. in 1951.
WORKS: *Andante* for oboe, harp and strings (1951); Cello Concerto (1952); *3 for 5* for woodwind quintet (1958); *Serenade* for orch. (1962); *Divertissement No. 1* for clarinet choir (1965); Sonata for trombone and piano (1966); *Divertissement No. 2* for string orch. (1968); *Lyric Suite* for euphonium and piano (1970); *Tetra Ergon* for bass trombone and piano (1972); band pieces; choruses.

White, Eric Walter, English writer on music; b. Bristol, Sept. 10, 1905. He studied at Oxford Univ.: was a member of the Secretariat of the League of Nations (1929–33), subsequently of the National Council of Social Service, London (1935–42), and of the Council for the Encouragement of the Arts Council of Great Britain (from 1946). He published a fundamental biography of Stravinsky (London, 1947), and a highly valuable annotated catalogue of Stravinsky's works (Berkeley and Los Angeles, 1966); a monograph, *Benjamin Britten* (London, 1948; new ed., 1954); *The Rise of English Opera* (London, 1951); numerous informative essays on modern composers.

White, Felix Harold, English composer; b. London, April 27, 1884; d. there, Jan. 31, 1945. He was entirely self-taught, except for some piano lessons from his mother. His overture *Shylock* was performed in London in 1907; other works for orch. include the symph. poems *Astarte Syriaca* and *The Deserted Village,* a polonaise, 2 rhapsodies, etc.; he also wrote chamber music, choral works, about 250 songs, 60 part-songs, 80 piano pieces, etc. He publ. a *Dictionary of Musical Terms;* edited piano works of Scriabin for the Belaieff publ. firm.

White, John, American organist and composer; b. West Springfield, Mass., March 12, 1855; d. Bad Nauheim, July 18, 1902. He studied organ with Dudley Buck in N.Y. and August Haupt in Berlin; composition with Rheinberger in Munich. He was organist of the Church of the Ascension, N.Y., from 1887 to 1896; then went back to Germany. He publ. a *Missa solemnis,* a *Requiem,* a *Te Deum;* many Latin hymns for mixed chorus a cappella; and an oratorio, *Alpha and Omega.*

White, John Reeves, American musicologist and conductor; b. Houston, Mississippi, May 2, 1924. He stud-

ied at the Cincinnati Cons. (1941–43); also took courses at the Cons. National de Musique in Paris (1945); obtained his M.A. at Colorado College in 1948, and his Ph.D. at the Univ. of Indiana in 1952; also received the degree of Dr. of Natural Philosophy at the Institute of Neurophenomenology, Amherst (1975). He held the teaching posts at Colorado College (1947–52), Univ. of Richmond (1953–61), and at Indiana Univ. (1961–66 and 1970–71); in 1971 was appointed to the faculty of Hunter College. From 1966 to 1970 he conducted concerts of the N.Y. Pro Musica; produced reconstructions of several Medieval and Renaissance dramatic works, among them *An Entertainment for Elizabeth,* a 16th-century court masque; *The Play of the Risen Christ,* a 13th-century liturgical drama; *The Play of Mary,* a 14th-century liturgical drama; etc.; served as specialist on cetacean vocalization at the N.Y. Zoological Society and was a member of the N.Y. Institute for Comparative Neurophenomenology; edited *The Keyboard Tablature of Johannes of Lublin* (6 vols., Corpus of Early Keyboard Music No. 6, American Inst. of Musicology, 1964–67), *François Dandrieu, Harpsichord Music* (Pennsylvania State Univ., 1965), *Michelangelo Rossi, Complete Keyboard Works* (Corpus of Early Keyboard Music No. 16, 1967), *The Arts between the Wars. A Symposium* (with John Dos Passos and Harriet Fitzgerald, 1964).

White, Maude Valérie, English composer; b. Dieppe, France (of English parents), June 23, 1855; d. London, Nov. 2, 1937. She studied with W. S. Rockstro; entered the Royal Academy of Music in 1876; was elected Mendelssohn Scholar in 1879 (the first woman to win this honor); then continued her studies under Sir G. Macfarren, and later with R. Fuchs in Vienna. She traveled extensively through Europe and South America; lived in London, and for some years in Florence. She wrote a number of attractive songs to English, German, French, and Italian texts; a vocal quintet to Heine's poem, *Du bist wie eine Blume;* an album of piano pieces, *Pictures from Abroad; Naissance d'amour,* for cello and piano; etc. Publ. her memoirs, *Friends and Memories* (London, 1914) and *My Indian Summer* (London, 1932).

White, Michael, American composer; b. Chicago, March 6, 1931. He studied at the Chicago Musical College and at the Juilliard School of Music, N.Y., with Peter Mennin. In 1963 he received a Guggenheim Fellowship and lived in Italy.
WORKS: *Fantasy* for orch. (1957); *Suite* for orch. (1959); *Gloria* for chorus and orch. (1960); *The Diary of Anne Frank* for soprano and orch. (1960); *Prelude and Ostinato* for string orch. (1960); *The Dybbuk,* opera (1960–62); *Sleep, Little Lord* for children's chorus and strings (1961); an opera, *Through the Looking Glass,* after Lewis Carroll (1965); choruses; songs.

White, Paul, American violinist, composer and conductor; b. Bangor, Maine, Aug. 22, 1895; d. Henrietta, near Rochester, N.Y., May 31, 1973. He studied theory at the New England Cons. of Music, Boston; then took violin lessons with Eugène Ysaÿe in Cincinnati; also studied conducting with Eugene Goossens in Rochester, N.Y. In 1929 he was appointed associate conductor of the Rochester Civic Orch. He composed *Pagan Festival Overture* (Rochester, N.Y., April 28, 1936); *Andante and Rondo,* for cello and orch. (1945); *5 Miniatures* for piano, including the popular *Mosquito Dance;* various pieces of chamber music.

White, Robert, one of the most important English composers of the 16th century; b. c.1535; d. London, Nov., 1574. He studied music for several years, obtaining the degree of Mus. Bac. at Cambridge Univ. on Dec. 13, 1560; appointed Master of the choristers at Ely Cathedral in 1561, retaining this post until 1565; then master of the choristers at Westminster Abbey, from 1570. He composed Latin services and motets, English anthems, etc. Some of his works are reprinted in *Tudor Church Music 5* (1926).

White, William, English composer of the 17th century; d. c.1660. He wrote fantasies, pavans, and other court dance tunes for viols. Apparently he was held in some esteem, for his name is mentioned by Simpson in *Principles of Practicle Musick* (1665) and by Thomas Mace in *Musick's Monument* (1676).

White, William C., American bandleader and march composer; b. Centerville, Utah, Sept. 29, 1881; d. Tenafly, New Jersey, Sept. 30, 1964. He studied violin at the New England Cons. in Boston and later at the Institute of Musical Arts in N.Y., graduating in 1914. He was a member of the 10th U.S. Coast Artillery Band (1907–12) and later led the Mecca Temple Band (1919–20) and Almes Temple Band in Washington (1921–28). He then served for many years as principal of the Army Music School on Governors Island. He composed several marches, among them the popular *American Doughboy;* publ. *A History of Military Music in America* (1943); *Military Band Arranging;* and *Tone Building and Intonation Studies for Military Bands.*

Whitehill, Clarence Eugene, American bass; b. on a farm near Parnell, Iowa, Nov. 5, 1871; d. New York, Dec. 19, 1932. He studied with H. D. Phelps in Chicago; earned his living as a clerk in an express office, and also sang in churches; then went to Paris in 1896, where he studied with Giraudet and Sbriglia; he was the first American male singer to be engaged at the Opéra-Comique (1900); then was a member of Henry Savage's Grand English Opera Co. at the Metropolitan Opera House in the autumn of 1900; went for further study to Stockhausen in Frankfurt, and from there to Bayreuth, where he studied the entire Wagner repertory with Cosima Wagner; after engagements in Germany, he became a member of the Cologne Opera (1903–08), the Metropolitan Opera (1909–10), the Chicago Opera (1911–15), and again at the Metropolitan Opera (1914–32).

Whitehouse, William Edward, English cellist; b. London, May 20, 1859; d. there, Jan. 12, 1935. He studied at the Royal Academy of Music in London; joined its faculty after graduation. From 1889 until 1904 he was cellist in the London Trio, with Achille Simonetti (violin) and Amina Goodwin (piano), with whom he toured all over Europe. He was greatly esteemed as a teacher; among his pupils were Felix Salmond and Beatrice Harrison. He wrote a number of attractive cello pieces (*Allegro perpetuo, Remembrance, Serenade,* etc.) and edited several cello works of the 18th century. He published a memoir, *Recollections of a Violoncellist* (London, 1930).

Whiteman, Paul, celebrated American conductor of popular music; b. Denver, Col., March 28, 1890; d. Doylestown, Pa., Dec. 29, 1967. He played viola in the Denver Symph. Orch. and later in the San Francisco People's Symph. Orch.; in 1917–18 he was conductor of a 40-piece band in the U.S. Navy. He then formed a hotel orch. in Santa Barbara, Calif., and began to develop a style of playing known as "symphonic jazz," which soon made him famous. On Feb. 12, 1924, he gave a concert in Aeolian Hall, N.Y., at which he introduced Gershwin's *Rhapsody in Blue,* written for his orch., with Gershwin himself as soloist. In 1926 he made a tour in Europe. While not himself a jazz musician, he was popularly known as the "King of Jazz," and frequently featured at his concerts such notables of the jazz world as Bix Beiderbecke, Frank Trumbauer, and Benny Goodman; Bing Crosby achieved his early fame as a member of Paul Whiteman's Rhythm Boys. Whiteman established the Whiteman Awards, made annually for "symphonic jazz" compositions written by Americans. He published the books *Jazz* (with M. M. McBride; N.Y., 1926), *How to Be a Bandleader* (with L. Lieber; N.Y., 1941), and *Records for the Millions* (N.Y., 1948).

Whithorne, Emerson, American composer; b. Cleveland, Sept. 6, 1884; d. Lyme, Conn., March 25, 1958. His name was **Whittern;** he had it legally changed in 1918 to Whithorne (the original family name of his paternal grandfather). He studied in Cleveland with J. H. Rogers; embarked on a musical career at the age of 15, and appeared as pianist on the Chautauqua circuit for 2 seasons. In 1904 he went to Vienna and took piano lessons with Leschetizky and composition with Robert Fuchs; in 1905–07 he was a pupil of Artur Schnabel. In 1907 he married pianist-composer **Ethel Leginska,** acting as her impresario in Germany until 1909; they were separated in 1912, and divorced in 1916. Between 1907 and 1915, Whithorne lived mainly in London; studied Chinese and Japanese music from materials in the British Museum, and wrote several pieces based on oriental tunes (*Adventures of a Samurai;* settings for *The Yellow Jacket; The Typhoon*). Returning to America, he became editor for the Art Publication Society of St. Louis (1915–20); then settled in N.Y. and devoted himself entirely to composition; was an active member of the League of Composers, N.Y. In his music he assumed a militantly modernistic attitude; wrote several pieces in the fashionable "machine music" style.

WORKS: for orch.: *The Rain* (Detroit, Feb. 22, 1913); *The Aeroplane* (Birmingham, England, Jan. 30, 1926; orchestral version of the piano piece written in 1920, one of the earliest examples of "machine music"); *Saturday's Child,* to poems by Countee Cullen, for mezzo-soprano, tenor, and small orch. (N.Y., March 13, 1926); *New York Days and Nights* (Philadelphia, July 30, 1926; originally for piano); *Poem* for piano and orch. (Chicago, Feb. 4, 1927); *Fata Morgana,* symph. poem (N.Y., Oct. 11, 1928); incidental music to Eugene O'Neill's *Marco Millions* (1928); Symph. No. 1 (1929; Cincinnati, Jan. 12, 1934); *The Dream Pedlar,* symph. poem (Los Angeles, Jan. 15, 1931); Violin Concerto (Chicago, Nov. 12, 1931); *Fandango* (N.Y., April 19, 1932); *Moon Trail,* symph. poem (Boston, Dec. 15, 1933); Symph. No. 2 (Cincinnati, March 19, 1937); *Sierra Morena* (N.Y., May 7, 1938); Piano Quintet (N.Y., Dec. 19, 1926) and other chamber music; piano pieces; songs.

BIBLIOGRAPHY: J. T. Howard, *Emerson Whithorne* (N.Y., 1929); R. Hammond, "Emerson Whithorne," *Modern Music* (Jan.-Feb. 1931).

Whiting, Arthur Battelle, American composer and pianist; nephew of **George E. Whiting;** b. Cambridge, Mass., June 20, 1861; d. Beverly, Mass., July 20, 1936. He studied in Boston with Sherwood (piano), Maas (harmony), and Chadwick (composition). In 1883 he went to Munich and took courses at the Cons. there with Rheinberger. Returning to the U.S., he stayed in Boston until 1895, when he settled in N.Y.; from 1907, gave educational chamber music concerts at Yale, Harvard, Princeton, and Columbia; in 1911 he inaugurated a series of concerts of early music, playing the harpsichord, other artists being Constance Edson (violin), Georges Barrère (flute), and Paul Kéfer (viola da gamba).

WORKS: *Concert Overture* (Boston, Feb. 5, 1886); Piano Concerto (Boston, Nov. 16, 1888, composer soloist); *Fantasie,* for piano and orch. (Boston, March 5, 1897; composer soloist); *Suite* for strings and 4 horns (Boston, March 13, 1891); Piano Quintet; String Quartet; Piano Trio; Violin Sonata; a number of piano pieces: *6 Bagatelles, Suite moderne, 3 Characteristic Waltzes;* also *Melodious Technical Studies; Pianoforte Pedal Studies* (with text in English and German); musical settings from the *Rubáiyát of Omar Khayyám* for baritone; anthems; etc.

BIBLIOGRAPHY: R. Hughes, *Contemporary American Composers* (Boston, 1900; pp. 283-91); D. G. Mason, "Arthur Whiting," *Musical Quarterly* (Jan. 1937); D. G. Mason, *Music in My Time* (N.Y., 1938, pp. 65-80); *National Cyclopedia of American Biography* (vol. 27, pp. 46-47).

Whiting, George Elbridge, American organist and composer; b. Holliston, Mass., Sept. 14, 1840; d. Cambridge, Mass., Oct. 14, 1923. He began to study with his brother Amos, a church organist, and played in public at the age of 13; at 17 he became organist of the North Congregational Church at Hartford; studied with George W. Morgan in N.Y.,; then went to England, where he became a pupil of W. T. Best of Liverpool (1863). Returning to America, he became organist at St. Joseph's in Albany, where the famous soprano Emma Albani sang in his choir. He then moved to Boston, where he was organist at King's Chapel; in 1874 he went to Berlin and studied harmony with Haupt and orchestration with Radecke. Settling finally in Boston, he taught the organ at the New England Cons. (until 1879, and again from 1883 to 1897). In the interim he was a teacher at the Cincin-

nati College of Music (1880-83). He was renowned as a teacher and composer of organ music; publ. *The Organist* (Boston, 1870) and *The First 6 Months on the Organ* (1871). He also wrote many sacred works: 2 Masses; Vesper Services; a *Te Deum;* the secular cantatas *The Tale of the Viking, Dream Pictures, March of the Monks of Bangor, Midnight, Henry of Navarre;* the 1-act opera *Lenora,* to an Italian libretto (1893); Symph.; an overture to Tennyson's *The Princess;* Piano Concerto; *Suite* for cello and orch.; piano pieces; songs.

BIBLIOGRAPHY: L. C. Elson, *The History of American Music* (N.Y., 1904; pp. 265-67).

Whitmer, Thomas Carl, American organist and composer; b. Altoona, Pa., June 24, 1873; d. Poughkeepsie, N.Y., May 30, 1959. He studied piano with C. Jarvis, organ with S. P. Warren, and composition with W. W. Gilchrist. He was director of the School of Music, Stephens College, Columbia, Mo. (1899-1909); director of music at the Pennsylvania College for Women, Pittsburgh (1909-16); organist and choirmaster of the Sixth Presbyterian Church, Pittsburgh (1916-32); then taught privately in N.Y.

WORKS: *Poem of Life,* for piano and orch. (1914); *A Syrian Night,* ballet suite for orch. (Philadelphia Orch., Pittsburgh, Feb. 17, 1919); *When God Laughed,* for chorus a cappella (1932); *Radiations over a 13th Century Theme,* for string orch. (1935); *Supper at Emmaus,* choral suite (Pittsburgh, Feb. 21, 1939); cantata, *Chant Me the Poem That Comes from the Soul of America,* after Walt Whitman (Pittsburgh, Feb. 19, 1942); 1-act opera, *Oh, Isabel* (1951); chamber music; piano pieces; songs; also published the books *The Way of My Heart and Mind* (Pittsburgh, 1920) and *The Art of Improvisation: A Handbook of Principles and Methods* (N.Y., 1934; revised ed., 1941).

Whitney, Myron William, American bass; b. Ashby, Mass., Sept. 5, 1836; d. Sandwich, Mass., Sept. 19, 1910. He was a pupil of E. H. Frost in Boston, Randegger in London, and Vannucini in Florence. He sang in concert and oratorio in America and Great Britain; was a member of the Boston Ideal Opera Co. (1879) and the American Opera Co. (1885-86); retired in 1900. His son, **Myron Whitney, Jr.** (1872-1954), a baritone, traveled as joint artist with Melba and Nordica; for many years taught singing at the New England Cons., Boston.

BIBLIOGRAPHY: H. C. Lahee, *Famous Singers of Today and Yesterday* (Boston, 1898; pp. 322-23).

Whitney, Robert, American conductor; b. Newcastle-on-the-Tyne, England (of an American father and an English mother), July 9, 1904. He studied with Leo Sowerby in Chicago; took lessons in conducting with Eric De Lamarter. In 1937 he was engaged as conductor of the Louisville Philharmonic (later renamed the Louisville Orchestra); a munificent grant from the Rockefeller Foundation enabled the Louisville Orch. to commission works from American and foreign composers, each to be paid a set fee of $1,000; the project proved highly successful, and the Louisville Orch. was able to give first performances of works by Honegger, Milhaud, Malipiero, Petrassi, Krenek, Dallapiccola, Toch, Chávez, Villa-Lobos, Ginastera, Schuman, Virgil Thomson, Cowell, Piston, Sessions, Antheil, Creston, Mennin, and others; recorded 189 contemporary symphonic works on Louisville Orch. Records; after completing his tenure as conductor in 1967, he was in charge of various special projects at the School of Music at the Univ. of Louisville. Among his own compositions are: *Concerto Grosso* (1934); Symph. in E minor (1936); *Sospiri di Roma* for chorus and orch. (1941); *Concertino* (1960).

BIBLIOGRAPHY: Hope Stoddard, *Symphony Conductors of the U.S.A.* (N.Y., 1957; pp. 248–56).

Whittaker, Howard, American composer; b. Lakewood, Ohio, Dec. 19, 1922. He studied with Herbert Elwell in Cleveland; in 1948 he was appointed director of the Cleveland Music School Settlement. He has written a piano concerto, 2 string quartets, a piano sonata, works for organ and songs. His *Two Murals for Orchestra,* inspired by paintings of Orozco, was performed for the first time by the Cleveland Orch. on March 31, 1960. In most of his works he applies modified serial procedures, but refuses to abandon tonality.

Whittaker, William Gillies, English choral conductor and composer; b. Newcastle-on-the-Tyne, July 23, 1876; d. Orkney Islands, July 5, 1944. He studied organ and singing; conducted various choral societies in Newcastle and London; in 1929 he was appointed prof. at the Univ. of Glasgow. He edited *North Country Folk Tunes,* for voice and piano (2 vols.); *Oxford Choral Songs;* sonatas of John Blow; church cantatas of Bach; etc.; author of *Fugitive Notes on Certain Cantatas and the Motets of J. S. Bach* (London, 1924)), *Class Singing* (London, 1925), *Collected Essays* (London, 1940); publ. *Time Exercises* for piano; received Carnegie Publication awards for his piano quintet, *Among the Northumbrian Hills,* and for his *A Lyke Wake Dirge,* for chorus and orch. (1924); also composed piano pieces and songs.

Whittall, Gertrude Clarke, American patron of music and literature; b. Bellevue, Neb., Oct. 7, 1867; d. Washington, D.C., June 29, 1965. Her maiden name was **Clarke;** she married Matthew John Whittall on June 4, 1906. In 1935 she donated to the Library of Congress, Washington, D.C., a quartet of Stradivari instruments—2 violins (including the famous "Betts"), a viola, and a cello—together with 4 Tourte bows; she added another Stradivari violin (the "Ward") and another Tourte bow in 1937. In 1936 she established an endowment fund in the Library of Congress to provide public concerts at which these instruments would be used, and in 1938 the Whittall Pavilion in the Library was built to house them and to serve other purposes in the musical life of the Library. In subsequent years, she continued to add to her gifts to the Library on behalf of both music and literature; one series enabled the Whittall Foundation to acquire many valuable autograph manuscripts of composers from Bach to Schoenberg, and in particular the finest single group of Brahms manuscripts gathered anywhere in the world.

BIBLIOGRAPHY: W. D. Orcutt, *The Stradivari Me-*morial *at Washington* (Washington, 1938); E. N. Waters, *Autograph Musical Scores in the Whittall Foundation Collection* (Washington, 1951).

Whittenberg, Charles, American composer; b. St. Louis, July 6, 1927. He studied with Burrill Phillips and Bernard Rogers at the Eastman School of Music in Rochester, N.Y. (1944–48); in 1962 he became affiliated with the Columbia-Princeton Electronic Music Center; in 1967 he was appointed associate prof. of music at the Univ. of Connecticut in Storrs, where he became director of Contemporary Music Projects. He received Guggenheim fellowships in 1963 and 1964 and the prize of the American Academy in Rome (1965–66).

WORKS: *Dialogue and Aria* for flute and piano (1956); *Electronic Study* for cello and tape (1960); *Structures* for 2 pianos (1961); *Fantasy* for wind quintet (1961); *Electronic Study II* for double bass and tape (1962); *Triptych* for brass quintet (1962); *Event* for chamber orch. (1963; N.Y., April 28, 1964); *Identities and Variations* for piano (1963); Chamber Concerto for violin and 7 instrumentalists (1963); *Duo-Divertimento* for flute and double bass (1963); *Composition* for cello and piano (1963); *3 Pieces* for solo cello (1963); Variations for 9 players (1964–65); String Quartet in one movement (1965); *Polyphony* for solo trumpet (1965); *3 Compositions* for piano (1967, revised 1969); *Conversations* for solo double bass (1967); Sextet (1967); *Games of Five* for wind quintet (1968); *Iambi* for 2 oboes (1968); Concerto for brass quintet (1968–69); *A due* for flutes and percussion (1969); *Correlations* for orch. (1969); *From John Donne: A Sacred Triptych* for 8 solo voices (1970–71).

Whittlesey, Walter Rose, American music librarian; b. Hartford, Conn., Jan. 5, 1861; d. Washington, D.C., April 9, 1936. Upon the opening of the new building of the Library of Congress (Sept. 1, 1897), he took charge of the musical copyright deposits which formed the basis of the present music collection; when O. G. Sonneck was appointed 1st chief of the Music Division, Whittlesey became his assistant; after Sonneck's resignation (1917) he was acting chief (until 1921); retired 1932. He publ. *Catalogue of First Editions of Stephen C. Foster* (1915; with O. G. Sonneck).

Whythorne, Thomas, English song composer; b. c.1528; d. Aug., 1595. He studied at Oxford Univ.; about 1553 he traveled through Europe and collected German, Austrian, and Neapolitan songs. Upon return to London he published a collection of 76 original songs under the title, *Songes, for three, fower and five voyces* (London, 1571); these were among the earliest sets of secular vocal pieces published in England. In 1590 Whythorne brought out another collection, comprising 52 vocal duos. His autobiography, discovered in 1950, was publ. in Oxford in 1961 in his original phonetic spelling, and reprinted in modern spelling in 1963, ed. by J. M. Osborn.

BIBLIOGRAPHY: Peter Warlock, *Thomas Whythorne: An Unknown Elizabethan Composer* (Oxford, 1927).

Wichmann, Hermann, German composer; b. Berlin, Oct. 24, 1824; d. Rome, Sept., 1905. He was a pupil of Taubert, Mendelssohn, and Spohr; lived most of his life in Berlin. He composed 7 string quartets; a string quintet; a piano trio; a violin sonata; several piano sonatas; publ. a collection of essays, *Gesammelte Aufsätze* (2 vols.; 1884, 1887), and *Frohes und Ernstes aus meinem Leben* (Leipzig, 1898).

Wichtl, Georg, German violinist and composer; b. Trostberg, Feb. 2, 1805; d. Bunzlau, June 3, 1877. He studied in Munich; was a violinist and conductor in various orchestras in Silesia; wrote an opera, *Almaïda;* an oratorio, *Die Auferstehung und Himmelfahrt Jesu;* symphonies and overtures; a string quartet; 6 trios for 2 violins and cello; 3 trios for 3 violins; 6 duets for violin and cello; many instructive pieces for violin.

Wickede, Friedrich von, German composer; b. Dömitz-on-Elbe, July 28, 1834; d. Schwerin, Sept. 11, 1904. He studied with J. Vieth; held various government posts; composition was his avocation. He wrote 2 operas, *Ingo* and *Per aspera ad astra;* piano pieces; songs (which were praised by the critics).

Wickenhauser, Richard, Austrian composer; b. Brünn, Feb. 7, 1867; d. Vienna, July 1, 1936. He studied at the Leipzig Cons. with Jadassohn and Paul; won a state stipend in 1894 (awarded by Brahms and Hanslick); conducted choral societies in Brünn, Graz, and Vienna; from 1907 was conductor of the Vienna Singakademie. He publ. *Sang fahrender Schüler* for male chorus and orch.; *Suite* for string orch.; Violin Sonata; Cello Sonata; *10 Choralvorspiele* for organ; numerous male choruses a cappella and songs; also *Anton Bruckners Symphonien* (Leipzig, 1927).

Wickham, Florence, American contralto singer; b. Beaver, Pa., 1880; d. New York, Oct. 20, 1962. She studied in Philadelphia; then went to Germany, where she was a pupil of Franz Emerich in Berlin. After making appearances in Wiesbaden and Munich, she sang the role of Kundry in *Parsifal* in Henry W. Savage's touring opera troupe in America (1904–05). She was a member of the Metropolitan Opera Co. from 1909 to 1912. Subsequently she retired from the stage and took up composition; wrote an operetta, *Rosalynd,* after Shakespeare's *As You Like It* (1938); also songs; lived mostly in New York.

Widmann, Benedikt, German music pedagogue; b. Bräunlingen, near Donaueschingen, March 5, 1820; d. Frankfurt, March 4, 1910. He was active in music instruction in Frankfurt; publ. several manuals: *Formenlehre der Instrumentalmusik* (1862); *Katechismus der allgemeinen Musiklehre* (2nd ed., 1879); *Grundzüge der musikalischen Klanglehre* (1868); *Praktischer Lehrgang für einen rationellen Gesangunterricht; Handbüchlein der Harmonie-, Melodie- und Formenlehre* (5th ed., 1889); *Generalbass-Übungen* (1859; 5th ed., 1893); *Die kunsthistorische Entwicklung des Männerchors* (1884); *Alberich Zwyssig als Komponist* (1905); etc.

Widmann, Erasmus, German composer and theorist; b. Hall, Württemberg, 1572; d. Rotenburg, Oct. 1634. After serving as cantor in Graz and Weickersheim, he became a schoolmaster at Rotenburg (1614). He wrote church music and some instrumental dance suites; publ. a treatise, *Praecepta musicae Latino-Germanica* (Nuremberg, 1615).

BIBLIOGRAPHY: G. Reichert, *Erasmus Widmann: Leben und Werk* (Tübingen, 1940).

Widmann, Joseph Viktor, Swiss writer and journalist; b. Nennowitz, Moravia, Feb. 20, 1842; d. Bern, Nov. 6, 1911. He was brought to Switzerland as a child; became engaged in the literary profession; was well known as a dramatist; from 1880 he was literary editor of the *Berner Bund;* wrote librettos. He was a friend of Brahms, and publ. *Johannes Brahms in Erinnerungen* (Berlin, 1898; new ed., Basel, 1947).

BIBLIOGRAPHY: E. and M. Widmann, *Joseph Viktor Widmann* (2 vols.; 1922, 1924); M. Waser, *Josef Viktor Widmann* (Leipzig, 1927).

Widor, Charles-Marie (-Jean-Albert), distinguished French organist, pedagogue, and composer; b. Lyons, Feb. 21, 1844; d. Paris, March 12, 1937. His father, an Alsatian of Hungarian descent, was organist at the church of St.-François, Lyons; as a boy, Widor was a skillful improviser on the organ; studied later in Brussels under Lemmens (organ) and Fétis (composition). Still a youth, he was appointed organist at his father's church in Lyons (1860), and gained high repute by concerts in provincial French cities. In 1869 he obtained the important post of organist at St.-Sulpice in Paris, holding it for more than 60 years, retiring in 1934. On April 19, 1934, he played at St. Sulpice his *Pièce mystique,* composed at the age of 90. In 1890 he succeeded César Franck as prof. of organ at the Paris Cons.; in 1896 became prof. of counterpoint, fugue, and composition. He was active also as a music critic for *L'Estafette* under the pen name *Aulétès;* also conducted the oratorio society Concordia. In 1910 he was elected a member of the Institute, of which he became permanent secretary in 1913. He had many distinguished pupils, including Albert Schweitzer, with whom he collaborated in editing the first 5 vols. of a definitive 8-vol. ed. of J. S. Bach's organ works (brought out by G. Schirmer, N.Y.); also edited the collection *L'Orgue moderne.* As a composer he wrote copiously in many forms, but is known best for his organ music, especially his 8 "symphonies" (suites); also the *Symphonie gothique* (op. 70) and the *Symphonie romaine* (op. 73).

WORKS: operas (all produced in Paris): *Maître Ambrose* (Opéra-Comique, May 6, 1886); *Les Pêcheurs de Saint-Jean* (Opéra-Comique, Dec. 26, 1905; his most successful opera); *Nerto* (Opéra, Oct. 27, 1924); incidental music to *Conte d'avril,* after Shakespeare's *Twelfth Night* (Odéon, Sept. 22, 1885); *Les Jacobites* (Nov. 21, 1885); etc.; a ballet, *La Korrigane* (Opéra, Dec. 1, 1880); symph. poem, *Une Nuit de Valpurgis* (London, April 19, 1888, composer conducting); 3 symphonies; *Symphonie antique* (with organ and final chorus); *Sinfonia sacra* (with organ); *Ouverture espagnole;* 2 piano concertos; Cello Concerto; *Fantaisie* for piano and orch.; *Choral et variations* for harp and orch.; chamber music; 2 piano quintets; String Quartet; Piano Trio; *Soirs d'Alsace* for piano trio; 2 violin sonatas; *Suite* for cello and piano; Cello Sonata; *Trois Valses* for cello and piano; *Trois Pièces* for cello and piano; for piano: *Airs de ballet; La Prière; Caprice; Trois Valses; Impromptu; Six Morceaux; Prélude, andante et finale; Scènes de bal; Six Valses caractéristiques; Douze Feuillets d'album; Dans les bois; Romance; Suite polonaise; Suite* in B minor; *Suite écossaise;* vocal music: Mass for 2 choirs and 2 organs; *Psalm 83* for chorus and string quintet; *Psalm 112* for 2 choirs, 2 organs, and orch.; *Tu es Petrus* for double chorus and organ; *Sacerdos et Pontifex* for chorus and organ; other church music; *Chant séculaire* for soprano, chorus, and orchestra; several song cycles, duets, choruses a cappella. He edited Berlioz's *Traité de l'instrumentation et d'orchestration modernes,* and wrote a supplement, *Technique de l'orchestre moderne* (1904; 2nd ed., 1906; in English, London, 1906 and 1946); published *Initiation musicale* (1923); *L'Orgue moderne* (1929); etc.

BIBLIOGRAPHY: H. Reynaud, *L'Œuvre de Charles-Marie Widor* (Lyons, 1900); J. F. E. Rupp, *Charles-Marie Widor und sein Werk* (Bremen, 1912); Isidor Philipp, "Charles-Marie Widor," *Musical Quarterly* (April 1944).

Wiechowicz, Stanislaw, Polish composer; b. Kroszyce, Nov. 27, 1893; d. Cracow, May 12, 1963. He studied successively in Cracow, Dresden, St. Petersburg and Paris; taught at the Poznán Cons. (1921–39); from 1945 to his death, taught at the State College of Music in Cracow.

WORKS: *Babie lato,* symph. poem (1922); *Chmiel (The Hopvine),* symph. scherzo (1926); *Ulegalki* for orch. (1944); *Kasia (Kitty),* folk suite for 2 clarinets and string orch. (1946); *Koncert staromiejski (Old Town Concerto)* for string orch. (1954); *Pastoralki,* recitation for chorus and orch. (1927); *Kantata romantyczna* (1930); *Kantata zniwna* (1948); *A czemuześ nie przyjechal? (Why Did You Not Come?),* rustic scene for chorus and orch. (1948); *List do Marc Chagalla (Letter to Marc Chagall),* dramatic rhapsody for soprano, mezzo-soprano, 2 narrators, chorus and orch. (1961); *Zstap, Golebico (O Dove, Descend),* cantata (1962–63); choruses.

Wieck, Alwin, German pianist; brother of **Clara Schumann**; b. Leipzig, Aug. 27, 1821; d. there, Oct. 21, 1885. He studied piano with his father, and violin with David; was a member of the Italian Opera orch. at St. Petersburg; then taught piano in Dresden. He publ. *Materialien zu F. Wiecks Pianoforte-Methodik* and *Vademecum perpetuum für den ersten Pianoforte-Unterricht nach F. Wiecks Methode;* also piano pieces.

Wieck, Friedrich, German pianist; father of **Clara Schumann**; b. Pretzsch, near Torgau, Aug. 18, 1785; d. Loschwitz, near Dresden, Oct. 6, 1873. He studied theology at Wittenberg, and at the same time pursued musical studies in private; established a piano factory and a circulating music library in Leipzig, but gave up both in order to devote himself to teaching the piano, in which profession he had extraordinary success.

Among his pupils were his daughters **Clara** and **Marie,** his son **Alwin,** Hans von Bülow, Fritz Spindler, Isidor Seiss, and Gustav Merkel. He was also Robert Schumann's teacher, but opposed bitterly Schumann's marriage to Clara. He settled in Dresden in 1840. In 1843 Mendelssohn offered him a professorship at the newly established Leipzig Cons., but Wieck declined. Wieck's first wife (*née* Tromlitz) was the mother of Clara Schumann and Alwin; after her divorce she married Bargiel, the father of Woldemar Bargiel; Marie Wieck was the daughter by Wieck's second wife, Clementine Fechner. He publ. 2 books of piano studies, and also *Clavier und Gesang* (1853; 3rd ed., 1878; also in English) and *Musikalische Bauernsprüche* (2nd ed., 1875, by Marie Wieck).

BIBLIOGRAPHY: A. von Meichsner, *Friedrich Wieck und seine beiden Töchter Clara und Marie* (Leipzig, 1875); A. Kohut, *Friedrich Wieck* (Dresden, 1887); V. Joss, *Friedrich Wieck und sein Verhältnis zu Robert Schumann* (Dresden, 1900); V. Joss, *Der Musikpädagoge Friedrich Wieck und seine Familie* (Dresden, 1902); Marie Wieck, *Aus dem Kreise Weick-Schumann* (Dresden, 1912; 2nd augmented ed., 1914).

Wieck, Marie, German pianist, daughter of **Friedrich Wieck**; b. Leipzig, Jan. 17, 1832; d. Dresden, Nov. 2, 1916. She studied with her father; at the age of 11 made her debut at a concert of her half-sister, **Clara Schumann;** appointed court pianist to the Prince of Hohenzollern in 1858; after tours of Germany, England, and Scandinavia, she settled in Dresden as a teacher of piano and singing; made prof. in 1914. Her last public appearance was with the Dresden Philharmonic Orch. in Nov., 1915, playing the Schumann Concerto. She publ. piano pieces and songs; edited her father's *Pianoforte-Studien;* and wrote *Aus dem Kreise Wieck-Schumann* (1912; 2nd augmented ed., 1914).

Wiedebein, Gottlob, German organist and conductor; b. Eilenstadt, July 27, 1779; d. Brunswick, April 17, 1854. After studying in Magdeburg, he settled in Brunswick as organist. He enjoyed a great reputation; Schumann sought his advice. He wrote some excellent lieder; was in correspondence with Beethoven, Schumann, and other composers; part of this correspondence was publ. in various German sources: *Die Musik* (1911), *Zeitschrift für Bücherfreunde* (1913), etc.

Wiedemann, Ernst Johann, German composer and teacher; b. Hohengiersdorf, Silesia, March 28, 1797; d. Potsdam, Dec. 7, 1873. From 1818 to 1852 he was organist of the Roman Catholic Church in Berlin; founded and conducted 2 singing societies there; composed a *Te Deum* for soli, chorus, and orch., Masses, motets, and hymns.

Wiederkehr, Jacob Christian Michael, Alsatian composer; b. Strasbourg, April 28, 1739; d. Paris, April 1823. From 1783 he was in Paris; played cello at the Concert Spirituel; bassoon at the Théâtre-Lyrique; trombone at the Opéra; taught singing at the Cons. (1795–1802). He composed 12 *concertantes* for wind instruments; 2 quintets and 10 quartets for strings; 6 quintets for piano and wind instruments; 6 pianos trios; 6 violin sonatas; etc.

Wiegand, (Josef Anton) Heinrich, German bass; b. Fränkisch-Crumbach in the Odenwald, Sept. 9, 1842; d. Frankfurt, May 28, 1899. He studied voice privately in Paris; became a member of the opera at Zürich in 1870; then sang in Cologne, and from 1873 to 1877 was leading bass at Frankfurt. In 1877 he toured America with the Adams-Pappenheim troupe; then was in Leipzig (1878–82); sang at the Vienna Court Opera (1882–84); then was engaged at Hamburg. He also appeared in the *Nibelung* cycle in Berlin (1881) and London (1882).

Wiehmayer, (Johann) Theodor, German pianist; b. Marienfeld, Jan. 7, 1870; d. Starnberg, March 15, 1947. He studied at the Leipzig Cons. under Jadassohn (composition) and Reinecke (piano). After his debut in Leipzig (1890) he undertook a successful tour in Sweden; then settled in Leipzig as a teacher, also giving concerts in other towns; 1902–06, teacher of piano in the Leipzig Cons.; from 1908 to 1925 at the Stuttgart Cons. Author of *Muskialische Rhythmik und Metrik* (1917) and *Musikalische Foremenlehre in Analysen* (1927); publ. technical studies for piano.

Wiel, Taddeo, Italian musicologist and composer; b. Oderzo, Treviso, Sept. 24, 1849; d. Venice, Feb. 17, 1920. He studied in Venice; became assistant librarian at San Marco; publ. valuable papers on Venetian music history: *I Codici contariniani nella R. Biblioteca di San Marco in Venezia* (1888); *I Teatri musicali veneziani del settecento* (1897); *Francesco Cavalli Musical* (Venice, 1914).

Wielhorsky, Count Mikhail, Russian patron of arts; b. Volynia, Nov. 12, 1788; d. Moscow, Sept. 9, 1856. His home in St. Petersburg was the gathering place of the most eminent musicians of the time. He wrote a string quartet and some songs, one of which, *Autrefois,* was arranged for piano by Liszt (1843). His brother, **Matvey Wielhorsky** (1794–1866), was a cellist; a distant relative, **Joseph Wielhorsky** (1817–92), wrote piano pieces and songs (48 op. numbers).

Wieniawski, Adam Tadeusz, Polish composer, nephew of **Henri** and **Joseph Wieniawski;** b. Warsaw, Nov. 27, 1879; d. Bydgoszcz, April 21, 1950. He studied in Warsaw with Melcer and Noskowski; then in Berlin with Bargiel, and in Paris with Vincent d'Indy, Fauré, and Gédalge. He fought in the French Army during World War I; returned to Warsaw in 1923; was appointed director of the Chopin School of Music in 1928.
WORKS: operas: *Megae* (Warsaw, Dec. 28, 1912); *Wyzwolony* (Warsaw, 1928); *Król Kochanek* (Warsaw, March 19, 1931); the ballets *Lalita* and *Le Festin chez Hérode* (1927); symph. poems *Kamaralmazan* (Paris, 1910) and *Princesse Baudour; Suite Polonaise* for orch. (1913); *Obrazki,* piano suite (also for orch.); arrangements of folksongs.

Wieniawski, Henryk (Henri), famous Polish violinist; b. Lublin, July 10, 1835; d. Moscow, March 31, 1880. His mother, Regina Wolff-Wieniawska, was a talented pianist; on the advice of her brother, **Eduard Wolff,** pianist and composer who lived in France, she took Henryk to Paris, where he entered the Cons. at the age of 8, first in Clavel's class, and the following year, in the advanced class of Massart. At the age of 11 he graduated with 1st prize in violin, an unprecedented event in the annals of the Paris Cons. He gave his 1st concert in St. Petersburg on March 31, 1848, and played 3 more concerts there; then played in Finland and the Baltic provinces; after several successful appearances in Warsaw, he returned in 1849 to Paris, where he studied composition with Hippolyte Collet at the Cons., graduating (again with 1st prize) in 1850. He then traveled with his brother **Joseph** in Russia (1850–55); in 1859, appointed solo violinst to the Czar; taught at the newly founded St. Petersburg Cons. (1862–67); played the viola in the Ernst String Quartet. In 1872 he went on a tour of the U.S. with Anton Rubinstein; one of the featured works was Beethoven's *Kreutzer Sonata,* which they performed about 70 times. When Rubinstein returned to Europe, Wieniawski continued his American tour, which included California. He returned to Europe in 1874, gave several concerts with Rubinstein in Paris, and in the same year succeeded Vieuxtemps as prof. of violin playing at the Brussels Cons., resigning in 1877 owing to an increasingly grave heart condition; suffered a heart attack during a concert in Berlin in 1878, but still agreed to play several concerts in Moscow, where he remained until his death at the age of 44. He was married to Isobel Hampton, an Englishwoman; their youngest daughter Irene wrote music under the pen name **Poldowski.** He was undoubtedly one of the greatest violinists of the 19th century; he possessed a virtuoso technique and an extraordinary range of dynamics. He was equally distinguished as a chamber-music player. Many of his compositions are in the repertory of every violinist; of these the most famous are concerto in D minor; *Légende* for violin and orch.; *Souvenir de Moscou,* on Russian themes, for violin and orch.; and *Le Carnaval russe,* for violin and piano. Other works include (for violin and orch.): Concerto in F-sharp minor; *Polonaise; Scherzo-Tarentelle; Fantaisie brillante* (on themes from Gounod's *Faust*); *Polonaise brillante;* for violin and piano: *Caprice fantastique, Souvenir der Posen; Adagio élégiaque; Capriccio-Valse; Romance sans paroles et Rondo élégant;* 2 mazurkas; *Gigue; Études-Caprices* for 2 violins; etc. With his brother Joseph he wrote *Allegro de sonate* and *Grand duo polonais.*
BIBLIOGRAPHY: A. Desfossez, *Henri Wieniawski: esquisse* (The Hague, 1856); J. Reiss, *Henryk Wieniawski* (Warsaw, 1931); I. Yampolski, *Henryk Wieniawski* (Moscow, 1955); W. Reiss, *H. Wieniawski* (Cracow, 1962).

Wieniawski, Joseph, Polish pianist and composer, brother of **Henryk Wieniawski;** b. Lublin, May 23, 1837; d. Brussels, Nov. 11, 1912. He studied at the Paris Cons. with Zimmerman, Marmontel, and Alkan (piano), and LeCouppey (composition); in 1851 he went on tour with his brother, Henryk; studied with

Liszt at Weimar (1855–56), and returned to Paris in 1858. In 1866 he settled in Moscow as a teacher at the Cons., but soon established a piano school of his own, which flourished. In 1875–76 he was director of the Warsaw Music Society; then settled in Brussels, teaching at the Cons. He also made numerous concert tours throughout Europe.

WORKS: *Suite romantique,* for orch.; *Guillaume le Taciturne,* overture; Piano Concerto; String Quartet; Piano Trio; *Grand duo polonais,* for piano and violin (with his brother); Cello Sonata; *Fantasia,* for 2 pianos; for piano solo: 4 polonaises; 5 waltzes; Sonata in B minor; mazurkas; *Fantaisie et fugue; Sur l'Océan; Barcarole; Ballade; Notturno; Barcarole-Caprice, Romanze-Etüde,* etc.; also *24 Études de mécanisme et de style.*

BIBLIOGRAPHY: L. Delcroix, *Joseph Wieniawski. Notices biographiques et anecdotiques* (Brussels, 1908).

Wieprecht, Friedrich Wilhelm, German trombonist and inventor; b. Aschersleben, Aug. 8, 1802; d. Berlin, Aug. 4, 1872. He studied in Dresden and Leipzig, where he was already famous as a trombonist. He invented the bass tuba (1835, with the instrument maker Moritz), the bathyphon, a sort of bass clarinet (1839, with Skorra), the "piangendo" on brass instruments with pistons, and an improved contrabass bassoon; his claim of priority over Sax, in the invention of the saxhorns, was not upheld by the courts.

BIBLIOGRAPHY: A. Kalkbrenner, *F. W. Wieprecht* (1888).

Wier, Albert Ernest, American music editor; b. Chelsea, Mass., July 22, 1879; d. Brooklyn, Sept. 8, 1945. He studied music at the New England Cons. and at Harvard Univ.; from 1900 was music ed. for various publishing firms in N.Y.; brought out a large number of collections and arrangements: *Whole World Music Series, The Pianist's Music Shelf, The Violinist's Music Shelf, Young Folks' Music Library, Radio Music Library,* etc.; devised the "arrow signal" system, in which arrows and other markings are added to orchestral scores to identify the main themes; using this system he issued numerous collections: *Classic Violin Concertos, The 9 Symphonies of Beethoven, The Symphonies of Brahms and Tschaikowsky, The Valkyrie,* etc.; also ed. *The Macmillan Encyclopedia of Music and Musicians* (1938; withdrawn from circulation owing to an excessive number of demonstrable errors) and other reference works of questionable scholarship.

Wiesengrund-Adorno, Theodor. See **Adorno, Theodor.**

Wigglesworth, Frank, American composer; b. Boston, March 3, 1918. He studied at Columbia Univ. and at Converse College, Spartanburg, South Carolina; also took lessons in New York with Henry Cowell and Otto Luening. He was in the U.S. Army Air Force during World War II; then taught at Columbia Univ. (1947–51) and Queens College (1954–55). He is a great-nephew of Mrs. Elizabeth Sprague Coolidge.

WORKS: 2 symphonies (1955; 1958); *Creation,* for chorus and small orch. (1940); *New England Concerto,* for violin and strings (1941); *The Plunger,* for soprano, flute, viola, cello, and piano (1941); Trio for flute, banjo, and harp (1942); *Jeremiah,* for baritone, chorus, and orch. (1942); *Sleep Becalmed,* for chorus and orch., after Dylan Thomas (1948); *3 Movements* for string orch. (1949); *Telesis,* for chamber orch. and percussion (1949); *Serenade* for flute, viola, and guitar (1952); Brass Quintet (1957).

Wihan, Hans (Hanuš), Czech cellist; b. Politz, near Braunau, Bohemia, June 5, 1855; d. Prague, May 1, 1920. He studied at the Prague Cons.; as a young man, he became instructor of cello at the Mozarteum, Salzburg; then was chamber musician in various courts in Germany; in 1880 he became member of the private string quartet of King Ludwig of Bavaria, and frequently played at Wagner's soirées at Wahnfried; from 1888 he was prof. of cello at the Prague Cons. In 1891 he formed the Bohemian String Quartet, selecting his four most talented pupils (Karel Hoffmann, Josef Suk, Oscar Nedbal, and Otto Berger); after Berger's retirement, owing to ill health, in 1897, Wihan himself took his place as cellist (until 1914); the Bohemian String Quartet for years enjoyed the highest reputation.

Wihtol (Vitols), Joseph, foremost Latvian composer and pedagogue; b. Volmar, July 26, 1863; d. Lübeck, April 24, 1948. He studied at the St. Petersburg Cons. (1880–86) with Rimsky-Korsakov; after graduation, was engaged as instructor there; succeeded Rimsky-Korsakov in 1908 as prof. of composition; among his students were Prokofiev and Miaskovsky. He was also music critic for the German daily *St. Petersburger Zeitung.* In 1918 he left St. Petersburg; was for a season director of the Latvian Opera in Riga; in 1919 founded the National Cons. there; many Latvian composers were his students. As the Soviet armies approached Riga (1944), Wihtol went to Germany, remaining there until his death. In his music he followed the harmonic practices of the Russian school, but often employed Latvian folksong patterns. Most of his works were publ. by Belaieff.

WORKS: Symphony (St. Petersburg, Dec. 17, 1887); *La Fête Ligho,* symph. tableau (1890); *Beverinas dziedonis (The Bard of Beverin),* for chorus and orch. (1891); *Ouverture dramatique* (1895); *Gaismas pils (The Castle of Light),* for chorus and orch. (1899); *Upe un cilvēka dzīve (River and Human Life),* for chorus (1903); *Spriditis,* Latvian fairy tale for orch. (1908); the cantatas *Song* (1908) and *Aurora Borealis* (1914); arrangements of 200 Latvian songs for voice and piano and for piano solo (2 books; 1906, 1919); many Latvian choral ballads; a string quartet; *10 Chants populaires lettons,* "miniature paraphrases" for piano; songs.

BIBLIOGRAPHY: O. Gravitis, *Latvian Composers* (Riga, 1955; in Russian; pp. 30–39); a volume of reminiscences, articles and letters of Wihtol were published in Russian in Leningrad (1969).

Wijdeveld, Wolfgang, Dutch composer and pianist; b. The Hague, May 9, 1910. He is the son of the noted Dutch architect Hendricus Wijdeveld. He studied piano with Willem Andriessen, theory with Sem Dresden, and violin with Kint at the Amsterdam Cons.; also took private lessons in composition with Willem Pijper. He was director of the Cons. at Zwolle (1940-46); taught piano at the Utrecht Cons. (1946-76); was music critic for the Amsterdam newspaper *Het Vrije Volk* (1956-68). He toured the U.S. in 1939 with the Yvonne Georgi Ballet as a pianist and composer; gave concerts and seminars at 15 North American universities (1962-63).

WORKS: *Psalm 150* for chorus and orch. (1950); *Concertstük* for wind quintet and strings (1952); *Matrooslied* for chorus and small orch. (1966); Wind Quintet (1934); Trio for flute, oboe, and bassoon (1958); Concerto for Guitar and String Trio (1960); Sonata for 2 violins and piano (1952); Violin Sonata (1948); *Sonatine Simple* for violin and piano (1952); *Introduction and Caprice* for violin and piano (1956); Flute Sonatina (1948); *Snarenspel* for guitar and piano (1958); Sonatina for solo accordion (1963); 3 piano sonatas: No. 1 (1940), No. 2 (1956), and No. 3, *For Americans* (1963); 2 piano sonatinas (1946, 1953); *Escapades* for piano (1944-45); *Kermesse*, ballet music for 2 pianos (1935); *Notebooks I, II, III, IV* for piano (1968-69); *Notebook V* for harpsichord (1968); *Introduction and Gigue* for organ (1949); *3 Songs*, after Walt Whitman, for 2 voices, violin, viola, clarinet, and piano (1949); other songs.

Wijk, Arnold. See **Wyk, Arnold van.**

Wiklund, Adolf, Swedish composer and conductor; b. Langserud, June 5, 1879; d. Stockholm, April 2, 1950. He studied with J. Lindegren (composition) and R. Andersson (piano) at the Stockholm Cons.; was granted a state fellowhip for study abroad; took lessons with James Kwast in Berlin (piano); was engaged as opera coach in Berlin; returning to Sweden in 1911, he became 2nd conductor of the Stockholm Opera; then led the Stockholm Court Orch. (1923-25) and the Concert Society (1925-38); was also guest conductor in London and Jena. He composed a symph. (1922); 2 piano concertos (1906; 1916); a *Konzertstück* for piano and orch. (1902); a symph. poem, *Sommarnatt och soluppgang* (1918); *Little Suite* for orch. (1928); *3 Pieces* for string orch. (1924); a violin sonata (1906); several albums of lyric pieces for piano; songs.

Wikmanson, Johan, Swedish organist and composer; b. Stockholm, Dec. 28, 1753; d. there, Jan. 10, 1800. He was trained as an engineer, but also studied music; played organ in Stockholm churches; took composition lessons with J. M. Kraus. He wrote 5 string quartets; 2 piano sonatas; songs. His style closely approximates that of Haydn.

BIBLIOGRAPHY: G. S. Möner, *Johan Wikmanson* (Stockholm, 1952).

Wilbye, John, one of the greatest English madrigalists; b. Diss, Norfolk, 1574 (baptized March 7); d. Colchester, Sept., 1638. From 1595 until 1628 he was resident musician at Hengrave Hall, the home of Sir Thomas Kytson, near Bury St. Edmunds. After the death of Lady Kytson (1628), Wilbye settled in Colchester. He made frequent visits to London, where the

Kytsons had a town house. His 1st book of madrigals (for 3, 4, 5, and 6 voices) appeared in 1598 (reprinted London, 1841); it contains 30 compositions; his 2nd book, containing 34 madrigals (also for 3 to 6 voices) came out in 1609 (reprinted London, 1846). To Leighton's *Teares or Lamentations* (1614) he contributed 2 hymns, and for *The Triumphes of Oriana* he wrote a 6-part madrigal, *The Lady Oriana*. His madrigals were reprinted in vols. 6/7 of *The English Madrigal School.*

BIBLIOGRAPHY: E. H. Fellowes, *The English Madrigal Composers* (1921; 2nd ed., 1948); H. Heurich, *John Wilbye in seinen Madrigalen* (Augsburg, 1931); P. Johnson, *Form and Transformation in the Music and Poetry of the English Renaissance* (New Haven, 1972); D. Brown, *Wilbye* (Oxford Studies of Composers 11; London, 1974).

Wilckens, Friedrich, Austrian pianist and composer; b. Liezen, April 13, 1899. He studied piano with Lalewicz in Vienna and composition with Franz Schreker there and in Berlin (1916-20); in 1933 he settled in Seefeld. As a ballet pianist, he made 17 tours in the U.S. and 3 tours in South America. He wrote several ballets (*Himmel und Erde, Schwingender Tempel,* etc.), film music; piano pieces. He retired in 1960 and lived in Tyrol.

Wildberger, Jacques, Swiss composer; b. Basel, Jan. 3, 1922. He studied piano at the Basel Cons., and took lessons in composition with Wladimir Vogel (1948-52); then went to Germany, where he was active as a music teacher in Karlsruhe (1956-66); in 1967 he was appointed a lecturer in harmony and instrumentation at the Basel Musical Academy. In his music he observes the formal traditions of the Baroque, but develops a highly intricate system of interrelated tones, intervals, and rhythms, resulting in a *sui generis* serial system, with a total emancipation of dissonances.

WORKS: Quartet for flute, clarinet, violin, and cello (1952); *Tre mutazioni* for chamber orch. (1953); Trio for oboe, clarinet, and bassoon (1953); *Vom Kommen und Gehen des Menschen,* cantata (1954); *Concertrum* for harpsichord (1956); *Ihr meint, das Leben sei kurz,* cantata for chorus and 10 instruments (1957); *Intensio—Centrum—Remissio* for orch. (1958); *Zeitebenen* for 8 instruments (1958); *Musik* for cello and piano (1960); *Musik* for 22 solo strings (1960); *Rondeau* for solo oboe (1962); *Épitaphe pour Evariste Galois,* "documented action" commemorating a mathematical genius killed in a duel at the age of 20, scored for narrator, soprano, baritone, speaking chorus, tape, and orch. (1962; Basel, May 20, 1964); Oboe Concerto (1963); *In My End is My Beginning,* cantata after T. S. Eliot, for soprano, tenor, and chamber orch. (1964); *Mouvements* for orch. (1964); Quartet for flute, oboe, harp, and piano (1967); *Rencontres* for flute and piano (1967); *La Notte,* trittico for tape, mezzo-soprano, and 5 instruments (1967); *Contratempi* for solo flute and 4 orch. groups (1970); *Double Refrain* for flute, English horn, guitar, and tape (1972); *Pour les neuf doigts* for solo oboe (1973); *Vision fugitive* for piano (1973); *Die Stimme, die alte, schwächer werdende Stimme* for soprano, cello, tape, and orch.

(1974); *Diario* for solo clarinet (1975); *Prismes* for solo saxophone (1975); *Schattenwerk* for organ (1976).

Wilder, Alec, American composer; b. Rochester, N.Y., Feb. 16, 1907. He studied composition with Herbert Inch and Edward Royce; was then active in New York City as a composer for the theater, radio, and films; wrote popular songs and arranged music for Frank Sinatra, Judy Garland, Perry Como, Peggy Lee, and the bands of Benny Goodman and Jimmy Dorsey. Wilder excels particularly in short operas scored for a limited ensemble of singers and instruments and suitable for performance in schools; most of his serious compositions, especially his chamber music, are in an affable, hedonistic, and ingratiating style.
WORKS: operas, operettas, musical comedies and theater cantatas, including *The Lowland Sea* (1951), *Sunday Excursion* (1952), *Cumberland Fair* (1953), *Miss Chicken Little* (1953), *The Opening, Kittiwake Island* (1954), *Ellen* (1955), *The Impossible Forest, The Churkendoose, Racketty Packetty House,* and *Herman Ermine in Rabbit Town; 8 Songs* for voice and orch. (Rochester, June 8, 1928); *Symphonic Piece* for orch. (Rochester, June 3, 1929); a ballet, *Juke Box* (1942); *Suite* for clarinet and strings (1947); Concerto for Oboe and Strings (1950); *Beginner's Luck* for wind ensemble (1953); 2 concertos for horn and chamber orch. (1954, 1960); 4 works entitled *An Entertainment:* No. 1 for wind ensemble (1961), No. 2 for orch., No. 3 for wind ensemble, and No. 4 for horn and chamber orch. (1971); 2 concertos for trumpet and wind ensemble; Concerto for Tuba and Wind Ensemble; *Suite* for horn and strings (1965); *Suite* for saxophone and strings (1965); Concerto for Saxophone and Chamber Orch. (1967); *Air* for horn and small wind ensemble (1968); *Children's Plea for Peace* for narrator, chorus and orch. (1969); Concerto for Euphonium and Wind Ensemble (1971). Chamber music: Nonet for brass (1969); 10 wind quintets (1953–72); 4 brass quintets; quintets, quartets, trios, duets (many called *Suites*) for numerous wind and brass instruments; 2 flute sonatas (1958, 1962); Clarinet Sonata (1963); 3 bassoon sonatas (1964, 1968, 1973); Saxophone Sonata (1960); 3 horn sonatas (1954, 1957, 1965); sonatas for viola, cello, string bass, oboe, English horn, trumpet, trombone, bass trombone, euphonium, and tuba; piano pieces (Sonata; *12 Mosaics; A Debutante's Diary; Neurotic Goldfish; Walking Home in the Spring,* etc.); many songs. He wrote the book *American Popular Song. The Great Innovations, 1900–1950* (N.Y., 1972).

Wilder, (Jérôme Albert) Victor (van), Belgian writer on music; b. Wetteren, near Ghent, Aug. 21, 1835; d. Paris, Sept. 8, 1892. He was a journalist; contributed articles to various publications in Paris, where he settled; wrote librettos; translated Wagner's texts into French, including *Der Ring des Nibelungen;* wrote *Mozart, l'homme et l'artiste* (Paris, 1880; English transl., 1908) and *Beethoven, sa vie et ses œuvres* (Paris, 1883).

Wilderer, Johann Hugo von, German composer; b. in Bavaria, c.1670; d. Mannheim, 1724 (buried, June 7, 1724). He studied with Legrenzi in Venice; was court organist in Düsseldorf and Mannheim. He wrote operas to Italian libretti; of these, *La Forza del Giusto* had a modicum of success. He also composed sacred music.
BIBLIOGRAPHY: G. Steffen, *Johann Hugo Wilderer* (Cologne, 1960).

Wildgans, Friedrich, Austrian composer; b. Vienna, June 5, 1913; d. Mödling, near Vienna, Nov. 7, 1965. He studied with J. Marx; taught at the Salzburg Mozarteum (1934–36); then played clarinet at the Vienna Opera; 1945–47, prof. at the Vienna State Academy of Music. He has written music in all genres, in an ultramodern style, eventually adopting the 12-tone technique. In 1946 he married the Austrian soprano **Ilona Steingruber.**
WORKS: opera, *Der Baum der Erkenntniss* (1935); choral symph. *Mayakovsky* (1946); *Sinfonia Austriaca;* 2 clarinet concertos; 3 piano sonatas; chamber music and choruses; author of *Entwicklung der Musik in Österreich im 20. Jahrhundert* (Vienna, 1950).

Wilding-White, Raymond, American composer; b. Caterham, Surrey, England, Oct. 9, 1922. He studied at the Juilliard School of Music, N.Y. (1947–49) and at the New England Cons. (1949–51); spent the summers of 1949, 1950, and 1951 at Tanglewood studying with Ibert, Dallapiccola, and Copland. He was a producer-director of radio and TV in Boston (1951–56); held the Kulas Chair of Music at Case Institute of Technology in Cleveland (1961–67); in 1967 was appointed to the faculty of DePaul Univ. in Chicago, where he founded a multimedia ensemble, "The Loop Group."
WORKS: a ballet, *The Trees,* for wind quartet, brass, percussion, and piano (1949); a chamber opera, *The Tub,* for soloists and piano (1952); *The Selfish Giant,* fable for television (1952; Cleveland, 1965); *The Lonesome Valley,* ballet for organ and percussion (1960); opera, *Yerma* (1962); *Monday Morning at the Gargoyle Works,* "action-piece" for 5 performers (1968); Piano Concerto (1949); *Even Now,* variations for baritone and orch. (1954); Concertante for violin, horn, and strings (1963); *Bandmusic* for concert band (1966); *Haiku* for soprano, tenor and instruments (1967); *Whatzit* No. 4 (for Louis Lane) for orch. and tape (1969); 10 other *Whatzits,* mostly for a particular solo performer, usually accompanied by tape (1967–75); String Quartet (1948); Piano Sonata (1950); Violin Sonata (1956); *Variations* for chamber organ and string trio (1959); *Paraphernalia,* a regalia of madrigalia from Pound, for chorus, trumpet, oboe, clarinet, violin, and harpsichord (1959); *For Mallets* for percussion ensemble (1962); *5 Fragments* for jazz ensemble (1966); *Movement* for string quartet (1973); songs; a cappella works; electronic pieces.

Wilhelm, Carl Friedrich, German choral composer; b. Schmalkalden, Sept. 5, 1815; d. there, Aug. 26, 1873. From 1839 to 1864 he was director of the Crefeld Liedertafel, for which he composed many men's choruses, among them *Die Wacht am Rhein,* which became a national song of the Germans; it was first performed by the Liedertafel on June 11, 1854, and first publ. in the *Chorliedersammlung* of Erk and Greef (Essen, 1854). In 1860 he received the title of "Royal

Prussian Music Director"; in 1870 he was granted a pension of 3,000 marks.

BIBLIOGRAPHY: K. Gollmick, *C. F. Wilhelm* (Frankfurt, 1848); W. Buchner, *C. F. Wilhelm* (Leipzig, 1874); G. Rogati, *Carl Wilhelm* (dissertation; Bonn, 1827).

Wilhelmj, August (Emil Daniel Ferdinand), famous violin virtuoso; b. Usingen, Germany, Sept. 21, 1845; d. London, Jan. 22, 1908. He received his earliest instruction in music from his mother, who was an amateur pianist; then studied violin with Konrad Fischer, court musician at Wiesbaden; made his 1st appearance there as a child prodigy on Jan. 8, 1854. In 1861, at the recommendation of Liszt, he was sent to the Leipzig Cons., where he studied with Ferdinand David (violin), Hauptmann and Richter (theory); in 1864 he went to Frankfurt for an additional course with Raff; in 1865 he began his concert career, touring Switzerland; then played in Holland and England (1866), France and Italy (1867), Russia, Switzerland, France, and Belgium (1869), England, Scotland, and Ireland (1869–70); then traveled through Holland, Scandinavia, Germany, and Austria (1871–74), to England (1875–77), and America (1878), making a 4-year tour of the world to South America, Australia, and Asia (1878–82). In 1876 he was concertmaster of the Bayreuth orch. at the production of *Der Ring des Nibelungen.* For several years he lived chiefly at Biebrich-am-Rhine, where he established (with R. Niemann) a master school for violin playing. In 1886 he moved to Blasewitz, near Dresden; in 1894 was appointed prof. of violin playing in the Guildhall School of Music, London. His first wife, whom he married in 1866, was Baroness Liphardt, a niece of Ferdinand David; in 1895 he married the pianist **Mariella Mausch.** He made a famous arrangement of Bach's air from the orch. *Suite* in D major which became known as the *Air on the G String* (Bach's original bore no such specification); also arranged Wagner's *Träume* for violin and orch.; wrote a cadenza to Beethoven's violin concerto; further composed for violin and orch. 2 *Konzertstücke* (No. 2, *In Memoriam*), *Alla Polacca,* and theme and variations (after 2 caprices of Paganini); *Romanze* for piano; songs. With James Brown he publ. *A Modern School for the Violin* (6 parts).

BIBLIOGRAPHY: E. Frassinesi, *August Wilhelmj Violinista. Memorie* (Mirandola, 1913); E. Wagner, *Der Geigerkönig August Wilhelmj* (Homburg, 1928).

Wilhem (real name **Bocquillon**), **Guillaume-Louis,** French music educator; b. Paris, Dec. 18, 1781; d. there, April 26, 1842. The son of an army officer, he himself entered active service at the age of 12; but from 1795–1801 studied at the school of Liancourt, and then for 2 years in the Paris Cons. He taught music in the military school of Saint-Cyr, and in 1810 was appointed teacher of music at the Lycée Napoléon (later Collège Henri IV), occupying this position until death. The system of *enseignement mutuel* (mutual instruction), which had been introduced into the popular schools of France, attracted Wilhem's attention; in 1815 he began to apply it in music teaching and met with such marked success that in 1819 he was chosen to organize a system of music instruction

for the primary schools in Paris; was appointed singing teacher to the Polytechnique in 1820, and director of a Normal School of Music. In 1833 he conceived the idea of instituting regular reunions of the pupils in one grand chorus to which he gave the name of "Orphéon." In 1835 he was made director general of music instruction in all primary schools of Paris, and was created a Chevalier of the Legion of Honor. Besides his school classes, he formed classes of adults, chiefly workingmen, in which the success of his system was equally conspicuous, and which later, under the name of "Orphéons," included several popular singing societies. He publ. numerous songs and choruses; also a collection of a cappella choruses, *Orphéon,* in 5 (later 10) vols.; and 4 textbooks.

BIBLIOGRAPHY: E. Niboyet, *Notice historique sur la vie et les ouvrages de G. L. B. Wilhem* (Paris, 1843); J. A. La Fage, *Notice sur Bocquillon-Wilhem* (Paris, 1845).

Wilke, Christian Friedrich Gottlieb, German organist and organ builder; b. Spandau, March 13, 1769; d. Treuenbrietzen, Aug. 1, 1848. He was organist in Spandau from 1791; in 1821, government expert on organ building. He publ. *Beiträge zur Geschichte der neuen Orgelbaukunst* (1846); *Über Wichtigkeit und Unentbehrlichkeit der Orgelmixturen* (1839).

Wilkes, Josué Teófilo, Argentine composer and musicologist; b. Buenos Aires, Jan. 8, 1883; d. there, Jan. 10, 1968. He studied with Alberto Williams; in 1908 went to Europe for further study; took some lessons from Liapunov in St. Petersburg, and also at the Schola Cantorum in Paris; returned to Argentina in 1914; for many years taught music in primary schools in Buenos Aires. He made a special study of Gregorian Chant; also transcribed and harmonized old colonial songs; composed 3 operas, *Nuite persane* (1916–20), *Por el cetro y la corona,* Byzantine tragedy after *Bajazet* of Racine (1924), *El Horoscopo* (after Calderón; 1926–27); a secular oratorio, *La Cautiva;* a symph. trilogy, *Humahuaca* (1911–14); a string octet; other chamber music; songs; *50 Canciones populares cuyanas* (arranged and harmonized), *Cancionero musical rioplatense* (Argentine dances). With I. Guerrero Cárpena he published *Formas musicales rioplatenses* (Buenos Aires, 1946).

Willaert, Adrian, important Flemish composer; b. Bruges, c.1490; d. Venice, Dec. 8, 1562. He went to Paris in 1514 to study law; studied music there with Jean Mouton; then traveled in Italy. He was in the service of Duke Alfonso I d'Este at Ferrara in 1522; in the spring of 1525 was attached to the court of Ippolito II d'Este, Archbishop of Milan. He became maestro di cappella at St. Mark's in Venice on Dec. 12, 1527; with the exception of 2 visits to Flanders (1542 and 1556), he remained in Venice, where he established a singing school, which flourished; among his famous pupils were Zarlino, Cipriano de Rore, and Andrea Gabrieli. He is justly regarded as the founder of the great Venetian school of composition; the style of writing for 2 antiphonal choirs (prompted by the 2 opposed organs of St. Mark's Cathedral) was initiated by Willaert; he was one of the greatest masters of the madrigal and of the instrumental *ricercar;* also publ. motets, *canzone*, vesper psalms, and Masses. His *Sämtliche Werke* were edited by H. Zenck as vol. 9 of *Publication älterer Musik;* his *Opera omnia,* edited by H. Zenck and W. Gerstenberg, in 15 vols. as *Corpus mensurabilis musicae* 3 (American Institute of Musicology); Zenck also publ. *9 ricercari per sonar con tre stromenti* (Mainz, 1933); other reprints are found in Blume's *Das Chorwerk* 59 and 105 (ed. by Wiora and Hertzmann).

BIBLIOGRAPHY: Ch. Carton, *Notice sur Adr. Willaert* (Bruges, 1849); E. Gregoir, *A. Willaert* (Antwerp, 1869); A. Averkamp, "Adrian Willaert," *Tijdschrift der Vereeniging voor Nederlandsche Muziekgeschiedenis* (1922); H. Zenck, *Studien zu A. Willaert* (Leipzig, 1929); E. Hertzmann, *Adrian Willaert in der weltlichen Vokalmusik seiner Zeit* (Leipzig, 1931); Otto Gombosi, in *Zeitschrift für Musikwissenschaft* XVI/54; R. Lenaerts, *Notes sur Adrian Willaert* (Brussels, 1935); René Vannes, *Dictionnaire des musiciens* (Brussels, 1947); G. Reese, *Music in the Renaissance* (N.Y., 1954).

Willan, Healey, eminent English-born Canadian composer, organist and music educator; b. Balham, Surrey, Oct. 12, 1880; d. Toronto, Feb. 16, 1968. He received his musical training at St. Saviour's Choir School in Eastbourne (1888–1895); was a church organist in London until 1913, when he went to Canada as head of the theory department at the Royal Cons. in Toronto; was vice-principal there (1920–36). In 1914 he was appointed lecturer and examiner at the Univ. of Toronto; 1937, prof. of music; retired in 1950; was also the Univ. organist (1932–64) and organist of St. Mary Magdalene Church in Toronto from 1921 until his death; founder and conductor of the Tudor Singers (1934–39). In 1956 he was awarded the historic Lambeth Doctorate by the Archbishop of Canterbury, and in 1967 was the first musician to receive the Companion of the Order of Canada. He was greatly esteemed as a pedagogue.

WORKS: 2 radio operas, *Transit through Fire* (1941–42; Canadian Radio, March 8, 1942) and *Deirdre* (1943–45; Canadian Radio, April 20, 1946; revised in 1962 and 1965; first stage performance, Toronto, 1965); a historical pageant, *Brébeuf and His Brethren* (CBC Radio, Sept. 26, 1943); several ballad-operas; 2 symphonies: No. 1 (Toronto, Oct. 8, 1936); and No. 2 (1941, revised 1948; Toronto, May 18, 1950); Piano Concerto (Montreal, Aug. 24, 1944; revised 1949); *Agincourt Song* for chorus and small orch. (1929); *Overture to an Unwritten Comedy* (1951); several ceremonial pieces, including *Coronation March* for orch. (1937), *Te Deum Laudamus* for chorus and small orch. (1937), *Coronation Suite* for chorus and orch. (1952), *Royal Salute* for orch. (1959), and *Centennial March* for orch. (1967); *Royce Hall Suite* for symph. band (1949); 2 violin sonatas (1920, 1923); several character pieces for piano; organ works; carols and hymn tunes; church services; motets a cappella; anthems with organ accompaniment; many other choral works; songs; arrangements of Canadian and British songs; school manuals. See catalogue by Giles Bryant, *Healey Willan* (Toronto, 1972).

Willeke, Willem, Dutch-American cellist; b. The Hague, Sept. 29, 1879; d. Pittsfield, Mass., Nov. 26, 1950. He studied cello in Holland; then was cellist in various German orchestras; also at the Vienna Opera (under Mahler). In 1908 he came to the U.S. and joined the Kneisel Quartet, with which he remained until its disbandment in 1917; taught at the Institute of Musical Art, N.Y.; then was appointed director of the Berkshire Music Colony, in Pittsfield, Mass., where he remained until his death.

Willent-Bordogni, Jean-Baptiste-Joseph, French bassoon virtuoso; b. Douai, Dec. 8, 1809; d. Paris, May 11, 1852. He studied with Delcambre at the Paris Cons.; played the bassoon in the orch. of the Théâtre Italien in Paris; married the daughter of the singing teacher Bordogni (1834) and added her name to his; taught at the Brussels Cons.; in 1848 was appointed to the faculty of the Paris Cons. He wrote a number of works for the bassoon, and publ. a method for it; also brought out 2 operas in Brussels: *Le Moine* (1844) and *Van Dyck* (1845).

Williams, Alberto, foremost Argentine composer; b. Buenos Aires, Nov. 23, 1862; d. there, June 17, 1952. He was a grandson of an Englishman; his maternal grandfather, **Amancio Alcorta**, was one of Argentina's early composers. Williams studied composition at the Paris Cons. with Guiraud, Durand, and Godard, piano with Mathias (a pupil of Chopin), and organ and counterpoint with César Franck. He returned to Argentina in 1889; founded the Alberto Williams Cons. in 1893; also organized branches in provincial towns of Argentina, numbering more than 100; founded a music publishing firm La Quena (also a music magazine of that name). He was the most prolific composer of Argentina; 112 op. numbers were publ. by La Quena. The greatest influence in his music was that of César Franck, but modernistic usages are found in his application of whole-tone scales, parallel chord progressions, etc. In many of his works he used characteristic melorhythms of Argentina; composed a number of piano pieces in Argentinian song and dance forms (milongas, gatos, cielitos, etc.).

WORKS: 9 symphonies, all performed for the first time in Buenos Aires: No. 1 (Nov. 25, 1907); No. 2, *La Bruja de las montañas* (Sept. 9, 1910); No. 3, *La Selva sagrada* (Dec. 8, 1934); No. 4, *El Ataja-Caminos* (Dec. 15, 1935); No. 5, *El Corazón de la Muñeca* (Nov. 29, 1936); No. 6, *La Muerte del Cometa* (Nov. 26, 1937); No. 7, *Eterno reposo* (Nov. 26, 1937); several suites of Argentinian dances; 3 violin sonatas, Cello Sonata; Piano Trio; a great number of piano albums, the last of which was *En el parque* (1952). He composed 136 opus numbers in all. He also publ. numerous didactic works and several books of poetry. A complete catalogue of his works is found in vol. 2 of *Composers of the Americas* publ. by the Pan American Union, Washington, D.C. (1956; pp. 138-55).

BIBLIOGRAPHY: Z. R. Lacoigne, *Alberto Williams; Músico argentino* (Buenos Aires, 1942); *Homenajes a Alberto Williams,* containing messages and opinions of musicians on the occasion of his 80th birthday (Buenos Aires, 1942); N. Slonimsky, "Alberto Williams: Father of Argentinian Music," *Musical Amer-*

ica (Jan. 10, 1942); V. A. Risolía, *Alberto Williams, curriculum vitae* (Buenos Aires, 1944).

Williams, Charles Francis Abdy, English writer on music; b. Dawlisch, Devonshire, July 16, 1855; d. Milford, near Lymington, Feb. 27, 1923. While pursuing his studies at Trinity College, Cambridge, he played violin and viola in the orch. of the Cambridge Univ. Musical Society; then went to New Zealand, where he was church organist in Auckland; returning to England in 1881, he took the degree of Mus. Bac. at Oxford (1889) and Cambridge (1891); 1895–1901, was director of music at the Greek Theatre at Bradfield College, where he wrote choruses in ancient Greek modes for the productions of Greek tragedies. Retiring from teaching in 1901, he devoted himself to scholarly work; in 1904 he introduced the Solesmes system of performing plainchant at the priests' seminary in Capri, which won him recognition from the Pope.

WRITINGS: *A Short Historical Account of the Degrees in Music at Oxford and Cambridge* (1893); *Bach* (1900; new ed., 1934) and *Handel* (1901; new ed. 1935; in the series The Master Musicians); *The Story of the Organ* (1903); *The Story of Notation* (1903); *The Story of Organ Music* (1905); *The Rhythm of Modern Music* (1909); *The Aristoxenian Theory of Musical Rhythm* (1911); essays on Greek music and plainchant in various journals.

Williams, Charles Lee, English organist and composer; b. Winchester, May 1, 1853; d. Gloucester, Aug. 29, 1935. He was a pupil of Dr. Arnold at the Cathedral of Winchester; from 1872 filled various posts as organist and choirmaster in Ireland and England; conducted several of the "Three Choirs Festivals" held at Gloucester; after 1898 became active in the educational field. He composed the cantatas *Gethsemane, Bethany, A Harvest Song, A Dedication,* etc.; much church music; brought out (with H. G. Chance) a continuation (1895, covering the years 1864–94) of D. Lysons's *Origin and Progress of the Meeting of the Three Choirs of Gloucester, Worcester, and Hereford* (1812, covering the years 1724–1811; supplemental vol. by John Amott in 1865, covering the years 1812–64); in 1931 brought out, with H. G. Chance and T. Hannan-Clark, a further continuation (covering the years 1895–1930) of the work, under the title *Annals of the Three Choirs.*

Williams, Christopher à Becket, English composer and writer on music; b. Dorchester, July 2, 1890; d. London, Nov. 3, 1956. He studied at Keble College, Oxford; was in the British Army during World War I; subsequently traveled in Europe, Asia, and America; wrote 2 travel books, 3 novels, etc.; also contributed to musical periodicals. He composed several orchestral suites: *5 Impressions, Pepperpot Suite, Welsh Suite, Theme and Derivations* for strings, etc.; 3 violin sonatas; a cello sonata; 2 piano sonatas; several piano suites.

Williams, David Christmas, Welsh conductor and composer; b. Llanwrtyd, Sept. 12, 1871; d. there, March 21, 1926. He studied with J. Parry at the South Wales School of Music; conducted various music societies in Wales; wrote a cantata, *The Sands of Lavan,* which received a prize at Cardiff (1893); *The Battle of the Severn,* for chorus and orch.; *Psalms of Praise;* men's choruses; songs; piano piece.

Williams, Frederic Arthur, American pianist, composer, and pedagogue; b. Oberlin, Ohio, March 3, 1869; d. Cleveland, July 31, 1942. He studied piano and composition with W. G. Smith and others in Cleveland; subsequently occupied various teaching posts in Ohio. He wrote about 250 pieces for piano; also some songs. His technical publications for piano include *Wrist and Forearm Studies* and *Octave and Chord Studies.*

Williams, Harry Evan, American tenor; b. Mineral Ridge, Ohio, Sept. 7, 1867; d. Akron, Ohio, May 24, 1918. Originally he worked in a mine and steel mill; then studied singing in Cleveland and N.Y.; made his debut at the Worchester, Mass., Festival of 1896, and then sang in oratorio at many other festivals; gave nearly 1000 recitals.

Williams, John Gerrard, English composer; b. London, Dec. 10, 1888; d. Oxted, Surrey, March 7, 1947. He was an architect by profession, but took some lessons in music from Richard Walthew, and soon began to compose; presented a concert of his works (chamber music, piano pieces, and songs) in London on March 27, 1922. He wrote a ballad opera, *Kate, the Cabin-Boy* (London, 1924); 2 operettas; a ballet, *The Wings of Horus* (1928); *3 Miniatures* and *Elegiac Rhapsody* for orch.; 2 string quartets; many songs and part-songs.

Williams, John M., American pianist and pedagogue; b. on a plantation in Washington County, Texas, Jan. 1, 1884; d. Los Angeles, Dec. 6, 1974. He studied in N.Y. and Chicago; since 1913 lectured on musical pedagogy to music teachers in the major cities of the U.S., Canada, England, and Scotland. His teaching material has had world-wide distribution, having been publ. in Great Britain, Australia, Cuba, and South America (Spanish editions). Some ten million copies of his various piano books have been sold. Among his teaching publications are the *Grade by Grade* and *Year by Year* books; *Child's First Music Book; Nothing Easier or Adventures of Ten Little Fingers in Mother Goose Land: First Book for the Adult Beginner.*

Williams, John T., American composer; b. Flushing, N.Y., Feb. 8, 1932. He studied piano with Rosina Lhévinne at the Juilliard School of Music in New York; then moved to Los Angeles, where he took composition lessons with Mario Castelnuovo-Tedesco. In his instrumental music he adopts a modified serial method of composition; he is also influenced by jazz. His works include an *Essay for Strings* (1966), a Sinfonietta for winds, a flute concerto, a violin concerto, and various pieces of chamber music.

Williams, Joseph, English music publisher; he was the son of Lucy Williams, who established a printing shop in London in 1808. Joseph Williams continued the business; was succeeded in 1883 by his son, **Joseph Benjamin Williams** (who publ. some of his own pieces under the *nom de plum* of **Florian Pascal**); the business was incorporated as Joseph Williams, Ltd., in 1900. Upon the death of J. B. Williams, his son, **Florian Williams,** became head of the company. Joseph Williams, Ltd. specialized in publishing contemporary English music; also brought out Elizabethan works.

BIBLIOGRAPHY: Florian Williams, "After Forty Years. Recollections of a Music Publisher," *Musical Opinion* (Feb.-Dec. 1940).

Williams, Ralph Vaughan.. See **Vaughan Williams, Ralph.**

Williams, Spencer, American composer of popular music; b. New Orleans, Oct. 14, 1889; d. New York, July 14, 1965. He played piano in night clubs in New Orleans, Chicago and New York; wrote songs in the slow rhythmic manner of the New Orleans blues. In 1932 he went to Europe for a prolonged stay; lived in Paris (where he was accompanist for Josephine Baker), London, and Stockholm; returned to the U.S. in 1957. His most famous song is *Basin Street Blues* (1928); wrote many blues and other songs: *Tishomingo Blues* (1917), *Arkansas Blues, Mississippi Blues, Royal Garden Blues;* his *Mahogany Hall Stomp* became a perennial favorite.

Williamson, John Finley, American choral conductor; b. Canton, Ohio, June 23, 1887; d. Toledo, Ohio, May 28, 1964. He studied singing with Witherspoon and Bispham in N.Y.; organ with Karl Straube in Leipzig. In 1921 he founded the Westminster Choir, and in 1926, the Westminster Choir School (later College) at Princeton, N.J.; was its president until 1958, when he resigned. With his choir he gave 1000 concerts in America; also made 2 European tours; edited the *Westminster Series* of choral music.

Williamson, Malcolm, Australian composer; b. Sydney, Nov. 21, 1931. He studied composition with Eugene Goossens at the Sydney Cons. (1944-51); in 1953 went to London, where he took lessons with Elisabeth Lutyens and Erwin Stein (1953-57); learned to play the organ and was employed as a church organist in England (1955-60); visited the U.S. in 1970, and was composer-in-residence at Westminster Choir College in Princeton, N.J. for an academic season; then returned to England. In 1975 he became Master of the Queen's Musick; in 1976 he received the order of Commander of the British Empire (CBE); in 1977 was elected president of the Royal Philharmonic Orch.

WORKS: OPERAS: *Our Man in Havana,* after Graham Greene's novel (London, July 2, 1963); *The English Eccentrics,* chamber opera (Aldeburgh Festival, June 11, 1964); *The Happy Prince,* children's opera after Oscar Wilde (Farnham, May 22, 1965); *Julius Caesar Jones,* children's opera for children's voices and 3 adults (London, Jan. 4, 1966); *The Violins of St. Jacques,* in 3-acts (London, Nov. 29, 1966); *Dunstan and the Devil,* chamber opera (Cookham, May 19, 1967); *The Growing Castle,* chamber opera for 4 sing-

ers, piano, harpsichord, tubular chimes, and drums, after Strindberg's *Dream Play,* (Dynevor Festival, Aug. 13, 1968, with the composer alternately at the piano and at the harpsichord); *Lucky-Peter's Journey,* after Strindberg's fairy-tale play (1969); *The Stone Wall* (London, Sept. 18, 1971); *Genesis* (1971; London, April 23, 1973); *The Red Sea* (1972); *The Death of Cuchulain* (1972); and *The Winter Star* (1972); a choral operatic sequence, *The Brilliant and the Dark,* for women's voices and orch. (1969); 3 cassations for audience, and orch.: *The Moonrakers* (1967; Brighton, April 22, 1967), *Knights in Shining Armour* (1968; Brighton, April 19, 1968) and *The Snow Wolf* (Brighton, April 30, 1968). BALLETS: *The Display,* dance symphony in 4 movements (Adelaide Festival, March 14, 1964); *Sun into Darkness* (London, April 13, 1966). FOR ORCH.: *Elevanti,* Symph. No. 1 (1956-57); *Santiago de Espada,* overture (1958); 3 piano concertos (1958; with string orch., 1960; 1961); Organ Concerto (1961); *Sinfonietta Concertante* for 3 trumpets, piano, and strings (1959-61); Violin Concerto (Bath, England, June 15, 1965, Yehudi Menuhin soloist); Sinfonietta (1965); *Concerto Grosso* for orch. (London, Aug. 28, 1965); *Symphonic Variations* (Edinburgh, Sept. 9, 1965); Symph. No. 2 (Bristol, Oct. 29, 1969); *Epitaphs for Edith Sitwell* for strings (1969; originally for organ, 1965); Concerto for 2 pianos and strings (1972); *The Icy Mirror* for soloists, chorus and orch. (Cheltenham Festival, July 9, 1972); *Ode to Music* for chorus, echo chorus, and orch. (London, Feb. 3, 1973); *Hammerskjöld Portrait* for soprano and strings (London, July 30, 1974). CHAMBER MUSIC: *Variations* for cello and piano (1964); Concerto for 2 pianos (8 hands) and wind quintet (1965); *Serenade* for flute, piano, and string trio (1967). FOR KEYBOARD: 2 piano sonatas (1958, revised 1971-72); *5 Preludes* for piano (1966); 2-Piano Sonata (1967); Piano Quintet (1968); Symphony for organ (1960). FOR VOICE: choruses, including *Symphony for Voices* a cappella (1960) and *The Musicians of Bremen* (1972).

BIBLIOGRAPHY: James Murdoch, *Australian Contemporary Composers* (Melbourne, 1972; pp. 205-209).

Willis, Henry, English organ builder; b. London, April 27, 1821; d. there, Feb. 11, 1901. As a youth he worked for John Gray (later Gray & Davidson), and still during his apprenticeship he invented the special manual and pedal couplers which he later used in his own instruments; from 1842 to 1845 he worked for Evans at Cheltenham, and in 1845 established his own business in London. He rebuilt the organ in the Gloucester Cathedral; exhibited a large organ at the Crystal Palace in 1851, which won the Council Medal, and was installed in the Winchester Cathedral; he subsequently was commissioned to build the great organ in St. George's Hall, Liverpool (1855). In 1878 he took his sons **Vincent** and **Henry** into partnership, adopting the firm name of "Henry Willis & Sons"; he became generally known as "Father Willis." Willis himself regarded the organ in St. Paul's, which he built in 1891, as his masterpiece (77 speaking stops, 19 couplers). After the founder's death in 1901, his son Henry Willis became the head of the business, and soon took his son, also named **Henry Willis,** into partnership. They built the organ in the Liverpool Cathedral (167 speaking stops, 48 couplers) in 1912–14; this organ was the largest in the world at the time.

Willis Music Co., American music publishers. The business was founded by **Charles H. Willis** at Cincinnati in 1899, in association with his son **William H. Willis.** The firm became known as W. H. Willis & Co.; after absorption of G. B. Jennings & Co. in 1910 it was incorporated as the Willis Music Co. On July 1, 1919, the business was acquired by Gustave Schirmer of New York. The company specialized in educational publications.

Willis, Richard Storrs, American composer and writer on music; b. Boston, Feb. 10, 1819; d. Detroit, May 7, 1900. He was a brother of the poet Nathaniel Parker Willis; studied at Yale Univ., where he was president of the Beethoven Society (1837), for which he wrote choruses and instrumental pieces. He then went to Germany, and studied theory with Schnyder von Wartensee in Frankfurt and with Hauptmann in Leipzig. Returning. to New York, he edited the periodical *The Musical World* (1852–60); brought out the collections *Church Chorals and Choir Studies* (N.Y., 1850) and *Our Church Music* (N.Y., 1856); also composed student songs and patriotic hymns, later collected as *Waif of Song* and publ. in Paris in 1876.

Willman, Allan, American composer and pianist; b. Hinckley, Illinois, May 11, 1909. He studied at the Chicago Musical College (M.M., 1930); then took lessons with Nadia Boulanger in Paris (1935). In 1936 he joined the faculty of the Univ. of Wyoming. His works include *Idyl* for orch. (1930); *Solitude* for orch. (1930; Boston, Symph., April 20, 1936); *A Ballade of the Night* for voice and string quartet (1936); numerous piano pieces and songs.

Willmers, Rudolf, pianist and composer; b. Copenhagen, Oct. 31, 1821; d. Vienna, Aug. 24, 1878. His father, a Danish agriculturist, sent him to Germany at the age of 13 to study science, but Willmers turned to music; took lessons with Hummel for 2 years and with Fr. Schneider for a year; became a concert pianist and toured successfully in Germany and Austria; was much acclaimed in Paris and London (1846–47); in 1866 settled in Vienna. His technical specialty was the performance of "chains of trills" for which he was famous. He wrote a number of brilliant piano solos: *Six études; Sérénade érotique* (for the left hand); *Sehnsucht am Meere; Un Jour d'été en Norvège; Deux études de concert (La Pompa di festa* and *La Danza delle Baccanti); Sonata héroïque; Tarantella giocosa; La Sylphide; Trilletkenen; Aus der Geisterwelt,* tremolo-caprice; *Allegro symphonique;* he also composed some chamber music.
BIBLIOGRAPHY: T. de L***, "Notice sur la vie et les travaux artistiques de R. Willmers," *Archives des Hommes du Jour* (April 1847; also separately).

Willner, Arthur, pianist and composer; b. Teplice, Czechoslovakia, March 5, 1881; d. London, April 7, 1959. He studied at Leipzig Cons. and in Munich. From 1904 to 1924 he taught at the Stern Cons. in Berlin; from 1924 to 1938 he lived in Vienna; in 1938

settled in London. His list of works includes more than 100 op. numbers: a symph., a cello concerto, a piano concerto, 5 string quartets, 4 violin sonatas, 3 sonatas for violin and piano, 4 piano sonatas and several character pieces, choral works, organ works, songs.

Willson, Meredith, American composer; b. Mason City, Iowa, May 18, 1902. He played the flute in a local orch. at the age of 11, and in 1916 was sent to N.Y., where he studied flute with Georges Barrère. In 1919 he joined Sousa's band as flutist, touring with it until 1922. From 1923 to 1928 he was flutist in the N.Y. Philharmonic. He then entered the field of radio as conductor and composer. For the 30th anniversary of the San Francisco earthquake he composed his first symph. and conducted its première with the San Francisco Symph. Orch. on April 19, 1936; his 2nd Symph. was presented by the Los Angeles Philharmonic on April 4, 1940. Other works include a symph. poem *The Jervis Bay* (1942); *Symphonic Variations on an American Theme; O. O. McIntyre Suite* for orch. (San Francisco, 1936); *Anthem of the Atomic Age* for chorus; many pieces for band. Then he devoted himself mainly to popular music, with ever increasing success, culminating in the production of his musical revue *The Music Man,* which opened on Broadway on Dec. 19, 1957. He published an autobiography, *And There I Stood with My Piccolo* (N.Y., 1948); *Eggs I Have Laid* (N.Y., 1955); *But He Doesn't Know the Territory* (descriptive of the origin of his musical, *The Music Man;* N.Y., 1959).

Willy. Pen name for **Gauthier-Villars, Henri.**

Wilm, Nicolai von, German pianist and composer; b. Riga, March 4, 1834; d. Wiesbaden, Feb. 20, 1911. He studied with Plaidy, Hauptmann, and Richter at the Leipzig Cons.; then in 1857 went to Riga as theater conductor, and in 1860 proceeded to St. Petersburg, where he became instructor at the Imperial Nicolayevsky Institute; returned to Germany in 1875 and lived mostly in Dresden and Wiesbaden.
WORKS: A highly prolific composer (243 opus numbers), he is best known through his chamber music; wrote a string sextet, a string quartet, a piano trio, a cello sonata, 2 violin sonatas, a sonata for violin and harp; numerous pieces for piano solo: *Kleine Suite, Herbstfrüchte, Im russischen Dorf, Stimmungen, Dorf- und Waldidyllen, Musikalisches Dekameron;* etc.; for piano 4 hands: *Eine Nordlandfahrt, Reisebilder aus Schlesien, Musikalische Federzeichnungen, Kalendarium,* etc.; also variations and other pieces for 2 pianos; men's choruses; songs.

Wilms, Jan Willem, composer; b. Witzhelden, Schwarzburg-Sondershausen, March 30, 1772; d. Amsterdam, July 19, 1847. He received his early musical training from his father. In 1791 he went to Amsterdam, where he appeared as pianist and harpist. He composed 2 piano concertos, 2 flute concertos, 2 string quartets, 2 piano trios, 3 violin sonatas, 2 flute sonatas, a clarinet concerto; also 3 symphonies. He was the author of the Dutch national song *Wien Neerlandsch bloed door d'aderen vloeit* (1815).

Wilsing, Daniel Friedrich Eduard, German composer; b. Hörde, near Dortmund, Oct. 21, 1809; d. Berlin, May 2, 1893. He was organist in Wesel from 1829 to 1834; then moved to Berlin. He composed an oratorio in 2 parts, *Jesus Christus* (produced in Bonn in 1889, by Wilsing's pupil Arnold Mendelssohn); a *De profundis a* 16, which won the gold medal for art at Berlin; piano sonatas; songs.

Wilson, Charles M., Canadian composer; b. Toronto, May 8, 1931. He attended the Univ. of Toronto (D. Mus., 1954); during two successive summers studied composition with Lukas Foss (1950) and Carlos Chávez (1951) at the Berkshire Music School at Tanglewood; also studied conducting there with Leonard Bernstein. From 1962 to 1970 he was head of the music department at Guelph Collegiate Vocational Institute. His music is contrapuntally dense and dissonant but the formal element is perserved in Baroque structures.
WORKS: 2 operas: *Heloïse and Abelard* (Toronto, Sept. 8, 1973); *Kamouraska* (1975); church opera, *The Summoning of Everyman* (Halifax, April 6, 1973); a children's opera, *The Selfish Giant* (Toronto, Dec. 20, 1973); 3 string quartets (1950, 1968, 1975); Symphony in A (1954); *Sonata da Chiesa* for oboe and strings (1960); String Trio (1963); *The Angels of the Earth,* oratorio (1966; Guelph, June 19, 1967); *En Guise d'Orphée* for baritone and string orch. (1968); *Phrases from Orpheus,* mixed-media score for chorus and dancers (Guelph Spring, Ontario, May 10, 1971); *Concerto 5x4x3* for string quintet, woodwind quartet, and brass trio (1970); *Sinfonia* for double orch. (Toronto, March 3, 1973); *Image out of Season* for chorus and brass quintet (1973); *Cristo Paremus Canticam* for chorus and orch. (Hamilton, Dec. 2, 1973); *Symphonic Perspectives,* subtitled *Kingsmere* (Ottawa, Oct. 4, 1974); *Missa Brevis* for chorus and organ (1975).

Wilson, Domingo Santa Cruz. See **Santa Cruz Wilson, Domingo.**

Wilson, Grenville Dean, American composer; b. Plymouth, Conn., Jan. 26, 1833; d. Nyack, N.Y., Sept. 20, 1897. He was taught piano by his mother; then studied theory with A. W. Johnson in Boston; some of his piano pieces were publ. before he was 10 years old. In 1871 he was head of the music dept. of Rockland Institute, Nyack; in 1877 he organized the Nyack Symph. Society. He publ. 178 pieces, chiefly for piano, some of which were popular (*The Shepherd-boy, Wayside Chapel, Chapel in the Mountains, Moonlight on the Hudson, Voix du matin,* etc.).

Wilson, John, English lutenist and song writer; b. (probably in Faversham, Kent) April 5, 1595; d. London, Feb. 22, 1674. He was musically gifted; at the age of 19, wrote music for *The Maske of Flowers.* According to some indications, he participated as a singer in a production of Shakespeare's *Much Ado About Nothing* (as Jacke Wilson). In 1635 he was made one of the King's Musicians; was in favor with Charles I, whom he followed to Oxford during the civil war in 1644, and was made D. Mus. by Oxford Univ. on March 10, 1645; he was "Musick Professor" there from 1656 until 1661. Upon the Restoration he resumed his post at court, and on Oct. 22, 1662 became successor of Henry Lawes as a Gentleman of the Chapel Royal. He publ. *Psalterium Carolinum* (London, 1657), *Cheerfull Ayres or Ballads* (Oxford, 1660); wrote several songs to Shakespeare's words. Some of his songs were included in Playford's *Select Musicall Ayres and Dialogues* (1652, 1653), *Select Ayres and Dialogues* (1659), *Catch that catch can: or the Musical Companion* (1667), and *The Treasury of Musick* (1669).
BIBLIOGRAPHY: E. R. Rimbault, *Who was "Jacke Wilson," the Singer of Shakespeare's Stage?* (London, 1846); E. F. Hart, "Caroline Lyrics and Contemporary Song-Books," *Library* (June 1953); V. H. Duckles, "The 'Curious' Art of John Wilson," *Journal of the American Musicological Society* (Summer 1954).

Wilson, Mortimer, American organist and composer; b. Chariton, Iowa, Aug. 6, 1876; d. New York, Jan. 27, 1932. He studied organ with Middelschulte in Chicago; composition with F. G. Gleason; in 1907 went to Leipzig to study with Max Reger. Returning to America in 1911, he became conductor of the Atlanta Philharmonic Orch. (until 1915); then taught at various music schools; settled in N.Y. He wrote 5 symphonies; an overture *New Orleans; Concerto Grosso* for strings; 2 piano trios; 3 violin sonatas; *Echoes from Childhood* and *Romance* for violin and piano; etc. Author of *The Rhetoric of Music* (Lincoln, Nebr., 1907) and *Harmonic and Melodic Technical Studies;* publ. *A series of work tables prepared for students of harmony* (1921).

Wilson, Olly, black American composer; b. St. Louis, Sept. 9, 1937. He was educated at Washington Univ., St. Louis (B.M., 1959), at the Univ. of Illinois (Mus. M., 1960), and at the Univ. of Iowa, where his teachers were Robert Sykes, Robert Kelley, and Phillip Bezanson (Ph.D., 1964). In 1971–72 he traveled in West Africa to study indigenous music; then devoted himself to teaching and composition; was on the faculty of Florida Univ. (1960–62 and 1964–65); at Oberlin Cons. of Music (1965–70), and later at the Univ. of California, Berkeley.
WORKS: *Prelude and Line Study* for woodwind quartet (1959); Trio for flute, cello, and piano (1959); String Quartet (1960); *Wry Fragments* for tenor and percussion (1961); Violin Sonata (1961); *Dance Suite* for wind ensemble (1962); *Soliloquy* for bass viol (1962); Sextet (1963); *Three Movements* for orch. (1964); *Piece for Four,* for flute, trumpet, double bass, and piano (1966); *In Memoriam Martin Luther King, Jr.* for chorus and electronic sound (1968); *Voices* for orch. (1970); *The 18 Hands of Jerome Harris,* an electronic ballet (1971); *Akwan* for piano, electronic piano and orch. (1972); *Black Martyrs,* electronic composition (1972); *Spirit Song* for soprano, chorus, and orch. (1973); *Sometimes* for tenor and tape (1976); Piano Trio (1977).

Wilson, Philip, English singer and music editor; b. Hove, Sussex, Nov. 29, 1886; d. London, July 26, 1924. After studying singing in London, he went to Australia in 1913 as a vocal teacher at the Sydney Cons.;

returning to England in 1920, he gave historical recitals, especially of Elizabethan songs. With Peter Warlock (Philip Heseltine) he edited *English Ayres, Elizabethan and Jacobean,* and *Chromatic Tunes* for 1606; also edited *The Musical Proverbs* (London, 1924) from the "Lekingfelde" manuscript.

Wilson, Richard, American composer; b. Cleveland, May 15, 1941. He studied piano with Leonard Shure and cello with Ernst Silberstein. In 1959 he entered Harvard Univ., where he took courses in music with Randall Thompson, G. W. Woodworth, and Robert Moevs (A.B., 1963, *magna cum laude*); subsequently enrolled at Rutgers Univ. (M.A., 1966). In 1966 he was appointed to the faculty of Vassar College.

WORKS: *Suite for 5 Players* (1963); Trio for oboe, violin, and cello (1964); *A Dissolve* for women's voices (1968); String Quartet No. 1 (1968); *Music for violin and cello* (1969); Quartet for flutes, double bass, and harpsichord (1969); *Initiation* for orch. (1970); *Music for solo cello* (1971); *Music for solo flute* (1972); Wind Quintet (1974); String Quartet No. 2 (1977).

Wiltberger, August, German composer; brother of **Heinrich Wiltberger;** b. Sobernheim, April 17, 1850; d. Stuttgart, Dec. 2, 1928. He was engaged as music teacher in various towns in Alsace; wrote a number of sacred works; a secular cantata, *Barbarossas Erwachen;* chamber music; organ pieces; author of *Harmonielehre; zum Gebrauch in Lehrerbildungsanstalten* (1906; 3rd ed., 1912).

Wiltberger, Heinrich, German composer and teacher; brother of **August Wiltberger;** b. Sobernheim, Aug. 17, 1841; d. Colmar, May 26, 1916. He studied with his father, an organist; taught in various music schools in Alsace; his setting of Alsatian folksongs for male chorus were very popular. He also wrote a *Märchen* for string orch.; a Requiem; several Masses; brought out collections of Latin and German hymns; publ. *Der Gesangsunterricht in der Volksschule* (1907).

Wimberger, Gerhard, Austrian composer; b. Vienna, Aug. 30, 1923. He studied in Salzburg; took courses at the Mozarteum there. He wrote several comic operas: *Schaubundengeschichte* (Mannheim, 1954); *Der Handschuh* (Frankfurt, 1955); *La Battaglia* (Schwetzingen, 1960); also *Kantate vom Sport* (1953); Concerto for piano and 15 string instruments (1955); *Divertimento* for string orch.. (1956); *Loga-Rhythmen* for orch. (1956); *Figuren und Phantasien* for orch. (1957); *Risonanze* for 3 orchestral groups (Berlin, Jan. 31, 1968); *Ars Amatoria,* to texts from Ovid, for voices, chorus, jazz combo and orch. (Vienna, Feb. 7, 1969); *Lebensregeln,* a "catechism with music" (Munich, Aug. 27, 1972); *Multiplay* for 23 players (1974).

Winderstein, Hans (Wilhelm Gustav), German conductor; b. Lüneburg, Oct. 29, 1856; d. Giessen, June 23, 1925. He studied at the Leipzig Cons. with H. Schradieck (violin) and Richter (theory); also played in the Gewandhaus Orch. He conducted the concerts of the Philharmonic Societies of Nuremberg and Fürth (1890–93); then was conductor of the newly established Philharmonic Orch. at Munich, and of the Kaim Concerts (1893–96). In 1896 he organized the Winderstein Orch. in Leipzig, which he conducted until 1919; from 1920 conducted summer concerts in Bad Nauheim. He composed a *Trauermarsch, Valse-Caprice,* and *Ständchen* for orch.; violin pices; piano pieces.

Windgassen, Wolfgang, French-born German tenor; b. Annemasse, Haute Savoie, June 26, 1914; d. Stuttgart, Sept. 8, 1974. He studied singing with his father, a renowned vocal teacher in Stuttgart, where the family moved when he was very young. After military service during the war, he joined the Stuttgart Opera; in 1951 he was engaged at the Wagner Bayreuth Festival and attained great acclaim as a "Heldentenor" in Wagner's operas; was also brilliantly successful in such roles as Radames in *Aida* and Don José in *Carmen.* He was engaged by the Metropolitan Opera in New York in 1957 to sing Siegmund and Siegfried in Wagner's tetralogy; he was also active as opera director.

BIBLIOGRAPHY: B. W. Wessling, *Wolfgang Windgassen* (Bremen, 1967).

Winding, August (Henrik), Danish pianist and composer; b. Taaro, March 24, 1835; d. Copenhagen, June 16, 1899. He studied with Gade; was appointed prof. at the Copenhagen Cons. in 1867; from 1891 till his death was its director. He composed a symphony; *Nordische Ouvertüre;* Piano Concerto; cadenzas to Beethoven's piano concertos and to many of Mozart's; String Sextet; Piano Quartet; 2 violin sonatas; many piano pieces (*Drei Fantasiestücke, Reisebilder, Ländliche Szenen, Studien und Stimmungen, Idyllen und Legenden, Albumblätter,* etc.); songs.

Windingstad, Ole, Norwegian-American conductor; b. Sandefjord, May 18, 1886; d. Kingston, N.Y., June 3, 1959. He graduated from the Oslo Cons. in 1902; then studied at the Leipzig Cons.; settled in America in 1913, and established the Scandinavian Symph. Orch., which he conducted until 1929; also conducted the Brooklyn Symph. Orch. (1930–32), the Knickerbocker Symph. Orch. in Albany, N.Y. (1937–39), the New Orleans Symph. Orch. (1940–44), and the Albany Symph. Orch. (1945–48). In 1929 he was decorated with the Norwegian Order of Saint Olaf. He composed a symphony (1913); a cantata, *The Skald of Norway* (1929); *The Tides,* for orch. (Albany, Feb. 13, 1938; composer conducting); many minor pieces.

Windsperger, Lothar, German composer; b. Ampfing, Oct. 22, 1885; d. Wiesbaden, May 30, 1935. He studied with R. Louis and others in Munich; from 1913, was in Mainz as artistic adviser to music publisher B. Schott's Söhne. Among his works are a symphony; *Lumen amoris,* symph. fantasy; a piano concerto; a violin concerto; *Missa Symphonica;* Requiem; chamber music; piano pieces; organ pieces; songs.

Windt, Herbert, German composer; b. Senftenberg, Sept. 15, 1894; d. Deisenhofen, Nov. 22, 1965. He studied piano as a child; then took courses in music theory with Klatte and Schreker in Berlin. In 1923 he obtained the Mendelssohn Prize; in 1936 he was awarded the Olympic Prize for his work *Marathon 1936.*

WORKS: *Andromache,* opera, to his own libretto (Berlin, March 16, 1932); cantata, *Flug zum Niederwald* (1935); chamber symph., *Andante religioso* for voice and 35 instruments (1921); numerous film scores.

Wingham, Thomas, English piano teacher and composer; b. London, Jan. 5, 1846; d. there, March 24, 1893. He studied with Sterndale Bennett at the Royal Academy of Music; became prof. of piano playing there in 1871; also served as church organist. He composed 2 Masses, motets, offertories, and other church music; also 4 symphonies; 6 overtures; *Concert-Capriccio* for piano and orch.; 2 string quartets; a septet for piano, strings, and wind instruments; songs.

Winham, Godfrey, British-American composer and computer specialist; b. London, Dec. 11, 1934; d. Princeton, N.J., April 26, 1975. He studied composition and composition at the Royal Academy of Music in London; in 1954 went to the U.S. where he took courses at Princeton Univ. (A.B., 1956; M.F.A., 1958); received his Ph.D. degree there for the thesis entitled *Composition with Arrays* (1965); then joined the staff as lecturer on electronic music and computer composition. In 1969 he worked on the computerized synthesis of music and speech. Apart from his programmed compositions on a computer, he wrote 2 string quartets, *The Habit of Perfection* for voice and string quartet, and several piano pieces. He was married to the American singer **Bethany Beardslee.**

Winkelmann, Hermann, German tenor; b. Brunswick, March 8, 1849; d. Vienna, Jan. 18, 1912. He started out as a piano maker, but became interested in singing; made a successful debut at Sondershausen (1875), and then sang at Altenburg, Darmstadt, and Hamburg. His interpretation of Tannhäuser and Lohengrin (in special engagements at Vienna) induced Richter to recommend him to Wagner, who chose him to create Parsifal at Bayreuth (July 26, 1882). From 1883 to 1906, when he retired on a pension, he was one of the brightest stars of the Vienna Opera, where one of his most brilliant achievements was the performance of the role of Tristan (with Materna as Isolde) in the Vienna première (Oct. 4, 1883). In 1884 he sang in the U.S. at the Wagner festivals given by Theodore Thomas in New York, Boston, Philadelphia, Cincinnati, and Chicago.

Winkler, Alexander, Russian composer and pianist; b. Kharkov, March 3, 1865; d. Besançon, Aug. 6, 1935. He studied with Duvernoy in Paris, and with Leschetizky (piano) and Navrátil (composition) in Vienna. Returning to Russia, he became a piano teacher in his native city (1890–96); then was prof. at the St. Petersburg Cons. (1907–24); among his students was Prokofiev. In 1924 he emigrated to France and became director of the Besançon Cons. He composed an overture, *En Bretagne;* orchestral variations on a Russian folksong, and on a Finnish folksong; a string quintet; 3 string quartets; a piano quartet; a piano trio; a viola sonata; several albums of piano pieces; songs.

Winkler, Peter K., American composer; b. Los Angeles, Jan. 26, 1943. He studied at the Univ. of California in Berkeley (A.B., 1964) and at Princeton Univ. (M.A., 1966). His works include *Etude* for 2 horns (1964); String Quartet (1967); *Praise of Silence* for soprano, chorus, instruments, and tape (1969); incidental music for plays, radio and television.

Winner, Septimus, American composer of popular music; b. Philadelphia, May 11, 1827; d. there, Nov. 22, 1902. He learned to play the violin; married at 20 and opened a music store in Philadelphia, where he began giving lessons on the violin, guitar, and banjo. In 1854 he wrote his best-known song, *Listen to the Mocking Bird* (based on a melody originated by his Negro errand boy, "Whistling Dick" Milburn), selling the copyright for 5 dollars; in his lifetime the song sold 20 million copies. In 1862 he wrote *Give Us Back Our Old Commander: Little Mac, the People's Pride,* voicing a widespread sentiment for the return of Gen. McClellan; the song was regarded as subversive and Winner was arraigned, but soon released; later the song, slightly altered, was used for Grant's presidential campaign. Winner also wrote the song *Whispering Hope,* which became extremely popular. He was a pioneer in bringing music to the masses; wrote over 200 volumes of music, including many instructive works, for 23 different instruments, and made about 2,000 arrangements for violin and piano. He used the pen name **Alice Hawthorne** (in honor of his mother, Mary Ann Hawthorne) for many of his songs, including *Listen to the Mocking Bird.*

BIBLIOGRAPHY: C. E. Claghorn, *The Mocking Bird: The Life and Diary of Its Author, Sep. Winner* (Philadelphia, 1937).

Winograd, Arthur, American cellist and conductor; b. New York, April 22, 1920. He studied at the New England Cons. (1937–40) and at the Curtis Institute (1940–41); played the cello in the Boston Symphony (1940–41) and in the NBC Symph. Orch. (1942–43); then was a member of the Juilliard String Quartet; joined the faculty of the Juilliard School of Music (1946–55) and later began to conduct. He was the conductor of the Birmingham, Alabama Symph. Orch. (1960–64); in 1964 he was appointed conductor and music director of the Hartford, Conn. Symph. Orch.

Winogron, Blanche, American pianist; b. New York, May 8, 1911. She studied at Hunter College and later took composition lessons with Henry Holden Huss, Stefan Wolpe, and Felix Salzer. In 1968 she was appointed to the faculty of the New England Cons. of Music in Boston. She published a number of teaching pieces for piano.

Winter, Peter, German composer; b. Mannheim (baptized Aug. 28), 1754; d. Munich, Oct. 17, 1825. He was a violinist in the Electoral orch. at the age of 11; studied with Abbé Vogler; in 1776 became music director at the court theater; went with the court to Munich in 1778; was appointed court conductor in 1798 and held this post until his death. In Munich he brought out a number of operas, of which the most important were: *Helena und Paris* (Feb. 5, 1782), *Der Bettelstudent*

(Feb. 2, 1785), *Marie von Montalban* (Jan. 28, 1800), and *Colmal* (Sept. 15, 1809). Frequent leaves of absence from Munich enabled him to travel; in Venice he produced his operas *Catone in Utica* (1791), *I Sacrifizi di Creta* (1792), *I Fratelli rivali* (1793), and *Belisa* (1794). In Vienna he brought out *Das unterbrochene Opferfest* (June 14, 1796; his most successful opera; produced all over Europe), *Babylons Pyramiden* (Oct. 25, 1797), and *Das Labirint* (June 12, 1798); in Paris he produced his only French opera, *Tamerlan* (Sept. 14, 1802); in London, the Italian operas *La Grotta di Calipso* (May 31, 1803), *Il Trionfo dell'amor fraterno* (March 22, 1804), *Il Ratto di Proserpina* (May 3, 1804), and *Zaira* (Jan. 29, 1805); in Milan, *Maometto II* (Jan. 28, 1817), *I due Valdomiri* (Dec. 26, 1817), and *Etelinda* (March 23, 1817). He also wrote several ballets; 3 oratorios and 17 sacred cantatas for the Munich court chapel; 26 Masses and a vast amount of other church music; 9 symphonies (including the grand choral symph. *Die Schlacht*); overtures; 2 septets; 6 string quartets; 2 string quintets; concertos for clarinet, for bassoon, and other instruments with orch.; and a *Vollständige Singschule* in 3 parts. Some of his chamber music was republished by Riemann in the *Denkmäler der Tonkunst in Bayern* 27 and 28 (15 and 16; with a thematic catalogue).

BIBLIOGRAPHY: V. Frensdorf, *Peter Winter als Opernkomponist* (dissertation; Erlangen, 1908); E. Löffler, *Die Messen Peter Winters* (Frankfurt, 1928).

Winterberger, Alexander, German pianist and composer; b. Weimar, Aug. 14, 1834; d. Leipzig, Sept. 23, 1914. He studied at the Leipzig Cons. (1848) and with Liszt. In 1861 he went to Vienna; in 1869, became piano prof. at the St. Petersburg Cons.; returned to Leipzig in 1872 and remained there as teacher and music critic. He publ. some piano pieces: *Alinen-Tänze* (waltzes, mazurkas, minuets, etc.), *Concert-Étude, Valse-Caprice, Concert-Adagio;* songs; German and Slavonic duets.

BIBLIOGRAPHY: O. Foerster, *Alexander Winterberger. Seine Werke, sein Leben* (Hannover, 1905; with a list of works).

Winterfeld, Carl von, German writer on music; b. Berlin, Jan. 28, 1784; d. there, Feb. 19, 1852. He studied law at the Univ. of Halle; then occupied juridical positions in Breslau and Berlin. He collected a valuable library of old music, which he donated to the Library of Berlin.

WRITINGS: *Palestrina* (1832); *J. Gabrieli und sein Zeitalter* (1834; 3 vols.); *Über K. Fr. Chr. Faschs geistliche Gesangswerke* (1839); *Dr. Martin Luthers deutsche geistliche Lieder* (1840); *Der evangelische Kirchengesang und sein Verhältnis zur Kunst des Tonsatzes* (1843–47; 3 vols.); *Über Herstellung des Gemeinde- und Chorgesangs in der evangelischen Kirche* (1848); *Zur Geschichte heiliger Tonkunst* (2 parts; 1850, 1852); *Musiktreiben und Musikempfindungen im 16. und 17. Jahrhundert* (1851); *Alceste von Lulli, Händel und Gluck* (1851); *Allegorisch-poetische Festopern am Kaiserlichen Hofe zu Wien in der letzten Hälfte des 17. Jahrhunderts* (1852).

BIBLIOGRAPHY: A. Prüfer, *Briefwechsel zwischen*

Carl von Winterfeld und Eduard Krüger (Leipzig, 1898).

Winter-Hjelm, Otto, Norwegian organist and composer; b. Christiania, Oct. 8, 1837; d. there, May 3, 1931. He studied with H. Kjerulf in Christiana, and with Kullak and Wüerst in Berlin. He was organist in the Trefoldighetskirke in Christiania from 1874 till 1921; wrote music criticism in the *Aftenposten* (1887–1913).

WORKS: Symph. No. 1 (Christiania, Sept. 27, 1862); Symph. No. 2 (1862; first performed, Christiania, March 18, 1916); many choruses for men's voices; edited *50 Melodier til Hauges og Landstads Salmebøger* and *50 Salmemelodier* for piano; also church music. Publ. *Af Kristiania teaterliv i den seneste tid* (essays; Christiania, 1875).

Winternitz, Emanuel, eminent Austrian-American musicologist, art historian, and museum curator; b. Vienna, Aug. 4, 1898. He served in the Austrian Army (1916–18); then studied law at the Univ. of Vienna (LL.D., 1922); was visiting lecturer in philosophy of law at the Univ. of Hamburg (1923); then served as corporation lawyer in Vienna (1929–38). After the annexation of Austria by Nazi Germany (1938) he emigrated to the U.S.; devoted himself mainly to lecturing on art; was Peripatetic Prof. for the Carnegie Foundation. In 1941 he joined the staff of the Metropolitan Museum of Art, N.Y., for the reorganization of the Crosby Brown Collection of Musical Instruments; served as its curator until 1973. He gave lectures in music history at Yale Univ. (1949–60); in 1971 was appointed to the faculty of the Graduate Center of the City Univ. of N.Y. In 1976 he was awarded the Austrian Cross of Honor for Science and Art. He published the informative books, *Musical Autographs, from Monteverdi to Hindemith* (2 vols., Princeton, N.J., 1955); *Die schönsten Musikinstrumente des Abendlandes* (Munich, 1966; in English as *Musical Instruments of the Western World*, N.Y., 1967); and *Musical Instruments and Their Symbolism in Western Art* (N.Y., 1967).

Wintzer, Richard, German composer; b. Nauendorf, near Halle, March 9, 1866; d. Berlin, Aug. 14, 1952. He studied painting, and also music (with Bargiel); lived mostly in Berlin, and was active as painter, composer, and music critic. He wrote 2 operas, *Die Willis* (1895) and *Marienkind* (1905); *Auf hohen Bergen*, for baritone solo, chorus, and orch.; some fine songs *(Ernste Gesänge, Kinderlieder, Sturmlieder);* piano pieces. He also publ. *Menschen von anderem Schlage* (1912) and an autobiography.

BIBLIOGRAPHY: H. Killer, "Richard Wintzer, ein Leben zwischen den Künsten," *Musik* (March 1941).

Wiora, Walter, renowned German musicologist; b. Katowice, Dec. 30, 1906. He studied musicology in Berlin with Abert, Blume, Gurlitt, Hornbostel, H. J. Moser, Schering, Schünemann, and J. Wolf. He served in the German Army during World War II; after 1945 he was in charge of the German Folk Music Archives in Freiburg-im-Breisgau. In 1958 he succeeded Friedrich Blume as prof. at Kiel Univ. In

1962-63 he was visiting prof. at Columbia Univ. in N.Y.; from 1964 to 1972 he was prof. of musicology at the Univ. of Saarland, Saarbrücken; since 1955 he has been a member of the International Folk Music Council. A Festschrift in his honor was published in 1967, in Kassel, containing a list of his publications. His principal achievement is research in the field of German folk music.

WRITINGS: *Zur Frühgeschichte der Musik in den Alpenländern* (Basel, 1949); *Das echte Volkslied* (Heidelberg, 1950); *Europäischer Volksgesang: gemeinsame Formen in charakteristischen Abwandlungen* (Cologne, 1952); a biography of Bruckner (Freiburg, 1952); *Die rheinisch-bergischen Melodien bei Zuccalmaglio und Brahms* (Bad Godesberg, 1953); and *Europäische Volksmusik und abendländische Tonkunst*, vol. 1 in the series *Die Musik im alten und neuen Europa* (Kassel, 1957; a work of fundamental significance); *Die vier Weltalter der Musik* (Stuttgart, 1961; in English, *The Four Ages of Music*, N.Y., 1965); *Das deutsche Lied. Zur Geschichte und Asthetik einer musikalischen Gattung* (Wolfenbüttel, 1971); with M. Gosebruch and C. Wolters, *Methoden der Kunst- und Musikwissenschaft* (Munich, 1970).

Wirén, Dag Ivar, prominent Swedish composer; b. Noraberg, Örebro, Oct. 15, 1905. He studied at the Stockholm Cons. with Oskar Lindberg and Ernest Ellberg (1926-31); then in Paris with Leonid Sabaneyev (1932-34). He returned to Sweden in 1934, and was music critic for the *Svenka Morgonbladet* (1938-46); was vice-president of the Society of Swedish Composers (1947-63). His early music was influenced by Scandinavian Romanticism; later he adopted a more sober and more cosmopolitan neo-Classicism, stressing the symmetry of formal structure; in his thematic procedures he adopts the method of systematic intervallic metamorphosis rather than development and variation.

WORKS: *Serenade* for strings (1937); ballet, *Oscarbalen (Oscarian Ball,* 1949); television ballet, *Den elaka drottningen (The Wicked Queen,* 1960; Swedish television performance, Nov. 22, 1961); 2 radio operettas, *Blått, gult, rött* (1940; inspired by Churchill's famous speech containing the phrase "Blood, sweat, tears") and *Den glada patiensen* (1941); 2 concert overtures (1931, 1940); 5 symphonies: No. 1 (1932), No. 2 (1939), No. 3 (1943-44); No. 4 (1951-52), No. 5 (1964; Stockholm, Dec. 5, 1964); *Sinfonietta* for orch. (1933-34); Cello Concerto (1936); *Little Suite* for orch. (1941); *Romantic Suite* for orch. (1945); Violin Concerto (1945-46); Piano Concerto (1947-50); *Divertimento* for orch. (1954-57); *Triptyk* for orch. (1958); *Music* for strings (1966-67; Stockholm, Jan. 12, 1968); Flute Concertino (1972); 3 string quartets (1930; 1935; 1941-45; 1952-53; 1969-70); *Theme and Variations* for piano (1933); 2 piano trios (1933, 1961); Violin Sonatina (1939); *5 Ironic Miniatures* for piano (1942-45); Piano Sonatina (1950); Quartet for flute, oboe, clarinet, and cello (1956); *5 Improvisations* for piano (1959); *Little Serenade* for guitar (1964); Wind Quintet (1971); *Little Piano Suite* (1971); incidental music for many plays and films; songs.

BIBLIOGRAPHY: M. Pergament, "Dag Wirén," *Svenska tonsättare* (Stockholm, 1943, pp. 154-59).

Wirth, Emanuel, Bohemian violinist; b. Luditz, Bohemia, Oct. 18, 1842; d. Berlin, Jan. 5, 1923. He was a pupil of Kittl at the Prague Cons.; then taught at the Cons. of Rotterdam, and was concertmaster of the local orch.; succeeded Rappoldi as viola player in the Joachim String Quartet, in Berlin; subsequently formed his own trio, with R. Hausmann (cello) and H. Barth (piano), presenting numerous concerts in Germany.

Wirth, Friedrich Moritz, German writer on music; b. Euba, near Chemnitz, Sept. 14, 1849; d. Leipzig, April 26, 1917. He studied classical philology and philosophy at the Univ. of Leipzig, where he lived. His writings include *Drohender Untergang Bayreuths* (1887); *Wagner-Museum und Zukunft des Wagnertums* (1894); *Der Ring des Nibelungen als Wotandrama* (1912); *Parsifal in neuem Lichte* (1914).

Wirth, Helmut, German musicologist and composer; b. Kiel, Oct. 10, 1912. He studied composition with R. Oppel, and musicology with Fritz Stein and Blume; Dr. phil. 1937, at Kiel Univ., with the dissertation, *Joseph Haydn als Dramatiker* (Wolfenbüttel, 1940); from 1936, was active on the Hamburg Radio. He composed a *Goldoni Suite,* chamber orch. (1939), an oboe sonata (1940), and harpsichord sonata (1946), many songs.

Wirth, Herman Felix, Dutch music scholar; b. Utrecht, May 6, 1885. He studied at the Cons. of Utrecht, and later with Hugo Riemann in Leipzig (1906-07). After teaching at the Brussels Cons. he taught at the Univ. of Berlin (1933-38); in 1955 he went to Marburg, where he became absorbed in the study of Christian religions; published *Um den Ursinn des Menschsein* (Vienna, 1960), dealing with subjects of primordial beliefs. He edited works by Dutch masters of the 17th century.

Wise, Michael, English singer and composer; b. Wiltshire, c.1648; d. Salisbury, Aug. 24, 1687. After an apprenticeship under Cooke at the Chapel Royal in London, he was appointed, at the age of 20, organist of Salisbury Cathedral; in 1676 he became Gentleman of the Chapel Royal; in 1687 he was appointed master of the choristers of St. Paul's Cathedral. He was killed by a watchman during a street dispute. He wrote anthems, church services, and catches; 6 of his anthems are included in Boyce's *Cathedral Music;* other pieces are found in various collections of the 17th century.

Wiske, Charles Mortimer, American choral conductor; b. Bennington, Vt., Jan. 12, 1853; d. Lewiston, Maine, July 9, 1934. He studied piano and organ; was engaged by Theodore Thomas to drill the mass chorus (3,000 voices) for the N.Y. May Festival of 1882, and was also chorusmaster during a series of Wagner festivals given by Thomas in the U.S. in 1884; subsequently conducted the N.Y. Chorus Society and various choruses in Paterson and Newark, N.J.

Wislocki, Stanislaw, Polish conductor and composer; b. Rzeszów, July 7, 1921. He studied music in Lwów and then in Rumania; conducted the Poznań Philh.

(1947-58); conducted the National Philh. in Warsaw (1961-67); also taught conducting at the State College of Music in Warsaw. He ceased composing in 1955. He composed a symph. (1944); *4 Poems* for tenor and chamber orch. (1944); *Symphonic Nocturne* (1947); Piano Concerto (1948-49); *Symphonic Ballad* (1950); *Symfonia tańcu (Symphony on Dancing,* 1952).

Wissmer, Pierre, Swiss composer; b. Geneva, Oct. 30, 1915. He studied with Roger-Ducasse at the Paris Cons. and with Daniel-Lesur at the Schola Cantorum; in 1963 he was appointed honorary director of the Schola Cantorum. He writes affable and pleasingly dissonant music in a natural contrapuntal idiom which is never congested by polyphonic superfluities. WORKS: radio opera, *Marion ou La Belle au tricorne* (Geneva, Radio Suisse Romaine, April 16, 1947); comic opera, *Capitaine Bruno* (Geneva, Nov. 9, 1952); opéra bouffe *Léonidas ou La Cruauté mentale* (Paris, Sept. 12, 1958); ballet, *Le Beau Dimanche* (1939; Geneva, March 20, 1944); *Alerte, puits 21* (Geneva, 1964); *Christina et les chimères* (French Television, 1967); *Naïades,* for narrator, soli, chorus and orch. (Geneva, Jan. 21, 1942); *Le Quatrième mage,* oratorio (Paris, Oct. 14, 1969); 5 symphonies (1938, 1951, 1955, 1962, 1969); *Divertissement sur un choral,* for 11 instruments (Geneva, Dec. 8, 1939); *Mouvement* for string orch. (Geneva, Feb. 1, 1940); symph. suite, *Antoine et Cléopâtre* (Geneva, Oct. 2, 1946); overture, *La Mandrellina* (Geneva, April 16, 1952); 2 string quartets (1937 and 1949); *Sérénade* for oboe, clarinet, and bassoon (1938); Sonatina for clarinet and piano (1941); Sonatina for violin and piano (1946); Piano Sonata (1949); *Concerto valcrosiano* for orch. (1966); 2 piano concertos (1937, 1948); 2 violin concertos (1944, 1954); Guitar Concerto (1957); Clarinet Concerto (1960); Trumpet Concerto (1961); Oboe Concerto (1963); *Concertino-Crosière* for flute, string orch., and piano (1966); Wind Quintet (1966); *Quadrige* for flute, violin, cello, and piano (1961); *Cantique en l'ounour dou grand santlouis, rei de franco et patroun de vaucros de cuers* for chorus with piano or organ (1971); songs; choruses.

Wiszniewski, Zbigniew, Polish composer; b. Lwów, July 30, 1922. He studied composition with Sikorski at the Cons. in Lódź (1948-52); taught at the Warsaw Cons. (1954); in 1957 was appointed director of the Polish Radio in Warsaw. WORKS: 3 radio operas: *Neffru* (1958-59; Warsaw, 1959); *Tak jakby (As if,* 1968-70; Warsaw, 1970) and *Paternoster* (1972; Warsaw, 1972); 2 ballets: *Obywatel walc* (1955) and *Ad hominem* (1962); 2 oratorios: *Genesis* (1967-68) and *Brothers* (1970-72); 2 cantatas: *Aubade* (1960) and *Sichel versäumter Stunden* (1971); *Tre pezzi della tradizione* for 3-part chorus and orch. (1964); Oboe Concerto (1951); Symph. (1954); Concerto for Clarinet and String Orch. (1968-70); 2 string quartets (1954, 1957); Trio for oboe, harp, and viola (1963); Solo Violin Sonata (1963); *Kammermusik I* for oboe, oboe d'amore, English horn, and bassoon (1965); *II* (1966); and *IV, Little Symphony,* for 10 instruments (1972-73); Duo for flute and viola (1966); *Cadenza* for percussion (1969); Quartet for flute, horn, piano, and double bass (1972); *Pezzo concer-*

tante for flute and 3 percussionists (1975); piano pieces.

Wit, Paul de, Dutch cellist; b. Maestricht, Jan. 4, 1852; d. Leipzig, Dec. 10, 1925. In 1880 he founded (with O. Laffert) the *Zeitschrift für Instrumentenbau;* opened a museum of musical instruments at Leipzig in 1886, but sold his collections to the Berlin Hochschule für Musik in 1888 and 1891; he then made a 3rd collection, which he sold in 1906 to Heyer of Cologne. Wit was a fine player on the viola da gamba, as well as a cellist. He published *Geigenzettel alter Meister vom 16. bis zur Mitte des 19. Jahrhunderts* (1902; 2nd ed., 1910); *Weltadressbuch der gesammten Musikinstrumenten-Industrie* (1903; 8th ed., 1912); *Katalog des musikhistorischen Museums von P. de Wie* (1903).

Witek, Anton, Bohemian violinist; b. Saaz, Bohemia, Jan. 7, 1872; d. Winchester, Mass., Aug. 19, 1933. He studied violin with his father and with A. Bennewitz at the Prague Cons. From 1894 to 1910 he was concertmaster of the Berlin Philharmonic; in 1895 he formed a duo with the Danish pianist **Vita Gerhardt** (1868-1925), whom he later married (1910). In 1910 he was engaged as concertmaster of the Boston Symph. Orch. (until 1918); from 1920 to 1925 he was in Germany; then returned to America. After the death of his first wife (1925), he married the American violinist **Alma Rosengrein.** He published *Fingered Octaves* (1919).

Witherspoon, Herbert, American bass, b. Buffalo, N.Y., July 21, 1873; d. New York, May 10, 1935. He studied with Horatio Parker at Yale Univ., and also took lessons with MacDowell in N.Y. He then studied singing with Bouhy in Paris, Henry Wood in London, and G. B. Lamperti in Berlin. Returning to America, he made his concert debut at New Haven (Oct. 21, 1895); made 2 tours of England as oratorio singer; his American opera debut occurred at the Metropolitan Opera House as Titurel in *Parsifal* (Nov. 26, 1908); then devoted himself to teaching; in 1925 became president of the Chicago Musical College; 1931, president of the Cincinnati Cons. of Music; in 1933 he returned to N.Y., and in May, 1935, was chosen to succeed Gatti-Casazza as general manager of the Metropolitan Opera Co., but he died suddenly of a heart attack. He published *Singing: A Treatise for Teachers and Students* (N.Y., 1925), and *36 Lessons in Singing for Teacher and Student* (Chicago, 1930).

Witkowski, Georges-Martin, French composer; b. Mostaganem, Algeria, Jan. 6, 1867 (of a French father and a Polish mother); d. Lyons, Aug. 12, 1943. He was educated at the military school of St.-Cyr; began music study with Vincent d'Indy at the Schola Cantorum; later left for the army and settled in Lyons, where he founded the Société des Grands Concerts in 1905 for the production of oratorios. In 1924 he was appointed director of the Lyons Cons. WORKS: the opera, *La Princesse lointaine* after Rostand (Paris, March 26, 1934); 2 symphonies (1900; 1910); *Poème de la maison,* for solo voices, chorus, and orch. (Lyons, Jan. 25, 1919); *Mon lac,* for piano and orch. (Lyons, Nov. 20, 1921); for voice and orch.:

4 Poèmes de Cœur Innombrable (1925), *3 Poèmes de Ronsard* (1935), *Paysage rêvé* (1937); *Introduction et Danse* for violin and orch. (Paris, Oct. 10, 1937); Piano Quintet (1897); String Quartet (1902); Violin Sonata (1907).

BIBLIOGRAPHY: M. Boucher, "G.-M. Witkowski," *Revue Musicale* (March 1926).

Witt, Franz Xaver, German composer of church music; b. Walderbach, Feb. 9, 1834; d. Schatzhofen, Dec. 2, 1888. He studied with Proske and Schrems in Regensberg; took holy orders in 1856. In 1866 he established and edited the *Fliegende Blätter für katholische Kirchenmusik* and *Musica sacra;* in 1868 he founded the Allgemeiner deutscher Cäcilienverein for the improvement of Catholic church music, which, while opposing the introduction of orchestral instruments into the church, helped to arouse interest in the great masterpieces of church music. In his own early Masses, Witt employed the orch. Besides numerous Masses, he publ. 2 Requiems, many litanies, offertories, motets, and hymns (55 opus numbers); also some secular men's choruses; author of *Der Zustand der katholischen Kirchenmusik* (1865); *Über das Dirigieren der katholischen Kirchenmusik;* and *Das bayerische Kultusministerium* (1886); his articles are collected in a centennial vol., *Ausgewählte Anfsätze zur Kirchenmusik* (Cologne, 1934).

BIBLIOGRAPHY: A. Walter, *Dr. Franz Witt. Ein Lebensbild* (Regensburg, 1889); 2nd ed., 1906; includes a full list of works).

Witt, Friedrich, German violinist and composer; b. Hallenbergstetten, Württemberg, Nov. 8, 1770; d. Würzburg, Jan. 3, 1836. At the age of 19, he was engaged as violinist in the orch. of Prince von Oettingen; from 1802 he was Kapellmeister at Würzburg, at first to the Prince-Bishop, then to the Grand Duke, finally to the city. It was Witt who composed the so-called "Jena Symphony," misattributed to Beethoven (see H. C. Robbins Landon's article in the *Music Review* for May 1957). Other works by Witt include the historical opera, *Palma* (Frankfurt, 1804); the comic opera *Das Fischerweib* (Würzburg, 1806); the oratorios *Der leidende Heiland* (Würzburg, 1802) and *Die Auferstehung Jesu;* Masses and cantatas; 9 symphonies; music for wind band; Septet for clarinet, horn, bassoon, and strings; Quintet for piano and winds; Flute Concerto, etc.

Witt, Theodor de, German music editor and composer; b. Wesel, May 9, 1823; d. Rome, Dec. 1, 1855. He studied organ with his father. When Liszt visited Witt's native town he became interested in the talented boy, and gave a concert for his benefit to enable him to study in Berlin (under Dehn). At 22 Witt developed tuberculosis and was sent to Italy; there he made a detailed study of church music; edited the first 4 vols. of Breitkopf & Härtel's complete edition of Palestrina's works. His own works include a piano sonata and some vocal pieces.

Wittassek, Johann Nepomuk August, Bohemian pianist and composer; b. Hořín, March 23, 1770; d. Prague, Dec. 7, 1839. The son of a schoolmaster, he received a good education; took music lessons with F. X. Dušek and J. A. Koželuch in Prague; succeeded Koželuch in 1814 as musical director at the Prague Cathedral; was appointed director of the School for Organists in Prague in 1830. He wrote an opera, *David*, brought out in Prague; 4 piano concertos; concertos for violin, for clarinet, and for bassoon; 6 string quartets; 4 violin sonatas; much church music.

Witte, Georg Hendrik, Dutch organist and composer; b. Utrecht, Nov. 16, 1843; d. Essen, Feb. 1, 1929. He studied at The Hague; then at the Leipzig Cons. with Moscheles and Plaidy (piano), Hauptmann and Reinecke (composition). In 1871 he was appointed conductor of the Musikverein at Essen, which post he held for 40 years, retiring in 1911. He wrote *Der Essener Musikverein 1838 bis 1913* (1913). His works include a cello concerto; a choral work, *An die Sonne;* a piano quartet; numerous piano pieces; also songs.

Wittinger, Robert, Austrian-born German composer; b. Knittelfeld, April 10, 1945. He grew up in Hungary, and studied there with Zsolt Durkó; then went to West Germany to live. His technique of composition is sonoristic, with sound blocks forming thematic groups, while the continuity is achieved by Baroque formulas; the titles of his pieces are indicative of their construction (Dissociations, Concentrations, Compensations, Irreversibilities, Divergences, Montage, Tendencies, Tensions, Symmetrical Structures, etc.).

WORKS: *Dissoziazioni* for orch. (1964); *Consonante* for English horn and orch. (1965); *Espressioni,* ballet music (1966); *Concentrazione* for orch. (1966); *Compensazioni* for small orch. (1967); *Irreversibilitazione* for cello and orch. (1967); *Om* for orch. (1968); *Divergenti* for orch. (West Berlin, Oct. 4, 1970); *Sinfonia* for string orch. (1970); *Costellazioni* for cymbal, chamber orch. and full orch. (Stuttgart, Sept. 25, 1971); *Montaggio,* concerto No. 1 for small orch. (1972); *Relazioni* for 7 soloists and orch. (West Berlin, April 11, 1972); Concerto for oboe, harp, and string orch. (1972); *Concerto Lirico* for orch. (1977); *Concerto Entusiastico* for orch. (1977); *Sinfonia II* for orch. (1977-78); 4 string quartets (1964; 1966; 1970; 1977); *Concentrazioni,* wind quintet (1965); *Itrospezioni* for solo bassoon (1967); *Tendenze* for piano, cello, and percussion (1970); *Tensioni,* wind quintet (1970); *Tolleranza* for oboe, celeste, and percussion (1970); 6 *Strutture simmetriche,* each for a different solo instrument (1970); *Catalizzazioni* for 24 vocalists and 7 instrumentalists (1972); *Sillogismo* for violin and percussion (1974).

Wittgenstein, Count Friedrich Ernst. See **Sayn-Wittgenstein-Berleburg.**

Wittgenstein, Paul, Austrian pianist; b. Vienna, Nov. 5, 1887; d. Manhasset, Long Island, N.Y., March 3, 1961. He was of a musical family; studied piano with Josef Labor and Leschetizky; made his 1st public appearance as pianist in 1913, in Vienna. He lost his right arm in World War I, at the Russian front; was prisoner of war in Omsk, Siberia; repatriated in 1916. He then developed an extraordinary technique for left hand alone, and performed a concerto specially composed for him by his teacher, Josef Labor. He subsequently commissioned left-hand piano concertos from Richard Strauss, Ravel, Prokofiev, Korngold, Benjamin Britten, and other composers, of which he gave the world premières (except the Prokofiev concerto, which he found unsuitable). He appeared in the major musical centers in Europe; toured America in 1934; in 1939 settled in New York. He was a brother of the famous philosopher Ludwig Wittgenstein.

Witting, Karl, German violinist and composer; b. Jülich, Sept. 8, 1823; d. Dresden, June 28, 1907. He studied in Paris under A. Reichel; returned to Germany in 1855, living in Berlin, Hamburg, and Glogau, and finally settling in Dresden in 1861 as a teacher. He publ. a cello sonata, instructive pieces for violin and piano, a *Violinschule;* edited a collection, *Die Kunst des Violinspiels* (8 books) and a collection of duets for 2 violins (4 books); wrote *Musikalisches Wörterbuch* (1887); *Geschichte des Violinspiels* (1900), and analyses for Breitkopf and Härtel's *Konzertführer.*

Wodell, Frederick William, British-American choral conductor and composer; b. London, Dec. 17, 1859; d. St. Petersburg, Fla., Feb. 13, 1938. He studied piano, voice, and composition with various teachers in London; settling in the U.S., he was for many years conductor of the People's Choral Union in Boston; also taught singing there. He composed a cantata, *The American Flag,* for tenor, baritone, men's chorus, and orch.; many anthems, songs, etc.; published *Choir and Chorus Conducting* (Philadelphia, 1901; 12th ed., 1931), and *How to Sing by Note* (1915).

Woehl, Waldemar, German music editor and educator; b. Lipine, near Bethuen, Prussia, Aug. 31, 1902. He studied with his father, and later in Berlin at the Akademie für Kirchen- und Schulmusik with Max Seiffert, Thiel, and Jöde; taught at the Folkwangschule in Essen; during World War II, led the Musikschule für Jugend und Volk in Villach, Austria; eventually settled in Soyen, Bavaria, as teacher and flute maker; started a movement for the restoration of vertical flutes (recorders). He published *Melodielehre* (Leipzig, 1929); *Klavierbuch für den Anfang* (Berlin, 1932); *Das Bach-Buch für Klavierspieler* (Berlin, 1932); *Musik für Blockflöten* (4 vols.; Hannover, 1930–34); a method, *Blockflötenschule* (1930); *Kurze Spielanweisung für das Scheitholz* (1951); composed numerous pieces for the recorder and for ensembles of recorders; edited much 18th-century chamber music.

Wohlfahrt, Franz, German piano pedagogue; son of **Heinrich Wohlfahrt;** b. Frauenpriesnitz, March 7, 1833; d. Gohlis, Feb. 14, 1884. He taught at Leipzig; published many piano studies, some of which have become standard exercises.

Wohlfahrt, Heinrich, German piano pedagogue; b. Kössnitz, near Apolda, Dec. 16, 1797; d. Connewitz, near Leipzig, May 9, 1883. He studied with Häser at Weimar; was cantor and tutor in Thuringian towns; taught at Jena and (from 1867) Leipzig. WRITINGS: *Kinder-Klavierschule* (24 editions),

Der erste Klavierunterricht, Der Klavierfreund (36 children's studies), *Klavierübungen, Grössere und rein praktische Elementar-Klavierschule, Schule der Fingermechanik, Anthologische Klavierschule, Theoretischpraktische Modulationsschule* (English transl., Boston, 1878), *Vorschule der Harmonielehre, Wegweiser zum Componiren für Musik-Dilettanten* (English transl., Boston, 1859); also 3 children's sonatas; *Kleine Leute;* etc.

Wohlgemuth, Gustav, German composer and choral conductor; b. Leipzig, Dec. 2, 1863; d. there, March 2, 1937. He studied at the Leipzig Cons.; in 1891 he founded the Leipziger Männerchor, which he conducted for many years; later also conducted other choral societies in Leipzig; was editor (1907–26) of the *Deutsche Sängerbundeszeitung;* published some 100 male choruses (some with orch.).
BIBLIOGRAPHY: *Gustav Wohlgemuth, sein Leben und Wirken* (Leipzig, 1934), a collection of articles.

Woikowski-Biedau, Viktor Hugo von, German composer; b. Nieder-Arnsdorf, near Schweidnitz, Sept. 2, 1866; d. Berlin, Jan. 1, 1935. He studied music with Wilhelm Berger in Berlin; was employed in the government statistics bureau.
WORKS: the operas *Helga* (Wiesbaden, 1904), *Der lange Kerl* (Berlin, 1906), and *Das Nothemd* (Dessau, 1913); 3 melodramas, *Jung Olaf, Der Todspieler,* and *Die Mette von Marienburg;* 4 ballads for baritone and orch., *Die Jüdin von Worms, Der Triumph des Lebens, Rahab, die Jerichonitin,* and *Jan van Jühren; Aus einem Menschenleben* for violin and piano; several song cycles (*Frühlingslieder, Lebensträume, Schiffslieder, Königslieder, Pagen-Balladen, Osterzauber, Des Sultans Gesetz,* etc.).

Woldemar, Michel, French violinist and composer; b. Orléans, June 17, 1750; d. Clermont-Ferrand, Dec. 19, 1815. He studied with Lolli; for some years was conductor for a traveling theatrical troupe. By adding a 5th string *(c)* to the violin, he obtained an instrument that he called "violon-alto," because it included the viola range, and for which he wrote a concerto. He also publ. 3 violin concertos, a string quartet, duos for 2 violins and for violin and viola; *Sonates fantomagiques* for violin (*L'Ombre de Lolli, de Mestrino, de Pugnani, de Tartini);* 12 grand solos; *6 Rêves ou Caprices; Caprices ou Études; Le Nouveau Labyrinth pour violon,* followed by studies in double stops; *Le Nouvel Art de l'archet; Étude élémentaire de l'archet moderne;* variations on *Les Folies d'Espagne,* etc.; methods for violin, viola, and clarinet; also a system of musical stenography *(Tableau mélotachigraphique)* and a method of musical correspondence (*Notographie).*

Wöldike, Mogens, Danish organist and conductor; b. Copenhagen, July 5, 1897. He studied with Carl Nielsen; was organist and choirmaster in several Copenhagen churches; in 1937 he became conductor of the radio madrigal chorus; toured with it in Scandinavia, England, and Italy; also director for the series of records *Masterpieces of Music before 1750* in collaboration with W. W. Norton & Co. and the Haydn Society of Vienna and Copenhagen. From 1959 to 1972 he served as organist of the Copenhagen Cathedral.

Wolf, Ernst Wilhelm, German composer; b. Grossenbehringen, near Gotha, 1735 (baptized Feb. 25); d. Weimar, 1792 (buried Dec. 1). In 1772 he became Kapellmeister to the music-loving Duchess of Saxe-Weimar, Anna Amalia.

WORKS: about 20 operas, of which the most successful were *Das Rosenfest* (Weimar, 1770) and *Die Dorfdeputierten* (Berlin, June 15, 1772); other works include Passion oratorios and Easter cantatas; 6 piano concertos; 4 quintets for piano, flute, violin, viola, and cello; 6 string quartets; 7 books of piano sonatas, each containing 6 numbers; in manuscript are 15 symphonies, 17 partitas, 12 piano concertos, and much chamber music. He also wrote *Kleine musikalische Reise* (1782) and *Musikalischer Unterricht* (1788; 2nd ed., 1804).

BIBLIOGRAPHY: J. Brockt, *Ernst Wilhelm Wolf* (dissertation; Striegau, 1927).

Wolf, Ferdinand, Austrian writer in literature and music; b. Vienna, Dec. 8, 1896; d. there, Feb. 18, 1866, as librarian of the Imperial Library. His book *Über die Lais, Sequenzen und Leiche, Ein Beitrag zur Geschichte der rhythmischen Formen und Singweisen der Volkslieder und der volksmässigen Kirchen- und Kunstlieder im Mittelalter* (Heidelberg, 1841) is a valuable compendium.

Wolf, Hugo, Austrian composer, one of the greatest masters of the German Lied. b. Windisch-Gräz, March 13, 1860; d. Vienna, Feb. 22, 1903. He studied piano and violin with his father, an amateur musician; then took lessons from Sebastian Weixler, a schoolmaster. In 1870 he was sent to Graz, where he entered a primary school, but left after a single semester and was enrolled in the Seminary at the Benedictine monastery of St. Paul in Carinthia; in 1873 he went to a Gymnasium in Marburg; in 1875 he moved to Vienna, where he became a pupil at the Cons., studying piano with Wilhelm Schenner and harmony with Robert Fuchs. When Wagner visited Vienna in 1875, Wolf went to see him, bringing along some of his compositions; the fact that Wagner received him at all, and even said a few words of encouragement, gave Wolf great impetus towards further composition. But he was incapable of submitting himself to academic discipline, and soon difficulties arose between him and the Cons. authorities. He openly expressed his dissatisfaction with the teaching of Franz Krenn (who was also the teacher of Mahler), and was so impertinent to the director, Josef Hellmesberger, that he was expelled. In March, 1877, he returned to his native town, but after a few months at home decided to go to Vienna again; there he managed to support himself by giving music lessons to children in the homes of friends. By that time he was composing diligently, writing songs to texts by his favorite poets—Goethe, Lenau, Heine. An unhappy encounter with Brahms, who advised him to study counterpoint before attempting to compose, embittered him, and he became determined to follow his own musical inclinations without seeking further advice. After a brief (and un-

successful) employment as chorusmaster in Salzburg (1881), he secured in 1883 the position of music critic of the weekly *Wiener Salonblatt.* He took this opportunity to indulge his professional frustration by attacking those not sympathetic with new trends in music; he poured invective of extraordinary virulence on Brahms, thus antagonizing the influential Hanslick and other admirers of Brahms. But he also formed a coterie of staunch friends, who had faith in his ability. Yet he was singularly unsuccessful in his repeated attempts to secure performances for his works. He submitted a string quartet to the celebrated Rosé Quartet, but it was rejected. Finally, Hans Richter accepted for the Vienna Philharmonic his symph. poem *Penthesilea,* but the public performance was a fiasco, and Wolf even accused Richter of deliberately sabotaging the work; later he reorchestrated the score, eliminating certain crudities of the early version. In 1887 he resigned as music critic of the *Wiener Salonblatt* and devoted himself entirely to composition. He became convinced that he was creating the greatest masterpieces of song since Schubert and Schumann, and stated his conviction in plain terms in his letters. In historical perspective, his self-appraisal has proved remarkably accurate, but psychologists may well wonder whether Wolf was not consciously trying to give himself the needed encouragement by what must have seemed to him a wild exaggeration. However, a favorable turn in his fortunes came in 1889, when his 27 songs to words by Mörike and 10 songs to words by Eichendorff appeared in print. There followed 25 Goethe songs in 1890, and the album of exquisite songs after Heyse and Geibel, *Spanisches Liederbuch,* in 1891, as well as 6 songs to poems of Keller, *Alte Weisen.* The singer Ferdinand Jäger became a champion of Wolf's music, and gave repeated performances of his songs at the meetings of the Vienna Wagner-Verein. Soon Wolf's name became known in Germany; he presented concerts of his own works in Berlin, Darmstadt, Mannheim, and other musical centers. He completed the 1st part of his great cycle of 22 songs, *Italienisches Liederbuch,* in 1891, and composed the 2nd part (24 songs) in 5 weeks, in the spring of 1896. In 1897 he wrote the *3 Gedichte von Michelangelo.* While Wolf could compose songs with a facility and degree of excellence that were truly astounding, he labored painfully on his orchestral works. His early symph. was never completed, nor was a violin concerto; the work on *Penthesilea* took him a disproportionately long time. In 1895 he undertook the composition of his opera, *Der Corregidor,* to the famous tale by Alarcón, *El Sombrero de tres picos,* and, working feverishly, completed the vocal score with piano accompaniment in a few months. The orchestration took him a much longer time. *Der Corregidor* had its première in Mannheim on June 7, 1896, but it proved a disappointment, The opera was ineffective dramatically, and the orchestration was weak. Wolf subsequently revised the score, and in its new version *Der Corregidor* was brought out in Strasbourg on April 29, 1898. He never completed his 2nd opera, *Manuel Venegas* (also after Alarcón); fragments were presented in concert form on March 1, 1903. In the meantime, his fame grew. A Hugo Wolf-Verein was organized at Berlin in 1896, and did excellent work in furthering performances of Wolf's songs in Germany. Even more effective was the Hugo Wolf-Verein in Vienna, founded by Michel Haberlandt on April 22, 1897 (disbanded in 1906). Amidst these encouraging signs of recognition, tragedy struck. A supposed rebuke administered to Wolf by Mahler, at that time the newly appointed director of the Vienna Opera, who had been considering a performance of *Der Corregidor*, precipitated in him a mental breakdown. He declared to friends that Mahler had been relieved of his post, and that he, Wolf, was appointed director of the Vienna Opera in Mahler's stead. On Sept. 20, 1897, he was placed in a private mental institution; after a favorable remission, he was discharged (Jan. 24, 1898), and traveled in Italy and Austria. After his return to Vienna, symptoms of mental derangement manifested themselves in even greater degree. He attempted suicide by throwing himself into a lake, and then was committed to a state asylum at his own request. (A parallel with Schumann's case forcibly suggests itself). He remained in confinement, gradually lapsing into complete irrationality. He died at the age of 42, and was buried near the graves of Schubert and Beethoven; a monument was unveiled on Oct. 20, 1904.

Wolf's significance in music history rests on his songs, about 300 in number, many of them published posthumously. The sobriquet "the Wagner of the Lied" may well be justified in regard to involved contrapuntal texture and chromatic harmony, for Wolf accepted the Wagnerian idiom through natural affinity as well as by clear choice. The elaboration of the accompaniment, and the incorporation of the vocal line into the contrapuntal scheme of the whole, are Wagnerian traits. But with these external similarities, Wolf's dependence on Wagner's models ceases. In his intimate penetration of the poetic spirit of the text, Wolf appears a legitimate successor of Schubert and Schumann. Wolf's songs are symphonic poems in miniature, artistically designed and admirably arranged for voice and piano, the combination in which he was a master.

WORKS: THE STAGE: incidental music to Isben's *Das Fest auf Solhaug* (Vienna, Nov. 21, 1891); *Der Corregidor*, 4-act comedy opera, after Alarcón's *El Sombrero de tres picos* (Mannheim, June 7, 1896; revised version, Strasbourg, Arpil 29, 1898); *Manuel Venegas*, 3-act tragic opera, text after Alarcón's *El Niño de la Bola* (fragments performed in concert form, Mannheim, March 1, 1903.)

CHORAL WORKS: *6 geistliche a cappella Chöre* (1881; ed. by E. Thomas; arranged for men's voices by Max Reger); *Christnacht* for solo voices, chorus, and orch. (1886–89); *Elfenlied* for soprano solo, chorus, and orch. (1889–91); *Dem Vaterland* for male chorus and orch. (1890; many revisions).

INSTRUMENTAL WORKS: String Quartet in D minor (1878–84); *Penthesilea*, symph. poem after Kleist (1883–85); *Italienische Serenade* (1892; a transcription of the *Serenade* in G major for string quartet, 1887); fragments from an early symph. in D minor and from a violin concerto.

SONGS: *12 Lieder aus der Jugendzeit* (1888); *Lieder nach verschiedenen Dichtern*, 31 songs (1877–97); *Gedichte von Mörike*, 53 songs (1888); *Gedichte von Eichendorff*, 20 songs (1886–88); *Gedichte von Goethe*, 51 songs (1888–89); *Spanisches Liederbuch*, 44 songs after Geibel and Heyse (1889–90); *Italienisches Liederbuch*, 46 songs after Heyse, in 2 parts: 22 songs (1890–91), 24 songs (1896). 20 of the songs were orchestrated by Wolf; others by Max Reger. 40 previously unpublished songs, mostly of the earliest period, were publ. in Leipzig in 1936, in 4 vols. as *Nachgelassene Werke*, edited by R. Haas and H. Schultz. Wolf's collected writings were brought out by R. Batka and H. Werner as *Hugo Wolfs musikalische Kritiken* (Leipzig, 1911). A complete edition of the songs was publ. by Peters (Leipzig, 1935). A complete works edition was begun by the Internationalen Hugo Wolf-Gesellschaft, under the direction of H. Janick, in 1960, reaching 18 vols. by 1978. For an index of his works, see P. Müller, *H. W. Verzeichnis seiner Werke* (Leipzig, 1908). An English transl. of the texts of all of Wolf's solo songs was publ. by Henry S. Drinker (N.Y., 1949).

BIBLIOGRAPHY: BIOGRAPHY: P. Müller, "Erinnerungen an Hugo Wolf," *Die Musik* (March-April 1903); M. Haberlandt, *Hugo Wolf. Erinnerungen und Gedanken* (Leipzig, 1903; 2nd ed., Darmstadt, 1911); E. Decsey, *Hugo Wolf* (4 vols., Berlin, 1903–06; new ed. in 1 vol., 1919; the standard work for facts and sources); P. Müller, *Hugo Wolf* (Berlin, 1904); E. Schmitz, *Hugo Wolf* (Leipzig, 1906); E. Newman, *Hugo Wolf* (London, 1907); M. Morold, *Hugo Wolf* (Leipzig, 1912; 2nd ed., 1920); H. Werner, *Hugo Wolf in Maierling* (Leipzig, 1913) and *Der Hugo Wolf-Verein in Wien* (Regensburg, 1922); G. Shur, *Erinnerungen an Hugo Wolf* (Regensburg, 1922); H. Werner, *Hugo Wolf in Perchtoldsdorf* (Regensburg, 1925) and *Hugo Wolf und der wiener akademische Wagner-Verein* (Regensburg, 1926); K. Grunsky, *Hugo Wolf* (Leipzig, 1928); B. B. Viterbi, *Hugo Wolf* (in Italian; Rome, 1931); H. Schouten, *Hugo Wolf: Mensch en Componist* (in Dutch; Amsterdam, 1935); A. von Ehrmann, *Hugo Wolf. Sein Leben in Bildern* (Leipzig, 1937); R. Litterscheid, *Hugo Wolf* (Potsdam, 1939); M. von Graedener-Hattingberg, *Hugo Wolf: vom Wesen und Werk des grössten Liedschöpfers* (Vienna and Leipzig, 1941; revised, 1953); A. von Ehrmann, "Johannes Brahms and Hugo Wolf: A Biographical Parallel," *Musical Quarterly* (Oct. 1943); A. Orel, *Hugo Wolf* (Vienna, 1947); W. Reich, *Hugo Wolf-Rhapsodie* (Zürich, 1947); F. Walker, *Hugo Wolf: A Biography* (London, 1951); N. Loeser, *Wolf* (Haarlem, 1955).

CRITICISM, APPRECIATION: *Gesammelte Aufsäte über Hugo Wolf* (2 vols.; Vienna, 1898, 1899); E. von Hellmer, *Der Corregidor. Kritische und biographische Beiträge zu seiner Würdigung* (Vienna, 1900); K. Heckel, *Hugo Wolf in seinem Verhältnis zu Richard Wagner* (Munich, 1905); K. Grunsky, *Hugo Wolf-Fest in Stuttgart* (Stuttgart, 1906); *Hugo Wolf-Programme für alle Stimmlagen* (Leipzig, 1907); R. Rolland, *Musiciens d'aujourd'hui* (1908; in English, N.Y., 1914); O. Bie, *Das deutsche Lied* (Berlin, 1926; pp. 199–246); K. Varges, *Der Musikkritiker, Hugo Wolf* (Magdeburg, 1934); V. O. Ludwig, *Mörike in der Lyrik von Hugo Wolf* (Bern and Leipzig, 1935); G. Bieri, *Die Lieder von Hugo Wolf* (Bern, 1935); A. Maecklenburg, "Hugo Wolf and Anton Bruckner," *Musical Quarterly* (July 1938); R. Hernried, "Hugo Wolf's *Corregidor* at Mannheim," *Musical Quarterly* (Jan. 1940); F. Walker,

"The History of Wolf's *Italian Serenade,*" *Music Review* (Aug. 1947); E. Sams, *The Songs of Hugo Wolf* (N.Y., 1962); Rita Egger, *Die Deklamationsrhythmik Hugo Wolfs in historischer Sicht* (Tutzing, 1963).

CORRESPONDENCE: E. von Hellmer, *Hugo Wolfs Briefe an Emil Kauffman* (Berlin, 1903); M. Haberlandt, *Hugo Wolfs Briefe an Hugo Faisst* (Stuttgart, 1904); P. Müller, "Ungedruckte Briefe von Hugo Wolf an Paul Müller," *Jahrbuch Peters* (1904); H. Werner, *H. Wolfs Briefe an Oskar Grohe* (Berlin, 1905); E. von Hellmer, *Hugo Wolf. Eine Persönlichkeit in Briefen* (Leipzig, 1912; family letters); *Wolfs Briefe an Rosa Mayreder* (Vienna, 1921); H. Nonveiller, *Wolfs Briefe an Heinrich Potpeschnigg* (Stuttgart, 1923); H. Werner, *Wolfs Briefe an Henriette Lang* (Regensburg, 1923); H. Werner, "Some Unpublished Letters of Hugo Wolf," *Monthly Musical Record* (1927).

Wolf, Johannes, eminent German musicologist; b. Berlin, April 17, 1869; d. Munich, May 25, 1947. He studied musicology with Philipp Spitta at the Univ. of Berlin. From 1902 to 1922 he taught musicology at Berlin Univ. He was co-editor of the *Sammelbände der Internationalen Musik-Gesellschaft* (1899–1904). In 1943 he went to live in Gmein; in 1946, in Munich. He made a particular study of medieval music, and especially the history of notation.
WRITINGS: *Geschichte der Mensural-Notation von 1250–1460 nach den theoretischen und praktischen Quellen* (3 parts, 1904; very important); "Deutsche Lieder des 15. Jahrhunderts," "Liliencron-Festschrift," (1910); *Handbuch der Notationskunde* (Part I, 1913; Part II, 1919); *Die Tonschriften* (1924); *Kleine Musikgeschichte* (1925), with musical examples in *Alte Sing- und Spielmusik* (1926–31; 2nd ed. in 1 vol., 1931; the examples only, as *Music of Earlier Times,* N.Y., 1950); *Zur Geschichte der Musikabteilung der Staatsbibliothek* (1930); *Geschichte der Musik in allgemeinverständlicher Form* (3 vols.; Leipzig, 1925–29; 2nd ed. of vol. II, 1934); etc. For the *Denkmäler deutscher Tonkunst* he selected vocal works of Joh. Rud. Ahle (vol. 5) and Rhaw's *Newe deutsche Geistliche Gesenge* (vol. 34); for the *Denkmäler der Tonkunst in Österreich,* Isaac's secular works (vols. 28 and 32 [14.i and 16.i]); for the *Vereeniging voor Nederlandsche Muziekgeschiedenis,* the complete works of Obrecht (from 1908; 30 vols.) and a collection of Dutch songs of the 16th century; also ed. the *Musica Practica* of Ramos de Pareja (Beiheft 2 of the Internationale Musik-Gesellschaft, 1901); the *Squarcialupi Codex* (publ. posthumously, 1955); the publications of the Paul Hirsch Library, including Luther's *Deutsche Messe* (Kassel, 1934); *Musikalische Schrifttafeln* (Bückeburg, 1927). A "Johannes Wolf-Festschrift" was published in 1929, ed. by Lott, Osthoff, and Wolffheim.
BIBLIOGRAPHY: Otto Gombosi, "Johannes Wolf," *Musical Quarterly* (April 1948); Otto Kinkeldey, "Johannes Wolf," *Journal of the American Musicological Society* (Spring 1948).

Wolf, Ludwig, German pianist and composer; b. Frankfurt, 1804; d. Vienna, Aug. 6, 1859. He studied composition with Seyfried; was skillful both as pianist and violinist; composed 3 string quartets; a piano quartet; 4 string trios; many other works in manuscript.

Wolf, Wilhelm, German pianist; b. Breslau, April 22, 1838; d. Berlin, Jan. 8, 1913. He studied with Th. Kullak; in 1881 established himself in Berlin as a teacher; contributed to musical periodicals; wrote *Musik-Ästhetik in kurzer und gemeinfasslicher Darstellung* (2 vols., 1895, 1906); a collection of essays appeared as *Gesammelte musikästhetische Aufsätze* (1894).

Wolf-Ferrari, Ermanno, famous Italian opera composer; b. Venice, Jan. 12, 1876; d. there, Jan. 21, 1948. His mother was Italian; his father was a well-known German painter. Wolf-Ferrari was sent to Rome to study art, but became interested in opera and decided to devote himself to music; accordingly, he was sent to Munich, where he studied with Rheinberger (1893–95). In 1899 he returned to Venice, where his oratorio *La Sulamite* was successfully performed. This was followed by the production of his first opera, *Cenerentola* (1900). From 1902 to 1907 he was director of the Liceo Benedetto Marcello in Venice; then taught at the Salzburg Mozarteum; lived mostly in Neu-Biberg, near Munich; obtained his first success with the production of the comic opera, *Le Donne curiose* (Munich, 1903); the next opera, *I quattro rusteghi* (Munich, 1906), was also well received; there followed his little masterpiece, *Il Segreto di Susanna,* a 1-act opera buffa in the style of the Italian "verismo" (Susanna's secret being not infidelity, as her husband suspected, but indulgence in surreptitious smoking). Turning towards grand opera, he wrote *I Gioielli della Madonna (The Jewels of the Madonna);* it was brought out at Berlin in 1911, and soon became a repertory piece everywhere; he continued to compose, but his later operas failed to match the appeal of his early creations.
WORKS: OPERAS: *Cenerentola* (Venice, Feb. 22, 1900; in Bremen as *Aschenbrödel,* Jan. 31, 1902); *Le Donne curiose* (Munich, Nov. 27, 1903; in German as *Die neugierigen Frauen;* in Italian, N.Y., Jan. 3, 1912); *I quattro rusteghi* (Munich, March 19, 1906; in German as *Die vier Grobiane); Il Segreto di Susanna* (Munich, Dec. 4, 1909; in German as *Susannens Geheimnis;* in Italian, N.Y., March 14, 1911); *I Gioielli della Madonna* (Berlin, Dec. 23, 1911; in German as *Der Schmuck der Madonna;* in Italian, Chicago, Jan. 16, 1912; in English, as *The Jewels of the Madonna,* N.Y., Oct. 14, 1913); *L'Amatore medico,* after Molière (Dresden, Dec. 4, 1913; in German, as *Der Liebhaber als Arzt;* in Italian, N.Y., Metropolitan Opera, March 25, 1914); *Gli Amanti sposi* (Venice, Feb. 19, 1925; *Veste di cielo* (Munich, April 21, 1927); in German as *Das Himmelsklied); Sly,* after the prologue to Shakespeare's *The Taming of the Shrew* (Milan, La Scala, Dec. 29, 1927); in Iialian as *La Leggenda del dormiente risvegliato); La Vedova scaltra,* after Goldoni (Rome, March 5, 1931); *Il Campiello,* after Goldoni (Milan, Feb. 12, 1936); *La Dama boba,* after Lope de Vega (Milan, Feb. 1m 1939); *Gli dei a Tebe* (Hannover, June 5, 1943; in German as *Der Kuckuck in Theben);* also a revision of Mozart's *Idomemeo* (Munich, June 15, 1931).
OTHER WORKS: *La Sulamite,* biblical cantata (1889);

Talitha kumi, mystery for solo voices, chorus, and orch. (1900); *La Vita nuova,* after Dante, oratorio (Munich, Feb. 21, 1903; N.Y., Dec. 4, 1907); *Serenade* for string orch.; *Kammersymphonie* (1901); *Idillio-concertino* for oboe, string orch., and 2 horns (Venice Festival, 1932); *Suite-concertino* for bassoon, string orch., and 2 horns (Rome, March 26, 1933); *Suite veneziana,* for orch. (1936); *Arabeschi* for orch. (1937); *Divertimento* for orch. (1938); *Kleines Konzert* for English horn and orch. (posthumous; Salzburg, Jan. 18, 1955); 2 violin sonatas; 2 piano trios; a string quartet; a piano quintet; piano pieces; songs.
    BIBLIOGRAPHY: H. Teibler, *Ermanno Wolf-Ferrari* (Leipzig, 1906); E. L. Stahl, *Ermanno Wolf-Ferrari* (Salzburg, 1936); R. de Rensis, *Ermanno Wolf-Ferrari, la sua vita d'artista* (Milan, 1937); A. C. Grisson, *Ermanno Wolf-Ferrari: Lebensbeschreibung* (Regensburg, 1941).

Wolfe, Jacques, American composer and teacher; b. Botoshan, Rumania, April 29, 1896. He was brought to the U.S. as a child; studied music in N.Y. at the Institute of Musical Art with Goetschius, Robinson, and Friskin (graduated in 1915). During World War I he was a clarinetist in the 50th Infantry Band; then was sent to North Carolina, where he studied Negro spirituals. Many of his songs are in the manner of spirituals; some of them acquired popularity *(De Glory Road, Gwine to Hebb'n, Halleluja Rhythm, Short'nin' Bread,* etc.); he also wrote *Betsy's Boy, The Hand-Organ Man, Sailormen, British Children's Prayer;* numerous choral works; piano pieces.

Wolfe, Stanley, American music educator and composer; b. Brooklyn, Feb. 7, 1924. After service in the U.S. Army during World War II, he enrolled at the Juilliard School of Music in New York, studying composition with William Bergsma, Vincent Persichetti and Peter Mennin (B.S., 1952; M.S., 1955); then joined its faculty; in 1963 was appointed director of the Juilliard Extension Division.
    WORKS: *Adagio* for woodwind quintet (1948); Symph. No. 1 (1954); Symph. No. 2 (1955); *Three Profiles* for piano (1955); *Lincoln Square Overture* (1957); Symph. No. 3 (Albuquerque, Nov. 18, 1959); Symph. No. 4 (Albuquerque, Dec. 7, 1966); *Variations* for orch. (1967); Symph. No. 5 (N.Y., April 2, 1971).

Wolfes, Felix, German-American pianist and conductor; b. Hannover, Sept. 2, 1892; d. Boston, March 28, 1971. He studied at the Leipzig Cons. with Max Reger (theory) and R. Teichmüller (piano); later in Strasbourg with Pfitzner (composition); conducted opera at Breslau, Essen, and Dortmund (until 1933); then went to France; in 1938 came to the U.S. and was appointed assistant conductor at the Metropolitan Opera House; subsequently joined the faculty of the New England Cons. in Boston as vocal teacher.

Wolff, Albert (Louis), French conductor; b. Paris, Jan. 19, 1884; d. Paris, Feb. 20, 1970. He studied at the Paris Cons.; in 1908 became chorusmaster at the Opéra-Comique, and was appointed conductor there in 1911; from 1919 to 1921 he was conductor of the French repertory at the Metropolitan Opera House;

conducted the world première of his opera *L'Oiseau bleu* there on Dec. 27, 1919. In 1922 he succeeded Messager as 1st conductor at the Opéra-Comique; from 1928 to 1934, conductor of the Concerts Lamoureux in Paris; from 1934 to 1940, of the Concerts Pasdeloup; toured in South America (1940–45); then returned to Paris; continued to conduct occasionally at the Opéra-Comique.
    BIBLIOGRAPHY: S. Wolff, "Albert Wolff, Doyen de l'Opéra-Comique," *Le Guide du Concert et du Disque* (Oct. 3, 1958).

Wolff, Auguste (Désiré Bernard), French pianist and piano manufacturer; b. Paris, May 3, 1821; d. there, Feb. 3, 1887. He studied piano with Zimmerman at the Paris Cons. and composition with Halévy; after a few years of teaching, he joined the firm of the piano maker Camille Pleyel in 1852, succeeding him as head on 1855; the firm then became known as Pleyel-Wolff & Cie.

Wolff, Christian, American composer of the avant-garde; b. Nice, France, March 8, 1934; came to the U.S. in 1941. He studied piano in New York; took lessons in composition with John Cage. He studied classical languages at Harvard Univ.; received his Ph.D. in comparative literature in 1963. In 1962 he was appointed instructor in Greek and Latin at Harvard. He evolved a curiously static method of composition, using drastically restricted numbers of pitches. His only structural resources became arithmetical progressions of rhythmic values and the expressive use of rests. He used 3 different pitches in his Duo for violin and piano; 4 different pitches in the Trio for flute, cello, and trumpet (1951); 9 in a piano piece called *For Piano I.* Beginning in 1957 he introduced into his works various degrees of free choice; sometimes the players are required to react to the musical activities of their partners according to unforeseen cues.
    WORKS: Trio for flute, cello, and trumpet (1951); *Nine* for 9 instruments (1951); *For 6 or 7 Players* (1959); *Summer* for string quartet (1961); *Duo for Violinist and Pianist* (1961); *For 5 or 10 Players* (1962); *In Between Pieces,* for 3 players (1963); *For 1, 2 or 3 People* (1964); Septet, for any instruments (1964); piano pieces, entitled *For Piano I, For Piano II, Duo for Pianists I and II,* for 2 pianos, 4 hands; *Duet I* for piano, 4 hands; *Duet II,* for piano and horn; *Snowdrop* for harpsichord (1970); *You Blew It* for chorus (1971).

Wolff, Christoph, eminent German musicologist; b. Solingen, May 24, 1940. He studied church music in Berlin and in Freiburg im Bresgau; took courses in musicology at the Univ. of Berlin; obtained his degree of Dr. phil. for the dissertation, *Der stile antico in der Musik J. S. Bachs* (Wiesbaden, 1968). He was lecturer at the Univ. of Toronto, Canada (1968–69); then prof. of musicology at Columbia Univ. (1970–76); in 1976 was appointed to the faculty of Harvard Univ. He has particularly distinguished himself by innovative research into formative elements in Bach's works; among his many contributions to these problems are "Der Terminus *Ricercar* in Bachs *Musikalisches Op-*

fer," *Bach-Jahrbuch*, 1967, and "New Research on Bach's *Musical Offering*," in the *Musical Quarterly*, 1971. He was elected editor of *Bach-Jahrbuch* in 1974; edited volumes of the *Neue Bach-Ausgabe* (V/2, *Goldberg Variations;* 14 Canons; VIII/1: *Musical Offering;* Canons); the *Neue Mozart-Ausgabe* (V/15, 2-3; Piano Concertos), and the *Hindemith-Gesamtausgabe*.

Wolff, Édouard, Polish pianist and composer; b. Warsaw, Sept. 15, 1816; d. Paris, Oct. 16, 1880. He studied in Warsaw with Zawadski (piano) and Elsner (composition); then was a piano pupil of Würfel in Vienna. In 1835 he settled in Paris, and became an esteemed teacher; he was a friend of Chopin, and imitated him in his piano music. He publ. 350 opus numbers for piano, among them several albums of études; a waltz, *La Favorite; Chansons polonaises originales; Tarentelle; Chansons bacchiques;* a piano concerto; also 30 celebrated duos for piano and violin (with de Bériot), and 8 more (with Vieuxtemps). His sister, **Regina Wolff,** a pianist, was the mother of violinist **Henryk Wieniawski.**

Wolff, Erich, Austrian pianist; b. Vienna, Dec. 3, 1874; d. New York, March 20, 1913 (while on a concert tour). He studied in Vienna with Anton Door (piano); lived in Vienna, and (from 1906) in Berlin; became well known as an excellent accompanist of singers. A volume of 60 of his German songs was publ. posthumously, eliciting great praise. He also wrote a violin concerto and some chamber music.

Wolff, Ernst Victor, German pianist and harpsichordist; b. Berlin, Aug. 6, 1889; d. East Lansing, Michigan, Aug. 21, 1960. He studied piano with Ph. Scharwenka in Berlin; musicology at the Univ. of Berlin; Dr. phil. there with the dissertation *Robert Schumanns Lieder in ersten und späteren Fassungen* (Leipzig, 1914); was active in Germany as harpsichord player; lived mostly in Berlin until 1933; then went to London, and in 1936 settled in N.Y.; in 1947 joined the faculty of Michigan State Univ. He published *With Reason and Rhyme* (New Haven, 1957).

Wolff, Hellmuth Christian, Swiss musicologist and composer; b. Zürich, May 23, 1906. He studied musicology in Berlin with Abert, Schering, Blume, and Sachs; received his Dr. phil. with a dissertation *Die venezianische Oper in der 2. Hälfte des 17. Jahrhunderts* (Berlin, 1937); in 1947 he was appointed prof. of musicology at the Univ. of Leipzig; beginning in 1956 he devoted a great deal of his time to painting, and exhibited in Leipzig and other German cities.
WORKS: Oboe Concerto (1933); *Inferno 1944,* symph. poem (1946); Piano Concerto (1948); Violin Concerto (1948); several scenic oratorios; chamber music; choruses.
WRITINGS: *Die Musik der alten Niederländer* (Leipzig, 1956); *Die Händel-Oper auf der modernen Bühne* (Leipzig, 1957); *Die Oper* (3 vols.; Cologne, 1971-72; also in English); *Originale Gesangsimprovisationen des 16. bis 18. Jahrhundert* (Cologne, 1972; also in English).

Wolff, Hermann, German concert manager; b. Cologne, Sept. 4, 1845; d. Berlin, Feb. 3, 1902. He was a pupil of Franz Kroll and Wüerst; was editor of the *Neue Berliner Musikzeitung* (1878-79); co-editor of the *Musikwelt.* In 1881 he founded the Hermann Wolff Concert Management, which became famous; it was later styled H. Wolf & J. Sachs (until 1935). He also composed piano pieces and songs.
BIBLIOGRAPHY: E. Stargardt-Wolff, *Wegbereiter grosser Musiker* (Berlin, 1954).

Wolff, Max, Austrian operetta composer; b. Moravia, Feb., 1840; d. Vienna, March 23, 1886. He studied music with Marx and Dessoff; became a successful composer of operettas, of which the following were produced in Vienna; *Die Pilger* (Sept. 6, 1872); *Die Porträt-Dame* (March 1, 1877); *Césarine* (Dec. 13, 1878).

Wolff, Werner, German conductor and writer on music; b. Berlin, Oct. 2, 1883; d. Rüschlikon, Switzerland, Nov. 23, 1961. He was the son of the concert manager **Hermann Wolff.** He studied music with Klatte; conducted opera in Vienna, Prague, Danzig, and Düsseldorf; from 1917 to 1932 was a conductor of the Hamburg State Opera. In 1938 he emigrated to the U.S.; taught at Wesleyan College, Tennessee; was conductor of the Chattanooga Opera Association (1943-59). He composed symphonic and chamber music; piano pieces, and songs. He published, in English, *Anton Bruckner: Rustic Genius* (N.Y., 1942; revised German ed. as *Anton Bruckner: Genie und Einfall,* Zürich, 1948).

Wolffheim, Werner (Joachim), German musicologist; b. Berlin, Aug. 1, 1877; d. there, Oct. 26, 1930. While studying jurisprudence in Munich and Berlin (1895-98), he took courses in musicology with Sandberger and Fleischer; later studied with Kretzschmar and Johannes Wolf. With H. Springer and Max Schneider he was co-editor of *Miscellanea bio-bibliographica* (supplement to Eitner's *Quellen-Lexikon*); edited the piano concertos for Breitkopf & Härtel's complete ed. of Haydn's works, and prepared (with Kretzschmar) a new ed. of Spitta's life of Bach. He formed a valuable music library (catalogue in 2 vols.), which he sold in 1928-29.

Wölfl (Woelfl, Wölffl), Joseph, Austrian pianist and composer; b. Salzburg, Dec. 24, 1773; d. London, May 21, 1812. He was a pupil of Leopold Mozart and Michael Haydn; served as a chorister at the Salzburg Cathedral (1783-86); was then in Vienna (1970-92) and Warsaw (1793); again in Vienna from 1795; was considered Beethoven's rival as a pianist; in 1798 he married the actress Therese Klemm. Traveling through Germany, he gave numerous concerts as pianist, reaching Paris in 1801; there he settled for several years; produced 2 French operas and was acclaimed as a piano virtuoso. In 1805 he went to London, and almost immediately established himself in favor of the public as pianist and teacher. He was, however, of an eccentric disposition, and became involved in all sorts of trouble. He died in obscurity at the age of 38. In his professional life, he emphasized the sensational element; gave fanciful titles to his works; named one of his piano sonatas *Ne plus ultra,* and claimed that it was the most difficult piece ever written.

WORKS: operas: *Der Höllenberg* (Vienna, Nov. 21, 1795), *Der Kopf ohne Mann* (Vienna, Dec. 3, 1798), *Das schöne Milchmädchen* (Vienna, Jan. 5, 1797), *Das trojanische Pferd* (Vienna, 1797), *L'Amour romanesque* (Paris, 1804), *Fernando, ou Les Maures* (Pairs, 1805); the ballets *La Surprise de Diane* (London, Dec. 21, 1805), and *Alzire* (London, Jan. 27, 1807); 7 piano concertos, including *Le Calme* and *Concerto militaire;* other publ. compositions are 2 symphonies; 9 string quartets; 12 piano trios; 2 trios for 2 clarinets and bassoon; 42 violin sonatas; 58 piano sonatas; 24 sets of variations for piano; a *Méthode de piano* (with 100 studies); sonatas for 4 hands; waltzes; polonaises, rondos, fantasias, etc.; also songs. Some of his piano pieces were publ. in monthly issues, under the title *The Harmonic Budget* (London, 1810).

BIBLIOGRAPHY: R. Duval, "Un Rival de Beethoven: Joseph Woelfl," *Rivista Musicale Italiana* (1898; also separately, Turin, 1898); R. Baum, *Joseph Wölfl. Leben, Klavierwerke, Klavierkammermusik und Klavierkonzerte* (Kassel, 1928).

Wolfram, Joseph Maria, Bohemian composer; b. Dobrzan, July 21, 1789; d. Teplitz, Sept. 30, 1839. He studied with J. A. Koželuch in Prague; moved to Vienna, as music teacher; then became a government official at Theusing, and mayor of Teplitz (1824). He brought out several successful operas: *Maja und Alpino* (Prague, May 24, 1826), *Der Bergmönch* (Dresden, March 14, 1830), *Das Schloss Candra* (Dresden, Dec. 1, 1832); a *Missa nuptialis* and some piano pieces and songs by him were published.

Wolfrum, Philipp, German musicologist and composer; b. Schwarzenbach-am-Wald, Dec. 17, 1854; d. Samaden, May 8, 1919. He was a pupil of Rheinberger and Wüllner in Munich; received his Dr. phil. degree at Leipzig Univ. in 1890 with the dissertation, *Die Entstehung und erste Entwickelung des deutschen evangelischen Kirchenliedes in musikalischer Beziehung.* He published *Joh. Seb. Bach* (2 vols., 1906; 2nd ed. of vol. 1, 1910); *Die evangelische Kirchenmusik: Ihr Stand und ihre Weiterentwicklung* (1914); *Luther und Bach* (1917); *Luther und die Musik* (1918).

WORKS: *Ein Weihnachtsmysterium,* a Christmas play, for chorus and orch. (1899); *Das grosse Hallelujah,* for male chorus and orch.; Piano Quartet; String Quartet; Piano Trio; Cello Sonata; 3 organ sonatas; edited *Der evangelische Kirchenchor* (collection of 44 hymns) and *Pfälzisches Melodienbuch.*

BIBLIOGRAPHY: K. Hasse, "Philipp Wolfrum," *Zeitschrift für Musikwissenschaft* (1919).

Wolfurt, Kurt von, German composer; b. Lettin, Sept. 7, 1880; d. Munich, Feb. 25, 1957. He studied science at the universities of Dorpat, Leipzig, and Munich; then took lessons in composition with Max Reger in Munich, where he settled. He composed the opera *Dame Kobold* (Kassel, March 14, 1940); *Faust,* after Goethe, for soprano, chorus, and orch.; *Gesang des Meeres,* symph. poem; *Concerto grosso;* Piano

Concerto; chamber music; etc. He published monographs on Mussorgsky (Stuttgart, 1927) and Tchaikovsky (Zürich, 1951).

BIBLIOGRAPHY: special issue of *Zeitschrift für Musik* (Oct. 1940).

Wolgast, Johannes, German musicologist; b. Kiel, July 2, 1891; d. Leipzig, Oct. 24, 1932. He studied with Riemann, Straube, and Pembaur in Leipzig; was in the German Army during World War I; after the Armistice, continued his studies with Schering and Abert in Berlin; Dr. phil., 1923, with the dissertation, *Georg Böhm;* then taught at the Kirchenmusik-Institut in Leipzig and at the Leipzig Cons.; edited the collected works of Georg Böhm (2 vols.; 1927, 1932); compiled various useful catalogues; contributed articles to German musical magazines.

Wolkenstein, Oswald von, one of the last of the Minnesänger; b. Burg Wolkenstein, Grödener Tal (Tyrol), 1377; d. Meran, Aug. 2, 1445. He led an adventurous life, traveling through Russia, Persia, Greece, Spain, France, Italy (with King Ruprecht in 1401), etc. For several years (from 1415) he was in the service of King (later Emperor) Sigismund, whom he accompanied to the Council of Constance. The musical settings that he devised for his poems are notable for their genuine melodic quality; some of them are in 2-part and 3-part counterpoint; there are also examples of canonic imitation. His works were edited by Schatz and Koller for the *Denkmäler der Tonkunst in Österreich* 18 (9.i).

BIBLIOGRAPHY: J. Beyrich, *Untersuchungen über des Stil Oswalds von Wolkenstein* (Leipzig, 1910); W. Türler, *Stilistische Studien zu Oswald von Wolkenstein* (Heidelberg, 1920); J. Schatz, *Sprache und Wortschatz Oswalds von Wolkenstein* (Vienna, 1930); A. Wolkenstein-Rodenegg, *Oswald von Wolkenstein* (Innsbruck, 1930); W. Salmen, "Werdegang und Lebensfülle des Oswald Wolkenstein," *Musica Disciplina* (1953).

Wollanck, Friedrich, German composer; b. Berlin, Nov. 3, 1782; d. there, Sept. 6, 1831. He was a lawyer and held a government position as counsellor of the city court in Berlin. His works include an opera, *Der Alpenhirt* (Berlin, 1811); a "Liederspiel," *Thibaut von Lowis;* 2 Masses; a Requiem and other church music; more than 100 songs; 33 parts-songs; 3 string quartets; 2 string sextets; other chamber music; piano sonatas.

Wolle, John Frederick, American choral conductor and organist; b. Bethlehem, Pennsylvania, April 4, 1863; d. there, Jan. 12, 1933. He went to Germany to study with Rheinberger in Munich (1884–85); upon return to the U.S. served as organist at the Moravian Church in Bethlehem (1885–1905); in 1900 he inaugurated the Bach Choir in Bethlehem, which became famous for its fine performances.

BIBLIOGRAPHY: R. Walters, *The Bethlehem Bach Choir* (Boston, 1918); R. Walters, "Bach at Bethlehem, Pennsylvania," *Musical Quarterly* (1935); M. A. DeWolfe Howe, "Venite in Bethlehem," *Musical Quarterly* (April 1942).

Wolle, Peter, Moravian minister, bishop, and composer; b. New Herrnhut, St. Thomas, West Indies, Jan. 5, 1792; d. Bethlehem, Pa., Nov. 14, 1871. He was consecrated to the episcopacy on Sept. 26, 1845. He left several compositions; edited the *Moravian Tune Book* (1836). One of his anthems, for double chorus with strings and organ, is included in the series, *Music of the Moravians in America,* published by the N.Y. Public Library (1939).
BIBLIOGRAPHY: A. G. Rau and H. T. David, *A Catalogue of Music by American Moravians* (Bethlehem, 1938).

Wollenhaupt, Hermann Adolf, German pianist and composer; b. Schkeuditz, near Leipzig, Sept. 27, 1827; d. New York, Sept. 18, 1863. He studied in Leipzig with Julius Knorr (piano) and Moritz Hauptmann (composition). In 1845 he settled in N.Y.; made a reputation as a concert pianist and teacher. He wrote about 100 brilliant piano pieces, among them *Galop di bravura, Valses styriennes, Improvisation, Nocturne,* and *Scherzo brillante;* he also made numerous transcriptions and arrangements.

Wollgandt, Edgar, German violinist and teacher; b. Wiesbaden, July 18, 1880; d. Halle, Dec. 25, 1949. He studied violin with H. Heermann in Frankfurt; in 1903 became concertmaster of the Gewandhaus Orch.; Leipzig; also was 1st violin of the Gewandhaus Quartet. He taught for many years in Leipzig, and in 1947 became prof. of the Musik Hochschule in Halle.

Wolpe, Stefan, significant modern composer; b. Berlin, Aug. 25, 1902; d. New York, April 4, 1972. He studied music theory with Paul Juon and Franz Schreker at the Berlin Hochschule für Musik (1919–24). After graduation, he became associated with choral and theatrical groups in Berlin, promoting social causes; composed songs on revolutionary themes. With the advent of the anti-Semitic Nazi regime, he went to Vienna, where he took lessons with Anton von Webern; then traveled to Palestine; taught music theory at the Jerusalem Cons. In 1938 he emigrated to the U.S., where he devoted himself mainly to teaching; was on the faculty of the Settlement Music School in Philadelphia (1946–48); at the Philadelphia Academy of Music (1949–52); at Black Mountain College, North Carolina (1952–56); and at Long Island Univ. (1957–68). He also taught privately. Among his students were Elmer Bernstein, Ezra Laderman, Ralph Shapey, David Tudor, and Morton Feldman. He was married successively to Ola Okuniewska, a painter, in 1927, to **Irma Schoenberg,** the Rumanian pianist, in 1934, and to Hilda Morley, the poetess, in 1948. In his style of composition, he attempted to reconcile the contradictions of triadic tonality (which he cultivated during his early period of writing "proletarian" music), atonality without procrustean dodecaphony, and serialism of contrasts obtained by intervallic contraction and expansion, metrical alteration, and dynamic variegation; superadded to these were explorations of Jewish cantillation and infatuation with jazz. Remarkably enough, the very copiousness of these resources contributed to a clearly identifiable idiom.
WORKS: operas: *Schöne Geschichten* (1927–29), *Zeus und Elida* (1928); *Cantata about Sport* (1952); *Street Music* for baritone, speaker and 5 instruments, to Wolpe's own text (1963–68); Cantata to texts by Hölderlin, Herodotus, and Robert Creeley (1963–68); incidental music: *Da liegt Hund begraben* (1932); *The Good Woman of Setzuan,* to a play by Bertolt Brecht (1953); *The Exception and the Rule* to a play by Bertolt Brecht (1960); for orch.: *Passacaglia* (1957); *The Man from Midian,* ballet suite (1942); Symphony (1955–56; revised 1964); *Chamber Piece No. 1,* for 14 players (1964); *Chamber Piece No. 2,* for 14 players (1965–66); chamber music: *Duo in Hexachord* for oboe and clarinet (1936); Oboe Sonata (1941); Violin Sonata (1949); Quartet for trumpet, saxophone, percussion, and piano (1950); Oboe Quartet (1955); Quintet with voice for baritone, clarinet, horn, cello, harp, and piano (1956–57); Trio for flute, cello, and piano (1964); *From Here on Farther* for clarinet, bass clarinet, violin, and piano (1969); String Quartet (1969); *Piece* for trumpet and 7 instruments (1971); for piano: *March and Variations* for 2 pianos (1933); *4 Studies on Basic Rows* (1935–36); *Toccata* (1941); *Enactments* for 3 pianos (1950–53); *Broken Sequences* (1969). He contributed numerous articles to German and American music magazines.
BIBLIOGRAPHY: Marion Bauer, "Stefan Wolpe," *Modern Music* (1940); Herbert Sucoff, *Catalogue and Evaluation of the Work of Stefan Wolpe* (N.Y., 1969).

Wolpert, Franz Alfons, German composer and theorist; b. Wiesentheid, Oct. 11, 1917. He sang in the Cathedral Choir in Regensburg, and studied there at a church seminary; took lessons in composition with Wolf-Ferrari in Salzburg (1939–41). He taught music at the Mozarteum (1941–50); then was engaged as music teacher in Überlingen, where he settled.
WORKS: song cycles to words by Uhland, Lenau and Goethe; 2 violin sonatas; 2 viola sonatas; 2 cello sonatas; clarinet trio; 2 piano sonatas; *Das Göttliche* for soprano chorus and orch.; cantata after Goethe (1961); 15 Shakespeare sonnets for bass and piano (1949–68). He published *Neue Harmonik* (Regensburg, 1952; new enlarged edition, Wilhelmshaven, 1972).

Wolstenholme, William, blind English organist and composer; b. Blackburn, Lancashire, Feb. 24, 1865; d. London, July 23, 1931. He entered the College for Blind Sons of Gentlemen in Worcester at the age of 9; studied with Dr. Done, the Cathedral organist there; Mus. Bac., Oxford, 1887; subsequently filled various posts as church organist in Blackburn, and (from 1902) in London. In 1908 he visited the U.S.
WORKS: *Lord Ullin's Daughter,* cantata; *Sir Humphrey Gilbert,* ballad for women's voices; *To Take the Air,* madrigal; *Suite* in F for string orch.; about 100 compositions for organ; Wind Quintet; Piano Quartet; 2 string quartets; Piano Trio; Violin Sonata; piano pieces: *Impromptu-Polonaise, Marche humoresque, Fantasy-Intermezzo,* etc.; songs and part-songs.
BIBLIOGRAPHY: F. H. Wood, "William Wolstenholme," *Musical Times* (1931).

Wolzogen, Alfred, Freiherr von, German writer on music; b. Frankfurt, May 27, 1823; d. San Remo, Jan.

14, 1883. From 1868 he was Intendant of the court theater at Schwerin. Author of *Über Theater und Musik* (Breslau, 1860); *Über die szenische Darstellung von Mozarts "Don Giovanni"* (1860); *Wilhelmine Schröder-Devrient* (Leipzig, 1863); new German versions of Mozart's *Don Giovanni* and *Schauspieldirektor;* also articles in periodicals.

Wolzogen, Ernst, Freiherr von, German poet and musical journalist; son of **Alfred von Wolzogen** and half-brother of **Hans von Wolzogen;** b. Breslau, April 23, 1855; d. Munich, July 30, 1934. He studied at the Universities of Strasbourg and Leipzig. In 1901 he established in Berlin (with O. J. Bierbaum and F. Wedekind) the "Überbrettl," a kind of artistic cabaret for the production of dramatic pieces, pantomimes, poems with recitation and music, etc., most of them reflecting or satirizing contemporary German life; Oskar Straus provided most of the music, and Schoenberg contributed some of the numbers; 2 journals, *Das moderne Brettl* and *Bühne und Brettl,* were published for a year or so to promote the ideas of the enterprise, but the cabaret closed after 2 sensationally successful seasons. Ernst von Wolzogen published 2 books dealing with music: *Der Kraftmayr* (1897; humorous novel with Liszt as the central figure; English transl. as *Florian Mayr,* 1914) and *Ansichten und Aussichten* (1908; essays). His wife, **Elsa Laura** (*née* **Seeman von Mangern**), became known as a singer, making a specialty of songs with lute accompaniment; with her husband she made a tour of the U.S. (1910–11); publ. 7 vols. of folksongs with lute accompaniment *(Meine Lieder zur Laute).*
BIBLIOGRAPHY: A. Hertwig, *Ernst von Wolzogens "Überbrettl" in Wort und Bild* (Berlin, 1901).

Wolzogen, Hans, Freiherr von, German writer on music and authority on Wagner; b. Potsdam, Nov. 13, 1848; d. Bayreuth, June 2, 1938. He studied mythology and comparative philology in Berlin (1868–71); then devoted himself to literature; in 1878, at Wagner's invitation, he became editor of the *Bayreuther Blätter* and lived in Bayreuth most of his life. He popularized the term "Leitmotif" first used by F. W. Jähns, in his "Motive in Wagners *Götterdämmerung,"* published in the *Musikalisches Wochenblatt* in 1887 (Wagner's preferred term was "Grundthema").
WRITINGS: *Der Nibelungenmythos in Sage und Literatur* (1876); *Thematischer Lietfaden durch die Musik von R. Wagners Festspiel "Der Ring des Nibelungen"* (1876; 4th ed. as *Erläuterungen zu R. Wagners Nibelungendrama,* 1878); *Die Tragödie in Bayreuth und ihr Satyrspiel* (1876; 5th ed., 1881); *Poetische Lautsymbolik. Psychische Wirkungen der Sprachlaute aus R. Wagners "Ring des Nibelungen"* (1876; 3rd ed., 1897); *Grundlage und Aufgabe des allgemeinen Patronatvereins zur Pflege und Erhaltung der Bühnenfestspiele in Bayreuth* (1877); *Die Sprache in Wagners Dichtungen* (1877; 2nd ed., 1881); *R. Wagners Tristan und Isolde* (1880); *Unsre Zeit und unsre Kunst* (1881); *Was ist Stil? was will Wagner?* (1881); *Die Religion des Mitleidens* (1882); *Parsifal. Ein thematischer Leitfaden* (1882; 21st printing, 1914); *R. Wagners Heldengestalten erläutert* (2nd ed., 1886); *Wagneriana* (1888); *R. Wagner und die Tierwelt;* *auch eine Biographie* (1890, 3rd ed., 1910); *Wagners Lebensbericht* (1884; the original work of "The Work and Mission of My Life," published 1879 in the *North American Review,* under Wagner's name); *Erinnerungen an R. Wagner* (1883); *Die Idealisierung des Theaters* (1885); *Grossmeister deutscher Musik* (1897); "Wagner-Brevier," *Die Musik* (1904); *R. Wagner* (1905; in Remer's series *Die Dichtung); Musikalisch-dramatische Parallelen* (1906); *E. T. A. Hoffmann und R. Wagner* (1906); *Aus R. Wagners Geisteswelt* (1908); *Kunst und Kirche* (1913); *E. T. A. Hoffmann, der deutsche Geisterseher* (1922); *Lebensbilder* (autobiographical; 1923); *Wagner und seine Werke* (1924); *Wohltäterin Musik* (1925); *Musik und Theater* (1929); edited Wagner's *Ausgewählte Schriften über Staat und Kunst und Religion* (1902; 3rd ed., 1914) and *Entwürfe zu "Die Meistersinger," "Tristan und Isolde" und "Parsifal"* (1907).

Wonder, Stevie, black American rock singer (real name **Steveland Judkins Hardaway**); b. Saginaw, Michigan, May 13, 1950. He was blind from birth; learned to play the drums and piano; improvised his first song, *Lonely Boy,* at the age of 10, and at 12 he composed *Fingertips,* which became a hit. Possessed by that indefinable gift of song, he rapidly advanced in the rosters of popular success; the shows at which he sings, accompanying himself at the piano, have become great moneymakers. Among his pop hits are *Living for the City, You Are the Sunshine of My Life, My Cherie Amour, I Was Made to Love Her,* and *Uptight.*

Wood, Charles, Irish organist and composer; b. Armagh, June 15, 1866; d. Cambridge, England, July 12, 1926. He studied at the Royal College of Music in London, and subsequently taught harmony there; received his Mus. Doc. degree, Cambridge, 1894. In 1924 he succeeded Stanford as prof. of music at Cambridge Univ. He wrote 6 string quartets (mostly in an Irish manner); vocal works with orch.: *Ode on Time* (1898), *Dirge for Two Veterans* (1901), *Song of the Tempest* (1902), *Ballad of Dundee* (1904); church music; edited a collection of Irish folksongs (1897).

Wood, David Duffie, blind American organist; b. Pittsburgh, March 2, 1838; d. Philadelphia, March 27, 1910. Having lost his eyesight by an accident at the age of 3, he was educated at the Penn. Institute for the Blind; from 1858 till his death he was instructor of music there. He was a fine organist; wrote anthems and songs. Published *A Dictionary of Musical Terms, for the Use of the Blind* (Philadelphia, 1869).

Wood, Haydn, English violinist and composer; b. Slaithwaite, March 25, 1882; d. London, March 11, 1959. He entered the Royal College of Music in London at 15; studied there with Fernández Arbós (violin) and Stanford (composition); later studied with César Thomson in Brussels. His works include 8 overtures, 8 rhapsodies, for band, 18 orchestral studies, 31 entr'actes for orch., 12 violin solos, 2 flute pieces, 3 accordion solos, and about 200 songs.

Wood, Sir Henry J., eminent English conductor; b. London, March 3, 1869; d. Hitchin, Herts, Aug. 19, 1944. Of musical parentage, he was taught to play the piano by his mother; participated in family musicales from the age of 6; he was equally precocious on the organ; at the age of 10 he often acted as deputy organist, and gave organ recitals at the Fisheries Exhibition (1883) and at the Inventions Exhibition (1885). In 1886 he entered the Royal Academy of Music, where his teachers were Prout, Steggall, Macfarren, and Garcia; won 4 medals. In 1888 he brought out some of his songs; then composed light operas and cantatas. But soon his ambition crystallized in the direction of conducting; he traveled with an opera company in 1889; then became assistant conductor at the Savoy Theatre (1890); was engaged as conductor for various other operatic enterprises. On Oct. 6, 1895 he began his 1st series of Promenade Concerts (the famous "Proms") in Queen's Hall, London, with an orch. of about 100 members. Their success was so conspicuous that a new series of concerts was inaugurated on Jan. 30, 1897, under Wood's direction, and flourished from the beginning. In 1899 he founded the Nottingham Orch.; also was appointed conductor of the Wolverhampton Festival Choral Society (1900), of the Sheffield Festival (1902-11), and of the Norwich Festival (1908). In 1904 he conducted in N.Y. He was married to Olga Urusova, a Russian noblewoman, and became greatly interested in Russian music, which he performed frequently at his concerts. He adopted a Russian pseudonym, **Paul Klenovsky,** for his compositions and arrangements, and supplied an imaginary biography of his alter ego for use in program notes. His wife died in 1909, and Wood married Muriel Greatorex in 1911. He was knighted in 1911. In 1918 he was offered the conductorship of the Boston Symph. Orch. as successor to Muck, but declined. In 1923 he was appointed prof. of conducting and orchestral playing at the Royal Academy of Music. In 1925 he conducted in California; in 1926 received the degree of Mus. Doc. *(honoris causa)* from Oxford Univ. Wood continued to conduct the Promenade Concerts almost to the end of his life, presenting the last concert on July 28, 1944. Among his popular arrangements are Chopin's *Marche Funèbre,* some works by Bach, and the *Trumpet Voluntary* (mistakenly attributed to Purcell, but actually by Jeremiah Clarke). He publ. *The Gentle Art of Singing* (4 vols.; 1927-28) and *About Conducting* (London, 1945), and edited the *Handbook of Miniature Orchestral and Chamber Music Scores* for J. W. Chester & Co. (1937); wrote an autobiography, *My Life and Music* (London, 1938).

BIBLIOGRAPHY: Rosa Newmarch, *Henry J. Wood,* in the Living Masters of Music series (London, 1904); R. Hill and others, *Sir Henry Wood: Fifty Years of the "Proms"* (London, 1944); J. Wood, *The Last Years of Henry J. Wood* (London, 1954; with a foreword by Sir Malcolm Sargent); Reginald Pound, *Sir Henry Wood: A Biography* (London, 1969).

Wood, Hugh, English composer; b. Parbold, near Wigan, Lancashire, June 27, 1932. He studied theory and composition with Anthony Milner, Iain Hamilton and Mátyás Seiber in London (1957-60); taught at Morley College in London (1958-67) and at the Royal Academy of Music (1962-65); was a composer-in-residence at the Univ. of Glasgow (1966-70); in 1971 he was appointed a lecturer at the Univ. of Liverpool.

WORKS: *Variations* for viola and piano (1957-59); *4 Songs* for mezzo-soprano, clarinet, violin, and cello (1959-61); Trio for flute, viola, and piano (1961); 3 string quartets (1962, 1970, 1978); *3 Pieces* for piano (1960-63); *Scenes from "Comus,"* after Milton, for soprano, tenor, and orch. (1962-65; London, Aug. 2, 1965); Quintet for clarinet, horn, violin, cello, and piano (1967); Cello Concerto (1965-69; London, Aug. 26, 1969); Chamber Concerto (1970-71; London, Nov. 27, 1971); Violin Concerto (1970-72; Liverpool, Sept. 19, 1972); *Song Cycle to Poems of Neruda* for high voice and chamber orch. (1973; London, Feb. 18, 1974).

Wood, Joseph, American composer; b. Pittsburgh, May 12, 1915. He studied with Bernard Wagenaar at the Juilliard School, N.Y., graduating in 1949, and with Otto Luening at Columbia Univ. (M.A., 1950). In 1950 he was appointed prof. in composition at the Oberlin Cons. of Music in Ohio. His music is couched in a modern Romantic vein; upon occasion he applies serial techniques.

WORKS: an opera *The Mother* (1945); 3 symphonies (1939, 1952, 1958); Piano Trio (1937); Viola Sonata (1938); String Quartet (1942); Violin Sonata (1947); Piano Quintet (1956); *Divertimento* for piano and chamber orch. (1959); choruses; incidental music for theatrical plays; piano pieces; songs.

Wood, Mary Knight, American pianist and composer; b. Easthampton, Mass., April 7, 1857; d. Florence, Dec. 20, 1944. She studied in Boston with B. J. Lang and in N.Y. with Huss; married A. B. Mason and went to live in Florence, where she remained for many years until her death. She published about 30 songs, among them *Ashes of Roses, In Harbor,* and *Poppies.*

Wood, Thomas, English composer and author; b. Chorley, Lancashire, Nov. 28, 1892; d. Bures, Essex, Nov. 19, 1950. He was educated at Exeter College, Oxford; then studied at the Royal Academy of Music with Stanford; was music director at Tonbridge School (1919-24); lecturer and precentor at Exeter College (1924-29). His extensive travels took him to the Far East and to the Arctic; his familiarity with the sea was reflected in many of his compositions (for chorus and orch.), such as *40 Singing Seamen* (1925), *Master Mariners* (1927), *Merchantmen* (1934), and in *A Seaman's Overture* (for orch., 1927). He edited vol. II of the *Oxford Song Book* (1928; 3rd ed., 1937). His books include *Music and Boyhood* (1925) and the autobiographical *True Thomas* (1936); also published *Cobbers* (on his Australian tour of 1930-32), which became highly popular in England, and a sequel to it, *Cobbers Campaigning* (1940).

BIBLIOGRAPHY: N. Coghill, "Thomas Wood," *Music & Letters* (April 1951).

Wood, William G., Irish organist; brother of **Charles Wood;** b. Armagh, Jan. 16, 1859; d. London, Sept. 25, 1895. He studied at the Royal Academy of Music in London; from 1886 till his death he was organist and music master at the Highgate Grammar School. He composed some fine organ music (3 canons, a sonata, *Fantasia and Fugue, Introduction and Allegro, Minuet and Trio,* etc.).

Woodbury, Arthur, American composer; b. Kimball, Nebraska, June 20, 1930. He studied at the Univ. of Idaho (B.S., 1951; M.M., 1955); also attended the Univ. of California, Berkeley (1957–58). A bassoon player by profession, he was a member of various orchestras; also played the saxophone. In 1963 he joined the staff of the Univ. of California, Davis. His early works are written in a traditional modern idiom; later he branched out as a composer of experimental music, cultivating electronic and aleatory techniques.

WORKS: Woodwind Quartet (1955); Symphony (1958); *Autobiography: Patricia Belle,* for soprano, electronic instruments, and an amplified chamber ensemble (1968); *Remembrances* for violin, saxophone, and vibraphone (1968); *Recall,* a theater piece (1969); *An Evening of the Music of Neil Jansen, A Put-on,* for tape, utilizing the Moog synthesizer (1969); *Werner Vonbrawnasaurus Rex* for tape, slide guitar, electric piano, and music synthesizer (1970).

Woodbury (original name **Woodberry**), **Isaac Baker,** American composer of songs; b. Beverly, Mass., Oct. 23, 1819; d. Charleston, S. C., Oct. 26, 1858. Originally a blacksmith, he took up music, going to Europe in 1838 for study in Paris and London; upon his return he settled in Boston. From 1850 to his death he was an editor of a New York music magazine published successively as *American Monthly Musical Review, Musical Pioneer,* etc. His collection of sacred songs, *The Dulcimer,* enjoyed great popularity; he also compiled a *Collection of Church Music* for the Boston Music Educational Society (1842) and *The Choral* (1845); published *Woodbury's Self-Instructor in Musical Composition and Thorough-Bass,* and many secular songs.

BIBLIOGRAPHY: F. J. Metcalf, *American Writers and Compilers of Sacred Music* (1925); *Dictionary of American Biography.*

Wood-Hill, Mabel, American composer; b. Brooklyn, March 12, 1870; d. Stamford, Conn., March 1, 1954. She was educated at Smith College and at Columbia Univ., where she studied composition with Rybner. She wrote songs and choruses; orchestrated pieces by Couperin *(Louis XIV Suite)* and Bach. Her pantomime, *The Adventures of Pinocchio,* was performed for the 1st time in N.Y. on April 13, 1931.

Woodhouse, George, English pianist; b. Cradley Heath, near Birmingham, Dec. 16, 1877; d. Southsea, Jan. 4, 1954. He studied in Birmingham and later took piano lessons with Leschetizky in Vienna. He established his own piano school in London; published *The Artist at the Piano* (London, 1910), *Creative Technique* (London, 1922), *From Keyboard to Music* (London, 1949), and *A Realistic Approach to Piano Playing* (London, 1953).

Woodman, Raymond Huntington, American organist and composer; b. Brooklyn, Jan. 18, 1861; d. there,

Dec. 25, 1943. He studied piano with his father; theory with Dudley Buck; then went to Paris, where he took lessons in organ playing from César Franck (1888). He filled various posts as church organist and teacher in N.Y.; also taught theory and conducted a choral society in Brooklyn. He published about 150 compositions, among them anthems, organ pieces, piano pieces *(Romance, The Brook, Spring Song, Three Album-Leaves,* etc.); songs, of which *A Birthday* was especially successful.

Woods, Francis Cunningham, English organist and composer; b. London, Aug. 29, 1862; d. there, Sept. 21, 1929. He studied at the National Training School for Music under Sullivan, Prout, Stainer, and Cowen; after serving as organist at Brasenose College and Exeter College, was private organist to the Duke of Marlborough (1891–94); then prof. of organ and lecturer at Oxford Univ. (1890–95); in 1896 succeeded William G. Wood as organist and music master of the Highgate Grammar School, London. He composed *King Harold,* a "historical cantata"; *Greyport Legend,* a ballad for baritone, men's chorus, and orch.; *Old May-Day,* cantata for women's voices and piano; *The Lords of Labor,* ode; some orchestral pieces; songs.

Woodworth, George Wallace, American choral conductor and music educator; b. Boston, Nov. 6, 1902; d. Cambridge, Mass., July 18, 1969. He was educated at Harvard Univ. (B.A., 1924; M.A., 1926); also studied at the Royal Academy of Music in London (1927–28). In 1925 he joined the staff of the music dept. at Harvard; prof. in 1948. In 1925 he became conductor of the Radcliffe Choral Society; in 1934, conductor of the Harvard Glee Club; in 1940, Harvard Univ. organist and choirmaster for the Harvard Univ. Chapel, resigning all these posts in 1958 to devote himself to teaching. He conducted the Harvard-Radcliffe Chorus on a transcontinental tour in 1954, and the Harvard Glee Club on its European tour in 1956. He published *The World of Music* (Cambridge, Mass., 1964).

Wooldridge, David, English composer, conductor and writer on music; b. Seal, Kent, Aug. 24, 1927. He is a grandson of the English musicologist **Henry Ellis Wooldridge** and godson of Rachmaninoff, from whom he received some friendly piano lessons at the age of 4. He began studying the violin at the age of 6; at 16 made his conducting debut; in 1952 he graduated from the Univ. of London, *summa cum laude;* was then apprenticed to Clemens Krauss at the Vienna State Opera; in 1954 he became junior conductor at the Bavarian State Opera. In 1956–58 he was in the U.S. as guest conductor in Minneapolis, Cincinnati, Cleveland, and Rochester; from 1961 to 1965 conducted the Lebanese National Orch. in Beirut; then was conductor of the Cape Town Symph., South Africa (1965–67); subsequently was visiting prof. at Indiana Univ. (1968–69); at Grinnell College, Iowa (1971); Univ. of California, Santa Cruz (1972); Wabash College, Indiana (1976); and Univ. of California, Riverside (1977); concurrently was music director, Bridgewater, Conn., Concert Association (1973–78).

WORKS: Viola Concerto (1949); ballet, *Les Parapluies* (1956); Cello Concerto (1957); ballet, *Octet*

(1958); *Suite Libanaise* (1962); *Four Armenian Dances* (1964); *Partita* for small orch. (1967); *Partita* for large orch. (1968); ballet, *Movements* (1970); symph. poem, *The Legend of Lillanonah* (1975); opera, *The Duchess of Amalfi* (1978); incidental music; film scores. He published the books *Conductor's World* (N.Y., 1970) and *From the Steeples and Mountains,* a biography of Charles Ives (N.Y., 1974).

Wooldridge, Harry Ellis, English musicologist; b. Winchester, March 28, 1845; d. London, Feb. 13, 1917. While studying at Trinity College, Oxford (1860–64), he became deeply interested in painting and music; entered the Royal Academy of Fine Arts in 1865, at the same time beginning his researches regarding early music in the libraries of Oxford and London; from 1895 till his death he was Slade Prof. of Fine Arts at Oxford Univ.

WRITINGS: *The English Metrical Psalter* (1890); *The Polyphonic Period,* being vols. I and II of the *Oxford History of Music* (1901, 1905; 2nd ed., revised by P. C. Buck, 1929–32); radically revised Chappell's *Popular Music of the Olden Times,* and published it under the title *Old English Popular Music* (2 vols., 1893); also edited *Early English Harmony* (2 vols., 1897, 1913; pieces from the 10th to 15th centuries); *The Yattendon Hymnal* (1899; with R. Bridges); Purcell's sacred compositions (vols. 13, 14, and 18 of Novello's ed. of Purcell's complete works).

Wooler, Alfred, American music teacher and composer; b. Shipley, Yorkshire, May 11, 1867; d. Lake Winola, Pa., Aug. 7, 1937. He settled in the U.S. as a youth, and studied at the Univ. of Pennsylvania; taught harmony at Scranton, Buffalo, and N.Y.; also conducted choral societies. He composed about 250 anthems, songs, and part-songs; also piano pieces.

Woolf, Benjamin Edward, American composer and music critic; b. London, Feb. 16, 1836; d. Boston, Feb. 7, 1901. He was taken to America as a child; studied organ with W. R. Bristow in N.Y.; in 1870 he settled in Boston, where he wrote on music and drama in the Boston *Globe* and the Boston *Herald.* He composed the "operatic comedietta" *Lawn Tennis, or Djakh and Djill* (Boston, 1880); the comic opera, *Pounce & Co.* (Boston, 1883); an operetta, *Westward Ho!* (Boston, Dec. 31, 1894); also some chamber music and piano pieces.

Woolhouse, Wesley S. B., English mathematician and writer on musical subjects; b. North Shields, May 6, 1809; d. London, Aug. 12, 1893. He was head assistant at the Nautical Almanach Establishment. He published *Essay on Musical Intervals, Harmonics, and the Temperament of the Musical Scale* (1835; new ed., 1888); *A Catechism of Music* (1843); *Treatise on Singing.* He owned a fine collection of violins.

Woollen, Russell, American composer; b. Hartford, Conn., Jan. 7, 1923. He studied for the priesthood; attended the Pius X School of Liturgical Music, N.Y.; in 1948 studied Gregorian Chant at the Benedictine Abbey at Solesmes. He was ordained a priest of the Hartford Diocese, in 1947; was released by his Bishop in

1964, and was married twice (1971, 1977). He received his B.A. from St. Mary's Univ., Baltimore in (1944); M.A., Romance Languages, of the Catholic Univ. of America, Washington, D.C. (1948); he had private lessons in piano and organ; studied composition with Franz Wasner of the Trapp Family Singers, with Nicolas Nabokov at the Peabody Cons. in Baltimore (1949–51), with Nadia Boulanger in Paris (1951), and with Walter Piston at Harvard Univ. (1953–55). He was a member of the music faculty of Catholic Univ. of America (1948–62) and of Howard Univ. (1969–74); in 1956 was appointed staff keyboard artist of the National Symph., Washington, D.C.

WORKS: opera, *The Decorator* (N.Y., Catholic Univ. May 24, 1959); Symph. No. 1 (1957–58); Symph. No. 2 (1978); Piano Quartet (1952); Quartet for flute and strings (1953); Woodwind Quintet (1955); Piano Trio (1957); *Suite* for flute & strings (1966); Trio for flute, oboe and harpsichord (1967); *Fantasy* for flute and harpsichord (1968); Sonata for trombone and piano (1972); Quartet for woodwinds (1975); *2 Pieces* for piano and orch. (1962–76); 16 Masses; numerous choral works; 40 Duets on *Au Clair de la Lune* for recorders.

Woollett, Henri (Henry) Edouard, French composer; b. (of English parentage) Le Havre, Aug. 13, 1864; d. there, Oct. 9, 1936. He studied in Paris with Pugno (piano) and Massenet (composition); returning to Le Havre he established himself as a teacher; among his students were André Caplet and Honegger. His music is of a lyrical nature, in the manner of his teacher Massenet.

WORKS: *La Rose de Sharon,* "poème lyrique" for orch. (1895); *Konzertstück* for cello and orch. (1911); String Quartet (1929); 2 violin sonatas (1908, 1922); Viola Sonata; Flute Sonata; Cello Sonata; many piano pieces in a Romantic vein (*Nocturnes et pastorales, Pièces intimes, À travers la vie, Au jardin de France, Préludes et valses*); many attractive songs. He published *Petit traité de prosodie* (Paris, 1903) and *Histoire de la musique depuis l'antiquité jusqu'à nos jours* (4 vols., Paris, 1909–25).

Wordsworth, William, English composer; b. London, Dec. 17, 1908. He studied with his father; then with Sir Donald Tovey in Edinburgh. He began to compose rather late in life; his music is marked by a certain austerity in the deployment of thematic materials.

WORKS: *Sinfonia* for strings (1936); *3 Pastoral Sketches* for orch. (1937); *Theme and Variations* for orch. (1941); 5 symphonies (1944, 1947–48, 1951, 1953, 1959–60); Piano Concerto (1946); *Divertimento* for orch. (1954); Violin Concerto (1955); Sinfonietta for small orch. (1957); *Variations on a Scottish Theme* for small orch. (1962); Cello Concerto (1963); *A Highland Overture* (1964); *Jubilation* for orch. (1965); *Conflict,* overture (1968); *Sinfonia Semplice* for amateur string orch. (1969); *Valediction* for orch. (1969); *A Pattern of Love* for low voice and string orch. (1969–70); *Spring Festival Overture* (1970); *Symposium* for solo violin, strings, and percussion (1972); *The Houseless Dead,* after D. H. Lawrence, for baritone, chorus and orch. (1939); an oratorio, *Dies Domini* (1942–44); *Lucifer Yields* for soloists, chorus, and orch. (1949); *A Vision* for women's chorus and strings (1950); *A Song of Praise* for chorus and orch. (1956); a dramatic cantata, *The Two Brigs* (1971); *The Solitary Reaper* for soprano, piano and clarinet (1973); 6 string quartets (1943, 1946, 1948, 1950, 1955, 1964); 2 cello sonatas (1937, 1959); 2 violin sonatas (1944, 1967); String Trio (1945); Piano Quartet (1948); Piano Trio (1949); Oboe Quartet (1949); Clarinet Quintet (1952); Wind Trio (1953); Piano Quintet (1959); Sonata for solo cello (1961); Violin Sonatina (1961); *Dialogue* for horn and piano (1965); piano pieces, including a Sonata (1939); songs.

Work, Henry Clay, American composer of popular songs; b. Middletown, Conn., Oct. 1, 1832; d. Hartford, June 8, 1884. He was a printer by trade; entirely self-taught in music; his first success was *We are coming, Sister Mary;* other well-known songs are *Grandfather's Clock; Father, Come Home; Shadows on the Floor;* his Civil War song *Marching through Georgia* became celebrated; other songs of the Civil War were *Drafted into the Army; God Save the Nation; Song of a Thousand Years; Wake, Nicodemus; Kingdom Coming,* etc.
BIBLIOGRAPHY: R. S. Hill, "The Mysterious Chord of Henry Clay Work," *Notes* (March-June 1953).

Wormser, André (Alphonse-Toussaint), French composer; b. Paris, Nov. 1, 1851; d. there, Nov. 4, 1926. He studied at the Paris Cons. with Marmontel (piano) and Bazin (theory); won 1st prize for piano in 1872, and the Grand Prix de Rome in 1875 with the cantata *Clytemnestre.* His most successful work was the pantomime, or "wordless opera," *L'Enfant prodigue* (Paris, June 14, 1890); also composed other stage works, orchestral works, men's choruses, songs, and piano pieces.

Wörner, Karl Heinrich, German musicologist; b. Waldorf, near Heidelberg, Jan. 6, 1910; d. Heiligenkirchen, near Detmold, Aug. 11, 1969. He studied musicology in Berlin with Schünemann and Schering, and conducting with Julius Prüwer; received the degree of Dr. phil. at Berlin Univ. with the dissertation *Beiträge zur Geschichte des Leitmotivs in der Oper,* published in the *Zeitschrift für Musikwissenschaft* (Dec. 1931); was critic for the *B. Z. am Mittag;* then (1935–40) opera conductor at Stettin, Magdeburg, and Frankfurt. He was in the German Army during World War II; 1944–46, prisoner of war in the U.S. Returning to Germany in 1946, he was active as lecturer. From 1954 to 1958 he was on the staff of B. Schott's Söhne (Mainz); 1958, on the faculty of the Folkwangschule in Essen.
WRITINGS: *Mendelssohn* (Wiesbaden, 1947); *Musik der Gegenwart* (Mainz, 1949); *Schumann* (Zürich, 1949); *Musiker-Worte* (Baden-Baden, 1949); *Geschichte der Musik* (Göttingen, 1954); *Neue Musik in der Entscheidung* (Mainz, 1954); *Gotteswort und Magie; die Oper "Moses und Aron" von Arnold Schönberg* (Heidelberg, 1959); *Das Zeitalter der thematischen Prozesse in der Geschichte der Musik* (1969); *Die Musik in der Geistesgeschichte* (1970).

Woronoff, Wladimir, Russian-born Belgian composer; b. St. Petersburg, Jan. 5, 1903. He studied violin as a child; left Russia after the Revolution and settled in Belgium in 1922; took lessons in composition with André Souris in Brussels. In 1954 he destroyed most of his early works, including the ballet *Le Masque de la mort rouge, Suite de Bruxelles* for orch., and a *Concert lyrique* for piano and orch.; revised most of remaining scores. His catalogue of extant works after this self-auto-da-fe can boast of the following: *La Foule* for bass, chorus, and orch. (1934, revised 1965); *Annas et le Lépreux* for low voice and piano (1946); *Les Douze,* 3 fragments from the poem by Alexander Blok, for low voice, and orch. or piano (1921–63); *Strophes concertantes* for piano and orch. (1964); *Lueur tournante* for narrator and orch. (1967); *Tripartita* for viola and chamber orch. (1970); *Vallées* for 2 pianos (1971).

Worp, Johannes, Dutch organist, composer, and arranger; b. Broek, Dec. 24, 1821; d. Groningen, April 21, 1891. He studied in Amsterdam, where he was active as church organist; then went to Leipzig, where he took a course with Moscheles; returning to Holland, he became organist at Groningen. He published valuable organ works and methods, which have gone through numerous editions: *De Melodieën der Evangelische Gezangen* for organ, piano, and chorus; *De Melodieën der Psalmen en Lof- en Bedezangen* for organ, piano, and chorus (20th printing, 1947); the manual, *Algemeene Muziekleer* (13th printing, 1932, revised by Sem Dresden); *Kleine Muziekleer* for schools; *Eerste en tweede Zangboekje* for schools; *De zingende Kinderwereld* (songs for children; many editions); *Volksliedjes uit het Land der Liefde;* etc.

Worzischek (Voříšek), Johann Hugo, Bohemian composer; b. Wamberg, Bohemia, May 11, 1791; d. Vienna, Nov. 19, 1825. He studied with his father and with Tomaschek in Prague, where he lived from 1801; in 1813 he went to Vienna and became known as a pianist; in 1818 he was appointed conductor of the Gesellschaft der Musikfreunde; having studied law, he obtained a post in the civil service in 1822, but abandoned it after a year, when he was made court organist. He composed symphonies, choral works with orch., a piano concerto, etc.; of more interest are his piano pieces, especially the *Rhapsodies* (1818) and *Impromptus* (1822), because Schubert was strongly influenced by them. A Piano Sonata in B minor (1820) shows kinship with Beethoven, whom he knew intimately.

Wöss, Josef Venantius von, Austrian musicologist; b. Cattaro, Dalmatia, June 13, 1863; d. Vienna, Oct. 22, 1943. He received his first musical instruction from his mother and an uncle; studied composition at the Vienna Cons. with Franz Krenn; wrote music criticism for *Musica Divina;* later in the editorial dept. of the Universal Edition, for which he edited the collection *Deutsche Meisterlieder.*
WORKS: the operas *Lenzlüge* (Elberfeld, 1905) and *Flaviennes Abenteuer* (Breslau, 1910); *Heiliges Lied,* for male chorus and orch.; *Serenade,* for orch.; *Sakuntala,* overture; Piano Sextet; sacred music (a *Te Deum*

and 2 Masses); motets with orch.; songs *(Sulamith, 4 slawische Lieder, 4 orientalische Gesänge,* etc.). He made the piano scores of Mahler's *Das klagende Lied, Lied von der Erde,* and symphonies Nos. 3, 4, 8, and 9; edited Bruckner's symphonies; publ. *Die Modulation* (Vienna, 1921).

Wöss, Kurt, Austrian conductor; b. Linz, May 2, 1914. He studied conducting with Felix Weingartner in Vienna, and also pursued musicological studies at the Univ. of Vienna with Haas, Lach, Orel and Wellesz; taught an orchestra class at the Vienna Academy (1938-40); after the war, he conducted the Tonkünstler-Orch. in Vienna (1948-51); subsequently went to Japan, where he conducted the Nippon Philharmonic Orch. in Tokyo (1951-54). From 1956 to 1960 he was principal conductor of the Victorian Symph. Orch. in Melbourne and of the Australian National Opera; in 1961 he returned to Linz, where he became music director of the Bruckner Orch. (1966-74). In 1974 he went again to Japan, where he was appointed music director of the Fumiwara Opera in Tokyo; also was conductor of the Tokyo Philharmonic. He published *Ratschläge zur Aufführung der Symphonien Anton Bruckners* (Linz, 1974).

Wotquenne, Alfred, Belgian musicologist; b. Lobbes, Jan. 25, 1867; d. Antibes, France, Sept. 25, 1939. He studied at the Brussels Cons. with Mailly (organ), and Joseph Dupont and Gevaert (theory); from 1894 to 1919 was librarian, secretary, and inspector of studies at the Brussels Cons.; then moved to Antibes in southern France, where in 1921 he became maître de chapelle.
WRITINGS: *Catalogue de la bibliothèque du Cons. Royal de Musique de Bruxelles* (vol. I, 1894; with a supplement, *Libretti d'opéras et d'oratorios italiens du XVIIᵉ siècle,* 1901; II, 1902; III, 1908; IV, 1912; V, 1914); *Baldassare Galuppi* (1899; 2nd augmented ed., 1902, as *Baldassare Galuppi. Étude bibliographique sur ses œuvres dramatiques); Thematisches Verzeichnis der Werke von Chr. W. v. Gluck* (1904); *Catalogue thématique des œuvres de C. Ph. E. Bach* (1905); *Table alphabétique des morceaux mesurés contenus dans les œuvres dramatiques de Zeno, Metastasio et Goldoni* (1905); *Étude bibliographique sur le compositeur napolitain Luigi Rossi* (1909; with thematic catalogue). He prepared a card catalogue of 18,000 Italian "cantate da camera" of the 18th century; edited *Chansons italiennes de la fin du XVIᵉ siècle* (canzonette a 4); continued the collections begun by Gevaert, *Répertoire classique du chant français* and *Répertoire français de l'ancien chant classique,* and edited a new collection, *Répertoire Wotquenne* (4 vols. publ.); also ed. violin sonatas of Tartini, Veracini, and others; composed much sacred music. The manuscripts of several important bibliographies in his collection were bought out by the Library of Congress in 1929; these comprise *Répertoire des textes publiés par les éditeurs parisiens Ballard; Histoire musicale et chronologique du Théâtre de la Foire depuis 1680 jusqu'à 1762; Histoire du nouveau Théâtre-Italien à Paris (1718-1762);* etc. A large part of his private music library was also bought by the Library of Congress.

Wouters, (François) Adolphe, Belgian organist and composer; b. Brussels, May 28, 1849; d. there, April 16, 1924. He studied at the Brussels Cons.; then taught piano there (1871-1920); from 1868 he was also organist at Notre-Dame-de-Finistère and maître de chapelle at Saint-Nicolas. He composed church music, men's choruses, technical studies and transcriptions for piano, etc.

Woyrsch, Felix von, composer and conductor; b. Troppau, Silesia, Oct. 8, 1860; d. Altona-Hamburg, March 20, 1944. He studied with A. Chevallier in Hamburg, but was chiefly self-taught. In 1894 he settled in Altona as conductor of the Kirchenchor, the Singakademie (from 1895), and the municipal symph. concerts and Volkskonzerte (from 1903); from 1895 to 1903 he was organist of the Friedenskirche, then of the Johanniskirche.
WORKS: Operas, *Der Pfarrer von Meudon* (Hamburg, 1886); *Der Weiberkrieg* (Hamburg, 1890); *Wikingerfahrt* (Nuremberg, 1896). For orch.: symph. prologue to *Divina Commedia; Skaldische Rhapsodie,* for violin and orch.; 2 symphonies; *3 Böcklin-Phantasien (Die Toteninsel, Der Eremit, Im Spiel der Wellen); Hamlet,* overture. Vocal works with orch.: *Da Jesus auf Erden ging,* a mystery play (Hamburg, Jan. 29, 1917; one of his best works); *Geburt Jesu, Deutscher Heerbann, Der Vandalen, Auszug, Passions-Oratorium, Sapphische Ode an Aphrodite, Totentanz, Da lachte schön Sigrid, Wollt' er nur fragen, Edward.* Chamber music: Piano Quintet; String Quartet. For piano: *3 Notturnos; 2 Walzer; Walzer* (4 hands); *Theme and Variations; 4 Impromptus; Improvisationen; Metamorphosen.* He also composed song cycles *(Persische Lieder, Spanisches Liederbuch, 10 Rattenfängerlieder);* edited *Deutsche Volkslieder* (14th-16th centuries), and choral works of Heinrich Schütz for practical use (3 vols.).

Woytowicz, Boleslaw, Polish pianist and composer; b. Dunajowce, Podolia, Dec. 5, 1899. He studied piano with Michalowski; composition with Statkowski and Maliszewski; obtained a diploma at the Chopin College of Music in Warsaw as a concert pianist; then went to Paris where he took lessons in composition with Nadia Boulanger (1930-32). In 1945 he was appointed prof. of piano and composition at the State College of Music in Katowice.
WORKS: *Kolysanka (Cradle Song)* for soprano, flute, clarinet, bassoon, and harp (1931); 2 string quartets (1932, 1953); Piano Concerto (1932); *Zalobny poema (Funeral Poem)* for orch. (1935); a ballet, *Powrót* (1937); 3 symphonies: No. 1 (1938), No. 2 (1945; Cracow, Sept. 27, 1946), and No. 3, *Concertante,* for piano and orch. (1963); *Kantata na pochwale pracy* (Cantata in Praise of Labor, 1948); *12 Etudes* for piano (1948); *Symphonic Sketches* for orch. (1949); a cantata, *Prorok (The Prophet,* 1950); Flute Sonata (1952); *Lamento* for soprano, piano and clarinet (1960); *10 Etudes* for piano (1960); *Little Piano Sonata* (1974).

Wrangel, Vasily, Baron, Russian composer; b. St. Petersburg, June 25, 1862; d. there, March 10, 1901. A functionary at the Ministry of Home Affairs, he was a musician by avocation; took several courses at the St.

Petersburg Cons. His songs, many of which were published, attracted singers by their artless melodic quality, and enjoyed some popularity for a time; he also wrote a ballet, *The Mikado's Daughter* (St. Petersburg, Dec. 1, 1897).

Wranitzky, Anton, Bohemian violinist and composer; b. Neureisch, Moravia, June 13, 1761; d. Vienna, Aug. 6, 1820. He studied with his older brother **Paul Wranitzky;** also had lessons in Vienna with Albrechtsberger, Haydn, and Mozart. In 1794 he was appointed Kapellmeister to Prince Lobkowitz at his castle in Bohemia, and later (1808) in Vienna. He wrote 15 violin concertos; much chamber music; marches; dances.

Wranitzky, Paul, Bohemian violinist and composer; brother of **Anton Wranitzky;** b. Neureisch, Moravia, Dec. 30, 1756; d. Vienna, Sept. 26, 1808. After studying in various provincial towns of Moravia, he went to Vienna in 1776, where he was a pupil of Joseph Martin Kraus. In 1780 he became a member of Prince Esterházy's orch. at Eisenstadt; in 1790 became concertmaster of the Vienna Opera, and retained this position until his death. His opera *Oberon, König der Elfen* was given with excellent success in Vienna on Nov. 7, 1789; other operas and Singspiele by him produced in Vienna were *Rudolf von Felseck* (Oct. 6, 1792); *Merkur, der Heurat-Stifter* (Feb. 21, 1793); *Das Fest der Lazzaroni* (Feb. 4, 1794); *Die gute Mutter* (May 11, 1795); *Johanna von Montfaucon* (Jan. 25, 1799); *Der Schreiner* (July 18, 1799); *Mitgefühl* (April 21, 1804); *Die Erkenntlichkeit* (July 22, 1805). He also produced numerous ballets; wrote incidental music to several plays; composed a great deal of instrumental music, including 22 symphonies; 5 concertos for various instruments with orch.; 6 quintets; 47 string quartets; 12 quartets for flute and strings; 3 piano quartets, and string trios.

Wrede, Ferdinand, German pianist and composer; b. Brökel, Hannover, July 28, 1827; d. Frankfurt-on-the-Oder, Jan. 20, 1899. He studied with Marschner and Litolff; then was active as singing teacher and choral conductor; wrote men's choruses and songs.

Wrightson, Herbert James, English-American composer and teacher; b. Sunderland, England, Dec. 20, 1869; d. West Lebanon, N.Y., Dec. 24, 1949. He studied at the Leipzig Cons. with Jadassohn and Reinecke. In 1897 he settled in the U.S.; taught in Philadelphia, Chicago, etc. His works include a symphony; 15 organ pieces; 29 piano pieces; 2 melodramas for speaker with music; 144 songs, of which nearly 100 were published. His hymns are included in various hymnals. He published *Elements of the Theory of Music* (Boston, 1921).

Wuensch, Gerhard, Austrian-born Canadian composer; b. Vienna, Dec. 23, 1925. He received a Dr. phil. degree from the Univ. of Vienna in 1950, and artist diploma in composition and piano from the State Academy of Music, Vienna, in 1952; studied music theory with Paul Pisk at the Univ. of Texas (1954). He then occupied teaching positions at Butler Univ. in Indianapolis (1956-63), at the Univ. of Toronto (1964-69), and at the Univ. of Calgary (1969-73); in 1973 was appointed to the faculty of the Univ. of Western Ontario in London, Ontario. He writes in an affable modernistic vein in neo-Classical forms.

WORKS: a ballet, *Labyrinth* (1957); a musical comedy, *Il Pomo d'Oro* (1958); *Nocturne* for orch. (1956); *Variations on a Dorian Hexachord* for orch. (1959); *Caribbean Rhapsody* for symph. band (1959); symph. No. 1 (1959); Piano Concerto (1961); *Ballad* for trumpet and orch. (1962); *Symphonia Sacra* for soloists, chorus, brass and perc. (1965); Symph. for brass and percussion (1967); Concerto for Piano and Chamber Orch. (1971); *Scherzo* for piano and wind ensemble (1971); *6 Guises* for narrator, winds and percussion (1972); Trio for clarinet, bassoon, and piano (1948); 2 string quartets (1955, 1963); *Mosaic* for brass quartet (1959); *Partita* for horn and piano (1961); *Viola Sonatina* (1963); *Ricercare* for 8 horns and organ (1963); 2 wind quintets (1963, 1967); Horn Sonata (1964); *Music for 7 brasses* (1966); Trumpet Sonata (1966); Sextet for horns (1966); *Suite* for trumpet and organ (1970); *Music in 4 Dimensions* for brass, harp and percussion (1970); Piano Trio (1971); *Variations* for clarinet and piano (1971); *Prelude, Aria and Fugue* for accordion and string quartet (1971); *Saxophone Sonata* (1971); *6 Songs* for voice, flute, and accordion (1970); piano pieces: *Esquisse* (1950), *Canzona and Toccata* (1963), 2 sonatinas (1969); organ pieces: *Toccata Piccola* (1963), *Sonata breve* (1963); solo accordion pieces: *4 Mini-Suites* (1968), *Sonata da camera* (1970), *Monologue* (1972), *Diversions* (1972); choruses.

Wüerst, Richard (Ferdinand), German composer; b. Berlin, Feb. 22, 1824; d. there, Oct. 9, 1881. He studied violin with Ferdinand David at the Leipzig Cons., where he also took lessons with Mendelssohn. He then taught at Kullak's Neue Akademie der Tonkunst in Berlin. As music critic for the *Berliner Fremdenblatt* he exercised considerable influence; published *Leitfaden der Elementartheorie der Musik* (1867; English transl. as *Elementary Theory of Music and Treatment of Chords*, Boston, 1893). As a composer he was a follower of Mendelssohn.

WORKS: the operas *Der Rotmantel* (Berlin, 1848), *Vineta* (Bratislava, Dec. 21, 1862), *Eine Künstlerreise* (with Winterfeld; Berlin, 1868), *Faublas* (Berlin, 1873), *A-ing-fo-hi* (Berlin, Jan. 28, 1878); *Die Offiziere der Kaiserin* (Berlin, 1878); cantata *Der Wasserneck;* 3 symphonies; *Ein Märchen,* symph. fantasy; *Variations sur une chanson nègre de Kentucky,* for orch. (on Stephen Foster's *My Old Kentucky Home); Sous le balcon,* a serenade for string orch. with cello obbligato; *Russische Suite* for string orch. with violin obbligato; *Tanz der Mücken, Fliegen und Käfer,* an orchestral scherzo; Piano Trio; Cello Sonata; 3 string quartets; various violin pieces; songs; vocal duets and terzets.

Wüllner, Franz, important German pianist, conductor, and composer; b. Münster, Jan. 28, 1832; d. Braunfels-on-the-Lahn, Sept. 7, 1902. He studied with Schindler in Münster and Frankfurt. In 1854 he went to Munich; was teacher at the Munich Cons. (1856-58); then municipal music director at Aachen (1858-64). He returned to Munich in 1864; succeeded

Hans von Bülow as conductor of the Munich court theater in 1869. Under unfavorable conditions (against Wagner's wishes) he prepared and conducted the first performance of *Das Rheingold* (Sept. 22, 1869) and *Die Walküre* (June 26, 1870). In 1877 he became court conductor at Dresden; in 1882 Schuch was promoted to take his place; thereafter Wüllner conducted the Berlin Philharmonic (1883–84), and on Oct. 1, 1884, succeeded Hiller as director of the Cologne Cons., later becoming also municipal music director, posts he held until his death. He was highly regarded as a choral composer; published the valuable book of vocal exercises, *Chorübungen der Münchener Musikschule* (1867; new ed. by E. Schwickerath, Munich, 1931).

WORKS: vocal with orch.: *Die Flucht der heiligen Familie; Heinrich der Finkler; Deutscher Siegesgesang; Lied und Leben; Psalm 98; Psalm 127;* church music; songs. He was a friend of Brahms.

BIBLIOGRAPHY: O. Klauwell, *Studien und Erinnerungen* (Langensalza, 1906); E. Wolff, ed., *Johannes Brahms im Briefwechsel mit Franz Wüllner* (Berlin, 1922; with a list of works); J. Wüllner, "Johannes Brahms in seiner Lebensfreundschaft mit Franz Wüllner," *Die Musik* (March 1942).

Wüllner, Ludwig, distinguished German singer; son of **Franz Wüllner;** b. Münster, Aug. 19, 1858; d. Berlin, March 19, 1938. He studied Germanic philology at the universities of Munich, Berlin, and Strasbourg; taught Germanic philology at the Akademie in Münster (1884–87), and sang occasionally in concert; his musical training began only in 1887, when he took a course of study at the Cologne Cons. A second change of vocation brought him to the Meiningen court theater, where he appeared as an actor of heroic parts in the spoken drama (1889–95); became friendly with Brahms, who commended his singing of German folksongs. In 1895 he gave song recitals in Berlin with such acclaim that he decided to devote himself mainly to lieder. He then made tours of all Europe, arousing tremendous enthusiasm; his first recital in N.Y. (Nov. 15, 1908) was a sensational success, and he followed it by one extensive tour of the U.S. and then another (1909–10). His peculiar distinction was his ability to give an actor's impersonation of the character of each song, introducing an element of drama on the concert stage.

BIBLIOGRAPHY: F. Ludwig, *L. Wüllner. Sein Leben und seine Kunst* (Leipzig, 1931).

Wunderer, Alexander, Austrian oboist, composer, and teacher; b. Vienna, April 11, 1877; d. Zinkenbach, near St. Gilgen (Salzkammergut), Dec. 29, 1955. He taught the oboe and other wind instruments at the State Academy of Music in Vienna (1919–37); wrote chamber music; was co-author of a book on orchestration. After 1945 he taught oboe classes at the Salzburg Mozarteum.

Wunsch, Hermann, German composer; b. Neuss, Aug. 9, 1884; d. Berlin, Dec. 21, 1954. He studied in Düsseldorf and Cologne, and later at the Hochschule für Musik in Berlin, where he subsequently taught (prof., 1945). He composed 6 symphonies, of which the 5th won the Schubert Memorial Prize (German section) of the Columbia Phonograph Co. contest (Schubert Centennial, 1928). Other works include the chamber operas *Bianca* (Weimar, May 22, 1927), *Don Juans Sohn* (Weimar, 1928), and *Franzosenzeit* (Schwerin, 1933); 2 Masses; *Südpolkantate* for chorus and orch.; *Helden* for chorus and orch. (Berlin, 1941); 3 violin concertos; Concerto for piano and small orch.; *Kleine Lustspielsuite* for orch.; *Fest auf Monbijou,* suite for chamber orch.; *Erntelied,* a symph. with a concluding chorus.

Wünsch, Walther, Austrian ethnomusicologist; b. Gablonz, July 23, 1908. He studied the theory of folk music with Becking in Prague; received his doctorate for the dissertation *Die Geigentechnik der jugoslawischen Guslaren* (Brno, 1934); subsequently worked in the Institute of Acoustics in Berlin; in 1943 he completed graduate studies at the Univ. of Vienna, despite the difficult war conditions. After the end of the war he was active mainly as a chamber music player. In 1960 he joined the faculty of the Univ. of Graz, and later was appointed prof. at the Institute of Ethnomusicology at the Hochschule für Musik in Graz. He published several important studies on ethnomusicology, including *Heldensänger in Südosteuropa* (Leipzig, 1937).

Wuorinen, Charles, American composer; b. New York, June 9, 1938. He studied piano at home; composition at Columbia Univ. with Otto Luening. He worked as an accompanist; sang countertenor parts in choral groups. From 1964 to 1971 he taught composition at Columbia Univ. In 1972 he joined the music faculty of the Manhattan School of Music. At the age of 16 he received a N.Y. Philharmonic Young Composers Award; several other awards and grants followed, among them the Lili Boulanger Memorial Award (1960). His mode of composition reposes on strictly rational formal principles, while his materials are discriminately derived from available modern resources and incorporate serial procedures. He has written 3 symphonies; 3 chamber concertos; other chamber music of varied contents; choruses; electronic pieces. Other works include *Orchestral and Electronic Exchanges* (1965) combining pre-recorded music with a live performance; 1st Piano Concerto (1966); String Trio (1968); *Contrafactum* for orch. (1969); *Time's Encomium* for electronic media, produced through the Mark II Synthesizer (1969; received the Pulitzer Prize); 2 piano sonatas (1969, 1976); *1851: A Message to Denmark Hill,* for baritone, flute, cello, and piano (1970); *Variations* for unaccompanied cello (1970); *A Song to the Lute in Musicke* for voice and piano (1970); *Ringing Changes* for percussion ensemble (1970); *Chamber Concerto* for tuba, 12 winds, 12 drums (1970); String Quartet (1971); Concerto for amplified violin and orch. (Tanglewood, Boston Symph., Aug. 4, 1972); 2nd Piano Concerto, for amplified piano and orch. (N.Y. Philharmonic, Dec. 6, 1974, composer soloist); an opera, *The W. of Babylon* (1975); *Hyperion* for 12 instruments (1975); Percussion Symphony (1976); *The Winds* (1977).

Würfel, Wilhelm, Bohemian pianist and composer; b. Plǎnany, near Kolín, May 6, 1790; d. Vienna, April 23, 1832. He taught at the Warsaw Cons., where Chopin was one of his students in organ playing; in 1826 he became assistant conductor at the Kärthnertor Theater in Vienna. His opera *Rübezahl* was produced in Vienna on March 10, 1825 with excellent success and enjoyed popularity for some years; he also wrote many piano pieces in a bravura style.

Wurlitzer, Rudolph H., American instrument dealer; b. Cincinnati, Dec. 30, 1873; d. there, May 27, 1948. He was the son of the founder of the Wurlitzer Co. (established 1856); studied violin at the Cincinnati College of Music and later in Berlin with Emanuel Wirth. He became secretary-treasurer of the Wurlitzer Co. in 1899; later vice-president, and finally president. In 1929 the company purchased 64 string instruments from the Rodman Wanamaker Collection, including some fine specimens. Several richly illustrated catalogues of string instruments in the Wurlitzer Collection have been issued: *Old Master Violins, Violas, Violoncellos* (Cincinnati, 1915); *Masterpieces of the Great Violin Makers* (N.Y., 1917; 2nd ed., 1918); *Rare Violins, Violas, Violoncellos of the 17th, 18th, and 19th Centuries* (N.Y., 1931); *Rare Bows for Violin, Viola, Violoncello, by Makers of the 18th and 19th Centuries* (N.Y., 1931); *Rare Violas by Celebrated Makers of the 16th–19th Centuries* (N.Y., 1940).

Wurm, Marie, noted English pianist; b. Southampton, May 18, 1860; d. Munich, Jan. 21, 1938. She studied piano with Raff and Clara Schumann in Germany; returning to England, she took theory lessons with Stanford and Arthur Sullivan. She was quite successful as a concert pianist in England and Germany; in 1925 she settled in Munich. Her avocation was conducting; she organized a women's orchestra in Berlin, and conducted its inaugural concert on Oct. 10, 1899, arousing considerable curiosity. She also was an ambitious composer.
WORKS: an opera *Die Mitschuldigen* (Leipzig, 1923); Piano Concerto; String Quartet; Violin Sonata; Cello Sonata; Piano Sonata; numerous piano pieces *(Valse de concert, Barcarolle, Sylph Dance, Suite,* gavottes, mazurkas, etc.); published *Das ABC der Musik,* and *Praktische Vorschule zur Caland-Lehre.* Her sisters, **Adela Wurm** and **Mathilda Wurm,** who made their careers in England, changed their last name to **Verne** in order to exorcise the vermicular sound of the original German family name, as pronounced in English.

Würz, Anton, German composer and musicologist; b. Munich, July 14, 1903; studied with Sandberger at the Munich Univ.; was music critic of the *Münchner Telegraph-Zeitung* (1927–45). His works include several song cycles, to words by Rilke, Eichendorff, etc.; a string quintet; 4 string quartets; a string trio; a violin sonata; a viola sonata; published numerous opera and operetta guide books for the Reclam ed.

Würz, Richard, German music critic and pedagogue; b. Munich, Feb. 15, 1885; d. there, Feb. 2, 1965. He took private lessons with Max Reger (1903–06); in 1907 he became a music critic of the *Münchner Neueste Nachrichte,* holding this position until 1945; was also active as a music teacher in Munich. He composed a number of choruses and piano pieces; published a monograph on Max Reger (Munich, 1920).
BIBLIOGRAPHY: W. Zentner, "Richard Würz," *Neue Musikzeitschrift* (Jan. 1950).

Wüst, Philipp, German conductor; b. Oppau, May 3, 1894; d. Saarbrücken, Nov. 1, 1975. He took private lessons in piano and composition with Ernst Toch in Berlin; beginning in 1928 he filled engagements as opera conductor in Saarbrücken, Bremerhaven, and Oldenburg. From 1936 to 1943 he was music director in Breslau, and later in Stuttgart. In 1946 he moved to Saarbrücken, where he taught at the Hochschule für Musik, and also conducted at the opera theater there; in 1969 he was named its honorary member.

Wustmann, Rudolf, German musicologist; b. Leipzig, Jan. 5, 1872; d. Bühlau, near Dresden, Aug. 15, 1916. He was the son of the bibliographer Gustav Wustmann; studied philology, history, and musicology (with Kretzschmar) at the Universities of Munich and Leipzig; was a teacher of academic subjects in Leipzig (1895–1900); later lived in Bolzano, Italy, and finally in Bühlau, devoting himself to philological and historical research. He published *Musikalische Bilder* (Leipzig, 1907); *Musikgeschichte Leipzigs* (Leipzig, 1909; vol. I only, up to the middle of the 17th century; vols. II and III written by Schering); *J. S. Bachs Kantatentexte* (Leipzig, 1913); *Die Hofweise Walthers von der Vogelweide* (Strasbourg, 1913); numerous articles in German musical periodicals.

Wyk, Arnold van, South African composer; b. Calvinia, Cape Province, April 26, 1916. He studied at the Stellenbosch Univ., near Cape Town (1936–38); then went to London, where he attended the Royal Academy of Music (1938–43). From 1939 to 1944 he worked with the British Broadcasting Corporation; went back to South Africa in 1946; taught there at the Univ. of Cape Town (1949–61); in 1961 joined the faculty of Stellenbosch Univ.
WORKS: *Southern Cross,* for orch. (1943); Symph. No. 1 (1944); *Christmas Oratorio* (1947); *Rhapsody* for orch. (Cape Town Festival, March 4, 1952); Symph. No. 2 (Cape Town Festival, March 13, 1952); *5 Elegies* for string quartet (1941); the song cycle *Liefde en Verlatenheid* (Festival of the International Society for Contemporary Music, Haifa, May 31, 1954); String Quartet No. 1 (1957); symph. suite, *Primavera* (1960); symph. variations, *Masquerade,* on a South African folk song (1964); choruses; songs; piano pieces.
BIBLIOGRAPHY: H. Ferguson, "Arnold van Wyk: Recently Published Works," *Tempo* (Summer 1958).

Wykes, Robert, American flutist and composer; b. Aliquippa, Pennsylvania, May 19, 1926. He studied at the Eastman School of Music (M.M., 1950) and at the Univ. of Illinois (Dr. of Mus. Arts, 1955). Trained as a flute player, he was a member of the St. Louis Symph. Orch. (1963–65). In 1965 he was appointed prof. of music at Washington Univ., St. Louis.

WORKS: *The Prankster*, chamber opera (Bowling Green, Ohio, Jan. 12, 1952); String Sextet (1958); Piano Quintet (1959); *Horizons* for orch. (1964); *Wave Forms and Pulses* for orch. (1964); *The Shape of Time* for orch. (1965); *Man Against Machine* for chamber group (1966); *In Common Cause* for strings, trumpet, English horn, and percussion (1966); *Towards Time's Receiving* for orch. (St. Louis, April 7, 1972); *4 American Indian Lyrics* for chorus (1957); also music for documentary films.

Wylde, Henry, English conductor, composer and educator; b. Bushey, Herts, May 22, 1822; d. London, March 13, 1890. He was the son of **Henry Wylde**, London organist and composer of glees. He studied piano with Moscheles and Cipriani Potter at the Royal Academy of Music in London. In 1852 he founded in London the New Philharmonic Society, and conducted its concerts in cooperation with Spohr, until 1858, when he took complete charge of its concerts (until 1879). In 1861 he founded the London Academy of Music; supervised the building of St. George's Hall (1867) to house it. In 1863 he became prof. of music there, retaining this post until his death.

WORKS: *Paradise Lost*, oratorio after Milton (London, May 11, 1853); Piano Concerto (London, April 14, 1852); songs; piano pieces. Books: *The Science of Music* (1865); *Music in Its Art-Mysteries* (1867); *Modern Counterpoint in Major Keys* (1873); *Occult Principles of Music* (1881); *Music as an Educator* (1882); *The Evolution of the Beautiful in Sound* (1888).

Wyman, Addison P., American violinist and composer; b. Cornish, N.Y., June 23, 1832; d. Washington, Pennsylvania, April 15, 1872. He was active as a violin teacher, and founded a music school at Claremont, N.Y., in 1869. He also published a number of popular piano pieces, with romantic titles *(Silvery Waves, Woodland Echoes, Moonlight Musings, Music among the Pines,* etc.).

Wyner, Yehudi, American composer, son of composer **Lazar Weiner** (whose name he phonetically changed to Wyner); b. Calgary, Canada, June 1, 1929. He followed his parents to the U.S.; enrolled in the Juilliard School of Music in N.Y., graduating in 1946; then entered Yale Univ., where his principal teacher was Richard Donovan; obtained his A.B. in 1950; B. Mus., 1951; M. Mus., 1953; he also acquired the M.A. degree from Harvard Univ. After occupying several temporary teaching posts, he joined the staff of Yale Univ. in 1963; was appointed chairman of the music dept. there in 1969. In 1976 he joined the faculty of the Berkshire Music Center in Tanglewood. His music is expressively vigesimosecular in its structural sobriety and melorhythmic aggressiveness; his serial techniques, anchored in tritones and major sevenths, are mitigated by a certain combinatorial harmoniousness; formally, he follows neo-Baroque practices.

WORKS: *Dance Variations* for wind octet (1953); Piano Sonata (1954); *Concerto Duo* for violin and piano (1957); *3 Informal Pieces* for violin and piano (1961); *Friday Evening Service* for cantor, chorus and organ (1963); *Torah Service* (1966); *Da Camera* for piano and orch. (1967); *Cadenza* for clarinet and harpsichord (1969); *De Novo* for cello and small ensemble (1971); *Canto Cantabile* for soprano and concert band (1972); *Intermedio* for soprano and string orch. (1974); *Dances of Atonement* for violin and piano (1976).

Wyschnegradsky, Ivan, foremost composer of microtonal music; b. St. Petersburg, May 16, 1893. He studied composition with Nicolas Sokoloff at the St. Petersburg Cons.; emigrated after the Russian Revolution, and in 1920 settled in Paris. He devoted virtually his entire musical career to the exploration and creative realization of music in quarter-tones and other microtonal intervals; had a quarter-tone piano constructed for him; also published a guide, *Manuel d'harmonie à quarts de ton* (Paris, 1932). On Nov. 10, 1945, he presented in Paris a concert of his music, at which he conducted the first performance of his *Cosmos*, for 4 pianos, with each pair tuned at quarter-tones. The Canadian composer Bruce Mather took interest in Wyschnegradsky's music and gave a concert of his works at McGill Univ., Montreal, that included 3 world premières (Feb. 10, 1977). But with the exception of these rare events, Wyschnegradsky remains a figure of legend; few performances of his music are ever given in Europe or America.

WORKS (all in quarter-tones unless otherwise shown): *La Journée de l'existence* for narrator, *ad lib.* chorus, and orch., in half-tones (1916–17; revised 1927 and 1940); *Chant douloureux et étude* for violin and piano (1928); *Chant funèbre* for strings and 2 harps (1922); *7 Variations on the note C* for 2 pianos (1918–20; performed in 1945 as *5 Variations,* then 2 more variations were added); *Chant Nocturne* for violin and 2 pianos (1923, revised 1972); 2 string quartets (1924, 1931–32); *2 Choruses* for voices and 4 pianos (1926); *Prélude et fugue sur un chant de l'Evangile rouge* for string quartet (1927); *Prélude et Danse* for 2 pianos (1928); *Ainsi parlait Zarathoustra* for orch. (1929–30; arranged for 4 pianos, 1936); *2 Études de Concert* for piano (1931; arranged for 2 pianos, 1936); *Étude en forme de scherzo* for 2 pianos (1932); *Prélude et Fugue* for 2 pianos (1933); *24 Préludes* for 2 pianos (1934, revised 1958–60); *4 Fragments Symphoniques* for 4 pianos (1934, final version 1968; 1937; 1946; 1956); *Linnite,* pantomime for 3 female voices and 4 pianos (1937); *Acte chorégraphique* for bass-baritone, chorus, and 4 pianos (1938–40, revised 1958–59); *Cosmos* for 4 pianos (1940); *Prélude et Fugue* for 3 pianos (1945); *2 Fugues* for 2 pianos (1951); *5 Variations sans thème et conclusion* for orch. (1951–52); *Sonate en un mouvement* for viola and 2 pianos (1956); *Transparences I* and *II* for Ondes Martenot and 2 pianos (1956, 1963); *Arc-en-ciel* for 6 pianos (1956); *Étude sur le carré magique sonore* for piano (1956; based on the "magic square" principle of cyclical structure, written in a tempered scale without quarter-tones); *Étude tricesimoprimal* for Fokker-organ (1959; for Dutch physicist Adriaan Fokker's 31-tone organ); *Composition* for string quartet (1960); *2 Pièces* for microtonal piano (1960); *Étude sur les mouvements Rotatoires* for 4 pianos (1961, orchestrated 1964); *2 Compositions:* No. 1 for 3 pianos and No. 2 for 2 pianos (1962); *Prélude et étude* for microtonal piano (1966); *Intégrations* for 2 pianos (1967); *L'éter-*

nel étranger for soloists, chorus, 4 pianos and percussion (1939–68); *Symphonie en un mouvement* for orch. (1969); *Dialogue à trois* for 3 pianos (1972; sixth-tones).

BIBLIOGRAPHY: Claude Ballif, ed., "Ivan Wyschnegradsky, L'ultrachromatisme, et les espaces non octaviants," special issue of *La Revue Musicale* (1972–73).

Wyss, Niklaus, Swiss conductor; b. Zürich, Nov. 5, 1936. He studied piano and violin in Zürich; conducting in Brussels and Rome. He is active mainly in Italy, Switzerland, and Holland.

Wyttenbach, Jurg, Swiss pianist and composer; b. Bern, Dec. 2, 1935. He studied composition at the Bern Cons.; later in Paris with Lefébure and Calvet (1955–57). In 1962 he became a prof. of piano at the Bern Cons. His music pursues the median line of European modernism, marked by a strong rhythmic pulse, dissonant counterpoint, and atonal diversions, without falling into the bottomless pit of dodecaphony.

WORKS: 4 works of "instrumental theater": *Execution ajournee I–III* (1969–70) and *Kunststücke, die Zeit totzuschlagen (Tricks to Kill Time,* 1972); Piano Concerto (1959, revised 1973); Sonata for solo oboe (1961); *3 Movements* for oboe, harp, and piano (1962); a ballet, *Der Gefesselte* (Heidelberg, 1962); *Divisions* for piano and 9 solo strings (1964); *De Metalli,* for baritone and orch. (1964–65); *Anrufungen und Ausbruch* for 28 woodwinds and brass (1966); *Nachspiel* for 2 pianos (1966); *Paraphrase* for a narrator, a flutist, and a pianist (1967–68); *Conteste* for chamber orch. (1969); *3 Pieces* for piano (1969); *Ad libitum* for one or two flutes (1969).

Wyzewa, Théodore de (real name **Wyzewski**), noted musicologist; b. Kalushin, Russian Poland, Sept. 12, 1862; d. Paris, April 7, 1917. In 1869 his parents settled in Châtelleraut, France, where he received his education; in 1884 he founded in Paris, with Édouard Dujardin, the *Revue Wagnérienne,* which, until it ceased publication in 1888, did much to advance the cause of Wagner in France. His importance as a musicologist rests upon his researches concerning the life and work of Mozart, about whom he published new facts in "Recherches sur la Jeunesse de Mozart," in the *Revue des Deux Mondes* (1904–05), and in *W. A. Mozart. Sa vie musicale et son œuvre de l'enfance à la pleine maturité* (with G. de Saint-Foix; 2 vols., Paris, 1912; 3 more vols. added by Saint-Foix in 1937, in 1940, and in 1946). He also wrote *Beethoven et Wagner* (Paris, 1898; new ed., 1914); edited 20 piano sonatas of Clementi with a biographical notice (vol. I, Paris, 1917; vol. II, posthumous, brought out by Henry Expert).

X

Xanrof, Léon, French composer of popular music; b. Paris, Dec. 9, 1867; d. there, May 17, 1953. His real name was **Léon Fourneau;** Xanrof is an anagram of its Latin equivalent *(fornax).* He was a lawyer by profession; from 1890 produced light stage pieces in the Paris theaters; the chansonette *Le Fiacre,* which he wrote for Yvette Guilbert, achieved great popularity. He also contributed music criticism to various Paris papers.

Xenakis, Iannis, eminent avant-garde theorist and composer of Greek descent; b. Braila, Rumania, May 29, 1922. At the age of 10 he was taken by his family to Greece, where he began to study engineering, but became involved in the Greek resistance movement against the Nazi occupation forces; was wounded in a skirmish. In 1947 he went to France; studied architecture with Le Corbusier and became his assistant (1948–60); during the same period he took lessons in composition with Honegger and Milhaud at the École Normale de Musique in Paris and with Messiaen at the Paris Cons. (1950–53). He acted as a helper of Le Corbusier in the design of the Philips Pavillion at the 1958 World's Fair in Brussels; met Varèse, who was then working on his *Poème électronique* for the exhibit, and received from him some stimulating advice on the creative potentialities of the electronic medium. During his entire career, Xenakis strove to connect mathematical concepts with the organization of a musical composition, using the theory of sets, symbolic logic, and probabilistic calculus; promulgated the stochastic method, which is teleologically directed and deterministic, as distinct from a purely aleatory handling of data. He published a comprehensive volume dealing with these procedures, *Musiques formelles* (Paris, 1963; in English, N.Y., 1971). He was founder and director of the Centre d'Études Mathématiques et Automatiques Musicales in Paris, and founder-director of the Center for Mathematical and Automated Music at Indiana Univ. in the U.S., where he served on the faculty from 1967 to 1972. His influence on the development of advanced composition in Europe and America is considerable; several composers adopted his theories and imitated the scientific sounding titles of some of his compositions. Xenakis uses Greek words for the titles of virtually all of his works to stress the philosophical derivation of modern science and modern arts from classical Greek concepts; in some cases he uses computer symbols for titles.

WORKS: *Metastasis* for 61 instruments (1953–54; Donaueschingen, Oct. 15, 1955); *Pithoprakta* for 50 instruments (1955–56; Munich, March 8, 1957); *Achorripsis* for 21 instruments (1956–57; Brussels, July 20, 1958); *Diamorphoses* for tape (1957); *Concret PH* for tape (1957); *Analogiques A & B* for 9 strings and tape (1959); *Syrmos (Chain of Events)* for 18 strings (1959); *Duel,* a musical game for 2 "antagonistic" conductors and 2 orchestras, playing different material, mathematically based on game theory, with the audience determining the winning orch. (1959; Radio Hilversum, Oct., 1971); *Orient-Occident* for tape (1960); *Herma (Foundation)* for piano (1960–61); *ST/*

48—1,240162 (1956–62; ST = stochastic; 48 = number of players; 1 = 1st work for this contingent; 240162 = 24 January 1962, date on which the work, derived from earlier sketches, was finally calculated by the IBM 7090 electronic computer in Paris as programmed probabilistically by Xenakis); *ST/10—1,080262* (1956–62; ST = stochastic; 10 = number of players; 1 = 1st work of this contingent; 080262 = 8 February 1962, date on which this work was finally electronically calculated; a version of this work for string quartet is entitled *ST/4); Morsima-Amorsima* (Morsima = that which come by Fate; Amorsima = that which does not come by Fate) for violin, cello, double bass, and piano (1956–62); *Atrées (Law of Necessity)* for 10 players (1956–62; written in homage to Blaise Pascal and calculated by the 7090 computer, with some license); *Stratégie,* musical game for 2 conductors and 2 orchestras (1959–62; Venice Festival, April 23, 1963; Bruno Maderna's orch. won over that of Konstantin Simonovic); *Bohor I* and *II* for tape (1962, 1975); *Polla Ta Dhina (Many Are the Wonders)* for children's choir and small orch., to a text of Sophocles' *Antigone* (1962); *Eonta* (neuter plural of the present participle of the verb "to be" in the Ionian dialect, the title being in Cypriot syllabic characters of Creto-Mycenean origin) for piano, 2 trumpets, and 3 tenor trombones (1963–64); *Hiketides (The Suppliants),* stage music for 50 women's voices, 10 instruments, and percussion, after Aeschylus (1964); *Akrata (Pure)* for 16 wind instruments (1964–65; Oxford, June 28, 1966); *Terretektorh (Action of Construction)* for 88 players scattered among the audience (1965–66; Royan Fest. of Cont. Music, April 3, 1966); *Oresteia,* incidental music for Aeschylus' tragedy, for chorus and chamber orch. (1965–66; also a concert suite); *Nomos Alpha (Law Alpha)* for solo cello (1966); *Polytope de Montréal,* light and sound spectacle for the Montreal EXPO '67, for 4 small, identical orchestras (1967); *Nuits* for 12 mixed voices a cappella (1967); *Medea,* stage music for male chorus and instrumental ensemble (1967); *Nomos Gamma* for 98 players scattered among the audience (1967–68; Royan Fest., April 3, 1969); *Kraanerg (Perfection of Energy),* ballet music for tape and orch. (1968–69; Ottawa, June 2, 1969); *Anaktoria* for 8 instruments (1969); *Persephassa* for 6 percussionists scattered among the audience (1969); *Synaphai* for 1 or 2 pianos, and orch. (1969); *Hibiki-Hana-Ma,* 12-channel electroacoustic music distributed kinematically over 800 loudspeakers, for the Osaka EXPO '70 (1969–70; also a 4-channel version); *Charisma* for clarinet and cello (1971); *Aroura* for 12 strings (1971); *Persepolis,* light and sound spectacle with 8- or 4-channel electroacoustic music (1971); *Antikhthon,* ballet music for orch. (1971; Bonn, Sept. 21, 1974); *Linaia-Agon* for horn, tenor trombone, and tuba (1972); *Mikka* for solo violin (1972); *Polytope de Cluny,* version of *Polytope de Montréal,* for 4-channel tape (1972); *Eridanos* for 8 brasses and 10 string instruments or their multiples (1973; La Rochelle Fest., 1973); *Evryali,* for piano (1973); *Cendrées* for chorus and orch. (1974; Lisbon,

June 18, 1974); *Erikhthon* for piano and orch. (1974; Paris, May, 1974); *Gmeeoorh* for organ (1974); *Noomena* for orch. (1974; Paris, Oct. 16, 1974); *Empreintes* for orch. (1975; La Rochelle Fest., June 29, 1975); *Phlegra* for 11 instruments (1975; London, Jan. 28, 1976); *Psappha* for solo percussion (1975); *N'shima* for 2 horns, 2 trombones, cello, and 2 mezzo-soprani (1975); *Theraps* for solo double bass (1975–76); *Khoaï* for solo harpsichord (1976); *Retours—Windungen* for 12 cellists (1976; Bonn, Dec. 20, 1976); *Dmaathen* for oboe and percussion (1976); *Epei* for English horn, clarinet, trumpet, 2 tenor trombones, and double bass (1976); *Mikka S* for solo violin (1976).

Xyndas, Spyridon, Greek composer; b. Corfu, June 8, 1812; d. Athens, Nov. 25, 1896. He studied in Italy; composed many attractive popular Greek songs; several operas to Italian librettos (*Il Conte Giuliano, I due pretendenti,* etc.); also *The Parliamentary Candidate* (Athens, March 1888), which was probably the first opera with a Greek text. He became blind toward the end of his life.

Y

Yamada, Kôsçak, eminent Japanese composer and conductor; b. Tokyo, June 9, 1886; d. there, Dec. 29, 1965. He studied at the Imperial Academy of Music in Tokyo; then in Berlin with Max Bruch (1909–13). Returning to Japan in 1914, he organized the Tokyo Philharmonic Orch. On Oct. 16, 1918, he conducted a program of Japanese music in Carnegie Hall, N.Y., including some of his own works (*Festival of Autumn, The Dark Gate, Flower of Madara,* and an *Oriental Suite*); appeared as guest conductor in the U.S. until 1921; in 1930, and again in 1933, he conducted in Russia; in 1937 he toured Europe. Most of his manuscripts were destroyed during the air raid on Tokyo on May 25, 1945; several scores have been restored from the extant orchestral parts.

WORKS: operas: *Alladine et Palomides,* after Maeterlinck (1913), *The Depraved Heavenly Maiden* (1908; Tokyo, Dec. 3, 1929); *Ayame* (*The Sweet Flag;* Tokyo, Feb. 24, 1935), *The Black Ships* (Tokyo, 1940), *Yoake* (*The Dawn;* Nov. 28, 1940), *Hsiang Fei* (1946); cantatas: *Bonno-Koru* (Tokyo, Oct. 9, 1931) and *The Dawn of the Orient* (Tokyo, July 7, 1941); Symph. (Tokyo, Dec. 6, 1914); *Ode to Meiji* for chorus and orch. (Tokyo, April 26, 1925); *Homage to Showa,* symph. poem (Tokyo, May 13, 1939); *Kamikaze,* symph. suite (1944); chamber music; nearly 1,000 choral pieces and songs.

Yamash'ta, Stomu (really **Yamashita, Tsutomu**), Japanese virtuoso percussionist and composer; b. Kyoto, March 10, 1947. He was trained in music by his father; played piano in his infancy, and drums at puberty; in early adolescence became a timpanist for the Kyoto Philharmonic and Osaka Philharmonic; also worked in several film studios in Tokyo; at the same time he was active in sports; won the speed skating championship of Japan for his age group. At 16 he went to London for further study; later went to the U.S. as a scholarship student at Interlochen Arts Academy; continued his musical education in Boston, N.Y., and Chicago. Returning to Japan he gave solo performances as a percussionist; developed a phenomenal degree of equilibristic prestidigitation synchronously manipulating a plethora of drums and a congregation of Oriental bells and gongs, while rotating 360° from the center of a circle to reach the prescribed percussionable objects. As a composer he cultivates a manner of controlled improvisation marked by constantly shifting meters. In 1970 he formed the Red Buddha Theater (an ensemble of 36 actors, musicians and dancers) for which he composed 2 musical pageants, *Man from the East* (1971) and *Rain Mountain* (1973). Other works: a ballet, *Fox* (1968); *Hito* for 3 instruments, any instruments (1970); *Prisms* for solo percussion (1970); *Red Buddha* for chamber ensemble (1971); percussion scores for some 77 Japanese films, as well as for Ken Russell's *The Devils* (with Peter Maxwell Davies, 1971) and Robert Altman's *Images* (1972).

Yampolsky, Izrail, Russian musicologist and lexicographer; b. Kiev, Nov. 21, 1905; d. Moscow, Sept. 20, 1976. He studied violin; then entered the Moscow Cons. where he took courses in advanced music theory with Miaskovsky and Glière; subsequently taught violin (1931–49) and gave lectures in music history there. A fine and diligent research scholar, he published a number of excellent monographs dealing mainly with violin and violinists: *Foundations of Violin Fingering* (Moscow, 1933; 3rd expanded edition, 1955; in English, London, 1967); *Henryk Wieniawski* (Moscow, 1955); *Enescu* (Moscow, 1956; also in Rumanian, Bucharest, 1959); *Music of Yugoslavia* (Moscow, 1958); *Paganini* (Moscow, 1961; 2nd ed., 1968); *David Oistrakh* (Moscow, 1964); *Fritz Kreisler* (1975). He was co-editor, with Boris Steinpress, of the one-volume reference work, *Encyclopedic Music Dictionary* (Moscow, 1959; revised, 1966). He was acting editor-in-chief of the first 3 volumes of the 5-volume *Musical Encyclopedia* (Moscow, 1973, 1974, 1976).

Yannay, Yehuda, Rumanian-born Israeli-American composer of hypermodern tendencies; b. Timisoara, May 26, 1937. He went to Israel in 1951, and studied composition with Boscovich (1959–64); received a Fulbright travel grant and went to the U.S., where he studied composition with Arthur Berger and Harold Shapero at Brandeis Univ. (M.F.A., 1966); attended summer classes of Gunther Schuller at the Berkshire Music Center in Tanglewood (1965); later studied composition at the Univ. of Illinois, Urbana (1968–70). In 1970 he joined the faculty of the Univ. of Wisconsin at Milwaukee; organized there a group called "Music from Almost Yesterday Ensemble" with the intention of producing music of the problematic future and that of the tenable yesteryear. In his own composition, he liberates himself from all prejudices of the past, present, and future. He invented an elastic nylon string monochord which he named, with a commendable eschewment of obsolescent modesty, "Yannaychord." Most of his creations are public exhibitions of a theatrical nature, in which all arts and human actions are united and all social conventions scorned, spurned, or both; the pugnacious determination to "épater les bourgeois" motivates his productions in the deluded hopes that the bourgeois will be epatated beyond endurance and precipitate a physical encounter of the kind that animated the fabled exhibitions of the futurists of yore.

WORKS: *Variations* for 2 flutes (1970); *The Chain of Proverbs* for choir, recorders, and percussion (1962); *Sefiroth* (*Spheres*) for soprano, flute, clarinet, bass clarinet, harp, prepared piano, and percussion (1963); *Incantations* for voices, keyboard and the piano interior (1964); *Interconnections* for 14 instruments (1965); *Mirkamim,* textures of sound for orch. of 84 solo instruments (1967); *Per se,* chamber concerto (1968; Chicago, Nov. 10, 1970); *Coloring Book for the Harpist,* playing with combs (1969); *Wraphap* for amplified actress lying upon a large aluminum sheet, and strumming the Yannaychord (1969); *Houdini's Ninth* for double bass and escape artist (straitjacketed to his instrument), while a recording plays the "Hymn to Joy" from Beethoven's Ninth Symphony and 2 hospital orderlies supervise the soloist

(1969); Concerto for audience, orch., and 29 red, yellow, and green slides monitoring the involuntary participants (1971); *3 Events: The Urbana (Illinois) Crystal Lake Park Gathering, Piano without Pianist,* and *The Vestibule Peep-In-Pipe-Out* (1968–71); *Bug Piece* for any irritants capable of bugging the captive audience, the bugging being symbolized by the projection on a screen of a centipede, a millipede, or fornicating ants, or any other terrestrial arthropods (1972); *A Noiseless Patient Spider,* for women's chorus a cappella (1975); *American Sonorama,* ballet score derived from sounds of the more obnoxious speeches by singularly illiterate politicians (1975–76); *The Decline and Fall of the Sonata in B-flat,* symbolic theater sketch (1970–76).

Yardumian, Richard, American composer; b. (of Armenian parents) Philadelphia, April 5, 1917; self-taught in music. His compositions reflect the spirit of Armenian folksongs and religious melodies. His *Armenian Suite* for orch. was performed for the 1st time by the Philadelphia Orch. on March 5, 1954. Other symph. works (also brought out by the Philadelphia Orch.) are *Desolate City* (April 6, 1945); Violin Concerto (March 30, 1951); Piano Concerto (Philadelphia, Jan. 3, 1958); Symph. No. 1 (Philadelphia, Dec. 1, 1961); Symph. No. 2 *(Psalms)* for orch. and contralto (Philadelphia, Nov. 13, 1964); *Come Creator Spirit,* Mass for contralto, chorus, and orch. (1966); an oratorio, *Abraham* (1971); *Chorales* (1977).

Yarustovsky, Boris, eminent Soviet musicologist; b. Moscow, May 14, 1911; d. there, July 1978. He studied music history and musicology at the Moscow Cons., graduating in 1941; obtained his degree of Dr. of Arts in 1953 with a dissertation, *Some Problems of the Dramaturgy of Classical Russian Operas.* Further publications: *Tchaikovsky, Life and Works* (Moscow, 1940); *Operatic Dramaturgy of Tchaikovsky* (Moscow, 1947); *Stravinsky, Life and Works* (Moscow, 1963); *Music of the New World* (Moscow, 1964).

Yashirō, Akio, Japanese composer; b. Tokyo, Sept. 10, 1929. He studied piano with Leonid Kreutzer and composition with Moroi, Ikenouchi, and Ifukube at the National Univ. of Tokyo, graduating in 1951; then went to Paris and took lessons with Nadia Boulanger, Tony Aubin, Henri Challan, and Messiaen (1951–56). Returning to Japan, he joined the music faculty of the Univ. of Tokyo.
WORKS: String Quartet (1954–55); Sonata for 2 flutes and piano (1957–58); Symphony (Tokyo, June 9, 1958); Cello Concerto (Tokyo, June 24, 1960); Piano Sonata (1960); Piano Concerto (Tokyo, Nov. 5, 1967); *Ouverture de Fête* for brass ensemble (performed at the opening ceremony of 14th Winter Olympic Games, Sapporo, Feb. 3, 1972).

Yasser, Joseph, Russian-American organist and musicologist; b. Lódź, Poland, April 16, 1893. He studied at the Moscow Cons., graduating in 1917 as organist; after several years of teaching organ in Moscow and Siberia, he reached Shanghai in 1922, and conducted a choral society there; subsequently emigrated to the U.S.; served as organist at Temple Rodeph Sholom,

N.Y. (1929–59); held various positions in American musicological groups. His most important contribution to music theory was *A Theory of Evolving Tonality* (N.Y., 1932), in which he proffered an ingenious hypothesis as to the origin of the pentatonic and heptatonic scales, and, operating by inductive reasoning, suggested that the ultimate western scale would contain 19 degrees. He contributed several articles to the *Musical Quarterly* (April, July, 1937 and July, 1938) dealing with quartal harmony, which were published in a separate edition (N.Y., 1938).
BIBLIOGRAPHY: Albert Weisser, compiler, *Joseph Yasser: An Annotated Bibliography of His Selected Writings and Lectures* (N.Y., 1970).

Yates, Peter B., Canadian-American writer on music; b. Toronto, Nov. 30, 1909; d. New York, Feb. 25, 1976. He studied at Princeton Univ. (B.A., 1931); married the pianist **Frances Mullen** in 1933. From 1937 to 1962 he was a functionary at the California Dept. of Employment in Los Angeles, but this bureaucratic occupation did not preclude his activities as a musical catalyst. In 1939 he inaugurated on the rooftop of his house in the Silver Lake district of Los Angeles a chamber concert series which was to become an important cultural enterprise in subcultural California, under the name Evenings on the Roof; he served as coordinator of these concerts from 1939 to 1954, when they were moved to a larger auditorium in downtown Los Angeles and became known as Monday Evening Concerts. In 1968 he was appointed chairman of the music department at the State Univ. of New York's College at Buffalo. He published *An Amateur at the Keyboard, Twentieth-Century Music,* and a collection of poems.

Yavorsky, Boleslav, Russian pianist and music theorist; b. Saratov, June 22, 1877; d. Kharkov, Nov. 26, 1942. He studied piano and composition with Taneyev in Moscow; in 1906 founded a People's Cons. there. From 1916–1921 he taught at the Kiev Cons.; then went to Moscow. His theory of aural gravitation as the determining factor of the formation of modes is embodied in his publications *Structure of Musical Speech* (Moscow, 1908), *Exercises in Schematic Formation of Modal Rhythm* (Moscow, 1915) and several monographs. He was also active in the field of general musical education, and his methods influenced Soviet practice in pedagogy. Vol. 1 of the collected edition of his articles and letters was published in Moscow in 1964.

Yoffe, Shlomo, Polish-born Israeli composer; b. Warsaw, May 19, 1909. He studied in Poland and Czechoslovakia; went to Palestine in 1930; studied with Partos and Boscovich at the Music Academies of Jerusalem and Tel Aviv; was director of the Studio for Music Education for Gilboa and Bet-Shean (1953–73).
WORKS: *Ruth,* symph. suite (1954); 3 symphonies (1955, 1957, 1958); Violin Concerto (1956); *Views of the Emek,* symph. suite (1958); *Symphonic Poem on Jewish Themes* (1959); *Divertimento* for orch. (1959); Cello Concertino (1959); Oboe Concerto (1960); Concerto for Strings (1961); *3 Pieces* for horn and strings (1966); *Fantasia Concertante* for brass quartet and

orch. (1968); *Beit-Alfa*, symph. poem (1972); *Introduction, Dance and Finale* for chamber orch. (1972); *Sobu Zion*, overture (1973); *5 Sketches of Old Jerusalem* for chamber orch. (1973); *Fantasy* for oboe and chamber orch. (1975); 6 cantatas: *Alilot Hagilboa* (1954), *Erez Hanegev* (1955), *Alu* (1958), *Shaalu Shelom Yerushalayim* (1967), *Religious Cantata* (1969) and *Psalm CXX* (1974); Quartet for 2 flutes, cello, and piano (1957); 2 string quartets (1961, 1969); *Fantasy* for string quartet (1966); *Chamber Concerto* for violin and 10 players (1966); *Affettuoso* for 2 flutes (1966); Brass Quartet (1967); *Musica concertante* for clarinet and 3 percussionists (1973); *4 Miniatures* for wind quintet (1973); *Etude* for 13 players (1974); *Serenata* for wind quintet (1975); *5 Songs* for soprano and 13 players (1975); *Nonetto*, fantasy for strings (1976); choruses.

Yon, Pietro Alessandro, Italian-American organist and composer; b. Settimo Vittone, Aug. 8, 1886; d. Huntington, L.I., N.Y., Nov. 22, 1943. He studied with Fumagalli at the Milan Cons.; then at the Turin Cons. (1901–04), and at the Santa Cecilia in Rome with Remigio Renzi (organ) and Sgambati (piano), graduating in 1905; subsequently served as organist at St. Peter's, Rome (1905–07). In 1907 he emigrated to the U.S.; from 1907 to 1919, and again from 1921 to 1926, was organist at St. Francis-Xavier's, N.Y.; then was appointed organist of St. Patrick's Cathedral, N.Y., a post he held until his death. He became a naturalized U.S. citizen in 1921. He was greatly esteemed as an organist and teacher; composed numerous organ pieces, of which *Gesù Bambino* (1917) became popular and was published in various instrumental and vocal arrangements; he also wrote an oratorio *The Triumph of St. Patrick* (N.Y., April 29, 1934); several Masses and other religious services. A novel based on his life, *The Heavens Heard Him*, written by V. B. Hammann and M. C. Yon, was published in N.Y. in 1963.

Yonge (Young), Nicholas, English musician; b. Lewes; d. London (buried Oct. 23), 1619; was a chorister at St. Paul's Cathedral. He translated and arranged a number of Italian madrigals, which he publ. in 2 books under the general title *Musica Transalpina* (1588; 1597).
BIBLIOGRAPHY: A. Obertello, *Madrigali italiani in Inghilterra* (Milan, 1949).

York, Francis Lodowick, American organist and teacher; b. Ontonagon, Mich., March 9, 1861; d. there, Jan. 13, 1955. He studied piano in Boston and Detroit; in 1892 went to Paris to study with Guilmant; upon return to the U.S. he devoted himself to teaching. He published the manuals, *Harmony Simplified* (1897) and *Counterpoint Simplified* (1907).

Yossifov, Alexander, Bulgarian composer; b. Sofia, Aug. 12, 1940. He studied composition with Vladigerov and conducting with Iliev at the Bulgarian State Cons. in Sofia, graduating in 1966.
WORKS: an opera, *Back to the Beginning*; 3 ballets: *Wings of Friendship* (1969), *The Woman Partisan* (1969) and *Student's Farewell Ball* (1969); 2 orato-

rios: *Homeland* (1966) and *The Great White Road* (1969); 5 nationalistic cantatas; *Revolution*, overture (1964); 2 symph. tales: *The Wolf and the Seven Kids* (1966) and *Little Red Riding Hood* (1969); 4 symphonies: No. 1, *Sinfonietta* (1966), No. 2 (1970), No. 3, *Bulgarian Blood*, for bass and orch. (1973) and No. 4 (1974); Concerto for 2 pianos, string orch., and percussion (1970); Piano Concerto (1971–72); *Festive Overture* (1974).

Yost, Gaylord, American violinist and composer; b. Fayette, Ohio, Jan. 28, 1888; d. Wauseon, Ohio, Oct. 10, 1958. After studying music in Toledo and Detroit, he went to Berlin where he took violin lessons with Issaye Barmas. Upon returning to the U.S. he organized the Yost String Quartet (1925). He taught at Indiana College of Music, Indianapolis (1915–21), and at the Pittsburgh Music Institute (1921–43). In 1951 he turned to politics and journalism; became editor and publisher of the *Fayette Review*, founded by his father. In 1954 he was elected mayor of Fayette, serving until 1957. He published *The Yost System*, in 8 vols. (1932; an abridged ed. as *The Yost Violin Method* in 3 vols.); also *Basic Principles of Violin Playing* (1940).

Yost, Michel, famous French clarinetist; b. Paris, 1754; d. there, July 5, 1786. He studied with Beer; wrote 14 clarinet concertos; 30 quartets for clarinet and strings; 8 books of duos for clarinets; *Airs variés* for clarinet with viola and bass.

Youdin, Mikhail, Russian composer; b. St. Petersburg, Sept. 29, 1893; d. Kazan, Feb. 8, 1948. He studied at the St. Petersburg Cons., graduating in 1923; joined its staff as instructor in 1926. He went to Kazan in 1942, and taught at the Cons. there until his death.
WORKS: opera *Farida* (1943); cantata *Song of Spring and Joy* (Leningrad, Nov. 25, 1936); *Heroic Oratorio* (1937); *Poem 1926* for orch. (Leningrad, March 30, 1927); other symph. pieces; 2 string quartets; piano sonata; organ toccata; choruses; songs; arrangements of folksongs.

Youll, Henry, English composer; flourished c.1600. He publ. *Canzonets to three voyces* (1608), a collection of 24 vocal pieces (*Slow, slow, fresh fount*, to Ben Jonson's words; *Pipe, shepherds, pipe*; etc.). It was republished in *The English Madrigal School* (vol. 28).

Youmans, Vincent, American composer of popular music; b. New York, Sept. 27, 1898; d. Denver, Colo., April 5, 1946. He took piano lessons as a child, but was apprenticed by his father to enter business; he served as a messenger in a Wall Street bank; then enlisted in the U.S. Navy; also played the piano in a Navy band; wrote a song *Hallelujah* which was picked up by John Philip Sousa, who performed it with his own bands; later it was incorporated by Youmans in his musical *Hit the Deck*. After World War I, Youmans earned a living as a song plugger for publishers in N.Y. He produced 2 musical comedies *Two Little Girls in Blue* (1922) and *Wildflower* (1923); both were moderately successful, but he achieved fame with his next production, *No No Nanette*; it opened in Detroit on April 21, 1924; was next staged in Chicago on May 5, 1924, and after a 49-week run there, moved to London where it was produced on March 11, 1925; it finally reached Broadway on Sept. 16, 1925, and proved to be one of the most beguiling and most enduring American musicals; its hit song, *Tea for Two,* became a perennial favorite all over the world. (Shostakovich arranged it in 1927 for a salon orch. under the title *Tahiti Trot.*) There followed several other successful musicals: *A Night Out* (1925), *Oh! Please* (1926), *Hit the Deck* (1927), *Rainbow* (1928), *Great Day* (1929), and *Through the Years* (1932). In 1933 Youmans went to Hollywood to complete his score for the film *Flying Down to Rio.* Because of an increasingly aggravated tubercular condition, he retired to Denver in the hope of recuperation in its then unpolluted environment, and remained there until his death. Among his songs the following were hits: *Bambalina; I Want to Be Happy; Hallelujah; Sometimes I'm Happy; Great Day; Without a Song; Time on My Hands; Through the Years; Oh, Me, Oh, My, Oh, You; Carioca; Orchids in the Moonlight; Drums in My Heart; More Than You Know; Rise 'n' Shine.*

Young, Anthony, English organist and composer; b. c.1685; d. after 1720. He was organist at various churches in London; wrote numerous songs; he is chiefly known as one of the composers falsely credited with the authorship of the tune of *God Save the Queen.*

Young, Cecilia, English singer; b. London, c.1710; d. there, Oct. 6, 1789. She made her appearance at the Drury Lane Theatre on March 4, 1730; in 1735 was engaged by Handel for his opera company; married **T. A. Arne** on March 15, 1737; went with him to Dublin in 1742, and sang soprano parts in his works presented there (*Comus, Judgment of Paris, Alfred,* etc.).

Young, Douglas, English composer; b. London, June 18, 1947. He studied at the Royal College of Music with Anthony Milner (composition) and Anthony Hopkins (piano) in 1966. He composes mostly instrumental music. Among his works are Sonata for horn and piano (1965); *Sonnet* for orch. (1967); Sonata for violin, viola, and cello (1968); *The Listeners,* ballet (London, Dec. 13, 1969); piano pieces for children.

Young, La Monte, American composer of the extreme avant-garde; b. Bern, Idaho, Oct. 14, 1935. He studied clarinet and saxophone with William Green in Los Angeles; then took courses in composition with John Vincent and Leonard Stein at the Univ. of California, Los Angeles (1956–57), and later at Berkeley (1957–60); subsequently worked with Richard Maxfield at the New School for Social Research in N.Y. (1960–61). In 1963 he married the artist and illustrator Marian Zazeela, and gave a number of audio-visual performances with her in a series of "Sound/Light Environments" in Europe and America. In 1970 he visited India to study Eastern philosophy and train himself physically, mentally, and vocally for cosmic awareness, gradually arriving at the realization that any human, subhuman, or inhuman activity constitutes art; in his *Composition 1990* he starts a fire on the stage while releasing captive butterflies in the

hall. In his attempt to overcome the terrestrial limitations he has decreed for himself a circadian period of 26 hours. He achieves timelessness by declaring, "this piece of music may play without stopping for thousands of years." Several of his works consist solely of imperious commands: "Push the piano to the wall; push it through the wall; keep pushing," or, more succinctly, "Urinate." He edited *An Anthology of Chance Operations, Concept Art, Anti-Art, etc.* (N.Y., 1963); his own contribution to it was a line drawn in India ink on a 3 x 5 filing card.

ASCERTAINABLE WORKS: *5 Little Pieces* for string quartet (1956); *For Guitar* (1958); String Trio (1958); *Poem for Tables, Chairs, and Benches* (moving furniture about; Univ. of California, Berkeley, Jan. 5, 1960); *Arabic Numeral (any Integer)* for gong or piano (1960); *Studies in the Bowed Disc* for gong (1963); *The Well-Tuned Piano* (1964); *The Tortoise Droning Selected Pitches from the Holy Numbers of the Two Black Tigers, the Green Tiger and the Hermit* (N.Y., Oct. 30, 1964) and *The Tortoise Recalling the Drone of the Holy Numbers as They Were Revealed in the Dreams of the Whirlwind and the Obsidian Gong, Illuminated by the Sawmill, the Green Sawtooth Ocelot, and the High-Tension Line Stepdown Transformer* (N.Y., Dec. 12, 1964); an arbitrary number of pieces of "conceptual" music and tape recordings of his own monophonous vocalizing achieved by both inspiration and expiration so that the vocal line is maintained indefinitely; various physical exercises with or without audible sounds. His *Selected Writings* were published in Munich in 1969.

Young, Percy Marshall, English writer on music; b. Northwich, Cheshire, May 17, 1912. He studied organ at Selwyn College at Cambridge (B.A., 1933); then went to Dublin where he graduated from Trinity College in 1937; upon his return to England he took courses with C. B. Rootham and E. J. Dent in Cambridge; subsequently occupied various teaching posts; from 1944 to 1966 was Director of Music at the College of Technology in Wolverhampton. He published a number of arrangements of old English songs, and also composed some vocal pieces; but he is known principally for his scholarly biographical studies and essays.

WRITINGS: *Handel* (London, 1947); *The Oratorios of Handel* (London, 1953); *A Critical Dictionary of Composers and Their Music* (London, 1954; in America as *Biographical Dictionary of Composers*); *Elgar, O.M. A Study of a Musician* (London, 1955; revised ed., 1972); *The Story of Song* (London, 1955); *Instrumental Music* (London, 1955); *In Search of Music* (London, 1956); *Concerto* (London, 1957); *Tragic Muse. The Life and Works of Robert Schumann* (1961; revised, 1967); *Symphony* (London, 1957); *Music Makers of Today* (London, 1958); *The Choral Tradition: An Historical and Analytical Survey from the 16th Century to the Present Day* (London, 1962); *Zoltán Kodály* (London, 1964); *Britten* (London, 1966); *A History of British Music* (London, 1967); *Great Ideas in Music* (London, 1967); *Keyboard Musicians of the World* (London, 1967); *Debussy* (London, 1969); *The Bachs, 1500–1850* (London, 1970); *Sir Arthur Sullivan* (London, 1971); *A Concise History of Music* (London,

1974). He edited *Sir Edward Elgar. Letters and Other Writings* (London, 1956).

Young, Polly (Mary), English singer; b. London, c.1745; d. there, Sept. 20, 1799. She lived in Dublin with her aunt, the singer **Cecilia Young** (Mrs. T. A. Arne), and made her debut as a singer upon her return to London in 1762. In 1766 she married the composer **François-Hippolyte Barthélémon;** their daughter, Cecilia Maria (Mrs. Henslowe), was a talented musician.

Young, Victor, American pianist and composer; b. Bristol, Tenn., April 9, 1889; d. Ossining, N.Y., Sept. 2, 1968. He studied piano with Isidor Philipp in Paris; toured in England and the U.S. as accompanist to prominent singers; held various teaching positions; was music director in Thomas A. Edison's Experimental Laboratory in West Orange, N.J., conducting tonal tests and making piano recordings under Edison's personal supervision (1919–27). He wrote the musical score for one of the earliest sound motion pictures, *In Old California;* composed some 300 film scores altogether; also wrote, for orch., *Scherzetto; Jeep; In the Great Smokies; Charm Assembly Line Ballet;* etc.; piano pieces (including *Under a Spanish Moon*); songs (*Gossip, Cuckoo Clock,* etc.).

Young, Victor, American composer of popular music; b. Chicago, Aug. 8, 1900; d. Palm Springs, Calif., Nov. 10, 1956. As a youth he was sent to Poland, where he studied violin at the Warsaw Cons., and made his debut with the Warsaw Philharmonic. He returned to Chicago in 1914, and after further study, became active on the radio. In 1935 he went to Hollywood, where he wrote film music. Some of his songs became famous (*Sweet Sue, Street of Dreams, Can't We Talk It Over, My Romance, Ghost of a Chance, Love Letters, Golden Earrings, Stella by Starlight, My Foolish Heart, Song of Delilah,* etc.). Shortly before his death, he completed the musical score for the motion picture *Around the World in 80 Days* (1956).

Young, William, English violinist, flutist, and composer; date of birth unknown; d. London, Dec. 21, 1671. He was attached to the court of the Archduke Ferdinand Karl in Innsbruck, where he published a book of 30 *Sonate a 3, 4, 5 voci con allemande, corranti* (1653). In 1660 he was a flutist in the private orch. of Charles II in London. The following year he also played the violin. Other pieces by Young include *Ayre, Almain and 2 Sarabands* in Playford's *Musick's Recreation on the Lyra Viola* (1652), and *Fantasies for 3 viols* in Playford's *Treasury of Musick* (1669); numerous manuscripts are in the Bodleian Library, Oxford; Gresham College, London; Corporation Music Library, Manchester; and in some private collections.
BIBLIOGRAPHY: W. Gillies Whittaker, *The Concerted Music of William Young* (Oxford, 1931).

Youssoupoff, Prince Nicolas, Russian musical dilettante and writer on musical subjects; b. St. Petersburg, 1827; d. Baden-Baden, Aug. 3, 1891. He studied violin with Vieuxtemps, and was an eager collector of violin literature; had a private orch. in his palace in St. Petersburg, but lived abroad for many years. He composed a programmatic symph., *Gonzalvo de Córdova,* with violin obbligato; *Concerto symphonique* for violin and orch.; several pieces for violin and piano (*Féeries de la scène, Hallucination, Chant d'amour, Plainte, Saltimbanques,* etc.); published an interesting book on violin making, *Luthomonographie, historique et raisonnée* (Frankfurt, 1856; printed in French in Munich) and *Musique sacrée suivie d'un choix de morceaux de chants d'église* (Paris, 1862, as vol. I of a projected *Histoire de la musique en Russie;* contains a valuable study of Russian neumes and examples of traditional chants). Themes from Youssoupoff's *Ballet d'Espagne* were used by Bériot for a group of 6 violin duets.

Yradier, Sebastián, Spanish composer; b. Sauciego, Álava, Jan. 20, 1809; d. Vitoria, Dec. 6, 1865. He composed theater music; after 1851 became singing master to the Empress Eugénie in Paris; for some time lived in Cuba. He published a number of melodious songs in a Spanish manner; one of them, *El Arreglito,* subtitled *Chanson havanaise,* was used by Bizet for the famous Habanera in *Carmen;* Bizet retained the key and the pattern of the accompaniment, making minor changes in the melody to adjust it to French words. Yradier's other songs that became famous are *La Paloma* and *Ay Chiquita!* In Paris he published 2 collections, *Echo d'Espagne* (8 songs) and *Fleurs d'Espagne* (25 songs).
BIBLIOGRAPHY: E. Istel, *Bizet und "Carmen"* (Stuttgart, 1927); J. Tiersot, "Bizet and Spanish Music," *Musical Quarterly* (Oct. 1927).

Yriarte, Tomás de, Spanish poet and musician; b. Orotava, Tenerife, Canary Islands, Sept. 18, 1750; d. Santa María, near Cádiz, Sept. 17, 1791. He was secretary at the Chancellery of State in Madrid and chief archivist at the Ministry of War. His literary works include a long didactic poem, *La Música* (Madrid, 1779; English transl., 1807). He composed tonadillas and some vocal and instrumental music.
BIBLIOGRAPHY: E. Cotarelo y Mori, *Yriarte y su época* (Madrid, 1897); J. Subirá, *El Compositor Yriarte ye el cultivo español del melólogo,* 2 vols. (Madrid, 1949–50).

Ysaÿe, Eugène, famous Belgian violinst, conductor, and composer; b. Liège, July 16, 1858; d. Brussels, May 12, 1931. At the age of 5 he began to study violin with his father, a theater conductor; at the age of 7 he was enrolled at the Cons. of Liège as a pupil of Désiré Heynberg; then studied with Rodolphe Massart there; in 1867 he obtained 2nd prize for violin playing (sharing it with Ovide Musin); in 1866, 1st prize for violin and chamber music. Still a very young boy, he played in his father's orchestras; in 1876 he was sent to Brussels to study with Henryk Wieniawski, and later was also a pupil of Vieuxtemps. After a sojourn in Bordeaux, he became concertmaster of Bilse's orch. in Berlin; appeared as soloist as Pauline Lucca's concerts in Cologne and Aachen; in Germany he met Anton Rubinstein, who took him to Russia, where he spent 2 winters; also toured Norway. In 1883 he settled in Paris, where he met César Franck, Vincent d'Indy, etc. and gave successful concerts; formed a duo with the pianist Raoul Pugno, and started a long series of concerts with him, establishing a new standard of excellence. On Sept. 26, 1886 he married Louise Bourdeau; César Franck dedicated his violin sonata to them as a wedding present; Ysaÿe's interpretation of this work made it famous. In 1886 he was named prof. at the Cons. of Brussels (resigned in 1898); in 1886 he also organized the Ysaÿe Quartet (with Crickboom, Léon Van Hout, and Joseph Jacob); Debussy dedicated his string quartet to Ysaÿe's group, which gave it its first performance at the Société Nationale, Paris, on Dec. 29, 1893. In 1889 he made successful appearances in England; on Nov. 16, 1894, he made his American debut, playing the Beethoven Violin Concerto with the N.Y. Philharmonic, and created a sensation by his virtuosity. He revisited America many times, with undiminished acclaim. He began his career as a conductor in 1894 and established his own orch. in Brussels, the "Société des Concerts Ysaÿe." When the Germans invaded Belgium in 1914 he fled to London, where he remained during World War I. On April 5, 1918, he made his American debut as conductor with the Cincinnati Symph. Orch., and also led the Cincinnati May Festival in that year. His success was so great that he was offered the permanent position as conductor of the Cincinnati Symph. Orch., which he held from 1918 to 1922. He then returned to Belgium and resumed leadership of the "Société des Concerts Ysaÿe." After the death of his 1st wife, he married, on July 9, 1927, an American pupil, Jeannette Dincin (b. Brooklyn, Aug. 26, 1902).

Ysaÿe's style of playing is best described as heroic; but his art was equally convincing in the expression of moods of exquisite delicacy and tenderness; his frequent employment of "tempo rubato" produced an effect of elasticity without distorting the melodic line. Ysaÿe was also a composer. His works include 8 violin concertos; 6 violin sonatas; *Poème nocturne,* for violin, cello, and strings; *Les Harmonies du soir,* for string quartet and string orch.; *Divertimento* for violin and orch.; *Méditation* for cello and string orch.; *Chant d'hiver* for violin and chamber orch.; *Trio de concert,* for 2 violins, viola, and orch.; *Amitié,* for 2 violins and orch. At the age of 70 he began the composition of an opera in the Walloon language, *Piér li Houïeu (Peter the Miner),* which was produced in Liège on March 4, 1931, in the presence of the composer, who was brought to the theater in an invalid's chair, suffering from the extreme ravages of diabetes, which had necessitated the amputation of his left foot. He began the composition of a 2nd Walloon opera, *L'Avierge di Piér (La Vierge de Pierre),* but had no time to complete it. In 1937 Queen Elisabeth of Belgium inaugurated the annual Prix International Eugène Ysaÿe in Brussels; the first winner was the famous Russian violinist, David Oistrakh.

BIBLIOGRAPHY: M. Pincherle, *Feuillets d'histoire du violon* (Paris, 1927); J. Quitin, *Eugène Ysaÿe: Étude biographique et critique* (Brussels, 1938); E. Christen, *Ysaÿe* (Geneva, 1946; 2nd ed., 1947); Antoine Ysaÿe and B. Ratcliffe, *Ysaÿe: His Life, Work and Influence* (London, 1947); Antoine Ysaÿe, *Eugène Ysaÿe: sa vie d'après les documents receuillis par son*

fils (Brussels, 1948; a considerably altered version of the preceding).

Ysaÿe, Théophile, Belgian pianist and composer; brother of **Eugène Ysaÿe;** b. Verviers, March 2, 1865; d. Nice, March 24, 1918. He was a pupil at the Liège Cons.; then studied at the Kullak Academy in Berlin, and also took lessons from César Franck in Paris; returning to Belgium, he became director of the Académie de Musique in Brussels; was noted as a fine ensemble player, and gave sonata recitals with his brother; during the latter's absence on tours, he also conducted the "Société des Concerts Ysaÿe" in Brussels. After the invasion of Belgium in 1914, he went with his brother to London; fearful of the Zeppelin air raids on London, he went to Nice, where he remained until his death. He was a prolific composer; his brother conducted a concert of Théophile's works in Brussels, on Nov. 6, 1904, including the premières of his Symph. in F major and the symph. poem *Le Cygne.* Other works are: Piano Concerto; symph. poems *(Les Abeilles, La Forêt et l'Oiseau); Fantaisie sur un thème populaire wallon,* for orch.; Piano Quintet; piano pieces; a Requiem.

Yttrehus, Rolv, American composer; b. Duluth, March 12, 1926. He studied at the Univ. of Minnesota (1946–50); then enrolled in the Univ. of Michigan 1950–53), obtaining his M.M.; went to Europe, where he took lessons with Brustad in Oslo (1953–54) and with Nadia Boulanger in Paris (1954–55); upon return home had satisfying sessions with Sessions (1957–60) at Princeton Univ.; then went to Rome and had instruction in advanced composition with Petrassi at the Santa Cecilia Academy (1960–62). Back in the U.S., he held several teaching positions: at the Univ. of Missouri (1963–68), at Purdue Univ. (1968–69), at the Univ. of Wisconsin in Oshkosh (1969–77), and, from 1977, at Rutgers Univ. He ditched the scores written in the first 35 years of his life as deciduous juvenilia; in his later works he cultivated distributive serialism, in which each note, each interval, and each rhythmic unit stands in an esoteric but surmisable relationship with other individual note groups.

WORKS: *Music* for winds, percussion, and viola (1961); *Espressioni* for orch. (1962); *Music* for winds, percussion, cello, and voices (1969); Sextet for trumpet, horn, violin, double bass, piano, and percussion (1969–70; revised 1974); *Angstwagen* for soprano and percussion (1971); Quintet for violin, cello, flute, clarinet, and piano (1973); *Gradus Ad Parnassum,* on texts by Nietzsche and J. J. Fux, for soprano, chamber ensemble, and tape (1974–77).

Yuasa, Joji, Japanese composer; b. Koriyama, Aug. 12, 1929. He was a medical student at Keio Univ.; studied composition in the "experimental workshop" in Tokyo (1951–57). In 1968 he received a Japan Society Fellowship for a lecture tour throughout the U.S. and Europe. In 1969 he was one of the organizers of the "Crosstalk Festival" of Japanese and American mulitmedia works in Tokyo and Osaka; was a member of the "tranSonic" composers group, in association with Ichiyanagi, Matsudaira, Takemitsu, and others. In his productions he adopts the most advanced multimedia techniques.

WORKS: *Projection* for 7 players (1955); *Cosmos Haptic* for piano (1957); *Projection Topologic* for piano (1959); *Aoi no Ue,* musique concrète (1961); *Interpenetration* for 2 flutes (1963); *Projection Esemplastic* for electronic media (1964); *Kansoku* for voices (1965); *Projection* for cello and piano (1967); *Projection* for several kotos and orch. (1967); *Projection* for electric guitars (1968); *Projection* for string quartet (1970); *Triplicity* for double bass (1970); *Questions* for chorus (1971); *On the Keyboard* for piano (1971); *Interposiplaytion I* for flute, piano, and percussion (1972) and *II* for flute, harp and percussion (1973); *Chronoplastic* for orch. (1972; Tokyo, Nov. 15, 1972); *Territory* for marimba, flute, clarinet, percussion, and double bass (1974); *Time of Orchestral Time* for orch. (1976).

Yun, Isang, important Korean composer; b. Tong Young, Sept. 17, 1917. He studied Western music in Korea (1935-37) and in Japan (1941-43). After the end of the war he taught music in South Korean schools; in 1956 went to Berlin, where he took lessons in composition with Boris Blacher and Josef Rufer at the Berlin Musikhochschule. He settled permanently in Berlin, where he produced several successful theatrical works, marked by a fine expressionistic and coloristic quality, and written in an idiom of euphonious dissonance. His career was dramatically interrupted when on June 17, 1967, he and his wife were brutally abducted from West Berlin by the secret police agents of South Korea, and forced to board a plane for Seoul, where they were brought to trial for sedition; he was sentenced to life imprisonment; his wife was given 3 years in jail. This act of lawlessness perpetrated on the territory of another country prompted an indignant protest by the government of West Germany, which threatened to cut off its substantial economic aid to South Korea; 23 celebrated musicians, including Igor Stravinsky, issued a vigorous letter of protest. As a result of this moral and material pressure, South Korea released Yun and his wife after nearly two years of detention, and they returned to Germany. In 1970 he was appointed a prof. at the Hochschule für Musik in Berlin.

WORKS: opera: *Der Traum des Liu-Tung* (Berlin, Sept. 25, 1965); *Die Witwe des Schmetterlings* (completed by him in his Seoul prison cell and produced *in absentia* in Bonn on Dec. 9, 1967; English version as *Butterfly Widow,* Northwestern Univ., Evanston, Ill., Feb. 27, 1970), *Träume* (an amalgam of the previous 2 operas: Nuremberg, Feb. 23, 1969), *Geisterliebe* (1969-70; Kiel, Germany, June 20, 1971) and *Sim Tjong* (1971-72; Munich, Aug. 1, 1972); *Symphonische Szene* (1960); *Bara,* for orch. (1960); *Colloides sonores* for string orch. (1961); *Fluktuationen* for orch. (1964; Berlin, Feb. 10, 1965); *Réak* for orch. (Donaueschingen, Oct. 23, 1966); *Dimensionen* for orch. (Nuremberg, Oct. 22, 1971); *Konzertante Figuren* for small orch. (1972; Hamburg, Nov. 30, 1973); *Ouvertüre* (1973-74); Cello Concerto (Royan, March 25, 1976); Concerto for flute and small orch. (1977); Double Concerto for oboe, harp and small orch. (1977); *Om mani padme hum,* cycle for soprano, baritone, chorus and orch. (1964; Hannover, Jan. 30, 1965); *Namo* for 3 sopranos and orch. (Berlin, May 4, 1971); *Der weise Mann,* cantata after P. Salomo, for baritone, chorus, and small orch. (1977); *Musik* for 7 instruments (1959); String Quartet No. 3 (1959; Nos. 1 and 2 are withdrawn); *Loyang* for chamber ensemble (1962); *Gasa* for violin and piano (1963); *Garak* for flute and piano (1963); *Nore* for cello and piano (1964); *Riul* for clarinet and piano (1968); *Images* for flute, oboe, violin, and cello (1968); *Glissées* for solo cello (1970); *Piri* for solo oboe (1971); *Gagok* for guitar, percussion, and voice (1972); Trio for flute, oboe, and violin (1972-73); *Memory* for mezzo-soprano, baritone, narrator, and percussion (1974); *Etüden* for solo flute (1974); *Harmonia* for 13 or 16 winds, harp and percussion (1974); *An der Schwelle,* 2 sonnets for baritone, female chorus, organ, and instruments (1975); *Rondell* for oboe, clarinet, and bassoon (1975); Piano Trio (1972-75); *Pièce concertante* for chamber ensemble (1976); Duo for viola and piano (1976); *Königliches Thema* for solo violin (1976); *5 Pieces* for piano (1959); *Shao Yang Yin* for harpsichord (1966); *Tuyaux sonores* for organ (1967); *Fragment* for organ (1975).

Yuon, Paul. See **Juon, Paul.**

Yurgenson, Peter. See **Jurgenson, Pyotr.**

Yussupov, Prince Nicolas. See **Youssoupoff, Prince Nicolas.**

Yvain, Maurice, French composer of musical comedies; b. Paris, Feb. 12, 1891; d. there, July 28, 1965. Among his successful productions are *Ta bouche* (1922), *Pas sur la bouche* (1925), *Bouche à bouche* (1936), and film scores (*Rien qu'un baiser; J'ai tant d'amour,* etc.). He also produced a ballet, *Blanche neige* (Paris Opéra, Nov. 14, 1951).

Yzac, Heinrich. See **Isaac, Heinrich.**

Z

Zabaleta, Nicanor, Spanish harpist; b. San Sebastian, Jan. 7, 1907. He went to Paris to study with Marcel Tournier; toured in Europe, South America, and the U.S. He is noted for his efforts to increase the number of works available for the harp, both by bringing to light neglected compositions of old composers, and by prompting modern composers to write music for the harp. In 1958 he made a long European tour as soloist with leading orchestras.

Zabalza y Olaso, Don Dámaso, Spanish composer and pianist; b. Irurita, Navarra, Dec. 11, 1833; d. Madrid, Feb. 25, 1894. He studied with Mariano García; in 1858 settled in Madrid as a piano teacher at the National Cons. He published a number of piano pieces, many of which became very popular; also piano studies that were used at the Paris Cons., in Italy, and in Spain.

Zabel, Albert Heinrich, German harpist; b. Berlin, Feb. 22, 1834; d. St. Petersburg, Feb. 16, 1910. He studied at the Institut für Kirchenmusik in Berlin; toured Germany, Russia, England, and America with Gungl's orch. In 1862 he joined the staff of the newly-founded St. Petersburg Cons., and held that post until his death. He composed a harp concerto and numerous short pieces for the harp (*Élégie fantastique, Légende, Marguérite au rouet, Am Springbrunnen, Chanson du pêcheur, Warum?, Murmure de cascade,* etc.); published a harp method (in German, French, and English), and a pamphlet, *A Word to Composers about the Practical Employment of the Harp in the Orchestra* (St. Petersburg, 1899; in Russian and German).

Zabrack, Harold, American pianist and composer; b. St. Louis, June 30, 1929. He studied piano with Rudolph Ganz at the Chicago Musical College (M.M., 1951); composition with Nadia Boulanger at Fontainebleau. In 1955-57 he held a Fulbright grant for travel in Europe; gave concerts in West Germany. Returning to St. Louis, he became active as concert pianist and teacher.
WORKS: *Piano Variations* (1959); 2 Duets for viola and oboe (1961); Piano Sonata (1964); Piano Concerto No. 1 (St. Louis, April 5, 1964, composer soloist); Piano Concerto No. 2 (1965).

Zacconi, Lodovico, Italian music theorist; b. Pesaro, June 11, 1555; d. Fiorenzuola, near Pesaro, March 23, 1627. He was a pupil of Baccusi and A. Gabrieli in Venice; studied theology in Pavia, entered the Order of St. Augustine, and became maestro di cappella at the monastery of his order in Venice; was tenor in the court chapel at Graz (1585), and at Munich (1591-95); then returned to Venice. His chief work, *Prattica di Musica,* in 2 parts (Venice, 1592, 1619), contains treatises on mensural theory and counterpoint, detailed descriptions of contemporary musical instruments, and explanations for executing the ornaments in vocal polyphonic music. He also wrote 4 books of *Canoni musicali,* with comments and solutions (publ. by F. Vatielli, Pesaro, 1905); *Ricercari* for organ and 2 collections of examples of counterpoint are still in manuscript. His manuscript autobiography (written in 1626) is in the library of the Liceo Musicale, Bologna.
BIBLIOGRAPHY: F. Chrysander, "L. Zacconi als Lehrer des Kunstgesanges," *Vierteljahrsschrift für Musikwissenschaft* (vols. 7, 9, 10; 1891-94; with an epitome of the autobiography); F. Vatielli, *Un Musicista pesarese nel secolo XVI* (Pesaro, 1904); H. Kretzschmar, "L. Zacconis Leben auf Grund seiner Autobiographie," *Jahrbuch der Musikbibliothek Peters* (1910); F. Vatielli, *Notizie su la vita e le opere di L. Zacconi* (Pesaro, 1912).

Zach, Jan, Czech composer; b. Czellakowitz, Nov. 13, 1699; d. Ellwangen, May 24, 1773. He studied with Czernohorsky in Prague; held the appointment of court Kapellmeister in Mainz (1745-56). He wrote church music; also concertos and orchestral works in a style resembling that of the Mannheim School.
BIBLIOGRAPHY: K. M. Komma, *Johann Zach und die tschechischen Musiker im deutschen Umbruch des 18. Jahrhunderts* (dissertation; Kassel, 1938).

Zach, Max (Wilhelm), Austrian conductor and viola player; b. Lwów, Aug. 31, 1864; d. St. Louis, Feb. 3, 1921. He studied violin with Grün, harmony with Fuchs, and composition with Krenn at the Vienna Cons. In 1886 he emigrated to the U.S., and played the first viola in the Boston Symph. Orch.; also was the violist in the Adamowski Quartet; for 10 seasons conducted the Boston Pops (1887-97). In 1907 he was appointed conductor of the St. Louis Symph. Orch., and held this post until his death.

Zacharewitsch, Michael, Russian-English violinist; b. Ostrov, Aug. 26, 1879; d. London, Dec. 20, 1953. He studied with Ševčik in Prague, and later with Ysaÿe in Brussels. He went to London in 1903, and became a British subject in 1915; toured Australia, New Zealand, and South Africa. He wrote *The New Art of Violin Playing* (1934), and composed *Dunkirk* (1945), for violin and orch., as well as violin exercises.

Zachau (Zachow), Friedrich Wilhelm, German organist and composer; b. Leipzig, Nov. 19, 1663; d. Halle, Aug. 14, 1712. He studied with his father, who was town musician in Leipzig, and learned to play the organ, violin, oboe, and harpsichord. From 1684 to his death he was organist of the Liebfrauenkirche in Halle, where Handel studied with him as a boy. Max Seiffert published Zachau's works in the *Denkmäler deutscher Tonkunst* (vols. 21, 22); organ pieces, chorale settings, etc., were publ. in Breitkopf & Härtel's *Sammlung von Präludien, Fugen, . . .* and in *Organum.*

Zádor, Eugen, Hungarian-American composer; b. Bátaszék, Nov. 5, 1894; d. Hollywood, April 4, 1977. (In the U.S. he Americanized his name to **Eugene Zador.**) He studied music with a local teacher; in 1911 he enrolled in the Vienna Cons.; studied composition with Richard Heuberger; in 1913 he went to Leipzig, where he took a course with Max Reger; also attended classes in musicology with Hermann Abert and Arnold Schering; continued musicological studies with Fritz Volbach at the Univ. of Münster; in 1921 obtained his degree of Dr. phil. with a dissertation *Wesen und Form der symphonischen Dichtung von Liszt bis Strauss.* He settled in Vienna and taught at the Neues Konservatorium there. Following the *Anschluss* of Austria by the Nazi regime in 1938, Zádor emigrated to the U.S.; settled in Hollywood, where he became successful and prosperous as an orchestrator of film scores; made some 120 orchestrations in all; at the same time he continued to compose music in every conceivable genre. Zádor was a master of musical sciences, excelling in euphonious modern harmonies, and an expert weaver of contrapuntal voices; his colorful writing for instruments was exemplary. He possessed a special skill in handling Hungarian folk motives in variation form; in this, he followed the tradition of Liszt. During his European period he composed some fashionable "machine music," as demonstrated with particular effect in his *Sinfonia tecnica.*

WORKS: OPERAS: *Diana* (Budapest, Dec. 22, 1923); *A holtak szigete* (*The Island of the Dead;* Budapest, March 29, 1928); *X-mal Rembrandt* (referring to the multiple copies of Rembrandt's self-portraits; Gera, May 24, 1930); *Asra* (Budapest, Feb. 15, 1936); *Christoph Columbus* (N.Y., Oct. 8, 1939); *Revisor* (*Inspector General,* after Gogol, 1928; revised and reorchestrated, and finally brought to performance for the first time in Los Angeles, June 11, 1971); *The Virgin and the Fawn* (Los Angeles, Oct. 24, 1964); *The Magic Chair* (Baton Rouge, Louisiana, May 14, 1966); *The Scarlet Mill* (Brooklyn, Oct. 26, 1968).

FOR ORCH.: symph. poems, *Bánk bán* (1918); 4 symphonies: No. 1, *Romantische Symphonie* (1922); No. 2, *Sinfonia tecnica* (Paris, May 26, 1932); No. 3, *Tanzsymphonie* (Budapest, Feb. 8, 1937); No. 4, *Children's Symphony* (1941); *Variations on a Hungarian Folksong* (Vienna, Feb. 9, 1927; his most successful work of this type); *Rondo* (Vienna, 1934); *Hungarian Caprice* (Budapest, Feb. 1, 1935, followed by numerous performances in Europe and America); *Pastorale and Tarantella* (Chicago, Feb. 5, 1942); *Biblical Triptych* (Chicago, Dec. 9, 1943); *Elegie and Dance* (Philadelphia, March 12, 1954); *Divertimento for strings* (1955); *Fugue-Fantasia* (1958); *Rhapsody* (Los Angeles, Feb. 5, 1961); *Christmas Overture* (1961); *The Remarkable Adventure of Henry Bold,* for narrator and orch. (Beverly Hills, Calif., Oct. 24, 1963); *Variations on a Merry Theme* (1963; Birmingham, Alabama, Jan. 12, 1965); *5 Contrasts for Orchestra* (Philadelphia, Jan. 8, 1965); Trombone Concerto (Rochester, Michigan, July 20, 1967); *Rhapsody* for cimbalom and orch. (Los Angeles, Nov. 2, 1969); *Studies for Orchestra* (Detroit, Nov. 12, 1970); *Fantasia Hungarica* for double bass and orch. (1970); *Hungarian Scherzo* for orch. (1975).

CHAMBER MUSIC: *Chamber Concerto* for strings, 2 horns, and piano (1930); *Piano Quintet* (1933); *Suite for brass* (1961); *Suite for 8 celli* (1966); *Suite for woodwind quintet* (1972); *Brass Quintet* (1973). .

FOR CHORUS: *Cantata tecnica* (1961); *Scherzo domestico* (1961); *Triptych* (1964).

Songs; piano pieces; ballet, *Maschinenmensch* (1934).

BIBLIOGRAPHY: Donald Tovey, *Essays in Musical Analysis* (vol. VI; London, 1939); Leslie Zador, *Eugene Zador. A Catalogue of His Works* (San Diego, Calif., 1978).

Zadora, Michael, American pianist and composer; b. New York (of Polish parents), June 14, 1882; d. there, June 30, 1946. He studied with his father; then at the Paris Cons. (1899), and later with Leschetizky and Busoni. He taught a master class at the Lwów Cons. (1911–12); then at the Institute of Musical Art in N.Y. (1913–14). He transcribed for piano several organ and violin works by Buxtehude and Bach; also composed piano pieces, songs, etc.

Zafred, Mario, Italian composer and conductor; b. Trieste, Feb. 21, 1922. He studied with Pizzetti at the Santa Cecilia Academy in Rome; was music critic of *Unità* (1949–56) and *Giustizia* (1956–63); then conducted opera in Trieste and in Rome. In conformity with his political philosophy of Communism, he renounced the modernistic trends of his musical environment and wrote music in an idiom accessible to the common people.

WORKS: operas: *Amleto* (Rome, 1961), and *Wallenstein* (Rome, 1965); 7 symphonies (1943, 1944, 1949, 1950, 1954, 1958, 1970); *Sinfonia breve* for string orch. (1955); Flute Concerto (1951); Violin Concerto (1953); Triple Concerto for violin, cello, piano and orch. (1954); Harp Concerto (1956); Viola Concerto (1957); Cello Concerto (1958); Piano Concerto (1960); Concerto for 2 pianos and orch. (1961); *Metamorfosi* for orch. (1964); Concerto for Strings (1969); String Sextet (1967); Wind Quintet (1952); 4 string quartets (1941, 1947, 1948, 1953); 3 piano trios (1942, 1945, 1954); 4 piano sonatas (1941, 1943, 1950, 1960); numerous choruses and solo songs.

Zagiba, Franz, Slovak music scholar; b. Rosenau, Oct. 20, 1912; d. Vienna, Aug. 12, 1977. He studied music and philology at the Univ. of Vienna, and in 1947 joined its staff; in 1973 was named full prof. there. He published *Die Musikdenkmäler der Franziskanerklöster in der Ostslowakei* (Prague, 1940); *Geschichte der slowakischen Musik* (vol. I, Bratislava, 1943; in Czech, with German summary); *Opernführer* (Bratislava, 1947); *Chopin und Wien* (Vienna, 1951); *Tschaikovskij, Leben und Werk* (Zürich, 1953); *Johann L. Bella (1843–1936) und das wiener Musikleben* (Vienna, 1955); *Zur Errichtung einer Chopin-Gedächtnisstätte in Wien* (Vienna, 1970); numerous valuable articles dealing with music in Slovakia and historical developments in Slavic music.

Zagwijn, Henri, Dutch composer; b. Nieuwer-Amstel, July 17, 1878; d. The Hague, Oct. 23, 1954. He had no formal education in music, but followed the trends of Impressionism and wrote music in the modern French style. In 1916 he was appointed teacher at the Rotterdam Academy of Music; in 1918, founded (with Sem Dresden) the Society of Modern Composers in the Netherlands; later settled in The Hague. He was a follower of Rudolf Steiner's anthroposophic movement, and published a book, *De Muziek in het licht der an-*

throposophie (1925); also published a biography of Debussy (The Hague, 1940).

WORKS: *Auferstehung,* an overture (1918); 2 concertantes for piano and orch. (1939; 1946); Harp Concerto (1948); String Sextet (1932); Quintet for flute, violin, viola, cello, and harp (1937); Trio for flute, oboe, and clarinet (1944); Trio for violin, viola, and cello (1946); Quintet for flute, oboe, clarinet, horn, and bassoon (1948); Trio for flute, oboe, and clarinet (1949); 2 string quartets; several albums of piano pieces; choral works; a number of songs; *Musik zur Eurhythmie* (6 books of piano pieces for eurhythmic exercises).

BIBLIOGRAPHY: W. Paap, "Henri Zagwijn," *Mens en Melodie* (Sept. 1948; Nov. 1954).

Zahn, Johannes, German composer and music scholar; b. Espenbach, Aug. 1, 1817; d. Neudettelsau, Feb. 17, 1895. He was a student of theology at Munich and Berlin; director of the teachers' seminary at Altdorf (1854–88). In 1875 he founded the periodical *Siona* for liturgy and church music. He published a valuable work, *Die Melodien der deutschen evangelischen Kirchenlieder, aus den Quellen geschöpft und mitgetheilt* (6 vols., 1889–93); *Sonntagsschulbuch für die lutherischen Gemeinden Nordamerikas* (1894); and various other scholarly and didactic works on church music.

Zajc, Ivan. See **Zaytz, Giovanni von.**

Zajic, Florian, Bohemian violinist; b. Unhoscht, May 4, 1853; d. Berlin, May 17, 1926. He studied at the Prague Cons.; then was a theater violinist in various German cities; in 1891 he became violin teacher at the Stern Cons., Berlin; gave sonata recitals; published 30 études for violin.

Zajíček, Jeronym, Czech-American composer; b. Krásné Březno, Nov. 10, 1926. He studied musicology at the Charles Univ. in Prague (1946–49); then left Czechoslovakia and served as program director of the Czech section of Radio Free Europe in Munich (1950–52). He emigrated to the U.S. in 1952; studied composition with K. Jirák at Roosevelt Univ. in Chicago (1955–58) and later with Paul Pisk (1959–60). In 1964 he was appointed instructor in composition and conducting at the Chicago City College in the Loop. He became an American citizen in 1957. His music mirrors the lyrical traditions of his Czech heritage.

WORKS: Variations for piano (1956–57); Piano Trio (1957); Clarinet Sonata (1957); Sinfonietta (1958); Violin Sonata (1961); String Quartet (1962–63); Concertino for flute and string orch. (1963–64; Chicago, Feb. 26, 1967); *Intrada and Processionale* for brass, timpani, and organ (1970); Cello Sonata (1975); songs.

Zak, Yakov, Soviet pianist; b. Odessa, Nov. 20, 1913; d. Moscow, June 28, 1976. He was a student of Neuhaus at the Moscow Cons., graduating in 1935. At the International Competition for pianists in Warsaw in 1937 he received first prize and a special award of a posthumous mask of Chopin for his performance of a Chopin mazurka. He joined the faculty of the Moscow Cons. in 1935; became head of the piano dept. there in

1965. As a concert pianist Zak toured all over Europe. He played in the U.S. in 1965 and 1967, and was acclaimed for his Soviet-like virtuosity.

Zakharov, Vladimir, Soviet composer of songs; b. Bogodukhov, on the Don Basin, Oct. 18, 1901; d. Moscow, July 13, 1956. He studied at the Rostov Cons.; after 1932, devoted himself mainly to the composition of mass songs, derived from the polyphonic essence of Russian folk music and employing asymmetric meters. Of these songs, *Two Falcons* and *Who can tell?* attained immense popularity in Russia. He received several prizes and was awarded the Order of Lenin.

Zamara, Antonio, Italian harpist; b. Milan, June 13, 1829; d. Hietzing, near Vienna, Nov. 11, 1901. He studied with Sechter in Vienna; for nearly 50 years was 1st harpist at the Kärntnertor Theater; for many years also was prof. at the Vienna Cons. He published a *Harfenschule* (4 books); a number of pieces for harp solo (*Barcarolle, La Rêveuse, Chant du berceau, L'Absence, Marche des Croates,* etc.); also pieces for harp and cello (*Élégie, L'Addio,* etc.) and transcriptions of operatic airs for 2 harps.

Zampieri, Giusto, Italian writer on music; b. Trieste, Nov. 6, 1879; d. Pavia, June 8, 1950. He was prof. of music history at the Cons. of Milan (1908–23); then at the Univ. of Pavia. He published *Il Pianoforte* (Milan, 1912), *F. Gafurio* (Pavia, 1925), and other books.

Zandonai, Riccardo, Italian composer; b. Sacco, Trentino, May 30, 1883; d. Pesaro, June 5, 1944. He was a pupil of Gianferrari at Rovereto (1893–98); then studied with Mascagni at the Liceo Rossini in Pesaro. He graduated in 1902; for his final examination he composed a symph. poem for solo voices, chorus, and orch., *Il Ritorno di Odisseo.* He then turned to opera, which remained his favored genre throughout his career. His first opera was *Il Grillo del focolare,* based on *The Cricket on the Hearth* of Dickens, which was produced in Turin on Nov. 28, 1908, with excellent success. With his next opera, *Conchita,* after the novel *La Femme et le pantin* by Pierre Louÿs (Milan, Oct. 14, 1911), he established himself as an important Italian composer; the title role was created by the soprano **Tarquinia Tarquini,** whom Zandonai married in 1917. *Conchita* received its American première in San Francisco on Sept. 28, 1912; as *La Femme et le pantin* it was given at the Opéra-Comique, Paris, on March 11, 1929. Zandonai's reputation was enhanced by subsequent works, notably *Francesca da Rimini,* after Gabriele d'Annunzio (Turin, Feb. 19, 1914; Metropolitan Opera, N.Y., Dec. 22, 1916), but a previous opera, *Melenis* (Milan, Nov. 13, 1912), was unsuccessful. During World War I Zandonai participated in the political agitation for the return of former Italian provinces; wrote a student hymn calling for the redemption of Trieste (1915). His other operas were: *La Via della finestra* (Pesaro, July 27, 1919; revised version, Trieste, Jan. 18, 1923); *Giulietta e Romeo* (Rome, Feb. 14, 1922); *I Cavalieri di Ekebù* (Milan, March 7, 1925); *Giuliano* (Naples, Feb. 4, 1928); *Una Partita* (Milan, Jan. 19, 1933); and *La Farsa amorosa,* after Alarcón's *El Sombrero de tres picos* (Rome, Feb. 22, 1933). He further wrote the symph. poems *Primavera in Val di Sole* (1908), *Patria lontana* (1918), *Fra gli alberghi delle Dolomiti* (1932); *Concerto romantico* for violin and orch. (1921); *Concerto andaloso* for cello and small orch. (1937); *Rapsodia trentina* for orch. (1937); *Messa da Requiem;* some chamber music. In 1939 he was appointed director of the Liceo Rossini in Pesaro, remaining there for the rest of his life.

BIBLIOGRAPHY: "Bibliografia delle opere musicali di Riccardo Zandonai," *Bollettino Bibliografico Musicale* (Dec. 1931); V. Bonajuti Tarquini, *Riccardo Zandonai, nel ricordo dei suoi intimi* (Milan, 1951).

Zandt, Marie Van. See **Van Zandt, Marie.**

Zanella, Amilcare, Italian composer; b. Monticelli d'Ongina, Piacenza, Sept. 26, 1873; d. Pesaro, Jan. 9, 1949. He studied with Andreotti in Cremona, then with Bottesini at the Parma Cons., graduating in 1891. In 1892 he went to South America as pianist and opera conductor; returning to Italy in 1901, he organized his own orch., giving symph. concerts in the principal Italian cities and introducing his own works. He then was director of the Parma Cons. (1903–05); succeeded Mascagni as director of the Liceo Rossini in Pesaro in 1905, and held this post until 1939, when he was succeeded by Zandonai.

WORKS: operas: *Aura* (Pesaro, Aug. 27, 1910), *La Sulamita* (Piacenza, Feb. 11, 1926), and *Il Revisore,* after Gogol (Trieste, Feb. 20, 1940); Symphony; 2 symph. poems, *Fede* and *Vita; Festa campestre, Danza paesana* for orch.; *Fantasia e Fugato* for piano and orch.; Nonet for strings, woodwind instruments, and piano; Piano Trio; a number of piano pieces (*Due Leggende, Passero solitario, Canto d'anima, Ansia,* etc.).

BIBLIOGRAPHY: *Amilcare Zanella, artista, uomo, educatore,* a compendium (Ferrara, 1932); A. Dioli and M. F. Nobili, *La Vita e l'art di Amilcare Zanella* (Bergamo, 1941).

Zanettini, Antonio. See **Gianettini, Antonio.**

Zang, Johann Heinrich, German organist and composer; b. Zella St. Blasii, near Gotha, April 13, 1733; d. Würzburg, Aug. 18, 1811. As a youth he was trained by Bach in Leipzig (for 2 years); composed and engraved *Die singende Muse am Main* (1776); wrote *Kunst- und Handwerksbuch,* Part II of which is *Der vollkommene Orgelmacher, oder Lehre von der Orgel und Windprobe* (1804). In manuscript are church cantatas, organ trios, piano sonatas, etc.

Zanger (Zangerus), Johannes, Austrian theologian and musician; b. Innsbruck, 1517; d. Braunschweig, April 5, 1587. He was a pupil of Heinrich Finck, Arnold von Bruck, and others in Vienna; then studied law in Prague and in Cologne. In 1542 he joined the Protestant church, and occupied positions as cantor, rector, and pastor in Braunschweig. He published *Musicae practicae praecepta* (Leipzig, 1554).

BIBLIOGRAPHY: H. J. Moser, "Johannes Zanger's *Praecepta,*" *Musica Disciplina* 5 (1951).

Zangius, Nikolaus, German organist and composer; b. c.1570; d. Berlin, c.1618. He was chamber musician in Brunswick (1597), church organist in Danzig (1602–05); then in Prague (1609), in Vienna, and finally in Berlin (from 1612). He composed a cappella chorus, motets, and a number of quodlibets. His *Cantiones sacrae* and 3-part German songs are reprinted in the *Denkmäler der Tonkunst in Österreich* 87.

BIBLIOGRAPHY: Joh. Sachs, *N. Zangius weltliche Lieder* (dissertation; Vienna, 1934).

Zanten, Cornelia Van. See **Van Zanten, Cornelia.**

Zappa, Frank, a versatile rock musician; b. Baltimore, Dec. 21, 1940. His family moved to California, where he managed to squeak through a few grades of a permissive high school. He played drums; in 1964 formed his own group, "Mothers of Invention." He cultivated higher learning to the extent of actually spending a few hours a week in libraries; in music he claimed to be a subliminal disciple of Varèse. He made much more money than any of the modern greats by giving multimedia spectacles in which he and his group assaulted the eardrums with 200-decibel noises. His record albums began selling big, and Zappa's name, itself onomatopoeic in its suggestions of instant zap, became a household word in the frug-besotted catacombs of Southern California, thence spreading its sound and odor across the Union and even across the Atlantic. It is his esthetic credo that classical music is the "province of old ladies and faggots."

Zarate, Eliodoro Ortíz de, Chilean composer; b. Valparaiso, Dec. 29, 1865; d. Santiago, June 27, 1953. He studied in his native city, and at the Milan Cons., graduating in 1888. Returning to Chile, he brought out his opera (to his own libretto in Italian), *La Fioraia di Lugano* (Santiago, Nov. 1, 1895), which was one of the earliest operas, if not the first, by a Chilean composer that was produced in Santiago.

Zarębski (Zarembski), Juliusz, Polish pianist and composer; b. Zhitomir, Feb. 28, 1854; d. there, Sept. 15, 1885. He studied piano with Dachs at the Vienna Cons., and later enrolled in the St. Petersburg Cons. (1872–74). In 1875 he joined Liszt in Weimar; from 1880 to 1885 he taught piano at the Brussels Cons. As a composer, he is known primarily for his effective salon pieces, in the manner of Chopin, among them *Suite polonaise, Ballade, Sérénade burlesque, Berceuse, À travers Pologne, Sérénade espagnole.*

BIBLIOGRAPHY: T. Strumillo, *Juliusz Zarębski* (Cracow, 1954).

Zaremba, Nikolai, Russian composer and pedagogue; b. near Vitebsk, June 15, 1821; d. St. Petersburg, April 8, 1879. He studied piano and cello; then went to Berlin where he took lessons with Adolf Marx. When the St. Petersburg Cons. was founded in 1862, he was engaged as teacher of composition; from 1867 to 1871 he was its director. He was the first to teach music theory using Russian terminology rather than the prevalent German nomenclature; among his students was Tchaikovsky. In his musical views Zaremba was extremely conservative; he was also apt to connect harmony rules with religious notions (such as piety being expressed by major keys, and sin and corruption by minor keys). Mussorgsky ridiculed Zaremba in his satirical piece *Rayok*, in which he illustrated Zaremba's classical tastes by a mock quotation from Handel.

Zariņš, Margeris, Latvian composer; b. Jaunpiebalga, May 24, 1910; he studied composition in Riga with Wihtol; also took lessons in piano and organ. From 1956 to 1968 he was Secretary General of the Union of Latvian Composers. In his works he stylizes the elements of Latvian folksongs; he is particularly successful in his operas on contemporary subjects, often with a satirical tilt. In his *Opera uz lankuma (Opera in Town Square,* 1970) he attempted to revive the early Soviet attempts to bring theatrical spectacles into the streets.

WORKS: operas: *Kungs un spēlmanītis (The King and the Little Musician,* 1939); *Uz jauno krastu (To New Shores,* 1955); *Zalās dzirnavas (The Green Mill,* 1958); *Nabaqu opera (Beggar's Opera,* 1964); *Sveta Mauricija brīnumdarbs (Miracle of St. Mauritius,* 1964); *Opera uz lankuma (Opera in Town Square,* 1970); oratorios: *Valmieras varoni (The Heroes of Valmiera,* 1950); *Mahagoni (Mahagonny),* a propaganda work denouncing the Western colonial policies in Africa (1965); Piano Concerto (1937); *Greek Vases* for piano and orch. (1946; revised 1960); numerous choruses based on Latvian folksongs; film music.

BIBLIOGRAPHY: L. Krasinska, *Margeris Zariņš* (Riga, 1960).

Zarlino, Gioseffo (Zarlinus Clodiensis), important Italian music theorist and composer; b. Chioggia, probably in April, 1517; d. Venice, Feb. 14, 1590. He entered the Franciscan order in 1539, and in 1541 went to Venice, where he became a pupil of Willaert. In 1565 he succeeded his fellow-pupil Cipriano de Rore as maestro di cappella at San Marco, holding this position until his death; also held the office of chaplain at San Severo. He was greatly esteemed not only as a teacher but also as a composer; indeed, Foscarini describes him as "the famous regenerator of music in all Italy." Most of Zarlino's manuscripts are lost; his extant works comprise *21 Modulationes 6 vocum* (Venice, 1566; edited by Zarlino's pupil, Usberti; *3 Lectiones pro mortuis* (part of a collection of motets *a* 4 by Cipriano de Rore and others; published by Scotto, Venice 1563), and a Mass (manuscript in the library of the Liceo Filarmonico in Bologna). 2 motets *a* 5 were published by L. Torchi in *L'Arte Musicale in Italia* (vol. I).

Zarlino's lasting significance lies in his theoretical works, particularly the *Istituzioni armoniche* (in 4 sections; Venice, 1558; republ. 1562, 1573), in which Zarlino treats the major and minor thirds as inversions within a fifth, and consequently, the major and minor triads as mutual mirror reflections of component intervals, thus anticipating the modern dualism of Rameau, Tartini, Hauptmann, and Riemann; also gives lucid and practical demonstrations of double counterpoint and canon, illustrated by numerous musical examples; while adhering to the system of 12 modes, he places the Ionian, rather than the Dorian mode, at the head of the list, thus pointing towards the emergence of the major scale as the preponderant

mode; gives 10 rules for proper syllabification of the text in musical settings; suggests equal temperament for the tuning of the lute. In 1571 he published *Dimostrationi armoniche,* in the form of 5 dialogues between Willaert and his disciples and friends. Zarlino's theories were attacked, with a violence uncommon even for the polemical spirit of the age, by Vincenzo Galilei, one of his former pupils, in *Dialogo della musica antica e della moderna* (Florence, 1581) and *Discorso intorno alle opere di Gioseffo Zarlino* (Florence, 1589). In reply to the first of Galilei's books, Zarlino publ. *Sopplimenti musicali* (Venice, 1588). Collected works of Zarlino (4 vols.), published in Venice in 1589, included, in addition to his former books, also a theological tract, *Trattato della pazienza.* Books III-IV of the *Istituzioni armoniche* are publ. in English transl. in O. Strunk, *Source Readings in Music History* (N.Y., 1950).

BIBLIOGRAPHY: G. Ravagnan, *Elogio di G. Zarlino* (Venice, 1819); G. Caffi, *Narrazione della vita e delle opere del prete Gioseffo Zarlino* (Venice, 1836); G. Caffi, *Storia della musica sacra nella già cappella di San Marco in Venezia* (Venice, 1854; vol. I); H. Riemann, *Geschichte der Musiktheorie* (2nd ed., 1921); V. Bellenio, *Gioseffo Zarlino* (Chioggia, 1884); F. Högler, "Bemerkungen zu Zarlinos Theorie," *Zeitschrift für Musikwissenschaft* 9 (1926); H. Zenck, "Zarlinos *Istituzioni armoniche,*" ibid. 13 (1930); G. Reese, *Music in the Renaissance* (N.Y., 1954); R. Flury, *Gioseffo Zarlino als Komponist* (Winterthur, 1962).

Zarotus, Antonio, Italian music printer, active in Milan. He printed a *Missale Romanum* dated April 26, 1476, in which he used for the first time movable type for the music (the type is in Gothic style). This incunabulum was published 6 months earlier than the Missale of Ulrich Han, at one time considered the earliest specimen of music printed from movable type.

BIBLIOGRAPHY: Otto Kinkeldey, "Music and Music Printing in Incunabula," *Papers of the Bibliographic Society of America* (1932).

Zarzycki, Alexander, Polish pianist and composer; b. Lwów , Feb. 21, 1834; d. Warsaw, Nov. 1, 1895. He studied in Lwów and later in Paris (1856-61) with Reber; gave brilliant concerts in France, Germany, Austria, and Poland; was director of the Warsaw Music Society (1866-74). In 1879 he became director of the Warsaw Cons. He wrote effective piano pieces (nocturnes, mazurkas, waltzes, etc.); also a piano concerto; *Grande Polonaise* for piano with orch.; *Introduction et Cracovienne* for violin and orch.; *Suite polonaise* for orch.; *Mazourka* in G major for violin with orch. (very popular); also 2 albums of songs.

Zaslawsky, Georges, Russian-American conductor; b. Kiev, Feb. 15, 1880; d. New York, Jan. 28, 1953. He studied violin with Leopold Auer, and composition with Liadov, at the St. Petersburg Cons. In 1922 he emigrated to the U.S.; made his debut as conductor at a special concert in Carnegie Hall, N.Y., April 12, 1926; in 1927 founded and conducted a "Beethoven Symph. Orch." in N.Y., which was discontinued after a few concerts. He also conducted in South America.

Zavertal, Ladislao, Italian bandmaster (of Bohemian extraction); b. Milan, Sept. 29, 1849; d. Cadenabbia, Jan. 29, 1942. He was the son of the clarinetist **Wenceslas Hugo Zavertal** (1821–1899). After studying at home he went to Treviso (where he produced an opera) and then to Milan (1869). In 1871 he went to Glasgow, where he conducted various orchestral groups; in 1881 he became bandmaster of the Royal Artillery Band at Woolwich; from 1895 to 1905 he conducted Sunday band concerts in the Albert Hall, London, which enjoyed considerable popularity. He returned to Italy in 1906. He was a voluminous composer; wrote operas, symphonies, and band pieces; received various honors from the goverments of England, Italy, Greece, Serbia, and Turkey.

BIBLIOGRAPHY: A. Faraone, *Il Commendatore Ladislao Zavertal* (Treviso, 1929); H. G. Farmer, *Ladislao Zavertal: His Life and Work* (London, 1949); H. G. Farmer, *Cavaliere Zavertal and the Royal Artillery Band* (London, 1951).

Zay, (William) Henri, American singing teacher and composer; b. Findlay, Ohio, March 20, 1869; d. New York, Nov. 2, 1927. He studied at the Cleveland Cons. and at the Royal Academy of Music in London. Returning to the U.S., he established himself as a voice specialist, gradually evolving and perfecting his own method, published as *Practical Psychology of Voice and of Life* (N.Y., 1917; reprinted, 1945); composed *Cosmic Conception* for orch., and several song cycles.

Zaytz, Giovanni von (real name **Ivan Zajc**), Croatian composer; b. Fiume, Aug. 3, 1831; d. Zagreb, Dec. 16, 1914. He was trained by his father, a bandmaster in the Austrian Army; then in Milan by Lauro Rossi. Returning to Fiume, he conducted the municipal band; then was theater conductor in Vienna (1862–70). Upon entering professional life, he changed his name to Giovanni von Zaytz. In 1870 he settled in Zagreb; was conductor of the Zagreb Opera (1870–89) and director of the Cons. there (until 1908). He composed about 1200 works of all descriptions (among them 20 operas), and was the author of the first Croatian national opera, *Nikola Šubrič Zrinski* (Zagreb, Nov. 4, 1876). He also wrote several Italian operas, of which *Amelia, ossia Il Bandito* (Fiume, April 14, 1860) enjoyed considerable popularity. Other operas and operettas (all produced by him in Vienna) are: *Mannschaft an Bord* (Dec. 15, 1863); *Fitzliputzli* (Nov. 5, 1864); *Die Lazzaroni vom Stanzel* (May 4, 1865); *Die Hexe von Boissy* (April 24, 1866); *Nachtschwärmer* (Nov. 10, 1866); *Das Rendezvous in der Schweiz* (April 3, 1867); *Das Gaugericht* (Sept. 14, 1867); *Nach Mekka* (Jan. 11, 1868); *Somnambula* (Jan. 25, 1868); *Schützen von Einst und Jetzt* (July 25, 1868); *Meister Puff* (May 22, 1869); and *Der gefangene Amor* (Sept. 12, 1874). In addition he wrote incidental music for 23 plays; 60 cantatas; 250 choral works, sacred and secular; 40 overtures; symphonic poems; more than 200 songs.

Zbar, Michel, French composer; b. Clermont-Ferrand, April 24, 1942. He studied at the Paris Cons. with Olivier Messiaen and Tony Aubin, graduating in 1967; also worked with Pierre Schaeffer at the Groupe de Recherches Musicales of the Paris Radio. In 1968 he won the competition for the Prix de Rome with his *Tragédie d'Hamlet*. Other works include *Tropismes* for violin and orch. (1969); *Incandescences* for soprano, speaker and orch. (1970); *Swingle Novae* for the Swingle Singers, chorus, and 5 instrumental groups (1970); *Apex II* for chamber orch. (1971); *Negative—Positive* for Ondes Martenot, electric guitar, and percussion (Orléans, France, March 23, 1973).

Zbinden, Julien-François, Swiss composer; b. Rolle, Nov. 11, 1917. He studied at the Cons. of Lausanne; then was a pupil of Marie Panthès (piano) and René Gerber (composition) (1934–38). After playing in jazz orchestras, he became a pianist and assistant director of the Radio Lausanne in 1947; in 1956 he joined the Service Musical of Radio-Television Suisse Romande; in 1973 he became president of the Association of Swiss Musicians.

WORKS: an opera, *Fait divers* (1960); a farce-ballet, *La Pantoufle*, for 5 soloists and 2 pianos (1958); 4 "pièces radiophoniques": *Microbus 666* (1955), *Le Petit Garçon de l'autobus* (1958), *Esperanto* (1961) and *Ethiopiques* (1971–72); Piano Concerto (1944); Concertino for trumpet, string, and timpani (1946); *Divertissement* for double bass and orch. (1948); *Concerto da camera* for piano and string orch. (1950–51); 2 symphonies (1953, 1951–57); *Fantaisie* for flute and chamber orch. (1954); *Suite française* for string orch. (1954); *Rhapsodie* for violin and orch. (1956); *Jazzific 59–16* for jazz group and strings (1958); *Ballade* for bassoon and orch. (1961); *Concerto breve* for cello and orch. (1962); Violin Concerto (1962–64); *Orchalau-Concerto* for orch. (1962); *Lémanic 70*, overture (1970); Concerto for Orch. (1977); *Terra Dei*, oratorio (1966–67); *Monophrases* for chorus, 2 pianos, and 6 percussionists (1970); *Jardins*, suite for baritone, soprano, and orch. (1974); Septet (1947); String Trio (1949); Trio for trumpet, horn, and trombone (1949); Violin Sonata (1950); *3 Pieces* for 4 horns (1953); *Partita* for violin and cello (1954); *Prelude, Fugue and Postlude* for trumpet and piano (1963), Capriccio for flute, English horn, bassoon, violin, and harpsichord (1968); *Sonate en Trio* for 2 violas de gamba and harpsichord (1969); *Dialogue* for trumpet and organ (1972–73); *Introduction and Scherzo-Valse* for flute and harp (1974).

BIBLIOGRAPHY: H. Jaccard, *Initiation à la musique contemporaine. Trios compositeurs vaudois: Raffaele d'Alessandro, Constantin Regamey, Julien-François Zbinden* (Lausanne, 1955).

Zdravković, Živojin, Serbian conductor; b. Belgrade, Nov. 24, 1914. He studied music theory at the Belgrade Music Academy and conducting with Talich in Prague. He conducted the Belgrade Radio Orch. (1948–51); was assistant conductor of the Belgrade Philharmonic (1951–61); in 1961 became its music director. In the 1960's he toured as guest conductor in the Near East, South America, Brazil and the U.S.

Zecchi, Adone, Italian composer and conductor; b. Bologna, July 23, 1904. He studied composition with Franco Alfano at the Liceo Musicale in Bologna, graduating in 1926; in 1930 he established the Orchestra Bolognese de Camera, and also organized the choral group Corale Euridice, which he led from 1927 to 1943; in 1942 he was appointed to the faculty of Bologna Cons. In his compositions he follows the path of Italian neo-Classicism, but applies dodecaphonic formulas in some of his music.

WORKS: *Partita* for orch. (1933); *Toccata, Ricercare e Finale* for orch. (1941); *Due Astrazioni in forma di fuga* for small ensemble (Copenhagen, Festival of the International Society for Contemporary Music, June 2, 1947); *Requiem* for chorus and orch. (1946); *Caleidofonia* for violin, piano, and orch. (1963); *Trattenimento musicale* for 11 groups of string instruments (1969). He published a number of manuals on choral conducting, including a reference work: *Il coro nella storia e dizionario dei nomi e dei termini* (Bologna, 1960) and *Il direttore di coro* (Milan, 1965). In collaboration with R. Allorto he brought out *Educazione musicale* (Milan, 1962); *Canti natalizi di altri paesi* (Milan, 1965); *Canti natalizi italiani* (Milan, 1965); *Canti della vecchia America* (Milan, 1966); and *Il mondo della musica* (Milan, 1969).

Zecchi, Carlo, Italian pianist and conductor; b. Rome, July 8, 1903. He studied piano with Artur Schnabel and Busoni in Berlin; began his concert career as a pianist at the age of 17, and in 1931 made a tour of the U.S. In 1938 he became interested in conducting and made excellent progress in his new career; appeared as guest conductor in Vienna, Amsterdam, London, and Leningrad; also made tours as conductor in the U.S., South America, and Japan.

Zech, Frederick, American pianist and composer; b. Philadelphia, May 10, 1858; d. San Francisco, Oct. 25, 1926. After preliminary training as a pianist in San Francisco, he went to Berlin where he studied at Kullak's Music School; returning to San Francisco, he held classes in advanced piano playing; also tried to conduct symphony concerts there. He composed 4 symphonies and 4 symph. poems (*The Eve of St. Agnes; Lamia; The Raven,* after Poe; and *The Wreck of the Hesperus,* after Longfellow); 4 piano concertos; Violin Concerto; Cello Concerto; Piano Quintet; 2 string quartets; Piano Trio; 3 violin sonatas; Cello Sonata; Flute Sonata; 2 clarinet sonatas; also composed the light operas *La Paloma* and *Wa-Kin-Yon, or The Passing of the Red Man.*

Zechlin, Ruth, German composer; b. Grosshartmannsdorf, near Freiberg, June 22, 1926. She studied with J. N. David at the Leipzig Hochschule für Musik (1943–49); in 1950 was appointed to the faculty of the Hochschule für Musik in East Berlin.

WORKS: an opera, *Reineke Fuchs* (1968); an oratorio, *Wenn der Wacholder blüht* (1961); *Lidice-Kantata* (1958); Violin Concerto (1963); 3 symphonies (1965, 1966, 1972); 2 chamber symphonies (1967, 1974); *Lineare Meditationen* for string orch. (1969); *Polyphone Meditationen* for string orch. (1969); *Thema mit 5 Veränderungen* for orch. (1971); *Emotionen* for orch. (1971); Trio for oboe, viola, and cello (1957); 5 string quartets (1959, 1965, 1971, 1971, 1974); *Thoughts on a Piano Piece by Prokofiev* for piano and 10 solo instruments (1968); *Exercitien* for

flute and harpsichord (1974); *Stationen* for wind quintet and keyboard instruments (1974); *Kontrapunkte* and *Epitaphe* for harpsichord (1971, 1974).

Zeckwer, Camille, American pianist and composer; b. Philadelphia, June 26, 1875; d. Southampton, N.Y., Aug. 7, 1924. He was educated by his father, **Richard Zeckwer,** and had the good fortune of taking composition lessons in N.Y. with Dvořák during the latter's stay in America; then went to Berlin in quest of more musical education and studied with Philipp Scharwenka; returning to Philadelphia, he began teaching young Americans what he was taught by old Germans. Like his father, he composed a number of unnecessary orchestral and other pieces; his symph. poem *Sohrab and Rustum* was performed in Philadelphia on Feb. 4, 1916; he performed his Piano Concerto thrice with the Philadelphia Orch. (1899, 1904, and 1914); wrote an opera, *Jane and Janetta,* but could not secure a production for it.

Zeckwer, Richard, German-American pianist and composer; b. Stendal, April 30, 1850; d. Philadelphia, Dec. 30, 1922. He studied piano with Moscheles, and theory with Hauptmann, Richter, and Reinecke at the Leipzig Cons. In 1870 he emigrated to the U.S., and settled in Philadelphia as a piano teacher and church organist. He composed a couple of unnecessary concert overtures and a number of perishable songs; published a purported guide, *A Scientific Investigation of Piano-Touch* (1902).

Zeerleder, Niklaus, Swiss cleric and theorist; b. Bern, July 5, 1628; d. Kirchberg, July 5, 1691. He was cantor in Bern, and later in Kirchberg. He published a singing instruction book, *Musica figuralis oder Kurtze Gründliche Underweysung der Sing Kunst* (Bern, 1658).

Zehnder, Max, Swiss composer; b. Turgi, Canton Aargau, Nov. 17, 1901; d. St. Gallen, July 16, 1972. He studied at the Zürich Cons. and later became active in various capacities as conductor, singing teacher, and instructor in church music. He wrote much religious music; also composed some instrumental pieces in the traditional vein, including a Concerto for Flute, Oboe, and Strings (1945); String Quartet (1928); String Trio (1933); vocal solos with orchestral accompaniment.

Zeidman, Boris, Soviet composer and pedagogue; b. St. Petersburg, Feb. 10, 1908. He studied composition at the Leningrad Cons. with Maximilian Steinberg, graduating in 1931; then taught music in various schools in Russia, in Azerbaijan and Uzbekistan. He performed an important educational service in these regions, formerly deficient in music culture, as teacher and adviser.

WORKS: operas: *The People's Wrath* (Baku, Dec. 28, 1941); *Son of the Regiment* (Baku, Feb. 23, 1955); *Zainab and Omon* (1958); *The Russians* (1970); the ballets: *The Gold Key* (1955); *The Dragon and the Sun* (1964); for orch.: *Songs of Struggle* (1966); and *Days of Spring* (1971); 2 piano concertos (1931, 1935); Violin Concerto (1968); Viola Concerto (1938); Cello Concerto (1948); Bassoon Concerto (1938); several pieces of chamber music; songs; an album of 24 children's pieces for piano; teaching collections.

Zeinally, Assaf, Azerbaijan composer; b. Derbent, April 5, 1909; d. Baku, Oct. 27, 1932. He studied cello and trumpet at the Baku Cons., graduating in 1931, but died a year later at the age of 23. He was a highly promising musician; his particular merit was the attempt to compose music in classical forms on folk themes; in this manner he wrote several violin pieces, a children's suite for piano and many songs to words by native poets.

BIBLIOGRAPHY: Kh. Melikov, *Assaf Zeinally* (Baku, 1956; 2nd ed., 1969).

Zeisl, Eric, Austrian-American composer; b. Vienna, May 18, 1905; d. Los Angeles, Feb. 18, 1959. A son of prosperous parents who owned a coffeehouse, he entered the Vienna State Academy of Music at 14; published his first songs at 16. In 1934 he won the Austrian State Prize for his *Requiem Concertante.* After the seizure of Austria by the Nazis in 1938, he fled to Paris, and at the outbreak of the War in 1939, went to the U.S.: in 1941 he settled in Los Angeles; in 1945 he became an American citizen. He taught at the Southern California School of Music; from 1949 until his death he was on the staff at Los Angeles City College. Increasingly conscious in exile of his Jewish heritage, he selected biblical themes for his stage works; death interrupted the composition of his major work, a music drama *Job;* Hebraic cantillation is basic to this period. His style of composition reflects the late Romantic school of Vienna, imbued with poetic melancholy with a relief provided by eruptions of dancing optimism. He was at best in his song cycles.

WORKS: children's opera *Die Fahrt ins Wunderland* (Vienna, 1934); *Leonce und Lena* (1937; Los Angeles, 1952); the ballets, *Pierrot in der Flasche* (Vienna Radio, 1935); *Uranium 235* (1946); *Naboth's Vineyard* (1953); *Jacob und Rachel* (1954); for orch.: *Kleine Symphonie* (Vienna Radio, May 30, 1937); *Passacaglia-Fantasie* (Vienna, Nov. 4, 1937); *November,* suite for chamber orch. (N.Y., Jan. 25, 1941); *Cossack Dance* (from the unfinished music drama *Job,* Hollywood, Aug. 18, 1946); *Return of Ulysses,* suite for chamber orch. (Chicago, Nov. 17, 1948); *Variations and Fugue on Christmas Carols* (1950); Piano Concerto (1951); *Concerto grosso* for cello and orch. (1956); chamber music: Trio for flute, viola, and harp (1956); Violin Sonata (1950); Viola Sonata (1950); Cello Sonata (1951); vocal works: *Requiem ebraico* (1945); *Mondbilder* for baritone and orch. (1928); choruses; the song cycles *Kinderlieder* for soprano; and *6 Lieder* for baritone.

BIBLIOGRAPHY: Malcolm S. Cole, "Eric Zeisl: The Rediscovery of an Emigré Composer," *Musical Quarterly* (April 1978).

Zeisler, Fannie (Bloomfield), noted pianist; b. Bielitz, Austrian Silesia, July 16, 1863; d. Chicago, Aug. 20, 1927. Her original name was **Blumenfeld;** it was changed to Bloomfield when the family settled in Chicago in 1868. Her first teachers there were Carl Wolfsohn and Bernhard Ziehn. She made her concert debut in Chicago on Feb. 26, 1875; in 1878 she went to Vienna, where she studied with Leschetizky (1878–83). From 1883 until 1893 she played annually in the U.S.; in 1893 she made a tour of Germany and Austria, which established her reputation as one of the best women pianists; other European tours followed in 1894–95, 1898, 1902–03, 1911–12, and the spring of 1914. She then returned to Chicago; made her farewell appearance there on Feb. 25, 1925, in a special concert to mark her golden jubilee. On Oct. 18, 1885, she married Sigmund Zeisler, a Chicago lawyer.

BIBLIOGRAPHY: *Dictionary of American Biography.*

Zelenka, Istvan, Hungarian composer; b. Budapest, July 30, 1936. He studied music in Budapest and later took a course with Hanns Jelinek in Vienna; in 1962 he went to Geneva, where he became an acoustical engineer. His works, all in an experimental style, with the application of serial and electronic techniques, include a chamber opera, *Ein Zwischenspiel* (1960); *Conversionen* for 3 string quartets, piano, harmonium, and harpsichord (1961); *Décors* for chamber orch. (1962); *Biais* for chamber orch., spatially and serially divided into 3 autochthonic groups (1963); *Hommage à Joan Miró* for orch. (1965).

Zelenka, Jan Dismas, Bohemian composer; b. Louňovice, Oct. 16, 1679; d. Dresden, Dec. 23, 1745. He received his general education in Prague; in 1710 he joined the court orch. in Dresden, playing the double bass; then studied with Fux in Vienna and with Lotti in Italy (1716). In 1719 he returned to Dresden, where he became assistant to Heinichen, succeeding him in 1729; he was named court Kapellmeister in 1733. He was a prolific composer; wrote much church music, including 21 Masses, 3 Requiems, and many motets; 3 Italian oratorios, etc.; a melodrama *De Sancto Venceslao;* also an interesting overture entitled *Hypocondria.*

BIBLIOGRAPHY: M. Fürstenau, *Zur Geschichte der Musik und des Theaters am Hofe zu Dresden,* vol. II (Dresden, 1862).

Zeleński, Wladislaw, Polish composer and pedagogue; b. Grodkowice, near Cracow, July 6, 1837; d. Cracow, Jan. 23, 1921. He studied with Mirecki in Cracow, Krejči in Prague, and Reber in Paris. He returned to Poland in 1871; was theory teacher at the Warsaw Cons. (1872–81). In 1887 he organized the Cracow Cons., and remained its director until his death; he also taught piano and theory there. As a pedagogue, he enjoyed a very high reputation; among his pupils were Stojowski, Opienski, and Szopski.

WORKS: operas: *Konrad Wallenrold* (Lwów, Feb. 26, 1885), *Goplana* (Cracow, July 23, 1896), *Janek* (Lwów, Oct. 4, 1900), *Stara baśń* (Lwów, March 14, 1907); 2 symphonies; 2 overtures; piano concerto; 7 cantatas; 2 Masses; motets for men's voices; 2 violin sonatas; a piano trio; 2 string quartets; a string sextet; a piano quartet; 3 piano sonatas; about 80 songs to Polish words; a number of piano pieces (*Valse-caprice, Humoreske und Gavotte, Grand scherzo de concert, Grosse Polonaise, Moments d'un carnaval,* etc.); 25 preludes for organ.

BIBLIOGRAPHY: F. Szopski, *W. Zeleński* (Warsaw,

1928); Z. Jachimecki, *Wladislaw Zeleński; zycie i twórczość, 1837-1921* (Cracow, 1952).

Železný, Lubomír, Czech composer; b. Ostrava, March 16, 1925. He studied composition with Karel Janeček at the Prague Cons. (1945-48) and with Bořkovec at the Prague Academy of Musical Arts (1948-50). He worked in the music department of Prague Radio before 1951; arranged songs for the Vit Nejedlý Army Artistic Ensemble (1951-56).
WORKS: 2 *Gavottes* for orch. (1954); 2 violin concertos (1958-59; 1974-75); 2 symphonies: No. 1, for large orch. (1961-62), and No. 2, for small orch. (1970); Concerto for flute, strings, and piano (1966); *Concertant Music* for viola, strings, and piano (1969); *Festive March* for orch. (1971); *Brigand Songs* for tenor and orch. (1958); Flute Sonata (1943); Trio for flute, viola, and cello (1946); 2 violin sonatas (1948, 1971); Quartet for flute, violin, viola, and cello (1948); 2 string quartets (1959-60, 1968); Piano Trio (1966); Quintet for 2 violins, clarinet, viola, and cello (1969); Wind Quintet (1970); choruses; songs.

Zelinka, Jan Evangelista, Czech composer; b. Prague, Jan. 13, 1893; d. there, June 30, 1969. He studied music with his father, an organist, and later with J. B. Foerster, Suk, Novák and Ostrčil.
WORKS: operas: *Dceruška hostinského* (*The Tavernkeeper's Little Daughter*; Prague, Feb. 24, 1925); *Devátá Louka* (*The Ninth Meadow*; Prague, Sept. 19, 1931); *Odchod dona Quijota* (*Departure of Don Quixote*, 1936); *Paličatý švec* (*The Stubborn Cobbler*; Prague, March 28, 1944); *Meluzína* (*The Wailing Wind*; Pilsen, April 15, 1950); the radio opera *Námluvy bez konce* (*Endless Wooing*; Czech radio, Jan. 27, 1950); *Masopustní noc* (*Shrovetide Night*, 1956); *Lásky žal i smích*, after Goldoni (*Love's Woe and Laughter*, 1958); *Škola pro ženy*, after Molière (*School for Wives*, 1959); *Blouznivé jaro* (*A Fanciful Spring*, 1960); the satirical opera *Dřevený kůň* (*The Wooden Horse*, 1962-63); a ballet pantomime, *Skleněná panna* (*The Glass Doll*, 1927; Prague, July 2, 1928); a scenic melodrama, *Srdce na prázdninách* (*Heart on a Fishhook*, 1932; Brno, Jan. 28, 1938); for orch.: *Overture to a Renaissance Comedy* (1919); *Pariz—Glotton*, overture burleske (1931); *Weekend,* suite (1939); *Sinfonia Rustica* (1956); *A Slovak Summer* (1959); *Musichetta primaverale* for chamber orch. (1962); *Satiricon,* suite (1964); numerous cantatas; much chamber music, including 2 nonets: *Capriccio* (1937) and *Cassation* (1943); *Late Summer,* a piano trio (1949); *Sonata leggera* for saxophone and piano (1962); Piano Sonata (1926); organ pieces; songs and incidental music.

Zeljenka, Ilja, Slovak composer; b. Bratislava, Dec. 21, 1932. He studied composition with Cikker, piano with Macudzinski, and esthetics with Ferenczy at the Bratislava Academy of Music and Dramatic Arts (1951-56). He was a dramaturgist of the Slovak Philharmonic in Bratislava (1957-61) and lecturer for the Bratislava Broadcasting station (1961-68); in 1961 he and Ivan Statdrucker established at the Czech Radio in Bratislava the first electronic music studio in Czechoslovakia. After a period of infatuation with hedonistic simplicity laced with permissible discords, he turned towards modern sonorism, including electronics.
WORKS: *Suite* for small orch. (1952); 2 piano quintets (1953, 1959); 3 symphonies (1954; for string orch., 1960; 1975); *Dramatic Overture* (1955); *Bagatelles* for piano (1955); *Ballad* for chorus and orch. (1957); 2 piano sonatas (1958, 1975); *Oswieczym,* melodrama on the tragedy of the infamous Nazi concentration camp, for 2 narrators, 2 choruses, and orch. (1960; Bratislava, April 29, 1965); *7 Compositional Studies* for chamber ensemble (1962); a ballet, *Cosmos* (1962-63); 2 string quartets (1963, 1976); *Štruktúry (Structures)* for orch. (1964); *Metamorphoses XV,* after Ovid, for speaker and 9 instruments (1964); *Polymetric Quartet* for 4 piano parts (1965); *Hudba (Music)* for chorus and orch. (1965); Piano Concerto (1966); *Zaklínadlá (Incantations)* for chorus and orch. (1967); *Hry (Games),* musical dada for 13 singers playing bells and drums (1968); *Musica polymetrica* for 4 string quartets (1970); *Meditation* for orch. (1971); Violin Concerto (1974); Piano Trio (1975); *Elegy* for chamber orch. (1975).

Zelle, Friedrich, German musicologist; b. Berlin, Jan. 24, 1845; d. there, Sept. 10, 1927. He studied piano with Kullak, composition with Geyer and Bellermann; taught at the Humboldt Akademie in Berlin (1875-92) and later was director of the Berlin Realschule (1893-1915). He edited Hassler's *Lustgarten* (1887), J. W. Franck's *Choral-kantate* (1890), and Keiser's opera *Jodelet* (1892); also Passions by Sebastiani and Theile for the *Denkmäler deutscher Tonkunst* 17.
WRITINGS: *Beiträge zur Geschichte der ältesten deutschen Oper: I, J. W. Franck* (1889), II, *Joh. Theile und N. A. Strungk* (1891), III, *J. Ph. Förtsch* (1893); *Die Singweisen der ältesten evangelischen Lieder* (1899, 1900); *Theorie der Musik* (1880); *Das erste evangelische Choralbuch* [Osiander, 1586] (1913); *Das älteste lutherische Hausgesangbuch* [the so-called *Färbefass-Enchiridion* of 1524] (1903); *Ballettstücke aus Keiserschen Opern* (1890).

Zeller, Karl, Austrian composer of operettas; b. St. Peter-in-der-Au, July 19, 1842; d. Baden, near Vienna, Aug. 17, 1898. He was an official in the Austrian Ministry of Education. Although following music only as an avocation, he became one of the most popular operetta composers of the day, winning extraordinary success with his *Der Vogelhändler* (Vienna, Jan. 10, 1891) and *Der Obersteiger* (Vienna, Jan. 5, 1894). Other successfull operettas (all produced in Vienna) were *Joconde* (March 18, 1876), *Die Carbonari* (Nov. 27, 1880), *Der Vagabund* (Oct. 30, 1886), and *Der Kellermeister* (Dec. 21, 1901).
BIBLIOGRAPHY: C. W. Zeller, *Mein Vater Karl Zeller* (St. Plöten, 1942).

Zellner, Julius, Austrian pianist and composer; b. Vienna, May 18, 1832; d. Mürzzuschlag, July 28, 1900. He was first engaged in a mercantile career, but abandoned it for music; became successful in Vienna as teacher and composer.
WORKS: 2 symphonies; *Melusine,* symph. suite; Piano Concerto; Piano Quartet; 3 piano trios; 2 cello sonatas; 2 violin sonatas; a number of piano pieces

(*Adagio und Allegro appassionato; Zwei kleine Suiten; Zwei Sonatinen;* etc.); piano pieces 4 hands (*Drei deutsche Tänze,* etc.); also a puppet play, *Wasserkaspar.*

Zellner, Leopold Alexander, Austrian organist and music editor; b. Agram, Sept. 23, 1823; d. Vienna, Nov. 24, 1894. He studied with his father, organist of the Agram Cathedral; at 15 became a church organist; taught music in Vienna; founded and edited the *Blätter für Theater, Musik und bildende Kunst* (1855-68). In 1868 he became prof. of harmony at the Vienna Cons.; wrote a method for the harmonium, and made improvements in its mechanism; published instructive pieces; also composed choruses and chamber music; ed. violin sonatas by Nardini and Vivaldi with additional piano parts. His lectures were published as *Vorträge über Akustik* (2 vols.; 1892) and *Vorträge über Orgelbau* (1893).

Zelter, Carl Friedrich, eminent German composer and teacher; b. Berlin, Dec. 11, 1758; d. there, May 15, 1832. The son of a mason, he was brought up in the same trade, but his musical inclinations soon asserted themselves; he studied organ, and at the age of 18 had a cantata of his composition performed in a church; then he became a pupil of C. F. C. Fasch and Kirnberger; was engaged as music director in Rellstab's Liebhaber-Konzerte; in 1786 he brought out a funeral cantata on the death of Frederick the Great; in 1791 he joined the Singverein (later Singakademie) conducted by Fasch, often acting as his deputy, and succeeding him in 1800. He was elected associate ("Assessor") of the Akademie in 1806; prof. in 1809. In 1807 he organized a Ripienschule for orchestral practice; and in 1809 he founded in Berlin the Liedertafel, a pioneer men's choral society which became famous; similar organizations were subsequently formed throughout Germany, and later in America. Zelter composed about 100 men's choruses for the Liedertafel. In 1822 he founded the Royal Institute for Church Music, of which he was director until his death (the Institute was later reorganized as the Akademie für Kirchen- und Schulmusik). Goethe greatly admired Zelter's musical settings of his poems, preferring them to Schubert's and Beethoven's; this predilection led to their friendship, which was reflected in a voluminous correspondence, *Briefwechsel zwischen Goethe und Zelter* (ed. in 6 vols. by F. W. Riemer, Berlin, 1833-34; ed. in 3 vols. by L. Geiger, Leipzig, 1906; ed. in 4 vols. by M. Hecker, Leipzig, 1913; English transl. by A. D. Coleridge, London, 1887). His songs are historically important, since they form a link between old ballad types and the new art of the lied, which found its flowering in Schubert and Schumann. Zelter's settings of Goethe's *König von Thule* and of *Es ist ein Schuss gefallen* became extremely popular. Other songs were publ. in collections of 12 each (1796 and 1801), followed by other albums: *Sämtliche Lieder, Balladen, Romanzen* (1810 et seq.), *Neue Sammlung* (1821), and *6 deutsche Lieder* (1827). New editions were brought out by Jöde (1930), Landshoff (1932), etc.; the cantatas *Johanna Sebus* and *Die Gunst des Augenblicks* were published by Müller-Blattau. He published a biography of Fasch (Berlin, 1801). Zelter's autobiography was first publ. under the title, *C. F. Zelter. Eine Lebensbeschreibung nach autobiographischen Manuscripten,* edited by W. Rintel; then as *C. F. Zelter. Darstellungen seines Lebens* (Weimar, 1931).

BIBLIOGRAPHY: W. Bornemann, *Die Zeltersche Liedertafel in Berlin* (Berlin, 1851); L. Sieber, *C. F. Zelter und der deutsche Männergesang* (Basel, 1862); H. Kuhlo, *Geschichte der Zelterschen Liedertafel von 1809-1909* (Berlin, 1909); G. R. Kruse, *Zelter* (Leipzig, 1915); J. W. Schottländer, "Zelters Beziehungen zu den Komponisten seiner Zeit," *Zeitschrift für Musikwissenschaft* 15; H. J. Moser, "Goethes Dichtung in der neueren Musik," *Goethe-Jahrbuch* (1931); J. Müller-Blattau, "Goethe und die Kantate," *Jahrbuch Peters* (1931); G. Schünemann, *C. F. Zelter, der Begründer der preussischen Musikpflege* (Berlin, 1932); G. Wittmann, *Das klavierbegleitete Sololied C. F. Zelters* (dissertation, Giessen, 1936); G. Schünemann, *C. F. Zelter: der Mensch und sein Werk* (Berlin, 1937); S. Holtzmann, ed., *C. F. Zelter im Spiegel seines Briefwechsel mit Goethe* (Weimar, 1957); W. Reich, ed., *C. F. Zelter, Selbstdarstellung,* a collection of documents (Zürich, 1958); K. H. Taubert, *Carl Friedrich Zelter. Ein Leben durch das Handwerk für die Musik* (Berlin, 1958).

Zemlinsky, Alexander von, eminent Austrian composer, conductor, and teacher; b. Vienna (of Polish parentage), Oct. 14, 1871; d. Larchmont, N.Y., March 15, 1942. He studied at the Vienna Cons. with Door (piano), Krenn, Robert Fuchs and J. N. Fuchs (composition); was encouraged by Brahms, who expressed a favorable opinion of his early chamber music. In 1900 he obtained the post of conductor of the Karlstheater in Vienna; in 1906 became conductor of the Vienna Volksoper; 1908, at the Vienna Opera. In 1909 he was engaged as conductor at the Mannheim Opera; from 1911 to 1927, conducted at the German Opera in Prague; also taught composition and conducting at the Prague College of Music. From 1927 to 1932 he was conductor of the Berlin State Opera; in 1933 returned to Vienna; also made guest appearances in Spain, Russia, etc. After the *Anschluss* in 1938 he emigrated to the U.S. He was the teacher of Schoenberg, who married his sister. Zemlinsky was greatly admired as a musician, teacher and composer; Schoenberg was particularly appreciative of him.

WORKS: OPERAS: *Sarema* (Munich, Oct. 10, 1897); *Es war einmal* (his most successful work; Vienna, Jan. 22, 1900, Mahler conducting); *Kleider machen Leute* (Vienna, Oct. 2, 1910); *Eine florentinische Tragödie* (Stuttgart, Jan. 30, 1917); *Der Zwerg* (Cologne, May 28, 1922); *Der Kreidekreis* (Zürich, Oct. 14, 1933). FOR ORCH.: Symph. No. 1 (1892; Vienna, Feb. 10, 1893); *Frühlingsbegräbnis* for chorus, soloists, and orch. (1896; Vienna, Feb. 11, 1900); Symph. No. 2 (1897; Vienna, March 5, 1899; won the Beethoven Prize of the Vienna Gesellschaft der Musikfreunde); Symph. No. 3 (1902-03); *Lyrische Symphonie* for soprano, baritone, and orch. (1922; Prague, June 5, 1924); *Symphonische Gesänge* for voice and orch. (1929); *Sinfonietta* (1934). CHAMBER MUSIC: Piano Quartet (1892); Trio for piano, clarinet, and cello (1896); 4 string quartets (1896, 1915, 1924, 1936); choruses; piano pieces; songs.

BIBLIOGRAPHY: Special issue of *Der Auftakt* 1 (Prague, 1921); Lawrence A. Ongley, "The Works of Alexander Zemlinsky: A Chronological List," *Notes* (Dec. 1977).

Zenatello, Giovanni, Italian tenor; b. Verona, Feb. 22, 1876; d. New York, Feb. 11, 1949. He was originally trained as a baritone and sang in minor opera companies in Italy; then went to Milan, where he took lessons from Moretti and changed his voice to tenor; made his debut in Naples as Canio in *Pagliacci* in 1901; sang the role of Pinkerton in the first performance of Puccini's *Madama Butterfly* (La Scala, Milan, Feb. 17, 1904); in 1905 he sang at Covent Garden, London; on Nov. 4, 1907 made his American debut in N.Y. as Enzo Grimaldo in Ponchielli's *La Gioconda*. From 1909 to 1912, and again in 1913-14, he was the leading tenor of the Boston Opera Co.; during the season of 1912-13 he sang with the Chicago Opera Co; also traveled with various touring opera companies in South America, Spain, and Russia. He eventually settled in N.Y. as a singing teacher, maintaining a studio with his wife, the contralto **Maria Gay,** whom he married in 1913. Together, they trained many famous singers, among them Lily Pons and Nino Martini.

Zenck, Hermann, German musicologist; b. Karlsruhe, March 19, 1898; d. Freiburg-im-Breisgau, Dec. 2, 1950. He studied with Ordenstein at the Karlsruhe Cons.; later in Heidelberg (with Kroyer), in Munich and Leipzig (Dr. phil., 1924); then became assistant at the Institute for Musicology in Leipzig, where he also taught at the Cons. In 1932 he joined the faculty of the Univ. of Göttingen; in 1943, went to Freiburg-im-Breisgau as prof. at the Univ. there. He edited the periodical *Musik und Volk;* was editor of works by Willaert (2 vols. publ. in 1937; vol. 3 in 1950); and Sixtus Dietrich (1942); also edited the *Megalynodia* of Praetorius (1934); Johann Schultz's *Musikalischer Lustgarten* (1937); Handel's Italian cantatas, etc. Published the books *Marienklage und Osterspiel des Wolfenbüttler Codex* (Hamburg, 1927) and *Sixtus Dietrich* (Leipzig, 1928).

Zenger, Max, German composer and conductor; b. Munich, Feb. 2, 1837; d. there, Nov. 18, 1911. He studied in Munich and Leipzig; in 1860 became theater conductor in Regensburg; in 1869, musical director of the Munich Court Opera; then was court conductor at Karlsruhe (1872-78); conductor of the Munich Oratorio Society (1878-85) and other choral societies there. WORKS: operas: *Die Foscari* (Munich, 1863), *Ruy Blas* (Mannheim, 1868), *Wieland der Schmied* (Munich, 1880; revised, 1894), *Eros und Psyche* (Munich, 1901); oratorio *Kain*, after Byron (Munich, 1867; often performed elsewhere in Germany); secular cantata *Die Heinzelmännchen;* 2 ballets for King Ludwig II of Bavaria, *Venus und Adonis* and *Les Plaisirs de l'île enchantée* (1881); 2 Gretchen scenes from *Faust* for soprano and small orch.; *Zwei Konzertstücke* for mixed chorus and string orch.; *Altgriechisches Liederspiel* for soprano solo, chorus, and orch.; *Die Kraniche des Ibikus*, melodrama with orch.; *Die deutsche Flotte* for men's chorus and orch.; a symph.; *Tragische Ouvertüre; Adagio concertante* for cello and orch.; a

piano trio; a cello sonata; choruses; piano pieces; songs. He wrote the valuable *Entstehung und Entwicklung der Instrumentalmusik* (Langensalza, 1906) and *Geshichte der Münchener Oper* (posthumous; ed. by Th. Kroyer, 1923).

Zeno, Apostolo, famous Italian opera librettist; b. Venice, Dec. 11, 1668; d. there, Nov. 11, 1750. In 1710 he founded the *Giornale dei Letterati d'Italia;* in 1718 was appointed court poet at Vienna; returned to Venice in 1729. The total number of librettos written by him (some in collaboration with Pietro Pariati) is 71; they were collected and edited by Gasparo Gozzi as *Poesie drammatiche di Apostolo Zeno* (10 vols.), Venice, 1744; reprinted in 11 vols. at Orléans, 1785-86). A man of great knowledge and culture, he was also an ardent numismatist; his large collection of coins was exhibited at Vienna in 1955.

BIBLIOGRAPHY: A. Wotquenne, *Libretti d'opéras et d'oratorios italiens du XVIIme siècle* (Brussels, 1901); A. Wotquenne, *Table alphabétique des morceaux mesurés contenus dans les œuvres dramatiques de Zeno, Metastasio et Goldoni* (Leipzig, 1905; also in German); M. Fehr, *Apostolo Zeno und seine Reform des Operntexts* (dissertation, Zürich, 1912); O. G. Sonneck, *Catalogue of Opera Librettos Printed before 1800* (2 vols.; Washington, 1914); R. Giazotto, "Apostolo Zeno, Pietro Metastasio e la critica del settecento," *Rivista Musicale Italiana* (1946); M. F. Robinson, *Naples and Neapolitan Opera* (London, 1972).

Zepler, Bogumil, German composer; b. Breslau, May 6, 1858; d. Krummhübel im Riesengebirge, Aug. 17, 1918. He studied architecture in Berlin, then medicine at the Univ. of Breslau (M.D., 1884); later began the study of music with H. Urban in Berlin; attracted attention in 1891 with *Cavalleria Berolina*, a parody on Mascagni's *Cavalleria Rusticana;* wrote stage music for Ernst von Wolzogen's artistic cabaret, "Überbrettl" (1901-02); also wrote a parody on Strauss' *Salome*. He further composed the comic operas *Der Brautmarkt zu Hira* (Berlin, 1892), *Der Vicomte von Letorières* (Hamburg, 1899), *Die Bäder von Lucca* (Berlin, 1905), *Monsieur Bonaparte* (Leipzig, 1911); several operettas (*Diogenes, Pick und Pocket, Die Liebesfestung,* etc.); a serious 1-act opera, *Nacht* (Bern, 1901); 2 pantomines, *Die Galgenfrist* and *Die Geisterbraut;* songs (*Rokokolieder,* etc.).

Zerrahn, Carl, German-American conductor; b. Malchow, Mecklenburg, July 28, 1826; d. Milton, Mass., Dec. 29, 1909. He studied in Rostock, Hannover and Berlin; after the revolutionary events of 1848, he emigrated to the U.S. and settled in Boston, then a center of German musical culture in America. He played the flute in the Germania Orch.; then became a professional conductor. For 42 years (1854-96) he led the concerts of the Handel and Haydn Society in Boston, and also conducted the Boston Philharmonic (1855-63) and the Harvard Musical Association (1865-82). He was music director, from 1866-1897, of the prestigious Music Festivals in Worcester, Mass., and choral director for the famous Peace Jubilee Concerts in Boston in 1869 and 1872, leading the huge choruses assembled on these occasions. He was also for many years teacher of harmony and singing at the New England Cons. (until 1898).

BIBLIOGRAPHY: *Dictionary of American Biography.*

Zeuner, Charles (real name **Heinrich Christoph**), German-American organist; b. Eisleben, Saxony, Sept. 20, 1795; d. (suicide) Philadelphia, Nov. 7, 1857. He studied in Erfurt. About 1830 he settled in Boston, where he became organist at Park Street Church; also organist of the Handel and Haydn Society (1830–37), and briefly its president (1838–39). He then went to Philadelphia, where he served as church organist. He composed one of the earliest American oratorios, *The Feast of Tabernacles* (Boston, May 3, 1837); published *Church Music, Consisting of New and Original Anthems, Motets and Chants* (1831); *The American Harp* (1832); *The Ancient Lyre,* a book of hymn tunes (1834 and several later eds.); *Organ Voluntaries* (1840); contributed to Lowell Mason's *Lyra Sacra* (1832); some of his compositions are also included in *The Psaltery,* ed. by Mason and Webb (1845). For an account of his suicide, see the *New York Musical Review and Gazette* for Nov. 14, 1857.

BIBLIOGRAPHY: F. J. Metcalf, *American Writers and Compilers of Sacred Music* (1925); *Dictionary of American Biography.*

Zeuner, Karl Traugott, German pianist and composer; b. Dresden, April 28, 1775; d. Paris, Jan. 24, 1841. He studied with Türk in Halle and Clementi in Russia; gave concerts and taught in Paris, Vienna, St. Petersburg, and Dresden. He composed 2 piano concertos; 3 string quartets; variations on a Russian theme for piano, violin, and cello; polonaises, fantasias, etc., for piano; these pieces were much in vogue in his time.

Zganec, Vinko, Croatian enthnomusicologist; b. Vratišinci, Jan. 22, 1890; d. Zagreb, Dec. 12, 1976. He studied law at the Univ. of Zagreb; then became interested in song collecting; traveled in the countryside gathering native melodies; published several albums of harmonizations of these songs and numerous articles in Croatian, German, and American music journals dealing with specific aspects of Croatian songs; in his analyses of their structure he applied modern methods of ethnomusicology.

Zhelobinsky, Valery, Russian composer; b. Tambov, Jan. 27, 1913; d. Leningrad, Aug. 13, 1946. He received elementary musical training in Tambov; then entered the Leningrad Cons. as a student of Vladimir Shcherbachev (1928–32). He gave piano recitals, playing his own compositions; taught at the Tambov Music School; then returned to Leningrad. During his brief span of life, he composed several operas in a fine Romantic manner, as well as symphonies and chamber music.

WORKS: operas: *Kamarinsky Muzhik* (Leningrad, Sept. 15, 1933), *Her Saint's Day* (Leningrad, Feb. 22, 1935), *Mother,* after Maxim Gorky (Leningrad, Dec. 30, 1938); operetta *The Last Ball* (Leningrad, March 30, 1939); 6 symphonies: No. 1 (1930); No. 2, *To the Memory of Revolutionary Victims* (1932); No. 3, *Dra-*

matic Symphony (Moscow, Dec. 17, 1939); No. 4 (Moscow, May 30, 1943); No. 5 (1944); No. 6 (1946); 3 piano concertos (1933, 1934, 1939); Violin Concerto (1934); *Romantic Poem* for violin and orch. (1939); *24 Preludes* for piano; 2 children's albums for piano; film music.

Zhiganov, Nazib, Russian composer of Tatar heritage; b. Uralsk, Jan. 15, 1911. He was brought up in an orphan asylum; educated in a music school in Kazan; went to Moscow where he studied in a technological school; then took courses with Litinsky at the Moscow Cons., graduating in 1938. In 1945 he was appointed director and prof. of the newly founded Cons. of Kazan. In his music he set for himself the task of creating a new national Tatar school of composition, following the harmonic and instrumental precepts of the Russian National School; wrote several successful operas, symphonies and symphonic suites on Tatar themes.

WORKS: operas: *Katchkyn* (Kazan, June 17, 1939); *Irek (Liberty;* Kazan, Feb. 24, 1940); *Altyntchetch (The Golden-Haired;* Kazan, July 12, 1941); *Ildar* (Kazan, Nov. 7, 1942); *Tulyak* (Kazan, July 27, 1945); *Namus (Honor;* Kazan, June 25, 1950); the ballet *Zugra* (Kazan, May 17, 1946); *Two Legends* (1970); cantata, *My Republic* (1960); operatic monologue *Dzhalil* (1950); 4 symphonies (1937, 1968, 1971, 1973); several suites on Tatar themes; chamber music; piano pieces; songs.

BIBLIOGRAPHY: Y. Girshman, *Nazib Zhiganov* (Moscow, 1957).

Zhitomirsky, Alexander, Russian composer and pedagogue; b. Kherson, May 23, 1881; d. Leningrad, Dec. 16, 1937. He took violin lessons in Odessa and in Vienna; also studied piano. Returning to Russia, he entered the St. Petersburg Cons. as a student of Rimsky-Korsakov, Liadov, and Glazunov, graduating in 1910; from 1915 to 1937 he was on its faculty, as instructor in composition and orchestration. Among his pupils were the Soviet conductors Melik-Pashayev and Gauck, and the composers Veprik, Tchishko, and others. In his own compositons, he followed the style and manner of the Russian National School; he wrote a Violin Concerto (1937); String Quartet (1923); a number of songs and choruses.

Zhivotov, Alexei, Russian composer; b. Kazan, Nov. 14, 1904; d. Leningrad, Aug. 27, 1964. He studied at the Leningrad Cons. with Vladimir Shcherbachev, graduating in 1930. During the siege of Leningrad by the Nazis (1941–42), he remained in the city and was awarded a medal for valor. Most of his music is set in a lyrical-dramatic vein; he also wrote patriotic songs and choruses.

WORKS: for orch.: *Dance Suite* (1935); *Romantic Poem* (1940); *Heroic Poem* (1946); *Theater Suite* (1949); vocal works: *The West,* song cycle with orchestral accompaniment (1932); *Lyric Etudes* (1934); *Spring* (1942); *Happiness* (1943); *Songs of Leningrad* (1944); film music.

Zhukovsky, Herman, Ukrainian composer; b. Radzivilovo, Volynya, Nov. 13, 1913; d. Kiev, March 15, 1976. He studied piano and composition at the Kiev

Cons., graduating in 1941; from 1951 to 1958 he taught music theory there. He wrote operas, ballets, symphonic music and other works in an approved style of socialist realism, using authentic Ukrainian song patterns for his materials, but a crisis supervened in his steady progress when his opera *From the Bottom of My Heart* (Moscow, Jan. 16, 1951) was viciously attacked by the cultural authorities of the Soviet government for alleged ideological and musical aberrations; he revised the score, and the new version was approved. His other operas are *Marina* (Kiev, March 12, 1939); *The First Spring* (1960); *Contrasts of Centuries*, operatic trilogy (1967); a monodrama for baritone, *A Soldier's Wife* (1968); ballets: *Rostislava* (1955); *Forest Song* (Moscow, May 1, 1961); several political cantatas: *Oath of the World Youth* (1951); *My Fatherland* (1949); several orchestral suites, chamber music; film scores.

Ziani, Marco Antonio, Italian composer, nephew of Pietro Andrea Ziani; b. Venice, c.1653; d. Vienna, Jan. 22, 1715. In 1700 he became vice Kapellmeister at the Vienna court; in 1712, Kapellmeister. He composed 45 operas and serenades, of which the following were produced in Vienna: *Il Giordano pio* (July 26, 1700); *Gli Ossequi della notte* (July 22, 1701); *Temistocle* (June 9, 1701); *La Fuga dell'invidia* (Nov. 15, 1701); *Il Romolo* (June 9, 1702); *Cajo Popilio* (June 9, 1704); *L' Ercole vincitore dell'invidia* (March 19, 1706); *Meleagro* (Aug. 16, 1706); *Chilonida* (April 21, 1709); *Il Campidoglio ricuperato* (July 26, 1709); *L'Atenaide* (with Negri and Caldara; Nov. 19, 1714). He also composed church music.

Ziani, Pietro Andrea, Italian organist and composer, uncle of **Marco Antonio Ziani;** b. Venice, c.1620; d. Naples, Feb. 12, 1684. In 1669 he succeeded Cavalli as 2nd organist at San Marco, Venice; went to Naples in 1676; in 1677 he entered the service of Empress Eleonora at Vienna; pensioned in 1684. He wrote 23 operas, including *Le Fortune di Rodope, e di Damira* (Venice, Carnival of 1657), *L'Antigona delusa da Alceste* (Venice, Jan. 15, 1660), *La Congiura del vizio contra la virtù* (Vienna, Nov. 15, 1663), and *La Circe* (Vienna, June 9, 1665); oratorio, *Le Lagrime della Vergine* (Venice, 1662); *Sacrae laudes a 5* (1659); sonatas for 3, 4, 5, or 6 instruments (1691); church music; etc.

BIBLIOGRAPHY: H. Kretzschmar, "Weitere Beiträge zur Geschichte der venezianischen Oper," *Jahrbuch der Bibliothek Peters* (1910).

Zich, Jaroslav, Czech musicologist and composer, son of **Otakar Zich;** b. Prague, Jan. 17, 1912. He studied with his father and with J. B. Foerster (1928–31); went to Charles Univ. in Prague, obtaining a Ph.D. in 1936; then devoted himself to administrative work and program directing at the Prague Radio; in 1952 was appointed to the faculty at the Academy of Musical Arts, Prague.

WORKS: *Letmý host (The Temporary Guest),* cycle of songs with orch. (1932); Duo for violin and cello (1932); String Quartet (1932); *Romance helgolandská,* melodrama with orch. (1934); *U muziky (At the Dance),* 9 dances on folk motifs for octet (1940); *Rhapsody* for cello and orch. (1956); Wind Quintet

(1965). He published the manuals *Instrumentation in Groups* (Prague, 1957) and *Chapters of Musical Aesthetics* (Prague, 1974).

Zich, Otakar, Czech composer and musicologist; father of **Jaroslav Zich;** b: Králové Městec, March 25, 1879; d. Oubĕnice, near Benešov, July 9, 1934. He was educated at Charles Univ. in Prague (1897–1901; Ph.D., 1902); appointed lecturer there in 1911; in 1920, prof. of esthetics at Masaryk Univ. in Brno; in 1924 he again became a member of the staff of Charles Univ., where he remained until his death.

WORKS: opera: *Malířský nápad (Painter's Whim;* Prague, March 11, 1910); *Vina (Guilt,* Prague, March 14, 1922); *Preciézky,* after Molière's *Les Précieuses ridicules* (Prague, May 11, 1926); also cantatas, song cycles, part-songs, etc. Compiled *Vojenský spěvník československý* (unaccompanied melodies; Prague, 1922).

BIBLIOGRAPHY: J. Hutter, *Otakar Zich a jeho "Vina"* (Prague, 1922).

Zichy, Géza, Count Vasony-Keö, Hungarian left-hand pianist and composer; b. Sztára Castle, July 22, 1849; d. Budapest, Jan. 14, 1924. He studied with Volkmann and Liszt. At the age of 14 he lost his right arm in a hunting accident, and, refusing to give up music, developed his left-hand technique to the point of virtuosity; also made arrangements for left hand. On several occasions he played in public with Liszt an arrangement of the *Rákóczy March* for 3 hands. From 1875 to 1918 he was president of the National Cons. in Budapest; was also intendant of the National Theater and Opera there (1890–94). He composed operas, produced at Budapest: *A vár története (Castle Story;* May 16, 1888), *Alár* (April 11, 1896), *Roland mester* (Jan. 10, 1899), and a dramatic trilogy on the life of Rákóczi: *Nemo* (March 30, 1905), *Rákóczi Ferenc* (Jan. 30, 1909), and *Rodostó* (March 20, 1912); a ballet, *Gemma* (Prague, 1903); a cantata, *Dolores* (1889); Piano Concerto (1902); Piano Sonata; studies and piano pieces for the left hand alone; songs; etc. He publ. an autobiography, *Aus meinem Leben* (German ed., 3 vols., 1911–20).

Ziehn, Bernhard, noted German-American music theorist and teacher; b. Erfurt, Jan. 20, 1845; d. Chicago, Sept. 8, 1912. He studied in Erfurt; was a school teacher in Mühlhausen; in 1868 he emigrated to the U.S., taught German, mathematics, and music theory at the German Lutheran School in Chicago (1868–71); subsequently became a private music teacher and established himself as a theorist. His "enharmonic law," built on the principle of functional equality of chords, is an original contribution to the theory of harmony.

WRITINGS: *System der Übungen für Clavierspieler* (1881); *Ein Lehrgang für den ersten Clavierunterricht* (1881); *Harmonie- und Modulationslehre* (1887; 2nd ed., 1909; completely recast and published in English as *Manual of Harmony: Theoretical and Practical,* 1907; valuable for the choice and range of the examples); *Five- and Six-Part Harmonies* (1911); *Canonical Studies; a New Technic in Composition* (1912; in both English and German); a collection of his articles was published by the German-American Historical

Society of Illinois, as *Gesammelte Aufsätze zur Geschichte und Theorie der Musik* (Chicago, 1927).

BIBLIOGRAPHY: W. Sargeant, "Bernhard Ziehn, Precursor," *Musical Quarterly* (April 1933); H. J. Moser, *Bernhard Ziehn: der deutsch-amerikanische Musiktheoretiker* (Bayreuth, 1950); *Dictionary of American Biography*.

Ziehrer, Karl Michael, Austrian bandleader and composer of operettas; b. Vienna, May 2, 1843; d. there, Nov. 14, 1922. Entirely self-taught in music, he organized in 1863 a dance orch., with which he made tours of Austria and Germany, introducing his own pieces; with an enlarged orch. (50 players) he established a regular series of popular concerts in Vienna, which met with great success; in 1907 he was appointed music director of the court balls. He wrote nearly 600 marches and dances for orch. (some very popular: *Meeresleuchten, Evatöchter, Donauwalzer, Alt-Wien, Ziehrereien,* etc.) and produced in Vienna a number of operettas: *Wiener Kinder* (Feb. 19, 1881); *Mahomeds Paradies* (Feb. 26, 1866); *König Jerôme* (Nov. 28, 1878); *Ein Deutschmeister* (Nov. 30, 1888); *Der schöne Rigo* (May 24, 1898); *Die Landstreicher,* his best work (July 29, 1899); *Die drei Wünsche* (March 9, 1901); *Der Fremdenführer* (Oct. 11, 1902); *Der Schätzmeister* (Dec. 10, 1904); *Fesche Geister* (July 7, 1905); *Am Lido* (Aug. 31, 1907); *Ein tolles Mädel* (Nov. 8, 1907); *Der Liebeswalzer* (Oct. 24, 1908); *Die Gaukler* (Sept. 6, 1909); *Herr und Frau Biedermeier* (Oct. 5, 1910); *In 50 Jahren* (Jan. 7, 1911); *Fürst Casimir* (Sept. 13, 1913); *Der Husarengeneral* (Oct. 3, 1913); *Das dumme Herz* (Feb. 27, 1914); *Die verliebte Eskadron* (July 11, 1920).

Zielinski, Jaroslaw de, Polish-American pianist; b. Lubycza Królewska, Galicia, March 31, 1844; d. Santa Barbara, Calif., July 25, 1922. He studied piano with Mikuli in Lwów and Schulhoff in Vienna; took part in the Polish uprising against Russia in 1863, was severely wounded; went to the U.S. in 1864, enlisted in a Massachusetts regiment, and served to the end of the Civil War; subsequently was active as pianist and teacher in New York, Detroit, and Buffalo; eventually settled in California, where he founded the Zielinski Trio Club. He published some graceful piano music (*Prelude, At the Spring, Gavotte, Minuet, Bourrée, Dreams,* mazurkas, etc.).

Zika, Richard, Czech violinist and composer; b. Vsetín, Moravia, Jan. 9, 1897; d. Prague, Nov. 10, 1947. He studied with his father, and later took courses at the Prague Cons.; was 1st violinist in the Prague Quartet (1920–32), and then (1932–46) in the Ondříček Quartet; in 1946 became prof. at the Prague Academy of Musical Arts. He composed some quartet music.

Zilcher, Hermann, German composer; b. Frankfurt, Aug. 18, 1881; d. Würzburg, Jan. 1, 1948. He studied piano with his father, Paul Zilcher, a music teacher; later at Hoch's Cons. in Frankfurt, with Kwast (piano), Knorr and B. Scholz (composition). From 1901 to 1905 he was in Berlin as concert pianist and teacher; 1905–08, taught piano at Hoch's Cons., Frankfurt; from 1908 to 1920, was prof. at the Akademie der Tonkunst in Munich; from 1920, director of the Würzburg Cons. and conductor of the symph. concerts there. He toured as pianist, and in the U.S. (1905, with Franz von Vecsey).

WORKS: incidental music for several Shakespearian plays: *As You Like It* (1917), *The Winter's Tale* (1919), *The Taming of the Shrew* (1926), and *A Comedy of Errors* (1934); the comic opera *Doktor Eisenbart* (Mannheim, 1922); *Liebesmesser,* oratorio (Strasbourg, 1913); 5 symphonies (No. 5, 1947; performed posthumously, Hamburg, Feb. 11, 1948); Double Concerto for 2 violins and orch.; Violin Concerto; Piano Concerto; chamber music; many piano pieces; about 150 songs; etc.

BIBLIOGRAPHY: W. Altmann, *Hermann Zilcher* (Leipzig, 1907); H. Oppenheim, *Hermann Zilcher* (Munich, 1921).

Zillig, Winfried, German conductor and composer; b. Würzburg, April 1, 1905; d. Hamburg, Dec. 17, 1963. He studied with Schoenberg in Vienna and Berlin; from 1928 to 1943 conducted opera in Oldenburg, Düsseldorf, Essen; 1947–51, conductor of the Hesse Radio.

WORKS: the operas *Rossknecht* (Düsseldorf, Feb. 11, 1933), *Das Opfer* (Hamburg, Nov. 12, 1937), *Die Windsbraut* (Leipzig, May 12, 1941), *Troilus und Cressida* (Düsseldorf, Feb. 3, 1951), *Chorfantasie* for chorus and orch. (Frankfurt, May 30, 1952); opera *Das Verlöbnis* (Linz, Nov. 23, 1963); Cello Concerto; several string quartets and other chamber music; songs; piano pieces. He published *Variationen über neue Musik* (Munich, 1959); *Die neue Musik: Linien und Porträts* (Munich, 1963).

Ziloti, Alexander. See **Siloti, Alexander.**

Zimbalist, Efrem, eminent Russian-American violinist and pedagogue; b. Rostov-on-the-Don, April 21, 1889. He studied violin with his father, an orchestral musician; from 1901 to 1907 he was a pupil of Leopold Auer at the St. Petersburg Cons., graduating with the gold medal. He made a highly successful European appearance as soloist in Berlin, Nov. 7, 1907. In 1911 he emigrated to the U.S.; made his American debut with the Boston Symph. Orch. on Oct. 27, 1911, playing the first American performance of Glazunov's Violin Concerto. In 1914 he married the singer **Alma Gluck,** who died in 1938; his second wife, whom he married in 1943, was Mary Louise Curtis Bok, founder of the Curtis Institute of Music in Philadelphia; he was director of the Curtis Institute from 1941 to 1968. After Mrs. Zimbalist's death in 1970, he moved to Reno, Nevada, to live with his daughter. His son, Efrem Zimbalist, Jr., is a well-known actor. Zimbalist was also a composer. He wrote the opera *Landara* (Philadelphia, April 6, 1956); a musical comedy, *Honeydew* (N.Y., 1920); *Slavonic Dances,* for violin and orch. (1911); *American Rhapsody,* for orch. (Chicago, March 3, 1936; revised version, Philadelphia, Feb. 5, 1943); *Portrait of an Artist,* symph. poem (Philadelphia, Dec. 7, 1945); Violin Concerto (1947); Cello Concerto (1969); String Quartet; Violin Sonata; *Concert Phantasy on Le Coq d'or* for violin and piano; *Sarasa-*

teana, for violin and piano; songs; etc. He published *One Hour's Daily Exercise* for violin.

Zimmer, Friedrich, German composer of church music; son of **Friedrich August Zimmer;** b. Gardelegen, Sept. 22, 1855; d. Giessen, Dec. 5, 1919. He studied theology; published several collections of Lutheran hymns; composed choruses and songs for children. He was greatly esteemed as an educator.
BIBLIOGRAPHY: W. Stölten, *Friedrich Zimmer, ein deutscher Volkserzieher* (1933).

Zimmer, Friedrich August, German organist and music educator; b. Herrengosserstädt, Thuringia, Feb. 26, 1826; d. Berlin, Feb. 8, 1899. He studied in Weissenfels; then devoted himself principally to teaching. He published the manuals *Elementarmusiklehre,* a *Violin-Schule,* and *Die Orgel.*

Zimmer, Ján, significant Czech composer; b. Ružomberok, May 16, 1926. He studied piano at the Bratislava Cons. and composition with Ferenc Farkas at the Liszt Musical Academy in Budapest. An accomplished pianist, he limits himself to the performance of his own compositions, either at solo concerts or with orchestras.
WORKS: 4 piano sonatas (1948, 1961, 1965, 1971); *2 Tatras Suites,* for piano (1951–52, 1956); Concerto for solo piano (1956); *2 Pieces* for 2 pianos, 8 hands (1969); *Two by Piano* for piano, 4 hands (1973); 6 piano concertos: No. 1 (1949, Bratislava, March 14, 1950); No. 2 (1952); No. 3 (1958; Bratislava, Jan. 14, 1960); No. 4 (1960; Bratislava, Oct. 11, 1962); No. 5, for left hand alone (1964; Bratislava, June 3, 1965); No. 6 (1972); Concerto for 2 pianos and orch. (1967; Bratislava, Nov. 3, 1968); *Concerto Grosso* for 2 pianos, 2 string orchestras and percussion (1950–51); *Rhapsody* for piano and orch. (1954); Concertino for piano and strings (1955; Prague, Feb. 17, 1957); *Small Fantasy* for piano and orch. (1960); 9 symphonies: No. 1 (1955; Bratislava, Dec. 2, 1956); No. 2 (1957–58); No. 3 (1959); No. 4, for soprano, tenor, mixed chorus, and orch. (1959; Bratislava, Feb. 2, 1961); No. 5 (1961; Bratislava, March 3, 1963); No. 6, *Improvisata* (1964–65); No. 7 (1966; Bratislava, March 4, 1967); No. 8 (1971); No. 9 (1973); Piano Quintet (1949–50); *Magnificat,* cantata (1951); *The Peace,* for male choir and orch. (1954); Violin Concerto (1953; Bratislava, May 4, 1956); *Insurrection,* cantata (1954); Concerto for organ, strings, and percussion (1957; Bratislava, Dec. 5, 1957); *Ahasver,* opera (1957–; unfinished); *Suite* for violin and piano (1957); Solo Violin Sonata (1958); *Fantasy and Toccata* for organ (1958); *Strečno,* symph. poem (1958); String Quartet (1960); *The Dove of Peace,* small cantata (1960); Concerto for solo organ (1960); *Concerto da Camera* for oboe and strings (1962); *Oedipus Rex,* opera (1963–64); *The Dead Do Not Return,* oratorio (1968); *French Suite* for chamber orch. (1968); Organ Sonata (1970); *Héraklés,* opera (1972); songs; music for films.

Zimmerman, Pierre-Joseph-Guillaume, famous French piano teacher and composer; b. Paris, March 19, 1785; d. there, Oct. 29, 1853. The son of a Paris piano maker, he entered the Paris Cons. in 1798, studying under Boieldieu, Rey, Catel, and Cherubini; won 1st prize for piano in 1800, and for harmony in 1802; became piano prof. at the Cons. in 1816, and was pensioned in 1848. Among his many pupils were Alkan, Marmontel, Lacombe, Ambroise Thomas, and César Franck.
WORKS: opera *L'Enlèvement* (Paris, Oct. 26, 1830); 2 piano concertos; Piano Sonata; 24 études; etc. His chief work is the *Encyclopédie du Pianiste,* a complete method for piano, Part III of which is a treatise on harmony and counterpoint.
BIBLIOGRAPHY: J. B. Labat, *Zimmerman et l'École française de piano* (Paris, 1865).

Zimmermann, Agnes, German-English pianist and composer; b. Cologne, July 5, 1845; d. London, Nov. 14, 1925. As a young girl she went to England, and studied at the Royal Academy of Music in London with Ernst Pauer (piano) and G. Macfarren (composition). She made her debut at the Crystal Palace on Dec. 5, 1863; toured England with excellent success; was praised for her fine renditions of classical works. She edited the sonatas of Mozart and Beethoven and the complete piano works of Schumann (for Novello). She was also a competent composer; wrote a piano trio; 3 violin sonatas; a cello sonata, and many playable piano pieces.
BIBLIOGRAPHY: Lady Arbuthnot, "In Memoriam Agnes Zimmerman," *Musical Times* (1926).

Zimmermann, Anton, Austrian composer; b. Pressburg, 1741; d. there, Oct. 16, 1781. He served for many years as organist at the Pressburg Cathedral; wrote a Songspiel, *Andromeda und Perseus* (produced in Vienna on April 23, 1781); published 9 violin sonatas and a programmatic piece, *Die Belagerung von Valenciennes* for violin and piano; 6 string quartets; 6 violin duos; and other pieces.

Zimmermann, Bernd Alois, important German composer; b. Bliesheim, near Cologne, March 20, 1918; d. (suicide) Königsdorf, Aug. 10, 1970. He studied philology at the universities of Bonn, Cologne and Berlin, and earned his living by playing in dance bands. He then took courses in composition in Cologne with Philipp Jarnach; attended lectures of Wolfgang Fortner and René Leibowitz at the summer courses of new music in Darmstadt. He subsequently worked in radio; in 1958 he was appointed lecturer in composition at the Hochschule für Musik at Cologne. Plagued by failing eyesight and obsessed with notions of death, he reflected these moods in his own music of the final period; his *Requiem für einen jungen Dichter* was written to texts by various poets, all of whom committed suicide; he killed himself shortly after the completion of this morbid score. His own idiom of composition is mainly Expressionistic, with a melodic line of anguished chromaticism which does not preclude the observance of strict formal structures in his instrumental works. While in his lifetime he was primarily known to limited music circles in Germany, the significance of his music began to be realized after his death.
WORKS: *Alagoana (Caprichos Brasileiros),* ballet (1940–43, 1947–50; Essen, Dec. 17, 1955; ballet suite,

Hamburg, Nov. 21, 1953); *Lob der Torheit (In Praise of Folly),* burlesque cantata after Goethe (1948; Cologne, May 25, 1948); Concerto for String Orch. (1948; rescoring of a discarded string trio of 1942-43); Violin Sonata (1949); Violin Concerto (1949-50; Baden-Baden, Dec. 10, 1950; an orchestration and revision of the Violin Sonata); *Rheinische Kirmestänze* for 13 winds (1950, revised 1962); Solo Violin Sonata (1951); Symphony in one movement (1947-52, revised 1953; Brussels, Nov. 20, 1953); *Enchiridion,* small piece for piano (1949-52); Concerto for oboe and small orch. (1952; Donaueschingen Fest., Oct., 1952); *Kontraste,* music for an imaginary ballet, for orch. (1953; orch. suite, Hamburg, 1953; ballet, Bielefeld, April 24, 1954); *Nobody Knows de Trouble I See,* concerto for trumpet and orch. (1954; Hamburg, Oct. 11, 1955); Solo Viola Sonata (1955); *Konfigurationen,* 8 pieces for piano (1954-56); *Perspektiven,* music for an imaginary ballet, for 2 pianos (1955; ballet version, Düsseldorf, June 2, 1957); *Canto di speranza,* cantata for cello and small orch. (1952-57; Baden-Baden radio, July 28, 1958); *Omnia tempus habent,* cantata for soprano and 17 instruments (1957); *Impromptu* for orch. (1958); *Vocal Symphony* for 5 soloists and orch. (1959; scenes from the opera *Die Soldaten); Die Soldaten (The Soldiers),* opera in 4 acts after J. M. R. Lenz (1958-60, revised 1963-64; Cologne, Feb. 15, 1965); Solo Cello Sonata (1959-60); *Dialoge,* Concerto for 2 pianos and orch., in homage to Debussy (1960, revised 1965; original version, Cologne radio, Dec. 5, 1960); *Présence,* "ballet blanc" in 5 scenes for piano trio (1961; Darmstadt Sept. 8, 1961); *Antophonen* for viola and 25 instrumentalists, some of whom speak a text drawn from Joyce, Dante, Dostoyevsky, Camus and Novalis (1961; Zürich, 1966); *5 capricci di G. Frescobaldi "La Frescobalda"* for 3 recorders, oboe d'amore, 3 viola da gamba, lute, 3 trumpets, and 3 trombones (1962); *Tempus loquendi,* "pezzi ellittici" for flauto grande, flute in G, and bass flute solo, for one performer (1963); *Monologe* for 2 pianos (1960-64; version of *Dialoge);* Concerto for cello and orch., in the form of a "pas de trois" (1965-66; concert version, Strasbourg, April 8, 1968; ballet version, Wuppertal, May 12, 1968); *Tratto I* and *II* for tape (in the form of a choreographic study, 1966; 1968); *Musique pour les soupers du Roi Ubu,* "ballet noir" in 7 parts and an entrée, for orch. (1966; Düsseldorf, 1968); *Intercomunicazione* for cello and piano (1967); *Ode to Eleutheria* for music from Death Dances from music for the radio play *Die Befristeten (The Numbered),* for jazz quintet (1967); *Photoptosis,* prelude for orch. (1968; Gelsenkirchen, Feb. 19, 1969); *Requiem für einen jungen Dichter (Requiem for a Young Poet),* "lingual" for narrator, soprano and baritone soloists, 3 choruses, tape, orch., jazz combo, and organ, to texts drawn from various poems, articles and news reports (1967-69; Düsseldorf, Dec. 11, 1969); 4 short *Studies* for solo cello (1970); *Stille und Umkehr (Stillness and Return),* sketch for orch. (1970; Nuremberg, March 19, 1971); *Ich wandte mich und sah an alles Unrecht das geschah unter der Sonne (I Come Again to Contemplate All the Oppression That is Committed Under the Sun),* "Ecclesiatical action" for 2 narrators, solo bass and orch. (1970; Kiel, Sept. 2, 1972).

Zimmermann, Louis, Dutch violinist and composer; b. Groningen, July 19, 1873; d. Amsterdam, March 6, 1954. He studied at the Leipzig Cons. with Hans Sitt and Carl Reinecke; also with Eugène Ysaÿe in Brussels. He was a member of the Concertgebouw Orch. in Amsterdam (1899-1904); taught violin at the Royal College of Music, London (1904-1909); then rejoined the Concertgebouw as its concertmaster, retiring in 1940. He wrote numerous violin pieces; also cadenzas for the violin concertos by Beethoven and Brahms.

Zinck, Benedikt Friedrich, German composer; b. Husum, Holstein, May 23, 1743; d. Ludwigslust, Mecklenburg, June 23, 1801. He was a church organist; in 1783 became court musician at Ludwigslust. Among his works are several symphonies, harpsichord sonatas, chamber music.

Zinck, Harnack Otto Conrad, German composer, brother of **Benedikt Friedrich Zinck;** b. Husum, Holstein, July 2, 1746; d. Copenhagen, Feb. 15, 1832. He was organist in Hamburg; then joined his brother at Ludwigslust, but left in 1787 for Copenhagen, where he was church organist and teacher; there he produced an opera to a Danish text, *Selim og Mirza* (Copenhagen, Feb. 1, 1790); also composed several oratorios, instrumental music, etc.; published *Die nördliche Harfe* (Copenhagen, 1801; on Scandinavian music) and *Vorlesungen über Musik und ihre nützlichste Anwendung* (Copenhagen, 1813).

Zingarelli, Nicola Antonio, Italian composer; b. Naples, April 4, 1752; d. Torre del Greco, near Naples, May 5, 1837. He studied at the Cons. di Loreto, Naples, with Fenaroli and Speranza (composition); also studied violin. His first stage work, *I quattro pazzi,* was performed at the Cons. in 1768. After finishing school in 1769 he earned his living as a violin teacher. He spent much time traveling throughout Italy, supervising the production of his operas. In 1792 he was appointed maestro di cappella at the Cathedral of Milan; in 1794, at the Santa Casa in Loreto; in 1804, at the Sistine Chapel in the Vatican, Rome. In 1811, for refusing to conduct a Te Deum to celebrate the birthday of Napoleon's son, the "King of Rome," he was imprisoned at Civitavecchia, later transported to Paris by order of Napoleon, who set him at liberty and liberally paid him for a Mass written in Paris. As Fioravanti had meanwhile become maestro at St. Peter's, Zingarelli went to Naples, and in 1813 became director of the royal Collegio di Musica; in 1816 he succeeded Paisiello as maestro at the Naples Cathedral. He was renowned as a teacher; Bellini, Mercadante, Carlo Conti, Lauro Rossi, Morlacchi, and Sir Michael Costa were his students. His operas, interpreted by the finest singers of the time (Catalani, Crescentini, Grassini, Marchesi, and Rubinelli), were highly successful. His facility was such that he was able to write an opera in a week. He wrote 37 operas in all. WORKS: operas (produced at La Scala, Milan): *Alsinda* (Feb. 22, 1785); *Ifigenia in Aulide* (Jan. 27, 1787); *La Morte de Cesare* (Dec. 26, 1790); *Pirro, re d'Epiro* (Dec. 26, 1791); *Il Mercato di Monfregoso* (Sept. 22, 1792); *La Secchia rapita* (Sept. 7, 1793); *Artaserse* (Dec. 26, 1793); *Giulietta e Romeo,* after

Shakespeare (Jan. 30, 1796; his best known work; staged all over Europe, and also in N.Y., with considerable success, but disappeared from the repertory after Zingarelli's death); *Meleagro* (Jan., 1798); *Il Ritratto* (Oct. 12, 1799); *Clitennestra* (Dec. 26, 1800); other operas: *Antigono* (Mantua, April 13, 1786); *Alzira* (Florence, Sept. 7, 1794); *Il Conte di Saldagna* (Venice, Dec. 26, 1794); *Orazi e Curiazi* (Naples, Nov. 4, 1795); *La Morte di Mitridate* (Venice, May 27, 1797); *Il Ratto delle Sabine* (Venice, Dec. 26, 1799); *Edipo a Colono* (Venice, Dec. 26, 1802); *La Distruzione di Gerusalemme* (Florence, Nov. 27, 1803); *L'Oracolo sannita* (Naples, Oct. 11, 1806); *Il Ritorno di Serse* (Modena, July 16, 1808); *Baldovino* (Rome, Feb. 11, 1811); *Berenice, regina d'Armenia* (Rome, Nov. 12, 1811). Oratorios: *Pimmalione* (Naples, 1779), *Ero* (Milan, 1786), *Telemaco* (Milan, 1787), *Il Trionfo di David* (Naples, 1788), *Francesca da Rimini* (Rome, 1804), *Tancredi al sepolcro di Clorinda* (Naples, 1805), and *La Fuga in Egitto* (Naples, 1837); a vast amount of church music; the Cons. di Loreto contains 541 manuscripts by Zingarelli, in a collection known as "Annuale di Zingarelli" (or "Annuale di Loreto"), including a series of Masses for every day in the year; a 4-part Miserere "alla Palestrina" (1827); 73 Magnificats, 28 Stabat Maters, 21 Credos, many Te Deums, motets, hymns, etc.; also solfeggi, arias, organ sonatas, some chamber music.

BIBLIOGRAPHY: R. Liberatore, *Necrologia di N. Zingarelli* (Naples, 1837); A. Schmid, *Joseph Haydn und N. Zingarelli* (Vienna, 1847); F. Florimo, in vol. II of *La Scuola musicale de Napoli* (Naples, 1880); S. di Giacomo, "Il fiero Zingarelli," *Musica d'Oggi* (June 1923); P. Dotto, "N. Zingarelli," *Musica d'Oggi* (July 1941).

Zingel, Rudolf Ewald, German organist and composer; b. Liegnitz, Sept. 5, 1876; d. there, Feb. 20, 1944. He studied at the Hochschule für Musik in Berlin; then was active as church organist and choral conductor in Berlin and in Frankfurt-on-the-Oder. He wrote 2 operas, *Margot* (Frankfurt-on-the-Oder, 1902) and *Persepolis* (Rostock, 1909); an operetta, *Liebeszauber* (Stralsund, 1908); a symph. poem, *Freudvoll und liedvoll;* a secular oratorio, *Der wilde Jäger;* several sacred cantatas for men's chorus and string orch.; numerous piano pieces and songs.

Zinkeisen, Konrad Ludwig Dietrich, German violinist and composer; b. Hannover, June 3, 1779; d. Brunswick, Nov. 28, 1838. He was trained by his father, and by Rode at Wolfenbüttel; played 1st violin under Forkel at the Academic Concerts in Göttingen; in 1819 he was appointed chamber musician in the Brunswick court orch. He wrote 6 violin concertos, 4 orch. overtures, 3 string quartets; concertos for oboe, for clarinet, for basset horn, for bassoon, and various other pieces for solo instruments with orch.; music for military band; choral works.

Zinman, David, American conductor; b. New York, July 9, 1936. He studied at the Oberlin Cons. (B.M., 1958) and at the Univ. of Minnesota (M.A., 1963); took a course in conducting with Pierre Monteux in his summer school in Maine, and from 1961 to 1964 was his assistant. From 1964 to 1969 he was regular conductor of the Nederland Kamerorkest in Holland, and also appeared as guest conductor in the U.S., Japan, South Africa. In 1977 he was appointed conductor and music director of the Rochester, N.Y., Philharmonic.

Zinnen, Jean-Antoine, Luxembourg composer; b. Neuenbourg, April 25, 1827; d. Neuilly-sur-Seine, May 16, 1898. He was the composer of the National Hymn of Luxembourg (1864); wrote several operettas. In 1881 he went to Paris, After his death, his remains were brought to Luxembourg. A postage stamp in his honor was issued in 1950.

Zipoli, Domenico, Italian composer and organist; b. Prato, Oct. 16, 1688; d. Córdoba, Argentina, Jan. 2, 1726. He went to Rome as a young man; was organist at the Jesuit Church there. His oratorios *Sant' Antonio di Padova* (1712) and *Santa Caterina, vergine e martire* (1714) were presented in Rome. In 1716 he published *Sonate d'intavolatura per organo e cimbalo.* He joined the Jesuit order at Seville in 1716; in 1717 went to South America, where he became organist of the Jesuit Church in Córdoba, Argentina. Walsh of London reprinted parts of the *Sonate d'intavolatura* under the titles *Six Suits of Italian Lessons for the Harpsichord* and *Third Collection of Toccatas, Vollentarys and Fugues.*

BIBLIOGRAPHY: L. Ayestarán, *Domenico Zipoli, el gran compositor y organista romano del 1700 en el Rio de La Plata* (Montevideo, 1941; radically revised and amplified, Montevideo, 1962; basic study establishing biographical facts); A. Salazar, "El Caso de Domenico Zipoli," *Nuestra Musica* (Mexico, May 1946; arguing against the identification of the immigrant organist Zipoli with the composer); V. de Rubertis, "Dove e quando nacque e morì Domenico Zipoli," *Rivista Musicale Italiana* (April-June 1951).

Zipp, Friedrich, German composer and pedagogue; b. Frankfurt, June 20, 1914. He studied at Hoch's Cons. in Frankfurt and with Armin Knab in Berlin; in 1947 was appointed to the faculty of the Musikhochschule in Frankfurt; also served as organist there. He composed *Musik* for orch. (1936); *Sinfonietta* for youth orch. (1958); *Kirchensuite* for string orch. (1962); *Au clair de la lune* for oboe and piano (1963); numerous choral pieces and songs. He published *Vom Wesen der Musik* (Heidelberg, 1974).

Zítek, Otakar, Czech music critic and composer; b. Prague, Nov. 5, 1892; d. Bratislava, April 28, 1955. He studied composition with Novák at the Vienna Cons. and musicology with Guido Adler and Grädener at the Vienna Univ. Upon graduation he wrote music criticism for the *Hudební Revue* and the *Lidové Noviny* in Prague; gave lectures on opera at the Prague Cons.; then was administrator at the National Theater in Brno (1921–29); taught at the Brno Cons. (1931–39). In 1939–41 he was placed in the Buchenwald concentration camp, but was released and worked as theater director in Pilsen (1941–43); supervised opera theaters in Prague and Brno (1946–49). He composed the operas *Vznesene srdce (The Exalted Heart;* 1918) and *Pád Petra Králence (The Downfall of Peter Králence;*

Brno, March 23, 1923); a ballet after Wilde's *Birthday of the Infanta* (Pilsen, 1942); *Město,* a symph. poem (1925); songs; etc. He published *O novou zpevohru (On New Opera;* Prague, 1920).

Živković, Milenko, Serbian composer; b. Belgrade, May 25, 1901; d. there, June 29, 1964. He studied law in Belgrade and music at the Leipzig Cons. with Grabner and at the Schola Cantorum in Paris with Vincent d'Indy. Returning to Belgrade, he taught at the Academy of Music until 1960. A follower of the national school of composition, he wrote music permeated with ethnic Balkan melorhythms. His works include: *Symphonic Prologue* (Belgrade, April 16, 1935); *Zelena Godina (Green Year),* folk ballet scenes for orch. (Belgrade, April 27, 1937); several suites of Yugoslav dances for piano, and numerous choruses.

Zmeskall, Nikolaus, Baron von Domanovecz, Hungarian diplomat and musical amateur; b. Lestine, 1759 (baptized Nov. 20, 1759); d. Vienna, June 23, 1833. He served as secretary of the Hungarian Chancellery in Vienna, and was an intimate friend of Beethoven, who dedicated to him the String Quartet op. 95. Zmeskall was also a composer in his own right; he wrote 14 string quartets and other instrumental music.
BIBLIOGRAPHY: A. Sandberger, *Beethovens Freund Zmeskall als Komponist* (Munich, 1924); C. Pidoll, *Verklungenes Spiel: Erinnerungen des Herrn Nikolaus Zmeskall* (Innsbruck, 1949).

Znosko-Borovsky, Alexander, Russian composer; b. Kiev, Feb. 27, 1908. He studied violin and composition at the Kiev Cons.; then was active as composer for films (1931–41). In 1941 he left Kiev, threatened by the Nazi invasion, and went to Ashkhabad, Turkmenia; was instrumental in promoting indigenous music culture there; several of his works are based on Turkmenian themes.
WORKS: ballet, *Akpamyk* (Ashkhabad, April 14, 1945); cantata, *Our Victory* (Kiev, May 8, 1946); 3 symphonies (1958, 1960, 1967); a symph. poem, *Kiev* (Kiev, March 9, 1949); Violin Concerto (Kiev, Dec. 17, 1955); symph. poem, *At the Mausoleum* (1960); a String Quartet on Ukrainian themes (1937); a String Quartet in Turkemian themes (1942); Sonata for unaccompanied violin (1950); *Scherzo* for 3 trombones (1938); various pieces for different instruments.

Zoeller, Carl, German-British composer; b. Berlin, March 28, 1840; d. London, July 13, 1889. He studied violin with Hubert Ries in Berlin; after traveling in Germany with various opera troupes as violinist, he went to London, settling there in 1873; in 1879, he became bandmaster of the 7th (Queen's Own) Hussars. In England he often performed on the viola d'amore; published *The Viole d'Amour, Its Origin and History, and Art of Playing It.* He composed an operetta, *The Missing Heir,* and a serious music drama, *Mary Stuart of Fotheringay;* a violin concerto; songs.

Zoellner, Joseph, Sr., American violinist; b. Brooklyn, Feb. 2, 1862; d. Los Angeles, Jan. 24, 1950. He studied violin; traveled to Europe, with a prolonged stay in Brussels (1907–12) where he organized, with his two

sons and a daughter, the Zoellner Quartet. From 1912 to 1922, they lived in N.Y.; in 1922 Zoellner founded with his children the Zoellner Cons. of Music in Los Angeles.

Zoilo, Annibale, Italian composer; b. Rome, c.1537; d. Loreto, 1592. He was maestro di cappella at San Luigi dei Francesi from 1561 to 1566; at San Giovanni in Laterano from Jan. 1568 to June 1570. In 1570 he became a singer in the Papal Choir, Rome (until 1581); then was at the Cathedral of Todi; returning to Rome, he entered the service of Cardinal Sirleto (until 1584); subsequently became maestro at the Santa Casa in Loreto (till June 30, 1592). In 1577 he and Palestrina were entrusted with the revision of the Roman Gradual *(Editio Medicaea).* He published *Madrigali a 4 e 5 voci* (Rome, 1563); *Salve Regina* for 12 voices is in Constantini's *Selectae Cantiones excellentissimorum auctorum* (Rome, 1614); various compositions in other collections, published between 1567 and 1616.
BIBLIOGRAPHY: R. Casimiri, "Anibale Zoilo e la sua famiglia: nouvi documenti biografici," *Note d'Archivio* (Jan.-April 1940).

Zöllner, Carl Friedrich, German choral conductor and composer; b. Mittelhausen, March 17, 1800; d. Leipzig, Sept. 25, 1860. He studied at the Thomasschule, Leipzig; became a vocal instructor and began writing male choruses; in 1833 he founded in Leipzig a "Liedertafel" known as the Zöllner-Verein, a male choral society modeled after Zelter's Berlin organization; after Zöllner's death, several choral societies were united to form the Zöllner-Bund. Zöllner was one of the most successful German composers of part-songs for male choruses; he also wrote for mixed chorus, and songs with piano accompaniment.
BIBLIOGRAPHY: R. Hänsch, *Der Liedermeister Carl Friedrich Zöllner* (Dresden, 1927).

Zöllner, Heinrich, German composer; b. Öls, Silesia, May 5, 1792; d. Wandsbeck, near Hamburg, July 2, 1836. He toured Germany as an organist; for a while lived in Vienna; in 1833 settled in Hamburg. He wrote an opera, *Kunz von Kauffungen* (Vienna, March 27, 1826); a melodrama, *Ein Uhr;* published Masses, motets, psalms, part-songs, organ pieces, a piano sonata, piano pieces, etc.

Zöllner, Heinrich, German composer, son of **Carl Friedrich Zöllner;** b. July 4, 1854; d. Freiburg-im-Breisgau, May 4, 1941. He studied at the Leipzig Cons., where his teachers were Reinecke, Jadassohn, Richter, and Wenzel (1875–77); then went to Dorpat, Russia, where he was music director at the local university; in 1885 he went to Cologne, where he taught at the Cologne Cons. and conducted choruses. In 1890 he was engaged to lead the Deutscher Liederkranz in N.Y.; in 1898 he returned to Germany; from 1902 to 1907 he taught composition at the Leipzig Cons.; from 1907 to 1914 he was conductor at the Flemish Opera in Antwerp; subsequently settled in Freiburg.
WORKS: He wrote 10 operas of which the following were produced: *Frithjof* (Cologne, 1884), *Die lustigen Chinesinnen* (Cologne, 1886), *Faust* (Munich, Oct.

19, 1887), *Matteo Falcone* (N.Y., 1894), *Der Überfall* (Dresden, Sept. 7, 1895), *Die versunkene Glocke* (Berlin, July 8, 1899; his best opera), *Der Schützenkönig* (Leipzig, 1903), *Zigeuner* (Stuttgart, 1912); the musical comedy *Das hölzerne Schwert* (Kassel, 1897); a great number of choral works with orch.; also 3 symphonies and some chamber music. He published a poem *Beethoven in Bonn. Ein Sang vom Rhein* (1898).

BIBLIOGRAPHY: E. Segnitz, *Heinrich Zöllner* (Leipzig, 1907).

Zolotarev, Vasily, eminent Russian composer and pedagogue; b. Taganrog, March 7, 1872; d. Moscow, May 25, 1964. (His name is pronounced Zolotaryóv). He studied violin and music theory at the Imperial Court Chapel in St. Petersburg; from 1893 to 1897 he took composition lessons with Balakirev; then entered the St. Petersburg Cons. in the class of Rimsky-Korsakov, graduating in 1900; received the Rubinstein Prize for his cantata *Paradise and Peri.* He subsequently held various teaching positions: instructor of violin at the Court Chapel (1897–1900); teacher of composition at the Rostov Music School (1906–08), at the Moscow Cons. (1908–18), the Ekaterinodar Cons. (1918–1924), the Odessa Cons. (1924–26), the Kiev Musico-Dramatic Institute (1926–31), the Sverdlovsk Music School (1931–33), and the Minsk Cons. (1933–41); after 1945 lived in Moscow. In 1955 he was awarded the Order of Lenin. Several well-known Soviet composers were his pupils, among them, Polovinkin, Dankevich, and Vainberg. In his music Zolotarev continued the line of the National Russian School of composition, based on broad diatonic melos, mellifluous euphonious harmonies, and in his operas, a resonant flow of choral singing.

WORKS: the operas *The Decembrists* (Moscow, Dec. 27, 1925) and *Ak-Gul,* on Uzbek themes (1942); ballet, *Lake Prince* (Minsk, Jan. 15, 1949); 7 symphonies: No. 1 (1902); No. 2 (1905); No. 3 (1935); No. 4 (1936); No. 5 (1942); No. 6 (1943); No. 7 (1962); overture, *Fête villageoise; Rhapsodie hébraïque,* for orch.; symph. suites: *Moldavian Suite* (1926), *Uzbek Suite* (1931), *Tadzhik Suite* (1932), *Belorussian Suite* (1936); Cello Concerto (1943); 6 string quartets (1899, 1902, 1907, 1912, 1916, 1945); Piano Quintet (1904); String Quintet (1904); Piano Trio (1905); Violin Sonata (1922); 2 piano sonatas (1903; 1919); many songs. He publ. a manual on the fugue (Moscow, 1932).

BIBLIOGRAPHY: V. Zolotarev, *Reminiscences About My Great Pupils, Friends and Colleagues* (Moscow, 1957); S. Nisievich, *V. Zolotarev* (Moscow, 1964).

Zoltán, Aladár, Rumanian composer; b. Mărtiniş-Harghita, May 31, 1929. He studied with Jodál and Demian at the Cluj Cons. (1946–53); in 1960 he was appointed secretary of the Tîrgu-Mureş branch of the Union of Rumanian Composers, and in 1965 was elected director of the Tîrgu-Mureş Philharmonic.

WORKS: for the stage: in Hungarian, *Biborkáne Iánya (The Marriage,* 1962); in Rumanian, *Poarta de sur* (1963); in French, *Coutumes d'hiver* (1969) and *Les "Marieurs" de Bihor* (1971); 4 cantatas; *5 Lyrical Songs* for tenor and orch. (1963); *Divertissement* for 2 clarinets and strings (1952); 2 symphonies (1961,

1971); *Dansuri de pe Mureş* for orch. (1968); *Suite Piccola* for orch. (1970); *Nonet* (1953); Bassoon Sonata (1955); String Quartet (1965); *Suite Piccola* for piano (1964–69); choruses; songs.

Zopff, Hermann, German music critic and composer; b. Glogau, June 1, 1826; d. Leipzig, July 12, 1883. He studied agriculture, then music (at the Stern Cons. in Berlin); founded an "Opernakademie" and an "Orchesterverein" in Berlin; in 1864 he settled in Leipzig as co-editor of the *Neue Zeitschrift für Musik,* becoming editor-in-chief in 1868. He published *Ratschläge für angehende Dirigenten* (1861; 3rd ed., 1922) and *Grundzüge einer Theorie der Oper* (Leipzig, 1868). His compositions include a symph. poem, *Wilhelm Tell; Drei Idyllen* for small orch.; *Gesangsstück* for cello and orch.; *Asträa, oder Das Evangelium der Tat* for solo voices, chorus, and orch.; piano pieces; male choruses; songs. His 2 operas, *Makkabäus* and *Mohammed,* were published but not produced.

Zoras, Leonidas, Greek composer and conductor; b. Sparta, March 8, 1905. He studied law at the Univ. of Athens; at the same time took conducting lessons with Mitropoulos, and studied composition with Kalomiris, Lavrangas, and Riadis. From 1926 to 1938 he taught music theory at the Odeon Music School; from 1938 to 1940 he lived in Berlin, where he took lessons in composition with Grabner and Blacher; in 1940 he returned to Athens and conducted the Athens Opera until 1958, when he took residence in Berlin. He wrote an opera *Elektra* (1969); the ballet, *Violanto* (1931); *Night Song* for cello solo and chamber orch. (1927); *Legend* for orch. (1936); Symphony (1947); Concertino for violin and 11 woodwind instruments (1950); String Quartet (1969); Violin Sonata (1950); numerous piano pieces, choruses, and songs.

Zorzor, Ştefan, Rumanian composer; b. Oradea, April 4, 1932. He studied with Chirescu, Negrea, I. Dumitrescu, Ciortea, Andricu, Olah, and Mendelsohn at the Bucharest Cons. (1951–52, 1956–61); then occupied teaching positions in Bucharest.

WORKS: *Ţara mea (My Country),* cantata for female chorus and small orch. (1956); Piano Sonata (1959); 3 string quartets (1960, 1962, 1968); Violin Sonata (1963); Concerto for Orch. (1965); *Nocturne* for orch. (1966); Wind Quintet (1968); *Heteroquintet* for flute, violin, cello, piano, and percussion (1969); *Circulara,* experimental music for 5 different instruments (1969); *Pièces diverses* for piano (1967–72); choruses.

Zouhar, Zdeněk, Czech composer; b. Kotvrdovice, Feb. 8, 1927. He studied with Jan Kunc (1948–50) and A. Moyzes (1950–51) in Bratislava. He was head of the music department of the Brno Univ. library (1953–61); in 1962 was appointed to the faculty at the Janáček Music Academy in Brno. In his music he makes multifarious use of modern techniques, including a fairly orthodox dodecaphony.

WORKS: *Spring Suite* for 3 violins (1949); *Prelude and Epilogue* for solo cello (1949); *Aulularia,* suite, for chamber ensemble (1956); *Partita* for organ (1956); *Prelude* for 2 pianos (1957); *Midnight Mass* for soloists, chorus, orch., and organ (1957); *151,* music for wind quintet (1958); *Sportovní stránky (Sports Pages),* suite for orch. (1959); Trio for flute, clarinet, and bass clarinet (1961); *3 Studies* for 4 horns (1963); *Divertimento* for 4 winds and percussion (1965); *Variations* for oboe and piano (1965); *Music* for strings (1966); 2 string quartets (1966, 1972); *Symphonic Triptych* (1967; Brno Radio, Nov. 29, 1967); *Music* for wind quintet (1968); *Triple Concerto* for clarinet, trumpet, trombone and orch. (1970); a chamber radio opera, *Metamorphosis* (1971).

Zschocher, Johann, noted German piano pedagogue; b. Leipzig, May 16, 1821. d. there, Jan. 6, 1897. He was a pupil of Iwan Knorr, Th. Kullak, Henselt, and Liszt. In 1846 he founded the Zschocher'sches Musik-Institut in Leipzig, which became a flourishing music school, still active in the 20th century.

Zsolt, Nándor, Hungarian violinist and composer; b. Esztergom, May 12, 1887; d. Budapest, June 25, 1936. He studied violin with Hubay in Budapest; in 1908 went to London, where he participated in chamber music concerts; returning to Budapest, he became a violin teacher. His piano quintet (1914) was awarded a prize. He also wrote a symph.; many violin pieces (*Valse Caprice, Berceuse, Enchaînée, Satyr et Dryade,* etc.).
BIBLIOGRAPHY: Cyril Scott, "Nándor Zsolt," *Monthly Musical Record* (1915).

Zubiaurre (y Urionabarrenechea), Valentí, Spanish composer; b. Villa de Garay, Feb. 13, 1837; d. Madrid, Jan. 13, 1914. He was a chorister at Bilbao; at the age of 16 he undertook a voyage to South America; he returned to Spain in 1866, and took music lessons wiht Hilarión Eslava. He wrote a considerable number of sacred works; then turned to opera; received 1st national prize with his opera *Fernando el Emplazado* (Madrid, May 12, 1871). In 1875 was named 2nd maestro at the Royal Chapel in Madrid, and in 1878 succeeded Eslava as 1st maestro; in the same year he was appointed prof. at the Madrid Cons. His 2nd opera, *Ledia,* was produced with considerable success in Madrid, on April 22, 1877. He also composed several zarzuelas, a symph., a potpourri of Basque folksongs, choruses.

Zucca, Mana. See **Mana–Zucca.**

Zuccalmaglio, Anton Wilhelm Florentin von, German collector of folksongs and writer on music; b. Waldbröl, April 12, 1803; d. Nachrodt, near Grüna, Westphalia, March 23, 1869. The son of a physician, who was a musical amateur, he learned music at home; contributed to the *Neue Zeitschrift für Musik* during Schumann's editorship, under the pseudonyms **Wilhelm von Waldbrühl** and **Dorfküster Wedel;** published 2 collections of folksongs, in 1829 and 1836 (with E. Baumstark); then brought out (with A. Kretzschmer) the important compilation, *Deutsche Volkslieder mit ihren Originalweisen* (2 vols.; 1838, 1840; reprint, Hildesheim, 1969). However, these songs are only partly authentic; a few melodies were composed by Zuccalmaglio himself; others were com-

bined from various sources; the texts were frequently rearranged. Brahms made use of the collection for his arrangements of German folksongs.
BIBLIOGRAPHY: M. Friedlaender, "Zuccalmaglio und das Volkslied," *Jahrbuch der Bibliothek Peters* (1918); W. Wiora, "Die Herkunft der Melodien in Kretzschmers und Zuccalmaglios Sammlung," *Jahrbuch für Volksliedforschung* (1941), revised and publ. as *Die rheinisch-bergischen Melodien bei Zuccalmaglio und Brahms* (Bad Godesberg, 1953).

Zuchert, Leon, Russian-born Canadian composer; b. Poltava, May 4, 1904. He emigrated to Canada in 1929; played viola in several orchestras in Canada and the U.S.; was principal violinist and assistant conductor of the Halifax Symph. Orch. (1963–65, 1967–69). He is autodidact as composer.
WORKS: *My Canadian Travels* for orch. (1938); 2 symphonies (1948–50, 1959–62); *Quetico,* symph. suite (1957); *Oriental Romance* for small orch. (1960); *Dniepr,* cantata (1961); *Song in Brass* for voice, solo viola, and orch. without woodwinds (1964); *Divertimento Orientale* for oboe and string orch. (1965); *Two Moods in One* for string orch. (1968); *My Paintings* for string orch. (1969); *Impressions of Teneriffe,* symph. suite (1970); *Fantasia on Ukrainian Themes* for orch. (1973); *In the Gleam of Northern Lights,* choreographic oratorio (1974); *Two Spanish Meditations* for orch. or piano (1975); 3 string quartets (1965, 1971, 1972); *Little Prince in Montreal* for wind quintet (1968); *Psychedelic Suite* for brass quintet (1968); *Short Suite* for trumpet or clarinet or viola, and piano (1974); *Suite* for solo bassoon (1975). Concerto for bassoon and string orch. (1976); *Elegy* for orch. (1977).

Zuelli, Guglielmo, Italian composer; b. Reggio Emilia, Oct. 20, 1859; d. Milan, Oct. 8, 1941. He studied with A. Busi and L. Mancinelli in Bologna; after teaching and conducting in various provincial towns, he became director of the Cons. in Palermo (1894–1911), of the Parma Cons. (1911–29), and of the Liceo Musicale of Alessandria, Piedmont (1929–33); then retired.
WORKS: the opera *La Fata del Nord* (Milan, May 4, 1884; Sonzogno prize); opera-ballet *Il Profeta di Korassan; Inno alla Notte* for solo voices, chorus, and orch.; 2 symphonies; *Un Saluto al mare,* symph. suite (its 3rd movement, *Festa delle sirene,* became extremely popular as a separate piece); *Il Canto del Coaro Romagnuolo* for orch.; String Quartet; minor pieces for strings; fugues for organ; songs; etc. He published *Gioacchino Rossini: Pagine segrete* (Bologna, 1922).

Zukerman, Pinchas, Israeli violinist; b. Tel Aviv, July 16, 1948. He began playing violin at the age of 6; then was sent for further study to the Juilliard School of Music in New York, where he took lessons with the renowned violin teacher Ivan Galamian (1962–67). In 1967 he won the Leventritt prize; then toured in America and Europe. On April 3, 1971 he made an auspicious N.Y. debut. His playing is distinguished by an innate emotional élan and a modern virtuoso technique.

Zweig, Fritz, Bohemian conductor; b. Olomouc, Moravia, Sept. 8, 1893. He studied with Schoenberg in Vienna; then devoted himself to opera conducting; was on the staff of the Mannheim Opera (1912–14 and 1919–21); music director at Barmen-Elberfeld (1921–23); conducted opera in Berlin (1923–33); at the German Opera in Prague (1934–38); then appeared in Paris and London; in 1940 emigrated to America; in 1942 settled in Hollywood as a teacher.

Zwilich, Ellen Taaffe, American composer; b. Miami, Florida, April 30, 1939. She studied at Florida State Univ. graduating in 1960 (M.M., 1962); then moved to N.Y.; took violin lessons with Ivan Galamian; enrolled at the Juilliard School of Music, N.Y., and had semiweekly sessions with Sessions there; was the first woman to receive a doctorate in composition from that school (1975).
WKS: *Einsame Nacht,* after Hesse, song cycle for baritone and piano (1971); *Im Nebel,* after Hesse, for altrato and piano (1972); *Symposium* for orch. (1973; Juilliard Orch., Jan. 31, 1975, Pierre Boulez conducting); *Impromptus* for solo harp (1973); Violin Sonata (1973); *Trompeten* for soprano and piano (19; *Allison* for chamber ensemble (1974); String Quartet (1974); *Clarino Quartet* for 4 trumpets (1977); Violin Concerto (1975–77).

Zwischer, Bruno, German pianist and pedagogue; b. Egenhain, May 15, 1838; d. Oberlössnitz, near Dresden, March 4, 1905. He studied piano with Julius in Dresden and with Moscheles in Leipzig; also took lessons with Plaidy. He subsequently taught piano at the Leipzig Cons. (1875–96); then settled in Dresden where he became a successful piano teacher. He published a manual *Klavier-Technik* (which be-

came extremely successful; was also published in English under the title *Technical Exercises Systematically).* He further published *Musikalische Verzierungen,* which contains practical exercises and theoretical notations pertaining to the proper performance of ornamentation.

Zwyssig, Alberich, Swiss composer; b. Bauen, Nov. 17, 1808; d. in the Cistercian monastery at Mehrerau, Nov. 18, 1854. He entered the Order of the Cistercians in 1826, giving up his real name Joseph for the monastic name Alberich; he was Kapellmeister in the monasteries of Wettingen, Zug, Wurmbach, and (shortly before his death) Mehrerau. *His Schweizer Psalm* for men's chorus a cappella (1841) attained great popularity, and in 1961 was named as a *pro tempore* national anthem of Switzerland. He further composed many sacred and secular choruses, and church music with organ accompaniment.
BIBLIOGRAPHY: B. Widmann, *Alberich Zwyssig als Komponist* (Bregenz, 1905); H. Meng, *Alberich Zwyssig, 1808–1854; Gedenkschrift* (Wettingen, 1954).

Zykan, Otto M., Austrian pianist and composer; b. Vienna, April 29, 1935. He studied piano and composition at the Vienna Academy of Music; in 1958 he won 1st prize at the Darmstadt Competition for young pianists and started on a successful concert career, specializing in modern music. His own compositions reveal a strong influence of Anton von Webern, but he does not exclude tonal, and even triadic, combinations and accepts formal periodicity in structure. His compositions include String Quartet (1956); *Loblied der Kreaturen,* cantata (1961); *3 Sätze* for percussion, wind instruments and piano (1962).